# TEXAS CRIMINAL AND TRAFFIC LAW MANUAL

## 2011-2012 EDITION

With statutory amendments through
the 82nd Legislative First Called Session, 2011

## QUESTIONS ABOUT THIS PUBLICATION?

For CUSTOMER SERVICE ASSISTANCE concerning replacement pages, shipments, billing, reprint permission, or other matters,

    please call Customer Service Department at 800-833-9844
    email *customer.support@lexisnexis.com*
    or visit our interactive customer service website at *www.lexisnexis.com/printcdsc*

For EDITORIAL **content questions** concerning this publication,

    email: *LEpublications@lexisnexis.com*

For **information on other LEXISNEXIS MATTHEW BENDER publications**,

    please call us at 877-461-8801
    or visit our online bookstore at *www.lexisnexis.com/bookstore*

---

ISBN: 978-1-4224-9392-2 (soft cover)
     978-1-4224-9393-9 (looseleaf)

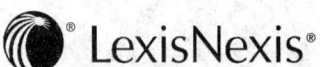

Matthew Bender & Company, Inc.
Editorial Offices
701 E. Water Street
Charlottesville, VA 22902
800-446-3410
www.lexisnexis.com

Product Number 3352518 (soft cover)
            3110114 (looseleaf)

Know the law to enforce the law.

## Save 20% on these Texas Law Enforcement Titles*

**Texas Criminal and Traffic Law Manual on Flash Drive, 2011 – 2012 Edition**

This flash drive contains the entire text of the book so that officers can quickly and easily search and find the most relevant results. Its 1 GB of memory allows for saving of documents with notes, department guidelines and reports.

~~$65~~ **$52    Now available in eBook format!**
1 flash drive, replaced biennially, Pub. #33525, ISBN 9781422493892

**Texas Criminal and Traffic Law Field Guide, 2011 – 2012 Edition**

Includes the most commonly referenced elements of key statutes--essential to officers while in the field!

~~$17~~ **$13.60    Now available in eBook format!**
1 volume, spiral bound, replaced biennially, Pub. #31081, ISBN 9781422494301

**Texas Traffic Laws, 2011 Edition**

Covers traffic laws most important to law enforcement officers; is a must-have for the traffic enforcement specialist.

~~$27~~ **$21.60    Now available in eBook format!**
1 volume, softbound, replaced biennially, Pub. #31121, ISBN 9781422494271

**Texas Law Enforcement Handbook: Contemporary Criminal Procedure**

*Larry E. Holtz, Warren J Spencer*
The most trusted and dependable commentary on Texas criminal procedure, vital for victory in the courtroom.

~~$44~~ **$35.20    Now available in eBook format!**
1 volume, softbound with CD-ROM, replaced biennially, Pub. #31105, ISBN 9781422485125

**Civil Process for Texas**

*John Steinsiek*
Used in the courtroom and the classroom, the author offers this incredibly concise and useful reference outlining laws, case law affecting application of law and practical tips.

~~$32~~ **$25.60    Now available in eBook format!**
1 volume, spiral bound, replaced annually, Pub. #36185, ISBN 9781422495667

*Find titles covering subjects like DUI, search and seizure, K-9 and more at www.lexisnexis.com/lawenforcement.*

**New in 2011!**
*We are pleased to offer LexisNexis® eBooks for Texas law enforcement. To learn more, call 800.223.1940 or visit www.lexisnexis.com/ebooks.*

## ORDER TODAY!

GO TO the LexisNexis® Store:
**www.lexisnexis.com/txbooks**

CALL toll-free **800.223.1940**
*(mention code JCM147459)*

 LexisNexis®

# FOREWORD

We are pleased to offer to the legal and law enforcement community the 2011–2012 edition of **Texas Criminal and Traffic Law Manual.** This compilation of selected laws is fully up to date through the 2011 Legislative Session. We have included a "Table of Amendments," covering 2011 legislation. This volume is intended to be used throughout 2011, 2012, and 2013, until publication of the 2013–2014 edition in September 2013.

We are indebted to the Texas Department of Public Safety, which provided us with direction and guidance in developing the contents of this volume.

We are committed to providing attorneys and other professionals with the most comprehensive, current, and useful publications available. We publish a number of publications covering various topics of Texas law as well as publications in neighboring jurisdictions. Please refer to the cross advertisements at the front of this edition and to our website www.lexisnexis.com/lawenforcement for a list of available titles.

We actively solicit your comments and suggestions. If you believe that there are statutes that should be included (or excluded), or if you have suggestions regarding any other improvements please write to: LexisNexis Custom Legal Publishing, 701 E. Water Street, Charlottesville, VA, 22902; call us toll-free at 1-800-833-9844; fax us toll-free at 1-800-643-1280; visit our website at http://www.lexisnexis.com; or Email us at lepublications@lexisnexis.com. By providing us with your informed comments, we can better provide you with a working tool that increases in value each year.

August 2011

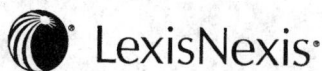

# TABLE OF CONTENTS

# TABLE OF AMENDMENTS

---

*Editor's Note. — Several sections listed below were affected by the 1st Called Session of the 82nd Legislature. At the time this book was printed, act chapter numbers had not been assigned. Therefore, act chapter numbers do not appear in this table for sections affected by the 1st C.S.

| Section | Effect | Chapter | Section | Effect | Chapter |
|---------|--------|---------|---------|--------|---------|
| 17.42 | Amended | 420 | 42.12 | Amended | 515 |
| 18.01 | Amended | 66 | 42.12 | Amended | 542 |
| 18.05 | Amended | 1163 | 42.12 | Amended | 671 |
| 18.07 | Amended | 772 | 42.12 | Amended | 694 |
| 18.20 | Amended | 85 | 42.12 | Amended | 957 |
| 18.21 | Amended | 316 | 42.12 | Amended | 961 |
| 18.21 | Amended | 620 | 42.12 | Amended | 984 |
| 20.011 | Amended | 1031 | 42.12 | Amended | 1119 |
| 20.011 | Amended | 1341 | 42.12 | Amended | 1280 |
| 20.02 | Amended | 1031 | 42.12 | Amended | 1322 |
| 20.02 | Amended | 1341 | 42.15 | Amended | 464 |
| 20.151 | New | 1031 | 42.24 | New | 491 |
| 20.151 | New | 1341 | 44.2811 | New | 731 |
| 20.22 | Amended | 278 | 45.0215 | Amended | 1322 |
| 26.04 | Amended | 671 | 45.0216 | Amended | 1322 |
| 26.04 | Amended | 984 | 45.0217 | New | 731 |
| 26.044 | Amended | 984 | 45.037 | Amended | 395 |
| 26.045 | New | 984 | 45.041 | Amended | 464 |
| 26.047 | New | 984 | 45.0492 | New | 227 |
| 26.05 | Amended | 984 | 45.0492 | New | 777 |
| 26.052 | Amended | 1343 | 45.051 | Amended | 227 |
| 27.18 | Amended | 1031 | 45.051 | Amended | 777 |
| 27.18 | Amended | 1341 | 45.051 | Amended | 914 |
| 27.19 | Amended | 665 | 45.0511 | Amended | 973 |
| 37.07 | Amended | 620 | 45.054 | Amended | 1098 |
| 38.07 | Amended | 1 | 45.055 | Amended | 1098 |
| 38.071 | Amended | 1 | 45.056 | Amended | 868 |
| 38.072 | Amended | 1 | 45.056 | Amended | 1055 |
| 38.073 | Amended | 1031 | 45.056 | Amended | 1098 |
| 38.073 | Amended | 1341 | 45.057 | Amended | 777 |
| 38.074 | New | 1227 | 45.061 | New | 1322 |
| 38.20 | New | 219 | 46.03 | Amended | 787 |
| 38.37 | Amended | 1 | 46B.004 | Amended | 822 |
| 38.43 | Amended | 91 | 46B.009 | Amended | 718 |
| 38.43 | Amended | 1248 | 46B.009 | Amended | 822 |
| 38.45 | Amended | 1322 | 46B.0095 | Amended | 718 |
| 38.46 | New | 104 | 46B.0095 | Amended | 822 |
| 38.46 | New | 591 | 46B.010 | Amended | 718 |
| 39.01 | Amended | 104 | 46B.010 | Amended | 822 |
| 39.026 | New | 104 | 46B.022 | Amended | 822 |
| 39.12 | Amended | 104 | 46B.024 | Amended | 822 |
| 39.15 | Amended | 1322 | 46B.025 | Amended | 822 |
| 42.01 | Amended | 91 | 46B.071 | Amended | 822 |
| 42.017 | Amended | 134 | 46B.072 | Amended | 822 |
| 42.0182 | New | 68 | 46B.073 | Amended | 822 |
| 42.0182 | New | 327 | 46B.0755 | New | 822 |
| 42.025 | New | 1280 | 46B.077 | Amended | 822 |
| 42.03 | Amended | 718 | 46B.079 | Amended | 822 |
| 42.03 | Amended | 822 | 46B.080 | Amended | 822 |
| 42.032 | Amended | 491 | 46B.084 | Amended | 822 |
| 42.0372 | New | 515 | 46B.086 | Amended | 822 |
| 42.12 | Amended | 1 | 46B.101 | Amended | 822 |
| 42.12 | Amended | 91 | 46B.151 | Amended | 822 |
| 42.12 | Amended | 134 | 46C.003 | New | 787 |
| 42.12 | Amended | 170 | 48.01 | Amended | 1053 |
| 42.12 | Amended | 327 | 49.13 | Repealed | 950 |
| 42.12 | Amended | 493 | 49.25 | Amended | 1341 |

xi TABLE OF AMENDMENTS

| Section | Effect | Chapter |
|---|---|---|
| 58.403 | Amended | 85 |
| 59.004 | Amended | 1322 |
| 61.002 | Amended | 1322 |
| 71.0021 | Amended | 872 |
| 82.002 | Amended | 110 |
| 82.002 | Amended | 632 |
| 82.002 | Amended | 872 |
| 82.009 | Amended | 632 |
| 83.006 | Amended | 632 |
| 83.007 | Repealed | 632 |
| 84.002 | Amended | 1163 |
| 84.006 | New | 59 |
| 85.001 | Amended | 627 |
| 85.021 | Amended | 136 |
| 85.022 | Amended | 136 |
| 85.025 | Amended | 627 |
| 85.026 | Amended | 632 |
| 85.042 | Amended | 327 |
| 85.065 | Amended | 632 |
| 87.002 | Amended | 627 |
| 160.512 | New | 1221 |
| 232.0135 | Amended | 508 |
| 232.014 | Amended | 508 |
| 261.001 | Amended | 1 |
| 261.3013 | New | 598 |
| 262.010 | New | 598 |
| 262.1015 | Amended | 598 |
| 262.1015 | Amended | 222 |
| 262.1095 | New | 490 |
| 262.2015 | Amended | 1 |

**Government Code**

| Section | Effect | Chapter |
|---|---|---|
| 411.0206 | Amended | 796 |
| 411.049 | New | 889 |
| 411.053 | Amended | 91 |
| 411.0625 | New | 205 |
| 411.0971 | New | 455 |
| 411.190 | Amended | 91 |
| 411.201 | Amended | *1st C.S. |
| 411.203 | Amended | 1058 |
| 411.351 | Amended | 737 |
| 411.421 | New | 1234 |
| 411.422 | New | 1234 |
| 420A.001 | New | 1201 |
| 420A.002 | New | 1201 |
| 420A.003 | New | 1201 |
| 420A.004 | New | 1201 |
| 420A.005 | New | 1201 |
| 420A.006 | New | 1201 |
| 420A.007 | New | 1201 |
| 420A.008 | New | 1201 |
| 420A.009 | New | 1201 |
| 420A.010 | New | 1201 |
| 420A.011 | New | 1201 |
| 508.181 | Amended | 1123 |
| 508.187 | Amended | 515 |
| 508.192 | New | 1025 |

| Section | Effect | Chapter |
|---|---|---|
| 508.251 | Amended | 546 |
| 508.281 | Amended | 1025 |

**Health and Safety Code**

| Section | Effect | Chapter |
|---|---|---|
| 365.012 | Amended | 430 |
| 365.035 | New | 1124 |
| 382.209 | Amended | 91 |
| 382.209 | Amended | 347 |
| 382.210 | Amended | 347 |
| 382.213 | Amended | 91 |
| 382.213 | Amended | 347 |
| 382.218 | Amended | 1163 |
| 431.202 | Amended | 973 |
| 431.206 | Amended | 973 |
| 431.244 | Amended | 1317 |
| 481.061 | Amended | 1228 |
| 481.061 | Amended | 1342 |
| 481.074 | Amended | 91 |
| 481.074 | Amended | 1228 |
| 481.074 | Amended | 1342 |
| 481.075 | Amended | 1228 |
| 481.075 | Amended | 1342 |
| 481.076 | Amended | 1228 |
| 481.076 | Amended | 1342 |
| 481.0761 | Amended | 1228 |
| 481.103 | Amended | 784 |
| 481.1031 | New | 170 |
| 481.111 | Amended | 170 |
| 481.113 | Amended | 170 |
| 481.1161 | New | 170 |
| 481.1285 | New | 1200 |
| 481.129 | Amended | 1200 |
| 481.134 | Amended | 170 |
| 486.001 | Amended | 742 |
| 486.014 | Amended | 742 |
| 486.0141 | New | 742 |
| 486.0142 | New | 742 |
| 486.0143 | New | 742 |
| 486.0144 | New | 742 |
| 486.0145 | New | 742 |
| 486.0146 | New | 742 |
| 486.015 | Amended | 742 |
| 784.001 | New | 651 |
| 784.002 | New | 651 |
| 784.003 | New | 651 |
| 784.004 | New | 651 |
| 841.002 | Amended | 1201 |
| 841.007 | Amended | 1201 |
| 841.021 | Amended | 1201 |
| 841.022 | Amended | 1201 |
| 841.023 | Amended | 1201 |
| 841.082 | Amended | 1201 |
| 841.083 | Amended | 1201 |
| 841.084 | Amended | 1201 |
| 841.101 | Amended | 1201 |
| 841.141 | Amended | 1201 |
| 841.142 | Amended | 1201 |

| Section | Effect | Chapter | Section | Effect | Chapter |
|---|---|---|---|---|---|
| 841.147 | Amended | 1201 | 2302.201 | Amended | 1136 |
| 841.150 | Amended | 1201 | 2302.204 | Amended | 1296 |
| 841.151 | New | 1201 | 2302.354 | New | 1296 |
| | | | 2303.1511 | Amended | 353 |
| **Local Government Code** | | | 2303.154 | Amended | 353 |
| 133.107 | Amended | 984 | 2303.160 | Amended | 353 |
| | | | 2305.007 | Amended | 117 |
| **Natural Resources Code** | | | 2308.002 | Amended | 353 |
| 151.052 | New | 23 | 2308.057 | Amended | 353 |
| | | | 2308.159 | Amended | 353 |
| **Occupations Code** | | | 2308.204 | Repealed | 353 |
| 1701.306 | Amended | 1224 | 2308.206 | Repealed | 353 |
| 1701.310 | Amended | 1224 | 2308.2065 | New | 353 |
| 1701.312 | Amended | 855 | 2308.209 | Amended | 1163 |
| 1701.313 | Amended | 855 | 2308.255 | Amended | 353 |
| 1701.351 | Amended | 602 | 2308.2555 | Amended | 91 |
| 1701.352 | Amended | 855 | 2308.2555 | Amended | 353 |
| 1701.353 | Amended | 1224 | 2308.256 | Amended | 91 |
| 1701.358 | New | 1224 | 2308.256 | Repealed | 353 |
| 1701.402 | Amended | 91 | 2308.2565 | New | 353 |
| 1701.402 | Amended | 855 | 2308.301 | Amended | 353 |
| 1701.405 | Amended | 855 | 2308.302 | Amended | 353 |
| 1701.452 | Amended | 399 | 2308.401 | Amended | 353 |
| 1701.4525 | Amended | 399 | 2308.402 | Amended | 353 |
| 1701.454 | Amended | 399 | 2308.404 | Amended | 353 |
| 1701.455 | Amended | 399 | 2308.451 | Amended | 91 |
| 1701.553 | Amended | 855 | 2308.453 | Amended | 91 |
| 1956.001 | Amended | 1234 | 2308.454 | Amended | 91 |
| 1956.003 | Amended | 1234 | 2308.455 | Amended | 91 |
| 1956.004 | New | 1234 | 2308.456 | Amended | 91 |
| 1956.015 | Amended | 1234 | 2308.458 | Amended | 353 |
| 1956.016 | New | 1234 | 2308.504 | Amended | 353 |
| 1956.017 | New | 1234 | 2308.505 | Amended | 353 |
| 1956.032 | Amended | 1234 | | | |
| 1956.033 | Amended | 1234 | **Penal Code** | | |
| 1956.0331 | New | 1234 | 1.07 | Amended | 839 |
| 1956.034 | Amended | 1234 | 3.03 | Amended | 1 |
| 1956.035 | Amended | 1234 | 12.35 | Amended | 122 |
| 1956.036 | Amended | 1234 | 12.42 | Amended | 1 |
| 1956.037 | Amended | 1234 | 12.42 | Amended | 122 |
| 1956.038 | Amended | 1234 | 12.42 | Amended | 834 |
| 1956.040 | Amended | 1234 | 12.42 | Amended | 1119 |
| 1956.051 | Amended | 1298 | 12.425 | New | 834 |
| 1956.0511 | New | 1298 | 15.031 | Amended | 1 |
| 1956.060 | Amended | 1298 | 16.01 | Amended | 814 |
| 1956.0611 | New | 1298 | 16.02 | Amended | 85 |
| 1956.0612 | New | 1298 | 19.03 | Amended | 1209 |
| 1956.0613 | New | 1298 | 20.05 | Amended | 223 |
| 1956.0614 | New | 1298 | 20A.01 | Amended | 1 |
| 1956.0615 | New | 1298 | 20A.02 | Amended | 1 |
| 1956.063 | Amended | 1298 | 20A.03 | New | 122 |
| 1956.064 | Amended | 1298 | 21.02 | Amended | 1 |
| 1956.067 | Amended | 1298 | 21.12 | Amended | 761 |
| 1956.069 | Amended | 1298 | 22.021 | Amended | 1 |
| 1956.103 | Amended | 1234 | 22.04 | Amended | 620 |
| 1956.151 | Amended | 1234 | 25.01 | Amended | 222 |
| 1956.202 | Amended | 1234 | 25.03 | Amended | 840 |
| 2002.054 | Amended | 124 | | | |

# TABLE OF AMENDMENTS

| Section | Effect | Chapter | Section | Effect | Chapter |
|---------|--------|---------|---------|--------|---------|
| 501.111 | Amended | 1296 | 502.008 | Repealed | 1296 |
| 501.113 | Amended | 1296 | 502.010 | Amended | 1296 |
| 501.114 | Amended | 1296 | 502.0021 | Amended | 1296 |
| 501.115 | Amended | 117 | 502.0023 | Amended | 1296 |
| 501.115 | Amended | 1296 | 502.040 | Amended | 1296 |
| 501.116 | Amended | 1296 | 502.041 | Amended | 1296 |
| 501.117 | Amended | 813 | 502.042 | Amended | 1296 |
| 501.134 | Amended | 1296 | 502.043 | Amended | 1296 |
| 501.135 | Amended | 1296 | 502.044 | Amended | 1296 |
| 501.138 | Amended | 1296 | 502.045 | Amended | 1296 |
| 501.145 | Amended | 1296 | 502.046 | Amended | 1296 |
| 501.146 | Amended | 1296 | 502.047 | Amended | 1296 |
| 501.147 | Amended | 1296 | 502.048 | Amended | 1296 |
| 501.148 | Amended | 1296 | 502.055 | Amended | 1296 |
| 501.152 | Amended | 1296 | 502.057 | Amended | 1296 |
| 501.153 | Amended | 1296 | 502.058 | Amended | 1296 |
| 501.154 | Amended | 1296 | 502.059 | Amended | 1296 |
| 501.155 | Amended | 1296 | 502.060 | Amended | 1296 |
| 501.158 | Amended | 1296 | 502.0074 | Repealed | 1296 |
| 501.161 | Amended | 1296 | 502.0075 | Repealed | 1296 |
| 501.162 | New | 1296 | 502.090 | Amended | 1296 |
| 501.163 | New | 1296 | 502.091 | Amended | 1296 |
| 501.171 | New | 1290 | 502.092 | Amended | 1296 |
| 501.171 | Amended | 1296 | 502.093 | Amended | 1296 |
| 501.172 | New | 1290 | 502.094 | Amended | 1296 |
| 501.172 | Amended | 1296 | 502.095 | Amended | 1296 |
| 501.173 | New | 1290 | 502.104 | Repealed | 1296 |
| 501.173 | Amended | 1296 | 502.105 | Repealed | 1296 |
| 501.174 | New | 1290 | 502.140 | Amended | 1296 |
| 501.174 | Amended | 1296 | 502.142 | Amended | 1296 |
| 501.175 | New | 1290 | 502.143 | Amended | 1296 |
| 501.175 | Amended | 1296 | 502.144 | Amended | 1296 |
| 501.176 | New | 1290 | 502.145 | Amended | 1296 |
| 501.176 | New | 1296 | 502.146 | Amended | 1296 |
| 501.177 | New | 1290 | 502.151 | Amended | 1290 |
| 501.177 | Amended | 1296 | 502.154 | Repealed | 1296 |
| 501.178 | New | 1290 | 502.163 | Amended | 1035 |
| 501.178 | Amended | 1296 | 502.167 | Amended | 700 |
| 501.179 | New | 1290 | 502.175 | Repealed | 1296 |
| 501.179 | Amended | 1296 | 502.177 | Repealed | 1296 |
| 501.0234 | Amended | 1296 | 502.185 | Amended | 1094 |
| 501.0235 | New | 1296 | 502.189 | Amended | 554 |
| 501.0275 | Amended | 1296 | 502.190 | Amended | 1296 |
| 501.0276 | Amended | 1296 | 502.191 | Amended | 1296 |
| 501.0331 | Amended | 1296 | 502.192 | New | 1296 |
| 501.0332 | Amended | 1296 | 502.193 | Amended | 1296 |
| 501.0721 | Amended | 1296 | 502.194 | Amended | 1296 |
| 501.0925 | New | 1136 | 502.195 | Amended | 1296 |
| 501.0935 | New | 1136 | 502.196 | Amended | 1296 |
| 501.1001 | Amended | 1296 | 502.197 | Amended | 1296 |
| 501.1002 | Amended | 1296 | 502.198 | Amended | 1296 |
| 501.1003 | Amended | 1296 | 502.206 | Repealed | 1296 |
| 501.09111 | Amended | 1296 | 502.00211 | Amended | 1296 |
| 501.09112 | Amended | 1296 | 502.251 | Amended | 1296 |
| 501.09113 | Amended | 1296 | 502.252 | Amended | 1296 |
| 502.001 | Amended | 1296 | 502.253 | Amended | 1296 |
| 502.002 | Amended | 1290 | 502.254 | Amended | 1296 |

# TABLE OF AMENDMENTS

| Section | Effect | Chapter | Section | Effect | Chapter |
|---------|--------|---------|---------|--------|---------|
| 504.516 | New | 1296 | 521.007 | New | *1st C.S. |
| 504.614 | Amended | 1296 | 521.025 | Amended | 195 |
| 504.615 | Amended | 1296 | 521.041 | Amended | *1st C.S. |
| 504.616 | Amended | 1296 | 521.042 | Amended | 689 |
| 504.624 | Repealed | 1296 | 521.054 | Amended | 91 |
| 504.629 | Repealed | 1296 | 521.061 | Amended | 91 |
| 504.634 | Repealed | 1296 | 521.062 | Amended | 91 |
| 504.642 | Amended | 1296 | 521.063 | New | 468 |
| 504.643 | Repealed | 1296 | 521.101 | Amended | *1st C.S. |
| 504.647 | Amended | 1296 | 521.103 | Amended | *1st C.S. |
| 504.649 | Repealed | 1296 | 521.121 | Amended | *1st C.S. |
| 504.650 | Repealed | 1296 | 521.121 | Amended | 91 |
| 504.653 | Repealed | 1296 | 521.142 | Amended | *1st C.S. |
| 504.655 | Repealed | 1296 | 521.142 | Amended | 91 |
| 504.659 | Amended | 91 | 521.142 | Amended | 273 |
| 504.659 | Amended | 1296 | 521.147 | Amended | 167 |
| 504.662 | New | 63 | 521.148 | Amended | 554 |
| 504.701 | Repealed | 1296 | 521.204 | Amended | 1160 |
| 504.702 | Amended | 1296 | 521.223 | Amended | 1121 |
| 504.801 | Amended | 1296 | 521.248 | Amended | 426 |
| 504.802 | Amended | 1296 | 521.271 | Amended | *1st C.S. |
| 504.851 | Amended | 1296 | 521.271 | Amended | 1160 |
| 504.851 | Amended | 1296 | 521.272 | Amended | *1st C.S. |
| 504.853 | Amended | 1296 | 521.295 | Amended | 1160 |
| 504.854 | Amended | 1296 | 521.296 | Amended | 1160 |
| 504.855 | New | 1296 | 521.401 | Amended | 554 |
| 504.901 | New | 1296 | 521.402 | Amended | 554 |
| 504.941 | New | 1296 | 521.421 | Amended | *1st C.S. |
| 504.942 | New | 1296 | 521.421 | Amended | 554 |
| 504.943 | New | 1296 | 521.422 | Amended | 554 |
| 504.944 | Amended | 1296 | 521.426 | Amended | 1133 |
| 504.945 | New | 1296 | 521.1211 | New | 441 |
| 504.3011 | Amended | 1296 | 521.1235 | New | 273 |
| 504.4061 | Amended | 1296 | 521.1425 | Amended | *1st C.S. |
| 504.6011 | Amended | 1296 | 521.1811 | New | 598 |
| 520-B-sc | Amended | 1296 | 521.2461 | New | 426 |
| 520-C-sc | Repealed | 1296 | 521.2462 | New | 426 |
| 520-D-sc | Repealed | 1296 | 521.2711 | Amended | *1st C.S. |
| 520.003 | New | 1290 | 521A-c | New | 123 |
| 520.003 | New | 1296 | 521A.001 | New | 123 |
| 520.004 | New | 1290 | 522.005 | Amended | *1st C.S. |
| 520.004 | New | 1296 | 522.030 | Amended | *1st C.S. |
| 520.005 | Amended | 1290 | 522.033 | Amended | *1st C.S. |
| 520.005 | Amended | 1296 | 522.034 | Amended | 554 |
| 520.006 | Amended | 1290 | 522.052 | Amended | *1st C.S. |
| 520.006 | Amended | 1296 | 542.0081 | New | 812 |
| 520.007 | Amended | 1296 | 542.402 | Amended | 1286 |
| 520.008 | Amended | 1296 | 544.002 | Amended | 216 |
| 520.009 | Amended | 1296 | 544.007 | Amended | 485 |
| 520.0091 | Amended | 1296 | 544.013 | New | 1345 |
| 520.0092 | Amended | 1296 | 545.157 | Amended | 229 |
| 520.0093 | Amended | 1296 | 545.301 | Amended | 229 |
| 520.013 | Repealed | 1296 | 545.352 | Amended | 265 |
| 520.015 | New | 1296 | 545.353 | Amended | 259 |
| 520.016 | Amended | 1296 | 545.353 | Amended | 265 |
| 520.034 | Repealed | 1296 | 545.354 | Amended | 265 |
| 520.051 | Amended | 1296 | 545.355 | Amended | 265 |

| Section | Effect | Chapter | Section | Effect | Chapter |
|---------|--------|---------|---------|--------|---------|
| 545.356 | Amended | 265 | 623.002 | New | 1345 |
| 545.356 | Amended | 1016 | 623.003 | New | 1345 |
| 545.358 | Amended | 265 | 623.011 | Amended | 700 |
| 545.362 | Amended | 265 | 623.012 | Amended | 1345 |
| 545.424 | Amended | 1160 | 623.016 | Amended | 1345 |
| 545.425 | Amended | 774 | 623.051 | Amended | 1345 |
| 545.3531 | Repealed | 259 | 623.052 | Amended | 1345 |
| 545.3561 | New | 216 | 623.071 | Amended | 941 |
| 545.4145 | New | 1172 | 623.075 | Amended | 1345 |
| 546.007 | New | 490 | 623.076 | Amended | 1345 |
| 547.304 | Amended | 1345 | 623.078 | Amended | 1345 |
| 547.305 | Amended | 229 | 623.080 | Amended | 1345 |
| 547.606 | Amended | 752 | 623.093 | Amended | 1345 |
| 547.616 | New | 739 | 623.096 | Amended | 1345 |
| 547.701 | Amended | 451 | 623.099 | Amended | 1345 |
| 548.052 | Amended | 91 | 623.100 | Amended | 1345 |
| 548.052 | Amended | 729 | 623.0112 | Amended | 1345 |
| 548.052 | Amended | 1296 | 623.126 | Amended | 1345 |
| 548.258 | Amended | 973 | 623.142 | Amended | 1345 |
| 548.506 | Amended | 1202 | 623.145 | Amended | 1345 |
| 548.507 | Amended | 1202 | 623.146 | Amended | 1345 |
| 548.508 | Amended | 91 | 623.163 | Amended | 1345 |
| 548.3065 | Amended | 1202 | 623.0181 | New | 941 |
| 548.4045 | New | 1202 | 623.192 | Amended | 1345 |
| 548.6015 | New | 1202 | 623.195 | Amended | 1345 |
| 548.6035 | New | 1202 | 623.196 | Amended | 1345 |
| 548.6036 | New | 1202 | 623.210 | Amended | 967 |
| 550.025 | Amended | 680 | 623.211 | Amended | 967 |
| 550.064 | Amended | 689 | 623.212 | Amended | 967 |
| 551-F-sc | Amended | 1296 | 623.212 | Amended | 1345 |
| 551.301 | Amended | 91 | 623.215 | Amended | 1345 |
| 551.351 | Amended | 91 | 623.219 | Amended | 967 |
| 551.353 | Amended | 91 | 623.230 | Amended | 613 |
| 551.401 | Amended | 1296 | 623.232 | Amended | 613 |
| 551.404 | Amended | 1296 | 623.233 | Amended | 1345 |
| 553.002 | Amended | 216 | 623.234 | Amended | 613 |
| 601.052 | Amended | 91 | 623.235 | Amended | 613 |
| 621.001 | Amended | 1345 | 623.235 | Amended | 1345 |
| 621.003 | Amended | 1345 | 623.253 | Amended | 1345 |
| 621.004 | Amended | 1345 | 623.304 | Amended | 1345 |
| 621.006 | Amended | 1345 | 623.0711 | New | 941 |
| 621.008 | New | 1345 | 643.253 | Amended | 274 |
| 621.102 | Amended | 571 | 644.101 | Amended | 249 |
| 621.102 | Amended | 1345 | 644.101 | Amended | 1163 |
| 621.202 | Amended | 1345 | 644.202 | Amended | 1163 |
| 621.301 | Amended | 1345 | 681.003 | Amended | 91 |
| 621.352 | Amended | 1345 | 681.003 | Amended | 1291 |
| 621.353 | Amended | 700 | 681.005 | Amended | 1296 |
| 621.356 | Amended | 1345 | 681.008 | Amended | 91 |
| 621.504 | Amended | 1345 | 681.008 | Amended | 339 |
| 621.4015 | Amended | 1163 | 681.008 | Amended | 709 |
| 622.001 | Amended | 1345 | 681.012 | Amended | 1296 |
| 622.002 | New | 1345 | 681.0111 | Amended | 756 |
| 622.013 | Amended | 1345 | 683.001 | Amended | 720 |
| 622.134 | Amended | 1345 | 683.011 | Amended | 720 |
| 622.955 | New | 390 | 683.012 | Amended | 720 |
| 623.001 | Amended | 1345 | 683.013 | Amended | 720 |

# TABLE OF AMENDMENTS

| Section | Effect | Chapter | Section | Effect | Chapter |
|---------|--------|---------|---------|--------|---------|
| 683.014 | Amended | 720 | 707.017 | Amended | 91 |
| 683.015 | Amended | 720 | 708.106 | New | 551 |
| 683.015 | Amended | 1181 | 708.157 | Amended | 711 |
| 683.016 | Amended | 1163 | 708.159 | New | 711 |
| 683.071 | Amended | 720 | 724.015 | Amended | 674 |
| 683.071 | Amended | 753 | 728.002 | Amended | 553 |
| 683.074 | Amended | 720 | 730.005 | Amended | 869 |
| 683.076 | Amended | 720 | 730.007 | Amended | 869 |
| 702.002 | Repealed | 871 | **Water Code** | | |
| 702.003 | Amended | 1094 | 26.3574 | Amended | 1021 |
| 706.005 | Amended | 1171 | | | |

# HIGHLIGHTS OF THE
# 2011 TEXAS LEGISLATIVE SESSION

## ALCOHOLIC BEVERAGES

### Minors

There is no penalty for consumption or possession of alcohol by a minor if the minor was the first person to request emergency medical assistance in response to the possible alcohol overdose of the minor or another person, and remained on the scene until the medical assistance arrived, and cooperated with medical assistance and law enforcement personnel. [*Alcoholic Beverage Code* §§ 106.04, 106.05]

## ANIMALS

### Cockfighting

A person commits an offense if the person knowingly:

- causes a cock to fight with another cock;
- participates in the earnings of a cockfight;
- uses or permits another to use any real estate, building, room, tent, arena, or other property for cockfighting;
- owns or trains a cock with the intent that the cock be used in an exhibition of cockfighting;
- manufactures, buys, sells, barters, exchanges, possesses, advertises, or otherwise offers a gaff, slasher, or other sharp implement designed for attachment to a cock with the intent that the implement be used in cockfighting; or
- attends as a spectator an exhibition of cockfighting.

The first two offenses are state jail felonies; the third, fourth and fifth are Class A misdemeanors; the sixth is a Class C misdemeanor (or a Class A misdemeanor if a second or subsequent conviction). [*Penal Code* § 42.105]

## ASSAULT

### Intoxication Assault

Intoxication assault is a felony of the second degree if it is shown on the trial of the offense that the person caused serious bodily injury to another in the nature of a traumatic brain injury that results in a persistent vegetative state. [*Penal Code* § 49.09]

## BURGLARY

### Locksmith Tools

"Mechanical security device" means a device designed or manufactured for use by a locksmith to perform services for a customer who seeks entry to a structure, motor vehicle, or other property. It is unlawful to possess a mechanical security device with the intent to use the device in the commission of an offense. It is also unlawful, with knowledge of its character and with the intent to use a mechanical security device or aid or permit another to use the device in the commission of an offense, to manufacture, adapt, sell, install, or set up the device. [*Penal Code* § 16.01]

## COMPUTER CRIME

### Online Impersonation

Online impersonation includes using the name or persona of another to create a commercial social networking site or other Internet website without obtaining the other person's consent and with the intent to harm, defraud, intimidate, or threaten any person. [*Penal Code* § 33.07]

### Unlawful Access

Penalties are increased for accessing a computer without consent if previously convicted of two or more computer crimes, or if the computer accessed is owned by the government or a critical infrastructure facility. [*Penal Code* § 33.02]

## CRIMES AGAINST CHILDREN

### Custodial Interference

A person commits an offense if the person takes or retains a child under 18 outside of the U.S. with the intent to deprive a person entitled to possession of or access to the child of that possession or access and without the permission of that person. [*Penal Code* § 25.03]

### Employment Harmful to Children

Employment harmful to children is now a state jail felony if a second conviction, or a felony of the third degree if a third or subsequent conviction. The offense is a felony of the first degree if the child is younger than 14 at the time of the offense. [*Penal Code* § 43.251]

## Jurisdiction

An offense under Penal Code Title 5 (offenses against the person) involving a victim younger than 18, or an offense under Penal Code § 25.03 (custodial interference) that results in bodily injury to a child younger than 18, may be prosecuted in the county in which:

- an element of the offense was committed,
- the defendant is apprehended,
- the victim resides, or
- the defendant resides.

[*Code of Criminal Procedure* Art. 13.075]

## Restitution

The court shall order a defendant convicted of trafficking of persons or compelling prostitution to pay restitution in an amount equal to the cost of necessary rehabilitation, including medical, psychiatric, and psychological care and treatment, for any victim of the offense who is under 18. [*Code of Criminal Procedure* Art. 42.0372]

## Sale or Purchase of Child

Sale or purchase of a child is now felony of the second degree if the defendant commits the offense with intent to commit an offense under Penal Code § 20A.02, 43.02 or 43.05. [*Penal Code* § 25.08]

## CRIMINAL PROCEDURE

### Arrest Warrants

A sheriff may, but is no longer required, to report to the National Crime Information Center each warrant or capias issued for a defendant charged with a misdemeanor who fails to appear in court when summoned. [*Code of Criminal Procedure* Art. 2.195]

To obtain an arrest warrant, a person may appear before the magistrate in person or the person's image may be presented to the magistrate through an electronic broadcast system. In the latter case, a recording of the communication must be made. If the defendant is charged with the offense, the recording must be preserved until the defendant is acquitted of the offense, or all appeals relating to the offense have been exhausted. [*Code of Criminal Procedure* Art. 15.03]

### Contact with Victim

If a defendant's sentence includes a term of confinement or imprisonment, the convicting court may, as part of the sentence, prohibit the defendant from contacting, during the term of the defendant's confinement or imprisonment, the victim of the offense of which the defendant is convicted or a member of the victim's family. [*Code of Criminal Procedure* Art. 42.24]

### Fines

When imposing a fine and costs in a misdemeanor case, if the court determines that the defendant is unable to immediately pay the fine and costs, the court shall allow the defendant to pay the fine and costs in specified portions at designated intervals. [*Code of Criminal Procedure* Art. 42.15]

When imposing a fine and costs, if the justice or judge determines that the defendant is unable to immediately pay the fine and costs, the justice or judge shall allow the defendant to pay the fine and costs in specified portions at designated intervals. [*Code of Criminal Procedure* Art. 45.041]

### Search Warrants

If a warrant is issued to search for and seize data or information contained in or on a computer, disk drive, flash drive, cell phone, or other electronic, communication, or data storage device, the warrant is considered to have been executed within 3 days if the device was seized before the expiration of the time allowed. Any data or information contained in or on a device seized may be recovered and analyzed after the expiration of the 3-day limitation on the warrant. [*Code of Criminal Procedure* Art. 18.07]

### Suspect Identification

Each law enforcement agency must adopt, implement, and as necessary amend a detailed written policy regarding the administration of photograph and live lineup identification procedures. The agency may use the model policy under this section, or its own policy that, at a minimum, conforms to the requirements of this section. [*Code of Criminal Procedure* Art. 38.20]

## DISORDERLY CONDUCT

### Defined

Several forms of disorderly conduct (including making unreasonable noise and fighting) are not criminal offenses when committed by a student in the sixth grade or a lower grade level on a public school campus during school hours. [*Penal Code* § 42.01]

### Funerals

It is unlawful to picket within 1,000 feet of a funeral during the period beginning three hours before the service begins and ending three hours after the service is completed. [*Penal Code* § 42.055]

## DOMESTIC VIOLENCE

### Protective Orders

In a hearing on an application for a protective order, a statement made by a child 12 or younger that describes alleged family violence against the child is admissible as evidence in the same manner that a child's statement regarding alleged abuse against the child is admissible under § 104.006 in a suit affecting the parent-child relationship. [*Family Code* § 84.006]

A protective order may prohibit a person from removing a pet, companion animal or assistance animal from the possession of a person named in the order. An order also may prohibit a person from harming, threatening or interfering with the care, custody or control of a pet, companion animal or assistance animal a person protected by the order or a member of that person's family or household. [*Family Code* §§ 85.021, 85.022]

A court may render a protective order effective for a period that exceeds 2 years if it finds that the subject of the order:

- caused serious bodily injury,
- has been subject to two or more previous orders.

[*Family Code* § 85.025]

A person subject to a protective order commits an offense by harming, threatening or interfering with the care, custody or control of a pet, companion animal or assistance animal possessed by a person protected by the order. [*Penal Code* § 25.07]

## DRUGS

### Classification

Penalty Group 2 now includes any compound structurally derived from 2-aminopropanal by substitution at the 1-position with any monocyclic or fused-polycyclic ring system, e.g. Mephedrone, Flephedrone, Methylone, MDPV, alpha-PVP or Butylone. [*Health & Safety Code* § 481.103]

### Synthetic Cannabinoids ("Spice")

A new Penalty Group, 2-A, is created for synthetic cannabinoids. [*Health & Safety Code* § 481.1031]

Knowing possession of synthetic cannabinoids is a Class B misdemeanor if the amount possessed is 2 ounces or less, a Class A misdemeanor if more than 2 ounces but less than 4 ounces, a state jail felony if more than 4 ounces but 5 pounds or less, a felony of the third degree if more than 5 pounds but 50 pounds or less, a felony of the second degree if more than 50 pounds but 2,000 pounds or less, or life or 5-99 years imprisonment and a $50,000 fine if more than 2,000 pounds. [*Health & Safety Code* § 481.1161]

## FIREARMS

### Watercraft

It is unlawful to carry a handgun in a watercraft if:

- the handgun is in plain view;
- the person is engaged in criminal activity (other than a boating offense);
- the person is prohibited from owning a firearm; or
- the person is a member of a criminal street gang.

[*Penal Code* § 46.02]

## FRAUD

### False Statement Regarding Child Custody Determination

It is a felony of the third degree to knowingly make a false statement relating to a child custody determination made in a foreign country during a hearing held under Chapter 152 or Subchapter I, Chapter 153, Family Code. [*Penal Code* § 37.14]

### Fictitious Military Record

A person commits an offense by using or claiming to hold a military record that the person knows is fraudulent, is fictitious or has otherwise not been granted or assigned to the person, or has been revoked, in an advertisement or with intent to obtain a benefit. Violation is a Class C misdemeanor. [*Penal Code* § 32.54]

### Paternity Tests

It is a felony of the third degree to alter, destroy, conceal, fabricate, or falsify genetic evidence in a proceeding to adjudicate parentage, including inducing another person to provide a specimen with the intent to affect the outcome of the proceeding. [*Family Code* § 160.512]

## HOMICIDE

### Capital Murder

Murder of a child under 10 (not 6) is now capital murder. [*Penal Code* § 19.03]

### Deferred Judgment

A judge may grant deferred judgment in a murder case if the defendant did not cause the death of the deceased, did not intend to kill the deceased or another, and did not anticipate that a human life would be taken. [*Code of Criminal Procedure* Art. 42.12]

## HUMAN TRAFFICKING

### Continuous Human Trafficking

A person commits an offense if, during a period that is 30 or more days in duration, the person engages two or more times in conduct that constitutes an offense under § 20A.02. The offense is a felony of the first degree punishable by 25 – 99 years imprisonment. [*Penal Code* § 20A.03]

### Defined

A person commits an offense by trafficking another person and, through force, fraud or coercion, causing the trafficked person to engage in a prostitution-related offense, or by receiving a benefit from the same.

It is also an offense to traffic a child with the intent that the trafficked child engage in forced labor or services, or to traffic a child and cause the child to engage in, or be the victim of, a sexual offense, or to benefit from the same. [*Penal Code* § 20A.02]

### Protective Order

A victim of a trafficking offense (or a parent or guardian of a victim of a victim under 18 or a prosecuting attorney) may apply for a protective order without regard to the relationship between the applicant and the alleged offender. [*Code of Criminal Procedure* Art. 7B.01]

### Smuggling of Persons

A person commits the offense of smuggling of persons by intentionally using a motor vehicle, aircraft, or watercraft to transport an individual with the intent to:

• conceal the individual from a peace officer or special investigator; or

• flee from a person the actor knows is a peace officer or special investigator attempting to lawfully arrest or detain the actor.

The offense is a state jail felony, or a felony of the third degree if done for pecuniary benefit or in a manner that creates a substantial likelihood that the transported individual will suffer serious bodily injury or death. It is an affirmative defense to prosecution under this section that the actor is related to the transported individual within the second degree of consanguinity or, at the time of the offense, within the second degree of affinity. [*Penal Code* § 20.05]

## LITTER

### Discarding Lighted Materials

It is a misdemeanor to discard lighted litter, including a match, cigarette, or cigar, onto open-space land, a private road or the right-of-way of a private road, a public highway or other public road or the right-of-way of a public highway or other public road, or a railroad right-of-way, when a fire ignites as a result. [*Health & Safety Code* § 365.012]

### Riverbeds

It is a Class C misdemeanor to knowingly possesses a glass container within the boundaries of a state-owned riverbed in a county that is located within 85 miles of an international border, and in which at least four rivers are located. It is a defense that the person:

• did not transport the glass container into the boundaries of the riverbed,

• possessed the glass container only for the purpose of lawfully disposing of the glass container in a designated waste receptacle, or

• was the owner of property adjacent to the section of the riverbed where the person possessed the glass container.

[*Health & Safety Code* § 365.035]

## MISSING PERSONS

### AMBER Alerts

The existing AMBER alert system is expanded to include a public alert mechanism for an adult with a diagnosed intellectual developmental disability who goes missing. [*Government Code* § 411.352, et seq.]

## OBSTRUCTION OF JUSTICE

### Escape

It is a crime to escape from custody when lawfully detained for an offense. [*Penal Code* § 38.06]

### Evading Arrest

Evading arrest is now a felony of the third degree if the defendant uses a tire deflation device against the officer while the actor is in flight (or a felony of the second degree if another suffers serious bodily injury as a result of the use of the device), or a state jail felony if the defendant uses a watercraft. [*Penal Code* § 38.04]

### Tampering with a Witness

Tampering with a witness is a felony of the third degree, except that if the official proceeding is part of the prosecution of a criminal case, an offense under this section is the same category of offense as the most serious offense charged in that criminal case. However, if the most serious offense charged is a capital felony, an offense under this section is a felony of the first degree. If conduct that constitutes an offense under this section also constitutes an offense under any other law, the defendant may be prosecuted under this section, the other law, or both. [*Penal Code* § 36.05]

## RULES OF THE ROAD

### Accidents

A driver approaching a stationary tow truck displaying flashing lights must move to a nonadjacent lane, if available, and slow to a speed at least 20 mph less than the posted speed limit. [*Transportation Code* § 545.157]

The governing body of a municipality by ordinance may give a designated official with transportation engineering experience establishing speed limits discretion to temporarily lower a prima facie speed limit for a highway or part of a highway in the municipality, including a highway of the state highway system, at the site of an investigation using vehicular accident reconstruction. [*Transportation Code* § 545.3561]

The driver of a vehicle involved in an accident resulting in damage only to a structure adjacent to a highway must:

- take reasonable steps to locate and notify the owner or person in charge of the property of the accident and of driver's name and address and the registration number of the vehicle;
- if requested and available, show his or her driver's license to the owner or person in charge of the property; and
- report the accident if required by Transportation Code § 550.061.

[*Transportation Code* § 550.025]

### Disabled Parking Placards

It is unlawful to alter a genuine disabled parking placard, or to knowingly park a vehicle displaying an altered placard in a parking space or area designated specifically for persons with disabilities. [*Transportation Code* § 681.0111]

### Driver's License

Failure to carry and exhibit a driver's license is now a Class A misdemeanor if operating a vehicle without insurance and cause or at fault in an accident resulting in serious bodily injury or death to another. [*Transportation Code* § 521.025]

A hardship license must be suspended if the holder commits two or more moving violations within a 12-month period. [*Transportation Code* § 521.223]

### DWI

DWI with an alcohol concentration level of 0.15 or more is now a Class A misdemeanor. [*Penal Code* § 49.04]

Before requesting a person to submit to the taking of a specimen, the officer shall inform the person orally and in writing that if the person refuses to submit to the taking of a specimen, the officer may apply for a warrant authorizing a specimen to be taken from the person. [*Transportation Code* § 724.015]

### Emissions Inspection

A person commits an offense if, in connection with a required emissions inspection of a motor vehicle, the person knowingly:

- places or causes to be placed on a motor vehicle an inspection certificate if the vehicle does not meet the emissions requirements established by DPS or the person has not inspected the vehicle;
- manipulates an emissions test result; or
- uses or causes to be used emissions data from another motor vehicle as a substitute for the motor vehicle being inspected;

The offense is a Class B misdemeanor, first offense, or a Class A misdemeanor, second or subsequent offense, or a state jail felony if done with intent to defraud or harm another.

It is a Class C misdemeanor, in connection with a required emissions inspection of a motor vehicle, to knowingly bypass or circumvent a fuel cap test. [*Transportation Code* § 548.6035]

### Licenses

A peace officer may be issued a driver's license that omits the officer's actual residence address and includes, as an alternative, an address that is in the same municipality or county as the residence. [*Transportation Code* § 521.1211]

### Radar Interference Devices

A person, other than a law enforcement officer in the discharge of official duties, may not use, attempt to use, install, operate, or attempt to operate a radar interference device in a motor vehicle operated by the person. It is also unlawful to purchase, sell, or offer for sale a radar interference device to be used in a manner described above. Violation of this section is a Class C misdemeanor. [*Transportation Code* § 547.616]

### Towing

It is unlawful to operate a motor vehicle on a highway or street when a child younger than 18 occupies a boat or personal watercraft being drawn by the vehicle. This section does not apply to a vehicle in a parade, or being driven on a beach. [*Transportation Code* § 545.4145]

### Traffic Signals

An operator of a vehicle facing a traffic-control signal, other than a freeway entrance ramp control signal or a pedestrian hybrid beacon, that does not display an indication in any of the signal heads shall stop as provided by Transportation Code § 544.010 as if the intersection had a stop sign. [*Transportation Code* § 544.007]

## SEXUAL OFFENSES

### Prostitution

A first offender prostitution prevention program is created. [*Health & Safety Code* § 169.100, et seq.]

Prostitution is a felony of the third degree if the person solicited is at least 14 but less than 18, or a felony of the second degree if the person solicited is under 14. [*Penal Code* § 43.02]

### Sexual Assault

A court may issue a protective order to a victim of sexual assault of any age, regardless of whether or not there is the threat of further harm by the alleged offender. [*Code of Criminal Procedure* Art. 7A.03]

A second or subsequent conviction for aggravated sexual assault (or a conviction for aggravated sexual assault following a conviction for aggravated assault) is now punishable by life imprisonment without parole. [*Penal Code* § 12.42]

### Sex Offenders

A defendant convicted of Indecency with a Child or Sexual Assault need not register as a sex offender if the victim or intended victim was at least 15, the defendant was not more than 4 years older than the victim or intended victim, and the defendant is not a threat public safety. [*Code of Criminal Procedure* Art. 42.12]

### "Sexting"

It is a defense to possession of child pornography that the material falls under § 43.261. [*Penal Code* § 43.26]

A minor commits an offense by knowingly or intentionally promoting visual material depicting a minor (including the actor) engaging in sexual conduct by electronic means if the actor produced the visual material or knows that another minor produced the visual material. The offense is a Class C misdemeanor; or a Class B misdemeanor if a second offense or promoted the visual material with intent to harass, annoy, alarm, abuse, torment, embarrass, or offend another; or a Class A misdemeanor third or subsequent conviction (or second conviction with intent to harass or embarrass).

It is an affirmative defense that the pictures were distributed only between two persons not more than 2 years apart in age, who were in a dating relationship, or between two married persons.

It is also an offense for a minor to possesses such visual material if the actor produced the visual material or knows that another minor produced the visual material. The offense is a Class C misdemeanor, first offense; a Class B misdemeanor, second offense; or a Class A misdemeanor, third or subsequent offense.

It is a defense to this offense that the actor did not produce or solicit the visual material, possessed the material only after receiving it from another minor, and destroyed the material within a reasonable time after receiving it. [*Penal Code* § 43.261]

## STALKING

### Defined

Stalking now includes threatening an individual with whom the victim has a dating relationship. [*Penal Code* § 42.072]

### Jurisdiction

The offense of stalking may be prosecuted in any county in which an element of the offense occurred. [*Code of Criminal Procedure* Art. 13.36]

### Protective Orders

A victim of stalking may file for a protective order. [*Code of Criminal Procedure* Arts. 6.09, 7A.01]

## THEFT

### Automated Teller Machines (ATMs)

Theft of an ATM or the contents or components of an ATM is now a felony of the second degree. [*Penal Code* § 31.03]

### Identity Theft

It is a Class B misdemeanor to obtain the financial sight order or payment card information of another by use of an electronic, photographic, visual imaging, recording, or other device capable of accessing, reading, recording, capturing, copying, imaging, scanning, reproducing, or storing in any manner the financial sight order or payment card information, knowing that he is not entitled to obtain or possess that financial information. It is a Class A misdemeanor to transfer such information to a third party. [*Penal Code* § 31.17]

### Shoplifting

Theft is increased to the next higher level of offense if the defendant intentionally, knowingly, or recklessly:

- caused a fire exit alarm to sound or otherwise become activated,
- deactivated or otherwise prevented a fire exit alarm or retail theft detector from sounding, or
- used a shielding or deactivation instrument to prevent or attempt to prevent detection of the offense by a retail theft detector.

[*Penal Code* § 31.03]

Organized retail theft is a Class B misdemeanor if the total value of the merchandise involved in the activity is less than $50, or a Class A misdemeanor if the total value is $50 or more but less than $500, a state jail felony if the total value is $500 or more but less than $1,500, a felony of the third degree if the total value is $1,500 or more but less than $20,000, a felony of the second degree if the total value is $20,000 or more but less than $100,000, or a felony of the first degree if the value is $100,000 or more. The penalty is increased to the next higher level of offense if the defendant intentionally, knowingly, or recklessly:

- caused a fire exit alarm to sound or otherwise become activated,
- deactivated or otherwise prevented a fire exit alarm or retail theft detector from sounding, or
- used a shielding or deactivation instrument to prevent or attempt to prevent detection of the offense by a retail theft detector.

[*Penal Code* § 31.16]

### Timber

A person commits an offense by harvesting standing timber with knowledge that the harvesting is without the permission of the owner of the standing timber, or by causing another person to harvest standing timber without the permission of the owner of the standing timber. The offense is:

- a state jail felony if it is shown on the trial of the offense that the value of the timber harvested is at least $500 but less than $20,000;
- a felony of the third degree if it is shown on the trial of the offense that the value of the timber harvested is at least $20,000 but less than $100,000;
- a felony of the second degree if it is shown on the trial of the offense that the value of the timber harvested is at least $100,000 but less than $200,000; or
- a felony of the first degree if it is shown on the trial of the offense that the value of the timber harvested is at least $200,000.

[*Natural Resources Code* § 151.052]

## VICTIMS' RIGHTS

### Notification

The attorney representing the state, as far as reasonably practical, must give to the victim of a crime (or the guardian of a victim or close relative of a deceased victim) notice of the existence and terms of any plea bargain agreement to be presented to the court. [*Code of Criminal Procedure* Art. 56.08]

## WEAPONS

### Prohibited Weapons

It is a state jail felony to intentionally or knowingly possess, manufacture, transport, repair or sell a tire deflation device. [*Penal Code* § 46.05]

# TEXAS LEGAL GUIDELINES

*Editor's Note: This is a general overview of criminal procedure law. It should be used to achieve understanding of basic principles but is not to be relied upon for guidance in a specific application. It is not to be used as a substitute for the opinion or advice of the appropriate legal counsel for the reader's department. To the extent possible, the information is current. However, very recent statutory and case law developments may not be covered.*

# I. INTRODUCTION

The Bill of Rights to the federal Constitution, and corresponding provisions in each state's constitution, provide citizens with certain fundamental safeguards from intrusive governmental conduct. Particularly relevant to situations involving a criminal suspect or defendant are the Fourth, Fifth, Sixth and, to a lesser extent, the Fourteenth Amendments. As a preliminary matter, the reader should note that the federal Bill of Rights, as ultimately interpreted by the Supreme Court, guarantees U.S. citizens enumerated fundamental freedoms and provides the constitutionally required minimum levels of protection. Under the principles of federalism, state courts are free, in interpreting their respective state constitutions, to afford greater protection to state citizens, and, in fact, Texas courts have found that article I, § 9 of the Texas constitution, although similarly worded to the federal Constitution, provides greater protections. See *Heitman v. State,* 815 S.W.2d 681 (Tex. Crim. App. 1991).

The Fourth Amendment guarantees the people the right to be secure in their persons, houses, papers and effects against unreasonable searches and seizures. This amendment also provides that no search or arrest warrants shall be issued, except those based on probable cause and which particularly describe both the place to be searched and the person or things to be seized.

The Fifth Amendment provides (in pertinent part) that no person shall be compelled to be a witness against oneself in a criminal case. The Supreme Court has also found that an integral part of an accused's right to be free from compelled incrimination is a judicially created right to have counsel present and a right to refuse to answer questions during a custodial interrogation, even though the Constitution does not specifically provide such a safeguard.

The Sixth Amendment provides that a defendant in a criminal case—and a suspect in a criminal investigation when the investigation has focused on him or her or has reached a critical stage—shall enjoy the right to counsel to aid in his or her defense.

The Fifth and Fourteenth Amendments provide that no person shall be deprived of life, liberty or property without the due process of law. In the context of the rights of a criminal suspect, this provision has been construed as offering protection against certain fundamentally unfair governmental conduct, particularly the use of suggestive, prejudicial or discriminatory identification procedures.

The ramifications of constitutional violations impact not only a law enforcement officers' efforts to enforce the law and obtain the conviction of criminal offenders, but also may lead to monetary sanctions against individual officers and the particular department employing them. Evidence seized in violation of the foregoing principles (whether it is physical evidence, *e.g.,* contraband, or testimonial evidence, *e.g.,* a statement or confession) generally cannot be introduced into evidence in any subsequent trial. The evidence will be excluded by the operation of a doctrine known as the exclusionary rule. The mechanism by which the use of evidence is denied to prosecutors is called suppression. Moreover, officers who violate a person's constitutional rights may be civilly liable to that person in monetary damages. Officers, or the municipalities for which they work when they act in a manner inconsistent with their lawful authority, may also be held accountable for such damages.

## II. DETENTION AND ARREST

### A. Levels of Encounters

When reviewing the legality of police interactions with citizens, courts initially assess the nature and extent of the contact. To aid in this analysis, interactions, or encounters, are divided into three conceptual categories. First, there are encounters of a consensual nature. This has sometimes been called the "common law right to inquire." This is a right to ask a question, enjoyed by all citizens, whether they work in law enforcement or not.

Occupying the next tier of encounters are interactions of a more intrusive character. These are encounters commonly called detentions, investigatory stops or *Terry* stops. The justifications offered by law enforcement for this more forceful contact must be based on facts that are specific and articulable and lead to a rational inference or a reasonable suspicion that criminal activity is being undertaken.

The final level of encounter is a formal arrest. To justify this action, law enforcement officials must possess a higher degree of suspicion, *i.e.,* "probable cause" to believe that a crime is being, or has been, perpetrated and that a specific person committed it.

This initial categorization of encounters is essential to a determination of the rights of the individual. If the encounter was consensual, the Constitution is not implicated because no seizure of a person, within the meaning of the Fourth Amendment, has taken place. However, if the encounter rises to the level of a detention or a full-scale arrest, then that person has been seized, and law enforcement conduct will be judged according to the standards of the Fourth Amendment. The person seized can then avail himself or herself of the Amendment's protections.

## B. Consensual Encounters—Right of Inquiry

The basic premise underlying a consensual encounter is that it is voluntary. Such an encounter is an interaction based on consent and is terminable by either party. Law enforcement officers do not infringe on a citizen's Fourth Amendment rights by merely approaching him or her at random in a public place in order to ask a few questions, as long as a reasonable person would understand that he or she could refuse to cooperate and excuse themselves from the exchange, if they choose to do so. Simply identifying oneself as an officer or asking for someone's name and identification is not an unreasonable intrusion or a seizure within the meaning of the Fourth Amendment. Courts reason that merely asking a few further questions, without more, does not constitute a seizure of the person. This is an important distinction; if the person has not been constitutionally seized, then the Fourth Amendment is not implicated and no constitutional violation can occur. A constitutional seizure occurs when the officer, by means of physical force, coercion or show of authority, has in some way restrained the freedom of a citizen so that a

reasonable person in the suspect's position would no longer feel as though he or she were free to leave. Detentions and arrests are viewed as seizures of a person. These actions are reviewed under the Fourth Amendment's reasonableness standard and are subject to constitutional controls.

The objective test in a consensual encounter is whether a reasonable person would think that he or she were free to go. The following are suggestions for the law enforcement officer to establish a consensual encounter: (i) ask the citizen:

- "May I talk to you?"
- "Can I have a minute of your time?"
- "Do you mind if I search you for drugs?"
- "Would you mind showing me what's in your hand?"
- "May I look in your purse/luggage?"

or (ii) simply walk up to a citizen in a public place and start a conversation. There is no requirement that a citizen be informed of the right to refuse consent to an encounter. *In re D.G.,* 96 S.W.3d 465 (Tex. App.-Austin 2002).

In *Michigan v. Chesternut,* 486 U.S. 567 (1988), defendant was not seized when an officer accelerated his patrol car and began to drive alongside defendant. The officer did not activate his siren or flashers, did not command defendant to halt, did not display a weapon, and did not drive aggressively so as to block defendant's path.

In *Barnes v. State,* 870 S.W.2d 74 (Tex. App.-Houston [1st Dist.] 1993), defendant was a passenger in a car parked along a curb outside an apartment complex, talking with a man sitting on the curb who happened to be a known drug dealer holding a brown paper bag. There was no seizure when an officer pulled up behind the car at a slanted angle, approached the car on foot, and asked the driver and defendant how they were doing, what they were doing in the area, and if they lived there. The encounter became a seizure only when the officer asked defendant to step out of the car (after seeing something in his mouth).

The courts will probably rule that what the officer thought was a consensual encounter was in fact a detention if the officer does one or more of the following:

- displays a weapon;
- uses a harsh, accusatorial tone of voice;
- orders the citizen to do something, *e.g.,* "Stop," "Open your hands," "Don't move," "Stay right there," or "Come over here";
- blocks the individual's path with his or her body or a police vehicle;

• tells the individual that he or she is a suspect;
• physically touches the individual;
• retains the individual's property (drivers' license, airline ticket or other personal property belonging to the individual).

See, *e.g., Crain v. State,* 315 S.W.3d 43 (Tex. Crim. App. 2010) (officer seized defendant when he called out from his patrol car "Come over here and talk to me" and shined the car's spotlight on defendant); State v. Garcia-Cantu, 253 S.W.3d 236 (Tex. Crim. App. 2008) (defendant seized when officer parked 10 feet behind and "boxed in" defendant's truck, shined his vehicle's spotlight on the truck, then walked up to it in an "authoritative" manner holding a large flashlight at shoulder-level); *Salcido v. State,* 758 S.W.2d 261 (Tex. Crim. App. 1988) (defendant seized when officer placed a hand on his shoulder); *Sheppard v. State,* 895 S.W.2d 823 (Tex. App.-Corpus Christi 1995) (seizure when officer in full raid gear exited his vehicle, approached defendant, and said, "Just sit tight, bud."); *Molina v. State,* 654 S.W.2d 468 (Tex. App.-San Antonio 1988) (although there was no seizure when officer initially approached defendant at a bus stop and asked his name, the encounter became a forcible investigative detention when the officer took defendant's Social Security card and radioed in for a warrants check on his name); *Herrera v. State,* 665 S.W.2d 497 (Tex. App.-Amarillo 1983) (defendant seized when at least six uniformed, armed officers drove up, surrounding his vehicle in a parking lot, and told him they wanted to question him regarding a murder).

A seizure does not occur until either the suspect complies with a "show of authority" by police or there is an application of physical force (however slight) to the suspect by police. *California v. Hodari D.,* 499 U.S. 621 (1991); *Johnson v. State,* 912 S.W.2d 227 (Tex. Crim. App. 1995).

A stop of a moving vehicle constitutes a seizure of both the driver and any passengers, even if the purpose of the stop is limited and the resulting detention quite brief. *Brendlin v. California,* 551 U.S. 249 (2007); *Berkemer v. McCarty,* 468 U.S. 420 (1984).

A stop of a moving vehicle is a seizure within the meaning of the Fourth Amendment, "even though the purpose of the stop is limited and the detention brief." *Berkemer v. McCarty,* 468 U.S. 420 (1984).

A seizure occurs when a person in a parked car complies with a police order to roll down the window, open the door, or get out of the car. *Ebarb v. State,* 598 S.W.2d 842 (Tex. Crim. App. 1979).

However, there is no detention if an officer merely approaches a parked vehicle and knocks on the window. *Merideth v. State,* 603 S.W.2d 872 (Tex. Crim. App. 1980).

Often an officer will approach a person in a public place (*i.e.* airport, bus station, train, plane or bus, etc.). The officer needs no reasonable suspicion to ask questions, or ask for a person's identification, as long as a reasonable person would understand that he or she could refuse to cooperate. *Florida v. Bostick,* 501 U.S. 429 (1991).

For example, in *U.S. v. Drayton,* 536 U.S. 194 (2002), defendant was not seized when officers boarded a bus and began questioning the passengers, even when an officer asked consent to search his bag. Although the officers displayed their badges, they did not brandish weapons or make intimidating moves. They gave the passengers no reason to believe that they were required to answer the officers' questions, and they left the aisle free so that passengers could exit the bus. Only one officer did the questioning, and he spoke in a polite, quiet (not authoritative) voice: "Nothing he said would suggest to a reasonable person that he or she was barred from leaving the bus or otherwise terminating the encounter."

Compare with *Jackson v. State,* 77 S.W.3d 921 (Tex. App.-Houston [14th Dist.] 2002). Two officers approached defendant at Houston International Airport because she was walking in a nervous manner and was overly protective of her bag. While one officer stayed back, the other approached defendant, identified herself as an officer, and asked to speak with her, adding that defendant did not have to talk to her if defendant did not wish to do so. When defendant agreed to speak with her, the officer asked in a "normal, quiet" tone of voice where she was going, if the trip was for business or pleasure, and if she had checked any luggage. As the conversation progressed, she also asked to see her ticket and eventually asked for consent to search her bag. Neither officer touched defendant, displayed a weapon, or took her to a secluded area. Defendant was not threatened, either overtly or through tone of voice. She was told that she was free to terminate the encounter. This was not a seizure.

Note: It is important for the law enforcement officer to remember that in a consensual encounter the officer does not have to give the citizen *Miranda* warnings. Once an arrest is made, or there is a detention equivalent to arrest, the person must be advised of his or her *Miranda* rights if the officer plans on questioning the person while he or she is in custody (see below).

## C. Detentions and Investigatory Stops

The next conceptual category in the hierarchy of encounters involves interactions that courts refer to as investigatory stops, temporary detentions or *Terry* stops. The U.S. Supreme Court articulated the standard officers require as a justification for this more intrusive action in *Terry v. Ohio,* 392 U.S. 1 (1968). The Court held that when an officer observes specific and articulable events which give rise to a reasonable suspicion that illegal activity may be underway then the officer is justified in detaining and questioning the individual. The requisite suspicion must derive from facts and inferences from those facts. Such suspicions cannot lead to a mere hunch that something is amiss. More is needed. The facts producing the officer's suspicions must be objectively reasonable at the time, taking into account all of the circumstances attendant to the encounter. Note that the observations made by the officer to justify a *Terry* stop need not be as convincing as information that would create "probable cause" for arrest.

In the *Terry* case, the Court also held that when a law enforcement officer has a reasonable suspicion that illegal activity may be under way and the suspect has been detained, the officer is entitled to conduct a limited pat-down, or frisk, of the outer garments of the detainee to determine whether the suspect is armed or possesses an item that could be used to harm the officer. The requirements for, and the parameters of, this limited search are discussed below. The legal standard for the stop is reasonable suspicion to believe the detainee is somehow engaged in unlawful activity. The legal standard for the frisk, unlike the stop, relates to fear that the suspect is armed with a deadly weapon.

### 1. Reasonable Suspicion.

a. **In General.** The level of doubt needed to permit this more intrusive type of encounter (*i.e.,* a *Terry* stop) is phrased as "reasonable suspicion of criminal activity." This suspicion must be reasonable to a judge or jury looking at the encounter in hindsight, not suspicion that was subjectively reasonable to the officer at the time. To ascertain if the suspicion was, in fact, reasonable, one must look to all the circumstances surrounding the encounter. The facts known by the officer are relevant here (*e.g.,* the suspect was arrested for burglary two months ago or an all-points bulletin just came out for a murder only two blocks away), as well as his or her observations (*e.g.,* the suspect was stumbling or slurring words or seemed nervous when the officer spoke to him)

and experience (*e.g.,* "I've been a cop for fifteen years and I know what a drug deal looks like."). When taken together these elements must coalesce and point to a conclusion that a circumspect, judicious person would come to, namely, that some form of criminal endeavor was afoot. The facts given to support the suspicion must be detailed. The officer must be able to state them in a clear and concise fashion. A mere intuition or instinctive feeling, standing alone, is insufficient. Facts are needed to bolster the conclusion that the suspicion was reasonable. Assuming there was adequate justification for the stop, the means of investigation employed must be reasonably related to the suspicion created. Moreover, the detention must last no longer than reasonably necessary to dispel or confirm the suspicion (15 to 30 minutes is the time frame courts seem to routinely permit, although substantially longer detentions have been upheld, and shorter ones have been found excessive).

Note: If the officers do not have a justification for making the initial stop (*i.e.,* at least a reasonable suspicion that criminal activity is underway), everything that may happen afterwards (*e.g.,* guns or drugs are found) will be of no consequence. Any evidence that might have been used against the suspect becomes tainted by the police misconduct and will be suppressed as the result, or fruit, of an unconstitutional detention. This is known as the exclusionary rule.

b. **Factors to Consider.** For the professional officer, an important point to note is that an individual fact or observation alone may be as consistent with innocuous, perfectly lawful conduct and activities, as it is with criminal enterprise. Courts consistently look at the combination of several different observations, each of which when isolated may appear innocent, but when taken together would lead to a reasonable impression that illegal activities are taking place.

Investigatory stops are routinely conducted in a variety of factual settings. The process of detaining and questioning a person is not limited to an "on-the-street" scenario, where an officer detains and questions a pedestrian. Investigatory stops are permissible in situations involving vehicles and motorists as well. An officer may briefly detain and question the driver or passengers of a vehicle if he has a reasonable suspicion that the occupants are involved in criminal activity. Following a lawful stop an officer may, as a matter of course, order the driver and any passengers to step out of the vehicle, even without any particularized suspicion that the vehicle occupants are armed or may otherwise pose a threat to the officer.

c. **Investigatory Stops.** The police may briefly detain and question a person upon a reasonable suspicion, short of probable cause for arrest, that the person is involved in criminal activity. What is, or is not, reasonable suspicion depends on balancing, weighing and meshing a variety of factors, taking into account the particular factual setting with which an officer is confronted. Some factors commonly cited by courts when determining the existence or absence of reasonable suspicion are as follows:

(1) A prior criminal record does not create a reasonable suspicion that there is current criminal activity. However, if that knowledge is coupled with other concrete facts or observations, an officer may rely on the combination to create a reasonable suspicion of present criminal activity.

(2) An officer's awareness that a crime was recently committed in the vicinity is a pertinent consideration. Standing alone, however, this knowledge does not create a reasonable suspicion that an individual who happens to be in that area, a short time later, was the perpetrator.

(3) A suspect's presence in a high-crime area, or an area known for drug trafficking, standing alone, is not a basis for reasonable suspicion. But a suspect's presence in such an area is an articulable fact. Coupled with other more solid observations, such presence can create reasonable suspicion that the suspect is engaged in the unlawful activity for which the neighborhood is known.

(4) Evasive conduct, furtive gestures, concealing or attempting to conceal one's identity are criteria an officer may weigh in assessing if his suspicion is reasonable. However, each individual observation, without more, will not create a reasonable suspicion of criminal endeavor.

(5) The time of day or night in which the individual is observed is relevant. However, merely being out in public at a late hour, without more, will not justify a stop.

(6) Information given to an officer by a third party, an informant, is generally insufficient by itself to create reasonable suspicion. However, when this information is corroborated by officers through independent investigation, or there is extraneous evidence that the informant is reliable and truthful, reasonable suspicion may be based on the tip. An officer may also rely on a flyer or bulletin describing a suspect and disseminated by another law enforcement agency as a source for reasonable suspicion. The officer relying on the bulletin does not have to demonstrate personal knowledge of the facts necessary to justify the stop. However, the party issuing the bulletin or flyer must have facts in his or her possession which would support a finding of reasonable suspicion. Moreover, the scope of the stop made by the officer relying on the bulletin may be no more intrusive than that the issuing agency would have been justified in conducting.

d. **Legality of a Stop.** A determination that an officer possessed reasonable suspicion, justifying a detention, is only the first step in determining the legality of a stop. A reviewing court will ask initially if the officer's action was justified at its inception, and secondly whether it was reasonably related in scope to the circumstances which justified the interference in the first place. An examination of the scope of the stop addresses the following: (i) the length of the detention, and (ii) the methods employed during the stop. The duration of, and methods employed during the stop must be tailored to serve the purpose of confirming or alleviating the officer's suspicions. If those concerns are confirmed, and an officer's observations during the detention create probable cause, an arrest may be made. If the suspicions are dispelled, then the suspect should be let go. The detention must be sufficiently limited in temporal duration to satisfy the conditions of an investigative seizure. The nature of the questioning and level of force employed during the detention must be similarly limited. Even though the initial stop was justified, if the detention exceeds the scope authorized by its justification, i.e., "reasonable suspicion of criminal activity," it will be deemed an illegal stop, and any incriminating evidence found thereafter will not be admissible in court.

e. **Justification for a Detention.**

(1) **Flight.** A suspect's flight, when confronted with police presence, may give the officer reasonable suspicion to pursue and detain the suspect. Note, however, that not all conduct that merely avoids contact with law enforcement is considered flight from law enforcement.

See, *e.g.*, *Illinois v. Wardlow*, 528 U.S. 119 (2000). Two uniformed officers were in the last car of a four-car police caravan that converged on an area of Chicago known for heavy narcotics trafficking, in order to investigate drug transactions. The officers observed defendant, who was standing next to a building holding an opaque bag, look at the police caravan, then run in the opposite direction. Given the character of the area and defendant's headlong flight ("the consummate act of evasion"), the officers had reasonable suspicion to stop him.

Compare with *Livingston v. State,* 739 S.W.2d 311 (Tex. Crim. App. 1987), *cert. denied,* 487 U.S. 1210 (1988). At around 9:00 p.m., an unidentified man told two Houston officers of a shooting in a nearby Weingarten store parking lot. Moments later, the officers saw defendant emerge from the dimly lit, isolated area behind the store. He was not carrying any grocery bags. As soon as he saw the officers' patrol car, he turned and walked in the opposite direction. The officers could see that his pants were ripped from knee to crotch and he was sweating profusely. Based on all these observations, they had reasonable suspicion to stop and question him.

See also *Salazar v. State,* 805 S.W.2d 538 (Tex. App.-Fort Worth 1991). At around 5:30 a.m., officers were called to the scene of a burglary in progress at unit 13D in Dry Dock Apartments. When the first officer arrived, he saw a small car parked outside the apartment. Defendant was inside the car, but he ducked down upon seeing the officer. He then repeatedly looked over the seat, only to duck down again upon still seeing the officer. The officer radioed his colleagues about this suspicious behavior, and his colleagues then had reasonable suspicion for an investigatory stop.

In *Worley v. State,* 912 S.W.2d 869 (Tex. App-Fort Worth 1995), police saw a car parked outside a known drug house. The driver, still in the vehicle, gave the officers "a good hard stare." Soon after, defendant walked out of the house, his attention focused on something in his cupped left hand. As defendant drew nearer, the officers could see that the something was a handful of capsules. Defendant was concentrating on them so hard he did not see the officers until he was almost at the curb. When he finally did look up and notice the officers, he "froze and stared at them." One of the officers later testified defendant "was looking real nervous, looking scared." One of the officers approached on foot, and when he was within arm's reach, defendant clinched his left hand to conceal the capsules and began to turn away. The officer then had reasonable suspicion to seize defendant by grabbing his arm.

(2) **High-Crime Area.** Presence in a high-crime area, when coupled with observations of suspicious activity, can create reasonable suspicion.

See, *e.g., King v. State,* 35 S.W.3d 740 (Tex. App.-Houston [1st Dist.] 2002). An officer was patrolling a high-crime area where he had made many prior drug arrests when he saw defendant's truck stopped in the middle of the road. Several men stood at the passenger side, but ran away as the patrol car drove up. The officer knew from his training and experience that drug transactions are often conducted in this manner (right in the middle of the road). Therefore, he had reasonable suspicion to stop the truck and briefly question defendant regarding his identity, itinerary, and immediate activity.

Compare with *Davis v. State,* 905 S.W.2d 655 (Tex. App.-Texarkana 1995). Two officers were patrolling a high-crime area of the city in an unmarked car one evening when the defendant attempted to "flag down" the officers as they drove by. The officers stopped, and defendant approached their car. However, as soon as he recognized one of the officers, he walked away. The officers knew dealers frequently flag down unfamiliar cars to sell their drugs, so, therefore, they had reasonable suspicion to stop defendant.

See also *Jones v. State,* 962 S.W.2d 158 (Tex. App.-Fort Worth 1998). An Arlington officer was on patrol at around 1:00 a.m. when he saw defendant and another man walking in the vicinity of some south Arlington apartments that had been the scene of recent burglaries. The unidentified man was carrying a large box-like object on his shoulder. The officer made a brief U-turn and lost sight of the men, but soon spotted defendant again and the object lying on the ground nearby (which the officer could then see was a microwave). The officer had a reasonable suspicion that defendant was involved in a burglary and thus was justified in making a stop.

Compare with *Bailey v. State,* 629 S.W.2d 189 (Tex. App.-Dallas 1982). At 12:15 a.m., an officer was on patrol outside a 7-11 store closed for construction. This was an unlighted high-crime area where there had been previous burglaries at other construction sites in the vicinity. Defendant's vehicle was stopped in front of the store, and defendant was transferring objects from one box to another on the front seat. The officer had reasonable suspicion for a temporary detention.

(3) **Officer's Experience.** Officers are entitled to rely on their own knowledge and experience in forming reasonable suspicion. Knowledge of an earlier crime in the area, coupled with observation of suspicious conduct, can justify a detention.

See, e.g., *Curtis v. State,* 238 S.W.3d 376 (Tex. Crim. App. 2007). At around 1:00 a.m., two officers saw defendant's car weave twice across "the inside fog line" (the left-most white line along the shoulder) and once across "the broken lane divider line" in the span of "several hundred yards." The officers had extensive experience and training in detecting drunk drivers, and knew such weaving to be a sign of intoxication. The officers had reasonable suspicion for a stop.

See also *Tanner v. State,* 228 S.W.3d 852 (Tex. App.-Austin 2007). At around 3:00 a.m., an officer on routine patrol saw defendant and a young woman pushing bicycles out from a dark area behind a bar. The officer knew the bar had been closed for at least an hour. Because the officer "made an on-the-spot observation of conduct that, by any standard, is unusual and highly consistent with criminal behavior," he had reasonable suspicion to stop and question the pair.

But see *Parks v. State,* 330 S.W.3d 675 (Tex. App.-San Antonio 2010), where officers did not have reasonable suspicion to stop four young men solely because they had blue rags hanging from their pockets, which the officers associated with gang membership. There was no individualized suspicion linking the men to any criminal activity.

Knowledge of an earlier crime in the area, coupled with observation of suspicious conduct, can justify a detention.

See, *e.g., Balentine v. State,* 71 S.W.3d 763 (Tex. Crim. App. 2002). Amarillo officers responded to a shots-fired call at 2:26 a.m. in a residential, low-traffic area. While searching the area, they saw defendant, two houses down from the complainant's home and walking away at a brisk pace with his hands in his pockets. He appeared nervous and was constantly looking over his shoulder. The officers had reasonable suspicion to detain him for questioning.

Compare with *Hammond v. State,* 664 S.W.2d 838 (Tex. App.-Corpus Christi 1984). At around 11:00 p.m., an officer heard a report of a burglary on Vine Street but was not assigned the call. Shortly thereafter, he was called to a disturbance at another address on Vine. While turning onto that street, he saw defendant "kind of run" in front of his patrol car, carrying a television. Reasonable suspicion was established for a stop.

In *Thomas v. State,* 297 S.W.3d 458 (Tex. App.-Houston [14th Dist.] 2009), a group of persons were robbed at gunpoint outside a Fulshear restaurant by five to seven men. The suspects were described as black or Hispanic men, wearing bulky dark or black clothing, and one wearing bright red shoes. Within an hour, an officer saw two black men walking together about a block

from the restaurant. One of the men wore bright red shoes, and the other wore black pants, black shoes and a white shirt like an undershirt with no jacket (despite the fact it was a cold February night). It was reasonable to believe the men might be connected to the earlier robbery, so the officer was justified in stopping and frisking both of them.

In *Malone v. State,* 734 S.W.2d 50 (Tex. App.-Houston [1st Dist.] 1987), an officer received a dispatch reporting a robbery-in-progress at the J.C. Penney's in the Almoda Mall at 10:45 on a Sunday morning. He arrived within 6 minutes and saw defendant walking through the parking lot, about 110 yards from the store. Because it was Sunday, the officer knew that the store was closed until noon. No one else was in sight in the parking lot. Moreover, defendant was wearing black gloves, even though it was a warm September day, and was carrying a flashlight in broad daylight. The officer had reasonable suspicion to stop defendant to determine if he was involved in the reported crime.

Compare with *Pennywell v. State,* 1127 S.W.3d 149 (Tex. App.-Houston [1st Dist.] 2003). An officer responded to a burglary at an apartment complex; the dispatcher described the burglar as a black male traveling on foot. The officer soon saw defendant, a black male, carrying a large bag capable of holding items taken during the burglary. The officer initiated a consensual encounter, asking defendant if he lived in the complex. Defendant said he was "just visiting." When asked who he was visiting, he said, "a friend," but could not recall this unnamed friend's apartment number. The officer then had reasonable suspicion to detain defendant in the back of his patrol car while he investigated further.

In *Sheffield v. State,* 647 S.W.2d 413 (Tex. App.-Austin 1983), two University of Texas officers saw the male defendant walk out of a student building at a "very fast pace" while going through a ladies wallet. The officers knew of a theft in the area the previous day by a man who appeared similar to defendant. Reasonable suspicion was established for a stop.

In *State v. Lopez,* 148 S.W.3d 586 (Tex. App.-Fort Worth 2004), officers responded to a call reporting that painting equipment had been stolen from the back of a couple's truck, which was parked in front of their home. While speaking with the complainants in their front yard, defendant and a companion drove by very slowly in a pick-up truck. The complainants stated that they had seen the same truck (or what they thought was the same truck-it was dark out) drive by slowly several times that night. The investigating officer was assigned to the burglary unit, and he knew it was common for burglars to return to the scene of the crime if they found particular equipment to steal the first time. He therefore had reasonable suspicion to stop and question defendant regarding the burglary.

See also *Hurtado v. State,* 881 S.W.2d 738 (Tex. App.-Houston [1st Dist.] 1994). An officer checked a car's license tag and learned that there were several outstanding arrest warrants for various people associated with the tag. He then had reasonable suspicion to stop the car to determine if the driver was named in any of the warrants.

(4) **Tips.** Information provided by someone outside the circles of law enforcement may provide sufficient justification for a stop if it carries with it sufficient indicia of reliability. Factors that bolster the reliability of information may include: the reliability and reputation of the person providing the tip; corroboration of the details contained in the tip by independent police work; and the extent to which any information provided by the informant has proved to be accurate or useful in the past.

For example, in *Carmouche v. State,* 10 S.W.3d 323 (Tex. Crim. App. 2000), a confidential informant (CI) phoned a narcotics investigator with the Texas Department of Public Safety. The investigator recognized her because she had provided accurate information about at least eight of her co-defendants in a pending federal drug conspiracy case. The CI said that she and defendant (whom she only described as a black male with "sleepy" eyes) would drive from Houston to Nacogdoches that evening, and that defendant would be carrying approximately 10 ounces of cocaine. She also stated that defendant would be renting a car, but she could not provide a description. The investigator asked her to stop at a specific gas station in Corrigan so he could identify her. At 8:45 that evening, the CI and a black male (later identified as defendant) pulled into the specified gas station. Because of the CI's previous history of reliability, police had reasonable suspicion to stop the car and investigate further.

In *Williams v. State,* 924 S.W.2d 189 (Tex. App.-Eastland 1996), a CI tipped a deputy that there was an "oversized black male at Ron's Place dealing crack cocaine." The CI identified this man as "Brian" and described his clothing. The deputy had "been associated with" this CI for about one year, and information received from him in the

past had proved reliable. Moreover, Ron's Place was known for drug activity. When the deputy arrived at the bar, he saw defendant (who matched the CI's description) standing outside. A car pulled up, and defendant knelt down to reach into the vehicle. This is conduct consistent with a drug transaction. Under the totality of the circumstances, the tip was sufficiently reliable to establish reasonable suspicion for a stop.

In *Reynolds v. State,* 962 S.E.2d 307 (Tex. App.-Houston [14th Dist.] 1998), a CI met with a Houston officer in person. He gave his phone number, but would not give his name. He told the officer that defendant Larry Reynolds, a black male who drove a green convertible Buick with a specified license plate, would transport crack cocaine to Goodhope and Rebecca Streets "right now" or soon. The officer searched that area, but did not see a green Buick convertible; however, a records check revealed that such a vehicle was registered to defendant at his residence on Goodhope. The officer drove to the residence and saw the described Buick parked outside. While he waited, a black male (later identified as defendant) left the residence, got into the Buick, and drove off in the direction of Rebecca Street. Because the CI had given his tip in person and accurately predicted defendant's future behavior, his tip gave the officer reasonable suspicion for a stop.

In *Turley v. State,* 242 S.W.3d 178 (Tex. App.-Fort Worth 2007), an officer received a call from a gas station clerk named Angela at around 3:00 a.m. (The officer knew Angela immediately because he often stopped at her station.) Angela told the officer that defendant had almost hit a gas pump while driving into the gas station parking lot; when he entered the store, she immediately smelled alcohol on him and suspected he was intoxicated. Angela described defendant's car, including the license plate number. The officer arrived at the station 2 to 3 minutes later, and quickly located defendant's vehicle. Even though he observed no traffic violations, he stopped it. The Court ruled that the officer had reasonable suspicion, based on Angela's tip. The officer "knew" Angela—at least her first name and place of work—so she could be held accountable if she gave false information. Moreover, she relayed events she had observed first-hand, and continued to observe as she called. This added to her reliability. There was no indication that Angela was a paid informant, which might decrease her reliability. Finally, her description of the car was sufficiently detailed to allow the officer to identify defendant immediately.

See also *Bilyeu v. State,* 136 S.W.3d 691 (Tex. App.-Texarkana 2004). Two officers were taking a break at a convenience store at around 2:00 a.m. when an unidentified man approached them to say he had seen a woman asleep at the wheel of a gold Mercedes-Benz stopped at a green light four blocks away. While speaking with the officers, the man noticed the same car "creeping past their location" (doing 10 m.p.h. in a 35 m.p.h. zone) and pointed it out to the officers. The officers followed the car and stopped it, even though they had seen no traffic violations personally. The Court held that the tip in this case established reasonable suspicion. Although the man in the convenience store did not give his name, he was in his vehicle when he approached the officers, so he could have been identified by his license plate number, if the officers deemed it necessary. Because he provided this information directly and in person, the officers could judge his demeanor, and he was more reliable than an anonymous caller. Moreover, the officers were in Addison, an area known for its restaurants and bars, around closing time. The vehicle's slow speed further corroborated the tip. Therefore, the stop was reasonable.

(5) **Anonymous Tips.** An anonymous tip, if corroborated by other observations and supported by indicia of reliability, can create reasonable suspicion.

See, *e.g., Alabama v. White,* 496 U.S. 325 (1990). Montgomery police received an anonymous tip stating that defendant, carrying a brown briefcase filled with cocaine, would leave a specific unit of an apartment building and travel in her brown Plymouth station wagon, which had a broken taillight, to a specific motel. Police watched the apartment complex, and saw a brown Plymouth wagon with a broken taillight. They then watched defendant, empty-handed, exit the specified apartment, get into the car and drive directly toward the motel. Even though not every detail in the tip turned out to be totally correct, the partial corroboration by police alone provided reasonable suspicion for a stop.

In *Glenn v. State,* 967 S.W.2d 467 (Tex. App.-Amarillo 1998), an anonymous caller told Lubbock police that, within the past hour, he had been to defendant's residence (#72 at the Fairway Villa Apartment Complex) and observed white powder packaged in plastic baggies in the rear hatchback portion of defendant's white Ford Mustang. The caller went on to say that defendant would leave to sell these amphetamines within the next couple of hours. The officer who took the call spoke with an investigator from the South Plains Narcotics Task Force, who said that the tip was consistent with his knowledge of defendant (gained through informants and other police sources). About 45 minutes after the call, surveillance was set up outside defendant's apartment (where a white Mustang was indeed parked outside). About an hour and a half later, defendant left the apartment and began to drive away in the Mustang. Because the unnamed caller accurately predicted future behavior and the officer was able to confirm all the facts given in the call but the presence of drugs, police had reasonable suspicion to stop and detain the car until a drug dog could be brought to sniff it.

See also *Zane v. State,* 84 S.W.3d 733 (Tex. App.-Houston [1st Dist.] 2002). Police received an anonymous tip that two black men were selling drugs near a gray car at 138 Goodson, an area known for drugs. An officer was dispatched to the scene, where he saw defendant and another black man under a tree near a gray Cadillac. As the officer approached, the other man handed defendant something, and defendant began to quickly walk away. The presence of the men and their evasive conduct sufficiently corroborated the tip to establish reasonable suspicion.

But see *Florida v. J.L.,* 529 U.S. 266 (2000). An anonymous caller to Miami-Dade County police stated that a young black male dressed in a plaid shirt who was standing at a specified bus stop was carrying a gun. Officers arrived at the bus stop approximately six minutes later, and saw three black males, one of whom (defendant) was wearing a plaid shirt. Other than the tip, the officers had no reason to suspect any of the three of criminal activity. They saw no firearm, nor any threatening or unusual movements. However, the tip carried no indicia of reliability. It provided no predictive information, and, therefore, no means to test the caller's credibility. The caller neither explained how he knew defendant had a gun nor supplied any basis for believing that he had "inside information" about defendant. Therefore, the officers lacked reasonable suspicion, so that their stop of defendant was illegal.

Compare with *Johnson v. State,* 146 S.W.3d 719 (Tex. App.-Texarkana 2004). An anonymous caller told police that a black male, accompanied by two black females and driving a 1999 black Ford Taurus with a specified license plate, was involved in possible drug activity at a particular apartment complex. Although police knew this to be a place where drug deals regularly occurred, they had never had information connecting this activity to defendant. Less than an hour after the tip was received, an officer saw the described car leaving the parking lot of the apartment complex; defendant was in the car alone. Because there was no prediction of future activity or corroboration of illegal activity by the officer, this tip did not establish reasonable suspicion.

(6) **"Erratic" Driving.** Driving in an erratic manner in and of itself justifies a stop. An officer does not violate the Fourth Amendment by stopping and questioning someone who just committed a traffic violation in the officer's presence. Moreover, routine traffic infractions, even minor ones, can provide the requisite reasonable suspicion to stop a vehicle. For example, stops have been upheld when:

- the dealer-installed license plate frame on a vehicle entirely covered the phrase "THE LONE STAR STATE" and partially obscured the word "Texas" and a depiction of the space shuttle on its license plate (*State v. Johnson,* 219 S.W.3d 386 (Tex. Crim. App. 2007));
- a van's license plate was defective—even driving during daylight—when the van's headlamps and auxiliary lamps were on (*Palacios v. State,* 319 S.W.3d 68 (Tex. App.-San Antonio 2010));
- a Jeep Cherokee was swerving within its lane for half a mile along an interstate at 3:00 a.m., even though there was no actual traffic violation (*State v. Alderete,* 314 S.W.3d 469 (Tex. App.- El Paso 2010));
- an officer heard squealing tires, and looked up to see light smoke coming from the tires of defendant's car as it fishtailed about 2 feet outside its lane of traffic (*Fernandez v. State,* 306 S.W.3d 354 (Tex. App.-Fort Worth 2010));
- a driver made a right turn without signaling, even though he was travelling in a turn-only lane (*Wehring v. State,* 276 S.W.3d 666 (Tex. App.-Texarkana 2008));
- a driver weaved within his own lane (*Mitchell v. State,* 187 S.W.3d 113 (Tex. App.-Waco 2006));
- a driver changed lanes without activating his car's blinker until he was already across the yellow center stripe (*Coleman v. State,* 188 S.W.3d 708 (Tex. App.-Tyler 2005));
- a driver was following too closely, "right up on another car," and, in the officer's opinion, would not have been able to stop safely had that other car stopped or slowed (*Stoker v. State,* 170 S.W.3d 807 (Tex. App.-Tyler 2005));

- there is a violation of the seatbelt statute (*Morrison v. State,* 71 S.W.3d 821 (Tex. App.-Corpus Christi 2002)).

But see *Richardson v. State,* 39 S.W.3d 634 (Tex. App.-Amarillo 2000) (driving slowly, standing alone, does not justify a stop).

Note: **Roadblocks and Checkpoints.** Roadblocks and checkpoints are used to make temporary stops. Law enforcement agencies set up road blocks and checkpoints for a variety of reasons: checking the validity of driver's licenses and registrations, determining if the vehicle meets safety inspection minimums, deciding if the car has the necessary municipal parking permit, apprehending intoxicated drivers, etc. The U.S. Supreme Court has upheld the Fourth Amendment constitutionality of sobriety checkpoints that meet certain guidelines. *Michigan Dep't of Public Safety v. Sitz,* 496 U.S. 444 (1990). In Texas, however, because no governing body has ever authorized a statewide procedure for DWI roadblocks, they are not permitted. *Holt v. State,* 887 S.W.2d 16 (Tex. Crim. App. 1994). In *Holt,* the Court also suggested that such roadblocks may be barred under the Texas Constitution, but did not rule specifically on that issue.

(7) **Drug Courier Profiles.** Profiles of drug couriers are relied on by officers to identify potential suspects. Generally, a match to the profile alone does not create reasonable suspicion to detain the suspect. The officer must observe other conduct or circumstances that sufficiently heighten his suspicion. Often, undercover officers will survey airport or bus terminals for individuals matching a certain profile. Factors utilized in compiling this profile may include: (i) a journey that originated in a source city for narcotics, or a short round trip, with a brief stay in such a city; (ii) the suspect carrying a hard-sided suitcase; (iii) the suspect appearing nervous when questioned; (iv) tickets that were paid for in cash; (v) the suspect providing inconsistent or wavering answers to inquiries; (vi) furtive movements (*e.g.,* glancing over one's shoulder, not making eye contact, etc.). See *U.S. v. Sokolow,* 490 U.S. 1 (1989); *Crockett v. State,* 803 S.W.2d 308 (Tex. Crim. App. 1991).

In a typical scenario, a suspect matching the profile is approached by officers and asked a few questions. Often, a threshold issue in such cases is the nature of the questioning. If the encounter is consensual, then no Fourth Amendment concerns arise. If, however, the officers' suspicions are aroused and a more aggressive investigatory posture is assumed, the encounter may escalate into a *Terry* type detention, and the scope of the encounter must conform to constitutional guidelines. The method employed by investigating officers should be of the least intrusive means reasonably necessary to verify or dispel the officer's suspicion in a short period of time. Although the initial stop may be justified, it may become so protracted, exceeding a time limit that the officer would reasonably need to confirm or dispel his or her suspicions about possible trafficking activity, that it becomes unreasonable. To pass constitutional muster, a detention not only must be justified at its inception, but also must be reasonably related in scope to the circumstances that justified it in the first instance.

If, and when, such an encounter progresses into a full-blown detention, another frequently adjudicated question involves the seizure of a suspect's luggage, purse, handbag or other personal item. The general rule is that officers may effect a temporary seizure if they have reasonable suspicion that the luggage contains contraband. The seizure must be brief, and related in duration to dispelling any suspicion about what the luggage contains. *U.S. v. Place,* 462 U.S. 696 (1983). Frequently, the luggage is subjected to a sniff-test (by a dog trained to recognize, by smell, the presence of narcotics or other drugs) or officers try to obtain consent to search the luggage. In such cases, a distinction must be drawn between detaining and actually opening and searching a container. Although police may temporarily detain a container based upon reasonable suspicion, they generally may not open it without a warrant, or some recognized exception to the warrant requirement.

(8) **"Pretext"** Stops. Pretext stop cases typically involve officers who have a hunch that the driver or passenger of a car is committing a given crime, *e.g.,* possession of narcotics. However, nothing they have observed rises to the level of reasonable suspicion necessary to stop the car. The police then observe the motorist commit a minor traffic violation, and use this infraction, "the claimed pretext," to stop the vehicle and pursue a more intrusive line of investigation. In the adjudicated cases, the pretext stop search typically leads to the discovery of contraband wholly unrelated to the reason for the stop. In *Whren v. U.S.,* 517 U.S. 806 (1996), the U.S. Supreme Court held that "Ulterior motives do not invalidate police conduct that is justified on the basis of probable cause to believe a violation of

the law has occurred." The true motivating factor behind the stop is irrelevant. As long as there is probable cause to believe the rules of the road have been violated, a detention under such circumstances is lawful. A suspect may not claim that he or she was illegally detained merely because an officer had a hunch that a different, more serious crime was being committed, although the officer lacked proof for that proposition and intended to find evidence of that crime during the stop. If there is an objectively valid reason for the stop, even one involving a minor traffic infraction, subjective intentions are irrelevant. The Court did note that a stop motivated by an intent to single out members of a suspect class, such as race, would, however, be impermissible.

Texas courts have adopted the *Whren* standard. See *Gordon v. State,* 801 S.W.2d 899 (Tex. Crim. App. 1990).

The *Whren* standard applies to arrests as well as investigatory stops—an arrest is valid as long as there was objective probable cause, even if the officer had a different subjective motivation for making the arrest. *Arkansas v. Sullivan,* 532 U.S. 769 (2001) (arrest for driving without registration or proof of insurance and carrying a weapon valid when supported by probable cause, even if the officer's "true" purpose for making the arrest was to search defendant's car for drugs). An arrest is valid even if the criminal offense for which probable cause actually exists is not "closely related" to the offense stated by the officer at the time of arrest. *Devenpeck v. Alford,* 543 U.S. 146 (2004).

(9) **Witnesses.** Police may stop persons who (or a vehicle whose occupants) are potential witnesses to a crime, if such stops are reasonable under the circumstances. To effect such a stop, there must be a known and specific crime of grave public concern under investigation, and the stop must be appropriately tailored to fit investigatory needs and only minimally interfere with the liberty of the persons stopped. *Gipson v. State,* 268 S.W.3d 185 (Tex. App.-Corpus Christi 2008).

In *Gipson, supra,* officers were dispatched to a Wal-Mart where a robbery had taken place at 3:28 a.m. According to the dispatcher, the suspect was last seen running through a wooded area, southwest of the Wal-Mart, directly in front of the store. An officer who arrived within a minute or two of the dispatch saw a single vehicle, a blue Toyota, preparing to exit the parking lot. The officer blocked the vehicle and questioned its occupants, thinking they were potential witnesses. He quickly discovered that one passenger was, in fact, the robber. The Court upheld this stop based on the above factors. The crime at issue at the time of detainment was robbery, an offense so grave it is classified as a second-degree felony. "[The] stop advanced this grave public concern to a significant degree because the stop was being used to obtain information from individuals who were in the vicinity of the crime at the time it occurred, and were thus possible witnesses to the crime." The stop was "also more than appropriately tailored to fit investigatory needs." The officer "not only stopped the Toyota in the parking lot where the robbery occurred, but he stopped it in a specific area of the parking lot where he knew the suspect was last seen fleeing." Finally, the stop interfered only minimally with the liberty of the Toyota's occupants.

2. **Search Incident to a Detention.** During an investigatory detention, an officer may come to reasonably believe that the persons with whom he is dealing may be armed and presently dangerous, and where nothing in the encounter serves to dispel his reasonable fear for his own or another's safety, he is entitled to conduct a carefully limited search of the outer clothing to discover weapons which might be used to assault him. *Terry v. Ohio,* 392 U.S. 1 (1968). Be aware that there is no requirement that the officer "feel scared" or testify as to his or her fear for a pat-down to be valid. However, a pat-down will not be justified if simply done as a matter of routine (for example, every time a suspect is placed in a patrol car, regardless of whether or not the suspect is believed to be armed). *O'Hara v. State,* 27 S.W.3d 548 (Tex. Crim. App. 2000).

See, *e.g., State v. Castleberry,* 2011 Tex. Crim. App. LEXIS 283 (Tex. Crim. App. 2011). At around 3:00 a.m., a Dallas officer was patrolling the Cedar Springs-Lemmon-Maple area, which he described as having one of the "higher crime rates" in the city—recently, police had caught quite a few burglars in the vicinity. He noticed defendant and another man walking behind a closed business in an area lit only by ambient light. The officer approached the pair and asked for identification. Defendant responded by reaching toward his waistband. He was told to put his hands above his head, but again made a movement toward his waistband. The officer knew weapons are commonly carried there, under an untucked shirt. He then had reasonable suspicion both to detain the men and pat them down.

In *Williams v. State,* 629 S.W.2d 146 (Tex. App.-Dallas 1982), defendant was stopped based on a tip that he had a gun. When the officer called

for defendant to pull his hands out of his pockets, defendant initially removed only the left hand. Following a second officer, he withdrew his right hand slowly. The officer had reasonable suspicion justifying a frisk.

In *Hill v. State,* 303 S.W.3d 863 (Tex. App.-Fort Worth 2009), officers were patrolling the east side of Forth Worth following a rash of robberies. They watched defendant's SUV pull into the back of a McDonalds parking lot and stop, but no one got out of the vehicle. The SUV then drove off and stopped at a convenience store a block away— again, no one exited. When it drove off again, the officers initiated a stop for an unsignaled turn. Defendant (the driver) and the front seat passenger both opened their doors and got out of the vehicle immediately—the officers later described this conduct as "out of the ordinary." Defendant then "reach[ed] towards his shirt, kind of reaching under the shirt on his back," as if retrieving a weapon. Given this suspicious conduct, the officers had reasonable suspicion to pat-down defendant.

See also *Spight v. State,* 76 S.W.3d 761 (Tex. App.-Houston [1st Dist.] 2002). A lone state trooper stopped defendant for speeding late at night on a dark stretch of I-10. Defendant was very nervous during the stop. His hands were shaking tremendously, he handed over his license before being asked, and he hesitated and seemed unsure of his answers to the trooper's questions. He remained nervous even when told he would only be issued a warning. When asked, defendant admitted to a previous arrest on "gun charges" and consented to a search of his car. In the back seat, the officer found a brick-shaped object wrapped in cellophane. Closer inspection revealed the object to be over $10,000 in cash. Defendant claimed he planned to use the money to buy a car, but began moving backward as he spoke. At this point, the totality of the circumstances—defendant's nervousness, his previous arrest, his apparent involvement with drugs or other illegal activity (as evidenced by the large sum of cash)—justified a pat-down for the trooper's safety.

In *Glazner v. State,* 175 S.W.3d 262 (Tex. Crim. App. 2005), a deputy stopped defendant, who was leaving a convenience store, after noticing that the registration on defendant's vehicle had expired. While explaining why he stopped him and asking for his license, the deputy noticed a clip on defendant's pocket which he suspected was connected to a knife. The deputy then had reasonable suspicion for a pat-down.

Compare with *O'Hara v. State, supra,* where a pat-down was justified when a lone officer stopped defendant at 3:30 a.m. for malfunctioning clearance lights, and defendant was wearing a "belt knife." Even after defendant voluntarily removed the knife, it was possible he had other weapons concealed.

In *Hitchcock v. State,* 118 S.W.3d 844 (Tex. App.-Texarkana 2003), officers were patrolling an apartment complex parking lot at around 1:30 a.m. when they saw three people sitting in a car with the lights out. Having received earlier reports of suspicious activity in the area, they decided to investigate, and one officer knocked on the front passenger-side window. When the occupants rolled the window down, the officer could smell burning marijuana. He asked all three occupants to step out. When they did, the backseat passenger fled. While another officer pursued him, the remaining officers had reasonable suspicion to pat-down the two remaining occupants.

But see *Guevera v. State,* 6 S.W.3d 759 (Tex. App.-Houston [1st Dist.] 1999). An anonymous tipster alleged that defendant would arrive at a donut shop with cocaine in his pocket and the intent to sell it. When defendant arrived at the specified shop in the van described by the unnamed informant, police had reasonable suspicion for a stop. However, they did not have reasonable suspicion to pat defendant down. The informant never alleged that defendant would be armed or dangerous, and the amount of cocaine involved was small, so there was no reason to suspect defendant was a "big-time" dealer. Moreover, the stop took place in broad daylight in a public parking lot, and defendant was cooperative throughout.

See also *Tucker v. State,* 135 S.W.3d 920 (Tex. App.-Amarillo 2004). After stopping defendant for speeding, an officer did not have reasonable suspicion to frisk him when defendant was cooperative, did not appear to be under the influence of intoxicating substances, and made no furtive gestures or attempt to flee. Although there was a large bulge in defendant's fanny pack, the officer did not testify that it resembled the outline of a firearm, knife, or other particular weapon, and conceded that a fanny pack was "not necessarily a storage place for a ... weapon." Because the officer had no reasonable fear defendant was armed and dangerous, a pat-down was not justified.

The scope of the search must be strictly limited, so that the officer seeks only items that could be used to harm him or her.

See *Davis v. State,* 829 S.W.2d 218 (Tex. Crim. App. 1992), where an officer exceeded scope of a valid pat-down by opening a matchbox, because that is not a place where as suspect could hide a dangerous weapon.

See also *Baldwin v. State,* 278 S.W.3d 367 (Tex. Crim. App. 2009), where an officer went beyond the bounds of a lawful pat-down search when he removed defendant's wallet to check his identification. "Though an officer may ask a defendant to identify himself during a valid investigative detention, that does not automatically mean that the officer can search a defendant's person to obtain or confirm his identity." Similarly, an officer may not search the contents of a suspect's cell phone based solely on reasonable suspicion—the officer must have either the suspect's consent or probable cause to arrest. *United States v. Zavala,* 541 F.3d 562 (5th Cir. 2008).

In *State v. Williams,* 312 S.W.3d 276 (Tex. App.-Houston [14th Dist.] 2010), defendant was a rear seat passenger in a car stopped for a defective taillight. The driver was arrested after a pat-down found numerous prescription pills on his person—the driver then said that defendant had a steak knife, and she had been threatening to stab the other passengers. As the officer was a male and defendant a female, he did not want to pat her down. Instead, he asked her to "kind of reach underneath [her bra] and just pull it out a little bit and kind of shake it a little bit ... and maneuver it." (Because defendant was relatively well-endowed—"more than average"—the officer was concerned she may have concealed the steak knife in her bra.) Defendant initially refused and cried, but after a second request complied. When she did, numerous pills fell out. The Court ruled this search unconstitutional. The Court found that the officer's reluctance to pat-down a female did not justify broadening the scope of this search beyond a simple frisk, noting that a pat-down would not have been dangerous or ineffective and that no legal authority prohibits the pat-down of a female suspect by a male officer. The pills were suppressed.

If a weapon is found during a pat-down, the officer may seize the item, and retain it, if its possession is unlawful. If the officer determines that the suspect is not armed, the purpose of the frisk is satisfied and the probing can proceed no further. However, if in the frisking procedure an object is detected, in a pocket or under clothing, that is clearly not a weapon, but rather, and just as obviously, contraband, the item may be seized. The rule here is that officers conducting a Terry frisk are entitled to seize any item whose contour, shape or mass make its identity immediately apparent as contraband. The officer must be able to instantly tell the item is contraband, without resorting to further manipulation of the item. This corollary is sometimes called the "plain feel" doctrine. *Minnesota v. Dickerson,* 508 U.S. 366 (1993).

*Minnesota v. Dickerson, supra,* set out the three requirements for "plain feel." First, the officer must have some independent constitutional justification for placing his or her hands on the person. Second, the officer must have lawful reason to touch the area in question, i.e., reasonable suspicion of finding a weapon there. Third, upon touching the area, the officer must, through the process of touching, garner probable cause to believe the object that he or she is touching constitutes evidence of crime, or contraband. The probable cause must be reasonably contemporaneous with the initial touching. Any evidence obtained as a result of an illegal pat-down or frisk is inadmissible under the "Exclusionary Rule."

See *Graham v. State,* 893 S.W.2d 4 (Tex. App.-Dallas 1994). During a pat-down, an officer noticed an object in defendant's watch pocket that "felt sort of puffy, [and] made sort of a crackling sound..." Because the object did not feel like a weapon, the officer continued his frisk; however, he then went back to the pocket and began to rub it, later testifying, "You could distinctly feel two objects in there, you know, if you pinched on them enough you could tell that [sic] felt like little capsules or pills or something like that." Because the officer did not immediately recognize the objects as pills in cellophane, but first had to manipulate them, there was no valid plain feel seizure.

In *U.S. v. Campbell,* 178 F.2d 345 (5th Cir. 1999), officers saw defendant, a suspect in a bank robbery the day before, leaving a residence in a high-crime area, headed toward the apparent getaway car. They had good reason to think he was armed, and were justified in frisking him. During this pat-down, the searching officer felt a "large bulge" in defendant's right front pants pocket, that he reasonably feared might be "some type of weapon[.]" He therefore lawfully removed a large wad of cash (over $1,400), a gold jewelry box, and some change from defendant's pocket.

Compare with *U.S. v. Majors,* 328 F.3d 791 (5th Cir. 2003). During a pat-down, an officer felt a large bulge in the left pocket of defendant's baggy shorts. It was "bigger than a softball" and "in between hard and soft." The officer could not tell

if there was a weapon within the bulge and was justified in emptying the pocket (he lawfully seized what turned out to be a large bag with several smaller bags of cocaine).

See also *Griffin v. State,* 215 S.W.3d 403 (Tex. Crim. App. 2007). A reliable confidential-informant told an investigator that defendant was dealing crack cocaine. The investigator knew that just two days earlier, defendant had been arrested for possession of a small amount of cocaine residue found in a "long plastic tube." About five minutes after receiving the tip, the investigator intercepted defendant, then stopped and frisked him. The investigator felt two long cylindrical tubes in defendant's left front pocket—he could tell this without having to "squeeze, slide, [or] otherwise manipulate" them. He immediately recognized these as contraband, based on his knowledge that defendant had used these types of containers to carry narcotics just two days earlier. The investigator's seizure of the tubes was therefore lawful.

But see *Campbell v. State,* 864 S.W.2d 223 (Tex. App.-Waco 1993). During a frisk, an officer felt a film canister in defendant's pocket. He opened it and found cocaine. The Court ruled this search illegal, because the film canister did not feel like a weapon, and when the officer touched it he felt nothing to indicate it held anything more incriminating than film.

In *Dew v. State,* 214 S.W.3d 459 (Tex. App.-Eastland 2005), defendant was stopped for two driving violations. He claimed he did not have his driver's license with him. However, during a pat-down, an officer felt a bulge in defendant's pocket that was clearly a wallet. The officer was justified under the "plain feel" doctrine in removing the wallet, so he could search it for some form of identification.

The safety concerns that underlie the *Terry* exception have relevance not only to detentions on the street or in a public place, but also to the detention of automobile drivers and passengers as well. The U.S. Supreme Court has noted that "roadside encounters between police and suspects are especially hazardous, and danger may arise from the possible presence of weapons in the area surrounding a suspect." Thus, the search of the passenger compartment of an automobile, limited to those areas in which a weapon may be placed or hidden, is permissible if the police officer possesses a reasonable belief based on specific and articulable facts which, taken together with the rational inferences from those facts, reasonably warrant the officer to believe that the suspect is dangerous and may gain immediate control of a weapon. *Michigan v. Long,* 463 U.S. 1032 (1983). The search must be limited in scope to the area that the suspect can reach easily, sometimes called the "zone within the wingspan" or "grabbable area." A *Long* search may be valid even when the motorist is outside the vehicle and under armed guard. *Maztzke v. State,* 93 S.W.3d 536 (Tex. App.-Texarkana 2002).

For safety reasons, following a lawful stop an officer may, as a matter of course, order the driver and any passengers to step out of the vehicle. *Pennsylvania v. Mimms,* 434 U.S. 106 (1977); *Maryland v. Wilson,* 519 U.S. 408 (1997). An officer may also pat-down a driver or passenger during a traffic stop if there is reasonable suspicion to believe they may be armed and dangerous. *Arizona v. Johnson,* 555 U.S. 323 (2009).

3. **Reasonable Suspicion and Probable Cause.** The facts and observations divulged during an investigatory detention may lead to "probable cause" to arrest the person detained. However, the officer must possess facts sufficient to support crossing the threshold between mere reasonable suspicion to detain and question, and full probable cause to arrest, before the latter action may be taken. If the investigating officer does not yet possess facts sufficient to create probable cause to believe the detainee has committed a crime, yet restrains the liberty of the detainee in a manner consistent with a formal arrest, the detention, even if initially lawful, becomes illegal. For example, transporting a suspect involuntarily to a stationhouse for further questioning without probable cause to link him with a crime violates the detainee's Fourth Amendment rights. This more intrusive step in the investigatory process requires probable cause and cannot be justified on reasonable suspicion alone. Courts look to the extent of the restriction on an individual's freedom and movement, to determine if the restraint is more consistent with a detention, or a full-blown arrest. For example, although the use of handcuffs on a suspect is a "hallmark" of a formal arrest and is generally considered a watershed, where a temporary detention becomes an arrest, a suspect nonetheless may be handcuffed or similarly restrained during a temporary detention, if the circumstances warrant. *State v. Sheppard,* 271 S.W.3d 281 (Tex. Crim. App. 2008).

One of the most common pitfalls in the area of reasonable suspicions and probable cause is the timing of an officer's arrest. In his or her zeal, an officer frequently acts prematurely and, as a result, nullifies what might have been a valid arrest. Thus, an officer may have grounds to approach an individual to question him or her and may even have reason to stop a person in order to obtain information. Certain officers, based on a "hunch" or a "gut feeling" that the individual is "dirty," will search or arrest the individual before they legally have grounds to do so. Many officers feel that the results of the search will justify the police activity. However, the courts have made it quite clear that a bad arrest or a bad search cannot be salvaged or corrected by what the officer recovers from the suspect.

Therefore an officer must proceed with care when approaching an individual on the street or in a car. The officer may only intrude upon the individual's privacy to the extent permitted. The officer can only act in relation to the information he or she possesses at that time. If the information he or she possesses does not constitute probable cause to arrest, the officer must not act prematurely and cannot take the person into custody. A law enforcement officer should proceed with questioning, surveillance, or other appropriate police work that can culminate in probable cause.

4. **Detention and Seizure of Property.** Persons and vehicles are not the only potential subjects of a temporary detention. Officers may temporarily seize and detain items of personal property when they possess a reasonable suspicion that the property is connected with criminal activity. The detention must last no longer than reasonably necessary for the purpose of determining if the item is in fact linked to a criminal endeavor. If a brief investigation reveals that it is not, then the property should be returned to the owner. The Fourth Amendment protects property as well as privacy. *Soldal v. Cook Co.,* 506 U.S. 538 (1992). Therefore, similar to the seizure of an individual, "seizures of property are subject to Fourth Amendment scrutiny." *Soldal, supra.* This is true even when no search within the meaning of the Amendment has taken place.

Property is detained most often when the police wish to detain luggage or a package to search it for drugs. Often there is a slight delay to obtain a drug-sniffing dog. Items also may be held to search for weapons, explosive material or other contraband. Although in many cases the police will not need full probable cause for the detention of the property, in all cases the police will need some type of objective justification.

A detention of property may be deemed more reasonable if the police allow the owner of the object to leave. The police should then arrange a way to get the detained item back to that individual if their suspicions turn out to be baseless.

A "seizure" of property occurs when "there is some meaningful interference with an individual's possessory interests in that property." *U.S. v. Jacobsen,* 466 U.S. 109 (1984).

Note: *In U.S. v. Bond,* 529 U.S. 334 (2000), the U.S. Supreme Court held that warrantless "squeezing" or other physical manipulation by police of luggage in the overhead compartment of a vehicle or other publicly accessible space—as opposed to mere visual inspection—violates the Fourth Amendment. Although passengers must expect some "casual contact" with their bags by other passengers, they also have a reasonable expectation that their privacy will not be invaded by the other passengers feeling their bags in an exploratory manner.

## D. Exclusionary Rule

1. **Judicially Created.** The federal exclusionary rule is a judicially created doctrine designed to protect those rights embodied in the Fourth Amendment. *Mapp v. Ohio,* 367 U.S. 643 (1961). In addition, there is a broader exclusionary rule in Texas created by statute. *Tex. Code Crim. Proc.* art. 38.23.

2. **Application.** The federal exclusionary rule is applicable only to constitutional violations by governmental actors, not an individual who is not an agent of the government. See *U.S. v. Jacobsen,* 466 U.S. 109 (1984). However, the Texas exclusionary rule (as created under *Tex. Code Crim. Proc.* art. 38.23) applies even to private individuals *not* acting as agents of the government. *Tex. Code Crim. Proc.* art. 38.23; *State v. Johnson,* 939 S.W.2d 586 (Tex. Crim. App. 1996).

3. **Purpose.** The federal exclusionary rule serves as a deterrent to unlawful police conduct. *U.S. v. Leon,* 468 U.S. 897 (1984).

## E. Probable Cause

1. **In General.** In a pre-trial, investigatory context, probable cause is the highest constitutional degree of suspicion (in a trial, or guilt phase context, the "beyond a reasonable doubt" standard would be an even higher level of skepticism, bordering on certainty of guilt). Probable cause does not mean that the arrestee actually committed the suspected crime, or that the officer possesses enough proof to convict the suspect at a trial, or even that the arrestee will go to trial for

the alleged offense. It does mean that at the time of the arrest, a prudent, objective person, in the position of the officer, taking into account his or her experience, knowledge and observations, would reasonably believe that a crime has been or is being committed. When probable cause determinations, whether made by a magistrate or an officer in the field, are challenged, the outcome will often depend on the presence or absence of one seemingly insignificant factor. As with factors used in a reasonable suspicion analysis, when an isolated factor is viewed alone, it may seem trivial. When analyzed with all of the other circumstances surrounding the arrest, it may lead a reviewing court to conclude the conduct was reasonable, and that the challenged arrest was based on probable cause.

In a warrantless arrest situation a police officer will be making the initial probable cause determination. Since probable cause is a somewhat nebulous concept, courts have tried to provide guidance. The U.S. Supreme Court has stated that "[i]n determining probable cause, evidence required to establish guilt is not necessary, but on the other hand, good faith on the part of the arresting officers is not enough, and probable cause exists if the facts and circumstances known to the officer warrant a prudent man in believing that the offense has been committed." *Henry v. U.S.,* 361 U.S. 98 (1959).

2. **Legal Definition.** "Probable cause" (sometimes called "reasonable cause") is a standard of proof greater than that of reasonable suspicion needed for a detention. It does not rise to the level of proof needed to obtain a conviction. Probable cause to arrest may exist (as determined later by a reviewing court) even if the arresting officer subjectively did not believe he had sufficient facts to constitute probable cause, as long as the objective standard is met. An arrest may be effectuated pursuant to a validly executed warrant, or without, provided probable cause exists.

The highest (most invasive) level of contact a law enforcement officer may have with a citizen is "probable cause to arrest." An officer may make a warrantless arrest if he or she has probable cause. Probable cause is the officer's knowledge of facts and circumstances based on reasonable, trustworthy information sufficient to warrant a prudent person to believe that the suspect has committed an offense.

"Probable cause" means that an officer need not have information which excludes every conceivable possibility of innocence. Probable cause depends upon probabilities, not certainties. Thus, it must appear to the officer that it is at least more probable than not that a crime has taken place, and that the one arrested is its perpetrator. Conduct equally compatible with guilt or innocence will not constitute probable cause.

The subsequent determination of the guilt or innocence of the person arrested does not determine the legality of the arrest. *Michigan v. DeFillippo,* 443 U.S. 31 (1979).

Because probable cause depends on the facts of each case, probable cause may or may not be found in certain instances.

3. **Cautions to Observe (Warrantless Arrest).** As every officer knows, our society is overrun with drugs. Many people rely on the police to fight this "war" against drug activity. The police officer must resist the temptation to use whatever means possible in fighting this "war." Courts will not tolerate a violation of constitutional rights merely because it occurs in the fight against drugs.

Thus, while an exchange of money for a glassine envelope, tinfoil packet or small vial with white powder will constitute probable cause for an arrest in most cases, not every exchange will permit an arrest. An officer may feel that if he or she sees an exchange for any object, the courts will back him or her up should he or she make an arrest. This is not so. An officer must still have reason to believe that he or she is observing a sale of drugs. Should the officer observe an exchange of an object he or she cannot see, the officer should not move in to make an arrest, unless there are other factors that make it probable that drugs are being transferred.

The officer cannot use the "high-crime area" factor as a crutch to make the arrest. Most geographical areas today can be considered high-crime areas, and that fact, in and of itself, will not turn an improper arrest for drugs into a valid arrest. An officer may feel that he or she knows from past experience that the individual has no other reason to be in this area than to buy or sell drugs. However, that fact by itself will not be enough probable cause to justify an arrest.

4. **Identification of Suspect Required.** An officer must be sure that the description of a suspect is sufficiently detailed before he or she can effectuate an arrest. If the description is too vague or general, the officer should refrain from making the mistake of arresting the suspect prematurely. Instead he or she should ask the suspect certain questions or keep the suspect under surveillance. Obviously, if those procedures are not practical, the officer should use common

sense and take reasonable steps to keep the suspect under observation.

The victim is the best source of identification of a suspect. The courts will assume that the victim is reliable and obviously knows what he or she is talking about. Unless a police officer has reason not to believe a victim (*i.e.,* if he or she exhibits emotional or mental problems), the officer can rely on the victim for sufficient identification and probable cause to make an arrest, without having to verify the information. *Casarez v. State,* 504 S.W.2d 847 (Tex. Crim. App. 1974).

See *Romero v. State,* 709 S.W.2d 53 (Tex. App.-Fort Worth 1986). An officer responded to a family disturbance call. He found the defendant's ex-wife with a cut lip, blood in her hair, scratches on her arm, and a swollen right eye; she said that defendant had come over and hit her. She then showed the officer a recent picture of defendant and described his vehicle. Less than an hour later, the officer found defendant near the described vehicle, a block away from the victim's home. He had probable cause to arrest.

A police officer can also rely on a citizen who is not the victim of a crime, to provide information which will constitute probable cause to make an arrest. While the courts have also found this type of citizen to be trustworthy, an officer must still verify that the citizen knows what he or she is talking about. This is known as the citizen's "basis of knowledge."

Occasionally a victim will tell a police officer that he or she is not absolutely certain of an identification or that a person only looks like the perpetrator of the crime. This information is usually insufficient to provide an officer with probable cause. However, probable cause will exist if the victim picks out a suspect's photograph.

5. **Informants.** When a police officer relies upon a confidential informant for information, there are certain points that the officer must keep in mind. Before the courts will find probable cause based on the informant's information, the officer must be sure that the tip is reliable. Two important components of this determination include both the informant's "credibility" and "basis of knowledge."

In order to establish an informant's "credibility," an officer should determine the following: (i) whether the informant came forward in the past with accurate information; (ii) whether the informant is making a declaration against his or her penal interest; (iii) whether the officer can confirm details of the informant's story; (iv) whether the informant is an ordinary citizen who provides information solely to help solve a crime or prevent a future crime.

In order to establish an informant's "basis of knowledge," the officer must consider the following: (i) whether the informant spoke from personal knowledge; (ii) whether the officer observed conduct directly involving the criminal activity about which the informant gave information.

If, under the totality of the circumstances—including the informant's "credibility" and "basis of knowledge"—the reliability of the tip can be established by the officer, probable cause for an arrest will exist.

Be aware that an anonymous tip, standing alone, will not establish probable cause to arrest; there must be additional facts corroborating the tip. *Amores v. State,* 816 S.W.3d 407 (Tex. Crim. App. 1991).

6. **Other Basis for Probable Cause.** When a police officer relies on information from fellow police officers or from official police sources, he or she is entitled to assume that the "sending" officer has "probable cause" and that the information is reliable and accurate. However, an officer should also realize that if he or she acts on information that has become stale or outdated before the arrest (*i.e.,* an outdated arrest warrant, parole warrant, stolen car report, etc.), the arrest will be voided by the courts. Note that a failure to make a diligent search for the defendant when acting on a warrant can invalidate an arrest.

"Probable cause" can come from a variety of sources. A police officer can obtain information from a defendant's accomplice. An officer can utilize fingerprints at the scene of a crime or even information from a conversation heard through a wall to obtain the necessary information for an arrest.

## F. Arrest

1. **Defined.** The most invasive level of encounter a law enforcement officer may have with a citizen is the formal arrest. Courts look to a variety of factors to determine whether an arrest has taken place, or whether a temporary detention has escalated into a formal arrest. Criteria employed in this evaluation include: (i) whether the initial encounter was consensual; (ii) the duration or scope of the encounter, not only regarding the length of the detention, but also with respect to the degree of intrusiveness; (iii) an officer's statement that an individual is not free to leave, and what a reasonable suspect in a similar situation would believe regarding his

liberty; (iv) whether the officer in some way restrained the suspect, and the nature and extent of that restraint; (v) the level of physical force threatened or employed; (vi) whether weapons or dogs were used to restrain, coerce, or intimidate the suspect; (vii) the number of officers conducting the stop, and the nature of their questioning; (viii) whether or not the individual was transported to another location; (ix) whether the encounter took place in public view, or in a private or secluded area.

For purposes of constitutional analysis, as with a *Terry* detention, when a suspect is formally arrested, he has been seized for Fourth Amendment purposes, thus calling constitutional protections into play. However, unlike the limited intrusion imposed during a *Terry* stop, an arrest imposes the greatest restraint on an individual's liberty short of incarceration, and a higher level of skepticism—probable cause—must be demonstrated.

2. **Warrantless Arrests.**

a. **In Public Places.** In Texas, there can be no warrantless arrest absent statutory authority. *Heath v. Boyd,* 175 S.W.2d 214 (Tex. 1943); *State v. Steelman,* 93 S.W.3d 102 (Tex. Crim. App. 2002).

An officer may make a warrantless arrest for any offense committed within his presence or view. *Tex. Code Crim. Proc.* art. 14.01(b). An officer may also arrest for a felony or breach of the peace committed within the presence or view of a magistrate, if the magistrate so directs. *Tex. Code Crim. Proc.* art. 14.02.

An offense is committed within an officer's "presence" when "any one of his senses afford him an awareness of its occurrence." However, the information afforded to the officer must give him reason to believe a *particular* suspect committed the offense before an arrest can be made. *State v. Steelman, supra* (when defendant stepped out of his house and officers could smell marijuana in the air, but not on defendant himself, they did not have probable cause to arrest him).

An officer may also make a warrantless arrest when a person is found in a "suspicious place" and the circumstances reasonably show that the person has committed a felony, disorderly conduct, breach of the peace or public intoxication, or is about to commit some offense against the laws. *Tex. Code Crim. Proc.* art. 14.03(a)(1).

Few, if any, places are suspicious in and of themselves. There must be additional facts to arouse justifiable suspicion. *Johnson v. State,* 722 S.W.2d 417 (Tex. Crim. App. 1986). The determination that a place is "suspicious" is highly fact-specific. *Holland v. State,* 788 S.W.2d 112 (Tex. App.-Dallas 1990). The time between the commission of the crime and the apprehension of the suspect is an "important factor" in determining if a place is suspicious. *Dyar v. State,* 125 S.W.3d 460 (Tex. Crim. App. 2003).

A place can be suspicious because (i) an eyewitness or officer connected the place to the crime; (ii) a crime occurred there or police reasonably believe a crime occurred there; (iii) there is specific evidence directly connecting the defendant or the place with the crime; or (iv) the defendant's behavior indicates that the place is suspicious. *Goldberg v. State,* 95 S.W.3d 345 (Tex. App.-Houston [1st Dist.] 2002).

See, *e.g., Dyar v. State, supra* (hospital a suspicious place when defendant was taken there following a single-car accident on New Year's Eve and showed signs of intoxication); *Adams v. State,* 552 S.W.2d 812 (Tex. Crim. App. 1977) (defendant's car a suspicious place when he drove it at 12:15 a.m. near the motel room of a known fence with the trunk open and a television in plain view inside); *Mitchell v. State,* 756 S.W.2d 71 (Tex. App.-Texarkana 1988) ("The presence of a stolen vehicle in [defendant's] yard [could] reasonably be considered to qualify the yard and house as a suspicious place"); *Wilson v. State,* 722 S.W.2d 3 (Tex. App.-Dallas 1986) (defendant's apartment a suspicious place when a car registered to him was used in a bank robbery and his apartment manager identified him from a composite drawing of the robber); *Thomas v. State,* 681 S.W.2d 672 (Tex. App.-Houston [14th Dist.] 1984) (street in a neighborhood where a least one home had been recently burglarized suspicious when three men were walking down it carrying a television); *Douglas v. State,* 679 S.W.2d 790 (Tex. App.-Fort Worth 1984) (defendant's house was a suspicious place when a dead body was found lying in the front yard and defendant had been seen near the body, had put something in a car parked outside the house, and had then run back inside after being seen by a witness); *Battles v. State,* 626 S.W.2d 149 (Tex. App.-Fort Worth 1981) (defendant was in a suspicious place when he was found in the complainant's home with a gun in his hand after a call for discharge of a firearm).

An officer may also make a warrantless arrest at any public place if the officer has probable cause to believe (i) a suspect has assaulted another causing bodily injury, if there is probable cause to believe there is danger of further bodily injury; (ii) for violation of a protective order; or (iii) for an assault resulting in bodily injury to a family or household member. *Tex. Code Crim. Proc.* art. 14.03(a)(2)-(4).

An arrest for a felony committed outside the officer's presence may also be made if: (i) a credible person alleges that the crime was committed, and (ii) the suspect is about to escape. *Tex. Code Crim. Proc.* art. 14.04. The State must prove by a clear showing that the suspect was about to escape, so that there was no time to procure an arrest warrant. *Fry v. State,* 639 S.W.2d 463 (Tex. Crim. App. 1982).

Any person, including an officer, may arrest a suspect if there is probable cause to believe the suspect is in possession of stolen property. *Tex. Code Crim. Proc.* art. 18.16.

The Fourth Amendment does not prohibit a custodial arrest for a minor, fine-only offense. *Atwater v. City of Lago Vista,* 532 U.S. 318 (2001) (upholding arrest of motorist for failure to wear a seatbelt). However, in lieu of making an arrest for a Class C misdemeanor (other than public intoxication), an officer may issue a citation to the person that contains written notice of the time and place the person must appear before a magistrate, the name and address of the person charged, and the offense charged. *Tex. Code Crim. Proc.* art. 14.06. In lieu of making an arrest for public intoxication, an officer may release the suspect if (i) the officer believes detention in a penal facility is unnecessary for the protection of the suspect or others and (ii) the individual is released to the care of an adult who agrees to assume responsibility or the suspect verbally agrees to enter a treatment program. *Tex. Code Crim. Proc.* art. 14.031.

If a person who commits one of the following resides in the county where the offense occurred, and the offense is a Class A or B misdemeanor, an officer may issue a citation rather than taking the person before a magistrate:

- Possession of 4 ounces or less of marihuana (Health & Safety Code § 481.121(b)(1)-(2))
- Criminal mischief involving pecuniary loss less than $500 (Penal Code § 28.03(b)(2))
- Graffiti involving pecuniary loss less than $500 (Penal Code § 28.08(b)(1))
- Theft of property with a value less than $500 (Penal Code § 31.03(e)(2)(a))
- Theft of services with a value less than $500 (Penal Code § 31.03(e)(2))
- Contraband in a correctional facility (Penal Code § 38.114)
- Driving while license invalid (Transportation Code § 521.457)

Tex. Code Crim. Proc. art. 14.06.

b. **Justification for a Warrantless Arrest.** Statements made by a co-offender or accomplice can lead to probable cause for the arrest of his or her partner, when such a statement is against the maker's penal interest, or is corroborated by the police through their own independent line of investigation. When the statement given implicates the maker in wrongdoing, courts may attach greater weight to it. It is sometimes said that statements against penal interest carry their own indicia of reliability because it is unlikely and unnatural for persons to falsely incriminate themselves.

Information that comes from a source outside of law enforcement circles, from private citizens or police informers, may demonstrate facts sufficient to establish probable cause. To determine if an informant's tip supports a probable cause finding, courts will employ a totality of the circumstances analysis and examine all of the attendant factors, including the veracity and reliability of the informant, and the basis of the informant's knowledge. No one aspect of the tip or information, or the person giving it, is determinative on the issue of probable cause, but rather the sum of all the circumstances concerning the tip and the person making it must be examined. (See discussion under **Informants,** above).

Police are entitled to rely on facts garnered by those with whom they work. When more than one officer is working on a particular case, a reviewing court will take into account all of the information known to all of the officers on the case (not just the information known to the one who made the arrest) to determine if there was probable cause to arrest. This is known as the "fellow officer rule." Probable cause may rest upon the collective knowledge of police where there is some degree of communication among them, rather than solely on the information possessed by the officer who made the arrest. If probable cause is possessed by one officer, and the officer communicates with a second officer, then that second officer may arrest although he or she does not have independent probable cause.

Flight, nervousness or evasive maneuvers when confronted with police presence, although not sufficient to create probable cause when standing alone, may create probable cause for arrest if coupled with a suspicion centering on the suspect.

See, *e.g., Guzman v. State,* 955 S.W.3d 85 (Tex. Crim. App. 1997). An Austin officer was patrolling the 1700 block of East First Street, an area well-known for drug trafficking. He saw a pedestrian flag down a car, the trade an object taken out of his mouth for cash from the motorist. The officer quickly detained the pedestrian, who told police he knew where they could "get a lot more heroin" and said he had seen defendant, a Hispanic male in a brown leather jacket, with balloons of heroin in his mouth. Shortly thereafter, this new informant pointed defendant out to police. Officers walked toward defendant, and yelled, "Hey, stop." Defendant "kind of turned and looked at [the officers] and started walking faster." As the officers closed in on him, he began swallowing. At this point, the officers had probable cause to arrest for possession of a controlled substance.

In *Muniz v. State,* 672 S.W.2d 804 (Tex. Crim. App. 1984), a burglary was reported at 12:45 p.m. Shortly thereafter, an officer saw two males who matched the descriptions of the burglars given by a witness walking down the street three blocks from the site of the break-in. After the pair saw the officer's patrol car, they "started throwing things out of their pockets" and walking "at a fast walk." The officer had probable cause to arrest the men for the burglary.

Compare with *Pyles v. State,* 755 S.W.2d 98 (Tex. Crim. App. 1988). A Dallas County officer was shot at around 1:00 a.m. while investigating the burglary of a grocery store. The other officers who arrived on the scene were unable to locate the suspect. A reserve deputy who had been called out to assist in the search set up surveillance in an unmarked car almost two miles from the grocery store. At around 4:00 a.m., the officer saw defendant walking toward him, from the direction of the crime scene. Defendant was covered in mud, his clothing was torn, and his right hand was swollen and bloody. When the deputy confronted him, he attempted to turn and walk away. The deputy had probable cause to arrest.

See also *Hughes v. State,* 24 S.W.3d 833 (Tex. Crim. App. 2000), undercover officers staked out the parking lot of a Dallas theater following a rash of robberies and burglaries. They noticed defendant and his partner, Michael English, walking through the lot toward the theater. Just 10 minutes later, they saw both men walking quickly back toward their car. Defendant walked 20 to 30 feet behind English, who was hunched over, concealing a "large bulge" beneath his shirt. (There had been no such bulge minutes before.) After both men entered the car, they quickly accelerated, exiting the parking lot at a high rate of speed. One of the officers followed clandestinely, and observed the car reach speeds up to 90 m.p.h. Soon thereafter, police discovered that the bodies of two theater patrons had been found, apparently dead of gunshot wounds. At this point, the officer had probable cause to arrest defendant and English.

Facts officers turn up through their own investigations, or by their own observations, can form the basis of probable cause.

See, *e.g., Butler v. State,* 825 S.W.2d 727 (Tex. App.-Houston [14th Dist.] 1992). An officer on routine patrol in a residential area saw a car parked illegally, facing south in a north-bound lane. He pulled up next to the car, intending to give it a warning. As he looked inside the car, he could see clear plastic baggies containing crack cocaine on the passenger side of the front seat (as a member of the narcotics unit, he had seen the drug several times and recognized it). He then had probable cause to arrest the car's occupants.

In *Brown v. State,* 986 S.W.2d 50 (Tex. App.-Dallas 1999), two officers on routine patrol observed a vehicle listed on their "hot sheet," a printout of all the vehicles reported stolen in the city. They stopped the car and confirmed through the National Crime Information Center that it had been reported stolen. At this point, they had probable cause to arrest its occupants.

In *Beverly v. State,* 792 S.W.2d 103 (Tex. Crim. App. 1990), an officer had probable cause to arrest defendant for trespass when he saw defendant get out of his car at an apartment complex and knew that defendant was on a list of "trespass warned" loiterers compiled by management.

See also *Johnson v. State,* 171 S.W.3d 643 (Tex. App.-Houston [14th Dist.] 2005). Around 10:00 p.m., two Harris County deputies were flagged down by a citizen. The citizen stated that he had been chasing an armadillo between two nearby houses; while searching for the armadillo, he had peered through a wooden fence surrounding the back yard of a house and saw his neighbor standing in the lighted kitchen processing cocaine. The deputies went to the house indicated by the citizen. From outside the fence surrounding the yard, they could see through a large kitchen window and glass patio door. They observed a triple beam scale in an upper cabinet, and knew from experience that triple beam scales are commonly used in the processing and sale of narcotics. They also saw a box of baking soda near the scale—baking soda is commonly used in the creation and "cutting" of crack cocaine. The Court noted that "[w]hile baking soda is a common in most kitchens, triple beam scales are not. The

chance of randomly observing a box of baking soda in close proximity to a triple beam scale while passing behind a residence is extremely remote[.]" Therefore, the deputies had probable cause to arrest defendant for crack cocaine manufacture.

If the officer actually observes someone committing an offense, then there is probable cause to make an arrest. Even if the officer does not witness the actual acts that constitute the offense, circumstantial evidence may create probable cause to believe the crime has been committed.

In *Dyar v. State,* 125 S.W.3d 460 (Tex. Crim. App. 2003), defendant was brought to a hospital following a single-car accident on New Year's Eve. While interviewing defendant in the hospital, an officer noticed that his speech was slurred (so that many of his answers were unintelligible), his eyes were red and glassy, and there was a strong smell of alcohol emanating from him. The officer had probable cause to arrest defendant for DWI, even though he had not seen him driving.

In *McGee v. State,* 105 S.W.3d 609 (Tex. Crim. App.), *cert. denied,* 540 U.S. 1004 (2003), a Houston officer received a tip from a concerned citizen that three men were selling drugs at Fleming and Cool Wood. He went to that location and saw three men who matched the citizen's description. As he approached the trio, he could smell the odor of marijuana and saw blue smoke surrounding the men; based on his training and experience, he associated blue smoke with marijuana. In addition, there was a marijuana cigarette on the ground next to defendant, and an odor of marijuana emanating from him. The officer had probable cause to arrest defendant for possession of marijuana.

In *Maryland v. Pringle,* 540 U.S. 366 (2003), a car with three male occupants was stopped for speeding in the early morning hours. When the driver retrieved his license from the glove compartment, an officer noticed a large amount of cash. Because he found this suspicious, the officer asked for and received consent to search the car. Police found $763 in the glove compartment and five glassine bags of cocaine between the back-seat armrest and the back-seat. All three men denied ownership of the drug. Because the cocaine was accessible to all the men, it was reasonable to infer all three had knowledge of, and exercised domain and control over, it. Police therefore had probable cause to arrest all three occupants, including defendant, the front-seat passenger.

c. **Warrantless Arrest at a Residence.** A distinction must be drawn between a warrantless arrest made in a public place, and one made in a residence. Historically, the home has enjoyed nearly sacrosanct status in American and English common law. Courts have long held that the home's threshold should not be crossed without significant justification. As a consequence of this long standing judicial respect for the integrity and privacy of the home, courts have held that in the absence of exigent circumstances or consent (see below), a law enforcement official may not make a warrantless entry into a person's home to effect his or her arrest. Note, however, that a suspect cannot avoid a lawful warrantless public arrest already set in motion by retreating into his or her home. *U.S. v. Santana,* 427 U.S. 38 (1976).

The requirement of a warrant for an in-home arrest applies as well to the arrest of a suspect in a motel or hotel room where the suspect has set up a temporary residence. For similar reasons, if the police are to search in the home of a third party for a suspect for whose arrest they already have a warrant, they must obtain a search warrant before entering the third party's home, absent exigent circumstances or consent. *Steagald v. U.S.,* 451 U.S. 204 (1981).

The possession of an arrest warrant provides officers with the authority to arrest an individual within his or her own home, and limited authority to enter the dwelling for that purpose, if police have reason to believe that the subject of the warrant is inside at the time of entry. *Payton v. New York,* 445 U.S. 573 (1980). In determining whether a suspect is home, police should consider the totality of the circumstances, including the presence of a car outside, the hour and day, the observation of lights or other electrical devices in use inside, the suspect's employment status, and the presence of visitors. Police may take into account the fact that the suspect may be trying to hide and are not required to rely on statements that the suspect is not home. *Green v. State,* 78 S.W.3d 604 (Tex. App.-Fort Worth 2002).

The result of these rules is that if a suspect is to be arrested in a residence, a warrant must be obtained first, or the State will be forced to show that exigent circumstances or another applicable exception justified the otherwise illegal entry. If this burden is not met the arrest will be quashed. Any evidence the State hopes to use as a result of the arrest may be suppressed.

The penalty for an unlawful arrest in a defendant's dwelling is the suppression of anything seized at the time of the arrest, either from the defendant or in the dwelling, and any statements made at the time of the arrest inside the home. However, if the officers in fact had probable cause to arrest, a confession obtained *after* the illegal warrantless entry to effect the arrest, or other evidence found outside the home, is not necessarily inadmissible at trial. *New York v. Harris,* 495 U.S. 14 (1990).

d. **Exceptions to the Warrant Requirement for Residence Arrest.**

(1) **Exigent Circumstances.** Generally, exigent circumstances are explained as those surrounding a fast moving, often tense series of events which call for quick and decisive law enforcement action. These are factors that allow law enforcement agents to conduct a warrantless arrest, based on probable cause, when there exists an urgent need for official action and time to secure a warrant is not available. Factors considered in determining if exigent circumstances are present include (*Dorman v. U.S.,* 435 F.2d 385 (D.C. Cir. 1970)): (i) if the offense was violent in nature; (ii) a reasonable belief the suspect is armed; (iii) the level of certainty that the suspect committed the offense; (iv) the level of certainty that the suspect is in the building; (v) evidence indicating that the suspect is a flight risk; (vi) the time of day; (vii) the level of force officers need to obtain entry to the premises.

The police generally must be unable to obtain a warrant in the time necessary to meet and defuse the situation, or at the very least, contacting a magistrate must be extremely impractical (*e.g.,* late hour, remote location). In such situations, the requirement of a warrant may be excused. The presence of these extreme circumstances mandates the compelling need for quick activity and makes warrantless in-home arrests reasonable within the meaning of the Fourth Amendment. If such circumstances were not present, a warrant would be required. Often cited examples of the risks created when officers hesitate in making a warrantless in-home arrest and instead seek to obtain a warrant before acting include the following: (i) the risk of injury or death to officers or bystanders; (ii) the potential destruction or concealment of valuable evidence; or (iii) the possibility that the suspect may flee and elude capture.

A police officer can enter a premises without a warrant to protect individuals in distress, to assist victims of crimes that have just occurred, or to investigate suspicious signs of impending danger. There are three basic requirements for such action: (i) the police must have reasonable cause to believe that there is an emergency at hand and an immediate need for their assistance for the protection of life or property; (ii) the search must not be primarily motivated by an intent to arrest and seize evidence; and (iii) there must be some reasonable basis to associate the emergency with the area or property to be searched. See *In re J.D.,* 68 S.W.3d 775 (Tex. App.-San Antonio 2001). Once the police respond and enter a premises pursuant to this exigency, they have the right to "restore or maintain the status quo during the emergency to control the dangerous or dynamic situation." This right enables the officer to take a number of intrusive actions ranging from a command to halt to a seizure of an individual. During the investigation of an emergency situation, the police may search for weapons to protect themselves and others and may look for injured or missing persons.

In *Brigham City v. Stuart,* 547 U.S. 398 (2006), four officers responded to a loud party at a residence at around 3:00 a.m. When they arrived, they heard sounds of an altercation occurring inside—"thumping and crashing" as well as people yelling "stop, stop" and "get off me." The officers looked in the front window but saw nothing; because the sounds seemed to be coming from the back of the house, they proceeded down the driveway to investigate further. From the end of the driveway, they could see two juveniles drinking beer in the back yard. When they entered the back yard, they saw an altercation taking place in the kitchen through a screen door and windows. "[F]our adults were attempting, with some difficulty, to restrain a juvenile." The juvenile, fists clenched, eventually "broke free, swung a fist and struck one of the adults in the face." That adult then spit blood into the sink. The other three adults continued to restrain the juvenile, pressing him against a refrigerator with such force that it slid across the floor. The officers called out, but were ignored. They then entered the residence and broke up the fight. The adults were arrested for contributing to the delinquency of a minor (because of the juveniles outside with beer), disorderly conduct and intoxication. The U.S. Supreme Court upheld this warrantless entry under the Fourth Amendment. The officers were confronted with ongoing violence. They had an objectively reasonable belief that "both the injured adult might need help and that the violence in the kitchen was just beginning." The Court noted that police are not required to wait until someone is unconscious (or semi-conscious) before entering: "The role of a peace officer in-

cludes preventing violence and restoring order, not simply rendering first aid to casualties; an officer is not like a boxing (or hockey) referee, poised to stop a bout only if it becomes too one-sided."

(2) **Hot Pursuit.** Hot pursuit can be thought of as a specific application of the general exigent circumstances exception. In *Warden v. Hayden,* 387 U.S. 294 (1967), the U.S. Supreme Court held that if police were in hot pursuit of a fleeing suspect, they were entitled to make a warrantless entry to effectuate the arrest if they had probable cause to believe the suspect committed a felony, and they believed he entered a specific dwelling. However, in *Welsh v. Wisconsin,* 466 U.S. 740 (1984), the Court held this exception was almost always inapplicable when the suspect commits a traffic offense or other non-jailable infraction. See also *Randolph v. State,* 152 S.W.3d 764 (Tex. Crim. App. 2004). To justify a warrantless in-home arrest based on this exception, the State must generally demonstrate that (i) the pursuit was undertaken immediately after the crime (*i.e.,* it was "hot"), and (ii) there was a continuity of pursuit from the crime to the place of arrest.

(3) **Consent.** A third exception to the warrant requirement for an in-home arrest comes into play when police officers are first given permission to enter the premises and then arrest a suspect inside. Valid consent to enter may be given by the owner, or one entitled to possession of the premises, or one with common control or joint access to the premises for most purposes. Valid consent is that which is given voluntarily (*i.e.,* in the absence of overbearing conduct on the part of the law enforcement officials seeking permission). Consent may be either actually given, or implied from conduct or acts. The validity, or voluntariness, of consent is determined by examining all of the facts and circumstances surrounding the encounter.

(4) **Family Violence Calls.** An officer who investigates an alleged act or responds to a disturbance call that may involve family violence must advise any possible adult victim of all reasonable means to prevent further family violence, including giving written notice of a victim's legal rights and remedies and the availability of shelter or other community services. *Tex. Code Crim. Proc.* art. 5.04. The officer may, at his or her discretion, stay with a victim of family violence to protect the victim and allow the victim to take the personal property of the victim or of a child in the care of the victim to a place of safety in an orderly manner; in such cases, the officer is not liable for

any act or omission that arises in connection with providing the assistance or determining whether to provide the assistance, or for the wrongful appropriation of any personal property by the victim. *Tex. Code Crim. Proc.* art. 5.045.

Following a family violence incident or a disturbance call that may involve family violence, the responding officer must make a written report describing the incident. *Tex. Code Crim. Proc.* art. 5.05.

3. **Arrests Pursuant to Warrant.** The essential difference between arrests with a warrant and those without involves where a person may be arrested. When acting pursuant to a warrant, police are entitled to arrest a suspect anywhere. This is not so, absent exigent circumstances, in the case of a warrantless arrest. Another distinction is that in a situation where an arrest is made with a warrant, the existence of probable cause is determined by a neutral and detached magistrate, who places his or her independent judgment between a perhaps overzealous law enforcement official and the citizenry. In a situation where an arrest is made without a warrant, probable cause is determined by the officer in the field.

a. **Contents of the Arrest Warrant.** The arrest warrant must be in the name of the State of Texas, specify the name of the person to be arrested (or, if unknown, some reasonably definite description of the person), name the offense the person is accused of committing, and be signed by the magistrate with his or her office named in the body of the warrant or in connection with his or her signature. *Tex. Code Crim. Proc.* art. 15.02.

b. **Delay in Making Arrest.** A criminal suspect has no constitutional right to be arrested. There is no requirement that once law enforcement possesses probable cause to arrest, they do so immediately. However, a gap between the commission of the offense, or the time law enforcement becomes aware of it, and the arrest may be so protracted that it violates the Due Process Clause of the Fourteenth Amendment. Although the Sixth Amendment guarantees a defendant the right to a speedy trial, it does not guarantee the right to a speedy arrest. However, an inordinate delay between the time a crime is committed and the time a defendant is arrested or indicted may violate Due Process guarantees. To prevail on such a claim, a defendant must show that (i) the delay caused actual and substantial prejudice to the defendant, and (ii) the delay was the product of deliberate action or inaction by law enforcement in order to gain a tactical advantage.

To demonstrate prejudice the defendant must show that real and tangible harm was done to his defense. The mere passage of time, and its effects, is not sufficient. The fact that "memories will dim, witnesses become inaccessible, and evidence will be lost" during the gap is inadequate to demonstrate the defendant cannot receive a fair trial and insufficient to show a Due Process violation. *U.S. v. Marion,* 404 U.S. 307 (1971).

c. **Execution of the Arrest Warrant.** An arrest warrant issued by any county or district clerk or by any magistrate may be executed in any county in the State. *Tex. Code Crim. Proc.* art. 15.06. An arrest warrant may be served at any time of the day or night. *Tex. Code Crim. Proc.* art. 15.23.

The officer need not have physical possession of the warrant before making the arrest, but must show the warrant to the arrestee as soon as possible, if the arrestee so requests. If the officer does not possess the warrant at the time of arrest, the arrestee must be informed of the offense charged and the fact that a warrant has been issued. *Tex. Code Crim. Proc.* art. 15.26.

A "media ride-along," where a reporter and photographer accompanied police while an arrest warrant was served in a suspect's home, violated the U.S. Constitution. *Wilson v. Layne,* 526 U.S. 603 (1999).

d. **Knock-and-Announce Rule.** When executing an arrest warrant, law enforcement officers should knock on the door of a residence or business, announce their purpose and authority, and give the occupants a reasonable opportunity to answer before forcing their way inside. *Tex. Code Crim. Proc.* art. 15.25. However, there is no constitutional mandate that an officer must knock and announce before entering a dwelling in every instance. In situations where exigent circumstances are present, an unannounced entry may be reasonable (*e.g.,* presence of weapons that may put officers at peril, the destruction of evidence, etc.). "A no-knock entry is justified when the police have a reasonable suspicion that knocking and announcing their presence, under the particular circumstances, would be dangerous or futile, or that it would inhibit the effective investigation of the crime." *Richards v. Wisconsin,* 520 U.S. 385 (1997). Police are not required to possess the higher standard of probable cause to believe that exigent circumstances exist, but only the less stringent standard of reasonable suspicion. The failure to knock and announce is not a per se constitutional violation. There are no rigid rules to determine when an unannounced entry will be excused. The constitutionality of the entry will be judged on the particular facts and circumstances of each case. However, the failure to knock and announce may render an entry unreasonable, and therefore unconstitutional, when there is no showing of exigent circumstances that justify the failure to first knock.

e. **Protective Sweep.** In *Maryland v. Buie,* 494 U.S. 325 (1990), the U.S. Supreme Court held that when police make an arrest at a residence, they may conduct a warrantless search of the arrest scene, known as a "protective sweep." The extent of the sweep is limited to a brief cursory visual inspection of the premises. The Court reasoned that it is reasonable for officers to safeguard themselves by ensuring that no others are present who could injure them. It is important to note this is not a general crime scene exception to the warrant requirement but rather a doctrine that may be used to justify a warrantless search in particularized circumstances. A sweep is permissible only "when the searching officer possesses a reasonable belief based on specific and articulable facts that the area to be swept harbors an individual posing a danger to those on the arrest scene."

See, *e.g., Ramirez v. State,* 105 S.W.3d 730 (Tex. App.-Austin 2003). An officer went to defendant's residence to investigate a report that he was selling marijuana. Defendant's young son answered the door and said his father was in the garage. The officer went around to the garage door and knocked. When defendant opened the door, the officer could see a set of scales with marijuana seeds and residue and a large green pipe on a table, as well as rolling papers and baggies on the floor; he could also smell the odor of fresh marijuana. Defendant stepped outside to speak with the officer, closing the door behind him. While they were speaking, another man, Pedro Reynosa, came out of the garage, leaving the door partially open behind him. The officer recognized Reynosa as someone who "had been handled for weapons before," and was a suspect in an assault that took place a week earlier. The officer frisked both men, and found a knife on Reynosa. The garage was lighted poorly, and the partially open door blocked the officer's view. Moreover, he did not know if there were any more adults inside, but did know that one of the adults who had been inside was armed. He therefore made a valid *Buie* sweep of the garage after arresting both men, to ensure the safety of him-

self and the other officers on the scene. However, the officer exceeded the scope of a valid *Buie* sweep when he looked inside a portable cooler, as this container was far to small to conceal a person.

See also *Beaver v. State,* 942 S.W.2d 626 (Tex. App.-Tyler 1996). Police served an arrest warrant and a search warrant for drugs at defendant's radiator shop. Defendant was not present when they arrived. However, officers saw an unknown individual going in and out of the mobile home where defendant resided, approximately 200 feet from the shop. The officers went to the mobile home, knocked on the door, and were invited in by defendant. They entered to find defendant sitting at a table, drinking beer with another individual. Because the officers did not know exactly how many people were in the trailer, they were justified in conducting a sweep of the adjoining rooms, to ensure that no one was waiting to ambush them. The Court noted with favor that the officers did not look in drawers or other closed areas, and that the search lasted less than a minute.

f. **Use of Force to Effect Arrest.** The general rule is that reasonable force may be used to place a suspect under arrest. The permissible quantum of force employed varies from situation to situation. A reasonable level of force in one context, may be unreasonable in another, and vice versa. Regardless the essential principle remains that the force used must be reasonable under the particular circumstances surrounding the arrest. The analysis applied by courts to determine the reasonableness of an officer's actions, focuses on the police conduct, viewed objectively, in light of the circumstances confronting the officers at the time, without regard to their subjective intent or motivation. Factors a court will weigh include the severity of the crime at issue, whether the suspect posed an immediate threat to the officers or others, and whether the suspect was actively resisting arrest or attempting to evade arrest by flight. *Graham v. Connor,* 490 U.S. 386 (1989). The ultimate inquiry is whether a reasonable officer, confronted with the same circumstances, would have reacted in the same way.

In some situations, the use of deadly force is reasonable within the meaning of the Fourth Amendment. Deadly force does not mean force that necessarily results in the death of the suspect, but rather a level of force that is reasonably likely to cause death or serious bodily injury. The U.S. Supreme Court has described the circumstances under which the use of deadly force may be reasonable for purposes of Fourth Amendment analysis, and therefore permissible. In *Tennessee v. Garner,* 471 U.S. 1 (1985), the Court stated "Where the officer has probable cause to believe that the suspect poses a threat of serious physical harm, either to the officer or to others, it is not constitutionally unreasonable to prevent escape by using deadly force." Thus, if the suspect threatens the officer with a weapon or there is probable cause to believe that he has committed a crime involving the "infliction or threatened infliction of serious physical harm," the use of deadly force is permissible. If the officer does not have probable cause to believe the above, reasonable, non-deadly force must be used to effect the arrest.

### G. Procedure After Arrest

When an individual is the subject of a warrantless arrest, he or she is entitled to a prompt judicial determination of probable cause to arrest without unnecessary delay (if he or she has been arrested pursuant to a warrant, a judge has already made a probable cause determination as a prerequisite to issuing the warrant). A prompt determination means that judicial hearing must be held as soon as is reasonably feasible. However, a finding must be made within 48 hours of the arrest. *County of Riverside v. McLaughlin,* 500 U.S. 44 (1991); see also *Tex. Code Crim. Pro.* art. 14.06. A hearing provided within 48 hours may violate the promptness requirement if the arrested individual can prove that the probable cause determination was delayed in an unreasonable manner. Examples of unreasonable delays are ones for the purpose of gathering additional evidence against the defendant, or motivated by ill will toward the defendant. The judicial probable cause determination may be combined with other proceedings, like an arraignment. If the State fails to provide a determination within this 48-hour window, the burden of proof shifts to the government to demonstrate the existence of an emergency or other extraordinary circumstances justifying the delay.

Note: The government cannot justify the failure to provide a determination within 48 hours on the basis of an intervening weekend (*e.g.,* a person arrested on Thursday not given a hearing until Monday).

An individual arrested pursuant to a warrant must also be brought before a magistrate within 48 hours, to be informed of the accusation against him or her and of his or her rights. Be aware that this may be done via two-way closed circuit television. *Tex. Code Crim. Pro.* art. 15.17.

When a student (or person believed to be a student) at a public primary or secondary school is arrested for a felony, unlawful restraint, indecent exposure, deadly conduct, terroristic threat, street gang activity, sale or possession of drugs or paraphernalia, or unlawful possession of a weapon, the arresting law enforcement agency must orally notify the superintendent in the arrestee's school district within 24 hours of the arrest, or on the next school day. Within seven days after the date the oral notice is given, the agency must mail written notification, marked "PERSONAL and CONFIDENTIAL" on the mailing envelope, to the superintendent. When a student at a private primary or secondary school is arrested for one of the above offenses, the agency must make the oral and written notifications to the principal of that school. *Tex. Code Crim. Proc.* art. 15.27.

## III. CRIMINAL LIABILITY

In order for criminal liability to attach, a person must engage in a course of conduct during which two factors coincide: a voluntary act committed by the accused and a culpable mental state, existing at the time of the act, *e.g.,* negligently, recklessly, knowingly, or intentionally. Conduct is intentional when it is the actor's conscious objective to engage in that conduct. Conduct is knowing when the actor is aware that that he or she is engaging in that conduct, or that the conduct is reasonably certain to cause a particular result. Conduct is reckless when the actor is aware of but consciously disregards a substantial and unjustifiable risk, and that disregard involves a gross deviation from the standard of care an ordinary person would exercise. Conduct is criminally negligent when the ought to be aware of a substantial and unjustifiable risk, and that disregard involves a gross deviation from the standard of care an ordinary person would exercise. An act may, in some instances, be an omission to perform a duty that the law imposes. There are certain offenses that do not require a mental state coinciding with an act to create criminal liability; the act alone, regardless of the state of mind of the defendant when he committed the act, is sufficient to constitute the completed crime. These are called strict liability crimes.

## IV. SEARCH & SEIZURE

The Fourth Amendment mandates that citizens shall be free from unreasonable searches and seizures. What type of governmental conduct is deemed unreasonable, and therefore unconstitutional, is determined by the particular facts and circumstances of each case. However, some hard and fast rules do provide guidance. First and foremost among these is the core principle that all searches, unless conducted pursuant to a warrant, are per se unreasonable, therefore unconstitutional. There are, however, certain well-crafted exceptions to the warrant requirement, permitting warrantless searches when the requirements of the relevant exception are met. These are discussed below.

## A. The Search Warrant

The Fourth Amendment requires that a search warrant be issued by a magistrate or judge who must, after receiving an oath or affirmation from the warrant applicant, make an independent, neutral and detached determination whether probable cause exists to believe that particularly described property will be found at a particular place.

When applying for a warrant, an officer must present an affidavit that contains facts that support a finding of "probable cause." The warrant and the affidavit or testimony on which it is based must be legally sufficient, *i.e.,* they must contain facts that show a crime was committed, and facts that indicate why evidence will be found in a given place. Cursory assertions and bare-bones allegations will not support a warrant.

A criminal defendant may challenge the validity of a warrant, or the sufficiency of an affidavit, on constitutional grounds, or may allege the warrant does not fulfill the requirements of the warrant statute. A constitutional challenge would, for example, involve assertions that the facts as alleged do not establish "probable cause," or that the warrant did not "particularly" describe the place to be searched, et al., as required by the Fourth Amendment. A statutory challenge would involve allegations that the procedures required by the statute were not complied with. See *Hunter v. State,* 92 S.W.3d 596 (Tex. App.-Waco 2002) where a warrant was invalid when the officer failed to sign to the supporting affidavit.

If the defendant shows that a search warrant contains false statements made by the affiant either knowingly or with reckless disregard for the truth, then the remaining information in the affidavit must independently establish probable cause, or else the warrant will be invalid. *Franks v. Delaware,* 438 U.S. 154 (1978); *Harris v. State,* 227 S.W.3d 83 (Tex. Crim. App. 2007).

An affidavit for a search warrant may be sealed if the judge finds a compelling state interest to do so. *Tex. Code Crim. Pro.* art. 18.011.

## B. Neutral and Detached Magistrate

The warrant must be issued by a removed, impartial judge. This requirement is premised on the notion "that a warrant authorized by a neutral and detached judicial officer is a more reliable safeguard against improper searches than the hurried judgment of a law enforcement officer engaged in the often competitive enterprise of ferreting out crime." *Lo-Ji Sales Inc. v. New York,* 442 U.S. 319 (1979). *In Lo-Ji,* the warrant was invalid when the magistrate who issued it went along on the raid he had authorized, and determined only when he saw certain materials what was obscene, and therefore what was to be seized. Similarly, where a warrant was issued by the state Attorney General, who was also actively involved in the investigation, and later prosecuted the case at trial, the initial probable cause determination was patently improper, for it was not made by an impartial and remote observer. *Coolidge v. New Hampshire,* 403 U.S. 443 (1971). To ensure the requisite neutrality, the issuing judge must not play a role in the investigation or the search itself.

Be aware that Justices of the Peace may not issue an evidentiary warrant under Article 18.02(10), *Code of Criminal Procedure,* although they may issue all other types of warrant included in that article, to be served within the geographical limits of the J.P.'s county. Tex. Code of Crim. Proc. Art. 18.01(c); *State v. Acosta,* 99 S.W.3d 301 (Tex. App.-Corpus Christi 2003); *Bitner v. State,* 135 S.W.3d 906 (Tex. App.-Fort Worth 2004).

## C. Probable Cause Required—Justification for Issuance of a Search Warrant

The probable cause standard for issuance of a search warrant is essentially the same as that for arrest, the difference being that police must have probable cause to believe that a crime has been committed, and they can find certain evidence in a particular place. *State v. Ozuna,* 88 S.W.3d 307 (Tex. App.-San Antonio 2002). When making a probable cause determination, the issuing magistrate is entitled to consider all the circumstances surrounding an alleged crime, *i.e.,* "the totality of the circumstances." There has to be, however, more than mere conjecture involved. Facts, real and demonstrable, must back up the allegations and assertions. Positive proof of an illegal endeavor and the location of incriminating evidence are not required, but rather a showing that there is a probability of criminal activity, and proof thereof in a specific location. The facts relied upon by the magistrate must be contained within the four corners of the affidavit. *Smith v. State,* 207 S.W.3d 787 (Tex. Crim. App. 2006).

Three specific concepts, regarding sources of information, or the nature and quality of the information itself, pose special problems for courts when ascertaining the existence of probable cause: (i) the use of third party informants, rather than direct observation or personal knowledge; (ii) the facts relied upon may be too old or no longer accurate (staleness); (iii) the facts relied upon establish that a crime may take place, and evidence of that crime may be found in a certain place in the future, but not at present (anticipatory warrants).

1. **Informants.** Rarely do law enforcement officers rely on their own direct observations to provide the underlying facts supporting a warrant. In many, if not most cases, a third party will provide documentation of a crime's commission, and detail where evidence or contraband can be found. To determine if an informant's tip supports a probable cause finding, courts will employ a totality of the circumstances analysis and examine all of the attendant factors, including the veracity and reliability of the informant, and the basis of the informant's knowledge, as well as the extent to which that information can be or has been corroborated and verified. *Illinois v. Gates,* 462 U.S. 213 (1983); *Bower v. State,* 769 S.W.2d 887 (Tex. Crim. App. 1989).

No one aspect of the tip or information, or the person giving it, is determinative on the issue of probable cause. A question regarding the informant's veracity may be compensated for by strong evidence confirming the way in which the informant obtained his or her information, or verification that the facts he or she relayed are accurate, or some other factors indicating the informant's reliability. Even so, some broad generalizations may be made. Generally, the information provided by a non-confidential informant will be given greater deference than that provided by a confidential informant, who asks that his or her identity be kept secret. Courts reason that if someone is willing to expose themselves to public scrutiny, then the information they pass on is likely more reliable than information given by someone who is reluctant to associate their identity with the tip.

Information given by a witness to or victim of a crime is likely to be perceived as more trustworthy than information given anonymously, or even by a known police informant. Generally, if other factors point to the conclusion that a witness's or victim's tip is reliable (*i.e.,* some corroboration), and there is no evidence that calls his or her motives for giving information into question, there will not be an inquiry into that informant's credibility or veracity. Moreover, witness and victim informers have not had the opportunity to build up a reputation for giving solid information to the authorities, as they have had no reason to do so. There is no past conduct by which to gauge their propensity for honesty. Witness and victim informers generally have nothing to gain by giving information to police, other than the satisfaction of knowing they may help solve a crime, or prevent the commission of another.

Statements against an informant's penal interest, i.e. which implicate him or herself in a crime, also carry a presumption of reliability, because courts reason it is unlikely and unnatural for persons to falsely incriminate themselves.

Regardless of who provides the information, the court will ultimately employ the same analysis, examining the totality of the circumstances; the informant's reputation for truthfulness, his or her dependability, and the circumstances under which he or she obtained the information.

See, *e.g., Blake v. State,* 125 S.W.3d 717 (Tex. App.-Houston [1st Dist.] 2003). A Texas City officer received information from a confidential-informant (CI) that persons living at 1024 Pin Oak in Dickinson were in possession of methamphetamine, cocaine, and crack cocaine. The officer had successfully executed several search warrants in the past based on this CI's information. The CI had also provided information to an agent with the Galveston County Narcotics Task Force which "resulted in the arrest of numerous defendant and the seizure of crack cocaine, marijuana, and currency." Therefore, the CI was credible and reliable. In addition, the CI claimed to have been in the suspect residence within the past two days, and described the glass ware, tubes, and microwaves used to manufacture the methamphetamine, as well as the strong smell of chemicals that permeated the residence. Thus the informant's basis of knowledge was clearly first-hand, personal observation. The CI's tips established probable cause to search the Pin Oak residence.

Compare with *Brown v. State,* 243 S.W.3d 141 (Tex. App.-Eastland 2007). An Abilene officer received information from a CI regarding defendant. In the previous 2 years, this CI has provided the officer with information leading to the arrest of five drug offenders. The CI was also a prior drug abuser, so he was familiar with controlled substances. The CI stated that within the past 48 hours, he had been inside defendant's home and observed defendant in possession of a quantity of an off-white rock-like substance defendant purported to be crack cocaine. Because the CI had a history of reliability, the officer had probable cause for a warrant to search defendant's home.

In *State v. Hackleman,* 919 S.W.2d 440 (Tex. App.-Austin 1996), following his detention, a CI told Austin police that he had purchased methamphetamine for at least two years from Deborah Ann Reel (later identified as defendant's girlfriend) and a man he knew only as "David" (later identified as defendant Davis Hackleman) from their residence at 1708 Ferguson Lane. The CI added that, two weeks earlier, Reel had told him that someone had broken into the couple's residence and stolen a safe containing thousands of dollars, jewelry, and drugs. An officer checked police records and confirmed that Deborah Ann Reel had reported a burglary at the Ferguson Lane residence earlier in the month; she reported that $5,000 and jewelry had been taken. "David Hackleman" was listed as a witness to the crime. Further checking revealed that, a year earlier, Reel herself had been arrested for burglary; after she was transported to jail, two vials and five baggies of methamphetamine were found in the back seat of the patrol car that transported her. In addition, defendant had three convictions for possession of a controlled substance; a phone call revealed that one of these convictions stemmed from an attempt to set up a covert meth lab in Liberty County. Although this was the CI's first time giving information, the statement that he had purchased methamphetamine over a period of two years was against his penal interest, which bolstered his veracity. Moreover, his basis of knowledge was first-hand, personal observation, not rumor or hearsay. His knowledge of the details of the burglary corroborated and added credence to his report, as did the officer's confirmation of Keel and defendant's criminal histories. Police had probable cause for a warrant to search the Ferguson Lane residence.

In *Barton v. State,* 962 S.W.3d 132 (Tex. App.-Beaumont 1997), an officer with the San Jacinto County Sheriff's Department met with a CI who had called 911. The CI said he/she lived with defendant and had been on the premises within the past 24 hours, then gave the officer a package wrapped in cellophane and tape. The officer recognized this packaging as the type commonly used to conceal cocaine; he cut open the package and found a white powdery substance later confirmed to be cocaine. The CI said the package came from an outbuilding on defendant's property, and that several more packages wrapped in the same manner could be found there. Although the CI's veracity was not specifically noted, the CI's basis of knowledge more than made up for any deficiency therein—the CI lived with defendant and had personally been on the premises where drugs were stored within the past day. Furthermore, the "reliability" of the information provided was proven to a significant degree when the officer tested the contents of the package provided to him by the informant, with the results confirming that the package indeed contained cocaine. The totality of the circumstances established probable cause for a warrant to search defendant's property for drugs.

In *Flores v. State,* 319 S.W.3d 697 (Tex. Crim. App. 2010), a Hayes County officer received an call from a concerned citizen reporting drug activity at a residence on Ramona Circle in San Marcos. The caller wished to remain anonymous for personal safety. Although the caller could not give an exact address, he stated that a black F-150 truck and gold Firebird were usually parked outside and that defendant Felix Flores resided there with his girlfriend, a white female he knew only as "Tiffany." The caller claimed to have observed a quantity of cocaine inside the residence in the past. The officer drove to Ramona Circle and found a residence with a black F-150 and gold Firebird parked outside. A license plate check revealed the truck was registered to Felix Flores. A utility subscriber check of the residence revealed the residence's account was in the name of "Tiffany Wardell"; a check of Ms Wardell's license indicated she lived at the residence. Police then performed two trash pulls, warrantless searches of trash left outside the curtilage for collection. The first pull discovered two empty packs of rolling papers and a plastic bag with a small amount of marijuana residue; the second pull, four days later, located several marijuana stems, seeds and marijuana residue. The officer's investigation sufficiently confirmed the anonymous caller's tip, giving police probable cause to obtain a warrant.

See also *State v. Long,* 137 S.W.3d 726 (Tex. App.-Waco 2004). A Navarro County deputy received information from a CI regarding the manufacture of methamphetamine at defendant's residence. The CI claimed defendant used the "Nazi lab" method of manufacture in a bedroom in the southwest corner of the home, keeping his lab equipment in a hole in the ground next to his house, then removing it when needed. The level of detail the CI gave regarding the method of manufacture indicated that the CI was familiar enough with methamphetamine to recognize the drug. Thus the CI had a strong basis of knowledge. The deputy had been to defendant's house within the past two months to follow up an arson investigation, and had smelled a strong odor of ether near the southwest corner at that time. Because ether is often used in the manufacture of methamphetamine, this corroborated the CI's tip. Under the totality of the circumstances, probable cause was established for a search warrant.

But see *Serrano v. State,* 123 S.W.3d 53 (Tex. App.-Austin 2003). A CI who had provided reliable information in the past told a detective that defendant Daniel Serrano, a 25-year-old Hispanic male, was dealing cocaine in the Austin area; he added that Daniel had a brother, Earnest. Using public records, the detective confirmed that a 25-year-old named Daniel Serrano lived in Austin with his brother Earnest. However, even though the CI had a track record of reliability, this tip did not establish probable cause. The tip was conclusory—there was no assertion that the information given was based on the CI's personal knowledge or observation. The CI gave no dates of drug sales or specific addresses where sales were made. Nor was there any indication of the amount of drugs involved or the price charged. In addition to this failure to establish the CI's basis of knowledge, the affidavit failed to mention where the crime was being committed other than "the 'Austin, Travis County' area." The CI did not say he had been at defendant's residence, so there was no nexus between the cocaine defendant was allegedly selling and his residence. Finally, because there was no indication when the drug sales took place, or when CI obtained his information, or when the detective received the tip, the information might have been stale. The warrant issued based on this tip was invalid.

2. **Staleness.** If there is an appreciable delay between the occurrence of the circumstances that create probable cause and the time a warrant is issued, the facts supporting the probable cause determination may become "stale," in that, although the alleged facts may have once supported a probable cause determination, presently, they may not. Courts reason that information demon-

strating that evidence of a crime could once be found in a given location, does not mean that evidence of a crime may necessarily be found there now. Stale information creates the mere suspicion crime has been committed, and does not rise to the level of probable cause.

Staleness depends on more than simply the number of days between the issuance of the warrant and the observations on which it is based, although that is one factor to consider. The issuing court must also weigh the character of the criminal activity under investigation, of the criminal, of the thing to be seized, and of the place to be searched, in order to determine if the evidence sought is still likely at the place it was once observed. *Ellis v. State,* 677 S.W.2d 129 (Tex. App.-Dallas 1984).

3. **Anticipatory Warrants.** An "anticipatory warrant" is a warrant authorizing a search at some future time. When applying for an anticipatory warrant, the affiant-officer is, in essence, asserting that probable cause does not exist presently, but will exist following the occurrence of some "triggering event" (for example, controlled delivery of a package containing contraband). Anticipatory warrants are constitutional. To obtain such a warrant, the affidavit must provide facts establishing a fair probability that evidence of a crime or contraband will be found at the place to be searched if the triggering condition occurs, and probable cause to believe that the triggering condition will occur. *U.S. v. Grubbs,* 547 U.S. 90 (2006).

In *Grubbs,* defendant purchased a videotape of child pornography from a website operated by an undercover postal inspector. Authorities arranged a controlled delivery of the videotape, then obtained a search warrant for defendant's home; the affidavit in support of the warrant specifically provided that the warrant was not to be executed "unless and until the parcel has been delivered by a person(s) and has been physically taken into the residence." After defendant's wife signed for the videotape, the warrant was lawfully executed. The affidavit in this case clearly established that contraband would be present in defendant's home once the videotape was delivered—child porn is obviously illegal. In addition, there was probable cause to believe this condition would be satisfied; although it was possible defendant might have refused delivery, he was unlikely to do so after having ordered the videotape. Therefore, this was a valid anticipatory warrant.

The Fourth Amendment does not require that the triggering condition be set forth in the warrant itself, although that is the better practice. *U.S. v. Grubbs, supra.*

Although anticipatory warrants have been upheld under the federal Fourth Amendment, be aware that Texas courts have yet to address their validity under the state constitution. See *State v. Toone,* 872 S.W.2d 750 (Tex. Crim. App. 1994).

### D. Particularity Requirement

The Fourth Amendment requires that a warrant specifically name both the places to be searched and the items to be seized. The purpose of this particularity requirement is to prevent general searches, *i.e.,* a rummaging for incriminating evidence without cause. The warrant must state the items and the places with distinctiveness, so that the officer executing the warrant will have no question, and no room for guesswork or discretionary choices, as to where he or she is to search, and for what they are looking. A valid warrant authorizes the executing officer to look for a particular item in any place it could logically be found (*e.g.,* narcotics may be reasonably expected to be found in a dresser drawer; a stolen Harley Davidson motorcycle, on the other hand, would not). However, the particularity requirement limits any arbitrary decisions as to what items may be seized. The warrant and the supporting affidavit may generally be read together to arrive at a sufficiently particular description.

The particularity requirement has two prongs: (i) a particularly described place, and (ii) particularly described items.

1. **Places to Be Searched.** The warrant must describe the location to be searched so that officers can, with reasonable effort, ascertain and identify the place authorized. Generally, a description containing the address as it would appear on a mailing envelope, along with the name of the resident, and a cursory listing of the physical appearance of the building itself, is sufficient for single unit dwellings. A problem arises, however, when the place to be searched is in a multi-unit structure, like an apartment in a complex, or an office in a professional building. The general rule is that the description must describe the specific sub-unit to be searched, not the whole building. If the description merely lists the address of a building, which itself contains many residences or offices, and the law enforcement agents executing the warrant have no means to determine which of the individual units is to be searched, the warrant may be invalid.

2. **Items to Be Seized.** The degree of particularity with which the items must be described will fluctuate, depending on the nature and individual attributes of the subject items. However, a certain minimum level of specificity will always be required. For example, generic descriptions of contraband, such as "controlled and dangerous substances" or "all controlled substances" or "narcotic drugs," etc., are generally held to be sufficient descriptions, if the affidavit suggests the presence of more than one drug.

In *Groh v. Ramirez,* 540 U.S. 551 (2004), a search warrant was plainly invalid when it provided no description of the type of evidence sought. The fact that the *application* for the warrant adequately described the "things to be seized" did not save it, because there were no words in the warrant incorporating other documents by reference and the application did not accompany the warrant (it had been sealed). Even though the search was conducted with restraint and only items listed in the application were seized, the search was unlawful.

### E. Execution of the Search Warrant

1. **Time of Service.** In general, a search warrant must be executed within three whole days, exclusive of its day of issuance and day of execution. *Tex. Code Crim. Proc.* Art. 18.07. This means three *calendar* days—a warrant may be executed up until midnight of the last day, even if more than 72 hours have passed since its issuance. *Gonzalez v. State,* 768 S.W.2d 436 (Tex. App.-Houston [1st Dist.] 1989). However, officers have up to 15 whole days to execute a warrant solely to search for and seize a blood or saliva sample from a specific person for DNA analysis and comparison. *Tex. Code Crim. Proc.* Art. 18.07.

A search warrant may be served at any time of the day or night.

The timing of the search is generally within the discretion of police officers—for example, they may delay a search until an individual arrives or leaves the location involved. *Allen v. State,* 249 S.W.3d 680 (Tex. App.-Austin 2008).

2. **Knock or No-Knock.** As a matter of course, when executing a search warrant, law enforcement officers should knock on the door of a residence or business, announce their purpose and authority, and give the occupants a reasonable opportunity to answer before forcing their way inside. The amount of time police must wait to enter after knocking depends on the totality of the circumstances. *U.S. v. Banks,* 540 U.S. 31 (2003). In *Banks,* a 15 to 20 second delay between

knocking and entry was held reasonable when police were searching for cocaine, which is easily disposable. The Court noted that police served the warrant during the middle of the day, when occupants would likely be up and around, and that a prudent dealer would keep cocaine near a commode or kitchen sink, meaning 15 to 20 seconds would likely be enough time for defendant to get in a position to rid his residence of cocaine. See also *Jeffrey v. State,* 169 S.W.3d 439 (Tex. App.-Texarkana 2005), where a mere 5-second delay before entry was justified when deputies with a warrant to search for crack cocaine heard people inside the residence running immediately after they knocked.

However, there is no constitutional mandate that an officer must knock and announce before entering a dwelling in every instance. In situations where exigent circumstances are present, an unannounced entry may be reasonable (*e.g.,* presence of weapons that may put officers at peril, the destruction of evidence, etc.). "A no-knock entry is justified when the police have a reasonable suspicion that knocking and announcing their presence, under the particular circumstances, would be dangerous or futile, or that it would inhibit the effective investigation of the crime." *Richards v. Wisconsin,* 520 U.S. 385 (1997). See also *Wilson v. Arkansas,* 514 U.S. 927 (1995); *U.S. v. Ramirez,* 523 U.S. 65 (1998). Police are not required to possess the higher standard of probable cause to believe that exigent circumstances exist, but only the less stringent standard of reasonable suspicion. The failure to knock and announce is not a per se constitutional violation, and there are no rigid rules to determine when an unannounced entry will be excused; rather, the constitutionality of the entry will be judged on the particular facts and circumstances of each case. Nevertheless, the failure to knock and announce may render an entry unreasonable, and therefore unconstitutional, where there is no showing of exigent circumstances that justify the failure to first knock.

In *White v. State,* 155 S.W.3d 927 (Tex. App.-Amarillo 2005), police made a valid no-knock entry when they personally knew that defendant had consumed methamphetamine (a drug that causes erratic and violent behavior) and possessed firearms in his trailer, so their lives may have been endangered by announcing their presence before entering.

See also *Marsh v. State,* 115 S.W.3d 709 (Tex. App.-Austin 2003). A SWAT team executing arrest and search warrants at defendant's home was justified in making a no-knock entry. The officers had reliable information that defendant possessed both a 9mm Glock and an SKS assault rifle, and knew he had a history of weapons charges. Moreover, at the time defendant was out on bond for a first-degree felony offense and had been armed with a firearm at the time of arrest. Most importantly, the officers had evidence that defendant was capable of aggressive, violent behavior on slight provocation-the current arrest warrant was issued after defendant beat the victim to death with a baseball bat because of the victim's alleged misbehavior toward defendant's girlfriend on a nightclub dance floor.

But see *Brown v. State,* 115 S.W.3d 633 (Tex. App.- Waco 2003), where a no-knock entry was not justified when their was no testimony that the residents of the house to be searched had a violent nature or possessed weapons, nor any testimony that methamphetamine (the object of the search) is easy to destroy or that the residents were in the process of destroying the drug.

Police need only knock-and-announce when entry is forcible; the rule does not apply if officers gain entry to a house without using force, even if entry is accomplished by a ruse. For example, there was no violation of the knock-and-announce rule when an officer posing as a hotel maintenance worker knocked on the door to defendant's room and announced he was there to fix the air conditioner. When defendant opened the door, other officers swept in and executed a valid search warrant. The Court found that although the first officer had not identified himself as with the police, the warrant was nonetheless lawfully executed. *Martinez v. State,* 220 S.W.3d 183 (Tex. App.-Austin 2007).

Although officers should make every effort to comply with the knock-and-announce rule, in *Hudson v. Michigan,* 547 U.S. 586 (2006), the U.S. Supreme Court held that evidence seized pursuant to a valid search warrant is not subject to suppression under the Exclusionary Rule solely because the officers executing the warrant entered in violation of the knock-and-announce requirement. The Court did note that officers who violate the rule still face the threat of possible civil remedies (such as a lawsuit under 42 U.S.C. § 1983) or internal discipline by their employer.

3. **Scope of the Search.** When executing a search warrant, officers are entitled to search the entire named premises for the items listed, and any closed containers, drawers, closets, etc., where they have probable cause to believe those items may be found. "A lawful search of fixed

premises generally extends to the entire area in which the object of the search may be found and is not limited by the possibility that separate acts of entry or opening may be required to complete the search. Thus, a warrant that authorizes an officer to search a home for illegal weapons also provides authority to open closets, chests, drawers and containers in which the weapon might be found. A warrant to open a footlocker to search for marijuana would also authorize the opening of packages found inside." *U.S. v. Ross,* 456 U.S. 798 (1982).

A warrant for a specified premises generally extends to any outbuildings within the curtilage of the property, as well as the main residence—for example, a detached garage, a tool shed or a chicken coop. *Long v. State,* 132 S.W.3d 443 (Tex. Crim. App. 2004); *Affatato v. State,* 169 S.W.3d 313 (Tex. App.-Austin 2005). But see *Matthews v. State,* 165 S.W.3d 104 (Tex. App.-Fort Worth), where a search warrant for a house and the curtilage thereof did not justify a search of a truck parked along the curb outside the house; the street and sidewalk separating the truck from the house were public areas not within its curtilage.

In addition, a valid warrant implicitly carries with it the limited authority to detain the occupants of the premises, or recall and similarly detain those seen leaving, while a proper search is conducted. *Michigan v. Summers,* 452 U.S. 692 (1981). Officers may detain anyone found in the residence, regardless of whether or not the occupant is a suspect named in the warrant, and may use reasonable force in detaining the occupants. *Muehler v. Mena,* 544 U.S. 93 (2005) (police justified in handcuffing woman for two to three hours while executing search warrant for weapons at the residence of a suspected gang member). See also *Illinois v. McArthur,* 531 U.S. 326 (2001), where the U.S. Supreme Court held that police could detain defendant on the front porch outside his home for two hours while they obtained a search warrant when they had probable cause to believe that marijuana was hidden inside the home, and that defendant would destroy this contraband if allowed to enter unescorted. (The Court noted with favor that this detention lasted only long enough for police, acting with diligence, to obtain a warrant.)

However, the authority to detain those present but not named in the warrant does not include the authority to search those persons, absent specific instruction in the warrant or an independent justification for the search. *Ybarra v. Illi-*

*nois,* 444 U.S. 85 (1979); *Lippert v. State,* 664 S.W.2d 712 (Tex. Crim. App. 1984). For example, in *Ybarra,* a warrant issued to search a bar for narcotics gave the police authority to search the bartender who was named in the warrant, but not a patron who just happened to be there.

Police violated the Fourth Amendment when they allowed members of the media to accompany them while executing a search warrant. *Hanlon v. Berger,* 526 U.S. 808 (1999).

When executing a warrant, officers may seize contraband or other evidence not listed in the warrant, in plain view, if the requirements of that doctrine are met. (See a complete discussion under **Plain View Doctrine,** below).

4. **Property Seized.** Whenever officers seize property pursuant to a warrant, they must prepare a written inventory of the property taken. A copy of this inventory, along with a copy of the warrant itself, must be given to the owner, if present, or a person in possession of the place searched. If no one is present, these items should be left at the place. *Tex. Code Crim. Proc.* art. 18.06(b). A copy of the inventory must also be given to the magistrate when the warrant is returned. *Tex. Code Crim. Proc.* art. 18.10.

When law enforcement agents seize property pursuant to a search warrant, Due Process requires that they give notice so that the owner can pursue any remedies available for return under state law; however, agents are not required to give owners notice of state law remedies established by published, generally available statutes and case law. *City of West Covina v. Perkins,* 525 U.S. 234 (1999).

## F. Search of Containers

Regardless of whether the subject of a search is a container, like a briefcase, purse, suitcase or footlocker, instead of a house, car, office building or person, the general rule is the same; a warrant must be obtained before the container may be opened. The Fourth Amendment "proscribes—except in certain well defined circumstances—the search of that property unless accomplished pursuant to a judicial warrant issued on probable cause." *U.S. v. Ross,* 456 U.S. 798 (1982). These "well-defined circumstances," *e.g.,* a search incident to arrest or a booking search, are discussed under **Warrantless Searches,** below. The rationale advanced in this situation is similar to the reasoning behind the rule requiring warrants for the search of a home. When an individual manifests an expectation that certain items remain private, by placing them in a closed container, it is unreasonable for the government to intrude on that expectation of privacy without the protections of a warrant, based on a clear showing of probable cause. When dealing with items of personalty, the procedure prior to a search may be somewhat different, in that it is permissible to briefly detain personal property, based on a reasonable suspicion that it contains contraband.

A crucial, and often dispositive distinction must be made between closed containers seized and detained from the possession of a person, and those containers taken from an automobile. If the container is found in an automobile, the police may almost always open and search the container without a warrant, if they have probable cause to think the container, or the car transporting it, contains contraband.

## G. Exceptions to the Warrant Requirement (Warrantless Searches)

The general rule is that all searches and seizures conducted without a warrant are presumptively unreasonable and therefore unconstitutional. To justify a warrantless search, the State must show that the search falls into one of the narrowly drawn exceptions to warrant requirement. Courts have, however, crafted a few specifically established and well-delineated exceptions to the general principle, and they are discussed in detail, below.

1. **Exigent Circumstances.** The situations that often fall under the exigent circumstances exception can be grouped into three general categories. An exigency exists if: (i) there is a good chance evidence—either contraband, instrumentalities used in the crime, or the fruits of the crime—is being or will be destroyed or concealed; (ii) it is likely a suspect will flee; (iii) there is a real danger to people. The rationale advanced for permitting warrantless searches under such circumstances is that extreme situations dictate that police act quickly, where there is no time to secure a warrant. The warrant requirement may be dispensed with when officers take actions that are necessary responses to an emergency situation. Courts permit warrantless searches where officers have probable cause and a qualifying set of circumstances.

2. **Destruction or Removal of Evidence.** Where police have a reasonable belief that evidence is being or about to be destroyed, a warrantless entry may be permitted under this exception. Where the police have an objectively reasonable fear that the evidence is being or about to be destroyed and a reasonable belief that

there are people within the home presently capable of destroying or hiding the evidence, and the officer's fear is of an immediate or imminent destruction, the requirements of the exception are met. In order to invoke this exception, the State must demonstrate that the seized evidence is of an "evanescent" nature (*i.e.,* an easily destructible item, like narcotics, which can be easily burned, secreted or flushed).

See, *e.g., Wisenbaker v. State,* 311 S.W.3d 57 (Tex. App.-San Antonio 2010). A Boerne officer was dispatched to defendant's residence following a complaint from a neighbor that defendant and some friends were smoking marijuana inside. The neighbor showed the officer a hole in a privacy fence surrounding the residence; the officer look through and could see through a sliding glass door that opened to the patio approximately 10 feet away. Inside the house, he could see defendant holding a marijuana pipe. Rather than take the time to obtain a search warrant, the officer decided to perform a "knock-and-talk." He approached the front door, where a sign read, "Go around, use the other door." He then walked a sidewalk around the house back to the patio. When he arrived there, he could still see defendant on the couch, holding the pipe. There was now a "thick cloud of smoke inside the room" and the officer could smell an odor of burnt marijuana coming from inside the home. The officer made eye contact with the defendant, who immediately appeared startled and looked as if he was attempting to either hide the pipe or get up from the couch. The officer opened the sliding glass door and entered the house—he saw and seized a bag of marijuana, pipes and other paraphernalia on a coffee table. The Court upheld warrantless entry. Exigent circumstances existed because evidence of a crime—the marijuana itself—could easily be destroyed by the act of smoking it.

See also *Effler v. State,* 115 S.W.3d 696 (Tex. App.-Eastland 2003). Officers responded to a report of unusual odors emanating from defendant's trailer home. Upon arrival, they detected a strong odor of anhydrous ammonia and ether, both commonly present during the manufacture of methamphetamine. As they approached the trailer, they heard the sound of someone running inside. After the officers knocked, defendant's guest opened the door. When the officers asked permission to enter, the guest turned around quickly and started running. At this point, the officers made a lawful warrantless entry to prevent the possible destruction of any methamphetamine or manufacturing equipment inside the trailer.

Note: The fact that the grounds for arrest involve narcotics, standing alone, does not create an exigent circumstance. The arrest of a narcotics suspect on his front doorstep, without any indication drugs are being hidden or destroyed, will not justify the arresting officers conducting a warrantless search of the arrestee's home for narcotics.

3. **Flight of the Suspect.** If police have evidence demonstrating a suspect is an immediate flight risk, and has the present ability to flee the jurisdiction, a warrantless entry may be permitted to apprehend that suspect before flight.

4. **Safety of the Officer or Others.** If the officer believes that the suspect is armed and presents a real and immediate danger to the officers or other people, a warrantless entry is permitted.

See, *e.g., Barocio v. State,* 158 S.W.3d 498 (Tex. Crim. App. 2005). While on patrol, two Harris County deputies noticed a car parked facing the wrong direction in front of a home, with the driver's door open and keys in the ignition. When the deputies approached the home to investigate, they saw pry marks on the front door lock and a surveillance camera aimed at the front door. After they knocked on the front door, they heard a lot of noise inside, and also detected an odor of burnt marijuana (one of the deputies later testified that it is not unusual for burglars to smoke marijuana while committing break-ins). After several minutes, defendant finally answered the door, but refused to provide identification to the deputies, despite repeated requests. The deputies had probable cause to make a warrantless entry to investigate what appeared to be a burglary-in-progress. (Although the deputies eventually learned there was no burglary because this was, in fact, defendant's home, they lawfully seized marijuana found in plain view.)

When police come upon the scene of a homicide, they may make a "prompt warrantless search of the area to see if there are other victims or if a killer is still on the premises." *Mincey v. Arizona,* 437 U.S. 385 (1978). However, there is no general "murder scene" exception to the warrant requirement, and police may not continue to search for evidence once the crime scene has been secured. *Flippo v. West Virginia,* 528 U.S. 11 (1999).

5. **Hot Pursuit.** This doctrine may be analyzed as a specific application of the exigent circumstance doctrine discussed above. A warrantless entry of a private dwelling will be allowed when police are in hot pursuit of a suspect who they have probable cause to believe committed a felony. The pursuing officers must also have probable cause to believe the suspect entered a specific dwelling. After following the suspect into a dwelling, the police may seize contraband, weapons, instrumentalities or fruits of crime that are in plain view.

This exception generally applies only to suspects who have committed an offense punishable by confinement. If the police are pursuing a suspect for a non-jailable offense, hot pursuit ordinarily will not apply. *Welsh v. Wisconsin,* 466 U.S. 740 (1984); *Randolph v. State,* 152 S.W.3d 764 (Tex. Crim. App. 2004).

6. **Search Incident to Arrest.** Upon the lawful arrest of a person, the arresting officer is entitled to search not only the person of the arrestee, but also the area that was in the immediate control of the suspect prior to the arrest. *Wallace v. State,* 467 S.W.2d 608 (Tex. Crim. App. 1971). This exception is premised on the notion that the arrest of a suspect, when based on probable cause, is per se reasonable with respect to the Fourth Amendment. Since this intrusion on an individual's freedom is by definition lawful, a search incident to the arrest requires no additional justification. It is the fact of the arrest that establishes the authority to search. Notice that the arrest must be lawful, i.e., based on probable cause. If the arrest is later deemed improper, all evidence seized incident to that arrest will be suppressed. Under this exception, a search of all effects in the suspect's possession is permissible. However, as mentioned, the scope of the search must be limited to the suspect's person, or what is in, or potentially could be in, the suspect's immediate control. Courts say that a region is within the immediate control of the suspect when he or she might immediately and easily gain possession of a weapon or destructible evidence from that area. *Chimel v. California,* 395 U.S. 752 (1969).

The search may precede the arrest, as long as probable cause for the arrest exists independently of what is found during the search and probable cause to arrest exists before the search is conducted. In other words, an officer may not use the fruits of a search as the basis for the arrest of the suspect, and then seek to justify the search as one incident to the arrest. *Rawlings v. Kentucky,* 448 U.S. 98 (1980); *Weide v. State,* 157 S.W.3d 87 (Tex. App.-Austin 2005).

A proper search incident to an arrest should be conducted contemporaneously with the arrest, i.e., immediately preceding or succeeding that actual physical act of arrest. However, a search of articles in the possession of the defendant at the time of arrest may not only be conducted at the time of the arrest, but may instead be conducted later, and at a different location, if a reasonable explanation for the delay is put forth. *U.S. v. Edwards,* 415 U.S. 800 (1974) (delay of ten hours between arrest and station house search permissible).

The warrantless seizure of a suspect's clothing subsequent to a legal arrest, while the suspect is in custody or detention, is permissible. *Young v. State,* 283 S.W.3d 854 (Tex. Crim. App. 2009).

Police may retrieve call records and text messages from an arrestee's cell phone incident to arrest. *U.S. v. Finley,* 477 F.3d 250 (5th Cir. 2007).

In *Edwards, supra,* the Court also noted that a search incident to arrest extends to the clothing worn by the arrestee.

When police arrest the driver of or a passenger in a vehicle, officers may search the passenger compartment of the vehicle incident to the arrest, but only if:

- the arrestee is within "reaching distance" of the passenger compartment at the time of the search, **or**
- it is reasonable to believe the vehicle contains evidence of the offense of arrest.

*Arizona v. Gant,* 556 U.S. __ (2009). If the arrestee has already been handcuffed and placed in the back of a patrol car, then a search of the vehicle is no longer justified because the arrestee is no longer capable of accessing any weapon potentially hidden inside, unless police reasonable expect to find evidence of the crime for which the arrest was made in the vehicle. While police can generally expect to find evidence following a drug arrest (e.g. more drugs, paraphernalia), a search is not allowed following a traffic violation (for example, driving with a suspended license) as no evidence of such offenses could be concealed inside the vehicle. Under *New York v. Belton,* 453 U.S. 454 (1981), the scope of a vehicle search incident to arrest includes the entire passenger compartment, and all containers located therein, locked or unlocked.

See, *e.g., Daves v. State,* 327 S.W.3d 289 (Tex. App.-Eastland 2010). A Midland officer stopped a driver for running a red light and changing lanes in an intersection. The officer smelled alcohol on the driver's breath, and ordered him out of the car to perform field sobriety tests. In an ill-conceived attempt to prove he was sober, the driver devised his own test, and tried to walk on his hands. As he did so, various items fell out of his pocket to the ground—including a purple marijuana pipe. He was arrested for possession of drug paraphernalia, handcuffed, and secured in the officer's patrol car. Because the officer had reason to believe he might find evidence related to the offense of possession of drug paraphernalia—for example, marijuana the driver intended to smoke in the pipe—a search incident to arrest of the passenger compartment was lawful under *Gant.*

In *State v. Ogeda,* 315 S.W.3d 664 (Tex. App.-Dallas 2010), an officer saw defendant and her boyfriend parked in a car outside an after-hours club. The officer knew that, because the club did not sell alcohol, patrons often drank or did drugs outside in their vehicles before entering. Defendant got out of the car, stumbling, car keys in hand; she yelled to her boyfriend to "hurry up" because the "cops" were behind them. The officer approached to initiate a conversation with defendant. He smelled an odor of alcohol on her breath, and saw her pupils were constricted and her hands were shaking. She also had difficulty answering questions. The officer arrested defendant for public intoxication, fearing she might pose a danger to others if she tried to drive or to herself if she remained in that condition in the surrounding high-crime area. Because the officer could reasonably expect to find evidence of intoxication (alcohol) in defendant's car, he was justified in searching the passenger compartment incident to the arrest. A bottle of GHB he found in the passenger door panel was lawfully seized.

As long as the above criteria are met, a search is allowed even when the arrestee is a "recent occupant" who has already stepped out of the vehicle when the officer first makes contact. *Thornton v. U.S.,* 541 U.S. 615 (2004). However, a search is not allowed during a routine traffic stop where only a traffic citation is issued and no formal arrest is made. *Knowles v. Iowa,* 525 U.S. 113 (1998).

7. **Emergency Aid.** Under this doctrine, a police officer can enter a premises without a warrant to protect individuals in distress, to assist victims of crimes that have just occurred or to investigate suspicious signs of impending danger. Warrantless entry is lawful if done to assist persons who are seriously injured or threatened with serious injury. *Brigham City v. Stuart,* 547 U.S. 398 (2006). This exigency, therefore, is based

on the officer's obligation to protect life and property.

There are three basic requirements for the application of the emergency doctrine: (i) the police must have reasonable cause to believe that there is an emergency at hand and an immediate need for their assistance for the protection of life or property; (ii) the search must not be primarily motivated by an intent to arrest and seize evidence; and (iii) there must be some reasonable basis to associate the emergency with the area or property to be searched. See *In re J.D.*, 68 S.W.3d 775 (Tex. App.-San Antonio 2001). Once the police respond and enter a premises pursuant to this exigency, they have the right to "restore or maintain the status quo during the emergency to control the dangerous or dynamic situation." This right enables the officer to take a number of intrusive actions ranging from a command to halt to a seizure of an individual. During the investigation of an emergency situation, the police may search for weapons to protect themselves and others and may look for injured or missing persons.

See, *e.g., State v. Cantwell*, 85 S.W.3d 849 (Tex. App.-Waco 2002). Police responded to a dispatch to defendant's home. They found the front door off its hinges and could hear defendant and his wife causing a disturbance inside. Warrantless entry was lawful.

Compare with *Shepherd v. State*, 230 S.W.3d 738 (Tex. App.-Houston (14th Dist.) 2007). Defendant's neighbor of 16 years called police because defendant's front door was open while his van was missing from the driveway. This was unusual, as she knew defendant typically used the garage door for entry and exit, and never left the front door open. Another neighbor had walked up to the house and called out to defendant, but received no response. Two officers arrived at the house and did the same, but again received no answer. Both officers later testified that, based on their experience, open-door calls to residences can involve assault victims or persons otherwise injured inside. The officers were justified in making a warrantless sweep of the house, to check for anyone possibly requiring medical assistance. Because they were inside the home lawfully, they made a valid seizure of a bag of marijuana they saw in plain view on a living room table.

In *Michigan v. Fisher*, 558 U.S. __ (2009), Brownstown, Michigan, officers responded to a complaint of a disturbance—a man was reportedly "going crazy" at a residence. Upon arrival, the officers found a household in considerable chaos: a pickup truck in the driveway with its front smashed, damaged fenceposts along the side of the property, and three broken house windows, the glass still on the ground outside. The officers also noticed blood on the hood of the pickup and on clothes inside of it, as well as on one of the doors to the house. Through a window, the officers could see defendant inside, screaming and throwing things. The back door was locked, and a couch had been placed to block the front door. The officers knocked, but defendant would not answer. They saw defendant had a cut on his hand and asked if he needed medical help, but defendant ignored these questions and demanded, with accompanying profanity, that they get a search warrant. One of the officers then pushed his way inside. The U.S. Supreme Court ruled that this warrantless entry was justified under the "Emergency Aid" doctrine because of defendant's violent behavior. Although the officers had not seen defendant hit anyone, they did see him throwing things, and it was objectively reasonable to believe that these projectiles might have a human target (perhaps a spouse or a child), or that defendant would hurt himself in the course of his rage.

See also *In re J.D., supra*. Officers responded at around 8:00 a.m. to a report of two juveniles carrying a rifle in the vicinity of an elementary school. While searching the alley where they had last been seen, a witness approached and said that he saw the juveniles enter a yard on the other side of the alley and thought they may have gone into the adjoining house. As the officers approached the house, they heard loud noises from within that "sounded like running and an object hitting the wall." The front door had been tampered with; the screen was torn, the window was broken, and the door was slightly ajar. Police had probable cause to believe a burglary was in progress, and made a valid warrantless entry to investigate.

In *Gipson v. State*, 82 S.W.3d 715 (Tex. App.-Waco 2002), the victim's 9-year-old daughter was locked out of their home. The victim had made no arrangements for her care, and the daughter was forced to spend the night with a neighbor. The victim's mother called the house repeatedly that day and the next; the phone rang initially, but was then continuously busy. Police had responded to a domestic violence call a year earlier where defendant had assaulted the victim, and had arrested defendant following another incident just two weeks earlier. Because police reasonably feared that the victim was in need of immediate medical assistance inside the home, warrantless entry was justified.

In Rauscher v. State, 129 S.W.3d 714 (Tex. App.-Houston [1st Dist.] 2004), An apartment leasing agent contacted police to report a foul odor coming from the apartment shared by defendant and his wife; several residents had complained, and one (a former police officer) said it smelled like a dead body. Neither defendant nor his wife answered the phone when the leasing agent called, and when she tried to use the master key to enter, she found the locks had been changed. Neighbors reported having heard the couple argue, and although defendant had been seen at the apartments recently, his wife had not. An officer went to the apartment and knocked on the door, but received no answer. He, too, could smell the foul odor, but he could not positively identify it. The officer then forced his way in and made a warrantless sweep of the apartment. The Court upheld this entry because, given the information available, it was reasonable for the officer to believe that defendant's wife was within the apartment and in need of immediate aid. (Although no one was inside, the officer did find several cats, a large volume of cat feces, and a large number of marijuana plants; although he did not seize any evidence at that time, his observations served as the basis for a valid search warrant.)

But see Gonzalez v. State, 148 S.W.3d 702 (Tex. App.-Austin 2004). Police responded to a 911 call from an apartment shared by defendant and his brother, Alexander, to find Alexander outside the apartment with a stab wound. Alexander was agitated and evasive with his answers, and would not tell police what had happened. Although defendant was not present, a female friend of Alexander (who had dialed 911) was; she told the officers she did not know what happened, but that Alexander had been depressed and the wound might be self-inflicted. Before being taken to the hospital, Alexander gave his friend a set of keys and asked her to lock up the apartment. Police stopped her from doing so, then entered and made a warrantless sweep, finding drugs. The Court found this entry was not lawful. Police had no evidence anyone else (either the perpetrator, if someone besides Alexander himself, or another stabbing victim) was inside the apartment. Moreover, defendant's request that the door be locked was reasonable as a common sense precaution, and should not have been viewed as an attempt to keep police from evidence in the apartment.

When a homeowner makes a 911 call and requests immediate assistance because of an emergency, he is indicating his consent to (i) the arrival and entry of the responding officers to resolve that emergency and, (ii) absent any evidence of the revocation of that consent, an objectively reasonable limited investigation by the responding officers into the emergency that the homeowner reported. Johnson v. State, 226 S.W.3d 439 (Tex. Crim. App. 2007). Therefore, in Johnson, warrantless entry into defendant's home was lawful after she called 911 and told the dispatcher that she had just shot her husband in self-defense.

Note: **Firefighters.** Firefighters may make a warrantless entry into a burning building and seize any evidence of arson in plain view. They may also remain for a reasonable time after the blaze is extinguished to investigate its cause. However, additional entries to investigate must be made pursuant to the warrant proceedings governing administrative searches. Michigan v. Tyler, 436 U.S. 499 (1978).

8. **Consent.** A tool often employed by law enforcement officers is to simply ask a suspect for permission to search his or her person, car or residence. If the request is granted, the individual has in effect waived his or her privacy interest in the area searched. This being so, a lawful, warrantless search may be conducted pursuant to consent given by the suspect. Balentine v. State, 71 S.W.2d 763 (Tex. Crim. App. 2002). Valid consent may be rendered verbally (express consent), or inferred from the conduct or actions of the person from whom the police seek consent (implied consent).

Permission to search may also be obtained from a third party who possesses common authority over, or other sufficient relationship to, the premises or effects sought to be inspected. Moreover, even where the party granting permission does not in fact have legally sufficient control over the premises, the consent may nonetheless be valid if the officer reasonably believes that the party had common control. Illinois v. Rodriguez, 497 U.S. 177 (1990).

A parent can consent to a search of a child's room (even if the child is no longer a minor) if the parent routinely enters the room. Alameda v. State, 235 S.W.3d 218 (Tex. Crim. App. 2007). See also Hubert v. State, 312 S.W.3d 554 (Tex. Crim. App. 2010), where defendant's grandfather could consent to a search of the bedroom defendant used when the grandfather was the exclusive owner of the home and opened the door for police. Similarly, spouses generally have common authority over marital property. *Howard v. State,* 239 S.W.3d 359 (Tex. App.-San Antonio 2007) (wife could consent to search of husband's truck, even though she never drove it and, in fact, could not even drive it because of its manual transmission, when she nevertheless had access to the unlocked truck).

But see *McNairy v. State,* 835 S.W.2d 101 (Tex. Crim. App. 1991) (as a general rule, a landlord cannot consent to a search of a tenant's premises); *Riordan v. State,* 905 S.W.2d 765 (Tex. App.-Austin 1995) (defendant's mother-in-law, who was in his home babysitting, could not consent to a search of a drawer in the master bedroom, when she told police she lived in a separate house and the drawer contained only men's clothing).

When one co-occupant of a residence consents to a search, but another co-occupant is also physically present and expressly objects to the search, then any subsequent search and seizure is unreasonable and invalid as to the objecting party. *Georgia v. Randolph,* 547 U.S. 103 (2006). In *Randolph,* defendant's wife called police regarding a domestic disturbance. When officers arrived, defendant was not home, but his wife alleged that he had a cocaine habit, and that he had drug paraphernalia in the house. While officers were speaking with defendant's wife, defendant returned home. He denied he had a drug habit, but also refused to consent to a search of the residence. Undeterred, the officer who asked defendant for consent then turned to defendant's wife and asked her; she readily agreed to let him search, leading the officer to a bedroom, where the officer saw a section of a drinking straw covered with a powdery residue. Because defendant had been present at the start of the search and objected to it, the contraband the officer observed could not be used against him. Compare with *Odom v. State,* 200 S.W.3d 333 (Tex. App.-Corpus Christi 2006), where a search of a building where defendant had been living for three months was unlawful when defendant's brother-in-law, who claimed to own the building, consented to a search, but defendant, who was present during the search, expressly objected and demanded that the officers obtain a warrant. But see *Beall v. State,* 237 S.W.3d 841 (Tex. App.-Fort Worth 2007), where a search of a motel room was valid when one co-occupant consented while the other was in the shower; because the other co-

occupant was not present, he could not object, even though he was close by.

To be valid, consent must be given voluntarily. Courts will examine the circumstances under which the consent was given and ascertain if it was rendered intentionally and deliberately. Courts will inquire if the permission was the product of an essentially free and unconstrained choice by its maker. In making this determination, a court will consider whether the suspect was in custody; whether the suspect was informed of the right to refuse consent; the suspect's age, education and intelligence; the constitutional advice given to the suspect; the length of any detention; the repetitiveness of questioning; and the use of physical punishment. *Laney v. State,* 76 S.W.3d 524 (Tex. App.-Houston [14th Dist.] 2002). Under Texas law, the State has the burden of proof to show by clear and convincing evidence that the consent to search was freely and voluntarily given. *Montanez v. State,* 195 S.W.3d 242 (Tex. Crim. App. 2006).

There is no requirement that officers tell an individual he or she has a right to refuse permission to search. While an individual's knowledge, or lack thereof, concerning his or her right to refuse permission is a factor to be considered in assessing the voluntariness of any consent given, it is not dispositive, and the State need not prove such knowledge for consent to be effective. *U.S. v. Drayton,* 536 U.S. 194 (2002); *State v. Kelly,* 204 S.W.3d 808 (Tex. Crim. App. 2006). Similarly, following a valid traffic stop, there is no requirement that an officer tell an individual that he or she is free to leave before asking for permission to search his or her vehicle. *Ohio v. Robinette,* 519 U.S. 33 (1996). Also be aware that reading of Miranda rights is not required as a precondition for obtaining consent to search. *Cleveland v. State,* 177 S.W.3d 374 (Tex. App.-Houston [1st Dist.] 2005).

Consent to a search is not rendered involuntary merely because the suspect has been placed under arrest at the time consent is given. *Harrison v. State,* 205 S.W.3d 549 (Tex. Crim. App. 2006).

The search must be limited to those areas to which the defendant actually or implicitly gives permission to search. The scope of the search is generally determined with reference to that which the officer is seeking, i.e., to areas or containers where the stated subject of the search could be located. In *Florida v. Jimeno,* 500 U.S. 248 (1991), the Court approved the search of a paper bag, found on the floor of a car, for narcotics, after the defendant had given consent to a general search of his car. The Court concluded that, based on these facts, it was reasonable for the searching officer to believe the scope of the consent given permitted him to open the bag. The defendant knew the purpose of the search was to look for drugs, and it was objectively reasonable to assume drugs could be found there.

Compare with *U.S. v. Rich,* 992 F.2d 502 (5th Cir. 1993). During a stop for a burned out license plate light, a state trooper asked defendant, "Do you have any narcotics or weapons in your truck?" He then asked, "Can I have a look in your truck?" Defendant said yes. Because of the open-ended nature of the question, defendant effectively consented to a search of the entire vehicle, including a closed suitcase found inside.

In *Lemons v. State,* 298 S.W.3d 658 (Tex. App.-Tyler 2009), a father contacted police to complain that defendant had taken inappropriate pictures of his 14-year-old daughter. Officers went to question defendant at his place of employment. One of the officers asked defendant if he could see his cell phone. Defendant responded by handing the phone over. The officer examined the calling information on the phone, then hit the "camera" button. As a result, he observed several pictures stored on the phone, including one of the 14-year-old girl lying naked on a bed. The Court found it reasonable to conclude that defendant's surrender of his phone in response to the officer's "open-ended request" implied a "grant of equally unbridled consent for the [officer] to examine the phone and the information contained therein." The Court also noted defendant did not object to the search as it was taking place. The scope of the search was within defendant's consent.

See also *State v. Garrett,* 177 S.W.3d 652 (Tex. App.-Houston [1st Dist.] 2005). During a traffic stop for speeding and mud flap violations, a state trooper asked defendant if he could search defendant's truck for any "illegal contraband." Defendant said, "Yes," and did not limit his consent to any particular area of the truck. Because defendant's consent was so open-ended, the Court concluded that the trooper did not exceed its scope by removing the driver's side door panel and looking inside (where he found nine balls of cocaine, three ecstasy pills, two sacks of clomiphene citrate pills, one bottle of liquid steroids and two baggies of powder cocaine).

But see *Stokvis v. State,* 147 S.W.3d 669 (Tex. App.-Amarillo 2004). The male driver of a pick-up truck consented to a search of the vehicle. This consent did not extend to defendant's purse, which she had left on the passenger seat, because

defendant was the only woman in the truck and the officer never asked for her consent or told her he planned to search the purse.

See also *Bagby v. State,* 119 S.W.3d 446 (Tex. App.-Tyler 2003). A deputy responded to a disturbance call. Defendant's neighbor said he had heard a sound like a .22 gunshot, saw his car window was shot out, then saw defendant "hunker down." Defendant denied shooting out the window, saying he had been in his shed the entire time. When asked, he did admit that he owned .22 weapons, which were in his shed. He agreed to let the deputy inspect the weapons to see if they had been fired recently, but added that he did not want his property searched. When the deputy entered the shed, he immediately saw a small amount of marijuana in plain view. Then, after inspecting the weapons, he continued to search the shed, finding more drugs. The Court held that while the marijuana was lawfully seized, all the contraband found after the deputy had completed his inspection of the firearms had to be suppressed, because the officer exceeded the scope of defendant's consent by remaining in the shed after the stated purpose of the search had been accomplished.

If, in an attempt to gain consent to search a residence, officers mislead a person by saying or implying they have a warrant and will search anyway, when in reality they do not, any permission given is invalid. *Bumper v. North Carolina,* 391 U.S. 543 (1968), *Cisneros v. State,* 165 S.W.3d 853 (Tex. App.-Texarkana 2005). However, the threat to obtain a warrant, while bearing on the voluntariness of consent, is not treated the same. Stating that a warrant can and will be obtained, if police in fact have the requisite grounds, will not automatically vitiate an ensuing consent. *U.S. v. Tompkins,* 130 F.3d 117 (5th Cir. 1997), *cert. denied,* 523 U.S. 1036 (1998).

9. **Inventory and Booking.** As long as pre-existing, standardized procedures are followed, police may conduct a warrantless search of a lawfully impounded automobile and its contents (*i.e.,* Inventory). Similarly, a lawful warrantless search of an arrestee, and containers in his or her possession, may be made prior to incarceration (*i.e.,* Booking). These exceptions are premised on the notion that the police are, in addition to their other duties, fulfilling a caretaking role. They are protecting the property of the arrestee from loss or theft or vandalism, and other fellow detainees from the possibility of assault if a weapon is smuggled in. They are also protecting themselves from possible charges of theft. Courts caution,

however, that the extent of the search must be tailored to serve these objectives. An inventory or booking search must not be a ruse for a general rummaging in order to discover incriminating evidence.

With respect to the legitimacy of inventory searches, courts have found that reasonable departmental regulations relating to inventory procedures, when carried out in good faith, satisfy the Constitution. *South Dakota v. Opperman,* 428 U.S. 364 (1976). The presence of preexisting and standardized procedures, as well as the absence of bad faith on the part of officers conducting the search, guard against the threat of using an inventory search as a pretext for looking for contraband or other evidence of crime without any individualized suspicion.

Under the federal Fourth Amendment, officers conducting an inventory search may open closed containers found in the vehicle and inventory their contents. *Colorado v. Burtine,* 479 U.S. 367 (1987). However, in *Autran v. State,* 887 S.W.2d 31 (Tex. Crim. App. 1994), a three-judge panel of the Texas Court of Criminal Appeals ruled that, under Article I, § 9 of the Texas Constitution, a search of closed containers would not be presumed reasonable solely because it is done as part of an inventory. Note that because this was not a majority opinion, some lower courts have questioned the continued vitality of this decision. See *Jurdi v. State,* 980 S.W.2d 904 (Tex. App.-Fort Worth 1998); *Hatcher v. State,* 916 S.W.2d 643 (Tex. App.-Texarkana 1996).

The vehicle searched must lawfully be in police custody (*i.e.,* there are sufficient grounds for impoundment) at the time of the search. Police may not "routinely" impound a vehicle solely because the driver has been arrested. *Benavides v. State,* 600 S.W.2d 809 (Tex. Crim. App. 1980). Some of the reasons impoundment would be justified include: (i) the vehicle is stolen; (ii) the vehicle is abandoned; (iii) the vehicle is a traffic hazard or is so mechanically unsound as to be a traffic hazard; (iv) the driver has been arrested *and* there is no alternative to impoundment (such as a passenger who can drive); (v) the vehicle is illegally parked; (vi) removal is necessary due to an accident; or (vii) the driver consents to impoundment. *Benavides v. State, supra.*

Similar to an inventory search, the search of an arrestee and his or her personal effects, including closed containers, prior to incarceration is reasonable under the Fourth Amendment. "A stationhouse search of every item carried on or by the person who has lawfully been taken into custody by the police" is permissible. *Illinois v. Lafayette,* 462 U.S. 640 (1983). In *Lafayette,* police arrested the defendant and transported him to the precinct headquarters. At the time he was carrying a shoulder bag. The bag was opened, emptied, and found to contain contraband. The defendant argued that the search exceeded the scope of a permissible booking search. The Supreme Court disagreed, reasoning that the search served the important government interests of protecting the property of the arrestee, as well as protecting the police department from false claims. A routine booking and search is a reasonable way to promote these interests, and thus is valid under the Fourth Amendment.

10. **Automobiles.** If police have probable cause to believe a moveable car contains contraband or evidence of a crime, they may lawfully conduct a search of the entire automobile, and any containers which could reasonably be expected to contain contraband, whether open or closed, without first securing a warrant. *Keehn v. State,* 279 S.W.3d 330 (Tex. Crim. App. 2009). This exception applies to all containers, whether owned by the driver or a passenger, and regardless of whether or not there is individualized probable cause to search a specific container. *Wyoming v. Houghton,* 526 U.S. 295 (1999) (after officer saw a syringe in plain view in the driver's pocket, he was entitled to search purse belonging to back seat passenger for narcotics). As long as there is probable cause to search the automobile, officers need not show facts establishing exigency. *Maryland v. Dyson,* 527 U.S. 465 (1999); *State v. Guzman,* 959 S.W.2d 631 (Tex. Crim. App. 1998).

See, *e.g., State v. Crawford,* 120 S.W.3d 508 (Tex. App.-Dallas 2003). An officer approached defendant at a gas pump in response to a reckless driver call. The officer immediately saw that defendant's eyes were "bloodshot and glassy" and noticed "a light odor of burned marijuana coming from [defendant]." The car's window was open, and as the officer passed it, he could detect "the strong odor of burned marijuana coming from inside the vehicle." The officer had probable cause to believe he would find drugs in the vehicle, so he was justified in conducting a warrantless search of it.

In *Blaylock v. State,* 125 S.W.3d 702 (Tex. App.-Texarkana 2003), a named informant told a Kilgore detective that she could arrange a drug deal with defendant, from whom she had purchased cocaine on several prior occasions. Forty minutes later, she called the detective back to say that she had arranged the purchase of 2 ounces of cocaine, and that defendant would deliver it within 20 minutes to a specified convenience store, adding that he would have the drug hidden under the hood of the car. When defendant arrived at the store as predicted, police could search his car without first obtaining a warrant.

See also *Dixon v. State,* 206 S.W.3d 613 (Tex. Crim. App. 2006). A confidential-informant (CI) phones an Abilene officer one morning to tell the officer that he had just observed defendant in possession of an off-white, rock-like substance that was purported to be crack cocaine to him. The CI said the rocks of cocaine were in a car, and gave the car's license plate number and location (an area of the city known for drug dealing). The officer had known this CI for over a year—although he was being paid and had a history of misdemeanor offenses, the information he provided was always shown to be true and had led to arrests of at least five drug offenders. Therefore, the officer believed him to be reliable and trustworthy. Less than an hour later, the officer drove to the neighborhood indicated by the CI, where he saw the vehicle described by the CI parked along the side of the road near a school. Defendant, who the officer knew from prior drug dealing incidents, was sitting inside the vehicle. Because the CI had a prior history of reliability, and because the officer managed to confirm every detail he provided except the presence of rocks of crack, probable cause was established for a warrantless search of the car.

Compare with *U.S. v. Reyes,* 792 F.2d 536 (5th Cir. 1986). A U.S. Customs investigator in Presidio received a call from a CI he had known for two years. The CI alleged that within the past 24 hours he had personally seen a large amount of cocaine in the motel room and vehicle of a Mexican man named Daniel. He further explained that "Daniel" was staying in Room 414 of the Holiday Inn on Highway 80 and drove a black and silver Chevrolet Blazer with temporary California tags. The investigator referred this tip to an Odessa officer, who went to the Holiday Inn to investigate. Outside Room 414, he saw a Hispanic man loading suitcases and gun cases into a black and silver Blazer. He then went into the office and confirmed that Room 414 had been occupied by a "Daniel Reyes." While he was still in the motel office, defendant walked in, identified himself as Daniel Reyes in Room 414, and said he wanted to check out. This information sufficiently corroborated the tip to establish probable cause. Moreover, because defendant was leaving, it was reasonable to assume that he had

transferred all of the cocaine he was alleged to possess from his room into the Blazer. Therefore, a warrantless search of the vehicle was lawful.

In *Keehn v. State, supra,* an officer looked inside a minivan parked in a residential driveway as he was walking to the front door to question the suspects in an unrelated matter. He saw a 5-gallon propane tank in the back of the minivan; the "cutting of the tank" had a bluish-greenish discoloration. Based on his experience, the officer concluded that the tank held anhydrous ammonia, which he knew is used in the manufacture of methamphetamine. He lawfully seized the tank under the automobile exception.

In *Stone v. State,* 147 S.W.3d 657 (Tex. App-Amarillo 2005), defendant was a passenger in a car stopped for lack of an inspection certificate. The officer asked her to step out of the vehicle, and she did, leaving her purse lying open on the passenger seat. Outside the vehicle, the officer could see that defendant had red, scabby needle tracks from her wrists to her elbows. The officer asked defendant if she used methamphetamine, and she replied that she had three days earlier. However, the officer could see a purple "Crown Royal" bag in defendant's purse. He had found narcotics and drug paraphernalia in Crown Royal bags on many occasions in the past. He therefore had probable cause to remove the bag from the purse and search it without a warrant.

In *U.S. v. McBee,* 659 F.2d 1302 (5th Cir. 1981), a bank was robbed one morning by a lone male in a blue-hooded sweatshirt. Immediately after the crime, a private citizen in a nearby office reported seeing a man in a sweat shirt enter the bank, leave as the alarm sounded, and then flee in a maroon Buick Regal with a specified dealer tag. Fifteen minutes to a half-hour after the robbery, an officer found a matching Buick parked on a street two or three miles from the bank. It was unoccupied, but the officer could see a blue sweatshirt inside. Warm air was coming from the grill, indicating the car had been parked recently. Police had probable cause for a warrantless search of the vehicle.

But see *Jenkins v. State,* 76 S.W.3d 709 (Tex. App.-Corpus Christi 2002), were the fact that defendant "appeared to be moving around, shuffling inside the car" during a traffic stop, without any other suspicious circumstances or reliable information suggesting his involvement in criminal activity, did not justify a warrantless search of his car.

Historically, this exception to the warrant requirement was premised on the notion that a car is readily mobile. As such, there is a potential exigency, in that a vehicle containing contraband may be driven from the jurisdiction before officers have an opportunity to secure a warrant. More recently, courts have focused on the pervasive government regulation of automobiles. Because the State has a hand in so many facets of automobile ownership and use (*e.g.,* licensing, registration, emission and safety inspections, *et al.* ), one's expectation of privacy in the solitude of his or her automobile and its contents is diminished. Automobiles, in our society, do not occupy the same sacrosanct position courts attribute to the home. With a lessened privacy interest, a greater intrusion becomes more reasonable, and permissible under the Fourth Amendment.

Note: **Canine Searches.** The Fourth Amendment does not require that police have a reasonable, articulable suspicion of criminal activity before allowing a well-trained narcotics detection dog to sniff the exterior of a vehicle during a lawful traffic stop, as long as this does not extend the duration of the stop. *Illinois v. Caballes,* 543 U.S. 405 (2005); *Haas v. State,* 172 S.W.3d 42 (Tex. App.-Waco 2005). An alert by a drug dog establishes probable cause to search a vehicle. *LeBlanc v. State,* 138 S.W.3d 603 (Tex. App.-Houston [14th Dist.] 2004).

Stopping a car for a minor traffic violation, without more, will not create probable cause to believe the car contains contraband and justify a search of the vehicle. The officer must have a reasonable belief that a more serious crime has been committed, and probable cause to think that evidence of it can be found in the car.

The search need not be contemporaneous with the seizure of the vehicle. *U.S. v. Johns,* 469 U.S. 478 (1985) (valid search of containers found in truck three days after vehicle seized).

Stated broadly, police have justification to conduct a warrantless search of a car, or an area or container within the car, in the following circumstances:

(i) the entire car, including the trunk and any closed containers, when the car is readily mobile and they possess probable cause to believe the car contains contraband or the fruits and instrumentalities of crime;

(ii) the area within an occupant's immediate control, to ensure the officer's safety during a *Terry* stop;

(iii) the entire passenger area of the car when they place an occupant of the car under arrest **if** the arrestee is within reaching distance of the passenger compartment at the time of the search **or** it is reasonable to believe the vehicle contains evidence of the offense of arrest;

(iv) the entire car, and generally any closed containers, as part of an inventory procedure when the car has been impounded;

(v) the entire car, when it has been abandoned or someone attempts to drive it across an international border;

(vi) the entire car, when valid consent has been given, or specific areas or containers, when permission to search has been limited to those areas.

The effective officer should keep these principles in mind when making the decision to act without a warrant. Although the rule remains that warrantless searches are per se invalid, warrantless searches are permissible in a variety of situations. However, the justifications permitting warrantless searches differ. The thorough officer should make sure that the circumstances with which he or she is confronted fit within the aforementioned exceptions, before deciding on a course of action.

Note: **Other Vehicles.** Watercraft are considered similar to automobiles, and searches of watercraft may be conducted under the same circumstances that would justify a search of an automobile. *U.S. v. Villamonte-Marquez,* 462 U.S. 579 (1983). Upon a showing of probable cause, police can make a warrantless search of a mobile home in a public place, if it is being used for transportation rather than as a residence. In making this determination, officers should consider: the location of the mobile home, whether it is truly mobile (or, for example, on blocks); whether the vehicle is licensed; whether it is connected to utilities; and whether it has convenient access to a public road. *California v. Carney,* 471 U.S. 386 (1985).

11. **Administrative Searches.** Searches and seizures may be undertaken by a state and its agents wholly apart from those pursued by law enforcement agencies. The constraints imposed by the Constitution apply to the state and federal governments and their subdivisions or agents. The U.S. Supreme Court has never limited the Amendment's prohibition on unreasonable searches and seizures to operations conducted by the police. Rather, the Court has long spoken of the Fourth Amendment's strictures as restraints imposed upon "governmental action"—that is, upon "the activities of sovereign authority." *New Jersey v. T.L.O., 469 U.S. 325 (1985).*

Detailed below are U.S. Supreme Court cases assessing the constitutionality of searches of an administrative character. In these instances, the Court has upheld searches in several situations where no law enforcement officials were involved, but where those individuals conducting the search could be deemed agents of a state or political subdivision (*i.e.*, intermediaries acting at the state's behest or in some way advancing the state's agenda), and their actions thus subject to constitutional limitations.

These warrantless intrusions by state actors are justified by the rationale that particular situations may involve special needs of the government. The special needs doctrine concerns governmental objectives that go beyond the normal day to day needs of law enforcement agencies. If special governmental needs are demonstrated, a reviewing court will balance the privacy interests of the individual against the magnitude of the state's need, to determine if a warrant, or at least some level of individualized suspicion (*i.e.*, probable cause or reasonable suspicion) is required to justify a search in each particular context.

The Court approved a warrantless search by school officials of schoolchildren, *New Jersey v. T.L.O., supra;* warrantless drug tests on student athletes, *Vernonia Sch. Dist. 47j v. Acton,* 515 U.S. 646 (1995), and students engaged in competitive extracurricular activities, *Bd. of Educ. of Indep. Sch. Dist. No. 92 of Pottawatomie Co. v. Earls,* 536 U.S. 822 (2002); a warrantless search by an employer of employees' desks, offices, or file cabinets, *O'Conner v. Ortega,* 480 U.S. 709 (1987); a warrantless search of a probationer's home, *Griffin v. Wisconsin,* 483 U.S. 868 (1987); mandatory warrantless drug testing of both railway employees, *Skinner v. Railway Labor Executives Ass'n,* 489 U.S. 602 (1989), and customs officials, *Nat'l Treasury Employees Union v. Von Raab,* 489 U.S. 656 (1989).

However, in *Chandler v. Miller,* 520 U.S. 305 (1997), the Court struck down a Georgia statutory provision requiring that candidates for specified state political offices pass a urinalysis drug test within 30 days prior to qualifying for election. The Court reasoned that Georgia had failed to show a special need important enough to override the individual privacy interests of the candidates. The Court found that the "certification requirement is not well designed to identify candidates who violate anti-drug laws" and that the statute failed to show any concrete danger posed by a state official possibly using drugs. See also *Ferguson v. City of Charleston,* 532 U.S. 67 (2001), where the Court struck down a policy which required state hospital employees to perform drug tests on urine samples taken from pregnant women (without the informed consent of the women), then to report positive results to police, who arrested the women if they refused to enter a drug treatment program. The Court found that the "central and indispensable" purpose of this policy was to generate evidence for law enforcement purposes, not to provide medical treatment, and noted that police were actively involved in the development of this policy as well as its day-to-day administration.

## V. EXPECTATION OF PRIVACY

In *Katz v. U.S.,* 389 U.S. 347 (1967), the U.S. Supreme Court held that the Fourth Amendment safeguards against unreasonable searches and seizures only extend to those places or objects with respect to which a person has exhibited some expectation of privacy. This expectation is one which society is prepared to recognize as reasonable. There are three varieties of property to which courts have consistently held no reasonable privacy expectation applies, and to which no constitutional protections will attach. These are: objects in open fields, objects placed in plain view, and objects that have been abandoned. These places can be searched, and items in those areas seized, without first securing a warrant.

The Supreme Court has noted that "the touchstone" of any claimed Fourth Amendment violation is always the reasonableness of the government's intrusion upon a citizen's personal security. It is often said that the Fourth Amendment does not prohibit all searches and seizures, only unreasonable ones. The threshold question in determining if government conduct is reasonable, is inquiring whether a legitimate privacy interest has been invaded. In *Katz, supra,* the Court spelled out the analysis that will be used to determine when Fourth Amendment protections are implicated, and when they are not. The Constitution will protect people from government intrusion only with respect to those areas and items for which they subjectively have an expectation of privacy and only when that expectation is plainly one that society is prepared to recognize as reasonable. The Fourth Amendment protects "people—and not simply areas—against unreasonable searches and seizures." The Court noted that an expectation of privacy will vary from person to person, and place to place, reasoning that "objects, activities or statements that one exposes to outsiders may fall outside the protection of the Fourth Amendment because (one) has displayed them freely and has not shown an intention of keeping them private. One may also exhibit an expectation of privacy in an item, even though he or she takes it to a public place, if his or her acts manifest an intent to keep the item private." If no privacy violation occurred, the Fourth Amendment is not implicated, and there is no need to further examine government conduct. Likewise, if one person's privacy concerns have been trodden upon, other individuals whose interests were not interfered with do not have legal grounds, or standing, to challenge the government's conduct, and that conduct need not be analyzed.

If, however, a privacy violation has occurred, the courts will proceed to examine the conduct in question, and endeavor to determine if it was reasonable under the circumstances. If the actions are deemed reasonable, they are legal; if unreasonable, they are unconstitutional, bringing the specter of suppression and civil liability into the forefront. To aid in this reasonableness determination, courts employ a balancing analysis. On one side of the scale rests a person's privacy concerns regarding his home, body and possessions. On the other side of the scale rests the government's interest in advancing or promoting the law enforcement conduct in question. If the privacy interest is weighty (*e.g.,* the inviolability of one's home), then intrusive government conduct is less likely to be reasonable under the circumstances. If, on the other hand, the government interest is significant (*e.g.,* curtailing the drug epidemic), and the individual's privacy interest is lessened (*e.g.,* items that may be carried about in one's car), then more intrusive government action is more likely to be deemed constitutionally reasonable under the circumstances.

Nonetheless, there remains a judicial preference for warrants, and the general rule remains that warrantless searches are per se unreasonable. The Supreme Court has provided some clear-cut guidelines in specific instances, the so-called "bright-line rules" (*e.g.,* requirement of a warrant for an in-home arrest, search of a passenger compartment when the occupant is arrested, etc.) Courts routinely state that they are hesitant to pronounce far-reaching rules of universal applicability. Rather, there is an increasing tendency to evaluate each case on its own facts, and resort to the balancing test to determine the reasonableness, and hence the constitutionality, of any given law enforcement action. There are many circumstances to which no precedent applies. In cases that fall beyond the confines of these "bright-line" rules, where government conduct is in the periphery, or gray area of Fourth Amendment law, courts are increasingly likely to employ the balancing test. The outcome, obviously, will vary depending on the unique circumstances of each factual setting. In these cases, rather than employing a rule requiring a warrant for virtually all law enforcement actions, subject to limited exceptions, courts will instead employ the above criteria to answer the question begged by the Fourth Amendment: Was the conduct reasonable?

The following doctrines concern areas, and objects within those areas, or classes of property, with respect to which courts have consistently held individuals do not have a reasonable expectation of privacy. Because there is no privacy expectation, no search, within the meaning of the Constitution, can take place; *i.e.,* the Fourth Amendment is not implicated, there is no need to examine government acts, and no basis for suppression of evidence seized.

## A. Plain View Doctrine

Under the plain view doctrine, the warrantless seizure of a piece of evidence that is in plain view is permissible when three criteria are met. First, the evidence must be seen from a lawful vantage point, *i.e.,* the officer must have a legal justification for his place of observation. Second, it must be immediately apparent to the viewer that the object observed is incriminating evidence. In other words, the observing officer must have probable cause to believe the evidence in question is contraband or incriminating evidence and should need no further investigation of the object or item in question to realize its evidentiary value. Finally, the officer must have a right of lawful access to the evidence before seizing it. *Horton v. California,* 496 U.S. 128 (1990); *Keehn v. State,* 279 S.W.3d 330 (Tex. Crim. App. 2009).

In *Hill v. State,* 303 S.W.3d 863 (Tex. App.-Fort Worth 2009), officers were patrolling the east side of Forth Worth following a rash of robberies. They watched defendant's SUV pull into the back of a McDonalds parking lot and stop, but no one got out of the vehicle. The SUV then drove off and stopped at a convenience store a block away—again, no one exited. When it drove off again, the officers initiated a stop for an unsignaled turn. Defendant (the driver) and the front seat passenger both opened their doors and got out of the vehicle immediately, leaving their doors open—

the officers later described this conduct as "out of the ordinary." Defendant then "reach[ed] towards his shirt, kind of reaching under the shirt on his back," as if retrieving a weapon. The officers quickly frisked and handcuffed defendant. Because of the dark tint on the windows, they could not see if anyone was in the SUV. While checking to see if there were any other passengers, one of the officers saw a brown paper bag wedged between the driver's seat and center console. Inside the bag, the officer could see a clear plastic baggie holding an off-white rock-like substance he believed to be crack cocaine. Because the officer was justified in looking inside the SUV for his own safety, and because the illegal nature of the crack cocaine was immediately apparent, the officer made a valid plain view seizure of the bag.

The incriminating nature of the item need only be "immediately apparent" before it is seized, not necessarily when police first lay eyes on it—as long as the probable cause to believe that the item in plain view constitutes contraband arises while the police are still lawfully on the premises, and their "further investigation" into the nature of the item does not entail an additional and unjustified search of (*i.e.,* a greater physical intrusion than originally justified), or presence on the premises (*i.e.,* a longer intrusion than originally justified), the item may be lawfully seized. *State v. Dobbs,* 323 S.W.3d 184 (Tex. Crim. App. 2010).

In *Dobbs,* officers were executing a search warrant for marijuana and cocaine in defendant's home. They found two sets of golf clubs in the middle of the floor in a bedroom—the clubs looked brand new. On a shelf in the bedroom closet, they found T-shirts with the logo of the Los Rios Country Club embroidered on them. At the time of discovery, the officers lacked probable cause to connect the clubs or shirts to any crime, but they were suspicious. They contacted dispatch to inquire if there had been any recent burglaries, particularly of country clubs. They learned the Los Rios Country Club had indeed reported a theft of golf merchandise. Because the officers were justified in looking in the bedroom and closet under the search warrant, and still lawfully on the premises searching for drugs when they learned of the stolen merchandise, this was a valid plain view seizure.

The theory behind the plain view doctrine is that when a police officer is conducting a lawful search and comes across an item or object that is not the object of a search, but is plainly incriminating, then the officer may seize that item. The justification for such a warrantless seizure is not a lack of privacy interest in the item (probable cause to believe that the object or item is contraband, evidence, or fruits or instrumentality of a crime is necessary), but that there is no intrusion beyond that which is already justified.

The importance of the plain view doctrine is that, technically, when conducting a search, an officer may seize only those objects or items described in a warrant or, in a warrantless search, those objects or items which the officer is lawfully authorized to seize under an exception to the warrant requirement. Thus, without the plain view doctrine, an officer searching an automobile for weapons would be forced to ignore evidence that was not a weapon. However, under the plain view doctrine, a seizure of other evidence is lawful.

Use of a flashlight to view an object does not make a plain view seizure unlawful. *Walter v. State,* 28 S.W.3d 541 (Tex. Crim. App. 2000). However, police cannot use a device which is not in general public use to explore details of the home that would previously have been unknowable without physical intrusion without first obtaining a warrant. *Kyllo v. U.S.,* 533 U.S. 27 (2001) (warrantless police use of a thermal imager, which measured the amount of heat emanating from different areas of defendant's house, violated the Fourth Amendment).

Similar to plain view is the theory of open view. However, in open view an officer needs no justification for his or her vantage point in that the object or item is in a place in which no person could have a reasonable expectation of privacy. Thus, there is no search being conducted when an officer finds an object or item in open view.

"The seizure of property in plain view involves no invasion of privacy and is presumptively reasonable, assuming that there is probable cause to associate the property with criminal activity." *Payton v. New York,* 445 U.S. 573 (1980). This doctrine is premised on the notion that if an article is already in plain view, the owner of the property has not manifested any expectation of privacy in the object. Often, the critical factor in deciding the applicability of the doctrine to the admission of proffered evidence, involves a determination of whether or not the seizing officers are lawfully in the position from which they view the seized item. As long as law enforcement officials have a proper justification for being where they conduct their observation, and have a right of access to the item seized, they may seize all contraband, fruits, and instrumentalities of crime, or those items that they have probable cause to believe are contraband, fruits, or instrumentalities of crime. Adequate justifications for being at a given vantage point would include being in a public area (*e.g.,* street, or business open to the public), working under the authority of a warrant, or where the intrusion that brings the police within plain view of the evidence is supported by one of the exceptions to the warrant requirement (*e.g.,* hot pursuit or exigent circumstances). A proper justification for the officers being where they are viewing from, in essence, means that the officer did not violate the defendant's constitutional rights in establishing his or her vantage point. To fall within the purview of this exception, the discovery of the incriminating items need not be inadvertent (*i.e.,* the seizing officer can be operating under the assumption that incriminating evidence will be found, or have an idea of what he or she will find), but the incriminating nature of the item must be immediately apparent. See *Ramos v. State,* 934 S.W.2d 358 (Tex. Crim. App. 1996).

Courts sometimes draw a distinction between items seized in "plain" view and items seized in "open" view. Under this analysis, items in plain view are in a constitutionally protected area (*i.e.,* one in which there is a reasonable expectation of privacy). When these items are seized the question a reviewing court will ask is, once the item has been seen, is there a justification, like a warrant or an applicable exception, that will permit access? Or, if the item is seen from a constitutionally protected area, is there a justification for the law enforcement personnel being in that protected area? For example, if contraband is seen in plain view, and the officer is justified in being at his vantage point, it does not always mean the contraband is subject to immediate seizure. If the contraband is in a home, or in the curtilage, and seen from without, a warrant must be procured, absent an applicable exception to the warrant requirement, before the home can be entered and the evidence seized. Items in open view, on the other hand, are items seen in an area that is not constitutionally protected (*i.e.,* where there is no reasonable expectation of privacy). Examples often cited are objects in open fields, on the body of a person, in a public building, or in a car. In this respect, the open view doctrine is essentially identical to the open fields concept, discussed below.

## B. Areas and Items Surrounding the Home

The home is clearly a bastion of Fourth Amendment rights. The area around the home, often referred to as the "curtilage," also enjoys protection. This includes areas such as the garage, garden, or the immediate yard. However, courts have held that the area outside the curtilage is not worthy of the same protection.

1. **Curtilage.** The sanctity of one's home is at the core of Fourth Amendment rights. While objects in open areas do not receive the benefit of Fourth Amendment protections, courts have also ruled that constitutional safeguards will extend to zones immediately outside the home, an area called the curtilage. The extent of the curtilage is determined by factors that bear upon whether an individual reasonably may expect that the area in question should be treated as the home itself. Courts look to see if the area is used for the "intimate activity associated with the sanctity of a man's home and the privacies of life." The analysis employed by courts entails an examination of four factors: (i) the proximity of the area claimed to be curtilage to the home; (ii) whether the area is enclosed, for example, by a fence or hedge; (iii) the types of activities for which the homeowner uses the area; and (iv) the measures taken by the resident to guard the area from observation by people passing by. *U.S. v. Dunn,* 480 U.S. 294, *reh'g denied,* 481 U.S. 1024 (1987).

As a consequence of the interplay between these two doctrines, the home and the curtilage are protected by the Constitution, and a warrant will generally be required to enter and search them. The open areas that surround those private protected zones do not occupy the same position of reverence and are not accorded the same protections.

There is no reasonable expectation of privacy in odors emanating from the curtilage. In *Rodriguez v. State,* 106 S.W.3d 224 (Tex. App.-Houston [1st Dist.] 2003), the Court upheld a warrantless sniff search of defendant's front door by a drug dog. The door was the main entrance to the house and was not enclosed or protected from observation by passersby, and the dog's action did not expose non-contraband items, activity, or information that would otherwise remain hidden from public view. Compare with *Romo v. State,* 315 S.W.3d 565 (Tex. App.-Fort Worth 2010), where the Court upheld a sniff search of the area around defendant's garage door by a trained narcotics-detection dog. The garage was accessible by public alleyway, and not enclosed by any fencing or barrier that would prevent access by the general public. The Court also held that an alert by a drug dog outside a residence, standing alone, established sufficient probable cause to search that home.

2. **Aerial Search.** Courts have found that it is unreasonable to have a privacy expectation in the aerial view of one's property. This is due to the fact that any private citizen may obtain such a view. Since there is no protected privacy interest in the view, police may conduct aerial searches without a warrant. *Dow Chemicals Co. v. U.S.,* 476 U.S. 227 (1986).

3. **Open Fields.** Courts have said that people cannot maintain a reasonable expectation of privacy as to items placed in open fields, or concerning activities conducted there. Because there is no intrusion on a constitutionally protected zone of privacy, the Fourth Amendment is not implicated when law enforcement officials survey structures found, or activities conducted, in an open field. Because the Fourth Amendment does not protect open fields, the examination of objects therein does not constitute a search, and neither a warrant, nor any exception to the warrant requirement, need be shown to justify the seizure of articles in an open field. *Oliver v. U.S.,* 466 U.S. 170 (1984); *Davidson v. State,* 249 S.W.3d 709 (Tex. App.-Austin 2008).

An "open field" need not be "open" or a "field" as those terms are commonly used; the term includes any unoccupied or undeveloped area outside the curtilage of a dwelling. *Davidson, supra.* The type of land a court may deem an open field will depend on the unique circumstances of each parcel. A variety of circumstantial factors will be examined to determine if the area is treated as a non-private area, or if the owner has manifested a privacy interest, or has exhibited an intent to keep outsiders away. The presence or absence of "No Trespassing" signs, and the extent to which such a policy is enforced, is relevant in this determination, as is the presence or absence of a fence or hedge surrounding the field, and the extent to which the owner controls access to the field by use of a gate or chain across an entry lane.

Courts have held that it is generally unreasonable to have an expectation of privacy in open areas of land. Even if the land shows evidence of an expectation of privacy, the courts will still only look at the reasonableness of that expectation.

4. **Abandoned Items or Garbage.** When property has been abandoned, it no longer falls within the area of protection afforded by the Fourth Amendment, and therefore can be searched or seized without a warrant or any other justification. When determining if property has been abandoned, courts will analyze the actions of the individual alleged to have discarded the article. The focus is not whether the defendant relinquished dominion and control of the property with respect to his or her possession, as would be the case if the ownership of the item were in dispute, but rather, whether the individual has relinquished any reasonable expectation of privacy in the article. An intent to abandon may be inferred from the suspect's words, actions, or other objective facts. *Morrison v. State,* 71 S.W.3d 821 (Tex. App.-Corpus Christi 2002). When police conduct is lawful (*e.g.,* they have a lawful right to approach and question a person) and a suspect discards an item in a public place, then he or she can be said to have abandoned that item. Police may secure the item and, if incriminating, retain it for use later as evidence, without fear of the suspect claiming that the evidence was seized from him or her unlawfully.

See, *e.g., Garcia v. State,* 769 S.W.2d 345 (Tex. App.-Houston [1st Dist.] 1989). A Harris County judge approached defendant at an apartment complex (the judge had seen defendant on his street near midnight on the same night that a playhouse was stolen from his front porch). Defendant was holding what appeared to be a shirt or a rag. Because he feared defendant might be concealing a weapon in the rag, the judge showed his judicial identification, asked defendant to place the object he was holding on the ground, then requested defendant's identification. Defendant hesitated for about 45 seconds, then threw the rag over a brick wall lined with barbed wire. The judge drew his gun, ordered defendant to the ground, and handcuffed him. He and an officer then searched behind the wall (they first had to drive around the block to get into the property from the front entrance), where they found syringes wrapped in the rag defendant had thrown. Because defendant could not have climbed over the wall or simply walked around it to retrieve the syringes, the Court found they were abandoned. Because the judge had at least reasonable suspicion for a detention, the abandonment was not forced, and the syringes could lawfully be seized without a warrant.

Compare with *Morrison v. State, supra.* Following a valid traffic stop, defendant dropped cocaine out a window to the roadside of a public street.

Because the drug was abandoned, he could not object to the officer's recovery of it.

In *Shelly v. State,* 101 S.W.3d 606 (Tex. App.-Houston [1st Dist.] 2003), two officers pulled into the Tour-Inn Motel, a low-budget motel with a history of problems with narcotics and prostitution, at around 2:00 a.m. While walking around the parking lot, they saw a car stopped with its engine running; two males were asleep in the back seat, while no one was in the front seat. At about this same time, the officers heard a commotion coming from Room 3. They looked over to see defendant in the doorway, cursing and shouting, with a cell phone to his ear and what appeared to be a baggie of crack cocaine in his hand. When defendant turned to face the officers, one of them called out, "Say man, come here." Defendant responded by dropping the baggie of cocaine and running. Because defendant did not comply with the officers and they did not physically touch him, there was not yet a seizure; therefore, the baggie was abandoned, and could be lawfully seized without a warrant.

Conversely, if officers do not have a justification for their initial actions (*e.g.,* detaining without reasonable suspicion), and the item is discarded in response to this unlawful activity, the evidence may be suppressed as the fruit of illegal law enforcement activity. In this instance, courts say that the unlawful police action forced the abandonment.

See, *e.g., Comer v. State,* 754 S.W.2d 656 (Tex. Crim. App. 1986), where although defendant dropped a syringe and attempted to kick it under his truck as he exited the vehicle, legally there was no "abandonment" of the syringe because police did not have reasonable suspicion to stop the truck in the first place.

When an individual abandons an item of personal property, he relinquishes a reasonable expectation of privacy in the discarded item. This is true whether an individual is putting trash to the curb or dropping evidence while fleeing from police. A showing of actual intent to abandon is not necessary. It is only necessary to show that the individual asserting a privacy interest in the property in question had relinquished sufficient control over the property so that he no longer had any reasonable expectation of privacy in the object or item. See *Flores v. State,* 319 S.W.3d 697 (Tex. Crim. App. 2010) (renounce any expectation of privacy in garbage left outside the curtilage of the home for collection).

Compare with *Hudson v. State,* 205 S.W.3d 600 (Tex. App.-Waco 2006). Defendant, who had been placed under arrest, was brought to an interrogation room for questioning regarding a burglary. During the interrogation, police gave him a can of Dr. Pepper to drink. Also during questioning, an investigator asked defendant to give a DNA sample via a mouth swab, but he refused. When the jailers came to return defendant to his cell, he smashed the now-empty Dr. Pepper can and tossed it in a trash bin. As soon as defendant left, the investigator retrieved the can and submitted it for DNA analysis. Because defendant had thrown the can away of his own volition, it was abandoned, and he could no longer object to law enforcement tests of it. See also *Wright v. State,* 253 S.W.3d 287 (Tex. Crim. App. 2008).

See also *Mondragon-Garcia v. State,* 129 S.W.3d 674 (Tex. App.-Eastland 2004). Federal agents had defendant's motel room under surveillance; one of the agents called the room and asked defendant to come out and talk. A short time later, the door to the room opened, and defendant came out wearing only his bikini underwear; he looked at the agents, then took off running. He was quickly captured and arrested due to his status as an illegal immigrant. A subsequent warrantless search of the room found drugs and the weapon used in a murder. The Court found that, because defendant left the door ajar after he ran and left behind his clothes and drugs in plain view, he "was clearly trying to escape and disassociate himself from the motel room and its contents." Because the circumstances indicated that he "voluntarily left and relinquished his interest in the property," he no longer had a reasonable expectation of privacy in the room or its contents. The evidence found had been abandoned, and was lawfully seized.

5. **Disclaimer of Ownership.** If a defendant disclaims ownership of property or any possessory interest, police may use such a denial as sufficient proof of either an intent to abandon the property or a lack of ownership of the property.

See, *e.g., State v. Velasquez,* 994 S.W.2d 676 (Tex. Crim. App. 1999). An officer saw defendant board a Greyhound bus carrying a black duffel bag. Before the bus was ready to leave, the officer and his partner (both in plain clothes) also boarded the bus and began to hold consensual interviews with the passengers. Without blocking defendant in, the officer squatted down next to defendant and asked—in addition to a few insignificant questions—to see his ticket and identification. He then asked if defendant had any luggage, to which defendant replied that he did not, even though the black bag he had carried on was in the seat next to him. The officer asked if it was his, and defendant replied, "No, that's not my bag." When the officer went to grab the bag, defendant placed his hands across it and asked, "What are you doing?" The officer said, "I'm getting this bag. Is this your bag?" Defendant replied, "Uh, no, it's not." Because defendant disclaimed any ownership interest in the bag, it was effectively abandoned, and he could no longer legally object to the officer's search. Therefore, the marihuana the officer found in the bag was admissible.

## C. The Caretaker Function

The "caretaker function" was first developed by the U.S. Supreme Court in *Cady v. Dombrowski,* 413 U.S. 433 (1973). The concept of the "caretaker function" is that the police are not always involved in the adversarial process of arresting criminals. Sometimes the police may act in other ways to help the public. This may be to render assistance to individuals in need or to provide protection for the rights and property of members of the general public. The "caretaker function" also applies to certain acts performed by police to secure a suspect's rights or property. The Courts will examine the reasonableness of any such act. However, probable cause is not necessary. Evidence that is found during such acts will be admissible.

In determining whether a citizen truly needs assistance, a court will examine the totality of circumstances, including (i) the nature and level of distress exhibited by the individual, (ii) the location of the individual, (iii) whether or not the individual was alone or had access to assistance independent of that offered by the officer, and (iv) to what extent the individual—if not assisted—presented a danger to himself or others. *Wright v. State,* 7 S.W.3d 148 (Tex. Crim. App. 1999).

See, *e.g., Hulit v. State,* 947 S.W.2d 707 (Tex. App.-Fort Worth 1997), *aff'd,* 982 S.W.2d 431 (Tex. Crim. App. 1998). A Benbrook officer received a report of a woman possibly having a heart attack in her vehicle at 2:00 a.m. When the officer arrived on the scene, he saw a pick-up truck stopped in the left turn lane of an interstate service road, 50 feet short of an intersection. Defendant was slumped over the steering wheel of the truck (although the defendant was a man, from a distance, his features could be mistaken for a woman's). The officer turned on his emergency lights and rapped on the truck's window in order to wake defendant up. When defendant finally woke up, his obvious intoxicated condition led to his arrest for DWI. Because the officer was solely concerned with the driver's medical condition, his conduct fell within the caretaker doctrine and did not have to be supported by probable cause.

Compare with *Doiron v. State,* 283 S.W.3d 71 (Tex. App.-Beaumont 2009). At around 1:00 a.m., an officer saw defendant's Honda Civic traveling slowly along a street, brake lights blinking intermittently. Defendant was the sole occupant. He stopped the car, opened the door, and began vomiting. The officer made a valid caretaker stop, to determine if defendant needed medical assistance.

In *Morfin v. State,* 34 S.W.3d 664 (Tex. App.-San Antonio 2000), an officer on routine patrol saw a car stopped just one block away from a high-crime area. It was dark out and the officer could reasonably conclude that the occupants were in danger if the car was inoperable. Therefore, he was justified under the caretaker doctrine in approaching the car to see if the occupants were in need of assistance.

See also *Ortega v. State,* 974 S.W.3d 361 (Tex. App.-San Antonio 1998), where a stop was justified under the caretaker doctrine when defendant was driving a 17-year-old vehicle only 18 to 20 m.p.h. in a 50 m.p.h. zone in the early morning hours. The officer had a reasonable, legitimate concern that defendant was having vehicle problems. Compare with *Bilyeu v. State,* 136 S.W.3d 691 (Tex. App-Texarkana 2004) (fact that defendant was traveling 10 m.p.h. in a 35 m.p.h. zone justified a caretaker stop). But see *Corbin v. State,* 85 S.W.3d 272 (Tex. Crim. App. 2002), where the court found that driving 13 m.p.h. below the speed limit, with no other violations, does not justify a caretaker stop.

The Caretaker Doctrine can also justify warrantless entry into a home. See *Laney v. State,* 117 S.W.3d 854 (Tex. Crim. App. 2003). Shortly after midnight, deputies responded to a dispute between neighbors at defendant's mobile home park. While the deputies were speaking with his neighbors, defendant came out of his trailer, approached the officers, and explained that he had turned off the electricity to a neighbor's trailer in retaliation for the neighbor doing the same to him. Defendant was placed in the back of a patrol car pending possible charges for criminal mischief. While the deputies continued their investigation, two young boys came out of defendant's darkened trailer onto the front porch. When asked if these were his sons, defendant said they were not. One of the boys, who appeared to be about 10-years-old, made eye contact with a deputy and then went back inside. The deputies then asked defendant if he had ever been arrested, and he admitted that he had, for indecency with a child. Because defendant was possibly going to jail, the deputies had a responsibility to get the children out of the trailer and find out who their parents were. As they approached the trailer, one of the boys came out. He said the other boy, his brother, was in a back bedroom. The deputies called out to the other boy, but received no response. One deputy then entered to find the boy. While searching with a flashlight, he saw sexually explicit pictures of young boys on a shelf; he did not touch the pictures, but instead led the boy out of the trailer. His observations later served as the basis for a search warrant. The Court upheld the deputy's entry as a valid caretaker search; his actions were directed solely toward securing the well-being of the child, not toward continuing the investigation of defendant.

## VI. THE EXCLUSIONARY RULE

The frequent result of unconstitutional actions by law enforcement is the imposition of a judicially created remedy—banning the use of evidence gathered under such circumstances—called suppression. The exclusionary rule mandates that all evidence obtained by searches and seizures violative of the rights of an accused are inadmissible against that person in a subsequent trial. The rule is premised on the notion that if private, constitutionally protected areas can be searched, and items taken unlawfully are used to obtain a conviction, the protections of the Fourth Amendment are of little, if any, value. The exclusionary rule is in essence an enforcement mechanism, serving to give teeth to constitutional guarantees. The rule bars the use of all forms of illegally obtained evidence. Physical evidence as well as statements are subject to suppression, if they derive from an unconstitutional act, such as an unlawful arrest, illegal search or coercive interrogation. If law enforcement officials come by evidence through exploitation of their illegal conduct, the evidence is said to be "tainted," and evidence tainted by illegal conduct on the part of law enforcement is inadmissible against an accused.

The exclusionary rule applies not only to the illegally obtained evidence itself, but also bars the use of evidence derived from the initially obtained illegal evidence, because of the initial illegality. This derivative, or secondary evidence, including an officer's testimony based on knowl-

edge garnered as a result of the illegal conduct, is often referred to as the "fruit of the poisonous tree." To invoke the protection of the "poisonous tree" principle, the defendant must first demonstrate there was a primary illegality (*i.e.,* an unconstitutional search or arrest, or a coerced confession), and secondly, a nexus, or connection, between the illegality and the derivative evidence. The nexus between the illegal act and the subject evidence must be so strong that police can be said to have obtained the evidence only by an exploitation of their illegal actions. If another event or outside factor weakens the connection between the illegality and the evidence, a principle referred to as attenuation, so that the evidence can no longer be said to be a by-product of the unlawful conduct, then suppression is not appropriate. The attenuating factor removes the stigma of the illegal law enforcement action, so that denying the admission of the seized evidence does not serve the deterrent purposes of the exclusionary rule.

The exclusionary rule is not mandated by the language of the Constitution. It is, rather, a judicially created remedy. Exclusion is appropriate where the underlying purposes of the Bill of Rights (*i.e.,* freedom from unbridled government intrusion) are best served. The rule prohibiting the use of illegally obtained evidence has its roots in the notion that we live in a society governed by the rule of law, not rule by law. If a government is not held to the standards found in the document that created it, then how can a government expect citizens to respect and abide by its pronouncements? Moreover, the rule is not designed to penalize officers for their mistakes or oversights, or to hamper their legitimate efforts. "The criminal does not go free because the constable blundered, but because the Constitution prohibits securing the evidence against" the defendant. *People v. Cahan,* 282 P.2d 905 (Cal. 1955). However, the rule does serve as a deterrent, in that it discourages officers from obtaining evidence in an illegal manner. If the evidence cannot be used to obtain a conviction, then the incentive to obtain it disappears. Put another way, law enforcement is encouraged to respect constitutional guarantees in evidence gathering, for only evidence taken in accordance with those principles will be of any use.

Note: **Inevitable Discovery.** Under the Fourth Amendment, "if the prosecution can establish by a preponderance of the evidence that the information ultimately or inevitably would have been discovered by lawful means then the deterrence rationale has so little basis that the evidence should be received." *Nix v. Williams,* 467 U.S. 431 (1984) For example, in Nix, even though police illegally obtained from a suspect the location of the body of a child he had murdered, the body was admissible when a 200-member search party was scheduled to search in the area where the body was found. Because of this, there was an extremely good chance the body would have eventually been found without the suspect's aid. However, in Texas, because of the statutory restrictions of *Tex. Code Crim. Proc.* art. 38.23(a), the "inevitable discovery" doctrine is not recognized. *Garcia v. State,* 829 S.W.3d 796 (Tex. Crim. App. 1992).

Note: **Independent Source.** The Fourth Amendment permits the introduction of evidence initially discovered during, or as a consequence of, an unlawful search, "but later obtained independently from lawful activities untainted by the initial illegality." *Murray v. U.S.,* 487 U.S. 533 (1988) (seizure of marijuana pursuant to warrant upheld even though police had illegally entered place to be searched, when no mention of the illegal entry was made in the warrant application and the warrant was based solely on facts accumulated prior to the illegal entry. The seizure was not a result of the illegal entry, but rather the result of a warrant issued pursuant to an independent finding of probable cause). Much like the "inevitable discovery" doctrine, this doctrine violates *Tex. Code Crim. Proc.* art. 38.23(a). *State v. Daugherty,* 931 S.W.2d 269 (Tex. Crim. App. 1996).

### A. The "Good Faith" Exception.

Under the Fourth Amendment, when an officer, operating in good faith, bases an arrest on a violation of a criminal statute or ordinance, and that statute is later deemed unconstitutional, retroactively rendering the arrest illegal, evidence discovered incident to that arrest will not be suppressed. *U.S. v. Leon,* 468 U.S. 897 (1984). Similarly, evidence will not be suppressed when an officer conducts a search or arrest in reasonable, good faith reliance on a warrant issued by a neutral and detached magistrate, and that warrant is later found defective or technically deficient. See *Arizona v. Evans,* 514 U.S. 1 (1995).

In Texas, a version of the good faith exception has been codified by statute at *Tex. Code Crim. Proc.* art. 38.23. This statutory exception is more restrictive than the federal exception. It will only save evidence seized by an officer acting in good faith reliance on a warrant based upon probable cause. Thus, if the warrant relied upon was supported by probable cause, the evidence seized will be suppressed even if the officer relied upon it in good faith. *Gordon v. State,* 801 S.W.2d 899 (Tex. Crim. App. 1990).

In *Dunn v. State,* 951 S.W.3d 478 (Tex. Crim. App. 1997), an arrest warrant supported by probable cause was upheld even though the magistrate had inadvertently failed to sign it.

## VII. LIABILITY

### A. Criminal Liability

Law enforcement officers may be held criminally liable under both 18 U.S.C. § 241 and 18 U.S.C. § 242. However, neither section provides individual relief for the party whose rights were violated.

Under 18 U.S.C. § 241, a law enforcement officer is liable if he or she enters into a conspiracy to deprive any citizen of any right or privilege guaranteed by the Constitution. For this section, the only act that is necessary for a violation is an act in furtherance of the conspiracy. The penalty under this section is up to 10 years in prison and/or up to a $10,000 fine. If death results then the prison term may be for life.

18 U.S.C. 242 makes it an offense for a law enforcement officer to act under color of law to willfully deprive any inhabitant of the United States of rights guaranteed by the Constitution or laws of the United States. Under color of law means under the pretense of law. The penalty under this section is up to 1 year in jail and/or up to a $1,000 fine.

### B. Civil Liability

Under Title 42, Chapter 21, Subchapter 1, § 1983 of the United States Code (commonly referred to as a "§ 1983" action), any person who, under pretense of law, deprives another of any constitutional right, "shall be liable to the party injured in an action at law, suit in equity, or other proper proceeding for redress."

Under this section the U.S. Supreme Court has held that an officer (and the department) may be sued for money damages by the victim of an unlawful arrest. *Malley v. Briggs,* 475 U.S. 335 (1986). Furthermore, the same civil liability for an objectively unreasonable arrest will apply to an objectively unreasonable search. *Anderson v. Creighton,* 483 U.S. 635 (1987).

It is important to note that a police officer's intent in making a false arrest is not material to an action for deprivation of civil rights brought under this statute. *Caballero v. City of Concord,* 956 F.2d 204 (9th Cir. 1992).

Once probable cause to arrest is established, a law enforcement officer cannot be held liable for false arrest under state laws or for deprivation of civil rights under this statute. *Hunter v. Clardy,* 558 F.2d 290 (5th Cir. 1977). Any collateral bad motive or intent on the part of the arresting officer is immaterial.

Qualified immunity is an affirmative defense against § 1983 claims. Its purpose is to shield public officials from undue interference with their duties and from potentially disabling threats of liability where the official acts objectively and reasonably in the good faith performance of his or her duties. The defense provides immunity from suit, not merely liability. *Saucier v. Katz,* 533 U.S. 194 (2001).

Some examples of the types of cases which have been brought under this statute are: (i) failure to advise grounds for arrest and detention, *Tilson v. Forrest City Police Dep't,* 28 F.3d 802 (8th Cir. 1994), *cert. denied,* 514 U.S. 1004 (1995); (ii) detaining the person arrested for too long a period, *Tilson v. Forrest City Police Dep't, supra;* (iii) use of unreasonable or excessive force during arrest or detention, *Elliott v. Leavitt,* 99 F.3d 640 (4th Cir. 1996); (iv) unlawful search and seizure by police, *Brouhard v. Lee,* 125 F.3d 656 (8th Cir. 1997); (v) interrogation in violation of a suspect's right to remain silent, *Cooper v. Dupink,* 963 F.2d 1220 (9th Cir.), cert. denied, 506 U.S. 953 (1992). But see *Scott v. Harris,* 550 U.S. 372 (2007) (actions undertaken by police to terminate a dangerous high-speed car chase that threatens the lives of innocent by-standers—such as bumping the fleeing vehicle—do not create liability under § 1983 even when such actions place the fleeing motorist at risk of death or serious bodily injury); *Town of Castle Rock v. Gonzales,* 545 U.S. 748 (2005) (no liability under § 1983 when police failed to arrest the plaintiff's husband for violation of a temporary restraining order).

Title 42 U.S.C. § 1985(3) is the conspiracy counterpart of § 1983. This section makes any person, who conspires with another to deprive a third person of any constitutional right, liable to that third person for damages. The violated individual may sue one or all of the conspirators.

Title 42 U.S.C. § 1983 provides that every person who, under color of law, deprives another of any rights, privileges and immunities secured by the Constitution shall be liable to the party injured. Actions by a suspect, an arrestee or

defendant may be premised, for example, on a claim of an unlawful arrest, the use of excessive force, a coerced confession, or an illegal search. See *Quinones v. Szorc,* 771 F.2d 289 (7th Cir. 1985); *Munson v. Friske,* 754 F.2d 683 (7th Cir. 1985); *Mass v. McClenahan,* 893 F. Supp. 225 (S.D.N.Y. 1995).

Individual officers and the municipality, but not the state, in which they work may be rendered liable under this section. See, *e.g., Bd. of County Comm'rs of Bryan Co., Okl. v. Brown,* 520 U.S. 397 (1997), where the plaintiff sought to sue the county for alleged excessive force used by a deputy. The plaintiff's theory of recovery was that the county, and its agent, in this case the sheriff who hired the deputy, were negligent in hiring the deputy. She maintained that a brief background check would have revealed that there was a strong likelihood, based on the deputy's past behavior, that he would routinely use excessive force. The Supreme Court disagreed, reasoning that a county or municipality cannot be liable under § 1983 merely because they employ a tort feasor. The plaintiff must show that there was a policy or custom of employing tort feasors. Moreover, the plaintiff must demonstrate a causal link between the municipality's conduct and the alleged injury. Here, the plaintiff did not prove any culpability on the part of the municipality. The State itself cannot be a defendant in a § 1983 action. The Court has ruled that a state, unlike a municipality, a county, or an individual officer, is not a person within the meaning of the statute, and therefore not amenable to suit.

Courts will, and routinely do, provide immunity from liability under this section. Immunity from suit "is the rule, not the exception." The doctrine of qualified immunity protects law enforcement officers to the extent that their discretionary actions do not clearly violate a suspect's federal statutory or constitutional rights. To raise a triable "§ 1983" claim, the plaintiff must initially demonstrate that the rights allegedly transgressed were clearly established at the time of the alleged violation. In other words, in order for conduct to fall outside the scope of the qualified immunity doctrine and render an officer or his or her employer liable, the plaintiff must demonstrate it would be clear to a reasonable officer in that position that his or her actions are offending a well-settled constitutional or statutory right. Conversely, if the officer objectively, reasonably, and in good faith performs his or her duties, he or she will be shielded from a damage claim. An officer is immune for harm resulting from his or her actions, for example, if a reasonable officer could have believed a search to be lawful in light of clearly established law and the information the searching officers possessed, or if a reasonable officer would have believed there was probable cause to arrest. See *Anderson v. Creighton, supra.*

In addition to suits under § 1983, officers may be liable for damages resulting from their unlawful actions in suits based on state law tort principles.

## VIII. FIFTH AMENDMENT RIGHTS AND PRIVILEGES

The Fifth Amendment of the U.S. Constitution contains numerous rights and privileges. However, two of particular importance in the area of police procedure are the privilege against self-incrimination and the right to an attorney during any custodial police interrogation. The privilege against self-incrimination may also be called the right to remain silent. The remedy for police violation of these rights is exclusion of all evidence obtained as a result of the violation. Also, individual officers may be liable in a civil or criminal context, or both, if found in violation of these rights.

The Fifth Amendment's prohibition against compelled self-incrimination requires that any custodial interrogation be preceded by advice to the suspect that he or she has the right to remain silent and also the right to the presence of an attorney. The Fifth Amendment itself does not mandate that *Miranda* warnings be given. Instead, the warnings, and the suppression of statements given by a custodial suspect in the absence of the warnings, are enforcement mechanisms, employed by the courts to preserve the essence of the right guaranteed by the amendment. The result of the rule is that custodial suspect, not given these warnings prior to an interrogation, may not have any statements he or she may make during that interrogation, used against him or her in a subsequent prosecution.

Moreover, if the suspect indicates that he or she wishes to remain silent, the interrogation must cease immediately, although the questioning generally may be resumed later. If the suspect requests counsel, the interrogation must cease until an attorney is present. Furthermore, if a suspect indicates he or she wants to deal with the police only through counsel, officers may not resume questioning unless the suspect initiates the contact and indicates he or she wishes to

proceed without the benefit of counsel. To this extent, police conduct is determined by which right the suspect invokes. If the suspect invokes the right to counsel, an attorney must be provided, and the police cannot initiate further communications with the suspect without counsel present, unless the suspect approaches the officers and personally reinitiates the interrogation. If however, the suspect invokes the right to remain silent, police may generally reinitiate questioning after a break and after fresh warnings are administered, if the request that questioning cease is initially honored. New warnings at the resumption of questioning may not always be required. If the court finds that the initial warnings are not too remote, and still sufficiently fresh to apprise the suspect of his or her rights, subsequent warnings may not be necessary.

Apart from these court created rules, the Fifth Amendment, by its terms, prohibits the State from forcing a criminal defendant into self-incrimination. Notice that the statements or evidence that a suspect is compelled to give must be testimonial or communicative in nature to fall under the Fifth Amendment's protection. The Fifth Amendment prohibits the State from marshaling evidence against a defendant only by "the cruel expedient of compelling it from his [or her] own mouth." Coercing a suspect into confessing, taking a statement prior to reading a custodial suspect *Miranda* warnings, or failing to honor a request for counsel or to remain silent, are methods by which courts have determined law enforcement may offend the guarantees of the Fifth Amendment. However, even if potentially incriminating, the following statements are not considered testimonial: statements used for voice exemplars; answers to general on-the-scene questions during routine investigatory stops; answers to routine booking questions prior to incarceration. Moreover, the privilege does not prohibit the State from compelling a suspect to provide what may ultimately be used as evidence against him or her in another fashion. Therefore, a suspect does not have a privilege against revealing the color of his or her eyes, skin, the way his or her face looks, or the way he or she is dressed, his or her fingerprints or measurements, assuming a particular posture or stance, or making a specific gesture. These displays, which certainly may point to the suspect's identity and guilt, and in that regard be incriminating, are nonetheless real or physical evidence as opposed to testimonial, and a suspect may be compelled to show these physical attributes.

## A. *Miranda* Rights

Suspects must be informed of their Fifth Amendment rights once they are in custody. Any statement made by a suspect in custody before he or she is apprised of these rights will be inadmissible. These rights must be presented to the suspect due to the fact that the U.S. Supreme Court has held that being interrogated while in custody is an inherently coercive situation. In Texas, suspects must be informed of the following:

- You have the right to remain silent and not make any statement at all and any statement you make may be used against you in court.
- Any statement you make may be used as evidence against you in court.
- You have the right to have a lawyer present to advise you prior to and during any questioning.
- If you cannot afford a lawyer, you have the right to have a lawyer appointed to advise you prior to and during any questioning
- You have the right to terminate this interview at any time.

*Miranda v. Arizona,* 384 U.S. 436 (1966); *Tex. Code Crim. Proc.* art. 38.22(2).

Be aware that although "technical noncompliance" with this section will not result in suppression of a statement, the better practice is to use the precise language of the statute. *Garcia v. State,* 919 S.W.2d 370 (Tex. Crim. App. 1994).

A suspect is entitled to the *Miranda* rights regardless of the nature or severity of the offense. *Berkemer v. McCarty,* 468 U.S. 420 (1984).

Note: **Juveniles.** When a child is taken into custody, police must notify the child's parent or guardian and the office or official designated by the juvenile board of the fact that the child has been taken into custody and the reason for this action. *Tex. Family Code* § 52.02(b). Failure to do so may result in suppression of the juvenile's statement. See *State v. Simpson,* 51 S.W.3d 633 (Tex. App.-Tyler 2000); In re R.R., 931 S.W.2d 11 (Tex. App.-Corpus Christi 1996). If a child is in a detention facility or other place of confinement, in the custody of an officer, or in the possession of the Department of Protective and Regulatory Services and suspected to have engaged in conduct that violates a penal law, for any statement by the child to be admissible the child must receive a warning from a magistrate outlining the *Miranda* rights and the child's right to end the interview out at any time. *Tex. Family Code* § 51.095.

## B. Custody and Interrogation

A suspect is only accorded the *Miranda* protections during a custodial interrogation. Both elements (*i.e.,* custody and interrogation) must be present before the requirement that the *Miranda* warning be given arises.

1. **Interrogation.** Interrogation is referred to as questioning initiated by law enforcement officers—either direct questioning or its functional equivalent. The term interrogation refers not only to express questioning, but also to any words or actions on the part of the police (other than those normally attendant to arrest and custody, *e.g.,* "routine booking questions") that the police should reasonably expect to elicit an incriminating response. *Rhode Island v. Innis,* 446 U.S. 291 (1980); *Moran v. State,* 213 S.W.3d 917 (Tex. Crim. App. 2007).

Because consent to a search is not an "incriminating statement," request for consent to search does not constitute interrogation. *Smith v. Wainwright,* 581 F.2d 1149 (5th Cir. 1978).

Spontaneous, volunteered statements are not subject to the *Miranda* requirement. *Camarillo v. State,* 82 S.W.3d 529 (Tex. App.-Austin 2002).

As mentioned above, "routine booking questions" do not constitute interrogation, and need not be preceded by *Miranda* warnings. See *Pennsylvania v. Muniz,* 496 U.S. 582 (1990) (questions regarding a suspect's name, address, height, weight, eye color, date of birth and current age do not qualify as custodial interrogation).

2. **Custody.** The warnings must be read to suspects in custody. If statements are made in a non-custodial setting, no warnings are required. Hence a defendant cannot later attempt to bar the use of his or her statements at trial on the ground that they were elicited without the benefit of the *Miranda* warnings. Custody is a legal status during which the suspect has been formally arrested or deprived of his or her freedom of action in any significant way, i.e. to a degree normally associated with formal arrest. *Stansbury v. California,* 511 U.S. 318 (1994); *Estrada v. State,* 313 S.W.3d 274 (Tex. Crim. App. 2010). Whether or not a suspect is in custody for purposes of Miranda warnings is an objective determination, based on all of the components of the setting, and determined on the basis of how a reasonable person in the suspect's situation would understand the circumstances. A custodial setting is not determined with reference to a suspect's belief that he or she is in police custody, or by a subjective belief on the part of the interrogating officers that they have placed the sus-

pect in custody, unless that fact has been communicated to the suspect.

In *Gardner v. State,* 306 S.W.3d 274 (Tex. Crim. App. 2009), the Texas Court of Criminal Appeals noted that the following situations generally constitute custody: (i) when the suspect is physically deprived of his or her freedom of action in any significant way; (ii) when the officer tells the suspect he or she cannot leave; (iii) when the officer creates a situation that would lead a reasonable person to believe that his or her freedom of movement has been significantly restricted; and (iv) when there is probable cause to arrest and the officer does not tell the suspect that he or she is free to leave.

See *Ramirez v. State,* 105 S.W.3d 730 (Tex. App.-Austin 2003). An officer went to defendant's residence to investigate a report that he was selling marijuana. Defendant's young son answered the door and said his father was in the garage. The officer went around to the garage door and knocked. When defendant opened the door, the officer could see a set of scales with marijuana seeds and residue and a large green pipe on a table, as well as rolling papers and baggies on the floor; he could also smell the odor of fresh marijuana. The officer immediately frisked defendant, handcuffed him, and told him, "You are being detained. I can see the marihuana in there. I can see residue, the drug paraphernalia." He then asked, "Is there anything else I'm going to find in there that's illegal, any more marihuana?" The Court found that defendant was in custody when the officer asked this question. Defendant was physically deprived his freedom of action in a significant way when he was handcuffed and frisked. In addition, the officer told him he was being detained. Finally, the officer told defendant that he had seen contraband in the garage. No reasonable person in defendant's position would feel free to leave. Defendant should have been *Mirandized* before the officer interrogated him by asking about the presence of more contraband.

But see *Vessels v. State,* 938 S.W.2d 485 (Tex. App.-El Paso 1996). Defendant was not in custody when he made several incriminating statements in a hospital while receiving treatment for a gunshot wound to the hand. He was not handcuffed or physically restrained in any way, nor was he told that he was forbidden from leaving the hospital. No guard was posted, and he was not told he was under arrest.

See also *Garcia v. State,* 237 S.W.3d 833 (Tex. App.-Amarillo 2007). Defendant, a teacher at a Coronado high school, was the owner of a vehicle connected to a hit-and-run accident. He voluntarily agreed to accompany an officer to the school cafeteria to discuss the accident. The subsequent conversation lasted less than 18 minutes, and the two were not alone in the cafeteria. Defendant was initially questioned as a witness—the officer believed defendant's girlfriend had been driving, and did not consider him a suspect until he admitted he had been the driver. The Court concluded this was not a custodial situation, so *Miranda* warnings were not required.

Note: A suspect not under formal arrest may nonetheless be in custody for *Miranda* purposes.

Similar to an arrest situation, in determining whether an individual was in custody for *Miranda* purposes, courts will not try to determine the subjective intent of the officers involved. Whether a person is in custody for *Miranda* purposes depends on whether the person is physically denied his or her freedom of action in any significant way or is placed in a situation in which he or she reasonably believes that his or her freedom of action or movement is restricted. Thus, police need not give *Miranda* warnings to an individual who is not restrained in any way and freely accompanies them to the police station. *California v. Beheler,* 463 U.S. 1121 (1983); *Dowthitt v. State* 931 S.W.2d 244 (Tex. Crim. App. 1996).

See, *e.g., Williams v. State,* 82 S.W.3d 557 (Tex. App.-San Antonio 2002). Two detectives located defendant at a friend's house and asked to speak with him privately. They then asked him to give his version of the events surrounding a murder (his accomplice had already given a statement). They told defendant that he was not under arrest or obligated to discuss the case, but he nonetheless agreed to an interview. The detectives gave him a ride to the station, but he was not handcuffed or *Mirandized.* Once in the interview room at the station, he was offered food and cigarettes, and was again told that he was not under arrest and that he was free to leave at any time. After he gave his statement, he was allowed to read it and make corrections, after which he was given a ride home. The Court concluded that defendant was not in custody, so that his unwarned statement was admissible.

Compare with *Rathbun v. State,* 96 S.W.3d 563 (Tex. App.-Texarkana 2002). Longview officers arrived at defendant's home to serve a search warrant. After explaining that they were only there to gather evidence and that he was not under arrest, they asked him to come to the police station for questioning. Defendant agreed to do so, and drove himself to the station, "so that he would have a ride." Once at the station, he initialed a statement reading, "Longview Police Department. Voluntary Statement. Not Under Arrest." His movements were not restricted during the two-hour interview, and he never asked to leave. He was told he was not under arrest at least twice during the interview, and in fact was allowed to return home and was not arrested until three weeks later. Defendant was not in custody for *Miranda* purposes.

See also *Rodgers v. State,* 111 S.W.3d 236 (Tex. App.-Texarkana 2003). After being taken to the hospital, defendant's cousin alleged that he had assaulted and tried to rape her. When defendant arrived at the hospital, an officers asked him to come down to the Mineola Police Department. Defendant agreed, and volunteered to ride with the officer because he did not have his own vehicle. He rode in the front seat of the officer's unmarked patrol car. He was not handcuffed, and the car did not have a restraining cage. At the station, defendant went in through the front door, not the sally port, and was allowed to smoke throughout the interview. At one point, the officer left defendant alone in his office while he went to make coffee; he left the door open and unlocked. The Court concluded that defendant was not in custody, and thus not entitled to *Miranda* warnings, during this interview.

But see *Jeffley v. State,* 38 S.W.3d 847 (Tex. App.-Houston [14th Dist.] 2001). The 15 year-old defendant agreed to accompany officers to the police station for questioning regarding a murder. Although both his mother and grandmother were at home with him when he was first approached, neither accompanied him to the station. Once at the station, police did not tell defendant he was free to leave or make arrangements for him to return home as they had promised. The interview was lengthy—almost four hours—and, during questioning, defendant was confronted with discrepancies in his statements. The Court concluded that defendant was in custody.

See also *State v. Vasquez,* 305 S.W.3d 289 (Tex. App.-Corpus Christi 2009), where an investigator and deputy investigating a murder approached defendant at his home and "said [he] had to" go to the sheriff's department for questioning. Defendant was only told he was free to go after he had given a written statement. The Court concluded that defendant was in custody.

Merely informing an individual of his or her *Miranda* rights does not necessarily create an in-custody situation. *Rodriguez v. State,* 939 S.W.2d 211 (Tex. App.-Austin 1997).

A motorist stopped for an ordinary traffic violation is not in custody for *Miranda* purposes. *Pennsylvania v. Bruder,* 488 U.S. 9 (1988). See also *Griffith v. State,* 55 S.W.3d 598 (Tex. Crim. App. 2001) (questions normally associated with the processing of a DWI arrestee, such as a request to take a BAC test, need not be preceded by *Miranda* rights). However, a motorist who is subsequently arrested, or otherwise placed in custody, must be given *Miranda* warnings prior to any questioning. Otherwise, any statements by the defendant may be inadmissible. *Berkemer v. McCarty,* 468 U.S. 420 (1984). See, *e.g., Alford v. State,* 22 S.W.3d 669 (Tex. App.-Fort Worth 2000) (during a traffic stop for weaving, defendant was put on the ground and handcuffed, and, therefore, his un*Mirandized* response when asked if he had been drinking was inadmissible).

Note: **Incarcerated Suspects.** A suspect who already has been incarcerated is not necessarily in custody for *Miranda purposes,* even though he or she is obviously not free to get up and leave during questioning. Some extra degree of restraint beyond that inherent in a prison setting must be imposed upon the inmate to force him or her to participate in the interrogation before *Miranda* warnings will be required. The factors a court will consider include:

- the language used to summon the inmate for questioning;
- the physical surroundings of the interrogation;
- the extent to which the inmate is confronted with evidence of his guilt; and
- additional pressure exerted to detain the inmate.

*Herrera v. State,* 241 S.W.3d 520 (Tex. Crim. App. 2007). As long as the Sixth Amendment right to counsel has not yet attached, an undercover officer posing as an inmate is not required to give *Miranda* warnings before questioning an incarcerated suspect. *Illinois v. Perkins,* 496 U.S. 292 (1990). However, once the suspect has been indicted and Sixth Amendment right has attached, such questioning is improper. *Patterson v. Illinois,* 487 U.S. 285 (1988).

3. **Recording Requirement.** Pursuant to *Tex. Code Crim. Proc.* art. 38.22(3), police must make an electronic record of any statement made

by a suspect while in custody. Failure to do so will render the statement inadmissible. *Davidson v. State,* 25 S.W.3d 183 (Tex. Crim. App. 2003) (noting that this is true of statements made both in-state *and* out-of-state). However, § 38.22(5) effectively exempts non-custodial statements from recording requirements. *Morris v. State,* 897 S.W.2d 528 (Tex. App.-El Paso 1995). Be aware that the failure to record may be disregarded if the error does not affect the defendant's substantial rights, i.e., it has no substantial or injurious effect on the jury's verdict. *Hernandez v. State,* 114 S.W.3d 58 (Tex. App.-Fort Worth 2003).

### C. Invocation of Rights

After a suspect has been informed of his or her rights, the police may wish to ask the suspect questions. It is at this point that suspects must invoke their right to remain silent and/or their right to have counsel present. A suspect that does not invoke either right will be subject to further questioning. Note that if the suspect gives a response to questioning that is ambiguous but may be construed as invoking either the right to remain silent or the right to counsel, the officers conducting the questioning are not required to clarify the response, and may continue questioning. Officers must stop all questioning only if there is an unambiguous, unequivocal request for counsel. *Davis v. U.S.,* 512 U.S. 452 (1994) ("Maybe I should talk to a lawyer" was not an unequivocal request for counsel, so continued questioning by police was upheld).

Compare with *Davis v. State,* 313 S.W.3d 317 (Tex. Crim. App. 2010) ("I should have an attorney" was too ambiguous to be a request for counsel when defendant subsequently asked detectives why he should help them); *Dinkins v. State,* 894 S.W.2d 330 (Tex. Crim. App. 1995) (when defendant said "Maybe I should talk to someone" [emphasis added]—not specifically a lawyer—and asked a detective what an attorney might ask him to do, there was no unequivocal invocation); *Russell v. State,* 727 S.W.2d 573 (Tex. Crim. App. 1987) (no invocation when defendant asked detectives if they thought an attorney was "necessary"); *Loredo v. State,* 130 S.W.3d 275 (Tex. App.-Houston [14th Dist.] 2004) ("Can I ask for a lawyer now?" ambiguous).

But see *State v. Gobert,* 275 S.W.3d 888 (Tex. Crim. App. 2009) ("I don't want to give up any right, though, if I don't got no lawyer" adequately communicated suspect's desire to deal with police only though, or at least in the presence of, counsel); *Jamial v. State,* 787 S.W.2d 372 (Tex. Crim.

App. 1990) ("Now it's time for me to call my lawyer" was a clear, unequivocal invocation of the right to counsel).

Asking to speak to someone other than a lawyer—for example, a parent or a probation officer—does not constitute invocation of the right to counsel. *In re H.V.,* 252 S.W.3d 319 (Tex. 2008).

In *Nichols v. State,* 754 S.W.2d 185 (Tex. Crim App. 1988), *cert. denied,* 488 U.S. 1019 (1989), defendant did not invoke his right to counsel when, as he was being arrested, he asked a friend (not the arresting officer) to call his attorney. But see *In re H.V., supra,* where a 16-year-old arrestee's statement that he "wanted his mother to ask for an attorney" was a sufficient invocation; there was no way to construe that as anything other than an expression of desire for the assistance of counsel.

In *Connecticut v. Barrett,* 479 U.S. 523 (1987), continued questioning was proper when defendant said he would not give a *written* statement regarding a sexual assault without an attorney present, but added he had "no problem" talking about the incident. See also *Dowthitt v. State,* 931 S.W.2d 244 (Tex. Crim. App. 1996) (defendant did not unequivocally invoke his right to remain silent by telling police "I can't say no more than that. I need to rest."); *Franks v. State,* 90 S.W.3d 771 (Tex. App.-Fort Worth 2002) ("I don't want to talk anymore, I'm tired" too ambiguous to invoke right to silence).

1. **Right to Remain Silent.** When a suspect informs the police that he or she wishes not to speak then the police must "scrupulously honor" the suspect's right to remain silent. At this point all questioning must cease and the police are not allowed to say or do anything that is intended to elicit a response from the suspect or that is likely to elicit a response from the suspect. *Marshall v. State,* 210 S.W.3d 618 (Tex. Crim. App. 2006). If they do elicit a response, then such response will be inadmissible.

As long as police "scrupulously honor" the suspect's invocation of the right to remain silent and immediately cease questioning, they may start questioning again later, after the passage of a "significant period" of time. However, this new round of questioning should concern a different topic than the earlier questioning. When and if questioning does resume, the suspect should be re-informed or reminded of the *Miranda* rights. Of course, the suspect may once again refuse to speak. *Michigan v. Mosley,* 423 U.S. 96 (1975).

2. **Right to Counsel.** When a suspect invokes his or her right to counsel all questioning must

cease immediately, and police may not initiate any new questioning until the suspect meets with an attorney. *Minnick v. Mississippi,* 498 U.S. 146 (1990); *Davis v. State,* 313 S.W.3d 317 (Tex. Crim. App. 2010). This is true whether the questioning is for the original offense or a different offense. *Arizona v. Roberson,* 486 U.S. 675 (1988). Any single officer's knowledge that defendant has requested counsel is imputed to every other state agent, whether or not they actually know of the waiver. *Herron v. State,* 86 S.W.3d 621 (Tex. Crim. App. 2002). The only way that the police may then speak to the suspect without an attorney is if the suspect initiates the conversation. *Davis v. State, supra.* However, for any statement to be admissible, the police will still have to show that the suspect waived his or her rights. *Arizona v. Edwards,* 451 U.S. 477 (1981).

In *Herron v. State, supra,* defendant's initial statement to an officer was suppressed because, unbeknownst to the questioning officer, he had already invoked his right to counsel. However, sometime after he gave this statement, he waved the officer over and said that while the first statement was true, he had "left something out" and wanted to talk further. Therefore, defendant initiated a new conversation, and, while his first statement was inadmissible, this second statement was admissible.

Be aware that "initiates the conversation" is a term of art, and does not necessarily mean the first person who speaks. Routine inquiries by a suspect, such as asking for a drink of water or to use the telephone, will not constitute an initiation of conversation justifying continued questioning by police. Instead, the suspect must convey a desire "to open up a general discussion relating directly or indirectly to the criminal investigation." Similarly, routine inquiries by police do not violate a suspect's right to counsel. *Oregon v. Bradshaw,* 462 U.S. 1039 (1983). In *Bradshaw,* after defendant invoked his right to counsel, he asked, "well what's going to happen to me now?" This question evidenced a desire to open up a generalized discussion about the investigation, so police could question him and obtain a valid waiver of his rights.

As long as the Sixth Amendment right to counsel has not yet attached, the failure of police to inform a suspect who is in custody that a third party (such as a relative) has retained counsel for him, or even that an attorney has made efforts to contact him, will not vitiate a waiver of *Miranda* rights by the suspect, because "[e]vents occurring outside the presence of the suspect and entirely unknown to him surely can have no bearing on the capacity to comprehend and relinquish a constitutional right." *Moran v. Burbine,* 475 U.S. 412 (1986). Be aware that the Texas Court of Criminal Appeals has never formally adopted this standard (see *Goodwin v. State,* 799 S.W.2d 719 (Tex. Crim. App. 1990)), although intermediate Texas courts have. See, *e.g., Terrell v. State,* 891 S.W.2d 307 (Tex. App.-El Paso 1994).

The U.S. Supreme Court has ruled that when a suspect who has requested an attorney is released from pretrial custody for 14 days or more, then the Edwards rule no longer applies. After a 14-day break in custody, police may attempt to once again initiate questioning even though the suspect is not accompanied by an attorney. *Maryland v. Shatzer,* 559 U.S. __ (2010).

3. **Waiver.** Once a custodial suspect has been given the Miranda warnings, he or she can, of course, waive his or her right to be silent or to counsel, and decide to talk to the police. If the suspect voluntarily waives these rights, police may continue to question until the suspect requests an attorney, or effectively renounces his or her waiver and relates that he or she wishes to remain silent. In *North Carolina v. Butler,* 441 U.S. 369 (1979), the U.S. Supreme Court held that courts may find a valid waiver even if the defendant only implicitly waives his or her Miranda rights. A suspect who has received and understood the Miranda warnings, and has not invoked his Miranda rights, waives the right to remain silent by making an uncoerced statement to the police. *Berghuis v. Thompkins,* 560 U.S. __ (2010).

A suspect may waive his or her Fourth Amendment rights at any time. However, the prosecution will be asked to show that any such waiver was not only knowing and voluntary, but that the suspect understood the right that he or she was waiving. *Tex. Code Crim. Proc.* art. 38.22(2)(b); *Joseph v. State,* 309 S.W.3d 20 (Tex. Crim. App. 2010). In checking to see that a waiver was legally sufficient, the courts will look at the totality of the circumstances surrounding the confession, including the suspect's background and experience (*e.g.,* age, level of education, prior experience with the criminal justice system, physical and emotional condition), as well as the conduct of police (*e.g.,* whether the suspect was advised of constitutional rights, the length of the detention, whether questioning was repeated or prolonged, whether there was physical punishment or deprivation of food or sleep). The State has the burden of showing by a preponderance of the evidence that the waiver was voluntary. *Colorado v. Connelly,* 479 U.S. 157 (1986); *Joseph v. State, supra.* Suspects who are in pain, intoxicated or on drugs may not be able to give a knowing, intelligent and voluntary waiver. See *Nichols v. State,* 754 S.W.2d 185 (Tex. Crim App. 1988), *cert. denied,* 488 U.S. 1019 (1989) (although intoxication does not automatically render a confession inadmissible, it will if the intoxication rendered the suspect incapable of making an independent, informed choice). Waivers obtained by improper means, such as suggesting that the suspect may receive some specific benefit by talking, are invalid.

A suspect may invoke or re-invoke either the right to remain silent or the right to counsel at any time and police must act accordingly.

Voluntariness and coercion are different sides of the same coin. If a confession or statement has been coerced, or taken from a custodial suspect in the absence of *Miranda* warnings, there was no waiver. The statement is involuntary, and therefore not the product of a free relinquishment of a known right, and hence not allowed in evidence at a trial. Conversely, if a confession or statement is voluntary, the suspect has either impliedly or expressly waived his rights, and the statement or confession has not been coerced, and it, and any other incriminating evidence deriving from it, is admissible.

A waiver of Fifth Amendment rights is not invalid solely because police do not inform the suspect of the potential subjects that might be covered in the interrogation before questioning begins. *Colorado v. Spring,* 479 U.S. 564 (1987). Similarly, there is no requirement that police inform the suspect of all the crimes he could possibly be charged with prior to the interrogation. *Corwin v. State,* 870 S.W.2d 23 (Tex. Crim. App. 1993).

One way in which a defendant may attempt to show his or her statement was involuntary is to show that actual physical or psychological force was used to coerce the confession (*e.g.,* actual or threatened bodily harm, or threats of adverse consequences).

See, *e.g., Arizona v. Fulmiante,* 499 U.S. 279 (1991) (a credible threat of physical violence will render a subsequent statement involuntary); *Lynumm v. Illinois,* 372 U.S. 528 (1963) (defendant's confession involuntary when police told her that her state financial aid would be cut off and her six children taken from her unless she "cooperated" with them).

See also *Contreras v. State,* 312 S.W.3d 566 (Tex. Crim. App. 2010). Defendant was the subject of an investigation into the death of an infant who had been under his care. Detectives confronted defendant with the child's autopsy report and told him that if he was not the killer, it "would be" or "could be" his wife. They also stated that if his wife was arrested, Child Protective Services would take their children away. Later, a detective told defendant, "Come on, you're not going to let your wife go to jail for something you did ... if it wasn't you, then it means your wife had to have done it." The detective added that if defendant confessed, his wife would not be arrested. However, police never had probable cause to arrest defendant's wife—all the evidence pointed to defendant being the only caregiver of the deceased child when the fatal wounds were inflicted. Therefore, the unjustified threat to arrest defendant's wife rendered his ensuing confession involuntary.

A defendant may also attempt to show that the atmosphere surrounding the interrogation was so inherently coercive that his or her will was overborne, and the statement or confession was given involuntarily (*e.g.,* suspect was denied sleep, food and drink, use of restroom facilities, handcuffed, or left alone for extended periods).

Another way a defendant may demonstrate involuntariness is to show that a promise of leniency was made, and in return for his or her cooperation, the defendant was told that his or her punishment would be less severe. To prevail, the defendant must show that the promise was (i) positive, (ii) made or sanctioned by someone with apparent authority, (iii) of some benefit to the defendant, and (iv) of such a character as would likely cause a person to speak untruthfully. *Garcia v. State,* 919 S.W.2d 370 (Tex. Crim App. 1994).

See *Sterling v. State,* 800 S.W.2d 513 (Tex. Crim. App. 1990) (statement inadmissible when defendant was told it could be used "for or against" him and when defendant was told "they might go easy on him" if he made a statement).

The promise must cause the statement. Mere exhortations to tell the truth or promises to tell the prosecution of any cooperation will not render a subsequent statement involuntary.

See *Garcia v. State, supra* (confession voluntary even when detective told defendant that "if he talked to me about [a robbery], I'd do whatever I could to help him out...I told him I'd talk to the D.A.[,]" because the detective made no specific promises); Brown v. State, 657 S.W.2d 797 (Tex.

Crim. App. 1983) (confession not induced merely because officer tells defendant "it would be best for him to go ahead and make a statement" or "it would be better to get his business straight"); *Sorola v. State,* 674 S.W.2d 809 (Tex. App.-San Antonio 1984) (mere fact that officer told defendant he would inform D.A. as to his cooperation or lack thereof did not render confession involuntary).

If police violate *Texas Penal Code* § 37.09 (Tampering with or Fabricating Physical Evidence), then any statement obtained through that violation must be suppressed, even if it was "voluntary" under federal constitutional standards. *Wilson v. State,* 311 S.W.3d 452 (Tex. Crim. App. 2010). In *Wilson,* defendant was under investigation for murder. Using an old forensic lab report as a template, a detective fabricated a false lab report on his computer that stated defendant's fingerprints had been found on a magazine clip at the crime scene. In fact, no legible prints had been recovered. When confronted with the fake document, defendant confessed to the murder. This confession was inadmissible because the detective's actions were prohibited by § 37.09.

As long as a suspect's un*Mirandized* statements were voluntary, statements voluntarily made by the suspect after the *Miranda* rights are read are admissible (even though the earlier unwarned statements must be suppressed). *Oregon v. Elstad,* 470 U.S. 298 (1985); *Corwin v. State, supra.* However, police may not use a "two-step" interview technique where they deliberately interview a suspect without reading the *Miranda* warnings until a confession is obtained, then, although that statement is inadmissible at trial, use facts gleaned from it to direct questioning during a successive post-*Miranda* interview. *Missouri v. Seibert,* 542 U.S. 600 (2004). See, e.g., *Martinez v. State,* 272 S.W.3d 615 (Tex. Crim. App. 2008), where defendant's statements were inadmissible when police first administered a polygraph exam without *Mirandizing* him or telling him he could end the exam at any time or that the results were inadmissible, then told him he "failed" the test, read him his rights, and questioned him again. The Court concluded that the polygraph was "used in a calculated way to undermine the *Miranda* warning."

### D. Actions Not Protected by the Fifth Amendment

The Fifth Amendment only provides protection for suspects from being forced to give testimony that is self-incriminating. Suspects may still be forced to provide evidence that is not testimonial in nature. Thus suspects may be forced to provide answers to booking questions, such as name, address, and telephone number. Suspects may also be forced to allow the taking of physical evidence such as voice exemplars, handwriting samples, blood samples, hair samples, or evidence of physical characteristics. *Schmerber v. California,* 384 U.S. 757 (1966). Texas courts have also allowed videotaped dexterity tests, as well as other conduct on videotape as long as it is not testimonial evidence. *Miffleton v. State,* 777 S.W.2d 76 (Tex. Crim. App. 1989); see also *Jones v. State,* 795 S.W.2d 171 (Tex. Crim. App. 1990) (audio tracks of tapes of DWI stops also admissible).

Although the Fifth Amendment allows the taking of such evidence, the Fourth Amendment and its protections (*i.e.* the warrant requirement) may still be implicated. See *Kinsley v. State,* 81 S.W.3d 478 (Tex. App.-Dallas 2002) (taking of blood from a suspect constitutes a search and seizure).

In *U.S. v. Patane,* 542 U.S. 630 (2004), the U.S. Supreme Court held that when a suspect's un*Mirandized* statements lead police to physical evidence, that evidence is admissible even though the underlying statements themselves are not.

### E. Public Safety Exception

In certain limited circumstances, suspects may be questioned without first being *Mirandized* pursuant to the "Public Safety Exception." This doctrine was first announced by the U.S. Supreme Court in *New York v. Quarles,* 467 U.S. 649 (1984). In that case, an officer entered a supermarket in pursuit of defendant following a report that defendant had raped a woman. Upon seeing the officer, defendant turned and ran to the rear of the store. The officer followed, and although he lost sight of defendant for several seconds, he found him again and apprehended him. The victim had alleged defendant was carrying a gun, and when the officer frisked him, he discovered that defendant was wearing an empty shoulder holster. After handcuffing defendant, the officer asked him where the gun was. Defendant nodded in the direction of some empty cartons and responded, "the gun is over there." As other officers arrived, the first officer retrieved a loaded .38-caliber revolver from one of the cartons, then formally placed defendant under arrest and read him his *Miranda* rights.

There is no question that defendant was in custody—he was in handcuffs surrounded by four police officers. And asking where a gun just used in a crime is located will likely elicit an incriminating response. Nevertheless, the Court held that there is a "public safety" exception to the requirement that *Miranda* warnings be given before a suspect's answers may be admitted into evidence. The Court noted that police were confronted with the immediate necessity of ascertaining the whereabouts of a gun they had every reason to believe defendant had just removed from his empty holster and discarded somewhere in the store. "So long as the gun was concealed somewhere in the supermarket, with its actual whereabouts unknown, it obviously posed more than one danger to the public safety: an accomplice might make use of it, a customer or employee might later come upon it." In such situations, if police were required to recite the *Miranda* warning before questioning, suspects in defendant's position might well be deterred from responding. The Court concluded that "the need for answers to questions in a situation posing a threat to the public safety outweighs the need for the prophylactic rule protecting the Fifth Amendment's privilege against self-incrimination." The Court reasoned that "police officers can and will distinguish almost instinctively between questions necessary to secure their own safety or the safety of the public and questions designed solely to elicit testimonial evidence from a suspect." If the question is motivated primarily out of concern for the officer's safety, or that of the public at large, rather than a deliberate attempt to obtain an incriminating statement, there is no reason to bar the statement's subsequent use against its maker. Thus, the gun in the *Quarles* case was not suppressed, even though it was recovered as a direct result of defendant's un*Mirandized* statement.

## IX. SIXTH AMENDMENT RIGHT TO COUNSEL

The Sixth Amendment right to counsel differs from the Fifth Amendment right to counsel in three principal ways. First, the right attaches when the criminal justice process has reached a critical stage, at the initiation of the prosecution, rather than during a custodial interrogation. A prosecution is initiated, for example, when:
- formal charges are filed,
- a preliminary hearing is held,
- an indictment or information is filed, or
- an arraignment is held.

*Brewer v. Williams,* 430 U.S. 387 (1977). So, for example, there is a right to have counsel present during a post arraignment line-up. But, the stage of the proceeding and the nature of the confrontation must be "trial-like" for the right to be implicated (*e.g.,* there is no Sixth Amendment right to counsel when police bring in a witness to examine a photo spread, because the accused is not being confronted).

Secondly, the Sixth Amendment right to counsel is offense specific. Once the right has attached for a given charge, the suspect cannot be questioned about that charge without counsel present. The suspect can, however, be questioned regarding other offenses for which the Sixth Amendment right has not yet attached without violating that provision. *McNeil v. Wisconsin,* 501 U.S. 171 (1991). Suspects can even be questioned regarding an offense which is "factually related" to the offense for which this right has been invoked, as long as the offenses are not the same for Double Jeopardy purposes. *Texas v. Cobb,* 532 U.S. 162 (2001); *Cobb v. State,* 85 S.W.3d 258 (Tex. Crim. App. 2002). On the other hand, the *Miranda* Fifth Amendment right to counsel is not offense specific. If a suspect has invoked his or her Fifth Amendment right to have counsel present during a custodial interrogation, he or she cannot be questioned regarding *any* offense without counsel present. Of course, the suspect may waive the Sixth Amendment right to counsel, provided the waiver is knowing, intelligent and voluntary. This right to counsel is safeguarded by the exclusionary rule as well. If a statement is obtained in violation of the Sixth Amendment, it, and any other evidence that may come to light as a result of the statement, will be suppressed.

Finally, unlike the Fifth Amendment right to counsel, a waiver of the Sixth Amendment right to counsel is not valid if police fail to inform the suspect that an attorney is trying to reach him or her. *Patterson v. Illinois,* 487 U.S. 285 (1988). However, once the Sixth Amendment is attached and the suspect is *actually* represented by counsel, then the suspect's attorney must be informed of any questioning. *Holloway v. State,* 780 S.W.2d 787 (Tex. Crim. App. 1989).

## X. SUSPECT IDENTIFICATION

Frequently, the State will attempt to elicit at trial, identification testimony from a witness to a crime who has made an out-of-court identification of the defendant. Typically, the testimony culminates in the witness pointing to the defendant in court and identifying him or her as the perpetrator. The defendant may challenge the admission of this testimony, claiming that the in-court identification was in fact the result of a suggestive, prior out-of-court identification orchestrated by law enforcement. The Fourteenth Amendment provides that no person shall lose his or her life, liberty or property without due process of law. The "Due Process Clause" protects a suspect from police identification procedures that are so impermissibly suggestive as to create a very substantial likelihood of irreparable misidentification. *Simmons v. U.S.,* 390 U.S. 377 (1968); *Stewart v. State,* 198 S.W.2d 60 (Tex. App.-Ft. Worth 2006).

A lineup is considered unduly suggestive if other participants are greatly dissimilar in appearance from the suspect. A suspect may be greatly dissimilar in appearance from the other participants because of his distinctly different appearance, race, hair color, height, or age. However, minor discrepancies between line-up participants do not render a line-up impermissibly suggestive. *McClenton v. State,* 167 S.W.3d 86 (Tex. App.-Waco 2005).

A suspect can challenge an identification by raising the issue of impermissible suggestiveness. If the requisite showing is made, a hearing will be held, after which the judge will make a ruling regarding the admissibility of testimony concerning the identification. To determine which practices are so unfairly suggestive as to deprive a suspect of Due Process, a court looks to the totality of the circumstances surrounding the out-of-court identification.

See, *e.g., Delk v. State,* 855 S.W.2d 700 (Tex. Crim. App. 1993), *cert. denied,* 510 U.S. 987 (1993) (impermissibly suggestive when police presented a witness with a single photo and told her the subject was under indictment for the murder of her husband); *Turner v. State,* 614 S.W.2d 144 (Tex. Crim. App. 1981) (photo array impermissibly suggestive when defendant's photos appeared three times in the eleven-photo array, only one other photo besides the defendant's three was in color, and defendant was the only one pictured in jail clothes); *Mendiola v. State,* 269 S.W.3d 144 (Tex. App.-Fort Worth 2008) (photo spread violated constitutional requirements when photo of defendant "both larger and darker" than the others and filled more of the space provided for photos); *Gonzalez v. State,* 752 S.W.2d 695 (Tex. App.-Houston [1st Dist.] 1988) (photo array impermissibly suggestive when defendant's photo was the only "mug shot" containing the location of a custodial facility and an identification number); *Tapley v. State,* 673 S.W.2d 284 (Tex. App.-San Antonio 1984) (photo

array impermissibly suggestive when defendant was an Anglo male pictured with all Mexican-Americans and was the only one pictured with a fair complexion).

But see *Garcia v. State,* 563 S.W.2d 925 (Tex. Crim. App. 1978). A five-man line-up was not found impermissibly suggestive, even though defendant was the tallest participant by several inches. All five men were Mexican-American and had dark hair, three of the five, including defendant, had mustaches, and four of the five, including defendant, had tattoos on their arms. See also *Page v. State,* 125 S.W.3d 640 (Tex. App.-Houston [1st Dist.] 2003) ("Slight differences in the background color and brightness of photographs [used in an array] are insignificant.").

An photo array is impermissible if it includes a picture taken during an illegal arrest; however, a subsequent in-court identification may still be admissible. *U.S. v. Crews,* 445 U.S. 463 (1980); *Pinchon v. State,* 683 S.W.2d 422 (Tex. Crim. App. 1984).

A line-up or photo array is not rendered suggestive merely because the complainant is informed that it includes a "suspect," because a witness would normally assume this to be the case (else why even bother with the procedure?). *Harris v. State,* 827 S.W.2d 949 (Tex. Crim. App.), *cert. denied,* 506 U.S. 942 (1992).

Even if an identification procedure is found to be unnecessarily suggestive, the resulting identification may still be admissible, if the reliability of the witness who made it can be independently established. Factors a court will consider in determining reliability include:

- the opportunity of the witness to view the defendant during the crime;
- the level of attention the witness was paying to the defendant;
- the accuracy of descriptions of the defendant made by the witness prior to the suggestive procedure;
- the witness' level of certainty in his or her identification; and
- the time between the crime and confrontation.

*Neil v. Biggers,* 409 U.S. 188 (1972); *Luna v. State,* 268 S.W.2d 594 (Tex. Crim. App. 2008).

See, *e.g., Powell v. State,* 837 S.W.2d 809 (Tex. App.-Houston [1st Dist.] 1992). The victim was robbed at gunpoint outside a Pearland convenience store, and defendant was quickly apprehended just a few blocks away. The victim went to this location and, while driving past in a patrol car, identified defendant, who stood handcuffed by himself, as the robber. This procedure was impermissibly suggestive. Nevertheless, the victim's identification was admissible because there was no likelihood of misidentification. Defendant "stuck" his gun in the victim's stomach for 15-20 seconds, and the victim watched his face throughout the mugging (1-1 ½ minutes from the time defendant first approached to when he fled) from about two feet away. The victim was wearing his glasses, so his vision was 20/20, and the lighting outside the store was "very good." The victim's attention was focused on defendant for obvious reasons, and, finally, he made his identification no more than 10 minutes after the hold-up.

Compare with *State v. Booker,* 291 S.W.3d 100 (Tex. App.-Eastland 2009). Defendant held up a carhop at a Sonic Drive-In at gunpoint after she delivered defendant's food. The victim later told police that her assailant had acne on his face, as well as braided hair. Twelve days later, police showed the victim a photographic lineup—of the six men pictured in the array, only defendant had acne marks on his face. Because of this the Court found that the identification procedure may have been impermissibly suggestive. However, the victim got a clear look at the robber's face, standing less than two feet from him. Although it was after 8:00 p.m., the Drive-In was well-lit and the robber wore nothing to cover his face. The victim focused her attention on the robber's face during the hold-up, and testified she had "no doubt" defendant was the man who robbed her. Thus the evidence supported a conclusion that her identification was based on her memory from the night of the crime, so that the suggestive lineup did not give rise to a very substantial likelihood of misidentification.

In *Turner v. State, supra,* a rape took place over 30 minutes in a lighted room, after the victim had initially seen the rapist on a porch with a floodlight. Before being shown the suggestive photo line-up discussed above, the victim went through at least six mug shot books, meticulously screening the pictures and offering comments about hair or facial features to explain why she rejected each photo. The victim never identified anyone but defendant as her attacker, and she made her identification just one month after the crime. The Court concluded that the victim had a basis for her in-court identification independent of the tainted photo array, and it was therefore admissible.

In *Burkett v. State,* 127 S.W.3d 83 (Tex. App.-Houston [1st Dist.] 2003), defendant exposed himself to the victim while sitting in his car in the parking lot of a grocery store, at around 11:40 a.m. Eleven days later, the victim was shown a six-photo array. After she identified defendant, the officer conducting the array told her she had a "good memory." The Court found that the officer's comment did not taint the victim's subsequent in-court identification, because her first identification was made immediately and without hesitation. The Court went on to state, however, that even if the statement could influence an in-court identification, in this case such an identification would be admissible under the *Biggers* test. The victim had adequate opportunity to view defendant—she had a clear view of him as his car was "right next to hers" for 15 to 20 seconds and the encounter took place in broad daylight. She "paid a lot of attention" to defendant, as evidenced by the fact that she could recall the license plate and bumper stickers on his vehicle, and accurately described his height, approximate age, dark frizzy hair, and mustache. Although she failed to mention the extensive tattoos on defendant's arms, she said this was because she paid more attention to his face and what he was doing, because she was embarrassed by his actions. At the photo array, she identified defendant without hesitation, then did so again at trial. Finally, only six months had passed between the incident and the trial.

See also *Johnigan v. State,* 69 S.W.3d 749 (Tex. App.-Tyler 2002). A confidential-informant (CI) purchased crack cocaine from a man named "Marcus" (whom he later identified as defendant) in a private home. After the buy, the CI was shown a single, driver's license photo of defendant, to which he stated, "That's him." The Court found that this single photograph "line-up" was impermissibly suggestive. However, the Court found that the CI's identification was still admissible. He had ample opportunity to view defendant during the drug transaction; he met defendant outside the house at midday, stood face-to-face and shook hands with him, then followed him inside where they discussed the deal for several minutes. The CI had worked with the police for over 11 years, and he was trained to carefully scrutinize features to remember them for later identification. Finally, the CI made his identification "just a matter of minutes" after completing the drug buy.

But see *Loserth v. State,* 985 S.W.2d 536 (Tex. App.-San Antonio 1998). At 3:20 a.m., a murder victim's neighbor heard a scream followed by a crash. He looked to see a man exit the victim's balcony by jumping 26 feet to the ground. Two and a half months after the murder, the witness was shown a single photo of defendant, whom he identified as the jumper. This procedure was impermissibly suggestive. In evaluating whether the identification was still reliable, the Court noted that the witness's degree of attention had been high. As an Air Force patrolman, he was used to being up at such a late hour, and he had been studying when he heard the loud scream and became curious to see what was going on. Moreover, the witness was certain in his identification. However, he had a very limited opportunity to view the man jumping from the balcony; he was 88 feet away and only saw the man for 5 seconds or so. More importantly, prior to being shown the photo, the only description the witness could give of the suspect was "tall and thin," wearing dark clothes. He could not even tell the man's race, and could not recall further details despite repeated questioning by police, even under hypnosis. This description was so vague that it could apply to thousands of men in the area. In addition, although the witness made his identification from the photo 2 ½ months after the murder, he did not make his in-court identification until almost 2 years after the crime. The Court concluded that there was no clear and convincing evidence to find that this in-court identification had an origin independent of the taint of the suggestive procedure, and, therefore, it was inadmissible.

## XI. FOREIGN NATIONALS

Pursuant to Article 36 of the Vienna Convention, when a foreign national (including an illegal alien or alien with a "green card") is arrested or detained, he or she must be informed without delay of the right to have the consular officials of his or her home country notified and the right to communicate with those consular officials. This notice should be given in addition to, not instead of, the *Miranda* warnings.

Brief, routine detentions, such as for a traffic violation or accident investigation, do not trigger this requirement. However, if the foreign national is required to accompany a law enforcement officer to a place of detention or is detained for a number of hours or overnight, the consular notification requirement will apply.

In addition, when a foreign national from one of the following countries is arrested or detained, the nearest consular officials must be notified without delay, *regardless* of the person's wishes. These countries include the following:

Algeria
Anguilla
Antigua and Barbuda
Armenia
Azerbaijan
Bahamas
Barbados
Belarus
Belize
Bermuda
British Virgin Islands
Brunei
Bulgaria
China (but not "Republic of China," i.e. Taiwan)
Costa Rica
Cyprus
Czech Republic
Dominica
Fiji
Gambia
Georgia
Ghana
Grenada
Guyana
Hong Kong
Hungary
Jamaica
Kazakhstan
Kiribati
Kuwait
Kyrgyzstan
Malaysia
Malta
Mauritius
Moldova
Mongolia
Montserrat
Nigeria
Philippines
Poland (nonpermanent residents only)
Romania
Russia
St. Kitts and Nevis
St. Lucia
St. Vincent and Grenadines
Seychelles
Sierra Leone
Singapore
Slovakia
Tajikistan
Tanzania
Tonga
Trinidad and Tobago
Tunisia
Turkmenistan

Turks and Caicos Islands
Tuvalu
Ukraine
United Kingdom
USSR (passports may still be in use)
Uzbekistan
Zambia
Zimbabwe

Note: Under no circumstances should any information indicating that a foreign national may have applied for asylum in the United States or elsewhere be disclosed to that person's government.

The following statement is suggested by the U.S. Department of State when consular notification is at the foreign national's option:

*As a non-U.S. citizen who is being arrested or detained, you are entitled to have us notify your country's consular representatives here in the United States. A consular official from your country may be able to help you obtain legal counsel and may contact your family and visit you in detention, among other things. If you want us to notify your country's consular officials, you can request this notification now or at any time in the future. After your consular officials are notified, they may call or visit you.*

*Do you want us to notify your country's consular officials?*

The following statement is suggested by the U.S. Department of State when consular notification is mandatory:

*Because of your nationality, we are required to notify your country's consular representatives here in the United States that you have been arrested or detained. After your consular officials are notified, they may call or visit you. You are not required to accept their assistance, but they may be able to help you obtain legal counsel and may contact your family and visit you in detention, among other things. We will be notifying your country's consular officials as soon as possible.*

Telephone and fax numbers of the foreign embassies and consulates in the United States and translations of the above statements into selected languages are available at the U.S. Department of State website http://travel.state.gov.

Although law enforcement officers should make every effort to comply with these requirements, suppression of evidence or a suspect's statement is not an available remedy for a violation of the Vienna Convention. *Sanchez-Llamas v. Oregon,* 548 U.S. 331 (2006); *Rocha v. State, 16 S.W.3d 1 (Tex. Crim. App. 2000).*

# PENAL CODE

Penal Code

# TITLE 1
# INTRODUCTORY PROVISIONS

## CHAPTER 1
## GENERAL PROVISIONS

### Sec. 1.01.  Short Title.

This code shall be known and may be cited as the Penal Code.

(Enacted by Acts 1973, 63rd Leg., ch. 399 (S.B. 34), § 1, effective January 1, 1974; am. Acts 1993, 73rd Leg., ch. 900 (S.B. 1067), § 1.01, effective September 1, 1994.)

### Sec. 1.02.  Objectives of Code.

The general purposes of this code are to establish a system of prohibitions, penalties, and correctional measures to deal with conduct that unjustifiably and inexcusably causes or threatens harm to those individual or public interests for which state protection is appropriate. To this end, the provisions of this code are intended, and shall be construed, to achieve the following objectives:

(1)  to insure the public safety through:

(A)  the deterrent influence of the penalties hereinafter provided;

(B)  the rehabilitation of those convicted of violations of this code; and

(C)  such punishment as may be necessary to prevent likely recurrence of criminal behavior;

(2)  by definition and grading of offenses to give fair warning of what is prohibited and of the consequences of violation;

(3)  to prescribe penalties that are proportionate to the seriousness of offenses and that permit recognition of differences in rehabilitation possibilities among individual offenders;

(4)  to safeguard conduct that is without guilt from condemnation as criminal;

(5)  to guide and limit the exercise of official discretion in law enforcement to prevent arbitrary or oppressive treatment of persons suspected, accused, or convicted of offenses; and

(6)  to define the scope of state interest in law enforcement against specific offenses and to systematize the exercise of state criminal jurisdiction.

(Enacted by Acts 1973, 63rd Leg., ch. 399 (S.B. 34), § 1, effective January 1, 1974; am. Acts 1993, 73rd Leg., ch. 900 (S.B. 1067), § 1.01, effective September 1, 1994.)

### Sec. 1.03.  Effect of Code.

(a)  Conduct does not constitute an offense unless it is defined as an offense by statute, municipal ordinance, order of a county commissioners court, or rule authorized by and lawfully adopted under a statute.

(b)  The provisions of Titles 1, 2, and 3 apply to offenses defined by other laws, unless the statute defining the offense provides otherwise; however, the punishment affixed to an offense defined outside this code shall be applicable unless the punishment is classified in accordance with this code.

(c)  This code does not bar, suspend, or otherwise affect a right or liability to damages, penalty, forfeiture, or other remedy authorized by law to be recovered or enforced in a civil suit for conduct this code defines as an offense, and the civil injury is not merged in the offense.

(Enacted by Acts 1973, 63rd Leg., ch. 399 (S.B. 34), § 1, effective January 1, 1974; am. Acts 1993, 73rd Leg., ch. 900 (S.B. 1067), § 1.01, effective September 1, 1994.)

### Sec. 1.04.  Territorial Jurisdiction.

(a)  This state has jurisdiction over an offense that a person commits by his own conduct or the conduct of another for which he is criminally responsible if:

(1)  either the conduct or a result that is an element of the offense occurs inside this state;

(2)  the conduct outside this state constitutes an attempt to commit an offense inside this state;

(3)  the conduct outside this state constitutes a conspiracy to commit an offense inside this state, and an act in furtherance of the conspiracy occurs inside this state; or

(4)  the conduct inside this state constitutes an attempt, solicitation, or conspiracy to com-

mit, or establishes criminal responsibility for the commission of, an offense in another jurisdiction that is also an offense under the laws of this state.

(b) If the offense is criminal homicide, a "result" is either the physical impact causing death or the death itself. If the body of a criminal homicide victim is found in this state, it is presumed that the death occurred in this state. If death alone is the basis for jurisdiction, it is a defense to the exercise of jurisdiction by this state that the conduct that constitutes the offense is not made criminal in the jurisdiction where the conduct occurred.

(c) An offense based on an omission to perform a duty imposed on an actor by a statute of this state is committed inside this state regardless of the location of the actor at the time of the offense.

(d) This state includes the land and water and the air space above the land and water over which this state has power to define offenses.
(Enacted by Acts 1973, 63rd Leg., ch. 399 (S.B. 34), § 1, effective January 1, 1974; am. Acts 1993, 73rd Leg., ch. 900 (S.B. 1067), § 1.01, effective September 1, 1994.)

## Sec. 1.05. Construction of Code.

(a) The rule that a penal statute is to be strictly construed does not apply to this code. The provisions of this code shall be construed according to the fair import of their terms, to promote justice and effect the objectives of the code.

(b) Unless a different construction is required by the context, Sections 311.011, 311.012, 311.014, 311.015, and 311.021 through 311.032 of Chapter 311, Government Code (Code Construction Act), apply to the construction of this code.

(c) In this code:

(1) a reference to a title, chapter, or section without further identification is a reference to a title, chapter, or section of this code; and

(2) a reference to a subchapter, subsection, subdivision, paragraph, or other numbered or lettered unit without further identification is a reference to a unit of the next-larger unit of this code in which the reference appears.
(Enacted by Acts 1973, 63rd Leg., ch. 399 (S.B. 34), § 1, effective January 1, 1974; am. Acts 1985, 69th Leg., ch. 479 (S.B. 813), § 69, effective September 1, 1985; am. Acts 1993, 73rd Leg., ch. 900 (S.B. 1067), § 1.01, effective September 1, 1994.)

## Sec. 1.06. Computation of Age.

A person attains a specified age on the day of the anniversary of his birthdate.

(Enacted by Acts 1973, 63rd Leg., ch. 399 (S.B. 34), § 1, effective January 1, 1974; am. Acts 1993, 73rd Leg., ch. 900 (S.B. 1067), § 1.01, effective September 1, 1994.)

## Sec. 1.07. Definitions.

(a) In this code:

(1) "Act" means a bodily movement, whether voluntary or involuntary, and includes speech.

(2) "Actor" means a person whose criminal responsibility is in issue in a criminal action. Whenever the term "suspect" is used in this code, it means "actor."

(3) "Agency" includes authority, board, bureau, commission, committee, council, department, district, division, and office.

(4) "Alcoholic beverage" has the meaning assigned by Section 1.04, Alcoholic Beverage Code.

(5) "Another" means a person other than the actor.

(6) "Association" means a government or governmental subdivision or agency, trust, partnership, or two or more persons having a joint or common economic interest.

(7) "Benefit" means anything reasonably regarded as economic gain or advantage, including benefit to any other person in whose welfare the beneficiary is interested.

(8) "Bodily injury" means physical pain, illness, or any impairment of physical condition.

(9) "Coercion" means a threat, however communicated:

(A) to commit an offense;

(B) to inflict bodily injury in the future on the person threatened or another;

(C) to accuse a person of any offense;

(D) to expose a person to hatred, contempt, or ridicule;

(E) to harm the credit or business repute of any person; or

(F) to take or withhold action as a public servant, or to cause a public servant to take or withhold action.

(10) "Conduct" means an act or omission and its accompanying mental state.

(11) "Consent" means assent in fact, whether express or apparent.

(12) "Controlled substance" has the meaning assigned by Section 481.002, Health and Safety Code.

(13) "Corporation" includes nonprofit corporations, professional associations created pursuant to statute, and joint stock companies.

(14) "Correctional facility" means a place designated by law for the confinement of a person arrested for, charged with, or convicted of a criminal offense. The term includes:

(A) a municipal or county jail;

(B) a confinement facility operated by the Texas Department of Criminal Justice;

(C) a confinement facility operated under contract with any division of the Texas Department of Criminal Justice; and

(D) a community corrections facility operated by a community supervision and corrections department.

(15) "Criminal negligence" is defined in Section 6.03 (Culpable Mental States).

(16) "Dangerous drug" has the meaning assigned by Section 483.001, Health and Safety Code.

(17) "Deadly weapon" means:

(A) a firearm or anything manifestly designed, made, or adapted for the purpose of inflicting death or serious bodily injury; or

(B) anything that in the manner of its use or intended use is capable of causing death or serious bodily injury.

(18) "Drug" has the meaning assigned by Section 481.002, Health and Safety Code.

(19) "Effective consent" includes consent by a person legally authorized to act for the owner. Consent is not effective if:

(A) induced by force, threat, or fraud;

(B) given by a person the actor knows is not legally authorized to act for the owner;

(C) given by a person who by reason of youth, mental disease or defect, or intoxication is known by the actor to be unable to make reasonable decisions; or

(D) given solely to detect the commission of an offense.

(20) "Electric generating plant" means a facility that generates electric energy for distribution to the public.

(21) "Electric utility substation" means a facility used to switch or change voltage in connection with the transmission of electric energy for distribution to the public.

(22) "Element of offense" means:

(A) the forbidden conduct;

(B) the required culpability;

(C) any required result; and

(D) the negation of any exception to the offense.

(23) "Felony" means an offense so designated by law or punishable by death or confinement in a penitentiary.

(24) "Government" means:

(A) the state;

(B) a county, municipality, or political subdivision of the state; or

(C) any branch or agency of the state, a county, municipality, or political subdivision.

(25) "Harm" means anything reasonably regarded as loss, disadvantage, or injury, including harm to another person in whose welfare the person affected is interested.

(26) "Individual" means a human being who is alive, including an unborn child at every stage of gestation from fertilization until birth.

(27) [Repealed by Acts 2009, 81st Leg., ch. 87 (S.B. 1969), § 25.144, effective September 1, 2009.]

(28) "Intentional" is defined in Section 6.03 (Culpable Mental States).

(29) "Knowing" is defined in Section 6.03 (Culpable Mental States).

(30) "Law" means the constitution or a statute of this state or of the United States, a written opinion of a court of record, a municipal ordinance, an order of a county commissioners court, or a rule authorized by and lawfully adopted under a statute.

(31) "Misdemeanor" means an offense so designated by law or punishable by fine, by confinement in jail, or by both fine and confinement in jail.

(32) "Oath" includes affirmation.

(33) "Official proceeding" means any type of administrative, executive, legislative, or judicial proceeding that may be conducted before a public servant.

(34) "Omission" means failure to act.

(35) "Owner" means a person who:

(A) has title to the property, possession of the property, whether lawful or not, or a greater right to possession of the property than the actor; or

(B) is a holder in due course of a negotiable instrument.

(36) "Peace officer" means a person elected, employed, or appointed as a peace officer under Article 2.12, Code of Criminal Procedure, Section 51.212 or 51.214, Education Code, or other law.

(37) "Penal institution" means a place designated by law for confinement of persons arrested for, charged with, or convicted of an offense.

(38) "Person" means an individual, corporation, or association.

(39) "Possession" means actual care, custody, control, or management.

(40) "Public place" means any place to which the public or a substantial group of the public has access and includes, but is not limited to, streets, highways, and the common areas of schools, hospitals, apartment houses, office buildings, transport facilities, and shops.

(41) "Public servant" means a person elected, selected, appointed, employed, or otherwise designated as one of the following, even if he has not yet qualified for office or assumed his duties:

(A) an officer, employee, or agent of government;

(B) a juror or grand juror; or

(C) an arbitrator, referee, or other person who is authorized by law or private written agreement to hear or determine a cause or controversy; or

(D) an attorney at law or notary public when participating in the performance of a governmental function; or

(E) a candidate for nomination or election to public office; or

(F) a person who is performing a governmental function under a claim of right although he is not legally qualified to do so.

(42) "Reasonable belief" means a belief that would be held by an ordinary and prudent man in the same circumstances as the actor.

(43) "Reckless" is defined in Section 6.03 (Culpable Mental States).

(44) "Rule" includes regulation.

(45) "Secure correctional facility" means:

(A) a municipal or county jail; or

(B) a confinement facility operated by or under a contract with any division of the Texas Department of Criminal Justice.

(46) "Serious bodily injury" means bodily injury that creates a substantial risk of death or that causes death, serious permanent disfigurement, or protracted loss or impairment of the function of any bodily member or organ.

(46-a) "Sight order" means a written or electronic instruction to pay money that is authorized by the person giving the instruction and that is payable on demand or at a definite time by the person being instructed to pay. The term includes a check, an electronic debit, or an automatic bank draft.

(46-b) "Federal special investigator" means a person described by Article 2.122, Code of Criminal Procedure.

(47) "Swear" includes affirm.

(48) "Unlawful" means criminal or tortious or both and includes what would be criminal or tortious but for a defense not amounting to justification or privilege.

(49) "Death" includes, for an individual who is an unborn child, the failure to be born alive.

(b) The definition of a term in this code applies to each grammatical variation of the term.
(Enacted by Acts 1973, 63rd Leg., ch. 399 (S.B. 34), § 1, effective January 1, 1974; am. Acts 1975, 64th Leg., ch. 342 (S.B. 127), § 1, effective September 1, 1975; am. Acts 1977, 65th Leg., ch. 848 (H.B. 2007), § 1, effective August 29, 1977; am. Acts 1979, 66th Leg., ch. 530 (S.B. 952), § 1, effective August 27, 1979; am. Acts 1979, 66th Leg., ch. 655 (S.B. 846), § 1, effective September 1, 1979; am. Acts 1987, 70th Leg., ch. 167 (S.B. 892), § 5.01(a)(43), effective September 1, 1987; am. Acts 1989, 71st Leg., ch. 997 (H.B. 832), § 1, effective August 28, 1989; am. Acts 1991, 72nd Leg., ch. 543 (H.B. 1801), § 1, effective September 1, 1991; am. Acts 1993, 73rd Leg., ch. 900 (S.B. 1067), § 1.01, effective September 1, 1994; am. Acts 2003, 78th Leg., ch. 822 (S.B. 319), § 2.01, effective September 1, 2003; am. Acts 2009, 81st Leg., ch. 87 (S.B. 1969), § 25.144, effective September 1, 2009; am. Acts 2009, 81st Leg., ch. 421 (H.B. 2031), § 1, effective September 1, 2009; am. Acts 2011, 82nd Leg., ch. 839 (H.B. 3423), § 1, effective September 1, 2011.)

## Sec. 1.08. Preemption.

No governmental subdivision or agency may enact or enforce a law that makes any conduct covered by this code an offense subject to a criminal penalty. This section shall apply only as long as the law governing the conduct proscribed by this code is legally enforceable.
(Enacted by Acts 1973, 63rd Leg., ch. 399 (S.B. 34), § 1, effective January 1, 1974; am. Acts 1993, 73rd Leg., ch. 900 (S.B. 1067), § 1.01, effective September 1, 1994.)

## Sec. 1.09. Concurrent Jurisdiction Under This Code to Prosecute Offenses That Involve State Property.

With the consent of the appropriate local county or district attorney, the attorney general has concurrent jurisdiction with that consenting local prosecutor to prosecute under this code any offense an element of which occurs on state property or any offense that involves the use, unlawful appropriation, or misapplication of state property, including state funds.

Penal Code

(Enacted by Acts 2007, 80th Leg., ch. 378 (S.B. 563), § 1, effective June 15, 2007.)

## CHAPTER 2
## BURDEN OF PROOF

Section
2.01.    Proof Beyond a Reasonable Doubt.
2.02.    Exception.
2.03.    Defense.
2.04.    Affirmative Defense.
2.05.    Presumption.

### Sec. 2.01.  Proof Beyond a Reasonable Doubt.

All persons are presumed to be innocent and no person may be convicted of an offense unless each element of the offense is proved beyond a reasonable doubt. The fact that he has been arrested, confined, or indicted for, or otherwise charged with, the offense gives rise to no inference of guilt at his trial.
(Enacted by Acts 1973, 63rd Leg., ch. 399 (S.B. 34), § 1, effective January 1, 1974; am. Acts 1993, 73rd Leg., ch. 900 (S.B. 1067), § 1.01, effective September 1, 1994.)

### Sec. 2.02.  Exception.

(a) An exception to an offense in this code is so labeled by the phrase: "It is an exception to the application of ... ."

(b) The prosecuting attorney must negate the existence of an exception in the accusation charging commission of the offense and prove beyond a reasonable doubt that the defendant or defendant's conduct does not fall within the exception.

(c) This section does not affect exceptions applicable to offenses enacted prior to the effective date of this code.
(Enacted by Acts 1973, 63rd Leg., ch. 399 (S.B. 34), § 1, effective January 1, 1974; am. Acts 1993, 73rd Leg., ch. 900 (S.B. 1067), § 1.01, effective September 1, 1994.)

### Sec. 2.03.  Defense.

(a) A defense to prosecution for an offense in this code is so labeled by the phrase: "It is a defense to prosecution ... ."

(b) The prosecuting attorney is not required to negate the existence of a defense in the accusation charging commission of the offense.

(c) The issue of the existence of a defense is not submitted to the jury unless evidence is admitted supporting the defense.

(d) If the issue of the existence of a defense is submitted to the jury, the court shall charge that

a reasonable doubt on the issue requires that the defendant be acquitted.

(e) A ground of defense in a penal law that is not plainly labeled in accordance with this chapter has the procedural and evidentiary consequences of a defense.
(Enacted by Acts 1973, 63rd Leg., ch. 399 (S.B. 34), § 1, effective January 1, 1974; am. Acts 1993, 73rd Leg., ch. 900 (S.B. 1067), § 1.01, effective September 1, 1994.)

### Sec. 2.04.  Affirmative Defense.

(a) An affirmative defense in this code is so labeled by the phrase: "It is an affirmative defense to prosecution ... ."

(b) The prosecuting attorney is not required to negate the existence of an affirmative defense in the accusation charging commission of the offense.

(c) The issue of the existence of an affirmative defense is not submitted to the jury unless evidence is admitted supporting the defense.

(d) If the issue of the existence of an affirmative defense is submitted to the jury, the court shall charge that the defendant must prove the affirmative defense by a preponderance of evidence.
(Enacted by Acts 1973, 63rd Leg., ch. 399 (S.B. 34), § 1, effective January 1, 1974; am. Acts 1993, 73rd Leg., ch. 900 (S.B. 1067), § 1.01, effective September 1, 1994.)

### Sec. 2.05.  Presumption.

(a) Except as provided by Subsection (b), when this code or another penal law establishes a presumption with respect to any fact, it has the following consequences:

(1) if there is sufficient evidence of the facts that give rise to the presumption, the issue of the existence of the presumed fact must be submitted to the jury, unless the court is satisfied that the evidence as a whole clearly precludes a finding beyond a reasonable doubt of the presumed fact; and

(2) if the existence of the presumed fact is submitted to the jury, the court shall charge the jury, in terms of the presumption and the specific element to which it applies, as follows:

(A) that the facts giving rise to the presumption must be proven beyond a reasonable doubt;

(B) that if such facts are proven beyond a reasonable doubt the jury may find that the element of the offense sought to be presumed exists, but it is not bound to so find;

(C) that even though the jury may find the existence of such element, the state must prove beyond a reasonable doubt each of the other elements of the offense charged; and

(D) if the jury has a reasonable doubt as to the existence of a fact or facts giving rise to the presumption, the presumption fails and the jury shall not consider the presumption for any purpose.

(b) When this code or another penal law establishes a presumption in favor of the defendant with respect to any fact, it has the following consequences:

(1) if there is sufficient evidence of the facts that give rise to the presumption, the issue of the existence of the presumed fact must be submitted to the jury unless the court is satisfied that the evidence as a whole clearly precludes a finding beyond a reasonable doubt of the presumed fact; and

(2) if the existence of the presumed fact is submitted to the jury, the court shall charge the jury, in terms of the presumption, that:

(A) the presumption applies unless the state proves beyond a reasonable doubt that the facts giving rise to the presumption do not exist;

(B) if the state fails to prove beyond a reasonable doubt that the facts giving rise to the presumption do not exist, the jury must find that the presumed fact exists;

(C) even though the jury may find that the presumed fact does not exist, the state must prove beyond a reasonable doubt each of the elements of the offense charged; and

(D) if the jury has a reasonable doubt as to whether the presumed fact exists, the presumption applies and the jury must consider the presumed fact to exist.

(Enacted by Acts 1973, 63rd Leg., ch. 399 (S.B. 34), § 1, effective January 1, 1974; am. Acts 1975, 64th Leg., ch. 342 (S.B. 127), § 2, effective September 1, 1975; am. Acts 1993, 73rd Leg., ch. 900 (S.B. 1067), § 1.01, effective September 1, 1994; am. Acts 2005, 79th Leg., ch. 288 (H.B. 823), § 2, effective September 1, 2005.)

## Sec. 2.06. Prima Facie Case [Repealed].

Repealed by Acts 1975, 64th Leg., ch. 342 (S.B. 127), § 16, effective September 1, 1975.
(Enacted by Acts 1973, 63rd Leg., ch. 399 (S.B. 34), § 1, effective January 1, 1974.)

# CHAPTER 3
# MULTIPLE PROSECUTIONS

**Section**

## Sec. 3.01. Definition.

In this chapter, "criminal episode" means the commission of two or more offenses, regardless of whether the harm is directed toward or inflicted upon more than one person or item of property, under the following circumstances:

(1) the offenses are committed pursuant to the same transaction or pursuant to two or more transactions that are connected or constitute a common scheme or plan; or

(2) the offenses are the repeated commission of the same or similar offenses.

(Enacted by Acts 1973, 63rd Leg., ch. 399 (S.B. 34), § 1, effective January 1, 1974; am. Acts 1987, 70th Leg., ch. 387 (H.B. 684), § 1, effective September 1, 1987; am. Acts 1993, 73rd Leg., ch. 900 (S.B. 1067), § 1.01, effective September 1, 1994.)

## Sec. 3.02. Consolidation and Joinder of Prosecutions.

(a) A defendant may be prosecuted in a single criminal action for all offenses arising out of the same criminal episode.

(b) When a single criminal action is based on more than one charging instrument within the jurisdiction of the trial court, the state shall file written notice of the action not less than 30 days prior to the trial.

(c) If a judgment of guilt is reversed, set aside, or vacated, and a new trial ordered, the state may not prosecute in a single criminal action in the new trial any offense not joined in the former prosecution unless evidence to establish probable guilt for that offense was not known to the appropriate prosecuting official at the time the first prosecution commenced.

(Enacted by Acts 1973, 63rd Leg., ch. 399 (S.B. 34), § 1, effective January 1, 1974; am. Acts 1993, 73rd Leg., ch. 900 (S.B. 1067), § 1.01, effective September 1, 1994.)

## Sec. 3.03. Sentences for Offenses Arising Out of Same Criminal Episode.

(a) When the accused is found guilty of more than one offense arising out of the same criminal episode prosecuted in a single criminal action, a sentence for each offense for which he has been found guilty shall be pronounced. Except as provided by Subsection (b), the sentences shall run concurrently.

(b) If the accused is found guilty of more than one offense arising out of the same criminal episode, the sentences may run concurrently or consecutively if each sentence is for a conviction of:

(1) an offense:

(A) under Section 49.07 or 49.08, regardless of whether the accused is convicted of violations of the same section more than once or is convicted of violations of both sections; or

(B) for which a plea agreement was reached in a case in which the accused was charged with more than one offense listed in Paragraph (A), regardless of whether the accused is charged with violations of the same section more than once or is charged with violations of both sections;

(2) an offense:

(A) under Section 33.021 or an offense under Section 21.02, 21.11, 22.011, 22.021, 25.02, or 43.25 committed against a victim younger than 17 years of age at the time of the commission of the offense regardless of whether the accused is convicted of violations of the same section more than once or is convicted of violations of more than one section; or

(B) for which a plea agreement was reached in a case in which the accused was charged with more than one offense listed in Paragraph (A) committed against a victim younger than 17 years of age at the time of the commission of the offense regardless of whether the accused is charged with violations of the same section more than once or is charged with violations of more than one section;

(3) an offense:

(A) under Section 21.15 or 43.26, regardless of whether the accused is convicted of violations of the same section more than once or is convicted of violations of both sections; or

(B) for which a plea agreement was reached in a case in which the accused was charged with more than one offense listed in Paragraph (A), regardless of whether the accused is charged with violations of the

same section more than once or is charged with violations of both sections;

(4) an offense for which the judgment in the case contains an affirmative finding under Article 42.0197, Code of Criminal Procedure; or

(5) an offense:

(A) under Section 20A.02 or 43.05, regardless of whether the accused is convicted of violations of the same section more than once or is convicted of violations of both sections; or

(B) for which a plea agreement was reached in a case in which the accused was charged with more than one offense listed in Paragraph (A), regardless of whether the accused is charged with violations of the same section more than once or is charged with violations of both sections.

(b-1) Subsection (b)(4) does not apply to a defendant whose case was transferred to the court under Section 54.02, Family Code.

(Enacted by Acts 1973, 63rd Leg., ch. 399 (S.B. 34), § 1, effective January 1, 1974; am. Acts 1993, 73rd Leg., ch. 900 (S.B. 1067), § 1.01, effective September 1, 1994; am. Acts 1995, 74th Leg., ch. 596 (H.B. 93), § 1, effective September 1, 1995; am. Acts 1997, 75th Leg., ch. 667 (S.B. 381), § 2, effective September 1, 1997; am. Acts 2005, 79th Leg., ch. 527 (H.B. 904), § 1, effective September 1, 2005; am. Acts 2007, 80th Leg., ch. 593 (H.B. 8), § 3.47, effective September 1, 2007; am. Acts 2007, 80th Leg., ch. 1291 (S.B. 6), § 6, effective September 1, 2007; am. Acts 2009, 81st Leg., ch. 1130 (H.B. 2086), § 21, effective September 1, 2009; am. Acts 2011, 82nd Leg., ch. 1 (S.B. 24), § 6.01, effective September 1, 2011.)

## Sec. 3.04. Severance.

(a) Whenever two or more offenses have been consolidated or joined for trial under Section 3.02, the defendant shall have a right to a severance of the offenses.

(b) In the event of severance under this section, the provisions of Section 3.03 do not apply, and the court in its discretion may order the sentences to run either concurrently or consecutively.

(c) The right to severance under this section does not apply to a prosecution for offenses described by Section 3.03(b) unless the court determines that the defendant or the state would be unfairly prejudiced by a joinder of offenses, in which event the judge may order the offenses to be tried separately or may order other relief as justice requires.

(Enacted by Acts 1973, 63rd Leg., ch. 399 (S.B. 34), § 1, effective January 1, 1974; am. Acts 1993, 73rd Leg., ch. 900 (S.B. 1067), § 1.01, effective September 1, 1994; am. Acts 1997, 75th Leg., ch. 667 (S.B. 381), § 3, effective September 1, 1997; am. Acts 2005, 79th Leg., ch. 527 (H.B. 904), § 2, effective September 1, 2005.)

# TITLE 2
# GENERAL PRINCIPLES OF CRIMINAL RESPONSIBILITY

## CHAPTER 6
## CULPABILITY GENERALLY

Section
6.01.       Requirement of Voluntary Act or Omission.
6.02.       Requirement of Culpability.
6.03.       Definitions of Culpable Mental States.
6.04.       Causation: Conduct and Results.

### Sec. 6.01.  Requirement of Voluntary Act or Omission.

(a) A person commits an offense only if he voluntarily engages in conduct, including an act, an omission, or possession.

(b) Possession is a voluntary act if the possessor knowingly obtains or receives the thing possessed or is aware of his control of the thing for a sufficient time to permit him to terminate his control.

(c) A person who omits to perform an act does not commit an offense unless a law as defined by Section 1.07 provides that the omission is an offense or otherwise provides that he has a duty to perform the act.
(Enacted by Acts 1973, 63rd Leg., ch. 399 (S.B. 34), § 1, effective January 1, 1974; am. Acts 1975, 64th Leg., ch. 342 (S.B. 127), § 3, effective September 1, 1975; am. Acts 1993, 73rd Leg., ch. 3 (S.B. 146), § 1, effective February 25, 1993; am. Acts 1993, 73rd Leg., ch. 900 (S.B. 1067), § 1.01, effective September 1, 1994.)

### Sec. 6.02.  Requirement of Culpability.

(a) Except as provided in Subsection (b), a person does not commit an offense unless he intentionally, knowingly, recklessly, or with criminal negligence engages in conduct as the definition of the offense requires.

(b) If the definition of an offense does not prescribe a culpable mental state, a culpable mental state is nevertheless required unless the definition plainly dispenses with any mental element.

(c) If the definition of an offense does not prescribe a culpable mental state, but one is nevertheless required under Subsection (b), intent, knowledge, or recklessness suffices to establish criminal responsibility.

(d) Culpable mental states are classified according to relative degrees, from highest to lowest, as follows:

(1) intentional;

(2) knowing;

(3) reckless;

(4) criminal negligence.

(e) Proof of a higher degree of culpability than that charged constitutes proof of the culpability charged.

(f) An offense defined by municipal ordinance or by order of a county commissioners court may not dispense with the requirement of a culpable mental state if the offense is punishable by a fine exceeding the amount authorized by Section 12.23.
(Enacted by Acts 1973, 63rd Leg., ch. 399 (S.B. 34), § 1, effective January 1, 1974; am. Acts 1993, 73rd Leg., ch. 900 (S.B. 1067), § 1.01, effective September 1, 1994; am. Acts 2005, 79th Leg., ch. 1219 (H.B. 970), § 1, effective September 1, 2005.)

### Sec. 6.03.  Definitions of Culpable Mental States.

(a) A person acts intentionally, or with intent, with respect to the nature of his conduct or to a result of his conduct when it is his conscious objective or desire to engage in the conduct or cause the result.

(b) A person acts knowingly, or with knowledge, with respect to the nature of his conduct or to circumstances surrounding his conduct when he is aware of the nature of his conduct or that the circumstances exist. A person acts knowingly, or with knowledge, with respect to a result of his conduct when he is aware that his conduct is reasonably certain to cause the result.

(c) A person acts recklessly, or is reckless, with respect to circumstances surrounding his conduct or the result of his conduct when he is aware of but consciously disregards a substantial and unjustifiable risk that the circumstances exist or the result will occur. The risk must be of such a nature and degree that its disregard constitutes a gross deviation from the standard of care that an ordinary person would exercise under all the circumstances as viewed from the actor's standpoint.

(d) A person acts with criminal negligence, or is criminally negligent, with respect to circumstances surrounding his conduct or the result of his conduct when he ought to be aware of a substantial and unjustifiable risk that the circumstances exist or the result will occur. The risk must be of such a nature and degree that the failure to perceive it constitutes a gross deviation from the standard of care that an ordinary person would exercise under all the circumstances as viewed from the actor's standpoint.

(Enacted by Acts 1973, 63rd Leg., ch. 399 (S.B. 34), § 1, effective January 1, 1974; am. Acts 1993, 73rd Leg., ch. 900 (S.B. 1067), § 1.01, effective September 1, 1994.)

## Sec. 6.04.   Causation: Conduct and Results.

(a) A person is criminally responsible if the result would not have occurred but for his conduct, operating either alone or concurrently with another cause, unless the concurrent cause was clearly sufficient to produce the result and the conduct of the actor clearly insufficient.

(b) A person is nevertheless criminally responsible for causing a result if the only difference between what actually occurred and what he desired, contemplated, or risked is that:

(1) a different offense was committed; or

(2) a different person or property was injured, harmed, or otherwise affected.

(Enacted by Acts 1973, 63rd Leg., ch. 399 (S.B. 34), § 1, effective January 1, 1974; am. Acts 1993, 73rd Leg., ch. 900 (S.B. 1067), § 1.01, effective September 1, 1994.)

## CHAPTER 7
## CRIMINAL RESPONSIBILITY FOR CONDUCT OF ANOTHER

### Subchapter A. Complicity

## SUBCHAPTER A
## COMPLICITY

### Sec. 7.01.   Parties to Offenses.

(a) A person is criminally responsible as a party to an offense if the offense is committed by his own conduct, by the conduct of another for which he is criminally responsible, or by both.

(b) Each party to an offense may be charged with commission of the offense.

(c) All traditional distinctions between accomplices and principals are abolished by this section, and each party to an offense may be charged and convicted without alleging that he acted as a principal or accomplice.

(Enacted by Acts 1973, 63rd Leg., ch. 399 (S.B. 34), § 1, effective January 1, 1974; am. Acts 1993, 73rd Leg., ch. 900 (S.B. 1067), § 1.01, effective September 1, 1994.)

### Sec. 7.02.   Criminal Responsibility for Conduct of Another.

(a) A person is criminally responsible for an offense committed by the conduct of another if:

(1) acting with the kind of culpability required for the offense, he causes or aids an innocent or nonresponsible person to engage in conduct prohibited by the definition of the offense;

(2) acting with intent to promote or assist the commission of the offense, he solicits, encourages, directs, aids, or attempts to aid the other person to commit the offense; or

(3) having a legal duty to prevent commission of the offense and acting with intent to promote or assist its commission, he fails to make a reasonable effort to prevent commission of the offense.

(b) If, in the attempt to carry out a conspiracy to commit one felony, another felony is committed by one of the conspirators, all conspirators are guilty of the felony actually committed, though having no intent to commit it, if the offense was committed in furtherance of the unlawful purpose and was one that should have been anticipated as a result of the carrying out of the conspiracy.

(Enacted by Acts 1973, 63rd Leg., ch. 399 (S.B. 34), § 1, effective January 1, 1974; am. Acts 1993, 73rd Leg., ch. 900 (S.B. 1067), § 1.01, effective September 1, 1994.)

## Sec. 7.03. Defenses Excluded.

In a prosecution in which an actor's criminal responsibility is based on the conduct of another, the actor may be convicted on proof of commission of the offense and that he was a party to its commission, and it is no defense:

(1) that the actor belongs to a class of persons that by definition of the offense is legally incapable of committing the offense in an individual capacity; or

(2) that the person for whose conduct the actor is criminally responsible has been acquitted, has not been prosecuted or convicted, has been convicted of a different offense or of a different type or class of offense, or is immune from prosecution.

(Enacted by Acts 1973, 63rd Leg., ch. 399 (S.B. 34), § 1, effective January 1, 1974; am. Acts 1993, 73rd Leg., ch. 900 (S.B. 1067), § 1.01, effective September 1, 1994.)

## Secs. 7.04 to 7.20 [Reserved for expansion].

## SUBCHAPTER B
## CORPORATIONS AND ASSOCIATIONS

## Sec. 7.21. Definitions.

In this subchapter:

(1) "Agent" means a director, officer, employee, or other person authorized to act in behalf of a corporation or association.

(2) "High managerial agent" means:

(A) a partner in a partnership;

(B) an officer of a corporation or association;

(C) an agent of a corporation or association who has duties of such responsibility that his conduct reasonably may be assumed to represent the policy of the corporation or association.

(Enacted by Acts 1973, 63rd Leg., ch. 399 (S.B. 34), § 1, effective January 1, 1974; am. Acts 1993, 73rd Leg., ch. 900 (S.B. 1067), § 1.01, effective September 1, 1994.)

## Sec. 7.22. Criminal Responsibility of Corporation or Association.

(a) If conduct constituting an offense is performed by an agent acting in behalf of a corporation or association and within the scope of his office or employment, the corporation or association is criminally responsible for an offense defined:

(1) in this code where corporations and associations are made subject thereto;

(2) by law other than this code in which a legislative purpose to impose criminal responsibility on corporations or associations plainly appears; or

(3) by law other than this code for which strict liability is imposed, unless a legislative purpose not to impose criminal responsibility on corporations or associations plainly appears.

(b) A corporation or association is criminally responsible for a felony offense only if its commission was authorized, requested, commanded, performed, or recklessly tolerated by:

(1) a majority of the governing board acting in behalf of the corporation or association; or

(2) a high managerial agent acting in behalf of the corporation or association and within the scope of his office or employment.

(Enacted by Acts 1973, 63rd Leg., ch. 399 (S.B. 34), § 1, effective January 1, 1974; am. Acts 1975, 64th Leg., ch. 342 (S.B. 127), § 4, effective September 1, 1975; am. Acts 1993, 73rd Leg., ch. 900 (S.B. 1067), § 1.01, effective September 1, 1994.)

## Sec. 7.23. Criminal Responsibility of Person for Conduct in Behalf of Corporation or Association.

(a) An individual is criminally responsible for conduct that he performs in the name of or in behalf of a corporation or association to the same extent as if the conduct were performed in his own name or behalf.

(b) An agent having primary responsibility for the discharge of a duty to act imposed by law on a corporation or association is criminally responsible for omission to discharge the duty to the same extent as if the duty were imposed by law directly on him.

(c) If an individual is convicted of conduct constituting an offense performed in the name of or on behalf of a corporation or association, he is subject to the sentence authorized by law for an individual convicted of the offense.

(Enacted by Acts 1973, 63rd Leg., ch. 399 (S.B. 34), § 1, effective January 1, 1974; am. Acts 1993,

73rd Leg., ch. 900 (S.B. 1067), § 1.01, effective September 1, 1994.)

## Sec. 7.24.  Defense to Criminal Responsibility of Corporation or Association.

It is an affirmative defense to prosecution of a corporation or association under Section 7.22(a)(1) or (a)(2) that the high managerial agent having supervisory responsibility over the subject matter of the offense employed due diligence to prevent its commission.

(Enacted by Acts 1973, 63rd Leg., ch. 399 (S.B. 34), § 1, effective January 1, 1974; am. Acts 1975, 64th Leg., ch. 342 (S.B. 127), § 5, effective September 1, 1975; am. Acts 1993, 73rd Leg., ch. 900 (S.B. 1067), § 1.01, effective September 1, 1994.)

# CHAPTER 8
# GENERAL DEFENSES TO CRIMINAL RESPONSIBILITY

**Section**

## Sec. 8.01.  Insanity.

(a) It is an affirmative defense to prosecution that, at the time of the conduct charged, the actor, as a result of severe mental disease or defect, did not know that his conduct was wrong.

(b) The term "mental disease or defect" does not include an abnormality manifested only by repeated criminal or otherwise antisocial conduct.

(Enacted by Acts 1973, 63rd Leg., ch. 399 (S.B. 34), § 1, effective January 1, 1974; am. Acts 1983, 68th Leg., ch. 454 (S.B. 7), § 1, effective August 29, 1983; am. Acts 1993, 73rd Leg., ch. 900 (S.B. 1067), § 1.01, effective September 1, 1994.)

## Sec. 8.02.  Mistake of Fact.

(a) It is a defense to prosecution that the actor through mistake formed a reasonable belief about a matter of fact if his mistaken belief negated the kind of culpability required for commission of the offense.

(b) Although an actor's mistake of fact may constitute a defense to the offense charged, he may nevertheless be convicted of any lesser included offense of which he would be guilty if the fact were as he believed.

(Enacted by Acts 1973, 63rd Leg., ch. 399 (S.B. 34), § 1, effective January 1, 1974; am. Acts 1993, 73rd Leg., ch. 900 (S.B. 1067), § 1.01, effective September 1, 1994.)

## Sec. 8.03.  Mistake of Law.

(a) It is no defense to prosecution that the actor was ignorant of the provisions of any law after the law has taken effect.

(b) It is an affirmative defense to prosecution that the actor reasonably believed the conduct charged did not constitute a crime and that he acted in reasonable reliance upon:

(1) an official statement of the law contained in a written order or grant of permission by an administrative agency charged by law with responsibility for interpreting the law in question; or

(2) a written interpretation of the law contained in an opinion of a court of record or made by a public official charged by law with responsibility for interpreting the law in question.

(c) Although an actor's mistake of law may constitute a defense to the offense charged, he may nevertheless be convicted of a lesser included offense of which he would be guilty if the law were as he believed.

(Enacted by Acts 1973, 63rd Leg., ch. 399 (S.B. 34), § 1, effective January 1, 1974; am. Acts 1993, 73rd Leg., ch. 900 (S.B. 1067), § 1.01, effective September 1, 1994.)

## Sec. 8.04.  Intoxication.

(a) Voluntary intoxication does not constitute a defense to the commission of crime.

(b) Evidence of temporary insanity caused by intoxication may be introduced by the actor in mitigation of the penalty attached to the offense for which he is being tried.

(c) When temporary insanity is relied upon as a defense and the evidence tends to show that such insanity was caused by intoxication, the court shall charge the jury in accordance with the provisions of this section.

(d) For purposes of this section "intoxication" means disturbance of mental or physical capacity resulting from the introduction of any substance into the body.

(Enacted by Acts 1973, 63rd Leg., ch. 399 (S.B. 34), § 1, effective January 1, 1974; am. Acts 1993, 73rd Leg., ch. 900 (S.B. 1067), § 1.01, effective September 1, 1994.)

Penal Code

## Sec. 8.05. Duress.

(a) It is an affirmative defense to prosecution that the actor engaged in the proscribed conduct because he was compelled to do so by threat of imminent death or serious bodily injury to himself or another.

(b) In a prosecution for an offense that does not constitute a felony, it is an affirmative defense to prosecution that the actor engaged in the proscribed conduct because he was compelled to do so by force or threat of force.

(c) Compulsion within the meaning of this section exists only if the force or threat of force would render a person of reasonable firmness incapable of resisting the pressure.

(d) The defense provided by this section is unavailable if the actor intentionally, knowingly, or recklessly placed himself in a situation in which it was probable that he would be subjected to compulsion.

(e) It is no defense that a person acted at the command or persuasion of his spouse, unless he acted under compulsion that would establish a defense under this section.

(Enacted by Acts 1973, 63rd Leg., ch. 399 (S.B. 34), § 1, effective January 1, 1974; am. Acts 1993, 73rd Leg., ch. 900 (S.B. 1067), § 1.01, effective September 1, 1994.)

## Sec. 8.06. Entrapment.

(a) It is a defense to prosecution that the actor engaged in the conduct charged because he was induced to do so by a law enforcement agent using persuasion or other means likely to cause persons to commit the offense. Conduct merely affording a person an opportunity to commit an offense does not constitute entrapment.

(b) In this section "law enforcement agent" includes personnel of the state and local law enforcement agencies as well as of the United States and any person acting in accordance with instructions from such agents.

(Enacted by Acts 1973, 63rd Leg., ch. 399 (S.B. 34), § 1, effective January 1, 1974; am. Acts 1993, 73rd Leg., ch. 900 (S.B. 1067), § 1.01, effective September 1, 1994.)

## Sec. 8.07. Age Affecting Criminal Responsibility.

(a) A person may not be prosecuted for or convicted of any offense that the person committed when younger than 15 years of age except:

(1) perjury and aggravated perjury when it appears by proof that the person had sufficient discretion to understand the nature and obligation of an oath;

(2) a violation of a penal statute cognizable under Chapter 729, Transportation Code, except for conduct for which the person convicted may be sentenced to imprisonment or confinement in jail;

(3) a violation of a motor vehicle traffic ordinance of an incorporated city or town in this state;

(4) a misdemeanor punishable by fine only;

(5) a violation of a penal ordinance of a political subdivision;

(6) a violation of a penal statute that is, or is a lesser included offense of, a capital felony, an aggravated controlled substance felony, or a felony of the first degree for which the person is transferred to the court under Section 54.02, Family Code, for prosecution if the person committed the offense when 14 years of age or older; or

(7) a capital felony or an offense under Section 19.02 for which the person is transferred to the court under Section 54.02(j)(2)(A), Family Code.

(b) Unless the juvenile court waives jurisdiction under Section 54.02, Family Code, and certifies the individual for criminal prosecution or the juvenile court has previously waived jurisdiction under that section and certified the individual for criminal prosecution, a person may not be prosecuted for or convicted of any offense committed before reaching 17 years of age except an offense described by Subsections (a)(1)—(5).

(c) No person may, in any case, be punished by death for an offense committed while the person was younger than 18 years.

(Enacted by Acts 1973, 63rd Leg., ch. 399 (S.B. 34), § 1, effective January 1, 1974; am. Acts 1975, 64th Leg., ch. 693 (S.B. 247), § 24, effective September 1, 1975; am. Acts 1987, 70th Leg., ch. 1040 (S.B. 17), § 26, effective September 1, 1987; am. Acts 1989, 71st Leg., ch. 1245 (H.B. 535), § 3, effective September 1, 1989; am. Acts 1991, 72nd Leg., ch. 169 (H.B. 944), § 3, effective September 1, 1991; am. Acts 1993, 73rd Leg., ch. 900 (S.B. 1067), § 1.01, effective September 1, 1994; am. Acts 1995, 74th Leg., ch. 262 (H.B. 327), § 77, effective January 1, 1996; am. Acts 1997, 75th Leg., ch. 165 (S.B. 898), § 30.236, effective September 1, 1997; am. Acts 1997, 75th Leg., ch. 822 (S.B. 81), § 4, effective September 1, 1997; am. Acts 1997, 75th Leg., ch. 1086 (H.B. 1550), § 42, effective September 1, 1997; am. Acts 2001, 77th Leg., ch. 1297 (H.B. 1118), § 68, effective September 1, 2001; am. Acts 2003, 78th Leg., ch. 283 (H.B. 2319), § 52, effective September 1, 2003; am. Acts 2005, 79th Leg., ch. 787 (S.B. 60), § 2, effective September 1, 2005; am. Acts 2005, 79th Leg., ch. 949 (H.B. 1575), § 45, effective September 1, 2005; am. Acts 2009, 81st Leg., ch. 311 (H.B. 558), § 5, effective September 1, 2009.)

# CHAPTER 9
# JUSTIFICATION EXCLUDING CRIMINAL RESPONSIBILITY

## SUBCHAPTER A
## GENERAL PROVISIONS

### Sec. 9.01.   Definitions.

In this chapter:

(1) "Custody" has the meaning assigned by Section 38.01.

(2) "Escape" has the meaning assigned by Section 38.01.

(3) "Deadly force" means force that is intended or known by the actor to cause, or in the manner of its use or intended use is capable of causing, death or serious bodily injury.

(4) "Habitation" has the meaning assigned by Section 30.01.

(5) "Vehicle" has the meaning assigned by Section 30.01.

(Enacted by Acts 1973, 63rd Leg., ch. 399 (S.B. 34), § 1, effective January 1, 1974; am. Acts 1993, 73rd Leg., ch. 900 (S.B. 1067), § 1.01, effective September 1, 1994; am. Acts 1997, 75th Leg., ch. 293 (H.B. 975), § 1, effective September 1, 1997; am. Acts 2007, 80th Leg., ch. 1 (S.B. 378), § 1, effective September 1, 2007.)

### Sec. 9.02.   Justification As a Defense.

It is a defense to prosecution that the conduct in question is justified under this chapter.

(Enacted by Acts 1973, 63rd Leg., ch. 399 (S.B. 34), § 1, effective January 1, 1974; am. Acts 1993, 73rd Leg., ch. 900 (S.B. 1067), § 1.01, effective September 1, 1994.)

### Sec. 9.03.   Confinement As Justifiable Force.

Confinement is justified when force is justified by this chapter if the actor takes reasonable measures to terminate the confinement as soon as he knows he safely can unless the person confined has been arrested for an offense.

(Enacted by Acts 1973, 63rd Leg., ch. 399 (S.B. 34), § 1, effective January 1, 1974; am. Acts 1993, 73rd Leg., ch. 900 (S.B. 1067), § 1.01, effective September 1, 1994.)

### Sec. 9.04.   Threats As Justifiable Force.

The threat of force is justified when the use of force is justified by this chapter. For purposes of this section, a threat to cause death or serious bodily injury by the production of a weapon or otherwise, as long as the actor's purpose is limited to creating an apprehension that he will use deadly force if necessary, does not constitute the use of deadly force.

(Enacted by Acts 1973, 63rd Leg., ch. 399 (S.B. 34), § 1, effective January 1, 1974; am. Acts 1993, 73rd Leg., ch. 900 (S.B. 1067), § 1.01, effective September 1, 1994.)

### Sec. 9.05.   Reckless Injury of Innocent Third Person.

Even though an actor is justified under this chapter in threatening or using force or deadly force against another, if in doing so he also

recklessly injures or kills an innocent third person, the justification afforded by this chapter is unavailable in a prosecution for the reckless injury or killing of the innocent third person.
(Enacted by Acts 1973, 63rd Leg., ch. 399 (S.B. 34), § 1, effective January 1, 1974; am. Acts 1993, 73rd Leg., ch. 900 (S.B. 1067), § 1.01, effective September 1, 1994.)

### Sec. 9.06. Civil Remedies Unaffected.

The fact that conduct is justified under this chapter does not abolish or impair any remedy for the conduct that is available in a civil suit.
(Enacted by Acts 1973, 63rd Leg., ch. 399 (S.B. 34), § 1, effective January 1, 1974; am. Acts 1993, 73rd Leg., ch. 900 (S.B. 1067), § 1.01, effective September 1, 1994.)

### Secs. 9.07 to 9.20 [Reserved for expansion].

## SUBCHAPTER B
## JUSTIFICATION GENERALLY

### Sec. 9.21. Public Duty.

(a) Except as qualified by Subsections (b) and (c), conduct is justified if the actor reasonably believes the conduct is required or authorized by law, by the judgment or order of a competent court or other governmental tribunal, or in the execution of legal process.

(b) The other sections of this chapter control when force is used against a person to protect persons (Subchapter C), to protect property (Subchapter D), for law enforcement (Subchapter E), or by virtue of a special relationship (Subchapter F).

(c) The use of deadly force is not justified under this section unless the actor reasonably believes the deadly force is specifically required by statute or unless it occurs in the lawful conduct of war. If deadly force is so justified, there is no duty to retreat before using it.

(d) The justification afforded by this section is available if the actor reasonably believes:

(1) the court or governmental tribunal has jurisdiction or the process is lawful, even though the court or governmental tribunal lacks jurisdiction or the process is unlawful; or

(2) his conduct is required or authorized to assist a public servant in the performance of his official duty, even though the servant exceeds his lawful authority.

(Enacted by Acts 1973, 63rd Leg., ch. 399 (S.B. 34), § 1, effective January 1, 1974; am. Acts 1993, 73rd Leg., ch. 900 (S.B. 1067), § 1.01, effective September 1, 1994.)

### Sec. 9.22. Necessity.

Conduct is justified if:

(1) the actor reasonably believes the conduct is immediately necessary to avoid imminent harm;

(2) the desirability and urgency of avoiding the harm clearly outweigh, according to ordinary standards of reasonableness, the harm sought to be prevented by the law proscribing the conduct; and

(3) a legislative purpose to exclude the justification claimed for the conduct does not otherwise plainly appear.

(Enacted by Acts 1973, 63rd Leg., ch. 399 (S.B. 34), § 1, effective January 1, 1974; am. Acts 1993, 73rd Leg., ch. 900 (S.B. 1067), § 1.01, effective September 1, 1994.)

### Secs. 9.23 to 9.30 [Reserved for expansion].

## SUBCHAPTER C
## PROTECTION OF PERSONS

### Sec. 9.31. Self-Defense.

(a) Except as provided in Subsection (b), a person is justified in using force against another when and to the degree the actor reasonably believes the force is immediately necessary to protect the actor against the other's use or attempted use of unlawful force. The actor's belief that the force was immediately necessary as described by this subsection is presumed to be reasonable if the actor:

(1) knew or had reason to believe that the person against whom the force was used:

(A) unlawfully and with force entered, or was attempting to enter unlawfully and with force, the actor's occupied habitation, vehicle, or place of business or employment;

(B) unlawfully and with force removed, or was attempting to remove unlawfully and with force, the actor from the actor's habitation, vehicle, or place of business or employment; or

(C) was committing or attempting to commit aggravated kidnapping, murder, sexual assault, aggravated sexual assault, robbery, or aggravated robbery;

(2) did not provoke the person against whom the force was used; and

(3) was not otherwise engaged in criminal activity, other than a Class C misdemeanor that is a violation of a law or ordinance regulating traffic at the time the force was used.

(b) The use of force against another is not justified:

(1) in response to verbal provocation alone;

(2) to resist an arrest or search that the actor knows is being made by a peace officer, or by a person acting in a peace officer's presence and at his direction, even though the arrest or search is unlawful, unless the resistance is justified under Subsection (c);

(3) if the actor consented to the exact force used or attempted by the other;

(4) if the actor provoked the other's use or attempted use of unlawful force, unless:

(A) the actor abandons the encounter, or clearly communicates to the other his intent to do so reasonably believing he cannot safely abandon the encounter; and

(B) the other nevertheless continues or attempts to use unlawful force against the actor; or

(5) if the actor sought an explanation from or discussion with the other person concerning the actor's differences with the other person while the actor was:

(A) carrying a weapon in violation of Section 46.02; or

(B) possessing or transporting a weapon in violation of Section 46.05.

(c) The use of force to resist an arrest or search is justified:

(1) if, before the actor offers any resistance, the peace officer (or person acting at his direction) uses or attempts to use greater force than necessary to make the arrest or search; and

(2) when and to the degree the actor reasonably believes the force is immediately necessary to protect himself against the peace officer's (or other person's) use or attempted use of greater force than necessary.

(d) The use of deadly force is not justified under this subchapter except as provided in Sections 9.32, 9.33, and 9.34.

(e) A person who has a right to be present at the location where the force is used, who has not provoked the person against whom the force is used, and who is not engaged in criminal activity at the time the force is used is not required to retreat before using force as described by this section.

(f) For purposes of Subsection (a), in determining whether an actor described by Subsection (e) reasonably believed that the use of force was necessary, a finder of fact may not consider whether the actor failed to retreat.

(Enacted by Acts 1973, 63rd Leg., ch. 399 (S.B. 34), § 1, effective January 1, 1974; am. Acts 1993, 73rd Leg., ch. 900 (S.B. 1067), § 1.01, effective September 1, 1994; am. Acts 1995, 74th Leg., ch. 190 (H.B. 981), § 1, effective September 1, 1995; am. Acts 2007, 80th Leg., ch. 1 (S.B. 378), § 2, effective September 1, 2007.)

## Sec. 9.32. Deadly Force in Defense of Person.

(a) A person is justified in using deadly force against another:

(1) if the actor would be justified in using force against the other under Section 9.31; and

(2) when and to the degree the actor reasonably believes the deadly force is immediately necessary:

(A) to protect the actor against the other's use or attempted use of unlawful deadly force; or

(B) to prevent the other's imminent commission of aggravated kidnapping, murder, sexual assault, aggravated sexual assault, robbery, or aggravated robbery.

(b) The actor's belief under Subsection (a)(2) that the deadly force was immediately necessary as described by that subdivision is presumed to be reasonable if the actor:

(1) knew or had reason to believe that the person against whom the deadly force was used:

(A) unlawfully and with force entered, or was attempting to enter unlawfully and with force, the actor's occupied habitation, vehicle, or place of business or employment;

(B) unlawfully and with force removed, or was attempting to remove unlawfully and with force, the actor from the actor's habitation, vehicle, or place of business or employment; or

(C) was committing or attempting to commit an offense described by Subsection (a)(2)(B);

(2) did not provoke the person against whom the force was used; and

(3) was not otherwise engaged in criminal activity, other than a Class C misdemeanor that is a violation of a law or ordinance regulating traffic at the time the force was used.

(c) A person who has a right to be present at the location where the deadly force is used, who has not provoked the person against whom the deadly force is used, and who is not engaged in criminal activity at the time the deadly force is used is not required to retreat before using deadly force as described by this section.

(d) For purposes of Subsection (a)(2), in determining whether an actor described by Subsection (c) reasonably believed that the use of deadly force was necessary, a finder of fact may not consider whether the actor failed to retreat.
(Enacted by Acts 1973, 63rd Leg., ch. 399 (S.B. 34), § 1, effective January 1, 1974; am. Acts 1983, 68th Leg., ch. 977 (H.B. 2008), § 5, effective September 1, 1983; am. Acts 1993, 73rd Leg., ch. 900 (S.B. 1067), § 1.01, effective September 1, 1994; am. Acts 1995, 74th Leg., ch. 235 (H.B. 94), § 1, effective September 1, 1995; am. Acts 2007, 80th Leg., ch. 1 (S.B. 378), § 3, effective September 1, 2007.)

### Sec. 9.33. Defense of Third Person.

A person is justified in using force or deadly force against another to protect a third person if:

(1) under the circumstances as the actor reasonably believes them to be, the actor would be justified under Section 9.31 or 9.32 in using force or deadly force to protect himself against the unlawful force or unlawful deadly force he reasonably believes to be threatening the third person he seeks to protect; and

(2) the actor reasonably believes that his intervention is immediately necessary to protect the third person.
(Enacted by Acts 1973, 63rd Leg., ch. 399 (S.B. 34), § 1, effective January 1, 1974; am. Acts 1993, 73rd Leg., ch. 900 (S.B. 1067), § 1.01, effective September 1, 1994.)

### Sec. 9.34. Protection of Life or Health.

(a) A person is justified in using force, but not deadly force, against another when and to the degree he reasonably believes the force is immediately necessary to prevent the other from committing suicide or inflicting serious bodily injury to himself.

(b) A person is justified in using both force and deadly force against another when and to the degree he reasonably believes the force or deadly force is immediately necessary to preserve the other's life in an emergency.
(Enacted by Acts 1973, 63rd Leg., ch. 399 (S.B. 34), § 1, effective January 1, 1974; am. Acts 1993,

73rd Leg., ch. 900 (S.B. 1067), § 1.01, effective September 1, 1994.)

### Secs. 9.35 to 9.40 [Reserved for expansion].

### SUBCHAPTER D
### PROTECTION OF PROPERTY

### Sec. 9.41. Protection of One's Own Property.

(a) A person in lawful possession of land or tangible, movable property is justified in using force against another when and to the degree the actor reasonably believes the force is immediately necessary to prevent or terminate the other's trespass on the land or unlawful interference with the property.

(b) A person unlawfully dispossessed of land or tangible, movable property by another is justified in using force against the other when and to the degree the actor reasonably believes the force is immediately necessary to reenter the land or recover the property if the actor uses the force immediately or in fresh pursuit after the dispossession and:

(1) the actor reasonably believes the other had no claim of right when he dispossessed the actor; or

(2) the other accomplished the dispossession by using force, threat, or fraud against the actor.
(Enacted by Acts 1973, 63rd Leg., ch. 399 (S.B. 34), § 1, effective January 1, 1974; am. Acts 1993, 73rd Leg., ch. 900 (S.B. 1067), § 1.01, effective September 1, 1994.)

### Sec. 9.42. Deadly Force to Protect Property.

A person is justified in using deadly force against another to protect land or tangible, movable property:

(1) if he would be justified in using force against the other under Section 9.41; and

(2) when and to the degree he reasonably believes the deadly force is immediately necessary:

(A) to prevent the other's imminent commission of arson, burglary, robbery, aggravated robbery, theft during the nighttime, or criminal mischief during the nighttime; or

(B) to prevent the other who is fleeing immediately after committing burglary, robbery, aggravated robbery, or theft during the nighttime from escaping with the property; and

(3) he reasonably believes that:

(A) the land or property cannot be protected or recovered by any other means; or

(B) the use of force other than deadly force to protect or recover the land or property would expose the actor or another to a substantial risk of death or serious bodily injury.

(Enacted by Acts 1973, 63rd Leg., ch. 399 (S.B. 34), § 1, effective January 1, 1974; am. Acts 1993, 73rd Leg., ch. 900 (S.B. 1067), § 1.01, effective September 1, 1994.)

## Sec. 9.43.  Protection of Third Person's Property.

A person is justified in using force or deadly force against another to protect land or tangible, movable property of a third person if, under the circumstances as he reasonably believes them to be, the actor would be justified under Section 9.41 or 9.42 in using force or deadly force to protect his own land or property and:

(1) the actor reasonably believes the unlawful interference constitutes attempted or consummated theft of or criminal mischief to the tangible, movable property; or

(2) the actor reasonably believes that:

(A) the third person has requested his protection of the land or property;

(B) he has a legal duty to protect the third person's land or property; or

(C) the third person whose land or property he uses force or deadly force to protect is the actor's spouse, parent, or child, resides with the actor, or is under the actor's care.

(Enacted by Acts 1973, 63rd Leg., ch. 399 (S.B. 34), § 1, effective January 1, 1974; am. Acts 1993, 73rd Leg., ch. 900 (S.B. 1067), § 1.01, effective September 1, 1994.)

## Sec. 9.44.  Use of Device to Protect Property.

The justification afforded by Sections 9.41 and 9.43 applies to the use of a device to protect land or tangible, movable property if:

(1) the device is not designed to cause, or known by the actor to create a substantial risk of causing, death or serious bodily injury; and

(2) use of the device is reasonable under all the circumstances as the actor reasonably believes them to be when he installs the device.

(Enacted by Acts 1973, 63rd Leg., ch. 399 (S.B. 34), § 1, effective January 1, 1974; am. Acts 1975,

64th Leg., ch. 342 (S.B. 127), § 6, effective September 1, 1975; am. Acts 1993, 73rd Leg., ch. 900 (S.B. 1067), § 1.01, effective September 1, 1994.)

## Secs. 9.45 to 9.50 [Reserved for expansion].

## SUBCHAPTER E
## LAW ENFORCEMENT

## Sec. 9.51.  Arrest and Search.

(a) A peace officer, or a person acting in a peace officer's presence and at his direction, is justified in using force against another when and to the degree the actor reasonably believes the force is immediately necessary to make or assist in making an arrest or search, or to prevent or assist in preventing escape after arrest, if:

(1) the actor reasonably believes the arrest or search is lawful or, if the arrest or search is made under a warrant, he reasonably believes the warrant is valid; and

(2) before using force, the actor manifests his purpose to arrest or search and identifies himself as a peace officer or as one acting at a peace officer's direction, unless he reasonably believes his purpose and identity are already known by or cannot reasonably be made known to the person to be arrested.

(b) A person other than a peace officer (or one acting at his direction) is justified in using force against another when and to the degree the actor reasonably believes the force is immediately necessary to make or assist in making a lawful arrest, or to prevent or assist in preventing escape after lawful arrest if, before using force, the actor manifests his purpose to and the reason for the arrest or reasonably believes his purpose and the reason are already known by or cannot reasonably be made known to the person to be arrested.

(c) A peace officer is justified in using deadly force against another when and to the degree the peace officer reasonably believes the deadly force is immediately necessary to make an arrest, or to prevent escape after arrest, if the use of force would have been justified under Subsection (a) and:

(1) the actor reasonably believes the conduct for which arrest is authorized included the use or attempted use of deadly force; or

(2) the actor reasonably believes there is a substantial risk that the person to be arrested will cause death or serious bodily injury to the actor or another if the arrest is delayed.

(d) A person other than a peace officer acting in a peace officer's presence and at his direction is justified in using deadly force against another when and to the degree the person reasonably believes the deadly force is immediately necessary to make a lawful arrest, or to prevent escape after a lawful arrest, if the use of force would have been justified under Subsection (b) and:

(1) the actor reasonably believes the felony or offense against the public peace for which arrest is authorized included the use or attempted use of deadly force; or

(2) the actor reasonably believes there is a substantial risk that the person to be arrested will cause death or serious bodily injury to another if the arrest is delayed.

(e) There is no duty to retreat before using deadly force justified by Subsection (c) or (d).

(f) Nothing in this section relating to the actor's manifestation of purpose or identity shall be construed as conflicting with any other law relating to the issuance, service, and execution of an arrest or search warrant either under the laws of this state or the United States.

(g) Deadly force may only be used under the circumstances enumerated in Subsections (c) and (d).

(Enacted by Acts 1973, 63rd Leg., ch. 399 (S.B. 34), § 1, effective January 1, 1974; am. Acts 1993, 73rd Leg., ch. 900 (S.B. 1067), § 1.01, effective September 1, 1994.)

## Sec. 9.52. Prevention of Escape from Custody.

The use of force to prevent the escape of an arrested person from custody is justifiable when the force could have been employed to effect the arrest under which the person is in custody, except that a guard employed by a correctional facility or a peace officer is justified in using any force, including deadly force, that he reasonably believes to be immediately necessary to prevent the escape of a person from the correctional facility.

(Enacted by Acts 1973, 63rd Leg., ch. 399 (S.B. 34), § 1, effective January 1, 1974; am. Acts 1993, 73rd Leg., ch. 900 (S.B. 1067), § 1.01, effective September 1, 1994.)

## Sec. 9.53. Maintaining Security in Correctional Facility.

An officer or employee of a correctional facility is justified in using force against a person in custody when and to the degree the officer or employee reasonably believes the force is necessary to maintain the security of the correctional facility, the safety or security of other persons in custody or employed by the correctional facility, or his own safety or security.

(Enacted by Acts 1987, 70th Leg., ch. 512 (H.B. 527), § 1, effective September 1, 1987; am. Acts 1993, 73rd Leg., ch. 900 (S.B. 1067), § 1.01, effective September 1, 1994.)

## Secs. 9.54 to 9.60 [Reserved for expansion].

## SUBCHAPTER F
## SPECIAL RELATIONSHIPS

## Sec. 9.61. Parent—Child.

(a) The use of force, but not deadly force, against a child younger than 18 years is justified:

(1) if the actor is the child's parent or stepparent or is acting in loco parentis to the child; and

(2) when and to the degree the actor reasonably believes the force is necessary to discipline the child or to safeguard or promote his welfare.

(b) For purposes of this section, "in loco parentis" includes grandparent and guardian, any person acting by, through, or under the direction of a court with jurisdiction over the child, and anyone who has express or implied consent of the parent or parents.

(Enacted by Acts 1973, 63rd Leg., ch. 399 (S.B. 34), § 1, effective January 1, 1974; am. Acts 1993, 73rd Leg., ch. 900 (S.B. 1067), § 1.01, effective September 1, 1994.)

## Sec. 9.62. Educator—Student.

The use of force, but not deadly force, against a person is justified:

(1) if the actor is entrusted with the care, supervision, or administration of the person for a special purpose; and

(2) when and to the degree the actor reasonably believes the force is necessary to further the special purpose or to maintain discipline in a group.

(Enacted by Acts 1973, 63rd Leg., ch. 399 (S.B. 34), § 1, effective January 1, 1974; am. Acts 1993, 73rd Leg., ch. 900 (S.B. 1067), § 1.01, effective September 1, 1994.)

## Sec. 9.63. Guardian—Incompetent.

The use of force, but not deadly force, against a mental incompetent is justified:

(1) if the actor is the incompetent's guardian or someone similarly responsible for the general care and supervision of the incompetent; and

(2) when and to the degree the actor reasonably believes the force is necessary:

(A) to safeguard and promote the incompetent's welfare; or

(B) if the incompetent is in an institution for his care and custody, to maintain discipline in the institution.

(Enacted by Acts 1973, 63rd Leg., ch. 399 (S.B. 34), § 1, effective January 1, 1974; am. Acts 1993, 73rd Leg., ch. 900 (S.B. 1067), § 1.01, effective September 1, 1994.)

# TITLE 3
# PUNISHMENTS

## CHAPTER 12
## PUNISHMENTS

## SUBCHAPTER A
## GENERAL PROVISIONS

### Sec. 12.01.   Punishment in Accordance with Code.

(a) A person adjudged guilty of an offense under this code shall be punished in accordance with this chapter and the Code of Criminal Procedure.

(b) Penal laws enacted after the effective date of this code shall be classified for punishment purposes in accordance with this chapter.

(c) This chapter does not deprive a court of authority conferred by law to forfeit property, dissolve a corporation, suspend or cancel a license or permit, remove a person from office, cite for contempt, or impose any other civil penalty. The civil penalty may be included in the sentence.

(Enacted by Acts 1973, 63rd Leg., ch. 399 (S.B. 34), § 1, effective January 1, 1974; am. Acts 1993, 73rd Leg., ch. 900 (S.B. 1067), § 1.01, effective September 1, 1994.)

### Sec. 12.02.   Classification of Offenses.

Offenses are designated as felonies or misdemeanors.

(Enacted by Acts 1973, 63rd Leg., ch. 399 (S.B. 34), § 1, effective January 1, 1974; am. Acts 1993, 73rd Leg., ch. 900 (S.B. 1067), § 1.01, effective September 1, 1994.)

### Sec. 12.03.   Classification of Misdemeanors.

(a) Misdemeanors are classified according to the relative seriousness of the offense into three categories:

(1) Class A misdemeanors;

(2) Class B misdemeanors;

(3) Class C misdemeanors.

(b) An offense designated a misdemeanor in

this code without specification as to punishment or category is a Class C misdemeanor.

(c) Conviction of a Class C misdemeanor does not impose any legal disability or disadvantage. (Enacted by Acts 1973, 63rd Leg., ch. 399 (S.B. 34), § 1, effective January 1, 1974; am. Acts 1993, 73rd Leg., ch. 900 (S.B. 1067), § 1.01, effective September 1, 1994.)

### Sec. 12.04. Classification of Felonies.

(a) Felonies are classified according to the relative seriousness of the offense into five categories:

(1) capital felonies;

(2) felonies of the first degree;

(3) felonies of the second degree;

(4) felonies of the third degree; and

(5) state jail felonies.

(b) An offense designated a felony in this code without specification as to category is a state jail felony.

(Enacted by Acts 1973, 63rd Leg., ch. 399 (S.B. 34), § 1, effective January 1, 1974; am. Acts 1973, 63rd Leg., ch. 426 (H.B. 200), art. 2, § 3, effective January 1, 1974; am. Acts 1993, 73rd Leg., ch. 900 (S.B. 1067), § 1.01, effective September 1, 1994.)

### Secs. 12.05 to 12.20 [Reserved for expansion].

## SUBCHAPTER B
## ORDINARY MISDEMEANOR PUNISHMENTS

### Sec. 12.21. Class A Misdemeanor.

An individual adjudged guilty of a Class A misdemeanor shall be punished by:

(1) a fine not to exceed $4,000;

(2) confinement in jail for a term not to exceed one year; or

(3) both such fine and confinement.

(Enacted by Acts 1973, 63rd Leg., ch. 399 (S.B. 34), § 1, effective January 1, 1974; am. Acts 1991, 72nd Leg., ch. 108 (H.B. 407), § 1, effective September 1, 1991; am. Acts 1993, 73rd Leg., ch. 900 (S.B. 1067), § 1.01, effective September 1, 1994.)

### Sec. 12.22. Class B Misdemeanor.

An individual adjudged guilty of a Class B misdemeanor shall be punished by:

(1) a fine not to exceed $2,000;

(2) confinement in jail for a term not to exceed 180 days; or

(3) both such fine and confinement.

(Enacted by Acts 1973, 63rd Leg., ch. 399 (S.B. 34), § 1, effective January 1, 1974; am. Acts 1991, 72nd Leg., ch. 108 (H.B. 407), § 1, effective September 1, 1991; am. Acts 1993, 73rd Leg., ch. 900 (S.B. 1067), § 1.01, effective September 1, 1994.)

### Sec. 12.23. Class C Misdemeanor.

An individual adjudged guilty of a Class C misdemeanor shall be punished by a fine not to exceed $500.

(Enacted by Acts 1973, 63rd Leg., ch. 399 (S.B. 34), § 1, effective January 1, 1974; am. Acts 1991, 72nd Leg., ch. 108 (H.B. 407), § 1, effective September 1, 1991; am. Acts 1993, 73rd Leg., ch. 900 (S.B. 1067), § 1.01, effective September 1, 1994.)

### Secs. 12.24 to 12.30 [Reserved for expansion].

## SUBCHAPTER C
## ORDINARY FELONY PUNISHMENTS

### Sec. 12.31. Capital Felony.

(a) An individual adjudged guilty of a capital felony in a case in which the state seeks the death penalty shall be punished by imprisonment in the Texas Department of Criminal Justice for life without parole or by death. An individual adjudged guilty of a capital felony in a case in which the state does not seek the death penalty shall be punished by imprisonment in the Texas Department of Criminal Justice for:

(1) life, if the individual's case was transferred to the court under Section 54.02, Family Code; or

(2) life without parole.

(b) In a capital felony trial in which the state seeks the death penalty, prospective jurors shall be informed that a sentence of life imprisonment without parole or death is mandatory on conviction of a capital felony. In a capital felony trial in which the state does not seek the death penalty, prospective jurors shall be informed that the state is not seeking the death penalty and that:

(1) a sentence of life imprisonment is mandatory on conviction of the capital felony, if the case was transferred to the court under Section 54.02, Family Code; or

(2) a sentence of life imprisonment without parole is mandatory on conviction of the capital felony.

(Enacted by Acts 1973, 63rd Leg., ch. 426 (H.B. 200), art. 2, § 2, effective January 1, 1974; am.

Acts 1991, 72nd Leg., ch. 652 (H.B. 9), § 12, effective September 1, 1991; am. Acts 1991, 72nd Leg., ch. 838 (S.B. 880), § 4, effective September 1, 1991; am. Acts 1993, 73rd Leg., ch. 900 (S.B. 1067), § 1.01, effective September 1, 1994; am. Acts 2005, 79th Leg., ch. 787 (S.B. 60), § 1, effective September 1, 2005; am. Acts 2009, 81st Leg., ch. 87 (S.B. 1969), § 25.145, effective September 1, 2009; am. Acts 2009, 81st Leg., ch. 765 (S.B. 839), § 1, effective September 1, 2009.)

## Sec. 12.32.   First Degree Felony Punishment.

(a) An individual adjudged guilty of a felony of the first degree shall be punished by imprisonment in the Texas Department of Criminal Justice for life or for any term of not more than 99 years or less than 5 years.

(b) In addition to imprisonment, an individual adjudged guilty of a felony of the first degree may be punished by a fine not to exceed $10,000. (Enacted by Acts 1973, 63rd Leg., ch. 399 (S.B. 34), § 1, effective January 1, 1974; am. Acts 1973, 63rd Leg., ch. 426 (H.B. 200), art. 2, § 2, effective January 1, 1974 (renumbered from Sec. 12.31); am. Acts 1979, 66th Leg., ch. 488 (H.B. 1117), § 1, effective September 1, 1979; am. Acts 1993, 73rd Leg., ch. 900 (S.B. 1067), § 1.01, effective September 1, 1994; am. Acts 2009, 81st Leg., ch. 87 (S.B. 1969), § 25.146, effective September 1, 2009.)

## Sec. 12.33.   Second Degree Felony Punishment.

(a) An individual adjudged guilty of a felony of the second degree shall be punished by imprisonment in the Texas Department of Criminal Justice for any term of not more than 20 years or less than 2 years.

(b) In addition to imprisonment, an individual adjudged guilty of a felony of the second degree may be punished by a fine not to exceed $10,000. (Enacted by Acts 1973, 63rd Leg., ch. 399 (S.B. 34), § 1, effective January 1, 1974; am. Acts 1973, 63rd Leg., ch. 426 (H.B. 200), art. 2, § 2, effective January 1, 1974 (renumbered from Sec. 12.32); am. Acts 1993, 73rd Leg., ch. 900 (S.B. 1067), § 1.01, effective September 1, 1994; am. Acts 2009, 81st Leg., ch. 87 (S.B. 1969), § 25.147, effective September 1, 2009.)

## Sec. 12.34.   Third Degree Felony Punishment.

(a) An individual adjudged guilty of a felony of the third degree shall be punished by imprison-ment in the Texas Department of Criminal Justice for any term of not more than 10 years or less than 2 years.

(b) In addition to imprisonment, an individual adjudged guilty of a felony of the third degree may be punished by a fine not to exceed $10,000. (Enacted by Acts 1973, 63rd Leg., ch. 399 (S.B. 34), § 1, effective January 1, 1974; am. Acts 1973, 63rd Leg., ch. 426 (H.B. 200), art. 2, § 2, effective January 1, 1974 (renumbered from Sec. 12.33); am. Acts 1989, 71st Leg., ch. 785 (H.B. 2335), § 4.01, effective September 1, 1989; am. Acts 1990, 71st Leg., 6th C.S., ch. 25 (S.B. 41), § 7, effective June 18, 1990; am. Acts 1993, 73rd Leg., ch. 900 (S.B. 1067), § 1.01, effective September 1, 1994; am. Acts 2009, 81st Leg., ch. 87 (S.B. 1969), § 25.148, effective September 1, 2009.)

## Sec. 12.35.   State Jail Felony Punishment.

(a) Except as provided by Subsection (c), an individual adjudged guilty of a state jail felony shall be punished by confinement in a state jail for any term of not more than two years or less than 180 days.

(b) In addition to confinement, an individual adjudged guilty of a state jail felony may be punished by a fine not to exceed $10,000.

(c) An individual adjudged guilty of a state jail felony shall be punished for a third degree felony if it is shown on the trial of the offense that:

(1) a deadly weapon as defined by Section 1.07 was used or exhibited during the commission of the offense or during immediate flight following the commission of the offense, and that the individual used or exhibited the deadly weapon or was a party to the offense and knew that a deadly weapon would be used or exhibited; or

(2) the individual has previously been finally convicted of any felony:

(A) under Section 20A.03 or 21.02 or listed in Section 3g(a)(1), Article 42.12, Code of Criminal Procedure; or

(B) for which the judgment contains an affirmative finding under Section 3g(a)(2), Article 42.12, Code of Criminal Procedure. (Enacted by Acts 1993, 73rd Leg., ch. 900 (S.B. 1067), § 1.01, effective September 1, 1994; am. Acts 2007, 80th Leg., ch. 593 (H.B. 8), § 3.48, effective September 1, 2007; am. Acts 2011, 82nd Leg., ch. 122 (H.B. 3000), § 13, effective September 1, 2011.)

**Secs. 12.36 to 12.40 [Reserved for expansion].**

## SUBCHAPTER D
## EXCEPTIONAL SENTENCES

### Sec. 12.41.  Classification of Offenses Outside This Code.

For purposes of this subchapter, any conviction not obtained from a prosecution under this code shall be classified as follows:

(1) "felony of the third degree" if imprisonment in the Texas Department of Criminal Justice or another penitentiary is affixed to the offense as a possible punishment;

(2) "Class B misdemeanor" if the offense is not a felony and confinement in a jail is affixed to the offense as a possible punishment;

(3) "Class C misdemeanor" if the offense is punishable by fine only.

(Enacted by Acts 1973, 63rd Leg., ch. 399 (S.B. 34), § 1, effective January 1, 1974; am. Acts 1993, 73rd Leg., ch. 900 (S.B. 1067), § 1.01, effective September 1, 1994; am. Acts 2009, 81st Leg., ch. 87 (S.B. 1969), § 25.149, effective September 1, 2009.)

### Sec. 12.42.  Penalties for Repeat and Habitual Felony Offenders on Trial for First, Second, or Third Degree Felony.

(a) Except as provided by Subsection (c)(2), if it is shown on the trial of a felony of the third degree that the defendant has previously been finally convicted of a felony other than a state jail felony punishable under Section 12.35(a), on conviction the defendant shall be punished for a felony of the second degree.

(b) Except as provided by Subsection (c)(2) or (c)(4), if it is shown on the trial of a felony of the second degree that the defendant has previously been finally convicted of a felony other than a state jail felony punishable under Section 12.35(a), on conviction the defendant shall be punished for a felony of the first degree.

(c) (1) If it is shown on the trial of a felony of the first degree that the defendant has previously been finally convicted of a felony other than a state jail felony punishable under Section 12.35(a), on conviction the defendant shall be punished by imprisonment in the Texas Department of Criminal Justice for life, or for any term of not more than 99 years or less than 15 years. In addition to imprisonment, an individual may be punished by a fine not to exceed $10,000.

(2) Notwithstanding Subdivision (1), a defendant shall be punished by imprisonment in the Texas Department of Criminal Justice for life if:

(A) the defendant is convicted of an offense:

(i) under Section 20A.02(a)(7) or (8), 21.11(a)(1), 22.021, or 22.011, Penal Code;

(ii) under Section 20.04(a)(4), Penal Code, if the defendant committed the offense with the intent to violate or abuse the victim sexually; or

(iii) under Section 30.02, Penal Code, punishable under Subsection (d) of that section, if the defendant committed the offense with the intent to commit a felony described by Subparagraph (i) or (ii) or a felony under Section 21.11, Penal Code; and

(B) the defendant has been previously convicted of an offense:

(i) under Section 43.25 or 43.26, Penal Code, or an offense under Section 43.23, Penal Code, punishable under Subsection (h) of that section;

(ii) under Section 20A.02(a)(7) or (8), 21.02, 21.11, 22.011, 22.021, or 25.02, Penal Code;

(iii) under Section 20.04(a)(4), Penal Code, if the defendant committed the offense with the intent to violate or abuse the victim sexually;

(iv) under Section 30.02, Penal Code, punishable under Subsection (d) of that section, if the defendant committed the offense with the intent to commit a felony described by Subparagraph (ii) or (iii); or

(v) under the laws of another state containing elements that are substantially similar to the elements of an offense listed in Subparagraph (i), (ii), (iii), or (iv).

(3) Notwithstanding Subdivision (1) or (2), a defendant shall be punished for a capital felony if it is shown on the trial of an offense under Section 22.021 otherwise punishable under Subsection (f) of that section that the defendant has previously been finally convicted of:

(A) an offense under Section 22.021 that was committed against a victim described by Section 22.021(f)(1) or was committed against a victim described by Section 22.021(f)(2) and in a manner described by Section 22.021(a)(2)(A); or

(B) an offense that was committed under the laws of another state that:

(i) contains elements that are substantially similar to the elements of an offense under Section 22.021; and

(ii) was committed against a victim described by Section 22.021(f)(1) or was committed against a victim described by Section 22.021(f)(2) and in a manner substantially similar to a manner described by Section 22.021(a)(2)(A).

(4) Notwithstanding Subdivision (1) or (2), a defendant shall be punished by imprisonment in the Texas Department of Criminal Justice for life without parole if it is shown on the trial of an offense under Section 21.02 or 22.021 that the defendant has previously been finally convicted of:

(A) an offense under Section 20A.03 or 21.02 or 22.021; or

(B) an offense that was committed under the laws of another state and that contains elements that are substantially similar to the elements of an offense under 20A.03 or Section 21.02 or 22.021.

(5) A previous conviction for a state jail felony punishable under Section 12.35(a) may not be used for enhancement purposes under Subdivision (2).

(d) Except as provided by Subsection (c)(2) or (c)(4), if it is shown on the trial of a felony offense other than a state jail felony punishable under Section 12.35(a) that the defendant has previously been finally convicted of two felony offenses, and the second previous felony conviction is for an offense that occurred subsequent to the first previous conviction having become final, on conviction the defendant shall be punished by imprisonment in the Texas Department of Criminal Justice for life, or for any term of not more than 99 years or less than 25 years. A previous conviction for a state jail felony punishable under Section 12.35(a) may not be used for enhancement purposes under this subsection.

(e) [Repealed by Acts 2011, 82nd Leg., ch. 834 (H.B. 3384), § 6, effective September 1, 2011.]

(f) For the purposes of Subsections (a), (b), (c)(1), and (e), an adjudication by a juvenile court under Section 54.03, Family Code, that a child engaged in delinquent conduct on or after January 1, 1996, constituting a felony offense for which the child is committed to the Texas Youth Commission under Section 54.04(d)(2), (d)(3), or (m), Family Code, or Section 54.05(f), Family Code, is a final felony conviction.

(g) For the purposes of Subsection (c)(2):

(1) a defendant has been previously convicted of an offense listed under Subsection (c)(2)(B) if the defendant was adjudged guilty of the offense or entered a plea of guilty or nolo contendere in return for a grant of deferred adjudication, regardless of whether the sentence for the offense was ever imposed or whether the sentence was probated and the defendant was subsequently discharged from community supervision; and

(2) a conviction under the laws of another state for an offense containing elements that are substantially similar to the elements of an offense listed under Subsection (c)(2)(B) is a conviction of an offense listed under Subsection (c)(2)(B).

(Enacted by Acts 1973, 63rd Leg., ch. 399 (S.B. 34), § 1, effective January 1, 1974; am. Acts 1983, 68th Leg., ch. 339 (H.B. 1048), § 1, effective September 1, 1983; am. Acts 1985, 69th Leg., ch. 582 (S.B. 574), § 1, effective September 1, 1985; am. Acts 1993, 73rd Leg., ch. 900 (S.B. 1067), § 1.01, effective September 1, 1994; am. Acts 1995, 74th Leg., ch. 250 (S.B. 45), § 1, effective September 1, 1995; am. Acts 1995, 74th Leg., ch. 262 (H.B. 327), § 78, effective January 1, 1996; am. Acts 1995, 74th Leg., ch. 318 (S.B. 15), § 1, effective January 1, 1996; am. Acts 1997, 75th Leg., ch. 665 (S.B. 46), §§ 1, 2, effective September 1, 1997; am. Acts 1997, 75th Leg., ch. 667 (S.B. 381), § 4, effective September 1, 1997; am. Acts 1999, 76th Leg., ch. 62 (S.B. 1368), § 15.01, effective September 1, 1999; am. Acts 2003, 78th Leg., ch. 283 (H.B. 2319), § 53, effective September 1, 2003; am. Acts 2003, 78th Leg., ch. 1005 (H.B. 236), § 2, effective September 1, 2003; am. Acts 2007, 80th Leg., ch. 340 (S.B. 75), §§ 1-4, effective September 1, 2007; am. Acts 2007, 80th Leg., ch. 593 (H.B. 8), §§ 1.14-1.16, effective September 1, 2007; am. Acts 2009, 81st Leg., ch. 87 (S.B. 1969), § 25.150, effective September 1, 2009; am. Acts 2011, 82nd Leg., ch. 1 (S.B. 24), § 6.02, effective September 1, 2011; am. Acts 2011, 82nd Leg., ch. 122 (H.B. 3000), § 14, effective September 1, 2011; am. Acts 2011, 82nd Leg., ch. 834 (H.B. 3384), §§ 1—4, 6, effective September 1, 2011; am. Acts 2011, 82nd Leg., ch. 1119 (H.B. 3), §§ 3, 4, effective September 1, 2011.)

## Sec. 12.422.  Imposition of Substance Abuse Felony Punishment [Deleted].

Deleted by Acts 1993, 73rd Leg., ch. 900 (S.B. 1067), § 1.01, effective September 1, 1993. (Enacted by Acts 1991, 72nd Leg., 2nd C.S., ch. 10 (H.B. 93), § 19.01, effective October 1, 1992.)

### Sec. 12.425. Penalties for Repeat and Habitual Felony Offenders on Trial for State Jail Felony.

(a) If it is shown on the trial of a state jail felony punishable under Section 12.35(a) that the defendant has previously been finally convicted of two state jail felonies punishable under Section 12.35(a), on conviction the defendant shall be punished for a felony of the third degree.

(b) If it is shown on the trial of a state jail felony punishable under Section 12.35(a) that the defendant has previously been finally convicted of two felonies other than a state jail felony punishable under Section 12.35(a), and the second previous felony conviction is for an offense that occurred subsequent to the first previous conviction having become final, on conviction the defendant shall be punished for a felony of the second degree.

(c) If it is shown on the trial of a state jail felony for which punishment may be enhanced under Section 12.35(c) that the defendant has previously been finally convicted of a felony other than a state jail felony punishable under Section 12.35(a), on conviction the defendant shall be punished for a felony of the second degree.

(Enacted by Acts 2011, 82nd Leg., ch. 834 (H.B. 3384), § 5, effective September 1, 2011.)

### Sec. 12.43. Penalties for Repeat and Habitual Misdemeanor Offenders.

(a) If it is shown on the trial of a Class A misdemeanor that the defendant has been before convicted of a Class A misdemeanor or any degree of felony, on conviction he shall be punished by:

(1) a fine not to exceed $4,000;

(2) confinement in jail for any term of not more than one year or less than 90 days; or

(3) both such fine and confinement.

(b) If it is shown on the trial of a Class B misdemeanor that the defendant has been before convicted of a Class A or Class B misdemeanor or any degree of felony, on conviction he shall be punished by:

(1) a fine not to exceed $2,000;

(2) confinement in jail for any term of not more than 180 days or less than 30 days; or

(3) both such fine and confinement.

(c) If it is shown on the trial of an offense punishable as a Class C misdemeanor under Section 42.01 or 49.02 that the defendant has been before convicted under either of those sections three times or three times for any combination of those offenses and each prior offense was committed in the 24 months preceding the date of commission of the instant offense, the defendant shall be punished by:

(1) a fine not to exceed $2,000;

(2) confinement in jail for a term not to exceed 180 days; or

(3) both such fine and confinement.

(d) If the punishment scheme for an offense contains a specific enhancement provision increasing punishment for a defendant who has previously been convicted of the offense, the specific enhancement provision controls over this section.

(Enacted by Acts 1973, 63rd Leg., ch. 399 (S.B. 34), § 1, effective January 1, 1974; am. Acts 1993, 73rd Leg., ch. 900 (S.B. 1067), § 1.01, effective September 1, 1994; am. Acts 1995, 74th Leg., ch. 318 (S.B. 15), § 2, effective September 1, 1995; am. Acts 1999, 76th Leg., ch. 564 (S.B. 430), § 1, effective September 1, 1999.)

### Sec. 12.44. Reduction of State Jail Felony Punishment to Misdemeanor Punishment.

(a) A court may punish a defendant who is convicted of a state jail felony by imposing the confinement permissible as punishment for a Class A misdemeanor if, after considering the gravity and circumstances of the felony committed and the history, character, and rehabilitative needs of the defendant, the court finds that such punishment would best serve the ends of justice.

(b) At the request of the prosecuting attorney, the court may authorize the prosecuting attorney to prosecute a state jail felony as a Class A misdemeanor.

(Enacted by Acts 1973, 63rd Leg., ch. 399 (S.B. 34), § 1, effective January 1, 1974; am. Acts 1989, 71st Leg., ch. 785 (H.B. 2335), § 4.02, effective September 1, 1989; am. Acts 1993, 73rd Leg., ch. 900 (S.B. 1067), § 1.01, effective September 1, 1994; am. Acts 1995, 74th Leg., ch. 318 (S.B. 15), § 3, effective September 1, 1995; am. Acts 2005, 79th Leg., ch. 1276 (H.B. 2296), § 1, effective September 1, 2005.)

### Sec. 12.45. Admission of Unadjudicated Offense.

(a) A person may, with the consent of the attorney for the state, admit during the sentencing hearing his guilt of one or more unadjudicated offenses and request the court to take each into account in determining sentence for the offense or offenses of which he stands adjudged guilty.

(b) Before a court may take into account an admitted offense over which exclusive venue lies in another county or district, the court must obtain permission from the prosecuting attorney with jurisdiction over the offense.

(c) If a court lawfully takes into account an admitted offense, prosecution is barred for that offense.

(Enacted by Acts 1973, 63rd Leg., ch. 399 (S.B. 34), § 1, effective January 1, 1974; am. Acts 1983, 68th Leg., ch. 649 (S.B. 1137), § 1, effective August 29, 1983; am. Acts 1993, 73rd Leg., ch. 900 (S.B. 1067), § 1.01, effective September 1, 1994.)

### Sec. 12.46.  Use of Prior Convictions.

The use of a conviction for enhancement purposes shall not preclude the subsequent use of such conviction for enhancement purposes.

(Enacted by Acts 1979, 66th Leg., ch. 459 (H.B. 671), § 1, effective June 7, 1979; am. Acts 1993, 73rd Leg., ch. 900 (S.B. 1067), § 1.01, effective September 1, 1994.)

### Sec. 12.47.  Penalty If Offense Committed Because of Bias or Prejudice.

(a) If an affirmative finding under Article 42.014, Code of Criminal Procedure, is made in the trial of an offense other than a first degree felony or a Class A misdemeanor, the punishment for the offense is increased to the punishment prescribed for the next highest category of offense. If the offense is a Class A misdemeanor, the minimum term of confinement for the offense is increased to 180 days. This section does not apply to the trial of an offense of injury to a disabled individual under Section 22.04, if the affirmative finding in the case under Article 42.014, Code of Criminal Procedure, shows that the defendant intentionally selected the victim because the victim was disabled.

(b) The attorney general, if requested to do so by a prosecuting attorney, may assist the prosecuting attorney in the investigation or prosecution of an offense committed because of bias or prejudice. The attorney general shall designate one individual in the division of the attorney general's office that assists in the prosecution of criminal cases to coordinate responses to requests made under this subsection.

(Enacted by Acts 1993, 73rd Leg., ch. 987 (S.B. 456), § 1, effective September 1, 1993; am. Acts 1997, 75th Leg., ch. 751 (H.B. 1333), § 1, effective September 1, 1997; am. Acts 2001, 77th Leg., ch.

85 (H.B. 587), § 1.01, effective September 1, 2001.)

### Sec. 12.48.  Certain Offenses Resulting in Loss to Nursing and Convalescent Homes.

If it is shown on the trial of an offense under Chapter 31 or 32 that, as a result of a loss incurred because of the conduct charged, a trustee was appointed and emergency assistance funds, other than funds used to pay the expenses of the trustee, were used for a nursing or convalescent home under Subchapter D, Chapter 242, Health and Safety Code, the punishment for the offense is increased to the punishment prescribed for the next higher category of offense except that a felony of the first degree is punished as a felony of the first degree.

(Enacted by Acts 1999, 76th Leg., ch. 439 (S.B. 1197), § 4, effective September 1, 1999.)

### Sec. 12.49.  Penalty If Controlled Substance Used to Commit Offense.

If the court makes an affirmative finding under Article 42.012, Code of Criminal Procedure, in the punishment phase of the trial of an offense under Chapter 29, Chapter 31, or Title 5, other than a first degree felony or a Class A misdemeanor, the punishment for the offense is increased to the punishment prescribed for the next highest category of offense. If the offense is a Class A misdemeanor, the minimum term of confinement for the offense is increased to 180 days.

(Enacted by Acts 1999, 76th Leg., ch. 417 (S.B. 1100), § 2(a), effective September 1, 1999; am. Acts 2001, 77th Leg., ch. 1420 (H.B. 2812), §§ 21.001(93), 21.002(15), effective September 1, 2001 (renumbered from Sec. 12.48).)

### Sec. 12.50.  Penalty If Offense Committed in Disaster Area or Evacuated Area.

(a) Subject to Subsection (c), the punishment for an offense described by Subsection (b) is increased to the punishment prescribed for the next higher category of offense if it is shown on the trial of the offense that the offense was committed in an area that was, at the time of the offense:

(1) subject to a declaration of a state of disaster made by:

(A) the president of the United States under the Robert T. Stafford Disaster Relief and Emergency Assistance Act (42 U.S.C. Section 5121 et seq.);

(B) the governor under Section 418.014, Government Code; or

(C) the presiding officer of the governing body of a political subdivision under Section 418.108, Government Code; or

(2) subject to an emergency evacuation order.

(b) The increase in punishment authorized by this section applies only to an offense under:

(1) Section 22.01;

(2) Section 29.02;

(3) Section 30.02; and

(4) Section 31.03.

(c) If an offense listed under Subsection (b)(1) or (4) is punishable as a Class A misdemeanor, the minimum term of confinement for the offense is increased to 180 days. If an offense listed under Subsection (b)(3) or (4) is punishable as a felony of the first degree, the punishment for that offense may not be increased under this section.

(d) It is a defense to a charge under Subsection (b)(4) that the conduct in question meets the elements of necessity outlined in Section 9.22.

(e) For purposes of this section, "emergency evacuation order" means an official statement issued by the governing body of this state or a political subdivision of this state to recommend or require the evacuation of all or part of the population of an area stricken or threatened with a disaster.

(Enacted by Acts 2009, 81st Leg., ch. 731 (S.B. 359), § 1, effective September 1, 2009.)

## SUBCHAPTER E
## CORPORATIONS AND ASSOCIATIONS

## Sec. 12.51. Authorized Punishments for Corporations and Associations.

(a) If a corporation or association is adjudged guilty of an offense that provides a penalty consisting of a fine only, a court may sentence the corporation or association to pay a fine in an amount fixed by the court, not to exceed the fine provided by the offense.

(b) If a corporation or association is adjudged guilty of an offense that provides a penalty including imprisonment, or that provides no specific penalty, a court may sentence the corporation or association to pay a fine in an amount fixed by the court, not to exceed:

(1) $20,000 if the offense is a felony of any category;

(2) $10,000 if the offense is a Class A or Class B misdemeanor;

(3) $2,000 if the offense is a Class C misdemeanor; or

(4) $50,000 if, as a result of an offense classified as a felony or Class A misdemeanor, an individual suffers serious bodily injury or death.

(c) In lieu of the fines authorized by Subsections (a), (b)(1), (b)(2), and (b)(4), if a court finds that the corporation or association gained money or property or caused personal injury or death, property damage, or other loss through the commission of a felony or Class A or Class B misdemeanor, the court may sentence the corporation or association to pay a fine in an amount fixed by the court, not to exceed double the amount gained or caused by the corporation or association to be lost or damaged, whichever is greater.

(d) In addition to any sentence that may be imposed by this section, a corporation or association that has been adjudged guilty of an offense may be ordered by the court to give notice of the conviction to any person the court deems appropriate.

(e) On conviction of a corporation or association, the court shall notify the attorney general of that fact.

(Enacted by Acts 1973, 63rd Leg., ch. 399 (S.B. 34), § 1, effective January 1, 1974; am. Acts 1977, 65th Leg., ch. 768 (S.B. 787), § 1, effective June 16, 1977; am. Acts 1987, 70th Leg., ch. 1085 (S.B. 1277), § 1, effective September 1, 1987; am. Acts 1993, 73rd Leg., ch. 900 (S.B. 1067), § 1.01, effective September 1, 1994.)

# TITLE 4
# INCHOATE OFFENSES

## CHAPTER 15
## PREPARATORY OFFENSES

**Section**

## Sec. 15.01.   Criminal Attempt.

(a) A person commits an offense if, with specific intent to commit an offense, he does an act amounting to more than mere preparation that tends but fails to effect the commission of the offense intended.

(b) If a person attempts an offense that may be aggravated, his conduct constitutes an attempt to commit the aggravated offense if an element that aggravates the offense accompanies the attempt.

(c) It is no defense to prosecution for criminal attempt that the offense attempted was actually committed.

(d) An offense under this section is one category lower than the offense attempted, and if the offense attempted is a state jail felony, the offense is a Class A misdemeanor.

(Enacted by Acts 1973, 63rd Leg., ch. 399 (S.B. 34), § 1, effective January 1, 1974; am. Acts 1975, 64th Leg., ch. 203 (H.B. 284), § 4, effective September 1, 1975; am. Acts 1993, 73rd Leg., ch. 900 (S.B. 1067), § 1.01, effective September 1, 1994.)

## Sec. 15.02.   Criminal Conspiracy. (14)

(a) A person commits criminal conspiracy if, with intent that a felony be committed:

(1) he agrees with one or more persons that they or one or more of them engage in conduct that would constitute the offense; and

(2) he or one or more of them performs an overt act in pursuance of the agreement.

(b) An agreement constituting a conspiracy may be inferred from acts of the parties.

(c) It is no defense to prosecution for criminal conspiracy that:

(1) one or more of the coconspirators is not criminally responsible for the object offense;

(2) one or more of the coconspirators has been acquitted, so long as two or more coconspirators have not been acquitted;

(3) one or more of the coconspirators has not been prosecuted or convicted, has been convicted of a different offense, or is immune from prosecution;

(4) the actor belongs to a class of persons that by definition of the object offense is legally incapable of committing the object offense in an individual capacity; or

(5) the object offense was actually committed.

(d) An offense under this section is one category lower than the most serious felony that is the object of the conspiracy, and if the most serious felony that is the object of the conspiracy is a state jail felony, the offense is a Class A misdemeanor.

(Enacted by Acts 1973, 63rd Leg., ch. 399 (S.B. 34), § 1, effective January 1, 1974; am. Acts 1993, 73rd Leg., ch. 900 (S.B. 1067), § 1.01, effective September 1, 1994.)

## Sec. 15.03.   Criminal Solicitation.

(a) A person commits an offense if, with intent that a capital felony or felony of the first degree be committed, he requests, commands, or attempts to induce another to engage in specific conduct that, under the circumstances surrounding his conduct as the actor believes them to be, would constitute the felony or make the other a party to its commission.

(b) A person may not be convicted under this section on the uncorroborated testimony of the person allegedly solicited and unless the solicitation is made under circumstances strongly corroborative of both the solicitation itself and the actor's intent that the other person act on the solicitation.

(c) It is no defense to prosecution under this section that:

(1) the person solicited is not criminally responsible for the felony solicited;

(2) the person solicited has been acquitted, has not been prosecuted or convicted, has been convicted of a different offense or of a different type or class of offense, or is immune from prosecution;

(3) the actor belongs to a class of persons that by definition of the felony solicited is legally incapable of committing the offense in an individual capacity; or

(4) the felony solicited was actually committed.

(d) An offense under this section is:

(1) a felony of the first degree if the offense solicited is a capital offense; or

(2) a felony of the second degree if the offense solicited is a felony of the first degree.

(Enacted by Acts 1973, 63rd Leg., ch. 399 (S.B. 34), § 1, effective January 1, 1974; am. Acts 1993, 73rd Leg., ch. 462 (H.B. 24), § 1, effective September 1, 1993; am. Acts 1993, 73rd Leg., ch. 900 (S.B. 1067), § 1.01, effective September 1, 1994.)

## Sec. 15.031. Criminal Solicitation of a Minor.

(a) A person commits an offense if, with intent that an offense listed by Section 3g(a)(1), Article 42.12, Code of Criminal Procedure, be committed, the person requests, commands, or attempts to induce a minor to engage in specific conduct that, under the circumstances surrounding the actor's conduct as the actor believes them to be, would constitute an offense listed by Section 3g(a)(1), Article 42.12, or make the minor a party to the commission of an offense listed by Section 3g(a)(1), Article 42.12.

(b) A person commits an offense if, with intent that an offense under Section 20A.02(a)(7) or (8), 21.02, 21.11, 22.011, 22.021, 43.02, 43.05(a)(2), or 43.25 be committed, the person by any means requests, commands, or attempts to induce a minor or another whom the person believes to be a minor to engage in specific conduct that, under the circumstances surrounding the actor's conduct as the actor believes them to be, would constitute an offense under one of those sections or would make the minor or other believed by the person to be a minor a party to the commission of an offense under one of those sections.

(c) A person may not be convicted under this section on the uncorroborated testimony of the minor allegedly solicited unless the solicitation is made under circumstances strongly corroborative of both the solicitation itself and the actor's intent that the minor act on the solicitation.

(d) It is no defense to prosecution under this section that:

(1) the minor solicited is not criminally responsible for the offense solicited;

(2) the minor solicited has been acquitted, has not been prosecuted or convicted, has been convicted of a different offense or of a different type or class of offense, or is immune from prosecution;

(3) the actor belongs to a class of persons that by definition of the offense solicited is legally incapable of committing the offense in an individual capacity; or

(4) the offense solicited was actually committed.

(e) An offense under this section is one category lower than the solicited offense, except that an offense under this section is the same category as the solicited offense if it is shown on the trial of the offense that the actor:

(1) was at the time of the offense 17 years of age or older and a member of a criminal street gang, as defined by Section 71.01; and

(2) committed the offense with the intent to:

(A) further the criminal activities of the criminal street gang; or

(B) avoid detection as a member of a criminal street gang.

(f) In this section, "minor" means an individual younger than 17 years of age.

(Enacted by Acts 1995, 74th Leg., ch. 262 (H.B. 327), § 79, effective January 1, 1996; am. Acts 1999, 76th Leg., ch. 1415 (H.B. 2145), § 22(a), effective September 1, 1999; am. Acts 2007, 80th Leg., ch. 593 (H.B. 8), § 3.49, effective September 1, 2007; am. Acts 2009, 81st Leg., ch. 1130 (H.B. 2086), § 2, effective September 1, 2009; am. Acts 2011, 82nd Leg., ch. 1 (S.B. 24), § 6.03, effective September 1, 2011.)

## Sec. 15.04. Renunciation Defense.

(a) It is an affirmative defense to prosecution under Section 15.01 that under circumstances manifesting a voluntary and complete renunciation of his criminal objective the actor avoided commission of the offense attempted by abandoning his criminal conduct or, if abandonment was insufficient to avoid commission of the offense, by taking further affirmative action that prevented the commission.

(b) It is an affirmative defense to prosecution under Section 15.02 or 15.03 that under circumstances manifesting a voluntary and complete renunciation of his criminal objective the actor countermanded his solicitation or withdrew from the conspiracy before commission of the object offense and took further affirmative action that prevented the commission of the object offense.

(c) Renunciation is not voluntary if it is motivated in whole or in part:

(1) by circumstances not present or apparent at the inception of the actor's course of conduct that increase the probability of detection or

apprehension or that make more difficult the accomplishment of the objective; or

(2) by a decision to postpone the criminal conduct until another time or to transfer the criminal act to another but similar objective or victim.

(d) Evidence that the defendant renounced his criminal objective by abandoning his criminal conduct, countermanding his solicitation, or withdrawing from the conspiracy before the criminal offense was committed and made substantial effort to prevent the commission of the object offense shall be admissible as mitigation at the hearing on punishment if he has been found guilty of criminal attempt, criminal solicitation, or criminal conspiracy; and in the event of a finding of renunciation under this subsection, the punishment shall be one grade lower than that provided for the offense committed.
(Enacted by Acts 1973, 63rd Leg., ch. 399 (S.B. 34), § 1, effective January 1, 1974; am. Acts 1993, 73rd Leg., ch. 900 (S.B. 1067), § 1.01, effective September 1, 1994.)

### Sec. 15.05.  No Offense.

Attempt or conspiracy to commit, or solicitation of, a preparatory offense defined in this chapter is not an offense.
(Enacted by Acts 1973, 63rd Leg., ch. 399 (S.B. 34), § 1, effective January 1, 1974; am. Acts 1993, 73rd Leg., ch. 900 (S.B. 1067), § 1.01, effective September 1, 1994.)

## CHAPTER 16
## CRIMINAL INSTRUMENTS, INTERCEPTION OF WIRE OR ORAL COMMUNICATION, AND INSTALLATION OF TRACKING DEVICE

### Sec. 16.01.  Unlawful Use of Criminal Instrument or Mechanical Security Device.

(a) A person commits an offense if:

(1) the person possesses a criminal instrument or mechanical security device with the intent to use the instrument or device in the commission of an offense; or

(2) with knowledge of its character and with the intent to use a criminal instrument or mechanical security device or aid or permit another to use the instrument or device in the commission of an offense, the person manufactures, adapts, sells, installs, or sets up the instrument or device.

(b) For the purpose of this section:

(1) "Criminal instrument" means anything, the possession, manufacture, or sale of which is not otherwise an offense, that is specially designed, made, or adapted for use in the commission of an offense.

(2) "Mechanical security device" means a device designed or manufactured for use by a locksmith to perform services for a customer who seeks entry to a structure, motor vehicle, or other property.

(c) An offense under Subsection (a)(1) is one category lower than the offense intended. An offense under Subsection (a)(2) is a state jail felony.
(Enacted by Acts 1973, 63rd Leg., ch. 399 (S.B. 34), § 1, effective January 1, 1974; am. Acts 1975, 64th Leg., ch. 342 (S.B. 127), § 7, effective September 1, 1975; am. Acts 1993, 73rd Leg., ch. 900 (S.B. 1067), § 1.01, effective September 1, 1994; am. Acts 2011, 82nd Leg., ch. 814 (H.B. 2577), § 1, effective September 1, 2011.)

### Sec. 16.02.  Unlawful Interception, Use, or Disclosure of Wire, Oral, or Electronic Communications.

(a) In this section, "computer trespasser," "covert entry," "communication common carrier," "contents," "electronic communication," "electronic, mechanical, or other device," "immediate life-threatening situation," "intercept," "investigative or law enforcement officer," "member of a law enforcement unit specially trained to respond to and deal with life-threatening situations," "oral communication," "protected computer," "readily accessible to the general public," and "wire communication" have the meanings given those terms in Article 18.20, Code of Criminal Procedure.

(b) A person commits an offense if the person:

(1) intentionally intercepts, endeavors to intercept, or procures another person to intercept or endeavor to intercept a wire, oral, or electronic communication;

(2) intentionally discloses or endeavors to disclose to another person the contents of a wire, oral, or electronic communication if the person knows or has reason to know the information was obtained through the interception of a wire, oral, or electronic communication in violation of this subsection;

(3) intentionally uses or endeavors to use the contents of a wire, oral, or electronic communication if the person knows or is reckless about whether the information was obtained through the interception of a wire, oral, or electronic communication in violation of this subsection;

(4) knowingly or intentionally effects a covert entry for the purpose of intercepting wire, oral, or electronic communications without court order or authorization; or

(5) intentionally uses, endeavors to use, or procures any other person to use or endeavor to use any electronic, mechanical, or other device to intercept any oral communication when the device:

(A) is affixed to, or otherwise transmits a signal through a wire, cable, or other connection used in wire communications; or

(B) transmits communications by radio or interferes with the transmission of communications by radio.

(c) It is an affirmative defense to prosecution under Subsection (b) that:

(1) an operator of a switchboard or an officer, employee, or agent of a communication common carrier whose facilities are used in the transmission of a wire or electronic communication intercepts a communication or discloses or uses an intercepted communication in the normal course of employment while engaged in an activity that is a necessary incident to the rendition of service or to the protection of the rights or property of the carrier of the communication, unless the interception results from the communication common carrier's use of service observing or random monitoring for purposes other than mechanical or service quality control checks;

(2) an officer, employee, or agent of a communication common carrier provides information, facilities, or technical assistance to an investigative or law enforcement officer who is authorized as provided by this section to intercept a wire, oral, or electronic communication;

(3) a person acting under color of law intercepts:

(A) a wire, oral, or electronic communication, if the person is a party to the communication or if one of the parties to the communication has given prior consent to the interception;

(B) a wire, oral, or electronic communication, if the person is acting under the authority of Article 18.20, Code of Criminal Procedure; or

(C) a wire or electronic communication made by a computer trespasser and transmitted to, through, or from a protected computer, if:

(i) the interception did not acquire a communication other than one transmitted to or from the computer trespasser;

(ii) the owner of the protected computer consented to the interception of the computer trespasser's communications on the protected computer; and

(iii) actor was lawfully engaged in an ongoing criminal investigation and the actor had reasonable suspicion to believe that the contents of the computer trespasser's communications likely to be obtained would be material to the investigation;

(4) a person not acting under color of law intercepts a wire, oral, or electronic communication, if:

(A) the person is a party to the communication; or

(B) one of the parties to the communication has given prior consent to the interception, unless the communication is intercepted for the purpose of committing an unlawful act;

(5) a person acting under color of law intercepts a wire, oral, or electronic communication if:

(A) oral or written consent for the interception is given by a magistrate before the interception;

(B) an immediate life-threatening situation exists;

(C) the person is a member of a law enforcement unit specially trained to:

(i) respond to and deal with life-threatening situations; or

(ii) install electronic, mechanical, or other devices; and

(D) the interception ceases immediately on termination of the life-threatening situation;

(6) an officer, employee, or agent of the Federal Communications Commission intercepts a

Penal Code

communication transmitted by radio or discloses or uses an intercepted communication in the normal course of employment and in the discharge of the monitoring responsibilities exercised by the Federal Communications Commission in the enforcement of Chapter 5, Title 47, United States Code;

(7) a person intercepts or obtains access to an electronic communication that was made through an electronic communication system that is configured to permit the communication to be readily accessible to the general public;

(8) a person intercepts radio communication, other than a cordless telephone communication that is transmitted between a cordless telephone handset and a base unit, that is transmitted:

(A) by a station for the use of the general public;

(B) to ships, aircraft, vehicles, or persons in distress;

(C) by a governmental, law enforcement, civil defense, private land mobile, or public safety communications system that is readily accessible to the general public, unless the radio communication is transmitted by a law enforcement representative to or from a mobile data terminal;

(D) by a station operating on an authorized frequency within the bands allocated to the amateur, citizens band, or general mobile radio services; or

(E) by a marine or aeronautical communications system;

(9) a person intercepts a wire or electronic communication the transmission of which causes harmful interference to a lawfully operating station or consumer electronic equipment, to the extent necessary to identify the source of the interference;

(10) a user of the same frequency intercepts a radio communication made through a system that uses frequencies monitored by individuals engaged in the provision or the use of the system, if the communication is not scrambled or encrypted; or

(11) a provider of electronic communications service records the fact that a wire or electronic communication was initiated or completed in order to protect the provider, another provider furnishing service towards the completion of the communication, or a user of that service from fraudulent, unlawful, or abusive use of the service.

(d) A person commits an offense if the person:

(1) intentionally manufactures, assembles, possesses, or sells an electronic, mechanical, or other device knowing or having reason to know that the device is designed primarily for nonconsensual interception of wire, electronic, or oral communications and that the device or a component of the device has been or will be used for an unlawful purpose; or

(2) places in a newspaper, magazine, handbill, or other publication an advertisement of an electronic, mechanical, or other device:

(A) knowing or having reason to know that the device is designed primarily for nonconsensual interception of wire, electronic, or oral communications;

(B) promoting the use of the device for the purpose of nonconsensual interception of wire, electronic, or oral communications; or

(C) knowing or having reason to know that the advertisement will promote the use of the device for the purpose of nonconsensual interception of wire, electronic, or oral communications.

(e) It is an affirmative defense to prosecution under Subsection (d) that the manufacture, assembly, possession, or sale of an electronic, mechanical, or other device that is designed primarily for the purpose of nonconsensual interception of wire, electronic, or oral communication is by:

(1) a communication common carrier or a provider of wire or electronic communications service or an officer, agent, or employee of or a person under contract with a communication common carrier or provider acting in the normal course of the provider's or communication carrier's business;

(2) an officer, agent, or employee of a person under contract with, bidding on contracts with, or doing business with the United States or this state acting in the normal course of the activities of the United States or this state;

(3) a member of the Department of Public Safety who is specifically trained to install wire, oral, or electronic communications intercept equipment; or

(4) a member of a local law enforcement agency that has an established unit specifically designated to respond to and deal with life-threatening situations.

(e-1) It is a defense to prosecution under Subsection (d)(1) that the electronic, mechanical, or other device is possessed by a person authorized to possess the device under Section 500.008, Government Code, or Section 242.103, Human Resources Code.

(f) An offense under this section is a felony of the second degree, unless the offense is committed under Subsection (d) or (g), in which event the offense is a state jail felony.

(g) A person commits an offense if, knowing that a government attorney or an investigative or law enforcement officer has been authorized or has applied for authorization to intercept wire, electronic, or oral communications, the person obstructs, impedes, prevents, gives notice to another of, or attempts to give notice to another of the interception.

(h) [Repealed by Acts 2005, 79th Leg., ch. 889 (S.B. 1551), § 1, effective June 17, 2005.]
(Enacted by Acts 1981, 67th Leg., ch. 275 (H.B. 360), § 2, effective August 31, 1981; am. Acts 1983, 68th Leg., ch. 864 (H.B. 1291), §§ 1-3, effective June 19, 1983; am. Acts 1989, 71st Leg., ch. 1166 (H.B. 910), § 16, effective September 1, 1989; am. Acts 1993, 73rd Leg., ch. 790 (S.B. 510), § 16, effective September 1, 1993; am. Acts 1993, 73rd Leg., ch. 900 (S.B. 1067), § 1.01, effective September 1, 1994; am. Acts 1997, 75th Leg., ch. 1051 (S.B. 1120), § 9, effective September 1, 1997; am. Acts 2001, 77th Leg., ch. 1270 (S.B. 1345), § 11, effective September 1, 2001; am. Acts 2003, 78th Leg., ch. 678 (H.B. 2474), § 1, effective September 1, 2003; am. Acts 2005, 79th Leg., ch. 889 (S.B. 1551), § 1, effective June 17, 2005; am. Acts 2009, 81st Leg., ch. 1169 (H.B. 3228), § 9, effective September 1, 2009; am. Acts 2011, 82nd Leg., ch. 85 (S.B. 653), § 3.023, effective September 1, 2011.)

## Sec. 16.021. Illegal Interception [Deleted].

Deleted by Acts 1993, 73rd Leg., ch. 900 (S.B. 1067), § 1.01, effective Septemer 1, 1994.
(Enacted by Acts 1985, 69th Leg., ch. 959 (S.B. 797), § 8, effective September 1, 1985.)

## Sec. 16.03. Unlawful Use of Pen Register or Trap and Trace Device.

(a) A person commits an offense if the person knowingly installs or uses a pen register or trap and trace device to record or decode electronic or other impulses for the purpose of identifying telephone numbers dialed or otherwise transmitted on a telephone line.

(b) In this section, "authorized peace officer," "communications common carrier," "pen register," and "trap and trace device" have the meanings assigned by Article 18.21, Code of Criminal Procedure.

(c) It is an affirmative defense to prosecution under Subsection (a) that the actor is:

(1) an officer, employee, or agent of a communications common carrier and the actor installs or uses a device or equipment to record a number dialed from or to a telephone instrument in the normal course of business of the carrier for purposes of:

(A) protecting property or services provided by the carrier; or

(B) assisting another who the actor reasonably believes to be a peace officer authorized to install or use a pen register or trap and trace device under Article 18.21, Code of Criminal Procedure;

(2) an officer, employee, or agent of a lawful enterprise and the actor installs or uses a device or equipment while engaged in an activity that:

(A) is a necessary incident to the rendition of service or to the protection of property of or services provided by the enterprise; and

(B) is not made for the purpose of gathering information for a law enforcement agency or private investigative agency, other than information related to the theft of communication or information services provided by the enterprise; or

(3) a person authorized to install or use a pen register or trap and trace device under Article 18.21, Code of Criminal Procedure.

(d) An offense under this section is a state jail felony.
(Enacted by Acts 1985, 69th Leg., ch. 587 (H.B. 10), § 6, effective August 26, 1985; am. Acts 1989, 71st Leg., ch. 958 (H.B. 241), § 2, effective September 1, 1989; am. Acts 1993, 73rd Leg., ch. 900 (S.B. 1067), § 1.01, effective September 1, 1994; am. Acts 1997, 75th Leg., ch. 1051 (S.B. 1120), § 10, effective September 1, 1997.)

## Sec. 16.04. Unlawful Access to Stored Communications.

(a) In this section, "electronic communication," "electronic storage," "user," and "wire communication" have the meanings assigned to those terms in Article 18.21, Code of Criminal Procedure.

(b) A person commits an offense if the person obtains, alters, or prevents authorized access to a wire or electronic communication while the communication is in electronic storage by:

(1) intentionally obtaining access without authorization to a facility through which a wire

or electronic communications service is provided; or

(2) intentionally exceeding an authorization for access to a facility through which a wire or electronic communications service is provided.

(c) Except as provided by Subsection (d), an offense under Subsection (b) is a Class A misdemeanor.

(d) If committed to obtain a benefit or to harm another, an offense is a state jail felony.

(e) It is an affirmative defense to prosecution under Subsection (b) that the conduct was authorized by:

(1) the provider of the wire or electronic communications service;

(2) the user of the wire or electronic communications service;

(3) the addressee or intended recipient of the wire or electronic communication; or

(4) Article 18.21, Code of Criminal Procedure.

(Enacted by Acts 1989, 71st Leg., ch. 958 (H.B. 241), § 3, effective September 1, 1989; am. Acts 1993, 73rd Leg., ch. 900 (S.B. 1067), § 1.01, effective September 1, 1994; am. Acts 1997, 75th Leg., ch. 1051 (S.B. 1120), § 11, effective September 1, 1997.)

### Sec. 16.05. Illegal Divulgence of Public Communications.

(a) In this section, "electronic communication," "electronic communications service," and "electronic communications system" have the meanings given those terms in Article 18.20, Code of Criminal Procedure.

(b) A person who provides electronic communications service to the public commits an offense if the person knowingly divulges the contents of a communication to another who is not the intended recipient of the communication.

(c) It is an affirmative defense to prosecution under Subsection (b) that the actor divulged the contents of the communication:

(1) as authorized by federal or state law;

(2) to a person employed, authorized, or whose facilities are used to forward the communication to the communication's destination; or

(3) to a law enforcement agency if the contents reasonably appear to pertain to the commission of a crime.

(d) Except as provided by Subsection (e), an offense under Subsection (b) that involves a scrambled or encrypted radio communication is a state jail felony.

(e) If committed for a tortious or illegal purpose or to gain a benefit, an offense under Subsection (b) that involves a radio communication that is not scrambled or encrypted:

(1) is a Class A misdemeanor if the communication is not a public land mobile radio service communication or a paging service communication; or

(2) is a Class C misdemeanor if the communication is a public land mobile radio service communication or a paging service communication.

(f) [Repealed by Acts 1997, 75th Leg., ch. 1051 (S.B. 1120), § 13, effective September 1, 1997.]
(Enacted by Acts 1989, 71st Leg., ch. 1166 (H.B. 910), § 17, effective September 1, 1989; am. Acts 1990, 71st Leg., 6th C.S., ch. 12 (S.B. 51), § 2(24), effective September 6, 1990 (renumbered from Sec. 16.04); am. Acts 1993, 73rd Leg., ch. 900 (S.B. 1067), § 1.01, effective September 1, 1994; am. Acts 1997, 75th Leg., ch. 1051 (S.B. 1120), §§ 12, 13, effective September 1, 1997.)

### Sec. 16.06. Unlawful Installation of Tracking Device.

(a) In this section:

(1) "Electronic or mechanical tracking device" means a device capable of emitting an electronic frequency or other signal that may be used by a person to identify, monitor, or record the location of another person or object.

(2) "Motor vehicle" has the meaning assigned by Section 501.002, Transportation Code.

(b) A person commits an offense if the person knowingly installs an electronic or mechanical tracking device on a motor vehicle owned or leased by another person.

(c) An offense under this section is a Class A misdemeanor.

(d) It is an affirmative defense to prosecution under this section that the person:

(1) obtained the effective consent of the owner or lessee of the motor vehicle before the electronic or mechanical tracking device was installed;

(2) assisted another whom the person reasonably believed to be a peace officer authorized to install the device in the course of a criminal investigation or pursuant to an order of a court to gather information for a law enforcement agency; or

(3) was a private investigator licensed under Chapter 1702, Occupations Code, who installed the device:

(A) with written consent:

    (i) to install the device given by the owner or lessee of the motor vehicle; and

    (ii) to enter private residential property, if that entry was necessary to install the device, given by the owner or lessee of the property; or

(B) pursuant to an order of or other authorization from a court to gather information.

(e) This section does not apply to a peace officer who installed the device in the course of a criminal investigation or pursuant to an order of a court to gather information for a law enforcement agency.

(Enacted by Acts 1999, 76th Leg., ch. 728 (H.B. 1001), § 1, effective September 1, 1999; am. Acts 2001, 77th Leg., ch. 1420 (H.B. 2812), § 14.828, effective September 1, 2001; am. Acts 2009, 81st Leg., ch. 1122 (H.B. 1659), § 1, effective September 1, 2009.)

# TITLE 5
# OFFENSES AGAINST THE PERSON

## CHAPTER 19
## CRIMINAL HOMICIDE

## Sec. 19.01. Types of Criminal Homicide.

(a) A person commits criminal homicide if he intentionally, knowingly, recklessly, or with criminal negligence causes the death of an individual.

(b) Criminal homicide is murder, capital murder, manslaughter, or criminally negligent homicide.

(Enacted by Acts 1973, 63rd Leg., ch. 399 (S.B. 34), § 1, effective January 1, 1974; am. Acts 1973, 63rd Leg., ch. 426 (H.B. 200), art. 2, § 1, effective January 1, 1974; am. Acts 1993, 73rd Leg., ch. 900 (S.B. 1067), § 1.01, effective September 1, 1994.)

## Sec. 19.02. Murder.

(a) In this section:

    (1) "Adequate cause" means cause that would commonly produce a degree of anger, rage, resentment, or terror in a person of ordinary temper, sufficient to render the mind incapable of cool reflection.

    (2) "Sudden passion" means passion directly caused by and arising out of provocation by the individual killed or another acting with the person killed which passion arises at the time of the offense and is not solely the result of former provocation.

(b) A person commits an offense if he:

    (1) intentionally or knowingly causes the death of an individual;

    (2) intends to cause serious bodily injury and commits an act clearly dangerous to human life that causes the death of an individual; or

    (3) commits or attempts to commit a felony, other than manslaughter, and in the course of and in furtherance of the commission or attempt, or in immediate flight from the commission or attempt, he commits or attempts to commit an act clearly dangerous to human life that causes the death of an individual.

(c) Except as provided by Subsection (d), an offense under this section is a felony of the first degree.

(d) At the punishment stage of a trial, the defendant may raise the issue as to whether he caused the death under the immediate influence of sudden passion arising from an adequate cause. If the defendant proves the issue in the affirmative by a preponderance of the evidence, the offense is a felony of the second degree.

(Enacted by Acts 1973, 63rd Leg., ch. 399 (S.B. 34), § 1, effective January 1, 1974; am. Acts 1973, 63rd Leg., ch. 426 (H.B. 200), art. 2, § 1, effective January 1, 1974; am. Acts 1993, 73rd Leg., ch. 900 (S.B. 1067), § 1.01, effective September 1, 1994.)

## Sec. 19.03. Capital Murder.

(a) A person commits an offense if the person commits murder as defined under Section 19.02(b)(1) and:

    (1) the person murders a peace officer or fireman who is acting in the lawful discharge of an official duty and who the person knows is a peace officer or fireman;

    (2) the person intentionally commits the murder in the course of committing or attempt-

ing to commit kidnapping, burglary, robbery, aggravated sexual assault, arson, obstruction or retaliation, or terroristic threat under Section 22.07(a)(1), (3), (4), (5), or (6);

(3) the person commits the murder for remuneration or the promise of remuneration or employs another to commit the murder for remuneration or the promise of remuneration;

(4) the person commits the murder while escaping or attempting to escape from a penal institution;

(5) the person, while incarcerated in a penal institution, murders another:

(A) who is employed in the operation of the penal institution; or

(B) with the intent to establish, maintain, or participate in a combination or in the profits of a combination;

(6) the person:

(A) while incarcerated for an offense under this section or Section 19.02, murders another; or

(B) while serving a sentence of life imprisonment or a term of 99 years for an offense under Section 20.04, 22.021, or 29.03, murders another;

(7) the person murders more than one person:

(A) during the same criminal transaction; or

(B) during different criminal transactions but the murders are committed pursuant to the same scheme or course of conduct;

(8) the person murders an individual under 10 years of age; or

(9) the person murders another person in retaliation for or on account of the service or status of the other person as a judge or justice of the supreme court, the court of criminal appeals, a court of appeals, a district court, a criminal district court, a constitutional county court, a statutory county court, a justice court, or a municipal court.

(b) An offense under this section is a capital felony.

(c) If the jury or, when authorized by law, the judge does not find beyond a reasonable doubt that the defendant is guilty of an offense under this section, he may be convicted of murder or of any other lesser included offense.

(Enacted by Acts 1973, 63rd Leg., ch. 426 (H.B. 200), art. 2, § 1, effective January 1, 1974; am. Acts 1983, 68th Leg., ch. 977 (H.B. 2008), § 6, effective September 1, 1983; am. Acts 1985, 69th Leg., ch. 44 (H.B. 8), § 1, effective September 1,

1985; am. Acts 1991, 72nd Leg., ch. 652 (H.B. 9), § 13, effective September 1, 1991; am. Acts 1993, 73rd Leg., ch. 715 (S.B. 818), § 1, effective September 1, 1993; am. Acts 1993, 73rd Leg., ch. 887 (S.B. 13), § 1, effective September 1, 1993; am. Acts 1993, 73rd Leg., ch. 900 (S.B. 1067), § 1.01, effective September 1, 1994; am. Acts 2003, 78th Leg., ch. 388 (H.B. 11), § 1, effective September 1, 2003; am. Acts 2005, 79th Leg., ch. 428 (S.B. 1791), § 1, effective September 1, 2005; am. Acts 2011, 82nd Leg., ch. 1209 (S.B. 377), § 1, effective September 1, 2011.)

## Sec. 19.04. Manslaughter.

(a) A person commits an offense if he recklessly causes the death of an individual.

(b) An offense under this section is a felony of the second degree.

(Enacted by Acts 1973, 63rd Leg., ch. 399 (S.B. 34), § 1, effective January 1, 1974; am. Acts 1973, 63rd Leg., ch. 426 (H.B. 200), art. 2, § 1, effective January 1, 1974 (renumbered from Sec. 19.03); am. Acts 1987, 70th Leg., ch. 307 (S.B. 120), § 1, effective September 1, 1987; am. Acts 1993, 73rd Leg., ch. 900 (S.B. 1067), § 1.01, effective September 1, 1994 (renumbered from Sec. 19.05).)

## Sec. 19.05. Criminally Negligent Homicide.

(a) A person commits an offense if he causes the death of an individual by criminal negligence.

(b) An offense under this section is a state jail felony.

(Enacted by Acts 1973, 63rd Leg., ch. 399 (S.B. 34), § 1, effective January 1, 1974; am. Acts 1973, 73rd Leg., ch. 426 (H.B. 200), art. 2, § 1, effective January 1, 1974 (renumbered from Sec. 19.06); am. Acts 1993, 73rd Leg., ch. 900 (S.B. 1067), § 1.01, effective September 1, 1994 (renumbered from Sec. 19.07).)

## Sec. 19.06. Applicability to Certain Conduct.

This chapter does not apply to the death of an unborn child if the conduct charged is:

(1) conduct committed by the mother of the unborn child;

(2) a lawful medical procedure performed by a physician or other licensed health care provider with the requisite consent, if the death of the unborn child was the intended result of the procedure;

(3) a lawful medical procedure performed by a physician or other licensed health care pro-

Penal Code

vider with the requisite consent as part of an assisted reproduction as defined by Section 160.102, Family Code; or

(4) the dispensation of a drug in accordance with law or administration of a drug prescribed in accordance with law.

(Enacted by Acts 2003, 78th Leg., ch. 822 (S.B. 319), § 2.02, effective September 1, 2003.)

### Sec. 19.07.  Criminally Negligent Homicide [Renumbered].

Renumbered to Tex. Penal Code § 19.05 by Acts 1993, 73rd Leg., ch. 900 (S.B. 1067), § 1.01, effective September 1, 1994.

## CHAPTER 20
## KIDNAPPING, UNLAWFUL RESTRAINT, AND SMUGGLING OF PERSONS

### Sec. 20.01.  Definitions.

In this chapter:

(1) "Restrain" means to restrict a person's movements without consent, so as to interfere substantially with the person's liberty, by moving the person from one place to another or by confining the person. Restraint is "without consent" if it is accomplished by:

(A) force, intimidation, or deception; or

(B) any means, including acquiescence of the victim, if:

(i) the victim is a child who is less than 14 years of age or an incompetent person and the parent, guardian, or person or institution acting in loco parentis has not acquiesced in the movement or confinement; or

(ii) the victim is a child who is 14 years of age or older and younger than 17 years of age, the victim is taken outside of the state and outside a 120-mile radius from the victim's residence, and the parent, guardian, or person or institution acting in loco parentis has not acquiesced in the movement.

(2) "Abduct" means to restrain a person with intent to prevent his liberation by:

(A) secreting or holding him in a place where he is not likely to be found; or

(B) using or threatening to use deadly force.

(3) "Relative" means a parent or stepparent, ancestor, sibling, or uncle or aunt, including an adoptive relative of the same degree through marriage or adoption.

(4) "Person" means an individual, corporation, or association.

(5) Notwithstanding Section 1.07, "individual" means a human being who has been born and is alive.

(Enacted by Acts 1973, 63rd Leg., ch. 399 (S.B. 34), § 1, effective January 1, 1974; am. Acts 1993, 73rd Leg., ch. 900 (S.B. 1067), § 1.01, effective September 1, 1994; am. Acts 1999, 76th Leg., ch. 790 (H.B. 1428), § 1, effective September 1, 1999; am. Acts 2003, 78th Leg., ch. 822 (S.B. 319), § 2.03, effective September 1, 2003.)

### Sec. 20.02.  Unlawful Restraint.

(a) A person commits an offense if he intentionally or knowingly restrains another person.

(b) It is an affirmative defense to prosecution under this section that:

(1) the person restrained was a child younger than 14 years of age;

(2) the actor was a relative of the child; and

(3) the actor's sole intent was to assume lawful control of the child.

(c) An offense under this section is a Class A misdemeanor, except that the offense is:

(1) a state jail felony if the person restrained was a child younger than 17 years of age; or

(2) a felony of the third degree if:

(A) the actor recklessly exposes the victim to a substantial risk of serious bodily injury;

(B) the actor restrains an individual the actor knows is a public servant while the public servant is lawfully discharging an official duty or in retaliation or on account of an exercise of official power or performance of an official duty as a public servant; or

(C) the actor while in custody restrains any other person.

(d) It is no offense to detain or move another under this section when it is for the purpose of effecting a lawful arrest or detaining an individual lawfully arrested.

(e) It is an affirmative defense to prosecution under this section that:

(1) the person restrained was a child who is 14 years of age or older and younger than 17 years of age;

(2) the actor does not restrain the child by force, intimidation, or deception; and

(3) the actor is not more than three years older than the child.

(Enacted by Acts 1973, 63rd Leg., ch. 399 (S.B. 34), § 1, effective January 1, 1974; am. Acts 1993, 73rd Leg., ch. 900 (S.B. 1067), § 1.01, effective September 1, 1994; am. Acts 1997, 75th Leg., ch. 707 (S.B. 1835), §§ 1(b), 2, effective September 1, 1997; am. Acts 1999, 76th Leg., ch. 790 (H.B. 1428), § 2, effective September 1, 1999; am. Acts 2001, 77th Leg., ch. 524 (H.B. 2098), § 1, effective September 1, 2001.)

## Sec. 20.03. Kidnapping.

(a) A person commits an offense if he intentionally or knowingly abducts another person.

(b) It is an affirmative defense to prosecution under this section that:

(1) the abduction was not coupled with intent to use or to threaten to use deadly force;

(2) the actor was a relative of the person abducted; and

(3) the actor's sole intent was to assume lawful control of the victim.

(c) An offense under this section is a felony of the third degree.

(Enacted by Acts 1973, 63rd Leg., ch. 399 (S.B. 34), § 1, effective January 1, 1974; am. Acts 1993, 73rd Leg., ch. 900 (S.B. 1067), § 1.01, effective September 1, 1994.)

## Sec. 20.04. Aggravated Kidnapping.

(a) A person commits an offense if he intentionally or knowingly abducts another person with the intent to:

(1) hold him for ransom or reward;

(2) use him as a shield or hostage;

(3) facilitate the commission of a felony or the flight after the attempt or commission of a felony;

(4) inflict bodily injury on him or violate or abuse him sexually;

(5) terrorize him or a third person; or

(6) interfere with the performance of any governmental or political function.

(b) A person commits an offense if the person intentionally or knowingly abducts another person and uses or exhibits a deadly weapon during the commission of the offense.

(c) Except as provided by Subsection (d), an offense under this section is a felony of the first degree.

(d) At the punishment stage of a trial, the defendant may raise the issue as to whether he voluntarily released the victim in a safe place. If the defendant proves the issue in the affirmative by a preponderance of the evidence, the offense is a felony of the second degree.

(Enacted by Acts 1973, 63rd Leg., ch. 399 (S.B. 34), § 1, effective January 1, 1974; am. Acts 1993, 73rd Leg., ch. 900 (S.B. 1067), § 1.01, effective September 1, 1994; am. Acts 1995, 74th Leg., ch. 318 (S.B. 15), § 4, effective September 1, 1995.)

## Sec. 20.05. Smuggling of Persons.

(a) A person commits an offense if the person intentionally uses a motor vehicle, aircraft, or watercraft to transport an individual with the intent to:

(1) conceal the individual from a peace officer or special investigator; or

(2) flee from a person the actor knows is a peace officer or special investigator attempting to lawfully arrest or detain the actor.

(b) Except as provided by Subsection (c), an offense under this section is a state jail felony.

(c) An offense under this section is a felony of the third degree if the actor commits the offense:

(1) for pecuniary benefit; or

(2) in a manner that creates a substantial likelihood that the transported individual will suffer serious bodily injury or death.

(d) It is an affirmative defense to prosecution under this section that the actor is related to the transported individual within the second degree of consanguinity or, at the time of the offense, within the second degree of affinity.

(e) If conduct constituting an offense under this section also constitutes an offense under another section of this code, the actor may be prosecuted under either section or under both sections.

(Enacted by Acts 1999, 76th Leg., ch. 1014 (H.B. 2879), § 1, effective September 1, 1999; am. Acts 2011, 82nd Leg., ch. 223 (H.B. 260), § 2, effective September 1, 2011.)

## CHAPTER 20A
## TRAFFICKING OF PERSONS

**Section**
20A.01.   Definitions.
20A.02.   Trafficking of Persons.
20A.03.   Continuous Trafficking of Persons.

## Sec. 20A.01. Definitions.

In this chapter:

(1) "Child" means a person younger than 18 years of age.

(2) "Forced labor or services" means labor or services, other than labor or services that con-

stitute sexual conduct, that are performed or provided by another person and obtained through an actor's use of force, fraud, or coercion.

(3) "Sexual conduct" has the meaning assigned by Section 43.25.

(4) "Traffic" means to transport, entice, recruit, harbor, provide, or otherwise obtain another person by any means.

(Enacted by Acts 2003, 78th Leg., ch. 641 (H.B. 2096), § 2, effective September 1, 2003; am. Acts 2007, 80th Leg., ch. 258 (S.B. 11), § 16.01, effective September 1, 2007; am. Acts 2007, 80th Leg., ch. 849 (H.B. 1121), § 4, effective June 15, 2007; am. Acts 2011, 82nd Leg., ch. 1 (S.B. 24), § 1.01, effective September 1, 2011.)

## Sec. 20A.02.  Trafficking of Persons.

(a) A person commits an offense if the person knowingly:

(1) traffics another person with the intent that the trafficked person engage in forced labor or services;

(2) receives a benefit from participating in a venture that involves an activity described by Subdivision (1), including by receiving labor or services the person knows are forced labor or services;

(3) traffics another person and, through force, fraud, or coercion, causes the trafficked person to engage in conduct prohibited by:

(A) Section 43.02 (Prostitution);

(B) Section 43.03 (Promotion of Prostitution);

(C) Section 43.04 (Aggravated Promotion of Prostitution); or

(D) Section 43.05 (Compelling Prostitution);

(4) receives a benefit from participating in a venture that involves an activity described by Subdivision (3) or engages in sexual conduct with a person trafficked in the manner described in Subdivision (3);

(5) traffics a child with the intent that the trafficked child engage in forced labor or services;

(6) receives a benefit from participating in a venture that involves an activity described by Subdivision (5), including by receiving labor or services the person knows are forced labor or services;

(7) traffics a child and by any means causes the trafficked child to engage in, or become the victim of, conduct prohibited by:

(A) Section 21.02 (Continuous Sexual Abuse of Young Child or Children);

(B) Section 21.11 (Indecency with a Child);

(C) Section 22.011 (Sexual Assault);

(D) Section 22.021 (Aggravated Sexual Assault);

(E) Section 43.02 (Prostitution);

(F) Section 43.03 (Promotion of Prostitution);

(G) Section 43.04 (Aggravated Promotion of Prostitution);

(H) Section 43.05 (Compelling Prostitution);

(I) Section 43.25 (Sexual Performance by a Child);

(J) Section 43.251 (Employment Harmful to Children); or

(K) Section 43.26 (Possession or Promotion of Child Pornography); or

(8) receives a benefit from participating in a venture that involves an activity described by Subdivision (7) or engages in sexual conduct with a child trafficked in the manner described in Subdivision (7).

(b) Except as otherwise provided by this subsection, an offense under this section is a felony of the second degree. An offense under this section is a felony of the first degree if:

(1) the applicable conduct constitutes an offense under Subsection (a)(5), (6), (7), or (8), regardless of whether the actor knows the age of the child at the time the actor commits the offense; or

(2) the commission of the offense results in the death of the person who is trafficked.

(c) If conduct constituting an offense under this section also constitutes an offense under another section of this code, the actor may be prosecuted under either section or under both sections.

(d) If the victim of an offense under Subsection (a)(7)(A) is the same victim as a victim of an offense under Section 21.02, a defendant may not be convicted of the offense under Section 21.02 in the same criminal action as the offense under Subsection (a)(7)(A) unless the offense under Section 21.02:

(1) is charged in the alternative;

(2) occurred outside the period in which the offense alleged under Subsection (a)(7)(A) was committed; or

(3) is considered by the trier of fact to be a lesser included offense of the offense alleged under Subsection (a)(7)(A).

(Enacted by Acts 2003, 78th Leg., ch. 641 (H.B. 2096), § 2, effective September 1, 2003; am. Acts 2007, 80th Leg., ch. 258 (S.B. 11), § 16.02, effective September 1, 2007; am. Acts 2007, 80th Leg., ch. 849 (H.B. 1121), § 5, effective June 15, 2007; am. Acts 2009, 81st Leg., ch. 1002 (H.B. 4009), § 7, effective September 1, 2009; am. Acts 2011, 82nd Leg., ch. 1 (S.B. 24), § 1.02, effective September 1, 2011.)

### Sec. 20A.03.  Continuous Trafficking of Persons.

(a) A person commits an offense if, during a period that is 30 or more days in duration, the person engages two or more times in conduct that constitutes an offense under Section 20A.02.

(b) If a jury is the trier of fact, members of the jury are not required to agree unanimously on which specific conduct engaged in by the defendant constituted an offense under Section 20A.02 or on which exact date the defendant engaged in that conduct. The jury must agree unanimously that the defendant, during a period that is 30 or more days in duration, engaged in conduct that constituted an offense under Section 20A.02.

(c) If the victim of an offense under Subsection (a) is the same victim as a victim of an offense under Section 20A.02, a defendant may not be convicted of the offense under Section 20A.02 in the same criminal action as the offense under Subsection (a), unless the offense under Section 20A.02:

(1) is charged in the alternative;

(2) occurred outside the period in which the offense alleged under Subsection (a) was committed; or

(3) is considered by the trier of fact to be a lesser included offense of the offense alleged under Subsection (a).

(d) A defendant may not be charged with more than one count under Subsection (a) if all of the conduct that constitutes an offense under Section 20A.02 is alleged to have been committed against the same victim.

(e) An offense under this section is a felony of the first degree, punishable by imprisonment in the Texas Department of Criminal Justice for life or for any term of not more than 99 years or less than 25 years.

(Enacted by Acts 2011, 82nd Leg., ch. 122 (H.B. 3000), § 1, effective September 1, 2011.)

## CHAPTER 21
## SEXUAL OFFENSES

### Sec. 21.01.  Definitions.

In this chapter:

(1) "Deviate sexual intercourse" means:

(A) any contact between any part of the genitals of one person and the mouth or anus of another person; or

(B) the penetration of the genitals or the anus of another person with an object.

(2) "Sexual contact" means, except as provided by Section 21.11, any touching of the anus, breast, or any part of the genitals of another person with intent to arouse or gratify the sexual desire of any person.

(3) "Sexual intercourse" means any penetration of the female sex organ by the male sex organ.

(4) "Spouse" means a person to whom a person is legally married under Subtitle A, Title 1, Family Code, or a comparable law of another jurisdiction.

(Enacted by Acts 1973, 63rd Leg., ch. 399 (S.B. 34), § 1, effective January 1, 1974; am. Acts 1979, 66th Leg., ch. 168 (H.B. 43), § 1, effective August 27, 1979; am. Acts 1981, 67th Leg., ch. 96 (H.B. 364), § 3, effective September 1, 1981; am. Acts 1993, 73rd Leg., ch. 900 (S.B. 1067), § 1.01, effective September 1, 1994; am. Acts 2001, 77th Leg., ch. 739 (S.B. 932), § 1, effective September 1, 2001; am. Acts 2005, 79th Leg., ch. 268 (S.B. 6), § 1.124, effective September 1, 2005.)

### Sec. 21.02.  Continuous Sexual Abuse of Young Child or Children.

(a) In this section, "child" has the meaning assigned by Section 22.011(c).

(b) A person commits an offense if:

(1) during a period that is 30 or more days in duration, the person commits two or more acts

of sexual abuse, regardless of whether the acts of sexual abuse are committed against one or more victims; and

(2) at the time of the commission of each of the acts of sexual abuse, the actor is 17 years of age or older and the victim is a child younger than 14 years of age.

(c) For purposes of this section, "act of sexual abuse" means any act that is a violation of one or more of the following penal laws:

(1) aggravated kidnapping under Section 20.04(a)(4), if the actor committed the offense with the intent to violate or abuse the victim sexually;

(2) indecency with a child under Section 21.11(a)(1), if the actor committed the offense in a manner other than by touching, including touching through clothing, the breast of a child;

(3) sexual assault under Section 22.011;

(4) aggravated sexual assault under Section 22.021;

(5) burglary under Section 30.02, if the offense is punishable under Subsection (d) of that section and the actor committed the offense with the intent to commit an offense listed in Subdivisions (1)—(4);

(6) sexual performance by a child under Section 43.25;

(7) trafficking of persons under Section 20A.02(a)(7) or (8); and

(8) compelling prostitution under Section 43.05(a)(2).

(d) If a jury is the trier of fact, members of the jury are not required to agree unanimously on which specific acts of sexual abuse were committed by the defendant or the exact date when those acts were committed. The jury must agree unanimously that the defendant, during a period that is 30 or more days in duration, committed two or more acts of sexual abuse.

(e) A defendant may not be convicted in the same criminal action of an offense listed under Subsection (c) the victim of which is the same victim as a victim of the offense alleged under Subsection (b) unless the offense listed in Subsection (c):

(1) is charged in the alternative;

(2) occurred outside the period in which the offense alleged under Subsection (b) was committed; or

(3) is considered by the trier of fact to be a lesser included offense of the offense alleged under Subsection (b).

(f) A defendant may not be charged with more than one count under Subsection (b) if all of the

specific acts of sexual abuse that are alleged to have been committed are alleged to have been committed against a single victim.

(g) It is an affirmative defense to prosecution under this section that the actor:

(1) was not more than five years older than:

(A) the victim of the offense, if the offense is alleged to have been committed against only one victim; or

(B) the youngest victim of the offense, if the offense is alleged to have been committed against more than one victim;

(2) did not use duress, force, or a threat against a victim at the time of the commission of any of the acts of sexual abuse alleged as an element of the offense; and

(3) at the time of the commission of any of the acts of sexual abuse alleged as an element of the offense:

(A) was not required under Chapter 62, Code of Criminal Procedure, to register for life as a sex offender; or

(B) was not a person who under Chapter 62 had a reportable conviction or adjudication for an offense under this section or an act of sexual abuse as described by Subsection (c).

(h) An offense under this section is a felony of the first degree, punishable by imprisonment in the Texas Department of Criminal Justice for life, or for any term of not more than 99 years or less than 25 years.

(Enacted by Acts 2007, 80th Leg., ch. 593 (H.B. 8), § 1.17, effective September 1, 2007; am. Acts 2011, 82nd Leg., ch. 1 (S.B. 24), § 6.04, effective September 1, 2011.)

## Sec. 21.03. Aggravated Rape [Repealed].

Repealed by Acts 1983, 68th Leg., ch. 977 (H.B. 2008), § 12, effective September 1, 1983.

(Enacted by Acts 1973, 63rd Leg., ch. 399 (S.B. 34), § 1, effective January 1, 1974; am. Acts 1981, 67th Leg., ch. 96 (H.B. 364), § 1, effective September 1, 1981; am. Acts 1981, 67th Leg., ch. 202 (S.B. 126), § 1, effective September 1, 1981.)

## Sec. 21.04. Sexual Abuse [Repealed].

Repealed by Acts 1983, 68th Leg., ch. 977 (H.B. 2008), § 12, effective September 1, 1983.

(Enacted by Acts 1973, 63rd Leg., ch. 399 (S.B. 34), § 1, effective January 1, 1974; am. Acts 1975, 64th Leg., ch. 203 (H.B. 284), § 2, effective September 1, 1975.)

Penal Code

## Sec. 21.05. Aggravated Sexual Abuse [Repealed].

Repealed by Acts 1983, 68th Leg., ch. 977 (H.B. 2008), § 12, effective September 1, 1983.

(Enacted by Acts 1973, 63rd Leg., ch. 399 (S.B. 34), § 1, effective January 1, 1974; am. Acts 1981, 67th Leg., ch. 96 (H.B. 364), § 2, effective September 1, 1981; am. Acts 1981, 67th Leg., ch. 202 (S.B. 126), § 2, effective September 1, 1981.)

## Sec. 21.06. Homosexual Conduct.

(a) A person commits an offense if he engages in deviate sexual intercourse with another individual of the same sex.

(b) An offense under this section is a Class C misdemeanor.

(Enacted by Acts 1973, 63rd Leg., ch. 399 (S.B. 34), § 1, effective January 1, 1974; am. Acts 1993, 73rd Leg., ch. 900 (S.B. 1067), § 1.01, effective September 1, 1994.)

### STATUTORY NOTES

**Editor's notes.** — This section was declared unconstitutional by *Lawrence v. Texas*, 539 U.S. 558, 123 S. Ct. 2472, 156 L. Ed. 2d 508, 2003 U.S. LEXIS 5013 (2003). On remand, the trial court judgments were reversed and the complaints dismissed by Lawrence v. State, Nos. 14-99-00109-CR and 14-99-00111-CR, 2003 Tex. App. Lexis 9191 (Tex. App—Houston [14th Dist.] Oct. 30, 2003, no pet. (unpublished mem. op.).

## Sec. 21.07. Public Lewdness.

(a) A person commits an offense if he knowingly engages in any of the following acts in a public place or, if not in a public place, he is reckless about whether another is present who will be offended or alarmed by his:

(1) act of sexual intercourse;

(2) act of deviate sexual intercourse;

(3) act of sexual contact; or

(4) act involving contact between the person's mouth or genitals and the anus or genitals of an animal or fowl.

(b) An offense under this section is a Class A misdemeanor.

(Enacted by Acts 1973, 63rd Leg., ch. 399 (S.B. 34), § 1, effective January 1, 1974; am. Acts 1993, 73rd Leg., ch. 900 (S.B. 1067), § 1.01, effective September 1, 1994.)

## Sec. 21.08. Indecent Exposure.

(a) A person commits an offense if he exposes his anus or any part of his genitals with intent to arouse or gratify the sexual desire of any person, and he is reckless about whether another is present who will be offended or alarmed by his act.

(b) An offense under this section is a Class B misdemeanor.

(Enacted by Acts 1973, 63rd Leg., ch. 399 (S.B. 34), § 1, effective January 1, 1974; am. Acts 1983, 68th Leg., ch. 924 (H.B. 1686), § 1, effective September 1, 1983; am. Acts 1993, 73rd Leg., ch. 900 (S.B. 1067), § 1.01, effective September 1, 1994.)

## Sec. 21.09. Rape of a Child [Repealed].

Repealed by Acts 1983, 68th Leg., ch. 977 (H.B. 2008), § 12, effective September 1, 1983.

(Enacted by Acts 1973, 63rd Leg., ch. 399 (S.B. 34), § 1, effective January 1, 1974; am. Acts 1975, 64th Leg., ch. 342 (S.B. 127), § 8, effective September 1, 1975.)

## Sec. 21.10. Sexual Abuse of a Child [Repealed].

Repealed by Acts 1983, 68th Leg., ch. 977 (H.B. 2008), § 12, effective September 1, 1983.

(Enacted by Acts 1973, 63rd Leg., ch. 399 (S.B. 34), § 1, effective January 1, 1974.)

## Sec. 21.11. Indecency with a Child.

(a) A person commits an offense if, with a child younger than 17 years of age, whether the child is of the same or opposite sex, the person:

(1) engages in sexual contact with the child or causes the child to engage in sexual contact; or

(2) with intent to arouse or gratify the sexual desire of any person:

(A) exposes the person's anus or any part of the person's genitals, knowing the child is present; or

(B) causes the child to expose the child's anus or any part of the child's genitals.

(b) It is an affirmative defense to prosecution under this section that the actor:

(1) was not more than three years older than the victim and of the opposite sex;

(2) did not use duress, force, or a threat against the victim at the time of the offense; and

(3) at the time of the offense:

(A) was not required under Chapter 62, Code of Criminal Procedure, to register for life as a sex offender; or

(B) was not a person who under Chapter 62 had a reportable conviction or adjudication for an offense under this section.

(b-1) It is an affirmative defense to prosecution under this section that the actor was the spouse of the child at the time of the offense.

(c) In this section, "sexual contact" means the following acts, if committed with the intent to arouse or gratify the sexual desire of any person:

(1) any touching by a person, including touching through clothing, of the anus, breast, or any part of the genitals of a child; or

(2) any touching of any part of the body of a child, including touching through clothing, with the anus, breast, or any part of the genitals of a person.

(d) An offense under Subsection (a)(1) is a felony of the second degree and an offense under Subsection (a)(2) is a felony of the third degree. (Enacted by Acts 1973, 63rd Leg., ch. 399 (S.B. 34), § 1, effective January 1, 1974; am. Acts 1981, 67th Leg., ch. 202 (S.B. 126), § 3, effective September 1, 1981; am. Acts 1987, 70th Leg., ch. 1028 (H.B. 2575), § 1, effective September 1, 1987; am. Acts 1993, 73rd Leg., ch. 900 (S.B. 1067), § 1.01, effective September 1, 1994; am. Acts 1999, 76th Leg., ch. 1415 (H.B. 2145), § 23, effective September 1, 1999; am. Acts 2001, 77th Leg., ch. 739 (S.B. 932), § 2, effective September 1, 2001; am. Acts 2009, 81st Leg., ch. 260 (H.B. 549), § 1, effective September 1, 2009.)

## Sec. 21.12.  Improper Relationship Between Educator and Student.

(a) An employee of a public or private primary or secondary school commits an offense if the employee:

(1) engages in sexual contact, sexual intercourse, or deviate sexual intercourse with a person who is enrolled in a public or private primary or secondary school at which the employee works;

(2) holds a certificate or permit issued as provided by Subchapter B, Chapter 21, Education Code, or is a person who is required to be licensed by a state agency as provided by Section 21.003(b), Education Code, and engages in sexual contact, sexual intercourse, or deviate sexual intercourse with a person the employee knows is:

(A) enrolled in a public primary or secondary school in the same school district as the school at which the employee works; or

(B) a student participant in an educational activity that is sponsored by a school district or a public or private primary or secondary school, if:

(i) students enrolled in a public or private primary or secondary school are the primary participants in the activity; and

(ii) the employee provides education services to those participants; or

(3) engages in conduct described by Section 33.021, with a person described by Subdivision (1), or a person the employee knows is a person described by Subdivision (2)(A) or (B), regardless of the age of that person.

(b) An offense under this section is a felony of the second degree.

(b-1) It is an affirmative defense to prosecution under this section that:

(1) the actor was the spouse of the enrolled person at the time of the offense; or

(2) the actor was not more than three years older than the enrolled person and, at the time of the offense, the actor and the enrolled person were in a relationship that began before the actor's employment at a public or private primary or secondary school.

(c) If conduct constituting an offense under this section also constitutes an offense under another section of this code, the actor may be prosecuted under either section or both sections.

(d) The name of a person who is enrolled in a public or private primary or secondary school and involved in an improper relationship with an educator as provided by Subsection (a) may not be released to the public and is not public information under Chapter 552, Government Code. (Enacted by Acts 2003, 78th Leg., ch. 224 (H.B. 532), § 1, effective September 1, 2003; am. Acts 2007, 80th Leg., ch. 610 (H.B. 401), § 1, effective September 1, 2007; am. Acts 2007, 80th Leg., ch. 772 (H.B. 3659), § 1, effective September 1, 2007; am. Acts 2009, 81st Leg., ch. 260 (H.B. 549), § 2, effective September 1, 2009; am. Acts 2011, 82nd Leg., ch. 761 (H.B. 1610), § 3, effective September 1, 2011.)

## Sec. 21.13.  Evidence of Previous Sexual Conduct [Renumbered].

Renumbered to Tex. Penal Code § 22.065 by Acts 1983, 68th Leg., ch. 977 (H.B. 2008), § 4, effective September 1, 1983.

## Sec. 21.14.  Sexual Exploitation by Mental Health Services Provider [Deleted].

Deleted by Acts 1993, 73rd Leg., ch. 900 (S.B. 1067), § 1.01, effective September 1, 1994. (Enacted by Acts 1993, 73rd Leg., ch. 573 (S.B. 210), § 2.02, effective September 1, 1993.)

Penal Code

### Sec. 21.15. Improper Photography or Visual Recording.

(a) In this section, "promote" has the meaning assigned by Section 43.21.

(b) A person commits an offense if the person:

(1) photographs or by videotape or other electronic means records, broadcasts, or transmits a visual image of another at a location that is not a bathroom or private dressing room:

(A) without the other person's consent; and

(B) with intent to arouse or gratify the sexual desire of any person;

(2) photographs or by videotape or other electronic means records, broadcasts, or transmits a visual image of another at a location that is a bathroom or private dressing room:

(A) without the other person's consent; and

(B) with intent to:

(i) invade the privacy of the other person; or

(ii) arouse or gratify the sexual desire of any person; or

(3) knowing the character and content of the photograph, recording, broadcast, or transmission, promotes a photograph, recording, broadcast, or transmission described by Subdivision (1) or (2).

(c) An offense under this section is a state jail felony.

(d) If conduct that constitutes an offense under this section also constitutes an offense under any other law, the actor may be prosecuted under this section or the other law.

(e) For purposes of Subsection (b)(2), a sign or signs posted indicating that the person is being photographed or that a visual image of the person is being recorded, broadcast, or transmitted is not sufficient to establish the person's consent under that subdivision.

(Enacted by Acts 2001, 77th Leg., ch. 458 (H.B. 73), § 1, effective September 1, 2001; am. Acts 2003, 78th Leg., ch. 500 (H.B. 1060), § 1, effective September 1, 2003; am. Acts 2007, 80th Leg., ch. 306 (H.B. 1804), § 1, effective September 1, 2007.)

# CHAPTER 22
## ASSAULTIVE OFFENSES

### Sec. 22.01. Assault.

(a) A person commits an offense if the person:

(1) intentionally, knowingly, or recklessly causes bodily injury to another, including the person's spouse;

(2) intentionally or knowingly threatens another with imminent bodily injury, including the person's spouse; or

(3) intentionally or knowingly causes physical contact with another when the person knows or should reasonably believe that the other will regard the contact as offensive or provocative.

(b) An offense under Subsection (a)(1) is a Class A misdemeanor, except that the offense is a felony of the third degree if the offense is committed against:

(1) a person the actor knows is a public servant while the public servant is lawfully discharging an official duty, or in retaliation or on account of an exercise of official power or performance of an official duty as a public servant;

(2) a person whose relationship to or association with the defendant is described by Section 71.0021(b), 71.003, or 71.005, Family Code, if:

(A) it is shown on the trial of the offense that the defendant has been previously convicted of an offense under this chapter, Chapter 19, or Section 20.03, 20.04, 21.11, or 25.11 against a person whose relationship to or association with the defendant is described by Section 71.0021(b), 71.003, or 71.005, Family Code; or

(B) the offense is committed by intentionally, knowingly, or recklessly impeding the normal breathing or circulation of the blood of the person by applying pressure to the person's throat or neck or by blocking the person's nose or mouth;

(3) a person who contracts with government to perform a service in a facility as defined by Section 1.07(a)(14), Penal Code, or Section 51.02(13) or (14), Family Code, or an employee of that person:

(A) while the person or employee is engaged in performing a service within the scope of the contract, if the actor knows the person or employee is authorized by government to provide the service; or

(B) in retaliation for or on account of the person's or employee's performance of a service within the scope of the contract;

(4) a person the actor knows is a security officer while the officer is performing a duty as a security officer; or

(5) a person the actor knows is emergency services personnel while the person is providing emergency services.

(b-1) Notwithstanding Subsection (b)(2), an offense under Subsection (a)(1) is a felony of the second degree if:

(1) the offense is committed against a person whose relationship to or association with the defendant is described by Section 71.0021(b), 71.003, or 71.005, Family Code;

(2) it is shown on the trial of the offense that the defendant has been previously convicted of an offense under this chapter, Chapter 19, or Section 20.03, 20.04, or 21.11 against a person whose relationship to or association with the defendant is described by Section 71.0021(b), 71.003, or 71.005, Family Code; and

(3) the offense is committed by intentionally, knowingly, or recklessly impeding the normal breathing or circulation of the blood of the person by applying pressure to the person's throat or neck or by blocking the person's nose or mouth.

(c) An offense under Subsection (a)(2) or (3) is a Class C misdemeanor, except that the offense is:

(1) a Class A misdemeanor if the offense is committed under Subsection (a)(3) against an elderly individual or disabled individual, as those terms are defined by Section 22.04; or

(2) a Class B misdemeanor if the offense is committed by a person who is not a sports participant against a person the actor knows is a sports participant either:

(A) while the participant is performing duties or responsibilities in the participant's capacity as a sports participant; or

(B) in retaliation for or on account of the participant's performance of a duty or responsibility within the participant's capacity as a sports participant.

(d) For purposes of Subsection (b), the actor is presumed to have known the person assaulted was a public servant, a security officer, or emergency services personnel if the person was wearing a distinctive uniform or badge indicating the person's employment as a public servant or status as a security officer or emergency services personnel.

(e) In this section:

(1) "Emergency services personnel" includes firefighters, emergency medical services personnel as defined by Section 773.003, Health and Safety Code, and other individuals who, in the course and scope of employment or as a volunteer, provide services for the benefit of the general public during emergency situations.

(2) [Repealed by Acts 2005, 79th Leg., ch. 788 (S.B. 91), § 6, effective September 1, 2005.]

(3) "Security officer" means a commissioned security officer as defined by Section 1702.002, Occupations Code, or a noncommissioned security officer registered under Section 1702.221, Occupations Code.

(4) "Sports participant" means a person who participates in any official capacity with respect to an interscholastic, intercollegiate, or other organized amateur or professional athletic competition and includes an athlete, referee, umpire, linesman, coach, instructor, administrator, or staff member.

(f) For the purposes of Subsections (b)(2)(A) and (b-1)(2):

(1) a defendant has been previously convicted of an offense listed in those subsections committed against a person whose relationship to or association with the defendant is described by Section 71.0021(b), 71.003, or 71.005, Family Code, if the defendant was adjudged guilty of the offense or entered a plea of guilty or nolo contendere in return for a grant of deferred adjudication, regardless of whether the sentence for the offense was ever

imposed or whether the sentence was probated and the defendant was subsequently discharged from community supervision; and

(2) a conviction under the laws of another state for an offense containing elements that are substantially similar to the elements of an offense listed in those subsections is a conviction of the offense listed.

(g) If conduct constituting an offense under this section also constitutes an offense under another section of this code, the actor may be prosecuted under either section or both sections. (Enacted by Acts 1973, 63rd Leg., ch. 399 (S.B. 34), § 1, effective January 1, 1974; am. Acts 1977, 65th Leg., 1st C.S., ch. 2 (S.B. 9), §§ 12, 13, effective July 22, 1977; am. Acts 1979, 66th Leg., ch. 135 (H.B. 901), §§ 1, 2, effective August 27, 1979; am. Acts 1979, 66th Leg., ch. 164 (S.B. 529), § 2, effective September 1, 1979; am. Acts 1983, 68th Leg., ch. 977 (H.B. 2008), § 1, effective September 1, 1983; am. Acts 1987, 70th Leg., ch. 1052 (S.B. 298), § 2.08, effective September 1, 1987; am. Acts 1989, 71st Leg., ch. 739 (H.B. 1230), §§ 1-3, effective September 1, 1989; am. Acts 1991, 72nd Leg., ch. 14 (S.B. 404), § 284(23)-(26), effective September 1, 1991; am. Acts 1991, 72nd Leg., ch. 334 (H.B. 1188), § 1, effective September 1, 1991; am. Acts 1991, 72nd Leg., ch. 366 (H.B. 391), § 1, effective September 1, 1991; am. Acts 1993, 73rd Leg., ch. 900 (S.B. 1067), § 1.01, effective September 1, 1994; am. Acts 1995, 74th Leg., ch. 318 (S.B. 15), § 5, effective September 1, 1995; am. Acts 1995, 74th Leg., ch. 659 (S.B. 134), § 1, effective September 1, 1995; am. Acts 1997, 75th Leg., ch. 165 (S.B. 898), §§ 27.01, 31.01(68), effective September 1, 1997; am. Acts 1999, 76th Leg., ch. 62 (S.B. 1368), § 15.02(a), effective September 1, 1999; am. Acts 1999, 76th Leg., ch. 1158 (S.B. 24), § 1, effective September 1, 1999; am. Acts 2003, 78th Leg., ch. 294 (H.B. 2525), § 1, effective September 1, 2003; am. Acts 2003, 78th Leg., ch. 1019 (H.B. 565), §§ 1, 2, effective September 1, 2003; am. Acts 2003, 78th Leg., ch. 1028 (H.B. 716), § 1, effective September 1, 2003; am. Acts 2005, 79th Leg., ch. 728 (H.B. 2018), §§ 16.001, 16.002, effective September 1, 2005; am. Acts 2005, 79th Leg., ch. 788 (S.B. 91), §§ 1, 2, and 6, effective September 1, 2005; am. Acts 2007, 80th Leg., ch. 623 (H.B. 495), §§ 1, 2, effective September 1, 2007; am. Acts 2009, 81st Leg., ch. 427 (H.B. 2066), § 1, effective September 1, 2009; am. Acts 2009, 81st Leg., ch. 665 (H.B. 2240), § 2, effective September 1, 2009.)

## Sec. 22.011.   Sexual Assault.

(a) A person commits an offense if the person:

(1) intentionally or knowingly:

(A) causes the penetration of the anus or sexual organ of another person by any means, without that person's consent;

(B) causes the penetration of the mouth of another person by the sexual organ of the actor, without that person's consent; or

(C) causes the sexual organ of another person, without that person's consent, to contact or penetrate the mouth, anus, or sexual organ of another person, including the actor; or

(2) intentionally or knowingly:

(A) causes the penetration of the anus or sexual organ of a child by any means;

(B) causes the penetration of the mouth of a child by the sexual organ of the actor;

(C) causes the sexual organ of a child to contact or penetrate the mouth, anus, or sexual organ of another person, including the actor;

(D) causes the anus of a child to contact the mouth, anus, or sexual organ of another person, including the actor; or

(E) causes the mouth of a child to contact the anus or sexual organ of another person, including the actor.

(b) A sexual assault under Subsection (a)(1) is without the consent of the other person if:

(1) the actor compels the other person to submit or participate by the use of physical force or violence;

(2) the actor compels the other person to submit or participate by threatening to use force or violence against the other person, and the other person believes that the actor has the present ability to execute the threat;

(3) the other person has not consented and the actor knows the other person is unconscious or physically unable to resist;

(4) the actor knows that as a result of mental disease or defect the other person is at the time of the sexual assault incapable either of appraising the nature of the act or of resisting it;

(5) the other person has not consented and the actor knows the other person is unaware that the sexual assault is occurring;

(6) the actor has intentionally impaired the other person's power to appraise or control the other person's conduct by administering any substance without the other person's knowledge;

(7) the actor compels the other person to submit or participate by threatening to use force or violence against any person, and the other person believes that the actor has the ability to execute the threat;

(8) the actor is a public servant who coerces the other person to submit or participate;

(9) the actor is a mental health services provider or a health care services provider who causes the other person, who is a patient or former patient of the actor, to submit or participate by exploiting the other person's emotional dependency on the actor;

(10) the actor is a clergyman who causes the other person to submit or participate by exploiting the other person's emotional dependency on the clergyman in the clergyman's professional character as spiritual adviser; or

(11) the actor is an employee of a facility where the other person is a resident, unless the employee and resident are formally or informally married to each other under Chapter 2, Family Code.

(c) In this section:

(1) "Child" means a person younger than 17 years of age.

(2) "Spouse" means a person who is legally married to another.

(3) "Health care services provider" means:

(A) a physician licensed under Subtitle B, Title 3, Occupations Code;

(B) a chiropractor licensed under Chapter 201, Occupations Code;

(C) a physical therapist licensed under Chapter 453, Occupations Code;

(D) a physician assistant licensed under Chapter 204, Occupations Code; or

(E) a registered nurse, a vocational nurse, or an advanced practice nurse licensed under Chapter 301, Occupations Code.

(4) "Mental health services provider" means an individual, licensed or unlicensed, who performs or purports to perform mental health services, including a:

(A) licensed social worker as defined by Section 505.002, Occupations Code;

(B) chemical dependency counselor as defined by Section 504.001, Occupations Code;

(C) licensed professional counselor as defined by Section 503.002, Occupations Code;

(D) licensed marriage and family therapist as defined by Section 502.002, Occupations Code;

(E) member of the clergy;

(F) psychologist offering psychological services as defined by Section 501.003, Occupations Code; or

(G) special officer for mental health assignment certified under Section 1701.404, Occupations Code.

(5) "Employee of a facility" means a person who is an employee of a facility defined by Section 250.001, Health and Safety Code, or any other person who provides services for a facility for compensation, including a contract laborer.

(d) It is a defense to prosecution under Subsection (a)(2) that the conduct consisted of medical care for the child and did not include any contact between the anus or sexual organ of the child and the mouth, anus, or sexual organ of the actor or a third party.

(e) It is an affirmative defense to prosecution under Subsection (a)(2):

(1) that the actor was the spouse of the child at the time of the offense; or

(2) that:

(A) the actor was not more than three years older than the victim and at the time of the offense:

(i) was not required under Chapter 62, Code of Criminal Procedure, to register for life as a sex offender; or

(ii) was not a person who under Chapter 62, Code of Criminal Procedure, had a reportable conviction or adjudication for an offense under this section; and

(B) the victim:

(i) was a child of 14 years of age or older; and

(ii) was not a person whom the actor was prohibited from marrying or purporting to marry or with whom the actor was prohibited from living under the appearance of being married under Section 25.01.

(f) An offense under this section is a felony of the second degree, except that an offense under this section is a felony of the first degree if the victim was a person whom the actor was prohibited from marrying or purporting to marry or with whom the actor was prohibited from living under the appearance of being married under Section 25.01.

(Enacted by Acts 1983, 68th Leg., ch. 977 (H.B. 2008), § 3, effective September 1, 1983; am. Acts 1985, 69th Leg., ch. 557 (H.B. 2139), § 1, effective September 1, 1985; am. Acts 1987, 70th Leg., ch. 1029 (H.B. 2576), § 1, effective September 1, 1987; am. Acts 1991, 72nd Leg., ch. 662 (H.B.

263), § 1, effective September 1, 1991; am. Acts 1993, 73rd Leg., ch. 900 (S.B. 1067), § 1.01, effective September 1, 1994; am. Acts 1995, 74th Leg., ch. 273 (S.B. 286), § 1, effective September 1, 1995; am. Acts 1995, 74th Leg., ch. 318 (S.B. 15), § 6, effective September 1, 1995; am. Acts 1997, 75th Leg., ch. 1031 (S.B. 542), §§ 1, 2, effective September 1, 1997; am. Acts 1997, 75th Leg., ch. 1286 (S.B. 185), § 1, effective September 1, 1997; am. Acts 1999, 76th Leg., ch. 1102 (H.B. 3479), § 3, effective September 1, 1999; am. Acts 1999, 76th Leg., ch. 1415 (H.B. 2145), § 24, effective September 1, 1999; am. Acts 2001, 77th Leg., ch. 1420 (H.B. 2812), § 14.829, effective September 1, 2001; am. Acts 2003, 78th Leg., ch. 155 (S.B. 825), §§ 1, 2, effective September 1, 2003; am. Acts 2003, 78th Leg., ch. 528 (H.B. 1246), § 1, effective September 1, 2003; am. Acts 2003, 78th Leg., ch. 553 (H.B. 1483), § 2.017, effective February 1, 2004; am. Acts 2005, 79th Leg., ch. 268 (S.B. 6), § 4.02, effective September 1, 2005; am. Acts 2009, 81st Leg., ch. 260 (H.B. 549), §§ 3, 4, effective September 1, 2009.)

### Sec. 22.012.  Intentionally Exposing Another to AIDS or HIV [Deleted].

Deleted by Acts 1993, 73rd Leg., ch. 900 (S.B. 1067), § 1.01, effective September 1, 1994. (Enacted by Acts 1989, 71st Leg., ch. 1195 (S.B. 959), § 14, effective September 1, 1989; am. Acts 1991, 72nd Leg., ch. 14 (S.B. 404), § 284(10), effective September 1, 1991.)

### Sec. 22.015.  Coercing, Soliciting, or Inducing Gang Membership [Repealed].

Repealed by Acts 2009, 81st Leg., ch. 435 (H.B. 2187), § 3, effective September 1, 2009. (Enacted by Acts 1999, 76th Leg., ch. 708 (H.B. 861), § 1, effective September 1, 1999.)

### Sec. 22.02.  Aggravated Assault.

(a) A person commits an offense if the person commits assault as defined in Section 22.01 and the person:

(1) causes serious bodily injury to another, including the person's spouse; or

(2) uses or exhibits a deadly weapon during the commission of the assault.

(b) An offense under this section is a felony of the second degree, except that the offense is a felony of the first degree if:

(1) the actor uses a deadly weapon during the commission of the assault and causes seri-

ous bodily injury to a person whose relationship to or association with the defendant is described by Section 71.0021(b), 71.003, or 71.005, Family Code;

(2) regardless of whether the offense is committed under Subsection (a)(1) or (a)(2), the offense is committed:

(A) by a public servant acting under color of the servant's office or employment;

(B) against a person the actor knows is a public servant while the public servant is lawfully discharging an official duty, or in retaliation or on account of an exercise of official power or performance of an official duty as a public servant;

(C) in retaliation against or on account of the service of another as a witness, prospective witness, informant, or person who has reported the occurrence of a crime; or

(D) against a person the actor knows is a security officer while the officer is performing a duty as a security officer; or

(3) the actor is in a motor vehicle, as defined by Section 501.002, Transportation Code, and:

(A) knowingly discharges a firearm at or in the direction of a habitation, building, or vehicle;

(B) is reckless as to whether the habitation, building, or vehicle is occupied; and

(C) in discharging the firearm, causes serious bodily injury to any person.

(c) The actor is presumed to have known the person assaulted was a public servant or a security officer if the person was wearing a distinctive uniform or badge indicating the person's employment as a public servant or status as a security officer.

(d) In this section, "security officer" means a commissioned security officer as defined by Section 1702.002, Occupations Code, or a noncommissioned security officer registered under Section 1702.221, Occupations Code.

(Enacted by Acts 1973, 63rd Leg., ch. 399 (S.B. 34), § 1, effective January 1, 1974; am. Acts 1979, 66th Leg., ch. 164 (S.B. 529), § 3, effective September 1, 1979; am. Acts 1979, 66th Leg., ch. 655 (S.B. 846), § 2, effective September 1, 1979; am. Acts 1983, 68th Leg., ch. 79 (S.B. 173), § 1, effective September 1, 1983; am. Acts 1983, 68th Leg., ch. 977 (H.B. 2008), § 2, effective September 1, 1983; am. Acts 1985, 69th Leg., ch. 223 (S.B. 447), § 1, effective September 1, 1985; am. Acts 1987, 70th Leg., ch. 18 (S.B. 251), § 3, effective April 14, 1987; am. Acts 1987, 70th Leg., ch. 1101 (S.B. 341), § 12, effective September 1,

1987; am. Acts 1989, 71st Leg., ch. 939 (H.B. 9), §§ 1-3, effective September 1, 1989; am. Acts 1991, 72nd Leg., ch. 334 (H.B. 1188), § 2, effective September 1, 1991; am. Acts 1991, 72nd Leg., ch. 903 (H.B. 806), § 1, effective September 1, 1991; am. Acts 1993, 73rd Leg., ch. 900 (S.B. 1067), § 1.01, effective September 1, 1994; am. Acts 2003, 78th Leg., ch. 1019 (H.B. 565), § 3, effective September 1, 2003; am. Acts 2005, 79th Leg., ch. 788 (S.B. 91), § 3, effective September 1, 2005; am. Acts 2009, 81st Leg., ch. 594 (H.B. 176), § 2, effective September 1, 2009.)

## Sec. 22.021. Aggravated Sexual Assault.

(a) A person commits an offense:

(1) if the person:

(A) intentionally or knowingly:

(i) causes the penetration of the anus or sexual organ of another person by any means, without that person's consent;

(ii) causes the penetration of the mouth of another person by the sexual organ of the actor, without that person's consent; or

(iii) causes the sexual organ of another person, without that person's consent, to contact or penetrate the mouth, anus, or sexual organ of another person, including the actor; or

(B) intentionally or knowingly:

(i) causes the penetration of the anus or sexual organ of a child by any means;

(ii) causes the penetration of the mouth of a child by the sexual organ of the actor;

(iii) causes the sexual organ of a child to contact or penetrate the mouth, anus, or sexual organ of another person, including the actor;

(iv) causes the anus of a child to contact the mouth, anus, or sexual organ of another person, including the actor; or

(v) causes the mouth of a child to contact the anus or sexual organ of another person, including the actor; and

(2) if:

(A) the person:

(i) causes serious bodily injury or attempts to cause the death of the victim or another person in the course of the same criminal episode;

(ii) by acts or words places the victim in fear that any person will become the victim of an offense under Section 20A.02(a)(3), (4), (7), or (8) or that death, serious bodily injury, or kidnapping will be imminently inflicted on any person;

(iii) by acts or words occurring in the presence of the victim threatens to cause any person to become the victim of an offense under Section 20A.02(a)(3), (4), (7), or (8) or to cause the death, serious bodily injury, or kidnapping of any person;

(iv) uses or exhibits a deadly weapon in the course of the same criminal episode;

(v) acts in concert with another who engages in conduct described by Subdivision (1) directed toward the same victim and occurring during the course of the same criminal episode; or

(vi) administers or provides flunitrazepam, otherwise known as rohypnol, gamma hydroxybutyrate, or ketamine to the victim of the offense with the intent of facilitating the commission of the offense;

(B) the victim is younger than 14 years of age; or

(C) the victim is an elderly individual or a disabled individual.

(b) In this section:

(1) "Child" has the meaning assigned by Section 22.011(c).

(2) "Elderly individual" and "disabled individual" have the meanings assigned by Section 22.04(c).

(c) An aggravated sexual assault under this section is without the consent of the other person if the aggravated sexual assault occurs under the same circumstances listed in Section 22.011(b).

(d) The defense provided by Section 22.011(d) applies to this section.

(e) An offense under this section is a felony of the first degree.

(f) The minimum term of imprisonment for an offense under this section is increased to 25 years if:

(1) the victim of the offense is younger than six years of age at the time the offense is committed; or

(2) the victim of the offense is younger than 14 years of age at the time the offense is committed and the actor commits the offense in a manner described by Subsection (a)(2)(A).

(Enacted by Acts 1983, 68th Leg., ch. 977 (H.B. 2008), § 3, effective September 1, 1983; am. Acts 1987, 70th Leg., ch. 573 (H.B. 161), § 1, effective September 1, 1987; am. Acts 1987, 70th Leg., 2nd C.S., ch. 16 (S.B. 35), § 1, effective September 1, 1987; am. Acts 1993, 73rd Leg., ch. 900 (S.B.

1067), § 1.01, effective September 1, 1994; am. Acts 1995, 74th Leg., ch. 318 (S.B. 15), § 7, effective September 1, 1995; am. Acts 1997, 75th Leg., ch. 1286 (S.B. 185), § 2, effective September 1, 1997; am. Acts 1999, 76th Leg., ch. 417 (S.B. 1100), § 1, effective September 1, 1999; am. Acts 2001, 77th Leg., ch. 459 (H.B. 139), § 5, effective September 1, 2001; am. Acts 2003, 78th Leg., ch. 528 (H.B. 1246), § 2, effective September 1, 2003; am. Acts 2003, 78th Leg., ch. 896 (S.B. 837), § 1, effective September 1, 2003; am. Acts 2007, 80th Leg., ch. 593 (H.B. 8), § 1.18, effective September 1, 2007; am. Acts 2011, 82nd Leg., ch. 1 (S.B. 24), § 6.05, effective September 1, 2011.)

## Sec. 22.03. Deadly Assault on Law Enforcement or Corrections Officer, Member or Employee of Board of Pardons and Paroles, Court Participant, Probation Personnel, or Employee of Texas Youth Commission [Deleted].

Deleted by Acts 1993, 73rd Leg., ch. 900 (S.B. 1067), § 1.01, effective September 1, 1994.
(Enacted by Acts 1973, 63rd Leg., ch. 399 (S.B. 34), § 1, effective January 1, 1974; am. Acts 1979, 66th Leg., ch. 655 (S.B. 846), § 3, effective September 1, 1979; am. Acts 1983, 68th Leg., ch. 79 (S.B. 173), § 2, effective September 1, 1983; am. Acts 1985, 69th Leg., ch. 256 (H.B. 833), § 1, effective September 1, 1985; am. Acts 1987, 70th Leg., ch. 18 (S.B. 251), § 4, effective April 14, 1987; am. Acts 1987, 70th Leg., ch. 1101 (S.B. 341), § 13, effective September 1, 1987; am. Acts 1989, 71st Leg., ch. 2 (S.B. 221), § 12.01, effective August 28, 1989; am. Acts 1989, 71st Leg., ch. 939 (H.B. 9), §§ 4, 5, effective September 1, 1989; am. Acts 1991, 72nd Leg., ch. 334 (H.B. 1188), § 3, effective September 1, 1991; am. Acts 1991, 72nd Leg., ch. 903 (H.B. 806), §§ 2-4, effective September 1, 1991.)

## Sec. 22.04. Injury to a Child, Elderly Individual, or Disabled Individual.

(a) A person commits an offense if he intentionally, knowingly, recklessly, or with criminal negligence, by act or intentionally, knowingly, or recklessly by omission, causes to a child, elderly individual, or disabled individual:

(1) serious bodily injury;

(2) serious mental deficiency, impairment, or injury; or

(3) bodily injury.

(a-1) A person commits an offense if the person is an owner, operator, or employee of a group home, nursing facility, assisted living facility, intermediate care facility for persons with mental retardation, or other institutional care facility and the person intentionally, knowingly, recklessly, or with criminal negligence by omission causes to a child, elderly individual, or disabled individual who is a resident of that group home or facility:

(1) serious bodily injury;

(2) serious mental deficiency, impairment, or injury; or

(3) bodily injury.

(b) An omission that causes a condition described by Subsection (a)(1), (2), or (3) or (a-1)(1), (2), or (3) is conduct constituting an offense under this section if:

(1) the actor has a legal or statutory duty to act; or

(2) the actor has assumed care, custody, or control of a child, elderly individual, or disabled individual.

(c) In this section:

(1) "Child" means a person 14 years of age or younger.

(2) "Elderly individual" means a person 65 years of age or older.

(3) "Disabled individual" means a person older than 14 years of age who by reason of age or physical or mental disease, defect, or injury is substantially unable to protect himself from harm or to provide food, shelter, or medical care for himself.

(4) [Repealed by Acts 2011, 82nd Leg., ch. 620 (S.B. 688), § 11, effective September 1, 2011.]

(d) For purposes of an omission that causes a condition described by Subsection (a)(1), (2), or (3), the actor has assumed care, custody, or control if he has by act, words, or course of conduct acted so as to cause a reasonable person to conclude that he has accepted responsibility for protection, food, shelter, and medical care for a child, elderly individual, or disabled individual. For purposes of an omission that causes a condition described by Subsection (a-1)(1), (2), or (3), the actor acting during the actor's capacity as owner, operator, or employee of a group home or facility described by Subsection (a-1) is considered to have accepted responsibility for protection, food, shelter, and medical care for the child, elderly individual, or disabled individual who is a resident of the group home or facility.

(e) An offense under Subsection (a)(1) or (2) or (a-1)(1) or (2) is a felony of the first degree when the conduct is committed intentionally or knowingly. When the conduct is engaged in recklessly, the offense is a felony of the second degree.

(f) An offense under Subsection (a)(3) or (a-1)(3) is a felony of the third degree when the conduct is committed intentionally or knowingly, except that an offense under Subsection (a)(3) is a felony of the second degree when the conduct is committed intentionally or knowingly and the victim is a disabled individual residing in a center, as defined by Section 555.001, Health and Safety Code, or in a facility licensed under Chapter 252, Health and Safety Code, and the actor is an employee of the center or facility whose employment involved providing direct care for the victim. When the conduct is engaged in recklessly, the offense is a state jail felony.

(g) An offense under Subsection (a) is a state jail felony when the person acts with criminal negligence. An offense under Subsection (a-1) is a state jail felony when the person, with criminal negligence and by omission, causes a condition described by Subsection (a-1)(1), (2), or (3).

(h) A person who is subject to prosecution under both this section and another section of this code may be prosecuted under either or both sections. Section 3.04 does not apply to criminal episodes prosecuted under both this section and another section of this code. If a criminal episode is prosecuted under both this section and another section of this code and sentences are assessed for convictions under both sections, the sentences shall run concurrently.

(i) It is an affirmative defense to prosecution under Subsection (b)(2) that before the offense the actor:

(1) notified in person the child, elderly individual, or disabled individual that he would no longer provide any of the care described by Subsection (d); and

(2) notified in writing the parents or person other than himself acting in loco parentis to the child, elderly individual, or disabled individual that he would no longer provide any of the care described by Subsection (d); or

(3) notified in writing the Department of Protective and Regulatory Services that he would no longer provide any of the care set forth in Subsection (d).

(j) Written notification under Subsection (i)(2) or (i)(3) is not effective unless it contains the name and address of the actor, the name and address of the child, elderly individual, or disabled individual, the type of care provided by the actor, and the date the care was discontinued.

(k) It is a defense to prosecution under this section that the act or omission consisted of:

(1) reasonable medical care occurring under the direction of or by a licensed physician; or

(2) emergency medical care administered in good faith and with reasonable care by a person not licensed in the healing arts.

(l) It is an affirmative defense to prosecution under this section:

(1) that the act or omission was based on treatment in accordance with the tenets and practices of a recognized religious method of healing with a generally accepted record of efficacy;

(2) for a person charged with an act of omission causing to a child, elderly individual, or disabled individual a condition described by Subsection (a)(1), (2), or (3) that:

(A) there is no evidence that, on the date prior to the offense charged, the defendant was aware of an incident of injury to the child, elderly individual, or disabled individual and failed to report the incident; and

(B) the person:

(i) was a victim of family violence, as that term is defined by Section 71.004, Family Code, committed by a person who is also charged with an offense against the child, elderly individual, or disabled individual under this section or any other section of this title;

(ii) did not cause a condition described by Subsection (a)(1), (2), or (3); and

(iii) did not reasonably believe at the time of the omission that an effort to prevent the person also charged with an offense against the child, elderly individual, or disabled individual from committing the offense would have an effect; or

(3) that:

(A) the actor was not more than three years older than the victim at the time of the offense; and

(B) the victim was a child at the time of the offense.

(Enacted by Acts 1973, 63rd Leg., ch. 399 (S.B. 34), § 1, effective January 1, 1974; am. Acts 1977, 65th Leg., ch. 819 (H.B. 1089), § 1, effective August 29, 1977; am. Acts 1979, 66th Leg., ch. 162 (S.B. 394), § 1, effective August 27, 1979; am. Acts 1981, 67th Leg., ch. 202 (S.B. 126), § 4, effective September 1, 1981; am. Acts 1981, 67th Leg., ch. 604 (H.B. 1459), § 1, effective September 1, 1981; am. Acts 1989, 71st Leg., ch. 357 (S.B. 1154), § 1, effective September 1, 1989; am.

Acts 1991, 72nd Leg., ch. 497 (S.B. 1436), § 1, effective September 1, 1991; am. Acts 1993, 73rd Leg., ch. 900 (S.B. 1067), § 1.01, effective September 1, 1994; am. Acts 1995, 74th Leg., ch. 76 (S.B. 959), § 8.139, effective September 1, 1995; am. Acts 1999, 76th Leg., ch. 62 (S.B. 1368), § 15.02(b), effective September 1, 1999; am. Acts 2005, 79th Leg., ch. 268 (S.B. 6), § 1.125(a), effective September 1, 2005; am. Acts 2005, 79th Leg., ch. 949 (H.B. 1575), § 46, effective September 1, 2005; am. Acts 2009, 81st Leg., ch. 284 (S.B. 643), § 38, effective June 11, 2009; am. Acts 2011, 82nd Leg., ch. 620 (S.B. 688), §§ 5, 11, effective September 1, 2011.)

### Sec. 22.041. Abandoning or Endangering Child.

(a) In this section, "abandon" means to leave a child in any place without providing reasonable and necessary care for the child, under circumstances under which no reasonable, similarly situated adult would leave a child of that age and ability.

(b) A person commits an offense if, having custody, care, or control of a child younger than 15 years, he intentionally abandons the child in any place under circumstances that expose the child to an unreasonable risk of harm.

(c) A person commits an offense if he intentionally, knowingly, recklessly, or with criminal negligence, by act or omission, engages in conduct that places a child younger than 15 years in imminent danger of death, bodily injury, or physical or mental impairment.

(c-1) For purposes of Subsection (c), it is presumed that a person engaged in conduct that places a child in imminent danger of death, bodily injury, or physical or mental impairment if:

(1) the person manufactured, possessed, or in any way introduced into the body of any person the controlled substance methamphetamine in the presence of the child;

(2) the person's conduct related to the proximity or accessibility of the controlled substance methamphetamine to the child and an analysis of a specimen of the child's blood, urine, or other bodily substance indicates the presence of methamphetamine in the child's body; or

(3) the person injected, ingested, inhaled, or otherwise introduced a controlled substance listed in Penalty Group 1, Section 481.102, Health and Safety Code, into the human body when the person was not in lawful possession of the substance as defined by Section 481.002(24) of that code.

(d) Except as provided by Subsection (e), an offense under Subsection (b) is:

(1) a state jail felony if the actor abandoned the child with intent to return for the child; or

(2) a felony of the third degree if the actor abandoned the child without intent to return for the child.

(e) An offense under Subsection (b) is a felony of the second degree if the actor abandons the child under circumstances that a reasonable person would believe would place the child in imminent danger of death, bodily injury, or physical or mental impairment.

(f) An offense under Subsection (c) is a state jail felony.

(g) It is a defense to prosecution under Subsection (c) that the act or omission enables the child to practice for or participate in an organized athletic event and that appropriate safety equipment and procedures are employed in the event.

(h) It is an exception to the application of this section that the actor voluntarily delivered the child to a designated emergency infant care provider under Section 262.302, Family Code.
(Enacted by Acts 1985, 69th Leg., ch. 791 (S.B. 175), § 1, effective September 1, 1985; am. Acts 1989, 71st Leg., ch. 904 (S.B. 748), § 1, effective September 1, 1989; am. Acts 1993, 73rd Leg., ch. 900 (S.B. 1067), § 1.01, effective September 1, 1994; am. Acts 1997, 75th Leg., ch. 687 (S.B. 612), § 1, effective September 1, 1997; am. Acts 1999, 76th Leg., ch. 1087 (H.B. 3423), § 3, effective September 1, 1999; am. Acts 2001, 77th Leg., ch. 809 (H.B. 706), § 7, effective September 1, 2001; am. Acts 2005, 79th Leg., ch. 282 (H.B. 164), § 10, effective August 1, 2005; am. Acts 2007, 80th Leg., ch. 840 (H.B. 946), § 2, effective September 1, 2007.)

### Sec. 22.05. Deadly Conduct.

(a) A person commits an offense if he recklessly engages in conduct that places another in imminent danger of serious bodily injury.

(b) A person commits an offense if he knowingly discharges a firearm at or in the direction of:

(1) one or more individuals; or

(2) a habitation, building, or vehicle and is reckless as to whether the habitation, building, or vehicle is occupied.

(c) Recklessness and danger are presumed if the actor knowingly pointed a firearm at or in the direction of another whether or not the actor believed the firearm to be loaded.

(d) For purposes of this section, "building," "habitation," and "vehicle" have the meanings assigned those terms by Section 30.01.

(e) An offense under Subsection (a) is a Class A misdemeanor. An offense under Subsection (b) is a felony of the third degree.

(Enacted by Acts 1973, 63rd Leg., ch. 399 (S.B. 34), § 1, effective January 1, 1974; am. Acts 1993, 73rd Leg., ch. 900 (S.B. 1067), § 1.01, effective September 1, 1994.)

### Sec. 22.06. Consent As Defense to Assaultive Conduct.

(a) The victim's effective consent or the actor's reasonable belief that the victim consented to the actor's conduct is a defense to prosecution under Section 22.01 (Assault), 22.02 (Aggravated Assault), or 22.05 (Deadly Conduct) if:

(1) the conduct did not threaten or inflict serious bodily injury; or

(2) the victim knew the conduct was a risk of:

(A) his occupation;

(B) recognized medical treatment; or

(C) a scientific experiment conducted by recognized methods.

(b) The defense to prosecution provided by Subsection (a) is not available to a defendant who commits an offense described by Subsection (a) as a condition of the defendant's or the victim's initiation or continued membership in a criminal street gang, as defined by Section 71.01.

(Enacted by Acts 1973, 63rd Leg., ch. 399 (S.B. 34), § 1, effective January 1, 1974; am. Acts 1993, 73rd Leg., ch. 900 (S.B. 1067), § 1.01, effective September 1, 1994; am. Acts 2007, 80th Leg., ch. 273 (H.B. 184), § 1, effective September 1, 2007.)

### Sec. 22.065. Evidence of Previous Sexual Conduct [Repealed].

Repealed by the Texas Court of Criminal Appeals pursuant to Acts 1985, 69th Leg., ch. 685 (H.B. 13), § 9.

(Enacted by Acts 1975, 64th Leg., ch. 203 (H.B. 284), § 3, effective September 1, 1975; am. Acts 1983, 68th Leg., ch. 977 (H.B. 2008), § 4, effective September 1, 1983 (renumbered from Sec. 21.13).)

### Sec. 22.07. Terroristic Threat.

(a) A person commits an offense if he threatens to commit any offense involving violence to any person or property with intent to:

(1) cause a reaction of any type to his threat by an official or volunteer agency organized to deal with emergencies;

(2) place any person in fear of imminent serious bodily injury;

(3) prevent or interrupt the occupation or use of a building, room, place of assembly, place to which the public has access, place of employment or occupation, aircraft, automobile, or other form of conveyance, or other public place;

(4) cause impairment or interruption of public communications, public transportation, public water, gas, or power supply or other public service;

(5) place the public or a substantial group of the public in fear of serious bodily injury; or

(6) influence the conduct or activities of a branch or agency of the federal government, the state, or a political subdivision of the state.

(b) An offense under Subsection (a)(1) is a Class B misdemeanor.

(c) An offense under Subsection (a)(2) is a Class B misdemeanor, except that the offense is a Class A misdemeanor if the offense:

(1) is committed against a member of the person's family or household or otherwise constitutes family violence; or

(2) is committed against a public servant.

(d) An offense under Subsection (a)(3) is a Class A misdemeanor, unless the actor causes pecuniary loss of $1,500 or more to the owner of the building, room, place, or conveyance, in which event the offense is a state jail felony.

(e) An offense under Subsection (a)(4), (a)(5), or (a)(6) is a felony of the third degree.

(f) In this section:

(1) "Family" has the meaning assigned by Section 71.003, Family Code.

(2) "Family violence" has the meaning assigned by Section 71.004, Family Code.

(3) "Household" has the meaning assigned by Section 71.005, Family Code.

(g) For purposes of Subsection (d), the amount of pecuniary loss is the amount of economic loss suffered by the owner of the building, room, place, or conveyance as a result of the prevention or interruption of the occupation or use of the building, room, place, or conveyance.

(Enacted by Acts 1973, 63rd Leg., ch. 399 (S.B. 34), § 1, effective January 1, 1974; am. Acts 1979, 66th Leg., ch. 530 (S.B. 952), § 2, effective August 27, 1979; am. Acts 1993, 73rd Leg., ch. 900 (S.B. 1067), § 1.01, effective September 1, 1994; am. Acts 2003, 78th Leg., ch. 139 (S.B. 408), § 1, effective September 1, 2003; am. Acts 2003, 78th

Leg., ch. 388 (H.B. 11), § 2, effective September 1, 2003; am. Acts 2003, 78th Leg., ch. 446 (H.B. 616), § 1, effective September 1, 2003; am. Acts 2005, 79th Leg., ch. 728 (H.B. 2018), § 16.003, effective September 1, 2005.)

### Sec. 22.08. Aiding Suicide.

(a) A person commits an offense if, with intent to promote or assist the commission of suicide by another, he aids or attempts to aid the other to commit or attempt to commit suicide.

(b) An offense under this section is a Class C misdemeanor unless the actor's conduct causes suicide or attempted suicide that results in serious bodily injury, in which event the offense is a state jail felony.

(Enacted by Acts 1973, 63rd Leg., ch. 399 (S.B. 34), § 1, effective January 1, 1974; am. Acts 1993, 73rd Leg., ch. 900 (S.B. 1067), § 1.01, effective September 1, 1994.)

### Sec. 22.09. Tampering with Consumer Product.

(a) In this section:

(1) "Consumer Product" means any product offered for sale to or for consumption by the public and includes "food" and "drugs" as those terms are defined in Section 431.002, Health and Safety Code.

(2) "Tamper" means to alter or add a foreign substance to a consumer product to make it probable that the consumer product will cause serious bodily injury.

(b) A person commits an offense if he knowingly or intentionally tampers with a consumer product knowing that the consumer product will be offered for sale to the public or as a gift to another.

(c) A person commits an offense if he knowingly or intentionally threatens to tamper with a consumer product with the intent to cause fear, to affect the sale of the consumer product, or to cause bodily injury to any person.

(d) An offense under Subsection (b) is a felony of the second degree unless a person suffers serious bodily injury, in which event it is a felony of the first degree. An offense under Subsection (c) is a felony of the third degree.

(Enacted by Acts 1983, 68th Leg., ch. 481 (S.B. 160), § 1, effective September 1, 1983; am. Acts 1989, 71st Leg., ch. 1008 (H.B. 972), § 1, effective September 1, 1989; am. Acts 1991, 72nd Leg., ch. 14 (S.B. 404), § 284(32), effective September 1, 1991; am. Acts 1993, 73rd Leg., ch. 900 (S.B. 1067), § 1.01, effective September 1, 1994.)

### Sec. 22.10. Leaving a Child in a Vehicle.

(a) A person commits an offense if he intentionally or knowingly leaves a child in a motor vehicle for longer than five minutes, knowing that the child is:

(1) younger than seven years of age; and

(2) not attended by an individual in the vehicle who is 14 years of age or older.

(b) An offense under this section is a Class C misdemeanor.

(Enacted by Acts 1984, 68th Leg., 2nd C.S., ch. 24 (H.B. 90), § 1, effective October 2, 1984; am. Acts 1993, 73rd Leg., ch. 900 (S.B. 1067), § 1.01, effective September 1, 1994.)

### Sec. 22.11. Harassment by Persons in Certain Correctional Facilities; Harassment of Public Servant.

(a) A person commits an offense if, with the intent to assault, harass, or alarm, the person:

(1) while imprisoned or confined in a correctional or detention facility, causes another person to contact the blood, seminal fluid, vaginal fluid, saliva, urine, or feces of the actor, any other person, or an animal; or

(2) causes another person the actor knows to be a public servant to contact the blood, seminal fluid, vaginal fluid, saliva, urine, or feces of the actor, any other person, or an animal while the public servant is lawfully discharging an official duty or in retaliation or on account of an exercise of the public servant's official power or performance of an official duty.

(b) An offense under this section is a felony of the third degree.

(c) If conduct constituting an offense under this section also constitutes an offense under another section of this code, the actor may be prosecuted under either section.

(d) In this section, "correctional or detention facility" means:

(1) a secure correctional facility; or

(2) a "secure correctional facility" or a "secure detention facility" as defined by Section 51.02, Family Code, operated by or under contract with a juvenile board or the Texas Youth Commission or any other facility operated by or under contract with that commission.

(e) For purposes of Subsection (a)(2), the actor is presumed to have known the person was a public servant if the person was wearing a distinctive uniform or badge indicating the person's employment as a public servant.

(Enacted by Acts 1999, 76th Leg., ch. 335 (H.B. 1713), § 1, effective September 1, 1999; am. Acts 2003, 78th Leg., ch. 878 (S.B. 729), § 1, effective September 1, 2003; am. Acts 2003, 78th Leg., ch. 1006 (H.B. 274), § 1, effective September 1, 2003; am. Acts 2005, 79th Leg., ch. 543 (H.B. 1095), §§ 1, 2, effective September 1, 2005; am. Acts 2005, 79th Leg., ch. 543 (H.B. 1095), § 2, effective September 1, 2005.)

### Sec. 22.12. Applicability to Certain Conduct.

This chapter does not apply to conduct charged as having been committed against an individual who is an unborn child if the conduct is:

(1) committed by the mother of the unborn child;

(2) a lawful medical procedure performed by a physician or other health care provider with the requisite consent;

(3) a lawful medical procedure performed by a physician or other licensed health care provider with the requisite consent as part of an assisted reproduction as defined by Section 160.102, Family Code; or

(4) the dispensation of a drug in accordance with law or administration of a drug prescribed in accordance with law.

(Enacted by Acts 2003, 78th Leg., ch. 822 (S.B. 319), § 2.04, effective September 1, 2003.)

# TITLE 6

# OFFENSES AGAINST THE FAMILY

## CHAPTER 25
## OFFENSES AGAINST THE FAMILY

### Sec. 25.01. Bigamy.

(a) An individual commits an offense if:

(1) he is legally married and he:

(A) purports to marry or does marry a person other than his spouse in this state, or any other state or foreign country, under circumstances that would, but for the actor's prior marriage, constitute a marriage; or

(B) lives with a person other than his spouse in this state under the appearance of being married; or

(2) he knows that a married person other than his spouse is married and he:

(A) purports to marry or does marry that person in this state, or any other state or foreign country, under circumstances that would, but for the person's prior marriage, constitute a marriage; or

(B) lives with that person in this state under the appearance of being married.

(b) For purposes of this section, "under the appearance of being married" means holding out that the parties are married with cohabitation and an intent to be married by either party.

(c) It is a defense to prosecution under Subsection (a)(1) that the actor reasonably believed at the time of the commission of the offense that the actor and the person whom the actor married or purported to marry or with whom the actor lived under the appearance of being married were legally eligible to be married because the actor's prior marriage was void or had been dissolved by death, divorce, or annulment. For purposes of this subsection, an actor's belief is reasonable if the belief is substantiated by a certified copy of a death certificate or other signed document issued by a court.

(d) For the purposes of this section, the lawful wife or husband of the actor may testify both for or against the actor concerning proof of the original marriage.

(e) An offense under this section is a felony of the third degree, except that if at the time of the commission of the offense, the person whom the actor marries or purports to marry or with whom the actor lives under the appearance of being married is:

(1) 17 years of age, the offense is a felony of the second degree; or

(2) 16 years of age or younger, the offense is a felony of the first degree.

(Enacted by Acts 1973, 63rd Leg., ch. 399 (S.B. 34), § 1, effective January 1, 1974; am. Acts 1993, 73rd Leg., ch. 900 (S.B. 1067), § 1.01, effective September 1, 1994; am. Acts 2005, 79th Leg., ch. 268 (S.B. 6), § 4.03, effective September 1, 2005; am. Acts 2011, 82nd Leg., ch. 222 (H.B. 253), § 4, effective September 1, 2011.)

### Sec. 25.02. Prohibited Sexual Conduct.

(a) A person commits an offense if the person engages in sexual intercourse or deviate sexual intercourse with another person the actor knows to be, without regard to legitimacy:

(1) the actor's ancestor or descendant by blood or adoption;

(2) the actor's current or former stepchild or stepparent;

(3) the actor's parent's brother or sister of the whole or half blood;

(4) the actor's brother or sister of the whole or half blood or by adoption;

(5) the children of the actor's brother or sister of the whole or half blood or by adoption; or

(6) the son or daughter of the actor's aunt or uncle of the whole or half blood or by adoption.

(b) For purposes of this section:

(1) "Deviate sexual intercourse" means any contact between the genitals of one person and the mouth or anus of another person with intent to arouse or gratify the sexual desire of any person.

(2) "Sexual intercourse" means any penetration of the female sex organ by the male sex organ.

(c) An offense under this section is a felony of the third degree, unless the offense is committed under Subsection (a)(1), in which event the offense is a felony of the second degree.

(Enacted by Acts 1973, 63rd Leg., ch. 399 (S.B. 34), § 1, effective January 1, 1974; am. Acts 1993, 73rd Leg., ch. 900 (S.B. 1067), § 1.01, effective September 1, 1994; am. Acts 2005, 79th Leg., ch. 268 (S.B. 6), § 4.04, effective September 1, 2005; am. Acts 2009, 81st Leg., ch. 673 (H.B. 2385), § 1, effective September 1, 2009.)

### Sec. 25.03. Interference with Child Custody.

(a) A person commits an offense if the person takes or retains a child younger than 18 years of age:

(1) when the person knows that the person's taking or retention violates the express terms of a judgment or order, including a temporary order, of a court disposing of the child's custody;

(2) when the person has not been awarded custody of the child by a court of competent jurisdiction, knows that a suit for divorce or a civil suit or application for habeas corpus to dispose of the child's custody has been filed, and takes the child out of the geographic area of the counties composing the judicial district if the court is a district court or the county if the court is a statutory county court, without the permission of the court and with the intent to deprive the court of authority over the child; or

(3) outside of the United States with the intent to deprive a person entitled to possession of or access to the child of that possession or access and without the permission of that person.

(b) A noncustodial parent commits an offense if, with the intent to interfere with the lawful custody of a child younger than 18 years, the noncustodial parent knowingly entices or persuades the child to leave the custody of the custodial parent, guardian, or person standing in the stead of the custodial parent or guardian of the child.

(c) It is a defense to prosecution under Subsection (a)(2) that the actor returned the child to the geographic area of the counties composing the judicial district if the court is a district court or the county if the court is a statutory county court, within three days after the date of the commission of the offense.

(c-1) It is an affirmative defense to prosecution under Subsection (a)(3) that:

(1) the taking or retention of the child was pursuant to a valid order providing for possession of or access to the child; or

(2) notwithstanding any violation of a valid order providing for possession of or access to the child, the actor's retention of the child was due only to circumstances beyond the actor's control and the actor promptly provided notice or made reasonable attempts to provide notice of those circumstances to the other person entitled to possession of or access to the child.

(c-2) Subsection (a)(3) does not apply if, at the time of the offense, the person taking or retaining the child:

(1) was entitled to possession of or access to the child; and

(2) was fleeing the commission or attempted commission of family violence, as defined by

Section 71.004, Family Code, against the child or the person.

(d) An offense under this section is a state jail felony.

(Enacted by Acts 1973, 63rd Leg., ch. 399 (S.B. 34), § 1, effective January 1, 1974; am. Acts 1979, 66th Leg., ch. 527 (S.B. 886), § 1, effective August 27, 1979; am. Acts 1987, 70th Leg., ch. 444 (H.B. 113), § 1, effective September 1, 1987; am. Acts 1989, 71st Leg., ch. 830 (S.B. 388), § 1, effective September 1, 1989; am. Acts 1993, 73rd Leg., ch. 900 (S.B. 1067), § 1.01, effective September 1, 1994; am. Acts 2001, 77th Leg., ch. 332 (H.B. 2621), § 1, effective May 24, 2001; am. Acts 2007, 80th Leg., ch. 272 (H.B. 95), § 1, effective September 1, 2007; am. Acts 2011, 82nd Leg., ch. 840 (H.B. 3439), § 2, effective September 1, 2011; am. Acts 2011, 82nd Leg., ch. 1100 (S.B. 1551), § 3, effective September 1, 2011.)

## Sec. 25.031.  Agreement to Abduct from Custody.

(a) A person commits an offense if the person agrees, for remuneration or the promise of remuneration, to abduct a child younger than 18 years of age by force, threat of force, misrepresentation, stealth, or unlawful entry, knowing that the child is under the care and control of a person having custody or physical possession of the child under a court order, including a temporary order, or under the care and control of another person who is exercising care and control with the consent of a person having custody or physical possession under a court order, including a temporary order.

(b) An offense under this section is a state jail felony.

(Enacted by Acts 1987, 70th Leg., ch. 444 (H.B. 113), § 3, effective September 1, 1987; am. Acts 1993, 73rd Leg., ch. 900 (S.B. 1067), § 1.01, effective September 1, 1994; am. Acts 2007, 80th Leg., ch. 272 (H.B. 95), § 2, effective September 1, 2007.)

## Sec. 25.04.  Enticing a Child.

(a) A person commits an offense if, with the intent to interfere with the lawful custody of a child younger than 18 years, he knowingly entices, persuades, or takes the child from the custody of the parent or guardian or person standing in the stead of the parent or guardian of such child.

(b) An offense under this section is a Class B misdemeanor, unless it is shown on the trial of the offense that the actor intended to commit a felony against the child, in which event an offense under this section is a felony of the third degree. (Enacted by Acts 1973, 63rd Leg., ch. 399 (S.B. 34), § 1, effective January 1, 1974; am. Acts 1993, 73rd Leg., ch. 900 (S.B. 1067), § 1.01, effective September 1, 1994; am. Acts 1999, 76th Leg., ch. 685 (H.B. 668), § 7, effective September 1, 1999.)

## Sec. 25.05.  Criminal Nonsupport.

(a) An individual commits an offense if the individual intentionally or knowingly fails to provide support for the individual's child younger than 18 years of age, or for the individual's child who is the subject of a court order requiring the individual to support the child.

(b) For purposes of this section, "child" includes a child born out of wedlock whose paternity has either been acknowledged by the actor or has been established in a civil suit under the Family Code or the law of another state.

(c) Under this section, a conviction may be had on the uncorroborated testimony of a party to the offense.

(d) It is an affirmative defense to prosecution under this section that the actor could not provide support for the actor's child.

(e) The pendency of a prosecution under this section does not affect the power of a court to enter an order for child support under the Family Code.

(f) An offense under this section is a state jail felony.

(Enacted by Acts 1973, 63rd Leg., ch. 399 (S.B. 34), § 1, effective January 1, 1974; am. Acts 1987, 70th Leg., 2nd C.S., ch. 73 (H.B. 167), § 13, effective November 1, 1987; am. Acts 1993, 73rd Leg., ch. 900 (S.B. 1067), § 1.01, effective September 1, 1994; am. Acts 2001, 77th Leg., ch. 375 (H.B. 2610), § 1, effective May 25, 2001.)

## Sec. 25.06.  Harboring Runaway Child.

(a) A person commits an offense if he knowingly harbors a child and he is criminally negligent about whether the child:

(1) is younger than 18 years; and

(2) has escaped from the custody of a peace officer, a probation officer, the Texas Youth Council, or a detention facility for children, or is voluntarily absent from the child's home without the consent of the child's parent or guardian for a substantial length of time or without the intent to return.

(b) It is a defense to prosecution under this section that the actor was related to the child within the second degree by consanguinity or affinity, as determined under Chapter 573, Government Code.

(c) It is a defense to prosecution under this section that the actor notified:

(1) the person or agency from which the child escaped or a law enforcement agency of the presence of the child within 24 hours after discovering that the child had escaped from custody; or

(2) a law enforcement agency or a person at the child's home of the presence of the child within 24 hours after discovering that the child was voluntarily absent from home without the consent of the child's parent or guardian.

(d) An offense under this section is a Class A misdemeanor.

(e) On the receipt of a report from a peace officer, probation officer, the Texas Youth Council, a foster home, or a detention facility for children that a child has escaped its custody or upon receipt of a report from a parent, guardian, conservator, or legal custodian that a child is missing, a law enforcement agency shall immediately enter a record of the child into the National Crime Information Center.

(Enacted by Acts 1979, 66th Leg., ch. 558 (H.B. 1375), § 1, effective September 1, 1979; am. Acts 1983, 68th Leg., ch. 831 (H.B. 1061), § 1, effective September 1, 1983; am. Acts 1991, 72nd Leg., ch. 561 (H.B. 1345), § 40, effective August 26, 1991; am. Acts 1993, 73rd Leg., ch. 900 (S.B. 1067), § 1.01, effective September 1, 1994 (renumbered from Sec. 25.07); am. Acts 1995, 74th Leg., ch. 76 (S.B. 959), § 5.95(27), effective September 1, 1995.)

## Sec. 25.07. Violation of Certain Court Orders or Conditions of Bond in a Family Violence Case.

(a) A person commits an offense if, in violation of a condition of bond set in a family violence case and related to the safety of the victim or the safety of the community, an order issued under Article 17.292, Code of Criminal Procedure, an order issued under Section 6.504, Family Code, Chapter 83, Family Code, if the temporary ex parte order has been served on the person, or Chapter 85, Family Code, or an order issued by another jurisdiction as provided by Chapter 88, Family Code, the person knowingly or intentionally:

(1) commits family violence or an act in furtherance of an offense under Section 22.011, 22.021, or 42.072;

(2) communicates:

(A) directly with a protected individual or a member of the family or household in a threatening or harassing manner;

(B) a threat through any person to a protected individual or a member of the family or household; or

(C) in any manner with the protected individual or a member of the family or household except through the person's attorney or a person appointed by the court, if the violation is of an order described by this subsection and the order prohibits any communication with a protected individual or a member of the family or household;

(3) goes to or near any of the following places as specifically described in the order or condition of bond:

(A) the residence or place of employment or business of a protected individual or a member of the family or household; or

(B) any child care facility, residence, or school where a child protected by the order or condition of bond normally resides or attends;

(4) possesses a firearm; or

(5) harms, threatens, or interferes with the care, custody, or control of a pet, companion animal, or assistance animal that is possessed by a person protected by the order.

(b) For the purposes of this section:

(1) "Family violence," "family," "household," and "member of a household" have the meanings assigned by Chapter 71, Family Code.

(2) "Firearm" has the meaning assigned by Chapter 46.

(3) "Assistance animal" has the meaning assigned by Section 121.002, Human Resources Code.

(c) If conduct constituting an offense under this section also constitutes an offense under another section of this code, the actor may be prosecuted under either section or under both sections.

(d) Reconciliatory actions or agreements made by persons affected by an order do not affect the validity of the order or the duty of a peace officer to enforce this section.

(e) A peace officer investigating conduct that may constitute an offense under this section for a violation of an order may not arrest a person protected by that order for a violation of that order.

(f) It is not a defense to prosecution under this section that certain information has been excluded, as provided by Section 85.007, Family Code, or Article 17.292, Code of Criminal Procedure, from an order to which this section applies.

(g) An offense under this section is a Class A misdemeanor unless it is shown on the trial of the offense that the defendant has previously been convicted under this section two or more times or has violated the order or condition of bond by committing an assault or the offense of stalking, in which event the offense is a third degree felony. (Enacted by Acts 1983, 68th Leg., ch. 631 (S.B. 997), § 3, effective September 1, 1983; am. Acts 1985, 69th Leg., ch. 583 (S.B. 869), § 3, effective September 1, 1985; am. Acts 1987, 70th Leg., ch. 170 (S.B. 1111), § 1, effective September 1, 1987; am. Acts 1987, 70th Leg., ch. 677 (S.B. 887), § 8, effective September 1, 1987; am. Acts 1989, 71st Leg., ch. 614 (S.B. 171), §§ 23—26, effective September 1, 1989; am. Acts 1989, 71st Leg., ch. 739 (H.B. 1230), §§ 4—7, effective September 1, 1989; am. Acts 1991, 72nd Leg., ch. 366 (H.B. 391), § 2, effective September 1, 1991; am. Acts 1993, 73rd Leg., ch. 900 (S.B. 1067), § 1.01, effective September 1, 1994 (renumbered from Sec. 25.08); am. Acts 1995, 74th Leg., ch. 658 (S.B. 129), §§ 2, 3, effective June 14, 1995; am. Acts 1995, 74th Leg., ch. 660 (S.B. 135), § 1, effective September 1, 1995; am. Acts 1995, 74th Leg., ch. 1024 (H.B. 418), § 23, effective September 1, 1995; am. Acts 1997, 75th Leg., ch. 1 (S.B. 97), § 2, effective January 28, 1997; am. Acts 1997, 75th Leg., ch. 1193 (S.B. 1253), § 21, effective September 1, 1997; am. Acts 1999, 76th Leg., ch. 62 (S.B. 1368), § 15.02(c), effective September 1, 1999; am. Acts 2001, 77th. Leg., ch. 23 (S.B. 199), § 1, effective September 1, 2001; am. Acts 2003, 78th Leg., ch. 134 (S.B. 317), § 1, effective September 1, 2003; am. Acts 2007, 80th Leg., ch. 66 (S.B. 584), § 2, effective May 11, 2007; am. Acts 2007, 80th Leg., ch. 1113 (H.B. 3692), §§ 1, 2, effective January 1, 2008; am. Acts 2009, 81st Leg., ch. 87 (S.B. 1969), § 19.001, effective September 1, 2009; am. Acts 2011, 82nd Leg., ch. 136 (S.B. 279), §§ 3, 4, effective September 1, 2011.)

## Sec. 25.071.   Violation of Protective Order Preventing Offense Caused by Bias or Prejudice.

(a) A person commits an offense if, in violation of an order issued under Article 6.08, Code of Criminal Procedure, the person knowingly or intentionally:

(1) commits an offense under Title 5 or Section 28.02, 28.03, or 28.08 and commits the offense because of bias or prejudice as described by Article 42.014, Code of Criminal Procedure;

(2) communicates:

(A) directly with a protected individual in a threatening or harassing manner;

(B) a threat through any person to a protected individual; or

(C) in any manner with the protected individual, if the order prohibits any communication with a protected individual; or

(3) goes to or near the residence or place of employment or business of a protected individual.

(b) If conduct constituting an offense under this section also constitutes an offense under another section of this code, the actor may be prosecuted under either section or under both sections.

(c) A peace officer investigating conduct that may constitute an offense under this section for a violation of an order may not arrest a person protected by that order for a violation of that order.

(d) An offense under this section is a Class A misdemeanor unless it is shown on the trial of the offense that the defendant has previously been convicted under this section two or more times or has violated the protective order by committing an assault, in which event the offense is a third degree felony.
(Enacted by Acts 2001, 77th Leg., ch. 85 (H.B. 587), § 3.02, effective September 1, 2001.)

## Sec. 25.08.   Sale or Purchase of Child.

(a) A person commits an offense if he:

(1) possesses a child younger than 18 years of age or has the custody, conservatorship, or guardianship of a child younger than 18 years of age, whether or not he has actual possession of the child, and he offers to accept, agrees to accept, or accepts a thing of value for the delivery of the child to another or for the possession of the child by another for purposes of adoption; or

(2) offers to give, agrees to give, or gives a thing of value to another for acquiring or maintaining the possession of a child for the purpose of adoption.

(b) It is an exception to the application of this section that the thing of value is:

(1) a fee or reimbursement paid to a child-placing agency as authorized by law;

(2) a fee paid to an attorney, social worker, mental health professional, or physician for

services rendered in the usual course of legal or medical practice or in providing adoption counseling;

(3) a reimbursement of legal or medical expenses incurred by a person for the benefit of the child; or

(4) a necessary pregnancy-related expense paid by a child-placing agency for the benefit of the child's parent during the pregnancy or after the birth of the child as permitted by the minimum standards for child-placing agencies and Department of Protective and Regulatory Services rules.

(c) An offense under this section is a felony of the third degree, except that the offense is a felony of the second degree if the actor commits the offense with intent to commit an offense under Section 20A.02, 43.02, 43.05, or 43.25.

(Enacted by Acts 1977, 65th Leg., ch. 38 (S.B. 217), § 1, effective March 30, 1977; am. Acts 1981, 67th Leg., ch. 514 (H.B. 42), § 1, effective September 1, 1981; am. Acts 1987, 70th Leg., ch. 167 (S.B. 892), § 5.01(a)(44), effective September 1, 1987 (renumbered from Sec. 25.06); am. Acts 1993, 73rd Leg., ch. 900 (S.B. 1067), § 1.01, effective September 1, 1994 (renumbered from Sec. 25.11); am. Acts 2001, 77th Leg., ch. 134 (H.B. 1634), § 1, effective September 1, 2001; am. Acts 2003, 78th Leg., ch. 1005 (H.B. 236), § 3, effective September 1, 2003; am. Acts 2011, 82nd Leg., ch. 515 (H.B. 2014), § 4.01, effective September 1, 2011.)

## Sec. 25.09.   Advertising for Placement of Child.

(a) A person commits an offense if the person advertises in the public media that the person will place a child for adoption or will provide or obtain a child for adoption.

(b) This section does not apply to a licensed child-placing agency that is identified in the advertisement as a licensed child-placing agency.

(c) An offense under this section is a Class A misdemeanor unless the person has been convicted previously under this section, in which event the offense is a felony of the third degree.

(d) In this section:

(1) "Child" has the meaning assigned by Section 101.003, Family Code.

(2) "Public media" has the meaning assigned by Section 38.01. The term also includes communications through the use of the Internet or another public computer network.

(Enacted by Acts 1997, 75th Leg., ch. 561 (H.B. 1091), § 31, effective September 1, 1997.)

## Sec. 25.10.   Interference with Rights of Guardian of the Person.

(a) In this section:

(1) "Possessory right" means the right of a guardian of the person to have physical possession of a ward and to establish the ward's legal domicile, as provided by Section 767(1), Texas Probate Code.

(2) "Ward" has the meaning assigned by Section 601, Texas Probate Code.

(b) A person commits an offense if the person takes, retains, or conceals a ward when the person knows that the person's taking, retention, or concealment interferes with a possessory right with respect to the ward.

(c) An offense under this section is a state jail felony.

(d) This section does not apply to a governmental entity where the taking, retention, or concealment of the ward was authorized by Subtitle E, Title 5, Family Code, or Chapter 48, Human Resources Code.

(Enacted by Acts 2003, 78th Leg., ch. 549 (H.B. 1470), § 32, effective September 1, 2003.)

## Sec. 25.11.   Continuous Violence Against the Family.

(a) A person commits an offense if, during a period that is 12 months or less in duration, the person two or more times engages in conduct that constitutes an offense under Section 22.01(a)(1) against another person or persons whose relationship to or association with the defendant is described by Section 71.0021(b), 71.003, or 71.005, Family Code.

(b) If the jury is the trier of fact, members of the jury are not required to agree unanimously on the specific conduct in which the defendant engaged that constituted an offense under Section 22.01(a)(1) against the person or persons described by Subsection (a) or the exact date when that conduct occurred. The jury must agree unanimously that the defendant, during a period that is 12 months or less in duration, two or more times engaged in conduct that constituted an offense under Section 22.01(a)(1) against the person or persons described by Subsection (a).

(c) A defendant may not be convicted in the same criminal action of another offense the victim of which is an alleged victim of the offense under Subsection (a) and an element of which is any conduct that is alleged as an element of the offense under Subsection (a) unless the other offense:

(1) is charged in the alternative;

(2) occurred outside the period in which the offense alleged under Subsection (a) was committed; or

(3) is considered by the trier of fact to be a lesser included offense of the offense alleged under Subsection (a).

(d) A defendant may not be charged with more than one count under Subsection (a) if all of the specific conduct that is alleged to have been engaged in is alleged to have been committed against a single victim or members of the same household, as defined by Section 71.005, Family Code.

(e) An offense under this section is a felony of the third degree.

(Enacted by Acts 2009, 81st Leg., ch. 665 (H.B. 2240), § 1, effective September 1, 2009.)

# TITLE 7
# OFFENSES AGAINST PROPERTY

## CHAPTER 28
## ARSON, CRIMINAL MISCHIEF, AND OTHER PROPERTY DAMAGE OR DESTRUCTION

## Sec. 28.01.  Definitions.

In this chapter:

(1) "Habitation" means a structure or vehicle that is adapted for the overnight accommodation of persons and includes:

(A) each separately secured or occupied portion of the structure or vehicle; and

(B) each structure appurtenant to or connected with the structure or vehicle.

(2) "Building" means any structure or enclosure intended for use or occupation as a habitation or for some purpose of trade, manufacture, ornament, or use.

(3) "Property" means:

(A) real property;

(B) tangible or intangible personal property, including anything severed from land; or

(C) a document, including money, that represents or embodies anything of value.

(4) "Vehicle" includes any device in, on, or by which any person or property is or may be propelled, moved, or drawn in the normal course of commerce or transportation.

(5) "Open-space land" means real property that is undeveloped for the purpose of human habitation.

(6) "Controlled burning" means the burning of unwanted vegetation with the consent of the owner of the property on which the vegetation is located and in such a manner that the fire is controlled and limited to a designated area.

(Enacted by Acts 1973, 63rd Leg., ch. 399 (S.B. 34), § 1, effective January 1, 1974; am. Acts 1979, 66th Leg., ch. 588 (S.B. 254), § 1, effective September 1, 1979; am. Acts 1989, 71st Leg., ch. 31 (S.B. 12), § 1, effective September 1, 1989; am. Acts 1993, 73rd Leg., ch. 900 (S.B. 1067), § 1.01, effective September 1, 1994.)

## Sec. 28.02.  Arson.

(a) A person commits an offense if the person starts a fire, regardless of whether the fire continues after ignition, or causes an explosion with intent to destroy or damage:

(1) any vegetation, fence, or structure on open-space land; or

(2) any building, habitation, or vehicle:

(A) knowing that it is within the limits of an incorporated city or town;

(B) knowing that it is insured against damage or destruction;

(C) knowing that it is subject to a mortgage or other security interest;

(D) knowing that it is located on property belonging to another;

(E) knowing that it has located within it property belonging to another; or

(F) when the person is reckless about whether the burning or explosion will endanger the life of some individual or the safety of the property of another.

(a-1) A person commits an offense if the person recklessly starts a fire or causes an explosion while manufacturing or attempting to manufacture a controlled substance and the fire or explosion damages any building, habitation, or vehicle.

(a-2) A person commits an offense if the person intentionally starts a fire or causes an explosion and in so doing:

(1) recklessly damages or destroys a building belonging to another; or

(2) recklessly causes another person to suffer bodily injury or death.

(b) It is an exception to the application of Subsection (a)(1) that the fire or explosion was a part of the controlled burning of open-space land.

(c) It is a defense to prosecution under Subsection (a)(2)(A) that prior to starting the fire or causing the explosion, the actor obtained a permit or other written authorization granted in accordance with a city ordinance, if any, regulating fires and explosions.

(d) An offense under Subsection (a) is a felony of the second degree, except that the offense is a felony of the first degree if it is shown on the trial of the offense that:

(1) bodily injury or death was suffered by any person by reason of the commission of the offense; or

(2) the property intended to be damaged or destroyed by the actor was a habitation or a place of assembly or worship.

(e) An offense under Subsection (a-1) is a state jail felony, except that the offense is a felony of the third degree if it is shown on the trial of the offense that bodily injury or death was suffered by any person by reason of the commission of the offense.

(f) An offense under Subsection (a-2) is a state jail felony.

(g) If conduct that constitutes an offense under Subsection (a-1) or that constitutes an offense under Subsection (a-2) also constitutes an offense under another subsection of this section or another section of this code, the actor may be prosecuted under Subsection (a-1) or Subsection (a-2), under the other subsection of this section, or under the other section of this code.

(Enacted by Acts 1973, 63rd Leg., ch. 399 (S.B. 34), § 1, effective January 1, 1974; am. Acts 1979, 66th Leg., ch. 588 (S.B. 254), § 2, effective September 1, 1979; am. Acts 1981, 67th Leg., ch. 425 (H.B. 927), § 1, effective September 1, 1981; am. Acts 1989, 71st Leg., ch. 31 (S.B. 12), § 2, effective September 1, 1989; am. Acts 1993, 73rd Leg., ch. 900 (S.B. 1067), § 1.01, effective September 1, 1994; am. Acts 1997, 75th Leg., ch. 1006 (S.B. 78), § 1, effective September 1, 1997; am. Acts 2001, 77th Leg., ch. 976 (H.B. 171), § 1, effective September 1, 2001; am. Acts 2005, 79th Leg., ch. 960 (H.B. 1634), § 1, effective September 1, 2005; am.

Acts 2009, 81st Leg., ch. 1168 (H.B. 3224), § 1, effective September 1, 2009.)

## Sec. 28.03.   Criminal Mischief.

(a) A person commits an offense if, without the effective consent of the owner:

(1) he intentionally or knowingly damages or destroys the tangible property of the owner;

(2) he intentionally or knowingly tampers with the tangible property of the owner and causes pecuniary loss or substantial inconvenience to the owner or a third person; or

(3) he intentionally or knowingly makes markings, including inscriptions, slogans, drawings, or paintings, on the tangible property of the owner.

(b) Except as provided by Subsections (f) and (h), an offense under this section is:

(1) a Class C misdemeanor if:

(A) the amount of pecuniary loss is less than $50; or

(B) except as provided in Subdivision (3)(A) or (3)(B), it causes substantial inconvenience to others;

(2) a Class B misdemeanor if the amount of pecuniary loss is $50 or more but less than $500;

(3) a Class A misdemeanor if:

(A) the amount of pecuniary loss is $500 or more but less than $1,500; or

(B) the actor causes in whole or in part impairment or interruption of any public water supply, or causes to be diverted in whole, in part, or in any manner, including installation or removal of any device for any such purpose, any public water supply, regardless of the amount of the pecuniary loss;

(4) a state jail felony if the amount of pecuniary loss is:

(A) $1,500 or more but less than $20,000;

(B) less than $1,500, if the property damaged or destroyed is a habitation and if the damage or destruction is caused by a firearm or explosive weapon;

(C) less than $1,500, if the property was a fence used for the production or containment of:

(i) cattle, bison, horses, sheep, swine, goats, exotic livestock, or exotic poultry; or

(ii) game animals as that term is defined by Section 63.001, Parks and Wildlife Code; or

(D) less than $20,000 and the actor causes wholly or partly impairment or interruption of public communications, public transportation, public gas or power supply, or other public service, or causes to be diverted wholly, partly, or in any manner, including installation or removal of any device for any such purpose, any public communications or public gas or power supply;

(5) a felony of the third degree if the amount of the pecuniary loss is $20,000 or more but less than $100,000;

(6) a felony of the second degree if the amount of pecuniary loss is $100,000 or more but less than $200,000; or

(7) a felony of the first degree if the amount of pecuniary loss is $200,000 or more.

(c) For the purposes of this section, it shall be presumed that a person who is receiving the economic benefit of public communications, public water, gas, or power supply, has knowingly tampered with the tangible property of the owner if the communication or supply has been:

(1) diverted from passing through a metering device; or

(2) prevented from being correctly registered by a metering device; or

(3) activated by any device installed to obtain public communications, public water, gas, or power supply without a metering device.

(d) The terms "public communication, public transportation, public gas or power supply, or other public service" and "public water supply" shall mean, refer to, and include any such services subject to regulation by the Public Utility Commission of Texas, the Railroad Commission of Texas, or the Texas Natural Resource Conservation Commission or any such services enfranchised by the State of Texas or any political subdivision thereof.

(e) When more than one item of tangible property, belonging to one or more owners, is damaged, destroyed, or tampered with in violation of this section pursuant to one scheme or continuing course of conduct, the conduct may be considered as one offense, and the amounts of pecuniary loss to property resulting from the damage to, destruction of, or tampering with the property may be aggregated in determining the grade of the offense.

(f) An offense under this section is a state jail felony if the damage or destruction is inflicted on a place of worship or human burial, a public monument, or a community center that provides medical, social, or educational programs and the amount of the pecuniary loss to real property or to tangible personal property is less than $20,000.

(g) In this section:

(1) "Explosive weapon" means any explosive or incendiary device that is designed, made, or adapted for the purpose of inflicting serious bodily injury, death, or substantial property damage, or for the principal purpose of causing such a loud report as to cause undue public alarm or terror, and includes:

(A) an explosive or incendiary bomb, grenade, rocket, and mine;

(B) a device designed, made, or adapted for delivering or shooting an explosive weapon; and

(C) a device designed, made, or adapted to start a fire in a time-delayed manner.

(2) "Firearm" has the meaning assigned by Section 46.01.

(3) "Institution of higher education" has the meaning assigned by Section 61.003, Education Code.

(4) "Aluminum wiring" means insulated or noninsulated wire or cable that consists of at least 50 percent aluminum, including any tubing or conduit attached to the wire or cable.

(5) "Bronze wiring" means insulated or noninsulated wire or cable that consists of at least 50 percent bronze, including any tubing or conduit attached to the wire or cable.

(6) "Copper wiring" means insulated or noninsulated wire or cable that consists of at least 50 percent copper, including any tubing or conduit attached to the wire or cable.

(7) "Transportation communications equipment" means:

(A) an official traffic-control device, railroad sign or signal, or traffic-control signal, as those terms are defined by Section 541.304, Transportation Code; or

(B) a sign, signal, or device erected by a railroad, public body, or public officer to direct the movement of a railroad train, as defined by Section 541.202, Transportation Code.

(8) "Transportation communications device" means any item attached to transportation communications equipment, including aluminum wiring, bronze wiring, and copper wiring.

(h) An offense under this section is a state jail felony if the amount of the pecuniary loss to real property or to tangible personal property is $1,500 or more but less than $20,000 and the damage or destruction is inflicted on a public or

**Penal Code**

private elementary school, secondary school, or institution of higher education.

(i) Notwithstanding Subsection (b), an offense under this section is a felony of the first degree if the property is livestock and the damage is caused by introducing bovine spongiform encephalopathy, commonly known as mad cow disease, or a disease described by Section 161.041(a), Agriculture Code. In this subsection, "livestock" has the meaning assigned by Section 161.001, Agriculture Code.

(j) Notwithstanding Subsection (b), an offense under this section is a felony of the third degree if:

(1) the tangible property damaged, destroyed, or tampered with is transportation communications equipment or a transportation communications device; and

(2) the amount of the pecuniary loss to the tangible property is less than $100,000.

(Enacted by Acts 1973, 63rd Leg., ch. 399 (S.B. 34), § 1, effective January 1, 1974; am. Acts 1981, 67th Leg., ch. 29 (S.B. 211), § 1, effective August 31, 1981; am. Acts 1983, 68th Leg., ch. 497 (S.B. 283), § 1, effective September 1, 1983; am. Acts 1985, 69th Leg., ch. 352 (H.B. 95), § 1, effective September 1, 1985; am. Acts 1989, 71st Leg., ch. 559 (H.B. 1416), § 1, effective June 14, 1989; am. Acts 1989, 71st Leg., ch. 1253 (H.B. 1777), § 1, effective September 1, 1989; am. Acts 1989, 71st Leg., 1st C.S., ch. 42 (H.B. 103), § 1, effective September 1, 1989; am. Acts 1993, 73rd Leg., ch. 900 (S.B. 1067), § 1.01, effective September 1, 1994; am. Acts 1995, 74th Leg., ch. 76 (S.B. 959), § 11.280, effective September 1, 1995; am. Acts 1997, 75th Leg., ch. 1083 (H.B. 1370), § 1, effective September 1, 1997; am. Acts 1999, 76th Leg., ch. 686 (H.B. 690), § 1, effective September 1, 1999; am. Acts 2001, 77th Leg., ch. 747 (S.B. 1174), § 1, effective September 1, 2001; am. Acts 2001, 77th Leg., ch. 976 (H.B. 171), § 2, effective September 1, 2001; am. Acts 2003, 78th Leg., ch. 1280 (H.B. 240), § 1, effective September 1, 2003; am. Acts 2007, 80th Leg., ch. 690 (H.B. 1767), §§ 1, 2, effective September 1, 2007; am. Acts 2009, 81st Leg., ch. 638 (H.B. 1614), § 1, effective September 1, 2009.)

### Sec. 28.04. Reckless Damage or Destruction.

(a) A person commits an offense if, without the effective consent of the owner, he recklessly damages or destroys property of the owner.

(b) An offense under this section is a Class C misdemeanor.

(Enacted by Acts 1973, 63rd Leg., ch. 399 (S.B. 34), § 1, effective January 1, 1974; am. Acts 1993, 73rd Leg., ch. 900 (S.B. 1067), § 1.01, effective September 1, 1994.)

### Sec. 28.05. Actor's Interest in Property.

It is no defense to prosecution under this chapter that the actor has an interest in the property damaged or destroyed if another person also has an interest that the actor is not entitled to infringe.

(Enacted by Acts 1973, 63rd Leg., ch. 399 (S.B. 34), § 1, effective January 1, 1974; am. Acts 1993, 73rd Leg., ch. 900 (S.B. 1067), § 1.01, effective September 1, 1994.)

### Sec. 28.06. Amount of Pecuniary Loss.

(a) The amount of pecuniary loss under this chapter, if the property is destroyed, is:

(1) the fair market value of the property at the time and place of the destruction; or

(2) if the fair market value of the property cannot be ascertained, the cost of replacing the property within a reasonable time after the destruction.

(b) The amount of pecuniary loss under this chapter, if the property is damaged, is the cost of repairing or restoring the damaged property within a reasonable time after the damage occurred.

(c) The amount of pecuniary loss under this chapter for documents, other than those having a readily ascertainable market value, is:

(1) the amount due and collectible at maturity less any part that has been satisfied, if the document constitutes evidence of a debt; or

(2) the greatest amount of economic loss that the owner might reasonably suffer by virtue of the destruction or damage if the document is other than evidence of a debt.

(d) If the amount of pecuniary loss cannot be ascertained by the criteria set forth in Subsections (a) through (c), the amount of loss is deemed to be greater than $500 but less than $1,500.

(e) If the actor proves by a preponderance of the evidence that he gave consideration for or had a legal interest in the property involved, the value of the interest so proven shall be deducted from:

(1) the amount of pecuniary loss if the property is destroyed; or

(2) the amount of pecuniary loss to the extent of an amount equal to the ratio the value of

the interest bears to the total value of the property, if the property is damaged.

(Enacted by Acts 1973, 63rd Leg., ch. 399 (S.B. 34), § 1, effective January 1, 1974; am. Acts 1983, 68th Leg., ch. 497 (S.B. 283), § 2, effective September 1, 1983; am. Acts 1993, 73rd Leg., ch. 900 (S.B. 1067), § 1.01, effective September 1, 1994.)

## Sec. 28.07. Interference with Railroad Property.

(a) In this section:

(1) "Railroad property" means:

(A) a train, locomotive, railroad car, caboose, work equipment, rolling stock, safety device, switch, or connection that is owned, leased, operated, or possessed by a railroad; or

(B) a railroad track, rail, bridge, trestle, or right-of-way owned or used by a railroad.

(2) "Tamper" means to move, alter, or interfere with railroad property.

(b) A person commits an offense if the person:

(1) throws an object or discharges a firearm or weapon at a train or rail-mounted work equipment; or

(2) without the effective consent of the owner:

(A) enters or remains on railroad property, knowing that it is railroad property;

(B) tampers with railroad property;

(C) places an obstruction on a railroad track or right-of-way; or

(D) causes in any manner the derailment of a train, railroad car, or other railroad property that moves on tracks.

(c) An offense under Subsection (b)(1) is a Class B misdemeanor unless the person causes bodily injury to another, in which event the offense is a felony of the third degree.

(d) An offense under Subsection (b)(2)(A) is a Class C misdemeanor.

(e) An offense under Subsection (b)(2)(B), (b)(2)(C), or (b)(2)(D) is a Class C misdemeanor unless the person causes pecuniary loss, in which event the offense is:

(1) a Class B misdemeanor if the amount of pecuniary loss is $20 or more but less than $500;

(2) a Class A misdemeanor if the amount of pecuniary loss is $500 or more but less than $1,500;

(3) a state jail felony if the amount of pecuniary loss is $1,500 or more but less than $20,000;

(4) a felony of the third degree if the amount of the pecuniary loss is $20,000 or more but less than $100,000;

(5) a felony of the second degree if the amount of pecuniary loss is $100,000 or more but less than $200,000; or

(6) a felony of the first degree if the amount of the pecuniary loss is $200,000 or more.

(f) The conduct described in Subsection (b)(2)(A) is not an offense under this section if it is undertaken by an employee of the railroad or by a representative of a labor organization which represents or is seeking to represent the employees of the railroad as long as the employee or representative has a right to engage in such conduct under the Railway Labor Act (45 U.S.C. Section 151 et seq.).

(Enacted by Acts 1989, 71st Leg., ch. 908 (S.B. 789), § 1, effective September 1, 1989; am. Acts 1993, 73rd Leg., ch. 900 (S.B. 1067), § 1.01, effective September 1, 1994.)

## Sec. 28.08. Graffiti.

(a) A person commits an offense if, without the effective consent of the owner, the person intentionally or knowingly makes markings, including inscriptions, slogans, drawings, or paintings, on the tangible property of the owner with:

(1) paint;

(2) an indelible marker; or

(3) an etching or engraving device.

(b) Except as provided by Subsection (d), an offense under this section is:

(1) a Class B misdemeanor if the amount of pecuniary loss is less than $500;

(2) a Class A misdemeanor if the amount of pecuniary loss is $500 or more but less than $1,500;

(3) a state jail felony if the amount of pecuniary loss is $1,500 or more but less than $20,000;

(4) a felony of the third degree if the amount of pecuniary loss is $20,000 or more but less than $100,000;

(5) a felony of the second degree if the amount of pecuniary loss is $100,000 or more but less than $200,000; or

(6) a felony of the first degree if the amount of pecuniary loss is $200,000 or more.

(c) When more than one item of tangible property, belonging to one or more owners, is marked in violation of this section pursuant to one scheme or continuing course of conduct, the conduct may be considered as one offense, and the amounts of pecuniary loss to property resulting from the marking of the property may be aggregated in determining the grade of the offense.

(d) An offense under this section is a state jail felony if:

(1) the marking is made on a school, an institution of higher education, a place of worship or human burial, a public monument, or a community center that provides medical, social, or educational programs; and

(2) the amount of the pecuniary loss to real property or to tangible personal property is less than $20,000.

(e) In this section:

(1) "Aerosol paint" means an aerosolized paint product.

(2) "Etching or engraving device" means a device that makes a delineation or impression on tangible property, regardless of the manufacturer's intended use for that device.

(3) "Indelible marker" means a device that makes a mark with a paint or ink product that is specifically formulated to be more difficult to erase, wash out, or remove than ordinary paint or ink products.

(4) "Institution of higher education" has the meaning assigned by Section 481.134, Health and Safety Code.

(5) "School" means a private or public elementary or secondary school.

(Enacted by Acts 1997, 75th Leg., ch. 593 (S.B. 758), § 1, effective September 1, 1997; am. Acts 1999, 76th Leg., ch. 166 (H.B. 152), §§ 1, 2, effective September 1, 1999; am. Acts 1999, 76th Leg., ch. 695 (H.B. 751), § 1, effective September 1, 1999; am. Acts 2001, 77th Leg., ch. 1420 (H.B. 2812), § 16.001, effective September 1, 2001; am. Acts 2009 81st Leg., ch. 639 (H.B. 1633), § 4, effective September 1, 2009.)

# CHAPTER 29
# ROBBERY

## Sec. 29.01.  Definitions.

In this chapter:

(1) "In the course of committing theft" means conduct that occurs in an attempt to commit, during the commission, or in immediate flight after the attempt or commission of theft.

(2) "Property" means:

(A) tangible or intangible personal property including anything severed from land; or

(B) a document, including money, that represents or embodies anything of value.

(Enacted by Acts 1973, 63rd Leg., ch. 399 (S.B. 34), § 1, effective January 1, 1974; am. Acts 1993, 73rd Leg., ch. 900 (S.B. 1067), § 1.01, effective September 1, 1994.)

## Sec. 29.02.  Robbery.

(a) A person commits an offense if, in the course of committing theft as defined in Chapter 31 and with intent to obtain or maintain control of the property, he:

(1) intentionally, knowingly, or recklessly causes bodily injury to another; or

(2) intentionally or knowingly threatens or places another in fear of imminent bodily injury or death.

(b) An offense under this section is a felony of the second degree.

(Enacted by Acts 1973, 63rd Leg., ch. 399 (S.B. 34), § 1, effective January 1, 1974; am. Acts 1993, 73rd Leg., ch. 900 (S.B. 1067), § 1.01, effective September 1, 1994.)

## Sec. 29.03.  Aggravated Robbery.

(a) A person commits an offense if he commits robbery as defined in Section 29.02, and he:

(1) causes serious bodily injury to another;

(2) uses or exhibits a deadly weapon; or

(3) causes bodily injury to another person or threatens or places another person in fear of imminent bodily injury or death, if the other person is:

(A) 65 years of age or older; or

(B) a disabled person.

(b) An offense under this section is a felony of the first degree.

(c) In this section, "disabled person" means an individual with a mental, physical, or developmental disability who is substantially unable to protect himself from harm.

(Enacted by Acts 1973, 63rd Leg., ch. 399 (S.B. 34), § 1, effective January 1, 1974; am. Acts 1989, 71st Leg., ch. 357 (S.B. 1154), § 2, effective September 1, 1989; am. Acts 1993, 73rd Leg., ch. 900 (S.B. 1067), § 1.01, effective September 1, 1994.)

## CHAPTER 30
## BURGLARY AND CRIMINAL TRESPASS

## Sec. 30.01. Definitions.

In this chapter:

(1) "Habitation" means a structure or vehicle that is adapted for the overnight accommodation of persons, and includes:

(A) each separately secured or occupied portion of the structure or vehicle; and

(B) each structure appurtenant to or connected with the structure or vehicle.

(2) "Building" means any enclosed structure intended for use or occupation as a habitation or for some purpose of trade, manufacture, ornament, or use.

(3) "Vehicle" includes any device in, on, or by which any person or property is or may be propelled, moved, or drawn in the normal course of commerce or transportation, except such devices as are classified as "habitation."

(Enacted by Acts 1973, 63rd Leg., ch. 399 (S.B. 34), § 1, effective January 1, 1974; am. Acts 1993, 73rd Leg., ch. 900 (S.B. 1067), § 1.01, effective September 1, 1994.)

## Sec. 30.02. Burglary.

(a) A person commits an offense if, without the effective consent of the owner, the person:

(1) enters a habitation, or a building (or any portion of a building) not then open to the public, with intent to commit a felony, theft, or an assault; or

(2) remains concealed, with intent to commit a felony, theft, or an assault, in a building or habitation; or

(3) enters a building or habitation and commits or attempts to commit a felony, theft, or an assault.

(b) For purposes of this section, "enter" means to intrude:

(1) any part of the body; or

(2) any physical object connected with the body.

(c) Except as provided in Subsection (d), an offense under this section is a:

(1) state jail felony if committed in a building other than a habitation; or

(2) felony of the second degree if committed in a habitation.

(d) An offense under this section is a felony of the first degree if:

(1) the premises are a habitation; and

(2) any party to the offense entered the habitation with intent to commit a felony other than felony theft or committed or attempted to commit a felony other than felony theft.

(Enacted by Acts 1973, 63rd Leg., ch. 399 (S.B. 34), § 1, effective January 1, 1974; am. Acts 1993, 73rd Leg., ch. 900 (S.B. 1067), § 1.01, effective September 1, 1994; am. Acts 1995, 74th Leg., ch. 318 (S.B. 15), § 8, effective September 1, 1995; am. Acts 1999, 76th Leg., ch. 727 (H.B. 998), § 1, effective September 1, 1999.)

## Sec. 30.03. Burglary of Coin-Operated or Coin Collection Machines.

(a) A person commits an offense if, without the effective consent of the owner, he breaks or enters into any coin-operated machine, coin collection machine, or other coin-operated or coin collection receptacle, contrivance, apparatus, or equipment used for the purpose of providing lawful amusement, sales of goods, services, or other valuable things, or telecommunications with intent to obtain property or services.

(b) For purposes of this section, "entry" includes every kind of entry except one made with the effective consent of the owner.

(c) An offense under this section is a Class A misdemeanor.

(Enacted by Acts 1973, 63rd Leg., ch. 399 (S.B. 34), § 1, effective January 1, 1974; am. Acts 1987, 70th Leg., ch. 62 (S.B. 701), § 1, effective September 1, 1987; am. Acts 1993, 73rd Leg., ch. 900 (S.B. 1067), § 1.01, effective September 1, 1994.)

## Sec. 30.04. Burglary of Vehicles.

(a) A person commits an offense if, without the effective consent of the owner, he breaks into or enters a vehicle or any part of a vehicle with intent to commit any felony or theft.

(b) For purposes of this section, "enter" means to intrude:

(1) any part of the body; or

(2) any physical object connected with the body.

(c) For purposes of this section, a container or trailer carried on a rail car is a part of the rail car.

(d) An offense under this section is a Class A misdemeanor, except that:

(1) the offense is a Class A misdemeanor with a minimum term of confinement of six months if it is shown on the trial of the offense that the defendant has been previously convicted of an offense under this section; and

(2) the offense is a state jail felony if:

(A) it is shown on the trial of the offense that the defendant has been previously convicted two or more times of an offense under this section; or

(B) the vehicle or part of the vehicle broken into or entered is a rail car.

(d-1) For the purposes of Subsection (d), a defendant has been previously convicted under this section if the defendant was adjudged guilty of the offense or entered a plea of guilty or nolo contendere in return for a grant of deferred adjudication, regardless of whether the sentence for the offense was ever imposed or whether the sentence was probated and the defendant was subsequently discharged from community supervision.

(e) It is a defense to prosecution under this section that the actor entered a rail car or any part of a rail car and was at that time an employee or a representative of employees exercising a right under the Railway Labor Act (45 U.S.C. Section 151 et seq.).

(Enacted by Acts 1973, 63rd Leg., ch. 399 (S.B. 34), § 1, effective January 1, 1974; am. Acts 1993, 73rd Leg., ch. 900 (S.B. 1067), § 1.01, effective September 1, 1994; am. Acts 1999, 76th Leg., ch. 916 (H.B. 2231), § 1, effective September 1, 1999; am. Acts 2007, 80th Leg., ch. 308 (H.B. 1887), § 1, effective September 1, 2007.)

## Sec. 30.05.  Criminal Trespass.

(a) A person commits an offense if the person enters or remains on or in property of another, including residential land, agricultural land, a recreational vehicle park, a building, or an aircraft or other vehicle, without effective consent and the person:

(1) had notice that the entry was forbidden; or

(2) received notice to depart but failed to do so.

(b) For purposes of this section:

(1) "Entry" means the intrusion of the entire body.

(2) "Notice" means:

(A) oral or written communication by the owner or someone with apparent authority to act for the owner;

(B) fencing or other enclosure obviously designed to exclude intruders or to contain livestock;

(C) a sign or signs posted on the property or at the entrance to the building, reasonably likely to come to the attention of intruders, indicating that entry is forbidden;

(D) the placement of identifying purple paint marks on trees or posts on the property, provided that the marks are:

(i) vertical lines of not less than eight inches in length and not less than one inch in width;

(ii) placed so that the bottom of the mark is not less than three feet from the ground or more than five feet from the ground; and

(iii) placed at locations that are readily visible to any person approaching the property and no more than:

(a) 100 feet apart on forest land; or

(b) 1,000 feet apart on land other than forest land; or

(E) the visible presence on the property of a crop grown for human consumption that is under cultivation, in the process of being harvested, or marketable if harvested at the time of entry.

(3) "Shelter center" has the meaning assigned by Section 51.002, Human Resources Code.

(4) "Forest land" means land on which the trees are potentially valuable for timber products.

(5) "Agricultural land" has the meaning assigned by Section 75.001, Civil Practice and Remedies Code.

(6) "Superfund site" means a facility that:

(A) is on the National Priorities List established under Section 105 of the federal Comprehensive Environmental Response, Compensation, and Liability Act of 1980 (42 U.S.C. Section 9605); or

(B) is listed on the state registry established under Section 361.181, Health and Safety Code.

(7) "Critical infrastructure facility" means one of the following, if completely enclosed by a fence or other physical barrier that is obviously designed to exclude intruders:

(A) a chemical manufacturing facility;

(B) a refinery;

(C) an electrical power generating facility, substation, switching station, electrical control center, or electrical transmission or distribution facility;

(D) a water intake structure, water treatment facility, wastewater treatment plant, or pump station;

(E) a natural gas transmission compressor station;

(F) a liquid natural gas terminal or storage facility;

(G) a telecommunications central switching office;

(H) a port, railroad switching yard, trucking terminal, or other freight transportation facility;

(I) a gas processing plant, including a plant used in the processing, treatment, or fractionation of natural gas; or

(J) a transmission facility used by a federally licensed radio or television station.

(8) "Protected freshwater area" has the meaning assigned by Section 90.001, Parks and Wildlife Code.

(9) "Recognized state" means another state with which the attorney general of this state, with the approval of the governor of this state, negotiated an agreement after determining that the other state:

(A) has firearm proficiency requirements for peace officers; and

(B) fully recognizes the right of peace officers commissioned in this state to carry weapons in the other state.

(10) "Recreational vehicle park" means a tract of land that has rental spaces for two or more recreational vehicles, as defined by Section 522.004, Transportation Code.

(11) "Residential land" means real property improved by a dwelling and zoned for or otherwise authorized for single-family or multifamily use.

(c) [Repealed by Acts 2009, 81st Leg., ch. 1138 (H.B. 2609), § 4, effective September 1, 2009.]

(d) An offense under this section is:

(1) a Class B misdemeanor, except as provided by Subdivisions (2) and (3);

(2) a Class C misdemeanor, except as provided by Subdivision (3), if the offense is committed:

(A) on agricultural land and within 100 feet of the boundary of the land; or

(B) on residential land and within 100 feet of a protected freshwater area; and

(3) a Class A misdemeanor if:

(A) the offense is committed:

(i) in a habitation or a shelter center;

(ii) on a Superfund site; or

(iii) on or in a critical infrastructure facility; or

(B) the person carries a deadly weapon during the commission of the offense.

(e) It is a defense to prosecution under this section that the actor at the time of the offense was:

(1) a firefighter or emergency medical services personnel, as defined by Section 773.003, Health and Safety Code, acting in the lawful discharge of an official duty under exigent circumstances;

(2) a person who was:

(A) an employee or agent of:

(i) an electric utility, as defined by Section 31.002, Utilities Code;

(ii) a telecommunications provider, as defined by Section 51.002, Utilities Code;

(iii) a video service provider or cable service provider, as defined by Section 66.002, Utilities Code;

(iv) a gas utility, as defined by Section 101.003 or 121.001, Utilities Code; or

(v) a pipeline used for the transportation or sale of oil, gas, or related products; and

(B) performing a duty within the scope of that employment or agency; or

(3) a person who was:

(A) employed by or acting as agent for an entity that had, or that the person reasonably believed had, effective consent or authorization provided by law to enter the property; and

(B) performing a duty within the scope of that employment or agency.

(f) It is a defense to prosecution under this section that:

(1) the basis on which entry on the property or land or in the building was forbidden is that entry with a handgun was forbidden; and

(2) the person was carrying a concealed handgun and a license issued under Subchapter H, Chapter 411, Government Code, to carry a concealed handgun of the same category the person was carrying.

(g) It is a defense to prosecution under this section that the actor entered a railroad switching yard or any part of a railroad switching yard and was at that time an employee or a representative of employees exercising a right under the Railway Labor Act (45 U.S.C. Section 151 et seq.).

(h) At the punishment stage of a trial in which the attorney representing the state seeks the increase in punishment provided by Subsection (d)(3)(A)(iii), the defendant may raise the issue as to whether the defendant entered or remained on or in a critical infrastructure facility as part of a peaceful or lawful assembly, including an attempt to exercise rights guaranteed by state or federal labor laws. If the defendant proves the issue in the affirmative by a preponderance of the evidence, the increase in punishment provided by Subsection (d)(3)(A)(iii) does not apply.

(i) This section does not apply if:

(1) the basis on which entry on the property or land or in the building was forbidden is that entry with a handgun or other weapon was forbidden; and

(2) the actor at the time of the offense was a peace officer, including a commissioned peace officer of a recognized state, or a special investigator under Article 2.122, Code of Criminal Procedure, regardless of whether the peace officer or special investigator was engaged in the actual discharge of an official duty while carrying the weapon.

(j) [Repealed by Acts 2009, 81st Leg., ch. 1138 (H.B. 2609), § 4, effective September 1, 2009.] (Enacted by Acts 1973, 63rd Leg., ch. 399 (S.B. 34), § 1, effective January 1, 1974; am. Acts 1979, 66th Leg., ch. 530 (S.B. 952), § 3, effective August 27, 1979; am. Acts 1981, 67th Leg., ch. 596 (H.B. 717), § 1, effective September 1, 1981; am. Acts 1989, 71st Leg., ch. 139 (S.B. 571), § 1, effective September 1, 1989; am. Acts 1991, 72nd Leg., ch. 308 (H.B. 50), § 1, effective September 1, 1991; am. Acts 1993, 73rd Leg., ch. 24 (H.B. 288), § 1, effective September 1, 1993; am. Acts 1993, 73rd Leg., ch. 900 (S.B. 1067), § 1.01, effective September 1, 1994; am. Acts 1997, 75th Leg., ch. 1229 (H.B. 793), §§ 1, 2, effective September 1, 1997; am. Acts 1999, 76th Leg., ch. 161 (S.B. 1558), § 1, effective September 1, 1999; am. Acts 1999, 76th Leg., ch. 169 (H.B. 436), §§ 1, 2, effective September 1, 1999; am. Acts 1999, 76th Leg., ch. 765 (H.B. 1265), §§ 1, 2, effective September 1, 1999; am. Acts 2001, 77th Leg., ch. 1420 (H.B. 2812), §§ 16.002, 21.001(94), effective September 1, 2001; am. Acts 2003, 78th Leg., ch. 1078 (H.B. 1872), § 1, effective September 1, 2003; am. Acts 2003, 78th Leg., ch. 1178 (S.B. 501), § 1, effective September 1, 2003; am. Acts 2003, 78th Leg., ch. 1276 (H.B. 3507), § 14B.001, effective September 1, 2003; am. Acts 2005, 79th Leg., ch. 1093 (H.B. 2110), § 3, effective September 1, 2005; am. Acts 2005, 79th Leg., ch. 1337 (S.B. 9), §§ 20, 21 effective June 18, 2005; am. Acts 2007, 80th Leg., ch. 921 (H.B. 3167), §§ 17.001(61), 17.002(13), effective September 1, 2007; am. Acts 2009, 81st Leg., ch. 1138 (H.B. 2609), §§ 1-4, effective September 1, 2009; am. Acts 2011, 82nd Leg., ch. 91 (S.B. 1303), § 20.001, effective September 1, 2011.)

## Sec. 30.06.  Trespass by Holder of License to Carry Concealed Handgun.

(a) A license holder commits an offense if the license holder:

(1) carries a handgun under the authority of Subchapter H, Chapter 411, Government Code, on property of another without effective consent; and

(2) received notice that:

(A) entry on the property by a license holder with a concealed handgun was forbidden; or

(B) remaining on the property with a concealed handgun was forbidden and failed to depart.

(b) For purposes of this section, a person receives notice if the owner of the property or someone with apparent authority to act for the owner provides notice to the person by oral or written communication.

(c) In this section:

(1) "Entry" has the meaning assigned by Section 30.05(b).

(2) "License holder" has the meaning assigned by Section 46.035(f).

(3) "Written communication" means:

(A) a card or other document on which is written language identical to the following: "Pursuant to Section 30.06, Penal Code (trespass by holder of license to carry a concealed handgun), a person licensed under Subchapter H, Chapter 411, Government Code (concealed handgun law), may not enter this property with a concealed handgun"; or

(B) a sign posted on the property that:

(i) includes the language described by Paragraph (A) in both English and Spanish;

(ii) appears in contrasting colors with block letters at least one inch in height; and

(iii) is displayed in a conspicuous manner clearly visible to the public.

(d) An offense under this section is a Class A misdemeanor.

(e) It is an exception to the application of this section that the property on which the license holder carries a handgun is owned or leased by a governmental entity and is not a premises or other place on which the license holder is prohibited from carrying the handgun under Section 46.03 or 46.035.

(Enacted by Acts 1997, 75th Leg., ch. 1261 (H.B. 2909), § 23, effective September 1, 1997; am. Acts 1999, 76th Leg., ch. 62 (S.B. 1368), § 9.24, effective September 1, 1999; am. Acts 2003, 78th Leg., ch. 1178 (S.B. 501), § 2, effective September 1, 2003.)

# CHAPTER 31
## THEFT

## Sec. 31.01.  Definitions.

In this chapter:

(1) "Deception" means:

(A) creating or confirming by words or conduct a false impression of law or fact that is likely to affect the judgment of another in the transaction, and that the actor does not believe to be true;

(B) failing to correct a false impression of law or fact that is likely to affect the judgment of another in the transaction, that the actor previously created or confirmed by words or conduct, and that the actor does not now believe to be true;

(C) preventing another from acquiring information likely to affect his judgment in the transaction;

(D) selling or otherwise transferring or encumbering property without disclosing a lien, security interest, adverse claim, or other legal impediment to the enjoyment of the property, whether the lien, security interest, claim, or impediment is or is not valid, or is or is not a matter of official record; or

(E) promising performance that is likely to affect the judgment of another in the transaction and that the actor does not intend to perform or knows will not be performed, except that failure to perform the promise in issue without other evidence of intent or knowledge is not sufficient proof that the actor did not intend to perform or knew the promise would not be performed.

(2) "Deprive" means:

(A) to withhold property from the owner permanently or for so extended a period of time that a major portion of the value or enjoyment of the property is lost to the owner;

(B) to restore property only upon payment of reward or other compensation; or

(C) to dispose of property in a manner that makes recovery of the property by the owner unlikely.

(3) "Effective consent" includes consent by a person legally authorized to act for the owner. Consent is not effective if:

(A) induced by deception or coercion;

(B) given by a person the actor knows is not legally authorized to act for the owner;

(C) given by a person who by reason of youth, mental disease or defect, or intoxication is known by the actor to be unable to make reasonable property dispositions;

(D) given solely to detect the commission of an offense; or

(E) given by a person who by reason of advanced age is known by the actor to have a diminished capacity to make informed and rational decisions about the reasonable disposition of property.

(4) "Appropriate" means:

(A) to bring about a transfer or purported transfer of title to or other nonpossessory interest in property, whether to the actor or another; or

(B) to acquire or otherwise exercise control over property other than real property.

(5) "Property" means:

(A) real property;

(B) tangible or intangible personal property including anything severed from land; or

(C) a document, including money, that represents or embodies anything of value.

(6) "Service" includes:

(A) labor and professional service;

(B) telecommunication, public utility, or transportation service;

(C) lodging, restaurant service, and entertainment; and

(D) the supply of a motor vehicle or other property for use.

(7) "Steal" means to acquire property or service by theft.

(8) "Certificate of title" has the meaning assigned by Section 501.002, Transportation Code.

(9) "Used or secondhand motor vehicle" means a used motor vehicle, as that term is defined by Section 501.002, Transportation Code.

(10) "Elderly individual" has the meaning assigned by Section 22.04(c).

(11) "Retail merchandise" means one or more items of tangible personal property displayed, held, stored, or offered for sale in a retail establishment.

(12) "Retail theft detector" means an electrical, mechanical, electronic, or magnetic device used to prevent or detect shoplifting and includes any article or component part essential to the proper operation of the device.

(13) "Shielding or deactivation instrument" means any item or tool designed, made, or adapted for the purpose of preventing the detection of stolen merchandise by a retail theft detector. The term includes a metal-lined or foil-lined shopping bag and any item used to remove a security tag affixed to retail merchandise.

(14) "Fire exit alarm" has the meaning assigned by Section 793.001, Health and Safety Code.

(Enacted by Acts 1973, 63rd Leg., ch. 399 (S.B. 34), § 1, effective January 1, 1974Acts 1975, 64th Leg., ch. 342 (S.B. 127), § 9, effective September 1, 1975; am. Acts 1985, 69th Leg., ch. 901 (H.B. 1365), § 2, effective September 1, 1985; am. Acts 1993, 73rd Leg., ch. 900 (S.B. 1067), § 1.01, effective September 1, 1994; am. Acts 1997, 75th Leg., ch. 165 (S.B. 898), § 30.237, effective September 1, 1997; am. Acts 2003, 78th Leg., ch. 432 (H.B. 420), § 1, effective September 1, 2003; am. Acts 2011, 82nd Leg., ch. 323 (H.B. 2482), § 1, effective September 1, 2011.)

## Sec. 31.02.  Consolidation of Theft Offenses.

Theft as defined in Section 31.03 constitutes a single offense superseding the separate offenses previously known as theft, theft by false pretext, conversion by a bailee, theft from the person, shoplifting, acquisition of property by threat, swindling, swindling by worthless check, embezzlement, extortion, receiving or concealing embezzled property, and receiving or concealing stolen property.

(Enacted by Acts 1973, 63rd Leg., ch. 399 (S.B. 34), § 1, effective January 1, 1974; am. Acts 1993, 73rd Leg., ch. 900 (S.B. 1067), § 1.01, effective September 1, 1994.)

## Sec. 31.03.  Theft.

(a) A person commits an offense if he unlawfully appropriates property with intent to deprive the owner of property.

(b) Appropriation of property is unlawful if:

(1) it is without the owner's effective consent;

(2) the property is stolen and the actor appropriates the property knowing it was stolen by another; or

(3) property in the custody of any law enforcement agency was explicitly represented by any law enforcement agent to the actor as being stolen and the actor appropriates the property believing it was stolen by another.

(c) For purposes of Subsection (b):

(1) evidence that the actor has previously participated in recent transactions other than, but similar to, that which the prosecution is based is admissible for the purpose of showing knowledge or intent and the issues of knowledge or intent are raised by the actor's plea of not guilty;

(2) the testimony of an accomplice shall be corroborated by proof that tends to connect the actor to the crime, but the actor's knowledge or intent may be established by the uncorroborated testimony of the accomplice;

(3) an actor engaged in the business of buying and selling used or secondhand personal property, or lending money on the security of personal property deposited with the actor, is presumed to know upon receipt by the actor of stolen property (other than a motor vehicle subject to Chapter 501, Transportation Code) that the property has been previously stolen from another if the actor pays for or loans against the property $25 or more (or consideration of equivalent value) and the actor knowingly or recklessly:

(A) fails to record the name, address, and physical description or identification number of the seller or pledgor;

(B) fails to record a complete description of the property, including the serial number, if reasonably available, or other identifying characteristics; or

(C) fails to obtain a signed warranty from the seller or pledgor that the seller or pledgor has the right to possess the property. It is the express intent of this provision that the presumption arises unless the actor complies with each of the numbered requirements;

(4) for the purposes of Subdivision (3)(A), "identification number" means driver's license number, military identification number, identification certificate, or other official number capable of identifying an individual;

(5) stolen property does not lose its character as stolen when recovered by any law enforcement agency;

(6) an actor engaged in the business of obtaining abandoned or wrecked motor vehicles or parts of an abandoned or wrecked motor vehicle for resale, disposal, scrap, repair, rebuilding, demolition, or other form of salvage is presumed to know on receipt by the actor of stolen property that the property has been previously stolen from another if the actor knowingly or recklessly:

(A) fails to maintain an accurate and legible inventory of each motor vehicle component part purchased by or delivered to the actor, including the date of purchase or delivery, the name, age, address, sex, and driver's license number of the seller or person making the delivery, the license plate number of the motor vehicle in which the part was delivered, a complete description of the part, and the vehicle identification number of the motor vehicle from which the part was removed, or in lieu of maintaining an inventory, fails to record the name and certificate of inventory number of the person who dismantled the motor vehicle from which the part was obtained;

(B) fails on receipt of a motor vehicle to obtain a certificate of authority, sales receipt, or transfer document as required by Chapter 683, Transportation Code, or a certificate of title showing that the motor vehicle is not subject to a lien or that all recorded liens on the motor vehicle have been released; or

(C) fails on receipt of a motor vehicle to immediately remove an unexpired license plate from the motor vehicle, to keep the plate in a secure and locked place, or to maintain an inventory, on forms provided by the Texas Department of Motor Vehicles, of license plates kept under this paragraph, including for each plate or set of plates the license plate number and the make, motor number, and vehicle identification number of the motor vehicle from which the plate was removed;

(7) an actor who purchases or receives a used or secondhand motor vehicle is presumed to know on receipt by the actor of the motor vehicle that the motor vehicle has been previously stolen from another if the actor knowingly or recklessly:

(A) fails to report to the Texas Department of Motor Vehicles the failure of the person who sold or delivered the motor vehicle to the actor to deliver to the actor a properly executed certificate of title to the motor vehicle at the time the motor vehicle was delivered; or

(B) fails to file with the county tax assessor-collector of the county in which the actor received the motor vehicle, not later than the 20th day after the date the actor received the motor vehicle, the registration license receipt and certificate of title or evidence of title delivered to the actor in accordance with Subchapter D, Chapter 520, Transportation Code, at the time the motor vehicle was delivered;

(8) an actor who purchases or receives from any source other than a licensed retailer or distributor of pesticides a restricted-use pesticide or a state-limited-use pesticide or a compound, mixture, or preparation containing a restricted-use or state-limited-use pesticide is presumed to know on receipt by the actor of the pesticide or compound, mixture, or preparation that the pesticide or compound, mixture, or preparation has been previously stolen from another if the actor:

(A) fails to record the name, address, and physical description of the seller or pledgor;

(B) fails to record a complete description of the amount and type of pesticide or compound, mixture, or preparation purchased or received; and

(C) fails to obtain a signed warranty from the seller or pledgor that the seller or pledgor has the right to possess the property; and

(9) an actor who is subject to Section 409, Packers and Stockyards Act (7 U.S.C. Section 228b), that obtains livestock from a commission merchant by representing that the actor will make prompt payment is presumed to have

induced the commission merchant's consent by deception if the actor fails to make full payment in accordance with Section 409, Packers and Stockyards Act (7 U.S.C. Section 228b).

(d) It is not a defense to prosecution under this section that:

(1) the offense occurred as a result of a deception or strategy on the part of a law enforcement agency, including the use of an undercover operative or peace officer;

(2) the actor was provided by a law enforcement agency with a facility in which to commit the offense or an opportunity to engage in conduct constituting the offense; or

(3) the actor was solicited to commit the offense by a peace officer, and the solicitation was of a type that would encourage a person predisposed to commit the offense to actually commit the offense, but would not encourage a person not predisposed to commit the offense to actually commit the offense.

(e) Except as provided by Subsection (f), an offense under this section is:

(1) a Class C misdemeanor if the value of the property stolen is less than:

(A) $50; or

(B) $20 and the defendant obtained the property by issuing or passing a check or similar sight order in a manner described by Section 31.06;

(2) a Class B misdemeanor if:

(A) the value of the property stolen is:

(i) $50 or more but less than $500; or

(ii) $20 or more but less than $500 and the defendant obtained the property by issuing or passing a check or similar sight order in a manner described by Section 31.06;

(B) the value of the property stolen is less than:

(i) $50 and the defendant has previously been convicted of any grade of theft; or

(ii) $20, the defendant has previously been convicted of any grade of theft, and the defendant obtained the property by issuing or passing a check or similar sight order in a manner described by Section 31.06; or

(C) the property stolen is a driver's license, commercial driver's license, or personal identification certificate issued by this state or another state;

(3) a Class A misdemeanor if the value of the property stolen is $500 or more but less than $1,500;

(4) a state jail felony if:

(A) the value of the property stolen is $1,500 or more but less than $20,000, or the property is less than 10 head of sheep, swine, or goats or any part thereof under the value of $20,000;

(B) regardless of value, the property is stolen from the person of another or from a human corpse or grave, including property that is a military grave marker;

(C) the property stolen is a firearm, as defined by Section 46.01;

(D) the value of the property stolen is less than $1,500 and the defendant has been previously convicted two or more times of any grade of theft;

(E) the property stolen is an official ballot or official carrier envelope for an election; or

(F) the value of the property stolen is less than $20,000 and the property stolen is:

(i) aluminum;

(ii) bronze;

(iii) copper; or

(iv) brass;

(5) a felony of the third degree if the value of the property stolen is $20,000 or more but less than $100,000, or the property is:

(A) cattle, horses, or exotic livestock or exotic fowl as defined by Section 142.001, Agriculture Code, stolen during a single transaction and having an aggregate value of less than $100,000; or

(B) 10 or more head of sheep, swine, or goats stolen during a single transaction and having an aggregate value of less than $100,000;

(6) a felony of the second degree if:

(A) the value of the property stolen is $100,000 or more but less than $200,000; or

(B) the value of the property stolen is less than $200,000 and the property stolen is an automated teller machine or the contents or components of an automated teller machine; or

(7) a felony of the first degree if the value of the property stolen is $200,000 or more.

(f) An offense described for purposes of punishment by Subsections (e)(1)—(6) is increased to the next higher category of offense if it is shown on the trial of the offense that:

(1) the actor was a public servant at the time of the offense and the property appropriated came into the actor's custody, possession, or control by virtue of his status as a public servant;

(2) the actor was in a contractual relationship with government at the time of the offense and the property appropriated came into the actor's custody, possession, or control by virtue of the contractual relationship;

(3) the owner of the property appropriated was at the time of the offense:

(A) an elderly individual; or

(B) a nonprofit organization;

(4) the actor was a Medicare provider in a contractual relationship with the federal government at the time of the offense and the property appropriated came into the actor's custody, possession, or control by virtue of the contractual relationship; or

(5) during the commission of the offense, the actor intentionally, knowingly, or recklessly:

(A) caused a fire exit alarm to sound or otherwise become activated;

(B) deactivated or otherwise prevented a fire exit alarm or retail theft detector from sounding; or

(C) used a shielding or deactivation instrument to prevent or attempt to prevent detection of the offense by a retail theft detector.

(g) For the purposes of Subsection (a), a person is the owner of exotic livestock or exotic fowl as defined by Section 142.001, Agriculture Code, only if the person qualifies to claim the animal under Section 142.0021, Agriculture Code, if the animal is an estray.

(h) In this section:

(1) "Restricted-use pesticide" means a pesticide classified as a restricted-use pesticide by the administrator of the Environmental Protection Agency under 7 U.S.C. Section 136a, as that law existed on January 1, 1995, and containing an active ingredient listed in the federal regulations adopted under that law (40 C.F.R. Section 152.175) and in effect on that date.

(2) "State-limited-use pesticide" means a pesticide classified as a state-limited-use pesticide by the Department of Agriculture under Section 76.003, Agriculture Code, as that section existed on January 1, 1995, and containing an active ingredient listed in the rules adopted under that section (4 TAC Section 7.24) as that section existed on that date.

(3) "Nonprofit organization" means an organization that is exempt from federal income taxation under Section 501(a), Internal Revenue Code of 1986, by being described as an exempt organization by Section 501(c)(3) of that code.

(4) "Automated teller machine" means an unstaffed electronic information processing device that, at the request of a user, performs a financial transaction through the direct transmission of electronic impulses to a financial institution or through the recording of electronic impulses or other indicia of a transaction for delayed transmission to a financial institution. The term includes an automated banking machine.

(i) For purposes of Subsection (c)(9), "livestock" and "commission merchant" have the meanings assigned by Section 147.001, Agriculture Code.

(j) With the consent of the appropriate local county or district attorney, the attorney general has concurrent jurisdiction with that consenting local prosecutor to prosecute an offense under this section that involves the state Medicaid program.

(Enacted by Acts 1973, 63rd Leg., ch. 399 (S.B. 34), § 1, effective January 1, 1974; am. Acts 1975, 64th Leg., ch. 342 (S.B. 127), § 10, effective September 1, 1975; am. Acts 1977, 65th Leg., ch. 349 (S.B. 310), § 1, effective August 29, 1977; am. Acts 1981, 67th Leg., ch. 298 (S.B. 372), § 1, effective September 1, 1981; am. Acts 1981, 67th Leg., ch. 455 (H.B. 1965), § 1, effective June 11, 1981; am. Acts 1983, 68th Leg., ch. 497 (S.B. 283), § 3, effective September 1, 1983; am. Acts 1983, 68th Leg., ch. 558 (S.B. 651), § 11, effective September 1, 1983; am. Acts 1983, 68th Leg., ch. 741 (H.B. 171), § 1, effective September 1, 1983; am. Acts 1985, 69th Leg., ch. 599 (S.B 30), § 1, effective September 1, 1985; am. Acts 1985, 69th Leg., ch. 901 (H.B. 1365), § 1, effective September 1, 1985; am. Acts 1987, 70th Leg., ch. 167 (S.B. 892), § 5.01(a)(45), effective September 1, 1987; am. Acts 1989, 71st Leg., ch. 245 (H.B. 524), § 1, September 1, 1989; am. Acts 1989, 71st Leg., ch. 724 (S.B. 1814), §§ 2, 3, effective September 1, 1989; am. Acts 1991, 72nd Leg., ch. 14 (S.B. 404), § 284(80), effective September 1, 1991; am. Acts 1991, 72nd Leg., ch. 565 (S.B. 4), § 1, effective September 1, 1991; am. Acts 1993, 73rd Leg., ch. 203 (H.B. 608), §§ 4, 5, effective September 1, 1993; am. Acts 1993, 73rd Leg., ch. 900 (S.B. 1067), § 1.01, effective September 1, 1994; am. Acts 1995, 74th Leg., ch. 318 (S.B. 15), § 9, effective September 1, 1995; am. Acts 1995, 74th Leg., ch. 734 (H.B. 1957), § 1, effective September 1, 1995; am. Acts 1995, 74th Leg., ch. 843 (S.B. 676), § 1, effective September 1, 1995; am. Acts 1997, 75th Leg., ch. 165 (S.B. 898),

§§ 30.238, 31.01(69), effective September 1, 1997; am. Acts. 1997, 75th Leg., ch. 1153 (S.B. 30), § 7.01, effective September 1, 1997; am. Acts 2001, 77th. Leg., ch. 1276 (S.B. 1747), § 1, effective September 1, 2001; am. Acts 2003, 78th Leg., ch. 198 (H.B. 2292), § 2.136, effective September 1, 2003; am. Acts 2003, 78th Leg., ch. 257 (H.B. 1743), § 13, effective September 1, 2003; am. Acts 2003, 78th Leg., ch. 393 (H.B. 54), § 20, effective September 1, 2003; am. Acts 2003, 78th Leg., ch. 432 (H.B. 420), § 2, effective September 1, 2003; am. Acts 2007, 80th Leg., ch. 304 (H.B. 1766), § 1, effective September 1, 2007; am. Acts 2009, 81st Leg., ch. 70 (H.B. 1282), § 1, effective September 1, 2009; am. Acts 2009, 81st Leg., ch. 105 (H.B. 1466), § 1, effective May 23, 2009; am. Acts 2009, 81st Leg., ch. 139 (S.B. 1163), § 1, effective September 1, 2009; am. Acts 2009, 81st Leg., ch. 295 (H.B. 348), § 1, effective September 1, 2009; am. Acts 2009, 81st Leg., ch. 903 (H.B. 671), §§ 1, 2, effective September 1, 2009; am. Acts 2009, 81st Leg., ch. 933 (H.B. 3097), § 3J.01, effective September 1, 2009; am. Acts 2011, 82nd Leg., ch. 120 (S.B. 887), §§ 1, 2, effective September 1, 2011; am. Acts 2011, 82nd Leg., ch. 323 (H.B. 2482), § 2, effective September 1, 2011; am. Acts 2011, 82nd Leg., ch. 1234 (S.B. 694), § 21, effective September 1, 2011.)

## Sec. 31.04.  Theft of Service.

(a) A person commits theft of service if, with intent to avoid payment for service that the actor knows is provided only for compensation:

(1) the actor intentionally or knowingly secures performance of the service by deception, threat, or false token;

(2) having control over the disposition of services of another to which the actor is not entitled, the actor intentionally or knowingly diverts the other's services to the actor's own benefit or to the benefit of another not entitled to the services;

(3) having control of personal property under a written rental agreement, the actor holds the property beyond the expiration of the rental period without the effective consent of the owner of the property, thereby depriving the owner of the property of its use in further rentals; or

(4) the actor intentionally or knowingly secures the performance of the service by agreeing to provide compensation and, after the service is rendered, fails to make full payment after receiving notice demanding payment.

(b) For purposes of this section, intent to avoid payment is presumed if:

(1) the actor absconded without paying for the service or expressly refused to pay for the service in circumstances where payment is ordinarily made immediately upon rendering of the service, as in hotels, campgrounds, recreational vehicle parks, restaurants, and comparable establishments;

(2) the actor failed to make payment under a service agreement within 10 days after receiving notice demanding payment;

(3) the actor returns property held under a rental agreement after the expiration of the rental agreement and fails to pay the applicable rental charge for the property within 10 days after the date on which the actor received notice demanding payment; or

(4) the actor failed to return the property held under a rental agreement:

(A) within five days after receiving notice demanding return, if the property is valued at less than $1,500; or

(B) within three days after receiving notice demanding return, if the property is valued at $1,500 or more.

(c) For purposes of Subsections (a)(4), (b)(2), and (b)(4), notice shall be notice in writing, sent by registered or certified mail with return receipt requested or by telegram with report of delivery requested, and addressed to the actor at his address shown on the rental agreement or service agreement.

(d) If written notice is given in accordance with Subsection (c), it is presumed that the notice was received no later than five days after it was sent.

(d-1) For purposes of Subsection (a)(4):

(1) if the compensation is or was to be paid on a periodic basis, the intent to avoid payment for a service may be formed at any time during or before a pay period; and

(2) the partial payment of wages alone is not sufficient evidence to negate the actor's intent to avoid payment for a service.

(e) An offense under this section is:

(1) a Class C misdemeanor if the value of the service stolen is less than $20;

(2) a Class B misdemeanor if the value of the service stolen is $20 or more but less than $500;

(3) a Class A misdemeanor if the value of the service stolen is $500 or more but less than $1,500;

(4) a state jail felony if the value of the service stolen is $1,500 or more but less than $20,000;

(5) a felony of the third degree if the value of the service stolen is $20,000 or more but less than $100,000;

(6) a felony of the second degree if the value of the service stolen is $100,000 or more but less than $200,000; or

(7) a felony of the first degree if the value of the service stolen is $200,000 or more.

(f) Notwithstanding any other provision of this code, any police or other report of stolen vehicles by a political subdivision of this state shall include on the report any rental vehicles whose renters have been shown to such reporting agency to be in violation of Subsection (b)(2) and shall indicate that the renting agency has complied with the notice requirements demanding return as provided in this section.

(g) It is a defense to prosecution under this section that:

(1) the defendant secured the performance of the service by giving a post-dated check or similar sight order to the person performing the service; and

(2) the person performing the service or any other person presented the check or sight order for payment before the date on the check or sight order.

(Enacted by Acts 1973, 63rd Leg., ch. 399 (S.B. 34), § 1, effective January 1, 1974; am. Acts 1977, 65th Leg., ch. 429 (S.B. 489), § 1, effective August 29, 1977; am. Acts 1983, 68th Leg., ch. 497 (S.B. 283), § 4, effective September 1, 1983; am. Acts 1991, 72nd Leg., ch. 565 (S.B. 4), § 15, effective September 1, 1991; am. Acts 1993, 73rd Leg., ch. 900 (S.B. 1067), § 1.01, effective September 1, 1994; am. Acts 1995, 74th Leg., ch. 479 (S.B. 919), § 1, effective August 28, 1995; am. Acts 1999, 76th Leg., ch. 843 (H.B. 1798), § 1, effective September 1, 1999; am. Acts 2001, 77th Leg., ch. 1245 (S.B. 437), §§ 1, 2, effective September 1, 2001; am. Acts 2003, 78th Leg., ch. 419 (H.B. 275), § 1, effective September 1, 2003; am. Acts 2011, 82nd Leg., ch. 141 (S.B. 1024), § 1, effective September 1, 2011.)

## Sec. 31.05. Theft of Trade Secrets.

(a) For purposes of this section:

(1) "Article" means any object, material, device, or substance or any copy thereof, including a writing, recording, drawing, sample, specimen, prototype, model, photograph, microorganism, blueprint, or map.

(2) "Copy" means a facsimile, replica, photograph, or other reproduction of an article or a note, drawing, or sketch made of or from an article.

(3) "Representing" means describing, depicting, containing, constituting, reflecting, or recording.

(4) "Trade secret" means the whole or any part of any scientific or technical information, design, process, procedure, formula, or improvement that has value and that the owner has taken measures to prevent from becoming available to persons other than those selected by the owner to have access for limited purposes.

(b) A person commits an offense if, without the owner's effective consent, he knowingly:

(1) steals a trade secret;

(2) makes a copy of an article representing a trade secret; or

(3) communicates or transmits a trade secret.

(c) An offense under this section is a felony of the third degree.

(Enacted by Acts 1973, 63rd Leg., ch. 399 (S.B. 34), § 1, effective January 1, 1974; am. Acts 1993, 73rd Leg., ch. 900 (S.B. 1067), § 1.01, effective September 1, 1994.)

## Sec. 31.06. Presumption for Theft by Check.

(a) If the actor obtained property or secured performance of service by issuing or passing a check or similar sight order for the payment of money, when the issuer did not have sufficient funds in or on deposit with the bank or other drawee for the payment in full of the check or order as well as all other checks or orders then outstanding, it is prima facie evidence of his intent to deprive the owner of property under Section 31.03 (Theft) including a drawee or third-party holder in due course who negotiated the check or to avoid payment for service under Section 31.04 (Theft of Service) (except in the case of a postdated check or order) if:

(1) he had no account with the bank or other drawee at the time he issued the check or order; or

(2) payment was refused by the bank or other drawee for lack of funds or insufficient funds, on presentation within 30 days after issue, and the issuer failed to pay the holder in full within 10 days after receiving notice of that refusal.

(b) For purposes of Subsection (a)(2) or (f)(3), notice may be actual notice or notice in writing that:

(1) is sent by:

(A) first class mail, evidenced by an affidavit of service; or

(B) registered or certified mail with return receipt requested;

(2) is addressed to the issuer at the issuer's address shown on:

(A) the check or order;

(B) the records of the bank or other drawee; or

(C) the records of the person to whom the check or order has been issued or passed; and

(3) contains the following statement:

"This is a demand for payment in full for a check or order not paid because of a lack of funds or insufficient funds. If you fail to make payment in full within 10 days after the date of receipt of this notice, the failure to pay creates a presumption for committing an offense, and this matter may be referred for criminal prosecution."

(c) If written notice is given in accordance with Subsection (b), it is presumed that the notice was received no later than five days after it was sent.

(d) Nothing in this section prevents the prosecution from establishing the requisite intent by direct evidence.

(e) Partial restitution does not preclude the presumption of the requisite intent under this section.

(f) If the actor obtained property by issuing or passing a check or similar sight order for the payment of money, the actor's intent to deprive the owner of the property under Section 31.03 (Theft) is presumed, except in the case of a postdated check or order, if:

(1) the actor ordered the bank or other drawee to stop payment on the check or order;

(2) the bank or drawee refused payment to the holder on presentation of the check or order within 30 days after issue;

(3) the owner gave the actor notice of the refusal of payment and made a demand to the actor for payment or return of the property; and

(4) the actor failed to:

(A) pay the holder within 10 days after receiving the demand for payment; or

(B) return the property to the owner within 10 days after receiving the demand for return of the property.

(Enacted by Acts 1973, 63rd Leg., ch. 399 (S.B. 34), § 1, effective January 1, 1974; am. Acts 1991, 72nd Leg., ch. 543 (H.B. 1801), § 2, effective September 1, 1991; am. Acts 1993, 73rd Leg., ch.

900 (S.B. 1067), § 1.01, effective September 1, 1994; am. Acts 1995, 74th Leg., ch. 753 (H.B. 576), § 1, effective September 1, 1995; am. Acts 2007, 80th Leg., ch. 976 (S.B. 548), § 1, effective September 1, 2007.)

### Sec. 31.07. Unauthorized Use of a Vehicle.

(a) A person commits an offense if he intentionally or knowingly operates another's boat, airplane, or motor-propelled vehicle without the effective consent of the owner.

(b) An offense under this section is a state jail felony.

(Enacted by Acts 1973, 63rd Leg., ch. 399 (S.B. 34), § 1, effective January 1, 1974; am. Acts 1993, 73rd Leg., ch. 900 (S.B. 1067), § 1.01, effective September 1, 1994.)

### Sec. 31.08. Value.

(a) Subject to the additional criteria of Subsections (b) and (c), value under this chapter is:

(1) the fair market value of the property or service at the time and place of the offense; or

(2) if the fair market value of the property cannot be ascertained, the cost of replacing the property within a reasonable time after the theft.

(b) The value of documents, other than those having a readily ascertainable market value, is:

(1) the amount due and collectible at maturity less that part which has been satisfied, if the document constitutes evidence of a debt; or

(2) the greatest amount of economic loss that the owner might reasonably suffer by virtue of loss of the document, if the document is other than evidence of a debt.

(c) If property or service has value that cannot be reasonably ascertained by the criteria set forth in Subsections (a) and (b), the property or service is deemed to have a value of $500 or more but less than $1,500.

(d) If the actor proves by a preponderance of the evidence that he gave consideration for or had a legal interest in the property or service stolen, the amount of the consideration or the value of the interest so proven shall be deducted from the value of the property or service ascertained under Subsection (a), (b), or (c) to determine value for purposes of this chapter.

(Enacted by Acts 1973, 63rd Leg., ch. 399 (S.B. 34), § 1, effective January 1, 1974; am. Acts 1983, 68th Leg., ch. 497 (S.B. 283), § 5, effective September 1, 1983; am. Acts 1993, 73rd Leg., ch. 900 (S.B. 1067), § 1.01, effective September 1, 1994.)

## Sec. 31.09. Aggregation of Amounts Involved in Theft.

When amounts are obtained in violation of this chapter pursuant to one scheme or continuing course of conduct, whether from the same or several sources, the conduct may be considered as one offense and the amounts aggregated in determining the grade of the offense.

(Enacted by Acts 1973, 63rd Leg., ch. 399 (S.B. 34), § 1, effective January 1, 1974; am. Acts 1993, 73rd Leg., ch. 900 (S.B. 1067), § 1.01, effective September 1, 1994.)

## Sec. 31.10. Actor's Interest in Property.

It is no defense to prosecution under this chapter that the actor has an interest in the property or service stolen if another person has the right of exclusive possession of the property.

(Enacted by Acts 1973, 63rd Leg., ch. 399 (S.B. 34), § 1, effective January 1, 1974; am. Acts 1993, 73rd Leg., ch. 900 (S.B. 1067), § 1.01, effective September 1, 1994.)

## Sec. 31.11. Tampering with Identification Numbers.

(a) A person commits an offense if the person:

(1) knowingly or intentionally removes, alters, or obliterates the serial number or other permanent identification marking on tangible personal property; or

(2) possesses, sells, or offers for sale tangible personal property and:

(A) the actor knows that the serial number or other permanent identification marking has been removed, altered, or obliterated; or

(B) a reasonable person in the position of the actor would have known that the serial number or other permanent identification marking has been removed, altered, or obliterated.

(b) It is an affirmative defense to prosecution under this section that the person was:

(1) the owner or acting with the effective consent of the owner of the property involved;

(2) a peace officer acting in the actual discharge of official duties; or

(3) acting with respect to a number assigned to a vehicle by the Texas Department of Transportation or the Texas Department of Motor Vehicles, as applicable, and the person was:

(A) in the actual discharge of official duties as an employee or agent of the department; or

(B) in full compliance with the rules of the department as an applicant for an assigned number approved by the department.

(c) Property involved in a violation of this section may be treated as stolen for purposes of custody and disposition of the property.

(d) An offense under this section is a Class A misdemeanor.

(e) In this section, "vehicle" has the meaning given by Section 541.201, Transportation Code.

(Enacted by Acts 1979, 66th Leg., ch. 191 (S.B. 116), § 1, effective September 1, 1979; am. Acts 1983, 68th Leg., ch. 741 (H.B. 171), § 2, effective September 1, 1983; am. Acts 1991, 72nd Leg., ch. 113 (S.B. 589), § 1, effective September 1, 1991; am. Acts 1993, 73rd Leg., ch. 900 (S.B. 1067), § 1.01, effective September 1, 1994; am. Acts 1997, 75th Leg., ch. 165 (S.B. 898), § 30.239, effective September 1, 1997; am. Acts 2009, 81st Leg., ch. 933 (H.B. 3097), § 3J.02, effective September 1, 2009.)

## Sec. 31.12. Theft of or Tampering with Multichannel Video or Information Services.

(a) A person commits an offense if, without the authorization of the multichannel video or information services provider, the person intentionally or knowingly:

(1) makes or maintains a connection, whether physically, electrically, electronically, or inductively, to:

(A) a cable, wire, or other component of or media attached to a multichannel video or information services system; or

(B) a television set, videotape recorder, or other receiver attached to a multichannel video or information system;

(2) attaches, causes to be attached, or maintains the attachment of a device to:

(A) a cable, wire, or other component of or media attached to a multichannel video or information services system; or

(B) a television set, videotape recorder, or other receiver attached to a multichannel video or information services system;

(3) tampers with, modifies, or maintains a modification to a device installed by a multichannel video or information services provider; or

(4) tampers with, modifies, or maintains a modification to an access device or uses that access device or any unauthorized access device to obtain services from a multichannel video or information services provider.

(b) In this section:

(1) "Access device," "connection," and "device" mean an access device, connection, or device wholly or partly designed to make intelligible an encrypted, encoded, scrambled, or other nonstandard signal carried by a multichannel video or information services provider.

(2) "Encrypted, encoded, scrambled, or other nonstandard signal" means any type of signal or transmission not intended to produce an intelligible program or service without the use of a device, signal, or information provided by a multichannel video or information services provider.

(3) "Multichannel video or information services provider" means a licensed cable television system, video dialtone system, multichannel multipoint distribution services system, direct broadcast satellite system, or other system providing video or information services that are distributed by cable, wire, radio frequency, or other media.

(c) This section does not prohibit the manufacture, distribution, sale, or use of satellite receiving antennas that are otherwise permitted by state or federal law.

(d) An offense under this section is a Class C misdemeanor unless it is shown on the trial of the offense that the actor:

(1) has been previously convicted one time of an offense under this section, in which event the offense is a Class B misdemeanor, or convicted two or more times of an offense under this section, in which event the offense is a Class A misdemeanor; or

(2) committed the offense for remuneration, in which event the offense is a Class A misdemeanor, unless it is also shown on the trial of the offense that the actor has been previously convicted two or more times of an offense under this section, in which event the offense is a Class A misdemeanor with a minimum fine of $2,000 and a minimum term of confinement of 180 days.

(e) For the purposes of this section, each connection, attachment, modification, or act of tampering is a separate offense.

(Enacted by Acts 1995, 74th Leg., ch. 318 (S.B. 15), § 10, effective September 1, 1995; am. Acts 1999, 76th Leg., ch. 858 (H.B. 1876), § 1, effective September 1, 1999.)

## Sec. 31.13. Manufacture, Distribution, or Advertisement of Multichannel Video or Information Services Device.

(a) A person commits an offense if the person for remuneration intentionally or knowingly manufactures, assembles, modifies, imports into the state, exports out of the state, distributes, advertises, or offers for sale, with an intent to aid in the commission of an offense under Section 31.12, a device, a kit or part for a device, or a plan for a system of components wholly or partly designed to make intelligible an encrypted, encoded, scrambled, or other nonstandard signal carried or caused by a multichannel video or information services provider.

(b) In this section, "device," "encrypted, encoded, scrambled, or other nonstandard signal," and "multichannel video or information services provider" have the meanings assigned by Section 31.12.

(c) This section does not prohibit the manufacture, distribution, advertisement, offer for sale, or use of satellite receiving antennas that are otherwise permitted by state or federal law.

(d) An offense under this section is a Class A misdemeanor.

(Enacted by Acts 1995, 74th Leg., ch. 318 (S.B. 15), § 10, effective September 1, 1995; am. Acts 1999, 76th Leg., ch. 858 (H.B. 1876), § 2, effective September 1, 1999.)

## Sec. 31.14. Sale or Lease of Multichannel Video or Information Services Device.

(a) A person commits an offense if the person intentionally or knowingly sells or leases, with an intent to aid in the commission of an offense under Section 31.12, a device, a kit or part for a device, or a plan for a system of components wholly or partly designed to make intelligible an encrypted, encoded, scrambled, or other nonstandard signal carried or caused by a multichannel video or information services provider.

(b) In this section, "device," "encrypted, encoded, scrambled, or other nonstandard signal," and "multichannel video or information services provider" have the meanings assigned by Section 31.12.

(c) This section does not prohibit the sale or lease of satellite receiving antennas that are otherwise permitted by state or federal law without providing notice to the comptroller.

(d) An offense under this section is a Class A misdemeanor.

(Enacted by Acts 1999, 76th Leg., ch. 858 (H.B. 1876), § 3, effective September 1, 1999.)

## Sec. 31.15. Possession, Manufacture, or Distribution of Certain Instruments Used to Commit Retail Theft.

(a) [Repealed by Acts 2011, 82nd Leg., ch. 323 (H.B. 2482), § 4, effective September 1, 2011.]

(b) A person commits an offense if, with the intent to use the instrument to commit theft, the person:

(1) possesses a shielding or deactivation instrument; or

(2) knowingly manufactures, sells, offers for sale, or otherwise distributes a shielding or deactivation instrument.

(c) An offense under this section is a Class A misdemeanor.

(Enacted by Acts 2001, 77th Leg., ch. 109 (S.B. 966), § 1, effective September 1, 2001; am. Acts 2011, 82nd Leg., ch. 323 (H.B. 2482), § 4, effective September 1, 2011.)

## Sec. 31.16. Organized Retail Theft.

(a) [Repealed by Acts 2011, 82nd Leg., ch. 323 (H.B. 2482), § 4, effective September 1, 2011.]

(b) A person commits an offense if the person intentionally conducts, promotes, or facilitates an activity in which the person receives, possesses, conceals, stores, barters, sells, or disposes of:

(1) stolen retail merchandise; or

(2) merchandise explicitly represented to the person as being stolen retail merchandise.

(c) An offense under this section is:

(1) a Class B misdemeanor if the total value of the merchandise involved in the activity is less than $50;

(2) a Class A misdemeanor if the total value of the merchandise involved in the activity is $50 or more but less than $500;

(3) a state jail felony if the total value of the merchandise involved in the activity is $500 or more but less than $1,500;

(4) a felony of the third degree if the total value of the merchandise involved in the activity is $1,500 or more but less than $20,000;

(5) a felony of the second degree if the total value of the merchandise involved in the activity is $20,000 or more but less than $100,000; or

(6) a felony of the first degree if the total value of the merchandise involved in the activity is $100,000 or more.

(d) An offense described for purposes of punishment by Subsections (c)(1)—(5) is increased to the next higher category of offense if it is shown on the trial of the offense that:

(1) the person organized, supervised, financed, or managed one or more other persons engaged in an activity described by Subsection (b); or

(2) during the commission of the offense, a person engaged in an activity described by Subsection (b) intentionally, knowingly, or recklessly:

(A) caused a fire exit alarm to sound or otherwise become activated;

(B) deactivated or otherwise prevented a fire exit alarm or retail theft detector from sounding; or

(C) used a shielding or deactivation instrument to prevent or attempt to prevent detection of the offense by a retail theft detector.

(e) [Repealed by Acts 2011, 82nd Leg., ch. 323 (H.B. 2482), § 4, effective September 1, 2011.]

(Enacted by Acts 2007, 80th Leg., ch. 1274 (H.B. 3584), § 1, effective September 1, 2007; am. Acts 2011, 82nd Leg., ch. 323 (H.B. 2482), §§ 3, 4, effective September 1, 2011.)

## Sec. 31.17. Unauthorized Acquisition or Transfer of Certain Financial Information.

(a) In this section:

(1) "Check" has the meaning assigned by Section 3.104, Business & Commerce Code.

(2) "Credit card" and "debit card" have the meanings assigned by Section 32.31.

(3) "Financial sight order or payment card information" means financial information that is:

(A) contained on either side of a check or similar sight order, check card, debit card, or credit card; or

(B) encoded on the magnetic strip or stripe of a check card, debit card, or credit card.

(b) A person commits an offense if the person, knowing that the person is not entitled to obtain or possess that financial information:

(1) obtains the financial sight order or payment card information of another by use of an electronic, photographic, visual imaging, recording, or other device capable of accessing, reading, recording, capturing, copying, imaging, scanning, reproducing, or storing in any manner the financial sight order or payment card information; or

(2) transfers to a third party information obtained as described by Subdivision (1).

(c) An offense under Subsection (b)(1) is a Class B misdemeanor. An offense under Subsection (b)(2) is a Class A misdemeanor.

(d) If conduct that constitutes an offense under this section also constitutes an offense under any other law, the actor may be prosecuted under this section or the other law.

(Enacted by Acts 2011, 82nd Leg., ch. 260 (H.B. 1215), § 1, effective September 1, 2011.)

# CHAPTER 32
# FRAUD

### Subchapter A. General Provisions

# SUBCHAPTER A
# GENERAL PROVISIONS

## Sec. 32.01.  Definitions.

In this chapter:

(1) "Financial institution" means a bank, trust company, insurance company, credit union, building and loan association, savings and loan association, investment trust, investment company, or any other organization held out to the public as a place for deposit of funds or medium of savings or collective investment.

(2) "Property" means:

(A) real property;

(B) tangible or intangible personal property including anything severed from land; or

(C) a document, including money, that represents or embodies anything of value.

(3) "Service" includes:

(A) labor and professional service;

(B) telecommunication, public utility, and transportation service;

(C) lodging, restaurant service, and entertainment; and

(D) the supply of a motor vehicle or other property for use.

(4) "Steal" means to acquire property or service by theft.

(Enacted by Acts 1973, 63rd Leg., ch. 399 (S.B. 34), § 1, effective January 1, 1974; am. Acts 1993, 73rd Leg., ch. 900 (S.B. 1067), § 1.01, effective September 1, 1994.)

## Sec. 32.02.  Value.

(a) Subject to the additional criteria of Subsections (b) and (c), value under this chapter is:

(1) the fair market value of the property or service at the time and place of the offense; or

(2) if the fair market value of the property cannot be ascertained, the cost of replacing the property within a reasonable time after the offense.

(b) The value of documents, other than those having a readily ascertainable market value, is:

(1) the amount due and collectible at maturity less any part that has been satisfied, if the document constitutes evidence of a debt; or

(2) the greatest amount of economic loss that the owner might reasonably suffer by virtue of loss of the document, if the document is other than evidence of a debt.

(c) If property or service has value that cannot be reasonably ascertained by the criteria set forth in Subsections (a) and (b), the property or service is deemed to have a value of $500 or more but less than $1,500.

(d) If the actor proves by a preponderance of the evidence that he gave consideration for or had a legal interest in the property or service stolen, the amount of the consideration or the value of the interest so proven shall be deducted from the value of the property or service ascertained under Subsection (a), (b), or (c) to determine value for purposes of this chapter.

(Enacted by Acts 1973, 63rd Leg., ch. 399 (S.B. 34), § 1, effective January 1, 1974; am. Acts 1993, 73rd Leg., ch. 900 (S.B. 1067), § 1.01, effective September 1, 1994.)

## Sec. 32.03. Aggregation of Amounts Involved in Fraud.

When amounts are obtained in violation of this chapter pursuant to one scheme or continuing course of conduct, whether from the same or several sources, the conduct may be considered as one offense and the amounts aggregated in determining the grade of offense.

(Enacted by Acts 1973, 63rd Leg., ch. 399 (S.B. 34), § 1, effective January 1, 1974; am. Acts 1993, 73rd Leg., ch. 900 (S.B. 1067), § 1.01, effective September 1, 1994.)

## Secs. 32.04 to 32.20 [Reserved for expansion].

### SUBCHAPTER B
### FORGERY

## Sec. 32.21. Forgery.

(a) For purposes of this section:

(1) "Forge" means:

(A) to alter, make, complete, execute, or authenticate any writing so that it purports:

(i) to be the act of another who did not authorize that act;

(ii) to have been executed at a time or place or in a numbered sequence other than was in fact the case; or

(iii) to be a copy of an original when no such original existed;

(B) to issue, transfer, register the transfer of, pass, publish, or otherwise utter a writing that is forged within the meaning of Paragraph (A); or

(C) to possess a writing that is forged within the meaning of Paragraph (A) with intent to utter it in a manner specified in Paragraph (B).

(2) "Writing" includes:

(A) printing or any other method of recording information;

(B) money, coins, tokens, stamps, seals, credit cards, badges, and trademarks; and

(C) symbols of value, right, privilege, or identification.

(b) A person commits an offense if he forges a writing with intent to defraud or harm another.

(c) Except as provided by Subsections (d), (e), and (e-1), an offense under this section is a Class A misdemeanor.

(d) An offense under this section is a state jail felony if the writing is or purports to be a will, codicil, deed, deed of trust, mortgage, security instrument, security agreement, credit card, check, authorization to debit an account at a financial institution, or similar sight order for payment of money, contract, release, or other commercial instrument.

(e) An offense under this section is a felony of the third degree if the writing is or purports to be:

(1) part of an issue of money, securities, postage or revenue stamps;

(2) a government record listed in Section 37.01(2)(C); or

(3) other instruments issued by a state or national government or by a subdivision of either, or part of an issue of stock, bonds, or other instruments representing interests in or claims against another person.

(e-1) An offense under this section is increased to the next higher category of offense if it is shown on the trial of the offense that the offense was committed against an elderly individual as defined by Section 22.04.

(f) A person is presumed to intend to defraud or harm another if the person acts with respect to two or more writings of the same type and if each writing is a government record listed in Section 37.01(2)(C).

(Enacted by Acts 1973, 63rd Leg., ch. 399 (S.B. 34), § 1, effective January 1, 1974; am. Acts 1991, 72nd Leg., ch. 113 (S.B. 589), § 2, effective September 1, 1991; am. Acts 1993, 73rd Leg., ch. 900 (S.B. 1067), § 1.01, effective September 1, 1994; am. Acts 1997, 75th Leg., ch. 189 (H.B. 1185), § 1, effective May 21, 1997; am. Acts 2003, 78th Leg., ch. 1104 (H.B. 2248), § 1, effective September 1, 2003; am. Acts 2009, 81st Leg., ch. 670 (H.B. 2328), § 1, effective September 1, 2009.)

## Sec. 32.22. Criminal Simulation.

(a) A person commits an offense if, with intent to defraud or harm another:

(1) he makes or alters an object, in whole or in part, so that it appears to have value because of age, antiquity, rarity, source, or authorship that it does not have;

(2) he possesses an object so made or altered, with intent to sell, pass, or otherwise utter it; or

(3) he authenticates or certifies an object so made or altered as genuine or as different from what it is.

(b) An offense under this section is a Class A misdemeanor.

(Enacted by Acts 1973, 63rd Leg., ch. 399 (S.B. 34), § 1, effective January 1, 1974; am. Acts 1993, 73rd Leg., ch. 900 (S.B. 1067), § 1.01, effective September 1, 1994.)

## Sec. 32.23.  Trademark Counterfeiting.

(a) In this section:

(1) "Counterfeit mark" means a mark that is identical to or substantially indistinguishable from a protected mark the use or production of which is not authorized by the owner of the protected mark.

(2) "Identification mark" means a data plate, serial number, or part identification number.

(3) **[2 Versions: Effective Until September 1, 2012]** "Protected mark" means a trademark or service mark or an identification mark that is:

(A) registered with the secretary of state;

(B) registered on the principal register of the United States Patent and Trademark Office;

(C) registered under the laws of another state; or

(D) protected by Section 16.30, Business & Commerce Code, or by 36 U.S.C. Section 371 et seq.

(3) **[2 Versions: Effective September 1, 2012]** "Protected mark" means a trademark or service mark or an identification mark that is:

(A) registered with the secretary of state;

(B) registered on the principal register of the United States Patent and Trademark Office;

(C) registered under the laws of another state; or

(D) protected by Section 16.105, Business & Commerce Code, or by 36 U.S.C. Section 371 et seq.

(4) "Retail value" means the actor's regular selling price for a counterfeit mark or an item or service that bears or is identified by a counterfeit mark, except that if an item bearing a counterfeit mark is a component of a finished product, the retail value means the actor's regular selling price of the finished product on or in which the component is used, distributed, or sold.

(5) **[2 Versions: Effective Until September 1, 2012]** "Service mark" has the meaning assigned by Section 16.01, Business & Commerce Code.

(5) **[2 Versions: Effective September 1, 2012]** "Service mark" has the meaning assigned by Section 16.001, Business & Commerce Code.

(6) **[2 Versions: Effective Until September 1, 2012]** "Trademark" has the meaning assigned by Section 16.01, Business & Commerce Code.

(6) **[2 Versions: Effective September 1, 2012]** "Trademark" has the meaning assigned by Section 16.001, Business & Commerce Code.

(b) A person commits an offense if the person intentionally manufactures, displays, advertises, distributes, offers for sale, sells, or possesses with intent to sell or distribute a counterfeit mark or an item or service that:

(1) bears or is identified by a counterfeit mark; or

(2) the person knows or should have known bears or is identified by a counterfeit mark.

(c) A state or federal certificate of registration of intellectual property is prima facie evidence of the facts stated in the certificate.

(d) For the purposes of Subsection (e), when items or services are the subject of counterfeiting in violation of this section pursuant to one scheme or continuing course of conduct, the conduct may be considered as one offense and the retail value of the items or services aggregated in determining the grade of offense.

(e) An offense under this section is a:

(1) Class C misdemeanor if the retail value of the item or service is less than $20;

(2) Class B misdemeanor if the retail value of the item or service is $20 or more but less than $500;

(3) Class A misdemeanor if the retail value of the item or service is $500 or more but less than $1,500;

(4) state jail felony if the retail value of the item or service is $1,500 or more but less than $20,000;

(5) felony of the third degree if the retail value of the item or service is $20,000 or more but less than $100,000;

(6) felony of the second degree if the retail value of the item or service is $100,000 or more but less than $200,000; or

(7) felony of the first degree if the retail value of the item or service is $200,000 or more. (Enacted by Acts 1997, 75th Leg., ch. 1161 (S.B. 228), § 2, effective September 1, 1997; am. Acts 2011, 82nd Leg., ch. 563 (H.B. 3141), § 2, effective September 1, 2012.)

## Sec. 32.24. Stealing or Receiving Stolen Check or Similar Sight Order.

(a) A person commits an offense if the person steals an unsigned check or similar sight order or, with knowledge that an unsigned check or similar sight order has been stolen, receives the check or sight order with intent to use it, to sell it, or to transfer it to a person other than the person from whom the check or sight order was stolen.

(b) An offense under this section is a Class A misdemeanor. (Enacted by Acts 1999, 76th Leg., ch. 1413 (H.B. 2125), § 1, effective September 1, 1999.)

## Secs. 32.25 to 32.30 [Reserved for expansion].

### *SUBCHAPTER C*
### *CREDIT*

## Sec. 32.31. Credit Card or Debit Card Abuse.

(a) For purposes of this section:

(1) "Cardholder" means the person named on the face of a credit card or debit card to whom or for whose benefit the card is issued.

(2) "Credit card" means an identification card, plate, coupon, book, number, or any other device authorizing a designated person or bearer to obtain property or services on credit. The term includes the number or description of the device if the device itself is not produced at the time of ordering or obtaining the property or service.

(3) "Expired credit card" means a credit card bearing an expiration date after that date has passed.

(4) "Debit card" means an identification card, plate, coupon, book, number, or any other device authorizing a designated person or bearer to communicate a request to an unmanned teller machine or a customer convenience terminal or obtain property or services by debit to an account at a financial institution.

The term includes the number or description of the device if the device itself is not produced at the time of ordering or obtaining the benefit.

(5) "Expired debit card" means a debit card bearing as its expiration date a date that has passed.

(6) "Unmanned teller machine" means a machine, other than a telephone, capable of being operated by a customer, by which a customer may communicate to a financial institution a request to withdraw a benefit for himself or for another directly from the customer's account or from the customer's account under a line of credit previously authorized by the institution for the customer.

(7) "Customer convenience terminal" means an unmanned teller machine the use of which does not involve personnel of a financial institution.

(b) A person commits an offense if:

(1) with intent to obtain a benefit fraudulently, he presents or uses a credit card or debit card with knowledge that:

(A) the card, whether or not expired, has not been issued to him and is not used with the effective consent of the cardholder; or

(B) the card has expired or has been revoked or cancelled;

(2) with intent to obtain a benefit, he uses a fictitious credit card or debit card or the pretended number or description of a fictitious card;

(3) he receives a benefit that he knows has been obtained in violation of this section;

(4) he steals a credit card or debit card or, with knowledge that it has been stolen, receives a credit card or debit card with intent to use it, to sell it, or to transfer it to a person other than the issuer or the cardholder;

(5) he buys a credit card or debit card from a person who he knows is not the issuer;

(6) not being the issuer, he sells a credit card or debit card;

(7) he uses or induces the cardholder to use the cardholder's credit card or debit card to obtain property or service for the actor's benefit for which the cardholder is financially unable to pay;

(8) not being the cardholder, and without the effective consent of the cardholder, he possesses a credit card or debit card with intent to use it;

(9) he possesses two or more incomplete credit cards or debit cards that have not been issued to him with intent to complete them without the effective consent of the issuer. For

purposes of this subdivision, a card is incomplete if part of the matter that an issuer requires to appear on the card before it can be used, other than the signature of the cardholder, has not yet been stamped, embossed, imprinted, or written on it;

(10) being authorized by an issuer to furnish goods or services on presentation of a credit card or debit card, he, with intent to defraud the issuer or the cardholder, furnishes goods or services on presentation of a credit card or debit card obtained or retained in violation of this section or a credit card or debit card that is forged, expired, or revoked; or

(11) being authorized by an issuer to furnish goods or services on presentation of a credit card or debit card, he, with intent to defraud the issuer or a cardholder, fails to furnish goods or services that he represents in writing to the issuer that he has furnished.

(c) It is presumed that a person who used a revoked, cancelled, or expired credit card or debit card had knowledge that the card had been revoked, cancelled, or expired if he had received notice of revocation, cancellation, or expiration from the issuer. For purposes of this section, notice may be either notice given orally in person or by telephone, or in writing by mail or by telegram. If written notice was sent by registered or certified mail with return receipt requested, or by telegram with report of delivery requested, addressed to the cardholder at the last address shown by the records of the issuer, it is presumed that the notice was received by the cardholder no later than five days after sent.

(d) An offense under this section is a state jail felony, except that the offense is a felony of the third degree if it is shown on the trial of the offense that the offense was committed against an elderly individual as defined by Section 22.04. (Enacted by Acts 1973, 63rd Leg., ch. 399 (S.B. 34), § 1, effective January 1, 1974; am. Acts 1993, 73rd Leg., ch. 900 (S.B. 1067), § 1.01, effective September 1, 1994; am. Acts 2003, 78th Leg., ch. 1104 (H.B. 2248), §§ 2, 3, effective September 1, 2003; am. Acts 2005, 79th Leg., ch. 1054 (H.B. 1323), § 1, effective September 1, 2005; am. Acts 2009, 81st Leg., ch. 670 (H.B. 2328), § 2, effective September 1, 2009.)

## Sec. 32.32. False Statement to Obtain Property or Credit or in the Provision of Certain Services.

(a) For purposes of this section, "credit" includes:

(1) a loan of money;

(2) furnishing property or service on credit;

(3) extending the due date of an obligation;

(4) comaking, endorsing, or guaranteeing a note or other instrument for obtaining credit;

(5) a line or letter of credit;

(6) a credit card, as defined in Section 32.31 (Credit Card or Debit Card Abuse); and

(7) a mortgage loan.

(b) A person commits an offense if he intentionally or knowingly makes a materially false or misleading written statement to obtain property or credit, including a mortgage loan.

(b-1) A person commits an offense if the person intentionally or knowingly makes a materially false or misleading written statement in providing an appraisal of real property for compensation.

(c) An offense under this section is:

(1) a Class C misdemeanor if the value of the property or the amount of credit is less than $50;

(2) a Class B misdemeanor if the value of the property or the amount of credit is $50 or more but less than $500;

(3) a Class A misdemeanor if the value of the property or the amount of credit is $500 or more but less than $1,500;

(4) a state jail felony if the value of the property or the amount of credit is $1,500 or more but less than $20,000;

(5) a felony of the third degree if the value of the property or the amount of credit is $20,000 or more but less than $100,000;

(6) a felony of the second degree if the value of the property or the amount of credit is $100,000 or more but less than $200,000; or

(7) a felony of the first degree if the value of the property or the amount of credit is $200,000 or more.

(d) The following agencies shall assist a prosecuting attorney of the United States or of a county or judicial district of this state, a county or state law enforcement agency of this state, or a federal law enforcement agency in the investigation of an offense under this section involving a mortgage loan:

(1) the office of the attorney general;

(2) the Department of Public Safety;

(3) the Texas Department of Insurance;

(4) the Office of Consumer Credit Commissioner;

(5) the Texas Department of Banking;

(6) the credit union department;

(7) the Department of Savings and Mortgage Lending;

(8) the Texas Real Estate Commission;

(9) the Texas Appraiser Licensing and Certification Board; and

(10) the Texas Department of Housing and Community Affairs.

(e) With the consent of the appropriate local county or district attorney, the attorney general has concurrent jurisdiction with that consenting local prosecutor to prosecute an offense under this section that involves a mortgage loan.

(Enacted by Acts 1973, 63rd Leg., ch. 399 (S.B. 34), § 1, effective January 1, 1974; am. Acts 1993, 73rd Leg., ch. 900 (S.B. 1067), § 1.01, effective September 1, 1994; am. Acts 1995, 74th Leg., ch. 76 (S.B. 959), § 14.50, effective September 1, 1995; am. Acts 2001, 77th Leg., ch. 1245 (S.B. 437), § 3, effective September 1, 2001; am. Acts 2007, 80th Leg., ch. 285 (H.B. 716), § 5, effective September 1, 2007; am. Acts 2009, 81st Leg., ch. 709 (H.B. 2840), §§ 4, 5, effective September 1, 2009.)

## Sec. 32.33. Hindering Secured Creditors.

(a) For purposes of this section:

(1) "Remove" means transport, without the effective consent of the secured party, from the state in which the property was located when the security interest or lien attached.

(2) "Security interest" means an interest in personal property or fixtures that secures payment or performance of an obligation.

(b) A person who has signed a security agreement creating a security interest in property or a mortgage or deed of trust creating a lien on property commits an offense if, with intent to hinder enforcement of that interest or lien, he destroys, removes, conceals, encumbers, or otherwise harms or reduces the value of the property.

(c) For purposes of this section, a person is presumed to have intended to hinder enforcement of the security interest or lien if, when any part of the debt secured by the security interest or lien was due, he failed:

(1) to pay the part then due; and

(2) if the secured party had made demand, to deliver possession of the secured property to the secured party.

(d) An offense under Subsection (b) is a:

(1) Class C misdemeanor if the value of the property destroyed, removed, concealed, encumbered, or otherwise harmed or reduced in value is less than $20;

(2) Class B misdemeanor if the value of the property destroyed, removed, concealed, encumbered, or otherwise harmed or reduced in value is $20 or more but less than $500;

(3) Class A misdemeanor if the value of the property destroyed, removed, concealed, encumbered, or otherwise harmed or reduced in value is $500 or more but less than $1,500;

(4) state jail felony if the value of the property destroyed, removed, concealed, encumbered, or otherwise harmed or reduced in value is $1,500 or more but less than $20,000;

(5) felony of the third degree if the value of the property destroyed, removed, concealed, encumbered, or otherwise harmed or reduced in value is $20,000 or more but less than $100,000;

(6) felony of the second degree if the value of the property destroyed, removed, concealed, encumbered, or otherwise harmed or reduced in value is $100,000 or more but less than $200,000; or

(7) felony of the first degree if the value of the property destroyed, removed, concealed, encumbered, or otherwise harmed or reduced in value is $200,000 or more.

(e) A person who is a debtor under a security agreement, and who does not have a right to sell or dispose of the secured property or is required to account to the secured party for the proceeds of a permitted sale or disposition, commits an offense if the person sells or otherwise disposes of the secured property, or does not account to the secured party for the proceeds of a sale or other disposition as required, with intent to appropriate (as defined in Chapter 31) the proceeds or value of the secured property. A person is presumed to have intended to appropriate proceeds if the person does not deliver the proceeds to the secured party or account to the secured party for the proceeds before the 11th day after the day that the secured party makes a lawful demand for the proceeds or account. An offense under this subsection is:

(1) a Class C misdemeanor if the proceeds obtained from the sale or other disposition are money or goods having a value of less than $20;

(2) a Class B misdemeanor if the proceeds obtained from the sale or other disposition are money or goods having a value of $20 or more but less than $500;

(3) a Class A misdemeanor if the proceeds obtained from the sale or other disposition are money or goods having a value of $500 or more but less than $1,500;

(4) a state jail felony if the proceeds obtained from the sale or other disposition are money or goods having a value of $1,500 or more but less than $20,000;

(5) a felony of the third degree if the proceeds obtained from the sale or other disposition are money or goods having a value of $20,000 or more but less than $100,000;

(6) a felony of the second degree if the proceeds obtained from the sale or other disposition are money or goods having a value of $100,000 or more but less than $200,000; or

(7) a felony of the first degree if the proceeds obtained from the sale or other disposition are money or goods having a value of $200,000 or more.

(Enacted by Acts 1973, 63rd Leg., ch. 399 (S.B. 34), § 1, effective January 1, 1974; am. Acts 1979, 66th Leg., ch. 232 (H.B. 838), § 1, effective September 1, 1979; am. Acts 1985, 69th Leg., ch. 914 (H.B. 1741), § 5, effective September 1, 1985; am. Acts 1993, 73rd Leg., ch. 900 (S.B. 1067), § 1.01, effective September 1, 1994.)

## Sec. 32.34.  Fraudulent Transfer of a Motor Vehicle.

(a) In this section:

(1) "Lease" means the grant of use and possession of a motor vehicle for consideration, whether or not the grant includes an option to buy the vehicle.

(2) "Motor vehicle" means a device in, on, or by which a person or property is or may be transported or drawn on a highway, except a device used exclusively on stationary rails or tracks.

(3) "Security interest" means an interest in personal property or fixtures that secures payment or performance of an obligation.

(4) "Third party" means a person other than the actor or the owner of the vehicle.

(5) "Transfer" means to transfer possession, whether or not another right is also transferred, by means of a sale, lease, sublease, lease assignment, or other property transfer.

(b) A person commits an offense if the person acquires, accepts possession of, or exercises control over the motor vehicle of another under a written or oral agreement to arrange for the transfer of the vehicle to a third party and:

(1) knowing the vehicle is subject to a security interest, lease, or lien, the person transfers the vehicle to a third party without first obtaining written authorization from the vehicle's secured creditor, lessor, or lienholder;

(2) intending to defraud or harm the vehicle's owner, the person transfers the vehicle to a third party;

(3) intending to defraud or harm the vehicle's owner, the person disposes of the vehicle in a manner other than by transfer to a third party; or

(4) the person does not disclose the location of the vehicle on the request of the vehicle's owner, secured creditor, lessor, or lienholder.

(c) For the purposes of Subsection (b)(2), the actor is presumed to have intended to defraud or harm the motor vehicle's owner if the actor does not take reasonable steps to determine whether or not the third party is financially able to pay for the vehicle.

(d) It is a defense to prosecution under Subsection (b)(1) that the entire indebtedness secured by or owed under the security interest, lease, or lien is paid or satisfied in full not later than the 30th day after the date that the transfer was made.

(e) It is not a defense to prosecution under Subsection (b)(1) that the motor vehicle's owner has violated a contract creating a security interest, lease, or lien in the motor vehicle.

(f) An offense under Subsection (b)(1), (b)(2), or (b)(3) is:

(1) a state jail felony if the value of the motor vehicle is less than $20,000; or

(2) a felony of the third degree if the value of the motor vehicle is $20,000 or more.

(g) An offense under Subsection (b)(4) is a Class A misdemeanor.

(Enacted by Acts 1989, 71st Leg., ch. 954 (H.B. 220), § 1, effective September 1, 1989; am. Acts 1993, 73rd Leg., ch. 900 (S.B. 1067), § 1.01, effective September 1, 1994 (renumbered from Sec. 32.36).)

## Sec. 32.35.  Credit Card Transaction Record Laundering.

(a) In this section:

(1) "Agent" means a person authorized to act on behalf of another and includes an employee.

(2) "Authorized vendor" means a person authorized by a creditor to furnish property, service, or anything else of value upon presentation of a credit card by a cardholder.

(3) "Cardholder" means the person named on the face of a credit card to whom or for whose benefit the credit card is issued, and includes the named person's agents.

(4) "Credit card" means an identification card, plate, coupon, book, number, or any other

device authorizing a designated person or bearer to obtain property or services on credit. It includes the number or description on the device if the device itself is not produced at the time of ordering or obtaining the property or service.

(5) "Creditor" means a person licensed under Chapter 342, Finance Code, a bank, savings and loan association, credit union, or other regulated financial institution that lends money or otherwise extends credit to a cardholder through a credit card and that authorizes other persons to honor the credit card.

(b) A person commits an offense if the person is an authorized vendor who, with intent to defraud the creditor or cardholder, presents to a creditor, for payment, a credit card transaction record of a sale that was not made by the authorized vendor or the vendor's agent.

(c) A person commits an offense if, without the creditor's authorization, the person employs, solicits, or otherwise causes an authorized vendor or the vendor's agent to present to a creditor, for payment, a credit card transaction record of a sale that was not made by the authorized vendor or the vendor's agent.

(d) It is presumed that a person is not the agent of an authorized vendor if a fee is paid or offered to be paid by the person to the authorized vendor in connection with the vendor's presentment to a creditor of a credit card transaction record.

(e) An offense under this section is a:

(1) Class C misdemeanor if the amount of the record of a sale is less than $20;

(2) Class B misdemeanor if the amount of the record of a sale is $20 or more but less than $500;

(3) Class A misdemeanor if the amount of the record of a sale is $500 or more but less than $1,500;

(4) state jail felony if the amount of the record of a sale is $1,500 or more but less than $20,000;

(5) felony of the third degree if the amount of the record of a sale is $20,000 or more but less than $100,000;

(6) felony of the second degree if the amount of the record of a sale is $100,000 or more but less than $200,000; or

(7) felony of the first degree if the amount of the record of a sale is $200,000 or more. (Enacted by Acts 1991, 72nd Leg., ch. 792 (H.B. 1030), § 1, effective August 26, 1991; am. Acts 1993, 73rd Leg., ch. 900 (S.B. 1067), § 1.01,

effective September 1, 1994 (renumbered from Sec. 32.37); am. Acts 1997, 75th Leg., ch. 1396 (H.B. 1971), § 38, effective September 1, 1997; am. Acts 1999, 76th Leg., ch. 62 (S.B. 1368), § 7.83, effective September 1, 1999.)

### Sec. 32.36. Fraudulent Transfer of a Motor Vehicle [Renumbered].

Renumbered to Tex. Penal Code § 32.34 by Acts 1993, 73rd Leg., ch. 900 (S.B. 1067), § 1.01, effective September 1, 1994.

### Sec. 32.37. Credit Card Transaction Record Laundering [Renumbered].

Renumbered to Tex. Penal Code § 32.35 by Acts 1993, 73rd Leg., ch. 900 (S.B. 1067), § 1.01, effective September 1, 1994.

### Secs. 32.38 to 32.40 [Reserved for expansion].

## SUBCHAPTER D
## OTHER DECEPTIVE PRACTICES

### Sec. 32.41. Issuance of Bad Check.

(a) A person commits an offense if he issues or passes a check or similar sight order for the payment of money knowing that the issuer does not have sufficient funds in or on deposit with the bank or other drawee for the payment in full of the check or order as well as all other checks or orders outstanding at the time of issuance.

(b) This section does not prevent the prosecution from establishing the required knowledge by direct evidence; however, for purposes of this section, the issuer's knowledge of insufficient funds is presumed (except in the case of a post-dated check or order) if:

(1) he had no account with the bank or other drawee at the time he issued the check or order; or

(2) payment was refused by the bank or other drawee for lack of funds or insufficient funds on presentation within 30 days after issue and the issuer failed to pay the holder in full within 10 days after receiving notice of that refusal.

(c) Notice for purposes of Subsection (b)(2) may be actual notice or notice in writing that:

(1) is sent by:

(A) first class mail, evidenced by an affidavit of service; or

(B) registered or certified mail with return receipt requested;

(2) is addressed to the issuer at the issuer's address shown on:

    (A) the check or order;

    (B) the records of the bank or other drawee; or

    (C) the records of the person to whom the check or order has been issued or passed; and

(3) contains the following statement:

"This is a demand for payment in full for a check or order not paid because of a lack of funds or insufficient funds. If you fail to make payment in full within 10 days after the date of receipt of this notice, the failure to pay creates a presumption for committing an offense, and this matter may be referred for criminal prosecution."

(d) If notice is given in accordance with Subsection (c), it is presumed that the notice was received no later than five days after it was sent.

(e) A person charged with an offense under this section may make restitution for the bad checks. Restitution shall be made through the prosecutor's office if collection and processing were initiated through that office. In other cases restitution may be, with the approval of the court in which the offense is filed:

(1) made through the court; or

(2) collected by a law enforcement agency if a peace officer of that agency executes a warrant against the person charged with the offense.

(f) Except as otherwise provided by this subsection, an offense under this section is a Class C misdemeanor. If the check or similar sight order that was issued or passed was for a child support payment the obligation for which is established under a court order, the offense is a Class B misdemeanor.

(g) An offense under this section is not a lesser included offense of an offense under Section 31.03 or 31.04.

(Enacted by Acts 1973, 63rd Leg., ch. 399 (S.B. 34), § 1, effective January 1, 1974; am. Acts 1983, 68th Leg., ch. 911 (H.B. 1606), § 1, effective August 29, 1983; am. Acts 1987, 70th Leg., ch. 687 (S.B. 1083), § 2, effective June 18, 1987; am. Acts 1989, 71st Leg., ch. 1038 (H.B. 803), § 1, effective June 16, 1989; am. Acts 1993, 73rd Leg., ch. 900 (S.B. 1067), § 1.01, effective September 1, 1994; am. Acts 1995, 74th Leg., ch. 753 (H.B. 576), § 2, effective September 1, 1995; am. Acts 1997, 75th Leg., ch. 702 (S.B. 1594), § 14, effective September 1, 1997; am. Acts 2007, 80th Leg., ch. 976 (S.B. 548), § 2, effective September 1, 2007; am. Acts 2007, 80th Leg., ch. 1393 (H.B. 485), § 1, effective September 1, 2007.)

## Sec. 32.42. Deceptive Business Practices.

(a) For purposes of this section:

(1) "Adulterated" means varying from the standard of composition or quality prescribed by law or set by established commercial usage.

(2) "Business" includes trade and commerce and advertising, selling, and buying service or property.

(3) "Commodity" means any tangible or intangible personal property.

(4) "Contest" includes sweepstake, puzzle, and game of chance.

(5) "Deceptive sales contest" means a sales contest:

    (A) that misrepresents the participant's chance of winning a prize;

    (B) that fails to disclose to participants on a conspicuously displayed permanent poster (if the contest is conducted by or through a retail outlet) or on each card game piece, entry blank, or other paraphernalia required for participation in the contest (if the contest is not conducted by or through a retail outlet):

        (i) the geographical area or number of outlets in which the contest is to be conducted;

        (ii) an accurate description of each type of prize;

        (iii) the minimum number and minimum amount of cash prizes; and

        (iv) the minimum number of each other type of prize; or

    (C) that is manipulated or rigged so that prizes are given to predetermined persons or retail establishments. A sales contest is not deceptive if the total value of prizes to each retail outlet is in a uniform ratio to the number of game pieces distributed to that outlet.

(6) "Mislabeled" means varying from the standard of truth or disclosure in labeling prescribed by law or set by established commercial usage.

(7) "Prize" includes gift, discount, coupon, certificate, gratuity, and any other thing of value awarded in a sales contest.

(8) "Sales contest" means a contest in connection with the sale of a commodity or service by which a person may, as determined by

drawing, guessing, matching, or chance, receive a prize and which is not regulated by the rules of a federal regulatory agency.

(9) "Sell" and "sale" include offer for sale, advertise for sale, expose for sale, keep for the purpose of sale, deliver for or after sale, solicit and offer to buy, and every disposition for value.

(b) A person commits an offense if in the course of business he intentionally, knowingly, recklessly, or with criminal negligence commits one or more of the following deceptive business practices:

(1) using, selling, or possessing for use or sale a false weight or measure, or any other device for falsely determining or recording any quality or quantity;

(2) selling less than the represented quantity of a property or service;

(3) taking more than the represented quantity of property or service when as a buyer the actor furnishes the weight or measure;

(4) selling an adulterated or mislabeled commodity;

(5) passing off property or service as that of another;

(6) representing that a commodity is original or new if it is deteriorated, altered, rebuilt, reconditioned, reclaimed, used, or secondhand;

(7) representing that a commodity or service is of a particular style, grade, or model if it is of another;

(8) advertising property or service with intent:

(A) not to sell it as advertised, or

(B) not to supply reasonably expectable public demand, unless the advertising adequately discloses a time or quantity limit;

(9) representing the price of property or service falsely or in a way tending to mislead;

(10) making a materially false or misleading statement of fact concerning the reason for, existence of, or amount of a price or price reduction;

(11) conducting a deceptive sales contest; or

(12) making a materially false or misleading statement:

(A) in an advertisement for the purchase or sale of property or service; or

(B) otherwise in connection with the purchase or sale of property or service.

(c) An offense under Subsections (b)(1), (b)(2), (b)(3), (b)(4), (b)(5), and (b)(6) is:

(1) a Class C misdemeanor if the actor commits an offense with criminal negligence and if he has not previously been convicted of a deceptive business practice; or

(2) a Class A misdemeanor if the actor commits an offense intentionally, knowingly, recklessly or if he has been previously convicted of a Class B or C misdemeanor under this section.

(d) An offense under Subsections (b)(7), (b)(8), (b)(9), (b)(10), (b)(11), and (b)(12) is a Class A misdemeanor.

(Enacted by Acts 1973, 63rd Leg., ch. 399 (S.B. 34), § 1, effective January 1, 1974; am. Acts 1975, 64th Leg., ch. 508 (H.B. 652), §§ 1, 2, effective September 1, 1975; am. Acts 1993, 73rd Leg., ch. 900 (S.B. 1067), § 1.01, effective September 1, 1994.)

## Sec. 32.43. Commercial Bribery.

(a) For purposes of this section:

(1) "Beneficiary" means a person for whom a fiduciary is acting.

(2) "Fiduciary" means:

(A) an agent or employee;

(B) a trustee, guardian, custodian, administrator, executor, conservator, receiver, or similar fiduciary;

(C) a lawyer, physician, accountant, appraiser, or other professional advisor; or

(D) an officer, director, partner, manager, or other participant in the direction of the affairs of a corporation or association.

(b) A person who is a fiduciary commits an offense if, without the consent of his beneficiary, he intentionally or knowingly solicits, accepts, or agrees to accept any benefit from another person on agreement or understanding that the benefit will influence the conduct of the fiduciary in relation to the affairs of his beneficiary.

(c) A person commits an offense if he offers, confers, or agrees to confer any benefit the acceptance of which is an offense under Subsection (b).

(d) An offense under this section is a state jail felony.

(e) In lieu of a fine that is authorized by Subsection (d), and in addition to the imprisonment that is authorized by that subsection, if the court finds that an individual who is a fiduciary gained a benefit through the commission of an offense under Subsection (b), the court may sentence the individual to pay a fine in an amount fixed by the court, not to exceed double the value of the benefit gained. This subsection does not affect the application of Section 12.51(c) to an offense under this section committed by a corporation or association.

(Enacted by Acts 1973, 63rd Leg., ch. 399 (S.B. 34), § 1, effective January 1, 1974; am. Acts 1983, 68th Leg., ch. 357 (H.B. 2352), § 1, effective September 1, 1983; am. Acts 1993, 73rd Leg., ch. 900 (S.B. 1067), § 1.01, effective September 1, 1994.)

### Sec. 32.44.  Rigging Publicly Exhibited Contest.

(a) A person commits an offense if, with intent to affect the outcome (including the score) of a publicly exhibited contest:

(1) he offers, confers, or agrees to confer any benefit on, or threatens harm to:

(A) a participant in the contest to induce him not to use his best efforts; or

(B) an official or other person associated with the contest; or

(2) he tampers with a person, animal, or thing in a manner contrary to the rules of the contest.

(b) A person commits an offense if he intentionally or knowingly solicits, accepts, or agrees to accept any benefit the conferring of which is an offense under Subsection (a).

(c) An offense under this section is a Class A misdemeanor.

(Enacted by Acts 1973, 63rd Leg., ch. 399 (S.B. 34), § 1, effective January 1, 1974; am. Acts 1993, 73rd Leg., ch. 900 (S.B. 1067), § 1.01, effective September 1, 1994.)

### Sec. 32.441.  Illegal Recruitment of an Athlete.

(a) A person commits an offense if, without the consent of the governing body or a designee of the governing body of an institution of higher education, the person intentionally or knowingly solicits, accepts, or agrees to accept any benefit from another on an agreement or understanding that the benefit will influence the conduct of the person in enrolling in the institution and participating in intercollegiate athletics.

(b) A person commits an offense if he offers, confers, or agrees to confer any benefit the acceptance of which is an offense under Subsection (a).

(c) It is an exception to prosecution under this section that the person offering, conferring, or agreeing to confer a benefit and the person soliciting, accepting, or agreeing to accept a benefit are related within the second degree of consanguinity or affinity, as determined under Chapter 573, Government Code.

(d) It is an exception to prosecution under Subsection (a) that, not later than the 60th day

after the date the person accepted or agreed to accept a benefit, the person contacted a law enforcement agency and furnished testimony or evidence about the offense.

(e) An offense under this section is a:

(1) Class C misdemeanor if the value of the benefit is less than $20;

(2) Class B misdemeanor if the value of the benefit is $20 or more but less than $500;

(3) Class A misdemeanor if the value of the benefit is $500 or more but less than $1,500;

(4) state jail felony if the value of the benefit is $1,500 or more but less than $20,000;

(5) felony of the third degree if the value of the benefit is $20,000 or more but less than $100,000;

(6) felony of the second degree if the value of the benefit is $100,000 or more but less than $200,000; or

(7) felony of the first degree if the value of the benefit is $200,000 or more.

(Enacted by Acts 1989, 71st Leg., ch. 125 (S.B. 429), § 1, effective September 1, 1989; am. Acts 1991, 72nd Leg., ch. 561 (H.B. 1345), § 41, effective August 26, 1991; am. Acts 1993, 73rd Leg., ch. 900 (S.B. 1067), § 1.01, effective September 1, 1994; am Acts 1995, 74th Leg., ch. 76 (S.B. 959), § 5.95(27), effective September 1, 1995.)

### Sec. 32.45.  Misapplication of Fiduciary Property or Property of Financial Institution.

(a) For purposes of this section:

(1) "Fiduciary" includes:

(A) a trustee, guardian, administrator, executor, conservator, and receiver;

(B) an attorney in fact or agent appointed under a durable power of attorney as provided by Chapter XII, Texas Probate Code;

(C) any other person acting in a fiduciary capacity, but not a commercial bailee unless the commercial bailee is a party in a motor fuel sales agreement with a distributor or supplier, as those terms are defined by Section 153.001, Tax Code; and

(D) an officer, manager, employee, or agent carrying on fiduciary functions on behalf of a fiduciary.

(2) "Misapply" means deal with property contrary to:

(A) an agreement under which the fiduciary holds the property; or

(B) a law prescribing the custody or disposition of the property.

(b) A person commits an offense if he intentionally, knowingly, or recklessly misapplies property he holds as a fiduciary or property of a financial institution in a manner that involves substantial risk of loss to the owner of the property or to a person for whose benefit the property is held.

(c) An offense under this section is:

(1) a Class C misdemeanor if the value of the property misapplied is less than $20;

(2) a Class B misdemeanor if the value of the property misapplied is $20 or more but less than $500;

(3) a Class A misdemeanor if the value of the property misapplied is $500 or more but less than $1,500;

(4) a state jail felony if the value of the property misapplied is $1,500 or more but less than $20,000;

(5) a felony of the third degree if the value of the property misapplied is $20,000 or more but less than $100,000;

(6) a felony of the second degree if the value of the property misapplied is $100,000 or more but less than $200,000; or

(7) a felony of the first degree if the value of the property misapplied is $200,000 or more.

(d) An offense described for purposes of punishment by Subsections (c)(1)-(6) is increased to the next higher category of offense if it is shown on the trial of the offense that the offense was committed against an elderly individual as defined by Section 22.04.

(e) With the consent of the appropriate local county or district attorney, the attorney general has concurrent jurisdiction with that consenting local prosecutor to prosecute an offense under this section that involves the state Medicaid program.

(Enacted by Acts 1973, 63rd Leg., ch. 399 (S.B. 34), § 1, effective January 1, 1974; am. Acts 1991, 72nd Leg., ch. 565 (S.B. 4), § 2, effective September 1, 1991; am. Acts 1993, 73rd Leg., ch. 900 (S.B. 1067), § 1.01, effective September 1, 1994; am. Acts 1997, 75th Leg., ch. 1036 (S.B. 665), § 14, effective September 1, 1997; am. Acts 2001, 77th Leg., ch. 1047 (H.B. 1813), § 1, effective September 1, 2001; am. Acts 2003, 78th Leg., ch. 198 (H.B. 2292), § 2.137, effective September 1, 2003; am. Acts 2003, 78th Leg., ch. 257 (H.B. 1743), § 14, effective September 1, 2003; am. Acts 2003, 78th Leg., ch. 432 (H.B. 420), § 3, effective September 1, 2003; am. Acts 2005, 79th Leg., ch. 728 (H.B. 2018), § 23.001(77), effective September 1, 2005.)

## Sec. 32.46. Securing Execution of Document by Deception.

(a) A person commits an offense if, with intent to defraud or harm any person, he, by deception:

(1) causes another to sign or execute any document affecting property or service or the pecuniary interest of any person; or

(2) causes or induces a public servant to file or record any purported judgment or other document purporting to memorialize or evidence an act, an order, a directive, or process of:

(A) a purported court that is not expressly created or established under the constitution or the laws of this state or of the United States;

(B) a purported judicial entity that is not expressly created or established under the constitution or laws of this state or of the United States; or

(C) a purported judicial officer of a purported court or purported judicial entity described by Paragraph (A) or (B).

(b) An offense under Subsection (a)(1) is a:

(1) Class C misdemeanor if the value of the property, service, or pecuniary interest is less than $20;

(2) Class B misdemeanor if the value of the property, service, or pecuniary interest is $20 or more but less than $500;

(3) Class A misdemeanor if the value of the property, service, or pecuniary interest is $500 or more but less than $1,500;

(4) state jail felony if the value of the property, service, or pecuniary interest is $1,500 or more but less than $20,000;

(5) felony of the third degree if the value of the property, service, or pecuniary interest is $20,000 or more but less than $100,000;

(6) felony of the second degree if the value of the property, service, or pecuniary interest is $100,000 or more but less than $200,000; or

(7) felony of the first degree if the value of the property, service, or pecuniary interest is $200,000 or more.

(c) An offense under Subsection (a)(2) is a state jail felony.

(c-1) An offense described for purposes of punishment by Subsections (b)(1)—(6) and (c) is increased to the next higher category of offense if it is shown on the trial of the offense that the offense was committed against an elderly individual as defined by Section 22.04 or involves the state Medicaid program.

(d) In this section:

(1) "Deception" has the meaning assigned by Section 31.01.

(2) "Document" includes electronically stored data or other information that is retrievable in a readable, perceivable form.

(e) With the consent of the appropriate local county or district attorney, the attorney general has concurrent jurisdiction with that consenting local prosecutor to prosecute an offense under this section that involves the state Medicaid program.

(Enacted by Acts 1973, 63rd Leg., ch. 399 (S.B. 34), § 1, effective January 1, 1974; am. Acts 1993, 73rd Leg., ch. 900 (S.B. 1067), § 1.01, effective September 1, 1994; am. Acts 1997, 75th Leg., ch. 189 (H.B. 1185), § 2, effective May 21, 1997; am. Acts 2003, 78th Leg., ch. 198 (H.B. 2292), § 2.138, effective September 1, 2003; am. Acts 2003, 78th Leg., ch. 257 (H.B. 1743), § 15, effective September 1, 2003; am. Acts 2003, 78th Leg., ch. 432 (H.B. 420), § 4, effective September 1, 2003; am. Acts 2007, 80th Leg., ch. 127 (S.B. 1694), § 4, effective September 1, 2007; am. Acts 2011, 82nd Leg., ch. 620 (S.B. 688), § 6, effective September 1, 2011.)

### Sec. 32.47. Fraudulent Destruction, Removal, or Concealment of Writing.

(a) A person commits an offense if, with intent to defraud or harm another, he destroys, removes, conceals, alters, substitutes, or otherwise impairs the verity, legibility, or availability of a writing, other than a governmental record.

(b) For purposes of this section, "writing" includes:

(1) printing or any other method of recording information;

(2) money, coins, tokens, stamps, seals, credit cards, badges, trademarks;

(3) symbols of value, right, privilege, or identification; and

(4) universal product codes, labels, price tags, or markings on goods.

(c) Except as provided in Subsection (d), an offense under this section is a Class A misdemeanor.

(d) An offense under this section is a state jail felony if the writing:

(1) is a will or codicil of another, whether or not the maker is alive or dead and whether or not it has been admitted to probate; or

(2) is a deed, mortgage, deed of trust, security instrument, security agreement, or other writing for which the law provides public recording or filing, whether or not the writing has been acknowledged.

(Enacted by Acts 1973, 63rd Leg., ch. 399 (S.B. 34), § 1, effective January 1, 1974; am. Acts 1993, 73rd Leg., ch. 900 (S.B. 1067), § 1.01, effective September 1, 1994; am. Acts 2001, 77th Leg., ch. 21 (S.B. 923), § 1, effective September 1, 2001.)

### Sec. 32.48. Simulating Legal Process.

(a) A person commits an offense if the person recklessly causes to be delivered to another any document that simulates a summons, complaint, judgment, or other court process with the intent to:

(1) induce payment of a claim from another person; or

(2) cause another to:

(A) submit to the putative authority of the document; or

(B) take any action or refrain from taking any action in response to the document, in compliance with the document, or on the basis of the document.

(b) Proof that the document was mailed to any person with the intent that it be forwarded to the intended recipient is a sufficient showing that the document was delivered.

(c) It is not a defense to prosecution under this section that the simulating document:

(1) states that it is not legal process; or

(2) purports to have been issued or authorized by a person or entity who did not have lawful authority to issue or authorize the document.

(d) If it is shown on the trial of an offense under this section that the simulating document was filed with, presented to, or delivered to a clerk of a court or an employee of a clerk of a court created or established under the constitution or laws of this state, there is a rebuttable presumption that the document was delivered with the intent described by Subsection (a).

(e) Except as provided by Subsection (f), an offense under this section is a Class A misdemeanor.

(f) If it is shown on the trial of an offense under this section that the defendant has previously been convicted of a violation of this section, the offense is a state jail felony.

(Enacted by Acts 1997, 75th Leg., ch. 189 (H.B. 1185), § 3, effective May 21, 1997.)

### Sec. 32.49. Refusal to Execute Release of Fraudulent Lien or Claim.

(a) A person commits an offense if, with intent to defraud or harm another, the person:

(1) owns, holds, or is the beneficiary of a purported lien or claim asserted against real or personal property or an interest in real or personal property that is fraudulent, as described by Section 51.901(c), Government Code; and

(2) not later than the 21st day after the date of receipt of actual or written notice sent by either certified or registered mail, return receipt requested, to the person's last known address, or by telephonic document transfer to the recipient's current telecopier number, requesting the execution of a release of the fraudulent lien or claim, refuses to execute the release on the request of:

(A) the obligor or debtor; or

(B) any person who owns any interest in the real or personal property described in the document or instrument that is the basis for the lien or claim.

(b) A person who fails to execute a release of the purported lien or claim within the period prescribed by Subsection (a)(2) is presumed to have had the intent to harm or defraud another.

(c) An offense under this section is a Class A misdemeanor.

(Enacted by Acts 1997, 75th Leg., ch. 189 (H.B. 1185), § 4, effective May 21, 1997.)

## Sec. 32.50. Deceptive Preparation and Marketing of Academic Product.

(a) For purposes of this section:

(1) "Academic product" means a term paper, thesis, dissertation, essay, report, recording, work of art, or other written, recorded, pictorial, or artistic product or material submitted or intended to be submitted by a person to satisfy an academic requirement of the person.

(2) "Academic requirement" means a requirement or prerequisite to receive course credit or to complete a course of study or degree, diploma, or certificate program at an institution of higher education.

(3) "Institution of higher education" means an institution of higher education or private or independent institution of higher education as those terms are defined by Section 61.003, Education Code, or a private postsecondary educational institution as that term is defined by Section 61.302, Education Code.

(b) A person commits an offense if, with intent to make a profit, the person prepares, sells, offers or advertises for sale, or delivers to another person an academic product when the person knows, or should reasonably have known, that a person intends to submit or use the academic product to satisfy an academic requirement of a person other than the person who prepared the product.

(c) A person commits an offense if, with intent to induce another person to enter into an agreement or obligation to obtain or have prepared an academic product, the person knowingly makes or disseminates a written or oral statement that the person will prepare or cause to be prepared an academic product to be sold for use in satisfying an academic requirement of a person other than the person who prepared the product.

(d) It is a defense to prosecution under this section that the actor's conduct consisted solely of action taken as an employee of an institution of higher education in providing instruction, counseling, or tutoring in research or writing to students of the institution.

(e) It is a defense to prosecution under this section that the actor's conduct consisted solely of offering or providing tutorial or editing assistance to another person in connection with the other person's preparation of an academic product to satisfy the other person's academic requirement, and the actor does not offer or provide substantial preparation, writing, or research in the production of the academic product.

(f) It is a defense to prosecution under this section that the actor's conduct consisted solely of typing, transcribing, or reproducing a manuscript for a fee, or of offering to do so.

(g) An offense under this section is a Class C misdemeanor.

(Enacted by Acts 1997, 75th Leg., ch. 730 (H.B. 762), § 1, effective September 1, 1997; am. Acts 1999, 76th Leg., ch. 62 (S.B. 1368), § 19.01(88), effective September 1, 1999 (renumbered from Sec. 32.49).)

## Sec. 32.51. Fraudulent Use or Possession of Identifying Information.

(a) (1) "Identifying information" means information that alone or in conjunction with other information identifies a person, including a person's:

(A) name and date of birth;

(B) unique biometric data, including the person's fingerprint, voice print, or retina or iris image;

(C) unique electronic identification number, address, routing code, or financial institution account number;

(D) telecommunication identifying information or access device; and

(E) social security number or other government-issued identification number.

(2) "Telecommunication access device" means a card, plate, code, account number, personal identification number, electronic serial number, mobile identification number, or other telecommunications service, equipment, or instrument identifier or means of account access that alone or in conjunction with another telecommunication access device may be used to:

(A) obtain money, goods, services, or other thing of value; or

(B) initiate a transfer of funds other than a transfer originated solely by paper instrument.

(b) A person commits an offense if the person, with the intent to harm or defraud another, obtains, possesses, transfers, or uses an item of:

(1) identifying information of another person without the other person's consent;

(2) information concerning a deceased natural person, including a stillborn infant or fetus, that would be identifying information of that person were that person alive, if the item of information is obtained, possessed, transferred, or used without legal authorization; or

(3) identifying information of a child younger than 18 years of age.

(b-1) For the purposes of Subsection (b), the actor is presumed to have the intent to harm or defraud another if the actor possesses:

(1) the identifying information of three or more other persons;

(2) information described by Subsection (b)(2) concerning three or more deceased persons; or

(3) information described by Subdivision (1) or (2) concerning three or more persons or deceased persons.

(b-2) The presumption established under Subsection (b-1) does not apply to a business or other commercial entity or a government agency that is engaged in a business activity or governmental function that does not violate a penal law of this state.

(c) An offense under this section is:

(1) a state jail felony if the number of items obtained, possessed, transferred, or used is less than five;

(2) a felony of the third degree if the number of items obtained, possessed, transferred, or used is five or more but less than 10;

(3) a felony of the second degree if the number of items obtained, possessed, transferred, or used is 10 or more but less than 50; or

(4) a felony of the first degree if the number of items obtained, possessed, transferred, or used is 50 or more.

(c-1) An offense described for purposes of punishment by Subsections (c)(1)—(3) is increased to the next higher category of offense if it is shown on the trial of the offense that the offense was committed against an elderly individual as defined by Section 22.04.

(d) If a court orders a defendant convicted of an offense under this section to make restitution to the victim of the offense, the court may order the defendant to reimburse the victim for lost income or other expenses, other than attorney's fees, incurred as a result of the offense.

(e) If conduct that constitutes an offense under this section also constitutes an offense under any other law, the actor may be prosecuted under this section, the other law, or both.

(Enacted by Acts 1999, 76th Leg., ch. 1159 (S.B. 46), § 1, effective September 1, 1999; am. Acts 2003, 78th Leg., ch. 1104 (H.B. 2248), § 4, effective September 1, 2003; am. Acts 2007, 80th Leg., ch. 631 (H.B. 649), § 1, effective September 1, 2007; am. Acts 2007, 80th Leg., ch. 1163 (H.B. 126), § 1, effective September 1, 2007; am. Acts 2007, 80th Leg., ch. 1173 (H.B. 460), §§ 1, 2, effective September 1, 2007; am. Acts 2009, 81st Leg., ch. 87 (S.B. 1969), § 19.002, effective September 1, 2009; am. Acts 2009, 81st Leg., ch. 670 (H.B. 2328), § 3, effective September 1, 2009; am. Acts 2011, 82nd Leg., ch. 276 (H.B. 1529), § 1, effective September 1, 2011.)

### Sec. 32.52. Fraudulent, Substandard, or Fictitious Degree.

(a) In this section, "fraudulent or substandard degree" has the meaning assigned by Section 61.302, Education Code.

(b) A person commits an offense if the person:

(1) uses or claims to hold a postsecondary degree that the person knows:

(A) is a fraudulent or substandard degree;

(B) is fictitious or has otherwise not been granted to the person; or

(C) has been revoked; and

(2) uses or claims to hold that degree:

(A) in a written or oral advertisement or other promotion of a business; or

(B) with the intent to:

(i) obtain employment;

(ii) obtain a license or certificate to practice a trade, profession, or occupation;

(iii) obtain a promotion, a compensation or other benefit, or an increase in compensation or other benefit, in employment or in the practice of a trade, profession, or occupation;

(iv) obtain admission to an educational program in this state; or

(v) gain a position in government with authority over another person, regardless of whether the actor receives compensation for the position.

(c) An offense under this section is a Class B misdemeanor.

(d) If conduct that constitutes an offense under this section also constitutes an offense under any other law, the actor may be prosecuted under this section or the other law.

(Enacted by Acts 2005, 79th Leg., ch. 1039 (H.B. 1173), § 8, effective September 1, 2005.)

## Sec. 32.53. Exploitation of Child, Elderly Individual, or Disabled Individual.

(a) In this section:

(1) "Child," "elderly individual," and "disabled individual" have the meanings assigned by Section 22.04.

(2) "Exploitation" means the illegal or improper use of a child, elderly individual, or disabled individual or of the resources of a child, elderly individual, or disabled individual for monetary or personal benefit, profit, or gain.

(b) A person commits an offense if the person intentionally, knowingly, or recklessly causes the exploitation of a child, elderly individual, or disabled individual.

(c) An offense under this section is a felony of the third degree.

(d) A person who is subject to prosecution under both this section and another section of this code may be prosecuted under either or both sections. Section 3.04 does not apply to criminal episodes prosecuted under both this section and another section of this code. If a criminal episode is prosecuted under both this section and another section of this code and sentences are assessed for convictions under both sections, the sentences shall run concurrently.

(e) With the consent of the appropriate local county or district attorney, the attorney general has concurrent jurisdiction with that consenting local prosecutor to prosecute an offense under this section that involves the Medicaid program.

(Enacted by Acts 2011, 82nd Leg., ch. 620 (S.B. 688), § 7, effective September 1, 2011.)

## Sec. 32.54. Fraudulent or Fictitious Military Record.

(a) In this section:

(1) "Military record" means an enlistment record, occupation specialty, medal, award, decoration, or certification obtained by a person through the person's service in the armed forces of the United States or the state military forces.

(2) "State military forces" has the meaning assigned by Section 431.001, Government Code.

(b) A person commits an offense if the person:

(1) uses or claims to hold a military record that the person knows:

(A) is fraudulent;

(B) is fictitious or has otherwise not been granted or assigned to the person; or

(C) has been revoked; and

(2) uses or claims to hold that military record:

(A) in a written or oral advertisement or other promotion of a business; or

(B) with the intent to:

(i) obtain priority in receiving services or resources under Subchapter G, Chapter 302, Labor Code;

(ii) qualify for a veteran's employment preference under Chapter 657, Government Code;

(iii) obtain a license or certificate to practice a trade, profession, or occupation;

(iv) obtain a promotion, compensation, or other benefit, or an increase in compensation or other benefit, in employment or in the practice of a trade, profession, or occupation;

(v) obtain a benefit, service, or donation from another person;

(vi) obtain admission to an educational program in this state; or

(vii) gain a position in state government with authority over another person, regardless of whether the actor receives compensation for the position.

(c) An offense under this section is a Class C misdemeanor.

(d) If conduct that constitutes an offense under this section also constitutes an offense under any other law, the actor may be prosecuted under this section or the other law.

(Enacted by Acts 2011, 82nd Leg., ch. 386 (S.B. 431), § 1, effective September 1, 2011.)

### Sec. 32.55.   Insurance Claim Fraud [Deleted].

Deleted by Acts 1993, 73rd Leg., ch. 900 (S.B. 1067), § 13.02, effective September 1, 1994. (Enacted by Acts 1993, 73rd Leg., ch. 904 (S.B. 208), § 1, effective September 1, 1993.)

### Sec. 32.71.   Embezzlement; Unauthorized Issuance; False Entry [Deleted].

Deleted by Acts 1993, 73rd Leg., ch. 900 (S.B. 1067), § 1.01, effective September 1, 1994. (Enacted by Acts 1989, 71st Leg., ch. 780 (S.B. 607), § 118, effective September 1, 1989; am. Acts 1993, 73rd Leg., ch. 1050 (S.B. 396), § 11, effective August 30, 1993.)

### Sec. 32.72.   False Information; Suppressing Evidence [Deleted].

Deleted by Acts 1993, 73rd Leg., ch. 900 (S.B. 1067), § 1.01, effective September 1, 1994. (Enacted by Acts 1989, 71st Leg., ch. 780 (S.B. 607), § 118, effective September 1, 1989; am. Acts 1993, 73rd Leg., ch. 1050 (S.B. 396), § 12, effective August 30, 1993.)

## CHAPTER 33
## COMPUTER CRIMES

### Sec. 33.01.   Definitions.

In this chapter:

(1) "Access" means to approach, instruct, communicate with, store data in, retrieve or intercept data from, alter data or computer software in, or otherwise make use of any resource of a computer, computer network, computer program, or computer system.

(2) "Aggregate amount" means the amount of:

(A) any direct or indirect loss incurred by a victim, including the value of money, property, or service stolen or rendered unrecoverable by the offense; or

(B) any expenditure required by the victim to verify that a computer, computer network, computer program, or computer system was not altered, acquired, damaged, deleted, or disrupted by the offense.

(3) "Communications common carrier" means a person who owns or operates a telephone system in this state that includes equipment or facilities for the conveyance, transmission, or reception of communications and who receives compensation from persons who use that system.

(4) "Computer" means an electronic, magnetic, optical, electrochemical, or other high-speed data processing device that performs logical, arithmetic, or memory functions by the manipulations of electronic or magnetic impulses and includes all input, output, processing, storage, or communication facilities that are connected or related to the device.

(5) "Computer network" means the interconnection of two or more computers or computer systems by satellite, microwave, line, or other communication medium with the capability to transmit information among the computers.

(6) "Computer program" means an ordered set of data representing coded instructions or statements that when executed by a computer cause the computer to process data or perform specific functions.

(7) "Computer services" means the product of the use of a computer, the information stored in the computer, or the personnel supporting the computer, including computer time, data processing, and storage functions.

(8) "Computer system" means any combination of a computer or computer network with the documentation, computer software, or physical facilities supporting the computer or computer network.

(9) "Computer software" means a set of computer programs, procedures, and associated documentation related to the operation of a computer, computer system, or computer network.

(10) "Computer virus" means an unwanted computer program or other set of instructions inserted into a computer's memory, operating system, or program that is specifically constructed with the ability to replicate itself or to affect the other programs or files in the computer by attaching a copy of the unwanted program or other set of instructions to one or more computer programs or files.

Penal Code

(10-a) "Critical infrastructure facility" means:

(A) a chemical manufacturing facility;

(B) a refinery;

(C) an electrical power generating facility, substation, switching station, electrical control center, or electrical transmission or distribution facility;

(D) a water intake structure, water treatment facility, wastewater treatment plant, or pump station;

(E) a natural gas transmission compressor station;

(F) a liquid natural gas terminal or storage facility;

(G) a telecommunications central switching office;

(H) a port, railroad switching yard, trucking terminal, or other freight transportation facility;

(I) a gas processing plant, including a plant used in the processing, treatment, or fractionation of natural gas;

(J) a transmission facility used by a federally licensed radio or television station; or

(K) a cable television or video service provider headend.

(11) "Data" means a representation of information, knowledge, facts, concepts, or instructions that is being prepared or has been prepared in a formalized manner and is intended to be stored or processed, is being stored or processed, or has been stored or processed in a computer. Data may be embodied in any form, including but not limited to computer printouts, magnetic storage media, laser storage media, and punchcards, or may be stored internally in the memory of the computer.

(12) "Effective consent" includes consent by a person legally authorized to act for the owner. Consent is not effective if:

(A) induced by deception, as defined by Section 31.01, or induced by coercion;

(B) given by a person the actor knows is not legally authorized to act for the owner;

(C) given by a person who by reason of youth, mental disease or defect, or intoxication is known by the actor to be unable to make reasonable property dispositions;

(D) given solely to detect the commission of an offense; or

(E) used for a purpose other than that for which the consent was given.

(13) "Electric utility" has the meaning assigned by Section 31.002, Utilities Code.

(14) "Harm" includes partial or total alteration, damage, or erasure of stored data, interruption of computer services, introduction of a computer virus, or any other loss, disadvantage, or injury that might reasonably be suffered as a result of the actor's conduct.

(14-a) "Identifying information" has the meaning assigned by Section 32.51.

(15) "Owner" means a person who:

(A) has title to the property, possession of the property, whether lawful or not, or a greater right to possession of the property than the actor;

(B) has the right to restrict access to the property; or

(C) is the licensee of data or computer software.

(16) "Property" means:

(A) tangible or intangible personal property including a computer, computer system, computer network, computer software, or data; or

(B) the use of a computer, computer system, computer network, computer software, or data.

(Enacted by Acts 1985, 69th Leg., ch. 600 (S.B. 72), § 1, effective September 1, 1985; am. Acts 1989, 71st Leg., ch. 306 (H.B. 2312), § 1, effective September 1, 1989; am. Acts 1993, 73rd Leg., ch. 900 (S.B. 1067), § 1.01, effective September 1, 1994; am. Acts 1997, 75th Leg., ch. 306 (H.B. 1482), § 1, effective September 1, 1997; am. Acts 1999, 76th Leg., ch. 62 (S.B. 1368), § 18.44, effective September 1, 1999; am. Acts 2011, 82nd Leg., ch. 1044 (H.B. 3396), § 1, effective September 1, 2011.)

## Sec. 33.02. Breach of Computer Security.

(a) A person commits an offense if the person knowingly accesses a computer, computer network, or computer system without the effective consent of the owner.

(b) An offense under Subsection (a) is a Class B misdemeanor, except that the offense is a state jail felony if:

(1) the defendant has been previously convicted two or more times of an offense under this chapter; or

(2) the computer, computer network, or computer system is owned by the government or a critical infrastructure facility.

(b-1) A person commits an offense if with the intent to defraud or harm another or alter, dam-

Penal Code

age, or delete property, the person knowingly accesses a computer, computer network, or computer system without the effective consent of the owner.

(b-2) An offense under Subsection (b-1) is:

(1) a state jail felony if the aggregate amount involved is less than $20,000;

(2) a felony of the third degree if the aggregate amount involved is $20,000 or more but less than $100,000;

(3) a felony of the second degree if:

(A) the aggregate amount involved is $100,000 or more but less than $200,000;

(B) the aggregate amount involved is any amount less than $200,000 and the computer, computer network, or computer system is owned by the government or a critical infrastructure facility; or

(C) the actor obtains the identifying information of another by accessing only one computer, computer network, or computer system; or

(4) a felony of the first degree if:

(A) the aggregate amount involved is $200,000 or more; or

(B) the actor obtains the identifying information of another by accessing more than one computer, computer network, or computer system.

(c) When benefits are obtained, a victim is defrauded or harmed, or property is altered, damaged, or deleted in violation of this section, whether or not in a single incident, the conduct may be considered as one offense and the value of the benefits obtained and of the losses incurred because of the fraud, harm, or alteration, damage, or deletion of property may be aggregated in determining the grade of the offense.

(d) A person who is subject to prosecution under this section and any other section of this code may be prosecuted under either or both sections.

(e) It is a defense to prosecution under this section that the person acted with the intent to facilitate a lawful seizure or search of, or lawful access to, a computer, computer network, or computer system for a legitimate law enforcement purpose.

(Enacted by Acts 1985, 69th Leg., ch. 600 (S.B. 72), § 1, effective September 1, 1985; am. Acts 1989, 71st Leg., ch. 306 (H.B. 2312), § 2, effective September 1, 1989; am. Acts 1993, 73rd Leg., ch. 900 (S.B. 1067), § 1.01, effective September 1, 1994; am. Acts 1997, 75th Leg., ch. 306 (H.B. 1482), § 2, effective September 1, 1997; am. Acts

2001, 77th Leg., ch. 1411 (S.B. 917), § 1, effective September 1, 2001; am. Acts 2011, 82nd Leg., ch. 1044 (H.B. 3396), § 2, effective September 1, 2011.)

## Sec. 33.021.  Online Solicitation of a Minor.

(a) In this section:

(1) "Minor" means:

(A) an individual who represents himself or herself to be younger than 17 years of age; or

(B) an individual whom the actor believes to be younger than 17 years of age.

(2) "Sexual contact," "sexual intercourse," and "deviate sexual intercourse" have the meanings assigned by Section 21.01.

(3) "Sexually explicit" means any communication, language, or material, including a photographic or video image, that relates to or describes sexual conduct, as defined by Section 43.25.

(b) A person who is 17 years of age or older commits an offense if, with the intent to arouse or gratify the sexual desire of any person, the person, over the Internet, by electronic mail or text message or other electronic message service or system, or through a commercial online service, intentionally:

(1) communicates in a sexually explicit manner with a minor; or

(2) distributes sexually explicit material to a minor.

(c) A person commits an offense if the person, over the Internet, by electronic mail or text message or other electronic message service or system, or through a commercial online service, knowingly solicits a minor to meet another person, including the actor, with the intent that the minor will engage in sexual contact, sexual intercourse, or deviate sexual intercourse with the actor or another person.

(d) It is not a defense to prosecution under Subsection (c) that:

(1) the meeting did not occur;

(2) the actor did not intend for the meeting to occur; or

(3) the actor was engaged in a fantasy at the time of commission of the offense.

(e) It is a defense to prosecution under this section that at the time conduct described by Subsection (b) or (c) was committed:

(1) the actor was married to the minor; or

(2) the actor was not more than three years older than the minor and the minor consented to the conduct.

(f) An offense under Subsection (b) is a felony of the third degree, except that the offense is a felony of the second degree if the minor is younger than 14 years of age or is an individual whom the actor believes to be younger than 14 years of age at the time of the commission of the offense. An offense under Subsection (c) is a felony of the second degree.

(g) If conduct that constitutes an offense under this section also constitutes an offense under any other law, the actor may be prosecuted under this section, the other law, or both.

(Enacted by Acts 2005, 79th Leg., ch. 1273 (H.B. 2228), § 1, effective June 18, 2005; am. Acts 2007, 80th Leg., ch. 610 (H.B. 401), § 2, effective September 1, 2007; am. Acts 2007, 80th Leg., ch. 1291 (S.B. 6), § 7, effective September 1, 2007.)

## Sec. 33.03. Defenses.

It is an affirmative defense to prosecution under Section 33.02 that the actor was an officer, employee, or agent of a communications common carrier or electric utility and committed the proscribed act or acts in the course of employment while engaged in an activity that is a necessary incident to the rendition of service or to the protection of the rights or property of the communications common carrier or electric utility.

(Enacted by Acts 1985, 69th Leg., ch. 600 (S.B. 72), § 1, effective September 1, 1985; am. Acts 1993, 73rd Leg., ch. 900 (S.B. 1067), § 1.01, effective September 1, 1994 (renumbered from Sec. 33.04).)

## Sec. 33.04. Assistance by Attorney General.

The attorney general, if requested to do so by a prosecuting attorney, may assist the prosecuting attorney in the investigation or prosecution of an offense under this chapter or of any other offense involving the use of a computer.

(Enacted by Acts 1985, 69th Leg., ch. 600 (S.B. 72), § 1, effective September 1, 1985; am. Acts 1993, 73rd Leg., ch. 900 (S.B. 1067), § 1.01, effective September 1, 1994 (renumbered from Sec. 33.05).)

## Sec. 33.05. Tampering with Direct Recording Electronic Voting Machine.

(a) In this section:

(1) "Direct recording electronic voting machine" has the meaning assigned by Section 121.003, Election Code.

(2) "Measure" has the meaning assigned by Section 1.005, Election Code.

(b) A person commits an offense if the person knowingly accesses a computer, computer network, computer program, computer software, or computer system that is a part of a voting system that uses direct recording electronic voting machines and by means of that access:

(1) prevents a person from lawfully casting a vote;

(2) changes a lawfully cast vote;

(3) prevents a lawfully cast vote from being counted; or

(4) causes a vote that was not lawfully cast to be counted.

(c) An offense under this section does not require that the votes as affected by the person's actions described by Subsection (b) actually be the votes used in the official determination of the outcome of the election.

(d) An offense under this section is a felony of the first degree.

(e) Notwithstanding Section 15.01(d), an offense under Section 15.01(a) is a felony of the third degree if the offense the actor intends to commit is an offense under this section.

(f) With the consent of the appropriate local county or district attorney, the attorney general has concurrent jurisdiction with that consenting local prosecutor to investigate or prosecute an offense under this section.

(Enacted by Acts 2005, 79th Leg., ch. 470 (H.B. 56), § 1, effective September 1, 2005; am. Acts 2009, 81st Leg., ch. 503 (S.B. 927), § 1, effective September 1, 2009.)

## Sec. 33.07. Online Impersonation.

(a) A person commits an offense if the person, without obtaining the other person's consent and with the intent to harm, defraud, intimidate, or threaten any person, uses the name or persona of another person to:

(1) create a web page on a commercial social networking site or other Internet website; or

(2) post or send one or more messages on or through a commercial social networking site or other Internet website, other than on or through an electronic mail program or message board program.

(b) A person commits an offense if the person sends an electronic mail, instant message, text message, or similar communication that references a name, domain address, phone number, or other item of identifying information belonging to any person:

(1) without obtaining the other person's consent;

(2) with the intent to cause a recipient of the communication to reasonably believe that the other person authorized or transmitted the communication; and

(3) with the intent to harm or defraud any person.

(c) An offense under Subsection (a) is a felony of the third degree. An offense under Subsection (b) is a Class A misdemeanor, except that the offense is a felony of the third degree if the actor commits the offense with the intent to solicit a response by emergency personnel.

(d) If conduct that constitutes an offense under this section also constitutes an offense under any other law, the actor may be prosecuted under this section, the other law, or both.

(e) It is a defense to prosecution under this section that the actor is any of the following entities or that the actor's conduct consisted solely of action taken as an employee of any of the following entities:

(1) a commercial social networking site;

(2) an Internet service provider;

(3) an interactive computer service, as defined by 47 U.S.C. Section 230;

(4) a telecommunications provider, as defined by Section 51.002, Utilities Code; or

(5) a video service provider or cable service provider, as defined by Section 66.002, Utilities Code.

(f) In this section:

(1) "Commercial social networking site" means any business, organization, or other similar entity operating a website that permits persons to become registered users for the purpose of establishing personal relationships with other users through direct or real-time communication with other users or the creation of web pages or profiles available to the public or to other users. The term does not include an electronic mail program or a message board program.

(2) "Identifying information" has the meaning assigned by Section 32.51.

(Enacted by Acts 2009, 81st Leg., ch. 911 (H.B. 2003), § 1, effective September 1, 2009; am. Acts 2011, 82nd Leg., ch. 282 (H.B. 1666), §§ 1, 2, effective September 1, 2011.)

# CHAPTER 33A
# TELECOMMUNICATIONS CRIMES

**Section**

## Sec. 33A.01.   Definitions.

In this chapter:

(1) "Counterfeit telecommunications access device" means a telecommunications access device that is false, fraudulent, not issued to a legitimate telecommunications access device subscriber account, or otherwise unlawful or invalid.

(2) "Counterfeit telecommunications device" means a telecommunications device that has been altered or programmed alone or with another telecommunications device to acquire, intercept, receive, or otherwise facilitate the use of a telecommunications service without the authority or consent of the telecommunications service provider and includes a clone telephone, clone microchip, tumbler telephone, tumbler microchip, or wireless scanning device capable of acquiring, intercepting, receiving, or otherwise facilitating the use of a telecommunications service without immediate detection.

(3) "Deliver" means to actually or constructively sell, give, loan, or otherwise transfer a telecommunications device, or a counterfeit telecommunications device or any telecommunications plans, instructions, or materials, to another person.

(4) "Publish" means to communicate information or make information available to another person orally, in writing, or by means of telecommunications and includes communicating information on a computer bulletin board or similar system.

(5) "Telecommunications" means the origination, emission, transmission, or reception of data, images, signals, sounds, or other intelli-

gence or equivalence of intelligence over a communications system by any method, including an electronic, magnetic, optical, digital, or analog method.

(6) "Telecommunications access device" means an instrument, device, card, plate, code, account number, personal identification number, electronic serial number, mobile identification number, counterfeit number, or financial transaction device that alone or with another telecommunications access device can acquire, intercept, provide, receive, use, or otherwise facilitate the use of a telecommunications device, counterfeit telecommunications device, or telecommunications service.

(7) "Telecommunications device" means any instrument, equipment, machine, or device that facilitates telecommunications and includes a computer, computer chip or circuit, telephone, pager, personal communications device, transponder, receiver, radio, modem, or device that enables use of a modem.

(8) "Telecommunications service" means the provision, facilitation, or generation of telecommunications through the use of a telecommunications device or telecommunications access device over a telecommunications system.

(9) "Value of the telecommunications service obtained or attempted to be obtained" includes the value of:

(A) a lawful charge for telecommunications service avoided or attempted to be avoided;

(B) money, property, or telecommunications service lost, stolen, or rendered unrecoverable by an offense; and

(C) an expenditure incurred by a victim to verify that a telecommunications device or telecommunications access device or telecommunications service was not altered, acquired, damaged, or disrupted as a result of an offense.

(Enacted by Acts 1997, 75th Leg., ch. 306 (H.B. 1482), § 3, effective September 1, 1997.)

## Sec. 33A.02. Unauthorized Use of Telecommunications Service.

(a) A person commits an offense if the person is an officer, shareholder, partner, employee, agent, or independent contractor of a telecommunications service provider and the person knowingly and without authority uses or diverts telecommunications service for the person's own benefit or to the benefit of another.

(b) An offense under this section is:

(1) a Class B misdemeanor if the value of the telecommunications service used or diverted is less than $500;

(2) a Class A misdemeanor if:

(A) the value of the telecommunications service used or diverted is $500 or more but less than $1,500; or

(B) the value of the telecommunications service used or diverted is less than $500 and the defendant has been previously convicted of an offense under this chapter;

(3) a state jail felony if:

(A) the value of the telecommunications service used or diverted is $1,500 or more but less than $20,000; or

(B) the value of the telecommunications service used or diverted is less than $1,500 and the defendant has been previously convicted two or more times of an offense under this chapter;

(4) a felony of the third degree if the value of the telecommunications service used or diverted is $20,000 or more but less than $100,000;

(5) a felony of the second degree if the value of the telecommunications service used or diverted is $100,000 or more but less than $200,000; or

(6) a felony of the first degree if the value of the telecommunications service used or diverted is $200,000 or more.

(c) When telecommunications service is used or diverted in violation of this section pursuant to one scheme or continuing course of conduct, whether or not in a single incident, the conduct may be considered as one offense and the values of the service used or diverted may be aggregated in determining the grade of the offense.

(Enacted by Acts 1997, 75th Leg., ch. 306 (H.B. 1482), § 3, effective September 1, 1997.)

## Sec. 33A.03. Manufacture, Possession, or Delivery of Unlawful Telecommunications Device.

(a) A person commits an offense if the person manufactures, possesses, delivers, offers to deliver, or advertises:

(1) a counterfeit telecommunications device; or

(2) a telecommunications device that is intended to be used to:

(A) commit an offense under Section 33A.04; or

Penal Code

(B) conceal the existence or place of origin or destination of a telecommunications service.

(b) A person commits an offense if the person delivers, offers to deliver, or advertises plans, instructions, or materials for manufacture of:

(1) a counterfeit telecommunications device; or

(2) a telecommunications device that is intended to be used to commit an offense under Subsection (a).

(c) An offense under this section is a felony of the third degree.

(d) It is a defense to prosecution under this section that the person was an officer, agent, or employee of a telecommunications service provider who engaged in the conduct for the purpose of gathering information for a law enforcement investigation related to an offense under this chapter.

(Enacted by Acts 1997, 75th Leg., ch. 306 (H.B. 1482), § 3, effective September 1, 1997.)

## Sec. 33A.04.    Theft of Telecommunications Service.

(a) A person commits an offense if the person knowingly obtains or attempts to obtain telecommunications service to avoid or cause another person to avoid a lawful charge for that service by using:

(1) a telecommunications access device without the authority or consent of the subscriber or lawful holder of the device or pursuant to an agreement for an exchange of value with the subscriber or lawful holder of the device to allow another person to use the device;

(2) a counterfeit telecommunications access device;

(3) a telecommunications device or counterfeit telecommunications device; or

(4) a fraudulent or deceptive scheme, pretense, method, or conspiracy, or other device or means, including a false, altered, or stolen identification.

(b) An offense under this section is:

(1) a Class B misdemeanor if the value of the telecommunications service obtained or attempted to be obtained is less than $500;

(2) a Class A misdemeanor if:

(A) the value of the telecommunications service obtained or attempted to be obtained is $500 or more but less than $1,500; or

(B) the value of the telecommunications service obtained or attempted to be obtained

is less than $500 and the defendant has been previously convicted of an offense under this chapter;

(3) a state jail felony if:

(A) the value of the telecommunications service obtained or attempted to be obtained is $1,500 or more but less than $20,000; or

(B) the value of the telecommunications service obtained or attempted to be obtained is less than $1,500 and the defendant has been previously convicted two or more times of an offense under this chapter;

(4) a felony of the third degree if the value of the telecommunications service obtained or attempted to be obtained is $20,000 or more but less than $100,000;

(5) a felony of the second degree if the value of the telecommunications service obtained or attempted to be obtained is $100,000 or more but less than $200,000; or

(6) a felony of the first degree if the value of the telecommunications service obtained or attempted to be obtained is $200,000 or more.

(c) When telecommunications service is obtained or attempted to be obtained in violation of this section pursuant to one scheme or continuing course of conduct, whether or not in a single incident, the conduct may be considered as one offense and the values of the service obtained or attempted to be obtained may be aggregated in determining the grade of the offense.

(Enacted by Acts 1997, 75th Leg., ch. 306 (H.B. 1482), § 3, effective September 1, 1997.)

## Sec. 33A.05.    Publication of Telecommunications Access Device.

(a) A person commits an offense if the person with criminal negligence publishes a telecommunications access device or counterfeit telecommunications access device that is designed to be used to commit an offense under Section 33A.04.

(b) Except as otherwise provided by this subsection, an offense under this section is a Class A misdemeanor. An offense under this section is a felony of the third degree if the person has been previously convicted of an offense under this chapter.

(Enacted by Acts 1997, 75th Leg., ch. 306 (H.B. 1482), § 3, effective September 1, 1997.)

## Sec. 33A.06.    Assistance by Attorney General.

The attorney general, if requested to do so by a prosecuting attorney, may assist the prosecuting attorney in the investigation or prosecution of an offense under this chapter or of any other offense involving the use of telecommunications equipment, services, or devices.

(Enacted by Acts 1997, 75th Leg., ch. 306 (H.B. 1482), § 3, effective September 1, 1997.)

# CHAPTER 34
# MONEY LAUNDERING

**Section**
34.01.    Definitions.
34.02.    Money Laundering.
34.021.   Protection from Civil Liability.
34.03.    Assistance by Attorney General.

## Sec. 34.01.  Definitions.

In this chapter:

(1) "Criminal activity" means any offense, including any preparatory offense, that is:

(A) classified as a felony under the laws of this state or the United States; or

(B) punishable by confinement for more than one year under the laws of another state.

(2) "Funds" includes:

(A) coin or paper money of the United States or any other country that is designated as legal tender and that circulates and is customarily used and accepted as a medium of exchange in the country of issue;

(B) United States silver certificates, United States Treasury notes, and Federal Reserve System notes;

(C) an official foreign bank note that is customarily used and accepted as a medium of exchange in a foreign country and a foreign bank draft; and

(D) currency or its equivalent, including an electronic fund, personal check, bank check, traveler's check, money order, bearer negotiable instrument, bearer investment security, bearer security, or certificate of stock in a form that allows title to pass on delivery.

(3) "Financial institution" has the meaning assigned by Section 32.01.

(4) "Proceeds" means funds acquired or derived directly or indirectly from, produced through, or realized through:

(A) an act; or

(B) conduct that constitutes an offense under Section 151.7032, Tax Code.

(Enacted by Acts 1993, 73rd Leg., ch. 761 (H.B. 354), § 2, effective September 1, 1993; am. Acts 2005, 79th Leg., ch. 1162 (H.B. 3376), § 1, effective September 1, 2005; am. Acts 2011, 82nd Leg.,

ch. 68 (S.B. 934), § 7, effective September 1, 2011.)

## Sec. 34.02.  Money Laundering.

(a) A person commits an offense if the person knowingly:

(1) acquires or maintains an interest in, conceals, possesses, transfers, or transports the proceeds of criminal activity;

(2) conducts, supervises, or facilitates a transaction involving the proceeds of criminal activity;

(3) invests, expends, or receives, or offers to invest, expend, or receive, the proceeds of criminal activity or funds that the person believes are the proceeds of criminal activity; or

(4) finances or invests or intends to finance or invest funds that the person believes are intended to further the commission of criminal activity.

(a-1) Knowledge of the specific nature of the criminal activity giving rise to the proceeds is not required to establish a culpable mental state under this section.

(b) For purposes of this section, a person is presumed to believe that funds are the proceeds of or are intended to further the commission of criminal activity if a peace officer or a person acting at the direction of a peace officer represents to the person that the funds are proceeds of or are intended to further the commission of criminal activity, as applicable, regardless of whether the peace officer or person acting at the peace officer's direction discloses the person's status as a peace officer or that the person is acting at the direction of a peace officer.

(c) It is a defense to prosecution under this section that the person acted with intent to facilitate the lawful seizure, forfeiture, or disposition of funds or other legitimate law enforcement purpose pursuant to the laws of this state or the United States.

(d) It is a defense to prosecution under this section that the transaction was necessary to preserve a person's right to representation as guaranteed by the Sixth Amendment of the United States Constitution and by Article 1, Section 10, of the Texas Constitution or that the funds were received as bona fide legal fees by a licensed attorney and at the time of their receipt, the attorney did not have actual knowledge that the funds were derived from criminal activity.

(e) An offense under this section is:

(1) a state jail felony if the value of the funds is $1,500 or more but less than $20,000;

(2) a felony of the third degree if the value of the funds is $20,000 or more but less than $100,000;

(3) a felony of the second degree if the value of the funds is $100,000 or more but less than $200,000; or

(4) a felony of the first degree if the value of the funds is $200,000 or more.

(f) For purposes of this section, if proceeds of criminal activity are related to one scheme or continuing course of conduct, whether from the same or several sources, the conduct may be considered as one offense and the value of the proceeds aggregated in determining the classification of the offense.

(g) For purposes of this section, funds on deposit at a branch of a financial institution are considered the property of that branch and any other branch of the financial institution.

(h) If conduct that constitutes an offense under this section also constitutes an offense under any other law, the actor may be prosecuted under this section, the other law, or both.

(Enacted by Acts 1993, 73rd Leg., ch. 761 (H.B. 354), § 2, effective September 1, 1993; am. Acts 2005, 79th Leg., ch. 1162 (H.B. 3376), § 2, effective September 1, 2005.)

## Sec. 34.021.  Protection from Civil Liability.

Notwithstanding Section 1.03(c), a financial institution or an agent of the financial institution acting in a manner described by Section 34.02(c) is not liable for civil damages to a person who:

(1) claims an ownership interest in funds involved in an offense under Section 34.02; or

(2) conducts with the financial institution or an insurer, as defined by Article 1.02, Insurance Code, a transaction concerning funds involved in an offense under Section 34.02.

(Enacted by Acts 2005, 79th Leg., ch. 1162 (H.B. 3376), § 3, effective September 1, 2005.)

## Sec. 34.03.  Assistance by Attorney General.

The attorney general, if requested to do so by a prosecuting attorney, may assist in the prosecution of an offense under this chapter.

(Enacted by Acts 1993, 73rd Leg., ch. 761 (H.B. 354), § 2, effective September 1, 1993.)

# CHAPTER 35
# INSURANCE FRAUD

## Sec. 35.01.  Definitions.

In this chapter:

(1) "Insurance policy" means a written instrument in which is provided the terms of any certificate of insurance, binder of coverage, contract of insurance, benefit plan, nonprofit hospital service plan, motor club service plan, surety bond, cash bond, or any other alternative to insurance authorized by Chapter 601, Transportation Code. The term includes any instrument authorized to be regulated by the Texas Department of Insurance.

(2) "Insurer" has the meaning assigned by Article 1.02, Insurance Code.

(3) "Statement" means an oral or written communication or a record or documented representation of fact made to an insurer. The term includes computer-generated information.

(4) "Value of the claim" means the total dollar amount of a claim for payment under an insurance policy or, as applicable, the value of the claim determined under Section 35.025.

(Enacted by Acts 1995, 74th Leg., ch. 621 (H.B. 1487), § 1, effective September 1, 1995; am. Acts 2001, 77th Leg., ch. 1420 (H.B. 2812), § 14.830, effective September 1, 2001; am. Acts 2003, 78th Leg., ch. 1276 (H.B. 3507), § 10A.541, effective September 1, 2003; am. Acts 2005, 79th Leg., ch. 1162 (H.B. 3376), § 4, effective September 1, 2005.)

## Sec. 35.015.  Materiality.

A statement is material for the purposes of this chapter, regardless of the admissibility of the statement at trial, if the statement could have affected:

(1) the eligibility for coverage or amount of the payment on a claim for payment under an insurance policy; or

Penal Code

(2) the decision of an insurer whether to issue an insurance policy.
(Enacted by Acts 2005, 79th Leg., ch. 1162 (H.B. 3376), § 4, effective September 1, 2005.)

## Sec. 35.02.  Insurance Fraud.

(a) A person commits an offense if, with intent to defraud or deceive an insurer, the person, in support of a claim for payment under an insurance policy:

(1) prepares or causes to be prepared a statement that:

(A) the person knows contains false or misleading material information; and

(B) is presented to an insurer; or

(2) presents or causes to be presented to an insurer a statement that the person knows contains false or misleading material information.

(a-1) A person commits an offense if the person, with intent to defraud or deceive an insurer and in support of an application for an insurance policy:

(1) prepares or causes to be prepared a statement that:

(A) the person knows contains false or misleading material information; and

(B) is presented to an insurer; or

(2) presents or causes to be presented to an insurer a statement that the person knows contains false or misleading material information.

(b) A person commits an offense if, with intent to defraud or deceive an insurer, the person solicits, offers, pays, or receives a benefit in connection with the furnishing of goods or services for which a claim for payment is submitted under an insurance policy.

(c) An offense under Subsection (a) or (b) is:

(1) a Class C misdemeanor if the value of the claim is less than $50;

(2) a Class B misdemeanor if the value of the claim is $50 or more but less than $500;

(3) a Class A misdemeanor if the value of the claim is $500 or more but less than $1,500;

(4) a state jail felony if the value of the claim is $1,500 or more but less than $20,000;

(5) a felony of the third degree if the value of the claim is $20,000 or more but less than $100,000;

(6) a felony of the second degree if the value of the claim is $100,000 or more but less than $200,000; or

(7) a felony of the first degree if:

(A) the value of the claim is $200,000 or more; or

(B) an act committed in connection with the commission of the offense places a person at risk of death or serious bodily injury.

(d) An offense under Subsection (a-1) is a state jail felony.

(e) The court shall order a defendant convicted of an offense under this section to pay restitution, including court costs and attorney's fees, to an affected insurer.

(f) If conduct that constitutes an offense under this section also constitutes an offense under any other law, the actor may be prosecuted under this section, the other law, or both.

(g) For purposes of this section, if the actor proves by a preponderance of the evidence that a portion of the claim for payment under an insurance policy resulted from a valid loss, injury, expense, or service covered by the policy, the value of the claim is equal to the difference between the total claim amount and the amount of the valid portion of the claim.

(h) If it is shown on the trial of an offense under this section that the actor submitted a bill for goods or services in support of a claim for payment under an insurance policy to the insurer issuing the policy, a rebuttable presumption exists that the actor caused the claim for payment to be prepared or presented.
(Enacted by Acts 1995, 74th Leg., ch. 621 (H.B. 1487), § 1, effective September 1, 1995; am. Acts 2003, 78th Leg., ch. 605 (H.B. 1838), § 1, effective September 1, 2003; am. Acts 2005, 79th Leg., ch. 1162 (H.B. 3376), § 4, effective September 1, 2005.)

## Sec. 35.025.  Value of Claim.

(a) Except as provided by Subsection (b) and subject to Subsection (c), for the purposes of Section 35.02(c), if the value of a claim is not readily ascertainable, the value of the claim is:

(1) the fair market value, at the time and place of the offense, of the goods or services that are the subject of the claim; or

(2) the cost of replacing the goods or services that are the subject of the claim within a reasonable time after the claim.

(b) If goods or services that are the subject of a claim cannot be reasonably ascertained under Subsection (a), the goods or services are considered to have a value of $500 or more but less than $1,500.

(c) If the actor proves by a preponderance of the evidence that a portion of the claim for payment under an insurance policy resulted from a valid loss, injury, expense, or service covered by the policy, the value of the claim is equal to the difference between the total claim amount and the amount of the valid portion of the claim.
(Enacted by Acts 2005, 79th Leg., ch. 1162 (H.B. 3376), § 4, effective September 1, 2005.)

## Sec. 35.03. Aggregation and Multiple Offenses.

(a) When separate claims in violation of this chapter are communicated to an insurer or group of insurers pursuant to one scheme or continuing course of conduct, the conduct may be considered as one offense and the value of the claims aggregated in determining the classification of the offense. If claims are aggregated under this subsection, Subsection (b) shall not apply.

(b) When three or more separate claims in violation of this chapter are communicated to an insurer or group of insurers pursuant to one scheme or continuing course of conduct, the conduct may be considered as one offense, and the classification of the offense shall be one category higher than the most serious single offense proven from the separate claims, except that if the most serious offense is a felony of the first degree, the offense is a felony of the first degree. This subsection shall not be applied if claims are aggregated under Subsection (a).
(Enacted by Acts 1995, 74th Leg., ch. 621 (H.B. 1487), § 1, effective September 1, 1995.)

## Sec. 35.04. Jurisdiction of Attorney General.

(a) The attorney general may offer to an attorney representing the state in the prosecution of an offense under Section 35.02 the investigative, technical, and litigation assistance of the attorney general's office.

(b) The attorney general may prosecute or assist in the prosecution of an offense under Section 35.02 on the request of the attorney representing the state described by Subsection (a).

(Enacted by Acts 1995, 74th Leg., ch. 621 (H.B. 1487), § 1, effective September 1, 1995.)

# CHAPTER 35A
# MEDICAID FRAUD

**Section**
35A.01. Definitions.
35A.02. Medicaid Fraud.

## Sec. 35A.01. Definitions.

In this chapter:

(1) "Claim" has the meaning assigned by Section 36.001, Human Resources Code.

(2) "Fiscal agent" has the meaning assigned by Section 36.001, Human Resources Code.

(3) "Health care practitioner" has the meaning assigned by Section 36.001, Human Resources Code.

(4) "Managed care organization" has the meaning assigned by Section 36.001, Human Resources Code.

(5) "Medicaid program" has the meaning assigned by Section 36.001, Human Resources Code.

(6) "Medicaid recipient" has the meaning assigned by Section 36.001, Human Resources Code.

(7) "Physician" has the meaning assigned by Section 36.001, Human Resources Code.

(8) "Provider" has the meaning assigned by Section 36.001, Human Resources Code.

(9) "Service" has the meaning assigned by Section 36.001, Human Resources Code.

(10) "High managerial agent" means a director, officer, or employee who is authorized to act on behalf of a provider and has duties of such responsibility that the conduct of the director, officer, or employee reasonably may be assumed to represent the policy or intent of the provider.
(Enacted by Acts 2005, 79th Leg., ch. 806 (S.B. 563), § 16, effective September 1, 2005; am. Acts 2011, 82nd Leg., ch. 620 (S.B. 688), § 8, effective September 1, 2011.)

## Sec. 35A.02. Medicaid Fraud.

(a) A person commits an offense if the person:

(1) knowingly makes or causes to be made a false statement or misrepresentation of a ma-

terial fact to permit a person to receive a benefit or payment under the Medicaid program that is not authorized or that is greater than the benefit or payment that is authorized;

(2) knowingly conceals or fails to disclose information that permits a person to receive a benefit or payment under the Medicaid program that is not authorized or that is greater than the benefit or payment that is authorized;

(3) knowingly applies for and receives a benefit or payment on behalf of another person under the Medicaid program and converts any part of the benefit or payment to a use other than for the benefit of the person on whose behalf it was received;

(4) knowingly makes, causes to be made, induces, or seeks to induce the making of a false statement or misrepresentation of material fact concerning:

(A) the conditions or operation of a facility in order that the facility may qualify for certification or recertification required by the Medicaid program, including certification or recertification as:

(i) a hospital;

(ii) a nursing facility or skilled nursing facility;

(iii) a hospice;

(iv) an intermediate care facility for the mentally retarded;

(v) an assisted living facility; or

(vi) a home health agency; or

(B) information required to be provided by a federal or state law, rule, regulation, or provider agreement pertaining to the Medicaid program;

(5) except as authorized under the Medicaid program, knowingly pays, charges, solicits, accepts, or receives, in addition to an amount paid under the Medicaid program, a gift, money, a donation, or other consideration as a condition to the provision of a service or product or the continued provision of a service or product if the cost of the service or product is paid for, in whole or in part, under the Medicaid program;

(6) knowingly presents or causes to be presented a claim for payment under the Medicaid program for a product provided or a service rendered by a person who:

(A) is not licensed to provide the product or render the service, if a license is required; or

(B) is not licensed in the manner claimed;

(7) knowingly makes or causes to be made a claim under the Medicaid program for:

(A) a service or product that has not been approved or acquiesced in by a treating physician or health care practitioner;

(B) a service or product that is substantially inadequate or inappropriate when compared to generally recognized standards within the particular discipline or within the health care industry; or

(C) a product that has been adulterated, debased, mislabeled, or that is otherwise inappropriate;

(8) makes a claim under the Medicaid program and knowingly fails to indicate the type of license and the identification number of the licensed health care provider who actually provided the service;

(9) knowingly enters into an agreement, combination, or conspiracy to defraud the state by obtaining or aiding another person in obtaining an unauthorized payment or benefit from the Medicaid program or a fiscal agent;

(10) is a managed care organization that contracts with the Health and Human Services Commission or other state agency to provide or arrange to provide health care benefits or services to individuals eligible under the Medicaid program and knowingly:

(A) fails to provide to an individual a health care benefit or service that the organization is required to provide under the contract;

(B) fails to provide to the commission or appropriate state agency information required to be provided by law, commission or agency rule, or contractual provision; or

(C) engages in a fraudulent activity in connection with the enrollment of an individual eligible under the Medicaid program in the organization's managed care plan or in connection with marketing the organization's services to an individual eligible under the Medicaid program;

(11) knowingly obstructs an investigation by the attorney general of an alleged unlawful act under this section or under Section 32.039, 32.0391, or 36.002, Human Resources Code; or

(12) knowingly makes, uses, or causes the making or use of a false record or statement to conceal, avoid, or decrease an obligation to pay or transmit money or property to this state under the Medicaid program.

(b) An offense under this section is:

(1) a Class C misdemeanor if the amount of any payment or the value of any monetary or in-kind benefit provided or claim for payment made under the Medicaid program, directly or indirectly, as a result of the conduct is less than $50;

(2) a Class B misdemeanor if the amount of any payment or the value of any monetary or in-kind benefit provided or claim for payment made under the Medicaid program, directly or indirectly, as a result of the conduct is $50 or more but less than $500;

(3) a Class A misdemeanor if the amount of any payment or the value of any monetary or in-kind benefit provided or claim for payment made under the Medicaid program, directly or indirectly, as a result of the conduct is $500 or more but less than $1,500;

(4) a state jail felony if:

(A) the amount of any payment or the value of any monetary or in-kind benefit provided or claim for payment made under the Medicaid program, directly or indirectly, as a result of the conduct is $1,500 or more but less than $20,000;

(B) the offense is committed under Subsection (a)(11); or

(C) it is shown on the trial of the offense that the amount of the payment or value of the benefit described by this subsection cannot be reasonably ascertained;

(5) a felony of the third degree if:

(A) the amount of any payment or the value of any monetary or in-kind benefit provided or claim for payment made under the Medicaid program, directly or indirectly, as a result of the conduct is $20,000 or more but less than $100,000; or

(B) it is shown on the trial of the offense that the defendant submitted more than 25 but fewer than 50 fraudulent claims under the Medicaid program and the submission of each claim constitutes conduct prohibited by Subsection (a);

(6) a felony of the second degree if:

(A) the amount of any payment or the value of any monetary or in-kind benefit provided or claim for payment made under the Medicaid program, directly or indirectly, as a result of the conduct is $100,000 or more but less than $200,000; or

(B) it is shown on the trial of the offense that the defendant submitted 50 or more fraudulent claims under the Medicaid program and the submission of each claim constitutes conduct prohibited by Subsection (a); or

(7) a felony of the first degree if the amount of any payment or the value of any monetary or in-kind benefit provided or claim for payment made under the Medicaid program, directly or indirectly, as a result of the conduct is $200,000 or more.

(c) If conduct constituting an offense under this section also constitutes an offense under another section of this code or another provision of law, the actor may be prosecuted under either this section or the other section or provision or both this section and the other section or provision.

(d) When multiple payments or monetary or in-kind benefits are provided under the Medicaid program as a result of one scheme or continuing course of conduct, the conduct may be considered as one offense and the amounts of the payments or monetary or in-kind benefits aggregated in determining the grade of the offense.

(e) The punishment prescribed for an offense under this section, other than the punishment prescribed by Subsection (b)(7), is increased to the punishment prescribed for the next highest category of offense if it is shown beyond a reasonable doubt on the trial of the offense that the actor was a provider or high managerial agent at the time of the offense.

(f) With the consent of the appropriate local county or district attorney, the attorney general has concurrent jurisdiction with that consenting local prosecutor to prosecute an offense under this section that involves the Medicaid program. (Enacted by Acts 2005, 79th Leg., ch. 806 (S.B. 563), § 16, effective September 1, 2005; am. Acts 2007, 80th Leg., ch. 127 (S.B. 1694), § 5, effective September 1, 2007; am. Acts 2011, 82nd Leg., ch. 398 (S.B. 544), § 8, effective September 1, 2011; am. Acts 2011, 82nd Leg., ch. 620 (S.B. 688), § 9, effective September 1, 2011.)

# TITLE 8
# OFFENSES AGAINST PUBLIC ADMINISTRATION

## CHAPTER 36
## BRIBERY AND CORRUPT INFLUENCE

## Sec. 36.01. Definitions.

In this chapter:

(1) "Custody" means:

(A) detained or under arrest by a peace officer; or

(B) under restraint by a public servant pursuant to an order of a court.

(2) "Party official" means a person who holds any position or office in a political party, whether by election, appointment, or employment.

(3) "Benefit" means anything reasonably regarded as pecuniary gain or pecuniary advantage, including benefit to any other person in whose welfare the beneficiary has a direct and substantial interest.

(4) "Vote" means to cast a ballot in an election regulated by law.

(Enacted by Acts 1973, 63rd Leg., ch. 399 (S.B. 34), § 1, effective January 1, 1974; am. Acts 1975, 64th Leg., ch. 342 (S.B. 127), § 11, effective September 1, 1975; am. Acts 1983, 68th Leg., ch. 558 (S.B. 651), § 1, effective September 1, 1983; am. Acts 1989, 71st Leg., ch. 67 (H.B. 594), § 2, effective September 1, 1989; am. Acts 1991, 72nd Leg., ch. 304 (S.B. 1), § 4.01, effective January 1, 1992; am. Acts 1991, 72nd Leg., ch. 565 (S.B. 4), § 3, effective September 1, 1991; am. Acts 1993, 73rd Leg., ch. 900 (S.B. 1067), § 1.01, effective September 1, 1994.)

## Sec. 36.02. Bribery.

(a) A person commits an offense if he intentionally or knowingly offers, confers, or agrees to confer on another, or solicits, accepts, or agrees to accept from another:

(1) any benefit as consideration for the recipient's decision, opinion, recommendation, vote, or other exercise of discretion as a public servant, party official, or voter;

(2) any benefit as consideration for the recipient's decision, vote, recommendation, or other exercise of official discretion in a judicial or administrative proceeding;

(3) any benefit as consideration for a violation of a duty imposed by law on a public servant or party official; or

(4) any benefit that is a political contribution as defined by Title 15, Election Code, or that is an expenditure made and reported in accordance with Chapter 305, Government Code, if the benefit was offered, conferred, solicited, accepted, or agreed to pursuant to an express agreement to take or withhold a specific exercise of official discretion if such exercise of official discretion would not have been taken or withheld but for the benefit; notwithstanding any rule of evidence or jury instruction allowing factual inferences in the absence of certain evidence, direct evidence of the express agreement shall be required in any prosecution under this subdivision.

(b) It is no defense to prosecution under this section that a person whom the actor sought to influence was not qualified to act in the desired way whether because he had not yet assumed office or he lacked jurisdiction or for any other reason.

(c) It is no defense to prosecution under this section that the benefit is not offered or conferred or that the benefit is not solicited or accepted until after:

(1) the decision, opinion, recommendation, vote, or other exercise of discretion has occurred; or

(2) the public servant ceases to be a public servant.

(d) It is an exception to the application of Subdivisions (1), (2), and (3) of Subsection (a) that the benefit is a political contribution as defined by Title 15, Election Code, or an expenditure made and reported in accordance with Chapter 305, Government Code.

(e) An offense under this section is a felony of the second degree.

(Enacted by Acts 1973, 63rd Leg., ch. 399 (S.B. 34), § 1, effective January 1, 1974; am. Acts 1975,

64th Leg., ch. 342 (S.B. 127), § 11, effective September 1, 1975; am. Acts 1983, 68th Leg., ch. 558 (S.B. 651), § 2, effective September 1, 1983; am. Acts 1991, 72nd Leg., ch. 304 (S.B. 1), § 4.02, effective January 1, 1992; am. Acts 1993, 73rd Leg., ch. 900 (S.B. 1067), § 1.01, effective September 1, 1994.)

## Sec. 36.03. Coercion of Public Servant or Voter.

(a) A person commits an offense if by means of coercion he:

(1) influences or attempts to influence a public servant in a specific exercise of his official power or a specific performance of his official duty or influences or attempts to influence a public servant to violate the public servant's known legal duty; or

(2) influences or attempts to influence a voter not to vote or to vote in a particular manner.

(b) An offense under this section is a Class A misdemeanor unless the coercion is a threat to commit a felony, in which event it is a felony of the third degree.

(c) It is an exception to the application of Subsection (a)(1) of this section that the person who influences or attempts to influence the public servant is a member of the governing body of a governmental entity, and that the action that influences or attempts to influence the public servant is an official action taken by the member of the governing body. For the purposes of this subsection, the term "official action" includes deliberations by the governing body of a governmental entity.

(Enacted by Acts 1973, 63rd Leg., ch. 399 (S.B. 34), § 1, effective January 1, 1974; am. Acts 1989, 71st Leg., ch. 67 (H.B. 594), §§ 1, 3, effective September 1, 1989; am. Acts 1993, 73rd Leg., ch. 900 (S.B. 1067), § 1.01, effective September 1, 1994.)

## Sec. 36.04. Improper Influence.

(a) A person commits an offense if he privately addresses a representation, entreaty, argument, or other communication to any public servant who exercises or will exercise official discretion in an adjudicatory proceeding with an intent to influence the outcome of the proceeding on the basis of considerations other than those authorized by law.

(b) For purposes of this section, "adjudicatory proceeding" means any proceeding before a court

or any other agency of government in which the legal rights, powers, duties, or privileges of specified parties are determined.

(c) An offense under this section is a Class A misdemeanor.

(Enacted by Acts 1973, 63rd Leg., ch. 399 (S.B. 34), § 1, effective January 1, 1974; am. Acts 1993, 73rd Leg., ch. 900 (S.B. 1067), § 1.01, effective September 1, 1994.)

## Sec. 36.05. Tampering with Witness.

(a) A person commits an offense if, with intent to influence the witness, he offers, confers, or agrees to confer any benefit on a witness or prospective witness in an official proceeding or coerces a witness or prospective witness in an official proceeding:

(1) to testify falsely;

(2) to withhold any testimony, information, document, or thing;

(3) to elude legal process summoning him to testify or supply evidence;

(4) to absent himself from an official proceeding to which he has been legally summoned; or

(5) to abstain from, discontinue, or delay the prosecution of another.

(b) A witness or prospective witness in an official proceeding commits an offense if he knowingly solicits, accepts, or agrees to accept any benefit on the representation or understanding that he will do any of the things specified in Subsection (a).

(c) It is a defense to prosecution under Subsection (a)(5) that the benefit received was:

(1) reasonable restitution for damages suffered by the complaining witness as a result of the offense; and

(2) a result of an agreement negotiated with the assistance or acquiescence of an attorney for the state who represented the state in the case.

(d) An offense under this section is a felony of the third degree, except that if the official proceeding is part of the prosecution of a criminal case, an offense under this section is the same category of offense as the most serious offense charged in that criminal case.

(e) Notwithstanding Subsection (d), if the most serious offense charged is a capital felony, an offense under this section is a felony of the first degree.

(f) If conduct that constitutes an offense under this section also constitutes an offense under any

other law, the actor may be prosecuted under this section, the other law, or both.
(Enacted by Acts 1973, 63rd Leg., ch. 399 (S.B. 34), § 1, effective January 1, 1974; am. Acts 1993, 73rd Leg., ch. 900 (S.B. 1067), § 1.01, effective September 1, 1994; am. Acts 1997, 75th Leg., ch. 721 (H.B. 312), § 1, effective September 1, 1997; am. Acts 2011, 82nd Leg., ch. 770 (H.B. 1856), § 1, effective September 1, 2011.)

## Sec. 36.06. Obstruction or Retaliation.

(a) A person commits an offense if he intentionally or knowingly harms or threatens to harm another by an unlawful act:

(1) in retaliation for or on account of the service or status of another as a:

(A) public servant, witness, prospective witness, or informant; or

(B) person who has reported or who the actor knows intends to report the occurrence of a crime; or

(2) to prevent or delay the service of another as a:

(A) public servant, witness, prospective witness, or informant; or

(B) person who has reported or who the actor knows intends to report the occurrence of a crime.

(b) In this section:

(1) "Honorably retired peace officer" means a peace officer who:

(A) did not retire in lieu of any disciplinary action;

(B) was eligible to retire from a law enforcement agency or was ineligible to retire only as a result of an injury received in the course of the officer's employment with the agency; and

(C) is entitled to receive a pension or annuity for service as a law enforcement officer or is not entitled to receive a pension or annuity only because the law enforcement agency that employed the officer does not offer a pension or annuity to its employees.

(2) "Informant" means a person who has communicated information to the government in connection with any governmental function.

(3) "Public servant" includes an honorably retired peace officer.

(c) An offense under this section is a felony of the third degree unless the victim of the offense was harmed or threatened because of the victim's service or status as a juror, in which event the offense is a felony of the second degree.

(Enacted by Acts 1973, 63rd Leg., ch. 399 (S.B. 34), § 1, effective January 1, 1974; am. Acts 1983, 68th Leg., ch. 558 (S.B. 651), § 4, effective September 1, 1983; am. Acts 1989, 71st Leg., ch. 557 (H.B. 3201), § 1, effective September 1, 1989; am. Acts 1993, 73rd Leg., ch. 900 (S.B. 1067), § 1.01, effective September 1, 1994; am. Acts 1997, 75th Leg., ch. 239 (H.B. 806), § 1, effective September 1, 1997; am. Acts 2001, 77th Leg., ch. 835 (H.B. 1181), § 1, effective September 1, 2001; am. Acts 2003, 78th Leg., ch. 246 (H.B. 1458), § 1, effective September 1, 2003.)

## Sec. 36.07. Acceptance of Honorarium.

(a) A public servant commits an offense if the public servant solicits, accepts, or agrees to accept an honorarium in consideration for services that the public servant would not have been requested to provide but for the public servant's official position or duties.

(b) This section does not prohibit a public servant from accepting transportation and lodging expenses in connection with a conference or similar event in which the public servant renders services, such as addressing an audience or engaging in a seminar, to the extent that those services are more than merely perfunctory, or from accepting meals in connection with such an event.

(b-1) Transportation, lodging, and meals described by Subsection (b) are not political contributions as defined by Title 15, Election Code.

(c) An offense under this section is a Class A misdemeanor.

(Enacted by Acts 1991, 72nd Leg., ch. 304 (S.B. 1), § 4.03, effective January 1, 1992; am. Acts 1993, 73rd Leg., ch. 900 (S.B. 1067), § 1.01, effective September 1, 1994; am. Acts 2011, 82nd Leg., ch. 56 (S.B. 1269), § 1, effective September 1, 2011.)

## Sec. 36.08. Gift to Public Servant by Person Subject to His Jurisdiction.

(a) A public servant in an agency performing regulatory functions or conducting inspections or investigations commits an offense if he solicits, accepts, or agrees to accept any benefit from a person the public servant knows to be subject to regulation, inspection, or investigation by the public servant or his agency.

(b) A public servant in an agency having custody of prisoners commits an offense if he solicits, accepts, or agrees to accept any benefit from a person the public servant knows to be in his custody or the custody of his agency.

(c) A public servant in an agency carrying on civil or criminal litigation on behalf of government commits an offense if he solicits, accepts, or agrees to accept any benefit from a person against whom the public servant knows litigation is pending or contemplated by the public servant or his agency.

(d) A public servant who exercises discretion in connection with contracts, purchases, payments, claims, or other pecuniary transactions of government commits an offense if he solicits, accepts, or agrees to accept any benefit from a person the public servant knows is interested in or likely to become interested in any contract, purchase, payment, claim, or transaction involving the exercise of his discretion.

(e) A public servant who has judicial or administrative authority, who is employed by or in a tribunal having judicial or administrative authority, or who participates in the enforcement of the tribunal's decision, commits an offense if he solicits, accepts, or agrees to accept any benefit from a person the public servant knows is interested in or likely to become interested in any matter before the public servant or tribunal.

(f) A member of the legislature, the governor, the lieutenant governor, or a person employed by a member of the legislature, the governor, the lieutenant governor, or an agency of the legislature commits an offense if he solicits, accepts, or agrees to accept any benefit from any person.

(g) A public servant who is a hearing examiner employed by an agency performing regulatory functions and who conducts hearings in contested cases commits an offense if the public servant solicits, accepts, or agrees to accept any benefit from any person who is appearing before the agency in a contested case, who is doing business with the agency, or who the public servant knows is interested in any matter before the public servant. The exception provided by Section 36.10(b) does not apply to a benefit under this subsection.

(h) An offense under this section is a Class A misdemeanor.

(i) A public servant who receives an unsolicited benefit that the public servant is prohibited from accepting under this section may donate the benefit to a governmental entity that has the authority to accept the gift or may donate the benefit to a recognized tax-exempt charitable organization formed for educational, religious, or scientific purposes.
(Enacted by Acts 1973, 63rd Leg., ch. 399 (S.B. 34), § 1, effective January 1, 1974; am. Acts 1975, 64th Leg., ch. 342 (S.B. 127), § 11, effective September 1, 1975; am. Acts 1983, 68th Leg., ch. 558 (S.B. 651), § 5, effective September 1, 1983; am. Acts 1991, 72nd Leg., ch. 304 (S.B. 1), § 4.04, effective January 1, 1992; am. Acts 1993, 73rd Leg., ch. 900 (S.B. 1067), § 1.01, effective September 1, 1994.)

## Sec. 36.09.   Offering Gift to Public Servant.

(a) A person commits an offense if he offers, confers, or agrees to confer any benefit on a public servant that he knows the public servant is prohibited by law from accepting.

(b) An offense under this section is a Class A misdemeanor.
(Enacted by Acts 1973, 63rd Leg., ch. 399 (S.B. 34), § 1, effective January 1, 1974; am. Acts 1993, 73rd Leg., ch. 900 (S.B. 1067), § 1.01, effective September 1, 1994.)

## Sec. 36.10.   Non-Applicable.

(a) Sections 36.08 (Gift to Public Servant) and 36.09 (Offering Gift to Public Servant) do not apply to:

(1) a fee prescribed by law to be received by a public servant or any other benefit to which the public servant is lawfully entitled or for which he gives legitimate consideration in a capacity other than as a public servant;

(2) a gift or other benefit conferred on account of kinship or a personal, professional, or business relationship independent of the official status of the recipient; or

(3) a benefit to a public servant required to file a statement under Chapter 572, Government Code, or a report under Title 15, Election Code, that is derived from a function in honor or appreciation of the recipient if:

(A) the benefit and the source of any benefit in excess of $50 is reported in the statement; and

(B) the benefit is used solely to defray the expenses that accrue in the performance of duties or activities in connection with the office which are nonreimbursable by the state or political subdivision;

(4) a political contribution as defined by Title 15, Election Code;

(5) a gift, award, or memento to a member of the legislative or executive branch that is required to be reported under Chapter 305, Government Code;

(6) an item with a value of less than $50, excluding cash or a negotiable instrument as described by Section 3.104, Business & Commerce Code;

(7) an item issued by a governmental entity that allows the use of property or facilities owned, leased, or operated by the governmental entity; or

(8) transportation, lodging, and meals described by Section 36.07(b).

(b) Section 36.08 (Gift to Public Servant) does not apply to food, lodging, transportation, or entertainment accepted as a guest and, if the donee is required by law to report those items, reported by the donee in accordance with that law.

(c) Section 36.09 (Offering Gift to Public Servant) does not apply to food, lodging, transportation, or entertainment accepted as a guest and, if the donor is required by law to report those items, reported by the donor in accordance with that law.

(d) Section 36.08 (Gift to Public Servant) does not apply to a gratuity accepted and reported in accordance with Section 11.0262, Parks and Wildlife Code. Section 36.09 (Offering Gift to Public Servant) does not apply to a gratuity that is offered in accordance with Section 11.0262, Parks and Wildlife Code.

(Enacted by Acts 1973, 63rd Leg., ch. 399 (S.B. 34), § 1, effective January 1, 1974; am. Acts 1975, 64th Leg., ch. 342 (S.B. 127), § 11, effective September 1, 1975; am. Acts 1981, 67th Leg., ch. 738 (H.B. 1466), § 1, effective January 1, 1982; am. Acts 1983, 68th Leg., ch. 558 (S.B. 651), § 6, effective September 1, 1983; am. Acts 1987, 70th Leg., ch. 472 (H.B. 612), § 60, effective September 1, 1987; am. Acts 1991, 72nd Leg., ch. 304 (S.B. 1), § 4.05, effective January 1, 1992; am. Acts 1993, 73rd Leg., ch. 900 (S.B. 1067), § 1.01, effective September 1, 1994; am. Acts 1995, 74th Leg., ch. 76 (S.B. 959), § 5.95(38), effective September 1, 1995; am. Acts 2005, 79th Leg., ch. 639 (H.B. 2685), § 2, effective September 1, 2005; am. Acts 2011, 82nd Leg., ch. 56 (S.B. 1269), § 2, effective September 1, 2011.)

# CHAPTER 37
# PERJURY AND OTHER FALSIFICATION

## Sec. 37.01. Definitions.

In this chapter:

(1) "Court record" means a decree, judgment, order, subpoena, warrant, minutes, or other document issued by a court of:

(A) this state;

(B) another state;

(C) the United States;

(D) a foreign country recognized by an act of congress or a treaty or other international convention to which the United States is a party;

(E) an Indian tribe recognized by the United States; or

(F) any other jurisdiction, territory, or protectorate entitled to full faith and credit in this state under the United States Constitution.

(2) "Governmental record" means:

(A) anything belonging to, received by, or kept by government for information, including a court record;

(B) anything required by law to be kept by others for information of government;

(C) a license, certificate, permit, seal, title, letter of patent, or similar document issued by government, by another state, or by the United States;

(D) a standard proof of motor vehicle liability insurance form described by Section 601.081, Transportation Code, a certificate of an insurance company described by Section 601.083 of that code, a document purporting to be such a form or certificate that is not issued by an insurer authorized to write motor vehicle liability insurance in this state, an electronic submission in a form described by Section 502.153(i), Transportation Code, or an evidence of financial responsibility described by Section 601.053 of that code;

(E) an official ballot or other election record; or

(F) the written documentation a mobile food unit is required to obtain under Section 437.0074, Health and Safety Code.

(3) "Statement" means any representation of fact.

(Enacted by Acts 1973, 63rd Leg., ch. 399 (S.B. 34), § 1, effective January 1, 1974; am. Acts 1991, 72nd Leg., ch. 113 (S.B. 589), § 3, effective September 1, 1991; am. Acts 1993, 73rd Leg., ch. 900 (S.B. 1067), § 1.01, effective September 1, 1994; am. Acts 1997, 75th Leg., ch. 189 (H.B. 1185), § 5, effective May 21, 1997; am. Acts 1997, 75th Leg., ch. 823 (S.B. 89), § 3, effective September 1, 1997; am. Acts 1999, 76th Leg., ch. 659 (H.B. 319), § 1, effective September 1, 1999; am. Acts 2003, 78th Leg., ch. 393 (H.B. 54), § 21, effective September 1, 2003; am. Acts 2007, 80th Leg., ch. 1276 (H.B. 3672), § 2, effective September 1, 2007.)

## Sec. 37.02.  Perjury.

(a) A person commits an offense if, with intent to deceive and with knowledge of the statement's meaning:

(1) he makes a false statement under oath or swears to the truth of a false statement previously made and the statement is required or authorized by law to be made under oath; or

(2) he makes a false unsworn declaration under Chapter 132, Civil Practice and Remedies Code.

(b) An offense under this section is a Class A misdemeanor.

(Enacted by Acts 1973, 63rd Leg., ch. 399 (S.B. 34), § 1, effective January 1, 1974; am. Acts 1993,

73rd Leg., ch. 900 (S.B. 1067), § 1.01, effective September 1, 1994.)

## Sec. 37.03.  Aggravated Perjury.

(a) A person commits an offense if he commits perjury as defined in Section 37.02, and the false statement:

(1) is made during or in connection with an official proceeding; and

(2) is material.

(b) An offense under this section is a felony of the third degree.

(Enacted by Acts 1973, 63rd Leg., ch. 399 (S.B. 34), § 1, effective January 1, 1974; am. Acts 1993, 73rd Leg., ch. 900 (S.B. 1067), § 1.01, effective September 1, 1994.)

## Sec. 37.04.  Materiality.

(a) A statement is material, regardless of the admissibility of the statement under the rules of evidence, if it could have affected the course or outcome of the official proceeding.

(b) It is no defense to prosecution under Section 37.03 (Aggravated Perjury) that the declarant mistakenly believed the statement to be immaterial.

(c) Whether a statement is material in a given factual situation is a question of law.

(Enacted by Acts 1973, 63rd Leg., ch. 399 (S.B. 34), § 1, effective January 1, 1974; am. Acts 1993, 73rd Leg., ch. 900 (S.B. 1067), § 1.01, effective September 1, 1994.)

## Sec. 37.05.  Retraction.

It is a defense to prosecution under Section 37.03 (Aggravated Perjury) that the actor retracted his false statement:

(1) before completion of the testimony at the official proceeding; and

(2) before it became manifest that the falsity of the statement would be exposed.

(Enacted by Acts 1973, 63rd Leg., ch. 399 (S.B. 34), § 1, effective January 1, 1974; am. Acts 1993, 73rd Leg., ch. 900 (S.B. 1067), § 1.01, effective September 1, 1994.)

## Sec. 37.06.  Inconsistent Statements.

An information or indictment for perjury under Section 37.02 or aggravated perjury under Section 37.03 that alleges that the declarant has made statements under oath, both of which cannot be true, need not allege which statement is false. At the trial the prosecution need not prove which statement is false.

(Enacted by Acts 1973, 63rd Leg., ch. 399 (S.B. 34), § 1, effective January 1, 1974; am. Acts 1993, 73rd Leg., ch. 900 (S.B. 1067), § 1.01, effective September 1, 1994.)

## Sec. 37.07.  Irregularities No Defense.

(a) It is no defense to prosecution under Section 37.02 (Perjury) or 37.03 (Aggravated Perjury) that the oath was administered or taken in an irregular manner, or that there was some irregularity in the appointment or qualification of the person who administered the oath.

(b) It is no defense to prosecution under Section 37.02 (Perjury) or 37.03 (Aggravated Perjury) that a document was not sworn to if the document contains a recital that it was made under oath, the declarant was aware of the recital when he signed the document, and the document contains the signed jurat of a public servant authorized to administer oaths.

(Enacted by Acts 1973, 63rd Leg., ch. 399 (S.B. 34), § 1, effective January 1, 1974; am. Acts 1993, 73rd Leg., ch. 900 (S.B. 1067), § 1.01, effective September 1, 1994.)

## Sec. 37.08.  False Report to Peace Officer, Federal Special Investigator, or Law Enforcement Employee.

(a) A person commits an offense if, with intent to deceive, he knowingly makes a false statement that is material to a criminal investigation and makes the statement to:

(1) a peace officer or federal special investigator conducting the investigation; or

(2) any employee of a law enforcement agency that is authorized by the agency to conduct the investigation and that the actor knows is conducting the investigation.

(b) In this section, "law enforcement agency" has the meaning assigned by Article 59.01, Code of Criminal Procedure.

(c) An offense under this section is a Class B misdemeanor.

(Enacted by Acts 1973, 63rd Leg., ch. 399 (S.B. 34), § 1, effective January 1, 1974; am. Acts 1993, 73rd Leg., ch. 900 (S.B. 1067), § 1.01, effective September 1, 1994; am. Acts 1997, 75th Leg., ch. 925 (S.B. 329), § 1, effective September 1, 1997; am. Acts 2011, 82nd Leg., ch. 839 (H.B. 3423), §§ 2, 3, effective September 1, 2011.)

## Sec. 37.081.  False Report Regarding Missing Child or Missing Person.

(a) A person commits an offense if, with intent to deceive, the person knowingly:

(1) files a false report of a missing child or missing person with a law enforcement officer or agency; or

(2) makes a false statement to a law enforcement officer or other employee of a law enforcement agency relating to a missing child or missing person.

(b) An offense under this section is a Class C misdemeanor.

(Enacted by Acts 1999, 76th Leg., ch. 200 (H.B. 605), § 3, effective September 1, 1999.)

## Sec. 37.09.  Tampering with or Fabricating Physical Evidence.

(a) A person commits an offense if, knowing that an investigation or official proceeding is pending or in progress, he:

(1) alters, destroys, or conceals any record, document, or thing with intent to impair its verity, legibility, or availability as evidence in the investigation or official proceeding; or

(2) makes, presents, or uses any record, document, or thing with knowledge of its falsity and with intent to affect the course or outcome of the investigation or official proceeding.

(b) This section shall not apply if the record, document, or thing concealed is privileged or is the work product of the parties to the investigation or official proceeding.

(c) An offense under Subsection (a) or Subsection (d)(1) is a felony of the third degree, unless the thing altered, destroyed, or concealed is a human corpse, in which case the offense is a felony of the second degree. An offense under Subsection (d)(2) is a Class A misdemeanor.

(c-1) It is a defense to prosecution under Subsection (a) or (d)(1) that the record, document, or thing was visual material prohibited under Section 43.261 that was destroyed as described by Subsection (f)(3)(B) of that section.

(d) A person commits an offense if the person:

(1) knowing that an offense has been committed, alters, destroys, or conceals any record, document, or thing with intent to impair its verity, legibility, or availability as evidence in any subsequent investigation of or official proceeding related to the offense; or

(2) observes a human corpse under circumstances in which a reasonable person would

believe that an offense had been committed, knows or reasonably should know that a law enforcement agency is not aware of the existence of or location of the corpse, and fails to report the existence of and location of the corpse to a law enforcement agency.

(e) In this section, "human corpse" has the meaning assigned by Section 42.08.

(Enacted by Acts 1973, 63rd Leg., ch. 399 (S.B. 34), § 1, effective January 1, 1974; am. Acts 1991, 72nd Leg., ch. 565 (S.B. 4), § 4, effective September 1, 1991; am. Acts 1993, 73rd Leg., ch. 900 (S.B. 1067), § 1.01, effective September 1, 1994; am. Acts 1997, 75th Leg., ch. 1284 (S.B. 160), § 1, effective September 1, 1997; am. Acts 2007, 80th Leg., ch. 287 (H.B. 872), § 1, effective September 1, 2007; am. Acts 2011, 82nd Leg., ch. 1322 (S.B. 407), § 1, effective September 1, 2011.)

## Sec. 37.10.  Tampering with Governmental Record.

(a) A person commits an offense if he:

(1) knowingly makes a false entry in, or false alteration of, a governmental record;

(2) makes, presents, or uses any record, document, or thing with knowledge of its falsity and with intent that it be taken as a genuine governmental record;

(3) intentionally destroys, conceals, removes, or otherwise impairs the verity, legibility, or availability of a governmental record;

(4) possesses, sells, or offers to sell a governmental record or a blank governmental record form with intent that it be used unlawfully;

(5) makes, presents, or uses a governmental record with knowledge of its falsity; or

(6) possesses, sells, or offers to sell a governmental record or a blank governmental record form with knowledge that it was obtained unlawfully.

(b) It is an exception to the application of Subsection (a)(3) that the governmental record is destroyed pursuant to legal authorization or transferred under Section 441.204, Government Code. With regard to the destruction of a local government record, legal authorization includes compliance with the provisions of Subtitle C, Title 6, Local Government Code.

(c) (1) Except as provided by Subdivisions (2), (3), and (4) and by Subsection (d), an offense under this section is a Class A misdemeanor unless the actor's intent is to defraud or harm another, in which event the offense is a state jail felony.

(2) An offense under this section is a felony of the third degree if it is shown on the trial of the offense that the governmental record was:

(A) a public school record, report, or assessment instrument required under Chapter 39, Education Code, or was a license, certificate, permit, seal, title, letter of patent, or similar document issued by government, by another state, or by the United States, unless the actor's intent is to defraud or harm another, in which event the offense is a felony of the second degree;

(B) a written report of a medical, chemical, toxicological, ballistic, or other expert examination or test performed on physical evidence for the purpose of determining the connection or relevance of the evidence to a criminal action; or

(C) a written report of the certification, inspection, or maintenance record of an instrument, apparatus, implement, machine, or other similar device used in the course of an examination or test performed on physical evidence for the purpose of determining the connection or relevance of the evidence to a criminal action.

(3) An offense under this section is a Class C misdemeanor if it is shown on the trial of the offense that the governmental record is a governmental record that is required for enrollment of a student in a school district and was used by the actor to establish the residency of the student.

(4) An offense under this section is a Class B misdemeanor if it is shown on the trial of the offense that the governmental record is a written appraisal filed with an appraisal review board under Section 41.43(a-1), Tax Code, that was performed by a person who had a contingency interest in the outcome of the appraisal review board hearing.

(d) An offense under this section, if it is shown on the trial of the offense that the governmental record is described by Section 37.01(2)(D), is:

(1) a Class B misdemeanor if the offense is committed under Subsection (a)(2) or Subsection (a)(5) and the defendant is convicted of presenting or using the record;

(2) a felony of the third degree if the offense is committed under:

(A) Subsection (a)(1), (3), (4), or (6); or

(B) Subsection (a)(2) or (5) and the defendant is convicted of making the record; and

(3) a felony of the second degree, notwithstanding Subdivisions (1) and (2), if the actor's

intent in committing the offense was to defraud or harm another.

(e) It is an affirmative defense to prosecution for possession under Subsection (a)(6) that the possession occurred in the actual discharge of official duties as a public servant.

(f) It is a defense to prosecution under Subsection (a)(1), (a)(2), or (a)(5) that the false entry or false information could have no effect on the government's purpose for requiring the governmental record.

(g) A person is presumed to intend to defraud or harm another if the person acts with respect to two or more of the same type of governmental records or blank governmental record forms and if each governmental record or blank governmental record form is a license, certificate, permit, seal, title, or similar document issued by government.

(h) If conduct that constitutes an offense under this section also constitutes an offense under Section 32.48 or 37.13, the actor may be prosecuted under any of those sections.

(i) With the consent of the appropriate local county or district attorney, the attorney general has concurrent jurisdiction with that consenting local prosecutor to prosecute an offense under this section that involves the state Medicaid program.

(j) It is not a defense to prosecution under Subsection (a)(2) that the record, document, or thing made, presented, or used displays or contains the statement "NOT A GOVERNMENT DOCUMENT" or another substantially similar statement intended to alert a person to the falsity of the record, document, or thing, unless the record, document, or thing displays the statement diagonally printed clearly and indelibly on both the front and back of the record, document, or thing in solid red capital letters at least one-fourth inch in height.

(Enacted by Acts 1973, 63rd Leg., ch. 399 (S.B. 34), § 1, effective January 1, 1974; am. Acts 1989, 71st Leg., ch. 1248 (H.B. 1285), § 66, effective September 1, 1989; am. Acts 1991, 72nd Leg., ch. 113 (S.B. 589), § 4, effective September 1, 1991; am. Acts 1991, 72nd Leg., ch. 565 (S.B. 4), § 5, effective September 1, 1991; am. Acts 1993, 73rd Leg., ch. 900 (S.B. 1067), § 1.01, effective September 1, 1994; am. Acts 1997, 75th Leg., ch. 189 (H.B. 1185), § 6, effective May 21, 1997; am. Acts 1997, 75th Leg., ch. 823 (S.B. 89), § 4, effective September 1, 1997; am. Acts 1999, 76th Leg., ch. 659 (H.B. 319), § 2, effective September 1, 1999; am. Acts 1999, 76th Leg., ch. 718 (H.B. 926), § 1,

effective September 1, 1999; am. Acts 2001, 77th Leg., ch. 771 (S.B. 1800), § 3, effective June 13, 2001; am. Acts 2003, 78th Leg., ch. 198 (H.B. 2292), § 2.139, effective September 1, 2003; am. Acts 2003, 78th Leg., ch. 257 (H.B. 1743), § 16, effective September 1, 2003; am. Acts 2005, 79th Leg., ch. 1364 (H.B. 126), § 1, effective June 18, 2005; am. Acts 2007, 80th Leg., ch. 1085 (H.B. 3024), § 2, effective September 1, 2007; am. Acts 2009, 81st Leg., ch. 73 (H.B. 1813), § 1, effective September 1, 2009; am. Acts 2009, 81st Leg., ch. 1130 (H.B. 2086), § 31, effective September 1, 2009.)

## Sec. 37.101. Fraudulent Filing of Financing Statement.

(a) A person commits an offense if the person knowingly presents for filing or causes to be presented for filing a financing statement that the person knows:

(1) is forged;

(2) contains a material false statement; or

(3) is groundless.

(b) An offense under Subsection (a)(1) is a felony of the third degree, unless it is shown on the trial of the offense that the person had previously been convicted under this section on two or more occasions, in which event the offense is a felony of the second degree. An offense under Subsection (a)(2) or (a)(3) is a Class A misdemeanor, unless the person commits the offense with the intent to defraud or harm another, in which event the offense is a state jail felony.

(Enacted by Acts 1997, 75th Leg., ch. 189 (H.B. 1185), § 10, effective May 21, 1997.)

## Sec. 37.11. Impersonating Public Servant.

(a) A person commits an offense if he:

(1) impersonates a public servant with intent to induce another to submit to his pretended official authority or to rely on his pretended official acts; or

(2) knowingly purports to exercise any function of a public servant or of a public office, including that of a judge and court, and the position or office through which he purports to exercise a function of a public servant or public office has no lawful existence under the constitution or laws of this state or of the United States.

(b) An offense under this section is a felony of the third degree.

(Enacted by Acts 1973, 63rd Leg., ch. 399 (S.B. 34), § 1, effective January 1, 1974; am. Acts 1993,

73rd Leg., ch. 900 (S.B. 1067), § 1.01, effective September 1, 1994; am. Acts 1997, 75th Leg., ch. 189 (H.B. 1185), § 7, effective May 21, 1997.)

## Sec. 37.12.   False Identification As Peace Officer; Misrepresentation of Property.

(a) A person commits an offense if:

(1) the person makes, provides to another person, or possesses a card, document, badge, insignia, shoulder emblem, or other item bearing an insignia of a law enforcement agency that identifies a person as a peace officer or a reserve law enforcement officer; and

(2) the person who makes, provides, or possesses the item bearing the insignia knows that the person so identified by the item is not commissioned as a peace officer or reserve law enforcement officer as indicated on the item.

(b) It is a defense to prosecution under this section that:

(1) the card, document, badge, insignia, shoulder emblem, or other item bearing an insignia of a law enforcement agency clearly identifies the person as an honorary or junior peace officer or reserve law enforcement officer, or as a member of a junior posse;

(2) the person identified as a peace officer or reserve law enforcement officer by the item bearing the insignia was commissioned in that capacity when the item was made; or

(3) the item was used or intended for use exclusively for decorative purposes or in an artistic or dramatic presentation.

(c) In this section, "reserve law enforcement officer" has the same meaning as is given that term in Section 1701.001, Occupations Code.

(d) A person commits an offense if the person intentionally or knowingly misrepresents an object as property belonging to a law enforcement agency.

(e) An offense under this section is a Class B misdemeanor.

(Enacted by Acts 1983, 68th Leg., ch. 1075 (H.B. 2398), § 1, effective September 1, 1983; am. Acts 1987, 70th Leg., ch. 514 (H.B. 592), § 1, effective September 1, 1987; am. Acts 1993, 73rd Leg., ch. 900 (S.B. 1067), § 1.01, effective September 1, 1994; am. Acts 2001, 77th Leg., ch. 1420 (H.B. 2812), § 14.831, effective September 1, 2001.)

## Sec. 37.13.   Record of a Fraudulent Court.

(a) A person commits an offense if the person makes, presents, or uses any document or other record with:

(1) knowledge that the document or other record is not a record of a court created under or established by the constitution or laws of this state or of the United States; and

(2) the intent that the document or other record be given the same legal effect as a record of a court created under or established by the constitution or laws of this state or of the United States.

(b) An offense under this section is a Class A misdemeanor, except that the offense is a felony of the third degree if it is shown on the trial of the offense that the defendant has previously been convicted under this section on two or more occasions.

(c) If conduct that constitutes an offense under this section also constitutes an offense under Section 32.48 or 37.10, the actor may be prosecuted under any of those sections.

(Enacted by Acts 1997, 75th Leg., ch. 189 (H.B. 1185), § 8, effective May 21, 1997.)

## Sec. 37.14.   False Statement Regarding Child Custody Determination Made in Foreign Country.

(a) For purposes of this section, "child custody determination" has the meaning assigned by Section 152.102, Family Code.

(b) A person commits an offense if the person knowingly makes or causes to be made a false statement relating to a child custody determination made in a foreign country during a hearing held under Chapter 152 or Subchapter I, Chapter 153, Family Code.

(c) An offense under this section is a felony of the third degree.

(Enacted by Acts 2011, 82nd Leg., ch. 92 (S.B. 1490), § 3, effective September 1, 2011.)

# CHAPTER 38
# OBSTRUCTING GOVERNMENTAL OPERATION

## Sec. 38.01. Definitions.

In this chapter:

(1) "Custody" means:

(A) under arrest by a peace officer or under restraint by a public servant pursuant to an order of a court of this state or another state of the United States; or

(B) under restraint by an agent or employee of a facility that is operated by or under contract with the United States and that confines persons arrested for, charged with, or convicted of criminal offenses.

(2) "Escape" means unauthorized departure from custody or failure to return to custody following temporary leave for a specific purpose or limited period or leave that is part of an intermittent sentence, but does not include a violation of conditions of community supervision or parole other than conditions that impose a period of confinement in a secure correctional facility.

(3) "Economic benefit" means anything reasonably regarded as an economic gain or advantage, including accepting or offering to accept employment for a fee, accepting or offering to accept a fee, entering into a fee contract, or accepting or agreeing to accept money or anything of value.

(4) "Finance" means to provide funds or capital or to furnish with necessary funds.

(5) "Fugitive from justice" means a person for whom a valid arrest warrant has been issued.

(6) "Governmental function" includes any activity that a public servant is lawfully authorized to undertake on behalf of government.

(7) "Invest funds" means to commit money to earn a financial return.

(8) "Member of the family" means anyone related within the third degree of consanguinity or affinity, as determined under Chapter 573, Government Code.

(9) "Qualified nonprofit organization" means a nonprofit organization that meets the following conditions:

(A) the primary purposes of the organization do not include the rendition of legal services or education regarding legal services;

(B) the recommending, furnishing, paying for, or educating persons regarding legal services is incidental and reasonably related to the primary purposes of the organization;

(C) the organization does not derive a financial benefit from the rendition of legal services by a lawyer; and

(D) the person for whom the legal services are rendered, and not the organization, is recognized as the client of a lawyer.

(10) "Public media" means a telephone directory or legal directory, newspaper or other periodical, billboard or other sign, radio or television broadcast, recorded message the public may access by dialing a telephone number, or a written communication not prohibited by Section 38.12(d).

(11) "Solicit employment" means to communicate in person or by telephone with a prospective client or a member of the prospective client's family concerning professional employment within the scope of a professional's license, registration, or certification arising out of a particular occurrence or event, or series of occurrences or events, or concerning an existing problem of the prospective client within the scope of the professional's license, registration, or certification, for the purpose of providing professional services to the prospective client, when neither the person receiving the communication nor anyone acting on that person's behalf has requested the communication. The term does not include a communication initiated by a family member of the person receiv-

ing a communication, a communication by a professional who has a prior or existing professional-client relationship with the person receiving the communication, or communication by an attorney for a qualified nonprofit organization with the organization's members for the purpose of educating the organization's members to understand the law, to recognize legal problems, to make intelligent selection of legal counsel, or to use available legal services. The term does not include an advertisement by a professional through public media.

(12) "Professional" means an attorney, chiropractor, physician, surgeon, private investigator, or any other person licensed, certified, or registered by a state agency that regulates a health care profession.
(Enacted by Acts 1973, 63rd Leg., ch. 399 (S.B. 34), § 1, effective January 1, 1974; am. Acts 1989, 71st Leg., ch. 866 (S.B. 843), § 1, effective September 1, 1989; am. Acts 1991, 72nd Leg., ch. 14 (S.B. 404), § 284(14), effective September 1, 1991; am. Acts 1991, 72nd Leg., ch. 561 (H.B. 1345), § 42, effective August 26, 1991; am. Acts 1993, 73rd Leg., ch. 723 (S.B. 1227), § 1, effective September 1, 1993; am. Acts 1993, 73rd Leg., ch. 900 (S.B. 1067), § 1.01, effective September 1, 1994; am. Acts 1995, 74th Leg., ch. 76 (S.B. 959), § 5.95(27), effective September 1, 1995; am. Acts 1995, 74th Leg., ch. 321 (H.B. 2162), § 1.103, effective September 1, 1995; am. Acts 1997, 75th Leg., ch. 293 (H.B. 975), § 2, effective September 1, 1997; am. Acts 1997, 75th Leg., ch. 750 (H.B. 1327), § 1, effective September 1, 1997.)

## Sec. 38.02.   Failure to Identify.

(a) A person commits an offense if he intentionally refuses to give his name, residence address, or date of birth to a peace officer who has lawfully arrested the person and requested the information.

(b) A person commits an offense if he intentionally gives a false or fictitious name, residence address, or date of birth to a peace officer who has:

(1) lawfully arrested the person;

(2) lawfully detained the person; or

(3) requested the information from a person that the peace officer has good cause to believe is a witness to a criminal offense.

(c) Except as provided by Subsections (d) and (e), an offense under this section is:

(1) a Class C misdemeanor if the offense is committed under Subsection (a); or

(2) a Class B misdemeanor if the offense is committed under Subsection (b).

(d) If it is shown on the trial of an offense under this section that the defendant was a fugitive from justice at the time of the offense, the offense is:

(1) a Class B misdemeanor if the offense is committed under Subsection (a); or

(2) a Class A misdemeanor if the offense is committed under Subsection (b).

(e) If conduct that constitutes an offense under this section also constitutes an offense under Section 106.07, Alcoholic Beverage Code, the actor may be prosecuted only under Section 106.07.
(Enacted by Acts 1973, 63rd Leg., ch. 399 (S.B. 34), § 1, effective January 1, 1974; am. Acts 1987, 70th Leg., ch. 869 (H.B. 826), § 1, effective September 1, 1987; am. Acts 1991, 72nd Leg., ch. 821 (S.B. 64), § 1, effective September 1, 1991; am. Acts 1993, 73rd Leg., ch. 900 (S.B. 1067), § 1.01, effective September 1, 1994; am. Acts 2003, 78th Leg., ch. 1009 (H.B. 325), § 1, effective September 1, 2003.)

## Sec. 38.03.   Resisting Arrest, Search, or Transportation.

(a) A person commits an offense if he intentionally prevents or obstructs a person he knows is a peace officer or a person acting in a peace officer's presence and at his direction from effecting an arrest, search, or transportation of the actor or another by using force against the peace officer or another.

(b) It is no defense to prosecution under this section that the arrest or search was unlawful.

(c) Except as provided in Subsection (d), an offense under this section is a Class A misdemeanor.

(d) An offense under this section is a felony of the third degree if the actor uses a deadly weapon to resist the arrest or search.
(Enacted by Acts 1973, 63rd Leg., ch. 399 (S.B. 34), § 1, effective January 1, 1974; am. Acts 1991, 72nd Leg., ch. 277 (H.B. 504), §§ 1, 2, effective September 1, 1991; am. Acts 1993, 73rd Leg., ch. 900 (S.B. 1067), § 1.01, effective September 1, 1994.)

## Sec. 38.04.   Evading Arrest or Detention.

(a) A person commits an offense if he intentionally flees from a person he knows is a peace officer or federal special investigator attempting lawfully to arrest or detain him.

(b) An offense under this section is a Class A misdemeanor, except that the offense is:

(1) a state jail felony if the actor has been previously convicted under this section;

(2) a felony of the third degree if:

(A) the actor uses a vehicle or watercraft while the actor is in flight;

(B) another suffers serious bodily injury as a direct result of an attempt by the officer or investigator from whom the actor is fleeing to apprehend the actor while the actor is in flight; or

(C) the actor uses a tire deflation device against the officer while the actor is in flight; or

(3) a felony of the second degree if:

(A) another suffers death as a direct result of an attempt by the officer from whom the actor is fleeing to apprehend the actor while the actor is in flight; or

(B) another suffers serious bodily injury as a direct result of the actor's use of a tire deflation device while the actor is in flight.

(c) In this section:

(1) "Vehicle" has the meaning assigned by Section 541.201, Transportation Code.

(2) **[2 Versions: As added by Acts 2011, 82nd Leg., ch. 391]** "Watercraft" has the meaning assigned by Section 49.01.

(2) **[2 Versions: As added by Acts 2011, 82nd Leg., ch. 920]** "Tire deflation device" has the meaning assigned by Section 46.01.

(d) A person who is subject to prosecution under both this section and another law may be prosecuted under either or both this section and the other law.

(Enacted by Acts 1973, 63rd Leg., ch. 399 (S.B. 34), § 1, effective January 1, 1974; am. Acts 1987, 70th Leg., ch. 504 (H.B. 280), § 1, effective September 1, 1987; am. Acts 1989, 71st Leg., ch. 126 (S.B. 916), § 1, effective September 1, 1989; am. Acts 1993, 73rd Leg., ch. 900 (S.B. 1067), § 1.01, effective September 1, 1994; am. Acts 1995, 74th Leg., ch. 708 (S.B. 281), § 1, effective September 1, 1995; am. Acts 1997, 75th Leg., ch. 165 (S.B. 898), § 30.240, effective September 1, 1997; am. Acts 2001, 77th Leg., ch. 1334 (H.B. 2798), § 3, effective September 1, 2001; am. Acts 2001, 77th Leg., ch. 1480 (S.B. 215), § 1, effective September 1, 2001; am. Acts 2009, 81st Leg., ch. 1400 (H.B. 221), § 4, effective September 1, 2009; am. Acts 2011, 82nd Leg., ch. 391 (S.B. 496), § 1, effective September 1, 2011; am. Acts 2011, 82nd Leg., ch. 839 (H.B. 3423), § 4, effective September 1, 2011;

am. Acts 2011, 82nd Leg., ch. 920 (S.B. 1416), § 3, effective September 1, 2011.)

## Sec. 38.05. Hindering Apprehension or Prosecution.

(a) A person commits an offense if, with intent to hinder the arrest, prosecution, conviction, or punishment of another for an offense or, with intent to hinder the arrest, detention, adjudication, or disposition of a child for engaging in delinquent conduct that violates a penal law of the state, or with intent to hinder the arrest of another under the authority of a warrant or capias, he:

(1) harbors or conceals the other;

(2) provides or aids in providing the other with any means of avoiding arrest or effecting escape; or

(3) warns the other of impending discovery or apprehension.

(b) It is a defense to prosecution under Subsection (a)(3) that the warning was given in connection with an effort to bring another into compliance with the law.

(c) Except as provided by Subsection (d), an offense under this section is a Class A misdemeanor.

(d) An offense under this section is a felony of the third degree if the person who is harbored, concealed, provided with a means of avoiding arrest or effecting escape, or warned of discovery or apprehension is under arrest for, charged with, or convicted of a felony, including an offense under Section 62.102, Code of Criminal Procedure, or is in custody or detention for, is alleged in a petition to have engaged in, or has been adjudicated as having engaged in delinquent conduct that violates a penal law of the grade of felony, including an offense under Section 62.102, Code of Criminal Procedure, and the person charged under this section knew that the person they harbored, concealed, provided with a means of avoiding arrest or effecting escape, or warned of discovery or apprehension is under arrest for, charged with, or convicted of a felony, or is in custody or detention for, is alleged in a petition to have engaged in, or has been adjudicated as having engaged in delinquent conduct that violates a penal law of the grade of felony.

(Enacted by Acts 1973, 63rd Leg., ch. 399 (S.B. 34), § 1, effective January 1, 1974; am. Acts 1991, 72nd Leg., ch. 748 (H.B. 377), § 1, effective September 1, 1991; am. Acts 1993, 73rd Leg., ch. 900 (S.B. 1067), § 1.01, effective September 1, 1994;

am. Acts 1995, 74th Leg., ch. 318 (S.B. 15), § 11, effective September 1, 1995; am. Acts 2005, 79th Leg., ch. 607 (H.B. 2104), § 1, effective September 1, 2005; am. Acts 2007, 80th Leg., ch. 593 (H.B. 8), § 1.19, effective September 1, 2007.)

### Sec. 38.06. Escape.

(a) A person commits an offense if the person escapes from custody when the person is:

(1) under arrest for, lawfully detained for, charged with, or convicted of an offense;

(2) in custody pursuant to a lawful order of a court;

(3) detained in a secure detention facility, as that term is defined by Section 51.02, Family Code; or

(4) in the custody of a juvenile probation officer for violating an order imposed by the juvenile court under Section 52.01, Family Code.

(b) Except as provided in Subsections (c), (d), and (e), an offense under this section is a Class A misdemeanor.

(c) An offense under this section is a felony of the third degree if the actor:

(1) is under arrest for, charged with, or convicted of a felony;

(2) is confined or lawfully detained in a secure correctional facility or law enforcement facility; or

(3) is committed to or lawfully detained in a secure correctional facility, as defined by Section 51.02, Family Code, other than a halfway house, operated by or under contract with the Texas Youth Commission.

(d) An offense under this section is a felony of the second degree if the actor to effect his escape causes bodily injury.

(e) An offense under this section is a felony of the first degree if to effect his escape the actor:

(1) causes serious bodily injury; or

(2) uses or threatens to use a deadly weapon.

(Enacted by Acts 1973, 63rd Leg., ch. 399 (S.B. 34), § 1, effective January 1, 1974; am. Acts 1985, 69th Leg., ch. 328 (H.B. 1055), § 1, effective September 1, 1985; am. Acts 1993, 73rd Leg., ch. 900 (S.B. 1067), § 1.01, effective September 1, 1994 (renumbered from Sec. 38.07); am. Acts 1999, 76th Leg., ch. 526 (S.B. 152), § 1, effective September 1, 1999; am. Acts 2007, 80th Leg., ch. 908 (H.B. 2884), § 38, effective September 1, 2007; am. Acts 2011, 82nd Leg., ch. 1330 (S.B. 844), § 1, effective September 1, 2011.)

### Sec. 38.07. Permitting or Facilitating Escape.

(a) An official or employee of a correctional facility commits an offense if he knowingly permits or facilitates the escape of a person in custody.

(b) A person commits an offense if he knowingly causes or facilitates the escape of one who is in custody pursuant to:

(1) an allegation or adjudication of delinquency; or

(2) involuntary commitment for mental illness under Subtitle C, Title 7, Health and Safety Code, or for chemical dependency under Chapter 462, Health and Safety Code.

(c) Except as provided in Subsections (d) and (e), an offense under this section is a Class A misdemeanor.

(d) An offense under this section is a felony of the third degree if the person in custody:

(1) was under arrest for, charged with, or convicted of a felony; or

(2) was confined in a correctional facility other than a secure correctional facility after conviction of a felony.

(e) An offense under this section is a felony of the second degree if:

(1) the actor or the person in custody used or threatened to use a deadly weapon to effect the escape; or

(2) the person in custody was confined in a secure correctional facility after conviction of a felony.

(f) In this section, "correctional facility" means:

(1) any place described by Section 1.07(a)(14); or

(2) a "secure correctional facility" or "secure detention facility" as those terms are defined by Section 51.02, Family Code.

(Enacted by Acts 1973, 63rd Leg., ch. 399 (S.B. 34), § 1, effective January 1, 1974; am. Acts 1993, 73rd Leg., ch. 900 (S.B. 1067), § 1.01, effective September 1, 1994 (renumbered from Sec. 38.08); am. Acts 2007, 80th Leg., ch. 908 (H.B. 2884), § 39, effective September 1, 2007.)

### Sec. 38.08. Effect of Unlawful Custody.

It is no defense to prosecution under Section 38.06 or 38.07 that the custody was unlawful. (Enacted by Acts 1973, 63rd Leg., ch. 399 (S.B. 34), § 1, effective January 1, 1974; am. Acts 1993, 73rd Leg., ch. 900 (S.B. 1067), § 1.01, effective

September 1, 1994 (renumbered from Sec. 38.09).)

## Sec. 38.09. Implements for Escape.

(a) A person commits an offense if, with intent to facilitate escape, he introduces into a correctional facility, or provides a person in custody or an inmate with, a deadly weapon or anything that may be useful for escape.

(b) An offense under this section is a felony of the third degree unless the actor introduced or provided a deadly weapon, in which event the offense is a felony of the second degree.

(c) In this section, "correctional facility" means:

(1) any place described by Section 1.07(a)(14); or

(2) a "secure correctional facility" or "secure detention facility" as those terms are defined by Section 51.02, Family Code.

(Enacted by Acts 1973, 63rd Leg., ch. 399 (S.B. 34), § 1, effective January 1, 1974; am. Acts 1993, 73rd Leg., ch. 900 (S.B. 1067), § 1.01, effective September 1, 1994 (renumbered from Sec. 38.10); am. Acts 2007, 80th Leg., ch. 908 (H.B. 2884), § 40, effective September 1, 2007.)

## Sec. 38.10. Bail Jumping and Failure to Appear.

(a) A person lawfully released from custody, with or without bail, on condition that he subsequently appear commits an offense if he intentionally or knowingly fails to appear in accordance with the terms of his release.

(b) It is a defense to prosecution under this section that the appearance was incident to community supervision, parole, or an intermittent sentence.

(c) It is a defense to prosecution under this section that the actor had a reasonable excuse for his failure to appear in accordance with the terms of his release.

(d) Except as provided in Subsections (e) and (f), an offense under this section is a Class A misdemeanor.

(e) An offense under this section is a Class C misdemeanor if the offense for which the actor's appearance was required is punishable by fine only.

(f) An offense under this section is a felony of the third degree if the offense for which the actor's appearance was required is classified as a felony.

(Enacted by Acts 1973, 63rd Leg., ch. 399 (S.B. 34), § 1, effective January 1, 1974; am. Acts 1993,

73rd Leg., ch. 900 (S.B. 1067), § 1.01, effective September 1, 1994 (renumbered from Sec. 38.11).)

## Sec. 38.11. Prohibited Substances and Items in Correctional Facility.

(a) A person commits an offense if the person provides, or possesses with the intent to provide:

(1) an alcoholic beverage, controlled substance, or dangerous drug to a person in the custody of a correctional facility, except on the prescription of a practitioner;

(2) a deadly weapon to a person in the custody of a correctional facility;

(3) a cellular telephone or other wireless communications device or a component of one of those devices to a person in the custody of a correctional facility;

(4) money to a person confined in a correctional facility; or

(5) a cigarette or tobacco product to a person confined in a correctional facility, except that if the facility is a local jail regulated by the Commission on Jail Standards, the person commits an offense only if providing the cigarette or tobacco product violates a rule or regulation adopted by the sheriff or jail administrator that:

(A) prohibits the possession of a cigarette or tobacco product by a person confined in the jail; or

(B) places restrictions on:

(i) the possession of a cigarette or tobacco product by a person confined in the jail; or

(ii) the manner in which a cigarette or tobacco product may be provided to a person confined in the jail.

(b) A person commits an offense if the person takes an alcoholic beverage, controlled substance, or dangerous drug into a correctional facility.

(c) A person commits an offense if the person takes a controlled substance or dangerous drug on property owned, used, or controlled by a correctional facility.

(d) A person commits an offense if the person:

(1) possesses a controlled substance or dangerous drug while in a correctional facility or on property owned, used, or controlled by a correctional facility; or

(2) possesses a deadly weapon while in a correctional facility.

(e) It is an affirmative defense to prosecution under Subsection (b), (c), or (d)(1) that the person possessed the alcoholic beverage, controlled substance, or dangerous drug pursuant to a prescription issued by a practitioner or while delivering the beverage, substance, or drug to a warehouse, pharmacy, or practitioner on property owned, used, or controlled by the correctional facility. It is an affirmative defense to prosecution under Subsection (d)(2) that the person possessing the deadly weapon is a peace officer or is an officer or employee of the correctional facility who is authorized to possess the deadly weapon while on duty or traveling to or from the person's place of assignment.

(f) In this section:

(1) "Practitioner" has the meaning assigned by Section 481.002, Health and Safety Code.

(2) "Prescription" has the meaning assigned by Section 481.002, Health and Safety Code.

(3) "Cigarette" has the meaning assigned by Section 154.001, Tax Code.

(4) "Tobacco product" has the meaning assigned by Section 155.001, Tax Code.

(5) "Component" means any item necessary for the current, ongoing, or future operation of a cellular telephone or other wireless communications device, including a subscriber identity module card or functionally equivalent portable memory chip, a battery or battery charger, and any number of minutes that have been purchased or for which a contract has been entered into and during which a cellular telephone or other wireless communications device is capable of transmitting or receiving communications.

(6) "Correctional facility" means:

(A) any place described by Section 1.07(a)(14)(A), (B), or (C); or

(B) a secure correctional facility or secure detention facility, as defined by Section 51.02, Family Code.

(g) An offense under this section is a felony of the third degree.

(h) Notwithstanding Section 15.01(d), if a person commits the offense of criminal attempt to commit an offense under Subsection (a), (b), or (c), the offense committed under Section 15.01 is a felony of the third degree.

(i) It is an affirmative defense to prosecution under Subsection (b) that the actor:

(1) is a duly authorized member of the clergy with rights and privileges granted by an ordaining authority that includes administration of a religious ritual or ceremony requiring the presence or consumption of an alcoholic beverage; and

(2) takes four ounces or less of an alcoholic beverage into the correctional facility and personally consumes all of the alcoholic beverage or departs from the facility with any portion of the beverage not consumed.

(j) A person commits an offense if the person, while confined in a correctional facility, possesses a cellular telephone or other wireless communications device or a component of one of those devices.

(k) A person commits an offense if, with the intent to provide to or make a cellular telephone or other wireless communications device or a component of one of those devices available for use by a person in the custody of a correctional facility, the person:

(1) acquires a cellular telephone or other wireless communications device or a component of one of those devices to be delivered to the person in custody;

(2) provides a cellular telephone or other wireless communications device or a component of one of those devices to another person for delivery to the person in custody; or

(3) makes a payment to a communication common carrier, as defined by Article 18.20, Code of Criminal Procedure, or to any communication service that provides to its users the ability to send or receive wire or electronic communications.

(Enacted by Acts 1991, 72nd Leg., 2nd C.S., ch. 10 (H.B. 55), § 5.01, effective October 1, 1991; am. Acts 1993, 73rd Leg., ch. 900 (S.B. 1067), § 1.01, effective September 1, 1994 (renumbered from Sec. 38.112); am. Acts 1999, 76th Leg., ch. 362 (H.B. 2593), § 1, effective September 1, 1999; am. Acts 1999, 76th Leg., ch. 649 (H.B. 163), § 1, effective September 1, 1999; am. Acts 2003, 78th Leg., ch. 470 (H.B. 864), §§ 1-3, effective September 1, 2003; am. Acts 2005, 79th Leg., ch. 499 (H.B. 549), § 1, effective June 17, 2005; am. Acts 2005, 79th Leg., ch. 949 (H.B. 1575), §§ 47, 48, effective September 1, 2005; am. Acts 2005, 79th Leg., ch. 1092 (H.B. 2077), § 1, effective September 1, 2005; am. Acts 2009, 81st Leg., ch. 1169 (H.B. 3228), § 1, effective September 1, 2009.)

## Sec. 38.111. Improper Contact with Victim.

(a) A person commits an offense if the person, while confined in a correctional facility after being charged with or convicted of an offense listed in Article 62.001(5), Code of Criminal Procedure, contacts by letter, telephone, or any other means, either directly or through a third party, a victim of the offense or a member of the victim's family, if:

(1) the victim was younger than 17 years of age at the time of the commission of the offense for which the person is confined; and

(2) the director of the correctional facility has not, before the person makes contact with the victim:

(A) received written and dated consent to the contact from:

(i) a parent of the victim;

(ii) a legal guardian of the victim;

(iii) the victim, if the victim is 17 years of age or older at the time of giving the consent; or

(iv) a member of the victim's family who is 17 years of age or older; and

(B) provided the person with a copy of the consent.

(b) The person confined in a correctional facility may not give the written consent required under Subsection (a)(2)(A).

(c) It is an affirmative defense to prosecution under this section that the contact was:

(1) indirect contact made through an attorney representing the person in custody; and

(2) solely for the purpose of representing the person in a criminal proceeding.

(d) An offense under this section is a Class A misdemeanor unless the actor is confined in a correctional facility after being convicted of a felony described by Subsection (a), in which event the offense is a felony of the third degree.

(e) In this section, "correctional facility" means:

(1) any place described by Section 1.07(a)(14); or

(2) a "secure correctional facility" or "secure detention facility" as those terms are defined by Section 51.02, Family Code.

(Enacted by Acts 2001, 77th Leg., ch. 1337 (H.B. 2890), § 1, effective September 1, 2001; am. Acts 2005, 79th Leg., ch. 1008 (H.B. 867), § 2.11, effective September 1, 2005; am. Acts 2007, 80th Leg., ch. 908 (H.B. 2884), § 41, effective September 1, 2007.)

### Sec. 38.112. Violation of Protective Order Issued on Basis of Sexual Assault.

(a) A person commits an offense if, in violation of an order issued under Chapter 7A, Code of Criminal Procedure, the person knowingly:

(1) communicates directly or indirectly with the applicant or any member of the applicant's family or household in a threatening or harassing manner;

(2) goes to or near the residence, place of employment or business, or child-care facility or school of the applicant or any member of the applicant's family or household; or

(3) possesses a firearm.

(b) If conduct constituting an offense under this section also constitutes an offense under another section of this code, the actor may be prosecuted under either section or under both sections.

(c) An offense under this section is a Class A misdemeanor.

(Enacted by Acts 2003, 78th Leg., ch. 836 (S.B. 433), § 3, effective September 1, 2003.)

### Sec. 38.113. Unauthorized Absence from Community Corrections Facility, County Correctional Center, or Assignment Site.

(a) A person commits an offense if the person:

(1) is sentenced to or is required as a condition of community supervision or correctional programming to submit to a period of detention or treatment in a community corrections facility or county correctional center;

(2) fails to report to or leaves the facility, the center, or a community service assignment site as directed by the court, community supervision and corrections department supervising the person, or director of the facility or center in which the person is detained or treated, as appropriate; and

(3) in failing to report or leaving acts without the approval of the court, the community supervision and corrections department supervising the person, or the director of the facility or center in which the person is detained or treated.

(b) An offense under this section is a state jail felony.

(Enacted by Acts 1993, 73rd Leg., ch. 900 (S.B. 1067), § 1.01, effective September 1, 1994; am. Acts 1995, 74th Leg., ch. 318 (S.B. 15), § 12, effective September 1, 1995.)

### Sec. 38.114. Contraband in Correctional Facility.

(a) A person commits an offense if the person:

(1) provides contraband to an inmate of a correctional facility;

(2) otherwise introduces contraband into a correctional facility; or

(3) possesses contraband while confined in a correctional facility.

(b) In this section, "contraband":

(1) means:

(A) any item not provided by or authorized by the operator of the correctional facility; or

(B) any item provided by or authorized by the operator of the correctional facility that has been altered to accommodate a use other than the originally intended use; and

(2) does not include any item specifically prohibited under Section 38.11.

(c) An offense under this section is a Class C misdemeanor, unless the offense is committed by an employee or a volunteer of the correctional facility, in which event the offense is a Class B misdemeanor.

(d) In this section, "correctional facility" means:

(1) any place described by Section 1.07(a)(14); or

(2) a "secure correctional facility" or "secure detention facility" as those terms are defined by Section 51.02, Family Code.

(Enacted by Acts 2005, 79th Leg., ch. 499 (H.B. 549), § 2, effective June 17, 2005; am. Acts 2007, 80th Leg., ch. 908 (H.B. 2884), § 42, effective September 1, 2007.)

## Sec. 38.12. Barratry and Solicitation of Professional Employment.

(a) A person commits an offense if, with intent to obtain an economic benefit the person:

(1) knowingly institutes a suit or claim that the person has not been authorized to pursue;

(2) solicits employment, either in person or by telephone, for himself or for another;

(3) pays, gives, or advances or offers to pay, give, or advance to a prospective client money or anything of value to obtain employment as a professional from the prospective client;

(4) pays or gives or offers to pay or give a person money or anything of value to solicit employment;

(5) pays or gives or offers to pay or give a family member of a prospective client money or anything of value to solicit employment; or

(6) accepts or agrees to accept money or anything of value to solicit employment.

(b) A person commits an offense if the person:

(1) knowingly finances the commission of an offense under Subsection (a);

(2) invests funds the person knows or believes are intended to further the commission of an offense under Subsection (a); or

(3) is a professional who knowingly accepts employment within the scope of the person's license, registration, or certification that results from the solicitation of employment in violation of Subsection (a).

(c) It is an exception to prosecution under Subsection (a) or (b) that the person's conduct is authorized by the Texas Disciplinary Rules of Professional Conduct or any rule of court.

(d) A person commits an offense if the person:

(1) is an attorney, chiropractor, physician, surgeon, or private investigator licensed to practice in this state or any person licensed, certified, or registered by a health care regulatory agency of this state; and

(2) with the intent to obtain professional employment for the person or for another, provides or knowingly permits to be provided to an individual who has not sought the person's employment, legal representation, advice, or care a written communication or a solicitation, including a solicitation in person or by telephone, that:

(A) concerns an action for personal injury or wrongful death or otherwise relates to an accident or disaster involving the person to whom the communication or solicitation is provided or a relative of that person and that was provided before the 31st day after the date on which the accident or disaster occurred;

(B) concerns a specific matter and relates to legal representation and the person knows or reasonably should know that the person to whom the communication or solicitation is directed is represented by a lawyer in the matter;

(C) concerns an arrest of or issuance of a summons to the person to whom the communication or solicitation is provided or a relative of that person and that was provided before the 31st day after the date on which the arrest or issuance of the summons occurred;

(D) concerns a lawsuit of any kind, including an action for divorce, in which the person to whom the communication or solicitation is provided is a defendant or a relative of that person, unless the lawsuit in which the person is named as a defendant has been on file for more than 31 days before the date on which the communication or solicitation was provided;

(E) is provided or permitted to be provided by a person who knows or reasonably should know that the injured person or relative of the injured person has indicated a desire not to be contacted by or receive communications or solicitations concerning employment;

(F) involves coercion, duress, fraud, overreaching, harassment, intimidation, or undue influence; or

(G) contains a false, fraudulent, misleading, deceptive, or unfair statement or claim.

(e) For purposes of Subsection (d)(2)(E), a desire not to be contacted is presumed if an accident report reflects that such an indication has been made by an injured person or that person's relative.

(f) An offense under Subsection (a) or (b) is a felony of the third degree.

(g) Except as provided by Subsection (h), an offense under Subsection (d) is a Class A misdemeanor.

(h) An offense under Subsection (d) is a felony of the third degree if it is shown on the trial of the offense that the defendant has previously been convicted under Subsection (d).

(i) Final conviction of felony barratry is a serious crime for all purposes and acts, specifically including the State Bar Rules and the Texas Rules of Disciplinary Procedure.
(Enacted by Acts 1973, 63rd Leg., ch. 399 (S.B. 34), § 1, effective January 1, 1974; am. Acts 1989, 71st Leg., ch. 866 (S.B. 843), § 2, effective September 1, 1989; am. Acts 1993, 73rd Leg., ch. 723 (S.B. 1227), § 2, effective September 1, 1993; am. Acts 1993, 73rd Leg., ch. 900 (S.B. 1067), § 1.01, effective September 1, 1994; am. Acts 1997, 75th Leg., ch. 750 (H.B. 1327), § 2, effective September 1, 1997; am. Acts 2009, 81st Leg., ch. 1252 (H.B. 148), § 1, effective September 1, 2009.)

## Sec. 38.122. Falsely Holding Oneself Out As a Lawyer.

(a) A person commits an offense if, with intent to obtain an economic benefit for himself or herself, the person holds himself or herself out as a lawyer, unless he or she is currently licensed to practice law in this state, another state, or a foreign country and is in good standing with the State Bar of Texas and the state bar or licensing authority of any and all other states and foreign countries where licensed.

(b) An offense under Subsection (a) of this section is a felony of the third degree.

(c) Final conviction of falsely holding oneself out to be a lawyer is a serious crime for all purposes and acts, specifically including the State Bar Rules.
(Enacted by Acts 1993, 73rd Leg., ch. 723 (S.B. 1227), § 5, effective September 1, 1993.)

## Sec. 38.123. Unauthorized Practice of Law.

(a) A person commits an offense if, with intent to obtain an economic benefit for himself or herself, the person:

(1) contracts with any person to represent that person with regard to personal causes of action for property damages or personal injury;

(2) advises any person as to the person's rights and the advisability of making claims for personal injuries or property damages;

(3) advises any person as to whether or not to accept an offered sum of money in settlement of claims for personal injuries or property damages;

(4) enters into any contract with another person to represent that person in personal injury or property damage matters on a contingent fee basis with an attempted assignment of a portion of the person's cause of action; or

(5) enters into any contract with a third person which purports to grant the exclusive right to select and retain legal counsel to represent the individual in any legal proceeding.

(b) This section does not apply to a person currently licensed to practice law in this state, another state, or a foreign country and in good standing with the State Bar of Texas and the state bar or licensing authority of any and all other states and foreign countries where licensed.

(c) Except as provided by Subsection (d) of this section, an offense under Subsection (a) of this section is a Class A misdemeanor.

(d) An offense under Subsection (a) of this section is a felony of the third degree if it is shown on the trial of the offense that the defendant has previously been convicted under Subsection (a) of this section.
(Enacted by Acts 1993, 73rd Leg., ch. 723 (S.B. 1227), § 5, effective September 1, 1993.)

## Sec. 38.13. Hindering Proceedings by Disorderly Conduct.

(a) A person commits an offense if he intentionally hinders an official proceeding by noise or violent or tumultuous behavior or disturbance.

(b) A person commits an offense if he recklessly hinders an official proceeding by noise or violent or tumultuous behavior or disturbance and continues after explicit official request to desist.

(c) An offense under this section is a Class A misdemeanor.

(Enacted by Acts 1973, 63rd Leg., ch. 399 (S.B. 34), § 1, effective January 1, 1974; am. Acts 1993, 73rd Leg., ch. 900 (S.B. 1067), § 1.01, effective September 1, 1994.)

## Sec. 38.14. Taking or Attempting to Take Weapon from Peace Officer, Federal Special Investigator, Employee or Official of Correctional Facility, Parole Officer, Community Supervision and Corrections Department Officer, or Commissioned Security Officer.

(a) In this section:

(1) "Firearm" has the meanings assigned by Section 46.01.

(2) "Stun gun" means a device designed to propel darts or other projectiles attached to wires that, on contact, will deliver an electrical pulse capable of incapacitating a person.

(3) "Commissioned security officer" has the meaning assigned by Section 1702.002(5), Occupations Code.

(b) A person commits an offense if the person intentionally or knowingly and with force takes or attempts to take from a peace officer, federal special investigator, employee or official of a correctional facility, parole officer, community supervision and corrections department officer, or commissioned security officer the officer's, investigator's, employee's, or official's firearm, nightstick, stun gun, or personal protection chemical dispensing device with the intention of harming the officer, investigator, employee, or official or a third person.

(c) The actor is presumed to have known that the peace officer, federal special investigator, employee or official of a correctional facility, parole officer, community supervision and corrections department officer, or commissioned security officer was a peace officer, federal special investigator, employee or official of a correctional facility, parole officer, community supervision and corrections department officer, or commissioned security officer if:

(1) the officer, investigator, employee, or official was wearing a distinctive uniform or badge indicating his employment; or

(2) the officer, investigator, employee, or official identified himself as a peace officer, fed-

eral special investigator, employee or official of a correctional facility, parole officer, community supervision and corrections department officer, or commissioned security officer.

(d) It is a defense to prosecution under this section that the defendant took or attempted to take the weapon from a peace officer, federal special investigator, employee or official of a correctional facility, parole officer, community supervision and corrections department officer, or commissioned security officer who was using force against the defendant or another in excess of the amount of force permitted by law.

(e) An offense under this section is:

(1) a felony of the third degree, if the defendant took a weapon described by Subsection (b) from an officer, investigator, employee, or official described by that subsection; and

(2) a state jail felony, if the defendant attempted to take a weapon described by Subsection (b) from an officer, investigator, employee, or official described by that subsection.

(Enacted by Acts 1989, 71st Leg., ch. 986 (H.B. 731), § 1, effective September 1, 1989; am. Acts 1990, 71st Leg., 6th C.S., ch. 12 (S.B. 51), § 2(25), effective September 6, 1990 (renumbered from Sec. 38.16); am. Acts 1993, 73rd Leg., ch. 900 (S.B. 1067), § 1.01, effective September 1, 1994 (renumbered from Sec. 38.17); am. Acts 1999, 76th Leg., ch. 714 (H.B. 635), § 1, effective September 1, 1999; am. Acts 2001, 77th Leg., ch. 322 (H.B. 1600), § 1, effective September 1, 2001; am. Acts 2005, 79th Leg., ch. 1201 (H.B. 582), § 1, effective September 1, 2005; am. Acts 2009, 81st Leg., ch. 394 (H.B. 1721), §§ 1, 2, effective September 1, 2009; am. Acts 2009, 81st Leg., ch. 942 (H.B. 3147), §§ 1—3, effective September 1, 2009; am. Acts 2011, 82nd Leg., ch. 839 (H.B. 3423), §§ 5, 6, effective September 1, 2011.)

## Sec. 38.15. Interference with Public Duties.

(a) A person commits an offense if the person with criminal negligence interrupts, disrupts, impedes, or otherwise interferes with:

(1) a peace officer while the peace officer is performing a duty or exercising authority imposed or granted by law;

(2) a person who is employed to provide emergency medical services including the transportation of ill or injured persons while the person is performing that duty;

(3) a fire fighter, while the fire fighter is fighting a fire or investigating the cause of a fire;

Penal Code

(4) an animal under the supervision of a peace officer, corrections officer, or jailer, if the person knows the animal is being used for law enforcement, corrections, prison or jail security, or investigative purposes;

(5) the transmission of a communication over a citizen's band radio channel, the purpose of which communication is to inform or inquire about an emergency;

(6) an officer with responsibility for animal control in a county or municipality, while the officer is performing a duty or exercising authority imposed or granted under Chapter 821 or 822, Health and Safety Code; or

(7) a person who:

(A) has responsibility for assessing, enacting, or enforcing public health, environmental, radiation, or safety measures for the state or a county or municipality;

(B) is investigating a particular site as part of the person's responsibilities under Paragraph (A);

(C) is acting in accordance with policies and procedures related to the safety and security of the site described by Paragraph (B); and

(D) is performing a duty or exercising authority imposed or granted under the Agriculture Code, Health and Safety Code, Occupations Code, or Water Code.

(b) An offense under this section is a Class B misdemeanor.

(c) It is a defense to prosecution under Subsection (a)(1) that the conduct engaged in by the defendant was intended to warn a person operating a motor vehicle of the presence of a peace officer who was enforcing Subtitle C, Title 7, Transportation Code.

(d) It is a defense to prosecution under this section that the interruption, disruption, impediment, or interference alleged consisted of speech only.

(e) In this section, "emergency" means a condition or circumstance in which an individual is or is reasonably believed by the person transmitting the communication to be in imminent danger of serious bodily injury or in which property is or is reasonably believed by the person transmitting the communication to be in imminent danger of damage or destruction.

(Enacted by Acts 1989, 71st Leg., ch. 1162 (H.B. 507), § 1, effective September 1, 1989; am. Acts 1990, 71st Leg., 6th C.S., ch. 12 (S.B. 51), § 2(26), effective September 6, 1990 (renumbered from Sec. 38.16); am. Acts 1993, 73rd Leg., ch. 900

(S.B. 1067), § 1.01, effective September 1, 1994 (renumbered from Sec. 38.18); am. Acts 1997, 75th Leg., ch. 165 (S.B. 898), § 30.241, effective September 1, 1997; am. Acts 2005, 79th Leg., ch. 1212 (H.B. 825), § 1, effective September 1, 2005; am. Acts 2007, 80th Leg., ch. 1251 (H.B. 2703), § 1, effective September 1, 2007.)

## Sec. 38.151. Interference with Police Service Animals.

(a) In this section:

(1) "Area of control" includes a vehicle, trailer, kennel, pen, or yard.

(2) "Handler or rider" means a peace officer, corrections officer, or jailer who is specially trained to use a police service animal for law enforcement, corrections, prison or jail security, or investigative purposes.

(3) "Police service animal" means a dog, horse, or other domesticated animal that is specially trained for use by a handler or rider.

(b) A person commits an offense if the person recklessly:

(1) taunts, torments, or strikes a police service animal;

(2) throws an object or substance at a police service animal;

(3) interferes with or obstructs a police service animal or interferes with or obstructs the handler or rider of a police service animal in a manner that:

(A) inhibits or restricts the handler's or rider's control of the animal; or

(B) deprives the handler or rider of control of the animal;

(4) releases a police service animal from its area of control;

(5) enters the area of control of a police service animal without the effective consent of the handler or rider, including placing food or any other object or substance into that area;

(6) injures or kills a police service animal; or

(7) engages in conduct likely to injure or kill a police service animal, including administering or setting a poison, trap, or any other object or substance.

(c) An offense under this section is:

(1) a Class C misdemeanor if the person commits an offense under Subsection (b)(1);

(2) a Class B misdemeanor if the person commits an offense under Subsection (b)(2);

(3) a Class A misdemeanor if the person commits an offense under Subsection (b)(3), (4), or (5);

(4) except as provided by Subdivision (5), a state jail felony if the person commits an offense under Subsection (b)(6) or (7) by injuring a police service animal or by engaging in conduct likely to injure the animal; or

(5) a felony of the second degree if the person commits an offense under Subsection (b)(6) or (7) by:

(A) killing a police service animal or engaging in conduct likely to kill the animal;

(B) injuring a police service animal in a manner that materially and permanently affects the ability of the animal to perform as a police service animal; or

(C) engaging in conduct likely to injure a police service animal in a manner that would materially and permanently affect the ability of the animal to perform as a police service animal.

(Enacted by Acts 2001, 77th Leg., ch. 979 (H.B. 280), § 1, effective September 1, 2001; am. Acts 2007, 80th Leg., ch. 1331 (S.B. 1562), § 5, effective September 1, 2007.)

## Sec. 38.152. Interference with Radio Frequency Licensed to Government Entity.

(a) A person commits an offense if, without the effective consent of the law enforcement agency, fire department, or emergency medical services provider, the person intentionally interrupts, disrupts, impedes, jams, or otherwise interferes with a radio frequency that is licensed by the Federal Communications Commission to a government entity and is used by the law enforcement agency, fire department, or emergency medical services provider.

(b) An offense under this section is a Class A misdemeanor, except that the offense is a state jail felony if the actor committed the offense with the intent to:

(1) facilitate the commission of another offense; or

(2) interfere with the ability of a law enforcement agency, a fire department, or an emergency medical services provider to respond to an emergency.

(c) In this section:

(1) "Emergency" has the meaning assigned by Section 38.15.

(2) "Emergency medical services provider" has the meaning assigned by Section 773.003, Health and Safety Code.

(3) "Law enforcement agency" has the meaning assigned by Article 59.01, Code of Criminal Procedure.

(d) If conduct constituting an offense under this section also constitutes an offense under another section of this code, the actor may be prosecuted under either section or under both sections.

(Enacted by Acts 2009, 81st Leg., ch. 1222 (S.B. 1273), § 1, effective September 1, 2009.)

## Sec. 38.16. Preventing Execution of Civil Process.

(a) A person commits an offense if he intentionally or knowingly by words or physical action prevents the execution of any process in a civil cause.

(b) It is an exception to the application of this section that the actor evaded service of process by avoiding detection.

(c) An offense under this section is a Class C misdemeanor.

(Enacted by Acts 1995, 74th Leg., ch. 318 (S.B. 15), § 13, effective September 1, 1995.)

## Sec. 38.17. Failure to Stop or Report Aggravated Sexual Assault of Child.

(a) A person, other than a person who has a relationship with a child described by Section 22.04(b), commits an offense if:

(1) the actor observes the commission or attempted commission of an offense prohibited by Section 21.02 or 22.021(a)(2)(B) under circumstances in which a reasonable person would believe that an offense of a sexual or assaultive nature was being committed or was about to be committed against the child;

(2) the actor fails to assist the child or immediately report the commission of the offense to a peace officer or law enforcement agency; and

(3) the actor could assist the child or immediately report the commission of the offense without placing the actor in danger of suffering serious bodily injury or death.

(b) An offense under this section is a Class A misdemeanor.

(Enacted by Acts 1999, 76th Leg., ch. 1344 (H.B. 628), § 1, effective September 1, 1999; am. Acts 2007, 80th Leg., ch. 593 (H.B. 8), § 3.50, effective September 1, 2007.)

## Sec. 38.171. Failure to Report Felony.

(a) A person commits an offense if the person:

(1) observes the commission of a felony under circumstances in which a reasonable person would believe that an offense had been

committed in which serious bodily injury or death may have resulted; and

(2) fails to immediately report the commission of the offense to a peace officer or law enforcement agency under circumstances in which:

(A) a reasonable person would believe that the commission of the offense had not been reported; and

(B) the person could immediately report the commission of the offense without placing himself or herself in danger of suffering serious bodily injury or death.

(b) An offense under this section is a Class A misdemeanor.

(Enacted by Acts 2003, 78th Leg., ch. 1009 (H.B. 325), § 2, effective September 1, 2003.)

## Sec. 38.18. Use of Accident Report Information and Other Information for Pecuniary Gain.

(a) This section applies to:

(1) information described by Section 550.065(a), Transportation Code;

(2) information reported under Chapter 772, Health and Safety Code, other than information that is confidential under that chapter; and

(3) information contained in a dispatch log, a towing record, or a record of a 9-1-1 service provider, other than information that is confidential under Chapter 772, Health and Safety Code.

(b) A person commits an offense if:

(1) the person obtains information described by Subsection (a) from the Department of Public Safety of the State of Texas or other governmental entity; and

(2) the information is subsequently used for the direct solicitation of business or employment for pecuniary gain by:

(A) the person;

(B) an agent or employee of the person; or

(C) the person on whose behalf the information was requested.

(c) A person who employs or engages another to obtain information described by Subsection (a) from the Department of Public Safety or other governmental entity commits an offense if the person subsequently uses the information for direct solicitation of business or employment for pecuniary gain.

(d) An offense under this section is a Class B misdemeanor.

(Enacted by Acts 2001, 77th Leg., ch. 1032 (H.B. 1544), § 1, effective September 1, 2001.)

## Sec. 38.19. Failure to Provide Notice and Report of Death of Resident of Institution.

(a) A superintendent or general manager of an institution commits an offense if, as required by Article 49.24 or 49.25, Code of Criminal Procedure, the person fails to:

(1) provide notice of the death of an individual under the care, custody, or control of or residing in the institution;

(2) submit a report on the death of the individual; or

(3) include in the report material facts known or discovered by the person at the time the report was filed.

(b) An offense under this section is a Class B misdemeanor.

(Enacted by Acts 2003, 78th Leg., ch. 894 (S.B. 826), § 4, effective September 1, 2003.)

## CHAPTER 39
## ABUSE OF OFFICE

## Sec. 39.01. Definitions.

In this chapter:

(1) "Law relating to a public servant's office or employment" means a law that specifically applies to a person acting in the capacity of a public servant and that directly or indirectly:

(A) imposes a duty on the public servant; or

(B) governs the conduct of the public servant.

(2) "Misuse" means to deal with property contrary to:

(A) an agreement under which the public servant holds the property;

(B) a contract of employment or oath of office of a public servant;

(C) a law, including provisions of the General Appropriations Act specifically relating to government property, that prescribes the manner of custody or disposition of the property; or

(D) a limited purpose for which the property is delivered or received.

(Enacted by Acts 1993, 73rd Leg., ch. 900 (S.B. 1067), § 1.01, September 1, 1994.)

## Sec. 39.015. Concurrent Jurisdiction to Prosecute Offenses Under This Chapter.

With the consent of the appropriate local county or district attorney, the attorney general has concurrent jurisdiction with that consenting local prosecutor to prosecute an offense under this chapter.

(Enacted by Acts 2007, 80th Leg., ch. 378 (S.B. 563), § 2, effective June 15, 2007.)

## Sec. 39.02. Abuse of Official Capacity.

(a) A public servant commits an offense if, with intent to obtain a benefit or with intent to harm or defraud another, he intentionally or knowingly:

(1) violates a law relating to the public servant's office or employment; or

(2) misuses government property, services, personnel, or any other thing of value belonging to the government that has come into the public servant's custody or possession by virtue of the public servant's office or employment.

(b) An offense under Subsection (a)(1) is a Class A misdemeanor.

(c) An offense under Subsection (a)(2) is:

(1) a Class C misdemeanor if the value of the use of the thing misused is less than $20;

(2) a Class B misdemeanor if the value of the use of the thing misused is $20 or more but less than $500;

(3) a Class A misdemeanor if the value of the use of the thing misused is $500 or more but less than $1,500;

(4) a state jail felony if the value of the use of the thing misused is $1,500 or more but less than $20,000;

(5) a felony of the third degree if the value of the use of the thing misused is $20,000 or more but less than $100,000;

(6) a felony of the second degree if the value of the use of the thing misused is $100,000 or more but less than $200,000; or

(7) a felony of the first degree if the value of the use of the thing misused is $200,000 or more.

(d) A discount or award given for travel, such as frequent flyer miles, rental car or hotel discounts, or food coupons, are not things of value belonging to the government for purposes of this section due to the administrative difficulty and cost involved in recapturing the discount or award for a governmental entity.

(e) If separate transactions that violate Subsection (a)(2) are conducted pursuant to one scheme or continuing course of conduct, the conduct may be considered as one offense and the value of the use of the things misused in the transactions may be aggregated in determining the classification of the offense.

(f) The value of the use of a thing of value misused under Subsection (a)(2) may not exceed:

(1) the fair market value of the thing at the time of the offense; or

(2) if the fair market value of the thing cannot be ascertained, the cost of replacing the thing within a reasonable time after the offense.

(Enacted by Acts 1973, 63rd Leg., ch. 399 (S.B. 34), § 1, effective January 1, 1974; am. Acts 1983, 68th Leg., ch. 558 (S.B. 651), § 7, effective September 1, 1983; am. Acts 1993, 73rd Leg., ch. 900 (S.B. 1067), § 1.01, effective September 1, 1994 (renumbered from Sec. 39.01); am. Acts 2009, 81st Leg., ch. 82 (S.B. 828), § 1, effective September 1, 2009.)

## Sec. 39.021. Violations of the Civil Rights of a Prisoner [Renumbered].

Renumbered to Tex. Penal Code § 39.04 by Acts 1993, 73rd Leg., ch. 900 (S.B. 1067), § 1.01, effective September 1, 1994.

## Sec. 39.022. Failure to Report Death of Prisoner [Renumbered].

Renumbered to Tex. Penal Code § 39.05 by Acts 1993, 73rd Leg., ch. 900 (S.B. 1067), § 1.01, effective September 1, 1994.

## Sec. 39.03. Official Oppression.

(a) A public servant acting under color of his office or employment commits an offense if he:

(1) intentionally subjects another to mistreatment or to arrest, detention, search, seizure, dispossession, assessment, or lien that he knows is unlawful;

(2) intentionally denies or impedes another in the exercise or enjoyment of any right, privilege, power, or immunity, knowing his conduct is unlawful; or

(3) intentionally subjects another to sexual harassment.

(b) For purposes of this section, a public servant acts under color of his office or employment if he acts or purports to act in an official capacity or takes advantage of such actual or purported capacity.

(c) In this section, "sexual harassment" means unwelcome sexual advances, requests for sexual favors, or other verbal or physical conduct of a sexual nature, submission to which is made a term or condition of a person's exercise or enjoyment of any right, privilege, power, or immunity, either explicitly or implicitly.

(d) An offense under this section is a Class A misdemeanor.

(Enacted by Acts 1973, 63rd Leg., ch. 399 (S.B. 34), § 1, effective January 1, 1974; am. Acts 1989, 71st Leg., ch. 1217 (H.B. 370), § 1, effective September 1, 1989; am. Acts 1991, 72nd Leg., ch. 16 (S.B. 232), § 19.01(34), effective August 26, 1991; am. Acts 1993, 73rd Leg., ch. 900 (S.B. 1067), § 1.01, effective September 1, 1994 (renumbered from Sec. 39.02).)

## Sec. 39.04. Violations of the Civil Rights of Person in Custody; Improper Sexual Activity with Person in Custody.

(a) An official of a correctional facility, an employee of a correctional facility, a person other than an employee who works for compensation at a correctional facility, a volunteer at a correctional facility, or a peace officer commits an offense if the person intentionally:

(1) denies or impedes a person in custody in the exercise or enjoyment of any right, privilege, or immunity knowing his conduct is unlawful; or

(2) engages in sexual contact, sexual intercourse, or deviate sexual intercourse with an individual in custody or, in the case of an individual in the custody of the Texas Youth Commission, employs, authorizes, or induces the individual to engage in sexual conduct or a sexual performance.

(b) An offense under Subsection (a)(1) is a Class A misdemeanor. An offense under Subsection (a)(2) is a state jail felony, except that an offense under Subsection (a)(2) is a felony of the second degree if the offense is committed against:

(1) an individual in the custody of the Texas Youth Commission; or

(2) a juvenile offender detained in or committed to a correctional facility the operation of which is financed primarily with state funds.

(c) This section shall not preclude prosecution for any other offense set out in this code.

(d) The Attorney General of Texas shall have concurrent jurisdiction with law enforcement agencies to investigate violations of this statute involving serious bodily injury or death.

(e) In this section:

(1) "Correctional facility" means:

(A) any place described by Section 1.07(a)(14); or

(B) a "secure correctional facility" or "secure detention facility" as defined by Section 51.02, Family Code.

(2) "Custody" means the detention, arrest, or confinement of an adult offender or the detention or the commitment of a juvenile offender to a facility operated by or under a contract with the Texas Youth Commission or a facility operated by or under contract with a juvenile board.

(3) "Sexual contact," "sexual intercourse," and "deviate sexual intercourse" have the meanings assigned by Section 21.01.

(4) "Sexual conduct" and "performance" have the meanings assigned by Section 43.25.

(5) "Sexual performance" means any performance or part thereof that includes sexual conduct by an individual.

(f) An employee of the Texas Department of Criminal Justice, the Texas Youth Commission, or a local juvenile probation department commits an offense if the employee engages in sexual contact, sexual intercourse, or deviate sexual intercourse with an individual who the employee knows is under the supervision of the department, commission, or probation department but not in the custody of the department, commission, or probation department.

(g) An offense under Subsection (f) is a state jail felony.

(h) It is an affirmative defense to prosecution under Subsection (f) that the actor was the spouse of the individual at the time of the offense.

(Enacted by Acts 1979, 66th Leg., ch. 618 (S.B. 546), § 1, effective September 1, 1979; am. Acts 1983, 68th Leg., ch. 558 (S.B. 651), § 8, effective September 1, 1983; am. Acts 1987, 70th Leg., ch. 18 (S.B. 251), § 5, effective April 14, 1987; am. Acts 1993, 73rd Leg., ch. 900 (S.B 1067), § 1.01, effective September 1, 1994 (renumbered from Sec. 39.021); am. Acts 1997, 75th Leg., ch. 1406 (H.B. 2283), § 1, effective September 1, 1997; am.

Acts 1999, 76th Leg., ch. 158 (S.B. 894), §§ 1-3, effective September 1, 1999; am. Acts 2001, 77th Leg., ch. 1070 (H.B. 2097), § 1, effective September 1, 2001; am. Acts 2001, 77th Leg., ch. 1297 (H.B. 1118), § 69, effective September 1, 2001; am. Acts 2007, 80th Leg., ch. 263 (S.B. 103), §§ 62, 63, effective June 8, 2007; am. Acts 2007, 80th Leg., ch. 378 (S.B. 563), § 3, effective June 15, 2007; am. Acts 2007, 80th Leg., ch. 908 (H.B. 2884), § 43, effective September 1, 2007; am. Acts 2009, 81st Leg., ch. 87 (S.B. 1969), § 19.003, effective September 1, 2009; am. Acts 2009, 81st Leg., ch. 260 (H.B. 549), § 5, effective September 1, 2009.)

## Sec. 39.05.   Failure to Report Death of Prisoner.

(a) A person commits an offense if the person is required to conduct an investigation and file a report by Article 49.18, Code of Criminal Procedure, and the person fails to investigate the death, fails to file the report as required, or fails to include in a filed report facts known or discovered in the investigation.

(b) A person commits an offense if the person is required by Section 501.055, Government Code, to:

(1) give notice of the death of an inmate and the person fails to give the notice; or

(2) conduct an investigation and file a report and the person:

(A) fails to conduct the investigation or file the report; or

(B) fails to include in the report facts known to the person or discovered by the person in the investigation.

(c) An offense under this section is a Class B misdemeanor.

(Enacted by Acts 1983, 68th Leg., ch. 441 (H.B. 1954), § 2, effective September 1, 1983; am. Acts 1993, 73rd Leg., ch. 900 (S.B. 1067), § 1.01, effective September 1, 1994 (renumbered from Sec. 39.022); am. Acts 1995, 74th Leg., ch. 321 (H.B. 2162), § 1.104, effective September 1, 1995.)

## Sec. 39.06.   Misuse of Official Information.

(a) A public servant commits an offense if, in reliance on information to which he has access by virtue of his office or employment and that has not been made public, he:

(1) acquires or aids another to acquire a pecuniary interest in any property, transaction, or enterprise that may be affected by the information;

(2) speculates or aids another to speculate on the basis of the information; or

(3) as a public servant, including as a principal of a school, coerces another into suppressing or failing to report that information to a law enforcement agency.

(b) A public servant commits an offense if with intent to obtain a benefit or with intent to harm or defraud another, he discloses or uses information for a nongovernmental purpose that:

(1) he has access to by means of his office or employment; and

(2) has not been made public.

(c) A person commits an offense if, with intent to obtain a benefit or with intent to harm or defraud another, he solicits or receives from a public servant information that:

(1) the public servant has access to by means of his office or employment; and

(2) has not been made public.

(d) In this section, "information that has not been made public" means any information to which the public does not generally have access, and that is prohibited from disclosure under Chapter 552, Government Code.

(e) Except as provided by Subsection (f), an offense under this section is a felony of the third degree.

(f) An offense under Subsection (a)(3) is a Class C misdemeanor.

(Enacted by Acts 1973, 63rd Leg., ch. 399 (S.B. 34), § 1, effective January 1, 1974; am. Acts 1983, 68th Leg., ch. 558 (S.B. 651), § 9, effective September 1, 1983; am. Acts 1987, 70th Leg., ch. 30 (H.B. 288), § 1, effective September 1, 1987; am. Acts 1987, 70th Leg., 2nd C.S., ch. 43 (H.B. 123), § 3, effective October 20, 1987; am. Acts 1989, 71st Leg., ch. 927 (S.B. 1070), § 1, effective August 28, 1989; am. Acts 1993, 73rd Leg., ch. 900 (S.B. 1067), § 1.01, effective September 1, 1994 (renumbered from Sec. 39.03); am. Acts 1995, 74th Leg., ch. 76 (S.B. 959), §§ 5.95(90), 14.52, effective September 1, 1995.)

# TITLE 9
# OFFENSES AGAINST PUBLIC ORDER AND DECENCY

## CHAPTER 42
## DISORDERLY CONDUCT AND RELATED OFFENSES

## Sec. 42.01.  Disorderly Conduct.

(a) A person commits an offense if he intentionally or knowingly:

(1) uses abusive, indecent, profane, or vulgar language in a public place, and the language by its very utterance tends to incite an immediate breach of the peace;

(2) makes an offensive gesture or display in a public place, and the gesture or display tends to incite an immediate breach of the peace;

(3) creates, by chemical means, a noxious and unreasonable odor in a public place;

(4) abuses or threatens a person in a public place in an obviously offensive manner;

(5) makes unreasonable noise in a public place other than a sport shooting range, as defined by Section 250.001, Local Government Code, or in or near a private residence that he has no right to occupy;

(6) fights with another in a public place;

(7) discharges a firearm in a public place other than a public road or a sport shooting range, as defined by Section 250.001, Local Government Code;

(8) displays a firearm or other deadly weapon in a public place in a manner calculated to alarm;

(9) discharges a firearm on or across a public road;

(10) exposes his anus or genitals in a public place and is reckless about whether another may be present who will be offended or alarmed by his act; or

(11) for a lewd or unlawful purpose:

(A) enters on the property of another and looks into a dwelling on the property through any window or other opening in the dwelling;

(B) while on the premises of a hotel or comparable establishment, looks into a guest room not the person's own through a window or other opening in the room; or

(C) while on the premises of a public place, looks into an area such as a restroom or shower stall or changing or dressing room that is designed to provide privacy to a person using the area.

(b) It is a defense to prosecution under Subsection (a)(4) that the actor had significant provocation for his abusive or threatening conduct.

(c) For purposes of this section:

(1) an act is deemed to occur in a public place or near a private residence if it produces its offensive or proscribed consequences in the public place or near a private residence; and

(2) a noise is presumed to be unreasonable if the noise exceeds a decibel level of 85 after the person making the noise receives notice from a magistrate or peace officer that the noise is a public nuisance.

(d) An offense under this section is a Class C misdemeanor unless committed under Subsection (a)(7) or (a)(8), in which event it is a Class B misdemeanor.

(e) It is a defense to prosecution for an offense under Subsection (a)(7) or (9) that the person who discharged the firearm had a reasonable fear of bodily injury to the person or to another by a dangerous wild animal as defined by Section 822.101, Health and Safety Code.

(f) Subsections (a)(1), (2), (3), (5), and (6) do not apply to a person who, at the time the person engaged in conduct prohibited under the applicable subdivision, was a student in the sixth grade or a lower grade level, and the prohibited conduct occurred at a public school campus during regular school hours.

(Enacted by Acts 1973, 63rd Leg., ch. 399 (S.B. 34), § 1, effective January 1, 1974; am. Acts 1977, 65th Leg., ch. 89 (H.B. 293), §§ 1, 2, effective August 29, 1977; am. Acts 1983, 68th Leg., ch. 800 (H.B. 747), § 1, effective September 1, 1983; am. Acts 1991, 72nd Leg., ch. 145 (S.B. 215), § 2, effective August 26, 1991; am. Acts 1993, 73rd Leg., ch. 900 (S.B. 1067), § 1.01, effective September 1, 1994; am. Acts 1995, 74th Leg., ch. 318 (S.B. 15), § 14, effective September 1, 1995; am. Acts 2001, 77th Leg., ch. 54 (H.B. 1362), § 4, effective September 1, 2001; am. Acts 2003, 78th Leg., ch. 389 (H.B. 12), § 1, effective September 1, 2003; am. Acts 2011, 82nd Leg., ch. 691 (H.B. 359), § 6, effective September 1, 2011.)

### Sec. 42.015.  Discharge of Firearm in Certain Metropolitan Areas [Deleted].

Deleted by Acts 1993, 73rd Leg., ch. 900 (S.B. 1067), § 13.02, effective September 1, 1994. (Enacted by Acts 1993, 73rd Leg., ch. 857 (S.B. 145), § 1, effective September 1, 1993.)

### Sec. 42.02.  Riot.

(a) For the purpose of this section, "riot" means the assemblage of seven or more persons resulting in conduct which:

(1) creates an immediate danger of damage to property or injury to persons;

(2) substantially obstructs law enforcement or other governmental functions or services; or

(3) by force, threat of force, or physical action deprives any person of a legal right or disturbs any person in the enjoyment of a legal right.

(b) A person commits an offense if he knowingly participates in a riot.

(c) It is a defense to prosecution under this section that the assembly was at first lawful and when one of those assembled manifested an intent to engage in conduct enumerated in Subsection (a), the actor retired from the assembly.

(d) It is no defense to prosecution under this section that another who was a party to the riot has been acquitted, has not been arrested, prosecuted, or convicted, has been convicted of a different offense or of a different type or class of offense, or is immune from prosecution.

(e) Except as provided in Subsection (f), an offense under this section is a Class B misdemeanor.

(f) An offense under this section is an offense of the same classification as any offense of a higher grade committed by anyone engaged in the riot if the offense was:

(1) in the furtherance of the purpose of the assembly; or

(2) an offense which should have been anticipated as a result of the assembly.

(Enacted by Acts 1973, 63rd Leg., ch. 399 (S.B. 34), § 1, effective January 1, 1974; am. Acts 1993, 73rd Leg., ch. 900 (S.B. 1067), § 1.01, effective September 1, 1994.)

### Sec. 42.03.  Obstructing Highway or Other Passageway.

(a) A person commits an offense if, without legal privilege or authority, he intentionally, knowingly, or recklessly:

(1) obstructs a highway, street, sidewalk, railway, waterway, elevator, aisle, hallway, entrance, or exit to which the public or a substantial group of the public has access, or any other place used for the passage of persons, vehicles, or conveyances, regardless of the means of creating the obstruction and whether the obstruction arises from his acts alone or from his acts and the acts of others; or

(2) disobeys a reasonable request or order to move issued by a person the actor knows to be or is informed is a peace officer, a fireman, or a person with authority to control the use of the premises:

(A) to prevent obstruction of a highway or any of those areas mentioned in Subdivision (1); or

(B) to maintain public safety by dispersing those gathered in dangerous proximity to a fire, riot, or other hazard.

(b) For purposes of this section, "obstruct" means to render impassable or to render passage unreasonably inconvenient or hazardous.

(c) An offense under this section is a Class B misdemeanor.

(Enacted by Acts 1973, 63rd Leg., ch. 399 (S.B. 34), § 1, effective January 1, 1974; am. Acts 1993, 73rd Leg., ch. 900 (S.B. 1067), § 1.01, effective September 1, 1994.)

### Sec. 42.04.  Defense When Conduct Consists of Speech or Other Expression.

(a) If conduct that would otherwise violate Section 42.01(a)(5) (Unreasonable Noise), 42.03 (Obstructing Passageway), or 42.055 (Funeral Service Disruptions) consists of speech or other communication, of gathering with others to hear or observe such speech or communication, or of gathering with others to picket or otherwise express in a nonviolent manner a position on social, economic, political, or religious questions, the actor must be ordered to move, disperse, or otherwise remedy the violation prior to his arrest if he has not yet intentionally harmed the interests of others which those sections seek to protect.

(b) The order required by this section may be given by a peace officer, a fireman, a person with authority to control the use of the premises, or any person directly affected by the violation.

(c) It is a defense to prosecution under Section 42.01(a)(5), 42.03, or 42.055:

(1) that in circumstances in which this section requires an order no order was given;

(2) that an order, if given, was manifestly unreasonable in scope; or

(3) that an order, if given, was promptly obeyed.

(Enacted by Acts 1973, 63rd Leg., ch. 399 (S.B. 34), § 1, effective January 1, 1974; am. Acts 1993, 73rd Leg., ch. 900 (S.B. 1067), § 1.01, effective September 1, 1994; am. Acts 2006, 79th Leg., 3rd C.S., ch. 2 (H.B. 97), § 2, effective May 19, 2006.)

## Sec. 42.05. Disrupting Meeting or Procession.

(a) A person commits an offense if, with intent to prevent or disrupt a lawful meeting, procession, or gathering, he obstructs or interferes with the meeting, procession, or gathering by physical action or verbal utterance.

(b) An offense under this section is a Class B misdemeanor.

(Enacted by Acts 1973, 63rd Leg., ch. 399 (S.B. 34), § 1, effective January 1, 1974; am. Acts 1993, 73rd Leg., ch. 900 (S.B. 1067), § 1.01, effective September 1, 1994.)

## Sec. 42.055. Funeral Service Disruptions.

(a) In this section:

(1) "Facility" means a building at which any portion of a funeral service takes place, including a funeral parlor, mortuary, private home, or established place of worship.

(2) "Funeral service" means a ceremony, procession, or memorial service, including a wake or viewing, held in connection with the burial or cremation of the dead.

(3) "Picketing" means:

(A) standing, sitting, or repeated walking, riding, driving, or other similar action by a person displaying or carrying a banner, placard, or sign;

(B) engaging in loud singing, chanting, whistling, or yelling, with or without noise amplification through a device such as a bullhorn or microphone; or

(C) blocking access to a facility or cemetery being used for a funeral service.

(b) A person commits an offense if, during the period beginning three hours before the service begins and ending three hours after the service is completed, the person engages in picketing within 1,000 feet of a facility or cemetery being used for a funeral service.

(c) An offense under this section is a Class B misdemeanor.

(Enacted by Acts 2006, 79th Leg., 3rd C.S., ch. 2 (H.B. 97), § 1, effective May 19, 2006; am. Acts 2007, 80th Leg., ch. 256 (H.B. 1093), § 1, effective June 4, 2007; am. Acts 2011, 82nd Leg., ch. 716 (H.B. 718), § 1, effective September 1, 2011.)

## Sec. 42.06. False Alarm or Report.

(a) A person commits an offense if he knowingly initiates, communicates or circulates a report of a present, past, or future bombing, fire, offense, or other emergency that he knows is false or baseless and that would ordinarily:

(1) cause action by an official or volunteer agency organized to deal with emergencies;

(2) place a person in fear of imminent serious bodily injury; or

(3) prevent or interrupt the occupation of a building, room, place of assembly, place to which the public has access, or aircraft, automobile, or other mode of conveyance.

(b) An offense under this section is a Class A misdemeanor unless the false report is of an emergency involving a public primary or secondary school, public communications, public transportation, public water, gas, or power supply or other public service, in which event the offense is a state jail felony.

(Enacted by Acts 1973, 63rd Leg., ch. 399 (S.B. 34), § 1, effective January 1, 1974; am. Acts 1979, 66th Leg., ch. 530 (S.B. 952), § 4, effective August 27, 1979; am. Acts 1993, 73rd Leg., ch. 900 (S.B. 1067), § 1.01, effective September 1, 1994.)

## Sec. 42.061. Silent or Abusive Calls to 9-1-1 Service.

(a) In this section "9-1-1 service" and "public safety answering point" or "PSAP" have the meanings assigned by Section 772.001, Health and Safety Code.

(b) A person commits an offense if the person makes a telephone call to 9-1-1 when there is not an emergency and knowingly or intentionally:

(1) remains silent; or

(2) makes abusive or harassing statements to a PSAP employee.

(c) A person commits an offense if the person knowingly permits a telephone under the person's control to be used by another person in a manner described in Subsection (b).

(d) An offense under this section is a Class B misdemeanor.

(Enacted by Acts 1989, 71st Leg., ch. 582 (H.B. 2489), § 1, effective September 1, 1989; am. Acts 1991, 72nd Leg., ch. 14 (S.B. 404), § 284(2), effective September 1, 1991; am. Acts 1993, 73rd Leg., ch. 900 (S.B. 1067), § 1.01, effective September 1, 1994.)

## Sec. 42.062. Interference with Emergency Telephone Call.

(a) An individual commits an offense if the individual knowingly prevents or interferes with another individual's ability to place an emergency telephone call or to request assistance in an emergency from a law enforcement agency, medical facility, or other agency or entity the primary purpose of which is to provide for the safety of individuals.

(b) An individual commits an offense if the individual recklessly renders unusable a telephone that would otherwise be used by another individual to place an emergency telephone call or to request assistance in an emergency from a law enforcement agency, medical facility, or other agency or entity the primary purpose of which is to provide for the safety of individuals.

(c) An offense under this section is a Class A misdemeanor, except that the offense is a state jail felony if the actor has previously been convicted under this section.

(d) In this section, "emergency" means a condition or circumstance in which any individual is or is reasonably believed by the individual making a telephone call to be in fear of imminent assault or in which property is or is reasonably believed by the individual making the telephone call to be in imminent danger of damage or destruction.

(Enacted by Acts 2001, 77th Leg., ch. 690 (S.B. 18), § 1, effective September 1, 2001; am. Acts 2003, 78th Leg., ch. 460 (H.B. 778), § 1, effective September 1, 2003; am. Acts 2003, 78th Leg., ch. 1164 (S.B. 176), § 1, effective September 1, 2003.)

## Sec. 42.07. Harassment.

(a) A person commits an offense if, with intent to harass, annoy, alarm, abuse, torment, or embarrass another, he:

(1) initiates communication by telephone, in writing, or by electronic communication and in the course of the communication makes a comment, request, suggestion, or proposal that is obscene;

(2) threatens, by telephone, in writing, or by electronic communication, in a manner reasonably likely to alarm the person receiving the threat, to inflict bodily injury on the person or to commit a felony against the person, a member of his family or household, or his property;

(3) conveys, in a manner reasonably likely to alarm the person receiving the report, a false report, which is known by the conveyor to be false, that another person has suffered death or serious bodily injury;

(4) causes the telephone of another to ring repeatedly or makes repeated telephone communications anonymously or in a manner reasonably likely to harass, annoy, alarm, abuse, torment, embarrass, or offend another;

(5) makes a telephone call and intentionally fails to hang up or disengage the connection;

(6) knowingly permits a telephone under the person's control to be used by another to commit an offense under this section; or

(7) sends repeated electronic communications in a manner reasonably likely to harass, annoy, alarm, abuse, torment, embarrass, or offend another.

(b) In this section:

(1) "Electronic communication" means a transfer of signs, signals, writing, images, sounds, data, or intelligence of any nature transmitted in whole or in part by a wire, radio, electromagnetic, photoelectronic, or photo-optical system. The term includes:

(A) a communication initiated by electronic mail, instant message, network call, or facsimile machine; and

(B) a communication made to a pager.

(2) "Family" and "household" have the meaning assigned by Chapter 71, Family Code.

(3) "Obscene" means containing a patently offensive description of or a solicitation to commit an ultimate sex act, including sexual intercourse, masturbation, cunnilingus, fellatio, or anilingus, or a description of an excretory function.

(c) An offense under this section is a Class B misdemeanor, except that the offense is a Class A misdemeanor if the actor has previously been convicted under this section.

(Enacted by Acts 1973, 63rd Leg., ch. 399 (S.B. 34), § 1, effective January 1, 1974; am. Acts 1983, 68th Leg., ch. 411 (H.B. 838), § 1, effective September 1, 1983; am. Acts 1993, 73rd Leg., ch. 10 (S.B. 25), § 1, effective March 19, 1993; am. Acts 1993, 73rd Leg., ch. 900 (S.B. 1067), § 1.01, effective September 1, 1994; am. Acts 1995, 74th Leg., ch. 657 (S.B. 126), § 1, effective June 14, 1995; am. Acts 1999, 76th Leg., ch. 62 (S.B. 1368), § 15.02(d), effective September 1, 1999; am. Acts 2001, 77th Leg., ch. 1222 (S.B. 139), § 1, effective September 1, 2001.)

### STATUTORY NOTES

**Editor's notes.** — Subsection (a)(7) was declared unconstitutional by *Karenev v. State*, 258 S.W.3d 210, 2008 Tex. App. LEXIS 2407 (Tex. App.—Fort Worth 2008, pet. granted).

## Sec. 42.071. Stalking [Repealed].

Repealed by Acts 1997, 75th Leg., ch. 1 (S.B. 97), § 10, effective January 28, 1997.

(Enacted by Acts 1995, 74th Leg., ch. 657 (S.B. 126), § 2, effective June 14, 1995.)

## Sec. 42.072. Stalking.

(a) A person commits an offense if the person, on more than one occasion and pursuant to the same scheme or course of conduct that is directed specifically at another person, knowingly engages in conduct that:

(1) the actor knows or reasonably believes the other person will regard as threatening:

(A) bodily injury or death for the other person;

(B) bodily injury or death for a member of the other person's family or household or for an individual with whom the other person has a dating relationship; or

(C) that an offense will be committed against the other person's property;

(2) causes the other person, a member of the other person's family or household, or an individual with whom the other person has a dating relationship to be placed in fear of bodily injury or death or fear that an offense will be committed against the other person's property; and

(3) would cause a reasonable person to fear:

(A) bodily injury or death for himself or herself;

(B) bodily injury or death for a member of the person's family or household or for an individual with whom the person has a dating relationship; or

(C) that an offense will be committed against the person's property.

(b) An offense under this section is a felony of the third degree, except that the offense is a felony of the second degree if the actor has previously been convicted of an offense under this section or of an offense under any of the following laws that contains elements that are substantially similar to the elements of an offense under this section:

(1) the laws of another state;

(2) the laws of a federally recognized Indian tribe;

(3) the laws of a territory of the United States; or

(4) federal law.

(c) For purposes of this section, a trier of fact may find that different types of conduct described by Subsection (a), if engaged in on more than one occasion, constitute conduct that is engaged in pursuant to the same scheme or course of conduct.

(d) In this section, "dating relationship," "family," "household," and "member of a household" have the meanings assigned by Chapter 71, Family Code.

(Enacted by Acts 1997, 75th Leg., ch. 1 (S.B. 97), § 1, effective January 28, 1997; am. Acts 1999, 76th Leg., ch. 62 (S.B. 1368), § 15.02(e), effective September 1, 1999; am. Acts 2001, 77th Leg., ch. 1222 (S.B. 139), § 2, effective September 1, 2001; am. Acts 2011, 82nd Leg., ch. 591 (S.B. 82), § 1, effective September 1, 2011.)

## Sec. 42.08. Abuse of Corpse.

(a) A person commits an offense if the person, without legal authority, knowingly:

(1) disinters, disturbs, damages, dissects, in whole or in part, carries away, or treats in an offensive manner a human corpse;

(2) conceals a human corpse knowing it to be illegally disinterred;

(3) sells or buys a human corpse or in any way traffics in a human corpse;

(4) transmits or conveys, or procures to be transmitted or conveyed, a human corpse to a place outside the state; or

(5) vandalizes, damages, or treats in an offensive manner the space in which a human corpse has been interred or otherwise permanently laid to rest.

(b) An offense under this section is a Class A misdemeanor.

(c) In this section, "human corpse" includes:

(1) any portion of a human corpse;

(2) the cremated remains of a human corpse; or

(3) any portion of the cremated remains of a human corpse.

(d) If conduct constituting an offense under this section also constitutes an offense under another section of this code, the actor may be prosecuted under either section or both sections.

(e) It is a defense to prosecution under this section that the actor:

(1) as a member or agent of a cemetery organization, removed or damaged anything that had been placed in or on any portion of the organization's cemetery in violation of the rules of the organization; or

(2) removed anything:

(A) placed in the cemetery in violation of the rules of the cemetery organization; or

(B) placed in the cemetery by or with the cemetery organization's consent but that, in the organization's judgment, had become wrecked, unsightly, or dilapidated.

(f) In this section, "cemetery" and "cemetery organization" have the meanings assigned by Section 711.001, Health and Safety Code.
(Enacted by Acts 1973, 63rd Leg., ch. 399 (S.B. 34), § 1, effective January 1, 1974; am. Acts 1993, 73rd Leg., ch. 900 (S.B. 1067), § 1.01, effective September 1, 1994 (renumbered from Sec. 42.10); am. Acts 2005, 79th Leg., ch. 1025 (H.B. 1012), § 1, effective June 18, 2005.)

## Sec. 42.09.   Cruelty to Livestock Animals.

(a) A person commits an offense if the person intentionally or knowingly:

(1) tortures a livestock animal;

(2) fails unreasonably to provide necessary food, water, or care for a livestock animal in the person's custody;

(3) abandons unreasonably a livestock animal in the person's custody;

(4) transports or confines a livestock animal in a cruel and unusual manner;

(5) administers poison to a livestock animal, other than cattle, horses, sheep, swine, or goats, belonging to another without legal authority or the owner's effective consent;

(6) causes one livestock animal to fight with another livestock animal or with an animal as defined by Section 42.092;

(7) uses a live livestock animal as a lure in dog race training or in dog coursing on a racetrack;

(8) trips a horse; or

(9) seriously overworks a livestock animal.

(b) In this section:

(1) "Abandon" includes abandoning a livestock animal in the person's custody without making reasonable arrangements for assumption of custody by another person.

(2) "Cruel manner" includes a manner that causes or permits unjustified or unwarranted pain or suffering.

(3) "Custody" includes responsibility for the health, safety, and welfare of a livestock animal subject to the person's care and control, regardless of ownership of the livestock animal.

(4) "Depredation" has the meaning assigned by Section 71.001, Parks and Wildlife Code.

(5) "Livestock animal" means:

(A) cattle, sheep, swine, goats, ratites, or poultry commonly raised for human consumption;

(B) a horse, pony, mule, donkey, or hinny;

(C) native or nonnative hoofstock raised under agriculture practices; or

(D) native or nonnative fowl commonly raised under agricultural practices.

(6) "Necessary food, water, or care" includes food, water, or care provided to the extent required to maintain the livestock animal in a state of good health.

(7) "Torture" includes any act that causes unjustifiable pain or suffering.

(8) "Trip" means to use an object to cause a horse to fall or lose its balance.

(c) An offense under Subsection (a)(2), (3), (4), or (9) is a Class A misdemeanor, except that the offense is a state jail felony if the person has previously been convicted two times under this section, two times under Section 42.092, or one time under this section and one time under Section 42.092. An offense under Subsection (a)(1), (5), (6), (7), or (8) is a state jail felony, except that the offense is a felony of the third degree if the person has previously been convicted two times under this section, two times under Section 42.092, or one time under this section and one time under Section 42.092.

(d) It is a defense to prosecution under Subsection (a)(8) that the actor tripped the horse for the purpose of identifying the ownership of the horse or giving veterinary care to the horse.

(e) It is a defense to prosecution for an offense under this section that the actor was engaged in bona fide experimentation for scientific research.

(f) It is an exception to the application of this section that the conduct engaged in by the actor is a generally accepted and otherwise lawful:

(1) form of conduct occurring solely for the purpose of or in support of:

  (A) fishing, hunting, or trapping; or

  (B) wildlife management, wildlife or depredation control, or shooting preserve practices as regulated by state and federal law; or

(2) animal husbandry or agriculture practice involving livestock animals.

(g) This section does not create a civil cause of action for damages or enforcement of this section. (Enacted by Acts 1973, 63rd Leg., ch. 399 (S.B. 34), § 1, effective January 1, 1974; am. Acts 1975, 64th Leg., ch. 342 (S.B. 127), § 12, effective September 1, 1975; am. Acts 1985, 69th Leg., ch. 549 (H.B. 1912), § 1, September 1, 1985; am. Acts 1991, 72nd Leg., ch. 78 (S.B. 17), § 1, effective August 26, 1991; am. Acts 1993, 73rd Leg., ch. 900 (S.B. 1067), § 1.01, effective September 1, 1994 (renumbered from Sec. 42.11); am. Acts 1995, 74th Leg., ch. 318 (S.B. 15), § 15, effective September 1, 1995; am. Acts 1997, 75th Leg., ch. 1283 (S.B. 143), § 1, effective September 1, 1997; am. Acts 2001, 77th Leg., ch. 54 (H.B. 1362), § 3, effective September 1, 2001; am. Acts 2001, 77th Leg., ch. 450 (S.B. 653), § 1, effective September 1, 2001; am. Acts 2003, 78th Leg., ch. 1275 (H.B. 3506), § 2(116), effective September 1, 2003; am. Acts 2007, 80th Leg., ch. 886 (H.B. 2328), § 1, effective September 1, 2007.)

## Sec. 42.091. Attack on Assistance Animal.

(a) A person commits an offense if the person intentionally, knowingly, or recklessly attacks, injures, or kills an assistance animal.

(b) A person commits an offense if the person intentionally, knowingly, or recklessly incites or permits an animal owned by or otherwise in the custody of the actor to attack, injure, or kill an assistance animal and, as a result of the person's conduct, the assistance animal is attacked, injured, or killed.

(c) An offense under this section is a:

(1) Class A misdemeanor if the actor or an animal owned by or otherwise in the custody of the actor attacks an assistance animal;

(2) state jail felony if the actor or an animal owned by or otherwise in the custody of the actor injures an assistance animal; or

(3) felony of the third degree if the actor or an animal owned by or otherwise in the custody of the actor kills an assistance animal.

(d) A court shall order a defendant convicted of an offense under Subsection (a) to make restitution to the owner of the assistance animal for:

(1) related veterinary or medical bills;

(2) the cost of:

  (A) replacing the assistance animal; or

  (B) retraining an injured assistance animal by an organization generally recognized by agencies involved in the rehabilitation of persons with disabilities as reputable and competent to provide special equipment for or special training to an animal to help a person with a disability; and

(3) any other expense reasonably incurred as a result of the offense.

(e) In this section:

(1) "Assistance animal" has the meaning assigned by Section 121.002, Human Resources Code.

(2) "Custody" has the meaning assigned by Section 42.09.

(Enacted by Acts 2003, 78th Leg., ch. 710 (H.B. 2881), § 2, effective September 1, 2003.)

## Sec. 42.092. Cruelty to Nonlivestock Animals.

(a) In this section:

(1) "Abandon" includes abandoning an animal in the person's custody without making reasonable arrangements for assumption of custody by another person.

(2) "Animal" means a domesticated living creature, including any stray or feral cat or dog, and a wild living creature previously captured. The term does not include an uncaptured wild living creature or a livestock animal.

(3) "Cruel manner" includes a manner that causes or permits unjustified or unwarranted pain or suffering.

(4) "Custody" includes responsibility for the health, safety, and welfare of an animal subject to the person's care and control, regardless of ownership of the animal.

(5) "Depredation" has the meaning assigned by Section 71.001, Parks and Wildlife Code.

(6) "Livestock animal" has the meaning assigned by Section 42.09.

(7) "Necessary food, water, care, or shelter" includes food, water, care, or shelter provided to the extent required to maintain the animal in a state of good health.

(8) "Torture" includes any act that causes unjustifiable pain or suffering.

(b) A person commits an offense if the person intentionally, knowingly, or recklessly:

(1) tortures an animal or in a cruel manner kills or causes serious bodily injury to an animal;

(2) without the owner's effective consent, kills, administers poison to, or causes serious bodily injury to an animal;

(3) fails unreasonably to provide necessary food, water, care, or shelter for an animal in the person's custody;

(4) abandons unreasonably an animal in the person's custody;

(5) transports or confines an animal in a cruel manner;

(6) without the owner's effective consent, causes bodily injury to an animal;

(7) causes one animal to fight with another animal, if either animal is not a dog;

(8) uses a live animal as a lure in dog race training or in dog coursing on a racetrack; or

(9) seriously overworks an animal.

(c) An offense under Subsection (b)(3), (4), (5), (6), or (9) is a Class A misdemeanor, except that the offense is a state jail felony if the person has previously been convicted two times under this section, two times under Section 42.09, or one time under this section and one time under Section 42.09. An offense under Subsection (b)(1), (2), (7), or (8) is a state jail felony, except that the offense is a felony of the third degree if the person has previously been convicted two times under this section, two times under Section 42.09, or one time under this section and one time under Section 42.09.

(d) It is a defense to prosecution under this section that:

(1) the actor had a reasonable fear of bodily injury to the actor or to another person by a dangerous wild animal as defined by Section 822.101, Health and Safety Code; or

(2) the actor was engaged in bona fide experimentation for scientific research.

(e) It is a defense to prosecution under Subsection (b)(2) or (6) that:

(1) the animal was discovered on the person's property in the act of or after injuring or killing the person's livestock animals or damaging the person's crops and that the person killed or injured the animal at the time of this discovery; or

(2) the person killed or injured the animal within the scope of the person's employment as a public servant or in furtherance of activities or operations associated with electricity transmission or distribution, electricity generation or operations associated with the generation of electricity, or natural gas delivery.

(f) It is an exception to the application of this section that the conduct engaged in by the actor is a generally accepted and otherwise lawful:

(1) form of conduct occurring solely for the purpose of or in support of:

(A) fishing, hunting, or trapping; or

(B) wildlife management, wildlife or depredation control, or shooting preserve practices as regulated by state and federal law; or

(2) animal husbandry or agriculture practice involving livestock animals.

(g) This section does not create a civil cause of action for damages or enforcement of the section. (Enacted by Acts 2007, 80th Leg., ch. 886 (H.B. 2328), § 2, effective September 1, 2007.)

## Sec. 42.10. Dog Fighting.

(a) A person commits an offense if the person intentionally or knowingly:

(1) causes a dog to fight with another dog;

(2) participates in the earnings of or operates a facility used for dog fighting;

(3) uses or permits another to use any real estate, building, room, tent, arena, or other property for dog fighting;

(4) owns or possesses dog-fighting equipment with the intent that the equipment be used to train a dog for dog fighting or in furtherance of dog fighting;

(5) owns or trains a dog with the intent that the dog be used in an exhibition of dog fighting; or

(6) attends as a spectator an exhibition of dog fighting.

(b) In this section:

(1) "Dog fighting" means any situation in which one dog attacks or fights with another dog.

(2) "Dog-fighting equipment" has the meaning assigned by Article 18.18(g), Code of Criminal Procedure.

(c) A conviction under Subsection (a)(2) or (3) may be had upon the uncorroborated testimony of a party to the offense.

(d) It is a defense to prosecution under Subsection (a)(1) that the actor caused a dog to fight with another dog to protect livestock, other property, or a person from the other dog, and for no other purpose.

(e) An offense under Subsection (a)(4), (5), or (6) is a Class A misdemeanor. An offense under Subsection (a)(1), (2), or (3) is a state jail felony. (Enacted by Acts 1983, 68th Leg., ch. 305 (S.B. 557), § 1, effective September 1, 1983; am. Acts 1993, 73rd Leg., ch. 900 (S.B. 1067), § 1.01, effective September 1, 1994 (renumbered from Sec. 42.111); am. Acts 2007, 80th Leg., ch. 644

(H.B. 916), § 1, effective September 1, 2007; am. Acts 2009, 81st Leg., ch. 1357 (S.B. 554), § 1, effective September 1, 2009.)

## Sec. 42.105. Cockfighting.

(a) In this section:

(1) "Bridle" means a leather device designed to fit over the head and beak of a cock to prevent the cock from injuring another cock.

(2) "Cock" means the male of any type of domestic fowl.

(3) "Cockfighting" means any situation in which one cock attacks or fights with another cock.

(4) "Gaff" means an artificial steel spur designed to attach to the leg of a cock to replace or supplement the cock's natural spur.

(5) "Slasher" means a steel weapon resembling a curved knife blade designed to attach to the foot of a cock.

(b) A person commits an offense if the person knowingly:

(1) causes a cock to fight with another cock;

(2) participates in the earnings of a cockfight;

(3) uses or permits another to use any real estate, building, room, tent, arena, or other property for cockfighting;

(4) owns or trains a cock with the intent that the cock be used in an exhibition of cockfighting;

(5) manufactures, buys, sells, barters, exchanges, possesses, advertises, or otherwise offers a gaff, slasher, or other sharp implement designed for attachment to a cock with the intent that the implement be used in cockfighting; or

(6) attends as a spectator an exhibition of cockfighting.

(c) It is an affirmative defense to prosecution under this section that the actor's conduct:

(1) occurred solely for the purpose of or in support of breeding cocks for poultry shows in which a cock is judged by the cock's physical appearance; or

(2) was incidental to collecting bridles, gaffs, or slashers.

(d) An affirmative defense to prosecution is not available under Subsection (c) if evidence shows that the actor is also engaging in use of the cocks for cockfighting.

(e) It is a defense to prosecution for an offense under this section that:

(1) the actor was engaged in bona fide experimentation for scientific research; or

(2) the conduct engaged in by the actor is a generally accepted and otherwise lawful animal husbandry or agriculture practice involving livestock animals.

(f) It is an exception to the application of Subsection (b)(6) that the actor is 15 years of age or younger at the time of the offense.

(g) An offense under Subsection (b)(1) or (2) is a state jail felony. An offense under Subsection (b)(3), (4), or (5) is a Class A misdemeanor. An offense under Subsection (b)(6) is a Class C misdemeanor, except that the offense is a Class A misdemeanor if it is shown on the trial of the offense that the person has been previously convicted of an offense under that subdivision.
(Enacted by Acts 2011, 82nd Leg., ch. 952 (H.B. 1043), § 1, effective September 1, 2011.)

## Sec. 42.11. Destruction of Flag.

(a) A person commits an offense if the person intentionally or knowingly damages, defaces, mutilates, or burns the flag of the United States or the State of Texas.

(b) In this section, "flag" means an emblem, banner, or other standard or a copy of an emblem, standard, or banner that is an official or commonly recognized depiction of the flag of the United States or of this state and is capable of being flown from a staff of any character or size. The term does not include a representation of a flag on a written or printed document, a periodical, stationery, a painting or photograph, or an article of clothing or jewelry.

(c) It is an exception to the application of this section that the act that would otherwise constitute an offense is done in conformity with statutes of the United States or of this state relating to the proper disposal of damaged flags.

(d) An offense under this section is a Class A misdemeanor.
(Enacted by Acts 1989, 71st Leg., 1st C.S., ch. 27 (S.B. 80), § 1, effective September 1, 1989; am. Acts 1993, 73rd Leg., ch. 900 (S.B. 1067), § 1.01, effective September 1, 1994 (renumbered from Sec. 42.14).)

## Sec. 42.111. Dog Fighting [Renumbered].

Renumbered to Tex. Penal Code § 42.10 by Acts 1993, 73rd Leg., ch. 900 (S.B. 1067), § 1.01, effective September 1, 1994.

## Sec. 42.12. Discharge of Firearm in Certain Municipalities.

(a) A person commits an offense if the person recklessly discharges a firearm inside the corporate limits of a municipality having a population of 100,000 or more.

(b) An offense under this section is a Class A misdemeanor.

(c) If conduct constituting an offense under this section also constitutes an offense under another section of this code, the person may be prosecuted under either section.

(d) Subsection (a) does not affect the authority of a municipality to enact an ordinance which prohibits the discharge of a firearm.

(Enacted by Acts 1995, 74th Leg., ch. 663 (S.B. 68), § 1, effective September 1, 1995.)

### Sec. 42.13.  Use of Laser Pointers.

(a) A person commits an offense if the person knowingly directs a light from a laser pointer at a uniformed safety officer, including a peace officer, security guard, firefighter, emergency medical service worker, or other uniformed municipal, state, or federal officer.

(b) In this section, "laser pointer" means a device that emits a visible light amplified by the stimulated emission of radiation.

(c) An offense under this section is a Class C misdemeanor.

(Enacted by Acts 2003, 78th Leg., ch. 467 (H.B. 831), § 1, effective September 1, 2003.)

### Sec. 42.14.  Illumination of Aircraft by Intense Light.

(a) A person commits an offense if:

(1) the person intentionally directs a light from a laser pointer or other light source at an aircraft; and

(2) the light has an intensity sufficient to impair the operator's ability to control the aircraft.

(b) It is an affirmative defense to prosecution under this section that the actor was using the light to send an emergency distress signal.

(c) An offense under this section is a Class C misdemeanor unless the intensity of the light impairs the operator's ability to control the aircraft, in which event the offense is a Class A misdemeanor.

(d) If conduct that constitutes an offense under this section also constitutes an offense under any other law, the actor may be prosecuted under this section or the other law.

(e) In this section, "laser pointer" has the meaning assigned by Section 42.13.

(Enacted by Acts 2007, 80th Leg., ch. 680 (H.B. 1586), § 1, effective September 1, 2007.)

# CHAPTER 43
# PUBLIC INDECENCY

### Subchapter A. Prostitution

## *SUBCHAPTER A*
## *PROSTITUTION*

### Sec. 43.01.  Definitions.

In this subchapter:

(1) "Deviate sexual intercourse" means any contact between the genitals of one person and the mouth or anus of another person.

(2) "Prostitution" means the offense defined in Section 43.02.

(3) "Sexual contact" means any touching of the anus, breast, or any part of the genitals of another person with intent to arouse or gratify the sexual desire of any person.

(4) "Sexual conduct" includes deviate sexual intercourse, sexual contact, and sexual intercourse.

(5) "Sexual intercourse" means any penetration of the female sex organ by the male sex organ.

(Enacted by Acts 1973, 63rd Leg., ch. 399 (S.B. 34), § 1, effective January 1, 1974; am. Acts 1979, 66th Leg., ch. 168 (H.B. 43), § 2, effective August 27, 1979; am. Acts 1993, 73rd Leg., ch. 900 (S.B. 1067), § 1.01, effective September 1, 1994.)

### Sec. 43.02.  Prostitution.

(a) A person commits an offense if he knowingly:

(1) offers to engage, agrees to engage, or engages in sexual conduct for a fee; or

(2) solicits another in a public place to engage with him in sexual conduct for hire.

(b) An offense is established under Subsection (a)(1) whether the actor is to receive or pay a fee. An offense is established under Subsection (a)(2) whether the actor solicits a person to hire him or offers to hire the person solicited.

(c) An offense under this section is a Class B misdemeanor, except that the offense is:

(1) a Class A misdemeanor if the actor has previously been convicted one or two times of an offense under this section;

(2) a state jail felony if the actor has previously been convicted three or more times of an offense under this section;

(3) a felony of the third degree if the person solicited is 14 years of age or older and younger than 18 years of age; or

(4) a felony of the second degree if the person solicited is younger than 14 years of age.

(d) It is a defense to prosecution under this section that the actor engaged in the conduct that constitutes the offense because the actor was the victim of conduct that constitutes an offense under Section 20A.02.

(Enacted by Acts 1973, 63rd Leg., ch. 399 (S.B. 34), § 1, effective January 1, 1974; am. Acts 1977, 65th Leg., ch. 286 (H.B. 678), § 1, effective May 27, 1977; am. Acts 1993, 73rd Leg., ch. 900 (S.B. 1067), § 1.01, effective September 1, 1994; am. Acts 2001, 77th Leg., ch. 987 (H.B. 460), § 1, effective September 1, 2001; am. Acts 2009, 81st Leg., ch. 1002 (H.B. 4009), § 8, effective September 1, 2009; am. Acts 2011, 82nd Leg., ch. 515 (H.B. 2014), § 4.02, effective September 1, 2011.)

## Sec. 43.03.  Promotion of Prostitution.

(a) A person commits an offense if, acting other than as a prostitute receiving compensation for personally rendered prostitution services, he or she knowingly:

(1) receives money or other property pursuant to an agreement to participate in the proceeds of prostitution; or

(2) solicits another to engage in sexual conduct with another person for compensation.

(b) An offense under this section is a Class A misdemeanor.

(Enacted by Acts 1973, 63rd Leg., ch. 399 (S.B. 34), § 1, effective January 1, 1974; am. Acts 1977, 65th Leg., ch. 287 (H.B. 679), § 1, effective May 27, 1977; am. Acts 1993, 73rd Leg., ch. 900 (S.B. 1067), § 1.01, effective September 1, 1994.)

## Sec. 43.04.  Aggravated Promotion of Prostitution.

(a) A person commits an offense if he knowingly owns, invests in, finances, controls, supervises, or manages a prostitution enterprise that uses two or more prostitutes.

(b) An offense under this section is a felony of the third degree.

(Enacted by Acts 1973, 63rd Leg., ch. 399 (S.B. 34), § 1, effective January 1, 1974; am. Acts 1993, 73rd Leg., ch. 900 (S.B. 1067), § 1.01, effective September 1, 1994.)

## Sec. 43.05.  Compelling Prostitution.

(a) A person commits an offense if the person knowingly:

(1) causes another by force, threat, or fraud to commit prostitution; or

(2) causes by any means a child younger than 18 years to commit prostitution, regardless of whether the actor knows the age of the child at the time the actor commits the offense.

(b) An offense under Subsection (a)(1) is a felony of the second degree. An offense under Subsection (a)(2) is a felony of the first degree.

(Enacted by Acts 1973, 63rd Leg., ch. 399 (S.B. 34), § 1, effective January 1, 1974; am. Acts 1993, 73rd Leg., ch. 900 (S.B. 1067), § 1.01, effective September 1, 1994; am. Acts 2009, 81st Leg., ch. 1002 (H.B. 4009), § 9, effective September 1, 2009; am. Acts 2011, 82nd Leg., ch. 1 (S.B. 24), § 1.03, effective September 1, 2011.)

## Sec. 43.06.  Accomplice Witness: Testimony and Immunity.

(a) A party to an offense under this subchapter may be required to furnish evidence or testify about the offense.

(b) A party to an offense under this subchapter may not be prosecuted for any offense about which he is required to furnish evidence or testify, and the evidence and testimony may not be used against the party in any adjudicatory proceeding except a prosecution for aggravated perjury.

(c) For purposes of this section, "adjudicatory proceeding" means a proceeding before a court or any other agency of government in which the legal rights, powers, duties, or privileges of specified parties are determined.

(d) A conviction under this subchapter may be had upon the uncorroborated testimony of a party to the offense.

(Enacted by Acts 1973, 63rd Leg., ch. 399 (S.B. 34), § 1, effective January 1, 1974; am. Acts 1993,

73rd Leg., ch. 900 (S.B. 1067), § 1.01, effective September 1, 1994.)

## Sec. 43.07. [Reserved for expansion].

### SUBCHAPTER B
### OBSCENITY

## Sec. 43.21.  Definitions.

(a) In this subchapter:

(1) "Obscene" means material or a performance that:

(A) the average person, applying contemporary community standards, would find that taken as a whole appeals to the prurient interest in sex;

(B) depicts or describes:

(i) patently offensive representations or descriptions of ultimate sexual acts, normal or perverted, actual or simulated, including sexual intercourse, sodomy, and sexual bestiality; or

(ii) patently offensive representations or descriptions of masturbation, excretory functions, sadism, masochism, lewd exhibition of the genitals, the male or female genitals in a state of sexual stimulation or arousal, covered male genitals in a discernibly turgid state or a device designed and marketed as useful primarily for stimulation of the human genital organs; and

(C) taken as a whole, lacks serious literary, artistic, political, and scientific value.

(2) "Material" means anything tangible that is capable of being used or adapted to arouse interest, whether through the medium of reading, observation, sound, or in any other manner, but does not include an actual three dimensional obscene device.

(3) "Performance" means a play, motion picture, dance, or other exhibition performed before an audience.

(4) "Patently offensive" means so offensive on its face as to affront current community standards of decency.

(5) "Promote" means to manufacture, issue, sell, give, provide, lend, mail, deliver, transfer, transmit, publish, distribute, circulate, disseminate, present, exhibit, or advertise, or to offer or agree to do the same.

(6) "Wholesale promote" means to manufacture, issue, sell, provide, mail, deliver, transfer, transmit, publish, distribute, circulate, disseminate, or to offer or agree to do the same for purpose of resale.

(7) "Obscene device" means a device including a dildo or artificial vagina, designed or marketed as useful primarily for the stimulation of human genital organs.

(b) If any of the depictions or descriptions of sexual conduct described in this section are declared by a court of competent jurisdiction to be unlawfully included herein, this declaration shall not invalidate this section as to other patently offensive sexual conduct included herein.

(Enacted by Acts 1973, 63rd Leg., ch. 399 (S.B. 34), § 1, effective January 1, 1974; am. Acts 1975, 64th Leg., ch. 163 (H.B. 589), § 1, effective September 1, 1975; am. Acts 1979, 66th Leg., ch. 778 (H.B. 1741), § 1, effective September 1, 1979; am. Acts 1993, 73rd Leg., ch. 900 (S.B. 1067), § 1.01, effective September 1, 1994.)

## Sec. 43.22.  Obscene Display or Distribution.

(a) A person commits an offense if he intentionally or knowingly displays or distributes an obscene photograph, drawing, or similar visual representation or other obscene material and is reckless about whether a person is present who will be offended or alarmed by the display or distribution.

(b) An offense under this section is a Class C misdemeanor.

(Enacted by Acts 1973, 63rd Leg., ch. 399 (S.B. 34), § 1, effective January 1, 1974; am. Acts 1993, 73rd Leg., ch. 900 (S.B. 1067), § 1.01, effective September 1, 1994.)

## Sec. 43.23.  Obscenity.

(a) A person commits an offense if, knowing its content and character, he wholesale promotes or possesses with intent to wholesale promote any obscene material or obscene device.

(b) Except as provided by Subsection (h), an offense under Subsection (a) is a state jail felony.

(c) A person commits an offense if, knowing its content and character, he:

(1) promotes or possesses with intent to promote any obscene material or obscene device; or

(2) produces, presents, or directs an obscene performance or participates in a portion thereof that is obscene or that contributes to its obscenity.

(d) Except as provided by Subsection (h), an offense under Subsection (c) is a Class A misdemeanor.

(e) A person who promotes or wholesale promotes obscene material or an obscene device or possesses the same with intent to promote or wholesale promote it in the course of his business is presumed to do so with knowledge of its content and character.

(f) A person who possesses six or more obscene devices or identical or similar obscene articles is presumed to possess them with intent to promote the same.

(g) It is an affirmative defense to prosecution under this section that the person who possesses or promotes material or a device proscribed by this section does so for a bona fide medical, psychiatric, judicial, legislative, or law enforcement purpose.

(h) The punishment for an offense under Subsection (a) is increased to the punishment for a felony of the third degree and the punishment for an offense under Subsection (c) is increased to the punishment for a state jail felony if it is shown on the trial of the offense that obscene material that is the subject of the offense visually depicts activities described by Section 43.21(a)(1)(B) engaged in by:

(1) a child younger than 18 years of age at the time the image of the child was made;

(2) an image that to a reasonable person would be virtually indistinguishable from the image of a child younger than 18 years of age; or

(3) an image created, adapted, or modified to be the image of an identifiable child.

(i) In this section, "identifiable child" means a person, recognizable as an actual person by the person's face, likeness, or other distinguishing characteristic, such as a unique birthmark or other recognizable feature:

(1) who was younger than 18 years of age at the time the visual depiction was created, adapted, or modified; or

(2) whose image as a person younger than 18 years of age was used in creating, adapting, or modifying the visual depiction.

(j) An attorney representing the state who seeks an increase in punishment under Subsection (h)(3) is not required to prove the actual identity of an identifiable child.

(Enacted by Acts 1973, 63rd Leg., ch. 399 (S.B. 34), § 1, effective January 1, 1974; am. Acts 1979, 66th Leg., ch. 778 (H.B. 1741), § 2, effective September 1, 1979; am. Acts 1993, 73rd Leg., ch. 900 (S.B. 1067), § 1.01, effective September 1, 1994; am. Acts 2003, 78th Leg., ch. 1005 (H.B. 236), § 1, effective September 1, 2003.)

## Sec. 43.24. Sale, Distribution, or Display of Harmful Material to Minor.

(a) For purposes of this section:

(1) "Minor" means an individual younger than 18 years.

(2) "Harmful material" means material whose dominant theme taken as a whole:

(A) appeals to the prurient interest of a minor, in sex, nudity, or excretion;

(B) is patently offensive to prevailing standards in the adult community as a whole with respect to what is suitable for minors; and

(C) is utterly without redeeming social value for minors.

(b) A person commits an offense if, knowing that the material is harmful:

(1) and knowing the person is a minor, he sells, distributes, exhibits, or possesses for sale, distribution, or exhibition to a minor harmful material;

(2) he displays harmful material and is reckless about whether a minor is present who will be offended or alarmed by the display; or

(3) he hires, employs, or uses a minor to do or accomplish or assist in doing or accomplishing any of the acts prohibited in Subsection (b)(1) or (b)(2).

(c) It is an affirmative defense to prosecution under this section that the sale, distribution, or exhibition was by a person having scientific, educational, governmental, or other similar justification.

(c-1) It is a defense to prosecution under this section that the actor was the spouse of the minor at the time of the offense.

(d) An offense under this section is a Class A misdemeanor unless it is committed under Subsection (b)(3) in which event it is a felony of the third degree.

(Enacted by Acts 1973, 63rd Leg., ch. 399 (S.B. 34), § 1, effective January 1, 1974; am. Acts 1993, 73rd Leg., ch. 900 (S.B. 1067), § 1.01, effective September 1, 1994; am. Acts 2011, 82nd Leg., ch. 497 (H.B. 1344), § 1, effective September 1, 2011.)

## Sec. 43.25. Sexual Performance by a Child.

(a) In this section:

(1) "Sexual performance" means any performance or part thereof that includes sexual conduct by a child younger than 18 years of age.

(2) "Sexual conduct" means sexual contact, actual or simulated sexual intercourse, deviate sexual intercourse, sexual bestiality, masturbation, sado-masochistic abuse, or lewd exhibition of the genitals, the anus, or any portion of the female breast below the top of the areola.

(3) "Performance" means any play, motion picture, photograph, dance, or other visual representation that can be exhibited before an audience of one or more persons.

(4) "Produce" with respect to a sexual performance includes any conduct that directly contributes to the creation or manufacture of the sexual performance.

(5) "Promote" means to procure, manufacture, issue, sell, give, provide, lend, mail, deliver, transfer, transmit, publish, distribute, circulate, disseminate, present, exhibit, or advertise or to offer or agree to do any of the above.

(6) "Simulated" means the explicit depiction of sexual conduct that creates the appearance of actual sexual conduct and during which a person engaging in the conduct exhibits any uncovered portion of the breasts, genitals, or buttocks.

(7) "Deviate sexual intercourse" and "sexual contact" have the meanings assigned by Section 43.01.

(b) A person commits an offense if, knowing the character and content thereof, he employs, authorizes, or induces a child younger than 18 years of age to engage in sexual conduct or a sexual performance. A parent or legal guardian or custodian of a child younger than 18 years of age commits an offense if he consents to the participation by the child in a sexual performance.

(c) An offense under Subsection (b) is a felony of the second degree, except that the offense is a felony of the first degree if the victim is younger than 14 years of age at the time the offense is committed.

(d) A person commits an offense if, knowing the character and content of the material, he produces, directs, or promotes a performance that includes sexual conduct by a child younger than 18 years of age.

(e) An offense under Subsection (d) is a felony of the third degree, except that the offense is a felony of the second degree if the victim is younger than 14 years of age at the time the offense is committed.

(f) It is an affirmative defense to a prosecution under this section that:

(1) the defendant was the spouse of the child at the time of the offense;

(2) the conduct was for a bona fide educational, medical, psychological, psychiatric, judicial, law enforcement, or legislative purpose; or

(3) the defendant is not more than two years older than the child.

(g) When it becomes necessary for the purposes of this section or Section 43.26 to determine whether a child who participated in sexual conduct was younger than 18 years of age, the court or jury may make this determination by any of the following methods:

(1) personal inspection of the child;

(2) inspection of the photograph or motion picture that shows the child engaging in the sexual performance;

(3) oral testimony by a witness to the sexual performance as to the age of the child based on the child's appearance at the time;

(4) expert medical testimony based on the appearance of the child engaging in the sexual performance; or

(5) any other method authorized by law or by the rules of evidence at common law.

(Enacted by Acts 1977, 65th Leg., ch. 381 (H.B. 1269), § 1, effective June 10, 1977; am. Acts 1979, 66th Leg., ch. 779 (H.B. 1742), § 1, effective September 1, 1979; am. Acts 1985, 69th Leg., ch. 530 (H.B. 626), § 1, effective September 1, 1985; am. Acts 1993, 73rd Leg., ch. 900 (S.B. 1067), § 1.01, effective September 1, 1994; am. Acts 1999, 76th Leg., ch. 1415 (H.B. 2145), § 22(b), effective September 1, 1999; am. Acts 2003, 78th Leg., ch. 1005 (H.B. 236), §§ 4, 5, effective September 1, 2003; am. Acts 2007, 80th Leg., ch. 593 (H.B. 8), § 1.20, effective September 1, 2007.)

## Sec. 43.251. Employment Harmful to Children.

(a) In this section:

(1) "Child" means a person younger than 18 years of age.

(2) "Massage" has the meaning assigned to the term "massage therapy" by Section 455.001, Occupations Code.

(3) "Massage establishment" has the meaning assigned by Section 455.001, Occupations Code.

(4) "Nude" means a child who is:

(A) entirely unclothed; or

(B) clothed in a manner that leaves uncovered or visible through less than fully opaque clothing any portion of the breasts below the top of the areola of the breasts, if the child is female, or any portion of the genitals or buttocks.

(5) "Sexually oriented commercial activity" means a massage establishment, nude studio, modeling studio, love parlor, or other similar commercial enterprise the primary business of which is the offering of a service that is intended to provide sexual stimulation or sexual gratification to the customer.

(6) "Topless" means a female child clothed in a manner that leaves uncovered or visible through less than fully opaque clothing any portion of her breasts below the top of the areola.

(b) A person commits an offense if the person employs, authorizes, or induces a child to work:

(1) in a sexually oriented commercial activity; or

(2) in any place of business permitting, requesting, or requiring a child to work nude or topless.

(c) **[2 Versions: As amended by Acts 2011, 82nd Leg., ch. 515]** An offense under this section is a felony of the second degree, except that the offense is a felony of the first degree if the child is younger than 14 years of age at the time the offense is committed.

(c) **[2 Versions: As amended by Acts 2011, 82nd Leg., ch. 938]** An offense under this section is a Class A misdemeanor, except that the offense is:

(1) a state jail felony if it is shown on the trial of the offense that the defendant has been previously convicted one time of an offense under this section; and

(2) a felony of the third degree if it is shown on the trial of the offense that the defendant has been previously convicted two or more times of an offense under this section.

(Enacted by Acts 1987, 70th Leg., ch. 783 (H.B. 1904), § 1, effective August 31, 1987; am. Acts 1993, 73rd Leg., ch. 900 (S.B. 1067), § 1.01, effective September 1, 1994; am. Acts 2001, 77th Leg., ch. 1420 (H.B. 2812), § 14.832, effective September 1, 2001; am. Acts 2011, 82nd Leg., ch. 515 (H.B. 2014), § 4.03, effective September 1, 2011; am. Acts 2011, 82nd Leg., ch. 938 (H.B. 290), § 1, effective September 1, 2011.)

## Sec. 43.26. Possession or Promotion of Child Pornography.

(a) A person commits an offense if:

(1) the person knowingly or intentionally possesses visual material that visually depicts a child younger than 18 years of age at the time the image of the child was made who is engaging in sexual conduct; and

(2) the person knows that the material depicts the child as described by Subdivision (1).

(b) In this section:

(1) "Promote" has the meaning assigned by Section 43.25.

(2) "Sexual conduct" has the meaning assigned by Section 43.25.

(3) "Visual material" means:

(A) any film, photograph, videotape, negative, or slide or any photographic reproduction that contains or incorporates in any manner any film, photograph, videotape, negative, or slide; or

(B) any disk, diskette, or other physical medium that allows an image to be displayed on a computer or other video screen and any image transmitted to a computer or other video screen by telephone line, cable, satellite transmission, or other method.

(c) The affirmative defenses provided by Section 43.25(f) also apply to a prosecution under this section.

(d) An offense under Subsection (a) is a felony of the third degree.

(e) A person commits an offense if:

(1) the person knowingly or intentionally promotes or possesses with intent to promote material described by Subsection (a)(1); and

(2) the person knows that the material depicts the child as described by Subsection (a)(1).

(f) A person who possesses visual material that contains six or more identical visual depictions of a child as described by Subsection (a)(1) is presumed to possess the material with the intent to promote the material.

(g) An offense under Subsection (e) is a felony of the second degree.

(h) It is a defense to prosecution under Subsection (a) or (e) or that the actor is a law enforcement officer or a school administrator who:

(1) possessed the visual material in good faith solely as a result of an allegation of a violation of Section 43.261;

(2) allowed other law enforcement or school administrative personnel to access the material only as appropriate based on the allegation described by Subdivision (1); and

(3) took reasonable steps to destroy the material within an appropriate period following the allegation described by Subdivision (1).

(Enacted by Acts 1985, 69th Leg., ch. 530 (H.B. 626), § 2, effective September 1, 1985; am. Acts 1989, 71st Leg., ch. 361 (S.B. 1191), § 1, effective September 1, 1989; am. Acts 1989, 71st Leg., ch. 968 (H.B. 377), § 1, effective September 1, 1989; am. Acts 1993, 73rd Leg., ch. 900 (S.B. 1067), § 1.01, effective September 1, 1994; am. Acts 1995, 74th Leg., ch. 76 (S.B. 959), § 14.51, effective September 1, 1995; am. Acts 1997, 75th Leg., ch. 933 (S.B. 674), § 1, effective September 1, 1997; am. Acts 1999, 76th Leg., ch. 1415 (H.B. 2145), § 22(c), effective September 1, 1999; am. Acts 2011, 82nd Leg., ch. 1322 (S.B. 407), § 2, effective September 1, 2011.)

## Sec. 43.261. Electronic Transmission of Certain Visual Material Depicting Minor.

(a) In this section:

(1) "Dating relationship" has the meaning assigned by Section 71.0021, Family Code.

(2) "Minor" means a person younger than 18 years of age.

(3) "Produce" with respect to visual material includes any conduct that directly contributes to the creation or manufacture of the material.

(4) "Promote" has the meaning assigned by Section 43.25.

(5) "Sexual conduct" has the meaning assigned by Section 43.25.

(6) "Visual material" has the meaning assigned by Section 43.26.

(b) A person who is a minor commits an offense if the person intentionally or knowingly:

(1) by electronic means promotes to another minor visual material depicting a minor, including the actor, engaging in sexual conduct, if the actor produced the visual material or knows that another minor produced the visual material; or

(2) possesses in an electronic format visual material depicting another minor engaging in sexual conduct, if the actor produced the visual material or knows that another minor produced the visual material.

(c) An offense under Subsection (b)(1) is a Class C misdemeanor, except that the offense is:

(1) a Class B misdemeanor if it is shown on the trial of the offense that the actor:

(A) promoted the visual material with intent to harass, annoy, alarm, abuse, torment, embarrass, or offend another; or

(B) except as provided by Subdivision (2)(A), has previously been convicted one time of any offense under this section; or

(2) a Class A misdemeanor if it is shown on the trial of the offense that the actor has previously been:

(A) convicted one or more times of an offense punishable under Subdivision (1)(A); or

(B) convicted two or more times of any offense under this section.

(d) An offense under Subsection (b)(2) is a Class C misdemeanor, except that the offense is:

(1) a Class B misdemeanor if it is shown on the trial of the offense that the actor has previously been convicted one time of any offense under this section; or

(2) a Class A misdemeanor if it is shown on the trial of the offense that the actor has previously been convicted two or more times of any offense under this section.

(e) It is an affirmative defense to prosecution under this section that the visual material:

(1) depicted only the actor or another minor:

(A) who is not more than two years older or younger than the actor and with whom the actor had a dating relationship at the time of the offense; or

(B) who was the spouse of the actor at the time of the offense; and

(2) was promoted or received only to or from the actor and the other minor.

(f) It is a defense to prosecution under Subsection (b)(2) that the actor:

(1) did not produce or solicit the visual material;

(2) possessed the visual material only after receiving the material from another minor; and

(3) destroyed the visual material within a reasonable amount of time after receiving the material from another minor.

(g) If conduct that constitutes an offense under this section also constitutes an offense under another law, the defendant may be prosecuted under this section, the other law, or both.

(h) Notwithstanding Section 51.13, Family Code, a finding that a person has engaged in conduct in violation of this section is considered a conviction for the purposes of Subsections (c) and (d).

(Enacted by Acts 2011, 82nd Leg., ch. 1322 (S.B. 407), § 3, effective September 1, 2011.)

## Sec. 43.27. Duty to Report.

(a) For purposes of this section, "visual material" has the meaning assigned by Section 43.26.

(b) A business that develops or processes visual material and determines that the material may be evidence of a criminal offense under this subchapter shall report the existence of the visual material to a local law enforcement agency.

(Enacted by Acts 2003, 78th Leg., ch. 1005 (H.B. 236), § 6, effective September 1, 2003.)

Penal Code

# TITLE 10
# OFFENSES AGAINST PUBLIC HEALTH, SAFETY, AND MORALS

## CHAPTER 46
## WEAPONS

## Sec. 46.01. Definitions.

In this chapter:

(1) "Club" means an instrument that is specially designed, made, or adapted for the purpose of inflicting serious bodily injury or death by striking a person with the instrument, and includes but is not limited to the following:

    (A) blackjack;

    (B) nightstick;

    (C) mace;

    (D) tomahawk.

(2) "Explosive weapon" means any explosive or incendiary bomb, grenade, rocket, or mine, that is designed, made, or adapted for the purpose of inflicting serious bodily injury, death, or substantial property damage, or for the principal purpose of causing such a loud report as to cause undue public alarm or terror, and includes a device designed, made, or adapted for delivery or shooting an explosive weapon.

(3) "Firearm" means any device designed, made, or adapted to expel a projectile through a barrel by using the energy generated by an explosion or burning substance or any device

readily convertible to that use. Firearm does not include a firearm that may have, as an integral part, a folding knife blade or other characteristics of weapons made illegal by this chapter and that is:

    (A) an antique or curio firearm manufactured before 1899; or

    (B) a replica of an antique or curio firearm manufactured before 1899, but only if the replica does not use rim fire or center fire ammunition.

(4) "Firearm silencer" means any device designed, made, or adapted to muffle the report of a firearm.

(5) "Handgun" means any firearm that is designed, made, or adapted to be fired with one hand.

(6) "Illegal knife" means a:

    (A) knife with a blade over five and one-half inches;

    (B) hand instrument designed to cut or stab another by being thrown;

    (C) dagger, including but not limited to a dirk, stiletto, and poniard;

    (D) bowie knife;

    (E) sword; or

    (F) spear.

(7) "Knife" means any bladed hand instrument that is capable of inflicting serious bodily injury or death by cutting or stabbing a person with the instrument.

(8) "Knuckles" means any instrument that consists of finger rings or guards made of a hard substance and that is designed, made, or adapted for the purpose of inflicting serious bodily injury or death by striking a person with a fist enclosed in the knuckles.

(9) "Machine gun" means any firearm that is capable of shooting more than two shots automatically, without manual reloading, by a single function of the trigger.

(10) "Short-barrel firearm" means a rifle with a barrel length of less than 16 inches or a shotgun with a barrel length of less than 18 inches, or any weapon made from a shotgun or

rifle if, as altered, it has an overall length of less than 26 inches.

(11) "Switchblade knife" means any knife that has a blade that folds, closes, or retracts into the handle or sheath and that opens automatically by pressure applied to a button or other device located on the handle or opens or releases a blade from the handle or sheath by the force of gravity or by the application of centrifugal force. The term does not include a knife that has a spring, detent, or other mechanism designed to create a bias toward closure and that requires exertion applied to the blade by hand, wrist, or arm to overcome the bias toward closure and open the knife.

(12) "Armor-piercing ammunition" means handgun ammunition that is designed primarily for the purpose of penetrating metal or body armor and to be used principally in pistols and revolvers.

(13) "Hoax bomb" means a device that:

(A) reasonably appears to be an explosive or incendiary device; or

(B) by its design causes alarm or reaction of any type by an official of a public safety agency or a volunteer agency organized to deal with emergencies.

(14) "Chemical dispensing device" means a device, other than a small chemical dispenser sold commercially for personal protection, that is designed, made, or adapted for the purpose of dispensing a substance capable of causing an adverse psychological or physiological effect on a human being.

(15) "Racetrack" has the meaning assigned that term by the Texas Racing Act (Article 179e, Vernon's Texas Civil Statutes).

(16) "Zip gun" means a device or combination of devices that was not originally a firearm and is adapted to expel a projectile through a smooth-bore or rifled-bore barrel by using the energy generated by an explosion or burning substance.

(17) "Tire deflation device" means a device, including a caltrop or spike strip, that, when driven over, impedes or stops the movement of a wheeled vehicle by puncturing one or more of the vehicle's tires. The term does not include a traffic control device that:

(A) is designed to puncture one or more of a vehicle's tires when driven over in a specific direction; and

(B) has a clearly visible sign posted in close proximity to the traffic control device

that prohibits entry or warns motor vehicle operators of the traffic control device.

(Enacted by Acts 1973, 63rd Leg., ch. 399 (S.B. 34), § 1, effective January 1, 1974; am. Acts 1975, 64th Leg., ch. 342 (S.B. 127), § 13, effective September 1, 1975; am. Acts 1983, 68th Leg., ch. 457 (S.B. 22), § 1, effective September 1, 1983; am. Acts 1983, 68th Leg., ch. 852 (H.B. 1208), § 1, effective September 1, 1983; am. Acts 1987, 70th Leg., ch. 167 (S.B. 892), § 5.01(a)(46), effective September 1, 1987; am. Acts 1989, 71st Leg., ch. 749 (H.B. 1293), § 1, effective September 1, 1989; am. Acts 1991, 72nd Leg., ch. 229 (H.B. 816), § 1, effective September 1, 1991; am. Acts 1993, 73rd Leg., ch. 900 (S.B. 1067), § 1.01, effective September 1, 1994; am. Acts 1999, 76th Leg., ch. 1445 (H.B. 2825), § 1, effective September 1, 1999; am. Acts 2007, 80th Leg., ch. 921 (H.B. 3167), § 12A.001, effective September 1, 2007; am. Acts 2009, 81st Leg., ch. 1199 (H.B. 4456), § 1, effective September 1, 2009; am. Acts 2011, 82nd Leg., ch. 920 (S.B. 1416), § 1, effective September 1, 2011.)

## Sec. 46.02.　Unlawful Carrying Weapons.

(a) A person commits an offense if the person intentionally, knowingly, or recklessly carries on or about his or her person a handgun, illegal knife, or club if the person is not:

(1) on the person's own premises or premises under the person's control; or

(2) inside of or directly en route to a motor vehicle or watercraft that is owned by the person or under the person's control.

(a-1) A person commits an offense if the person intentionally, knowingly, or recklessly carries on or about his or her person a handgun in a motor vehicle or watercraft that is owned by the person or under the person's control at any time in which:

(1) the handgun is in plain view; or

(2) the person is:

(A) engaged in criminal activity, other than a Class C misdemeanor that is a violation of a law or ordinance regulating traffic or boating;

(B) prohibited by law from possessing a firearm; or

(C) a member of a criminal street gang, as defined by Section 71.01.

(a-2) For purposes of this section, "premises" includes real property and a recreational vehicle that is being used as living quarters, regardless of whether that use is temporary or permanent. In this subsection, "recreational vehicle" means a motor vehicle primarily designed as temporary living quarters or a vehicle that contains temporary living quarters and is designed to be towed by a motor vehicle. The term includes a travel trailer, camping trailer, truck camper, motor home, and horse trailer with living quarters.

(a-3) For purposes of this section, "watercraft" means any boat, motorboat, vessel, or personal watercraft, other than a seaplane on water, used or capable of being used for transportation on water.

(b) Except as provided by Subsection (c), an offense under this section is a Class A misdemeanor.

(c) An offense under this section is a felony of the third degree if the offense is committed on any premises licensed or issued a permit by this state for the sale of alcoholic beverages.

(Enacted by Acts 1973, 63rd Leg., ch. 399 (S.B. 34), § 1, effective January 1, 1974; am. Acts 1975, 64th Leg., ch. 49 (H.B. 717), § 1, effective April 15, 1975; am. Acts 1975, 64th Leg., ch. 342 (S.B. 127), § 14, effective September 1, 1975; am. Acts 1975, 64th Leg., ch. 494 (H.B. 431), § 2, effective June 19, 1975; am. Acts 1977, 65th Leg., ch. 746 (S.B. 428), § 26, effective August 29, 1977; am. Acts 1981, 67th Leg., ch. 552 (H.B. 1321), § 1, effective August 31, 1981; am. Acts 1983, 68th Leg., ch. 931 (H.B. 1708), § 1, effective August 29, 1983; am. Acts 1987, 70th Leg., ch. 262 (S.B. 1161), § 21, effective September 1, 1987; am. Acts 1987, 70th Leg., ch. 873 (H.B. 888), § 25, effective September 1, 1987; am. Acts 1991, 72nd Leg., ch. 168 (S.B. 443), § 1, effective September 1, 1991; am. Acts 1993, 73rd Leg., ch. 900 (S.B. 1067), § 1.01, effective September 1, 1994; am. Acts 1995, 74th Leg., ch. 229 (S.B. 60), § 2, effective September 1, 1995; am. Acts 1995, 74th Leg., ch. 318 (S.B. 15), § 16, effective September 1, 1995; am. Acts 1995, 74th Leg., ch. 754 (H.B. 713), § 15, effective September 1, 1995; am. Acts 1995, 74th Leg., ch. 790 (S.B. 1542), § 16, effective September 1, 1995; am. Acts 1995, 74th Leg., ch. 998 (S.B. 538), § 3, effective September 1, 1995; am. Acts 1997, 75th Leg., ch. 165 (S.B. 898), § 10.02, effective September 1, 1997; am. Acts 1997, 75th Leg., ch. 1221 (H.B. 311), § 1, effective September 1, 1997; am. Acts 1997, 75th Leg., ch. 1261 (H.B. 2909), § 24, effective September 1, 1997; am. Acts 2007, 80th Leg., ch. 693 (H.B. 1815), § 1, effective September 1, 2007; am. Acts 2011, 82nd Leg., ch. 679 (H.B. 25), § 1, effective September 1, 2011.)

## Sec. 46.03.　Places Weapons Prohibited.

(a) A person commits an offense if the person intentionally, knowingly, or recklessly possesses or goes with a firearm, illegal knife, club, or prohibited weapon listed in Section 46.05(a):

(1) on the physical premises of a school or educational institution, any grounds or building on which an activity sponsored by a school or educational institution is being conducted, or a passenger transportation vehicle of a school or educational institution, whether the school or educational institution is public or private, unless pursuant to written regulations or written authorization of the institution;

(2) on the premises of a polling place on the day of an election or while early voting is in progress;

(3) on the premises of any government court or offices utilized by the court, unless pursuant to written regulations or written authorization of the court;

(4) on the premises of a racetrack;

(5) in or into a secured area of an airport; or

(6) within 1,000 feet of premises the location of which is designated by the Texas Department of Criminal Justice as a place of execution under Article 43.19, Code of Criminal Procedure, on a day that a sentence of death is set to be imposed on the designated premises and the person received notice that:

(A) going within 1,000 feet of the premises with a weapon listed under this subsection was prohibited; or

(B) possessing a weapon listed under this subsection within 1,000 feet of the premises was prohibited.

(b) It is a defense to prosecution under Subsections (a)(1)—(4) that the actor possessed a firearm while in the actual discharge of his official duties as a member of the armed forces or national guard or a guard employed by a penal institution, or an officer of the court.

(c) In this section:

(1) "Premises" has the meaning assigned by Section 46.035.

(2) "Secured area" means an area of an airport terminal building to which access is controlled by the inspection of persons and property under federal law.

(d) It is a defense to prosecution under Subsection (a)(5) that the actor possessed a firearm or club while traveling to or from the actor's place of assignment or in the actual discharge of duties as:

(1) a member of the armed forces or national guard;

(2) a guard employed by a penal institution; or

(3) a security officer commissioned by the Texas Private Security Board if:

(A) the actor is wearing a distinctive uniform; and

(B) the firearm or club is in plain view; or

(4) a security officer who holds a personal protection authorization under Chapter 1702, Occupations Code, provided that the officer is either:

(A) wearing the uniform of a security officer, including any uniform or apparel described by Section 1702.323(d), Occupations Code, and carrying the officer's firearm in plain view; or

(B) not wearing the uniform of a security officer and carrying the officer's firearm in a concealed manner.

(e) It is a defense to prosecution under Subsection (a)(5) that the actor checked all firearms as baggage in accordance with federal or state law or regulations before entering a secured area.

(f) It is not a defense to prosecution under this section that the actor possessed a handgun and was licensed to carry a concealed handgun under Subchapter H, Chapter 411, Government Code.

(g) An offense under this section is a third degree felony.

(h) It is a defense to prosecution under Subsection (a)(4) that the actor possessed a firearm or club while traveling to or from the actor's place of assignment or in the actual discharge of duties as a security officer commissioned by the Texas Board of Private Investigators and Private Security Agencies, if:

(1) the actor is wearing a distinctive uniform; and

(2) the firearm or club is in plain view.

(i) It is an exception to the application of Subsection (a)(6) that the actor possessed a firearm or club:

(1) while in a vehicle being driven on a public road; or

(2) at the actor's residence or place of employment.

(Enacted by Acts 1973, 63rd Leg., ch. 399 (S.B. 34), § 1, effective January 1, 1974; am. Acts 1983, 68th Leg., ch. 508 (S.B. 354), § 1, effective August 29, 1983; am. Acts 1989, 71st Leg., ch. 749 (H.B. 1293), § 2, effective September 1, 1989; am. Acts 1991, 72nd Leg., ch. 203 (S.B. 1234), § 2.79, effective September 1, 1991; am. Acts 1991, 72nd Leg., ch. 386 (H.B. 2263), § 71, effective August 26, 1991; am. Acts 1991, 72nd Leg., ch. 433 (H.B. 44), § 1, effective September 1, 1991; am. Acts 1991, 72nd Leg., ch. 554 (S.B. 1186), § 50, effective September 1, 1991; am. Acts 1993, 73rd Leg., ch. 900 (S.B. 1067), § 1.01, effective September 1, 1994 (renumbered from Sec. 46.04); am. Acts 1995, 74th Leg., ch. 229 (S.B. 60), § 3, effective September 1, 1995; am. Acts 1995, 74th Leg., ch. 260 (S.B. 1), § 42, effective May 30, 1995; am. Acts 1995, 74th Leg., ch. 318 (S.B. 15), § 17, effective September 1, 1995; am. Acts 1995, 74th Leg., ch. 790 (S.B. 1542), § 17, effective September 1, 1995; am. Acts 1997, 75th Leg., ch. 165 (S.B. 898), §§ 10.03, 31.01(70), effective September 1, 1997; am. Acts 1997, 75th Leg., ch. 1043 (S.B. 1001), § 1, effective September 1, 1997; am Acts 1997, 75th Leg., ch. 1221 (H.B. 311), §§ 2, 3, effective June 20, 1997; am. Acts. 1997, 75th Leg., ch. 1261 (H.B. 2909), § 25, effective September 1, 1997; am. Acts 2001, 77th Leg., ch. 1060 (H.B. 1925), §§ 1, 2, effective September 1, 2001; am. Acts 2003, 78th. Leg., ch. 1178 (S.B. 501), § 3, effective September 1, 2003; am. Acts 2009, 81st Leg., ch. 1146 (H.B. 2730), § 4B.21, effective September 1, 2009.)

## Sec. 46.035.  Unlawful Carrying of Handgun by License Holder.

(a) A license holder commits an offense if the license holder carries a handgun on or about the license holder's person under the authority of Subchapter H, Chapter 411, Government Code, and intentionally fails to conceal the handgun.

(b) A license holder commits an offense if the license holder intentionally, knowingly, or recklessly carries a handgun under the authority of Subchapter H, Chapter 411, Government Code, regardless of whether the handgun is concealed, on or about the license holder's person:

(1) on the premises of a business that has a permit or license issued under Chapter 25, 28, 32, 69, or 74, Alcoholic Beverage Code, if the business derives 51 percent or more of its income from the sale or service of alcoholic beverages for on-premises consumption, as determined by the Texas Alcoholic Beverage Commission under Section 104.06, Alcoholic Beverage Code;

(2) on the premises where a high school, collegiate, or professional sporting event or interscholastic event is taking place, unless the license holder is a participant in the event and a handgun is used in the event;

(3) on the premises of a correctional facility;

(4) on the premises of a hospital licensed under Chapter 241, Health and Safety Code, or on the premises of a nursing home licensed under Chapter 242, Health and Safety Code, unless the license holder has written authorization of the hospital or nursing home administration, as appropriate;

(5) in an amusement park; or

(6) on the premises of a church, synagogue, or other established place of religious worship.

(c) A license holder commits an offense if the license holder intentionally, knowingly, or recklessly carries a handgun under the authority of Subchapter H, Chapter 411, Government Code, regardless of whether the handgun is concealed, at any meeting of a governmental entity.

(d) A license holder commits an offense if, while intoxicated, the license holder carries a handgun under the authority of Subchapter H, Chapter 411, Government Code, regardless of whether the handgun is concealed.

(e) A license holder who is licensed as a security officer under Chapter 1702, Occupations Code, and employed as a security officer commits an offense if, while in the course and scope of the security officer's employment, the security officer violates a provision of Subchapter H, Chapter 411, Government Code.

(f) In this section:

(1) "Amusement park" means a permanent indoor or outdoor facility or park where amusement rides are available for use by the public that is located in a county with a population of more than one million, encompasses at least 75 acres in surface area, is enclosed with access only through controlled entries, is open for operation more than 120 days in each calendar year, and has security guards on the premises at all times. The term does not include any public or private driveway, street, sidewalk or walkway, parking lot, parking garage, or other parking area.

(2) "License holder" means a person licensed to carry a handgun under Subchapter H, Chapter 411, Government Code.

(3) "Premises" means a building or a portion of a building. The term does not include any public or private driveway, street, sidewalk or walkway, parking lot, parking garage, or other parking area.

(g) An offense under Subsection (a), (b), (c), (d), or (e) is a Class A misdemeanor, unless the offense is committed under Subsection (b)(1) or (b)(3), in which event the offense is a felony of the third degree.

(h) It is a defense to prosecution under Subsection (a) that the actor, at the time of the commission of the offense, displayed the handgun under circumstances in which the actor would have been justified in the use of deadly force under Chapter 9.

(h-1) [2 Versions: As added by Acts 2007, 80th Leg., ch. 1214] It is a defense to prosecution under Subsections (b) and (c) that the actor, at the time of the commission of the offense, was:

(1) an active judicial officer, as defined by Section 411.201, Government Code; or

(2) a bailiff designated by the active judicial officer and engaged in escorting the officer.

(h-1) [2 Versions: As added by Acts 2007, 80th Leg., ch. 1222] It is a defense to prosecution under Subsections (b)(1), (2), and (4)—(6), and (c) that at the time of the commission of the offense, the actor was:

(1) a judge or justice of a federal court;

(2) an active judicial officer, as defined by Section 411.201, Government Code; or

(3) a district attorney, assistant district attorney, criminal district attorney, assistant criminal district attorney, county attorney, or assistant county attorney.

(i) Subsections (b)(4), (b)(5), (b)(6), and (c) do not apply if the actor was not given effective notice under Section 30.06.

(j) Subsections (a) and (b)(1) do not apply to a historical reenactment performed in compliance with the rules of the Texas Alcoholic Beverage Commission.

(k) It is a defense to prosecution under Subsection (b)(1) that the actor was not given effective notice under Section 411.204, Government Code. (Enacted by Acts 1995, 74th Leg., ch. 229 (S.B. 60), § 4, effective September 1, 1995; am. Acts 1997, 75th Leg., ch. 165 (S.B. 898), § 10.04, effective September 1, 1997; am. Acts 1997, 75th Leg., ch. 1261 (H.B. 2909), §§ 26, 27, effective September 1, 1997; am. Acts 2001, 77th Leg., ch. 1420 (H.B. 2812), § 14.833, effective September 1, 2001; am. Acts 2005, 79th Leg., ch. 976 (H.B. 1813), § 3, effective September 1, 2005; am. Acts 2007, 80th Leg., ch. 1214 (H.B. 1889), § 2, effective June 15, 2007; am. Acts 2007, 80th Leg., ch. 1222 (H.B. 2300), § 5, effective June 15, 2007; am. Acts 2009, 81st Leg., ch. 687 (H.B. 2664), § 1, effective September 1, 2009.)

### Sec. 46.04. Unlawful Possession of Firearm. — Felon in possession

(a) A person who has been convicted of a felony commits an offense if he possesses a firearm:

(1) after conviction and before the fifth anniversary of the person's release from confinement following conviction of the felony or the person's release from supervision under community supervision, parole, or mandatory supervision, whichever date is later; or

(2) after the period described by Subdivision (1), at any location other than the premises at which the person lives.

*Any firearm until 5 years after Release from confinement/supervision whichever later + only @ home*

(b) A person who has been convicted of an offense under Section 22.01, punishable as a Class A misdemeanor and involving a member of the person's family or household, commits an offense if the person possesses a firearm before the fifth anniversary of the later of:

(1) the date of the person's release from confinement following conviction of the misdemeanor; or

(2) the date of the person's release from community supervision following conviction of the misdemeanor.

(c) A person, other than a peace officer, as defined by Section 1.07, actively engaged in employment as a sworn, full-time paid employee of a state agency or political subdivision, who is subject to an order issued under Section 6.504 or Chapter 85, Family Code, under Article 17.292 or Chapter 7A, Code of Criminal Procedure, or by another jurisdiction as provided by Chapter 88, Family Code, commits an offense if the person possesses a firearm after receiving notice of the order and before expiration of the order.

(d) In this section, "family," "household," and "member of a household" have the meanings assigned by Chapter 71, Family Code.

(e) An offense under Subsection (a) is a felony of the third degree. An offense under Subsection (b) or (c) is a Class A misdemeanor.

(f) For the purposes of this section, an offense under the laws of this state, another state, or the United States is, except as provided by Subsection (g), a felony if, at the time it is committed, the offense:

(1) is designated by a law of this state as a felony;

(2) contains all the elements of an offense designated by a law of this state as a felony; or

(3) is punishable by confinement for one year or more in a penitentiary.

(g) An offense is not considered a felony for purposes of Subsection (f) if, at the time the person possesses a firearm, the offense:

(1) is not designated by a law of this state as a felony; and

(2) does not contain all the elements of any offense designated by a law of this state as a felony.

(Enacted by Acts 1973, 63rd Leg., ch. 399 (S.B. 34), § 1, effective January 1, 1974; am. Acts 1993, 73rd Leg., ch. 900 (S.B. 1067), § 1.01, effective September 1, 1994 (renumbered from Sec. 46.05); am. Acts 2001, 77th Leg., ch. 23 (S.B. 199), § 2, effective September 1, 2001; am. Acts 2003, 78th Leg., ch. 836 (S.B. 433), § 4, effective September 1, 2003; am. Acts 2009, 81st Leg., ch. 1146 (H.B. 2730), § 11.24, effective September 1, 2009.)

### Sec. 46.041. Unlawful Possession of Metal or Body Armor by Felon.

(a) In this section, "metal or body armor" means any body covering manifestly designed, made, or adapted for the purpose of protecting a person against gunfire.

(b) A person who has been convicted of a felony commits an offense if after the conviction the person possesses metal or body armor.

(c) An offense under this section is a felony of the third degree.

(Enacted by Acts 2001, 77th Leg., ch. 452 (H.B. 84), § 1, effective September 1, 2001.)

### Sec. 46.05. Prohibited Weapons.

(a) A person commits an offense if the person intentionally or knowingly possesses, manufactures, transports, repairs, or sells:

(1) an explosive weapon;

(2) a machine gun;

(3) a short-barrel firearm;

(4) a firearm silencer;

(5) a switchblade knife;

(6) knuckles;

(7) armor-piercing ammunition;

(8) a chemical dispensing device;

(9) a zip gun; or

(10) a tire deflation device.

*46.03*

(b) It is a defense to prosecution under this section that the actor's conduct was incidental to the performance of official duty by the armed forces or national guard, a governmental law enforcement agency, or a correctional facility.

(c) It is a defense to prosecution under this section that the actor's possession was pursuant to registration pursuant to the National Firearms Act, as amended.

(d) It is an affirmative defense to prosecution under this section that the actor's conduct:

(1) was incidental to dealing with a switch-blade knife, springblade knife, short-barrel firearm, or tire deflation device solely as an antique or curio;

(2) was incidental to dealing with armor-piercing ammunition solely for the purpose of making the ammunition available to an organization, agency, or institution listed in Subsection (b); or

(3) was incidental to dealing with a tire deflation device solely for the purpose of making the device available to an organization, agency, or institution listed in Subsection (b).

(e) An offense under Subsection (a)(1), (2), (3), (4), (7), (8) or (9) is a felony of the third degree. An offense under Subsection (a)(10) is a state jail felony. An offense under Subsection (a)(5) or (6) is a Class A misdemeanor.

(f) It is a defense to prosecution under this section for the possession of a chemical dispensing device that the actor is a security officer and has received training on the use of the chemical dispensing device by a training program that is:

(1) provided by the Commission on Law Enforcement Officer Standards and Education; or

(2) approved for the purposes described by this subsection by the Texas Private Security Board of the Department of Public Safety.

(g) In Subsection (f), "security officer" means a commissioned security officer as defined by Section 1702.002, Occupations Code, or a noncommissioned security officer registered under Section 1702.221, Occupations Code.

(Enacted by Acts 1973, 63rd Leg., ch. 399 (S.B. 34), § 1, effective January 1, 1974; am. Acts 1975, 64th Leg., ch. 342 (S.B. 127), § 15, effective September 1, 1975; am. Acts 1983, 68th Leg., ch. 457 (S.B. 22), § 2, effective September 1, 1983; am. Acts 1983, 68th Leg., ch. 852 (H.B. 1208), § 2, effective September 1, 1983; am. Acts 1987, 70th Leg., ch. 167 (S.B. 892), § 5.01(a)(47), effective September 1, 1987; am. Acts 1991, 72nd Leg., ch. 229 (H.B. 816), § 2, effective September 1, 1991; am. Acts 1993, 73rd Leg., ch. 900 (S.B. 1067), § 1.01, effective September 1, 1994 (renumbered from Sec. 46.06); am. Acts 2003, 78th Leg., ch. 1071 (H.B. 1661), § 1, effective September 1, 2003; am. Acts 2005, 79th Leg., ch. 1035 (H.B. 1132), § 2.01, effective September 1, 2005; am. Acts 2005, 79th Leg., ch. 1278 (H.B. 2303), § 7, effective September 1, 2005; am. Acts 2011, 82nd Leg., ch. 920 (S.B. 1416), § 2, effective September 1, 2011.)

## Sec. 46.06. Unlawful Transfer of Certain Weapons.

(a) A person commits an offense if the person:

(1) sells, rents, leases, loans, or gives a handgun to any person knowing that the person to whom the handgun is to be delivered intends to use it unlawfully or in the commission of an unlawful act;

(2) intentionally or knowingly sells, rents, leases, or gives or offers to sell, rent, lease, or give to any child younger than 18 years any firearm, club, or illegal knife;

(3) intentionally, knowingly, or recklessly sells a firearm or ammunition for a firearm to any person who is intoxicated;

(4) knowingly sells a firearm or ammunition for a firearm to any person who has been convicted of a felony before the fifth anniversary of the later of the following dates:

(A) the person's release from confinement following conviction of the felony; or

(B) the person's release from supervision under community supervision, parole, or mandatory supervision following conviction of the felony;

(5) sells, rents, leases, loans, or gives a handgun to any person knowing that an active protective order is directed to the person to whom the handgun is to be delivered; or

(6) knowingly purchases, rents, leases, or receives as a loan or gift from another a handgun while an active protective order is directed to the actor.

(b) In this section:

(1) "Intoxicated" means substantial impairment of mental or physical capacity resulting from introduction of any substance into the body.

(2) "Active protective order" means a protective order issued under Title 4, Family Code, that is in effect. The term does not include a temporary protective order issued before the court holds a hearing on the matter.

(c) It is an affirmative defense to prosecution under Subsection (a)(2) that the transfer was to a minor whose parent or the person having legal custody of the minor had given written permission for the sale or, if the transfer was other than a sale, the parent or person having legal custody had given effective consent.

(d) An offense under this section is a Class A misdemeanor, except that an offense under Subsection (a)(2) is a state jail felony if the weapon that is the subject of the offense is a handgun.

Penal Code

(Enacted by Acts 1973, 63rd Leg., ch. 399 (S.B. 34), § 1, effective January 1, 1974; am. Acts 1985, 69th Leg., ch. 686 (H.B. 85), § 1, effective September 1, 1985; am. Acts 1993, 73rd Leg., ch. 900 (S.B. 1067), § 1.01, effective September 1, 1994 (renumbered from Sec. 46.07); am. Acts 1995, 74th Leg., ch. 324 (S.B. 130), § 1, effective January 1, 1996; am. Acts 1997, 75th Leg., ch. 1193 (S.B. 1253), § 22, effective September 1, 1997; am. Acts 1997, 75th Leg., ch. 1304 (S.B. 548), § 1, effective September 1, 1997; am. Acts 1999, 76th Leg., ch. 62 (S.B. 1368), § 15.02(f), effective September 1, 1999.)

### Sec. 46.07.  Interstate Purchase.

A resident of this state may, if not otherwise precluded by law, purchase firearms, ammunition, reloading components, or firearm accessories in another state. This authorization is enacted in conformance with 18 U.S.C. Section 922(b)(3)(A).

DISREGARD

(Enacted by Acts 1973, 63rd Leg., ch. 399 (S.B. 34), § 1, effective January 1, 1974; am. Acts 1993, 73rd Leg., ch. 900 (S.B. 1067), § 1.01, effective September 1, 1994 (renumbered from Sec. 46.08); am. Acts 2009, 81st Leg., ch. 280 (S.B. 1188), § 1, effective May 30, 2009.)

### Sec. 46.08.  Hoax Bombs.

(a) A person commits an offense if the person knowingly manufactures, sells, purchases, transports, or possesses a hoax bomb with intent to use the hoax bomb to:

(1) make another believe that the hoax bomb is an explosive or incendiary device; or

(2) cause alarm or reaction of any type by an official of a public safety agency or volunteer agency organized to deal with emergencies.

(b) An offense under this section is a Class A misdemeanor.

(Enacted by Acts 1983, 68th Leg., ch. 852 (H.B. 1208), § 3, effective September 1, 1983; am. Acts 1993, 73rd Leg., ch. 900 (S.B. 1067), § 1.01, effective September 1, 1994 (renumbered from Sec. 46.09).)

### Sec. 46.09.  Components of Explosives.

(a) A person commits an offense if the person knowingly possesses components of an explosive weapon with the intent to combine the components into an explosive weapon for use in a criminal endeavor.

(b) An offense under this section is a felony of the third degree.

(Enacted by Acts 1983, 68th Leg., ch. 852 (H.B. 1208), § 4, effective September 1, 1983; am. Acts 1993, 73rd Leg., ch. 900 (S.B. 1067), § 1.01, effective September 1, 1994 (renumbered from Sec. 46.10).)

### Sec. 46.10.  Deadly Weapon in Penal Institution.

(a) A person commits an offense if, while confined in a penal institution, he intentionally, knowingly, or recklessly:

(1) carries on or about his person a deadly weapon; or

(2) possesses or conceals a deadly weapon in the penal institution.

(b) It is an affirmative defense to prosecution under this section that at the time of the offense the actor was engaged in conduct authorized by an employee of the penal institution.

(c) A person who is subject to prosecution under both this section and another section under this chapter may be prosecuted under either section.

(d) An offense under this section is a felony of the third degree.

(Enacted by Acts 1985, 69th Leg., ch. 46 (S.B. 185), § 1, effective September 1, 1985; am. Acts 1987, 70th Leg., ch. 714 (H.B. 412), § 1, effective September 1, 1987; am. Acts 1993, 73rd Leg., ch. 900 (S.B. 1067), § 1.01, effective September 1, 1993 (renumbered from Sec. 46.11).)

### Sec. 46.11.  Penalty If Offense Committed Within Weapon-Free School Zone.  DISREGARD

(a) Except as provided by Subsection (b), the punishment prescribed for an offense under this chapter is increased to the punishment prescribed for the next highest category of offense if it is shown beyond a reasonable doubt on the trial of the offense that the actor committed the offense in a place that the actor knew was:

(1) within 300 feet of the premises of a school; or

(2) on premises where:

(A) an official school function is taking place; or

(B) an event sponsored or sanctioned by the University Interscholastic League is taking place.

(b) This section does not apply to an offense under Section 46.03(a)(1).

(c) In this section:

(1) "Premises" has the meaning assigned by Section 481.134, Health and Safety Code.

(2) "School" means a private or public elementary or secondary school.

(Enacted by Acts 1995, 74th Leg., ch. 320 (S.B. 840), § 1, effective September 1, 1995; am. Acts 1997, 75th Leg., ch. 1063 (S.B. 1539), § 10, effective September 1, 1997; am. Acts 2011, 82nd Leg., ch. 91 (S.B. 1303), § 20.002, effective September 1, 2011.)

## Sec. 46.12. Maps As Evidence of Location or Area. DISREGARD

(a) In a prosecution of an offense for which punishment is increased under Section 46.11, a map produced or reproduced by a municipal or county engineer for the purpose of showing the location and boundaries of weapon-free zones is admissible in evidence and is prima facie evidence of the location or boundaries of those areas if the governing body of the municipality or county adopts a resolution or ordinance approving the map as an official finding and record of the location or boundaries of those areas.

(b) A municipal or county engineer may, on request of the governing body of the municipality or county, revise a map that has been approved by the governing body of the municipality or county as provided by Subsection (a).

(c) A municipal or county engineer shall file the original or a copy of every approved or revised map approved as provided by Subsection (a) with the county clerk of each county in which the area is located.

(d) This section does not prevent the prosecution from:

(1) introducing or relying on any other evidence or testimony to establish any element of an offense for which punishment is increased under Section 46.11; or

(2) using or introducing any other map or diagram otherwise admissible under the Texas Rules of Evidence.

(Enacted by Acts 1995, 74th Leg., ch. 320 (S.B. 840), § 2, effective September 1, 1995; am. Acts 2005, 79th Leg., ch. 728 (H.B. 2018), § 16.004, effective September 1, 2005.)

## Sec. 46.13. Making a Firearm Accessible to a Child.

(a) In this section:

(1) "Child" means a person younger than 17 years of age.

(2) "Readily dischargeable firearm" means a firearm that is loaded with ammunition, whether or not a round is in the chamber.

(3) "Secure" means to take steps that a reasonable person would take to prevent the access to a readily dischargeable firearm by a child, including but not limited to placing a firearm in a locked container or temporarily rendering the firearm inoperable by a trigger lock or other means.

(b) A person commits an offense if a child gains access to a readily dischargeable firearm and the person with criminal negligence:

(1) failed to secure the firearm; or

(2) left the firearm in a place to which the person knew or should have known the child would gain access.

(c) It is an affirmative defense to prosecution under this section that the child's access to the firearm:

(1) was supervised by a person older than 18 years of age and was for hunting, sporting, or other lawful purposes;

(2) consisted of lawful defense by the child of people or property;

(3) was gained by entering property in violation of this code; or

(4) occurred during a time when the actor was engaged in an agricultural enterprise.

(d) Except as provided by Subsection (e), an offense under this section is a Class C misdemeanor.

(e) An offense under this section is a Class A misdemeanor if the child discharges the firearm and causes death or serious bodily injury to himself or another person.

(f) A peace officer or other person may not arrest the actor before the seventh day after the date on which the offense is committed if:

(1) the actor is a member of the family, as defined by Section 71.003, Family Code, of the child who discharged the firearm; and

(2) the child in discharging the firearm caused the death of or serious injury to the child.

(g) A dealer of firearms shall post in a conspicuous position on the premises where the dealer conducts business a sign that contains the following warning in block letters not less than one inch in height:

"IT IS UNLAWFUL TO STORE, TRANSPORT, OR ABANDON AN UNSECURED FIREARM IN A PLACE WHERE CHILDREN ARE LIKELY TO BE AND CAN OBTAIN ACCESS TO THE FIREARM."

(Enacted by Acts 1995, 74th Leg., ch. 83 (H.B. 44), § 1, effective September 1, 1995; am. Acts 1999,

Penal Code

76th Leg., ch. 62 (S.B. 1368), § 15.02 (g), effective September 1, 1999.)

## Sec. 46.14.  Firearm Smuggling.

(a) A person commits an offense if the person knowingly engages in the business of transporting or transferring a firearm that the person knows was acquired in violation of the laws of any state or of the United States. For purposes of this subsection, a person is considered to engage in the business of transporting or transferring a firearm if the person engages in that conduct:

(1) on more than one occasion; or

(2) for profit or any other form of remuneration.

(b) An offense under this section is a felony of the third degree, unless it is shown on the trial of the offense that the offense was committed with respect to three or more firearms in a single criminal episode, in which event the offense is a felony of the second degree.

(c) This section does not apply to a peace officer who is engaged in the actual discharge of an official duty.

(d) If conduct that constitutes an offense under this section also constitutes an offense under any other law, the actor may be prosecuted under this section, the other law, or both.

(Enacted by Acts 2009, 81st Leg., ch. 153 (S.B. 2225), § 1, effective September 1, 2009.)

## Sec. 46.15.  Nonapplicability.

(a) Sections 46.02 and 46.03 do not apply to:

(1) peace officers or special investigators under Article 2.122, Code of Criminal Procedure, and neither section prohibits a peace officer or special investigator from carrying a weapon in this state, including in an establishment in this state serving the public, regardless of whether the peace officer or special investigator is engaged in the actual discharge of the officer's or investigator's duties while carrying the weapon;

(2) parole officers and neither section prohibits an officer from carrying a weapon in this state if the officer is:

(A) engaged in the actual discharge of the officer's duties while carrying the weapon; and

(B) in compliance with policies and procedures adopted by the Texas Department of Criminal Justice regarding the possession of a weapon by an officer while on duty;

(3) community supervision and corrections department officers appointed or employed un-

der Section 76.004, Government Code, and neither section prohibits an officer from carrying a weapon in this state if the officer is:

(A) engaged in the actual discharge of the officer's duties while carrying the weapon; and

(B) authorized to carry a weapon under Section 76.0051, Government Code;

(4) [2 Versions: Effective Until September 28, 2011] a judge or justice of a federal court, the supreme court, the court of criminal appeals, a court of appeals, a district court, a criminal district court, a constitutional county court, a statutory county court, a justice court, or a municipal court who is licensed to carry a concealed handgun under Subchapter H, Chapter 411, Government Code;

(4) [2 Versions: Effective September 28, 2011] an active judicial officer as defined by Section 411.201, Government Code, who is licensed to carry a concealed handgun under Subchapter H, Chapter 411, Government Code;

(5) an honorably retired peace officer or federal criminal investigator who holds a certificate of proficiency issued under Section 1701.357, Occupations Code, and is carrying a photo identification that:

(A) verifies that the officer honorably retired after not less than 15 years of service as a commissioned officer; and

(B) is issued by a state or local law enforcement agency;

(6) a district attorney, criminal district attorney, municipal attorney, or county attorney who is licensed to carry a concealed handgun under Subchapter H, Chapter 411, Government Code;

(7) an assistant district attorney, assistant criminal district attorney, or assistant county attorney who is licensed to carry a concealed handgun under Subchapter H, Chapter 411, Government Code;

(8) a bailiff designated by an active judicial officer as defined by Section 411.201, Government Code, who is:

(A) licensed to carry a concealed handgun under Chapter 411, Government Code; and

(B) engaged in escorting the judicial officer; or

(9) a juvenile probation officer who is authorized to carry a firearm under Section 142.006, Human Resources Code.

(b) Section 46.02 does not apply to a person who:

(1) is in the actual discharge of official duties as a member of the armed forces or state military forces as defined by Section 431.001, Government Code, or as a guard employed by a penal institution;

(2) is traveling;

(3) is engaging in lawful hunting, fishing, or other sporting activity on the immediate premises where the activity is conducted, or is en route between the premises and the actor's residence, motor vehicle, or watercraft, if the weapon is a type commonly used in the activity;

(4) holds a security officer commission issued by the Texas Private Security Board, if the person is engaged in the performance of the person's duties as an officer commissioned under Chapter 1702, Occupations Code, or is traveling to or from the person's place of assignment and is wearing the officer's uniform and carrying the officer's weapon in plain view;

(5) acts as a personal protection officer and carries the person's security officer commission and personal protection officer authorization, if the person:

    (A) is engaged in the performance of the person's duties as a personal protection officer under Chapter 1702, Occupations Code, or is traveling to or from the person's place of assignment; and

    (B) is either:

      (i) wearing the uniform of a security officer, including any uniform or apparel described by Section 1702.323(d), Occupations Code, and carrying the officer's weapon in plain view; or

      (ii) not wearing the uniform of a security officer and carrying the officer's weapon in a concealed manner;

(6) is carrying a concealed handgun and a valid license issued under Subchapter H, Chapter 411, Government Code, to carry a concealed handgun of the same category as the handgun the person is carrying;

(7) holds an alcoholic beverage permit or license or is an employee of a holder of an alcoholic beverage permit or license if the person is supervising the operation of the permitted or licensed premises; or

(8) is a student in a law enforcement class engaging in an activity required as part of the class, if the weapon is a type commonly used in the activity and the person is:

    (A) on the immediate premises where the activity is conducted; or

    (B) en route between those premises and the person's residence and is carrying the weapon unloaded.

(c) The provision of Section 46.02 prohibiting the carrying of a club does not apply to a noncommissioned security guard at an institution of higher education who carries a nightstick or similar club, and who has undergone 15 hours of training in the proper use of the club, including at least seven hours of training in the use of the club for nonviolent restraint. For the purposes of this subsection, "nonviolent restraint" means the use of reasonable force, not intended and not likely to inflict bodily injury.

(d) The provisions of Section 46.02 prohibiting the carrying of a firearm or carrying of a club do not apply to a public security officer employed by the adjutant general under Section 431.029, Government Code, in performance of official duties or while traveling to or from a place of duty.

(e) The provisions of Section 46.02 prohibiting the carrying of an illegal knife do not apply to an individual carrying a bowie knife or a sword used in a historical demonstration or in a ceremony in which the knife or sword is significant to the performance of the ceremony.

(f) Section 46.03(a)(6) does not apply to a person who possesses a firearm or club while in the actual discharge of official duties as:

    (1) a member of the armed forces or state military forces, as defined by Section 431.001, Government Code; or

    (2) an employee of a penal institution.

(g) The provisions of Sections 46.02 and 46.03 prohibiting the possession or carrying of a club do not apply to an animal control officer who holds a certificate issued under Section 829.006, Health and Safety Code, and who possesses or carries an instrument used specifically for deterring the bite of an animal while the officer is in the performance of official duties under the Health and Safety Code or is traveling to or from a place of duty.

(h) [Repealed by Acts 2007, 80th Leg., ch. 693 (H.B. 1815), § 3(1), effective September 1, 2007.]

(i) [Repealed by Acts 2007, 80th Leg., ch. 693 (H.B. 1815), § 3(2), effective September 1, 2007.]

(j) The provisions of Section 46.02 prohibiting the carrying of a handgun do not apply to an individual who carries a handgun as a participant in a historical reenactment performed in accordance with the rules of the Texas Alcoholic Beverage Commission.

(Enacted by Acts 1995, 74th Leg., ch. 318 (S.B. 15), § 18, effective September 1, 1995; am. Acts

1997, 75th Leg., ch. 1221 (H.B. 331), § 4, effective June 20, 1997; am. Acts 1997, 75th Leg., ch. 1261 (H.B. 2909), § 28, effective September 1, 1997; am. Acts 1999, 76th Leg., ch. 62 (S.B. 1368), § 9.25, effective September 1, 1999; am. Acts 1999, 76th Leg., ch. 1445 (H.B. 2825), § 2, effective September 1, 1999; am. Acts 2001, 77th Leg., ch. 1060 (H.B. 1925), § 3, effective September 1, 2001; am. Acts 2003, 78th Leg., ch. 325 (S.B. 117), § 2, effective September 1, 2003; am. Acts 2003, 78th Leg., ch. 421 (H.B. 284), § 1, effective September 1, 2003; am. Acts 2003, 78th Leg., ch. 795 (S.B. 103), § 1, effective June 20, 2003; am. Acts 2005, 79th Leg., ch. 288 (H.B. 823), § 1, effective September 1, 2005; am. Acts 2005, 79th Leg., ch. 728 (H.B. 2018), § 23.001(78), effective September 1, 2005; am. Acts 2005, 79th Leg., ch. 976 (H.B. 1813), § 4, effective September 1, 2005; am. Acts 2005, 79th Leg., ch. 1093 (H.B. 2110), §§ 1, 4, effective September 1, 2005; am. Acts 2005, 79th Leg., ch. 1179 (H.B. 578), §§ 2, 3, effective September 1, 2005; am. Acts 2007, 80th Leg., ch. 647 (H.B. 964), § 1, effective September 1, 2007; am. Acts 2007, 80th Leg., ch. 693 (H.B. 1815), §§ 2, 3(1), 3(2), effective September 1, 2007; am. Acts 2007, 80th Leg., ch. 921 (H.B. 3167), § 17.001(62), effective September 1, 2007; am. Acts 2007, 80th Leg., ch. 1048 (H.B. 2101), § 3, effective September 1, 2007; am. Acts 2007, 80th Leg., ch. 1214 (H.B. 1889), § 1, effective June 15, 2007; am. Acts 2007, 80th Leg., ch. 1222 (H.B. 2300), § 6, effective June 15, 2007; am. Acts 2009, 81st Leg., ch. 299 (H.B. 405), § 1, effective June 19, 2009; am. Acts 2009, 81st Leg., ch. 794 (S.B. 1237), § 4, effective June 19, 2009; am. Acts 2009, 81st Leg., ch. 1146 (H.B. 2730), § 4B.22, effective September 1, 2009; am. Acts 2011, 82nd Leg., ch. 679 (H.B. 25), § 2, effective September 1, 2011; am. Acts 2011, 82nd Leg., 1st C.S., (H.B. 79), § 13.02, effective September 28, 2011.)

# CHAPTER 47
# GAMBLING

## Sec. 47.01. Definitions.

In this chapter:

(1) "Bet" means an agreement to win or lose something of value solely or partially by chance. A bet does not include:

(A) contracts of indemnity or guaranty, or life, health, property, or accident insurance;

(B) an offer of a prize, award, or compensation to the actual contestants in a bona fide contest for the determination of skill, speed, strength, or endurance or to the owners of animals, vehicles, watercraft, or aircraft entered in a contest; or

(C) an offer of merchandise, with a value not greater than $25, made by the proprietor of a bona fide carnival contest conducted at a carnival sponsored by a nonprofit religious, fraternal, school, law enforcement, youth, agricultural, or civic group, including any nonprofit agricultural or civic group incorporated by the state before 1955, if the person to receive the merchandise from the proprietor is the person who performs the carnival contest.

(2) "Bookmaking" means:

(A) to receive and record or to forward more than five bets or offers to bet in a period of 24 hours;

(B) to receive and record or to forward bets or offers to bet totaling more than $1,000 in a period of 24 hours; or

(C) a scheme by three or more persons to receive, record, or forward a bet or an offer to bet.

(3) "Gambling place" means any real estate, building, room, tent, vehicle, boat, or other property whatsoever, one of the uses of which is the making or settling of bets, bookmaking, or the conducting of a lottery or the playing of gambling devices.

(4) "Gambling device" means any electronic, electromechanical, or mechanical contrivance not excluded under Paragraph (B) that for a consideration affords the player an opportunity to obtain anything of value, the award of which is determined solely or partially by chance, even though accompanied by some skill, whether or not the prize is automatically paid by the contrivance. The term:

(A) includes, but is not limited to, gambling device versions of bingo, keno, blackjack, lottery, roulette, video poker, or similar electronic, electromechanical, or mechanical games, or facsimiles thereof, that operate by chance or partially so, that as a result of the play or operation of the game award credits or free games, and that record the number of free games or credits so awarded and the cancellation or removal of the free games or credits; and

(B) does not include any electronic, electromechanical, or mechanical contrivance designed, made, and adapted solely for bona fide amusement purposes if the contrivance rewards the player exclusively with noncash merchandise prizes, toys, or novelties, or a representation of value redeemable for those items, that have a wholesale value available from a single play of the game or device of not more than 10 times the amount charged to play the game or device once or $5, whichever is less.

(5) "Altered gambling equipment" means any contrivance that has been altered in some manner, including, but not limited to, shaved dice, loaded dice, magnetic dice, mirror rings, electronic sensors, shaved cards, marked cards, and any other equipment altered or designed to enhance the actor's chances of winning.

(6) "Gambling paraphernalia" means any book, instrument, or apparatus by means of which bets have been or may be recorded or registered; any record, ticket, certificate, bill, slip, token, writing, scratch sheet, or other means of carrying on bookmaking, wagering pools, lotteries, numbers, policy, or similar games.

(7) "Lottery" means any scheme or procedure whereby one or more prizes are distributed by chance among persons who have paid or promised consideration for a chance to win anything of value, whether such scheme or procedure is called a pool, lottery, raffle, gift, gift enterprise, sale, policy game, or some other name.

(8) "Private place" means a place to which the public does not have access, and excludes, among other places, streets, highways, restaurants, taverns, nightclubs, schools, hospitals, and the common areas of apartment houses, hotels, motels, office buildings, transportation facilities, and shops.

(9) "Thing of value" means any benefit, but does not include an unrecorded and immediate right of replay not exchangeable for value.
(Enacted by Acts 1973, 63rd Leg., ch. 399 (S.B. 34), § 1, effective January 1, 1974; am. Acts 1987, 70th Leg., ch. 313 (S.B. 342), §§ 1, 2, effective September 1, 1987; am. Acts 1989, 71st Leg., ch. 396 (S.B. 807), § 1, effective June 14, 1989; am.

Acts 1993, 73rd Leg., ch. 774 (S.B. 522), § 1, effective August 30, 1993; am. Acts 1993, 73rd Leg., ch. 900 (S.B. 1067), § 1.01, effective September 1, 1994; am. Acts 1995, 74th Leg., ch. 318 (S.B. 15), § 19, effective September 1, 1995.)

## Sec. 47.02. Gambling.
(a) A person commits an offense if he:

(1) makes a bet on the partial or final result of a game or contest or on the performance of a participant in a game or contest;

(2) makes a bet on the result of any political nomination, appointment, or election or on the degree of success of any nominee, appointee, or candidate; or

(3) plays and bets for money or other thing of value at any game played with cards, dice, balls, or any other gambling device.

(b) It is a defense to prosecution under this section that:

(1) the actor engaged in gambling in a private place;

(2) no person received any economic benefit other than personal winnings; and

(3) except for the advantage of skill or luck, the risks of losing and the chances of winning were the same for all participants.

(c) It is a defense to prosecution under this section that the actor reasonably believed that the conduct:

(1) was permitted under Chapter 2001, Occupations Code;

(2) was permitted under Chapter 2002, Occupations Code;

(3) consisted entirely of participation in the state lottery authorized by the State Lottery Act (Chapter 466, Government Code);

(4) was permitted under the Texas Racing Act (Article 179e, Vernon's Texas Civil Statutes); or

(5) consisted entirely of participation in a drawing for the opportunity to participate in a hunting, fishing, or other recreational event conducted by the Parks and Wildlife Department.

(d) An offense under this section is a Class C misdemeanor.

(e) It is a defense to prosecution under this section that a person played for something of value other than money using an electronic, electromechanical, or mechanical contrivance excluded from the definition of "gambling device" under Section 47.01(4)(B).
(Enacted by Acts 1973, 63rd Leg., ch. 399 (S.B. 34), § 1, effective January 1, 1974; am. Acts 1981,

67th Leg., 1st C.S., ch. 11 (H.B. 3), § 43, effective November 10, 1981; am. Acts 1989, 71st Leg., ch. 957 (H.B. 240), § 2, effective January 1, 1990; am. Acts 1991, 72nd Leg., 1st C.S., ch. 6 (H.B. 54), § 3, effective November 5, 1991; am. Acts 1993, 73rd Leg., ch. 107 (H.B. 947), § 4.04, effective August 30, 1993; am. Acts 1993, 73rd Leg., ch. 774 (S.B. 522), § 2, effective August 30, 1993; am. Acts 1993, 73rd Leg., ch. 900 (S.B. 1067), § 1.01, effective September 1, 1994; am. Acts 1995, 74th Leg., ch. 76 (S.B. 959), § 14.53, effective September 1, 1995; am. Acts 1995, 74th Leg., ch. 318 (S.B. 15), § 20, effective September 1, 1995; am. Acts 1995, 74th Leg., ch. 931 (H.B. 2216), § 79, effective June 16, 1995; am. Acts 1997, 75th Leg., ch. 1256 (H.B. 2542), § 124, effective September 1, 1997; am. Acts 2001, 77th Leg., ch. 1420 (H.B. 2812), § 14.834, effective September 1, 2001.)

### Sec. 47.03.  Gambling Promotion.

(a) A person commits an offense if he intentionally or knowingly does any of the following acts:

(1) operates or participates in the earnings of a gambling place;

(2) engages in bookmaking;

(3) for gain, becomes a custodian of anything of value bet or offered to be bet;

(4) sells chances on the partial or final result of or on the margin of victory in any game or contest or on the performance of any participant in any game or contest or on the result of any political nomination, appointment, or election or on the degree of success of any nominee, appointee, or candidate; or

(5) for gain, sets up or promotes any lottery or sells or offers to sell or knowingly possesses for transfer, or transfers any card, stub, ticket, check, or other device designed to serve as evidence of participation in any lottery.

(b) An offense under this section is a Class A misdemeanor.

(Enacted by Acts 1973, 63rd Leg., ch. 399 (S.B. 34), § 1, effective January 1, 1974; am. Acts 1987, 70th Leg., ch. 313 (S.B. 342), § 3, effective September 1, 1987; am. Acts 1993, 73rd Leg., ch. 900 (S.B. 1067), § 1.01, effective September 1, 1994.)

### Sec. 47.04.  Keeping a Gambling Place.

(a) A person commits an offense if he knowingly uses or permits another to use as a gambling place any real estate, building, room, tent, vehicle, boat, or other property whatsoever owned by him or under his control, or rents or lets any such property with a view or expectation that it be so used.

(b) It is an affirmative defense to prosecution under this section that:

(1) the gambling occurred in a private place;

(2) no person received any economic benefit other than personal winnings; and

(3) except for the advantage of skill or luck, the risks of losing and the chances of winning were the same for all participants.

(c) An offense under this section is a Class A misdemeanor.

(Enacted by Acts 1973, 63rd Leg., ch. 399 (S.B. 34), § 1, effective January 1, 1974; am. Acts 1977, 65th Leg., ch. 251 (H.B. 1124), § 1, effective August 29, 1977; am. Acts 1989, 71st Leg., ch. 1030 (H.B. 141), § 1, effective September 1, 1989; am. Acts 1993, 73rd Leg., ch. 900 (S.B. 1067), § 1.01, effective September 1, 1994.)

### Sec. 47.05.  Communicating Gambling Information.

(a) A person commits an offense if, with the intent to further gambling, he knowingly communicates information as to bets, betting odds, or changes in betting odds or he knowingly provides, installs, or maintains equipment for the transmission or receipt of such information.

(b) It is an exception to the application of Subsection (a) that the information communicated is intended for use in placing a lawful wager under Article 11, Texas Racing Act (Article 179e, Vernon's Texas Civil Statutes), and is not communicated in violation of Section 14.01 of that Act.

(c) An offense under this section is a Class A misdemeanor.

(Enacted by Acts 1973, 63rd Leg., ch. 399 (S.B. 34), § 1, effective January 1, 1974; am. Acts 1993, 73rd Leg., ch. 900 (S.B. 1067), § 1.01, effective September 1, 1994.)

### Sec. 47.06.  Possession of Gambling Device, Equipment, or Paraphernalia.

(a) A person commits an offense if, with the intent to further gambling, he knowingly owns, manufactures, transfers, or possesses any gambling device that he knows is designed for gambling purposes or any equipment that he knows is designed as a subassembly or essential part of a gambling device.

(b) A person commits an offense if, with the intent to further gambling, he knowingly owns, manufactures, transfers commercially, or possesses any altered gambling equipment that he knows is designed for gambling purposes or any equipment that he knows is designed as a subassembly or essential part of such device.

(c) A person commits an offense if, with the intent to further gambling, the person knowingly owns, manufactures, transfers commercially, or possesses gambling paraphernalia.

(d) It is a defense to prosecution under Subsections (a) and (c) that:

(1) the device, equipment, or paraphernalia is used for or is intended for use in gambling that is to occur entirely in a private place;

(2) a person involved in the gambling does not receive any economic benefit other than personal winnings; and

(3) except for the advantage of skill or luck, the chance of winning is the same for all participants.

(e) An offense under this section is a Class A misdemeanor.

(f) It is a defense to prosecution under Subsection (a) or (c) that the person owned, manufactured, transferred, or possessed the gambling device, equipment, or paraphernalia for the sole purpose of shipping it to another jurisdiction where the possession or use of the device, equipment, or paraphernalia was legal.

(g) A district or county attorney is not required to have a search warrant or subpoena to inspect a gambling device or gambling equipment or paraphernalia on an ocean-going vessel that enters the territorial waters of this state to call at a port in this state.

(Enacted by Acts 1973, 63rd Leg., ch. 399 (S.B. 34), § 1, effective January 1, 1974; am. Acts 1977, 65th Leg., ch. 251 (H.B. 1124), § 2, effective August 29, 1977; am. Acts 1977, 65th Leg., ch. 741 (S.B. 210), § 1, effective August 29, 1977; am. Acts 1987, 70th Leg., ch. 167 (S.B. 892), § 5.01(a)(48), effective September 1, 1987; am. Acts 1987, 70th Leg., ch. 458 (H.B. 359), § 1, effective September 1, 1987; am. Acts 1989, 71st Leg., ch. 1030 (H.B. 141), § 2, effective September 1, 1989; am. Acts 1991, 72nd Leg., ch. 44 (S.B. 247), § 1, effective August 26, 1991; am. Acts 1991, 72nd Leg., ch. 315 (H.B. 1715), § 1, effective September 1, 1991; am. Acts 1991, 72nd Leg., 1st C.S., ch. 6 (H.B. 54), § 4, effective November 5, 1991; am. Acts 1993, 73rd Leg., ch. 107 (H.B. 947), § 4.05, effective August 30, 1993; am. Acts 1993, 73rd Leg., ch. 284 (H.B. 1587), § 30, effective September 1 1993; am. Acts 1993, 73rd Leg.,

ch. 900 (S.B. 1067), § 1.01, effective September 1, 1994.)

## Sec. 47.07.  Evidence.

In any prosecution under this chapter in which it is relevant to prove the occurrence of a sporting event, a published report of its occurrence in a daily newspaper, magazine, or other periodically printed publication of general circulation shall be admissible in evidence and is prima facie evidence that the event occurred.

(Enacted by Acts 1973, 63rd Leg., ch. 399 (S.B. 34), § 1, effective January 1, 1974; am. Acts 1993, 73rd Leg., ch. 900 (S.B. 1067), § 1.01, effective September 1, 1994 (renumbered from Sec. 47.08).)

## Sec. 47.08.  Testimonial Immunity.

(a) A party to an offense under this chapter may be required to furnish evidence or testify about the offense.

(b) A party to an offense under this chapter may not be prosecuted for any offense about which he is required to furnish evidence or testify, and the evidence and testimony may not be used against the party in any adjudicatory proceeding except a prosecution for aggravated perjury.

(c) For purposes of this section, "adjudicatory proceeding" means a proceeding before a court or any other agency of government in which the legal rights, powers, duties, or privileges of specified parties are determined.

(d) A conviction under this chapter may be had upon the uncorroborated testimony of a party to the offense.

(Enacted by Acts 1973, 63rd Leg., ch. 399 (S.B. 34), § 1, effective January 1, 1974; am. Acts 1993, 73rd Leg., ch. 900 (S.B. 1067), § 1.01, effective September 1, 1994 (renumbered from Sec. 47.09).)

## Sec. 47.09.  Other Defenses.

(a) It is a defense to prosecution under this chapter that the conduct:

(1) was authorized under:

(A) Chapter 2001, Occupations Code;

(B) Chapter 2002, Occupations Code; or

(C) the Texas Racing Act (Article 179e, Vernon's Texas Civil Statutes);

(2) consisted entirely of participation in the state lottery authorized by Chapter 466, Government Code; or

(3) was a necessary incident to the operation of the state lottery and was directly or indirectly authorized by:

(A) Chapter 466, Government Code;

(B) the lottery division of the Texas Lottery Commission;

(C) the Texas Lottery Commission; or

(D) the director of the lottery division of the Texas Lottery Commission.

(b) It is an affirmative defense to prosecution under Sections 47.04, 47.06(a), and 47.06(c) that the gambling device, equipment, or paraphernalia is aboard an ocean-going vessel that enters the territorial waters of this state to call at a port in this state if:

(1) before the vessel enters the territorial waters of this state, the district attorney or, if there is no district attorney, the county attorney for the county in which the port is located receives notice of the existence of the device, equipment, or paraphernalia on board the vessel and of the anticipated dates on which the vessel will enter and leave the territorial waters of this state;

(2) at all times while the vessel is in the territorial waters of this state all devices, equipment, or paraphernalia are disabled, electronically or by another method, from a remote and secured area of the vessel in a manner that allows only the master or crew of the vessel to remove any disabling device;

(3) at all times while the vessel is in the territorial waters of this state any disabling device is not removed except for the purposes of inspecting or repairing the device, equipment, or paraphernalia; and

(4) the device, equipment, or paraphernalia is not used for gambling or other gaming purposes while the vessel is in the territorial waters of this state.

(Enacted by Acts 1993, 73rd Leg., ch. 900 (S.B. 1067), § 1.01, effective September 1, 1994; am. Acts 1995, 74th Leg., ch. 76 (S.B. 959), § 14.54, effective September 1, 1995; am. Acts 1997, 75th Leg., ch. 111 (H.B. 449), § 1, effective May 16, 1997; am. Acts 1997, 75th Leg., ch. 1035 (S.B. 645), § 55, effective June 19, 1997; am. Acts 1999, 76th Leg., ch. 844 (H.B. 1802), § 1, effective September 1, 1999; am. Acts 2001, 77th Leg., ch. 1420 (H.B. 2812), § 14.835, effective September 1, 2001.)

### Sec. 47.10. American Documentation of Vessel Required.

If 18 U.S.C. Section 1082 is repealed, the affirmative defenses provided by Section 47.09(b) apply only if the vessel is documented under the laws of the United States.

(Enacted by Acts 1989, 71st Leg., ch. 1030 (H.B. 141), § 4, effective September 1, 1989; am. Acts 1990, 71st Leg., 6th C.S., ch. 12 (S.B. 51), § 2(27), effective September 6, 1990 (renumbered from Sec. 47.12); am. Acts 1993, 73rd Leg., ch. 900 (S.B. 1067), § 1.01, effective September 1, 1994 (renumbered from Sec. 47.13).)

### Sec. 47.11. Pari-Mutuel Wagering on Certain Races [Deleted].

Deleted by Acts 1993, 73rd Leg., ch. 900 (S.B. 1067), § 1.01, effective September 1, 1994.
(Enacted by Acts 1986, 69th Leg., ch. 19 (S.B. 15), § 2, effective December 4, 1986.)

### Sec. 47.111. Public Hunting Drawing [Deleted].

Deleted by Acts 1993, 73rd Leg., ch. 900 (S.B. 1067), § 13.02, effective September 1, 1994.
(Enacted by Acts 1993, 73rd Leg., ch. 635 (H.B. 1417), § 9, effective September 1, 1993.)

### Sec. 47.12. Raffle by Nonprofit Organization [Deleted].

Deleted by Acts 1993, 73rd Leg., ch. 900 (S.B. 1067), § 1.01, effective September 1, 1994.
(Enacted by Acts 1989, 71st Leg., ch. 957 (H.B. 240), § 3, effective January 1, 1990.)

### Sec. 47.13. American Documentation of Vessel Required [Renumbered].

Renumbered to Tex. Penal Code § 47.10 by Acts 1993, 73rd Leg., ch. 900 (S.B. 1067), § 1.01, effective September 1, 1994.

### Sec. 47.14. State Lottery [Deleted].

Deleted by Acts 1993, 73rd Leg., ch. 900 (S.B. 1067), § 1.01, effective September 1, 1994.
(Enacted by Acts 1991, 72nd Leg., 1st C.S., ch. 6 (H.B. 54), § 5, effective November 5, 1991; am. Acts 1993, 73rd Leg., ch. 107 (H.B. 947), § 4.06, effective August 30, 1993; am. Acts 1993, 73rd

Leg., ch. 284 (H.B. 1587), § 31, effective September 1, 1993.)

# CHAPTER 48
## CONDUCT AFFECTING PUBLIC HEALTH

**Section**

## Sec. 48.01.   Smoking Tobacco.

(a) A person commits an offense if he is in possession of a burning tobacco product or smokes tobacco in a facility of a public primary or secondary school or an elevator, enclosed theater or movie house, library, museum, hospital, transit system bus, or intrastate bus, as defined by Section 541.201, Transportation Code, plane, or train which is a public place.

(b) It is a defense to prosecution under this section that the conveyance or public place in which the offense takes place does not have prominently displayed a reasonably sized notice that smoking is prohibited by state law in such conveyance or public place and that an offense is punishable by a fine not to exceed $500.

(c) All conveyances and public places set out in Subsection (a) of Section 48.01 shall be equipped with facilities for extinguishment of smoking materials and it shall be a defense to prosecution under this section if the conveyance or public place within which the offense takes place is not so equipped.

(d) It is an exception to the application of Subsection (a) if the person is in possession of the burning tobacco product or smokes tobacco exclusively within an area designated for smoking tobacco or as a participant in an authorized theatrical performance.

(e) An area designated for smoking tobacco on a transit system bus or intrastate plane or train must also include the area occupied by the operator of the transit system bus, plane, or train.

(f) An offense under this section is punishable as a Class C misdemeanor.
(Enacted by Acts 1975, 64th Leg., ch. 290 (S.B. 59), § 1, effective September 1, 1975; am. Acts 1991, 72nd Leg., ch. 108 (H.B. 407), § 2, effective September 1, 1991; am. Acts 1993, 73rd Leg., ch. 900 (S.B. 1067), § 1.01, effective September 1, 1994; am. Acts 1997, 75th Leg., ch. 165 (S.B. 898), § 30.242, effective September 1, 1997.)

## Sec. 48.015.   Prohibitions Relating to Certain Cigarettes.

(a) A person may not acquire, hold, own, possess, or transport for sale or distribution in this state or import or cause to be imported into this state for sale or distribution in this state:

(1) cigarettes that do not comply with all applicable requirements imposed by or under federal law and implementing regulations; or

(2) cigarettes to which stamps may not be affixed under Section 154.0415, Tax Code, other than cigarettes lawfully imported or brought into the state for personal use and cigarettes lawfully sold or intended to be sold as duty-free merchandise by a duty-free sales enterprise in accordance with 19 U.S.C. Section 1555(b), as amended.

(b) A person who commits an act prohibited by Subsection (a), knowing or having reason to know that the person is doing so, is guilty of a Class A misdemeanor.
(Enacted by Acts 2001, 77th Leg., ch. 1104 (H.B. 2378), § 6, effective September 1, 2001.)

## Sec. 48.02.   Prohibition of the Purchase and Sale of Human Organs.

(a) "Human organ" means the human kidney, liver, heart, lung, pancreas, eye, bone, skin, fetal tissue, or any other human organ or tissue, but does not include hair or blood, blood components (including plasma), blood derivatives, or blood reagents.

(b) A person commits an offense if he or she knowingly or intentionally offers to buy, offers to sell, acquires, receives, sells, or otherwise transfers any human organ for valuable consideration.

(c) It is an exception to the application of this section that the valuable consideration is: (1) a fee paid to a physician or to other medical personnel for services rendered in the usual course of medical practice or a fee paid for hospital or other clinical services; (2) reimbursement of legal or medical expenses incurred for the benefit of the ultimate receiver of the organ; or (3) reimbursement of expenses of travel, housing, and lost wages incurred by the donor of a human organ in connection with the donation of the organ.

(d) A violation of this section is a Class A misdemeanor.
(Enacted by Acts 1985, 69th Leg., ch. 40 (S.B. 33), § 1, effective August 26, 1985; am. Acts 1993, 73rd Leg., ch. 900 (S.B. 1067), § 1.01, effective September 1, 1994.)

Penal Code

# CHAPTER 49
# INTOXICATION AND ALCOHOLIC
# BEVERAGE OFFENSES

## Sec. 49.01.  Definitions.

In this chapter:

(1) "Alcohol concentration" means the number of grams of alcohol per:

(A)  210 liters of breath;

(B)  100 milliliters of blood; or

(C)  67 milliliters of urine.

(2) "Intoxicated" means:

(A)  not having the normal use of mental or physical faculties by reason of the introduction of alcohol, a controlled substance, a drug, a dangerous drug, a combination of two or more of those substances, or any other substance into the body; or

(B)  having an alcohol concentration of 0.08 or more.

(3) "Motor vehicle" has the meaning assigned by Section 32.34(a).

(4) "Watercraft" means a vessel, one or more water skis, an aquaplane, or another device used for transporting or carrying a person on water, other than a device propelled only by the current of water.

(5) "Amusement ride" has the meaning assigned by Section 2151.002, Occupations Code.

(6) "Mobile amusement ride" has the meaning assigned by Section 2151.002, Occupations Code.

(Enacted by Acts 1993, 73rd Leg., ch. 900 (S.B. 1067), § 1.01, effective September 1, 1994; am. Acts 1999, 76th Leg., ch. 234 (S.B. 114), § 1, effective September 1, 1999; am. Acts 1999, 76th Leg., ch. 1364 (H.B. 1059), § 8, effective January 1, 2000; am. Acts 2001, 77th Leg., ch. 1420 (H.B. 2812), § 14.707, effective September 1, 2001.)

## Sec. 49.02.  Public Intoxication.

(a) A person commits an offense if the person appears in a public place while intoxicated to the degree that the person may endanger the person or another.

(a-1) For the purposes of this section, a premises licensed or permitted under the Alcoholic Beverage Code is a public place.

(b) It is a defense to prosecution under this section that the alcohol or other substance was administered for therapeutic purposes and as a part of the person's professional medical treatment by a licensed physician.

(c) Except as provided by Subsection (e), an offense under this section is a Class C misdemeanor.

(d) An offense under this section is not a lesser included offense under Section 49.04.

(e) An offense under this section committed by a person younger than 21 years of age is punishable in the same manner as if the minor committed an offense to which Section 106.071, Alcoholic Beverage Code, applies.

(Enacted by Acts 1993, 73rd Leg., ch. 900 (S.B. 1067), § 1.01, effective September 1, 1994; am. Acts 1997, 75th Leg., ch. 1013 (S.B. 35), § 12, effective September 1, 1997; am. Acts 2007, 80th Leg., ch. 68 (H.B. 904), § 25, effective September 1, 2007.)

## Sec. 49.03.  Consumption or Possession of Alcoholic Beverage in Motor Vehicle [Repealed].

Repealed by Acts 2001, 77th Leg., ch. 969 (H.B. 5), § 10, effective September 1, 2001.

(Enacted by Acts 1993, 73rd Leg., ch. 900 (S.B. 1067), § 1.01, effective September 1, 1994.)

## Sec. 49.031.  Possession of Alcoholic Beverage in Motor Vehicle.

(a) In this section:

(1) "Open container" means a bottle, can, or other receptacle that contains any amount of alcoholic beverage and that is open, that has been opened, that has a broken seal, or the contents of which are partially removed.

(2) "Passenger area of a motor vehicle" means the area of a motor vehicle designed for the seating of the operator and passengers of the vehicle. The term does not include:

(A)  a glove compartment or similar storage container that is locked;

(B)  the trunk of a vehicle; or

(C)  the area behind the last upright seat of the vehicle, if the vehicle does not have a trunk.

(3) "Public highway" means the entire width between and immediately adjacent to the boundary lines of any public road, street, highway, interstate, or other publicly maintained way if any part is open for public use for the purpose of motor vehicle travel. The term includes the right-of-way of a public highway.

(b) A person commits an offense if the person knowingly possesses an open container in a passenger area of a motor vehicle that is located on a public highway, regardless of whether the vehicle is being operated or is stopped or parked. Possession by a person of one or more open containers in a single criminal episode is a single offense.

(c) It is an exception to the application of Subsection (b) that at the time of the offense the defendant was a passenger in:

(1) the passenger area of a motor vehicle designed, maintained, or used primarily for the transportation of persons for compensation, including a bus, taxicab, or limousine; or

(2) the living quarters of a motorized house coach or motorized house trailer, including a self-contained camper, a motor home, or a recreational vehicle.

(d) An offense under this section is a Class C misdemeanor.

(e) A peace officer charging a person with an offense under this section, instead of taking the person before a magistrate, shall issue to the person a written citation and notice to appear that contains the time and place the person must appear before a magistrate, the name and address of the person charged, and the offense charged. If the person makes a written promise to appear before the magistrate by signing in duplicate the citation and notice to appear issued by the officer, the officer shall release the person.
(Enacted by Acts 2001, 77th Leg., ch. 969 (H.B. 5), § 2, effective September 1, 2001.)

## Sec. 49.04. Driving While Intoxicated.

(a) A person commits an offense if the person is intoxicated while operating a motor vehicle in a public place.

(b) Except as provided by Subsections (c) and (d) and Section 49.09, an offense under this section is a Class B misdemeanor, with a minimum term of confinement of 72 hours.

(c) If it is shown on the trial of an offense under this section that at the time of the offense the person operating the motor vehicle had an open container of alcohol in the person's immediate possession, the offense is a Class B misdemeanor, with a minimum term of confinement of six days.

(d) If it is shown on the trial of an offense under this section that an analysis of a specimen of the person's blood, breath, or urine showed an alcohol concentration level of 0.15 or more at the time the analysis was performed, the offense is a Class A misdemeanor.
(Enacted by Acts 1993, 73rd Leg., ch. 900 (S.B. 1067), § 1.01, effective September 1, 1994; am. Acts 1995, 74th Leg., ch. 76 (S.B. 959), § 14.55, effective September 1, 1995; am. Acts 2011, 82nd Leg., ch. 960 (H.B. 1199), § 2, effective September 1, 2011.)

## Sec. 49.045. Driving While Intoxicated with Child Passenger.

(a) A person commits an offense if:

(1) the person is intoxicated while operating a motor vehicle in a public place; and

(2) the vehicle being operated by the person is occupied by a passenger who is younger than 15 years of age.

(b) An offense under this section is a state jail felony.
(Enacted by Acts 2003, 78th Leg., ch. 787 (S.B. 45), § 1, effective September 1, 2003.)

## Sec. 49.05. Flying While Intoxicated.

(a) A person commits an offense if the person is intoxicated while operating an aircraft.

(b) Except as provided by Section 49.09, an offense under this section is a Class B misdemeanor, with a minimum term of confinement of 72 hours.
(Enacted by Acts 1993, 73rd Leg., ch. 900 (S.B. 1067), § 1.01, effective September 1, 1994.)

## Sec. 49.06. Boating While Intoxicated.

(a) A person commits an offense if the person is intoxicated while operating a watercraft.

(b) Except as provided by Section 49.09, an offense under this section is a Class B misdemeanor, with a minimum term of confinement of 72 hours.
(Enacted by Acts 1993, 73rd Leg., ch. 900 (S.B. 1067), § 1.01, effective September 1, 1994.)

## Sec. 49.065. Assembling or Operating an Amusement Ride While Intoxicated.

(a) A person commits an offense if the person is intoxicated while operating an amusement ride or while assembling a mobile amusement ride.

(b) Except as provided by Subsection (c) and Section 49.09, an offense under this section is a

Class B misdemeanor with a minimum term of confinement of 72 hours.

(c) If it is shown on the trial of an offense under this section that at the time of the offense the person operating the amusement ride or assembling the mobile amusement ride had an open container of alcohol in the person's immediate possession, the offense is a Class B misdemeanor with a minimum term of confinement of six days. (Enacted by Acts 1999, 76th Leg., ch. 1364 (H.B. 1059), § 9, effective January 1, 2000.)

## Sec. 49.07. Intoxication Assault.

(a) A person commits an offense if the person, by accident or mistake:

> INTOXICATION =
> NO MENTAL STATE
>
> EXAMPLE: TRAFFIC ACCIDENT
> WHERE FATALITIES EXIST →
> GO w/ THIS TO ↑ ABILITY TO
> CONVICT w/o MENTAL STATE

effective January 1, 2000; am. Acts 2007, 80th Leg., ch. 662 (H.B. 12124), § 2, effective September 1, 2007.)

## Sec. 49.08. Intoxication Manslaughter.

(a) A person commits an offense if the person:

(1) operates a motor vehicle in a public place, operates an aircraft, a watercraft, or an amusement ride, or assembles a mobile amusement ride; and

(2) is intoxicated and by reason of that intoxication causes the death of another by accident or mistake.

(b) Except as provided by Section 49.09, an offense under this section is a felony of the second degree.

(Enacted by Acts 1993, 73rd Leg., ch. 900 (S.B. 1067), § 1.01, effective September 1, 1994; am. Acts 1999, 76th Leg., ch. 1364 (H.B. 1059), § 11,

effective January 1, 2000; am. Acts 2007, 80th Leg., ch. 662 (H.B. 1212), § 3, effective September 1, 2007.)

## Sec. 49.09. Enhanced Offenses and Penalties.

(a) Except as provided by Subsection (b), an offense under Section 49.04, 49.05, 49.06, or 49.065 is a Class A misdemeanor, with a minimum term of confinement of 30 days, if it is shown on the trial of the offense that the person has previously been convicted one time of an offense relating to the operating of a motor vehicle while intoxicated, an offense of operating an aircraft while intoxicated, an offense of operating a watercraft while intoxicated, or an offense of operating or assembling an amusement ride while intoxicated.

(b) An offense under Section 49.04, 49.05, 49.06, or 49.065 is a felony of the third degree if it is shown on the trial of the offense that the person has previously been convicted:

(1) one time of an offense under Section 49.08 or an offense under the laws of another state if the offense contains elements that are substantially similar to the elements of an offense under Section 49.08; or

(2) two times of any other offense relating to the operating of a motor vehicle while intoxicated, operating an aircraft while intoxicated, operating a watercraft while intoxicated, or operating or assembling an amusement ride while intoxicated.

(b-1) An offense under Section 49.07 is a felony of the second degree if it is shown on the trial of the offense that the person caused serious bodily injury to a peace officer, a firefighter, or emergency medical services personnel while in the actual discharge of an official duty.

(b-2) An offense under Section 49.08 is a felony of the first degree if it is shown on the trial of the offense that the person caused the death of a person described by Subsection (b-1).

(b-3) For the purposes of Subsection (b-1):

(1) "Emergency medical services personnel" has the meaning assigned by Section 773.003, Health and Safety Code.

(2) "Firefighter" means:

(A) an individual employed by this state or by a political or legal subdivision of this state who is subject to certification by the Texas Commission on Fire Protection; or

(B) a member of an organized volunteer fire-fighting unit that:

(i) renders fire-fighting services without remuneration; and

(ii) conducts a minimum of two drills each month, each at least two hours long.

(b-4) An offense under Section 49.07 is a felony of the second degree if it is shown on the trial of the offense that the person caused serious bodily injury to another in the nature of a traumatic brain injury that results in a persistent vegetative state.

(c) For the purposes of this section:

(1) "Offense relating to the operating of a motor vehicle while intoxicated" means:

(A) an offense under Section 49.04 or 49.045;

(B) an offense under Section 49.07 or 49.08, if the vehicle operated was a motor vehicle;

(C) an offense under Article 6701*l*-1, Revised Statutes, as that law existed before September 1, 1994;

(D) an offense under Article 6701*l*-2, Revised Statutes, as that law existed before January 1, 1984;

(E) an offense under Section 19.05(a)(2), as that law existed before September 1, 1994, if the vehicle operated was a motor vehicle; or

(F) an offense under the laws of another state that prohibit the operation of a motor vehicle while intoxicated.

(2) "Offense of operating an aircraft while intoxicated" means:

(A) an offense under Section 49.05;

(B) an offense under Section 49.07 or 49.08, if the vehicle operated was an aircraft;

(C) an offense under Section 1, Chapter 46, Acts of the 58th Legislature, Regular Session, 1963 (Article 46f-3, Vernon's Texas Civil Statutes), as that law existed before September 1, 1994;

(D) an offense under Section 19.05(a)(2), as that law existed before September 1, 1994, if the vehicle operated was an aircraft; or

(E) an offense under the laws of another state that prohibit the operation of an aircraft while intoxicated.

(3) "Offense of operating a watercraft while intoxicated" means:

(A) an offense under Section 49.06;

(B) an offense under Section 49.07 or 49.08, if the vehicle operated was a watercraft;

(C) an offense under Section 31.097, Parks and Wildlife Code, as that law existed before September 1, 1994;

(D) an offense under Section 19.05(a)(2), as that law existed before September 1, 1994, if the vehicle operated was a watercraft; or

(E) an offense under the laws of another state that prohibit the operation of a watercraft while intoxicated.

(4) "Offense of operating or assembling an amusement ride while intoxicated" means:

(A) an offense under Section 49.065;

(B) an offense under Section 49.07 or 49.08, if the offense involved the operation or assembly of an amusement ride; or

(C) an offense under the law of another state that prohibits the operation of an amusement ride while intoxicated or the assembly of a mobile amusement ride while intoxicated.

(d) For the purposes of this section, a conviction for an offense under Section 49.04, 49.045, 49.05, 49.06, 49.065, 49.07, or 49.08 that occurs on or after September 1, 1994, is a final conviction, whether the sentence for the conviction is imposed or probated.

(e), (f) [Repealed by Acts 2005, 79th Leg., ch. 996 (H.B. 51), § 3, effective September 1, 2005.]

(g) A conviction may be used for purposes of enhancement under this section or enhancement under Subchapter D, Chapter 12, but not under both this section and Subchapter D.

(h) This subsection applies only to a person convicted of a second or subsequent offense relating to the operating of a motor vehicle while intoxicated committed within five years of the date on which the most recent preceding offense was committed. The court shall enter an order that requires the defendant to have a device installed, on each motor vehicle owned or operated by the defendant, that uses a deep-lung breath analysis mechanism to make impractical the operation of the motor vehicle if ethyl alcohol is detected in the breath of the operator, and that requires that before the first anniversary of the ending date of the period of license suspension under Section 521.344, Transportation Code, the defendant not operate any motor vehicle that is not equipped with that device. The court shall require the defendant to obtain the device at the defendant's own cost on or before that ending date, require the defendant to provide evidence to the court on or before that ending date that the device has been installed on each appropriate vehicle, and order the device to remain installed on each vehicle until the first anniversary of that ending date. If the court determines the offender is unable to pay for the device, the court may impose a reasonable payment schedule not to extend beyond the first anniversary of the date of installation. The Department of Public Safety shall approve devices for use under this subsection. Section 521.247, Transportation Code, applies to the approval of a device under this subsection and the consequences of that approval. Failure to comply with an order entered under this subsection is punishable by contempt. For the purpose of enforcing this subsection, the court that enters an order under this subsection retains jurisdiction over the defendant until the date on which the device is no longer required to remain installed. To the extent of a conflict between this subsection and Section 13(i), Article 42.12, Code of Criminal Procedure, this subsection controls.

(Enacted by Acts 1993, 73rd Leg., ch. 900 (S.B. 1067), § 1.01, effective September 1, 1994; am. Acts 1995, 74th Leg., ch. 76 (S.B. 959), § 14.56, effective September 1, 1995; am. Acts 1995, 74th Leg., ch. 318 (S.B. 15), § 21, effective September 1, 1995; am. Acts 1999, 76th Leg., ch. 1364 (H.B. 1059), §§ 12, 13, effective January 1, 2000; am. Acts 2001, 77th Leg.,ch. 648 (H.B. 2250), §§ 1, 2, effective September 1, 2001; am. Acts 2001, 77th Leg., ch. 969 (H.B. 5), § 3, effective September 1, 2001; am. Acts 2003, 78th Leg., ch. 787 (S.B. 45), § 2, effective September 1, 2003; am. Acts 2003, 78th Leg., ch. 1275 (H.B. 3506), § 2(117), effective September 1, 2003; am. Acts 2005, 79th Leg., ch. 996 (H.B. 51), §§ 1, 3,effective September 1, 2005; am. Acts 2007, 80th Leg., ch. 662 (H.B. 1212), § 4, effective September 1, 2007; am. Acts 2011, 82nd Leg., ch. 960 (H.B. 1199), § 3, effective September 1, 2011.)

### Sec. 49.10.  No Defense.

In a prosecution under Section 49.03, 49.04, 49.045, 49.05, 49.06, 49.065, 49.07, or 49.08, the fact that the defendant is or has been entitled to use the alcohol, controlled substance, drug, dangerous drug, or other substance is not a defense. (Enacted by Acts 1993, 73rd Leg., ch. 900 (S.B. 1067), § 1.01, effective September 1, 1994; am. Acts 1999, 76th Leg., ch. 1364 (H.B. 1059), § 14, effective January 1, 2000; am. Acts 2003, 78th Leg., ch. 787 (S.B. 45), § 3, effective September 1, 2003.)

### Sec. 49.11.  Proof of Mental State Unnecessary.

(a) Notwithstanding Section 6.02(b), proof of a culpable mental state is not required for conviction of an offense under this chapter.

(b) Subsection (a) does not apply to an offense under Section 49.031. (Enacted by Acts 1995, 74th Leg., ch. 318 (S.B. 15), § 22, effective September 1, 1995; am. Acts 2001, 77th Leg., ch. 969 (H.B. 5), § 4, effective September 1, 2001.)

### Sec. 49.12.  Applicability to Certain Conduct.

Sections 49.07 and 49.08 do not apply to injury to or the death of an unborn child if the conduct charged is conduct committed by the mother of the unborn child. (Enacted by Acts 2003, 78th Leg., ch. 822 (S.B. 319), § 2.05, effective September 1, 2003.)

# TITLE 11
# ORGANIZED CRIME

## CHAPTER 71
## ORGANIZED CRIME

### Sec. 71.01.  Definitions.

In this chapter,

(a) "Combination" means three or more persons who collaborate in carrying on criminal activities, although:

(1) participants may not know each other's identity;

(2) membership in the combination may change from time to time; and

(3) participants may stand in a wholesal-

er-retailer or other arm's-length relationship in illicit distribution operations.

(b) "Conspires to commit" means that a person agrees with one or more persons that they or one or more of them engage in conduct that would constitute the offense and that person and one or more of them perform an overt act in pursuance of the agreement. An agreement constituting conspiring to commit may be inferred from the acts of the parties.

(c) "Profits" means property constituting or derived from any proceeds obtained, directly or indirectly, from an offense listed in Section 71.02.

(d) "Criminal street gang" means three or more persons having a common identifying sign or symbol or an identifiable leadership who continuously or regularly associate in the commission of criminal activities.

(Enacted by Acts 1977, 65th Leg., ch. 346 (S.B. 151), § 1, effective June 10, 1977; am. Acts 1989, 71st Leg., ch. 782 (H.B. 5), § 1, effective September 1, 1989; am. Acts 1991, 72nd Leg., ch. 555 (H.B. 549), § 1, effective September 1, 1991; am. Acts 1993, 73rd Leg., ch. 900 (S.B. 1067), § 1.01, effective September 1, 1994; am. Acts 1995, 74th Leg., ch. 318 (S.B. 15), § 23, effective September 1, 1995.)

## Sec. 71.02. Engaging in Organized Criminal Activity.

(a) A person commits an offense if, with the intent to establish, maintain, or participate in a combination or in the profits of a combination or as a member of a criminal street gang, the person commits or conspires to commit one or more of the following:

(1) murder, capital murder, arson, aggravated robbery, robbery, burglary, theft, aggravated kidnapping, kidnapping, aggravated assault, aggravated sexual assault, sexual assault, forgery, deadly conduct, assault punishable as a Class A misdemeanor, burglary of a motor vehicle, or unauthorized use of a motor vehicle;

(2) any gambling offense punishable as a Class A misdemeanor;

(3) promotion of prostitution, aggravated promotion of prostitution, or compelling prostitution;

(4) unlawful manufacture, transportation, repair, or sale of firearms or prohibited weapons;

(5) unlawful manufacture, delivery, dispensation, or distribution of a controlled substance or dangerous drug, or unlawful possession of a controlled substance or dangerous drug through forgery, fraud, misrepresentation, or deception;

(5-a) causing the unlawful delivery, dispensation, or distribution of a controlled substance or dangerous drug in violation of Subtitle B, Title 3, Occupations Code;

(6) any unlawful wholesale promotion or possession of any obscene material or obscene device with the intent to wholesale promote the same;

(7) any offense under Subchapter B, Chapter 43, depicting or involving conduct by or directed toward a child younger than 18 years of age;

(8) any felony offense under Chapter 32;

(9) any offense under Chapter 36;

(10) any offense under Chapter 34, 35, or 35A;

(11) any offense under Section 37.11(a);

(12) any offense under Chapter 20A;

(13) any offense under Section 37.10;

(14) any offense under Section 38.06, 38.07, 38.09, or 38.11;

(15) any offense under Section 42.10;

(16) any offense under Section 46.06(a)(1) or 46.14; or

(17) **[2 Versions: As added by Acts 2011, 82nd Leg., ch. 68]** any offense classified as a felony under the Tax Code.

(17) **[2 Versions: As added by Acts 2011, 82nd Leg., ch. 223]** any offense under Section 20.05.

(b) Except as provided in Subsections (c) and (d), an offense under this section is one category higher than the most serious offense listed in Subsection (a) that was committed, and if the most serious offense is a Class A misdemeanor, the offense is a state jail felony, except that if the most serious offense is a felony of the first degree, the offense is a felony of the first degree.

(c) Conspiring to commit an offense under this section is of the same degree as the most serious offense listed in Subsection (a) that the person conspired to commit.

(d) At the punishment stage of a trial, the defendant may raise the issue as to whether in voluntary and complete renunciation of the offense he withdrew from the combination before commission of an offense listed in Subsection (a) and made substantial effort to prevent the commission of the offense. If the defendant proves the issue in the affirmative by a preponderance of the evidence the offense is the same category of offense as the most serious offense listed in Subsection (a) that is committed, unless the defendant is convicted of conspiring to commit the offense, in which event the offense is one category lower than the most serious offense that the defendant conspired to commit.

(Enacted by Acts 1977, 65th Leg., ch. 346 (S.B. 151), § 1, effective June 10, 1977; am. Acts 1981, 67th Leg., ch. 587 (H.B. 21), §§ 1-3, effective September 1, 1981; am. Acts 1989, 71st Leg., ch. 782 (H.B. 5), § 2, effective September 1, 1989; am. Acts 1991, 72nd Leg., ch. 555 (H.B. 549), § 1, effective September 1, 1991; am. Acts 1993, 73rd Leg., ch. 761 (H.B. 354), § 3, effective September 1 1993; am. Acts 1993, 73rd Leg., ch. 900 (S.B. 1067), § 1.01, effective September 1, 1994; am. Acts 1995, 74th Leg., ch. 318 (S.B. 15), § 24, effective September 1, 1995; am. Acts 1997, 75th Leg., ch. 189 (H.B. 1185), § 9, effective May 21, 1997; am. Acts 1999, 76th Leg., ch. 685 (H.B. 668), § 8, effective September 1, 1999; am. Acts 2003, 78th Leg., ch. 641 (H.B. 2096), § 3, effective September 1, 2003; am. Acts 2005, 79th Leg., ch. 1162 (H.B. 3376), § 5, effective September 1, 2005; am. Acts 2007, 80th Leg., ch. 1163 (H.B. 126), § 2, effective September 1, 2007; am. Acts 2009, 81st Leg., ch. 153 (S.B. 2225), § 2, effective September 1, 2009; am. Acts 2009, 81st Leg., ch. 1130 (H.B. 2086), § 1, effective September 1, 2009; am. Acts 2009, 81st Leg., ch. 1357 (S.B. 554), § 2, effective September 1, 2009; am. Acts 2011, 82nd Leg., ch. 68 (S.B. 934), § 8, effective September 1, 2011; am. Acts 2011, 82nd Leg., ch. 91 (S.B. 1303), § 20.003, effective September 1, 2011; am. Acts 2011, 82nd Leg., ch. 223 (H.B. 260), § 3, effective September 1, 2011; am. Acts 2011, 82nd Leg., ch. 620 (S.B. 688), § 10, effective September 1, 2011; am. Acts 2011, 82nd Leg., ch. 1200 (S.B. 158), §§ 3, 4, effective September 1, 2011.)

### Sec. 71.021.   Violation of Court Order Enjoining Organized Criminal Activity.

(a) A person commits an offense if the person knowingly violates a temporary or permanent order issued under Section 125.065(a) or (b), Civil Practice and Remedies Code.

(b) If conduct constituting an offense under this section also constitutes an offense under another section of this code, the actor may be prosecuted under either section or under both sections.

(c) An offense under this section is a Class A misdemeanor.

(Enacted by Acts 1995, 74th Leg., ch. 584 (S.B. 1090), § 1, effective September 1, 1995.)

### Sec. 71.022.   Coercing, Inducing, or Soliciting Membership in a Criminal Street Gang.

(a) A person commits an offense if the person knowingly causes, enables, encourages, recruits, or solicits another person to become a member of a criminal street gang which, as a condition of initiation, admission, membership, or continued membership, requires the commission of any conduct which constitutes an offense punishable as a Class A misdemeanor or a felony.

(a-1) A person commits an offense if, with intent to coerce, induce, or solicit a child to actively participate in the activities of a criminal street gang, the person:

(1) threatens the child or a member of the child's family with imminent bodily injury; or

(2) causes bodily injury to the child or a member of the child's family.

(b) Except as provided by Subsection (c), an offense under this section is a felony of the third degree.

(c) A second or subsequent offense under this section is a felony of the second degree.

(d) In this section:

(1) "Child" means an individual younger than 17 years of age.

(2) "Family" has the meaning assigned by Section 71.003, Family Code.

(Enacted by Acts 1999, 76th Leg., ch. 1555 (S.B. 1579), § 1, effective September 1, 1999; am. Acts 2009, 81st Leg., ch. 435 (H.B. 2187), §§ 1, 2, effective September 1, 2009.)

### Sec. 71.023.   Directing Activities of Certain Criminal Street Gangs.

(a) A person commits an offense if the person knowingly initiates, organizes, plans, finances, directs, manages, or supervises a criminal street gang or members of a criminal street gang with the intent to benefit, promote, or further the interests of the criminal street gang or to increase the person's standing, position, or status in the criminal street gang.

(b) An offense under this section is a felony of the first degree.

(c) Notwithstanding Section 71.01, in this section, "criminal street gang" means:

(1) an organization that:

(A) has more than 10 members whose names are included in an intelligence database under Chapter 61, Code of Criminal Procedure;

(B) has a hierarchical structure that has been documented in an intelligence database under Chapter 61, Code of Criminal Procedure;

(C) engages in profit-sharing among two or more members of the organization; and

(D) in one or more regions of this state served by different regional councils of government, continuously or regularly engages in conduct:

(i) that constitutes an offense listed in Section 3g(a)(1), Article 42.12, Code of Criminal Procedure;

(ii) in which it is alleged that a deadly weapon is used or exhibited during the commission of or immediate flight from the commission of any felony offense; or

(iii) that is punishable as a felony of the first or second degree under Chapter 481, Health and Safety Code; or

(2) an organization that, in collaboration with an organization described by Subdivision (1), engages in conduct or commits an offense or conspires to engage in conduct or commit an offense described by Subdivision (1)(D).

(Enacted by Acts 2009, 81st Leg., ch. 1130 (H.B. 2086), § 3, effective September 1, 2009.)

## Sec. 71.028. Gang-Free Zones.

(a) In this section:

(1) "Institution of higher education," "playground," "premises," "school," "video arcade facility," and "youth center" have the meanings assigned by Section 481.134, Health and Safety Code.

(2) "Shopping mall" means an enclosed public walkway or hall area that connects retail, service, or professional establishments.

(b) This section applies to an offense listed in Section 71.02(a)(1), (4), or (7), other than burglary, theft, burglary of a motor vehicle, or unauthorized use of a motor vehicle.

(c) Except as provided by Subsection (d), the punishment prescribed for an offense described by Subsection (b) is increased to the punishment prescribed for the next highest category of offense if the actor is 17 years of age or older and it is shown beyond a reasonable doubt on the trial of the offense that the actor committed the offense at a location that was:

(1) in, on, or within 1,000 feet of any:

(A) real property that is owned, rented, or leased by a school or school board;

(B) premises owned, rented, or leased by an institution of higher education;

(C) premises of a public or private youth center; or

(D) playground;

(2) in, on, or within 300 feet of any:

(A) shopping mall;

(B) movie theater;

(C) premises of a public swimming pool; or

(D) premises of a video arcade facility; or

(3) on a school bus.

(d) The punishment for an offense described by Subsection (b) may not be increased under this section if the offense is punishable under Section 71.02 as a felony of the first degree.

(Enacted by Acts 2009, 81st Leg., ch. 1130 (H.B. 2086), § 3, effective September 1, 2009.)

## Sec. 71.029. Maps As Evidence of Location or Area.

(a) In a prosecution of an offense for which punishment is increased under Section 71.028, a map produced or reproduced by a municipal or county engineer for the purpose of showing the location and boundaries of gang-free zones is admissible in evidence and is prima facie evidence of the location or boundaries of those zones if the governing body of the municipality or county adopts a resolution or ordinance approving the map as an official finding and record of the location or boundaries of those zones.

(b) A municipal or county engineer may, on request of the governing body of the municipality or county, revise a map that has been approved by the governing body of the municipality or county as provided by Subsection (a).

(c) A municipal or county engineer shall file the original or a copy of every approved or revised map approved as provided by Subsection (a) with the county clerk of each county in which the zone is located.

(d) This section does not prevent the prosecution from:

(1) introducing or relying on any other evidence or testimony to establish any element of an offense for which punishment is increased under Section 71.028; or

(2) using or introducing any other map or diagram otherwise admissible under the Texas Rules of Evidence.

(Enacted by Acts 2009, 81st Leg., ch. 1130 (H.B. 2086), § 3, effective September 1, 2009.)

## Sec. 71.03. Defenses Excluded.

It is no defense to prosecution under Section 71.02 that:

(1) one or more members of the combination are not criminally responsible for the object offense;

(2) one or more members of the combination have been acquitted, have not been prosecuted or convicted, have been convicted of a different offense, or are immune from prosecution;

(3) a person has been charged with, acquitted, or convicted of any offense listed in Subsection (a) of Section 71.02; or

(4) once the initial combination of three or more persons is formed there is a change in the number or identity of persons in the combination as long as two or more persons remain in the combination and are involved in a continuing course of conduct constituting an offense under this chapter.

(Enacted by Acts 1977, 65th Leg., ch. 346 (S.B. 151), § 1, effective June 10, 1977; am. Acts 1993, 73rd Leg., ch. 900 (S.B. 1067), § 1.01, effective September 1, 1994.)

## Sec. 71.04. Testimonial Immunity.

(a) A party to an offense under this chapter may be required to furnish evidence or testify about the offense.

(b) No evidence or testimony required to be furnished under the provisions of this section nor any information directly or indirectly derived from such evidence or testimony may be used against the witness in any criminal case, except a prosecution for aggravated perjury or contempt. (Enacted by Acts 1977, 65th Leg., ch. 346 (S.B. 151), § 1, effective June 10, 1977; am. Acts 1993, 73rd Leg., ch. 900 (S.B. 1067), § 1.01, effective September 1, 1994.)

## Sec. 71.05. Renunciation Defense.

(a) It is an affirmative defense to prosecution under Section 71.02 that under circumstances manifesting a voluntary and complete renunciation of the actor's criminal objective, the actor withdrew from the combination before commission of an offense listed in Section 71.02(a) and took further affirmative action that prevented the commission of the offense.

(b) For the purposes of this section and Subsection (d) of Section 71.02, renunciation is not voluntary if it is motivated in whole or in part:

(1) by circumstances not present or apparent at the inception of the actor's course of conduct that increase the probability of detection or apprehension or that make more difficult the accomplishment of the objective; or

(2) by a decision to postpone the criminal conduct until another time or to transfer the criminal act to another but similar objective or victim.

(c) Evidence that the defendant withdrew from the combination before commission of an offense listed in Section 71.02(a) and made substantial effort to prevent the commission of an offense listed in Section 71.02(a) shall be admissible as mitigation at the hearing on punishment if the actor has been found guilty under Section 71.02 and in the event of a finding of renunciation under this subsection, the punishment shall be one grade lower than that provided under Section 71.02.

(Enacted by Acts 1977, 65th Leg., ch. 346 (S.B. 151), § 1, effective June 10, 1977; am. Acts 1981, 67th Leg., ch. 587 (H.B. 21), §§ 4, 5, effective September 1, 1981; am. Acts 1993, 73rd Leg., ch. 761 (H.B. 354), § 4, effective September 1 1993; am. Acts 1993, 73rd Leg., ch. 900 (S.B. 1067), § 1.01, effective September 1, 1994; am. Acts 2011, 82nd Leg., ch. 1200 (S.B. 158), §§ 5, 6, effective September 1, 2011.)

# CODE OF CRIMINAL PROCEDURE

## TITLE 2
## CODE OF CRIMINAL PROCEDURE

Criminal Procedure

# TITLE 1
# CODE OF CRIMINAL PROCEDURE OF 1965

## Introductory

## CHAPTER 1
## GENERAL PROVISIONS

## Art. 1.01. Short Title.

This Act shall be known, and may be cited, as the "Code of Criminal Procedure".
(Enacted by Acts 1965, 59th Leg., ch. 722 (S.B. 107), § 1, effective January 1, 1966.)

## Art. 1.02. Effective Date.

This Code shall take effect and be in force on and after January 1, 1966. The procedure herein prescribed shall govern all criminal proceedings instituted after the effective date of this Act and all proceedings pending upon the effective date hereof insofar as are applicable.
(Enacted by Acts 1965, 59th Leg., ch. 722 (S.B. 107), § 1, effective January 1, 1966.)

## Art. 1.03. Objects of this Code.

This Code is intended to embrace rules applicable to the prevention and prosecution of of-fenses against the laws of this State, and to make the rules of procedure in respect to the prevention and punishment of offenses intelligible to the officers who are to act under them, and to all persons whose rights are to be affected by them. It seeks:

1. To adopt measures for preventing the commission of crime;

2. To exclude the offender from all hope of escape;

3. To insure a trial with as little delay as is consistent with the ends of justice;

4. To bring to the investigation of each of-fense on the trial all the evidence tending to produce conviction or acquittal;

5. To insure a fair and impartial trial; and

6. The certain execution of the sentence of the law when declared.
(Enacted by Acts 1965, 59th Leg., ch. 722 (S.B. 107), § 1, effective January 1, 1966.)

## Art. 1.04. Due Course of Law.

No citizen of this State shall be deprived of life, liberty, property, privileges or immunities, or in any manner disfranchised, except by the due course of the law of the land.
(Enacted by Acts 1965, 59th Leg., ch. 722 (S.B. 107), § 1, effective January 1, 1966.)

## Art. 1.05. Rights of Accused.

In all criminal prosecutions the accused shall have a speedy public trial by an impartial jury. He shall have the right to demand the nature and cause of the accusation against him, and to have a copy thereof. He shall not be compelled to give evidence against himself. He shall have the right of being heard by himself, or counsel, or both; shall be confronted with the witnesses against him, and shall have compulsory process for obtaining witnesses in his favor. No person shall be held to answer for a felony unless on indictment of a grand jury.
(Enacted by Acts 1965, 59th Leg., ch. 722 (S.B. 107), § 1, effective January 1, 1966.)

## Art. 1.051. Right to Representation by Counsel.

(a) A defendant in a criminal matter is entitled to be represented by counsel in an adversarial judicial proceeding. The right to be represented by counsel includes the right to consult in private with counsel sufficiently in advance of a proceeding to allow adequate preparation for the proceeding.

(b) For the purposes of this article and Articles 26.04 and 26.05 of this code, "indigent" means a person who is not financially able to employ counsel.

(c) An indigent defendant is entitled to have an attorney appointed to represent him in any adversary judicial proceeding that may result in punishment by confinement and in any other criminal proceeding if the court concludes that the interests of justice require representation. Except as otherwise provided by this subsection, if an indigent defendant is entitled to and requests appointed counsel and if adversarial judicial proceedings have been initiated against the defendant, a court or the courts' designee authorized under Article 26.04 to appoint counsel for indigent defendants in the county shall appoint counsel as soon as possible, but not later than the end of the third working day after the date on which the court or the courts' designee receives the defendant's request for appointment of counsel. In a county with a population of 250,000 or more, the court or the courts' designee shall appoint counsel as required by this subsection as soon as possible, but not later than the end of the first working day after the date on which the court or the courts' designee receives the defendant's request for appointment of counsel.

(d) An eligible indigent defendant is entitled to have the trial court appoint an attorney to represent him in the following appellate and postconviction habeas corpus matters:

(1) an appeal to a court of appeals;

(2) an appeal to the Court of Criminal Appeals if the appeal is made directly from the trial court or if a petition for discretionary review has been granted;

(3) a habeas corpus proceeding if the court concludes that the interests of justice require representation; and

(4) any other appellate proceeding if the court concludes that the interests of justice require representation.

(e) An appointed counsel is entitled to 10 days to prepare for a proceeding but may waive the preparation time with the consent of the defendant in writing or on the record in open court. If a nonindigent defendant appears without counsel at a proceeding after having been given a reasonable opportunity to retain counsel, the court, on 10 days' notice to the defendant of a dispositive setting, may proceed with the matter without securing a written waiver or appointing counsel. If an indigent defendant who has refused appointed counsel in order to retain private counsel appears without counsel after having been given an opportunity to retain counsel, the court, after giving the defendant a reasonable opportunity to request appointment of counsel or, if the defendant elects not to request appointment of counsel, after obtaining a waiver of the right to counsel pursuant to Subsections (f) and (g), may proceed with the matter on 10 days' notice to the defendant of a dispositive setting.

(f) A defendant may voluntarily and intelligently waive in writing the right to counsel. A waiver obtained in violation of Subsection (f-1) or (f-2) is presumed invalid.

(f-1) In any adversary judicial proceeding that may result in punishment by confinement, the attorney representing the state may not:

(1) initiate or encourage an attempt to obtain from a defendant who is not represented by counsel a waiver of the right to counsel; or

(2) communicate with a defendant who has requested the appointment of counsel, unless the court or the court's designee authorized under Article 26.04 to appoint counsel for indigent defendants in the county has denied the request and, subsequent to the denial, the defendant:

(A) has been given a reasonable opportunity to retain and has failed to retain private counsel; or

(B) waives or has waived the opportunity to retain private counsel.

(f-2) In any adversary judicial proceeding that may result in punishment by confinement, the court may not direct or encourage the defendant to communicate with the attorney representing the state until the court advises the defendant of the right to counsel and the procedure for requesting appointed counsel and the defendant has been given a reasonable opportunity to request appointed counsel. If the defendant has requested appointed counsel, the court may not direct or encourage the defendant to communicate with the attorney representing the state unless the court or the court's designee authorized under Article 26.04 to appoint counsel for indigent defendants in the county has denied the request and, subsequent to the denial, the defendant:

(1) has been given a reasonable opportunity to retain and has failed to retain private counsel; or

(2) waives or has waived the opportunity to retain private counsel.

(g) If a defendant wishes to waive the right to counsel for purposes of entering a guilty plea or proceeding to trial, the court shall advise the defendant of the nature of the charges against the defendant and, if the defendant is proceeding to trial, the dangers and disadvantages of self-representation. If the court determines that the waiver is voluntarily and intelligently made, the court shall provide the defendant with a statement substantially in the following form, which, if signed by the defendant, shall be filed with and become part of the record of the proceedings:

"I have been advised this _____ day of _____, 2 _____, by the (name of court) Court of my right to representation by counsel in the case pending against me. I have been further advised that if I am unable to afford counsel, one will be appointed for me free of charge. Understanding my right to have counsel appointed for me free of charge if I am not financially able to employ counsel, I wish to waive that right and request the court to proceed with my case without an attorney being appointed for me. I hereby waive my right to counsel. (signature of defendant)"

(h) A defendant may withdraw a waiver of the right to counsel at any time but is not entitled to repeat a proceeding previously held or waived solely on the grounds of the subsequent appointment or retention of counsel. If the defendant withdraws a waiver, the trial court, in its discretion, may provide the appointed counsel 10 days to prepare.

(i) Except as otherwise provided by this subsection, if an indigent defendant is entitled to and requests appointed counsel and if adversarial judicial proceedings have not been initiated against the defendant, a court or the courts' designee authorized under Article 26.04 to appoint counsel for indigent defendants in the county shall appoint counsel immediately following the expiration of three working days after the date on which the court or the courts' designee receives the defendant's request for appointment of counsel. If adversarial judicial proceedings are initiated against the defendant before the expiration of the three working days, the court or the courts' designee shall appoint counsel as provided by Subsection (c). In a county with a population of 250,000 or more, the court or the courts' designee shall appoint counsel as required by this subsection immediately following the expiration of one working day after the date on which the court or the courts' designee receives the defendant's request for appointment of counsel. If adversarial judicial proceedings are initiated against the defendant before the expiration of the one working day, the court or the courts' designee shall appoint counsel as provided by Subsection (c).

(j) Notwithstanding any other provision of this section, if an indigent defendant is released from custody prior to the appointment of counsel under this section, appointment of counsel is not required until the defendant's first court appearance or when adversarial judicial proceedings are initiated, whichever comes first.

(k) A court or the courts' designee may without unnecessary delay appoint new counsel to represent an indigent defendant for whom counsel is appointed under Subsection (c) or (i) if:

(1) the defendant is subsequently charged in the case with an offense different from the offense with which the defendant was initially charged; and

(2) good cause to appoint new counsel is stated on the record as required by Article 26.04(j)(2).

(Enacted by Acts 1987, 70th Leg., ch. 979 (S.B. 1108), § 1, effective September 1, 1987; am. Acts 2001, 77th Leg., ch. 906 (S.B. 7), § 2, effective January 1, 2002; am. Acts 2007, 80th Leg., ch. 463 (H.B. 1178), § 1, effective September 1, 2007.)

## Art. 1.052. Signed Pleadings of Defendant.

(a) A pleading, motion, and other paper filed for or on behalf of a defendant represented by an attorney must be signed by at least one attorney of record in the attorney's name and state the attorney's address. A defendant who is not represented by an attorney must sign any pleading, motion, or other paper filed for or on the defendant's behalf and state the defendant's address.

(b) The signature of an attorney or a defendant constitutes a certificate by the attorney or defendant that the person has read the pleading, motion, or other paper and that to the best of the person's knowledge, information, and belief formed after reasonable inquiry that the instrument is not groundless and brought in bad faith or groundless and brought for harassment, unnecessary delay, or other improper purpose.

(c) If a pleading, motion, or other paper is not signed, the court shall strike it unless it is signed promptly after the omission is called to the attention of the attorney or defendant.

(d) An attorney or defendant who files a fictitious pleading in a cause for an improper purpose described by Subsection (b) or who makes a statement in a pleading that the attorney or defendant knows to be groundless and false to obtain a delay of the trial of the cause or for the purpose of harassment shall be held guilty of contempt.

(e) If a pleading, motion, or other paper is signed in violation of this article, the court, on motion or on its own initiative, after notice and hearing, shall impose an appropriate sanction, which may include an order to pay to the other party or parties to the prosecution or to the general fund of the county in which the pleading, motion, or other paper was filed the amount of reasonable expenses incurred because of the filing of the pleading, motion, or other paper, including reasonable attorney's fees.

(f) A court shall presume that a pleading, motion, or other paper is filed in good faith. Sanctions under this article may not be imposed except for good cause stated in the sanction order.

(g) A plea of "not guilty" or "no contest" or "nolo contendere" does not constitute a violation of this article. An allegation that an event took place or occurred on or about a particular date does not constitute a violation of this article.

(h) In this article, "groundless" means without basis in law or fact and not warranted by a good faith argument for the extension, modification, or reversal of existing law.
(Enacted by Acts 1997, 75th Leg., ch. 189 (H.B. 1185), § 11, effective May 21, 1997.)

## Art. 1.06. Searches and Seizures.

The people shall be secure in their persons, houses, papers and possessions from all unreasonable seizures or searches. No warrant to search any place or to seize any person or thing shall issue without describing them as near as may be, nor without probable cause supported by oath or affirmation.
(Enacted by Acts 1965, 59th Leg., ch. 722 (S.B. 107), § 1, effective January 1, 1966.)

## Art. 1.07. Right to Bail.

All prisoners shall be bailable unless for capital offenses when the proof is evident. This provision shall not be so construed as to prevent bail after indictment found upon examination of the evidence, in such manner as may be prescribed by law.
(Enacted by Acts 1965, 59th Leg., ch. 722 (S.B. 107), § 1, effective January 1, 1966.)

## Art. 1.08. Habeas Corpus.

The writ of habeas corpus is a writ of right and shall never be suspended.
(Enacted by Acts 1965, 59th Leg., ch. 722 (S.B. 107), § 1, effective January 1, 1966.)

## Art. 1.09. Cruelty Forbidden.

Excessive bail shall not be required, nor excessive fines imposed, nor cruel or unusual punishment inflicted.
(Enacted by Acts 1965, 59th Leg., ch. 722 (S.B. 107), § 1, effective January 1, 1966.)

## Art. 1.10. Jeopardy.

No person for the same offense shall be twice put in jeopardy of life or liberty; nor shall a person be again put upon trial for the same offense, after a verdict of not guilty in a court of competent jurisdiction.
(Enacted by Acts 1965, 59th Leg., ch. 722 (S.B. 107), § 1, effective January 1, 1966.)

## Art. 1.11. Acquittal a Bar.

An acquittal of the defendant exempts him from a second trial or a second prosecution for the same offense, however irregular the proceedings may have been; but if the defendant shall have been acquitted upon trial in a court having no jurisdiction of the offense, he may be prosecuted again in a court having jurisdiction.
(Enacted by Acts 1965, 59th Leg., ch. 722 (S.B. 107), § 1, effective January 1, 1966.)

## Art. 1.12. Right to Jury.

The right of trial by jury shall remain inviolate.
(Enacted by Acts 1965, 59th Leg., ch. 722 (S.B. 107), § 1, effective January 1, 1966.)

## Art. 1.13. Waiver of Trial by Jury.

(a) The defendant in a criminal prosecution for any offense other than a capital felony case in which the state notifies the court and the defendant that it will seek the death penalty shall have the right, upon entering a plea, to waive the right of trial by jury, conditioned, however, that, except as provided by Article 27.19, the waiver must be made in person by the defendant in writing in open court with the consent and approval of the court, and the attorney representing the state. The consent and approval by the court shall be entered of record on the minutes of the court, and the consent and approval of the attorney representing the state shall be in writing, signed by that attorney, and filed in the papers of the cause before the defendant enters the defendant's plea.

(b) In a capital felony case in which the attorney representing the State notifies the court and the defendant that it will not seek the death penalty, the defendant may waive the right to trial by jury but only if the attorney representing the State, in writing and in open court, consents to the waiver.

(c) A defendant may agree to waive a jury trial regardless of whether the defendant is represented by an attorney at the time of making the waiver, but before a defendant charged with a felony who has no attorney can agree to waive the jury, the court must appoint an attorney to represent him.

(Enacted by Acts 1965, 59th Leg., ch. 722 (S.B. 107), § 1, effective January 1, 1966; am. Acts 1991, 72nd Leg., ch. 652 (H.B. 9), § 1, effective September 1, 1991; am. Acts 1997, 75th Leg., ch. 285 (H.B. 515), § 1, effective September 1, 1997; am. Acts 2011, 82nd Leg., ch. 1031 (H.B. 2847), § 1, effective September 1, 2011.)

### Art. 1.14. Waiver of Rights.

(a) The defendant in a criminal prosecution for any offense may waive any rights secured him by law except that a defendant in a capital felony case may waive the right of trial by jury only in the manner permitted by Article 1.13(b) of this code.

(b) If the defendant does not object to a defect, error, or irregularity of form or substance in an indictment or information before the date on which the trial on the merits commences, he waives and forfeits the right to object to the defect, error, or irregularity and he may not raise the objection on appeal or in any other postconviction proceeding. Nothing in this article prohibits a trial court from requiring that an objection to an indictment or information be made at an earlier time in compliance with Article 28.01 of this code.

(Enacted by Acts 1965, 59th Leg., ch. 722 (S.B. 107), § 1, effective January 1, 1966; am. Acts 1967, 60th Leg., ch. 659 (S.B. 145), § 1, effective August 28, 1967; am. Acts 1973, 63rd Leg., ch. 426 (H.B. 200), art. 3, § 5, effective June 14, 1973; am. Acts 1985, 69th Leg., ch. 577 (S.B. 169), § 1, effective December 1, 1985; am. Acts 1991, 72nd Leg., ch. 652 (H.B. 9), § 2, effective September 1, 1991.)

### Art. 1.141. Waiver of Indictment for Noncapital Felony.

A person represented by legal counsel may in open court or by written instrument voluntarily waive the right to be accused by indictment of any offense other than a capital felony. On waiver as provided in this article, the accused shall be charged by information.

(Enacted by Acts 1971, 62nd Leg., ch. 260 (S.B. 116), § 1, effective May 19, 1971.)

### Art. 1.15. Jury in Felony.

No person can be convicted of a felony except upon the verdict of a jury duly rendered and recorded, unless the defendant, upon entering a plea, has in open court in person waived his right of trial by jury in writing in accordance with Articles 1.13 and 1.14; provided, however, that it shall be necessary for the state to introduce evidence into the record showing the guilt of the defendant and said evidence shall be accepted by the court as the basis for its judgment and in no event shall a person charged be convicted upon his plea without sufficient evidence to support the same. The evidence may be stipulated if the defendant in such case consents in writing, in open court, to waive the appearance, confrontation, and cross-examination of witnesses, and further consents either to an oral stipulation of the evidence and testimony or to the introduction of testimony by affidavits, written statements of witnesses, and any other documentary evidence in support of the judgment of the court. Such waiver and consent must be approved by the court in writing, and be filed in the file of the papers of the cause.

(Enacted by Acts 1965, 59th Leg., ch. 722 (S.B. 107), § 1, effective January 1, 1966; am. Acts 1967, 60th Leg., ch. 659 (S.B. 145), § 2, effective August 28, 1967; am. Acts 1971, 62nd Leg., ch. 996 (H.B. 1034), § 1, effective June 15, 1971; am. Acts 1973, 63rd Leg., ch. 426 (H.B. 200), art. 3, § 5, effective June 14, 1973; am. Acts 1991, 72nd Leg., ch. 652 (H.B. 9), § 3, effective September 1, 1991.)

### Art. 1.16. Liberty of Speech and Press.

Every person shall be at liberty to speak, write or publish his opinion on any subject, being liable for the abuse of that privilege; and no law shall ever be passed curtailing the liberty of speech or of the press. In prosecutions for the publication of papers investigating the conduct of officers or men in public capacity, or when the matter published is proper for public information, the truth thereof may be given in evidence. In all indictments for libels, the jury shall have the right to determine the law and the facts, under the direction of the court, as in other cases.

**Criminal Procedure**

(Enacted by Acts 1965, 59th Leg., ch. 722 (S.B. 107), § 1, effective January 1, 1966.)

### Art. 1.17. Religious Belief.

No person shall be disqualified to give evidence in any court of this State on account of his religious opinions, or for the want of any religious belief; but all oaths or affirmations shall be administered in the mode most binding upon the conscience, and shall be taken subject to the pains and penalties of perjury.
(Enacted by Acts 1965, 59th Leg., ch. 722 (S.B. 107), § 1, effective January 1, 1966.)

### Art. 1.18. Outlawry and Transportation.

No citizen shall be outlawed, nor shall any person be transported out of the State for any offense committed within the same.
(Enacted by Acts 1965, 59th Leg., ch. 722 (S.B. 107), § 1, effective January 1, 1966.)

### Art. 1.19. Corruption of Blood, Etc.

No conviction shall work corruption of blood or forfeiture of estate.
(Enacted by Acts 1965, 59th Leg., ch. 722 (S.B. 107), § 1, effective January 1, 1966.)

### Art. 1.20. Conviction of Treason.

No person shall be convicted of treason except on the testimony of two witnesses to the same overt act, or on confession in open court.
(Enacted by Acts 1965, 59th Leg., ch. 722 (S.B. 107), § 1, effective January 1, 1966.)

### Art. 1.21. Privilege of Legislators.

Senators and Representatives shall, except in cases of treason, felony or breach of the peace, be privileged from arrest during the session of the Legislature, and in going to and returning from the same, allowing one day for every twenty miles such member may reside from the place at which the Legislature is convened.
(Enacted by Acts 1965, 59th Leg., ch. 722 (S.B. 107), § 1, effective January 1, 1966.)

### Art. 1.22. Privilege of Voters [Repealed].

Repealed by Acts 1985, 69th Leg., ch. 211 (S.B. 616), § 9(a)(6), effective January 1, 1986.

### Art. 1.23. Dignity of State.

All justices of the Supreme Court, judges of the Court of Criminal Appeals, justices of the Courts of Appeals and judges of the District Courts, shall, by virtue of their offices, be conservators of the peace throughout the State. The style of all writs and process shall be "The State of Texas". All prosecutions shall be carried on "in the name and by authority of The State of Texas", and conclude, "against the peace and dignity of the State".
(Enacted by Acts 1965, 59th Leg., ch. 722 (S.B. 107), § 1, effective January 1, 1966; am. Acts 1981, 67th Leg., ch. 291 (S.B. 265), § 97, effective September 1, 1981.)

### Art. 1.24. Public Trial.

The proceedings and trials in all courts shall be public.
(Enacted by Acts 1965, 59th Leg., ch. 722 (S.B. 107), § 1, effective January 1, 1966.)

### Art. 1.25. Confronted by Witnesses.

The defendant, upon a trial, shall be confronted with the witnesses, except in certain cases provided for in this Code where depositions have been taken.
(Enacted by Acts 1965, 59th Leg., ch. 722 (S.B. 107), § 1, effective January 1, 1966.)

### Art. 1.26. Construction of This Code.

The provisions of this Code shall be liberally construed, so as to attain the objects intended by the Legislature: The prevention, suppression and punishment of crime.
(Enacted by Acts 1965, 59th Leg., ch. 722 (S.B. 107), § 1, effective January 1, 1966.)

### Art. 1.27. Common Law Governs.

If this Code fails to provide a rule of procedure in any particular state of case which may arise, the rules of the common law shall be applied and govern.
(Enacted by Acts 1965, 59th Leg., ch. 722 (S.B. 107), § 1, effective January 1, 1966.)

# CHAPTER 2
# GENERAL DUTIES OF OFFICERS

## Art. 2.01. Duties of District Attorneys.

Each district attorney shall represent the State in all criminal cases in the district courts of his district and in appeals therefrom, except in cases where he has been, before his election, employed adversely. When any criminal proceeding is had before an examining court in his district or before a judge upon habeas corpus, and he is notified of the same, and is at the time within his district, he shall represent the State therein, unless prevented by other official duties. It shall be the primary duty of all prosecuting attorneys, including any special prosecutors, not to convict, but to see that justice is done. They shall not suppress facts or secrete witnesses capable of establishing the innocence of the accused.
(Enacted by Acts 1965, 59th Leg., ch. 722 (S.B. 107), § 1, effective January 1, 1966; am. Acts 1981, 67th Leg., ch. 291 (S.B. 265), § 98, effective September 1, 1981.)

## Art. 2.02. Duties of County Attorneys.

The county attorney shall attend the terms of court in his county below the grade of district court, and shall represent the State in all criminal cases under examination or prosecution in said county; and in the absence of the district attorney he shall represent the State alone and, when requested, shall aid the district attorney in the prosecution of any case in behalf of the State in the district court. He shall represent the State in cases he has prosecuted which are appealed.
(Enacted by Acts 1965, 59th Leg., ch. 722 (S.B. 107), § 1, effective January 1, 1966; am. Acts 1981, 67th Leg., ch. 291 (S.B. 265), § 99, effective September 1, 1981.)

## Art. 2.021. Duties of Attorney General.

The attorney general may offer to a county or district attorney the assistance of the attorney general's office in the prosecution of an offense described by Article 60.051(g) the victim of which is younger than 17 years of age at the time the offense is committed. On request of a county or district attorney, the attorney general shall assist in the prosecution of an offense described by Article 60.051(g) the victim of which is younger than 17 years of age at the time the offense is committed. For purposes of this article, assistance includes investigative, technical, and litigation assistance of the attorney general's office.
(Enacted by Acts 2007, 80th Leg., ch. 593 (H.B. 8), § 1.02, effective September 1, 2007.)

Criminal Procedure

## Art. 2.022. Assistance of Texas Rangers.

(a) The attorney representing the state may request the Texas Rangers division of the Department of Public Safety to provide assistance to a local law enforcement agency investigating an offense that:

(1) is alleged to have been committed by an elected officer of the political subdivision served by the local law enforcement agency; and

(2) on conviction or adjudication, would subject the elected officer to registration as a sex offender under Chapter 62.

(b) For purposes of this article, "assistance" includes investigative, technical, and administrative assistance.

(Enacted by Acts 2009, 81st Leg., ch. 431 (H.B. 2130), § 1, effective June 19, 2009.)

## Art. 2.025. Special Duty of District or County Attorney Relating to Child Support.

If a district or county attorney receives money from a person who is required by a court order to pay child support through a local registry or the Title IV-D agency and the money is presented to the attorney as payment for the court-ordered child support, the attorney shall transfer the money to the local registry or Title IV-D agency designated as the place of payment in the child support order.

(Enacted by Acts 1999, 76th Leg., ch. 40 (S.B. 118), § 1, effective September 1, 1999.)

## Art. 2.03. Neglect of Duty.

(a) It shall be the duty of the attorney representing the State to present by information to the court having jurisdiction, any officer for neglect or failure of any duty enjoined upon such officer, when such neglect or failure can be presented by information, whenever it shall come to the knowledge of said attorney that there has been a neglect or failure of duty upon the part of said officer; and he shall bring to the notice of the grand jury any act of violation of law or neglect or failure of duty upon the part of any officer, when such violation, neglect or failure is not presented by information, and whenever the same may come to his knowledge.

(b) It is the duty of the trial court, the attorney representing the accused, the attorney representing the state and all peace officers to so conduct themselves as to insure a fair trial for both the state and the defendant, not impair the presumption of innocence, and at the same time afford the public the benefits of a free press.

(Enacted by Acts 1965, 59th Leg., ch. 722 (S.B. 107), § 1, effective January 1, 1966; am. Acts 1967, 60th Leg., ch. 659 (S.B. 145), § 3, effective August 28, 1967.)

## Art. 2.04. Shall Draw Complaints.

Upon complaint being made before a district or county attorney that an offense has been committed in his district or county, he shall reduce the complaint to writing and cause the same to be signed and sworn to by the complainant, and it shall be duly attested by said attorney.

(Enacted by Acts 1965, 59th Leg., ch. 722 (S.B. 107), § 1, effective January 1, 1966.)

## Art. 2.05. When Complaint Is Made.

If the offense be a misdemeanor, the attorney shall forthwith prepare an information based upon such complaint and file the same in the court having jurisdiction; provided, that in counties having no county attorney, misdemeanor cases may be tried upon complaint alone, without an information, provided, however, in counties having one or more criminal district courts an information must be filed in each misdemeanor case. If the offense be a felony, he shall forthwith file the complaint with a magistrate of the county.

(Enacted by Acts 1965, 59th Leg., ch. 722 (S.B. 107), § 1, effective January 1, 1966.)

## Art. 2.06. May Administer Oaths.

For the purpose mentioned in the two preceding Articles, district and county attorneys are authorized to administer oaths.

(Enacted by Acts 1965, 59th Leg., ch. 722 (S.B. 107), § 1, effective January 1, 1966.)

## Art. 2.07. Attorney Pro Tem.

(a) Whenever an attorney for the state is disqualified to act in any case or proceeding, is absent from the county or district, or is otherwise unable to perform the duties of his office, or in any instance where there is no attorney for the state, the judge of the court in which he represents the state may appoint any competent attorney to perform the duties of the office during the absence or disqualification of the attorney for the state.

(b) Except as otherwise provided by this subsection, if the appointed attorney is also an attorney for the state, the duties of the appointed office are additional duties of his present office, and he is not entitled to additional compensation. Nothing herein shall prevent a commissioners court of a county from contracting with another commissioners court to pay expenses and reimburse compensation paid by a county to an attorney for the state who is appointed to perform additional duties.

(b-1) An attorney for the state who is not disqualified to act may request the court to permit him to recuse himself in a case for good cause and upon approval by the court is disqualified.

(c) If the appointed attorney is not an attorney for the state, he is qualified to perform the duties of the office for the period of absence or disqualification of the attorney for the state on filing an oath with the clerk of the court. He shall receive compensation in the same amount and manner as an attorney appointed to represent an indigent person.

(d) In this article, "attorney for the state" means a county attorney, a district attorney, or a criminal district attorney.

(e) In Subsections (b) and (c) of this article, "attorney for the state" includes an assistant attorney general.

(f) In Subsection (a) of this article, "competent attorney" includes an assistant attorney general.

(g) An attorney appointed under Subsection (a) of this article to perform the duties of the office of an attorney for the state in a justice or municipal court may be paid a reasonable fee for performing those duties.

(Enacted by Acts 1965, 59th Leg., ch. 722 (S.B. 107), § 1, effective January 1, 1966; am. Acts 1967, 60th Leg., ch. 659 (S.B. 145), § 4, effective August 28, 1967; am. Acts 1973, 63rd Leg., ch. 154 (H.B. 759), § 1, effective May 23, 1973; am. Acts 1987, 70th Leg., ch. 918 (H.B. 163), § 1, effective August 31, 1987; am. Acts 1995, 74th Leg., ch. 785 (S.B. 1379), § 1, effective September 1, 1995; am. Acts 1999, 76th Leg., ch. 1545 (S.B. 1230), § 1, effective September 1, 1999.)

## Art. 2.08. Disqualified.

(a) District and county attorneys shall not be of counsel adversely to the State in any case, in any court, nor shall they, after they cease to be such officers, be of counsel adversely to the State in any case in which they have been of counsel for the State.

(b) A judge of a court in which a district or county attorney represents the State shall declare the district or county attorney disqualified for purposes of Article 2.07 on a showing that the

attorney is the subject of a criminal investigation by a law enforcement agency if that investigation is based on credible evidence of criminal misconduct for an offense that is within the attorney's authority to prosecute. A disqualification under this subsection applies only to the attorney's access to the criminal investigation pending against the attorney and to any prosecution of a criminal charge resulting from that investigation.

(Enacted by Acts 1965, 59th Leg., ch. 722 (S.B. 107), § 1, effective January 1, 1966; am. Acts 2011, 82nd Leg., ch. 977 (H.B. 1638), § 1, effective September 1, 2011.)

## Art. 2.09. [Effective until January 1, 2012] Who Are Magistrates.

Each of the following officers is a magistrate within the meaning of this Code: The justices of the Supreme Court, the judges of the Court of Criminal Appeals, the justices of the Courts of Appeals, the judges of the District Court, the magistrates appointed by the judges of the district courts of Bexar County, Dallas County, or Tarrant County that give preference to criminal cases, the criminal law hearing officers for Harris County appointed under Subchapter L, Chapter 54, Government Code, the criminal law hearing officers for Cameron County appointed under Subchapter BB, Chapter 54, Government Code, the magistrates appointed by the judges of the district courts of Lubbock County, Nolan County, or Webb County, the magistrates appointed by the judges of the criminal district courts of Dallas County or Tarrant County, the masters appointed by the judges of the district courts and the county courts at law that give preference to criminal cases in Jefferson County, the magistrates appointed by the judges of the district courts and the statutory county courts of Brazos County, Nueces County, or Williamson County, the magistrates appointed by the judges of the district courts and statutory county courts that give preference to criminal cases in Travis County, the criminal magistrates appointed by the Brazoria County Commissioners Court, the criminal magistrates appointed by the Burnet County Commissioners Court, the county judges, the judges of the county courts at law, judges of the county criminal courts, the judges of statutory probate courts, the associate judges appointed by the judges of the statutory probate courts under Subchapter G, Chapter 54, Government Code, the associate judges appointed by the judge of a district court under Subchapter II, Chapter 54, Government Code, the magistrates appointed under Subchapter JJ, Chapter 54, Government Code, the justices of the peace, and the mayors and recorders and the judges of the municipal courts of incorporated cities or towns.

(Enacted by Acts 1965, 59th Leg., ch. 722 (S.B. 107), § 1, effective January 1, 1966; am. Acts 1981, 67th Leg., ch. 291 (S.B. 265), § 100, effective September 1, 1981; am. Acts 1983, 68th Leg., ch. 204 (S.B. 781), § 1, effective August 29, 1983; am. Acts 1989, 71st Leg., ch. 25 (S.B. 577), § 2, effective August 28, 1989; am. Acts 1989, 71st Leg., ch. 79 (S.B. 38), § 1, effective May 15, 1989; am. Acts 1989, 71st Leg., ch. 916 (S.B. 515), § 1, effective September 1, 1989; am. Acts 1989, 71st Leg., ch. 1068 (H.B. 4722), § 2, effective August 28, 1989; am. Acts 1991, 72nd Leg., ch. 16 (S.B. 232), § 4.01, effective August 26, 1991; am. Acts 1993, 73rd Leg., ch. 224 (H.B. 2113), § 2, effective August 30, 1993; am. Acts 1993, 73rd Leg., ch. 413 (S.B. 667), § 1, effective September 1, 1993; am. Acts 1993, 73rd Leg., ch. 468 (H.B. 567), § 1, effective June 9, 1993; am. Acts 1993, 73rd Leg., ch. 577 (H.B. 965), § 2, effective August 30, 1993; am. Acts 1999, 76th Leg., ch. 586 (S.B. 611), § 2, effective June 18, 1999; am. Acts 1999, 76th Leg., ch. 1503 (S.B. 294), § 2, effective September 1, 1999; am. Acts 2003, 78th Leg., ch. 979 (S.B. 1794), § 1, effective September 1, 2003; am. Acts 2003, 78th Leg., ch. 1066 (H.B. 1539), § 9, effective September 1, 2003; am. Acts 2005, 79th Leg., ch. 109 (S.B. 552), § 2, effective May 20, 2005; am. Acts 2005, 79th Leg., ch. 767 (H.B. 3485), § 2, effective September 1, 2005; am. Acts 2005, 79th Leg., ch. 1331 (H.B. 3541), § 1, effective September 1, 2005; am. Acts 2007, 80th Leg., ch. 1141 (H.B. 4107), § 1, effective September 1, 2007; am. Acts 2009, 81st Leg., ch. 646 (H.B. 1750), § 2, effective June 19, 2009; am. Acts 2009, 81st Leg., ch. 964 (H.B. 3554), § 2, effective June 19, 2009; am. Acts 2011, 82nd Leg., ch. 863 (H.B. 3844), § 2, effective June 17, 2011; am. Acts 2011, 82nd Leg., ch. 995 (H.B. 2132), § 2, effective June 17, 2011.)

### Art. 2.09. [Effective January 1, 2012] Who Are Magistrates.

Each of the following officers is a magistrate within the meaning of this Code: The justices of the Supreme Court, the judges of the Court of Criminal Appeals, the justices of the Courts of Appeals, the judges of the District Court, the magistrates appointed by the judges of the dis-

trict courts of Bexar County, Dallas County, or Tarrant County that give preference to criminal cases, the criminal law hearing officers for Harris County appointed under Subchapter L, Chapter 54, Government Code, the criminal law hearing officers for Cameron County appointed under Subchapter BB, Chapter 54, Government Code, the magistrates or associate judges appointed by the judges of the district courts of Lubbock County, Nolan County, or Webb County, the magistrates appointed by the judges of the criminal district courts of Dallas County or Tarrant County, the associate judges appointed by the judges of the district courts and the county courts at law that give preference to criminal cases in Jefferson County, the associate judges appointed by the judges of the district courts and the statutory county courts of Brazos County, Nueces County, or Williamson County, the magistrates appointed by the judges of the district courts and statutory county courts that give preference to criminal cases in Travis County, the criminal magistrates appointed by the Brazoria County Commissioners Court, the criminal magistrates appointed by the Burnet County Commissioners Court, the county judges, the judges of the county courts at law, judges of the county criminal courts, the judges of statutory probate courts, the associate judges appointed by the judges of the statutory probate courts under Chapter 54A, Government Code, the associate judges appointed by the judge of a district court under Chapter 54A, Government Code, the magistrates appointed under Subchapter JJ, Chapter 54, Government Code, as added by H.B. No. 2132, Acts of the 82nd Legislature, Regular Session, 2011, the justices of the peace, and the mayors and recorders and the judges of the municipal courts of incorporated cities or towns.

(Enacted by Acts 1965, 59th Leg., ch. 722 (S.B. 107), § 1, effective January 1, 1966; am. Acts 1981, 67th Leg., ch. 291 (S.B. 265), § 100, effective September 1, 1981; am. Acts 1983, 68th Leg., ch. 204 (S.B. 781), § 1, effective August 29, 1983; am. Acts 1989, 71st Leg., ch. 25 (S.B. 577), § 2, effective August 28, 1989; am. Acts 1989, 71st Leg., ch. 79 (S.B. 38), § 1, effective May 15, 1989; am. Acts 1989, 71st Leg., ch. 916 (S.B. 515), § 1, effective September 1, 1989; am. Acts 1989, 71st Leg., ch. 1068 (H.B. 4722), § 2, effective August 28, 1989; am. Acts 1991, 72nd Leg., ch. 16 (S.B. 232), § 4.01, effective August 26, 1991; am. Acts 1993, 73rd Leg., ch. 224 (H.B. 2113), § 2, effective August 30, 1993; am. Acts 1993, 73rd Leg., ch. 413 (S.B. 667), § 1, effective September 1, 1993;

am. Acts 1993, 73rd Leg., ch. 468 (H.B. 567), § 1, effective June 9, 1993; am. Acts 1993, 73rd Leg., ch. 577 (H.B. 965), § 2, effective August 30, 1993; am. Acts 1999, 76th Leg., ch. 586 (S.B. 611), § 2, effective June 18, 1999; am. Acts 1999, 76th Leg., ch. 1503 (S.B. 294), § 2, effective September 1, 1999; am. Acts 2003, 78th Leg., ch. 979 (S.B. 1794), § 1, effective September 1, 2003; am. Acts 2003, 78th Leg., ch. 1066 (H.B. 1539), § 9, effective September 1, 2003; am. Acts 2005, 79th Leg., ch. 109 (S.B. 552), § 2, effective May 20, 2005; am. Acts 2005, 79th Leg., ch. 767 (H.B. 3485), § 2, effective September 1, 2005; am. Acts 2005, 79th Leg., ch. 1331 (H.B. 3541), § 1, effective September 1, 2005; am. Acts 2007, 80th Leg., ch. 1141 (H.B. 4107), § 1, effective September 1, 2007; am. Acts 2009, 81st Leg., ch. 646 (H.B. 1750), § 2, effective June 19, 2009; am. Acts 2009, 81st Leg., ch. 964 (H.B. 3554), § 2, effective June 19, 2009; am. Acts 2011, 82nd Leg., ch. 863 (H.B. 3844), § 2, effective June 17, 2011; am. Acts 2011, 82nd Leg., ch. 995 (H.B. 2132), § 2, effective June 17, 2011; am. Acts 2011, 82nd Leg., 1st C.S., (H.B. 79), § 6.06, effective January 1, 2012.)

## Art. 2.10. Duty of Magistrates.

It is the duty of every magistrate to preserve the peace within his jurisdiction by the use of all lawful means; to issue all process intended to aid in preventing and suppressing crime; to cause the arrest of offenders by the use of lawful means in order that they may be brought to punishment. (Enacted by Acts 1965, 59th Leg., ch. 722 (S.B. 107), § 1, effective January 1, 1966.)

## Art. 2.11. Examining Court.

When the magistrate sits for the purpose of inquiring into a criminal accusation against any person, this is called an examining court. (Enacted by Acts 1965, 59th Leg., ch. 722 (S.B. 107), § 1, effective January 1, 1966.)

## Art. 2.12. Who Are Peace Officers.

The following are peace officers:

(1) sheriffs, their deputies, and those reserve deputies who hold a permanent peace officer license issued under Chapter 1701, Occupations Code;

(2) constables, deputy constables, and those reserve deputy constables who hold a permanent peace officer license issued under Chapter 1701, Occupations Code;

(3) marshals or police officers of an incorporated city, town, or village, and those reserve municipal police officers who hold a permanent peace officer license issued under Chapter 1701, Occupations Code;

(4) rangers and officers commissioned by the Public Safety Commission and the Director of the Department of Public Safety;

(5) investigators of the district attorneys', criminal district attorneys', and county attorneys' offices;

(6) law enforcement agents of the Texas Alcoholic Beverage Commission;

(7) each member of an arson investigating unit commissioned by a city, a county, or the state;

(8) officers commissioned under Section 37.081, Education Code, or Subchapter E, Chapter 51, Education Code;

(9) officers commissioned by the General Services Commission;

(10) law enforcement officers commissioned by the Parks and Wildlife Commission;

(11) airport police officers commissioned by a city with a population of more than 1.18 million located primarily in a county with a population of 2 million or more that operates an airport that serves commercial air carriers;

(12) airport security personnel commissioned as peace officers by the governing body of any political subdivision of this state, other than a city described by Subdivision (11), that operates an airport that serves commercial air carriers;

(13) municipal park and recreational patrolmen and security officers;

(14) security officers and investigators commissioned as peace officers by the comptroller;

(15) officers commissioned by a water control and improvement district under Section 49.216, Water Code;

(16) officers commissioned by a board of trustees under Chapter 54, Transportation Code;

(17) investigators commissioned by the Texas Medical Board;

(18) officers commissioned by:

(A) the board of managers of the Dallas County Hospital District, the Tarrant County Hospital District, the Bexar County Hospital District, or the El Paso County Hospital District under Section 281.057, Health and Safety Code; and

(B) the board of directors of the Ector County Hospital District under Section 1024.117, Special District Local Laws Code;

*Criminal Procedure*

(19) county park rangers commissioned under Subchapter E, Chapter 351, Local Government Code;

(20) investigators employed by the Texas Racing Commission;

(21) officers commissioned under Chapter 554, Occupations Code;

(22) officers commissioned by the governing body of a metropolitan rapid transit authority under Section 451.108, Transportation Code, or by a regional transportation authority under Section 452.110, Transportation Code;

(23) investigators commissioned by the attorney general under Section 402.009, Government Code;

(24) security officers and investigators commissioned as peace officers under Chapter 466, Government Code;

(25) an officer employed by the Department of State Health Services under Section 431.2471, Health and Safety Code;

(26) officers appointed by an appellate court under Subchapter F, Chapter 53, Government Code;

(27) officers commissioned by the state fire marshal under Chapter 417, Government Code;

(28) an investigator commissioned by the commissioner of insurance under Section 701.104, Insurance Code;

(29) apprehension specialists and inspectors general commissioned by the Texas Juvenile Justice Department as officers under Sections 242.102 and 243.052, Human Resources Code;

(30) officers appointed by the inspector general of the Texas Department of Criminal Justice under Section 493.019, Government Code;

(31) investigators commissioned by the Commission on Law Enforcement Officer Standards and Education under Section 1701.160, Occupations Code;

(32) commission investigators commissioned by the Texas Private Security Board under Section 1702.061(f), Occupations Code;

(33) the fire marshal and any officers, inspectors, or investigators commissioned by an emergency services district under Chapter 775, Health and Safety Code;

(34) officers commissioned by the State Board of Dental Examiners under Section 254.013, Occupations Code, subject to the limitations imposed by that section;

(35) investigators commissioned by the Texas Juvenile Justice Department as officers under Section 221.011, Human Resources Code; and

(36) the fire marshal and any related officers, inspectors, or investigators commissioned by a county under Subchapter B, Chapter 352, Local Government Code.

(Enacted by Acts 1965, 59th Leg., ch. 722 (S.B. 107), § 1, effective January 1, 1966; am. Acts 1967, 60th Leg., ch. 659 (S.B. 145), § 5, effective August 28, 1967; am. Acts 1971, 62nd Leg., ch. 246 (H.B. 468), § 3, effective May 17, 1971; am. Acts 1973, 63rd Leg., ch. 7 (H.B. 82), § 2, effective August 27, 1973; am. Acts 1973, 63rd Leg., ch. 459 (S.B. 769), § 1, effective August 27, 1973; am. Acts 1975, 64th Leg., ch. 204 (H.B. 341), § 1, effective September 1, 1975; am. Acts 1977, 65th Leg., ch. 227 (S.B. 719), § 2, effective May 24, 1977; am. Acts 1977, 65th Leg., ch. 396 (S.B. 146), § 1, effective August 29, 1977; am. Acts 1983, 68th Leg., ch. 114 (S.B. 346), § 1, effective May 17, 1983; am. Acts 1983, 68th Leg., ch. 699 (S.B. 1352), § 11, effective June 19, 1983; am. Acts 1983, 68th Leg., ch. 867 (H.B. 1304), § 2, effective June 19, 1983; am. Acts 1983, 68th Leg., ch. 974 (H.B. 1999), § 11, effective August 29, 1983; am. Acts 1985, 69th Leg., ch. 384 (H.B. 1248), § 2, effective August 26, 1985; am. Acts 1985, 69th Leg., ch. 907 (H.B. 1592), § 6, effective September 1, 1985; am. Acts 1986, 69th Leg., 2nd C.S., ch. 19 (S.B. 15), § 4, effective December 4, 1986; am. Acts 1987, 70th Leg., ch. 262 (S.B. 1161), § 20, effective September 1, 1987; am. Acts 1987, 70th Leg., ch. 350 (H.B. 791), § 1, effective August 31, 1987; am. Acts 1989, 71st Leg., ch. 277 (H.B. 2780), § 4, effective June 14, 1989; am. Acts 1989, 71st Leg., ch. 794 (H.B. 427), § 1, effective August 28, 1989; am. Acts 1989, 71st Leg., ch. 1104 (S.B. 1190), § 4, effective June 16, 1989; am. Acts 1991, 72nd Leg., ch. 16 (S.B. 232), § 4.02, effective August 26, 1991; am. Acts 1991, 72nd Leg., ch. 228 (H.B. 693), § 1, effective September 1, 1991; am. Acts 1991, 72nd Leg., ch. 287 (S.B. 1222), § 24, effective September 1, 1991; am. Acts 1991, 72nd Leg., ch. 386 (H.B. 2263), § 70, effective August 26, 1991; am. Acts 1991, 72nd Leg., ch. 446 (S.B. 411), § 1, effective June 11, 1991; am. Acts 1991, 72nd Leg., ch. 544 (S.B. 1816), § 1, effective August 26, 1991; am. Acts 1991, 72nd Leg., ch. 545 (H.B. 2140), § 2, effective August 26, 1991; am. Acts 1991, 72nd Leg., ch. 597 (S.B. 992), § 57, effective September 1, 1991; am. Acts 1991, 72nd Leg., ch. 853 (S.B. 1412), § 2, effective September 1, 1991; am. Acts 1991, 72nd Leg., 1st C.S., ch. 6 (H.B. 54), § 6, effective November 5, 1991; am. Acts 1991, 72nd Leg., 1st

C.S., ch. 14 (H.B. 169), § 3.01, effective November 12, 1991; am. Acts 1993, 73rd Leg., ch. 107 (H.B. 947), § 4.07, effective August 30, 1993; am. Acts 1993, 73rd Leg., ch. 116 (H.B. 635), § 1, effective August 30, 1993; am. Acts 1993, 73rd Leg., ch. 339 (S.B. 563), § 2, effective September 1, 1993; am. Acts 1993, 73rd Leg., ch. 695 (S.B. 841), § 2, effective September 1, 1993; am. Acts 1993, 73rd Leg., ch. 912 (S.B. 1110), § 25, effective September 1, 1993; am. Acts 1995, 74th Leg., ch. 260 (S.B. 1), § 10, effective May 30, 1995; am. Acts 1995, 74th Leg., ch. 621 (H.B. 1487), § 2, effective September 1, 1995; am. Acts 1995, 74th Leg., ch. 729 (H.B. 1275), § 1, effective August 28, 1995; am. Acts 1997, 75th Leg., ch. 1423 (H.B. 2841), § 4.01, effective September 1, 1997; am. Acts 1999, 76th Leg., ch. 90 (H.B. 957), § 1, effective September 1, 1999; am. Acts 1999, 76th Leg., ch. 322 (H.B. 1112), § 2, effective May 29, 1999; am. Acts 1999, 76th Leg., ch. 882 (H.B. 2023), § 2, effective June 18, 1999; am. Acts 1999, 76th Leg., ch. 974 (H.B. 2617), § 37, effective September 1, 1999; am. Acts 2001, 77th Leg., ch. 272 (S.B. 1167), § 7, effective September 1, 2001; am. Acts 2001, 77th Leg., ch. 442 (S.B. 1123), § 1, effective September 1, 2001; am. Acts 2001, 77th Leg., ch. 669 (H.B. 2810), § 8, effective September 1, 2001; am. Acts 2001, 77th Leg., ch. 1420 (H.B. 2812), § 3.001), effective September 1, 2001; am. Acts 2003, 78th Leg., ch. 235, effective September 1, 2003; am. Acts 2003, 78th Leg., ch. 474 (H.B. 875), § 1, effective June 20, 2003; am. Acts 2003, 78th Leg., ch. 930 (S.B. 1022), § 12, effective September 1, 2003; am. Acts 2005, 79th Leg., ch. 728 (H.B. 2018), § 4.001, effective September 1, 2005; am. Acts 2007, 80th Leg., ch. 263 (S.B. 103), § 1, effective June 8, 2007; am. Acts 2007, 80th Leg., ch. 838 (H.B. 914), § 1, effective June 15, 2007; am. Acts 2007, 80th Leg., ch. 908 (H.B. 2884), § 1, effective September 1, 2007; am. Acts 2007, 80th Leg., ch. 1172 (H.B. 434), § 1, effective June 15, 2007; am. Acts 2009, 81st Leg., ch. 1164 (H.B. 3201), § 1, effective June 19, 2009; am. Acts 2011, 82nd Leg., ch. 85 (S.B. 653), § 3.001, effective September 1, 2011; am. Acts 2011, 82nd Leg., ch. 402 (S.B. 601), § 2, effective June 17, 2011; am. Acts 2011, 82nd Leg., ch. 584 (H.B. 3815), § 2, effective June 17, 2011; am. Acts 2011, 82nd Leg., ch. 1163 (H.B. 2702), § 5, effective September 1, 2011.)

## Art. 2.121. Railroad Peace Officers.

(a) The director of the Department of Public Safety may appoint up to 250 railroad peace officers who are employed by a railroad company to aid law enforcement agencies in the protection of railroad property and the protection of the persons and property of railroad passengers and employees.

(b) Except as provided by Subsection (c) of this article, a railroad peace officer may make arrests and exercise all authority given peace officers under this code when necessary to prevent or abate the commission of an offense involving injury to passengers and employees of the railroad or damage to railroad property or to protect railroad property or property in the custody or control of the railroad.

(c) A railroad peace officer may not issue a traffic citation for a violation of Chapter 521, Transportation Code, or Subtitle C, Title 7, Transportation Code.

(d) A railroad peace officer is not entitled to state benefits normally provided by the state to a peace officer.

(e) A person may not serve as a railroad peace officer for a railroad company unless:

(1) the Texas Railroad Association submits the person's application for appointment and certification as a railroad peace officer to the director of the Department of Public Safety and to the executive director of the Commission on Law Enforcement Officer Standards and Education;

(2) the director of the department issues the person a certificate of authority to act as a railroad peace officer; and

(3) the executive director of the commission determines that the person meets minimum standards required of peace officers by the commission relating to competence, reliability, education, training, morality, and physical and mental health and issues the person a license as a railroad peace officer; and

(4) the person has met all standards for certification as a peace officer by the Commission on Law Enforcement Officer Standards and Education.

(f) For good cause, the director of the department may revoke a certificate of authority issued under this article and the executive director of the commission may revoke a license issued under this article. Termination of employment with a railroad company, or the revocation of a railroad peace officer license, shall constitute an automatic revocation of a certificate of authority to act as a railroad peace officer.

(g) A railroad company is liable for any act or omission by a person serving as a railroad peace

*Criminal Procedure*

officer for the company that is within the person's scope of employment. Neither the state nor any political subdivision or agency of the state shall be liable for any act or omission by a person appointed as a railroad peace officer. All expenses incurred by the granting or revocation of a certificate of authority to act as a railroad peace officer shall be paid by the employing railroad company.

(h) A railroad peace officer who is a member of a railroad craft may not perform the duties of a member of any other railroad craft during a strike or labor dispute.

(i) The director of the department and the executive director of the commission shall have the authority to promulgate rules necessary for the effective administration and performance of the duties and responsibilities delegated to them by this article.

(Enacted by Acts 1985, 69th Leg., ch. 531 (H.B. 740), § 1, effective June 12, 1985; am. Acts 1999, 76th Leg., ch. 62 (S.B. 1368), § 3.01, effective September 1, 1999.)

## Art. 2.122. Special Investigators.

(a) The following named criminal investigators of the United States shall not be deemed peace officers, but shall have the powers of arrest, search, and seizure under the laws of this state as to felony offenses only:

(1) Special Agents of the Federal Bureau of Investigation;

(2) Special Agents of the Secret Service;

(3) Special Agents of the United States Immigration and Customs Enforcement;

(4) Special Agents of the Bureau of Alcohol, Tobacco, Firearms and Explosives;

(5) Special Agents of the United States Drug Enforcement Administration;

(6) Inspectors of the United States Postal Inspection Service;

(7) Special Agents of the Criminal Investigation Division of the Internal Revenue Service;

(8) Civilian Special Agents of the United States Naval Criminal Investigative Service;

(9) Marshals and Deputy Marshals of the United States Marshals Service;

(10) Special Agents of the United States Department of State, Bureau of Diplomatic Security;

(11) Special Agents of the Treasury Inspector General for Tax Administration; and

(12) [2 Versions: As added by Acts 2011, 82nd Leg., ch. 1223] Special Agents of the Office of Inspector General of the United States Social Security Administration.

(12) [2 Versions: As added by Acts 2011, 82nd Leg., ch. 1319] Special Agents of the Office of Inspector General of the United States Department of Veterans Affairs.

(b) A person designated as a special policeman by the Federal Protective Services division of the General Services Administration under 40 U.S.C. Section 318 or 318d is not a peace officer but has the powers of arrest and search and seizure as to any offense under the laws of this state.

(c) A Customs and Border Protection Officer or Border Patrol Agent of the United States Customs and Border Protection or an immigration enforcement agent or deportation officer of the Department of Homeland Security is not a peace officer under the laws of this state but, on the premises of a port facility designated by the commissioner of the United States Customs and Border Protection as a port of entry for arrival in the United States by land transportation from the United Mexican States into the State of Texas or at a permanent established border patrol traffic check point, has the authority to detain a person pending transfer without unnecessary delay to a peace officer if the agent or officer has probable cause to believe that the person has engaged in conduct that is a violation of Section 49.02, 49.04, 49.07, or 49.08, Penal Code, regardless of whether the violation may be disposed of in a criminal proceeding or a juvenile justice proceeding.

(d) A commissioned law enforcement officer of the National Park Service is not a peace officer under the laws of this state, except that the officer has the powers of arrest, search, and seizure as to any offense under the laws of this state committed within the boundaries of a national park or national recreation area. In this subsection, "national park or national recreation area" means a national park or national recreation area included in the National Park System as defined by 16 U.S.C. Section 1c(a).

(e) A Special Agent or Law Enforcement Officer of the United States Forest Service is not a peace officer under the laws of this state, except that the agent or officer has the powers of arrest, search, and seizure as to any offense under the laws of this state committed within the National Forest System. In this subsection, "National Forest System" has the meaning assigned by 16 U.S.C. Section 1609.

(f) Security personnel working at a commercial nuclear power plant, including contract security personnel, trained and qualified under a security plan approved by the United States Nuclear

Regulatory Commission, are not peace officers under the laws of this state, except that such personnel have the powers of arrest, search, and seizure, including the powers under Section 9.51, Penal Code, while in the performance of their duties on the premises of a commercial nuclear power plant site or under agreements entered into with local law enforcement regarding areas surrounding the plant site.

(g) In addition to the powers of arrest, search, and seizure under Subsection (a), a Special Agent of the Secret Service protecting a person described by 18 U.S.C. Section 3056(a) or investigating a threat against a person described by 18 U.S.C. Section 3056(a) has the powers of arrest, search, and seizure as to:

(1) misdemeanor offenses under the laws of this state; and

(2) any criminal offense under federal law.
(Enacted by Acts 1985, 69th Leg., ch. 543 (H.B. 1351), § 1, effective September 1, 1985; am. Acts 1987, 70th Leg., ch. 503 (H.B. 279), § 1, effective August 31, 1987 (renumbered from art. 2.121); am. Acts 1987, 70th Leg., ch. 854 (H.B. 41), § 1, effective August 31, 1987 (renumbered from art. 2.121); am. Acts 1989, 71st Leg., ch. 841 (S.B. 567), § 1, effective June 14, 1989; am. Acts 1993, 73rd Leg., ch. 927 (H.B. 1182), § 1, effective June 19, 1993; am. Acts 1997, 75th Leg., ch. 290 (H.B. 870), § 1, effective May 26, 1997; am. Acts 1997, 75th Leg., ch. 717 (H.B. 253), § 1, effective June 17, 1997; am. Acts 1999, 76th Leg., ch. 197 (H.B. 525), § 1, effective May 24, 1999; am. Acts 1999, 76th Leg., ch. 628 (S.B. 965), § 1, effective June 18, 1999; am. Acts 1999, 76th Leg., ch. 863 (H.B. 1907), § 1, effective June 18, 1999; am. Acts 2001, 77th Leg., ch. 1420 (H.B. 2812), § 21.001(7), effective September 1, 2001; am. Acts 2003, 78th Leg., ch. 1237 (S.B. 1517), § 1, effective June 20, 2003; am. Acts 2005, 79th Leg., ch. 1337 (S.B. 9), § 5, effective June 18, 2005; am. Acts 2009, 81st Leg., ch. 732 (S.B. 390), § 1, effective September 1, 2009; am. Acts 2011, 82nd Leg., ch. 1223 (S.B. 530), § 1, effective June 17, 2011; am. Acts 2011, 82nd Leg., ch. 1319 (S.B. 150), § 1, effective June 17, 2011.)

### Art. 2.123. Adjunct Police Officers.

(a) Within counties under 200,000 population, the chief of police of a municipality or the sheriff of the county, if the institution is outside the corporate limits of a municipality, that has jurisdiction over the geographical area of a private institution of higher education, provided the governing board of such institution consents, may appoint up to 50 peace officers who are commissioned under Section 51.212, Education Code, and who are employed by a private institution of higher education located in the municipality or county, to serve as adjunct police officers of the municipality or county. Officers appointed under this article shall aid law enforcement agencies in the protection of the municipality or county in a geographical area that is designated by agreement on an annual basis between the appointing chief of police or sheriff and the private institution.

(b) The geographical area that is subject to designation under Subsection (a) of this article may include only the private institution's campus area and an area that:

(1) is adjacent to the campus of the private institution;

(2) does not extend further than a distance of one mile from the perimeter of the campus of the private institution; and

(3) is inhabited primarily by students or employees of the private institution.

(c) A peace officer serving as an adjunct police officer may make arrests and exercise all authority given peace officers under this code only within the geographical area designated by agreement between the appointing chief of police or sheriff and the private institution.

(d) A peace officer serving as an adjunct police officer has all the rights, privileges, and immunities of a peace officer but is not entitled to state compensation and retirement benefits normally provided by the state to a peace officer.

(e) A person may not serve as an adjunct police officer for a municipality or county unless:

(1) the institution of higher education submits the person's application for appointment and certification as an adjunct police officer to the chief of police of the municipality or, if outside a municipality, the sheriff of the county that has jurisdiction over the geographical area of the institution;

(2) the chief of police of the municipality or sheriff of the county to whom the application was made issues the person a certificate of authority to act as an adjunct police officer; and

(3) the person undergoes any additional training required for that person to meet the training standards of the municipality or county for peace officers employed by the municipality or county.

(f) For good cause, the chief of police or sheriff may revoke a certificate of authority issued under this article.

*Criminal Procedure*

Criminal Procedure

(g) A private institution of higher education is liable for any act or omission by a person while serving as an adjunct police officer outside of the campus of the institution in the same manner as the municipality or county governing that geographical area is liable for any act or omission of a peace officer employed by the municipality or county. This subsection shall not be construed to act as a limitation on the liability of a municipality or county for the acts or omissions of a person serving as an adjunct police officer.

(h) The employing institution shall pay all expenses incurred by the municipality or county in granting or revoking a certificate of authority to act as an adjunct police officer under this article.

(i) This article does not affect any duty of the municipality or county to provide law enforcement services to a geographical area designated under Subsection (a) of this article.
(Enacted by Acts 1987, 70th Leg., ch. 1128 (H.B. 957), § 1, effective August 31, 1987.)

## Art. 2.124. Peace Officers from Adjoining States.

(a) A commissioned peace officer of a state of the United States of America adjoining this state, while the officer is in this state, has under this subsection the same powers, duties, and immunities as a peace officer of this state who is acting in the discharge of an official duty, but only:

(1) during a time in which:

(A) the peace officer from the adjoining state has physical custody of an inmate or criminal defendant and is transporting the inmate or defendant from a county in the adjoining state that is on the border between the two states to a hospital or other medical facility in a county in this state that is on the border between the two states; or

(B) the peace officer has physical custody of the inmate or defendant and is returning the inmate or defendant from the hospital or facility to the county in the adjoining state; and

(2) to the extent necessary to:

(A) maintain physical custody of the inmate or defendant while transporting the inmate or defendant; or

(B) regain physical custody of the inmate or defendant if the inmate or defendant escapes while being transported.

(b) A commissioned peace officer of a state of the United States of America adjoining this state, while the officer is in this state, has under this subsection the same powers, duties, and immunities as a peace officer of this state who is acting in the discharge of an official duty, but only in a municipality some part of the municipal limits of which are within one mile of the boundary between this state and the adjoining state and only at a time the peace officer is regularly assigned to duty in a county, parish, or municipality that adjoins this state. A peace officer described by this subsection may also as part of the officer's powers in this state enforce the ordinances of a Texas municipality described by this subsection but only after the governing body of the municipality authorizes that enforcement by majority vote at an open meeting.
(Enacted by Acts 1995, 74th Leg., ch. 156 (H.B. 1155), § 1, effective May 19, 1995; am. Acts 1999, 76th Leg., ch. 107 (H.B. 165), § 1, effective September 1, 1999.)

## Art. 2.125. Special Rangers of Texas and Southwestern Cattle Raisers Association.

(a) The director of the Department of Public Safety may appoint up to 50 special rangers who are employed by the Texas and Southwestern Cattle Raisers Association to aid law enforcement agencies in the investigation of the theft of livestock or related property.

(b) Except as provided by Subsection (c) of this article, a special ranger may make arrests and exercise all authority given peace officers under this code when necessary to prevent or abate the commission of an offense involving livestock or related property.

(c) A special ranger may not issue a traffic citation for a violation of Chapter 521, Transportation Code, or Subtitle C, Title 7, Transportation Code.

(d) A special ranger is not entitled to state benefits normally provided by the state to a peace officer.

(e) A person may not serve as a special ranger unless:

(1) the Texas and Southwestern Cattle Raisers Association submits the person's application for appointment and certification as a special ranger to the director of the Department of Public Safety and to the executive director of the Commission on Law Enforcement Officer Standards and Education;

(2) the director of the department issues the person a certificate of authority to act as a special ranger;

(3) the executive director of the commission determines that the person meets minimum standards required of peace officers by the commission relating to competence, reliability, education, training, morality, and physical and mental health and issues the person a license as a special ranger; and

(4) the person has met all standards for certification as a peace officer by the Commission on Law Enforcement Officer Standards and Education.

(f) For good cause, the director of the department may revoke a certificate of authority issued under this article and the executive director of the commission may revoke a license issued under this article. Termination of employment with the association, or the revocation of a special ranger license, shall constitute an automatic revocation of a certificate of authority to act as a special ranger.

(g) The Texas and Southwestern Cattle Raisers Association is liable for any act or omission by a person serving as a special ranger for the association that is within the person's scope of employment. Neither the state nor any political subdivision or agency of the state shall be liable for any act or omission by a person appointed as a special ranger. All expenses incurred by the granting or revocation of a certificate of authority to act as a special ranger shall be paid by the association.

(h) The director of the department and the executive director of the commission shall have the authority to promulgate rules necessary for the effective administration and performance of the duties and responsibilities delegated to them by this article.

(Enacted by Acts 2005, 79th Leg., ch. 209 (H.B. 1695), § 1, effective September 1, 2005.)

### Art. 2.126. Peace Officers Commissioned by the Alabama-Coushatta Indian Tribe.

(a) The tribal council of the Alabama-Coushatta Indian Tribe is authorized to employ and commission peace officers for the purpose of enforcing state law within the boundaries of the tribe's reservation.

(b) Within the boundaries of the tribe's reservation, a peace officer commissioned under this article:

(1) is vested with all the powers, privileges, and immunities of peace officers;

(2) may, in accordance with Chapter 14, arrest without a warrant any person who violates a law of the state; and

(3) may enforce all traffic laws on streets and highways.

(c) Outside the boundaries of the tribe's reservation, a peace officer commissioned under this article is vested with all the powers, privileges, and immunities of peace officers and may arrest any person who violates any law of the state if the peace officer:

(1) is summoned by another law enforcement agency to provide assistance; or

(2) is assisting another law enforcement agency.

(d) Any officer assigned to duty and commissioned under this article shall take and file the oath required of peace officers and shall execute and file a good and sufficient bond in the sum of $1,000, payable to the governor, with two or more good and sufficient sureties, conditioned that the officer will fairly, impartially, and faithfully perform the duties as may be required of the officer by law. The bond may be sued on from time to time in the name of the person injured until the whole amount is recovered.

(e) Any person commissioned under this article must:

(1) meet the minimum standards required of peace officers by the commission relating to competence, reliability, education, training, morality, and physical and mental health; and

(2) meet all standards for certification as a peace officer by the Commission on Law Enforcement Officer Standards and Education.

(f) A peace officer commissioned under this article is not entitled to state benefits normally provided by the state to a peace officer.

(Enacted by Acts 2011, 82nd Leg., ch. 1344 (S.B. 1378), § 1, effective September 1, 2011.)

### Art. 2.13. Duties and Powers.

(a) It is the duty of every peace officer to preserve the peace within the officer's jurisdiction. To effect this purpose, the officer shall use all lawful means.

(b) The officer shall:

(1) in every case authorized by the provisions of this Code, interfere without warrant to prevent or suppress crime;

(2) execute all lawful process issued to the officer by any magistrate or court;

(3) give notice to some magistrate of all offenses committed within the officer's jurisdiction, where the officer has good reason to believe there has been a violation of the penal law; and

(4) arrest offenders without warrant in every case where the officer is authorized by law, in order that they may be taken before the proper magistrate or court and be tried.

(c) It is the duty of every officer to take possession of a child under Article 63.009(g).

(Enacted by Acts 1965, 59th Leg., ch. 722 (S.B. 107), § 1, effective January 1, 1966; am. Acts 1999, 76th Leg., ch. 685 (H.B. 668), § 1, effective September 1, 1999; am. Acts 2003, 78th Leg., ch. 1276 (H.B. 3507), § 5.0005, effective September 1, 2003.)

## Art. 2.131. Racial Profiling Prohibited.

A peace officer may not engage in racial profiling.

(Enacted by Acts 2001, 77th Leg., ch. 947 (S.B. 1074), § 1, effective September 1, 2001.)

## Art. 2.132. Law Enforcement Policy on Racial Profiling.

(a) In this article:

(1) "Law enforcement agency" means an agency of the state, or of a county, municipality, or other political subdivision of the state, that employs peace officers who make motor vehicle stops in the routine performance of the officers' official duties.

(2) "Motor vehicle stop" means an occasion in which a peace officer stops a motor vehicle for an alleged violation of a law or ordinance.

(3) "Race or ethnicity" means of a particular descent, including Caucasian, African, Hispanic, Asian, Native American, or Middle Eastern descent.

(b) Each law enforcement agency in this state shall adopt a detailed written policy on racial profiling. The policy must:

(1) clearly define acts constituting racial profiling;

(2) strictly prohibit peace officers employed by the agency from engaging in racial profiling;

(3) implement a process by which an individual may file a complaint with the agency if the individual believes that a peace officer employed by the agency has engaged in racial profiling with respect to the individual;

(4) provide public education relating to the agency's complaint process;

(5) require appropriate corrective action to be taken against a peace officer employed by the agency who, after an investigation, is shown to have engaged in racial profiling in violation of the agency's policy adopted under this article;

(6) require collection of information relating to motor vehicle stops in which a citation is issued and to arrests made as a result of those stops, including information relating to:

(A) the race or ethnicity of the individual detained;

(B) whether a search was conducted and, if so, whether the individual detained consented to the search; and

(C) whether the peace officer knew the race or ethnicity of the individual detained before detaining that individual; and

(7) require the chief administrator of the agency, regardless of whether the administrator is elected, employed, or appointed, to submit an annual report of the information collected under Subdivision (6) to:

(A) the Commission on Law Enforcement Officer Standards and Education; and

(B) the governing body of each county or municipality served by the agency, if the agency is an agency of a county, municipality, or other political subdivision of the state.

(c) The data collected as a result of the reporting requirements of this article shall not constitute prima facie evidence of racial profiling.

(d) On adoption of a policy under Subsection (b), a law enforcement agency shall examine the feasibility of installing video camera and transmitter-activated equipment in each agency law enforcement motor vehicle regularly used to make motor vehicle stops and transmitter-activated equipment in each agency law enforcement motorcycle regularly used to make motor vehicle stops. If a law enforcement agency installs video or audio equipment as provided by this subsection, the policy adopted by the agency under Subsection (b) must include standards for reviewing video and audio documentation.

(e) A report required under Subsection (b)(7) may not include identifying information about a peace officer who makes a motor vehicle stop or about an individual who is stopped or arrested by a peace officer. This subsection does not affect the collection of information as required by a policy under Subsection (b)(6).

(f) On the commencement of an investigation by a law enforcement agency of a complaint described by Subsection (b)(3) in which a video or audio recording of the occurrence on which the complaint is based was made, the agency shall promptly provide a copy of the recording to the peace officer who is the subject of the complaint on written request by the officer.

(g) On a finding by the Commission on Law Enforcement Officer Standards and Education that the chief administrator of a law enforcement agency intentionally failed to submit a report required under Subsection (b)(7), the commission shall begin disciplinary procedures against the chief administrator.

(Enacted by Acts 2001, 77th Leg., ch. 947 (S.B. 1074), § 1, effective September 1, 2001; am. Acts 2009, 81st Leg., ch. 1172 (H.B. 3389), § 25, effective September 1, 2009.)

## Art. 2.133. Reports Required for Motor Vehicle Stops.

(a) In this article, "race or ethnicity" has the meaning assigned by Article 2.132(a).

(b) A peace officer who stops a motor vehicle for an alleged violation of a law or ordinance shall report to the law enforcement agency that employs the officer information relating to the stop, including:

(1) a physical description of any person operating the motor vehicle who is detained as a result of the stop, including:

(A) the person's gender; and

(B) the person's race or ethnicity, as stated by the person or, if the person does not state the person's race or ethnicity, as determined by the officer to the best of the officer's ability;

(2) the initial reason for the stop;

(3) whether the officer conducted a search as a result of the stop and, if so, whether the person detained consented to the search;

(4) whether any contraband or other evidence was discovered in the course of the search and a description of the contraband or evidence;

(5) the reason for the search, including whether:

(A) any contraband or other evidence was in plain view;

(B) any probable cause or reasonable suspicion existed to perform the search; or

(C) the search was performed as a result of the towing of the motor vehicle or the arrest of any person in the motor vehicle;

(6) whether the officer made an arrest as a result of the stop or the search, including a statement of whether the arrest was based on a violation of the Penal Code, a violation of a traffic law or ordinance, or an outstanding warrant and a statement of the offense charged;

(7) the street address or approximate location of the stop; and

(8) whether the officer issued a written warning or a citation as a result of the stop.

(Enacted by Acts 2001, 77th Leg., ch. 947 (S.B. 1074), § 1, effective September 1, 2001; am. Acts 2009, 81st Leg., ch. 1172 (H.B. 3389), § 26, effective September 1, 2009.)

## Art. 2.134. Compilation and Analysis of Information Collected.

(a) In this article:

(1) "Motor vehicle stop" has the meaning assigned by Article 2.132(a).

(2) "Race or ethnicity" has the meaning assigned by Article 2.132(a).

(b) A law enforcement agency shall compile and analyze the information contained in each report received by the agency under Article 2.133. Not later than March 1 of each year, each law enforcement agency shall submit a report containing the incident-based data compiled during the previous calendar year to the Commission on Law Enforcement Officer Standards and Education and, if the law enforcement agency is a local law enforcement agency, to the governing body of each county or municipality served by the agency.

(c) A report required under Subsection (b) must be submitted by the chief administrator of the law enforcement agency, regardless of whether the administrator is elected, employed, or appointed, and must include:

(1) a comparative analysis of the information compiled under Article 2.133 to:

(A) evaluate and compare the number of motor vehicle stops, within the applicable jurisdiction, of persons who are recognized as racial or ethnic minorities and persons who are not recognized as racial or ethnic minorities; and

(B) examine the disposition of motor vehicle stops made by officers employed by the agency, categorized according to the race or ethnicity of the affected persons, as appropriate, including any searches resulting from stops within the applicable jurisdiction; and

(2) information relating to each complaint filed with the agency alleging that a peace officer employed by the agency has engaged in racial profiling.

(d) A report required under Subsection (b) may not include identifying information about a peace officer who makes a motor vehicle stop or about an individual who is stopped or arrested by a peace officer. This subsection does not affect the reporting of information required under Article 2.133(b)(1).

(e) The Commission on Law Enforcement Officer Standards and Education, in accordance with Section 1701.162, Occupations Code, shall develop guidelines for compiling and reporting information as required by this article.

(f) The data collected as a result of the reporting requirements of this article shall not constitute prima facie evidence of racial profiling.

(g) On a finding by the Commission on Law Enforcement Officer Standards and Education that the chief administrator of a law enforcement agency intentionally failed to submit a report required under Subsection (b), the commission shall begin disciplinary procedures against the chief administrator.

(Enacted by Acts 2001, 77th Leg., ch. 947 (S.B. 1074), § 1, effective September 1, 2001; am. Acts 2009, 81st Leg., ch. 1172 (H.B. 3389), § 27, effective September 1, 2009.)

## Art. 2.135. Partial Exemption for Agencies Using Video and Audio Equipment.

(a) A peace officer is exempt from the reporting requirement under Article 2.133 and the chief administrator of a law enforcement agency, regardless of whether the administrator is elected, employed, or appointed, is exempt from the compilation, analysis, and reporting requirements under Article 2.134 if:

(1) during the calendar year preceding the date that a report under Article 2.134 is required to be submitted:

(A) each law enforcement motor vehicle regularly used by an officer employed by the agency to make motor vehicle stops is equipped with video camera and transmitter-activated equipment and each law enforcement motorcycle regularly used to make motor vehicle stops is equipped with transmitter-activated equipment; and

(B) each motor vehicle stop made by an officer employed by the agency that is capable of being recorded by video and audio or audio equipment, as appropriate, is recorded by using the equipment; or

(2) the governing body of the county or municipality served by the law enforcement agency, in conjunction with the law enforcement agency, certifies to the Department of Public Safety, not later than the date specified by rule by the department, that the law enforcement agency needs funds or video and audio equipment for the purpose of installing video and audio equipment as described by Subsection (a)(1)(A) and the agency does not receive from the state funds or video and audio equipment sufficient, as determined by the department, for the agency to accomplish that purpose.

(b) Except as otherwise provided by this subsection, a law enforcement agency that is exempt from the requirements under Article 2.134 shall retain the video and audio or audio documentation of each motor vehicle stop for at least 90 days after the date of the stop. If a complaint is filed with the law enforcement agency alleging that a peace officer employed by the agency has engaged in racial profiling with respect to a motor vehicle stop, the agency shall retain the video and audio or audio record of the stop until final disposition of the complaint.

(c) This article does not affect the collection or reporting requirements under Article 2.132.

(d) In this article, "motor vehicle stop" has the meaning assigned by Article 2.132(a).

(Enacted by Acts 2001, 77th Leg., ch. 947 (S.B. 1074), § 1, effective September 1, 2001; am. Acts 2009, 81st Leg., ch. 1172 (H.B. 3389), § 28, effective September 1, 2009.)

## Art. 2.136. Liability.

A peace officer is not liable for damages arising from an act relating to the collection or reporting of information as required by Article 2.133 or under a policy adopted under Article 2.132.

(Enacted by Acts 2001, 77th Leg., ch. 947 (S.B. 1074), § 1, effective September 1, 2001.)

## Art. 2.137. Provision of Funding or Equipment.

(a) The Department of Public Safety shall adopt rules for providing funds or video and audio equipment to law enforcement agencies for the purpose of installing video and audio equipment as described by Article 2.135(a)(1)(A), including specifying criteria to prioritize funding or equipment provided to law enforcement agencies. The criteria may include consideration of tax effort, financial hardship, available revenue, and budget surpluses. The criteria must give priority to:

(1) law enforcement agencies that employ peace officers whose primary duty is traffic enforcement;

(2) smaller jurisdictions; and

(3) municipal and county law enforcement agencies.

(b) The Department of Public Safety shall collaborate with an institution of higher education to identify law enforcement agencies that need funds or video and audio equipment for the purpose of installing video and audio equipment as described by Article 2.135(a)(1)(A). The collaboration may include the use of a survey to assist in developing criteria to prioritize funding or equipment provided to law enforcement agencies.

(c) To receive funds or video and audio equipment from the state for the purpose of installing video and audio equipment as described by Article 2.135(a)(1)(A), the governing body of a county or municipality, in conjunction with the law enforcement agency serving the county or municipality, shall certify to the Department of Public Safety that the law enforcement agency needs funds or video and audio equipment for that purpose.

(d) On receipt of funds or video and audio equipment from the state for the purpose of installing video and audio equipment as described by Article 2.135(a)(1)(A), the governing body of a county or municipality, in conjunction with the law enforcement agency serving the county or municipality, shall certify to the Department of Public Safety that the law enforcement agency has installed video and audio equipment as described by Article 2.135(a)(1)(A) and is using the equipment as required by Article 2.135(a)(1).
(Enacted by Acts 2001, 77th Leg., ch. 947 (S.B. 1074), § 1, effective September 1, 2001.)

## Art. 2.138. Rules.

The Department of Public Safety may adopt rules to implement Articles 2.131—2.137.
(Enacted by Acts 2001, 77th Leg., ch. 947 (S.B. 1074), § 1, effective September 1, 2001.)

## Art. 2.1385. Civil Penalty.

(a) If the chief administrator of a local law enforcement agency intentionally fails to submit the incident-based data as required by Article 2.134, the agency is liable to the state for a civil penalty in the amount of $1,000 for each violation. The attorney general may sue to collect a civil penalty under this subsection.

(b) From money appropriated to the agency for the administration of the agency, the executive director of a state law enforcement agency that intentionally fails to submit the incident-based data as required by Article 2.134 shall remit to the comptroller the amount of $1,000 for each violation.

(c) Money collected under this article shall be deposited in the state treasury to the credit of the general revenue fund.
(Enacted by Acts 2009, 81st Leg., ch. 1172 (H.B. 3389), § 29, effective September 1, 2009.)

## Art. 2.14. May Summon Aid.

Whenever a peace officer meets with resistance in discharging any duty imposed upon him by law, he shall summon a sufficient number of citizens of his county to overcome the resistance; and all persons summoned are bound to obey.
(Enacted by Acts 1965, 59th Leg., ch. 722 (S.B. 107), § 1, effective January 1, 1966.)

## Art. 2.15. Person Refusing to Aid.

The peace officer who has summoned any person to assist him in performing any duty shall report such person, if he refuse to obey, to the proper district or county attorney, in order that he may be prosecuted for the offense.
(Enacted by Acts 1965, 59th Leg., ch. 722 (S.B. 107), § 1, effective January 1, 1966.)

## Art. 2.16. Neglecting to Execute Process.

If any sheriff or other officer shall wilfully refuse or fail from neglect to execute any summons, subpoena or attachment for a witness, or any other legal process which it is made his duty by law to execute, he shall be liable to a fine for contempt not less than ten nor more than two hundred dollars, at the discretion of the court. The payment of such fine shall be enforced in the same manner as fines for contempt in civil cases.
(Enacted by Acts 1965, 59th Leg., ch. 722 (S.B. 107), § 1, effective January 1, 1966.)

## Art. 2.17. Conservator of the Peace.

Each sheriff shall be a conservator of the peace in his county, and shall arrest all offenders against the laws of the State, in his view or hearing, and take them before the proper court for examination or trial. He shall quell and suppress all assaults and batteries, affrays, insurrections and unlawful assemblies. He shall apprehend and commit to jail all offenders, until an examination or trial can be had.
(Enacted by Acts 1965, 59th Leg., ch. 722 (S.B. 107), § 1, effective January 1, 1966.)

## Art. 2.18. Custody of Prisoners.

When a prisoner is committed to jail by warrant from a magistrate or court, he shall be placed in jail by the sheriff. It is a violation of duty on the part of any sheriff to permit a defendant so committed to remain out of jail, except that he may, when a defendant is committed for want of bail, or when he arrests in a bailable case, give the person arrested a reasonable time to procure bail; but he shall so guard the accused as to prevent escape.
(Enacted by Acts 1965, 59th Leg., ch. 722 (S.B. 107), § 1, effective January 1, 1966.)

## Art. 2.19. Report As to Prisoners.

On the first day of each month, the sheriff shall give notice, in writing, to the district or county attorney, where there be one, as to all prisoners in his custody, naming them, and of the authority under which he detains them.
(Enacted by Acts 1965, 59th Leg., ch. 722 (S.B. 107), § 1, effective January 1, 1966.)

## Art. 2.195. Report of Warrant or Capias Information.

Not later than the 30th day after the date the court clerk issues the warrant or capias, the sheriff:

(1) shall report to the national crime information center each warrant or capias issued for a defendant charged with a felony who fails to appear in court when summoned; and

(2) may report to the national crime information center each warrant or capias issued for a defendant charged with a misdemeanor other than a Class C misdemeanor who fails to appear in court when summoned.
(Enacted by Acts 2009, 81st Leg., ch. 578 (S.B. 2438), § 1, effective June 19, 2009; am. Acts 2011, 82nd Leg., ch. 531 (H.B. 2472), § 1, effective September 1, 2011.)

## Art. 2.20. Deputy.

Wherever a duty is imposed by this Code upon the sheriff, the same duty may lawfully be performed by his deputy. When there is no sheriff in a county, the duties of that office, as to all proceedings under the criminal law, devolve upon the officer who, under the law, is empowered to discharge the duties of sheriff, in case of vacancy in the office.
(Enacted by Acts 1965, 59th Leg., ch. 722 (S.B. 107), § 1, effective January 1, 1966.)

## Art. 2.21. Duty of Clerks.

(a) In a criminal proceeding, a clerk of the district or county court shall:

(1) receive and file all papers;

(2) receive all exhibits at the conclusion of the proceeding;

(3) issue all process;

(4) accept and file electronic documents received from the defendant, if the clerk accepts electronic documents from an attorney representing the state;

(5) accept and file digital multimedia evidence received from the defendant, if the clerk accepts digital multimedia evidence from an attorney representing the state; and

(6) perform all other duties imposed on the clerk by law.

(a-1) A district clerk is exempt from the requirements of Subsections (a)(4) and (5) if the electronic filing system used by the clerk for accepting electronic documents or electronic digital media from an attorney representing the state does not have the capability of accepting electronic filings from a defendant and the system was established or procured before June 1, 2009. If the electronic filing system described by this subsection is substantially upgraded or is replaced with a new system, the exemption provided by this subsection is no longer applicable.

(b) At any time during or after a criminal proceeding, the court reporter shall release for safekeeping any firearm or contraband received as an exhibit in that proceeding to:

(1) the sheriff; or

(2) in a county with a population of 500,000 or more, the law enforcement agency that collected, seized, or took possession of the firearm or contraband or produced the firearm or contraband at the proceeding.

(c) The sheriff or the law enforcement agency, as applicable, shall receive and hold the exhibits consisting of firearms or contraband and release them only to the person or persons authorized by the court in which such exhibits have been received or dispose of them as provided by Chapter 18.

(d) In this article, "eligible exhibit" means an exhibit filed with the clerk that:

(1) is not a firearm or contraband;

(2) has not been ordered by the court to be returned to its owner; and

(3) is not an exhibit in another pending criminal action.

(e) An eligible exhibit may be disposed of as provided by this article:

(1) on or after the first anniversary of the date on which a conviction becomes final in the case, if the case is a misdemeanor or a felony for which the sentence imposed by the court is five years or less; or

(2) on or after the second anniversary of the date on which a conviction becomes final in the case, if the case is a non-capital felony for which the sentence imposed by the court is greater than five years.

(f) Subject to Subsections (g), (h), (i), and (j), a clerk may dispose of an eligible exhibit or may deliver the eligible exhibit to the county purchasing agent for disposal as surplus or salvage property under Section 263.152, Local Government Code, if on the date provided by Subsection (e) the clerk has not received a request for the exhibit from either the attorney representing the state in the case or the attorney representing the defendant.

(f-1) Notwithstanding Section 263.156, Local Government Code, or any other law, the commissioners court shall remit 50 percent of any proceeds of the disposal of an eligible exhibit as surplus or salvage property as described by Subsection (f), less the reasonable expense of keeping the exhibit before disposal and the costs of that disposal, to each of the following:

(1) the county treasury, to be used only to defray the costs incurred by the district clerk of the county for the management, maintenance, or destruction of eligible exhibits in the county; and

(2) the state treasury to the credit of the compensation to victims of crime fund established under Subchapter B, Chapter 56.

(g) A clerk in a county with a population of less than two million must provide written notice by mail to the attorney representing the state in the case and the attorney representing the defendant before disposing of an eligible exhibit.

(h) The notice under Subsection (g) of this article must:

(1) describe the eligible exhibit;

(2) give the name and address of the court holding the exhibit; and

(3) state that the eligible exhibit will be disposed of unless a written request is received by the clerk before the 31st day after the date of notice.

(i) If a request is not received by a clerk covered by Subsection (g) before the 31st day after the date of notice, the clerk may dispose of the eligible exhibit in the manner permitted by this article, including the delivery of the eligible exhibit for disposal as surplus or salvage property as described by Subsection (f).

(j) If a request is timely received, the clerk shall deliver the eligible exhibit to the person making the request if the court determines the requestor is the owner of the eligible exhibit.

(k) In this article, "digital multimedia evidence" means evidence stored or transmitted in a binary form and includes data representing documents, audio, video metadata, and any other information attached to a digital file.

(Enacted by Acts 1965, 59th Leg., ch. 722 (S.B. 107), § 1, effective January 1, 1966; am. Acts 1979, 66th Leg., ch. 119 (S.B. 653), § 1, effective August 27, 1979; am. Acts 1993, 73rd Leg., ch. 967 (H.B. 665), § 1, effective September 1, 1993; am. Acts 1999, 76th Leg., ch. 580 (S.B. 577), § 1, effective September 1, 1999; am. Acts 2005, 79th Leg., ch. 1026 (H.B. 1048), § 1, effective September 1, 2005; am. Acts 2009, 81st Leg., ch. 795 (S.B. 1259), § 10, effective June 19, 2009; am. Acts 2009, 81st Leg., ch. 829 (S.B. 1774), § 1, effective September 1, 2009; am. Acts 2011, 82nd Leg., ch. 911 (S.B. 1228), § 1, effective June 17, 2011; am. Acts 2011, 82nd Leg., ch. 1163 (H.B. 2702), § 6, effective September 1, 2011.)

### Art. 2.211. Hate Crime Reporting.

In addition to performing duties required by Article 2.21, a clerk of a district or county court in which an affirmative finding under Article 42.014 is requested shall report that request to the Texas Judicial Council, along with a statement as to whether the request was granted by the court and, if so, whether the affirmative finding was entered in the judgment in the case. The clerk shall make the report required by this article not later than the 30th day after the date the judgment is entered in the case.

(Enacted by Acts 2001, 77th Leg., ch. 85 (H.B. 587), § 4.01, effective September 1, 2001.)

### Art. 2.22. Power of Deputy Clerks.

Whenever a duty is imposed upon the clerk of the district or county court, the same may be lawfully performed by his deputy.

(Enacted by Acts 1965, 59th Leg., ch. 722 (S.B. 107), § 1, effective January 1, 1966.)

### Art. 2.23. Report to Attorney General.

(a) The clerks of the district and county courts shall, when requested in writing by the Attorney

General, report to the Attorney General not later than the 10th day after the date the request is received, and in the form prescribed by the Attorney General, information in court records that relates to a criminal matter, including information requested by the Attorney General for purposes of federal habeas review.

(b) A state agency or the office of an attorney representing the state shall, when requested in writing by the Attorney General, provide to the Attorney General any record that is needed for purposes of federal habeas review. The agency or office must provide the record not later than the 10th day after the date the request is received and in the form prescribed by the Attorney General.

(c) A district court, county court, state agency, or office of an attorney representing the state may not restrict or delay the reproduction or delivery of a record requested by the Attorney General under this article.

(Enacted by Acts 1965, 59th Leg., ch. 722 (S.B. 107), § 1, effective January 1, 1966; am. Acts 2005, 79th Leg., ch. 933 (H.B. 646), § 1, effective September 1, 2005.)

## Art. 2.24. Authenticating Officer.

(a) The governor may appoint an authenticating officer, in accordance with Subsection (b) of this article, and delegate to that officer the power to sign for the governor or to use the governor's facsimile signature for signing any document that does not have legal effect under this code unless it is signed by the governor.

(b) To appoint an authenticating officer under this article, the governor shall file with the secretary of state a document that contains:

(1) the name of the person to be appointed as authenticating officer and a copy of the person's signature;

(2) the types of documents the authenticating officer is authorized to sign for the governor; and

(3) the types of documents on which the authenticating officer is authorized to use the governor's facsimile signature.

(c) The governor may revoke an appointment made under this article by filing with the secretary of state a document that expressly revokes the appointment of the authenticating agent.

(d) If an authenticating officer signs a document described in Subsection (a) of this article, the officer shall sign in the following manner: "_____, Authenticating Officer for Governor _____."

(e) If a provision of this code requires the governor's signature on a document before that document has legal effect, the authorized signature of the authenticating officer or an authorized facsimile signature of the governor gives the document the same legal effect as if it had been signed manually by the governor.

(Enacted by Acts 1983, 68th Leg., ch. 684 (S.B. 1308), § 1, effective June 19, 1983.)

## Art. 2.25. Reporting Certain Aliens to Federal Government.

A judge shall report to the United States Immigration and Naturalization Service a person who has been convicted in the judge's court of a crime or has been placed on deferred adjudication for a felony and is an illegal criminal alien as defined by Section 493.015(a), Government Code.

(Enacted by Acts 1995, 74th Leg., ch. 85 (S.B. 279), § 2, effective May 16, 1995.)

## Art. 2.26. Digital Signature and Electronic Documents.

(a) In this section, "digital signature" means an electronic identifier intended by the person using it to have the same force and effect as the use of a manual signature.

(b) An electronically transmitted document issued or received by a court or a clerk of the court in a criminal matter is considered signed if a digital signature is transmitted with the document.

(b-1) An electronically transmitted document is a written document for all purposes and exempt from any additional writing requirement under this code or any other law of this state.

(c) This section does not preclude any symbol from being valid as a signature under other applicable law, including Section 1.201(39), Business & Commerce Code.

(d) The use of a digital signature under this section is subject to criminal laws pertaining to fraud and computer crimes, including Chapters 32 and 33, Penal Code.

(Enacted by Acts 1999, 76th Leg., ch. 701 (H.B. 806), § 1, effective August 30, 1999; am. Acts 2005, 79th Leg., ch. 312 (S.B. 611), §§ 1, 2, effective June 17, 2005.)

## Art. 2.27. Investigation of Certain Reports Alleging Abuse.

(a) On receipt of a report that is assigned the highest priority in accordance with rules adopted by the Department of Family and Protective

Services under Section 261.301(d), Family Code, and that alleges an immediate risk of physical or sexual abuse of a child that could result in the death of or serious harm to the child by a person responsible for the care, custody, or welfare of the child, a peace officer from the appropriate local law enforcement agency shall investigate the report jointly with the department or with the agency responsible for conducting an investigation under Subchapter E, Chapter 261, Family Code. As soon as possible after being notified by the department of the report, but not later than 24 hours after being notified, the peace officer shall accompany the department investigator in initially responding to the report.

(b) On receipt of a report of abuse or neglect or other complaint of a resident of a nursing home, convalescent home, or other related institution under Section 242.126(c)(1), Health and Safety Code, the appropriate local law enforcement agency shall investigate the report as required by Section 242.135, Health and Safety Code.

(Enacted by Acts 2001, 77th Leg., ch. 492 (H.B. 1267), § 1, effective September 1, 2001; am. Acts 2003, 78th Leg., ch. 867 (S.B. 669), § 2, effective September 1, 2003; am. Acts 2003, 78th Leg., ch. 1210 (S.B. 1074), § 5, effective September 1, 2003; am. Acts 2011, 82nd Leg., ch. 91 (S.B. 1303), § 6.001, effective September 1, 2011.)

### Art. 2.271. Investigation of Certain Reports Alleging Abuse, Neglect, or Exploitation.

Notwithstanding Article 2.27, on receipt of a report of abuse, neglect, exploitation, or other complaint of a resident of a nursing home, convalescent home, or other related institution or an assisted living facility, under Section 260A.007(c)(1), Health and Safety Code, the appropriate local law enforcement agency shall investigate the report as required by Section 260A.017, Health and Safety Code.

(Enacted by Acts 2011, 82nd Leg., 1st C.S., (S.B. 7), § 1.05(d), effective September 28, 2011.)

### Art. 2.28. Duties Regarding Misused Identity.

On receipt of information to the effect that a person's identifying information was falsely given by a person arrested as the arrested person's identifying information, the local law enforcement agency responsible for collecting identifying information on arrested persons in the county in which the arrest was made shall:

(1) notify the person that:

(A) the person's identifying information was misused by another person arrested in the county;

(B) the person may file a declaration with the Department of Public Safety under Section 411.0421, Government Code; and

(C) the person is entitled to expunction of information contained in criminal records and files under Chapter 55 of this code; and

(2) notify the Department of Public Safety regarding:

(A) the misuse of the identifying information;

(B) the actual identity of the person arrested, if known by the agency; and

(C) whether the agency was able to notify the person whose identifying information was misused.

(Enacted by Acts 2003, 78th Leg., ch. 339 (S.B. 566), § 1, effective September 1, 2003.)

### Art. 2.29. Report Required in Connection with Fraudulent Use or Possession of Identifying Information.

(a) A peace officer to whom an alleged violation of Section 32.51, Penal Code, is reported shall make a written report to the law enforcement agency that employs the peace officer that includes the following information:

(1) the name of the victim;

(2) the name of the suspect, if known;

(3) the type of identifying information obtained, possessed, transferred, or used in violation of Section 32.51, Penal Code; and

(4) the results of any investigation.

(b) On the victim's request, the law enforcement agency shall provide the report created under Subsection (a) to the victim. In providing the report, the law enforcement agency shall redact any otherwise confidential information that is included in the report, other than the information described by Subsection (a).

(Enacted by Acts 2005, 79th Leg., ch. 294 (S.B. 122), § 1(a), effective September 1, 2005.)

### Art. 2.295. Report Required in Connection with Unauthorized Acquisition or Transfer of Certain Financial Information.

(a) A peace officer to whom an alleged violation of Section 31.17, Penal Code, is reported shall make a written report to the law enforcement agency that employs the peace officer that includes the following information:

(1) the name of the victim;

(2) the name of the suspect, if known;

(3) the type of financial sight order or payment card information obtained or transferred in violation of Section 31.17, Penal Code; and

(4) the results of any investigation.

(b) On the victim's request, the law enforcement agency shall provide the report created under Subsection (a) to the victim. In providing the report, the law enforcement agency shall redact any otherwise confidential information that is included in the report, other than the information described by Subsection (a).

(Enacted by Acts 2011, 82nd Leg., ch. 260 (H.B. 1215), § 2, effective September 1, 2011.)

## Art. 2.30. Report Concerning Certain Assaultive or Terroristic Offenses.

(a) This article applies only to the following offenses:

(1) assault under Section 22.01, Penal Code;

(2) aggravated assault under Section 22.02, Penal Code;

(3) sexual assault under Section 22.011, Penal Code;

(4) aggravated sexual assault under Section 22.021, Penal Code; and

(5) terroristic threat under Section 22.07, Penal Code.

(b) A peace officer who investigates the alleged commission of an offense listed under Subsection (a) shall prepare a written report that includes the information required under Article 5.05(a).

(c) On request of a victim of an offense listed under Subsection (a), the local law enforcement agency responsible for investigating the commission of the offense shall provide the victim, at no cost to the victim, with any information that is:

(1) contained in the written report prepared under Subsection (b);

(2) described by Article 5.05(a)(1) or (2); and

(3) not exempt from disclosure under Chapter 552, Government Code, or other law.

(Enacted by Acts 2007, 80th Leg., ch. 1057 (H.B. 2210), § 1, effective September 1, 2007.)

## Art. 2.31. [2 Versions: As added by Acts 2011, 82nd Leg., ch. 176] County Jailers.

If a jailer licensed under Chapter 1701, Occupations Code, has successfully completed a training program provided by the sheriff, the jailer may execute lawful process issued to the jailer by any magistrate or court on a person confined in the jail at which the jailer is employed to the same extent that a peace officer is authorized to execute process under Article 2.13(b)(2), including:

(1) a warrant under Chapter 15, 17, or 18;

(2) a capias under Chapter 17 or 23;

(3) a subpoena under Chapter 20 or 24; or

(4) an attachment under Chapter 20 or 24.

(Enacted by Acts 2011, 82nd Leg., ch. 176 (S.B. 604), § 1, effective September 1, 2011.)

## Art. 2.31. [2 Versions: As added by Acts 2011, 82nd Leg., ch. 1341] County Jailers.

A jailer licensed under Chapter 1701, Occupations Code, may execute lawful process issued to the jailer by any magistrate or court on a person confined in the jail at which the jailer is employed to the same extent that a peace officer is authorized to execute process under Article 2.13(b)(2), including:

(1) a warrant under Chapter 15, 17, or 18;

(2) a capias under Chapter 17 or 23;

(3) a subpoena under Chapter 20 or 24; or

(4) an attachment under Chapter 20 or 24.

(Enacted by Acts 2011, 82nd Leg., ch. 1341 (S.B. 1233), § 2, effective June 17, 2011.)

# CHAPTER 3
# DEFINITIONS

## Art. 3.01. Words and Phrases.

All words, phrases and terms used in this Code are to be taken and understood in their usual acceptation in common language, except where specially defined.

(Enacted by Acts 1965, 59th Leg., ch. 722 (S.B. 107), § 1, effective January 1, 1966; am. Acts 1975, 64th Leg., ch. 341 (S.B. 122), § 1, effective June 19, 1975.)

## Art. 3.02. Criminal Action.

A criminal action is prosecuted in the name of the State of Texas against the accused, and is conducted by some person acting under the authority of the State, in accordance with its laws.

(Enacted by Acts 1965, 59th Leg., ch. 722 (S.B. 107), § 1, effective January 1, 1966.)

## Art. 3.03. Officers.

The general term "officers" includes both magistrates and peace officers.

(Enacted by Acts 1965, 59th Leg., ch. 722 (S.B. 107), § 1, effective January 1, 1966.)

## Art. 3.04. Official Misconduct.

In this code:

(1) "Official misconduct" means an offense that is an intentional or knowing violation of a law committed by a public servant while acting in an official capacity as a public servant.

(2) "Public servant" has the meaning assigned by Section 1.07, Penal Code.

(Enacted by Acts 1993, 73rd Leg., ch. 900 (S.B. 1067), § 1.03, effective September 1, 1994.)

## Art. 3.05. Racial Profiling.

In this code, "racial profiling" means a law enforcement-initiated action based on an individual's race, ethnicity, or national origin rather than on the individual's behavior or on information identifying the individual as having engaged in criminal activity.

(Enacted by Acts 2001, 77th Leg., ch. 947 (S.B. 1074), § 2, effective September 1, 2001.)

# Courts and Criminal Jurisdiction

## CHAPTER 4
## COURTS AND CRIMINAL JURISDICTION

## Art. 4.01. What Courts Have Criminal Jurisdiction.

The following courts have jurisdiction in criminal actions:

1. The Court of Criminal Appeals;
2. Courts of appeals;
3. The district courts;
4. The criminal district courts;
5. The magistrates appointed by the judges of the district courts of Bexar County, Dallas County, Tarrant County, or Travis County that give preference to criminal cases and the magistrates appointed by the judges of the criminal district courts of Dallas County or Tarrant County;
6. The county courts;
7. All county courts at law with criminal jurisdiction;
8. County criminal courts;
9. Justice courts;
10. Municipal courts; and
11. The magistrates appointed by the judges of the district courts of Lubbock County.

(Enacted by Acts 1965, 59th Leg., ch. 722 (S.B. 107), § 1, effective January 1, 1966; am. Acts 1981, 67th Leg., ch. 291 (S.B. 265), § 101, effective September 1, 1981; am. Acts 1983, 68th Leg., ch. 204 (S.B. 781), § 2, effective August 29, 1983; am. Acts 1989, 71st Leg., ch. 25 (S.B. 577), § 3, effective August 28, 1989; am. Acts 1989, 71st Leg., ch. 79 (S.B. 38), § 2, effective May 15, 1989; am. Acts 1989, 71st Leg., ch. 1068 (S.B. 264), § 3, effective August 28, 1989; am. Acts 1991, 72nd Leg., ch. 16 (S.B. 232), § 4.03, effective August 26, 1991; am. Acts 1993, 73rd Leg., ch. 413 (S.B. 667), § 2, effective September 1, 1993.)

## Art. 4.02. Existing Courts Continued.

No existing courts shall be abolished by this Code and shall continue with the jurisdiction, organization, terms and powers currently existing unless otherwise provided by law.

(Enacted by Acts 1965, 59th Leg., ch. 722 (S.B. 107), § 1, effective January 1, 1966.)

## Art. 4.03. Courts of Appeals.

The Courts of Appeals shall have appellate jurisdiction coextensive with the limits of their respective districts in all criminal cases except those in which the death penalty has been assessed. This Article shall not be so construed as to embrace any case which has been appealed from any inferior court to the county court, the county criminal court, or county court at law, in which the fine imposed or affirmed by the county court, the county criminal court or county court at law

does not exceed one hundred dollars, unless the sole issue is the constitutionality of the statute or ordinance on which the conviction is based.
(Enacted by Acts 1965, 59th Leg., ch. 722 (S.B. 107), § 1, effective January 1, 1966; am. Acts 1981, 67th Leg., ch. 291 (S.B. 265), § 102, effective September 1, 1981; am. Acts 2011, 82nd Leg., ch. 1324 (S.B. 480), § 1, effective June 17, 2011.)

## Art. 4.04. Court of Criminal Appeals.

Sec. 1. The Court of Criminal Appeals and each judge thereof shall have, and is hereby given, the power and authority to grant and issue and cause the issuance of writs of habeas corpus, and, in criminal law matters, the writs of mandamus, procedendo, prohibition, and certiorari. The court and each judge thereof shall have, and is hereby given, the power and authority to grant and issue and cause the issuance of such other writs as may be necessary to protect its jurisdiction or enforce its judgments.

Sec. 2. The Court of Criminal Appeals shall have, and is hereby given, final appellate and review jurisdiction in criminal cases coextensive with the limits of the state, and its determinations shall be final. The appeal of all cases in which the death penalty has been assessed shall be to the Court of Criminal Appeals. In addition, the Court of Criminal Appeals may, on its own motion, with or without a petition for such discretionary review being filed by one of the parties, review any decision of a court of appeals in a criminal case. Discretionary review by the Court of Criminal Appeals is not a matter of right, but of sound judicial discretion.
(Enacted by Acts 1965, 59th Leg., ch. 722 (S.B. 107), § 1, effective January 1, 1966; am. Acts 1971, 62nd Leg., ch. 831 (S.B. 132), § 6, effective August 30, 1971; am. Acts 1981, 67th Leg., ch. 291 (S.B. 265), § 103, effective September 1, 1981.)

## Art. 4.05. Jurisdiction of District Courts.

District courts and criminal district courts shall have original jurisdiction in criminal cases of the grade of felony, of all misdemeanors involving official misconduct, and of misdemeanor cases transferred to the district court under Article 4.17 of this code.
(Enacted by Acts 1965, 59th Leg., ch. 722 (S.B. 107), § 1, effective January 1, 1966; am. Acts 1983, 68th Leg., ch. 303 (S.B. 1), § 5, effective January 1, 1984.)

## Art. 4.06. When Felony Includes Misdemeanor.

Upon the trial of a felony case, the court shall hear and determine the case as to any grade of offense included in the indictment, whether the proof shows a felony or a misdemeanor.
(Enacted by Acts 1965, 59th Leg., ch. 722 (S.B. 107), § 1, effective January 1, 1966.)

## Art. 4.07. Jurisdiction of County Courts.

The county courts shall have original jurisdiction of all misdemeanors of which exclusive original jurisdiction is not given to the justice court, and when the fine to be imposed shall exceed five hundred dollars.
(Enacted by Acts 1965, 59th Leg., ch. 722 (S.B. 107), § 1, effective January 1, 1966; am. Acts 1991, 72nd Leg., ch. 108 (H.B. 407), § 3, effective September 1, 1991.)

## Art. 4.08. Appellate Jurisdiction of County Courts.

The county courts shall have appellate jurisdiction in criminal cases of which justice courts and other inferior courts have original jurisdiction.
(Enacted by Acts 1965, 59th Leg., ch. 722 (S.B. 107), § 1, effective January 1, 1966.)

## Art. 4.09. Appeals from Inferior Court.

If the jurisdiction of any county court has been transferred to the district court or to a county court at law, then an appeal from a justice or other inferior court will lie to the court to which such appellate jurisdiction has been transferred.
(Enacted by Acts 1965, 59th Leg., ch. 722 (S.B. 107), § 1, effective January 1, 1966.)

## Art. 4.10. To Forfeit Bail Bonds.

County courts and county courts at law shall have jurisdiction in the forfeiture and final judgment of all bail bonds and personal bonds taken in criminal cases of which said courts have jurisdiction.
(Enacted by Acts 1965, 59th Leg., ch. 722 (S.B. 107), § 1, effective January 1, 1966.)

## Art. 4.11. Jurisdiction of Justice Courts.

(a) Justices of the peace shall have original jurisdiction in criminal cases:

(1) punishable by fine only or punishable by:

(A) a fine; and

(B) as authorized by statute, a sanction not consisting of confinement or imprisonment; or

(2) arising under Chapter 106, Alcoholic Beverage Code, that do not include confinement as an authorized sanction.

(b) The fact that a conviction in a justice court has as a consequence the imposition of a penalty or sanction by an agency or entity other than the court, such as a denial, suspension, or revocation of a privilege, does not affect the original jurisdiction of the justice court.

(c) A justice court has concurrent jurisdiction with a municipal court in criminal cases that arise in the municipality's extraterritorial jurisdiction and that arise under an ordinance of the municipality applicable to the extraterritorial jurisdiction under Section 216.902, Local Government Code.

(Enacted by Acts 1965, 59th Leg., ch. 722 (S.B. 107), § 1, effective January 1, 1966; am. Acts 1991, 72nd Leg., ch. 108 (H.B. 407), § 4, effective September 1, 1991; am. Acts 1995, 74th Leg., ch. 449 (H.B. 1648), § 1, effective September 1, 1995; am. Acts 1997, 75th Leg., ch. 533 (H.B. 1291), § 1, effective September 1, 1997; am. Acts 1997, 75th Leg., ch. 1013 (S.B. 35), § 38, effective September 1, 1997; am. Acts 2007, 80th Leg., ch. 612 (H.B. 413), § 13, effective September 1, 2007.)

## Art. 4.12. Misdemeanor Cases; Precinct in Which Defendant to Be Tried in Justice Court.

(a) Except as otherwise provided by this article, a misdemeanor case to be tried in justice court shall be tried:

(1) in the precinct in which the offense was committed;

(2) in the precinct in which the defendant or any of the defendants reside;

(3) with the written consent of the state and each defendant or the defendant's attorney, in any other precinct within the county; or

(4) if the offense was committed in a county with a population of 3.3 million or more, in any precinct in the county that is adjacent to the precinct in which the offense was committed.

(b) In any misdemeanor case in which the offense was committed in a precinct where there is no qualified justice court, then trial shall be held:

(1) in the next adjacent precinct in the same county which has a duly qualified justice court; or

(2) in the precinct in which the defendant may reside.

(c) In any misdemeanor case in which each justice of the peace in the precinct where the offense was committed is disqualified for any reason, such case may be tried in the next adjoining precinct in the same county having a duly qualified justice of the peace.

(d) A defendant who is taken before a magistrate in accordance with Article 15.18 may waive trial by jury and enter a written plea of guilty or nolo contendere.

(e) **[Effective January 1, 2012]** The justices of the peace in each county shall, by majority vote, adopt local rules of administration regarding the transfer of a pending misdemeanor case from one precinct to a different precinct.

(Enacted by Acts 1965, 59th Leg., ch. 722 (S.B. 107), § 1, effective January 1, 1966; am. Acts 1999, 76th Leg., ch. 1545 (S.B. 1230), § 2, effective September 1, 1999; am. Acts 2001, 77th Leg., ch. 145 (S.B. 219), § 1, effective September 1, 2001; am. Acts 2011, 82nd Leg., ch. 1086 (S.B. 1200), § 1, effective September 1, 2011; am. Acts 2011, 82nd Leg., 1st C.S., (H.B. 79), § 5.05, effective January 1, 2012.)

## Art. 4.13. Justice May Forfeit Bond.

A justice of the peace shall have the power to take forfeitures of all bonds given for the appearance of any party at his court, regardless of the amount.

(Enacted by Acts 1965, 59th Leg., ch. 722 (S.B. 107), § 1, effective January 1, 1966.)

## Art. 4.14. Jurisdiction of Municipal Court.

(a) A municipal court, including a municipal court of record, shall have exclusive original jurisdiction within the territorial limits of the municipality in all criminal cases that:

(1) arise under the ordinances of the municipality; and

(2) are punishable by a fine not to exceed:

(A) $2,000 in all cases arising under municipal ordinances that govern fire safety, zoning, or public health and sanitation, including dumping of refuse; or

(B) $500 in all other cases arising under a municipal ordinance.

(b) The municipal court shall have concurrent jurisdiction with the justice court of a precinct in which the municipality is located in all criminal cases arising under state law that:

(1) arise within the territorial limits of the municipality and are punishable by fine only, as defined in Subsection (c) of this article; or

(2) arise under Chapter 106, Alcoholic Beverage Code, and do not include confinement as an authorized sanction.

(c) In this article, an offense which is punishable by "fine only" is defined as an offense that is punishable by fine and such sanctions, if any, as authorized by statute not consisting of confinement in jail or imprisonment.

(d) The fact that a conviction in a municipal court has as a consequence the imposition of a penalty or sanction by an agency or entity other than the court, such as a denial, suspension, or revocation of a privilege, does not affect the original jurisdiction of the municipal court.

(e) The municipal court has jurisdiction in the forfeiture and final judgment of all bail bonds and personal bonds taken in criminal cases of which the court has jurisdiction.

(f) A municipality with a population of 1.9 million or more and another municipality contiguous to that municipality may enter into an agreement providing concurrent jurisdiction for the municipal courts of either jurisdiction for all criminal cases arising from offenses under state law that are:

(1) committed on the boundary of those municipalities or within 200 yards of that boundary; and

(2) punishable by fine only.

(g) A municipality may enter into an agreement with a contiguous municipality or a municipality with boundaries that are within one-half mile of the municipality seeking to enter into the agreement to establish concurrent jurisdiction of the municipal courts in the municipalities and provide original jurisdiction to a municipal court in which a case is brought as if the municipal court were located in the municipality in which the case arose, for:

(1) all cases in which either municipality has jurisdiction under Subsection (a); and

(2) cases that arise under Section 821.022, Health and Safety Code, or Section 25.094, Education Code.

(Enacted by Acts 1965, 59th Leg., ch. 722 (S.B. 107), § 1, effective January 1, 1966; am. Acts 1983, 68th Leg., ch. 601 (S.B. 856), § 3, effective September 1, 1983; am. Acts 1985, 69th Leg., ch. 329 (H.B. 1070), § 3, effective September 1, 1985; am. Acts 1987, 70th Leg., ch. 641 (H.B. 2220), § 2, effective September 1, 1987; am. Acts 1987, 70th Leg., ch. 680 (S.B. 920), § 1, effective September 1, 1987; am. Acts 1995, 74th Leg., ch. 449 (H.B. 1648), § 3, effective September 1, 1995; am. Acts 1997, 75th Leg., ch. 533 (H.B. 1291), § 2,

effective September 1, 1997; am. Acts 1997, 75th Leg., ch. 1013 (S.B. 35), § 39, effective September 1, 1997; am. Acts 2009, 81st Leg., ch. 230 (S.B. 1504), § 1, effective September 1, 2009; am. Acts 2011, 82nd Leg., ch. 76 (H.B. 984), § 2, effective May 19, 2011.)

## Art. 4.15. May Sit at Any Time.

Justice courts and corporation courts may sit at any time to try criminal cases over which they have jurisdiction. Any case in which a fine may be assessed shall be tried in accordance with the rules of evidence and this Code.

(Enacted by Acts 1965, 59th Leg., ch. 722 (S.B. 107), § 1, effective January 1, 1966.)

## Art. 4.16. Concurrent Jurisdiction.

When two or more courts have concurrent jurisdiction of any criminal offense, the court in which an indictment or a complaint shall first be filed shall retain jurisdiction except as provided in Article 4.12.

(Enacted by Acts 1965, 59th Leg., ch. 722 (S.B. 107), § 1, effective January 1, 1966.)

## Art. 4.17. Transfer of Certain Misdemeanors.

On a plea of not guilty to a misdemeanor offense punishable by confinement in jail, entered in a county court of a judge who is not a licensed attorney, on the motion of the state or the defendant, the judge may transfer the case to a district court having jurisdiction in the county or to a county court at law in the county presided over by a judge who is a licensed attorney. The judge may make the transfer on his own motion. The attorney representing the state in the case in county court shall continue the prosecution in the court to which the case is transferred. Provided, in no case may any such case be transferred to a district court except with the written consent of the judge of the district court to which the transfer is sought.

(Enacted by Acts 1983, 68th Leg., ch. 303 (S.B. 1), § 6, effective January 1, 1984; am. Acts 1989, 71st Leg., ch. 295 (H.B. 2247), § 1, effective September 1, 1989.)

## Art. 4.18. Claim of Underage.

(a) A claim that a district court or criminal district court does not have jurisdiction over a person because jurisdiction is exclusively in the juvenile court and that the juvenile court could not waive jurisdiction under Section 8.07(a), Penal Code, or did not waive jurisdiction under Section 8.07(b), Penal Code, must be made by written motion in bar of prosecution filed with the court in which criminal charges against the person are filed.

(b) The motion must be filed and presented to the presiding judge of the court:

(1) if the defendant enters a plea of guilty or no contest, before the plea;

(2) if the defendant's guilt or punishment is tried or determined by a jury, before selection of the jury begins; or

(3) if the defendant's guilt is tried by the court, before the first witness is sworn.

(c) Unless the motion is not contested, the presiding judge shall promptly conduct a hearing without a jury and rule on the motion. The party making the motion has the burden of establishing by a preponderance of the evidence those facts necessary for the motion to prevail.

(d) A person may not contest the jurisdiction of the court on the ground that the juvenile court has exclusive jurisdiction if:

(1) the person does not file a motion within the time requirements of this article; or

(2) the presiding judge finds under Subsection (c) that a motion made under this article does not prevail.

(e) An appellate court may review a trial court's determination under this article, if otherwise authorized by law, only after conviction in the trial court.

(f) A court that finds that it lacks jurisdiction over a case because exclusive jurisdiction is in the juvenile court shall transfer the case to the juvenile court as provided by Section 51.08, Family Code.

(g) This article does not apply to a claim of a defect or error in a discretionary transfer proceeding in juvenile court. A defendant may appeal a defect or error only as provided by Article 44.47. (Enacted by Acts 1995, 74th Leg., ch. 262 (H.B. 327), § 80, effective January 1, 1996; am. Acts 1999, 76th Leg., ch. 1477 (H.B. 3517), § 27, effective September 1, 1999; am. Acts 1999, 76th Leg., ch. 1477 (H.B. 3517), § 28, effective September 1, 1999.)

### Art. 4.19. Transfer of Child.

Notwithstanding the order of a juvenile court to detain a child in a certified juvenile detention facility under Section 54.02(h), Family Code, the judge of the criminal court having jurisdiction over the child may order the child to be trans-

ferred to another facility and treated as an adult as provided by this code.
(Enacted by Acts 2011, 82nd Leg., ch. 1087 (S.B. 1209), § 5, effective September 1, 2011.)

# Prevention and Suppression of Offenses

## CHAPTER 5
## FAMILY VIOLENCE PREVENTION

### Art. 5.01. Legislative Statement.

(a) Family violence is a serious danger and threat to society and its members. Victims of family violence are entitled to the maximum protection from harm or abuse or the threat of harm or abuse as is permitted by law.

(b) In any law enforcement, prosecutorial, or judicial response to allegations of family violence, the responding law enforcement or judicial officers shall protect the victim, without regard to the relationship between the alleged offender and victim.
(Enacted by Acts 1985, 69th Leg., ch. 583 (S.B. 869), § 1, effective September 1, 1985.)

### Art. 5.02. Definitions.

In this chapter, "family violence," "family," "household," and "member of a household" have the meanings assigned by Chapter 71, Family Code.
(Enacted by Acts 1985, 69th Leg., ch. 583 (S.B. 869), § 1, effective September 1, 1985; am. Acts 2003, 78th Leg., ch. 1276 (H.B. 3507), § 7.002, effective September 1, 2003.)

### Art. 5.03. Family or Household Relationship Does Not Create an Exception to Official Duties.

A general duty prescribed for an officer by Chapter 2 of this code is not waived or excepted in any family violence case or investigation because of a family or household relationship between an alleged violator and the victim of family violence. A peace officer's or a magistrate's duty to prevent the commission of criminal offenses, including acts of family violence, is not waived or excepted because of a family or household relationship between the potential violator and victim. (Enacted by Acts 1985, 69th Leg., ch. 583 (S.B. 869), § 1, effective September 1, 1985.)

### Art. 5.04. Duties of Peace Officers.

(a) The primary duties of a peace officer who investigates a family violence allegation or who responds to a disturbance call that may involve family violence are to protect any potential victim of family violence, enforce the law of this state, enforce a protective order from another jurisdiction as provided by Chapter 88, Family Code, and make lawful arrests of violators.

(a-1) A peace officer who investigates a family violence allegation or who responds to a disturbance call that may involve family violence shall determine whether the address of the persons involved in the allegation or call matches the address of a current licensed foster home or verified agency foster home listed in the Texas Crime Information Center.

(b) A peace officer who investigates a family violence allegation or who responds to a disturbance call that may involve family violence shall advise any possible adult victim of all reasonable means to prevent further family violence, including giving written notice of a victim's legal rights and remedies and of the availability of shelter or other community services for family violence victims.

(c) A written notice required by Subsection (b) of this article is sufficient if it is in substantially the following form with the required information in English and in Spanish inserted in the notice:

### "NOTICE TO ADULT VICTIMS OF FAMILY VIOLENCE

"It is a crime for any person to cause you any physical injury or harm EVEN IF THAT PERSON IS A MEMBER OR FORMER MEMBER OF YOUR FAMILY OR HOUSEHOLD.

"Please tell the investigating peace officer:

"IF you, your child, or any other household resident has been injured; or

"IF you feel you are going to be in danger when the officer leaves or later.

"You have the right to:

"ASK the local prosecutor to file a criminal complaint against the person committing family violence; and

"APPLY to a court for an order to protect you (you should consult a legal aid office, a prosecuting attorney, or a private attorney). If a family or household member assaults you and is arrested, you may request that a magistrate's order for emergency protection be issued. Please inform the investigating officer if you want an order for emergency protection. You need not be present when the order is issued. You cannot be charged a fee by a court in connection with filing, serving, or entering a protective order. For example, the court can enter an order that:

"(1) the abuser not commit further acts of violence;

"(2) the abuser not threaten, harass, or contact you at home;

"(3) directs the abuser to leave your household; and

"(4) establishes temporary custody of the children and directs the abuser not to interfere with the children or any property.

"A VIOLATION OF CERTAIN PROVISIONS OF COURT-ORDERED PROTECTION (such as (1) and (2) above) MAY BE A FELONY.

"CALL THE FOLLOWING VIOLENCE SHELTERS OR SOCIAL ORGANIZATIONS IF YOU NEED PROTECTION:

"_____

"_____."

(Enacted by Acts 1985, 69th Leg., ch. 583 (S.B. 869), § 1, effective September 1, 1985; am. Acts 1991, 72nd Leg., ch. 366 (H.B. 391), § 4, effective September 1, 1991; am. Acts 1995, 74th Leg., ch. 1024 (H.B. 418), § 24, effective September 1, 1995; am. Acts 1997, 75th Leg., ch. 610 (S.B. 550), § 2, effective September 1, 1997; am. Acts 1997, 75th Leg., ch. 1193 (S.B. 1253), § 23, effective September 1, 1997; am. Acts 2007, 80th Leg., ch. 524 (S.B. 723), § 2, effective June 16, 2007.)

### Art. 5.045. Standby Assistance; Liability.

(a) In the discretion of a peace officer, the officer may stay with a victim of family violence to protect the victim and allow the victim to take the personal property of the victim or of a child in the care of the victim to a place of safety in an orderly manner.

(b) A peace officer who provides assistance under Subsection (a) of this article is not:

(1) civilly liable for an act or omission of the officer that arises in connection with providing the assistance or determining whether to provide the assistance; or

(2) civilly or criminally liable for the wrongful appropriation of any personal property by the victim.

(Enacted by Acts 1995, 74th Leg., ch. 565 (S.B. 284), § 1, effective June 14, 1995.)

## Art. 5.05. Reports and Records.

(a) A peace officer who investigates a family violence incident or who responds to a disturbance call that may involve family violence shall make a written report, including but not limited to:

    (1) the names of the suspect and complainant;

    (2) the date, time, and location of the incident;

    (3) any visible or reported injuries;

    (4) a description of the incident and a statement of its disposition; and

    (5) whether the suspect is a member of the state military forces or is serving in the armed forces of the United States in an active-duty status.

(a-1) In addition to the written report required under Subsection (a), a peace officer who investigates a family violence incident or who responds to a disturbance call that may involve family violence shall make a report to the Department of Family and Protective Services if the location of the incident or call, or the known address of a person involved in the incident or call, matches the address of a current licensed foster home or a verified agency foster home as listed in the Texas Crime Information Center. The report under this subsection may be made orally or electronically and must:

    (1) include the information required by Subsection (a); and

    (2) be filed with the Department of Family and Protective Services within 24 hours of the beginning of the investigation or receipt of the disturbance call.

(a-2) If a suspect is identified as being a member of the military, as described by Subsection (a)(5), the peace officer shall provide written notice of the incident or disturbance call to the staff judge advocate at Joint Force Headquarters or the provost marshal of the military installation to which the suspect is assigned with the intent that the commanding officer will be notified, as applicable.

(b) Each local law enforcement agency shall establish a departmental code for identifying and retrieving family violence reports as outlined in Subsection (a) of this section. A district or county attorney or an assistant district or county attorney exercising authority in the county where the law enforcement agency maintains records under this section is entitled to access to the records. The Department of Family and Protective Services is entitled to access the records relating to any person who is 14 years of age or older and who resides in a licensed foster home or a verified agency foster home.

(c) In order to ensure that officers responding to calls are aware of the existence and terms of protective orders, each municipal police department and sheriff shall establish procedures within the department or office to provide adequate information or access to information for law enforcement officers of the names of persons protected by a protective order and of persons to whom protective orders are directed.

(d) Each law enforcement officer shall accept a certified copy of an original or modified protective order as proof of the validity of the order and it is presumed the order remains valid unless:

    (1) the order contains a termination date that has passed;

    (2) it is more than one year after the date the order was issued; or

    (3) the law enforcement officer has been notified by the clerk of the court vacating the order that the order has been vacated.

(e) A peace officer who makes a report under Subsection (a) of this article shall provide information concerning the incident or disturbance to the bureau of identification and records of the Department of Public Safety for its recordkeeping function under Section 411.042, Government Code. The bureau shall prescribe the form and nature of the information required to be reported to the bureau by this article.

(f) On request of a victim of an incident of family violence, the local law enforcement agency responsible for investigating the incident shall provide the victim, at no cost to the victim, with any information that is:

    (1) contained in the written report prepared under Subsection (a);

    (2) described by Subsection (a)(1) or (2); and

    (3) not exempt from disclosure under Chapter 552, Government Code, or other law.

(Enacted by Acts 1985, 69th Leg., ch. 583 (S.B. 869), § 1, effective September 1, 1985; am. Acts 1989, 71st Leg., ch. 614 (S.B. 171), § 27, effective September 1, 1989; am. Acts 1989, 71st Leg., ch. 739 (H.B. 1230), § 8, effective September 1, 1989; am. Acts 1993, 73rd Leg., ch. 900 (S.B. 1067),

§ 8.01, effective September 1, 1993; am. Acts 2007, 80th Leg., ch. 1057 (H.B. 2210), § 2, effective September 1, 2007; am. Acts 2011, 82nd Leg., ch. 327 (H.B. 2624), § 2, effective September 1, 2011.)

### Art. 5.06. Duties of Prosecuting Attorneys and Courts.

(a) Neither a prosecuting attorney nor a court may:

(1) dismiss or delay any criminal proceeding that involves a prosecution for an offense that constitutes family violence because a civil proceeding is pending or not pending; or

(2) require proof that a complaining witness, victim, or defendant is a party to a suit for the dissolution of a marriage or a suit affecting the parent-child relationship before presenting a criminal allegation to a grand jury, filing an information, or otherwise proceeding with the prosecution of a criminal case.

(b) A prosecuting attorney's decision to file an application for a protective order under Chapter 71, Family Code, should be made without regard to whether a criminal complaint has been filed by the applicant. A prosecuting attorney may require the applicant to provide information for an offense report, relating to the facts alleged in the application, with a local law enforcement agency.

(c) The prosecuting attorney having responsibility under Section 71.04(c), Family Code, for filing applications for protective orders under Chapter 71, Family Code, shall provide notice of that responsibility to all law enforcement agencies within the jurisdiction of the prosecuting attorney for the prosecuting attorney.

(Enacted by Acts 1985, 69th Leg., ch. 583 (S.B. 869), § 1, effective September 1, 1985; am. Acts 1989, 71st Leg., ch. 614 (S.B. 171), § 28, effective September 1, 1989; am. Acts 1989, 71st Leg., ch. 739 (H.B. 1230), § 9, effective September 1, 1989; am. Acts 1995, 74th Leg., ch. 564 (S.B. 283), § 2, effective September 1, 1995; am. Acts 1995, 74th Leg., ch. 1024 (H.B. 418), § 25, effective September 1, 1995.)

### Art. 5.07. Venue for Protective Order Offenses.

The venue for an offense under Section 25.07, Penal Code, is in the county in which the order was issued or, without regard to the identity or location of the court that issued the protective order, in the county in which the offense was committed.

(Enacted by Acts 1989, 71st Leg., ch. 614 (S.B. 171), § 29, effective September 1, 1989; enacted by Acts 1989, 71st Leg., ch. 739 (H.B. 1230), § 10, effective September 1, 1989; am. Acts 1995, 74th Leg., ch. 76 (S.B. 959), § 14.16, effective September 1, 1995.)

### Art. 5.08. Mediation in Family Violence Cases.

Notwithstanding Article 26.13(g) or Section 11(a)(16), Article 42.12, of this code, in a criminal prosecution arising from family violence, as that term is defined by Section 71.004, Family Code, a court shall not refer or order the victim or the defendant involved to mediation, dispute resolution, arbitration, or other similar procedures.

(Enacted by Acts 1999, 76th Leg., ch. 389 (S.B. 1124), § 1, effective August 30, 1999.)

# CHAPTER 6
## PREVENTING OFFENSES BY THE ACT OF MAGISTRATES AND OTHER OFFICERS; EDUCATION CONCERNING CONSEQUENCES OF CERTAIN OFFENSES

### Art. 6.01. When Magistrate Hears Threat.

It is the duty of every magistrate, when he may have heard, in any manner, that a threat has been made by one person to do some injury to himself or the person or property of another, including the person or property of his spouse, immediately to give notice to some peace officer, in order that such peace officer may use lawful means to prevent the injury.

(Enacted by Acts 1965, 59th Leg., ch. 722 (S.B. 107), § 1, effective January 1, 1966; am. Acts 1979, 66th Leg., ch. 164 (S.B. 529), § 1, effective September 1, 1979.)

## Art. 6.02. Threat to Take Life.

If, within the hearing of a magistrate, one person shall threaten to take the life of another, including that of his spouse, or himself, the magistrate shall issue a warrant for the arrest of the person making the threat, or in case of emergency, he may himself immediately arrest such person.

(Enacted by Acts 1965, 59th Leg., ch. 722 (S.B. 107), § 1, effective January 1, 1966; am. Acts 1979, 66th Leg., ch. 164 (S.B. 529), § 1, effective September 1, 1979.)

## Art. 6.03. On Attempt to Injure.

Whenever, in the presence or within the observation of a magistrate, an attempt is made by one person to inflict an injury upon himself or to the person or property of another, including the person or property of his spouse, it is his duty to use all lawful means to prevent the injury. This may be done, either by verbal order to a peace officer to interfere and prevent the injury, or by the issuance of an order of arrest against the offender, or by arresting the offender; for which purpose he may call upon all persons present to assist in making the arrest.

(Enacted by Acts 1965, 59th Leg., ch. 722 (S.B. 107), § 1, effective January 1, 1966; am. Acts 1979, 66th Leg., ch. 164 (S.B. 529), § 1, effective September 1, 1979.)

## Art. 6.04. May Compel Offender to Give Security.

When the person making such threat is brought before a magistrate, he may compel him to give security to keep the peace, or commit him to custody.

(Enacted by Acts 1965, 59th Leg., ch. 722 (S.B. 107), § 1, effective January 1, 1966.)

## Art. 6.05. Duty of Peace Officer As to Threats.

It is the duty of every peace officer, when he may have been informed in any manner that a threat has been made by one person to do some injury to himself or to the person or property of another, including the person or property of his spouse, to prevent the threatened injury, if within his power; and, in order to do this, he may call in aid any number of citizens in his county. He may take such measures as the person about to be injured might for the prevention of the offense.

(Enacted by Acts 1965, 59th Leg., ch. 722 (S.B. 107), § 1, effective January 1, 1966; am. Acts 1979, 66th Leg., ch. 164 (S.B. 529), § 1, effective September 1, 1979.)

## Art. 6.06. Peace Officer to Prevent Injury.

Whenever, in the presence of a peace officer, or within his view, one person is about to commit an offense against the person or property of another, including the person or property of his spouse, or injure himself, it is his duty to prevent it; and, for this purpose the peace officer may summon any number of the citizens of his county to his aid. The peace officer must use the amount of force necessary to prevent the commission of the offense, and no greater.

(Enacted by Acts 1965, 59th Leg., ch. 722 (S.B. 107), § 1, effective January 1, 1966; am. Acts 1979, 66th Leg., ch. 164 (S.B. 529), § 1, effective September 1, 1979.)

## Art. 6.07. Conduct of Peace Officer.

The conduct of peace officers, in preventing offenses about to be committed in their presence, or within their view, is to be regulated by the same rules as are prescribed to the action of the person about to be injured. They may use all force necessary to repel the aggression.

(Enacted by Acts 1965, 59th Leg., ch. 722 (S.B. 107), § 1, effective January 1, 1966.)

## Art. 6.08. Protective Order Prohibiting Offense Caused by Bias or Prejudice.

(a) At any proceeding in which the defendant appears in constitutional county court, statutory county court, or district court that is related to an offense under Title 5, Penal Code, or Section 28.02, 28.03, or 28.08, Penal Code, in which it is alleged that the defendant committed the offense because of bias or prejudice as described by Article 42.014, a person may request the court to render a protective order under Title 4, Family Code, for the protection of the person.

(b) The court shall render a protective order in the manner provided by Title 4, Family Code, if, in lieu of the finding that family violence occurred and is likely to occur in the future as required by Section 85.001, Family Code, the court finds that probable cause exists to believe that an offense under Title 5, Penal Code, or Section 28.02, 28.03, or 28.08, Penal Code, occurred, that the defendant committed the offense because of bias or prejudice, and that the nature of the scheme or course of conduct engaged in by the defendant in the commission of the offense indicates that the

**Criminal Procedure**

defendant is likely to engage in the future in conduct prohibited by Title 5, Penal Code, or Section 28.02, 28.03, or 28.08, Penal Code, and committed because of bias or prejudice.

(c) The procedure for the enforcement of a protective order under Title 4, Family Code, applies to the fullest extent practicable to the enforcement of a protective order under this article, including provisions relating to findings, contents, duration, warning, delivery, law enforcement duties, and modification, except that:

(1) the printed statement on the warning must refer to the prosecution of subsequent offenses committed because of bias or prejudice;

(2) the court shall require a constable to serve a protective order issued under this article; and

(3) the clerk of the court shall forward a copy of a protective order issued under this article to the Department of Public Safety with a designation indicating that the order was issued to prevent offenses committed because of bias or prejudice.

(d) For an original or modified protective order rendered under this article, on receipt of the order from the clerk of the court, a law enforcement agency shall immediately, but not later than the 10th day after the date the order is received, enter the information required by Section 411.042(b)(6), Government Code, into the statewide law enforcement information system maintained by the Department of Public Safety.
(Enacted by Acts 2001, 77th Leg., ch. 85 (H.B. 587), § 3.01, effective September 1, 2001.)

### Art. 6.09. [2 Versions: As added by Acts 2011, 82nd Leg., ch. 981] Stalking Protective Order.

(a) At any proceeding related to an offense under Section 42.072, Penal Code, in which the defendant appears before the court, a person may request the court to render a protective order under Title 4, Family Code, for the protection of the person. The request is made by filing "An Application for a Protective Order" in the same manner as an application for a protective order under Title 4, Family Code.

(b) The court shall render a protective order in the manner provided by Title 4, Family Code, if, in lieu of the finding that family violence occurred and is likely to occur in the future as required by Section 85.001, Family Code, the court finds that probable cause exists to believe that an offense

under Section 42.072, Penal Code, occurred and that the nature of the scheme or course of conduct engaged in by the defendant in the commission of the offense indicates that the defendant is likely to engage in the future in conduct prohibited by Section 42.072(a)(1), (2), or (3), Penal Code.

(c) The procedure for the enforcement of a protective order under Title 4, Family Code, applies to the fullest extent practicable to the enforcement of a protective order under this article, including provisions relating to findings, contents, duration, warning, delivery, law enforcement duties, and modification.
(Enacted by Acts 2011, 82nd Leg., ch. 981 (H.B. 1721), § 1, effective September 1, 2011.)

### Art. 6.09. [2 Versions: As added by Acts 2011, 82nd Leg., ch. 1322] Educational Programs Concerning Certain Offenses Committed by Minors; Mandatory Court Attendance.

(a) In this article, "parent" means a natural or adoptive parent, managing or possessory conservator, or legal guardian. The term does not include a parent whose parental rights have been terminated.

(b) This article applies to a defendant who has not had the disabilities of minority removed and has been charged with an offense under Section 43.261, Penal Code.

(c) The judge of a county court:

(1) must take the defendant's plea in open court; and

(2) shall issue a summons to compel the defendant's parent to be present during:

(A) the taking of the defendant's plea; and

(B) all other proceedings relating to the case.

(d) If a county court finds that a defendant has committed an offense under Section 43.261, Penal Code, the court may enter an order requiring the defendant to attend and successfully complete an educational program described by Section 37.218, Education Code, or another equivalent educational program.

(e) A court that enters an order under Subsection (d) shall require the defendant or the defendant's parent to pay the cost of attending an educational program under Subsection (d) if the court determines that the defendant or the defendant's parent is financially able to make payment.
(Enacted by Acts 2011, 82nd Leg., ch. 1322 (S.B. 407), § 6, effective September 1, 2011.)

# CHAPTER 7
# PROCEEDINGS BEFORE MAGISTRATES TO PREVENT OFFENSES

## Art. 7.01. Shall Issue Warrant.

Whenever a magistrate is informed upon oath that an offense is about to be committed against the person or property of the informant, or of another, or that any person has threatened to commit an offense, the magistrate shall immediately issue a warrant for the arrest of the accused; that he may be brought before such magistrate or before some other named in the warrant.

(Enacted by Acts 1965, 59th Leg., ch. 722 (S.B. 107), § 1, effective January 1, 1966.)

## Art. 7.02. Appearance Bond Pending Peace Bond Hearing.

In proceedings under this Chapter, the accused shall have the right to make an appearance bond; such bond shall be conditioned as appearance bonds in other cases, and shall be further conditioned that the accused, pending the hearing, will not commit such offense and that he will keep the peace toward the person threatened or about to be injured, and toward all others, pending the hearing. Should the accused enter into such appearance bond, such fact shall not constitute any evidence of the accusation brought against him at the hearing on the merits before the magistrate.

(Enacted by Acts 1965, 59th Leg., ch. 722 (S.B. 107), § 1, effective January 1, 1966.)

## Art. 7.03. Accused Brought Before Magistrate.

When the accused has been brought before the magistrate, he shall hear proof as to the accusation, and if he be satisfied that there is just reason to apprehend that the offense was intended to be committed, or that the threat was seriously made, he shall make an order that the accused enter into bond in such sum as he may in his discretion require, conditioned that he will not commit such offense, and that he will keep the peace toward the person threatened or about to be injured, and toward all others named in the bond for any period of time, not to exceed one year from the date of the bond. The magistrate shall admonish the accused that if the accused violates a condition of the bond, the court, in addition to ordering forfeiture of the bond, may punish the accused for contempt under Section 21.002(c), Government Code.

(Enacted by Acts 1965, 59th Leg., ch. 722 (S.B. 107), § 1, effective January 1, 1966; am. Acts 1997, 75th Leg., ch. 773 (H.B. 1968), § 1, effective September 1, 1997.)

## Art. 7.04. Form of Peace Bond.

Such bond shall be sufficient if it be payable to the State of Texas, conditioned as required in said order of the magistrate, be for some certain sum, and be signed by the defendant and his surety or sureties and dated, and the provisions of Article 17.02 permitting the deposit of current United States money in lieu of sureties is applicable to this bond. No error of form shall vitiate such bond, and no error in the proceedings prior to the execution of the bond shall be a defense in a suit thereon.

(Enacted by Acts 1965, 59th Leg., ch. 722 (S.B. 107), § 1, effective January 1, 1966.)

## Art. 7.05. Oath of Surety; Bond Filed.

The officer taking such bond shall require the sureties of the accused to make oath as to the value of their property as pointed out with regard to bail bonds. Such officer shall forthwith deposit such bond and oaths in the office of the clerk of the county where such bond is taken.

(Enacted by Acts 1965, 59th Leg., ch. 722 (S.B. 107), § 1, effective January 1, 1966.)

## Art. 7.06. Amount of Bail.

The magistrate, in fixing the amount of such bonds, shall be governed by the pecuniary circumstances of the accused and the nature of the offense threatened or about to be committed.

(Enacted by Acts 1965, 59th Leg., ch. 722 (S.B. 107), § 1, effective January 1, 1966.)

## Art. 7.07. Surety May Exonerate Himself.

A surety upon any such bond may, at any time before a breach thereof, exonerate himself from the obligations of the same by delivering to any magistrate of the county where such bond was taken, the person of the defendant; and such magistrate shall in that case again require of the defendant bond, with other security in the same amount as the first bond; and the same proceeding shall be had as in the first instance, but the one year's time shall commence to run from the date of the first order.

(Enacted by Acts 1965, 59th Leg., ch. 722 (S.B. 107), § 1, effective January 1, 1966.)

## Art. 7.08. Failure to Give Bond.

If the defendant fail to give bond, he shall be committed to jail for one year from the date of the first order requiring such bond.

(Enacted by Acts 1965, 59th Leg., ch. 722 (S.B. 107), § 1, effective January 1, 1966.)

## Art. 7.09. Discharge of Defendant.

A defendant committed for failing to give bond shall be discharged by the officer having him in custody, upon giving the required bond, or at the expiration of the time for which he has been committed.

(Enacted by Acts 1965, 59th Leg., ch. 722 (S.B. 107), § 1, effective January 1, 1966.)

## Art. 7.10. May Discharge Defendant.

If the magistrate believes from the evidence that there is no good reason to apprehend that the offense was intended or will be committed, or that no serious threat was made by the defendant, he shall discharge the accused, and may, in his discretion, tax the cost of the proceeding against the party making the complaint.

(Enacted by Acts 1965, 59th Leg., ch. 722 (S.B. 107), § 1, effective January 1, 1966.)

## Art. 7.11. Bond of Person Charged with Libel [Repealed].

Repealed by Acts 1973, 63rd Leg., ch. 399 (S.B. 34), § 3(b), effective January 1, 1974.

(Enacted by Acts 1965, 59th Leg., ch. 722 (S.B. 107), § 1, effective January 1, 1966.)

## Art. 7.12. Destruction of Libel [Repealed].

Repealed by Acts 1973, 63rd Leg., ch. 399 (S.B. 34), § 3(b), effective January 1, 1974.

(Enacted by Acts 1965, 59th Leg., ch. 722 (S.B. 107), § 1, effective January 1, 1966.)

## Art. 7.13. When the Defendant Has Committed a Crime.

If it appears from the evidence before the magistrate that the defendant has committed a criminal offense, the same proceedings shall be had as in other cases where parties are charged with crime.

(Enacted by Acts 1965, 59th Leg., ch. 722 (S.B. 107), § 1, effective January 1, 1966.)

## Art. 7.14. Costs.

If the accused is found subject to the charge and required to give bond, the costs of the proceedings shall be adjudged against him.

(Enacted by Acts 1965, 59th Leg., ch. 722 (S.B. 107), § 1, effective January 1, 1966.)

## Art. 7.15. May Order Protection.

When, from the nature of the case and the proof offered to the magistrate, it may appear necessary and proper, he shall have a right to order any peace officer to protect the person or property of any individual threatened; and such peace officer shall have the right to summon aid by requiring any number of citizens of his county to assist in giving the protection.

(Enacted by Acts 1965, 59th Leg., ch. 722 (S.B. 107), § 1, effective January 1, 1966.)

## Art. 7.16. Suit on Bond.

A suit to forfeit any bond taken under the provisions of this Chapter shall be brought in the name of the State by the district or county attorney in the county where the bond was taken.

(Enacted by Acts 1965, 59th Leg., ch. 722 (S.B. 107), § 1, effective January 1, 1966.)

## Art. 7.17. Limitation and Procedure.

Suits upon such bonds shall be commenced within two years from the breach of the same, and not thereafter, and shall be governed by the same rules as civil actions, except that the sureties may be sued without joining the principal. To entitle the State to recover, it shall only be necessary to prove that the accused violated any condition of said bond. The full amount of such bond may be recovered of the accused and the sureties.

(Enacted by Acts 1965, 59th Leg., ch. 722 (S.B. 107), § 1, effective January 1, 1966.)

## Art. 7.18. Contempt.

Violation of a condition of bond imposed under this chapter is punishable by:

    (1) forfeiture of the bond;

    (2) imposition of the fine and confinement for contempt under Section 21.002(c), Government Code; or

    (3) both forfeiture of the bond and imposition of the fine and confinement.

(Enacted by Acts 1997, 75th Leg., ch. 773 (H.B. 1968), § 2, effective September 1, 1997.)

## CHAPTER 7A
## PROTECTIVE ORDER FOR CERTAIN VICTIMS OF TRAFFICKING OR SEXUAL ASSAULT
## [2 VERSIONS: AS AMENDED BY ACTS 2011, 82ND LEG., CH. 1]

## Art. 7A.01. Application for Protective Order.

(a) The following persons may file an application for a protective order under this chapter without regard to the relationship between the applicant and the alleged offender:

    (1) a person who is the victim of an offense under Section 21.02, 21.11, 22.011, or 22.021, Penal Code;

    (2) a person who is the victim of an offense under Section 20A.02(a)(3), (4), (7), or (8) or Section 43.05, Penal Code;

    (3) a parent or guardian acting on behalf of a person younger than 18 years of age who is the victim of an offense listed in Subdivision (1) or (2); or

    (4) a prosecuting attorney acting on behalf of a person described by Subdivision (1) or (2).

(b) An application for a protective order under this chapter may be filed in a district court, juvenile court having the jurisdiction of a district court, statutory county court, or constitutional county court in:

    (1) the county in which the applicant resides; or

    (2) the county in which the alleged offender resides.

(Enacted by Acts 2003, 78th Leg., ch. 836 (S.B. 433), § 1, effective September 1, 2003; am. Acts 2007, 80th Leg., ch. 593 (H.B. 8), § 3.05, effective September 1, 2007; am. Acts 2007, 80th Leg., ch. 882 (H.B. 1988), § 1, effective September 1, 2007; am. Acts 2011, 82nd Leg., ch. 1 (S.B. 24), § 2.02, effective September 1, 2011.)

## Art. 7A.02. Temporary Ex Parte Order.

If the court finds from the information contained in an application for a protective order that there is a clear and present danger of a sexual assault or other harm to the applicant, the court, without further notice to the alleged offender and without a hearing, may enter a temporary ex parte order for the protection of the applicant or any other member of the applicant's family or household.

(Enacted by Acts 2003, 78th Leg., ch. 836 (S.B. 433), § 1, effective September 1, 2003.)

## Art. 7A.03. Required Findings; Issuance of Protective Order.

(a) At the close of a hearing on an application for a protective order under this chapter, the court shall find whether there are reasonable grounds to believe that the applicant is the victim of a sexual assault.

(b) If the court finds reasonable grounds to believe that the applicant is the victim of a sexual assault, the court shall issue a protective order that includes a statement of the required findings.

(Enacted by Acts 2003, 78th Leg., ch. 836 (S.B. 433), § 1, effective September 1, 2003; am. Acts 2007, 80th Leg., ch. 882 (H.B. 1988), § 2, effective September 1, 2007; am. Acts 2011, 82nd Leg., ch. 238 (H.B. 649), § 1, effective September 1, 2011.)

## Art. 7A.035. Hearsay Statement of Child Victim.

In a hearing on an application for a protective order under this chapter, a statement that is made by a child younger than 14 years of age who is the victim of an offense under Section 21.02, 21.11, 22.011, or 22.021, Penal Code, and that describes the offense committed against the child is admissible as evidence in the same manner that a child's statement regarding alleged abuse against the child is admissible under Section 104.006, Family Code, in a suit affecting the parent-child relationship.

(Enacted by Acts 2011, 82nd Leg., ch. 981 (H.B. 1721), § 2, effective September 1, 2011.)

Criminal Procedure

## Art. 7A.04. Application of Other Law.

To the extent applicable, except as otherwise provided by this chapter, Title 4, Family Code, applies to a protective order issued under this chapter.

(Enacted by Acts 2003, 78th Leg., ch. 836 (S.B. 433), § 1, effective September 1, 2003.)

## Art. 7A.05. Conditions Specified by Order.

(a) In a protective order issued under this chapter, the court may:

(1) order the alleged offender to take action as specified by the court that the court determines is necessary or appropriate to prevent or reduce the likelihood of future harm to the applicant or a member of the applicant's family or household; or

(2) prohibit the alleged offender from:

(A) communicating directly or indirectly with the applicant or any member of the applicant's family or household in a threatening or harassing manner;

(B) going to or near the residence, place of employment or business, or child-care facility or school of the applicant or any member of the applicant's family or household;

(C) engaging in conduct directed specifically toward the applicant or any member of the applicant's family or household, including following the person, that is reasonably likely to harass, annoy, alarm, abuse, torment, or embarrass the person; and

(D) possessing a firearm, unless the alleged offender is a peace officer, as defined by Section 1.07, Penal Code, actively engaged in employment as a sworn, full-time paid employee of a state agency or political subdivision.

(b) In an order under Subsection (a)(2)(B), the court shall specifically describe each prohibited location and the minimum distance from the location, if any, that the alleged offender must maintain. This subsection does not apply to an order with respect to which the court has received a request to maintain confidentiality of information revealing the locations.

(c) In a protective order, the court may suspend a license to carry a concealed handgun issued under Section 411.177, Government Code, that is held by the alleged offender.

(Enacted by Acts 2003, 78th Leg., ch. 836 (S.B. 433), § 1, effective September 1, 2003.)

## Art. 7A.06. Warning on Protective Order.

(a) Each protective order issued under this chapter, including a temporary ex parte order, must contain the following prominently displayed statements in boldfaced type, capital letters, or underlined:

"A PERSON WHO VIOLATES THIS ORDER MAY BE PUNISHED FOR CONTEMPT OF COURT BY A FINE OF AS MUCH AS $500 OR BY CONFINEMENT IN JAIL FOR AS LONG AS SIX MONTHS, OR BOTH."

"NO PERSON, INCLUDING A PERSON WHO IS PROTECTED BY THIS ORDER, MAY GIVE PERMISSION TO ANYONE TO IGNORE OR VIOLATE ANY PROVISION OF THIS ORDER. DURING THE TIME IN WHICH THIS ORDER IS VALID, EVERY PROVISION OF THIS ORDER IS IN FULL FORCE AND EFFECT UNLESS A COURT CHANGES THE ORDER."

"IT IS UNLAWFUL FOR ANY PERSON, OTHER THAN A PEACE OFFICER, AS DEFINED BY SECTION 1.07, PENAL CODE, ACTIVELY ENGAGED IN EMPLOYMENT AS A SWORN, FULL-TIME PAID EMPLOYEE OF A STATE AGENCY OR POLITICAL SUBDIVISION, WHO IS SUBJECT TO A PROTECTIVE ORDER TO POSSESS A FIREARM OR AMMUNITION."

(b) Each protective order issued under this chapter, except for a temporary ex parte order, must contain the following prominently displayed statement in boldfaced type, capital letters, or underlined:

"A VIOLATION OF THIS ORDER BY COMMISSION OF AN ACT PROHIBITED BY THE ORDER MAY BE PUNISHABLE BY A FINE OF AS MUCH AS $4,000 OR BY CONFINEMENT IN JAIL FOR AS LONG AS ONE YEAR, OR BOTH. AN ACT THAT RESULTS IN A SEPARATE OFFENSE MAY BE PROSECUTED AS A SEPARATE OFFENSE IN ADDITION TO A VIOLATION OF THIS ORDER."

(Enacted by Acts 2003, 78th Leg., ch. 836 (S.B. 433), § 1, effective September 1, 2003.)

## Art. 7A.07. Duration of Protective Order.

(a) A protective order issued under Article 7A.03 may be effective for the duration of the lives of the offender and victim or for any shorter period stated in the order. If a period is not stated in the order, the order is effective until the second anniversary of the date the order was issued.

(b) A victim who is 17 years of age or older or a parent or guardian acting on behalf of a victim who is younger than 17 years of age may file at any time an application with the court to rescind the protective order.

(c) If a person who is the subject of a protective order issued under Article 7A.03 is confined or imprisoned on the date the protective order is due to expire under Subsection (a), the period for which the order is effective is extended, and the order expires on the first anniversary of the date the person is released from confinement or imprisonment.

(d) To the extent of any conflict with Section 85.025, Family Code, this article prevails.

(Enacted by Acts 2007, 80th Leg., ch. 882 (H.B. 1988), § 3, effective September 1, 2007; am. Acts 2011, 82nd Leg., ch. 238 (H.B. 649), § 2, effective September 1, 2011.)

## CHAPTER 7A
## PROTECTIVE ORDER FOR VICTIM OF SEXUAL ASSAULT OR STALKING
## [2 VERSIONS: AS AMENDED BY ACTS 2011, 82ND LEG., CH. 135]

### Art. 7A.01. Application for Protective Order.

(a) A person who is the victim of an offense under Section 21.02, 21.11, 22.011, 22.021, or 42.072, Penal Code, a parent or guardian acting on behalf of a person younger than 17 years of age who is the victim of such an offense, or a prosecuting attorney acting on behalf of the person may file an application for a protective order under this chapter without regard to the relationship between the applicant and the alleged offender.

(b) An application for a protective order under this chapter may be filed in a district court, juvenile court having the jurisdiction of a district court, statutory county court, or constitutional county court in:

(1) the county in which the applicant resides; or

(2) the county in which the alleged offender resides.

(Enacted by Acts 2003, 78th Leg., ch. 836 (S.B. 433), § 1, effective September 1, 2003; am. Acts 2007, 80th Leg., ch. 593 (H.B. 8), § 3.05, effective September 1, 2007; am. Acts 2007, 80th Leg., ch. 882 (H.B. 1988), § 1, effective September 1, 2007; am. Acts 2011, 82nd Leg., ch. 135 (S.B. 250), § 2, effective September 1, 2011.)

### Art. 7A.02. Temporary Ex Parte Order.

If the court finds from the information contained in an application for a protective order that there is a clear and present danger of sexual assault, stalking, or other harm to the applicant, the court, without further notice to the alleged offender and without a hearing, may enter a temporary ex parte order for the protection of the applicant or any other member of the applicant's family or household.

(Enacted by Acts 2003, 78th Leg., ch. 836 (S.B. 433), § 1, effective September 1, 2003; am. Acts 2011, 82nd Leg., ch. 135 (S.B. 250), § 3, effective September 1, 2011.)

### Art. 7A.03. [2 Versions: As amended by Acts 2011, 82nd Leg., ch. 135] Required Findings; Issuance of Protective Order.

(a) At the close of a hearing on an application for a protective order under this chapter, the court shall find whether there are reasonable grounds to believe that the applicant is the victim of:

(1) sexual assault and:

(A) is younger than 18 years of age; or

(B) regardless of age, is the subject of a threat that reasonably places the applicant in fear of further harm from the alleged offender; or

(2) stalking.

(b) If the court makes a finding described by Subsection (a)(1) or (2), the court shall issue a protective order that includes a statement of the required findings.

(Enacted by Acts 2003, 78th Leg., ch. 836 (S.B. 433), § 1, effective September 1, 2003; am. Acts 2007, 80th Leg., ch. 882 (H.B. 1988), § 2, effective September 1, 2007; am. Acts 2011, 82nd Leg., ch. 135 (S.B. 250), § 4, effective September 1, 2011.)

**Art. 7A.03. [2 Versions: As amended by Acts 2011, 82nd Leg., ch. 238] Required Findings; Issuance of Protective Order.**

(a) At the close of a hearing on an application for a protective order under this chapter, the court shall find whether there are reasonable grounds to believe that the applicant is the victim of a sexual assault.

(b) If the court finds reasonable grounds to believe that the applicant is the victim of a sexual assault, the court shall issue a protective order that includes a statement of the required findings.

(Enacted by Acts 2003, 78th Leg., ch. 836 (S.B. 433), § 1, effective September 1, 2003; am. Acts 2007, 80th Leg., ch. 882 (H.B. 1988), § 2, effective September 1, 2007; am. Acts 2011, 82nd Leg., ch. 238 (H.B. 649), § 1, effective September 1, 2011.)

**Art. 7A.035. Hearsay Statement of Child Victim.**

In a hearing on an application for a protective order under this chapter, a statement that is made by a child younger than 14 years of age who is the victim of an offense under Section 21.02, 21.11, 22.011, or 22.021, Penal Code, and that describes the offense committed against the child is admissible as evidence in the same manner that a child's statement regarding alleged abuse against the child is admissible under Section 104.006, Family Code, in a suit affecting the parent-child relationship.

(Enacted by Acts 2011, 82nd Leg., ch. 981 (H.B. 1721), § 2, effective September 1, 2011.)

**Art. 7A.04. Application of Other Law.**

To the extent applicable, except as otherwise provided by this chapter, Title 4, Family Code, applies to a protective order issued under this chapter.

(Enacted by Acts 2003, 78th Leg., ch. 836 (S.B. 433), § 1, effective September 1, 2003.)

**Art. 7A.05. Conditions Specified by Order.**

(a) In a protective order issued under this chapter, the court may:

(1) order the alleged offender to take action as specified by the court that the court determines is necessary or appropriate to prevent or reduce the likelihood of future harm to the applicant or a member of the applicant's family or household; or

(2) prohibit the alleged offender from:

(A) communicating directly or indirectly with the applicant or any member of the applicant's family or household in a threatening or harassing manner;

(B) going to or near the residence, place of employment or business, or child-care facility or school of the applicant or any member of the applicant's family or household;

(C) engaging in conduct directed specifically toward the applicant or any member of the applicant's family or household, including following the person, that is reasonably likely to harass, annoy, alarm, abuse, torment, or embarrass the person; and

(D) possessing a firearm, unless the alleged offender is a peace officer, as defined by Section 1.07, Penal Code, actively engaged in employment as a sworn, full-time paid employee of a state agency or political subdivision.

(b) In an order under Subsection (a)(2)(B), the court shall specifically describe each prohibited location and the minimum distance from the location, if any, that the alleged offender must maintain. This subsection does not apply to an order with respect to which the court has received a request to maintain confidentiality of information revealing the locations.

(c) In a protective order, the court may suspend a license to carry a concealed handgun issued under Section 411.177, Government Code, that is held by the alleged offender.

(Enacted by Acts 2003, 78th Leg., ch. 836 (S.B. 433), § 1, effective September 1, 2003.)

**Art. 7A.06. Warning on Protective Order.**

(a) Each protective order issued under this chapter, including a temporary ex parte order, must contain the following prominently displayed statements in boldfaced type, capital letters, or underlined:

"A PERSON WHO VIOLATES THIS ORDER MAY BE PUNISHED FOR CONTEMPT OF COURT BY A FINE OF AS MUCH AS $500 OR BY CONFINEMENT IN JAIL FOR AS LONG AS SIX MONTHS, OR BOTH."

"NO PERSON, INCLUDING A PERSON WHO IS PROTECTED BY THIS ORDER, MAY GIVE PERMISSION TO ANYONE TO IGNORE OR VIOLATE ANY PROVISION OF THIS ORDER. DURING THE TIME IN WHICH THIS ORDER IS VALID, EVERY PROVISION OF THIS OR-

DER IS IN FULL FORCE AND EFFECT UNLESS A COURT CHANGES THE ORDER."

"IT IS UNLAWFUL FOR ANY PERSON, OTHER THAN A PEACE OFFICER, AS DEFINED BY SECTION 1.07, PENAL CODE, ACTIVELY ENGAGED IN EMPLOYMENT AS A SWORN, FULL-TIME PAID EMPLOYEE OF A STATE AGENCY OR POLITICAL SUBDIVISION, WHO IS SUBJECT TO A PROTECTIVE ORDER TO POSSESS A FIREARM OR AMMUNITION."

(b) Each protective order issued under this chapter, except for a temporary ex parte order, must contain the following prominently displayed statement in boldfaced type, capital letters, or underlined:

"A VIOLATION OF THIS ORDER BY COMMISSION OF AN ACT PROHIBITED BY THE ORDER MAY BE PUNISHABLE BY A FINE OF AS MUCH AS $4,000 OR BY CONFINEMENT IN JAIL FOR AS LONG AS ONE YEAR, OR BOTH. AN ACT THAT RESULTS IN A SEPARATE OFFENSE MAY BE PROSECUTED AS A SEPARATE OFFENSE IN ADDITION TO A VIOLATION OF THIS ORDER."

(Enacted by Acts 2003, 78th Leg., ch. 836 (S.B. 433), § 1, effective September 1, 2003.)

## Art. 7A.07. Duration of Protective Order.

(a) A protective order issued under Article 7A.03 may be effective for the duration of the lives of the offender and victim or for any shorter period stated in the order. If a period is not stated in the order, the order is effective until the second anniversary of the date the order was issued.

(b) A victim who is 17 years of age or older or a parent or guardian acting on behalf of a victim who is younger than 17 years of age may file at any time an application with the court to rescind the protective order.

(c) If a person who is the subject of a protective order issued under Article 7A.03 is confined or imprisoned on the date the protective order is due to expire under Subsection (a), the period for which the order is effective is extended, and the order expires on the first anniversary of the date the person is released from confinement or imprisonment.

(d) To the extent of any conflict with Section 85.025, Family Code, this article prevails.

(Enacted by Acts 2007, 80th Leg., ch. 882 (H.B. 1988), § 3, effective September 1, 2007; am. Acts 2011, 82nd Leg., ch. 238 (H.B. 649), § 2, effective September 1, 2011.)

## CHAPTER 7B
## PROTECTIVE ORDER FOR VICTIM OF TRAFFICKING OF PERSONS

## Art. 7B.01. Application for Protective Order.

(a) A person who is the victim of an offense under Section 20A.02, Penal Code, a parent or guardian acting on behalf of a person younger than 18 years of age who is the victim of such an offense, or a prosecuting attorney acting on behalf of the person may file an application for a protective order under this chapter without regard to the relationship between the applicant and the offender or alleged offender.

(b) An application for a protective order under this chapter may be filed in a district court, juvenile court having the jurisdiction of a district court, statutory county court, or constitutional county court in:

(1) the county in which the applicant resides; or

(2) the county in which the offender or alleged offender resides.

(Enacted by Acts 2011, 82nd Leg., ch. 1008 (H.B. 2329), § 1, effective September 1, 2011.)

## Art. 7B.02. Temporary Ex Parte Order.

If the court finds from the information contained in an application for a protective order that there is a clear and present danger that the alleged offender will traffic the applicant in a manner that constitutes an offense under Section 20A.02, Penal Code, or that the victim will otherwise suffer harm described by that section, the court, without further notice to the offender or alleged offender and without a hearing, may enter a temporary ex parte order for the protection of the applicant or any other member of the applicant's family or household.

(Enacted by Acts 2011, 82nd Leg., ch. 1008 (H.B. 2329), § 1, effective September 1, 2011.)

## Art. 7B.03. Required Findings; Issuance of Temporary Pretrial Protective

Criminal Procedure

## Order.

(a) At the close of a hearing on an application for a protective order under this chapter, the court shall find whether there are reasonable grounds to believe that the applicant is the victim of an offense for which the subject of the protective order has been charged under Section 20A.02, Penal Code, and:

(1) is younger than 18 years of age; or

(2) regardless of age, is the subject of a threat that reasonably places the applicant in fear of further harm from the alleged offender.

(b) If the court finds reasonable grounds to believe that the applicant is the victim of an offense for which the subject of the protective order has been charged under Section 20A.02, Penal Code, and is younger than 18 years of age, or regardless of age, the subject of a threat that reasonably places the applicant in fear of further harm from the alleged offender, the court shall issue a temporary protective order that includes a statement of the required findings, to be effective until the date the alleged offender is convicted or acquitted, or until the date on which the case involving the offense under Section 20A.02, Penal Code, is finally disposed.

(Enacted by Acts 2011, 82nd Leg., ch. 1008 (H.B. 2329), § 1, effective September 1, 2011.)

## Art. 7B.04. Required Findings; Issuance of Post-Trial Protective Order.

(a) At the close of a hearing on an application for a protective order under this chapter, the court shall find whether there are reasonable grounds to believe that the applicant is the victim of an offense for which the subject of the protective order has been convicted under Section 20A.02, Penal Code, and:

(1) is younger than 18 years of age; or

(2) regardless of age, is the subject of a threat that reasonably places the applicant in fear of further harm from the alleged offender.

(b) If the court finds reasonable grounds to believe that the applicant is the victim of an offense for which the subject of the protective order has been convicted under Section 20A.02, Penal Code, and is younger than 18 years of age, or regardless of age, the subject of a threat that reasonably places the applicant in fear of further harm from the offender, the court shall issue a protective order that includes a statement of the required findings.

(Enacted by Acts 2011, 82nd Leg., ch. 1008 (H.B. 2329), § 1, effective September 1, 2011.)

## Art. 7B.05. Application of Other Law.

To the extent applicable, except as otherwise provided by this chapter, Title 4, Family Code, applies to a protective order issued under this chapter.

(Enacted by Acts 2011, 82nd Leg., ch. 1008 (H.B. 2329), § 1, effective September 1, 2011.)

## Art. 7B.06. Conditions Specified by Order.

(a) In a protective order issued under this chapter, the court may:

(1) order the offender or alleged offender to take action as specified by the court that the court determines is necessary or appropriate to prevent or reduce the likelihood of future harm to the applicant or a member of the applicant's family or household; or

(2) prohibit the offender or alleged offender from:

(A) communicating directly or indirectly with the applicant or any member of the applicant's family or household in a threatening or harassing manner;

(B) going to or near the residence, place of employment or business, or child-care facility or school of the applicant or any member of the applicant's family or household;

(C) engaging in conduct directed specifically toward the applicant or any member of the applicant's family or household, including following the person, that is reasonably likely to harass, annoy, alarm, abuse, torment, or embarrass the person; and

(D) possessing a firearm, unless the alleged offender is a peace officer, as defined by Section 1.07, Penal Code, actively engaged in employment as a sworn, full-time paid employee of a state agency or political subdivision.

(b) In an order under Subsection (a)(2)(B), the court shall specifically describe each prohibited location and the minimum distance from the location, if any, that the offender or alleged offender must maintain. This subsection does not apply to an order with respect to which the court has received a request to maintain confidentiality of information revealing the locations.

(c) In a protective order, the court may suspend a license to carry a concealed handgun issued under Section 411.177, Government Code, that is held by the offender or alleged offender.

(Enacted by Acts 2011, 82nd Leg., ch. 1008 (H.B. 2329), § 1, effective September 1, 2011.)

### Art. 7B.07. Warning on Protective Order.

(a) Each protective order issued under this chapter, including a temporary ex parte order, must contain the following prominently displayed statements in boldfaced type, capital letters, or underlined:

"A PERSON WHO VIOLATES THIS ORDER MAY BE PUNISHED FOR CONTEMPT OF COURT BY A FINE OF AS MUCH AS $500 OR BY CONFINEMENT IN JAIL FOR AS LONG AS SIX MONTHS, OR BOTH."

"NO PERSON, INCLUDING A PERSON WHO IS PROTECTED BY THIS ORDER, MAY GIVE PERMISSION TO ANYONE TO IGNORE OR VIOLATE ANY PROVISION OF THIS ORDER. DURING THE TIME IN WHICH THIS ORDER IS VALID, EVERY PROVISION OF THIS ORDER IS IN FULL FORCE AND EFFECT UNLESS A COURT CHANGES THE ORDER."

"IT MAY BE UNLAWFUL FOR ANY PERSON, OTHER THAN A PEACE OFFICER, AS DEFINED BY SECTION 1.07, PENAL CODE, ACTIVELY ENGAGED IN EMPLOYMENT AS A SWORN, FULL-TIME PAID EMPLOYEE OF A STATE AGENCY OR POLITICAL SUBDIVISION, WHO IS SUBJECT TO A PROTECTIVE ORDER TO POSSESS A FIREARM OR AMMUNITION."

(b) Each protective order issued under this chapter, except for a temporary ex parte order, must contain the following prominently displayed statement in boldfaced type, capital letters, or underlined:

"A VIOLATION OF THIS ORDER BY COMMISSION OF AN ACT PROHIBITED BY THE ORDER MAY BE PUNISHABLE BY A FINE OF AS MUCH AS $4,000 OR BY CONFINEMENT IN JAIL FOR AS LONG AS ONE YEAR, OR BOTH. AN ACT THAT RESULTS IN A SEPARATE OFFENSE MAY BE PROSECUTED AS A SEPARATE OFFENSE IN ADDITION TO A VIOLATION OF THIS ORDER."

(Enacted by Acts 2011, 82nd Leg., ch. 1008 (H.B. 2329), § 1, effective September 1, 2011.)

### Art. 7B.08. Duration of Post-Trial Protective Order.

(a) A protective order issued under Article 7B.04 may be effective for the duration of the lives of the offender and victim as provided by Subsection (b), or for any shorter period stated in the order. If a period is not stated in the order, the order is effective until the second anniversary of the date the order was issued.

(b) A protective order issued under Article 7B.04 may be effective for the duration of the lives of the offender and victim only if the court finds reasonable cause to believe that the victim is the subject of a threat that reasonably places the victim in fear of further harm from the alleged offender.

(c) A victim who is 18 years of age or older or a parent or guardian acting on behalf of a victim who is younger than 18 years of age may file at any time an application with the court to rescind the protective order.

(d) To the extent of any conflict with Section 85.025, Family Code, this article prevails.
(Enacted by Acts 2011, 82nd Leg., ch. 1008 (H.B. 2329), § 1, effective September 1, 2011.)

## CHAPTER 8
## SUPPRESSION OF RIOTS AND OTHER DISTURBANCES

### Art. 8.01. Officer May Require Aid.

When any officer authorized to execute process is resisted, or when he has sufficient reason to believe that he will meet with resistance in executing the same, he may command as many of the citizens of his county as he may think proper; and the sheriff may call any military company in the county to aid him in overcoming the resistance, and if necessary, in seizing and arresting the persons engaged in such resistance.
(Enacted by Acts 1965, 59th Leg., ch. 722 (S.B. 107), § 1, effective January 1, 1966.)

### Art. 8.02. Military Aid in Executing Process.

If it be represented to the Governor in such manner as to satisfy him that the power of the county is not sufficient to enable the sheriff to execute process, he may, on application, order any military company of volunteers or militia company from another county to aid in overcoming such resistance.
(Enacted by Acts 1965, 59th Leg., ch. 722 (S.B. 107), § 1, effective January 1, 1966.)

## Art. 8.03. Military Aid in Suppressing Riots.

Whenever, for the purpose of suppressing riots or unlawful assemblies, the aid of military or militia companies is called, they shall obey the orders of the civil officer who is engaged in suppressing the same.
(Enacted by Acts 1965, 59th Leg., ch. 722 (S.B. 107), § 1, effective January 1, 1966.)

## Art. 8.04. Dispersing Riot.

Whenever a number of persons are assembled together in such a manner as to constitute a riot, according to the penal law of the State, it is the duty of every magistrate or peace officer to cause such persons to disperse. This may either be done by commanding them to disperse or by arresting the persons engaged, if necessary, either with or without warrant.
(Enacted by Acts 1965, 59th Leg., ch. 722 (S.B. 107), § 1, effective January 1, 1966.)

## Art. 8.05. Officer May Call Aid.

In order to enable the officer to disperse a riot, he may call to his aid the power of the county in the same manner as is provided where it is necessary for the execution of process.
(Enacted by Acts 1965, 59th Leg., ch. 722 (S.B. 107), § 1, effective January 1, 1966.)

## Art. 8.06. Means Adopted to Suppress.

The officer engaged in suppressing a riot, and those who aid him are authorized and justified in adopting such measures as are necessary to suppress the riot, but are not authorized to use any greater degree of force than is requisite to accomplish that object.
(Enacted by Acts 1965, 59th Leg., ch. 722 (S.B. 107), § 1, effective January 1, 1966.)

## Art. 8.07. Unlawful Assembly.

The Articles of this Chapter relating to the suppression of riots apply equally to an unlawful assembly and other unlawful disturbances, as defined by the Penal Code.
(Enacted by Acts 1965, 59th Leg., ch. 722 (S.B. 107), § 1, effective January 1, 1966.)

## Art. 8.08. Suppression at Election.

To suppress riots, unlawful assemblies and other disturbances at elections, any magistrate may appoint a sufficient number of special constables. Such appointments shall be made to each special constable, shall be in writing, dated and signed by the magistrate, and shall recite the purposes for which such appointment is made, and the length of time it is to continue. Before the same is delivered to such special constable, he shall take an oath before the magistrate to suppress, by lawful means, all riots, unlawful assemblies and breaches of the peace of which he may receive information, and to act impartially between all parties and persons interested in the result of the election.
(Enacted by Acts 1965, 59th Leg., ch. 722 (S.B. 107), § 1, effective January 1, 1966.)

## Art. 8.09. Power of Special Constable.

Special constables so appointed shall, during the time for which they are appointed, exercise the powers and perform the duties properly belonging to peace officers.
(Enacted by Acts 1965, 59th Leg., ch. 722 (S.B. 107), § 1, effective January 1, 1966.)

# CHAPTER 9
# OFFENSES INJURIOUS TO PUBLIC HEALTH

**Article**
9.01.    Trade Injurious to Health.
9.02.    Refusal to Give Bond.
9.03.    Requisites of Bond.
9.04.    Suit upon Bond.
9.05.    Proof.
9.06.    Unwholesome Food.

## Art. 9.01. Trade Injurious to Health.

After an indictment or information has been presented against any person for carrying on a trade, business or occupation injurious to the health of those in the neighborhood, the court shall have power, on the application of anyone interested, and after hearing proof both for and against the accused, to restrain the defendant, in such penalty as may be deemed proper, from carrying on such trade, business or occupation, or may make such order respecting the manner and place of carrying on the same as may be deemed advisable; and if upon trial, the defendant be convicted, the restraint shall be made perpetual, and the party shall be required to enter into bond, with security, not to continue such trade, business or occupation to the detriment of the health of such neighborhood, or of any other neighborhood within the county.
(Enacted by Acts 1965, 59th Leg., ch. 722 (S.B. 107), § 1, effective January 1, 1966.)

## Art. 9.02. Refusal to Give Bond.

If the party refuses to give bond when required under the provisions of the preceding Article, the court may either commit him to jail, or make an order requiring the sheriff to seize upon the implements of such trade, business or occupation, or the goods and property used in conducting such trade, business or occupation, and destroy the same.

(Enacted by Acts 1965, 59th Leg., ch. 722 (S.B. 107), § 1, effective January 1, 1966.)

## Art. 9.03. Requisites of Bond.

Such bond shall be payable to the State of Texas, in a reasonable amount to be fixed by the court, conditioned that the defendant will not carry on such trade, business or occupation, naming the same, at such place, naming the place, or at any other place in the county, to the detriment of the health of the neighborhood. The bond shall be signed by the defendant and his sureties and dated, and shall be approved by the court taking the same, and filed in such court.

(Enacted by Acts 1965, 59th Leg., ch. 722 (S.B. 107), § 1, effective January 1, 1966.)

## Art. 9.04. Suit upon Bond.

Any such bond, upon the breach thereof, may be sued upon by the district or county attorney, in the name of the State of Texas, within two years after such breach, and not afterwards; and such suits shall be governed by the same rules as civil actions.

(Enacted by Acts 1965, 59th Leg., ch. 722 (S.B. 107), § 1, effective January 1, 1966.)

## Art. 9.05. Proof.

It shall be sufficient proof of the breach of any such bond to show that the party continued after executing the same, to carry on the trade, business or occupation which he bound himself to discontinue; and the full amount of such bond may be recovered of the defendant and his sureties.

(Enacted by Acts 1965, 59th Leg., ch. 722 (S.B. 107), § 1, effective January 1, 1966.)

## Art. 9.06. Unwholesome Food.

After conviction for selling unwholesome food or adulterated medicine, the court shall enter and issue an order to the sheriff or other proper officer to seize and destroy such as remains in the hands of the defendant.

(Enacted by Acts 1965, 59th Leg., ch. 722 (S.B. 107), § 1, effective January 1, 1966.)

# CHAPTER 10
# OBSTRUCTIONS OF PUBLIC HIGHWAYS

## Art. 10.01. Order to Remove.

After prosecution begun against any person for obstructing any highway, any one, in behalf of the public, may apply to the county judge of the county in which such highway is situated; and upon hearing proof, such judge, either in term time or in vacation, may issue his written order to the sheriff or other proper officer of the county, directing him to remove the obstruction. Before the issuance of such order, the applicant therefor shall give bond with security in an amount to be fixed by the judge, to indemnify the accused, in case of his acquittal, for the loss he sustains. Such bond shall be approved by the county judge and filed with the papers in the cause.

(Enacted by Acts 1965, 59th Leg., ch. 722 (S.B. 107), § 1, effective January 1, 1966.)

## Art. 10.02. Bond of Applicant.

If the defendant be acquitted after a trial upon the merits of the case, he may maintain a civil action against the applicant and his sureties upon such bond, and may recover the full amount of the bond, or such damages, less than the full amount thereof, as may be assessed by a court or jury; provided, he shows on the trial that the place was not in fact, at the time he placed the obstruction or impediment thereupon, a public highway established by proper authority, but was in fact his own property or in his lawful possession.

(Enacted by Acts 1965, 59th Leg., ch. 722 (S.B. 107), § 1, effective January 1, 1966.)

## Art. 10.03. Removal.

Upon the conviction of a defendant for obstructing a public highway, if such obstruction still exists, the court shall order the sheriff or other proper officer to forthwith remove the same at the cost of the defendant, to be taxed and collected as other costs in the case.

(Enacted by Acts 1965, 59th Leg., ch. 722 (S.B. 107), § 1, effective January 1, 1966.)

# Habeas Corpus

## CHAPTER 11
## HABEAS CORPUS

## Art. 11.01.  What Writ Is.

The writ of habeas corpus is the remedy to be used when any person is restrained in his liberty. It is an order issued by a court or judge of competent jurisdiction, directed to any one having a person in his custody, or under his restraint, commanding him to produce such person, at a time and place named in the writ, and show why he is held in custody or under restraint.

(Enacted by Acts 1965, 59th Leg., ch. 722 (S.B. 107), § 1, effective January 1, 1966.)

## Art. 11.02.  To Whom Directed.

The writ runs in the name of "The State of Texas". It is addressed to a person having another under restraint, or in his custody, describing, as near as may be, the name of the office, if any, of the person to whom it is directed, and the name of the person said to be detained. It shall fix the time and place of return, and be signed by the judge, or by the clerk with his seal, where issued by a court.

(Enacted by Acts 1965, 59th Leg., ch. 722 (S.B. 107), § 1, effective January 1, 1966.)

## Art. 11.03.  Want of Form.

The writ of habeas corpus is not invalid, nor shall it be disobeyed for any want of form, if it substantially appear that it is issued by competent authority, and the writ sufficiently show the object of its issuance.

(Enacted by Acts 1965, 59th Leg., ch. 722 (S.B. 107), § 1, effective January 1, 1966.)

## Art. 11.04.  Construction.

Every provision relating to the writ of habeas corpus shall be most favorably construed in order to give effect to the remedy, and protect the rights of the person seeking relief under it.

(Enacted by Acts 1965, 59th Leg., ch. 722 (S.B. 107), § 1, effective January 1, 1966.)

## Art. 11.05. By Whom Writ May Be Granted.

The Court of Criminal Appeals, the District Courts, the County Courts, or any Judge of said Courts, have power to issue the writ of habeas corpus; and it is their duty, upon proper motion, to grant the writ under the rules prescribed by law.

(Enacted by Acts 1965, 59th Leg., ch. 722 (S.B. 107), § 1, effective January 1, 1966.)

## Art. 11.051. Filing Fee Prohibited.

Notwithstanding any other law, a clerk of a court may not require a filing fee from an individual who files an application or petition for a writ of habeas corpus.

(Enacted by Acts 1999, 76th Leg., ch. 392 (H.B. 149), § 1, effective August 30, 1999.)

## Art. 11.06. Returnable to Any County.

Before indictment found, the writ may be made returnable to any county in the State.

(Enacted by Acts 1965, 59th Leg., ch. 722 (S.B. 107), § 1, effective January 1, 1966.)

## Art. 11.07. Procedure After Conviction Without Death Penalty.

Sec. 1. This article establishes the procedures for an application for writ of habeas corpus in which the applicant seeks relief from a felony judgment imposing a penalty other than death.

Sec. 2. After indictment found in any felony case, other than a case in which the death penalty is imposed, and before conviction, the writ must be made returnable in the county where the offense has been committed.

Sec. 3. (a) After final conviction in any felony case, the writ must be made returnable to the Court of Criminal Appeals of Texas at Austin, Texas.

(b) An application for writ of habeas corpus filed after final conviction in a felony case, other than a case in which the death penalty is imposed, must be filed with the clerk of the court in which the conviction being challenged was obtained, and the clerk shall assign the application to that court. When the application is received by that court, a writ of habeas corpus, returnable to the Court of Criminal Appeals, shall issue by operation of law. The clerk of that court shall make appropriate notation thereof, assign to the case a file number (ancillary to that of the conviction being challenged), and forward a copy of the applica-

tion by certified mail, return receipt requested, or by personal service to the attorney representing the state in that court, who shall answer the application not later than the 15th day after the date the copy of the application is received. Matters alleged in the application not admitted by the state are deemed denied.

(c) Within 20 days of the expiration of the time in which the state is allowed to answer, it shall be the duty of the convicting court to decide whether there are controverted, previously unresolved facts material to the legality of the applicant's confinement. Confinement means confinement for any offense or any collateral consequence resulting from the conviction that is the basis of the instant habeas corpus. If the convicting court decides that there are no such issues, the clerk shall immediately transmit to the Court of Criminal Appeals a copy of the application, any answers filed, and a certificate reciting the date upon which that finding was made. Failure of the court to act within the allowed 20 days shall constitute such a finding.

(d) If the convicting court decides that there are controverted, previously unresolved facts which are material to the legality of the applicant's confinement, it shall enter an order within 20 days of the expiration of the time allowed for the state to reply, designating the issues of fact to be resolved. To resolve those issues the court may order affidavits, depositions, interrogatories, additional forensic testing, and hearings, as well as using personal recollection. The state shall pay the cost of additional forensic testing ordered under this subsection, except that the applicant shall pay the cost of the testing if the applicant retains counsel for purposes of filing an application under this article. The convicting court may appoint an attorney or a magistrate to hold a hearing and make findings of fact. An attorney so appointed shall be compensated as provided in Article 26.05 of this code. It shall be the duty of the reporter who is designated to transcribe a hearing held pursuant to this article to prepare a transcript within 15 days of its conclusion. After the convicting court makes findings of fact or approves the findings of the person designated to make them, the clerk of the convicting court shall immediately transmit to the Court of Criminal Appeals, under one cover, the application, any answers filed, any motions filed, transcripts of all depositions and hearings, any affidavits, and any other matters such as official records used by the court in resolving issues of fact.

(e) For the purposes of Subsection (d), "additional forensic testing" does not include forensic DNA testing as provided for in Chapter 64.

Sec. 4. (a) If a subsequent application for writ of habeas corpus is filed after final disposition of an initial application challenging the same conviction, a court may not consider the merits of or grant relief based on the subsequent application unless the application contains sufficient specific facts establishing that:

(1) the current claims and issues have not been and could not have been presented previously in an original application or in a previously considered application filed under this article because the factual or legal basis for the claim was unavailable on the date the applicant filed the previous application; or

(2) by a preponderance of the evidence, but for a violation of the United States Constitution no rational juror could have found the applicant guilty beyond a reasonable doubt.

(b) For purposes of Subsection (a)(1), a legal basis of a claim is unavailable on or before a date described by Subsection (a)(1) if the legal basis was not recognized by and could not have been reasonably formulated from a final decision of the United States Supreme Court, a court of appeals of the United States, or a court of appellate jurisdiction of this state on or before that date.

(c) For purposes of Subsection (a)(1), a factual basis of a claim is unavailable on or before a date described by Subsection (a)(1) if the factual basis was not ascertainable through the exercise of reasonable diligence on or before that date.

Sec. 5. The Court of Criminal Appeals may deny relief upon the findings and conclusions of the hearing judge without docketing the cause, or may direct that the cause be docketed and heard as though originally presented to said court or as an appeal. Upon reviewing the record the court shall enter its judgment remanding the applicant to custody or ordering his release, as the law and facts may justify. The mandate of the court shall issue to the court issuing the writ, as in other criminal cases. After conviction the procedure outlined in this Act shall be exclusive and any other proceeding shall be void and of no force and effect in discharging the prisoner.

Sec. 6. Upon any hearing by a district judge by virtue of this Act, the attorney for applicant, and the state, shall be given at least seven full days' notice before such hearing is held.

Sec. 7. When the attorney for the state files an answer, motion, or other pleading relating to an application for a writ of habeas corpus or the court issues an order relating to an application for a writ of habeas corpus, the clerk of the court shall mail or deliver to the applicant a copy of the answer, motion, pleading, or order.

(Enacted by Acts 1965, 59th Leg., ch. 722 (S.B. 107), § 1, effective January 1, 1966; am. Acts 1967, 60th Leg., ch. 659 (S.B. 145), § 7, effective August 28, 1967; am. Acts 1973, 63rd Leg., ch. 465 (H.B. 702), § 2, effective June 14, 1973; am. Acts 1977, 65th Leg., ch. 789 (S.B. 1070), § 1, effective August 29, 1977; am. Acts 1979, 66th Leg., ch. 451 (S.B. 856), § 1, effective September 1, 1979; am. Acts 1995, 74th Leg., ch. 319 (S.B. 440), § 5, effective September 1, 1995; am. Acts 1999, 76th Leg., ch. 580 (S.B. 577), § 2, effective September 1, 1999; am. Acts 2007, 80th Leg., ch. 1006 (H.B. 681), § 1, effective September 1, 2007.)

## Art. 11.071. Procedure in Death Penalty Case.

### Sec. 1. Application to Death Penalty Case.

Notwithstanding any other provision of this chapter, this article establishes the procedures for an application for a writ of habeas corpus in which the applicant seeks relief from a judgment imposing a penalty of death.

### Sec. 2. Representation by Counsel.

(a) An applicant shall be represented by competent counsel unless the applicant has elected to proceed pro se and the convicting trial court finds, after a hearing on the record, that the applicant's election is intelligent and voluntary.

(b) If a defendant is sentenced to death the convicting court, immediately after judgment is entered under Article 42.01, shall determine if the defendant is indigent and, if so, whether the defendant desires appointment of counsel for the purpose of a writ of habeas corpus. If the defendant desires appointment of counsel for the purpose of a writ of habeas corpus, the court shall appoint the office of capital writs to represent the defendant as provided by Subsection (c).

(c) At the earliest practical time, but in no event later than 30 days, after the convicting court makes the findings required under Subsections (a) and (b), the convicting court shall appoint the office of capital writs or, if the office of capital writs does not accept or is prohibited from accepting an appointment under Section 78.054, Government Code, other competent counsel under Subsection (f), unless the applicant elects to proceed pro se or is represented by retained counsel. On appointing counsel under this section, the convicting court shall immediately notify the court of criminal appeals of the appointment, including in the notice a copy of the judgment and the name, address, and telephone number of the appointed counsel.

(d) [Repealed by Acts 2009, 81st Leg., ch. 781 (S.B. 1091), § 11, effective January 1, 2010.]

(e) If the court of criminal appeals denies an applicant relief under this article, an attorney appointed under this section to represent the applicant shall, not later than the 15th day after the date the court of criminal appeals denies relief or, if the case is filed and set for submission, the 15th day after the date the court of criminal appeals issues a mandate on the initial application for a writ of habeas corpus under this article, move for the appointment of counsel in federal habeas review under 18 U.S.C. Section 3599. The attorney shall immediately file a copy of the motion with the court of criminal appeals, and if the attorney fails to do so, the court may take any action to ensure that the applicant's right to federal habeas review is protected, including initiating contempt proceedings against the attorney.

(f) If the office of capital writs does not accept or is prohibited from accepting an appointment under Section 78.054, Government Code, the convicting court shall appoint counsel from a list of competent counsel maintained by the presiding judges of the administrative judicial regions under Section 78.056, Government Code. The convicting court shall reasonably compensate as provided by Section 2A an attorney appointed under this section, other than an attorney employed by the office of capital writs, regardless of whether the attorney is appointed by the convicting court or was appointed by the court of criminal appeals under prior law. An attorney appointed under this section who is employed by the office of capital writs shall be compensated in accordance with Subchapter B, Chapter 78, Government Code.

### Sec. 2A. State Reimbursement; County Obligation.

(a) The state shall reimburse a county for compensation of counsel under Section 2, other than for compensation of counsel employed by the office of capital writs, and for payment of expenses under Section 3, regardless of whether counsel is employed by the office of capital writs. The total amount of reimbursement to which a county is entitled under this section for an application under this article may not exceed $25,000. Compensation and expenses in excess of the $25,000 reimbursement provided by the state are the obligation of the county.

(b) A convicting court seeking reimbursement for a county shall certify to the comptroller of public accounts the amount of compensation that the county is entitled to receive under this section. The comptroller of public accounts shall issue a warrant to the county in the amount certified by the convicting court, not to exceed $25,000.

(c) The limitation imposed by this section on the reimbursement by the state to a county for compensation of counsel and payment of reasonable expenses does not prohibit a county from compensating counsel and reimbursing expenses in an amount that is in excess of the amount the county receives from the state as reimbursement, and a county is specifically granted discretion by this subsection to make payments in excess of the state reimbursement.

(d) The comptroller shall reimburse a county for the compensation and payment of expenses of an attorney appointed by the court of criminal appeals under prior law. A convicting court seeking reimbursement for a county as permitted by this subsection shall certify the amount the county is entitled to receive under this subsection for an application filed under this article, not to exceed a total amount of $25,000.

### Sec. 3. Investigation of Grounds for Application.

(a) On appointment, counsel shall investigate expeditiously, before and after the appellate record is filed in the court of criminal appeals, the factual and legal grounds for the filing of an application for a writ of habeas corpus.

(b) Not later than the 30th day before the date the application for a writ of habeas corpus is filed with the convicting court, counsel may file with the convicting court an ex parte, verified, and confidential request for prepayment of expenses, including expert fees, to investigate and present potential habeas corpus claims. The request for expenses must state:

(1) the claims of the application to be investigated;

(2) specific facts that suggest that a claim of possible merit may exist; and

(3) an itemized list of anticipated expenses for each claim.

(c) The court shall grant a request for expenses in whole or in part if the request for expenses is timely and reasonable. If the court denies in whole or in part the request for expenses, the court shall briefly state the reasons for the denial in a written order provided to the applicant.

(d) Counsel may incur expenses for habeas corpus investigation, including expenses for experts, without prior approval by the convicting court or the court of criminal appeals. On presentation of a claim for reimbursement, which may be presented ex parte, the convicting court shall order reimbursement of counsel for expenses, if the expenses are reasonably necessary and reasonably incurred. If the convicting court denies in whole or in part the request for expenses, the court shall briefly state the reasons for the denial in a written order provided to the applicant. The applicant may request reconsideration of the denial for reimbursement by the convicting court.

(e) Materials submitted to the court under this section are a part of the court's record.

(f) This section applies to counsel's investigation of the factual and legal grounds for the filing of an application for a writ of habeas corpus, regardless of whether counsel is employed by the office of capital writs.

### Sec. 4. Filing of Application.

(a) An application for a writ of habeas corpus, returnable to the court of criminal appeals, must be filed in the convicting court not later than the 180th day after the date the convicting court appoints counsel under Section 2 or not later than the 45th day after the date the state's original brief is filed on direct appeal with the court of criminal appeals, whichever date is later.

(b) The convicting court, before the filing date that is applicable to the applicant under Subsection (a), may for good cause shown and after notice and an opportunity to be heard by the attorney representing the state grant one 90-day extension that begins on the filing date applicable to the defendant under Subsection (a). Either party may request that the court hold a hearing on the request. If the convicting court finds that the applicant cannot establish good cause justifying the requested extension, the court shall make a finding stating that fact and deny the request for the extension.

(c) An application filed after the filing date that is applicable to the applicant under Subsection (a) or (b) is untimely.

(d) If the convicting court receives an untimely application or determines that after the filing date that is applicable to the applicant under Subsection (a) or (b) no application has been filed, the convicting court immediately, but in any event within 10 days, shall send to the court of criminal appeals and to the attorney representing the state:

(1) a copy of the untimely application, with a statement of the convicting court that the application is untimely, or a statement of the convicting court that no application has been filed within the time periods required by Subsections (a) and (b); and

(2) any order the judge of the convicting court determines should be attached to an untimely application or statement under Subdivision (1).

(e) A failure to file an application before the filing date applicable to the applicant under Subsection (a) or (b) constitutes a waiver of all grounds for relief that were available to the applicant before the last date on which an application could be timely filed, except as provided by Section 4A.

### Sec. 4A. Untimely Application; Application Not Filed.

(a) On command of the court of criminal appeals, a counsel who files an untimely application or fails to file an application before the filing date applicable under Section 4(a) or (b) shall show cause as to why the application was untimely filed or not filed before the filing date.

(b) At the conclusion of the counsel's presentation to the court of criminal appeals, the court may:

(1) find that good cause has not been shown and dismiss the application;

(2) permit the counsel to continue representation of the applicant and establish a new filing date for the application, which may be not more than 180 days from the date the court permits the counsel to continue representation; or

(3) appoint new counsel to represent the applicant and establish a new filing date for the application, which may be not more than 270 days after the date the court appoints new counsel.

(c) The court of criminal appeals may hold in contempt counsel who files an untimely application or fails to file an application before the date required by Section 4(a) or (b). The court of criminal appeals may punish as a separate instance of contempt each day after the first day on which the counsel fails to timely file the application. In addition to or in lieu of holding counsel in contempt, the court of criminal appeals may enter an order denying counsel compensation under Section 2A.

(d) If the court of criminal appeals establishes a new filing date for the application, the court of criminal appeals shall notify the convicting court of that fact and the convicting court shall proceed under this article.

(e) Sections 2A and 3 apply to compensation and reimbursement of counsel appointed under Subsection (b)(3) in the same manner as if counsel had been appointed by the convicting court, unless the attorney is employed by the office of capital writs, in which case the compensation of that attorney is governed by Subchapter B, Chapter 78, Government Code.

(f) Notwithstanding any other provision of this article, the court of criminal appeals shall appoint counsel and establish a new filing date for application, which may be no later than the 270th day after the date on which counsel is appointed, for each applicant who before September 1, 1999, filed an untimely application or failed to file an application before the date required by Section 4(a) or (b). Section 2A applies to the compensation and payment of expenses of counsel appointed by the court of criminal appeals under this subsection, unless the attorney is employed by the office of capital writs, in which case the compensation of that attorney is governed by Subchapter B, Chapter 78, Government Code.

### Sec. 5. Subsequent Application.

(a) If a subsequent application for a writ of habeas corpus is filed after filing an initial application, a court may not consider the merits of or grant relief based on the subsequent application unless the application contains sufficient specific facts establishing that:

(1) the current claims and issues have not been and could not have been presented previously in a timely initial application or in a previously considered application filed under this article or Article 11.07 because the factual or legal basis for the claim was unavailable on the date the applicant filed the previous application;

(2) by a preponderance of the evidence, but for a violation of the United States Constitution no rational juror could have found the applicant guilty beyond a reasonable doubt; or

(3) by clear and convincing evidence, but for a violation of the United States Constitution no rational juror would have answered in the state's favor one or more of the special issues that were submitted to the jury in the appli-

cant's trial under Article 37.071, 37.0711, or 37.072.

(b) If the convicting court receives a subsequent application, the clerk of the court shall:

(1) attach a notation that the application is a subsequent application;

(2) assign to the case a file number that is ancillary to that of the conviction being challenged; and

(3) immediately send to the court of criminal appeals a copy of:

(A) the application;

(B) the notation;

(C) the order scheduling the applicant's execution, if scheduled; and

(D) any order the judge of the convicting court directs to be attached to the application.

(c) On receipt of the copies of the documents from the clerk, the court of criminal appeals shall determine whether the requirements of Subsection (a) have been satisfied. The convicting court may not take further action on the application before the court of criminal appeals issues an order finding that the requirements have been satisfied. If the court of criminal appeals determines that the requirements have not been satisfied, the court shall issue an order dismissing the application as an abuse of the writ under this section.

(d) For purposes of Subsection (a)(1), a legal basis of a claim is unavailable on or before a date described by Subsection (a)(1) if the legal basis was not recognized by or could not have been reasonably formulated from a final decision of the United States Supreme Court, a court of appeals of the United States, or a court of appellate jurisdiction of this state on or before that date.

(e) For purposes of Subsection (a)(1), a factual basis of a claim is unavailable on or before a date described by Subsection (a)(1) if the factual basis was not ascertainable through the exercise of reasonable diligence on or before that date.

(f) If an amended or supplemental application is not filed within the time specified under Section 4(a) or (b), the court shall treat the application as a subsequent application under this section.

### Sec. 6. Issuance of Writ.

(a) If a timely application for a writ of habeas corpus is filed in the convicting court, a writ of habeas corpus, returnable to the court of criminal appeals, shall issue by operation of law.

(b) If the convicting court receives notice that the requirements of Section 5 for consideration of a subsequent application have been met, a writ of habeas corpus, returnable to the court of criminal appeals, shall issue by operation of law.

(b-1) If the convicting court receives notice that the requirements of Section 5(a) for consideration of a subsequent application have been met and if the applicant has not elected to proceed pro se and is not represented by retained counsel, the convicting court shall appoint, in order of priority:

(1) the attorney who represented the applicant in the proceedings under Section 5, if the attorney seeks the appointment;

(2) the office of capital writs, if the office represented the applicant in the proceedings under Section 5 or otherwise accepts the appointment; or

(3) counsel from a list of competent counsel maintained by the presiding judges of the administrative judicial regions under Section 78.056, Government Code, if the office of capital writs:

(A) did not represent the applicant as described by Subdivision (2); or

(B) does not accept or is prohibited from accepting the appointment under Section 78.054, Government Code.

(b-2) Regardless of whether the subsequent application is ultimately dismissed, compensation and reimbursement of expenses for counsel appointed under Subsection (b-1) shall be provided as described by Section 2, 2A, or 3, including compensation for time previously spent and reimbursement of expenses previously incurred with respect to the subsequent application.

(c) The clerk of the convicting court shall:

(1) make an appropriate notation that a writ of habeas corpus was issued;

(2) assign to the case a file number that is ancillary to that of the conviction being challenged; and

(3) send a copy of the application by certified mail, return receipt requested, to the attorney representing the state in that court.

(d) The clerk of the convicting court shall promptly deliver copies of documents submitted to the clerk under this article to the applicant and the attorney representing the state.

**Sec. 7. Answer to Application.**

(a) The state shall file an answer to the application for a writ of habeas corpus not later than the 120th day after the date the state receives notice of issuance of the writ. The state shall serve the answer on counsel for the applicant or, if the applicant is proceeding pro se, on the applicant. The state may request from the convicting court an extension of time in which to answer the application by showing particularized justifying circumstances for the extension, but in no event may the court permit the state to file an answer later than the 180th day after the date the state receives notice of issuance of the writ.

(b) Matters alleged in the application not admitted by the state are deemed denied.

**Sec. 8. Findings of Fact Without Evidentiary Hearing.**

(a) Not later than the 20th day after the last date the state answers the application, the convicting court shall determine whether controverted, previously unresolved factual issues material to the legality of the applicant's confinement exist and shall issue a written order of the determination.

(b) If the convicting court determines the issues do not exist, the parties shall file proposed findings of fact and conclusions of law for the court to consider on or before a date set by the court that is not later than the 30th day after the date the order is issued.

(c) After argument of counsel, if requested by the court, the convicting court shall make appropriate written findings of fact and conclusions of law not later than the 15th day after the date the parties filed proposed findings or not later than the 45th day after the date the court's determination is made under Subsection (a), whichever occurs first.

(d) The clerk of the court shall immediately send to:

(1) the court of criminal appeals a copy of the:

(A) application;

(B) answer;

(C) orders entered by the convicting court;

(D) proposed findings of fact and conclusions of law; and

(E) findings of fact and conclusions of law entered by the court; and

(2) counsel for the applicant or, if the applicant is proceeding pro se, to the applicant, a copy of:

(A) orders entered by the convicting court;

(B) proposed findings of fact and conclusions of law; and

(C) findings of fact and conclusions of law entered by the court.

**Sec. 9. Hearing.**

(a) If the convicting court determines that controverted, previously unresolved factual issues material to the legality of the applicant's confinement exist, the court shall enter an order, not later than the 20th day after the last date the state answers the application, designating the issues of fact to be resolved and the manner in which the issues shall be resolved. To resolve the issues, the court may require affidavits, depositions, interrogatories, and evidentiary hearings and may use personal recollection.

(b) The convicting court shall hold the evidentiary hearing not later than the 30th day after the date on which the court enters the order designating issues under Subsection (a). The convicting court may grant a motion to postpone the hearing, but not for more than 30 days, and only if the court states, on the record, good cause for delay.

(c) The presiding judge of the convicting court shall conduct a hearing held under this section unless another judge presided over the original capital felony trial, in which event that judge, if qualified for assignment under Section 74.054 or 74.055, Government Code, may preside over the hearing.

(d) The court reporter shall prepare a transcript of the hearing not later than the 30th day after the date the hearing ends and file the transcript with the clerk of the convicting court.

(e) The parties shall file proposed findings of fact and conclusions of law for the convicting court to consider on or before a date set by the court that is not later than the 30th day after the date the transcript is filed. If the court requests argument of counsel, after argument the court shall make written findings of fact that are necessary to resolve the previously unresolved facts and make conclusions of law not later than the 15th day after the date the parties file proposed findings or not later than the 45th day after the date the court reporter files the transcript, whichever occurs first.

(f) The clerk of the convicting court shall immediately transmit to:

(1) the court of criminal appeals a copy of:

(A) the application;

(B) the answers and motions filed;

(C) the court reporter's transcript;

(D) the documentary exhibits introduced into evidence;

(E) the proposed findings of fact and conclusions of law;

(F) the findings of fact and conclusions of law entered by the court;

(G) the sealed materials such as a confidential request for investigative expenses; and

(H) any other matters used by the convicting court in resolving issues of fact; and

(2) counsel for the applicant or, if the applicant is proceeding pro se, to the applicant, a copy of:

(A) orders entered by the convicting court;

(B) proposed findings of fact and conclusions of law; and

(C) findings of fact and conclusions of law entered by the court.

(g) The clerk of the convicting court shall forward an exhibit that is not documentary to the court of criminal appeals on request of the court.

**Sec. 10. Rules of Evidence.**

The Texas Rules of Criminal Evidence apply to a hearing held under this article.

**Sec. 11. Review by Court of Criminal Appeals.**

The court of criminal appeals shall expeditiously review all applications for a writ of habeas corpus submitted under this article. The court may set the cause for oral argument and may request further briefing of the issues by the applicant or the state. After reviewing the record, the court shall enter its judgment remanding the applicant to custody or ordering the applicant's release, as the law and facts may justify.

(Enacted by Acts 1995, 74th Leg., ch. 319 (S.B. 440), § 1, effective September 1, 1995; am. Acts 1997, 75th Leg., ch. 1336 (S.B. 1728), §§ 1-5, effective September 1, 1997; am. Acts 1999, 76th Leg., ch. 803 (H.B. 1516), §§ 1-10, effective September 1, 1999; am. Acts 2003, 78th Leg., ch. 315 (H.B. 3306), §§ 1-3, effective September 1, 2003; am. Acts 2005, 79th Leg., ch. 787 (S.B. 60), § 13, effective September 1, 2005; am. Acts 2005, 79th Leg., ch. 965 (H.B. 1701), § 5, effective September 1, 2005; am. Acts 2007, 80th Leg., ch. 593 (H.B. 8), § 3.06, effective September 1, 2007; am. Acts 2009, 81st Leg., ch. 781 (S.B. 1091), §§ 2-5, effective September 1, 2009; am. Acts 2009, 81st Leg., ch. 781 (S.B. 1091), § 11, effective January 1, 2010; am. Acts 2011, 82nd Leg., ch. 1139 (H.B. 1646), § 1, effective September 1, 2011.)

# Art. 11.072. Procedure in Community Supervision Case.

**Sec. 1.** This article establishes the procedures for an application for a writ of habeas corpus in a felony or misdemeanor case in which the applicant seeks relief from an order or a judgment of conviction ordering community supervision.

**Sec. 2.** (a) An application for a writ of habeas corpus under this article must be filed with the clerk of the court in which community supervision was imposed.

(b) At the time the application is filed, the applicant must be, or have been, on community supervision, and the application must challenge the legal validity of:

(1) the conviction for which or order in which community supervision was imposed; or

(2) the conditions of community supervision.

Sec. 3. (a) An application may not be filed under this article if the applicant could obtain the requested relief by means of an appeal under Article 44.02 and Rule 25.2, Texas Rules of Appellate Procedure.

(b) An applicant seeking to challenge a particular condition of community supervision but not the legality of the conviction for which or the order in which community supervision was imposed must first attempt to gain relief by filing a motion to amend the conditions of community supervision.

(c) An applicant may challenge a condition of community supervision under this article only on constitutional grounds.

Sec. 4. (a) When an application is filed under this article, a writ of habeas corpus issues by operation of law.

(b) At the time the application is filed, the clerk of the court shall assign the case a file number ancillary to that of the judgment of conviction or order being challenged.

Sec. 5. (a) Immediately on filing an application, the applicant shall serve a copy of the application on the attorney representing the state, by either certified mail, return receipt requested, or personal service.

(b) The state may file an answer within the period established by Subsection (c), but is not required to file an answer.

(c) The state may not file an answer after the 30th day after the date of service, except that for good cause the convicting court may grant the state one 30-day extension.

(d) Any answer, motion, or other document filed by the state must be served on the applicant by certified mail, return receipt requested, or by personal service.

(e) Matters alleged in the application not admitted by the state are considered to have been denied.

Sec. 6. (a) Not later than the 60th day after the day on which the state's answer is filed, the trial court shall enter a written order granting or denying the relief sought in the application.

(b) In making its determination, the court may order affidavits, depositions, interrogatories, or a hearing, and may rely on the court's personal recollection.

(c) If a hearing is ordered, the hearing may not be held before the eighth day after the day on which the applicant and the state are provided notice of the hearing.

(d) The court may appoint an attorney or magistrate to hold a hearing ordered under this section and make findings of fact. An attorney appointed under this subsection is entitled to compensation as provided by Article 26.05.

Sec. 7. (a) If the court determines from the face of an application or documents attached to the application that the applicant is manifestly entitled to no relief, the court shall enter a written order denying the application as frivolous. In any other case, the court shall enter a written order including findings of fact and conclusions of law. The court may require the prevailing party to submit a proposed order.

(b) At the time an order is entered under this section, the clerk of the court shall immediately, by certified mail, return receipt requested, send a copy of the order to the applicant and to the state.

Sec. 8. If the application is denied in whole or part, the applicant may appeal under Article 44.02 and Rule 31, Texas Rules of Appellate Procedure. If the application is granted in whole or part, the state may appeal under Article 44.01 and Rule 31, Texas Rules of Appellate Procedure.

Sec. 9. (a) If a subsequent application for a writ of habeas corpus is filed after final disposition of an initial application under this article, a court may not consider the merits of or grant relief based on the subsequent application unless the application contains sufficient specific facts establishing that the current claims and issues have not been and could not have been presented previously in an original application or in a previously considered application filed under this article because the factual or legal basis for the claim was unavailable on the date the applicant filed the previous application.

(b) For purposes of Subsection (a), a legal basis of a claim is unavailable on or before a date described by that subsection if the legal basis was not recognized by and could not have been reasonably formulated from a final decision of the United States Supreme Court, a court of appeals of the United States, or a court of appellate jurisdiction of this state on or before that date.

(c) For purposes of Subsection (a), a factual basis of a claim is unavailable on or before a date described by that subsection if the factual basis was not ascertainable through the exercise of reasonable diligence on or before that date.

(Enacted by Acts 2003, 78th Leg., ch. 587 (H.B. 1713), § 1, effective June 20, 2003.)

## Art. 11.08. Applicant Charged with Felony.

If a person is confined after indictment on a charge of felony, he may apply to the judge of the court in which he is indicted; or if there be no judge within the district, then to the judge of any district whose residence is nearest to the court house of the county in which the applicant is held in custody.

(Enacted by Acts 1965, 59th Leg., ch. 722 (S.B. 107), § 1, effective January 1, 1966.)

## Art. 11.09. Applicant Charged with Misdemeanor.

If a person is confined on a charge of misdemeanor, he may apply to the county judge of the county in which the misdemeanor is charged to have been committed, or if there be no county judge in said county, then to the county judge whose residence is nearest to the courthouse of the county in which the applicant is held in custody.

(Enacted by Acts 1965, 59th Leg., ch. 722 (S.B. 107), § 1, effective January 1, 1966.)

## Art. 11.10. Proceedings Under the Writ.

When motion has been made to a judge under the circumstances set forth in the two preceding Articles, he shall appoint a time when he will examine the cause of the applicant, and issue the writ returnable at that time, in the county where the offense is charged in the indictment or information to have been committed. He shall also specify some place in the county where he will hear the motion.

(Enacted by Acts 1965, 59th Leg., ch. 722 (S.B. 107), § 1, effective January 1, 1966.)

## Art. 11.11. Early Hearing.

The time so appointed shall be the earliest day which the judge can devote to hearing the cause of the applicant.

(Enacted by Acts 1965, 59th Leg., ch. 722 (S.B. 107), § 1, effective January 1, 1966.)

## Art. 11.12. Who May Present Petition.

Either the party for whose relief the writ is intended, or any person for him, may present a petition to the proper authority for the purpose of obtaining relief.

(Enacted by Acts 1965, 59th Leg., ch. 722 (S.B. 107), § 1, effective January 1, 1966.)

## Art. 11.13. Applicant.

The word applicant, as used in this Chapter, refers to the person for whose relief the writ is asked, though the petition may be signed and presented by any other person.

(Enacted by Acts 1965, 59th Leg., ch. 722 (S.B. 107), § 1, effective January 1, 1966.)

## Art. 11.14. Requisites of Petition.

The petition must state substantially:

1. That the person for whose benefit the application is made is illegally restrained in his liberty, and by whom, naming both parties, if their names are known, or if unknown, designating and describing them;

2. When the party is confined or restrained by virtue of any writ, order or process, or under color of either, a copy shall be annexed to the petition, or it shall be stated that a copy cannot be obtained;

3. When the confinement or restraint is not by virtue of any writ, order or process, the petition may state only that the party is illegally confined or restrained in his liberty;

4. There must be a prayer in the petition for the writ of habeas corpus; and

5. Oath must be made that the allegations of the petition are true, according to the belief of the petitioner.

(Enacted by Acts 1965, 59th Leg., ch. 722 (S.B. 107), § 1, effective January 1, 1966.)

## Art. 11.15. Writ Granted Without Delay.

The writ of habeas corpus shall be granted without delay by the judge or court receiving the petition, unless it be manifest from the petition itself, or some documents annexed to it, that the party is entitled to no relief whatever.

(Enacted by Acts 1965, 59th Leg., ch. 722 (S.B. 107), § 1, effective January 1, 1966.)

Criminal Procedure

## Art. 11.16. Writ May Issue Without Motion.

A judge of the district or county court who has knowledge that any person is illegally confined or restrained in his liberty within his district or county may, if the case be one within his jurisdiction, issue the writ of habeas corpus, without any motion being made for the same.

(Enacted by Acts 1965, 59th Leg., ch. 722 (S.B. 107), § 1, effective January 1, 1966.)

## Art. 11.17. Judge May Issue Warrant of Arrest.

Whenever it appears by satisfactory evidence to any judge authorized to issue such writ that any one is held in illegal confinement or custody, and there is good reason to believe that he will be carried out of the State, or suffer some irreparable injury before he can obtain relief in the usual course of law, or whenever the writ of habeas corpus has been issued and disregarded, the said judge may issue a warrant to any peace officer, or to any person specially named by said judge, directing him to take and bring such person before such judge, to be dealt with according to law.

(Enacted by Acts 1965, 59th Leg., ch. 722 (S.B. 107), § 1, effective January 1, 1966.)

## Art. 11.18. May Arrest Detainer.

Where it appears by the proof offered, under circumstances mentioned in the preceding Article, that the person charged with having illegal custody of the prisoner is, by such act, guilty of an offense against the law, the judge may, in the warrant, order that he be arrested and brought before him; and upon examination, he may be committed, discharged, or held to bail, as the law and the nature of the case may require.

(Enacted by Acts 1965, 59th Leg., ch. 722 (S.B. 107), § 1, effective January 1, 1966.)

## Art. 11.19. Proceedings Under the Warrant.

The officer charged with the execution of the warrant shall bring the persons therein mentioned before the judge or court issuing the same, who shall inquire into the cause of the imprisonment or restraint, and make an order thereon, as in cases of habeas corpus, either remanding into custody, discharging or admitting to bail the party so imprisoned or restrained.

(Enacted by Acts 1965, 59th Leg., ch. 722 (S.B. 107), § 1, effective January 1, 1966.)

## Art. 11.20. Officer Executing Warrant.

The same power may be exercised by the officer executing the warrant in cases arising under the foregoing Articles as is exercised in the execution of warrants of arrest.

(Enacted by Acts 1965, 59th Leg., ch. 722 (S.B. 107), § 1, effective January 1, 1966.)

## Art. 11.21. Constructive Custody.

The words "confined", "imprisoned", "in custody", "confinement", "imprisonment", refer not only to the actual, corporeal and forcible detention of a person, but likewise to any coercive measures by threats, menaces or the fear of injury, whereby one person exercises a control over the person of another, and detains him within certain limits.

(Enacted by Acts 1965, 59th Leg., ch. 722 (S.B. 107), § 1, effective January 1, 1966.)

## Art. 11.22. Restraint.

By "restraint" is meant the kind of control which one person exercises over another, not to confine him within certain limits, but to subject him to the general authority and power of the person claiming such right.

(Enacted by Acts 1965, 59th Leg., ch. 722 (S.B. 107), § 1, effective January 1, 1966.)

## Art. 11.23. Scope of Writ.

The writ of habeas corpus is intended to be applicable to all such cases of confinement and restraint, where there is no lawful right in the person exercising the power, or where, though the power in fact exists, it is exercised in a manner or degree not sanctioned by law.

(Enacted by Acts 1965, 59th Leg., ch. 722 (S.B. 107), § 1, effective January 1, 1966.)

## Art. 11.24. One Committed in Default of Bail.

Where a person has been committed to custody for failing to enter into bond, he is entitled to the writ of habeas corpus, if it be stated in the petition that there was no sufficient cause for requiring bail, or that the bail required is excessive. If the proof sustains the petition, it will entitle the party to be discharged, or have the bail reduced.

(Enacted by Acts 1965, 59th Leg., ch. 722 (S.B. 107), § 1, effective January 1, 1966.)

### Art. 11.25. Person Afflicted with Disease.

When a judge or court authorized to grant writs of habeas corpus shall be satisfied, upon investigation, that a person in legal custody is afflicted with a disease which will render a removal necessary for the preservation of life, an order may be made for the removal of the prisoner to some other place where his health will not be likely to suffer; or he may be admitted to bail when it appears that any species of confinement will endanger his life.
(Enacted by Acts 1965, 59th Leg., ch. 722 (S.B. 107), § 1, effective January 1, 1966.)

### Art. 11.26. Who May Serve Writ.

The service of the writ may be made by any person competent to testify.
(Enacted by Acts 1965, 59th Leg., ch. 722 (S.B. 107), § 1, effective January 1, 1966.)

### Art. 11.27. How Writ May Be Served and Returned.

The writ may be served by delivering a copy of the original to the person who is charged with having the party under restraint or in custody, and exhibiting the original, if demanded; if he refuse to receive it, he shall be informed verbally of the purport of the writ. If he refuses admittance to the person wishing to make the service, or conceals himself, a copy of the writ may be fixed upon some conspicuous part of the house where such person resides or conceals himself, or of the place where the prisoner is confined; and the person serving the writ of habeas corpus shall, in all cases, state fully, in his return, the manner and the time of the service of the writ.
(Enacted by Acts 1965, 59th Leg., ch. 722 (S.B. 107), § 1, effective January 1, 1966.)

### Art. 11.28. Return Under Oath.

The return of a writ of habeas corpus, under the provisions of the preceding Article, if made by any person other than an officer, shall be under oath.
(Enacted by Acts 1965, 59th Leg., ch. 722 (S.B. 107), § 1, effective January 1, 1966.)

### Art. 11.29. Must Make Return.

The person on whom the writ of habeas corpus is served shall immediately obey the same, and make the return required by law upon the copy of the original writ served on him, and this, whether the writ be directed to him or not.

(Enacted by Acts 1965, 59th Leg., ch. 722 (S.B. 107), § 1, effective January 1, 1966.)

### Art. 11.30. How Return Is Made.

The return is made by stating in plain language upon the copy of the writ or some paper connected with it:

1. Whether it is true or not, according to the statement of the petition, that he has in his custody, or under his restraint, the person named or described in such petition;

2. By virtue of what authority, or for what cause, he took and detains such person;

3. If he had such person in his custody or under restraint at any time before the service of the writ, and has transferred him to the custody of another, he shall state particularly to whom, at what time, for what reason or by what authority he made such transfer;

4. He shall annex to his return the writ or warrant, if any, by virtue of which he holds the person in custody; and

5. The return must be signed and sworn to by the person making it.
(Enacted by Acts 1965, 59th Leg., ch. 722 (S.B. 107), § 1, effective January 1, 1966.)

### Art. 11.31. Applicant Brought Before Judge.

The person on whom the writ is served shall bring before the judge the person in his custody, or under his restraint, unless it be made to appear that by reason of sickness he cannot be removed; in which case, another day may be appointed by the judge or court for hearing the cause, and for the production of the person confined; or the application may be heard and decided without the production of the person detained, by the consent of his counsel.
(Enacted by Acts 1965, 59th Leg., ch. 722 (S.B. 107), § 1, effective January 1, 1966.)

### Art. 11.32. Custody Pending Examination.

When the return of the writ has been made, and the applicant brought before the court, he is no longer detained on the original warrant or process, but under the authority of the habeas corpus. The safekeeping of the prisoner, pending the examination or hearing, is entirely under the direction and authority of the judge or court issuing the writ, or to which the return is made. He may be bailed from day to day, or be remanded to the same jail whence he came, or to any other place of safekeeping under the control of the judge or court, till the case is finally determined. (Enacted by Acts 1965, 59th Leg., ch. 722 (S.B. 107), § 1, effective January 1, 1966.)

### Art. 11.33. Court Shall Allow Time.

The court or judge granting the writ of habeas corpus shall allow reasonable time for the production of the person detained in custody. (Enacted by Acts 1965, 59th Leg., ch. 722 (S.B. 107), § 1, effective January 1, 1966.)

### Art. 11.34. Disobeying Writ.

When service has been made upon a person charged with the illegal custody of another, if he refuses to obey the writ and make the return required by law, or, if he refuses to receive the writ, or conceals himself, the court or judge issuing the writ shall issue a warrant directed to any officer or other suitable person willing to execute the same, commanding him to arrest the person charged with the illegal custody or detention of another, and bring him before such court or judge. When such person has been arrested and brought before the court or judge, if he still refuses to return the writ, or does not produce the person in his custody, he shall be committed to jail and remain there until he is willing to obey the writ of habeas corpus, and until he pays all the costs of the proceeding. (Enacted by Acts 1965, 59th Leg., ch. 722 (S.B. 107), § 1, effective January 1, 1966.)

### Art. 11.35. Further Penalty for Disobeying Writ.

Any person disobeying the writ of habeas corpus shall also be liable to a civil action at the suit of the party detained, and shall pay in such suit fifty dollars for each day of illegal detention and restraint, after service of the writ. It shall be deemed that a person has disobeyed the writ who detains a prisoner a longer time than three days after service thereof, unless where further time is allowed in the writ for making the return thereto. (Enacted by Acts 1965, 59th Leg., ch. 722 (S.B. 107), § 1, effective January 1, 1966.)

### Art. 11.36. Applicant May Be Brought Before Court.

In case of disobedience of the writ of habeas corpus, the person for whose relief it is intended may also be brought before the court or judge having competent authority, by an order for that purpose, issued to any peace officer or other proper person specially named. (Enacted by Acts 1965, 59th Leg., ch. 722 (S.B. 107), § 1, effective January 1, 1966.)

### Art. 11.37. Death, Etc., Sufficient Return of Writ.

It is a sufficient return of the writ of habeas corpus that the person, once detained, has died or escaped, or that by some superior force he has been taken from the custody of the person making the return; but where any such cause shall be assigned, the court or judge shall proceed to hear testimony; and the facts stated in the return shall be proved by satisfactory evidence. (Enacted by Acts 1965, 59th Leg., ch. 722 (S.B. 107), § 1, effective January 1, 1966.)

### Art. 11.38. When a Prisoner Dies.

When a prisoner confined in jail, or who is in legal custody, shall die, the officer having charge of him shall forthwith report the same to a justice of the peace of the county, who shall hold an inquest to ascertain the cause of his death. All the proceedings had in such cases shall be reduced to writing, certified and returned as in other cases of inquest; a certified copy of which shall be sufficient proof of the death of the prisoner at the hearing of a motion under habeas corpus. (Enacted by Acts 1965, 59th Leg., ch. 722 (S.B. 107), § 1, effective January 1, 1966.)

### Art. 11.39. Who Shall Represent the State.

If neither the county nor the district attorney be present, the judge may appoint some qualified practicing attorney to represent the State, who shall be paid the same fee allowed district attorneys for like services. (Enacted by Acts 1965, 59th Leg., ch. 722 (S.B. 107), § 1, effective January 1, 1966.)

### Art. 11.40. Prisoner Discharged.

The judge or court before whom a person is brought by writ of habeas corpus shall examine the writ and the papers attached to it; and if no legal cause be shown for the imprisonment or restraint, or if it appear that the imprisonment or restraint, though at first legal, cannot for any cause be lawfully prolonged, the applicant shall be discharged. (Enacted by Acts 1965, 59th Leg., ch. 722 (S.B. 107), § 1, effective January 1, 1966.)

### Art. 11.41. Where Party Is Indicted for Capital Offense.

If it appears by the return and papers attached that the party stands indicted for a capital offense, the judge or court having jurisdiction of the case shall, nevertheless, proceed to hear such testimony as may be offered on the part of the State and the applicant, and may either remand or admit him to bail, as the law and the facts may justify.

(Enacted by Acts 1965, 59th Leg., ch. 722 (S.B. 107), § 1, effective January 1, 1966.)

### Art. 11.42. If Court Has No Jurisdiction.

If it appear by the return and papers attached that the judge or court has no jurisdiction, such court or judge shall at once remand the applicant to the person from whose custody he has been taken.

(Enacted by Acts 1965, 59th Leg., ch. 722 (S.B. 107), § 1, effective January 1, 1966.)

### Art. 11.43. Presumption of Innocence.

No presumption of guilt arises from the mere fact that a criminal accusation has been made before a competent authority.

(Enacted by Acts 1965, 59th Leg., ch. 722 (S.B. 107), § 1, effective January 1, 1966.)

### Art. 11.44. Action of Court upon Examination.

The judge or court, after having examined the return and all documents attached, and heard the testimony offered on both sides, shall, according to the facts and circumstances of the case, proceed either to remand the party into custody, admit him to bail or discharge him; provided, that no defendant shall be discharged after indictment without bail.

(Enacted by Acts 1965, 59th Leg., ch. 722 (S.B. 107), § 1, effective January 1, 1966.)

### Art. 11.45. Void or Informal.

If it appears that the applicant is detained or held under a warrant of commitment which is informal, or void; yet, if from the document on which the warrant was based, or from the proof on the hearing of the habeas corpus, it appears that there is probable cause to believe that an offense has been committed by the prisoner, he shall not be discharged, but shall be committed or held to bail.

(Enacted by Acts 1965, 59th Leg., ch. 722 (S.B. 107), § 1, effective January 1, 1966.)

### Art. 11.46. If Proof Shows Offense.

Where, upon an examination under habeas corpus, it appears to the court or judge that there is probable cause to believe that an offense has been committed by the prisoner, he shall not be discharged, but shall be committed or admitted to bail.

(Enacted by Acts 1965, 59th Leg., ch. 722 (S.B. 107), § 1, effective January 1, 1966.)

### Art. 11.47. May Summon Magistrate.

To ascertain the grounds on which an informal or void warrant has been issued, the judge or court may cause to be summoned the magistrate who issued the warrant, and may, by an order, require him to bring with him all the papers and proceedings touching the matter. The attendance of such magistrate and the production of such papers may be enforced by warrant of arrest.

(Enacted by Acts 1965, 59th Leg., ch. 722 (S.B. 107), § 1, effective January 1, 1966.)

### Art. 11.48. Written Issue Not Necessary.

It shall not be necessary, on the trial of any cause arising under habeas corpus, to make up a written issue, though it may be done by the applicant for the writ. He may except to the sufficiency of, or controvert the return or any part thereof, or allege any new matter in avoidance. If written denial on his part be not made, it shall be considered, for the purpose of investigation, that the statements of said return are contested by a denial of the same; and the proof shall be heard accordingly, both for and against the applicant for relief.

(Enacted by Acts 1965, 59th Leg., ch. 722 (S.B. 107), § 1, effective January 1, 1966.)

### Art. 11.49. Order of Argument.

The applicant shall have the right by himself or counsel to open and conclude the argument upon the trial under habeas corpus.

(Enacted by Acts 1965, 59th Leg., ch. 722 (S.B. 107), § 1, effective January 1, 1966.)

### Art. 11.50. Costs.

The judge trying the cause under habeas corpus may make such order as is deemed right concerning the cost of bringing the defendant before him, and all other costs of the proceeding, awarding the same either against the person to whom the writ was directed, the person seeking relief, or may award no costs at all.

(Enacted by Acts 1965, 59th Leg., ch. 722 (S.B. 107), § 1, effective January 1, 1966.)

### Art. 11.51. Record of Proceedings.

If a writ of habeas corpus be made returnable before a court in session, all the proceedings had shall be entered of record by the clerk thereof, as in any other case in such court. When the motion is heard out of the county where the offense was committed, or in the Court of Criminal Appeals, the clerk shall transmit a certified copy of all the proceedings upon the motion to the clerk of the court which has jurisdiction of the offense.
(Enacted by Acts 1965, 59th Leg., ch. 722 (S.B. 107), § 1, effective January 1, 1966.)

### Art. 11.52. Proceedings Had in Vacation.

If the return is made and the proceedings had before a judge of a court in vacation, he shall cause all of the proceedings to be written, shall certify to the same, and cause them to be filed with the clerk of the court which has jurisdiction of the offense, who shall keep them safely.
(Enacted by Acts 1965, 59th Leg., ch. 722 (S.B. 107), § 1, effective January 1, 1966.)

### Art. 11.53. Construing the Two Preceding Articles.

The two preceding Articles refer only to cases where an applicant is held under accusation for some offense; in all other cases the proceedings had before the judge shall be filed and kept by the clerk of the court hearing the case.
(Enacted by Acts 1965, 59th Leg., ch. 722 (S.B. 107), § 1, effective January 1, 1966.)

### Art. 11.54. Court May Grant Necessary Orders.

The court or judge granting a writ of habeas corpus may grant all necessary orders to bring before him the testimony taken before the examining court, and may issue process to enforce the attendance of witnesses.
(Enacted by Acts 1965, 59th Leg., ch. 722 (S.B. 107), § 1, effective January 1, 1966.)

### Art. 11.55. Meaning of "Return".

The word "return", as used in this Chapter, means the report made by the officer or person charged with serving the writ of habeas corpus, and also the answer made by the person served with such writ.
(Enacted by Acts 1965, 59th Leg., ch. 722 (S.B. 107), § 1, effective January 1, 1966.)

### Art. 11.56. Effect of Discharge Before Indictment.

Where a person, before indictment found against him, has been discharged or held to bail on habeas corpus by order of a court or judge of competent jurisdiction, he shall not be again imprisoned or detained in custody on an accusation for the same offense, until after he shall have been indicted, unless surrendered by his bail.
(Enacted by Acts 1965, 59th Leg., ch. 722 (S.B. 107), § 1, effective January 1, 1966.)

### Art. 11.57. Writ After Indictment.

Where a person once discharged or admitted to bail is afterward indicted for the same offense for which he has been once arrested, he may be committed on the indictment, but shall be again entitled to the writ of habeas corpus, and may be admitted to bail, if the facts of the case render it proper; but in cases where, after indictment is found, the cause of the defendant has been investigated on habeas corpus, and an order made, either remanding him to custody, or admitting him to bail, he shall neither be subject to be again placed in custody, unless when surrendered by his bail, nor shall he be again entitled to the writ of habeas corpus, except in the special cases mentioned in this Chapter.
(Enacted by Acts 1965, 59th Leg., ch. 722 (S.B. 107), § 1, effective January 1, 1966.)

### Art. 11.58. Person Committed for a Capital Offense.

If the accusation against the defendant for a capital offense has been heard on habeas corpus before indictment found, and he shall have been committed after such examination, he shall not be entitled to the writ, unless in the special cases mentioned in Articles 11.25 and 11.59.
(Enacted by Acts 1965, 59th Leg., ch. 722 (S.B. 107), § 1, effective January 1, 1966.)

### Art. 11.59. Obtaining Writ a Second Time.

A party may obtain the writ of habeas corpus a second time by stating in a motion therefor that since the hearing of his first motion important testimony has been obtained which it was not in his power to produce at the former hearing. He shall also set forth the testimony so newly discovered; and if it be that of a witness, the affidavit of the witness shall also accompany such motion.
(Enacted by Acts 1965, 59th Leg., ch. 722 (S.B. 107), § 1, effective January 1, 1966.)

### Art. 11.60. Refusing to Execute Writ.

Any officer to whom a writ of habeas corpus, or other writ, warrant or process authorized by this Chapter shall be directed, delivered or tendered, who refuses to execute the same according to his directions, or who wantonly delays the service or execution of the same, shall be liable to fine as for contempt of court.

(Enacted by Acts 1965, 59th Leg., ch. 722 (S.B. 107), § 1, effective January 1, 1966.)

### Art. 11.61. Refusal to Obey Writ.

Any one having another in his custody, or under his power, control or restraint who refuses to obey a writ of habeas corpus, or who evades the service of the same, or places the person illegally detained under the control of another, removes him, or in any other manner attempts to evade the operation of the writ, shall be dealt with as provided in Article 11.34 of this Code.

(Enacted by Acts 1965, 59th Leg., ch. 722 (S.B. 107), § 1, effective January 1, 1966.)

### Art. 11.62. Refusal to Give Copy of Process.

Any jailer, sheriff or other officer who has a prisoner in his custody and refuses, upon demand, to furnish a copy of the process under which he holds the person, is guilty of an offense, and shall be dealt with as provided in Article 11.34 of this Code for refusal to return the writ therein required.

(Enacted by Acts 1965, 59th Leg., ch. 722 (S.B. 107), § 1, effective January 1, 1966.)

### Art. 11.63. Held Under Federal Authority.

No person shall be discharged under the writ of habeas corpus who is in custody by virtue of a commitment for any offense exclusively cognizable by the courts of the United States, or by order or process issuing out of such courts in cases where they have jurisdiction, or who is held by virtue of any legal engagement or enlistment in the army, or who, being rightfully subject to the rules and articles of war, is confined by any one legally acting under the authority thereof, or who is held as a prisoner of war under the authority of the United States.

(Enacted by Acts 1965, 59th Leg., ch. 722 (S.B. 107), § 1, effective January 1, 1966.)

### Art. 11.64. Application of Chapter.

This Chapter applies to all cases of habeas corpus for the enlargement of persons illegally held in custody or in any manner restrained in their personal liberty, for the admission of prisoners to bail, and for the discharge of prisoners before indictment upon a hearing of the testimony. Instead of a writ of habeas corpus in other cases heretofore used, a simple order shall be substituted.

(Enacted by Acts 1965, 59th Leg., ch. 722 (S.B. 107), § 1, effective January 1, 1966.)

### Art. 11.65. Bond for Certain Applicants.

(a) This article applies to an applicant for a writ of habeas corpus seeking relief from the judgment in a criminal case, other than an applicant seeking relief from a judgment imposing a penalty of death.

(b) On making proposed findings of fact and conclusions of law jointly stipulated to by the applicant and the state, or on approving proposed findings of fact and conclusions of law made by an attorney or magistrate appointed by the court to perform that duty and jointly stipulated to by the applicant and the state, the convicting court may order the release of the applicant on bond, subject to conditions imposed by the convicting court, until the applicant is denied relief, remanded to custody, or ordered released.

(c) For the purposes of this chapter, an applicant released on bond under this article remains restrained in his liberty.

(d) Article 44.04(b) does not apply to the release of an applicant on bond under this article.

(Enacted by Acts 2003, 78th Leg., ch. 197 (S.B. 1948), § 1, effective June 2, 2003.)

## Limitation and Venue

## CHAPTER 12
## LIMITATION

### Art. 12.01. Felonies.

Except as provided in Article 12.03, felony indictments may be presented within these limits, and not afterward:

(1) no limitation:

(A) murder and manslaughter;

(B) sexual assault under Section 22.011(a)(2), Penal Code, or aggravated sexual assault under Section 22.021(a)(1)(B), Penal Code;

(C) sexual assault, if during the investigation of the offense biological matter is collected and subjected to forensic DNA testing and the testing results show that the matter does not match the victim or any other person whose identity is readily ascertained;

(D) continuous sexual abuse of young child or children under Section 21.02, Penal Code;

(E) indecency with a child under Section 21.11, Penal Code;

(F) an offense involving leaving the scene of an accident under Section 550.021, Transportation Code, if the accident resulted in the death of a person; or

(G) **[2 Versions: As added by Acts 2011, 82nd Leg., ch. 1]** trafficking of persons under Section 20A.02(a)(7) or (8), Penal Code;

(G) **[2 Versions: As added by Acts 2011, 82nd Leg., ch. 122]** continuous trafficking of persons under Section 20A.03, Penal Code;

(2) ten years from the date of the commission of the offense:

(A) theft of any estate, real, personal or mixed, by an executor, administrator, guardian or trustee, with intent to defraud any creditor, heir, legatee, ward, distributee, beneficiary or settlor of a trust interested in such estate;

(B) theft by a public servant of government property over which he exercises control in his official capacity;

(C) forgery or the uttering, using or passing of forged instruments;

(D) injury to an elderly or disabled individual punishable as a felony of the first degree under Section 22.04, Penal Code;

(E) sexual assault, except as provided by Subdivision (1);

(F) arson;

(G) trafficking of persons under Section 20A.02(a)(1), (2), (3), or (4), Penal Code; or

(H) compelling prostitution under Section 43.05(a)(1), Penal Code;

(3) seven years from the date of the commission of the offense:

(A) misapplication of fiduciary property or property of a financial institution;

(B) securing execution of document by deception;

(C) a felony violation under Chapter 162, Tax Code;

(D) false statement to obtain property or credit under Section 32.32, Penal Code;

(E) money laundering;

(F) credit card or debit card abuse under Section 32.31, Penal Code;

(G) fraudulent use or possession of identifying information under Section 32.51, Penal Code; or

(H) **[2 Versions: As added by Acts 2011, 82nd Leg., ch. 222]** bigamy under Section 25.01, Penal Code, except as provided by Subdivision (6);

(H) **[2 Versions: As added by Acts 2011, 82nd Leg., ch. 620]** Medicaid fraud under Section 35A.02, Penal Code;

(4) five years from the date of the commission of the offense:

(A) theft or robbery;

(B) except as provided by Subdivision (5), kidnapping or burglary;

(C) injury to an elderly or disabled individual that is not punishable as a felony of the first degree under Section 22.04, Penal Code;

(D) abandoning or endangering a child; or

(E) insurance fraud;

(5) if the investigation of the offense shows that the victim is younger than 17 years of age at the time the offense is committed, 20 years from the 18th birthday of the victim of one of the following offenses:

(A) sexual performance by a child under Section 43.25, Penal Code;

(B) aggravated kidnapping under Section 20.04(a)(4), Penal Code, if the defendant committed the offense with the intent to violate or abuse the victim sexually; or

(C) burglary under Section 30.02, Penal Code, if the offense is punishable under Subsection (d) of that section and the defendant committed the offense with the intent to commit an offense described by Subdivision (1)(B) or (D) of this article or Paragraph (B) of this subdivision;

(6) **[2 Versions: As amended by Acts 2011, 82nd Leg., ch. 1]** ten years from the 18th birthday of the victim of the offense:

(A) trafficking of persons under Section 20A.02(a)(5) or (6), Penal Code;

(B) injury to a child under Section 22.04, Penal Code; or

(C) compelling prostitution under Section 43.05(a)(2), Penal Code; or

(6) **[2 Versions: As amended by Acts 2011, 82nd Leg., ch. 222]** ten years from the 18th birthday of the victim of the offense:

(A) injury to a child under Section 22.04, Penal Code; or

(B) bigamy under Section 25.01, Penal Code, if the investigation of the offense shows that the person, other than the legal spouse of the defendant, whom the defendant marries or purports to marry or with whom the defendant lives under the appearance of being married is younger than 18 years of age at the time the offense is committed; or

(7) three years from the date of the commission of the offense: all other felonies.

(Enacted by Acts 1965, 59th Leg., ch. 722 (S.B. 107), § 1, effective January 1, 1966; am. Acts 1973, 63rd Leg., ch. 399 (S.B. 34), § 2(B), effective January 1, 1974; am. Acts 1975, 64th Leg., ch. 203 (H.B. 284), § 5, effective September 1, 1975; am. Acts 1983, 68th Leg., ch. 85 (S.B. 343), § 1, effective September 1, 1983; am. Acts 1983, 68th Leg., ch. 977 (H.B. 2008), § 7, effective September 1, 1983; am. Acts 1985, 69th Leg., ch. 330 (H.B. 1149), § 1, effective August 26, 1985; am. Acts 1987, 70th Leg., ch. 716 (H.B. 494), § 1, effective September 1, 1987; am. Acts 1991, 72nd Leg., ch. 565 (S.B. 4), § 6, effective September 1, 1991; am. Acts 1995, 74th Leg., ch. 476 (S.B. 698), § 1, effective September 1, 1995; am. Acts 1997, 75th Leg., ch. 740 (H.B. 921), § 1, effective September 1, 1997; am. Acts 1999, 76th Leg., ch. 39 (S.B. 70), § 1, effective September 1, 1999; am. Acts 1999, 76th Leg., ch. 1285 (S.B. 1547), § 33, effective September 1, 2000; am. Acts 2001, 77th Leg., ch. 12 (H.B. 656), § 1, effective September 1, 2001; am. Acts 2001, 77th Leg., ch. 1479 (S.B. 214), § 1, effective September 1, 2001; am. Acts 2001, 77th Leg., ch. 1482 (S.B. 328), § 1, effective September 1, 2001; am. Acts 2003, 78th Leg., ch. 371 (S.B. 1460), § 6, effective September 1, 2003; am. Acts 2003, 78th Leg., ch. 1276 (H.B. 3507), § 5.001, effective September 1, 2003; am. Acts 2005, 79th Leg., ch. 1162 (H.B. 3376), § 6, effective September 1, 2005; am. Acts 2007, 80th Leg., ch. 285 (H.B. 716), § 6, effective September 1, 2007; am. Acts 2007, 80th Leg., ch. 593 (H.B. 8), § 1.03, effective September 1, 2007; am. Acts 2007, 80th Leg., ch. 640 (H.B. 887), § 1, effective September 1, 2007; am. Acts 2007, 80th Leg., ch. 841 (H.B. 959), § 1, effective September 1, 2007; am. Acts 2009, 81st Leg., ch. 87 (S.B. 1969), § 6.001, effective September 1, 2009; am. Acts 2009, 81st Leg., ch. 1227 (S.B. 1495), § 38, effective September 1, 2009; am. Acts 2011, 82nd Leg., ch. 1 (S.B. 24), § 2.03, effective September 1, 2011; am. Acts 2011, 82nd Leg., ch. 122 (H.B. 3000), § 2, effective September 1, 2011; am. Acts 2011, 82nd Leg., ch. 222 (H.B. 253), § 1, effective September 1, 2011; am. Acts 2011, 82nd Leg., ch. 620 (S.B. 688), § 1, effective September 1, 2011.)

## Art. 12.02. Misdemeanors.

(a) An indictment or information for any Class A or Class B misdemeanor may be presented within two years from the date of the commission of the offense, and not afterward.

(b) A complaint or information for any Class C misdemeanor may be presented within two years from the date of the commission of the offense, and not afterward.

(Enacted by Acts 1965, 59th Leg., ch. 722 (S.B. 107), § 1, effective January 1, 1966; am. Acts 1973, 63rd Leg., ch. 399 (S.B. 34), § 2(B), effective January 1, 1974; am. Acts 2009, 81st Leg., ch. 472 (S.B. 410), § 1, effective September 1, 2009.)

## Art. 12.03. Aggravated Offenses, Attempt, Conspiracy, Solicitation, Organized Criminal Activity.

(a) The limitation period for criminal attempt is the same as that of the offense attempted.

(b) The limitation period for criminal conspiracy or organized criminal activity is the same as that of the most serious offense that is the object of the conspiracy or the organized criminal activity.

(c) The limitation period for criminal solicitation is the same as that of the felony solicited.

(d) Except as otherwise provided by this chapter, any offense that bears the title "aggravated" shall carry the same limitation period as the primary crime.

(Enacted by Acts 1965, 59th Leg., ch. 722 (S.B. 107), § 1, effective January 1, 1966; am. Acts 1973, 63rd Leg., ch. 399 (S.B. 34), § 2(B), effective January 1, 1974; am. Acts 1987, 70th Leg., ch. 1133 (H.B. 349), § 1, effective September 1, 1987; am. Acts 1997, 75th Leg., ch. 740 (H.B. 921), § 2, effective September 1, 1997.)

## Art. 12.04. Computation.

The day on which the offense was committed and the day on which the indictment or information is presented shall be excluded from the computation of time.

(Enacted by Acts 1965, 59th Leg., ch. 722 (S.B. 107), § 1, effective January 1, 1966; am. Acts

1973, 63rd Leg., ch. 399 (S.B. 34), § 2(B), effective January 1, 1974.)

## Art. 12.05. Absence from State and Time of Pendency of Indictment, Etc., Not Computed.

(a) The time during which the accused is absent from the state shall not be computed in the period of limitation.

(b) The time during the pendency of an indictment, information, or complaint shall not be computed in the period of limitation.

(c) The term "during the pendency," as used herein, means that period of time beginning with the day the indictment, information, or complaint is filed in a court of competent jurisdiction, and ending with the day such accusation is, by an order of a trial court having jurisdiction thereof, determined to be invalid for any reason.

(Enacted by Acts 1965, 59th Leg., ch. 722 (S.B. 107), § 1, effective January 1, 1966; am. Acts 1973, 63rd Leg., ch. 399 (S.B. 34), § 2(B), effective January 1, 1974.)

## Art. 12.06. An Indictment Is "Presented," When.

An indictment is considered as "presented" when it has been duly acted upon by the grand jury and received by the court.

(Enacted by Acts 1965, 59th Leg., ch. 722 (S.B. 107), effective January 1, 1966; am. Acts 1973, 63rd Leg., ch. 399 (S.B. 34), § 2(B), effective January 1, 1974.)

## Art. 12.07. An Information Is "Presented," When.

An information is considered as "presented," when it has been filed by the proper officer in the proper court.

(Enacted by Acts 1965, 59th Leg., ch. 722 (S.B. 107), § 1, effective January 1, 1966; am. Acts 1973, 63rd Leg., ch. 399 (S.B. 34), § 2(B), effective January 1, 1974.)

## Art. 12.08. An Indictment Is "Presented," When [Deleted].

Deleted by Acts 1973, 63rd Leg., ch. 399 (S.B. 34), § 2(B), effective January 1, 1974.

## Art. 12.09. An Information Is "Presented," When [Deleted].

Deleted by Acts 1973, 63rd Leg., ch. 399 (S.B. 34), § 2(B), effective January 1, 1974.

# CHAPTER 13
## VENUE

## Art. 13.01. Offenses Committed Outside This State.

Offenses committed wholly or in part outside this State, under circumstances that give this State jurisdiction to prosecute the offender, may be prosecuted in any county in which the offender is found or in any county in which an element of the offense occurs.

(Enacted by Acts 1965, 59th Leg., ch. 722 (S.B. 107), § 1, effective January 1, 1966; am. Acts 1973, 63rd Leg., ch. 399 (S.B. 34), § 2(C), effective January 1, 1974.)

## Art. 13.02. Forgery.

Forgery may be prosecuted in any county where the writing was forged, or where the same was used or passed, or attempted to be used or passed, or deposited or placed with another person, firm, association, or corporation either for collection or credit for the account of any person, firm, association or corporation. In addition, a forging and uttering, using or passing of forged instruments in writing which concern or affect the title to land in this State may be prosecuted in the county in which such land, or any part thereof, is situated.

(Enacted by Acts 1965, 59th Leg., ch. 722 (S.B. 107), § 1, effective January 1, 1966; am. Acts 1973, 63rd Leg., ch. 399 (S.B. 34), § 2(C), effective January 1, 1974.)

## Art. 13.03. Perjury.

Perjury and aggravated perjury may be prosecuted in the county where committed, or in the county where the false statement is used or attempted to be used.

(Enacted by Acts 1965, 59th Leg., ch. 722 (S.B. 107), § 1, effective January 1, 1966; am. Acts 1973, 63rd Leg., ch. 399 (S.B. 34), § 2(C), effective January 1, 1974.)

## Art. 13.04. On the Boundaries of Counties.

An offense committed on the boundaries of two or more counties, or within four hundred yards thereof, may be prosecuted and punished in any one of such counties and any offense committed on the premises of any airport operated jointly by two municipalities and situated in two counties may be prosecuted and punished in either county.

(Enacted by Acts 1965, 59th Leg., ch. 722 (S.B. 107), § 1, effective January 1, 1966; am. Acts 1973, 63rd Leg., ch. 399 (S.B. 34), § 2(C), effective January 1, 1974; am. Acts 1973, 63rd Leg.,

ch. 454 (S.B. 657), art. 2, § 1, effective January 1, 1974; am. Acts 1981, 67th Leg., ch. 534 (H.B. 641), § 1, effective August 31, 1981.)

## Art. 13.045. On the Boundaries of Certain Municipalities.

An offense punishable by fine only that is committed on the boundary, or within 200 yards of the boundary, of contiguous municipalities that have entered into an agreement authorized by Article 4.14(f) and Section 29.003(h), Government Code, may be prosecuted in either of those municipalities.

(Enacted by Acts 2009, 81st Leg., ch. 230 (S.B. 1504), § 2, effective September 1, 2009.)

## Art. 13.05. Criminal Homicide Committed Outside This State.

The offense of criminal homicide committed wholly or in part outside this State, under circumstances that give this State jurisdiction to prosecute the offender, may be prosecuted in the county where the injury was inflicted, or in the county where the offender was located when he inflicted the injury, or in the county where the victim died or the body was found.

(Enacted by Acts 1965, 59th Leg., ch. 722 (S.B. 107), § 1, effective January 1, 1966; am. Acts 1973, 63rd Leg., ch. 399 (S.B. 34), § 2(C), effective January 1, 1974.)

## Art. 13.06. Committed on a Boundary Stream.

If an offense be committed upon any river or stream, the boundary of this State, it may be prosecuted in the county the boundary of which is upon such stream or river, and the county seat of which is nearest the place where the offense was committed.

(Enacted by Acts 1965, 59th Leg., ch. 722 (S.B. 107), § 1, effective January 1, 1966; am. Acts 1973, 63rd Leg., ch. 399 (S.B. 34), § 2(C), effective January 1, 1974.)

## Art. 13.07. Injured in One County and Dying in Another.

If a person receives an injury in one county and dies in another by reason of such injury, the offender may be prosecuted in the county where the injury was received or where the death occurred, or in the county where the dead body is found.

(Enacted by Acts 1965, 59th Leg., ch. 722 (S.B. 107), § 1, effective January 1, 1966; am. Acts

1973, 63rd Leg., ch. 399 (S.B. 34), § 2(C), effective January 1, 1974.)

## Art. 13.075. Child Injured in One County and Residing in Another.

An offense under Title 5, Penal Code, involving a victim younger than 18 years of age, or an offense under Section 25.03, Penal Code, that results in bodily injury to a child younger than 18 years of age, may be prosecuted in the county:

   (1) in which an element of the offense was committed;

   (2) in which the defendant is apprehended;

   (3) in which the victim resides; or

   (4) in which the defendant resides.

(Enacted by Acts 2011, 82nd Leg., ch. 1100 (S.B. 1551), § 1, effective September 1, 2011.)

## Art. 13.08. Theft; Organized Retail Theft.

(a) Where property is stolen in one county and removed to another county, the offender may be prosecuted either in the county in which the property was stolen or in any other county through or into which the property was removed.

(b) An offense under Section 31.16, Penal Code, may be prosecuted in any county in which an underlying theft could have been prosecuted as a separate offense.

(Enacted by Acts 1965, 59th Leg., ch. 722 (S.B. 107), § 1, effective January 1, 1966; am. Acts 1973, 63rd Leg., ch. 399 (S.B. 34), § 2, effective January 1, 1974; am. Acts 2007, 80th Leg., ch. 1274 (H.B. 3584), § 2(C), effective September 1, 2007; am. Acts 2011, 82nd Leg., ch. 433 (S.B. 1103), § 1, effective September 1, 2011.)

## Art. 13.09. Hindering Secured Creditors.

If secured property is taken from one county and unlawfully disposed of in another county or state, the offender may be prosecuted either in the county in which such property was disposed of, or in the county from which it was removed, or in the county in which the security agreement is filed.

(Enacted by Acts 1965, 59th Leg., ch. 722 (S.B. 107), § 1, effective January 1, 1966; am. Acts 1973, 63rd Leg., ch. 399 (S.B. 34), § 2(C), effective January 1, 1974.)

## Art. 13.10. Persons Acting Under Authority of This State.

An offense committed outside this State by any officer acting under the authority of this State, under circumstances that give this state jurisdiction to prosecute the offender, may be prosecuted in the county of his residence or, if a nonresident of this State, in Travis County.

(Enacted by Acts 1965, 59th Leg., ch. 722 (S.B. 107), § 1, effective January 1, 1966; am. Acts 1973, 63rd Leg., ch. 399 (S.B. 34), § 2(C), effective January 1, 1974.)

## Art. 13.11. On Vessels.

An offense committed on board a vessel which is at the time upon any navigable water within the boundaries of this State, may be prosecuted in any county through which the vessel is navigated in the course of her voyage, or in the county where the voyage commences or terminates.

(Enacted by Acts 1965, 59th Leg., ch. 722 (S.B. 107), § 1, effective January 1, 1966; am. Acts 1973, 63rd Leg., ch. 399 (S.B. 34), § 2(C), effective January 1, 1974.)

## Art. 13.12. [2 Versions: As amended by Acts 2011, 82nd Leg., ch. 1] Trafficking of Persons, False Imprisonment, and Kidnapping.

Venue for trafficking of persons, false imprisonment, and kidnapping is in:

   (1) the county in which the offense was committed; or

   (2) any county through, into, or out of which the person trafficked, falsely imprisoned, or kidnapped may have been taken.

(Enacted by Acts 1965, 59th Leg., ch. 722 (S.B. 107), § 1, effective January 1, 1966; am. Acts 1973, 63rd Leg., ch. 399 (S.B. 34), § 2(C), effective January 1, 1974; am. Acts 2011, 82nd Leg., ch. 1 (S.B. 24), § 2.04, effective September 1, 2011.)

## Art. 13.12. [2 Versions: As amended by Acts 2011, 82nd Leg., ch. 223] False Imprisonment, Kidnapping, and Smuggling of Persons.

Venue for false imprisonment, kidnapping, and smuggling of persons is in either the county in which the offense was committed, or in any county through, into, or out of which the person falsely imprisoned, kidnapped, or transported may have been taken.

(Enacted by Acts 1965, 59th Leg., ch. 722 (S.B. 107), § 1, effective January 1, 1966; am. Acts 1973, 63rd Leg., ch. 399 (S.B. 34), § 2(C), effective January 1, 1974; am. Acts 2011, 82nd Leg., ch. 223 (H.B. 260), § 4, effective September 1, 2011.)

## Art. 13.13. Conspiracy.

Criminal conspiracy may be prosecuted in the county where the conspiracy was entered into, in the county where the conspiracy was agreed to be executed, or in any county in which one or more of the conspirators does any act to effect an object of the conspiracy. If the object of the conspiracy is an offense classified as a felony under the Tax Code, regardless of whether the offense was committed, the conspiracy may be prosecuted in any county in which venue is proper under the Tax Code for the offense. If a conspiracy was entered into outside this State under circumstances that give this State jurisdiction to prosecute the offender, the offender may be prosecuted in the county where the conspiracy was agreed to be executed, in the county where any one of the conspirators was found, or in Travis County.

(Enacted by Acts 1965, 59th Leg., ch. 722 (S.B. 107), § 1, effective January 1, 1966; am. Acts 1973, 63rd Leg., ch. 399 (S.B. 34), § 2(C), effective January 1, 1974; am. Acts 2011, 82nd Leg., ch. 68 (S.B. 934), § 1, effective September 1, 2011.)

## Art. 13.14. Bigamy.

Bigamy may be prosecuted:

(1) in the county where the bigamous marriage occurred;

(2) in any county in this State in which the parties to such bigamous marriage may live or cohabit together as man and wife; or

(3) in any county in this State in which a party to the bigamous marriage not charged with the offense resides.

(Enacted by Acts 1965, 59th Leg., ch. 722 (S.B. 107), § 1, effective January 1, 1966; am. Acts 1973, 63rd Leg., ch. 399 (S.B. 34), § 2(C), effective January 1, 1974; am. Acts 1989, 71st Leg., ch. 1112 (H.B. 1582), § 1, effective August 28, 1989.)

## Art. 13.15. Sexual Assault.

Sexual assault may be prosecuted in the county in which it is committed, in the county in which the victim is abducted, or in any county through or into which the victim is transported in the course of the abduction and sexual assault. When it shall come to the knowledge of any district judge whose court has jurisdiction under this Article that sexual assault has probably been committed, he shall immediately, if his court be in session, and if not in session, then, at the first term thereafter in any county of the district, call the attention of the grand jury thereto; and if the

court be in session, but the grand jury has been discharged, he shall immediately recall the grand jury to investigate the accusation. The district courts are authorized and directed to change the venue in such cases whenever it shall be necessary to secure a speedy trial.

(Enacted by Acts 1965, 59th Leg., ch. 722 (S.B. 107), § 1, effective January 1, 1966; am. Acts 1973, 63rd Leg., ch. 399 (S.B. 34), § 2(C), effective January 1, 1974; am. Acts 1977, 65th Leg., ch. 262 (H.B. 1963), § 1, effective May 25, 1977; am. Acts 1981, 67th Leg., ch. 707 (H.B. 646), § 4(17), effective August 31, 1981; am. Acts 1983, 68th Leg., ch. 977 (H.B. 2008), § 7, effective September 1, 1983.)

## Art. 13.16. Criminal Nonsupport.

Criminal nonsupport may be prosecuted in the county where the offended spouse or child is residing at the time the information or indictment is presented.

(Enacted by Acts 1965, 59th Leg., ch. 722 (S.B. 107), § 1, effective January 1, 1966; am. Acts 1973, 63rd Leg., ch. 399 (S.B. 34), § 2(C), effective January 1, 1974.)

## Art. 13.17. Proof of Venue.

In all cases mentioned in this Chapter, the indictment or information, or any pleading in the case, may allege that the offense was committed in the county where the prosecution is carried on. To sustain the allegation of venue, it shall only be necessary to prove by the preponderance of the evidence that by reason of the facts in the case, the county where such prosecution is carried on has venue.

(Enacted by Acts 1965, 59th Leg., ch. 722 (S.B. 107), § 1, effective January 1, 1966; am. Acts 1973, 63rd Leg., ch. 399 (S.B. 34), § 2(C), effective January 1, 1974.)

## Art. 13.18. Other Offenses.

If venue is not specifically stated, the proper county for the prosecution of offenses is that in which the offense was committed.

(Enacted by Acts 1965, 59th Leg., ch. 722 (S.B. 107), effective January 1, 1966; am. Acts 1973, 63rd Leg., ch. 399 (S.B. 34), § 2(C), effective January 1, 1974.)

## Art. 13.19. Where Venue Cannot Be Determined.

If an offense has been committed within the state and it cannot readily be determined within which county or counties the commission took place, trial may be held in the county in which the defendant resides, in the county in which he is apprehended, or in the county to which he is extradited.

(Enacted by Acts 1965, 59th Leg., ch. 722 (S.B. 107), § 1, effective January 1, 1966; am. Acts 1973, 63rd Leg., ch. 399 (S.B. 34), § 2(C), effective January 1, 1974.)

### Art. 13.20. Venue by Consent.

The trial of all felony cases, without a jury, may, with the consent of the defendant in writing, his attorney, and the attorney for the state, be held in any county within the judicial district or districts for the county where venue is otherwise authorized by law.

(Enacted by Acts 1975, 64th Leg., ch. 91 (H.B. 154), § 1, effective September 1, 1975.)

### Art. 13.21. Organized Criminal Activity.

The offense of engaging in organized criminal activity may be prosecuted in any county in which any act is committed to effect an objective of the combination or, if the prosecution is based on a criminal offense classified as a felony under the Tax Code, in any county in which venue is proper under the Tax Code for the offense.

(Enacted by Acts 1977, 65th Leg., ch. 346 (S.B. 151), § 2, effective June 10, 1977; am. Acts 2011, 82nd Leg., ch. 68 (S.B. 934), § 2, effective September 1, 2011.)

### Art. 13.22. Possession and Delivery of Marihuana.

An offense of possession or delivery of marihuana may be prosecuted in the county where the offense was committed or with the consent of the defendant in a county that is adjacent to and in the same judicial district as the county where the offense was committed.

(Enacted by Acts 1979, 66th Leg., ch. 10 (S.B. 216), § 1, effective March 7, 1979.)

### Art. 13.23. Unauthorized Use of a Vehicle.

An offense of unauthorized use of a vehicle may be prosecuted in any county where the unauthorized use of the vehicle occurred or in the county in which the vehicle was originally reported stolen.

(Enacted by Acts 1985, 69th Leg., ch. 719 (H.B. 1391), § 1, effective August 26, 1985.)

### Art. 13.24. Illegal Recruitment of Athletes.

An offense of illegal recruitment of an athlete may be prosecuted in any county in which the offense was committed or in the county in which is located the institution of higher education in which the athlete agreed to enroll or was influenced to enroll.

(Enacted by Acts 1989, 71st Leg., ch. 125 (S.B. 429), § 2, effective September 1, 1989.)

### Art. 13.25. Computer Crimes.

(a) In this section "access," "computer," "computer network," "computer program," "computer system," and "owner" have the meanings assigned to those terms by Section 33.01, Penal Code.

(b) An offense under Chapter 33, Penal Code, may be prosecuted in:

    (1) the county of the principal place of business of the owner or lessee of a computer, computer network, or computer system involved in the offense;

    (2) any county in which a defendant had control or possession of:

        (A) any proceeds of the offense; or

        (B) any books, records, documents, property, negotiable instruments, computer programs, or other material used in furtherance of the offense; or

    (3) any county from which, to which, or through which access to a computer, computer network, computer program, or computer system was made in violation of Chapter 33, whether by wires, electromagnetic waves, microwaves, or any other means of communication.

(Enacted by Acts 1989, 71st Leg., ch. 306 (H.B. 2312), § 4, effective September 1, 1989; am. Acts 1991, 72nd Leg., ch. 16, § 19.01(1), effective August 26, 1991 (renumbered from art. 13.24); am. Acts 1993, 73rd Leg., ch. 900 (S.B. 1067), § 3.01, effective September 1, 1994; am. Acts 1997, 75th Leg., ch. 306 (H.B. 1482), § 4, effective September 1, 1997.)

### Art. 13.26. Telecommunications Crimes.

An offense under Chapter 33A, Penal Code, may be prosecuted in the county in which the telecommunications service originated or terminated or in the county to which the bill for the telecommunications service was or would have been delivered.

(Enacted by Acts 1997, 75th Leg., ch. 306 (H.B. 1482), § 5, effective September 1, 1997.)

### Art. 13.27. Simulating Legal Process.

An offense under Section 32.46, 32.48, 32.49, or 37.13, Penal Code, may be prosecuted either in the county from which any material document was sent or in the county in which it was delivered.

(Enacted by Acts 1997, 75th Leg., ch. 189 (H.B. 1185), § 12, effective May 21, 1997; am. Acts 1999, 76th Leg., ch. 62 (S.B. 1368), § 19.01(6), effective September 1, 1999 (renumbered from art. 13.26).)

### Art. 13.271. Prosecution of Mortgage Fraud.

(a) In this article, "real estate transaction" means a sale, lease, trade, exchange, gift, grant, or other conveyance of a real property interest.

(b) Any offense under Chapter 32, Penal Code, that involves a real estate transaction may be prosecuted in:

    (1) the county where the property is located; or

    (2) any county in which part of the transaction occurred, including the generation of documentation supporting the transaction.

(c) An offense under Section 32.46, 32.48, or 32.49, Penal Code, that involves a real estate transaction may also be prosecuted in any county authorized by Article 13.27.

(Enacted by Acts 2011, 82nd Leg., ch. 389 (S.B. 485), § 1, effective September 1, 2011.)

### Art. 13.28. Escape; Unauthorized Absence.

An offense of escape under Section 38.06, Penal Code, or unauthorized absence under Section 38.113, Penal Code, may be prosecuted in:

    (1) the county in which the offense of escape or unauthorized absence was committed; or

    (2) the county in which the defendant committed the offense for which the defendant was placed in custody, detained, or required to submit to treatment.

(Enacted by Acts 2003, 78th Leg., ch. 392 (H.B. 42), § 1, effective September 1, 2003.)

### Art. 13.29. Fraudulent Use or Possession of Identifying Information.

An offense under Section 32.51, Penal Code, may be prosecuted in any county in which the offense was committed or in the county of resi-

dence for the person whose identifying information was fraudulently obtained, possessed, transferred, or used.

(Enacted by Acts 2003, 78th Leg., ch. 415, effective September 1, 2003; am. Acts 2005, 79th Leg., ch. 728 (H.B. 2018), § 23.001(7), effective September 1, 2005 (renumbered from art. 13.28).)

### Art. 13.295. Unauthorized Acquisition or Transfer of Certain Financial Information.

An offense under Section 31.17, Penal Code, may be prosecuted in any county in which the offense was committed or in the county of residence of the person whose financial sight order or payment card information was unlawfully obtained or transferred.

(Enacted by Acts 2011, 82nd Leg., ch. 260 (H.B. 1215), § 3, effective September 1, 2011.)

### Art. 13.30. Fraudulent, Substandard, or Fictitious Degree.

An offense under Section 32.52, Penal Code, may be prosecuted in the county in which an element of the offense occurs or in Travis County.

(Enacted by Acts 2005, 79th Leg., ch. 1039 (H.B. 1173), § 9, effective September 1, 2005.)

### Art. 13.31. Failure to Comply with Sex Offender Registration Statute.

An offense under Chapter 62 may be prosecuted in:

    (1) any county in which an element of the offense occurs;

    (2) the county in which the person subject to Chapter 62 last registered, verified registration, or otherwise complied with a requirement of Chapter 62;

    (3) the county in which the person required to register under Chapter 62 has indicated that the person intends to reside, regardless of whether the person establishes or attempts to establish residency in that county;

    (4) any county in which the person required to register under Chapter 62 is placed under custodial arrest for an offense subsequent to the person's most recent reportable conviction or adjudication under Chapter 62; or

    (5) the county in which the person required to register under Chapter 62 resides or is found by a peace officer, regardless of how long the person has been in the county or intends to stay in the county.

(Acts 2005, 79th Leg., ch. 1008 (H.B. 867), § 1.02, effective September 1, 2005; am. Acts 2007, 80th

Leg., ch. 921 (H.B. 3167), § 17.001(8), effective September 1, 2007 (renumbered from art. 13.30); am. Acts 2009, 81st Leg., ch. 661 (H.B. 2153), § 1, effective September 1, 2009.)

### Art. 13.315. Failure to Comply with Sexually Violent Predator Civil Commitment Requirement.

An offense under Section 841.085, Health and Safety Code, may be prosecuted in the county in which any element of the offense occurs or in Montgomery County.
(Enacted by Acts 2007, 80th Leg., ch. 1219 (H.B. 2034), § 10, effective September 1, 2007.)

### Art. 13.32. Misapplication of Certain Property.

(a) An offender who misapplies property held as a fiduciary or property of a financial institution in one county and removes the property to another county may be prosecuted in the county where the offender misapplied the property, in any other county through or into which the offender removed the property, or, as applicable, in the county in which the fiduciary was appointed to serve.

(b) An offense related to misapplication of construction trust funds under Chapter 162, Property Code, must be prosecuted in the county where the construction project is located.
(Enacted by Acts 2005, 79th Leg., ch. 1275 (H.B. 2294), § 1, effective September 1, 2005; am. Acts 2007, 80th Leg., ch. 921 (H.B. 3167), § 17.001(9), effective September 1, 2007 (renumbered from art. 13.30).)

### Art. 13.34. Certain Offenses Committed Against a Child Committed to the Texas Youth Commission.

An offense described by Article 104.003(a) committed by an employee or officer of the Texas Youth Commission or a person providing services under a contract with the commission against a child committed to the commission may be prosecuted in:

(1) any county in which an element of the offense occurred; or

(2) Travis County.
(Enacted by Acts 2009, 81st Leg., ch. 947 (H.B. 3316), § 1, effective September 1, 2009; enacted by Acts 2009, 81st Leg., ch. 1187 (H.B. 3689), § 4.001, effective June 19, 2009.)

### Art. 13.35. Money Laundering.

Money laundering may be prosecuted in the county in which the offense was committed as provided by Article 13.18 or, if the prosecution is based on a criminal offense classified as a felony under the Tax Code, in any county in which venue is proper under the Tax Code for the offense.
(Enacted by Acts 2011, 82nd Leg., ch. 68 (S.B. 934), § 3, effective September 1, 2011.)

### Art. 13.36. Stalking.

The offense of stalking may be prosecuted in any county in which an element of the offense occurred.
(Enacted by Acts 2011, 82nd Leg., ch. 591 (S.B. 82), § 2, effective September 1, 2011.)

## Arrest, Commitment and Bail

## CHAPTER 14
## ARREST WITHOUT WARRANT

### Art. 14.01. Offense Within View.

(a) A peace officer or any other person, may, without a warrant, arrest an offender when the offense is committed in his presence or within his view, if the offense is one classed as a felony or as an offense against the public peace.

(b) A peace officer may arrest an offender without a warrant for any offense committed in his presence or within his view.
(Enacted by Acts 1965, 59th Leg., ch. 722 (S.B. 107), § 1, effective January 1, 1966; am. Acts 1967, 60th Leg., ch. 659 (S.B. 145), § 8, effective August 28, 1967.)

### Art. 14.02. Within View of Magistrate.

A peace officer may arrest, without warrant, when a felony or breach of the peace has been committed in the presence or within the view of a magistrate, and such magistrate verbally orders the arrest of the offender.
(Enacted by Acts 1965, 59th Leg., ch. 722 (S.B. 107), § 1, effective January 1, 1966.)

## Art. 14.03. Authority of Peace Officers.

(a) Any peace officer may arrest, without warrant:

(1) persons found in suspicious places and under circumstances which reasonably show that such persons have been guilty of some felony, violation of Title 9, Chapter 42, Penal Code, breach of the peace, or offense under Section 49.02, Penal Code, or threaten, or are about to commit some offense against the laws;

(2) persons who the peace officer has probable cause to believe have committed an assault resulting in bodily injury to another person and the peace officer has probable cause to believe that there is danger of further bodily injury to that person;

(3) persons who the peace officer has probable cause to believe have committed an offense defined by Section 25.07, Penal Code (violation of Protective Order), or by Section 38.112, Penal Code (violation of Protective Order issued on basis of sexual assault), if the offense is not committed in the presence of the peace officer;

(4) persons who the peace officer has probable cause to believe have committed an offense involving family violence;

(5) persons who the peace officer has probable cause to believe have prevented or interfered with an individual's ability to place a telephone call in an emergency, as defined by Section 42.062(d), Penal Code, if the offense is not committed in the presence of the peace officer; or

(6) a person who makes a statement to the peace officer that would be admissible against the person under Article 38.21 and establishes probable cause to believe that the person has committed a felony.

(b) A peace officer shall arrest, without a warrant, a person the peace officer has probable cause to believe has committed an offense under Section 25.07, Penal Code (violation of Protective Order), or Section 38.112, Penal Code (violation of Protective Order issued on basis of sexual assault), if the offense is committed in the presence of the peace officer.

(c) If reasonably necessary to verify an allegation of a violation of a protective order or of the commission of an offense involving family violence, a peace officer shall remain at the scene of the investigation to verify the allegation and to prevent the further commission of the violation or of family violence.

(d) A peace officer who is outside his jurisdiction may arrest, without warrant, a person who commits an offense within the officer's presence or view, if the offense is a felony, a violation of Chapter 42 or 49, Penal Code, or a breach of the peace. A peace officer making an arrest under this subsection shall, as soon as practicable after making the arrest, notify a law enforcement agency having jurisdiction where the arrest was made. The law enforcement agency shall then take custody of the person committing the offense and take the person before a magistrate in compliance with Article 14.06 of this code.

(e) The justification for conduct provided under Section 9.21, Penal Code, applies to a peace officer when the peace officer is performing a duty required by this article.

(f) In this article, "family violence" has the meaning assigned by Section 71.004, Family Code.

(g) (1) A peace officer listed in Subdivision (1), (2), or (5), Article 2.12, who is licensed under Chapter 1701, Occupations Code, and is outside of the officer's jurisdiction may arrest without a warrant a person who commits any offense within the officer's presence or view, other than a violation of Subtitle C, Title 7, Transportation Code.

(2) A peace officer listed in Subdivision (3), Article 2.12, who is licensed under Chapter 1701, Occupations Code, and is outside of the officer's jurisdiction may arrest without a warrant a person who commits any offense within the officer's presence or view, except that an officer described in this subdivision who is outside of that officer's jurisdiction may arrest a person for a violation of Subtitle C, Title 7, Transportation Code, only if the offense is committed in the county or counties in which the municipality employing the peace officer is located.

(3) A peace officer making an arrest under this subsection shall as soon as practicable after making the arrest notify a law enforcement agency having jurisdiction where the arrest was made. The law enforcement agency shall then take custody of:

(A) the person committing the offense and take the person before a magistrate in compliance with Article 14.06; and

(B) any property seized during or after the arrest as if the property had been seized by a peace officer of that law enforcement agency.

(Enacted by Acts 1965, 59th Leg., ch. 722 (S.B. 107), § 1, effective January 1, 1966; am. Acts 1967, 60th Leg., ch. 659 (S.B. 145), § 9, effective August 28, 1967; am. Acts 1981, 67th Leg., ch.

442 (H.B. 1743), § 1, effective August 31, 1981; am. Acts 1985, 69th Leg., ch. 583 (S.B. 869), § 2, effective September 1, 1985; am. Acts 1987, 70th Leg., ch. 68 (S.B. 82), § 1, effective September 1, 1987; am. Acts 1989, 71st Leg., ch. 740 (H.B. 1231), § 1, effective August 28, 1989; am. Acts 1991, 72nd Leg., ch. 542 (H.B. 1563), § 9, effective September 1, 1991; am. Acts 1993, 73rd Leg., ch. 900 (S.B. 1067), § 3.02, effective September 1, 1994; am. Acts 1995, 74th Leg., ch. 76 (S.B. 959), § 14.17, effective September 1, 1995; am. Acts 1995, 74th Leg., ch. 829 (H.B. 2614), § 1, effective August 28, 1995; am. Acts 1999, 76th Leg., ch. 62 (S.B. 1368), § 3.02, effective September 1, 1999; am. Acts 1999, 76th Leg., ch. 210 (H.B. 1121), § 2, effective May 24, 1999; am. Acts 2003, 78th Leg., ch. 460 (H.B. 778), § 2, effective September 1, 2003; am. Acts 2003, 78th Leg., ch. 836 (S.B. 433), § 2, effective September 1, 2003; am. Acts 2003, 78th Leg., ch. 897 (S.B. 840), § 1, effective September 1, 2003; am. Acts 2003, 78th Leg., ch. 989 (S.B. 1896), § 1, effective September 1, 2003; am. Acts 2003, 78th Leg., ch. 1164 (S.B. 176), § 2, effective September 1, 2003; am. Acts 2003, 78th Leg., ch. 1276 (H.B. 3507), § 7.002(d), effective September 1, 2003; am. Acts 2005, 79th Leg., ch. 728 (H.B. 2018), § 4.002, effective September 1, 2005; am. Acts 2005, 79th Leg., ch. 788 (S.B. 91), §§ 4, 5, effective September 1, 2005; am. Acts 2005, 79th Leg., ch. 847 (S.B. 907), § 1, effective September 1, 2005; am. Acts 2005, 79th Leg., ch. 1015 (H.B. 915), § 1, effective September 1, 2005.)

### Art. 14.031. Public Intoxication.

(a) In lieu of arresting an individual who is not a child, as defined by Section 51.02, Family Code, and who commits an offense under Section 49.02, Penal Code, a peace officer may release the individual if:

(1) the officer believes detention in a penal facility is unnecessary for the protection of the individual or others; and

(2) the individual:

(A) is released to the care of an adult who agrees to assume responsibility for the individual; or

(B) verbally consents to voluntary treatment for chemical dependency in a program in a treatment facility licensed and approved by the Texas Commission on Alcohol and Drug Abuse, and the program admits the individual for treatment.

(b) A magistrate may release from custody an individual who is not a child, as defined by Section 51.02, Family Code, and who is arrested under Section 49.02, Penal Code, if the magistrate determines the individual meets the conditions required for release in lieu of arrest under Subsection (a) of this article.

(c) The release of an individual under Subsection (a) or (b) of this article to an alcohol or drug treatment program may not be considered by a peace officer or magistrate in determining whether the individual should be released to such a program for a subsequent incident or arrest under Section 49.02, Penal Code.

(d) A peace officer and the agency or political subdivision that employs the peace officer may not be held liable for damage to persons or property that results from the actions of an individual released under Subsection (a) or (b) of this article.

(Enacted by Acts 1993, 73rd Leg., ch. 900 (S.B. 1067), § 1.04, effective September 1, 1994; am. Acts 2009, 81st Leg., ch. 311 (H.B. 558), § 1, effective September 1, 2009.)

### Art. 14.04. When Felony Has Been Committed.

Where it is shown by satisfactory proof to a peace officer, upon the representation of a credible person, that a felony has been committed, and that the offender is about to escape, so that there is no time to procure a warrant, such peace officer may, without warrant, pursue and arrest the accused.

(Enacted by Acts 1965, 59th Leg., ch. 722 (S.B. 107), § 1, effective January 1, 1966.)

### Art. 14.05. Rights of Officer.

In each case enumerated where arrests may be lawfully made without warrant, the officer or person making the arrest is justified in adopting all the measures which he might adopt in cases of arrest under warrant, except that an officer making an arrest without a warrant may not enter a residence to make the arrest unless:

(1) a person who resides in the residence consents to the entry; or

(2) exigent circumstances require that the officer making the arrest enter the residence without the consent of a resident or without a warrant.

(Enacted by Acts 1965, 59th Leg., ch. 722 (S.B. 107), § 1, effective January 1, 1966; am. Acts 1987, 70th Leg., ch. 532 (H.B. 1175), § 1, effective August 31, 1987.)

## Art. 14.051. Arrest by Peace Officer from Other Jurisdiction.

(a) A peace officer commissioned and authorized by another state to make arrests for felonies who is in fresh pursuit of a person for the purpose of arresting that person for a felony may continue the pursuit into this state and arrest the person.

(b) In this article, "fresh pursuit" means a pursuit without unreasonable delay by a peace officer of a person the officer reasonably suspects has committed a felony.

(Enacted by Acts 1989, 71st Leg., ch. 997 (H.B. 832), § 2, effective August 28, 1989.)

## Art. 14.06. Must Take Offender Before Magistrate.

(a) Except as otherwise provided by this article, in each case enumerated in this Code, the person making the arrest or the person having custody of the person arrested shall take the person arrested or have him taken without unnecessary delay, but not later than 48 hours after the person is arrested, before the magistrate who may have ordered the arrest, before some magistrate of the county where the arrest was made without an order, or, to provide more expeditiously to the person arrested the warnings described by Article 15.17 of this Code, before a magistrate in any other county of this state. The magistrate shall immediately perform the duties described in Article 15.17 of this Code.

(b) A peace officer who is charging a person, including a child, with committing an offense that is a Class C misdemeanor, other than an offense under Section 49.02, Penal Code, may, instead of taking the person before a magistrate, issue a citation to the person that contains written notice of the time and place the person must appear before a magistrate, the name and address of the person charged, the offense charged, and the following admonishment, in boldfaced or underlined type or in capital letters:

"If you are convicted of a misdemeanor offense involving violence where you are or were a spouse, intimate partner, parent, or guardian of the victim or are or were involved in another, similar relationship with the victim, it may be unlawful for you to possess or purchase a firearm, including a handgun or long gun, or ammunition, pursuant to federal law under 18 U.S.C. Section 922(g)(9) or Section 46.04(b), Texas Penal Code. If you have any questions whether these laws make it illegal for you to possess or purchase a firearm, you should consult an attorney."

(c) If the person resides in the county where the offense occurred, a peace officer who is charging a person with committing an offense that is a Class A or B misdemeanor may, instead of taking the person before a magistrate, issue a citation to the person that contains written notice of the time and place the person must appear before a magistrate of this state as described by Subsection (a), the name and address of the person charged, and the offense charged.

(d) Subsection (c) applies only to a person charged with committing an offense under:

(1) Section 481.121, Health and Safety Code, if the offense is punishable under Subsection (b)(1) or (2) of that section;

(1-a) Section 481.1161, Health and Safety Code, if the offense is punishable under Subsection (b)(1) or (2) of that section;

(2) Section 28.03, Penal Code, if the offense is punishable under Subsection (b)(2) of that section;

(3) Section 28.08, Penal Code, if the offense is punishable under Subsection (b)(1) of that section;

(4) Section 31.03, Penal Code, if the offense is punishable under Subsection (e)(2)(A) of that section;

(5) Section 31.04, Penal Code, if the offense is punishable under Subsection (e)(2) of that section;

(6) Section 38.114, Penal Code, if the offense is punishable as a Class B misdemeanor; or

(7) Section 521.457, Transportation Code.

(Enacted by Acts 1965, 59th Leg., ch. 722 (S.B. 107), § 1, effective January 1, 1966; am. Acts 1967, 60th Leg., ch. 659 (S.B. 145), § 10, effective August 28, 1967; am. Acts 1987, 70th Leg., ch. 455 (H.B. 249), § 1, effective August 31, 1987; am. Acts 1991, 72nd Leg., ch. 84 (S.B. 883), § 1, effective September 1, 1991; am. Acts 1993, 73rd Leg., ch. 900 (S.B. 1067), § 1.05, effective September 1, 1994; am. Acts 1995, 74th Leg., ch. 262 (H.B. 327), § 81, effective January 1, 1996; am. Acts 2001, 77th Leg., ch. 906 (S.B. 7), § 3, effective January 1, 2002; am. Acts 2005, 79th Leg., ch. 1094 (H.B. 2120), § 1, effective September 1, 2005; am. Acts 2007, 80th Leg., ch. 320 (H.B. 2391), § 1, effective September 1, 2007; am. Acts 2009, 81st Leg., ch. 1379 (S.B. 1236), § 1, effective September 1, 2009; am. Acts 2011, 82nd Leg., ch. 170 (S.B. 331), § 7, effective September 1, 2011.)

Criminal Procedure

# CHAPTER 15
# ARREST UNDER WARRANT

## Art. 15.01. Warrant of Arrest.

A "warrant of arrest" is a written order from a magistrate, directed to a peace officer or some other person specially named, commanding him to take the body of the person accused of an offense, to be dealt with according to law.

(Enacted by Acts 1965, 59th Leg., ch. 722 (S.B. 107), § 1, effective January 1, 1966.)

## Art. 15.02. Requisites of Warrant.

It issues in the name of "The State of Texas", and shall be sufficient, without regard to form, if it have these substantial requisites:

1. It must specify the name of the person whose arrest is ordered, if it be known, if unknown, then some reasonably definite description must be given of him.

2. It must state that the person is accused of some offense against the laws of the State, naming the offense.

3. It must be signed by the magistrate, and his office be named in the body of the warrant, or in connection with his signature.

(Enacted by Acts 1965, 59th Leg., ch. 722 (S.B. 107), § 1, effective January 1, 1966.)

## Art. 15.03. Magistrate May Issue Warrant or Summons.

(a) A magistrate may issue a warrant of arrest or a summons:

1. In any case in which he is by law authorized to order verbally the arrest of an offender;

2. When any person shall make oath before the magistrate that another has committed some offense against the laws of the State; and

3. In any case named in this Code where he is specially authorized to issue warrants of arrest.

(b) A summons may be issued in any case where a warrant may be issued, and shall be in the same form as the warrant except that it shall summon the defendant to appear before a magistrate at a stated time and place. The summons shall be served upon a defendant by delivering a copy to him personally, or by leaving it at his dwelling house or usual place of abode with some person of suitable age and discretion then residing therein or by mailing it to the defendant's last known address. If a defendant fails to appear in response to the summons a warrant shall be issued.

(c) For purposes of Subdivision 2, Subsection (a), a person may appear before the magistrate in person or the person's image may be presented to the magistrate through an electronic broadcast system.

(d) A recording of the communication between the person and the magistrate must be made if the person's image is presented through an electronic broadcast system under Subsection (c). If the defendant is charged with the offense, the recording must be preserved until:

(1) the defendant is acquitted of the offense; or

(2) all appeals relating to the offense have been exhausted.

(e) The counsel for the defendant may obtain a copy of the recording on payment of an amount reasonably necessary to cover the costs of reproducing the recording.

(f) In this article, "electronic broadcast system" means a two-way electronic communication of image and sound between a person and magistrate and includes secure Internet videoconferencing.

(Enacted by Acts 1965, 59th Leg., ch. 722 (S.B. 107), § 1, effective January 1, 1966; am. Acts 2011, 82nd Leg., ch. 248 (H.B. 976), § 1, effective June 17, 2011.)

## Art. 15.04. Complaint.

The affidavit made before the magistrate or district or county attorney is called a "complaint" if it charges the commission of an offense.
(Enacted by Acts 1965, 59th Leg., ch. 722 (S.B. 107), § 1, effective January 1, 1966.)

## Art. 15.05. Requisites of Complaint.

The complaint shall be sufficient, without regard to form, if it have these substantial requisites:

1. It must state the name of the accused, if known, and if not known, must give some reasonably definite description of him.

2. It must show that the accused has committed some offense against the laws of the State, either directly or that the affiant has good reason to believe, and does believe, that the accused has committed such offense.

3. It must state the time and place of the commission of the offense, as definitely as can be done by the affiant.

4. It must be signed by the affiant by writing his name or affixing his mark.

(Enacted by Acts 1965, 59th Leg., ch. 722 (S.B. 107), § 1, effective January 1, 1966.)

## Art. 15.051. Requiring Polygraph Examination of Complainant Prohibited.

(a) A peace officer or an attorney representing the state may not require a polygraph examination of a person who charges or seeks to charge in a complaint the commission of an offense under Section 21.02, 21.11, 22.011, 22.021, or 25.02, Penal Code.

(b) If a peace officer or an attorney representing the state requests a polygraph examination of a person who charges or seeks to charge in a complaint the commission of an offense listed in Subsection (a), the officer or attorney must inform the complainant that the examination is not required and that a complaint may not be dismissed solely:

(1) because a complainant did not take a polygraph examination; or

(2) on the basis of the results of a polygraph examination taken by the complainant.

(c) A peace officer or an attorney representing the state may not take a polygraph examination of a person who charges or seeks to charge the commission of an offense listed in Subsection (a) unless the officer or attorney provides the information in Subsection (b) to the person and the person signs a statement indicating the person understands the information.

(d) A complaint may not be dismissed solely:

(1) because a complainant did not take a polygraph examination; or

(2) on the basis of the results of a polygraph examination taken by the complainant.

(Enacted by Acts 1995, 74th Leg., ch. 24 (S.B. 222), § 1, effective September 1, 1995; am. Acts 1997, 75th Leg., ch. 608 (S.B. 467), § 1, effective September 1, 1997; am. Acts 2007, 80th Leg., ch. 593 (H.B. 8), § 3.07, effective September 1, 2007.)

## Art. 15.06. Warrant Extends to Every Part of the State.

A warrant of arrest, issued by any county or district clerk, or by any magistrate (except mayors of an incorporated city or town), shall extend to any part of the State; and any peace officer to whom said warrant is directed, or into whose hands the same has been transferred, shall be authorized to execute the same in any county in this State.
(Enacted by Acts 1965, 59th Leg., ch. 722 (S.B. 107), § 1, effective January 1, 1966; am. Acts 1985, 69th Leg., ch. 666 (S.B. 1257), § 1, effective June 14, 1985.)

## Art. 15.07. Warrant Issued by Other Magistrate.

When a warrant of arrest is issued by any mayor of an incorporated city or town, it cannot be executed in another county than the one in which it issues, except:

1. It be endorsed by a judge of a court of record, in which case it may be executed anywhere in the State; or

2. If it be endorsed by any magistrate in the county in which the accused is found, it may be executed in such county. The endorsement may be: "Let this warrant be executed in the county of ...". Or, if the endorsement is made by a judge of a court of record, then the endorsement may be: "Let this warrant be executed in any county of the State of Texas". Any other words of the same meaning will be sufficient. The endorsement shall be dated, and signed officially by the magistrate making it.

(Enacted by Acts 1965, 59th Leg., ch. 722 (S.B. 107), § 1, effective January 1, 1966; am. Acts 1985, 69th Leg., ch. 666 (S.B. 1257), § 2, effective June 14, 1985.)

## Art. 15.08. Warrant May Be Forwarded.

A warrant of arrest may be forwarded by any method that ensures the transmission of a duplicate of the original warrant, including secure facsimile transmission or other secure electronic means or a telegraph transmission from any telegraph office to another in this State. If issued by any magistrate named in Article 15.06, the peace officer receiving the same shall execute it without delay. If it be issued by any other magistrate than is named in Article 15.06, the peace officer receiving the same shall proceed with it to the nearest magistrate of the peace officer's county, who shall endorse thereon, in substance, these words:

"Let this warrant be executed in the county of _____", which endorsement shall be dated and signed officially by the magistrate making the same.

(Enacted by Acts 1965, 59th Leg., ch. 722 (S.B. 107), § 1, effective January 1, 1966; am. Acts 2009, 81st Leg., ch. 345 (H.B. 1060), § 1, effective September 1, 2009.)

### Art. 15.09. Complaint May Be Forwarded.

A complaint in accordance with Article 15.05, may be forwarded as provided by Article 15.08 to any magistrate in the State; and the magistrate who receives the same shall forthwith issue a warrant for the arrest of the accused; and the accused, when arrested, shall be dealt with as provided in this Chapter in similar cases.

(Enacted by Acts 1965, 59th Leg., ch. 722 (S.B. 107), § 1, effective January 1, 1966; am. Acts 2009, 81st Leg., ch. 345 (H.B. 1060), § 1, effective September 1, 2009.)

### Art. 15.10. Copy to Be Deposited.

A certified copy of the original warrant or complaint, certified to by the magistrate issuing or taking the same, shall be deposited with the manager of the telegraph office from which the same is to be forwarded, taking precedence over other business, to the place of its destination or to the telegraph office nearest thereto, precisely as it is written, including the certificate of the seal attached.

(Enacted by Acts 1965, 59th Leg., ch. 722 (S.B. 107), § 1, effective January 1, 1966.)

### Art. 15.11. Duty of Telegraph Manager.

When a warrant or complaint is received at a telegraph office for delivery, it shall be delivered to the party to whom it is addressed as soon as practicable, written on the proper blanks of the telegraph company and certified to by the man-

ager of the telegraph office as being a true and correct copy of the warrant or complaint received at his office.

(Enacted by Acts 1965, 59th Leg., ch. 722 (S.B. 107), § 1, effective January 1, 1966.)

### Art. 15.12. Warrant or Complaint Must Be Under Seal.

No manager of a telegraph office shall receive and forward a warrant or complaint unless the same shall be certified to under the seal of a court of record or by a justice of the peace, with the certificate under seal of the district or county clerk of his county that he is a legally qualified justice of the peace of such county; nor shall it be lawful for any magistrate to endorse a warrant received by telegraph, or issue a warrant upon a complaint received by telegraph, unless all the requirements of the law in relation thereto have been fully complied with.

(Enacted by Acts 1965, 59th Leg., ch. 722 (S.B. 107), § 1, effective January 1, 1966.)

### Art. 15.13. Telegram Prepaid.

Whoever presents a warrant or complaint to the manager of a telegraph office to be forwarded by telegraph, shall pay for the same in advance, unless, by the rules of the company, it may be sent collect.

(Enacted by Acts 1965, 59th Leg., ch. 722 (S.B. 107), § 1, effective January 1, 1966.)

### Art. 15.14. Arrest After Dismissal Because of Delay.

If a prosecution of a defendant is dismissed under Article 32.01, the defendant may be rearrested for the same criminal conduct alleged in the dismissed prosecution only upon presentation of indictment or information for the offense and the issuance of a capias subsequent to the indictment or information.

(Enacted by Acts 1997, 75th Leg., ch. 289 (H.B. 749), § 3, effective May 26, 1997.)

### Art. 15.15. Private Person Executing Warrant [Repealed].

Repealed by Acts 1991, 72nd Leg., ch. 446 (S.B. 411), § 2, effective June 11, 1991.

### Art. 15.16. How Warrant Is Executed.

(a) The officer or person executing a warrant of arrest shall without unnecessary delay take the person or have him taken before the magistrate who issued the warrant or before the magistrate named in the warrant, if the magistrate is in the same county where the person is arrested. If the issuing or named magistrate is in another county, the person arrested shall without unnecessary delay be taken before some magistrate in the county in which he was arrested.

(b) Notwithstanding Subsection (a), to provide more expeditiously to the person arrested the warnings described by Article 15.17, the officer or person executing the arrest warrant may as permitted by that article take the person arrested before a magistrate in a county other than the county of arrest.

(Enacted by Acts 1965, 59th Leg., ch. 722 (S.B. 107), § 1, effective January 1, 1966; am. Acts 1967, 60th Leg., ch. 659 (S.B. 145), § 11, effective August 28, 1967; am. Acts 2005, 79th Leg., ch. 1094 (H.B. 2120), § 2, effective September 1, 2005.)

## Art. 15.17. Duties of Arresting Officer and Magistrate.

(a) In each case enumerated in this Code, the person making the arrest or the person having custody of the person arrested shall without unnecessary delay, but not later than 48 hours after the person is arrested, take the person arrested or have him taken before some magistrate of the county where the accused was arrested or, to provide more expeditiously to the person arrested the warnings described by this article, before a magistrate in any other county of this state. The arrested person may be taken before the magistrate in person or the image of the arrested person may be presented to the magistrate by means of an electronic broadcast system. The magistrate shall inform in clear language the person arrested, either in person or through the electronic broadcast system, of the accusation against him and of any affidavit filed therewith, of his right to retain counsel, of his right to remain silent, of his right to have an attorney present during any interview with peace officers or attorneys representing the state, of his right to terminate the interview at any time, and of his right to have an examining trial. The magistrate shall also inform the person arrested of the person's right to request the appointment of counsel if the person cannot afford counsel. The magistrate shall inform the person arrested of the procedures for requesting appointment of counsel. If the person does not speak and understand the English language or is deaf, the magistrate shall inform the person in a manner consistent

with Articles 38.30 and 38.31, as appropriate. The magistrate shall ensure that reasonable assistance in completing the necessary forms for requesting appointment of counsel is provided to the person at the same time. If the person arrested is indigent and requests appointment of counsel and if the magistrate is authorized under Article 26.04 to appoint counsel for indigent defendants in the county, the magistrate shall appoint counsel in accordance with Article 1.051. If the magistrate is not authorized to appoint counsel, the magistrate shall without unnecessary delay, but not later than 24 hours after the person arrested requests appointment of counsel, transmit, or cause to be transmitted to the court or to the courts' designee authorized under Article 26.04 to appoint counsel in the county, the forms requesting the appointment of counsel. The magistrate shall also inform the person arrested that he is not required to make a statement and that any statement made by him may be used against him. The magistrate shall allow the person arrested reasonable time and opportunity to consult counsel and shall, after determining whether the person is currently on bail for a separate criminal offense, admit the person arrested to bail if allowed by law. A recording of the communication between the arrested person and the magistrate shall be made. The recording shall be preserved until the earlier of the following dates: (1) the date on which the pretrial hearing ends; or (2) the 91st day after the date on which the recording is made if the person is charged with a misdemeanor or the 120th day after the date on which the recording is made if the person is charged with a felony. The counsel for the defendant may obtain a copy of the recording on payment of a reasonable amount to cover costs of reproduction. For purposes of this subsection, "electronic broadcast system" means a two-way electronic communication of image and sound between the arrested person and the magistrate and includes secure Internet videoconferencing.

(b) After an accused charged with a misdemeanor punishable by fine only is taken before a magistrate under Subsection (a) and the magistrate has identified the accused with certainty, the magistrate may release the accused without bond and order the accused to appear at a later date for arraignment in the applicable justice court or municipal court. The order must state in writing the time, date, and place of the arraignment, and the magistrate must sign the order. The accused shall receive a copy of the order on release. If an accused fails to appear as required by the order, the judge of the court in which the accused is required to appear shall issue a warrant for the arrest of the accused. If the accused is arrested and brought before the judge, the judge may admit the accused to bail, and in admitting the accused to bail, the judge should set as the amount of bail an amount double that generally set for the offense for which the accused was arrested. This subsection does not apply to an accused who has previously been convicted of a felony or a misdemeanor other than a misdemeanor punishable by fine only.

(c) When a deaf accused is taken before a magistrate under this article or Article 14.06 of this Code, an interpreter appointed by the magistrate qualified and sworn as provided in Article 38.31 of this Code shall interpret the warning required by those articles in a language that the accused can understand, including but not limited to sign language.

(d) If a magistrate determines that a person brought before the magistrate after an arrest authorized by Article 14.051 of this code was arrested unlawfully, the magistrate shall release the person from custody. If the magistrate determines that the arrest was lawful, the person arrested is considered a fugitive from justice for the purposes of Article 51.13 of this code, and the disposition of the person is controlled by that article.

(e) In each case in which a person arrested is taken before a magistrate as required by Subsection (a), a record shall be made of:

(1) the magistrate informing the person of the person's right to request appointment of counsel;

(2) the magistrate asking the person whether the person wants to request appointment of counsel; and

(3) whether the person requested appointment of counsel.

(f) A record required under Subsection (e) may consist of written forms, electronic recordings, or other documentation as authorized by procedures adopted in the county under Article 26.04(a).

(g) If a person charged with an offense punishable as a misdemeanor appears before a magistrate in compliance with a citation issued under Article 14.06(b) or (c), the magistrate shall perform the duties imposed by this article in the same manner as if the person had been arrested and brought before the magistrate by a peace officer. After the magistrate performs the duties imposed by this article, the magistrate except for good cause shown may release the person on personal bond. If a person who was issued a citation under Article 14.06(c) fails to appear as required by that citation, the magistrate before which the person is required to appear shall issue a warrant for the arrest of the accused.

(Enacted by Acts 1965, 59th Leg., ch. 722 (S.B. 107), § 1, effective January 1, 1966; am. Acts 1967, 60th Leg., ch. 659 (S.B. 145), § 12, effective August 28, 1967; am. Acts 1979, 66th Leg., ch. 186 (H.B. 1521), § 3, effective May 15, 1979; am. Acts 1987, 70th Leg., ch. 455 (H.B. 249), § 2, effective August 31, 1987; am. Acts 1989, 71st Leg., ch. 467 (H.B. 1929), § 1, effective August 28, 1989; am. Acts 1989, 71st Leg., ch. 977 (H.B. 646), §§ 1, 3, effective August 28, 1989; am. Acts 1991, 72nd Leg., ch. 16 (S.B. 232), § 19.01(2), effective August 26, 1991; am. Acts 2001, 77th Leg., ch. 906 (S.B. 7), § 4, effective January 1, 2002; am. Acts 2001, 77th Leg., ch. 1281 (S.B. 1807), § 1, effective September 1, 2001; am. Acts 2001, 77th Leg., ch. 906 (S.B. 7), § 4, effective January 1, 2002; am. Acts 2005, 79th Leg., ch. 1094 (H.B. 2120), § 3, effective September 1, 2005; am. Acts 2007, 80th Leg., ch. 320 (H.B. 2391), § 2, effective September 1, 2007; am. Acts 2009, 81st Leg., ch. 735 (S.B. 415), § 1, effective September 1, 2009.)

## Art. 15.18. Arrest for Out-of-County Offense.

(a) A person arrested under a warrant issued in a county other than the one in which the person is arrested shall be taken before a magistrate of the county where the arrest takes place or, to provide more expeditiously to the arrested person the warnings described by Article 15.17, before a magistrate in any other county of this state, including the county where the warrant was issued. The magistrate shall:

(1) take bail, if allowed by law, and, if without jurisdiction, immediately transmit the bond taken to the court having jurisdiction of the offense; or

(2) in the case of a person arrested under warrant for an offense punishable by fine only, accept a written plea of guilty or nolo contendere, set a fine, determine costs, accept payment of the fine and costs, give credit for time served, determine indigency, or, on satisfaction of the judgment, discharge the defendant, as the case may indicate.

(b) Before the 11th business day after the date a magistrate accepts a written plea of guilty or nolo contendere in a case under Subsection (a)(2), the magistrate shall, if without jurisdiction, transmit to the court having jurisdiction of the offense:

    (1) the written plea;

    (2) any orders entered in the case; and

    (3) any fine or costs collected in the case.

(c) The arrested person may be taken before a magistrate by means of an electronic broadcast system as provided by and subject to the requirements of Article 15.17.

(d) This article does not apply to an arrest made pursuant to a capias pro fine issued under Chapter 43 or Article 45.045.

(Enacted by Acts 1965, 59th Leg., ch. 722 (S.B. 107), § 1, effective January 1, 1966; am. Acts 2001, 77th Leg., ch. 145 (S.B. 219), § 2, effective September 1, 2001; am. Acts 2005, 79th Leg., ch. 1094 (H.B. 2120), § 4, effective September 1, 2005; am. Acts 2007, 80th Leg., ch. 1263 (H.B. 3060), § 1, effective September 1, 2007.)

### Art. 15.19. Notice of Arrest.

(a) If the arrested person fails or refuses to give bail, as provided in Article 15.18, the arrested person shall be committed to the jail of the county where the person was arrested; and the magistrate committing the arrested person shall immediately provide notice to the sheriff of the county in which the offense is alleged to have been committed regarding:

    (1) the arrest and commitment, which notice may be given by telegraph, mail, or other written means or by secure facsimile transmission or other secure electronic means; and

    (2) whether the person was also arrested under a warrant issued under Section 508.251, Government Code.

(b) If a person is arrested and taken before a magistrate in a county other than the county in which the arrest is made and if the person is remanded to custody, the person may be confined in a jail in the county in which the magistrate serves for a period of not more than 72 hours after the arrest before being transferred to the county jail of the county in which the arrest occurred.

(Enacted by Acts 1965, 59th Leg., ch. 722 (S.B. 107), § 1, effective January 1, 1966; am. Acts 1987, 70th Leg., 2nd C.S., ch. 40 (H.B. 109), § 1, effective October 20, 1987; am. Acts 2005, 79th Leg., ch. 1094 (H.B. 2120), § 5, effective September 1, 2005; am. Acts 2007, 80th Leg., ch. 1308 (S.B. 909), § 1, effective June 15, 2007; am. Acts 2009, 81st Leg., ch. 345 (H.B. 1060), § 2, effective September 1, 2009.)

### Art. 15.20. Duty of Sheriff Receiving Notice.

(a) Subject to Subsection (b), the sheriff receiving the notice of arrest and commitment under Article 15.19 shall forthwith go or send for the arrested person and have the arrested person brought before the proper court or magistrate.

(b) A sheriff who receives notice under Article 15.19(a)(2) of a warrant issued under Section 508.251, Government Code, shall have the arrested person brought before the proper magistrate or court before the 11th day after the date the person is committed to the jail of the county in which the person was arrested.

(Enacted by Acts 1965, 59th Leg., ch. 722 (S.B. 107), § 1, effective January 1, 1966; am. Acts 2007, 80th Leg., ch. 1308 (S.B. 909), § 2, effective June 15, 2007.)

### Art. 15.21. Prisoner Discharged If Not Timely Demanded.

If the proper office of the county where the offense is alleged to have been committed does not demand the arrested person and take charge of the arrested person before the 11th day after the date the person is committed to the jail of the county in which the person is arrested, the arrested person shall be discharged from custody.

(Enacted by Acts 1965, 59th Leg., ch. 722 (S.B. 107), § 1, effective January 1, 1966; am. Acts 2007, 80th Leg., ch. 1308 (S.B. 909), § 2, effective June 15, 2007.)

### Art. 15.22. When a Person Is Arrested.

A person is arrested when he has been actually placed under restraint or taken into custody by an officer or person executing a warrant of arrest, or by an officer or person arresting without a warrant.

(Enacted by Acts 1965, 59th Leg., ch. 722 (S.B. 107), § 1, effective January 1, 1966.)

### Art. 15.23. Time of Arrest.

An arrest may be made on any day or at any time of the day or night.

(Enacted by Acts 1965, 59th Leg., ch. 722 (S.B. 107), § 1, effective January 1, 1966.)

### Art. 15.24. What Force May Be Used.

In making an arrest, all reasonable means are permitted to be used to effect it. No greater force, however, shall be resorted to than is necessary to secure the arrest and detention of the accused.

(Enacted by Acts 1965, 59th Leg., ch. 722 (S.B. 107), § 1, effective January 1, 1966.)

Criminal Procedure

## Art. 15.25. May Break Door.

In case of felony, the officer may break down the door of any house for the purpose of making an arrest, if he be refused admittance after giving notice of his authority and purpose.

(Enacted by Acts 1965, 59th Leg., ch. 722 (S.B. 107), § 1, effective January 1, 1966.)

## Art. 15.26. Authority to Arrest Must Be Made Known.

In executing a warrant of arrest, it shall always be made known to the accused under what authority the arrest is made. The warrant shall be executed by the arrest of the defendant. The officer need not have the warrant in his possession at the time of the arrest, provided the warrant was issued under the provisions of this Code, but upon request he shall show the warrant to the defendant as soon as possible. If the officer does not have the warrant in his possession at the time of arrest he shall then inform the defendant of the offense charged and of the fact that a warrant has been issued. The arrest warrant, and any affidavit presented to the magistrate in support of the issuance of the warrant, is public information, and beginning immediately when the warrant is executed the magistrate's clerk shall make a copy of the warrant and the affidavit available for public inspection in the clerk's office during normal business hours. A person may request the clerk to provide copies of the warrant and affidavit on payment of the cost of providing the copies.

(Enacted by Acts 1965, 59th Leg., ch. 722 (S.B. 107), § 1, effective January 1, 1966; am. Acts 1967, 60th Leg., ch. 659 (S.B. 145), § 13, effective August 28, 1967; am. Acts 2003, 78th Leg., ch. 390 (H.B. 13), § 1, effective September 1, 2003.)

## Art. 15.27. Notification to Schools Required.

(a) A law enforcement agency that arrests any person or refers a child to the office or official designated by the juvenile board who the agency believes is enrolled as a student in a public primary or secondary school, for an offense listed in Subsection (h), shall attempt to ascertain whether the person is so enrolled. If the law enforcement agency ascertains that the individual is enrolled as a student in a public primary or secondary school, the head of the agency or a person designated by the head of the agency shall orally notify the superintendent or a person designated by the superintendent in the school district in which the student is enrolled of that arrest or referral within 24 hours after the arrest or referral is made, or before the next school day, whichever is earlier. If the law enforcement agency cannot ascertain whether the individual is enrolled as a student, the head of the agency or a person designated by the head of the agency shall orally notify the superintendent or a person designated by the superintendent in the school district in which the student is believed to be enrolled of that arrest or detention within 24 hours after the arrest or detention, or before the next school day, whichever is earlier. If the individual is a student, the superintendent or the superintendent's designee shall immediately notify all instructional and support personnel who have responsibility for supervision of the student. All personnel shall keep the information received in this subsection confidential. The State Board for Educator Certification may revoke or suspend the certification of personnel who intentionally violate this subsection. Within seven days after the date the oral notice is given, the head of the law enforcement agency or the person designated by the head of the agency shall mail written notification, marked "PERSONAL and CONFIDENTIAL" on the mailing envelope, to the superintendent or the person designated by the superintendent. The written notification must include the facts contained in the oral notification, the name of the person who was orally notified, and the date and time of the oral notification. Both the oral and written notice shall contain sufficient details of the arrest or referral and the acts allegedly committed by the student to enable the superintendent or the superintendent's designee to determine whether there is a reasonable belief that the student has engaged in conduct defined as a felony offense by the Penal Code. The information contained in the notice shall be considered by the superintendent or the superintendent's designee in making such a determination.

(a-1) The superintendent or a person designated by the superintendent in the school district shall send to a school district employee having direct supervisory responsibility over the student the information contained in the confidential notice under Subsection (a).

(b) On conviction, deferred prosecution, or deferred adjudication or an adjudication of delinquent conduct of an individual enrolled as a student in a public primary or secondary school, for an offense or for any conduct listed in Subsection (h) of this article, the office of the prosecuting attorney acting in the case shall orally notify the superintendent or a person designated by the superintendent in the school district in which the student is enrolled of the conviction or adjudication and whether the student is required to register as a sex offender under Chapter 62. Oral notification must be given within 24 hours of the time of the order or before the next school day, whichever is earlier. The superintendent shall, within 24 hours of receiving notification from the office of the prosecuting attorney, or before the next school day, whichever is earlier, notify all instructional and support personnel who have regular contact with the student. Within seven days after the date the oral notice is given, the office of the prosecuting attorney shall mail written notice, which must contain a statement of the offense of which the individual is convicted or on which the adjudication, deferred adjudication, or deferred prosecution is grounded and a statement of whether the student is required to register as a sex offender under Chapter 62.

(c) A parole, probation, or community supervision office, including a community supervision and corrections department, a juvenile probation department, the paroles division of the Texas Department of Criminal Justice, and the Texas Youth Commission, having jurisdiction over a student described by Subsection (a), (b), or (e) who transfers from a school or is subsequently removed from a school and later returned to a school or school district other than the one the student was enrolled in when the arrest, referral to a juvenile court, conviction, or adjudication occurred shall within 24 hours of learning of the student's transfer or reenrollment, or before the next school day, whichever is earlier, notify the superintendent or a person designated by the superintendent of the school district to which the student transfers or is returned or, in the case of a private school, the principal or a school employee designated by the principal of the school to which the student transfers or is returned of the arrest or referral in a manner similar to that provided for by Subsection (a) or (e)(1), or of the conviction or delinquent adjudication in a manner similar to that provided for by Subsection (b) or (e)(2). The superintendent of the school district to which the student transfers or is returned or, in the case of a private school, the principal of the school to which the student transfers or is returned shall, within 24 hours of receiving notification under this subsection or before the next school day, whichever is earlier, notify all instructional and support personnel who have regular contact with the student.

(d) [Repealed by Acts 2007, 80th Leg., ch. 1240 (H.B. 2532), § 5, effective June 15, 2007 and Acts 2007, 80th Leg., ch. 1291 (S.B. 6), § 8, effective September 1, 2007.]

(e) (1) A law enforcement agency that arrests, or refers to a juvenile court under Chapter 52, Family Code, an individual who the law enforcement agency knows or believes is enrolled as a student in a private primary or secondary school shall make the oral and written notifications described by Subsection (a) to the principal or a school employee designated by the principal of the school in which the student is enrolled.

(2) On conviction, deferred prosecution, or deferred adjudication or an adjudication of delinquent conduct of an individual enrolled as a student in a private primary or secondary school, the office of prosecuting attorney shall make the oral and written notifications described by Subsection (b) of this article to the principal or a school employee designated by the principal of the school in which the student is enrolled.

(3) The principal of a private school in which the student is enrolled or a school employee designated by the principal shall send to a school employee having direct supervisory responsibility over the student the information contained in the confidential notice, for the same purposes as described by Subsection (a-1) of this article.

(f) A person who receives information under this article may not disclose the information except as specifically authorized by this article. A person who intentionally violates this article commits an offense. An offense under this subsection is a Class C misdemeanor.

(g) The office of the prosecuting attorney or the office or official designated by the juvenile board shall, within two working days, notify the school district that removed a student to a disciplinary alternative education program under Section 37.006, Education Code, if:

(1) prosecution of the student's case was refused for lack of prosecutorial merit or insufficient evidence and no formal proceedings, deferred adjudication, or deferred prosecution will be initiated; or

(2) the court or jury found the student not guilty or made a finding the child did not engage in delinquent conduct or conduct indicating a need for supervision and the case was dismissed with prejudice.

(h) This article applies to any felony offense and the following misdemeanors:

(1) an offense under Section 20.02, 21.08, 22.01, 22.05, 22.07, or 71.02, Penal Code;

(2) the unlawful use, sale, or possession of a controlled substance, drug paraphernalia, or marihuana, as defined by Chapter 481, Health and Safety Code; or

(3) the unlawful possession of any of the weapons or devices listed in Sections 46.01(1)—(14) or (16), Penal Code, or a weapon listed as a prohibited weapon under Section 46.05, Penal Code.

(i) A person may substitute electronic notification for oral notification where oral notification is required by this article. If electronic notification is substituted for oral notification, any written notification required by this article is not required.

(j) The notification provisions of this section concerning a person who is required to register as a sex offender under Chapter 62 do not lessen the requirement of a person to provide any additional notification prescribed by that chapter.

(k) Oral or written notice required under this article must include all pertinent details of the offense or conduct, including details of any:

(1) assaultive behavior or other violence;

(2) weapons used in the commission of the offense or conduct; or

(3) weapons possessed during the commission of the offense or conduct.

(l) If a school district board of trustees learns of a failure by the superintendent of the district or a district principal to provide a notice required under Subsection (a), (a-1), or (b), the board of trustees shall report the failure to the State Board for Educator Certification. If the governing body of a private primary or secondary school learns of a failure by the principal of the school to provide a notice required under Subsection (e), and the principal holds a certificate issued under Subchapter B, Chapter 21, Education Code, the governing body shall report the failure to the State Board for Educator Certification.

(m) If the superintendent of a school district in which the student is enrolled learns of a failure of the head of a law enforcement agency or a person designated by the head of the agency to provide a notification under Subsection (a), the superintendent or principal shall report the failure to notify to the Commission on Law Enforcement Officer Standards and Education.

(n) If a juvenile court judge or official designated by the juvenile board learns of a failure by

the office of the prosecuting attorney to provide a notification required under Subsection (b) or (g), the official shall report the failure to notify to the elected prosecuting attorney responsible for the operation of the office.

(o) If the supervisor of a parole, probation, or community supervision department officer learns of a failure by the officer to provide a notification under Subsection (c), the supervisor shall report the failure to notify to the director of the entity that employs the officer.

(Enacted by Acts 1993, 73rd Leg., ch. 461 (H.B. 23), § 1, effective September 1, 1993; am. Acts 1995, 74th Leg., ch. 76 (S.B. 959), § 14.18, effective September 1, 1995; am. Acts 1995, 74th Leg., ch. 626 (H.B. 1687), § 1, effective August 28, 1995; am. Acts 1997, 75th Leg., ch. 165 (S.B. 898), § 12.02, effective September 1, 1997; am. Acts 1997, 75th Leg., ch. 1015 (S.B. 133), §§ 12, 13, 14, effective June 19, 1997; am. Acts 1997, 75th Leg., ch. 1233 (H.B. 1150), § 1, effective June 20, 1997; am. Acts 2001, 77th Leg., ch. 1297 (H.B. 1118), §§ 48, 49, effective September 1, 2001; am. Acts 2003, 78th Leg., ch. 1055 (H.B. 1314), §§ 25, 26, 27, effective June 20, 2003; am. Acts 2005, 79th Leg., ch. 949 (H.B. 1575), § 31, effective September 1, 2005; am. Acts 2007, 80th Leg., ch. 492 (S.B. 230), § 1, effective June 16, 2007; am. Acts 2007, 80th Leg., ch. 1240 (H.B. 2532), §§ 4, 5, effective June 15, 2007; am. Acts 2007, 80th Leg., ch. 1291 (S.B. 6), §§ 1, 8, effective September 1, 2007; am. Acts 2009, 81st Leg., ch. 87 (S.B. 1969), § 6.002, effective September 1, 2009; am. Acts 2011, 82nd Leg., ch. 992 (H.B. 1907), §§ 1, 2, effective September 1, 2011.)

# CHAPTER 16
## THE COMMITMENT OR DISCHARGE OF THE ACCUSED

## Art. 16.01. Examining Trial.

When the accused has been brought before a magistrate for an examining trial that officer shall proceed to examine into the truth of the accusation made, allowing the accused, however, sufficient time to procure counsel. In a proper case, the magistrate may appoint counsel to represent an accused in such examining trial only, to be compensated as otherwise provided in this Code. The accused in any felony case shall have the right to an examining trial before indictment in the county having jurisdiction of the offense, whether he be in custody or on bail, at which time the magistrate at the hearing shall determine the amount or sufficiency of bail, if a bailable case. If the accused has been transferred for criminal prosecution after a hearing under Section 54.02, Family Code, the accused may be granted an examining trial at the discretion of the court.
(Enacted by Acts 1965, 59th Leg., ch. 722 (S.B. 107), § 1, effective January 1, 1966; am. Acts 1987, 70th Leg., ch. 140 (S.B. 218), § 4, effective September 1, 1987.)

## Art. 16.02. Examination Postponed.

The magistrate may at the request of either party postpone the examination to procure testimony; but the accused shall in the meanwhile be detained in custody unless he give bail to be present from day to day before the magistrate until the examination is concluded, which he may do in all cases except murder and treason.
(Enacted by Acts 1965, 59th Leg., ch. 722 (S.B. 107), § 1, effective January 1, 1966.)

## Art. 16.03. Warning to Accused.

Before the examination of the witnesses, the magistrate shall inform the accused that it is his right to make a statement relative to the accusation brought against him, but at the same time shall also inform him that he cannot be compelled to make any statement whatever, and that if he does make such statement, it may be used in evidence against him.
(Enacted by Acts 1965, 59th Leg., ch. 722 (S.B. 107), § 1, effective January 1, 1966.)

## Art. 16.04. Voluntary Statement.

If the accused desires to make a voluntary statement, he may do so before the examination of any witness, but not afterward. His statement shall be reduced to writing by or under the direction of the magistrate, or by the accused or his counsel, and shall be signed by the accused by affixing his name or mark, but shall not be sworn to by him. The magistrate shall attest by his own certificate and signature to the execution and signing of the statement.
(Enacted by Acts 1965, 59th Leg., ch. 722 (S.B. 107), § 1, effective January 1, 1966.)

## Art. 16.05. Witness Placed Under Rule [Repealed].

Repealed by Texas Court of Criminal Appeals pursuant to Acts 1985, 69th Leg., ch. 685 (H.B. 13), § 9.

## Art. 16.06. Counsel May Examine Witness.

The counsel for the State, and the accused or his counsel may question the witnesses on direct or cross examination. If no counsel appears for the State the magistrate may examine the witnesses.
(Enacted by Acts 1965, 59th Leg., ch. 722 (S.B. 107), § 1, effective January 1, 1966.)

## Art. 16.07. Same Rules of Evidence As on Final Trial.

The same rules of evidence shall apply to and govern a trial before an examining court that apply to and govern a final trial.
(Enacted by Acts 1965, 59th Leg., ch. 722 (S.B. 107), § 1, effective January 1, 1966.)

## Art. 16.08. Presence of the Accused.

The examination of each witness shall be in the presence of the accused.
(Enacted by Acts 1965, 59th Leg., ch. 722 (S.B. 107), § 1, effective January 1, 1966.)

## Art. 16.09. Testimony Reduced to Writing.

The testimony of each witness shall be reduced to writing by or under the direction of the magistrate, and shall then be read over to the witness, or he may read it over himself. Such corrections shall be made in the same as the witness may direct; and he shall then sign the same by affixing thereto his name or mark. All the testimony thus taken shall be certified to by the

*Criminal Procedure*

magistrate. In lieu of the above provision, a statement of facts authenticated by State and defense counsel and approved by the presiding magistrate may be used to preserve the testimony of witnesses.
(Enacted by Acts 1965, 59th Leg., ch. 722 (S.B. 107), § 1, effective January 1, 1966.)

### Art. 16.10. Attachment for Witness.

The magistrate has the power in all cases, where a witness resides or is in the county where the prosecution is pending, to issue an attachment for the purpose of enforcing the attendance of such witness; this he may do without having previously issued a subpoena for that purpose.
(Enacted by Acts 1965, 59th Leg., ch. 722 (S.B. 107), § 1, effective January 1, 1966.)

### Art. 16.11. Attachment to Another County.

The magistrate may issue an attachment for a witness to any county in the State, when affidavit is made by the party applying therefor that the testimony of the witness is material to the prosecution, or the defense, as the case may be; and the affidavit shall further state the facts which it is expected will be proved by the witness; and if the facts set forth are not considered material by the magistrate, or if they be admitted to be true by the adverse party, the attachment shall not issue.
(Enacted by Acts 1965, 59th Leg., ch. 722 (S.B. 107), § 1, effective January 1, 1966.)

### Art. 16.12. Witness Need Not Be Tendered His Witness Fees or Expenses.

A witness attached need not be tendered his witness fees or expenses.
(Enacted by Acts 1965, 59th Leg., ch. 722 (S.B. 107), § 1, effective January 1, 1966.)

### Art. 16.13. Attachment Executed Forthwith.

The officer receiving the attachment shall execute it forthwith by bringing before the magistrate the witness named therein, unless such witness shall give bail for his appearance before the magistrate at the time and place required by the writ.
(Enacted by Acts 1965, 59th Leg., ch. 722 (S.B. 107), § 1, effective January 1, 1966.)

### Art. 16.14. Postponing Examination.

After examining the witness in attendance, if it appear to the magistrate that there is other important testimony which may be had by a postponement, he shall, at the request of the prosecutor or of the defendant, postpone the hearing for a reasonable time to enable such testimony to be procured; but in such case the accused shall remain in the custody of the proper officer until the day fixed for such further examination. No postponement shall take place, unless a sworn statement be made by the defendant, or the prosecutor, setting forth the name and residence of the witness, and the facts which it is expected will be proved. If it be testimony other than that of a witness, the statement made shall set forth the nature of the evidence. If the magistrate is satisfied that the testimony is not material, or if the same be admitted to be true by the adverse party, the postponement shall be refused.
(Enacted by Acts 1965, 59th Leg., ch. 722 (S.B. 107), § 1, effective January 1, 1966.)

### Art. 16.15. Who May Discharge Capital Offense.

The examination of one accused of a capital offense shall be conducted by a justice of the peace, county judge, county court at law, or county criminal court. The judge may admit to bail, except in capital cases where the proof is evident.
(Enacted by Acts 1965, 59th Leg., ch. 722 (S.B. 107), § 1, effective January 1, 1966.)

### Art. 16.16. If Insufficient Bail Has Been Taken.

Where it is made to appear by affidavit to a judge of the Court of Criminal Appeals, a justice of a court of appeals, or to a judge of the district or county court, that the bail taken in any case is insufficient in amount, or that the sureties are not good for the amount, or that the bond is for any reason defective or insufficient, such judge shall issue a warrant of arrest, and require of the defendant sufficient bond and security, according to the nature of the case.
(Enacted by Acts 1965, 59th Leg., ch. 722 (S.B. 107), § 1, effective January 1, 1966; am. Acts 1981, 67th Leg., ch. 291 (S.B. 265), § 104, effective September 1, 1981.)

## Art. 16.17. Decision of Judge.

After the examining trial has been had, the judge shall make an order committing the defendant to the jail of the proper county, discharging him or admitting him to bail, as the law and facts of the case may require. Failure of the judge to make or enter an order within 48 hours after the examining trial has been completed operates as a finding of no probable cause and the accused shall be discharged.

(Enacted by Acts 1965, 59th Leg., ch. 722 (S.B. 107), § 1, effective January 1, 1966.)

## Art. 16.18. When No Safe Jail.

If there is no safe jail in the county in which the prosecution is carried on, the magistrate may commit defendant to the nearest safe jail in any other county.

(Enacted by Acts 1965, 59th Leg., ch. 722 (S.B. 107), § 1, effective January 1, 1966.)

## Art. 16.19. Warrant in Such Case.

The commitment in the case mentioned in the preceding Article shall be directed to the sheriff of the county to which the defendant is sent, but the sheriff of the county from which the defendant is taken shall be required to deliver the prisoner into the hands of the sheriff to whom he is sent.

(Enacted by Acts 1965, 59th Leg., ch. 722 (S.B. 107), § 1, effective January 1, 1966.)

## Art. 16.20. "Commitment".

A "commitment" is an order signed by the proper magistrate directing a sheriff to receive and place in jail the person so committed. It will be sufficient if it have the following requisites:

1. That it run in the name of "The State of Texas";

2. That it be addressed to the sheriff of the county to the jail of which the defendant is committed;

3. That it state in plain language the offense for which the defendant is committed, and give his name, if it be known, or if unknown, contain an accurate description of the defendant;

4. That it state to what court and at what time the defendant is to be held to answer;

5. When the prisoner is sent out of the county where the prosecution arose, the warrant of commitment shall state that there is no safe jail in the proper county; and

6. If bail has been granted, the amount of bail shall be stated in the warrant of commitment.

(Enacted by Acts 1965, 59th Leg., ch. 722 (S.B. 107), § 1, effective January 1, 1966.)

## Art. 16.21. Duty of Sheriff As to Prisoners.

Every sheriff shall keep safely a person committed to his custody. He shall use no cruel or unusual means to secure this end, but shall adopt all necessary measures to prevent the escape of a prisoner. He may summon a guard of sufficient number, in case it becomes necessary to prevent an escape from jail, or the rescue of a prisoner.

(Enacted by Acts 1965, 59th Leg., ch. 722 (S.B. 107), § 1, effective January 1, 1966.)

## Art. 16.22. Early Identification of Defendant Suspected of Having Mental Illness or Mental Retardation.

(a) (1) Not later than 72 hours after receiving credible information that may establish reasonable cause to believe that a defendant committed to the sheriff's custody has a mental illness or is a person with mental retardation, including observation of the defendant's behavior immediately before, during, and after the defendant's arrest and the results of any previous assessment of the defendant, the sheriff shall provide written or electronic notice of the information to the magistrate. On a determination that there is reasonable cause to believe that the defendant has a mental illness or is a person with mental retardation, the magistrate, except as provided by Subdivision (2), shall order the local mental health or mental retardation authority or another qualified mental health or mental retardation expert to:

    (A) collect information regarding whether the defendant has a mental illness as defined by Section 571.003, Health and Safety Code, or is a person with mental retardation as defined by Section 591.003, Health and Safety Code, including information obtained from any previous assessment of the defendant; and

    (B) provide to the magistrate a written assessment of the information collected under Paragraph (A).

(2) The magistrate is not required to order the collection of information under Subdivision (1) if the defendant in the year preceding the defendant's applicable date of arrest has been determined to have a mental illness or to be a person with mental retardation by the local mental health or mental retardation authority

or another mental health or mental retardation expert described by Subdivision (1). A court that elects to use the results of that previous determination may proceed under Subsection (c).

(3) If the defendant fails or refuses to submit to the collection of information regarding the defendant as required under Subdivision (1), the magistrate may order the defendant to submit to an examination in a mental health facility determined to be appropriate by the local mental health or mental retardation authority for a reasonable period not to exceed 21 days. The magistrate may order a defendant to a facility operated by the Department of State Health Services or the Department of Aging and Disability Services for examination only on request of the local mental health or mental retardation authority and with the consent of the head of the facility. If a defendant who has been ordered to a facility operated by the Department of State Health Services or the Department of Aging and Disability Services for examination remains in the facility for a period exceeding 21 days, the head of that facility shall cause the defendant to be immediately transported to the committing court and placed in the custody of the sheriff of the county in which the committing court is located. That county shall reimburse the facility for the mileage and per diem expenses of the personnel required to transport the defendant calculated in accordance with the state travel regulations in effect at the time.

(b) A written assessment of the information collected under Subsection (a)(1)(A) shall be provided to the magistrate not later than the 30th day after the date of any order issued under Subsection (a) in a felony case and not later than the 10th day after the date of any order issued under that subsection in a misdemeanor case, and the magistrate shall provide copies of the written assessment to the defense counsel, the prosecuting attorney, and the trial court. The written assessment must include a description of the procedures used in the collection of information under Subsection (a)(1)(A) and the applicable expert's observations and findings pertaining to:

(1) whether the defendant is a person who has a mental illness or is a person with mental retardation;

(2) whether there is clinical evidence to support a belief that the defendant may be incompetent to stand trial and should undergo a complete competency examination under Subchapter B, Chapter 46B; and

(3) recommended treatment.

(c) After the trial court receives the applicable expert's written assessment relating to the defendant under Subsection (b) or elects to use the results of a previous determination as described by Subsection (a)(2), the trial court may, as applicable:

(1) resume criminal proceedings against the defendant, including any appropriate proceedings related to the defendant's release on personal bond under Article 17.032;

(2) resume or initiate competency proceedings, if required, as provided by Chapter 46B or other proceedings affecting the defendant's receipt of appropriate court-ordered mental health or mental retardation services, including proceedings related to the defendant's receipt of outpatient mental health services under Section 574.034, Health and Safety Code; or

(3) consider the written assessment during the punishment phase after a conviction of the offense for which the defendant was arrested, as part of a presentence investigation report, or in connection with the impositions of conditions following placement on community supervision, including deferred adjudication community supervision.

(d) This article does not prevent the applicable court from, before, during, or after the collection of information regarding the defendant as described by this article:

(1) releasing a mentally ill or mentally retarded defendant from custody on personal or surety bond; or

(2) ordering an examination regarding the defendant's competency to stand trial.

(Enacted by Acts 1993, 73rd Leg., ch. 900 (S.B. 1067), § 3.05, effective September 1, 1994; am. Acts 1997, 75th Leg., ch. 312 (H.B. 1747), § 1, effective September 1, 1997; am. Acts 2001, 77th Leg., ch. 828 (H.B. 1071), § 1, effective September 1, 2001; am. Acts 2003, 78th Leg., ch. 35 (S.B. 1057), § 2, effective January 1, 2004; am. Acts 2007, 80th Leg., ch. 1307 (S.B. 867), § 1, effective September 1, 2007; am. Acts 2009, 81st Leg., ch.

1228 (S.B. 1557), § 1, effective September 1, 2009.)

# CHAPTER 17
# BAIL

## Art. 17.01. Definition of "Bail".

"Bail" is the security given by the accused that he will appear and answer before the proper court the accusation brought against him, and includes a bail bond or a personal bond.

(Enacted by Acts 1965, 59th Leg., ch. 722 (S.B. 107), § 1, effective January 1, 1966.)

## Art. 17.02. Definition of "Bail Bond".

A "bail bond" is a written undertaking entered into by the defendant and the defendant's sureties for the appearance of the principal therein before a court or magistrate to answer a criminal accusation; provided, however, that the defendant on execution of the bail bond may deposit with the custodian of funds of the court in which the prosecution is pending current money of the United States in the amount of the bond in lieu of having sureties signing the same. Any cash funds deposited under this article shall be receipted for by the officer receiving the funds and, on order of the court, be refunded, after the defendant complies with the conditions of the defendant's bond, to:

   (1) any person in the name of whom a receipt was issued, in the amount reflected on the face of the receipt, including the defendant if a receipt was issued to the defendant; or

(2) the defendant, if no other person is able to produce a receipt for the funds.
(Enacted by Acts 1965, 59th Leg., ch. 722 (S.B. 107), § 1, effective January 1, 1966; am. Acts 2011, 82nd Leg., ch. 978 (H.B. 1658), § 1, effective September 1, 2011.)

## Art. 17.025. Officers Taking Bail Bond.

A jailer licensed under Chapter 1701, Occupations Code, is considered to be an officer for the purposes of taking a bail bond and discharging any other related powers and duties under this chapter.
(Enacted by Acts 2011, 82nd Leg., ch. 736 (H.B. 1070), § 1, effective June 17, 2011.)

## Art. 17.03. Personal Bond.

(a) Except as provided by Subsection (b) of this article, a magistrate may, in the magistrate's discretion, release the defendant on his personal bond without sureties or other security.

(b) Only the court before whom the case is pending may release on personal bond a defendant who:

(1) is charged with an offense under the following sections of the Penal Code:

(A) Section 19.03 (Capital Murder);

(B) Section 20.04 (Aggravated Kidnapping);

(C) Section 22.021 (Aggravated Sexual Assault);

(D) Section 22.03 (Deadly Assault on Law Enforcement or Corrections Officer, Member or Employee of Board of Pardons and Paroles, or Court Participant);

(E) Section 22.04 (Injury to a Child, Elderly Individual, or Disabled Individual);

(F) Section 29.03 (Aggravated Robbery);

(G) Section 30.02 (Burglary);

(H) Section 71.02 (Engaging in Organized Criminal Activity);

(I) Section 21.02 (Continuous Sexual Abuse of Young Child or Children); or

(J) Section 20A.03 (Continuous Trafficking of Persons);

(2) is charged with a felony under Chapter 481, Health and Safety Code, or Section 485.033, Health and Safety Code, punishable by imprisonment for a minimum term or by a maximum fine that is more than a minimum term or maximum fine for a first degree felony; or

(3) does not submit to testing for the presence of a controlled substance in the defendant's body as requested by the court or magistrate under Subsection (c) of this article or submits to testing and the test shows evidence of the presence of a controlled substance in the defendant's body.

(c) When setting a personal bond under this chapter, on reasonable belief by the investigating or arresting law enforcement agent or magistrate of the presence of a controlled substance in the defendant's body or on the finding of drug or alcohol abuse related to the offense for which the defendant is charged, the court or a magistrate shall require as a condition of personal bond that the defendant submit to testing for alcohol or a controlled substance in the defendant's body and participate in an alcohol or drug abuse treatment or education program if such a condition will serve to reasonably assure the appearance of the defendant for trial.

(d) The state may not use the results of any test conducted under this chapter in any criminal proceeding arising out of the offense for which the defendant is charged.

(e) Costs of testing may be assessed as court costs or ordered paid directly by the defendant as a condition of bond.

(f) In this article, "controlled substance" has the meaning assigned by Section 481.002, Health and Safety Code.

(g) The court may order that a personal bond fee assessed under Section 17.42 be:

(1) paid before the defendant is released;

(2) paid as a condition of bond;

(3) paid as court costs;

(4) reduced as otherwise provided for by statute; or

(5) waived.
(Enacted by Acts 1965, 59th Leg., ch. 722 (S.B. 107), § 1, effective January 1, 1966; am. Acts 1989, 71st Leg., ch. 374 (S.B. 376), § 1, effective September 1, 1989; am. Acts 1991, 72nd Leg., ch. 14 (S.B. 404), §§ 284(45), (57), effective September 1, 1991; am. Acts 1995, 74th Leg., ch. 76 (S.B. 959), § 14.19, effective September 1, 1995; am. Acts 2007, 80th Leg., ch. 593 (H.B. 8), § 3.08, effective September 1, 2007; am. Acts 2011, 82nd Leg., ch. 122 (H.B. 3000), § 3, effective September 1, 2011.)

## Art. 17.031. Release on Personal Bond.

(a) Any magistrate in this state may release a defendant eligible for release on personal bond under Article 17.03 of this code on his personal bond where the complaint and warrant for arrest does not originate in the county wherein the accused is arrested if the magistrate would have had jurisdiction over the matter had the complaint arisen within the county wherein the magistrate presides. The personal bond may not be revoked by the judge of the court issuing the warrant for arrest except for good cause shown.

(b) If there is a personal bond office in the county from which the warrant for arrest was issued, the court releasing a defendant on his personal bond will forward a copy of the personal bond to the personal bond office in that county. (Enacted by Acts 1971, 62nd Leg., ch. 787 (H.B. 1202), § 1, effective June 8, 1971; am. Acts 1989, 71st Leg., ch. 374 (S.B. 376), § 2, effective September 1, 1989.)

### Art. 17.032. Release on Personal Bond of Certain Mentally Ill Defendants.

(a) In this article, "violent offense" means an offense under the following sections of the Penal Code:

(1) Section 19.02 (murder);

(2) Section 19.03 (capital murder);

(3) Section 20.03 (kidnapping);

(4) Section 20.04 (aggravated kidnapping);

(5) Section 21.11 (indecency with a child);

(6) Section 22.01(a)(1)(assault);

(7) Section 22.011 (sexual assault);

(8) Section 22.02 (aggravated assault);

(9) Section 22.021 (aggravated sexual assault);

(10) Section 22.04 (injury to a child, elderly individual, or disabled individual);

(11) Section 29.03 (aggravated robbery);

(12) Section 21.02 (continuous sexual abuse of young child or children); or

(13) Section 20A.03 (continuous trafficking of persons).

(b) A magistrate shall release a defendant on personal bond unless good cause is shown otherwise if the:

(1) defendant is not charged with and has not been previously convicted of a violent offense;

(2) defendant is examined by the local mental health or mental retardation authority or another mental health expert under Article 16.22 of this code;

(3) applicable expert, in a written assessment submitted to the magistrate under Article 16.22:

(A) concludes that the defendant has a mental illness or is a person with mental retardation and is nonetheless competent to stand trial; and

(B) recommends mental health treatment for the defendant; and

(4) magistrate determines, in consultation with the local mental health or mental retardation authority, that appropriate community-based mental health or mental retardation services for the defendant are available through the Texas Department of Mental Health and Mental Retardation under Section 534.053, Health and Safety Code, or through another mental health or mental retardation services provider.

(c) The magistrate, unless good cause is shown for not requiring treatment, shall require as a condition of release on personal bond under this article that the defendant submit to outpatient or inpatient mental health or mental retardation treatment as recommended by the local mental health or mental retardation authority if the defendant's:

(1) mental illness or mental retardation is chronic in nature; or

(2) ability to function independently will continue to deteriorate if the defendant is not treated.

(d) In addition to a condition of release imposed under Subsection (c) of this article, the magistrate may require the defendant to comply with other conditions that are reasonably necessary to protect the community.

(e) In this article, a person is considered to have been convicted of an offense if:

(1) a sentence is imposed;

(2) the person is placed on community supervision or receives deferred adjudication; or

(3) the court defers final disposition of the case.

(Enacted by Acts 1993, 73rd Leg., ch. 900 (S.B. 1067), § 3.06, effective September 1, 1994; am. Acts 1995, 74th Leg., ch. 76 (S.B. 959), § 14.20, effective September 1, 1995; am. Acts 1997, 75th Leg., ch. 312 (H.B. 1747), § 2, effective September 1, 1997; am. Acts 2001, 77th Leg., ch. 828 (H.B. 1071), § 2, effective September 1, 2001; am. Acts 2007, 80th Leg., ch. 593 (H.B. 8), § 3.09, effective September 1, 2007; am. Acts 2009, 81st Leg., ch. 1228 (S.B. 1557), § 2, effective September 1, 2009; am. Acts 2011, 82nd Leg., ch. 122 (H.B. 3000), § 4, effective September 1, 2011.)

### Art. 17.033. Release on Bond of Certain Persons Arrested Without a War-

**rant.**

(a) Except as provided by Subsection (c), a person who is arrested without a warrant and who is detained in jail must be released on bond, in an amount not to exceed $5,000, not later than the 24th hour after the person's arrest if the person was arrested for a misdemeanor and a magistrate has not determined whether probable cause exists to believe that the person committed the offense. If the person is unable to obtain a surety for the bond or unable to deposit money in the amount of the bond, the person must be released on personal bond.

(a-1) **[Expires September 1, 2013]** Notwithstanding Subsection (a) and except as provided by Subsection (c), a person who, in a county with a population of three million or more, is arrested without a warrant and who is detained in jail must be released on bond, in an amount not to exceed $5,000, not later than the 36th hour after the person's arrest if the person was arrested for a misdemeanor and a magistrate has not determined whether probable cause exists to believe that the person committed the offense.

(b) Except as provided by Subsection (c), a person who is arrested without a warrant and who is detained in jail must be released on bond, in an amount not to exceed $10,000, not later than the 48th hour after the person's arrest if the person was arrested for a felony and a magistrate has not determined whether probable cause exists to believe that the person committed the offense. If the person is unable to obtain a surety for the bond or unable to deposit money in the amount of the bond, the person must be released on personal bond.

(c) On the filing of an application by the attorney representing the state, a magistrate may postpone the release of a person under Subsection (a), (a-1), or (b) for not more than 72 hours after the person's arrest. An application filed under this subsection must state the reason a magistrate has not determined whether probable cause exists to believe that the person committed the offense for which the person was arrested.

(d) The time limits imposed by Subsections (a), (a-1), and (b) do not apply to a person arrested without a warrant who is taken to a hospital, clinic, or other medical facility before being taken before a magistrate under Article 15.17. For a person described by this subsection, the time limits imposed by Subsections (a), (a-1), and (b) begin to run at the time, as documented in the records of the hospital, clinic, or other medical facility, that a physician or other medical profes-sional releases the person from the hospital, clinic, or other medical facility.

(e) **[Expires September 1, 2013]** Subsection (a-1) and this subsection expire on September 1, 2013.
(Enacted by Acts 2001, 77th Leg., ch. 906 (S.B. 7), § 5(a), effective January 1, 2002; am. Acts 2003, 78th Leg., ch. 298 (H.B. 2795), § 1 effective June 18, 2003; am. Acts 2011, 82nd Leg., ch. 1350 (H.B. 1173), § 1, effective September 1, 2011.)

## Art. 17.0331. [Expires September 1, 2013] Impact Study.

(a) This article applies only to a county with a population of three million or more.

(b) Each county to which this article applies shall conduct an impact study to determine the effect of Article 17.033(a-1) on the county's ability to control and process the county's misdemeanor caseload, including a specific assessment of the effect of that subsection on:

(1) the average number of hours a person who is arrested for a misdemeanor is detained in jail before being released on bond;

(2) bonding practices, including the number of persons released on personal bond;

(3) the inmate population in a county jail and in each municipal jail located in the county;

(4) the number of arrests for misdemeanor offenses;

(5) public safety;

(6) costs to the criminal justice system; and

(7) the number of applications filed by the attorney representing the state under Article 17.033(c).

(c) The county shall also determine whether a more cost-effective method of controlling and processing misdemeanor caseloads exists than an extension of the period for which a person may be detained after a misdemeanor arrest.

(d) Not later than October 15, 2012, the county must file the impact study with:

(1) the commissioners court of the county;

(2) the Senate Committee on Criminal Justice;

(3) the Senate Committee on Jurisprudence; and

(4) the House Criminal Jurisprudence Committee.

(e) The county shall make the results of the impact study available to the public.

(f) This article expires on September 1, 2013.
(Enacted by Acts 2011, 82nd Leg., ch. 1350 (H.B. 1173), § 2, effective September 1, 2011.)

## Art. 17.04. Requisites of a Personal Bond.

A personal bond is sufficient if it includes the requisites of a bail bond as set out in Article 17.08, except that no sureties are required. In addition, a personal bond shall contain:

(1) the defendant's name, address, and place of employment;

(2) identification information, including the defendant's:

(A) date and place of birth;

(B) height, weight, and color of hair and eyes;

(C) driver's license number and state of issuance, if any; and

(D) nearest relative's name and address, if any; and

(3) the following oath sworn and signed by the defendant:

"I swear that I will appear before (the court or magistrate) at (address, city, county) Texas, on the (date), at the hour of (time, a.m. or p.m.) or upon notice by the court, or pay to the court the principal sum of (amount) plus all necessary and reasonable expenses incurred in any arrest for failure to appear."

(Enacted by Acts 1965, 59th Leg., ch. 722 (S.B. 107), § 1, effective January 1, 1966; am. Acts 1987, 70th Leg., ch. 623 (H.B. 1827), § 1, effective September 1, 1987.)

## Art. 17.045. Bail Bond Certificates.

A bail bond certificate with respect to which a fidelity and surety company has become surety as provided in the Automobile Club Services Act, or for any truck and bus association incorporated in this state, when posted by the person whose signature appears thereon, shall be accepted as bail bond in an amount not to exceed $200 to guarantee the appearance of such person in any court in this state when the person is arrested for violation of any motor vehicle law of this state or ordinance of any municipality in this state, except for the offense of driving while intoxicated or for any felony, and the alleged violation was committed prior to the date of expiration shown on such bail bond certificate.

(Enacted by Acts 1969, 61st Leg., ch. 697 (S.B. 507), § 2, effective September 1, 1969.)

## Art. 17.05. When a Bail Bond Is Given.

A bail bond is entered into either before a magistrate, upon an examination of a criminal accusation, or before a judge upon an application

under habeas corpus; or it is taken from the defendant by a peace officer or jailer if authorized by Article 17.20, 17.21, or 17.22.

(Enacted by Acts 1965, 59th Leg., ch. 722 (S.B. 107), § 1, effective January 1, 1966; am. Acts 1971, 62nd Leg., ch. 1006 (H.B. 1325), § 1, effective August 30, 1971; am. Acts 2011, 82nd Leg., ch. 736 (H.B. 1070), § 2, effective June 17, 2011.)

## Art. 17.06. Corporation As Surety.

Wherever in this Chapter, any person is required or authorized to give or execute any bail bond, such bail bond may be given or executed by such principal and any corporation authorized by law to act as surety, subject to all the provisions of this Chapter regulating and governing the giving of bail bonds by personal surety insofar as the same is applicable.

(Enacted by Acts 1965, 59th Leg., ch. 722 (S.B. 107), § 1, effective January 1, 1966.)

## Art. 17.07. Corporation to File with County Clerk Power of Attorney Designating Agent.

(a) Any corporation authorized by the law of this State to act as a surety, shall before executing any bail bond as authorized in the preceding Article, first file in the office of the county clerk of the county where such bail bond is given, a power of attorney designating and authorizing the named agent, agents or attorney of such corporation to execute such bail bonds and thereafter the execution of such bail bonds by such agent, agents or attorney, shall be a valid and binding obligation of such corporation.

(b) A corporation may limit the authority of an agent designated under Subsection (a) by specifying the limitation in the power of attorney that is filed with the county clerk.

(Enacted by Acts 1965, 59th Leg., ch. 722 (S.B. 107), § 1, effective January 1, 1966; am. Acts 2011, 82nd Leg., ch. 769 (H.B. 1823), § 1, effective September 1, 2011.)

## Art. 17.08. Requisites of a Bail Bond.

A bail bond must contain the following requisites:

1. That it be made payable to "The State of Texas";

2. That the defendant and his sureties, if any, bind themselves that the defendant will appear before the proper court or magistrate to answer the accusation against him;

3. If the defendant is charged with a felony, that it state that he is charged with a felony. If

the defendant is charged with a misdemeanor, that it state that he is charged with a misdemeanor;

4. That the bond be signed by name or mark by the principal and sureties, if any, each of whom shall write thereon his mailing address;

5. That the bond state the time and place, when and where the accused binds himself to appear, and the court or magistrate before whom he is to appear. The bond shall also bind the defendant to appear before any court or magistrate before whom the cause may thereafter be pending at any time when, and place where, his presence may be required under this Code or by any court or magistrate, but in no event shall the sureties be bound after such time as the defendant receives an order of deferred adjudication or is acquitted, sentenced, placed on community supervision, or dismissed from the charge;

6. The bond shall also be conditioned that the principal and sureties, if any, will pay all necessary and reasonable expenses incurred by any and all sheriffs or other peace officers in rearresting the principal in the event he fails to appear before the court or magistrate named in the bond at the time stated therein. The amount of such expense shall be in addition to the principal amount specified in the bond. The failure of any bail bond to contain the conditions specified in this paragraph shall in no manner affect the legality of any such bond, but it is intended that the sheriff or other peace officer shall look to the defendant and his sureties, if any, for expenses incurred by him, and not to the State for any fees earned by him in connection with the rearresting of an accused who has violated the conditions of his bond.

(Enacted by Acts 1965, 59th Leg., ch. 722 (S.B. 107), effective January 1, 1966; am. Acts 1999, 76th Leg., ch. 1506 (S.B. 403), § 1, effective September 1, 1999.)

## Art. 17.085. Notice of Appearance Date.

The clerk of a court that does not provide online Internet access to that court's criminal case records shall post in a designated public place in the courthouse notice of a prospective criminal court docket setting as soon as the court notifies the clerk of the setting.

(Enacted by Acts 2007, 80th Leg., ch. 1038 (H.B. 1801), § 1, effective September 1, 2007; am. Acts 2011, 82nd Leg., ch. 278 (H.B. 1573), § 1, effective September 1, 2011.)

## Art. 17.09. Duration; Original and Subsequent Proceedings; New Bail.

Sec. 1. Where a defendant, in the course of a criminal action, gives bail before any court or person authorized by law to take same, for his personal appearance before a court or magistrate, to answer a charge against him, the said bond shall be valid and binding upon the defendant and his sureties, if any, thereon, for the defendant's personal appearance before the court or magistrate designated therein, as well as before any other court to which same may be transferred, and for any and all subsequent proceedings had relative to the charge, and each such bond shall be so conditioned except as hereinafter provided.

Sec. 2. When a defendant has once given bail for his appearance in answer to a criminal charge, he shall not be required to give another bond in the course of the same criminal action except as herein provided.

Sec. 3. Provided that whenever, during the course of the action, the judge or magistrate in whose court such action is pending finds that the bond is defective, excessive or insufficient in amount, or that the sureties, if any, are not acceptable, or for any other good and sufficient cause, such judge or magistrate may, either in term-time or in vacation, order the accused to be rearrested, and require the accused to give another bond in such amount as the judge or magistrate may deem proper. When such bond is so given and approved, the defendant shall be released from custody.

Sec. 4. Notwithstanding any other provision of this article, the judge or magistrate in whose court a criminal action is pending may not order the accused to be rearrested or require the accused to give another bond in a higher amount because the accused:

(1) withdraws a waiver of the right to counsel; or

(2) requests the assistance of counsel, appointed or retained.

(Enacted by Acts 1965, 59th Leg., ch. 722 (S.B. 107), § 1, effective January 1, 1966; am. Acts 2007, 80th Leg., ch. 463 (H.B. 1178), § 2, effective September 1, 2007.)

## Art. 17.091. Notice of Certain Bail Reductions Required.

Before a judge or magistrate reduces the amount of bail set for a defendant charged with an offense listed in Section 3g, Article 42.12, an offense described by Article 62.001(5), or an offense under Section 20A.03, Penal Code, the judge or magistrate shall provide:

(1) to the attorney representing the state, reasonable notice of the proposed bail reduction; and

(2) on request of the attorney representing the state or the defendant or the defendant's counsel, an opportunity for a hearing concerning the proposed bail reduction.

(Enacted by Acts 2005, 79th Leg., ch. 671 (S.B. 56), § 1, effective September 1, 2005; am. Acts 2007, 80th Leg., ch. 593 (H.B. 8), § 3.10, effective September 1, 2007; am. Acts 2011, 82nd Leg., ch. 122 (H.B. 3000), § 5, effective September 1, 2011.)

## Art. 17.10. Disqualified Sureties.

(a) A minor may not be surety on a bail bond, but the accused party may sign as principal.

(b) A person, for compensation, may not be a surety on a bail bond written in a county in which a county bail bond board regulated under Chapter 1704, Occupations Code, does not exist unless the person, within two years before the bail bond is given, completed in person at least eight hours of continuing legal education in criminal law courses or bail bond law courses that are:

(1) approved by the State Bar of Texas; and

(2) offered by an accredited institution of higher education in this state.

(c) A person, for compensation, may not act as a surety on a bail bond if the person has been finally convicted of:

(1) a misdemeanor involving moral turpitude; or

(2) a felony.

(Enacted by Acts 1965, 59th Leg., ch. 722 (S.B. 107), § 1, effective January 1, 1966; am. Acts 2005, 79th Leg., ch. 743 (H.B. 2767), § 1, effective September 1, 2005; am. Acts 2011, 82nd Leg., ch. 769 (H.B. 1823), § 2, effective September 1, 2011.)

## Art. 17.11. How Bail Bond Is Taken.

Sec. 1. Every court, judge, magistrate or other officer taking a bail bond shall require evidence of the sufficiency of the security offered; but in every case, one surety shall be sufficient, if it be made to appear that such surety is worth at least double the amount of the sum for which he is bound, exclusive of all property exempted by law from execution, and of debts or other encumbrances; and that he is a resident of this state, and has property therein liable to execution worth the sum for which he is bound.

Sec. 2. Provided, however, any person who has signed as a surety on a bail bond and is in default thereon shall thereafter be disqualified to sign as a surety so long as he is in default on said bond. It shall be the duty of the clerk of the court wherein such surety is in default on a bail bond, to notify in writing the sheriff, chief of police, or other peace officer, of such default. A surety shall be deemed in default from the time execution may be issued on a final judgment in a bond forfeiture proceeding under the Texas Rules of Civil Procedure, unless the final judgment is superseded by the posting of a supersedeas bond.

(Enacted by Acts 1965, 59th Leg., ch. 722 (S.B. 107), § 1, effective January 1, 1966; am. Acts 1967, 60th Leg., ch. 659 (S.B. 145), § 14, effective August 28, 1967; am. Acts 1999, 76th Leg., ch. 1506 (S.B. 403), § 2, effective September 1, 1999.)

## Art. 17.12. Exempt Property.

The property secured by the Constitution and laws from forced sale shall not, in any case, be held liable for the satisfaction of bail, either as to principal or sureties, if any.

(Enacted by Acts 1965, 59th Leg., ch. 722 (S.B. 107), § 1, effective January 1, 1966.)

## Art. 17.13. Sufficiency of Sureties Ascertained.

To test the sufficiency of the security offered to any bail bond, unless the court or officer taking the same is fully satisfied as to its sufficiency, the following oath shall be made in writing and subscribed by the sureties: "I, do swear that I am worth, in my own right, at least the sum of (here insert the amount in which the surety is bound), after deducting from my property all that which is exempt by the Constitution and Laws of the State from forced sale, and after the payment of all my debts of every description, whether individual or security debts, and after satisfying all encumbrances upon my property which are known to me; that I reside in ... County, and have property in this State liable to execution worth said amount or more.

(Dated ... , and attested by the judge of the court, clerk, magistrate or sheriff.)"

Such affidavit shall be filed with the papers of the proceedings.
(Enacted by Acts 1965, 59th Leg., ch. 722 (S.B. 107), § 1, effective January 1, 1966.)

## Art. 17.14. Affidavit Not Conclusive.

Such affidavit shall not be conclusive as to the sufficiency of the security; and if the court or officer taking the bail bond is not fully satisfied as to the sufficiency of the security offered, further evidence shall be required before approving the same.
(Enacted by Acts 1965, 59th Leg., ch. 722 (S.B. 107), § 1, effective January 1, 1966.)

## Art. 17.141. Eligible Bail Bond Sureties in Certain Counties.

In a county in which a county bail bond board regulated under Chapter 1704, Occupations Code, does not exist, the sheriff may post a list of eligible bail bond sureties whose security has been determined to be sufficient. Each surety listed under this article must file annually a sworn financial statement with the sheriff.
(Enacted by Acts 2005, 79th Leg., ch. 743 (H.B. 2767), § 2, effective September 1, 2005.)

## Art. 17.15. Rules for Fixing Amount of Bail.

The amount of bail to be required in any case is to be regulated by the court, judge, magistrate or officer taking the bail; they are to be governed in the exercise of this discretion by the Constitution and by the following rules:

1. The bail shall be sufficiently high to give reasonable assurance that the undertaking will be complied with.

2. The power to require bail is not to be so used as to make it an instrument of oppression.

3. The nature of the offense and the circumstances under which it was committed are to be considered.

4. The ability to make bail is to be regarded, and proof may be taken upon this point.

5. The future safety of a victim of the alleged offense and the community shall be considered.
(Enacted by Acts 1965, 59th Leg., ch. 722 (S.B. 107), § 1, effective January 1, 1966; am. Acts 1985, 69th Leg., ch. 588 (H.B. 235), § 2, effective September 1, 1985; am. Acts 1993, 73rd Leg., ch. 396, § 1, effective September 1, 1993.)

## Art. 17.151. Release Because of Delay.

Sec. 1. A defendant who is detained in jail pending trial of an accusation against him must be released either on personal bond or by reducing the amount of bail required, if the state is not ready for trial of the criminal action for which he is being detained within:

(1) 90 days from the commencement of his detention if he is accused of a felony;

(2) 30 days from the commencement of his detention if he is accused of a misdemeanor punishable by a sentence of imprisonment in jail for more than 180 days;

(3) 15 days from the commencement of his detention if he is accused of a misdemeanor punishable by a sentence of imprisonment for 180 days or less; or

(4) five days from the commencement of his detention if he is accused of a misdemeanor punishable by a fine only.

Sec. 2. The provisions of this article do not apply to a defendant who is:

(1) serving a sentence of imprisonment for another offense while the defendant is serving that sentence;

(2) being detained pending trial of another accusation against the defendant as to which the applicable period has not yet elapsed;

(3) incompetent to stand trial, during the period of the defendant's incompetence; or

(4) being detained for a violation of the conditions of a previous release related to the safety of a victim of the alleged offense or to the safety of the community under this article.

Sec. 3. [Repealed by Acts 2005, 79th Leg., ch. 110 (S.B. 599), § 2, effective September 1, 2005.]
(Enacted by Acts 1977, 65th Leg., ch. 787 (S.B. 1043), § 2, effective July 1, 1978; am. Acts 2005, 79th Leg., ch. 110 (S.B. 599), § 1, effective September 1, 2005; am. Acts 2005, 79th Leg., ch. 110 (S.B. 599), § 2, effective September 1, 2005.)

## Art. 17.152. Denial of Bail for Violation of Certain Court Orders or Conditions of Bond in a Family Violence Case.

(a) In this article, "family violence" has the meaning assigned by Section 71.004, Family Code.

(b) Except as otherwise provided by Subsection (d), a person who commits an offense under Section 25.07, Penal Code, related to a violation of a condition of bond set in a family violence case and whose bail in the case under Section 25.07, Penal Code, or in the family violence case is revoked or forfeited for a violation of a condition of bond may be taken into custody and, pending trial or other court proceedings, denied release on bail if following a hearing a judge or magistrate determines by a preponderance of the evidence that the person violated a condition of bond related to:

    (1) the safety of the victim of the offense under Section 25.07, Penal Code, or the family violence case, as applicable; or

    (2) the safety of the community.

(c) Except as otherwise provided by Subsection (d), a person who commits an offense under Section 25.07, Penal Code, other than an offense related to a violation of a condition of bond set in a family violence case, may be taken into custody and, pending trial or other court proceedings, denied release on bail if following a hearing a judge or magistrate determines by a preponderance of the evidence that the person committed the offense.

(d) A person who commits an offense under Section 25.07(a)(3), Penal Code, may be held without bail under Subsection (b) or (c), as applicable, only if following a hearing the judge or magistrate determines by a preponderance of the evidence that the person went to or near the place described in the order or condition of bond with the intent to commit or threaten to commit:

    (1) family violence; or

    (2) an act in furtherance of an offense under Section 42.072, Penal Code.

(e) In determining whether to deny release on bail under this article, the judge or magistrate may consider:

    (1) the order or condition of bond;

    (2) the nature and circumstances of the alleged offense;

    (3) the relationship between the accused and the victim, including the history of that relationship;

    (4) any criminal history of the accused; and

    (5) any other facts or circumstances relevant to a determination of whether the accused poses an imminent threat of future family violence.

(f) A person arrested for committing an offense under Section 25.07, Penal Code, shall without unnecessary delay and after reasonable notice is given to the attorney representing the state, but not later than 48 hours after the person is arrested, be taken before a magistrate in accordance with Article 15.17. At that time, the magistrate shall conduct the hearing and make the determination required by this article.
(Enacted by Acts 2007, 80th Leg., ch. 1113 (H.B. 3692), § 3, effective January 1, 2008.)

## Art. 17.153. Denial of Bail for Violation of Condition of Bond Where Child Alleged Victim.

(a) This article applies to a defendant charged with a felony offense under any of the following provisions of the Penal Code, if committed against a child younger than 14 years of age:

    (1) Chapter 21 (Sexual Offenses);

    (2) Section 25.02 (Prohibited Sexual Conduct);

    (3) Section 43.25 (Sexual Performance by a Child);

    (4) Section 20A.02 (Trafficking of Persons), if the defendant is alleged to have:

        (A) trafficked the child with the intent or knowledge that the child would engage in sexual conduct, as defined by Section 43.25, Penal Code; or

        (B) benefited from participating in a venture that involved a trafficked child engaging in sexual conduct, as defined by Section 43.25, Penal Code; or

    (5) Section 43.05(a)(2)(Compelling Prostitution).

(b) A defendant described by Subsection (a) who violates a condition of bond set under Article 17.41 and whose bail in the case is revoked for the violation may be taken into custody and denied release on bail pending trial if, following a hearing, a judge or magistrate determines by a preponderance of the evidence that the defendant violated a condition of bond related to the safety of the victim of the offense or the safety of the community. If the magistrate finds that the violation occurred, the magistrate may revoke the defendant's bond and order that the defendant be immediately returned to custody. Once the defendant is placed in custody, the revocation of the defendant's bond discharges the sureties on the bond, if any, from any future liability on the bond. A discharge under this subsection from any future liability on the bond does not discharge any surety from liability for previous forfeitures on the bond.
(Enacted by Acts 2009, 81st Leg., ch. 982 (H.B. 3751), § 2, effective September 1, 2009; am. Acts 2011, 82nd Leg., ch. 515 (H.B. 2014), § 2.01, effective September 1, 2011.)

## Art. 17.16. Discharge of Liability; Surrender or Incarceration of Principal Before Forfeiture; Verification of Incarceration.

(a) A surety may before forfeiture relieve the surety of the surety's undertaking by:

Criminal Procedure

(1) surrendering the accused into the custody of the sheriff of the county where the prosecution is pending; or

(2) delivering to the sheriff of the county in which the prosecution is pending and to the office of the prosecuting attorney an affidavit stating that the accused is incarcerated in federal custody, in the custody of any state, or in any county of this state.

(b) On receipt of an affidavit described by Subsection (a)(2), the sheriff of the county in which the prosecution is pending shall verify whether the accused is incarcerated as stated in the affidavit. If the sheriff verifies the statement in the affidavit, the sheriff shall notify the magistrate before which the prosecution is pending of the verification.

(c) On a verification described by this article, the sheriff shall place a detainer against the accused with the appropriate officials in the jurisdiction in which the accused is incarcerated. On receipt of notice of a verification described by this article, the magistrate before which the prosecution is pending shall direct the clerk of the court to issue a capias for the arrest of the accused, except as provided by Subsection (d).

(d) A capias for the arrest of the accused is not required if:

(1) a warrant has been issued for the accused's arrest and remains outstanding; or

(2) the issuance of a capias would otherwise be unnecessary for the purpose of taking the accused into custody.

(e) For the purposes of Subsection (a)(2) of this article, the bond is discharged and the surety is absolved of liability on the bond on the verification of the incarceration of the accused.

(f) An affidavit described by Subsection (a)(2) and the documentation of any verification obtained under Subsection (b) must be:

(1) filed in the court record of the underlying criminal case in the court in which the prosecution is pending or, if the court record does not exist, in a general file maintained by the clerk of the court; and

(2) delivered to the office of the prosecuting attorney.

(g) A surety is liable for all reasonable and necessary expenses incurred in returning the accused into the custody of the sheriff of the county in which the prosecution is pending.
(Enacted by Acts 1965, 59th Leg., ch. 722 (S.B. 107), § 1, effective January 1, 1966; am. Acts 1987, 70th Leg., ch. 1047 (S.B. 185), § 1, effective June 20, 1987; am. Acts 2011, 82nd Leg., ch. 87 (S.B. 877), § 1, effective May 19, 2011.)

## Art. 17.17. When Surrender Is Made During Term.

If a surrender of the accused be made during a term of the court to which he has bound himself to appear, the sheriff shall take him before the court; and if he is willing to give other bail, the court shall forthwith require him to do so. If he fails or refuses to give bail, the court shall make an order that he be committed to jail until the bail is given, and this shall be a sufficient commitment without any written order to the sheriff. (Enacted by Acts 1965, 59th Leg., ch. 722 (S.B. 107), § 1, effective January 1, 1966.)

## Art. 17.18. Surrender in Vacation.

When the surrender is made at any other time than during the session of the court, the sheriff may take the necessary bail bond, but if the defendant fails or refuses to give other bail, the sheriff shall take him before the nearest magistrate; and such magistrate shall issue a warrant of commitment, reciting the fact that the accused has been once admitted to bail, has been surrendered, and now fails or refuses to give other bail. (Enacted by Acts 1965, 59th Leg., ch. 722 (S.B. 107), § 1, effective January 1, 1966.)

## Art. 17.19. Surety May Obtain a Warrant.

(a) Any surety, desiring to surrender his principal and after notifying the principal's attorney, if the principal is represented by an attorney, in a manner provided by Rule 21a, Texas Rules of Civil Procedure, of the surety's intention to surrender the principal, may file an affidavit of such intention before the court or magistrate before which the prosecution is pending. The affidavit must state:

(1) the court and cause number of the case;

(2) the name of the defendant;

(3) the offense with which the defendant is charged;

(4) the date of the bond;

(5) the cause for the surrender; and

(6) that notice of the surety's intention to surrender the principal has been given as required by this subsection.

(b) In a prosecution pending before a court, if the court finds that there is cause for the surety to surrender the surety's principal, the court shall issue a capias for the principal. In a prosecution pending before a magistrate, if the magistrate finds that there is cause for the surety to surrender the surety's principal, the magistrate shall issue a warrant of arrest for the principal: It is an affirmative defense to any liability on the bond that:

(1) the court or magistrate refused to issue a capias or warrant of arrest for the principal; and

(2) after the refusal to issue the capias or warrant of arrest, the principal failed to appear.

(c) If the court or magistrate before whom the prosecution is pending is not available, the surety may deliver the affidavit to any other magistrate in the county and that magistrate, on a finding of cause for the surety to surrender the surety's principal, shall issue a warrant of arrest for the principal.

(d) An arrest warrant or capias issued under this article shall be issued to the sheriff of the county in which the case is pending, and a copy of the warrant or capias shall be issued to the surety or his agent.

(e) An arrest warrant or capias issued under this article may be executed by a peace officer, a security officer, or a private investigator licensed in this state.

(Enacted by Acts 1965, 59th Leg., ch. 722 (S.B. 107), § 1, effective January 1, 1966; am. Acts 1987, 70th Leg., ch. 1047 (S.B. 185), § 2, effective June 20, 1987; am. Acts 1989, 71st Leg., ch. 374 (S.B. 376), § 3, effective September 1, 1989; am. Acts 1999, 76th Leg., ch. 1506 (S.B. 403), § 3, effective September 1, 1999; am. Acts 2003, 78th Leg., ch. 942 (S.B. 1336), § 4, effective June 20, 2003; am. Acts 2007, 80th Leg., ch. 1263 (H.B. 3060), § 2, effective September 1, 2007.)

### Art. 17.20. Bail in Misdemeanor.

In cases of misdemeanor, the sheriff or other peace officer, or a jailer licensed under Chapter 1701, Occupations Code, may, whether during the term of the court or in vacation, where the officer has a defendant in custody, take of the defendant a bail bond.

(Enacted by Acts 1965, 59th Leg., ch. 722 (S.B. 107), § 1, effective January 1, 1966; am. Acts 1971, 62nd Leg., ch. 1006 (H.B. 1325), § 1, effective August 30, 1971; am. Acts 2011, 82nd Leg., ch. 736 (H.B. 1070), § 3, effective June 17, 2011.)

### Art. 17.21. Bail in Felony.

In cases of felony, when the accused is in custody of the sheriff or other officer, and the court before which the prosecution is pending is in session in the county where the accused is in custody, the court shall fix the amount of bail, if it is a bailable case and determine if the accused is eligible for a personal bond; and the sheriff or other peace officer, unless it be the police of a city, or a jailer licensed under Chapter 1701, Occupations Code, is authorized to take a bail bond of the accused in the amount as fixed by the court, to be approved by such officer taking the same, and will thereupon discharge the accused from custody. The defendant and the defendant's sureties are not required to appear in court.

(Enacted by Acts 1965, 59th Leg., ch. 722 (S.B. 107), § 1, effective January 1, 1966; am. Acts 2011, 82nd Leg., ch. 736 (H.B. 1070), § 4, effective June 17, 2011.)

### Art. 17.22. May Take Bail in Felony.

In a felony case, if the court before which the same is pending is not in session in the county where the defendant is in custody, the sheriff or other peace officer, or a jailer licensed under Chapter 1701, Occupations Code, who has the defendant in custody may take the defendant's bail bond in such amount as may have been fixed by the court or magistrate, or if no amount has been fixed, then in such amount as such officer may consider reasonable.

(Enacted by Acts 1965, 59th Leg., ch. 722 (S.B. 107), § 1, effective January 1, 1966; am. Acts 2011, 82nd Leg., ch. 736 (H.B. 1070), § 5, effective June 17, 2011.)

### Art. 17.23. Sureties Severally Bound.

In all bail bonds taken under any provision of this Code, the sureties shall be severally bound. Where a surrender of the principal is made by one or more of them, all the sureties shall be considered discharged.

(Enacted by Acts 1965, 59th Leg., ch. 722 (S.B. 107), § 1, effective January 1, 1966.)

### Art. 17.24. General Rules Applicable.

All general rules in the Chapter are applicable to bail defendant before an examining court.

(Enacted by Acts 1965, 59th Leg., ch. 722 (S.B. 107), § 1, effective January 1, 1966.)

### Art. 17.25. Proceedings When Bail Is Granted.

After a full examination of the testimony, the magistrate shall, if the case be one where bail may properly be granted and ought to be re-

quired, proceed to make an order that the accused execute a bail bond with sufficient security, conditioned for his appearance before the proper court.
(Enacted by Acts 1965, 59th Leg., ch. 722 (S.B. 107), § 1, effective January 1, 1966.)

### Art. 17.26. Time Given to Procure Bail.

Reasonable time shall be given the accused to procure security.
(Enacted by Acts 1965, 59th Leg., ch. 722 (S.B. 107), § 1, effective January 1, 1966.)

### Art. 17.27. When Bail Is Not Given.

If, after the allowance of a reasonable time, the security be not given, the magistrate shall make an order committing the accused to jail to be kept safely until legally discharged; and he shall issue a commitment accordingly.
(Enacted by Acts 1965, 59th Leg., ch. 722 (S.B. 107), § 1, effective January 1, 1966.)

### Art. 17.28. When Ready to Give Bail.

If the party be ready to give bail, the magistrate shall cause to be prepared a bond, which shall be signed by the accused and his surety or sureties, if any.
(Enacted by Acts 1965, 59th Leg., ch. 722 (S.B. 107), § 1, effective January 1, 1966.)

### Art. 17.29. Accused Liberated.

(a) When the accused has given the required bond, either to the magistrate or the officer having him in custody, he shall at once be set at liberty.

(b) Before releasing on bail a person arrested for an offense under Section 42.072, Penal Code, or a person arrested or held without warrant in the prevention of family violence, the law enforcement agency holding the person shall make a reasonable attempt to give personal notice of the imminent release to the victim of the alleged offense or to another person designated by the victim to receive the notice. An attempt by an agency to give notice to the victim or the person designated by the victim at the victim's or person's last known telephone number or address, as shown on the records of the agency, constitutes a reasonable attempt to give notice under this subsection. If possible, the arresting officer shall collect the address and telephone number of the victim at the time the arrest is made and shall communicate that information to the agency holding the person.

(c) A law enforcement agency or an employee of a law enforcement agency is not liable for damages arising from complying or failing to comply with Subsection (b) of this article.

(d) In this article, "family violence" has the meaning assigned by Section 71.004, Family Code.
(Enacted by Acts 1965, 59th Leg., ch. 722 (S.B. 107), § 1, effective January 1, 1966; am. Acts 1995, 74th Leg., ch. 656 (S.B. 124), § 1, effective June 14, 1995; am. Acts 1995, 74th Leg., ch. 661 (S.B. 223), § 1, effective August 28, 1995; am. Acts 1997, 75th Leg., ch. 1 (S.B. 97), § 3, effective January 28, 1997; am. Acts 2003, 78th Leg., ch. 1276 (H.B. 3507), § 7.002(e), effective September 1, 2003.)

### Art. 17.291. Further Detention of Certain Persons.

(a) In this article:

(1) "family violence" has the meaning assigned to that phrase by Section 71.004, Family Code; and

(2) "magistrate" has the meaning assigned to it by Article 2.09 of this code.

(b) Article 17.29 does not apply when a person has been arrested or held without a warrant in the prevention of family violence if there is probable cause to believe the violence will continue if the person is immediately released. The head of the agency arresting or holding such a person may hold the person for a period of not more than four hours after bond has been posted. This detention period may be extended for an additional period not to exceed 48 hours, but only if authorized in a writing directed to the person having custody of the detained person by a magistrate who concludes that:

(1) the violence would continue if the person is released; and

(2) if the additional period exceeds 24 hours, probable cause exists to believe that the person committed the instant offense and that, during the 10-year period preceding the date of the instant offense, the person has been arrested:

(A) on more than one occasion for an offense involving family violence; or

(B) for any other offense, if a deadly weapon, as defined by Section 1.07, Penal Code, was used or exhibited during commission of the offense or during immediate flight after commission of the offense.
(Enacted by Acts 1991, 72nd Leg., ch. 552 (S.B. 409), § 2, effective June 16, 1991; am. Acts 1999,

76th Leg., ch. 1341 (H.B. 577), § 1, effective September 1, 1999; am. Acts 2003, 78th Leg., ch. 1276 (H.B. 3507), § 7.002(f), effective September 1, 2003.)

## Art. 17.292. Magistrate's Order for Emergency Protection.

(a) At a defendant's appearance before a magistrate after arrest for an offense involving family violence or an offense under Section 22.011, 22.021, or 42.072, Penal Code, the magistrate may issue an order for emergency protection on the magistrate's own motion or on the request of:

    (1) the victim of the offense;

    (2) the guardian of the victim;

    (3) a peace officer; or

    (4) the attorney representing the state.

(b) At a defendant's appearance before a magistrate after arrest for an offense involving family violence, the magistrate shall issue an order for emergency protection if the arrest is for an offense that also involves:

    (1) serious bodily injury to the victim; or

    (2) the use or exhibition of a deadly weapon during the commission of an assault.

(c) The magistrate in the order for emergency protection may prohibit the arrested party from:

    (1) committing:

        (A) family violence or an assault on the person protected under the order; or

        (B) an act in furtherance of an offense under Section 42.072, Penal Code;

    (2) communicating:

        (A) directly with a member of the family or household or with the person protected under the order in a threatening or harassing manner; or

        (B) a threat through any person to a member of the family or household or to the person protected under the order;

    (3) going to or near:

        (A) the residence, place of employment, or business of a member of the family or household or of the person protected under the order; or

        (B) the residence, child care facility, or school where a child protected under the order resides or attends; or

    (4) possessing a firearm, unless the person is a peace officer, as defined by Section 1.07, Penal Code, actively engaged in employment as a sworn, full-time paid employee of a state agency or political subdivision.

(c-1) In addition to the conditions described by Subsection (c), the magistrate in the order for emergency protection may impose a condition described by Article 17.49(b) in the manner provided by that article, including ordering a defendant's participation in a global positioning monitoring system or allowing participation in the system by an alleged victim or other person protected under the order.

(d) The victim of the offense need not be present in court when the order for emergency protection is issued.

(e) In the order for emergency protection the magistrate shall specifically describe the prohibited locations and the minimum distances, if any, that the party must maintain, unless the magistrate determines for the safety of the person or persons protected by the order that specific descriptions of the locations should be omitted.

(f) To the extent that a condition imposed by an order for emergency protection issued under this article conflicts with an existing court order granting possession of or access to a child, the condition imposed under this article prevails for the duration of the order for emergency protection.

(f-1) To the extent that a condition imposed by an order issued under this article conflicts with a condition imposed by an order subsequently issued under Chapter 85, Subtitle B, Title 4, Family Code, or under Title 1 or Title 5, Family Code, the condition imposed by the order issued under the Family Code prevails.

(f-2) To the extent that a condition imposed by an order issued under this article conflicts with a condition imposed by an order subsequently issued under Chapter 83, Subtitle B, Title 4, Family Code, the condition imposed by the order issued under this article prevails unless the court issuing the order under Chapter 83, Family Code:

    (1) is informed of the existence of the order issued under this article; and

    (2) makes a finding in the order issued under Chapter 83, Family Code, that the court is superseding the order issued under this article.

(g) An order for emergency protection issued under this article must contain the following statements printed in bold-face type or in capital letters:

"A VIOLATION OF THIS ORDER BY COMMISSION OF AN ACT PROHIBITED BY THE ORDER MAY BE PUNISHABLE BY A FINE OF AS MUCH AS $4,000 OR BY CONFINEMENT IN JAIL FOR AS LONG AS ONE YEAR OR BY BOTH. AN ACT THAT RESULTS IN FAMILY VIOLENCE OR A STALKING OFFENSE MAY BE PROSECUTED AS A SEPARATE MISDE-

MEANOR OR FELONY OFFENSE. IF THE ACT IS PROSECUTED AS A SEPARATE FELONY OFFENSE, IT IS PUNISHABLE BY CONFINEMENT IN PRISON FOR AT LEAST TWO YEARS. THE POSSESSION OF A FIREARM BY A PERSON, OTHER THAN A PEACE OFFICER, AS DEFINED BY SECTION 1.07, PENAL CODE, ACTIVELY ENGAGED IN EMPLOYMENT AS A SWORN, FULL-TIME PAID EMPLOYEE OF A STATE AGENCY OR POLITICAL SUBDIVISION, WHO IS SUBJECT TO THIS ORDER MAY BE PROSECUTED AS A SEPARATE OFFENSE PUNISHABLE BY CONFINEMENT OR IMPRISONMENT.

"NO PERSON, INCLUDING A PERSON WHO IS PROTECTED BY THIS ORDER, MAY GIVE PERMISSION TO ANYONE TO IGNORE OR VIOLATE ANY PROVISION OF THIS ORDER. DURING THE TIME IN WHICH THIS ORDER IS VALID, EVERY PROVISION OF THIS ORDER IS IN FULL FORCE AND EFFECT UNLESS A COURT CHANGES THE ORDER."

(h) The magistrate issuing an order for emergency protection under this article shall send a copy of the order to the chief of police in the municipality where the member of the family or household or individual protected by the order resides, if the person resides in a municipality, or to the sheriff of the county where the person resides, if the person does not reside in a municipality. If the victim of the offense is not present when the order is issued, the magistrate issuing the order shall order an appropriate peace officer to make a good faith effort to notify, within 24 hours, the victim that the order has been issued by calling the victim's residence and place of employment. The clerk of the court shall send a copy of the order to the victim.

(i) If an order for emergency protection issued under this article prohibits a person from going to or near a child care facility or school, the magistrate shall send a copy of the order to the child care facility or school.

(j) An order for emergency protection issued under this article is effective on issuance, and the defendant shall be served a copy of the order in open court. An order for emergency protection issued under Subsection (a) or (b)(1) of this article remains in effect up to the 61st day but not less than 31 days after the date of issuance. An order for emergency protection issued under Subsection (b)(2) of this article remains in effect up to the 91st day but not less than 61 days after the date of issuance. After notice to each affected party and a hearing, the issuing court may mod-

ify all or part of an order issued under this article if the court finds that:

(1) the order as originally issued is unworkable;

(2) the modification will not place the victim of the offense at greater risk than did the original order; and

(3) the modification will not in any way endanger a person protected under the order.

(k) To ensure that an officer responding to a call is aware of the existence and terms of an order for emergency protection issued under this article, each municipal police department and sheriff shall establish a procedure within the department or office to provide adequate information or access to information for peace officers of the names of persons protected by an order for emergency protection issued under this article and of persons to whom the order is directed. The police department or sheriff may enter an order for emergency protection issued under this article in the department's or office's record of outstanding warrants as notice that the order has been issued and is in effect.

(*l*) In the order for emergency protection, the magistrate shall suspend a license to carry a concealed handgun issued under Subchapter H, Chapter 411, Government Code, that is held by the defendant.

(m) In this article:

(1) "Family," "family violence," and "household" have the meanings assigned by Chapter 71, Family Code.

(2) "Firearm" has the meaning assigned by Chapter 46, Penal Code.

(n) On motion, notice, and hearing, or on agreement of the parties, an order for emergency protection issued under this article may be transferred to the court assuming jurisdiction over the criminal act giving rise to the issuance of the emergency order for protection. On transfer, the criminal court may modify all or part of an order issued under this subsection in the same manner and under the same standards as the issuing court under Subsection (j).

(Enacted by Acts 1995, 74th Leg., ch. 658 (S.B. 129), § 1, effective June 14, 1995; am. Acts 1997, 75th Leg., ch. 1 (S.B. 97), § 4, effective January 28, 1997; am. Acts 1997, 75th Leg., ch. 610 (S.B. 550), § 1, effective September 1, 1997; am. Acts 1999, 76th Leg., ch. 514 (S.B. 23), § 1, effective September 1, 1999; am. Acts 1999, 76th Leg., ch. 1412 (H.B. 2124), § 1, effective September 1, 1999; am. Acts 2001, 77th Leg., ch. 23 (S.B. 199), § 4, effective September 1, 2001; am. Acts 2003,

78th Leg., ch. 424 (H.B. 297), § 1, effective September 1, 2003; am. Acts 2005, 79th Leg., ch. 361 (S.B. 1275), § 1, effective June 17, 2005; am. Acts 2007, 80th Leg., ch. 66 (S.B. 584), § 1, effective May 11, 2007; am. Acts 2009, 81st Leg., ch. 1146 (H.B. 2730), § 11.20, effective September 1, 2009; am. Acts 2009, 81st Leg., ch. 1276 (H.B. 1506), § 1, effective September 1, 2009.)

### Art. 17.293. Delivery of Order for Emergency Protection to Other Persons.

The magistrate or the clerk of the magistrate's court issuing an order for emergency protection under Article 17.292 that suspends a license to carry a concealed handgun shall immediately send a copy of the order to the appropriate division of the Department of Public Safety at its Austin headquarters. On receipt of the order suspending the license, the department shall:

(1) record the suspension of the license in the records of the department;

(2) report the suspension to local law enforcement agencies, as appropriate; and

(3) demand surrender of the suspended license from the license holder.

(Enacted by Acts 1999, 76th Leg., ch. 1412 (H.B. 2124), § 2, effective September 1, 1999.)

### Art. 17.30. Shall Certify Proceedings.

The magistrate, before whom an examination has taken place upon a criminal accusation, shall certify to all the proceedings had before him, as well as where he discharges, holds to bail or commits, and transmit them, sealed up, to the court before which the defendant may be tried, writing his name across the seals of the envelope. The voluntary statement of the defendant, the testimony, bail bonds, and every other proceeding in the case, shall be thus delivered to the clerk of the proper court, without delay.

(Enacted by Acts 1965, 59th Leg., ch. 722 (S.B. 107), § 1, effective January 1, 1966.)

### Art. 17.31. Duty of Clerks Who Receive Such Proceedings.

If the proceedings be delivered to a district clerk, he shall keep them safely and deliver the same to the next grand jury. If the proceedings are delivered to a county clerk, he shall without delay deliver them to the district or county attorney of his county.

(Enacted by Acts 1965, 59th Leg., ch. 722 (S.B. 107), § 1, effective January 1, 1966.)

### Art. 17.32. In Case of No Arrest.

Upon failure from any cause to arrest the accused the magistrate shall file with the proper clerk the complaint, warrant of arrest, and a list of the witnesses.

(Enacted by Acts 1965, 59th Leg., ch. 722 (S.B. 107), § 1, effective January 1, 1966.)

### Art. 17.33. Request Setting of Bail.

The accused may at any time after being confined request a magistrate to review the written statements of the witnesses for the State as well as all other evidence available at that time in determining the amount of bail. This setting of the amount of bail does not waive the defendant's right to an examining trial as provided in Article 16.01.

(Enacted by Acts 1965, 59th Leg., ch. 722 (S.B. 107), § 1, effective January 1, 1966.)

### Art. 17.34. Witnesses to Give Bond.

Witnesses for the State or defendant may be required by the magistrate, upon the examination of any criminal accusation before him, to give bail for their appearance to testify before the proper court. A personal bond may be taken of a witness by the court before whom the case is pending.

(Enacted by Acts 1965, 59th Leg., ch. 722 (S.B. 107), § 1, effective January 1, 1966.)

### Art. 17.35. Security of Witness.

The amount of security to be required of a witness is to be regulated by his pecuniary condition, character and the nature of the offense with respect to which he is a witness.

(Enacted by Acts 1965, 59th Leg., ch. 722 (S.B. 107), § 1, effective January 1, 1966.)

### Art. 17.36. Effect of Witness Bond.

The bond given by a witness for his appearance has the same effect as a bond of the accused and may be forfeited and recovered upon in the same manner.

(Enacted by Acts 1965, 59th Leg., ch. 722 (S.B. 107), § 1, effective January 1, 1966.)

### Art. 17.37. Witness May Be Committed.

A witness required to give bail who fails or refuses to do so shall be committed to jail as in other cases of a failure to give bail when required, but shall be released from custody upon giving such bail.

(Enacted by Acts 1965, 59th Leg., ch. 722 (S.B. 107), § 1, effective January 1, 1966.)

## Art. 17.38. Rules Applicable to All Cases of Bail.

The rules in this Chapter respecting bail are applicable to all such undertakings when entered into in the course of a criminal action, whether before or after an indictment, in every case where authority is given to any court, judge, magistrate, or other officer, to require bail of a person accused of an offense, or of a witness in a criminal action. (Enacted by Acts 1965, 59th Leg., ch. 722 (S.B. 107), § 1, effective January 1, 1966.)

## Art. 17.39. Records of Bail.

A magistrate or other officer who sets the amount of bail or who takes bail shall record in a well-bound book the name of the person whose appearance the bail secures, the amount of bail, the date bail is set, the magistrate or officer who sets bail, the offense or other cause for which the appearance is secured, the magistrate or other officer who takes bail, the date the person is released, and the name of the bondsman, if any. (Enacted by Acts 1977, 65th Leg., ch. 618 (H.B. 1214), § 1, effective August 29, 1977.)

## Art. 17.40. Conditions Related to Victim or Community Safety.

(a) To secure a defendant's attendance at trial, a magistrate may impose any reasonable condition of bond related to the safety of a victim of the alleged offense or to the safety of the community.

(b) At a hearing limited to determining whether the defendant violated a condition of bond imposed under Subsection (a), the magistrate may revoke the defendant's bond only if the magistrate finds by a preponderance of the evidence that the violation occurred. If the magistrate finds that the violation occurred, the magistrate shall revoke the defendant's bond and order that the defendant be immediately returned to custody. Once the defendant is placed in custody, the revocation of the defendant's bond discharges the sureties on the bond, if any, from any future liability on the bond. A discharge under this subsection from any future liability on the bond does not discharge any surety from liability for previous forfeitures on the bond. (Enacted by Acts 1999, 76th Leg., ch. 768 (H.B. 1321), § 1, effective September 1, 1999; am. Acts 2007, 80th Leg., ch. 1113 (H.B. 3692), § 4, effective January 1, 2008.)

## Art. 17.41. Condition Where Child Alleged Victim.

(a) This article applies to a defendant charged with an offense under any of the following provisions of the Penal Code, if committed against a child younger than 14 years of age:

(1) Chapter 21 (Sexual Offenses) or 22 (Assaultive Offenses);

(2) Section 25.02 (Prohibited Sexual Conduct); or

(3) Section 43.25 (Sexual Performance by a Child).

(b) Subject to Subsections (c) and (d), a magistrate shall require as a condition of bond for a defendant charged with an offense described by Subsection (a) that the defendant not:

(1) directly communicate with the alleged victim of the offense; or

(2) go near a residence, school, or other location, as specifically described in the bond, frequented by the alleged victim.

(c) A magistrate who imposes a condition of bond under this article may grant the defendant supervised access to the alleged victim.

(d) To the extent that a condition imposed under this article conflicts with an existing court order granting possession of or access to a child, the condition imposed under this article prevails for a period specified by the magistrate, not to exceed 90 days. (Enacted by Acts 1985, 69th Leg., ch. 595 (H.B. 1378), § 1, effective September 1, 1985; am. Acts 1995, 74th Leg., ch. 76 (S.B. 959), § 14.21, effective September 1, 1995; am. Acts 2009, 81st Leg., ch. 982 (H.B. 3751), § 1, effective September 1, 2009.)

## Art. 17.42. Personal Bond Office.

Sec. 1. Any county, or any judicial district with jurisdiction in more than one county, with the approval of the commissioners court of each county in the district, may establish a personal bond office to gather and review information about an accused that may have a bearing on whether he will comply with the conditions of a personal bond and report its findings to the court before which the case is pending.

Sec. 2. (a) The commissioners court of a county that establishes the office or the district and county judges of a judicial district that establishes the office may employ a director of the office.

(b) The director may employ the staff authorized by the commissioners court of the county or the commissioners court of each county in the judicial district.

Sec. 3. If a judicial district establishes an office, each county in the district shall pay its pro rata share of the costs of administering the office according to its population.

Sec. 4. (a) If a court releases an accused on personal bond on the recommendation of a personal bond office, the court shall assess a personal bond fee of $20 or three percent of the amount of the bail fixed for the accused, whichever is greater. The court may waive the fee or assess a lesser fee if good cause is shown.

(b) Fees collected under this article may be used solely to defray expenses of the personal bond office, including defraying the expenses of extradition.

(c) Fees collected under this article shall be deposited in the county treasury, or if the office serves more than one county, the fees shall be apportioned to each county in the district according to each county's pro rata share of the costs of the office.

Sec. 5 (a) A personal bond pretrial release office established under this article shall:

(1) prepare a record containing information about any accused person identified by case number only who, after review by the office, is released by a court on personal bond;

(2) update the record on a monthly basis; and

(3) file a copy of the record in the office of the clerk of the county court in any county served by the office.

(b) In preparing a record under Subsection (a), the office shall include in the record a statement of:

(1) the offense with which the person is charged;

(2) the dates of any court appearances scheduled in the matter that were previously unattended by the person;

(3) whether a warrant has been issued for the person's arrest for failure to appear in accordance with the terms of the person's release;

(4) whether the person has failed to comply with conditions of release on personal bond; and

(5) the presiding judge or magistrate who authorized the personal bond.

(c) This section does not apply to a personal bond pretrial release office that on January 1, 1995, was operated by a community corrections and supervision department.

Sec. 6. (a) Not later than April 1 of each year, a personal bond office established under this article shall submit to the commissioners court or district and county judges that established the office an annual report containing information about the operations of the office during the preceding year.

(b) In preparing an annual report under Subsection (a), the office shall include in the report a statement of:

(1) the office's operating budget;

(2) the number of positions maintained for office staff;

(3) the number of accused persons who, after review by the office, were released by a court on personal bond; and

(4) the number of persons described by Subdivision (3):

(A) who were convicted of the same offense or of any felony within the six years preceding the date on which charges were filed in the matter pending during the person's release;

(B) who failed to attend a scheduled court appearance;

(C) for whom a warrant was issued for the person's arrest for failure to appear in accordance with the terms of the person's release; or

(D) who were arrested for any other offense while on the personal bond.

(c) This section does not apply to a personal bond pretrial release office that on January 1, 1995, was operated by a community corrections and supervision department.

(Enacted by Acts 1989, 71st Leg., ch. 2 (S.B. 221), § 5.01(a), effective August 28, 1989; am. Acts 1989, 71st Leg., ch. 1080, § 1, effective September 1, 1989; am. Acts 1995, 74th Leg., ch. 318 (S.B. 15), § 44, effective September 1, 1995; am. Acts 2011, 82nd Leg., ch. 420 (S.B. 882), § 1, effective June 17, 2011.)

### Art. 17.43. Home Curfew and Electronic Monitoring As Condition.

(a) A magistrate may require as a condition of release on personal bond that the defendant submit to home curfew and electronic monitoring under the supervision of an agency designated by the magistrate.

(b) Cost of monitoring may be assessed as court costs or ordered paid directly by the defendant as a condition of bond.

(Enacted by Acts 1989, 71st Leg., ch. 374 (S.B. 376), § 4, effective September 1, 1989.)

## Art. 17.44. Home Confinement, Electronic Monitoring, and Drug Testing As Condition.

(a) A magistrate may require as a condition of release on bond that the defendant submit to:

(1) home confinement and electronic monitoring under the supervision of an agency designated by the magistrate; or

(2) testing on a weekly basis for the presence of a controlled substance in the defendant's body.

(b) In this article, "controlled substance" has the meaning assigned by Section 481.002, Health and Safety Code.

(c) The magistrate may revoke the bond and order the defendant arrested if the defendant:

(1) violates a condition of home confinement and electronic monitoring;

(2) refuses to submit to a test for controlled substances or submits to a test for controlled substances and the test indicates the presence of a controlled substance in the defendant's body; or

(3) fails to pay the costs of monitoring or testing for controlled substances, if payment is ordered under Subsection (e) as a condition of bond and the magistrate determines that the defendant is not indigent and is financially able to make the payments as ordered.

(d) The community justice assistance division of the Texas Department of Criminal Justice may provide grants to counties to implement electronic monitoring programs authorized by this article.

(e) The cost of electronic monitoring or testing for controlled substances under this article may be assessed as court costs or ordered paid directly by the defendant as a condition of bond.

(Enacted by Acts 1989, 71st Leg., ch. 785 (H.B. 2335), § 4.03, effective September 1, 1989; am. Acts 1991, 72nd Leg., ch. 14 (S.B. 404), § 284(46), effective September 1, 1991; am. Acts 1991, 72nd Leg., ch. 16 (S.B. 232), § 19.01(3), effective August 26, 1991 (renumbered from art. 17.42); am. Acts 2009, 81st Leg., ch. 163 (S.B. 1506), § 1, effective September 1, 2009.)

## Art. 17.441. Conditions Requiring Motor Vehicle Ignition Interlock.

(a) Except as provided by Subsection (b), a magistrate shall require on release that a defendant charged with a subsequent offense under Sections 49.04—49.06, Penal Code, or an offense under Section 49.07 or 49.08 of that code:

(1) have installed on the motor vehicle owned by the defendant or on the vehicle most regularly driven by the defendant, a device that uses a deep-lung breath analysis mechanism to make impractical the operation of a motor vehicle if ethyl alcohol is detected in the breath of the operator; and

(2) not operate any motor vehicle unless the vehicle is equipped with that device.

(b) The magistrate may not require the installation of the device if the magistrate finds that to require the device would not be in the best interest of justice.

(c) If the defendant is required to have the device installed, the magistrate shall require that the defendant have the device installed on the appropriate motor vehicle, at the defendant's expense, before the 30th day after the date the defendant is released on bond.

(d) The magistrate may designate an appropriate agency to verify the installation of the device and to monitor the device. If the magistrate designates an agency under this subsection, in each month during which the agency verifies the installation of the device or provides a monitoring service the defendant shall pay a fee to the designated agency in the amount set by the magistrate. The defendant shall pay the initial fee at the time the agency verifies the installation of the device. In each subsequent month during which the defendant is required to pay a fee the defendant shall pay the fee on the first occasion in that month that the agency provides a monitoring service. The magistrate shall set the fee in an amount not to exceed $10 as determined by the county auditor, or by the commissioners court of the county if the county does not have a county auditor, to be sufficient to cover the cost incurred by the designated agency in conducting the verification or providing the monitoring service, as applicable in that county.

(Enacted by Acts 1995, 74th Leg., ch. 318 (S.B. 15), § 45, effective September 1, 1995; am. Acts 1999, 76th Leg., ch. 537 (S.B. 205), § 1, effective September 1, 1999.)

## Art. 17.45. Conditions Requiring AIDS and HIV Instruction.

A magistrate may require as a condition of bond that a defendant charged with an offense under Section 43.02, Penal Code, receive counseling or education, or both, relating to acquired immune deficiency syndrome or human immunodeficiency virus.

(Enacted by Acts 1989, 71st Leg., ch. 1195 (S.B. 959), § 8, effective September 1, 1989; am. Acts 1991, 72nd Leg., ch. 16 (S.B. 232), § 19.01(4), effective August 26, 1991 (renumbered from art. 17.42).)

## Art. 17.46. Conditions for a Defendant Charged with Stalking.

(a) A magistrate may require as a condition of release on bond that a defendant charged with an offense under Section 42.072, Penal Code, may not:

(1) communicate directly or indirectly with the victim; or

(2) go to or near the residence, place of employment, or business of the victim or to or near a school, day-care facility, or similar facility where a dependent child of the victim is in attendance.

(b) If the magistrate requires the prohibition contained in Subsection (a)(2) of this article as a condition of release on bond, the magistrate shall specifically describe the prohibited locations and the minimum distances, if any, that the defendant must maintain from the locations.

(Enacted by Acts 1993, 73rd Leg., ch. 10 (S.B. 25), § 2, effective March 19, 1993; am. Acts 1995, 74th Leg., ch. 657 (S.B. 126), § 3, effective June 14, 1995; am. Acts 1997, 75th Leg., ch. 1 (S.B. 97), § 5, effective January 28, 1997.)

## Art. 17.47. Conditions Requiring Submission of Specimen.

(a) A magistrate may require as a condition of release on bail or bond of a defendant that the defendant provide to a local law enforcement agency one or more specimens for the purpose of creating a DNA record under Subchapter G, Chapter 411, Government Code.

(b) A magistrate shall require as a condition of release on bail or bond of a defendant described by Section 411.1471(a), Government Code, that the defendant provide to a local law enforcement agency one or more specimens for the purpose of creating a DNA record under Subchapter G, Chapter 411, Government Code.

(Enacted by Acts 2001, 77th Leg., ch. 1490 (S.B. 638), § 5, effective September 1, 2001; am. Acts 2005, 79th Leg., ch. 1224 (H.B. 1068), § 17, effective September 1, 2005.)

## Art. 17.48. Posttrial Actions.

A convicting court on entering a finding favorable to a convicted person under Article 64.04,

after a hearing at which the attorney representing the state and the counsel for the defendant are entitled to appear, may release the convicted person on bail under this chapter pending the conclusion of court proceedings or proceedings under Section 11, Article IV, Texas Constitution, and Article 48.01.

(Enacted by Acts 2001, 77th Leg., ch. 2 (S.B. 3), § 3, effective April 5, 2001; am. Acts 2003, 78th Leg., ch. 1275 (H.B. 3506), § 2(6), effective September 1, 2003 (renumbered from art. 17.47).)

## Art. 17.49. Conditions for Defendant Charged with Offense Involving Family Violence.

(a) In this article:

(1) "Family violence" has the meaning assigned by Section 71.004, Family Code.

(2) "Global positioning monitoring system" means a system that electronically determines and reports the location of an individual through the use of a transmitter or similar device carried or worn by the individual that transmits latitude and longitude data to a monitoring entity through global positioning satellite technology. The term does not include a system that contains or operates global positioning system technology, radio frequency identification technology, or any other similar technology that is implanted in or otherwise invades or violates the individual's body.

(b) A magistrate may require as a condition of release on bond that a defendant charged with an offense involving family violence:

(1) refrain from going to or near a residence, school, place of employment, or other location, as specifically described in the bond, frequented by an alleged victim of the offense;

(2) carry or wear a global positioning monitoring system device and, except as provided by Subsection (h), pay the costs associated with operating that system in relation to the defendant; or

(3) except as provided by Subsection (h), if the alleged victim of the offense consents after receiving the information described by Subsection (d), pay the costs associated with providing the victim with an electronic receptor device that:

(A) is capable of receiving the global positioning monitoring system information from the device carried or worn by the defendant; and

(B) notifies the victim if the defendant is at or near a location that the defendant has been ordered to refrain from going to or near under Subdivision (1).

(c) Before imposing a condition described by Subsection (b)(1), a magistrate must afford an alleged victim an opportunity to provide the magistrate with a list of areas from which the victim would like the defendant excluded and shall consider the victim's request, if any, in determining the locations the defendant will be ordered to refrain from going to or near. If the magistrate imposes a condition described by Subsection (b)(1), the magistrate shall specifically describe the locations that the defendant has been ordered to refrain from going to or near and the minimum distances, if any, that the defendant must maintain from those locations.

(d) Before imposing a condition described by Subsection (b)(3), a magistrate must provide to an alleged victim information regarding:

(1) the victim's right to participate in a global positioning monitoring system or to refuse to participate in that system and the procedure for requesting that the magistrate terminate the victim's participation;

(2) the manner in which the global positioning monitoring system technology functions and the risks and limitations of that technology, and the extent to which the system will track and record the victim's location and movements;

(3) any locations that the defendant is ordered to refrain from going to or near and the minimum distances, if any, that the defendant must maintain from those locations;

(4) any sanctions that the court may impose on the defendant for violating a condition of bond imposed under this article;

(5) the procedure that the victim is to follow, and support services available to assist the victim, if the defendant violates a condition of bond or if the global positioning monitoring system equipment fails;

(6) community services available to assist the victim in obtaining shelter, counseling, education, child care, legal representation, and other assistance available to address the consequences of family violence; and

(7) the fact that the victim's communications with the court concerning the global positioning monitoring system and any restrictions to be imposed on the defendant's movements are not confidential.

(e) In addition to the information described by Subsection (d), a magistrate shall provide to an alleged victim who participates in a global posi-

tioning monitoring system under this article the name and telephone number of an appropriate person employed by a local law enforcement agency whom the victim may call to request immediate assistance if the defendant violates a condition of bond imposed under this article.

(f) In determining whether to order a defendant's participation in a global positioning monitoring system under this article, the magistrate shall consider the likelihood that the defendant's participation will deter the defendant from seeking to kill, physically injure, stalk, or otherwise threaten the alleged victim before trial.

(g) An alleged victim may request that the magistrate terminate the victim's participation in a global positioning monitoring system at any time. The magistrate may not impose sanctions on the victim for requesting termination of the victim's participation in or refusing to participate in a global positioning monitoring system under this article.

(h) If the magistrate determines that a defendant is indigent, the magistrate may, based on a sliding scale established by local rule, require the defendant to pay costs under Subsection (b)(2) or (3) in an amount that is less than the full amount of the costs associated with operating the global positioning monitoring system in relation to the defendant or providing the victim with an electronic receptor device.

(i) If an indigent defendant pays to an entity that operates a global positioning monitoring system the partial amount ordered by a magistrate under Subsection (h), the entity shall accept the partial amount as payment in full. The county in which the magistrate who enters an order under Subsection (h) is located is not responsible for payment of any costs associated with operating the global positioning monitoring system in relation to an indigent defendant.

(j) A magistrate that imposes a condition described by Subsection (b)(1) or (2) shall order the entity that operates the global positioning monitoring system to notify the court and the appropriate local law enforcement agency if a defendant violates a condition of bond imposed under this article.

(k) A magistrate that imposes a condition described by Subsection (b) may only allow or require the defendant to execute or be released under a type of bond that is authorized by this chapter.

(l) This article does not limit the authority of a magistrate to impose any other reasonable condi-

tions of bond or enter any orders of protection under other applicable statutes.
(Enacted by Acts 2009, 81st Leg., ch. 1276 (H.B. 1506), § 2, effective September 1, 2009.)

# CHAPTER 17A
## CORPORATIONS AND ASSOCIATIONS

## Art. 17A.01. Application and Definitions.

(a) This chapter sets out some of the procedural rules applicable to the criminal responsibility of corporations and associations. Where not in conflict with this chapter, the other chapters of this code apply to corporations and associations.

(b) In this code, unless the context requires a different definition:

(1) "Agent" means a director, officer, employee, or other person authorized to act in behalf of a corporation or association.

(2) "Association" means a government or governmental subdivision or agency, trust, partnership, or two or more persons having a joint or common economic interest.

(3) "High managerial agent" means:

(A) an officer of a corporation or association;

(B) a partner in a partnership; or

(C) an agent of a corporation or association who has duties of such responsibility that his conduct may reasonably be assumed to represent the policy of the corporation or association.

(4) "Person," "he," and "him" include corporation and association.

(Enacted by Acts 1973, 63rd Leg., ch. 399 (S.B. 34), § 2(D), effective January 1, 1974.)

## Art. 17A.02. Allegation of Name.

(a) In alleging the name of a defendant corporation, it is sufficient to state in the complaint, indictment, or information the corporate name, or to state any name or designation by which the corporation is known or may be identified. It is not necessary to allege that the defendant was lawfully incorporated.

(b) In alleging the name of a defendant association it is sufficient to state in the complaint, indictment, or information the association's name, or to state any name or designation by which the association is known or may be identified, or to state the name or names of one or more members of the association, referring to the unnamed members as "others." It is not necessary to allege the legal form of the association.

(Enacted by Acts 1973, 63rd Leg., ch. 399 (S.B. 34), § 2(D), effective January 1, 1974.)

## Art. 17A.03. Summoning Corporation or Association.

(a) When a complaint is filed or an indictment or information presented against a corporation or association, the court or clerk shall issue a summons to the corporation or association. The summons shall be in the same form as a capias except that:

(1) it shall summon the corporation or association to appear before the court named at the place stated in the summons; and

(2) it shall be accompanied by a certified copy of the complaint, indictment, or information; and

(3) it shall provide that the corporation or association appear before the court named at or before 10 a.m. of the Monday next after the expiration of 20 days after it is served with summons, except when service is made upon the secretary of state or the Commissioner of Insurance, in which instance the summons shall provide that the corporation or association appear before the court named at or before 10 a.m. of the Monday next after the expiration of 30 days after the secretary of state or the Commissioner of Insurance is served with summons.

(b) No individual may be arrested upon a complaint, indictment, information, judgment, or sentence against a corporation or association.

(Enacted by Acts 1973, 63rd Leg., ch. 399 (S.B. 34), § 2(D), effective January 1, 1974; am. Acts 1987, 70th Leg., ch. 46 (S.B. 357), § 10, effective September 1, 1987.)

## Art. 17A.04. Service on Corporation.

(a) Except as provided in Paragraph (d) of this article, a peace officer shall serve a summons on a corporation by personally delivering a copy of it to the corporation's registered agent. However, if a registered agent has not been designated, or cannot with reasonable diligence be found at the registered office, then the peace officer shall serve the summons by personally delivering a copy of it to the president or a vice-president of the corporation.

(b) If the peace officer certifies on the return that he diligently but unsuccessfully attempted to effect service under Paragraph (a) of this article, or if the corporation is a foreign corporation that has no certificate of authority, then he shall serve the summons on the secretary of state by personally delivering a copy of it to him, or to the deputy secretary of state, or to any clerk in charge of the corporation department of his office. On receipt of the summons copy, the secretary of state shall immediately forward it by certified or registered mail, return receipt requested, addressed to the defendant corporation at its registered or principal office in the state or country under whose law it was incorporated.

(c) The secretary of state shall keep a permanent record of the date and time of receipt and his disposition of each summons served under Paragraph (b) of this article together with the return receipt.

(d) The method of service on a corporation regulated under the Insurance Code is governed by that code.

(Enacted by Acts 1973, 63rd Leg., ch. 399 (S.B. 34), § 2(D), effective January 1, 1974; am. Acts 2005, 79th Leg., ch. 41 (H.B. 297), § 15, effective September 1, 2005.)

## Art. 17A.05. Service on Association.

(a) Except as provided in Paragraph (b) of this article, a peace officer shall serve a summons on an association by personally delivering a copy of it:

    (1) to a high managerial agent at any place where business of the association is regularly conducted; or

    (2) if the peace officer certifies on the return that he diligently but unsuccessfully attempted to serve a high managerial agent, to any employee of suitable age and discretion at any place where business of the association is regularly conducted; or

    (3) if the peace officer certifies on the return that he diligently but unsuccessfully attempted to serve a high managerial agent, or employee of suitable age and discretion, to any member of the association.

(b) The method of service on an association regulated under the Insurance Code is governed by that code.

(Enacted by Acts 1973, 63rd Leg., ch. 399 (S.B. 34), § 2(D), effective January 1, 1974.)

## Art. 17A.06. Appearance.

(a) In all criminal actions instituted against a corporation or association, in which original jurisdiction is in a district or county-level court:

    (1) appearance is for the purpose of arraignment;

    (2) the corporation or association has 10 full days after the day the arraignment takes place and before the day the trial begins to file written pleadings.

(b) In all criminal actions instituted against a corporation or association, in which original jurisdiction is in a justice court or corporation court:

    (1) appearance is for the purpose of entering a plea; and

    (2) 10 full days must elapse after the day of appearance before the corporation or association may be tried.

(Enacted by Acts 1973, 63rd Leg., ch. 399 (S.B. 34), § 2(D), effective January 1, 1974.)

## Art. 17A.07. Presence of Corporation or Association.

(a) A defendant corporation or association appears through counsel.

(b) If a corporation or association does not appear in response to summons, or appears but fails or refuses to plead:

    (1) it is deemed to be present in person for all purposes; and

    (2) the court shall enter a plea of not guilty in its behalf; and

    (3) the court may proceed with trial, judgment, and sentencing.

(c) If, having appeared and entered a plea in response to summons, a corporation or association is absent without good cause at any time during later proceedings:

    (1) it is deemed to be present in person for all purposes; and

    (2) the court may proceed with trial, judgment, or sentencing.

(Enacted by Acts 1973, 63rd Leg., ch. 399 (S.B. 34), § 2(D), effective January 1, 1974.)

## Art. 17A.08. Probation.

The benefits of the adult probation laws shall not be available to corporations and associations.

(Enacted by Acts 1973, 63rd Leg., ch. 399 (S.B. 34), § 2(D), effective January 1, 1974.)

## Art. 17A.09. Notifying Attorney General of Corporation's Conviction.

If a corporation is convicted of an offense, or if a high managerial agent is convicted of an offense committed in the conduct of the affairs of the corporation, the court shall notify the attorney general in writing of the conviction when it becomes final and unappealable. The notice shall include:

(1) the corporation's name, and the name of the corporation's registered agent and the address of the registered office, or the high managerial agent's name and address, or both; and

(2) certified copies of the judgment and sentence and of the complaint, information, or indictment on which the judgment and sentence were based.

(Enacted by Acts 1973, 63rd Leg., ch. 399 (S.B. 34), § 2(D), effective January 1, 1974.)

# Search Warrants

## CHAPTER 18
## SEARCH WARRANTS

## Art. 18.01. Search Warrant.

(a) A "search warrant" is a written order, issued by a magistrate and directed to a peace officer, commanding him to search for any property or thing and to seize the same and bring it before such magistrate or commanding him to search for and photograph a child and to deliver to the magistrate any of the film exposed pursuant to the order.

(b) No search warrant shall issue for any purpose in this state unless sufficient facts are first presented to satisfy the issuing magistrate that probable cause does in fact exist for its issuance. A sworn affidavit setting forth substantial facts establishing probable cause shall be filed in every instance in which a search warrant is requested. Except as provided by Article 18.011, the affidavit is public information if executed, and the magistrate's clerk shall make a copy of the affidavit available for public inspection in the clerk's office during normal business hours.

(c) A search warrant may not be issued under Article 18.02(10) unless the sworn affidavit required by Subsection (b) sets forth sufficient facts to establish probable cause: (1) that a specific offense has been committed, (2) that the specifically described property or items that are to be searched for or seized constitute evidence of that offense or evidence that a particular person committed that offense, and (3) that the property or items constituting evidence to be searched for or seized are located at or on the particular person, place, or thing to be searched. Except as provided by Subsections (d), (i), and (j), only a judge of a municipal court of record or a county court who is an attorney licensed by the State of Texas, a statutory county court judge, a district court judge, a judge of the Court of Criminal Appeals, including the presiding judge, a justice of the Supreme Court of Texas, including the chief justice, or a magistrate with jurisdiction over criminal cases serving a district court may issue warrants under Article 18.02(10).

(d) Only the specifically described property or items set forth in a search warrant issued under

Subdivision (10) of Article 18.02 of this code or property, items or contraband enumerated in Subdivisions (1) through (9) or in Subdivision (12) of Article 18.02 of this code may be seized. A subsequent search warrant may be issued pursuant to Subdivision (10) of Article 18.02 of this code to search the same person, place, or thing subjected to a prior search under Subdivision (10) of Article 18.02 of this code only if the subsequent search warrant is issued by a judge of a district court, a court of appeals, the court of criminal appeals, or the supreme court.

(e) A search warrant may not be issued under Subdivision (10) of Article 18.02 of this code to search for and seize property or items that are not described in Subdivisions (1) through (9) of that article and that are located in an office of a newspaper, news magazine, television station, or radio station, and in no event may property or items not described in Subdivisions (1) through (9) of that article be legally seized in any search pursuant to a search warrant of an office of a newspaper, news magazine, television station, or radio station.

(f) A search warrant may not be issued pursuant to Article 18.021 of this code unless the sworn affidavit required by Subsection (b) of this article sets forth sufficient facts to establish probable cause:

(1) that a specific offense has been committed;

(2) that a specifically described person has been a victim of the offense;

(3) that evidence of the offense or evidence that a particular person committed the offense can be detected by photographic means; and

(4) that the person to be searched for and photographed is located at the particular place to be searched.

(g) A search warrant may not be issued under Subdivision (12), Article 18.02, of this code unless the sworn affidavit required by Subsection (b) of this article sets forth sufficient facts to establish probable cause that a specific felony offense has been committed and that the specifically described property or items that are to be searched for or seized constitute contraband as defined in Article 59.01 of this code and are located at or on the particular person, place, or thing to be searched.

(h) Except as provided by Subsection (i) of this article, a warrant under Subdivision (12), Article 18.02 of this code may only be issued by:

(1) a judge of a municipal court of record who is an attorney licensed by the state;

(2) a judge of a county court who is an attorney licensed by the state; or

(3) judge of a statutory county court, district court, the court of criminal appeals, or the supreme court.

(i) In a county that does not have a judge of a municipal court of record who is an attorney licensed by the state, a county court judge who is an attorney licensed by the state, or a statutory county court judge, any magistrate may issue a search warrant under Subdivision (10) or Subdivision (12) of Article 18.02 of this code. This subsection is not applicable to a subsequent search warrant under Subdivision (10) of Article 18.02 of this code.

(j) Any magistrate who is an attorney licensed by this state may issue a search warrant under Article 18.02(10) to collect a blood specimen from a person who:

(1) is arrested for an offense under Section 49.04, 49.045, 49.05, 49.06, 49.065, 49.07, or 49.08, Penal Code; and

(2) refuses to submit to a breath or blood alcohol test.

(Enacted by Acts 1965, 59th Leg., ch. 722 (S.B. 107), § 1, effective January 1, 1966; am. Acts 1973, 63rd Leg., ch. 399 (S.B. 34), § 2, effective January 1, 1974; am. Acts 1977, 65th Leg., ch. 237 (S.B. 156), § 1, effective May 25, 1977; am. Acts 1979, 66th Leg., ch. 505 (H.B. 2091), § 1, effective September 1, 1979; am. Acts 1979, 66th Leg., ch. 536 (S.B. 1202), § 1, effective June 11, 1979; am. Acts 1981, 67th Leg., ch. 289 (S.B. 242), §§ 3, 4, effective September 1, 1981; am. Acts 1981, 67th Leg., ch. 755 (H.B. 2153), § 1, effective September 1, 1981; am. Acts 1987, 70th Leg., ch. 686 (S.B. 1077), § 1, effective September 1, 1987; am. Acts 1989, 71st Leg., 1st C.S., ch. 12 (H.B. 404), § 2, effective October 18, 1989; am. Acts 1991, 72nd Leg., ch. 73 (H.B. 597), § 1, effective May 9, 1991; am. Acts 1995, 74th Leg., ch. 670 (S.B. 1349), § 1, effective September 1, 1995; am. Acts 1997, 75th Leg., ch. 604 (S.B. 224), § 1, effective September 1, 1997; am. Acts 1999, 76th Leg., ch. 167 (H.B. 234), § 1, effective August 30, 1999; am. Acts 1999, 76th Leg., ch. 1469 (H.B. 3229), § 1, effective June 19, 1999; am. Acts 2001, 77th Leg., ch. 1395 (H.B. 1999), § 1, effective June 16, 2001; am. Acts 2007, 80th Leg., ch. 355 (S.B. 244), § 1, effective September 1, 2007; am. Acts 2007, 80th Leg., ch. 748 (H.B. 3131), § 1, effective September 1, 2007; am. Acts 2009, 81st Leg., ch. 1348 (S.B. 328), § 5, effective September 1, 2009; am. Acts 2011, 82nd Leg., ch. 66 (S.B. 483), § 3, effective September 1, 2011.)

**Art. 18.011. Sealing of Affidavit.**

(a) An attorney representing the state in the prosecution of felonies may request a district judge or the judge of an appellate court to seal an affidavit presented under Article 18.01(b). The judge may order the affidavit sealed if the attorney establishes a compelling state interest in that:

(1) public disclosure of the affidavit would jeopardize the safety of a victim, witness, or confidential informant or cause the destruction of evidence; or

(2) the affidavit contains information obtained from a court-ordered wiretap that has not expired at the time the attorney representing the state requests the sealing of the affidavit.

(b) An order sealing an affidavit under this section expires on the 31st day after the date on which the search warrant for which the affidavit was presented is executed. After an original order sealing an affidavit is issued under this article, an attorney representing the state in the prosecution of felonies may request, and a judge may grant, before the 31st day after the date on which the search warrant for which the affidavit was presented is executed, on a new finding of compelling state interest, one 30-day extension of the original order.

(c) On the expiration of an order issued under Subsection (b) and any extension, the affidavit must be unsealed.

(d) An order issued under this section may not:

(1) prohibit the disclosure of information relating to the contents of a search warrant, the return of a search warrant, or the inventory of property taken pursuant to a search warrant; or

(2) affect the right of a defendant to discover the contents of an affidavit.

(Enacted by Acts 2007, 80th Leg., ch. 355 (S.B. 244), § 2, effective September 1, 2007.)

**Art. 18.02. Grounds for Issuance.**

A search warrant may be issued to search for and seize:

(1) property acquired by theft or in any other manner which makes its acquisition a penal offense;

(2) property specially designed, made, or adapted for or commonly used in the commission of an offense;

(3) arms and munitions kept or prepared for the purposes of insurrection or riot;

(4) weapons prohibited by the Penal Code;

(5) gambling devices or equipment, altered gambling equipment, or gambling paraphernalia;

(6) obscene materials kept or prepared for commercial distribution or exhibition, subject to the additional rules set forth by law;

(7) a drug, controlled substance, immediate precursor, chemical precursor, or other controlled substance property, including an apparatus or paraphernalia kept, prepared, or manufactured in violation of the laws of this state;

(8) any property the possession of which is prohibited by law;

(9) implements or instruments used in the commission of a crime;

(10) property or items, except the personal writings by the accused, constituting evidence of an offense or constituting evidence tending to show that a particular person committed an offense;

(11) persons; or

(12) contraband subject to forfeiture under Chapter 59 of this code.

(Enacted by Acts 1965, 59th Leg., ch. 722 (S.B. 107), § 1, effective January 1, 1966; am. Acts 1973, 63rd Leg., ch. 399 (S.B. 34), § 2(E), effective January 1, 1974; am. Acts 1977, 65th Leg., ch. 237 (S.B. 156), § 2, effective May 25, 1977; am. Acts 1981, 67th Leg., ch. 755 (H.B. 2153), § 5, effective September 1, 1981; am. Acts 1989, 71st Leg., 1st C.S., ch. 12 (H.B. 65), § 3, effective October 18, 1989; am. Acts 2003, 78th Leg., ch. 1099 (H.B. 2192), § 16, effective September 1, 2003.)

**Art. 18.021. Issuance of Search Warrant to Photograph Injured Child.**

(a) A search warrant may be issued to search for and photograph a child who is alleged to be the victim of the offenses of injury to a child as prohibited by Section 22.04, Penal Code; sexual assault of a child as prohibited by Section 22.011(a), Penal Code; aggravated sexual assault of a child as prohibited by Section 22.021, Penal Code; or continuous sexual abuse of young child or children as prohibited by Section 21.02, Penal Code.

(b) The officer executing the warrant may be accompanied by a photographer who is employed by a law enforcement agency and who acts under the direction of the officer executing the warrant. The photographer is entitled to access to the child in the same manner as the officer executing the warrant.

(c) In addition to the requirements of Subdivisions (1) and (4) of Article 18.04 of this code, a warrant issued under this article shall identify, as near as may be, the child to be located and photographed, shall name or describe, as near as may be, the place or thing to be searched, and shall command any peace officer of the proper county to search for and cause the child to be photographed.

(d) After having located and photographed the child, the peace officer executing the warrant shall take possession of the exposed film and deliver it forthwith to the magistrate. The child may not be removed from the premises on which he or she is located except under Subchapters A and B, Chapter 262, Family Code.

(e) A search warrant under this section shall be executed by a peace officer of the same sex as the alleged victim or, if the officer is not of the same sex as the alleged victim, the peace officer must be assisted by a person of the same sex as the alleged victim. The person assisting an officer under this subsection must be acting under the direction of the officer and must be with the alleged victim during the taking of the photographs.

(Enacted by Acts 1981, 67th Leg., ch. 289 (S.B. 242), § 2, effective September 1, 1981; am. Acts 1983, 68th Leg., ch. 977 (H.B. 2008), § 8, effective September 1, 1983; am. Acts 1997, 75th Leg., ch. 165 (S.B. 898), § 7.01, effective September 1, 1997; am. Acts 2007, 80th Leg., ch. 593 (H.B. 8), § 3.11, effective September 1, 2007.)

## Art. 18.03. Search Warrant May Order Arrest.

If the facts presented to the magistrate under Article 18.02 of this chapter also establish the existence of probable cause that a person has committed some offense under the laws of this state, the search warrant may, in addition, order the arrest of such person.

(Enacted by Acts 1965, 59th Leg., ch. 722 (S.B. 107), § 1, effective January 1, 1966; am. Acts 1973, 63rd Leg., ch. 399 (S.B. 34), § 2(E), effective January 1, 1974.)

## Art. 18.04. Contents of Warrant.

A search warrant issued under this chapter shall be sufficient if it contains the following requisites:

(1) that it run in the name of "The State of Texas";

(2) that it identify, as near as may be, that which is to be seized and name or describe, as

near as may be, the person, place, or thing to be searched;

(3) that it command any peace officer of the proper county to search forthwith the person, place, or thing named; and

(4) that it be dated and signed by the magistrate.

(Enacted by Acts 1965, 59th Leg., ch. 722 (S.B. 107), § 1, effective January 1, 1966; am. Acts 1973, 63rd Leg., ch. 399 (S.B. 34), § 2(E), effective January 1, 1974.)

## Art. 18.05. Warrants for Fire, Health, and Code Inspections.

(a) Except as provided by Subsection (e) of this article, a search warrant may be issued to a fire marshal, health officer, or code enforcement official of the state or of any county, city, or other political subdivision for the purpose of allowing the inspection of any specified premises to determine the presence of a fire or health hazard or unsafe building condition or a violation of any fire, health, or building regulation, statute, or ordinance.

(b) A search warrant may not be issued under this article except upon the presentation of evidence of probable cause to believe that a fire or health hazard or violation or unsafe building condition is present in the premises sought to be inspected.

(c) In determining probable cause, the magistrate is not limited to evidence of specific knowledge, but may consider any of the following:

(1) the age and general condition of the premises;

(2) previous violations or hazards found present in the premises;

(3) the type of premises;

(4) the purposes for which the premises are used; and

(5) the presence of hazards or violations in and the general condition of premises near the premises sought to be inspected.

(d) Each city or county may designate one or more code enforcement officials for the purpose of being issued a search warrant as authorized by Subsection (a) of this article. A political subdivision other than a city or county may designate not more than one code enforcement official for the purpose of being issued a search warrant as authorized by Subsection (a) of this article only if the political subdivision routinely inspects premises to determine whether there is a fire or health hazard or unsafe building condition or a violation of fire, health, or building regulation, statute, or ordinance.

(e) A search warrant may not be issued under this article to a code enforcement official of a county with a population of 3.3 million or more for the purpose of allowing the inspection of specified premises to determine the presence of an unsafe building condition or a violation of a building regulation, statute, or ordinance.

(Enacted by Acts 1965, 59th Leg., ch. 722 (S.B. 107), § 1, effective January 1, 1966; am. Acts 1969, 61st Leg., ch. 502 (H.B. 643), § 1, effective September 1, 1969; am. Acts 1973, 63rd Leg., ch. 399 (S.B. 34), § 2(E), effective January 1, 1974 (renumbered from art. 18.011); am. Acts 1989, 71st Leg., ch. 382 (S.B. 498), § 1, effective August 28, 1989; am. Acts 2007, 80th Leg., ch. 769 (H.B. 3558), § 1, effective September 1, 2007; am. Acts 2011, 82nd Leg., ch. 1163 (H.B. 2702), § 7, effective September 1, 2011.)

### Art. 18.06. Execution of Warrants.

(a) A peace officer to whom a search warrant is delivered shall execute it without delay and forthwith return it to the proper magistrate. It must be executed within three days from the time of its issuance, and shall be executed within a shorter period if so directed in the warrant by the magistrate.

(b) On searching the place ordered to be searched, the officer executing the warrant shall present a copy of the warrant to the owner of the place, if he is present. If the owner of the place is not present but a person who is present is in possession of the place, the officer shall present a copy of the warrant to the person. Before the officer takes property from the place, he shall prepare a written inventory of the property to be taken. He shall legibly endorse his name on the inventory and present a copy of the inventory to the owner or other person in possession of the property. If neither the owner nor a person in possession of the property is present when the officer executes the warrant, the officer shall leave a copy of the warrant and the inventory at the place.

(Enacted by Acts 1965, 59th Leg., ch. 722 (S.B. 107), § 1, effective January 1, 1966; am. Acts 1973, 63rd Leg., ch. 399 (S.B. 34), § 2(E), effective January 1, 1974; am. Acts 1981, 67th Leg., ch. 755 (H.B. 2153), § 2, effective September 1, 1981.)

### Art. 18.07. Days Allowed for Warrant to Run.

(a) The time allowed for the execution of a search warrant, exclusive of the day of its issuance and of the day of its execution, is:

(1) 15 whole days if the warrant is issued solely to search for and seize specimens from a specific person for DNA analysis and comparison, including blood and saliva samples; or

(2) three whole days if the warrant is issued for a purpose other than that described by Subdivision (1).

(b) The magistrate issuing a search warrant under this chapter shall endorse on the search warrant the date and hour of its issuance.

(c) If a warrant is issued to search for and seize data or information contained in or on a computer, disk drive, flash drive, cellular telephone, or other electronic, communication, or data storage device, the warrant is considered to have been executed within the time allowed under Subsection (a) if the device was seized before the expiration of the time allowed. Notwithstanding any other law, any data or information contained in or on a device seized may be recovered and analyzed after the expiration of the time allowed under Subsection (a).

(Enacted by Acts 1965, 59th Leg., ch. 722 (S.B. 107), § 1, effective January 1, 1966; am. Acts 1973, 63rd Leg., ch. 399 (S.B. 34), § 2(E), effective January 1, 1974; am. Acts 2009, 81st Leg., ch. 761 (S.B. 743), § 1, effective September 1, 2009; am. Acts 2011, 82nd Leg., ch. 772 (H.B. 1891), § 1, effective September 1, 2011.)

### Art. 18.08. Power of Officer Executing Warrant.

In the execution of a search warrant, the officer may call to his aid any number of citizens in this county, who shall be bound to aid in the execution of the same.

(Enacted by Acts 1965, 59th Leg., ch. 722 (S.B. 107), § 1, effective January 1, 1966; am. Acts 1973, 63rd Leg., ch. 399 (S.B. 34), § 2(E), effective January 1, 1974.)

### Art. 18.09. Shall Seize Accused and Property.

When the property which the officer is directed to search for and seize is found he shall take possession of the same and carry it before the magistrate. He shall also arrest any person whom he is directed to arrest by the warrant and

**Criminal Procedure**

immediately take such person before the magistrate. For purposes of this chapter, "seizure," in the context of property, means the restraint of property, whether by physical force or by a display of an officer's authority, and includes the collection of property or the act of taking possession of property.
(Enacted by Acts 1965, 59th Leg., ch. 722 (S.B. 107), § 1, effective January 1, 1966; am. Acts 1973, 63rd Leg., ch. 399 (S.B. 34), § 2(E), effective January 1, 1974; am. Acts 2005, 79th Leg., ch. 1026 (H.B. 1048), § 2, effective September 1, 2005.)

### Art. 18.095. Seizure of Circuit Board of Gambling Device, Equipment, or Paraphernalia.

For purposes of this chapter, an officer directed under a search warrant to search for and seize a gambling device or equipment, altered gambling equipment, or gambling paraphernalia in the discretion of the officer may:

(1) seize only the programmable main circuit board of the device, equipment, or paraphernalia if that circuit board is designed as a subassembly or essential part of the device, equipment, or paraphernalia to provide the information necessary for the device, equipment, or paraphernalia to operate as a gambling device or equipment, altered gambling equipment, or gambling paraphernalia;

(2) carry the circuit board before the magistrate; and

(3) retain custody of the circuit board as the property seized pursuant to the warrant as required under this chapter.
(Enacted by Acts 2009, 81st Leg., ch. 898 (H.B. 358), § 1, effective September 1, 2009.)

### Art. 18.10. How Return Made.

Upon returning the search warrant, the officer shall state on the back of the same, or on some paper attached to it, the manner in which it has been executed and shall likewise deliver to the magistrate a copy of the inventory of the property taken into his possession under the warrant. The officer who seized the property shall retain custody of it until the magistrate issues an order directing the manner of safekeeping the property. The property may not be removed from the county in which it was seized without an order approving the removal, issued by a magistrate in the county in which the warrant was issued; provided, however, nothing herein shall prevent

the officer, or his department, from forwarding any item or items seized to a laboratory for scientific analysis.
(Enacted by Acts 1965, 59th Leg., ch. 722 (S.B. 107), § 1, effective January 1, 1966; am. Acts 1973, 63rd Leg., ch. 399 (S.B. 34), § 2(E), effective January 1, 1974; am. Acts 1981, 67th Leg., ch. 755 (H.B. 2153), § 3, effective September 1, 1981.)

### Art. 18.11. Custody of Property Found.

Property seized pursuant to a search warrant shall be kept as provided by the order of a magistrate issued in accordance with Article 18.10 of this code.
(Enacted by Acts 1965, 59th Leg., ch. 722 (S.B. 107), § 1, effective January 1, 1966; am. Acts 1973, 63rd Leg., ch. 399 (S.B. 34), § 2(E), effective January 1, 1974; am. Acts 1981, 67th Leg., ch. 755 (H.B. 2153), § 4, effective September 1, 1981.)

### Art. 18.12. Magistrate Shall Investigate.

The magistrate, upon the return of a search warrant, shall proceed to try the questions arising upon the same, and shall take testimony as in other examinations before him.
(Enacted by Acts 1965, 59th Leg., ch. 722 (S.B. 107), § 1, effective January 1, 1966; am. Acts 1973, 63rd Leg., ch. 399 (S.B. 34), § 2(E), effective January 1, 1974.)

### Art. 18.13. Shall Discharge Defendant.

If the magistrate be not satisfied, upon investigation, that there was good ground for the issuance of the warrant, he shall discharge the defendant and order restitution of the property taken from him, except for criminal instruments. In such case, the criminal instruments shall be kept by the sheriff subject to the order of the proper court.
(Enacted by Acts 1965, 59th Leg., ch. 722 (S.B. 107), § 1, effective January 1, 1966; am. Acts 1973, 63rd Leg., ch. 399 (S.B. 34), § 2(E), effective January 1, 1974.)

### Art. 18.14. Examining Trial.

The magistrate shall proceed to deal with the accused as in other cases before an examining court if he is satisfied there was good ground for issuing the warrant.
(Enacted by Acts 1965, 59th Leg., ch. 722 (S.B. 107), § 1, effective January 1, 1966; am. Acts

1973, 63rd Leg., ch. 399 (S.B. 34), § 2(E), effective January 1, 1974.)

## Art. 18.15. Certify Record to Proper Court.

The magistrate shall keep a record of all the proceedings had before him in cases of search warrants, and shall certify the same and deliver them to the clerk of the court having jurisdiction of the case, before the next term of said court, and accompany the same with all the original papers relating thereto, including the certified schedule of the property seized.

(Enacted by Acts 1965, 59th Leg., ch. 722 (S.B. 107), § 1, effective January 1, 1966; am. Acts 1973, 63rd Leg., ch. 399 (S.B. 34), § 2(E), effective January 1, 1974.)

## Art. 18.16. Preventing Consequences of Theft.

Any person has a right to prevent the consequences of theft by seizing any personal property that has been stolen and bringing it, with the person suspected of committing the theft, if that person can be taken, before a magistrate for examination, or delivering the property and the person suspected of committing the theft to a peace officer for that purpose. To justify a seizure under this article, there must be reasonable ground to believe the property is stolen, and the seizure must be openly made and the proceedings had without delay.

(Enacted by Acts 1965, 59th Leg., ch. 722 (S.B. 107), § 1, effective January 1, 1966; am. Acts 1973, 63rd Leg., ch. 399 (S.B. 34), § 2(E), effective January 1, 1974; am. Acts 2001, 77th Leg., ch. 109 (S.B. 966), § 2, effective September 1, 2001.)

## Art. 18.17. Disposition of Abandoned or Unclaimed Property.

(a) All unclaimed or abandoned personal property of every kind, other than contraband subject to forfeiture under Chapter 59 of this code and whiskey, wine and beer, seized by any peace officer in the State of Texas which is not held as evidence to be used in any pending case and has not been ordered destroyed or returned to the person entitled to possession of the same by a magistrate, which shall remain unclaimed for a period of 30 days shall be delivered for disposition to a person designated by the municipality or the purchasing agent of the county in which the property was seized. If a peace officer of a munic-

ipality seizes the property, the peace officer shall deliver the property to a person designated by the municipality. If any other peace officer seizes the property, the peace officer shall deliver the property to the purchasing agent of the county. If the county has no purchasing agent, then such property shall be disposed of by the sheriff of the county.

(b) The county purchasing agent, the person designated by the municipality, or the sheriff of the county, as the case may be, shall mail a notice to the last known address of the owner of such property by certified mail. Such notice shall describe the property being held, give the name and address of the officer holding such property, and shall state that if the owner does not claim such property within 90 days from the date of the notice such property will be disposed of and the proceeds, after deducting the reasonable expense of keeping such property and the costs of the disposition, placed in the treasury of the municipality or county giving the notice.

(c) If the property has a fair market value of $500 or more and the owner or the address of the owner is unknown, the person designated by the municipality, the county purchasing agent, or the sheriff, as the case may be, shall cause to be published once in a paper of general circulation in the municipality or county a notice containing a general description of the property held, the name of the owner if known, the name and address of the officer holding such property, and a statement that if the owner does not claim such property within 90 days from the date of the publication such property will be disposed of and the proceeds, after deducting the reasonable expense of keeping such property and the costs of the disposition, placed in the treasury of the municipality or county disposing of the property. If the property has a fair market value of less than $500 and the owner or the address of the owner is unknown, the person designated by the municipality, the county purchasing agent, or the sheriff may sell or donate the property. The person designated by the municipality, the purchasing agent, or the sheriff shall deposit the sale proceeds, after deducting the reasonable expense of keeping the property and costs of the sale, in the treasury of the municipality or county selling or donating the property.

(d) The sale under this article of any property that has a fair market value of $500 or more shall be preceded by a notice published once at least 14 days prior to the date of such sale in a newspaper of general circulation in the municipality or county where the sale is to take place, stating the general description of the property, the names of the owner if known, and the date and place that such sale will occur. This article does not require disposition by sale.

(e) The real owner of any property disposed of shall have the right to file a claim to the proceeds with the commissioners court of the county or with the governing body of the municipality in which the disposition took place. A claim by the real owner must be filed not later than the 30th day after the date of disposition. If the claim is allowed by the commissioners court or the governing body of the municipality, the municipal or county treasurer shall pay the owner such funds as were paid into the treasury of the municipality or county as proceeds of the disposition. If the claim is denied by the commissioners court or the governing body or if said court or body fails to act upon such claim within 90 days, the claimant may sue the municipal or county treasurer in a court of competent jurisdiction in the county, and upon sufficient proof of ownership, recover judgment against such municipality or county for the recovery of the proceeds of the disposition.

(f) For the purposes of this article:

(1) "Person designated by a municipality" means an officer or employee of a municipality who is designated by the municipality to be primarily responsible for the disposition of property under this article.

(2) "Property held as evidence" means property related to a charge that has been filed or to a matter that is being investigated for the filing of a charge.

(g) If the provisions of this section have been met and the property is scheduled for disposition, the municipal or county law enforcement agency that originally seized the property may request and have the property converted to agency use. The agency at any time may transfer the property to another municipal or county law enforcement agency for the use of that agency. The agency last using the property shall return the property to the person designated by the municipality, county purchasing agent, or sheriff, as the case may be, for disposition when the agency has completed the intended use of the property.

(h) If the abandoned or unclaimed personal property is money, the person designated by the municipality, the county purchasing agent, or the sheriff of the county, as appropriate, may, after giving notice under Subsection (b) or (c) of this article, deposit the money in the treasury of the municipality or county giving notice without con-

ducting the sale as required by Subsection (d) of this article.

(i) While offering the property for sale under this article, if a person designated by a municipality, county purchasing agent, or sheriff considers any bid as insufficient, the person, agent, or sheriff may decline the bid and reoffer the property for sale.

(j) Chapters 72, 74, 75, and 76, Property Code, do not apply to unclaimed or abandoned property to which this article applies.

(Enacted by Acts 1965, 59th Leg., ch. 722 (S.B. 107), § 1, effective January 1, 1966; am. Acts 1967, 60th Leg., ch. 659 (S.B. 145), § 15, effective August 27, 1967; am. Acts 1973, 63rd Leg., ch. 399 (S.B. 34), § 2(E), effective January 1, 1974; am. Acts 1987, 70th Leg., ch. 1002 (H.B. 2187), § 1, effective September 1, 1987; am. Acts 1989, 71st Leg., 1st C.S., ch. 12 (H.B. 65), § 4, effective October 18, 1989; am. Acts 1991, 72nd Leg., ch. 254 (S.B. 422), § 1, effective June 5, 1991; am. Acts 1993, 73rd Leg., ch. 157 (S.B. 191), § 1, effective September 1, 1993; am. Acts 1993, 73rd Leg., ch. 321 (H.B. 772), §§ 1—4, effective May 28, 1993; am. Acts 1995, 74th Leg., ch. 76 (S.B. 959), §§ 3.01—3.05, effective September 1, 1995; am. Acts 2001, 77th Leg., ch. 402 (H.B. 1265), § 18, effective September 1, 2001.)

### Art. 18.18. Disposition of Gambling Paraphernalia, Prohibited Weapon, Criminal Instrument, and Other Contraband.

(a) Following the final conviction of a person for possession of a gambling device or equipment, altered gambling equipment, or gambling paraphernalia, for an offense involving a criminal instrument, for an offense involving an obscene device or material, for an offense involving child pornography, or for an offense involving a scanning device or re-encoder, the court entering the judgment of conviction shall order that the machine, device, gambling equipment or gambling paraphernalia, instrument, obscene device or material, child pornography, or scanning device or re-encoder be destroyed or forfeited to the state. Not later than the 30th day after the final conviction of a person for an offense involving a prohibited weapon, the court entering the judgment of conviction on its own motion, on the motion of the prosecuting attorney in the case, or on the motion of the law enforcement agency initiating the complaint on notice to the prosecuting attorney in the case if the prosecutor fails to move for the order shall order that the prohibited weapon be destroyed or forfeited to the law enforcement agency that initiated the complaint. If the court fails to enter the order within the time required by this subsection, any magistrate in the county in which the offense occurred may enter the order. Following the final conviction of a person for an offense involving dog fighting, the court entering the judgment of conviction shall order that any dog-fighting equipment be destroyed or forfeited to the state. Destruction of dogs, if necessary, must be carried out by a veterinarian licensed in this state or, if one is not available, by trained personnel of a humane society or an animal shelter. If forfeited, the court shall order the contraband delivered to the state, any political subdivision of the state, or to any state institution or agency. If gambling proceeds were seized, the court shall order them forfeited to the state and shall transmit them to the grand jury of the county in which they were seized for use in investigating alleged violations of the Penal Code, or to the state, any political subdivision of the state, or to any state institution or agency.

(b) If there is no prosecution or conviction following seizure, the magistrate to whom the return was made shall notify in writing the person found in possession of the alleged gambling device or equipment, altered gambling equipment or gambling paraphernalia, gambling proceeds, prohibited weapon, obscene device or material, child pornography, scanning device or re-encoder, criminal instrument, or dog-fighting equipment to show cause why the property seized should not be destroyed or the proceeds forfeited. The magistrate, on the motion of the law enforcement agency seizing a prohibited weapon, shall order the weapon destroyed or forfeited to the law enforcement agency seizing the weapon, unless a person shows cause as to why the prohibited weapon should not be destroyed or forfeited. A law enforcement agency shall make a motion under this section in a timely manner after the time at which the agency is informed in writing by the attorney representing the state that no prosecution will arise from the seizure.

(c) The magistrate shall include in the notice a detailed description of the property seized and the total amount of alleged gambling proceeds; the name of the person found in possession; the address where the property or proceeds were seized; and the date and time of the seizure.

(d) The magistrate shall send the notice by registered or certified mail, return receipt requested, to the person found in possession at the address where the property or proceeds were seized. If no one was found in possession, or the possessor's address is unknown, the magistrate shall post the notice on the courthouse door.

(e) Any person interested in the alleged gambling device or equipment, altered gambling equipment or gambling paraphernalia, gambling proceeds, prohibited weapon, obscene device or material, child pornography, scanning device or re-encoder, criminal instrument, or dog-fighting equipment seized must appear before the magistrate on the 20th day following the date the notice was mailed or posted. Failure to timely appear forfeits any interest the person may have in the property or proceeds seized, and no person after failing to timely appear may contest destruction or forfeiture.

(f) If a person timely appears to show cause why the property or proceeds should not be destroyed or forfeited, the magistrate shall conduct a hearing on the issue and determine the nature of property or proceeds and the person's interest therein. Unless the person proves by a preponderance of the evidence that the property or proceeds is not gambling equipment, altered gambling equipment, gambling paraphernalia, gambling device, gambling proceeds, prohibited weapon, obscene device or material, child pornography, criminal instrument, scanning device or re-encoder, or dog-fighting equipment and that he is entitled to possession, the magistrate shall dispose of the property or proceeds in accordance with Paragraph (a) of this article.

(g) For purposes of this article:

(1) "criminal instrument" has the meaning defined in the Penal Code;

(2) "gambling device or equipment, altered gambling equipment or gambling paraphernalia" has the meaning defined in the Penal Code;

(3) "prohibited weapon" has the meaning defined in the Penal Code;

(4) "dog-fighting equipment" means:

(A) equipment used for training or handling a fighting dog, including a harness, treadmill, cage, decoy, pen, house for keeping a fighting dog, feeding apparatus, or training pen;

(B) equipment used for transporting a fighting dog, including any automobile, or other vehicle, and its appurtenances which are intended to be used as a vehicle for transporting a fighting dog;

(C) equipment used to promote or advertise an exhibition of dog fighting, including a printing press or similar equipment, paper, ink, or photography equipment; or

(D) a dog trained, being trained, or intended to be used to fight with another dog;

(5) "obscene device" and "obscene" have the meanings assigned by Section 43.21, Penal Code;

(6) "re-encoder" has the meaning assigned by Section 522.001, Business & Commerce Code;

(7) "scanning device" has the meaning assigned by Section 522.001, Business & Commerce Code; and

(8) "obscene material" and "child pornography" include digital images and the media and equipment on which those images are stored.

(h) No provider of an electronic communication service or of a remote computing service to the public shall be held liable for an offense involving obscene material or child pornography under this section on account of any action taken in good faith in providing that service.

(Enacted by Acts 1965, 59th Leg., ch. 722 (S.B. 107), § 1, effective January 1, 1966; am. Acts 1973, 63rd Leg., ch. 399 (S.B. 34), § 2(E), effective January 1, 1974; am. Acts 1983, 68th Leg., ch. 305 (S.B. 557), §§ 2, 3, effective September 1, 1983; am. Acts 1983, 68th Leg., ch. 351 (H.B. 1643), § 1, effective September 1, 1983; am. Acts 1987, 70th Leg., ch. 167 (S.B. 892), § 5.01(a)(6), effective September 1, 1987; am. Acts 1987, 70th Leg., ch. 980 (S.B. 1115), § 1, effective September 1, 1987; am. Acts 1993, 73rd Leg., ch. 157 (S.B. 191), § 2, effective September 1, 1993; am. Acts 2003, 78th Leg., ch. 441 (H.B. 559), § 1, effective September 1, 2003; am. Acts 2003, 78th Leg., ch. 649 (H.B. 2138), § 2, effective September 1, 2003; am. Acts 2005, 79th Leg., ch. 522 (H.B. 839), §§ 1, 2, effective September 1, 2005; am. Acts 2007, 80th Leg., ch. 885 (H.B. 2278), § 2.13, effective April 1, 2009; am. Acts 2007, 80th Leg., ch. 921 (H.B. 3167), § 17.002(1), effective September 1, 2007.)

## Art. 18.181. Disposition of Explosive Weapons and Chemical Dispensing Devices.

(a) After seizure of an explosive weapon or chemical dispensing device, as these terms are defined in Section 46.01, Penal Code, a peace officer or a person acting at the direction of a peace officer shall:

(1) photograph the weapon in the position where it is recovered before touching or moving it;

(2) record the identification designations printed on a weapon if the markings are intact;

(3) if the weapon can be moved, move it to an isolated area in order to lessen the danger to the public;

(4) if possible, retain a portion of a wrapper or other packaging materials connected to the weapon;

(5) retain a small portion of the explosive material and submit the material to a laboratory for chemical analysis;

(6) separate and retain components associated with the weapon such as fusing and triggering mechanisms if those mechanisms are not hazardous in themselves;

(7) destroy the remainder of the weapon in a safe manner;

(8) at the time of destruction, photograph the destruction process and make careful observations of the characteristics of the destruction;

(9) after destruction, inspect the disposal site and photograph the site to record the destructive characteristics of the weapon; and

(10) retain components of the weapon and records of the destruction for use as evidence in court proceedings.

(b) Representative samples, photographs, and records made pursuant to this article are admissible in civil or criminal proceedings in the same manner and to the same extent as if the explosive weapon were offered in evidence, regardless of whether or not the remainder of the weapon has been destroyed. No inference or presumption of spoliation applies to weapons destroyed pursuant to this article.

(Enacted by Acts 1983, 68th Leg., ch. 852 (H.B. 1208), § 5, effective September 1, 1983.)

## Art. 18.182. Destruction of Vicious Dog [Repealed].

Repealed by Acts 1991, 72nd Leg., ch. 916 (H.B. 2065), § 3, effective September 1, 1991.

## Art. 18.183. Deposit of Money Pending Disposition.

(a) If money is seized by a law enforcement agency in connection with a violation of Chapter 47, Penal Code, the state or the political subdivision of the state that employs the law enforcement agency may deposit the money in an interest-bearing bank account in the jurisdiction of the agency that made seizure or in the county in which the money was seized until a final judgment is rendered concerning the violation.

(b) If a final judgment is rendered concerning a violation of Chapter 47, Penal Code, money seized in connection with the violation that has been placed in an interest-bearing bank account shall be distributed according to this chapter, with any interest being distributed in the same manner and used for the same purpose as the principal.

(Am. Acts 1987, 70th Leg., ch. 167 (S.B. 892), § 4.02(a), effective September 1, 1987; am. Acts 1989, 71st Leg., ch. 2 (S.B. 221), § 16.01(6), effective August 28, 1989 (renumbered from art. 18.182).)

## Art. 18.19. Disposition of Seized Weapons.

(a) Weapons seized in connection with an offense involving the use of a weapon or an offense under Penal Code Chapter 46 shall be held by the law enforcement agency making the seizure, subject to the following provisions, unless:

(1) the weapon is a prohibited weapon identified in Penal Code Chapter 46, in which event Article 18.18 of this code applies; or

(2) the weapon is alleged to be stolen property, in which event Chapter 47 of this code applies.

(b) When a weapon described in Paragraph (a) of this article is seized, and the seizure is not made pursuant to a search or arrest warrant, the person seizing the same shall prepare and deliver to a magistrate a written inventory of each weapon seized.

(c) If there is no prosecution or conviction for an offense involving the weapon seized, the magistrate to whom the seizure was reported shall, before the 61st day after the date the magistrate determines that there will be no prosecution or conviction, notify in writing the person found in possession of the weapon that the person is entitled to the weapon upon written request to the magistrate. The magistrate shall order the weapon returned to the person found in possession before the 61st day after the date the magistrate receives a request from the person. If the weapon is not requested before the 61st day after the date of notification, the magistrate shall, before the 121st day after the date of notification, order the weapon destroyed or forfeited to the state for use by the law enforcement agency holding the weapon or by a county forensic laboratory designated by the magistrate. If the magistrate does not order the return, destruction, or forfeiture of the weapon within the applicable period prescribed by this subsection, the law enforcement agency holding the weapon may request an order of destruction or forfeiture of the weapon from the magistrate.

(d) A person either convicted or receiving deferred adjudication under Chapter 46, Penal Code, is entitled to the weapon seized upon request to the court in which the person was convicted or placed on deferred adjudication. However, the court entering the judgment shall order the weapon destroyed or forfeited to the state for use by the law enforcement agency holding the weapon or by a county forensic laboratory designated by the court if:

(1) the person does not request the weapon before the 61st day after the date of the judgment of conviction or the order placing the person on deferred adjudication;

(2) the person has been previously convicted under Chapter 46, Penal Code;

(3) the weapon is one defined as a prohibited weapon under Chapter 46, Penal Code;

(4) the offense for which the person is convicted or receives deferred adjudication was committed in or on the premises of a playground, school, video arcade facility, or youth center, as those terms are defined by Section 481.134, Health and Safety Code; or

(5) the court determines based on the prior criminal history of the defendant or based on the circumstances surrounding the commission of the offense that possession of the seized weapon would pose a threat to the community or one or more individuals.

(e) If the person found in possession of a weapon is convicted of an offense involving the use of the weapon, before the 61st day after the date of conviction the court entering judgment of conviction shall order destruction of the weapon or forfeiture to the state for use by the law enforcement agency holding the weapon or by a county forensic laboratory designated by the court. If the court entering judgment of conviction does not order the destruction or forfeiture of the weapon within the period prescribed by this subsection, the law enforcement agency holding the weapon may request an order of destruction or forfeiture of the weapon from a magistrate.

(Enacted by Acts 1965, 59th Leg., ch. 722 (S.B. 107), § 1, effective January 1, 1966; am. Acts 1973, 63rd Leg., ch. 399 (S.B. 34), § 2(E), effective January 1, 1974; am. Acts 1987, 70th Leg., ch. 980 (S.B. 1115), § 2, effective September 1, 1987; am. Acts 1993, 73rd Leg., ch. 157 (S.B. 191), § 3, effective September 1, 1993; am. Acts 1995,

*Criminal Procedure*

74th Leg., ch. 318 (S.B. 15), § 46(a), effective September 1, 1995; am. Acts 2001, 77th Leg., ch. 1083 (H.B. 2184), § 1, effective September 1, 2001; am. Acts 2005, 79th Leg., ch. 509 (H.B. 705), § 1, effective September 1, 2005.)

## Art. 18.20. Detection, Interception, and Use of Wire, Oral, or Electronic Communications.

### Sec. 1. Definitions.

In this article:

(1) "Wire communication" means an aural transfer made in whole or in part through the use of facilities for the transmission of communications by the aid of wire, cable, or other like connection between the point of origin and the point of reception, including the use of such a connection in a switching station, furnished or operated by a person authorized to engage in providing or operating the facilities for the transmission of communications as a communications common carrier.

(2) "Oral communication" means an oral communication uttered by a person exhibiting an expectation that the communication is not subject to interception under circumstances justifying that expectation. The term does not include an electronic communication.

(3) "Intercept" means the aural or other acquisition of the contents of a wire, oral, or electronic communication through the use of an electronic, mechanical, or other device.

(4) "Electronic, mechanical, or other device" means a device that may be used for the nonconsensual interception of wire, oral, or electronic communications. The term does not include a telephone or telegraph instrument, the equipment or a facility used for the transmission of electronic communications, or a component of the equipment or a facility used for the transmission of electronic communications if the instrument, equipment, facility, or component is:

(A) furnished to the subscriber or user by a provider of wire or electronic communications service in the ordinary course of the provider's business and being used by the subscriber or user in the ordinary course of its business;

(B) furnished by a subscriber or user for connection to the facilities of a wire or electronic communications service for use in the ordinary course of the subscriber's or user's business;

(C) being used by a communications common carrier in the ordinary course of its business; or

(D) being used by an investigative or law enforcement officer in the ordinary course of the officer's duties.

(5) "Investigative or law enforcement officer" means an officer of this state or of a political subdivision of this state who is empowered by law to conduct investigations of or to make arrests for offenses enumerated in Section 4 of this article or an attorney authorized by law to prosecute or participate in the prosecution of the enumerated offenses.

(6) "Contents," when used with respect to a wire, oral, or electronic communication, includes any information concerning the substance, purport, or meaning of that communication.

(7) "Judge of competent jurisdiction" means a judge from the panel of nine active district judges with criminal jurisdiction appointed by the presiding judge of the court of criminal appeals as provided by Section 3 of this article.

(8) "Prosecutor" means a district attorney, criminal district attorney, or county attorney performing the duties of a district attorney, with jurisdiction in the county within an administrative judicial district described by Section 3(b).

(9) "Director" means the director of the Department of Public Safety or, if the director is absent or unable to serve, the assistant director of the Department of Public Safety.

(10) "Communication common carrier" means a person engaged as a common carrier for hire in the transmission of wire or electronic communications.

(11) "Aggrieved person" means a person who was a party to an intercepted wire, oral, or electronic communication or a person against whom the interception was directed.

(12) "Covert entry" means any entry into or onto premises which if made without a court order allowing such an entry under this Act, would be a violation of the Penal Code.

(13) "Residence" means a structure or the portion of a structure used as a person's home or fixed place of habitation to which the person indicates an intent to return after any temporary absence.

(14) "Pen register," "ESN reader," "trap and trace device," and "mobile tracking device" have the meanings assigned by Article 18.21.

(15) "Electronic communication" means a transfer of signs, signals, writing, images, sounds, data, or intelligence of any nature transmitted in whole or in part by a wire, radio, electromagnetic, photoelectronic, or photo-optical system. The term does not include:

(A) a wire or oral communication;

(B) a communication made through a tone-only paging device; or

(C) a communication from a tracking device.

(16) "User" means a person who uses an electronic communications service and is authorized by the provider of the service to use the service.

(17) "Electronic communications system" means a wire, radio, electromagnetic, photo-optical or photoelectronic facility for the transmission of wire or electronic communications, and any computer facility or related electronic equipment for the electronic storage of those communications.

(18) "Electronic communications service" means a service that provides to users of the service the ability to send or receive wire or electronic communications.

(19) "Readily accessible to the general public" means, with respect to a radio communication, a communication that is not:

(A) scrambled or encrypted;

(B) transmitted using modulation techniques whose essential parameters have been withheld from the public with the intention of preserving the privacy of the communication;

(C) carried on a subcarrier or other signal subsidiary to a radio transmission;

(D) transmitted over a communication system provided by a common carrier, unless the communication is a tone-only paging system communication;

(E) transmitted on frequencies allocated under Part 25, Subpart D, E, or F of Part 74, or Part 94 of the rules of the Federal Communications Commission, unless, in the case of a communication transmitted on a frequency allocated under Part 74 that is not exclusively allocated to broadcast auxiliary services, the communication is a two-way voice communication by radio; or

(F) an electronic communication.

(20) "Electronic storage" means:

(A) a temporary, intermediate storage of a wire or electronic communication that is in-cidental to the electronic transmission of the communication; or

(B) storage of a wire or electronic communication by an electronic communications service for purposes of backup protection of the communication.

(21) "Aural transfer" means a transfer containing the human voice at any point between and including the point of origin and the point of reception.

(22) "Immediate life-threatening situation" means a hostage, barricade, or other emergency situation in which a person unlawfully and directly:

(A) threatens another with death; or

(B) exposes another to a substantial risk of serious bodily injury.

(23) "Member of a law enforcement unit specially trained to respond to and deal with life-threatening situations" means a peace officer who, as evidenced by the submission of appropriate documentation to the Commission on Law Enforcement Officer Standards and Education:

(A) receives a minimum of 40 hours a year of training in hostage and barricade suspect situations; or

(B) has received a minimum of 24 hours of training on kidnapping investigations and is:

(i) the sheriff of a county with a population of 3.3 million or more or the sheriff's designee; or

(ii) the police chief of a police department in a municipality with a population of 500,000 or more or the police chief's designee.

(24) "Access," "computer," "computer network," "computer system," and "effective consent" have the meanings assigned by Section 33.01, Penal Code.

(25) "Computer trespasser" means a person who:

(A) is accessing a protected computer without effective consent of the owner; and

(B) has no reasonable expectation of privacy in any communication transmitted to, through, or from the protected computer. The term does not include a person who accesses the computer under an existing contractual relationship with the owner or operator of the protected computer.

(26) "Protected computer" means a computer, computer network, or computer system that is:

(A) owned by a financial institution or governmental entity; or

(B) used by or for a financial institution or governmental entity and conduct constituting an offense affects that use.

## Sec. 2. Prohibition of Use As Evidence of Intercepted Communications.

(a) The contents of an intercepted communication and evidence derived from an intercepted communication may be received in evidence in any trial, hearing, or other proceeding in or before any court, grand jury, department, officer, agency, regulatory body, legislative committee, or other authority of the United States or of this state or a political subdivision of this state unless:

(1) the communication was intercepted in violation of this article, Section 16.02, Penal Code, or federal law; or

(2) the disclosure of the contents of the intercepted communication or evidence derived from the communication would be in violation of this article, Section 16.02, Penal Code, or federal law.

(b) The contents of an intercepted communication and evidence derived from an intercepted communication may be received in a civil trial, hearing, or other proceeding only if the civil trial, hearing, or other proceeding arises out of a violation of a penal law.

(c) This section does not prohibit the use or admissibility of the contents of a communication or evidence derived from the communication if the communication was intercepted in a jurisdiction outside this state in compliance with the law of that jurisdiction.

## Sec. 3. Judges Authorized to Consider Interception Applications.

(a) The presiding judge of the court of criminal appeals, by order filed with the clerk of that court, shall appoint one district judge from each of the administrative judicial districts of this state to serve at his pleasure as the judge of competent jurisdiction within that administrative judicial district. The presiding judge shall fill vacancies, as they occur, in the same manner.

(b) Except as provided by Subsection (c), a judge appointed under Subsection (a) may act on an application for authorization to intercept wire, oral, or electronic communications if the judge is appointed as the judge of competent jurisdiction within the administrative judicial district in which the following is located:

(1) the site of:

(A) the proposed interception; or

(B) the interception device to be installed or monitored;

(2) the communication device to be intercepted;

(3) the billing, residential, or business address of the subscriber to the electronic communications service to be intercepted;

(4) the headquarters of the law enforcement agency that makes a request for or executes an order authorizing an interception; or

(5) the headquarters of the service provider.

(c) If the judge of competent jurisdiction for an administrative judicial district is absent or unable to serve or if exigent circumstances exist, the application may be made to the judge of competent jurisdiction in an adjacent administrative judicial district. Exigent circumstances does not include a denial of a previous application on the same facts and circumstances. To be valid, the application must fully explain the circumstances justifying application under this subsection.

## Sec. 4. Offenses for Which Interceptions May Be Authorized.

A judge of competent jurisdiction may issue an order authorizing interception of wire, oral, or electronic communications only if the prosecutor applying for the order shows probable cause to believe that the interception will provide evidence of the commission of:

(1) a felony under Section 19.02, 19.03, or 43.26, Penal Code;

(2) a felony under:

(A) Chapter 481, Health and Safety Code, other than felony possession of marihuana;

(B) Section 485.032, Health and Safety Code; or

(C) Chapter 483, Health and Safety Code;

(3) an offense under Section 20.03 or 20.04, Penal Code;

(4) an offense under Chapter 20A, Penal Code;

(5) an offense under Chapter 34, Penal Code, if the criminal activity giving rise to the proceeds involves the commission of an offense under Title 5, Penal Code, or an offense under federal law or the laws of another state containing elements that are substantially similar to the elements of an offense under Title 5;

(6) an offense under Section 38.11, Penal Code; or

(7) an attempt, conspiracy, or solicitation to commit an offense listed in this section.

**Sec. 5. Control of Intercepting Devices.**

(a) Except as otherwise provided by this section and Sections 8A and 8B, only the Department of Public Safety is authorized by this article to own, possess, install, operate, or monitor an electronic, mechanical, or other device. The Department of Public Safety may be assisted by an investigative or law enforcement officer or other person in the operation and monitoring of an interception of wire, oral, or electronic communications, provided that the officer or other person:

(1) is designated by the director for that purpose; and

(2) acts in the presence and under the direction of a commissioned officer of the Department of Public Safety.

(b) The director shall designate in writing the commissioned officers of the Department of Public Safety who are responsible for the possession, installation, operation, and monitoring of electronic, mechanical, or other devices for the department.

(c) The Texas Department of Criminal Justice may own electronic, mechanical, or other devices for a use or purpose authorized by Section 500.008, Government Code, and the inspector general of the Texas Department of Criminal Justice, a commissioned officer of that office, or another person acting in the presence and under the direction of a commissioned officer of that office may possess, install, operate, or monitor those devices as provided by Section 500.008.

(d) The Texas Juvenile Justice Department may own electronic, mechanical, or other devices for a use or purpose authorized by Section 242.103, Human Resources Code, and the inspector general of the Texas Juvenile Justice Department, a commissioned officer of that office, or another person acting in the presence and under the direction of a commissioned officer of that office may possess, install, operate, or monitor those devices as provided by Section 242.103.

**Sec. 6. Request for Application for Interception.**

(a) The director may, based on written affidavits, request in writing that a prosecutor apply for an order authorizing interception of wire, oral, or electronic communications.

(b) The head of a local law enforcement agency or, if the head of the local law enforce-ment agency is absent or unable to serve, the acting head of the local law enforcement agency may, based on written affidavits, request in writing that a prosecutor apply for an order authorizing interception of wire, oral, or electronic communications. Prior to the requesting of an application under this subsection, the head of a local law enforcement agency must submit the request and supporting affidavits to the director, who shall make a finding in writing whether the request and supporting affidavits establish that other investigative procedures have been tried and failed or they reasonably appear unlikely to succeed or to be too dangerous if tried, is feasible, is justifiable, and whether the Department of Public Safety has the necessary resources available. The prosecutor may file the application only after a written positive finding on all the above requirements by the director.

**Sec. 7. Authorization for Disclosure and Use of Intercepted Communications.**

(a) An investigative or law enforcement officer who, by any means authorized by this article, obtains knowledge of the contents of a wire, oral, or electronic communication or evidence derived from the communication may disclose the contents or evidence to another investigative or law enforcement officer, including a federal law enforcement officer or agent or a law enforcement officer or agent of another state, to the extent that the disclosure is appropriate to the proper performance of the official duties of the officer making or receiving the disclosure.

(b) An investigative or law enforcement officer who, by any means authorized by this article, obtains knowledge of the contents of a wire, oral, or electronic communication or evidence derived from the communication may use the contents or evidence to the extent the use is appropriate to the proper performance of his official duties.

(c) A person who receives, by any means authorized by this article, information concerning a wire, oral, or electronic communication or evidence derived from a communication intercepted in accordance with the provisions of this article may disclose the contents of that communication or the derivative evidence while giving testimony under oath in any proceeding held under the authority of the United States, of this state, or of a political subdivision of this state.

(d) An otherwise privileged wire, oral, or electronic communication intercepted in accordance with, or in violation of, the provisions of this article does not lose its privileged character and any evidence derived from such privileged communication against the party to the privileged communication shall be considered privileged also.

(e) When an investigative or law enforcement officer, while engaged in intercepting wire, oral, or electronic communications in a manner authorized by this article, intercepts wire, oral, or electronic communications relating to offenses other than those specified in the order of authorization, the contents of and evidence derived from the communication may be disclosed or used as provided by Subsections (a) and (b) of this section. Such contents and any evidence derived therefrom may be used under Subsection (c) of this section when authorized by a judge of competent jurisdiction where the judge finds, on subsequent application, that the contents were otherwise intercepted in accordance with the provisions of this article. The application shall be made as soon as practicable.

## Sec. 8. Application for Interception Authorization.

(a) To be valid, an application for an order authorizing the interception of a wire, oral, or electronic communication must be made in writing under oath to a judge of competent jurisdiction and must state the applicant's authority to make the application. An applicant must include the following information in the application:

(1) the identity of the prosecutor making the application and of the officer requesting the application;

(2) a full and complete statement of the facts and circumstances relied on by the applicant to justify his belief that an order should be issued, including:

(A) details about the particular offense that has been, is being, or is about to be committed;

(B) a particular description of the nature and location of the facilities from which or the place where the communication is to be intercepted;

(C) a particular description of the type of communication sought to be intercepted; and

(D) the identity of the person, if known, committing the offense and whose communications are to be intercepted;

(3) a full and complete statement as to whether or not other investigative procedures have been tried and failed or why they reasonably appear to be unlikely to succeed or to be too dangerous if tried;

(4) a statement of the period of time for which the interception is required to be maintained and, if the nature of the investigation is such that the authorization for interception should not automatically terminate when the described type of communication is first obtained, a particular description of facts establishing probable cause to believe that additional communications of the same type will occur after the described type of communication is obtained;

(5) a statement whether a covert entry will be necessary to properly and safely install the wiretapping or electronic surveillance or eavesdropping equipment and, if a covert entry is requested, a statement as to why such an entry is necessary and proper under the facts of the particular investigation, including a full and complete statement as to whether other investigative techniques have been tried and have failed or why they reasonably appear to be unlikely to succeed or to be too dangerous if tried or are not feasible under the circumstances or exigencies of time;

(6) a full and complete statement of the facts concerning all applications known to the prosecutor making the application that have been previously made to a judge for authorization to intercept wire, oral, or electronic communications involving any of the persons, facilities, or places specified in the application and of the action taken by the judge on each application; and

(7) if the application is for the extension of an order, a statement setting forth the results already obtained from the interception or a reasonable explanation of the failure to obtain results.

(b) The judge may, in an ex parte hearing in chambers, require additional testimony or documentary evidence in support of the application, and such testimony or documentary evidence shall be preserved as part of the application.

## Sec. 8A. Emergency Installation and Use of Intercepting Device.

(a) The prosecutor in a county in which an electronic, mechanical, or other device is to be installed or used to intercept wire, oral, or electronic communications shall designate in writing each peace officer in the county, other than a commissioned officer of the Department of Public Safety, who:

(1) is a member of a law enforcement unit specially trained to respond to and deal with life-threatening situations; and

(2) is authorized to possess such a device and responsible for the installation, operation, and monitoring of the device in an immediate life-threatening situation.

(b) A peace officer designated under Subsection (a) or under Section 5(b) may possess, install, operate, or monitor an electronic, mechanical, or other device to intercept wire, oral, or electronic communications if the officer:

(1) reasonably believes an immediate life-threatening situation exists that:

(A) is within the territorial jurisdiction of the officer or another officer the officer is assisting; and

(B) requires interception of communications before an order authorizing the interception can, with due diligence, be obtained under this section;

(2) reasonably believes there are sufficient grounds under this section on which to obtain an order authorizing the interception; and

(3) obtains oral or written consent to the interception before beginning the interception from:

(A) a judge of competent jurisdiction;

(B) a district judge for the county in which the device will be installed or used; or

(C) a judge or justice of a court of appeals or of a higher court.

(c) An official described in Subsection (b)(3) may give oral or written consent to the interception of communications under this section to provide evidence of the commission of a felony, or of a threat, attempt, or conspiracy to commit a felony, in an immediate life-threatening situation. Oral or written consent given under this section expires 48 hours after the grant of consent or at the conclusion of the emergency justifying the interception, whichever occurs first.

(d) If an officer installs or uses a device under Subsection (b), the officer shall:

(1) promptly report the installation or use to the prosecutor in the county in which the device is installed or used; and

(2) within 48 hours after the installation is complete or the interception begins, whichever occurs first, obtain a written order from a judge of competent jurisdiction authorizing the interception.

(e) A judge of competent jurisdiction under Section 3 or under Subsection (b) may issue a written order authorizing interception of communications under this section during the 48-hour period prescribed by Subsection (d)(2). A written order under this section expires on the 30th day after execution of the order or at the conclusion of the emergency that initially justified the interception, whichever occurs first. If an order is denied or is not issued within the 48-hour period, the officer shall terminate use of and remove the device promptly on the earlier of:

(1) the denial;

(2) the end of the emergency that initially justified the interception; or

(3) the expiration of 48 hours.

(f) The state may not use as evidence in a criminal proceeding any information gained through the use of a device installed under this section if authorization for the device is not sought or is sought but not obtained.

(g) A peace officer may certify to a communications common carrier that the officer is acting lawfully under this section.

**Sec. 8B. Detection of Cellular Telephone or Other Wireless Communications Device in Correctional or Detention Facility.**

(a) In this section, "correctional facility" has the meaning assigned by Section 39.04(e), Penal Code.

(b) Notwithstanding any other provision of this article or Article 18.21, the office of the inspector general of the Texas Department of Criminal Justice may:

(1) without a warrant, use electronic, mechanical, or other devices to detect the presence or use of a cellular telephone or other wireless communications device in a correctional facility;

(2) without a warrant, intercept, monitor, detect, or, as authorized by applicable federal laws and regulations, prevent the transmission of any communication transmitted through the use of a cellular telephone or other wireless communications device in a correctional facility; and

(3) use, to the extent authorized by law, any information obtained under Subdivision (2), including the contents of an intercepted

communication, in any criminal or civil proceeding before a court or other governmental agency or entity.

(c) Not later than the 30th day after the date on which the office of the inspector general uses an electronic, mechanical, or other device under Subsection (b), the inspector general shall report the use of the device to:

(1) a prosecutor with jurisdiction in the county in which the device was used; or

(2) the special prosecution unit established under Subchapter E, Chapter 41, Government Code, if that unit has jurisdiction in the county in which the device was used.

(d) When using an electronic, mechanical, or other device under Subsection (b), the office of the inspector general shall minimize the impact of the device on any communication that is not reasonably related to the detection of the presence or use of a cellular telephone or other wireless communications device in a correctional facility.

(e) A person confined in a correctional facility does not have an expectation of privacy with respect to the possession or use of a cellular telephone or other wireless communications device located on the premises of the facility. The person who is confined, and any person with whom that person communicates through the use of a cellular telephone or other wireless communications device, does not have an expectation of privacy with respect to the contents of any communication transmitted by the cellular telephone or wireless communications device.

### Sec. 9. Action on Application for Interception Order.

(a) On receipt of an application, the judge may enter an ex parte order, as requested or as modified, authorizing interception of wire, oral, or electronic communications if the judge determines from the evidence submitted by the applicant that:

(1) there is probable cause to believe that a person is committing, has committed, or is about to commit a particular offense enumerated in Section 4 of this article;

(2) there is probable cause to believe that particular communications concerning that offense will be obtained through the interception;

(3) normal investigative procedures have been tried and have failed or reasonably appear to be unlikely to succeed or to be too dangerous if tried;

(4) there is probable cause to believe that the facilities from which or the place where the wire, oral, or electronic communications are to be intercepted are being used or are about to be used in connection with the commission of an offense or are leased to, listed in the name of, or commonly used by the person; and

(5) a covert entry is or is not necessary to properly and safely install the wiretapping or electronic surveillance or eavesdropping equipment.

(b) An order authorizing the interception of a wire, oral, or electronic communication must specify:

(1) the identity of the person, if known, whose communications are to be intercepted;

(2) the nature and location of the communications facilities as to which or the place where authority to intercept is granted;

(3) a particular description of the type of communication sought to be intercepted and a statement of the particular offense to which it relates;

(4) the identity of the officer making the request and the identity of the prosecutor;

(5) the time during which the interception is authorized, including a statement of whether or not the interception will automatically terminate when the described communication is first obtained; and

(6) whether or not a covert entry or surreptitious entry is necessary to properly and safely install wiretapping, electronic surveillance, or eavesdropping equipment.

(c) On request of the applicant for an order authorizing the interception of a wire, oral, or electronic communication, the judge may issue a separate order directing that a provider of wire or electronic communications service, a communication common carrier, landlord, custodian, or other person furnish the applicant all information, facilities, and technical assistance necessary to accomplish the interception unobtrusively and with a minimum of interference with the services that the provider, carrier, landlord, custodian, or other person is providing the person whose communications are to be intercepted. Any provider of wire or electronic communications service, communication common carrier, landlord, custodian, or other person furnishing facilities or technical assistance is entitled to compensation by the applicant for reasonable expenses incurred in providing the facilities or assistance at the prevailing rates. The interception order may include an order to:

(1) install or use a pen register, ESN reader, trap and trace device, or mobile tracking device, or similar equipment that combines the function of a pen register and trap and trace device;

(2) disclose a stored communication, information subject to an administrative subpoena, or information subject to access under Article 18.21, Code of Criminal Procedure.

(d) An order entered pursuant to this section may not authorize the interception of a wire, oral, or electronic communication for longer than is necessary to achieve the objective of the authorization and in no event may it authorize interception for more than 30 days. The issuing judge may grant extensions of an order, but only on application for an extension made in accordance with Section 8 and the court making the findings required by Subsection (a). The period of extension may not be longer than the authorizing judge deems necessary to achieve the purposes for which it is granted and in no event may the extension be for more than 30 days. To be valid, each order and extension of an order must provide that the authorization to intercept be executed as soon as practicable, be conducted in a way that minimizes the interception of communications not otherwise subject to interception under this article, and terminate on obtaining the authorized objective or within 30 days, whichever occurs sooner. If the intercepted communication is in code or a foreign language and an expert in that code or language is not reasonably available during the period of interception, minimization may be accomplished as soon as practicable after the interception.

(e) An order entered pursuant to this section may not authorize a covert entry into a residence solely for the purpose of intercepting a wire or electronic communication.

(f) An order entered pursuant to this section may not authorize a covert entry into or onto a premises for the purpose of intercepting an oral communication unless:

(1) the judge, in addition to making the determinations required under Subsection (a) of this section, determines that:

(A) (i) the premises into or onto which the covert entry is authorized or the person whose communications are to be obtained has been the subject of a pen register previously authorized in connection with the same investigation;

(ii) the premises into or onto which the covert entry is authorized or the person whose communications are to be obtained has been the subject of an interception of wire or electronic communications previously authorized in connection with the same investigation; and

(iii) that such procedures have failed; or

(B) that the procedures enumerated in Paragraph (A) reasonably appear to be unlikely to succeed or to be too dangerous if tried or are not feasible under the circumstances or exigencies of time; and

(2) the order, in addition to the matters required to be specified under Subsection (b) of this section, specifies that the covert entry is for the purpose of intercepting oral communications of two or more persons and that there is probable cause to believe they are committing, have committed, or are about to commit a particular offense enumerated in Section 4 of this article.

(g) Whenever an order authorizing interception is entered pursuant to this article, the order may require reports to the judge who issued the order showing what progress has been made toward achievement of the authorized objective and the need for continued interception. Reports shall be made at any interval the judge requires.

(h) A judge who issues an order authorizing the interception of a wire, oral, or electronic communication may not hear a criminal prosecution in which evidence derived from the interception may be used or in which the order may be an issue.

**Sec. 9A. Interception Order for Communication by Specified Person.**

(a) The requirements of Sections 8(a)(2)(B) and 9(b)(2) relating to the specification of the facilities from which or the place where a communication is to be intercepted do not apply if:

(1) in the case of an application for an order authorizing the interception of an oral communication:

(A) the application contains a full and complete statement as to why the specification is not practical and identifies the person committing or believed to be committing the offense and whose communications are to be intercepted; and

(B) a judge of competent jurisdiction finds that the specification is not practical; and

(2) in the case of an application for an order authorizing the interception of a wire or electronic communication:

(A) the application identifies the person committing or believed to be committing the offense and whose communications are to be intercepted;

(B) a judge of competent jurisdiction finds that the applicant has made an adequate showing of probable cause to believe that the actions of the person identified in the application could have the effect of thwarting interception from a specified facility; and

(C) the authority to intercept a wire or electronic communication under the order is limited to a period in which it is reasonable to presume that the person identified in the application will be reasonably proximate to the interception device.

(b) A person implementing an order authorizing the interception of an oral communication that, in accordance with this section, does not specify the facility from which or the place where a communication is to be intercepted may begin interception only after the person ascertains the place where the communication is to be intercepted.

(c) A provider of wire or electronic communications that receives an order authorizing the interception of a wire or electronic communication that, in accordance with this section, does not specify the facility from which or the place where a communication is to be intercepted may move the court to modify or quash the order on the ground that the provider's assistance with respect to the interception cannot be performed in a timely or reasonable fashion. On notice to the state, the court shall decide the motion expeditiously.

## Sec. 10. Procedure for Preserving Intercepted Communications.

(a) The contents of a wire, oral, or electronic communication intercepted by means authorized by this article shall be recorded on tape, wire, or other comparable device. The recording of the contents of a wire, oral, or electronic communication under this subsection shall be done in a way that protects the recording from editing or other alterations.

(b) Immediately on the expiration of the period of the order and all extensions, if any, the recordings shall be made available to the judge issuing the order and sealed under his directions. Custody of the recordings shall be wherever the judge orders. The recordings may not be destroyed until at least 10 years after the date of expiration of the order and the last extension, if any. A recording may be destroyed only by order of the judge of competent jurisdiction for the administrative judicial district in which the interception was authorized.

(c) Duplicate recordings may be made for use or disclosure pursuant to Subsections (a) and (b), Section 7, of this article for investigations.

(d) The presence of the seal required by Subsection (b) of this section or a satisfactory explanation of its absence is a prerequisite for the use or disclosure of the contents of a wire, oral, or electronic communication or evidence derived from the communication under Subsection (c), Section 7, of this article.

## Sec. 11. Sealing of Orders and Applications.

The judge shall seal each application made and order granted under this article. Custody of the applications and orders shall be wherever the judge directs. An application or order may be disclosed only on a showing of good cause before a judge of competent jurisdiction and may not be destroyed until at least 10 years after the date it is sealed. An application or order may be destroyed only by order of the judge of competent jurisdiction for the administrative judicial district in which it was made or granted.

## Sec. 12. Contempt.

A violation of Section 10 or 11 of this article may be punished as contempt of court.

## Sec. 13. Notice and Disclosure of Interception to a Party.

(a) Within a reasonable time but not later than 90 days after the date an application for an order is denied or after the date an order or the last extension, if any, expires, the judge who granted or denied the application shall cause to be served on the persons named in the order or the application and any other parties to intercepted communications, if any, an inventory, which must include notice:

(1) of the entry of the order or the application;

(2) of the date of the entry and the period of authorized interception or the date of denial of the application; and

(3) that during the authorized period wire, oral, or electronic communications were or were not intercepted.

(b) The judge, on motion, may in his discretion make available to a person or his counsel for inspection any portion of an intercepted communication, application, or order that the judge determines, in the interest of justice, to disclose to that person.

(c) On an ex parte showing of good cause to the judge, the serving of the inventory required by this section may be postponed, but in no event may any evidence derived from an order under this article be disclosed in any trial, until after such inventory has been served.

### Sec. 14. Preconditions to Use As Evidence.

(a) The contents of an intercepted wire, oral, or electronic communication or evidence derived from the communication may not be received in evidence or otherwise disclosed in a trial, hearing, or other proceeding in a federal or state court unless each party, not later than the 10th day before the date of the trial, hearing, or other proceeding, has been furnished with a copy of the court order and application under which the interception was authorized or approved. This 10-day period may be waived by the judge if he finds that it is not possible to furnish the party with the information 10 days before the trial, hearing, or proceeding and that the party will not be prejudiced by the delay in receiving the information.

(b) An aggrieved person charged with an offense in a trial, hearing, or proceeding in or before a court, department, officer, agency, regulatory body, or other authority of the United States or of this state or a political subdivision of this state may move to suppress the contents of an intercepted wire, oral, or electronic communication or evidence derived from the communication on the ground that:

(1) the communication was unlawfully intercepted;

(2) the order authorizing the interception is insufficient on its face; or

(3) the interception was not made in conformity with the order.

(c) A person identified by a party to an intercepted wire, oral, or electronic communication during the course of that communication may move to suppress the contents of the communication on the grounds provided in Subsection (b) of this section or on the ground that the harm to the person resulting from his identification in court exceeds the value to the prosecution of the disclosure of the contents.

(d) The motion to suppress must be made before the trial, hearing, or proceeding unless there was no opportunity to make the motion or the person was not aware of the grounds of the motion. The hearing on the motion shall be held in camera upon the written request of the aggrieved person. If the motion is granted, the contents of the intercepted wire, oral, or electronic communication and evidence derived from the communication shall be treated as having been obtained in violation of this article. The judge, on the filing of the motion by the aggrieved person, shall make available to the aggrieved person or his counsel for inspection any portion of the intercepted communication or evidence derived from the communication that the judge determines, in the interest of justice, to make available.

(e) Any judge of this state, upon hearing a pretrial motion regarding conversations intercepted by wire pursuant to this article, or who otherwise becomes informed that there exists on such intercepted wire, oral, or electronic communication identification of a specific individual who is not a party or suspect to the subject of interception:

(1) shall give notice and an opportunity to be heard on the matter of suppression of references to that person if identification is sufficient so as to give notice; or

(2) shall suppress references to that person if identification is sufficient to potentially cause embarrassment or harm which outweighs the probative value, if any, of the mention of such person, but insufficient to require the notice provided for in Subdivision (1), above.

### Sec. 15. Reports Concerning Intercepted Wire, Oral, or Electronic Communications.

(a) Within 30 days after the date an order or the last extension, if any, expires or after the denial of an order, the issuing or denying judge shall report to the Administrative Office of the United States Courts:

(1) the fact that an order or extension was applied for;

(2) the kind of order or extension applied for;

(3) the fact that the order or extension was granted as applied for, was modified, or was denied;

(4) the period of interceptions authorized by the order and the number and duration of any extensions of the order;

(5) the offense specified in the order or application or extension;

(6) the identity of the officer making the request and the prosecutor; and

(7) the nature of the facilities from which or the place where communications were to be intercepted.

(b) In January of each year each prosecutor shall report to the Administrative Office of the United States Courts the following information for the preceding calendar year:

(1) the information required by Subsection (a) of this section with respect to each application for an order or extension made;

(2) a general description of the interceptions made under each order or extension, including the approximate nature and frequency of incriminating communications intercepted, the approximate nature and frequency of other communications intercepted, the approximate number of persons whose communications were intercepted, and the approximate nature, amount, and cost of the manpower and other resources used in the interceptions;

(3) the number of arrests resulting from interceptions made under each order or extension and the offenses for which arrests were made;

(4) the number of trials resulting from interceptions;

(5) the number of motions to suppress made with respect to interceptions and the number granted or denied;

(6) the number of convictions resulting from interceptions, the offenses for which the convictions were obtained, and a general assessment of the importance of the interceptions; and

(7) the information required by Subdivisions (2) through (6) of this subsection with respect to orders or extensions obtained.

(c) Any judge or prosecutor required to file a report with the Administrative Office of the United States Courts shall forward a copy of such report to the director of the Department of Public Safety. On or before March 1 of each year, the director shall submit to the governor; lieutenant governor; speaker of the house of representatives; chairman, senate jurisprudence committee; and chairman, house of representatives criminal jurisprudence committee a report of all intercepts as defined herein conducted pursuant to this article and terminated during the preceding calendar year. Such report shall include:

(1) the reports of judges and prosecuting attorneys forwarded to the director as required in this section;

(2) the number of Department of Public Safety personnel authorized to possess, install, or operate electronic, mechanical, or other devices;

(3) the number of Department of Public Safety and other law enforcement personnel who participated or engaged in the seizure of intercepts pursuant to this article during the preceding calendar year; and

(4) the total cost to the Department of Public Safety of all activities and procedures relating to the seizure of intercepts during the preceding calendar year, including costs of equipment, manpower, and expenses incurred as compensation for use of facilities or technical assistance provided to the department.

## Sec. 16. Recovery of Civil Damages Authorized.

(a) A person whose wire, oral, or electronic communication is intercepted, disclosed, or used in violation of this article, or in violation of Chapter 16, Penal Code, has a civil cause of action against any person who intercepts, discloses, or uses or solicits another person to intercept, disclose, or use the communication and is entitled to recover from the person:

(1) actual damages but not less than liquidated damages computed at a rate of $100 a day for each day of violation or $1,000, whichever is higher;

(2) punitive damages; and

(3) a reasonable attorney's fee and other litigation costs reasonably incurred.

(b) A good faith reliance on a court order or legislative authorization constitutes a complete defense to an action brought under this section.

(c) A person is subject to suit by the federal or state government in a court of competent jurisdiction for appropriate injunctive relief if the person engages in conduct that:

(1) constitutes an offense under Section 16.05, Penal Code, but is not for a tortious or illegal purpose or for the purpose of direct or indirect commercial advantage or private commercial gain; and

(2) involves a radio communication that is:

(A) transmitted on frequencies allocated under Subpart D of Part 74 of the rules of the Federal Communications Commission; and

(B) not scrambled or encrypted.

(d) A defendant is liable for a civil penalty of $500 if it is shown at the trial of the civil suit brought under Subsection (c) that the defendant:

(1) has been convicted of an offense under Section 16.05, Penal Code; or

(2) is found liable in a civil action brought under Subsection (a).

(e) Each violation of an injunction ordered under Subsection (c) is punishable by a fine of $500.

(f) The attorney general, or the county or district attorney of the county in which the conduct, as described by Subsection (c), is occurring, may file suit under Subsection (c) on behalf of the state.

(g) A computer trespasser or a user, aggrieved person, subscriber, or customer of a communications common carrier or electronic communications service does not have a cause of action against the carrier or service, its officers, employees, or agents, or other specified persons for providing information, facilities, or assistance as required by a good faith reliance on:

(1) legislative authority; or

(2) a court order, warrant, subpoena, or certification under this article.

### Sec. 17. Nonapplicability.

This article does not apply to conduct described as an affirmative defense under Section 16.02(c), Penal Code, except as otherwise specifically provided by that section.

Sec. 18. [Repealed by Acts 2005, 79th Leg., ch. 889 (S.B. 1551), § 2, effective June 17, 2005.]

(Enacted by Acts 1981, 67th Leg., ch. 275 (H.B. 360), § 1, effective August 31, 1981; am. Acts 1983, 68th Leg., ch. 864 (H.B. 1291), § 4, effective June 19, 1983; am. Acts 1985, 69th Leg., ch. 587 (H.B. 10), §§ 2—4, effective August 26, 1985; am. Acts 1989, 71st Leg., ch. 1166 (H.B. 910), §§ 1—15, effective September 1, 1989; am. Acts 1991, 72nd Leg., ch. 14 (S.B. 404), § 284(38), (57), effective September 1, 1991; am. Acts 1993, 73rd Leg., ch. 790 (S.B. 510), § 15, effective September 1, 1993; am. Acts 1993, 73rd Leg., ch. 900 (S.B. 1067), § 1.06, effective September 1, 1994; am. Acts 1997, 75th Leg., ch. 1051 (S.B. 1120), §§ 1—4, effective September 1, 1997; am. Acts 2001, 77th Leg., ch. 1270 (S.B. 1345), §§ 1—6, effective September 1, 2001; am. Acts 2003, 78th Leg., ch. 678 (H.B. 2474), §§ 2—7, effective September 1, 2003; am. Acts 2005, 79th Leg., ch. 390 (S.B. 1461), § 1, effective September 1, 2005; am. Acts 2005, 79th Leg., ch. 889 (S.B. 1551), § 2,

effective June 17, 2005; am. Acts 2007, 80th Leg., ch. 186 (S.B. 823), § 1, effective May 23, 2007; am. Acts 2007, 80th Leg., ch. 258 (S.B. 11), § 6.01, effective September 1, 2007; am. Acts 2009, 81st Leg., ch. 1130 (H.B. 2086), § 40, effective September 1, 2009; am. Acts 2009, 81st Leg., ch. 1169 (H.B. 3228), §§ 2—6, effective September 1, 2009; am. Acts 2009, 81st Leg., ch. 1237 (S.B. 2047), § 1, effective September 1, 2009; am. Acts 2009, 81st Leg., ch. 1356 (S.B. 537), § 1, effective September 1, 2009; am. Acts 2011, 82nd Leg., ch. 85 (S.B. 653), § 3.002, effective September 1, 2011.)

### Art. 18.21. Pen Registers and Trap and Trace Devices; Access to Stored Communications; Mobile Tracking Devices.

#### Sec. 1. Definitions.

In this article:

(1) "Aural transfer," "communication common carrier," "computer trespasser," "electronic communication," "electronic communications service," "electronic communications system," "electronic storage," "immediate life-threatening situation," "member of a law enforcement unit specially trained to respond to and deal with life-threatening situations," "readily accessible to the general public," "user," and "wire communication" have the meanings assigned by Article 18.20.

(2) "Authorized peace officer" means:

(A) a sheriff or a sheriff's deputy;

(B) a constable or deputy constable;

(C) a marshal or police officer of an incorporated city;

(D) a ranger or officer commissioned by the Public Safety Commission or the director of the Department of Public Safety;

(E) an investigator of a prosecutor's office;

(F) a law enforcement agent of the Alcoholic Beverage Commission;

(G) a law enforcement officer commissioned by the Parks and Wildlife Commission;

(H) an enforcement officer appointed by the inspector general of the Texas Department of Criminal Justice under Section 493.019, Government Code; or

(I) an investigator commissioned by the attorney general under Section 402.009, Government Code.

(3) "Department" means the Department of Public Safety.

(3-a) "Designated law enforcement office or agency" means:

**Criminal Procedure**

Criminal Procedure

(A) the sheriff's department of a county with a population of 3.3 million or more;

(B) a police department in a municipality with a population of 500,000 or more; or

(C) the office of inspector general of the Texas Department of Criminal Justice.

(4) "ESN reader" means a device that records the electronic serial number from the data track of a wireless telephone, cellular telephone, or similar communication device that transmits its operational status to a base site, if the device does not intercept the contents of a communication.

(5) "Mobile tracking device" means an electronic or mechanical device that permits tracking the movement of a person, vehicle, container, item, or object.

(6) "Pen register" means a device or process that records or decodes dialing, routing, addressing, or signaling information transmitted by an instrument or facility from which a wire or electronic communication is transmitted, if the information does not include the contents of the communication. The term does not include a device used by a provider or customer of a wire or electronic communication service in the ordinary course of the provider's or customer's business for purposes of:

(A) billing or recording as an incident to billing for communications services; or

(B) cost accounting, security control, or other ordinary business purposes.

(7) "Prosecutor" means a district attorney, criminal district attorney, or county attorney performing the duties of a district attorney.

(8) "Remote computing service" means the provision to the public of computer storage or processing services by means of an electronic communications system.

(9) "Supervisory official" means:

(A) an investigative agent or an assistant investigative agent who is in charge of an investigation;

(B) an equivalent person at an investigating agency's headquarters or regional office; and

(C) the principal prosecuting attorney of the state or of a political subdivision of the state or the first assistant or chief assistant prosecuting attorney in the office of either.

(10) "Trap and trace device" means a device or process that records an incoming electronic or other impulse that identifies the originating number or other dialing, routing, addressing, or signaling information reasonably likely to identify the source of a wire or electronic communication, if the information does not include the contents of the communication. The term does not include a device or telecommunications network used in providing:

(A) a caller identification service authorized by the Public Utility Commission of Texas under Subchapter E, Chapter 55, Utilities Code;

(B) the services referenced in Section 55.102(b), Utilities Code; or

(C) a caller identification service provided by a commercial mobile radio service provider licensed by the Federal Communications Commission.

**Sec. 2. Application and Order.**

(a) A prosecutor with jurisdiction in a county within a judicial district described by this subsection may file an application for the installation and use of a pen register, ESN reader, trap and trace device, or similar equipment that combines the function of a pen register and a trap and trace device with a district judge in the judicial district. The judicial district must be a district in which is located:

(1) the site of the proposed installation or use of the device or equipment;

(2) the site of the communication device on which the device or equipment is proposed to be installed or used;

(3) the billing, residential, or business address of the subscriber to the electronic communications service on which the device or equipment is proposed to be installed or used;

(4) the headquarters of:

(A) the office of the prosecutor filing an application under this section; or

(B) a law enforcement agency that requests the prosecutor to file an application under this section or that proposes to execute an order authorizing installation and use of the device or equipment; or

(5) the headquarters of a service provider ordered to install the device or equipment.

(b) A prosecutor may file an application under this section or under federal law on the prosecutor's own motion or on the request of an authorized peace officer, regardless of whether the officer is commissioned by the department. A prosecutor who files an application on the prosecutor's own motion or who files an application for the installation and use of a pen register, ESN reader, or similar equipment on the request of an authorized peace officer not commissioned by the department, other than an authorized peace officer employed by a designated law enforcement office or agency, must make the application personally and may not do so through an assistant or some other person acting on the prosecutor's behalf. A prosecutor may make an application through an assistant or other person acting on the prosecutor's behalf if the prosecutor files an application for the installation and use of:

(1) a pen register, ESN reader, or similar equipment on the request of:

(A) an authorized peace officer who is commissioned by the department; or

(B) an authorized peace officer of a designated law enforcement office or agency; or

(2) a trap and trace device or similar equipment on the request of an authorized peace officer, regardless of whether the officer is commissioned by the department.

(c) The application must:

(1) be made in writing under oath;

(2) include the name of the subscriber and the telephone number and location of the communication device on which the pen register, ESN reader, trap and trace device, or similar equipment will be used, to the extent that information is known or is reasonably ascertainable; and

(3) state that the installation and use of the device or equipment will likely produce information that is material to an ongoing criminal investigation.

(d) On presentation of the application, the judge may order the installation and use of the pen register, ESN reader, or similar equipment by an authorized peace officer commissioned by the department or an authorized peace officer of a designated law enforcement office or agency, and, on request of the applicant, the judge shall direct in the order that a communication common carrier or a provider of electronic communications service furnish all information, facilities, and technical assistance necessary to facilitate the installation and use of the device or equipment by the department or designated law enforcement office or agency unobtrusively and with a minimum of interference to the services provided by the carrier or service. The carrier or service is entitled to compensation at the prevailing rates for the facilities and assistance provided to the department or a designated law enforcement office or agency.

(e) On presentation of the application, the judge may order the installation and use of the trap and trace device or similar equipment by the communication common carrier or other person on the appropriate line. The judge may direct the communication common carrier or other person, including any landlord or other custodian of equipment, to furnish all information, facilities, and technical assistance necessary to install or use the device or equipment unobtrusively and with a minimum of interference to the services provided by the communication common carrier, landlord, custodian, or other person. Unless otherwise ordered by the court, the results of the trap and trace device or similar equipment shall be furnished to the applicant, designated by the court, at reasonable intervals during regular business hours, for the duration of the order. The carrier is entitled to compensation at the prevailing rates for the facilities and assistance provided to the designated law enforcement office or agency.

(f) Except as otherwise provided by this subsection, an order for the installation and use of a device or equipment under this section is valid for not more than 60 days after the earlier of the date the device or equipment is installed or the 10th day after the date the order is entered, unless the prosecutor applies for and obtains from the court an extension of the order before the order expires. The period of extension may not exceed 60 days for each extension granted, except that with the consent of the subscriber or customer of the service on which the device or equipment is used, the court may extend an order for a period not to exceed one year.

(g) The district court shall seal an application and order granted under this article.

(h) A peace officer is not required to file an application or obtain an order under this section before the officer makes an otherwise lawful search, with or without a warrant, to determine the contents of a caller identification message, pager message, or voice message that is contained within the memory of an end-user's identification, paging, or answering device.

(i) A peace officer of a designated law enforcement office or agency is authorized to possess, install, operate, or monitor a pen register, ESN reader, or similar equipment if the officer's name is on the list submitted to the director of the department under Subsection (k).

(j) Each designated law enforcement office or agency shall:

(1) adopt a written policy governing the application of this article to the office or agency; and

(2) submit the policy to the director of the department, or the director's designee, for approval.

(k) If the director of the department or the director's designee approves the policy submitted under Subsection (j), the inspector general of the Texas Department of Criminal Justice or the inspector general's designee, or the sheriff or chief of a designated law enforcement agency or the sheriff's or chief's designee, as applicable, shall submit to the director a written list of all officers in the designated law enforcement office or agency who are authorized to possess, install, monitor, or operate pen registers, ESN readers, or similar equipment.

(l) The department may conduct an audit of a designated law enforcement office or agency to ensure compliance with this article. If the department determines from the audit that the designated law enforcement office or agency is not in compliance with the policy adopted by the office or agency under Subsection (j) the department shall notify the office or agency in writing that it is not in compliance. If the department determines that the office or agency still is not in compliance with the policy 90 days after the date the office or agency receives written notice under this subsection, the office or agency loses the authority granted by this article until:

(1) the office or agency adopts a new written policy governing the application of this article to the office or agency; and

(2) the department approves the written policy.

(m) The inspector general of the Texas Department of Criminal Justice or the sheriff or chief of a designated law enforcement agency, as applicable, shall submit to the director of the department a written report of expenditures made by the designated law enforcement office or agency for the purchase and maintenance of a pen register, ESN reader, or similar equipment, authorized under this article. The director of the department shall report those expenditures publicly on an annual basis via the department's website, or other comparable means.

**Sec. 3. Emergency Installation and Use of Pen Register or Trap and Trace Device.**

(a) A peace officer authorized to possess, install, operate, or monitor a device under Section 8A, Article 18.20, may install and use a pen register or trap and trace device if the officer:

(1) reasonably believes an immediate life-threatening situation exists that:

(A) is within the territorial jurisdiction of the officer or another officer the officer is assisting; and

(B) requires the installation of a pen register or trap and trace device before an order authorizing the installation and use can, with due diligence, be obtained under this article; and

(2) reasonably believes there are sufficient grounds under this article on which to obtain an order authorizing the installation and use of a pen register or trap and trace device.

(b) If an officer installs or uses a pen register or trap and trace device under Subsection (a), the officer shall:

(1) promptly report the installation or use to the prosecutor in the county in which the device is installed or used; and

(2) within 48 hours after the installation is complete or the use of the device begins, whichever occurs first, obtain an order under Section 2 authorizing the installation and use.

(c) A judge may issue an order authorizing the installation and use of a device under this section during the 48-hour period prescribed by Subsection (b)(2). If an order is denied or is not issued within the 48-hour period, the officer shall terminate use of and remove the pen register or the trap and trace device promptly on the earlier of the denial or the expiration of 48 hours.

(d) The state may not use as evidence in a criminal proceeding any information gained through the use of a pen register or trap and trace device installed under this section if an authorized peace officer does not apply for or applies for but does not obtain authorization for the pen register or trap and trace device.

**Sec. 4. Requirements for Government Access to Stored Communications.**

(a) An authorized peace officer may require a provider of electronic communications service to disclose the contents of a wire communication or an electronic communication that has been in electronic storage for not longer than

180 days by obtaining a warrant.

(b) An authorized peace officer may require a provider of electronic communications service to disclose the contents of a wire communication or an electronic communication that has been in electronic storage for longer than 180 days:

(1) if notice is not being given to the subscriber or customer, by obtaining a warrant;

(2) if notice is being given to the subscriber or customer, by obtaining:

(A) an administrative subpoena authorized by statute;

(B) a grand jury subpoena; or

(C) a court order issued under Section 5 of this article; or

(3) as otherwise permitted by applicable federal law.

(c) (1) An authorized peace officer may require a provider of a remote computing service to disclose the contents of a wire communication or an electronic communication as described in Subdivision (2) of this subsection:

(A) if notice is not being given to the subscriber or customer, by obtaining a warrant issued under this code;

(B) if notice is being given to the subscriber or customer, by:

(i) an administrative subpoena authorized by statute;

(ii) a grand jury subpoena; or

(iii) a court order issued under Section 5 of this article; or

(C) as otherwise permitted by applicable federal law.

(2) Subdivision (1) of this subsection applies only to a wire communication or an electronic communication that is in electronic storage:

(A) on behalf of a subscriber or customer of the service and is received by means of electronic transmission from or created by means of computer processing of communications received by means of electronic transmission from the subscriber or customer; and

(B) solely for the purpose of providing storage or computer processing services to the subscriber or customer if the provider of the service is not authorized to obtain access to the contents of those communications for purposes of providing any service other than storage or computer processing.

(d) An authorized peace officer may require a provider of remote computing service to disclose records or other information pertaining to a subscriber or customer of the service, other than communications described in Subsection (c) of this section, without giving the subscriber or customer notice:

(1) by obtaining an administrative subpoena authorized by statute;

(2) by obtaining a grand jury subpoena;

(3) by obtaining a warrant;

(4) by obtaining the consent of the subscriber or customer to the disclosure of the records or information;

(5) by obtaining a court order under Section 5 of this article; or

(6) as otherwise permitted by applicable federal law.

(e) A provider of telephonic communications service shall disclose to an authorized peace officer, without any form of legal process, subscriber listing information, including name, address, and telephone number or similar access code that:

(1) the service provides to others in the course of providing publicly available directory or similar assistance; or

(2) is solely for use in the dispatch of emergency vehicles and personnel responding to a distress call directed to an emergency dispatch system or when the information is reasonably necessary to aid in the dispatching of emergency vehicles and personnel for the immediate prevention of death, personal injury, or destruction of property.

(f) A provider of telephonic communications service shall provide an authorized peace officer with the name of the subscriber of record whose published telephone number is provided to the service by an authorized peace officer.

**Sec. 5. Court Order to Obtain Access to Stored Communications.**

(a) A court shall issue an order authorizing disclosure of contents, records, or other information of a wire or electronic communication held in electronic storage if the court determines that there is reasonable belief that the information sought is relevant to a legitimate law enforcement inquiry.

(b) A court may grant a motion by the service provider to quash or modify the order issued under Subsection (a) of this section if the court determines that the information or records requested are unusually voluminous in nature or that compliance with the order would cause an undue burden on the provider.

## Sec. 6. Backup Preservation.

(a) A subpoena or court order for disclosure of the contents of an electronic communication in a remote computing service under Section 4(c) of this article may require that the service provider to whom the request is directed create a copy of the contents of the electronic communications sought by the subpoena or court order for the purpose of preserving those contents. The service provider may not inform the subscriber or customer whose communications are being sought that the subpoena or court order has been issued. The service provider shall create the copy not later than two business days after the date of the receipt by the service provider of the subpoena or court order.

(b) The service provider shall immediately notify the authorized peace officer who presented the subpoena or court order requesting the copy when the copy has been created.

(c) Except as provided by Section 7 of this article, the authorized peace officer shall notify the subscriber or customer whose communications are the subject of the subpoena or court order of the creation of the copy not later than three days after the date of the receipt of the notification from the service provider that the copy was created.

(d) The service provider shall release the copy to the requesting authorized peace officer not earlier than the 14th day after the date of the peace officer's notice to the subscriber or customer if the service provider has not:

(1) initiated proceedings to challenge the request of the peace officer for the copy; or

(2) received notice from the subscriber or customer that the subscriber or customer has initiated proceedings to challenge the request.

(e) The service provider may not destroy or permit the destruction of the copy until the information has been delivered to the designated law enforcement office or agency or until the resolution of any court proceedings, including appeals of any proceedings, relating to the subpoena or court order requesting the creation of the copy, whichever occurs last.

(f) An authorized peace officer who reasonably believes that notification to the subscriber or customer of the subpoena or court order would result in the destruction of or tampering with information sought may request the creation of a copy of the information. The peace officer's belief is not subject to challenge by the subscriber or customer or service provider.

(g) (1) A subscriber or customer who receives notification as described in Subsection (c) of this section may file a written motion to quash the subpoena or vacate the court order in the court that issued the subpoena or court order not later than the 14th day after the date of the receipt of the notice. The motion must contain an affidavit or sworn statement stating that:

(A) the applicant is a subscriber or customer of the service from which the contents of electronic communications stored for the subscriber or customer have been sought; and

(B) the applicant's reasons for believing that the information sought is not relevant to a legitimate law enforcement inquiry or that there has not been substantial compliance with the provisions of this article in some other respect.

(2) The subscriber or customer shall give written notice to the service provider of the challenge to the subpoena or court order. The authorized peace officer or designated law enforcement office or agency requesting the subpoena or court order shall be served a copy of the papers filed by personal delivery or by registered or certified mail.

(h) (1) The court shall order the authorized peace officer to file a sworn response to the motion filed by the subscriber or customer if the court determines that the subscriber or customer has complied with the requirements of Subsection (g) of this section. On request of the peace officer, the court may permit the response to be filed in camera. The court may conduct any additional proceedings the court considers appropriate if the court is unable to make a determination on the motion on the basis of the parties' initial allegations and response.

(2) The court shall rule on the motion as soon after the filing of the officer's response as practicable. The court shall deny the motion if the court finds that the applicant is not the subscriber or customer whose stored communications are the subject of the subpoena or court order or that there is reason to believe that the peace officer's inquiry is legitimate and that the communications sought are relevant to that inquiry. The court shall quash the subpoena or vacate the order if the court finds that the applicant is the

subscriber or customer whose stored communications are the subject of the subpoena or court order and that there is not a reason to believe that the communications sought are relevant to a legitimate law enforcement inquiry or that there has not been substantial compliance with the provisions of this article.

(3) A court order denying a motion or application under this section is not a final order and no interlocutory appeal may be taken from the denial.

### Sec. 7. Delay of Notification.

(a) An authorized peace officer seeking a court order to obtain information under Section 4 of this article may include a request for an order delaying the notification required under Section 4 of this article for a period not to exceed 90 days. The court shall grant the request if the court determines that there is reason to believe that notification of the existence of the court order may have an adverse result, as described in Subsection (c) of this section.

(b) An authorized peace officer who has obtained a subpoena authorized by statute or a grand jury subpoena to seek information under Section 4 of this article may delay the notification required under that section for a period not to exceed 90 days on the execution of a written certification of a supervisory official that there is reason to believe that notification of the existence of the subpoena may have an adverse result as described in Subsection (c) of this section. The peace officer shall maintain a true copy of the certification.

(c) In this section an "adverse result" means:

(1) endangering the life or physical safety of an individual;

(2) flight from prosecution;

(3) destruction of or tampering with evidence;

(4) intimidation of a potential witness; or

(5) otherwise seriously jeopardizing an investigation or unduly delaying a trial.

(d) A court may grant one or more extensions of the delay of notification provided by this section of up to 90 days on request or by certification by a supervisory official if the original requirements under Subsection (a) or (b) of this section are met for each extension.

(e) When the delay of notification under this section expires, the authorized peace officer shall serve, by personal delivery or registered or certified mail, the subscriber or customer a copy of the process or request together with notice that:

(1) states with reasonable specificity the nature of the law enforcement inquiry; and

(2) informs the subscriber or customer:

(A) that information stored for the subscriber or customer by the service provider named in the process or request was supplied to or requested by the peace officer and the date on which the information was supplied or requested;

(B) that notification to the subscriber or customer was delayed;

(C) of the name of the supervisory official who made the certification or the court that granted the request for the delay of notification; and

(D) of which provision of this article permitted the delay of notification.

### Sec. 8. Preclusion of Notification.

When an authorized peace officer seeking information under Section 4 of this article is not required to give notice to the subscriber or customer or is delaying notification under Section 7 of this article, the peace officer may apply to the court for an order commanding the service provider to whom a warrant, subpoena, or court order is directed not to disclose to any other person the existence of the warrant, subpoena, or court order. The order is effective for the period the court considers appropriate. The court shall enter the order if the court determines that there is reason to believe that notification of the existence of the warrant, subpoena, or court order will have an adverse result as described in Section 7(c) of this article.

### Sec. 9. Reimbursement of Costs.

(a) Except as provided by Subsection (c) of this section, an authorized peace officer who obtains information under this article shall reimburse the person assembling or providing the information for all costs that are reasonably necessary and that have been directly incurred in searching for, assembling, reproducing, or otherwise providing the information. These costs include costs arising from necessary disruption of normal operations of an electronic communications service or remote computing service in which the information may be stored.

(b) The authorized peace officer and the person providing the information may agree on the amount of reimbursement. If there is no agreement, the court that issued the order for production of the information shall determine the amount. If no court order was issued for production of the information, the court before which the criminal prosecution relating to the information would be brought shall determine the amount.

(c) Subsection (a) of this section does not apply to records or other information maintained by a communications common carrier that relate to telephone toll records or telephone listings obtained under Section 4(e) of this article unless the court determines that the amount of information required was unusually voluminous or that an undue burden was imposed on the provider.

**Sec. 10. No Cause of Action.**

A subscriber or customer of a wire or electronic communications or remote computing service does not have a cause of action against a wire or electronic communications or remote computing service, its officers, employees, agents, or other specified persons for providing information, facilities, or assistance as required by a court order, warrant, subpoena, or certification under this article.

**Sec. 11. Disclosure of Stored Communications.**

(a) Except as provided by Subsection (c) of this section, a provider of an electronic communications service may not knowingly divulge the contents of a communication that is in electronic storage.

(b) Except as provided by Subsection (c) of this section, a provider of remote computing service may not knowingly divulge the contents of any communication that is:

(1) in electronic storage;

(2) stored on behalf of a subscriber or customer of the service and is received by means of electronic transmission from or created by means of computer processing of communications received by means of electronic transmission from the subscriber or customer; and

(3) solely for the purpose of providing storage or computer processing services to the subscriber or customer if the provider of the service is not authorized to obtain access to the contents of those communications for purposes of providing any service other than storage or computer processing.

(c) A provider of an electronic communications or remote computing service may divulge the contents of an electronically stored communication:

(1) to an intended recipient of the communication or that person's agent;

(2) to the addressee or that person's agent;

(3) with the consent of the originator, to the addressee or the intended recipient of the communication, or the subscriber of a remote computing service;

(4) to a person whose facilities are used to transmit the communication to its destination or the person's employee or authorized representative;

(5) as may be necessary to provide the service or to protect the property or rights of the provider of the service;

(6) to a law enforcement agency if the contents were obtained inadvertently by the service provider and the contents appear to pertain to the commission of a crime; or

(7) as authorized under federal or other state law.

**Sec. 12. Cause of Action.**

(a) Except as provided by Section 10 of this article, a provider of electronic communications service or subscriber or customer of an electronic communications service aggrieved by a violation of this article has a civil cause of action if the conduct constituting the violation was committed knowingly or intentionally and is entitled to:

(1) injunctive relief;

(2) a reasonable attorney's fee and other litigation costs reasonably incurred; and

(3) the sum of the actual damages suffered and any profits made by the violator as a result of the violation or $1,000, whichever is more.

(b) The reliance in good faith on a court order, warrant, subpoena, or legislative authorization is a complete defense to any civil action brought under this article.

(c) A civil action under this section may be presented within two years after the date the claimant first discovered or had reasonable opportunity to discover the violation, and not afterward.

**Sec. 13. Exclusivity of Remedies.**

The remedies and sanctions described in this article are the exclusive judicial remedies and sanctions for a violation of this article other than a violation that infringes on a right of a party guaranteed by a state or federal constitution.

**Sec. 14. Mobile Tracking Devices.**

(a) A district judge may issue an order for the installation and use of a mobile tracking device in the same judicial district as the site of:

(1) the investigation; or

(2) the person, vehicle, container, item, or object the movement of which will be tracked by the mobile tracking device.

(b) The order may authorize the use of a mobile tracking device outside the judicial district but within the state, if the device is installed within the district.

(c) A district judge may issue the order only on the application of an authorized peace officer. An application must be written and signed and sworn to or affirmed before the judge. The affidavit must:

(1) state the name, department, agency, and address of the applicant;

(2) identify the vehicle, container, or item to which, in which, or on which the mobile tracking device is to be attached, placed, or otherwise installed;

(3) state the name of the owner or possessor of the vehicle, container, or item described in Subdivision (2);

(4) state the judicial jurisdictional area in which the vehicle, container, or item described in Subdivision (2) is expected to be found; and

(5) state the facts and circumstances that provide the applicant with a reasonable suspicion that:

(A) criminal activity has been, is, or will be committed; and

(B) the installation and use of a mobile tracking device is likely to produce information that is material to an ongoing criminal investigation of the criminal activity described in Paragraph (A).

(d) Within 72 hours after the time the mobile tracking device was activated in place on or within the vehicle, container, or item, the applicant shall notify in writing the judge who issued an order under this section.

(e) An order under this section expires not later than the 90th day after the date that the device has been activated in place on or within the vehicle, container, or item. For good cause shown, the judge may grant an extension for an additional 90-day period.

(f) The applicant shall remove or cause to be removed a mobile tracking device as soon as is practicable after the authorization period expires. If removal is not practicable, monitoring

of the device shall cease on expiration of the authorization order.

(g) This section does not apply to a global positioning or similar device installed in or on an item of property by the owner or with the consent of the owner of the property. A device described by this subsection may be monitored by a private entity in an emergency.

**Sec. 15. Subpoena Authority.**

(a) The director of the department or the director's designee, the inspector general of the Texas Department of Criminal Justice or the inspector general's designee, or the sheriff or chief of a designated law enforcement agency or the sheriff's or chief's designee may issue an administrative subpoena to a communications common carrier or an electronic communications service to compel the production of the carrier's or service's business records that:

(1) disclose information about:

(A) the carrier's or service's customers; or

(B) users of the services offered by the carrier or service; and

(2) are material to a criminal investigation.

(b) Not later than the 30th day after the date on which the administrative subpoena is issued under Subsection (a), the inspector general of the Texas Department of Criminal Justice or the sheriff or chief of a designated law enforcement agency, as applicable, shall report the issuance of the subpoena to the department.

(c) If, based on reports received under Subsection (b), the department determines that a designated law enforcement office or agency is not in compliance with the policy adopted by the office or agency under Section 2(j), the department shall notify the office or agency in writing that it is not in compliance. If the department determines that the office or agency still is not in compliance with the policy 90 days after the date the office or agency receives written notice under this subsection, the office or agency loses the authority granted by this article until:

(1) the office or agency adopts a new written policy governing the application of this article to the office or agency; and

(2) the department approves the written policy.

**Sec. 16. Limitation.**

A governmental agency authorized to install

and use a pen register under this article or other law must use reasonably available technology to only record and decode electronic or other impulses used to identify the numbers dialed, routed, addressed, or otherwise processed or transmitted by a wire or electronic communication so as to not include the contents of the communication.

(Enacted by Acts 1985, 69th Leg., ch. 587 (H.B. 10), § 5, effective August 26, 1985; am. Acts 1989, 71st Leg., ch. 958 (H.B. 241), § 1, effective September 1, 1989; am. Acts 1993, 73rd Leg., ch. 659 (S.B. 73), § 2, effective September 1, 1993; am. Acts 1995, 74th Leg., ch. 170 (S.B. 1158), § 1, effective August 28, 1995; am. Acts 1995, 74th Leg., ch. 318 (S.B. 15), § 47, effective September 1, 1995; am. Acts 1997, 75th Leg., ch. 1051 (S.B. 1120), §§ 5—8, effective September 1, 1997; am. Acts 1999, 76th Leg., ch. 62 (S.B. 1368), § 18.20, effective September 1, 1999; am. Acts 2001, 77th Leg., ch. 1270 (S.B. 1345), §§ 7—10, effective September 1, 2001; am. Acts 2003, 78th Leg., ch. 678 (H.B. 2474), §§ 8—11, effective September 1, 2003; am. Acts 2007, 80th Leg., ch. 186 (S.B. 823), §§ 2—4, effective May 23, 2007; am. Acts 2009, 81st Leg., ch. 1237 (S.B. 2047), §§ 2—5, effective September 1, 2009; am. Acts 2011, 82nd Leg., ch. 316 (H.B. 2354), §§ 1, 2, 3, 4, 5, effective September 1, 2011; am. Acts 2011, 82nd Leg., ch. 620 (S.B. 688), § 2, effective September 1, 2011.)

## Art. 18.22. Testing for Communicable Diseases Following Certain Arrests.

(a) A person who is arrested for a misdemeanor or felony and who during the commission of that offense or an arrest following the commission of that offense causes a peace officer to come into contact with the person's bodily fluids shall, at the direction of the court having jurisdiction over the arrested person, undergo a medical procedure or test designed to show or help show whether the person has a communicable disease. The court may direct the person to undergo the procedure or test on its own motion or on the request of the peace officer. If the person refuses to submit voluntarily to the procedure or test, the court shall require the person to submit to the procedure or test. Notwithstanding any other law, the person performing the procedure or test shall make the test results available to the local health authority, and the local health authority shall notify the peace officer of the test result. The

state may not use the fact that a medical procedure or test was performed on a person under this article, or use the results of the procedure or test, in any criminal proceeding arising out of the alleged offense.

(b) Testing under this article shall be conducted in accordance with written infectious disease control protocols adopted by the Texas Board of Health that clearly establish procedural guidelines that provide criteria for testing and that respect the rights of the arrested person and the peace officer.

(c) Nothing in this article authorizes a court to release a test result to a person other than a person specifically authorized by this article, and Section 81.103(d), Health and Safety Code, does not authorize that disclosure.

(Enacted by Acts 2001, 77th Leg., ch. 1480 (S.B. 215), § 2, effective September 1, 2001; am. Acts 2003, 78th Leg., ch. 1250 (S.B. 1835), § 1, effective September 1, 2003.)

## Art. 18.23. Expenses for Motor Vehicle Towed and Stored for Certain Purposes.

(a) A law enforcement agency that directs the towing and storage of a motor vehicle for an evidentiary or examination purpose shall pay the cost of the towing and storage.

(b) Subsection (a) applies whether the motor vehicle is taken to or stored on property that is:

(1) owned or operated by the law enforcement agency; or

(2) owned or operated by another person who provides storage services to the law enforcement agency, including:

(A) a governmental entity; and

(B) a vehicle storage facility, as defined by Section 2303.002, Occupations Code.

(c) Subsection (a) does not require a law enforcement agency to pay the cost of:

(1) towing or storing a motor vehicle for a purpose that is not an evidentiary or examination purpose, including towing or storing a vehicle that has been abandoned, illegally parked, in an accident, or recovered after being stolen; or

(2) storing a motor vehicle after the date the law enforcement agency authorizes the owner or operator of the property to which the vehicle was taken or on which the vehicle is stored to release the vehicle to the vehicle's owner.

(d) This subsection applies only to a motor

vehicle taken to or stored on property described by Subsection (b)(2). After a law enforcement agency authorizes the release of a motor vehicle held for an evidentiary or examination purpose, the owner or operator of the storage property may not refuse to release the vehicle to the vehicle's owner because the law enforcement agency has not paid the cost of the towing and storage.

(e) Subchapter J, Chapter 2308, Occupations Code, does not apply to a motor vehicle directed by a law enforcement agency to be towed and stored for an evidentiary or examination purpose. (Enacted by Acts 2005, 79th Leg., ch. 1197 (H.B. 480), § 1, effective September 1, 2005; am. Acts 2007, 80th Leg., ch. 1046 (H.B. 2094), § 3.01, effective September 1, 2007.)

## Art. 18.24. Custody of Property Found [Deleted].

Deleted by Acts 1973, 63rd Leg., ch. 399 (S.B. 34), § 2(E), effective January 1, 1974.

## Art. 18.25. Magistrate Shall Investigate [Deleted].

Deleted by Acts 1973, 63rd Leg., ch. 399 (S.B. 34), § 2(E), effective January 1, 1974.

## Art. 18.26. Shall Discharge Defendant [Deleted].

Deleted by Acts 1973, 63rd Leg., ch. 399 (S.B. 34), § 2(E), effective January 1, 1974.

## Art. 18.27. Schedule [Deleted].

Deleted by Acts 1973, 63rd Leg., ch. 399 (S.B. 34), § 2(E), effective January 1, 1974.

## Art. 18.28. Examining Trial [Deleted].

Deleted by Acts 1973, 63rd Leg., ch. 399 (S.B. 34), § 2(E), effective January 1, 1974.

## Art. 18.29. Certify Record to Proper Court [Deleted].

Deleted by Acts 1973, 63rd Leg., ch. 399 (S.B. 34), § 2(E), effective January 1, 1974.

## Art. 18.30. Sale of Unclaimed or Abandoned Property [Deleted].

Deleted by Acts 1973, 63rd Leg., ch. 399 (S.B.

34), § 2(E), effective January 1, 1974.
(Am. Acts 1967, 60th Leg., ch. 659 (S.B. 145), § 15, effective August 28, 1967.)

# After Commitment or Bail and Before the Trial

## CHAPTER 19
## ORGANIZATION OF THE GRAND JURY

Criminal Procedure

**Article**
19.42.   Personal Information About Grand Jurors.

## Art. 19.01. Appointment of Jury Commissioners; Selection Without Jury Commission.

(a) The district judge, at or during any term of court, shall appoint not less than three, nor more than five persons to perform the duties of jury commissioners, and shall cause the sheriff to notify them of their appointment, and when and where they are to appear. The district judge shall, in the order appointing such commissioners, designate whether such commissioners shall serve during the term at which selected or for the next succeeding term. Such commissioners shall receive as compensation for each day or part thereof they may serve the sum of Ten Dollars, and they shall possess the following qualifications:

1. Be intelligent citizens of the county and able to read and write the English language;

2. Be qualified jurors in the county;

3. Have no suit in said court which requires intervention of a jury;

4. Be residents of different portions of the county; and

5. The same person shall not act as jury commissioner more than once in any 12-month period.

(b) In lieu of the selection of prospective jurors by means of a jury commission, the district judge may direct that 20 to 125 prospective grand jurors be selected and summoned, with return on summons, in the same manner as for the selection and summons of panels for the trial of civil cases in the district courts. The judge shall try the qualifications for and excuses from service as a grand juror and impanel the completed grand jury in the same manner as provided for grand jurors selected by a jury commission.
(Enacted by Acts 1965, 59th Leg., ch. 722 (S.B. 107), § 1, effective January 1, 1966; am. Acts 1971, 62nd Leg., ch. 131 (H.B. 222), § 1, effective May 10, 1971; am. Acts 1979, 66th Leg., ch. 184 (H.B. 1436), § 1, effective September 1, 1979; am. Acts 1983, 68th Leg., ch. 514 (S.B. 380), § 1, effective June 19, 1983; am. Acts 1991, 72nd Leg., ch. 67 (H.B. 885), § 1, effective September 1, 1991; am. Acts 2001, 77th Leg., ch. 344 (S.B. 203), § 1, effective September 1, 2001.)

## Art. 19.02. Notified of Appointment.

The judge shall cause the proper officer to notify such appointees of such appointment, and when and where they are to appear.

(Enacted by Acts 1965, 59th Leg., ch. 722 (S.B. 107), § 1, effective January 1, 1966.)

## Art. 19.03. Oath of Commissioners.

When the appointees appear before the judge, he shall administer to them the following oath: "You do swear faithfully to discharge the duties required of you as jury commissioners; that you will not knowingly elect any man as juryman whom you believe to be unfit and not qualified; that you will not make known to any one the name of any juryman selected by you and reported to the court; that you will not, directly or indirectly, converse with any one selected by you as a juryman concerning the merits of any case to be tried at the next term of this court, until after said cause may be tried or continued, or the jury discharged".

(Enacted by Acts 1965, 59th Leg., ch. 722 (S.B. 107), § 1, effective January 1, 1966.)

## Art. 19.04. Instructed.

The jury commissioners, after they have been organized and sworn, shall be instructed by the judge in their duties and shall then retire in charge of the sheriff to a suitable room to be secured by the sheriff for that purpose. The clerk shall furnish them the necessary stationery, the names of those appearing from the records of the court to be exempt or disqualified from serving on the jury at each term, and the last assessment roll of the county.

(Enacted by Acts 1965, 59th Leg., ch. 722 (S.B. 107), § 1, effective January 1, 1966.)

## Art. 19.05. Kept Free from Intrusion.

The jury commissioners shall be kept free from the intrusion of any person during their session, and shall not separate without leave of the court until they complete their duties.

(Enacted by Acts 1965, 59th Leg., ch. 722 (S.B. 107), § 1, effective January 1, 1966.)

## Art. 19.06. Shall Select Grand Jurors.

The jury commissioners shall select not less than 15 nor more than 40 persons from the citizens of the county to be summoned as grand jurors for the next term of court, or the term of court for which said commissioners were selected to serve, as directed in the order of the court selecting the commissioners. The commissioners shall, to the extent possible, select grand jurors who the commissioners determine represent a broad cross-section of the population of the county, considering the factors of race, sex, and age. A commissioner is not qualified to be selected for or to serve as a grand juror during the term of court for which the commissioner is serving as a commissioner.

(Enacted by Acts 1965, 59th Leg., ch. 722 (S.B. 107), § 1, effective January 1, 1966; am. Acts 1967, 60th Leg., ch. 515 (H.B. 294), § 1, effective August 28, 1967; am. Acts 1979, 66th Leg., ch. 184 (H.B. 1436), § 4, effective September 1, 1979; am. Acts 2001, 77th Leg., ch. 344 (S.B. 203), § 2, effective September 1, 2001; am. Acts 2005, 79th Leg., ch. 801 (S.B. 451), § 1, effective September 1, 2005.)

## Art. 19.07. Extension Beyond Term of Period for Which Grand Jurors Shall Sit.

If prior to the expiration of the term for which the grand jury was impaneled, it is made to appear by a declaration of the foreman or of a majority of the grand jurors in open court, that the investigation by the grand jury of the matters before it cannot be concluded before the expiration of the term, the judge of the district court in which said grand jury was impaneled may, by the entry of an order on the minutes of said court, extend, from time to time, for the purpose of concluding the investigation of matters then before it, the period during which said grand jury shall sit, for not to exceed a total of ninety days after the expiration of the term for which it was impaneled, and all indictments pertaining thereto returned by the grand jury within said extended period shall be as valid as if returned before the expiration of the term. The extension of the term of a grand jury under this article does not affect the provisions of Article 19.06 relating to the selection and summoning of grand jurors for each regularly scheduled term.

(Enacted by Acts 1965, 59th Leg., ch. 722 (S.B. 107), § 1, effective January 1, 1966.)

## Art. 19.08. Qualifications.

No person shall be selected or serve as a grand juror who does not possess the following qualifications:

    1. The person must be a citizen of the state, and of the county in which the person is to serve, and be qualified under the Constitution and laws to vote in said county, provided that the person's failure to register to vote shall not be held to disqualify the person in this instance;

    2. The person must be of sound mind and good moral character;

    3. The person must be able to read and write;

    4. The person must not have been convicted of misdemeanor theft or a felony;

    5. The person must not be under indictment or other legal accusation for misdemeanor theft or a felony;

    6. The person must not be related within the third degree of consanguinity or second degree of affinity, as determined under Chapter 573, Government Code, to any person selected to serve or serving on the same grand jury;

    7. The person must not have served as grand juror or jury commissioner in the year before the date on which the term of court for which the person has been selected as grand juror begins;

    8. The person must not be a complainant in any matter to be heard by the grand jury during the term of court for which the person has been selected as a grand juror.

(Enacted by Acts 1965, 59th Leg., ch. 722 (S.B. 107), § 1, effective January 1, 1966; am. Acts 1969, 61st Leg., ch. 412 (S.B. 424), § 5, effective September 1, 1969; am. Acts 1981, 67th Leg., ch. 827 (H.B. 1288), § 5, effective August 31, 1981; am. Acts 1989, 71st Leg., ch. 1065 (S.B. 208), § 1, effective September 1, 1989; am. Acts 1991, 72nd Leg., ch. 561 (H.B. 1345), § 8, effective August 26, 1991; am. Acts 1995, 74th Leg., ch. 76 (S.B. 959), § 5.95(27), effective September 1, 1995; am. Acts 1999, 76th Leg., ch. 1177 (S.B. 216), § 1, effective September 1, 1999; am. Acts 2005, 79th Leg., ch. 801 (S.B. 451), § 2, effective September 1, 2005.)

## Art. 19.09. Names Returned.

The names of those selected as grand jurors by the commissioners shall be written upon a paper; and the fact that they were so selected shall be certified and signed by the jury commissioners, who shall place said paper, so certified and signed, in an envelope, and seal the same, and endorse thereon the words, "The list of grand jurors selected at ... term of the district court", the blank being for the month and year in which the term of the court began its session. The commissioners shall write their names across the seal of said envelope, direct the same to the district judge and deliver it to him in open court.

(Enacted by Acts 1965, 59th Leg., ch. 722 (S.B. 107), § 1, effective January 1, 1966.)

## Art. 19.10. List to Clerk.

The judge shall deliver the envelope containing the list of grand jurors to the clerk or one of his deputies in open court without opening the same. (Enacted by Acts 1965, 59th Leg., ch. 722 (S.B. 107), § 1, effective January 1, 1966.)

## Art. 19.11. Oath to Clerk.

Before the list of grand jurors is delivered to the clerk, the judge shall administer to the clerk and each of his deputies in open court the following oath: "You do swear that you will not open the jury lists now delivered you, nor permit them to be opened until the time prescribed by law; that you will not, directly or indirectly, converse with any one selected as a juror concerning any case or proceeding which may come before such juror for trial in this court at its next term". (Enacted by Acts 1965, 59th Leg., ch. 722 (S.B. 107), § 1, effective January 1, 1966.)

## Art. 19.12. Deputy Clerk Sworn.

Should the clerk subsequently appoint a deputy, such clerk shall administer to him the same oath, at the time of such appointment. (Enacted by Acts 1965, 59th Leg., ch. 722 (S.B. 107), § 1, effective January 1, 1966.)

## Art. 19.13. Clerk Shall Open Lists.

The grand jury may be convened on the first or any subsequent day of the term. The judge shall designate the day on which the grand jury is to be impaneled and notify the clerk of such date; and within thirty days of such date, and not before, the clerk shall open the envelope containing the list of grand jurors, make out a copy of the names of those selected as grand jurors, certify to it under his official seal, note thereon the day for which they are to be summoned, and deliver it to the sheriff. (Enacted by Acts 1965, 59th Leg., ch. 722 (S.B. 107), § 1, effective January 1, 1966.)

## Art. 19.14. Summoning.

The sheriff shall summon the persons named in the list at least three days, exclusive of the day of service, prior to the day on which the grand jury is to be impaneled, by giving personal notice to each juror of the time and place when and where he is to attend as a grand juror, or by leaving at his place of residence with a member of his family over sixteen years old, a written notice to such juror that he has been selected as a grand juror, and the time and place when and where he is to attend; or the judge, at his election, may direct the sheriff to summon the grand jurors by registered or certified mail. (Enacted by Acts 1965, 59th Leg., ch. 722 (S.B. 107), § 1, effective January 1, 1966; am. Acts 1993, 73rd Leg., ch. 268 (S.B. 248), § 5, effective September 1, 1993.)

## Art. 19.15. Return of Officer.

The officer executing such summons shall return the list on the day on which the grand jury is to be impaneled, with a certificate thereon of the date and manner of service upon each juror. If any of said jurors have not been summoned, he shall also state in his certificate the reason why they have not been summoned. (Enacted by Acts 1965, 59th Leg., ch. 722 (S.B. 107), § 1, effective January 1, 1966.)

## Art. 19.16. Absent Juror Fined.

A juror legally summoned, failing to attend without a reasonable excuse, may, by order of the court entered on the record, be fined not less than $100 nor more than $500. (Enacted by Acts 1965, 59th Leg., ch. 722 (S.B. 107), § 1, effective January 1, 1966; am. Acts 2009, 81st Leg., ch. 640 (H.B. 1665), § 2, effective September 1, 2009.)

## Art. 19.17. Failure to Select.

If for any reason a grand jury shall not be selected or summoned prior to the commencement of any term of court, or when none of those summoned shall attend, the district judge may at any time after the commencement of the term, in his discretion, direct a writ to be issued to the sheriff commanding him to summon a jury commission, selected by the court, which commission shall select not more than 40 persons, as provided by law, who shall serve as grand jurors. (Enacted by Acts 1965, 59th Leg., ch. 722 (S.B. 107), § 1, effective January 1, 1966; am. Acts 2001, 77th Leg., ch. 344 (S.B. 203), § 2, effective September 1, 2001.)

## Art. 19.18. If Less Than Fourteen Attend.

When less than fourteen of those summoned to serve as grand jurors are found to be in attendance and qualified to so serve, the court shall order the sheriff to summon such additional number of persons as may be deemed necessary to constitute a grand jury of twelve persons and two alternates.

(Enacted by Acts 1965, 59th Leg., ch. 722 (S.B. 107), § 1, effective January 1, 1966; am. Acts 1999, 76th Leg., ch. 1065 (H.B. 3230), § 1, effective September 1, 1999.)

### Art. 19.19. Jurors to Attend Forthwith.

The jurors provided for in the two preceding Articles shall be summoned in person to attend before the court forthwith.

(Enacted by Acts 1965, 59th Leg., ch. 722 (S.B. 107), § 1, effective January 1, 1966.)

### Art. 19.20. To Summon Qualified Persons.

Upon directing the sheriff to summon grand jurors not selected by the jury commissioners, the court shall instruct him that he must summon no person to serve as a grand juror who does not possess the qualifications prescribed by law.

(Enacted by Acts 1965, 59th Leg., ch. 722 (S.B. 107), § 1, effective January 1, 1966.)

### Art. 19.21. To Test Qualifications.

When as many as fourteen persons summoned to serve as grand jurors are in attendance upon the court, it shall proceed to test their qualifications as such.

(Enacted by Acts 1965, 59th Leg., ch. 722 (S.B. 107), § 1, effective January 1, 1966; am. Acts 1999, 76th Leg., ch. 1065 (H.B. 3230), § 2, effective September 1, 1999.)

### Art. 19.22. Interrogated.

Each person who is presented to serve as a grand juror shall, before being impaneled, be interrogated on oath by the court or under his direction, touching his qualifications.

(Enacted by Acts 1965, 59th Leg., ch. 722 (S.B. 107), § 1, effective January 1, 1966.)

### Art. 19.23. Mode of Test.

In trying the qualifications of any person to serve as a grand juror, he shall be asked:

1. Are you a citizen of this state and county, and qualified to vote in this county, under the Constitution and laws of this state?

2. Are you able to read and write?

3. Have you ever been convicted of a felony?

4. Are you under indictment or other legal accusation for theft or for any felony?

(Enacted by Acts 1965, 59th Leg., ch. 722 (S.B. 107), § 1, effective January 1, 1966; am. Acts 1969, 61st Leg., ch. 412 (S.B. 424), § 6, effective September 1, 1969.)

### Art. 19.24. Qualified Juror Accepted.

When, by the answer of the person, it appears to the court that he is a qualified juror, he shall be accepted as such, unless it be shown that he is not of sound mind or of good moral character, or unless it be shown that he is in fact not qualified to serve as a grand juror.

(Enacted by Acts 1965, 59th Leg., ch. 722 (S.B. 107), § 1, effective January 1, 1966.)

### Art. 19.25. Excuses from Service.

Any person summoned who does not possess the requisite qualifications shall be excused by the court from serving. The following qualified persons may be excused from grand jury service:

(1) a person older than 70 years;

(2) a person responsible for the care of a child younger than 18 years;

(3) a student of a public or private secondary school;

(4) a person enrolled and in actual attendance at an institution of higher education; and

(5) any other person that the court determines has a reasonable excuse from service.

(Enacted by Acts 1965, 59th Leg., ch. 722 (S.B. 107), § 1, effective January 1, 1966; am. Acts 1979, 66th Leg., ch. 184 (H.B. 1436), § 2, effective September 1, 1979; am. Acts 1999, 76th Leg., ch. 1177 (S.B. 216), § 2, effective September 1, 1999.)

### Art. 19.26. Jury Impaneled.

(a) When fourteen qualified jurors are found to be present, the court shall proceed to impanel the grand jury, unless a challenge is made, which may be to the array or to any particular person presented to serve as a grand juror or an alternate.

(b) The grand jury is composed of not more than twelve qualified jurors. In addition, the court shall qualify and impanel not more than two alternates to serve on disqualification or unavailability of a juror during the term of the grand jury. On learning that a grand juror has become disqualified or unavailable during the term of the grand jury, the attorney representing the state shall prepare an order for the court identifying the disqualified or unavailable juror, stating the basis for the disqualification or unavailability, dismissing the disqualified or unavailable juror from the grand jury, and naming one of the alternates as a member of the grand jury. The procedure established by this subsection may be used on disqualification or unavailability of a second grand juror during the term of

Criminal Procedure

the grand jury. For purposes of this subsection, a juror is unavailable if the juror is unable to participate fully in the duties of the grand jury because of the death of the juror or a physical or mental illness of the juror.

(Enacted by Acts 1965, 59th Leg., ch. 722 (S.B. 107), § 1, effective January 1, 1966; am. Acts 1999, 76th Leg., ch. 1065 (H.B. 3230), § 3, effective September 1, 1999; am. Acts 2003, 78th Leg., ch. 889 (S.B. 802), § 1, effective September 1, 2003.)

## Art. 19.27. Any Person May Challenge.

Before the grand jury has been impaneled, any person may challenge the array of jurors or any person presented as a grand juror. In no other way shall objections to the qualifications and legality of the grand jury be heard. Any person confined in jail in the county shall upon his request be brought into court to make such challenge.

(Enacted by Acts 1965, 59th Leg., ch. 722 (S.B. 107), § 1, effective January 1, 1966.)

## Art. 19.28. "Array".

By the "array" of grand jurors is meant the whole body of persons summoned to serve as such before they have been impaneled.

(Enacted by Acts 1965, 59th Leg., ch. 722 (S.B. 107), § 1, effective January 1, 1966.)

## Art. 19.29. "Impaneled" and "Panel".

A grand juror is said to be "impaneled" after his qualifications have been tried and he has been sworn. By "panel" is meant the whole body of grand jurors.

(Enacted by Acts 1965, 59th Leg., ch. 722 (S.B. 107), § 1, effective January 1, 1966.)

## Art. 19.30. Challenge to "Array".

A challenge to the "array" shall be made in writing for these causes only:

1. That those summoned as grand jurors are not in fact those selected by the method provided by Article 19.01(b) of this chapter or by the jury commissioners; and

2. In case of grand jurors summoned by order of the court, that the officer who summoned them had acted corruptly in summoning any one or more of them.

(Enacted by Acts 1965, 59th Leg., ch. 722 (S.B. 107), § 1, effective January 1, 1966; am. Acts 1979, 66th Leg., ch. 184 (H.B. 1436), § 3, effective September 1, 1979.)

## Art. 19.31. Challenge to Juror.

A challenge to a particular grand juror may be made orally for the following causes only:

1. That he is not a qualified juror; and

2. That he is the prosecutor upon an accusation against the person making the challenge.

(Enacted by Acts 1965, 59th Leg., ch. 722 (S.B. 107), § 1, effective January 1, 1966.)

## Art. 19.32. Summarily Decided.

When a challenge to the array or to any individual has been made, the court shall hear proof and decide in a summary manner whether the challenge be well-founded or not.

(Enacted by Acts 1965, 59th Leg., ch. 722 (S.B. 107), § 1, effective January 1, 1966.)

## Art. 19.33. Other Jurors Summoned.

The court shall order another grand jury to be summoned if the challenge to the array be sustained, or order the panel to be completed if by challenge to any particular grand juror their number be reduced below twelve.

(Enacted by Acts 1965, 59th Leg., ch. 722 (S.B. 107), § 1, effective January 1, 1966.)

## Art. 19.34. Oath of Grand Jurors.

When the grand jury is completed, the court shall appoint one of the number foreman; and the following oath shall be administered by the court, or under its direction, to the jurors: "You solemnly swear that you will diligently inquire into, and true presentment make, of all such matters and things as shall be given you in charge; the State's counsel, your fellows and your own, you shall keep secret, unless required to disclose the same in the course of a judicial proceeding in which the truth or falsity of evidence given in the grand jury room, in a criminal case, shall be under investigation. You shall present no person from envy, hatred or malice; neither shall you leave any person unpresented for love, fear, favor, affection or hope of reward; but you shall present things truly as they come to your knowledge, according to the best of your understanding, so help you God".

(Enacted by Acts 1965, 59th Leg., ch. 722 (S.B. 107), § 1, effective January 1, 1966.)

## Art. 19.35. To Instruct Jury.

The court shall instruct the grand jury as to their duty.

(Enacted by Acts 1965, 59th Leg., ch. 722 (S.B. 107), § 1, effective January 1, 1966.)

### Art. 19.36. Bailiffs Appointed.

The court and the district attorney may each appoint one or more bailiffs to attend upon the grand jury, and at the time of appointment, the following oath shall be administered to each of them by the court, or under its direction: "You solemnly swear that you will faithfully and impartially perform all the duties of bailiff of the grand jury, and that you will keep secret the proceedings of the grand jury, so help you God". Such bailiffs shall be compensated in a sum to be set by the commissioners court of said county.
(Enacted by Acts 1965, 59th Leg., ch. 722 (S.B. 107), § 1, effective January 1, 1966.)

### Art. 19.37. Bailiff's Duties.

A bailiff is to obey the instructions of the foreman, to summon all witnesses, and generally, to perform all such duties as the foreman may require of him. One bailiff shall be always with the grand jury, if two or more are appointed.
(Enacted by Acts 1965, 59th Leg., ch. 722 (S.B. 107), § 1, effective January 1, 1966.)

### Art. 19.38. Bailiff Violating Duty.

No bailiff shall take part in the discussions or deliberations of the grand jury nor be present when they are discussing or voting upon a question. The grand jury shall report to the court any violation of duty by a bailiff and the court may punish him for such violation as for contempt.
(Enacted by Acts 1965, 59th Leg., ch. 722 (S.B. 107), § 1, effective January 1, 1966.)

### Art. 19.39. Another Foreman Appointed.

If the foreman of the grand jury is from any cause absent or unable or disqualified to act, the court shall appoint in his place some other member of the body.
(Enacted by Acts 1965, 59th Leg., ch. 722 (S.B. 107), § 1, effective January 1, 1966.)

### Art. 19.40. Quorum.

Nine members shall be a quorum for the purpose of discharging any duty or exercising any right properly belonging to the grand jury.
(Enacted by Acts 1965, 59th Leg., ch. 722 (S.B. 107), § 1, effective January 1, 1966.)

### Art. 19.41. Reassembled.

A grand jury discharged by the court for the term may be reassembled by the court at any time during the term.

(Enacted by Acts 1965, 59th Leg., ch. 722 (S.B. 107), § 1, effective January 1, 1966; am. Acts 1999, 76th Leg., ch. 1065 (H.B. 3230), § 4, effective September 1, 1999.)

### Art. 19.42. Personal Information About Grand Jurors.

(a) Except as provided by Subsection (b), information collected by the court, court personnel, or prosecuting attorney during the grand jury selection process about a person who serves as a grand juror, including the person's home address, home telephone number, social security number, driver's license number, and other personal information, is confidential and may not be disclosed by the court, court personnel, or prosecuting attorney.

(b) On a showing of good cause, the court shall permit disclosure of the information sought to a party to the proceeding.
(Enacted by Acts 1999, 76th Leg., ch. 1177 (S.B. 216), § 3, effective September 1, 1999.)

## CHAPTER 20
## DUTIES AND POWERS OF THE GRAND JURY

### Art. 20.01. Grand Jury Room.

After the grand jury is organized they shall proceed to the discharge of their duties in a

suitable place which the sheriff shall prepare for their sessions.
(Enacted by Acts 1965, 59th Leg., ch. 722 (S.B. 107), § 1, effective January 1, 1966.)

### Art. 20.011. Who May Be Present in Grand Jury Room.

(a) Only the following persons may be present in a grand jury room while the grand jury is conducting proceedings:

(1) grand jurors;

(2) bailiffs;

(3) the attorney representing the state;

(4) witnesses while being examined or when necessary to assist the attorney representing the state in examining other witnesses or presenting evidence to the grand jury;

(5) interpreters, if necessary;

(6) a stenographer or person operating an electronic recording device, as provided by Article 20.012; and

(7) a person operating a video teleconferencing system for use under Article 20.151.

(b) Only a grand juror may be in a grand jury room while the grand jury is deliberating.
(Enacted by Acts 1995, 74th Leg., ch. 1011 (S.B. 1074), § 1, effective September 1, 1995; am. Acts 2011, 82nd Leg., ch. 1031 (H.B. 2847), § 2, effective September 1, 2011; am. Acts 2011, 82nd Leg., ch. 1341 (S.B. 1233), § 3, effective June 17, 2011.)

### Art. 20.012. Recording of Certain Testimony.

(a) Questions propounded by the grand jury or the attorney representing the state to a person accused or suspected and the testimony of that person to the grand jury shall be recorded either by a stenographer or by use of an electronic device capable of recording sound.

(b) The validity of a grand jury proceeding is not affected by an unintentional failure to record all or part of questions propounded or testimony made under Subsection (a).

(c) The attorney representing the state shall maintain possession of all records other than stenographer's notes made under this article and any typewritten transcription of those records, except as provided by Article 20.02.
(Enacted by Acts 1995, 74th Leg., ch. 1011 (S.B. 1074), § 1, effective September 1, 1995.)

### Art. 20.02. Proceedings Secret.

(a) The proceedings of the grand jury shall be secret.

(b) A grand juror, bailiff, interpreter, stenographer or person operating an electronic recording device, person preparing a typewritten transcription of a stenographic or electronic recording, or person operating a video teleconferencing system for use under Article 20.151 who discloses anything transpiring before the grand jury, regardless of whether the thing transpiring is recorded, in the course of the official duties of the grand jury, is liable to a fine as for contempt of the court, not exceeding $500, imprisonment not exceeding 30 days, or both the fine and imprisonment.

(c) A disclosure of a record made under Article 20.012, a disclosure of a typewritten transcription of that record, or a disclosure otherwise prohibited by Subsection (b) or Article 20.16 may be made by the attorney representing the state in performing the attorney's duties to a grand juror serving on the grand jury before whom the record was made, another grand jury, a law enforcement agency, or a prosecuting attorney, as permitted by the attorney representing the state and determined by the attorney as necessary to assist the attorney in the performance of the attorney's duties. The attorney representing the state shall warn any person the attorney authorizes to receive information under this subsection of the person's duty to maintain the secrecy of the information. Any person who receives information under this subsection and discloses the information for purposes other than those permitted by this subsection is subject to punishment for contempt in the same manner as persons who violate Subsection (b).

(d) The defendant may petition a court to order the disclosure of information otherwise made secret by this article or the disclosure of a recording or typewritten transcription under Article 20.012 as a matter preliminary to or in connection with a judicial proceeding. The court may order disclosure of the information, recording, or transcription on a showing by the defendant of a particularized need.

(e) A petition for disclosure under Subsection (d) must be filed in the district court in which the case is pending. The defendant must also file a copy of the petition with the attorney representing the state, the parties to the judicial proceeding, and any other persons required by the court to receive a copy of the petition. All persons receiving a petition under this subsection are entitled to appear before the court. The court shall provide interested parties with an opportunity to appear and present arguments for the continuation of or end to the requirement of secrecy.

(f) A person who receives information under Subsection (d) or (e) and discloses that information is subject to punishment for contempt in the same manner as a person who violates Subsection (b).

(g) The attorney representing the state may not disclose anything transpiring before the grand jury except as permitted by Subsections (c), (d), and (e).

(h) A subpoena or summons relating to a grand jury proceeding or investigation must be kept secret to the extent and for as long as necessary to prevent the unauthorized disclosure of a matter before the grand jury. This subsection may not be construed to limit a disclosure permitted by Subsection (c), (d), or (e).

(Enacted by Acts 1965, 59th Leg., ch. 722 (S.B. 107), § 1, effective January 1, 1966; am. Acts 1995, 74th Leg., ch. 1011 (S.B. 1074), § 2, effective September 1, 1995; am. Acts 2007, 80th Leg., ch. 628 (H.B. 587), § 1, effective September 1, 2007; am. Acts 2011, 82nd Leg., ch. 1031 (H.B. 2847), § 3, effective September 1, 2011; am. Acts 2011, 82nd Leg., ch. 1341 (S.B. 1233), § 4, effective June 17, 2011.)

### Art. 20.03. Attorney Representing State Entitled to Appear.

"The attorney representing the State" means the Attorney General, district attorney, criminal district attorney, or county attorney. The attorney representing the State, is entitled to go before the grand jury and inform them of offenses liable to indictment at any time except when they are discussing the propriety of finding an indictment or voting upon the same.

(Enacted by Acts 1965, 59th Leg., ch. 722 (S.B. 107), § 1, effective January 1, 1966.)

### Art. 20.04. Attorney May Examine Witnesses.

The attorney representing the State may examine the witnesses before the grand jury and shall advise as to the proper mode of interrogating them. No person other than the attorney representing the State or a grand juror may question a witness before the grand jury. No person may address the grand jury about a matter before the grand jury other than the attorney representing the State, a witness, or the accused or suspected person or the attorney for the accused or suspected person if approved by the State's attorney.

(Enacted by Acts 1965, 59th Leg., ch. 722 (S.B. 107), § 1, effective January 1, 1966; am. Acts 1989, 71st Leg., ch. 1065 (S.B. 108), § 2, effective September 1, 1989.)

### Art. 20.05. May Send for Attorney.

The grand jury may send for the attorney representing the state and ask his advice upon any matter of law or upon any question arising respecting the proper discharge of their duties.

(Enacted by Acts 1965, 59th Leg., ch. 722 (S.B. 107), § 1, effective January 1, 1966; am. Acts 1989, 71st Leg., ch. 1065 (S.B. 108), § 3, effective September 1, 1989.)

### Art. 20.06. Advice from Court.

The grand jury may also seek and receive advice from the court touching any matter before them, and for this purpose, shall go into court in a body; but they shall so guard the manner of propounding their questions as not to divulge the particular accusation that is pending before them; or they may propound their questions in writing, upon which the court may give them the desired information in writing.

(Enacted by Acts 1965, 59th Leg., ch. 722 (S.B. 107), § 1, effective January 1, 1966.)

### Art. 20.07. Foreman Shall Preside.

The foreman shall preside over the sessions of the grand jury, and conduct its business and proceedings in an orderly manner. He may appoint one or more members of the body to act as clerks for the grand jury.

(Enacted by Acts 1965, 59th Leg., ch. 722 (S.B. 107), § 1, effective January 1, 1966.)

### Art. 20.08. Adjournments.

The grand jury shall meet and adjourn at times agreed upon by a majority of the body; but they shall not adjourn, at any one time, for more than three days, unless by consent of the court. With the consent of the court, they may adjourn for a longer time, and shall as near as may be, conform their adjournments to those of the court.

(Enacted by Acts 1965, 59th Leg., ch. 722 (S.B. 107), § 1, effective January 1, 1966.)

### Art. 20.09. Duties of Grand Jury.

The grand jury shall inquire into all offenses liable to indictment of which any member may have knowledge, or of which they shall be informed by the attorney representing the State, or any other credible person.

(Enacted by Acts 1965, 59th Leg., ch. 722 (S.B. 107), § 1, effective January 1, 1966.)

## Art. 20.10. Attorney or Foreman May Issue Process.

The attorney representing the state, or the foreman, in term time or vacation, may issue a summons or attachment for any witness in the county where they are sitting; which summons or attachment may require the witness to appear before them at a time fixed, or forthwith, without stating the matter under investigation.

(Enacted by Acts 1965, 59th Leg., ch. 722 (S.B. 107), § 1, effective January 1, 1966.)

## Art. 20.11. Out-of-County Witnesses.

Sec. 1. The foreman or the attorney representing the State may, upon written application to the district court stating the name and residence of the witness and that his testimony is believed to be material, cause a subpoena or an attachment to be issued to any county in the State for such witness, returnable to the grand jury then in session, or to the next grand jury for the county from whence the same issued, as such foreman or attorney may desire. The subpoena may require the witness to appear and produce records and documents. An attachment shall command the sheriff or any constable of the county where the witness resides to serve the witness, and have him before the grand jury at the time and place specified in the writ.

Sec. 2. A subpoena or attachment issued pursuant to this article shall be served and returned in the manner prescribed in Chapter 24 of this code.

A witness subpoenaed pursuant to this article shall be compensated as provided in this code.

(Enacted by Acts 1965, 59th Leg., ch. 722 (S.B. 107), § 1, effective January 1, 1966; am. Acts 1973, 63rd Leg., ch. 350 (H.B. 692), § 1, effective June 12, 1973.)

## Art. 20.12. Attachment in Vacation.

The attorney representing the state may cause an attachment for a witness to be issued, as provided in the preceding Article, either in term time or in vacation.

(Enacted by Acts 1965, 59th Leg., ch. 722 (S.B. 107), § 1, effective January 1, 1966.)

## Art. 20.13. Execution of Process.

The bailiff or other officer who receives process to be served from a grand jury shall forthwith execute the same and return it to the foreman, if the grand jury be in session; and if the grand jury be not in session, the process shall be returned to the district clerk. If the process is returned not executed, the return shall state why it was not executed.

(Enacted by Acts 1965, 59th Leg., ch. 722 (S.B. 107), § 1, effective January 1, 1966.)

## Art. 20.14. Evasion of Process.

If it be made to appear satisfactorily to the court that a witness for whom an attachment has been issued to go before the grand jury is in any manner wilfully evading the service of such summons or attachment, the court may fine such witness, as for contempt, not exceeding five hundred dollars.

(Enacted by Acts 1965, 59th Leg., ch. 722 (S.B. 107), § 1, effective January 1, 1966.)

## Art. 20.15. When Witness Refuses to Testify.

When a witness, brought in any manner before a grand jury, refuses to testify, such fact shall be made known to the attorney representing the State or to the court; and the court may compel the witness to answer the question, if it appear to be a proper one, by imposing a fine not exceeding five hundred dollars, and by committing the party to jail until he is willing to testify.

(Enacted by Acts 1965, 59th Leg., ch. 722 (S.B. 107), § 1, effective January 1, 1966.)

## Art. 20.151. Certain Testimony by Video Teleconferencing.

(a) With the consent of the foreman of the grand jury and the attorney representing the state, a peace officer summoned to testify before the grand jury may testify through the use of a closed circuit video teleconferencing system that provides an encrypted, simultaneous, compressed full motion video and interactive communication of image and sound between the peace officer, the attorney representing the state, and the grand jury.

(b) In addition to being administered the oath described by Article 20.16(a), before being interrogated, a peace officer testifying through the use of a closed circuit video teleconferencing system under this article shall affirm that:

(1) no person other than a person in the grand jury room is capable of hearing the peace officer's testimony; and

(2) the peace officer's testimony is not being recorded or otherwise preserved by any person

at the location from which the peace officer is testifying.

(c) **[2 Versions: As added by Acts 2011, 82nd Leg., ch. 1031]** Testimony received from a peace officer under this article shall be recorded in the same manner as other testimony taken before the grand jury.

(c) **[2 Versions: As added by Acts 2011, 82nd Leg., ch. 1341]** Testimony received from a peace officer under this article shall be recorded and preserved.

(Enacted by Acts 2011, 82nd Leg., ch. 1031 (H.B. 2847), § 4, effective September 1, 2011; enacted by Acts 2011, 82nd Leg., ch. 1341 (S.B. 1233), § 5, effective June 17, 2011.)

### Art. 20.16. Oaths to Witnesses.

(a) The following oath shall be administered by the foreman, or under the foreman's direction, to each witness before being interrogated: "You solemnly swear that you will not reveal, by your words or conduct, and will keep secret any matter about which you may be interrogated or that you have observed during the proceedings of the grand jury, and that you will answer truthfully the questions asked of you by the grand jury, or under its direction, so help you God."

(b) A witness who reveals any matter about which the witness is interrogated or that the witness has observed during the proceedings of the grand jury, other than when required to give evidence thereof in due course, shall be liable to a fine as for contempt of court, not exceeding $500, and to imprisonment not exceeding six months.

(Enacted by Acts 1965, 59th Leg., ch. 722 (S.B. 107), § 1, effective January 1, 1966; am. Acts 1973, 63rd Leg., ch. 399 (S.B. 34), § 2(A), effective January 1, 1974; am. Acts 2007, 80th Leg., ch. 28 (S.B. 343), § 1, effective September 1, 2007.)

### Art. 20.17. How Suspect or Accused Questioned.

(a) The grand jury, in propounding questions to the person accused or suspected, shall first state the offense with which he is suspected or accused, the county where the offense is said to have been committed and as nearly as may be, the time of commission of the offense, and shall direct the examination to the offense under investigation.

(b) Prior to any questioning of an accused or suspected person who is subpoenaed to appear before the grand jury, the accused or suspected person shall be furnished a written copy of the warnings contained in Subsection (c) of this section and shall be given a reasonable opportunity to retain counsel or apply to the court for an appointed attorney and to consult with counsel prior to appearing before the grand jury.

(c) If an accused or suspected person is subpoenaed to appear before a grand jury prior to any questions before the grand jury, the person accused or suspected shall be orally warned as follows:

(1) "Your testimony before this grand jury is under oath";

(2) "Any material question that is answered falsely before this grand jury subjects you to being prosecuted for aggravated perjury";

(3) "You have the right to refuse to make answers to any question, the answer to which would incriminate you in any manner";

(4) "You have the right to have a lawyer present outside this chamber to advise you before making answers to questions you feel might incriminate you";

(5) "Any testimony you give may be used against you at any subsequent proceeding";

(6) "If you are unable to employ a lawyer, you have the right to have a lawyer appointed to advise you before making an answer to a question, the answer to which you feel might incriminate you."

(Enacted by Acts 1965, 59th Leg., ch. 722 (S.B. 107), § 1, effective January 1, 1966; am. Acts 1989, 71st Leg., ch. 1065 (S.B. 108), § 4, effective September 1, 1989.)

### Art. 20.18. How Witness Questioned.

When a felony has been committed in any county within the jurisdiction of the grand jury, and the name of the offender is known or unknown or where it is uncertain when or how the felony was committed, the grand jury shall first state to the witness called the subject matter under investigation, then may ask pertinent questions relative to the transaction in general terms and in such a manner as to determine whether he has knowledge of the violation of any particular law by any person, and if so, by what person.

(Enacted by Acts 1965, 59th Leg., ch. 722 (S.B. 107), § 1, effective January 1, 1966.)

### Art. 20.19. Grand Jury Shall Vote.

After all the testimony which is accessible to the grand jury shall have been given in respect to

Criminal Procedure

any criminal accusation, the vote shall be taken as to the presentment of an indictment, and if nine members concur in finding the bill, the foreman shall make a memorandum of the same with such data as will enable the attorney who represents the State to write the indictment. (Enacted by Acts 1965, 59th Leg., ch. 722 (S.B. 107), § 1, effective January 1, 1966.)

### Art. 20.20. Indictment Prepared.

The attorney representing the State shall prepare all indictments which have been found, with as little delay as possible, and deliver them to the foreman, who shall sign the same officially, and said attorney shall endorse thereon the names of the witnesses upon whose testimony the same was found.
(Acts 1965, 59th Leg., vol. 2, p. 317, ch. 722, effective January 1, 1966.)

### Art. 20.21. Indictment Presented.

When the indictment is ready to be presented, the grand jury shall through their foreman, deliver the indictment to the judge or clerk of the court. At least nine members of the grand jury must be present on such occasion.
(Enacted by Acts 1965, 59th Leg., ch. 722 (S.B. 107), § 1, effective January 1, 1966; am. Acts 1979, 66th Leg., ch. 463 (H.B. 794), § 1, effective June 7, 1979.)

### Art. 20.22. Presentment Entered of Record.

(a) The fact of a presentment of indictment by a grand jury shall be entered in the record of the court, if the defendant is in custody or under bond, noting briefly the style of the criminal action, the file number of the indictment, and the defendant's name.

(b) If the defendant is not in custody or under bond at the time of the presentment of indictment, the indictment may not be made public and the entry in the record of the court relating to the indictment must be delayed until the capias is served and the defendant is placed in custody or under bond.
(Enacted by Acts 1965, 59th Leg., ch. 722 (S.B. 107), § 1, effective January 1, 1966; am. Acts 1979, 66th Leg., ch. 463 (H.B. 794), § 2, effective June 7, 1979; am. Acts 1999, 76th Leg., ch. 580 (S.B. 577), § 3, effective September 1, 1999; am. Acts 2007, 80th Leg., ch. 628 (H.B. 587), § 2, effective September 1, 2007; am. Acts 2011, 82nd Leg., ch. 278 (H.B. 1573), § 2, effective September 1, 2011.)

# CHAPTER 21
# INDICTMENT AND INFORMATION

### Art. 21.01. "Indictment".

An "indictment" is the written statement of a grand jury accusing a person therein named of some act or omission which, by law, is declared to be an offense.
(Enacted by Acts 1965, 59th Leg., ch. 722 (S.B. 107), § 1, effective January 1, 1966.)

### Art. 21.011. Filing of Charging Instrument or Related Document in Electronic Form.

(a) An indictment, information, complaint, or other charging instrument or a related document in a criminal case may be filed in electronic form with a judge or clerk of the court authorized to receive the document.

(b) A judge or clerk of the court is authorized to receive for filing purposes an information, indictment, complaint, or other charging instrument or a related document in electronic form in accordance with Subchapter I, Chapter 51, Government Code, if:

(1) the document complies with the requirements that would apply if the document were filed in hard-copy form;

(2) the clerk of the court has the means to electronically store the document for the statutory period of record retention;

(3) the judge or clerk of the court is able to reproduce the document in hard-copy form on demand; and

(4) the clerk of the court is able to display or otherwise make the document available in electronic form to the public at no charge.

(c) The person filing the document and the person receiving the document must complete the electronic filing as provided by Section 51.804, Government Code.

(d) Notwithstanding Section 51.806, Government Code, an indictment, information, complaint, or other charging instrument or a related document transmitted in electronic form is exempt from a requirement under this code that the pleading be endorsed by a natural person. The requirement of an oath under this code is satisfied if:

(1) all or part of the document was sworn to; and

(2) the electronic form states which parts of the document were sworn to and the name of the officer administering the oath.

(e) An electronically filed document described by this section may be amended or modified in compliance with Chapter 28 or other applicable law. The amended or modified document must reflect that the original document has been superseded.

(f) This section does not affect the application of Section 51.318, Government Code, Section 118.052(3), Local Government Code, or any other law permitting the collection of fees for the provision of services related to court documents.
(Enacted by Acts 2005, 79th Leg., ch. 312 (S.B. 611), § 3, effective June 17, 2005.)

## Art. 21.02. Requisites of an Indictment.

An indictment shall be deemed sufficient if it has the following requisites:

1. It shall commence, "In the name and by authority of The State of Texas".

2. It must appear that the same was presented in the district court of the county where the grand jury is in session.

3. It must appear to be the act of a grand jury of the proper county.

4. It must contain the name of the accused, or state that his name is unknown and give a reasonably accurate description of him.

5. It must show that the place where the offense was committed is within the jurisdiction of the court in which the indictment is presented.

6. The time mentioned must be some date anterior to the presentment of the indictment, and not so remote that the prosecution of the offense is barred by limitation.

7. The offense must be set forth in plain and intelligible words.

8. The indictment must conclude, "Against the peace and dignity of the State".

9. It shall be signed officially by the foreman of the grand jury.
(Enacted by Acts 1965, 59th Leg., ch. 722 (S.B. 107), § 1, effective January 1, 1966.)

## Art. 21.03. What Should Be Stated.

Everything should be stated in an indictment which is necessary to be proved.
(Enacted by Acts 1965, 59th Leg., ch. 722 (S.B. 107), § 1, effective January 1, 1966.)

## Art. 21.04. The Certainty Required.

The certainty required in an indictment is such as will enable the accused to plead the judgment that may be given upon it in bar of any prosecution for the same offense.
(Enacted by Acts 1965, 59th Leg., ch. 722 (S.B. 107), § 1, effective January 1, 1966.)

## Art. 21.05. Particular Intent; Intent to Defraud.

Where a particular intent is a material fact in the description of the offense, it must be stated in the indictment; but in any case where an intent to defraud is required to constitute an offense, it shall be sufficient to allege an intent to defraud, without naming therein the particular person intended to be defrauded.
(Enacted by Acts 1965, 59th Leg., ch. 722 (S.B. 107), § 1, effective January 1, 1966.)

## Art. 21.06. Allegation of Venue.

When the offense may be prosecuted in either of two or more counties, the indictment may allege the offense to have been committed in the county where the same is prosecuted, or in any county or place where the offense was actually committed.

Criminal Procedure

(Enacted by Acts 1965, 59th Leg., ch. 722 (S.B. 107), § 1, effective January 1, 1966.)

## Art. 21.07. Allegation of Name.

In alleging the name of the defendant, or of any other person necessary to be stated in the indictment, it shall be sufficient to state one or more of the initials of the given name and the surname. When a person is known by two or more names, it shall be sufficient to state either name. When the name of the person is unknown to the grand jury, that fact shall be stated, and if it be the accused, a reasonably accurate description of him shall be given in the indictment.

(Enacted by Acts 1965, 59th Leg., ch. 722 (S.B. 107), § 1, effective January 1, 1966; am. Acts 1995, 74th Leg., ch. 830 (H.B. 2662), § 1, effective September 1, 1995.)

## Art. 21.08. Allegation of Ownership.

Where one person owns the property, and another person has the possession of the same, the ownership thereof may be alleged to be in either. Where property is owned in common, or jointly, by two or more persons, the ownership may be alleged to be in all or either of them. When the property belongs to the estate of a deceased person, the ownership may be alleged to be in the executor, administrator or heirs of such deceased person, or in any one of such heirs. Where the ownership of the property is unknown to the grand jury, it shall be sufficient to allege that fact. (Enacted by Acts 1965, 59th Leg., ch. 722 (S.B. 107), § 1, effective January 1, 1966; am. Acts 1967, 60th Leg., ch. 659 (S.B. 145), § 16, effective August 28, 1967.)

## Art. 21.09. Description of Property.

If known, personal property alleged in an indictment shall be identified by name, kind, number, and ownership. When such is unknown, that fact shall be stated, and a general classification, describing and identifying the property as near as may be, shall suffice. If the property be real estate, its general locality in the county, and the name of the owner, occupant or claimant thereof, shall be a sufficient description of the same. (Enacted by Acts 1965, 59th Leg., ch. 722 (S.B. 107), § 1, effective January 1, 1966; am. Acts 1975, 64th Leg., ch. 341 (S.B. 122), § 2, effective June 19, 1975.)

## Art. 21.10. "Felonious" and "Feloniously".

It is not necessary to use the words "felonious" or "feloniously" in any indictment. (Enacted by Acts 1965, 59th Leg., ch. 722 (S.B. 107), § 1, effective January 1, 1966.)

## Art. 21.11. Certainty; What Sufficient.

An indictment shall be deemed sufficient which charges the commission of the offense in ordinary and concise language in such a manner as to enable a person of common understanding to know what is meant, and with that degree of certainty that will give the defendant notice of the particular offense with which he is charged, and enable the court, on conviction, to pronounce the proper judgment; and in no case are the words "force and arms" or "contrary to the form of the statute" necessary. (Enacted by Acts 1965, 59th Leg., ch. 722 (S.B. 107), § 1, effective January 1, 1966.)

## Art. 21.12. Special and General Terms.

When a statute defining any offense uses special or particular terms, indictment on it may use the general term which, in common language, embraces the special term. To charge an unlawful sale, it is necessary to name the purchaser. (Enacted by Acts 1965, 59th Leg., ch. 722 (S.B. 107), § 1, effective January 1, 1966.)

## Art. 21.13. Act with Intent to Commit an Offense.

An indictment for an act done with intent to commit some other offense may charge in general terms the commission of such act with intent to commit such other offense. (Enacted by Acts 1965, 59th Leg., ch. 722 (S.B. 107), § 1, effective January 1, 1966.)

## Art. 21.14. Perjury and Aggravated Perjury.

(a) An indictment for perjury or aggravated perjury need not charge the precise language of the false statement, but may state the substance of the same, and no such indictment shall be held insufficient on account of any variance which does not affect the subject matter or general import of such false statement; and it is not necessary in such indictment to set forth the pleadings, records or proceeding with which the false statement is connected, nor the commission or authority of the court or person before whom the false statement was made; but it is sufficient to state the name of the court or public servant by whom the oath was administered with the allegation of the falsity of the matter on which the perjury or aggravated perjury is assigned.

(b) If an individual is charged with aggravated perjury before a grand jury, the indictment may not be entered by the grand jury before which the false statement was alleged to have been made. (Enacted by Acts 1965, 59th Leg., ch. 722 (S.B. 107), § 1, effective January 1, 1966; am. Acts 1973, 63rd Leg., ch. 399 (S.B. 34), § 2(A), effective January 1, 1974; am. Acts 1989, 71st Leg., ch. 1065 (S.B. 208), § 5, effective September 1, 1989.)

## Art. 21.15. Must Allege Acts of Recklessness or Criminal Negligence.

Whenever recklessness or criminal negligence enters into or is a part or element of any offense, or it is charged that the accused acted recklessly or with criminal negligence in the commission of an offense, the complaint, information, or indictment in order to be sufficient in any such case must allege, with reasonable certainty, the act or acts relied upon to constitute recklessness or criminal negligence, and in no event shall it be sufficient to allege merely that the accused, in committing the offense, acted recklessly or with criminal negligence. (Enacted by Acts 1965, 59th Leg., ch. 722 (S.B. 107), § 1, effective January 1, 1966; am. Acts 1973, 63rd Leg., ch. 399 (S.B. 34), § 2(A), effective January 1, 1974.)

## Art. 21.16. Certain Forms of Indictments.

The following form of indictments is sufficient: "In the name and by authority of the State of Texas: The grand jury of ... County, State of Texas, duly organized at the ... term, A.D. ... , of the district court of said county, in said court at said term, do present that ... (defendant) on the ... day of ... A.D. ... , in said county and State, did ... (description of offense) against the peace and dignity of the State.

     ... , Foreman of the grand jury." (Enacted by Acts 1965, 59th Leg., ch. 722 (S.B. 107), § 1, effective January 1, 1966.)

## Art. 21.17. Following Statutory Words.

Words used in a statute to define an offense need not be strictly pursued in the indictment; it is sufficient to use other words conveying the same meaning, or which include the sense of the statutory words.

(Enacted by Acts 1965, 59th Leg., ch. 722 (S.B. 107), § 1, effective January 1, 1966.)

## Art. 21.18. Matters of Judicial Notice.

Presumptions of law and matters of which judicial notice is taken (among which are included the authority and duties of all officers elected or appointed under the General Laws of this State) need not be stated in an indictment. (Enacted by Acts 1965, 59th Leg., ch. 722 (S.B. 107), § 1, effective January 1, 1966.)

## Art. 21.19. Defects of Form.

An indictment shall not be held insufficient, nor shall the trial, judgment or other proceedings thereon be affected, by reason of any defect of form which does not prejudice the substantial rights of the defendant. (Enacted by Acts 1965, 59th Leg., ch. 722 (S.B. 107), § 1, effective January 1, 1966.)

## Art. 21.20. "Information".

An "information" is a written statement filed and presented in behalf of the State by the district or county attorney, charging the defendant with an offense which may by law be so prosecuted. (Enacted by Acts 1965, 59th Leg., ch. 722 (S.B. 107), § 1, effective January 1, 1966.)

## Art. 21.21. Requisites of an Information.

An information is sufficient if it has the following requisites:

1. It shall commence, "In the name and by authority of the State of Texas";

2. That it appear to have been presented in a court having jurisdiction of the offense set forth;

3. That it appear to have been presented by the proper officer;

4. That it contain the name of the accused, or state that his name is unknown and give a reasonably accurate description of him;

5. It must appear that the place where the offense is charged to have been committed is within the jurisdiction of the court where the information is filed;

6. That the time mentioned be some date anterior to the filing of the information, and that the offense does not appear to be barred by limitation;

7. That the offense be set forth in plain and intelligible words;

8. That it conclude, "Against the peace and dignity of the State"; and

9. It must be signed by the district or county attorney, officially.

(Enacted by Acts 1965, 59th Leg., ch. 722 (S.B. 107), § 1, effective January 1, 1966.)

## Art. 21.22. Information Based upon Complaint.

No information shall be presented until affidavit has been made by some credible person charging the defendant with an offense. The affidavit shall be filed with the information. It may be sworn to before the district or county attorney who, for that purpose, shall have power to administer the oath, or it may be made before any officer authorized by law to administer oaths.

(Enacted by Acts 1965, 59th Leg., ch. 722 (S.B. 107), § 1, effective January 1, 1966.)

## Art. 21.23. Rules As to Indictment Apply to Information.

The rules with respect to allegations in an indictment and the certainty required apply also to an information.

(Enacted by Acts 1965, 59th Leg., ch. 722 (S.B. 107), § 1, effective January 1, 1966.)

## Art. 21.24. Joinder of Certain Offenses.

(a) Two or more offenses may be joined in a single indictment, information, or complaint, with each offense stated in a separate count, if the offenses arise out of the same criminal episode, as defined in Chapter 3 of the Penal Code.

(b) A count may contain as many separate paragraphs charging the same offense as necessary, but no paragraph may charge more than one offense.

(c) A count is sufficient if any one of its paragraphs is sufficient. An indictment, information, or complaint is sufficient if any one of its counts is sufficient.

(Enacted by Acts 1965, 59th Leg., ch. 722 (S.B. 107), § 1, effective January 1, 1966; am. Acts 1973, 63rd Leg., ch. 399 (S.B. 34), § 2(A), effective January 1, 1974.)

## Art. 21.25. When Indictment Has Been Lost, Etc.

When an indictment or information has been lost, mislaid, mutilated or obliterated, the district or county attorney may suggest the fact to the court; and the same shall be entered upon the minutes of the court. In such case, another indict-ment or information may be substituted, upon the written statement of such attorney that it is substantially the same as that which has been lost, mislaid, mutilated, or obliterated. Or another indictment may be presented, as in the first instance; and in such case, the period for the commencement of the prosecution shall be dated from the time of making such entry.

(Enacted by Acts 1965, 59th Leg., ch. 722 (S.B. 107), § 1, effective January 1, 1966.)

## Art. 21.26. Order Transferring Cases.

Upon the filing of an indictment in the district court which charges an offense over which such court has no jurisdiction, the judge of such court shall make an order transferring the same to such inferior court as may have jurisdiction, stating in such order the cause transferred and to what court transferred.

(Enacted by Acts 1965, 59th Leg., ch. 722 (S.B. 107), § 1, effective January 1, 1966.)

## Art. 21.27. Causes Transferred to Justice Court.

Causes over which justices of the peace have jurisdiction may be transferred to a justice of the peace at the county seat, or in the discretion of the judge, to a justice of the precinct in which the same can be most conveniently tried, as may appear by memorandum endorsed by the grand jury on the indictment or otherwise. If it appears to the judge that the offense has been committed in any incorporated town or city, the cause shall be transferred to a justice in said town or city, if there be one therein; and any justice to whom such cause may be transferred shall have jurisdiction to try the same.

(Enacted by Acts 1965, 59th Leg., ch. 722 (S.B. 107), § 1, effective January 1, 1966.)

## Art. 21.28. Duty on Transfer.

The clerk of the court, without delay, shall deliver the indictments in all cases transferred, together with all the papers relating to each case, to the proper court or justice, as directed in the order of transfer; and shall accompany each case with a certified copy of all the proceedings taken therein in the district court, and with a bill of the costs that have accrued therein in the district court. The said costs shall be taxed in the court in which said cause is tried, in the event of a conviction.

(Enacted by Acts 1965, 59th Leg., ch. 722 (S.B. 107), § 1, effective January 1, 1966.)

## Art. 21.29. Proceedings of Inferior Court.

Any case so transferred shall be entered on the docket of the court to which it is transferred. All process thereon shall be issued and the defendant tried as if the case had originated in the court to which it was transferred.

(Enacted by Acts 1965, 59th Leg., ch. 722 (S.B. 107), § 1, effective January 1, 1966.)

## Art. 21.30. Cause Improvidently Transferred.

When a cause has been improvidently transferred to a court which has no jurisdiction of the same, the court to which it has been transferred shall order it to be re-transferred to the proper court; and the same proceedings shall be had as in the case of the original transfer. In such case, the defendant and the witnesses shall be held bound to appear before the court to which the case has been re-transferred, the same as they were bound to appear before the court so transferring the same.

(Enacted by Acts 1965, 59th Leg., ch. 722 (S.B. 107), § 1, effective January 1, 1966.)

## Art. 21.31. Testing for AIDS and Certain Other Diseases.

(a) A person who is indicted for or who waives indictment for an offense under Section 21.02, 21.11(a)(1), 22.011, or 22.021, Penal Code, shall, at the direction of the court on the court's own motion or on the request of the victim of the alleged offense, undergo a standard diagnostic test approved by the United States Food and Drug Administration for human immunodeficiency virus (HIV) infection and other sexually transmitted diseases. If the person refuses to submit voluntarily to the test, the court shall require the person to submit to the test. On request of the victim of the alleged offense, the court shall order the defendant to undergo the test not later than 48 hours after an indictment for the offense is presented against the defendant or the defendant waives indictment. Except as provided by Subsection (b-1), the court may require a defendant previously required under this article to undergo a diagnostic test on indictment for an offense to undergo a subsequent test only after conviction of the offense. A person performing a test under this subsection shall make the test results available to the local health authority, and the local health authority shall be required to make the notification of the test results

to the victim of the alleged offense and to the defendant.

(a-1) If the victim requests the testing of the defendant and a law enforcement agency is unable to locate the defendant during the 48-hour period allowed for that testing under Subsection (a), the running of the 48-hour period is tolled until the law enforcement agency locates the defendant and the defendant is present in the jurisdiction.

(b) The court shall order a person who is charged with an offense under Section 22.11, Penal Code, to undergo in the manner provided by Subsection (a) a diagnostic test designed to show or help show whether the person has HIV, hepatitis A, hepatitis B, tuberculosis, or any other disease designated as a reportable disease under Section 81.048, Health and Safety Code. The person charged with the offense shall pay the costs of testing under this subsection.

(b-1) If the results of a diagnostic test conducted under Subsection (a) or (b) are positive for HIV, the court shall order the defendant to undergo any necessary additional testing within a reasonable time after the test results are released.

(c) The state may not use the fact that a test was performed on a person under Subsection (a) or use the results of a test conducted under Subsection (a) in any criminal proceeding arising out of the alleged offense.

(d) Testing under this article shall be conducted in accordance with written infectious disease control protocols adopted by the Texas Board of Health that clearly establish procedural guidelines that provide criteria for testing and that respect the rights of the person accused and any victim of the alleged offense.

(e) This article does not permit a court to release a test result to anyone other than those authorized by law, and the provisions of Section 81.103(d), Health and Safety Code, may not be construed to allow that disclosure.

(Enacted by Acts 1987, 70th Leg., 2nd C.S., ch. 55 (S.B. 66), § 3, effective October 20, 1987; am. Acts 1991, 72nd Leg., ch. 14 (S.B. 404), § 284(7), effective September 1, 1991; am. Acts 1993, 73rd Leg., ch. 811 (H.B. 2650), § 1, effective September 1, 1993; am. Acts 2005, 79th Leg., ch. 543 (H.B. 1095), § 3, effective September 1, 2005; am. Acts 2007, 80th Leg., ch. 593 (H.B. 8), § 3.12, effective September 1, 2007; am. Acts 2009, 81st Leg., ch. 418 (H.B. 1985), § 1, effective September 1, 2009.)

# CHAPTER 22
# FORFEITURE OF BAIL

## Art. 22.01. Bail Forfeited, When.

When a defendant is bound by bail to appear and fails to appear in any court in which such case may be pending and at any time when his personal appearance is required under this Code, or by any court or magistrate, a forfeiture of his bail and a judicial declaration of such forfeiture shall be taken in the manner provided in Article 22.02 of this Code and entered by such court.
(Enacted by Acts 1965, 59th Leg., ch. 722 (S.B. 107), § 1, effective January 1, 1966; am. Acts 1981, 67th Leg., ch. 312 (S.B. 727), § 2, effective August 31, 1981.)

## Art. 22.01a. Failure to Appear; Violation of Bail Bond [Repealed].

Repealed by Acts 1973, 63rd Leg., ch. 399 (S.B. 34), § 3(b), effective January 1, 1974.

## Art. 22.02. Manner of Taking a Forfeiture.

Bail bonds and personal bonds are forfeited in the following manner: The name of the defendant shall be called distinctly at the courthouse door, and if the defendant does not appear within a reasonable time after such call is made, judgment shall be entered that the State of Texas recover of the defendant the amount of money in which he is bound, and of his sureties, if any, the amount of money in which they are respectively bound, which judgment shall state that the same will be made final, unless good cause be shown why the defendant did not appear.

(Enacted by Acts 1965, 59th Leg., ch. 722 (S.B. 107), § 1, effective January 1, 1966.)

## Art. 22.021. Forfeiture After Violating Treatment Condition [Repealed].

Repealed by Acts 2007, 80th Leg., ch. 1113 (H.B. 3692), § 6, effective January 1, 2008.
(Acts 1983, 68th Leg., p. 3206, ch. 551, § 2, effective September 1, 1983.)

## Art. 22.03. Citation to Sureties.

(a) Upon entry of judgment, a citation shall issue forthwith notifying the sureties of the defendant, if any, that the bond has been forfeited, and requiring them to appear and show cause why the judgment of forfeiture should not be made final.

(b) A citation to a surety who is an individual shall be served to the individual at the address shown on the face of the bond or the last known address of the individual.

(c) A citation to a surety that is a corporation or other entity shall be served to the attorney designated for service of process by the corporation or entity under Chapter 804, Insurance Code.

(d) By filing the waiver or designation in writing with the clerk of the court, a surety may waive service of citation or may designate a person other than the surety or the surety's attorney to receive service of citation under this article. The waiver or designation is effective until a written revocation is filed with the clerk.
(Enacted by Acts 1965, 59th Leg., ch. 722 (S.B. 107), § 1, effective January 1, 1966; am. Acts 2005, 79th Leg., ch. 743 (H.B. 2767), § 3, effective September 1, 2005; am. Acts 2007, 80th Leg., ch. 657 (H.B. 1158), § 1, effective September 1, 2007.)

## Art. 22.035. Citation to Defendant Posting Cash Bond.

A citation to a defendant who posted a cash bond shall be served to the defendant at the address shown on the face of the bond or the last known address of the defendant.
(Enacted by Acts 2007, 80th Leg., ch. 657 (H.B. 1158), § 2, effective September 1, 2007.)

## Art. 22.04. Requisites of Citation.

A citation shall be sufficient if it be in the form provided for citations in civil cases in such court; provided, however, that a copy of the judgment of forfeiture entered by the court, a copy of the forfeited bond, and a copy of any power of attorney attached to the forfeited bond shall be attached to the citation and the citation shall notify the parties cited to appear and show cause why the judgment of forfeiture should not be made final.

(Enacted by Acts 1965, 59th Leg., ch. 722 (S.B. 107), § 1, effective January 1, 1966; am. Acts 2005, 79th Leg., ch. 743 (H.B. 2767), § 4, effective September 1, 2005.)

## Art. 22.05. Citation As in Civil Actions.

If service of citation is not waived under Article 22.03, a surety is entitled to notice by service of citation, the length of time and in the manner required in civil actions; and the officer executing the citation shall return the same as in civil actions. It shall not be necessary to give notice to the defendant unless he has furnished his address on the bond, in which event notice to the defendant shall be deposited in the United States mail directed to the defendant at the address shown on the bond or the last known address of the defendant.

(Enacted by Acts 1965, 59th Leg., ch. 722 (S.B. 107), § 1, effective January 1, 1966; am. Acts 2005, 79th Leg., ch. 743 (H.B. 2767), § 5, effective September 1, 2005; am. Acts 2007, 80th Leg., ch. 657 (H.B. 1158), § 3, effective September 1, 2007.)

## Art. 22.06. Citation by Publication.

Where the surety is a nonresident of the State, or where he is a transient person, or where his residence is unknown, the district or county attorney may, upon application in writing to the county clerk, stating the facts, obtain a citation to be served by publication; and the same shall be served by a publication and returned as in civil actions.

(Enacted by Acts 1965, 59th Leg., ch. 722 (S.B. 107), § 1, effective January 1, 1966.)

## Art. 22.07. Cost of Publication.

When service of citation is made by publication, the county in which the forfeiture has been taken shall pay the costs thereof, to be taxed as costs in the case.

(Enacted by Acts 1965, 59th Leg., ch. 722 (S.B. 107), § 1, effective January 1, 1966.)

## Art. 22.08. Service out of the State.

Service of a certified copy of the citation upon any absent or non-resident surety may be made outside of the limits of this State by any person competent to make oath of the fact; and the affidavit of such person, stating the facts of such service, shall be a sufficient return.

(Enacted by Acts 1965, 59th Leg., ch. 722 (S.B. 107), § 1, effective January 1, 1966.)

## Art. 22.09. When Surety Is Dead.

If the surety is dead at the time the forfeiture is taken, the forfeiture shall nevertheless be valid. The final judgment shall not be rendered where a surety has died, either before or after the forfeiture has been taken, unless his executor, administrator or heirs, as the case may be, have been cited to appear and show cause why the judgment should not be made final, in the same manner as provided in the case of the surety.

(Enacted by Acts 1965, 59th Leg., ch. 722 (S.B. 107), § 1, effective January 1, 1966.)

## Art. 22.10. Scire Facias Docket.

When a forfeiture has been declared upon a bond, the court or clerk shall docket the case upon the scire facias or upon the civil docket, in the name of the State of Texas, as plaintiff, and the principal and his sureties, if any, as defendants; and, except as otherwise provided by this chapter, the proceedings had therein shall be governed by the same rules governing other civil suits.

(Enacted by Acts 1965, 59th Leg., ch. 722 (S.B. 107), § 1, effective January 1, 1966; am. Acts 1981, 67th Leg., ch. 312 (S.B. 727), § 3, effective August 31, 1981; am. Acts 1999, 76th Leg., ch. 1506 (S.B. 403), § 4, effective September 1, 1999.)

## Art. 22.11. Sureties May Answer.

After the forfeiture of the bond, if the sureties, if any, have been duly notified, the sureties, if any, may answer in writing and show cause why the defendant did not appear, which answer may be filed within the time limited for answering in other civil actions.

(Enacted by Acts 1965, 59th Leg., ch. 722 (S.B. 107), § 1, effective January 1, 1966.)

## Art. 22.12. Proceedings Not Set Aside for Defect of Form.

The bond, the judgment declaring the forfeiture, the citation and the return thereupon, shall not be set aside because of any defect of form; but such defect of form may, at any time, be amended under the direction of the court.

(Enacted by Acts 1965, 59th Leg., ch. 722 (S.B. 107), § 1, effective January 1, 1966.)

Criminal Procedure

## Art. 22.12a. Powers of the Court [Renumbered].

Renumbered to Tex. Code Crim. Proc. art. 22.125 by Acts 1987, 70th Leg., ch. 167 (S.B. 892), § 5.02(1), effective September 1, 1987.

## Art. 22.125. Powers of the Court.

After a judicial declaration of forfeiture is entered, the court may proceed with the trial required by Article 22.14 of this code. The court may exonerate the defendant and his sureties, if any, from liability on the forfeiture, remit the amount of the forfeiture, or set aside the forfeiture only as expressly provided by this chapter. The court may approve any proposed settlement of the liability on the forfeiture that is agreed to by the state and by the defendant or the defendant's sureties, if any.

(Am. Acts 1981, 67th Leg., ch. 312 (S.B. 727), § 4, effective August 31, 1981; am. Acts 1987, 70th Leg., ch. 167 (S.B. 892), § 5.02(1), effective September 1, 1987 (renumbered from art. 22.12a); am. Acts 1999, 76th Leg., ch. 1506 (S.B. 403), § 5, effective September 1, 1999.)

## Art. 22.13. Causes Which Will Exonerate.

(a) The following causes, and no other, will exonerate the defendant and his sureties, if any, from liability upon the forfeiture taken:

1. That the bond is, for any cause, not a valid and binding undertaking in law. If it be valid and binding as to the principal, and one or more of his sureties, if any, they shall not be exonerated from liability because of its being invalid and not binding as to another surety or sureties, if any. If it be invalid and not binding as to the principal, each of the sureties, if any, shall be exonerated from liability. If it be valid and binding as to the principal, but not so as to the sureties, if any, the principal shall not be exonerated, but the sureties, if any, shall be.

2. The death of the principal before the forfeiture was taken.

3. The sickness of the principal or some uncontrollable circumstance which prevented his appearance at court, and it must, in every such case, be shown that his failure to appear arose from no fault on his part. The causes mentioned in this subdivision shall not be deemed sufficient to exonerate the principal and his sureties, if any, unless such principal appear before final judgment on the bond to answer the accusation against him, or show sufficient cause for not so appearing.

4. Failure to present an indictment or information at the first term of the court which may be held after the principal has been admitted to bail, in case where the party was bound over before indictment or information, and the prosecution has not been continued by order of the court.

5. The incarceration of the principal in any jurisdiction in the United States:

(A) in the case of a misdemeanor, at the time of or not later than the 180th day after the date of the principal's failure to appear in court; or

(B) in the case of a felony, at the time of or not later than the 270th day after the date of the principal's failure to appear in court.

(b) A surety exonerated under Subdivision 5, Subsection (a), remains obligated to pay costs of court, any reasonable and necessary costs incurred by a county to secure the return of the principal, and interest accrued on the bond amount from the date of the judgment nisi to the date of the principal's incarceration.

(Enacted by Acts 1965, 59th Leg., ch. 722 (S.B. 107), § 1, effective January 1, 1966; am. Acts 2003, 78th Leg., ch. 942 (S.B. 1336), § 1, effective June 20, 2003.)

## Art. 22.14. Judgment Final.

When, upon a trial of the issues presented, no sufficient cause is shown for the failure of the principal to appear, the judgment shall be made final against him and his sureties, if any, for the amount in which they are respectively bound; and the same shall be collected by execution as in civil actions. Separate executions shall issue against each party for the amount adjudged against him. The costs shall be equally divided between the sureties, if there be more than one.

(Enacted by Acts 1965, 59th Leg., ch. 722 (S.B. 107), § 1, effective January 1, 1966.)

## Art. 22.15. Judgment Final by Default.

When the sureties have been duly cited and fail to answer, and the principal also fails to answer within the time limited for answering in other civil actions, the court shall enter judgment final by default.

(Enacted by Acts 1965, 59th Leg., ch. 722 (S.B. 107), § 1, effective January 1, 1966.)

## Art. 22.16. Remittitur After Forfeiture.

(a) After forfeiture of a bond and before entry of a final judgment, the court shall, on written motion, remit to the surety the amount of the bond, after deducting the costs of court and any reasonable and necessary costs to the county for the return of the principal, and the interest accrued on the bond amount as provided by Subsection (c) if the principal is released on new bail in the case or the case for which bond was given is dismissed.

(b) For other good cause shown and before the entry of a final judgment against the bond, the court in its discretion may remit to the surety all or part of the amount of the bond after deducting the costs of court and any reasonable and necessary costs to the county for the return of the principal, and the interest accrued on the bond amount as provided by Subsection (c).

(c) For the purposes of this article, interest accrues on the bond amount from the date of forfeiture in the same manner and at the same rate as provided for the accrual of prejudgment interest in civil cases.

(Enacted by Acts 1965, 59th Leg., ch. 722 (S.B. 107), § 1, effective January 1, 1966; am. Acts 1981, 67th Leg., ch. 312 (S.B. 727), § 5, effective August 31, 1981; am. Acts 1987, 70th Leg., ch. 1047 (S.B. 185), § 3, effective June 20, 1987; am. Acts 2003, 78th Leg., ch. 942 (S.B. 1336), § 2, effective June 20, 2003.)

## Art. 22.17. Special Bill of Review.

(a) Not later than two years after the date a final judgment is entered in a bond forfeiture proceeding, the surety on the bond may file with the court a special bill of review. A special bill of review may include a request, on equitable grounds, that the final judgment be reformed and that all or part of the bond amount be remitted to the surety, after deducting the costs of court, any reasonable costs to the county for the return of the principal, and the interest accrued on the bond amount from the date of forfeiture. The court in its discretion may grant or deny the bill in whole or in part.

(b) For the purposes of this article, interest accrues on the bond amount from the date of:

(1) forfeiture to the date of final judgment in the same manner and at the same rate as provided for the accrual of prejudgment interest in civil cases; and

(2) final judgment to the date of the order for remittitur at the same rate as provided for the accrual of postjudgment interest in civil cases.

(Enacted by Acts 1987, 70th Leg., ch. 1047 (S.B. 185), § 4, effective June 20, 1987.)

## Art. 22.18. Limitation.

An action by the state to forfeit a bail bond under this chapter must be brought not later than the fourth anniversary of the date the principal fails to appear in court.

(Enacted by Acts 1999, 76th Leg., ch. 1506 (S.B. 403), § 6, effective September 1, 1999.)

# CHAPTER 23
# THE CAPIAS

## Art. 23.01. Definition of a "Capias".

In this chapter, a "capias" is a writ that is:

(1) issued by a judge of the court having jurisdiction of a case after commitment or bail and before trial, or by a clerk at the direction of the judge; and

(2) directed "To any peace officer of the State of Texas", commanding the officer to arrest a person accused of an offense and bring the arrested person before that court immediately or on a day or at a term stated in the writ.

(Enacted by Acts 1965, 59th Leg., ch. 722 (S.B. 107), § 1, effective January 1, 1966; am. Acts 2007, 80th Leg., ch. 1263 (H.B. 3060), § 3, effective September 1, 2007.)

## Art. 23.02. Its Requisites.

A capias shall be held sufficient if it have the following requisites:

1. That it run in the name of "The State of Texas";

2. That it name the person whose arrest is ordered, or if unknown, describe him;

3. That it specify the offense of which the defendant is accused, and it appear thereby

that he is accused of some offense against the penal laws of the State;

   4. That it name the court to which and the time when it is returnable; and

   5. That it be dated and attested officially by the authority issuing the same.

(Enacted by Acts 1965, 59th Leg., ch. 722 (S.B. 107), § 1, effective January 1, 1966.)

## Art. 23.03. Capias or Summons in Felony.

(a) A capias shall be issued by the district clerk upon each indictment for felony presented, after bail has been set or denied by the judge of the court. Upon the request of the attorney representing the State, a summons shall be issued by the district clerk. The capias or summons shall be delivered by the clerk or mailed to the sheriff of the county where the defendant resides or is to be found. A capias or summons need not issue for a defendant in custody or under bond.

(b) Upon the request of the attorney representing the State a summons instead of a capias shall issue. If a defendant fails to appear in response to the summons a capias shall issue.

(c) Summons. The summons shall be in the same form as the capias except that it shall summon the defendant to appear before the proper court at a stated time and place. The summons shall be served upon a defendant by delivering a copy to him personally, or by leaving it at his dwelling house or usual place of abode with some person of suitable age and discretion then residing therein or by mailing it to the defendant's last known address.

(d) A summons issued to any person must clearly and prominently state in English and in Spanish the following:

"It is an offense for a person to intentionally influence or coerce a witness to testify falsely or to elude legal process. It is also a felony offense to harm or threaten to harm a witness or prospective witness in retaliation for or on account of the service of the person as a witness or to prevent or delay the person's service as a witness to a crime."

(Enacted by Acts 1965, 59th Leg., ch. 722 (S.B. 107), § 1, effective January 1, 1966; am. Acts 1979, 66th Leg., ch. 463 (H.B. 794), § 3, effective June 7, 1979; am. Acts 1995, 74th Leg., ch. 67 (S.B. 128), § 1, effective September 1, 1995.)

## Art. 23.031. Issuance of Capias in Electronic Form.

A district clerk, county clerk, or court may issue in electronic form a capias for the failure of a person to appear before a court or comply with a court order.

(Enacted by Acts 2005, 79th Leg., ch. 312 (S.B. 611), § 4, effective June 17, 2005; am. Acts 2007, 80th Leg., ch. 1263 (H.B. 3060), § 4, effective September 1, 2007.)

## Art. 23.04. In Misdemeanor Case.

In misdemeanor cases, the capias or summons shall issue from a court having jurisdiction of the case on the filing of an information or complaint. The summons shall be issued only upon request of the attorney representing the State and on the determination of probable cause by the judge, and shall follow the same form and procedure as in a felony case.

(Enacted by Acts 1965, 59th Leg., ch. 722 (S.B. 107), § 1, effective January 1, 1966; am. Acts 2007, 80th Leg., ch. 1263 (H.B. 3060), § 5, effective September 1, 2007.)

## Art. 23.05. Capias After Forfeiture.

(a) If a forfeiture of bail is declared by a court or a surety surrenders a defendant under Article 17.19, a capias shall be immediately issued for the arrest of the defendant, and when arrested, in its discretion, the court may require the defendant, in order to be released from custody, to deposit with the custodian of funds of the court in which the prosecution is pending current money of the United States in the amount of the new bond as set by the court, in lieu of a surety bond, unless a forfeiture is taken and set aside under the third subdivision of Article 22.13, in which case the defendant and the defendant's sureties shall remain bound under the same bail.

(b) A capias issued under this article may be executed by a peace officer or by a private investigator licensed under Chapter 1702, Occupations Code.

(c) A capias under this article must be issued not later than the 10th business day after the date of the court's issuance of the order of forfeiture or order permitting surrender of the bond.

(d) The sheriff of each county shall enter a capias issued under this article into a local warrant system not later than the 10th business day after the date of issuance of the capias by the

clerk of court.
(Enacted by Acts 1965, 59th Leg., ch. 722 (S.B. 107), § 1, effective January 1, 1966; am. Acts 1971, 62nd Leg., ch. 740 (H.B. 50), § 1, effective August 30, 1971; am. Acts 1999, 76th Leg., ch. 1506 (S.B. 403), § 7, effective September 1, 1999; am. Acts 2001, 77th Leg., ch. 1420 (H.B. 2812), § 14.733, effective September 1, 2001; am. Acts 2003, 78th Leg., ch. 942 (S.B. 1336), § 5, effective June 20, 2003; am. Acts 2007, 80th Leg., ch. 1263 (H.B. 3060), § 6, effective September 1, 2007.)

## Art. 23.06. New Bail in Felony Case.

When a defendant who has been arrested for a felony under a capias has previously given bail to answer said charge, his sureties, if any, shall be released by such arrest, and he shall be required to give new bail.
(Enacted by Acts 1965, 59th Leg., ch. 722 (S.B. 107), § 1, effective January 1, 1966.)

## Art. 23.07. Capias Does Not Lose Its Force.

A capias shall not lose its force if not executed and returned at the time fixed in the writ, but may be executed at any time afterward, and return made. All proceedings under such capias shall be as valid as if the same had been executed and returned within the time specified in the writ.
(Acts 1965, 59th Leg., p. 317, ch. 722, § 1, effective January 1, 1966.)

## Art. 23.08. Reasons for Retaining Capias.

When the capias is not returned at the time fixed in the writ, the officer holding it shall notify the court from whence it was issued, in writing, of his reasons for retaining it.
(Enacted by Acts 1965, 59th Leg., ch. 722 (S.B. 107), § 1, effective January 1, 1966.)

## Art. 23.09. Capias to Several Counties.

Capiases for a defendant may be issued to as many counties as the district or county attorney may direct.
(Enacted by Acts 1965, 59th Leg., ch. 722 (S.B. 107), § 1, effective January 1, 1966.)

## Art. 23.10. Bail in Felony.

In cases of arrest for felony in the county where the prosecution is pending, during a term of court, the officer making the arrest may take bail as provided in Article 17.21.
(Enacted by Acts 1965, 59th Leg., ch. 722 (S.B. 107), § 1, effective January 1, 1966.)

## Art. 23.11. Sheriff May Take Bail in Felony.

In cases of arrest for felony less than capital, made during vacation or made in another county than the one in which the prosecution is pending, the sheriff may take bail; in such cases the amount of the bail bond shall be the same as is endorsed upon the capias; and if no amount be endorsed on the capias, the sheriff shall require a reasonable amount of bail. If it be made to appear by affidavit, made by any district attorney, county attorney, or the sheriff approving the bail bond, to a judge of the Court of Criminal Appeals, a justice of a court of appeals, or to a judge of the district or county court, that the bail taken in any case after indictment is insufficient in amount, or that the sureties are not good for the amount, or that the bond is for any reason defective or insufficient, such judge shall issue a warrant of arrest and require of the defendant sufficient bond, according to the nature of the case.
(Enacted by Acts 1965, 59th Leg., ch. 722 (S.B. 107), § 1, effective January 1, 1966; am. Acts 1981, 67th Leg., ch. 291 (S.B. 265), § 105, effective September 1, 1981.)

## Art. 23.12. Court Shall Fix Bail in Felony.

In felony cases which are bailable, the court shall, before adjourning, fix and enter upon the minutes the amount of the bail to be required in each case. The clerk shall endorse upon the capias the amount of bail required. In case of neglect to so comply with this Article, the arrest of the defendant, and the bail taken by the sheriff, shall be as legal as if there had been no such omission.
(Enacted by Acts 1965, 59th Leg., ch. 722 (S.B. 107), § 1, effective January 1, 1966.)

## Art. 23.13. Who May Arrest Under Capias.

A capias may be executed by any peace officer. In felony cases, the defendant must be delivered immediately to the sheriff of the county where the arrest is made together, with the writ under which he was taken.
(Enacted by Acts 1965, 59th Leg., ch. 722 (S.B. 107), § 1, effective January 1, 1966.)

Criminal Procedure

## Art. 23.14. Bail in Misdemeanor.

Any officer making an arrest under a capias in a misdemeanor may in term time or vacation take a bail bond of the defendant.
(Enacted by Acts 1965, 59th Leg., ch. 722 (S.B. 107), § 1, effective January 1, 1966.)

## Art. 23.15. Arrest in Capital Cases.

Where an arrest is made under a capias in a capital case, the sheriff shall confine the defendant in jail, and the capias shall, for that purpose, be a sufficient commitment. This Article is applicable when the arrest is made in the county where the prosecution is pending.
(Enacted by Acts 1965, 59th Leg., ch. 722 (S.B. 107), § 1, effective January 1, 1966.)

## Art. 23.16. Arrest in Capital Case in Another County.

In each capital case where a defendant is arrested under a capias in a county other than that in which the case is pending, the sheriff who arrests or to whom the defendant is delivered, shall convey him immediately to the county from which the capias issued and deliver him to the sheriff of such county.
(Enacted by Acts 1965, 59th Leg., ch. 722 (S.B. 107), § 1, effective January 1, 1966.)

## Art. 23.17. Return of Bail and Capias.

When an arrest has been made and a bail taken, such bond, together with the capias, shall be returned forthwith to the proper court.
(Enacted by Acts 1965, 59th Leg., ch. 722 (S.B. 107), § 1, effective January 1, 1966.)

## Art. 23.18. Return of Capias.

The return of the capias shall be made to the court from which it is issued. If it has been executed, the return shall state what disposition has been made of the defendant. If it has not been executed, the cause of the failure to execute it shall be fully stated. If the defendant has not been found, the return shall further show what efforts have been made by the officer to find him, and what information he has as to the defendant's whereabouts.
(Enacted by Acts 1965, 59th Leg., ch. 722 (S.B. 107), § 1, effective January 1, 1966.)

# CHAPTER 24
# SUBPOENA AND ATTACHMENT

## Art. 24.01. Issuance of Subpoenas.

(a) A subpoena may summon one or more persons to appear:

(1) before a court to testify in a criminal action at a specified term of the court or on a specified day; or

(2) on a specified day:

(A) before an examining court;

(B) at a coroner's inquest;

(C) before a grand jury;

(D) at a habeas corpus hearing; or

(E) in any other proceeding in which the person's testimony may be required in accordance with this code.

(b) The person named in the subpoena to summon the person whose appearance is sought must be:

(1) a peace officer; or

(2) a least 18 years old and, at the time the subpoena is issued, not a participant in the proceeding for which the appearance is sought.

(c) A person who is not a peace officer may not be compelled to accept the duty to execute a subpoena, but if he agrees in writing to accept that duty and neglects or refuses to serve or return the subpoena, he may be punished in accordance with Article 2.16 of this code.

(d) A court or clerk issuing a subpoena shall sign the subpoena and indicate on it the date it was issued, but the subpoena need not be under seal.

(Enacted by Acts 1965, 59th Leg., ch. 722 (S.B. 107), § 1, effective January 1, 1966; am. Acts 1981, 67th Leg., ch. 209 (S.B. 259), § 1, effective September 1, 1981.)

### Art. 24.011. Subpoenas; Child Witnesses.

(a) If a witness is younger than 18 years, the court may issue a subpoena directing a person having custody, care, or control of the child to produce the child in court.

(b) If a person, without legal cause, fails to produce the child in court as directed by a subpoena issued under this article, the court may impose on the person penalties for contempt provided by this chapter. The court may also issue a writ of attachment for the person and the child, in the same manner as other writs of attachment are issued under this chapter.

(c) If the witness is in a placement in the custody of the Texas Youth Commission, a juvenile secure detention facility, or a juvenile secure correctional facility, the court may issue a bench warrant or direct that an attachment issue to require a peace officer or probation officer to secure custody of the person at the placement and produce the person in court. When the person is no longer needed as a witness, the court shall order the peace officer or probation officer to return the person to the placement from which the person was released.

(d) The court may order that the person who is the witness be detained in a certified juvenile detention facility if the person is younger than 17 years of age. If the person is at least 17 years of age, the court may order that the person be detained without bond in an appropriate county facility for the detention of adults accused of criminal offenses.

(e) In this article, "secure detention facility" and "secure correctional facility" have the meanings assigned by Section 51.02, Family Code.

(Enacted by Acts 1987, 70th Leg., ch. 520 (H.B. 697), § 1, effective June 17, 1987; am. Acts 2005, 79th Leg., ch. 949 (H.B. 1575), § 32, effective September 1, 2005.)

### Art. 24.02. Subpoena Duces Tecum.

If a witness have in his possession any instrument of writing or other thing desired as evidence, the subpoena may specify such evidence and direct that the witness bring the same with him and produce it in court.

(Enacted by Acts 1965, 59th Leg., ch. 722 (S.B. 107), § 1, effective January 1, 1966.)

### Art. 24.03. Subpoena and Application Therefor.

(a) Before the clerk or his deputy shall be required or permitted to issue a subpoena in any felony case pending in any district or criminal district court of this State of which he is clerk or deputy, the defendant or his attorney or the State's attorney shall make an application in writing or by electronic means to such clerk for each witness desired. Such application shall state the name of each witness desired, the location and vocation, if known, and that the testimony of said witness is material to the State or to the defense. The application must be filed with the clerk and placed with the papers in the cause or, if the application is filed electronically, placed with any other electronic information linked to the number of the cause. The application must also be made available to both the State and the defendant. Except as provided by Subsection (b), as far as is practical such clerk shall include in one subpoena the names of all witnesses for the State and for defendant, and such process shall show that the witnesses are summoned for the State or for the defendant. When a witness has been served with a subpoena, attached or placed under bail at the instance of either party in a particular case, such execution of process shall inure to the benefit of the opposite party in such case in the event such opposite party desires to use such witness on the trial of the case, provided that when a witness has once been served with a subpoena, no further subpoena shall be issued for said witness.

(b) If the defendant is a member of a combination as defined by Section 71.01, Penal Code, the clerk shall issue for each witness a subpoena that does not include a list of the names of all other witnesses for the State or the defendant.

(Enacted by Acts 1965, 59th Leg., ch. 722 (S.B. 107), § 1, effective January 1, 1966; am. Acts

Criminal Procedure

1993, 73rd Leg., ch. 900 (S.B. 1067), § 10.01, effective September 1, 1993; am. Acts 1999, 76th Leg., ch. 580 (S.B. 577), § 4, effective September 1, 1999; am. Acts 1999, 76th Leg., ch. 614 (S.B. 851), § 2, effective June 18, 1999.)

### Art. 24.04. Service and Return of Subpoena.

(a) A subpoena is served by:

(1) reading the subpoena in the hearing of the witness;

(2) delivering a copy of the subpoena to the witness;

(3) electronically transmitting a copy of the subpoena, acknowledgment of receipt requested, to the last known electronic address of the witness; or

(4) mailing a copy of the subpoena by certified mail, return receipt requested, to the last known address of the witness unless:

(A) the applicant for the subpoena requests in writing that the subpoena not be served by certified mail; or

(B) the proceeding for which the witness is being subpoenaed is set to begin within seven business days after the date the subpoena would be mailed.

(b) The officer having the subpoena shall make due return thereof, showing the time and manner of service, if served under Subsection (a)(1) or (2) of this article, the acknowledgment of receipt, if served under Subsection (a)(3) of this article, or the return receipt, if served under Subsection (a)(4) of this article. If the subpoena is not served, the officer shall show in his return the cause of his failure to serve it. If receipt of an electronically transmitted subpoena is not acknowledged within a reasonable time or a mailed subpoena is returned undelivered, the officer shall use due diligence to locate and serve the witness. If the witness could not be found, the officer shall state the diligence he has used to find him, and what information he has as to the whereabouts of the witness.

(c) A subpoena served under Subsection (a)(3) of this article must be accompanied by notice that an acknowledgment of receipt of the subpoena must be made in a manner enabling verification of the person acknowledging receipt.

(Enacted by Acts 1965, 59th Leg., ch. 722 (S.B. 107), § 1, effective January 1, 1966; am. Acts 1979, 66th Leg., ch. 336 (S.B. 849), § 1, effective August 27, 1979; am. Acts 1995, 74th Leg., ch. 374 (H.B. 941), § 1, effective June 8, 1995; am.

Acts 1999, 76th Leg., ch. 580 (S.B. 577), § 5, effective September 1, 1999.)

### Art. 24.05. Refusing to Obey.

If a witness refuses to obey a subpoena, he may be fined at the discretion of the court, as follows: In a felony case, not exceeding five hundred dollars; in a misdemeanor case, not exceeding one hundred dollars.

(Enacted by Acts 1965, 59th Leg., ch. 722 (S.B. 107), § 1, effective January 1, 1966.)

### Art. 24.06. What Is Disobedience of a Subpoena.

It shall be held that a witness refuses to obey a subpoena:

1. If he is not in attendance on the court on the day set apart for taking up the criminal docket or on any day subsequent thereto and before the final disposition or continuance of the particular case in which he is a witness;

2. If he is not in attendance at any other time named in a writ; and

3. If he refuses without legal cause to produce evidence in his possession which he has been summoned to bring with him and produce.

(Enacted by Acts 1965, 59th Leg., ch. 722 (S.B. 107), § 1, effective January 1, 1966.)

### Art. 24.07. Fine Against Witness Conditional.

When a fine is entered against a witness for failure to appear and testify, the judgment shall be conditional; and a citation shall issue to him to show cause, at the term of the court at which said fine is entered, or at the first term thereafter, at the discretion of the judge of said court, why the same should not be final; provided, citation shall be served upon said witness in the manner and for the length of time prescribed for citations in civil cases.

(Enacted by Acts 1965, 59th Leg., ch. 722 (S.B. 107), § 1, effective January 1, 1966.)

### Art. 24.08. Witness May Show Cause.

A witness cited to show cause, as provided in the preceding Article, may do so under oath, in writing or verbally, at any time before judgment final is entered against him; but if he fails to show cause within the time limited for answering in civil actions, a judgment final by default shall be entered against him.

(Enacted by Acts 1965, 59th Leg., ch. 722 (S.B. 107), § 1, effective January 1, 1966.)

## Art. 24.09. Court May Remit Fine.

It shall be within the discretion of the court to judge of the sufficiency of an excuse rendered by a witness, and upon the hearing the court shall render judgment against the witness for the whole or any part of the fine, or shall remit the fine altogether, as to the court may appear proper and right. Said fine shall be collected as fines in misdemeanor cases.

(Enacted by Acts 1965, 59th Leg., ch. 722 (S.B. 107), § 1, effective January 1, 1966.)

## Art. 24.10. When Witness Appears and Testifies.

When a fine has been entered against a witness, but no trial of the cause takes place, and such witness afterward appears and testifies upon the trial thereof, it shall be discretionary with the judge, though no good excuse be rendered, to reduce the fine or remit it altogether; but the witness, in such case, shall, nevertheless, be adjudged to pay all the costs accruing in the proceeding against him by reason of his failure to attend.

(Enacted by Acts 1965, 59th Leg., ch. 722 (S.B. 107), § 1, effective January 1, 1966.)

## Art. 24.11. Requisites of an "Attachment".

An "attachment" is a writ issued by a clerk of a court under seal, or by any magistrate, or by the foreman of a grand jury, in any criminal action or proceeding authorized by law, commanding some peace officer to take the body of a witness and bring him before such court, magistrate or grand jury on a day named, or forthwith, to testify in behalf of the State or of the defendant, as the case may be. It shall be dated and signed officially by the officer issuing it.

(Enacted by Acts 1965, 59th Leg., ch. 722 (S.B. 107), § 1, effective January 1, 1966.)

## Art. 24.12. When Attachment May Issue.

When a witness who resides in the county of the prosecution has been duly served with a subpoena to appear and testify in any criminal action or proceeding fails to so appear, the State or the defendant shall be entitled to have an attachment issued forthwith for such witness.

(Enacted by Acts 1965, 59th Leg., ch. 722 (S.B. 107), § 1, effective January 1, 1966.)

## Art. 24.13. Attachment for Convict Witnesses.

All persons who have been or may be convicted in this state, and who are confined in an institution operated by the Texas Department of Criminal Justice or any jail in this state, shall be permitted to testify in person in any court for the state and the defendant when the presiding judge finds, after hearing, that the ends of justice require their attendance, and directs that an attachment issue to accomplish the purpose, notwithstanding any other provision of this code. Nothing in this article shall be construed as limiting the power of the courts of this state to issue bench warrants.

(Enacted by Acts 1965, 59th Leg., ch. 722 (S.B. 107), § 1, effective January 1, 1966; am. Acts 2009, 81st Leg., ch. 87 (S.B. 1969), § 25.013, effective September 1, 2009.)

## Art. 24.131. Notification to Department of Criminal Justice.

If after the Texas Department of Criminal Justice transfers a defendant or inmate to a county under Article 24.13 and before that person is returned to the department the person is released on bail or the charges on which the person was convicted and for which the person was transferred to the department are dismissed, the county shall immediately notify an officer designated by the department of the release on bail or the dismissal.

(Enacted by Acts 2001, 77th Leg., ch. 857 (H.B. 1659), § 1, effective June 14, 2001.)

## Art. 24.14. Attachment for Resident Witness.

When a witness resides in the county of the prosecution, whether he has disobeyed a subpoena or not, either in term-time or vacation, upon the filing of an affidavit with the clerk by the defendant or State's counsel, that he has good reason to believe, and does believe, that such witness is a material witness, and is about to move out of the county, the clerk shall forthwith issue an attachment for such witness; provided, that in misdemeanor cases, when the witness makes oath that he cannot give surety, the officer executing the attachment shall take his personal bond.

(Enacted by Acts 1965, 59th Leg., ch. 722 (S.B. 107), § 1, effective January 1, 1966.)

Criminal Procedure

### Art. 24.15. To Secure Attendance Before Grand Jury.

At any time before the first day of any term of the district court, the clerk, upon application of the State's attorney, shall issue a subpoena for any witness who resides in the county. If at the time such application is made, such attorney files a sworn application that he has good reason to believe and does believe that such witness is about to move out of the county, then said clerk shall issue an attachment for such witness to be and appear before said district court on the first day thereof to testify as a witness before the grand jury. Any witness so summoned, or attached, who shall fail or refuse to obey a subpoena or attachment, shall be punished by the court by a fine not exceeding five hundred dollars, to be collected as fines and costs in other criminal cases.

(Enacted by Acts 1965, 59th Leg., ch. 722 (S.B. 107), § 1, effective January 1, 1966.)

### Art. 24.16. Application for Out-County Witness.

Where, in misdemeanor cases in which confinement in jail is a permissible punishment, or in felony cases, a witness resides out of the county in which the prosecution is pending, the State or the defendant shall be entitled, either in term-time or in vacation, to a subpoena to compel the attendance of such witness on application to the proper clerk or magistrate. Such application shall be in the manner and form as provided in Article 24.03. Witnesses in such misdemeanor cases shall be compensated in the same manner as in felony cases. This Article shall not apply to more than one character witness in a misdemeanor case.

(Enacted by Acts 1965, 59th Leg., ch. 722 (S.B. 107), § 1, effective January 1, 1966.)

### Art. 24.17. Duty of Officer Receiving Said Subpoena.

The officer receiving said subpoena shall execute the same by delivering a copy thereof to each witness therein named. He shall make due return of said subpoena, showing therein the time and manner of executing the same, and if not executed, such return shall show why not executed, the diligence used to find said witness, and such information as the officer has as to the whereabouts of said witness.

(Enacted by Acts 1965, 59th Leg., ch. 722 (S.B. 107), § 1, effective January 1, 1966.)

### Art. 24.18. Subpoena Returnable Forthwith.

When a subpoena is returnable forthwith, the officer shall immediately serve the witness with a copy of the same; and it shall be the duty of said witness to immediately make his appearance before the court, magistrate or other authority issuing the same. If said witness makes affidavit of his inability from lack of funds to appear in obedience to said subpoena, the officer executing the same shall provide said witness, if said subpoena be issued as provided in Article 24.16, with the necessary funds or means to appear in obedience to said subpoena, taking his receipt therefor, and showing in his return on said subpoena, under oath, the amount furnished to said witness, together with the amount of his fees for executing said subpoena.

(Enacted by Acts 1965, 59th Leg., ch. 722 (S.B. 107), § 1, effective January 1, 1966.)

### Art. 24.19. Certificate to Officer.

The clerk, magistrate, or foreman of the grand jury issuing said process, immediately upon the return of said subpoena, if issued as provided in Article 24.16, shall issue to such officer a certificate for the amount furnished such witness, together with the amount of his fees for executing the same, showing the amount of each item; which certificate shall be approved by the district judge and recorded by the district clerk in a book kept for that purpose; and said certificate transmitted to the officer executing such subpoena, which amount shall be paid by the State, as costs are paid in other criminal matters.

(Enacted by Acts 1965, 59th Leg., ch. 722 (S.B. 107), § 1, effective January 1, 1966.)

### Art. 24.20. Subpoena Returnable at Future Date.

If the subpoena be returnable at some future date, the officer shall have authority to take bail of such witness for his appearance under said subpoena, which bond shall be returned with such subpoena, and shall be made payable to the State of Texas, in the amount in which the witness and his surety, if any, shall be bound and conditioned for the appearance of the witness at the time and before the court, magistrate or grand jury named in said subpoena, and shall be signed by the witness and his sureties. If the witness refuses to give bond, he shall be kept in custody until such time as he starts in obedience to said subpoena, when he shall be, upon affidavit being made, provided with funds necessary to appear in obedience to said subpoena.

(Enacted by Acts 1965, 59th Leg., ch. 722 (S.B. 107), § 1, effective January 1, 1966.)

### Art. 24.21. Stating Bail in Subpoena.

The court or magistrate issuing said subpoena may direct therein the amount of the bail to be required. The officer may fix the amount if not specified, and in either case, shall require sufficient security, to be approved by himself.

(Enacted by Acts 1965, 59th Leg., ch. 722 (S.B. 107), § 1, effective January 1, 1966.)

### Art. 24.22. Witness Fined and Attached.

If a witness summoned from without the county refuses to obey a subpoena, he shall be fined by the court or magistrate not exceeding five hundred dollars, which fine and judgment shall be final, unless set aside after due notice to show cause why it should not be final, which notice may immediately issue, requiring the defaulting witness to appear at once or at the next term of said court, in the discretion of the judge, to answer for such default. The court may cause to be issued at the same time an attachment for said witness, directed to the proper county, commanding the officer to whom said writ is directed to take said witness into custody and have him before said court at the time named in said writ; in which case such witness shall receive no fees, unless it appears to the court that such disobedience is excusable, when the witness may receive the same pay as if he had not been attached. Said fine when made final and all costs thereon shall be collected as in other criminal cases. Said fine and judgment may be set aside in vacation or at the time or any subsequent term of the court for good cause shown, after the witness testifies or has been discharged. The following words shall be written or printed on the face of such subpoena for out-county witnesses: "A disobedience of this subpoena is punishable by fine not exceeding five hundred dollars, to be collected as fines and costs in other criminal cases."

(Enacted by Acts 1965, 59th Leg., ch. 722 (S.B. 107), § 1, effective January 1, 1966.)

### Art. 24.23. Witness Released.

A witness who is in custody for failing to give bail shall be at once released upon giving bail required.

(Enacted by Acts 1965, 59th Leg., ch. 722 (S.B. 107), § 1, effective January 1, 1966.)

### Art. 24.24. Bail for Witness.

Witnesses on behalf of the State or defendant may, at the request of either party, be required to enter into bail in an amount to be fixed by the court to appear and testify in a criminal action; but if it shall appear to the court that any witness is unable to give security upon such bail, he shall be released without security.

(Enacted by Acts 1965, 59th Leg., ch. 722 (S.B. 107), § 1, effective January 1, 1966.)

### Art. 24.25. Personal Bond of Witness.

When it appears to the satisfaction of the court that personal bond of the witness will insure his attendance, no security need be required of him; but no bond without security shall be taken by any officer.

(Enacted by Acts 1965, 59th Leg., ch. 722 (S.B. 107), § 1, effective January 1, 1966.)

### Art. 24.26. Enforcing Forfeiture.

The bond of a witness may be enforced against him and his sureties, if any, in the manner pointed out in this Code for enforcing the bond of a defendant in a criminal case.

(Enacted by Acts 1965, 59th Leg., ch. 722 (S.B. 107), § 1, effective January 1, 1966.)

### Art. 24.27. No Surrender After Forfeiture.

The sureties of a witness have no right to discharge themselves by the surrender of the witness after the forfeiture of their bond.

(Enacted by Acts 1965, 59th Leg., ch. 722 (S.B. 107), § 1, effective January 1, 1966.)

### Art. 24.28. Uniform Act to Secure Attendance of Witnesses from Without State.

#### Sec. 1. Short Title.

This Act may be cited as the "Uniform Act to Secure the Attendance of Witnesses from Without the State in Criminal Proceedings".

#### Sec. 2. Definitions.

"Witness" as used in this Act shall include a person whose testimony is desired in any proceeding or investigation by a grand jury or in a criminal action, prosecution or proceeding.

The word "State" shall include any territory of the United States and the District of Columbia.

The word "summons" shall include a subpoena, order or other notice requiring the appearance of a witness.

### Sec. 3. Summoning witness in this State to testify in another State.

(a) If a judge of a court of record in any State which by its laws has made provision for commanding persons within that State to attend and testify in this State certifies under the seal of such court that there is a criminal prosecution pending in such court, or that a grand jury investigation has commenced or is about to commence, that a person being within this State is a material witness in such prosecution, or grand jury investigation, and that his presence will be required for a specified number of days, upon presentation of such certificate to any judge of a court of record in the county in which such person is, such judge shall fix a time and place for a hearing, and shall make an order directing the witness to appear at a time and place certain for the hearing.

(b) If at a hearing the judge determines that the witness is material and necessary, that it will not cause undue hardship to the witness to be compelled to attend and testify in the prosecution or a grand jury investigation in the other State, and that the laws of the State in which the prosecution is pending, or grand jury investigation has commenced or is about to commence, (and of any other State through which the witness may be required to pass by ordinary course of travel), will give to him protection from arrest and the service of civil and criminal process, he shall issue a summons, with a copy of the certificate attached, directing the witness to attend and testify in the court where the prosecution is pending, or where a grand jury investigation has commenced or is about to commence at a time and place specified in the summons. In any such hearing the certificate shall be prima facie evidence of all the facts stated therein.

(c) If said certificate recommends that the witness be taken into immediate custody and delivered to an officer of the requesting State to assure his attendance in the requesting State, such judge may, in lieu of notification of the hearing, direct that such witness be forthwith brought before him for said hearing; and the judge at the hearing being satisfied of the desirability of such custody and delivery, for which determination the certificate shall be prima facie proof of such desirability may, in lieu of issuing subpoena or summons, order that said witness be forthwith taken into custody and delivered to an officer of the requesting State.

(d) If the witness, who is summoned as above provided, after being paid or tendered by some properly authorized person the compensation for nonresident witnesses authorized and provided for by Article 35.27 of this Code, fails without good cause to attend and testify as directed in the summons, he shall be punished in the manner provided for the punishment of any witness who disobeys a summons issued from a court of record in this State.

### Sec. 4. Witness from another State summoned to testify in this State.

(a) If a person in any State, which by its laws has made provision for commanding persons within its borders to attend and testify in criminal prosecutions, or grand jury investigations commenced or about to commence, in this State, is a material witness in a prosecution pending in a court of record in this State, or in a grand jury investigation which has commenced or is about to commence, a judge of such court may issue a certificate under the seal of the court stating these facts and specifying the number of days the witness will be required. Said certificate may include a recommendation that the witness be taken into immediate custody and delivered to an officer of this State to assure his attendance in this State. This certificate shall be presented to a judge of a court of record in the county in which the witness is found.

(b) If the witness is summoned to attend and testify in this State he shall be tendered the compensation for nonresident witnesses authorized by Article 35.27 of this Code, together with such additional compensation, if any, required by the other State for compliance. A witness who has appeared in accordance with the provisions of the summons shall not be required to remain within this State a longer period of time than the period mentioned in the certificate, unless otherwise ordered by the court. If such witness, after coming into this State, fails without good cause to attend and testify as directed in the summons, he shall be punished in the manner provided for the punishment of any witness who disobeys a summons issued from a court of record in this State.

### Sec. 5. Exemption from arrest and service of process.

If a person comes into this State in obedience to a summons directing him to attend and testify in this State he shall not while in this State pursuant to such summons be subject to arrest or the service of process, civil or criminal, in connection with matters which arose before his entrance into this State under the summons.

If a person passes through this State while going to another State in obedience to a summons to attend and testify in that State or while returning therefrom, he shall not while so passing through this State be subject to arrest or the service of process, civil or criminal, in connection with matters which arose before his entrance into this State under the summons.

(Enacted by Acts 1965, 59th Leg., ch. 722 (S.B. 107), § 1, effective January 1, 1966; am. Acts 1973, 63rd Leg., ch. 477 (H.B. 844), § 1, effective August 27, 1973.)

## Art. 24.29. Uniform Act to Secure Rendition of Prisoners in Criminal Proceedings.

### Sec. 1. Short title.

This article may be cited as the "Uniform Act to Secure Rendition of Prisoners in Criminal Proceedings."

### Sec. 2. Definitions.

In this Act:

(1) "Penal institution" means a jail, prison, penitentiary, house of correction, or other place of penal detention.

(2) "State" means a state of the United States, the District of Columbia, the Commonwealth of Puerto Rico, and any territory of the United States.

(3) "Witness" means a person who is confined in a penal institution in a state and whose testimony is desired in another state in a criminal proceeding or investigation by a grand jury or in any criminal action before a court.

### Sec. 3. Summoning witness in this state to testify in another state.

(a) A judge of a state court of record in another state, which by its laws has made provision for commanding persons confined in penal institutions within that state to attend and testify in this state, may certify that:

(1) there is a criminal proceeding or investigation by a grand jury or a criminal action pending in the court;

(2) a person who is confined in a penal institution in this state may be a material witness in the proceeding, investigation, or action; and

(3) his presence will be required during a specified time.

(b) On presentation of the certificate to any judge having jurisdiction over the person confined and on notice to the attorney general, the judge in this state shall fix a time and place for a hearing and shall make an order directed to the person having custody of the prisoner requiring that the prisoner be produced before him at the hearing.

### Sec. 4. Court order.

(a) A judge may issue a transfer order if at the hearing the judge determines that:

(1) the witness may be material and necessary;

(2) his attending and testifying are not adverse to the interest of this state or to the health or legal rights of the witness;

(3) the laws of the state in which he is requested to testify will give him protection from arrest and the service of civil and criminal process because of any act committed prior to his arrival in the state under the order; and

(4) as a practical matter the possibility is negligible that the witness may be subject to arrest or to the service of civil or criminal process in any state through which he will be required to pass.

(b) If a judge issues an order under Subsection (a) of this section, the judge shall attach to the order a copy of a certificate presented under Section 3 of this Act. The order shall:

(1) direct the witness to attend and testify;

(2) except as provided by Subsection (c) of this section, direct the person having custody of the witness to produce him in the court where the criminal action is pending or where the grand jury investigation is pending at a time and place specified in the order; and

(3) prescribe such conditions as the judge shall determine.

(c) The judge, in lieu of directing the person having custody of the witness to produce him in the requesting jurisdiction's court, may direct and require in his order that:

(1) an officer of the requesting jurisdiction come to the Texas penal institution in which the witness is confined to accept custody of the witness for physical transfer to the requesting jurisdiction;

(2) the requesting jurisdiction provide proper safeguards on his custody while in transit;

(3) the requesting jurisdiction be liable for and pay all expenses incurred in producing and returning the witness, including but not limited to food, lodging, clothing, and medical care; and

(4) the requesting jurisdiction promptly deliver the witness back to the same or another Texas penal institution as specified

by the Texas Department of Criminal Justice at the conclusion of his testimony.

**Sec. 5. Terms and conditions.**

An order to a witness and to a person having custody of the witness shall provide for the return of the witness at the conclusion of his testimony, proper safeguards on his custody, and proper financial reimbursement or prepayment by the requesting jurisdiction for all expenses incurred in the production and return of the witness. The order may prescribe any other condition the judge thinks proper or necessary. The judge shall not require prepayment of expenses if the judge directs and requires the requesting jurisdiction to accept custody of the witness at the Texas penal institution in which the witness is confined and to deliver the witness back to the same or another Texas penal institution at the conclusion of his testimony. An order does not become effective until the judge of the state requesting the witness enters an order directing compliance with the conditions prescribed.

**Sec. 6. Exceptions.**

This Act does not apply to a person in this state who is confined as mentally ill or who is under sentence of death.

**Sec. 7. Prisoner from another state summoned to testify in this state.**

(a) If a person confined in a penal institution in any other state may be a material witness in a criminal action pending in a court of record or in a grand jury investigation in this state, a judge of the court may certify that:

(1) there is a criminal proceeding or investigation by a grand jury or a criminal action pending in the court;

(2) a person who is confined in a penal institution in the other state may be a material witness in the proceeding, investigation, or action; and

(3) his presence will be required during a specified time.

(b) The judge of the court in this state shall:

(1) present the certificate to a judge of a court of record in the other state having jurisdiction over the prisoner confined; and

(2) give notice that the prisoner's presence will be required to the attorney general of the state in which the prisoner is confined.

**Sec. 8. Compliance.**

A judge of the court in this state may enter an order directing compliance with the terms and conditions of an order specified in a certificate under Section 3 of this Act and entered by the judge of the state in which the witness is confined.

**Sec. 9. Exemption from arrest and service of process.**

If a witness from another state comes into or passes through this state under an order directing him to attend and testify in this or another state, while in this state pursuant to the order he is not subject to arrest or the service of civil or criminal process because of any act committed prior to his arrival in this state under the order.

**Sec. 10. Uniformity of interpretation.**

This Act shall be so construed as to effect its general purpose to make uniform the laws of those states which enact it.

(Enacted by Acts 1983, 68th Leg., ch. 240 (S.B. 162), § 1, effective August 29, 1983; am. Acts 2009, 81st Leg., ch. 87 (S.B. 1969), § 25.014, effective September 1, 2009.)

# CHAPTER 24A
# RESPONDING TO SUBPOENAS AND CERTAIN OTHER COURT ORDERS; PRESERVING CERTAIN INFORMATION

**Subchapter A. Responding to Subpoenas and Certain Other Court Orders**

## SUBCHAPTER A
## RESPONDING TO SUBPOENAS AND CERTAIN OTHER COURT ORDERS

### Art. 24A.001. Applicability of Subchapter.

This subchapter applies only to a subpoena, search warrant, or other court order that:

(1) relates to the investigation or prosecution of a criminal offense under Section 33.021, Penal Code; and

(2) is served on or issued with respect to an Internet service provider that provides service in this state.

(Enacted by Acts 2007, 80th Leg., ch. 1291 (S.B. 6), § 2, effective September 1, 2007.)

### Art. 24A.002. Response Required; Deadlilne for Response.

(a) Except as provided by Subsection (b), not later than the 10th day after the date on which an Internet service provider is served with or otherwise receives a subpoena, search warrant, or other court order described by Article 24A.001, the Internet service provider shall:

(1) fully comply with the subpoena, warrant, or order; or

(2) petition a court to excuse the Internet service provider from complying with the subpoena, warrant, or order.

(b) As soon as is practicable, and in no event later than the second business day after the date the Internet service provider is served with or otherwise receives a subpoena, search warrant, or other court order described by Article 24A.001, the Internet service provider shall fully comply with the subpoena, search warrant, or order if the subpoena, search warrant, or order indicates that full compliance is necessary to address a situation that threatens a person with death or other serious bodily injury.

(c) For the purposes of Subsection (a)(1), full compliance with the subpoena, warrant, or order includes:

(1) producing or providing, to the extent permitted under federal law, all documents or information requested under the subpoena, warrant, or order; or

(2) providing, to the extent permitted under federal law, electronic access to all documents or information requested under the subpoena, warrant, or order.

(Enacted by Acts 2007, 80th Leg., ch. 1291 (S.B. 6), § 2, effective September 1, 2007.)

### Art. 24A.003. Disobeying Subpoena, Warrant, or Order.

An Internet service provider that disobeys a subpoena, search warrant, or other court order described by Article 24A.001 and that was not excused from complying with the subpoena, warrant, or order under Article 24A.002(a)(2) may be punished in any manner provided by law.

(Enacted by Acts 2007, 80th Leg., ch. 1291 (S.B. 6), § 2, effective September 1, 2007.)

### Arts. 24A.004 to 24A.050. [Reserved for expansion].

## SUBCHAPTER B
## PRESERVING CERTAIN INFORMATION

### Art. 24A.051. Preserving Information.

(a) On written request of a law enforcement agency in this state or a federal law enforcement agency and pending the issuance of a subpoena or other court order described by Article 24A.001, an Internet service provider that provides service in this state shall take all steps necessary to preserve all records or other potential evidence in a criminal trial that is in the possession of the Internet service provider.

(b) Subject to Subsection (c), an Internet service provider shall preserve information under Subsection (a) for a period of 90 days after the date the Internet service provider receives the written request described by Subsection (a).

(c) An Internet service provider shall preserve information under Subsection (a) for the 90-day period immediately following the 90-day period described by Subsection (b) if the requesting law enforcement agency in writing requests an extension of the preservation period.

(Enacted by Acts 2007, 80th Leg., ch. 1291 (S.B. 6), § 2, effective September 1, 2007.)

## CHAPTER 25
## SERVICE OF A COPY OF THE INDICTMENT

### Art. 25.01. In Felony.

In every case of felony, when the accused is in custody, or as soon as he may be arrested, the clerk of the court where an indictment has been presented shall immediately make a certified copy of the same, and deliver such copy to the sheriff, together with a writ directed to such sheriff, commanding him forthwith to deliver such certified copy to the accused.

(Enacted by Acts 1965, 59th Leg., ch. 722 (S.B. 107), § 1, effective January 1, 1966.)

## Art. 25.02. Service and Return.

Upon receipt of such writ and copy, the sheriff shall immediately deliver such certified copy of the indictment to the accused and return the writ to the clerk issuing the same, with his return thereon, showing when and how the same was executed.

(Enacted by Acts 1965, 59th Leg., ch. 722 (S.B. 107), § 1, effective January 1, 1966.)

## Art. 25.03. If on Bail in Felony.

When the accused, in case of felony, is on bail at the time the indictment is presented, it is not necessary to serve him with a copy, but the clerk shall on request deliver a copy of the same to the accused or his counsel, at the earliest possible time.

(Enacted by Acts 1965, 59th Leg., ch. 722 (S.B. 107), § 1, effective January 1, 1966.)

## Art. 25.04. In Misdemeanor.

In misdemeanors, it shall not be necessary before trial to furnish the accused with a copy of the indictment or information; but he or his counsel may demand a copy, which shall be given as early as possible.

(Enacted by Acts 1965, 59th Leg., ch. 722 (S.B. 107), § 1, effective January 1, 1966.)

# CHAPTER 26
# ARRAIGNMENT

## Art. 26.01. Arraignment.

In all felony cases, after indictment, and all misdemeanor cases punishable by imprisonment, there shall be an arraignment.

(Enacted by Acts 1965, 59th Leg., ch. 722 (S.B. 107), § 1, effective January 1, 1966.)

## Art. 26.011. Waiver of Arraignment.

An attorney representing a defendant may present a waiver of arraignment, and the clerk of the court may not require the presence of the defendant as a condition of accepting the waiver.

(Enacted by Acts 2001, 77th Leg., ch. 818 (H.B. 840), § 1, effective June 14, 2001.)

## Art. 26.02. Purpose of Arraignment.

An arraignment takes place for the purpose of fixing his identity and hearing his plea.

(Enacted by Acts 1965, 59th Leg., ch. 722 (S.B. 107), § 1, effective January 1, 1966.)

## Art. 26.03. Time of Arraignment.

No arraignment shall take place until the expiration of at least two entire days after the day on which a copy of the indictment was served on the defendant, unless the right to such copy or to such delay be waived, or unless the defendant is on bail.

(Enacted by Acts 1965, 59th Leg., ch. 722 (S.B. 107), § 1, effective January 1, 1966.)

## Art. 26.04. Procedures for Appointing Counsel.

(a) The judges of the county courts, statutory county courts, and district courts trying criminal cases in each county, by local rule, shall adopt and publish written countywide procedures for timely and fairly appointing counsel for an indigent defendant in the county arrested for, charged with, or taking an appeal from a conviction of a misdemeanor punishable by confinement or a felony. The procedures must be consistent with this article and Articles 1.051, 15.17, 26.05, and 26.052. A court shall appoint an attorney from a public appointment list using a system of rotation, unless the court appoints an attorney under Subsection (f), (f-1), (h), or (i). The court shall appoint attorneys from among the next five names on the appointment list in the order in which the attorneys' names appear on the list, unless the court makes a finding of good cause on the record for appointing an attorney out of order. An attorney who is not appointed in the order in which the attorney's name appears on the list shall remain next in order on the list.

(b) Procedures adopted under Subsection (a) shall:

(1) authorize only the judges of the county courts, statutory county courts, and district courts trying criminal cases in the county, or the judges' designee, to appoint counsel for indigent defendants in the county;

(2) apply to each appointment of counsel made by a judge or the judges' designee in the county;

(3) ensure that each indigent defendant in the county who is charged with a misdemeanor punishable by confinement or with a felony and who appears in court without counsel has an opportunity to confer with appointed counsel before the commencement of judicial proceedings;

(4) require appointments for defendants in capital cases in which the death penalty is sought to comply with any applicable requirements under Articles 11.071 and 26.052;

(5) ensure that each attorney appointed from a public appointment list to represent an indigent defendant perform the attorney's duty owed to the defendant in accordance with the adopted procedures, the requirements of this code, and applicable rules of ethics; and

(6) ensure that appointments are allocated among qualified attorneys in a manner that is fair, neutral, and nondiscriminatory.

(c) Whenever a court or the courts' designee authorized under Subsection (b) to appoint counsel for indigent defendants in the county determines for purposes of a criminal proceeding that a defendant charged with or appealing a conviction of a felony or a misdemeanor punishable by confinement is indigent or that the interests of justice require representation of a defendant in the proceeding, the court or the courts' designee shall appoint one or more practicing attorneys to represent the defendant in accordance with this subsection and the procedures adopted under Subsection (a). If the court or the courts' designee determines that the defendant does not speak and understand the English language or that the defendant is deaf, the court or the courts' designee shall make an effort to appoint an attorney who is capable of communicating in a language understood by the defendant.

(d) A public appointment list from which an attorney is appointed as required by Subsection (a) shall contain the names of qualified attorneys, each of whom:

(1) applies to be included on the list;

(2) meets the objective qualifications specified by the judges under Subsection (e);

(3) meets any applicable qualifications specified by the Texas Indigent Defense Commission; and

(4) is approved by a majority of the judges who established the appointment list under Subsection (e).

(e) In a county in which a court is required under Subsection (a) to appoint an attorney from a public appointment list:

(1) the judges of the county courts and statutory county courts trying misdemeanor cases in the county, by formal action:

(A) shall:

(i) establish a public appointment list of attorneys qualified to provide representation in the county in misdemeanor cases punishable by confinement; and

(ii) specify the objective qualifications necessary for an attorney to be included on the list; and

(B) may establish, if determined by the judges to be appropriate, more than one appointment list graduated according to the degree of seriousness of the offense, the attorneys' qualifications, and whether representation will be provided in trial court proceedings, appellate proceedings, or both; and

(2) the judges of the district courts trying felony cases in the county, by formal action:

(A) shall:

(i) establish a public appointment list of attorneys qualified to provide representation in felony cases in the county; and

(ii) specify the objective qualifications necessary for an attorney to be included on the list; and

(B) may establish, if determined by the judges to be appropriate, more than one appointment list graduated according to the degree of seriousness of the offense, the attorneys' qualifications, and whether representation will be provided in trial court proceedings, appellate proceedings, or both.

(f) In a county in which a public defender's office is created or designated under Article 26.044, the court or the courts' designee may appoint that office to represent the defendant in accordance with guidelines established for the office.

(f-1) In a county in which a managed assigned counsel program is operated in accordance with Article 26.047, the managed assigned counsel program may appoint counsel to represent the defendant in accordance with the guidelines established for the program.

(g) A countywide alternative program for appointing counsel for indigent defendants in criminal cases is established by a formal action in which two-thirds of the judges of the courts designated under this subsection vote to establish the alternative program. An alternative program for appointing counsel in misdemeanor and felony cases may be established in the manner provided by this subsection by the judges of the county courts, statutory county courts, and district courts trying criminal cases in the county. An alternative program for appointing counsel in misdemeanor cases may be established in the manner provided by this subsection by the judges of the county courts and statutory county courts trying criminal cases in the county. An alternative program for appointing counsel in felony cases may be established in the manner provided by this subsection by the judges of the district courts trying criminal cases in the county. In a county in which an alternative program is established:

(1) the alternative program may:

(A) use a single method for appointing counsel or a combination of methods; and

(B) use a multicounty appointment list using a system of rotation; and

(2) the procedures adopted under Subsection (a) must ensure that:

(A) attorneys appointed using the alternative program to represent defendants in misdemeanor cases punishable by confinement:

(i) meet specified objective qualifications for that representation, which may be graduated according to the degree of seriousness of the offense and whether representation will be provided in trial court proceedings, appellate proceedings, or both; and

(ii) are approved by a majority of the judges of the county courts and statutory county courts trying misdemeanor cases in the county;

(B) attorneys appointed using the alternative program to represent defendants in felony cases:

(i) meet specified objective qualifications for that representation, which may be graduated according to the degree of seriousness of the offense and whether representation will be provided in trial court proceedings, appellate proceedings, or both; and

(ii) are approved by a majority of the judges of the district courts trying felony cases in the county;

(C) appointments for defendants in capital cases in which the death penalty is sought comply with the requirements of Article 26.052; and

(D) appointments are reasonably and impartially allocated among qualified attorneys.

(h) In a county in which an alternative program for appointing counsel is established as provided by Subsection (g) and is approved by the presiding judge of the administrative judicial region, a court or the courts' designee may appoint an attorney to represent an indigent defendant by using the alternative program. In establishing an alternative program under Subsection (g), the judges of the courts establishing the program may not, without the approval of the commissioners court, obligate the county by contract or by the creation of new positions that cause an increase in expenditure of county funds.

(i) A court or the courts' designee required under Subsection (c) to appoint an attorney to represent a defendant accused or convicted of a felony may appoint an attorney from any county located in the court's administrative judicial region.

(j) An attorney appointed under this article shall:

(1) make every reasonable effort to contact the defendant not later than the end of the first working day after the date on which the attorney is appointed and to interview the defendant as soon as practicable after the attorney is appointed;

(2) represent the defendant until charges are dismissed, the defendant is acquitted, appeals are exhausted, or the attorney is permitted or ordered by the court to withdraw as counsel for the defendant after a finding of good cause is entered on the record; and

(3) with respect to a defendant not represented by other counsel, before withdrawing as counsel for the defendant after a trial or the entry of a plea of guilty:

(A) advise the defendant of the defendant's right to file a motion for new trial and a notice of appeal;

(B) if the defendant wishes to pursue either or both remedies described by Paragraph (A), assist the defendant in requesting the prompt appointment of replacement counsel; and

(C) if replacement counsel is not appointed promptly and the defendant wishes to pursue an appeal, file a timely notice of appeal.

(k) A court may replace an attorney who violates Subsection (j)(1) with other counsel. A majority of the judges of the county courts and statutory county courts or the district courts, as appropriate, trying criminal cases in the county may remove from consideration for appointment an attorney who intentionally or repeatedly violates Subsection (j)(1).

(*l*) Procedures adopted under Subsection (a) must include procedures and financial standards for determining whether a defendant is indigent. The procedures and standards shall apply to each defendant in the county equally, regardless of whether the defendant is in custody or has been released on bail.

(m) In determining whether a defendant is indigent, the court or the courts' designee may consider the defendant's income, source of income, assets, property owned, outstanding obligations, necessary expenses, the number and ages of dependents, and spousal income that is available to the defendant. The court or the courts' designee may not consider whether the defendant has posted or is capable of posting bail, except to the extent that it reflects the defendant's financial circumstances as measured by the considerations listed in this subsection.

(n) A defendant who requests a determination of indigency and appointment of counsel shall:

(1) complete under oath a questionnaire concerning his financial resources;

(2) respond under oath to an examination regarding his financial resources by the judge or magistrate responsible for determining whether the defendant is indigent; or

(3) complete the questionnaire and respond to examination by the judge or magistrate.

(o) Before making a determination of whether a defendant is indigent, the court shall request the defendant to sign under oath a statement substantially in the following form: "On this ____ day of _____, 20 ____, I have been advised by the (name of the court) Court of my right to representation by counsel in connection with the charge pending against me. I am without means to employ counsel of my own choosing and I hereby request the court to appoint counsel for me. (signature of the defendant)"

(p) A defendant who is determined by the court to be indigent is presumed to remain indigent for the remainder of the proceedings in the case unless a material change in the defendant's financial circumstances occurs. If there is a material change in financial circumstances after a determination of indigency or nonindigency is made, the defendant, the defendant's counsel, or the attorney representing the state may move for reconsideration of the determination.

(q) A written or oral statement elicited under this article or evidence derived from the statement may not be used for any purpose, except to determine the defendant's indigency or to impeach the direct testimony of the defendant. This subsection does not prohibit prosecution of the defendant under Chapter 37, Penal Code.

(r) A court may not threaten to arrest or incarcerate a person solely because the person requests the assistance of counsel.

(Enacted by Acts 1965, 59th Leg., ch. 722 (S.B. 107), § 1, effective January 1, 1966; am. Acts 1987, 70th Leg., ch. 979 (S.B. 1108), § 2, effective September 1, 1987; am. Acts 2001, 77th Leg., ch. 906 (S.B. 7), § 6, effective January 1, 2002; am. Acts 2011, 82nd Leg., ch. 671 (S.B. 1681), § 1, effective September 1, 2011; am. Acts 2011, 82nd Leg., ch. 984 (H.B. 1754), § 7, effective September 1, 2011.)

### Art. 26.041. Assistance for Court-Appointed Counsel in Harris County [Repealed].

Repealed by Acts 2001, 77th Leg., ch. 906 (S.B. 7), § 15, effective January 1, 2002.

### Art. 26.042. Tarrant County Public Defender [Repealed].

Repealed by Acts 2001, 77th Leg., ch. 906 (S.B. 7), § 15, effective January 1, 2002.

### Art. 26.043. Public Defender in Wichita County [Repealed].

Repealed by Acts 2001, 77th Leg., ch. 906 (S.B. 7), § 15, effective January 1, 2002.

### Art. 26.044. Public Defender's Office.

(a) In this chapter:

(1) "Governmental entity" includes a county, a group of counties, a department of a county,

an administrative judicial region created by Section 74.042, Government Code, and any entity created under the Interlocal Cooperation Act as permitted by Chapter 791, Government Code.

(2) "Office of capital writs" means the office of capital writs established under Subchapter B, Chapter 78, Government Code.

(3) "Oversight board" means an oversight board established in accordance with Article 26.045.

(4) "Public defender's office" means an entity that:

(A) is either:

(i) a governmental entity; or

(ii) a nonprofit corporation operating under a written agreement with a governmental entity, other than an individual judge or court; and

(B) uses public funds to provide legal representation and services to indigent defendants accused of a crime or juvenile offense, as those terms are defined by Section 79.001, Government Code.

(b) The commissioners court of any county, on written approval of a judge of a county court, statutory county court, or district court trying criminal cases or cases under Title 3, Family Code, in the county, may create a department of the county or by contract may designate a nonprofit corporation to serve as a public defender's office. The commissioners courts of two or more counties may enter into a written agreement to jointly create or designate and jointly fund a regional public defender's office. In creating or designating a public defender's office under this subsection, the commissioners court shall specify or the commissioners courts shall jointly specify, if creating or designating a regional public defender's office:

(1) the duties of the public defender's office;

(2) the types of cases to which the public defender's office may be appointed under Article 26.04(f) and the courts in which an attorney employed by the public defender's office may be required to appear;

(3) if the public defender's office is a nonprofit corporation, the term during which the contract designating the public defender's office is effective and how that contract may be renewed on expiration of the term; and

(4) if an oversight board is established under Article 26.045 for the public defender's office, the powers and duties that have been delegated to the oversight board.

(b-1) The applicable commissioners court or commissioners courts shall require a written plan from a governmental entity serving as a public defender's office.

(c) Before contracting with a nonprofit corporation to serve as a public defender's office under Subsection (b), the commissioners court or commissioners courts shall solicit proposals for the public defender's office.

(c-1) A written plan under Subsection (b-1) or a proposal under Subsection (c) must include:

(1) a budget for the public defender's office, including salaries;

(2) a description of each personnel position, including the chief public defender position;

(3) the maximum allowable caseloads for each attorney employed by the public defender's office;

(4) provisions for personnel training;

(5) a description of anticipated overhead costs for the public defender's office;

(6) policies regarding the use of licensed investigators and expert witnesses by the public defender's office; and

(7) a policy to ensure that the chief public defender and other attorneys employed by the public defender's office do not provide representation to a defendant if doing so would create a conflict of interest that has not been waived by the client.

(d) After considering each proposal for the public defender's office submitted by a nonprofit corporation under Subsection (c), the commissioners court or commissioners courts shall select a proposal that reasonably demonstrates that the public defender's office will provide adequate quality representation for indigent defendants in the county or counties.

(e) The total cost of the proposal under Subsection (c) may not be the sole consideration in selecting a proposal.

(f) A public defender's office must be directed by a chief public defender who:

(1) is a member of the State Bar of Texas;

(2) has practiced law for at least three years; and

(3) has substantial experience in the practice of criminal law.

(g) A public defender's office is entitled to receive funds for personnel costs and expenses incurred in operating as a public defender's office in amounts fixed by the commissioners court and paid out of the appropriate county fund, or jointly fixed by the commissioners courts and proportionately paid out of each appropriate county fund if the public defender's office serves more than one county.

(h) A public defender's office may employ attorneys, licensed investigators, and other personnel necessary to perform the duties of the public defender's office as specified by the commissioners court or commissioners courts under Subsection (b)(1).

(i) Except as authorized by this article, the chief public defender and other attorneys employed by a public defender's office may not:

(1) engage in the private practice of criminal law; or

(2) accept anything of value not authorized by this article for services rendered under this article.

(j) A public defender's office may not accept an appointment under Article 26.04(f) if:

(1) a conflict of interest exists that has not been waived by the client;

(2) the public defender's office has insufficient resources to provide adequate representation for the defendant;

(3) the public defender's office is incapable of providing representation for the defendant in accordance with the rules of professional conduct; or

(4) the public defender's office shows other good cause for not accepting the appointment.

(k) The judge may remove from a case a person who violates a provision of Subsection (i).

(*l*) A public defender's office may investigate the financial condition of any person the public defender's office is appointed to represent. The public defender's office shall report the results of the investigation to the appointing judge. The judge may hold a hearing to determine if the person is indigent and entitled to representation under this article.

(m) If it is necessary that an attorney who is not employed by a public defender's office be appointed, the attorney is entitled to the compensation provided by Article 26.05 of this code.

(n) An attorney employed by a public defender's office may be appointed with respect to an application for a writ of habeas corpus only if:

(1) an attorney employed by the office of capital writs is not appointed in the case; and

(2) the attorney employed by the public defender's office is on the list of competent counsel maintained under Section 78.056, Government Code.

(Enacted by Acts 1985, 69th Leg., ch. 480 (S.B. 1228), § 17, effective September 1, 1985; am. Acts 1987, 70th Leg., ch. 167 (S.B. 892), § 4.03(a),

effective September 1, 1987; am. Acts 2001, 77th Leg., ch. 906 (S.B. 7), § 7, effective January 1, 2002; am. Acts 2005, 79th Leg., ch. 965 (H.B. 1701), § 6, effective September 1, 2005; am. Acts 2009, 81st Leg., ch. 781 (S.B. 1091), §§ 7, 8, effective September 1, 2009; am. Acts 2011, 82nd Leg., ch. 984 (H.B. 1754), §§ 8, 9, effective September 1, 2011.)

### Art. 26.045. Public Defender Oversight Board.

(a) The commissioners court of a county or the commissioners courts of two or more counties may establish an oversight board for a public defender's office created or designated in accordance with this chapter.

(b) The commissioners court or courts that establish an oversight board under this article shall appoint members of the board. Members may include one or more of the following:

(1) an attorney;

(2) the judge of a trial court in this state;

(3) a county commissioner;

(4) a county judge;

(5) a community representative; and

(6) a former client or a family member of a former client of the public defender's office for which the oversight board was established under this article.

(c) The commissioners court or courts may delegate to the board any power or duty of the commissioners court to provide oversight of the office under Article 26.044, including:

(1) recommending selection and removal of a chief public defender;

(2) setting policy for the office; and

(3) developing a budget proposal for the office.

(d) An oversight board established under this article may not gain access to privileged or confidential information.

(Enacted by Acts 2011, 82nd Leg., ch. 984 (H.B. 1754), § 10, effective September 1, 2011.)

### Art. 26.046. Public Defender in Webb County [Repealed].

Repealed by Acts 2001, 77th Leg., ch. 906 (S.B. 7), § 15, effective January 1, 2002.

### Art. 26.047. Managed Assigned Counsel Program.

(a) In this article:

(1) "Governmental entity" has the meaning assigned by Article 26.044.

(2) "Managed assigned counsel program" or "program" means a program operated with public funds:

(A) by a governmental entity, nonprofit corporation, or bar association under a written agreement with a governmental entity, other than an individual judge or court; and

(B) for the purpose of appointing counsel under Article 26.04 of this code or Section 51.10, Family Code.

(b) The commissioners court of any county, on written approval of a judge of the juvenile court of a county or a county court, statutory county court, or district court trying criminal cases in the county, may appoint a governmental entity, nonprofit corporation, or bar association to operate a managed assigned counsel program. The commissioners courts of two or more counties may enter into a written agreement to jointly appoint and fund a governmental entity, nonprofit corporation, or bar association to operate a managed assigned counsel program. In appointing an entity to operate a managed assigned counsel program under this subsection, the commissioners court shall specify or the commissioners courts shall jointly specify:

(1) the types of cases in which the program may appoint counsel under Article 26.04 of this code or Section 51.10, Family Code, and the courts in which the counsel appointed by the program may be required to appear; and

(2) the term of any agreement establishing a program and how the agreement may be terminated or renewed.

(c) The commissioners court or commissioners courts shall require a written plan of operation from an entity operating a program under this article. The plan of operation must include:

(1) a budget for the program, including salaries;

(2) a description of each personnel position, including the program's director;

(3) the maximum allowable caseload for each attorney appointed by the program;

(4) provisions for training personnel of the program and attorneys appointed under the program;

(5) a description of anticipated overhead costs for the program;

(6) a policy regarding licensed investigators and expert witnesses used by attorneys appointed under the program;

(7) a policy to ensure that appointments are reasonably and impartially allocated among qualified attorneys; and

(8) a policy to ensure that an attorney appointed under the program does not accept appointment in a case that involves a conflict of interest for the attorney that has not been waived by all affected clients.

(d) A program under this article must have a director. Unless the program uses a review committee appointed under Subsection (e), a program under this article must be directed by a person who:

(1) is a member of the State Bar of Texas;

(2) has practiced law for at least three years; and

(3) has substantial experience in the practice of criminal law.

(e) The governmental entity, nonprofit corporation, or bar association operating the program may appoint a review committee of three or more individuals to approve attorneys for inclusion on the program's public appointment list described by Subsection (f). Each member of the committee:

(1) must meet the requirements described by Subsection (d);

(2) may not be employed as a prosecutor; and

(3) may not be included on or apply for inclusion on the public appointment list described by Subsection (f).

(f) The program's public appointment list from which an attorney is appointed must contain the names of qualified attorneys, each of whom:

(1) applies to be included on the list;

(2) meets any applicable requirements specified by the procedure for appointing counsel adopted under Article 26.04(a) and the Texas Indigent Defense Commission; and

(3) is approved by the program director or review committee, as applicable.

(g) A court may replace an attorney appointed by the program for the same reasons and in the same manner described by Article 26.04(k).

(h) A managed assigned counsel program is entitled to receive funds for personnel costs and expenses incurred in amounts fixed by the commissioners court and paid out of the appropriate county fund, or jointly fixed by the commissioners courts and proportionately paid out of each appropriate county fund if the program serves more than one county.

(i) A managed assigned counsel program may employ personnel and enter into contracts necessary to perform the program's duties as specified by the commissioners court or commissioners courts under this article.

(Enacted by Acts 2011, 82nd Leg., ch. 984 (H.B. 1754), § 11, effective September 1, 2011.)

### Art. 26.048. Public Defender in Cherokee County [Repealed].

Repealed by Acts 2001, 77th Leg., ch. 906 (S.B. 7), § 15, effective January 1, 2002.

### Art. 26.049. Public Defender in Tom Green County [Repealed].

Repealed by Acts 2001, 77th Leg., ch. 906 (S.B. 7), § 15, effective January 1, 2002.

### Art. 26.050. Public Defender in 293rd and 365th Judicial Districts [Repealed].

Repealed by Acts 2001, 77th Leg., ch. 906 (S.B. 7), § 15, effective January 1, 2002.

### Art. 26.05. Compensation of Counsel Appointed to Defend.

(a) A counsel, other than an attorney with a public defender's office or an attorney employed by the office of capital writs, appointed to represent a defendant in a criminal proceeding, including a habeas corpus hearing, shall be paid a reasonable attorney's fee for performing the following services, based on the time and labor required, the complexity of the case, and the experience and ability of the appointed counsel:

(1) time spent in court making an appearance on behalf of the defendant as evidenced by a docket entry, time spent in trial, and time spent in a proceeding in which sworn oral testimony is elicited;

(2) reasonable and necessary time spent out of court on the case, supported by any documentation that the court requires;

(3) preparation of an appellate brief and preparation and presentation of oral argument to a court of appeals or the Court of Criminal Appeals; and

(4) preparation of a motion for rehearing.

(b) All payments made under this article shall be paid in accordance with a schedule of fees adopted by formal action of the judges of the county courts, statutory county courts, and district courts trying criminal cases in each county. On adoption of a schedule of fees as provided by this subsection, a copy of the schedule shall be sent to the commissioners court of the county.

(c) Each fee schedule adopted shall state reasonable fixed rates or minimum and maximum hourly rates, taking into consideration reasonable and necessary overhead costs and the availability of qualified attorneys willing to accept the stated rates, and shall provide a form for the appointed counsel to itemize the types of services performed. No payment shall be made under this article until the form for itemizing the services performed is submitted to the judge presiding over the proceedings or, if the county operates a managed assigned counsel program under Article 26.047, to the director of the program, and until the judge or director, as applicable, approves the payment. If the judge or director disapproves the requested amount of payment, the judge or director shall make written findings stating the amount of payment that the judge or director approves and each reason for approving an amount different from the requested amount. An attorney whose request for payment is disapproved or is not otherwise acted on by the 60th day after the date the request for payment is submitted may appeal the disapproval or failure to act by filing a motion with the presiding judge of the administrative judicial region. On the filing of a motion, the presiding judge of the administrative judicial region shall review the disapproval of payment or failure to act and determine the appropriate amount of payment. In reviewing the disapproval or failure to act, the presiding judge of the administrative judicial region may conduct a hearing. Not later than the 45th day after the date an application for payment of a fee is submitted under this article, the commissioners court shall pay to the appointed counsel the amount that is approved by the presiding judge of the administrative judicial region and that is in accordance with the fee schedule for that county.

(d) A counsel in a noncapital case, other than an attorney with a public defender's office, appointed to represent a defendant under this code shall be reimbursed for reasonable and necessary expenses, including expenses for investigation and for mental health and other experts. Expenses incurred with prior court approval shall be reimbursed in the same manner provided for capital cases by Articles 26.052(f) and (g), and expenses incurred without prior court approval shall be reimbursed in the manner provided for capital cases by Article 26.052(h).

(e) A majority of the judges of the county courts and statutory county courts or the district courts, as appropriate, trying criminal cases in the county may remove an attorney from consideration for appointment if, after a hearing, it is shown that the attorney submitted a claim for legal services not performed by the attorney.

(f) All payments made under this article shall be paid from the general fund of the county in which the prosecution was instituted or habeas corpus hearing held and may be included as costs of court.

(g) If the court determines that a defendant has financial resources that enable him to offset in part or in whole the costs of the legal services provided, including any expenses and costs, the court shall order the defendant to pay during the pendency of the charges or, if convicted, as court costs the amount that it finds the defendant is able to pay.

(h) Reimbursement of expenses incurred for purposes of investigation or expert testimony may be paid directly to a private investigator licensed under Chapter 1702, Occupations Code, or to an expert witness in the manner designated by appointed counsel and approved by the court.

(i) [Repealed by Acts 2011, 82nd Leg., ch. 984 (H.B. 1754), § 15(1), effective September 1, 2011.]

(Am. Acts 1965, 59th Leg., ch. 722 (S.B. 107), § 1, effective January 1, 1966; am. Acts 1969, 61st Leg., ch. 347 (H.B. 541), § 1, effective May 27, 1969; am. Acts 1971, 62nd Leg., ch. 520 (H.B. 1792), § 1, effective August 30, 1971; am. Acts 1973, 63rd Leg., ch. 426 (H.B. 200), art. 3, § 3, effective June 14, 1973; am. Acts 1981, 67th Leg., ch. 291 (S.B. 265), § 106, effective September 1, 1981; am. Acts 1987, 70th Leg., ch. 979 (S.B. 1108), § 3, effective September 1, 1987; am. Acts 1999, 76th Leg., ch. 837 (H.B. 1752), § 1, effective September 1, 1999; am. Acts 2001, 77th Leg., ch. 906 (S.B. 7), § 8, effective January 1, 2002; am. Acts 2001, 77th Leg., ch. 1420 (H.B. 2812), § 14.734, effective September 1, 2001; am. Acts 2007, 80th Leg., ch. 1014 (H.B. 1267), § 1, effective September 1, 2007; am. Acts 2009, 81st Leg., ch. 781 (S.B. 1091), § 9, effective September 1, 2009; am. Acts 2011, 82nd Leg., ch. 984 (H.B. 1754), §§ 12, 15(1), effective September 1, 2011.)

## Art. 26.05-1. Contribution from State in Certain Counties [Renumbered].

Renumbered to Tex. Code Crim. Proc. art. 26.056 by Acts 1987, 70th Leg., ch. 167 (S.B. 892), § 5.02(2), effective September 1, 1987.

## Art. 26.051. Indigent Inmate Defense.

(a) In this article:

(1) "Board" means the Texas Board of Criminal Justice.

(2) "Correctional institutions division" means the correctional institutions division of the Texas Department of Criminal Justice.

(b), (c) [Repealed by Acts 2007, 80th Leg., ch. 1014 (H.B. 1267), § 7, effective September 1, 2007.]

(d) A court shall:

(1) notify the board if it determines that a defendant before the court is indigent and is an inmate charged with an offense committed while in the custody of the correctional institutions division or a correctional facility authorized by Section 495.001, Government Code; and

(2) request that the board provide legal representation for the inmate.

(e) The board shall provide legal representation for inmates described by Subsection (d) of this section. The board may employ attorneys, support staff, and any other personnel required to provide legal representation for those inmates. All personnel employed under this article are directly responsible to the board in the performance of their duties. The board shall pay all fees and costs associated with providing legal representation for those inmates.

(f) [Repealed by Acts 1993, 73rd Leg., ch. 988 (S.B. 532), § 7.02, effective September 1, 1993.]

(g) The court shall appoint an attorney other than an attorney provided by the board if the court determines for any of the following reasons that a conflict of interest could arise from the use of an attorney provided by the board under Subsection (e) of this article:

(1) the case involves more than one inmate and the representation of more than one inmate could impair the attorney's effectiveness;

(2) the case is appealed and the court is satisfied that conflict of interest would prevent the presentation of a good faith allegation of ineffective assistance of counsel by a trial attorney provided by the board; or

(3) any conflict of interest exists under the Texas Disciplinary Rules of Professional Conduct of the State Bar of Texas that precludes representation by an attorney appointed by the board.

(h) When the court appoints an attorney other than an attorney provided by the board:

(1) except as otherwise provided by this article, the inmate's legal defense is subject to Articles 1.051, 26.04, 26.05, and 26.052, as applicable; and

(2) the county in which a facility of the correctional institutions division or a correctional facility authorized by Section 495.001, Government Code, is located shall pay from its general fund the total costs of the aggregate

amount allowed and awarded by the court for attorney compensation and expenses under Article 26.05 or 26.052, as applicable.

(i) The state shall reimburse a county for attorney compensation and expenses awarded under Subsection (h). A court seeking reimbursement for a county shall certify to the comptroller of public accounts the amount of compensation and expenses for which the county is entitled to be reimbursed under this article. Not later than the 60th day after the date the comptroller receives from the court the request for reimbursement, the comptroller shall issue a warrant to the county in the amount certified by the court.

(Am. Acts 1990, 71st Leg., 6th C.S., ch. 15 (H.B. 80), § 2, effective June 14, 1990; am. Acts 1991, 72nd Leg., ch. 719 (H.B. 2426), § 1, effective September 1, 1991; am. Acts 1993, 73rd Leg., ch. 988 (S.B. 532), § 7.01, effective September 1, 1993; am. Acts 1993, 73rd Leg., ch. 988 (S.B. 532), § 7.02, effective September 1, 1993; am. Acts 2007, 80th Leg., ch. 1014 (H.B. 1267), §§ 2, 3, 7, effective September 1, 2007.)

### Art. 26.052. Appointment of Counsel in Death Penalty Case; Reimbursement of Investigative Expenses.

(a) Notwithstanding any other provision of this chapter, this article establishes procedures in death penalty cases for appointment and payment of counsel to represent indigent defendants at trial and on direct appeal and to apply for writ of certiorari in the United States Supreme Court.

(b) If a county is served by a public defender's office, trial counsel and counsel for direct appeal or to apply for a writ of certiorari may be appointed as provided by the guidelines established by the public defender's office. In all other cases in which the death penalty is sought, counsel shall be appointed as provided by this article.

(c) A local selection committee is created in each administrative judicial region created under Section 74.042, Government Code. The administrative judge of the judicial region shall appoint the members of the committee. A committee shall have not less than four members, including:

(1) the administrative judge of the judicial region;

(2) at least one district judge;

(3) a representative from the local bar association; and

(4) at least one practitioner who is board certified by the State Bar of Texas in criminal law.

(d) (1) The committee shall adopt standards for the qualification of attorneys to be appointed to represent indigent defendants in capital cases in which the death penalty is sought.

(2) The standards must require that a trial attorney appointed as lead counsel to a capital case:

(A) be a member of the State Bar of Texas;

(B) exhibit proficiency and commitment to providing quality representation to defendants in death penalty cases;

(C) have not been found by a federal or state court to have rendered ineffective assistance of counsel during the trial or appeal of any capital case, unless the local selection committee determines under Subsection (n) that the conduct underlying the finding no longer accurately reflects the attorney's ability to provide effective representation;

(D) have at least five years of criminal law experience;

(E) have tried to a verdict as lead defense counsel a significant number of felony cases, including homicide trials and other trials for offenses punishable as second or first degree felonies or capital felonies;

(F) have trial experience in:

(i) the use of and challenges to mental health or forensic expert witnesses; and

(ii) investigating and presenting mitigating evidence at the penalty phase of a death penalty trial; and

(G) have participated in continuing legal education courses or other training relating to criminal defense in death penalty cases.

(3) The standards must require that an attorney appointed as lead appellate counsel in the direct appeal of a capital case:

(A) be a member of the State Bar of Texas;

(B) exhibit proficiency and commitment to providing quality representation to defendants in death penalty cases;

(C) have not been found by a federal or state court to have rendered ineffective assistance of counsel during the trial or appeal of any capital case, unless the local selection committee determines under Subsection (n) that the conduct underlying the finding no longer accurately reflects the attorney's ability to provide effective representation;

(D) have at least five years of criminal law experience;

(E) have authored a significant number of appellate briefs, including appellate briefs

Criminal Procedure

for homicide cases and other cases involving an offense punishable as a capital felony or a felony of the first degree or an offense described by Section 3g(a)(1), Article 42.12;

    (F) have trial or appellate experience in:

      (i) the use of and challenges to mental health or forensic expert witnesses; and

      (ii) the use of mitigating evidence at the penalty phase of a death penalty trial; and

    (G) have participated in continuing legal education courses or other training relating to criminal defense in appealing death penalty cases.

(4) The committee shall prominently post the standards in each district clerk's office in the region with a list of attorneys qualified for appointment.

(5) Not later than the second anniversary of the date an attorney is placed on the list of attorneys qualified for appointment in death penalty cases and each year following the second anniversary, the attorney must present proof to the committee that the attorney has successfully completed the minimum continuing legal education requirements of the State Bar of Texas, including a course or other form of training relating to criminal defense in death penalty cases or in appealing death penalty cases, as applicable. The committee shall remove the attorney's name from the list of qualified attorneys if the attorney fails to provide the committee with proof of completion of the continuing legal education requirements.

(e) The presiding judge of the district court in which a capital felony case is filed shall appoint two attorneys, at least one of whom must be qualified under this chapter, to represent an indigent defendant as soon as practicable after charges are filed, unless the state gives notice in writing that the state will not seek the death penalty.

(f) Appointed counsel may file with the trial court a pretrial ex parte confidential request for advance payment of expenses to investigate potential defenses. The request for expenses must state:

    (1) the type of investigation to be conducted;

    (2) specific facts that suggest the investigation will result in admissible evidence; and

    (3) an itemized list of anticipated expenses for each investigation.

(g) The court shall grant the request for advance payment of expenses in whole or in part if the request is reasonable. If the court denies in whole or in part the request for expenses, the court shall:

    (1) state the reasons for the denial in writing;

    (2) attach the denial to the confidential request; and

    (3) submit the request and denial as a sealed exhibit to the record.

(h) Counsel may incur expenses without prior approval of the court. On presentation of a claim for reimbursement, the court shall order reimbursement of counsel for the expenses, if the expenses are reasonably necessary and reasonably incurred.

(i) If the indigent defendant is convicted of a capital felony and sentenced to death, the defendant is entitled to be represented by competent counsel on appeal and to apply for a writ of certiorari to the United States Supreme Court.

(j) As soon as practicable after a death sentence is imposed in a capital felony case, the presiding judge of the convicting court shall appoint counsel to represent an indigent defendant on appeal and to apply for a writ of certiorari, if appropriate.

(k) The court may not appoint an attorney as counsel on appeal if the attorney represented the defendant at trial, unless:

    (1) the defendant and the attorney request the appointment on the record; and

    (2) the court finds good cause to make the appointment.

(*l*) An attorney appointed under this article to represent a defendant at trial or on direct appeal is compensated as provided by Article 26.05 from county funds. Advance payment of expenses anticipated or reimbursement of expenses incurred for purposes of investigation or expert testimony may be paid directly to a private investigator licensed under Chapter 1702, Occupations Code, or to an expert witness in the manner designated by appointed counsel and approved by the court.

(m) The local selection committee shall annually review the list of attorneys posted under Subsection (d) to ensure that each listed attorney satisfies the requirements under this chapter.

(n) At the request of an attorney, the local selection committee shall make a determination under Subsection (d)(2)(C) or (3)(C) as applicable, regarding an attorney's current ability to provide effective representation following a judicial finding that the attorney previously rendered ineffective assistance of counsel in a capital case.

(Enacted by Acts 1995, 74th Leg., ch. 319 (S.B. 440), § 2, effective September 1, 1995; am. Acts

1999, 76th Leg., ch. 837 (H.B. 1752), § 2, effective September 1, 1999; am. Acts 2001, 77th Leg., ch. 906 (S.B. 7), § 9, effective January 1, 2002; am. Acts 2001, 77th Leg., ch. 1420 (H.B. 2812), § 14.735, effective September 1, 2001; am. Acts 2005, 79th Leg., ch. 787 (S.B. 60), § 14, effective September 1, 2005; am. Acts 2005, 79th Leg., ch. 965 (H.B. 1701), § 7, effective September 1, 2005; am. Acts 2009, 81st Leg., ch. 32 (H.B. 2058), § 1, effective September 1, 2009; am. Acts 2011, 82nd Leg., ch. 1343 (S.B. 1308), § 1, effective September 1, 2011.)

### STATUTORY NOTES

**Editor's notes.** — Acts 2009, 81st Leg., ch. 32 (H.B. 2058), § 2 provides: "A local selection committee shall amend its standards as necessary to conform with the requirements of Article 26.052(d), Code of Criminal Procedure, as amended by this Act, not later than the 75th day after the effective date of this Act. An attorney appointed to a death penalty case on or after the 75th day after the effective date of this Act must meet the standards adopted in conformity with amended Article 26.052(d), Code of Criminal Procedure. An attorney appointed to a death penalty case before the 75th day after the effective date of this Act is covered by the law in effect when the attorney was appointed, and the former law is continued in effect for that purpose."

## Art. 26.053. Public Defender in Randall County.

(a) The Commissioners Court of Randall County may appoint an attorney to serve as a public defender. The public defender serves at the pleasure of the commissioners court.

(b) To be eligible for appointment as a public defender, a person must be a member of the State Bar of Texas.

(c) With the approval of the commissioners court, the public defender may employ assistant public defenders, investigators, secretaries, and other necessary personnel. An assistant public defender must be a licensed attorney and may perform the duties of a public defender under this article.

(d) A public defender's office consists of the public defender and the personnel employed by the public defender under Subsection (c).

(e) A public defender is entitled to receive an annual salary in an amount set by the commissioners court. Subchapter B, Chapter 152, Local Government Code, applies to the compensation of personnel and the payment of office expenses in the public defender's office.

(f) Except as authorized by this article, a public defender or an assistant public defender may not:

(1) engage in the private practice of law; or

(2) accept anything of value not authorized by this article for services rendered under this article.

(g) The commissioners court may remove a public defender or an assistant public defender who violates Subsection (f).

(h) The public defender or an assistant public defender shall represent each indigent person who is:

(1) charged with a criminal offense in Randall County punishable by confinement or imprisonment;

(2) a minor who is a party to a juvenile delinquency proceeding in the county; or

(3) entitled to representation under:

(A) Chapter 462, Health and Safety Code; or

(B) Subtitle C or D, Title 7, Health and Safety Code.

(i) If at any stage of the proceeding the judge determines that a conflict of interest exists between the public defender and the indigent person, the judge may appoint another attorney to represent the person. The attorney must be licensed to practice law in this state and is entitled to the compensation provided by Article 26.05.

(j) The public defender's office shall investigate the financial condition of any person the public defender is appointed to represent. The public defender's office shall report the results of the investigation to the appointing judge. The judge may hold a hearing to determine if the person is indigent and entitled to representation under this article.

(k) Except for the provisions relating to daily appearance fees, Article 26.05 applies to the public defender and an assistant public defender.

(*l*) The commissioners court may accept gifts and grants from any source to finance an adequate and effective public defender program. (Enacted by Acts 2001, 77th Leg., ch. 184 (S.B. 1789), § 1, effective May 18, 2001.)

## Art. 26.054. Public Defender in Potter County [Repealed].

Repealed by Acts 2001, 77th Leg., ch. 906 (S.B. 7), § 15, effective January 1, 2002.

## Art. 26.055. Contribution from State for Defense of Indigent Inmates [Repealed].

Repealed by Acts 2007, 80th Leg., ch. 1014 (H.B. 1267), § 7, effective September 1, 2007.

(Enacted by Acts 1975, 64th Leg., p. 168, ch. 72 (H.B. 1749), § 1, effective September 1, 1975; am. Acts 1985, 69th Leg., ch. 529 (H.B. 393), § 2, effective September 1, 1985; am. Acts 1987, 70th Leg., ch. 1049 (S.B. 245), § 52, effective September 1, 1987; am. Acts 1990, 71st Leg., 6th C.S., ch. 15 (H.B. 80), § 1, effective June 14, 1990.)

## Art. 26.056. Contribution from State in Certain Counties.

Sec. 1. A county in which a state training school for delinquent children is located shall pay from its general fund the first $250 of fees awarded for court-appointed counsel under Article 26.05 toward defending a child committed to the school from another county who is being prosecuted for a felony or misdemeanor in the county where the training school is located.

Sec. 2. If the fees awarded for counsel compensation are in excess of $250, the court shall certify the amount in excess of $250 to the Comptroller of Public Accounts of the State of Texas. The Comptroller shall issue a warrant to the court-appointed counsel in the amount certified to the comptroller by the court.

(Am. Acts 1967, 60th Leg., ch. 307 (H.B. 974), § 1, effective August 28, 1967; am. Acts 1987, 70th Leg., ch. 167 (S.B. 892), § 5.02(2), effective September 1, 1987 (renumbered from art. 26.05-1).)

## Art. 26.057. Cost of Employment of Counsel for Certain Minors.

If a juvenile has been transferred to a criminal court under Section 54.02, Family Code, and if a court appoints counsel for the juvenile under Article 26.04 of this code, the county that pays for the counsel has a cause of action against a parent or other person who is responsible for the support of the juvenile and is financially able to employ counsel for the juvenile but refuses to do so. The county may recover its cost of payment to the appointed counsel and may recover attorney's fees necessary to prosecute the cause of action against the parent or other person.

(Am. Acts 1987, 70th Leg., ch. 979 (S.B. 1108), § 4, effective September 1, 1987; am. Acts 1989, 71st Leg., ch. 2 (S.B. 221), § 16.01(8), effective August 28, 1989 (renumbered from art. 26.056).)

## Art. 26.058. Public Defender in Aransas County [Repealed].

Repealed by Acts 2001, 77th Leg., ch. 906 (S.B. 7), § 15, effective January 1, 2002.

## Art. 26.06. Elected Officials Not to Be Appointed.

No court may appoint an elected county, district or state official to represent a person accused of crime, unless the official has notified the court of his availability for appointment. If an official has notified the court of his availability and is appointed as counsel, he may decline the appointment if he determines that it is in the best interest of his office to do so. Nothing in this Code shall modify any statutory provision for legislative continuance.

(Enacted by Acts 1965, 59th Leg., ch. 722 (S.B. 107), § 1, effective January 1, 1966.)

## Art. 26.07. Name As Stated in Indictment.

When the defendant is arraigned, his name, as stated in the indictment, shall be distinctly called; and unless he suggest by himself or counsel that he is not indicted by his true name, it shall be taken that his name is truly set forth, and he shall not thereafter be allowed to deny the same by way of defense.

(Enacted by Acts 1965, 59th Leg., ch. 722 (S.B. 107), § 1, effective January 1, 1966.)

## Art. 26.08. If Defendant Suggests Different Name.

If the defendant, or his counsel for him, suggests that he bears some name different from that stated in the indictment, the same shall be noted upon the minutes of the court, the indictment corrected by inserting therein the name of the defendant as suggested by himself or his counsel for him, the style of the case changed so as to give his true name, and the cause proceed as if the true name had been first recited in the indictment.

(Enacted by Acts 1965, 59th Leg., ch. 722 (S.B. 107), § 1, effective January 1, 1966.)

## Art. 26.09. If Accused Refuses to Give His Real Name.

If the defendant alleges that he is not indicted by his true name, and refuses to say what his real name is, the cause shall proceed as if the name stated in the indictment were true; and the defendant shall not be allowed to contradict the same by way of defense.

(Enacted by Acts 1965, 59th Leg., ch. 722 (S.B. 107), § 1, effective January 1, 1966.)

## Art. 26.10. Where Name Is Unknown.

A defendant described as a person whose name is unknown may have the indictment so corrected as to give therein his true name.

(Enacted by Acts 1965, 59th Leg., ch. 722 (S.B. 107), § 1, effective January 1, 1966.)

## Art. 26.11. Indictment Read.

The name of the accused having been called, if no suggestion, such as is spoken of in the four preceding Articles, be made, or being made is disposed of as before directed, the indictment shall be read, and the defendant asked whether he is guilty or not, as therein charged.

(Enacted by Acts 1965, 59th Leg., ch. 722 (S.B. 107), § 1, effective January 1, 1966.)

## Art. 26.12. Plea of Not Guilty Entered.

If the defendant answers that he is not guilty, such plea shall be entered upon the minutes of the court; if he refuses to answer, the plea of not guilty shall in like manner be entered.

(Enacted by Acts 1965, 59th Leg., ch. 722 (S.B. 107), § 1, effective January 1, 1966.)

## Art. 26.13. Plea of Guilty.

(a) Prior to accepting a plea of guilty or a plea of nolo contendere, the court shall admonish the defendant of:

(1) the range of the punishment attached to the offense;

(2) the fact that the recommendation of the prosecuting attorney as to punishment is not binding on the court. Provided that the court shall inquire as to the existence of any plea bargaining agreements between the state and the defendant and, in the event that such an agreement exists, the court shall inform the defendant whether it will follow or reject such agreement in open court and before any finding on the plea. Should the court reject any such agreement, the defendant shall be permitted to withdraw his plea of guilty or nolo contendere;

(3) the fact that if the punishment assessed does not exceed the punishment recommended by the prosecutor and agreed to by the defendant and his attorney, the trial court must give its permission to the defendant before he may prosecute an appeal on any matter in the case except for those matters raised by written motions filed prior to trial;

(4) the fact that if the defendant is not a citizen of the United States of America, a plea of guilty or nolo contendere for the offense charged may result in deportation, the exclusion from admission to this country, or the denial of naturalization under federal law; and

(5) the fact that the defendant will be required to meet the registration requirements of Chapter 62, if the defendant is convicted of or placed on deferred adjudication for an offense for which a person is subject to registration under that chapter.

(b) No plea of guilty or plea of nolo contendere shall be accepted by the court unless it appears that the defendant is mentally competent and the plea is free and voluntary.

(c) In admonishing the defendant as herein provided, substantial compliance by the court is sufficient, unless the defendant affirmatively shows that he was not aware of the consequences of his plea and that he was misled or harmed by the admonishment of the court.

(d) The court may make the admonitions required by this article either orally or in writing. If the court makes the admonitions in writing, it must receive a statement signed by the defendant and the defendant's attorney that he understands the admonitions and is aware of the consequences of his plea. If the defendant is unable or refuses to sign the statement, the court shall make the admonitions orally.

(e) Before accepting a plea of guilty or a plea of nolo contendere, the court shall inquire as to whether a victim impact statement has been returned to the attorney representing the state and ask for a copy of the statement if one has been returned.

(f) The court must substantially comply with Subsection (e) of this article. The failure of the court to comply with Subsection (e) of this article is not grounds for the defendant to set aside the conviction, sentence, or plea.

(g) Before accepting a plea of guilty or a plea of nolo contendere and on the request of a victim of the offense, the court may assist the victim and the defendant in participating in a victim-offender mediation program.

(h) The court must substantially comply with Subsection (a)(5). The failure of the court to comply with Subsection (a)(5) is not a ground for the defendant to set aside the conviction, sentence, or plea.

(i) Notwithstanding this article, a court shall not order the state or any of its prosecuting attorneys to participate in mediation, dispute resolution, arbitration, or other similar procedures in relation to a criminal prosecution unless upon written consent of the state.

(Am. Acts 1965, 59th Leg., ch. 722 (S.B. 107), § 1, effective January 1, 1966; am. Acts 1973, 63rd Leg., ch. 399 (S.B. 34), § 2(A), effective January 1, 1974; am. Acts 1975, 64th Leg., ch. 341 (S.B. 122), § 3, effective June 19, 1975; am. Acts 1977, 65th Leg., ch. 280 (S.B. 937), § 1, effective August 29, 1977; am. Acts 1979, 66th Leg., ch. 524 (S.B. 854), § 1, effective September 1, 1979; am. Acts 1979, 66th Leg., ch. 561 (H.B. 1566), § 1, effective September 1, 1979; am. Acts 1985, 69th Leg., ch. 671 (S.B. 1348), § 1, effective June 14, 1985; am. Acts 1985, 69th Leg., ch. 685 (H.B. 13), § 8(a), effective August 26, 1985; am. Acts 1987, 70th Leg., ch. 443 (H.B. 95), § 1, effective August 31, 1987; am. Acts 1991, 72nd Leg., ch. 202 (S.B. 1407), § 1, effective September 1, 1991; am. Acts 1997, 75th Leg., ch. 670 (H.B. 156), § 4, effective September 1, 1997; am. Acts 1999, 76th Leg., ch. 425 (S.B. 1125), § 1, effective August 30, 1999; am. Acts 1999, 76th Leg., ch. 1415 (H.B. 2145), § 1, effective September 1, 1999; am. Acts 2001, 77th Leg., ch. 1420 (H.B. 2812), § 21.001(8), effective September 1, 2001; am. Acts 2005, 79th Leg., ch. 1008 (H.B. 867), § 1.03, effective September 1, 2005; am. Acts 2007, 80th Leg., ch. 125 (S.B. 1470), § 1, effective September 1, 2007; am. Acts 2009, 81st Leg., ch. 1379 (S.B. 1236), § 2, effective September 1, 2009.)

## Art. 26.14. Jury on Plea of Guilty.

Where a defendant in a case of felony persists in pleading guilty or in entering a plea of nolo contendere, if the punishment is not absolutely fixed by law, a jury shall be impaneled to assess the punishment and evidence may be heard to enable them to decide thereupon, unless the defendant in accordance with Articles 1.13 or 37.07 shall have waived his right to trial by jury. (Enacted by Acts 1965, 59th Leg., ch. 722 (S.B. 107), § 1, effective January 1, 1966.)

## Art. 26.15. Correcting Name.

In any case, the same proceedings shall be had with respect to the name of the defendant and the correction of the indictment or information as provided with respect to the same in capital cases. (Enacted by Acts 1965, 59th Leg., ch. 722 (S.B. 107), § 1, effective January 1, 1966.)

# CHAPTER 27
# THE PLEADING IN CRIMINAL ACTIONS

## Art. 27.01. Indictment or Information.

The primary pleading in a criminal action on the part of the State is the indictment or information.
(Enacted by Acts 1965, 59th Leg., ch. 722 (S.B. 107), § 1, effective January 1, 1966.)

## Art. 27.02. Defendant's Pleadings.

The pleadings and motions of the defendant shall be:

(1) A motion to set aside or an exception to an indictment or information for some matter of form or substance;

(2) A special plea as provided in Article 27.05 of this code;

(3) A plea of guilty;

(4) A plea of not guilty;

(5) A plea of nolo contendere, the legal effect of which shall be the same as that of a plea of guilty, except that such plea may not be used against the defendant as an admission in any civil suit based upon or growing out of the act upon which the criminal prosecution is based;

(6) An application for probation, if any;

(7) An election, if any, to have the jury assess the punishment if he is found guilty; and

Criminal Procedure

(8) Any other motions or pleadings that are by law permitted to be filed.

(Am. Acts 1965, 59th Leg., ch. 722 (S.B. 107), § 1, effective January 1, 1966; am. Acts 1967, 60th Leg., ch. 659 (S.B. 145), § 17, effective August 28, 1967; am. Acts 1973, 63rd Leg., ch. 399 (S.B. 34), § 2, effective January 1, 1974.)

### Art. 27.03. Motion to Set Aside Indictment.

In addition to any other grounds authorized by law, a motion to set aside an indictment or information may be based on the following:

1. That it appears by the records of the court that the indictment was not found by at least nine grand jurors, or that the information was not based upon a valid complaint;

2. That some person not authorized by law was present when the grand jury was deliberating upon the accusation against the defendant, or was voting upon the same; and

3. That the grand jury was illegally impaneled; provided, however, in order to raise such question on motion to set aside the indictment, the defendant must show that he did not have an opportunity to challenge the array at the time the grand jury was impaneled.

(Enacted by Acts 1965, 59th Leg., ch. 722 (S.B. 107), § 1, effective January 1, 1966.)

### Art. 27.04. Motion Tried by Judge.

An issue of fact arising upon a motion to set aside an indictment or information shall be tried by the judge without a jury.

(Enacted by Acts 1965, 59th Leg., ch. 722 (S.B. 107), § 1, effective January 1, 1966.)

### Art. 27.05. Defendant's Special Plea.

A defendant's only special plea is that he has already been prosecuted for the same or a different offense arising out of the same criminal episode that was or should have been consolidated into one trial, and that the former prosecution:

(1) resulted in acquittal;

(2) resulted in conviction;

(3) was improperly terminated; or

(4) was terminated by a final order or judgment for the defendant that has not been reversed, set aside, or vacated and that necessarily required a determination inconsistent with a fact that must be established to secure conviction in the subsequent prosecution.

(Am. Acts 1965, 59th Leg., ch. 722 (S.B. 107), § 1, effective January 1, 1966; am. Acts 1973, 63rd Leg., ch. 399 (S.B. 34), § 2(A), effective January 1, 1974.)

### Art. 27.06. Special Plea Verified.

Every special plea shall be verified by the affidavit of the defendant.

(Enacted by Acts 1965, 59th Leg., ch. 722 (S.B. 107), § 1, effective January 1, 1966.)

### Art. 27.07. Special Plea Tried.

All issues of fact presented by a special plea shall be tried by the trier of the facts on the trial on the merits.

(Enacted by Acts 1965, 59th Leg., ch. 722 (S.B. 107), § 1, effective January 1, 1966.)

### Art. 27.08. Exception to Substance of Indictment.

There is no exception to the substance of an indictment or information except:

1. That it does not appear therefrom that an offense against the law was committed by the defendant;

2. That it appears from the face thereof that a prosecution for the offense is barred by a lapse of time, or that the offense was committed after the finding of the indictment;

3. That it contains matter which is a legal defense or bar to the prosecution; and

4. That it shows upon its face that the court trying the case has no jurisdiction thereof.

(Enacted by Acts 1965, 59th Leg., ch. 722 (S.B. 107), § 1, effective January 1, 1966.)

### Art. 27.09. Exception to Form of Indictment.

Exceptions to the form of an indictment or information may be taken for the following causes only:

1. That it does not appear to have been presented in the proper court as required by law;

2. The want of any requisite prescribed by Articles 21.02 and 21.21.

3. That it was not returned by a lawfully chosen or empaneled grand jury.

(Enacted by Acts 1965, 59th Leg., ch. 722 (S.B. 107), § 1, effective January 1, 1966.)

### Art. 27.10. Written Pleadings.

All motions to set aside an indictment or information and all special pleas and exceptions shall be in writing.

(Enacted by Acts 1965, 59th Leg., ch. 722 (S.B. 107), § 1, effective January 1, 1966.)

Criminal Procedure

## Art. 27.11. Ten Days Allowed for Filing Pleadings.

In all cases the defendant shall be allowed ten entire days, exclusive of all fractions of a day after his arrest, and during the term of the court, to file written pleadings.

(Enacted by Acts 1965, 59th Leg., ch. 722 (S.B. 107), § 1, effective January 1, 1966.)

## Art. 27.12. Time After Service.

In cases where the defendant is entitled to be served with a copy of the indictment, he shall be allowed the ten days time mentioned in the preceding Article to file written pleadings after such service.

(Enacted by Acts 1965, 59th Leg., ch. 722 (S.B. 107), § 1, effective January 1, 1966.)

## Art. 27.13. Plea of Guilty or Nolo Contendere in Felony.

A plea of "guilty" or a plea of "nolo contendere" in a felony case must be made in open court by the defendant in person; and the proceedings shall be as provided in Articles 26.13, 26.14 and 27.02. If the plea is before the judge alone, same may be made in the same manner as is provided for by Articles 1.13 and 1.15.

(Enacted by Acts 1965, 59th Leg., ch. 722 (S.B. 107), § 1, effective January 1, 1966.)

## Art. 27.14. Plea of Guilty or Nolo Contendere in Misdemeanor.

(a) A plea of "guilty" or a plea of "nolo contendere" in a misdemeanor case may be made either by the defendant or his counsel in open court; in such case, the defendant or his counsel may waive a jury, and the punishment may be assessed by the court either upon or without evidence, at the discretion of the court.

(b) A defendant charged with a misdemeanor for which the maximum possible punishment is by fine only may, in lieu of the method provided in Subsection (a) of this article, mail or deliver in person to the court a plea of "guilty" or a plea of "nolo contendere" and a waiver of jury trial. The defendant may also request in writing that the court notify the defendant, at the address stated in the request, of the amount of an appeal bond that the court will approve. If the court receives a plea and waiver before the time the defendant is scheduled to appear in court, the court shall dispose of the case without requiring a court appearance by the defendant. If the court receives a plea and waiver after the time the defendant is scheduled to appear in court but at least five business days before a scheduled trial date, the court shall dispose of the case without requiring a court appearance by the defendant. The court shall notify the defendant either in person or by certified mail, return receipt requested, of the amount of any fine assessed in the case and, if requested by the defendant, the amount of an appeal bond that the court will approve. The defendant shall pay any fine assessed or give an appeal bond in the amount stated in the notice before the 31st day after receiving the notice.

(c) In a misdemeanor case for which the maximum possible punishment is by fine only, payment of a fine or an amount accepted by the court constitutes a finding of guilty in open court as though a plea of nolo contendere had been entered by the defendant and constitutes a waiver of a jury trial in writing.

(d) If written notice of an offense for which maximum possible punishment is by fine only or of a violation relating to the manner, time, and place of parking has been prepared, delivered, and filed with the court and a legible duplicate copy has been given to the defendant, the written notice serves as a complaint to which the defendant may plead "guilty," "not guilty," or "nolo contendere." If the defendant pleads "not guilty" to the offense or fails to appear based on the written notice, a complaint shall be filed that conforms to the requirements of Chapter 45 of this code, and that complaint serves as an original complaint. A defendant may waive the filing of a sworn complaint and elect that the prosecution proceed on the written notice of the charged offense if the defendant agrees in writing with the prosecution, signs the agreement, and files it with the court.

(e) (1) Before accepting a plea of guilty or a plea of nolo contendere by a defendant charged with a misdemeanor involving family violence, as defined by Section 71.004, Family Code, the court shall admonish the defendant by using the following statement:

"If you are convicted of a misdemeanor offense involving violence where you are or were a spouse, intimate partner, parent, or guardian of the victim or are or were involved in another, similar relationship with the victim, it may be unlawful for you to possess or purchase a firearm, including a handgun or long gun, or ammunition, pursuant to federal law under 18 U.S.C. Section 922(g)(9) or Section 46.04(b), Texas Penal Code. If you have any questions whether these laws make it illegal for you to possess or purchase a firearm, you should consult an attorney."

(2) The court may provide the admonishment under Subdivision (1) orally or in writing, except that if the defendant is charged with a misdemeanor punishable by fine only, the statement printed on a citation issued under Article 14.06(b) may serve as the court admonishment required by this subsection.

(Am. Acts 1965, 59th Leg., ch. 722 (S.B. 107), § 1, effective January 1, 1966; am. Acts 1967, 60th Leg., ch. 659 (S.B. 145), § 18, effective August 28, 1967; am. Acts 1977, 65th Leg., ch. 858 (H.B. 2257), § 1, effective June 16, 1977; am. Acts 1979, 66th Leg., ch. 207 (S.B. 518), § 1, effective September 1, 1979; am. Acts 1983, 68th Leg., ch. 273 (S.B. 335), § 1, effective September 1, 1983; am. Acts 1985, 69th Leg., ch. 87 (S.B. 392), § 1, effective September 1, 1985; am. Acts 2009, 81st Leg., ch. 473 (S.B. 413), § 1, effective September 1, 2009; am. Acts 2009, 81st Leg., ch. 1121 (H.B. 1544), § 1, effective September 1, 2009; am. Acts 2009, 81st Leg., ch. 1379 (S.B. 1236), § 3, effective September 1, 2009.)

## Art. 27.15. Change of Venue to Plead Guilty.

When in any county which is located in a judicial district composed of more than one county, a party is charged with a felony and the maximum punishment therefor shall not exceed fifteen years, and the district court of said county is not in session, such party may, if he desires to plead guilty, or enter a plea of nolo contendere, make application to the district judge of such district for a change of venue to the county in which said court is in session, and said district judge may enter an order changing the venue of said cause to the county in which the court is then in session, and the defendant may plead guilty or enter a plea of nolo contendere to said charge in said court to which the venue has been changed. (Enacted by Acts 1965, 59th Leg., ch. 722 (S.B. 107), § 1, effective January 1, 1966.)

## Art. 27.16. Plea of Not Guilty, How Made.

(a) The plea of not guilty may be made orally by the defendant or by his counsel in open court. If the defendant refuses to plead, the plea of not guilty shall be entered for him by the court.

(b) A defendant charged with a misdemeanor for which the maximum possible punishment is by fine only may, in lieu of the method provided in Subsection (a) of this article, mail to the court a plea of not guilty.

(Am. Acts 1965, 59th Leg., ch. 722 (S.B. 107), § 1, effective January 1, 1966; am. Acts 1977, 65th Leg., ch. 858 (H.B. 2257), § 2, effective June 16, 1977.)

## Art. 27.17. Plea of Not Guilty Construed.

The plea of not guilty shall be construed to be a denial of every material allegation in the indictment or information. Under this plea, evidence to establish the insanity of defendant, and every fact whatever tending to acquit him of the accusation may be introduced, except such facts as are proper for a special plea under Article 27.05. (Enacted by Acts 1965, 59th Leg., ch. 722 (S.B. 107), § 1, effective January 1, 1966.)

## Art. 27.18. Plea or Waiver of Rights by Closed Circuit Video Teleconferencing.

(a) Notwithstanding any provision of this code requiring that a plea or a waiver of a defendant's right be made in open court, a court may accept the plea or waiver by broadcast by closed circuit video teleconferencing to the court if:

(1) the defendant and the attorney representing the state file with the court written consent to the use of closed circuit video teleconferencing;

(2) the closed circuit video teleconferencing system provides for a simultaneous, compressed full motion video, and interactive communication of image and sound between the judge, the attorney representing the state, the defendant, and the defendant's attorney; and

(3) on request of the defendant, the defendant and the defendant's attorney are able to communicate privately without being recorded or heard by the judge or the attorney representing the state.

(b) On motion of the defendant or the attorney representing the state or in the court's discretion, the court may terminate an appearance by closed circuit video teleconferencing at any time during the appearance and require an appearance by the defendant in open court.

(c) [2 Versions: As amended by Acts 2011, 82nd Leg., ch. 1031] A record of the communication shall be made by a court reporter and preserved by the court reporter until all appellate proceedings have been disposed of. The defendant may obtain a copy of the record on payment of a reasonable amount to cover the costs of reproduction or, if the defendant is indigent, the court shall provide a copy to the defendant without charging a cost for the copy.

(c) **[2 Versions: As amended by Acts 2011, 82nd Leg., ch. 1341]** A recording of the communication shall be made and preserved until all appellate proceedings have been disposed of. A court reporter or court recorder is not required to transcribe or make a separate recording of a plea taken under this article unless an appeal is taken in the case and a party requests a transcript.

(c-1) **[2 Versions: As added by Acts 2011, 82nd Leg., ch. 1031]** The loss or destruction of or failure to make a record of a plea entered under this article is not alone sufficient grounds for a defendant to withdraw the defendant's plea or to request the court to set aside a conviction or sentence based on the plea.

(c-1) **[2 Versions: As added by Acts 2011, 82nd Leg., ch. 1341]** The defendant may obtain a copy of a recording made under Subsection (c) on payment of a reasonable amount to cover the costs of reproduction or, if the defendant is indigent, the court shall provide a copy to the defendant without charging a cost for the copy.

(c-2) The loss or destruction of or failure to make a video recording of a plea entered under this article is not alone sufficient grounds for a defendant to withdraw the defendant's plea or to request the court to set aside a conviction, sentence, or plea.

(d) A defendant who is confined in a county other than the county in which charges against the defendant are pending may use the teleconferencing method provided by this article or the electronic broadcast system authorized in Article 15.17 to enter a plea or waive a right in the court with jurisdiction over the case.

(e) A defendant who enters a plea or waiver under Subsection (d):

(1) consents to venue in the county in which the court receiving the plea or waiver is located; and

(2) waives any claim of error related to venue.

(f) Subsection (e) does not prohibit a court from granting a defendant's motion for a change of venue during the trial of the defendant.

(g) If a defendant enters a plea of guilty or nolo contendere under Subsection (d), the attorney representing the state may request at the time the plea is entered that the defendant submit a fingerprint of the defendant suitable for attachment to the judgment. On request for a finger-

print under this subsection, the county in which the defendant is confined shall obtain a fingerprint of the defendant and use first-class mail or other means acceptable to the attorney representing the state and the county to forward the fingerprint to the court accepting the plea.
(Enacted by Acts 1997, 75th Leg., ch. 1014 (S.B. 121), § 1, effective September 1, 1997; am. Acts 2005, 79th Leg., ch. 1094 (H.B. 2120), § 6, effective September 1, 2005; am. Acts 2011, 82nd Leg., ch. 1031 (H.B. 2847), § 5, effective September 1, 2011; am. Acts 2011, 82nd Leg., ch. 1341 (S.B. 1233), § 6, effective June 17, 2011.)

## Art. 27.19. Plea by Certain Defendants.

(a) Notwithstanding any other provision of this code, a court shall accept a plea of guilty or nolo contendere from a defendant who is confined in a penal institution if the plea is made:

(1) in accordance with the procedure established by Article 27.18; or

(2) in writing, including a writing delivered by United States mail or secure electronic or facsimile transmission, before the appropriate court having jurisdiction in the county in which the penal institution is located, provided that:

(A) the defendant is notified by the court of original jurisdiction of the right to counsel and the procedures for requesting appointment of counsel, and is provided a reasonable opportunity to request a court-appointed lawyer;

(B) if the defendant elects to proceed without counsel, the defendant must waive the right to counsel in accordance with Article 1.051;

(C) the defendant must waive the right to be present at the taking of the plea or to have counsel present, if the defendant has counsel; and

(D) if the defendant is charged with a felony, judgment and sentence are rendered in accordance with the conditions and the procedure established by Article 42.14(b).

(b) In this article, "penal institution" has the meaning assigned by Section 1.07, Penal Code.

(c) Before accepting a plea submitted under Subsection (a)(2), the court shall verify that the person submitting the plea is:

(1) the defendant named in the information or indictment; or

(2) a person with legal authority to act for the defendant named in the information or indictment.

(Enacted by Acts 2009, 81st Leg., ch. 291 (H.B. 107), § 1, effective September 1, 2009; am. Acts 2011, 82nd Leg., ch. 665 (S.B. 1522), § 1, effective September 1, 2011.)

## CHAPTER 28
## MOTIONS, PLEADINGS AND EXCEPTIONS

## Art. 28.01. Pre-trial.

Sec. 1. The court may set any criminal case for a pre-trial hearing before it is set for trial upon its merits, and direct the defendant and his attorney, if any of record, and the State's attorney, to appear before the court at the time and place stated in the court's order for a conference and hearing. The defendant must be present at the arraignment, and his presence is required during any pre-trial proceeding. The pre-trial hearing shall be to determine any of the following matters:

(1) Arraignment of the defendant, if such be necessary; and appointment of counsel to represent the defendant, if such be necessary;

(2) Pleadings of the defendant;

(3) Special pleas, if any;

(4) Exceptions to the form or substance of the indictment or information;

(5) Motions for continuance either by the State or defendant; provided that grounds for continuance not existing or not known at the time may be presented and considered at any time before the defendant announces ready for trial;

(6) Motions to suppress evidence—When a hearing on the motion to suppress evidence is granted, the court may determine the merits of said motion on the motions themselves, or upon opposing affidavits, or upon oral testimony, subject to the discretion of the court;

(7) Motions for change of venue by the State or the defendant; provided, however, that such motions for change of venue, if overruled at the pre-trial hearing, may be renewed by the State or the defendant during the voir dire examination of the jury;

(8) Discovery;

(9) Entrapment; and

(10) Motion for appointment of interpreter.

Sec. 2. When a criminal case is set for such pre-trial hearing, any such preliminary matters not raised or filed seven days before the hearing will not thereafter be allowed to be raised or filed, except by permission of the court for good cause shown; provided that the defendant shall have sufficient notice of such hearing to allow him not less than 10 days in which to raise or file such preliminary matters. The record made at such pre-trial hearing, the rulings of the court and the exceptions and objections thereto shall become a part of the trial record of the case upon its merits.

Sec. 3. The notice mentioned in Section 2 above shall be sufficient if given in any one of the following ways:

(1) By announcement made by the court in open court in the presence of the defendant or his attorney of record;

(2) By personal service upon the defendant or his attorney of record;

(3) By mail to either the defendant or his attorney of record deposited by the clerk in the mail at least six days prior to the date set for hearing. If the defendant has no attorney of record such notice shall be addressed to defendant at the address shown on his bond, if the bond shows such an address, and if not, it may be addressed to one of the sureties on his bond. If the envelope containing the notice is properly addressed, stamped and mailed, the state will not be required to show that it was received.

(Am. Acts 1965, 59th Leg., ch. 722 (S.B. 107), § 1, effective January 1, 1966; am. Acts 1967, 60th Leg., ch. 659 (S.B. 145), § 19, effective August 28, 1967; am. Acts 1973, 63rd Leg., ch. 399 (S.B. 34), § 2(A), effective January 1, 1974; am. Acts 1979, 66th Leg., ch. 113 (S.B. 449), § 1, effective August 27, 1979; am. Acts 1979, 66th Leg., ch. 209 (S.B. 548), § 2, effective August 27, 1979.)

## Art. 28.02. Order of Argument.

The counsel of the defendant has the right to open and conclude the argument upon all pleadings of the defendant presented for the decision of the judge.

(Enacted by Acts 1965, 59th Leg., ch. 722 (S.B. 107), § 1, effective January 1, 1966.)

### Art. 28.03. Process for Testimony on Pleadings.

When the matters involved in any written pleading depend in whole or in part upon testimony, and not altogether upon the record of the court, every process known to the law may be obtained on behalf of either party to procure such testimony; but there shall be no delay on account of the want of the testimony, unless it be shown to the satisfaction of the court that all the means given by the law have been used to procure the same.

(Enacted by Acts 1965, 59th Leg., ch. 722 (S.B. 107), § 1, effective January 1, 1966.)

### Art. 28.04. Quashing Charge in Misdemeanor.

If the motion to set aside or the exception to an indictment or information is sustained, the defendant in a misdemeanor case shall be discharged, but may be again prosecuted within the time allowed by law.

(Enacted by Acts 1965, 59th Leg., ch. 722 (S.B. 107), § 1, effective January 1, 1966.)

### Art. 28.05. Quashing Indictment in Felony.

If the motion to set aside or the exception to the indictment in cases of felony be sustained, the defendant shall not therefor be discharged, but may immediately be recommitted by order of the court, upon motion of the State's attorney or without motion; and proceedings may afterward be had against him as if no prosecution had ever been commenced.

(Enacted by Acts 1965, 59th Leg., ch. 722 (S.B. 107), § 1, effective January 1, 1966.)

### Art. 28.06. Shall Be Fully Discharged, When.

Where, after the motion or exception is sustained, it is made known to the court by sufficient testimony that the offense of which the defendant is accused will be barred by limitation before another indictment can be presented, he shall be fully discharged.

(Enacted by Acts 1965, 59th Leg., ch. 722 (S.B. 107), § 1, effective January 1, 1966.)

### Art. 28.061. Discharge for Delay.

If a motion to set aside an indictment, information, or complaint for failure to provide a speedy trial is sustained, the court shall discharge the defendant. A discharge under this article is a bar to any further prosecution for the offense discharged and for any other offense arising out of the same transaction, other than an offense of a higher grade that the attorney representing the state and prosecuting the offense that was discharged does not have the primary duty to prosecute.

(Enacted by Acts 1977, 65th Leg., ch. 787 (S.B. 1043), § 4, effective July 1, 1978; am. Acts 1987, 70th Leg., ch. 383 (H.B. 23), § 1, effective September 1, 1987; am. Acts 1997, 75th Leg., ch. 289 (H.B. 749), § 1, effective May 26, 1997.)

### Art. 28.07. If Exception Is That No Offense Is Charged.

If an exception to an indictment or information is taken and sustained upon the ground that there is no offense against the law charged therein, the defendant shall be discharged, unless an affidavit be filed accusing him of the commission of a penal offense.

(Enacted by Acts 1965, 59th Leg., ch. 722 (S.B. 107), § 1, effective January 1, 1966.)

### Art. 28.08. When Defendant Is Held by Order of Court.

If the motion to set aside the indictment or any exception thereto is sustained, but the court refuses to discharge the defendant, then at the expiration of ten days from the order sustaining such motions or exceptions, the defendant shall be discharged, unless in the meanwhile complaint has been made before a magistrate charging him with an offense, or unless another indictment has been presented against him for such offense.

(Enacted by Acts 1965, 59th Leg., ch. 722 (S.B. 107), § 1, effective January 1, 1966.)

### Art. 28.09. Exception on Account of Form or Substance.

If the exception to an indictment or information is sustained, the information or indictment may be amended if permitted by Article 28.10 of this code, and the cause may proceed upon the amended indictment or information.

(Am. Acts 1965, 59th Leg., ch. 722 (S.B. 107), § 1, effective January 1, 1966; am. Acts 1985, 69th Leg., ch. 577 (S.B. 169), § 1, effective December 1, 1985.)

## Art. 28.10. Amendment of Indictment or Information.

(a) After notice to the defendant, a matter of form or substance in an indictment or information may be amended at any time before the date the trial on the merits commences. On the request of the defendant, the court shall allow the defendant not less than 10 days, or a shorter period if requested by the defendant, to respond to the amended indictment or information.

(b) A matter of form or substance in an indictment or information may also be amended after the trial on the merits commences if the defendant does not object.

(c) An indictment or information may not be amended over the defendant's objection as to form or substance if the amended indictment or information charges the defendant with an additional or different offense or if the substantial rights of the defendant are prejudiced.

(Am. Acts 1965, 59th Leg., ch. 722 (S.B. 107), § 1, effective January 1, 1966; am. Acts 1985, 69th Leg., ch. 577 (S.B. 169), § 1.)

## Art. 28.11. How Amended.

All amendments of an indictment or information shall be made with the leave of the court and under its direction.

(Enacted by Acts 1965, 59th Leg., ch. 722 (S.B. 107), § 1, effective January 1, 1966.)

## Art. 28.12. Exception and Trial of Special Pleas.

When a special plea is filed by the defendant, the State may except to it for substantial defects. If the exception be sustained, the plea may be amended. If the plea be not excepted to, it shall be considered that issue has been taken upon the same. Such special pleas as set forth matter of fact proper to be tried by a jury shall be submitted and tried with a plea of not guilty.

(Enacted by Acts 1965, 59th Leg., ch. 722 (S.B. 107), § 1, effective January 1, 1966.)

## Art. 28.13. Former Acquittal or Conviction.

A former judgment of acquittal or conviction in a court of competent jurisdiction shall be a bar to any further prosecution for the same offense, but shall not bar a prosecution for any higher grade of offense over which said court had not jurisdiction, unless such judgment was had upon indictment or information, in which case the prosecution shall be barred for all grades of the offense.

(Enacted by Acts 1965, 59th Leg., ch. 722 (S.B. 107), § 1, effective January 1, 1966.)

## Art. 28.14. Plea Allowed.

Judgment shall, in no case, be given against the defendant where his motion, exception or plea is overruled; but in all cases the plea of not guilty may be made by or for him.

(Enacted by Acts 1965, 59th Leg., ch. 722 (S.B. 107), § 1, effective January 1, 1966.)

# CHAPTER 29
# CONTINUANCE

## Art. 29.01. By Operation of Law.

Criminal actions are continued by operation of law if:

(1) The individual defendant has not been arrested;

(2) A defendant corporation or association has not been served with summons; or

(3) There is not sufficient time for trial at that term of court.

(Am. Acts 1965, 59th Leg., ch. 722 (S.B. 107), § 1, effective January 1, 1966; am. Acts 1973, 63rd Leg., ch. 399 (S.B. 34), § 2(A), effective January 1, 1974.)

## Art. 29.011. Religious Holy Day.

(a) In this article:

(1) "Religious organization" means an organization that meets the standards for qualifying as a religious organization under Section 11.20, Tax Code.

(2) "Religious holy day" means a day on which the tenets of a religious organization prohibit its members from participating in secular activities, such as court proceedings.

(b) If a defendant, an attorney representing the defendant, or an attorney representing the state in a criminal action is required to appear at a court proceeding on a religious holy day observed by the person, the court shall continue the action.

(c) A defendant or attorney seeking a continuance must file with the court an affidavit stating:

(1) the grounds for the continuance; and

(2) that the person holds religious beliefs that prohibit him from taking part in a court proceeding on the day for which the continuance is sought.

(d) An affidavit filed under Subsection (c) of this article is proof of the facts stated and need not be corroborated.

(Enacted by Acts 1987, 70th Leg., ch. 825 (H.B. 2449), § 1, effective September 1, 1987.)

## Art. 29.012. Religious Holy Day.

(a) In this article:

(1) "Religious organization" means an organization that meets the standards for qualification as a religious organization under Section 11.20, Tax Code.

(2) "Religious holy day" means a day on which the tenets of a religious organization prohibit its members from participating in secular activities, such as court proceedings.

(b) If a juror in a criminal action is required to appear at a court proceeding on a religious holy day observed by the juror, the court or the court's designee shall recess the criminal action until the next day the court is in session after the conclusion of the holy day.

(c) A juror seeking a recess must file with the court before the final selection of the jury an affidavit stating:

(1) the grounds for the recess; and

(2) that the juror holds religious beliefs that prohibit him from taking part in a court proceeding on the day for which the recess is sought.

(d) An affidavit filed under Subsection (c) of this section is proof of the facts stated and need not be corroborated.

(Enacted by Acts 1987, 70th Leg., ch. 589 (H.B. 2408), § 1, effective August 31, 1987; enacted by Acts 1987, 70th Leg., ch. 825 (H.B. 2449), § 4, effective September 1, 1987.)

## Art. 29.02. By Agreement.

A criminal action may be continued by consent of the parties thereto, in open court, at any time on a showing of good cause, but a continuance may be only for as long as is necessary.

(Am. Acts 1965, 59th Leg., ch. 722 (S.B. 107), § 1, effective January 1, 1966; am. Acts 1977, 65th Leg., ch. 787 (S.B. 1043), § 3, effective July 1, 1978.)

## Art. 29.03. For Sufficient Cause Shown.

A criminal action may be continued on the written motion of the State or of the defendant, upon sufficient cause shown; which cause shall be fully set forth in the motion. A continuance may be only for as long as is necessary.

(Am. Acts 1965, 59th Leg., ch. 722 (S.B. 107), § 1, effective January 1, 1966; am. Acts 1977, 65th Leg., ch. 787 (S.B. 1043), § 3, effective July 1, 1978.)

## Art. 29.04. First Motion by State.

It shall be sufficient, upon the first motion by the State for a continuance, if the same be for the want of a witness, to state:

1. The name of the witness and his residence, if known, or that his residence is unknown;

2. The diligence which has been used to procure his attendance; and it shall not be considered sufficient diligence to have caused to be issued, or to have applied for, a subpoena, in cases where the law authorized an attachment to issue; and

3. That the testimony of the witness is believed by the applicant to be material for the State.

(Enacted by Acts 1965, 59th Leg., ch. 722 (S.B. 107), § 1, effective January 1, 1966.)

## Art. 29.05. Subsequent Motion by State.

On any subsequent motion for a continuance by the State, for the want of a witness, the motion, in addition to the requisites in the preceding Article, must show:

1. The facts which the applicant expects to establish by the witness, and it must appear to the court that they are material;

2. That the applicant expects to be able to procure the attendance of the witness at the next term of the court; and

3. That the testimony cannot be procured from any other source during the present term of the court.

(Enacted by Acts 1965, 59th Leg., ch. 722 (S.B. 107), § 1, effective January 1, 1966.)

Criminal Procedure

### Art. 29.06. First Motion by Defendant.

In the first motion by the defendant for a continuance, it shall be necessary, if the same be on account of the absence of a witness, to state:

1. The name of the witness and his residence, if known, or that his residence is not known.

2. The diligence which has been used to procure his attendance; and it shall not be considered sufficient diligence to have caused to be issued, or to have applied for, a subpoena, in cases where the law authorized an attachment to issue.

3. The facts which are expected to be proved by the witness, and it must appear to the court that they are material.

4. That the witness is not absent by the procurement or consent of the defendant.

5. That the motion is not made for delay.

6. That there is no reasonable expectation that attendance of the witness can be secured during the present term of court by a postponement of the trial to some future day of said term. The truth of the first, or any subsequent motion, as well as the merit of the ground set forth therein and its sufficiency shall be addressed to the sound discretion of the court called to pass upon the same, and shall not be granted as a matter of right. If a motion for continuance be overruled, and the defendant convicted, if it appear upon the trial that the evidence of the witness or witnesses named in the motion was of a material character, and that the facts set forth in said motion were probably true, a new trial should be granted, and the cause continued or postponed to a future day of the same term.

(Enacted by Acts 1965, 59th Leg., ch. 722 (S.B. 107), § 1, effective January 1, 1966.)

### Art. 29.07. Subsequent Motion by Defendant.

Subsequent motions for continuance on the part of the defendant shall, in addition to the requisites in the preceding Article, state also:

1. That the testimony cannot be procured from any other source known to the defendant; and

2. That the defendant has reasonable expectation of procuring the same at the next term of the court.

(Enacted by Acts 1965, 59th Leg., ch. 722 (S.B. 107), § 1, effective January 1, 1966.)

### Art. 29.08. Motion Sworn To.

All motions for continuance must be sworn to by a person having personal knowledge of the facts relied on for the continuance.

(Am. Acts 1965, 59th Leg., ch. 722 (S.B. 107), § 1, effective January 1, 1966; am. Acts 1981, 67th Leg., ch. 210 (S.B. 261), § 1, effective September 1, 1981.)

### Art. 29.09. Controverting Motion.

Any material fact stated, affecting diligence, in a motion for a continuance, may be denied in writing by the adverse party. The denial shall be supported by the oath of some credible person, and filed as soon as practicable after the filing of such motion.

(Enacted by Acts 1965, 59th Leg., ch. 722 (S.B. 107), § 1, effective January 1, 1966.)

### Art. 29.10. When Denial Is Filed.

When such denial is filed, the issue shall be tried by the judge; and he shall hear testimony by affidavits, and grant or refuse continuance, according to the law and facts of the case.

(Enacted by Acts 1965, 59th Leg., ch. 722 (S.B. 107), § 1, effective January 1, 1966.)

### Art. 29.11. Argument.

No argument shall be heard on a motion for a continuance, unless requested by the judge; and when argument is heard, the applicant shall have the right to open and conclude it.

(Enacted by Acts 1965, 59th Leg., ch. 722 (S.B. 107), § 1, effective January 1, 1966.)

### Art. 29.12. Bail Resulting from Continuance.

If a defendant in a capital case demand a trial, and it appears that more than one continuance has been granted to the State, and that the defendant has not before applied for a continuance, he shall be entitled to be admitted to bail, unless it be made to appear to the satisfaction of the court that a material witness of the State had been prevented from attendance by the procurement of the defendant or some person acting in his behalf.

(Enacted by Acts 1965, 59th Leg., ch. 722 (S.B. 107), § 1, effective January 1, 1966.)

### Art. 29.13. Continuance After Trial Is Begun.

A continuance or postponement may be granted on the motion of the State or defendant after the trial has begun, when it is made to appear to the

Criminal Procedure

satisfaction of the court that by some unexpected occurrence since the trial began, which no reasonable diligence could have anticipated, the applicant is so taken by surprise that a fair trial cannot be had.
(Enacted by Acts 1965, 59th Leg., ch. 722 (S.B. 107), § 1, effective January 1, 1966.)

### Art. 29.14. Consideration of Impact on Certain Victims.

(a) In this article, "victim" means the victim of an assault or sexual assault who is younger than 17 years of age or whose case involves family violence as defined by Section 71.004, Family Code.

(b) On request by the attorney representing the state, a court that considers a motion for continuance on the part of the defendant shall also consider the impact of the continuance on the victim. On request by the attorney representing the state or by counsel for the defendant, the court shall state on the record the reason for granting or denying the continuance.
(Enacted by Acts 2009, 81st Leg., ch. 664 (H.B. 2236), § 2, effective September 1, 2009.)

# CHAPTER 30
# DISQUALIFICATION OF THE JUDGE

### Art. 30.01. Causes Which Disqualify.

No judge or justice of the peace shall sit in any case where he may be the party injured, or where he has been of counsel for the State or the accused, or where the accused or the party injured may be connected with him by consanguinity or affinity within the third degree, as determined under Chapter 573, Government Code.
(Enacted by Acts 1965, 59th Leg., ch. 722 (S.B. 107), § 1, effective January 1, 1966; am. Acts 1991, 72nd Leg., ch. 561 (H.B. 1345), § 9, effective August 26, 1991; am. Acts 1995, 74th Leg., ch. 76 (S.B. 959), § 5.95(27), effective September 1, 1995.)

### Art. 30.02. District Judge Disqualified.

Whenever any case is pending in which the district judge or criminal district judge is disqualified from trying the case, no change of venue shall be made necessary thereby; but the judge presiding shall certify that fact to the presiding judge of the administrative judicial district in which the case is pending and the presiding judge of such administrative judicial district shall assign a judge to try such case in accordance with the provisions of Article 200a, V.A.C.S.
(Enacted by Acts 1965, 59th Leg., ch. 722 (S.B. 107), § 1, effective January 1, 1966.)

### Art. 30.03. County Judge Disqualified, Absent, or Disabled [Repealed].

Repealed by Acts 1999, 76th Leg., ch. 1388 (H.B. 1606), § 14, effective September 1, 1999. (Enacted by Acts 1965, 59th Leg., ch. 722 (S.B. 107), § 1, effective January 1, 1966; am. Acts 1975, 64th Leg., ch. 448 (S.B. 1074), § 1, effective June 19, 1975; am. Acts 1995, 74th Leg., ch. 782 (S.B. 1197), § 1, effective September 1, 1995.)

### Art. 30.04. Special Judge to Take Oath [Repealed].

Repealed by Acts 1999, 76th Leg., ch. 1388 (H.B. 1606), § 14, effective September 1, 1999. (Enacted by Acts 1965, 59th Leg., ch. 722 (S.B. 107), § 1, effective January 1, 1966; am. Acts 1975, 64th Leg., ch. 448 (S.B. 1074), § 2, effective June 19, 1975; am. Acts 1995, 74th Leg., ch. 456 (H.B. 2463), § 1, effective September 1, 1995; am. Acts 1995, 74th Leg., ch. 782 (S.B. 1197), § 2, effective September 1, 1995.)

### Art. 30.05. Record Made by Clerk [Repealed].

Repealed by Acts 1999, 76th Leg., ch. 1388 (H.B. 1606), § 14, effective September 1, 1999. (Enacted by Acts 1965, 59th Leg., ch. 722 (S.B. 107), § 1, effective January 1, 1966; am. Acts 1975, 64th Leg., ch. 448 (S.B. 1074), § 3, effective June 19, 1975; am. Acts 1995, 74th Leg., ch. 456 (H.B. 2463), § 2, effective September 1, 1995; am. Acts 1995, 74th Leg., ch. 782 (S.B. 1197), § 3, effective September 1, 1995.)

### Art. 30.06. Compensation [Repealed].

Repealed by Acts 1999, 76th Leg., ch. 1388 (H.B. 1606), § 14, effective September 1, 1999. (Enacted by Acts 1965, 59th Leg., ch. 722 (S.B. 107), § 1, effective January 1, 1966.)

### Art. 30.07. Justice Disqualified.

If a justice of the peace be disqualified from sitting in any criminal action pending before him, he shall transfer the same to any justice of the peace in the county who is not disqualified to try the case.

(Enacted by Acts 1965, 59th Leg., ch. 722 (S.B. 107), § 1, effective January 1, 1966.)

### Art. 30.08. Order of Transfer.

In cases provided for in the preceding Article, the order of transfer shall state the cause of the transfer, and name the court to which the transfer is made, and the time and place, when and where, the parties and witnesses shall appear before such court. The rules governing the transfer of cases from the district to inferior courts shall govern in the transfer of cases under the preceding Article.

(Enacted by Acts 1965, 59th Leg., ch. 722 (S.B. 107), § 1, effective January 1, 1966.)

## CHAPTER 31
## CHANGE OF VENUE

### Art. 31.01. On Court's Own Motion.

Whenever in any case of felony or misdemeanor punishable by confinement, the judge presiding shall be satisfied that a trial, alike fair and impartial to the accused and to the State, cannot, from any cause, be had in the county in which the case is pending, he may, upon his own motion, after due notice to accused and the State, and after hearing evidence thereon, order a change of venue to any county in the judicial district in which such county is located or in an adjoining district, stating in his order the grounds for such change of venue. The judge, upon his own motion, after ten days notice to the parties or their counsel, may order a change of venue to any county beyond an adjoining district; provided, however, an order changing venue to a county beyond an adjoining district shall be grounds for reversal if, upon timely contest by the defendant, the record of the contest affirmatively shows that any county in his own and the adjoining district is not subject to the same conditions which required the transfer.

(Enacted by Acts 1965, 59th Leg., ch. 722 (S.B. 107), § 1, effective January 1, 1966.)

### Art. 31.02. State May Have.

Whenever the district or county attorney shall represent in writing to the court before which any felony or misdemeanor case punishable by confinement, is pending, that, by reason of existing combinations or influences in favor of the accused, or on account of the lawless condition of affairs in the county, a fair and impartial trial as between the accused and the State cannot be safely and speedily had; or whenever he shall represent that the life of the prisoner, or of any witness, would be jeopardized by a trial in the county in which the case is pending, the judge shall hear proof in relation thereto, and if satisfied that such representation is well-founded and that the ends of public justice will be subserved thereby, he shall order a change of venue to any county in the judicial district in which such county is located or in an adjoining district.

(Enacted by Acts 1965, 59th Leg., ch. 722 (S.B. 107), § 1, effective January 1, 1966.)

### Art. 31.03. Granted on Motion of Defendant.

(a) A change of venue may be granted in any felony or misdemeanor case punishable by confinement on the written motion of the defendant, supported by his own affidavit and the affidavit of at least two credible persons, residents of the county where the prosecution is instituted, for either of the following causes, the truth and sufficiency of which the court shall determine:

1. That there exists in the county where the prosecution is commenced so great a prejudice against him that he cannot obtain a fair and impartial trial; and

2. That there is a dangerous combination against him instigated by influential persons, by reason of which he cannot expect a fair trial.

An order changing venue to a county beyond an adjoining district shall be grounds for reversal, if upon timely contest by defendant, the record of the contest affirmatively shows that any county in his own and the adjoining district is not subject to the same conditions which required the transfer.

(b) For the convenience of parties and witnesses, and in the interest of justice, the court upon motion of the defendant and with the consent of the attorney for the state may transfer the proceeding as to him to another district.

(c) The court upon motion of the defendant and with the consent of the attorney for the state may transfer the proceedings to another district in those cases wherein the defendant stipulates that a plea of guilty will be entered.

(Am. Acts 1965, 59th Leg., ch. 722 (S.B. 107), § 1, effective January 1, 1966; am. Acts 1979, 66th Leg., ch. 140 (H.B. 1319), § 1, effective August 27, 1979.)

## Art. 31.04. Motion May Be Controverted.

The credibility of the persons making affidavit for change of venue, or their means of knowledge, may be attacked by the affidavit of a credible person. The issue thus formed shall be tried by the judge, and the motion granted or refused, as the law and facts shall warrant.

(Enacted by Acts 1965, 59th Leg., ch. 722 (S.B. 107), § 1, effective January 1, 1966.)

## Art. 31.05. Clerk's Duties on Change of Venue.

Where an order for a change of venue of any court in any criminal cause in this State has been made the clerk of the court where the prosecution is pending shall make out a certified copy of the court's order directing such change of venue, together with a certified copy of the defendant's bail bond or personal bond, together with all the original papers in said cause and also a certificate of the said clerk under his official seal that such papers are the papers and all the papers on file in said court in said cause; and he shall transmit the same to the clerk of the court to which the venue has been changed.

(Enacted by Acts 1965, 59th Leg., ch. 722 (S.B. 107), § 1, effective January 1, 1966.)

## Art. 31.06. If Defendant Be in Custody.

When the venue is changed in any criminal action if the defendant be in custody, an order shall be made for his removal to the proper county, and his delivery to the sheriff thereof before the next succeeding term of the court of the county to which the case is to be taken, and he shall be delivered by the sheriff as directed in the order.

(Enacted by Acts 1965, 59th Leg., ch. 722 (S.B. 107), § 1, effective January 1, 1966.)

## Art. 31.07. Witness Need Not Again Be Summoned.

When the venue in a criminal action has been changed, it shall not be necessary to have the witnesses therein again subpoenaed, attached or bailed, but all the witnesses who have been subpoenaed, attached or bailed to appear and testify in the cause shall be held bound to appear before the court to which the cause has been transferred, as if there had been no such transfer.

(Enacted by Acts 1965, 59th Leg., ch. 722 (S.B. 107), § 1, effective January 1, 1966.)

## Art. 31.08. Return to County of Original Venue.

Sec. 1. (a) On the completion of a trial in which a change of venue has been ordered and after the jury has been discharged, the court, with the consent of counsel for the state and the defendant, may return the cause to the original county in which the indictment or information was filed. Except as provided by Subsection (b) of this section, all subsequent and ancillary proceedings, including the pronouncement of sentence after appeals have been exhausted, must be heard in the county in which the indictment or information was filed.

(b) A motion for new trial alleging jury misconduct must be heard in the county in which the cause was tried. The county in which the indictment or information was filed must pay the costs of the prosecution of the motion for new trial.

Sec. 2. (a) Except as provided by Subsection (b), on an order returning venue to the original county in which the indictment or information was filed, the clerk of the county in which the cause was tried shall:

(1) make a certified copy of the court's order directing the return to the original county;

(2) make a certified copy of the defendant's bail bond, personal bond, or appeal bond;

(3) gather all the original papers in the cause and certify under official seal that the papers are all the original papers on file in the court; and

(4) transmit the items listed in this section to the clerk of the court of original venue.

(b) This article does not apply to a proceeding in which the clerk of the court of original venue was present and performed the duties as clerk for the court under Article 31.09.

Sec. 3. Except for the review of a death sentence under Section 2(h), Article 37.071, or under Section 2(h), Article 37.072, an appeal taken in a cause returned to the original county under this article must be docketed in the appellate district in which the county of original venue is located.

(Am. Acts 1989, 71st Leg., ch. 824 (S.B. 344), § 1, effective September 1, 1989; am. Acts 1995, 74th Leg., ch. 651 (H.B. 2949), § 1, effective September 1, 1995; am. Acts 2007, 80th Leg., ch. 593 (H.B. 8), § 3.13, effective September 1, 2007.)

### Art. 31.09. Change of Venue; Use of Existing Services.

(a) If a change of venue in a criminal case is ordered under this chapter, the judge ordering the change of venue may, with the written consent of the prosecuting attorney, the defense attorney, and the defendant, maintain the original case number on its own docket, preside over the case, and use the services of the court reporter, the court coordinator, and the clerk of the court of original venue. The court shall use the courtroom facilities and any other services or facilities of the district or county to which venue is changed. A jury, if required, must consist of residents of the district or county to which venue is changed.

(b) Notwithstanding Article 31.05, the clerk of the court of original venue shall:

(1) maintain the original papers of the case, including the defendant's bail bond or personal bond;

(2) make the papers available for trial; and

(3) act as the clerk in the case.

(Enacted by Acts 1995, 74th Leg., ch. 651 (H.B. 2949), § 2, effective September 1, 1995.)

## Trial and Its Incidents

### CHAPTER 32
### DISMISSING PROSECUTIONS

### Art. 32.01. Defendant in Custody and No Indictment Presented.

When a defendant has been detained in custody or held to bail for his appearance to answer any criminal accusation, the prosecution, unless otherwise ordered by the court, for good cause shown, supported by affidavit, shall be dismissed and the bail discharged, if indictment or information be not presented against such defendant on or before the last day of the next term of the court which is held after his commitment or admission to bail or on or before the 180th day after the date of commitment or admission to bail, whichever date is later.

(Am. Acts 1965, 59th Leg., ch. 722 (S.B. 107), § 1, effective January 1, 1966; am. Acts 1997, 75th Leg., ch. 289 (H.B. 749), § 2, effective May 26, 1997; am. Acts 2005, 79th Leg., ch. 743 (H.B. 2767), § 6, effective September 1, 2005.)

### Art. 32.02. Dismissal by State's Attorney.

The attorney representing the State may, by permission of the court, dismiss a criminal action at any time upon filing a written statement with the papers in the case setting out his reasons for such dismissal, which shall be incorporated in the judgment of dismissal. No case shall be dismissed without the consent of the presiding judge.

(Enacted by Acts 1965, 59th Leg., ch. 722 (S.B. 107), § 1, effective January 1, 1966.)

### CHAPTER 32A
### SPEEDY TRIAL

### Art. 32A.01. Trial Priorities.

Insofar as is practicable, the trial of a criminal action shall be given preference over trials of civil cases, and the trial of a criminal action against a defendant who is detained in jail pending trial of the action shall be given preference over trials of other criminal actions.

(Enacted by Acts 1977, 65th Leg., ch. 787 (S.B. 1043), § 1, effective July 1, 1978.)

### Art. 32A.02. Time Limitations [Repealed].

Repealed by Acts 2005, 79th Leg., ch. 1019 (H.B. 969), § 2, effective June 18, 2005.

(Enacted by Acts 1977, 65th Leg., ch. 787 (S.B. 1043), § 1, effective July 1, 1978; am. Acts 1979, 66th Leg., ch. 3 (S.B. 106), § 1, effective September 1, 1979; am. Acts 1987, 70th Leg., ch. 383 (H.B. 23), § 2, effective September 1, 1987.)

### CHAPTER 33
### THE MODE OF TRIAL

### Art. 33.01. Jury Size.

(a) Except as provided by Subsection (b), in the district court, the jury shall consist of twelve qualified jurors. In the county court and inferior courts, the jury shall consist of six qualified jurors.

(b) In a trial involving a misdemeanor offense, a district court jury shall consist of six qualified jurors.

(Am. Acts 1965, 59th Leg., ch. 722 (S.B. 107), § 1, effective January 1, 1966; am. Acts 2003, 78th Leg., ch. 466 (H.B. 830), § 1, effective January 1, 2004.)

### Art. 33.011.  Alternate Jurors.

(a) In district courts, the judge may direct that not more than four jurors in addition to the regular jury be called and impaneled to sit as alternate jurors. In county courts, the judge may direct that not more than two jurors in addition to the regular jury be called and impaneled to sit as alternate jurors.

(b) Alternate jurors in the order in which they are called shall replace jurors who, prior to the time the jury renders a verdict on the guilt or innocence of the defendant and, if applicable, the amount of punishment, become or are found to be unable or disqualified to perform their duties or are found by the court on agreement of the parties to have good cause for not performing their duties. Alternate jurors shall be drawn and selected in the same manner, shall have the same qualifications, shall be subject to the same examination and challenges, shall take the same oath, and shall have the same functions, powers, facilities, security, and privileges as regular jurors. An alternate juror who does not replace a regular juror shall be discharged after the jury has rendered a verdict on the guilt or innocence of the defendant and, if applicable, the amount of punishment.

(Enacted by Acts 1983, 68th Leg., ch. 775 (H.B. 533), § 2, effective August 29, 1983; am. Acts 2007, 80th Leg., ch. 846 (H.B. 1086), § 1, effective September 1, 2007.)

### Art. 33.02.  Failure to Register.

Failure to register to vote shall not disqualify any person from jury service.

(Am. Acts 1965, 59th Leg., ch. 722 (S.B. 107), § 1, effective January 1, 1966; am. Acts 1981, 67th Leg., ch. 827 (H.B. 1288), § 6, effective August 31, 1981.)

### Art. 33.03.  Presence of Defendant.

In all prosecutions for felonies, the defendant must be personally present at the trial, and he must likewise be present in all cases of misde-meanor when the punishment or any part thereof is imprisonment in jail; provided, however, that in all cases, when the defendant voluntarily absents himself after pleading to the indictment or information, or after the jury has been selected when trial is before a jury, the trial may proceed to its conclusion. When the record in the appellate court shows that the defendant was present at the commencement, or any portion of the trial, it shall be presumed in the absence of all evidence in the record to the contrary that he was present during the whole trial. Provided, however, that the presence of the defendant shall not be required at the hearing on the motion for new trial in any misdemeanor case.

(Am. Acts 1965, 59th Leg., ch. 722 (S.B. 107), § 1, effective January 1, 1966; am. Acts 1979, 66th Leg., ch. 745 (H.B. 1135), § 1, effective August 27, 1979.)

### Art. 33.04.  May Appear by Counsel.

In other misdemeanor cases, the defendant may, by consent of the State's attorney, appear by counsel, and the trial may proceed without his personal presence.

(Enacted by Acts 1965, 59th Leg., ch. 722 (S.B. 107), § 1, effective January 1, 1966.)

### Art. 33.05.  On Bail During Trial.

If the defendant is on bail when the trial commences, such bail shall be considered as discharged if he is acquitted. If a verdict of guilty is returned against him, the discharge of his bail shall be governed by other provisions of this Code.

(Enacted by Acts 1965, 59th Leg., ch. 722 (S.B. 107), § 1, effective January 1, 1966.)

### Art. 33.06.  Sureties Bound in Case of Mistrial.

If there be a mistrial in a felony case, the original sureties, if any, of the defendant shall be still held bound for his appearance until they surrender him in accordance with the provisions of this Code.

(Enacted by Acts 1965, 59th Leg., ch. 722 (S.B. 107), § 1, effective January 1, 1966.)

### Art. 33.07.  Record of Criminal Actions.

Each clerk of a court of record having criminal jurisdiction shall keep a record in which shall be set down the style and file number of each criminal action, the nature of the offense, the names of counsel, the proceedings had therein, and the date of each proceeding.

(Enacted by Acts 1965, 59th Leg., ch. 722 (S.B. 107), § 1, effective January 1, 1966; am. Acts 2007, 80th Leg., ch. 628 (H.B. 587), § 3, effective September 1, 2007.)

### Art. 33.08. To Fix Day for Criminal Docket.

The district courts and county courts shall have control of their respective dockets as to the settings of criminal cases.

(Enacted by Acts 1965, 59th Leg., ch. 722 (S.B. 107), § 1, effective January 1, 1966.)

### Art. 33.09. Jury Drawn.

Jury panels, including special venires, for the trial of criminal cases shall be selected and summoned (with return on summons) in the same manner as the selection of panels for the trial of civil cases except as otherwise provided in this Code.

(Enacted by Acts 1965, 59th Leg., ch. 722 (S.B. 107), § 1, effective January 1, 1966.)

## CHAPTER 34
## SPECIAL VENIRE IN CAPITAL CASES

**Article**
34.01.    Special Venire.
34.02.    Additional Names Drawn.
34.03.    Instructions to Sheriff.
34.04.    Notice of List.
34.05.    Mechanical or Electronic Selection Method.

### Art. 34.01. Special Venire.

A "special venire" is a writ issued in a capital case by order of the district court, commanding the sheriff to summon either verbally or by mail such a number of persons, not less than 50, as the court may order, to appear before the court on a day named in the writ from whom the jury for the trial of such case is to be selected. Where as many as one hundred jurors have been summoned in such county for regular service for the week in which such capital case is set for trial, the judge of the court having jurisdiction of a capital case in which a motion for a special venire has been made, shall grant or refuse such motion for a special venire, and upon such refusal require the case to be tried by regular jurors summoned for service in such county for the week in which such capital case is set for trial and such additional talesmen as may be summoned by the sheriff upon order of the court as provided in Article 34.02 of this Code, but the clerk of such court shall furnish the defendant or his counsel a list of

the persons summoned as provided in Article 34.04.

(Enacted by Acts 1965, 59th Leg., ch. 722 (S.B. 107), § 1, effective January 1, 1966.)

### Art. 34.02. Additional Names Drawn.

In any criminal case in which the court deems that the veniremen theretofore drawn will be insufficient for the trial of the case, or in any criminal case in which the venire has been exhausted by challenge or otherwise, the court shall order additional veniremen in such numbers as the court may deem advisable, to be summoned as follows:

(a) In a jury wheel county, the names of those to be summoned shall be drawn from the jury wheel.

(b) In counties not using the jury wheel, the veniremen shall be summoned by the sheriff.

(Enacted by Acts 1965, 59th Leg., ch. 722 (S.B. 107), § 1, effective January 1, 1966.)

### Art. 34.03. Instructions to Sheriff.

When the sheriff is ordered by the court to summon persons upon a special venire whose names have not been selected under the Jury Wheel Law, the court shall, in every case, caution and direct the sheriff to summon such persons as have legal qualifications to serve on juries, informing him of what those qualifications are, and shall direct him, as far as he may be able to summon persons of good character who can read and write, and such as are not prejudiced against the defendant or biased in his favor, if he knows of such bias or prejudice.

(Enacted by Acts 1965, 59th Leg., ch. 722 (S.B. 107), § 1, effective January 1, 1966.)

### Art. 34.04. Notice of List.

No defendant in a capital case in which the state seeks the death penalty shall be brought to trial until he shall have had at least two days (including holidays) a copy of the names of the persons summoned as veniremen, for the week for which his case is set for trial except where he waives the right or is on bail. When such defendant is on bail, the clerk of the court in which the case is pending shall furnish such a list to the defendant or his counsel at least two days prior to the trial (including holidays) upon timely motion by the defendant or his counsel therefor at the office of such clerk, and the defendant shall not be brought to trial until such list has been furnished defendant or his counsel for at least two days

(including holidays). Where the venire is exhausted, by challenges or otherwise, and additional names are drawn, the defendant shall not be entitled to two days service of the names additionally drawn, but the clerk shall compile a list of such names promptly after they are drawn and if the defendant is not on bail, the sheriff shall serve a copy of such list promptly upon the defendant, and if on bail, the clerk shall furnish a copy of such list to the defendant or his counsel upon request, but the proceedings shall not be delayed thereby.
(Enacted by Acts 1965, 59th Leg., ch. 722 (S.B. 107), § 1, effective January 1, 1966; am. Acts 1991, 72nd Leg., ch. 652 (H.B. 9), § 4, effective September 1, 1991.)

### Art. 34.05. Mechanical or Electronic Selection Method.

A mechanical or electronic method of jury selection as provided by Chapter 62, Government Code, may be used under this chapter.
(Enacted by Acts 1995, 74th Leg., ch. 694 (H.B. 2951), § 1, effective September 1, 1995.)

## CHAPTER 35
## FORMATION OF THE JURY

### Art. 35.01. Jurors Called.

When a case is called for trial and the parties have announced ready for trial, the names of those summoned as jurors in the case shall be called. Those not present may be fined not less than $100 nor more than $500. An attachment may issue on request of either party for any absent summoned juror, to have him brought forthwith before the court. A person who is summoned but not present, may upon an appearance, before the jury is qualified, be tried as to his qualifications and impaneled as a juror unless challenged, but no cause shall be unreasonably delayed on account of his absence.
(Enacted by Acts 1965, 59th Leg., ch. 722 (S.B. 107), § 1, effective January 1, 1966; am. Acts 2009, 81st Leg., ch. 640 (H.B. 1665), § 3, effective September 1, 2009.)

### Art. 35.02. Sworn to Answer Questions.

To those present the court shall cause to be administered this oath: "You, and each of you, solemnly swear that you will make true answers to such questions as may be propounded to you by the court, or under its directions, touching your service and qualifications as a juror, so help you God."
(Enacted by Acts 1965, 59th Leg., ch. 722 (S.B. 107), § 1, effective January 1, 1966.)

### Art. 35.03. Excuses.

Sec. 1. Except as provided by Sections 2 and 3 of this article, the court shall then hear and determine excuses offered for not serving as a juror, including any claim of an exemption or a lack of qualification, and if the court considers the excuse sufficient, the court shall discharge the prospective juror or postpone the prospective juror's service to a date specified by the court, as appropriate.

Sec. 2. Under a plan approved by the commissioners court of the county in the same manner as a plan is approved for jury selection under Section 62.011, Government Code, in a case other than a capital felony case, the court's designee may hear and determine an excuse offered for not serving as a juror, including any claim of an exemption or a lack of qualification. The court's designee may discharge the prospective juror or postpone the prospective juror's service to a date specified by the court's designee, as appropriate, if:

(1) the court's designee considers the excuse sufficient; and

(2) the juror submits to the court's designee a statement of the ground of the exemption or lack of qualification or other excuse.

Sec. 3. A court or a court's designee may discharge a juror or postpone the juror's service on the basis of the juror's observation of a religious holy day or religious beliefs only if the juror provides an affidavit as required by Article 29.012(c) of this code.

(Enacted by Acts 1965, 59th Leg., ch. 722 (S.B. 107), § 1, effective January 1, 1966; am. Acts 1987, 70th Leg., ch. 589 (H.B. 2408), § 2, effective August 31, 1987; am. Acts 1987, 70th Leg., 2nd C.S., ch. 43 (H.B. 123), § 2, effective October 20, 1987; am. Acts 2005, 79th Leg., ch. 905 (H.B. 75), § 1, effective September 1, 2005.)

## Art. 35.04. Claiming Exemption.

Any person summoned as a juror who is exempt by law from jury service may establish his exemption without appearing in person by filing a signed statement of the ground of his exemption with the clerk of the court at any time before the date upon which he is summoned to appear.

(Enacted by Acts 1965, 59th Leg., ch. 722 (S.B. 107), § 1, effective January 1, 1966; am. Acts 1971, 62nd Leg., ch. 421 (H.B. 821), § 3, effective May 26, 1971.)

## Art. 35.05. Excused by Consent.

One summoned upon a special venire may by consent of both parties be excused from attendance by the court at any time before he is impaneled.

(Enacted by Acts 1965, 59th Leg., ch. 722 (S.B. 107), § 1, effective January 1, 1966.)

## Art. 35.06. Challenge to Array First Heard.

The court shall hear and determine a challenge to the array before interrogating those summoned as to their qualifications.

(Enacted by Acts 1965, 59th Leg., ch. 722 (S.B. 107), § 1, effective January 1, 1966.)

## Art. 35.07. Challenge to the Array.

Each party may challenge the array only on the ground that the officer summoning the jury has wilfully summoned jurors with a view to securing a conviction or an acquittal. All such challenges must be in writing setting forth distinctly the grounds of such challenge. When made by the defendant, it must be supported by his affidavit or the affidavit of any credible person. When such challenge is made, the judge shall hear evidence and decide without delay whether or not the challenge shall be sustained.

(Enacted by Acts 1965, 59th Leg., ch. 722 (S.B. 107), § 1, effective January 1, 1966.)

## Art. 35.08. When Challenge Is Sustained.

The array of jurors summoned shall be discharged if the challenge be sustained, and the court shall order other jurors to be summoned in their stead, and direct that the officer who summoned those so discharged, and on account of whose misconduct the challenge has been sustained shall not summon any other jurors in the case.

(Enacted by Acts 1965, 59th Leg., ch. 722 (S.B. 107), § 1, effective January 1, 1966.)

## Art. 35.09. List of New Venire.

When a challenge to the array has been sustained, the defendant shall be entitled, as in the first instance, to service of a copy of the list of names of those summoned by order of the court.

(Enacted by Acts 1965, 59th Leg., ch. 722 (S.B. 107), § 1, effective January 1, 1966.)

## Art. 35.10. Court to Try Qualifications.

When no challenge to the array has been made, or if made, has been over-ruled, the court shall proceed to try the qualifications of those present who have been summoned to serve as jurors.

(Enacted by Acts 1965, 59th Leg., ch. 722 (S.B. 107), § 1, effective January 1, 1966.)

## Art. 35.11. Preparation of List.

The trial judge, on the demand of the defendant or his attorney, or of the State's counsel, shall cause a sufficient number of jurors from which a jury may be selected to try the case to be randomly selected from the members of the general panel drawn or assigned as jurors in the case. The clerk shall randomly select the jurors by a computer or other process of random selection and shall write or print the names, in the order selected, on the jury list from which the jury is to be selected to try the case. The clerk shall deliver a copy of the list to the State's counsel and to the defendant or his attorney.

(Enacted by Acts 1965, 59th Leg., ch. 722 (S.B. 107), § 1, effective January 1, 1966; am. Acts 1991, 72nd Leg., ch. 337 (H.B. 1328), § 1, effective September 1, 1991.)

## Art. 35.12. Mode of Testing.

(a) In testing the qualification of a prospective juror after the juror has been sworn, the juror shall be asked by the court, or under its direction:

    1. Except for failure to register, are you a qualified voter in this county and state under the Constitution and laws of this state?

    2. Have you ever been convicted of theft or any felony?

    3. Are you under indictment or legal accusation for theft or any felony?

(b) In testing the qualifications of a prospective juror, with respect to whether the juror has been the subject of an order of nondisclosure or has a criminal history that includes information subject to that order, the juror may state only that the matter in question has been sealed.
(Enacted by Acts 1965, 59th Leg., ch. 722 (S.B. 107), § 1, effective January 1, 1966; am. Acts 1969, 61st Leg., ch. 412 (S.B. 424), § 2, effective September 1, 1969; am. Acts 1981, 67th Leg., ch. 827 (H.B. 1288), § 7, effective August 31, 1981; am. Acts 2005, 79th Leg., ch. 1309 (H.B. 3093), § 4, effective September 1, 2005.)

## Art. 35.13. Passing Juror for Challenge.

A juror in a capital case in which the state has made it known it will seek the death penalty, held to be qualified, shall be passed for acceptance or challenge first to the state and then to the defendant. Challenges to jurors are either peremptory or for cause.
(Enacted by Acts 1965, 59th Leg., ch. 722 (S.B. 107), § 1, effective January 1, 1966; am. Acts 1967, 60th Leg., ch. 659 (S.B. 145), § 20, effective August 28, 1967.)

## Art. 35.14. A Peremptory Challenge.

A peremptory challenge is made to a juror without assigning any reason therefor.
(Enacted by Acts 1965, 59th Leg., ch. 722 (S.B. 107), § 1, effective January 1, 1966.)

## Art. 35.15. Number of Challenges.

(a) In capital cases in which the State seeks the death penalty both the State and defendant shall be entitled to fifteen peremptory challenges. Where two or more defendants are tried together, the State shall be entitled to eight peremptory challenges for each defendant; and each defendant shall be entitled to eight peremptory challenges.

(b) In non-capital felony cases and in capital cases in which the State does not seek the death penalty, the State and defendant shall each be entitled to ten peremptory challenges. If two or more defendants are tried together each defendant shall be entitled to six peremptory challenges and the State to six for each defendant.

(c) The State and the defendant shall each be entitled to five peremptory challenges in a misdemeanor tried in the district court and to three in the county court, or county court at law. If two or more defendants are tried together, each defendant shall be entitled to three such challenges and the State to three for each defendant in either court.

(d) The State and the defendant shall each be entitled to one peremptory challenge in addition to those otherwise allowed by law if one or two alternate jurors are to be impaneled and two peremptory challenges if three or four alternate jurors are to be impaneled. The additional peremptory challenges provided by this subsection may be used against an alternate juror only, and the other peremptory challenges allowed by law may not be used against an alternate juror.
(Enacted by Acts 1965, 59th Leg., ch. 722 (S.B. 107), § 1, effective January 1, 1966; am. Acts 1973, 63rd Leg., ch. 426 (H.B. 200), art. 3, § 4, effective June 14, 1973; am. Acts 1983, 68th Leg., ch. 775 (H.B. 533), § 3, effective August 29, 1983; am. Acts 1991, 72nd Leg., ch. 652 (S.B. 9), § 5, effective September 1, 1991.)

## Art. 35.16. Reasons for Challenge for Cause.

(a) A challenge for cause is an objection made to a particular juror, alleging some fact which renders the juror incapable or unfit to serve on the jury. A challenge for cause may be made by either the state or the defense for any one of the following reasons:

    1. That the juror is not a qualified voter in the state and county under the Constitution and laws of the state; provided, however, the failure to register to vote shall not be a disqualification;

    2. That the juror has been convicted of misdemeanor theft or a felony;

    3. That the juror is under indictment or other legal accusation for misdemeanor theft or a felony;

    4. That the juror is insane;

    5. That the juror has such defect in the organs of feeling or hearing, or such bodily or mental defect or disease as to render the juror unfit for jury service, or that the juror is legally

blind and the court in its discretion is not satisfied that the juror is fit for jury service in that particular case;

6. That the juror is a witness in the case;

7. That the juror served on the grand jury which found the indictment;

8. That the juror served on a petit jury in a former trial of the same case;

9. That the juror has a bias or prejudice in favor of or against the defendant;

10. That from hearsay, or otherwise, there is established in the mind of the juror such a conclusion as to the guilt or innocence of the defendant as would influence the juror in finding a verdict. To ascertain whether this cause of challenge exists, the juror shall first be asked whether, in the juror's opinion, the conclusion so established will influence the juror's verdict. If the juror answers in the affirmative, the juror shall be discharged without further interrogation by either party or the court. If the juror answers in the negative, the juror shall be further examined as to how the juror's conclusion was formed, and the extent to which it will affect the juror's action; and, if it appears to have been formed from reading newspaper accounts, communications, statements or reports or mere rumor or hearsay, and if the juror states that the juror feels able, notwithstanding such opinion, to render an impartial verdict upon the law and the evidence, the court, if satisfied that the juror is impartial and will render such verdict, may, in its discretion, admit the juror as competent to serve in such case. If the court, in its discretion, is not satisfied that the juror is impartial, the juror shall be discharged;

11. That the juror cannot read or write.

No juror shall be impaneled when it appears that the juror is subject to the second, third or fourth grounds of challenge for cause set forth above, although both parties may consent. All other grounds for challenge may be waived by the party or parties in whose favor such grounds of challenge exist.

In this subsection "legally blind" shall mean having not more than 20/200 of visual acuity in the better eye with correcting lenses, or visual acuity greater than 20/200 but with a limitation in the field of vision such that the widest diameter of the visual field subtends an angle no greater than 20 degrees.

(b) A challenge for cause may be made by the State for any of the following reasons:

1. That the juror has conscientious scruples in regard to the infliction of the punishment of death for crime, in a capital case, where the State is seeking the death penalty;

2. That he is related within the third degree of consanguinity or affinity, as determined under Chapter 573, Government Code, to the defendant; and

3. That he has a bias or prejudice against any phase of the law upon which the State is entitled to rely for conviction or punishment.

(c) A challenge for cause may be made by the defense for any of the following reasons:

1. That he is related within the third degree of consanguinity or affinity, as determined under Chapter 573, Government Code, to the person injured by the commission of the offense, or to any prosecutor in the case; and

2. That he has a bias or prejudice against any of the law applicable to the case upon which the defense is entitled to rely, either as a defense to some phase of the offense for which the defendant is being prosecuted or as a mitigation thereof or of the punishment therefor.

(Enacted by Acts 1965, 59th Leg., ch. 722 (S.B. 107), § 1, effective January 1, 1966; am. Acts 1969, 61st Leg., ch. 412 (S.B. 424), § 3, effective September 1, 1969; am. Acts 1975, 64th Leg., ch. 202 (H.B. 159), § 2, effective September 1, 1975; am. Acts 1981, 67th Leg., ch. 827 (H.B. 1288), § 8, effective August 31, 1981; am. Acts 1983, 68th Leg., ch. 134 (H.B. 176), § 2, effective September 1, 1983; am. Acts 2005, 79th Leg., ch. 801 (S.B. 451), § 3, effective September 1, 2005.)

### Art. 35.17. Voir Dire Examination.

1. When the court in its discretion so directs, except as provided in Section 2, the state and defendant shall conduct the voir dire examination of prospective jurors in the presence of the entire panel.

2. In a capital felony case in which the State seeks the death penalty, the court shall propound to the entire panel of prospective jurors questions concerning the principles, as applicable to the case on trial, of reasonable doubt, burden of proof, return of indictment by grand jury, presumption of innocence, and opinion. Then, on demand of the State or defendant, either is entitled to examine each juror on voir dire individually and apart from the entire panel, and may further question the juror on the principles propounded by the court.

(Enacted by Acts 1965, 59th Leg., ch. 722 (S.B. 107), § 1, effective January 1, 1966; am. Acts

Criminal Procedure

1973, 63rd Leg., ch. 426 (H.B. 200), art. 3, § 5, effective June 14, 1973.)

## Art. 35.18. Other Evidence on Challenge.

Upon a challenge for cause, the examination is not confined to the answers of the juror, but other evidence may be heard for or against the challenge.
(Enacted by Acts 1965, 59th Leg., ch. 722 (S.B. 107), § 1, effective January 1, 1966.)

## Art. 35.19. Absolute Disqualification.

No juror shall be impaneled when it appears that he is subject to the second, third or fourth cause of challenge in Article 35.16, though both parties may consent.
(Enacted by Acts 1965, 59th Leg., ch. 722 (S.B. 107), § 1, effective January 1, 1966; am. Acts 1969, 61st Leg., ch. 412 (S.B. 424), § 4, effective September 1, 1969.)

## Art. 35.20. Names Called in Order.

In selecting the jury from the persons summoned, the names of such persons shall be called in the order in which they appear upon the list furnished the defendant. Each juror shall be tried and passed upon separately. A person who has been summoned, but who is not present, may, upon his appearance before the jury is completed, be tried as to his qualifications and impaneled as a juror, unless challenged, but no cause shall be unreasonably delayed on account of such absence.
(Enacted by Acts 1965, 59th Leg., ch. 722 (S.B. 107), § 1, effective January 1, 1966.)

## Art. 35.21. Judge to Decide Qualifications.

The court is the judge, after proper examination, of the qualifications of a juror, and shall decide all challenges without delay and without argument thereupon.
(Enacted by Acts 1965, 59th Leg., ch. 722 (S.B. 107), § 1, effective January 1, 1966.)

## Art. 35.22. Oath to Jury.

When the jury has been selected, the following oath shall be administered them by the court or under its direction: "You and each of you do solemnly swear that in the case of the State of Texas against the defendant, you will a true verdict render according to the law and the evidence, so help you God".
(Enacted by Acts 1965, 59th Leg., ch. 722 (S.B. 107), § 1, effective January 1, 1966.)

## Art. 35.23. Jurors May Separate.

The court may adjourn veniremen to any day of the term. When jurors have been sworn in a felony case, the court may, at its discretion, permit the jurors to separate until the court has given its charge to the jury. The court on its own motion may and on the motion of either party shall, after having given its charge to the jury, order that the jury not be allowed to separate, after which the jury shall be kept together, and not permitted to separate except to the extent of housing female jurors separate and apart from male jurors, until a verdict has been rendered or the jury finally discharged. Any person who makes known to the jury which party made the motion not to allow separation of the jury shall be punished for contempt of court. If such jurors are kept overnight, facilities shall be provided for female jurors separate and apart from the facilities provided for male jurors. In misdemeanor cases the court may, at its discretion, permit the jurors to separate at any time before the verdict. In any case in which the jury is permitted to separate, the court shall first give the jurors proper instructions with regard to their conduct as jurors when so separated.
(Enacted by Acts 1965, 59th Leg., ch. 722 (S.B. 107), § 1, effective January 1, 1966; am. Acts 1989, 71st Leg., ch. 825 (S.B. 351), § 1, effective September 1, 1989.)

## Art. 35.24. Special Pay for Veniremen [Repealed].

Repealed by Acts 1975, 64th Leg., ch. 510 (H.B. 671), § 2, effective September 1, 1975.

## Art. 35.25. Making Peremptory Challenge.

In non-capital cases and in capital cases in which the State's attorney has announced that he will not qualify the jury for, or seek the death penalty, the party desiring to challenge any juror peremptorily shall strike the name of such juror from the list furnished him by the clerk.
(Enacted by Acts 1965, 59th Leg., ch. 722 (S.B. 107), § 1, effective January 1, 1966.)

## Art. 35.26. Lists Returned to Clerk.

(a) When the parties have made or declined to make their peremptory challenges, they shall deliver their lists to the clerk. Except as provided in Subsection (b) of this section, the clerk shall, if the case be in the district court, call off the first twelve names on the lists that have not been stricken. If the case be in the county court, he shall call off the first six names on the lists that have not been stricken. Those whose names are called shall be the jury.

(b) In a capital case in which the state seeks the death penalty, the court may direct that two alternate jurors be selected and that the first fourteen names not stricken be called off by the clerk. The last two names to be called are the alternate jurors.

(Enacted by Acts 1965, 59th Leg., ch. 722 (S.B. 107), § 1, effective January 1, 1966; am. Acts 1981, 67th Leg., ch. 545 (H.B. 1167), § 1, effective June 12, 1981; am. Acts 1991, 72nd Leg., ch. 652 (S.B. 9), § 7, effective September 1, 1991.)

### Art. 35.261. Peremptory Challenges Based on Race Prohibited.

(a) After the parties have delivered their lists to the clerk under Article 35.26 of this code and before the court has impanelled the jury, the defendant may request the court to dismiss the array and call a new array in the case. The court shall grant the motion of a defendant for dismissal of the array if the court determines that the defendant is a member of an identifiable racial group, that the attorney representing the state exercised peremptory challenges for the purpose of excluding persons from the jury on the basis of their race, and that the defendant has offered evidence of relevant facts that tend to show that challenges made by the attorney representing the state were made for reasons based on race. If the defendant establishes a prima facie case, the burden then shifts to the attorney representing the state to give a racially neutral explanation for the challenges. The burden of persuasion remains with the defendant to establish purposeful discrimination.

(b) If the court determines that the attorney representing the state challenged prospective jurors on the basis of race, the court shall call a new array in the case.

(Enacted by Acts 1987, 70th Leg., ch. 751 (H.B. 65), § 1, effective August 31, 1987.)

### Art. 35.27. Reimbursement of Nonresident Witnesses.

**Sec. 1. Expenses for Nonresident Witnesses.** (a) Every person subpoenaed by either party or otherwise required or requested in writing by the prosecuting attorney or the court to appear for the purpose of giving testimony in a criminal proceeding who resides outside the state or the county in which the prosecution is pending shall be reimbursed by the state for the reasonable and necessary transportation, meal, and lodging expenses he incurs by reason of his attendance as a witness at such proceeding.

(b) The state may reimburse a witness for transportation only if the transportation is provided by a commercial transportation company or the witness uses the witness's personally owned or leased motor vehicle. In this article, "commercial transportation company" means an entity that offers transportation of people or goods to the public in exchange for compensation.

(c) The state may reimburse a witness for lodging only if the lodging is provided by a commercial lodging establishment. In this article, "commercial lodging establishment" means a motel, hotel, inn, apartment, or similar entity that offers lodging to the public in exchange for compensation.

**Sec. 2. Amount of Reimbursement for Expenses.** Any person seeking reimbursement as a witness shall make an affidavit setting out the transportation, meal, and lodging expenses necessitated by his travel to and from and attendance at the place he appeared to give testimony, together with the number of days that such travel and attendance made him absent from his place of residence. A reimbursement paid by the state to a witness for transportation, meal, or lodging expenses may not be paid at a rate that exceeds the maximum rates provided by law for state employees.

**Sec. 2A. Direct Payment of Transportation or Lodging Expenses.** If this article requires the state to reimburse a witness for transportation or lodging expenses, the state may instead directly pay a commercial transportation company or commercial lodging establishment for those expenses.

**Sec. 3. Other Expenses.** In addition to reimbursement or payment for transportation, meal, and lodging expenses, the comptroller, upon proper application by the attorney for the state, shall reimburse or pay the other expenses required by the laws of this state or the state from which the attendance of the witness is sought.

**Sec. 4. Application and Approval by Judge.** A reimbursement to a witness as provided by this article shall be paid by the state to the witness or his assignee. Claim shall be made by sworn application to the comptroller, a copy of which shall be filed with the clerk of the court, setting out the facts showing entitlement as provided in this article to the reimbursement, which application shall be presented for approval by the judge who presided over the court or empaneled the grand jury before whom the criminal proceeding was pending. No fee shall be required of any witness for the processing of his claim for reimbursement.

**Sec. 5. Payment by State.** The Comptroller of Public Accounts, upon receipt of a claim approved by the judge, shall examine it and, if he deems the claim in compliance with and authorized by this Article, draw his warrant on the State Treasury for the amount due the witness, or to any person to which the certificate has been assigned by the witness, but no warrant may issue to any assignee of a witness claim unless the assignment is made under oath and acknowledged before some person authorized to administer oaths, certified to by the officer, and under seal. If the appropriation for paying the account is exhausted, the Comptroller of Public Accounts shall file it away and issue a certificate in the name of the witness entitled to it, stating therein the amount of the claim. Each claim not filed in the office of the Comptroller of Public Accounts within twelve months from the date it became due and payable shall be forever barred.

**Sec. 6. Advance by State.** Funds required to be tendered to an out-of-state witness pursuant to Article 24.28 of this Code shall be paid by the Comptroller of Public Accounts into the registry of the Court in which the case is to be tried upon certification by the Court such funds are necessary to obtain attendance of said witness. The court shall then cause to be issued checks drawn upon the registry of the Court to secure the attendance of such witness. In the event that such funds are not used pursuant to this Act, the Court shall return the funds to the Comptroller of Public Accounts.

**Sec. 7. Advance by County.** The county in which a criminal proceeding is pending, upon request of the district attorney or other prosecutor charged with the duty of prosecution in the proceeding, may advance funds from its treasury to any witness who will be entitled to reimbursement under this article. The amount advanced may not exceed the amount that is reasonably necessary to enable the witness to attend as required or requested. However, the amount advanced may include sums in excess of the reimbursement provided for by this article if the excess is required for compliance with Section 4 of Article 24.28 in securing the attendance of a witness from another state under the Uniform

Act. A county that advances funds to a witness under this section is entitled to reimbursement by the state as an assignee of the witness.

**Sec. 8. Advance for Expenses for Witnesses of Indigent Defendant.** Upon application by a defendant shown to be indigent and a showing to the court of reasonable necessity and materiality for the testimony of a witness residing outside the State, the court shall act pursuant to Section 6 hereof to secure advance of funds necessary for the attendance of such witness.

**Sec. 9. Limitations.** A witness, when attached and conveyed by a sheriff or other officer, is not eligible to receive reimbursement of transportation, meal, or lodging expenses incurred while in the custody of the officer. A court, in its discretion, may limit the number of character witnesses allowed reimbursement under this article to not fewer than two for each defendant and two per defendant for the state.
(Enacted by Acts 1965, 59th Leg., ch. 722 (S.B. 107), § 1, effective January 1, 1966; am. Acts 1973, 63rd Leg., ch. 477 (H.B. 844), § 2, effective August 27, 1973; am. Acts 1979, 66th Leg., ch. 469 (H.B. 875), § 1, effective September 1, 1979; am. Acts 1993, 73rd Leg., ch. 449 (H.B. 1952), § 18, effective September 1, 1993.)

## Art. 35.28. When No Clerk.

In each instance in Article 35.27 in which the clerk of the court is authorized or directed to perform any act, the judge of such court shall perform the same if there is no clerk of the court.
(Enacted by Acts 1965, 59th Leg., ch. 722 (S.B. 107), § 1, effective January 1, 1966.)

## Art. 35.29. Personal Information About Jurors.

Information collected by the court or by a prosecuting attorney during the jury selection process about a person who serves as a juror, including the juror's home address, home telephone number, social security number, driver's license number, and other personal information, is confidential and may not be disclosed by the court, the prosecuting attorney, the defense counsel, or any court personnel except on application by a party in the trial or on application by a bona fide member of the news media acting in such capacity to the court in which the person is serving or did serve as a juror. On a showing of good cause, the court shall permit disclosure of the information sought.
(Enacted by Acts 1993, 73rd Leg., ch. 371 (S.B. 12), § 1, effective September 1, 1993.)

## CHAPTER 36
## THE TRIAL BEFORE THE JURY

## Art. 36.01. Order of Proceeding in Trial.

(a) A jury being impaneled in any criminal action, except as provided by Subsection (b) of this article, the cause shall proceed in the following order:

1. The indictment or information shall be read to the jury by the attorney prosecuting. When prior convictions are alleged for purposes of enhancement only and are not jurisdictional, that portion of the indictment or information reciting such convictions shall not be read until the hearing on punishment is held as provided in Article 37.07.

2. The special pleas, if any, shall be read by the defendant's counsel, and if the plea of not guilty is also relied upon, it shall also be stated.

3. The State's attorney shall state to the jury the nature of the accusation and the facts which are expected to be proved by the State in support thereof.

4. The testimony on the part of the State shall be offered.

5. The nature of the defenses relied upon and the facts expected to be proved in their support shall be stated by defendant's counsel.

6. The testimony on the part of the defendant shall be offered.

7. Rebutting testimony may be offered on the part of each party.

8. In the event of a finding of guilty, the trial shall then proceed as set forth in Article 37.07.

(b) The defendant's counsel may make the opening statement for the defendant immediately after the attorney representing the State makes the opening statement for the State. After the defendant's attorney concludes the defendant's opening statement, the State's testimony shall be offered. At the conclusion of the presentation of the State's testimony, the defendant's testimony shall be offered, and the order of proceedings shall continue in the manner described by Subsection (a) of this article.

(Enacted by Acts 1965, 59th Leg., ch. 722 (S.B. 107), § 1, effective January 1, 1966; am. Acts 1987, 70th Leg., ch. 519 (H.B. 679), § 1, effective September 1, 1987.)

## Art. 36.02. Testimony at Any Time.

The court shall allow testimony to be introduced at any time before the argument of a cause is concluded, if it appears that it is necessary to a due administration of justice.

(Enacted by Acts 1965, 59th Leg., ch. 722 (S.B. 107), § 1, effective January 1, 1966.)

## Art. 36.03. Invocation of Rule.

(a) Notwithstanding Rule 614, Texas Rules of Evidence, a court at the request of a party may order the exclusion of a witness who for the purposes of the prosecution is a victim, close relative of a deceased victim, or guardian of a victim only if the witness is to testify and the court determines that the testimony of the witness would be materially affected if the witness hears other testimony at the trial.

(b) On the objection of the opposing party, the court may require the party requesting exclusion of a witness under Subsection (a) to make an offer of proof to justify the exclusion.

(c) Subsection (a) does not limit the authority of the court on its own motion to exclude a witness or other person to maintain decorum in the courtroom.

(d) In this article:

(1) "Close relative of a deceased victim" and "guardian of a victim" have the meanings assigned by Article 56.01.

(2) "Victim" means a victim of any criminal offense.

(e) At the commencement of a trial, the court shall admonish each witness who is to testify as to those persons whom the court determines the witness may talk to about the case before the trial ends and those persons whom the witness may not talk to about the case. The court may punish as contempt a witness who violates the admonishment provided by the court.

(Enacted by Acts 2001, 77th Leg., ch. 1034 (H.B. 1572), § 1, effective September 1, 2001.)

## Art. 36.04. [Repealed].

Repealed by Texas Court of Criminal Appeals pursuant to Acts 1985, 69th Leg., ch. 685 (H.B. 13), § 9, effective September 1, 1986.

## Art. 36.05. Not to Hear Testimony.

Witnesses under rule shall be attended by an officer, and all their reasonable wants provided for, unless the court, in its discretion, directs that they be allowed to go at large; but in no case where the witnesses are under rule shall they be allowed to hear any testimony in the case.

(Enacted by Acts 1965, 59th Leg., ch. 722 (S.B. 107), § 1, effective January 1, 1966.)

## Art. 36.06. Instructed by the Court.

Witnesses, when placed under rule, shall be instructed by the court that they are not to converse with each other or with any other person about the case, except by permission of the court, and that they are not to read any report of or comment upon the testimony in the case while under rule. The officer who attends the witnesses shall report to the court at once any violation of its instructions, and the party violating the same shall be punished for contempt of court.

(Enacted by Acts 1965, 59th Leg., ch. 722 (S.B. 107), § 1, effective January 1, 1966.)

## Art. 36.07. Order of Argument.

The order of argument may be regulated by the presiding judge; but the State's counsel shall have the right to make the concluding address to the jury.

(Enacted by Acts 1965, 59th Leg., ch. 722 (S.B. 107), § 1, effective January 1, 1966.)

## Art. 36.08. Number of Arguments.

The court shall never restrict the argument in felony cases to a number of addresses less than two on each side.

(Enacted by Acts 1965, 59th Leg., ch. 722 (S.B. 107), § 1, effective January 1, 1966.)

## Art. 36.09. Severance on Separate Indictments.

Two or more defendants who are jointly or separately indicted or complained against for the same offense or any offense growing out of the same transaction may be, in the discretion of the court, tried jointly or separately as to one or more defendants; provided that in any event either defendant may testify for the other or on behalf of the state; and provided further, that in cases in which, upon timely motion to sever, and evidence introduced thereon, it is made known to the court that there is a previous admissible conviction against one defendant or that a joint trial would be prejudicial to any defendant, the court shall order a severance as to the defendant whose joint trial would prejudice the other defendant or defendants.

(Enacted by Acts 1965, 59th Leg., ch. 722 (S.B. 107), § 1, effective January 1, 1966; am. Acts 1967, 60th Leg., ch. 659 (S.B. 145), § 21, effective August 28, 1967.)

## Art. 36.10. Order of Trial.

If a severance is granted, the defendants may agree upon the order in which they are to be tried, but if they fail to agree, the court shall direct the order of the trial.

(Enacted by Acts 1965, 59th Leg., ch. 722 (S.B. 107), § 1, effective January 1, 1966.)

## Art. 36.11. Discharge Before Verdict.

If it appears during a trial that the court has no jurisdiction of the offense, or that the facts charged in the indictment do not constitute an offense, the jury shall be discharged. The accused shall also be discharged, but such discharge shall be no bar in any case to a prosecution before the proper court for any offense unless termination of the former prosecution was improper.

(Enacted by Acts 1965, 59th Leg., ch. 722 (S.B. 107), § 1, effective January 1, 1966; am. Acts 1973, 63rd Leg., ch. 399 (S.B. 34), § 2(A), effective January 1, 1974.)

## Art. 36.12. Court May Commit.

If the want of jurisdiction arises from the fact that the defendant is not liable to prosecution in the county where the indictment was presented, the court may in felony cases order the accused into custody for a reasonable length of time to await a warrant for his arrest from the proper county; or if the offense be bailable, may require him to enter into recognizance to answer before the proper court; in which case a certified copy of the recognizance shall be sent forthwith to the clerk of the proper court, to be enforced by that court in case of forfeiture.

(Enacted by Acts 1965, 59th Leg., ch. 722 (S.B. 107), § 1, effective January 1, 1966.)

## Art. 36.13. Jury Is Judge of Facts.

Unless otherwise provided in this Code, the jury is the exclusive judge of the facts, but it is bound to receive the law from the court and be governed thereby.

(Enacted by Acts 1965, 59th Leg., ch. 722 (S.B. 107), § 1, effective January 1, 1966.)

## Art. 36.14. Charge of Court.

Subject to the provisions of Article 36.07 in each felony case and in each misdemeanor case tried in a court of record, the judge shall, before the argument begins, deliver to the jury, except in pleas of guilty, where a jury has been waived, a written charge distinctly setting forth the law applicable to the case; not expressing any opinion as to the weight of the evidence, not summing up the testimony, discussing the facts or using any argument in his charge calculated to arouse the sympathy or excite the passions of the jury. Before said charge is read to the jury, the defendant or his counsel shall have a reasonable time to examine the same and he shall present his objections thereto in writing, distinctly specifying each ground of objection. Said objections may embody errors claimed to have been committed in the charge, as well as errors claimed to have been committed by omissions therefrom or in failing to charge upon issues arising from the facts, and in no event shall it be necessary for the defendant or his counsel to present special requested charges to preserve or maintain any error assigned to the charge, as herein provided. The requirement that the objections to the court's charge be in writing will be complied with if the objections are dictated to the court reporter in the presence of the court and the state's counsel, before the reading of the court's charge to the jury. Compliance with the provisions of this Article is all that is necessary to preserve, for review, the exceptions and objections presented to the charge and any amendment or modification thereof. In no event shall it be necessary for the defendant to except to the action of the court in over-ruling defendant's exceptions or objections to the charge.

(Enacted by Acts 1965, 59th Leg., ch. 722 (S.B. 107), § 1, effective January 1, 1966; am. Acts 1975, 64th Leg., ch. 253 (H.B. 207), § 1, effective September 1, 1975; am. Acts 1981, 67th Leg., ch. 537 (H.B. 864), § 1, effective June 12, 1981.)

## Art. 36.15. Requested Special Charges.

Before the court reads his charge to the jury, counsel on both sides shall have a reasonable time to present written instructions and ask that they be given to the jury. The requirement that the instructions be in writing is complied with if the instructions are dictated to the court reporter in the presence of the court and the state's counsel, before the reading of the court's charge to the jury. The court shall give or refuse these charges. The defendant may, by a special requested instruction, call the trial court's attention to error in the charge, as well as omissions therefrom, and no other exception or objection to the court's charge shall be necessary to preserve any error reflected by any special requested instruction which the trial court refuses.

Any special requested charge which is granted shall be incorporated in the main charge and shall be treated as a part thereof, and the jury shall not be advised that it is a special requested charge of either party. The judge shall read to the jury only such special charges as he gives.

When the defendant has leveled objections to the charge or has requested instructions or both, and the court thereafter modifies his charge and rewrites the same and in so doing does not respond to objections or requested charges, or any of them, then the objections or requested charges shall not be deemed to have been waived by the party making or requesting the same, but shall be deemed to continue to have been urged by the party making or requesting the same unless the contrary is shown by the record; no exception by the defendant to the action of the court shall be necessary or required in order to preserve for review the error claimed in the charge.

(Enacted by Acts 1965, 59th Leg., ch. 722 (S.B. 107), § 1, effective January 1, 1966; am. Acts 1979, 66th Leg., ch. 525 (S.B. 855), § 1, effective September 1, 1979; am. Acts 1981, 67th Leg., ch. 537 (H.B. 864), § 1, effective June 12, 1981.)

## Art. 36.16. Final Charge.

After the judge shall have received the objections to his main charge, together with any special charges offered, he may make such changes in his main charge as he may deem proper, and

the defendant or his counsel shall have the opportunity to present their objections thereto and in the same manner as is provided in Article 36.15, and thereupon the judge shall read his charge to the jury as finally written, together with any special charges given, and no further exception or objection shall be required of the defendant in order to preserve any objections or exceptions theretofore made. After the argument begins no further charge shall be given to the jury unless required by the improper argument of counsel or the request of the jury, or unless the judge shall, in his discretion, permit the introduction of other testimony, and in the event of such further charge, the defendant or his counsel shall have the right to present objections in the same manner as is prescribed in Article 36.15. The failure of the court to give the defendant or his counsel a reasonable time to examine the charge and specify the ground of objection shall be subject to review either in the trial court or in the appellate court.
(Enacted by Acts 1965, 59th Leg., ch. 722 (S.B. 107), § 1, effective January 1, 1966.)

### Art. 36.17. Charge Certified by Judge.

The general charge given by the court and all special charges given or refused shall be certified by the judge and filed among the papers in the cause.
(Enacted by Acts 1965, 59th Leg., ch. 722 (S.B. 107), § 1, effective January 1, 1966.)

### Art. 36.18. Jury May Take Charge.

The jury may take to their jury room the charges given by the court after the same have been filed. They shall not be permitted to take with them any charge or part thereof which the court has refused to give.
(Enacted by Acts 1965, 59th Leg., ch. 722 (S.B. 107), § 1, effective January 1, 1966.)

### Art. 36.19. Review of Charge on Appeal.

Whenever it appears by the record in any criminal action upon appeal that any requirement of Articles 36.14, 36.15, 36.16, 36.17 and 36.18 has been disregarded, the judgment shall not be reversed unless the error appearing from the record was calculated to injure the rights of defendant, or unless it appears from the record that the defendant has not had a fair and impartial trial. All objections to the charge and to the refusal of special charges shall be made at the time of the trial.

(Enacted by Acts 1965, 59th Leg., ch. 722 (S.B. 107), § 1, effective January 1, 1966.)

### Art. 36.20. [Repealed].

Repealed by Texas Court of Criminal Appeals pursuant to Acts 1985, 69th Leg., ch. 685 (H.B. 13), § 4, effective September 1, 1986.

### Art. 36.21. To Provide Jury Room.

The sheriff shall provide a suitable room for the deliberation of the jury and supply them with such necessary food and lodging as he can obtain. No intoxicating liquor shall be furnished them. In all cases wherein a jury consists partly of male jurors and partly of female jurors, the sheriff shall provide facilities for the female jurors separate and apart from the facilities provided for the male jurors.
(Enacted by Acts 1965, 59th Leg., ch. 722 (S.B. 107), § 1, effective January 1, 1966.)

### Art. 36.215. Recording of Jury Deliberations.

A person may not use any device to produce or make an audio, visual, or audio-visual broadcast, recording, or photograph of a jury while the jury is deliberating.
(Enacted by Acts 2003, 78th Leg., ch. 54 (S.B. 164), § 1, effective September 1, 2003.)

### Art. 36.22. Conversing with Jury.

No person shall be permitted to be with a jury while it is deliberating. No person shall be permitted to converse with a juror about the case on trial except in the presence and by the permission of the court.
(Enacted by Acts 1965, 59th Leg., ch. 722 (S.B. 107), § 1, effective January 1, 1966.)

### Art. 36.23. Violation of Preceding Article.

Any juror or other person violating the preceding Article shall be punished for contempt of court by confinement in jail not to exceed three days or by fine not to exceed one hundred dollars, or by both such fine and imprisonment.
(Enacted by Acts 1965, 59th Leg., ch. 722 (S.B. 107), § 1, effective January 1, 1966.)

### Art. 36.24. Officer Shall Attend Jury.

The sheriff of the county shall furnish the court with a bailiff during the trial of any case to attend the wants of the jury and to act under the direction of the court. If the person furnished by the sheriff is to be called as a witness in the case he may not serve as bailiff.

(Enacted by Acts 1965, 59th Leg., ch. 722 (S.B. 107), § 1, effective January 1, 1966.)

## Art. 36.25. Written Evidence.

There shall be furnished to the jury upon its request any exhibits admitted as evidence in the case.

(Enacted by Acts 1965, 59th Leg., ch. 722 (S.B. 107), § 1, effective January 1, 1966.)

## Art. 36.26. Foreman of Jury.

Each jury shall appoint one of its members foreman.

(Enacted by Acts 1965, 59th Leg., ch. 722 (S.B. 107), § 1, effective January 1, 1966.)

## Art. 36.27. Jury May Communicate with Court.

When the jury wishes to communicate with the court, it shall so notify the sheriff, who shall inform the court thereof. Any communication relative to the cause must be written, prepared by the foreman and shall be submitted to the court through the bailiff. The court shall answer any such communication in writing, and before giving such answer to the jury shall use reasonable diligence to secure the presence of the defendant and his counsel, and shall first submit the question and also submit his answer to the same to the defendant or his counsel or objections and exceptions, in the same manner as any other written instructions are submitted to such counsel, before the court gives such answer to the jury, but if he is unable to secure the presence of the defendant and his counsel, then he shall proceed to answer the same as he deems proper. The written instruction or answer to the communication shall be read in open court unless expressly waived by the defendant.

All such proceedings in felony cases shall be a part of the record and recorded by the court reporter.

(Enacted by Acts 1965, 59th Leg., ch. 722 (S.B. 107), § 1, effective January 1, 1966.)

## Art. 36.28. Jury May Have Witness Re-Examined or Testimony Read.

In the trial of a criminal case in a court of record, if the jury disagree as to the statement of any witness they may, upon applying to the court, have read to them from the court reporter's notes that part of such witness testimony or the partic-ular point in dispute, and no other; but if there be no such reporter, or if his notes cannot be read to the jury, the court may cause such witness to be again brought upon the stand and the judge shall direct him to repeat his testimony as to the point in dispute, and no other, as nearly as he can in the language used on the trial.

(Enacted by Acts 1965, 59th Leg., ch. 722 (S.B. 107), § 1, effective January 1, 1966.)

## Art. 36.29. If a Juror Dies or Becomes Disabled.

(a) Not less than twelve jurors can render and return a verdict in a felony case. It must be concurred in by each juror and signed by the foreman. Except as provided in Subsection (b), however, after the trial of any felony case begins and a juror dies or, as determined by the judge, becomes disabled from sitting at any time before the charge of the court is read to the jury, the remainder of the jury shall have the power to render the verdict; but when the verdict shall be rendered by less than the whole number, it shall be signed by every member of the jury concurring in it.

(b) If alternate jurors have been selected in a capital case in which the state seeks the death penalty and a juror dies or becomes disabled from sitting at any time before the charge of the court is read to the jury, the alternate juror whose name was called first under Article 35.26 of this code shall replace the dead or disabled juror. Likewise, if another juror dies or becomes disabled from sitting before the charge of the court is read to the jury, the other alternate juror shall replace the second juror to die or become disabled.

(c) After the charge of the court is read to the jury, if a juror becomes so sick as to prevent the continuance of the juror's duty and an alternate juror is not available, or if any accident of circumstance occurs to prevent the jury from being kept together under circumstances under which the law or the instructions of the court requires that the jury be kept together, the jury shall be discharged, except that on agreement on the record by the defendant, the defendant's counsel, and the attorney representing the state 11 members of a jury may render a verdict and, if punishment is to be assessed by the jury, assess punishment. If a verdict is rendered by less than the whole number of the jury, each member of the jury shall sign the verdict.

(d) After the jury has rendered a verdict on the guilt or innocence of the defendant and, if applicable, the amount of punishment, the court shall discharge an alternate juror who has not replaced a juror.

(Enacted by Acts 1965, 59th Leg., ch. 722 (S.B. 107), § 1, effective January 1, 1966; am. Acts 1981, 67th Leg., ch. 545 (H.B. 1167), § 2, effective June 12, 1981; am. Acts 1991, 72nd Leg., ch. 652 (H.B. 9), § 8, effective September 1, 1991; am. Acts 1997, 75th Leg., ch. 866 (H.B. 1684), § 1, effective September 1, 1997; am. Acts 2001, 77th Leg., ch. 1000 (H.B. 842), §§ 1, 2, effective September 1, 2001; am. Acts 2007, 80th Leg., ch. 846 (H.B. 1086), § 2, effective September 1, 2007; am. Acts 2009, 81st Leg., ch. 627 (H.B. 1321), § 1, effective September 1, 2009.)

## Art. 36.30. Discharging Jury in Misdemeanor.

If nine of the jury can be kept together in a misdemeanor case in the district court, they shall not be discharged. If more than three of the twelve are discharged, the entire jury shall be discharged.

(Enacted by Acts 1965, 59th Leg., ch. 722 (S.B. 107), § 1, effective January 1, 1966.)

## Art. 36.31. Disagreement of Jury.

After the cause is submitted to the jury, it may be discharged when it cannot agree and both parties consent to its discharge; or the court may in its discretion discharge it where it has been kept together for such time as to render it altogether improbable that it can agree.

(Enacted by Acts 1965, 59th Leg., ch. 722 (S.B. 107), § 1, effective January 1, 1966.)

## Art. 36.32. Receipt of Verdict and Final Adjournment.

During the trial of any case, the term shall be deemed to have been extended until such time as the jury has rendered its verdict or been discharged according to law.

(Enacted by Acts 1965, 59th Leg., ch. 722 (S.B. 107), § 1, effective January 1, 1966.)

## Art. 36.33. Discharge Without Verdict.

When a jury has been discharged, as provided in the four preceding Articles, without having rendered a verdict, the cause may be again tried at the same or another term.

(Enacted by Acts 1965, 59th Leg., ch. 722 (S.B. 107), § 1, effective January 1, 1966.)

# CHAPTER 37
# THE VERDICT

## Art. 37.01. Verdict.

A "verdict" is a written declaration by a jury of its decision of the issue submitted to it in the case.

(Enacted by Acts 1965, 59th Leg., ch. 722 (S.B. 107), § 1, effective January 1, 1966.)

## Art. 37.02. Verdict by Nine Jurors.

In misdemeanor cases in the district court, where one or more jurors have been discharged from serving after the cause has been submitted to them, if all the alternate jurors selected under Article 33.011 of this code have either been seated or discharged, and there be as many as nine of the jurors remaining, those remaining may render and return a verdict; but in such case, the verdict must be signed by each juror rendering it.

(Enacted by Acts 1965, 59th Leg., ch. 722 (S.B. 107), § 1, effective January 1, 1966; am. Acts 1983, 68th Leg., ch. 775 (H.B. 533), § 4, effective August 29, 1983.)

## Art. 37.03. In County Court.

In the county court the verdict must be concurred in by each juror.

(Enacted by Acts 1965, 59th Leg., ch. 722 (S.B. 107), § 1, effective January 1, 1966.)

## Art. 37.04. When Jury Has Agreed.

When the jury agrees upon a verdict, it shall be brought into court by the proper officer; and if it states that it has agreed, the verdict shall be read aloud by the judge, the foreman, or the clerk. If in proper form and no juror dissents therefrom, and neither party requests a poll of the jury, the verdict shall be entered upon the minutes of the court.

(Enacted by Acts 1965, 59th Leg., ch. 722 (S.B. 107), § 1, effective January 1, 1966; am. Acts 1981, 67th Leg., ch. 78 (S.B. 293), § 1, effective April 30, 1981.)

## Art. 37.05. Polling the Jury.

The State or the defendant shall have the right to have the jury polled, which is done by calling separately the name of each juror and asking him if the verdict is his. If all, when asked, answer in the affirmative, the verdict shall be entered upon the minutes; but if any juror answer in the negative, the jury shall retire again to consider its verdict.

(Enacted by Acts 1965, 59th Leg., ch. 722 (S.B. 107), § 1, effective January 1, 1966.)

## Art. 37.06. Presence of Defendant.

In felony cases the defendant must be present when the verdict is read unless his absence is wilful or voluntary. A verdict in a misdemeanor case may be received and read in the absence of the defendant.

(Enacted by Acts 1965, 59th Leg., ch. 722 (S.B. 107), § 1, effective January 1, 1966.)

## Art. 37.07. Verdict Must Be General; Separate Hearing on Proper Punishment.

**Sec. 1.** (a) The verdict in every criminal action must be general. When there are special pleas on which a jury is to find they must say in their verdict that the allegations in such pleas are true or untrue.

(b) If the plea is not guilty, they must find that the defendant is either guilty or not guilty, and, except as provided in Section 2, they shall assess the punishment in all cases where the same is not absolutely fixed by law to some particular penalty.

(c) If the charging instrument contains more than one count or if two or more offenses are consolidated for trial pursuant to Chapter 3 of the Penal Code, the jury shall be instructed to return a finding of guilty or not guilty in a separate verdict as to each count and offense submitted to them.

**Sec. 2.** (a) In all criminal cases, other than misdemeanor cases of which the justice court or

municipal court has jurisdiction, which are tried before a jury on a plea of not guilty, the judge shall, before argument begins, first submit to the jury the issue of guilt or innocence of the defendant of the offense or offenses charged, without authorizing the jury to pass upon the punishment to be imposed. If the jury fails to agree on the issue of guilt or innocence, the judge shall declare a mistrial and discharge the jury, and jeopardy does not attach in the case.

(b) Except as provided by Article 37.071 or 37.072, if a finding of guilty is returned, it shall then be the responsibility of the judge to assess the punishment applicable to the offense; provided, however, that (1) in any criminal action where the jury may recommend community supervision and the defendant filed his sworn motion for community supervision before the trial began, and (2) in other cases where the defendant so elects in writing before the commencement of the voir dire examination of the jury panel, the punishment shall be assessed by the same jury, except as provided in Section 3(c) of this article and in Article 44.29. If a finding of guilty is returned, the defendant may, with the consent of the attorney for the state, change his election of one who assesses the punishment.

(c) Punishment shall be assessed on each count on which a finding of guilty has been returned.

**Sec. 3. Evidence of prior criminal record in all criminal cases after a finding of guilty.** (a)(1) Regardless of the plea and whether the punishment be assessed by the judge or the jury, evidence may be offered by the state and the defendant as to any matter the court deems relevant to sentencing, including but not limited to the prior criminal record of the defendant, his general reputation, his character, an opinion regarding his character, the circumstances of the offense for which he is being tried, and, notwithstanding Rules 404 and 405, Texas Rules of Evidence, any other evidence of an extraneous crime or bad act that is shown beyond a reasonable doubt by evidence to have been committed by the defendant or for which he could be held criminally responsible, regardless of whether he has previously been charged with or finally convicted of the crime or act. A court may consider as a factor in mitigating punishment the conduct of a defendant while participating in a program under Chapter 17 as a condition of release on bail. Additionally, notwithstanding Rule 609(d), Texas Rules of Evidence, and subject to Subsection (h), evidence may be offered by the state and the defendant of an adjudication of delinquency based on a violation by the defendant of a penal law of the grade of:

(A) a felony; or

(B) a misdemeanor punishable by confinement in jail.

(2) Notwithstanding Subdivision (1), evidence may not be offered by the state to establish that the race or ethnicity of the defendant makes it likely that the defendant will engage in future criminal conduct.

(3) Regardless of the plea and whether the punishment is assessed by the judge or the jury, during the punishment phase of the trial of an offense under Section 35A.02, Penal Code, subject to the applicable rules of evidence, the state and the defendant may offer evidence not offered during the guilt or innocence phase of the trial concerning the total pecuniary loss to the Medicaid program caused by the defendant's conduct or, if applicable, the scheme or continuing course of conduct of which the defendant's conduct is part. Subject to the applicable rules of evidence, an employee of the Health and Human Services Commission's office of inspector general or the office of attorney general's Medicaid fraud control unit may testify concerning the total pecuniary loss to the Medicaid program. An employee who testifies under this subdivision is subject to cross-examination. Evidence offered under this subdivision may be considered by the judge or jury in ordering or recommending the amount of any restitution to be made to the Medicaid program or the appropriate punishment for the defendant.

(b) After the introduction of such evidence has been concluded, and if the jury has the responsibility of assessing the punishment, the court shall give such additional written instructions as may be necessary and the order of procedure and the rules governing the conduct of the trial shall be the same as are applicable on the issue of guilt or innocence.

(c) If the jury finds the defendant guilty and the matter of punishment is referred to the jury, the verdict shall not be complete until a jury verdict has been rendered on both the guilt or innocence of the defendant and the amount of punishment. In the event the jury shall fail to agree on the issue of punishment, a mistrial shall be declared only in the punishment phase of the trial, the jury shall be discharged, and no jeopardy shall attach. The court shall impanel another jury as soon as practicable to determine the issue of punishment.

(d) When the judge assesses the punishment, he may order an investigative report as contemplated in Section 9 of Article 42.12 of this code and after considering the report, and after the hearing of the evidence hereinabove provided for, he shall forthwith announce his decision in open court as to the punishment to be assessed.

(e) Nothing herein contained shall be construed as affecting the admissibility of extraneous offenses on the question of guilt or innocence.

(f) In cases in which the matter of punishment is referred to a jury, either party may offer into evidence the availability of community corrections facilities serving the jurisdiction in which the offense was committed.

(g) On timely request of the defendant, notice of intent to introduce evidence under this article shall be given in the same manner required by Rule 404(b), Texas Rules of Evidence. If the attorney representing the state intends to introduce an extraneous crime or bad act that has not resulted in a final conviction in a court of record or a probated or suspended sentence, notice of that intent is reasonable only if the notice includes the date on which and the county in which the alleged crime or bad act occurred and the name of the alleged victim of the crime or bad act. The requirement under this subsection that the attorney representing the state give notice applies only if the defendant makes a timely request to the attorney representing the state for the notice.

(h) Regardless of whether the punishment will be assessed by the judge or the jury, neither the state nor the defendant may offer before sentencing evidence that the defendant plans to undergo an orchiectomy.

(i) Evidence of an adjudication for conduct that is a violation of a penal law of the grade of misdemeanor punishable by confinement in jail is admissible only if the conduct upon which the adjudication is based occurred on or after January 1, 1996.

**Sec. 4.** (a) In the penalty phase of the trial of a felony case in which the punishment is to be assessed by the jury rather than the court, if the offense of which the jury has found the defendant guilty is listed in Section 3g(a)(1), Article 42.12, of this code or if the judgment contains an affirmative finding under Section 3g(a)(2), Article 42.12, of this code, unless the defendant has been convicted of an offense under Section 21.02, Penal Code, an offense under Section 22.021, Penal Code, that is punishable under Subsection (f) of that section, or a capital felony, the court shall charge the jury in writing as follows:

"Under the law applicable in this case, the defendant, if sentenced to a term of imprisonment, may earn time off the period of incarceration imposed through the award of good conduct time. Prison authorities may award good conduct time to a prisoner who exhibits good behavior, diligence in carrying out prison work assignments, and attempts at rehabilitation. If a prisoner engages in misconduct, prison authorities may also take away all or part of any good conduct time earned by the prisoner.

"It is also possible that the length of time for which the defendant will be imprisoned might be reduced by the award of parole.

"Under the law applicable in this case, if the defendant is sentenced to a term of imprisonment, he will not become eligible for parole until the actual time served equals one-half of the sentence imposed or 30 years, whichever is less, without consideration of any good conduct time he may earn. If the defendant is sentenced to a term of less than four years, he must serve at least two years before he is eligible for parole. Eligibility for parole does not guarantee that parole will be granted.

"It cannot accurately be predicted how the parole law and good conduct time might be applied to this defendant if he is sentenced to a term of imprisonment, because the application of these laws will depend on decisions made by prison and parole authorities.

"You may consider the existence of the parole law and good conduct time. However, you are not to consider the extent to which good conduct time may be awarded to or forfeited by this particular defendant. You are not to consider the manner in which the parole law may be applied to this particular defendant."

(b) In the penalty phase of the trial of a felony case in which the punishment is to be assessed by the jury rather than the court, if the offense is punishable as a felony of the first degree, if a prior conviction has been alleged for enhancement of punishment as provided by Section 12.42(b), (c)(1) or (2), or (d), Penal Code, or if the offense is a felony not designated as a capital felony or a felony of the first, second, or third degree and the maximum term of imprisonment that may be imposed for the offense is longer than 60 years, unless the offense of which the jury has found the defendant guilty is an offense that is punishable under Section 21.02(h), Penal Code, or is listed in Section 3g(a)(1), Article 42.12, of

this code or the judgment contains an affirmative finding under Section 3g(a)(2), Article 42.12, of this code, the court shall charge the jury in writing as follows:

"Under the law applicable in this case, the defendant, if sentenced to a term of imprisonment, may earn time off the period of incarceration imposed through the award of good conduct time. Prison authorities may award good conduct time to a prisoner who exhibits good behavior, diligence in carrying out prison work assignments, and attempts at rehabilitation. If a prisoner engages in misconduct, prison authorities may also take away all or part of any good conduct time earned by the prisoner.

"It is also possible that the length of time for which the defendant will be imprisoned might be reduced by the award of parole.

"Under the law applicable in this case, if the defendant is sentenced to a term of imprisonment, he will not become eligible for parole until the actual time served plus any good conduct time earned equals one-fourth of the sentence imposed or 15 years, whichever is less. Eligibility for parole does not guarantee that parole will be granted.

"It cannot accurately be predicted how the parole law and good conduct time might be applied to this defendant if he is sentenced to a term of imprisonment, because the application of these laws will depend on decisions made by prison and parole authorities.

"You may consider the existence of the parole law and good conduct time. However, you are not to consider the extent to which good conduct time may be awarded to or forfeited by this particular defendant. You are not to consider the manner in which the parole law may be applied to this particular defendant."

(c) In the penalty phase of the trial of a felony case in which the punishment is to be assessed by the jury rather than the court, if the offense is punishable as a felony of the second or third degree, if a prior conviction has been alleged for enhancement as provided by Section 12.42(a), Penal Code, or if the offense is a felony not designated as a capital felony or a felony of the first, second, or third degree and the maximum term of imprisonment that may be imposed for the offense is 60 years or less, unless the offense of which the jury has found the defendant guilty is listed in Section 3g(a)(1), Article 42.12, of this code or the judgment contains an affirmative finding under Section 3g(a)(2), Article 42.12, of

**Criminal Procedure**

this code, the court shall charge the jury in writing as follows:

"Under the law applicable in this case, the defendant, if sentenced to a term of imprisonment, may earn time off the period of incarceration imposed through the award of good conduct time. Prison authorities may award good conduct time to a prisoner who exhibits good behavior, diligence in carrying out prison work assignments, and attempts at rehabilitation. If a prisoner engages in misconduct, prison authorities may also take away all or part of any good conduct time earned by the prisoner.

"It is also possible that the length of time for which the defendant will be imprisoned might be reduced by the award of parole.

"Under the law applicable in this case, if the defendant is sentenced to a term of imprisonment, he will not become eligible for parole until the actual time served plus any good conduct time earned equals one-fourth of the sentence imposed. Eligibility for parole does not guarantee that parole will be granted.

"It cannot accurately be predicted how the parole law and good conduct time might be applied to this defendant if he is sentenced to a term of imprisonment, because the application of these laws will depend on decisions made by prison and parole authorities.

"You may consider the existence of the parole law and good conduct time. However, you are not to consider the extent to which good conduct time may be awarded to or forfeited by this particular defendant. You are not to consider the manner in which the parole law may be applied to this particular defendant."

(d) This section does not permit the introduction of evidence on the operation of parole and good conduct time laws.

(Enacted by Acts 1965, 59th Leg., ch. 722 (S.B. 107), § 1, effective January 1, 1966; am. Acts 1967, 60th Leg., ch. 659 (S.B. 145), § 22, effective August 28, 1967; am. Acts 1973, 63rd Leg., ch. 399 (S.B. 34), § 2(A), effective January 1, 1974; am. Acts 1973, 63rd Leg., ch. 426 (H.B. 200), art. 3, § 2, effective June 14, 1973; am. Acts 1981, 67th Leg., ch. 639 (H.B. 2107), § 1, effective September 1, 1981; am. Acts 1985, 69th Leg., ch. 291 (S.B. 148), § 1, effective September 1, 1985; am. Acts 1985, 69th Leg., ch. 576 (S.B. 37), § 1, effective September 1, 1985; am. Acts 1985, 69th Leg., ch. 685 (H.B. 13), § 8(b), effective August 26, 1985; am. Acts 1987, 70th Leg., ch. 66 (H.B. 475), § 1, effective May 6, 1987; am. Acts 1987, 70th Leg., ch. 179 (S.B. 43), § 2, effective August

31, 1987; am. Acts 1987, 70th Leg., ch. 385 (H.B. 682), § 19, effective September 1, 1987; am. Acts 1987, 70th Leg., ch. 386 (H.B. 683), § 1, effective September 1, 1987; am. Acts 1987, 70th Leg., ch. 1101 (S.B. 341), § 15, effective September 1, 1987; am. Acts 1989, 71st Leg., ch. 103 (S.B. 54), § 1; am. Acts 1989 71st Leg., ch. 785 (H.B. 2335), § 4.04, effective September 1, 1989; am. Acts 1990 71st Leg., 6th C.S., ch. 25 (S.B. 41), § 30, effective June 18, 1990; am. Acts 1993, 73rd Leg., ch. 900 (S.B. 1067), §§ 5.01, 5.02, 5.05, 5.06, effective September 1, 1993; am. Acts 1995, 74th Leg., ch. 262 (H.B. 327), § 82, effective January 1, 1996; am. Acts 1997, 75th Leg., ch. 144 (S.B. 123), § 2, effective May 20, 1997; am. Acts 1997, 75th Leg., ch. 1086 (H.B. 1550), § 31, effective September 1, 1997; am. Acts 1999, 76th Leg., ch. 62 (S.B. 1368), § 19.01(7), effective September 1, 1999; am. Acts 2001, 77th Leg., ch. 585 (S.B. 133), § 1, effective September 1, 2001; am. Acts 2005, 79th Leg., ch. 660 (H.B. 3265), §§ 1, 2, effective September 1, 2005; am. Acts 2005, 79th Leg., ch. 728 (H.B. 2018), § 4.003, effective September 1, 2005; am. Acts 2007, 80th Leg., ch. 593 (H.B. 8), §§ 3.14, 3.15, effective September 1, 2007; am. Acts 2011, 82nd Leg., ch. 620 (S.B. 688), § 3, effective September 1, 2011.)

## Art. 37.071. Procedure in Capital Case.

Sec. 1. If a defendant is found guilty in a capital felony case in which the state does not seek the death penalty, the judge shall sentence the defendant to life imprisonment without parole.

Sec. 2. (a)(1) If a defendant is tried for a capital offense in which the state seeks the death penalty, on a finding that the defendant is guilty of a capital offense, the court shall conduct a separate sentencing proceeding to determine whether the defendant shall be sentenced to death or life imprisonment without parole. The proceeding shall be conducted in the trial court and, except as provided by Article 44.29(c) of this code, before the trial jury as soon as practicable. In the proceeding, evidence may be presented by the state and the defendant or the defendant's counsel as to any matter that the court deems relevant to sentence, including evidence of the defendant's background or character or the circumstances of the offense that mitigates against the imposition of the death penalty. This subdivision shall not be construed to authorize the introduction of any evidence secured in violation of the Constitution of the United States or of the State of Texas. The state and the defendant or the defendant's counsel shall be permitted to present argument for or against sentence of death. The introduction of evidence of extraneous conduct is governed by the notice requirements of Section 3(g), Article 37.07. The court, the attorney representing the state, the defendant, or the defendant's counsel may not inform a juror or a prospective juror of the effect of a failure of a jury to agree on issues submitted under Subsection (c) or (e).

(2) Notwithstanding Subdivision (1), evidence may not be offered by the state to establish that the race or ethnicity of the defendant makes it likely that the defendant will engage in future criminal conduct.

(b) On conclusion of the presentation of the evidence, the court shall submit the following issues to the jury:

(1) whether there is a probability that the defendant would commit criminal acts of violence that would constitute a continuing threat to society; and

(2) in cases in which the jury charge at the guilt or innocence stage permitted the jury to find the defendant guilty as a party under Sections 7.01 and 7.02, Penal Code, whether the defendant actually caused the death of the deceased or did not actually cause the death of the deceased but intended to kill the deceased or another or anticipated that a human life would be taken.

(c) The state must prove each issue submitted under Subsection (b) of this article beyond a reasonable doubt, and the jury shall return a special verdict of "yes" or "no" on each issue submitted under Subsection (b) of this Article.

(d) The court shall charge the jury that:

(1) in deliberating on the issues submitted under Subsection (b) of this article, it shall consider all evidence admitted at the guilt or innocence stage and the punishment stage, including evidence of the defendant's background or character or the circumstances of the offense that militates for or mitigates against the imposition of the death penalty;

(2) it may not answer any issue submitted under Subsection (b) of this article "yes" unless it agrees unanimously and it may not answer any issue "no" unless 10 or more jurors agree; and

(3) members of the jury need not agree on what particular evidence supports a negative answer to any issue submitted under Subsection (b) of this article.

(e) (1) The court shall instruct the jury that if the jury returns an affirmative finding to

each issue submitted under Subsection (b), it shall answer the following issue:

Whether, taking into consideration all of the evidence, including the circumstances of the offense, the defendant's character and background, and the personal moral culpability of the defendant, there is a sufficient mitigating circumstance or circumstances to warrant that a sentence of life imprisonment without parole rather than a death sentence be imposed.

(2) The court shall:

(A) instruct the jury that if the jury answers that a circumstance or circumstances warrant that a sentence of life imprisonment without parole rather than a death sentence be imposed, the court will sentence the defendant to imprisonment in the Texas Department of Criminal Justice for life without parole; and

(B) charge the jury that a defendant sentenced to confinement for life without parole under this article is ineligible for release from the department on parole.

(f) The court shall charge the jury that in answering the issue submitted under Subsection (e) of this article, the jury:

(1) shall answer the issue "yes" or "no";

(2) may not answer the issue "no" unless it agrees unanimously and may not answer the issue "yes" unless 10 or more jurors agree;

(3) need not agree on what particular evidence supports an affirmative finding on the issue; and

(4) shall consider mitigating evidence to be evidence that a juror might regard as reducing the defendant's moral blameworthiness.

(g) If the jury returns an affirmative finding on each issue submitted under Subsection (b) and a negative finding on an issue submitted under Subsection (e)(1), the court shall sentence the defendant to death. If the jury returns a negative finding on any issue submitted under Subsection (b) or an affirmative finding on an issue submitted under Subsection (e)(1) or is unable to answer any issue submitted under Subsection (b) or (e), the court shall sentence the defendant to confinement in the Texas Department of Criminal Justice for life imprisonment without parole.

(h) The judgment of conviction and sentence of death shall be subject to automatic review by the Court of Criminal Appeals.

(i) This article applies to the sentencing procedure in a capital case for an offense that is committed on or after September 1, 1991. For the purposes of this section, an offense is committed on or after September 1, 1991, if any element of that offense occurs on or after that date.

(Enacted by Acts 1973, 63rd Leg., ch. 426 (H.B. 200), art. 3, § 1, effective June 14, 1973; am. Acts 1981, 67th Leg., ch. 725 (H.B. 1164), § 1, effective August 31, 1981; am. Acts 1985, 69th Leg., ch. 44 (H.B. 8), § 2, effective September 1, 1985; am. Acts 1991, 72nd Leg., ch. 562 (H.B. 2411), § 9, effective September 1, 1991; am. Acts 1991 72nd Leg., ch. 838 (S.B. 880), § 1, effective September 1, 1991; am. Acts 1993, 73rd Leg., ch. 781 (H.B. 798), § 1, effective August 30, 1993; am. Acts 1999, 76th Leg., ch. 140 (S.B. 39), § 1, effective September 1, 1999; am. Acts 2001, 77th Leg., ch. 585 (S.B. 133), § 2, effective September 1, 2001; am. Acts 2005, 79th Leg., ch. 399 (S.B. 1507), § 1, effective September 1, 2005; am. Acts 2005, 79th Leg., ch. 787 (S.B. 60), §§ 6—9, effective September 1, 2005; am. Acts 2009, 81st Leg., ch. 87 (S.B. 1969), §§ 25.015, 25.016, effective September 1, 2009.)

## Art. 37.0711. Procedure in Capital Case for Offense Committed Before September 1, 1991.

Sec. 1. This article applies to the sentencing procedure in a capital case for an offense that is committed before September 1, 1991, whether the sentencing procedure is part of the original trial of the offense, an award of a new trial for both the guilt or innocence stage and the punishment stage of the trial, or an award of a new trial only for the punishment stage of the trial. For the purposes of this section, an offense is committed before September 1, 1991, if every element of the offense occurs before that date.

Sec. 2. If a defendant is found guilty in a case in which the state does not seek the death penalty, the judge shall sentence the defendant to life imprisonment.

Sec. 3. (a)(1) If a defendant is tried for a capital offense in which the state seeks the death penalty, on a finding that the defendant is guilty of a capital offense, the court shall conduct a separate sentencing proceeding to determine whether the defendant shall be sentenced to death or life imprisonment. The proceeding shall be conducted in the trial court and, except as provided by Article 44.29(c) of this code, before the trial jury

as soon as practicable. In the proceeding, evidence may be presented as to any matter that the court deems relevant to sentence. This subdivision shall not be construed to authorize the introduction of any evidence secured in violation of the Constitution of the United States or of this state. The state and the defendant or the defendant's counsel shall be permitted to present argument for or against sentence of death.

(2) Notwithstanding Subdivision (1), evidence may not be offered by the state to establish that the race or ethnicity of the defendant makes it likely that the defendant will engage in future criminal conduct.

(b) On conclusion of the presentation of the evidence, the court shall submit the following three issues to the jury:

(1) whether the conduct of the defendant that caused the death of the deceased was committed deliberately and with the reasonable expectation that the death of the deceased or another would result;

(2) whether there is a probability that the defendant would commit criminal acts of violence that would constitute a continuing threat to society; and

(3) if raised by the evidence, whether the conduct of the defendant in killing the deceased was unreasonable in response to the provocation, if any, by the deceased.

(c) The state must prove each issue submitted under Subsection (b) of this section beyond a reasonable doubt, and the jury shall return a special verdict of "yes" or "no" on each issue submitted.

(d) The court shall charge the jury that:

(1) it may not answer any issue submitted under Subsection (b) of this section "yes" unless it agrees unanimously; and

(2) it may not answer any issue submitted under Subsection (b) of this section "no" unless 10 or more jurors agree.

(e) The court shall instruct the jury that if the jury returns an affirmative finding on each issue submitted under Subsection (b) of this section, it shall answer the following issue:

Whether, taking into consideration all of the evidence, including the circumstances of the offense, the defendant's character and background, and the personal moral culpability of the defendant, there is a sufficient mitigating circumstance or circumstances to warrant that a sentence of life imprisonment rather than a death sentence be imposed.

(f) The court shall charge the jury that, in answering the issue submitted under Subsection (e) of this section, the jury:

(1) shall answer the issue "yes" or "no";

(2) may not answer the issue "no" unless it agrees unanimously and may not answer the issue "yes" unless 10 or more jurors agree; and

(3) shall consider mitigating evidence that a juror might regard as reducing the defendant's moral blameworthiness.

(g) If the jury returns an affirmative finding on each issue submitted under Subsection (b) and a negative finding on the issue submitted under Subsection (e), the court shall sentence the defendant to death. If the jury returns a negative finding on any issue submitted under Subsection (b) or an affirmative finding on the issue submitted under Subsection (e) or is unable to answer any issue submitted under Subsection (b) or (e), the court shall sentence the defendant to confinement in the Texas Department of Criminal Justice for life.

(h) If a defendant is convicted of an offense under Section 19.03(a)(7), Penal Code, the court shall submit the issues under Subsections (b) and (e) of this section only with regard to the conduct of the defendant in murdering the deceased individual first named in the indictment.

(i) The court, the attorney for the state, or the attorney for the defendant may not inform a juror or prospective juror of the effect of failure of the jury to agree on an issue submitted under this article.

(j) The Court of Criminal Appeals shall automatically review a judgment of conviction and sentence of death not later than the 60th day after the date of certification by the sentencing court of the entire record, unless the Court of Criminal Appeals extends the time for an additional period not to exceed 30 days for good cause shown. Automatic review under this subsection has priority over all other cases before the Court of Criminal Appeals, and the court shall hear automatic reviews under rules adopted by the court for that purpose.

(Enacted by Acts 1993, 73rd Leg., ch. 781 (H.B. 798), § 2, effective August 30, 1993; am. Acts 1995, 74th Leg., ch. 76 (S.B. 959), § 14.22, effective September 1, 1995; am. Acts 2001, 77th Leg., ch. 585 (S.B. 133), § 3, effective September 1, 2001; am. Acts 2009, 81st Leg., ch. 87 (S.B. 1969), § 25.017, effective September 1, 2009.)

## Art. 37.072. Procedure in Repeat Sex Offender Capital Case.

Sec. 1. If a defendant is found guilty in a capital felony case punishable under Section 12.42(c)(3), Penal Code, in which the state does not seek the death penalty, the judge shall sentence the defendant to life imprisonment without parole.

Sec. 2. (a) (1) If a defendant is tried for an offense punishable under Section 12.42(c)(3), Penal Code, in which the state seeks the death penalty, on a finding that the defendant is guilty of a capital offense, the court shall conduct a separate sentencing proceeding to determine whether the defendant shall be sentenced to death or life imprisonment without parole. The proceeding shall be conducted in the trial court and, except as provided by Article 44.29(d) of this code, before the trial jury as soon as practicable. In the proceeding, evidence may be presented by the state and the defendant or the defendant's counsel as to any matter that the court considers relevant to sentence, including evidence of the defendant's background or character or the circumstances of the offense that mitigates against the imposition of the death penalty. This subdivision may not be construed to authorize the introduction of any evidence secured in violation of the Constitution of the United States or of the State of Texas. The state and the defendant or the defendant's counsel shall be permitted to present argument for or against sentence of death. The introduction of evidence of extraneous conduct is governed by the notice requirements of Section 3(g), Article 37.07. The court, the attorney representing the state, the defendant, or the defendant's counsel may not inform a juror or a prospective juror of the effect of a failure of a jury to agree on issues submitted under Subsection (b) or (e).

(2) Notwithstanding Subdivision (1), evidence may not be offered by the state to establish that the race or ethnicity of the defendant makes it likely that the defendant will engage in future criminal conduct.

(b) On conclusion of the presentation of the evidence, the court shall submit the following issues to the jury:

(1) whether there is a probability that the defendant would commit criminal acts of violence that would constitute a continuing threat to society; and

(2) in cases in which the jury charge at the guilt or innocence stage permitted the jury to find the defendant guilty as a party under Sections 7.01 and 7.02, Penal Code, whether the defendant actually engaged in the conduct prohibited by Section 22.021, Penal Code, or did not actually engage in the conduct prohibited by Section 22.021, Penal Code, but intended that the offense be committed against the victim or another intended victim.

(c) The state must prove beyond a reasonable doubt each issue submitted under Subsection (b) of this section, and the jury shall return a special verdict of "yes" or "no" on each issue submitted under Subsection (b) of this section.

(d) The court shall charge the jury that:

(1) in deliberating on the issues submitted under Subsection (b) of this section, it shall consider all evidence admitted at the guilt or innocence stage and the punishment stage, including evidence of the defendant's background or character or the circumstances of the offense that militates for or mitigates against the imposition of the death penalty;

(2) it may not answer any issue submitted under Subsection (b) of this section "yes" unless it agrees unanimously and it may not answer any issue "no" unless 10 or more jurors agree; and

(3) members of the jury need not agree on what particular evidence supports a negative answer to any issue submitted under Subsection (b) of this section.

(e) (1) The court shall instruct the jury that if the jury returns an affirmative finding to each issue submitted under Subsection (b), it shall answer the following issue:

Whether, taking into consideration all of the evidence, including the circumstances of the offense, the defendant's character and background, and the personal moral culpability of the defendant, there is a sufficient mitigating circumstance or circumstances to warrant that a sentence of life imprisonment without parole rather than a death sentence be imposed.

(2) The court shall:

(A) instruct the jury that if the jury answers that a circumstance or circumstances warrant that a sentence of life imprisonment without parole rather than a death sentence be imposed, the court will sentence the defendant to imprisonment in the Texas Department of Criminal Justice for life without parole; and

(B) charge the jury that a defendant sentenced to confinement for life without parole under this article is ineligible for release from the department on parole.

(f) The court shall charge the jury that in answering the issue submitted under Subsection (e) of this section, the jury:

(1) shall answer the issue "yes" or "no";

(2) may not answer the issue "no" unless it agrees unanimously and may not answer the issue "yes" unless 10 or more jurors agree;

(3) need not agree on what particular evidence supports an affirmative finding on the issue; and

(4) shall consider mitigating evidence to be evidence that a juror might regard as reducing the defendant's moral blameworthiness.

(g) If the jury returns an affirmative finding on each issue submitted under Subsection (b) and a negative finding on an issue submitted under Subsection (e)(1), the court shall sentence the defendant to death. If the jury returns a negative finding on any issue submitted under Subsection (b) or an affirmative finding on an issue submitted under Subsection (e)(1) or is unable to answer any issue submitted under Subsection (b) or (e), the court shall sentence the defendant to imprisonment in the Texas Department of Criminal Justice for life without parole.

(h) The judgment of conviction and sentence of death shall be subject to automatic review by the Court of Criminal Appeals.

(Enacted by Acts 2007, 80th Leg., ch. 593 (H.B. 8), § 1.04, effective September 1, 2007.)

## Art. 37.073. Repayment of Rewards.

(a) After a defendant has been convicted of a felony offense, the judge may order a defendant to repay all or part of a reward paid by a crime stoppers organization.

(b) In determining whether the defendant must repay the reward or part of the reward, the court shall consider:

(1) the ability of the defendant to make the payment and the financial hardship on the defendant to make the required payment; and

(2) the importance of the information to the prosecution of the defendant as provided by the arresting officer or the attorney for the state with due regard for the confidentiality of the crime stoppers organization records.

(c) In this article, "crime stoppers organization" means a crime stoppers organization, as

defined by Subdivision (2), Section 414.001, Government Code, that is approved by the Texas Crime Stoppers Council to receive payments of rewards under this article and Article 42.152.
(Enacted by Acts 1989, 71st Leg., ch. 611 (S.B. 611), § 1, effective September 1, 1989; am. Acts 1991, 72nd Leg., ch. 16 (S.B. 232), § 19.01(5), effective August 26, 1991 (renumbered from art. 37.072); am. Acts 1997, 75th Leg., ch. 700 (S.B. 1546), § 10, effective September 1, 1997; am. Acts 2009, 81st Leg., ch. 168 (H.B. 590), § 4, effective May 27, 2009.)

## Art. 37.08. Conviction of Lesser Included Offense.

In a prosecution for an offense with lesser included offenses, the jury may find the defendant not guilty of the greater offense, but guilty of any lesser included offense.
(Enacted by Acts 1965, 59th Leg., ch. 722 (S.B. 107), § 1, effective January 1, 1966; am. Acts 1973, 63rd Leg., ch. 399 (S.B. 34), § 2(A), effective January 1, 1974.)

## Art. 37.09. Lesser Included Offense.

An offense is a lesser included offense if:

(1) it is established by proof of the same or less than all the facts required to establish the commission of the offense charged;

(2) it differs from the offense charged only in the respect that a less serious injury or risk of injury to the same person, property, or public interest suffices to establish its commission;

(3) it differs from the offense charged only in the respect that a less culpable mental state suffices to establish its commission; or

(4) it consists of an attempt to commit the offense charged or an otherwise included offense.
(Enacted by Acts 1965, 59th Leg., ch. 722 (S.B. 107), § 1, effective January 1, 1966; am. Acts 1973, 63rd Leg., ch. 399 (S.B. 34), § 2(A), effective January 1, 1974.)

## Art. 37.10. Informal Verdict.

(a) If the verdict of the jury is informal, its attention shall be called to it, and with its consent the verdict may, under the direction of the court, be reduced to the proper form. If the jury refuses to have the verdict altered, it shall again retire to its room to deliberate, unless it manifestly appear that the verdict is intended as an acquittal; and in that case, the judgment shall be rendered accordingly, discharging the defendant.

(b) If the jury assesses punishment in a case and in the verdict assesses both punishment that is authorized by law for the offense and punishment that is not authorized by law for the offense, the court shall reform the verdict to show the punishment authorized by law and to omit the punishment not authorized by law. If the trial court is required to reform a verdict under this subsection and fails to do so, the appellate court shall reform the verdict as provided by this subsection.
(Enacted by Acts 1965, 59th Leg., ch. 722 (S.B. 107), § 1, effective January 1, 1966; am. Acts 1985, 69th Leg., ch. 442 (S.B. 1349), § 1, effective June 11, 1985.)

## Art. 37.11. Defendants Tried Jointly.

Where several defendants are tried together, the jury may convict each defendant it finds guilty and acquit others. If it agrees to a verdict as to one or more, it may find a verdict in accordance with such agreement, and if it cannot agree as to others, a mistrial may be entered as to them.
(Enacted by Acts 1965, 59th Leg., ch. 722 (S.B. 107), § 1, effective January 1, 1966.)

## Art. 37.12. Judgment on Verdict.

On each verdict of acquittal or conviction, the proper judgment shall be entered immediately. If acquitted, the defendant shall be at once discharged from all further liability upon the charge for which he was tried; provided that, in misdemeanor cases where there is returned a verdict, or a plea of guilty is entered and the punishment assessed is by fine only, the court may, on written request of the defendant and for good cause shown, defer judgment until some other day fixed by order of the court; but in no event shall the judgment be deferred for a longer period of time than six months. On expiration of the time fixed by the order of the court, the court or judge thereof, shall enter judgment on the verdict or plea and the same shall be executed as provided by Chapter 43 of this Code. Provided further, that the court or judge thereof, in the exercise of sound discretion may permit the defendant where judgment is deferred, to remain at large on his personal bond, or may require him to enter into bail bond in a sum at least double the amount of the assessed fine and costs, conditioned that the defendant and sureties, jointly and severally, will pay such fine and costs unless the defendant personally appears on the day, set in the order

and discharges the judgment in the manner provided by Chapter 43 of this Code; and for the enforcement of any judgment entered, all writs, processes and remedies of this Code are made applicable so far as necessary to carry out the provisions of this Article.
(Enacted by Acts 1965, 59th Leg., ch. 722 (S.B. 107), § 1, effective January 1, 1966.)

## Art. 37.13. If Jury Believes Accused Insane.

When a jury has been impaneled to assess the punishment upon a plea of guilty, it shall say in its verdict what the punishment is which it assesses; but if it is of the opinion that a person pleading guilty is insane, it shall so report to the court, and an issue as to that fact shall be tried before another jury; and if, upon such trial, it be found that the defendant is insane, such proceedings shall be had as directed in cases where a defendant becomes insane after conviction.
(Enacted by Acts 1965, 59th Leg., ch. 722 (S.B. 107), § 1, effective January 1, 1966.)

## Art. 37.14. Acquittal of Higher Offense As Jeopardy.

If a defendant, prosecuted for an offense which includes within it lesser offenses, be convicted of an offense lower than that for which he is indicted, and a new trial be granted him, or the judgment be arrested for any cause other than the want of jurisdiction, the verdict upon the first trial shall be considered an acquittal of the higher offense; but he may, upon a second trial, be convicted of the same offense of which he was before convicted, or any other inferior thereto.
(Enacted by Acts 1965, 59th Leg., ch. 722 (S.B. 107), § 1, effective January 1, 1966.)

## Art. 37.15. Texas Punishment Standards Commission [Expired].

Expired pursuant to Acts 1991, 72nd Leg., 2nd C.S., ch. 10 (H.B. 93), § 11.14, effective September 1, 1994.

# CHAPTER 38
# EVIDENCE IN CRIMINAL ACTIONS

## Art. 38.01. Texas Forensic Science Commission.

**Sec. 1. Creation.** The Texas Forensic Science Commission is created.

**Sec. 2. Definition.** In this article, "forensic analysis" has the meaning assigned by Article 38.35(a).

**Sec. 3. Composition.** (a) The commission is composed of the following nine members:

(1) four members appointed by the governor:

(A) two of whom must have expertise in the field of forensic science;

(B) one of whom must be a prosecuting attorney that the governor selects from a list of 10 names submitted by the Texas District and County Attorneys Association; and

(C) one of whom must be a defense attorney that the governor selects from a list of 10 names submitted by the Texas Criminal Defense Lawyers Association;

(2) three members appointed by the lieutenant governor:

(A) one of whom must be a faculty member or staff member of The University of Texas who specializes in clinical laboratory medicine selected from a list of 10 names submitted to the lieutenant governor by the chancellor of The University of Texas System;

(B) one of whom must be a faculty member or staff member of Texas A&M University who specializes in clinical laboratory medicine selected from a list of 10 names submitted to the lieutenant governor by the chancellor of The Texas A&M University System;

(C) one of whom must be a faculty member or staff member of Texas Southern University who has expertise in pharmaceutical laboratory research selected from a list of 10 names submitted to the lieutenant governor by the chancellor of Texas Southern University; and

(3) two members appointed by the attorney general:

(A) one of whom must be a director or division head of the University of North Texas Health Science Center at Fort Worth Missing Persons DNA Database; and

(B) one of whom must be a faculty or staff member of the Sam Houston State University College of Criminal Justice and have expertise in the field of forensic science or statistical analyses selected from a list of 10 names submitted to the lieutenant governor by the chancellor of Texas State University System.

(b) Each member of the commission serves a two-year term. The term of the members appointed under Subsections (a)(1) and (2) expires on September 1 of each odd-numbered year. The term of the members appointed under Subsection (a)(3) expires on September 1 of each even-numbered year.

(c) The governor shall designate a member of the commission to serve as the presiding officer.

**Sec. 4. Duties.** (a) The commission shall:

(1) develop and implement a reporting system through which accredited laboratories, facilities, or entities report professional negligence or misconduct;

(2) require all laboratories, facilities, or entities that conduct forensic analyses to report professional negligence or misconduct to the commission; and

(3) investigate, in a timely manner, any allegation of professional negligence or misconduct that would substantially affect the integrity of the results of a forensic analysis conducted by an accredited laboratory, facility, or entity.

(b) An investigation under Subsection (a)(3):

(1) must include the preparation of a written report that identifies and also describes the methods and procedures used to identify:

(A) the alleged negligence or misconduct;

(B) whether negligence or misconduct occurred; and

(C) any corrective action required of the laboratory, facility, or entity; and

(2) may include one or more:

(A) retrospective reexaminations of other forensic analyses conducted by the laboratory, facility, or entity that may involve the same kind of negligence or misconduct; and

(B) follow-up evaluations of the laboratory, facility, or entity to review:

(i) the implementation of any corrective action required under Subdivision (1)(C); or

(ii) the conclusion of any retrospective reexamination under Paragraph (A).

(c) The commission by contract may delegate the duties described by Subsections (a)(1) and (3) to any person the commission determines to be qualified to assume those duties.

(d) The commission may require that a laboratory, facility, or entity investigated under this section pay any costs incurred to ensure compliance with Subsection (b)(1).

(e) The commission shall make all investigation reports completed under Subsection (b)(1) available to the public. A report completed under Subsection (b)(1), in a subsequent civil or criminal proceeding, is not prima facie evidence of the information or findings contained in the report.

**Criminal Procedure**

**Sec. 5. Reimbursement.** A member of the commission may not receive compensation but is entitled to reimbursement for the member's travel expenses as provided by Chapter 660, Government Code, and the General Appropriations Act.

**Sec. 6. Assistance.** The Texas Legislative Council, the Legislative Budget Board, and The University of Texas at Austin shall assist the commission in performing the commission's duties.

**Sec. 7. Submission.** The commission shall submit any report received under Section 4(a)(2) and any report prepared under Section 4(b)(1) to the governor, the lieutenant governor, and the speaker of the house of representatives not later than December 1 of each even-numbered year.

(Acts 2005, 79th Leg., ch. 1224 (H.B. 1068), § 1, effective September 1, 2005.)

## Art. 38.02. Effect Under Public Information Law of Release of Certain Information.

A release of information by an attorney representing the state to defense counsel for a purpose relating to the pending or reasonably anticipated prosecution of a criminal case is not considered a voluntary release of information to the public for purposes of Section 552.007, Government Code, and does not waive the right to assert in the future that the information is excepted from required disclosure under Chapter 552, Government Code.

(Enacted by Acts 2009, 81st Leg., ch. 630 (H.B. 1360), § 1, effective June 19, 2009.)

## Art. 38.03. Presumption of Innocence.

All persons are presumed to be innocent and no person may be convicted of an offense unless each element of the offense is proved beyond a reasonable doubt. The fact that he has been arrested, confined, or indicted for, or otherwise charged with, the offense gives rise to no inference of guilt at his trial.

(Enacted by Acts 1965, 59th Leg., ch. 722 (S.B. 107), § 1, effective January 1, 1966; am. Acts 1981, 67th Leg., ch. 539 (H.B. 866), § 1, effective June 12, 1981.)

## Art. 38.04. Jury Are Judges of Facts.

The jury, in all cases, is the exclusive judge of the facts proved, and of the weight to be given to the testimony, except where it is provided by law that proof of any particular fact is to be taken as either conclusive or presumptive proof of the existence of another fact, or where the law directs that a certain degree of weight is to be attached to a certain species of evidence.

(Enacted by Acts 1965, 59th Leg., ch. 722 (S.B. 107), § 1, effective January 1, 1966.)

## Art. 38.05. Judge Shall Not Discuss Evidence.

In ruling upon the admissibility of evidence, the judge shall not discuss or comment upon the weight of the same or its bearing in the case, but shall simply decide whether or not it is admissible; nor shall he, at any stage of the proceeding previous to the return of the verdict, make any remark calculated to convey to the jury his opinion of the case.

(Enacted by Acts 1965, 59th Leg., ch. 722 (S.B. 107), § 1, effective January 1, 1966.)

## Art. 38.06. Persons Competent to Testify [Repealed].

Repealed by the Texas Court of Criminal Appeals pursuant to Acts 1985, 69th Leg., ch. 685 (H.B. 13), § 9, effective September 1, 1986.

(Enacted by Acts 1965, 59th Leg., ch. 722 (S.B. 107), § 1, effective January 1, 1966.)

## Art. 38.07. Testimony in Corroboration of Victim of Sexual Offense.

(a) A conviction under Chapter 21, Section 20A.02(a)(3), (4), (7), or (8), Section 22.011, or Section 22.021, Penal Code, is supportable on the uncorroborated testimony of the victim of the sexual offense if the victim informed any person, other than the defendant, of the alleged offense within one year after the date on which the offense is alleged to have occurred.

(b) The requirement that the victim inform another person of an alleged offense does not apply if at the time of the alleged offense the victim was a person:

(1) 17 years of age or younger;

(2) 65 years of age or older; or

(3) 18 years of age or older who by reason of age or physical or mental disease, defect, or injury was substantially unable to satisfy the person's need for food, shelter, medical care, or protection from harm.

(Enacted by Acts 1975, 64th Leg., ch. 203 (H.B. 284), § 6, effective September 1, 1975; am. Acts 1983, 68th Leg., ch. 382 (S.B. 838), § 1, effective September 1, 1983; am. Acts 1983, 68th Leg., ch. 977 (H.B. 2008), § 7, effective September 1, 1983;

am. Acts 1993, 73rd Leg., ch. 200 (H.B. 261), § 1, effective May 19, 1993; am. Acts 1993, 73rd Leg., ch. 900 (S.B. 1067), § 12.01, effective September 1, 1993; am. Acts 2001, 77th Leg., ch. 1018 (H.B. 1209), § 1, effective September 1, 2001; am. Acts 2011, 82nd Leg., ch. 1 (S.B. 24), § 2.05, effective September 1, 2011.)

## Art. 38.071. Testimony of Child Who Is Victim of Offense.

Sec. 1. This article applies only to a hearing or proceeding in which the court determines that a child younger than 13 years of age would be unavailable to testify in the presence of the defendant about an offense defined by any of the following sections of the Penal Code:

(1) Section 19.02 (Murder);

(2) Section 19.03 (Capital Murder);

(3) Section 19.04 (Manslaughter);

(4) Section 20.04 (Aggravated Kidnapping);

(5) Section 21.11 (Indecency with a Child);

(6) Section 22.011 (Sexual Assault);

(7) Section 22.02 (Aggravated Assault);

(8) Section 22.021 (Aggravated Sexual Assault);

(9) Section 22.04(e) (Injury to a Child, Elderly Individual, or Disabled Individual);

(10) Section 22.04(f) (Injury to a Child, Elderly Individual, or Disabled Individual), if the conduct is committed intentionally or knowingly;

(11) Section 25.02 (Prohibited Sexual Conduct);

(12) Section 29.03 (Aggravated Robbery);

(13) Section 43.25 (Sexual Performance by a Child);

(14) Section 21.02 (Continuous Sexual Abuse of Young Child or Children);

(15) Section 43.05(a)(2)(Compelling Prostitution); or

(16) Section 20A.02(a)(7) or (8) (Trafficking of Persons).

Sec. 2. (a) The recording of an oral statement of the child made before the indictment is returned or the complaint has been filed is admissible into evidence if the court makes a determination that the factual issues of identity or actual occurrence were fully and fairly inquired into in a detached manner by a neutral individual experienced in child abuse cases that seeks to find the truth of the matter.

(b) If a recording is made under Subsection (a) of this section and after an indictment is returned or a complaint has been filed, by motion of the attorney representing the state or the attorney representing the defendant and on the approval of the court, both attorneys may propound written interrogatories that shall be presented by the same neutral individual who made the initial inquiries, if possible, and recorded under the same or similar circumstances of the original recording with the time and date of the inquiry clearly indicated in the recording.

(c) A recording made under Subsection (a) of this section is not admissible into evidence unless a recording made under Subsection (b) is admitted at the same time if a recording under Subsection (b) was requested prior to the time of the hearing or proceeding.

Sec. 3. (a) On its own motion or on the motion of the attorney representing the state or the attorney representing the defendant, the court may order that the testimony of the child be taken in a room other than the courtroom and be televised by closed circuit equipment in the courtroom to be viewed by the court and the finder of fact. To the extent practicable, only the judge, the court reporter, the attorneys for the defendant and for the state, persons necessary to operate the equipment, and any person whose presence would contribute to the welfare and well-being of the child may be present in the room with the child during his testimony. Only the attorneys and the judge may question the child. To the extent practicable, the persons necessary to operate the equipment shall be confined to an adjacent room or behind a screen or mirror that permits them to see and hear the child during his testimony, but does not permit the child to see or hear them. The court shall permit the defendant to observe and hear the testimony of the child and to communicate contemporaneously with his attorney during periods of recess or by audio contact, but the court shall attempt to ensure that the child cannot hear or see the defendant. The court shall permit the attorney for the defendant adequate opportunity to confer with the defendant during cross-examination of the child. On application of the attorney for the defendant, the court may recess the proceeding before or during cross-examination of the child for a reasonable time to allow the attorney for the defendant to confer with defendant.

(b) The court may set any other conditions and limitations on the taking of the testimony that it finds just and appropriate, taking into consideration the interests of the child, the rights of the defendant, and any other relevant factors.

Sec. 4. (a) After an indictment has been returned or a complaint filed, on its own motion or on the motion of the attorney representing the state or the attorney representing the defendant, the court may order that the testimony of the child be taken outside the courtroom and be recorded for showing in the courtroom before the court and the finder of fact. To the extent practicable, only those persons permitted to be present at the taking of testimony under Section 3 of this article may be present during the taking of the child's testimony, and the persons operating the equipment shall be confined from the child's sight and hearing as provided by Section 3. The court shall permit the defendant to observe and hear the testimony of the child and to communicate contemporaneously with his attorney during periods of recess or by audio contact but shall attempt to ensure that the child cannot hear or see the defendant.

(b) The court may set any other conditions and limitations on the taking of the testimony that it finds just and appropriate, taking into consideration the interests of the child, the rights of the defendant, and any other relevant factors. The court shall also ensure that:

(1) the recording is both visual and aural and is recorded on film or videotape or by other electronic means;

(2) the recording equipment was capable of making an accurate recording, the operator was competent, the quality of the recording is sufficient to allow the court and the finder of fact to assess the demeanor of the child and the interviewer, and the recording is accurate and is not altered;

(3) each voice on the recording is identified;

(4) the defendant, the attorneys for each party, and the expert witnesses for each party are afforded an opportunity to view the recording before it is shown in the courtroom;

(5) before giving his testimony, the child was placed under oath or was otherwise admonished in a manner appropriate to the child's age and maturity to testify truthfully;

(6) the court finds from the recording or through an in camera examination of the child that the child was competent to testify at the time the recording was made; and

(7) only one continuous recording of the child was made or the necessity for pauses in the recordings or for multiple recordings is established at the hearing or proceeding.

(c) After a complaint has been filed or an indictment returned charging the defendant, on the motion of the attorney representing the state, the court may order that the deposition of the child be taken outside of the courtroom in the same manner as a deposition may be taken in a civil matter. A deposition taken under this subsection is admissible into evidence.

Sec. 5. (a) On the motion of the attorney representing the state or the attorney representing the defendant and on a finding by the court that the following requirements have been substantially satisfied, the recording of an oral statement of the child made before a complaint has been filed or an indictment returned is admissible into evidence if:

(1) no attorney or peace officer was present when the statement was made;

(2) the recording is both visual and aural and is recorded on film or videotape or by other electronic means;

(3) the recording equipment was capable of making an accurate recording, the operator of the equipment was competent, the quality of the recording is sufficient to allow the court and the finder of fact to assess the demeanor of the child and the interviewer, and the recording is accurate and has not been altered;

(4) the statement was not made in response to questioning calculated to lead the child to make a particular statement;

(5) every voice on the recording is identified;

(6) the person conducting the interview of the child in the recording is expert in the handling, treatment, and investigation of child abuse cases, present at the hearing or proceeding, called by the state, and subject to cross-examination;

(7) immediately after a complaint was filed or an indictment returned, the attorney representing the state notified the court, the defendant, and the attorney representing the defendant of the existence of the recording;

(8) the defendant, the attorney for the defendant, and the expert witnesses for the defendant were afforded an opportunity to view the recording before it is offered into evidence and, if a proceeding was requested as provided by Subsection (b) of this section, in a proceeding conducted before a district court judge but outside the presence of the

jury were afforded an opportunity to cross-examine the child as provided by Subsection (b) of this section from any time immediately following the filing of the complaint or the returning of an indictment charging the defendant until the date the hearing or proceeding begins;

(9) the recording of the cross-examination, if there is one, is admissible under Subsection (b) of this section;

(10) before giving his testimony, the child was placed under oath or was otherwise admonished in a manner appropriate to the child's age and maturity to testify truthfully;

(11) the court finds from the recording or through an in camera examination of the child that the child was competent to testify at the time that the recording was made; and

(12) only one continuous recording of the child was made or the necessity for pauses in the recordings or for multiple recordings has been established at the hearing or proceeding.

(b) On the motion of the attorney representing the defendant, a district court may order that the cross-examination of the child be taken and be recorded before the judge of that court at any time until a recording made in accordance with Subsection (a) of this section has been introduced into evidence at the hearing or proceeding. On a finding by the court that the following requirements were satisfied, the recording of the cross-examination of the child is admissible into evidence and shall be viewed by the finder of fact only after the finder of fact has viewed the recording authorized by Subsection (a) of this section if:

(1) the recording is both visual and aural and is recorded on film or videotape or by other electronic means;

(2) the recording equipment was capable of making an accurate recording, the operator of the equipment was competent, the quality of the recording is sufficient to allow the court and the finder of fact to assess the demeanor of the child and the attorney representing the defendant, and the recording is accurate and has not been altered;

(3) every voice on the recording is identified;

(4) the defendant, the attorney representing the defendant, the attorney representing the state, and the expert witnesses for the defendant and the state were afforded an opportunity to view the recording before the hearing or proceeding began;

(5) the child was placed under oath before the cross-examination began or was otherwise admonished in a manner appropriate to the child's age and maturity to testify truthfully; and

(6) only one continuous recording of the child was made or the necessity for pauses in the recordings or for multiple recordings was established at the hearing or proceeding.

(c) During cross-examination under Subsection (b) of this section, to the extent practicable, only a district court judge, the attorney representing the defendant, the attorney representing the state, persons necessary to operate the equipment, and any other person whose presence would contribute to the welfare and well-being of the child may be present in the room with the child during his testimony. Only the attorneys and the judge may question the child. To the extent practicable, the persons operating the equipment shall be confined to an adjacent room or behind a screen or mirror that permits them to see and hear the child during his testimony but does not permit the child to see or hear them. The court shall permit the defendant to observe and hear the testimony of the child and to communicate contemporaneously with his attorney during periods of recess or by audio contact, but shall attempt to ensure that the child cannot hear or see the defendant.

(d) Under Subsection (b) of this section the district court may set any other conditions and limitations on the taking of the cross-examination of a child that it finds just and appropriate, taking into consideration the interests of the child, the rights of the defendant, and any other relevant factors.

Sec. 6. If the court orders the testimony of a child to be taken under Section 3 or 4 of this article or if the court finds the testimony of the child taken under Section 2 or 5 of this article is admissible into evidence, the child may not be required to testify in court at the proceeding for which the testimony was taken, unless the court finds there is good cause.

Sec. 7. In making any determination of good cause under this article, the court shall consider the rights of the defendant, the interests of the child, the relationship of the defendant to the child, the character and duration of the alleged offense, any court finding related to the availability of the child to testify, the age, maturity, and emotional stability of the child, the time elapsed

Criminal Procedure

since the alleged offense, and any other relevant factors.

Sec. 8. (a) In making a determination of unavailability under this article, the court shall consider relevant factors including the relationship of the defendant to the child, the character and duration of the alleged offense, the age, maturity, and emotional stability of the child, and the time elapsed since the alleged offense, and whether the child is more likely than not to be unavailable to testify because:

(1) of emotional or physical causes, including the confrontation with the defendant; or

(2) the child would suffer undue psychological or physical harm through his involvement at the hearing or proceeding.

(b) A determination of unavailability under this article can be made after an earlier determination of availability. A determination of availability under this article can be made after an earlier determination of unavailability.

Sec. 9. If the court finds the testimony taken under Section 2 or 5 of this article is admissible into evidence or if the court orders the testimony to be taken under Section 3 or 4 of this article and if the identity of the perpetrator is a contested issue, the child additionally must make an in-person identification of the defendant either at or before the hearing or proceeding.

Sec. 10. In ordering a child to testify under this article, the court shall take all reasonable steps necessary and available to minimize undue psychological trauma to the child and to minimize the emotional and physical stress to the child caused by relevant factors, including the confrontation with the defendant and the ordinary participation of the witness in the courtroom.

Sec. 11. In a proceeding under Section 2, 3, or 4 or Subsection (b) of Section 5 of this article, if the defendant is not represented by counsel and the court finds that the defendant is not able to obtain counsel for the purposes of the proceeding, the court shall appoint counsel to represent the defendant at the proceeding.

Sec. 12. In this article, "cross-examination" has the same meaning as in other legal proceedings in the state.

Sec. 13. The attorney representing the state shall determine whether to use the procedure provided in Section 2 of this article or the procedure provided in Section 5 of this article.
(Enacted by Acts 1983, 68th Leg., ch. 599 (S.B. 836), § 1, effective August 29, 1983; am. Acts 1987, 70th Leg., ch. 998 (H.B. 2146), § 1, effective August 31, 1987; am. Acts 1987, 70th Leg., 2nd

C.S., ch. 55 (S.B. 66), § 1, effective October 20, 1987; am. Acts 1991, 72nd Leg., ch. 266 (S.B. 1083), § 1, effective September 1, 1991; am. Acts 1995, 74th Leg., ch. 76 (S.B. 959), § 14.24, effective September 1, 1995; am. Acts 2001, 77th Leg., ch. 338 (S.B. 24), §§ 1—8, effective September 1, 2001; am. Acts 2007, 80th Leg., ch. 593 (H.B. 8), § 3.16, effective September 1, 2007; am. Acts 2011, 82nd Leg., ch. 1 (S.B. 24), § 2.06, effective September 1, 2011.)

## Art. 38.072. Hearsay Statement of Certain Abuse Victims.

Sec. 1. This article applies to a proceeding in the prosecution of an offense under any of the following provisions of the Penal Code, if committed against a child younger than 14 years of age or a person with a disability:

(1) Chapter 21 (Sexual Offenses) or 22 (Assaultive Offenses);

(2) Section 25.02 (Prohibited Sexual Conduct);

(3) Section 43.25 (Sexual Performance by a Child);

(4) Section 43.05(a)(2) (Compelling Prostitution);

(5) Section 20A.02(a)(7) or (8) (Trafficking of Persons); or

(6) Section 15.01 (Criminal Attempt), if the offense attempted is described by Subdivision (1), (2), (3), (4), or (5) of this section.

Sec. 2(a) This article applies only to statements that describe the alleged offense that:

(1) were made by the child or person with a disability against whom the offense was allegedly committed; and

(2) were made to the first person, 18 years of age or older, other than the defendant, to whom the child or person with a disability made a statement about the offense.

(b) A statement that meets the requirements of Subsection (a) is not inadmissible because of the hearsay rule if:

(1) on or before the 14th day before the date the proceeding begins, the party intending to offer the statement:

(A) notifies the adverse party of its intention to do so;

(B) provides the adverse party with the name of the witness through whom it intends to offer the statement; and

(C) provides the adverse party with a written summary of the statement;

(2) the trial court finds, in a hearing conducted outside the presence of the jury, that

the statement is reliable based on the time, content, and circumstances of the statement; and

(3) the child or person with a disability testifies or is available to testify at the proceeding in court or in any other manner provided by law.

Sec. 3. In this article, "person with a disability" means a person 13 years of age or older who because of age or physical or mental disease, disability, or injury is substantially unable to protect the person's self from harm or to provide food, shelter, or medical care for the person's self. (Enacted by Acts 1985, 69th Leg., ch. 590 (H.B. 579), § 1, effective September 1, 1985; am. Acts 1995, 74th Leg., ch. 76 (S.B. 959), § 14.25, effective September 1, 1995; am. Acts 2009, 81st Leg., ch. 710 (H.B. 2846), § 1, effective September 1, 2009, am. Acts 2009, 81st Leg., ch. 284 (S.B. 643), § 1, effective June 11, 2009; am. Acts 2011, 82nd Leg., ch. 1 (S.B. 24), § 2.07, effective September 1, 2011.)

## Art. 38.073. Testimony of Inmate Witnesses.

In a proceeding in the prosecution of a criminal offense in which an inmate in the custody of the Texas Department of Criminal Justice is required to testify as a witness, any deposition or testimony of the inmate witness may be conducted by a video teleconferencing system in the manner described by Article 27.18.

(Am. Acts 2001, 77th Leg., ch. 788 (H.B. 176), § 2, effective June 14, 2001; am. Acts 2011, 82nd Leg., ch. 1031 (H.B. 2847), § 6, effective September 1, 2011; am. Acts 2011, 82nd Leg., ch. 1341 (S.B. 1233), § 7, effective June 17, 2011.)

## Art. 38.074. Testimony of Child in Prosecution of Offense.

**Sec. 1.** In this article:

(1) "Child " has the meaning assigned by Section 22.011(c), Penal Code.

(2) "Support person" means any person whose presence would contribute to the welfare and well-being of a child.

**Sec 2.** This article applies to the testimony of a child in any hearing or proceeding in the prosecution of any offense, other than the testimony of a child in a hearing or proceeding in a criminal case in which that child is the defendant.

**Sec. 3.** (a) A court shall:

(1) administer an oath to a child in a manner that allows the child to fully understand the child's duty to tell the truth;

(2) ensure that questions asked of the child are stated in language appropriate to the child's age;

(3) explain to the child that the child has the right to have the court notified if the child is unable to understand any question and to have a question restated in a form that the child does understand;

(4) ensure that a child testifies only at a time of day when the child is best able to understand the questions and to undergo the proceedings without being traumatized, including:

(A) limiting the duration of the child's testimony;

(B) limiting the timing of the child's testimony to the child's normal school hours; or

(C) ordering a recess during the child's testimony when necessary for the energy, comfort, or attention span of the child; and

(5) prevent intimidation or harassment of the child by any party and, for that purpose, rephrase as appropriate any question asked of the child.

(b) On the motion of any party, or a parent, managing conservator, guardian, or guardian ad litem of a child or special advocate for a child, the court shall allow the child to have a toy, blanket, or similar comforting item in the child's possession while testifying or allow a support person to be present in close proximity to the child during the child's testimony if the court finds by a preponderance of the evidence that:

(1) the child cannot reliably testify without the possession of the item or presence of the support person, as applicable; and

(2) granting the motion is not likely to prejudice the trier of fact in evaluating the child's testimony.

(c) A support person who is present during a child's testimony may not:

(1) obscure the child from the view of the defendant or the trier of fact;

(2) provide the child with an answer to any question asked of the child; or

(3) assist or influence the testimony of the child.

(d) The court may set any other conditions and limitations on the taking of the testimony of a child that it finds just and appropriate, considering the interests of the child, the rights of the defendant, and any other relevant factors.

(Enacted by Acts 2011, 82nd Leg., ch. 1227 (S.B. 578), § 1, effective September 1, 2011.)

### Art. 38.075. Corroboration of Certain Testimony Required.

(a) A defendant may not be convicted of an offense on the testimony of a person to whom the defendant made a statement against the defendant's interest during a time when the person was imprisoned or confined in the same correctional facility as the defendant unless the testimony is corroborated by other evidence tending to connect the defendant with the offense committed. In this subsection, "correctional facility" has the meaning assigned by Section 1.07, Penal Code.

(b) Corroboration is not sufficient for the purposes of this article if the corroboration only shows that the offense was committed.

(Enacted by Acts 2009, 81st Leg., ch. 1422 (S.B. 1681), § 1, effective September 1, 2009.)

### Art. 38.08. Defendant May Testify.

Any defendant in a criminal action shall be permitted to testify in his own behalf therein, but the failure of any defendant to so testify shall not be taken as a circumstance against him, nor shall the same be alluded to or commented on by counsel in the cause.

(Enacted by Acts 1965, 59th Leg., ch. 722 (S.B. 107), § 1, effective January 1, 1966.)

### Art. 38.09. Court May Determine Competency [Repealed].

Repealed by the Texas Court of Criminal Appeals pursuant to Acts 1985, 69th Leg., ch. 685 (H.B. 13), § 9, effective September 1, 1986.

(Enacted by Acts 1965, 59th Leg., ch. 722 (S.B. 107), § 1, effective January 1, 1966.)

### Art. 38.10. Exceptions to the Spousal Adverse Testimony Privilege.

The privilege of a person's spouse not to be called as a witness for the state does not apply in any proceeding in which the person is charged with:

(1) a crime committed against the person's spouse, a minor child, or a member of the household of either spouse; or

(2) an offense under Section 25.01, Penal Code (Bigamy).

(Enacted by Acts 1995, 74th Leg., ch. 67 (S.B. 128), § 2, effective September 1, 1995; am. Acts 2005, 79th Leg., ch. 268 (S.B. 6), § 4.01, effective September 1, 2005.)

### Art. 38.101. Communications by Drug Abusers.

A communication to any person involved in the treatment or examination of drug abusers by a person being treated voluntarily or being examined for admission to voluntary treatment for drug abuse is not admissible. However, information derived from the treatment or examination of drug abusers may be used for statistical and research purposes if the names of the patients are not revealed.

(Enacted by Acts 1971, 62nd Leg., ch. 983 (H.B. 840), § 2, effective June 15, 1971.)

### Art. 38.11. Journalist's Qualified Testimonial Privilege in Criminal Proceedings.

**Sec. 1. Definitions.** In this article:

(1) "Communication service provider" means a person or the parent, subsidiary, division, or affiliate of a person who transmits information chosen by a customer by electronic means, including:

(A) a telecommunications carrier, as defined by Section 3, Communications Act of 1934 (47 U.S.C. Section 153);

(B) a provider of information service, as defined by Section 3, Communications Act of 1934 (47 U.S.C. Section 153);

(C) a provider of interactive computer service, as defined by Section 230, Communications Act of 1934 (47 U.S.C. Section 230); and

(D) an information content provider, as defined by Section 230, Communications Act of 1934 (47 U.S.C. Section 230).

(2) "Journalist" means a person, including a parent, subsidiary, division, or affiliate of a person, who for a substantial portion of the person's livelihood or for substantial financial gain, gathers, compiles, prepares, collects, photographs, records, writes, edits, reports, investigates, processes, or publishes news or information that is disseminated by a news medium or communication service provider and includes:

(A) a person who supervises or assists in gathering, preparing, and disseminating the news or information; or

(B) notwithstanding the foregoing, a person who is or was a journalist, scholar, or researcher employed by an institution of higher education at the time the person obtained or prepared the requested information, or a person who at the time the person obtained or prepared the requested information:

　　(i) is earning a significant portion of the person's livelihood by obtaining or preparing information for dissemination by a news medium or communication service provider; or

　　(ii) was serving as an agent, assistant, employee, or supervisor of a news medium or communication service provider.

(3) "News medium" means a newspaper, magazine or periodical, book publisher, news agency, wire service, radio or television station or network, cable, satellite, or other transmission system or carrier or channel, or a channel or programming service for a station, network, system, or carrier, or an audio or audiovisual production company or Internet company or provider, or the parent, subsidiary, division, or affiliate of that entity, that disseminates news or information to the public by any means, including:

　　(A) print;

　　(B) television;

　　(C) radio;

　　(D) photographic;

　　(E) mechanical;

　　(F) electronic; and

　　(G) other means, known or unknown, that are accessible to the public.

(4) "Official proceeding" means any type of administrative, executive, legislative, or judicial proceeding that may be conducted before a public servant.

(5) "Public servant" means a person elected, selected, appointed, employed, or otherwise designated as one of the following, even if the person has not yet qualified for office or assumed the person's duties:

　　(A) an officer, employee, or agent of government;

　　(B) a juror or grand juror;

　　(C) an arbitrator, referee, or other person who is authorized by law or private written agreement to hear or determine a cause or controversy;

　　(D) an attorney or notary public when participating in the performance of a governmental function; or

　　(E) a person who is performing a governmental function under a claim of right, although the person is not legally qualified to do so.

**Sec. 2. Purpose.** The purpose of this article is to increase the free flow of information and pre-serve a free and active press and, at the same time, protect the right of the public to effective law enforcement and the fair administration of justice.

**Sec. 3. Privilege. (a)** Except as otherwise provided by this article, a judicial, legislative, administrative, or other body with the authority to issue a subpoena or other compulsory process may not compel a journalist to testify regarding or to produce or disclose in an official proceeding:

　　(1) any confidential or nonconfidential unpublished information, document, or item obtained or prepared while acting as a journalist; or

　　(2) the source of any information, document, or item described by Subdivision (1).

(b) A subpoena or other compulsory process may not compel the parent, subsidiary, division, or affiliate of a communication service provider or news medium to disclose the unpublished information, documents, or items or the source of any information, documents, or items that are privileged from disclosure under Subsection (a).

**Sec. 4. Privilege Concerning Confidential Sources.** (a) A journalist may be compelled to testify regarding or to disclose the confidential source of any information, document, or item obtained while acting as a journalist if the person seeking the testimony, production, or disclosure makes a clear and specific showing that the source of any information, document, or item:

　　(1) was observed by the journalist committing a felony criminal offense and the subpoenaing party has exhausted reasonable efforts to obtain from alternative sources the confidential source of any information, document, or item obtained or prepared while acting as a journalist;

　　(2) is a person who confessed or admitted to the journalist the commission of a felony criminal offense and the subpoenaing party has exhausted reasonable efforts to obtain from alternative sources the confidential source of any information, document, or item obtained or prepared while acting as a journalist;

　　(3) is a person for whom probable cause exists that the person participated in a felony criminal offense and the subpoenaing party has exhausted reasonable efforts to obtain from alternative sources the confidential source of any information, document, or item obtained or prepared while acting as a journalist; or

(4) disclosure of the confidential source is reasonably necessary to stop or prevent reasonably certain death or substantial bodily harm.

(b) If the alleged criminal conduct is the act of communicating, receiving, or possessing the information, document, or item, this section does not apply, and Section 5 governs the act.

(c) Notwithstanding Subsection (b), if the information, document, or item was disclosed or received in violation of a grand jury oath given to either a juror or a witness under Article 19.34 or 20.16, a journalist may be compelled to testify if the person seeking the testimony, production, or disclosure makes a clear and specific showing that the subpoenaing party has exhausted reasonable efforts to obtain from alternative sources the confidential source of any information, document, or item obtained. In this context, the court has the discretion to conduct an in camera hearing. The court may not order the production of the confidential source until a ruling has been made on the motion.

(d) An application for a subpoena of a journalist under Article 24.03, or a subpoena of a journalist issued by an attorney representing the state under Article 20.10 or 20.11, must be signed by the elected district attorney, elected criminal district attorney, or elected county attorney, as applicable. If the elected district attorney, elected criminal district attorney, or elected county attorney has been disqualified or recused or has resigned, the application for the subpoena or the subpoena must be signed by the person succeeding the elected attorney. If the elected officer is not in the jurisdiction, the highest ranking assistant to the elected officer must sign the subpoena.

**Sec. 5. Privilege Concerning Unpublished Information, Document, or Item and Nonconfidential Sources.** (a) After service of subpoena and an opportunity to be heard, a court may compel a journalist, a journalist's employer, or a person with an independent contract with a journalist to testify regarding or to produce or disclose any unpublished information, document, or item or the source of any information, document, or item obtained while acting as a journalist, other than as described by Section 4, if the person seeking the unpublished information, document, or item or the source of any information, document, or item makes a clear and specific showing that:

(1) all reasonable efforts have been exhausted to obtain the information from alternative sources; and

(2) the unpublished information, document, or item:

(A) is relevant and material to the proper administration of the official proceeding for which the testimony, production, or disclosure is sought and is essential to the maintenance of a claim or defense of the person seeking the testimony, production, or disclosure; or

(B) is central to the investigation or prosecution of a criminal case and based on something other than the assertion of the person requesting the subpoena, reasonable grounds exist to believe that a crime has occurred.

(b) The court, when considering an order to compel testimony regarding or to produce or disclose any unpublished information, document, or item or the source of any information, document, or item obtained while acting as a journalist, should consider the following factors, including but not limited to whether:

(1) the subpoena is overbroad, unreasonable, or oppressive;

(2) reasonable and timely notice was given of the demand for the information, document, or item;

(3) in this instance, the interest of the party subpoenaing the information outweighs the public interest in gathering and dissemination of news, including the concerns of the journalist; and

(4) the subpoena or compulsory process is being used to obtain peripheral, nonessential, or speculative information.

(c) A court may not consider a single factor under Subsection (b) as outcome-determinative in the decision whether to compel the testimony or the production or disclosure of the unpublished information, document, or item, or the source of any information, document, or item.

**Sec. 6. Notice.** An order to compel testimony, production, or disclosure to which a journalist has asserted a privilege under this article may be issued only after timely notice to the journalist, the journalist's employer, or a person who has an independent contract with the journalist and a hearing. The order must include clear and specific findings as to the showing made by the person seeking the testimony, production, or disclosure and the clear and specific evidence on which the court relied in issuing the court's order.

**Sec. 7. Publication of Privileged Information.** Publication or dissemination by a news medium or communication service provider of information, documents, or items privileged under this article is not a waiver of the journalist's privilege regarding sources and unpublished information, documents, or items.

**Sec. 8. Published Information.** This article does not apply to any information, document, or item that has at any time been published or broadcast by the journalist.

**Sec. 9. Reimbursement of Costs.** The subpoenaing party shall pay a journalist a reasonable fee for the journalist's time and costs incurred in providing the information, item, or document subpoenaed, based on the fee structure provided by Subchapter F, Chapter 552, Government Code.

(Enacted by Acts 2009, 81st Leg., ch. 29 (H.B. 670), § 2, effective May 13, 2009.)

## Art. 38.111. News Media Recordings.

Extrinsic evidence of the authenticity of evidence as a condition precedent to the admissibility of the evidence in a criminal proceeding is not required with respect to a recording that purports to be a broadcast by a radio or television station that holds a license issued by the Federal Communications Commission at the time of the recording. The court may take judicial notice of the recording license as provided by Rule 201, Texas Rules of Evidence.

(Enacted by Acts 2009, 81st Leg., ch. 29 (H.B. 670), § 2, effective May 13, 2009.)

## Art. 38.12. Religious Opinion.

No person is incompetent to testify on account of his religious opinion or for the want of any religious belief.

(Enacted by Acts 1965, 59th Leg., ch. 722 (S.B. 107), § 1, effective January 1, 1966.)

## Art. 38.13. Judge As a Witness [Repealed].

Repealed by the Texas Court of Criminal Appeals pursuant to Acts 1985, 69th Leg., ch. 685 (H.B. 13), § 9, effective September 1, 1986.

(Enacted by Acts 1965, 59th Leg., ch. 722 (S.B. 107), § 1, effective January 1, 1966.)

## Art. 38.14. Testimony of Accomplice.

A conviction cannot be had upon the testimony of an accomplice unless corroborated by other evidence tending to connect the defendant with the offense committed; and the corroboration is not sufficient if it merely shows the commission of the offense.

(Enacted by Acts 1965, 59th Leg., ch. 722 (S.B. 107), § 1, effective January 1, 1966.)

## Art. 38.141. Testimony of Undercover Peace Officer or Special Investigator.

(a) A defendant may not be convicted of an offense under Chapter 481, Health and Safety Code, on the testimony of a person who is not a licensed peace officer or a special investigator but who is acting covertly on behalf of a law enforcement agency or under the color of law enforcement unless the testimony is corroborated by other evidence tending to connect the defendant with the offense committed.

(b) Corroboration is not sufficient for the purposes of this article if the corroboration only shows the commission of the offense.

(c) In this article, "peace officer" means a person listed in Article 2.12, and "special investigator" means a person listed in Article 2.122.

(Enacted by Acts 2001, 77th Leg., ch. 1102 (H.B. 2351), § 1, effective September 1, 2001.)

## Art. 38.15. Two Witnesses in Treason.

No person can be convicted of treason except upon the testimony of at least two witnesses to the same overt act, or upon his own confession in open court.

(Enacted by Acts 1965, 59th Leg., ch. 722 (S.B. 107), § 1, effective January 1, 1966.)

## Art. 38.16. Evidence in Treason.

Evidence shall not be admitted in a prosecution for treason as to an overt act not expressly charged in the indictment; nor shall any person be convicted under an indictment for treason unless one or more overt acts are expressly charged therein.

(Enacted by Acts 1965, 59th Leg., ch. 722 (S.B. 107), § 1, effective January 1, 1966.)

## Art. 38.17. Two Witnesses Required.

In all cases where, by law, two witnesses, or one with corroborating circumstances, are required to authorize a conviction, if the requirement be not fulfilled, the court shall instruct the jury to render a verdict of acquittal, and they are bound by the instruction.

(Enacted by Acts 1965, 59th Leg., ch. 722 (S.B. 107), § 1, effective January 1, 1966.)

Criminal Procedure

## Art. 38.18. Perjury and Aggravated Perjury.

(a) No person may be convicted of perjury or aggravated perjury if proof that his statement is false rests solely upon the testimony of one witness other than the defendant.

(b) Paragraph (a) of this article does not apply to prosecutions for perjury or aggravated perjury involving inconsistent statements.
(Enacted by Acts 1965, 59th Leg., ch. 722 (S.B. 107), § 1, effective January 1, 1966; am. Acts 1973, 63rd Leg., ch. 399 (S.B. 34), § 2(A), effective January 1, 1974.)

## Art. 38.19. Intent to Defraud in Forgery.

In trials of forgery, it need not be proved that the defendant committed the act with intent to defraud any particular person. It shall be sufficient to prove that the forgery was, in its nature, calculated to injure or defraud any of the sovereignties, bodies corporate or politic, officers or persons, named in the definition of forgery in the Penal Code.
(Enacted by Acts 1965, 59th Leg., ch. 722 (S.B. 107), § 1, effective January 1, 1966.)

## Art. 38.20. Photograph and Live Lineup Identification Procedures.

**Sec. 1.** In this article, "institute" means the Bill Blackwood Law Enforcement Management Institute of Texas located at Sam Houston State University.

**Sec. 2.** This article applies only to a law enforcement agency of this state or of a county, municipality, or other political subdivision of this state that employs peace officers who conduct photograph or live lineup identification procedures in the routine performance of the officers' official duties.

**Sec. 3.** (a) Each law enforcement agency shall adopt, implement, and as necessary amend a detailed written policy regarding the administration of photograph and live lineup identification procedures in accordance with this article. A law enforcement agency may adopt:

(1) the model policy adopted under Subsection (b); or

(2) the agency's own policy that, at a minimum, conforms to the requirements of Subsection (c).

(b) The institute, in consultation with large, medium, and small law enforcement agencies and with law enforcement associations, scientific experts in eyewitness memory research, and appropriate organizations engaged in the development of law enforcement policy, shall develop, adopt, and disseminate to all law enforcement agencies in this state a model policy and associated training materials regarding the administration of photograph and live lineup identification procedures. The institute shall provide for a period of public comment before adopting the policy and materials.

(c) The model policy or any other policy adopted by a law enforcement agency under Subsection (a) must:

(1) be based on:

(A) credible field, academic, or laboratory research on eyewitness memory;

(B) relevant policies, guidelines, and best practices designed to reduce erroneous eyewitness identifications and to enhance the reliability and objectivity of eyewitness identifications; and

(C) other relevant information as appropriate; and

(2) address the following topics:

(A) the selection of photograph and live lineup filler photographs or participants;

(B) instructions given to a witness before conducting a photograph or live lineup identification procedure;

(C) the documentation and preservation of results of a photograph or live lineup identification procedure, including the documentation of witness statements, regardless of the outcome of the procedure;

(D) procedures for administering a photograph or live lineup identification procedure to an illiterate person or a person with limited English language proficiency;

(E) for a live lineup identification procedure, if practicable, procedures for assigning an administrator who is unaware of which member of the live lineup is the suspect in the case or alternative procedures designed to prevent opportunities to influence the witness;

(F) for a photograph identification procedure, procedures for assigning an administrator who is capable of administering a photograph array in a blind manner or in a manner consistent with other proven or supported best practices designed to prevent opportunities to influence the witness; and

(G) any other procedures or best practices supported by credible research or commonly accepted as a means to reduce erroneous eyewitness identifications and to enhance the objectivity and reliability of eyewitness identifications.

**Sec. 4.** (a) Not later than December 31 of each odd-numbered year, the institute shall review the model policy and training materials adopted under this article and shall modify the policy and materials as appropriate.

(b) Not later than September 1 of each even-numbered year, each law enforcement agency shall review its policy adopted under this article and shall modify that policy as appropriate.

**Sec. 5.** (a) Any evidence or expert testimony presented by the state or the defendant on the subject of eyewitness identification is admissible only subject to compliance with the Texas Rules of Evidence. Evidence of compliance with the model policy or any other policy adopted under this article or with the minimum requirements of this article is not a condition precedent to the admissibility of an out-of-court eyewitness identification.

(b) Notwithstanding Article 38.23 as that article relates to a violation of a state statute, a failure to conduct a photograph or live lineup identification procedure in substantial compliance with the model policy or any other policy adopted under this article or with the minimum requirements of this article does not bar the admission of eyewitness identification testimony in the courts of this state.

(Enacted by Acts 2011, 82nd Leg., ch. 219 (H.B. 215), § 1, effective September 1, 2011.)

## Art. 38.21. Statement.

A statement of an accused may be used in evidence against him if it appears that the same was freely and voluntarily made without compulsion or persuasion, under the rules hereafter prescribed.

(Enacted by Acts 1965, 59th Leg., ch. 722 (S.B. 107), § 1, effective January 1, 1966; am. Acts 1977, 65th Leg., ch. 348 (S.B. 157), § 1, effective August 29, 1977.)

## Art. 38.22. When Statements May Be Used.

**Sec. 1.** In this article, a written statement of an accused means a statement signed by the accused or a statement made by the accused in his own handwriting or, if the accused is unable to write, a statement bearing his mark, when the mark has been witnessed by a person other than a peace officer.

**Sec. 2.** No written statement made by an accused as a result of custodial interrogation is admissible as evidence against him in any criminal proceeding unless it is shown on the face of the statement that:

(a) the accused, prior to making the statement, either received from a magistrate the warning provided in Article 15.17 of this code or received from the person to whom the statement is made a warning that:

(1) he has the right to remain silent and not make any statement at all and that any statement he makes may be used against him at his trial;

(2) any statement he makes may be used as evidence against him in court;

(3) he has the right to have a lawyer present to advise him prior to and during any questioning;

(4) if he is unable to employ a lawyer, he has the right to have a lawyer appointed to advise him prior to and during any questioning; and

(5) he has the right to terminate the interview at any time; and

(b) the accused, prior to and during the making of the statement, knowingly, intelligently, and voluntarily waived the rights set out in the warning prescribed by Subsection (a) of this section.

**Sec. 3.** (a) No oral or sign language statement of an accused made as a result of custodial interrogation shall be admissible against the accused in a criminal proceeding unless:

(1) an electronic recording, which may include motion picture, video tape, or other visual recording, is made of the statement;

(2) prior to the statement but during the recording the accused is given the warning in Subsection (a) of Section 2 above and the accused knowingly, intelligently, and voluntarily waives any rights set out in the warning;

(3) the recording device was capable of making an accurate recording, the operator was competent, and the recording is accurate and has not been altered;

(4) all voices on the recording are identified; and

(5) not later than the 20th day before the date of the proceeding, the attorney representing the defendant is provided with a true, complete, and accurate copy of all recordings of the defendant made under this article.

Criminal Procedure

Criminal Procedure

(b) Every electronic recording of any statement made by an accused during a custodial interrogation must be preserved until such time as the defendant's conviction for any offense relating thereto is final, all direct appeals therefrom are exhausted, or the prosecution of such offenses is barred by law.

(c) Subsection (a) of this section shall not apply to any statement which contains assertions of facts or circumstances that are found to be true and which conduce to establish the guilt of the accused, such as the finding of secreted or stolen property or the instrument with which he states the offense was committed.

(d) If the accused is a deaf person, the accused's statement under Section 2 or Section 3(a) of this article is not admissible against the accused unless the warning in Section 2 of this article is interpreted to the deaf person by an interpreter who is qualified and sworn as provided in Article 38.31 of this code.

(e) The courts of this state shall strictly construe Subsection (a) of this section and may not interpret Subsection (a) as making admissible a statement unless all requirements of the subsection have been satisfied by the state, except that:

(1) only voices that are material are identified; and

(2) the accused was given the warning in Subsection (a) of Section 2 above or its fully effective equivalent.

Sec. 4. When any statement, the admissibility of which is covered by this article, is sought to be used in connection with an official proceeding, any person who swears falsely to facts and circumstances which, if true, would render the statement admissible under this article is presumed to have acted with intent to deceive and with knowledge of the statement's meaning for the purpose of prosecution for aggravated perjury under Section 37.03 of the Penal Code. No person prosecuted under this subsection shall be eligible for probation.

Sec. 5. Nothing in this article precludes the admission of a statement made by the accused in open court at his trial, before a grand jury, or at an examining trial in compliance with Articles 16.03 and 16.04 of this code, or of a statement that is the res gestae of the arrest or of the offense, or of a statement that does not stem from custodial interrogation, or of a voluntary statement, whether or not the result of custodial interrogation, that has a bearing upon the credibility of the accused as a witness, or of any other statement that may be admissible under law.

Sec. 6. In all cases where a question is raised as to the voluntariness of a statement of an accused, the court must make an independent finding in the absence of the jury as to whether the statement was made under voluntary conditions. If the statement has been found to have been voluntarily made and held admissible as a matter of law and fact by the court in a hearing in the absence of the jury, the court must enter an order stating its conclusion as to whether or not the statement was voluntarily made, along with the specific finding of facts upon which the conclusion was based, which order shall be filed among the papers of the cause. Such order shall not be exhibited to the jury nor the finding thereof made known to the jury in any manner. Upon the finding by the judge as a matter of law and fact that the statement was voluntarily made, evidence pertaining to such matter may be submitted to the jury and it shall be instructed that unless the jury believes beyond a reasonable doubt that the statement was voluntarily made, the jury shall not consider such statement for any purpose nor any evidence obtained as a result thereof. In any case where a motion to suppress the statement has been filed and evidence has been submitted to the court on this issue, the court within its discretion may reconsider such evidence in his finding that the statement was voluntarily made and the same evidence submitted to the court at the hearing on the motion to suppress shall be made a part of the record the same as if it were being presented at the time of trial. However, the state or the defendant shall be entitled to present any new evidence on the issue of the voluntariness of the statement prior to the court's final ruling and order stating its findings.

Sec. 7. When the issue is raised by the evidence, the trial judge shall appropriately instruct the jury, generally, on the law pertaining to such statement.

Sec. 8. Notwithstanding any other provision of this article, a written, oral, or sign language statement of an accused made as a result of a custodial interrogation is admissible against the accused in a criminal proceeding in this state if:

(1) the statement was obtained in another state and was obtained in compliance with the laws of that state or this state; or

(2) the statement was obtained by a federal law enforcement officer in this state or another state and was obtained in compliance with the laws of the United States.

(Enacted by Acts 1965, 59th Leg., ch. 722 (S.B. 107), § 1, effective January 1, 1966; am. Acts 1967, 60th Leg., ch. 659 (S.B. 145), § 23, effective August 28, 1967; am. Acts 1977, 65th Leg., ch. 348 (S.B. 157), § 2, effective August 29, 1977; am. Acts 1979, 66th Leg., ch. 186 (H.B. 1521), § 4, effective May 15, 1979; am. Acts 1979, 66th Leg., ch. 186 (H.B. 1521), § 5, effective May 15, 1979; am. Acts 1981, 67th Leg., ch. 271 (S.B. 121), § 1, effective September 1, 1981; am. Acts 1989, 71st Leg., ch. 777 (S.B. 55), §§ 1, 2, effective September 1, 1989; am. Acts 2001, 77th Leg., ch. 990 (H.B. 553), § 1, effective September 1, 2001.)

## Art. 38.23.  Evidence Not to Be Used.

(a)  No evidence obtained by an officer or other person in violation of any provisions of the Constitution or ~~~~ of ~~ State of T~~~ ~~ of the Constitution ~~~~~~~~ America, sh~~~~~~~~ the accused

In any ca~ issue herei~ if it believe~ evidence wa~ sions of thi~ jury shall ~ tained.

(b)  It is ~ section (a) ~ obtained by ~ objective g~ sued by a r~ cause.

(Enacted b~ 107), § 1, ~ 1987, 70th~ September 1, 1987.)

*[handwritten marginal note:]*
*Evidence not to be used CCP 38.23 (b)*
*- Good faith exception codified - Exception*
*- obtained by officer or other person*
*  in violation of Constitution of US & TX*
*LEON VS. US*
*- Good faith reliance → # LEO acting*
*upon warrant issued by neutral*
*magistrate acts in good faith*
*and evidence should not be*
*suppressed if warrant later found*
*to be defective    NOT IN TX*

## Art. 38.24.  Part of an Act, Declaration, Conversation or Writing [Repealed].

Repealed by the Texas Court of Criminal Appeals pursuant to Acts 1985, 69th Leg., ch. 685 (H.B. 13), § 9, effective September 1, 1986.
(Enacted by Acts 1965, 59th Leg., ch. 722 (S.B. 107), § 1, effective January 1, 1966.)

## Art. 38.25.  Written Part of Instrument Controls.

When an instrument is partly written and partly printed, the written shall control the printed portion when the two are inconsistent.
(Enacted by Acts 1965, 59th Leg., ch. 722 (S.B. 107), § 1, effective January 1, 1966.)

## Art. 38.26.  If Subscribing Witness Denies Execution [Repealed].

Repealed by the Texas Court of Criminal Appeals pursuant to Acts 1985, 69th Leg., ch. 685 (H.B. 13), § 9, effective September 1, 1986.
(Enacted by Acts 1965, 59th Leg., ch. 722 (S.B. 107), § 1, effective January 1, 1966.)

## Art. 38.27.  Evidence of Handwriting.

It is competent to give evidence of handwriting by comparison, made by experts or by the jury. Proof by comparison only shall not be sufficient to establish the handwriting of a witness who denies his signature under oath.
(Enacted by Acts 1965, 59th Leg., ch. 722 (S.B. 107), § 1, effective January 1, 1966.)

## Art. 38.28.  Attacking Testimony of His ~~~~ess [Repealed].

~~~~ by the Texas Court of Criminal Appeals pursuant to Acts 1985, 69th Leg., ch. 685 ~~~~ 9(b), effective September 1, 1986.
~~~~ Acts 1965, 59th Leg., ch. 722 (S.B. ~~~~fective January 1, 1966.)

## ~~~~. Indictment, Information or ~~~~t Not Admissible to Impeach ~~~~Repealed].

~~~~ by the Texas Court of Criminal Appeals pursuant to Acts 1985, 69th Leg., ch. 685 ~~~~ 9.
~~~~ Acts 1965, 59th Leg., ch. 722 (S.B. ~~~~fective January 1, 1966.)

## ~~~~.  Interpreter.

~~~~ a motion for appointment of an in~~~~ filed by any party or on motion of the ~~~~, ~~~~ny criminal proceeding, it is determined that a person charged or a witness does not understand and speak the English language, an interpreter must be sworn to interpret for the person charged or the witness. Any person may be subpoenaed, attached or recognized in any criminal action or proceeding, to appear before the proper judge or court to act as interpreter therein, under the same rules and penalties as are provided for witnesses. In the event that the only available interpreter is not considered to possess adequate interpreting skills for the particular situation or the interpreter is not familiar with use of slang, the person charged or witness may be permitted by the court to nominate another person to act as intermediary between the person charged or witness and the appointed interpreter during the proceedings.

(a-1) A qualified telephone interpreter may be sworn to interpret for the person in the trial of a Class C misdemeanor or a proceeding before a magistrate if an interpreter is not available to appear in person before the court or if the only available interpreter is not considered to possess adequate interpreting skills for the particular situation or is unfamiliar with the use of slang. In this subsection, "qualified telephone interpreter" means a telephone service that employs:

(1) licensed court interpreters as defined by Section 57.001, Government Code; or

(2) federally certified court interpreters.

(b) Except as provided by Subsection (c) of this article, interpreters appointed under the terms of this article will receive from the general fund of the county for their services a sum not to exceed $100 a day as follows: interpreters shall be paid not less than $15 nor more than $100 a day at the discretion of the judge presiding, and when travel of the interpreter is involved all the actual expenses of travel, lodging, and meals incurred by the interpreter pertaining to the case the interpreter is appointed to serve shall be paid at the same rate applicable to state employees.

(c) A county commissioners court may set a payment schedule and expend funds for the services of interpreters in excess of the daily amount of not less than $15 or more than $100 established by Subsection (b) of this article.

(Enacted by Acts 1965, 59th Leg., ch. 722 (S.B. 107), § 1, effective January 1, 1966; am. Acts 1979, 66th Leg., ch. 209 (S.B. 548), § 1, effective August 27, 1979; am. Acts 2005, 79th Leg., ch. 956 (H.B. 1601), § 1, effective September 1, 2005.)

## Art. 38.31. Interpreters for Deaf Persons.

(a) If the court is notified by a party that the defendant is deaf and will be present at an arraignment, hearing, examining trial, or trial, or that a witness is deaf and will be called at a hearing, examining trial, or trial, the court shall appoint a qualified interpreter to interpret the proceedings in any language that the deaf person can understand, including but not limited to sign language. On the court's motion or the motion of a party, the court may order testimony of a deaf witness and the interpretation of that testimony by the interpreter visually, electronically recorded for use in verification of the transcription of the reporter's notes. The clerk of the court shall include that recording in the appellate record if requested by a party under Article 40.09 of this Code.

(b) Following the filing of an indictment, information, or complaint against a deaf defendant, the court on the motion of the defendant shall appoint a qualified interpreter to interpret in a language that the defendant can understand, including but not limited to sign language, communications concerning the case between the defendant and defense counsel. The interpreter may not disclose a communication between the defendant and defense counsel or a fact that came to the attention of the interpreter while interpreting those communications if defense counsel may not disclose that communication or fact.

(c) In all cases where the mental condition of a person is being considered and where such person may be committed to a mental institution, and where such person is deaf, all of the court proceedings pertaining to him shall be interpreted by a qualified interpreter appointed by the court.

(d) A proceeding for which an interpreter is required to be appointed under this Article may not commence until the appointed interpreter is in a position not exceeding ten feet from and in full view of the deaf person.

(e) The interpreter appointed under the terms of this Article shall be required to take an oath that he will make a true interpretation to the person accused or being examined, which person is deaf, of all the proceedings of his case in a language that he understands; and that he will repeat said deaf person's answer to questions to counsel, court, or jury, in the English language, in his best skill and judgment.

(f) Interpreters appointed under this Article are entitled to a reasonable fee determined by the court after considering the recommendations of the Texas Commission for the Deaf and Hard of Hearing. When travel of the interpreter is involved all the actual expenses of travel, lodging, and meals incurred by the interpreter pertaining to the case he is appointed to serve shall be paid at the same rate applicable to state employees.

(g) In this Code:

(1) "Deaf person" means a person who has a hearing impairment, regardless of whether the person also has a speech impairment, that inhibits the person's comprehension of the proceedings or communication with others.

(2) "Qualified interpreter" means an interpreter for the deaf who holds a current legal certificate issued by the National Registry of Interpreters for the Deaf or a current court interpreter certificate issued by the Board for

Evaluation of Interpreters at the Department of Assistive or Rehabilitative Services.

(Enacted by Acts 1965, 59th Leg., ch. 722 (S.B. 107), § 1, effective January 1, 1966; am. Acts 1967, 60th Leg., ch. 105 (H.B. 36), § 2, effective August 28, 1967; am. Acts 1979, 66th Leg., ch. 186 (H.B. 1521), § 1, effective May 15, 1979; am. Acts 1987, 70th Leg., ch. 434 (S.B. 1346), § 1, effective June 17, 1987; am. Acts 1995, 74th Leg., ch. 835 (H.B. 2859), § 14, effective September 1, 1995; am. Acts 2005, 79th Leg., ch. 614 (H.B. 2200), § 11, effective September 1, 2006.)

## Art. 38.32. Presumption of Death.

(a) Upon introduction and admission into evidence of a valid certificate of death wherein the time of death of the decedent has been entered by a licensed physician, a presumption exists that death occurred at the time stated in the certificate of death.

(b) A presumption existing pursuant to Section (a) of this Article is sufficient to support a finding as to time of death but may be rebutted through a showing by a preponderance of the evidence that death occurred at some other time.

(Enacted by Acts 1969, 61st Leg., ch. 337 (H.B. 245), § 1, effective May 27, 1969.)

## Art. 38.33. Preservation and Use of Evidence of Certain Misdemeanor Convictions.

Sec. 1. The court shall order that a defendant who is convicted of a felony or a misdemeanor offense that is punishable by confinement in jail have a thumbprint of the defendant's right thumb rolled legibly on the judgment or the docket sheet in the case. The court shall order a defendant who is placed on probation under Section 5 of Article 42.12, Code of Criminal Procedure, for an offense described by this section to have a thumbprint of the defendant's right thumb rolled legibly on the order placing the defendant on probation. If the defendant does not have a right thumb, the defendant must have a thumbprint of the defendant's left thumb rolled legibly on the judgment, order, or docket sheet. The defendant must have a fingerprint of the defendant's index finger rolled legibly on the judgment, order, or docket sheet if the defendant does not have a right thumb or a left thumb. The judgment, order, or docket sheet must contain a statement that describes from which thumb or finger the print was taken, unless a rolled 10-finger print set was taken. A clerk or bailiff of the court or other person qual-

ified to take fingerprints shall take the thumbprint or fingerprint, either by use of the ink-rolled print method or by use of a live-scanning device that prints the thumbprint or fingerprint image on the judgment, order, or docket sheet.

Sec. 2. This article does not prohibit a court from including in the records of the case additional information to identify the defendant.

(Enacted by Acts 1979, 66th Leg., ch. 751 (H.B. 1275), § 1, effective September 1, 1979; am. Acts 1983, 68th Leg., ch. 303 (S.B. 1), § 7, effective January 1, 1984; am. Acts 1987, 70th Leg., ch. 721 (H.B. 635), § 1, effective September 1, 1987; am. Acts 1989, 71st Leg., ch. 603 (S.B. 60), § 1, effective September 1, 1989; am. Acts 1991, 72nd Leg., 2nd C.S., ch. 10 (H.B. 93), § 7.01, effective December 1, 1991.)

## Art. 38.34. Photographic Evidence in Theft Cases.

(a) In this article, "property" means any tangible personal property.

(b) A photograph of property that a person is alleged to have unlawfully appropriated with the intent to deprive the owner of the property is admissible into evidence under rules of law governing the admissibility of photographs. The photograph is as admissible in evidence as is the property itself.

(c) The provisions of Article 18.16 concerning the bringing of stolen property before a magistrate for examination are complied with if a photograph of the stolen property is brought before the magistrate.

(d) The defendant's rights of discovery and inspection of tangible physical evidence are satisfied if a photograph of the property is made available to the defendant by the state on order of any court having jurisdiction over the cause.

(Enacted by Acts 1985, 69th Leg., ch. 144 (S.B. 427), § 1, effective September 1, 1985; am. Acts 2009, 81st Leg., ch. 61 (H.B. 796), § 1, effective September 1, 2009.)

## Art. 38.35. Forensic Analysis of Evidence; Admissibility.

(a) In this article:

(1) "Crime laboratory" includes a public or private laboratory or other entity that conducts a forensic analysis subject to this article.

(2) "Criminal action" includes an investigation, complaint, arrest, bail, bond, trial, appeal, punishment, or other matter related to conduct proscribed by a criminal offense.

(3) "Director" means the public safety director of the Department of Public Safety.

(4) "Forensic analysis" means a medical, chemical, toxicologic, ballistic, or other expert examination or test performed on physical evidence, including DNA evidence, for the purpose of determining the connection of the evidence to a criminal action. The term includes an examination or test requested by a law enforcement agency, prosecutor, criminal suspect or defendant, or court. The term does not include:

(A) latent print examination;

(B) a test of a specimen of breath under Chapter 724, Transportation Code;

(C) digital evidence;

(D) an examination or test excluded by rule under Section 411.0205(c), Government Code;

(E) a presumptive test performed for the purpose of determining compliance with a term or condition of community supervision or parole and conducted by or under contract with a community supervision and corrections department, the parole division of the Texas Department of Criminal Justice, or the Board of Pardons and Paroles; or

(F) an expert examination or test conducted principally for the purpose of scientific research, medical practice, civil or administrative litigation, or other purpose unrelated to determining the connection of physical evidence to a criminal action.

(5) "Physical evidence" means any tangible object, thing, or substance relating to a criminal action.

(b) A law enforcement agency, prosecutor, or court may request a forensic analysis by a crime laboratory of physical evidence if the evidence was obtained in connection with the requesting entity's investigation or disposition of a criminal action and the requesting entity:

(1) controls the evidence;

(2) submits the evidence to the laboratory; or

(3) consents to the analysis.

(c) A law enforcement agency, other governmental agency, or private entity performing a forensic analysis of physical evidence may require the requesting law enforcement agency to pay a fee for such analysis.

(d) (1) Except as provided by Subsection (e), a forensic analysis of physical evidence under this article and expert testimony relating to the evidence are not admissible in a criminal action if, at the time of the analysis, the crime laboratory conducting the analysis was not accredited by the director under Section 411.0205, Government Code.

(2) If before the date of the analysis the director issues a certificate of accreditation under Section 411.0205, Government Code, to a crime laboratory conducting the analysis, the certificate is prima facie evidence that the laboratory was accredited by the director at the time of the analysis.

(e) A forensic analysis of physical evidence under this article and expert testimony relating to the evidence are not inadmissible in a criminal action based solely on the accreditation status of the crime laboratory conducting the analysis if the laboratory:

(A) except for making proper application, was eligible for accreditation by the director at the time of the examination or test; and

(B) obtains accreditation from the director before the time of testimony about the examination or test.

(f) This article does not apply to the portion of an autopsy conducted by a medical examiner or other forensic pathologist who is a licensed physician.

(Enacted by Acts 1991, 72nd Leg., ch. 298 (H.B. 413), § 1, effective September 1, 1991; am. Acts 2003, 78th Leg., ch. 698 (H.B. 2703), §§ 1—3, effective June 20, 2003; am. Acts 2005, 79th Leg., ch. 1224 (H.B. 1068), § 2, effective September 1, 2005.)

## Art. 38.36. Evidence in Prosecutions for Murder.

(a) In all prosecutions for murder, the state or the defendant shall be permitted to offer testimony as to all relevant facts and circumstances surrounding the killing and the previous relationship existing between the accused and the deceased, together with all relevant facts and circumstances going to show the condition of the mind of the accused at the time of the offense.

(b) In a prosecution for murder, if a defendant raises as a defense a justification provided by Section 9.31, 9.32, or 9.33, Penal Code, the defendant, in order to establish the defendant's reasonable belief that use of force or deadly force was immediately necessary, shall be permitted to offer:

(1) relevant evidence that the defendant had been the victim of acts of family violence committed by the deceased, as family violence is defined by Section 71.004, Family Code; and

(2) relevant expert testimony regarding the condition of the mind of the defendant at the time of the offense, including those relevant facts and circumstances relating to family violence that are the basis of the expert's opinion.

(Enacted by Acts 1993, 73rd Leg., ch. 900 (S.B. 1067), § 7.03, effective September 1, 1994; am. Acts 2003, 78th Leg., ch. 1276 (H.B. 3507), § 7.002(g), effective September 1, 2003.)

## Art. 38.37. Evidence of Extraneous Offenses or Acts.

Sec. 1. This article applies to a proceeding in the prosecution of a defendant for an offense, or an attempt or conspiracy to commit an offense, under the following provisions of the Penal Code:

(1) if committed against a child under 17 years of age:

(A) Chapter 21 (Sexual Offenses);

(B) Chapter 22 (Assaultive Offenses); or

(C) Section 25.02 (Prohibited Sexual Conduct); or

(2) if committed against a person younger than 18 years of age:

(A) Section 43.25 (Sexual Performance by a Child);

(B) Section 20A.02(a)(7) or (8); or

(C) Section 43.05(a)(2) (Compelling Prostitution).

Sec. 2. Notwithstanding Rules 404 and 405, Texas Rules of Evidence, evidence of other crimes, wrongs, or acts committed by the defendant against the child who is the victim of the alleged offense shall be admitted for its bearing on relevant matters, including:

(1) the state of mind of the defendant and the child; and

(2) the previous and subsequent relationship between the defendant and the child.

Sec. 3. On timely request by the defendant, the state shall give the defendant notice of the state's intent to introduce in the case in chief evidence described by Section 2 in the same manner as the state is required to give notice under Rule 404(b), Texas Rules of Evidence.

Sec. 4. This article does not limit the admissibility of evidence of extraneous crimes, wrongs, or acts under any other applicable law.

(Enacted by Acts 1995, 74th Leg., ch. 318 (S.B. 15), § 48(a), effective September 1, 1995; am. Acts 2005, 79th Leg., ch. 728 (H.B. 2018), § 4.004, effective September 1, 2005; am. Acts 2011, 82nd Leg., ch. 1 (S.B. 24), § 2.08, effective September 1, 2011.)

## Art. 38.38. Evidence Relating to Retaining Attorney.

Evidence that a person has contacted or retained an attorney is not admissible on the issue of whether the person committed a criminal offense. In a criminal case, neither the judge nor the attorney representing the state may comment on the fact that the defendant has contacted or retained an attorney in the case.

(Enacted by Acts 1995, 74th Leg., ch. 318 (S.B. 15), § 49, effective September 1, 1995.)

## Art. 38.39. Evidence in an Aggregation Prosecution with Numerous Victims.

In trials involving an allegation of a continuing scheme of fraud or theft alleged to have been committed against a large class of victims in an aggregate amount or value, it need not be proved by direct evidence that each alleged victim did not consent or did not effectively consent to the transaction in question. It shall be sufficient if the lack of consent or effective consent to a particular transaction or transactions is proven by either direct or circumstantial evidence.

(Enacted by Acts 2001, 77th Leg., ch. 1411 (S.B. 917), § 2, effective September 1, 2001.)

## Art. 38.40. Evidence of Pregnancy.

(a) In a prosecution for the death of or injury to an individual who is an unborn child, the prosecution shall provide medical or other evidence that the mother of the individual was pregnant at the time of the alleged offense.

(b) For the purpose of this section, "individual" has the meaning assigned by Section 1.07, Penal Code.

(Enacted by Acts 2003, 78th Leg., ch. 822 (S.B. 319), § 2.06, effective September 1, 2003.)

## Art. 38.41. Certificate of Analysis.

Sec. 1. A certificate of analysis that complies with this article is admissible in evidence on behalf of the state or the defendant to establish the results of a laboratory analysis of physical evidence conducted by or for a law enforcement agency without the necessity of the analyst personally appearing in court.

Sec. 2. This article does not limit the right of a party to summon a witness or to introduce admissible evidence relevant to the results of the analysis.

Sec. 3. A certificate of analysis under this article must contain the following information certified under oath:

(1) the names of the analyst and the laboratory employing the analyst;

(2) a statement that the laboratory employing the analyst is accredited by a nationally recognized board or association that accredits crime laboratories;

(3) a description of the analyst's educational background, training, and experience;

(4) a statement that the analyst's duties of employment included the analysis of physical evidence for one or more law enforcement agencies;

(5) a description of the tests or procedures conducted by the analyst;

(6) a statement that the tests or procedures used were reliable and approved by the laboratory employing the analyst; and

(7) the results of the analysis.

Sec. 4. Not later than the 20th day before the trial begins in a proceeding in which a certificate of analysis under this article is to be introduced, the certificate must be filed with the clerk of the court and a copy must be provided by fax, hand delivery, or certified mail, return receipt requested, to the opposing party. The certificate is not admissible under Section 1 if, not later than the 10th day before the trial begins, the opposing party files a written objection to the use of the certificate with the clerk of the court and provides a copy of the objection by fax, hand delivery, or certified mail, return receipt requested, to the offering party.

Sec. 5. A certificate of analysis is sufficient for purposes of this article if it uses the following form or if it otherwise substantially complies with this article:

## CERTIFICATE OF ANALYSIS

BEFORE ME, the undersigned authority, personally appeared _____, who being duly sworn, stated as follows:

My name is _____. I am of sound mind, over the age of 18 years, capable of making this affidavit, and personally acquainted with the facts stated in this affidavit.

I am employed by the _____, which was authorized to conduct the analysis referenced in this affidavit. Part of my duties for this laboratory involved the analysis of physical evidence for one or more law enforcement agencies. This laboratory is accredited by _____.

My educational background is as follows: (description of educational background)

My training and experience that qualify me to perform the tests or procedures referred to in this affidavit and determine the results of those tests or procedures are as follows: (description of training and experience)

I received the physical evidence listed on laboratory report no. _____ (attached) on the _____ day of _____, 20____. On the date indicated in the laboratory report, I conducted the following tests or procedures on the physical evidence: (description of tests and procedures)

The tests and procedures used were reliable and approved by the laboratory. The results are as indicated on the lab report.

_____
Affiant

SWORN TO AND SUBSCRIBED before me on the _____ day of _____, 20____.

_____
Notary Public, State of Texas

(Enacted by Acts 2003, 78th Leg., ch. 923 (S.B. 1129), § 1, effective September 1, 2003.)

## Art. 38.42. Chain of Custody Affidavit.

Sec. 1. A chain of custody affidavit that complies with this article is admissible in evidence on behalf of the state or the defendant to establish the chain of custody of physical evidence without the necessity of any person in the chain of custody personally appearing in court.

Sec. 2. This article does not limit the right of a party to summon a witness or to introduce admissible evidence relevant to the chain of custody.

Sec. 3. A chain of custody affidavit under this article must contain the following information stated under oath:

(1) the affiant's name and address;

(2) a description of the item of evidence and its container, if any, obtained by the affiant;

(3) the name of the affiant's employer on the date the affiant obtained custody of the physical evidence;

(4) the date and method of receipt and the name of the person from whom or location from which the item of physical evidence was received;

(5) the date and method of transfer and the name of the person to whom or location to which the item of physical evidence was transferred; and

(6) a statement that the item of evidence was transferred in essentially the same condition as received except for any minor change resulting from field or laboratory testing procedures.

Sec. 4. Not later than the 20th day before the trial begins in a proceeding in which a chain of custody affidavit under this article is to be introduced, the affidavit must be filed with the clerk of the court and a copy must be provided by fax, hand delivery, or certified mail, return receipt requested, to the opposing party. The affidavit is not admissible under Section 1 if, not later than the 10th day before the trial begins, the opposing party files a written objection to the use of the affidavit with the clerk of the court and provides a copy of the objection by fax, hand delivery, or certified mail, return receipt requested, to the offering party.

Sec. 5. A chain of custody affidavit is sufficient for purposes of this article if it uses the following form or if it otherwise substantially complies with this article:

## CHAIN OF CUSTODY AFFIDAVIT

BEFORE ME, the undersigned authority, personally appeared _____, who being by me duly sworn, stated as follows:

My name is _____. I am of sound mind, over the age of 18 years, capable of making this affidavit, and personally acquainted with the facts stated in this affidavit.

My address is _____.

On the _____ day of _____, 20____, I was employed by _____.

On that date, I came into possession of the physical evidence described as follows: (description of evidence)

I received the physical evidence from _____ (name of person or description of location) on the _____ day of _____, 20____, by _____ _____ (method of receipt).

This physical evidence was in a container described and marked as follows: (description of container)

I transferred the physical evidence to _____ (name of person or description of location) on the _____ day of _____, 20____, by _____ (method of delivery).

During the time that the physical evidence was in my custody, I did not make any changes or alterations to the condition of the physical evidence except for those resulting from field or laboratory testing procedures, and the physical evidence or a representative sample of the physical evidence was transferred in essentially the same condition as received.

_____
Affiant

SWORN TO AND SUBSCRIBED before me on the _____ day of _____, 20____.

_____
Notary Public, State of Texas

(Enacted by Acts 2003, 78th Leg., ch. 923 (S.B. 1129), § 1, effective September 1, 2003.)

## Art. 38.43. Evidence Containing Biological Material.

(a) In this article, "biological evidence" means:

(1) the contents of a sexual assault examination kit; or

(2) any item that contains blood, semen, hair, saliva, skin tissue, fingernail scrapings, bone, bodily fluids, or any other identifiable biological material that was collected as part of an investigation of an alleged felony offense or conduct constituting a felony offense that might reasonably be used to:

(A) establish the identity of the person committing the offense or engaging in the conduct constituting the offense; or

(B) exclude a person from the group of persons who could have committed the offense or engaged in the conduct constituting the offense.

(b) This article applies to a governmental or public entity or an individual, including a law enforcement agency, prosecutor's office, court, public hospital, or crime laboratory, that is charged with the collection, storage, preservation, analysis, or retrieval of biological evidence.

(c) An entity or individual described by Subsection (b) shall ensure that biological evidence collected pursuant to an investigation or prosecution of a felony offense or conduct constituting a felony offense is retained and preserved:

(1) for not less than 40 years, or until the applicable statute of limitations has expired, if there is an unapprehended actor associated with the offense; or

(2) in a case in which a defendant has been convicted, placed on deferred adjudication community supervision, or adjudicated as having engaged in delinquent conduct and there are no additional unapprehended actors associated with the offense:

(A) until the inmate is executed, dies, or is released on parole, if the defendant is convicted of a capital felony;

(B) until the defendant dies, completes the defendant's sentence, or is released on parole or mandatory supervision, if the defendant is sentenced to a term of confinement or imprisonment in the Texas Department of Criminal Justice;

(C) until the defendant completes the defendant's term of community supervision, including deferred adjudication community supervision, if the defendant is placed on community supervision;

(D) until the defendant dies, completes the defendant's sentence, or is released on parole, mandatory supervision, or juvenile probation, if the defendant is committed to the Texas Youth Commission; or

(E) until the defendant completes the defendant's term of juvenile probation, including a term of community supervision upon transfer of supervision to a criminal court, if the defendant is placed on juvenile probation.

(d) The attorney representing the state, clerk, or other officer in possession of biological evidence described by Subsection (a) may destroy the evidence, but only if the attorney, clerk, or officer by mail notifies the defendant, the last attorney of record for the defendant, and the convicting court of the decision to destroy the evidence and a written objection is not received by the attorney, clerk, or officer from the defendant, attorney of record, or court before the 91st day after the later of the following dates:

(1) the date on which the attorney representing the state, clerk, or other officer receives proof that the defendant received notice of the planned destruction of evidence; or

(2) the date on which notice of the planned destruction of evidence is mailed to the last attorney of record for the defendant.

(e) To the extent of any conflict, this article controls over Article 2.21.

(f) The Department of Public Safety shall adopt standards and rules authorizing a county with a population less than 100,000 to ensure the preservation of biological evidence by promptly delivering the evidence to the Department of Public Safety for storage in accordance with Section 411.053, Government Code, and department rules.

(g) The Department of Public Safety shall adopt standards and rules, consistent with best practices, relating to a person described by Subsection (b), that specify the manner of collection, storage, preservation, and retrieval of biological evidence.

(h) A person described by Subsection (b) may solicit and accept gifts, grants, donations, and contributions to support the collection, storage, preservation, retrieval, and destruction of biological evidence.
(Enacted by Acts 2001, 77th Leg., ch. 2 (S.B. 3), effective April 5, 2001; am. Acts 2005, 79th Leg., ch. 728 (H.B. 2018), § 23.001(8), effective September 1, 2005 (renumbered from art. 38.39); am. Acts 2009, 81st Leg., ch. 1179 (H.B. 3594), § 1, effective September 1, 2009; am. Acts 2011, 82nd Leg., ch. 91 (S.B. 1303), § 27.002(1), effective September 1, 2011; am. Acts 2011, 82nd Leg., ch. 1248 (S.B. 1616), § 1, effective June 17, 2011.)

### Art. 38.44. Admissibility of Electronically Preserved Document.

An electronically preserved document has the same legal significance and admissibility as if the document had been maintained in hard-copy form. If a party opposes admission of the document on the grounds that the document has been materially altered, the proponent of the document must disprove the allegation by a preponderance of the evidence.
(Enacted by Acts 2005, 79th Leg., ch. 312 (S.B. 611), § 5, effective June 17, 2005.)

### Art. 38.45. Evidence Depicting or Describing Abuse of or Sexual Conduct by Child or Minor.

(a) During the course of a criminal hearing or proceeding, the court may not make available or allow to be made available for copying or dissemination to the public property or material:

(1) that constitutes child pornography, as described by Section 43.26(a)(1), Penal Code;

(2) the promotion or possession of which is prohibited under Section 43.261, Penal Code; or

(3) that is described by Section 2 or 5, Article 38.071, of this code.

(b) The court shall place property or material described by Subsection (a) under seal of the court on conclusion of the criminal hearing or proceeding.

(c) The attorney representing the state shall be provided access to property or material described by Subsection (a). In the manner provided by Article 39.15, the defendant, the defendant's attorney, and any individual the defendant seeks to qualify to provide expert testimony at trial shall be provided access to property or material described by Subsection (a).

(d) A court that places property or material described by Subsection (a) under seal may issue

an order lifting the seal on a finding that the order is in the best interest of the public.
(Enacted by Acts 2009, 81st Leg., ch. 276 (S.B. 595), § 1, effective September 1, 2009; am. Acts 2011, 82nd Leg., ch. 1322 (S.B. 407), §§ 7, 8, effective September 1, 2011.)

### Art. 38.46. [2 Versions: As added by Acts 2011, 82nd Leg., ch. 104] Evidence in Aggregation Prosecution for Fraud or Theft Committed with Respect to Numerous Medicaid or Medicare Recipients.

In trials involving an allegation of a continuing scheme of fraud or theft that involves Medicaid or Medicare benefits and is alleged to have been committed with respect to a large class of Medicaid or Medicare recipients in an aggregate amount or value, the attorney representing the state is not required to prove by direct evidence that each Medicaid or Medicare recipient did not consent or effectively consent to a transaction in question. It is sufficient if the lack of consent or effective consent to a particular transaction or transactions is proven by either direct or circumstantial evidence.
(Enacted by Acts 2011, 82nd Leg., ch. 104 (S.B. 1680), § 1, effective September 1, 2011.)

### Art. 38.46. [2 Versions: As added by Acts 2011, 82nd Leg., ch. 591] Evidence in Prosecutions for Stalking.

(a) In a prosecution for stalking, each party may offer testimony as to all relevant facts and circumstances that would aid the trier of fact in determining whether the actor's conduct would cause a reasonable person to experience a fear described by Section 42.072(a)(3)(A), (B), or (C), Penal Code, including the facts and circumstances surrounding any existing or previous relationship between the actor and the alleged victim, a member of the alleged victim's family or household, or an individual with whom the alleged victim has a dating relationship.

(b) This article does not permit the presentation of character evidence that would otherwise be inadmissible under the Texas Rules of Evidence or other applicable law.
(Enacted by Acts 2011, 82nd Leg., ch. 591 (S.B. 82), § 3, effective September 1, 2011.)

## CHAPTER 39
## DEPOSITIONS AND DISCOVERY

### Art. 39.01. In Examining Trial.

When an examination takes place in a criminal action before a magistrate, the state or the defendant may have the deposition of any witness taken by any officer authorized by this chapter. The state or the defendant may not use the deposition for any purpose unless that party first acknowledges that the entire evidence or statement of the witness may be used for or against the defendant on the trial of the case, subject to all legal objections. The deposition of a witness duly taken before an examining trial or a jury of inquest and reduced to writing or recorded and then certified according to law, provided that the defendant and the defendant's attorney were present when that testimony was taken and that the defendant had the privilege afforded of cross-examining the witness, or taken at any prior trial of the defendant for the same offense, may be used by either the state or the defendant in the trial of the defendant's criminal case under the following circumstances:

When oath is made by the party using the deposition that the witness resides outside the state; or that since the witness's testimony was taken, the witness has died, or has removed beyond the limits of the state, or has been prevented from attending the court through the act or agency of the other party, or by the act or

agency of any person whose object was to deprive the state or the defendant of the benefit of the testimony; or that by reason of age or bodily infirmity, that witness cannot attend; or that the witness is a Medicaid or Medicare recipient or a caregiver or guardian of the recipient, and the recipient's Medicaid or Medicare account was charged for a product or service that was not provided or rendered to the recipient. When the testimony is sought to be used by the state, the oath may be made by any credible person. When sought to be used by the defendant, the oath must be made by the defendant in person.
(Enacted by Acts 1965, 59th Leg., ch. 722 (S.B. 107), § 1, effective January 1, 1966; am. Acts 2005, 79th Leg., ch. 1021 (H.B. 975), § 1, effective September 1, 2005; am. Acts 2011, 82nd Leg., ch. 104 (S.B. 1680), § 2, effective September 1, 2011.)

### Art. 39.02. Witness Depositions.

Depositions of witnesses may be taken by either the state or the defendant. When a party desires to take the deposition of a witness, the party shall file with the clerk of the court in which the case is pending an affidavit stating the facts necessary to constitute a good reason for taking the witness's deposition and an application to take the deposition. On the filing of the affidavit and application, and after notice to the opposing party, the court shall hear the application and determine if good reason exists for taking the deposition. The court shall base its determination and shall grant or deny the application on the facts made known at the hearing. This provision is limited to the purposes stated in Article 39.01.
(Enacted by Acts 1965, 59th Leg., ch. 722 (S.B. 107), § 1, effective January 1, 1966; am. Acts 1967, 60th Leg., ch. 659 (S.B. 145), § 24, effective August 28, 1967; am. Acts 2005, 79th Leg., ch. 1021 (H.B. 975), § 1, effective September 1, 2005.)

### Art. 39.025. Depositions of Elderly or Disabled Persons.

(a) In this article:
(1) "Disabled person" means a person with a disability as defined by Section 3, Americans with Disabilities Act (42 U.S.C. 12102).
(2) "Elderly person" means a person 65 years of age or older.
(b) The court shall order the attorney representing the state to take the deposition of an elderly or disabled person who is the alleged victim of or witness to an offense not later than the 60th day after the date on which the state files an application to take the deposition under Article 39.02.
(c) The attorney representing the state and the defendant or the defendant's attorney may, by written agreement filed with the court, extend the deadline for the taking of the deposition.
(d) The court shall grant any request by the attorney representing the state to extend the deadline for the taking of the deposition if a reason for the request is the unavailability, health, or well-being of the victim or witness.
(e) The Texas Rules of Civil Procedure govern the taking of the deposition, except to the extent of any conflict with this code or applicable court rules adopted for criminal proceedings, in which event this code and the rules for criminal proceedings govern. The attorney representing the state and the defendant or defendant's attorney may agree to modify the rules applicable to the deposition by written agreement filed with the court before the taking of the deposition.
(f) If a defendant is unavailable to attend a deposition because the defendant is confined in a correctional facility, the court shall issue any orders or warrants necessary to secure the defendant's presence at the deposition. The sheriff of the county in which a deposition under this subsection is to be taken shall provide a secure location for the taking of the deposition and sufficient law enforcement personnel to ensure the deposition is taken safely. The state's application to take a deposition or notice of deposition is not required to include the identity of any law enforcement agents the sheriff assigns to the deposition and may not serve as a basis for the defendant to object to the taking of the deposition.
(g) If a defendant is unavailable to attend a deposition for any reason other than confinement in a correctional facility, the defendant or defendant's attorney shall request a continuance from the court. The court may grant the continuance if the defendant or defendant's attorney demonstrates good cause for the continuance and that the request is not brought for the purpose of delay or avoidance. A defendant's failure to attend a deposition or request a continuance in accordance with this subsection constitutes a waiver of the defendant's right to be present at the deposition.
(Enacted by Acts 2009, 81st Leg., ch. 678 (H.B. 2465), § 1, effective September 1, 2009.)

## Art. 39.026. Depositions of Medicaid or Medicare Recipients or Caregivers.

(a) In this article:

(1) "Caregiver" means a person, including a guardian, who is authorized by law, contract, or familial relationship to care for a recipient.

(2) "Medicaid" means the state Medicaid program.

(3) "Medicaid recipient" has the meaning assigned by Section 36.001, Human Resources Code.

(4) "Medicare" means the federal health insurance program that is operated under the Health Insurance for the Aged Act (42 U.S.C. Section 1395 et seq.).

(5) "Medicare recipient" means an individual on whose behalf a person claims or receives a payment under Medicare, without regard to whether the individual was eligible for benefits under Medicare.

(6) "Recipient" means a Medicaid recipient or a Medicare recipient.

(b) The court may order the attorney representing the state to take the deposition of a recipient or caregiver who is the alleged victim of or witness to an offense constituting fraud or theft that involves Medicaid or Medicare benefits. Any order under this subsection must be issued not later than the 180th day after the date on which the state files an application to take the deposition under Article 39.02.

(c) On the motion of either party, the court may order the attorney representing the state to take the deposition of a recipient or caregiver by video recording. The person operating the video recording device must be available to testify regarding the authenticity of the video recording and the taking of the deposition in order for the video recording to be admissible.

(d) If the court finds that the video recording of the deposition is properly authenticated and that requiring the jury to view the entire recording would unnecessarily prolong the trial, the court may allow a party to offer the entire video recording into evidence without requiring the jury to view the entire video recording during the trial. This subsection does not preclude the attorney representing the state, the defendant, or the defendant's attorney from offering into evidence and playing for the jury a portion of a video-recorded deposition.

(e) The attorney representing the state and the defendant or the defendant's attorney, by written agreement filed with the court, may extend the deadline for the taking of the deposition.

(f) The court shall grant any request by the attorney representing the state to extend the deadline for the taking of the deposition if a reason for the request is the unavailability, health, or well-being of the recipient or caregiver.

(g) The Texas Rules of Civil Procedure govern the taking of the deposition, except that, to the extent of any conflict with this code or applicable court rules adopted for criminal proceedings, this code and the rules for criminal proceedings govern. The attorney representing the state and the defendant or the defendant's attorney may agree to modify the rules applicable to the deposition by written agreement filed with the court before the taking of the deposition.

(h) If a defendant is unavailable to attend a deposition because the defendant is confined in a correctional facility, the court shall issue any orders or warrants necessary to secure the defendant's presence at the deposition. The sheriff of the county in which a deposition is to be taken under this subsection shall provide a secure location for the taking of the deposition and sufficient law enforcement personnel to ensure that the deposition is taken safely. The state's application to take a deposition or notice of deposition is not required to include the identity of any law enforcement agent the sheriff assigns to the deposition under this subsection, and the defendant may not object to the taking of the deposition based solely on the state's omission of the identity of that agent.

(i) If a defendant is unavailable to attend a deposition for any reason other than confinement in a correctional facility, the defendant or the defendant's attorney shall request a continuance from the court. The court may grant the continuance if the defendant or the defendant's attorney demonstrates good cause for the continuance and that the request is not brought for the purpose of delay or avoidance. A defendant's failure to attend a deposition or request a continuance in accordance with this subsection constitutes a waiver of the defendant's right to be present at the deposition.

(Enacted by Acts 2011, 82nd Leg., ch. 104 (S.B. 1680), § 3, effective September 1, 2011.)

## Art. 39.03. Officers Who May Take the Deposition.

Upon the filing of such an affidavit and application, the court shall appoint, order or designate one of the following persons before whom such deposition shall be taken:

Criminal Procedure

1. A district judge.
2. A county judge.
3. A notary public.
4. A district clerk.
5. A county clerk.

Such order shall specifically name such person and the time when and place where such deposition shall be taken. Failure of a witness to respond thereto, shall be punishable by contempt by the court. Such deposition shall be oral or written, as the court shall direct.
(Enacted by Acts 1965, 59th Leg., ch. 722 (S.B. 107), § 1, effective January 1, 1966; am. Acts 1967, 60th Leg., ch. 659 (S.B. 145), § 25, effective August 28, 1967.)

## Art. 39.04. Applicability of Civil Rules.

The rules prescribed in civil cases for issuance of commissions, subpoenaing witnesses, taking the depositions of witnesses and all other formalities governing depositions shall, as to the manner and form of taking and returning the same and other formalities to the taking of the same, govern in criminal actions, when not in conflict with this Code.
(Enacted by Acts 1965, 59th Leg., ch. 722 (S.B. 107), § 1, effective January 1, 1966.)

## Art. 39.05. Objections.

The rules of procedure as to objections in depositions in civil actions shall govern in criminal actions when not in conflict with this Code.
(Enacted by Acts 1965, 59th Leg., ch. 722 (S.B. 107), § 1, effective January 1, 1966.)

## Art. 39.06. Written Interrogatories.

When any such deposition is to be taken by written interrogatories, such written interrogatories shall be filed with the clerk of the court, and a copy of the same served on all other parties or their counsel for the length of time and in the manner required for service of interrogatories in civil action, and the same procedure shall also be followed with reference to cross-interrogatories as that prescribed in civil actions.
(Enacted by Acts 1965, 59th Leg., ch. 722 (S.B. 107), § 1, effective January 1, 1966.)

## Art. 39.07. Certificate.

Where depositions are taken under commission in criminal actions, the officer or officers taking the same shall certify that the person deposing is the identical person named in the commission; or, if they cannot certify to the identity of the wit-

ness, there shall be an affidavit of some person attached to the deposition proving the identity of such witness, and the officer or officers shall certify that the person making the affidavit is known to them.
(Enacted by Acts 1965, 59th Leg., ch. 722 (S.B. 107), § 1, effective January 1, 1966; am. Acts 1967, 60th Leg., ch. 659 (S.B. 145), § 26, effective August 28, 1967.)

## Art. 39.08. Authenticating the Deposition.

The official seal and signature of the officer taking the deposition shall be attached to the certificate authenticating the deposition.
(Enacted by Acts 1965, 59th Leg., ch. 722 (S.B. 107), § 1, effective January 1, 1966.)

## Art. 39.09. Non-Resident Witnesses.

Depositions of a witness residing out of the State may be taken before a judge or before a commissioner of deeds and depositions for this State, who resides within the State where the deposition is to be taken, or before a notary public of the place where such deposition is to be taken, or before any commissioned officer of the armed services or before any diplomatic or consular officer. The deposition of a non-resident witness who may be temporarily within the State, may be taken under the same rules which apply to the taking of depositions of other witnesses in the State.
(Enacted by Acts 1965, 59th Leg., ch. 722 (S.B. 107), § 1, effective January 1, 1966.)

## Art. 39.10. Return.

In all cases the return of depositions may be made as provided in civil actions.
(Enacted by Acts 1965, 59th Leg., ch. 722 (S.B. 107), § 1, effective January 1, 1966.)

## Art. 39.11. Waiver.

The State and defense may agree upon a waiver of any formalities in the taking of a deposition other than that the taking of such deposition must be under oath.
(Enacted by Acts 1965, 59th Leg., ch. 722 (S.B. 107), § 1, effective January 1, 1966.)

## Art. 39.12. Predicate to Read.

Depositions taken in criminal actions shall not be read unless oath be made that the witness resides out of the state; or that since the deposition was taken, the witness has died; or that the witness has removed beyond the limits of the state; or that the witness has been prevented from attending the court through the act or agency of the defendant; or by the act or agency of any person whose object was to deprive the state or the defendant of the benefit of the testimony; or that by reason of age or bodily infirmity, the witness cannot attend; or that the witness is a Medicaid or Medicare recipient or a caregiver or guardian of the recipient, and the recipient's Medicaid or Medicare account was charged for a product or service that was not provided or rendered to the recipient. When the deposition is sought to be used by the state, the oath may be made by any credible person. When sought to be used by the defendant, the oath shall be made by the defendant in person.

(Enacted by Acts 1965, 59th Leg., ch. 722 (S.B. 107), § 1, effective January 1, 1966; am. by Acts 2011, 82nd Leg., ch. 104 (S.B. 1680), § 4, effective September 1, 2011.)

### Art. 39.13. Impeachment.

Nothing contained in the preceding Articles shall be construed as prohibiting the use of any such evidence for impeachment purposes under the rules of evidence heretofore existing at common law.

(Enacted by Acts 1965, 59th Leg., ch. 722 (S.B. 107), § 1, effective January 1, 1966.)

### Art. 39.14. Discovery.

(a) Upon motion of the defendant showing good cause therefor and upon notice to the other parties, except as provided by Article 39.15, the court in which an action is pending shall order the State before or during trial of a criminal action therein pending or on trial to produce and permit the inspection and copying or photographing by or on behalf of the defendant of any designated documents, papers, written statement of the defendant, (except written statements of witnesses and except the work product of counsel in the case and their investigators and their notes or report), books, accounts, letters, photographs, objects or tangible things not privileged, which constitute or contain evidence material to any matter involved in the action and which are in the possession, custody or control of the State or any of its agencies. The order shall specify the time, place and manner of making the inspection and taking the copies and photographs of any of the aforementioned documents or tangible evidence; provided, however, that the rights herein

granted shall not extend to written communications between the State or any of its agents or representatives or employees. Nothing in this Act shall authorize the removal of such evidence from the possession of the State, and any inspection shall be in the presence of a representative of the State.

(b) On motion of a party and on notice to the other parties, the court in which an action is pending may order one or more of the other parties to disclose to the party making the motion the name and address of each person the other party may use at trial to present evidence under Rules 702, 703, and 705, Texas Rules of Evidence. The court shall specify in the order the time and manner in which the other party must make the disclosure to the moving party, but in specifying the time in which the other party shall make disclosure the court shall require the other party to make the disclosure not later than the 20th day before the date the trial begins.

(Enacted by Acts 1965, 59th Leg., ch. 722 (S.B. 107), § 1, effective January 1, 1966; am. Acts 1999, 76th Leg., ch. 578 (S.B. 557), § 1, effective September 1, 1999; am. Acts 2005, 79th Leg., ch. 1019 (H.B. 969), § 1, effective June 18, 2005; am. Acts 2009, 81st Leg., ch. 276 (S.B. 595), § 2, effective September 1, 2009.)

### Art. 39.15. Discovery of Evidence Depicting or Describing Abuse of or Sexual Conduct by Child or Minor.

(a) In the manner provided by this article, a court shall allow discovery under Article 39.14 of property or material:

(1) that constitutes child pornography, as described by Section 43.26(a)(1), Penal Code;

(2) the promotion or possession of which is prohibited under Section 43.261, Penal Code; or

(3) that is described by Section 2 or 5, Article 38.071, of this code.

(b) Property or material described by Subsection (a) must remain in the care, custody, or control of the court or the state as provided by Article 38.45.

(c) A court shall deny any request by a defendant to copy, photograph, duplicate, or otherwise reproduce any property or material described by Subsection (a), provided that the state makes the property or material reasonably available to the defendant.

(d) For purposes of Subsection (c), property or material is considered to be reasonably available

Criminal Procedure

to the defendant if, at a facility under the control of the state, the state provides ample opportunity for the inspection, viewing, and examination of the property or material by the defendant, the defendant's attorney, and any individual the defendant seeks to qualify to provide expert testimony at trial.
(Enacted by Acts 2009, 81st Leg., ch. 276 (S.B. 595), § 3, effective September 1, 2009; am. Acts 2011, 82nd Leg., ch. 1322 (S.B. 407), §§ 9, 10, effective September 1, 2011.)

# Proceedings After Verdict

## CHAPTER 40
## NEW TRIALS

Article
40.001.     New Trial on Material Evidence.

### Art. 40.001. New Trial on Material Evidence.

A new trial shall be granted an accused where material evidence favorable to the accused has been discovered since trial.
(Enacted by Acts 1993, 73rd Leg., ch. 900 (S.B. 1067), § 11.01, effective September 1, 1993.)

### Art. 40.01. Definition of "New Trial" [Repealed].

Repealed by the Texas Court of Criminal Appeals pursuant to Acts 1985, 69th Leg., ch. 685 (H.B. 13), § 4, effective September 1, 1986.
(Enacted by Acts 1965, 59th Leg., ch. 722 (S.B. 107), § 1, effective January 1, 1966.)

### Art. 40.02. Granted Only to Accused [Repealed].

Repealed by the Texas Court of Criminal Appeals pursuant to Acts 1985, 69th Leg., ch. 685 (H.B. 13), § 4.
(Enacted by Acts 1965, 59th Leg., ch. 722 (S.B. 107), § 1, effective January 1, 1966.)

### Art. 40.03. Grounds for New Trial in Felony [Repealed].

Repealed by the Texas Court of Criminal Appeals pursuant to Acts 1985, 69th Leg., ch. 685 (H.B. 13), § 4.
(Enacted by Acts 1965, 59th Leg., ch. 722 (S.B. 107), § 1, effective January 1, 1966; am. Acts 1973, 63rd Leg., ch. 399 (S.B. 34), § 2(A), effective January 1, 1974; am. Acts 1973, 63rd Leg., ch. 426 (H.B. 200), Art. 3 § 5, effective June 14, 1973.)

### Art. 40.04. In Misdemeanors [Repealed].

Repealed by the Texas Court of Criminal Appeals pursuant to Acts 1985, 69th Leg., ch. 685 (H.B. 13), § 4.
(Enacted by Acts 1965, 59th Leg., ch. 722 (S.B. 107), § 1, effective January 1, 1966.)

### Art. 40.05. Time to Apply for New Trial; Amendment [Repealed].

Repealed by the Texas Court of Criminal Appeals pursuant to Acts 1985, 69th Leg., ch. 685 (H.B. 13), § 4.
(Enacted by Acts 1965, 59th Leg., ch. 722 (S.B. 107), § 1, effective January 1, 1966; am. Acts 1981, 67th Leg., ch. 291 (S.B. 265), § 107, effective September 1, 1981.)

### Art. 40.06. State May Controvert Motion [Repealed].

Repealed by the Texas Court of Criminal Appeals pursuant to Acts 1985, 69th Leg., ch. 685 (H.B. 13), § 4.
(Enacted by Acts 1965, 59th Leg., ch. 722 (S.B. 107), § 1, effective January 1, 1966.)

### Art. 40.07. Judge Not to Discuss Evidence [Repealed].

Repealed by the Texas Court of Criminal Appeals pursuant to Acts 1985, 69th Leg., ch. 685 (H.B. 13), § 4.
(Enacted by Acts 1965, 59th Leg., ch. 722 (S.B. 107), § 1, effective January 1, 1966.)

### Art. 40.08. Effect of a New Trial [Repealed].

Repealed by the Texas Court of Criminal Appeals pursuant to Acts 1985, 69th Leg., ch. 685 (H.B. 13), § 4.
(Enacted by Acts 1965, 59th Leg., ch. 722 (S.B. 107), § 1, effective January 1, 1966.)

### Art. 40.09. Record on Appeals [Repealed].

Repealed by the Texas Court of Criminal Appeals pursuant to Acts 1985, 69th Leg., ch. 685 (H.B. 13), § 4.
(Enacted by Acts 1965, 59th Leg., ch. 722 (S.B. 107), § 1, effective January 1, 1966; am. Acts 1967, 60th Leg., ch. 659 (S.B. 145), § 27, effective August 28, 1967; am. Acts 1973, 63rd Leg., ch. 460 (S.B. 780), § 2, effective August 27, 1973; am. Acts 1977, 65th Leg., ch. 236 (S.B. 155), §§ 1—3, effective May 25, 1977; am. Acts 1979, 66th Leg.,

ch. 204 (S.B. 442), § 1, effective August 27, 1979; am. Acts 1979, 66th Leg., ch. 324 (S.B. 439), § 1, effective August 27, 1979; am. Acts 1979, 66th Leg., ch. 390 (H.B. 1565), § 1, effective September 1, 1979; am. Acts 1981, 67th Leg., ch. 144 (S.B. 556), § 1, effective May 14, 1981; am. Acts 1981, 67th Leg., ch. 291 (S.B. 265), § 108, effective September 1, 1981; am. Acts 1983, 68th Leg., ch. 329 (H.B. 559), § 1, effective August 29, 1983.)

### Art. 40.10. Application of Civil Statutes [Repealed].

Repealed by the Texas Court of Criminal Appeals pursuant to Acts 1985, 69th Leg., ch. 685 (H.B. 13), § 4.

(Enacted by Acts 1965, 59th Leg., ch. 722 (S.B. 107), § 1, effective January 1, 1966; am. Acts 1981, 67th Leg., ch. 291 (S.B. 265), § 109, effective September 1, 1981.)

### Art. 40.11. Requirement for Filing Court Reporter's Notes [Repealed].

Repealed by the Texas Court of Criminal Appeals pursuant to Acts 1985, 69th Leg., ch. 685 (H.B. 13), § 4.

(Enacted by Acts 1983, 68th Leg., ch. 1018 (H.B. 2224), § 1, effective September 1, 1983.)

# CHAPTER 41
## ARREST OF JUDGMENT
## [REPEALED]

### Art. 41.01. Motion in Arrest of Judgment [Repealed].

Repealed by the Texas Court of Criminal Appeals pursuant to Acts 1985, 69th Leg., ch. 685 (H.B. 13), § 4.

(Enacted by Acts 1965, 59th Leg., ch. 722 (S.B. 107), § 1, effective January 1, 1966.)

### Art. 41.02. Time to Make Motion [Repealed].

Repealed by the Texas Court of Criminal Appeals pursuant to Acts 1985, 69th Leg., ch. 685 (H.B. 13), § 4.

(Enacted by Acts 1965, 59th Leg., ch. 722 (S.B. 107), § 1, effective January 1, 1966; am. Acts 1981, 67th Leg., ch. 291 (S.B. 265), § 110, effective September 1, 1981.)

### Art. 41.03. Granted for Substantial Defect [Repealed].

Repealed by the Texas Court of Criminal Appeals pursuant to Acts 1985, 69th Leg., ch. 685 (H.B. 13), § 4.

(Enacted by Acts 1965, 59th Leg., ch. 722 (S.B. 107), § 1, effective January 1, 1966.)

### Art. 41.04. Want of Form [Repealed].

Repealed by the Texas Court of Criminal Appeals pursuant to Acts 1985, 69th Leg., ch. 685 (H.B. 13), § 4.

(Enacted by Acts 1965, 59th Leg., ch. 722 (S.B. 107), § 1, effective January 1, 1966.)

### Art. 41.05. Effect of Arresting Judgment [Repealed].

Repealed by the Texas Court of Criminal Appeals pursuant to Acts 1985, 69th Leg., ch. 685 (H.B. 13), § 4.

(Enacted by Acts 1965, 59th Leg., ch. 722 (S.B. 107), § 1, effective January 1, 1966.)

# CHAPTER 42
## JUDGMENT AND SENTENCE

## Art. 42.01. Judgment.

Sec. 1. A judgment is the written declaration of the court signed by the trial judge and entered of record showing the conviction or acquittal of the defendant. The sentence served shall be based on the information contained in the judgment. The judgment shall reflect:

1. The title and number of the case;

2. That the case was called and the parties appeared, naming the attorney for the state, the defendant, and the attorney for the defendant, or, where a defendant is not represented by counsel, that the defendant knowingly, intelligently, and voluntarily waived the right to representation by counsel;

3. The plea or pleas of the defendant to the offense charged;

4. Whether the case was tried before a jury or a jury was waived;

5. The submission of the evidence, if any;

6. In cases tried before a jury that the jury was charged by the court;

7. The verdict or verdicts of the jury or the finding or findings of the court;

8. In the event of a conviction that the defendant is adjudged guilty of the offense as found by the verdict of the jury or the finding of the court, and that the defendant be punished in accordance with the jury's verdict or the court's finding as to the proper punishment;

9. In the event of conviction where death or any punishment is assessed that the defendant be sentenced to death, a term of confinement or community supervision, or to pay a fine, as the case may be;

10. In the event of conviction where the imposition of sentence is suspended and the defendant is placed on community supervision, setting forth the punishment assessed, the length of community supervision, and the conditions of community supervision;

11. In the event of acquittal that the defendant be discharged;

12. The county and court in which the case was tried and, if there was a change of venue in the case, the name of the county in which the prosecution was originated;

13. The offense or offenses for which the defendant was convicted;

14. The date of the offense or offenses and degree of offense for which the defendant was convicted;

15. The term of sentence;

16. The date judgment is entered;

17. The date sentence is imposed;

18. The date sentence is to commence and any credit for time served;

19. The terms of any order entered pursuant to Article 42.08 of this code that the defendant's sentence is to run cumulatively or concurrently with another sentence or sentences;

20. The terms of any plea bargain;

21. Affirmative findings entered pursuant to Subdivision (2) of Subsection (a) of Section 3g of Article 42.12 of this code;

22. The terms of any fee payment ordered under Article 42.151 of this code;

23. The defendant's thumbprint taken in accordance with Article 38.33 of this code;

24. In the event that the judge orders the defendant to repay a reward or part of a reward under Articles 37.073 and 42.152 of this code, a

statement of the amount of the payment or payments required to be made;

25. In the event that the court orders restitution to be paid to the victim, a statement of the amount of restitution ordered and:

(A) the name and address of a person or agency that will accept and forward restitution payments to the victim; or

(B) if the court specifically elects to have payments made directly to the crime victim, the name and permanent address of the victim at the time of judgment;

26. In the event that a presentence investigation is required by Section 9(a), (b), (h), or (i), Article 42.12 of this code, a statement that the presentence investigation was done according to the applicable provision;

27. In the event of conviction of an offense for which registration as a sex offender is required under Chapter 62, a statement that the registration requirement of that chapter applies to the defendant and a statement of the age of the victim of the offense;

28. The defendant's state identification number required by Section 60.052(a)(2), if that number has been assigned at the time of the judgment; and

29. The incident number required by Section 60.052(a)(4), if that number has been assigned at the time of the judgment.

Sec. 2. The judge may order the prosecuting attorney, or the attorney or attorneys representing any defendant, or the court clerk under the supervision of an attorney, to prepare the judgment, or the court may prepare the same.

Sec. 3. The provisions of this article shall apply to both felony and misdemeanor cases.

Sec. 4. The Office of Court Administration of the Texas Judicial System shall promulgate a standardized felony judgment form that conforms to the requirements of Section 1 of this article. A court entering a felony judgement [sic] shall use the form promulgated under this section.

Sec. 5. In addition to the information described by Section 1 of this article, the judgment should reflect affirmative findings entered pursuant to Article 42.013 of this code.

Sec. 6. In addition to the information described by Section 1 of this article, the judgment should reflect affirmative findings entered pursuant to Article 42.014 of this code.

Sec. 7. In addition to the information described by Section 1, the judgment should reflect affirmative findings entered pursuant to Article 42.015.

Sec. 8. In addition to the information described by Section 1, the judgment should reflect affirmative findings entered pursuant to Article 42.017.

Sec. 9. In addition to the information described by Section 1, the judgment should reflect affirmative findings entered pursuant to Article 42.0197.

Sec. 10. In addition to the information described by Section 1, the judgment should reflect affirmative findings entered pursuant to Article 42.0198.

(Enacted by Acts 1965, 59th Leg., ch. 722 (S.B. 107), § 1, effective January 1, 1966; am. Acts 1975, 64th Leg., ch. 95 (H.B. 253), § 1, effective September 1, 1975; am. Acts 1981, 67th Leg., ch. 291 (S.B. 265), § 111, effective September 1, 1981; am. Acts 1985, 69th Leg., ch. 344 (S.B. 845), § 1, effective January 1, 1986; am. Acts 1985, 69th Leg., ch. 344 (S.B. 845), § 2, effective June 10, 1985; am. Acts 1987, 70th Leg., ch. 110 (S.B. 26), § 2, effective August 31, 1987; am. Acts 1989, 71st Leg., ch. 360 (S.B. 1175), § 2, effective September 1, 1989; am. Acts 1989, 71st Leg., ch. 603 (S.B. 60), § 2, effective September 1, 1989; am. Acts 1989, 71st Leg., ch. 611 (S.B. 149), § 2, effective September 1, 1989; am. Acts 1989, 71st Leg., ch. 806 (H.B. 568), § 1, effective September 1, 1989; am. Acts 1991, 72nd Leg., ch. 16 (S.B. 232), § 4.04, effective August 26, 1991; am. Acts 1991, 72nd Leg., 2nd C.S., ch. 10 (H.B. 93), § 7.02, effective December 1, 1991; am. Acts 1993, 73rd Leg., ch. 900 (S.B. 1067), § 5.03, effective September 1, 1993; am. Acts 1993, 73rd Leg., ch. 900 (S.B. 1067), § 9.02, effective September 1, 1993; am. Acts 1993, 73rd Leg., ch. 987 (S.B. 456), § 4, effective September 1, 1993; am. Acts 1995, 74th Leg., ch. 258 (S.B. 267), § 9, effective September 1, 1995; am. Acts 1997, 75th Leg., ch. 668 (S.B. 875), § 2, effective September 1, 1997; am. Acts 1999, 76th Leg., ch. 580 (S.B. 577), § 6, effective September 1, 1999; am. Acts 1999, 76th Leg., ch. 1193 (S.B. 399), § 1, effective September 1, 1999; am. Acts 1999, 76th Leg., ch. 1415 (H.B. 2145), § 2, effective September 1, 1999; am. Acts 2001, 77th Leg., ch. 1159 (H.B. 2987), § 1, effective September 1, 2001; am. Acts 2005, 79th Leg., ch. 1218 (H.B. 967), § 1, effective September 1, 2005; am. Acts 2009, 81st Leg., ch. 1040 (H.B. 4464), § 1, effective September 1, 2009; am. Acts 2009, 81st Leg., ch. 1130 (H.B. 2086), § 15, effective September 1, 2009; am. Acts 2009, 81st Leg., ch. 1400 (H.B. 221), § 1, effective September 1, 2009; am. Acts 2011, 82nd Leg., ch. 91 (S.B. 1303), §§ 27.001(2), effective September 1, 2011.)

## Art. 42.011. Judgment Affecting an Officer or Jailer.

If a person licensed under Chapter 415, Government Code, is charged with the commission of a felony and a court that knows the person is licensed under that chapter convicts the person or places the person on community supervision, the clerk of the court shall send the Commission on Law Enforcement Officer Standards and Education, by mail or electronically, the license number of the person and a certified copy of the court's judgment reflecting that the person has been convicted or placed on community supervision. (Enacted by Acts 1995, 74th Leg., ch. 538 (S.B. 1337), § 10, effective September 1, 1995.)

## Art. 42.012. Finding That Controlled Substance Used to Commit Offense.

In the punishment phase of the trial of an offense under Chapter 29, Chapter 31, or Title 5, Penal Code, if the court determines beyond a reasonable doubt that the defendant administered or provided a controlled substance to the victim of the offense with the intent of facilitating the commission of the offense, the court shall make an affirmative finding of that fact and enter the affirmative finding in the judgment of that case. (Enacted by Acts 1999, 76th Leg., ch. 417 (S.B. 1100), § 2(b), effective September 1, 1999; am. Acts 2001, 77th Leg., ch. 1420 (H.B. 2812), § 21.001(9), effective September 1, 2001 (renumbered from art. 42.015).)

## Art. 42.013. Finding of Family Violence.

In the trial of an offense under Title 5, Penal Code, if the court determines that the offense involved family violence, as defined by Section 71.004, Family Code, the court shall make an affirmative finding of that fact and enter the affirmative finding in the judgment of the case. (Enacted by Acts 1993, 73rd Leg., ch. 900 (S.B. 1067), § 9.01, effective September 1, 1993; am. Acts 2003, 78th Leg., ch. 1276 (H.B. 3507), § 7.002(h), effective September 1, 2003.)

## Art. 42.0131. Required Notice for Persons Convicted of Misdemeanors Involving Family Violence.

If a person is convicted of a misdemeanor involving family violence, as defined by Section 71.004, Family Code, the court shall notify the person of the fact that it is unlawful for the person to possess or transfer a firearm or ammunition. (Enacted by Acts 2007, 80th Leg., ch. 125 (S.B. 1470), § 2, effective September 1, 2007.)

## Art. 42.014. Finding That Offense Was Committed Because of Bias or Prejudice.

(a) In the trial of an offense under Title 5, Penal Code, or Section 28.02, 28.03, or 28.08, Penal Code, the judge shall make an affirmative finding of fact and enter the affirmative finding in the judgment of the case if at the guilt or innocence phase of the trial, the judge or the jury, whichever is the trier of fact, determines beyond a reasonable doubt that the defendant intentionally selected the person against whom the offense was committed or intentionally selected property damaged or affected as a result of the offense because of the defendant's bias or prejudice against a group identified by race, color, disability, religion, national origin or ancestry, age, gender, or sexual preference.

(b) The sentencing judge may, as a condition of punishment, require attendance in an educational program to further tolerance and acceptance of others.

(c) In this article, "sexual preference" has the following meaning only: a preference for heterosexuality, homosexuality, or bisexuality. (Enacted by Acts 1993, 73rd Leg., ch. 987 (S.B. 456), § 5, effective September 1, 1993; am. Acts 1995, 74th Leg., ch. 318 (S.B. 15), § 50, effective September 1, 1995; am. Acts 2001, 77th Leg., ch. 85 (H.B. 587), § 1.02, effective September 1, 2001.)

## Art. 42.015. Finding of Age of Victim.

In the trial of an offense under Section 20.02, 20.03, or 20.04, Penal Code, or an attempt, conspiracy, or solicitation to commit one of those offenses, the judge shall make an affirmative finding of fact and enter the affirmative finding in the judgment in the case if the judge determines that the victim or intended victim was younger than 17 years of age at the time of the offense. (Enacted by Acts 1999, 76th Leg., ch. 417 (S.B. 1100), § 2(b), effective September 1, 1999; enacted by Acts 1999, 76th Leg., ch. 1193 (S.B. 399), § 2, effective September 1, 1999; enacted by Acts 1999, 76th Leg., ch. 1415 (H.B. 2145), § 3, effective September 1, 1999.)

## Art. 42.016. Special Driver's License or Identification Requirements for Cer-

**tain Sex Offenders.**

If a person is convicted of, receives a grant of deferred adjudication for, or is adjudicated as having engaged in delinquent conduct based on a violation of an offense for which a conviction or adjudication requires registration as a sex offender under Chapter 62, the court shall:

(1) issue an order requiring the Texas Department of Public Safety to include in any driver's license record or personal identification certificate record maintained by the department for the person an indication that the person is subject to the registration requirements of Chapter 62;

(2) require the person to apply to the Texas Department of Public Safety in person for an original or renewal driver's license or personal identification certificate not later than the 30th day after the date the person is released or the date the department sends written notice to the person of the requirements of Article 62.060, as applicable, and to annually renew the license or certificate;

(3) notify the person of the consequence of the conviction or order of deferred adjudication as it relates to the order issued under this article; and

(4) send to the Texas Department of Public Safety a copy of the record of conviction, a copy of the order granting deferred adjudication, or a copy of the juvenile adjudication, as applicable, and a copy of the order issued under this article.

(Enacted by Acts 1999, 76th Leg., ch. 1401 (H.B. 1939), § 1, effective September 1, 2000; am. Acts 2005, 79th Leg., ch. 1008 (H.B. 867), § 2.01, effective September 1, 2005.)

### Art. 42.017. Finding Regarding Age-Based Offense.

In the trial of an offense under Section 21.11 or 22.011, Penal Code, the judge shall make an affirmative finding of fact and enter the affirmative finding in the judgment in the case if the judge determines that:

(1) at the time of the offense, the defendant was not more than four years older than the victim or intended victim and the victim or intended victim was at least 15 years of age; and

(2) the conviction is based solely on the ages of the defendant and the victim or intended victim at the time of the offense.

(Enacted by Acts 2001, 77th Leg., ch. 1159 (H.B. 2987), § 2, effective September 1, 2001; am. Acts

2007, 80th Leg., ch. 593 (H.B. 8), § 3.17, effective September 1, 2007; am. Acts 2011, 82nd Leg., ch. 134 (S.B. 198), § 1, effective September 1, 2011.)

### Art. 42.018. Notice Provided by Clerk of Court.

(a) This article applies only:

(1) to conviction or deferred adjudication granted on the basis of:

(A) an offense under Title 5, Penal Code; or

(B) an offense on conviction of which a defendant is required to register as a sex offender under Chapter 62; and

(2) if the victim of the offense is under 18 years of age.

(b) Not later than the fifth day after the date a person who holds a certificate issued under Subchapter B, Chapter 21, Education Code, is convicted or granted deferred adjudication on the basis of an offense, the clerk of the court in which the conviction or deferred adjudication is entered shall provide to the State Board for Educator Certification written notice of the person's conviction or deferred adjudication, including the offense on which the conviction or deferred adjudication was based.

(Enacted by Acts 2003, 78th Leg., ch. 920 (S.B. 1109), § 2, effective June 20, 2003.)

### Art. 42.0181. Notice of Theft, Fraud, Money Laundering, or Insurance Fraud Provided by Clerk of Court.

Not later than the fifth day after the date a person who holds a certificate of authority, license, or other authority issued by the Texas Department of Insurance is convicted of or granted deferred adjudication for an offense under Chapter 31, 32, 34, or 35, Penal Code, the clerk of the court in which the conviction or order of deferred adjudication is entered shall provide to the Texas Department of Insurance written notice of the person's conviction or deferred adjudication, including the offense on which the conviction or deferred adjudication was based.

(Enacted by Acts 2005, 79th Leg., ch. 1162 (H.B. 3376), § 7, effective September 1, 2005.)

### Art. 42.0182. [2 Versions: As added by Acts 2011, 82nd Leg., ch. 68] Findings Regarding Tax Fraud.

(a) In the trial of an offense under the Tax Code or an offense under the Penal Code related to the administration of taxes, the state may file a written request with the court in which the indictment or information is pending for the court to make affirmative findings regarding the commission of tax fraud as described by Subsection (b). The state must provide a copy of the written request to the defendant before the date the trial begins.

(b) If the state requests affirmative findings in the manner required by Subsection (a), the court shall make the requested affirmative findings and enter the findings in the papers in the case if the court finds by clear and convincing evidence that:

(1) the defendant's failure to pay a tax or file a report when due, as required by Title 2 or 3, Tax Code, was a result of fraud or an intent to evade the tax;

(2) the defendant altered, destroyed, or concealed any record, document, or thing, or presented to the comptroller any altered or fraudulent record, document, or thing, or otherwise engaged in fraudulent conduct for the apparent purpose of affecting the course or outcome of an audit, investigation, redetermination, or other proceeding before the comptroller; or

(3) the defendant's failure to file a report under Chapter 162, Tax Code, or to pay a tax under that chapter when the tax became due is attributable to fraud or an intent to evade the application of Chapter 162, Tax Code, or a rule adopted under Chapter 111 or 162, Tax Code.

(Enacted by Acts 2011, 82nd Leg., ch. 68 (S.B. 934), § 4, effective September 1, 2011.)

### Art. 42.0182. [2 Versions: As added by Acts 2011, 82nd Leg., ch. 327] Notice of Family Violence Offenses Provided by Clerk of Court.

(a) This article applies only:

(1) to conviction or deferred adjudication granted on the basis of:

(A) an offense that constitutes family violence, as defined by Section 71.004, Family Code; or

(B) an offense under Title 5, Penal Code; and

(2) if the defendant is a member of the state military forces or is serving in the armed forces of the United States in an active-duty status.

(b) As soon as possible after the date on which the defendant is convicted or granted deferred adjudication on the basis of an offense, the clerk of the court in which the conviction or deferred adjudication is entered shall provide written notice of the conviction or deferred adjudication to the staff judge advocate at Joint Force Headquarters or the provost marshal of the military installation to which the defendant is assigned with the intent that the commanding officer will be notified, as applicable.

(Enacted by Acts 2011, 82nd Leg., ch. 327 (H.B. 2624), § 3, effective September 1, 2011.)

### Art. 42.019. Motor Fuel Theft.

(a) A judge shall enter an affirmative finding in the judgment in a case if the judge or jury, whichever is the finder of fact, determines beyond a reasonable doubt in the guilt or innocence phase of the trial of an offense under Section 31.03, Penal Code, that the defendant, in committing the offense:

(1) dispensed motor fuel into the fuel tank of a motor vehicle on the premises of an establishment at which motor fuel is offered for retail sale; and

(2) after dispensing the motor fuel, left the premises of the establishment without paying the establishment for the motor fuel.

(b) If a judge enters an affirmative finding as required by Subsection (a) and determines that the defendant has previously been convicted of an offense the judgment for which contains an affirmative finding under Subsection (a), the judge shall enter a special affirmative finding in the judgment in the case.

(Enacted by Acts 2001, 77th Leg., ch. 359 (S.B. 968), § 1, effective September 1, 2001.)

### Art. 42.0191. Finding Regarding Victims of Trafficking or Other Abuse.

(a) In the trial of an offense, on the motion of the attorney representing the state the judge shall make an affirmative finding of fact and enter the affirmative finding in the papers in the case if the judge determines that, regardless of whether the conduct at issue is the subject of the prosecution or part of the same criminal episode as the conduct that is the subject of the prosecution, a victim in the trial:

(1) is or has been a victim of a severe form of trafficking in persons, as defined by 22 U.S.C. Section 7102(8); or

(2) has suffered substantial physical or mental abuse as a result of having been a victim of criminal activity described by 8 U.S.C. Section 1101(a)(15)(U)(iii).

(b) That part of the papers in the case containing an affirmative finding under this article:

(1) must include specific information identifying the victim, as available;

(2) may not include information identifying the victim's location; and

(3) is confidential, unless written consent for the release of the affirmative finding is obtained from the victim or, if the victim is younger than 18 years of age, the victim's parent or guardian.

(Enacted by Acts 2007, 80th Leg., ch. 849 (H.B. 1121), § 1, effective June 15, 2007.)

## Art. 42.0197. Finding Regarding Gang-Related Conduct.

In the trial of an offense, on the motion of the attorney representing the state the judge shall make an affirmative finding of fact and enter the affirmative finding in the judgment in the case if the judge determines that the applicable conduct was engaged in as part of the activities of a criminal street gang as defined by Section 71.01, Penal Code.

(Enacted by Acts 2009, 81st Leg., ch. 1130 (H.B. 2086), § 16, effective September 1, 2009.)

## Art. 42.0198. Finding Regarding Delay in Arrest of Defendant.

In the trial of an offense under Section 19.02, 22.011, or 22.021, Penal Code, on the motion of the attorney representing the state the judge shall make an affirmative finding of fact regarding the number of months that elapsed, if any, between the date an arrest warrant was issued for the defendant following an indictment for the offense and the date the defendant was arrested for the offense. The judge shall enter the affirmative finding in the judgment in the case.

(Enacted by Acts 2009, 81st Leg., ch. 1400 (H.B. 221), § 2, effective September 1, 2009.)

## Art. 42.02. Sentence.

The sentence is that part of the judgment, or order revoking a suspension of the imposition of a sentence, that orders that the punishment be carried into execution in the manner prescribed by law.

(Enacted by Acts 1965, 59th Leg., ch. 722 (S.B. 107), § 1, effective January 1, 1966; am. Acts 1981, 67th Leg., ch. 291 (S.B. 265), § 112, effective September 1, 1981; am. Acts 1993, 73rd Leg., ch. 900 (S.B. 1067), § 5.03, effective September 1, 1993.)

## Art. 42.023. Judge May Consider Alternative Sentencing.

Before pronouncing sentence on a defendant

convicted of a criminal offense, the judge may consider whether the defendant should be committed for care and treatment under Section 462.081, Health and Safety Code.

(Enacted by Acts 1993, 73rd Leg., ch. 900 (S.B. 1067), § 5.03, effective September 1, 1993.)

## Art. 42.025. Sentencing Hearing at Secondary School.

(a) A judge may order the sentencing hearing of a defendant convicted of an offense involving possession, manufacture, or delivery of a controlled substance under Chapter 481, Health and Safety Code, to be held at a secondary school if:

(1) the judge determines that the sentencing hearing would have educational value to students due to the nature of the offense and its consequences;

(2) the defendant agrees;

(3) the school administration agrees; and

(4) appropriate measures are taken to ensure:

(A) the safety of the students; and

(B) a fair hearing for the defendant that complies with all applicable laws and rules.

(b) A judge may, at a secondary school, receive a plea of guilty or nolo contendere from a defendant charged with an offense described by Subsection (a) and place the defendant on deferred adjudication under Section 5, Article 42.12, if:

(1) the judge makes the determination that the proceeding would have educational value, as provided by Subsection (a)(1);

(2) the defendant and the school agree to the location of the proceeding, as provided by Subsections (a)(2) and (3); and

(3) appropriate measures are taken in regard to the safety of students and the rights of the defendant, as described by Subsection (a)(4).

(Enacted by Acts 2011, 82nd Leg., ch. 1280 (H.B. 1113), § 1, effective September 1, 2011.)

## Art. 42.03. Pronouncing Sentence; Time; Credit for Time Spent in Jail Between Arrest and Sentence or Pending Appeal.

Sec. 1. (a) Except as provided in Article 42.14, sentence shall be pronounced in the defendant's presence.

(b) The court shall permit a victim, close relative of a deceased victim, or guardian of a victim, as defined by Article 56.01 of this code, to appear in person to present to the court and to the defendant a statement of the person's views about the offense, the defendant, and the effect of the offense on the victim. The victim, relative, or guardian may not direct questions to the defendant while making the statement. The court reporter may not transcribe the statement. The statement must be made:

(1) after punishment has been assessed and the court has determined whether or not to grant community supervision in the case;

(2) after the court has announced the terms and conditions of the sentence; and

(3) after sentence is pronounced.

Sec. 2. (a) In all criminal cases the judge of the court in which the defendant is convicted shall give the defendant credit on the defendant's sentence for the time that the defendant has spent:

(1) in jail for the case, including confinement served as described by Article 46B.009 and excluding confinement served as a condition of community supervision, from the time of his arrest and confinement until his sentence by the trial court;

(2) in a substance abuse treatment facility operated by the Texas Department of Criminal Justice under Section 493.009, Government Code, or another court-ordered residential program or facility as a condition of deferred adjudication community supervision granted in the case if the defendant successfully completes the treatment program at that facility; or

(3) confined in a mental health facility or residential care facility as described by Article 46B.009.

(b) In all revocations of a suspension of the imposition of a sentence the judge shall enter the restitution or reparation due and owing on the date of the revocation.

Sec. 3. If a defendant appeals his conviction, is not released on bail, and is retained in a jail as provided in Section 7, Article 42.09, pending his appeal, the judge of the court in which the defendant was convicted shall give the defendant credit on his sentence for the time that the defendant has spent in jail pending disposition of his appeal. The court shall endorse on both the commitment and the mandate from the appellate court all credit given the defendant under this section, and the Texas Department of Criminal Justice shall grant the credit in computing the defendant's eligibility for parole and discharge.

Sec. 4. When a defendant who has been sentenced to imprisonment in the Texas Department of Criminal Justice has spent time in jail pending trial and sentence or pending appeal, the judge of the sentencing court shall direct the sheriff to attach to the commitment papers a statement assessing the defendant's conduct while in jail.

Secs. 5 and 6. [Repealed by Acts 1989, 71st Leg., ch. 785 (H.B. 2335), § 4.24, effective September 1, 1989.]

Secs. 7 and 8. [Deleted by Acts 1993, 73rd Leg., ch. 900 (S.B. 1067), § 5.03, effective September 1, 1993.]

(Enacted by Acts 1965, 59th Leg., ch. 722 (S.B. 107), § 1, effective January 1, 1966; am. Acts 1967, 60th Leg., ch. 659 (S.B. 145), § 28, effective August 28, 1967; am. Acts 1973, 63rd Leg., ch. 91 (H.B. 403), § 1, effective August 27, 1973; am. Acts 1977, 65th Leg., ch. 382 (H.B. 1322), § 1, effective August 29, 1977; am. Acts 1977, 65th Leg., p. 2076, ch. 827 (H.B. 1271), § 1, effective August 29, 1977; am. Acts 1981, 67th Leg., ch. 141 (S.B. 125), § 1, effective September 1, 1981; am. Acts 1981, 67th Leg., ch. 291 (S.B. 265), § 113, effective September 1, 1981; am. Acts 1981, 67th Leg., ch. 616 (H.B. 1695), § 1, effective August 31, 1981; am. Acts 1983, 68th Leg., ch. 586 (S.B. 779), § 4, effective August 29, 1983; am. Acts 1983, 68th Leg., ch. 809 (H.B. 855), § 1, effective August 29, 1983; am. Acts 1985, 69th Leg., ch. 232 (S.B. 1175), § 13, effective September 1, 1985; am. Acts 1989, 71st Leg., ch. 785 (H.B. 2335), § 4.06, effective June 15, 1989; am. Acts 1989, 71st Leg., ch. 785 (H.B. 2335), § 4.24, effective September 1, 1989; am. Acts 1989, 71st Leg., ch. 848 (S.B. 638), § 1, effective June 14, 1989; am. Acts 1989, 71st Leg., ch. 1040 (H.B. 1779), §§ 1, 2, effective August 28, 1989; am. Acts 1991, 72nd Leg., ch. 16 (S.B. 232), § 4.05, effective August 26, 1991; am. Acts 1991, 72nd Leg., ch. 278 (H.B. 520), § 1, effective June 5, 1991; am. Acts 1991, 72nd Leg., 2nd C.S., ch. 10 (H.B. 93), § 8.02, effective December 1, 1991; am. Acts 1991, 72nd Leg., 2nd C.S., ch. 10 (H.B. 93), §§ 14.01—14.04, 15.03, effective October 1, 1991; am. Acts 1993, 73rd Leg., ch. 900 (S.B. 1067), § 5.03, effective September 1, 1993; am. Acts 1995, 74th Leg., ch. 556 (S.B. 39), § 1, effective September 1, 1995; am. Acts 2003, 78th Leg., ch. 406 (H.B. 178), § 2, effective September 1, 2003; am. Acts 2007, 80th Leg., ch. 1205 (H.B. 1678), § 1, effective September 1, 2007; am. Acts 2009, 81st Leg., ch. 87 (S.B. 1969), § 25.018, effective September 1, 2009; am. Acts 2011, 82nd Leg., ch. 718 (H.B. 748), § 1, effective September 1, 2011; am. Acts 2011, 82nd Leg., ch. 822 (H.B. 2725), § 1, effective September 1, 2011.)

## Art. 42.031. Work Release Program.

Sec. 1. (a) The sheriff of each county may attempt to secure employment for each defendant sentenced to the county jail work release program under Article 42.034 and each defendant confined in the county jail awaiting transfer to the Texas Department of Criminal Justice.

(b) The employer of a defendant participating in a program under this article shall pay the defendant's salary to the sheriff. The sheriff shall deposit the salary into a special fund to be given to the defendant on his release after deducting:

(1) the cost to the county for the defendant's confinement during the pay period based on the average daily cost of confining defendants in the county jail, as determined by the commissioners court of the county;

(2) support of the defendant's dependents; and

(3) restitution to the victims of an offense committed by the defendant.

(c) At the time of sentencing or at a later date, the court sentencing a defendant may direct the sheriff not to deduct the cost described under Subdivision (1) of Subsection (b) of this section or to deduct only a specified portion of the cost if the court determines that the full deduction would cause a significant financial hardship to the defendant's dependents.

(d) If the sheriff does not find employment for a defendant who would otherwise be sentenced to imprisonment in the department, the sheriff shall:

(1) transfer the defendant to the sheriff of a county who agrees to accept the defendant as a participant in the county jail work release program; or

(2) retain the defendant in the county jail for employment as soon as possible in a jail work release program.

Sec. 2. A defendant participating in a program under this article shall be confined in the county jail or in another facility designated by the sheriff at all times except for:

(1) time spent at work and traveling to or from work; and

(2) time spent attending or traveling to or from an education or rehabilitation program approved by the sheriff.

Sec. 3. (a) The sheriff of each county shall classify each felon serving a sentence in the county jail work release program for the purpose of awarding good conduct time credit in the same manner as inmates of the Texas Department of Criminal Justice are classified under Chapter 498, Government Code, and shall award good conduct time in the same manner as the director of the department does in that chapter.

(b) If the sheriff determines that the defendant is conducting himself in a manner that is dangerous to inmates in the county jail or to society as a whole, the sheriff may remove the defendant from participation in the program pending a hearing before the sentencing court. At the hearing, if the court determines that the sheriff's assessment of the defendant's conduct is correct, the court may terminate the defendant's participation in the program and order the defendant to the term of imprisonment that the defendant would have received had he not entered the program. If the court determines that the sheriff's assessment is incorrect, the court shall order the sheriff to readmit the defendant to the program. A defendant shall receive as credit toward his sentence any time served as a participant in the program. (Enacted by Acts 1989, 71st Leg., ch. 2 (S.B. 221), § 5.03(a), effective August 28, 1989; am. Acts 1991, 72nd Leg., 2nd C.S., ch. 10 (H.B. 93), §§ 14.10, 14.11, effective October 1, 1991; am. Acts 1993, 73rd Leg., ch. 900 (S.B. 1067), § 5.03, effective September 1, 1993; am. Acts 2009, 81st Leg., ch. 87 (S.B. 1969), §§ 25.019, 25.020, effective September 1, 2009.)

## Art. 42.032. Good Conduct.

Sec. 1. To encourage county jail discipline, a distinction may be made to give orderly, industrious, and obedient defendants the comforts and privileges they deserve. The reward for good conduct may consist of a relaxation of strict county jail rules and extension of social privileges consistent with proper discipline.

Sec. 2. The sheriff in charge of each county jail may grant commutation of time for good conduct, industry, and obedience. A deduction not to exceed one day for each day of the original sentence actually served may be made for the term or terms of sentences if a charge of misconduct has not been sustained against the defendant.

Sec. 3. This article applies whether or not the judgment of conviction is a fine or jail sentence or both, but the deduction in time may not exceed one-third of the original sentence as to fines and court costs assessed in the judgment of conviction.

Sec. 4. A defendant serving two or more cumulative sentences shall be allowed commutation as if the sentences were one sentence.

Sec. 5. Any part or all of the commutation accrued under this article may be forfeited and taken away by the sheriff:

(1) for a sustained charge of misconduct in violation of any rule known to the defendant, including escape or attempt to escape, if the sheriff has complied with discipline proceedings as approved by the Commission on Jail Standards;

(2) on receipt by the sheriff of a certified copy of a final order of a state or federal court that dismisses as frivolous or malicious a lawsuit brought by a defendant while the defendant was in the custody of the sheriff; or

(3) if the defendant, in violation of an order entered under Article 42.24, contacts the victim of the offense for which the defendant is serving a sentence or a member of the victim's family.

Sec. 6. [Repealed by Acts 2009, 81st Leg., ch. 854 (S.B. 2340), § 7, effective June 19, 2009.]

Sec. 7. The sheriff shall keep a conduct record in card or ledger form and a calendar card on each defendant showing all forfeitures of commutation time and the reasons for the forfeitures.

(Enacted by Acts 1989, 71st Leg., ch. 2 (S.B. 221), § 5.04(a), effective August 28, 1989; am. Acts 1991, 72nd Leg., 2nd C.S., ch. 10 (H.B. 93), § 14.05, effective October 1, 1991; am. Acts 1993, 73rd Leg., ch. 900 (S.B. 1067), § 5.03, effective September 1, 1993; am. Acts 1999, 76th Leg., ch. 655 (H.B. 261), § 2(a), effective June 18, 1999; am. Acts 2009, 81st Leg., ch. 854 (S.B. 2340), § 7, effective June 19, 2009; am. Acts 2011, 82nd Leg., ch. 491 (H.B. 1028), § 2, effective September 1, 2011.)

## Art. 42.033. Sentence to Serve Time During Off-Work Hours.

(a) Where jail time has been awarded to a person sentenced for a misdemeanor or sentenced to confinement in the county jail for a felony or when a defendant is serving a period of confinement as a condition of community supervision, the trial judge, at the time of the pronouncement of sentence or at any time while the defendant is serving the sentence or period of confinement, when in the judge's discretion the ends of justice would best be served, may permit the defendant to serve the defendant's sentence or period of confinement intermittently during his off-work hours or on weekends. The judge may require bail of the defendant to ensure the faithful performance of the sentence or period of confinement. The judge may attach conditions regarding the employment, travel, and other conduct of the defendant during the performance of such a sentence or period of confinement.

(b) The court may impose as a condition to permitting a defendant to serve the jail time assessed or period of confinement intermittently an additional requirement that the defendant make any of the following payments to the court, agencies, or persons, or that the defendant execute a letter and direct it to the defendant's employer directing the employer to deduct from the defendant's salary an amount directed by the court, which is to be sent by the employer to the clerk of the court. The money received by the court under this section may be used to pay the following expenses as directed by the court:

(1) the support of the defendant's dependents, if necessary;

(2) the defendant's documented personal, business, and travel expenses;

(3) reimbursement of the general fund of the county for the maintenance of the defendant in jail; and

(4) installment payments on restitution, fines, and court costs ordered by the court.

(c) The condition imposed under Subsection (b) of this article is not binding on an employer, except that income withheld for child support is governed by Chapter 158, Family Code.

(d) The court may permit the defendant to serve the defendant's sentence or period of confinement intermittently in order for the defendant to continue employment if the court imposes confinement for failure to pay a fine or court costs, as punishment for criminal nonsupport under Section 25.05, Penal Code, or for contempt of a court order for periodic payments for the support of a child.

(e) The court may permit the defendant to seek employment or obtain medical, psychological, or substance abuse treatment or counseling or obtain training or needed education under the same terms and conditions that apply to employment under this article.

(Enacted by Acts 1989, 71st Leg., ch. 785 (H.B. 2335), § 4.07, effective September 1, 1989; am. Acts 1991, 72nd Leg., 2nd C.S., ch. 10 (H.B. 93), § 14.06, effective October 1, 1991; am. Acts 1993, 73rd Leg., ch. 900 (S.B. 1067), § 5.03, effective September 1, 1993; am. Acts 1997, 75th Leg., ch. 165 (S.B. 898), § 7.03, effective September 1, 1997.)

## Art. 42.034. County Jail Work Release Program.

(a) If jail time has been awarded to a person sentenced for a misdemeanor or sentenced to confinement in the county jail for a felony, the trial judge at the time of pronouncement of sentence or at any time while the defendant is serving the sentence, when in the judge's discretion the ends of justice would best be served, may require the defendant to serve an alternate term for the same period of time in the county jail work release program of the county in which the offense occurred, if the person is classified by the sheriff as a low-risk offender under the classification system developed by the Commission on Jail Standards under Section 511.009, Government Code.

(b) The sheriff shall provide a classification report for a defendant to a judge as necessary so that the judge can determine whether to require the defendant to participate in the work release program under this article.

(c) A defendant sentenced under this article who would otherwise be sentenced to confinement in jail may earn good conduct credit in the same manner as provided by Article 42.032 of this code, but only while actually confined.
(Enacted by Acts 1989, 71st Leg., ch. 785 (H.B. 2335), § 4.08, effective September 1, 1989; am. Acts 1991, 72nd Leg., 2nd C.S., ch. 10 (S.B. 35), § 14.07, effective October 1, 1991; am. Acts 1993, 73rd Leg., ch. 900 (S.B. 1067), § 5.03, effective September 1, 1993; am. Acts 1995, 74th Leg., ch. 722 (H.B. 179), § 1, effective September 1, 1995.)

## Art. 42.035. Electronic Monitoring; House Arrest.

(a) A court may require a defendant to serve all or part of a sentence of confinement in county jail by participating in an electronic monitoring program rather than being confined in the county jail, if the program:

(1) is operated by a community supervision and corrections department that serves the county in which the court is located and has been approved by the community justice assistance division of the Texas Department of Criminal Justice; or

(2) is operated by the commissioners court of the county, or by a private vendor under contract with the commissioners court, under Section 351.904, Local Government Code, if the defendant has not been placed on community supervision.

(b) A judge, at the time of the pronouncement of a sentence of confinement or at any time while the defendant is serving the sentence, on the judge's own motion or on the written motion of

the defendant, may permit the defendant to serve the sentence under house arrest, including electronic monitoring and any other conditions the court chooses to impose, during the person's off-work hours. The judge may require bail of the defendant to ensure the faithful performance of the sentence.

(c) The court may require the defendant to pay to the community supervision and corrections department or the county any reasonable cost incurred because of the defendant's participation in the house arrest program, including the cost of electronic monitoring.

(d) A defendant who submits to electronic monitoring or participates in the house arrest program under this article discharges a sentence of confinement in the same manner as if the defendant were confined in county jail.

(e) A court may revoke a defendant's participation in an electronic monitoring program and require the defendant to serve the remainder of the defendant's sentence of confinement in county jail if the defendant violates a condition imposed by a court under this article, including a condition requiring the defendant to pay for participating in the program under Subsection (c).
(Enacted by Acts 1989, 71st Leg., ch. 785 (H.B. 2335), § 4.09, effective September 1, 1989; am. Acts 1993, 73rd Leg., ch. 900 (S.B. 1067), § 5.03, effective September 1, 1993; am. Acts 2009, 81st Leg., ch. 854 (S.B. 2340), § 1, effective June 19, 2009.)

## Art. 42.036. Community Service.

(a) A court may require a defendant, other than a defendant convicted of an offense under Sections 49.04-49.08, Penal Code, to serve all or part of a sentence of confinement or period of confinement required as a condition of community supervision in county jail by performing community service rather than by being confined in county jail unless the sentence of confinement was imposed by the jury in the case.

(b) In its order requiring a defendant to participate in community service work, the court must specify:

(1) the number of hours the defendant is required to work; and

(2) the entity or organization for which the defendant is required to work.

(c) The court may order the defendant to perform community service work under this article only for a governmental entity or a nonprofit organization that provides services to the general public that enhance social welfare and the general well-being of the community. A governmental entity or nonprofit organization that accepts a defendant under this section to perform community service must agree to supervise the defendant in the performance of the defendant's work and report on the defendant's work to the community supervision and corrections department or court-related services office.

(d) The court may require bail of a defendant to ensure the defendant's faithful performance of community service and may attach conditions to the bail as it determines are proper.

(e) A court may not order a defendant who is employed to perform more than 16 hours per week of community service under this article unless the court determines that requiring the defendant to work additional hours does not work a hardship on the defendant or the defendant's dependents. A court may not order a defendant who is unemployed to perform more than 32 hours per week of community service under this article, but may direct the defendant to use the remaining hours of the week to seek employment.

(f) A defendant is considered to have served one day in jail for each eight hours of community service performed under this article.

(g) [Deleted by Acts 1993, 73rd Leg., ch. 900, § 5.03, effective September 1, 1993.]

(h) [Repealed by Acts 1995, 74th Leg., ch. 76, § 3.14, effective September 1, 1995.]
(Enacted by Acts 1989, 71st Leg., ch. 785 (H.B. 2335), § 4.10, effective September 1, 1989; am. Acts 1990, 71st Leg., 6th C.S., ch. 25 (S.B. 41), § 27, effective June 18, 1990; am. Acts 1991, 72nd Leg., 2nd C.S., ch. 10 (H.B. 93) §§ 14.08, 15.01, effective October 1, 1991; am. Acts 1993, 73rd Leg., ch. 201 (H.B. 294), § 2, effective August 30, 1993; am. Acts 1993, 73rd Leg., ch. 900 (S.B. 1067), § 5.03, effective September 1, 1993; am. Acts 1995, 74th Leg., ch. 76 (S.B. 959), § 3.14, effective September 1, 1995.)

### Art. 42.037. Restitution.

(a) In addition to any fine authorized by law, the court that sentences a defendant convicted of an offense may order the defendant to make restitution to any victim of the offense or to the compensation to victims of crime fund established under Subchapter B, Chapter 56, to the extent that fund has paid compensation to or on behalf of the victim. If the court does not order restitution or orders partial restitution under this subsection, the court shall state on the record

the reasons for not making the order or for the limited order.

(b) (1) If the offense results in damage to or loss or destruction of property of a victim of the offense, the court may order the defendant:

(A) to return the property to the owner of the property or someone designated by the owner; or

(B) if return of the property is impossible or impractical or is an inadequate remedy, to pay an amount equal to the greater of:

(i) the value of the property on the date of the damage, loss, or destruction; or

(ii) the value of the property on the date of sentencing, less the value of any part of the property that is returned on the date the property is returned.

(2) If the offense results in personal injury to a victim, the court may order the defendant to make restitution to:

(A) the victim for any expenses incurred by the victim as a result of the offense; or

(B) the compensation to victims of crime fund to the extent that fund has paid compensation to or on behalf of the victim.

(3) If the victim or the victim's estate consents, the court may, in addition to an order under Subdivision (2), order the defendant to make restitution by performing services instead of by paying money or make restitution to a person or organization, other than the compensation to victims of crime fund, designated by the victim or the estate.

(c) The court, in determining whether to order restitution and the amount of restitution, shall consider:

(1) the amount of the loss sustained by any victim and the amount paid to or on behalf of the victim by the compensation to victims of crime fund as a result of the offense; and

(2) other factors the court deems appropriate.

(d) If the court orders restitution under this article and the victim is deceased the court shall order the defendant to make restitution to the victim's estate.

(e) The court shall impose an order of restitution that is as fair as possible to the victim or to the compensation to victims of crime fund, as applicable. The imposition of the order may not unduly complicate or prolong the sentencing process.

(f) (1) The court may not order restitution for a loss for which the victim has received or will receive compensation only from a source other than the compensation to victims of crime fund. The court may, in the interest of justice, order restitution to any person who has compensated the victim for the loss to the extent the person paid compensation. An order of restitution shall require that all restitution to a victim or to the compensation to victims of crime fund be made before any restitution to any other person is made under the order.

(2) Any amount recovered by a victim from a person ordered to pay restitution in a federal or state civil proceeding is reduced by any amount previously paid to the victim by the person under an order of restitution.

(g) (1) The court may require a defendant to make restitution under this article within a specified period or in specified installments. If the court requires the defendant to make restitution in specified installments, in addition to the installment payments, the court may require the defendant to pay a one-time restitution fee of $12, $6 of which the court shall retain for costs incurred in collecting the specified installments and $6 of which the court shall order to be paid to the compensation to victims of crime fund.

(2) The end of the period or the last installment may not be later than:

(A) the end of the period of probation, if probation is ordered;

(B) five years after the end of the term of imprisonment imposed, if the court does not order probation; or

(C) five years after the date of sentencing in any other case.

(3) If the court does not provide otherwise, the defendant shall make restitution immediately.

(4) Except as provided by Subsection (n), the order of restitution must require the defendant to: (i) make restitution directly to the person or agency that will accept and forward restitution payments to the victim or other person eligible for restitution under this article, including the compensation to victims of crime fund; (ii) make restitution directly to the victim or other person eligible for restitution under this article, including the compensation to victims of crime fund; or (iii) deliver the amount or property due as restitution to a community supervision and corrections department for transfer to the victim or person.

(h) If a defendant is placed on community supervision or is paroled or released on mandatory supervision, the court or the parole panel shall order the payment of restitution ordered under this article as a condition of community supervision, parole, or mandatory supervision. The court may revoke community supervision and the parole panel may revoke parole or mandatory supervision if the defendant fails to comply with the order. In determining whether to revoke community supervision, parole, or mandatory supervision, the court or parole panel shall consider:

(1) the defendant's employment status;

(2) the defendant's current and future earning ability;

(3) the defendant's current and future financial resources;

(4) the willfulness of the defendant's failure to pay;

(5) any other special circumstances that may affect the defendant's ability to pay; and

(6) the victim's financial resources or ability to pay expenses incurred by the victim as a result of the offense.

(i) In addition to any other terms and conditions of probation imposed under Article 42.12, the court may require a probationer to reimburse the compensation to victims of crime fund created under Subchapter B, Chapter 56, for any amounts paid from that fund to or on behalf of a victim of the probationer's offense. In this subsection, "victim" has the meaning assigned by Article 56.32.

(j) The court may order a community supervision and corrections department to obtain information pertaining to the factors listed in Subsection (c) of this article. The probation officer shall include the information in the report required under Section 9(a), Article 42.12, of this code or a separate report, as the court directs. The court shall permit the defendant and the prosecuting attorney to read the report.

(k) The court shall resolve any dispute relating to the proper amount or type of restitution. The standard of proof is a preponderance of the evidence. The burden of demonstrating the amount of the loss sustained by a victim as a result of the offense is on the prosecuting attorney. The burden of demonstrating the financial resources of the defendant and the financial needs of the defendant and the defendant's dependents is on the defendant. The burden of demonstrating other matters as the court deems appropriate is on the party designated by the court as justice requires.

(l) Conviction of a defendant for an offense involving the act giving rise to restitution under this article estops the defendant from denying the essential allegations of that offense in any subsequent federal civil proceeding or state civil proceeding brought by the victim, to the extent consistent with state law.

(m) An order of restitution may be enforced by the state or a victim named in the order to receive the restitution in the same manner as a judgment in a civil action.

(n) If a defendant is convicted of or receives deferred adjudication for an offense under Section 25.05, Penal Code, if the child support order on which prosecution of the offense was based required the defendant to pay the support to a local registry or the Title IV-D agency, and if the court orders restitution under this article, the order of restitution must require the defendant to pay the child support in the following manner:

(1) during any period in which the defendant is under the supervision of a community supervision and corrections department, to the department for transfer to the local registry or Title IV-D agency designated as the place of payment in the child support order; and

(2) during any period in which the defendant is not under the supervision of a department, directly to the registry or agency described by Subdivision (1).

(o) The department may waive a supervision fee or an administrative fee imposed on an inmate under Section 508.182, Government Code, during any period in which the inmate is required to pay restitution under this article.

(p) (1) A court shall order a defendant convicted of an offense under Section 28.03(f), Penal Code, involving damage or destruction inflicted on a place of human burial or under Section 42.08, Penal Code, to make restitution in the amount described by Subsection (b)(1)(B) to a cemetery organization operating a cemetery affected by the commission of the offense.

(2) If a court orders an unemancipated minor to make restitution under Subsection (a) and the minor is financially unable to make the restitution, the court may order:

(A) the minor to perform a specific number of hours of community service to satisfy the restitution; or

(B) the parents or other person responsible for the minor's support to make the restitution in the amount described by Subsection (b)(1)(B).

(3) In this subsection, "cemetery" and "cemetery organization" have the meanings as-

signed by Section 711.001, Health and Safety Code.

(q) The court shall order a defendant convicted of an offense under Section 22.11, Penal Code, to make restitution to the victim of the offense or the victim's employer in an amount equal to the sum of any expenses incurred by the victim or employer to:

(1) test the victim for HIV, hepatitis A, hepatitis B, tuberculosis, or any other disease designated as a reportable disease under Section 81.048, Health and Safety Code; or

(2) treat the victim for HIV, hepatitis A, hepatitis B, tuberculosis, or any other disease designated as a reportable disease under Section 81.048, Health and Safety Code, the victim contracts as a result of the offense.

(r) [Reserved.]

(s) (1) A court shall order a defendant convicted of an offense under Section 28.08, Penal Code, to make restitution by:

(A) reimbursing the owner of the property for the cost of restoring the property; or

(B) with the consent of the owner of the property, personally restoring the property by removing or painting over any markings the defendant made.

(2) A court shall order a defendant convicted of an offense under Section 28.08, Penal Code, to make restitution to a political subdivision that owns public property or erects a street sign or official traffic-control device on which the defendant makes markings in violation of Section 28.08, Penal Code, by:

(A) paying an amount equal to the lesser of the cost to the political subdivision of replacing or restoring the public property, street sign, or official traffic-control device; or

(B) with the consent of the political subdivision, restoring the public property, street sign, or official traffic-control device by removing or painting over any markings made by the defendant on the property, sign, or device.

(3) If the court orders a defendant to make restitution under this subsection and the defendant is financially unable to make the restitution, the court may order the defendant to perform a specific number of hours of community service to satisfy the restitution.

(4) Notwithstanding Subsection (g)(4), a court shall direct a defendant ordered to make restitution under this subsection as a condition of community supervision to deliver the amount or property due as restitution to the

defendant's supervising officer for transfer to the owner. A parole panel shall direct a defendant ordered to make restitution under this subsection as a condition of parole or mandatory supervision to deliver the amount or property due as restitution to the defendant's supervising officer. The defendant's supervising officer shall notify the court when the defendant has delivered the full amount of restitution ordered.

(5) For purposes of this subsection, "official traffic-control device" has the meaning assigned by Section 541.304, Transportation Code.

(Enacted by Acts 1993, 73rd Leg., ch. 806 (H.B. 2179), § 1, effective September 1, 1993; am. Acts 1995, 74th Leg., ch. 76 (S.B. 959), § 5.95(111), effective September 1, 1995; am. Acts 1995, 74th Leg., ch. 318 (S.B. 15), § 51, effective September 1, 1995; am. Acts 1999, 76th Leg., ch. 40 (S.B. 118), §§ 2, 3, effective September 1, 1999; am. Acts 2001, 77th Leg., ch. 856 (H.B. 1649), § 10, effective September 1, 2001; am. Acts 2001, 77th Leg., ch. 1034 (H.B. 1572), § 2, effective September 1, 2001; am. Acts 2005, 79th Leg., ch. 543 (H.B. 1095), § 4, effective September 1, 2005; am. Acts 2005, 79th Leg., ch. 969 (H.B. 1751), § 1, effective September 1, 2005; am. Acts 2005, 79th Leg., ch. 1025 (H.B. 1012), § 2, effective June 18, 2005; am. Acts 2007, 80th Leg., ch. 921 (H.B. 3167), § 17.001(10), effective September 1, 2007; am. Acts 2007, 80th Leg., ch. 1053 (H.B. 2151), § 2, effective September 1, 2007; am. Acts 2009 81st Leg., ch. 87 (S.B. 1969), § 25.021, effective September 1, 2009; am. Acts 2009, 81st Leg., ch. 639 (H.B. 1633), § 1, effective September 1, 2009; am. Acts 2009, 81st Leg., ch. 1040 (H.B. 4464), § 2, effective September 1, 2009.)

### Art. 42.0371. Mandatory Restitution for Kidnapped or Abducted Children.

(a) The court shall order a defendant convicted of an offense under Chapter 20, Penal Code, or Section 25.03, 25.031, or 25.04, Penal Code, to pay restitution in an amount equal to the cost of necessary rehabilitation, including medical, psychiatric, and psychological care and treatment, for the victim of the offense if the victim is younger than 17 years of age.

(b) The court shall, after considering the financial circumstances of the defendant, specify in a restitution order issued under Subsection (a) the manner in which the defendant must pay the restitution.

(c) A restitution order issued under Subsection (a) may be enforced by the state or a victim named in the order to receive the restitution in the same manner as a judgment in a civil action.

(d) The court may hold a hearing, make findings of fact, and amend a restitution order issued under Subsection (a) if the defendant fails to pay the victim named in the order in the manner specified by the court.

(Enacted by Acts 1999, 76th Leg., ch. 657 (H.B. 302), § 1, effective September 1, 1999.)

### Art. 42.0372. Mandatory Restitution for Child Victims of Trafficking of Persons or Compelling Prostitution.

(a) The court shall order a defendant convicted of an offense under Section 20A.02 or 43.05(a)(2), Penal Code, to pay restitution in an amount equal to the cost of necessary rehabilitation, including medical, psychiatric, and psychological care and treatment, for any victim of the offense who is younger than 18 years of age.

(b) The court shall, after considering the financial circumstances of the defendant, specify in a restitution order issued under Subsection (a) the manner in which the defendant must pay the restitution.

(c) A restitution order issued under Subsection (a) may be enforced by the state, or by a victim named in the order to receive the restitution, in the same manner as a judgment in a civil action.

(d) The court may hold a hearing, make findings of fact, and amend a restitution order issued under Subsection (a) if the defendant fails to pay the victim named in the order in the manner specified by the court.

(Enacted by Acts 2011, 82nd Leg., ch. 515 (H.B. 2014), § 2.02, effective September 1, 2011.)

### Art. 42.038. Reimbursement for Confinement Expenses.

(a) In addition to any fine, cost, or fee authorized by law, a court that sentences a defendant convicted of a misdemeanor to serve a term of confinement in county jail and orders execution of the sentence may require the defendant to reimburse the county for the defendant's confinement at a rate of $25 a day.

(b) A court that requires a defendant convicted of a misdemeanor or placed on deferred adjudication for a misdemeanor to submit to a period of confinement in county jail as a condition of community supervision may also require as a condition of community supervision that the defendant reimburse the county for the defendant's confinement, with the amount of reimbursement determined as if the defendant were serving an executed sentence.

(c) A judge may not require reimbursement under this article if the judge determines the defendant is indigent based on the defendant's sworn statement or affidavit filed with the court. A court that requires reimbursement under this article may require the defendant to reimburse the county only for those days the defendant is confined after the date of conviction or on which a plea of guilty or nolo contendere was entered. The court may not require a defendant to reimburse the county for those days the defendant was confined after arrest and before the date of conviction or on which the plea of guilty or nolo contendere was entered.

(d) The court, in determining whether to order reimbursement under this article, shall consider:

(1) the defendant's employment status, earning ability, and financial resources; and

(2) any other special circumstances that may affect the defendant's ability to pay, including child support obligations and including any financial responsibilities owed by the defendant to dependents or restitution payments owed by the defendant to a victim.

(e) On the day on which a defendant who is required to reimburse the county under this article discharges an executed sentence of confinement or completes the period of confinement required as a condition of community supervision, the sheriff shall present to the defendant a bill computed by multiplying the daily rate of $25 times the number of days the defendant was confined in the county jail, not counting the day on which the execution of the sentence or the period of confinement began. For purposes of this subsection, a defendant who is confined in county jail for only a portion of a day is nonetheless considered to have been confined for the whole day.

(f) The court may require a defendant to reimburse the county under this article by paying to the sheriff the bill presented by the sheriff within a specified period or in specified installments. The end of the period or the last installment may not be later than:

(1) the end of the period of community supervision, if community supervision is ordered; or

(2) the fifth anniversary of the last day of the term of confinement, if the court does not order community supervision.

(Enacted by Acts 1999, 76th Leg., ch. 295 (S.B. 1276), § 1, effective September 1, 1999.)

## Art. 42.04. Sentence When Appeal Is Taken.

When a defendant is sentenced to death, no date shall be set for the execution of sentence until after the receipt by the clerk of the trial court of the mandate of affirmance of the court of criminal appeals.

(Enacted by Acts 1965, 59th Leg., ch. 722 (S.B. 107), § 1, effective January 1, 1966; am. Acts 1981, 67th Leg., ch. 291 (S.B. 265), § 114, effective September 1, 1981.)

## Art. 42.05. If Court Is About to Adjourn.

The time limit within which any act is to be done within the meaning of this Code shall not be affected by the expiration of the term of the court.

(Enacted by Acts 1965, 59th Leg., ch. 722 (S.B. 107), § 1, effective January 1, 1966.)

## Art. 42.07. Reasons to Prevent Sentence.

Before pronouncing sentence, the defendant shall be asked whether he has anything to say why the sentence should not be pronounced against him. The only reasons which can be shown, on account of which sentence cannot be pronounced, are:

1. That the defendant has received a pardon from the proper authority, on the presentation of which, legally authenticated, he shall be discharged.

2. That the defendant is incompetent to stand trial; and if evidence be shown to support a finding of incompetency to stand trial, no sentence shall be pronounced, and the court shall proceed under Chapter 46B; and

3. When a person who has been convicted escapes after conviction and before sentence and an individual supposed to be the same has been arrested he may before sentence is pronounced, deny that he is the person convicted, and an issue be accordingly tried before a jury, or before the court if a jury is waived, as to his identity.

(Enacted by Acts 1965, 59th Leg., ch. 722 (S.B. 107), § 1, effective January 1, 1966; am. Acts 1975, 64th Leg., ch. 415 (S.B. 901), § 3, effective June 19, 1975; am. Acts 1981, 67th Leg., ch. 291 (S.B. 265), § 115, effective September 1, 1981; am. Acts 2003, 78th Leg., ch. 35 (S.B. 1057), § 3, effective January 1, 2004.)

## Art. 42.08. Cumulative or Concurrent Sentence.

(a) When the same defendant has been convicted in two or more cases, judgment and sentence shall be pronounced in each case in the same manner as if there had been but one conviction. Except as provided by Sections (b) and (c) of this article, in the discretion of the court, the judgment in the second and subsequent convictions may either be that the sentence imposed or suspended shall begin when the judgment and the sentence imposed or suspended in the preceding conviction has ceased to operate, or that the sentence imposed or suspended shall run concurrently with the other case or cases, and sentence and execution shall be accordingly; provided, however, that the cumulative total of suspended sentences in felony cases shall not exceed 10 years, and the cumulative total of suspended sentences in misdemeanor cases shall not exceed the maximum period of confinement in jail applicable to the misdemeanor offenses, though in no event more than three years, including extensions of periods of community supervision under Section 22, Article 42.12, of this code, if none of the offenses are offenses under Chapter 49, Penal Code, or four years, including extensions, if any of the offenses are offenses under Chapter 49, Penal Code.

(b) If a defendant is sentenced for an offense committed while the defendant was an inmate in the Texas Department of Criminal Justice and serving a sentence for an offense other than a state jail felony and the defendant has not completed the sentence he was serving at the time of the offense, the judge shall order the sentence for the subsequent offense to commence immediately on completion of the sentence for the original offense.

(c) If a defendant has been convicted in two or more cases and the court suspends the imposition of the sentence in one of the cases, the court may not order a sentence of confinement to commence on the completion of a suspended sentence for an offense.

(Enacted by Acts 1965, 59th Leg., ch. 722 (S.B. 107), § 1, effective January 1, 1966; am. Acts 1985, 69th Leg., ch. 29 (S.B. 186), § 1, effective September 1, 1985; am. Acts 1987, 70th Leg., ch. 513 (H.B. 554), § 1, effective August 31, 1987; am. Acts 1989, 71st Leg., ch. 785 (H.B. 2335), § 4.11, effective September 1, 1989; am. Acts 1993, 73rd Leg., ch. 900 (S.B. 1067), § 5.03, effective September 1, 1993; am. Acts 2009, 81st Leg., ch. 87 (S.B. 1969), § 25.022, effective September 1, 2009.)

## Art. 42.09. Commencement of Sentence; Status During Appeal; Pen Packet.

Sec. 1. Except as provided in Sections 2 and 3, a defendant shall be delivered to a jail or to the Texas Department of Criminal Justice when his sentence is pronounced, or his sentence to death is announced, by the court. The defendant's sentence begins to run on the day it is pronounced, but with all credits, if any, allowed by Article 42.03.

Sec. 2. If a defendant appeals his conviction and is released on bail pending disposition of his appeal, when his conviction is affirmed, the clerk of the trial court, on receipt of the mandate from the appellate court, shall issue a commitment against the defendant. The officer executing the commitment shall endorse thereon the date he takes the defendant into custody and the defendant's sentence begins to run from the date endorsed on the commitment. The Texas Department of Criminal Justice shall admit the defendant named in the commitment on the basis of the commitment.

Sec. 3. If a defendant is convicted of a felony and sentenced to death, life, or a term of more than ten years in the Texas Department of Criminal Justice and he gives notice of appeal, he shall be transferred to the department on a commitment pending a mandate from the court of appeals or the Court of Criminal Appeals.

Sec. 4. If a defendant is convicted of a felony, is eligible for release on bail pending appeal under Article 44.04(b), and gives notice of appeal, he shall be transferred to the Texas Department of Criminal Justice on a commitment pending a mandate from the Court of Appeals or the Court of Criminal Appeals upon request in open court or upon written request to the sentencing court. Upon a valid transfer to the department under this section, the defendant may not thereafter be released on bail pending his appeal.

Sec. 5. If a defendant is transferred to the Texas Department of Criminal Justice pending appeal under Section 3 or 4, his sentence shall be computed as if no appeal had been taken if the appeal is affirmed.

Sec. 6. All defendants who have been transferred to the Texas Department of Criminal Justice pending the appeal of their convictions under this article shall be under the control and authority of the department for all purposes as if no appeal were pending.

Sec. 7. If a defendant is sentenced to a term of imprisonment in the Texas Department of Criminal Justice but is not transferred to the department under Section 3 or 4, the court, before the date on which it would lose jurisdiction under Section 6(a), Article 42.12, shall send to the department a document containing a statement of the date on which the defendant's sentence was pronounced and credits earned by the defendant under Article 42.03 as of the date of the statement.

Sec. 8. (a) A county that transfers a defendant to the Texas Department of Criminal Justice under this article shall deliver to an officer designated by the department:

(1) a copy of the judgment entered pursuant to Article 42.01, completed on a standardized felony judgment form described by Section 4 of that article;

(2) a copy of any order revoking community supervision and imposing sentence pursuant to Section 23, Article 42.12, including:

(A) any amounts owed for restitution, fines, and court costs, completed on a standardized felony judgment form described by Section 4, Article 42.01; and

(B) a copy of the client supervision plan prepared for the defendant by the community supervision and corrections department supervising the defendant, if such a plan was prepared;

(3) a written report that states the nature and the seriousness of each offense and that states the citation to the provision or provisions of the Penal Code or other law under which the defendant was convicted;

(4) a copy of the victim impact statement, if one has been prepared in the case under Article 56.03;

(5) a statement as to whether there was a change in venue in the case and, if so, the names of the county prosecuting the offense and the county in which the case was tried;

(6) if requested, information regarding the criminal history of the defendant, including the defendant's state identification number if the number has been issued;

(7) a copy of the indictment or information for each offense;

(8) a checklist sent by the department to the county and completed by the county in a manner indicating that the documents required by this subsection and Subsection (c) of this section accompany the defendant;

(9) if prepared, a copy of a presentence or postsentence investigation report prepared under Section 9, Article 42.12;

(10) a copy of any detainer, issued by an agency of the federal government, that is in the possession of the county and that has been placed on the defendant;

(11) if prepared, a copy of the defendant's Texas Uniform Health Status Update Form; and

(12) a written description of a hold or warrant, issued by any other jurisdiction, that the county is aware of and that has been placed on or issued for the defendant.

(b) The Texas Department of Criminal Justice shall not take a defendant into custody under this article until the designated officer receives the documents required by Subsections (a) and (c) of this section. The designated officer shall certify under the seal of the department the documents received under Subsections (a) and (c) of this section. A document certified under this subsection is self-authenticated for the purposes of Rules 901 and 902, Texas Rules of Evidence.

(c) A county that transfers a defendant to the Texas Department of Criminal Justice under this article shall also deliver to the designated officer any presentence or postsentence investigation report, revocation report, psychological or psychiatric evaluation of the defendant, including an evaluation prepared for the juvenile court before transferring the defendant to criminal court and contained in the criminal prosecutor's file, and available social or psychological background information relating to the defendant and may deliver to the designated officer any additional information upon which the judge or jury bases the punishment decision.

(d) The correctional institutions division of the Texas Department of Criminal Justice shall make documents received under Subsections (a) and (c) available to the parole division on the request of the parole division and shall, on release of a defendant on parole or to mandatory supervision, immediately provide the parole division with copies of documents received under Subsection (a). The parole division shall provide to the parole officer appointed to supervise the defendant a comprehensive summary of the information contained in the documents referenced in this section not later than the 14th day after the date of the defendant's release. The summary shall include a current photograph of the defendant and a complete set of the defendant's fingerprints. Upon written request from the county sheriff, the photograph and fingerprints shall be filed with the sheriff of the county to which the parolee is assigned if that county is not the county from which the parolee was sentenced.

(e) A county is not required to deliver separate documents containing information relating to citations to provisions of the Penal Code or other law and to changes of venue, as otherwise required by Subsections (a)(3) and (a)(5) of this article, if the standardized felony judgment form described by Section 4, Article 42.01, of this code is modified to require that information.

(f) Except as provided by Subsection (g) of this section, the county sheriff is responsible for ensuring that documents and information required by this section accompany defendants sentenced by district courts in the county to the Texas Department of Criminal Justice.

(g) If the presiding judge of the administrative judicial region in which the county is located determines that the county sheriff is unable to perform the duties required by Subsection (f) of this section, the presiding judge may impose those duties on:

(1) the district clerk; or

(2) the prosecutor of each district court in the county.

(h) If a parole panel releases on parole a person who is confined in a jail in this state, a federal correctional institution, or a correctional institution in another state, the Texas Department of Criminal Justice shall request the sheriff who would otherwise be required to transfer the person to the department to forward to the department the information described by Subsections (a) and (c) of this section. The sheriff shall comply with the request of the department. The department shall determine whether the information forwarded by the sheriff under this subsection contains a thumbprint taken from the person in the manner provided by Article 38.33 of this code and, if not, the department shall obtain a thumbprint taken in the manner provided by that article and shall forward the thumbprint to the department for inclusion with the information sent by the sheriff.

(i) A county may deliver the documents required under Subsections (a) and (c) of this section to the Texas Department of Criminal Justice by electronic means. For purposes of this subsection, "electronic means" means the transmission of data between word processors, data processors, or similar automated information equipment over dedicated cables, commercial lines, or other similar methods of transmission.

(j) If after a county transfers a defendant or inmate to the Texas Department of Criminal Justice the charges on which the defendant or inmate was convicted and for which the defendant or inmate was transferred are dismissed, the county shall immediately notify an officer designated by the department of the dismissal.

Sec. 9. A county that transfers a defendant to the Texas Department of Criminal Justice under this article may deliver to an officer designated by the department a certified copy of a final order of a state or federal court that dismisses as frivolous or malicious a lawsuit brought by the inmate while the inmate was confined in the county jail awaiting transfer to the department following conviction of a felony or revocation of community supervision, parole, or mandatory supervision. The county may deliver the copy to the department at the time of the transfer of the inmate or at any time after the transfer of the inmate.

(Enacted by Acts 1965, 59th Leg., ch. 722 (S.B. 107), § 1, effective January 1, 1966; am. Acts 1973, 63rd Leg., ch. 91 (H.B. 403), § 2, effective August 27, 1973; am. Acts 1977, 65th Leg., ch. 806 (H.B. 39), § 1, effective August 29, 1977; am. Acts 1981, 67th Leg., ch. 291 (S.B. 265), § 117, effective September 1, 1981; am. Acts 1983, 68th Leg., ch. 40 (S.B. 218), § 1, effective April 26, 1983; am. Acts 1983, 68th Leg., ch. 810 (H.B. 859), § 1, effective September 1, 1983; am. Acts 1985, 69th Leg., ch. 344 (S.B. 845), § 3, effective January 1, 1986; am. Acts 1987, 70th Leg., ch. 1049 (S.B. 245), § 53, effective September 1, 1987; am. Acts 1989, 71st Leg., ch. 33 (S.B. 192), § 2, effective April 26, 1989; am. Acts 1989, 71st Leg., ch. 785 (H.B. 2335), § 4.12, effective September 1, 1989; am. Acts 1991, 72nd Leg., 2nd C.S., ch. 10 (H.B. 93), § 11.05, effective August 29, 1991; am. Acts 1993, 73rd Leg., ch. 900 (S.B. 1067), § 5.03, effective September 1, 1993; am. Acts 1995, 74th Leg., ch. 321 (H.B. 2162), § 3.001, effective September 1, 1995; am. Acts 1995, 74th Leg., ch. 723 (H.B. 253), § 1, effective September 1, 1995; am. Acts 1999, 76th Leg., ch. 655 (H.B. 261), § 1, effective June 18, 1999; am. Acts 1999, 76th Leg., ch. 1188 (S.B. 365), § 1.42, effective September 1, 1999; am. Acts 1999, 76th Leg., ch. 1477 (H.B. 3517), § 29, effective September 1, 1999; am. Acts 2001, 77th Leg., ch. 214 (H.B. 261), § 1, effective May 22, 2001; am. Acts 2001, 77th Leg., ch. 453 (H.B. 1658), § 1, effective June 8, 2001; am. Acts 2003, 78th Leg., ch. 14 (H.B. 1236), § 1, effective September 1, 2003; am.

Acts 2005, 79th Leg., ch. 728 (H.B. 2018), § 4.005, effective September 1, 2005; am. Acts 2007, 80th Leg., ch. 1308 (S.B. 909), § 4, effective June 15, 2007; am. Acts 2009, 81st Leg., ch. 87 (S.B. 1969), §§ 25.023, 25.024, effective September 1, 2009; am. Acts 2009, 81st Leg., ch. 980 (H.B. 3671), § 1, effective September 1, 2009.)

## Art. 42.10. Satisfaction of Judgment As in Misdemeanor Convictions.

When a person is convicted of a felony, and the punishment assessed is only a fine or a term in jail, or both, the judgment may be satisfied in the same manner as a conviction for a misdemeanor is by law satisfied.

(Enacted by Acts 1965, 59th Leg., ch. 722 (S.B. 107), § 1, effective January 1, 1966.)

## Art. 42.11. Uniform Act for Out-of-State Probationer and Parolee Supervision [Repealed].

Repealed by Acts 2001, 77th Leg., ch. 543 (H.B. 2494), § 2, effective June 19, 2003.

(Enacted by Acts 1965, 59th Leg., ch. 722 (S.B. 107), § 1, effective January 1, 1966; am. Acts 1973, 63rd Leg., ch. 233 (S.B. 231), § 1, effective August 27, 1973; am. Acts 1977, 65th Leg., ch. 735 (S.B. 54), § 2(2.134), effective August 29, 1977; am. Acts 1985, 69th Leg., ch. 479 (S.B. 813), § 162, effective September 1, 1985; am. Acts 1987, 70th Leg., ch. 939 (H.B. 83), § 1, effective September 1, 1987; am. Acts 1991, 72nd Leg., 1st C.S., ch. 17 (H.B. 222), § 7.01(27), effective September 1, 1991; am. Acts 1995, 74th Leg., ch. 321 (H.B. 2162), §§ 3.002(a), (b), effective September 1, 1995; am. Acts 1997, 75th Leg., ch. 514 (S.B. 1609), § 1, effective May 31, 1997.)

## Art. 42.111. Deferral of Proceedings in Cases Appealed to County Court.

If a defendant convicted of a misdemeanor punishable by fine only appeals the conviction to a county court, on the trial in county court the defendant may enter a plea of guilty or nolo contendere to the offense. If the defendant enters a plea of guilty or nolo contendere, the court may defer further proceedings without entering an adjudication of guilt in the same manner as provided for the deferral of proceedings in justice court or municipal court under Article 45.051 of this code. This article does not apply to a misdemeanor case disposed of under Subchapter B, Chapter 543, Transportation Code, or a serious traffic violation as defined by Section 522.003, Transportation Code.

(Enacted by Acts 1989, 71st Leg., ch. 399 (S.B. 980), § 2, effective June 14, 1989; am. Acts 1999, 76th Leg., ch. 62 (S.B. 1368), § 3.03, effective September 1, 1999; am. Acts 1999, 76th Leg., ch. 1545 (S.B. 1230), § 62, effective September 1, 1999.)

## Art. 42.12. Community Supervision.

### Sec. 1. Purpose.

It is the purpose of this article to place wholly within the state courts the responsibility for determining when the imposition of sentence in certain cases shall be suspended, the conditions of community supervision, and the supervision of defendants placed on community supervision, in consonance with the powers assigned to the judicial branch of this government by the Constitution of Texas. It is the purpose of this article to remove from existing statutes the limitations, other than questions of constitutionality, that have acted as barriers to effective systems of community supervision in the public interest.

### Sec. 2. Definitions.

In this article:

(1) "Court" means a court of record having original criminal jurisdiction.

(2) "Community supervision" means the placement of a defendant by a court under a continuum of programs and sanctions, with conditions imposed by the court for a specified period during which:

(A) criminal proceedings are deferred without an adjudication of guilt; or

(B) a sentence of imprisonment or confinement, imprisonment and fine, or confinement and fine, is probated and the imposition of sentence is suspended in whole or in part.

(3) "Supervision officer" means a person appointed or employed under Section 76.004, Government Code, to supervise defendants placed on community supervision.

(4) "Electronic monitoring" includes voice tracking systems, position tracking systems, position location systems, biometric tracking systems, and any other electronic or telecommunications system that may be used to assist in the supervision of individuals under this article.

### Sec. 3. Judge Ordered Community Supervision.

(a) A judge, in the best interest of justice, the public, and the defendant, after conviction or a plea of guilty or nolo contendere, may suspend the imposition of the sentence and place the defendant on community supervision or impose a fine applicable to the offense and place the defendant on community supervision.

(b) In a felony case the minimum period of community supervision is the same as the minimum term of imprisonment applicable to the offense and the maximum period of community supervision is, subject to the extensions provided by Section 22:

   (1) 10 years, for a felony other than a third degree felony described by Subdivision (2); and

   (2) five years, for the following third degree felonies:

     (A) a third degree felony under Title 7, Penal Code, other than an offense under Section 33.021(c), Penal Code; and

     (B) a third degree felony under Chapter 481, Health and Safety Code.

(c) The maximum period of community supervision in a misdemeanor case is two years.

(d) A judge may increase the maximum period of community supervision in the manner provided by Section 22(c) or 22A of this article.

(e) A defendant is not eligible for community supervision under this section if the defendant:

   (1) is sentenced to a term of imprisonment that exceeds 10 years; or

   (2) is sentenced to serve a term of confinement under Section 12.35, Penal Code.

(f) The minimum period of community supervision for a felony described by Section 13B(b) is five years and the maximum period of supervision is 10 years.

(g) A judge shall not deny community supervision to a defendant based solely on the defendant's inability to speak, read, write, hear, or understand English.

(h) The minimum period of community supervision under this section for an offense under Section 30.04, Penal Code, punishable as a Class A misdemeanor with a minimum term of confinement of six months is one year.

## Sec. 3g. Limitation on Judge Ordered Community Supervision.

(a) The provisions of Section 3 of this article do not apply:

   (1) to a defendant adjudged guilty of an offense under:

     (A) Section 19.02, Penal Code (Murder);

     (B) Section 19.03, Penal Code (Capital murder);

     (C) Section 21.11(a)(1), Penal Code (Indecency with a child);

     (D) Section 20.04, Penal Code (Aggravated kidnapping);

     (E) Section 22.021, Penal Code (Aggravated sexual assault);

     (F) Section 29.03, Penal Code (Aggravated robbery);

     (G) Chapter 481, Health and Safety Code, for which punishment is increased under:

       (i) Section 481.140, Health and Safety Code; or

       (ii) Section 481.134(c), (d), (e), or (f), Health and Safety Code, if it is shown that the defendant has been previously convicted of an offense for which punishment was increased under any of those subsections;

     (H) Section 22.011, Penal Code (Sexual assault);

     (I) Section 22.04(a)(1), Penal Code (Injury to a child, elderly individual, or disabled individual), if the offense is punishable as a felony of the first degree and the victim of the offense is a child;

     (J) Section 43.25, Penal Code (Sexual performance by a child);

     (K) Section 15.03, Penal Code, if the offense is punishable as a felony of the first degree;

     (L) Section 43.05, Penal Code (Compelling prostitution); or

     (M) Section 20A.02, Penal Code (Trafficking of persons); or

   (2) to a defendant when it is shown that a deadly weapon as defined in Section 1.07, Penal Code, was used or exhibited during the commission of a felony offense or during immediate flight therefrom, and that the defendant used or exhibited the deadly weapon or was a party to the offense and knew that a deadly weapon would be used or exhibited on an affirmative finding under this subdivision, the trial court shall enter the finding in the judgment of the court. On an affirmative finding that the deadly weapon was a firearm, the court shall enter that finding in its judgment.

(b) If there is an affirmative finding under Subsection (a)(2) in the trial of a felony of the second degree or higher that the deadly weapon used or exhibited was a firearm and the defendant is granted community supervision, the court may order the defendant confined in the Texas Department of Criminal Justice for not less than 60 and not more than 120 days. At any time after the defendant has served 60 days in the custody of the department, the sentencing judge, on his own motion or on motion of the defendant, may order the defendant released to community supervision. The department shall release the defendant to community supervision after he has served 120 days.

**Sec. 4. Jury Recommended Community Supervision.**

(a) A jury that imposes confinement as punishment for an offense may recommend to the judge that the judge suspend the imposition of the sentence and place the defendant on community supervision. A judge shall suspend the imposition of the sentence and place the defendant on community supervision if the jury makes that recommendation in the verdict.

(b) If the jury recommends to the judge that the judge place the defendant on community supervision, the judge shall place the defendant on community supervision for any period permitted under Section 3(b) or 3(c) of this article, as appropriate.

(c) A judge may increase the maximum period of community supervision in the manner provided by Section 22(c) or Section 22A of this article.

(d) A defendant is not eligible for community supervision under this section if the defendant:

(1) is sentenced to a term of imprisonment that exceeds 10 years;

(2) is convicted of a state jail felony for which suspension of the imposition of the sentence occurs automatically under Section 15(a);

(3) does not file a sworn motion under Subsection (e) of this section or for whom the jury does not enter in the verdict a finding that the information contained in the motion is true;

(4) is convicted of an offense for which punishment is increased under Section 481.134(c), (d), (e), or (f), Health and Safety Code, if it is shown that the defendant has been previously convicted of an offense for which punishment was increased under any one of those subsections;

(5) is convicted of an offense listed in Section 3g(a)(1)(C), (E), or (H), if the victim of the offense was younger than 14 years of age at the time the offense was committed;

(6) is convicted of an offense listed in Section 3g(a)(1)(D), if the victim of the offense was younger than 14 years of age at the time

the offense was committed and the actor committed the offense with the intent to violate or abuse the victim sexually;

(7) is convicted of an offense listed in Section 3g(a)(1)(J); or

(8) is adjudged guilty of an offense under Section 19.02, Penal Code.

(e) A defendant is eligible for community supervision under this section only if before the trial begins the defendant files a written sworn motion with the judge that the defendant has not previously been convicted of a felony in this or any other state, and the jury enters in the verdict a finding that the information in the defendant's motion is true.

(f) The minimum period of community supervision under this section for an offense under Section 30.04, Penal Code, punishable as a Class A misdemeanor with a minimum term of confinement of six months is one year.

**Sec. 5. Deferred Adjudication; Community Supervision.**

(a) Except as provided by Subsection (d) of this section, when in the judge's opinion the best interest of society and the defendant will be served, the judge may, after receiving a plea of guilty or plea of nolo contendere, hearing the evidence, and finding that it substantiates the defendant's guilt, defer further proceedings without entering an adjudication of guilt, and place the defendant on community supervision. A judge may place on community supervision under this section a defendant charged with an offense under Section 21.11, 22.011, or 22.021, Penal Code, regardless of the age of the victim, or a defendant charged with a felony described by Section 13B(b) of this article, only if the judge makes a finding in open court that placing the defendant on community supervision is in the best interest of the victim. The failure of the judge to find that deferred adjudication is in the best interest of the victim is not grounds for the defendant to set aside the plea, deferred adjudication, or any subsequent conviction or sentence. After placing the defendant on community supervision under this section, the judge shall inform the defendant orally or in writing of the possible consequences under Subsection (b) of this section of a violation of community supervision. If the information is provided orally, the judge must record and maintain the judge's statement to the defendant. The failure of a judge to inform a defendant of possible consequences under Subsection (b) of this section is not a ground for reversal unless the defendant shows that he was harmed by the failure of the judge to provide the information. In a felony case, the period of community supervision may not exceed 10 years. For a defendant charged with a felony under Section 21.11, 22.011, or 22.021, Penal Code, regardless of the age of the victim, and for a defendant charged with a felony described by Section 13B(b) of this article, the period of community supervision may not be less than five years. In a misdemeanor case, the period of community supervision may not exceed two years. A judge may increase the maximum period of community supervision in the manner provided by Section 22(c) or 22A of this article. The judge may impose a fine applicable to the offense and require any reasonable conditions of community supervision, including mental health treatment under Section 11(d) of this article, that a judge could impose on a defendant placed on community supervision for a conviction that was probated and suspended, including confinement. The provisions of Section 15 of this article specifying whether a defendant convicted of a state jail felony is to be confined in a county jail or state jail felony facility and establishing the minimum and maximum terms of confinement as a condition of community supervision apply in the same manner to a defendant placed on community supervision after pleading guilty or nolo contendere to a state jail felony. However, upon written motion of the defendant requesting final adjudication filed within 30 days after entering such plea and the deferment of adjudication, the judge shall proceed to final adjudication as in all other cases.

(a-1) Before placing a defendant on deferred adjudication community supervision under this section, the court shall inform the defendant of the defendant's right to petition the court for an order of nondisclosure under Section 411.081, Government Code, unless the defendant is ineligible to pursue that right because of:

(1) the nature of the offense for which the defendant is placed on deferred adjudication community supervision; or

(2) the defendant's criminal history.

(b) On violation of a condition of community supervision imposed under Subsection (a) of this section, the defendant may be arrested and detained as provided in Section 21 of this article. The defendant is entitled to a hearing limited to the determination by the court of whether it proceeds with an adjudication of guilt on the original charge. This determination is reviewable in the same manner as a revocation hearing conducted under Section 21 of this article in a case in which an adjudication of guilt had not been deferred. After an adjudication of guilt, all proceedings, including assessment of punishment, pronouncement of sentence, granting of community supervision, and defendant's appeal continue as if the adjudication of guilt had not been deferred. A court assessing punishment after an adjudication of guilt of a defendant charged with a state jail felony may suspend the imposition of the sentence and place the defendant on community supervision or may order the sentence to be executed, regardless of whether the defendant has previously been convicted of a felony.

(c) On expiration of a community supervision period imposed under Subsection (a), if the judge has not proceeded to adjudication of guilt, the judge shall dismiss the proceedings against the defendant and discharge him. The judge may dismiss the proceedings and discharge a defendant, other than a defendant charged with an offense requiring the defendant to register as a sex offender under Chapter 62, prior to the expiration of the term of community supervision if in the judge's opinion the best interest of society and the defendant will be served. The judge may not dismiss the proceedings and discharge a defendant charged with an offense requiring the defendant to register under Chapter 62. Except as provided by Section 12.42(g), Penal Code, a dismissal and discharge under this section may not be deemed a conviction for the purposes of disqualifications or disabilities imposed by law for conviction of an offense. For any defendant who receives a dismissal and discharge under this section:

(1) upon conviction of a subsequent offense, the fact that the defendant had previously received community supervision with a deferred adjudication of guilt shall be admissible before the court or jury to be considered on the issue of penalty;

(2) if the defendant is an applicant for a license or is a licensee under Chapter 42, Human Resources Code, the Department of Family and Protective Services may consider the fact that the defendant previously has received community supervision with a deferred adjudication of guilt under this section in issuing, renewing, denying, or revoking a license under that chapter; and

Criminal Procedure

(3) if the defendant is a person who has applied for registration to provide mental health or medical services for the rehabilitation of sex offenders, the Council on Sex Offender Treatment may consider the fact that the defendant has received community supervision under this section in issuing, renewing, denying, or revoking a license or registration issued by that council.

(c-1) A judge who dismisses the proceedings against a defendant and discharges the defendant under Subsection (c) shall:

(1) provide the defendant with a copy of the order of dismissal and discharge; and

(2) if applicable, inform the defendant of the defendant's eligibility to petition the court for an order of nondisclosure under Section 411.081, Government Code, and the earliest date the defendant is eligible to file the petition for the order of nondisclosure.

(d) In all other cases the judge may grant deferred adjudication unless:

(1) the defendant is charged with an offense:

(A) under Sections 49.04—49.08, Penal Code; or

(B) for which punishment may be increased under Section 481.134(c), (d), (e), or (f), Health and Safety Code, if it is shown that the defendant has been previously convicted of an offense for which punishment was increased under any one of those subsections;

(2) the defendant:

(A) is charged with an offense under Section 21.11, 22.011, or 22.021, Penal Code, regardless of the age of the victim, or a felony described by Section 13B(b) of this article; and

(B) has previously been placed on community supervision for any offense under Paragraph (A) of this subdivision;

(3) the defendant is charged with an offense under:

(A) Section 21.02, Penal Code; or

(B) Section 22.021, Penal Code, that is punishable under Subsection (f) of that section or under Section 12.42(c)(3) or (4), Penal Code; or

(e) If a judge places on community supervision under this section a defendant charged with an offense under Section 20.02, 20.03, or 20.04, Penal Code, or an attempt, conspiracy, or solicitation to commit one of those offenses, the judge shall make an affirmative finding of fact and file a statement of that affirmative finding with the papers in the case if the judge determines that the victim or intended victim was younger than 17 years of age at the time of the offense.

(f) A record in the custody of the court clerk regarding a case in which a person is granted deferred adjudication is not confidential.

(g) If a judge places on community supervision under this section a defendant charged with an offense under Section 21.11 or 22.011, Penal Code, the judge shall make an affirmative finding of fact and file a statement of that affirmative finding with the papers in the case if the judge determines that:

(1) at the time of the offense, the defendant was not more than four years older than the victim or intended victim and the victim or intended victim was at least 15 years of age; and

(2) the charge to which the plea is entered under this section is based solely on the ages of the defendant and the victim or intended victim at the time of the offense.

(h) A court retains jurisdiction to hold a hearing under Subsection (b) and to proceed with an adjudication of guilt, regardless of whether the period of community supervision imposed on the defendant has expired, if before the expiration the attorney representing the state files a motion to proceed with the adjudication and a capias is issued for the arrest of the defendant.

(i) If a judge places on community supervision under this section a defendant charged with an offense, on the motion of the attorney representing the state the judge shall make an affirmative finding of fact and file a statement of that affirmative finding in the papers in the case if the judge determines that, regardless of whether the conduct at issue is the subject of the prosecution or part of the same criminal episode as the conduct that is the subject of the prosecution, a victim in the trial:

(1) is or has been a victim of a severe form of trafficking in persons, as defined by 22 U.S.C. Section 7102(8); or

(2) has suffered substantial physical or mental abuse as a result of having been a victim of criminal activity described by 8 U.S.C. Section 1101(a)(15)(U)(iii).

(j) That part of the papers in the case containing an affirmative finding under Subsection (i):

(1) must include specific information identifying the victim, as available;

(2) may not include information identifying the victim's location; and

(3) is confidential, unless written consent for the release of the affirmative finding is obtained from the victim or, if the victim is younger than 18 years of age, the victim's parent or guardian.

### Sec. 6. Continuing Court Jurisdiction in Felony Cases.

(a) For the purposes of this section, the jurisdiction of a court imposing a sentence requiring imprisonment in the Texas Department of Criminal Justice for an offense other than a state jail felony continues for 180 days from the date the execution of the sentence actually begins. Before the expiration of 180 days from the date the execution of the sentence actually begins, the judge of the court that imposed such sentence may on his own motion, on the motion of the attorney representing the state, or on the written motion of the defendant, suspend further execution of the sentence and place the defendant on community supervision under the terms and conditions of this article, if in the opinion of the judge the defendant would not benefit from further imprisonment and:

(1) the defendant is otherwise eligible for community supervision under this article; and

(2) the defendant had never before been incarcerated in a penitentiary serving a sentence for a felony.

(b) When the defendant or the attorney representing the state files a written motion requesting suspension by the judge of further execution of the sentence and placement of the defendant on community supervision, and when requested to do so by the judge, the clerk of the court shall request a copy of the defendant's record while imprisoned from the Texas Department of Criminal Justice or, if the defendant is confined in county jail, from the sheriff. Upon receipt of such request, the Texas Department of Criminal Justice or the sheriff shall forward to the judge, as soon as possible, a full and complete copy of the defendant's record while imprisoned or confined. When the defendant files a written motion requesting suspension of further execution of the sentence and placement on community supervision, he shall immediately deliver or cause to be delivered a true and correct copy of the motion to the office of the attorney representing the state.

(c) The judge may deny the motion without a hearing but may not grant the motion without holding a hearing and providing the attorney representing the state and the defendant the opportunity to present evidence on the motion.

### Sec. 7. Continuing Court Jurisdiction in Misdemeanor Cases.

(a) For the purposes of this section, the jurisdiction of the courts in this state in which a sentence requiring confinement in a jail is imposed for conviction of a misdemeanor shall continue for 180 days from the date the execution of the sentence actually begins. The judge of the court that imposed such sentence may on his own motion, on the motion of the attorney representing the state, or on the written motion of the defendant suspend further execution of the sentence and place the defendant on community supervision under the terms and conditions of this article, if in the opinion of the judge the defendant would not benefit from further confinement.

(b) When the defendant files a written motion with the court requesting suspension of further execution of the sentence and placement on community supervision or when requested to do so by the judge, the clerk of the court shall request a copy of the defendant's record while confined from the agency operating the jail where the defendant is confined. Upon receipt of such request, the agency operating the jail where the defendant is confined shall forward to the court as soon as possible a full and complete copy of the defendant's record while confined.

(c) The judge may deny the motion without a hearing but may not grant a motion without holding a hearing and allowing the attorney representing the state and the defendant to present evidence in the case.

### Sec. 8. State Boot Camp Program.

(a) For the purposes of this section, the jurisdiction of a court imposing a sentence requiring imprisonment in the Texas Department of Criminal Justice for an offense other than a state jail felony continues for 180 days from the date on which the convicted person is received into custody by the department. After the expiration of 75 days but prior to the expiration of 180 days from the date on which the convicted person is received into custody by the department, the judge of the court that imposed the sentence may suspend further execution of the sentence imposed and place the person on community supervision under the terms and conditions of this article, if in the opinion of the judge the person would not benefit from further imprisonment. The court shall clearly indicate in its order recommending the placement of the person in the state boot camp program that the court is not retaining jurisdiction over the person for the purposes of Section 6. A court may recommend a person for placement in the state boot camp program only if:

(1) the person is otherwise eligible for community supervision under this article;

(2) the person is 17 years of age or older but younger than 26 years and is physically and mentally capable of participating in a program that requires strenuous physical activity; and

(3) the person is not convicted of an offense punishable as a state jail felony.

(b) On the 76th day after the day on which the convicted person is received into custody by the department, the department shall send the convicting court the record of the person's progress, conduct, and conformity to department rules.

(c) The judge's recommendation that a person be placed in the state boot camp program created under Section 499.052, Government Code, does not give the court the power to hold the Texas Department of Criminal Justice or any officer or employee of the department in contempt of court for failure to adhere to that recommendation.

### Sec. 9. Presentence Investigations.

(a) Except as provided by Subsection (g) of this section, before the imposition of sentence by a judge in a felony case, and except as provided by Subsection (b) of this section, before the imposition of sentence by a judge in a misdemeanor case the judge shall direct a supervision officer to report to the judge in writing on the circumstances of the offense with which the defendant is charged, the amount of restitution necessary to adequately compensate a victim of the offense, the criminal and social history of the defendant, and any other information relating to the defendant or the offense requested by the judge. It is not necessary that the report contain a sentencing recommendation, but the report must contain a proposed client supervision plan describing programs and sanctions that the community supervision and corrections department would provide the defendant if the judge suspended the imposition of the sentence or granted deferred adjudication.

(b) The judge is not required to direct a supervision officer to prepare a report in a misdemeanor case if:

(1) the defendant requests that a report not be made and the judge agrees to the request; or

(2) the judge finds that there is sufficient information in the record to permit the meaningful exercise of sentencing discretion and the judge explains this finding on the record.

(c) The judge may not inspect a report and the contents of the report may not be disclosed to any person unless:

(1) the defendant pleads guilty or nolo contendere or is convicted of the offense; or

(2) the defendant, in writing, authorizes the judge to inspect the report.

(d) Unless waived by the defendant, at least 48 hours before sentencing a defendant, the judge shall permit the defendant or his counsel to read the presentence report.

(e) The judge shall allow the defendant or his attorney to comment on a presentence investigation or a postsentence report and, with the approval of the judge, introduce testimony or other information alleging a factual inaccuracy in the investigation or report.

(f) The judge shall allow the attorney representing the state access to any information made available to the defendant under this section.

(g) A judge is not required to direct an officer to prepare a presentence report in a felony case under this section if:

(1) punishment is to be assessed by a jury;

(2) the defendant is convicted of or enters a plea of guilty or nolo contendere to capital murder;

(3) the only available punishment is imprisonment; or

(4) the judge is informed that a plea bargain agreement exists, under which the defendant agrees to a punishment of imprisonment, and the judge intends to follow the agreement.

(h) On a determination by the judge that alcohol or drug abuse may have contributed to the commission of the offense, or in any case involving a second or subsequent offense under Section 49.04, Penal Code, committed within five years of the date on which the most recent preceding offense was committed, or a second or subsequent offense under Section 49.07 or 49.08 of that code that involves the operation of a motor vehicle, committed within five years of the date on which the most recent preceding offense was committed, the judge shall direct a supervision officer approved by the community supervision and corrections department or the judge or a person, program, or other agency approved by the Texas Commission on Alcohol and Drug Abuse, to conduct an evaluation to determine the appropriateness of, and a course of conduct necessary for, alcohol or drug rehabilitation for a defendant and to report that evaluation to the judge. The evaluation shall be made:

    (1) after arrest and before conviction, if requested by the defendant;

    (2) after conviction and before sentencing, if the judge assesses punishment in the case;

    (3) after sentencing and before the entry of a final judgment, if the jury assesses punishment in the case; or

    (4) after community supervision is granted, if the evaluation is required as a condition of community supervision under Section 13 of this article.

(i) A presentence investigation conducted on any defendant convicted of a felony offense who appears to the judge through its own observation or on suggestion of a party to have a mental impairment shall include a psychological evaluation which determines, at a minimum, the defendant's IQ and adaptive behavior score. The results of the evaluation shall be included in the report to the judge as required by Subsection (a) of this section.

(j) The judge by order may direct that any information and records that are not privileged and that are relevant to a report required by Subsection (a) or Subsection (k) of this section be released to an officer conducting a presentence investigation under Subsection (i) of this section or a postsentence report under Subsection (k) of this section. The judge may also issue a subpoena to obtain that information. A report and all information obtained in connection with a presentence investigation or postsentence report are confidential and may be released only:

    (1) to those persons and under those circumstances authorized under Subsections (d), (e), (f), (h), (k), and (*l*) of this section;

    (2) pursuant to Section 614.017, Health and Safety Code; or

    (3) as directed by the judge for the effective supervision of the defendant.

(k) If a presentence report in a felony case is not required under this section, the judge may direct the officer to prepare a postsentence report containing the same information that would have been required for the presentence report, other than a proposed client supervision plan and any information that is reflected in the judgment. If the postsentence report is ordered, the officer shall send the report to the clerk of the court not later than the 30th day after the date on which sentence is pronounced or deferred adjudication is granted, and the clerk shall deliver the postsentence report with the papers in the case to a designated officer of the Texas Department of Criminal Justice, as described by Section 8(a), Article 42.09.

(*l*) Each presentence investigation shall include information regarding whether the defendant is a current or former member of the state military forces or whether the defendant is currently serving or has previously served in the armed forces of the United States in an active-duty status. If the defendant has served in an active-duty status, the investigation shall additionally determine whether the defendant was deployed to a combat zone and whether the defendant may suffer from post-traumatic stress disorder or a traumatic brain injury. In addition, if available, a copy of the defendant's military discharge papers and military records must be included in the investigation report provided to the judge under Subsection (a) of this section.

(m) [Repealed by Acts 2003, 78th Leg., ch. 353 (S.B. 1054), § 5, effective September 1, 2003.]

**Sec. 9A. Sex Offenders: Presentence Investigation and Postsentence Treatment and Supervision.**

(a) In this section:

    (1) "Council" means the Council on Sex Offender Treatment.

    (2) "Sex offender" means a person who has been convicted or has entered a plea of guilty or nolo contendere for an offense under any one of the following provisions of the Penal Code:

        (A) Section 20.04(a)(4) (Aggravated Kidnapping), if the person committed the offense with the intent to violate or abuse the victim sexually;

        (B) Section 21.08 (Indecent Exposure);

        (C) Section 21.11 (Indecency with a Child);

        (D) Section 22.011 (Sexual Assault);

(E) Section 22.021 (Aggravated Sexual Assault);

(F) Section 25.02 (Prohibited Sexual Conduct);

(G) Section 30.02 (Burglary), if:

(i) the offense is punishable under Subsection (d) of that section; and

(ii) the person committed the offense with the intent to commit a felony listed in this subsection;

(H) Section 43.25 (Sexual Performance by a Child); or

(I) Section 43.26 (Possession or Promotion of Child Pornography).

(b) If the defendant is a sex offender, a supervision officer may release information in a presentence or postsentence report concerning the social and criminal history of the defendant to a person who:

(1) is licensed or certified in this state to provide mental health or medical services, including a:

(A) physician;

(B) psychiatrist;

(C) psychologist;

(D) licensed professional counselor;

(E) licensed marriage and family therapist; or

(F) certified social worker; and

(2) provides mental health or medical services for the rehabilitation of the defendant.

(c) If the defendant is a sex offender, the judge shall direct a supervision officer approved by the community supervision and corrections department or the judge or a person, program, or other agency approved by the council to evaluate the appropriateness of, and a course of conduct necessary for, treatment, specialized supervision, or rehabilitation of the defendant and to report the results of the evaluation to the judge. The judge may require the evaluation to use offense-specific standards of practice adopted by the council and may require the report to reflect those standards. The evaluation shall be made after conviction and before the entry of a final judgment or, if requested by the defendant, after arrest and before conviction.

## Sec. 10. Authority to Impose, Modify, or Revoke Community Supervision.

(a) Only the court in which the defendant was tried may grant community supervision, impose conditions, revoke the community supervision, or discharge the defendant, unless the judge has transferred jurisdiction of the case to another court with the latter's consent. Except as provided by Subsection (d) of this section, only the judge may alter conditions of community supervision. In a felony case, only the judge who originally sentenced the defendant may suspend execution thereof and place the defendant under community supervision pursuant to Section 6 of this article. If the judge who originally sentenced the defendant is deceased or disabled or if the office is vacant and the judge who originally sentenced the defendant is deceased or disabled or if the office is vacant and a motion is filed in accordance with Section 6 of this article, the clerk of the court shall promptly forward a copy of the motion to the presiding judge of the administrative judicial district for that court, who may deny the motion without a hearing or appoint a judge to hold a hearing on the motion.

(b) After a defendant has been placed on community supervision, jurisdiction of the case may be transferred to a court of the same rank in this state having geographical jurisdiction where the defendant is residing or where a violation of the conditions of community supervision occurs. Upon transfer, the clerk of the court of original jurisdiction shall forward a transcript of such portions of the record as the transferring judge shall direct to the court accepting jurisdiction, which latter court shall thereafter proceed as if the trial and conviction had occurred in that court.

(c) Any judge of a court having geographical jurisdiction where the defendant is residing or where a violation of the conditions of community supervision occurs may issue a warrant for his arrest, but the determination of action to be taken after arrest shall be only by the judge of the court having jurisdiction of the case at the time the action is taken.

(d) A judge that places a defendant on community supervision may authorize the supervision officer supervising the defendant or a magistrate appointed by the district courts in the county that give preference to criminal cases to modify the conditions of community supervision for the limited purpose of transferring the defendant to different programs within the community supervision continuum of programs and sanctions.

(e) If a supervision officer or magistrate modifies the conditions of community supervision, the officer or magistrate shall deliver a copy of the modified conditions to the defendant, shall file a copy of the modified conditions with the sentencing court, and shall note the date of delivery of the copy in the defendant's file. If the defendant agrees to the modification in writing, the officer or magistrate shall file a copy of the modified conditions with the district clerk and the conditions shall be enforced as modified. If the defendant does not agree to the modification in writing, the supervision officer or magistrate shall refer the case to the judge of the court for modification in the manner provided by Section 22 of this article.

### Sec. 11. Basic Conditions of Community Supervision.

(a) The judge of the court having jurisdiction of the case shall determine the conditions of community supervision and may, at any time during the period of community supervision, alter or modify the conditions. The judge may impose any reasonable condition that is designed to protect or restore the community, protect or restore the victim, or punish, rehabilitate, or reform the defendant. Conditions of community supervision may include, but shall not be limited to, the conditions that the defendant shall:

(1) Commit no offense against the laws of this State or of any other State or of the United States;

(2) Avoid injurious or vicious habits;

(3) Avoid persons or places of disreputable or harmful character, including any person, other than a family member of the defendant, who is an active member of a criminal street gang;

(4) Report to the supervision officer as directed by the judge or supervision officer and obey all rules and regulations of the community supervision and corrections department;

(5) Permit the supervision officer to visit the defendant at the defendant's home or elsewhere;

(6) Work faithfully at suitable employment as far as possible;

(7) Remain within a specified place;

(8) Pay the defendant's fine, if one is assessed, and all court costs whether a fine is assessed or not, in one or several sums;

(9) Support the defendant's dependents;

(10) Participate, for a time specified by the judge, in any community-based program, including a community-service work program under Section 16 of this article;

(11) Reimburse the county in which the prosecution was instituted for compensation paid to appointed counsel for defending the defendant in the case, if counsel was appointed, or if the defendant was represented by a public defender's office, in an amount that would have been paid to an appointed attorney had the county not had a public defender's office;

(12) Remain under custodial supervision in a community corrections facility, obey all rules and regulations of the facility, and pay a percentage of the defendant's income to the facility for room and board;

(13) Pay a percentage of the defendant's income to the defendant's dependents for their support while under custodial supervision in a community corrections facility;

(14) Submit to testing for alcohol or controlled substances;

(15) Attend counseling sessions for substance abusers or participate in substance abuse treatment services in a program or facility approved or licensed by the Department of State Health Services;

(16) With the consent of the victim of a misdemeanor offense or of any offense under Title 7, Penal Code, participate in victim-defendant mediation;

(17) Submit to electronic monitoring;

(18) Reimburse the compensation to victims of crime fund for any amounts paid from that fund to or on behalf of a victim, as defined by Article 56.32, of the defendant's offense or if no reimbursement is required, make one payment to the compensation to victims of crime fund in an amount not to exceed $50 if the offense is a misdemeanor or not to exceed $100 if the offense is a felony;

(19) Reimburse a law enforcement agency for the analysis, storage, or disposal of raw materials, controlled substances, chemical precursors, drug paraphernalia, or other materials seized in connection with the offense;

(20) Pay all or part of the reasonable and necessary costs incurred by the victim for psychological counseling made necessary by the offense or for counseling and education relating to acquired immune deficiency syndrome or human immunodeficiency virus made necessary by the offense;

(21) Make one payment in an amount not to exceed $50 to a crime stoppers organization as defined by Section 414.001, Government Code, and as certified by the Texas Crime Stoppers Council;

(22) Submit a DNA sample to the Department of Public Safety under Subchapter G, Chapter 411, Government Code, for the purpose of creating a DNA record of the defendant;

(23) In any manner required by the judge, provide public notice of the offense for which the defendant was placed on community supervision in the county in which the offense was committed; and

(24) Reimburse the county in which the prosecution was instituted for compensation paid to any interpreter in the case.

(b) A judge may not order a defendant to make any payments as a term or condition of community supervision, except for fines, court costs, restitution to the victim, and other conditions related personally to the rehabilitation of the defendant or otherwise expressly authorized by law. The court shall consider the ability of the defendant to make payments in ordering the defendant to make payments under this article.

(c) If the judge or jury places a defendant on community supervision, the judge shall require the defendant to demonstrate to the court whether the defendant has an educational skill level that is equal to or greater than the average skill level of students who have completed the sixth grade in public schools in this state. If the judge determines that the defendant has not attained that skill level, the judge shall require as a condition of community supervision that the defendant attain that level of educational skill, unless the judge determines that the defendant lacks the intellectual capacity or the learning ability to ever achieve that level of skill.

(d) If the judge places a defendant on community supervision and the defendant is determined to have a mental illness or be a person with mental retardation as provided by Article 16.22 or Chapter 46B or in a psychological evaluation conducted under Section 9(i) of this article, the judge may require the defendant as a condition of community supervision to submit to outpatient or inpatient mental health or mental retardation treatment if the:

(1) defendant's:

(A) mental impairment is chronic in nature; or

(B) ability to function independently will continue to deteriorate if the defendant does not receive mental health or mental retardation services; and

(2) judge determines, in consultation with a local mental health or mental retardation services provider, that appropriate mental health or mental retardation services for the defendant are available through the Texas Department of Mental Health and Mental Retardation under Section 534.053, Health and Safety Code, or through another mental health or mental retardation services provider.

(e) A judge granting community supervision to a defendant required to register as a sex offender under Chapter 62 shall require that the defendant, as a condition of community supervision:

(1) register under that chapter; and

(2) submit a DNA sample to the Department of Public Safety under Subchapter G, Chapter 411, Government Code, for the purpose of creating a DNA record of the defendant, unless the defendant has already submitted the required sample under other state law.

(f) A judge may not require a defendant to undergo an orchiectomy as a condition of community supervision.

(g) A judge who grants community supervision to a person may require the person to make one payment in an amount not to exceed $50 to a children's advocacy center established under Subchapter E, Chapter 264, Family Code, if the person is charged with or convicted of an offense under Section 21.11 or 22.011(a)(2), Penal Code.

(h) If a judge grants community supervision to a person convicted of an offense under Title 5, Penal Code, that the court determines involves family violence, the judge shall require the person to pay $100 to a family violence center that receives state or federal funds and that serves the county in which the court is located. In this subsection, "family violence" has the meaning assigned by Section 71.004, Family Code, and "family violence center" has the meaning assigned by Section 51.002, Human Resources Code.

(i) A judge who grants community supervision to a sex offender evaluated under Section 9A may require the sex offender as a condition of community supervision to submit to treatment, specialized supervision, or rehabilitation according to offense-specific standards of practice adopted by the Council on Sex Offender Treatment. On a finding that the defendant is financially able to make payment, the judge shall require the defendant to pay all or part of the reasonable and necessary costs of the treatment, supervision, or rehabilitation.

(j) A judge granting community supervision to a defendant convicted of a felony shall require that the defendant, as a condition of community supervision, provide a DNA sample under Subchapter G, Chapter 411, Government Code, for the purpose of creating a DNA record of the defendant, unless the defendant has already submitted the required sample under other state law.

(k) A court granting community supervision to a defendant convicted of an offense under Section 28.08, Penal Code, shall require as a condition of community supervision that the defendant perform:

(1) at least 15 hours of community service if the amount of pecuniary loss resulting from the commission of the offense is $50 or more but less than $500; or

(2) at least 30 hours of community service if the amount of pecuniary loss resulting from the commission of the offense is $500 or more.

(l) (1) If the court grants community supervision to a person convicted of an offense under Section 42.072, Penal Code, the court may require as a condition of community supervision that the person may not:

(A) communicate directly or indirectly with the victim; or

(B) go to or near the residence, place of employment, or business of the victim or to or near a school, day-care facility, or similar facility where a dependent child of the victim is in attendance.

(2) If the court requires the prohibition contained in Subdivision (1)(B) of this subsection as a condition of community supervision, the court shall specifically describe the prohibited locations and the minimum distances, if any, that the person must maintain from the locations.

(m) If a judge grants community supervision to a person convicted of an offense under Section 42.09, 42.091, 42.092, or 42.10, Penal Code, the judge may require the person to attend a responsible pet owner course sponsored by a municipal animal shelter, as defined by Section 823.001, Health and Safety Code, that:

(1) receives federal, state, county, or municipal funds; and

(2) serves the county in which the court is located.

### Sec. 12. Confinement As a Condition of Community Supervision.

(a) If a judge having jurisdiction of a misdemeanor case requires as a condition of community supervision that the defendant submit to a period of confinement in a county jail, the period of confinement may not exceed 30 days. If a judge having jurisdiction of a felony case requires as a condition of community supervision that the defendant submit to a period of confinement in a county jail, the period of confinement may not exceed 180 days.

(b) A judge that requires as a condition of community supervision that the defendant serve a term in a community corrections facility under Section 18 of this article may not impose a term of confinement under this section that, when added to the term imposed under Section 18, exceeds 24 months.

(c) A judge may impose confinement as a condition of community supervision under Subsection (a) of this section on placing the defendant on supervision or at any time during the supervision period. The judge may impose periods of confinement as a condition of community supervision in increments smaller than the maximum periods provided by Subsection (a) of this section but may not impose periods of confinement that if added together exceed the maximum periods provided by Subsection (a).

### Sec. 13. DWI Community Supervision.

(a) A judge granting community supervision to a defendant convicted of an offense under Chapter 49, Penal Code, shall require as a condition of community supervision that the defendant submit to:

(1) not less than 72 hours of continuous confinement in county jail if the defendant was punished under Section 49.09(a); not less than five days of confinement in county jail if the defendant was punished under Section 49.09(a) and was subject to Section 49.09(h); not less than 10 days of confinement in county jail if the defendant was punished under Section 49.09(b) or (c); or not less than 30 days of confinement in county jail if the defendant was convicted under Section 49.07; and

(2) an evaluation by a supervision officer or by a person, program, or facility approved by the Texas Commission on Alcohol and Drug Abuse for the purpose of having the facility prescribe and carry out a course of

conduct necessary for the rehabilitation of the defendant's drug or alcohol dependence condition.

(b) A judge granting community supervision to a defendant convicted of an offense under Section 49.08, Penal Code, shall require as a condition of community supervision that the defendant submit to a period of confinement of not less than 120 days.

(c) If the director of a facility to which a defendant is referred under Subdivision (2) of Subsection (a) of this section determines that the defendant is not making a good faith effort to participate in a program of rehabilitation, the director shall notify the judge that referred the defendant of that fact.

(d) If a judge requires as a condition of community supervision that the defendant participate in a prescribed course of conduct necessary for the rehabilitation of the defendant's drug or alcohol dependence condition, the judge shall require that the defendant pay for all or part of the cost of such rehabilitation based on the defendant's ability to pay. The judge may, in its discretion, credit such cost paid by the defendant against the fine assessed. In making a determination of a defendant's ability to pay the cost of rehabilitation under this subsection, the judge shall consider whether the defendant has insurance coverage that will pay for rehabilitation.

(e) The confinement imposed shall be treated as a condition of community supervision, and in the event of a sentence of confinement upon the revocation of community supervision, the term of confinement served may not be credited toward service of such subsequent confinement.

(f) If a judge grants community supervision to a defendant convicted of an offense under Sections 49.04—49.08, Penal Code, and if before receiving community supervision the defendant has not submitted to an evaluation under Section 9 of this article, the judge shall require the defendant to submit to the evaluation as a condition of community supervision. If the evaluation indicates to the judge that the defendant is in need of treatment for drug or alcohol dependency, the judge shall require the defendant to submit to that treatment as a condition of community supervision in a program or facility approved or licensed by the Texas Commission on Alcohol and Drug Abuse or in a program or facility that complies with standards established by the community jus-

tice assistance division of the Texas Department of Criminal Justice, after consultation by the division with the commission.

(g) A jury that recommends community supervision for a person convicted of an offense under Sections 49.04—49.08, Penal Code, may recommend that any driver's license issued to the defendant under Chapter 521, Transportation Code, not be suspended. This subsection does not apply to a person punished under Section 49.09(a) or (b), Penal Code, and subject to Section 49.09(h) of that code.

(h) If a person convicted of an offense under Sections 49.04—49.08, Penal Code, is placed on community supervision, the judge shall require, as a condition of the community supervision, that the defendant attend and successfully complete before the 181st day after the day community supervision is granted an educational program jointly approved by the Texas Commission on Alcohol and Drug Abuse, the Department of Public Safety, the Traffic Safety Section of the Texas Department of Transportation, and the community justice assistance division of the Texas Department of Criminal Justice designed to rehabilitate persons who have driven while intoxicated. The Texas Commission on Alcohol and Drug Abuse shall publish the jointly approved rules and shall monitor, coordinate, and provide training to persons providing the educational programs. The Texas Commission on Alcohol and Drug Abuse is responsible for the administration of the certification of approved educational programs and may charge a nonrefundable application fee for the initial certification of approval and for renewal of a certificate. The judge may waive the educational program requirement or may grant an extension of time to successfully complete the program that expires not later than one year after the beginning date of the person's community supervision, however, if the defendant by a motion in writing shows good cause. In determining good cause, the judge may consider but is not limited to: the defendant's school and work schedule, the defendant's health, the distance that the defendant must travel to attend an educational program, and the fact that the defendant resides out of state, has no valid driver's license, or does not have access to transportation. The judge shall set out the finding of good cause for waiver in the judgment. If a defendant is required, as a condition of community supervision, to attend an educational program or if the court waives the educational program requirement, the court clerk shall immediately report that fact to the Department of Public Safety, on a form prescribed by the department, for inclusion in the person's driving record. If the court grants an extension of time in which the person may complete the program, the court clerk shall immediately report that fact to the Department of Public Safety on a form prescribed by the department. The report must include the beginning date of the person's community supervision. Upon the person's successful completion of the educational program, the person's instructor shall give notice to the Department of Public Safety for inclusion in the person's driving record and to the community supervision and corrections department. The community supervision and corrections department shall then forward the notice to the court clerk for filing. If the Department of Public Safety does not receive notice that a defendant required to complete an educational program has successfully completed the program within the period required by this section, as shown on department records, the department shall revoke the defendant's driver's license, permit, or privilege or prohibit the person from obtaining a license or permit, as provided by Sections 521.344(e) and (f), Transportation Code. The Department of Public Safety may not reinstate a license suspended under this subsection unless the person whose license was suspended makes application to the department for reinstatement of the person's license and pays to the department a reinstatement fee of $100. The Department of Public Safety shall remit all fees collected under this subsection to the comptroller for deposit in the general revenue fund. This subsection does not apply to a defendant if a jury recommends community supervision for the defendant and also recommends that the defendant's driver's license not be suspended.

(i) If a person convicted of an offense under Sections 49.04—49.08, Penal Code, is placed on community supervision, the court may require as a condition of community supervision that the defendant have a device installed, on the motor vehicle owned by the defendant or on the vehicle most regularly driven by the defendant, that uses a deep-lung breath analysis mechanism to make impractical the operation of the motor vehicle if ethyl alcohol is detected in the breath of the operator and that the defendant not operate any motor vehicle that is not equipped with that device. If it is shown on the

trial of the offense that an analysis of a specimen of the person's blood, breath, or urine showed an alcohol concentration level of 0.15 or more at the time the analysis was performed, or if the person is convicted of an offense under Sections 49.04—49.06, Penal Code, and punished under Section 49.09(a) or (b), Penal Code, or of a second or subsequent offense under Section 49.07 or 49.08, Penal Code, and the person after conviction of either offense is placed on community supervision, the court shall require as a condition of community supervision that the defendant have the device installed on the appropriate vehicle and that the defendant not operate any motor vehicle unless the vehicle is equipped with that device. Before placing on community supervision a person convicted of an offense under Sections 49.04—49.08, Penal Code, the court shall determine from criminal history record information maintained by the Department of Public Safety whether the person has one or more previous convictions under Sections 49.04—49.08, Penal Code, or has one previous conviction under Sections 49.04—49.07, Penal Code, or one previous conviction under Section 49.08, Penal Code. If it is shown on the trial of the offense that an analysis of a specimen of the person's blood, breath, or urine showed an alcohol concentration level of 0.15 or more at the time the analysis was performed, or if the court determines that the person has one or more such previous convictions, the court shall require as a condition of community supervision that the defendant have that device installed on the motor vehicle owned by the defendant or on the vehicle most regularly driven by the defendant and that the defendant not operate any motor vehicle unless the vehicle is equipped with the device described in this subsection. The court shall require the defendant to obtain the device at the defendant's own cost before the 30th day after the date of conviction unless the court finds that to do so would not be in the best interest of justice and enters its findings on record. The court shall require the defendant to provide evidence to the court within the 30-day period that the device has been installed on the appropriate vehicle and order the device to remain installed on that vehicle for a period not less than 50 percent of the supervision period. If the court determines the offender is unable to pay for the device, the court may impose a reasonable payment schedule not to exceed twice the period of the court's order. The Department of Public Safety shall approve devices for use under this subsection. Section 521.247, Transportation Code, applies to the approval of a device under this subsection and the consequences of that approval. Notwithstanding the provisions of this section, if a person is required to operate a motor vehicle in the course and scope of the person's employment and if the vehicle is owned by the employer, the person may operate that vehicle without installation of an approved ignition interlock device if the employer has been notified of that driving privilege restriction and if proof of that notification is with the vehicle. This employment exemption does not apply, however, if the business entity that owns the vehicle is owned or controlled by the person whose driving privilege has been restricted. A previous conviction may not be used for purposes of restricting a person to the operation of a motor vehicle equipped with an interlock ignition device under this subsection if:

　(1) the previous conviction was a final conviction under Section 49.04, 49.045, 49.05, 49.06, 49.07, or 49.08, Penal Code, and was for an offense committed more than 10 years before the instant offense for which the person was convicted and placed on community supervision; and

　(2) the person has not been convicted of an offense under Section 49.04, 49.045, 49.05, 49.06, 49.07, or 49.08 of that code, committed within 10 years before the date on which the instant offense for which the person was convicted and placed on community supervision.

　(j) The judge shall require a defendant who is punished under Section 49.09, Penal Code, as a condition of community supervision, to attend and successfully complete an educational program for repeat offenders approved by the Texas Commission on Alcohol and Drug Abuse. The Texas Commission on Alcohol and Drug Abuse shall adopt rules and shall monitor, coordinate, and provide training to persons providing the educational programs. The Texas Commission on Alcohol and Drug Abuse is responsible for the administration of the certification of approved educational programs and may charge a nonrefundable application fee for initial certification of approval or for renewal of the certification. The judge may waive the educational program requirement only if the defendant by a motion in writing shows good

cause. In determining good cause, the judge may consider the defendant's school and work schedule, the defendant's health, the distance that the defendant must travel to attend an educational program, and whether the defendant resides out of state or does not have access to transportation. The judge shall set out the finding of good cause in the judgment. If a defendant is required, as a condition of community supervision, to attend an educational program, the court clerk shall immediately report that fact to the Department of Public Safety, on a form prescribed by the department, for inclusion in the defendant's driving record. The report must include the beginning date of the defendant's community supervision. On the defendant's successful completion of the educational program for repeat offenders, the defendant's instructor shall give notice to the Department of Public Safety for inclusion in the defendant's driving record and to the community supervision and corrections department. The community supervision and corrections department shall then forward the notice to the court clerk for filing. If the Department of Public Safety does not receive notice that a defendant required to complete an educational program has successfully completed the program for repeat offenders within the period required by the judge, as shown on department records, the department shall revoke the defendant's driver's license, permit, or privilege or prohibit the defendant from obtaining a license or permit, as provided by Sections 521.344(e) and (f), Transportation Code.

　(k) Notwithstanding Sections 521.344(d)–(i), Transportation Code, if the judge, under Subsection (h) or (j) of this section, permits or requires a defendant punished under Section 49.09, Penal Code, to attend an educational program as a condition of community supervision, or waives the required attendance for such a program, and the defendant has previously been required to attend such a program, or the required attendance at the program had been waived, the judge nonetheless shall order the suspension of the driver's license, permit, or operating privilege of that person for a period determined by the judge according to the following schedule:

　(1) not less than 90 days or more than 365 days, if the defendant is convicted under Sections 49.04—49.08, Penal Code;

　(2) not less than 180 days or more than two years, if the defendant is punished under Section 49.09(a) or (b), Penal Code; or

(3) not less than one year or more than two years, if the person is convicted of a second or subsequent offense under Sections 49.04—49.08, Penal Code, committed within five years of the date on which the most recent preceding offense was committed.

(*l*) If the Department of Public Safety receives notice that a defendant has been required or permitted to attend a subsequent educational program under Subsection (h), (j), or (k) of this section, although the previously required attendance had been waived, but the judge has not ordered a period of suspension, the department shall suspend the defendant's driver's license, permit, or operating privilege, or shall issue an order prohibiting the defendant from obtaining a license or permit for a period of 365 days.

(m) If a judge revokes the community supervision of a defendant for an offense under Section 49.04, Penal Code, or an offense involving the operation of a motor vehicle under Section 49.07, Penal Code, and the driver's license or privilege to operate a motor vehicle has not previously been ordered by the judge to be suspended, or if the suspension was previously probated, the judge shall suspend the license or privilege for a period provided under Subchapter O, Chapter 521, Transportation Code. The suspension shall be reported to the Department of Public Safety as provided under Section 521.347, Transportation Code.

(n) Notwithstanding any other provision of this section or other law, the judge who places on community supervision a defendant who was younger than 21 years of age at the time of the offense and was convicted for an offense under Sections 49.04—49.08, Penal Code, shall:

(1) order that the defendant's driver's license be suspended for 90 days beginning on the date that the person is placed on community supervision; and

(2) require as a condition of community supervision that the defendant not operate a motor vehicle unless the vehicle is equipped with the device described by Subsection (i) of this section.

### Sec. 13A. Community Supervision for Offense Committed Because of Bias or Prejudice.

(a) A court granting community supervision to a defendant convicted of an offense for which the court has made an affirmative finding under Article 42.014 shall require as a term of community supervision that the defendant:

(1) serve a term of not more than one year imprisonment in the Texas Department of Criminal Justice if the offense is a felony other than an offense under Section 19.02, Penal Code; or

(2) serve a term of not more than 90 days confinement in jail if the offense is a misdemeanor.

(b) The court may not grant community supervision on its own motion or on the recommendation of the jury to a defendant convicted of an offense for which the court has made an affirmative finding under Article 42.014 of this code if:

(1) the offense is murder under Section 19.02, Penal Code; or

(2) the defendant has been previously convicted of an offense for which the court made an affirmative finding under Article 42.014 of this code.

### Sec. 13B. Defendants Placed on Community Supervision for Sexual Offenses Against Children.

(a) If a judge grants community supervision to a defendant described by Subsection (b) and the judge determines that a child as defined by Section 22.011(c), Penal Code, was the victim of the offense, the judge shall establish a child safety zone applicable to the defendant by requiring as a condition of community supervision that the defendant:

(1) not:

(A) supervise or participate in any program that includes as participants or recipients persons who are 17 years of age or younger and that regularly provides athletic, civic, or cultural activities; or

(B) go in, on, or within 1,000 feet of a premises where children commonly gather, including a school, day-care facility, playground, public or private youth center, public swimming pool, or video arcade facility; and

(2) attend psychological counseling sessions for sex offenders with an individual or organization which provides sex offender treatment or counseling as specified by or approved by the judge or the community supervision and corrections department officer supervising the defendant.

(b) This section applies to a defendant placed on community supervision for an offense:

Criminal Procedure

(1) under Section 43.05(a)(2), 43.25, or 43.26, Penal Code;

(2) under Section 21.08, 21.11, 22.011, 22.021, or 25.02, Penal Code;

(3) under Section 20.04(a)(4), Penal Code, if the defendant committed the offense with the intent to violate or abuse the victim sexually;

(4) under Section 30.02, Penal Code, punishable under Subsection (d) of that section, if the defendant committed the offense with the intent to commit a felony listed in Subdivision (2) or (3) of this subsection; or

(5) under Section 20A.02, Penal Code, if the defendant:

(A) trafficked the victim with the intent or knowledge that the victim would engage in sexual conduct, as defined by Section 43.25, Penal Code; or

(B) benefited from participating in a venture that involved a trafficked victim engaging in sexual conduct, as defined by Section 43.25, Penal Code.

(c) A community supervision and corrections department officer who under Subsection (a)(2) specifies a sex offender treatment provider to provide counseling to a defendant shall contact the provider before the defendant is released, establish the date, time, and place of the first session between the defendant and the provider, and request the provider to immediately notify the officer if the defendant fails to attend the first session or any subsequent scheduled session.

(d) Notwithstanding Subsection (a)(1), a judge is not required to impose the conditions described by Subsection (a)(1) if the defendant is a student at a primary or secondary school.

(e) At any time after the imposition of a condition under Subsection (a)(1), the defendant may request the court to modify the child safety zone applicable to the defendant because the zone as created by the court:

(1) interferes with the ability of the defendant to attend school or hold a job and consequently constitutes an undue hardship for the defendant; or

(2) is broader than is necessary to protect the public, given the nature and circumstances of the offense.

(f) A community supervision and corrections department officer supervising a defendant described by Subsection (b) may permit the defendant to enter on an event-by-event basis into the child safety zone from which the defendant is otherwise prohibited from entering if:

(1) the defendant has served at least two years of the period of community supervision;

(2) the defendant enters the zone as part of a program to reunite with the defendant's family;

(3) the defendant presents to the officer a written proposal specifying where the defendant intends to go within the zone, why and with whom the defendant is going, and how the defendant intends to cope with any stressful situations that occur;

(4) the sex offender treatment provider treating the defendant agrees with the officer that the defendant should be allowed to attend the event; and

(5) the officer and the treatment provider agree on a chaperon to accompany the defendant and the chaperon agrees to perform that duty.

(g) Section 10(a) does not prohibit a community supervision and corrections department officer from altering a condition of community supervision by permitting a defendant to enter a child safety zone under Subsection (f).

(h) In this section, "playground," "premises," "school," "video arcade facility," and "youth center" have the meanings assigned by Section 481.134, Health and Safety Code.

(i) Notwithstanding Subsection (a)(1)(B), a requirement that a defendant not go in, on, or within 1,000 feet of certain premises does not apply to a defendant while the defendant is in or going immediately to or from a:

(1) community supervision and corrections department office;

(2) premises at which the defendant is participating in a program or activity required as a condition of community supervision;

(3) residential facility in which the defendant is required to reside as a condition of community supervision, if the facility was in operation as a residence for defendants on community supervision on June 1, 2003; or

(4) private residence at which the defendant is required to reside as a condition of community supervision.

**Sec. 13C. Community Supervision for Making a Firearm Accessible to a Child.**

(a) A court granting community supervision to a defendant convicted of an offense under Section 46.13, Penal Code, may require as a condition of community supervision that the defendant:

(1) provide an appropriate public service activity designated by the court; or

(2) attend a firearms safety course which meets or exceeds the requirements set by the National Rifle Association as of January 1, 1995, for a firearms safety course that requires not more than 17 hours of instruction.

(b) The court shall require the defendant to pay the cost of attending the firearms safety course under Subsection (a)(2).

## Sec. 13D. Defendants Placed on Community Supervision for Violent Offenses; Protecting Children.

(a) If a judge grants community supervision to a defendant convicted of an offense listed in Section 3g(a)(1) or for which the judgment contains an affirmative finding under Section 3g(a)(2), the judge, if the nature of the offense for which the defendant is convicted warrants the establishment of a child safety zone, may establish a child safety zone applicable to the defendant by requiring as a condition of community supervision that the defendant not:

(1) supervise or participate in any program that includes as participants or recipients persons who are 17 years of age or younger and that regularly provides athletic, civic, or cultural activities; or

(2) go in or on, or within a distance specified by the judge of, a premises where children commonly gather, including a school, day-care facility, playground, public or private youth center, public swimming pool, or video arcade facility.

(b) At any time after the imposition of a condition under Subsection (a), the defendant may request the judge to modify the child safety zone applicable to the defendant because the zone as created by the judge:

(1) interferes with the ability of the defendant to attend school or hold a job and consequently constitutes an undue hardship for the defendant; or

(2) is broader than is necessary to protect the public, given the nature and circumstances of the offense.

(c) This section does not apply to a defendant described by Section 13B.

(d) In this section, "playground," "premises," "school," "video arcade facility," and "youth center" have the meanings assigned by Section 481.134, Health and Safety Code.

## Sec. 13E. Electronic Monitoring of Certain Members of Criminal Street Gang Who Are Placed on Community Supervision.

(a) This section applies only to a defendant who:

(1) is identified as a member of a criminal street gang in an intelligence database established under Chapter 61; and

(2) has two or more times been previously convicted of, or received a grant of deferred adjudication community supervision or another functionally equivalent form of community supervision or probation for, a felony offense under the laws of this state, another state, or the United States.

(b) A court granting community supervision to a defendant described by Subsection (a) may, on the defendant's conviction of a felony offense, require as a condition of community supervision that the defendant submit to tracking under an electronic monitoring service or other appropriate technological service designed to track a person's location.

## Sec. 13F. Restrictions on Operation of Motor Vehicle for Defendants Convicted of Certain Organized Crime Offenses.

A court granting community supervision to a defendant convicted of an offense under Chapter 71, Penal Code, may impose as a condition of community supervision restrictions on the defendant's operation of a motor vehicle, including specifying:

(1) hours during which the defendant may not operate a motor vehicle; and

(2) locations at or in which the defendant may not operate a motor vehicle.

## Sec. 13G. Prohibitions on Internet Access for Certain Sex Offenders.

(a) This section applies only to a person who is required to register as a sex offender under Chapter 62, by court order or otherwise, and:

(1) is convicted of or receives a grant of deferred adjudication community supervision for a violation of Section 21.11, 22.011(a)(2), 22.021(a)(1)(B), 33.021, or 43.25, Penal Code;

(2) used the Internet or any other type of electronic device used for Internet access to commit the offense or engage in the conduct for which the person is required to register under Chapter 62; or

(3) is assigned a numeric risk level of three based on an assessment conducted under Article 62.007.

(b) If the court grants community supervision to a defendant described by Subsection (a), the court as a condition of community supervision shall prohibit the defendant from using the Internet to:

(1) access material that is obscene as defined by Section 43.21, Penal Code;

(2) access a commercial social networking site, as defined by Article 62.0061(f);

(3) communicate with any individual concerning sexual relations with an individual who is younger than 17 years of age; or

(4) communicate with another individual the defendant knows is younger than 17 years of age.

(c) The court may modify at any time the condition described by Subsection (b)(4) if:

(1) the condition interferes with the defendant's ability to attend school or become or remain employed and consequently constitutes an undue hardship for the defendant; or

(2) the defendant is the parent or guardian of an individual who is younger than 17 years of age and the defendant is not otherwise prohibited from communicating with that individual.

**Sec. 13H. Defendants Placed on Community Supervision for Electronic Transmission of Certain Visual Material.**

(a) In this section, "parent" means a natural or adoptive parent, managing or possessory conservator, or legal guardian. The term does not include a parent whose parental rights have been terminated.

(b) If a judge grants community supervision to a defendant who is convicted of or charged with an offense under Section 43.261, Penal Code, the judge may require as a condition of community supervision that the defendant attend and successfully complete an educational program described by Section 37.218, Education Code, or another equivalent educational program.

(c) The court shall require the defendant or the defendant's parent to pay the cost of attending an educational program under Subsection (b) if the court determines that the defendant or the defendant's parent is financially able to make payment.

**Sec. 14. [2 Versions: As amended by Acts 1993, 73rd Leg., ch. 165, § 1; Acts 1999, 76th Leg., ch. 910, § 1; Acts 2003, 78th Leg., ch. 353, §§ 4, 5; and Acts 2007, 80th Leg., ch. 113,**

**§ 1] Child Abusers and Family Violence Offenders; Special Conditions.**

(a) If the court grants probation to a person convicted of an offense described by Article 17.41(a) of this code, the court may require as a condition of probation that the defendant not directly communicate with the victim of the offense or go near a residence, school, or other location, as specifically described in the copy of terms and conditions, frequented by the victim. In imposing the condition, the court may grant the defendant supervised access to the victim. To the extent that a condition imposed under this subsection conflicts with an existing court order granting possession of or access to a child, the condition imposed under this subsection prevails for a period specified by the court granting probation, not to exceed 90 days.

(b) [Repealed by Acts 2003, 78th Leg., ch. 353 (S.B. 1054), § 6, effective September 1, 2003.]

(c) If the court grants community supervision to a person convicted of an offense involving family violence, as defined by Section 71.004, Family Code, the court may require the defendant, at the direction of the community supervision and corrections department officer, to:

(1) attend a battering intervention and prevention program as defined by Article 42.141;

(2) beginning on September 1, 2008, if the referral option under Subdivision (1) is not available, attend a program or counsel with a provider that has begun the accreditation process described by Subsection (c-1); or

(3) if the referral option under Subdivision (1) or, beginning on September 1, 2008, the referral option under Subdivision (2) is not available, attend counseling sessions for the elimination of violent behavior with a licensed counselor, social worker, or other professional who has completed family violence intervention training that the community justice assistance division of the Texas Department of Criminal Justice has approved, after consultation with the licensing authorities described by Chapters 152, 501, 502, 503, and 505, Occupations Code, and experts in the field of family violence.

(c-1) Beginning on September 1, 2009, a program or provider serving as a referral option for the courts under Subsection (c)(1) or (2) must be accredited under Section 4A, Article

42.141, as conforming to program guidelines under that article.

(c-2) If the court requires the defendant to attend counseling or a program, the court shall require the defendant to begin attendance not later than the 60th day after the date the court grants community supervision, notify the community supervision and corrections department officer of the name, address, and phone number of the counselor or program, and report the defendant's attendance to the officer. The court shall require the defendant to pay all the reasonable costs of the counseling sessions or attendance in the program on a finding that the defendant is financially able to make payment. If the court finds the defendant is unable to make payment, the court shall make the counseling sessions or enrollment in the program available without cost to the defendant. The court may also require the defendant to pay all or a part of the reasonable costs incurred by the victim for counseling made necessary by the offense, on a finding that the defendant is financially able to make payment. The court may order the defendant to make payments under this subsection for a period not to exceed one year after the date on which the order is entered.

**Sec. 14. [2 Versions: As amended by Acts 1993, 73rd Leg., ch. 900, § 4.01; Acts 1995, 74th Leg., ch. 76, § 3.09; Acts 1995, 74th Leg., ch. 321, §§ 3.004 and 3.005; Acts 1999, 76th Leg., ch. 1188, § 1.44; Acts 2003, 78th Leg., ch. 209, § 63; and Acts 2003, 78th Leg., ch. 1310, § 2] Substance Abuse Felony Program.**

(a) If a court places a defendant on community supervision under any provision of this article as an alternative to imprisonment, the judge may require as a condition of community supervision that the defendant serve a term of confinement and treatment in a substance abuse treatment facility operated by the Texas Department of Criminal Justice under Section 493.009, Government Code. A term of confinement and treatment imposed under this section must be an indeterminate term of not more than one year or less than 90 days.

(b) A judge may impose the condition of community supervision created under this section if:

(1) the judge places the defendant on community supervision under this article;

(2) the defendant is charged with or convicted of a felony other than:

(A) a felony under Section 21.11, 22.011, or 22.021, Penal Code; or

(B) criminal attempt of a felony under Section 21.11, 22.011, or 22.021, Penal Code; and

(3) the judge makes an affirmative finding that:

(A) drug or alcohol abuse significantly contributed to the commission of the crime or violation of community supervision; and

(B) the defendant is a suitable candidate for treatment, as determined by the suitability criteria established by the Texas Board of Criminal Justice under Section 493.009(b), Government Code.

(c) If a judge requires as a condition of community supervision that the defendant serve a term of confinement and treatment in a substance abuse treatment facility under this section, the judge shall also require as a condition of community supervision that on release from the facility the defendant:

(1) participate in a drug or alcohol abuse continuum of care treatment plan; and

(2) pay a fee in an amount established by the judge for residential aftercare required as part of the treatment plan.

(d) The Texas Commission on Alcohol and Drug Abuse shall develop the continuum of care treatment plan.

(e) **[2 Versions: As amended by Acts 2003, 78th Leg., ch. 209]** The clerk of a court that collects a fee imposed under Subsection (c)(2) shall deposit the fee to be sent to the comptroller as provided by Subchapter B, Chapter 133, Local Government Code, and the comptroller shall deposit the fee into the general revenue fund. In requiring the payment of a fee under Subsection (c)(2), the judge shall consider fines, fees, and other necessary expenses for which the defendant is obligated in establishing the amount of the fee. The judge may not:

(1) establish the fee in an amount that is greater than 25 percent of the defendant's gross income while the defendant is a participant in residential aftercare; or

(2) require the defendant to pay the fee at any time other than a time at which the defendant is both employed and a participant in residential aftercare.

(e) **[2 Versions: As amended by Acts 2003, 78th Leg., ch. 1310]** The clerk of a court that collects a fee imposed under Subsection (c)(2) shall remit the fee to the comptroller not later than the last day of the month following the end of the calendar quarter in which the fee is collected, and the comptroller shall deposit the fee into the general revenue fund. If the clerk does not collect a fee imposed under Subsection (c)(2), the clerk is not required to file any report required by the comptroller relating to the collection of the fee. In requiring the payment of a fee under Subsection (c)(2), the judge shall consider fines, fees, and other necessary expenses for which the defendant is obligated in establishing the amount of the fee. The judge may not:

(1) establish the fee in an amount that is greater than 25 percent of the defendant's gross income while the defendant is a participant in residential aftercare; or

(2) require the defendant to pay the fee at any time other than a time at which the defendant is both employed and a participant in residential aftercare.

### Sec. 15. Procedures Relating to State Jail Felony Community Supervision.

(a) (1) On conviction of a state jail felony under Section 481.115(b), 481.1151(b)(1), 481.116(b), 481.1161(b)(3), 481.121(b)(3), or 481.129(g)(1), Health and Safety Code, that is punished under Section 12.35(a), Penal Code, the judge shall suspend the imposition of the sentence and place the defendant on community supervision, unless the defendant has previously been convicted of a felony, other than a felony punished under Section 12.44(a), Penal Code, or unless the conviction resulted from an adjudication of the guilt of a defendant previously placed on deferred adjudication community supervision for the offense, in which event the judge may suspend the imposition of the sentence and place the defendant on community supervision or may order the sentence to be executed. The provisions of this subdivision requiring the judge to suspend the imposition of the sentence and place the defendant on community supervision do not apply to a defendant who:

(A) under Section 481.1151(b)(1), Health and Safety Code, possessed more than five abuse units of the controlled substance;

(B) under Section 481.1161(b)(3), Health and Safety Code, possessed more than one pound, by aggregate weight, including adulterants or dilutants, of the controlled substance; or

(C) under Section 481.121(b)(3), Health and Safety Code, possessed more than one pound of marihuana.

(2) On conviction of a state jail felony punished under Section 12.35(a), Penal Code, other than a state jail felony listed in Subdivision (1), the judge may suspend the imposition of the sentence and place the defendant on community supervision or may order the sentence to be executed.

(3) The judge may suspend in whole or in part the imposition of any fine imposed on conviction.

(b) The minimum period of community supervision a judge may impose under this section is two years. The maximum period of community supervision a judge may impose under this section is five years, except that the judge may extend the maximum period of community supervision under this section to not more than 10 years. A judge may extend a period of community supervision under this section at any time during the period of community supervision, or if a motion for revocation of community supervision is filed before the period of community supervision ends, before the first anniversary of the expiration of the period of community supervision.

(c) (1) A judge may impose any condition of community supervision on a defendant that the judge could impose on a defendant placed on supervision for an offense other than a state jail felony.

(2) Except as otherwise provided by Subdivision (3), a judge who places a defendant on community supervision for an offense listed in Subsection (a)(1) shall require the defendant to comply with substance abuse treatment conditions that are consistent with standards adopted by the Texas Board of Criminal Justice under Section 509.015, Government Code.

(3) A judge is not required to impose conditions described by Subdivision (2) if the judge makes an affirmative finding that the defendant does not require imposition of the conditions to successfully complete the period of community supervision.

(d) A judge may impose as a condition of community supervision that a defendant submit at the beginning of the period of community supervision to a term of confinement in a state jail felony facility for a term of not less than 90 days or more than 180 days, or a term of not less than 90 days or more than one year if the defendant is convicted of an offense punishable as a state jail felony under Section 481.112, 481.1121, 481.113, or 481.120, Health and Safety Code. A judge may not require a defendant to submit to both the term of confinement authorized by this subsection and a term of confinement under Section 5 or 12 of this article. For the purposes of this subsection, a defendant previously has been convicted of a felony regardless of whether the sentence for the previous conviction was actually imposed or was probated and suspended.

(e) If a defendant violates a condition of community supervision imposed on the defendant under this article and after a hearing under Section 21 of this article the judge modifies the defendant's community supervision, the judge may impose any sanction permitted by Section 22 of this article, except that if the judge requires a defendant to serve a period of confinement in a state jail felony facility as a modification of the defendant's community supervision, the minimum term of confinement is 90 days and the maximum term of confinement is 180 days.

(f) (1) If a defendant violates a condition of community supervision imposed on the defendant under this article and after a hearing under Section 21 of this article the judge revokes the defendant's community supervision, the judge shall dispose of the case in the manner provided by Section 23 of this article.

(2) The court retains jurisdiction over the defendant for the period during which the defendant is confined in a state jail. At any time after the 75th day after the date the defendant is received into the custody of a state jail, the judge on the judge's own motion, on the motion of the attorney representing the state, or on the motion of the defendant may suspend further execution of the sentence and place the defendant on community supervision under the conditions of this section.

(3) When the defendant or the attorney representing the state files a written motion requesting suspension by the judge of further execution of the sentence and placement of the defendant on community supervision, the clerk of the court, if requested to do so by the judge, shall request a copy of the defendant's record while confined from the facility director of the state jail felony facility in which the defendant is confined or, if the defendant is confined in county jail, from the sheriff. On

receipt of the request, the facility director or the sheriff shall forward to the judge, as soon as possible, a full and complete copy of the defendant's record while confined. When the defendant files a written motion requesting suspension of further execution of the sentence and placement on community supervision, he shall immediately deliver or cause to be delivered a true and correct copy of the motion to the office of the attorney representing the state. The judge may deny the motion without a hearing but may not grant the motion without holding a hearing and providing the attorney representing the state and the defendant the opportunity to present evidence on the motion.

(g) The facility director of a state jail felony facility shall report to a judge who orders a defendant confined in the facility as a condition of community supervision or as sanction imposed as a modification of community supervision under Subsection (e) not less than every 90 days on the defendant's programmatic progress, conduct, and conformity to the rules of the facility.

(h) (1) A defendant confined in a state jail felony facility does not earn good conduct time for time served in the facility but may be awarded diligent participation credit in accordance with Subdivision (6).

(2) A judge:

(A) may credit against any time a defendant is required to serve in a state jail felony facility time served by the defendant in a county jail from the time of the defendant's arrest and confinement until sentencing by the trial court; and

(B) shall credit against any time a defendant is required to serve in a state jail felony facility time served by the defendant in a substance abuse treatment facility operated by the Texas Department of Criminal Justice under Section 493.009, Government Code, or other court-ordered residential program or facility as a condition of deferred adjudication community supervision before sentencing, but only if the defendant successfully completes the treatment program in that facility.

(3) A judge shall credit against any time a defendant is subsequently required to serve in a state jail felony facility after revocation of community supervision any time served after sentencing by the defendant:

(A) in a state jail felony facility; or

(B) in a substance abuse treatment facility operated by the Texas Department of Criminal Justice under Section 493.009, Government Code, or another court-ordered residential program or facility if the defendant successfully completes the treatment program in that facility.

(4) For purposes of Subdivisions (5) and (6), "diligent participation" includes:

(A) successful completion of an educational, vocational, or treatment program;

(B) progress toward successful completion of an educational, vocational, or treatment program that was interrupted by illness, injury, or another circumstance outside the control of the defendant; and

(C) active involvement in a work program.

(5) For a defendant who has participated in an educational, vocational, treatment, or work program while confined in a state jail felony facility, not later than the 30th day before the date on which the defendant will have served 80 percent of the defendant's sentence, the Texas Department of Criminal Justice shall report to the sentencing court the number of days during which the defendant diligently participated in any educational, vocational, treatment, or work program. The contents of a report submitted under this subdivision are not subject to challenge by a defendant.

(6) A judge, based on the report received under Subdivision (5), may credit against any time a defendant is required to serve in a state jail felony facility additional time for each day the defendant actually served in the facility while diligently participating in an educational, vocational, treatment, or work program. A time credit under this subdivision may not exceed one-fifth of the amount of time the defendant is originally required to serve in the facility. A defendant may not be awarded a credit under this subdivision for any period during which the defendant is subject to disciplinary action. A time credit under this subdivision is a privilege and not a right.

(i) **[2 Versions: As added by Acts 2007, 80th Leg., ch. 617]** If a defendant is convicted of a state jail felony and the sentence is executed, the judge sentencing the defendant may release the defendant to a medical care facility or medical treatment program if the Texas Correctional Office on Offenders with Medical or Mental Impairments:

(1) identifies the defendant as being elderly, physically disabled, mentally ill, terminally ill, or mentally retarded or having a condition requiring long-term care; and

(2) in cooperation with the community supervision and corrections department serving the sentencing court, prepares for the defendant a medically recommended intensive supervision plan that:

(A) ensures appropriate supervision of the defendant; and

(B) requires the defendant to remain under the care of a physician at the facility or in the program.

(i) **[2 Versions: As added by Acts 2007, 80th Leg., ch. 1308]** If a defendant is convicted of a state jail felony and the sentence is executed, the judge sentencing the defendant may release the defendant to a medically suitable placement if the judge determines that the defendant does not constitute a threat to public safety and the Texas Correctional Office on Offenders with Medical or Mental Impairments:

(1) in coordination with the Correctional Managed Health Care Committee prepares a case summary and medical report that identifies the defendant as being elderly, physically disabled, mentally ill, terminally ill, or mentally retarded or having a condition requiring long-term care; and

(2) in cooperation with the community supervision and corrections department serving the sentencing court, prepares for the defendant a medically recommended intensive supervision and continuity of care plan that:

(A) ensures appropriate supervision of the defendant by the community supervision and corrections department; and

(B) requires the defendant to remain under the care of a physician at and reside in a medically suitable placement.

(j) **[2 Versions: As added by Acts 2007, 80th Leg., ch. 617]** If a defendant released to a medical care facility or medical treatment program under Subsection (i) violates the terms of that release, the judge may dispose of the matter as provided by Subsections (e) and (f)(1).

(j) **[2 Versions: As added by Acts 2007, 80th Leg., ch. 1308]** The Texas Correctional Office on Offenders with Medical or Mental

Impairments shall submit to a judge who releases a defendant to an appropriate medical care facility under Subsection (i) a quarterly status report concerning the defendant's medical and treatment status.

(k) If a defendant released to a medically suitable placement under Subsection (i) violates the terms of that release, the judge may dispose of the matter as provided by Subsections (e) and (f)(1).

**Sec. 15A. Enhanced Disorderly Conduct and Public Intoxication Offenses.**

On conviction of an offense for which punishment is enhanced under Section 12.43(c), Penal Code, the court may suspend the imposition of the sentence and place the defendant on community supervision if the court finds that the defendant would benefit from community supervision and enters its finding on the record. The judge may suspend in whole or in part the imposition of any fine imposed on conviction. All provisions of this article applying to a defendant placed on community supervision for a misdemeanor apply to a defendant placed on community supervision under this section, except that the court shall require the defendant as a condition of community supervision to:

(1) submit to diagnostic testing for addiction to alcohol or a controlled substance or drug;

(2) submit to a psychological assessment;

(3) if indicated as necessary by testing and assessment, participate in an alcohol or drug abuse treatment or education program; and

(4) pay the costs of testing, assessment, and treatment or education, either directly or as a court cost.

**Sec. 16. Community Service.**

(a) A judge may require as a condition of community supervision that the defendant work a specified number of hours at a community service project or projects for an organization or organizations approved by the judge and designated by the department. The judge may not require that a defendant work at a community service project if the judge determines and notes on the order placing the defendant on community supervision that:

(1) the defendant is physically or mentally incapable of participating in the project;

(2) participating in the project will work a hardship on the defendant or the defendant's dependents;

(3) the defendant is to be confined in a substance abuse punishment facility as a condition of community supervision; or

(4) there is other good cause shown.

(b) The amount of community service work ordered by the judge:

(1) may not exceed 1,000 hours for an offense classified as a first degree felony;

(2) may not exceed 800 hours for an offense classified as a second degree felony;

(3) may not exceed 600 hours for an offense classified as a third degree felony;

(4) may not exceed 400 hours for an offense classified as a state jail felony;

(5) may not:

(A) exceed 600 hours for an offense under Section 30.04, Penal Code, classified as a Class A misdemeanor; or

(B) exceed 200 hours for any other offense classified as a Class A misdemeanor or for any other misdemeanor for which the maximum permissible confinement, if any, exceeds six months or the maximum permissible fine, if any, exceeds $4,000; and

(6) may not exceed 100 hours for an offense classified as a Class B misdemeanor or for any other misdemeanor for which the maximum permissible confinement, if any, does not exceed six months and the maximum permissible fine, if any, does not exceed $4,000.

(c) A defendant required to perform community service under this section is not a state employee for the purposes of Article 8309g or 8309h, Revised Statutes.

(d) If the court makes an affirmative finding under Article 42.014 of this code, the judge may order the defendant to perform community service under this section at a project designated by the judge that primarily serves the person or group who was the target of the defendant. If the judge orders community service under this subsection the judge shall order the defendant to perform not less than:

(1) 100 hours of service if the offense is a misdemeanor; or

(2) 300 hours of service if the offense is a felony.

(e) A defendant required to perform community service under this section after conviction of an offense under Section 352.082, Local Government Code, shall perform 60 hours of service. The community service must consist of picking up litter in the county in which the defendant resides or working at a recycling facility if a program for performing that type of service is available in the community in which the court is located.

(f) In lieu of requiring a defendant to work a specified number of hours at a community service project or projects under Subsection (a), the judge may order a defendant to make a specified donation to a nonprofit food bank or food pantry in the community in which the defendant resides.

(g) If the judge orders a defendant placed on community supervision for an offense involving possession, manufacture, or delivery of a controlled substance under Chapter 481, Health and Safety Code, to perform community service, the judge may authorize the defendant to perform not more than 30 hours of community outreach under this subsection in lieu of hours of community service. Community outreach under this subsection consists of working in conjunction with a secondary school at the direction of the judge to educate students on the dangers and legal consequences of possessing, manufacturing, or delivering controlled substances. A secondary school is not required to allow a defendant to perform community outreach at that school. The judge may not authorize the defendant to perform hours of community outreach under this subsection in lieu of hours of community service if:

(1) the defendant is physically or mentally incapable of participating in community outreach; or

(2) the defendant is subject to registration as a sex offender under Chapter 62.

### Sec. 17. Change of Residence; Leaving the State.

(a) If, for good and sufficient reasons, a defendant desires to change his residence within the state, the change may be effected by application to the supervising supervision officer, which change shall be subject to the judge's consent and subject to such regulations as the judge may require in the absence of an officer in the locality to which the defendant is transferred.

(b) Any defendant who removes himself from the state without permission of the judge having jurisdiction of the case shall be considered a fugitive from justice and shall be subject to extradition as provided by law.

### Sec. 18. Community Corrections Facilities.

(a) In this section, "community corrections facility" has the meaning assigned by Section 509.001, Government Code.

(b) If a judge requires as a condition of community supervision or participation in a drug court program established under Chapter 469, Health and Safety Code, that the defendant serve a term in a community corrections facility, the term may not be more than 24 months.

(c) A defendant granted community supervision under this section may not earn good conduct credit for time spent in a community corrections facility or apply time spent in the facility toward completion of a prison sentence if the community supervision is revoked.

(d) As directed by the judge, the community corrections facility director shall file with the community supervision and corrections department director or administrator of a drug court program, as applicable, a copy of an evaluation made by the facility director of the defendant's behavior and attitude at the facility. The community supervision and corrections department director or program administrator shall examine the evaluation, make written comments on the evaluation that the director or administrator considers relevant, and file the evaluation and comments with the judge who granted community supervision to the defendant or placed the defendant in a drug court program. If the evaluation indicates that the defendant has made significant progress toward compliance with court-ordered conditions of community supervision or objectives of placement in the drug court program, as applicable, the court may release the defendant from the community corrections facility. A defendant who served a term in the facility as a condition of community supervision shall serve the remainder of the defendant's community supervision under any terms and conditions the court imposes under this article.

(e) No later than 18 months after the date on which a defendant is granted community supervision under this section, the community corrections facility director shall file with the community supervision and corrections department director a copy of an evaluation made by the director of the defendant's behavior and attitude at the center. The director shall examine the evaluation, make written comments on the evaluation that he considers relevant, and file the evaluation and comments with the judge who granted community supervision to the defendant. If the report indicates that the defendant has made significant progress toward court-ordered conditions of community supervision, the judge shall modify the judge's sentence and release the defendant in the same manner as provided by Subsection (d) of this section. If the report indicates that the defendant would benefit from continued participation in the community corrections facility program, the judge may order the defendant to remain at the community corrections facility for a period determined by the judge. If the report indicates that the defendant has not made significant progress toward rehabilitation, the judge may revoke community supervision and order the defendant to the term of confinement specified in the defendant's sentence.

(f) If ordered by the judge who placed the defendant on community supervision, a community corrections facility director shall attempt to place a defendant as a worker in a community-service project of a type described by Section 16 of this article.

(g) A defendant participating in a program under this article shall be confined in the community corrections facility at all times except for:

(1) time spent attending and traveling to and from an education or rehabilitation program as ordered by the court;

(2) time spent attending and traveling to and from a community-service project;

(3) time spent away from the facility for purposes described by this section; and

(4) time spent traveling to and from work, if applicable.

(h) A judge that requires as a condition of community supervision that the defendant serve a term in a community corrections facility may not impose a subsequent term in a community corrections facility or jail during the same supervision period that, when added to the terms previously imposed, exceeds 36 months.

(i) If a judge who places a defendant on community supervision under this section does not require the defendant to deliver the defendant's salary to the restitution center director, the employer of the defendant shall deliver the salary to the director. The director shall deposit the salary into a fund to be given to the defendant on release after deducting:

(1) the cost to the center for the defendant's food, housing, and supervision;

(2) necessary travel expense to and from work and community-service projects and other incidental expenses of the defendant;

(3) support of the defendant's dependents; and

(4) restitution to the victims of an offense committed by the defendant.

**Sec. 19. Fees.**

(a) Except as otherwise provided by this subsection, a judge granting community supervision shall fix a fee of not less than $25 and not more than $60 per month to be paid during the period of community supervision by the defendant to the court of original jurisdiction or, in the case of an intrastate transfer described by Section 10(b) of this article, to the court to which jurisdiction of the defendant's case is transferred. The judge may make payment of the fee a condition of granting or continuing the community supervision. The judge may waive or reduce the fee or suspend a monthly payment of the fee if the judge determines that payment of the fee would cause the defendant a significant financial hardship.

(b) A judge shall deposit any fee received under Subsection (a) of this section in the special fund of the county treasury, to be used for the same purposes for which state aid may be used under Chapter 76, Government Code.

(c) A judge receiving a defendant for supervision as authorized by Article 42.11 of this code may impose on the defendant any term of community supervision authorized by this article and may require the defendant to pay the fee authorized by Subsection (a) of this section. Fees received under this section shall be deposited in the same manner as required by Subsection (b) of this section.

(d) For the purpose of determining when fees due on conviction are to be paid to any officer or officers, the placing of the defendant on community supervision shall be considered a final disposition of the case, without the necessity of waiting for the termination of the period of community supervision.

(e) If the judge grants community supervision to a defendant convicted of an offense under Section 21.08, 21.11, 22.011, 22.021, 25.02, 43.25, or 43.26, Penal Code, the judge shall require as a condition of community supervision that the defendant pay to the community corrections and supervision department officer supervising the defendant a community supervision fee of $5 each month during the period of community supervision. The fee is in addition to court costs or any other fee imposed on the defendant.

(f) **[2 Versions: As amended by Acts 2003, 78th Leg., ch. 209]** A community corrections and supervision department shall deposit the fees collected under Subsection (e) of this section to be sent to the comptroller as provided by Subchapter B, Chapter 133, Local Government Code. The comptroller shall deposit e fee in the sexual assault program fund under Section 420.008, Government Code.

(f) **[2 Versions: As amended by Acts 2003, 78th Leg., ch. 1310]** A community corrections and supervision department shall remit fees collected under Subsection (e) of this section to the comptroller not later than the last day of the month following the end of the calendar quarter in which the fee is collected. The comptroller shall deposit the fee in the special revenue fund to the credit of the sexual assault program fund established under Section 44.0061, Health and Safety Code. If the department does not collect a fee imposed under Subsection (e), the department is not required to file any report required by the comptroller relating to the collection of the fee.

(g) A court to which jurisdiction of a defendant's case is transferred under Section 10(b) of this article shall enter an order directing the defendant to pay the monthly fee described by Subsection (a) of this section to that court in lieu of paying the monthly fee to the court of original jurisdiction. To the extent of any conflict between an order issued under this subsection and an order issued by a court of original jurisdiction, the order entered under this subsection prevails.

(h) [Repealed by Acts 2005, 79th Leg., ch. 1008 (H.B. 867), § 4.07, effective September 1, 2005.]

### Sec. 20. Reduction or Termination of Community Supervision.

(a) At any time after the defendant has satisfactorily completed one-third of the original community supervision period or two years of community supervision, whichever is less, the period of community supervision may be reduced or terminated by the judge. On completion of one-half of the original community supervision period or two years of community supervision, whichever is more, the judge shall review the defendant's record and consider whether to reduce or terminate the period of community supervision, unless the defendant is delinquent in paying required restitution, fines, costs, or fees that the defendant has the ability to pay or the defendant has not com-

pleted court-ordered counseling or treatment. Before reducing or terminating a period of community supervision or conducting a review under this section, the judge shall notify the attorney representing the state and the defendant or, if the defendant has an attorney, the defendant's attorney. If the judge determines that the defendant has failed to satisfactorily fulfill the conditions of community supervision, the judge shall advise the defendant in writing of the requirements for satisfactorily fulfilling those conditions. Upon the satisfactory fulfillment of the conditions of community supervision, and the expiration of the period of community supervision, the judge, by order duly entered, shall amend or modify the original sentence imposed, if necessary, to conform to the community supervision period and shall discharge the defendant. If the judge discharges the defendant under this section, the judge may set aside the verdict or permit the defendant to withdraw the defendant's plea, and shall dismiss the accusation, complaint, information or indictment against the defendant, who shall thereafter be released from all penalties and disabilities resulting from the offense or crime of which the defendant has been convicted or to which the defendant has pleaded guilty, except that:

(1) proof of the conviction or plea of guilty shall be made known to the judge should the defendant again be convicted of any criminal offense; and

(2) if the defendant is an applicant for a license or is a licensee under Chapter 42, Human Resources Code, the Health and Human Services Commission may consider the fact that the defendant previously has received community supervision under this article in issuing, renewing, denying, or revoking a license under that chapter.

(b) This section does not apply to a defendant convicted of an offense under Sections 49.04—49.08, Penal Code, a defendant convicted of an offense for which on conviction registration as a sex offender is required under Chapter 62, or a defendant convicted of a felony described by Section 3g.

### Sec. 20A. Time Credits for Completion of Certain Conditions of Community Supervision.

(a) This section applies only to a defendant who:

(1) is granted community supervision, including deferred adjudication community su-

pervision, for an offense punishable as a state jail felony or a felony of the third degree, other than an offense:

(A) under Chapter 49, Penal Code;

(B) involving family violence as defined by Section 71.004, Family Code;

(C) included as a "reportable conviction or adjudication" under Article 62.001(5); or

(D) under Section 20.03 or 28.02, Penal Code;

(2) is not delinquent in paying required fines, costs, or fees; and

(3) has fully satisfied any order to pay restitution to a victim.

(b) A defendant described by Subsection (a) is entitled to receive any combination of time credits toward the completion of the defendant's period of community supervision in accordance with this section if the court ordered the defendant as a condition of community supervision to:

(1) earn a certificate, diploma, or degree described by Subsection (c);

(2) make a payment described by Subsection (d); or

(3) complete a treatment or rehabilitation program described by Subsection (e).

(c) A defendant is entitled to time credits toward the completion of the defendant's period of community supervision for earning the following certificates, diplomas, or degrees:

(1) a high school diploma or high school equivalency certificate: 90 days; and

(2) an associate's degree: 120 days.

(d) A defendant is entitled to time credits toward the completion of the defendant's period of community supervision for the full payment of court costs, fines, attorney's fees, and restitution as follows:

(1) court costs: 15 days;

(2) fines: 30 days;

(3) attorney's fees: 30 days; and

(4) restitution: 60 days.

(e) A defendant is entitled to time credits toward the completion of the defendant's period of community supervision for the successful completion of treatment or rehabilitation programs as follows:

(1) alcohol or substance abuse counseling or treatment: 90 days;

(2) vocational, technical, or career education or training program: 60 days;

(3) parenting class or parental responsibility program: 30 days;

(4) anger management program: 30 days; and

(5) life skills training program: 30 days.

(f) A defendant's supervision officer shall notify the court if one or more time credits under this section, cumulated with the amount of the original community supervision period the defendant has completed, allow or require the court to conduct a review of the defendant's community supervision under Section 20. On receipt of the notice from the supervision officer, the court shall conduct the review of the defendant's community supervision to determine if the defendant is eligible for a reduction or termination of community supervision under Section 20, taking into account any time credits to which the defendant is entitled under this section when determining if the defendant has completed, as applicable:

(1) the lesser of one-third of the original community supervision period or two years of community supervision; or

(2) the greater of one-half of the original community supervision period or two years of community supervision.

(g) A court may order that some or all of the credit to which a defendant is entitled under this section be forfeited if, before the expiration of the original period or a reduced period of community supervision, the court:

(1) after a hearing under Section 21, finds that a defendant violated one or more conditions of community supervision; and

(2) modifies or continues the defendant's period of community supervision under Section 22 or revokes the defendant's community supervision under Section 23.

### Sec. 21. Violation of Community Supervision: Detention and Hearing.

(a) At any time during the period of community supervision the judge may issue a warrant for violation of any of the conditions of the community supervision and cause a defendant convicted under Section 43.02, Penal Code, or under Chapter 481, Health and Safety Code, or Sections 485.031 through 485.035, Health and Safety Code, or placed on deferred adjudication after being charged with one of those offenses, to be subject to the control measures of Section 81.083, Health and Safety Code, and to the court-ordered-management provisions of Subchapter G, Chapter 81, Health and Safety Code.

(b) At any time during the period of community supervision the judge may issue a warrant for violation of any of the conditions of the community supervision and cause the defendant to be arrested. Any supervision officer, police officer or other officer with power of arrest may arrest such defendant with or without a warrant upon the order of the judge to be noted on the docket of the court. Subject to Subsection (b-1), a defendant arrested under this subsection may be detained in the county jail or other appropriate place of confinement until he can be taken before the judge for a determination regarding the alleged violation. The arresting officer shall immediately report the arrest and detention to the judge.

(b-1) Without any unnecessary delay, but not later than 48 hours after the person is arrested, the arresting officer or the person with custody of the arrested person shall take the arrested person before the judge who ordered the arrest for the alleged violation of a condition of community supervision or, if the judge is unavailable, before a magistrate of the county in which the person was arrested. The judge or magistrate shall perform all appropriate duties and may exercise all appropriate powers as provided by Article 15.17 with respect to an arrest for a new criminal offense, except that only the judge who ordered the arrest for the alleged violation may authorize the person's release on bail. The arrested person may be taken before the judge or magistrate under this subsection by means of an electronic broadcast system as provided by and subject to the requirements of Article 15.17.

(b-2) If the defendant has not been released on bail as permitted under Subsection (b-1), on motion by the defendant the judge who ordered the arrest for the alleged violation of a condition of community supervision shall cause the defendant to be brought before the judge for a hearing on the alleged violation within 20 days of filing of said motion, and after a hearing without a jury, may either continue, extend, modify, or revoke the community supervision. A judge may revoke the community supervision of a defendant who is imprisoned in a penal institution without a hearing if the defendant in writing before a court of record in the jurisdiction where imprisoned waives his right to a hearing and to counsel, affirms that he has nothing to say as to why sentence should not be pronounced against him, and requests the judge to revoke community supervision and to pronounce sentence. In a felony case, the state may amend the motion to revoke community

supervision any time up to seven days before the date of the revocation hearing, after which time the motion may not be amended except for good cause shown, and in no event may the state amend the motion after the commencement of taking evidence at the hearing. The judge may continue the hearing for good cause shown by either the defendant or the state.

(c) In a community supervision revocation hearing at which it is alleged only that the defendant violated the conditions of community supervision by failing to pay compensation paid to appointed counsel, community supervision fees, or court costs, the state must prove by a preponderance of the evidence that the defendant was able to pay and did not pay as ordered by the judge. The court may order a community supervision and corrections department to obtain information pertaining to the factors listed under Article 42.037(h) of this code and include that information in the report required under Section 9(a) of this article or a separate report, as the court directs.

(d) A defendant has a right to counsel at a hearing under this section. The court shall appoint counsel for an indigent defendant in accordance with the procedures adopted under Article 26.04.

(e) A court retains jurisdiction to hold a hearing under Subsection (b) and to revoke, continue, or modify community supervision, regardless of whether the period of community supervision imposed on the defendant has expired, if before the expiration the attorney representing the state files a motion to revoke, continue, or modify community supervision and a capias is issued for the arrest of the defendant.

### Sec. 22. Continuation or Modification.

(a) If after a hearing under Section 21 of this article a judge continues or modifies community supervision after determining that the defendant violated a condition of community supervision, the judge may impose any other conditions the judge determines are appropriate, including:

(1) a requirement that the defendant perform community service for a number of hours specified by the court under Section 16 of this article, or an increase in the number of hours that the defendant has previously been required to perform under those sections in an amount not to exceed double the number of hours permitted by Section 16;

(2) an increase in the period of community supervision, in the manner described by Subsection (c) of this section;

(3) an increase in the defendant's fine, in the manner described by Subsection (d) of this section; or

(4) the placement of the defendant in a substance abuse felony punishment program operated under Section 493.009, Government Code, if:

(A) the defendant is convicted of a felony other than:

(i) a felony under Section 21.11, 22.011, or 22.021, Penal Code; or

(ii) criminal attempt of a felony under Section 21.11, 22.011, or 22.021, Penal Code; and

(B) the judge makes an affirmative finding that:

(i) drug or alcohol abuse significantly contributed to the commission of the crime or violation of community supervision; and

(ii) the defendant is a suitable candidate for treatment, as determined by the suitability criteria established by the Texas Board of Criminal Justice under Section 493.009(b), Government Code.

(b) If the judge imposes a sanction under Subsection (a)(4) of this section, the judge shall also impose a condition requiring the defendant on successful completion of the program to participate in a drug or alcohol abuse continuum of care program.

(c) The judge may extend a period of community supervision on a showing of good cause under this section as often as the judge determines is necessary, but the period of community supervision in a first, second, or third degree felony case may not exceed 10 years and, except as otherwise provided by this subsection, the period of community supervision in a misdemeanor case may not exceed three years. The judge may extend the period of community supervision in a misdemeanor case for any period the judge determines is necessary, not to exceed an additional two years beyond the three-year limit, if the defendant fails to pay a previously assessed fine, costs, or restitution and the judge determines that extending the period of supervision increases the likelihood that the defendant will fully pay the fine, costs, or restitution. A court may extend a period of community supervision under this section at any time during the period of super-

vision or, if a motion for revocation of community supervision is filed before the period of supervision ends, before the first anniversary of the date on which the period of supervision expires.

(d) A judge may impose a sanction on a defendant described by Subsection (a)(3) of this section by increasing the fine imposed on the defendant. The original fine imposed on the defendant and an increase in the fine imposed under this subsection may not exceed the maximum fine for the offense for which the defendant was sentenced. The judge shall deposit money received from an increase in the defendant's fine under this subsection in the special fund of the county treasury to be used for the same purposes for which state aid may be used under Chapter 76, Government Code.

**Sec. 22A. Extending Supervision Period for Sex Offenders.**

(a) If a defendant is placed on community supervision after receiving a grant of deferred adjudication for or being convicted of an offense under Section 21.11, 22.011, or 22.021, Penal Code, at any time during the period of community supervision, the judge may extend the period of community supervision as provided by this section.

(b) If at a hearing at which the defendant is provided the same rights as are provided a defendant at a hearing under Section 21 the judge determines that the defendant has not sufficiently demonstrated a commitment to avoid future criminal behavior and that the release of the defendant from supervision would endanger the public, the judge may extend the period of supervision for a period not to exceed 10 additional years.

(c) A judge may extend a period of community supervision under this section only once; however, the judge may extend a period of community supervision for a defendant under both Section 22(c) and this section, and the prohibition in Section 22(c) against a period of community supervision in a felony case exceeding 10 years does not apply to a defendant for whom community supervision is increased under this section or under both Section 22(c) and this section.

**Sec. 23. Revocation.**

(a) If community supervision is revoked after a hearing under Section 21 of this article, the judge may proceed to dispose of the case as if there had been no community supervision, or if the judge determines that the best interests of society and the defendant would be served by a shorter term of confinement, reduce the term of confinement originally assessed to any term of confinement not less than the minimum prescribed for the offense of which the defendant was convicted. The judge shall enter the amount of restitution or reparation owed by the defendant on the date of revocation in the judgment in the case.

(b) No part of the time that the defendant is on community supervision shall be considered as any part of the time that he shall be sentenced to serve, except that on revocation, the judge shall credit to the defendant time served by the defendant as a condition of community supervision in a substance abuse treatment facility operated by the Texas Department of Criminal Justice under Section 493.009, Government Code, or another court-ordered residential program or facility, but only if the defendant successfully completes the treatment program in that facility. The right of the defendant to appeal for a review of the conviction and punishment, as provided by law, shall be accorded the defendant at the time he is placed on community supervision. When he is notified that his community supervision is revoked for violation of the conditions of community supervision and he is called on to serve a sentence in a jail or in the Texas Department of Criminal Justice, he may appeal the revocation.

## Sec. 24. Due Diligence Defense.

For the purposes of a hearing under Section 5(b) or 21(b), it is an affirmative defense to revocation for an alleged failure to report to a supervision officer as directed or to remain within a specified place that a supervision officer, peace officer, or other officer with the power of arrest under a warrant issued by a judge for that alleged violation failed to contact or attempt to contact the defendant in person at the defendant's last known residence address or last known employment address, as reflected in the files of the department serving the county in which the order of community supervision was entered.

**Sec. 29.** [Repealed by Acts 1995, 74th Leg., ch. 76 (S.B. 959), § 3.15, effective September 1, 1995.]

(Enacted by Acts 1965, 59th Leg., ch. 722 (S.B. 107), § 1, effective January 1, 1966; am. Acts 1967, 60th Leg., ch. 659 (S.B. 145), § 29, effective August 28, 1967; am. Acts 1973, 63rd Leg., ch. 241 (S.B. 334), § 1, effective August 27, 1973; am. Acts 1973, 63rd Leg., ch. 447 (S.B. 335), § 1,

effective June 14, 1973; am. Acts 1973, 63rd Leg., ch. 464 (H.B. 545), § 1, effective June 14, 1973; am. Acts 1975, 64th Leg., ch. 110 (H.B. 669), § 1, effective September 1, 1975; am. Acts 1975, 64th Leg., ch. 231 (S.B. 382), § 1, effective September 1, 1975; am. Acts 1975, 64th Leg., ch. 341 (S.B. 122), § 4, effective June 19, 1975; am. Acts 1975, 64th Leg., ch. 467 (H.B. 9), § 1, effective June 19, 1975; am. Acts 1975, 64th Leg., ch. 468 (H.B. 10), § 1, effective September 1, 1975; am. Acts 1975, 64th Leg., ch. 692 (S.B. 240), § 1, effective September 1, 1975; am. Acts 1977, 65th Leg., ch. 22 (S.B. 150), § 1, effective August 29, 1977; am. Acts 1977, 65th Leg., ch. 47 (H.B. 97), § 1, effective April 5, 1977; am. Acts 1977, 65th Leg., ch. 306 (S.B. 695), §§ 1, 2, effective August 29, 1977; am. Acts 1977, 65th Leg., ch. 342 (S.B. 32), §§ 1, 2, effective August 29, 1977; am. Acts 1977, 65th Leg., ch. 343 (S.B. 39), § 2, effective September 1, 1978; am. Acts 1977, 65th Leg., ch. 347 (S.B. 152), §§ 1, 2, effective August 29, 1977; am. Acts 1977, 65th Leg., ch. 388 (S.B. 61), §§ 1, 2, effective August 29, 1977; am. Acts 1977, 65th Leg., ch. 735 (S.B. 54), § 2.133, effective August 29, 1977; am. Acts 1979, 66th Leg., ch. 139 (H.B. 1094), § 1, effective August 27, 1979; am. Acts 1979, 66th Leg., ch. 605 (S.B. 376), §§ 1, 2, 4, effective August 27, 1979; am. Acts 1981, 67th Leg., ch. 69 (S.B. 123), §§ 1—4, effective September 1, 1981; am. Acts 1981, 67th Leg., ch. 141 (S.B. 125), §§ 2—9, effective September 1, 1981; am. Acts 1981, 67th Leg., ch. 268 (H.B. 730), § 16, effective September 1, 1981; am. Acts 1981, 67th Leg., ch. 276 (H.B. 729), § 3, effective September 1, 2981; am. Acts 1981, 67th Leg., ch. 291 (S.B. 265), § 118, effective September 1, 1981; am. Acts 1981, 67th Leg., ch. 538 (H.B. 865), §§ 1, 2, effective June 12, 1981; am. Acts 1981, 67th Leg., ch. 544 (H.B. 1166), § 1, effective September 1, 1981; am. Acts 1981, 67th Leg., ch. 638 (H.B. 2106), § 1, effective September 1, 1981; am. Acts 1981, 67th Leg., ch. 639 (H.B. 2107), § 2, effective September 1, 1981; am. Acts 1983, 68th Leg., ch. 40 (S.B. 218), §§ 2, 3, effective April 26, 1983; am. Acts 1983, 68th Leg., ch. 232 (S.B. 396), §§ 1—5; am. Acts 1983, 68th Leg., ch. 237 (H.B. 658), §§ 1—4, effective August 29, 1983; am. Acts 1983, 68th Leg., ch. 303 (S.B. 1), §§ 8—13, effective January 1, 1984; am. Acts 1983, 68th Leg., ch. 325 (H.B. 411), § 2, effective September 1, 1983; am. Acts 1983, 68th Leg., ch. 343 (H.B. 1178), § 1, effective August 29, 1983; am. Acts 1983, 68th Leg., ch. 372 (S.B. 563), § 1, effective August 29, 1983; am. Acts 1983, 68th Leg., ch. 425 (H.B. 1191), § 25, effective August 29, 1983;

am. Acts 1983, 68th Leg., ch. 548 (S.B. 622), §§ 2, 3, effective June 19, 1983; am. Acts 1983, 68th Leg., ch. 747 (H.B. 242), § 1, effective June 19, 1983; am. Acts 1983, 68th Leg., ch. 762 (H.B. 413), § 1, effective August 29, 1983; am. Acts 1983, 68th Leg., ch. 811 (H.B. 861), § 1, effective August 29, 1983; am. Acts 1983, 68th Leg., ch. 863 (H.B. 1289), §§ 1, 2, effective August 29, 1983; am. Acts 1983, 68th Leg., ch. 897 (H.B. 1517), § 1, effective August 29, 1983; am. Acts 1983, 68th Leg., ch. 977 (H.B. 2008), §§ 9, 10, effective September 1, 1983; am. Acts 1985, 69th Leg., ch. 239 (H.B. 1593), §§ 24, 80(a), effective September 1, 1985; am. Acts 1985, 69th Leg., ch 255 (H.B. 826), § 1, effective June 4, 1985; am. Acts 1985, 69th Leg., ch. 427 (S.B. 589), § 1, effective September 1, 1985; am. Acts 1985, 69th Leg., ch. 479 (S.B. 813), § 163, effective September 1, 1985; am. Acts 1985, 69th Leg., ch. 481 (S.B. 59), § 1, effective August 26, 1985; am. Acts 1985, 69th Leg., ch. 508 (S.B. 842), § 1, effective August 26, 1985; am. Acts 1985, 69th Leg., ch. 554 (H.B. 2053), §§ 1, 2, effective August 26, 1985; am. Acts 1985, 69th Leg., ch. 588 (H.B. 235), § 3, effective September 1, 1985; am. Acts 1985, 69th Leg., ch. 595 (H.B. 1378), §§ 2, 3, effective September 1, 1985; am. Acts 1985, 69th Leg., ch. 632 (S.B. 601), § 13, effective September 1, 1985; am. Acts 1985, 69th Leg., ch. 714 (H.B. 1307), §§ 1, 2, 12, effective August 26, 1985; am. Acts 1985, 69th Leg., ch. 727 (H.B. 1569), § 1, effective January 1, 1986; am. Acts 1985, 69th Leg., ch. 729 (H.B. 1585), § 5, effective September 1, 1985; am. Acts 1985, 69th Leg., ch. 801 (S.B. 454), § 1, effective August 26, 1985; am. Acts 1985, 69th Leg., ch. 956 (S.B. 5), § 1, effective June 16, 1985; am. Acts 1987, 70th Leg., ch. 1 (S.B. 215), §§ 4—6, effective February 20, 1987; am. Acts 1987, 70th Leg., ch. 167 (S.B. 892), §§ 5.01(a)(7), 5.01(a)(8), effective September 1, 1987; am. Acts 1987, 70th Leg., ch. 441 (H.B. 56), § 1, effective September 1, 1987; am. Acts 1987, 70th Leg., ch. 473 (H.B. 655), § 3, effective September 1, 1987; am. Acts 1987, 70th Leg., ch. 507 (H.B. 313), §§ 1, 2, effective September 1, 1987; am. Acts 1987, 70th Leg., ch. 922 (H.B. 914), § 4, effective September 1, 1987; am. Acts 1987, 70th Leg., ch. 928 (H.B. 1300), § 1, effective September 1, 1987; am. Acts 1987, 70th Leg., ch. 930 (H.B. 1826), § 1, effective September 1, 1987; am. Acts 1987, 70th Leg., ch. 939 (H.B. 83), §§ 2—9, effective September 1, 1987; am. Acts 1987, 70th Leg., ch. 1049 (S.B. 245), § 54, effective September 1, 1987; am. Acts 1987, 70th Leg., ch. 1101 (S.B. 341), § 16, effective September 1, 1987; am.

Acts 1989, 71st Leg., ch. 2 (S.B. 221), §§ 5.02(a), 8.11(c), 16.01(9), 16.01(10), effective August 28, 1989; am. Acts 1989, 71st Leg., 1st C.S., ch. 6 (S.B. 29), § 1, effective January 1, 1990; am. Acts 1989, 71st Leg., 1st C.S., ch. 8 (S.B. 32), § 1, effective October 18, 1989; am. Acts 1989, 71st Leg., ch. 86 (S.B. 85), § 1, effective August 28, 1989; am. Acts 1989, 71st Leg., ch. 111 (S.B. 439), § 1, effective September 1, 1989; am. Acts 1989, 71st Leg., ch. 191 (S.B. 440), § 1, effective May 26, 1989; am. Acts 1989, 71st Leg., ch. 236 (H.B. 1935), § 11, effective April 1, 1990; am. Acts 1989, 71st Leg., ch. 260 (H.B. 2634), § 1, effective September 1, 1989; am. Acts 1989, 71st Leg., ch. 679 (S.B. 1237), §§ 1, 2, 3, effective September 1, 1989; am. Acts 1989, 71st Leg., ch. 785 (H.B. 2335), § 4.17, effective September 1, 1989; am. Acts 1989, 71st Leg., ch. 1040 (H.B. 1779), § 5, effective August 28, 1989; am. Acts 1989, 71st Leg., ch. 1074 (S.B. 1090), § 8, effective September 1, 1989; am. Acts 1989, 71st Leg., ch. 1135 (H.B. 3065), § 5, effective August 28, 1989; am. Acts 1989, 71st Leg., ch. 1195 (S.B. 959), §§ 9, 10, effective September 1, 1989; am. Acts 1990, 71st Leg., 6th C.S., ch. 25 (S.B. 41), §§ 8—12, 31, effective June 18, 1990; am. Acts 1991, 72nd Leg., ch. 14 (S.B. 404), §§ 284(8), 284(9), 284(52), 284(60), effective September 1, 1991; am. Acts 1991, 72nd Leg., ch. 202 (S.B. 1407), § 2, effective September 1, 1991; am. Acts 1991, 72nd Leg., ch. 285 (S.B. 853), § 1, effective September 1, 1991; am. Acts 1991, 72nd Leg., ch. 343 (H.B. 1674), § 1, effective August 26, 1991; am. Acts 1991, 72nd Leg., ch. 344 (H.B. 1675), § 1, effective June 5, 1991; am. Acts 1991, 72nd Leg., ch. 541 (H.B. 1459), § 1, effective September 1, 1991; am. Acts 1991, 72nd Leg., ch. 555 (H.B. 549), § 3, effective September 1, 1991; am. Acts 1991, 72nd Leg., ch. 572 (S.B. 259), § 2, effective September 1, 1991; am. Acts 1991, 72nd Leg., ch. 784 (H.B. 434), § 9, effective September 1, 1991; am. Acts 1991, 72nd Leg., ch. 900 (H.B. 154), § 3, effective August 26, 1991; am. Acts 1991, 72nd Leg., 2nd C.S., ch. 10 (H.B. 93), §§ 6.01, 8.01, 16.01, effective December 1, 1991; am. Acts 1991, 72nd Leg., 2nd C.S., ch. 10 (H.B. 93), §§ 15.01, 19.02, effective October 1, 1991; am. Acts 1993, 73rd Leg., ch. 10 (S.B. 25), § 3, effective March 19, 1993; am. Acts 1993, 73rd Leg., ch. 107 (H.B. 947), § 10.01(1), effective August 30, 1993; am. Acts 1993, 73rd Leg., ch. 165 (H.B. 119), § 1, effective September 1, 1993; am. Acts 1993, 73rd Leg., ch. 201 (H.B. 294), §§ 3, 4, effective August 30, 1993; am. Acts 1993, 73rd Leg., ch. 470 (H.B. 637), § 2, effective September 1, 1993; am. Acts 1993, 73rd Leg., ch. 662 (S.B.

371), §§ 1, 8, effective September 1, 1993; am. Acts 1993, 73rd Leg., ch. 790 (S.B. 510), §§ 30, 36, effective September 1, 1993; am. Acts 1993, 73rd Leg., ch. 796 (H.B. 1319), §§ 1, 2, effective September 1, 1993; am. Acts 1993, 73rd Leg., ch. 805 (H.B. 2178), § 7, effective August 30, 1993; am. Acts 1993, 73rd Leg., ch. 806 (H.B. 2179), §§ 2, 3, effective September 1, 1993; am. Acts 1993, 73rd Leg., ch. 886 (S.B. 1), § 15, effective January 1, 1995; am. Acts 1993, 73rd Leg., ch. 889 (S.B. 109), § 1, effective September 1, 1993; am. Acts 1993, 73rd Leg., ch. 900 (S.B. 1067), § 4.01, effective September 1, 1993; Sec. 15 added by Acts 1993, 73rd Leg., ch. 900 (S.B. 1067), § 4.01, effective September 1, 1994; am. Acts 1993, 73rd Leg., ch. 987 (S.B. 456), §§ 2, 3, effective September 1, 1993; am. Acts 1995, 74th Leg., ch. 76 (S.B. 959), §§ 3.06, 3.07(a), 3.07(b), 3.08, 3.09, 3.10, 3.11, 3.12(a), 3.12(b), 3.15, 3.16, 3.17, 3.18, 7.02, 7.13, 7.14, 7.15, effective September 1, 1995; am. Acts 1995, 74th Leg., ch. 83 (H.B. 44), § 2, effective September 1, 1995; am. Acts 1995, 74th Leg., ch. 256 (S.B. 111), §§ 1, 2, 3, effective September 1, 1995; am. Acts 1995, 74th Leg., ch. 257 (S.B. 149), § 1, effective September 1, 1995; am. Acts 1995, 74th Leg., ch. 258 (S.B. 267), § 10, effective September 1, 1995; am. Acts 1995, 74th Leg., ch. 260 (S.B. 1), §§ 14 to 16, effective May 30, 1995; am. Acts 1995, 74th Leg., ch. 318 (S.B. 15), §§ 52, 54 to 56, 57(a), 57(b), 58, 59, effective September 1, 1995; am. Acts 1995, 74th Leg., ch. 318 (S.B. 15), §§ 53, 60, 61, effective January 1, 1996; am. Acts 1995, 74th Leg., ch. 321 (H.B. 2162), §§ 3.003, 3.004, 3.005, 3.006, 3.007, 3.008, 3.020(a), effective September 1, 1995; am. Acts 1995, 74th Leg., ch. 595 (H.B. 40), § 2, effective September 1, 1995; am. Acts 1995, 74th Leg., ch. 657 (S.B. 126), § 4, effective June 14, 1995; am. Acts 1997, 75th Leg., ch. 1 (S.B. 97), § 6, effective January 28, 1997; am. Acts 1997, 75th Leg., ch. 144 (S.B. 123), § 3, effective May 20, 1997; am. Acts 1997, 75th Leg., ch. 165 (S.B. 898), §§ 12.03, 31.01(10), 31.01(11), effective September 1, 1997; am. Acts 1997, 75th Leg., ch. 312 (H.B. 1747), § 3, effective September 1, 1997; am. Acts 1997, 75th Leg., ch. 488 (S.B. 633), §§ 1 to 4, effective September 1, 1997; am. Acts 1997, 75th Leg., ch. 577 (H.B. 2119), § 18, effective September 1, 1997; am. Acts 1997, 75th Leg., ch. 667 (S.B. 381), § 1, effective September 1, 1997; am. Acts 1997, 75th Leg., ch. 668 (S.B. 875), §§ 3, 4, effective September 1, 1997; am. Acts 1997, 75th Leg., ch. 700 (S.B. 1546)§ 11, effective September 1, 1997; am. Acts 1997, 75th Leg., ch. 706 (S.B. 1827), § 1, effective September 1, 1997; am. Acts

1997, 75th Leg., ch. 745 (H.B. 1070), § 34, effective January 1, 1998; am. Acts 1997, 75th Leg., ch. 754 (H.B. 1467), § 1, effective September 1, 1997; am. Acts 1997, 75th Leg., ch. 1430 (H.B. 2918), §§ 1 to 5, effective September 1, 1997; am. Acts 1999, 76th Leg., ch. 27 (S.B. 461), § 1, effective September 1, 1999; am. Acts 1999, 76th Leg., ch. 56 (S.B. 660), § 1, effective September 1, 1999; am. Acts 1999, 76th Leg., ch. 62 (S.B. 1368), § 3.04, effective September 1, 1999; am. Acts 1999, 76th Leg., ch. 323 (H.B. 1162), § 1, effective September 1, 1999; am. Acts 1999, 76th Leg., ch. 564 (S.B. 430), § 2, effective September 1, 1999; am. Acts 1999, 76th Leg., ch. 580 (S.B. 577), §§ 7, 8, effective September 1, 1999; am. Acts 1999, 76th Leg., ch. 806 (H.B. 1535), § 1, effective September 1, 1999; am. Acts 1999, 76th Leg., ch. 910 (H.B. 2187), § 1, effective September 1, 1999; am. Acts 1999, 76th Leg., ch. 1105 (H.B. 3492), § 3, effective September 1, 1999; am. Acts 1999, 76th Leg., ch. 1188 (S.B. 365), §§ 1.43, 1.44, effective September 1, 1999; am. Acts 1999, 76th Leg., ch. 1193 (S.B. 399), § 3, effective September 1, 1999; am. Acts 1999, 76th Leg., ch. 1263 (S.B. 1215), § 1, effective September 1, 1999; am. Acts 1999, 76th Leg., ch. 1415 (H.B. 2145), §§ 4, 5(a), 5(b), 6(a), effective September 1, 1999; am. Acts 2001, 77th Leg., ch. 211 (S.B. 1380), § 1, effective September 1, 2001; am. Acts 2001, 77th Leg., ch. 786 (H.B. 156), § 2, effective June 14, 2001; am. Acts 2001, 77th Leg., ch. 969 (H.B. 5), §§ 8, 9, effective September 1, 2001; am. Acts 2001, 77th Leg., ch. 970 (H.B. 31), § 1, effective September 1, 2001; am. Acts 2001, 77th Leg., ch. 992 (H.B. 598), § 1, effective September 1, 2001; am. Acts 2001, 77th Leg., ch. 1159 (H.B. 2987), § 3, effective September 1, 2001; am. Acts 2001, 77th Leg., ch. 1351 (H.B. 3613), § 1, effective September 1, 2001; am. Acts 2001, 77th Leg., ch. 1420 (H.B. 2812), §§ 21.001(10), 21.001(11), effective September 1, 2001; am. Acts 2003, 78th Leg., ch. 35 (S.B. 1057), § 4, effective January 1, 2004; am. Acts 2003, 78th Leg., ch. 209 (H.B. 2424), §§ 63(a), 64(a), effective January 1, 2004; am. Acts 2003, 78th Leg., ch. 239 (H.B. 1180), § 1, effective September 1, 2003; am. Acts 2003, 78th Leg., ch. 250 (H.B. 1634), §§ 1 to 3, effective June 18, 2003; am. Acts 2003, 78th Leg., ch. 353 (S.B. 1054), §§ 1 to 6, effective September 1, 2003; am. Acts 2003, 78th Leg., ch. 892 (S.B. 810), § 20, effective September 1, 2003; am. Acts 2003, 78th Leg., ch. 1122 (H.B. 2668), § 1, effective September 1, 2003; am. Acts 2003, 78th Leg., ch. 1275 (H.B. 3506), § 3, effective September 1, 2003; am. Acts 2003, 78th Leg., ch. 1300 (S.B. 146), § 1, effective September 1, 2003; am. Acts 2003, 78th Leg., ch. 1310 (H.B. 2425), §§ 2, 3, effective September 1, 2003; am. Acts 2005, 79th Leg., ch. 210 (H.B. 1759), §§ 1, 2, effective September 1, 2005; am. Acts 2005, 79th Leg., ch. 500 (H.B. 550), § 1, effective September 1, 2005; am. Acts 2005, 79th Leg., ch. 904 (H.B. 39), § 3, effective September 1, 2005; am. Acts 2005, 79th Leg., ch. 956 (H.B. 1601), § 2, effective September 1, 2005; am. Acts 2005, 79th Leg., ch. 969 (H.B. 1751), § 2, effective September 1, 2005; am. Acts 2005, 79th Leg., ch. 996 (H.B. 51), § 2, effective September 1, 2005; am. Acts 2005, 79th Leg., ch. 1008 (H.B. 867), § 4.07, effective September 1, 2005; am. Acts 2005, 79th Leg., ch. 1139 (H.B. 2791), § 4, effective June 18, 2005; am. Acts 2005, 79th Leg., ch. 1188 (H.B. 157), § 1, effective September 1, 2005; am. Acts 2005, 79th Leg., ch. 1224 (H.B. 1068), § 18, effective September 1, 2005; am. Acts 2007, 80th Leg., ch. 113 (S.B. 44), § 1, effective September 1, 2007; am. Acts 2007, 80th Leg., ch. 308 (H.B. 1887), §§ 2, 3, effective September 1, 2007; am. Acts 2007, 80th Leg., ch. 405 (S.B. 877), § 1, effective September 1, 2007; am. Acts 2007, 80th Leg., ch. 593 (H.B. 8), §§ 1.05 to 1.07, effective September 1, 2007; am. Acts 2007, 80th Leg., ch. 604 (H.B. 312), § 1, effective September 1, 2007; am. Acts 2007, 80th Leg., ch. 617 (H.B. 431), § 1, effective September 1, 2007; am. Acts 2007, 80th Leg., ch. 849, § 2, effective June 15, 2007; am. Acts 2007, 80th Leg., ch. 1025 (H.B. 1610), § 1, effective September 1, 2007; am. Acts 2007, 80th Leg., ch. 1050 (H.B. 2115), § 1, effective September 1, 2007; am. Acts 2007, 80th Leg., ch. 1205 (H.B. 1678), §§ 2 to 8, effective September 1, 2007; am. Acts 2007, 80th Leg., ch. 1308 (S.B. 909), §§ 5 to 9, effective June 15, 2007; am. Acts 2009, 81st Leg., ch. 87 (S.B. 1969), §§ 6.003 to 6.005, 25.025 to 25.030, effective September 1, 2009; am. Acts 2009, 81st Leg., ch. 146 (S.B. 1832), § 1, effective September 1, 2009; am. Acts 2009, 81st Leg., ch. 168 (H.B. 590), § 5, effective May 27, 2009; am. Acts 2009, 81st Leg., ch. 639 (H.B. 1633), § 2, effective September 1, 2009; am. Acts 2009, 81st Leg., ch. 755 (S.B. 689), § 1, effective September 1, 2009; am. Acts 2009, 81st Leg., ch. 1130 (H.B. 2086), §§ 17, 18, effective September 1, 2009; am. Acts 2009, 81st Leg., ch. 1146 (H.B. 2730), § 16.04, effective September 1, 2009; am. Acts 2009, 81st Leg., ch. 1209 (S.B. 727), § 6, effective September 1, 2009; am. Acts 2009, 81st Leg., ch. 1228 (S.B. 1557), § 3, effective September 1, 2009; am. Acts 2009, 81st Leg., ch. 1339 (S.B. 82), § 1, effective September 1, 2009; am. Acts 2009, 81st Leg., ch. 1348 (S.B. 328), § 6, effective September 1, 2009; am. Acts 2011, 82nd Leg., ch. 1 (S.B. 24), § 2.09, effective September 1, 2011; am. Acts 2011, 82nd Leg., ch. 91 (S.B. 1303), § 27.001(3), effective September 1, 2011; am. Acts 2011, 82nd Leg., ch. 134 (S.B. 198), § 2, effective September 1, 2011; am. Acts 2011, 82nd Leg., ch. 170 (S.B. 331), § 8, effective September 1, 2011; am. Acts 2011, 82nd Leg., ch. 327 (H.B. 2624), § 4, effective September 1, 2011; am. Acts 2011, 82nd Leg., ch. 493 (H.B. 1106), § 1, effective September 1, 2011; am. Acts 2011, 82nd Leg., ch. 515 (H.B. 2014), § 2.03, effective September 1, 2011; am. Acts 2011, 82nd Leg., ch. 542 (H.B. 2649), § 1, effective September 1, 2011; am. Acts 2011, 82nd Leg., ch. 671 (S.B. 1681), § 2, effective September 1, 2011; am. Acts 2011, 82nd Leg., ch. 694 (H.B. 371), § 1, effective September 1, 2011; am. Acts 2011, 82nd Leg., ch. 957 (H.B. 1103), § 1, effective September 1, 2011; am. Acts 2011, 82nd Leg., ch. 961 (H.B. 1205), §§ 1, 2, effective September 1, 2011; am. Acts 2011, 82nd Leg., ch. 984 (H.B. 1754), § 13, effective September 1, 2011; am. Acts 2011, 82nd Leg., ch. 1119 (H.B. 3), § 1, effective September 1, 2011; am. Acts 2011, 82nd Leg., ch. 1280 (H.B. 1113), § 2, effective September 1, 2011; am. Acts 2011, 82nd Leg., ch. 1322 (S.B. 407), § 11, effective September 1, 2011.)

## Art. 42.122. Adult Probation Officers of the 222nd Judicial District; Salary and Allowances.

The adult probation officer of the 222nd Judicial District receives a salary of not less than $15,000 per annum. Also, the probation officer receives allowances, not to exceed the amount allowed by the federal government for traveling the most practical route to and from the place where the duties are discharged, for his necessary travel and hotel expenses. Upon the sworn statement of the officer, approved by the judge, the respective counties of the judicial district pay the expenses incurred for their regular or special term of court out of the general county fund. In lieu of travel allowances the commissioners court of each county, by agreement, may provide transportation under the same terms and conditions as provided for sheriffs.

(Enacted by Acts 1985, 69th Leg., ch. 480 (S.B. 1228), § 18, effective September 1, 1985.)

## Art. 42.13. [Repealed].

Repealed by Acts 1995, 74th Leg., ch. 76 (S.B. 959), § 7.10, effective September 1, 1995.

(Enacted by Acts 1965, 59th Leg., ch. 722 (S.B. 107), § 1, effective January 1, 1966; am. Acts 1967, 60th Leg., ch. 659 (S.B. 145), § 30, effective August 28, 1967; am. Acts 1975, 64th Leg., ch. 341 (S.B. 122), § 5, effective June 19, 1975; am. Acts 1977, 65th Leg., ch. 306 (S.B. 695), § 3, effective August 29, 1977; am. Acts 1977, 65th Leg., ch. 388 (S.B. 61), §§ 3, 4, effective August 29, 1977; am. Acts 1979, 66th Leg., ch. 26 (H.B. 588), §§ 1, 2, effective September 1, 1979; am. Acts 1979, 66th Leg., ch. 428 (H.B. 2184), § 31, effective August 27, 1979; am. Acts 1979, 66th Leg., ch. 605 (S.B. 376), § 5, effective August 27, 1979; am. Acts 1979, 66th Leg., ch. 654 (S.B. 844), § 1, effective August 27, 1979; am. Acts 1979, 66th Leg., ch. 807 (H.B. 2107), § 1, effective September 1, 1979; am. Acts 1981, 67th Leg., ch. 142 (S.B. 368), §§ 1, 2, effective January 1, 1982; am. Acts 1981, 67th Leg., ch. 291 (S.B. 265), § 119, effective September 1, 1981; am. Acts 1981, 67th Leg., ch. 544 (H.B. 1166), § 2, effective September 1, 1981; am. Acts 1983, 68th Leg., ch. 303 (S.B. 1), §§ 14—21, effective January 1, 1984; am. Acts 1983, 68th Leg., ch. 325 (H.B. 411), § 3, effective September 1, 1983; am. Acts 1983, 68th Leg., ch. 811 (H.B. 861), § 2, effective August 29, 1983; am. Acts 1983, 68th Leg., ch. 863 (H.B. 1289), § 2, effective August 29, 1983; am. Acts 1985, 69th Leg., ch. 239 (H.B. 1593), § 25, effective September 1, 1985; am. Acts 1985, 69th Leg., ch. 427 (S.B. 589), § 3, effective September 1, 1985; am. Acts 1985, 69th Leg., ch. 595 (H.B. 1378), § 4, effective September 1, 1985; am. Acts 1985, 69th Leg., ch. 632 (S.B. 601), §§ 14, 15, effective September 1, 1985; am. Acts 1987, 70th Leg., ch. 928 (H.B. 1300), § 3, effective September 1, 1987; am. Acts 1987, 70th Leg., ch. 939 (H.B. 83), § 24, effective September 1, 1987; am. Acts 1993, 73rd Leg., ch. 988 (S.B. 532), § 2.01, effective September 1, 1993; am. Acts 1995, 74th Leg., ch. 76 (S.B. 959), § 7.10, effective September 1, 1995; am. Acts 1995, 74th Leg., ch. 318 (S.B. 15), § 62, effective September 1, 1995; am. Acts 1995, 74th Leg., ch. 321 (H.B. 2162), §§ 3.009—3.013, effective September 1, 1995.)

## Art. 42.131. [Repealed].

Repealed by Acts 1995, 74th Leg., ch. 76 (S.B. 959),§ 7.12, effective September 1, 1995.
(Am. Acts 1993, 73rd Leg., ch. 809 (H.B. 2535), § 1, effective August 30, 1993; am. Acts 1993, 73rd Leg., ch. 988 (S.B. 532), § 2.02, effective September 1, 1993; am. Acts 1995, 74th Leg., ch.

76 (S.B. 959), § 17.01(3), effective September 1, 1995; am. Acts 1995, 74th Leg., ch. 185 (H.B. 592), § 1, effective May 23, 1995; am. Acts 1995, 74th Leg., ch. 217 (H.B. 2265), § 1, effective May 23, 1995; am. Acts 1995, 74th Leg., ch. 252 (S.B. 47), § 1, effective September 1, 1995; am. Acts 1995, 74th Leg., ch. 266 (S.B. 146), § 1, effective June 5, 1995; am. Acts 1995, 74th Leg., ch. 321 (H.B. 2162), §§ 3.014, 3.0151, effective September 1, 1995; am. Acts 1995, 74th Leg., ch. 611 (H.B. 1180), § 5, effective August 28, 1995.)

## Art. 42.14. In Absence of Defendant.

(a) In a misdemeanor case, the judgment and sentence may be rendered in the absence of the defendant.

(b) In a felony case, the judgment and sentence may be rendered in the absence of the defendant only if:

(1) the defendant is confined in a penal institution;

(2) the defendant is not charged with a felony offense:

(A) that is listed in Section 3g(a)(1), Article 42.12; or

(B) for which it is alleged that:

(i) a deadly weapon was used or exhibited during the commission of the offense or during immediate flight from the commission of the offense; and

(ii) the defendant used or exhibited the deadly weapon or was a party to the offense and knew that a deadly weapon would be used or exhibited;

(3) the defendant in writing before the appropriate court having jurisdiction in the county in which the penal institution is located:

(A) waives the right to be present at the rendering of the judgment and sentence or to have counsel present;

(B) affirms that the defendant does not have anything to say as to why the sentence should not be pronounced and that there is no reason to prevent the sentence under Article 42.07;

(C) states that the defendant has entered into a written plea agreement with the attorney representing the state in the prosecution of the case; and

(D) requests the court to pronounce sentence in the case in accordance with the plea agreement;

(4) the defendant and the attorney representing the state in the prosecution of the case

have entered into a written plea agreement that is made a part of the record in the case; and

(5) sentence is pronounced in accordance with the plea agreement.

(c) A judgment and sentence may be rendered under this article in the absence of the defendant only after the defendant is notified by the court of original jurisdiction of the right to counsel and the defendant requests counsel or waives the right to counsel in accordance with Article 1.051.

(d) In this article, "deadly weapon" and "penal institution" have the meanings assigned by Section 1.07, Penal Code.

(e) If a defendant enters a plea of guilty or nolo contendere under Article 27.19, the attorney representing the state may request at the time the plea is entered that the defendant submit a fingerprint of the defendant suitable for attachment to the judgment. On request for a fingerprint under this subsection, the county in which the defendant is confined shall obtain a fingerprint of the defendant and use first-class mail or other means acceptable to the attorney representing the state and the county to forward the fingerprint to the court accepting the plea. (Enacted by Acts 1965, 59th Leg., ch. 722 (S.B. 107), § 1, effective January 1, 1966; am. Acts 2009, 81st Leg., ch. 291 (H.B. 107), § 2, effective September 1, 2009.)

## Art. 42.141. Battering Intervention and Prevention Program.

**Sec. 1. Definitions.**

In this article:

(1) "Batterer" means a person who commits repeated acts of violence or who repeatedly threatens violence against another who is:

(A) related to the actor by affinity or consanguinity, as determined under Chapter 573, Government Code;

(B) is a former spouse of the actor; or

(C) resides or has resided in the same household with the actor.

(2) "Division" means the community justice assistance division of the Texas Department of Criminal Justice.

(3) "Family" has the meaning assigned by Section 71.003, Family Code.

(4) "Family violence" has the meaning assigned by Section 71.004, Family Code.

(5) "Shelter center" has the meaning assigned by Section 51.002, Human Resources Code.

(6) "Household" has the meaning assigned by Section 71.005, Family Code.

(7) "Program" means a battering intervention and prevention program that:

(A) meets:

(i) the guidelines adopted by the community justice assistance division of the Texas Department of Criminal Justice with the assistance of the statewide nonprofit organization described by Section 3(1); and

(ii) any other eligibility requirements adopted by the Texas Department of Criminal Justice; and

(B) provides, on a local basis to batterers referred by the courts for intervention, educational services and intervention designed to help the batterers stop their abusive behavior.

(8) "Project" means the statewide activities for the funding of battering intervention and prevention programs, the related community educational campaign, and education and research regarding such programs.

(9) "Responsive law enforcement climate" means an area where, in cases of family violence:

(A) the local law enforcement agency has a policy or record of arresting batterers; and

(B) the local criminal justice system:

(i) cooperates with the victim in filing protective orders; and

(ii) takes appropriate action against a person who violates protective orders.

**Sec. 2. Establishment.**

The battering intervention and prevention program is established in the division.

**Sec. 3. Duties of the Division.** The division shall:

(1) contract with a nonprofit organization that for the five-year period before the date on which a contract is to be signed has been involved in providing to shelter centers, law enforcement agencies, and the legal community statewide advocacy and technical assistance relating to family violence, with the contract requiring the nonprofit organization to perform the duties described in Section (4) of this article;

(2) seek the input of the statewide nonprofit organization described in Subdivision (1) in the development of standards for selection of programs for inclusion in the project and the review of proposals submitted by programs;

(3) issue requests for proposals for the programs and an educational campaign not later than January 1, 1990;

(4) award contracts for programs that are operated by nonprofit organizations and that take into consideration:

(A) a balanced geographical distribution of urban, rural, and suburban models; and

(B) the presence of a responsive law enforcement climate in the community;

(5) develop and monitor the project in cooperation with the nonprofit organization described by Subdivision (1);

(6) monitor the development of a community educational campaign in cooperation with the nonprofit organization described by Subdivision (1);

(7) assist the nonprofit organization described by Subdivision (1) in designing program evaluations and research activities;

(8) facilitate training of probation officers and other criminal justice professionals by the nonprofit organization described by Subdivision (1) and by programs;

(9) seek the assistance of the nonprofit organization described by Subdivision (1) in developing program guidelines and in accrediting programs and providers providing battering intervention and prevention services as conforming to those guidelines; and

(10) before adopting program guidelines under Section 4A:

(A) notify the licensing authorities described by Chapters 152, 501, 502, 503, and 505, Occupations Code, that the division is considering adopting program guidelines; and

(B) invite the licensing authorities to comment on the program guidelines.

**Sec. 4. Duties of the Nonprofit Organization.** The nonprofit organization with which the division contracts under Section 3(1) shall:

(1) assist the division in developing and issuing requests for proposals for the programs and the educational campaign;

(2) assist the division in reviewing the submitted proposals and making recommendations for proposals to be selected for funding;

(3) develop and monitor the project in cooperation with the division;

(4) provide technical assistance to programs to:

(A) develop appropriate services for batterers;

(B) train staff;

(C) improve coordination with shelter centers, the criminal justice system, the judiciary, law enforcement agencies, prosecutors, and other appropriate officials and support services;

(D) implement the community educational campaign; and

(E) participate in project administered program evaluation and research activities;

(5) provide technical assistance to the division to:

(A) develop and implement standards for selection of programs for inclusion in the project; and

(B) develop standards for selection of the community educational campaign described in Section 6 of this article;

(6) submit an annual written report to the division and to the legislature with recommendations for continuation, elimination, or changes in the project;

(7) evaluate the programs and the community educational campaign, including an analysis of the effectiveness of the project and the level of public awareness relating to family violence; and

(8) assist the division in developing program guidelines and in accrediting programs and providers providing battering intervention and prevention services as conforming to those guidelines.

**Sec. 4A. Adoption of Program Guidelines; Accreditation Process.** With the assistance of the statewide nonprofit organization described by Section 3(1) and after notifying the licensing authorities described by Section 3(10), the division shall adopt guidelines for programs and shall accredit programs and providers providing battering intervention and prevention services as conforming to those guidelines. The division shall collect from each program or provider that applies for accreditation under this section a one-time application fee in an amount set by the Texas Department of Criminal Justice.

**Sec. 5. Programs.**

(a) A program proposal must:

(1) describe the counseling or treatment the program will offer;

(2) include letters from a local law enforcement agency or agencies, courts, probation officers, and other community resources describing the community's commitment to improve the criminal justice system's response to victims and batterers and to cooperate with and interact in the programs' activities;

(3) include a letter from the local shelter center describing the support services available to victims of family violence in the community and the shelter's commitment to cooperate and work with the program; and

(4) describe the public education and local community outreach activities relating to family violence currently available in the community and a statement of commitment to participate on the local level in the public educational campaign described in Section 6 of this article.

(b) A program must:

(1) be situated in a county in which a shelter center is located;

(2) offer counseling or treatment in which the primary approach is direct intervention with the batterer, on an individual or group basis, but that does not require the victim of the family violence to participate in the counseling or treatment;

(3) offer training to law enforcement prosecutors, judges, probation officers, and others on the dynamics of family violence, treatment options, and program activities; and

(4) have a system for receiving referrals from the courts and for reporting to the court regarding batterers' compliance with the treatment program.

(c) This section does not preclude a program from serving a batterer other than one who was ordered by a court to participate in the program established under this subchapter.

## Sec. 6. Community Educational Campaign.

(a) The division, with assistance from the nonprofit organization, shall select the community educational campaign relating to family violence after the commission has selected the programs. The campaign is to be implemented in the areas covered by the programs.

(b) The campaign shall use a variety of media, including newspapers, radio, television, and billboards, and shall focus on:

(1) the criminality of acts of violence toward family members;

(2) the consequences of family violence crimes to the batterer; and

(3) eradicating public misconceptions of family violence.

## Sec. 7. Use of Legislative Appropriation.

Of a legislative appropriation for the project established under this article:

(1) not more than six percent may be used by the division for management and administration of the project;

(2) not more than 14 percent may be applied to the contract between the division and the nonprofit organization; and

(3) not more than three percent may be applied to the contract for the community educational campaign.

## Sec. 8. Contract Date.

The contract required under Section 3(a) of this article shall be signed not later than November 1, 1989.

(Enacted by Acts 1989, 71st Leg., ch. 785 (H.B. 2335), § 3.05, effective September 1, 1989; am. Acts 1991, 72nd Leg., ch. 561 (H.B. 1345), § 11, effective August 26, 1991; am. Acts 1995, 74th Leg., ch. 76 (S.B. 959), § 5.95(27), effective September 1, 1995; am. Acts 2003, 78th Leg., ch. 1276 (H.B. 3507), § 7.002(i), effective September 1, 2003; am. Acts 2007, 80th Leg., ch. 113 (S.B. 44), §§ 2, 3, effective September 1, 2007.)

## Art. 42.15. Fines and Costs.

(a) When the defendant is fined, the judgment shall be that the defendant pay the amount of the fine and all costs to the state.

(b) Subject to Subsection (c), when imposing a fine and costs, a court may direct a defendant:

(1) to pay the entire fine and costs when sentence is pronounced;

(2) to pay the entire fine and costs at some later date; or

(3) to pay a specified portion of the fine and costs at designated intervals.

(c) When imposing a fine and costs in a misdemeanor case, if the court determines that the defendant is unable to immediately pay the fine and costs, the court shall allow the defendant to pay the fine and costs in specified portions at designated intervals.

(Enacted by Acts 1965, 59th Leg., ch. 722 (S.B. 107), § 1, effective January 1, 1966; am. Acts 1971, 62nd Leg., ch. 987 (H.B. 887), § 1, effective June 15, 1971; am. Acts 2011, 82nd Leg., ch. 464 (H.B. 27), §§ 1, 2, effective September 1, 2011.)

## Art. 42.151. Fees for Abused Children's Counseling.

If a court orders a defendant to pay a fee under Article 37.072 of this code, the court shall assess the fee against the defendant in the same manner as other costs of prosecution are assessed against a defendant. The court may direct a defendant:

Criminal Procedure

(1) to pay the entire fee when sentence is pronounced;

(2) to pay the entire fee at some later date; or

(3) to pay a specified portion of the fee at designated intervals.

(Enacted by Acts 1989, 71st Leg., ch. 360 (S.B. 1175), § 3, effective September 1, 1989; enacted by Acts 1989, 71st Leg., ch. 611 (S.B. 149), § 3, effective September 1, 1989.)

## Art. 42.152. Repayment of Reward.

(a) If a judge orders a defendant to repay a reward or part of a reward under Article 37.073 of this code, the court shall assess this cost against the defendant in the same manner as other costs of prosecution are assessed against a defendant. The court may order the defendant to:

(1) pay the entire amount required when sentence is pronounced;

(2) pay the entire amount required at a later date specified by the court; or

(3) pay specified portions of the required amount at designated intervals.

(b) After receiving a payment from a person ordered to make the payment under this article, the clerk of the court or fee officer shall:

(1) make a record of the payment;

(2) deduct a one-time $7 processing fee from the reward repayment;

(3) forward the payment to the designated crime stoppers organization; and

(4) make a record of the forwarding of the payment.

(Enacted by Acts 1989, 71st Leg., ch. 611 (S.B. 149), § 3, effective September 1, 1989; am. Acts 1991, 72nd Leg., ch. 16 (S.B. 232), § 19.01(6), effective August 26, 1991 (renumbered from art. 42.151); am. Acts 1997, 75th Leg., ch. 700 (S.B. 1546), § 12, effective September 1, 1997.)

## Art. 42.16. On Other Judgment.

If the punishment is any other than a fine, the judgment shall specify it, and order it enforced by the proper process. It shall also adjudge the costs against the defendant, and order the collection thereof as in other cases.

(Enacted by Acts 1965, 59th Leg., ch. 722 (S.B. 107), § 1, effective January 1, 1966.)

## Art. 42.17. Transfer Under Treaty.

When a treaty is in effect between the United States and a foreign country providing for the transfer of convicted offenders who are citizens or nationals of foreign countries to the foreign coun-

tries of which they are citizens or nationals, the governor is authorized, subject to the terms of such treaty, to act on behalf of the State of Texas and to consent to the transfer of such convicted offenders under the provisions of Article IV, Section 11 of the Constitution of the State of Texas.

(Enacted by Acts 1977, 65th Leg., ch. 489 (S.B. 999), § 1, effective June 15, 1977.)

## Art. 42.18. [Repealed].

Repealed by Acts 1997, 75th Leg., ch. 165 (S.B. 898), § 12.22, effective September 1, 1997.

(Enacted by Acts 1985, 69th Leg., ch. 24 (S.B. 126), § 1; enacted by Acts 1985, 69th Leg., ch. 427 (S.B. 589), § 2, effective September 1, 1985; am. Acts 1986, 69th Leg., 3rd C.S., ch. 8 (S.B. 40), § 1, effective September 1, 1987; am. Acts 1987, 70th Leg., ch. 1 (S.B. 215), §§ 2, 3, 13, effective February 20, 1987; am. Acts 1987, 70th Leg., ch. 12 (S.B. 5), § 2, effective September 1, 1987; am. Acts 1987, 70th Leg., ch. 18 (S.B. 251), § 7, effective April 14, 1987; am. Acts 1987, 70th Leg., ch. 42 (H.B. 51), § 1, effective April 29, 1987; am. Acts 1987, 70th Leg., ch. 110 (S.B. 26), § 1, effective August 31, 1987; am. Acts 1987, 70th Leg., ch. 384 (H.B. 685), §§ 5, 6, effective September 1, 1987; am. Acts 1987, 70th Leg., ch. 441 (H.B. 56), § 2, effective September 1, 1987; am. Acts 1987, 70th Leg., ch. 449 (H.B. 150), § 1, effective August 31, 1987; am. Acts 1987, 70th Leg., ch. 926 (H.B. 1196), § 1, effective June 20, 1987; am. Acts 1987, 70th Leg., ch. 1101 (S.B. 341), §§ 1—11, effective September 1, 1987; am. Acts 1989, 71st Leg., ch. 212 (S.B. 1044), § 3.01, effective September 1, 1989; am. Acts 1989, 71st Leg., ch. 260 (H.B. 2634), § 2, effective September 1, 1989; am. Acts 1989, 71st Leg., ch. 584 (H.B. 2519), § 83, effective September 1, 1989; am. Acts 1989, 71st Leg., ch. 785 (H.B. 2335), § 5.01, effective September 1, 1989; am. Acts 1989, 71st Leg., 1st C.S., ch. 6 (S.B. 29), § 3, effective January 1, 1990; am. Acts 1993, 73rd Leg., ch. 805 (H.B. 2178), § 8, effective August 30, 1993; am. Acts 1993, 73rd Leg., ch. 809 (H.B. 2535), § 2, effective August 30, 1993; am. Acts 1993, 73rd Leg., ch. 888 (S.B. 16), § 2, effective September 1, 1993; am. Acts 1993, 73rd Leg., ch. 900 (S.B. 1067), §§ 6.01, 6.02, 6.03, effective September 1, 1993; am. Acts 1993, 73rd Leg., ch. 987 (S.B. 456), § 6, effective September 1, 1993; am. Acts 1993, 73rd Leg., ch. 988 (S.B. 532), §§ 3.03, 5.01, 10.01—10.14, 11.01—11.05, effective September 1, 1993; am. Acts 1995, 74th Leg., ch. 76 (S.B. 959), § 7.03, effective September 1,

1995; am. Acts 1995, 74th Leg., ch. 250 (S.B. 45), §§ 2, 3, effective September 1, 1995; am. Acts 1995, 74th Leg., ch. 253 (S.B. 48), § 1, effective September 1, 1995; am. Acts 1995, 74th Leg., ch. 256 (S.B. 111), § 4, effective September 1, 1995; am. Acts 1995, 74th Leg., ch. 258 (S.B. 267), §§ 12, 13, effective September 1, 1995; am. Acts 1995, 74th Leg., ch. 260 (S.B. 1), § 17, effective May 30, 1995; am. Acts 1995, 74th Leg., ch. 262 (H.B. 327), §§ 83, 84, effective January 1, 1996; am. Acts 1995, 74th Leg., ch. 263 (H.B. 1433), §§ 1, 2, effective September 1, 1996; am. Acts 1995, 74th Leg., ch. 318 (S.B. 15), § 64, effective September 1, 1995; am. Acts 1995, 74th Leg., ch. 321 (H.B. 2162), §§ 2.001—2.018, 2.022, effective September 1, 1995; am. Acts 1995, 74th Leg., ch. 657 (S.B. 126), § 5, effective June 14, 1995; am. Acts 1995, 74th Leg., ch. 996 (S.B. 452), §§ 10, 11(2), effective January 1, 1996; am. Acts 1997, 75th Leg., ch. 1 (S.B. 97), § 7, effective January 28, 1997; am. Acts 1997, 75th Leg., ch. 144 (S.B. 123), § 4, effective May 20, 1997; am. Acts 1997, 75th Leg., ch. 161 (H.B. 1386), §§ 1—11, effective September 1, 1997; am. Acts 1997, 75th Leg., ch. 188 (H.B. 1050), § 1, effective May 21, 1997; am. Acts 1997, 75th Leg., ch. 238 (H.B. 432), § 1, effective May 23, 1997; am. Acts 1997, 75th Leg., ch. 429 (H.B. 1112), §§ 1—3, effective January 1, 1998; am. Acts 1997, 75th Leg., ch. 478 (S.B. 66), § 2, effective September 1, 1997; am. Acts 1997, 75th Leg., ch. 480 (S.B. 113), §§ 1, 2, effective September 1, 1997; am. Acts 1997, 75th Leg., ch. 665 (S.B. 46), § 3, effective September 1, 1997; am. Acts 1997, 75th Leg., ch. 668 (S.B. 875), §§ 5, 6, 7, effective September 1, 1997; am. Acts 1997, 75th Leg., ch. 670 (H.B. 156), §§ 1—3, effective September 1, 1997; am. Acts 1997, 75th Leg., ch. 736 (H.B. 818), § 1, effective June 17, 1997; am. Acts 1997, 75th Leg., ch. 836 (H.B. 658), § 1, effective September 1, 1997; am. Acts 1997, 75th Leg., ch. 1423 (H.B. 2841), § 4.02, effective September 1, 1997; am. Acts 1997, 75th Leg., ch. 1430 (H.B. 2918), § 6(a), effective September 1, 1997.)

## Art. 42.19. Interstate Corrections Compact.

### Article I. Purpose and Policy

The party states, desiring by common action to fully utilize and improve their institutional facilities and provide adequate programs for the confinement, treatment, and rehabilitation of various types of offenders, declare that it is the policy of each of the party states to provide such facilities and programs on a basis of cooperation with one another, thereby serving the best interests of such offenders and of society and effecting economies in capital expenditures and operational costs. The purpose of this compact is to provide for the mutual development and execution of such programs of cooperation for the confinement, treatment, and rehabilitation of offenders with the most economical use of human and material resources.

### Article II. Definitions

As used in this compact, unless the context clearly requires otherwise:

(a) "State" means a state of the United States; the United States of America; a territory or possession of the United States; the District of Columbia; the commonwealth of Puerto Rico.

(b) "Sending state" means a state party to this compact in which conviction or court commitment was had.

(c) "Receiving state" means a state party to this compact to which an inmate is sent for confinement other than a state in which conviction or court commitment was had.

(d) "Inmate" means a male or female offender who is committed, under sentence to or confined in a penal or correctional institution.

(e) "Institution" means any penal or correctional facility, including but not limited to a facility for the mentally ill or mentally defective, in which inmates as defined in (d) above may lawfully be confined.

### Article III. Contracts

(a) Each party state may make one or more contracts with any one or more of the other party states for the confinement of inmates on behalf of a sending state in institutions situated within receiving states. Any such contract shall provide for:

1. Its duration.

2. Payments to be made to the receiving state by the sending state for inmate maintenance, extraordinary medical and dental expenses, and any participation in or receipt by inmates of rehabilitative or correctional services, facilities, programs, or treatment not reasonably included as part of normal maintenance.

3. Participation in programs of inmate employment, if any; the disposition or cred-

iting of any payments received by inmates on account thereof; and the crediting of proceeds from or disposal of any products resulting therefrom.

4. Delivery and retaking of inmates.

5. Such other matters as may be necessary and appropriate to fix the obligations, responsibilities, and rights of the sending and receiving states.

(b) The terms and provisions of this compact shall be a part of any contract entered into by the authority of or pursuant thereto, and nothing in any such contract shall be inconsistent therewith.

## Article IV. Procedures and Rights

(a) Whenever the duly constituted authorities in a state party to this compact, and which has entered into a contract pursuant to Article III, shall decide that confinement in, or transfer of an inmate to, an institution within the territory of another party state is necessary or desirable in order to provide adequate quarters and care or an appropriate program of rehabilitation or treatment, such official may direct that the confinement be within an institution within the territory of such other party state, the receiving state to act in that regard solely as agent for the sending state.

(b) The appropriate officials of any state party to this compact shall have access, at all reasonable times, to any institution in which it has a contractual right to confine inmates for the purpose of inspecting the facilities thereof and visiting such of its inmates as may be confined in the institution.

(c) Inmates confined in an institution pursuant to this compact shall at all times be subject to the jurisdiction of the sending state and may at any time be removed therefrom for transfer to a prison or other institution within the sending state, for transfer to another institution in which the sending state may have a contractual or other right to confine inmates, for release on probation or parole, for discharge, or for any other purpose permitted by the laws of the sending state. However, the sending state shall continue to be obligated to such payments as may be required pursuant to the terms of any contract entered into under the terms of Article III.

(d) Each receiving state shall provide regular reports to each sending state on the inmates of that sending state who are in institutions pursuant to this compact including a conduct record of each inmate and shall certify such record to the official designated by the sending state, in order that each inmate may have official review of his or her record in determining and altering the disposition of the inmate in accordance with the law which may obtain in the sending state and in order that the same may be a source of information for the sending state.

(e) All inmates who may be confined in an institution pursuant to this compact shall be treated in a reasonable and humane manner and shall be treated equally with such similar inmates of the receiving state as may be confined in the same institution. The fact of confinement in a receiving state shall not deprive any inmate so confined of any legal rights which the inmate would have had if confined in an appropriate institution of the sending state.

(f) Any hearing or hearings to which an inmate confined pursuant to this compact may be entitled by the laws of the sending state may be had before the appropriate authorities of the sending state, or of the receiving state if authorized by the sending state. The receiving state shall provide adequate facilities for such hearing as may be conducted by the appropriate officials of a sending state. In the event such hearing or hearings are had before officials of the receiving state, the governing law shall be that of the sending state and a record of the hearing or hearings as prescribed by the sending state shall be made. The record together with any recommendations of the hearing officials shall be transmitted forthwith to the official or officials before whom the hearing would have been had if it had taken place in the sending state. In any and all proceedings had pursuant to the provisions of this paragraph (f), the officials of the receiving state shall act solely as agents of the sending state and no final determination shall be made in any matter except by the appropriate officials of the sending state.

(g) Any inmate confined pursuant to this compact shall be released within the territory of the sending state unless the inmate and the sending and receiving states shall agree upon release in some other place. The sending state shall bear the cost of such return to its territory.

(h) Any inmate confined pursuant to this compact shall have any rights and all rights to participate in and derive any benefits or incur or be relieved of any obligations or have such obligations modified or his status changed on account of any action or proceeding in which he could have participated if confined in any appropriate institution of the sending state located within such state.

(i) The parent, guardian, trustee, or other person or persons entitled under the laws of the sending state to act for, advise, or otherwise function with respect to any inmate shall not be deprived of or restricted in his exercise of any power in respect of any inmate confined pursuant to the terms of this compact.

## Article V. Act Not Reviewable in Receiving State: Extradition

(a) Any decision of the sending state in respect of any matter over which it retains jurisdiction pursuant to this compact shall be conclusive upon and not reviewable within the receiving state, but if at the time the sending state seeks to remove an inmate from an institution in the receiving state there is pending against the inmate within such state any criminal charge or if the inmate is formally accused of having committed within such state a criminal offense, the inmate shall not be returned without the consent of the receiving state until discharged from prosecution or other form of proceeding, imprisonment, or detention for such offense. The duly accredited officer of the sending state shall be permitted to transport inmates pursuant to this compact through any and all states party to this compact without interference.

(b) An inmate who escapes from an institution in which he is confined pursuant to this compact shall be deemed a fugitive from the sending state and from the state in which the institution escaped from is situated. In the case of an escape to a jurisdiction other than the sending or receiving state, the responsibility for institution of extradition or rendition proceedings shall be that of the sending state, but nothing contained herein shall be construed to prevent or affect the activities of officers and agencies of any jurisdiction directed toward the apprehension and return of an escapee.

## Article VI. Federal Aid

Any state party to this compact may accept federal aid for use in connection with any institution or program, the use of which is or may be affected by this compact or any contract pursuant thereto. Any inmate in a receiving state pursuant to this compact may participate in any such federally aided program or activity for which the sending and receiving states have made contractual provision. However, if such program or activity is not part of the customary correctional regimen, the express consent of the appropriate official of the sending state shall be required therefor.

## Article VII. Entry into Force

This compact shall enter into force and become effective and binding upon the states so acting when it has been enacted into law by any two states. Thereafter, this compact shall enter into force and become effective and binding as to any other of such states upon similar action by such state.

## Article VIII. Withdrawal and Termination

This compact shall continue in force and remain binding upon a party state until it shall have enacted a statute repealing the compact and providing for the sending of formal written notice of withdrawal from the compact to the appropriate officials of all other party states. An actual withdrawal shall not take effect until one year after the notices provided in the statute have been sent. Such withdrawal shall not relieve the withdrawing state from its obligations assumed hereunder prior to the effective date of withdrawal. Before the effective date of withdrawal, a withdrawal state shall remove to its territory, at its own expense, such inmates as it may have confined pursuant to the provisions of this compact.

## Article IX. Other Arrangements Unaffected

Nothing contained in this compact shall be construed to abrogate or impair an agreement or other arrangement which a party state may have with a nonparty state for the confinement, rehabilitation, or treatment of inmates, nor to repeal any other laws of a party state authorizing the making of cooperative institutional arrangements.

## Article X. Construction and Severability

(a) The provisions of this compact shall be liberally construed and shall be severable. If any

Criminal Procedure

phrase, clause, sentence, or provision of this compact is declared to be contrary to the constitution of any participating state or of the United States or the applicability thereof to any government, agency, person, or circumstance is held invalid, the validity of the remainder of this compact and the applicability thereof to any government, agency, person, or circumstance shall not be affected thereby. If this compact shall be held contrary to the constitution of any state participating therein, the compact shall remain in full force and effect as to the remaining states and in full force and effect as to the state affected as to all severable matters.

(b) Powers. The director of the Texas Department of Criminal Justice is authorized and directed to do all things necessary or incidental to the carrying out of the compact in every particular.

(Enacted by Acts 1985, 69th Leg., ch. 24 (S.B. 126), § 1, effective January 1, 1986; am. Acts 1987, 70th Leg., ch. 167 (S.B. 892), § 5.01(a 9), effective September 1, 1987 (renumbered from art. 42.18); am. Acts 2009, 81st Leg., ch. 87 (S.B. 1969), § 25.031, effective September 1, 2009.)

## Art. 42.20. Immunities.

(a) An individual listed in Subsection (c) of this article and the governmental entity that the individual serves as an officer or employee are not liable for damages arising from an act or failure to act by the individual or governmental entity in connection with a community service program or work program established under this chapter or in connection with an inmate, offender, or releasee programmatic or nonprogrammatic activity, including work, educational, and treatment activities, if the act or failure to act:

(1) was performed pursuant to a court order or was otherwise performed in an official capacity; and

(2) was not performed with conscious indifference for the safety of others.

(b) Chapter 101, Civil Practice and Remedies Code, does not apply to a claim based on an act or a failure to act of an individual listed in Subsection (c) of this article or a governmental entity the officer serves as an officer or employee if the act or failure to act is in connection with a program described by Subsection (a) of this article.

(c) This article applies to:

(1) a director or employee of a community supervision and corrections department or a community corrections facility;

(2) a sheriff or employee of a sheriff's department;

(3) a county judge, county attorney, county commissioner, or county employee;

(4) a district judge, district attorney, or criminal district attorney;

(5) an officer or employee of a state agency; or

(6) an officer or employee of a political subdivision other than a county.

(Enacted by Acts 1993, 73rd Leg., ch. 900 (S.B. 1067), § 5.03, effective September 1, 1993; am. Acts 1995, 74th Leg., ch. 76 (S.B. 959), § 3.13, effective September 1, 1995; am. Acts 2003, 78th Leg., ch. 406 (H.B. 178), § 1, effective September 1, 2003.)

## Art. 42.21. Notice of Release of Family Violence Offenders.

(a) Before releasing a person convicted of a family violence offense, the entity holding the person shall make a reasonable attempt to give personal notice of the imminent release to the victim of the offense or to another person designated by the victim to receive the notice. An attempt by an entity to give notice to the victim or person designated by the victim at the victim's or person's last known telephone number or address, as shown on the records of the entity, constitutes a reasonable attempt to give notice under this subsection.

(b) An entity or an employee of an entity is not liable for damages arising from complying or failing to comply with Subsection (a) of this article.

(c) In this article, "family violence" has the meaning assigned by Section 71.004, Family Code.

(Enacted by Acts 1995, 74th Leg., ch. 661 (S.B. 223), § 2, effective August 28, 1995; am. Acts 2003, 78th Leg., ch. 1276 (H.B. 3507), § 7.002(j), effective September 1, 2003.)

## Art. 42.22. Restitution Liens.
### Sec. 1. Definitions.

In this article:

(1) "Department" means the Texas Department of Motor Vehicles.

(2) "Motor vehicle" has the meaning assigned by Chapter 501, Transportation Code.

(3) "State" means the State of Texas and all political subdivisions thereof.

(4) "Victim" means:

(A) a "close relative of a deceased victim," "guardian of a victim," or "victim," as those terms are defined by Article 56.01 of this code; or

(B) an individual who suffers damages as a result of another committing an offense under Section 38.04, Penal Code, in which the defendant used a motor vehicle while the defendant was in flight.

(5) "Personal property" means any property other than real property including all tangible and intangible types of property and including but not limited to copyrights, book rights, movie rights, patents, and trademarks acquired by the defendant prior to, during, and after conviction.

### Sec. 2. Lien Established.

(a) The victim of a criminal offense has a restitution lien to secure the amount of restitution to which the victim is entitled under the order of a court in a criminal case.

(b) The state also has a restitution lien to secure the:

(1) amount of fines or costs entered against a defendant in the judgment in a felony criminal case;

(2) amount of reimbursement for costs of:

(A) confinement ordered under Article 42.038; or

(B) notice provided under Article 62.056 or 62.201; and

(3) amount of damages incurred by the state as a result of the commission of an offense under Section 38.04, Penal Code, in which the defendant used a motor vehicle while the defendant was in flight.

### Sec. 3. Perfection.

(a) Except as provided by this section, a restitution lien attaches and is perfected when an affidavit to perfect the lien is filed in accordance with this article.

(b) If a lien established under this article is attached to a motor vehicle, the lien must be perfected in the manner provided by Chapter 501, Transportation Code, and the court that entered the order of restitution giving rise to the lien shall include in the order a requirement that the defendant surrender to the court evidence of current legal ownership of the motor vehicle and the title, if applicable, against which the lien attaches. A lien against a motor vehicle as provided by this article is not perfected until the defendant's title to the vehicle has been surrendered to the court and the department has issued a subsequent title that discloses on its face the fact that the vehicle is subject to a restitution lien established as provided by this article.

### Sec. 4. Judgment Required.

An affidavit to perfect a restitution lien may not be filed under this article until a court has ordered restitution or entered a judgment requiring the defendant to pay a fine or costs.

### Sec. 5. Persons Who May File.

The following persons may file an affidavit to perfect a restitution lien:

(1) the attorney representing the state in a criminal case in which a victim is determined by the court to be entitled to restitution or in which a defendant is ordered to pay fines or costs; or

(2) a victim in a criminal case determined by the court to be entitled to restitution.

### Sec. 6. Affidavit.

An affidavit to perfect a restitution lien must be signed by the attorney representing the state or a magistrate and must contain:

(1) the name and date of birth of the defendant whose property or other interests are subject to the lien;

(2) the residence or principal place of business of the person named in the lien, if known;

(3) the criminal proceeding giving rise to the lien, including the name of the court, the name of the case, and the court's file number for the case;

(4) the name and address of the attorney representing the state and the name of the person entitled to restitution;

(5) a statement that the notice is being filed under this article;

(6) the amount of restitution and the amount of fines and costs the defendant has been ordered to pay by the court;

(7) a statement that the amount of restitution owed at any one time may be less than the original balance and that the outstanding balance is reflected in the records of the clerk of the court hearing the criminal proceeding giving rise to the lien; and

(8) the vehicle description and vehicle identification number.

### Sec. 7. Filing.

(a) An affidavit to perfect a restitution lien may be filed with:

(1) the secretary of state;

(2) the department in the manner provided by Chapter 501, Transportation Code; or

(3) the county clerk of the county in which:

(A) the crime was committed;

(B) the defendant resides; or

(C) the property is located.

(b) The uniform fee for filing and indexing and for stamping a copy furnished by the state or victim to show the date and place of filing is $5.

(c) The secretary of state shall deposit the filing fee in the state treasury to the credit of the statutory filing fund solely to defray the costs of administration of this section. The department shall deposit the filing fee in the state treasury to the credit of the state highway fund to be used solely to defray the costs of administering this section.

(d) The county clerk shall immediately record the restitution lien in the judgment records of the county. The clerk shall note in the records the date and hour the lien is received.

(e) The secretary of state shall immediately file the restitution lien in the security interest and financing statement records of the secretary of state. The secretary of state shall note in the records the date and hour the lien is received.

(f) The department shall immediately file the restitution lien in the motor vehicle records of the department. The department shall note in the records the date and hour the lien is received.

(g) When a restitution lien is filed, the county clerk or secretary of state shall enter the restitution lien in an alphabetical index to the records in which the lien is filed showing:

(1) the name of the person entitled to restitution;

(2) the name of the defendant obligated to pay restitution, fines, or costs;

(3) the amount of the lien; and

(4) the name of the court that ordered restitution.

(h) A person who files an affidavit to perfect a restitution lien under this article shall notify in writing the clerk of the court entering the judgment creating the lien of all officers or entities with which the affidavit was filed.

**Sec. 8. Subject Property.**

A restitution lien extends to:

(1) any interest of the defendant in real property whether then owned or after-acquired located in a county in which the lien is perfected by the filing of an affidavit with the county clerk;

(2) any interest of the defendant in tangible or intangible personal property whether then owned or after-acquired other than a motor vehicle if the lien is perfected by the filing of the affidavit with the secretary of state; or

(3) any interest of the defendant in a motor vehicle whether then owned or after-acquired if the lien is perfected by the filing of the affidavit with the department.

**Sec. 9. Priority.**

The perfection of a restitution lien under this article is notice of the claim to all persons dealing with the defendant or the property identified in the affidavit perfecting the lien. Without regard to whether perfected before or after the perfection of a restitution lien filed and perfected under this article, a perfected real estate mortgage lien, a vendor's lien, a purchase money security interest, a chattel paper security interest, a lien on a motor vehicle perfected as provided by Chapter 501, Transportation Code, or a worker's lien perfected in the manner provided by law is superior and prior to a restitution lien filed and perfected under this article. Except as provided by this article, a perfected lien in favor of a victim is superior and prior to a lien perfected by the state under this article, and the perfected lien in favor of the state is superior and prior to the claim or interest of any other person, other than:

(1) a person who acquires a valid lien or security interest perfected before the perfection of the restitution lien;

(2) a bona fide purchaser who acquires an interest in the property, if personal property, before the filing of the restitution lien, to the extent that the purchaser gives value; or

(3) a bona fide purchaser for value who acquires and files for record an interest in the property, if real property, before the perfection of the restitution lien.

**Sec. 10. Payment.**

The clerk receiving a payment from a defendant ordered to pay restitution shall make payments to the person having an interest in the restitution lien on a schedule of not less than quarterly payments as determined by the clerk or agency.

**Sec. 11. Foreclosure.**

If a defendant fails to timely make a payment required by the order of the court entering the judgment creating the restitution lien, the person having an interest in the lien may file suit in a court of competent jurisdiction to foreclose the lien. If the defendant cures the default on or before the 20th day after the date the suit is filed and pays the person who files the suit costs of court and reasonable attorney's fees, the court may dismiss the suit without prejudice to the person. The person may refile the suit against the defendant if the defendant subsequently defaults.

### Sec. 12. Expiration; Records.

(a) A restitution lien expires on the 10th anniversary of the date the lien was filed or on the date the defendant satisfies the judgment creating the lien, whichever occurs first. The person having an interest in the lien may refile the lien before the date the lien expires. A lien that is refiled expires on the 10th anniversary of the date the lien was refiled or the date the defendant satisfies the judgment creating the lien, whichever occurs first.

(b) Failure to execute or foreclose the restitution lien does not cause dormancy of the lien.

(c) The clerk of the court entering the judgment creating the restitution lien shall maintain a record of the outstanding balance of restitution, fines, or costs owed. If the defendant satisfies the judgment, the clerk shall immediately execute and file for record a release of the restitution lien with all officers or entities with which the affidavit perfecting the lien was filed, as indicated by the notice received by the clerk under Section 7(h) of this article, unless a release was executed and filed by the person who filed the affidavit to perfect the lien.

(d) A partial release of a lien as to specific property may be executed by the attorney representing the state or a magistrate who signs an affidavit described by Section 6 of this article on payment of a sum determined to represent the defendant's interest in any property to which the lien may attach.

(Enacted by Acts 1995, 74th Leg., ch. 997 (S.B. 494), § 1, effective September 1, 1996; am. Acts 1997, 75th Leg., ch. 165 (S.B. 898), § 31.01(12), effective September 1, 1997 (renumbered from art. 42.21); am. Acts 1997, 75th Leg., ch. 1118 (H.B. 2830), § 1, effective September 1, 1997; am. Acts 1999, 76th Leg., ch. 295 (S.B. 1276), § 2, effective September 1, 1999; am. Acts 2001, 77th Leg., ch. 1334 (H.B. 2798), §§ 1, 2, effective September 1, 2001; am. Acts 2003, 78th Leg., ch. 1300 (S.B. 146), § 2, effective September 1, 2003; am. Acts 2005, 79th Leg., ch. 1008 (H.B. 867), § 2.02, effective September 1, 2005; am. Acts 2009, 81st Leg., ch. 933 (H.B. 3097), § 3B.01, effective September 1, 2009.)

### Art. 42.23. Notification of Court of Family Violence Conviction.

(a) In this article, "family violence" has the meaning assigned by Section 71.004, Family Code.

(b) If the attorney representing the state in a criminal case involving family violence learns that the defendant is subject to the jurisdiction of another court relating to an order that provides for the appointment of a conservator or that sets the terms and conditions of conservatorship or for possession of or access to a child, the attorney representing the state shall notify the court in which the defendant is being tried of the existence of the order and the identity of the court of continuing jurisdiction.

(c) On the conviction or entry of an order deferring adjudication of a defendant for an offense involving family violence, the convicting court or the court entering the order shall notify the court of continuing jurisdiction of the conviction or deferred adjudication.

(Enacted by Acts 2001, 77th Leg., ch. 1289 (H.B. 596), § 11, effective September 1, 2001.)

### Art. 42.24. Prohibiting Contact with Victim.

If a defendant's sentence includes a term of confinement or imprisonment, the convicting court may, as part of the sentence, prohibit the defendant from contacting, during the term of the defendant's confinement or imprisonment, the victim of the offense of which the defendant is convicted or a member of the victim's family.

(Enacted by Acts 2011, 82nd Leg., ch. 491 (H.B. 1028), § 1, effective September 1, 2011.)

## CHAPTER 43
### EXECUTION OF JUDGMENT

## Art. 43.01. Discharging Judgment for Fine.

(a) When the sentence against an individual defendant is for fine and costs, he shall be discharged from the same:

(1) when the amount thereof has been fully paid;

(2) when remitted by the proper authority;

(3) when he has remained in custody for the time required by law to satisfy the amount thereof; or

(4) when the defendant has discharged the amount of fines and costs in any other manner permitted by this code.

(b) When the sentence against a defendant corporation or association is for fine and costs, it shall be discharged from same:

(1) when the amount thereof has been fully paid;

(2) when the execution against the corporation or association has been fully satisfied; or

(3) when the judgment has been fully satisfied in any other manner.

(Enacted by Acts 1965, 59th Leg., ch. 722 (S.B. 107), § 1, effective January 1, 1966; am. Acts 1973, 63rd Leg., ch. 399 (S.B. 34), § 2(A), effective January 1, 1974; am. Acts 1993, 73rd Leg., ch. 900 (S.B. 1067), § 5.04, effective September 1, 1993.)

## Art. 43.015. Definitions.

In this chapter:

(1) "Capias" means a writ that is:

(A) issued by a court having jurisdiction of a case after judgment and sentence; and

(B) directed "To any peace officer of the State of Texas" and commanding the officer to arrest a person convicted of an offense and bring the arrested person before that court immediately or on a day or at a term stated in the writ.

(2) "Capias pro fine" means a writ that is:

(A) issued by a court having jurisdiction of a case after judgment and sentence for unpaid fines and costs; and

(B) directed "To any peace officer of the State of Texas" and commanding the officer to arrest a person convicted of an offense and bring the arrested person before that court immediately.

(Enacted by Acts 2007, 80th Leg., ch. 1263 (H.B. 3060), § 7, effective September 1, 2007.)

## Art. 43.02. Payable in Money.

All recognizances, bail bonds, and undertakings of any kind, whereby a party becomes bound to pay money to the State, and all fines and forfeitures of a pecuniary character, shall be collected in the lawful money of the United States only.

(Enacted by Acts 1965, 59th Leg., ch. 722 (S.B. 107), § 1, effective January 1, 1966.)

## Art. 43.021. Capias or Capias Pro Fine in Electronic Form.

A capias or capias pro fine may be issued in electronic form.

(Enacted by Acts 2007, 80th Leg., ch. 1263 (H.B. 3060), § 8, effective September 1, 2007.)

## Art. 43.03. Payment of Fine.

(a) If a defendant is sentenced to pay a fine or costs or both and the defendant defaults in payment, the court after a hearing under Subsection (d) of this article may order the defendant confined in jail until discharged as provided by law, may order the defendant to discharge the fines and costs in any other manner provided by Article 43.09 of this code, or may waive payment of the fines and costs as provided by Article 43.091. A certified copy of the judgment, sentence, and order is sufficient to authorize confinement under this subsection.

(b) A term of confinement for default in payment of fine or costs or both may not exceed the maximum term of confinement authorized for the offense for which the defendant was sentenced to pay the fine or costs or both. If a court orders a term of confinement for default in payment of fines or costs under this article at a time during which a defendant is serving another term of confinement for default or is serving a term of confinement for conviction of an offense, the term of confinement for default runs concurrently with the other term of confinement, unless the court orders the terms to run consecutively under Article 42.08 of this code.

(c) If a defendant is sentenced both to confinement and to pay a fine or costs or both, and he defaults in payment of either, a term of confinement for the default, when combined with the term of confinement already assessed, may not exceed the maximum term of confinement authorized for the offense for which the defendant was sentenced.

(d) A court may not order a defendant confined under Subsection (a) of this article unless the court at a hearing makes a written determination that:

(1) the defendant is not indigent and has failed to make a good faith effort to discharge the fines and costs; or

(2) the defendant is indigent and:

(A) has failed to make a good faith effort to discharge the fines and costs under Article 43.09(f); and

(B) could have discharged the fines and costs under Article 43.09 without experiencing any undue hardship.

(e) This article does not apply to a court governed by Chapter 45.

(f) For purposes of a hearing described by Subsection (d), a defendant may be brought before the court in person or by means of an electronic broadcast system through which an image of the defendant is presented to the court. For purposes of this subsection, "electronic broadcast system" means a two-way electronic communication of image and sound between the defendant and the court and includes secure Internet videoconferencing.

(Enacted by Acts 1965, 59th Leg., ch. 722 (S.B. 107), § 1, effective January 1, 1966; am. Acts 1971, 62nd Leg., ch. 987 (H.B. 887), § 2, effective June 15, 1971; am. Acts 1973, 63rd Leg., ch. 399 (S.B. 34), § 2(A), effective January 1, 1974; am. Acts 1993, 73rd Leg., ch. 900 (S.B. 1067), § 5.04, effective September 1, 1993; am. Acts 2001, 77th Leg., ch. 1111 (H.B. 2410), § 1, effective September 1, 2001; am. Acts 2007, 80th Leg., ch. 1263 (H.B. 3060), § 9, effective September 1, 2007; am. Acts 2009, 81st Leg., ch. 474 (S.B. 414), § 1, effective September 1, 2009.)

## Art. 43.04. If Defendant Is Absent.

When a judgment and sentence have been rendered against a defendant in the defendant's absence, the court may order a capias issued for the defendant's arrest. The sheriff shall execute the capias by bringing the defendant before the court or by placing the defendant in jail until the defendant can be brought before the court.

(Enacted by Acts 1965, 59th Leg., ch. 722 (S.B. 107), § 1, effective January 1, 1966; am. Acts 1971, 62nd Leg., ch. 987 (H.B. 887), § 3, effective June 15, 1971; am. Acts 2007, 80th Leg., ch. 1263 (H.B. 3060), § 10, effective September 1, 2007.)

## Art. 43.05. Capias Pro Fine Shall Recite.

(a) A capias pro fine issued for the arrest and commitment of a defendant convicted of a misdemeanor or felony, or found in contempt, the penalty for which includes a fine, shall recite the judgment and sentence and command a peace officer to immediately bring the defendant before the court.

(b) A capias pro fine authorizes a peace officer to place the defendant in jail until the business day following the date of the defendant's arrest if the defendant cannot be brought before the court immediately.

(Enacted by Acts 1965, 59th Leg., ch. 722 (S.B. 107), § 1, effective January 1, 1966; am. Acts 1971, 62nd Leg., ch. 987 (H.B. 887), § 4, effective June 15, 1971; am. Acts 2007, 80th Leg., ch. 1263 (H.B. 3060), § 11, effective September 1, 2007.)

## Art. 43.06. Capias or Capias Pro Fine May Issue to Any County.

A capias or capias pro fine may be issued to any county in the State, and shall be executed and returned as in other cases, but no bail shall be taken in such cases.

(Enacted by Acts 1965, 59th Leg., ch. 722 (S.B. 107), § 1, effective January 1, 1966; am. Acts 2007, 80th Leg., ch. 1263 (H.B. 3060), § 12, effective September 1, 2007.)

## Art. 43.07. Execution for Fine and Costs.

In each case of pecuniary fine, an execution may issue for the fine and costs, though a capias pro fine was issued for the defendant; and a capias pro fine may issue for the defendant though an execution was issued against the defendant's property. The execution shall be collected and returned as in civil actions. When the execution has been collected, the defendant shall be at once discharged; and whenever the fine and costs have been legally discharged in any way, the execution shall be returned satisfied.

(Enacted by Acts 1965, 59th Leg., ch. 722 (S.B. 107), § 1, effective January 1, 1966; am. Acts 2007, 80th Leg., ch. 1263 (H.B. 3060), § 13, effective September 1, 2007.)

## Art. 43.08. Further Enforcement of Judgment.

When a defendant has been committed to jail in default of the fine and costs adjudged against him, the further enforcement of such judgment and sentence shall be in accordance with the provisions of this Code.

(Enacted by Acts 1965, 59th Leg., ch. 722 (S.B. 107), § 1, effective January 1, 1966.)

## Art. 43.09. Fine Discharged.

(a) When a defendant is convicted of a misdemeanor and his punishment is assessed at a pecuniary fine or is confined in a jail after conviction of a felony for which a fine is imposed, if he is unable to pay the fine and costs adjudged against him, he may for such time as will satisfy the judgment be put to work in the county jail industries program, in the workhouse, or on the county farm, or public improvements and maintenance projects of the county or a political subdivision located in whole or in part in the county, as provided in the succeeding article; or if there be no such county jail industries program, workhouse, farm, or improvements and maintenance projects, he shall be confined in jail for a sufficient length of time to discharge the full amount of fine and costs adjudged against him; rating such confinement at $50 for each day and rating such labor at $50 for each day; provided, however, that the defendant may pay the pecuniary fine assessed against him at any time while he is serving at work in the county jail industries program, in the workhouse, or on the county farm, or on the public improvements and maintenance projects of the county or a political subdivision located in whole or in part in the county, or while he is serving his jail sentence, and in such instances he shall be entitled to the credit he has earned under this subsection during the time that he has served and he shall only be required to pay his balance of the pecuniary fine assessed against him. A defendant who performs labor under this article during a day in which he is confined is entitled to both the credit for confinement and the credit for labor provided by this article.

(b) In its discretion, the court may order that for each day's confinement served by a defendant under this article, the defendant receive credit toward payment of the pecuniary fine and credit toward payment of costs adjudged against the defendant. Additionally, the court may order that the defendant receive credit under this article for each day's confinement served by the defendant as punishment for the offense.

(c) In its discretion, the court may order that a defendant serving concurrent, but not consecutive, sentences for two or more misdemeanors may, for each day served, receive credit toward the satisfaction of costs and fines imposed for each separate offense.

(d) Notwithstanding any other provision of this article, in its discretion, the court or the sheriff of the county may grant an additional two days credit for each day served to any inmate participating in an approved work program under this article or a rehabilitation, restitution, or education program.

(e) A court in a county that operates an electronic monitoring program or contracts with a private vendor to operate an electronic monitoring program under Section 351.904, Local Government Code, or that is served by a community supervision and corrections department that operates an electronic monitoring program approved by the community justice assistance division of the Texas Department of Criminal Justice, may require a defendant who is unable to pay a fine or costs to discharge all or part of the fine or costs by participating in the program. A defendant who participates in an electronic monitoring program under this subsection discharges fines and costs in the same manner as if the defendant were confined in county jail.

(f) A court may require a defendant who is unable to pay a fine or costs to discharge all or part of the fine or costs by performing community service.

(g) In its order requiring a defendant to participate in community service work under Subsection (f) of this article, the court must specify:

(1) the number of hours the defendant is required to work; and

(2) whether the community supervision and corrections department or a court-related services office will perform the administrative duties required by the placement of the defendant in the community service program.

(h) The court may order the defendant to perform community service work under Subsection (f) of this article only for a governmental entity or a nonprofit organization that provides services to the general public that enhance social welfare and the general well-being of the community. A governmental entity or nonprofit organization that accepts a defendant under Subsection (f) of this article to perform community service must agree to supervise the defendant in the performance of the defendant's work and report on the defendant's work to the district probation department or court-related services office.

(i) The court may require bail of a defendant to ensure the defendant's faithful performance of community service under Subsection (f) of this article and may attach conditions to the bail as it determines are proper.

(j) A court may not order a defendant to perform more than 16 hours per week of community service under Subsection (f) of this article unless the court determines that requiring the defendant to work additional hours does not work a hardship on the defendant or the defendant's dependents.

(k) A defendant is considered to have discharged $100 of fines or costs for each eight hours of community service performed under Subsection (f) of this article.

(l) A sheriff, employee of a sheriff's department, county commissioner, county employee, county judge, an employee of a community corrections and supervision department, restitution center, or officer or employee of a political subdivision other than a county is not liable for damages arising from an act or failure to act in connection with manual labor performed by an inmate pursuant to this article if the act or failure to act:

(1) was performed pursuant to confinement or other court order; and

(2) was not intentional, wilfully or wantonly negligent, or performed with conscious indifference or reckless disregard for the safety of others.

(m) [Repealed by Acts 2007, 80th Leg., ch. 1263 (H.B. 3060), § 22, effective September 1, 2007.]

(n) This article does not apply to a court governed by Chapter 45.
(Enacted by Acts 1965, 59th Leg., ch. 722 (S.B. 107), § 1, effective January 1, 1966; am. Acts 1981, 67th Leg., ch. 143 (S.B. 430), § 1, effective May 14, 1981; am. Acts 1987, 70th Leg., ch. 347 (H.B. 631), § 1, effective September 1, 1987; am. Acts 1989, 71st Leg., ch. 753 (H.B. 1312), § 1, effective September 1, 1989; am. Acts 1989, 71st Leg., ch. 785 (H.B. 2335), § 4.13, effective September 1, 1989; am. Acts 1989, 71st Leg., ch. 1040 (H.B. 1779), §§ 3, 4, effective August 28, 1989;

am. Acts 1991, 72nd Leg., ch. 16 (S.B. 232), § 4.06, effective August 26, 1991; am. Acts 1991, 72nd Leg., ch. 900 (H.B. 154), § 1, effective August 26, 1991; am. Acts 1993, 73rd Leg., ch. 578 (H.B. 1056), § 2, effective June 11, 1993; am. Acts 1993, 73rd Leg., ch. 900 (S.B. 1067), § 5.04, effective September 1, 1993; am. Acts 1999, 76th Leg., ch. 1545 (S.B. 1230), § 3, effective September 1, 1999; am. Acts 2007, 80th Leg., ch. 1263 (H.B. 3060), §§ 14, 22, effective September 1, 2007; am. Acts 2009, 81st Leg., ch. 854 (S.B. 2340), § 2, effective June 19, 2009.)

## Art. 43.091. Waiver of Payment of Fines and Costs for Indigent Defendants.

A court may waive payment of a fine or cost imposed on a defendant who defaults in payment if the court determines that:

(1) the defendant is indigent; and

(2) each alternative method of discharging the fine or cost under Article 43.09 would impose an undue hardship on the defendant.
(Enacted by Acts 2001, 77th Leg., ch. 1111 (H.B. 2410), § 2, effective September 1, 2001; am. Acts 2007, 80th Leg., ch. 1263 (H.B. 3060), § 15, effective September 1, 2007.)

## Art. 43.10. Manual Labor.

Where the punishment assessed in a conviction for a misdemeanor is confinement in jail for more than one day or is only a pecuniary fine and the defendant is unable to pay the fine and costs adjudged against the defendant, or where the defendant is sentenced to jail for a felony or is confined in jail after conviction of a felony, the defendant shall be required to work in the county jail industries program or shall be required to do manual labor in accordance with the following rules and regulations:

1. Each commissioners court may provide for the erection of a workhouse and the establishment of a county farm in connection therewith for the purpose of utilizing the labor of defendants under this article;

2. Such farms and workhouses shall be under the control and management of the sheriff, and the sheriff may adopt such rules and regulations not inconsistent with the rules and regulations of the Commission on Jail Standards and with the laws as the sheriff deems necessary;

3. Such overseers and guards may be employed by the sheriff under the authority of the

commissioners court as may be necessary to prevent escapes and to enforce such labor, and they shall be paid out of the county treasury such compensation as the commissioners court may prescribe;

4. They shall be put to labor upon public works and maintenance projects, including public works and maintenance projects for a political subdivision located in whole or in part in the county. They may be put to labor upon maintenance projects for a cemetery that the commissioners court uses public funds, county employees, or county equipment to maintain under Section 713.028, Health and Safety Code. They may also be put to labor providing maintenance and related services to a nonprofit organization that qualifies for a tax exemption under Section 501(a), Internal Revenue Code of 1986, as an organization described by Section 501(c)(3) of that code, and is organized as a nonprofit corporation under the Texas Non-Profit Corporation Act (Article 1396-1.01 et seq., Vernon's Texas Civil Statutes), provided that, at the sheriff's request, the commissioners court determines that the nonprofit organization provides a public service to the county or to a political subdivision located in whole or in part in the county;

5. A defendant who from age, disease, or other physical or mental disability is unable to do manual labor shall not be required to work. The defendant's inability to do manual labor may be determined by a physician appointed for that purpose by the county judge or the commissioners court, who shall be paid for such service such compensation as said court may allow; and

6. For each day of manual labor, in addition to any other credits allowed by law, a defendant is entitled to have one day deducted from each sentence the defendant is serving.

(Enacted by Acts 1965, 59th Leg., ch. 722 (S.B. 107), § 1, effective January 1, 1966; am. Acts 1981, 67th Leg., ch. 708 (H.B. 647), § 1, effective August 31, 1981; am. Acts 1989, 71st Leg., ch. 753 (H.B. 1312), § 2, effective September 1, 1989; am. Acts 1989, 71st Leg., ch. 785 (H.B. 2335), § 4.14, effective September 1, 1989; am. Acts 1991, 72nd Leg., ch. 900 (H.B. 154), § 2, effective August 26, 1991; am. Acts 1991, 72nd Leg., 2nd C.S., ch. 10 (H.B. 93), § 14.09, effective October 1, 1991; am. Acts 1993, 73rd Leg., ch. 578 (H.B. 1056), § 3, effective June 11, 1993; am. Acts 1993, 73rd Leg., ch. 900 (S.B. 1067), § 5.04, effective September 1, 1993; am. Acts 1995, 74th Leg., ch. 76 (S.B. 959),

§ 3.19, effective September 1, 1995; am. Acts 1995, 74th Leg., ch. 321 (H.B. 2162), § 3.015, effective September 1, 1995; am. Acts 2005, 79th Leg., ch. 853 (S.B. 951), § 2, effective September 1, 2005; am. Acts 2005, 79th Leg., ch. 1187 (H.B. 129), § 1, effective June 18, 2005; am. Acts 2009, 81st Leg., ch. 854 (S.B. 2340), § 3, effective June 19, 2009.)

## Art. 43.101. Voluntary Work.

(a) A defendant who is confined in county jail before trial, after conviction of a misdemeanor, or after conviction of a felony or revocation of community supervision, parole, or mandatory supervision and awaiting transfer to the Texas Department of Criminal Justice may volunteer to participate in any work program operated by the sheriff that uses the labor of convicted defendants.

(b) The sheriff may accept a defendant as a volunteer under Subsection (a) if the defendant is not awaiting trial for an offense involving violence or is not awaiting transfer to the Texas Department of Criminal Justice after conviction of a felony involving violence, and if the sheriff determines that the inmate has not engaged previously in violent conduct and does not pose a security risk to the general public if allowed to participate in the work program.

(c) A defendant participating in a work program under this section is not an employee for the purposes of Chapter 501 or 504, Labor Code.

(d) For each day of volunteer work, in addition to any other credits allowed by law, the court or sheriff may deduct one day from each sentence imposed on the defendant in relation to the offense or violation of the terms of release for which the defendant was confined in county jail. (Enacted by Acts 1989, 71st Leg., ch. 753 (H.B. 1312), § 3, effective September 1, 1989; am. Acts 1993, 73rd Leg., ch. 86 (H.B. 864), § 1, effective August 30, 1993; am. Acts 1993, 73rd Leg., ch. 900 (S.B. 1067), § 5.04, effective September 1, 1993; am. Acts 1995, 74th Leg., ch. 76 (S.B. 959), § 3.20, effective September 1, 1995; am. Acts 2009, 81st Leg., ch. 87 (S.B. 1969), § 25.032, effective September 1, 2009; am. Acts 2009, 81st Leg., ch. 854 (S.B. 2340), § 4, effective June 19, 2009.)

## Art. 43.11. Authority for Confinement.

When, by the judgment and sentence of the court, a defendant is to be confined in jail, a certified copy of such judgment and sentence shall be sufficient authority for the sheriff to place such defendant in jail.

(Enacted by Acts 1965, 59th Leg., ch. 722 (S.B. 107), § 1, effective January 1, 1966; am. Acts 1993, 73rd Leg., ch. 900 (S.B. 1067), § 5.04, effective September 1, 1993.)

## Art. 43.12. Capias for Confinement [Repealed].

Repealed by Acts 2007, 80th Leg., ch. 1263 (H.B. 3060), § 22, effective September 1, 2007.

(Enacted by Acts 1965, 59th Leg., ch. 722 (S.B. 107), § 1, effective January 1, 1966; am. Acts 1993, 73rd Leg., ch. 900 (S.B. 1067), § 5.04, effective September 1, 1993.)

## Art. 43.13. Discharge of Defendant.

(a) A defendant who has remained in jail the length of time required by the judgment and sentence shall be discharged. The sheriff shall return the copy of the judgment and sentence, or the capias under which the defendant was imprisoned, to the proper court, stating how it was executed.

(b) A defendant convicted of a misdemeanor and sentenced to a term of confinement of more than 30 days discharges the defendant's sentence at any time between the hours of 6 a.m. and 7 p.m. on the day of discharge.

(Enacted by Acts 1965, 59th Leg., ch. 722 (S.B. 107), § 1, effective January 1, 1966; am. Acts 1997, 75th Leg., ch. 714 (H.B. 126), § 1, effective September 1, 1997.)

## Art. 43.131. Immunities.

(a) An individual listed in Subsection (c) of this article and the governmental entity that the individual serves as an officer or employee are not liable for damages arising from an act or failure to act by the individual or governmental entity in connection with a community service program or work program established under this chapter if the act or failure to act:

(1) was performed pursuant to a court order or was otherwise performed in an official capacity; and

(2) was not performed with conscious indifference for the safety of others.

(b) Chapter 101, Civil Practice and Remedies Code, does not apply to a claim based on an act or a failure to act of an individual listed in Subsection (c) of this article or a governmental entity the officer serves as an officer or employee if the act or failure to act is in connection with a program described by Subsection (a) of this article.

(c) This article applies to:

(1) a director or employee of a community supervision and corrections department or a community corrections facility;

(2) a sheriff or employee of a sheriff's department;

(3) a county judge, county commissioner, or county employee;

(4) an officer or employee of a state agency; or

(5) an officer or employee of a political subdivision other than a county.

(Enacted by Acts 1993, 73rd Leg., ch. 900 (S.B. 1067), § 5.04, effective September 1, 1993.)

## Art. 43.14. Execution of Convict.

Whenever the sentence of death is pronounced against a convict, the sentence shall be executed at any time after the hour of 6 p.m. on the day set for the execution, by intravenous injection of a substance or substances in a lethal quantity sufficient to cause death and until such convict is dead, such execution procedure to be determined and supervised by the director of the correctional institutions division of the Texas Department of Criminal Justice.

(Enacted by Acts 1965, 59th Leg., ch. 722 (S.B. 107), § 1, effective January 1, 1966; am. Acts 1977, 65th Leg., ch. 138 (H.B. 945), § 1, effective August 29, 1977; am. Acts 1981, 67th Leg., ch. 291 (S.B. 265), § 120, effective September 1, 1981; am. Acts 1991, 72nd Leg., ch. 652 (H.B. 9), § 11, effective September 1, 1991; am. Acts 1995, 74th Leg., ch. 319 (S.B. 440), § 3, effective September 1, 1995; am. Acts 2009, 81st Leg., ch. 87 (S.B. 1969), § 25.033, effective September 1, 2009.)

## Art. 43.141. Scheduling of Execution Date; Withdrawal; Modification.

(a) If an initial application under Article 11.071 is timely filed, the convicting court may not set an execution date before:

(1) the court of criminal appeals denies relief; or

(2) if the case is filed and set for submission, the court of criminal appeals issues a mandate.

(b) If an original application is not timely filed under Article 11.071 or good cause is not shown for an untimely application under Article 11.071, the convicting court may set an execution date.

(c) The first execution date may not be earlier than the 91st day after the date the convicting court enters the order setting the execution date.

A subsequent execution date may not be earlier than the 31st day after the date the convicting court enters the order setting the execution date.

(d) The convicting court may modify or withdraw the order of the court setting a date for execution in a death penalty case if the court determines that additional proceedings are necessary on:

(1) a subsequent or untimely application for a writ of habeas corpus filed under Article 11.071; or

(2) a motion for forensic testing of DNA evidence submitted under Chapter 64.

(e) If the convicting court withdraws the order of the court setting the execution date, the court shall recall the warrant of execution. If the court modifies the order of the court setting the execution date, the court shall recall the previous warrant of execution, and the clerk of the court shall issue a new warrant.

(Enacted by Acts 1995, 74th Leg., ch. 319 (S.B. 440), § 4, effective September 1, 1995; am. Acts 2003, 78th Leg., ch. 13 (H.B. 1011), § 6, effective September 1, 2003.)

### Art. 43.15. Warrant of Execution.

Whenever any person is sentenced to death, the clerk of the court in which the sentence is pronounced, shall within ten days after the court enters its order setting the date for execution, issue a warrant under the seal of the court for the execution of the sentence of death, which shall recite the fact of conviction, setting forth specifically the offense, the judgment of the court, the time fixed for his execution, and directed to the Director of the Department of Corrections at Huntsville, Texas, commanding him to proceed, at the time and place named in the order of execution, to carry the same into execution, as provided in the preceding Article, and shall deliver such warrant to the sheriff of the county in which such judgment of conviction was had, to be by him delivered to the said Director of the Department of Corrections, together with the condemned person if he has not previously been so delivered.

(Enacted by Acts 1965, 59th Leg., ch. 722 (S.B. 107), § 1, effective January 1, 1966; am. Acts 1981, 67th Leg., ch. 291 (S.B. 265), § 121, effective September 1, 1981.)

### Art. 43.16. Taken to Department of Corrections.

Immediately upon the receipt of such warrant, the sheriff shall transport such condemned person to the Director of the Department of Corrections, if he has not already been so delivered, and shall deliver him and the warrant aforesaid into the hands of the Director of the Department of Corrections and shall take from the Director of the Department of Corrections his receipt for such person and such warrant, which receipt the sheriff shall return to the office of the clerk of the court where the judgment of death was rendered. For his services, the sheriff shall be entitled to the same compensation as is now allowed by law to sheriffs for removing or conveying prisoners under the provisions of Section 4 of Article 1029 or 1030 of the Code of Criminal Procedure of 1925, as amended.

(Enacted by Acts 1965, 59th Leg., ch. 722 (S.B. 107), § 1, effective January 1, 1966; am. Acts 1981, 67th Leg., ch. 291 (S.B. 265), § 122, effective September 1, 1981.)

### Art. 43.17. Visitors.

Upon the receipt of such condemned person by the Director of the Department of Corrections, the condemned person shall be confined therein until the time for his or her execution arrives, and while so confined, all persons outside of said prison shall be denied access to him or her, except his or her physician, lawyer, and clergyperson, who shall be admitted to see him or her when necessary for his or her health or for the transaction of business, and the relatives and friends of the condemned person, who shall be admitted to see and converse with him or her at all proper times, under such reasonable rules and regulations as may be made by the Board of Directors of the Department of Corrections.

(Enacted by Acts 1965, 59th Leg., ch. 722 (S.B. 107), § 1, effective January 1, 1966; am. Acts 1979, 66th Leg., ch. 572 (H.B. 2118), § 1, effective August 27, 1979.)

### Art. 43.18. Executioner.

The director of the Texas Department of Criminal Justice shall designate an executioner to carry out the death penalty provided by law.

(Enacted by Acts 1965, 59th Leg., ch. 722 (S.B. 107), § 1, effective January 1, 1966; am. Acts 1975, 64th Leg., ch. 341 (S.B. 122), § 6, effective June 19, 1975; am. Acts 1977, 65th Leg., ch. 138 (H.B. 945), § 2, effective August 29, 1977; am. Acts 2009, 81st Leg., ch. 87 (S.B. 1969), § 25.034, effective September 1, 2009.)

Criminal Procedure

## Art. 43.19. Place of Execution.

The execution shall take place at a location designated by the Texas Department of Criminal Justice in a room arranged for that purpose.
(Enacted by Acts 1965, 59th Leg., ch. 722 (S.B. 107), § 1, effective January 1, 1966; am. Acts 1985, 69th Leg., ch. 250 (H.B. 667), § 1, effective August 26, 1985; am. Acts 2009, 81st Leg., ch. 87 (S.B. 1969), § 25.035, effective September 1, 2009.)

## Art. 43.20. Present at Execution.

The following persons may be present at the execution: the executioner, and such persons as may be necessary to assist him in conducting the execution; the Board of Directors of the Department of Corrections, two physicians, including the prison physician, the spiritual advisor of the condemned, the chaplains of the Department of Corrections, the county judge and sheriff of the county in which the Department of Corrections is situated, and any of the relatives or friends of the condemned person that he may request, not exceeding five in number, shall be admitted. No convict shall be permitted by the prison authorities to witness the execution.
(Enacted by Acts 1965, 59th Leg., ch. 722 (S.B. 107), § 1, effective January 1, 1966.)

## Art. 43.21. Escape After Sentence.

If the condemned escape after sentence and before his delivery to the Director of the Department of Corrections, and be not rearrested until after the time fixed for execution, any person may arrest and commit him to the jail of the county in which he was sentenced; and thereupon the court by whom the condemned was sentenced; either in term-time or vacation, on notice of such arrest being given by the sheriff, shall again appoint a time for the execution, not less than thirty days from such appointment, which appointment shall be by the clerk of said court immediately certified to the Director of the Department of Corrections and such clerk shall place such certificate in the hands of the sheriff, who shall deliver the same, together with the warrant aforesaid and the condemned person to the Director of the Department of Corrections, who shall receipt to the sheriff for the same and proceed at the appointed time to carry the sentence of death into execution as hereinabove provided.
(Enacted by Acts 1965, 59th Leg., ch. 722 (S.B. 107), § 1, effective January 1, 1966.)

## Art. 43.22. Escape from Department of Corrections.

If the condemned person escapes after his delivery to the Director of the Department of Corrections, and is not retaken before the time appointed for his execution, any person may arrest and commit him to the Director of the Department of Corrections whereupon the Director of the Department of Corrections shall certify the fact of his escape and recapture to the court in which sentence was passed; and the court, either in term-time or vacation, shall again appoint a time for the execution which shall not be less than thirty days from the date of such appointment; and thereupon the clerk of such court shall certify such appointment to the Director of the Department of Corrections, who shall proceed at the time so appointed to execute the condemned, as hereinabove provided. The sheriff or other officer or other person performing any service under this and the preceding Article shall receive the same compensation as is provided for similar services under the provisions of Articles 1029 or 1030 of the Code of Criminal Procedure of 1925, as amended. If for any reason execution is delayed beyond the date set, then the court which originally sentenced the defendant may set a later date for execution.
(Enacted by Acts 1965, 59th Leg., ch. 722 (S.B. 107), § 1, effective January 1, 1966.)

## Art. 43.23. Return of Director.

When the execution of sentence is suspended or respited to another date, same shall be noted on the warrant and on the arrival of such date, the Director of the Department of Corrections shall proceed with such execution; and in case of death of any condemned person before the time for his execution arrives, or if he should be pardoned or his sentence commuted by the Governor, no execution shall be had; but in such cases, as well as when the sentence is executed, the Director of the Department of Corrections shall return the warrant and certificate with a statement of any such act and his proceedings endorsed thereon, together with a statement showing what disposition was made of the dead body of the convict, to the clerk of the court in which the sentence was passed, who shall record the warrant and return in the minutes of the court.
(Enacted by Acts 1965, 59th Leg., ch. 722 (S.B. 107), § 1, effective January 1, 1966.)

Criminal Procedure

## Art. 43.24. Treatment of Condemned.

No torture, or ill treatment, or unnecessary pain, shall be inflicted upon a prisoner to be executed under the sentence of the law.
(Enacted by Acts 1965, 59th Leg., ch. 722 (S.B. 107), § 1, effective January 1, 1966.)

## Art. 43.25. Body of Convict.

The body of a convict who has been legally executed shall be embalmed immediately and so directed by the Director of the Department of Corrections. If the body is not demanded or requested by a relative or bona fide friend within forty-eight hours after execution then it shall be delivered to the Anatomical Board of the State of Texas, if requested by the Board. If the body is requested by a relative, bona fide friend, or the Anatomical Board of the State of Texas, such recipient shall pay a fee of not to exceed twenty-five dollars to the mortician for his services in embalming the body for which the mortician shall issue to the recipient a written receipt. When such receipt is delivered to the Director of the Department of Corrections, the body of the deceased shall be delivered to the party named in the receipt or his authorized agent. If the body is not delivered to a relative, bona fide friend, or the Anatomical Board of the State of Texas, the Director of the Department of Corrections shall cause the body to be decently buried, and the fee for embalming shall be paid by the county in which the indictment which resulted in conviction was found.
(Enacted by Acts 1965, 59th Leg., ch. 722 (S.B. 107), § 1, effective January 1, 1966.)

## Art. 43.26. Preventing Rescue.

The sheriff may, when he supposes there will be a necessity, order such number of citizens of his county, or request any military or militia company, to aid in preventing the rescue of a prisoner.
(Enacted by Acts 1965, 59th Leg., ch. 722 (S.B. 107), § 1, effective January 1, 1966.)

# Appeal and Writ of Error

## CHAPTER 44
## APPEAL AND WRIT OF ERROR

## Art. 44.01. Appeal by State.

(a) The state is entitled to appeal an order of a court in a criminal case if the order:

(1) dismisses an indictment, information, or complaint or any portion of an indictment, information, or complaint;

(2) arrests or modifies a judgment;

(3) grants a new trial;

(4) sustains a claim of former jeopardy;

(5) grants a motion to suppress evidence, a confession, or an admission, if jeopardy has not attached in the case and if the prosecuting attorney certifies to the trial court that the appeal is not taken for the purpose of delay and that the evidence, confession, or admission is of substantial importance in the case; or

(6) is issued under Chapter 64.

(b) The state is entitled to appeal a sentence in a case on the ground that the sentence is illegal.

(c) The state is entitled to appeal a ruling on a question of law if the defendant is convicted in the case and appeals the judgment.

(d) The prosecuting attorney may not make an appeal under Subsection (a) or (b) of this article later than the 20th day after the date on which the order, ruling, or sentence to be appealed is entered by the court.

(e) The state is entitled to a stay in the proceedings pending the disposition of an appeal under Subsection (a) or (b) of this article.

(f) The court of appeals shall give precedence in its docket to an appeal filed under Subsection (a) or (b) of this article. The state shall pay all costs of appeal under Subsection (a) or (b) of this article, other than the cost of attorney's fees for the defendant.

(g) If the state appeals pursuant to this article and the defendant is on bail, he shall be permitted to remain at large on the existing bail. If the defendant is in custody, he is entitled to reasonable bail, as provided by law, unless the appeal is from an order which would terminate the prosecution, in which event the defendant is entitled to release on personal bond.

(h) The Texas Rules of Appellate Procedure apply to a petition by the state to the Court of Criminal Appeals for review of a decision of a court of appeals in a criminal case.

(i) In this article, "prosecuting attorney" means the county attorney, district attorney, or criminal district attorney who has the primary responsibility of prosecuting cases in the court hearing the case and does not include an assistant prosecuting attorney.

(j) Nothing in this article is to interfere with the defendant's right to appeal under the procedures of Article 44.02 of this code. The defendant's right to appeal under Article 44.02 may be prosecuted by the defendant where the punishment assessed is in accordance with Subsection (a), Section 3d, Article 42.12 of this code, as well as any other punishment assessed in compliance with Article 44.02 of this code.

(k) The state is entitled to appeal an order granting relief to an applicant for a writ of habeas corpus under Article 11.072.

(*l*) The state is entitled to appeal an order entered under:

    (1) Subchapter G or H, Chapter 62, that exempts a person from complying with the requirements of Chapter 62; and

    (2) Subchapter I, Chapter 62, that terminates a person's obligation to register under Chapter 62.

(Enacted by Acts 1965, 59th Leg., ch. 722 (S.B. 107), § 1, effective January 1, 1966; am. Acts 1981, 67th Leg., ch. 291 (S.B. 265), § 123, effective September 1, 1981; am. Acts 1987, 70th Leg., ch. 382 (S.B. 762), § 1; am. Acts 2003, 78th Leg., ch. 13 (H.B. 1011), § 7, effective September 1, 2003; am. Acts 2003, 78th Leg., ch. 587 (H.B. 1713), § 2, effective June 20, 2003; am. Acts

2005, 79th Leg., ch. 1008 (H.B. 867), § 1.04, effective September 1, 2005; am. Acts 2007, 80th Leg., ch. 1038 (H.B. 1801), § 2, effective September 1, 2007.)

## Art. 44.02. Defendant May Appeal.

A defendant in any criminal action has the right of appeal under the rules hereinafter prescribed, provided, however, before the defendant who has been convicted upon either his plea of guilty or plea of nolo contendere before the court and the court, upon the election of the defendant, assesses punishment and the punishment does not exceed the punishment recommended by the prosecutor and agreed to by the defendant and his attorney may prosecute his appeal, he must have permission of the trial court, except on those matters which have been raised by written motion filed prior to trial. This article in no way affects appeals pursuant to Article 44.17 of this chapter.

(Enacted by Acts 1965, 59th Leg., ch. 722 (S.B. 107), § 1, effective January 1, 1966; am. Acts 1977, 65th Leg., ch. 351 (S.B. 334), § 1, effective August 29, 1977.)

## Art. 44.04. Bond Pending Appeal.

(a) Pending the determination of any motion for new trial or the appeal from any misdemeanor conviction, the defendant is entitled to be released on reasonable bail.

(b) The defendant may not be released on bail pending the appeal from any felony conviction where the punishment equals or exceeds 10 years confinement or where the defendant has been convicted of an offense listed under Section 3g(a)(1), Article 42.12, but shall immediately be placed in custody and the bail discharged.

(c) Pending the appeal from any felony conviction other than a conviction described in Subsection (b) of this section, the trial court may deny bail and commit the defendant to custody if there then exists good cause to believe that the defendant would not appear when his conviction became final or is likely to commit another offense while on bail, permit the defendant to remain at large on the existing bail, or, if not then on bail, admit him to reasonable bail until his conviction becomes final. The court may impose reasonable conditions on bail pending the finality of his conviction. On a finding by the court on a preponderance of the evidence of a violation of a condition, the court may revoke the bail.

(d) After conviction, either pending determination of any motion for new trial or pending final determination of the appeal, the court in which trial was had may increase or decrease the amount of bail, as it deems proper, either upon its own motion or the motion of the State or of the defendant.

(e) Any bail entered into after conviction and the sureties on the bail must be approved by the court where trial was had. Bail is sufficient if it substantially meets the requirements of this code and may be entered into and given at any term of court.

(f) In no event shall the defendant and the sureties on his bond be released from their liability on such bond or bonds until the defendant is placed in the custody of the sheriff.

(g) The right of appeal to the Court of Appeals of this state is expressly accorded the defendant for a review of any judgment or order made hereunder, and said appeal shall be given preference by the appellate court.

(h) If a conviction is reversed by a decision of a Court of Appeals, the defendant, if in custody, is entitled to release on reasonable bail, regardless of the length of term of imprisonment, pending final determination of an appeal by the state or the defendant on a motion for discretionary review. If the defendant requests bail before a petition for discretionary review has been filed, the Court of Appeals shall determine the amount of bail. If the defendant requests bail after a petition for discretionary review has been filed, the Court of Criminal Appeals shall determine the amount of bail. The sureties on the bail must be approved by the court where the trial was had. The defendant's right to release under this subsection attaches immediately on the issuance of the Court of Appeals' final ruling as defined by Tex.Cr.App.R. 209(c).

(Enacted by Acts 1965, 59th Leg., ch. 722 (S.B. 107), § 1, effective January 1, 1966; am. Acts 1977, 65th Leg., ch. 234 (S.B. 52), § 1, effective August 29, 1977; am. Acts 1981, 67th Leg., ch. 268 (H.B. 730), § 17, effective September 1, 1981; am. Acts 1981, 67th Leg., ch. 291 (S.B. 265), § 125, effective September 1, 1981; am. Acts 1983, 68th Leg., ch. 249 (S.B. 613), § 2, effective August 29, 1983; am. Acts 1983, 68th Leg., ch. 425 (H.B. 1191), § 26, effective August 29, 1983; am. Acts 1985, 69th Leg., ch. 968 (H.B. 44), § 1, effective August 26, 1985; am. Acts 1999, 76th Leg., ch. 546 (S.B. 306), § 1, effective September 1, 1999; am. Acts 2003, 78th Leg., ch. 942 (S.B. 1336), § 3, effective June 20, 2003.)

## Art. 44.041. Conditions in Lieu of Bond.

(a) If a defendant is confined in county jail pending appeal and is eligible for release on bond pending appeal but is financially unable to make bond, the court may release the defendant without bond pending the conclusion of the appeal only if the court determines that release under this article is reasonable given the circumstances of the defendant's offense and the sentence imposed.

(b) A court that releases a defendant under this article must require the defendant to participate in a program under Article 42.033, 42.034, 42.035, or 42.036 during the pendency of the appeal. A defendant required to participate in a program may receive credit toward completion of the defendant's sentence while participating in the program in the same manner and to the same extent provided by Article 42.033, 42.034, 42.035, or 42.036, as applicable.

(Enacted by Acts 1989, 71st Leg., ch. 785 (H.B. 2335), § 4.15, effective September 1, 1989; am. Acts 2009, 81st Leg., ch. 854 (S.B. 2340), § 5, effective June 19, 2009.)

## Art. 44.05. Receipt of Mandate [Repealed].

Repealed by Acts 1985, 69th Leg., ch. 685 (H.B. 13), § 4, effective September 1, 1986.

## Art. 44.06. Capias May Issue to Any County [Repealed].

Repealed by Acts 1985, 69th Leg., ch. 685 (H.B. 13), § 4, effective September 1, 1986.

## Art. 44.07. Right of Appeal Not Abridged.

The right of appeal, as otherwise provided by law, shall in no wise be abridged by any provision of this Chapter.

(Enacted by Acts 1965, 59th Leg., ch. 722 (S.B. 107), § 1, effective January 1, 1966.)

## Art. 44.10. Sheriff to Report Escape.

When any such escape occurs, the sheriff who had the prisoner in custody shall immediately report the fact under oath to the district or county attorney of the county in which the conviction was had, who shall forthwith forward such report to the State prosecuting attorney. Such report shall be sufficient evidence of the fact of such escape to authorize the dismissal of the appeal.

(Enacted by Acts 1965, 59th Leg., ch. 722 (S.B. 107), § 1, effective January 1, 1966.)

## Art. 44.12. Procedure As to Bail Pending Appeal.

The amount of any bail given in any felony or misdemeanor case to perfect an appeal from any court to the Court of Appeals shall be fixed by the court in which the judgment or order appealed from was rendered. The sufficiency of the security thereon shall be tested, and the same proceedings had in case of forfeiture, as in other cases regarding bail.

(Enacted by Acts 1965, 59th Leg., ch. 722 (S.B. 107), § 1, effective January 1, 1966; am. Acts 1981, 67th Leg., ch. 291 (S.B. 265), § 130, effective September 1, 1981.)

## Art. 44.13. [Repealed].

Repealed by Acts 1999, 76th Leg., ch. 1545 (S.B. 1230), § 75(a), effective September 1, 1999. (Enacted by Acts 1965, 59th Leg., ch. 722 (S.B. 107), § 1, effective January 1, 1966; am. Acts 1979, 66th Leg., ch. 207 (S.B. 518), § 2, effective September 1, 1979; am. Acts 1981, 67th Leg., ch. 443 (H.B. 1745), § 1, effective September 1, 1981.)

## Art. 44.14. [Renumbered].

Renumbered to Tex. Code Crim Proc. art. 45.0426 by Acts 1999, 76th Leg., ch. 1545 (S.B. 1230), § 42, effective September 1, 1999.

## Art. 44.15. Appellate Court May Allow New Bond.

When an appeal is taken from any court of this State, by filing a bond within the time prescribed by law in such cases, and the court to which appeal is taken determines that such bond is defective in form or substance, such appellate court may allow the appellant to amend such bond by filing a new bond, on such terms as the court may prescribe.

(Enacted by Acts 1965, 59th Leg., ch. 722 (S.B. 107), § 1, effective January 1, 1966.)

## Art. 44.16. Appeal Bond Given Within What Time.

If the defendant is not in custody, a notice of appeal as provided in Article 44.13 shall have no effect whatever until the required appeal bond has been given and approved. The appeal bond shall be given within ten days after the sentence of the court has been rendered, except as provided in Article 27.14 of this code.

(Enacted by Acts 1965, 59th Leg., ch. 722 (S.B. 107), § 1, effective January 1, 1966; am. Acts 1979, 66th Leg., ch. 207 (S.B. 518), § 3, effective September 1, 1979.)

## Art. 44.17. Appeal to County Court, How Conducted.

In all appeals to a county court from justice courts and municipal courts other than municipal courts of record, the trial shall be de novo in the trial in the county court, the same as if the prosecution had been originally commenced in that court. An appeal to the county court from a municipal court of record may be based only on errors reflected in the record.

(Enacted by Acts 1965, 59th Leg., ch. 722 (S.B. 107), § 1, effective January 1, 1966; am. Acts 1987, 70th Leg., ch. 641 (H.B. 2220), § 3, effective September 1, 1987.)

## Art. 44.18. Original Papers Sent Up.

In appeals from justice and corporation courts, all the original papers in the case, together with the appeal bond, if any, and together, with a certified transcript of all the proceedings had in the case before such court shall be delivered without delay to the clerk of the court to which the appeal was taken, who shall file the same and docket the case.

(Enacted by Acts 1965, 59th Leg., ch. 722 (S.B. 107), § 1, effective January 1, 1966.)

## Art. 44.181. Defect in Complaint.

(a) A court conducting a trial de novo based on an appeal from a justice or municipal court may dismiss the case because of a defect in the complaint only if the defendant objected to the defect before the trial began in the justice or municipal court.

(b) The attorney representing the state may move to amend a defective complaint before the trial de novo begins.

(Enacted by Acts 1995, 74th Leg., ch. 478 (S.B. 918), § 2, effective September 1, 1995; am. Acts 1999, 76th Leg., ch. 1545 (S.B. 1230), § 4, effective September 1, 1999.)

## Art. 44.19. Witnesses Not Again Summoned.

In the cases mentioned in the preceding Article, the witnesses who have been summoned or attached to appear in the case before the court below, shall appear before the court to which the appeal is taken without further process. In case of

their failure to do so, the same proceedings may be had as if they had been originally summoned or attached to appear before such court.
(Enacted by Acts 1965, 59th Leg., ch. 722 (S.B. 107), § 1, effective January 1, 1966.)

## Art. 44.20. Rules Governing Appeal Bonds.

The rules governing the taking and forfeiture of bail shall govern appeal bonds, and the forfeiture and collection of such appeal bonds shall be in the court to which such appeal is taken.
(Enacted by Acts 1965, 59th Leg., ch. 722 (S.B. 107), § 1, effective January 1, 1966.)

## Arts. 44.21 to 44.24. [Repealed].

## Art. 44.25. Cases Remanded.

The courts of appeals or the Court of Criminal Appeals may reverse the judgment in a criminal action, as well upon the law as upon the facts.
(Enacted by Acts 1965, 59th Leg., ch. 722 (S.B. 107), § 1, effective January 1, 1966; am. Acts 1981, 67th Leg., ch. 291 (S.B. 265), § 134, effective September 1, 1981.)

## Art. 44.251. Reformation of Sentence in Capital Case.

(a) The court of criminal appeals shall reform a sentence of death to a sentence of confinement in the Texas Department of Criminal Justice for life without parole if the court finds that there is legally insufficient evidence to support an affirmative answer to an issue submitted to the jury under Section 2(b), Article 37.071, or Section 2(b), Article 37.072.

(b) The court of criminal appeals shall reform a sentence of death to a sentence of confinement in the Texas Department of Criminal Justice for life without parole if:

(1) the court finds reversible error that affects the punishment stage of the trial other than a finding of insufficient evidence under Subsection (a); and

(2) within 30 days after the date on which the opinion is handed down, the date the court disposes of a timely request for rehearing, or the date that the United States Supreme Court disposes of a timely filed petition for writ of certiorari, whichever date is later, the prosecuting attorney files a motion requesting that the sentence be reformed to confinement for life without parole.

(c) If the court of criminal appeals finds reversible error that affects the punishment stage of the

trial only, as described by Subsection (b) of this article, and the prosecuting attorney does not file a motion for reformation of sentence in the period described by that subsection, the defendant shall receive a new sentencing trial in the manner required by Article 44.29(c) or (d), as applicable.

(d) The court of criminal appeals shall reform a sentence of death imposed under Section 12.42(c)(3), Penal Code, to a sentence of imprisonment in the Texas Department of Criminal Justice for life without parole if the United States Supreme Court:

(1) finds that the imposition of the death penalty under Section 12.42(c)(3), Penal Code, violates the United States Constitution; and

(2) issues an order that is not inconsistent with this article.

(Enacted by Acts 1981, 67th Leg., ch. 725 (H.B. 1164), § 2, effective August 31, 1981; am. Acts 1991, 72nd Leg., ch. 838 (S.B. 880), § 3, effective September 1, 1991; am. Acts 1993, 73rd Leg., ch. 781 (H.B. 798), § 3, effective August 30, 1993; am. Acts 2005, 79th Leg., ch. 787 (S.B. 60), § 10, effective September 1, 2005; am. Acts 2007, 80th Leg., ch. 593 (H.B. 8), § 3.18, effective September 1, 2007; am. Acts 2009, 81st Leg., ch. 87 (S.B. 1969), § 25.036, effective September 1, 2009.)

## Art. 44.2511. Reformation of Sentence in Capital Case for Offense Committed Before September 1, 1991.

(a) This article applies to the reformation of a sentence of death in a capital case for an offense committed before September 1, 1991. For purposes of this subsection, an offense is committed before September 1, 1991, if every element of the offense occurred before that date.

(b) The court of criminal appeals shall reform a sentence of death to a sentence of confinement in the Texas Department of Criminal Justice for life if the court finds that there is legally insufficient evidence to support an affirmative answer to an issue submitted to the jury under Section 3(b), Article 37.0711.

(c) The court of criminal appeals shall reform a sentence of death to a sentence of confinement in the Texas Department of Criminal Justice for life if:

(1) the court finds reversible error that affects the punishment stage of the trial other than a finding of insufficient evidence under Subsection (b); and

(2) within 30 days after the date on which the opinion is handed down, the date the court

disposes of a timely request for rehearing, or the date that the United States Supreme Court disposes of a timely filed petition for writ of certiorari, whichever date is later, the prosecuting attorney files a motion requesting that the sentence be reformed to confinement for life.

(d) If the court of criminal appeals finds reversible error that affects the punishment stage of the trial only, as described by Subsection (c), and the prosecuting attorney does not file a motion for reformation of sentence in the period described by that subsection, the defendant shall receive a new sentencing trial in the manner required by Article 44.29(c).

(Enacted by Acts 2005, 79th Leg., ch. 787 (S.B. 60), § 11, effective September 1, 2005; am. Acts 2009, 81st Leg., ch. 87 (S.B. 1969), § 25.037, effective September 1, 2009.)

## Art. 44.28. When Misdemeanor Is Affirmed.

In misdemeanor cases where there has been an affirmance, no proceedings need be had after filing the mandate, except to forfeit the bond of the defendant, or to issue a capias for the defendant, or an execution against his property, to enforce the judgment of the court, as if no appeal had been taken.

(Enacted by Acts 1965, 59th Leg., ch. 722 (S.B. 107), § 1, effective January 1, 1966.)

## Art. 44.281. Disposition of Fines and Costs When Misdemeanor Affirmed.

In misdemeanor cases affirmed on appeal from a municipal court, the fine imposed on appeal and the costs imposed on appeal shall be collected from the defendant, and the fine of the municipal court when collected shall be paid into the municipal treasury.

(Enacted by Acts 1965, 59th Leg., ch. 722 (S.B. 107), § 1, effective January 1, 1966; am. Acts 1999, 76th Leg., ch. 1545 (S.B. 1230), § 65, effective September 1, 1999 (renumbered from art. 45.11).)

## Art. 44.2811. Records Relating to Children Convicted of Fine-Only Misdemeanors.

All records and files and information stored by electronic means or otherwise, from which a record or file could be generated, relating to a child who is convicted of and has satisfied the judgment for a fine-only misdemeanor offense other than a traffic offense are confidential and may not be disclosed to the public except as provided under Article 45.0217(b). All records and files and information stored by electronic means or otherwise, from which a record or file could be generated, relating to a child whose conviction for a fine-only misdemeanor other than a traffic offense is affirmed are confidential upon satisfaction of the judgment and may not be disclosed to the public except as provided under Article 45.0217(b).

(Enacted by Acts 2011, 82nd Leg., ch. 731 (H.B. 961), § 1, effective June 17, 2011.)

## Art. 44.29. Effect of Reversal.

(a) Where the court of appeals or the Court of Criminal Appeals awards a new trial to the defendant on the basis of an error in the guilt or innocence stage of the trial or on the basis of errors in both the guilt or innocence stage of the trial and the punishment stage of the trial, the cause shall stand as it would have stood in case the new trial had been granted by the court below.

(b) If the court of appeals or the Court of Criminal Appeals awards a new trial to a defendant other than a defendant convicted of an offense under Section 19.03, Penal Code, only on the basis of an error or errors made in the punishment stage of the trial, the cause shall stand as it would have stood in case the new trial had been granted by the court below, except that the court shall commence the new trial as if a finding of guilt had been returned and proceed to the punishment stage of the trial under Subsection (b), Section 2, Article 37.07, of this code. If the defendant elects, the court shall empanel a jury for the sentencing stage of the trial in the same manner as a jury is empaneled by the court for other trials before the court. At the new trial, the court shall allow both the state and the defendant to introduce evidence to show the circumstances of the offense and other evidence as permitted by Section 3 of Article 37.07 of this code.

(c) If any court sets aside or invalidates the sentence of a defendant convicted of an offense under Section 19.03, Penal Code, and sentenced to death on the basis of any error affecting punishment only, the court shall not set the conviction aside but rather shall commence a new punishment hearing under Article 37.071 or Article 37.0711 of this code, as appropriate, as if a finding of guilt had been returned. The court shall empanel a jury for the sentencing stage of the trial in the same manner as a jury is to be empaneled by the court in other trials before the court for offenses under Section 19.03, Penal Code. At the new punishment hearing, the court shall permit both the state and the defendant to introduce evidence as permitted by Article 37.071 or Article 37.0711 of this code.

(d) If any court sets aside or invalidates the sentence of a defendant convicted of an offense punishable as a capital felony under Section 12.42(c)(3), Penal Code, and sentenced to death on the basis of any error affecting punishment only, the court shall not set the conviction aside but rather shall commence a new punishment hearing under Article 37.072, as if a finding of guilt had been returned. The court shall empanel a jury for the sentencing stage of the trial in the same manner as a jury is to be empaneled by the court in other trials before the court for the offense of which the defendant was convicted. At the new punishment hearing, the court shall permit both the state and the defendant to introduce evidence as permitted by Article 37.072.
(Enacted by Acts 1965, 59th Leg., ch. 722 (S.B. 107), § 1, effective January 1, 1966; am. Acts 1981, 67th Leg., ch. 291 (S.B. 265), § 137, effective September 1, 1981; am. Acts 1987, 70th Leg., ch. 179 (S.B. 43), § 1, effective August 31, 1987; am. Acts 1991, 72nd Leg., ch. 838 (S.B. 880), § 2, effective September 1, 1991; am. Acts 1993, 73rd Leg., ch. 781 (H.B. 798), § 4, effective August 30, 1993; am. Acts 2007, 80th Leg., ch. 593 (H.B. 8), § 3.19, effective September 1, 2007.)

## Art. 44.33. Hearing in Appellate Court.

(a) The Court of Criminal Appeals shall make rules of posttrial and appellate procedure as to the hearing of criminal actions not inconsistent with this Code. After the record is filed in the Court of Appeals or the Court of Criminal Appeals the parties may file such supplemental briefs as they may desire before the case is submitted to the court. Each party, upon filing any such supplemental brief, shall promptly cause true copy thereof to be delivered to the opposing party or to the latter's counsel. In every case at least two counsel for the defendant shall be heard in the Court of Appeals if such be desired by defendant. In every case heard by the Court of Criminal Appeals at least two counsel for the defendant shall be permitted oral argument if desired by the appellant.

(b) Appellant's failure to file his brief in the time prescribed shall not authorize a dismissal of the appeal by the Court of Appeals or the Court of Criminal Appeals, nor shall the Court of Appeals or the Court of Criminal Appeals, for such reason, refuse to consider appellant's case on appeal.
(Enacted by Acts 1965, 59th Leg., ch. 722 (S.B. 107), § 1, effective January 1, 1966; am. Acts 1981, 67th Leg., ch. 291 (S.B. 265), § 139, effective September 1, 1981.)

## Art. 44.35. Bail Pending Habeas Corpus Appeal.

In any habeas corpus proceeding in any court or before any judge in this State where the defendant is remanded to the custody of an officer and an appeal is taken to an appellate court, the defendant shall be allowed bail by the court or judge so remanding the defendant, except in capital cases where the proof is evident. The fact that such defendant is released on bail shall not be grounds for a dismissal of the appeal except in capital cases where the proof is evident.
(Enacted by Acts 1965, 59th Leg., ch. 722 (S.B. 107), § 1, effective January 1, 1966.)

## Art. 44.39. Appellant Detained by Other Than Officer.

If the appellant in a case of habeas corpus be detained by any person other than an officer, the sheriff receiving the mandate of the appellate court, shall immediately cause the person so held to be discharged; and the mandate shall be sufficient authority therefor.
(Enacted by Acts 1965, 59th Leg., ch. 722 (S.B. 107), § 1, effective January 1, 1966; am. Acts 1981, 67th Leg., ch. 291 (S.B. 265), § 144, effective September 1, 1981.)

## Art. 44.41. Who Shall Take Bail Bond.

When, by the judgment of the appellate court upon cases of habeas corpus, the applicant is ordered to give bail, such judgment shall be certified to the officer holding him in custody; and if such officer be the sheriff, the bail bond may be executed before him; if any other officer, he shall take the person detained before some magistrate, who may receive a bail bond, and shall file the same in the proper court of the proper county; and such bond may be forfeited and enforced as provided by law.
(Enacted by Acts 1965, 59th Leg., ch. 722 (S.B. 107), § 1, effective January 1, 1966; am. Acts 1981, 67th Leg., ch. 291 (S.B. 265), § 146, effective September 1, 1981.)

Criminal Procedure

## Art. 44.42. Appeal on Forfeitures.

An appeal may be taken by the defendant from every final judgment rendered upon a personal bond, bail bond or bond taken for the prevention or suppression of offenses, where such judgment is for twenty dollars or more, exclusive of costs, but not otherwise.

(Enacted by Acts 1965, 59th Leg., ch. 722 (S.B. 107), § 1, effective January 1, 1966.)

## Art. 44.43. Writ of Error.

The defendant may also have any such judgment as is mentioned in the preceding Article, and which may have been rendered in courts other than the justice and corporation courts, reviewed upon writ of error.

(Enacted by Acts 1965, 59th Leg., ch. 722 (S.B. 107), § 1, effective January 1, 1966.)

## Art. 44.44. Rules in Forfeitures.

In the cases provided for in the two preceding Articles, the proceeding shall be regulated by the same rules that govern civil actions where an appeal is taken or a writ of error sued out.

(Enacted by Acts 1965, 59th Leg., ch. 722 (S.B. 107), § 1, effective January 1, 1966.)

## Art. 44.45. Review by Court of Criminal Appeals.

(a) The Court of Criminal Appeals may review decisions of the court of appeals on its own motion. An order for review must be filed before the decision of the court of appeals becomes final as determined by Article 42.045.

(b) The Court of Criminal Appeals may review decisions of the court of appeals upon a petition for review.

(1) The state or a defendant in a case may petition the Court of Criminal Appeals for review of the decision of a court of appeals in that case.

(2) The petition shall be filed with the clerk of the court of appeals which rendered the decision within 30 days after the final ruling of the court of appeals.

(3) The petition for review shall be addressed to "The Court of Criminal Appeals of Texas," and shall state the name of the petitioning party and shall include a statement of the case and authorities and arguments in support of each ground for review.

(4) Upon filing a petition for review, the petitioning party shall cause a true copy to be delivered to the attorney representing the opposing party. The opposing party may file a reply to the petition with the Court of Criminal Appeals within 30 days after receipt of the petition from the petitioning party.

(5) Within 15 days after the filing of a petition for review, the clerk of the court of appeals shall note the filing on the record and forward the petition together with the original record and the opinion of the court of appeals to the Court of Criminal Appeals.

(6) The Court of Criminal Appeals shall either grant the petition and review the case or refuse the petition.

(7) Subsequent to granting the petition for review, the Court of Criminal Appeals may reconsider, set aside the order granting the petition, and refuse the petition as though the petition had never been granted.

(c) The Court of Criminal Appeals may promulgate rules pursuant to this article.

(d) Extensions of time for meeting the limits prescribed in Subdivisions (2) and (4) of Subsection (b) of this article may be granted by the Court of Criminal Appeals or a judge thereof for good cause shown on timely application to the Court of Criminal Appeals.

(Enacted by Acts 1981, 67th Leg., ch. 291 (S.B. 265), § 147, effective September 1, 1981; am. Acts 1983, 68th Leg., ch. 249 (S.B. 613), § 1, effective August 29, 1983; am. Acts 1987, 70th Leg., ch. 167 (S.B. 892), § 5.02(3), effective September 1, 1987.)

## Art. 44.46. Reversal of Conviction on the Basis of Service on Jury by a Disqualified Juror.

A conviction in a criminal case may be reversed on appeal on the ground that a juror in the case was absolutely disqualified from service under Article 35.19 of this code only if:

(1) the defendant raises the disqualification before the verdict is entered; or

(2) the disqualification was not discovered or brought to the attention of the trial court until after the verdict was entered and the defendant makes a showing of significant harm by the service of the disqualified juror.

(Enacted by Acts 1993, 73rd Leg., ch. 372 (S.B. 46), § 1, effective September 1, 1993.)

## Art. 44.47. Appeal of Transfer from Juvenile Court.

(a) A defendant may appeal an order of a juvenile court certifying the defendant to stand trial as an adult and transferring the defendant to a criminal court under Section 54.02, Family Code.

(b) A defendant may appeal a transfer under Subsection (a) only in conjunction with the appeal of a conviction of or an order of deferred adjudication for the offense for which the defendant was transferred to criminal court.

(c) An appeal under this section is a criminal matter and is governed by this code and the Texas Rules of Appellate Procedure that apply to a criminal case.

(d) An appeal under this article may include any claims under the law that existed before January 1, 1996, that could have been raised on direct appeal of a transfer under Section 54.02, Family Code.

(Enacted by Acts 1995, 74th Leg., ch. 262 (H.B. 327), § 85, effective January 1, 1996; am. Acts 2003, 78th Leg., ch. 283 (H.B. 2319), § 30, effective September 1, 2003.)

# Justice and Corporation Courts

## CHAPTER 45
## JUSTICE AND MUNICIPAL COURTS

### Subchapter A. General Provisions

## SUBCHAPTER A
## GENERAL PROVISIONS

### Art. 45.001. Objectives of Chapter.

The purpose of this chapter is to establish procedures for processing cases that come within the criminal jurisdiction of the justice courts and municipal courts. This chapter is intended and shall be construed to achieve the following objectives:

(1) to provide fair notice to a person appearing in a criminal proceeding before a justice or municipal court and a meaningful opportunity for that person to be heard;

(2) to ensure appropriate dignity in court procedure without undue formalism;

(3) to promote adherence to rules with sufficient flexibility to serve the ends of justice; and

(4) to process cases without unnecessary expense or delay.

(Enacted by Acts 1999, 76th Leg., ch. 1545 (S.B. 1230), § 6, effective September 1, 1999.)

### Art. 45.002. Application of Chapter.

Criminal proceedings in the justice and municipal courts shall be conducted in accordance with this chapter, including any other rules of procedure specifically made applicable to those proceedings by this chapter. If this chapter does not provide a rule of procedure governing any aspect of a case, the justice or judge shall apply the other general provisions of this code to the extent necessary to achieve the objectives of this chapter.

(Enacted by Acts 1999, 76th Leg., ch. 1545 (S.B. 1230), § 6, effective September 1, 1999.)

### Art. 45.003. Definition for Certain Prosecutions.

For purposes of dismissing a charge under Section 502.407 or 548.605, Transportation Code, "day" does not include Saturday, Sunday, or a legal holiday.

(Enacted by Acts 1999, 76th Leg., ch. 1545 (S.B. 1230), § 6, effective September 1, 1999.)

### Art. 45.01. Complaint [Repealed].

Repealed by Acts 1999, 76th Leg., ch. 1545 (S.B. 1230), § 75(a), effective September 1, 1999. (Enacted by Acts 1965, 59th Leg., ch. 722 (S.B. 107), § 1, effective January 1, 1966; am. Acts 1969, 61st Leg., ch. 520 (H.B. 758), § 1, effective June 10, 1969; am. Acts 1989, 71st Leg., ch. 600 (S.B. 48), § 1, effective June 14, 1989.)

## SUBCHAPTER B
## PROCEDURES FOR JUSTICE AND MUNICIPAL COURTS

### Art. 45.011. Rules of Evidence.

The rules of evidence that govern the trials of criminal actions in the district court apply to a criminal proceeding in a justice or municipal court.

(Enacted by Acts 1965, 59th Leg., ch. 722 (S.B. 107), § 1, effective January 1, 1966; am. Acts 1999, 76th Leg., ch. 1545 (S.B. 1230), § 8, effective September 1, 1999 (renumbered from art. 45.38).)

### Art. 45.012. Electronically Created Records.

(a) Notwithstanding any other provision of law, a document that is issued or maintained by a justice or municipal court or a notice or a citation issued by a law enforcement officer may be created by electronic means, including optical imaging, optical disk, digital imaging, or other electronic reproduction technique that does not permit changes, additions, or deletions to the originally created document.

(b) The court may use electronic means to:

(1) produce a document required by law to be written;

(2) record an instrument, paper, or notice that is permitted or required by law to be recorded or filed; or

(3) maintain a docket.

(c) The court shall maintain original documents as provided by law.

(d) An electronically recorded judgment has the same force and effect as a written signed judgment.

(e) A record created by electronic means is an original record or a certification of the original record.

(f) A printed copy of an optical image of the original record printed from an optical disk system is an accurate copy of the original record.

(g) A justice or municipal court shall have a court seal, the impression of which must be attached to all papers issued out of the court except subpoenas, and which must be used to authenticate the official acts of the clerk and of the recorder. A court seal may be created by electronic means, including optical imaging, optical disk, or other electronic reproduction technique that does not permit changes, additions, or deletions to an original document created by the same type of system.

Criminal Procedure

(h) A statutory requirement that a document contain the signature of any person, including a judge, clerk of the court, or defendant, is satisfied if the document contains that signature as captured on an electronic device.

(Enacted by Acts 1995, 74th Leg., ch. 735 (H.B. 1966), § 2, effective September 1, 1995; am. Acts 1999, 76th Leg., ch. 701 (H.B. 806), § 2, effective August 30, 1999; am. Acts 1999, 76th Leg., ch. 1545 (S.B. 1230), § 9, effective September 1, 1999 (renumbered from art. 45.021); am. Acts 2001, 77th Leg., ch. 1420 (H.B. 2812), § 21.001(12), effective September 1, 2001.)

## Art. 45.013. Filing with Clerk by Mail.

(a) Notwithstanding any other law, for the purposes of this chapter a document is considered timely filed with the clerk of a court if:

(1) the document is deposited with the United States Postal Service in a first class postage prepaid envelope properly addressed to the clerk on or before the date the document is required to be filed with the clerk; and

(2) the clerk receives the document not later than the 10th day after the date the document is required to be filed with the clerk.

(b) A legible postmark affixed by the United States Postal Service is prima facie evidence of the date the document is deposited with the United States Postal Service.

(c) In this article, "day" does not include Saturday, Sunday, or a legal holiday.

(Enacted by Acts 1999, 76th Leg., ch. 1545 (S.B. 1230), § 10, effective September 1, 1999.)

## Art. 45.014. Warrant of Arrest.

(a) When a sworn complaint or affidavit based on probable cause has been filed before the justice or municipal court, the justice or judge may issue a warrant for the arrest of the accused and deliver the same to the proper officer to be executed.

(b) The warrant is sufficient if:

(1) it is issued in the name of "The State of Texas";

(2) it is directed to the proper peace officer or some other person specifically named in the warrant;

(3) it includes a command that the body of the accused be taken, and brought before the authority issuing the warrant, at the time and place stated in the warrant;

(4) it states the name of the person whose arrest is ordered, if known, or if not known, it describes the person as in the complaint;

(5) it states that the person is accused of some offense against the laws of this state, naming the offense; and

(6) it is signed by the justice or judge, naming the office of the justice or judge in the body of the warrant or in connection with the signature of the justice or judge.

(c) Chapter 15 applies to a warrant of arrest issued under this article, except as inconsistent or in conflict with this chapter.

(d) In a county with a population of more than two million that does not have a county attorney, a justice or judge may not issue a warrant under this section for an offense under Section 32.41, Penal Code, unless the district attorney has approved the complaint or affidavit on which the warrant is based.

(Enacted by Acts 1965, 59th Leg., ch. 722 (S.B. 107), § 1, effective January 1, 1966; am. Acts 1999, 76th Leg., ch. 1545 (S.B. 1230), § 11, effective September 1, 1999 (renumbered from art. 45.18); am. Acts 2005, 79th Leg., ch. 644 (H.B. 2885), § 1, effective September 1, 2005.)

## Art. 45.015. Defendant Placed in Jail.

Whenever, by the provisions of this title, the peace officer is authorized to retain a defendant in custody, the peace officer may place the defendant in jail in accordance with this code or other law.

(Enacted by Acts 1965, 59th Leg., ch. 722 (S.B. 107), § 1, effective January 1, 1966; am. Acts 1999, 76th Leg., ch. 1545 (S.B. 1230), § 12, effective September 1, 1999 (renumbered from art. 45.43).)

## Art. 45.016. Bail.

The justice or judge may require the defendant to give bail to secure the defendant's appearance in accordance with this code. If the defendant fails to give bail, the defendant may be held in custody.

(Enacted by Acts 1965, 59th Leg., ch. 722 (S.B. 107), § 1, effective January 1, 1966; am. Acts 1999, 76th Leg., ch. 1545 (S.B. 1230), § 13, effective September 1, 1999 (renumbered from art. 45.41).)

## Art. 45.017. Criminal Docket.

(a) The justice or judge of each court, or, if directed by the justice or judge, the clerk of the court, shall keep a docket containing the following information:

(1) the style and file number of each criminal action;

(2) the nature of the offense charged;

(3) the plea offered by the defendant and the date the plea was entered;

(4) the date the warrant, if any, was issued and the return made thereon;

(5) the date the examination or trial was held, and if a trial was held, whether it was by a jury or by the justice or judge;

(6) the verdict of the jury, if any, and the date of the verdict;

(7) the judgment and sentence of the court, and the date each was given;

(8) the motion for new trial, if any, and the decision thereon; and

(9) whether an appeal was taken and the date of that action.

(b) The information in the docket may be processed and stored by the use of electronic data processing equipment, at the discretion of the justice of the peace or the municipal court judge. (Enacted by Acts 1965, 59th Leg., ch. 722 (S.B. 107), § 1, effective January 1, 1966; am. Acts 1989, 71st Leg., ch. 499 (H.B. 1101) § 1, effective August 28, 1989; am. Acts 1999, 76th Leg., ch. 1545 (S.B. 1230), § 14, effective September 1, 1999 (renumbered from art. 45.13).)

## Art. 45.018. Complaint.

(a) For purposes of this chapter, a complaint is a sworn allegation charging the accused with the commission of an offense.

(b) A defendant is entitled to notice of a complaint against the defendant not later than the day before the date of any proceeding in the prosecution of the defendant under the complaint. The defendant may waive the right to notice granted by this subsection. (Enacted by Acts 1999, 76th Leg., ch. 1545 (S.B. 1230), § 15, effective September 1, 1999.)

## Art. 45.019. Requisites of Complaint.

(a) A complaint is sufficient, without regard to its form, if it substantially satisfies the following requisites:

(1) it must be in writing;

(2) it must commence "In the name and by the authority of the State of Texas";

(3) it must state the name of the accused, if known, or if unknown, must include a reasonably definite description of the accused;

(4) it must show that the accused has committed an offense against the law of this state, or state that the affiant has good reason to believe and does believe that the accused has committed an offense against the law of this state;

(5) it must state the date the offense was committed as definitely as the affiant is able to provide;

(6) it must bear the signature or mark of the affiant; and

(7) it must conclude with the words "Against the peace and dignity of the State" and, if the offense charged is an offense only under a municipal ordinance, it may also conclude with the words "Contrary to the said ordinance".

(b) A complaint filed in justice court must allege that the offense was committed in the county in which the complaint is made.

(c) A complaint filed in municipal court must allege that the offense was committed in the territorial limits of the municipality in which the complaint is made.

(d) A complaint may be sworn to before any officer authorized to administer oaths.

(e) A complaint in municipal court may be sworn to before:

(1) the municipal judge;

(2) the clerk of the court or a deputy clerk;

(3) the city secretary; or

(4) the city attorney or a deputy city attorney.

(f) If the defendant does not object to a defect, error, or irregularity of form or substance in a charging instrument before the date on which the trial on the merits commences, the defendant waives and forfeits the right to object to the defect, error, or irregularity. Nothing in this article prohibits a trial court from requiring that an objection to a charging instrument be made at an earlier time.

(g) In a county with a population of more than two million that does not have a county attorney, a complaint for an offense under Section 32.41, Penal Code, must be approved by the district attorney, regardless of whether a collection proceeding is initiated by the district attorney under Section 32.41(e), Penal Code. (Enacted by Acts 1965, 59th Leg., ch. 722 (S.B. 107), § 1, effective January 1, 1966; am. Acts 1999, 76th Leg., ch. 1545 (S.B. 1230), § 16, effective September 1, 1999 (renumbered from art. 45.17); am. Acts 2005, 79th Leg., ch. 644 (H.B. 2885), § 2, effective September 1, 2005.)

## Art. 45.020. Appearance by Counsel.

(a) The defendant has a right to appear by counsel as in all other cases.

Criminal Procedure

(b) Not more than one counsel shall conduct either the prosecution or defense. State's counsel may open and conclude the argument.
(Enacted by Acts 1965, 59th Leg., ch. 722 (S.B. 107), § 1, effective January 1, 1966; am. Acts 1999, 76th Leg., ch. 1545 (S.B. 1230), § 17, effective September 1, 1999 (renumbered from art. 45.37).)

## Art. 45.02. Seal [Repealed].

Repealed by Acts 1999, 76th Leg., ch. 1545 (S.B. 1230), § 75(a), effective September 1, 1999. (Enacted by Acts 1965, 59th Leg., ch. 722 (S.B. 107), § 1, effective January 1, 1966; am. Acts 1995, 74th Leg., ch. 735 (H.B. 1966), § 1, effective September 1, 1995.)

## Art. 45.021. Pleadings.

All pleading of the defendant in justice or municipal court may be oral or in writing as the court may direct.
(Enacted by Acts 1965, 59th Leg., ch. 722 (S.B. 107), § 1, effective January 1, 1966; am. Acts 1999, 76th Leg., ch. 1545 (S.B. 1230), § 18, effective September 1, 1999 (renumbered from art. 45.33).)

## Art. 45.0215. Plea by Minor and Appearance of Parent.

(a) This article applies to a defendant who has not had the disabilities of minority removed and has been:

(1) charged with an offense other than an offense under Section 43.261, Penal Code, if the defendant is younger than 17 years of age; or

(2) charged with an offense under Section 43.261, Penal Code, if the defendant is younger than 18 years of age.

(a-1) The judge or justice:

(1) must take the defendant's plea in open court; and

(2) shall issue a summons to compel the defendant's parent, guardian, or managing conservator to be present during:

(A) the taking of the defendant's plea; and

(B) all other proceedings relating to the case.

(b) If the court is unable to secure the appearance of the defendant's parent, guardian, or managing conservator by issuance of a summons, the court may, without the defendant's parent, guardian, or managing conservator present, take the defendant's plea and proceed against the defendant.

(c) If the defendant resides in a county other than the county in which the alleged offense occurred, the defendant may, with leave of the judge of the court of original jurisdiction, enter the plea, including a plea under Article 45.052, before a judge in the county in which the defendant resides.

(d) A justice or municipal court shall endorse on the summons issued to a parent an order to appear personally at a hearing with the child. The summons must include a warning that the failure of the parent to appear may result in arrest and is a Class C misdemeanor.
(Enacted by Acts 1997, 75th Leg., ch. 193 (H.B. 1545) § 1, effective September 1, 1997; am. Acts 1999, 76th Leg., ch. 1545 (S.B. 1230), § 19, effective September 1, 1999 (renumbered from art. 45.331); am. Acts 2005, 79th Leg., ch. 949 (H.B. 1575), § 33, effective September 1, 2005; am. Acts 2011, 82nd Leg., ch. 1322 (S.B. 407), § 12, effective September 1, 2011.)

## Art. 45.0216. Expunction of Certain Conviction Records.

(a) In this article, "child" has the meaning assigned by Section 51.02, Family Code.

(b) A person may apply to the court in which the person was convicted to have the conviction expunged as provided by this article on or after the person's 17th birthday if:

(1) the person was convicted of not more than one offense described by Section 8.07(a)(4) or (5), Penal Code, while the person was a child; or

(2) the person was convicted only once of an offense under Section 43.261, Penal Code.

(c) The person must make a written request to have the records expunged. The request must be under oath.

(d) The request must contain the person's statement that the person was not convicted of any additional offense or found to have engaged in conduct indicating a need for supervision as described by Subsection (f)(1) or (2), as applicable.

(e) The judge shall inform the person and any parent in open court of the person's expunction rights and provide them with a copy of this article.

(f) The court shall order the conviction, together with all complaints, verdicts, sentences, and prosecutorial and law enforcement records, and any other documents relating to the offense, expunged from the person's record if the court finds that:

(1) for a person applying for the expunction of a conviction for an offense described by Section 8.07(a)(4) or (5), Penal Code, the person was not convicted of any other offense described by Section 8.07(a)(4) or (5), Penal Code, while the person was a child; and

(2) for a person applying for the expunction of a conviction for an offense described by Section 43.261, Penal Code, the person was not found to have engaged in conduct indicating a need for supervision described by Section 51.03(b)(7), Family Code, while the person was a child.

(f-1) After entry of an order under Subsection (f), the person is released from all disabilities resulting from the conviction and the conviction may not be shown or made known for any purpose.

(g) This article does not apply to any offense otherwise covered by:

(1) Chapter 106, Alcoholic Beverage Code;

(2) Chapter 161, Health and Safety Code; or

(3) Section 25.094, Education Code.

(h) Records of a person under 17 years of age relating to a complaint dismissed as provided by Article 45.051 or 45.052 may be expunged under this article.

(i) The justice or municipal court shall require a person who requests expungement under this article to pay a fee in the amount of $30 to defray the cost of notifying state agencies of orders of expungement under this article.

(j) The procedures for expunction provided under this article are separate and distinct from the expunction procedures under Chapter 55.

(Enacted by Acts 2001, 77th Leg., ch. 1297 (H.B. 1118), § 50, effective September 1, 2001; am. Acts 2005, 79th Leg., ch. 886 (S.B. 1426), § 2, effective September 1, 2005; am. Acts 2011, 82nd Leg., ch. 1322 (S.B. 407), §§ 13, 14, effective September 1, 2011.)

### Art. 45.0217. Confidential Records Related to the Conviction of a Child.

(a) Except as provided by Article 15.27 and Subsection (b), all records and files, including those held by law enforcement, and information stored by electronic means or otherwise, from which a record or file could be generated, relating to a child who is convicted of and has satisfied the judgment for a fine-only misdemeanor offense other than a traffic offense are confidential and may not be disclosed to the public.

(b) Information subject to Subsection (a) may be open to inspection only by:

(1) judges or court staff;

(2) a criminal justice agency for a criminal justice purpose, as those terms are defined by Section 411.082, Government Code;

(3) the Department of Public Safety;

(4) an attorney for a party to the proceeding;

(5) the child defendant; or

(6) the defendant's parent, guardian, or managing conservator.

(Enacted by Acts 2011, 82nd Leg., ch. 731 (H.B. 961), § 2, effective June 17, 2011.)

### Art. 45.022. Plea of Guilty or Nolo Contendere.

Proof as to the offense may be heard upon a plea of guilty or a plea of nolo contendere and the punishment assessed by the court.

(Enacted by Acts 1965, 59th Leg., ch. 722 (S.B. 107), § 1, effective January 1, 1966; am. Acts 1999, 76th Leg., ch. 1545 (S.B. 1230), § 20, effective September 1, 1999 (renumbered from art. 45.34).)

### Art. 45.023. Defendant's Plea.

After the jury is impaneled, or after the defendant has waived trial by jury, the defendant may:

(1) plead guilty or not guilty;

(2) enter a plea of nolo contendere; or

(3) enter the special plea of double jeopardy as described by Article 27.05.

(Enacted by Acts 1965, 59th Leg., ch. 722 (S.B. 107), § 1, effective January 1, 1966; am. Acts 1999, 76th Leg., ch. 1545 (S.B. 1230), § 21, effective September 1, 1999 (renumbered from art. 45.31).)

### Art. 45.024. Defendant's Refusal to Plead.

The justice or judge shall enter a plea of not guilty if the defendant refuses to plead.

(Enacted by Acts 1965, 59th Leg., ch. 722 (S.B. 107), § 1, effective January 1, 1966; am. Acts 1999, 76th Leg., ch. 1545 (S.B. 1230), § 22, effective September 1, 1999 (renumbered from art. 45.35).)

### Art. 45.025. Defendant May Waive Jury.

The accused may waive a trial by jury in writing. If the defendant waives a trial by jury, the justice or judge shall hear and determine the cause without a jury.

(Enacted by Acts 1965, 59th Leg., ch. 722 (S.B. 107), § 1, effective January 1, 1966; am. Acts

1999, 76th Leg., ch. 1545 (S.B. 1230), § 23, effective September 1, 1999 (renumbered from art. 45.24).)

## Art. 45.026. Jury Trial; Failure to Appear.

(a) A justice or municipal court may order a party who does not waive a jury trial in a justice or municipal court and who fails to appear for the trial to pay the costs incurred for impaneling the jury.

(b) The justice or municipal court may release a party from the obligation to pay costs under this section for good cause.

(c) An order issued by a justice or municipal court under this section may be enforced by contempt as prescribed by Section 21.002(c), Government Code.

(Enacted by Acts 1995, 74th Leg., ch. 122 (S.B. 1060), § 1, effective September 1, 1995; am. Acts 1999, 76th Leg., ch. 1545 (S.B. 1230), § 24, effective September 1, 1999 (renumbered from art. 45.251).)

## Art. 45.027. Jury Summoned.

(a) If the accused does not waive a trial by jury, the justice or judge shall issue a writ commanding the proper officer to summon a venire from which six qualified persons shall be selected to serve as jurors in the case.

(b) The jurors when so summoned shall remain in attendance as jurors in all cases that may come up for hearing until discharged by the court.

(c) Any person so summoned who fails to attend may be fined an amount not to exceed $100 for contempt.

(Enacted by Acts 1965, 59th Leg., ch. 722 (S.B. 107), § 1, effective January 1, 1966; am. Acts 1995, 74th Leg., ch. 802 (H.B. 1204), § 1, effective September 1, 1995; am. Acts 1999, 76th Leg., ch. 1545 (S.B. 1230), § 25, effective September 1, 1999 (renumbered from art. 45.25).)

## Art. 45.028. Other Jurors Summoned.

If, from challenges or any other cause, a sufficient number of jurors are not in attendance, the justice or judge shall order the proper officer to summon a sufficient number of qualified persons to form the jury.

(Enacted by Acts 1965, 59th Leg., ch. 722 (S.B. 107), § 1, effective January 1, 1966; am. Acts 1999, 76th Leg., ch. 1545 (S.B. 1230), § 26, effective September 1, 1999 (renumbered from art. 45.29).)

## Art. 45.029. Peremptory Challenges.

In all jury trials in a justice or municipal court, the state and each defendant in the case is entitled to three peremptory challenges.

(Enacted by Acts 1965, 59th Leg., ch. 722 (S.B. 107), § 1, effective January 1, 1966; am. Acts 1999, 76th Leg., ch. 1545 (S.B. 1230), § 27, effective September 1, 1999 (renumbered from art. 45.28).)

## Art. 45.03. Prosecutions [Renumbered].

Renumbered to Tex. Code Crim Proc. art. 45.201 by Acts 1999, 76th Leg., ch. 1545 (S.B. 1230), § 59, effective September 1, 1999.

## Art. 45.030. Formation of Jury.

The justice or judge shall form the jury and administer the appropriate oath in accordance with Chapter 35.

(Enacted by Acts 1965, 59th Leg., ch. 722 (S.B. 107), § 1, effective January 1, 1966; am. Acts 1999, 76th Leg., ch. 1545 (S.B. 1230), § 28, effective September 1, 1999 (amended and renumbered from art. 45.30).)

## Art. 45.031. Counsel for State Not Present.

If the state is not represented by counsel when the case is called for trial, the justice or judge may:

(1) postpone the trial to a date certain;

(2) appoint an attorney pro tem as provided by this code to represent the state; or

(3) proceed to trial.

(Enacted by Acts 1965, 59th Leg., ch. 722 (S.B. 107), § 1, effective January 1, 1966; am. Acts 1999, 76th Leg., ch. 1545 (S.B. 1230), § 29, effective September 1, 1999 (renumbered from art. 45.36).)

## Art. 45.032. Directed Verdict.

If, upon the trial of a case in a justice or municipal court, the state fails to prove a prima facie case of the offense alleged in the complaint, the defendant is entitled to a directed verdict of "not guilty."

(Enacted by Acts 1969, 61st Leg., ch. 520 (H.B. 758), § 2, effective June 10, 1969; am. Acts 1999, 76th Leg., ch. 1545 (S.B. 1230), § 30, effective September 1, 1999 (renumbered from art. 45.031).)

## Art. 45.033. Jury Charge.

The judge shall charge the jury. The charge may be made orally or in writing, except that the charge shall be made in writing if required by law.

(Enacted by Acts 1999, 76th Leg., ch. 1545 (S.B. 1230), § 31, effective September 1, 1999.)

## Art. 45.034. Jury Kept Together.

The jury shall retire in charge of an officer when the cause is submitted to them, and be kept together until they agree to a verdict, are discharged, or the court recesses.

(Enacted by Acts 1965, 59th Leg., ch. 722 (S.B. 107), § 1, effective January 1, 1966; am. Acts 1999, 76th Leg., ch. 1545 (S.B. 1230), § 32, effective September 1, 1999 (renumbered from art. 45.39).)

## Art. 45.035. Mistrial.

A jury shall be discharged if it fails to agree to a verdict after being kept together a reasonable time. If a jury is discharged because it fails to agree to a verdict, the justice or judge may impanel another jury as soon as practicable to try such cause.

(Enacted by Acts 1965, 59th Leg., ch. 722 (S.B. 107), § 1, effective January 1, 1966; am. Acts 1995, 74th Leg., ch. 1005 (S.B. 886), § 1, effective September 1, 1995; am. Acts 1999, 76th Leg., ch. 1545 (S.B. 1230), § 33, effective September 1, 1999 (renumbered from art. 45.40).)

## Art. 45.036. Verdict.

(a) When the jury has agreed on a verdict, the jury shall bring the verdict into court.

(b) The justice or judge shall see that the verdict is in proper form and shall render the proper judgment and sentence on the verdict.

(Enacted by Acts 1965, 59th Leg., ch. 722 (S.B. 107), § 1, effective January 1, 1966; am. Acts 1999, 76th Leg., ch. 1545 (S.B. 1230), § 34, effective September 1, 1999 (renumbered from art. 45.42).)

## Art. 45.037. Motion for New Trial.

A motion for a new trial must be made within five days after the rendition of judgment and sentence, and not afterward.

(Enacted by Acts 1965, 59th Leg., ch. 722 (S.B. 107), § 1, effective January 1, 1966; am. Acts 1999, 76th Leg., ch. 1545 (S.B. 1230), § 35, effective September 1, 1999 (renumbered from art.

45.45); am. Acts 2011, 82nd Leg., ch. 395 (S.B. 519), § 1, effective September 1, 2011.)

## Art. 45.038. New Trial Granted.

(a) Not later than the 10th day after the date that the judgment is entered, a justice or judge may, for good cause shown, grant the defendant a new trial, whenever the justice or judge considers that justice has not been done the defendant in the trial of the case.

(b) If a motion for a new trial is not granted before the 11th day after the date that the judgment is entered, the motion shall be considered denied.

(Enacted by Acts 1965, 59th Leg., ch. 722 (S.B. 107), § 1, effective January 1, 1966; am. Acts 1999, 76th Leg., ch. 1545 (S.B. 1230), § 36, effective September 1, 1999 (renumbered from art. 45.44).)

## Art. 45.039. Only One New Trial Granted.

Not more than one new trial shall be granted the defendant in the same case. When a new trial has been granted, the justice or judge shall proceed, as soon as practicable, to try the case again.

(Enacted by Acts 1965, 59th Leg., ch. 722 (S.B. 107), § 1, effective January 1, 1966; am. Acts 1999, 76th Leg., ch. 1545 (S.B. 1230), § 37, effective September 1, 1999 (renumbered from art. 45.46).)

## Art. 45.040. State Not Entitled to New Trial.

In no case shall the state be entitled to a new trial.

(Enacted by Acts 1965, 59th Leg., ch. 722 (S.B. 107), § 1, effective January 1, 1966; am. Acts 1999, 76th Leg., ch. 1545 (S.B. 1230), § 38, effective September 1, 1999 (amended and renumbered from art. 45.47).)

## Art. 45.04. Service of Process [Renumbered].

Renumbered to Tex. Code Crim Proc. art. 45.202 by Acts 1999, 76th Leg., ch. 1545 (S.B. 1230), § 60, effective September 1, 1999.

(Amended and renumbered to Art. 45.202 Acts 1999, 76th Leg., ch. 1545, effective September 1, 1999.)

## Art. 45.041. Judgment.

(a) The judgment and sentence, in case of conviction in a criminal action before a justice of the peace or municipal court judge, shall be that the defendant pay the amount of the fine and costs to the state.

(b) Subject to Subsection (b-2), the justice or judge may direct the defendant:

(1) to pay:

(A) the entire fine and costs when sentence is pronounced;

(B) the entire fine and costs at some later date; or

(C) a specified portion of the fine and costs at designated intervals;

(2) if applicable, to make restitution to any victim of the offense; and

(3) to satisfy any other sanction authorized by law.

(b-1) Restitution made under Subsection (b)(2) may not exceed $5,000 for an offense under Section 32.41, Penal Code.

(b-2) When imposing a fine and costs, if the justice or judge determines that the defendant is unable to immediately pay the fine and costs, the justice or judge shall allow the defendant to pay the fine and costs in specified portions at designated intervals.

(c) The justice or judge shall credit the defendant for time served in jail as provided by Article 42.03. The credit shall be applied to the amount of the fine and costs at the rate provided by Article 45.048.

(d) All judgments, sentences, and final orders of the justice or judge shall be rendered in open court.

(Enacted by Acts 1965, 59th Leg., ch. 722 (S.B. 107), § 1, effective January 1, 1966; am. Acts 1971, 62nd Leg., ch. 987 (H.B. 887), § 5, effective June 15, 1971; am. Acts 1999, 76th Leg., ch. 1545 (S.B. 1230), § 39, effective September 1, 1999 (renumbered from art. 45.50); am. Acts 2007, 80th Leg., ch. 1393 (H.B. 485), § 2, effective September 1, 2007; am. Acts 2011, 82nd Leg., ch. 464 (H.B. 27), § 3, effective September 1, 2011.)

### Art. 45.042. Appeal.

(a) Appeals from a justice or municipal court, including appeals from final judgments in bond forfeiture proceedings, shall be heard by the county court except in cases where the county court has no jurisdiction, in which counties such appeals shall be heard by the proper court.

(b) Unless the appeal is taken from a municipal court of record and the appeal is based on error reflected in the record, the trial shall be de novo.

(c) In an appeal from the judgment and sentence of a justice or municipal court, if the defendant is in custody, the defendant is to be committed to jail unless the defendant gives bail.

(Enacted by Acts 1965, 59th Leg., ch. 722 (S.B. 107), § 1, effective January 1, 1966; am. Acts 1999, 76th Leg., ch. 1545 (S.B. 1230), § 40, effective September 1, 1999 (renumbered from art. 45.10).)

### Art. 45.0425. Appeal Bond.

(a) If the court from whose judgment and sentence the appeal is taken is in session, the court must approve the bail. The amount of a bail bond may not be less than two times the amount of the fine and costs adjudged against the defendant, payable to the State of Texas. The bail may not in any case be for a sum less than $50. If the appeal bond otherwise meets the requirements of this code, the court without requiring a court appearance by the defendant shall approve the appeal bond in the amount the court under Article 27.14(b) notified the defendant would be approved.

(b) An appeal bond shall recite that in the cause the defendant was convicted and has appealed and be conditioned that the defendant shall make the defendant's personal appearance before the court to which the appeal is taken instanter, if the court is in session, or, if the court is not in session, at its next regular term, stating the time and place of that session, and there remain from day to day and term to term, and answer in the cause in the court.

(Enacted by Acts 1999, 76th Leg., ch. 1545 (S.B. 1230), § 41, effective September 1, 1999.)

### Art. 45.0426. Filing Bond Perfects Appeal.

(a) When the appeal bond has been filed with the justice or judge who tried the case not later than the 10th day after the date the judgment was entered, the appeal in such case shall be held to be perfected.

(b) If an appeal bond is not timely filed, the appellate court does not have jurisdiction over the case and shall remand the case to the justice or municipal court for execution of the sentence.

(c) An appeal may not be dismissed because the defendant failed to give notice of appeal in open court. An appeal by the defendant or the state may not be dismissed on account of any defect in the transcript.

(Enacted by Acts 1965, 59th Leg., ch. 722 (S.B. 107), § 1, effective January 1, 1966; am. Acts 1995, 74th Leg., ch. 478 (S.B. 918), § 1, effective September 1, 1995; am. Acts 1999, 76th Leg., ch. 1545 (S.B. 1230), § 42, effective September 1, 1999 (renumbered from art. 44.14).)

Criminal Procedure

## Art. 45.043. Effect of Appeal.

When a defendant files the appeal bond required by law with the justice or municipal court, all further proceedings in the case in the justice or municipal court shall cease.

(Enacted by Acts 1965, 59th Leg., ch. 722 (S.B. 107), § 1, effective January 1, 1966; am. Acts 1999, 76th Leg., ch. 1545 (S.B. 1230), § 43, effective September 1, 1999 (renumbered from art. 45.48).)

## Art. 45.044. Forfeiture of Cash Bond in Satisfaction of Fine.

(a) A justice or judge may enter a judgment of conviction and forfeit a cash bond posted by the defendant in satisfaction of the defendant's fine and cost if the defendant:

(1) has entered a written and signed plea of nolo contendere and a waiver of jury trial; and

(2) fails to appear according to the terms of the defendant's release.

(b) A justice or judge who enters a judgment of conviction and forfeiture under Subsection (a) of this article shall immediately notify the defendant in writing, by regular mail addressed to the defendant at the defendant's last known address, that:

(1) a judgment of conviction and forfeiture of bond was entered against the defendant on a date certain and the forfeiture satisfies the defendant's fine and costs in the case; and

(2) the defendant has a right to a new trial in the case if the defendant applies for the new trial not later than the 10th day after the date of judgment and forfeiture.

(c) Notwithstanding Article 45.037 of this code, the defendant may file a motion for a new trial within the period provided by Subsection (b) of this article, and the court shall grant the motion if the motion is made within that period. On the new trial, the court shall permit the defendant to withdraw the previously entered plea of nolo contendere and waiver of jury trial.

(Enacted by Acts 1993, 73rd Leg., ch. 109 (H.B. 521), § 1, effective May 9, 1993; am. Acts 1999, 76th Leg., ch. 1545 (S.B. 1230), § 44, effective September 1, 1999 (renumbered from art. 45.231).)

## Art. 45.045. Capias Pro Fine.

(a) If the defendant is not in custody when the judgment is rendered or if the defendant fails to satisfy the judgment according to its terms, the court may order a capias pro fine, as defined by Article 43.015, issued for the defendant's arrest. The capias pro fine shall state the amount of the judgment and sentence, and command the appropriate peace officer to bring the defendant before the court immediately or place the defendant in jail until the business day following the date of the defendant's arrest if the defendant cannot be brought before the court immediately.

(b) A capias pro fine may not be issued for an individual convicted for an offense committed before the individual's 17th birthday unless:

(1) the individual is 17 years of age or older;

(2) the court finds that the issuance of the capias pro fine is justified after considering:

(A) the sophistication and maturity of the individual;

(B) the criminal record and history of the individual; and

(C) the reasonable likelihood of bringing about the discharge of the judgment through the use of procedures and services currently available to the court; and

(3) the court has proceeded under Article 45.050 to compel the individual to discharge the judgment.

(c) This article does not limit the authority of a court to order a child taken into custody under Article 45.058 or 45.059.

(Enacted by Acts 1965, 59th Leg., ch. 722 (S.B. 107), § 1, effective January 1, 1966; am. Acts 1971, 62nd Leg., ch. 987 (H.B. 887), § 6, effective June 15, 1971; am. Acts 1999, 76th Leg., ch. 1545 (S.B. 1230), § 45, effective September 1, 1999 (renumbered from art. 45.51); am. Acts 2003, 78th Leg., ch. 283 (H.B. 2319), § 31, effective September 1, 2003; am. Acts 2007, 80th Leg., ch. 1263 (H.B. 3060), § 16, effective September 1, 2007.)

## Art. 45.046. Commitment.

(a) When a judgment and sentence have been entered against a defendant and the defendant defaults in the discharge of the judgment, the judge may order the defendant confined in jail until discharged by law if the judge at a hearing makes a written determination that:

(1) the defendant is not indigent and has failed to make a good faith effort to discharge the fine and costs; or

(2) the defendant is indigent and:

(A) has failed to make a good faith effort to discharge the fines and costs under Article 45.049; and

(B) could have discharged the fines and costs under Article 45.049 without experiencing any undue hardship.

(b) A certified copy of the judgment, sentence, and order is sufficient to authorize such confinement.

(c) For purposes of a hearing described by Subsection (a), a defendant may be brought before the court in person or by means of an electronic broadcast system through which an image of the defendant is presented to the court. For purposes of this subsection, "electronic broadcast system" means a two-way electronic communication of image and sound between the defendant and the court and includes secure Internet videoconferencing.

(Enacted by Acts 1965, 59th Leg., ch. 722 (S.B. 107), § 1, effective January 1, 1966; am. Acts 1971, 62nd Leg., ch. 987 (H.B. 887), § 7, effective June 15, 1971; am. Acts 1999, 76th Leg., ch. 1545 (S.B. 1230), § 46, effective September 1, 1999 (renumbered from art. 45.52); am. Acts 2007, 80th Leg., ch. 1263 (H.B. 3060), § 19, effective September 1, 2007; am. Acts 2009, 81st Leg., ch. 474 (S.B. 414), § 2, effective September 1, 2009.)

## Art. 45.047. Civil Collection of Fines After Judgment.

If after a judgment and sentence is entered the defendant defaults in payment of a fine, the justice or judge may order the fine and costs collected by execution against the defendant's property in the same manner as a judgment in a civil suit.

(Enacted by Acts 1999, 76th Leg., ch. 1545 (S.B. 1230), § 47, effective September 1, 1999.)

## Art. 45.048. Discharged from Jail.

(a) A defendant placed in jail on account of failure to pay the fine and costs shall be discharged on habeas corpus by showing that the defendant:

(1) is too poor to pay the fine and costs; or

(2) has remained in jail a sufficient length of time to satisfy the fine and costs, at the rate of not less than $50 for each period of time served, as specified by the convicting court in the judgment in the case.

(b) A convicting court may specify a period of time that is not less than eight hours or more than 24 hours as the period for which a defendant who fails to pay the fines and costs in the case must remain in jail to satisfy $50 of the fine and costs.

(Enacted by Acts 1965, 59th Leg., ch. 722 (S.B. 107), § 1, effective January 1, 1966; am. Acts 1981, 67th Leg., ch. 708 (H.B. 647), § 3, effective

August 31, 1981; am. Acts 1999, 76th Leg., ch. 1545 (S.B. 1230), § 48, effective September 1, 1999 (renumbered from art. 45.53); am. Acts 2001, 77th Leg., ch. 872 (H.B. 1955), § 1, effective September 1, 2001; am. Acts 2003, 78th Leg., ch. 209 (H.B. 2424), § 65(a), effective January 1, 2004.)

## Art. 45.049. Community Service in Satisfaction of Fine or Costs.

(a) A justice or judge may require a defendant who fails to pay a previously assessed fine or costs, or who is determined by the court to have insufficient resources or income to pay a fine or costs, to discharge all or part of the fine or costs by performing community service. A defendant may discharge an obligation to perform community service under this article by paying at any time the fine and costs assessed.

(b) In the justice's or judge's order requiring a defendant to participate in community service work under this article, the justice or judge must specify the number of hours the defendant is required to work.

(c) The justice or judge may order the defendant to perform community service work under this article only for a governmental entity or a nonprofit organization that provides services to the general public that enhance social welfare and the general well-being of the community. A governmental entity or nonprofit organization that accepts a defendant under this article to perform community service must agree to supervise the defendant in the performance of the defendant's work and report on the defendant's work to the justice or judge who ordered the community service.

(d) A justice or judge may not order a defendant to perform more than 16 hours per week of community service under this article unless the justice or judge determines that requiring the defendant to work additional hours does not work a hardship on the defendant or the defendant's dependents.

(e) A defendant is considered to have discharged not less than $50 of fines or costs for each eight hours of community service performed under this article.

(f) A sheriff, employee of a sheriff's department, county commissioner, county employee, county judge, justice of the peace, municipal court judge, or officer or employee of a political subdivision other than a county is not liable for damages arising from an act or failure to act in connection with manual labor performed by a defendant under this article if the act or failure to act:

    (1) was performed pursuant to court order; and

    (2) was not intentional, wilfully or wantonly negligent, or performed with conscious indifference or reckless disregard for the safety of others.

(g) This subsection applies only to a defendant who is charged with a traffic offense or an offense under Section 106.05, Alcoholic Beverage Code, and is a resident of this state. If under Article 45.051(b)(10), Code of Criminal Procedure, the judge requires the defendant to perform community service as a condition of the deferral, the defendant is entitled to elect whether to perform the required governmental entity or nonprofit organization community service in:

    (1) the county in which the court is located; or

    (2) the county in which the defendant resides, but only if the entity or organization agrees to:

        (A) supervise the defendant in the performance of the defendant's community service work; and

        (B) report to the court on the defendant's community service work.

(h) This subsection applies only to a defendant charged with an offense under Section 106.05, Alcoholic Beverage Code, who, under Subsection (g), elects to perform the required community service in the county in which the defendant resides. The community service must comply with Sections 106.071(d) and (e), Alcoholic Beverage Code, except that if the educational programs or services described by Section 106.071(e) are not available in the county of the defendant's residence, the court may order community service that it considers appropriate for rehabilitative purposes.

(i) A community supervision and corrections department or a court-related services office may provide the administrative and other services necessary for supervision of a defendant required to perform community service under this article. (Enacted by Acts 1993, 73rd Leg., ch. 298 (H.B. 930), § 1, effective May 27, 1993; am. Acts 1999, 76th Leg., ch. 1545 (S.B. 1230), § 49, effective September 1, 1999 (renumbered from art. 45.521); am. Acts 2003, 78th Leg., ch. 209 (H.B. 2424), § 66(a), effective January 1, 2004; am. Acts 2007, 80th Leg., ch. 1113 (H.B. 3692), § 5, effective September 1, 2007; am. Acts 2007, 80th Leg., ch. 1263 (H.B. 3060), § 17, effective September 1, 2007; am. Acts 2009, 81st Leg., ch. 87 (S.B. 1969), § 27.001(2), effective September 1, 2009.)

### Art. 45.0491. Waiver of Payment of Fines and Costs for Indigent Defendants.

A municipal court, regardless of whether the court is a court of record, or a justice court may waive payment of a fine or costs imposed on a defendant who defaults in payment if the court determines that:

    (1) the defendant is indigent; and

    (2) discharging the fine and costs under Article 45.049 would impose an undue hardship on the defendant.
(Enacted by Acts 2007, 80th Leg., ch. 1263 (H.B. 3060), § 18, effective September 1, 2007.)

### Art. 45.0492. [2 Versions: As added by Acts 2011, 82nd Leg., ch. 227] Community Service or Tutoring in Satisfaction of Fine or Costs for Certain Juvenile Defendants.

(a) This article applies only to a defendant younger than 17 years of age who is assessed a fine or costs for a Class C misdemeanor occurring in a building or on the grounds of the primary or secondary school at which the defendant was enrolled at the time of the offense.

(b) A justice or judge may require a defendant described by Subsection (a) to discharge all or part of the fine or costs by performing community service or attending a tutoring program that is satisfactory to the court. A defendant may discharge an obligation to perform community service or attend a tutoring program under this article by paying at any time the fine and costs assessed.

(c) In the justice's or judge's order requiring a defendant to participate in community service work or a tutoring program under this article, the justice or judge must specify the number of hours the defendant is required to work or attend tutoring.

(d) The justice or judge may order the defendant to perform community service work under this article only for a governmental entity or a nonprofit organization that provides services to the general public that enhance social welfare and the general well-being of the community. A governmental entity or nonprofit organization that accepts a defendant under this article to perform community service must agree to supervise the defendant in the performance of the defendant's work and report on the defendant's work to the justice or judge who ordered the community service.

(e) A tutoring program that accepts a defendant under this article must agree to supervise the defendant in the attendance of the tutoring program and report on the defendant's work to the justice or judge who ordered the tutoring.

(f) A justice or judge may not order a defendant to perform more than 16 hours of community service per week or attend more than 16 hours of tutoring per week under this article unless the justice or judge determines that requiring additional hours of work or tutoring does not cause a hardship on the defendant or the defendant's family. For purposes of this subsection, "family" has the meaning assigned by Section 71.003, Family Code.

(g) A defendant is considered to have discharged not less than $50 of fines or costs for each eight hours of community service performed or tutoring program attended under this article.

(h) A sheriff, employee of a sheriff's department, county commissioner, county employee, county judge, justice of the peace, municipal court judge, officer or employee of a political subdivision other than a county, nonprofit organization, or tutoring program is not liable for damages arising from an act or failure to act in connection with an activity performed by a defendant under this article if the act or failure to act:

(1) was performed pursuant to court order; and

(2) was not intentional, grossly negligent, or performed with conscious indifference or reckless disregard for the safety of others.

(i) A local juvenile probation department or a court-related services office may provide the administrative and other services necessary for supervision of a defendant required to perform community service under this article.

(Enacted by Acts 2011, 82nd Leg., ch. 227 (H.B. 350), § 1, effective September 1, 2011.)

### Art. 45.0492. [2 Versions: As added by Acts 2011, 82nd Leg., ch. 777] Community Service in Satisfaction of Fine or Costs for Certain Juvenile Defendants.

(a) This article applies only to a defendant younger than 17 years of age who is assessed a fine or costs for a Class C misdemeanor.

(b) A justice or judge may require a defendant described by Subsection (a) to discharge all or part of the fine or costs by performing community service. A defendant may discharge an obligation to perform community service under this article by paying at any time the fine and costs assessed.

(c) In the justice's or judge's order requiring a defendant to perform community service under this article, the justice or judge shall specify the number of hours of service the defendant is required to perform and may not order more than 200 hours of service.

(d) The justice or judge may order the defendant to perform community service work under this article only for a governmental entity or a nonprofit organization that provides services to the general public that enhance social welfare and the general well-being of the community. A governmental entity or nonprofit organization that accepts a defendant under this article to perform community service must agree to supervise the defendant in the performance of the defendant's work and report on the defendant's work to the justice or judge who ordered the community service.

(e) A justice or judge may not order a defendant to perform more than 16 hours of community service per week under this article unless the justice or judge determines that requiring additional hours of work does not cause a hardship on the defendant or the defendant's family. For purposes of this subsection, "family" has the meaning assigned by Section 71.003, Family Code.

(f) A sheriff, employee of a sheriff's department, county commissioner, county employee, county judge, justice of the peace, municipal court judge, or officer or employee of a political subdivision other than a county is not liable for damages arising from an act or failure to act in connection with community service performed by a defendant under this article if the act or failure to act:

(1) was performed pursuant to court order; and

(2) was not intentional, wilfully or wantonly negligent, or performed with conscious indifference or reckless disregard for the safety of others.

(g) A local juvenile probation department or a court-related services office may provide the administrative and other services necessary for supervision of a defendant required to perform community service under this article.

(Enacted by Acts 2011, 82nd Leg., ch. 777 (H.B. 1964), § 1, effective September 1, 2011.)

## Art. 45.050. Failure to Pay Fine; Contempt: Juveniles.

(a) In this article, "child" has the meaning assigned by Article 45.058(h).

(b) A justice or municipal court may not order the confinement of a child for:

(1) the failure to pay all or any part of a fine or costs imposed for the conviction of an offense punishable by fine only; or

(2) contempt of another order of a justice or municipal court.

(c) If a child fails to obey an order of a justice or municipal court under circumstances that would constitute contempt of court, the justice or municipal court, after providing notice and an opportunity to be heard, may:

(1) refer the child to the appropriate juvenile court for delinquent conduct for contempt of the justice or municipal court order; or

(2) retain jurisdiction of the case, hold the child in contempt of the justice or municipal court, and order either or both of the following:

(A) that the contemnor pay a fine not to exceed $500; or

(B) that the Department of Public Safety suspend the contemnor's driver's license or permit or, if the contemnor does not have a license or permit, to deny the issuance of a license or permit to the contemnor until the contemnor fully complies with the orders of the court.

(d) A justice or municipal court may hold a person in contempt and impose a remedy authorized by Subsection (c)(2) if:

(1) the person was convicted for an offense committed before the person's 17th birthday;

(2) the person failed to obey the order while the person was 17 years of age or older; and

(3) the failure to obey occurred under circumstances that constitute contempt of court.

(e) A justice or municipal court may hold a person in contempt and impose a remedy authorized by Subsection (c)(2) if the person, while younger than 17 years of age, engaged in conduct in contempt of an order issued by the justice or municipal court, but contempt proceedings could not be held before the person's 17th birthday.

(f) A court that orders suspension or denial of a driver's license or permit under Subsection (c)(2)(B) shall notify the Department of Public Safety on receiving proof of compliance with the orders of the court.

(g) A justice or municipal court may not refer a child who violates a court order while 17 years of age or older to a juvenile court for delinquency proceedings for contempt of court.

(Enacted by Acts 1995, 74th Leg., ch. 262 (H.B. 327), § 86, effective January 1, 1996; am. Acts 1999, 76th Leg., ch. 76 (H.B. 688), § 7, effective September 1, 1999; am. Acts 1999, 76th Leg., ch. 1545 (S.B. 1230), § 49, effective September 1, 1999 (renumbered from art. 45.522); am. Acts 2001, 77th Leg., ch. 1297 (H.B. 1118), § 51, effective September 1, 2001; am. Acts 2001, 77th Leg., ch. 1514 (S.B. 1432), § 8, effective September 1, 2001; am. Acts 2003, 78th Leg., ch. 283 (H.B. 2319), § 32, effective September 1, 2003; am. Acts 2003, 78th Leg., ch. 1276 (H.B. 3507), § 5.002, effective September 1, 2003.)

## Art. 45.05. Commitment [Repealed].

Repealed by Acts 1999, 76th Leg., ch. 1545 (S.B. 1230), § 75(a), effective September 1, 1999. (Enacted by Acts 1965, 59th Leg., ch. 722 (S.B. 107), § 1, effective January 1, 1966.)

## Art. 45.051. Suspension of Sentence and Deferral of Final Disposition.

(a) On a plea of guilty or nolo contendere by a defendant or on a finding of guilt in a misdemeanor case punishable by fine only and payment of all court costs, the judge may defer further proceedings without entering an adjudication of guilt and place the defendant on probation for a period not to exceed 180 days. In issuing the order of deferral, the judge may impose a special expense fee on the defendant in an amount not to exceed the amount of the fine that could be imposed on the defendant as punishment for the offense. The special expense fee may be collected at any time before the date on which the period of probation ends. The judge may elect not to impose the special expense fee for good cause shown by the defendant. If the judge orders the collection of a special expense fee, the judge shall require that the amount of the special expense fee be credited toward the payment of the amount of the fine imposed by the judge. An order of deferral under this subsection terminates any liability under a bail bond or an appearance bond given for the charge.

(a-1) Notwithstanding any other provision of law, as an alternative to requiring a defendant charged with one or more offenses to make payment of all court costs as required by Subsection (a), the judge may:

(1) allow the defendant to enter into an agreement for payment of those costs in installments during the defendant's period of probation;

(2) require an eligible defendant to discharge all or part of those costs by performing community service or attending a tutoring program under Article 45.049 or 45.0492; or

(3) take any combination of actions authorized by Subdivision (1) or (2).

(b) During the deferral period, the judge may require the defendant to:

(1) post a bond in the amount of the fine assessed to secure payment of the fine;

(2) pay restitution to the victim of the offense in an amount not to exceed the fine assessed;

(3) submit to professional counseling;

(4) submit to diagnostic testing for alcohol or a controlled substance or drug;

(5) submit to a psychosocial assessment;

(6) participate in an alcohol or drug abuse treatment or education program;

(7) pay the costs of any diagnostic testing, psychosocial assessment, or participation in a treatment or education program either directly or through the court as court costs;

(8) complete a driving safety course approved under Chapter 1001, Education Code, or another course as directed by the judge;

(9) present to the court satisfactory evidence that the defendant has complied with each requirement imposed by the judge under this article; and

(10) comply with any other reasonable condition.

(b-1) **[2 Versions: Effective Until January 1, 2012]** If the defendant is younger than 25 years of age and the offense committed by the defendant is a traffic offense classified as a moving violation:

(1) Subsection (b)(8) does not apply;

(2) during the deferral period, the judge shall require the defendant to complete a driving safety course approved under Chapter 1001, Education Code; and

(3) if the defendant holds a provisional license, during the deferral period the judge shall require that the defendant be examined by the Department of Public Safety as required by Section 521.161(b)(2), Transportation Code; a defendant is not exempt from the examination regardless of whether the defendant was examined previously.

(b-1) **[2 Versions: Effective January 1, 2012]** If the defendant is younger than 25 years of age and the offense committed by the defendant is a traffic offense classified as a moving violation:

(1) Subsection (b)(8) does not apply;

(2) during the deferral period, the judge:

(A) shall require the defendant to complete a driving safety course approved under Chapter 1001, Education Code; and

(B) may require the defendant to complete an additional driving safety course designed for drivers younger than 25 years of age and approved under Section 1001.111, Education Code; and

(3) if the defendant holds a provisional license, during the deferral period the judge shall require that the defendant be examined by the Department of Public Safety as required by Section 521.161(b)(2), Transportation Code; a defendant is not exempt from the examination regardless of whether the defendant was examined previously.

(b-2) A person examined as required by Subsection (b-1)(3) must pay a $10 examination fee.

(b-3) The fee collected under Subsection (b-2) must be deposited to the credit of a special account in the general revenue fund and may be used only by the Department of Public Safety for the administration of Chapter 521, Transportation Code.

(c) On determining that the defendant has complied with the requirements imposed by the judge under this article, the judge shall dismiss the complaint, and it shall be clearly noted in the docket that the complaint is dismissed and that there is not a final conviction.

(c-1) If the defendant fails to present within the deferral period satisfactory evidence of compliance with the requirements imposed by the judge under this article, the court shall:

(1) notify the defendant in writing, mailed to the address on file with the court or appearing on the notice to appear, of that failure; and

(2) require the defendant to appear at the time and place stated in the notice to show cause why the order of deferral should not be revoked.

(c-2) On the defendant's showing of good cause for failure to present satisfactory evidence of compliance with the requirements imposed by the judge under this article, the court may allow an additional period during which the defendant may present evidence of the defendant's compliance with the requirements.

(d) If on the date of a show cause hearing under Subsection (c-1) or, if applicable, by the conclusion of an additional period provided under Subsection (c-2) the defendant does not present satisfactory evidence that the defendant complied with the requirements imposed, the judge may impose the fine assessed or impose a lesser fine. The imposition of the fine or lesser fine constitutes a final conviction of the defendant. This subsection does not apply to a defendant required under Subsection (b-1) to complete a driving safety course approved under Chapter 1001, Education Code, or an examination under Section 521.161(b)(2), Transportation Code.

(d-1) If the defendant was required to complete a driving safety course or an examination under Subsection (b-1) and on the date of a show cause hearing under Subsection (c-1) or, if applicable, by the conclusion of an additional period provided under Subsection (c-2) the defendant does not present satisfactory evidence that the defendant completed that course or examination, the judge shall impose the fine assessed. The imposition of the fine constitutes a final conviction of the defendant.

(e) Records relating to a complaint dismissed as provided by this article may be expunged under Article 55.01. If a complaint is dismissed under this article, there is not a final conviction and the complaint may not be used against the person for any purpose.

(f) This article does not apply to:

(1) an offense to which Section 542.404, Transportation Code, applies; or

(2) a violation of a state law or local ordinance relating to motor vehicle control, other than a parking violation, committed by a person who:

(A) holds a commercial driver's license; or

(B) held a commercial driver's license when the offense was committed.

(Enacted by Acts 1981, 67th Leg., ch. 318 (S.B. 914), § 1, effective September 1, 1981; am. Acts 1987, 70th Leg., ch. 226 (S.B. 1422), § 1, effective September 1, 1987; am. Acts 1989, 71st Leg., ch. 399 (S.B. 980), § 1, effective June 14, 1989; am. Acts 1991, 72nd Leg., ch. 775 (H.B. 1342), § 19, effective September 1, 1991; am. Acts 1991, 72nd Leg., ch. 835 (S.B. 757), § 4, effective September 1, 1991; am. Acts 1993, 73rd Leg., ch. 900 (S.B. 1067), § 5.07, effective September 1, 1993; am. Acts 1999, 76th Leg., ch. 532 (S.B. 185), § 1, effective September 1, 1999; am. Acts 1999, 76th Leg., ch. 1387 (H.B. 1603), § 1, effective September 1, 1999; am. Acts 1999, 76th Leg., ch. 1545 (S.B. 1230), § 50, effective September 1, 1999 (renumbered from art. 45.54); am. Acts 2001, 77th Leg., ch. 1420 (H.B. 2812), § 3.002, effective September 1, 2001; am. Acts 2003, 78th Leg., ch. 991 (S.B. 1904), § 12, effective September 1,

2003; am. Acts 2003, 78th Leg., ch. 1182 (S.B. 631), § 1, effective September 1, 2003; am. Acts 2003, 78th Leg., 3rd C.S., ch. 8 (H.B. 2), §§ 4.01, 4.03, effective January 11, 2004; am. Acts 2005, 79th Leg., ch. 90 (S.B. 1005), § 1, effective September 1, 2005; am. Acts 2005, 79th Leg., ch. 281 (H.B. 2702), § 3.01, effective June 14, 2005; am. Acts 2005, 79th Leg., ch. 357 (S.B. 1257), § 6, effective September 1, 2005; am. Acts 2007, 80th Leg., ch. 508 (S.B. 545), § 1, effective September 1, 2007; am. Acts 2007, 80th Leg., ch. 714 (H.B. 2267), § 1, effective September 1, 2007; am. Acts 2007, 80th Leg., ch. 921 (H.B. 3167), § 3.001, effective September 1, 2007; am. Acts 2009, 81st Leg., ch. 1121 (H.B. 1544), § 2, effective September 1, 2009; am. Acts 2011, 82nd Leg., ch. 227 (H.B. 350), § 2, effective January 1, 2012; am. Acts 2011, 82nd Leg., ch. 777 (H.B. 1964), § 2, effective September 1, 2011; am. Acts 2011, 82nd Leg., ch. 914 (S.B. 1330), § 1, effective January 1, 2012.)

## Art. 45.0511. Driving Safety Course or Motorcycle Operator Course Dismissal Procedures.

(a) Except as provided by Subsection (a-1), this article applies only to an alleged offense that:

(1) is within the jurisdiction of a justice court or a municipal court;

(2) involves the operation of a motor vehicle; and

(3) is defined by:

(A) Section 472.022, Transportation Code;

(B) Subtitle C, Title 7, Transportation Code; or

(C) Section 729.001(a)(3), Transportation Code.

(a-1) If the defendant is younger than 25 years of age, this article applies to any alleged offense that:

(1) is within the jurisdiction of a justice court or a municipal court;

(2) involves the operation of a motor vehicle; and

(3) is classified as a moving violation.

(b) The judge shall require the defendant to successfully complete a driving safety course approved by the Texas Education Agency or a course under the motorcycle operator training and safety program approved by the designated state agency under Chapter 662, Transportation Code, if:

(1) the defendant elects driving safety course or motorcycle operator training course dismissal under this article;

(2) the defendant:

(A) has not completed an approved driving safety course or motorcycle operator training course, as appropriate, within the 12 months preceding the date of the offense; or

(B) does not have a valid Texas driver's license or permit, is a member, or the spouse or dependent child of a member, of the United States military forces serving on active duty, and has not completed a driving safety course or motorcycle operator training course, as appropriate, in another state within the 12 months preceding the date of the offense;

(3) the defendant enters a plea under Article 45.021 in person or in writing of no contest or guilty on or before the answer date on the notice to appear and:

(A) presents in person or by counsel to the court a request to take a course; or

(B) sends to the court by certified mail, return receipt requested, postmarked on or before the answer date on the notice to appear, a written request to take a course;

(4) the defendant:

(A) has a valid Texas driver's license or permit; or

(B) is a member, or the spouse or dependent child of a member, of the United States military forces serving on active duty;

(5) the defendant is charged with an offense to which this article applies, other than speeding at a speed of:

(A) 95 miles per hour or more; or

(B) 25 miles per hour or more over the posted speed limit; and

(6) the defendant provides evidence of financial responsibility as required by Chapter 601, Transportation Code.

(c) The court shall enter judgment on the defendant's plea of no contest or guilty at the time the plea is made, defer imposition of the judgment, and allow the defendant 90 days to successfully complete the approved driving safety course or motorcycle operator training course and present to the court:

(1) a uniform certificate of completion of the driving safety course or a verification of completion of the motorcycle operator training course;

(2) unless the judge proceeds under Subsection (c-1), the defendant's driving record as maintained by the Department of Public Safety, if any, showing that the defendant had not completed an approved driving safety

course or motorcycle operator training course, as applicable, within the 12 months preceding the date of the offense;

(3) an affidavit stating that the defendant was not taking a driving safety course or motorcycle operator training course, as applicable, under this article on the date the request to take the course was made and had not completed such a course that is not shown on the defendant's driving record within the 12 months preceding the date of the offense; and

(4) if the defendant does not have a valid Texas driver's license or permit and is a member, or the spouse or dependent child of a member, of the United States military forces serving on active duty, an affidavit stating that the defendant was not taking a driving safety course or motorcycle operator training course, as appropriate, in another state on the date the request to take the course was made and had not completed such a course within the 12 months preceding the date of the offense.

(c-1) In this subsection, "state electronic Internet portal" has the meaning assigned by Section 2054.003, Government Code. As an alternative to receiving the defendant's driving record under Subsection (c)(2), the judge, at the time the defendant requests a driving safety course or motorcycle operator training course dismissal under this article, may require the defendant to pay a fee in an amount equal to the sum of the amount of the fee established by Section 521.048, Transportation Code, and the state electronic Internet portal fee and, using the state electronic Internet portal, may request the Texas Department of Public Safety to provide the judge with a copy of the defendant's driving record that shows the information described by Section 521.047(b), Transportation Code. As soon as practicable and using the state electronic Internet portal, the Texas Department of Public Safety shall provide the judge with the requested copy of the defendant's driving record. The fee authorized by this subsection is in addition to any other fee required under this article. If the copy of the defendant's driving record provided to the judge under this subsection shows that the defendant has not completed an approved driving safety course or motorcycle operator training course, as appropriate, within the 12 months preceding the date of the offense, the judge shall allow the defendant to complete the appropriate course as provided by this article. The custodian of a municipal or county treasury who receives fees collected under this subsection shall keep a record of the fees and, without deduction or proration, forward the fees to the comptroller, with and in the manner required for other fees and costs received in connection with criminal cases. The comptroller shall credit fees received under this subsection to the Texas Department of Public Safety.

(d) Notwithstanding Subsections (b)(2) and (3), before the final disposition of the case, the court may grant a request to take a driving safety course or a motorcycle operator training course under this article.

(e) A request to take a driving safety course or motorcycle operator training course made at or before the time and at the place at which a defendant is required to appear in court is an appearance in compliance with the defendant's promise to appear.

(f) In addition to court costs and fees authorized or imposed by a law of this state and applicable to the offense, the court may:

(1) require a defendant requesting a course under Subsection (b) to pay an administrative fee set by the court to cover the cost of administering this article at an amount of not more than $10; or

(2) require a defendant requesting a course under Subsection (d) to pay a fee set by the court at an amount not to exceed the maximum amount of the fine for the offense committed by the defendant.

(g) A defendant who requests but does not take a course is not entitled to a refund of the fee.

(h) Fees collected by a municipal court shall be deposited in the municipal treasury. Fees collected by another court shall be deposited in the county treasury of the county in which the court is located.

(i) If a defendant requesting a course under this article fails to comply with Subsection (c), the court shall:

(1) notify the defendant in writing, mailed to the address on file with the court or appearing on the notice to appear, of that failure; and

(2) require the defendant to appear at the time and place stated in the notice to show cause why the evidence was not timely submitted to the court.

(j) If the defendant fails to appear at the time and place stated in the notice under Subsection (i), or appears at the time and place stated in the notice but does not show good cause for the defendant's failure to comply with Subsection (c), the court shall enter an adjudication of guilt and impose sentence.

(k) On a defendant's showing of good cause for failure to furnish evidence to the court, the court may allow an extension of time during which the defendant may present:

(1) a uniform certificate of course completion as evidence that the defendant successfully completed the driving safety course; or

(2) a verification of course completion as evidence that the defendant successfully completed the motorcycle operator training course.

(l) When a defendant complies with Subsection (c), the court shall:

(1) remove the judgment and dismiss the charge;

(2) report the fact that the defendant successfully completed a driving safety course or a motorcycle operator training course and the date of completion to the Texas Department of Public Safety for inclusion in the person's driving record; and

(3) state in that report whether the course was taken under this article to provide information necessary to determine eligibility to take a subsequent course under Subsection (b).

(m) The court may dismiss only one charge for each completion of a course.

(n) A charge that is dismissed under this article may not be part of a person's driving record or used for any purpose.

(o) An insurer delivering or issuing for delivery a motor vehicle insurance policy in this state may not cancel or increase the premium charged an insured under the policy because the insured completed a driving safety course or a motorcycle operator training course, or had a charge dismissed under this article.

(p) The court shall advise a defendant charged with a misdemeanor under Section 472.022, Transportation Code, Subtitle C, Title 7, Transportation Code, or Section 729.001(a)(3), Transportation Code, committed while operating a motor vehicle of the defendant's right under this article to successfully complete a driving safety course or, if the offense was committed while operating a motorcycle, a motorcycle operator training course. The right to complete a course does not apply to a defendant charged with:

(1) a violation of Section 545.066, 550.022, or 550.023, Transportation Code;

(2) a serious traffic violation; or

(3) an offense to which Section 542.404 or 729.004(b), Transportation Code, applies.

(q) A notice to appear issued for an offense to which this article applies must inform a defendant charged with an offense under Section

Criminal Procedure

472.022, Transportation Code, an offense under Subtitle C, Title 7, Transportation Code, or an offense under Section 729.001(a)(3), Transportation Code, committed while operating a motor vehicle of the defendant's right to complete a driving safety course or, if the offense was committed while operating a motorcycle, of the defendant's right to complete a motorcycle operator training course. The notice required by this subsection must read substantially as follows:

"You may be able to require that this charge be dismissed by successfully completing a driving safety course or a motorcycle operator training course. You will lose that right if, on or before your appearance date, you do not provide the court with notice of your request to take the course."

(r) If the notice required by Subsection (q) is not provided to the defendant charged with the offense, the defendant may continue to exercise the defendant's right to take a driving safety course or a motorcycle operator training course until the notice required by Subsection (q) is provided to the defendant or there is a final disposition of the case.

(s) This article does not apply to an offense committed by a person who:

(1) holds a commercial driver's license; or

(2) held a commercial driver's license when the offense was committed.

(t) An order of deferral under Subsection (c) terminates any liability under a bail bond or appearance bond given for the charge.

(u) The requirement of Subsection (b)(2) does not apply to a defendant charged with an offense under Section 545.412, Transportation Code, if the judge requires the defendant to attend and present proof that the defendant has successfully completed a specialized driving safety course that includes four hours of instruction that encourages the use of child passenger safety seat systems, and any driving safety course taken by the defendant under this section within the 12 months preceding the date of the offense did not include that training. The person's driving record under Subsection (c)(2) and the affidavit of the defendant under Subsection (c)(3) is required to include only previous or concurrent courses that included that training.

(Enacted by Acts 1999, 76th Leg., ch. 1545 (S.B. 1230), § 51, effective September 1, 1999; am. Acts 2001, 77th Leg., ch. 1420 (H.B. 2812), § 3.0021(a), effective September 1, 2001; am. Acts 2003, 78th Leg., ch. 991 (S.B. 1904), § 13, effective September 1, 2003; am. Acts 2003, 78th

Leg., ch. 1182 (S.B. 631), § 2, effective September 1, 2003; am. Acts 2003, 78th Leg., 3rd C.S., ch. 8 (H.B. 2), § 4.02, effective January 11, 2004; am. Acts 2005, 79th Leg., ch. 90 (S.B. 1005), § 2, effective September 1, 2005; am. Acts 2005, 79th Leg., ch. 357 (S.B. 1257), § 7, effective September 1, 2005; am. Acts 2005, 79th Leg., ch. 913 (H.B. 183), § 6, effective September 1, 2005; am. Acts 2005, 79th Leg., ch. 1194 (H.B. 370), § 1, effective September 1, 2005; am. Acts 2005, 79th Leg., ch. 1209 (H.B. 703), § 1, effective September 1, 2005; am. Acts 2007, 80th Leg., ch. 805 (S.B. 1083), § 1, effective September 1, 2007; am. Acts 2007, 80th Leg., ch. 829 (H.B. 586), § 1, effective September 1, 2007; am. Acts 2011, 82nd Leg., ch. 973 (H.B. 1504), § 1, effective June 17, 2011.)

## Art. 45.052. Dismissal of Misdemeanor Charge on Completion of Teen Court Program.

(a) A justice or municipal court may defer proceedings against a defendant who is under the age of 18 or enrolled full time in an accredited secondary school in a program leading toward a high school diploma for not more than 180 days if the defendant:

(1) is charged with an offense that the court has jurisdiction of under Article 4.11 or 4.14, Code of Criminal Procedure;

(2) pleads nolo contendere or guilty to the offense in open court with the defendant's parent, guardian, or managing conservator present;

(3) presents to the court an oral or written request to attend a teen court program; and

(4) has not successfully completed a teen court program in the two years preceding the date that the alleged offense occurred.

(b) The teen court program must be approved by the court.

(c) A defendant for whom proceedings are deferred under Subsection (a) shall complete the teen court program not later than the 90th day after the date the teen court hearing to determine punishment is held or the last day of the deferral period, whichever date is earlier. The justice or municipal court shall dismiss the charge at the time the defendant presents satisfactory evidence that the defendant has successfully completed the teen court program.

(d) A charge dismissed under this article may not be part of the defendant's criminal record or driving record or used for any purpose. However, if the charge was for a traffic offense, the court shall report to the Department of Public Safety that the defendant successfully completed the teen court program and the date of completion for inclusion in the defendant's driving record.

(e) The justice or municipal court may require a person who requests a teen court program to pay a fee not to exceed $10 that is set by the court to cover the costs of administering this article. Fees collected by a municipal court shall be deposited in the municipal treasury. Fees collected by a justice court shall be deposited in the county treasury of the county in which the court is located. A person who requests a teen court program and fails to complete the program is not entitled to a refund of the fee.

(f) A court may transfer a case in which proceedings have been deferred under this section to a court in another county if the court to which the case is transferred consents. A case may not be transferred unless it is within the jurisdiction of the court to which it is transferred.

(g) In addition to the fee authorized by Subsection (e) of this article, the court may require a child who requests a teen court program to pay a $10 fee to cover the cost to the teen court for performing its duties under this article. The court shall pay the fee to the teen court program, and the teen court program must account to the court for the receipt and disbursal of the fee. A child who pays a fee under this subsection is not entitled to a refund of the fee, regardless of whether the child successfully completes the teen court program.

(h) A justice or municipal court may exempt a defendant for whom proceedings are deferred under this article from the requirement to pay a court cost or fee that is imposed by another statute.

(i) Notwithstanding Subsection (e) or (g), a justice or municipal court that is located in the Texas-Louisiana border region, as defined by Section 2056.002, Government Code, may charge a fee of $20 under those subsections.
(Enacted by Acts 1989, 71st Leg., ch. 1031 (H.B. 198), § 1, effective September 1, 1989; am. Acts 1995, 74th Leg., ch. 598 (H.B. 330) § 1, effective September 1, 1995; am. Acts 1995, 74th Leg., ch. 748 (H.B. 120), § 2, effective September 1, 1995; am. Acts 1997, 75th Leg., ch. 165 (S.B. 198), § 31.01(13), effective September 1, 1997; am. Acts 1999, 76th Leg., ch. 76 (H.B. 688), § 6, effective September 1, 1999; am. Acts 1999, 76th Leg., ch. 1545 (S.B. 1230), § 52, effective September 1, 1999 (renumbered from art. 45.55); am. Acts 2001, 77th Leg., ch. 216 (H.B. 822), § 1,

effective September 1, 2001; am. Acts 2007, 80th Leg., ch. 910 (H.B. 2949), § 1, effective September 1, 2007.)

## Art. 45.053. Dismissal of Misdemeanor Charge on Commitment of Chemically Dependent Person.

(a) On a plea of guilty or nolo contendere by a defendant or on a finding of guilt in a misdemeanor case punishable by a fine only, a justice or municipal court may defer further proceedings for 90 days without entering an adjudication of guilt if:

(1) the court finds that the offense resulted from or was related to the defendant's chemical dependency; and

(2) an application for court-ordered treatment of the defendant is filed in accordance with Chapter 462, Health and Safety Code.

(b) At the end of the deferral period, the justice or municipal court shall dismiss the charge if satisfactory evidence is presented that the defendant was committed for and completed court-ordered treatment in accordance with Chapter 462, Health and Safety Code, and it shall be clearly noted in the docket that the complaint is dismissed and that there is not a final conviction.

(c) If at the conclusion of the deferral period satisfactory evidence that the defendant was committed for and completed court-ordered treatment in accordance with Chapter 462, Health and Safety Code, is not presented, the justice or municipal court may impose the fine assessed or impose a lesser fine. The imposition of a fine constitutes a final conviction of the defendant.

(d) Records relating to a complaint dismissed under this article may be expunged under Article 55.01 of this code. If a complaint is dismissed under this article, there is not a final conviction and the complaint may not be used against the person for any purpose.
(Enacted by Acts 1991, 72nd Leg., ch. 198 (H.B. 960), § 1, effective September 1, 1991; am. Acts 1999, 76th Leg., ch. 1545 (S.B. 1230), § 53, effective September 1, 1999 (renumbered from art. 45.56).)

## Art. 45.054. Failure to Attend School Proceedings.

(a) On a finding by a county, justice, or municipal court that an individual has committed an offense under Section 25.094, Education Code, the court has jurisdiction to enter an order that includes one or more of the following provisions requiring that:

Criminal Procedure

(1) the individual:

(A) attend school without unexcused absences;

(B) attend a preparatory class for the high school equivalency examination administered under Section 7.111, Education Code, if the court determines that the individual is too old to do well in a formal classroom environment; or

(C) if the individual is at least 16 years of age, take the high school equivalency examination administered under Section 7.111, Education Code;

(2) the individual attend a special program that the court determines to be in the best interest of the individual, including:

(A) an alcohol and drug abuse program;

(B) a rehabilitation program;

(C) a counseling program, including self-improvement counseling;

(D) a program that provides training in self-esteem and leadership;

(E) a work and job skills training program;

(F) a program that provides training in parenting, including parental responsibility;

(G) a program that provides training in manners;

(H) a program that provides training in violence avoidance;

(I) a program that provides sensitivity training; and

(J) a program that provides training in advocacy and mentoring;

(3) the individual and the individual's parent attend a class for students at risk of dropping out of school designed for both the individual and the individual's parent;

(4) the individual complete reasonable community service requirements; or

(5) for the total number of hours ordered by the court, the individual participate in a tutorial program covering the academic subjects in which the student is enrolled provided by the school the individual attends.

(a-1) On a finding by a juvenile court in a county with a population of less than 100,000 that the individual has engaged in conduct that violates Section 25.094, Education Code, the court has jurisdiction to enter an order that includes one or more of the provisions listed under Subsection (a).

(a-2) An order under Subsection (a) may not require a student to attend a juvenile justice alternative education program.

(b) An order under Subsection (a)(3) that requires the parent of an individual to attend a class for students at risk of dropping out of school is enforceable in the justice, municipal, or juvenile court by contempt.

(c) A court having jurisdiction under this article shall endorse on the summons issued to the parent of the individual who is the subject of the hearing an order directing the parent to appear personally at the hearing and directing the person having custody of the individual to bring the individual to the hearing.

(d) An individual commits an offense if the individual is a parent who fails to attend a hearing under this article after receiving notice under Subsection (c) that the individual's attendance is required. An offense under this subsection is a Class C misdemeanor.

(e) On the commencement of proceedings under this article, the court shall inform the individual who is the subject of the hearing and the individual's parent in open court of the individual's expunction rights and provide the individual and the individual's parent with a written copy of Article 45.055.

(f) In addition to any other order authorized by this article, the court may order the Department of Public Safety to suspend the driver's license or permit of the individual who is the subject of the hearing or, if the individual does not have a license or permit, to deny the issuance of a license or permit to the individual for a period specified by the court not to exceed 365 days.

(g) A dispositional order under this article is effective for the period specified by the court in the order but may not extend beyond the 180th day after the date of the order or beyond the end of the school year in which the order was entered, whichever period is longer.

(h) In this article, "parent" includes a person standing in parental relation.

(i) A county, justice, or municipal court shall dismiss the complaint against an individual alleging that the individual committed an offense under Section 25.094, Education Code, if:

(1) the court finds that the individual has successfully complied with the conditions imposed on the individual by the court under this article; or

(2) the individual presents to the court proof that the individual has obtained a high school diploma or a high school equivalency certificate.

(j) A county, justice, or municipal court may waive or reduce a fee or court cost imposed under this article if the court finds that payment of the fee or court cost would cause financial hardship. (Enacted by Acts 2001, 77th Leg., ch. 1514 (S.B. 1432), § 9, effective September 1, 2001; am. Acts 2003, 78th Leg., ch. 137 (S.B. 358), § 14, effective September 1, 2003; am. Acts 2003, 78th Leg., ch. 180 (H.B. 829), § 1, effective September 1, 2003; am. Acts 2007, 80th Leg., ch. 908 (H.B. 2884), § 2, effective September 1, 2007; am. Acts 2011, 82nd Leg., ch. 1098 (S.B. 1489), § 6, effective September 1, 2011.)

### Art. 45.055. Expunction of Conviction and Records in Failure to Attend School Cases.

(a) Except as provided by Subsection (e), an individual convicted of not more than one violation of Section 25.094, Education Code, may, on or after the individual's 18th birthday, apply to the court in which the individual was convicted to have the conviction and records relating to the conviction expunged.

(b) To apply for an expunction, the applicant must submit a written request that:

(1) is made under oath;

(2) states that the applicant has not been convicted of more than one violation of Section 25.094, Education Code; and

(3) is in the form determined by the applicant.

(c) The court may expunge the conviction and records relating to the conviction without a hearing or, if facts are in doubt, may order a hearing on the application. If the court finds that the applicant has not been convicted of more than one violation of Section 25.094, Education Code, the court shall order the conviction, together with all complaints, verdicts, sentences, and other documents relating to the offense, including any documents in the possession of a school district or law enforcement agency, to be expunged from the applicant's record. After entry of the order, the applicant is released from all disabilities resulting from the conviction, and the conviction may not be shown or made known for any purpose. The court shall inform the applicant of the court's decision on the application.

(d) The court shall require an individual who files an application under this article to pay a fee in the amount of $30 to defray the cost of notifying state agencies of orders of expunction under this article.

(e) A court shall expunge an individual's conviction under Section 25.094, Education Code, and records relating to a conviction, regardless of whether the individual has previously been convicted of an offense under that section, if:

(1) the court finds that the individual has successfully complied with the conditions imposed on the individual by the court under Article 45.054; or

(2) before the individual's 21st birthday, the individual presents to the court proof that the individual has obtained a high school diploma or a high school equivalency certificate.

(Enacted by Acts 2001, 77th Leg., ch. 1514 (S.B. 1432), § 9, effective September 1, 2001; am. Acts 2003, 78th Leg., ch. 137 (S.B. 358), § 15, effective September 1, 2003; am. Acts 2005, 79th Leg., ch. 886 (S.B. 1426), § 3, effective September 1, 2005; am. Acts 2011, 82nd Leg., ch. 1098 (S.B. 1489), § 7, effective September 1, 2011.)

### Art. 45.056. Juvenile Case Managers.

(a) On approval of the commissioners court, city council, school district board of trustees, juvenile board, or other appropriate authority, a county court, justice court, municipal court, school district, juvenile probation department, or other appropriate governmental entity may:

(1) employ a case manager to provide services in cases involving juvenile offenders before a court consistent with the court's statutory powers; or

(2) agree in accordance with Chapter 791, Government Code, to jointly employ a case manager.

(b) A local entity may apply or more than one local entity may jointly apply to the criminal justice division of the governor's office for reimbursement of all or part of the costs of employing one or more juvenile case managers from funds appropriated to the governor's office or otherwise available for that purpose. To be eligible for reimbursement, the entity applying must present to the governor's office a comprehensive plan to reduce juvenile crimes in the entity's jurisdiction that addresses the role of the case manager in that effort.

(c) A county or justice court on approval of the commissioners court or a municipality or municipal court on approval of the city council may employ one or more juvenile case managers to assist the court in administering the court's juvenile docket and in supervising its court orders in juvenile cases.

(d) Pursuant to Article 102.0174, the court or governing body may pay the salary and benefits of a juvenile case manager and the costs of training, travel, office supplies, and other necessary expenses relating to the position of the juvenile case manager from the juvenile case manager fund.

(e) [Repealed by Acts 2011, 82nd Leg., ch. 1098 (S.B. 1489), § 16, effective September 1, 2011.]

(f) **[2 Versions: As added by Acts 2011, 82nd Leg., ch. 868]** The governing body of the employing governmental entity under Subsection (a) shall adopt reasonable rules for juvenile case managers that provide:

(1) a code of ethics, and for the enforcement of the code of ethics;

(2) appropriate educational preservice and in-service training standards for juvenile case managers; and

(3) training in:

(A) the role of the juvenile case manager;

(B) case planning and management;

(C) applicable procedural and substantive law;

(D) courtroom proceedings and presentation;

(E) services to at-risk youth under Subchapter D, Chapter 264, Family Code;

(F) local programs and services for juveniles and methods by which juveniles may access those programs and services; and

(G) detecting and preventing abuse, exploitation, and neglect of juveniles.

(f) **[2 Versions: As added by Acts 2011, 82nd Leg., ch. 1055]** The juvenile case manager shall timely report to the judge who signed the order or judgment and, on request, to the judge assigned to the case or the presiding judge any information or recommendations relevant to assisting the judge in making decisions that are in the best interest of the child.

(g) **[2 Versions: As added by Acts 2011, 82nd Leg., ch. 868]** The employing court or governmental entity under this article shall implement the rules adopted under Subsection (f).

(g) **[2 Versions: As added by Acts 2011, 82nd Leg., ch. 1055]** The judge who is assigned to the case shall consult with the juvenile case manager who is supervising the case regarding:

(1) the child's home environment;

(2) the child's developmental, psychological, and educational status;

(3) the child's previous interaction with the justice system; and

(4) any sanctions available to the court that would be in the best interest of the child.

(h) **[2 Versions: As added by Acts 2011, 82nd Leg., ch. 868]** The commissioners court or governing body of the municipality that administers a juvenile case manager fund under Article 102.0174 shall require periodic review of juvenile case managers to ensure the implementation of the rules adopted under Subsection (f).

(h) **[2 Versions: As added by Acts 2011, 82nd Leg., ch. 1055]** Subsections (f) and (g) do not apply to:

(1) a part-time judge; or

(2) a county judge of a county court that has one or more appointed full-time magistrates under Section 54.1172, Government Code.

(Enacted by Acts 2001, 77th Leg., ch. 1514 (S.B. 1432), § 9, effective September 1, 2001; am. Acts 2003, 78th Leg., ch. 283 (H.B. 2319), § 33, effective September 1, 2003; am. Acts 2005, 79th Leg., ch. 949 (H.B. 1575), § 34, effective September 1, 2005; am. Acts 2011, 82nd Leg., ch. 868 (S.B. 61), §§ 1, 2, effective June 17, 2011; am. Acts 2011, 82nd Leg., ch. 1055 (S.B. 209), § 1, effective September 1, 2011; am. Acts 2011, 82nd Leg., ch. 1098 (S.B. 1489), § 16, effective September 1, 2011.)

## Art. 45.057. Offenses Committed by Juveniles.

(a) In this article:

(1) "Child" has the meaning assigned by Article 45.058(h).

(2) "Residence" means any place where the child lives or resides for a period of at least 30 days.

(3) "Parent" includes a person standing in parental relation, a managing conservator, or a custodian.

(b) On a finding by a justice or municipal court that a child committed an offense that the court has jurisdiction of under Article 4.11 or 4.14, the court has jurisdiction to enter an order:

(1) referring the child or the child's parent for services under Section 264.302, Family Code;

(2) requiring that the child attend a special program that the court determines to be in the best interest of the child and, if the program involves the expenditure of municipal or county funds, that is approved by the governing body of the municipality or county commissioners court, as applicable, including a rehabilitation, counseling, self-esteem and leadership, work and job skills training, job interviewing and work preparation, self-improvement, parent-

ing, manners, violence avoidance, tutoring, sensitivity training, parental responsibility, community service, restitution, advocacy, or mentoring program; or

　　(3) requiring that the child's parent do any act or refrain from doing any act that the court determines will increase the likelihood that the child will comply with the orders of the court and that is reasonable and necessary for the welfare of the child, including:

　　　　(A) attend a parenting class or parental responsibility program; and

　　　　(B) attend the child's school classes or functions.

　　(c) The justice or municipal court may order the parent, managing conservator, or guardian of a child required to attend a program under Subsection (b) to pay an amount not greater than $100 to pay for the costs of the program.

　　(d) A justice or municipal court may require a child, parent, managing conservator, or guardian required to attend a program, class, or function under this article to submit proof of attendance to the court.

　　(e) A justice or municipal court shall endorse on the summons issued to a parent an order to appear personally at the hearing with the child. The summons must include a warning that the failure of the parent to appear may result in arrest and is a Class C misdemeanor.

　　(f) An order under this article involving a child is enforceable under Article 45.050.

　　(g) A person commits an offense if the person is a parent, managing conservator, or guardian who fails to attend a hearing under this article after receiving an order under Subsection (e). An offense under this subsection is a Class C misdemeanor.

　　(h) A child and parent required to appear before the court have an obligation to provide the court in writing with the current address and residence of the child. The obligation does not end when the child reaches age 17. On or before the seventh day after the date the child or parent changes residence, the child or parent shall notify the court of the current address in the manner directed by the court. A violation of this subsection may result in arrest and is a Class C misdemeanor. The obligation to provide notice terminates on discharge and satisfaction of the judgment or final disposition not requiring a finding of guilt.

　　(i) If an appellate court accepts an appeal for a trial de novo, the child and parent shall provide the notice under Subsection (h) to the appellate court.

　　(j) The child and parent are entitled to written notice of their obligation under Subsections (h) and (i), which may be satisfied by being given a copy of those subsections by:

　　　　(1) the court during their initial appearance before the court;

　　　　(2) a peace officer arresting and releasing a child under Article 45.058(a) on release; and

　　　　(3) a peace officer that issues a citation under Section 543.003, Transportation Code, or Article 14.06(b) of this code.

　　(k) It is an affirmative defense to prosecution under Subsection (h) that the child and parent were not informed of their obligation under this article.

　　(*l*) Any order under this article is enforceable by the justice or municipal court by contempt.
(Enacted by Acts 2001, 77th Leg., ch. 1514 (S.B. 1432), § 9, effective September 1, 2001; am. Acts 2003, 78th Leg., ch. 283 (H.B. 2319), § 34, effective September 1, 2003; am. Acts 2011, 82nd Leg., ch. 777 (H.B. 1964), § 3, effective September 1, 2011.)

## Art. 45.058. Children Taken into Custody.

　　(a) A child may be released to the child's parent, guardian, custodian, or other responsible adult as provided by Section 52.02(a)(1), Family Code, if the child is taken into custody for an offense that a justice or municipal court has jurisdiction of under Article 4.11 or 4.14.

　　(b) A child described by Subsection (a) must be taken only to a place previously designated by the head of the law enforcement agency with custody of the child as an appropriate place of nonsecure custody for children unless the child:

　　　　(1) is released under Section 52.02(a)(1), Family Code; or

　　　　(2) is taken before a justice or municipal court.

　　(c) A place of nonsecure custody for children must be an unlocked, multipurpose area. A lobby, office, or interrogation room is suitable if the area is not designated, set aside, or used as a secure detention area and is not part of a secure detention area. A place of nonsecure custody may be a juvenile processing office designated under Section 52.025, Family Code, if the area is not locked when it is used as a place of nonsecure custody.

　　(d) The following procedures shall be followed in a place of nonsecure custody for children:

Criminal Procedure

(1) a child may not be secured physically to a cuffing rail, chair, desk, or other stationary object;

(2) the child may be held in the nonsecure facility only long enough to accomplish the purpose of identification, investigation, processing, release to parents, or the arranging of transportation to the appropriate juvenile court, juvenile detention facility, secure detention facility, justice court, or municipal court;

(3) residential use of the area is prohibited; and

(4) the child shall be under continuous visual supervision by a law enforcement officer or facility staff person during the time the child is in nonsecure custody.

(e) Notwithstanding any other provision of this article, a child may not, under any circumstances, be detained in a place of nonsecure custody for more than six hours.

(f) A child taken into custody for an offense that a justice or municipal court has jurisdiction of under Article 4.11 or 4.14 may be presented or detained in a detention facility designated by the juvenile court under Section 52.02(a)(3), Family Code, only if:

(1) the child's non-traffic case is transferred to the juvenile court by a justice or municipal court under Section 51.08(b), Family Code; or

(2) the child is referred to the juvenile court by a justice or municipal court for contempt of court under Article 45.050.

(g) Except as provided by Subsection (g-1), a law enforcement officer may issue a field release citation as provided by Article 14.06 in place of taking a child into custody for a traffic offense or an offense punishable by fine only.

(g-1) A law enforcement officer may issue a field release citation as provided by Article 14.06 in place of taking a child into custody for conduct constituting a violation of Section 49.02, Penal Code, only if the officer releases the child to the child's parent, guardian, custodian, or other responsible adult.

(h) In this article, "child" means a person who is:

(1) at least 10 years of age and younger than 17 years of age; and

(2) charged with or convicted of an offense that a justice or municipal court has jurisdiction of under Article 4.11 or 4.14.

(Enacted by Acts 2001, 77th Leg., ch. 1514 (S.B. 1432), § 9, effective September 1, 2001; am. Acts 2009, 81st Leg., ch. 311 (H.B. 558), § 2, effective September 1, 2009.)

## Art. 45.059. Children Taken into Custody for Violation of Juvenile Curfew or Order.

(a) A peace officer taking into custody a person younger than 17 years of age for violation of a juvenile curfew ordinance of a municipality or order of the commissioners court of a county shall, without unnecessary delay:

(1) release the person to the person's parent, guardian, or custodian;

(2) take the person before a justice or municipal court to answer the charge; or

(3) take the person to a place designated as a juvenile curfew processing office by the head of the law enforcement agency having custody of the person.

(b) A juvenile curfew processing office must observe the following procedures:

(1) the office must be an unlocked, multipurpose area that is not designated, set aside, or used as a secure detention area or part of a secure detention area;

(2) the person may not be secured physically to a cuffing rail, chair, desk, or stationary object;

(3) the person may not be held longer than necessary to accomplish the purposes of identification, investigation, processing, release to a parent, guardian, or custodian, or arrangement of transportation to school or court;

(4) a juvenile curfew processing office may not be designated or intended for residential purposes;

(5) the person must be under continuous visual supervision by a peace officer or other person during the time the person is in the juvenile curfew processing office; and

(6) a person may not be held in a juvenile curfew processing office for more than six hours.

(c) A place designated under this article as a juvenile curfew processing office is not subject to the approval of the juvenile board having jurisdiction where the governmental entity is located. (Enacted by Acts 2001, 77th Leg., ch. 1514 (S.B. 1432), § 9, effective September 1, 2001.)

## Art. 45.060. Unadjudicated Children, Now Adults; Notice on Reaching Age of Majority; Offense.

(a) Except as provided by Articles 45.058 and 45.059, an individual may not be taken into secured custody for offenses alleged to have occurred before the individual's 17th birthday.

(b) On or after an individual's 17th birthday, if the court has used all available procedures under this chapter to secure the individual's appearance to answer allegations made before the individual's 17th birthday, the court may issue a notice of continuing obligation to appear by personal service or by mail to the last known address and residence of the individual. The notice must order the individual to appear at a designated time, place, and date to answer the allegations detailed in the notice.

(c) Failure to appear as ordered by the notice under Subsection (b) is a Class C misdemeanor independent of Section 38.10, Penal Code, and Section 543.003, Transportation Code.

(d) It is an affirmative defense to prosecution under Subsection (c) that the individual was not informed of the individual's obligation under Articles 45.057(h) and (i) or did not receive notice as required by Subsection (b).

(e) A notice of continuing obligation to appear issued under this article must contain the following statement provided in boldfaced type or capital letters:

"WARNING: COURT RECORDS REVEAL THAT BEFORE YOUR 17TH BIRTHDAY YOU WERE ACCUSED OF A CRIMINAL OFFENSE AND HAVE FAILED TO MAKE AN APPEARANCE OR ENTER A PLEA IN THIS MATTER. AS AN ADULT, YOU ARE NOTIFIED THAT YOU HAVE A CONTINUING OBLIGATION TO APPEAR IN THIS CASE. FAILURE TO APPEAR AS REQUIRED BY THIS NOTICE MAY BE AN ADDITIONAL CRIMINAL OFFENSE AND RESULT IN A WARRANT BEING ISSUED FOR YOUR ARREST."

(Enacted by Acts 2003, 78th Leg., ch. 283 (H.B. 2319), § 35, effective September 1, 2003.)

## Art. 45.06. Fines and Special Expenses [Renumbered].

Renumbered to Tex. Code Crim. Proc. art. 45.203 by Acts 1999, 76th Leg., ch. 1545 (S.B. 1230), § 61, effective September 1, 1999.

## Art. 45.061. Proceedings Concerning Electronic Transmission of Certain Visual Material Depicting Minor.

(a) In this article, "parent" means a natural or adoptive parent, managing or possessory conservator, or legal guardian. The term does not include a parent whose parental rights have been terminated.

(b) If a justice or municipal court finds that a defendant has committed an offense under Sec-

tion 43.261, Penal Code, the court may enter an order requiring the defendant to attend and successfully complete an educational program described by Section 37.218, Education Code, or another equivalent educational program.

(c) A court that enters an order under Subsection (b) shall require the defendant or the defendant's parent to pay the cost of attending an educational program under Subsection (b) if the court determines that the defendant or the defendant's parent is financially able to make payment.

(Enacted by Acts 2011, 82nd Leg., ch. 1322 (S.B. 407), § 15, effective September 1, 2011.)

## Art. 45.07. Collection of Costs [Repealed].

Repealed by Acts 1999, 76th Leg., ch. 1545 (S.B. 1230), § 75(a), effective September 1, 1999. (Enacted by Acts 1965, 59th Leg., ch. 722 (S.B. 107), § 1, effective January 1, 1966.)

## Art. 45.08. Jury Fees [Repealed].

Repealed by Acts 1999, 76th Leg., ch. 1545 (S.B. 1230), § 75(a), effective September 1, 1999. (Enacted by Acts 1965, 59th Leg., ch. 722 (S.B. 107), § 1, effective January 1, 1966.)

## Art. 45.09. Officers' Fees [Repealed].

Repealed by Acts 1999, 76th Leg., ch. 1545 (S.B. 1230), § 75(a), effective September 1, 1999. (Enacted by Acts 1965, 59th Leg., ch. 722 (S.B. 107), § 1, effective January 1, 1966.)

## Art. 45.10. Appeal [Renumbered].

Renumbered to Tex. Code Crim Proc. art. 45.042 by Acts 1999, 76th Leg., ch. 1545 (S.B. 1230), § 40, effective September 1, 1999.

## SUBCHAPTER C
## PROCEDURES IN JUSTICE COURT

## Art. 45.101. Justice Court Prosecutions.

(a) All prosecutions in a justice court shall be conducted by the county or district attorney or a deputy county or district attorney.

(b) Except as otherwise provided by law, appeals from justice court may be prosecuted by the district attorney or a deputy district attorney with the consent of the county attorney.

(Enacted by Acts 1999, 76th Leg., ch. 1545 (S.B. 1230), § 55, effective September 1, 1999.)

## Art. 45.102. Offenses Committed in Another County.

Whenever complaint is made before any justice of the peace that a felony has been committed in any other than a county in which the complaint is made, the justice shall issue a warrant for the arrest of the accused, directed as in other cases, commanding that the accused be arrested and taken before any magistrate of the county where such felony is alleged to have been committed, forthwith, for examination as in other cases.
(Enacted by Acts 1965, 59th Leg., ch. 722 (S.B. 107), § 1, effective January 1, 1966; am. Acts 1999, 76th Leg., ch. 1545 (S.B. 1230), § 56, effective September 1, 1999 (renumbered from art. 45.21).)

## Art. 45.103. Warrant Without Complaint.

If a criminal offense that a justice of the peace has jurisdiction to try is committed within the view of the justice, the justice may issue a warrant for the arrest of the offender.
(Enacted by Acts 1965, 59th Leg., ch. 722 (S.B. 107), § 1, effective January 1, 1966; am. Acts 1999, 76th Leg., ch. 1545 (S.B. 1230), § 57, effective September 1, 1999 (renumbered from art. 45.15).)

## Art. 45.11. Disposition of Fees [Renumbered].

Renumbered to Tex. Code Crim. Proc. art. 44.281 by Acts 1999, 76th Leg., ch. 1545 (S.B. 1230), § 65, effective September 1, 1999.

## Art. 45.12. Contempt and Bail [Repealed].

Repealed by Acts 1999, 76th Leg., ch. 1545 (S.B. 1230), § 75(a), effective September 1, 1999. (Enacted by Acts 1965, 59th Leg., ch. 722 (S.B. 107), § 1, effective January 1, 1966; am. Acts 1971, 62nd Leg., ch. 831 (S.B. 132), § 5, effective August 30, 1971; am. Acts 1987, 70th Leg., ch. 641 (H.B. 2220), § 5, effective September 1, 1987.)

## Art. 45.13. Criminal Docket [Renumbered].

Renumbered to Tex. Code Crim. Proc. art. 45.017 by Acts 1999, 76th Leg., ch. 1545 (S.B. 1230), § 14, effective September 1, 1999.

## Art. 45.14. To File Transcript of Docket [Repealed].

Repealed by Acts 1989, 71st Leg., ch. 499 (H.B. 1101), § 2, effective August 28, 1989.
(Enacted by Acts 1965, 59th Leg., ch. 722 (S.B. 107), § 1, effective January 1, 1966.)

## Art. 45.15. Warrant Without Complaint [Renumbered].

Renumbered to Tex. Code Crim. Proc. art. 45.103 by Acts 1999, 76th Leg., ch. 1545 (S.B. 1230), § 57, effective September 1, 1999.

## Art. 45.16. Complaint Shall Be Written [Repealed].

Repealed by Acts 1999, 76th Leg., ch. 1545 (S.B. 1230), § 75(a), effective September 1, 1999. (Enacted by Acts 1965, 59th Leg., ch. 722 (S.B. 107), § 1, effective January 1, 1966.)

## Art. 45.17. What Complaint Must State [Renumbered].

Renumbered to Tex. Code Crim. Proc. art. 45.019 by Acts 1999, 76th Leg., ch. 1545 (S.B. 1230), § 16, effective September 1, 1999.

## Art. 45.18. Warrant Shall Issue [Renumbered].

Renumbered to Tex. Code Crim. Proc. art. 45.014 by Acts 1999, 76th Leg., ch. 1545 (S.B. 1230), § 11, effective September 1, 1999.

## Art. 45.19. Requisites of Warrant [Repealed].

Repealed by Acts 1999, 76th Leg., ch. 1545 (S.B. 1230), § 75(a), effective September 1, 1999. (Enacted by Acts 1965, 59th Leg., ch. 722 (S.B. 107), § 1, effective January 1, 1966.)

### SUBCHAPTER D
### PROCEDURES IN MUNICIPAL COURT

## Art. 45.20. [Repealed].

Repealed by Acts 1991, 72nd Leg., ch. 446 (S.B. 411), § 2, effective June 11, 1991.
(Enacted by Acts 1965, 59th Leg., ch. 722 (S.B. 107), § 1, effective January 1, 1966.)

## Art. 45.201. Municipal Prosecutions.

(a) All prosecutions in a municipal court shall be conducted by the city attorney of the municipality or by a deputy city attorney.

(b) The county attorney of the county in which

*Criminal Procedure*

the municipality is situated may, if the county attorney so desires, also represent the state in such prosecutions. In such cases, the county attorney is not entitled to receive any fees or other compensation for those services.

(c) With the consent of the county attorney, appeals from municipal court to a county court, county court at law, or any appellate court may be prosecuted by the city attorney or a deputy city attorney.

(d) It is the primary duty of a municipal prosecutor not to convict, but to see that justice is done.

(Enacted by Acts 1965, 59th Leg., ch. 722 (S.B. 107), § 1, effective January 1, 1966; am. Acts 1999, 76th Leg., ch. 1545 (S.B. 1230), § 59, effective September 1, 1999 (renumbered from art. 45.03).)

## Art. 45.202. Service of Process.

(a) All process issuing out of a municipal court may be served and shall be served when directed by the court, by a peace officer or marshal of the municipality within which it is situated, under the same rules as are provided by law for the service by sheriffs and constables of process issuing out of the justice court, so far as applicable.

(b) The peace officer or marshal may serve all process issuing out of a municipal court anywhere in the county in which the municipality is situated. If the municipality is situated in more than one county, the peace officer or marshal may serve the process throughout those counties.

(Enacted by Acts 1965, 59th Leg., ch. 722 (S.B. 107), § 1, effective January 1, 1966; am. Acts 1967, 60th Leg., ch. 523 (H.B. 738), § 1, effective August 28, 1967; am. Acts 1999, 76th Leg., ch. 1545 (S.B. 1230), § 60, effective September 1, 1999 (renumbered from art. 45.04).)

## Art. 45.203. Collection of Fines, Costs, and Special Expenses.

(a) The governing body of each municipality shall by ordinance prescribe rules, not inconsistent with any law of this state, as may be proper to enforce the collection of fines imposed by a municipal court. In addition to any other method of enforcement, the municipality may enforce the collection of fines by:

(1) execution against the property of the defendant; or

(2) imprisonment of the defendant.

(b) The governing body of a municipality may adopt such rules and regulations, not inconsis-

tent with any law of this state, concerning the practice and procedure in the municipal court as the governing body may consider proper.

(c) The governing body of each municipality may prescribe by ordinance the collection, after due notice, of a special expense, not to exceed $25 for the issuance and service of a warrant of arrest for an offense under Section 38.10, Penal Code, or Section 543.009, Transportation Code. Money collected from the special expense shall be paid into the municipal treasury for the use and benefit of the municipality.

(d) Costs may not be imposed or collected in criminal cases in municipal court by municipal ordinance.

(Enacted by Acts 1965, 59th Leg., ch. 722 (S.B. 107), § 1, effective January 1, 1966; am. Acts 1983, 68th Leg., ch. 389 (S.B. 1034), § 1, effective September 1, 1983; am. Acts 1987, 70th Leg., ch. 124 (S.B. 243), § 1, effective September 1, 1987; am. Acts 1995, 74th Leg., ch. 76 (S.B. 959), § 14.26, effective September 1, 1995; am. Acts 1999, 76th Leg., ch. 1545 (S.B. 1230), § 61, effective September 1, 1999 (renumbered from art. 45.06).)

## Art. 45.21. [Renumbered].

Renumbered to Tex. Code Crim. Proc. art. 45.102 by Acts 1999, 76th Leg., ch. 1545 (S.B. 1230), § 56, effective September 1, 1999.

(Enacted by Acts 1965, 59th Leg., ch. 722 (S.B. 107), § 1, effective January 1, 1966.)

## Art. 45.22. [Repealed].

Repealed by Acts 1999, 76th Leg., ch. 1545 (S.B. 1230), § 75(a), effective September 1, 1999.

(Enacted by Acts 1965, 59th Leg., ch. 722 (S.B. 107), § 1, effective January 1, 1966; am. Acts 1993, 73rd Leg., ch. 298 (H.B. 930), §§ 2, 3, effective May 27, 1993.)

## Art. 45.23. [Repealed].

Repealed by Acts 1999, 76th Leg., ch. 1545 (S.B. 1230), § 75(a), effective September 1, 1999.

(Enacted by Acts 1965, 59th Leg., ch. 722 (S.B. 107), § 1, effective January 1, 1966.)

## Art. 45.231. [Renumbered].

(Renumbered to Tex. Code Crim. Proc. art. 45.044 by Acts 1999, 76th Leg., ch. 1545 (S.B. 1230), § 44, effective September 1, 1999.)

## Art. 45.24. [Renumbered].

Renumbered to Tex. Code Crim. Proc. art. 45.025 by Acts 1999, 76th Leg., ch. 1545 (S.B. 1230), § 23, effective September 1, 1999.

(Enacted by Acts 1965, 59th Leg., ch. 722 (S.B. 107), § 1, effective January 1, 1966.)

### Art. 45.25. [Renumbered].

Renumbered to Tex. Code Crim. Proc. art. 45.027 by Acts 1999, 76th Leg., ch. 1545 (S.B. 1230), § 25, effective September 1, 1999.

(Enacted by Acts 1965, 59th Leg., ch. 722 (S.B. 107), § 1, effective January 1, 1966.)

### Art. 45.251. [Renumbered].

Renumbered to Tex. Code Crim. Proc. art. 45.026 by Acts 1999, 76th Leg., ch. 1545 (S.B. 1230), § 24, effective September 1, 1999.

### Art. 45.26. [Repealed].

Repealed by Acts 1999, 76th Leg., ch. 1545 (S.B. 1230), § 75(a), effective September 1, 1999.

(Enacted by Acts 1965, 59th Leg., ch. 722 (S.B. 107), § 1, effective January 1, 1966.)

### Art. 45.27. [Repealed].

Repealed by Acts 1999, 76th Leg., ch. 1545 (S.B. 1230), § 75(a), effective September 1, 1999.

(Enacted by Acts 1965, 59th Leg., ch. 722 (S.B. 107), § 1, effective January 1, 1966.)

### Art. 45.28. [Renumbered].

Renumbered to Tex. Code Crim. Proc. art. 45.029 by Acts 1999, 76th Leg., ch. 1545 (S.B. 1230), § 27, effective September 1, 1999.

(Enacted by Acts 1965, 59th Leg., ch. 722 (S.B. 107), § 1, effective January 1, 1966.)

### Art. 45.29. [Renumbered].

Renumbered to Tex. Code Crim. Proc. art. 45.028 by Acts 1999, 76th Leg., ch. 1545 (S.B. 1230), § 26, effective September 1, 1999.

(Enacted by Acts 1965, 59th Leg., ch. 722 (S.B. 107), § 1, effective January 1, 1966.)

### Art. 45.30. [Renumbered].

Renumbered to Tex. Code Crim. Proc. art. 45.030 by Acts 1999, 76th Leg., ch. 1545 (S.B. 1230), § 28, effective September 1, 1999.

(Enacted by Acts 1965, 59th Leg., ch. 722 (S.B. 107), § 1, effective January 1, 1966.)

### Art. 45.31. [Renumbered].

Renumbered to Tex. Code Crim. Proc. art. 45.023 by Acts 1999, 76th Leg., ch. 1545 (S.B. 1230), § 21, effective September 1, 1999.

(Enacted by Acts 1965, 59th Leg., ch. 722 (S.B. 107), § 1, effective January 1, 1966.)

### Art. 45.32. [Repealed].

Repealed by Acts 1999, 76th Leg., ch. 1545 (S.B. 1230), § 75(a), effective September 1, 1999. (Enacted by Acts 1965, 59th Leg., ch. 722 (S.B. 107), § 1, effective January 1, 1966; am. Acts 1973, 63rd Leg., ch. 399 (S.B. 34), § 2, effective January 1, 1974.)

### Art. 45.33. [Renumbered].

Renumbered to Tex. Code Crim. Proc. art. 45.021 by Acts 1999, 76th Leg., ch. 1545 (S.B. 1230), § 18, effective September 1, 1999.

(Enacted by Acts 1965, 59th Leg., ch. 722 (S.B. 107), § 1, effective January 1, 1966.)

### Art. 45.331. [Renumbered].

Renumbered to Tex. Code Crim. Proc. art. 45.0215 by Acts 1999, 76th Leg., ch. 1545 (S.B. 1230), § 19, effective September 1, 1999.

(Enacted by Acts 1965, 59th Leg., ch. 722 (S.B. 107), § 1, effective January 1, 1966.)

### Art. 45.34. [Renumbered].

Renumbered to Tex. Code Crim. Proc. art. 45.022 by Acts 1999, 76th Leg., ch. 1545 (S.B. 1230), § 20, effective September 1, 1999.

(Enacted by Acts 1965, 59th Leg., ch. 722 (S.B. 107), § 1, effective January 1, 1966.)

### Art. 45.35. [Renumbered].

Renumbered to Tex. Code Crim. Proc. art. 45.024 by Acts 1999, 76th Leg., ch. 1545 (S.B. 1230), § 22, effective September 1, 1999.

(Enacted by Acts 1965, 59th Leg., ch. 722 (S.B. 107), § 1, effective January 1, 1966.)

### Art. 45.36. [Renumbered].

Renumbered to Tex. Code Crim. Proc. art. 45.031 by Acts 1999, 76th Leg., ch. 1545 (S.B. 1230), § 29, effective September 1, 1999.

(Enacted by Acts 1965, 59th Leg., ch. 722 (S.B. 107), § 1, effective January 1, 1966.)

### Art. 45.37. [Renumbered].

Renumbered to Tex. Code Crim. Proc. art. 45.020 by Acts 1999, 76th Leg., ch. 1545 (S.B. 1230), § 17, effective September 1, 1999.

(Enacted by Acts 1965, 59th Leg., ch. 722 (S.B. 107), § 1, effective January 1, 1966.)

### Art. 45.38. [Renumbered].

Renumbered to Tex. Code Crim. Proc. art. 45.011 by Acts 1999, 76th Leg., ch. 1545 (S.B. 1230), § 8, effective September 1, 1999.

Criminal Procedure

(Enacted by Acts 1965, 59th Leg., ch. 722 (S.B. 107), § 1, effective January 1, 1966.)

### Art. 45.39. [Renumbered].

Renumbered to Tex. Code Crim. Proc. art. 45.034 by Acts 1999, 76th Leg., ch. 1545 (S.B. 1230), § 32, effective September 1, 1999. (Enacted by Acts 1965, 59th Leg., ch. 722 (S.B. 107), § 1, effective January 1, 1966.)

### Art. 45.40. [Renumbered].

Renumbered to Tex. Code Crim. Proc. art. 45.035 by Acts 1999, 76th Leg., ch. 1545 (S.B. 1230), § 33, effective September 1, 1999. (Enacted by Acts 1965, 59th Leg., ch. 722 (S.B. 107), § 1, effective January 1, 1966.)

### Art. 45.41. [Renumbered].

Renumbered to Tex. Code Crim. Proc. art. 45.016 by Acts 1999, 76th Leg., ch. 1545 (S.B. 1230), § 13, effective September 1, 1999. (Enacted by Acts 1965, 59th Leg., ch. 722 (S.B. 107), § 1, effective January 1, 1966.)

### Art. 45.42. [Renumbered].

Renumbered to Tex. Code Crim. Proc. art. 45.036 by Acts 1999, 76th Leg., ch. 1545 (S.B. 1230), § 34, effective September 1, 1999. (Enacted by Acts 1965, 59th Leg., ch. 722 (S.B. 107), § 1, effective January 1, 1966.)

### Art. 45.43. [Renumbered].

Renumbered to Tex. Code Crim. Proc. art. 45.015 by Acts 1999, 76th Leg., ch. 1545 (S.B. 1230), § 12, effective September 1, 1999. (Enacted by Acts 1965, 59th Leg., ch. 722 (S.B. 107), § 1, effective January 1, 1966.)

### Art. 45.44. [Renumbered].

Renumbered to Tex. Code Crim. Proc. art. 45.038 by Acts 1999, 76th Leg., ch. 1545 (S.B. 1230), § 36, effective September 1, 1999. (Enacted by Acts 1965, 59th Leg., ch. 722 (S.B. 107), § 1, effective January 1, 1966.)

### Art. 45.45. [Renumbered].

Renumbered to Tex. Code Crim. Proc. art. 45.037 by Acts 1999, 76th Leg., ch. 1545 (S.B. 1230), § 35, effective September 1, 1999. (Enacted by Acts 1965, 59th Leg., ch. 722 (S.B. 107), § 1, effective January 1, 1966.)

### Art. 45.46. [Renumbered].

Renumbered to Tex. Code Crim. Proc. art.

45.039 by Acts 1999, 76th Leg., ch. 1545 (S.B. 1230), § 37, effective September 1, 1999. (Enacted by Acts 1965, 59th Leg., ch. 722 (S.B. 107), § 1, effective January 1, 1966.)

### Art. 45.47. [Renumbered].

Renumbered to Tex. Code Crim. Proc. art. 45.040 by Acts 1999, 76th Leg., ch. 1545 (S.B. 1230), § 38, effective September 1, 1999. (Enacted by Acts 1965, 59th Leg., ch. 722 (S.B. 107), § 1, effective January 1, 1966.)

### Art. 45.48. [Renumbered].

Renumbered to Tex. Code Crim. Proc. art. 45.043 by Acts 1999, 76th Leg., ch. 1545 (S.B. 1230), § 43, effective September 1, 1999. (Enacted by Acts 1965, 59th Leg., ch. 722 (S.B. 107), § 1, effective January 1, 1966.)

### Art. 45.49. [Repealed].

Repealed by Acts 1999, 76th Leg., ch. 1545 (s.B. 1230), § 75(a), effective September 1, 1999. (Enacted by Acts 1965, 59th Leg., ch. 722 (S.B. 107), § 1, effective January 1, 1966; am. Acts 1995, 74th Leg., ch. 478 (S.B. 918), § 3, effective September 1, 1995.)

### Art. 45.50. [Renumbered].

Renumbered to Article 45.041 by Acts 1999, 76th Leg., ch. 1545 (S.B. 1230) § 39, effective September 1, 1999. (Enacted by Acts 1965, 59th Leg., ch. 722 (S.B. 107), § 1, effective January 1, 1966.)

### Art. 45.51. [Renumbered].

Renumbered to Article 45.045 by Acts 1999, 76th Leg., ch. 1545 (S.B. 1230), § 45, effective September 1, 1999. (Enacted by Acts 1965, 59th Leg., ch. 722 (S.B. 107), § 1, effective January 1, 1966.)

### Art. 45.52. [Renumbered].

Renumbered to Article 45.046 by Acts 1999, 76th Leg., ch. 1545 (S.B. 1230), § 46, effective September 1, 1999. (Enacted by Acts 1965, 59th Leg., ch. 722 (S.B. 107), § 1, effective January 1, 1966.)

### Art. 45.521. [Renumbered].

Renumbered to Article 45.049 by Acts 1999, 76th Leg., ch. 1545 (S.B. 1230), § 49, effective September 1, 1999.

## Art. 45.522. [Renumbered].

Renumbered to Article 45.050 by Acts 1999, 76th Leg., ch. 1545 (S.B. 1230), § 49, effective September 1, 1999.

## Art. 45.53. [Renumbered].

Renumbered to Article 45.048 by Acts 1999, 76th Leg., ch. 1545 (S.B. 1230), § 48, effective September 1, 1999.

(Enacted by Acts 1965, 59th Leg., ch. 722 (S.B. 107), § 1, effective January 1, 1966.)

## Art. 45.54. [Renumbered].

Renumbered to Article 45.051 by Acts 1999, 76th Leg., ch. 1545 (S.B. 1230), § 50, effective September 1, 1999.

## Art. 45.541. [Repealed].

Repealed by Acts 2001, 77th Leg., ch. 1420 (H.B. 2812), § 3.0021(b), effective September 1, 2001.

(Enacted by Acts 1999, 76th Leg., ch. 1387 (H.B. 1603), § 2, effective September 1, 1999.)

## Art. 45.55. [Renumbered].

Renumbered to Article 45.052 by Acts 1999, 76th Leg., ch, 1545 (S.B. 1230), § 52, effective September 1, 1999.

## Art. 45.56. [Renumbered].

Renumbered to Article 45.053 by Acts 1999, 76th Leg., ch. 1545 (S.B. 1230), § 53, effective September 1, 1999.

# Miscellaneous Proceedings

## CHAPTER 46
## INSANITY AS DEFENSE

Article
46.03.    Insanity Defense.
46.04.    Transportation to a Mental Health Facility or Residential Care Facility.
46.05.    Competency to Be Executed.

## Art. 46.01. [Repealed].

Repealed by Acts 1999, 76th Leg., ch. 561 (S.B. 421), § 8, effective September 1, 1999.

(Enacted by Acts 1965, 59th Leg., ch. 722 (S.B. 107), § 1, effective January 1, 1966; am. Acts 1967, 60th Leg., ch. 299 (H.B. 955), § 2, effective August 28, 1967.)

## Art. 46.02. Incompetency to Stand Trial [Repealed].

Repealed by Acts 2003, 78th Leg., ch. 35 (S.B.

1057), § 15, effective January 1, 2004.

(Enacted by Acts 1965, 59th Leg., ch. 722 (S.B. 107), § 1, effective January 1, 1966; am. Acts 1967, 60th Leg., ch. 299 (H.B. 955), § 1, effective August 28, 1967; am. Acts 1967, 60th Leg., ch. 659 (S.B. 145), § 33, effective August 28, 1967; am. Acts 1969, 61st Leg., ch. 554 (H.B. 1088), § 1, effective June 10, 1969; am. Acts 1969, 61st Leg., ch. 833 (S.B. 569), § 1, effective June 18, 1969; am. Acts 1971, 62nd Leg., ch. 995 (H.B. 1016), §§ 1, 2, effective August 30, 1971; am. Acts 1973, 63rd Leg., ch. 275 (S.B. 893), § 1, effective June 11, 1973; am. Acts 1973, 63rd Leg., ch. 468 (H.B. 727), § 1, effective August 27, 1973; am. Acts 1975, 64th Leg., ch. 415 (S.B. 901), § 1, effective June 19, 1975; am. Acts 1977, 65th Leg., ch. 596 (H.B. 951), § 1, effective September 1, 1977; am. Acts 1981, 67th Leg., ch. 291 (S.B. 265), § 148, effective September 1, 1981; am. Acts 1983, 68th Leg., ch. 54 (S.B. 302), §§ 1, 2, effective August 29, 1983; am. Acts 1983, 68th Leg., ch. 772 (H.B. 500), §§ 1—6, effective June 14, 1989; am. Acts 1999, 76th Leg., ch. 561 (S.B. 421), §§ 1—7, effective September 1, 1999; am. Acts 2001, 77th Leg., ch. 828 (H.B. 1071), §§ 3, 4, effective September 1, 2001.)

## Art. 46.03. Insanity Defense.

Secs. 1 to 3. [Repealed by Acts 2005, 79th Leg., ch. 831 (H.B. 837), § 1, effective September 1, 2005.]

## Disposition Following Acquittal by Reason of Insanity

Sec. 4(a) to (c) [Repealed by Acts 2005, 79th Leg., ch. 831 (H.B. 837), § 1, effective September 1, 2005.]

Sec 4. (1) to (7) [Repealed by Acts 2005, 79th Leg., ch. 831 (H.B. 837), § 1, effective September 1, 2005.]

Sec 4. (8) [Renumbered to Tex. Code Crim. Proc § 46C.003 by Acts 2011, 82nd Leg., ch. 787 (H.B. 2124), § 1, effective June 17, 2011.]

(Enacted by Acts 1975, 64th Leg., ch. 415 (S.B. 901), § 2, effective June 19, 1975; am. Acts 1977, 65th Leg., ch. 596 (H.B. 951), § 2, effective September 1, 1977; am. Acts 1983, 68th Leg., ch. 454 (S.B. 7), §§ 2, 3, effective August 29, 1983; am. Acts 1989, 71st Leg., ch. 393 (S.B. 754), §§ 7—9, effective June 14, 1989; am. Acts 2001, 77th Leg., ch. 985 (H.B. 434), § 1, effective September 1, 2001; am. Acts 2003, 78th Leg., ch. 35 (S.B. 1057), § 5, effective January 1, 2004; am. Acts 2005,

Criminal Procedure

79th Leg., ch. 485 (H.B. 291), § 1, effective September 1, 2005; am. Acts 2005, 79th Leg., ch. 831 (S.B. 837), § 1, effective September 1, 2005.)

## Art. 46.04. Transportation to a Mental Health Facility or Residential Care Facility.

### Sec. 1. Persons Accompanying Transport.

(a) A patient transported from a jail or detention facility to a mental health facility or a residential care facility shall be transported by a special officer for mental health assignment certified under Section 1701.404, Occupations Code, or by a sheriff or constable.

(b) The court ordering the transport shall require appropriate medical personnel to accompany the person transporting the patient, at the expense of the county from which the patient is transported, if there is reasonable cause to believe the patient will require medical assistance or will require the administration of medication during the transportation.

(c) A female patient must be accompanied by a female attendant.

### Sec. 2. Requirements for Transport.

The transportation of a patient from a jail or detention facility to a mental health facility or residential care facility must meet the following requirements:

(1) the patient must be transported directly to the facility within a reasonable amount of time and without undue delay;

(2) a vehicle used to transport the patient must be adequately heated in cold weather and adequately ventilated in warm weather;

(3) a special diet or other medical precautions recommended by the patient's physician must be followed;

(4) the person transporting the patient shall give the patient reasonable opportunities to get food and water and to use a bathroom; and

(5) the patient may not be transported with a state prisoner.

(Enacted by Acts 1999, 76th Leg., ch. 1512 (S.B. 539), § 6, effective September 1, 1999; am. Acts 2001, 77th Leg., ch. 1420 (H.B. 2812), § 14.736, effective September 1, 2001.)

## Art. 46.05. Competency to Be Executed.

(a) A person who is incompetent to be executed may not be executed.

(b) The trial court retains jurisdiction over motions filed by or for a defendant under this article.

(c) A motion filed under this article must identify the proceeding in which the defendant was convicted, give the date of the final judgment, set forth the fact that an execution date has been set if the date has been set, and clearly set forth alleged facts in support of the assertion that the defendant is presently incompetent to be executed. The defendant shall attach affidavits, records, or other evidence supporting the defendant's allegations or shall state why those items are not attached. The defendant shall identify any previous proceedings in which the defendant challenged the defendant's competency in relation to the conviction and sentence in question, including any challenge to the defendant's competency to be executed, competency to stand trial, or sanity at the time of the offense. The motion must be verified by the oath of some person on the defendant's behalf.

(d) On receipt of a motion filed under this article, the trial court shall determine whether the defendant has raised a substantial doubt of the defendant's competency to be executed on the basis of:

(1) the motion, any attached documents, and any responsive pleadings; and

(2) if applicable, the presumption of competency under Subsection (e).

(e) If a defendant is determined to have previously filed a motion under this article, and has previously been determined to be competent to be executed, the previous adjudication creates a presumption of competency and the defendant is not entitled to a hearing on the subsequent motion filed under this article, unless the defendant makes a prima facie showing of a substantial change in circumstances sufficient to raise a significant question as to the defendant's competency to be executed at the time of filing the subsequent motion under this article.

(f) If the trial court determines that the defendant has made a substantial showing of incompetency, the court shall order at least two mental health experts to examine the defendant using the standard described by Subsection (h) to determine whether the defendant is incompetent to be executed.

(g) If the trial court does not determine that the defendant has made a substantial showing of incompetency, the court shall deny the motion and may set an execution date as otherwise provided by law.

(h) A defendant is incompetent to be executed if the defendant does not understand:

(1) that he or she is to be executed and that the execution is imminent; and

(2) the reason he or she is being executed.

(i) Mental health experts who examine a defendant under this article shall provide within a time ordered by the trial court copies of their reports to the attorney representing the state, the attorney representing the defendant, and the court.

(j) By filing a motion under this article, the defendant waives any claim of privilege with respect to, and consents to the release of, all mental health and medical records relevant to whether the defendant is incompetent to be executed.

(k) The trial court shall determine whether, on the basis of reports provided under Subsection (i), the motion, any attached documents, any responsive pleadings, and any evidence introduced in the final competency hearing, the defendant has established by a preponderance of the evidence that the defendant is incompetent to be executed. If the court makes a finding that the defendant is not incompetent to be executed, the court may set an execution date as otherwise provided by law.

(*l*) Following the trial court's determination under Subsection (k) and on motion of a party, the clerk shall send immediately to the court of criminal appeals in accordance with Section 8(d), Article 11.071, the appropriate documents for that court's review and entry of a judgment of whether to adopt the trial court's order, findings, or recommendations issued under Subsection (g) or (k). The court of criminal appeals also shall determine whether any existing execution date should be withdrawn and a stay of execution issued while that court is conducting its review or, if a stay is not issued during the review, after entry of its judgment.

(*l*-1) Notwithstanding Subsection (l), the court of criminal appeals may not review any finding of the defendant's competency made by a trial court as a result of a motion filed under this article if the motion is filed on or after the 20th day before the defendant's scheduled execution date.

(m) If a stay of execution is issued by the court of criminal appeals, the trial court periodically shall order that the defendant be reexamined by mental health experts to determine whether the defendant is no longer incompetent to be executed.

(n) If the court of criminal appeals enters a judgment that a defendant is not incompetent to be executed, the court may withdraw any stay of execution issued under Subsection (l), and the trial court may set an execution date as otherwise provided by law.

(Enacted by Acts 1999, 76th Leg., ch. 654 (H.B. 245), § 1, effective September 1, 1999; am. Acts 2001, 77th Leg., ch. 1420 (H.B. 2812), § 21.001(13), effective September 1, 2001 (renumbered from art. 46.04); am. Acts 2007, 80th Leg., ch. 677 (H.B. 1545), § 1, effective September 1, 2007.)

# CHAPTER 46A
## AIDS AND HIV TESTING IN COUNTY AND MUNICIPAL JAILS

### Art. 46A.01. Testing; Segregation; Disclosure.

(a) In this article "AIDS" and "HIV" have the meanings assigned those terms by Section 81.101, Health and Safety Code.

(b) A county or municipality may test an inmate confined in the county or municipal jail or in a contract facility authorized by Article 5115d, Revised Statutes, or Article 5115e, Revised Statutes, to determine the proper medical treatment of the inmate or the proper social management of the inmate or other inmates in the jail or facility.

(c) If the county or municipality determines that an inmate has a positive test result for AIDS or HIV, the county or municipality may segregate the inmate from other inmates in the jail or facility.

(d) This article does not provide a duty to test for AIDS or HIV, and a cause of action does not arise under this article from a failure to test for AIDS or HIV.

(Enacted by Acts 1989, 71st Leg., ch. 1195 (S.B. 959), § 13, effective September 1, 1989; am. Acts 1991, 72nd Leg., ch. 14 (S.B. 404), § 284(10), effective September 1, 1991.)

# CHAPTER 46B
## INCOMPETENCY TO STAND TRIAL

### Subchapter A. General Provisions

## SUBCHAPTER A
## GENERAL PROVISIONS

### Art. 46B.001. Definitions.

In this chapter:

(1) "Department" means the Department of State Health Services.

(2) "Inpatient mental health facility" has the meaning assigned by Section 571.003, Health and Safety Code.

(3) "Local mental health authority" has the meaning assigned by Section 571.003, Health and Safety Code.

(4) "Local mental retardation authority" has the meaning assigned by Section 531.002, Health and Safety Code.

(5) "Mental health facility" has the meaning assigned by Section 571.003, Health and Safety Code.

(6) "Mental illness" has the meaning assigned by Section 571.003, Health and Safety Code.

(7) "Mental retardation" has the meaning assigned by Section 591.003, Health and Safety Code.

(8) "Residential care facility" has the meaning assigned by Section 591.003, Health and Safety Code.

(9) "Electronic broadcast system" means a two-way electronic communication of image and sound between the defendant and the court and includes secure Internet videoconferencing.

(Enacted by Acts 2003, 78th Leg., ch. 35 (S.B. 1057), § 1, effective January 1, 2004; am. Acts 2005, 79th Leg., ch. 324 (S.B. 679), § 1, effective September 1, 2005.)

## Art. 46B.002. Applicability.

This chapter applies to a defendant charged with a felony or with a misdemeanor punishable by confinement.

(Enacted by Acts 2003, 78th Leg., ch. 35 (S.B. 1057), § 1, effective January 1, 2004.)

## Art. 46B.003. Incompetency; Presumptions.

(a) A person is incompetent to stand trial if the person does not have:

(1) sufficient present ability to consult with the person's lawyer with a reasonable degree of rational understanding; or

(2) a rational as well as factual understanding of the proceedings against the person.

(b) A defendant is presumed competent to stand trial and shall be found competent to stand trial unless proved incompetent by a preponderance of the evidence.

(Enacted by Acts 2003, 78th Leg., ch. 35 (S.B. 1057), § 1, effective January 1, 2004.)

## Art. 46B.004. Raising Issue of Incompetency to Stand Trial.

(a) Either party may suggest by motion, or the trial court may suggest on its own motion, that the defendant may be incompetent to stand trial. A motion suggesting that the defendant may be incompetent to stand trial may be supported by affidavits setting out the facts on which the suggestion is made.

(b) If evidence suggesting the defendant may be incompetent to stand trial comes to the attention of the court, the court on its own motion shall suggest that the defendant may be incompetent to stand trial.

(c) On suggestion that the defendant may be incompetent to stand trial, the court shall deter-

mine by informal inquiry whether there is some evidence from any source that would support a finding that the defendant may be incompetent to stand trial.

(c-1) A suggestion of incompetency is the threshold requirement for an informal inquiry under Subsection (c) and may consist solely of a representation from any credible source that the defendant may be incompetent. A further evidentiary showing is not required to initiate the inquiry, and the court is not required to have a bona fide doubt about the competency of the defendant. Evidence suggesting the need for an informal inquiry may be based on observations made in relation to one or more of the factors described by Article 46B.024 or on any other indication that the defendant is incompetent within the meaning of Article 46B.003.

(d) If the court determines there is evidence to support a finding of incompetency, the court, except as provided by Subsection (e) and Article 46B.005(d), shall stay all other proceedings in the case.

(e) At any time during the proceedings under this chapter after the issue of the defendant's incompetency to stand trial is first raised, the court on the motion of the attorney representing the state may dismiss all charges pending against the defendant, regardless of whether there is any evidence to support a finding of the defendant's incompetency under Subsection (d) or whether the court has made a finding of incompetency under this chapter. If the court dismisses the charges against the defendant, the court may not continue the proceedings under this chapter, except that, if there is evidence to support a finding of the defendant's incompetency under Subsection (d), the court may proceed under Subchapter F. If the court does not elect to proceed under Subchapter F, the court shall discharge the defendant.

(Enacted by Acts 2003, 78th Leg., ch. 35 (S.B. 1057), § 1, effective January 1, 2004; am. Acts 2005, 79th Leg., ch. 324 (S.B. 679), § 2, effective September 1, 2005; am. Acts 2011, 82nd Leg., ch. 822 (H.B. 2725), § 2, effective September 1, 2011.)

## Art. 46B.005. Determining Incompetency to Stand Trial.

(a) If after an informal inquiry the court determines that evidence exists to support a finding of incompetency, the court shall order an examination under Subchapter B to determine whether the defendant is incompetent to stand trial in a criminal case.

(b) Except as provided by Subsection (c), the court shall hold a trial under Subchapter C before determining whether the defendant is incompetent to stand trial on the merits.

(c) A trial under this chapter is not required if:

(1) neither party's counsel requests a trial on the issue of incompetency;

(2) neither party's counsel opposes a finding of incompetency; and

(3) the court does not, on its own motion, determine that a trial is necessary to determine incompetency.

(d) If the issue of the defendant's incompetency to stand trial is raised after the trial on the merits begins, the court may determine the issue at any time before the sentence is pronounced. If the determination is delayed until after the return of a verdict, the court shall make the determination as soon as reasonably possible after the return. If a verdict of not guilty is returned, the court may not determine the issue of incompetency.

(Enacted by Acts 2003, 78th Leg., ch. 35 (S.B. 1057), § 1, effective January 1, 2004; am. Acts 2005, 79th Leg., ch. 324 (S.B. 679), § 3, effective September 1, 2005.)

## Art. 46B.006. Appointment of and Representation by Counsel.

(a) A defendant is entitled to representation by counsel before any court-ordered competency evaluation and during any proceeding at which it is suggested that the defendant may be incompetent to stand trial.

(b) If the defendant is indigent and the court has not appointed counsel to represent the defendant, the court shall appoint counsel as necessary to comply with Subsection (a).

(Enacted by Acts 2003, 78th Leg., ch. 35 (S.B. 1057), § 1, effective January 1, 2004.)

## Art. 46B.007. Admissibility of Statements and Certain Other Evidence.

A statement made by a defendant during an examination or trial on the defendant's incompetency, the testimony of an expert based on that statement, and evidence obtained as a result of that statement may not be admitted in evidence against the defendant in any criminal proceeding, other than at:

(1) a trial on the defendant's incompetency; or

(2) any proceeding at which the defendant first introduces into evidence a statement, testimony, or evidence described by this article.

(Enacted by Acts 2003, 78th Leg., ch. 35 (S.B. 1057), § 1, effective January 1, 2004; am. Acts 2005, 79th Leg., ch. 324 (S.B. 679), § 3, effective September 1, 2005.)

## Art. 46B.008. Rules of Evidence.

Notwithstanding Rule 101, Texas Rules of Evidence, the Texas Rules of Evidence apply to a trial under Subchapter C or other proceeding under this chapter whether the proceeding is before a jury or before the court.

(Enacted by Acts 2003, 78th Leg., ch. 35 (S.B. 1057), § 1, effective January 1, 2004; am. Acts 2005, 79th Leg., ch. 324 (S.B. 679), § 3, effective September 1, 2005.)

## Art. 46B.009. Time Credits.

A court sentencing a person convicted of a criminal offense shall credit to the term of the person's sentence each of the following periods for which the person may be confined in a mental health facility, residential care facility, or jail:

(1) any period of confinement that occurs pending a determination under Subchapter C as to the defendant's competency to stand trial; and

(2) any period of confinement that occurs between the date of any initial determination of the defendant's incompetency under that subchapter and the date the person is transported to jail following a final judicial determination that the person has been restored to competency.

(Enacted by Acts 2003, 78th Leg., ch. 35 (S.B. 1057), § 1, effective January 1, 2004; am. Acts 2005, 79th Leg., ch. 324 (S.B. 679), § 3, effective September 1, 2005; am. Acts 2007, 80th Leg., ch. 1307 (S.B. 867), § 2, effective September 1, 2007; am. Acts 2011, 82nd Leg., ch. 718 (H.B. 748), § 2, effective September 1, 2011; am. Acts 2011, 82nd Leg., ch. 822 (H.B. 2725), § 3, effective September 1, 2011.)

## Art. 46B.0095. [2 Versions: As amended by Acts 2011, 82nd Leg., ch. 718] Maximum Period of Commitment or Outpatient Treatment Program Participation Determined by Maximum Term for Offense.

(a) A defendant may not, under this chapter, be committed to a mental hospital or other inpatient or residential facility, ordered to participate in an outpatient treatment program, or subjected to both inpatient and outpatient treatment for a cumulative period that exceeds the maximum term provided by law for the offense for which the defendant was to be tried, except that if the defendant is charged with a misdemeanor and has been ordered only to participate in an outpatient treatment program under Subchapter D or E, the maximum period of restoration is two years.

(b) On expiration of the maximum restoration period under Subsection (a), the mental hospital or other inpatient or residential facility or outpatient treatment program provider identified in the most recent order of commitment or order of outpatient treatment program participation under this chapter shall assess the defendant to determine if civil proceedings under Subtitle C or D, Title 7, Health and Safety Code, are appropriate. The defendant may be confined for an additional period in a mental hospital or other inpatient or residential facility or ordered to participate for an additional period in an outpatient treatment program, as appropriate, only pursuant to civil commitment proceedings.

(c) The cumulative period described by Subsection (a):

(1) begins on the date the initial order of commitment or initial order for outpatient treatment program participation is entered under this chapter; and

(2) includes any time that, following the entry of an order described by Subdivision (1), the defendant is confined in a correctional facility, as defined by Section 1.07, Penal Code, while awaiting:

(A) transfer to a mental hospital or other inpatient or residential facility;

(B) release on bail to participate in an outpatient treatment program; or

(C) a criminal trial following any temporary restoration of the defendant's competency to stand trial.

(d) The court may credit to the cumulative period described by Subsection (a):

(1) any time that a defendant, following arrest for the offense for which the defendant was to be tried, is confined in a correctional facility, as defined by Section 1.07, Penal Code, before the initial order of commitment or initial order for outpatient treatment program participation is entered under this chapter; and

(2) any good conduct time the defendant has been granted under Article 42.032 in relation to

the defendant's confinement as described by Subdivision (1).

(Enacted by Acts 2007, 80th Leg., ch. 1307 (S.B. 867), § 2, effective September 1, 2007; am. Acts 2011, 82nd Leg., ch. 718 (H.B. 748), § 3, effective September 1, 2011.)

## Art. 46B.0095. [2 Versions: As amended by Acts 2011, 82nd Leg., ch. 822] Maximum Period of Commitment or Outpatient Treatment Program Participation Determined by Maximum Term for Offense.

(a) A defendant may not, under Subchapter D or E or any other provision of this chapter, be committed to a mental hospital or other inpatient or residential facility, ordered to participate in an outpatient treatment program, or subjected to both inpatient and outpatient treatment for a cumulative period that exceeds the maximum term provided by law for the offense for which the defendant was to be tried, except that if the defendant is charged with a misdemeanor and has been ordered only to participate in an outpatient treatment program under Subchapter D or E, the maximum period of restoration is two years.

(b) On expiration of the maximum restoration period under Subsection (a), the defendant may be confined for an additional period in a mental hospital or other inpatient or residential facility or ordered to participate for an additional period in an outpatient treatment program, as appropriate, only pursuant to civil proceedings conducted under Subtitle C or D, Title 7, Health and Safety Code, by a court with probate jurisdiction.

(c) The cumulative period described by Subsection (a):

(1) begins on the date the initial order of commitment or initial order for outpatient treatment program participation is entered under this chapter; and

(2) in addition to any inpatient or outpatient treatment periods described by Subsection (a), includes any time that, following the entry of an order described by Subdivision (1), the defendant is confined in a correctional facility, as defined by Section 1.07, Penal Code, or is otherwise in the custody of the sheriff during or while awaiting, as applicable:

(A) the defendant's transfer to a mental hospital or other inpatient or residential facility;

(B) the defendant's release on bail to participate in an outpatient treatment program; or

(C) a criminal trial following any temporary restoration of the defendant's competency to stand trial.

(d) The court shall credit to the cumulative period described by Subsection (a) any time that a defendant, following arrest for the offense for which the defendant was to be tried, is confined in a correctional facility, as defined by Section 1.07, Penal Code, before the initial order of commitment or initial order for outpatient treatment program participation is entered under this chapter.

(Enacted by Acts 2007, 80th Leg., ch. 1307 (S.B. 867), § 2, effective September 1, 2007; am. Acts 2011, 82nd Leg., ch. 822 (H.B. 2725), § 4, effective September 1, 2011.)

## Art. 46B.010. Mandatory Dismissal of Misdemeanor Charges.

If a court orders that a defendant charged with a misdemeanor punishable by confinement be committed to a mental hospital or other inpatient or residential facility, participate in an outpatient treatment program, or be subjected to both inpatient and outpatient treatment, and the defendant is not tried before the expiration of the maximum period of restoration described by Article 46B.0095:

(1) on the motion of the attorney representing the state, the court shall dismiss the charge; or

(2) **[2 Versions: As added by Acts 2011, 82nd Leg., ch. 718]** on the motion of the attorney representing the defendant, the court shall:

(A) set the matter to be heard not later than the 10th day after the date of filing of the motion; and

(B) dismiss the charge on a finding that the defendant was not tried before the expiration of the maximum period of restoration.

(2) **[2 Versions: As added by Acts 2011, 82nd Leg., ch. 822]** on the motion of the attorney representing the defendant and notice to the attorney representing the state, the court:

(A) shall set the matter to be heard not later than the 10th day after the date of filing of the motion; and

(B) may dismiss the charge on a finding that the defendant was not tried before the expiration of the maximum period of restoration.

(Enacted by Acts 2003, 78th Leg., ch. 35 (S.B. 1057), § 1, effective January 1, 2004; am. Acts

2007, 80th Leg., ch. 1307 (S.B. 867), § 2, effective September 1, 2007; am. Acts 2011, 82nd Leg., ch. 718 (H.B. 748), § 4, effective September 1, 2011; am. Acts 2011, 82nd Leg., ch. 822 (H.B. 2725), § 5, effective September 1, 2011.)

## Art. 46B.011. Appeals.

Neither the state nor the defendant is entitled to make an interlocutory appeal relating to a determination or ruling under Article 46B.005. (Enacted by Acts 2003, 78th Leg., ch. 35 (S.B. 1057), § 1, effective January 1, 2004; am. Acts 2005, 79th Leg., ch. 324 (S.B. 679), § 3, effective September 1, 2005.)

## Art. 46B.012. Compliance with Chapter.

The failure of a person to comply with this chapter does not provide a defendant with a right to dismissal of charges.

(Enacted by Acts 2003, 78th Leg., ch. 35 (S.B. 1057), § 1, effective January 1, 2004.)

## Art. 46B.013. Use of Electronic Broadcast System in Certain Proceedings Under This Chapter.

(a) A hearing may be conducted using an electronic broadcast system as permitted by this chapter and in accordance with the other provisions of this code if:

(1) written consent to the use of an electronic broadcast system is filed with the court by:

(A) the defendant or the attorney representing the defendant; and

(B) the attorney representing the state;

(2) the electronic broadcast system provides for a simultaneous, compressed full motion video, and interactive communication of image and sound between the judge, the attorney representing the state, the attorney representing the defendant, and the defendant; and

(3) on request of the defendant or the attorney representing the defendant, the defendant and the attorney representing the defendant are able to communicate privately without being recorded or heard by the judge or the attorney representing the state.

(b) On the motion of the defendant, the attorney representing the defendant, or the attorney representing the state or on the court's own motion, the court may terminate an appearance made through an electronic broadcast system at any time during the appearance and require an appearance by the defendant in open court.

(c) A recording of the communication shall be made and preserved until any appellate proceedings have been concluded. The defendant may obtain a copy of the recording on payment of a reasonable amount to cover the costs of reproduction or, if the defendant is indigent, the court shall provide a copy to the defendant without charging a cost for the copy.

(Enacted by Acts 2005, 79th Leg., ch. 324 (S.B. 679), § 4, effective September 1, 2005.)

## SUBCHAPTER B
## EXAMINATION

### Art. 46B.021. Appointment of Experts.

(a) On a suggestion that the defendant may be incompetent to stand trial, the court may appoint one or more disinterested experts to:

(1) examine the defendant and report to the court on the competency or incompetency of the defendant; and

(2) testify as to the issue of competency or incompetency of the defendant at any trial or hearing involving that issue.

(b) On a determination that evidence exists to support a finding of incompetency to stand trial, the court shall appoint one or more experts to perform the duties described by Subsection (a).

(c) An expert involved in the treatment of the defendant may not be appointed to examine the defendant under this article.

(d) The movant or other party as directed by the court shall provide to experts appointed under this article information relevant to a determination of the defendant's competency, including copies of the indictment or information, any supporting documents used to establish probable cause in the case, and previous mental health evaluation and treatment records.

(e) The court may appoint as experts under this chapter qualified psychiatrists or psychologists employed by the local mental health authority or local mental retardation authority. The local mental health authority or local mental retardation authority is entitled to compensation and reimbursement as provided by Article 46B.027.

(f) If a defendant wishes to be examined by an expert of the defendant's own choice, the court on timely request shall provide the expert with reasonable opportunity to examine the defendant.

(Enacted by Acts 2003, 78th Leg., ch. 35 (S.B. 1057), § 1, effective January 1, 2004.)

### Art. 46B.022. Experts: Qualifications.

(a) To qualify for appointment under this subchapter as an expert, a psychiatrist or psychologist must:

(1) as appropriate, be a physician licensed in this state or be a psychologist licensed in this state who has a doctoral degree in psychology; and

(2) have the following certification or training:

(A) as appropriate, certification by:

(i) the American Board of Psychiatry and Neurology with added or special qualifications in forensic psychiatry; or

(ii) the American Board of Professional Psychology in forensic psychology; or

(B) training consisting of:

(i) at least 24 hours of specialized forensic training relating to incompetency or insanity evaluations; and

(ii) at least eight hours of continuing education relating to forensic evaluations, completed in the 12 months preceding the appointment.

(b) In addition to meeting qualifications required by Subsection (a), to be appointed as an expert a psychiatrist or psychologist must have completed six hours of required continuing education in courses in forensic psychiatry or psychology, as appropriate, in either of the reporting periods in the 24 months preceding the appointment.

(c) A court may appoint as an expert a psychiatrist or psychologist who does not meet the requirements of Subsections (a) and (b) only if exigent circumstances require the court to base the appointment on professional training or experience of the expert that directly provides the expert with a specialized expertise to examine the defendant that would not ordinarily be possessed by a psychiatrist or psychologist who meets the requirements of Subsections (a) and (b).

(Enacted by Acts 2003, 78th Leg., ch. 35 (S.B. 1057), § 1, effective January 1, 2004; am. Acts 2011, 82nd Leg., ch. 822 (H.B. 2725), § 6, effective September 1, 2011.)

### Art. 46B.023. Custody Status.

During an examination under this subchapter, except as otherwise ordered by the court, the defendant shall be maintained under the same custody or status as the defendant was maintained under immediately before the examination began.

(Enacted by Acts 2003, 78th Leg., ch. 35 (S.B. 1057), § 1, effective January 1, 2004.)

## Art. 46B.024. Factors Considered in Examination.

During an examination under this subchapter and in any report based on that examination, an expert shall consider, in addition to other issues determined relevant by the expert, the following:

(1) the capacity of the defendant during criminal proceedings to:

(A) rationally understand the charges against the defendant and the potential consequences of the pending criminal proceedings;

(B) disclose to counsel pertinent facts, events, and states of mind;

(C) engage in a reasoned choice of legal strategies and options;

(D) understand the adversarial nature of criminal proceedings;

(E) exhibit appropriate courtroom behavior; and

(F) testify;

(2) as supported by current indications and the defendant's personal history, whether the defendant:

(A) has a mental illness; or

(B) is a person with mental retardation;

(3) whether the identified condition has lasted or is expected to last continuously for at least one year;

(4) the degree of impairment resulting from the mental illness or mental retardation, if existent, and the specific impact on the defendant's capacity to engage with counsel in a reasonable and rational manner; and

(5) if the defendant is taking psychoactive or other medication:

(A) whether the medication is necessary to maintain the defendant's competency; and

(B) the effect, if any, of the medication on the defendant's appearance, demeanor, or ability to participate in the proceedings.

(Enacted by Acts 2003, 78th Leg., ch. 35 (S.B. 1057), § 1, effective January 1, 2004; am. Acts 2011, 82nd Leg., ch. 822 (H.B. 2725), § 7, effective September 1, 2011.)

## Art. 46B.025. Expert's Report.

(a) An expert's report to the court must state an opinion on a defendant's competency or incompetency to stand trial or explain why the expert is unable to state such an opinion and must also:

(1) identify and address specific issues referred to the expert for evaluation;

(2) document that the expert explained to the defendant the purpose of the evaluation, the persons to whom a report on the evaluation is provided, and the limits on rules of confidentiality applying to the relationship between the expert and the defendant;

(3) in specific terms, describe procedures, techniques, and tests used in the examination, the purpose of each procedure, technique, or test, and the conclusions reached; and

(4) state the expert's clinical observations, findings, and opinions on each specific issue referred to the expert by the court, state the specific criteria supporting the expert's diagnosis, and state specifically any issues on which the expert could not provide an opinion.

(a-1) The expert's opinion on the defendant's competency or incompetency may not be based solely on the defendant's refusal to communicate during the examination.

(b) If in the opinion of an expert appointed under Article 46B.021 the defendant is incompetent to proceed, the expert shall state in the report:

(1) the symptoms, exact nature, severity, and expected duration of the deficits resulting from the defendant's mental illness or mental retardation, if any, and the impact of the identified condition on the factors listed in Article 46B.024;

(2) an estimate of the period needed to restore the defendant's competency, including whether the defendant is likely to be restored to competency in the foreseeable future; and

(3) prospective treatment options, if any, appropriate for the defendant.

(c) An expert's report may not state the expert's opinion on the defendant's sanity at the time of the alleged offense, if in the opinion of the expert the defendant is incompetent to proceed.

(d) The court shall direct an expert to provide the expert's report to the court and the appropriate parties in the form approved by the Texas Correctional Office on Offenders with Medical or Mental Impairments under Section 614.0032(b), Health and Safety Code.

(Enacted by Acts 2003, 78th Leg., ch. 35 (S.B. 1057), § 1, effective January 1, 2004; am. Acts 2005, 79th Leg., ch. 1269 (H.B. 2194), § 1, effective June 18, 2005; am. Acts 2011, 82nd Leg., ch. 822 (H.B. 2725), § 8, effective September 1, 2011.)

Criminal Procedure

## Art. 46B.026. Report Deadline.

(a) Except as provided by Subsection (b), an expert examining the defendant shall provide the report on the defendant's competency or incompetency to stand trial to the court, the attorney representing the state, and the attorney representing the defendant not later than the 30th day after the date on which the expert was ordered to examine the defendant and prepare the report.

(b) For good cause shown, the court may permit an expert to complete the examination and report and provide the report to the court and attorneys at a date later than the date required by Subsection (a).

(c) As soon as practicable after the court receives a report under this article, the court shall forward the report to the Texas Correctional Office on Offenders with Medical or Mental Impairments to enable that office to discharge its duties under Section 614.0032(b), Health and Safety Code.

(Enacted by Acts 2003, 78th Leg., ch. 35 (S.B. 1057), § 1, effective January 1, 2004; am. Acts 2005, 79th Leg., ch. 1269 (H.B. 2194), § 2, effective June 18, 2005.)

## Art. 46B.027. Compensation of Experts; Reimbursement of Facilities.

(a) For any appointment under this chapter, the county in which the indictment was returned or information was filed shall pay for services described by Articles 46B.021(a)(1) and (2). If those services are provided by an expert who is an employee of the local mental health authority or local mental retardation authority, the county shall pay the authority for the services.

(b) The county in which the indictment was returned or information was filed shall reimburse a facility that accepts a defendant for examination under this chapter for expenses incurred that are determined by the department to be reasonably necessary and incidental to the proper examination of the defendant.

(Enacted by Acts 2003, 78th Leg., ch. 35 (S.B. 1057), § 1, effective January 1, 2004.)

## SUBCHAPTER C
## INCOMPETENCY TRIAL

## Art. 46B.051. Trial Before Judge or Jury.

(a) If a court holds a trial to determine whether the defendant is incompetent to stand trial, on the request of either party or the motion of the court, a jury shall make the determination.

(b) The court shall make the determination of incompetency if a jury determination is not required by Subsection (a).

(c) If a jury determination is required by Subsection (a), a jury that has not been selected to determine the guilt or innocence of the defendant must determine the issue of incompetency.

(Enacted by Acts 2003, 78th Leg., ch. 35 (S.B. 1057), § 1, effective January 1, 2004; am. Acts 2005, 79th Leg., ch. 324 (S.B. 679), § 6, effective September 1, 2005.)

## Art. 46B.052. Jury Verdict.

(a) If a jury determination of the issue of incompetency to stand trial is required by Article 46B.051(a), the court shall require the jury to state in its verdict whether the defendant is incompetent to stand trial.

(b) The verdict must be concurred in by each juror.

(Enacted by Acts 2003, 78th Leg., ch. 35 (S.B. 1057), § 1, effective January 1, 2004.)

## Art. 46B.053. Procedure After Finding of Competency.

If the court or jury determines that the defendant is competent to stand trial, the court shall continue the trial on the merits. If a jury determines that the defendant is competent and the trial on the merits is to be held before a jury, the court shall continue the trial with another jury selected for that purpose.

(Enacted by Acts 2003, 78th Leg., ch. 35 (S.B. 1057), § 1, effective January 1, 2004; am. Acts 2005, 79th Leg., ch. 324 (S.B. 679), § 7, effective September 1, 2005.)

## Art. 46B.054. Uncontested Incompetency.

If the court finds that evidence exists to support a finding of incompetency to stand trial and the court and the counsel for each party agree that the defendant is incompetent to stand trial, the court shall proceed in the same manner as if a jury had been impaneled and had found the defendant incompetent to stand trial.

(Enacted by Acts 2003, 78th Leg., ch. 35 (S.B. 1057), § 1, effective January 1, 2004; am. Acts 2005, 79th Leg., ch. 324 (S.B. 679), § 7, effective September 1, 2005.)

## Art. 46B.055. Procedure After Finding of Incompetency.

If the defendant is found incompetent to stand trial, the court shall proceed under Subchapter D.

(Enacted by Acts 2003, 78th Leg., ch. 35 (S.B. 1057), § 1, effective January 1, 2004.)

## SUBCHAPTER D
## PROCEDURES AFTER DETERMINATION OF INCOMPETENCY

### Art. 46B.071. Options on Determination of Incompetency.

(a) Except as provided by Subsection (b), on a determination that a defendant is incompetent to stand trial, the court shall:

(1) commit the defendant to a facility under Article 46B.073; or

(2) release the defendant on bail under Article 46B.072.

(b) On a determination that a defendant is incompetent to stand trial and is unlikely to be restored to competency in the foreseeable future, the court shall:

(1) proceed under Subchapter E or F; or

(2) release the defendant on bail as permitted under Chapter 17.

(Enacted by Acts 2003, 78th Leg., ch. 35 (S.B. 1057), § 1, effective January 1, 2004; am. Acts 2011, 82nd Leg., ch. 822 (H.B. 2725), § 9, effective September 1, 2011.)

### Art. 46B.072. Release on Bail.

(a) This article applies only to a defendant who is subject to an initial restoration period based on Article 46B.071.

(a-1) Subject to conditions reasonably related to assuring public safety and the effectiveness of the defendant's treatment, if the court determines that a defendant found incompetent to stand trial is not a danger to others and may be safely treated on an outpatient basis with the specific objective of attaining competency to stand trial and if an appropriate outpatient treatment program is available for the defendant, the court:

(1) may release on bail a defendant found incompetent to stand trial with respect to a felony or may continue the defendant's release on bail; and

(2) shall release on bail a defendant found incompetent to stand trial with respect to a misdemeanor or shall continue the defendant's release on bail.

(b) The court shall order a defendant released on bail under Subsection (a-1) to participate in an outpatient treatment program for a period not to exceed 120 days.

(c) Notwithstanding Subsection (a-1), the court may order a defendant to participate in an outpatient treatment program under this article only if:

(1) the court receives and approves a comprehensive plan that:

(A) provides for the treatment of the defendant for purposes of competency restoration; and

(B) identifies the person who will be responsible for providing that treatment to the defendant; and

(2) the court finds that the treatment proposed by the plan will be available to and will be provided to the defendant.

(d) An order issued under this article may require the defendant to participate in:

(1) as appropriate, an outpatient treatment program administered by a community center or an outpatient treatment program administered by any other entity that provides outpatient competency restoration services; and

(2) an appropriate prescribed regimen of medical, psychiatric, or psychological care or treatment, including care or treatment involving the administration of psychoactive medication, including those required under Article 46B.086.

(Enacted by Acts 2003, 78th Leg., ch. 35 (S.B. 1057), § 1, effective January 1, 2004; am. Acts 2007, 80th Leg., ch. 1307 (S.B. 867), § 3, effective September 1, 2007; am. Acts 2011, 82nd Leg., ch. 822 (H.B. 2725), § 10, effective September 1, 2011.)

### Art. 46B.073. Commitment for Restoration to Competency.

(a) This article applies only to a defendant not released on bail who is subject to an initial restoration period based on Article 46B.071.

(b) For further examination and treatment toward the specific objective of the defendant attaining competency to stand trial, the court shall commit a defendant described by Subsection (a) to a mental health facility or residential care facility for the applicable period as follows:

(1) a period of not more than 60 days, if the defendant is charged with an offense punishable as a misdemeanor; or

(2) a period of not more than 120 days, if the defendant is charged with an offense punishable as a felony.

(c) If the defendant is charged with an offense listed in Article 17.032(a), other than an offense listed in Article 17.032(a)(6), or the indictment alleges an affirmative finding under Section 3g(a)(2), Article 42.12, the court shall enter an order committing the defendant to the maximum security unit of any facility designated by the department, to an agency of the United States operating a mental hospital, or to a Department of Veterans Affairs hospital.

(d) If the defendant is not charged with an offense described by Subsection (c) and the indictment does not allege an affirmative finding under Section 3g(a)(2), Article 42.12, the court shall enter an order committing the defendant to a mental health facility or residential care facility determined to be appropriate by the local mental health authority or local mental retardation authority.

(Enacted by Acts 2003, 78th Leg., ch. 35 (S.B. 1057), § 1, effective January 1, 2004; am. Acts 2005, 79th Leg., ch. 324 (S.B. 679), § 9, effective September 1, 2005; am. Acts 2007, 80th Leg., ch. 1307 (S.B. 867), § 4, effective September 1, 2007; am. Acts 2011, 82nd Leg., ch. 822 (H.B. 2725), § 11, effective September 1, 2011.)

### Art. 46B.074. Competent Testimony Required.

(a) A defendant may be committed to a mental health facility or residential care facility under this subchapter only on competent medical or psychiatric testimony provided by an expert qualified under Article 46B.022.

(b) The court may allow an expert to substitute the expert's report under Article 46B.025 for any testimony by the expert that may be required under this article.

(Enacted by Acts 2003, 78th Leg., ch. 35 (S.B. 1057), § 1, effective January 1, 2004; am. Acts 2005, 79th Leg., ch. 324 (S.B. 679), § 10, effective September 1, 2005.)

### Art. 46B.075. Transfer of Defendant to Facility or Outpatient Treatment Program.

An order issued under Article 46B.072 or 46B.073 must place the defendant in the custody of the sheriff for transportation to the facility or outpatient treatment program, as applicable, in which the defendant is to receive treatment for purposes of competency restoration.

(Enacted by Acts 2003, 78th Leg., ch. 35 (S.B. 1057), § 1, effective January 1, 2004; am. Acts

2007, 80th Leg., ch. 1307 (S.B. 867), § 5, effective September 1, 2007.)

### Art. 46B.0755. Procedures on Credible Evidence of Immediate Restoration.

(a) Notwithstanding any other provision of this subchapter, if the court receives credible evidence indicating that the defendant has been restored to competency at any time after the defendant's incompetency trial under Subchapter C but before the defendant is transported under Article 46B.075 to a mental health facility, residential care facility, or outpatient treatment program, as applicable, the court may appoint disinterested experts to reexamine the defendant in accordance with Subchapter B. The court is not required to appoint the same expert or experts who performed the initial examination of the defendant under that subchapter.

(b) If after a reexamination of the defendant the applicable expert's report states an opinion that the defendant remains incompetent, the court's order under Article 46B.072 or 46B.073 remains in effect, and the defendant shall be transported to the facility or outpatient treatment program as required by Article 46B.075. If after a reexamination of the defendant the applicable expert's report states an opinion that the defendant has been restored to competency, the court shall withdraw its order under Article 46B.072 or 46B.073 and proceed under Subsection (c) or (d).

(c) The court shall find the defendant competent to stand trial and proceed in the same manner as if the defendant had been found restored to competency at a hearing if:

(1) both parties agree that the defendant is competent to stand trial; and

(2) the court concurs.

(d) The court shall hold a hearing to determine whether the defendant has been restored to competency if any party fails to agree or if the court fails to concur that the defendant is competent to stand trial. If a court holds a hearing under this subsection, on the request of the counsel for either party or the motion of the court, a jury shall make the competency determination. For purposes of the hearing, incompetency is presumed, and the defendant's competency must be proved by a preponderance of the evidence. If after the hearing the defendant is again found to be incompetent to stand trial, the court shall issue a new order under Article 46B.072 or 46B.073, as appropriate based on the defendant's current condition.

(Enacted by Acts 2011, 82nd Leg., ch. 822 (H.B. 2725), § 12, effective September 1, 2011.)

### Art. 46B.076. Court's Order.

(a) If the defendant is found incompetent to stand trial, not later than the date of the order of commitment or of release on bail, as applicable, the court shall send a copy of the order to the facility of the department to which the defendant is committed or the outpatient treatment program to which the defendant is released. The court shall also provide to the facility or outpatient treatment program copies of the following made available to the court during the incompetency trial:

    (1) reports of each expert;

    (2) psychiatric, psychological, or social work reports that relate to the mental condition of the defendant;

    (3) documents provided by the attorney representing the state or the attorney representing the defendant that relate to the defendant's current or past mental condition;

    (4) copies of the indictment or information and any supporting documents used to establish probable cause in the case;

    (5) the defendant's criminal history record; and

    (6) the addresses of the attorney representing the state and the attorney representing the defendant.

(b) The court shall order that the transcript of all medical testimony received by the jury or court be promptly prepared by the court reporter and forwarded to the proper facility or outpatient treatment program.

(Enacted by Acts 2003, 78th Leg., ch. 35 (S.B. 1057), § 1, effective January 1, 2004; am. Acts 2005, 79th Leg., ch. 324 (S.B. 679), § 11, effective September 1, 2005; am. Acts 2007, 80th Leg., ch. 1307 (S.B. 867), § 5, effective September 1, 2007.)

### Art. 46B.077. Individual Treatment Program.

(a) The facility to which the defendant is committed or the outpatient treatment program to which the defendant is released on bail shall:

    (1) develop an individual program of treatment;

    (2) assess and evaluate whether the defendant is likely to be restored to competency in the foreseeable future; and

    (3) report to the court and to the local mental health authority or to the local mental retardation authority on the defendant's progress toward achieving competency.

(b) If the defendant is committed to an inpatient mental health facility or to a residential care facility, the facility shall report to the court at least once during the commitment period. If the defendant is released to a treatment program not provided by an inpatient mental health facility or a residential care facility, the treatment program shall report to the court:

    (1) not later than the 14th day after the date on which the defendant's treatment begins; and

    (2) until the defendant is no longer released to the treatment program, at least once during each 30-day period following the date of the report required by Subdivision (1).

(Enacted by Acts 2003, 78th Leg., ch. 35 (S.B. 1057), § 1, effective January 1, 2004; am. Acts 2007, 80th Leg., ch. 1307 (S.B. 867), § 6, effective September 1, 2007; am. Acts 2011, 82nd Leg., ch. 822 (H.B. 2725), § 13, effective September 1, 2011.)

### Art. 46B.078. Charges Subsequently Dismissed.

If the charges pending against a defendant are dismissed, the court that issued the order under Article 46B.072 or 46B.073 shall send a copy of the order of dismissal to the sheriff of the county in which the court is located and to the head of the facility or the provider of the outpatient treatment program, as appropriate. On receipt of the copy of the order, the facility or outpatient treatment program shall discharge the defendant into the care of the sheriff for transportation in the manner described by Article 46B.082.

(Enacted by Acts 2003, 78th Leg., ch. 35 (S.B. 1057), § 1, effective January 1, 2004; am. Acts 2007, 80th Leg., ch. 1307 (S.B. 867), § 7, effective September 1, 2007.)

### Art. 46B.079. Notice and Report to Court.

(a) The head of the facility or the provider of the outpatient treatment program, as appropriate, not later than the 15th day before the date on which the initial restoration period is to expire according to the terms of the order or under Article 46B.0095 or other applicable provisions of this chapter, shall notify the applicable court that the period is about to expire.

(b) The head of the facility or outpatient treatment program provider shall promptly notify the court when the head of the facility or outpatient treatment program provider believes that:

(1) the defendant has attained competency to stand trial; or

(2) the defendant is not likely to attain competency in the foreseeable future.

(c) When the head of the facility or outpatient treatment program provider gives notice to the court under Subsection (a) or (b), the head of the facility or outpatient treatment program provider also shall file a final report with the court stating the reason for the proposed discharge under this chapter and including a list of the types and dosages of medications prescribed for the defendant while the defendant was in the facility or participating in the outpatient treatment program. To enable any objection to the findings of the report to be made in a timely manner under Article 46B.084(a), the court shall provide copies of the report to the attorney representing the defendant and the attorney representing the state.

(d) If the head of the facility or outpatient treatment program provider notifies the court that the initial restoration period is about to expire, the notice may contain a request for an extension of the period for an additional period of 60 days and an explanation for the basis of the request. An explanation provided under this subsection must include a description of any evidence indicating a reduction in the severity of the defendant's symptoms or impairment.

(Enacted by Acts 2003, 78th Leg., ch. 35 (S.B. 1057), § 1, effective January 1, 2004; am. Acts 2005, 79th Leg., ch. 324 (S.B. 679), § 12, effective September 1, 2005; am. Acts 2007, 80th Leg., ch. 1307 (S.B. 867), § 7, effective September 1, 2007; am. Acts 2011, 82nd Leg., ch. 822 (H.B. 2725), § 14, effective September 1, 2011.)

### Art. 46B.080. Extension of Order.

(a) On a request of the head of a facility or a treatment program provider that is made under Article 46B.079(d) and notwithstanding any other provision of this subchapter, the court may enter an order extending the initial restoration period for an additional period of 60 days.

(b) The court may enter an order under Subsection (a) only if the court determines that:

(1) the defendant has not attained competency; and

(2) an extension of the initial restoration period will likely enable the facility or program to restore the defendant to competency within the period of the extension.

(c) The court may grant only one 60-day extension under this article in connection with the specific offense with which the defendant is charged.

(Enacted by Acts 2003, 78th Leg., ch. 35 (S.B. 1057), § 1, effective January 1, 2004; am. Acts 2005, 79th Leg., ch. 324 (S.B. 679), § 12, effective September 1, 2005; am. Acts 2007, 80th Leg., ch. 1307 (S.B. 867), § 7, effective September 1, 2007; am. Acts 2011, 82nd Leg., ch. 822 (H.B. 2725), § 15, effective September 1, 2011.)

### Art. 46B.081. Return to Court.

Subject to Article 46B.082(b), a defendant committed or released on bail under this subchapter shall be returned to the applicable court as soon as practicable after notice to the court is provided under Article 46B.079, but not later than the date of expiration of the period for restoration specified by the court under Article 46B.072 or 46B.073.

(Enacted by Acts 2003, 78th Leg., ch. 35 (S.B. 1057), § 1, effective January 1, 2004; am. Acts 2005, 79th Leg., ch. 324 (S.B. 679), § 13, effective September 1, 2005; am. Acts 2007, 80th Leg., ch. 1307 (S.B. 867), § 7, effective September 1, 2007.)

### Art. 46B.082. Transportation of Defendant.

(a) On notification from the court under Article 46B.078, the sheriff of the county in which the court is located or the sheriff's designee shall transport the defendant to the court.

(b) If before the 15th day after the date on which the court received notification under Article 46B.079 a defendant committed to a facility of the department or ordered to participate in an outpatient treatment program has not been transported to the court that issued the order under Article 46B.072 or 46B.073, as applicable, the head of the facility to which the defendant is committed or the provider of the outpatient treatment program in which the defendant is participating shall cause the defendant to be promptly transported to the court and placed in the custody of the sheriff of the county in which the court is located. The county in which the court is located shall reimburse the department for the mileage and per diem expenses of the personnel required to transport the defendant, calculated in accordance with rates provided in the General Appropriations Act for state employees.

(Enacted by Acts 2003, 78th Leg., ch. 35 (S.B. 1057), § 1, effective January 1, 2004; am. Acts 2007, 80th Leg., ch. 1307 (S.B. 867), § 7, effective September 1, 2007.)

## Art. 46B.083. Supporting Commitment Information Provided by Facility Head or Outpatient Treatment Program Provider.

(a) If the head of the facility or outpatient treatment program provider believes that the defendant is a person with mental illness and meets the criteria for court-ordered mental health services under Subtitle C, Title 7, Health and Safety Code, the head of the facility or the outpatient treatment program provider shall have submitted to the court a certificate of medical examination for mental illness.

(b) If the head of the facility or the outpatient treatment program provider believes that the defendant is a person with mental retardation, the head of the facility or the outpatient treatment program provider shall have submitted to the court an affidavit stating the conclusions reached as a result of the examination.

(Enacted by Acts 2003, 78th Leg., ch. 35 (S.B. 1057), § 1, effective January 1, 2004; am. Acts 2005, 79th Leg., ch. 324 (S.B. 679), § 14, effective September 1, 2005; am. Acts 2007, 80th Leg., ch. 1307 (S.B. 867), § 7, effective September 1, 2007.)

## Art. 46B.084. Proceedings on Return of Defendant to Court.

(a) On the return of a defendant to the court, the court shall make a determination with regard to the defendant's competency to stand trial. The court may make the determination based on the report filed under Article 46B.079(c) and on other medical information or personal history information relating to the defendant. A party may object in writing or in open court to the findings of the report not later than the 15th day after the date on which the court received notification under Article 46B.079. The court shall make the determination not later than the 20th day after the date on which the court received notification under Article 46B.079, regardless of whether a party objects to the report as described by this subsection and the issue is set for hearing under Subsection (b).

(b) If a party objects under Subsection (a), the issue shall be set for a hearing. The hearing is before the court, except that on motion by the defendant, the defense counsel, the prosecuting attorney, or the court, the hearing shall be held before a jury.

(b-1) If the hearing is before the court, the hearing may be conducted by means of an electronic broadcast system as provided by Article 46B.013. Notwithstanding any other provision of this chapter, the defendant is not required to be returned to the court with respect to any hearing that is conducted under this article in the manner described by this subsection.

(c) [Repealed by Acts 2007, 80th Leg., ch. 1307 (S.B. 867), § 21, effective September 1, 2007.]

(d) If the defendant is found competent to stand trial, criminal proceedings against the defendant may be resumed.

(e) If the defendant is found incompetent to stand trial and if all charges pending against the defendant are not dismissed, the court shall proceed under Subchapter E.

(f) If the defendant is found incompetent to stand trial and if all charges pending against the defendant are dismissed, the court shall proceed under Subchapter F.

(Enacted by Acts 2003, 78th Leg., ch. 35 (S.B. 1057), § 1, effective January 1, 2004; am. Acts 2005, 79th Leg., ch. 324 (S.B. 679), § 15, effective September 1, 2005; am. Acts 2007, 80th Leg., ch. 1307 (S.B. 867), §§ 8, 21, effective September 1, 2007; am. Acts 2011, 82nd Leg., ch. 822 (H.B. 2725), § 16, effective September 1, 2011.)

## Art. 46B.085. Subsequent Restoration Periods and Extensions of Those Periods Prohibited.

(a) The court may order only one initial period of restoration and one extension under this subchapter in connection with the same offense.

(b) After an initial restoration period and an extension are ordered as described by Subsection (a), any subsequent court orders for treatment must be issued under Subchapter E or F.

(Enacted by Acts 2003, 78th Leg., ch. 35 (S.B. 1057), § 1, effective January 1, 2004; am. Acts 2005, 79th Leg., ch. 324 (S.B. 679), § 16, effective September 1, 2005; am. Acts 2007, 80th Leg., ch. 1307 (S.B. 867), § 9, effective September 1, 2007.)

## Art. 46B.086. Court-Ordered Medications.

(a) This article applies only to a defendant:

(1) who is determined under this chapter to be incompetent to stand trial;

(2) who either:

(A) remains confined in a correctional facility, as defined by Section 1.07, Penal Code, for a period exceeding 72 hours while awaiting transfer to an inpatient mental health facility, a residential care facility, or an outpatient treatment program;

Criminal Procedure

(B) is committed to an inpatient mental health facility or a residential care facility for the purpose of competency restoration;

(C) is confined in a correctional facility while awaiting further criminal proceedings following competency restoration treatment; or

(D) is subject to Article 46B.072, if the court has made the determinations required by Subsection (a-1) of that article;

(3) for whom a correctional facility that employs or contracts with a licensed psychiatrist, an inpatient mental health facility, a residential care facility, or an outpatient treatment program provider has prepared a continuity of care plan that requires the defendant to take psychoactive medications; and

(4) who, after a hearing held under Section 574.106, Health and Safety Code, if applicable, has been found to not meet the criteria prescribed by Sections 574.106(a) and (a-1), Health and Safety Code, for court-ordered administration of psychoactive medications.

(b) If a defendant described by Subsection (a) refuses to take psychoactive medications as required by the defendant's continuity of care plan, the director of the correctional facility or outpatient treatment program provider, as applicable, shall notify the court in which the criminal proceedings are pending of that fact not later than the end of the next business day following the refusal. The court shall promptly notify the attorney representing the state and the attorney representing the defendant of the defendant's refusal. The attorney representing the state may file a written motion to compel medication. The motion to compel medication must be filed not later than the 15th day after the date a judge issues an order stating that the defendant does not meet the criteria for court-ordered administration of psychoactive medications under Section 574.106, Health and Safety Code, except that, for a defendant in an outpatient treatment program, the motion may be filed at any time.

(c) The court, after notice and after a hearing held not later than the 10th day after the motion to compel medication is filed, may authorize the director of the correctional facility or the program provider, as applicable, to have the medication administered to the defendant, by reasonable force if necessary. A hearing under this subsection may be conducted using an electronic broadcast system as provided by Article 46B.013.

(d) The court may issue an order under this article only if the order is supported by the testimony of two physicians, one of whom is the physician at or with the applicable correctional facility or outpatient treatment program who is prescribing the medication as a component of the defendant's continuity of care plan and another who is not otherwise involved in proceedings against the defendant. The court may require either or both physicians to examine the defendant and report on the examination to the court.

(e) The court may issue an order under this article if the court finds by clear and convincing evidence that:

(1) the prescribed medication is medically appropriate, is in the best medical interest of the defendant, and does not present side effects that cause harm to the defendant that is greater than the medical benefit to the defendant;

(2) the state has a clear and compelling interest in the defendant obtaining and maintaining competency to stand trial;

(3) no other less invasive means of obtaining and maintaining the defendant's competency exists; and

(4) the prescribed medication will not unduly prejudice the defendant's rights or use of defensive theories at trial.

(f) A statement made by a defendant to a physician during an examination under Subsection (d) may not be admitted against the defendant in any criminal proceeding, other than at:

(1) a hearing on the defendant's incompetency; or

(2) any proceeding at which the defendant first introduces into evidence the contents of the statement.

(g) For a defendant described by Subsection (a)(2)(A), an order issued under this article:

(1) authorizes the initiation of any appropriate mental health treatment for the defendant awaiting transfer; and

(2) does not constitute authorization to retain the defendant in a correctional facility for competency restoration treatment.

(Enacted by Acts 2003, 78th Leg., ch. 35 (S.B. 1057), § 1, effective January 1, 2004; am. Acts 2005, 79th Leg., ch. 717 (S.B. 465), § 8, effective June 17, 2005; am. Acts 2007, 80th Leg., ch. 1307 (S.B. 867), § 9, effective September 1, 2007; am. Acts 2009, 81st Leg., ch. 624 (H.B. 1233), § 4, effective June 19, 2009; am. Acts 2011, 82nd Leg., ch. 822 (H.B. 2725), § 17, effective September 1, 2011.)

## SUBCHAPTER E
## CIVIL COMMITMENT: CHARGES PENDING

### Art. 46B.101. Applicability.

This subchapter applies to a defendant against whom a court is required to proceed according to Article 46B.084(e) or according to the court's appropriate determination under Article 46B.071.

(Enacted by Acts 2003, 78th Leg., ch. 35 (S.B. 1057), § 1, effective January 1, 2004; am. Acts 2011, 82nd Leg., ch. 822 (H.B. 2725), § 18, effective September 1, 2011.)

### Art. 46B.102. Civil Commitment Hearing: Mental Illness.

(a) If it appears to the court that the defendant may be a person with mental illness, the court shall hold a hearing to determine whether the defendant should be court-ordered to mental health services under Subtitle C, Title 7, Health and Safety Code.

(b) Proceedings for commitment of the defendant to court-ordered mental health services are governed by Subtitle C, Title 7, Health and Safety Code, to the extent that Subtitle C applies and does not conflict with this chapter, except that the criminal court shall conduct the proceedings whether or not the criminal court is also the county court.

(c) If the court enters an order committing the defendant to a mental health facility, the defendant shall be:

(1) treated in conformity with Subtitle C, Title 7, Health and Safety Code, except as otherwise provided by this chapter; and

(2) released in conformity with Article 46B.107.

(d) In proceedings conducted under this subchapter for a defendant described by Subsection (a):

(1) an application for court-ordered temporary or extended mental health services may not be required;

(2) the provisions of Subtitle C, Title 7, Health and Safety Code, relating to notice of hearing do not apply; and

(3) appeals from the criminal court proceedings are to the court of appeals as in the proceedings for court-ordered inpatient mental health services under Subtitle C, Title 7, Health and Safety Code.

(Enacted by Acts 2003, 78th Leg., ch. 35 (S.B. 1057), § 1, effective January 1, 2004; am. Acts 2005, 79th Leg., ch. 324 (S.B. 679), § 18, effective September 1, 2005; am. Acts 2007, 80th Leg., ch. 1307 (S.B. 867), § 10, effective September 1, 2007.)

### Art. 46B.103. Civil Commitment Hearing: Mental Retardation.

(a) If it appears to the court that the defendant may be a person with mental retardation, the court shall hold a hearing to determine whether the defendant is a person with mental retardation.

(b) Proceedings for commitment of the defendant to a residential care facility are governed by Subtitle D, Title 7, Health and Safety Code, to the extent that Subtitle D applies and does not conflict with this chapter, except that the criminal court shall conduct the proceedings whether or not the criminal court is also a county court.

(c) If the court enters an order committing the defendant to a residential care facility, the defendant shall be:

(1) treated and released in accordance with Subtitle D, Title 7, Health and Safety Code, except as otherwise provided by this chapter; and

(2) released in conformity with Article 46B.107.

(d) In the proceedings conducted under this subchapter for a defendant described by Subsection (a):

(1) an application to have the defendant declared a person with mental retardation may not be required;

(2) the provisions of Subtitle D, Title 7, Health and Safety Code, relating to notice of hearing do not apply; and

(3) appeals from the criminal court proceedings are to the court of appeals as in the proceedings for commitment to a residential care facility under Subtitle D, Title 7, Health and Safety Code.

(Enacted by Acts 2003, 78th Leg., ch. 35 (S.B. 1057), § 1, effective January 1, 2004; am. Acts 2005, 79th Leg., ch. 324 (S.B. 679), § 19, effective September 1, 2005; am. Acts 2007, 80th Leg., ch. 1307 (S.B. 867), § 11, effective September 1, 2007.)

## Art. 46B.104. Civil Commitment Placement: Finding of Violence.

A defendant committed to a facility as a result of proceedings initiated under this chapter shall be committed to the maximum security unit of any facility designated by the department if:

(1) the defendant is charged with an offense listed in Article 17.032(a), other than an offense listed in Article 17.032(a)(6); or

(2) the indictment charging the offense alleges an affirmative finding under Section 3g(a)(2), Article 42.12.

(Enacted by Acts 2003, 78th Leg., ch. 35 (S.B. 1057), § 1, effective January 1, 2004; am. Acts 2005, 79th Leg., ch. 324 (S.B. 679), § 20, effective September 1, 2005; am. Acts 2007, 80th Leg., ch. 1307 (S.B. 867), § 12, effective September 1, 2007.)

## Art. 46B.105. Transfer Following Civil Commitment Placement.

(a) Unless a defendant is determined to be manifestly dangerous by a department review board, not later than the 60th day after the date the defendant arrives at the maximum security unit, the defendant shall be transferred to:

(1) a unit of an inpatient mental health facility other than a maximum security unit;

(2) a residential care facility; or

(3) a program designated by a local mental health authority or a local mental retardation authority.

(b) The commissioner of mental health and mental retardation shall appoint a review board of five members, including one psychiatrist licensed to practice medicine in this state and two persons who work directly with persons with mental illness or mental retardation, to determine whether the defendant is manifestly dangerous and, as a result of the danger the defendant presents, requires continued placement in a maximum security unit.

(c) The review board may not make a determination as to the defendant's need for treatment.

(d) A finding that the defendant is not manifestly dangerous is not a medical determination that the defendant no longer meets the criteria for involuntary civil commitment under Subtitle C or D, Title 7, Health and Safety Code.

(e) If the superintendent of the facility at which the maximum security unit is located disagrees with the determination, the matter shall be referred to the commissioner of mental health and mental retardation. The commissioner shall decide whether the defendant is manifestly dangerous.

(Enacted by Acts 2003, 78th Leg., ch. 35 (S.B. 1057), § 1, effective January 1, 2004; am. Acts 2005, 79th Leg., ch. 324 (S.B. 679), § 21, effective September 1, 2005.)

## Art. 46B.106. Civil Commitment Placement: No Finding of Violence.

(a) A defendant committed to a facility as a result of the proceedings initiated under this chapter, other than a defendant described by Article 46B.104, shall be committed to:

(1) a facility designated by the department; or

(2) an outpatient treatment program.

(b) A facility or outpatient treatment program may not refuse to accept a placement ordered under this article on the grounds that criminal charges against the defendant are pending.

(Enacted by Acts 2003, 78th Leg., ch. 35 (S.B. 1057), § 1, effective January 1, 2004; am. Acts 2005, 79th Leg., ch. 324 (S.B. 679), § 22, effective September 1, 2005; am. Acts 2007, 80th Leg., ch. 1307 (S.B. 867), § 13, effective September 1, 2007.)

## Art. 46B.107. Release of Defendant After Civil Commitment.

(a) The release from the department, an outpatient treatment program, or a facility of a defendant committed under this chapter is subject to disapproval by the committing court if the court or the attorney representing the state has notified the head of the facility or outpatient treatment provider, as applicable, to which the defendant has been committed that a criminal charge remains pending against the defendant.

(b) If the head of the facility or outpatient treatment provider to which a defendant has been committed under this chapter determines that the defendant should be released from the facility, the head of the facility or outpatient treatment provider shall notify the committing court and the sheriff of the county from which the defendant was committed in writing of the release not later than the 14th day before the date on which the facility or outpatient treatment provider intends to release the defendant.

(c) The head of the facility or outpatient treatment provider shall provide with the notice a written statement that states an opinion as to whether the defendant to be released has attained competency to stand trial.

(d) The court may, on motion of the attorney representing the state or on its own motion, hold a hearing to determine whether release is appropriate under the applicable criteria in Subtitle C or D, Title 7, Health and Safety Code. The court may conduct the hearing:

(1) at the facility; or

(2) by means of an electronic broadcast system as provided by Article 46B.013.

(e) If the court determines that release is not appropriate, the court shall enter an order directing the head of the facility or the outpatient treatment provider to not release the defendant.

(f) If an order is entered under Subsection (e), any subsequent proceeding to release the defendant is subject to this article.

(Enacted by Acts 2003, 78th Leg., ch. 35 (S.B. 1057), § 1, effective January 1, 2004; am. Acts 2005, 79th Leg., ch. 324 (S.B. 679), §§ 23, 24, effective September 1, 2005; am. Acts 2007, 80th Leg., ch. 1307 (S.B. 867), § 14, effective September 1, 2007.)

### Art. 46B.108. Redetermination of Competency.

(a) If criminal charges against a defendant found incompetent to stand trial have not been dismissed, the trial court at any time may determine whether the defendant has been restored to competency.

(b) An inquiry into restoration of competency under this subchapter may be made at the request of the head of the mental health facility, outpatient treatment provider, or residential care facility to which the defendant has been committed, the defendant, the attorney representing the defendant, or the attorney representing the state, or may be made on the court's own motion.

(Enacted by Acts 2003, 78th Leg., ch. 35 (S.B. 1057), § 1, effective January 1, 2004; am. Acts 2005, 79th Leg., ch. 324 (S.B. 679), § 25, effective September 1, 2005; am. Acts 2007, 80th Leg., ch. 1307 (S.B. 867), § 15, effective September 1, 2007.)

### Art. 46B.109. Request by Head of Facility or Outpatient Treatment Provider.

(a) The head of a facility or outpatient treatment provider to which a defendant has been committed as a result of a finding of incompetency to stand trial may request the court to determine that the defendant has been restored to competency.

(b) The head of the facility or outpatient treatment provider shall provide with the request a written statement that in their opinion the defendant is competent to stand trial.

(Enacted by Acts 2003, 78th Leg., ch. 35 (S.B. 1057), § 1, effective January 1, 2004; am. Acts 2007, 80th Leg., ch. 1307 (S.B. 867), § 16, effective September 1, 2007.)

### Art. 46B.110. Motion by Defendant, Attorney Representing Defendant, or Attorney Representing State.

(a) The defendant, the attorney representing the defendant, or the attorney representing the state may move that the court determine that the defendant has been restored to competency.

(b) A motion for a determination of competency may be accompanied by affidavits supporting the moving party's assertion that the defendant is competent.

(Enacted by Acts 2003, 78th Leg., ch. 35 (S.B. 1057), § 1, effective January 1, 2004; am. Acts 2005, 79th Leg., ch. 324 (S.B. 679), § 26, effective September 1, 2005.)

### Art. 46B.111. Appointment of Examiners.

On the filing of a request or motion to determine that the defendant has been restored to competency or on the court's decision on its own motion to inquire into restoration of competency, the court may appoint disinterested experts to examine the defendant in accordance with Subchapter B.

(Enacted by Acts 2003, 78th Leg., ch. 35 (S.B. 1057), § 1, effective January 1, 2004.)

### Art. 46B.112. Determination of Restoration with Agreement.

On the filing of a request or motion to determine that the defendant has been restored to competency or on the court's decision on its own motion to inquire into restoration of competency, the court shall find the defendant competent to stand trial and proceed in the same manner as if the defendant had been found restored to competency at a hearing if:

(1) both parties agree that the defendant is competent to stand trial; and

(2) the court concurs.

(Enacted by Acts 2003, 78th Leg., ch. 35 (S.B. 1057), § 1, effective January 1, 2004.)

### Art. 46B.113. Determination of Restoration Without Agreement.

(a) The court shall hold a hearing on a request by the head of a facility or outpatient treatment provider to which a defendant has been committed as a result of a finding of incompetency to stand trial to determine whether the defendant has been restored to competency.

(b) The court may hold a hearing on a motion to determine whether the defendant has been restored to competency or on the court's decision on its own motion to inquire into restoration of competency, and shall hold a hearing if a motion and any supporting material establish good reason to believe the defendant may have been restored to competency.

(c) If a court holds a hearing under this article, on the request of the counsel for either party or the motion of the court, a jury shall make the competency determination. If the competency determination will be made by the court rather than a jury, the court may conduct the hearing:

(1) at the facility; or

(2) by means of an electronic broadcast system as provided by Article 46B.013.

(d) If the head of a facility or outpatient treatment provider to which the defendant was committed as a result of a finding of incompetency to stand trial has provided an opinion that the defendant has regained competency, competency is presumed at a hearing under this subchapter and continuing incompetency must be proved by a preponderance of the evidence.

(e) If the head of a facility or outpatient treatment provider has not provided an opinion described by Subsection (d), incompetency is presumed at a hearing under this subchapter and the defendant's competency must be proved by a preponderance of the evidence.

(Enacted by Acts 2003, 78th Leg., ch. 35 (S.B. 1057), § 1, effective January 1, 2004; am. Acts 2005, 79th Leg., ch. 324 (S.B. 679), § 27, effective September 1, 2005; am. Acts 2007, 80th Leg., ch. 1307 (S.B. 867), § 17, effective September 1, 2007.)

### Art. 46B.114. Transportation of Defendant to Court.

If the hearing is not conducted at the facility to which the defendant has been committed under this chapter or conducted by means of an electronic broadcast system as described by this subchapter, an order setting a hearing to determine whether the defendant has been restored to competency shall direct that, as soon as practicable but not earlier than 72 hours before the date the hearing is scheduled, the defendant be placed in the custody of the sheriff of the county in which

the committing court is located or the sheriff's designee for transportation to the court. The sheriff or the sheriff's designee may not take custody of the defendant under this article until 72 hours before the date the hearing is scheduled. (Enacted by Acts 2003, 78th Leg., ch. 35 (S.B. 1057), § 1, effective January 1, 2004; am. Acts 2005, 79th Leg., ch. 324 (S.B. 679), § 28, effective September 1, 2005.)

### Art. 46B.115. Subsequent Redeterminations of Competency.

(a) If the court has made a determination that a defendant has not been restored to competency under this subchapter, a subsequent request or motion for a redetermination of competency filed before the 91st day after the date of that determination must:

(1) explain why the person making the request or motion believes another inquiry into restoration is appropriate; and

(2) provide support for the belief.

(b) The court may hold a hearing on a request or motion under this article only if the court first finds reason to believe the defendant's condition has materially changed since the prior determination that the defendant was not restored to competency.

(c) If the competency determination will be made by the court, the court may conduct the hearing at the facility to which the defendant has been committed under this chapter or may conduct the hearing by means of an electronic broadcast system as provided by Article 46B.013. (Enacted by Acts 2003, 78th Leg., ch. 35 (S.B. 1057), § 1, effective January 1, 2004; am. Acts 2005, 79th Leg., ch. 324 (S.B. 679), § 29, effective September 1, 2005.)

### Art. 46B.116. Disposition on Determination of Competency.

If the defendant is found competent to stand trial, the proceedings on the criminal charge may proceed. (Enacted by Acts 2003, 78th Leg., ch. 35 (S.B. 1057), § 1, effective January 1, 2004.)

### Art. 46B.117. Disposition on Determination of Incompetency.

If a defendant under order of commitment to a facility or outpatient treatment program is found to not have been restored to competency to stand trial, the court shall remand the defendant pursuant to that order of commitment, and, if applicable, order the defendant placed in the custody of the sheriff or the sheriff's designee for transportation back to the facility or outpatient treatment program.

(Enacted by Acts 2003, 78th Leg., ch. 35 (S.B. 1057), § 1, effective January 1, 2004; am. Acts 2005, 79th Leg., ch. 324 (S.B. 679), § 30, effective September 1, 2005; am. Acts 2007, 80th Leg., ch. 1307 (S.B. 867), § 18, effective September 1, 2007.)

## SUBCHAPTER F
## CIVIL COMMITMENT: CHARGES DISMISSED

### Art. 46B.151. Court Determination Related to Commitment.

(a) If a court is required by Article 46B.084(f) or by its appropriate determination under Article 46B.071 to proceed under this subchapter, or if the court is permitted by Article 46B.004(e) to proceed under this subchapter, the court shall determine whether there is evidence to support a finding that the defendant is either a person with mental illness or a person with mental retardation.

(b) If it appears to the court that there is evidence to support a finding of mental illness or mental retardation, the court shall enter an order transferring the defendant to the appropriate court for civil commitment proceedings and stating that all charges pending against the defendant in that court have been dismissed. The court may order the defendant:

(1) detained in jail or any other suitable place pending the prompt initiation and prosecution by the attorney for the state or other person designated by the court of appropriate civil proceedings to determine whether the defendant will be committed to a mental health facility or residential care facility; or

(2) placed in the care of a responsible person on satisfactory security being given for the defendant's proper care and protection.

(c) Notwithstanding Subsection (b), a defendant placed in a facility of the department pending civil hearing under this article may be detained in that facility only with the consent of the head of the facility and pursuant to an order of protective custody issued under Subtitle C, Title 7, Health and Safety Code.

(d) If the court does not detain or place the defendant under Subsection (b), the court shall release the defendant.

(Enacted by Acts 2003, 78th Leg., ch. 35 (S.B. 1057), § 1, effective January 1, 2004; am. Acts 2005, 79th Leg., ch. 324 (S.B. 679), § 32, effective September 1, 2005; am. Acts 2005, 79th Leg., ch. 324 (S.B. 679), § 33, effective September 1, 2005; am. Acts 2011, 82nd Leg., ch. 822 (H.B. 2725), § 19, effective September 1, 2011.)

## SUBCHAPTER G
## PROVISIONS APPLICABLE TO SUBCHAPTERS E AND F

### Art. 46B.171. Transcripts and Other Records.

(a) The court shall order that:

(1) a transcript of all medical testimony received in both the criminal proceedings and the civil commitment proceedings under Subchapter E or F be prepared as soon as possible by the court reporters; and

(2) copies of documents listed in Article 46B.076 accompany the defendant to the mental health facility, outpatient treatment program, or residential care facility.

(b) On the request of the defendant or the attorney representing the defendant, a mental health facility, an outpatient treatment program, or a residential care facility shall provide to the defendant or the attorney copies of the facility's records regarding the defendant.

(Enacted by Acts 2003, 78th Leg., ch. 35 (S.B. 1057), § 1, effective January 1, 2004; am. Acts 2005, 79th Leg., ch. 324 (S.B. 679), § 34, effective September 1, 2005; am. Acts 2007, 80th Leg., ch. 1307 (S.B. 867), § 19, effective September 1, 2007.)

## CHAPTER 46C
## INSANITY DEFENSE

**Subchapter A. General Provisions**

**Criminal Procedure**

## SUBCHAPTER A
## GENERAL PROVISIONS

### Art. 46C.001. Definitions.

In this chapter:

(1) "Commissioner" means the commissioner of state health services.

(2) "Department" means the Department of State Health Services.

(3) "Mental illness" has the meaning assigned by Section 571.003, Health and Safety Code.

(4) "Mental retardation" has the meaning assigned by Section 591.003, Health and Safety Code.

(5) "Residential care facility" has the meaning assigned by Section 591.003, Health and Safety Code.

(Enacted by Acts 2005, 79th Leg., ch. 831 (S.B. 837), § 2, effective September 1, 2005.)

### Art. 46C.002. Maximum Period of Commitment Determined by Maximum Term for Offense.

(a) A person acquitted by reason of insanity may not be committed to a mental hospital or other inpatient or residential care facility or ordered to receive outpatient or community-based treatment and supervision under Subchapter F for a cumulative period that exceeds the maximum term provided by law for the offense for which the acquitted person was tried.

(b) On expiration of that maximum term, the acquitted person may be further confined in a mental hospital or other inpatient or residential care facility or ordered to receive outpatient or community-based treatment and supervision only under civil commitment proceedings.

(Enacted by Acts 2005, 79th Leg., ch. 831 (S.B. 837), § 2, effective September 1, 2005.)

### Art. 46C.003. Victim Notification of Release.

If the court issues an order that requires the release of an acquitted person on discharge or on a regimen of outpatient care, the clerk of the court issuing the order, using the information provided on any victim impact statement received by the court under Article 56.03 or other information made available to the court, shall notify the victim or the victim's guardian or close relative of the release. Notwithstanding Article 56.03(f), the clerk of the court may inspect a victim impact statement for the purpose of notification under this article.

(Enacted by Acts 1975, 64th Leg., ch. 415 (S.B. 901), § 2, effective June 19, 1975; am. Acts 1977, 65th Leg., ch. 596 (H.B. 951), § 2, effective September 1, 1977; am. Acts 1983, 68th Leg., ch. 454 (S.B. 7), §§ 2, 3, effective August 29, 1983; am. Acts 1989, 71st Leg., ch. 393 (S.B. 754), §§ 7—9, effective June 14, 1989; am. Acts 2001, 77th Leg., ch. 985 (H.B. 434), § 1, effective September 1, 2001; am. Acts 2003, 78th Leg., ch. 35 (S.B. 1057), § 5, effective January 1, 2004; am. Acts 2005, 79th Leg., ch. 485 (H.B. 291), § 1, effective September 1, 2005; am. Acts 2005, 79th Leg., ch. 831 (S.B. 837), § 1, effective September 1, 2005; am. Acts 2011, 82nd Leg., ch. 787 (H.B. 2124), § 1, effective June 17, 2011 (renumbered from Art. 46.03, Art. 4(d)(8)).)).

### Arts. 46C.004 to 46C.050. [Reserved for expansion].

## SUBCHAPTER B
## RAISING THE INSANITY DEFENSE

### Art. 46C.051. Notice of Intent to Raise Insanity Defense.

(a) A defendant planning to offer evidence of the insanity defense must file with the court a notice of the defendant's intention to offer that evidence.

(b) The notice must:

(1) contain a certification that a copy of the notice has been served on the attorney representing the state; and

(2) be filed at least 20 days before the date the case is set for trial, except as described by Subsection (c).

(c) If before the 20-day period the court sets a pretrial hearing, the defendant shall give notice at the hearing.

(Enacted by Acts 2005, 79th Leg., ch. 831 (S.B. 837), § 2, effective September 1, 2005.)

### Art. 46C.052. Effect of Failure to Give Notice.

Unless notice is timely filed under Article 46C.051, evidence on the insanity defense is not admissible unless the court finds that good cause exists for failure to give notice.

(Enacted by Acts 2005, 79th Leg., ch. 831 (S.B. 837), § 2, effective September 1, 2005.)

### Arts. 46C.053 to 46C.100. [Reserved for expansion].

## SUBCHAPTER C
## COURT-ORDERED EXAMINATION AND REPORT

### Art. 46C.101. Appointment of Experts.

(a) If notice of intention to raise the insanity defense is filed under Article 46C.051, the court may, on its own motion or motion by the defendant, the defendant's counsel, or the attorney representing the state, appoint one or more disinterested experts to:

(1) examine the defendant with regard to the insanity defense; and

(2) testify as to the issue of insanity at any trial or hearing involving that issue.

(b) The court shall advise an expert appointed under this article of the facts and circumstances of the offense with which the defendant is charged and the elements of the insanity defense.

(Enacted by Acts 2005, 79th Leg., ch. 831 (S.B. 837), § 2, effective September 1, 2005.)

### Art. 46C.102. Experts: Qualifications.

(a) The court may appoint qualified psychiatrists or psychologists as experts under this chapter. To qualify for appointment under this subchapter as an expert, a psychiatrist or psychologist must:

(1) as appropriate, be a physician licensed in this state or be a psychologist licensed in this state who has a doctoral degree in psychology; and

(2) have the following certification or experience or training:

(A) as appropriate, certification by:

(i) the American Board of Psychiatry and Neurology with added or special qualifications in forensic psychiatry; or

(ii) the American Board of Professional Psychology in forensic psychology; or

(B) experience or training consisting of:

(i) at least 24 hours of specialized forensic training relating to incompetency or insanity evaluations;

(ii) at least five years of experience in performing criminal forensic evaluations for courts; and

(iii) eight or more hours of continuing education relating to forensic evaluations, completed in the 12 months preceding the appointment and documented with the court.

(b) In addition to meeting qualifications required by Subsection (a), to be appointed as an expert a psychiatrist or psychologist must have completed six hours of required continuing education in courses in forensic psychiatry or psychology, as appropriate, in the 24 months preceding the appointment.

(c) A court may appoint as an expert a psychiatrist or psychologist who does not meet the requirements of Subsections (a) and (b) only if exigent circumstances require the court to base the appointment on professional training or experience of the expert that directly provides the expert with a specialized expertise to examine the defendant that would not ordinarily be possessed by a psychiatrist or psychologist who meets the requirements of Subsections (a) and (b).

(Enacted by Acts 2005, 79th Leg., ch. 831 (S.B. 837), § 2, effective September 1, 2005.)

## Art. 46C.103. Competency to Stand Trial: Concurrent Appointment.

(a) An expert appointed under this subchapter to examine the defendant with regard to the insanity defense also may be appointed by the court to examine the defendant with regard to the defendant's competency to stand trial under Chapter 46B, if the expert files with the court separate written reports concerning the defendant's competency to stand trial and the insanity defense.

(b) Notwithstanding Subsection (a), an expert may not examine the defendant for purposes of determining the defendant's sanity and may not file a report regarding the defendant's sanity if in the opinion of the expert the defendant is incompetent to proceed.

(Enacted by Acts 2005, 79th Leg., ch. 831 (S.B. 837), § 2, effective September 1, 2005.)

## Art. 46C.104. Order Compelling Defendant to Submit to Examination.

(a) For the purposes described by this chapter, the court may order any defendant to submit to examination, including a defendant who is free on bail. If the defendant fails or refuses to submit to examination, the court may order the defendant to custody for examination for a reasonable period not to exceed 21 days. Custody ordered by the court under this subsection may include custody at a facility operated by the department.

(b) If a defendant who has been ordered to a facility operated by the department for examination remains in the facility for a period that exceeds 21 days, the head of that facility shall cause the defendant to be immediately transported to the committing court and placed in the custody of the sheriff of the county in which the committing court is located. That county shall reimburse the facility for the mileage and per diem expenses of the personnel required to transport the defendant, calculated in accordance with the state travel rules in effect at that time.

(c) The court may not order a defendant to a facility operated by the department for examination without the consent of the head of that facility.

(Enacted by Acts 2005, 79th Leg., ch. 831 (S.B. 837), § 2, effective September 1, 2005.)

## Art. 46C.105. Reports Submitted by Experts.

(a) A written report of the examination shall be submitted to the court not later than the 30th day after the date of the order of examination. The court shall provide copies of the report to the defense counsel and the attorney representing the state.

(b) The report must include a description of the procedures used in the examination and the examiner's observations and findings pertaining to the insanity defense.

(c) The examiner shall submit a separate report stating the examiner's observations and findings concerning:

(1) whether the defendant is presently a person with a mental illness and requires court-ordered mental health services under Subtitle C, Title 7, Health and Safety Code; or

(2) whether the defendant is presently a person with mental retardation.

(Enacted by Acts 2005, 79th Leg., ch. 831 (S.B. 837), § 2, effective September 1, 2005.)

## Art. 46C.106. Compensation of Experts.

(a) The appointed experts shall be paid by the county in which the indictment was returned or information was filed.

(b) The county in which the indictment was returned or information was filed shall reimburse a facility operated by the department that accepts a defendant for examination under this subchapter for expenses incurred that are determined by the department to be reasonably necessary and incidental to the proper examination of the defendant.

(Enacted by Acts 2005, 79th Leg., ch. 831 (S.B. 837), § 2, effective September 1, 2005.)

## Art. 46C.107. Examination by Expert of Defendant's Choice.

If a defendant wishes to be examined by an expert of the defendant's own choice, the court on timely request shall provide the examiner with reasonable opportunity to examine the defendant.

(Enacted by Acts 2005, 79th Leg., ch. 831 (S.B. 837), § 2, effective September 1, 2005.)

## Arts. 46C.108 to 46C.150. [Reserved for expansion].

## SUBCHAPTER D
## DETERMINATION OF ISSUE OF DEFENDANT'S SANITY

## Art. 46C.151. Determination of Sanity Issue by Jury.

(a) In a case tried to a jury, the issue of the defendant's sanity shall be submitted to the jury only if the issue is supported by competent evidence. The jury shall determine the issue.

(b) If the issue of the defendant's sanity is submitted to the jury, the jury shall determine and specify in the verdict whether the defendant is guilty, not guilty, or not guilty by reason of insanity.

(Enacted by Acts 2005, 79th Leg., ch. 831 (S.B. 837), § 2, effective September 1, 2005.)

## Art. 46C.152. Determination of Sanity Issue by Judge.

(a) If a jury trial is waived and if the issue is supported by competent evidence, the judge as trier of fact shall determine the issue of the defendant's sanity.

(b) The parties may, with the consent of the judge, agree to have the judge determine the issue of the defendant's sanity on the basis of introduced or stipulated competent evidence, or both.

(c) If the judge determines the issue of the defendant's sanity, the judge shall enter a finding of guilty, not guilty, or not guilty by reason of insanity.

(Enacted by Acts 2005, 79th Leg., ch. 831 (S.B. 837), § 2, effective September 1, 2005.)

## Art. 46C.153. General Provisions Relating to Determination of Sanity Issue by Judge or Jury.

(a) The judge or jury shall determine that a defendant is not guilty by reason of insanity if:

(1) the prosecution has established beyond a reasonable doubt that the alleged conduct constituting the offense was committed; and

(2) the defense has established by a preponderance of the evidence that the defendant was insane at the time of the alleged conduct.

(b) The parties may, with the consent of the judge, agree to both:

(1) dismissal of the indictment or information on the ground that the defendant was insane; and

(2) entry of a judgment of dismissal due to the defendant's insanity.

(c) An entry of judgment under Subsection (b)(2) has the same effect as a judgment stating that the defendant has been found not guilty by reason of insanity.

(Enacted by Acts 2005, 79th Leg., ch. 831 (S.B. 837), § 2, effective September 1, 2005.)

## Art. 46C.154. Informing Jury Regarding Consequences of Acquittal.

The court, the attorney representing the state, or the attorney for the defendant may not inform a juror or a prospective juror of the consequences to the defendant if a verdict of not guilty by reason of insanity is returned.

(Enacted by Acts 2005, 79th Leg., ch. 831 (S.B. 837), § 2, effective September 1, 2005.)

## Art. 46C.155. Finding of Not Guilty by Reason of Insanity Considered Acquittal.

(a) Except as provided by Subsection (b), a defendant who is found not guilty by reason of insanity stands acquitted of the offense charged and may not be considered a person charged with an offense.

(b) A defendant who is found not guilty by reason of insanity is not considered to be acquitted for purposes of Chapter 55.
(Enacted by Acts 2005, 79th Leg., ch. 831 (S.B. 837), § 2, effective September 1, 2005.)

### Art. 46C.156. Judgment.

(a) In each case in which the insanity defense is raised, the judgment must reflect whether the defendant was found guilty, not guilty, or not guilty by reason of insanity.

(b) If the defendant was found not guilty by reason of insanity, the judgment must specify the offense of which the defendant was found not guilty.

(c) If the defendant was found not guilty by reason of insanity, the judgment must reflect the finding made under Article 46C.157.
(Enacted by Acts 2005, 79th Leg., ch. 831 (S.B. 837), § 2, effective September 1, 2005.)

### Art. 46C.157. Determination Regarding Dangerous Conduct of Acquitted Person.

If a defendant is found not guilty by reason of insanity, the court immediately shall determine whether the offense of which the person was acquitted involved conduct that:

(1) caused serious bodily injury to another person;

(2) placed another person in imminent danger of serious bodily injury; or

(3) consisted of a threat of serious bodily injury to another person through the use of a deadly weapon.
(Enacted by Acts 2005, 79th Leg., ch. 831 (S.B. 837), § 2, effective September 1, 2005.)

### Art. 46C.158. Continuing Jurisdiction of Dangerous Acquitted Person.

If the court finds that the offense of which the person was acquitted involved conduct that caused serious bodily injury to another person, placed another person in imminent danger of serious bodily injury, or consisted of a threat of serious bodily injury to another person through the use of a deadly weapon, the court retains jurisdiction over the acquitted person until either:

(1) the court discharges the person and terminates its jurisdiction under Article 46C.268; or

(2) the cumulative total period of institutionalization and outpatient or community-based

treatment and supervision under the court's jurisdiction equals the maximum term provided by law for the offense of which the person was acquitted by reason of insanity and the court's jurisdiction is automatically terminated under Article 46C.269.
(Enacted by Acts 2005, 79th Leg., ch. 831 (S.B. 837), § 2, effective September 1, 2005.)

### Art. 46C.159. Proceedings Regarding Nondangerous Acquitted Person.

If the court finds that the offense of which the person was acquitted did not involve conduct that caused serious bodily injury to another person, placed another person in imminent danger of serious bodily injury, or consisted of a threat of serious bodily injury to another person through the use of a deadly weapon, the court shall proceed under Subchapter E.
(Enacted by Acts 2005, 79th Leg., ch. 831 (S.B. 837), § 2, effective September 1, 2005.)

### Art. 46C.160. Detention Pending Further Proceedings.

(a) On a determination by the judge or jury that the defendant is not guilty by reason of insanity, pending further proceedings under this chapter, the court may order the defendant detained in jail or any other suitable place for a period not to exceed 14 days.

(b) The court may order a defendant detained in a facility of the department or a facility of the Department of Aging and Disability Services under this article only with the consent of the head of the facility.
(Enacted by Acts 2005, 79th Leg., ch. 831 (S.B. 837), § 2, effective September 1, 2005.)

### Arts. 46C.161 to 46C.200. [Reserved for expansion].

### SUBCHAPTER E
### DISPOSITION FOLLOWING ACQUITTAL BY REASON OF INSANITY: NO FINDING OF DANGEROUS CONDUCT

### Art. 46C.201. Disposition: Nondangerous Conduct.

(a) If the court determines that the offense of which the person was acquitted did not involve conduct that caused serious bodily injury to another person, placed another person in imminent danger of serious bodily injury, or consisted of a threat of serious bodily injury to another person through the use of a deadly weapon, the court shall determine whether there is evidence to support a finding that the person is a person with a mental illness or with mental retardation.

(b) If the court determines that there is evidence to support a finding of mental illness or mental retardation, the court shall enter an order transferring the person to the appropriate court for civil commitment proceedings to determine whether the person should receive court-ordered mental health services under Subtitle C, Title 7, Health and Safety Code, or be committed to a residential care facility to receive mental retardation services under Subtitle D, Title 7, Health and Safety Code. The court may also order the person:

(1) detained in jail or any other suitable place pending the prompt initiation and prosecution of appropriate civil proceedings by the attorney representing the state or other person designated by the court; or

(2) placed in the care of a responsible person on satisfactory security being given for the acquitted person's proper care and protection.

(Enacted by Acts 2005, 79th Leg., ch. 831 (S.B. 837), § 2, effective September 1, 2005.)

### Art. 46C.202. Detention or Release.

(a) Notwithstanding Article 46C.201(b), a person placed in a department facility or a facility of the Department of Aging and Disability Services pending civil hearing as described by that subsection may be detained only with the consent of the head of the facility and under an Order of Protective Custody issued under Subtitle C or D, Title 7, Health and Safety Code.

(b) If the court does not detain or place the person under Article 46C.201(b), the court shall release the person.

(Enacted by Acts 2005, 79th Leg., ch. 831 (S.B. 837), § 2, effective September 1, 2005.)

### Arts. 46C.203 to 46C.250. [Reserved for expansion].

### SUBCHAPTER F
### DISPOSITION FOLLOWING ACQUITTAL BY REASON OF INSANITY: FINDING OF DANGEROUS CONDUCT

### Art. 46C.251. Commitment for Evaluation and Treatment; Report.

(a) The court shall order the acquitted person to be committed for evaluation of the person's present mental condition and for treatment to the maximum security unit of any facility designated by the department. The period of commitment under this article may not exceed 30 days.

(b) The court shall order that:

(1) a transcript of all medical testimony received in the criminal proceeding be prepared as soon as possible by the court reporter and the transcript be forwarded to the facility to which the acquitted person is committed; and

(2) the following information be forwarded to the facility and, as applicable, to the department or the Department of Aging and Disability Services:

(A) the complete name, race, and gender of the person;

(B) any known identifying number of the person, including social security number, driver's license number, or state identification number;

(C) the person's date of birth; and

(D) the offense of which the person was found not guilty by reason of insanity and a statement of the facts and circumstances surrounding the alleged offense.

(c) The court shall order that a report be filed with the court under Article 46C.252.

(d) To determine the proper disposition of the acquitted person, the court shall hold a hearing on disposition not later than the 30th day after the date of acquittal.

(Enacted by Acts 2005, 79th Leg., ch. 831 (S.B. 837), § 2, effective September 1, 2005.)

### Art. 46C.252. Report After Evaluation.

(a) The report ordered under Article 46C.251 must be filed with the court as soon as practicable before the hearing on disposition but not later than the fourth day before that hearing.

(b) The report in general terms must describe and explain the procedure, techniques, and tests used in the examination of the person.

(c) The report must address:

(1) whether the acquitted person has a mental illness or mental retardation and, if so, whether the mental illness or mental retardation is severe;

(2) whether as a result of any severe mental illness or mental retardation the acquitted person is likely to cause serious harm to another;

(3) whether as a result of any impairment the acquitted person is subject to commitment under Subtitle C or D, Title 7, Health and Safety Code;

(4) prospective treatment and supervision options, if any, appropriate for the acquitted person; and

(5) whether any required treatment and supervision can be safely and effectively provided as outpatient or community-based treatment and supervision.

(Enacted by Acts 2005, 79th Leg., ch. 831 (S.B. 837), § 2, effective September 1, 2005.)

## Art. 46C.253. Hearing on Disposition.

(a) The hearing on disposition shall be conducted in the same manner as a hearing on an application for involuntary commitment under Subtitle C or D, Title 7, Health and Safety Code, except that the use of a jury is governed by Article 46C.255.

(b) At the hearing, the court shall address:

(1) whether the person acquitted by reason of insanity has a severe mental illness or mental retardation;

(2) whether as a result of any mental illness or mental retardation the person is likely to cause serious harm to another; and

(3) whether appropriate treatment and supervision for any mental illness or mental retardation rendering the person dangerous to another can be safely and effectively provided as outpatient or community-based treatment and supervision.

(c) The court shall order the acquitted person committed for inpatient treatment or residential care under Article 46C.256 if the grounds required for that order are established.

(d) The court shall order the acquitted person to receive outpatient or community-based treatment and supervision under Article 46C.257 if the grounds required for that order are established.

(e) The court shall order the acquitted person transferred to an appropriate court for proceedings under Subtitle C or D, Title 7, Health and Safety Code, if the state fails to establish the grounds required for an order under Article 46C.256 or 46C.257 but the evidence provides a reasonable basis for believing the acquitted person is a proper subject for those proceedings.

(f) The court shall order the acquitted person discharged and immediately released if the evidence fails to establish that disposition under Subsection (c), (d), or (e) is appropriate.

(Enacted by Acts 2005, 79th Leg., ch. 831 (S.B. 837), § 2, effective September 1, 2005.)

## Art. 46C.254. Effect of Stabilization on Treatment Regimen.

If an acquitted person is stabilized on a treatment regimen, including medication and other treatment modalities, rendering the person no longer likely to cause serious harm to another, inpatient treatment or residential care may be found necessary to protect the safety of others only if:

(1) the person would become likely to cause serious harm to another if the person fails to follow the treatment regimen on an Order to Receive Outpatient or Community-Based Treatment and Supervision; and

(2) under an Order to Receive Outpatient or Community-Based Treatment and Supervision either:

(A) the person is likely to fail to comply with an available regimen of outpatient or community-based treatment, as determined by the person's insight into the need for medication, the number, severity, and controllability of side effects, the availability of support and treatment programs for the person from community members, and other appropriate considerations; or

(B) a regimen of outpatient or community-based treatment will not be available to the person.

(Enacted by Acts 2005, 79th Leg., ch. 831 (S.B. 837), § 2, effective September 1, 2005.)

## Art. 46C.255. Trial by Jury.

(a) The following proceedings under this chapter must be before the court, and the underlying matter determined by the court, unless the acquitted person or the state requests a jury trial or the court on its own motion sets the matter for jury trial:

(1) a hearing under Article 46C.253;

(2) a proceeding for renewal of an order under Article 46C.261;

(3) a proceeding on a request for modification or revocation of an order under Article 46C.266; and

(4) a proceeding seeking discharge of an acquitted person under Article 46C.268.

(b) The following proceedings may not be held before a jury:

(1) a proceeding to determine outpatient or community-based treatment and supervision under Article 46C.262; or

(2) a proceeding to determine modification or revocation of outpatient or community-based

treatment and supervision under Article 46C.267.

(c) If a hearing is held before a jury and the jury determines that the person has a mental illness or mental retardation and is likely to cause serious harm to another, the court shall determine whether inpatient treatment or residential care is necessary to protect the safety of others.

(Enacted by Acts 2005, 79th Leg., ch. 831 (S.B. 837), § 2, effective September 1, 2005.)

## Art. 46C.256. Order of Commitment to Inpatient Treatment or Residential Care.

(a) The court shall order the acquitted person committed to a mental hospital or other appropriate facility for inpatient treatment or residential care if the state establishes by clear and convincing evidence that:

(1) the person has a severe mental illness or mental retardation;

(2) the person, as a result of that mental illness or mental retardation, is likely to cause serious bodily injury to another if the person is not provided with treatment and supervision; and

(3) inpatient treatment or residential care is necessary to protect the safety of others.

(b) In determining whether inpatient treatment or residential care has been proved necessary, the court shall consider whether the evidence shows both that:

(1) an adequate regimen of outpatient or community-based treatment will be available to the person; and

(2) the person will follow that regimen.

(c) The order of commitment to inpatient treatment or residential care expires on the 181st day following the date the order is issued but is subject to renewal as provided by Article 46C.261. (Enacted by Acts 2005, 79th Leg., ch. 831 (S.B. 837), § 2, effective September 1, 2005.)

## Art. 46C.257. Order to Receive Outpatient or Community-Based Treatment and Supervision.

(a) The court shall order the acquitted person to receive outpatient or community-based treatment and supervision if:

(1) the state establishes by clear and convincing evidence that the person:

(A) has a severe mental illness or mental retardation; and

(B) as a result of that mental illness or mental retardation is likely to cause serious bodily injury to another if the person is not provided with treatment and supervision; and

(2) the state fails to establish by clear and convincing evidence that inpatient treatment or residential care is necessary to protect the safety of others.

(b) The order of commitment to outpatient or community-based treatment and supervision expires on the first anniversary of the date the order is issued but is subject to renewal as provided by Article 46C.261.

(Enacted by Acts 2005, 79th Leg., ch. 831 (S.B. 837), § 2, effective September 1, 2005.)

## Art. 46C.258. Responsibility of Inpatient or Residential Care Facility.

(a) The head of the facility to which an acquitted person is committed has, during the commitment period, a continuing responsibility to determine:

(1) whether the acquitted person continues to have a severe mental illness or mental retardation and is likely to cause serious harm to another because of any severe mental illness or mental retardation; and

(2) if so, whether treatment and supervision cannot be safely and effectively provided as outpatient or community-based treatment and supervision.

(b) The head of the facility must notify the committing court and seek modification of the order of commitment if the head of the facility determines that an acquitted person no longer has a severe mental illness or mental retardation, is no longer likely to cause serious harm to another, or that treatment and supervision can be safely and effectively provided as outpatient or community-based treatment and supervision.

(c) Not later than the 60th day before the date of expiration of the order, the head of the facility shall transmit to the committing court a psychological evaluation of the acquitted person, a certificate of medical examination of the person, and any recommendation for further treatment of the person. The committing court shall make the documents available to the attorneys representing the state and the acquitted person.

(Enacted by Acts 2005, 79th Leg., ch. 831 (S.B. 837), § 2, effective September 1, 2005.)

Criminal Procedure

## Art. 46C.259. Status of Committed Person.

If an acquitted person is committed under this subchapter, the person's status as a patient or resident is governed by Subtitle C or D, Title 7, Health and Safety Code, except that:

(1) transfer to a nonsecure unit is governed by Article 46C.260;

(2) modification of the order to direct outpatient or community-based treatment and supervision is governed by Article 46C.262; and

(3) discharge is governed by Article 46C.268.

(Enacted by Acts 2005, 79th Leg., ch. 831 (S.B. 837), § 2, effective September 1, 2005.)

## Art. 46C.260. Transfer of Committed Person to Nonsecure Facility.

(a) A person committed to a facility under this subchapter shall be committed to the maximum security unit of any facility designated by the department.

(b) A person committed under this subchapter shall be transferred to the maximum security unit immediately on the entry of the order of commitment.

(c) Unless the person is determined to be manifestly dangerous by a review board within the department, not later than the 60th day following the date of the person's arrival at the maximum security unit the person shall be transferred to a nonsecure unit of a facility designated by the department or the Department of Aging and Disability Services, as appropriate.

(d) The commissioner shall appoint a review board of five members, including one psychiatrist licensed to practice medicine in this state and two persons who work directly with persons with mental illnesses or with mental retardation, to determine whether the person is manifestly dangerous and, as a result of the danger the person presents, requires continued placement in a maximum security unit.

(e) If the head of the facility at which the maximum security unit is located disagrees with the determination, then the matter shall be referred to the commissioner. The commissioner shall decide whether the person is manifestly dangerous.

(Enacted by Acts 2005, 79th Leg., ch. 831 (S.B. 837), § 2, effective September 1, 2005.)

## Art. 46C.261. Renewal of Orders for Inpatient Commitment or Outpatient or Community-Based Treatment and Supervision.

(a) A court that orders an acquitted person committed to inpatient treatment or orders outpatient or community-based treatment and supervision annually shall determine whether to renew the order.

(b) Not later than the 30th day before the date an order is scheduled to expire, the institution to which a person is committed, the person responsible for providing outpatient or community-based treatment and supervision, or the attorney representing the state may file a request that the order be renewed. The request must explain in detail the reasons why the person requests renewal under this article. A request to renew an order committing the person to inpatient treatment must also explain in detail why outpatient or community-based treatment and supervision is not appropriate.

(c) The request for renewal must be accompanied by a certificate of medical examination for mental illness signed by a physician who examined the person during the 30-day period preceding the date on which the request is filed.

(d) On the filing of a request for renewal under this article, the court shall:

(1) set the matter for a hearing; and

(2) appoint an attorney to represent the person.

(e) The court shall act on the request for renewal before the order expires.

(f) If a hearing is held, the person may be transferred from the facility to which the acquitted person was committed to a jail for purposes of participating in the hearing only if necessary but not earlier than 72 hours before the hearing begins. If the order is renewed, the person shall be transferred back to the facility immediately on renewal of the order.

(g) If no objection is made, the court may admit into evidence the certificate of medical examination for mental illness. Admitted certificates constitute competent medical or psychiatric testimony, and the court may make its findings solely from the certificate and the detailed request for renewal.

(h) A court shall renew the order only if the court finds that the party who requested the renewal has established by clear and convincing evidence that continued mandatory supervision and treatment are appropriate. A renewed order authorizes continued inpatient commitment or outpatient or community-based treatment and supervision for not more than one year.

(i) The court, on application for renewal of an order for inpatient or residential care services, may modify the order to provide for outpatient or community-based treatment and supervision if the court finds the acquitted person has established by a preponderance of the evidence that treatment and supervision can be safely and effectively provided as outpatient or community-based treatment and supervision.
(Enacted by Acts 2005, 79th Leg., ch. 831 (S.B. 837), § 2, effective September 1, 2005.)

## Art. 46C.262. Court-Ordered Outpatient or Community-Based Treatment and Supervision After Inpatient Commitment.

(a) An acquitted person, the head of the facility to which the acquitted person is committed, or the attorney representing the state may request that the court modify an order for inpatient treatment or residential care to order outpatient or community-based treatment and supervision.

(b) The court shall hold a hearing on a request made by the head of the facility to which the acquitted person is committed. A hearing under this subsection must be held not later than the 14th day after the date of the request.

(c) If a request is made by an acquitted person or the attorney representing the state, the court must act on the request not later than the 14th day after the date of the request. A hearing under this subsection is at the discretion of the court, except that the court shall hold a hearing if the request and any accompanying material provide a basis for believing modification of the order may be appropriate.

(d) If a request is made by an acquitted person not later than the 90th day after the date of a hearing on a previous request, the court is not required to act on the request except on the expiration of the order or on the expiration of the 90-day period following the date of the hearing on the previous request.

(e) The court shall rule on the request during or as soon as practicable after any hearing on the request but not later than the 14th day after the date of the request.

(f) The court shall modify the commitment order to direct outpatient or community-based treatment and supervision if at the hearing the acquitted person establishes by a preponderance of the evidence that treatment and supervision can be safely and effectively provided as outpatient or community-based treatment and supervision.

(Enacted by Acts 2005, 79th Leg., ch. 831 (S.B. 837), § 2, effective September 1, 2005.)

## Art. 46C.263. Court-Ordered Outpatient or Community-Based Treatment and Supervision.

(a) The court may order an acquitted person to participate in an outpatient or community-based regimen of treatment and supervision:

(1) as an initial matter under Article 46C.253;

(2) on renewal of an order of commitment under Article 46C.261; or

(3) after a period of inpatient treatment or residential care under Article 46C.262.

(b) An acquitted person may be ordered to participate in an outpatient or community-based regimen of treatment and supervision only if:

(1) the court receives and approves an outpatient or community-based treatment plan that comprehensively provides for the outpatient or community-based treatment and supervision; and

(2) the court finds that the outpatient or community-based treatment and supervision provided for by the plan will be available to and provided to the acquitted person.

(c) The order may require the person to participate in a prescribed regimen of medical, psychiatric, or psychological care or treatment, and the regimen may include treatment with psychoactive medication.

(d) The court may order that supervision of the acquitted person be provided by the appropriate community supervision and corrections department or the facility administrator of a community center that provides mental health or mental retardation services.

(e) The court may order the acquitted person to participate in a supervision program funded by the Texas Correctional Office on Offenders with Medical or Mental Impairments.

(f) An order under this article must identify the person responsible for administering an ordered regimen of outpatient or community-based treatment and supervision.

(g) In determining whether an acquitted person should be ordered to receive outpatient or community-based treatment and supervision rather than inpatient care or residential treatment, the court shall have as its primary concern the protection of society.
(Enacted by Acts 2005, 79th Leg., ch. 831 (S.B. 837), § 2, effective September 1, 2005.)

## Art. 46C.264. Location of Court-Ordered Outpatient or Community-Based Treatment and Supervision.

(a) The court may order the outpatient or community-based treatment and supervision to be provided in any appropriate county where the necessary resources are available.

(b) This article does not supersede any requirement under the other provisions of this subchapter to obtain the consent of a treatment and supervision provider to administer the court-ordered outpatient or community-based treatment and supervision.

(Enacted by Acts 2005, 79th Leg., ch. 831 (S.B. 837), § 2, effective September 1, 2005.)

## Art. 46C.265. Supervisory Responsibility for Outpatient or Community-Based Treatment and Supervision.

(a) The person responsible for administering a regimen of outpatient or community-based treatment and supervision shall:

(1) monitor the condition of the acquitted person; and

(2) determine whether the acquitted person is complying with the regimen of treatment and supervision.

(b) The person responsible for administering a regimen of outpatient or community-based treatment and supervision shall notify the court ordering that treatment and supervision and the attorney representing the state if the person:

(1) fails to comply with the regimen; and

(2) becomes likely to cause serious harm to another.

(Enacted by Acts 2005, 79th Leg., ch. 831 (S.B. 837), § 2, effective September 1, 2005.)

## Art. 46C.266. Modification or Revocation of Order for Outpatient or Community-Based Treatment and Supervision.

(a) The court, on its own motion or the motion of any interested person and after notice to the acquitted person and a hearing, may modify or revoke court-ordered outpatient or community-based treatment and supervision.

(b) At the hearing, the court without a jury shall determine whether the state has established clear and convincing evidence that:

(1) the acquitted person failed to comply with the regimen in a manner or under circumstances indicating the person will become likely to cause serious harm to another if the person is provided continued outpatient or community-based treatment and supervision; or

(2) the acquitted person has become likely to cause serious harm to another if provided continued outpatient or community-based treatment and supervision.

(c) On a determination under Subsection (b), the court may take any appropriate action, including:

(1) revoking court-ordered outpatient or community-based treatment and supervision and ordering the person committed for inpatient or residential care; or

(2) imposing additional or more stringent terms on continued outpatient or community-based treatment.

(d) An acquitted person who is the subject of a proceeding under this article is entitled to representation by counsel in the proceeding.

(e) The court shall set a date for a hearing under this article that is not later than the seventh day after the applicable motion was filed. The court may grant one or more continuances of the hearing on the motion of a party or of the court and for good cause shown.

(Enacted by Acts 2005, 79th Leg., ch. 831 (S.B. 837), § 2, effective September 1, 2005.)

## Art. 46C.267. Detention Pending Proceedings to Modify or Revoke Order for Outpatient or Community-Based Treatment and Supervision.

(a) The state or the head of the facility or other person responsible for administering a regimen of outpatient or community-based treatment and supervision may file a sworn application with the court for the detention of an acquitted person receiving court-ordered outpatient or community-based treatment and supervision. The application must state that the person meets the criteria of Article 46C.266 and provide a detailed explanation of that statement.

(b) If the court determines that the application establishes probable cause to believe the order for outpatient or community-based treatment and supervision should be revoked, the court shall issue an order to an on-duty peace officer authorizing the acquitted person to be taken into custody and brought before the court.

(c) An acquitted person taken into custody under an order of detention shall be brought before the court without unnecessary delay.

(d) When an acquitted person is brought before the court, the court shall determine whether there is probable cause to believe that the order for outpatient or community-based treatment and supervision should be revoked. On a finding that probable cause for revocation exists, the court shall order the person held in protective custody pending a determination of whether the order should be revoked.

(e) An acquitted person may be detained under an order for protective custody for a period not to exceed 72 hours, excluding Saturdays, Sundays, legal holidays, and the period prescribed by Section 574.025(b), Health and Safety Code, for an extreme emergency.

(f) This subchapter does not affect the power of a peace officer to take an acquitted person into custody under Section 573.001, Health and Safety Code.

(Enacted by Acts 2005, 79th Leg., ch. 831 (S.B. 837), § 2, effective September 1, 2005.)

## Art. 46C.268. Advance Discharge of Acquitted Person and Termination of Jurisdiction.

(a) An acquitted person, the head of the facility to which the acquitted person is committed, the person responsible for providing the outpatient or community-based treatment and supervision, or the state may request that the court discharge an acquitted person from inpatient commitment or outpatient or community-based treatment and supervision.

(b) Not later than the 14th day after the date of the request, the court shall hold a hearing on a request made by the head of the facility to which the acquitted person is committed or the person responsible for providing the outpatient or community-based treatment and supervision.

(c) If a request is made by an acquitted person, the court must act on the request not later than the 14th day after the date of the request. A hearing under this subsection is at the discretion of the court, except that the court shall hold a hearing if the request and any accompanying material indicate that modification of the order may be appropriate.

(d) If a request is made by an acquitted person not later than the 90th day after the date of a hearing on a previous request, the court is not required to act on the request except on the expiration of the order or on the expiration of the 90-day period following the date of the hearing on the previous request.

(e) The court shall rule on the request during or shortly after any hearing that is held and in

any case not later than the 14th day after the date of the request.

(f) The court shall discharge the acquitted person from all court-ordered commitment and treatment and supervision and terminate the court's jurisdiction over the person if the court finds that the acquitted person has established by a preponderance of the evidence that:

(1) the acquitted person does not have a severe mental illness or mental retardation; or

(2) the acquitted person is not likely to cause serious harm to another because of any severe mental illness or mental retardation.

(Enacted by Acts 2005, 79th Leg., ch. 831 (S.B. 837), § 2, effective September 1, 2005.)

## Art. 46C.269. Termination of Court's Jurisdiction.

(a) The jurisdiction of the court over a person covered by this subchapter automatically terminates on the date when the cumulative total period of institutionalization and outpatient or community-based treatment and supervision imposed under this subchapter equals the maximum term of imprisonment provided by law for the offense of which the person was acquitted by reason of insanity.

(b) On the termination of the court's jurisdiction under this article, the person must be discharged from any inpatient treatment or residential care or outpatient or community-based treatment and supervision ordered under this subchapter.

(c) An inpatient or residential care facility to which a person has been committed under this subchapter or a person responsible for administering a regimen of outpatient or community-based treatment and supervision under this subchapter must notify the court not later than the 30th day before the court's jurisdiction over the person ends under this article.

(d) This subchapter does not affect whether a person may be ordered to receive care or treatment under Subtitle C or D, Title 7, Health and Safety Code.

(Enacted by Acts 2005, 79th Leg., ch. 831 (S.B. 837), § 2, effective September 1, 2005.)

## Art. 46C.270. Appeals.

(a) An acquitted person may appeal a judgment reflecting an acquittal by reason of insanity on the basis of the following:

(1) a finding that the acquitted person committed the offense; or

(2) a finding that the offense on which the prosecution was based involved conduct that:

(A) caused serious bodily injury to another person;

(B) placed another person in imminent danger of serious bodily injury; or

(C) consisted of a threat of serious bodily injury to another person through the use of a deadly weapon.

(b) Either the acquitted person or the state may appeal from:

(1) an Order of Commitment to Inpatient Treatment or Residential Care entered under Article 46C.256;

(2) an Order to Receive Outpatient or Community-Based Treatment and Supervision entered under Article 46C.257 or 46C.262;

(3) an order renewing or refusing to renew an Order for Inpatient Commitment or Outpatient or Community-Based Treatment and Supervision entered under Article 46C.261;

(4) an order modifying or revoking an Order for Outpatient or Community-Based Treatment and Supervision entered under Article 46C.266 or refusing a request to modify or revoke that order; or

(5) an order discharging an acquitted person under Article 46C.268 or denying a request for discharge of an acquitted person.

(c) An appeal under this subchapter may not be considered moot solely due to the expiration of an order on which the appeal is based.
(Enacted by Acts 2005, 79th Leg., ch. 831 (S.B. 837), § 2, effective September 1, 2005.)

# CHAPTER 47
# DISPOSITION OF STOLEN PROPERTY

## Art. 47.01. Subject to Order of Court.

(a) Except as provided by Subsection (b), an officer who comes into custody of property alleged to have been stolen shall hold it subject to the order of the proper court only if the ownership of the property is contested or disputed.

(b) An officer who comes into custody of property governed by Chapter 371, Finance Code, that is alleged to have been stolen shall hold the property subject to the order of the proper court regardless of whether the ownership of the property is contested or disputed.
(Enacted by Acts 1965, 59th Leg., ch. 722 (S.B. 107), § 1, effective January 1, 1966; am. Acts 1993, 73rd Leg., ch. 860 (S.B. 590), § 1, effective August 30, 1993; am. Acts 1999, 76th Leg., ch. 62 (S.B. 1368), § 3.07, effective September 1, 1999; am. Acts 2001, 77th Leg., ch. 752 (S.B. 1262), § 1, effective September 1, 2001.)

## Art. 47.01a. Restoration When No Trial Is Pending.

(a) If a criminal action relating to allegedly stolen property is not pending, a district judge, county court judge, statutory county court judge, or justice of the peace having jurisdiction as a magistrate in the county in which the property is held or a municipal judge having jurisdiction as a magistrate in the municipality in which the property is being held may hold a hearing to determine the right to possession of the property, upon the petition of an interested person, a county, a city, or the state. Jurisdiction under this section is based solely on jurisdiction as a criminal magistrate under this code and not jurisdiction as a civil court. The court shall:

(1) order the property delivered to whoever has the superior right to possession, without conditions; or

(2) on the filing of a written motion before trial by an attorney representing the state, order the property delivered to whoever has the superior right to possession, subject to the condition that the property be made available to the prosecuting authority should it be needed in future prosecutions; or

(3) order the property awarded to the custody of the peace officer, pending resolution of criminal investigations regarding the property.

(b) If it is shown in a hearing that probable cause exists to believe that the property was acquired by theft or by another manner that makes its acquisition an offense and that the identity of the actual owner of the property cannot be determined, the court shall order the peace officer to:

(1) deliver the property to a government agency for official purposes;

(2) deliver the property to a person authorized by Article 18.17 of this code to receive and dispose of the property; or

(3) destroy the property.

(c) At a hearing under Subsection (a) of this article, any interested person may present evidence showing that the property was not acquired by theft or another offense or that the person is entitled to possess the property. At the hearing, hearsay evidence is admissible.

(d) Venue for a hearing under this article is in any justice, county, statutory county, or district court in the county in which the property is seized or in any municipal court in any municipality in which the property is seized, except that the court may transfer venue to a court in another county on the motion of any interested party.

(Enacted by Acts 1977, 65th Leg., ch. 813 (H.B. 905), § 1, effective August 29, 1977; am. Acts 1987, 70th Leg., ch. 548 (S.B. 152), § 1, effective August 31, 1987; am. Acts 1993, 73rd Leg., ch. 860 (S.B. 590), § 1, effective August 30, 1993; am. Acts 1995, 74th Leg., ch. 184 (H.B. 523), § 3, effective May 23, 1995.)

## Art. 47.02. Restored on Trial.

(a) On the trial of any criminal action for theft or any other offense involving the illegal acquisition of property, the court trying the case shall order the property to be restored to the person appearing by the proof to be the owner of the property.

(b) On written consent of the prosecuting attorney, any magistrate having jurisdiction in the county in which a criminal action for theft or any other offense involving the illegal acquisition of property is pending may hold a hearing to determine the right to possession of the property. If it is proved to the satisfaction of the magistrate that any person is a true owner of the property alleged to have been stolen, and the property is under the control of a peace officer, the magistrate may, by written order, direct the property to be restored to that person.

(Enacted by Acts 1965, 59th Leg., ch. 722 (S.B. 107), § 1, effective January 1, 1966; am. Acts 1997, 75th Leg., ch. 1415 (H.B. 2592), § 1, effective September 1, 1997; am. Acts 2009, 81st Leg., ch. 613 (H.B. 796), § 2, effective September 1, 2009.)

## Art. 47.03. Schedule.

When an officer seizes property alleged to have been stolen, he shall immediately file a schedule of the same, and its value, with the court having jurisdiction of the case, certifying that the property has been seized by him, and the reason therefor. The officer shall notify the court of the names and addresses of each party known to the officer who has a claim to possession of the seized property.

(Enacted by Acts 1965, 59th Leg., ch. 722 (S.B. 107), § 1, effective January 1, 1966; am. Acts 1993, 73rd Leg., ch. 860 (S.B. 590), § 1, effective August 30, 1993.)

## Art. 47.04. Restored to Owner.

Upon an examining trial, if it is proven to the satisfaction of the court that any person is the true owner of property alleged to have been stolen, and which is in possession of a peace officer, the court may upon motion by the state, by written order direct the property to be restored to such owner subject to the conditions that such property shall be made available to the state or by order of any court having jurisdiction over the offense to be used for evidentiary purposes.

(Enacted by Acts 1965, 59th Leg., ch. 722 (S.B. 107), § 1, effective January 1, 1966; am. Acts 1993, 73rd Leg., ch. 860 (S.B. 590), § 1, effective August 30, 1993.)

## Art. 47.05. Bond Required.

If the court has any doubt as to the ownership of the property, the court may require a bond of the claimant for its re-delivery in case it should thereafter be shown not to belong to such claimant; or the court may, in its discretion, direct the property to be retained by the sheriff until further orders as to its possession. Such bond shall be in a sum equal to the value of the property, with sufficient security, payable to and approved by the county judge of the county in which the property is in custody. Such bond shall be filed in the office of the county clerk of such county, and in case of a breach thereof may be sued upon in such county by any claimant of the property; or by the county treasurer of such county.

(Enacted by Acts 1965, 59th Leg., ch. 722 (S.B. 107), § 1, effective January 1, 1966; am. Acts 1993, 73rd Leg., ch. 860 (S.B. 590), § 1, effective August 30, 1993.)

## Art. 47.06. Property Sold.

If the property is not claimed within 30 days from the conviction of the person accused of illegally acquiring it, the same procedure for its disposition as set out in Article 18.17 of this Code shall be followed.

(Enacted by Acts 1965, 59th Leg., ch. 722 (S.B. 107), § 1, effective January 1, 1966; am. Acts 1987, 70th Leg., ch. 66 (H.B. 475), § 2, effective May 6, 1987.)

### Art. 47.07. Owner May Recover.

The real owner of the property sold under the provisions of Article 47.06 may recover such property under the same terms as prescribed in Subsection (e) of Article 18.17 of this Code.
(Enacted by Acts 1965, 59th Leg., ch. 722 (S.B. 107), § 1, effective January 1, 1966; am. Acts 1987, 70th Leg., ch. 66 (H.B. 475), § 2, effective May 6, 1987.)

### Art. 47.08. Written Instrument.

If the property is a written instrument, it shall be deposited with the county clerk of the county where the proceedings are had, subject to the claim of any person who may establish his right thereto. The claimant of any such written instrument shall file his written sworn claim thereto with the county judge. If such judge be satisfied that such claimant is the real owner of the written instrument, the same shall be delivered to him. The county judge may, in his discretion, require a bond of such claimant, as in other cases of property claimed under any provision of this Chapter, and may also before such delivery require the written instrument to be recorded in the minutes of his court.
(Enacted by Acts 1965, 59th Leg., ch. 722 (S.B. 107), § 1, effective January 1, 1966.)

### Art. 47.09. Claimant to Pay Charges.

The claimant of the property, before he shall be entitled to have the same delivered to him, shall pay all reasonable charges for the safekeeping of the same while in the custody of the law, which charges shall be verified by the affidavit of the officer claiming the same, and determined by the court having jurisdiction thereof. If said charges are not paid, the property shall be sold as under execution; and the proceeds of sale, after the payment of said charges and costs of sale, paid to the owner of such property.
(Enacted by Acts 1965, 59th Leg., ch. 722 (S.B. 107), § 1, effective January 1, 1966; am. Acts 1993, 73rd Leg., ch. 860 (S.B. 590), § 1, effective August 30, 1993.)

### Art. 47.10. Charges of Officer.

When property is sold, and the proceeds of sale are ready to be paid into the county treasury, the amount of expenses for keeping the same and the costs of sale shall be determined by the county judge. The account thereof shall be in writing and verified by the officer claiming the same, with the approval of the county judge thereto for the amount allowed and shall be filed in the office of the county treasurer at the time of paying into his hands the balance of the proceeds of such sale.
(Enacted by Acts 1965, 59th Leg., ch. 722 (S.B. 107), § 1, effective January 1, 1966.)

### Art. 47.11. Scope of Chapter.

Each provision of this Chapter relating to stolen property applies as well to property acquired in any manner which makes the acquisition a penal offense.
(Enacted by Acts 1965, 59th Leg., ch. 722 (S.B. 107), § 1, effective January 1, 1966.)

### Art. 47.12. Appeal.

(a) Appeals from a hearing in a district court, county court, or statutory county court under Article 47.01a of this code shall be heard by a court of appeals. The appeal is governed by the applicable rules of procedure for appeals of civil cases to a court of appeals.

(b) Appeals from a hearing in a municipal court or justice court under Article 47.01a of this code shall be heard by a county court or statutory county court. The appeal is governed by the applicable rules of procedure for appeals for civil cases in justice courts to a county court or statutory county court.

(c) Only an interested person who appears at a hearing under this article may appeal, and such person must give an oral notice of appeal at the conclusion of the hearing and must post an appeal bond by the end of the next business day, exclusive of Saturdays, Sundays, and legal holidays.

(d) The court may require an appeal bond, in an amount determined appropriate by the court, but not to exceed twice the value of the property. The bond shall be made payable to the party who was awarded possession at the hearing, with sufficient sureties approved by the court, and conditioned that appellant will prosecute his appeal to conclusion.
(Enacted by Acts 1993, 73rd Leg., ch. 860 (S.B. 590), § 2, effective August 30, 1993.)

# CHAPTER 48
# PARDON AND PAROLE

## Art. 48.01. [2 Versions: Effective Until January 1, 2012, Contingent on Voter Approval — See Note] Governor May Pardon.

In all criminal cases, except treason and impeachment, the Governor shall have power, after conviction, on the written signed recommendation and advice of the Board of Pardons and Paroles, or a majority thereof, to grant reprieves and commutations of punishments and pardons; and upon the written recommendation and advice of a majority of the Board of Pardons and Paroles, he shall have the power to remit fines and forfeitures. The Governor shall have the power to grant one reprieve in any capital case for a period not to exceed 30 days; and he shall have power to revoke conditional pardons. With the advice and consent of the Legislature, the Governor may grant reprieves, commutations of punishment and pardons in cases of treason.

(Enacted by Acts 1965, 59th Leg., ch. 722 (S.B. 107), § 1, effective January 1, 1966; am. Acts 1995, 74th Leg., ch. 321 (H.B. 2162), § 2.019, effective September 1, 1995.)

### STATUTORY NOTES

**Editor's notes.** — Acts 2011, 82nd Leg., ch. 1053 (S.B. 144), § 2 provides: "This Act takes effect January 1, 2012, but only if the constitutional amendment proposed by the 82nd Legislature, Regular Session, 2011, authorizing the governor to grant a pardon to a person who successfully completes a term of deferred adjudication community supervision is approved by the voters. If that amendment is not approved by the voters, this Act has no effect."

## Art. 48.01. [2 Versions: Effective January 1, 2012, Contingent on Voter Approval — See Note] Governor May Pardon.

(a) In all criminal cases, except treason and impeachment, the Governor shall have power, after conviction or successful completion of a term of deferred adjudication community supervision, on the written signed recommendation and advice of the Board of Pardons and Paroles, or a majority thereof, to grant reprieves and commutations of punishments and pardons; and upon the written recommendation and advice of a majority of the Board of Pardons and Paroles, he shall have the power to remit fines and forfeitures. The Governor shall have the power to grant one reprieve in any capital case for a period not to exceed 30 days; and he shall have power to revoke conditional pardons. With the advice and consent of the Legislature, the Governor may grant reprieves, commutations of punishment and pardons in cases of treason.

(b) The Board of Pardons and Paroles may recommend that the Governor grant a pardon to a person who:

(1) is placed on deferred adjudication community supervision under Section 5, Article 42.12, and subsequently receives a discharge and dismissal under Section 5(c) of that article; and

(2) on or after the 10th anniversary of the date of discharge and dismissal, submits a written request to the board for a recommendation under this subsection.

(Enacted by Acts 1965, 59th Leg., ch. 722 (S.B. 107), § 1, effective January 1, 1966; am. Acts 1995, 74th Leg., ch. 321 (H.B. 2162), § 2.019, effective September 1, 1995; am. Acts 2011, 82nd Leg., ch. 1053 (S.B. 144), § 1, effective January 1, 2012.)

### STATUTORY NOTES

**Editor's notes.** — Acts 2011, 82nd Leg., ch. 1053 (S.B. 144), § 2 provides: "This Act takes effect January 1, 2012, but only if the constitutional amendment proposed by the 82nd Legislature, Regular Session, 2011, authorizing the governor to grant a pardon to a person who successfully completes a term of deferred adjudication community supervision is approved by the voters. If that amendment is not approved by the voters, this Act has no effect."

## Art. 48.02. Shall File Reasons.

When the Governor remits fines or forfeitures, or grants reprieves, commutation of punishment or pardons, he shall file in the office of Secretary of State his reasons therefor.

(Enacted by Acts 1965, 59th Leg., ch. 722 (S.B. 107), § 1, effective January 1, 1966.)

## Art. 48.03. Governor's Acts Under Seal.

All remissions of fines and forfeitures, and all reprieves, commutations of punishment and par-

dons, shall be signed by the Governor, and certified by the Secretary of State, under the state seal, and shall be forthwith obeyed by any officer to whom the same may be presented.
(Enacted by Acts 1965, 59th Leg., ch. 722 (S.B. 107), § 1, effective January 1, 1966; am. Acts 1993, 73rd Leg., ch. 300 H.B. 1463), § 26, effective August 30, 1993.)

## Art. 48.04. Power to Remit Fines and Forfeitures.

The Governor shall have the power to remit forfeitures of bail bonds.
(Enacted by Acts 1965, 59th Leg., ch. 722 (S.B. 107), § 1, effective January 1, 1966.)

## Art. 48.05. Restoration of Civil Rights.

(a) (1) An individual convicted of an offense described by Subdivision (2) of this subsection may, except as provided by Subsection (b) of this article, submit an application for restoration of any civil rights forfeited under the laws of this state as a result of the conviction.

(2) This article applies to:

(A) a federal offense, other than an offense involving:

(i) violence or the threat of violence;

(ii) drugs; or

(iii) firearms; and

(B) an offense under the laws of another country, other than an offense involving:

(i) violence or the threat of violence;

(ii) drugs; or

(iii) firearms, if the elements of the offense are substantially similar to elements of an offense under the laws of this state punishable as a felony.

(b) An individual may not apply for restoration of civil rights under this article unless:

(1) the individual has completed the sentence for the offense;

(2) the conviction occurred:

(A) three or more years before the date of application, if the offense is a federal offense; or

(B) two or more years before the date of application, if the offense is an offense under the laws of another country; and

(3) the individual has not been convicted at any other time of an offense under the laws of this state, another state, or the United States.

(c) An application for restoration of civil rights must contain:

(1) a completed application on a form adopted by the Board of Pardons and Paroles;

(2) three or more affidavits attesting to the good character of the applicant; and

(3) proof that the applicant has completed the sentence for the offense.

(d) The applicant must submit the application to:

(1) the sheriff of the county in which the applicant resides at the time of application or resided at the time of conviction of the offense, if the individual resided in this state at that time; or

(2) the Board of Pardons and Paroles.

(e) If an application is submitted to a sheriff, the sheriff shall review the application and recommend to the Board of Pardons and Paroles whether the individual's civil rights should be restored. If the sheriff recommends restoration of the individual's civil rights, the board may either:

(1) concur in the recommendation and forward the recommendation to the governor; or

(2) independently review the application to determine whether to recommend to the governor the restoration of the individual's civil rights.

(f) If the sheriff does not recommend the restoration of the individual's civil rights, the individual may apply directly to the Board of Pardons and Paroles.

(g) If an application is submitted to the Board of Pardons and Paroles without first being submitted to a sheriff, the board shall review the application and recommend to the governor as to whether the individual's civil rights should be restored.

(h) The Board of Pardons and Paroles may require or obtain additional information as necessary to perform a review under Subsection (e)(2) or Subsection (g) of this article.

(i) On receipt from the Board of Pardons and Paroles of a recommendation to restore the civil rights of an individual, the governor may either grant or deny the restoration of civil rights to the individual. If the governor grants the restoration of civil rights to the individual, the governor shall issue a certificate of restoration of civil rights.

(j) If an application under this article is denied by the Board of Pardons and Paroles or the governor, the individual may not file another application under this article before the first anniversary of the date of the denial.

(k) A restoration of civil rights under this article is a form of pardon that restores all civil rights under the laws of this state that an individual forfeits as a result of the individual's conviction of an offense, except as specifically provided in the certificate of restoration.

(Enacted by Acts 1993, 73rd Leg., ch. 900 (S.B. 1067), § 7.01(a), effective September 1, 1993; am. Acts 2001, 77th Leg., ch. 150 (S.B. 610), § 1, effective May 16, 2001.)

# CHAPTER 49
# INQUESTS UPON DEAD BODIES

### Subchapter A. Duties Performed by Justices of the Peace

# SUBCHAPTER A
# DUTIES PERFORMED BY JUSTICES OF THE PEACE

## Art. 49.01. Definitions.

In this article:

(1) "Autopsy" means a post mortem examination of the body of a person, including X-rays and an examination of the internal organs and structures after dissection, to determine the cause of death or the nature of any pathological changes that may have contributed to the death.

(2) "Inquest" means an investigation into the cause and circumstances of the death of a person, and a determination, made with or without a formal court hearing, as to whether the death was caused by an unlawful act or omission.

(3) "Inquest hearing" means a formal court hearing held to determine whether the death of a person was caused by an unlawful act or omission and, if the death was caused by an unlawful act or omission, to obtain evidence to form the basis of a criminal prosecution.

(4) "Institution" means any place where health care services are rendered, including a hospital, clinic, health facility, nursing home, extended-care facility, out-patient facility, foster-care facility, and retirement home.

(5) "Physician" means a practicing doctor of medicine or doctor of osteopathic medicine who is licensed by the Texas State Board of Medical Examiners under Subtitle B, Title 3, Occupations Code.

(Am. Acts 1987, 70th Leg., ch. 529 (H.B. 1104), § 1, effective September 1, 1987; am. Acts 1989, 71st Leg., ch. 72 (H.B. 1400), § 1, effective May 9, 1989; am. Acts 2001, 77th Leg., ch. 1420 (H.B. 2812), § 14.737, effective September 1, 2001.)

## Art. 49.02. Applicability.

This subchapter applies to the inquest into a death occurring in a county that does not have a medical examiner's office or that is not part of a medical examiner's district.

(Am. Acts 1987, 70th Leg., ch. 529 (H.B. 1104), § 1, effective September 1, 1987.)

## Art. 49.03. Powers and Duties.

The powers granted and duties imposed on a justice of the peace under this article are independent of the powers and duties of a law enforcement agency investigating a death.

(Am. Acts 1987, 70th Leg., ch. 529 (H.B. 1104), § 1, effective September 1, 1987.)

## Art. 49.04. Deaths Requiring an Inquest.

(a) A justice of the peace shall conduct an inquest into the death of a person who dies in the county served by the justice if:

(1) the person dies in prison under circumstances other than those described by Section 501.055(b), Government Code, or in jail;

(2) the person dies an unnatural death from a cause other than a legal execution;

(3) the body or a body part of a person is found, the cause or circumstances of death are unknown, and:

(A) the person is identified; or

(B) the person is unidentified;

(4) the circumstances of the death indicate that the death may have been caused by unlawful means;

(5) the person commits suicide or the circumstances of the death indicate that the death may have been caused by suicide;

(6) the person dies without having been attended by a physician;

(7) the person dies while attended by a physician who is unable to certify the cause of death and who requests the justice of the peace to conduct an inquest; or

(8) the person is a child younger than six years of age and an inquest is required by Chapter 264, Family Code.

(b) Except as provided by Subsection (c) of this section, a physician who attends the death of a person and who is unable to certify the cause of death shall report the death to the justice of the peace of the precinct where the death occurred and request that the justice conduct an inquest.

(c) If a person dies in a hospital or other institution and an attending physician is unable to certify the cause of death, the superintendent or general manager of the hospital or institution shall report the death to the justice of the peace of the precinct where the hospital or institution is located.

(d) A justice of the peace investigating a death described by Subsection (a)(3)(B) shall report the death to the missing children and missing persons information clearinghouse of the Department of Public Safety and the national crime information center not later than the 10th working day after the date the investigation began. (Am. Acts 1987, 70th Leg., ch. 529 (H.B. 1104), § 1, effective September 1, 1987; am. Acts 1995, 74th Leg., ch. 255 (S.B. 81), § 3, effective September 1, 1995; am. Acts 1995, 74th Leg., ch. 321 (H.B. 2162), § 1.105, effective September 1, 1995; am. Acts 1995, 74th Leg., ch. 878 (S.B. 1485), § 2, effective September 1, 1995; am. Acts 1997, 75th Leg., ch. 656 (H.B. 2693), § 1, effective September 1, 1997; am. Acts 1999, 76th Leg., ch. 785 (H.B. 1387), § 2, effective September 1, 1999; am.

Acts 2003, 78th Leg., ch. 826 (S.B. 356), § 1, effective September 1, 2003; am. Acts 2003, 78th Leg., ch. 1295 (H.B. 2989), § 1, effective September 1, 2003.)

## Art. 49.041. Reopening an Inquest.

A justice of the peace may reopen an inquest if, based on information provided by a credible person or facts within the knowledge of the justice of the peace, the justice of the peace determines that reopening the inquest may reveal a different cause or different circumstances of death. (Enacted by Acts 1997, 75th Leg., ch. 897 (H.B. 2845), § 1, effective September 1, 1997.)

## Art. 49.05. Time and Place of Inquest; Removal of Property and Body from Place of Death.

(a) A justice of the peace shall conduct an inquest immediately or as soon as practicable after the justice receives notification of the death.

(b) A justice of the peace may conduct an inquest:

(1) at the place where the death occurred;

(2) where the body was found; or

(3) at any other place determined to be reasonable by the justice.

(c) A justice of the peace may direct the removal of a body from the scene of death or move any part of the physical surroundings of a body only after a law enforcement agency is notified of the death and a peace officer has conducted an investigation or, if a law enforcement agency has not begun an investigation, a reasonable time has elapsed from the time the law enforcement agency was notified.

(d) A law enforcement agency that is notified of a death requiring an inquest under Article 49.04 of this code shall begin its investigation immediately or as soon as practicable after the law enforcement agency receives notification of the death.

(e) Except in emergency circumstances, a peace officer or other person conducting a death investigation for a law enforcement agency may not move the body or any part of the physical surroundings of the place of death without authorization from a justice of the peace.

(f) A person not authorized by law to move the body of a decedent or any part of the physical surroundings of the body commits an offense if the person tampers with a body that is subject to an inquest under Article 49.04 of this code or any part of the physical surroundings of the body. An

offense under this section is punishable by a fine in an amount not to exceed $500.
(Am. Acts 1987, 70th Leg., ch. 529 (H.B. 1104), § 1, effective September 1, 1987.)

## Art. 49.06. Hindering an Inquest.

(a) A person commits an offense if the person intentionally or knowingly hinders the entrance of a justice of the peace to a premises where a death occurred or a body is found.

(b) An offense under this article is a Class B misdemeanor.
(Am. Acts 1987, 70th Leg., ch. 529 (H.B. 1104), § 1, effective September 1, 1987.)

## Art. 49.07. Notification of Investigating Official.

(a) A physician or other person who has possession of a body or body part of a person whose death requires an inquest under Article 49.04 of this code shall immediately notify the justice of the peace who serves the precinct in which the body or body part was found.

(b) A peace officer who has been notified of the death of a person whose death requires an inquest under Article 49.04 of this code shall immediately notify the justice of the peace who serves the precinct in which the body or body part was found.

(c) (1) If the justice of the peace who serves the precinct in which the body or body part was found is not available to conduct an inquest, a person required to give notice under this article shall notify the nearest available justice of the peace serving the county in which the body or body part was found, and that justice of the peace shall conduct the inquest.

(2) If no justice of the peace serving the county in which the body or body part was found is available to conduct an inquest, a person required to give notice under this article shall notify the county judge, and the county judge shall initiate the inquest. The county judge may exercise any power and perform any duty otherwise granted to or imposed under this subchapter on the justice of the peace serving the county in which the body or body part was found, except that not later than the fifth day after the day on which the inquest is initiated, the county judge shall transfer all information obtained by the judge to the justice of the peace in whose precinct the body or body part was found for final disposition of the matter.

(d) A person commits an offense if the person is required by this article to give notice and intentionally or knowingly fails to give the notice. An offense under this subsection is a Class C misdemeanor.
(Am. Acts 1987, 70th Leg., ch. 529 (H.B. 1104), § 1, effective September 1, 1987; am. Acts 1997, 75th Leg., ch. 656 (H.B. 2693), § 2, effective September 1, 1997; am. Acts 2001, 77th Leg., ch. 229 (S.B. 164), § 1, effective May 22, 2001; am. Acts 2003, 78th Leg., ch. 826 (S.B. 356), § 2, effective September 1, 2003; am. Acts 2003, 78th Leg., ch. 1295 (H.B. 2989), § 2, effective September 1, 2003.)

## Art. 49.08. Information Leading to an Inquest.

A justice of the peace conducting an inquest may act on information the justice receives from any credible person or on facts within his knowledge.
(Am. Acts 1987, 70th Leg., ch. 529 (H.B. 1104), § 1, effective September 1, 1987.)

## Art. 49.09. Body Disinterred or Cremated.

(a) If a body or body part subject to investigation under Article 49.04 of this code is interred and an authorized person has not conducted an inquest required under this subchapter, a justice of the peace may direct the disinterment of the body or body part in order to conduct an inquest.

(b) A person may not cremate or direct the cremation of a body subject to investigation under Article 49.04 unless the body is identified and the person has received from the justice of the peace a certificate signed by the justice stating that:

(1) an autopsy was performed on the body under Article 49.10 of this code; or

(2) no autopsy was necessary.

(c) An owner or operator of a crematory shall retain a certificate received under Subsection (b) of this article for a period of 10 years from the date of cremation of the body named on the certificate.

(d) A person commits an offense if the person cremates or directs the cremation of a body without obtaining a certificate from a justice of the peace as required by Subsection (b) of this article. An offense under this section is a Class B misdemeanor.

(e) If the body of a deceased person is unidentified, a person may not cremate or direct the cremation of the body under this article. If the body is buried, the justice of the peace shall record and maintain for not less than 10 years all information pertaining to the body and the location of burial.

(Am. Acts 1987, 70th Leg., ch. 529 (H.B. 1104), § 1, effective September 1, 1987; am. Acts 1997, 75th Leg., ch. 656 (H.B. 2693), § 3, effective September 1, 1997; am. Acts 2003, 78th Leg., ch. 826 (S.B. 356), § 3, effective September 1, 2003; am. Acts 2003, 78th Leg., ch. 1295 (H.B. 2989), § 3, effective September 1, 2003.)

### Art. 49.10. Autopsies and Tests.

(a) At his discretion, a justice of the peace may obtain the opinion of a county health officer or a physician concerning the necessity of obtaining an autopsy in order to determine or confirm the nature and cause of a death.

(b) The commissioners court of the county shall pay a reasonable fee for a consultation obtained by a justice of the peace under Subsection (a) of this article.

(c) Except as required by Section 264.514, Family Code, for each body that is the subject of an inquest by a justice of the peace, the justice, in the justice's discretion, shall:

(1) direct a physician to perform an autopsy; or

(2) certify that no autopsy is necessary.

(d) A justice of the peace may not order a person to perform an autopsy on the body of a deceased person whose death was caused by Asiatic cholera, bubonic plague, typhus fever, or smallpox. A justice of the peace may not order a person to perform an autopsy on the body of a deceased person whose death was caused by a communicable disease during a public health disaster.

(e) A justice of the peace shall order an autopsy performed on a body if:

(1) the justice determines that an autopsy is necessary to determine or confirm the nature and cause of death;

(2) the deceased was a child younger than six years of age and the death is determined under Section 264.514, Family Code, to be unexpected or the result of abuse or neglect; or

(3) directed to do so by the district attorney, criminal district attorney, or, if there is no district or criminal district attorney, the county attorney.

(f) A justice of the peace shall request a physician to perform the autopsy.

(g) The commissioners court shall pay a reasonable fee to a physician performing an autopsy

on the order of a justice of the peace, if a fee is assessed.

(h) The commissioners court shall pay a reasonable fee for the transportation of a body to a place where an autopsy can be performed under this article if a justice of the peace orders the body to be transported to the place.

(i) If a justice of the peace determines that a complete autopsy is unnecessary to confirm or determine the cause of death, the justice may order a physician to take or remove from a body a sample of body fluids, tissues, or organs in order to determine the nature and cause of death. Except as provided by Subsection (j) of this article, a justice may not order any person other than a physician to take samples from the body of a deceased person.

(j) A justice of the peace may order a physician, qualified technician, paramedic, chemist, registered professional nurse, or licensed vocational nurse to take a specimen of blood from the body of a person who died as the result of a motor vehicle accident if the justice determines that circumstances indicate that the person may have been driving while intoxicated.

(k) A justice of the peace may order an investigative or laboratory test to determine the identity of a deceased person. After proper removal of a sample from a body, a justice may order any person specially trained in identification work to complete any tests necessary to determine the identity of the deceased person.

(l) A medical examination on an unidentified person shall include the following information to enable a timely and accurate identification of the person:

(1) all available fingerprints and palm prints;

(2) dental charts and radiographs (X-rays) of the person's teeth;

(3) frontal and lateral facial photographs with scale indicated;

(4) notation and photographs, with scale indicated, of a significant scar, mark, tattoo, or item of clothing or other personal effect found with or near the body;

(5) notation of antemortem medical conditions;

(6) notation of observations pertinent to the estimation of time of death; and

(7) precise documentation of the location of burial of the remains.

(m) A medical examination on an unidentified person may include the following information to enable a timely and accurate identification of the person:

(1) full body radiographs (X-rays); and

(2) hair specimens with roots.

(n) On discovering the body or body part of a deceased person in the circumstances described by Article 49.04(a)(3)(B), the justice of the peace may request the aid of a forensic anthropologist in the examination of the body or body part. The forensic anthropologist must hold a doctoral degree in anthropology with an emphasis in physical anthropology. The forensic anthropologist shall attempt to establish whether the body or body part is of a human or animal, whether evidence of childbirth, injury, or disease exists, and the sex, race, age, stature, and physical anomalies of the body or body part. The forensic anthropologist may also attempt to establish the cause, manner, and time of death.

(o) If a person is injured in one county and dies as a result of those injuries, with the death occurring in another county, the attorney representing the state in the prosecution of felonies in the county in which the injury occurred may request a justice of the peace in the county in which the death occurred to order an autopsy be performed on the body of the deceased person. If the justice of the peace orders that the autopsy be performed, the county in which the injury occurred shall reimburse the county in which the death occurred.

(Am. Acts 1987, 70th Leg., ch. 529 (H.B. 1104), § 1, effective September 1, 1987; am. Acts 1995, 74th Leg., ch. 255 (S.B. 81), § 4, effective September 1, 1995; am. Acts 1995, 74th Leg., ch. 878 (S.B. 1485), § 3, effective September 1, 1995; am. Acts 1997, 75th Leg., ch. 656 (H.B. 2693), § 4, effective June 11, 1997; am. Acts 1997, 75th Leg., ch. 1022 (S.B. 359), § 102, effective September 1, 1997; am. Acts 1997, 75th Leg., ch. 1301 (S.B. 502), § 1, effective September 1, 1997; am. Acts 1999, 76th Leg., ch. 1071 (H.B. 3265), § 1, effective August 30, 1999; am. Acts 1999, 76th Leg., ch. 1132 (H.B. 3775), § 1, effective September 1, 1999; am. Acts 2001, 77th Leg., ch. 237 (S.B. 370), § 1, effective May 22, 2001; am. Acts 2001, 77th Leg., ch. 240 (S.B. 600), § 1, effective September 1, 2001; am. Acts 2003, 78th Leg., ch. 198 (H.B. 2292), § 2.190, effective September 1, 2003; am. Acts 2003, 78th Leg., ch. 826 (S.B. 356), § 4, effective September 1, 2003; am. Acts 2003, 78th Leg., ch. 1295 (H.B. 2989), § 4, effective September 1, 2003.)

## Art. 49.11. Chemical Analysis.

(a) A justice of the peace may obtain a chemical analysis of a sample taken from a body in order to determine whether death was caused, in whole or in part, by the ingestion, injection, or introduction into the body of a poison or other chemical substance. A justice may obtain a chemical analysis under this article from a chemist, toxicologist, pathologist, or other medical expert.

(b) A justice of the peace shall obtain a chemical analysis under Subsection (a) of this article if requested to do so by the physician who performed an autopsy on the body.

(c) The commissioners court shall pay a reasonable fee to a person who conducts a chemical analysis at the request of a justice of the peace.

(Am. Acts 1987, 70th Leg., ch. 529 (H.B. 1104), § 1, effective September 1, 1987.)

## Art. 49.12. Liability of Person Performing Autopsy or Test.

A person who performs an autopsy or makes a test on a body on the order of a justice of the peace in the good faith belief that the order is valid is not liable for damages if the order is invalid.

(Am. Acts 1987, 70th Leg., ch. 529 (H.B. 1104), § 1, effective September 1, 1987.)

## Art. 49.13. [Repealed January 1, 2012] Consent to Autopsy.

(a) Consent for a physician to conduct an autopsy is sufficient if given by the following:

(1) if the deceased was married, the surviving spouse;

(2) if the deceased was married but not survived by a spouse, an adult child of the deceased;

(3) if the deceased was married but not survived by a spouse, and a child of the deceased is under the care of a guardian or a court, the guardian or court having care of the child; or

(4) if the deceased person was unmarried or is not survived by a spouse or a child, the following persons in the order stated:

(A) a parent;

(B) a guardian;

(C) the next of kin; or

(D) any person who assumes custody of and responsibility for the burial of the body.

(b) Notwithstanding Subsection (a), consent for a physician to conduct an autopsy is sufficient if given by the Texas Department of Criminal Justice or an authorized official of the department in accordance with Section 501.055, Government Code.

(Am. Acts 1987, 70th Leg., ch. 529 (H.B. 1104), § 1, effective September 1, 1987; am. Acts 1997, 75th Leg., ch. 1422 (H.B. 2827), § 4, effective June 20, 1997.)

### Art. 49.14. Inquest Hearing.

(a) A justice of the peace conducting an inquest may hold an inquest hearing if the justice determines that the circumstances warrant the hearing. The justice shall hold an inquest hearing if requested to do so by a district attorney or a criminal district attorney who serves the county in which the body was found.

(b) An inquest hearing may be held with or without a jury unless the district attorney or criminal district attorney requests that the hearing be held with a jury.

(c) A jury in an inquest hearing is composed of six persons. Jurors shall be summoned in the same manner as are jurors for county court. A juror who is properly summoned and fails to appear, other than a juror exempted by law, commits an offense. An offense under this subsection is punishable by a fine not to exceed $100.

(d) A justice of the peace may hold a public or a private inquest hearing. If a person has been arrested and charged with causing the death of the deceased, the defendant and the defendant's counsel are entitled to be present at the inquest hearing, examine witnesses, and introduce evidence.

(e) A justice of the peace may issue a subpoena to enforce the attendance of a witness at an inquest hearing and may issue an attachment for a person who is subpoenaed and fails to appear at the time and place cited on the subpoena.

(f) A justice of the peace may require bail of a witness to secure the appearance of the witness at an inquest hearing or before a grand jury, examining court, or other court investigating a death.

(g) The justice of the peace shall swear witnesses appearing at an inquest hearing. The justice and an attorney representing the state may examine witnesses at an inquest hearing. The justice shall direct that all sworn testimony be reduced to writing and the justice shall subscribe the transcription.

(h) Only the justice of the peace, a person charged in the death under investigation, the counsel for the person charged, and an attorney representing the state may question a witness at an inquest hearing.

(i) A justice of the peace may hold a person who disrupts the proceedings of an inquest hearing in contempt of court. A person who is found in contempt of court under this subsection may be fined in an amount not to exceed $100 and removed from court by a peace officer.

(Am. Acts 1987, 70th Leg., ch. 529 (H.B. 1104), § 1, effective September 1, 1987.)

### Art. 49.15. Inquest Record.

(a) A justice of the peace or other person authorized under this subchapter to conduct an inquest shall make an inquest record for each inquest he conducts. The inquest record must include a report of the events, proceedings, findings, and conclusions of the inquest. The record must also include any autopsy prepared in the case and all other papers of the case. All papers of the inquest record must be marked with the case number and be clearly indexed and be maintained in the office of the justice of the peace and be made available to the appropriate officials upon request.

(b) As part of the inquest record, the justice of the peace shall make and keep complete and permanent records of all inquest hearings. The inquest hearing records must include:

(1) the name of the deceased person or, if the person is unidentified, a description of the body;

(2) the time, date, and place where the body was found;

(3) the time, date, and place where the inquest was held;

(4) the name of every witness who testified at the inquest;

(5) the name of every person who provided to the justice information pertinent to the inquest;

(6) the amount of bail set for each witness and person charged in the death;

(7) a transcript of the testimony given by each witness at the inquest hearing;

(8) the autopsy report, if an autopsy was performed; and

(9) the name of every person arrested as a suspect in the death who appeared at the inquest and the details of that person's arrest.

(c) The commissioners court shall pay a reasonable fee to a person who records or transcribes sworn testimony during an inquest hearing.

(d) The justice of the peace shall certify a copy of the inquest summary report and deliver the certified copy in a sealed envelope to the clerk of the district court. The clerk of the district court shall retain the summary report subject to an order by the district court.

(Am. Acts 1987, 70th Leg., ch. 529 (H.B. 1104), § 1, effective September 1, 1987.)

### Art. 49.16. Orders and Death Certificates.

The justice of the peace or other person who conducts an inquest under this subchapter shall sign the death certificate and all orders made as a necessary part of the inquest.

(Am. Acts 1987, 70th Leg., ch. 529 (H.B. 1104), § 1, effective September 1, 1987.)

### Art. 49.17. Evidence.

A justice of the peace shall preserve all tangible evidence that the justice accumulates in the course of an inquest that tends to show the real cause of death or identify the person who caused the death. The justice shall:

(1) deposit the evidence with the appropriate law enforcement agency to be stored in the agency's property room for safekeeping; or

(2) deliver the evidence to the district clerk for safekeeping subject to the order of the court.

(Am. Acts 1987, 70th Leg., ch. 529 (H.B. 1104), § 1, effective September 1, 1987.)

### Art. 49.18. Death in Custody.

(a) If a person confined in a penal institution dies, the sheriff or other person in charge of the penal institution shall as soon as practicable inform the justice of the peace of the precinct where the penal institution is located of the death.

(b) If a person dies while in the custody of a peace officer or as a result of a peace officer's use of force or if a person incarcerated in a jail, correctional facility, or state juvenile facility dies, the director of the law enforcement agency of which the officer is a member or of the facility in which the person was incarcerated shall investigate the death and file a written report of the cause of death with the attorney general no later than the 30th day after the date on which the person in custody or the incarcerated person died. The director shall make a good faith effort to obtain all facts relevant to the death and include those facts in the report. The attorney general shall make the report, with the exception of any portion of the report that the attorney general determines is privileged, available to any interested person.

(c) Subsection (a) does not apply to a death that occurs in a facility operated by or under contract with the Texas Department of Criminal Justice. Subsection (b) does not apply to a death that occurs in a facility operated by or under contract with the Texas Department of Criminal Justice if the death occurs under circumstances described by Section 501.055(b)(2), Government Code.

(d) In this article:

(1) "Correctional facility" means a confinement facility or halfway house operated by or under contract with any division of the Texas Department of Criminal Justice.

(2) "In the custody of a peace officer" means:

(A) under arrest by a peace officer; or

(B) under the physical control or restraint of a peace officer.

(3) "State juvenile facility" means any facility or halfway house:

(A) operated by or under contract with the Texas Youth Commission; or

(B) described by Section 51.02(13) or (14), Family Code.

(Am. Acts 1987, 70th Leg., ch. 529 (H.B. 1104), § 1, effective September 1, 1987; am. Acts 1995, 74th Leg., ch. 321 (H.B. 2162), § 1.106, effective September 1, 1995; am. Acts 1997, 75th Leg., ch. 1422 (H.B. 2827), § 1, effective June 20, 1997; am. Acts 2003, 78th Leg., ch. 894 (S.B. 826), § 1, effective September 1, 2003.)

### Art. 49.19. Warrant of Arrest.

(a) A justice of the peace who is conducting an inquest of a death under this subchapter may issue a warrant for the arrest of a person suspected of causing the death if:

(1) the justice has knowledge that the person caused the death of the deceased;

(2) the justice receives an affidavit stating that the person caused the death; or

(3) evidence is adduced at an inquest hearing that shows probable cause to believe the person caused the death.

(b) A peace officer who receives an arrest warrant issued by a justice of the peace shall:

(1) execute the warrant without delay; and

(2) detain the person arrested until the person's discharge is ordered by the justice of the peace or other proper authority.

(c) A person who is charged in a death and arrested under a warrant of a justice of the peace shall remain in the custody of the arresting peace officer and may not be removed from the peace

officer's custody on the authority of a warrant from another magistrate. A person charged in a death who has not been arrested under a warrant of a justice of the peace may be arrested on the order of a magistrate other than the justice of the peace and examined by that magistrate while an inquest is pending.
(Am. Acts 1987, 70th Leg., ch. 529 (H.B. 1104), § 1, effective September 1, 1987.)

### Art. 49.20. Requisites of Warrant.

A warrant of arrest issued under Article 49.19 of this code is sufficient if it:

(1) is issued in the name of "The State of Texas";

(2) specifies the name of the person whose arrest is ordered or, if the person's name is unknown, reasonably describes the person;

(3) recites in plain language the offense with which the person is charged; and

(4) is signed and dated by a justice of the peace.
(Am. Acts 1987, 70th Leg., ch. 529 (H.B. 1104), § 1, effective September 1, 1987.)

### Art. 49.21. Commitment of Homicide Suspect.

At the conclusion of an inquest, if a justice of the peace finds that a person who has been arrested in the case caused or contributed to the death of the deceased, the justice may:

(1) commit the person to jail; or

(2) require the person to execute a bail bond with security for the person's appearance before the proper court to answer for the offense.
(Am. Acts 1987, 70th Leg., ch. 529 (H.B. 1104), § 1, effective September 1, 1987.)

### Art. 49.22. Sealing Premises of Deceased.

(a) If a body or body part that is subject to an inquest under Article 49.04 of this code is found on premises that were under the sole control of the deceased, a justice of the peace or other person authorized under this subchapter to conduct an inquest may direct that the premises be locked and sealed to prohibit entrance by any person other than a peace officer conducting an investigation of the death.

(b) Rent, utility charges, taxes, and all other reasonable expenses accruing against the property of the deceased during the time the premises of the deceased are locked and sealed under this article may be charged against the estate of the deceased.

(c) A person other than a peace officer commits an offense if the person tampers with or removes a lock or seal placed on premises under this article.

(d) An offense under this article is a Class B misdemeanor.
(Am. Acts 1987, 70th Leg., ch. 529 (H.B. 1104), § 1, effective September 1, 1987; am. Acts 1997, 75th Leg., ch. 656 (H.B. 2693), § 5, effective September 1, 1997; am. Acts 2003, 78th Leg., ch. 826 (S.B. 356), § 5, effective September 1, 2003; am. Acts 2003, 78th Leg., ch. 1295 (H.B. 2989), § 5, effective September 1, 2003.)

### Art. 49.23. Office of Death Investigator.

(a) The commissioners court of a county may establish an office of death investigator and employ one or more death investigators to provide assistance to those persons in the county who conduct inquests. A death investigator employed under this article is entitled to receive compensation from the county in an amount set by the commissioners court. A death investigator serves at the will of the commissioners court and on terms and conditions set by the commissioners court.

(b) To be eligible for employment as a death investigator, a person must have experience or training in investigative procedures concerning the circumstances, manner, and cause of the death of a deceased person.

(c) At the request of and under the supervision of a justice of the peace or other person conducting an inquest, a death investigator may assist the person conducting the inquest to investigate the time, place, and manner of death and lock and seal the premises of the deceased. A death investigator who assists in an inquest under this subsection shall make a complete report of the death investigator's activities, findings, and conclusions to the justice of the peace or other person conducting the inquest not later than eight hours after the death investigator completes the investigation.
(Am. Acts 1987, 70th Leg., ch. 529 (H.B. 1104), § 1, effective September 1, 1987.)

### Art. 49.24. Notification and Report of Death of Resident of Institution.

(a) A superintendent or general manager of an institution who is required by Article 49.04 to report to a justice of the peace the death of an individual under the care, custody, or control of or residing in the institution shall:

(1) notify the office of the attorney general of the individual's death within 24 hours of the death; and

(2) prepare and submit to the office of the attorney general a report containing all facts relevant to the individual's death within 72 hours of the death.

(b) The superintendent or general manager of the institution shall make a good faith effort to obtain all facts relevant to an individual's death and to include those facts in the report submitted under Subsection (a)(2).

(c) The office of the attorney general may investigate each death reported to the office by an institution that receives payments through the medical assistance program under Chapter 32, Human Resources Code.

(d) Except as provided by Subsection (e), the office of the attorney general shall make a report submitted under Subsection (a)(2) available to any interested person who submits a written request for access to the report.

(e) The office of the attorney general may deny a person access to a report or a portion of a report filed under Subsection (a)(2) if the office determines that the report or a portion of the report is:

(1) privileged from discovery; or

(2) exempt from required public disclosure under Chapter 552, Government Code.

(f) This article does not relieve a superintendent or general manager of an institution of the duty of making any other notification or report of an individual's death as required by law.

(g) For the purposes of this article, the definition of "institution" excludes hospitals.

(Enacted by Acts 2003, 78th Leg., ch. 894 (S.B. 826), § 2, effective September 1, 2003; am. Acts 2005, 79th Leg., ch. 392 (S.B. 1469), § 1, effective June 17, 2005.)

## SUBCHAPTER B
## DUTIES PERFORMED BY MEDICAL EXAMINERS

### Art. 49.25. Medical Examiners.
#### Sec. 1. Office Authorized.

Subject to the provisions of this Act, the Commissioners Court of any county having a population of more than one million and not having a reputable medical school as defined in Articles 4501 and 4503, Revised Civil Statutes of Texas, shall establish and maintain the office of medical examiner, and the Commissioners Court of any county may establish and provide for the maintenance of the office of medical examiner. Population shall be according to the last preceding federal census.

#### Sec. 1-a. Multi-County District; Joint Office.

(a) The commissioners courts of two or more counties may enter into an agreement to create a medical examiners district and to jointly operate and maintain the office of medical examiner of the district. The district must include the entire area of all counties involved. The counties within the district must, when taken together, form a continuous area.

(b) There may be only one medical examiner in a medical examiners district, although he may employ, within the district, necessary staff personnel. When a county becomes a part of a medical examiners district, the effect is the same within the county as if the office of medical examiner had been established in that county alone. The district medical examiner has all the powers and duties within the district that a medical examiner who serves in a single county has within that county.

(c) The commissioners court of any county which has become a part of a medical examiners district may withdraw the county from the district, but twelve months' notice of withdrawal must be given to the commissioners courts of all other counties in the district.

#### Sec. 2. Appointments and Qualifications.

The commissioners court shall appoint the medical examiner, who shall serve at the pleasure of the commissioners court. No person shall be appointed medical examiner unless he is a physician licensed by the State Board of Medical Examiners. To the greatest extent possible, the medical examiner shall be appointed from persons having training and experience in pathology, toxicology, histology and other medico-legal sciences. The medical examiner shall devote so much of his time and energy as is necessary in the performance of the duties conferred by this Article.

#### Sec. 3. Assistants.

The medical examiner may, subject to the approval of the commissioners court, employ such deputy examiners, scientific experts, trained technicians, officers and employees as may be necessary to the proper performance of the duties imposed by this Article upon the medical examiner.

#### Sec. 4. Salaries.

The commissioners court shall establish and pay the salaries and compensations of the medical examiner and his staff.

### Sec. 5. Offices.

The commissioners court shall provide the medical examiner and his staff with adequate office space and shall provide laboratory facilities or make arrangements for the use of existing laboratory facilities in the county, if so requested by the medical examiner.

### Sec. 6. Death Investigations.

(a) Any medical examiner, or his duly authorized deputy, shall be authorized, and it shall be his duty, to hold inquests with or without a jury within his county, in the following cases:

1. When a person shall die within twenty-four hours after admission to a hospital or institution or in prison or in jail;

2. When any person is killed; or from any cause dies an unnatural death, except under sentence of the law; or dies in the absence of one or more good witnesses;

3. When the body or a body part of a person is found, the cause or circumstances of death are unknown, and:

(A) the person is identified; or

(B) the person is unidentified;

4. When the circumstances of the death of any person are such as to lead to suspicion that he came to his death by unlawful means;

5. When any person commits suicide, or the circumstances of his death are such as to lead to suspicion that he committed suicide;

6. When a person dies without having been attended by a duly licensed and practicing physician, and the local health officer or registrar required to report the cause of death under Section 193.005, Health and Safety Code, does not know the cause of death. When the local health officer or registrar of vital statistics whose duty it is to certify the cause of death does not know the cause of death, he shall so notify the medical examiner of the county in which the death occurred and request an inquest;

7. When the person is a child who is younger than six years of age and the death is reported under Chapter 264, Family Code; and

8. When a person dies who has been attended immediately preceding his death by a duly licensed and practicing physician or physicians, and such physician or physicians are not certain as to the cause of death and are unable to certify with certainty the cause of death as required by Section 193.004, Health and Safety Code. In case of such uncertainty the attending physician or phy-

sicians, or the superintendent or general manager of the hospital or institution in which the deceased shall have died, shall so report to the medical examiner of the county in which the death occurred, and request an inquest.

(b) The inquests authorized and required by this Article shall be held by the medical examiner of the county in which the death occurred.

(c) In making such investigations and holding such inquests, the medical examiner or an authorized deputy may administer oaths and take affidavits. In the absence of next of kin or legal representatives of the deceased, the medical examiner or authorized deputy shall take charge of the body and all property found with it.

### Sec. 6a. Organ Transplant Donors; Notice; Inquests.

(a) When death occurs to an individual designated a prospective organ donor for transplantation by a licensed physician under circumstances requiring the medical examiner of the county in which death occurred, or the medical examiner's authorized deputy, to hold an inquest, the medical examiner, or a member of his staff will be so notified by the administrative head of the facility in which the transplantation is to be performed.

(b) When notified pursuant to Subsection (a) of this Section, the medical examiner or the medical examiner's deputy shall perform an inquest on the deceased prospective organ donor.

### Sec. 7. Reports of Death.

(a) Any police officer, superintendent or general manager of an institution, physician, or private citizen who shall become aware of a death under any of the circumstances set out in Section 6(a) of this Article, shall immediately report such death to the office of the medical examiner or to the city or county police departments; any such report to a city or county police department shall be immediately transmitted to the office of the medical examiner.

(b) A person investigating a death described by Subdivision 3(B) of Section 6(a) shall report the death to the missing children and missing persons information clearinghouse of the Department of Public Safety and the national crime information center not later than the 10th working day after the date the investigation began.

(c) A superintendent or general manager of an institution who reports a death under Subsection (a) must comply with the notice and reporting requirements of Article 49.24. The office of the attorney general has the same powers and duties provided the office under that article regarding the dissemination and investigation of the report.

**Sec. 8. Removal of Bodies.**

When any death under circumstances set out in Section 6 shall have occurred, the body shall not be disturbed or removed from the position in which it is found by any person without authorization from the medical examiner or authorized deputy, except for the purpose of preserving such body from loss or destruction or maintaining the flow of traffic on a highway, railroad or airport.

**Sec. 9. Autopsy.**

(a) If the cause of death shall be determined beyond a reasonable doubt as a result of the investigation, the medical examiner shall file a report thereof setting forth specifically the cause of death with the district attorney or criminal district attorney, or in a county in which there is no district attorney or criminal district attorney with the county attorney, of the county in which the death occurred. If in the opinion of the medical examiner an autopsy is necessary, or if such is requested by the district attorney or criminal district attorney, or county attorney where there is no district attorney or criminal district attorney, the autopsy shall be immediately performed by the medical examiner or a duly authorized deputy. In those cases where a complete autopsy is deemed unnecessary by the medical examiner to ascertain the cause of death, the medical examiner may perform a limited autopsy involving the taking of blood samples or any other samples of body fluids, tissues or organs, in order to ascertain the cause of death or whether a crime has been committed. In the case of a body of a human being whose identity is unknown, the medical examiner may authorize such investigative and laboratory tests and processes as are required to determine its identity as well as the cause of death. In performing an autopsy the medical examiner or authorized deputy may use the facilities of any city or county hospital within the county or such other facilities as are made available. Upon completion of the autopsy, the medical examiner shall file a report setting forth the findings in detail with the office of the district attorney or criminal district attorney of the county, or if there is no district attorney or criminal district attorney, with the county attorney of the county.

(b) A medical examination on an unidentified person shall include the following information to enable a timely and accurate identification of the person:

(1) all available fingerprints and palm prints;

(2) dental charts and radiographs (X-rays) of the person's teeth;

(3) frontal and lateral facial photographs with scale indicated;

(4) notation and photographs, with scale indicated, of a significant scar, mark, tattoo, or item of clothing or other personal effect found with or near the body;

(5) notation of antemortem medical conditions;

(6) notation of observations pertinent to the estimation of time of death; and

(7) precise documentation of the location of burial of the remains.

(c) A medical examination on an unidentified person may include the following information to enable a timely and accurate identification of the person:

(1) full body radiographs (X-rays); and

(2) hair specimens with roots.

**Sec. 10. Disinterments and Cremations.**

When a body upon which an inquest ought to have been held has been interred, the medical examiner may cause it to be disinterred for the purpose of holding such inquest.

Before any body, upon which an inquest is authorized by the provisions of this Article, can be lawfully cremated, an autopsy shall be performed thereon as provided in this Article, or a certificate that no autopsy was necessary shall be furnished by the medical examiner. Before any dead body can be lawfully cremated, the owner or operator of the crematory shall demand and be furnished with a certificate, signed by the medical examiner of the county in which the death occurred showing that an autopsy was performed on said body or that no autopsy thereon was necessary. It shall be the duty of the medical examiner to determine whether or not, from all the circumstances surrounding the death, an autopsy is necessary prior to issuing a certificate under the provisions of this section. No autopsy shall be required by the medical examiner as a prerequisite to cremation in case death is caused by the pestilential diseases of Asiatic cholera, bubonic plague, typhus fever, or smallpox. All certificates furnished to the owner or operator of a crematory by any medical examiner, under the terms of this Article, shall be preserved by such

Criminal Procedure

owner or operator of such crematory for a period of two years from the date of the cremation of said body. A medical examiner is not required to perform an autopsy on the body of a deceased person whose death was caused by a communicable disease during a public health disaster.

### Sec. 10a. Waiting Period Between Death and Cremation.

The body of a deceased person shall not be cremated within 48 hours after the time of death as indicated on the regular death certificate, unless the death certificate indicates death was caused by the pestilential diseases of Asiatic cholera, bubonic plague, typhus fever, or smallpox, or unless the time requirement is waived in writing by the county medical examiner or, in counties not having a county medical examiner, a justice of the peace. In a public health disaster, the commissioner of public health may designate other communicable diseases for which cremation within 48 hours of the time of death is authorized.

### Sec. 10b. Disposal of Unidentified Body.

If the body of a deceased person is unidentified, a person may not cremate or direct the cremation of the body under this article. If the body is buried, the investigating agency responsible for the burial shall record and maintain for not less than 10 years all information pertaining to the body and the location of burial.

### Sec. 11. Records.

The medical examiner shall keep full and complete records properly indexed, giving the name if known of every person whose death is investigated, the place where the body was found, the date, the cause and manner of death, and shall issue a death certificate. The full report and detailed findings of the autopsy, if any, shall be a part of the record. Copies of all records shall promptly be delivered to the proper district, county, or criminal district attorney in any case where further investigation is advisable. The records are subject to required public disclosure in accordance with Chapter 552, Government Code, except that a photograph or x-ray of a body taken during an autopsy is excepted from required public disclosure in accordance with Chapter 552, Government Code, but is subject to disclosure:

　(1) under a subpoena or authority of other law; or

　(2) if the photograph or x-ray is of the body of a person who died while in the custody of law enforcement.

### Sec. 12. Transfer of Duties of Justice of Peace.

When the commissioners court of any county shall establish the office of medical examiner, all powers and duties of justices of the peace in such county relating to the investigation of deaths and inquests shall vest in the office of the medical examiner. Any subsequent General Law pertaining to the duties of justices of the peace in death investigations and inquests shall apply to the medical examiner in such counties as to the extent not inconsistent with this Article, and all laws or parts of laws otherwise in conflict herewith are hereby declared to be inapplicable to this Article.

### Sec. 13. Use of Forensic Anthropologist.

On discovering the body or body part of a deceased person in the circumstances described by Subdivision 3(B) of Section 6(a), the medical examiner may request the aid of a forensic anthropologist in the examination of the body or body part. The forensic anthropologist must hold a doctoral degree in anthropology with an emphasis in physical anthropology. The forensic anthropologist shall attempt to establish whether the body or body part is of a human or animal, whether evidence of childbirth, injury, or disease exists, and the sex, race, age, stature, and physical anomalies of the body or body part. The forensic anthropologist may also attempt to establish the cause, manner, and time of death.

### Sec. 13A. Fees.

(a) A medical examiner may charge reasonable fees for services provided by the office of medical examiner under this article, including cremation approvals, court testimonies, consultations, and depositions.

(b) The commissioners court must approve the amount of the fee before the fee may be assessed. The fee may not exceed the amount necessary to provide the services described by Subsection (a).

(c) The fee may not be assessed against the county's district attorney or a county office.

### Sec. 14. Penalty.

(a) A person commits an offense if the person knowingly violates this article.

(b) An offense under this section is a Class B misdemeanor.

(Enacted by Acts 1965, 59th Leg., ch. 722 (S.B. 107), § 1, effective January 1, 1966; am. Acts 1969, 61st Leg., ch. 336 (H.B. 243), § 1, effective May 27, 1969; am. Acts 1969, 61st Leg., ch. 500 (H.B. 612), §§ 1—3, effective June 10, 1969; am. Acts 1971, 62nd Leg., ch. 270 (H.B. 172), § 1, effective August 30, 1971; am. Acts 1975, 64th Leg., ch. 562 (H.B. 1325), § 1, effective September 1, 1975; am. Acts 1995, 74th Leg., ch. 255 (S.B. 81), § 5, effective September 1, 1995; am. Acts 1995, 74th Leg., ch. 878 (S.B. 1485), § 4, effective September 1, 1995; am. Acts 1997, 75th Leg., ch. 656 (H.B. 2693), § 6, effective September 1, 1997; am. Acts 1999, 76th Leg., ch. 607 (S.B. 785), § 2, effective September 1, 1999; am. Acts 2003, 78th Leg., ch. 198 (H.B. 2292), § 2.191, effective September 1, 2003; am. Acts 2003, 78th Leg., ch. 826 (S.B. 356), §§ 6, 7, effective September 1, 2003; am. Acts 2003, 78th Leg., ch. 894 (S.B. 826), § 3, effective September 1, 2003; am. Acts 2003, 78th Leg., ch. 1295 (H.B. 2989), § 6, effective September 1, 2003; am. Acts 2003, 78th Leg., ch. 1295 (H.B. 2989), § 7, effective September 1, 2003; am. Acts 2011, 82nd Leg., ch. 1341 (S.B. 1233), § 8, effective June 17, 2011.)

## SUBCHAPTER C
## INFORMED CONSENT FOR POSTMORTEM EXAMINATION OR AUTOPSY

### Art. 49.31. Applicability.
This subchapter does not apply to an autopsy that:
(1) is ordered by the Texas Department of Criminal Justice or an authorized official of the department in accordance with Section 501.055, Government Code; or
(2) a justice of the peace or medical examiner determines is required under this chapter or other law.
(Enacted by Acts 2011, 82nd Leg., ch. 950 (H.B. 1009), § 2, effective September 1, 2011.)

### Art. 49.32. Consent to Postmortem Examination or Autopsy.
(a) Except as provided by Subsection (b) of this article, a physician may not perform, or assist in the performance of, a postmortem examination or autopsy on the body of a deceased person unless the physician obtains the written informed consent of a person authorized to provide consent under Article 49.33 of this code. The consent must be provided on the form prescribed under Article 49.34 of this code.
(b) If, after due diligence, a physician is unable to identify or contact a person authorized to give consent under Article 49.33 of this code, the physician may, as authorized by a medical examiner, justice of the peace, or county judge, as appropriate, perform a postmortem examination or autopsy on the body of a deceased person not less than 24 hours and not more than 48 hours from the time of the decedent's death or the time the physician or other person took possession of the body.
(Enacted by Acts 2011, 82nd Leg., ch. 950 (H.B. 1009), § 2, effective September 1, 2011.)

### Art. 49.33. Persons Authorized to Consent to Postmortem Examination or Autopsy.
(a) Subject to Subsections (b) and (c) of this article, consent for a postmortem examination or autopsy may be given by any member of the following classes of persons who is reasonably available, in the order of priority listed:
(1) the spouse of the decedent;
(2) the person acting as guardian of the person of the decedent at the time of death or the executor or administrator of the decedent's estate;
(3) the adult children of the decedent;
(4) the parents of the decedent; and
(5) the adult siblings of the decedent.
(b) If there is more than one member of a class listed in Subsection (a)(2), (3), (4), or (5) of this article entitled to give consent to a postmortem examination or autopsy, consent may be given by a member of the class unless another member of the class files an objection with the physician, medical examiner, justice of the peace, or county judge. If an objection is filed, the consent may be given only by a majority of the members of the class who are reasonably available.
(c) A person may not give consent under this article if, at the time of the decedent's death, a person in a class granted higher priority under Subsection (a) of this article is reasonably available to give consent or to file an objection to a postmortem examination or autopsy.
(Enacted by Acts 2011, 82nd Leg., ch. 950 (H.B. 1009), § 2, effective September 1, 2011.)

### Art. 49.34. Postmortem Examination or Autopsy Consent Form.
The commissioner of state health services, in consultation with the Texas Medical Board, shall prescribe a standard written consent form for a postmortem examination or autopsy. The form must:
(1) include the name of the hospital or other institution and the department that will perform the examination or autopsy;

(2) include a statement that the removal from the deceased person's body and retention by the physician of organs, fluids, prosthetic devices, or tissue may be required for purposes of comprehensive evaluation or accurate determination of a cause of death;

(3) provide the family of the deceased person with an opportunity to place restrictions or special limitations on the examination or autopsy;

(4) include a separate section regarding the disposition of organs, fluids, prosthetic devices, or tissue after the examination or autopsy, including a prioritized list of the persons authorized to control that disposition, as provided by Chapter 692A, Health and Safety Code;

(5) provide for documented and witnessed consent;

(6) allow authorization for the release of human remains to a funeral home or individual designated by the person giving consent for the postmortem examination or autopsy;

(7) include information regarding the rights described by Article 49.35 of this code;

(8) list the circumstances under which a medical examiner is required by law to conduct an investigation, inquest, or autopsy under Article 49.25 of this code;

(9) include a statement that the form is required by state law; and

(10) be written in plain language designed to be easily understood by the average person.
(Enacted by Acts 2011, 82nd Leg., ch. 950 (H.B. 1009), § 2, effective September 1, 2011.)

### Art. 49.35. Right to Nonaffiliated Physician.

(a) A person authorized to consent to a postmortem examination or autopsy under Article 49.33 of this code may request that a physician who is not affiliated with the hospital or other institution where the deceased person died:

(1) perform the postmortem examination or autopsy at another hospital or institution; or

(2) review the postmortem examination or autopsy conducted by a physician affiliated with the hospital or other institution where the deceased person died.

(b) A representative of the hospital or other institution shall inform the person of the person's right to request the performance or review of a postmortem examination or autopsy by a nonaffiliated physician under Subsection (a) before the person consents to the postmortem examination or autopsy.

(c) A person requesting a nonaffiliated physician to perform or review a postmortem examination or autopsy shall bear the additional costs incurred as a result of the nonaffiliated physician's performance or review of the examination or autopsy under Subsection (a) of this article.
(Enacted by Acts 2011, 82nd Leg., ch. 950 (H.B. 1009), § 2, effective September 1, 2011.)

## CHAPTER 50
## FIRE INQUESTS

### Art. 50.01. Investigations.

When an affidavit is made by a credible person before any justice of the peace that there is ground to believe that any building has been unlawfully set or attempted to be set on fire, such justice shall cause the truth of such complaint to be investigated.
(Enacted by Acts 1965, 59th Leg., ch. 722 (S.B. 107), § 1, effective January 1, 1966.)

### Art. 50.02. Proceedings.

The proceedings in such case shall be governed by the laws relating to inquests upon dead bodies. The officer conducting such investigations shall have the same powers as are conferred upon justices of the peace in the preceding Articles of this Chapter.
(Enacted by Acts 1965, 59th Leg., ch. 722 (S.B. 107), § 1, effective January 1, 1966.)

### Art. 50.03. Verdict in Fire Inquest.

The jury after inspecting the place in question and after hearing the testimony, shall deliver to the justice holding such inquest its written signed verdict in which it shall find and certify how and in what manner such fire happened or was attempted, and all the circumstances attending the same, and who are guilty thereof, and in what manner. If such a jury is unable to so ascertain, it shall find and certify accordingly.
(Enacted by Acts 1965, 59th Leg., ch. 722 (S.B. 107), § 1, effective January 1, 1966; am. Acts 1973, 63rd Leg., ch. 399 (S.B. 34), § 2(A), effective January 1, 1974.)

## Art. 50.04. Witnesses Bound Over.

If the jury finds that any building has been unlawfully set on fire or has been attempted so to be, the justice holding such inquest shall bind over the witnesses to appear and testify before the next grand jury of the county in which such offense was committed.

(Enacted by Acts 1965, 59th Leg., ch. 722 (S.B. 107), § 1, effective January 1, 1966.)

## Art. 50.05. Warrant for Accused.

If the person charged with the offense, if any, be not in custody, the justice of the peace shall issue a warrant for his arrest, and when arrested, such person shall be dealt with as in other like cases.

(Enacted by Acts 1965, 59th Leg., ch. 722 (S.B. 107), § 1, effective January 1, 1966.)

## Art. 50.06. Testimony Written Down.

In all such investigations, the testimony of all witnesses examined before the jury shall be reduced to writing by or under the direction of the justice and signed by each witness. Such testimony together with the verdict and all bail bonds taken in the case shall be certified to and returned by the justice to the next district or criminal district court of his county.

(Enacted by Acts 1965, 59th Leg., ch. 722 (S.B. 107), § 1, effective January 1, 1966.)

## Art. 50.07. Compensation.

The pay of the officers and jury making such investigation shall be the same as that allowed for the holding of an inquest upon a dead body, so far as applicable, and shall be paid in like manner.

(Enacted by Acts 1965, 59th Leg., ch. 722 (S.B. 107), § 1, effective January 1, 1966.)

# CHAPTER 51
# FUGITIVES FROM JUSTICE

## Art. 51.01. Delivered Up.

A person in any other State of the United States charged with treason or any felony who shall flee from justice and be found in this State, shall on demand of the executive authority of the State from which he fled, be delivered up, to be removed to the State having jurisdiction of the crime.

(Enacted by Acts 1965, 59th Leg., ch. 722 (S.B. 107), § 1, effective January 1, 1966.)

## Art. 51.02. To Aid in Arrest.

All peace officers of the State shall give aid in the arrest and detention of a fugitive from any other State that he may be held subject to a requisition by the Governor of the State from which he fled.

(Enacted by Acts 1965, 59th Leg., ch. 722 (S.B. 107), § 1, effective January 1, 1966.)

## Art. 51.03. Magistrate's Warrant.

When a complaint is made to a magistrate that any person within his jurisdiction is a fugitive from justice from another State, he shall issue a warrant of arrest directing a peace officer to apprehend and bring the accused before him.

(Enacted by Acts 1965, 59th Leg., ch. 722 (S.B. 107), § 1, effective January 1, 1966.)

## Art. 51.04. Complaint.

The complaint shall be sufficient if it recites:

1. The name of the person accused;
2. The State from which he has fled;
3. The offense committed by the accused;
4. That he has fled to this State from the State where the offense was committed; and
5. That the act alleged to have been committed by the accused is a violation of the penal law of the State from which he fled.

(Enacted by Acts 1965, 59th Leg., ch. 722 (S.B. 107), § 1, effective January 1, 1966.)

## Art. 51.05. Bail or Commitment.

When the accused is brought before the magistrate, he shall hear proof, and if satisfied that the accused is charged in another State with the offense named in the complaint, he shall require of him bail with sufficient security, in such amount as the magistrate deems reasonable, to appear before such magistrate at a specified time. In default of such bail, he may commit the defendant to jail to await a requisition from the Governor of the State from which he fled. A properly certified transcript of an indictment against the accused is sufficient to show that he is charged with the crime alleged. One arrested under the provisions of this title shall not be committed or held to bail for a longer time than ninety days. (Enacted by Acts 1965, 59th Leg., ch. 722 (S.B. 107), § 1, effective January 1, 1966.)

### Art. 51.06. Notice of Arrest.

The magistrate who held or committed such fugitive shall immediately notify the Secretary of State and the district or county attorney of his county of such fact and the date thereof, stating the name of such fugitive, the State from which he fled, and the crime with which he is charged; and such officers so notified shall in turn notify the Governor of the proper State. (Enacted by Acts 1965, 59th Leg., ch. 722 (S.B. 107), § 1, effective January 1, 1966.)

### Art. 51.07. Discharge.

A fugitive not arrested under a warrant from the Governor of this State before the expiration of ninety days from the day of his commitment or the date of the bail shall be discharged. (Enacted by Acts 1965, 59th Leg., ch. 722 (S.B. 107), § 1, effective January 1, 1966.)

### Art. 51.08. Second Arrest.

A person who has once been arrested under the provisions of this title and discharged under the provisions of the preceding Article or by habeas corpus shall not be again arrested upon a charge of the same offense, except by a warrant from the Governor of this State. (Enacted by Acts 1965, 59th Leg., ch. 722 (S.B. 107), § 1, effective January 1, 1966.)

### Art. 51.09. Governor May Demand Fugitive.

When the Governor deems it proper to demand a person who has committed an offense in this State and has fled to another State, he may commission any suitable person to take such requisition. The accused, if brought back to the State, shall be delivered up to the sheriff of the county in which it is alleged he has committed the offense. (Enacted by Acts 1965, 59th Leg., ch. 722 (S.B. 107), § 1, effective January 1, 1966.)

### Art. 51.10. Pay of Agent; Traveling Expenses.

**Sec. 1.** The officer or person so commissioned shall receive as compensation the actual and necessary traveling expenses upon requisition of the Governor to be allowed by such Governor and to be paid out of the State Treasury upon a certificate of the Governor reciting the services rendered and the allowance therefor.

**Sec. 2.** The commissioners court of the county where an offense is committed may in its discretion, on the request of the sheriff and the recommendation of the district attorney, pay the actual and necessary traveling expenses of the officer or person so commissioned out of any fund or funds not otherwise pledged. (Enacted by Acts 1965, 59th Leg., ch. 722 (S.B. 107), § 1, effective January 1, 1966.)

### Art. 51.11. Reward.

The Governor may offer a reward for the apprehension of one accused of a felony in this State who is evading arrest, by causing such offer to be published in such manner as he deems most likely to effect the arrest. The reward shall be paid out of the State Treasury to the person who becomes entitled to it upon a certificate of the Governor reciting the facts which entitle such person to receive it. (Enacted by Acts 1965, 59th Leg., ch. 722 (S.B. 107), § 1, effective January 1, 1966.)

### Art. 51.12. Sheriff to Report.

Each sheriff upon the close of any regular term of the district or criminal district court in his county, or within thirty days thereafter, shall make out and mail to the Director of the Department of Public Safety a certified list of all persons, who, after indictment for a felony, have fled from said county. Such lists shall contain the full name of each such fugitive, the offense with which he is charged, and a description giving his age, height, weight, color and occupation, the complexion of the skin and the color of eyes and hair, and any peculiarity in person, speech, manner or gait that may serve to identify such person so far as the sheriff may be able to give them. The Director of the Department of Public Safety shall prescribe and forward to all sheriffs the necessary blanks upon which are to be made the lists herein required. (Enacted by Acts 1965, 59th Leg., ch. 722 (S.B. 107), § 1, effective January 1, 1966.)

### Art. 51.13. Uniform Criminal Extradition Act.

#### Sec. 1. Definitions.

Where appearing in this Article, the term "Governor" includes any person performing the functions of Governor by authority of the laws of this State. The term "Executive Authority" includes the Governor, and any person performing the functions of Governor in a State other than this State, and the term "State", referring to a State other than this State, includes any other State organized or unorganized of the United States of America.

**Sec. 2. Fugitives from Justice; Duty of Governor.**

Subject to the provisions of this Article, the provisions of the Constitution of the United States controlling, and any and all Acts of Congress enacted in pursuance thereof, it is the duty of the Governor of this State to have arrested and delivered up to the Executive Authority of any other State of the United States any person charged in that State with treason, felony, or other crime, who has fled from justice and is found in this State.

**Sec. 3. Form of Demand.**

No demand for the extradition of a person charged with crime in another State shall be recognized by the Governor unless in writing, alleging, except in cases arising under Section 6, that the accused was present in the demanding State at the time of the commission of the alleged crime, and that thereafter he fled from the State, and accompanied by a copy of an indictment found or by information supported by affidavit in the State having jurisdiction of the crime, or by a copy of an affidavit before a magistrate there, together with a copy of any warrant which issued thereupon; or by a copy of a judgment of conviction or of a sentence imposed in execution thereof, together with a statement by the Executive Authority of the demanding State that the person claimed has escaped from confinement or has broken the terms of his bail, probation or parole. The indictment, information, or affidavit made before the magistrate must substantially charge the person demanded with having committed a crime under the law of that State; and the copy of indictment, information, affidavit, judgment of conviction or sentence must be authenticated by the Executive Authority making the demand; provided, however, that all such copies of the aforesaid instruments shall be in duplicate, one complete set of such instruments to be delivered to the defendant or to his attorney.

**Sec. 4. Governor May Investigate Case.**

When a demand shall be made upon the Governor of this State by the Executive Authority of another State for the surrender of a person so charged with crime, the Governor may call upon the Secretary of State, Attorney General or any prosecuting officer in this State to investigate or assist in investigating the demand, and to report to him the situation and circumstances of the person so demanded, and whether he ought to be surrendered.

**Sec. 5. Extradition of Persons Imprisoned or Awaiting Trial in Another State or Who Have Left the Demanding State Under Compulsion.**

When it is desired to have returned to this State a person charged in this State with a crime, and such person is imprisoned or is held under criminal proceedings then pending against him in another State, the Governor of this State may agree with the Executive Authority of such other State for the extradition of such person before the conclusion of such proceedings or his term of sentence in such other State, upon condition that such person be returned to such other State at the expense of this State as soon as the prosecution in this State is terminated.

The Governor of this State may also surrender on demand of the Executive Authority of any other State any person in this State who is charged in the manner provided in Section 23 of this Act with having violated the laws of the State whose Executive Authority is making the demand, even though such person left the demanding State involuntarily.

**Sec. 6. Extradition of Persons Not Present in Demanding State at Time of Commission of Crime.**

The Governor of this State may also surrender, on demand of the Executive Authority of any other State, any person in this State charged in such other State in the manner provided in Section 3 with committing an act in this State, or in a third State, intentionally resulting in a crime in the State whose Executive Authority is making the demand, and the provisions of this Article not otherwise inconsistent, shall apply to such cases, even though the accused was not in that State at the time of the commission of the crime, and has not fled therefrom.

**Sec. 7. Issue of Governor's Warrant of Arrest; Its Recitals.**

If the Governor decides that the demand should be complied with, he shall sign a warrant of arrest, which shall be sealed with the state seal and be directed to any peace officer or other person whom he may think fit to entrust with the execution thereof. The warrant must substantially recite the facts necessary to the validity of its issuance.

Criminal Procedure

### Sec. 8. Manner and Place of Execution.

Such warrant shall authorize the peace officer or other person to whom directed to arrest the accused at any time and any place where he may be found within the State and to command the aid of all peace officers and other persons in the execution of the warrant, and to deliver the accused, subject to the provisions of this Article to the duly authorized agent of the demanding State.

### Sec. 9. Authority of Arresting Officer.

Every such peace officer or other person empowered to make the arrest, shall have the same authority, in arresting the accused, to command assistance therein, as peace officers have by law in the execution of any criminal process directed to them, with like penalties against those who refuse their assistance.

### Sec. 10. Rights of Accused Person; Application for Writ of Habeas Corpus.

No person arrested upon such warrant shall be delivered over to the agent whom the Executive Authority demanding him shall have appointed to receive him unless he shall first be taken forthwith before a judge of a court of record in this State, who shall inform him of the demand made for his surrender and of the crime with which he is charged, and that he has the right to demand and procure legal counsel; and if the prisoner or his counsel shall state that he or they desire to test the legality of his arrest, the judge of such court of record shall fix a reasonable time to be allowed him within which to apply for a writ of habeas corpus. When such a writ is applied for, notice thereof, and of the time and place of hearing thereon, shall be given to the prosecuting officer of the county in which the arrest is made and in which the accused is in custody, and to the said agent of the demanding State.

### Sec. 11. Penalty for Non-Compliance with Preceding Section.

Any officer who shall deliver to the agent for extradition of the demanding State a person in his custody under the Governor's warrant, in wilful disobedience to Section 10 of this Act, shall be guilty of a misdemeanor and, on conviction, shall be fined not more than one thousand dollars or be imprisoned not more than six months, or both.

### Sec. 12. Confinement in Jail, When Necessary.

The officer or persons executing the Governor's warrant of arrest, or the agent of the demanding State to whom the prisoner may have been delivered may, when necessary, confine the prisoner in the jail of any county or city through which he may pass; and the keeper of such jail must receive and safely keep the prisoner until the officer or person having charge of him is ready to proceed on his route, such officer or person being chargeable with the expense of keeping.

The officer or agent of a demanding State to whom a prisoner may have been delivered following extradition proceedings in another State, or to whom a prisoner may have been delivered after waiving extradition in such other State, and who is passing through this State with such a prisoner for the purpose of immediately returning such prisoner to the demanding State may, when necessary, confine the prisoner in the jail of any county or city through which he may pass; and the keeper of such jail must receive and safely keep the prisoner until the officer or agent having charge of him is ready to proceed on his route, such officer or agent, however, being chargeable with the expense of keeping; provided, however, that such officer or agent shall produce and show to the keeper of such jail satisfactory written evidence of the fact that he is actually transporting such prisoner to the demanding State after a requisition by the Executive Authority of such demanding State. Such prisoner shall not be entitled to demand a new requisition while in this State.

### Sec. 13. Arrest Prior to Requisition.

Whenever any person within this State shall be charged on the oath of any credible person before any judge or magistrate of this State with the commission of any crime in any other State and except in cases arising under Section 6, with having fled from justice, or with having been convicted of a crime in that State and having escaped from confinement, or having broken the terms of his bail, probation or parole, or whenever complaint shall have been made before any judge or magistrate in this State setting forth on the affidavit of any credible person in another State that a crime has been committed in such other State and that the accused has been charged in such State with the commission of the crime, and except in cases arising under Section 6, has fled from justice, or with having been convicted of a crime in that State and having escaped from confinement, or having broken the terms of his bail, probation or parole and is believed to be in this State, the judge or magistrate shall issue a warrant directed to any peace officer commanding him to apprehend the person named therein, wherever he may be found in this State, and to bring him before the same or any other judge, magistrate or court who or which may be available in or convenient of access to the place where the arrest may be made, to answer the charge or complaint and affidavit, and a certified copy of the sworn charge or complaint and affidavit upon which the warrant is issued shall be attached to the warrant.

### Sec. 14. Arrest Without a Warrant.

The arrest of a person may be lawfully made also by any peace officer or private person, without a warrant upon reasonable information that the accused stands charged in the courts of a State with a crime punishable by death or imprisonment for a term exceeding one year, but when so arrested the accused must be taken before a judge or magistrate with all practicable speed and complaint must be made against him under oath setting forth the ground for the arrest as in the preceding section; and thereafter his answer shall be heard as if he had been arrested on a warrant.

### Sec. 15. Commitment to Await Requisition; Bail.

If from the examination before the judge or magistrate it appears that the person held is the person charged with having committed the crime alleged and except in cases arising under Section 6, that he has fled from justice, the judge or magistrate must, by warrant reciting the accusation, commit him to the county jail for such time not exceeding thirty days and specified in the warrant, as will enable the arrest of the accused to be made under a warrant of the Governor on a requisition of the Executive Authority of the State having jurisdiction of the offense, unless the accused give bail as provided in the next section, or until he shall be legally discharged.

### Sec. 16. Bail; In What Cases; Conditions of Bond.

Unless the offense with which the prisoner is charged is shown to be an offense punishable by death or life imprisonment under the laws of the State in which it was committed, a judge or magistrate in this State may admit the person arrested to bail by bond, with sufficient sureties and in such sum as he deems proper, conditioned for his appearance before him at a time specified in such bond, and for his surrender, to be arrested upon the warrant of the Governor in this State.

### Sec. 17. Extension of Time of Commitment; Adjournment.

If the accused is not arrested under warrant of the Governor by the expiration of the time specified in the warrant or bond, a judge or magistrate may discharge him or may recommit him for a further period not to exceed sixty days, or a judge or magistrate may again take bail for his appearance and surrender, as provided in Section 16, but within a period not to exceed sixty days after the date of such new bond.

### Sec. 18. Forfeiture of Bail.

If the prisoner is admitted to bail and fails to appear and surrender himself according to the conditions of his bond, the judge, or magistrate by proper order, shall declare the bond forfeited and order his immediate arrest without warrant if he be within this State. Recovery may be had on such bond in the name of the State as in the case of other bonds given by the accused in criminal proceedings within this State.

### Sec. 19. Persons Under Criminal Prosecution in This State at the Time of Requisition.

If a criminal prosecution has been instituted against such person under the laws of this State and is still pending, the Governor, in his discretion, either may surrender him on demand of the Executive Authority of another State or hold him until he has been tried and discharged or convicted and punished in this State.

### Sec. 20. Guilt or Innocence of Accused, When Inquired into.

The guilt or innocence of the accused as to the crime of which he is charged may not be inquired into by the Governor or in any proceeding after the demand for extradition accompanied by a charge of crime in legal form as above provided shall have been presented to the Governor, except as it may be involved in identifying the person held as the person charged with the crime.

### Sec. 21. Governor May Recall Warrant or Issue Alias.

The governor may recall his warrant of the arrest or may issue another warrant whenever he deems proper. Each warrant issued by the Governor shall expire and be of no force and effect when not executed within one year from the date thereof.

### Sec. 22. Fugitives from This State; Duty of Governor.

Whenever the Governor of this State shall demand a person charged with crime or with escaping from confinement or breaking the terms of his bail, probation or parole in this State, from the Executive Authority of any other State, or from the Chief Justice or an Associate Justice of the Supreme Court of the District of Columbia authorized to receive such demand under the laws of the United States, he shall issue a warrant under the state seal, to some agent, commanding him to receive the person so charged if delivered to him and convey him to the proper officer of the county in this State in which the offense was committed, or in which the prosecution for such offense is then pending.

**Sec. 23. Application for Issuance of Requisition; By Whom Made; Contents.**

1. When the return to this State of a person charged with crime in this State is required, the State's attorney shall present to the Governor his written motion for a requisition for the return of the person charged, in which motion shall be stated the name of the person so charged, the crime charged against him, the approximate time, place and circumstances of its commission, the State in which he is believed to be, including the location of the accused therein at the time the motion is made and certifying that, in the opinion of the said State's attorney the ends of justice require the arrest and return of the accused to this State for trial and that the proceeding is not instituted to enforce a private claim.

2. When the return to this State is required of a person who has been convicted of a crime in this State and has escaped from confinement, or broken the terms of his bail, probation or parole, the prosecuting attorney of the county in which the offense was committed, the parole board, or the warden of the institution or sheriff of the county, from which escape was made, shall present to the Governor a written application for a requisition for the return of such person, in which application shall be stated the name of the person, the crime of which he was convicted, the circumstances of his escape from confinement, or the circumstances of the breach of the terms of his bail, probation or parole, the State in which he is believed to be, including the location of the person therein at the time application is made.

3. The application shall be verified by affidavit, shall be executed in duplicate and shall be accompanied by two certified copies of the indictment returned, or information and affidavit filed, or of the complaint made to the judge or magistrate, stating the offense with which the accused is charged, or of the judgment of conviction or of the sentence. The prosecuting officer, parole board, warden or sheriff may also attach such further affidavits and other documents in duplicate as he shall deem proper to be submitted with such application. One copy of the application, with the action of the Governor indicated by endorsement thereon, and one of the certified copies of the indictment,

complaint, information, and affidavits, or of the judgment of conviction or of the sentence shall be filed in the office of the Governor. The other copies of all papers shall be forwarded with the Governor's requisition.

**Sec. 24. Costs and Expenses.**

In all cases of extradition, the commissioners court of the county where an offense is alleged to have been committed, or in which the prosecution is then pending may in its discretion, on request of the sheriff and the recommendation of the prosecuting attorney, pay the actual and necessary expenses of the officer or person commissioned to receive the person charged, out of any county fund or funds not otherwise pledged.

**Sec. 25. Immunity from Service of Process in Certain Civil Cases.**

A person brought into this State by, or after waiver of, extradition based on a criminal charge shall not be subject to service of personal process in civil actions arising out of the same facts as the criminal proceeding to answer which he is being or has been returned, until he has been convicted in the criminal proceeding, or if acquitted, until he has had reasonable opportunity to return to the State from which he was extradited.

**Sec. 25a. Written Waiver of Extradition Proceedings.**

Any person arrested in this State charged with having committed any crime in another State or alleged to have escaped from confinement, or broken the terms of his bail, probation, or parole may waive the issuance and service of the warrant provided for in Sections 7 and 8 and all other procedure incidental to extradition proceedings, by executing or subscribing in the presence of a judge or any court of record within this State a writing which states that he consents to return to the demanding State; provided, however, that before such waiver shall be executed or subscribed by such person it shall be the duty of such judge to inform such person of his rights to the issuance and service of a warrant of extradition and to obtain a writ of habeas corpus as provided for in Section 10.

If and when such consent has been duly executed it shall forthwith be forwarded to the office of the Governor of this State and filed therein. The judge shall direct the officer having such person in custody to deliver forthwith such person to the duly accredited agent or agents of the demanding State, and shall deliver or cause to be delivered to such agent or agents a copy of such consent; provided, however, that nothing in this section shall be deemed to limit the rights of the accused person to return voluntarily and without formality to the demanding State, nor shall this waiver procedure be deemed to be an exclusive procedure or to limit the powers, rights or duties of the officers of the demanding State or of this State.

### Sec. 25b. Non-Waiver by This State.

Nothing in this Act contained shall be deemed to constitute a waiver by this State of its right, power or privilege to try such demanded person for crime committed within this State, or of its right, power or privilege to regain custody of such person by extradition proceedings or otherwise for the purpose of trial, sentence or punishment for any crime committed within this State, nor shall any proceedings had under this Article which result, or fail to result in, extradition to be deemed a waiver by this State of any of its rights, privileges or jurisdiction in any way whatsoever.

### Sec. 26. No Right of Asylum, No Immunity from Other Criminal Prosecutions While in This State.

After a person has been brought back to this State by, or after waiver of extradition proceedings, he may be tried in this State for other crimes which he may be charged with having committed here as well as that specified in the requisition for his extradition.

### Sec. 27. Interpretation.

The provisions of this Article shall be interpreted and construed as to effectuate its general purposes to make uniform the law of those States which enact it.

(Enacted by Acts 1965, 59th Leg., ch. 722 (S.B. 107), § 1, effective January 1, 1966; am. Acts 1997, 75th Leg., ch. 701 (S.B. 1579), § 1, effective September 1, 1997.)

## Art. 51.14. Interstate Agreement on Detainers.

This article may be cited as the "Interstate Agreement on Detainers Act." This agreement on detainers is hereby enacted into law and entered into by this state with all other jurisdictions legally joined therein in the form substantially as follows:

The contracting states solemnly agree that:

### ARTICLE I.

The party states find that charges outstanding against a prisoner, detainers based on untried indictments, informations, or complaints, and difficulties in securing speedy trial of persons already incarcerated in other jurisdictions, produce uncertainties which obstruct programs of prisoner treatment and rehabilitation. Accordingly, it is the policy of the party states and the purpose of this agreement to encourage the expeditious and orderly disposition of such charges and determination of the proper status of any and all detainers based on untried indictments, informations, or complaints. The party states also find that proceedings with reference to such charges and detainers, when emanating from another jurisdiction, cannot properly be had in the absence of cooperative procedures. It is the further purpose of this agreement to provide such cooperative procedures.

### ARTICLE II.

As used is this agreement:

(a) "State" shall mean a state of the United States; the United States of America; a territory or possession of the United States; the District of Columbia; the Commonwealth of Puerto Rico.

(b) "Sending state" shall mean a state in which a prisoner is incarcerated at the time that he initiates a request for final disposition pursuant to Article III hereof or at the time that a request for custody or availability is initiated pursuant to Article IV hereof.

### ARTICLE III.

(a) Whenever a person has entered upon a term of imprisonment in a penal or correctional institution of a party state, and whenever during the continuance of the term of imprisonment there is pending in any other party state any untried indictment, information, or complaint on the basis of which a detainer has been lodged against the prisoner, he shall be brought to trial within 180 days after he shall have caused to be delivered to the prosecuting officer and the appropriate court of the prosecuting officer's jurisdiction written notice of the place of his imprisonment and his request for a final disposition to be made of the indictment, information, or complaint; provided that for good cause shown in open court, the prisoner or his counsel being present, the court having jurisdiction of the matter may grant any necessary or reasonable continuance. The request of the prisoner shall be accompanied by a certificate of the appropriate official having custody of the prisoner, stating the term of commitment under which the prisoner is being held, the time already served, the time remaining to be served on the sentence, the amount of good time earned, the time of parole eligibility of the prisoner, and any decision of the state parole agency relating to the prisoner.

(b) The written notice and request for final disposition referred to in Paragraph (a) hereof shall be given or sent by the prisoner to the warden, commissioner of corrections, or other official having custody of him, who shall promptly forward it together with the certificate to the appropriate prosecuting official and court by registered or certified mail, return receipt requested.

(c) The warden, commissioner of corrections, or other official having custody of the prisoner shall promptly inform him of the source and contents of any detainer lodged against him and shall also inform him of his right to make a request for final disposition of the indictment, information, or complaint on which the detainer is based.

(d) Any request for final disposition made by a prisoner pursuant to Paragraph (a) hereof shall operate as a request for final disposition of all untried indictments, informations, or complaints on the basis of which detainers have been lodged against the prisoner from the state to whose prosecuting official the request for final disposition is specifically directed. The warden, commissioner of corrections, or other official having custody of the prisoner shall forthwith notify all appropriate prosecuting officers and courts in the several jurisdictions within the state to which the prisoner's request for final disposition is being sent of the proceeding being initiated by the prisoner. Any notification sent pursuant to this paragraph shall be accompanied by copies of the prisoner's written notice, request, and the certificate. If trial is not had on any indictment, information, or complaint contemplated hereby prior to the return of the prisoner to the original place of imprisonment, such indictment, information, or complaint shall not be of any further force or effect, and the court shall enter an order dismissing the same with prejudice.

(e) Any request for final disposition made by a prisoner pursuant to Paragraph (a) hereof shall also be deemed to be a waiver of extradition with respect to any charge or proceeding contemplated thereby or included therein by reason of Paragraph (d) hereof, and a waiver of extradition to the receiving state to serve any sentence there imposed upon him after comple-

tion of his term of imprisonment in the sending state. The request for final disposition shall also constitute a consent by the prisoner to the production of his body in any court where his presence may be required in order to effectuate the purposes of this agreement and a further consent voluntarily to be returned to the original place of imprisonment in accordance with the provisions of this agreement. Nothing in this paragraph shall prevent the imposition of a concurrent sentence if otherwise permitted by law.

(f) Escape from custody by the prisoner subsequent to his execution of the request for final disposition referred to in Paragraph (a) hereof shall void the request.

## ARTICLE IV.

(a) The appropriate officer of the jurisdiction in which an untried indictment, information, or complaint is pending shall be entitled to have a prisoner against whom he has lodged a detainer and who is serving a term of imprisonment in any party state made available in accordance with Paragraph (a) of Article V hereof upon presentation of a written request for temporary custody or availability to the appropriate authorities of the state in which the prisoner is incarcerated; provided that the court having jurisdiction of such indictment, information, or complaint shall have duly approved, recorded, and transmitted the request; and provided further that there shall be a period of 30 days after receipt by the appropriate authorities before the request be honored, within which period the governor of the sending state may disapprove the request for temporary custody or availability, either upon his own motion or upon motion of the prisoner.

(b) Upon receipt of the officer's written request as provided in Paragraph (a) hereof, the appropriate authorities having the prisoner in custody shall furnish the officer with a certificate stating the term of commitment under which the prisoner is being held, the time already served, the time remaining to be served on the sentence, the amount of good time earned, the time of parole eligibility of the prisoner, and any decisions of the state parole agency relating to the prisoner. Said authorities simultaneously shall furnish all other officers and appropriate courts in the receiving state who have lodged detainers against the prisoner with similar certificates and with notices informing them of the request for custody or availability and of the reasons therefor.

(c) In respect of any proceeding made possible by this article, trial shall be commenced within 120 days of the arrival of the prisoner in the receiving state, but for good cause shown in open court, the prisoner or his counsel being present, the court having jurisdiction of the matter may grant any necessary or reasonable continuance.

(d) Nothing contained in this article shall be construed to deprive any prisoner of any right which he may have to contest the legality of his delivery as provided in Paragraph (a) hereof, but such delivery may not be opposed or denied on the ground that the executing authority of the sending state has not affirmatively consented to or ordered such delivery.

(e) If trial is not had on any indictment, information, or complaint contemplated hereby prior to the prisoner's being returned to the original place of imprisonment pursuant to Paragraph (e) of Article V hereof, such indictment, information, or complaint shall not be of any further force or effect, and the court shall enter an order dismissing the same with prejudice.

## ARTICLE V.

(a) In response to a request made under Article III or Article IV hereof, the appropriate authority in a sending state shall offer to deliver temporary custody of such prisoner to the appropriate authority in the state where such indictment, information, or complaint is pending against such person in order that speedy and efficient prosecution may be had. If the request for final disposition is made by the prisoner, the offer of temporary custody shall accompany the written notice provided for in Article III of this agreement. In the case of a federal prisoner, the appropriate authority in the receiving state shall be entitled to temporary custody as provided by this agreement or to the prisoner's presence in federal custody at the place of trial, whichever custodial arrangement may be approved by the custodian.

(b) The officer or other representative of a state accepting an offer of temporary custody shall present the following upon demand:

(1) proper identification and evidence of his authority to act for the state into whose temporary custody this prisoner is to be given;

(2) a duly certified copy of the indictment, information, or complaint on the basis of which the detainer has been lodged and on the basis of which the request for temporary custody of the prisoner has been made.

(c) If the appropriate authority shall refuse or fail to accept temporary custody of said person, or in the event that an action on the indictment, information, or complaint on the basis of which the detainer has been lodged is not brought to trial within the period provided in Article III or Article IV hereof, the appropriate court of the jurisdiction where the indictment, information, or complaint has been pending shall enter an order dismissing the same with prejudice, and any detainer based thereon shall cease to be of any force or effect.

(d) The temporary custody referred to in this agreement shall be only for the purpose of permitting prosecution on the charge or charges contained in one or more untried indictments, informations, or complaints which form the basis of the detainer or detainers or for prosecution on any other charge or charges arising out of the same transaction. Except for his attendance at court and while being transported to or from any place at which his presence may be required, the prisoner shall be held in a suitable jail or other facility regularly used for persons awaiting prosecution.

(e) At the earliest practicable time consonant with the purposes of this agreement, the prisoner shall be returned to the sending state.

(f) During the continuance of temporary custody or while the prisoner is otherwise being made available for trial as required by this agreement, time being served on the sentence shall continue to run but good time shall be earned by the prisoner only if, and to the extent that, the law and practice of the jurisdiction which imposed the sentence may allow.

(g) For all purposes other than that for which temporary custody as provided in this agreement is exercised, the prisoner shall be deemed to remain in the custody of and subject to the jurisdiction of the sending state and any escape from temporary custody may be dealt with in the same manner as an escape from the original place of imprisonment or in any other manner permitted by law.

(h) From the time that a party state receives custody of a prisoner pursuant to this agreement until such prisoner is returned to the territory and custody of the sending state, the state in which the one or more untried indictments, informations, or complaints are pending or in which trial is being had shall be responsible for the prisoner and shall also pay all costs of transporting, caring for, keeping, and returning the prisoner. The provisions of this paragraph shall govern unless the states concerned shall have entered into a supplementary agreement providing for a different allocation of costs and responsibilities as between or among themselves. Nothing herein contained shall be construed to alter or affect any internal relationship among the departments, agencies, and officers of and in the government of a party state, or between a party state and its subdivisions, as to the payment of costs, or responsibilities therefor.

## ARTICLE VI.

(a) In determining the duration and expiration dates of the time periods provided in Articles III and IV of this agreement, the running of said time periods shall be tolled whenever and for as long as the prisoner is unable to stand trial, as determined by the court having jurisdiction of the matter.

(b) No provision of this agreement, and no remedy made available by this agreement shall apply to any person who is adjudged to be mentally ill.

## ARTICLE VII.

Each state party to this agreement shall designate an officer who, acting jointly with like officers of other party states, shall promulgate rules and regulations to carry out more effectively the terms and provisions of this agreement, and who shall provide, within and without the state, information necessary to the effective operation of this agreement.

## ARTICLE VIII.

This agreement shall enter into full force and effect as to a party state when such state has enacted the same into law. A state party to this agreement may withdraw herefrom by enacting a statute repealing the same. However, the withdrawal of any state shall not affect the status of any proceedings already initiated by inmates or by state officers at the time such withdrawal takes effect, nor shall it affect their rights in respect thereof.

## ARTICLE IX.

(a) This agreement shall be liberally construed so as to effectuate its purposes. The provisions of this agreement shall be severable and if any phrase, clause, sentence, or provision of this agreement is declared to be contrary to the constitution of any party state or of the United States or the applicability thereof to any government, agency, person, or circumstance is held invalid, the validity of the remainder of this agreement and the applicability thereof to any government, agency, person, or circumstance shall not be affected thereby. If this agreement shall be held contrary to the constitution of any state party hereto, the agreement shall remain in full force and effect as to the remaining states and in full force and effect as to the state affected as to all severable matters.

(b) As used in this article, "appropriate court" means a court of record with criminal jurisdiction.

(c) All courts, departments, agencies, officers, and employees of this state and its political subdivisions are hereby directed to enforce this article and to cooperate with one another and with other party states in enforcing the agreement and effectuating its purpose.

(d) Any prisoner escapes from lawful custody while in another state as a result of the application of this article shall be punished as though such escape had occurred within this state.

(e) The governor is empowered to designate the officer who will serve as central administrator of and information agent for the agreement on detainers pursuant to the provisions of Article VII hereof.

(f) Copies of this article, upon its enactment, shall be transmitted to the governor of each state, the Attorney General and the Secretary of State of the United States, and the council of state governments.

(Enacted by Acts 1975, 64th Leg., ch. 343 (S.B. 130), § 1, effective June 19, 1975.)

# CHAPTER 52
# COURT OF INQUIRY

## Art. 52.01. Courts of Inquiry Conducted by District Judges.

(a) When a judge of any district court of this state, acting in his capacity as magistrate, has probable cause to believe that an offense has been committed against the laws of this state, he may request that the presiding judge of the administrative judicial district appoint a district judge to commence a Court of Inquiry. The judge, who shall be appointed in accordance with Subsection (b), may summon and examine any witness in relation to the offense in accordance with the rules hereinafter provided, which procedure is defined as a "Court of Inquiry".

(b) (1) Before requesting the presiding judge to appoint a district judge to commence a Court of Inquiry, a judge must enter into the minutes of his court a sworn affidavit stating the substantial facts establishing probable cause that a specific offense has been committed against the laws of this state.

(2) After the affidavit has been entered into the minutes of his court and a copy filed with the district clerk, the judge shall request the presiding judge of the administrative judicial district in which the affidavit is filed to appoint a judge to commence the Court of Inquiry. The judge appointed to commence the Court of Inquiry shall issue a written order commencing the Court of Inquiry and stating its scope. The presiding judge shall not name the judge who requests the Court of Inquiry to preside over the Court of Inquiry.

(c) The district or county attorney of the district or county in which the Court of Inquiry is held shall assist the district judge in conducting the Court of Inquiry. The attorney shall examine witnesses and evidence admitted before the court to determine if an offense has been committed and shall render other assistance to the judge as is necessary in the proceeding.

(d) If the Court of Inquiry pertains to the activities of the district or county attorney or to the attorney's office, deputies, or employees, or if the attorney is otherwise disqualified in the proceeding, the judge shall appoint one attorney pro tem to assist in the proceeding. In any other circumstance, the judge may appoint an attorney pro tem to assist in the proceeding.

(e) If more than one Court of Inquiry is commenced which pertains to the activities of a state governmental entity or public servant thereof, then, upon motion of the state governmental entity or public servant, made to the presiding judge or judges of the administrative judicial region or regions where the Courts of Inquiry have been commenced, the presiding judge or judges shall transfer the Courts of Inquiry to the presiding administrative judge of Travis County. The presiding administrative judge of Travis County shall consolidate the Courts of Inquiry for further proceedings and shall assign a district judge to preside over the consolidated Courts of Inquiry.

(Enacted by Acts 1965, 59th Leg., ch. 722 (S.B. 107), § 1, effective January 1, 1966; am. Acts 1967, 60th Leg., ch. 659 (S.B. 145), § 34, effective August 28, 1967; am. Acts 1987, 70th Leg., ch. 534 (H.B. 1219), § 1, effective September 1, 1987; am. Acts 1995, 74th Leg., ch. 318 (S.B. 15) § 65, effective September 1, 1995.)

## Art. 52.02. Evidence; Deposition; Affidavits.

At the hearing at a Court of Inquiry, evidence may be taken orally or by deposition, or, in the discretion of the judge, by affidavit. If affidavits are admitted, any witness against whom they may bear has the right to propound written interrogatories to the affiants or to file answering affidavits. The judge in hearing such evidence, at his discretion, may conclude not to sustain objections to all or to any portion of the evidence taken nor exclude same; but any of the witnesses or attorneys engaged in taking the testimony may have any objections they make recorded with the testimony and reserved for the action of any court in which such evidence is thereafter sought to be admitted, but such court is not confined to objections made at the taking of the testimony at the Court of Inquiry. Without restricting the foregoing, the judge may allow the introduction of any documentary or real evidence which he deems

Criminal Procedure

reliable, and the testimony adduced before any grand jury.

(Enacted by Acts 1965, 59th Leg., ch. 722 (S.B. 107), § 1, effective January 1, 1966; am. Acts 1967, 60th Leg., ch. 659 (S.B. 145), § 35, effective August 28, 1967.)

### Art. 52.03. Subpoenas.

The judge or his clerk has power to issue subpoenas which may be served within the same territorial limits as subpoenas issued in felony prosecutions or to summon witnesses before grand juries in this state.

(Enacted by Acts 1965, 59th Leg., ch. 722 (S.B. 107), § 1, effective January 1, 1966; am. Acts 1967, 60th Leg., ch. 659 (S.B. 145), § 36, effective August 28, 1967.)

### Art. 52.04. Rights of Witnesses.

(a) All witnesses testifying in any Court of Inquiry have the same rights as to testifying as do defendants in felony prosecutions in this state. Before any witness is sworn to testify in any Court of Inquiry, he shall be instructed by the judge that he is entitled to counsel; that he cannot be forced to testify against himself; and that such testimony may be taken down and used against him in a later trial or trials ensuing from the instant Court of Inquiry. Any witness or his counsel has the right to fully cross-examine any of the witnesses whose testimony bears in any manner against him.

(b) If the Court of Inquiry pertains to the activities of a state governmental entity or its officers or employees, the officers and employees of that state governmental entity shall be indemnified for attorney's fees incurred as a result of exercising the employees' or officers' right to counsel under Subsection (a) if:

(1) the officer or employee is found not guilty after a trial or appeal or the complaint, information, or indictment is dismissed without a plea of guilty or nolo contendere being entered; and

(2) the judge commencing the Court of Inquiry, or the judge to whom the Court of Inquiry was transferred pursuant to Article 52.01(e), determines that the complaint, information, or indictment presented against the person was dismissed because:

(A) the presentment was made on mistake, false information, or other similar basis, indicating absence of probable cause to believe, at the time of dismissal, the person committed the offense; or

(B) the complaint, information, or indictment was void.

(c) The county in which the affidavit under Article 52.01 was filed shall be responsible for any attorney's fees awarded under Subsection (b).

(Enacted by Acts 1965, 59th Leg., ch. 722 (S.B. 107), § 1, effective January 1, 1966; am. Acts 1967, 60th Leg., ch. 659 (S.B. 145), § 37, effective August 28, 1967; am. Acts 1995, 74th Leg., ch. 318 (S.B. 15), § 66, effective September 1, 1995.)

### Art. 52.05. Witness Must Testify.

A person may be compelled to give testimony or produce evidence when legally called upon to do so at any Court of Inquiry; however, if any person refuses or declines to testify or produce evidence on the ground that it may incriminate him under laws of this state, then the judge may, in his discretion, compel such person to testify or produce evidence but the person shall not be prosecuted or subjected to any penalty or forfeiture for, or on account of, any transaction, matter or thing concerning which he may be compelled to testify or produce evidence at such Court of Inquiry.

(Enacted by Acts 1965, 59th Leg., ch. 722 (S.B. 107), § 1, effective January 1, 1966; am. Acts 1967, 60th Leg., ch. 659 (S.B. 145), § 38, effective August 28, 1967.)

### Art. 52.06. Contempt.

Contempt of court in a Court of Inquiry may be punished by a fine not exceeding One Hundred Dollars ($100.00) and any witness refusing to testify may be attached and imprisoned until he does testify.

(Enacted by Acts 1965, 59th Leg., ch. 722 (S.B. 107), § 1, effective January 1, 1966.)

### Art. 52.07. Stenographic Record; Public Hearing.

All evidence taken at a Court of Inquiry shall be transcribed by the court reporter and all proceedings shall be open to the public.

(Enacted by Acts 1965, 59th Leg., ch. 722 (S.B. 107), § 1, effective January 1, 1966.)

### Art. 52.08. Criminal Prosecutions.

If it appear from a Court of Inquiry or any testimony adduced therein, that an offense has been committed, the Judge shall issue a warrant for the arrest of the offender as if complaint had been made and filed.

(Enacted by Acts 1965, 59th Leg., ch. 722 (S.B. 107), § 1, effective January 1, 1966.)

### Art. 52.09. Costs and Attorney's Fees.

(a) All costs incurred in conducting a Court of Inquiry, including compensation of an attorney pro tem, shall be borne by the county in which said Court of Inquiry is conducted; provided, however, that where the Attorney General of Texas has submitted a request in writing to the judge for the holding of such Court of Inquiry, then and in that event the costs shall be borne by the State of Texas and shall be taxed to the attorney general and paid in the same manner and from the same funds as other court costs.

(b) Assistance by a county or district attorney to a Court of Inquiry is a duty of the attorney's office, and the attorney may not receive a fee for the service. A county is not liable for attorney's fees claimed for assistance in a Court of Inquiry by any attorney other than an attorney pro tem appointed under Article 52.01(d) of this code.

(c) An attorney pro tem appointed under Article 52.01(d) of this code is entitled to compensation in the same manner as an attorney pro tem appointed under Article 2.07 of this code. The district judge shall set the compensation of the attorney pro tem based on the sworn testimony of the attorney or other evidence that is given in open court.

(Enacted by Acts 1965, 59th Leg., ch. 722 (S.B. 107), § 1, effective January 1, 1966; am. Acts 1967, 60th Leg., ch. 659 (S.B. 145), § 39, effective August 28, 1967; am. Acts 1987, 70th Leg., ch. 534 (H.B. 1219), § 1, effective September 1, 1987.)

## CHAPTER 53
## COSTS AND FEES

### Art. 53.01. Peace Officers [Repealed].

Repealed by Acts 1987, 70th Leg., ch. 167 (S.B. 892), § 4.01(b) effective September 1, 1987. (Enacted by Acts 1965, 59th Leg., ch. 722 (S.B. 107), § 1, effective January 1, 1966; am. Acts 1985, 69th Leg., ch. 239 (H.B. 1593), § 9, effective September 1, 1985.)

### Art. 53.02. Fees of Peace Officers [Repealed].

Repealed by Acts 1985, 69th Leg., ch. 269 (S.B. 854), § 5(1) effective September 1, 1985. (Enacted by Acts 1965, 59th Leg., ch. 722 (S.B. 107), § 1, effective January 1, 1966.)

### Art. 53.03. Fee of State's Attorney [Repealed].

Repealed by Acts 1987, 70th Leg., ch. 167 (S.B. 892), § 4.01(b) effective September 1, 1987. (Enacted by Acts 1965, 59th Leg., ch. 722 (S.B. 107), § 1, effective January 1, 1966.)

### Art. 53.04. Officers in Examining Court [Repealed].

Repealed by Acts 1987, 70th Leg., ch. 167 (S.B. 892), § 4.01(b) effective September 1, 1987. (Enacted by Acts 1965, 59th Leg., ch. 722 (S.B. 107), § 1, effective January 1, 1966.)

### Art. 53.05. In District and County Courts [Repealed].

Repealed by Acts 1987, 70th Leg., ch. 167 (S.B. 892), § 4.01(b) effective September 1, 1987. (Enacted by Acts 1965, 59th Leg., ch. 722 (S.B. 107), § 1, effective January 1, 1966.)

### Art. 53.06. Trial Fee [Repealed].

Repealed by Acts 1987, 70th Leg., ch. 167 (S.B. 892), § 4.01(b) effective September 1, 1987. (Enacted by Acts 1965, 59th Leg., ch. 722 (S.B. 107), § 1, effective January 1, 1966.)

### Art. 53.07. Justice of Peace Salary [Repealed].

Repealed by Acts 1985, 69th Leg., ch. 269 (S.B. 854), § 5(1) effective September 1, 1985. (Enacted by Acts 1965, 59th Leg., ch. 722 (S.B. 107), § 1, effective January 1, 1966.)

### Art. 53.08. Fee for Collecting and Processing Sight Order [Repealed].

Repealed by Acts 1987, 70th Leg., ch. 167 (S.B. 892), § 4.01(b) effective September 1, 1987. (Enacted by Acts 1979, 66th Leg., ch. 604 (S.B. 374), § 2, effective August 27, 1979.)

### Art. 53.09. Justice of Peace Costs in Counties over Two Million [Repealed].

Repealed by Acts 1987, 70th Leg., ch. 167 (S.B. 892), § 4.01(b) effective September 1, 1987. (Enacted by Acts 1983, 68th Leg., ch. 888 (H.B. 1460), § 1, effective August 29, 1983.)

### Art. 53.10. [Blank].

[Blank]

## Art. 53.11. Fees in Proceedings for Expunction of Criminal Records [Repealed].

Repealed by Acts 1987, 70th Leg., ch. 167 (S.B. 892), § 4.01(b) effective September 1, 1987.

(Am. Acts 1987, 70th Leg., ch. 167 (S.B. 892), § 5.01(a)(10), effective September 1, 1987 (renumbered from art. 53.08).)

## CHAPTER 54
## MISCELLANEOUS PROVISIONS

## Art. 54.01. Severability Clause.

If any provision, section or clause of this Act or application thereof to any person or circumstances is held invalid, such invalidity shall not affect other provisions or applications hereof which can be given effect without the invalid provision, section or clause, and to this end the provisions of this Act are declared to be severable. (Enacted by Acts 1965, 59th Leg., ch. 722 (S.B. 107), § 1, effective January 1, 1966.)

## Art. 54.02. Repealing Clause.

**Sec. 1.** (a) Except as otherwise provided in this Article 54.02, all laws relating to criminal procedure in this State that are not embraced, incorporated, or included in this Act and that have not been enacted during the Regular Session of the 59th Legislature are repealed.

(b) None of the following articles of the Code of Criminal Procedure of Texas, 1925, in force on the effective date of this Act, is repealed: 52; 52-1 through 52-161, both inclusive; 367D through 367K, both inclusive; 781B-1, 781B-2; 944 through 951, both inclusive; 1009 through 1035, both inclusive; 1037 through 1056, both inclusive; 1058 through 1064, both inclusive; and 1075 through 1082, both inclusive.

**Sec. 2.** (a) All laws and parts of laws relating to criminal procedure omitted from this Act have been intentionally omitted, and all additions to and changes in such procedure have been intentionally made. This Act shall be construed to be an independent Act of the Legislature, enacted under its caption, and the articles contained in this Act, as revised, rewritten, changed, combined, and codified, may not be construed as a continuation of former laws except as otherwise provided in this Act. The existing statutes of the Revised Civil Statutes of Texas, 1925, as amended, and of the Penal Code of Texas, 1925, as amended, which contain special or specific provisions of criminal procedure covering specific instances are not repealed by this Act.

(b) A person under recognizance or bond on the effective date of this Act continues under such recognizance or bond pending final disposition of any action pending against him.

(Enacted by Acts 1965, 59th Leg., ch. 722 (S.B. 107), § 1, effective January 1, 1966.)

## Art. 54.03. Emergency Clause.

The fact that the laws relating to criminal procedure in this State have not been completely revised and re-codified in more than a century past and the further fact that the administration of justice, in the field of criminal law, has undergone changes, through judicial construction and interpretation of constitutional provisions, which have been, in certain instances, modified or nullified, as the case may be, necessitates important changes requiring the revision or modernization of the laws relating to criminal procedure, and the further fact that it is desirous and desirable to strengthen, and to conform, various provisions in such laws to current interpretation and application, emphasizes the importance of this legislation and all of which, together with the crowded condition of the calendar in both Houses, create an emergency and an imperative public necessity that the Constitutional Rule requiring bills to be read on three several days be suspended, and said Rule is hereby suspended, and that this Act shall take effect and be in force and effect from and after 12 o'clock Meridian on the 1st day of January, Anno Domini, 1966, and it is so enacted. (Enacted by Acts 1965, 59th Leg., ch. 722 (S.B. 107), § 1, effective January 1, 1966.)

## CHAPTER 55
## EXPUNCTION OF CRIMINAL RECORDS

## Art. 55.01. Right to Expunction.

(a) A person who has been placed under a custodial or noncustodial arrest for commission of either a felony or misdemeanor is entitled to have all records and files relating to the arrest expunged if:

(1) the person is tried for the offense for which the person was arrested and is:

(A) acquitted by the trial court, except as provided by Subsection (c); or

(B) **[2 Versions: As amended by Acts 2011, 82nd Leg., ch. 690]** convicted and subsequently:

(i) pardoned for a reason other than that described by Subparagraph (ii); or

(ii) pardoned or otherwise granted relief on the basis of actual innocence with respect to that offense, if the applicable pardon or court order clearly indicates on its face that the pardon or order was granted or rendered on the basis of the person's actual innocence; or

(B) **[2 Versions: As amended by Acts 2011, 82nd Leg., ch. 894]** convicted and subsequently pardoned; or

(2) the person has been released and the charge, if any, has not resulted in a final conviction and is no longer pending and there was no court-ordered community supervision under Article 42.12 for the offense, unless the offense is a Class C misdemeanor, provided that:

(A) regardless of whether any statute of limitations exists for the offense and whether any limitations period for the offense has expired, an indictment or information charging the person with the commission of a misdemeanor offense based on the person's arrest or charging the person with the commission of any felony offense arising out of the same transaction for which the person was arrested:

(i) has not been presented against the person at any time following the arrest, and:

(a) at least 180 days have elapsed from the date of arrest if the arrest for which the expunction was sought was for an offense punishable as a Class C misdemeanor and if there was no felony charge arising out of the same transaction for which the person was arrested;

(b) at least one year has elapsed from the date of arrest if the arrest for which the expunction was sought was for an offense punishable as a Class B or A misdemeanor and if there was no felony charge arising out of the same transaction for which the person was arrested;

(c) at least three years have elapsed from the date of arrest if the arrest for which the expunction was sought was for an offense punishable as a felony or if there was a felony charge arising out of the same transaction for which the person was arrested; or

(d) the attorney representing the state certifies that the applicable arrest records and files are not needed for use in any criminal investigation or prosecution, including an investigation or prosecution of another person; or

(ii) if presented at any time following the arrest, was dismissed or quashed, and the court finds that the indictment or information was dismissed or quashed because the person completed a pretrial intervention program authorized under Section 76.011, Government Code, because the presentment had been made because of mistake, false information, or other similar reason indicating absence of probable cause at the time of the dismissal to believe the person committed the offense, or because the indictment or information was void; or

(B) prosecution of the person for the offense for which the person was arrested is no longer possible because the limitations period has expired.

(a-1) Notwithstanding any other provision of this article, a person may not expunge records and files relating to an arrest that occurs pursuant to a warrant issued under Section 21, Article 42.12

(a-2) Notwithstanding any other provision of this article, a person who intentionally or knowingly absconds from the jurisdiction after being released under Chapter 17 following an arrest is not eligible under Subsection (a)(2)(A)(i)(a), (b), or (c) or Subsection (a)(2)(B) for an expunction of the records and files relating to that arrest.

(b) Except as provided by Subsection (c), a district court may expunge all records and files relating to the arrest of a person who has been arrested for commission of a felony or misdemeanor under the procedure established under Article 55.02 if:

(1) the person is:

(A) tried for the offense for which the person was arrested;

(B) convicted of the offense; and

(C) acquitted by the court of criminal appeals or, if the period for granting a petition for discretionary review has expired, by a court of appeals; or

(2) an office of the attorney representing the state authorized by law to prosecute the offense for which the person was arrested recommends the expunction to the appropriate district court before the person is tried for the offense, regardless of whether an indictment or information has been presented against the person in relation to the offense.

(c) A court may not order the expunction of records and files relating to an arrest for an offense for which a person is subsequently acquitted, whether by the trial court, a court of appeals, or the court of criminal appeals, if the offense for which the person was acquitted arose out of a criminal episode, as defined by Section 3.01, Penal Code, and the person was convicted of or remains subject to prosecution for at least one other offense occurring during the criminal episode.

(d) A person is entitled to have any information that identifies the person, including the person's name, address, date of birth, driver's license number, and social security number, contained in records and files relating to the arrest of another person expunged if:

(1) the information identifying the person asserting the entitlement to expunction was falsely given by the person arrested as the arrested person's identifying information without the consent of the person asserting the entitlement; and

(2) the only reason for the information identifying the person asserting the entitlement being contained in the arrest records and files of the person arrested is that the information was falsely given by the person arrested as the arrested person's identifying information.

(Enacted by Acts 1977, 65th Leg., ch. 747 (S.B. 471), § 1, effective August 29, 1977; am. Acts 1979, 66th Leg., ch. 604 (S.B. 374), § 1, effective August 27, 1979; am Acts 1989, 71st Leg., ch. 803 (H.B. 526), § 1, effective September 1, 1989; am. Acts 1991, 72nd Leg., ch. 14 (S.B. 404), § 284(53), effective September 1, 1991; am. Acts 1993, 73rd Leg., ch. 900 (S.B. 1067), § 7.02(a), effective September 1, 1993; am. Acts 1999, 76th Leg., ch. 1236 (S.B. 840), § 1, effective August 30, 1999; enacted by Acts 2001, 77th Leg., ch. 945 (S.B.

1047), § 1, effective June 14, 2001; am. Acts 2001, 77th Leg., ch. 1021 (H.B. 1323), § 1, effective September 1, 2001; am. Acts 2003, 78th Leg., ch. 1236 (S.B. 1477), § 1, effective September 1, 2003; am. Acts 2005, 79th Leg., ch. 1309 (H.B. 3093), § 1, effective September 1, 2005; am. Acts 2009, 81st Leg., ch. 840, (S.B. 1940), § 5, effective June 19, 2009; am. Acts 2009, 81st Leg., ch. 1103, (H.B. 4833), § 17(b), effective September 1, 2009; am. Acts 2011, 82nd Leg., ch. 690 (H.B. 351), § 1, effective September 1, 2011; am. Acts 2011, 82nd Leg., ch. 894 (S.B. 462), § 1, effective September 1, 2011.)

## Art. 55.011. Right of Close Relative to Seek Expunction on Behalf of Deceased Person.

(a) In this article, "close relative of a deceased person" means the grandparent, parent, spouse, or adult brother, sister, or child of a deceased person.

(b) A close relative of a deceased person who, if not deceased, would be entitled to expunction of records and files under Article 55.01 may file on behalf of the deceased person an ex parte petition for expunction under Section 2 or 2a, Article 55.02. If the court finds that the deceased person would be entitled to expunction of any record or file that is the subject of the petition, the court shall enter an order directing expunction.

(Enacted by Acts 2009, 81st Leg., ch. 659 (H.B. 2002), § 1, effective June 19, 2009.)

## Art. 55.02. Procedure for Expunction.

Sec. 1. At the request of the defendant and after notice to the state, the trial court presiding over the case in which the defendant was acquitted, if the trial court is a district court, or a district court in the county in which the trial court is located shall enter an order of expunction for a person entitled to expunction under Article 55.01(a)(1)(A) not later than the 30th day after the date of the acquittal. Upon acquittal, the trial court shall advise the defendant of the right to expunction. The defendant shall provide to the district court all of the information required in a petition for expunction under Section 2(b). The attorney for the defendant in the case in which the defendant was acquitted, if the defendant was represented by counsel, or the attorney for the state, if the defendant was not represented by counsel, shall prepare the order for the court's signature.

Sec. 1a. (a) The trial court presiding over a case in which a defendant is convicted and subsequently granted relief or pardoned on the basis of actual innocence of the offense of which the defendant was convicted, if the trial court is a district court, or a district court in the county in which the trial court is located shall enter an order of expunction for a person entitled to expunction under Article 55.01(a)(1)(B)(ii) not later than the 30th day after the date the court receives notice of the pardon or other grant of relief. The person shall provide to the district court all of the information required in a petition for expunction under Section 2(b).

(b) The attorney for the state shall:

(1) prepare an expunction order under this section for the court's signature; and

(2) notify the Texas Department of Criminal Justice if the person is in the custody of the department.

(c) The court shall include in an expunction order under this section a listing of each official, agency, or other entity of this state or political subdivision of this state and each private entity that there is reason to believe has any record or file that is subject to the order. The court shall also provide in an expunction order under this section that:

(1) the Texas Department of Criminal Justice shall send to the court the documents delivered to the department under Section 8(a), Article 42.09; and

(2) the Department of Public Safety and the Texas Department of Criminal Justice shall delete or redact, as appropriate, from their public records all index references to the records and files that are subject to the expunction order.

(d) The court shall retain all documents sent to the court under Subsection (c)(1) until the statute of limitations has run for any civil case or proceeding relating to the wrongful imprisonment of the person subject to the expunction order.

Sec. 2. (a) A person who is entitled to expunction of records and files under Article 55.01(a)(1)(B)(i) or 55.01(a)(2) or a person who is eligible for expunction of records and files under Article 55.01(b) may file an ex parte petition for expunction in a district court for the county in which:

(1) the petitioner was arrested; or

(2) the offense was alleged to have occurred.

(b) The petition must be verified and must include the following or an explanation for why one or more of the following is not included:

(1) the petitioner's:

(A) full name;

(B) sex;

(C) race;

(D) date of birth;

(E) driver's license number;

(F) social security number; and

(G) address at the time of the arrest;

(2) the offense charged against the petitioner;

(3) the date the offense charged against the petitioner was alleged to have been committed;

(4) the date the petitioner was arrested;

(5) the name of the county where the petitioner was arrested and if the arrest occurred in a municipality, the name of the municipality;

(6) the name of the agency that arrested the petitioner;

(7) the case number and court of offense; and

(8) together with the applicable physical or e-mail addresses, a list of all:

(A) law enforcement agencies, jails or other detention facilities, magistrates, courts, prosecuting attorneys, correctional facilities, central state depositories of criminal records, and other officials or agencies or other entities of this state or of any political subdivision of this state;

(B) central federal depositories of criminal records that the petitioner has reason to believe have records or files that are subject to expunction; and

(C) private entities that compile and disseminate for compensation criminal history record information that the petitioner has reason to believe have information related to records or files that are subject to expunction.

(c) The court shall set a hearing on the matter no sooner than thirty days from the filing of the petition and shall give to each official or agency or other governmental entity named in the petition reasonable notice of the hearing by:

(1) certified mail, return receipt requested; or

(2) secure electronic mail, electronic transmission, or facsimile transmission.

(c-1) An entity described by Subsection (c) may be represented by the attorney responsible for providing the entity with legal representation in other matters.

Criminal Procedure

(d) If the court finds that the petitioner, or a person for whom an ex parte petition is filed under Subsection (e), is entitled to expunction of any records and files that are the subject of the petition, it shall enter an order directing expunction.

(e) The director of the Department of Public Safety or the director's authorized representative may file on behalf of a person described by Subsection (a) of this section or by Section 2a an ex parte petition for expunction in a district court for the county in which:

(1) the person was arrested; or

(2) the offense was alleged to have occurred.

(f) An ex parte petition filed under Subsection (e) must be verified and must include the following or an explanation for why one or more of the following is not included:

(1) the person's:

(A) full name;

(B) sex;

(C) race;

(D) date of birth;

(E) driver's license number;

(F) social security number; and

(G) address at the time of the arrest;

(2) the offense charged against the person;

(3) the date the offense charged against the person was alleged to have been committed;

(4) the date the person was arrested;

(5) the name of the county where the person was arrested and if the arrest occurred in a municipality, the name of the municipality;

(6) the name of the agency that arrested the person;

(7) the case number and court of offense; and

(8) together with the applicable physical or e-mail addresses, a list of all:

(A) law enforcement agencies, jails or other detention facilities, magistrates, courts, prosecuting attorneys, correctional facilities, central state depositories of criminal records, and other officials or agencies or other entities of this state or of any political subdivision of this state;

(B) central federal depositories of criminal records that the person has reason to believe have records or files that are subject to expunction; and

(C) private entities that compile and disseminate for compensation criminal history record information that the person has reason to believe have information relating to records or files that are subject to expunction.

Sec. 2a. (a) A person who is entitled to expunction of information contained in records and files under Article 55.01(d) may file an application for expunction with the attorney representing the state in the prosecution of felonies in the county in which the person resides.

(b) The application must be verified, include authenticated fingerprint records of the applicant, and include the following or an explanation for why one or more of the following is not included:

(1) the applicant's full name, sex, race, date of birth, driver's license number, social security number, and address at the time the person who falsely identified himself or herself as the applicant was arrested;

(2) the following information regarding the arrest:

(A) the date of arrest;

(B) the offense charged against the person arrested;

(C) the name of the county or municipality in which the arrest occurred; and

(D) the name of the arresting agency; and

(3) a statement that:

(A) the applicant is not the person arrested and for whom the arrest records and files were created; and

(B) the applicant did not give the person arrested consent to falsely identify himself or herself as the applicant.

(c) After verifying the allegations in an application received under Subsection (a), the attorney representing the state shall:

(1) include on the application information regarding the arrest that was requested of the applicant but was unknown by the applicant;

(2) forward a copy of the application to the district court for the county;

(3) together with the applicable physical or e-mail addresses, attach to the copy a list of all:

(A) law enforcement agencies, jails or other detention facilities, magistrates, courts, prosecuting attorneys, correctional facilities, central state depositories of criminal records, and other officials or agencies or other entities of this state or of any political subdivision of this state;

(B) central federal depositories of criminal records that are reasonably likely to have records or files containing information that is subject to expunction; and

(C) private entities that compile and disseminate for compensation criminal history record information that are reasonably likely to have records or files containing information that is subject to expunction; and

(4) request the court to enter an order directing expunction based on an entitlement to expunction under Article 55.01(d).

(d) On receipt of a request under Subsection (c), the court shall, without holding a hearing on the matter, enter a final order directing expunction.

Sec. 3. (a) In an order of expunction issued under this article, the court shall require any state agency that sent information concerning the arrest to a central federal depository to request the depository to return all records and files subject to the order of expunction. The person who is the subject of the expunction order or an agency protesting the expunction may appeal the court's decision in the same manner as in other civil cases.

(b) The order of expunction entered by the court shall have attached and incorporate by reference a copy of the judgment of acquittal and shall include:

(1) the following information on the person who is the subject of the expunction order:

(A) full name;

(B) sex;

(C) race;

(D) date of birth;

(E) driver's license number; and

(F) social security number;

(2) the offense charged against the person who is the subject of the expunction order;

(3) the date the person who is the subject of the expunction order was arrested;

(4) the case number and court of offense; and

(5) the tracking incident number (TRN) assigned to the individual incident of arrest under Article 60.07(b)(1) by the Department of Public Safety.

(c) When the order of expunction is final, the clerk of the court shall send a certified copy of the order to the Crime Records Service of the Department of Public Safety and to each official or agency or other governmental entity of this state or of any political subdivision of this state named in the order. The certified copy of the order must be sent by secure electronic mail, electronic transmission, or facsimile transmission or otherwise by certified mail, return receipt requested. In sending the order to a governmental entity named in the order, the clerk may elect to substitute hand delivery for certified mail under this subsection, but the clerk must receive a receipt for that hand-delivered order.

(c-1) The Department of Public Safety shall notify any central federal depository of criminal records by any means, including secure electronic mail, electronic transmission, or facsimile transmission, of the order with an explanation of the effect of the order and a request that the depository, as appropriate, either:

(1) destroy or return to the court the records in possession of the depository that are subject to the order, including any information with respect to the order; or

(2) comply with Section 5(f) pertaining to information contained in records and files of a person entitled to expunction under Article 55.01(d).

(c-2) The Department of Public Safety shall also provide, by secure electronic mail, electronic transmission, or facsimile transmission, notice of the order to any private entity that is named in the order or that purchases criminal history record information from the department. The notice must include an explanation of the effect of the order and a request that the entity destroy any information in the possession of the entity that is subject to the order. The department may charge to a private entity that purchases criminal history record information from the department a fee in an amount sufficient to recover costs incurred by the department in providing notice under this subsection to the entity.

(d) Any returned receipts received by the clerk from notices of the hearing and copies of the order shall be maintained in the file on the proceedings under this chapter.

Sec. 4. (a) If the state establishes that the person who is the subject of an expunction order is still subject to conviction for an offense arising out of the transaction for which the person was arrested because the statute of limitations has not run and there is reasonable cause to believe that the state may proceed against the person for the offense, the court may provide in its expunction order that the law enforcement agency and the prosecuting attorney responsible for investigating the offense may retain any records and files that are necessary to the investigation.

(a-1) The court shall provide in its expunction order that the applicable law enforcement agency and prosecuting attorney may retain the arrest records and files of any person who becomes entitled to an expunction of those records and files based on the expiration of a period described by Article 55.01(a)(2)(A)(i)(a), (b), or (c), but without the certification of the prosecuting attorney as described by Article 55.01(a)(2)(A)(i)(d).

(a-2) In the case of a person who is the subject of an expunction order on the basis of an acquittal, the court may provide in the expunction order that the law enforcement agency and the prosecuting attorney retain records and files if:

(1) the records and files are necessary to conduct a subsequent investigation and prosecution of a person other than the person who is the subject of the expunction order; or

(2) the state establishes that the records and files are necessary for use in:

(A) another criminal case, including a prosecution, motion to adjudicate or revoke community supervision, parole revocation hearing, mandatory supervision revocation hearing, punishment hearing, or bond hearing; or

(B) a civil case, including a civil suit or suit for possession of or access to a child.

(b) Unless the person who is the subject of the expunction order is again arrested for or charged with an offense arising out of the transaction for which the person was arrested or unless the court provides for the retention of records and files under Subsection (a-1) or (a-2), the provisions of Articles 55.03 and 55.04 apply to files and records retained under this section.

Sec. 5. (a) Except as provided by Subsections (f) and (g), on receipt of the order, each official or agency or other governmental entity named in the order shall:

(1) return all records and files that are subject to the expunction order to the court or in cases other than those described by Section 1a, if removal is impracticable, obliterate all portions of the record or file that identify the person who is the subject of the order and notify the court of its action; and

(2) delete from its public records all index references to the records and files that are subject to the expunction order.

(b) Except in the case of a person who is the subject of an expunction order on the basis of an acquittal or an expunction order based on an entitlement under Article 55.01(d), the court may give the person who is the subject of the order all records and files returned to it pursuant to its order.

(c) Except in the case of a person who is the subject of an expunction order based on an entitlement under Article 55.01(d) and except as provided by Subsection (g), if an order of expunction is issued under this article, the court records concerning expunction proceedings are not open for inspection by anyone except the person who is the subject of the order unless the order permits retention of a record under Section 4 of this article and the person is again arrested for or charged with an offense arising out of the transaction for which the person was arrested or unless the court provides for the retention of records and files under Section 4(a) of this article. The clerk of the court issuing the order shall obliterate all public references to the proceeding and maintain the files or other records in an area not open to inspection.

(d) Except in the case of a person who is the subject of an expunction order on the basis of an acquittal or an expunction order based on an entitlement under Article 55.01(d) and except as provided by Subsection (g), the clerk of the court shall destroy all the files or other records maintained under Subsection (c) not earlier than the 60th day after the date the order of expunction is issued or later than the first anniversary of that date unless the records or files were released under Subsection (b).

(d-1) Not later than the 30th day before the date on which the clerk destroys files or other records under Subsection (d), the clerk shall provide notice by mail, electronic mail, or facsimile transmission to the attorney representing the state in the expunction proceeding. If the attorney representing the state in the expunction proceeding objects to the destruction not later than the 20th day after receiving notice under this subsection, the clerk may not destroy the files or other records until the first anniversary of the date the order of expunction is issued or the first business day after that date.

(e) The clerk shall certify to the court the destruction of files or other records under Subsection (d) of this section.

(f) On receipt of an order granting expunction to a person entitled to expunction under Article 55.01(d), each official, agency, or other governmental entity named in the order:

(1) shall:

(A) obliterate all portions of the record or file that identify the petitioner; and

(B) substitute for all obliterated portions of the record or file any available information that identifies the person arrested; and

(2) may not return the record or file or delete index references to the record or file.

(g) Notwithstanding any other provision in this section, an official, agency, court, or other entity may retain receipts, invoices, vouchers, or similar records of financial transactions that arose from the expunction proceeding or prosecution of the underlying criminal cause in accordance with internal financial control procedures. An official, agency, court, or other entity that retains records under this subsection shall obliterate all portions of the record or the file that identify the person who is the subject of the expunction order.

(Enacted by Acts 1977, 65th Leg., ch. 747 (S.B. 471), § 1, effective August 29, 1977; am. Acts 1979, 66th Leg., ch. 604 (S.B. 374), § 1, effective August 27, 1979; am. Acts 1989, 71st Leg., ch. 803 (H.B. 526), §§ 2—4, effective September 1, 1989; am. Acts 1991, 72nd Leg., ch. 380 (H.B. 1548), § 1, effective August 26, 1991; am. Acts 1999, 76th Leg., ch. 1236 (S.B. 840), § 2, effective August 30, 1999; am. Acts 2001, 77th Leg., ch. 945 (S.B. 1047), §§ 2, 3, effective June 14, 2001; am. Acts 2001, 77th Leg., ch. 1021 ( H.B. 1323), § 2, effective September 1, 2001; am. Acts 2003, 78th Leg., ch. 339 (S.B. 566), §§ 2—4, 7, effective September 1, 2003; am. Acts 2003, 78th Leg., ch. 404 (H.B. 171), §§ 1, 2, effective September 1, 2003; am. Acts 2003, 78th Leg., ch. 1126 (H.B. 2725), § 1, effective June 20, 2003; am. Acts 2003, 78th Leg., ch. 1236 (S.B. 1477), § 2, effective September 1, 2003; am. Acts 2005, 79th Leg., ch. 177 (H.B. 413), §§ 1, 2, effective September 1, 2005; am. Acts 2005, 79th Leg., ch. 728 (H.B. 2018), § 4.006, effective September 1, 2005; am. Acts 2005, 79th Leg., ch. 1309 (H.B. 3093), § 2, effective September 1, 2005; am. Acts 2007, 80th Leg., ch. 120 (S.B. 1106), § 1, effective September 1, 2007; am. Acts 2007, 80th Leg., ch. 1017 (H.B. 1303), §§ 1—4, effective September 1, 2007; am. Acts 2011, 82nd Leg., ch. 91 (S.B. 1303), § 6.002, effective September 1, 2011; am. Acts 2011, 82nd Leg., ch. 278 (H.B. 1573), §§ 3, 4, effective September 1, 2011; am. Acts 2011, 82nd Leg., ch. 690 (H.B. 351), §§ 2, 3, 4, 5, 6, effective September 1, 2011; am. Acts 2011, 82nd Leg., ch. 894 (S.B. 462), § 2, effective September 1, 2011.)

## Art. 55.03. Effect of Expunction.

When the order of expunction is final:

(1) the release, maintenance, dissemination, or use of the expunged records and files for any purpose is prohibited;

(2) except as provided in Subdivision (3) of this article, the person arrested may deny the occurrence of the arrest and the existence of the expunction order; and

(3) the person arrested or any other person, when questioned under oath in a criminal proceeding about an arrest for which the records have been expunged, may state only that the matter in question has been expunged.

(Enacted by Acts 1977, 65th Leg., ch. 747 (S.B. 471), § 1, effective August 29, 1977; am. Acts 1979, 66th Leg., ch. 604 (S.B. 374), § 1, effective August 27, 1979; am. Acts 1999, 76th Leg., ch. 1236 (S.B. 840), § 3, effective August 30, 1999; am. Acts 2001, 77th Leg., ch. 1021 (H.B. 1323), § 3, effective September 1, 2001; am. Acts 2003, 78th Leg., ch. 1236 (S.B. 1477), § 3, effective September 1, 2003; am. Acts 2005, 79th Leg., ch. 790 (S.B. 166), § 1, effective June 17, 2005; am. Acts 2005, 79th Leg., ch. 919 (H.B. 269), § 1, effective June 18, 2005.)

## Art. 55.04. Violation of Expunction Order.

**Sec. 1.** A person who acquires knowledge of an arrest while an officer or employee of the state or of any agency or other entity of the state or any political subdivision of the state and who knows of an order expunging the records and files relating to that arrest commits an offense if he knowingly releases, disseminates, or otherwise uses the records or files.

**Sec. 2.** A person who knowingly fails to return or to obliterate identifying portions of a record or file ordered expunged under this chapter commits an offense.

**Sec. 3.** An offense under this article is a Class B misdemeanor.

(Enacted by Acts 1977, 65th Leg., ch. 747 (S.B. 471), § 1, effective August 29, 1977; am. Acts 1979, 66th Leg., ch. 604 (S.B. 374), § 1, effective August 27, 1979.)

## Art. 55.05. Notice of Right to Expunction.

On release or discharge of an arrested person, the person responsible for the release or discharge shall give him a written explanation of his rights under this chapter and a copy of the provisions of this chapter.

(Enacted by Acts 1977, 65th Leg., ch. 747 (S.B. 471), § 1, effective August 29, 1977; am. Acts 1979, 66th Leg., ch. 604 (S.B. 374), § 1, effective August 27, 1979.)

## Art. 55.06. License Suspensions and Revocations.

Records relating to the suspension or revocation of a driver's license, permit, or privilege to operate a motor vehicle may not be expunged under this chapter except as provided in Section 524.015, Transportation Code, or Section 724.048 of that code.

(Enacted by Acts 1993, 73rd Leg., ch. 886 (S.B. 1), § 16, effective January 1, 1995; am. Acts 1999, 76th Leg., ch. 62 (S.B. 1368), § 3.08, effective September 1, 1999; am. Acts 1999, 76th Leg., ch. 1236 (S.B. 840), § 4, effective August 30, 1999.)

## CHAPTER 56
## RIGHTS OF CRIME VICTIMS

### Subchapter A. Crime Victims' Rights

### Subchapter B. Crime Victims' Compensation

### Subchapter C. Address Confidentiality Program for Victims of Family Violence, Sexual Assault, or Stalking

## SUBCHAPTER A
## CRIME VICTIMS' RIGHTS

### Art. 56.01. Definitions.

In this chapter:

(1) "Close relative of a deceased victim" means a person who was the spouse of a deceased victim at the time of the victim's death or who is a parent or adult brother, sister, or child of the deceased victim.

(2) "Guardian of a victim" means a person who is the legal guardian of the victim, whether or not the legal relationship between the guardian and victim exists because of the age of the victim or the physical or mental incompetency of the victim.

(2-a) "Sexual assault" includes an offense under Section 21.02, Penal Code.

(3) "Victim" means a person who is the victim of the offense of sexual assault, kidnapping, aggravated robbery, trafficking of persons, or injury to a child, elderly individual, or disabled individual or who has suffered personal injury or death as a result of the criminal conduct of another.

(Enacted by Acts 1985, 69th Leg., ch. 588 (H.B. 235), § 1, effective September 1, 1985; am. Acts 2005, 79th Leg., ch. 66 (H.B. 1489), § 1, effective September 1, 2005; am. Acts 2005, 79th Leg., ch. 268 (S.B. 6), § 1.126, effective September 1, 2005; am. Acts 2007, 80th Leg., ch. 593 (H.B. 8), § 3.20, effective September 1, 2007; am. Acts 2009, 81st Leg., ch. 372 (H.B. 1372), § 1, effective June 19, 2009.)

## Art. 56.02. Crime Victims' Rights.

(a) A victim, guardian of a victim, or close relative of a deceased victim is entitled to the following rights within the criminal justice system:

(1) the right to receive from law enforcement agencies adequate protection from harm and threats of harm arising from cooperation with prosecution efforts;

(2) the right to have the magistrate take the safety of the victim or his family into consideration as an element in fixing the amount of bail for the accused;

(3) the right, if requested, to be informed:

(A) by the attorney representing the state of relevant court proceedings, including appellate proceedings, and to be informed if those proceedings have been canceled or rescheduled prior to the event; and

(B) by an appellate court of decisions of the court, after the decisions are entered but before the decisions are made public;

(4) the right to be informed, when requested, by a peace officer concerning the defendant's right to bail and the procedures in criminal investigations and by the district attorney's office concerning the general procedures in the criminal justice system, including general procedures in guilty plea negotiations and ar-

rangements, restitution, and the appeals and parole process;

(5) the right to provide pertinent information to a probation department conducting a presentencing investigation concerning the impact of the offense on the victim and his family by testimony, written statement, or any other manner prior to any sentencing of the offender;

(6) the right to receive information regarding compensation to victims of crime as provided by Subchapter B, including information related to the costs that may be compensated under that subchapter and the amount of compensation, eligibility for compensation, and procedures for application for compensation under that subchapter, the payment for a medical examination under Article 56.06 for a victim of a sexual assault, and when requested, to referral to available social service agencies that may offer additional assistance;

(7) the right to be informed, upon request, of parole procedures, to participate in the parole process, to be notified, if requested, of parole proceedings concerning a defendant in the victim's case, to provide to the Board of Pardons and Paroles for inclusion in the defendant's file information to be considered by the board prior to the parole of any defendant convicted of any crime subject to this subchapter, and to be notified, if requested, of the defendant's release;

(8) the right to be provided with a waiting area, separate or secure from other witnesses, including the offender and relatives of the offender, before testifying in any proceeding concerning the offender; if a separate waiting area is not available, other safeguards should be taken to minimize the victim's contact with the offender and the offender's relatives and witnesses, before and during court proceedings;

(9) the right to prompt return of any property of the victim that is held by a law enforcement agency or the attorney for the state as evidence when the property is no longer required for that purpose;

(10) the right to have the attorney for the state notify the employer of the victim, if requested, of the necessity of the victim's cooperation and testimony in a proceeding that may necessitate the absence of the victim from work for good cause;

(11) the right to counseling, on request, regarding acquired immune deficiency syndrome (AIDS) and human immunodeficiency virus (HIV) infection and testing for acquired im-

Criminal Procedure

mune deficiency syndrome (AIDS), human immunodeficiency virus (HIV) infection, antibodies to HIV, or infection with any other probable causative agent of AIDS, if the offense is an offense under Section 21.02, 21.11(a)(1), 22.011, or 22.021, Penal Code;

(12) the right to request victim-offender mediation coordinated by the victim services division of the Texas Department of Criminal Justice;

(13) the right to be informed of the uses of a victim impact statement and the statement's purpose in the criminal justice system, to complete the victim impact statement, and to have the victim impact statement considered:

(A) by the attorney representing the state and the judge before sentencing or before a plea bargain agreement is accepted; and

(B) by the Board of Pardons and Paroles before an inmate is released on parole;

(14) to the extent provided by Articles 56.06 and 56.065, for a victim of a sexual assault, the right to a forensic medical examination if, within 96 hours of the sexual assault, the assault is reported to a law enforcement agency or a forensic medical examination is otherwise conducted at a health care facility; and

(15) for a victim of an assault or sexual assault who is younger than 17 years of age or whose case involves family violence, as defined by Section 71.004, Family Code, the right to have the court consider the impact on the victim of a continuance requested by the defendant; if requested by the attorney representing the state or by counsel for the defendant, the court shall state on the record the reason for granting or denying the continuance.

(b) A victim, guardian of a victim, or close relative of a deceased victim is entitled to the right to be present at all public court proceedings related to the offense, subject to the approval of the judge in the case.

(c) The office of the attorney representing the state, and the sheriff, police, and other law enforcement agencies shall ensure to the extent practicable that a victim, guardian of a victim, or close relative of a deceased victim is afforded the rights granted by Subsection (a) of this article and, on request, an explanation of those rights.

(d) A judge, attorney for the state, peace officer, or law enforcement agency is not liable for a failure or inability to provide a right enumerated in this article. The failure or inability of any person to provide a right or service enumerated in this article may not be used by a defendant in a criminal case as a ground for appeal, a ground to set aside the conviction or sentence, or a ground in a habeas corpus petition. A victim, guardian of a victim, or close relative of a deceased victim does not have standing to participate as a party in a criminal proceeding or to contest the disposition of any charge.

(Enacted by Acts 1985, 69th Leg., ch. 588 (H.B. 235), § 1, effective September 1, 1985; am. Acts 1987, 70th Leg., ch. 433 (S.B. 1300), § 1, effective August 31, 1987; am. Acts 1987, 70th Leg., ch. 929 (H.B. 1552), § 1, effective September 1, 1987; am. Acts 1989, 71st Leg., ch. 996 (H.B. 828), § 1, effective September 1, 1989; am. Acts 1991, 72nd Leg., ch. 202 (S.B. 1407), § 3, effective September 1, 1991; am. Acts 1993, 73rd Leg., ch. 811 (H.B. 2650), § 3, effective September 1, 1993; am. Acts 1995, 74th Leg., ch. 76 (S.B. 959), § 5.95(108), effective September 1, 1995; am. Acts 2001, 77th Leg., ch. 1034 (H.B. 1572), § 3, effective September 1, 2001; am. Acts 2005, 79th Leg., ch. 498 (H.B. 544), § 1, effective September 1, 2005; am. Acts 2007, 80th Leg., ch. 593 (H.B. 8), § 3.21, effective September 1, 2007; am. Acts 2009, 81st Leg., ch. 664 (H.B. 2236), § 1, effective September 1, 2009; am. Acts 2009, 81st Leg., ch. 1140 (H.B. 2626), § 1, effective June 19, 2009.)

## Art. 56.03. Victim Impact Statement.

(a) The Texas Crime Victim Clearinghouse, with the participation of the community justice assistance division of the Texas Department of Criminal Justice and the Board of Pardons and Paroles, shall develop a form to be used by law enforcement agencies, prosecutors, and other participants in the criminal justice system to record the impact of an offense on a victim of the offense, guardian of a victim, or a close relative of a deceased victim and to provide the agencies, prosecutors, and participants with information needed to contact the victim, guardian, or relative if needed at any stage of a prosecution of a person charged with the offense. The Texas Crime Victim Clearinghouse, with the participation of the community justice assistance division of the Texas Department of Criminal Justice and the Board of Pardons and Paroles, shall also develop a victims' information booklet that provides a general explanation of the criminal justice system to victims of an offense, guardians of victims, and relatives of deceased victims.

(b) The victim impact statement must be in a form designed to inform a victim, guardian of a victim, or a close relative of a deceased victim with a clear statement of rights provided by Article 56.02 and to collect the following information:

(1) the name of the victim of the offense or, if the victim has a legal guardian or is deceased, the name of a guardian or close relative of the victim;

(2) the address and telephone number of the victim, guardian, or relative through which the victim, guardian of a victim, or a close relative of a deceased victim, may be contacted;

(3) a statement of economic loss suffered by the victim, guardian, or relative as a result of the offense;

(4) a statement of any physical or psychological injury suffered by the victim, guardian, or relative as a result of the offense, as described by the victim, guardian, relative, or by a physician or counselor;

(5) a statement of any psychological services requested as a result of the offense;

(6) a statement of any change in the victim's, guardian's, or relative's personal welfare or familial relationship as a result of the offense;

(7) a statement as to whether or not the victim, guardian, or relative wishes to be notified in the future of any parole hearing for the defendant and an explanation as to the procedures by which the victim, guardian, or relative may obtain information concerning the release of the defendant from the Texas Department of Criminal Justice; and

(8) any other information, other than facts related to the commission of the offense, related to the impact of the offense on the victim, guardian, or relative.

(c) The victim assistance coordinator, designated in Article 56.04(a) of this code, shall send to a victim, guardian of a victim, or close relative of a deceased victim a victim impact statement, a victims' information booklet, and an application for compensation under Subchapter B, Chapter 56, along with an offer to assist in completing those forms on request. The victim assistance coordinator, on request, shall explain the possible use and consideration of the victim impact statement at sentencing and future parole hearing of the offender.

(d) If a victim, guardian of a victim, or close relative of a deceased victim states on the victim impact statement that he wishes to be notified of parole proceedings, the victim, guardian, or relative is responsible for notifying the Board of Pardons and Paroles of any change of address.

(e) Prior to the imposition of a sentence by the court in a criminal case, the court, if it has received a victim impact statement, shall consider the information provided in the statement. Before sentencing the defendant, the court shall permit the defendant or his counsel a reasonable time to read the statement, excluding the victim's name, address, and telephone number, comment on the statement, and, with the approval of the court, introduce testimony or other information alleging a factual inaccuracy in the statement. If the court sentences the defendant to a term of community supervision, the court shall forward any victim's impact statement received in the case to the community supervision and corrections department supervising the defendant, along with the papers in the case.

(f) The court may not inspect a victim impact statement until after a finding of guilt or until deferred adjudication is ordered and the contents of the statement may not be disclosed to any person unless:

(1) the defendant pleads guilty or nolo contendere or is convicted of the offense; or

(2) the defendant in writing authorizes the court to inspect the statement.

(g) A victim impact statement is subject to discovery under Article 39.14 of this code before the testimony of the victim is taken only if the court determines that the statement contains exculpatory material.

(h) Not later than December 1 of each odd-numbered year, the Texas Crime Victim Clearinghouse, with the participation of the community justice assistance division of the Texas Department of Criminal Justice and the Board of Pardons and Paroles, shall update the victim impact statement form and any other information provided by the commission to victims, guardians of victims, and relatives of deceased victims, if necessary, to reflect changes in law relating to criminal justice and the rights of victims and guardians and relatives of victims.

(i) In addition to the information described by Subsections (b)(1)—(8), the victim impact statement must be in a form designed to collect information on whether, if the victim is a child, there is an existing court order granting to the defendant possession of or access to the victim. If information collected under this subsection indicates the defendant is granted access or possession under court order and the defendant is subsequently confined by the Texas Department of Criminal Justice as a result of the commission of the offense, the victim services office of the department shall contact the court issuing the order before the defendant is released from the department on parole or mandatory supervision. (Enacted by Acts 1985, 69th Leg., ch. 588 (H.B. 235), § 1, effective September 1, 1985; am. Acts 1987, 70th Leg., ch. 433 (S.B. 1300), § 2, effective August 31, 1987; am. Acts 1987, 70th Leg., ch. 929 (H.B. 1552), §§ 2, 3, effective September 1, 1987; am. Acts 1989, 71st Leg., ch. 996 (H.B. 828), § 1, effective September 1, 1989; am. Acts 1995, 74th Leg., ch. 76 § 5.95(108), effective September 1, 1995; am. Acts 1997, 75th Leg., ch. 670 (H.B. 156), § 5, effective September 1, 1997; am. Acts 2001, 77th Leg., ch. 1034 (H.B. 1572), § 4, effective September 1, 2001; am. Acts 2009, 81st Leg., ch. 87 (S.B. 1969), § 25.038, effective September 1, 2009.)

## Art. 56.04. Victim Assistance Coordinator; Crime Victim Liaison.

(a) The district attorney, criminal district attorney, or county attorney who prosecutes criminal cases shall designate a person to serve as victim assistance coordinator in that jurisdiction.

(b) The duty of the victim assistance coordinator is to ensure that a victim, guardian of a victim, or close relative of a deceased victim is afforded the rights granted victims, guardians, and relatives by Article 56.02 of this code. The victim assistance coordinator shall work closely with appropriate law enforcement agencies, prosecuting attorneys, the Board of Pardons and Paroles, and the judiciary in carrying out that duty.

(c) Each local law enforcement agency shall designate one person to serve as the agency's crime victim liaison. Each agency shall consult with the victim assistance coordinator in the office of the attorney representing the state to determine the most effective manner in which the crime victim liaison can perform the duties imposed on the crime victim liaison under this article.

(d) The duty of the crime victim liaison is to ensure that a victim, guardian of a victim, or close relative of a deceased victim is afforded the rights granted victims, guardians, or close relatives of deceased victims by Subdivisions (4), (6), and (9) of Article 56.02(a) of this code.

(e) The victim assistance coordinator shall send a copy of a victim impact statement to the court sentencing the defendant. If the court sentences the defendant to imprisonment in the Texas Department of Criminal Justice, it shall attach the copy of the victim impact statement to the commitment papers.

(f) The commissioners court may approve a program in which the crime victim liaison or victim assistance coordinator may offer not more than 10 hours of posttrial psychological counseling for a person who serves as a juror or an alternate juror in a criminal trial involving graphic evidence or testimony and who requests the posttrial psychological counseling not later than the 180th day after the date on which the jury in the trial is dismissed. The crime victim liaison or victim assistance coordinator may provide the counseling using a provider that assists local criminal justice agencies in providing similar services to victims.

(Enacted by Acts 1985, 69th Leg., ch. 588 (H.B. 235), § 1, effective September 1, 1985; am. Acts 1989, 71st Leg., ch. 996 (H.B. 828), § 3, effective September 1, 1989; am. Acts 1991, 72nd Leg., ch. 202 (S.B. 1407), § 4, effective September 1, 1991; am. Acts 2007, 80th Leg., ch. 1378 (S.B. 560), § 6, effective September 1, 2007; am. Acts 2009, 81st Leg., ch. 87 (S.B. 1969), § 25.039, effective September 1, 2009; am. Acts 2009, 81st Leg., ch. 93 (H.B. 608), § 1, effective September 1, 2009.)

## Art. 56.045. Presence of Advocate or Representative During Forensic Medical Examination.

(a) Before conducting a forensic medical examination of a person who consents to such an examination for the collection of evidence for an alleged sexual assault, the physician or other medical services personnel conducting the examination shall offer the person the opportunity to have an advocate from a sexual assault program as defined by Section 420.003, Government Code, who has completed a sexual assault training program described by Section 420.011(b), Government Code, present with the person during the examination, if the advocate is available at the time of the examination.

(b) The advocate may only provide the injured person with:

(1) counseling and other support services; and

(2) information regarding the rights of crime victims under Article 56.02.

(c) Notwithstanding Subsection (a), the advocate and the sexual assault program providing the advocate may not delay or otherwise impede the screening or stabilization of an emergency medical condition.

(d) The sexual assault program providing the advocate shall pay all costs associated with providing the advocate.

(e) Any individual or entity, including a health care facility, that provides an advocate with access to a person consenting to an examination under Subsection (a) is not subject to civil or criminal liability for providing that access. In this subsection, "health care facility" includes a hospital licensed under Chapter 241, Health and Safety Code.

(f) If a person alleging to have sustained injuries as the victim of a sexual assault was confined in a penal institution, as defined by Section 1.07, Penal Code, at the time of the alleged assault, the penal institution shall provide, at the person's request, a representative to be present with the person at any forensic medical examination conducted for the purpose of collecting and preserving evidence related to the investigation or prosecution of the alleged assault. The representative may only provide the injured person with counseling and other support services and with information regarding the rights of crime victims under Article 56.02 and may not delay or otherwise impede the screening or stabilization of an emergency medical condition. The representative must be approved by the penal institution and must be a:

    (1) psychologist;

    (2) sociologist;

    (3) chaplain;

    (4) social worker;

    (5) case manager; or

    (6) volunteer who has completed a sexual assault training program described by Section 420.011(b), Government Code.

(Enacted by Acts 2001, 77th Leg., ch. 1019 (H.B. 1234), § 1, effective September 1, 2001.)

## Art. 56.05. Reports Required.

(a) The Board of Pardons and Paroles, the community justice assistance division of the Texas Department of Criminal Justice, and the Texas Crime Victim Clearinghouse, designated as the planning body for the purposes of this article, shall develop a survey plan to maintain statistics on the numbers and types of persons to whom state and local agencies provide victim impact statements during each year.

(b) At intervals specified in the plan, the planning body may require any state or local agency to submit, in a form prescribed for the reporting of the information, statistical data on the num-

bers and types of persons to whom the agency provides victim impact statements and any other information required by the planning body. The form must be designed to protect the privacy of persons afforded rights under this chapter and to determine whether the selected agency or office is making a good faith effort to protect the rights of the persons served.

(c) The Texas Crime Victim Clearinghouse shall develop crime victim assistance standards and distribute those standards to law enforcement officers and attorneys representing the state to aid those officers and prosecutors in performing duties imposed by this chapter.

(Enacted by Acts 1985, 69th Leg., ch. 588 (H.B. 235), § 1, effective September 1, 1985; am. Acts 1989, 71st Leg., ch. 996 (H.B. 828), § 4, effective September 1, 1989; am. Acts 2009, 81st Leg., ch. 87 (S.B. 1969), § 25.040, effective September 1, 2009.)

## Art. 56.06. Medical Examination for Sexual Assault Victim Who Has Reported Assault; Costs.

(a) If a sexual assault is reported to a law enforcement agency within 96 hours of the assault, the law enforcement agency, with the consent of the victim, a person authorized to act on behalf of the victim, or an employee of the Department of Family and Protective Services, shall request a medical examination of the victim of the alleged assault for use in the investigation or prosecution of the offense. A law enforcement agency may decline to request a medical examination under this subsection only if the person reporting the sexual assault has made one or more false reports of sexual assault to any law enforcement agency and if there is no other evidence to corroborate the current allegations of sexual assault.

(b) If a sexual assault is not reported within the period described by Subsection (a), on receiving the consent described by that subsection the law enforcement agency may request a medical examination of a victim of an alleged sexual assault as considered appropriate by the agency.

(c) A law enforcement agency that requests a medical examination of a victim of an alleged sexual assault for use in the investigation or prosecution of the offense shall pay all costs of the examination. On application to the attorney general, the law enforcement agency is entitled to be reimbursed for the reasonable costs of that examination if the examination was performed by a

Criminal Procedure

physician or by a sexual assault examiner or sexual assault nurse examiner, as defined by Section 420.003, Government Code.

(d) A law enforcement agency or prosecuting attorney's office may pay all costs related to the testimony of a licensed health care professional in a criminal proceeding regarding the results of the medical examination or manner in which it was performed.

(e) This article does not require a law enforcement agency to pay any costs of treatment for injuries.

(Enacted by Acts 1989, 71st Leg., ch. 2 (S. B. 221), § 5.05(a), effective August 28, 1989; am. Acts 1991, 72nd Leg., ch. 75 (H.B. 861), § 1, effective September 1, 1991; am. Acts 2001, 77th Leg., ch. 1507 (H.B. 131), § 1, effective June 15, 2001; am. Acts 2005, 79th Leg., ch. 498 (H.B. 544), § 2, effective September 1, 2005; am. Acts 2009, 81st Leg., ch. 1140 (H.B. 2626), § 2, effective June 19, 2009.)

## Art. 56.065. Medical Examination for Sexual Assault Victim Who Has Not Reported Assault; Costs.

(a) In this article:

(1) "Crime laboratory" has the meaning assigned by Article 38.35.

(2) "Department" means the Department of Public Safety.

(3) "Sexual assault examiner" and "sexual assault nurse examiner" have the meanings assigned by Section 420.003, Government Code.

(b) This article applies to the following health care facilities that provide diagnosis or treatment services to victims of sexual assault:

(1) a general or special hospital licensed under Chapter 241, Health and Safety Code;

(2) a general or special hospital owned by this state;

(3) an outpatient clinic; and

(4) a private physician's office.

(c) In accordance with Subchapter B, Chapter 420, Government Code, and except as provided by Subsection (e), a health care facility shall conduct a forensic medical examination of the victim of an alleged sexual assault if:

(1) the victim arrives at the facility within 96 hours after the assault occurred;

(2) the victim consents to the examination; and

(3) at the time of the examination the victim has not reported the assault to a law enforcement agency.

(d) The department shall pay the appropriate fees, as set by attorney general rule, for the forensic portion of the medical examination and for the evidence collection kit if a physician, sexual assault examiner, or sexual assault nurse examiner conducts the forensic portion of the examination within 96 hours after the alleged sexual assault occurred. The attorney general shall reimburse the department for fees paid under this subsection.

(e) If a health care facility does not provide diagnosis or treatment services to victims of sexual assault, the facility shall refer a victim seeking a forensic medical examination under Subsection (c) to a health care facility that provides services to those victims.

(f) The department, consistent with Chapter 420, Government Code, may develop procedures regarding the submission or collection of additional evidence of the alleged sexual assault other than through an examination as described by this article.

(g) The department, consistent with Chapter 420, Government Code, shall develop procedures for the transfer and preservation of evidence collected under this article to a crime laboratory or other suitable location designated by the public safety director of the department. The receiving entity shall preserve the evidence until the earlier of:

(1) the second anniversary of the date the evidence was collected; or

(2) the date on which written consent to release the evidence is obtained as provided by Section 420.0735, Government Code.

(h) The victim may not be required to:

(1) participate in the investigation or prosecution of an offense as a condition of receiving a forensic medical examination under this article; or

(2) pay for the forensic portion of the medical examination or for the evidence collection kit.

(i) The attorney general and the department each shall adopt rules as necessary to implement this article.

(j) A communication or record that contains identifying information regarding a person who receives a forensic medical examination under this article and that is created by, provided to, or in the control or possession of the department is confidential for purposes of Section 552.101, Government Code. In this subsection, "identifying information" includes:

(1) information revealing the identity, personal history, or background of the person; or

(2) information concerning the victimization of the person.

(Enacted by Acts 2009, 81st Leg., ch. 1140 (H.B. 2626), § 3, effective June 19, 2009; am. Acts 2011, 82nd Leg., ch. 826 (H.B. 2966), § 1, effective June 17, 2011; am. Acts 2011, 82nd Leg., ch. 1105 (S.B. 1636), § 12, effective September 1, 2011.)

## Art. 56.07. Notification.

(a) At the initial contact or at the earliest possible time after the initial contact between the victim of a reported crime and the law enforcement agency having the responsibility for investigating that crime, that agency shall provide the victim a written notice containing:

(1) information about the availability of emergency and medical services, if applicable;

(2) notice that the victim has the right to receive information regarding compensation to victims of crime as provided by Subchapter B, Chapter 56, including information about:

(A) the costs that may be compensated under that Act and the amount of compensation, eligibility for compensation, and procedures for application for compensation under that Act;

(B) the payment for a medical examination for a victim of a sexual assault under Article 56.06 of this code; and

(C) referral to available social service agencies that may offer additional assistance;

(3) the name, address, and phone number of the law enforcement agency's victim assistance liaison;

(4) the address, phone number, and name of the crime victim assistance coordinator of the office of the attorney representing the state;

(5) the following statement:

"You may call the law enforcement agency's telephone number for the status of the case and information about victims' rights"; and

(6) the rights of crime victims under Article 56.02 of this code.

(b) At the same time a law enforcement agency provides notice under Subsection (a), the agency shall provide, if the agency possesses the relevant information, a referral to a sexual assault program as defined by Section 420.003, Government Code, and a written description of the services provided by that program. A sexual assault program may provide a written description of its services to a law enforcement agency.

(Enacted by Acts 1991, 72nd Leg., ch. 202 (S.B. 1407), § 5, effective September 1, 1991; am. Acts

1995, 74th Leg., ch. 76 (S.B. 959), § 5.95(108), effective September 1, 1995; am. Acts 2003, 78th Leg., ch. 788 (S.B. 51), § 1, effective June 20, 2003.)

## Art. 56.08. Notification of Rights by Attorney Representing the State.

(a) Not later than the 10th day after the date that an indictment or information is returned against a defendant for an offense, the attorney representing the state shall give to each victim of the offense a written notice containing:

(1) a brief general statement of each procedural stage in the processing of a criminal case, including bail, plea bargaining, parole restitution, and appeal;

(2) notification of the rights and procedures under this chapter;

(3) suggested steps the victim may take if the victim is subjected to threats or intimidation;

(4) notification of the right to receive information regarding compensation to victims of crime as provided by Subchapter B, including information about:

(A) the costs that may be compensated under Subchapter B, eligibility for compensation, and procedures for application for compensation under Subchapter B of this chapter;

(B) the payment for a medical examination for a victim of a sexual assault under Article 56.06; and

(C) referral to available social service agencies that may offer additional assistance;

(5) the name, address, and phone number of the local victim assistance coordinator;

(6) the case number and assigned court for the case;

(7) the right to file a victim impact statement with the office of the attorney representing the state and the Texas Department of Criminal Justice; and

(8) notification of the right of a victim, guardian of a victim, or close relative of a deceased victim, as defined by Section 508.117, Government Code, to appear in person before a member of the Board of Pardons and Paroles as provided by Section 508.153, Government Code.

(b) If requested by the victim, the attorney representing the state, as far as reasonably practical, shall give to the victim notice of any scheduled court proceedings, changes in that schedule, the filing of a request for continuance of a trial setting, and any plea agreements to be presented to the court.

(c) A victim who receives a notice under Subsection (a) and who chooses to receive other notice under law about the same case must keep the following persons informed of the victim's current address and phone number:

(1) the attorney representing the state; and

(2) the Texas Department of Criminal Justice if after sentencing the defendant is confined in the department.

(d) An attorney representing the state who receives information concerning a victim's current address and phone number shall immediately provide that information to the community supervision and corrections department supervising the defendant, if the defendant is placed on community supervision.

(e) The brief general statement describing the plea bargaining stage in a criminal trial required by Subsection (a)(1) shall include a statement that:

(1) the victim impact statement provided by the victim, guardian of a victim, or close relative of a deceased victim will be considered by the attorney representing the state in entering into the plea bargain agreement; and

(2) the judge before accepting the plea bargain is required under Section 26.13(e) to ask:

(A) whether a victim impact statement has been returned to the attorney; and

(B) if a statement has been returned, for a copy of the statement.

(Enacted by Acts 1991, 72nd Leg., ch. 202 (S.B. 1407), § 5, effective September 1, 1991; am. Acts 1995, 74th Leg., ch. 252 (S.B. 47), § 2, effective September 1, 1995; am. Acts 1995, 74th Leg., ch. 253 (S.B. 48), § 2, effective September 1, 1995; am. Acts 1997, 75th Leg., ch. 165 (S.B. 898), § 12.04, effective September 1, 1997; am. Acts 2001, 77th Leg., ch. 1034 (H.B. 1572), § 5, effective September 1, 2001; am. Acts 2009, 81st Leg., ch. 87 (S.B. 1969), § 25.041, effective September 1, 2009.)

### Art. 56.09. Victim's Right to Privacy.

As far as reasonably practical, the address of the victim may not be a part of the court file except as necessary to identify the place of the crime. The phone number of the victim may not be a part of the court file.

(Enacted by Acts 1991, 72nd Leg., ch. 202 (S.B. 1407), § 5, effective September 1, 1991.)

### Art. 56.10. Victim's Discovery Attendance.

Unless absolutely necessary, victims or witnesses who are not incarcerated may not be required to attend depositions in a correctional facility.

(Enacted by Acts 1991, 72nd Leg., ch. 202 (S.B. 1407), § 5, effective September 1, 1991.)

### Art. 56.11. Notification to Victim or Witness of Release or Escape of Defendant.

(a) The Texas Department of Criminal Justice or the sheriff, whichever has custody of the defendant in the case of a felony, or the sheriff in the case of a misdemeanor, shall notify the victim of the offense or a witness who testified against the defendant at the trial for the offense, other than a witness who testified in the course and scope of the witness's official or professional duties, whenever a defendant convicted of an offense described by Subsection (c):

(1) completes the defendant's sentence and is released; or

(2) escapes from a correctional facility.

(a-1) The Texas Department of Criminal Justice, in the case of an inmate released on parole or to mandatory supervision following a term of imprisonment for an offense described by Subsection (c), or a community supervision and corrections department supervising a defendant, in the case of a defendant convicted of an offense described by Subsection (c) and subsequently released on community supervision, shall notify a victim or witness described by Subsection (a) whenever the inmate or defendant, if subject to electronic monitoring as a condition of release, ceases to be electronically monitored.

(b) If the Texas Department of Criminal Justice is required by Subsection (a) to give notice to a victim or witness, the department shall also give notice to local law enforcement officials in the county in which the victim or witness resides.

(c) This article applies to a defendant convicted of:

(1) an offense under Title 5, Penal Code, that is punishable as a felony;

(2) an offense described by Section 508.187(a), Government Code, other than an offense described by Subdivision (1); or

(3) an offense involving family violence, stalking, or violation of a protective order or magistrate's order.

(d) It is the responsibility of a victim or witness desiring notification of the defendant's release to provide the Texas Department of Criminal Justice, the sheriff, or the community supervision and corrections department supervising the defendant, as appropriate, with the e-mail address, mailing address, and telephone number of the victim, witness, or other person through whom the victim or witness may be contacted and to notify the appropriate department or the sheriff of any change of address or telephone number of the victim, witness, or other person. Information obtained and maintained by the Texas Department of Criminal Justice, a sheriff, or a community supervision and corrections department under this subsection is privileged and confidential.

(e) The Texas Department of Criminal Justice, the sheriff, or the community supervision and corrections department supervising the defendant, as appropriate:

(1) shall make a reasonable attempt to give any notice required by Subsection (a) or (a-1):

(A) not later than the 30th day before the date the defendant completes the sentence and is released or ceases to be electronically monitored as a condition of release; or

(B) immediately if the defendant escapes from the correctional facility; and

(2) may give any notice required by Subsection (a) or (a-1) by e-mail, if possible.

(f) An attempt by the Texas Department of Criminal Justice, the sheriff, or the community supervision and corrections department supervising the defendant to give notice to a victim or witness at the victim's or witness's last known mailing address or, if notice via e-mail is possible, last known e-mail address, as shown on the records of the appropriate department or agency, constitutes a reasonable attempt to give notice under this article.

(g) Not later than immediately following the conviction of a defendant described by Subsection (c), the attorney who represented the state in the prosecution of the case shall notify in writing a victim or witness described by Subsection (a) of the victim's or witness's right to receive notice under this article.

(h) In this article:

(1) "Correctional facility" has the meaning assigned by Section 1.07, Penal Code.

(2) "Family violence" has the meaning assigned by Section 71.004, Family Code.

(Enacted by Acts 1993, 73rd Leg., ch. 10 (S.B. 25), § 6, effective March 19, 1993; am. Acts 1995, 74th Leg., ch. 657 (S.B. 126), § 6, effective June 14, 1995; am. Acts 1997, 75th Leg., ch. 1 (S.B. 97), § 8, effective January 28, 1997; am. Acts 1997, 75th Leg., ch. 670 (H.B. 156), § 6, effective September 1, 1997; am. Acts 2001, 77th Leg., ch. 978 (H.B. 223), § 3, effective September 1, 2001; am. Acts 2003, 78th Leg., ch. 1276 (H.B. 3507), § 7.002(k), effective September 1, 2003; am. Acts 2007, 80th Leg., ch. 458 (H.B. 963), § 1, effective September 1, 2007; am. Acts 2009, 81st Leg., ch. 618 (H.B. 1003), § 1, effective September 1, 2009.)

## Art. 56.12. Notification of Escape or Transfer.

(a) The Texas Department of Criminal Justice shall immediately notify the victim of an offense, the victim's guardian, or the victim's close relative, if the victim is deceased, if the victim, victim's guardian, or victim's close relative has notified the department as provided by Subsection (b), whenever the defendant:

(1) escapes from a facility operated by the department for the imprisonment of individuals convicted of felonies other than state jail felonies; or

(2) is transferred from the custody of a facility operated by the department for the imprisonment of individuals convicted of felonies other than state jail felonies to the custody of a peace officer under a writ of attachment or a bench warrant.

(a-1) The Texas Department of Criminal Justice shall immediately notify a witness who testified against a defendant at the trial for the offense for which the defendant is incarcerated, the witness's guardian, or the witness's close relative, if the witness is deceased, if the witness, witness's guardian, or witness's close relative has notified the department as provided by Subsection (b), whenever the defendant:

(1) escapes from a facility operated by the department for the imprisonment of individuals convicted of felonies other than state jail felonies; or

(2) is transferred from the custody of a facility operated by the department for the imprisonment of individuals convicted of felonies other than state jail felonies to the custody of a peace officer under a writ of attachment or a bench warrant.

(b) It is the responsibility of the victim, witness, guardian, or close relative desiring notification of a defendant's escape or transfer from custody under a writ of attachment or bench warrant to notify the Texas Department of Criminal Justice of the desire for notification and any change of address.

(c) In providing notice under Subsection (a)(2) or (a-1)(2), the department shall include the name, address, and telephone number of the peace officer receiving the defendant into custody. On returning the defendant to the custody of the department, the victim services division of the department shall notify the victim, witness, guardian, or close relative, as applicable, of that fact.

(d) In this article, "witness's close relative" means a person who was the spouse of the deceased witness at the time of the witness's death or who is a parent or adult brother, sister, or child of the deceased witness.

(Enacted by Acts 1995, 74th Leg., ch. 251 (S.B. 46), § 1, effective May 29, 1995; am. Acts 2001, 77th Leg., ch. 1034 (H.B. 1572), § 6, effective September 1, 2001; am. Acts 2007, 80th Leg., ch. 458 (H.B. 963), § 2, effective September 1, 2007; am. Acts 2009, 81st Leg., ch. 87 (S.B. 1969), § 25.042, effective September 1, 2009.)

### Art. 56.13.  Victim-Offender Mediation.

The victim services division of the Texas Department of Criminal Justice shall:

(1) train volunteers to act as mediators between victims, guardians of victims, and close relatives of deceased victims and offenders whose criminal conduct caused bodily injury or death to victims; and

(2) provide mediation services through referral of a trained volunteer, if requested by a victim, guardian of a victim, or close relative of a deceased victim.

(Enacted by Acts 2001, 77th Leg., ch. 1034 (H.B. 1572), § 7, effective September 1, 2001.)

### Art. 56.14.  Clearinghouse Annual Conference.

(a) The Texas Crime Victim Clearinghouse may conduct an annual conference to provide to participants in the criminal justice system training containing information on crime victims' rights.

(b) The clearinghouse may charge fees to persons attending the conference described by Subsection (a).

(Enacted by Acts 2001, 77th Leg., ch. 1034 (H.B. 1572), § 7, effective September 1, 2001.)

### Art. 56.15.  Computerized Database; Defendant Release Information.

The Texas Department of Criminal Justice shall:

(1) create and maintain a computerized database containing the release information and release date of a defendant described by Article 56.11(c); and

(2) allow a victim or witness entitled to notice under Article 56.11 or 56.12 to access via the Internet the computerized database maintained under Subdivision (1).

(Enacted by Acts 2007, 80th Leg., ch. 458 (H.B. 963), § 3, effective September 1, 2007.)

## SUBCHAPTER B
## CRIME VICTIMS' COMPENSATION

### Art. 56.31.  Short Title.

This subchapter may be cited as the Crime Victims' Compensation Act.

(Enacted by Acts 1993, 73rd Leg., ch. 268 (S.B. 248), § 6, effective September 1, 1993; am. Acts 1995, 74th Leg., ch. 76 (S.B. 959), § 5.84(a), effective September 1, 1995; am. Acts 1995, 74th Leg., ch. 779 (S.B. 1049), § 1, effective September 1, 1995.)

### Art. 56.311.  Legislative Findings and Intent.

The legislature recognizes that many innocent individuals suffer personal injury or death as a result of criminal acts. Crime victims and persons who intervene to prevent criminal acts often suffer disabilities, incur financial burdens, or become dependent on public assistance. The legislature finds that there is a need for the compensation of victims of crime and those who suffer personal injury or death in the prevention of crime or in the apprehension of criminals. It is the legislature's intent that the compensation of innocent victims of violent crime encourage greater public cooperation in the successful apprehension and prosecution of criminals.

(Enacted by Acts 1995, 74th Leg., ch. 779 (S.B. 1049), § 1, effective September 1, 1995.)

### Art. 56.32.  Definitions.

(a) In this subchapter:

(1) "Child" means an individual younger than 18 years of age who:

(A) is not married; or

(B) has not had the disabilities of minority removed for general purposes under Chapter 31, Family Code.

(2) "Claimant" means, except as provided by Subsection (b), any of the following individuals

who is entitled to file or has filed a claim for compensation under this subchapter:

(A) an authorized individual acting on behalf of a victim;

(B) an individual who legally assumes the obligation or who voluntarily pays medical or burial expenses of a victim incurred as a result of the criminally injurious conduct of another;

(C) a dependent of a victim who died as a result of criminally injurious conduct;

(D) an immediate family member or household member of a victim who:

(i) requires psychiatric care or counseling as a result of the criminally injurious conduct; or

(ii) as a result of the criminally injurious conduct, incurs with respect to a deceased victim expenses for traveling to and attending the victim's funeral or suffers wage loss from bereavement leave taken in connection with the death of that victim; or

(E) an authorized individual acting on behalf of an individual who is described by Subdivision (C) or (D) and who is a child.

(3) "Collateral source" means any of the following sources of benefits or advantages for pecuniary loss that a claimant or victim has received or that is readily available to the claimant or victim from:

(A) the offender under an order of restitution to the claimant or victim imposed by a court as a condition of community supervision;

(B) the United States, a federal agency, a state or any of its political subdivisions, or an instrumentality of two or more states, unless the law providing for the benefits or advantages makes them in excess of or secondary to benefits under this subchapter;

(C) social security, Medicare, or Medicaid;

(D) another state's or another country's crime victims' compensation program;

(E) workers' compensation;

(F) an employer's wage continuation program, not including vacation and sick leave benefits;

(G) proceeds of an insurance contract payable to or on behalf of the claimant or victim for loss that the claimant or victim sustained because of the criminally injurious conduct;

(H) a contract or self-funded program providing hospital and other health care services or benefits; or

(I) proceeds awarded to the claimant or victim as a result of third-party litigation.

(4) "Criminally injurious conduct" means conduct that:

(A) occurs or is attempted;

(B) poses a substantial threat of personal injury or death;

(C) is punishable by fine, imprisonment, or death, or would be punishable by fine, imprisonment, or death if the person engaging in the conduct possessed capacity to commit the conduct; and

(D) does not arise out of the ownership, maintenance, or use of a motor vehicle, aircraft, or water vehicle, unless the conduct is intended to cause personal injury or death or the conduct is in violation of Section 545.157 or 545.401, Transportation Code, and results in bodily injury or death, or is in violation of Section 550.021, Transportation Code, or one or more of the following sections of the Penal Code:

(i) Section 19.04 (manslaughter);

(ii) Section 19.05 (criminally negligent homicide);

(iii) Section 22.02 (aggravated assault);

(iv) Section 22.05 (deadly conduct);

(v) Section 49.04 (driving while intoxicated);

(vi) Section 49.05 (flying while intoxicated);

(vii) Section 49.06 (boating while intoxicated);

(viii) Section 49.07 (intoxication assault); or

(ix) Section 49.08 (intoxication manslaughter).

(5) "Dependent" means:

(A) a surviving spouse;

(B) a person who is a dependent, within the meaning of the Internal Revenue Code, of a victim; and

(C) a posthumous child of a deceased victim.

(6) "Household member" means an individual who resided in the same permanent household as the victim at the time that the criminally injurious conduct occurred and who is related by consanguinity or affinity to the victim.

(7) "Immediate family member" means an individual who is related to a victim within the second degree by affinity or consanguinity.

(8) "Intervenor" means an individual who goes to the aid of another and is killed or

injured in the good faith effort to prevent criminally injurious conduct, to apprehend a person reasonably suspected of having engaged in criminally injurious conduct, or to aid a peace officer.

(9) "Pecuniary loss" means the amount of expense reasonably and necessarily incurred as a result of personal injury or death for:

(A) medical, hospital, nursing, or psychiatric care or counseling, or physical therapy;

(B) actual loss of past earnings and anticipated loss of future earnings and necessary travel expenses because of:

(i) a disability resulting from the personal injury;

(ii) the receipt of medically indicated services related to the disability resulting from the personal injury; or

(iii) participation in or attendance at investigative, prosecutorial, or judicial processes related to the criminally injurious conduct and participation in or attendance at any postconviction or postadjudication proceeding relating to criminally injurious conduct;

(C) care of a child or dependent;

(D) funeral and burial expenses, including, for an immediate family member or household member of the victim, the necessary expenses of traveling to and attending the funeral;

(E) loss of support to a dependent, consistent with Article 56.41(b)(5);

(F) reasonable and necessary costs of cleaning the crime scene;

(G) reasonable replacement costs for clothing, bedding, or property of the victim seized as evidence or rendered unusable as a result of the criminal investigation;

(H) reasonable and necessary costs, as provided by Article 56.42(d), incurred by a victim of family violence or a victim of sexual assault who is assaulted in the victim's place of residence for relocation and housing rental assistance payments;

(I) for an immediate family member or household member of a deceased victim, bereavement leave of not more than 10 work days; and

(J) reasonable and necessary costs of traveling to and from a place of execution for the purpose of witnessing the execution, including one night's lodging near the place at which the execution is conducted.

(10) "Personal injury" means physical or mental harm.

(11) "Victim" means, except as provided by Subsection (c):

(A) an individual who:

(i) suffers personal injury or death as a result of criminally injurious conduct or as a result of actions taken by the individual as an intervenor, if the conduct or actions occurred in this state; and

(ii) is a resident of this state, another state of the United States, the District of Columbia, the Commonwealth of Puerto Rico, or a possession or territory of the United States;

(B) an individual who:

(i) suffers personal injury or death as a result of criminally injurious conduct or as a result of actions taken by the individual as an intervenor, if the conduct or actions occurred in a state or country that does not have a crime victims' compensation program that meets the requirements of Section 1403(b), Crime Victims Compensation Act of 1984 (42 U.S.C. Section 10602(b));

(ii) is a resident of this state; and

(iii) would be entitled to compensation under this subchapter if the criminally injurious conduct or actions had occurred in this state; or

(C) an individual who:

(i) suffers personal injury or death as a result of criminally injurious conduct caused by an act of international terrorism as defined by 18 U.S.C. Section 2331 committed outside of the United States; and

(ii) is a resident of this state.

(12) "Family violence" has the meaning assigned by Section 71.004(1), Family Code.

(13) "Victim-related services or assistance" means compensation, services, or assistance provided directly to a victim or claimant for the purpose of supporting or assisting the recovery of the victim or claimant from the consequences of criminally injurious conduct.

(b) In this subchapter "claimant" does not include a service provider.

(Enacted by Acts 1993, 73rd Leg., ch. 268 (S.B. 248), § 6, effective September 1, 1993; am. Acts 1993, 73rd Leg., ch. 805 (H.B. 2178), §§ 3, 4, effective August 30, 1993; am. Acts 1995, 74th Leg., ch. 76 (S.B. 959), §§ 5.84(a), 9.55, 14.27, effective September 1, 1995; am. Acts 1995, 74th Leg., ch. 779 (S.B. 1049), § 1, effective September 1, 1995; am. Acts 1997, 75th Leg., ch. 1434 (H.B.

3062), § 1, effective September 1, 1997; am. Acts 1999, 76th Leg., ch. 1470 (H.B. 3255), § 1, effective June 19, 1999; am. Acts 2001, 77th Leg., ch. 11 (H.B. 519), §§ 1, 2, effective September 1, 2001; am. Acts 2003, 78th Leg., ch. 1286 (H.B. 1895), § 1, effective September 1, 2003; am. Acts 2003, 78th Leg., ch. 1303 (S.B. 1015), § 2, effective June 21, 2003; am. Acts 2005, 79th Leg., ch. 66 (H.B. 1489), § 2, effective September 1, 2005; am. Acts 2005, 79th Leg., ch. 728 (H.B. 2018), § 4.007, effective September 1, 2005; am. Acts 2007, 80th Leg., ch. 1374 (S.B. 157), § 1, effective September 1, 2007.)

## Art. 56.33. Administration; Rules.

(a) The attorney general shall adopt rules consistent with this subchapter governing its administration, including rules relating to the method of filing claims and the proof of entitlement to compensation and the review of health care services subject to compensation under this chapter. Subchapters A and B, Chapter 2001, Government Code, except Sections 2001.004(3) and 2001.005, apply to the attorney general.

(b) The attorney general may delegate a power, duty, or responsibility given to the attorney general under this subchapter to a person in the attorney general's office.

(Enacted by Acts 1993, 73rd Leg., ch. 268 (S.B. 248), § 6, effective September 1, 1993; am. Acts 1995, 74th Leg., ch. 76 (S.B. 959), § 5.84(a), effective September 1, 1995; am. Acts 1995, 74th Leg., ch. 779 (S.B. 1049), § 1, effective September 1, 1995.)

## Art. 56.34. Compensation.

(a) The attorney general shall award compensation for pecuniary loss arising from criminally injurious conduct if the attorney general is satisfied by a preponderance of the evidence that the requirements of this subchapter are met.

(b) The attorney general, shall establish whether, as a direct result of criminally injurious conduct, a claimant or victim suffered personal injury or death that resulted in a pecuniary loss for which the claimant or victim is not compensated from a collateral source.

(c) The attorney general shall award compensation for health care services according to the medical fee guidelines prescribed by Subtitle A, Title 5, Labor Code.

(d) The attorney general, a claimant, or a victim is not liable for health care service charges in excess of the medical fee guidelines. A health care provider shall accept compensation from the attorney general as payment in full for the charges unless an investigation of the charges by the attorney general determines that there is a reasonable health care justification for the deviation from the guidelines.

(e) A claimant or victim is not liable for the balance of service charges left as a result of an adjustment of payment for the charges under Article 56.58.

(f) The compensation to victims of crime fund and the compensation to victims of crime auxiliary fund are the payers of last resort.

(Enacted by Acts 1993, 73rd Leg., ch. 268 (S.B. 248), § 6, effective September 1, 1993; am. Acts 1995, 74th Leg., ch. 76 (S.B. 959), § 5.84(a), effective September 1, 1995; am. Acts 1995, 74th Leg., ch. 779 (S.B. 1049), § 1, effective September 1, 1995; am. Acts 1997, 75th Leg., ch. 1434 (H.B. 3062), § 1, effective September 1, 1997.)

## Art. 56.35. Types of Assistance.

If the attorney general approves an application for compensation under Article 56.41, the attorney general shall determine what type of state assistance will best aid the claimant or victim. The attorney general may do one or more of the following:

(1) authorize cash payment or payments to or on behalf of a claimant or victim for pecuniary loss;

(2) refer a claimant or victim to a state agency for vocational or other rehabilitative services; or

(3) provide counseling services for a claimant or victim or contract with a private entity to provide counseling services.

(Enacted by Acts 1993, 73rd Leg., ch. 268 (S.B. 248), § 6, effective September 1, 1993; am. Acts 1995, 74th Leg., ch. 76 (S.B. 959), 5.84(a), effective September 1, 1995; am. Acts 1995, 74th Leg., ch. 779 (S.B. 1049), § 1, effective September 1, 1995.)

## Art. 56.36. Application.

(a) An applicant for compensation under this subchapter must apply in writing on a form prescribed by the attorney general.

(b) An application must be verified and must contain:

(1) the date on which the criminally injurious conduct occurred;

(2) a description of the nature and circumstances of the criminally injurious conduct;

(3) a complete financial statement, including:

(A) the cost of medical care or burial expenses and the loss of wages or support the claimant or victim has incurred or will incur; and

(B) the extent to which the claimant or victim has been indemnified for those expenses from a collateral source;

(4) if appropriate, a statement indicating the extent of a disability resulting from the injury incurred;

(5) an authorization permitting the attorney general to verify the contents of the application; and

(6) other information the attorney general requires.

(Enacted by Acts 1993, 73rd Leg., ch. 268 (S.B. 248), § 6, effective September 1, 1993; am. Acts 1995, 74th Leg., ch. 76 (S.B. 959), § 5.84(a), effective September 1, 1995; am. Acts 1995, 74th Leg., ch. 779 (S.B. 1049), § 1, effective September 1, 1995; am. Acts 1997, 75th Leg., ch. 1434 (H.B. 3062), § 1, effective September 1, 1997.)

### Art. 56.37. Time for Filing.

(a) Except as otherwise provided by this article, a claimant or victim must file an application not later than three years from the date of the criminally injurious conduct.

(b) The attorney general may extend the time for filing for good cause shown by the claimant or victim.

(c) If the victim is a child, the application must be filed within three years from the date the claimant or victim is made aware of the crime but not after the child is 21 years of age.

(d) If a claimant or victim presents medically documented evidence of a physical or mental incapacity that was incurred by the claimant or victim as a result of the criminally injurious conduct and that reasonably prevented the claimant or victim from filing the application within the limitations period under Subsection (a), the period of the incapacity is not included.

(e) For a claim that is based on criminally injurious conduct in violation of Chapter 19, Penal Code, the claimant must file an application not later than three years after the date the identity of the victim is established by a law enforcement agency.

(Enacted by Acts 1993, 73rd Leg., ch. 268 (S.B. 248), § 6, effective September 1, 1993; am. Acts 1993, 73rd Leg., ch. 805 (H.B. 2178), § 10, effective August 30, 1993; am. Acts 1995, 74th Leg., ch. 76 (S.B. 959), § 5.84(a), effective September 1, 1995; am. Acts 1995, 74th Leg., ch. 779 (S.B. 1049), § 1, effective September 1, 1995; am. Acts 1997, 75th Leg., ch. 1434 (H.B. 3062), § 1, effective September 1, 1997; am. Acts 2009, 81st Leg., ch. 496 (S.B. 808), § 1, effective September 1, 2009; am. Acts 2009, 81st Leg., ch. 716 (H.B. 2916), § 1, effective June 19, 2009.)

### Art. 56.38. Review; Verification.

(a) The attorney general shall appoint a clerk to review each application for compensation under Article 56.36 to ensure the application is complete. If an application is not complete, the clerk shall return it to the claimant or victim and give a brief statement showing the additional information required. Not later than the 30th day after receiving a returned application, a claimant or victim may:

(1) supply the additional information; or

(2) appeal the action to the attorney general, who shall review the application to determine whether it is complete.

(b) The attorney general may investigate an application.

(c) Incident to the attorney general's review, verification, and hearing duties under this subchapter, the attorney general may:

(1) subpoena witnesses and administer oaths to determine whether and the extent to which a claimant or victim qualifies for an award; and

(2) order a claimant or victim to submit to a mental or physical examination by a physician or psychologist or order an autopsy of a deceased victim as provided by Article 56.39, if the mental, physical, or emotional condition of a claimant or victim is material to a claim.

(d) On request by the attorney general and not later than the 14th business day after the date of the request, a law enforcement agency shall release to the attorney general all reports, including witness statements and criminal history record information, for the purpose of allowing the attorney general to determine whether a claimant or victim qualifies for an award and the extent of the qualification.

(Enacted by Acts 1993, 73rd Leg., ch. 268 (S.B. 248), § 6, effective September 1, 1993; am. Acts 1995, 74th Leg., ch. 76 (S.B. 959), § 5.84(a), effective September 1, 1995; am. Acts 1995, 74th Leg., ch. 779 (S.B. 1049), § 1, effective September 1, 1995.)

## Art. 56.385. Review of Health Care Services.

(a) The attorney general may review the actual or proposed health care services for which a claimant or victim seeks compensation in an application filed under Article 56.36.

(b) The attorney general may not compensate a claimant or victim for health care services that the attorney general determines are not medically necessary.

(c) The attorney general, a claimant, or a victim is not liable for a charge that is not medically necessary.

(Enacted by Acts 1995, 74th Leg., ch. 779 (S.B. 1049), § 1, effective September 1, 1995.)

## Art. 56.39. Mental or Physical Examination; Autopsy.

(a) An order for a mental or physical examination or an autopsy as provided by Article 56.38(c)(3) may be made for good cause shown on notice to the individual to be examined and to all persons who have appeared.

(b) An order shall:

(1) specify the time, place, manner, conditions, and scope of the examination or autopsy;

(2) specify the person by whom the examination or autopsy is to be made; and

(3) require the person making the examination or autopsy to file with the attorney general a detailed written report of the examination or autopsy.

(c) A report shall set out the findings of the person making the examination or autopsy, including:

(1) the results of any tests made; and

(2) diagnoses, prognoses, and other conclusions and reports of earlier examinations of the same conditions.

(d) On request of the individual examined, the attorney general shall furnish the individual with a copy of the report. If the victim is deceased, the attorney general on request shall furnish the claimant with a copy of the report.

(e) A physician or psychologist making an examination or autopsy under this article shall be compensated from funds appropriated for the administration of this subchapter.

(Enacted by Acts 1993, 73rd Leg., ch. 268 (S.B. 248), § 6, effective September 1, 1993; am. Acts 1995, 74th Leg., ch. 76 (S.B. 959), § 5.84(a), effective September 1, 1995; am. Acts 1995, 74th Leg., ch. 779 (S.B. 1049), § 1, effective September 1, 1995.)

## Art. 56.40. Hearings.

(a) The attorney general shall determine whether a hearing on an application for compensation under this subchapter is necessary.

(b) If the attorney general determines that a hearing is not necessary, the attorney general may approve the application in accordance with the provisions of Article 56.41.

(c) If the attorney general determines that a hearing is necessary or if the claimant or victim requests a hearing, the attorney general shall consider the application at a hearing at a time and place of the attorney general's choosing. The attorney general shall notify all interested persons not less than 10 days before the date of the hearing.

(d) At the hearing the attorney general shall:

(1) review the application for assistance and the report prepared under Article 56.39 and any other evidence obtained as a result of the attorney general's investigation; and

(2) receive other evidence that the attorney general finds necessary or desirable to evaluate the application properly.

(e) The attorney general may appoint hearing officers to conduct hearings or prehearing conferences under this subchapter.

(f) A hearing or prehearing conference is open to the public unless in a particular case the hearing officer or attorney general determines that the hearing or prehearing conference or a part of it should be held in private because a criminal suspect has not been apprehended or because it is in the interest of the claimant or victim.

(g) The attorney general may suspend the proceedings pending disposition of a criminal prosecution that has been commenced or is imminent, but may make an emergency award under Article 56.50.

(h) Subchapters C through H, Chapter 2001, Government Code, do not apply to the attorney general or the attorney general's orders and decisions.

(Enacted by Acts 1993, 73rd Leg., ch. 268 (S.B. 248), § 6, effective September 1, 1993; am. Acts 1995, 74th Leg., ch. 76 (S.B. 959), § 5.84(a), effective September 1, 1995; am. Acts 1995, 74th Leg., ch. 779 (S.B. 1049), § 1, effective September 1, 1995.)

## Art. 56.41. Approval of Claim.

(a) The attorney general shall approve an application for compensation under this subchapter if the attorney general finds by a preponderance of the evidence that grounds for compensation under this subchapter exist.

(b) The attorney general shall deny an application for compensation under this subchapter if:

(1) the criminally injurious conduct is not reported as provided by Article 56.46;

(2) the application is not made in the manner provided by Articles 56.36 and 56.37;

(3) the claimant or victim knowingly and willingly participated in the criminally injurious conduct;

(4) the claimant or victim is the offender or an accomplice of the offender;

(5) an award of compensation to the claimant or victim would benefit the offender or an accomplice of the offender;

(6) the claimant or victim was incarcerated in a penal institution, as defined by Section 1.07, Penal Code, at the time the offense was committed; or

(7) the claimant or victim knowingly or intentionally submits false or forged information to the attorney general.

(c) Except as provided by rules adopted by the attorney general to prevent the unjust enrichment of an offender, the attorney general may not deny an award otherwise payable to a claimant or victim because the claimant or victim:

(1) is an immediate family member of the offender; or

(2) resides in the same household as the offender.

(Enacted by Acts 1993, 73rd Leg., ch. 268 (S.B. 248), § 6, effective September 1, 1993; am. Acts 1995, 74th Leg., ch. 76 (S.B. 959), §§ 5.84(a), 14.28, effective September 1, 1995; am. Acts 1995, 74th Leg., ch. 779 (S.B. 1049), § 1, effective September 1, 1995; am. Acts 1997, 75th Leg., ch. 1434 (H.B. 3062), § 1, effective September 1, 1997; am. Acts 2005, 79th Leg., ch. 66 (H.B. 1489), § 3, effective September 1, 2005.)

## Art. 56.42. Limits on Compensation.

(a) Except as otherwise provided by this article, awards payable to a victim and all other claimants sustaining pecuniary loss because of injury or death of that victim may not exceed $50,000 in the aggregate.

(b) In addition to an award payable under Subsection (a), the attorney general may award an additional $75,000 for extraordinary pecuniary losses, if the personal injury to a victim is catastrophic and results in a total and permanent

disability to the victim, for lost wages and reasonable and necessary costs of:

(1) making a home or automobile accessible;

(2) obtaining job training and vocational rehabilitation;

(3) training in the use of special appliances;

(4) receiving home health care;

(5) durable medical equipment;

(6) rehabilitation technology; and

(7) long-term medical expenses incurred as a result of medically indicated treatment for the personal injury.

(c) The attorney general may by rule establish limitations on any other pecuniary loss compensated for under this subchapter, including limitations on pecuniary loss incurred as a result of a claimant's travel to and attendance of a deceased victim's funeral.

(d) A victim who is a victim of family violence or a victim of sexual assault who is assaulted in the victim's place of residence may receive a onetime-only assistance payment in an amount not to exceed:

(1) $2,000 to be used for relocation expenses, including expenses for rental deposit, utility connections, expenses relating to the moving of belongings, motor vehicle mileage expenses, and for out-of-state moves, transportation, lodging, and meals; and

(2) $1,800 to be used for housing rental expenses.

(e) An immediate family member or household member of a deceased victim may not receive more than $1,000 in lost wages as a result of bereavement leave taken by the family or household member.

(Enacted by Acts 1993, 73rd Leg., ch. 268 (S.B. 248), § 6, effective September 1, 1993; am. Acts 1995, 74th Leg., ch. 76 (S.B. 959), § 5.84(a), effective September 1, 1995; am. Acts 1995, 74th Leg., ch. 779 (S.B. 1049), § 1, effective September 1, 1995; am. Acts 1997, 75th Leg., ch. 1434 (H.B. 3062), § 1, effective September 1, 1997; am. Acts 1999, 76th Leg., ch. 1470 (H.B. 3255), § 2, effective June 19, 1999; am. Acts 2001, 77th Leg., ch. 11 (S.B. 519), § 3, effective September 1, 2001; am. Acts 2001, 77th Leg., ch. 274 (S.B. 1202), § 1, effective September 1, 2001; am. Acts 2003, 78th Leg., ch. 1286 (H.B. 1895), § 2, effective September 1, 2003.)

## Art. 56.43. Attorney Fees.

(a) As part of an order, the attorney general shall determine and award reasonable attorney's fees, commensurate with legal services rendered, to be paid by the state to the attorney representing the claimant or victim. Attorney fees shall not exceed 25 percent of the amount the attorney assisted the claimant or victim in obtaining. Where there is no dispute of the attorney general's determination of the amount of the award due to the claimant or victim and where no hearing is held, the attorney fee shall be the lesser of either 25 percent of the amount the attorney assisted the claimant or victim in obtaining or $300.

(b) Attorney fees may be denied on a finding that the claim or appeal is frivolous.

(c) An award of attorney fees is in addition to an award of compensation.

(d) An attorney may not contract for or receive an amount larger than that allowed under this article.

(e) Attorney fees may not be paid to an attorney of a claimant or victim unless an award is made to the claimant or victim.

(Enacted by Acts 1993, 73rd Leg., ch. 268 (S.B. 248), § 6, effective September 1, 1993; am. Acts 1993, 73rd Leg., ch. 805 (H.B. 2178), § 9, effective August 30, 1993; am. Acts 1995, 74th Leg., ch. 76 (S.B. 959), § 5.84(a), effective September 1, 1995; am. Acts 1995, 74th Leg., ch. 779 (S.B. 1049), § 1, effective September 1, 1995.)

## Art. 56.44. Payments.

(a) The attorney general may provide for the payment of an award in a lump sum or in installments. The attorney general shall provide that the part of an award equal to the amount of pecuniary loss accrued to the date of the award be paid in a lump sum. Except as provided in Subsection (b), the attorney general shall pay the part of an award for allowable expense that accrues after the award is made in installments.

(b) At the request of the claimant or victim, the attorney general may provide that an award for future pecuniary loss be paid in a lump sum if the attorney general finds that:

(1) paying the award in a lump sum will promote the interests of the claimant or victim; or

(2) the present value of all future pecuniary loss does not exceed $1,000.

(c) The attorney general may not provide for an award for future pecuniary loss payable in installments for a period for which the attorney general cannot reasonably determine the future pecuniary loss.

(d) The attorney general may make payments only to an individual who is a claimant or a victim or to a provider on the individual's behalf.

(Enacted by Acts 1993, 73rd Leg., ch. 268 (S.B. 248), § 6, effective September 1, 1993; am. Acts 1995, 74th Leg., ch. 76 (S.B. 959), § 5.84(a), effective September 1, 1995; am. Acts 1995, 74th Leg., ch. 779 (S.B. 1049), § 1, effective September 1, 1995; am. Acts 1997, 75th Leg., ch. 1434 (H.B. 3062), § 1, effective September 1, 1997.)

## Art. 56.45. Denial or Reduction of Award.

The attorney general may deny or reduce an award otherwise payable:

(1) if the claimant or victim has not substantially cooperated with an appropriate law enforcement agency;

(2) if the claimant or victim bears a share of the responsibility for the act or omission giving rise to the claim because of the claimant's or victim's behavior;

(3) to the extent that pecuniary loss is recouped from a collateral source; or

(4) if the claimant or victim was engaging in an activity that at the time of the criminally injurious conduct was prohibited by law or a rule made under law.

(Enacted by Acts 1993, 73rd Leg., ch. 268 (S.B. 248), § 6, effective September 1, 1993; am. Acts 1995, 74th Leg., ch. 76 (S.B. 959), § 5.84(a), effective September 1, 1995; am. Acts 1995, 74th Leg., ch. 779 (S.B. 1049), § 1, effective September 1, 1995; am. Acts 1997, 75th Leg., ch. 1434 (H.B. 3062), § 1, effective September 1, 1997.)

## Art. 56.46. Reporting of Crime.

(a) Except as otherwise provided by this article, a claimant or victim may not file an application unless the victim reports the criminally injurious conduct to the appropriate state or local public safety or law enforcement agency within a reasonable period of time, but not so late as to interfere with or hamper the investigation and prosecution of the crime after the criminally injurious conduct is committed.

(b) The attorney general may extend the time for reporting the criminally injurious conduct if the attorney general determines that the extension is justified by extraordinary circumstances.

(c) Subsection (a) does not apply if the victim is a child.

(Enacted by Acts 1993, 73rd Leg., ch. 268 (S.B. 248), § 6, effective September 1, 1993; am. Acts 1995, 74th Leg., ch. 76 (S.B. 959), § 5.84(a), effective September 1, 1995; am. Acts 1995, 74th Leg., ch. 779 (S.B. 1049), § 1, effective September

Criminal Procedure

1, 1995; am. Acts 1997, 75th Leg., ch. 1434 (H.B. 3062), § 1, effective September 1, 1997.)

### Art. 56.47. Reconsideration.

(a) The attorney general, on the attorney general's own motion or on request of a claimant or victim, may reconsider:

    (1) a decision to make or deny an award; or

    (2) the amount of an award.

(b) At least annually, the attorney general shall reconsider each award being paid in installments.

(c) An order on reconsideration may require a refund of an award if:

    (1) the award was obtained by fraud or mistake; or

    (2) newly discovered evidence shows the claimant or victim to be ineligible for the award under Article 56.41 or 56.45.

(Enacted by Acts 1993, 73rd Leg., ch. 268 § 6, effective September 1, 1993; am. Acts 1993, 73rd Leg., ch. 805 (H.B. 2178), § 6, effective August 30, 1993; am. Acts 1995, 74th Leg., ch. 76 (S.B. 959), §§ 5.84(a), 5.85(b), effective September 1, 1995; am. Acts 1995, 74th Leg., ch. 779 (S.B. 1049), § 1, effective September 1, 1995; am. Acts 1997, 75th Leg., ch. 1434 (H.B. 3062), § 1, effective September 1, 1997.)

### Art. 56.48. Judicial Review.

(a) Not later than the 40th day after the attorney general renders a final decision, a claimant or victim may file with the attorney general a notice of dissatisfaction with the decision. Not later than the 40th day after the claimant or victim gives notice, the claimant or victim shall bring suit in the district court having jurisdiction in the county in which:

    (1) the injury or death occurred;

    (2) the victim resided at the time the injury or death occurred; or

    (3) if the victim resided out of state at the time of the injury or death, in the county where the injury or death occurred or in a district court of Travis County.

(b) While judicial review of a decision by the attorney general is pending, the attorney general:

    (1) shall suspend payments to the claimant or victim; and

    (2) may not reconsider the award.

(c) The court shall determine the issues by trial de novo. The burden of proof is on the party who filed the notice of dissatisfaction.

(d) A court may award not more than 25 percent of the total recovery by the claimant or victim for attorney fees in the event of review.

(e) In computing a period under this article, if the last day is a legal holiday or Sunday, the last day is not counted, and the time is extended to include the next business day.

(Enacted by Acts 1993, 73rd Leg., ch. 268 (S.B. 248), § 6, effective September 1, 1993; am. Acts 1995, 74th Leg., ch. 76 (S.B. 959), § 5.84(a), effective September 1, 1995; am. Acts 1995, 74th Leg., ch. 779 (S.B. 1049), § 1, effective September 1, 1995; am. Acts 1997, 75th Leg., ch. 1434 (H.B. 3062), § 1, effective September 1, 1997.)

### Art. 56.49. Exemption; Assignability.

(a) An award is not subject to execution, attachment, garnishment, or other process, except that an award is not exempt from a claim of a creditor to the extent that the creditor provided products, services, or accommodations, the costs of which are included in the award.

(b) An assignment or agreement to assign a right to benefits for loss accruing in the future is unenforceable except:

    (1) an assignment of a right to benefits for loss of earnings is enforceable to secure payment of alimony, maintenance, or child support; and

    (2) an assignment of a right to benefits is enforceable to the extent that the benefits are for the cost of products, services, or accommodations:

        (A) made necessary by the injury or death on which the claim is based; and

        (B) provided or to be provided by the assignee.

(Enacted by Acts 1993, 73rd Leg., ch. 268 (S.B. 248), § 6, effective September 1, 1993; am. Acts 1995, 74th Leg., ch. 76 (S.B. 959), § 5.84(a), effective September 1, 1995; am. Acts 1995, 74th Leg., ch. 779 (S.B. 1049), § 1, effective September 1, 1995.)

### Art. 56.50. Emergency Award.

(a) The attorney general may make an emergency award if, before acting on an application for compensation under this subchapter, it appears likely that:

    (1) a final award will be made; and

    (2) the claimant or victim will suffer undue hardship if immediate economic relief is not obtained.

(b) An emergency award may not exceed $1,500.

(c) The amount of an emergency award shall be:

(1) deducted from the final award; or

(2) repaid by and recoverable from the claimant or victim to the extent the emergency award exceeds the final award.

(Enacted by Acts 1993, 73rd Leg., ch. 268 9S.B. 248), § 6, effective September 1, 1993; am. Acts 1995, 74th Leg., ch. 76 (S.B. 959), § 5.84(a), effective September 1, 1995; am. Acts 1995, 74th Leg., ch. 779 (S.B. 1049), § 1, effective September 1, 1995.)

## Art. 56.51. Subrogation.

If compensation is awarded under this subchapter, the state is subrogated to all the claimant's or victim's rights to receive or recover benefits for pecuniary loss to the extent compensation is awarded from a collateral source.

(Enacted by Acts 1993, 73rd Leg., ch. 268 (S.B. 248), § 6, effective September 1, 1993; am. Acts 1995, 74th Leg., ch. 76 (S.B. 959), § 5.84(a), effective September 1, 1995; am. Acts 1995, 74th Leg., ch. 779 (S.B. 1049), § 1, effective September 1, 1995.)

## Art. 56.52. Notice of Private Action.

(a) Before a claimant or victim may bring an action to recover damages related to criminally injurious conduct for which compensation under this subchapter is claimed or awarded, the claimant or victim must give the attorney general written notice of the proposed action. After receiving the notice, the attorney general shall promptly:

(1) join in the action as a party plaintiff to recover benefits awarded;

(2) require the claimant or victim to bring the action in the claimant's or victim's name as a trustee on behalf of the state to recover benefits awarded; or

(3) reserve the attorney general's rights and do neither in the proposed action.

(b) If the claimant or victim brings the action as trustee and recovers compensation awarded by the attorney general, the claimant or victim may deduct from the benefits recovered on behalf of the state the reasonable expenses of the suit, including attorney fees, expended in pursuing the recovery for the state. The claimant or victim must justify this deduction in writing to the attorney general on a form provided by the attorney general.

(c) A claimant or victim shall not settle or resolve any such action without written authorization to do so from the attorney general. No third party or agents, insurers, or attorneys for third parties shall participate in the settlement or resolution of such an action if they actually know, or should know, that the claimant or victim has received moneys from the fund and is subject to the subrogation provisions of this article. Any attempt by such third party, or agents, insurers, or attorneys of third parties to settle an action is void and shall result in no release from liability to the fund for any rights subrogated pursuant to this article. All such agents, insurers, and attorneys are personally liable to the fund for any moneys paid to a claimant or victim in violation of this subsection, up to the full amount of the fund's right to reimbursement. A claimant, victim, third party, or any agents, attorneys, or insurers of third parties who knowingly or intentionally fail to comply with the requirements of this chapter commits a Class B misdemeanor.

(d) A person adjudged guilty of a Class B misdemeanor shall be punished by:

(1) a fine not to exceed $500;

(2) confinement in jail for a term not to exceed 180 days; or

(3) both such fine and imprisonment.

(Enacted by Acts 1993, 73rd Leg., ch. 268 (S.B. 248), § 6, effective September 1, 1993; am. Acts 1993, 73rd Leg., ch. 805 (H.B. 2178), § 11, effective August 30, 1993; am. Acts 1995, 74th Leg., ch. 76 (S.B. 959), § 5.84(a), effective September 1, 1995; am. Acts 1995, 74th Leg., ch. 779 (S.B. 1049), § 1, effective September 1, 1995.)

## Art. 56.53. Annual Report.

Annually, the attorney general shall report to the governor and the legislature on the attorney general's activities, including a statistical summary of claims and awards made and denied. The reporting period is the state fiscal year. The attorney general shall file the report not later than the 100th day after the end of the fiscal year.

(Enacted by Acts 1993, 73rd Leg., ch. 268 (S.B. 248), § 6, effective September 1, 1993; am. Acts 1995, 74th Leg., ch. 76 (S.B. 959), § 5.84(a), effective September 1, 1995; am. Acts 1995, 74th Leg., ch. 779 (S.B. 1049), § 1, effective September 1, 1995.)

## Art. 56.54. Funds.

(a) The compensation to victims of crime fund and the compensation to victims of crime auxiliary fund are in the state treasury.

(b) Except as provided by Subsections (h), (i), (j), and (k) and Article 56.541, the compensation to victims of crime fund may be used only by the attorney general for the payment of compensation to claimants or victims under this subchapter. For purposes of this subsection, compensation to claimants or victims includes money allocated from the fund to the Crime Victims' Institute created by Section 96.65, Education Code, for the operation of the institute and for other expenses in administering this subchapter. The institute shall use money allocated from the fund only for the purposes of Sections 96.65, 96.651, and 96.652, Education Code.

(c) Except as provided by Subsections (h), (i), and (l), the compensation to victims of crime auxiliary fund may be used by the attorney general only for the payment of compensation to claimants or victims under this subchapter.

(d) The attorney general may not make compensation payments in excess of the amount of money available from the combined funds.

(e) General revenues may not be used for payments under this subchapter.

(f) The office of the attorney general is authorized to accept gifts, grants, and donations to be credited to the compensation to victims of crime fund and compensation to victims of crime auxiliary fund and shall file annually with the governor and the presiding officer of each house of the legislature a complete and detailed written report accounting for all gifts, grants, and donations received and disbursed, used, or maintained by the office for the attorney general that are credited to these funds.

(g) Money in the compensation to victims of crime fund or in the compensation to victims of crime auxiliary fund may be used only as provided by this subchapter and is not available for any other purpose. Section 403.095, Government Code, does not apply to the fund.

(h) An amount of money deposited to the credit of the compensation to victims of crime fund not to exceed one-quarter of the amount disbursed from that fund in the form of compensation payments during a fiscal year shall be carried forward into the next succeeding fiscal year and applied toward the amount listed in the next succeeding fiscal year's method of financing.

(i) If the sums available in the compensation to victims of crime fund are sufficient in a fiscal year to make all compensation payments, the attorney general may retain any portion of the fund that was deposited during the fiscal year that was in excess of compensation payments made during that fiscal year as an emergency reserve for the next fiscal year. Such emergency reserve may not

exceed $10,000,000. The emergency reserve fund may be used only to make compensation awards in claims and for providing emergency relief and assistance, including crisis intervention, emergency housing, travel, food, or expenses and technical assistance expenses incurred in the implementation of this subsection in incidents resulting from an act of mass violence or from an act of international terrorism as defined by 18 U.S.C. Section 2331, occurring in the state or for Texas residents injured or killed in an act of terrorism outside of the United States.

(j) The legislature may appropriate money in the compensation to victims of crime fund to administer the associate judge program under Subchapter C, Chapter 201, Family Code.

(k) The attorney general may use the compensation to victims of crime fund to reimburse a law enforcement agency for the reasonable costs of a medical examination that are incurred by the agency under Article 56.06.

(l) The attorney general may use the compensation to victims of crime auxiliary fund to cover costs incurred by the attorney general in administering the address confidentiality program established under Subchapter C.

(m) Not later than September 15 of each year, the attorney general, after consulting with the comptroller, shall certify the amount of money remaining in the compensation to victims of crime auxiliary fund at the end of the preceding state fiscal year. If the amount remaining in the fund exceeds $5 million, as soon as practicable after the date of certification, the attorney general may transfer from that excess amount in the compensation to victims of crime auxiliary fund to the compensation to victims of crime fund an amount that is not more than 50 percent of the excess amount in the auxiliary fund, to be used only for the purpose of making compensation payments during the fiscal year in which the amount is transferred.

(Enacted by Acts 1993, 73rd Leg., ch. 268 (S.B. 248), § 6, effective September 1, 1993; am. Acts 1993, 73rd Leg., ch. 805 (H.B. 2178), § 1, effective August 30, 1993; am. Acts 1995, 74th Leg., ch. 76 (S.B. 959), § 5.84(a), effective September 1, 1995; am. Acts 1995, 74th Leg., ch. 779 (S.B. 1049), § 1, effective September 1, 1995; am. Acts 1997, 75th Leg., ch. 1042 (S.B. 987), § 1, effective June 19, 1997; am. Acts 1997, 75th Leg., ch. 1042 (S.B. 987), § 2, effective September 1, 1997; am. Acts 1997, 75th Leg., ch. 1434 (H.B. 3062), § 1, effective September 1, 1997; am. Acts 1999, 76th Leg., ch. 1302 (S.B. 1735), § 13, effective September 1,

1999; am. Acts 2001, 77th Leg., ch. 1507 (H.B. 131), §§ 2, 3, effective June 15, 2001; am. Acts 2003, 78th Leg., ch. 927 (S.B. 1245), § 2, effective September 1, 2003; am. Acts 2007, 80th Leg., ch. 1295 (S.B. 74), § 2, effective June 15, 2007; am. Acts 2009, 81st Leg., ch. 532 (S.B. 1377), § 1, effective September 1, 2009.)

## Art. 56.541. Appropriation of Excess Money for Other Crime Victim Assistance.

(a) Not later than December 15 of each even-numbered year, the attorney general, after consulting with the comptroller, shall prepare forecasts and certify estimates of:

(1) the amount of money that the attorney general anticipates will be received from deposits made to the credit of the compensation to victims of crime fund during the next state fiscal biennium, other than deposits of:

(A) gifts, grants, and donations; and

(B) money received from the United States;

(2) the amount of money from the fund that the attorney general anticipates will be obligated during the next state fiscal biennium to comply with this chapter; and

(3) the amount of money in the fund that the attorney general anticipates will remain unexpended at the end of the current state fiscal year and that is available for appropriation in the next state fiscal biennium.

(b) At the time the attorney general certifies the estimates made under Subsection (a), the attorney general shall also certify for the next state fiscal biennium the amount of excess money in the compensation to victims of crime fund available for the purposes of Subsection (c), calculated by multiplying the amount estimated under Subsection (a)(2) by 105 percent, and subtracting that product from the sum of the amounts estimated under Subsections (a)(1) and (a)(3).

(c) For a state fiscal biennium, the legislature may appropriate from the compensation to victims of crime fund the amount of excess money in the fund certified for the biennium under Subsection (b) to state agencies that deliver or fund victim-related services or assistance.

(d) The attorney general and the comptroller shall cooperate in determining the proper allocation of the various sources of revenue deposited to the credit of the compensation to victims of crime fund for purposes of this article.

(e) The attorney general may use money appropriated from the compensation to victims of crime fund for grants or contracts supporting victim-related services or assistance, including support for private Texas nonprofit corporations that provide victim-related civil legal services directly to victims, immediate family members of victims, or claimants. A grant supporting victim-related services or assistance is governed by Chapter 783, Government Code.

(f) The attorney general shall adopt rules necessary to carry out this article.

(Enacted by Acts 1997, 75th Leg., ch. 1042 (S.B. 987), § 3, effective September 1, 1997; am. Acts 1999, 76th Leg., ch. 1077 (H.B. 3324), § 1, effective August 30, 1999; am. Acts 2005, 79th Leg., ch. 66 (H.B. 1489), § 3, effective September 1, 2005; am. Acts 2009, 81st Leg., ch. 532 (S.B. 1377), § 2, effective September 1, 2009.)

## Art. 56.542. Payments for Certain Disabled Peace Officers.

(a) In this article, "peace officer":

(1) means an individual elected, appointed, or employed to serve as a peace officer for a governmental entity under Article 2.12 or other law; and

(2) includes a former peace officer who because of an injury suffered while performing duties as a peace officer is entitled to receive payments under this article.

(b) If a peace officer employed by the state or a local governmental entity in this state sustains an injury as a result of criminally injurious conduct on or after September 1, 1989, in the performance of the officer's duties as a peace officer and presents evidence satisfactory to the attorney general that the officer's condition is a total disability resulting in permanent incapacity for work and that the total disability has persisted for more than 12 months, the officer is entitled to an annual payment equal to the difference between:

(1) any amounts received by the officer on account of the injury or disability from other sources of income, including settlements related to the injury or disability, insurance benefits, federal disability benefits, workers' compensation benefits, and benefits from another governmental entity, if those amounts do not exceed the amount described by Subdivision (2); and

(2) an amount equal to the officer's average annual salary during the officer's final three years as a peace officer.

(c) The amount of the payment under Subsection (b) is subject to an annual cost-of-living adjustment computed by the attorney general. The attorney general shall compute the amount of the cost-of-living adjustment by multiplying the amount of the annual payment received by the peace officer under this section during the previous year times the percentage by which the Consumer Price Index for All Urban Consumers published by the Bureau of Labor Statistics of the United States Department of Labor, or its successor index, increased during the previous calendar year.

(d) The attorney general shall compute the amount of an initial payment based on an injury suffered after September 1, 1989, by:

(1) computing the amount to which the officer is entitled under Subsection (b); and

(2) adding to that amount the cumulative successive cost-of-living adjustments for the intervening years computed from the date of the injury.

(e) To receive a payment under this section, a peace officer must furnish to the attorney general:

(1) proof that the injury was sustained in the performance of the applicant's duties as a peace officer and is a total disability resulting in permanent incapacity for work; and

(2) other information or evidence the attorney general requires.

(f) The attorney general may approve the application without a hearing or may conduct a hearing under Article 56.40. The decision of the attorney general is subject to judicial review under Article 56.48.

(g) The attorney general may appoint a panel of physicians to periodically review each application for assistance under this article to ensure the validity of the application and the necessity of continued assistance to the peace officer.

(h) The attorney general shall notify the comptroller of the attorney general's determination that a claim under this section is valid and justifies payment. On receipt of the notice, the comptroller shall issue a warrant to or in behalf of the claimant in the proper amount from amounts in the compensation to victims of crime fund. A payment under this section to or in behalf of a peace officer is payable as soon as possible after the attorney general notifies the comptroller.

(i) The attorney general and the comptroller by rule shall adopt a memorandum of understanding to establish procedures under which annual payments continue to a peace officer until continued assistance is no longer necessary.

(j) Article 56.37 does not apply to the filing of an application under this article. Other provisions of this chapter apply to this article to the extent applicable and consistent with this article.

(k) The limits on compensation imposed by Article 56.42 do not apply to payments made under this article, but the total aggregate amount of all annual payments made to an individual peace officer under this section may not exceed $200,000.

(l) A peace officer who is entitled to an annual payment under Subsection (b) may elect to receive the payment in:

(1) a single payment paid each year; or

(2) equal monthly installments.

(Enacted by Acts 2001, 77th Leg., ch. 1512 (S.B. 850), § 2, effective September 1, 2001; am. Acts 2005, 79th Leg., ch. 751 (H.B. 2823), § 1, effective June 17, 2005.)

### Art. 56.55. Court Costs [Repealed].

Repealed by Acts 2003, 78th Leg., ch. 209 (H.B. 2424), § 85(a)(1), effective January 1, 2004.
(Enacted by Acts 1993, 73rd Leg., ch. 268 (S.B. 248), § 6, effective September 1, 1993; am. Acts 1993, 73rd Leg., ch. 805 (H.B. 2178), § 5, effective August 30, 1993; am. Acts 1995, 74th Leg., ch. 76 (S.B. 959), § 5.84(a), effective September 1, 1995; am. Acts 1995, 74th Leg., ch. 779 (S.B. 1049), § 1, effective September 1, 1995.)

### Art. 56.56. Deposit and Remittance of Court Costs [Repealed].

Repealed by Acts 2003, 78th Leg., ch. 209 (H.B. 2424), § 85(a)(2), effective January 1, 2004.
(Enacted by Acts 1993, 73rd Leg., ch. 268 (S.B. 248), § 6, effective September 1, 1993; am. Acts 1995, 74th Leg., ch. 76 (S.B. 959), § 5.84(a), effective September 1, 1995; am. Acts 1995, 74th Leg., ch. 779 (S.B. 1049), § 1, effective September 1, 1995.)

### Art. 56.57. Deposit by Comptroller; Audit [Repealed].

Repealed by Acts 2003, 78th Leg., ch. 209 (H.B. 2424), § 85(a)(3), effective January 1, 2004.
(Enacted by Acts 1993, 73rd Leg., ch. 268 (S.B. 248), § 6, effective September 1, 1993; am. Acts 1993, 73rd Leg., ch. 805 (H.B. 2178), § 2, effective August 30, 1993; am. Acts 1995, 74th Leg., ch. 76 (S.B. 959), § 5.84(a), effective September 1, 1995; am. Acts 1995, 74th Leg., ch. 779 (S.B. 1049), § 1, effective September 1, 1995.)

## Art. 56.58. Adjustment of Awards and Payments.

(a) The attorney general shall establish a policy to adjust awards and payments so that the total amount of awards granted in each calendar year does not exceed the amount of money credited to the fund during that year.

(b) If the attorney general establishes a policy to adjust awards under Subsection (a), the attorney general, the claimant, or the victim is not liable for the amount of charges incurred in excess of the adjusted amount for the service on which the adjusted payment is determined.

(c) A service provider who accepts a payment that has been adjusted by a policy established under Subsection (a) agrees to accept the adjusted payment as payment in full for the service and is barred from legal action against the claimant or victim for collection.

(Enacted by Acts 1993, 73rd Leg., ch. 268 § 6, effective September 1, 1993; am. Acts 1995, 74th Leg., ch. 76 § 5.84(a), effective September 1, 1995; am. Acts 1995, 74th Leg., ch. 779 (S.B. 1049), § 1, effective September 1, 1995.)

## Art. 56.59. Attorney General Supervision of Collection of Costs; Failure to Comply [Repealed].

Repealed by Acts 2003, 78th Leg., ch. 209 (H.B. 2424), § 85(a)(4), effective January 1, 2004.

(Enacted by Acts 1993, 73rd Leg., ch. 268 (S.B. 248), § 6, effective September 1, 1993; am. Acts 1995, 74th Leg., ch. 76 (S.B. 959), § 5.84(a), effective September 1, 1995; am. Acts 1995, 74th Leg., ch. 779 (S.B. 1049), § 1, effective September 1, 1995.)

## Art. 56.60. Public Notice.

(a) A hospital licensed under the laws of this state shall display prominently in its emergency room posters giving notification of the existence and general provisions of this subchapter. The attorney general shall set standards for the location of the display and shall provide posters, application forms, and general information regarding this subchapter to each hospital and physician licensed to practice in this state.

(b) Each local law enforcement agency shall inform a claimant or victim of criminally injurious conduct of the provisions of this subchapter and make application forms available. The attorney general shall provide application forms and all other documents that local law enforcement agencies may require to comply with this article.

The attorney general shall set standards to be followed by local law enforcement agencies for this purpose and may require them to file with the attorney general a description of the procedures adopted by each agency to comply.

(Enacted by Acts 1993, 73rd Leg., ch. 268 (S.B. 248), § 6, effective September 1, 1993; am. Acts 1995, 74th Leg., ch. 76 (S.B. 959), § 5.84(a), effective September 1, 1995; am. Acts 1995, 74th Leg., ch. 779 (S.B. 1049), § 1, effective September 1, 1995.)

## Art. 56.61. Compensation for Certain Criminally Injurious Conduct Prohibited; Exception.

(a) Except as provided by Subsection (b), the attorney general may not award compensation for pecuniary loss arising from criminally injurious conduct that occurred before January 1, 1980.

(b) The attorney general may award compensation for pecuniary loss arising from criminally injurious conduct that occurred before January 1, 1980, if:

(1) the conduct was in violation of Chapter 19, Penal Code;

(2) **[2 Versions: As amended by Acts 2009, 81st Leg., ch. 496]** the identity of the victim is established by a law enforcement agency on or after September 1, 2009; and

(2) **[2 Versions: As amended by Acts 2009, 81st Leg., ch. 716]** the identity of the victim is established by a law enforcement agency on or after January 1, 2009, and the pecuniary loss was incurred with respect to the victim's funeral or burial on or after that date; and

(3) the claimant files the application for compensation within the limitations period provided by Article 56.37(e).

(Enacted by Acts 1993, 73rd Leg., ch. 268 (S.B. 248), § 6, effective September 1, 1993; am. Acts 1995, 74th Leg., ch. 76 (S.B. 959), § 5.84(a), effective September 1, 1995; am. Acts 1995, 74th Leg., ch. 779 (S.B. 1049), § 1, effective September 1, 1995; am. Acts 2009, 81st Leg., ch. 496 (S.B. 808), § 2, effective September 1, 2009; am. Acts 2009, 81st Leg., ch. 716 (H.B. 2916), § 2, effective June 19, 2009.)

## Art. 56.62. Public Letter of Reprimand.

(a) The attorney general may issue a letter of reprimand against an individual if the attorney general finds that the person has filed or has

Criminal Procedure

caused to be filed under this subchapter an application for benefits or claim for pecuniary loss that contains a statement or representation that the person knows to be false.

(b) The attorney general must give the person notice of the proposed action before issuing the letter.

(c) A person may challenge the denial of compensation and the issuance of a letter of reprimand in a contested case hearing under Chapter 2001, Government Code (Administrative Procedure Act).

(d) A letter of reprimand issued under this article is public information.
(Enacted by Acts 1995, 74th Leg., ch. 779 (S.B. 1049), § 1, effective September 1, 1995.)

## Art. 56.63. Civil Penalty.

(a) A person is subject to a civil penalty of not less than $2,500 or more than $25,000 for each application for compensation that:

(1) is filed under this subchapter by the person or is filed under this subchapter as a result of conduct of the person; and

(2) contains a material statement or representation that the person knows to be false.

(b) The attorney general shall institute and conduct the suit to collect the civil penalty authorized by this article on behalf of the state.

(c) A civil penalty recovered under this article shall be deposited to the credit of the compensation to victims of crime fund.

(d) The civil penalty authorized by this article is in addition to any other civil, administrative, or criminal penalty provided by law.

(e) In addition to the civil penalty authorized by this article, the attorney general may recover expenses incurred by the attorney general in the investigation, institution, and prosecution of the suit, including investigative costs, witness fees, attorney's fees, and deposition expenses.
(Enacted by Acts 1995, 74th Leg., ch. 779 (S.B. 1049), § 1, effective September 1, 1995.)

## Art. 56.64. Administrative Penalty.

(a) A person who presents to the attorney general under this subchapter, or engages in conduct that results in the presentation to the attorney general under this subchapter of, an application for compensation under this subchapter that contains a statement or representation the person knows to be false is liable to the attorney general for:

(1) the amount paid in reliance on the application and interest on that amount determined

at the rate provided by law for legal judgments and accruing from the date on which the payment was made;

(2) payment of an administrative penalty not to exceed twice the amount paid because of the false application for benefits or claim for pecuniary loss; and

(3) payment of an administrative penalty of not more than $10,000 for each item or service for which payment was claimed.

(b) In determining the amount of the penalty to be assessed under Subsection (a)(3), the attorney general shall consider:

(1) the seriousness of the violation;

(2) whether the person has previously submitted a false application for benefits or a claim for pecuniary loss; and

(3) the amount necessary to deter the person from submitting future false applications for benefits or claims for pecuniary loss.

(c) If the attorney general determines that a violation has occurred, the attorney general may issue a report that states the facts on which the determination is made and the attorney general's recommendation on the imposition of a penalty, including a recommendation on the amount of the penalty.

(d) The attorney general shall give written notice of the report to the person. Notice under this subsection may be given by certified mail and must:

(1) include a brief summary of the alleged violation;

(2) include a statement of the amount of the recommended penalty; and

(3) inform the person of the right to a hearing on:

(A) the occurrence of the violation;

(B) the amount of the penalty; or

(C) both the occurrence of the violation and the amount of the penalty.

(e) Not later than the 20th day after the date the person receives the notice, the person, in writing, may:

(1) accept the attorney general's determination and recommended penalty; or

(2) request in writing a hearing on:

(A) the occurrence of the violation;

(B) the amount of the penalty; or

(C) both the occurrence of the violation and the amount of the penalty.

(f) If the person accepts the determination and recommended penalty of the attorney general, the attorney general by order shall approve the determination and impose the recommended penalty.

(g) If the person requests a hearing as provided by Subsection (e) or fails to respond to the notice in a timely manner, the attorney general shall set a contested case hearing under Chapter 2001, Government Code (Administrative Procedure Act), and notify the person of the hearing. The administrative law judge shall make findings of facts and conclusions of law and promptly issue to the attorney general a proposal for a decision regarding the occurrence of the violation and the amount of a proposed penalty. Based on the findings of fact, conclusions of law, and proposal for a decision, the attorney general by order may:

(1) find that a violation has occurred and impose a penalty; or

(2) find that a violation has not occurred.

(h) Notice of the attorney general's order given to the person under Chapter 2001, Government Code, must include a statement of the right of the person to judicial review of the order.

(i) Not later than the 30th day after the date that the attorney general's order is final under Section 2001.144, Government Code, the person shall:

(1) pay the amount of the penalty;

(2) pay the amount of the penalty and file a petition for judicial review contesting:

(A) the occurrence of the violation;

(B) the amount of the penalty; or

(C) the occurrence of the violation and the amount of the penalty; or

(3) without paying the amount of the penalty, file a petition for judicial review contesting:

(A) the occurrence of the violation;

(B) the amount of the penalty; or

(C) the occurrence of the violation and the amount of the penalty.

(j) Within the 30-day period, a person who acts under Subsection (i)(3) may:

(1) stay enforcement of the penalty by:

(A) paying the amount of the penalty to the court for placement in an escrow account; or

(B) giving to the court a supersedeas bond that is approved by the court for the amount of the penalty and that is effective until all judicial review of the attorney general's order is final; or

(2) request the court to stay enforcement of the penalty by:

(A) filing with the court a sworn affidavit of the person stating that the person is financially unable to pay the amount of the penalty or to give the supersedeas bond; and

(B) delivering a copy of the affidavit to the attorney general by certified mail.

(k) On receipt by the attorney general of a copy of an affidavit under Subsection (j)(2), the attorney general may file with the court, not later than the fifth day after the date the copy is received, a contest to the affidavit. The court shall hold a hearing on the facts alleged in the affidavit as soon as practicable and shall stay the enforcement of the penalty on finding that the alleged facts are true. A person who files an affidavit under Subsection (j)(2) has the burden of proving that the person is financially unable to pay the amount of the penalty or to give a supersedeas bond.

(*l*) If the person does not pay the amount of the penalty and the enforcement of the penalty is not stayed, the attorney general may file suit for collection of the amount of the penalty.

(m) Judicial review of the order of the attorney general:

(1) is instituted by filing a petition as provided by Section 2001.176, Government Code; and

(2) is governed by the substantial evidence rule.

(n) If the court upholds the finding that a violation occurred, the court may order the person to pay the full or reduced amount of the penalty. If the court does not uphold the finding, the court shall order that no penalty is owed.

(o) If the person paid the amount of the penalty and if that amount is reduced or is not upheld by the court, the court shall order that the appropriate amount plus accrued interest be remitted to the person. The rate of the interest is the rate charged on loans to depository institutions by the New York Federal Reserve Bank, and the interest shall be paid for the period beginning on the date the penalty was paid and ending on the date the penalty is remitted. If the person gave a supersedeas bond and if the amount of the penalty is not upheld by the court, the court shall order the release of the bond. If the person gave a supersedeas bond and if the amount of the penalty is reduced, the court shall order the release of the bond after the person pays the amount.

(p) A penalty collected under this article shall be sent to the comptroller and deposited to the credit of the compensation to victims of crime fund.

(q) All proceedings under this article are subject to Chapter 2001, Government Code.

(r) In addition to the administrative penalty authorized by this article, the attorney general may recover all expenses incurred by the attorney general in the investigation, institution, and prosecution of the suit, including investigative costs, witness fees, attorney's fees, and deposition expenses.

(Enacted by Acts 1995, 74th Leg., ch. 779 (S.B. 1049), § 1, effective September 1, 1995.)

## SUBCHAPTER C
## ADDRESS CONFIDENTIALITY PROGRAM FOR VICTIMS OF FAMILY VIOLENCE, SEXUAL ASSAULT, OR STALKING

### Art. 56.81. Definitions.

In this subchapter:

(1) "Applicant" means a person who applies to participate in the program.

(2) "Family violence" has the meaning assigned by Section 71.004, Family Code.

(3) "Family violence shelter center" has the meaning assigned by Section 51.002, Human Resources Code.

(4) "Mail" means first class mail and any mail sent by a government agency. The term does not include a package, regardless of size or type of mailing.

(5) "Participant" means an applicant who is certified for participation in the program.

(6) "Program" means the address confidentiality program created under this subchapter.

(Enacted by Acts 2007, 80th Leg., ch. 1295 (S.B. 74), § 1, effective June 15, 2007.)

### Art. 56.82. Address Confidentiality Program.

(a) The attorney general shall establish an address confidentiality program, as provided by this subchapter, to assist a victim of family violence or an offense under Section 22.011, 22.021, 25.02, or 42.072, Penal Code, in maintaining a confidential address.

(b) The attorney general shall:

(1) designate a substitute post office box address that a participant may use in place of the participant's true residential, business, or school address;

(2) act as agent to receive service of process and mail on behalf of the participant; and

(3) forward to the participant mail received by the office of the attorney general on behalf of the participant.

(c) A summons, writ, notice, demand, or process may be served on the attorney general on behalf of the participant by delivery of two copies of the document to the office of the attorney general. The attorney general shall retain a copy of the summons, writ, notice, demand, or process and forward the original to the participant not later than the third day after the date of service on the attorney general.

(d) The attorney general shall make and retain a copy of the envelope in which certified mail is received on behalf of the participant.

(Enacted by Acts 2007, 80th Leg., ch. 1295 (S.B. 74), § 1, effective June 15, 2007.)

### Art. 56.83. Eligibility to Participate in Program.

(a) To be eligible to participate in the program, an applicant must:

(1) meet with a victim's assistance counselor from a state or local agency or other entity, whether for-profit or nonprofit that is identified by the attorney general as an entity that provides counseling and shelter services to victims of family violence;

(2) file an application for participation with the attorney general or a state or local agency or other entity identified by the attorney general under Subdivision (1);

(3) designate the attorney general as agent to receive service of process and mail on behalf of the applicant; and

(4) live at a residential address, or relocate to a residential address, that is unknown to the person who committed or is alleged to have committed the family violence or an offense under Section 22.011, 22.021, 25.02, or 42.072, Penal Code.

(b) An application under Subsection (a)(2) must contain:

(1) a signed, sworn statement by the applicant stating that the applicant fears for the safety of the applicant, the applicant's child, or another person in the applicant's household because of a threat of immediate or future harm caused by the person who committed or is alleged to have committed the family violence or an offense under Section 22.011, 22.021, 25.02, or 42.072, Penal Code;

(2) the applicant's true residential address and, if applicable, the applicant's business and school addresses; and

(3) a statement by the applicant of whether there is an existing court order or a pending

court case for child support or child custody or visitation that involves the applicant and, if so, the name and address of:

(A) the legal counsel of record; and

(B) each parent involved in the court order or pending case.

(c) An application under Subsection (a)(2) must be completed by the applicant in person at the state or local agency or other entity with which the application is filed. An applicant who knowingly or intentionally makes a false statement in an application under Subsection (a)(2) is subject to prosecution under Chapter 37, Penal Code.

(d) A state or local agency or other entity with which an application is filed under Subsection (a)(2) shall forward the application to the office of the attorney general.

(e) The attorney general by rule may establish additional eligibility requirements for participation in the program that are consistent with the purpose of the program as stated in Article 56.82(a). The attorney general may establish procedures for requiring an applicant, in appropriate circumstances, to submit with the application under Subsection (a)(2) independent documentary evidence of family violence or an offense under Section 22.011, 22.021, 25.02, or 42.072, Penal Code, in the form of:

(1) an active or recently issued protective order;

(2) an incident report or other record maintained by a law enforcement agency or official;

(3) a statement of a physician or other health care provider regarding the applicant's medical condition as a result of the family violence or offense; or

(4) a statement of a mental health professional, a member of the clergy, an attorney or other legal advocate, a trained staff member of a family violence center, or another professional who has assisted the applicant in addressing the effects of the family violence or offense.

(f) Any assistance or counseling provided by the attorney general or an employee or agent of the attorney general to an applicant does not constitute legal advice.

(Enacted by Acts 2007, 80th Leg., ch. 1295 (S.B. 74), § 1, effective June 15, 2007.)

## Art. 56.84. Certification; Expiration.

(a) The attorney general shall certify for participation in the program an applicant who satisfies the eligibility requirements under Article 56.83.

(b) A certification under this article expires on the third anniversary of the date of certification. (Enacted by Acts 2007, 80th Leg., ch. 1295 (S.B. 74), § 1, effective June 15, 2007.)

## Art. 56.85. Renewal.

To renew a certification under Article 56.84, a participant must satisfy the eligibility requirements under Article 56.83 as if the participant were originally applying for participation in the program.

(Enacted by Acts 2007, 80th Leg., ch. 1295 (S.B. 74), § 1, effective June 15, 2007.)

## Art. 56.86. Ineligibility and Cancellation.

(a) An applicant is ineligible for, and a participant may be excluded from, participation in the program if the applicant or participant knowingly makes a false statement on an application filed under Article 56.83(a)(2).

(b) A participant may be excluded from participation in the program if:

(1) mail forwarded to the participant by the attorney general is returned undeliverable on at least four occasions;

(2) the participant changes the participant's true residential address as provided in the application filed under Article 56.83(a)(2) and does not notify the attorney general of the change at least 10 days before the date of the change; or

(3) the participant changes the participant's name.

(Enacted by Acts 2007, 80th Leg., ch. 1295 (S.B. 74), § 1, effective June 15, 2007.)

## Art. 56.87. Withdrawal.

A participant may withdraw from the program by notifying the attorney general in writing of the withdrawal.

(Enacted by Acts 2007, 80th Leg., ch. 1295 (S.B. 74), § 1, effective June 15, 2007.)

## Art. 56.88. Confidentiality; Destruction of Information.

(a) Information relating to a participant:

(1) is confidential, except as provided by Article 56.90; and

(2) may not be disclosed under Chapter 552, Government Code.

(b) Except as provided by Article 56.82(d), the attorney general may not make a copy of any mail received by the office of the attorney general on behalf of the participant.

(c) The attorney general shall destroy all information relating to a participant on the third anniversary of the date participation in the program ends.

(Enacted by Acts 2007, 80th Leg., ch. 1295 (S.B. 74), § 1, effective June 15, 2007.)

## Art. 56.89. Acceptance of Substitute Address; Exemptions.

(a) Except as provided by Subsection (b), a state or local agency must accept the substitute post office box address designated by the attorney general if the substitute address is presented to the agency by a participant in place of the participant's true residential, business, or school address.

(b) The attorney general by rule may permit an agency to require a participant to provide the participant's true residential, business, or school address, if necessary for the agency to perform a duty or function that is imposed by law or administrative requirement.

(Enacted by Acts 2007, 80th Leg., ch. 1295 (S.B. 74), § 1, effective June 15, 2007.)

## Art. 56.90. Exceptions.

(a) The attorney general:

(1) shall disclose a participant's true residential, business, or school address if:

(A) requested by:

(i) a law enforcement agency;

(ii) the Department of Family and Protective Services for the purpose of conducting a child protective services investigation under Chapter 261, Family Code; or

(iii) the Department of State Health Services or a local health authority for the purpose of making a notification described by Article 21.31, Section 54.033, Family Code, or Section 81.051, Health and Safety Code; or

(B) required by court order; and

(2) may disclose a participant's true residential, business, or school address if:

(A) the participant consents to the disclosure; and

(B) the disclosure is necessary to administer the program.

(b) A person to whom a participant's true residential, business, or school address is disclosed under this section shall maintain the requested information in a manner that protects the confidentiality of the participant's true residential, business, or school address.

(Enacted by Acts 2007, 80th Leg., ch. 1295 (S.B. 74), § 1, effective June 15, 2007.)

## Art. 56.91. Liability.

(a) The attorney general or an agent or employee of the attorney general is immune from liability for any act or omission by the agent or employee in administering the program if the agent or employee was acting in good faith and in the course and scope of assigned responsibilities and duties.

(b) An agent or employee of the attorney general who does not act in good faith and in the course and scope of assigned responsibilities and duties in disclosing a participant's true residential, business, or school address is subject to prosecution under Chapter 39, Penal Code.

(Enacted by Acts 2007, 80th Leg., ch. 1295 (S.B. 74), § 1, effective June 15, 2007.)

## Art. 56.92. Program Information and Application Materials.

The attorney general shall make program information and application materials available online.

(Enacted by Acts 2007, 80th Leg., ch. 1295 (S.B. 74), § 1, effective June 15, 2007.)

## Art. 56.93. Rules.

The attorney general shall adopt rules to administer the program.

(Enacted by Acts 2007, 80th Leg., ch. 1295 (S.B. 74), § 1, effective June 15, 2007.)

# CHAPTER 57
# CONFIDENTIALITY OF IDENTIFYING INFORMATION OF SEX OFFENSE VICTIMS

## Art. 57.01. Definitions.

In this chapter:

(1) "Name" means the legal name of a person.

(2) "Pseudonym" means a set of initials or a fictitious name chosen by a victim to designate the victim in all public files and records concerning the offense, including police summary

reports, press releases, and records of judicial proceedings.

(3) "Public servant" has the meaning assigned by Subsection (a), Section 1.07, Penal Code.

(4) "Victim" means a person who was the subject of:

(A) an offense the commission of which leads to a reportable conviction or adjudication under Chapter 62; or

(B) an offense that is part of the same criminal episode, as defined by Section 3.01, Penal Code, as an offense described by Paragraph (A).

(Enacted by Acts 1987, 70th Leg., ch. 571 (S.B. 1392), § 1, effective September 1, 1987; am. Acts 1997, 75th Leg., ch. 680 (S.B. 48), § 1, effective September 1, 1997; am. Acts 2003, 78th Leg., ch. 451 (H.B. 670), § 1, effective September 1, 2003; am. Acts 2003, 78th Leg., ch. 1276 (H.B. 3507), § 5.0025, effective September 1, 2003.)

## Art. 57.02. Confidentiality of Files and Records.

(a) The Sexual Assault Prevention and Crisis Services Program of the office of the attorney general shall develop and distribute to all law enforcement agencies of the state a pseudonym form to record the name, address, telephone number, and pseudonym of a victim.

(b) A victim may choose a pseudonym to be used instead of the victim's name to designate the victim in all public files and records concerning the offense, including police summary reports, press releases, and records of judicial proceedings. A victim who elects to use a pseudonym as provided by this article must complete a pseudonym form developed under this article and return the form to the law enforcement agency investigating the offense.

(c) A victim who completes and returns a pseudonym form to the law enforcement agency investigating the offense may not be required to disclose the victim's name, address, and telephone number in connection with the investigation or prosecution of the offense.

(d) A completed and returned pseudonym form is confidential and may not be disclosed to any person other than a defendant in the case or the defendant's attorney, except on an order of a court of competent jurisdiction. The court finding required by Subsection (g) of this article is not required to disclose the confidential pseudonym form to the defendant in the case or to the defendant's attorney.

(e) If a victim completes and returns a pseudonym form to a law enforcement agency under this article, the law enforcement agency receiving the form shall:

(1) remove the victim's name and substitute the pseudonym for the name on all reports, files, and records in the agency's possession;

(2) notify the attorney for the state of the pseudonym and that the victim has elected to be designated by the pseudonym; and

(3) maintain the form in a manner that protects the confidentiality of the information contained on the form.

(f) An attorney for the state who receives notice that a victim has elected to be designated by a pseudonym shall ensure that the victim is designated by the pseudonym in all legal proceedings concerning the offense.

(g) A court of competent jurisdiction may order the disclosure of a victim's name, address, and telephone number only if the court finds that the information is essential in the trial of the defendant for the offense or the identity of the victim is in issue.

(h) Except as required or permitted by other law or by court order, a public servant or other person who has access to or obtains the name, address, telephone number, or other identifying information of a victim younger than 17 years of age may not release or disclose the identifying information to any person who is not assisting in the investigation, prosecution, or defense of the case. This subsection does not apply to the release or disclosure of a victim's identifying information by:

(1) the victim; or

(2) the victim's parent, conservator, or guardian, unless the parent, conservator, or guardian is a defendant in the case.

(i) [2 Versions: As added by Acts 2007, 80th Leg., ch. 619] This article does not prohibit the inspector general of the Texas Department of Criminal Justice from disclosing a victim's identifying information to an employee of the department if the victim is an inmate or state jail defendant confined in a facility operated by or under contract with the department.

(i) [2 Versions: As added by Acts 2007, 80th Leg., ch. 1217] This article does not prohibit the inspector general of the Texas Department of Criminal Justice from disclosing a victim's identifying information to the department's ombudsperson if the victim is an inmate or state jail defendant confined in a facility operated by or under contract with the department.

(Enacted by Acts 1987, 70th Leg., ch. 571 (S.B. 1392), § 1, effective September 1, 1987; am. Acts 2001, 77th Leg., ch. 1337 (H.B. 2890), § 3, effective September 1, 2001; am. Acts 2005, 79th Leg., ch. 93 (S.B. 1126), § 1, effective September 1, 2005; am. Acts 2007, 80th Leg., ch. 619 (H.B. 433), § 1, effective September 1, 2007; am. Acts 2007, 80th Leg., ch. 1217 (H.B. 1944), § 1, effective June 15, 2007.)

### Art. 57.03. Offense.

(a) A public servant with access to the name, address, or telephone number of a victim 17 years of age or older who has chosen a pseudonym under this chapter commits an offense if the public servant knowingly discloses the name, address, or telephone number of the victim to any person who is not assisting in the investigation or prosecution of the offense or to any person other than the defendant, the defendant's attorney, or the person specified in the order of a court of competent jurisdiction.

(b) Unless the disclosure is required or permitted by other law, a public servant or other person commits an offense if the person:

(1) has access to or obtains the name, address, or telephone number of a victim younger than 17 years of age; and

(2) knowingly discloses the name, address, or telephone number of the victim to any person who is not assisting in the investigation or prosecution of the offense or to any person other than the defendant, the defendant's attorney, or a person specified in an order of a court of competent jurisdiction.

(c) It is an affirmative defense to prosecution under Subsection (b) that the actor is:

(1) the victim; or

(2) the victim's parent, conservator, or guardian, unless the actor is a defendant in the case.

(c-1) **[2 Versions: As added by Acts 2007, 80th Leg., ch. 619]** It is an exception to the application of this article that:

(1) the person who discloses the name, address, or telephone number of a victim is the inspector general of the Texas Department of Criminal Justice;

(2) the victim is an inmate or state jail defendant confined in a facility operated by or under contract with the Texas Department of Criminal Justice; and

(3) the person to whom the disclosure is made is an employee of the department.

(c-1) **[2 Versions: As added by Acts 2007, 80th Leg., ch. 1217]** It is an exception to the application of this article that:

(1) the person who discloses the name, address, or telephone number of a victim is the inspector general of the Texas Department of Criminal Justice;

(2) the victim is an inmate or state jail defendant confined in a facility operated by or under contract with the department; and

(3) the person to whom the disclosure is made is the department's ombudsperson.

(d) An offense under this article is a Class C misdemeanor.

(Enacted by Acts 1987, 70th Leg., ch. 571 (S.B. 1392), § 1, effective September 1, 1987; am. Acts 2001, 77th Leg., ch. 1337 (H.B. 2890), § 4, effective September 1, 2001; am. Acts 2007, 80th Leg., ch. 619 (H.B. 433), § 2, effective September 1, 2007; am. Acts 2007, 80th Leg., ch. 1217 (H.B. 1944), § 2, effective June 15, 2007.)

# CHAPTER 57B
# CONFIDENTIALITY OF IDENTIFYING INFORMATION OF FAMILY VIOLENCE VICTIMS

### Art. 57B.01. Definitions.

In this chapter:

(1) "Name" means the legal name of a person.

(2) "Pseudonym" means a set of initials or a fictitious name chosen by a victim to designate the victim in all public files and records concerning the offense, including police summary reports, press releases, and records of judicial proceedings.

(3) "Public servant" has the meaning assigned by Subsection (a), Section 1.07, Penal Code.

(4) "Victim" means a person who is the subject of:

(A) an offense that allegedly constitutes family violence, as defined by Section 71.004, Family Code; or

(B) an offense that is part of the same criminal episode, as defined by Section 3.01,

Penal Code, as an offense described by Paragraph (A).

(Enacted by Acts 2007, 80th Leg., ch. 1295 (S.B. 74), § 3, effective June 15, 2007.)

## Art. 57B.02. Confidentiality of Files and Records.

(a) The office of the attorney general shall develop and distribute to all law enforcement agencies of the state a pseudonym form to record the name, address, telephone number, and pseudonym of a victim.

(b) A victim may choose a pseudonym to be used instead of the victim's name to designate the victim in all public files and records concerning the offense, including police summary reports, press releases, and records of judicial proceedings. A victim who elects to use a pseudonym as provided by this article must complete a pseudonym form developed under this article and return the form to the law enforcement agency investigating the offense.

(c) A victim who completes and returns a pseudonym form to the law enforcement agency investigating the offense may not be required to disclose the victim's name, address, and telephone number in connection with the investigation or prosecution of the offense.

(d) A completed and returned pseudonym form is confidential and may not be disclosed to any person other than a defendant in the case or the defendant's attorney, except on an order of a court of competent jurisdiction. The court finding required by Subsection (g) is not required to disclose the confidential pseudonym form to the defendant in the case or to the defendant's attorney.

(e) If a victim completes and returns a pseudonym form to a law enforcement agency under this article, the law enforcement agency receiving the form shall:

(1) remove the victim's name and substitute the pseudonym for the name on all reports, files, and records in the agency's possession;

(2) notify the attorney for the state of the pseudonym and that the victim has elected to be designated by the pseudonym; and

(3) maintain the form in a manner that protects the confidentiality of the information contained on the form.

(f) An attorney for the state who receives notice that a victim has elected to be designated by a pseudonym shall ensure that the victim is designated by the pseudonym in all legal proceedings concerning the offense.

(g) A court of competent jurisdiction may order the disclosure of a victim's name, address, and telephone number only if the court finds that the information is essential in the trial of the defendant for the offense or the identity of the victim is in issue.

(h) Except as required or permitted by other law or by court order, a public servant or other person who has access to or obtains the name, address, telephone number, or other identifying information of a victim younger than 17 years of age may not release or disclose the identifying information to any person who is not assisting in the investigation, prosecution, or defense of the case. This subsection does not apply to the release or disclosure of a victim's identifying information by:

(1) the victim; or

(2) the victim's parent, conservator, or guardian, unless the victim's parent, conservator, or guardian allegedly committed the offense described by Article 57B.01(4).

(Enacted by Acts 2007, 80th Leg., ch. 1295 (S.B. 74), § 3, effective June 15, 2007.)

## Art. 57B.03. Offense.

(a) A public servant with access to the name, address, or telephone number of a victim 17 years of age or older who has chosen a pseudonym under this chapter commits an offense if the public servant knowingly discloses the name, address, or telephone number of the victim to any person who is not assisting in the investigation or prosecution of the offense or to any person other than the defendant, the defendant's attorney, or the person specified in the order of a court of competent jurisdiction.

(b) Unless the disclosure is required or permitted by other law, a public servant or other person commits an offense if the person:

(1) has access to or obtains the name, address, or telephone number of a victim younger than 17 years of age; and

(2) knowingly discloses the name, address, or telephone number of the victim to any person who is not assisting in the investigation or prosecution of the offense or to any person other than the defendant, the defendant's attorney, or a person specified in an order of a court of competent jurisdiction.

(c) It is an affirmative defense to prosecution under Subsection (b) that the actor is:

(1) the victim; or

(2) the victim's parent, conservator, or guardian, unless the victim's parent, conserva-

Criminal Procedure

tor, or guardian allegedly committed the offense described by Article 57B.01(4).

(d) An offense under this article is a Class C misdemeanor.

(Enacted by Acts 2007, 80th Leg., ch. 1295 (S.B. 74), § 3, effective June 15, 2007.)

### Art. 57B.04. Applicability of Chapter to Department of Family and Protective Services.

Nothing in this chapter requires the Department of Family and Protective Services to use a pseudonym in a department report, file, or record relating to the abuse, neglect, or exploitation of a child or adult who may also be the subject of an offense described by Article 57B.01(4). To the extent permitted by law, the Department of Family and Protective Services and a department employee, as necessary in performing department duties, may disclose the name of a victim who elects to use a pseudonym under this chapter.

(Enacted by Acts 2007, 80th Leg., ch. 1295 (S.B. 74), § 3, effective June 15, 2007.)

### Art. 57B.05. Applicability of Chapter to Political Subdivisions.

Nothing in this chapter requires a political subdivision to use a pseudonym in a report, file, or record that is not:

(1) intended for distribution to the public; or

(2) the subject of an open records request under Chapter 552, Government Code.

(Enacted by Acts 2007, 80th Leg., ch. 1295 (S.B. 74), § 3, effective June 15, 2007.)

## CHAPTER 57C
## SEALING OF COURT RECORDS CONTAINING MEDICAL INFORMATION FOR CERTAIN CHILD VICTIMS

**Article**
57C.01.    Definitions.
57C.02.    Sealing of Records.

### Art. 57C.01. Definitions.

In this chapter:

(1) "Child" means a person who is younger than 18 years of age.

(2) "Medical records" means any information used or generated by health care providers, including records relating to emergency room treatment, rehabilitation therapy, or counseling.

(Enacted by Acts 2009, 81st Leg., ch. 1010 (H.B. 4136), § 1, effective June 19, 2009.)

### Art. 57C.02. Sealing of Records.

(a) Except as provided by Subsection (c), on a motion filed by a person described by Subsection (b), the court shall seal the medical records of a child who is a victim of an offense described by Section 1, Article 38.071.

(b) A motion under this article may be filed on the court's own motion or by:

(1) the attorney representing the state;

(2) the defendant; or

(3) the parent or guardian of the victim or, if the victim is no longer a child, the victim.

(c) The court is not required to seal the records described by this article on a finding of good cause after a hearing held under Subsection (d).

(d) The court shall grant the motion without a hearing unless the motion is contested not later than the seventh day after the date the motion is filed.

(e) Medical records sealed under this chapter are not open for inspection by any person except:

(1) on further order of the court after:

(A) notice to a parent or guardian of the victim whose information is sealed or, if the victim is no longer a child, notice to the victim; and

(B) a finding of good cause;

(2) in connection with a criminal or civil proceeding as otherwise provided by law; or

(3) on request of a parent or legal guardian of the victim whose information is being sealed or, if the victim is no longer a child, on request of the victim.

(f) A clerk of court is not liable for any failure to seal medical records after a motion under this chapter is granted, except on a showing of bad faith.

(Enacted by Acts 2009, 81st Leg., ch. 1010 (H.B. 4136), § 1, effective June 19, 2009.)

## CHAPTER 57D
## CONFIDENTIALITY OF IDENTIFYING INFORMATION OF VICTIMS OF TRAFFICKING OF PERSONS

**Article**
57D.01.    Definitions.
57D.02.    Confidentiality of Files and Records.
57D.03.    Offense.

### Art. 57D.01. Definitions.

In this chapter:

(1) "Name" means the legal name of a person.

(2) "Pseudonym" means a set of initials or a fictitious name chosen by a victim to designate the victim in all public files and records concerning the offense, including police summary reports, press releases, and records of judicial proceedings.

(3) "Public servant" has the meaning assigned by Section 1.07(a), Penal Code.

(4) "Victim" means a person who is the subject of:

(A) an offense under Section 20A.02, Penal Code; or

(B) an offense that is part of the same criminal episode, as defined by Section 3.01, Penal Code, as an offense under Section 20A.02, Penal Code.

(Enacted by Acts 2011, 82nd Leg., ch. 1008 (H.B. 2329), § 2, effective September 1, 2011.)

## Art. 57D.02. Confidentiality of Files and Records.

(a) The office of the attorney general shall develop and distribute to all law enforcement agencies of the state a pseudonym form to record the name, address, telephone number, and pseudonym of a victim.

(b) A victim may choose a pseudonym to be used instead of the victim's name to designate the victim in all public files and records concerning the offense, including police summary reports, press releases, and records of judicial proceedings. A victim who elects to use a pseudonym as provided by this article must complete a pseudonym form developed under this article and return the form to the law enforcement agency investigating the offense.

(c) A victim who completes and returns a pseudonym form to the law enforcement agency investigating the offense may not be required to disclose the victim's name, address, and telephone number in connection with the investigation or prosecution of the offense.

(d) A completed and returned pseudonym form is confidential and may not be disclosed to any person other than a defendant in the case or the defendant's attorney, except on an order of a court of competent jurisdiction. The court finding required by Subsection (g) is not required to disclose the confidential pseudonym form to the defendant in the case or to the defendant's attorney.

(e) If a victim completes and returns a pseudonym form to a law enforcement agency under this article, the law enforcement agency receiving the form shall:

(1) remove the victim's name and substitute the pseudonym for the name on all reports, files, and records in the agency's possession;

(2) notify the attorney for the state of the pseudonym and that the victim has elected to be designated by the pseudonym; and

(3) maintain the form in a manner that protects the confidentiality of the information contained on the form.

(f) An attorney for the state who receives notice that a victim has elected to be designated by a pseudonym shall ensure that the victim is designated by the pseudonym in all legal proceedings concerning the offense.

(g) A court of competent jurisdiction may order the disclosure of a victim's name, address, and telephone number only if the court finds that the information is essential in the trial of the defendant for the offense or the identity of the victim is in issue.

(h) Except as required or permitted by other law or by court order, a public servant or other person who has access to or obtains the name, address, telephone number, or other identifying information of a victim younger than 18 years of age may not release or disclose the identifying information to any person who is not assisting in the investigation, prosecution, or defense of the case. This subsection does not apply to the release or disclosure of a victim's identifying information by:

(1) the victim; or

(2) the victim's parent, conservator, or guardian, unless the victim's parent, conservator, or guardian allegedly committed the offense described by Article 57D.01(4).

(Enacted by Acts 2011, 82nd Leg., ch. 1008 (H.B. 2329), § 2, effective September 1, 2011.)

## Art. 57D.03. Offense.

(a) A public servant with access to the name, address, or telephone number of a victim 18 years of age or older who has chosen a pseudonym under this chapter commits an offense if the public servant knowingly discloses the name, address, or telephone number of the victim to any person who is not assisting in the investigation or prosecution of the offense or to any person other than the defendant, the defendant's attorney, or the person specified in the order of a court of competent jurisdiction.

(b) Unless the disclosure is required or permitted by other law, a public servant or other person commits an offense if the person:

(1) has access to or obtains the name, address, or telephone number of a victim younger than 18 years of age; and

(2) knowingly discloses the name, address, or telephone number of the victim to any person who is not assisting in the investigation or prosecution of the offense or to any person other than the defendant, the defendant's attorney, or a person specified in an order of a court of competent jurisdiction.

(c) It is an affirmative defense to prosecution under Subsection (b) that the actor is:

(1) the victim; or

(2) the victim's parent, conservator, or guardian, unless the victim's parent, conservator, or guardian allegedly committed the offense described by Article 57D.01(4).

(d) An offense under this article is a Class C misdemeanor.

(Enacted by Acts 2011, 82nd Leg., ch. 1008 (H.B. 2329), § 2, effective September 1, 2011.)

# CHAPTER 58
## SEALING FILES AND RECORDS OF CHILDREN
### [REPEALED]

### Art. 58.01. Sealing Files and Records of Children [Repealed].

Repealed by Acts 2001, 77th Leg., ch. 1297 (H.B. 1118), § 71(3), effective September 1, 2001. (Enacted by Acts 1987, 70th Leg., ch. 1040 (S.B. 17), § 27, effective September 1, 1987; am. Acts 1989, 71st Leg., ch. 2 (S.B. 221), § 16.01(11), effective August 28, 1989 (renumbered from art. 57.01); am. Acts 1997, 75th Leg., ch. 165 (S.B. 898), § 7.04, effective September 1, 1997.)

# CHAPTER 59
## FORFEITURE OF CONTRABAND

## Art. 59.01. Definitions.

In this chapter:

(1) "Attorney representing the state" means the prosecutor with felony jurisdiction in the county in which a forfeiture proceeding is held under this chapter or, in a proceeding for forfeiture of contraband as defined under Subdivision (2)(B)(v) of this article, the city attorney of a municipality if the property is seized in that municipality by a peace officer employed by that municipality and the governing body of the municipality has approved procedures for the city attorney acting in a forfeiture proceeding. In a proceeding for forfeiture of contraband as defined under Subdivision (2)(B)(vii) of this article, the term includes the attorney general.

(2) "Contraband" means property of any nature, including real, personal, tangible, or intangible, that is:

(A) used in the commission of:

(i) any first or second degree felony under the Penal Code;

(ii) any felony under Section 15.031(b), 20.05, 21.11, 38.04, or Chapter 43, 20A, 29, 30, 31, 32, 33, 33A, or 35, Penal Code;

(iii) any felony under The Securities Act (Article 581-1 et seq., Vernon's Texas Civil Statutes); or

(iv) any offense under Chapter 49, Penal Code, that is punishable as a felony of the third degree or state jail felony, if the defendant has been previously convicted three times of an offense under that chapter;

(B) used or intended to be used in the commission of:

(i) any felony under Chapter 481, Health and Safety Code (Texas Controlled Substances Act);

(ii) any felony under Chapter 483, Health and Safety Code;

(iii) a felony under Chapter 153, Finance Code;

(iv) any felony under Chapter 34, Penal Code;

(v) a Class A misdemeanor under Subchapter B, Chapter 365, Health and Safety

Code, if the defendant has been previously convicted twice of an offense under that subchapter;

(vi) any felony under Chapter 152, Finance Code;

(vii) any felony under Chapter 32, Human Resources Code, or Chapter 31, 32, 35A, or 37, Penal Code, that involves the state Medicaid program;

(viii) a Class B misdemeanor under Chapter 522, Business & Commerce Code;

(ix) a Class A misdemeanor under Section 306.051, Business & Commerce Code;

(x) any offense under Section 42.10, Penal Code;

(xi) any offense under Section 46.06(a)(1) or 46.14, Penal Code;

(xii) any offense under Chapter 71, Penal Code; or

(xiii) any offense under Section 20.05, Penal Code;

(C) the proceeds gained from the commission of a felony listed in Paragraph (A) or (B) of this subdivision, a misdemeanor listed in Paragraph (B)(viii), (x), (xi), or (xii) of this subdivision, or a crime of violence;

(D) acquired with proceeds gained from the commission of a felony listed in Paragraph (A) or (B) of this subdivision, a misdemeanor listed in Paragraph (B)(viii), (x), (xi), or (xii) of this subdivision, or a crime of violence;

(E) used to facilitate or intended to be used to facilitate the commission of a felony under Section 15.031 or 43.25, Penal Code; or

(F) used to facilitate or intended to be used to facilitate the commission of a felony under Section 20A.02 or Chapter 43, Penal Code.

(3) "Crime of violence" means:

(A) any criminal offense defined in the Penal Code or in a federal criminal law that results in a personal injury to a victim; or

(B) an act that is not an offense under the Penal Code involving the operation of a motor vehicle, aircraft, or water vehicle that results in injury or death sustained in an accident caused by a driver in violation of Section 550.021, Transportation Code.

(4) "Interest holder" means the bona fide holder of a perfected lien or a perfected security interest in property.

(5) "Law enforcement agency" means an agency of the state or an agency of a political subdivision of the state authorized by law to employ peace officers.

(6) "Owner" means a person who claims an equitable or legal ownership interest in property.

(7) "Proceeds" includes income a person accused or convicted of a crime or the person's representative or assignee receives from:

(A) a movie, book, magazine article, tape recording, phonographic record, radio or television presentation, telephone service, electronic media format, including an Internet website, or live entertainment in which the crime was reenacted; or

(B) the sale of tangible property the value of which is increased by the notoriety gained from the conviction of an offense by the person accused or convicted of the crime.

(8) "Seizure" means the restraint of property by a peace officer under Article 59.03(a) or (b) of this code, whether the officer restrains the property by physical force or by a display of the officer's authority, and includes the collection of property or the act of taking possession of property.

(9) "Depository account" means the obligation of a regulated financial institution to pay the account owner under a written agreement, including a checking account, savings account, money market account, time deposit, NOW account, or certificate of deposit.

(10) "Primary state or federal financial institution regulator" means the state or federal regulatory agency that chartered and comprehensively regulates a regulated financial institution.

(11) "Regulated financial institution" means a depository institution chartered by a state or federal government, the deposits of which are insured by the Federal Deposit Insurance Corporation or the National Credit Union Administration.

(Enacted by Acts 1989, 71st Leg., 1st C.S., ch. 12 (H.B. 65), § 1, effective October 18, 1989; am. Acts 1991, 72nd Leg., ch. 102 (H.B. 46), § 2, effective September 1, 1991; am. Acts 1993, 73rd Leg., ch. 761 (H.B. 354), § 5, effective September 1, 1993; am. Acts 1993, 73rd Leg., ch. 780 (H.B. 605), § 1, effective September 1, 1993; am. Acts 1993, 73rd Leg., ch. 828 (S.B. 1285), § 1, effective September 1, 1993; am. Acts 1995, 74th Leg., ch. 76 (S.B. 959), §§ 5.91, 5.95(112), effective September 1, 1995; am. Acts 1995, 74th Leg., ch. 621 (H.B. 1487), § 3, effective September 1, 1995; am. Acts 1995, 74th Leg., ch. 708 (S.B. 281), § 2, effective September 1, 1995; am. Acts 1997, 75th Leg., ch. 306 (H.B. 1482), § 6, effective September 1, 1997; am. Acts 1999, 76th Leg., ch. 62 (S.B. 1368), §§ 3.09, 7.48, effective September 1, 1999; am. Acts 2001, 77th Leg., ch. 124 (S.B. 795), § 1, effective September 1, 2001; am. Acts 2001, 77th Leg., ch. 438 (S.B. 626), § 1, effective September 1, 2001; am. Acts 2001, 77th Leg., ch. 467 (H.B. 510), § 1, effective September 1, 2001; am. Acts 2003, 78th Leg., ch. 198 (H.B. 2292), § 2.141, effective September 1, 2003; am. Acts 2003, 78th Leg., ch. 257 (H.B. 1743), § 17, effective September 1, 2003; am. Acts 2003, 78th Leg., ch. 428 (H.B. 406), § 1, effective September 1, 2003; am. Acts 2003, 78th Leg., ch. 649 (H.B. 2138), § 3, effective September 1, 2003; am. Acts 2003, 78th Leg., ch. 1005 (H.B. 236), § 7, effective September 1, 2003; am. Acts 2005, 79th Leg., ch. 617 (H.B. 2275), § 1, effective September 1, 2005; am. Acts 2005, 79th Leg., ch. 728 (H.B. 2018), § 4.008, effective September 1, 2005; am. Acts 2005, 79th Leg., ch. 944 (H.B. 840), §§ 1, 2, effective September 1, 2005; am. Acts 2005, 79th Leg., ch. 1026 (H.B. 1048), §§ 3, 4, effective September 1, 2005; am. Acts 2007, 80th Leg., ch. 127 (S.B. 1694), § 6, effective September 1, 2007; am. Acts 2007, 80th Leg., ch. 822 (H.B. 73), § 2, effective September 1, 2007; am. Acts 2007, 80th Leg., ch. 885 (H.B. 2278), § 2.14, effective April 1, 2009; am. Acts 2009, 81st Leg., ch. 87 (S.B. 1969), § 6.006, effective September 1, 2009; am. Acts 2009, 81st Leg., ch. 153 (S.B. 2225), § 3, effective September 1, 2009; am. Acts 2009, 81st Leg., ch. 1130 (H.B. 2086), § 11, effective September 1, 2009; am. Acts 2009, 81st Leg., ch. 1357 (S.B. 554), § 3, effective September 1, 2009; am. Acts 2011, 82nd Leg., ch. 91 (S.B. 1303), § 6.003, effective September 1, 2011; am. Acts 2011, 82nd Leg., ch. 223 (H.B. 260), § 5, effective September 1, 2011; am. Acts 2011, 82nd Leg., ch. 515 (H.B. 2014), § 2.04, effective September 1, 2011.)

### Art. 59.011. Election of Forfeiture Proceeding.

If property described by Article 59.01(2)(B)(x), (xi), or (xii) is subject to forfeiture under this chapter and Article 18.18, the attorney representing the state may proceed under either this chapter or that article.

(Enacted by Acts 2009, 81st Leg., ch. 153 (S.B. 2225), § 4, effective September 1, 2009; Enacted by Acts 2009, 81st Leg., ch. 1130 (H.B. 2086), § 12, effective September 1, 2009; Enacted by Acts 2009, 81st Leg., ch. 1357 (S.B. 554), § 4,

effective September 1, 2009; am. Acts 2011, 82nd Leg., ch. 91 (S.B. 1303), § 6.004, effective September 1, 2011.)

### Art. 59.02. Forfeiture of Contraband.

(a) Property that is contraband is subject to seizure and forfeiture under this chapter.

(b) Any property that is contraband other than property held as evidence in a criminal investigation or a pending criminal case, money, a negotiable instrument, or a security that is seized under this chapter may be replevied by the owner or interest holder of the property, on execution of a good and valid bond with sufficient surety in a sum equal to the appraised value of the property replevied. The bond may be approved as to form and substance by the court after the court gives notice of the bond to the authority holding the seized property. The bond must be conditioned:

(1) on return of the property to the custody of the state on the day of hearing of the forfeiture proceedings; and

(2) that the interest holder or owner of the property will abide by the decision that may be made in the cause.

(c) An owner or interest holder's interest in property may not be forfeited under this chapter if the owner or interest holder proves by a preponderance of the evidence that the owner or interest holder acquired and perfected the interest:

(1) before or during the act or omission giving rise to forfeiture or, if the property is real property, he acquired an ownership interest, security interest, or lien interest before a lis pendens notice was filed under Article 59.04(g) of this code and did not know or should not reasonably have known of the act or omission giving rise to the forfeiture or that it was likely to occur at or before the time of acquiring and perfecting the interest or, if the property is real property, at or before the time of acquiring the ownership interest, security interest, or lien interest; or

(2) after the act or omission giving rise to the forfeiture, but before the seizure of the property, and only if the owner or interest holder:

(A) was, at the time that the interest in the property was acquired, an owner or interest holder for value; and

(B) was without reasonable cause to believe that the property was contraband and did not purposefully avoid learning that the property was contraband.

(d) Notwithstanding any other law, if property is seized from the possession of an owner or interest holder who asserts an ownership interest, security interest, or lien interest in the property under applicable law, the owner or interest holder's rights remain in effect during the pendency of proceedings under this chapter as if possession of the property had remained with the owner or interest holder.

(e) On motion by any party or on the motion of the court, after notice in the manner provided by Article 59.04 of this code to all known owners and interest holders of property subject to forfeiture under this chapter, and after a hearing on the matter, the court may make appropriate orders to preserve and maintain the value of the property until a final disposition of the property is made under this chapter, including the sale of the property if that is the only method by which the value of the property may be preserved until final disposition.

(f) Any property that is contraband and has been seized by the Texas Department of Criminal Justice shall be forfeited to the department under the same rules and conditions as for other forfeitures.

(g) An individual, firm, corporation, or other entity insured under a policy of title insurance may not assert a claim or cause of action on or because of the policy if the claim or cause of action is based on forfeiture under this chapter and, at or before the time of acquiring the ownership of real property, security interest in real property, or lien interest against real property, the insured knew or reasonably should have known of the act or omission giving rise to the forfeiture or that the act or omission was likely to occur.

(h) (1) An owner or interest holder's interest in property may not be forfeited under this chapter if at the forfeiture hearing the owner or interest holder proves by a preponderance of the evidence that the owner or interest holder was not a party to the offense giving rise to the forfeiture and that the contraband:

(A) was stolen from the owner or interest holder before being used in the commission of the offense giving rise to the forfeiture;

(B) was purchased with:

(i) money stolen from the owner or interest holder; or

(ii) proceeds from the sale of property stolen from the owner or interest holder; or

(C) was used or intended to be used without the effective consent of the owner or

interest holder in the commission of the offense giving rise to the forfeiture.

(2) An attorney representing the state who has a reasonable belief that property subject to forfeiture is described by Subdivision (1) and who has a reasonable belief as to the identity of the rightful owner or interest holder of the property shall notify the owner or interest holder as provided by Article 59.04.

(3) An attorney representing the state is not liable in an action for damages resulting from an act or omission in the performance of the duties imposed by Subdivision (2).

(4) The exclusive remedy for failure by the attorney representing the state to provide the notice required under Subdivision (2) is submission of that failure as a ground for new trial in a motion for new trial or bill of review.

(i) The forfeiture provisions of this chapter apply to contraband as defined by Article 59.01(2)(B)(v) of this code only in a municipality with a population of 250,000 or more.

(Enacted by Acts 1989, 71st Leg., 1st C.S., ch. 12 (H.B. 65), § 1, effective October 18, 1989; am. Acts 1993, 73rd Leg., ch. 828 (S.B. 1285), § 2, effective September 1, 1993; am. Acts 2001, 77th Leg., ch. 438 (S.B. 626), § 2, effective September 1, 2001; am. Acts 2001, 77th Leg., ch. 929 (S.B. 563), § 1, effective September 1, 2001; am. Acts 2003, 78th Leg., ch. 1275 (H.B. 3506), § 2(9), effective September 1, 2003; am. Acts 2009, 81st Leg., ch. 87 (S.B. 1969), § 25.043, effective September 1, 2009.)

### Art. 59.03. Seizure of Contraband.

(a) Property subject to forfeiture under this chapter, other than property described by Article 59.12, may be seized by any peace officer under authority of a search warrant.

(b) Seizure of property subject to forfeiture may be made without warrant if:

(1) the owner, operator, or agent in charge of the property knowingly consents;

(2) the seizure is incident to a search to which the owner, operator, or agent in charge of the property knowingly consents;

(3) the property subject to seizure has been the subject of a prior judgment in favor of the state in a forfeiture proceeding under this chapter; or

(4) the seizure was incident to a lawful arrest, lawful search, or lawful search incident to arrest.

(c) A peace officer who seizes property under this chapter has custody of the property, subject only to replevy under Article 59.02 of this code or an order of a court. A peace officer who has custody of property shall provide the attorney representing the state with a sworn statement that contains a schedule of the property seized, an acknowledgment that the officer has seized the property, and a list of the officer's reasons for the seizure. Not later than 72 hours after the seizure, the peace officer shall:

    (1) place the property under seal;

    (2) remove the property to a place ordered by the court; or

    (3) require a law enforcement agency of the state or a political subdivision to take custody of the property and move it to a proper location.

(d) A person in the possession of property at the time a peace officer seizes the property under this chapter may at the time of seizure assert the person's interest in or right to the property. A peace officer, including the peace officer who seizes the property, may not request, require, or in any manner induce any person, including a person who asserts an interest in or right to the property, to execute a document purporting to waive the person's interest in or rights to property seized under this chapter.

(e) At any time before notice is filed under Article 59.04(b), an attorney representing the state may not request, require, or in any manner induce any person, including a person who asserts an interest in or right to property seized under this chapter, to execute a document purporting to waive the person's interest in or rights to the property.

(Enacted by Acts 1989, 71st Leg., 1st C.S., ch. 12 (H.B. 65), § 1, effective October 18, 1989; am. Acts 2001, 77th Leg., ch. 438 (S.B. 626), § 3, effective September 1, 2001; am. Acts 2001, 77th Leg., ch. 929 (S.B. 563), § 2, effective September 1, 2001; am. Acts 2011, 82nd Leg., ch. 1321 (S.B. 316), § 1, effective September 1, 2011.)

## Art. 59.04. Notification of Forfeiture Proceeding.

(a) If a peace officer seizes property under this chapter, the attorney representing the state shall commence proceedings under this section not later than the 30th day after the date of the seizure.

(b) A forfeiture proceeding commences under this chapter when the attorney representing the state files a notice of the seizure and intended forfeiture in the name of the state with the clerk of the district court in the county in which the

seizure is made. The attorney representing the state must attach to the notice the peace officer's sworn statement under Article 59.03 of this code or, if the property has been seized under Article 59.12(b), the statement of the terms and amount of the depository account or inventory of assets provided by the regulated financial institution to the peace officer executing the warrant in the manner described by Article 59.12(b). Except as provided by Subsection (c) of this article, the attorney representing the state shall cause certified copies of the notice to be served on the following persons in the same manner as provided for the service of process by citation in civil cases:

    (1) the owner of the property; and

    (2) any interest holder in the property.

(c) If the property is a motor vehicle, and if there is reasonable cause to believe that the vehicle has been registered under the laws of this state, the attorney representing the state shall ask the Texas Department of Motor Vehicles to identify from its records the record owner of the vehicle and any interest holder. If the addresses of the owner and interest holder are not otherwise known, the attorney representing the state shall request citation be served on such persons at the address listed with the Texas Department of Motor Vehicles. If the citation issued to such address is returned unserved, the attorney representing the state shall cause a copy of the notice of the seizure and intended forfeiture to be posted at the courthouse door, to remain there for a period of not less than 30 days. If the owner or interest holder does not answer or appear after the notice has been so posted, the court shall enter a judgment by default as to the owner or interest holder, provided that the attorney representing the state files a written motion supported by affidavit setting forth the attempted service. An owner or interest holder whose interest is forfeited in this manner shall not be liable for court costs. If the person in possession of the vehicle at the time of the seizure is not the owner or the interest holder of the vehicle, notification shall be provided to the possessor in the same manner specified for notification to an owner or interest holder.

(d) If the property is a motor vehicle and is not registered in this state, the attorney representing the state shall attempt to ascertain the name and address of the person in whose name the vehicle is licensed in another state. If the vehicle is licensed in a state that has a certificate of title law, the attorney representing the state shall request the appropriate agency of that state to identify the record owner of the vehicle and any interest holder.

(e) If a financing statement is required by law to be filed to perfect a security interest affecting the property, and if there is reasonable cause to believe that a financing statement has been filed, the attorney representing the state who commences the proceedings shall ask the appropriate official designated by Chapter 9, Business & Commerce Code, to identify the record owner of the property and the person who is an interest holder.

(f) If the property is an aircraft or a part of an aircraft, and if there is reasonable cause to believe that a perfected security instrument affects the property, the attorney representing the state shall request an administrator of the Federal Aviation Administration to identify from the records of that agency the record owner of the property and the holder of the perfected security instrument. The attorney representing the state shall also notify the Department of Public Safety in writing of the fact that an aircraft has been seized and shall provide the department with a description of the aircraft.

(g) If the property is real property, the attorney representing the state, not later than the third day after the date proceedings are commenced, shall file a lis pendens notice describing the property with the county clerk of each county in which the property is located.

(h) For all other property subject to forfeiture, if there is reasonable cause to believe that a perfected security instrument affects the property, the attorney representing the state shall make a good faith inquiry to identify the holder of the perfected security instrument.

(i) Except as provided by Section (c) of this article, the attorney representing the state who commences the proceedings shall cause the owner and any interest holder to be named as a party and to be served with citation as provided by the Texas Rules of Civil Procedure.

(j) A person who was in possession of the property at the time it was seized shall be made a party to the proceeding.

(k) If no person was in possession of the property at the time it was seized, and if the owner of the property is unknown, the attorney representing the state shall file with the clerk of the court in which the proceedings are pending an affidavit stating that no person was in possession of the property at the time it was seized and that the owner of the property is unknown. The clerk of

the court shall issue a citation for service by publication addressed to "The Unknown Owner of _____," filling in the blank space with a reasonably detailed description of the property subject to forfeiture. The citation must contain the other requisites prescribed by and be served as provided by Rules 114, 115, and 116, Texas Rules of Civil Procedure.

(*l*) Proceedings commenced under this chapter may not proceed to hearing unless the judge who is to conduct the hearing is satisfied that this article has been complied with and that the attorney representing the state will introduce into evidence at the hearing any answer received from an inquiry required by Subsections (c)—(h) of this article.

(Enacted by Acts 1989, 71st Leg., 1st C.S., ch. 12 (H.B. 65), § 1, effective October 18, 1989; am. Acts 1991, 72nd Leg., ch. 14 (S.B. 404), § 282, effective September 1, 1991; am. Acts 1995, 74th Leg., ch. 165 (S.B. 971), § 22(25), effective September 1, 1995; am. Acts 1995, 74th Leg., ch. 533 (S.B. 1217), § 1, effective September 1, 1995; am. Acts 2001, 77th Leg., ch. 438 (S.B. 626), § 4, effective September 1, 2001; am. Acts 2009, 81st Leg., ch. 933 (H.B. 3097), § 3B.02, effective September 1, 2009.)

## Art. 59.05. Forfeiture Hearing.

(a) All parties must comply with the rules of pleading as required in civil suits.

(b) All cases under this chapter shall proceed to trial in the same manner as in other civil cases. The state has the burden of proving by a preponderance of the evidence that property is subject to forfeiture.

(c) It is an affirmative defense to forfeiture under this chapter of property belonging to the spouse of a person whose acts gave rise to the seizure of community property that, because of an act of family violence, as defined by Section 71.004, Family Code, the spouse was unable to prevent the act giving rise to the seizure.

(d) A final conviction for an underlying offense is not a requirement for forfeiture under this chapter. An owner or interest holder may present evidence of a dismissal or acquittal of an underlying offense in a forfeiture proceeding, and evidence of an acquittal raises a presumption that the property or interest that is the subject of the hearing is nonforfeitable. This presumption can be rebutted by evidence that the owner or interest holder knew or should have known that the property was contraband.

(e) It is the intention of the legislature that asset forfeiture is remedial in nature and not a form of punishment. If the court finds that all or any part of the property is subject to forfeiture, the judge shall forfeit the property to the state, with the attorney representing the state as the agent for the state, except that if the court finds that the nonforfeitable interest of an interest holder in the property is valued in an amount greater than or substantially equal to the present value of the property, the court shall order the property released to the interest holder. If the court finds that the nonforfeitable interest of an interest holder is valued in an amount substantially less than the present value of the property and that the property is subject to forfeiture, the court shall order the property forfeited to the state with the attorney representing the state acting as the agent of the state, and making necessary orders to protect the nonforfeitable interest of the interest holder. On final judgment of forfeiture, the attorney representing the state shall dispose of the property in the manner required by Article 59.06 of this code.

(f) On forfeiture to the state of an amount greater than $2,500, the clerk of the court in which the forfeiture proceeding was held is entitled to court costs in that proceeding as in other civil proceedings unless the forfeiture violates federal requirements for multijurisdictional task force cases authorized under Chapter 362, Local Government Code. The procedure for collecting the costs is the procedure established under Subsections (a) and (c), Article 59.06.

(g) If property is seized at a federal checkpoint, the notice of seizure and intended forfeiture may be filed in and the proceeding may be held in:

(1) the county in which the seizure occurred; or

(2) with the consent of the owner, operator, or agent in charge of the property, a county that is adjacent to the county in which the seizure occurred, if both counties are in the same judicial district.

(Enacted by Acts 1989, 71st Leg., 1st C.S., ch. 12 (H.B. 65), § 1, effective October 18, 1989; am. Acts 1993, 73rd Leg., ch. 780 (H.B. 605), § 2, effective September 1, 1993; am. Acts 1995, 74th Leg., ch. 533 (S.B. 1217), § 2, effective September 1, 1995; am. Acts 1999, 76th Leg., ch. 582 (S.B. 579), § 1, effective September 1, 1999; am. Acts 2003, 78th Leg., ch. 1153 (H.B. 3377), § 1, effective September 1, 2003; am. Acts 2003, 78th Leg., ch. 1276 (H.B. 3507), § 7.002(l), effective September 1, 2003.)

## Art. 59.06. Disposition of Forfeited Property.

(a) Except as provided by Subsection (k), all forfeited property shall be administered by the attorney representing the state, acting as the agent of the state, in accordance with accepted accounting practices and with the provisions of any local agreement entered into between the attorney representing the state and law enforcement agencies. If a local agreement has not been executed, the property shall be sold on the 75th day after the date of the final judgment of forfeiture at public auction under the direction of the county sheriff, after notice of public auction as provided by law for other sheriff's sales. The proceeds of the sale shall be distributed as follows:

(1) to any interest holder to the extent of the interest holder's nonforfeitable interest;

(2) after any distributions under Subdivision (1), if the Title IV-D agency has filed a child support lien in the forfeiture proceeding, to the Title IV-D agency in an amount not to exceed the amount of child support arrearages identified in the lien; and

(3) the balance, if any, after the deduction of court costs to which a district court clerk is entitled under Article 59.05(f) and, after that deduction, the deduction of storage and disposal costs, to be deposited not later than the 30th day after the date of the sale in the state treasury to the credit of the general revenue fund.

(b) If a local agreement exists between the attorney representing the state and law enforcement agencies, the attorney representing the state may transfer the property to law enforcement agencies to maintain, repair, use, and operate the property for official purposes if the property is free of any interest of an interest holder. The agency receiving the forfeited property may purchase the interest of an interest holder so that the property can be released for use by the agency. The agency receiving the forfeited property may maintain, repair, use, and operate the property with money appropriated for current operations. If the property is a motor vehicle subject to registration under the motor vehicle registration laws of this state, the agency receiving the forfeited vehicle is considered to be the purchaser and the certificate of title shall issue to the agency. A law enforcement agency to which property is transferred under this subsection at any time may transfer or loan the property to any other municipal or county agency, a groundwater conservation district governed by Chapter 36, Water Code, or a school district for the use of that agency or district. A municipal or county agency, a groundwater conservation district, or a school district to which a law enforcement agency loans a motor vehicle under this subsection shall maintain any automobile insurance coverage for the vehicle that is required by law.

(b-1) If a loan is made by a sheriff's office or by a municipal police department, the commissioners court of the county in which the sheriff has jurisdiction or the governing body of the municipality in which the department has jurisdiction, as applicable, may revoke the loan at any time by notifying the receiving agency or district, by mail, that the receiving agency or district must return the loaned vehicle to the loaning agency before the seventh day after the date the receiving agency or district receives the notice.

(b-2) An agency that loans property under this article shall:

(1) keep a record of the loan, including the name of the agency or district to which the vehicle was loaned, the fair market value of the vehicle, and where the receiving agency or district will use the vehicle; and

(2) update the record when the information relating to the vehicle changes.

(c) If a local agreement exists between the attorney representing the state and law enforcement agencies, all money, securities, negotiable instruments, stocks or bonds, or things of value, or proceeds from the sale of those items, shall be deposited, after the deduction of court costs to which a district court clerk is entitled under Article 59.05(f), according to the terms of the agreement into one or more of the following funds:

(1) a special fund in the county treasury for the benefit of the office of the attorney representing the state, to be used by the attorney solely for the official purposes of his office;

(2) a special fund in the municipal treasury if distributed to a municipal law enforcement agency, to be used solely for law enforcement purposes, such as salaries and overtime pay for officers, officer training, specialized investigative equipment and supplies, and items used by officers in direct law enforcement duties;

(3) a special fund in the county treasury if distributed to a county law enforcement agency, to be used solely for law enforcement purposes; or

(4) a special fund in the state law enforcement agency if distributed to a state law enforcement agency, to be used solely for law enforcement purposes.

(c-1) Notwithstanding Subsection (a), the attorney representing the state and special rangers of the Texas and Southwestern Cattle Raisers Association who meet the requirements of Article 2.125 may enter into a local agreement that allows the attorney representing the state to transfer proceeds from the sale of forfeited property described by Subsection (c), after the deduction of court costs as described by that subsection, to a special fund established for the special rangers. Proceeds transferred under this subsection must be used by the special rangers solely for law enforcement purposes, such as training, essential equipment, and operating expenses. Any expenditures of the proceeds are subject to the audit provisions established under this article.

(c-2) Any postjudgment interest from money, securities, negotiable instruments, stocks or bonds, or things of value, or proceeds from the sale of those items, that are deposited in an interest-bearing bank account under Subsection (c) shall be used for the same purpose as the principal.

(c-3) Notwithstanding Subsection (a), with respect to forfeited property seized in connection with a violation of Chapter 481, Health and Safety Code (Texas Controlled Substances Act), by a peace officer employed by the Department of Public Safety, in a proceeding under Article 59.05 in which a default judgment is rendered in favor of the state, the attorney representing the state shall enter into a local agreement with the department that allows the attorney representing the state either to:

(1) transfer forfeited property to the department to maintain, repair, use, and operate for official purposes in the manner provided by Subsection (b); or

(2) allocate proceeds from the sale of forfeited property described by Subsection (c), after the deduction of court costs as described by that subsection, in the following proportions:

(A) 40 percent to a special fund in the department to be used solely for law enforcement purposes;

(B) 30 percent to a special fund in the county treasury for the benefit of the office of the attorney representing the state, to be used by the attorney solely for the official purposes of the attorney's office; and

(C) 30 percent to the general revenue fund.

(c-4) Notwithstanding Subsections (a) and (c-3), with respect to forfeited property seized in connection with a violation of Chapter 481, Health and Safety Code (Texas Controlled Substances Act), by the Department of Public Safety concurrently with any other law enforcement agency, in a proceeding under Article 59.05 in which a default judgment is rendered in favor of the state, the attorney representing the state may allocate property or proceeds in accordance with a memorandum of understanding between the law enforcement agencies and the attorney representing the state.

(d) Proceeds awarded under this chapter to a law enforcement agency or to the attorney representing the state may be spent by the agency or the attorney after a budget for the expenditure of the proceeds has been submitted to the commissioners court or governing body of the municipality. The budget must be detailed and clearly list and define the categories of expenditures, but may not list details that would endanger the security of an investigation or prosecution. Expenditures are subject to the audit and enforcement provisions established under this chapter. A commissioners court or governing body of a municipality may not use the existence of an award to offset or decrease total salaries, expenses, and allowances that the agency or the attorney receives from the commissioners court or governing body at or after the time the proceeds are awarded.

(d-1) The head of a law enforcement agency or an attorney representing the state may not use proceeds or property received under this chapter to:

(1) contribute to a political campaign;

(2) make a donation to any entity, except as provided by Subsection (d-2);

(3) pay expenses related to the training or education of any member of the judiciary;

(4) pay any travel expenses related to attendance at training or education seminars if the expenses violate generally applicable restrictions established by the commissioners court or governing body of the municipality, as applicable;

(5) purchase alcoholic beverages;

(6) make any expenditure not approved by the commissioners court or governing body of the municipality, as applicable, if the head of a law enforcement agency or attorney representing the state holds an elective office and:

(A) the deadline for filing an application for a place on the ballot as a candidate for reelection to that office in the general primary election has passed and the person did not file an application for a place on that ballot; or

(B) during the person's current term of office, the person was a candidate in a primary, general, or runoff election for reelection to that office and was not the prevailing candidate in that election; or

(7) increase a salary, expense, or allowance for an employee of the law enforcement agency or attorney representing the state who is budgeted by the commissioners court or governing body of the municipality unless the commissioners court or governing body first approves the increase.

(d-2) The head of a law enforcement agency or an attorney representing the state may use as an official purpose of the agency or attorney proceeds or property received under this chapter to make a donation to an entity that assists in:

(1) the detection, investigation, or prosecution of:

(A) criminal offenses; or

(B) instances of abuse, as defined by Section 261.001, Family Code;

(2) the provision of:

(A) mental health, drug, or rehabilitation services; or

(B) services for victims or witnesses of criminal offenses or instances of abuse described by Subdivision (1); or

(3) the provision of training or education related to duties or services described by Subdivision (1) or (2).

(e) On the sale of contraband under this article, the appropriate state agency shall issue a certificate of title to the recipient if a certificate of title is required for the property by other law.

(f) A final judgment of forfeiture under this chapter perfects the title of the state to the property as of the date that the contraband was seized or the date the forfeiture action was filed, whichever occurred first, except that if the property forfeited is real property, the title is perfected as of the date a notice of lis pendens is filed on the property.

(g) (1) All law enforcement agencies and attorneys representing the state who receive proceeds or property under this chapter shall account for the seizure, forfeiture, receipt, and specific expenditure of all the proceeds and property in an audit, which is to be performed annually by the commissioners court or governing body of a municipality, as appropriate. The annual period of the audit for a law enforcement agency is the fiscal year of the appropriate county or municipality and the annual period for an attorney representing the state is the state fiscal year. The audit must be completed on a form provided by the attorney general and must include a detailed report and explanation of all expenditures, including salaries and overtime pay, officer training, investigative equipment and supplies, and other items. Certified copies of the audit shall be delivered by the law enforcement agency or attorney representing the state to the attorney general not later than the 60th day after the date on which the annual period that is the subject of the audit ends.

(2) If a copy of the audit is not delivered to the attorney general within the period required by Subdivision (1), within five days after the end of the period the attorney general shall notify the law enforcement agency or the attorney representing the state of that fact. On a showing of good cause, the attorney general may grant an extension permitting the agency or attorney to deliver a copy of the audit after the period required by Subdivision (1) and before the 76th day after the date on which the annual period that is the subject of the audit ends. If the law enforcement agency or the attorney representing the state fails to establish good cause for not delivering the copy of the audit within the period required by Subdivision (1) or fails to deliver a copy of an audit within the extension period, the attorney general shall notify the comptroller of that fact.

(3) On notice under Subdivision (2), the comptroller shall perform the audit otherwise required by Subdivision (1). At the conclusion of the audit, the comptroller shall forward a copy of the audit to the attorney general. The law enforcement agency or attorney representing the state is liable to the comptroller for the costs of the comptroller in performing the audit.

(h) As a specific exception to the requirement of Subdivisions (1)—(3) of Subsection (c) of this article that the funds described by those subdivisions be used only for the official purposes of the attorney representing the state or for law enforcement purposes, on agreement between the attorney representing the state or the head of a law enforcement agency and the governing body of a political subdivision, the attorney representing the state or the head of the law enforcement agency shall comply with the request of the

governing body to deposit not more than a total of 10 percent of the gross amount credited to the attorney's or agency's fund into the treasury of the political subdivision. The governing body of the political subdivision shall, by ordinance, order, or resolution, use funds received under this subsection for:

(1) nonprofit programs for the prevention of drug abuse;

(2) nonprofit chemical dependency treatment facilities licensed under Chapter 464, Health and Safety Code;

(3) nonprofit drug and alcohol rehabilitation or prevention programs administered or staffed by professionals designated as qualified and credentialed by the Texas Commission on Alcohol and Drug Abuse; or

(4) financial assistance as described by Subsection (o).

(i) The governing body of a political subdivision may not use funds received under this subchapter for programs or facilities listed under Subsections (h)(1)—(3) if an officer of or member of the Board of Directors of the entity providing the program or facility is related to a member of the governing body, the attorney representing the state, or the head of the law enforcement agency within the third degree by consanguinity or the second degree by affinity.

(j) As a specific exception to Subdivision (4) of Subsection (c) of this article, the director of a state law enforcement agency may use not more than 10 percent of the amount credited to the special fund of the agency under that subdivision for the prevention of drug abuse and the treatment of persons with drug-related problems.

(k) (1) The attorney for the state shall transfer all forfeited property that is income from, or acquired with the income from, a movie, book, magazine article, tape recording, phonographic record, radio or television presentation, telephone service, electronic media format, including an Internet website, or live entertainment in which a crime is reenacted to the attorney general.

(2) The attorney for the state shall transfer to the attorney general all income from the sale of tangible property the value of which is increased by the notoriety gained from the conviction of an offense by the person accused or convicted of the crime, minus the deduction authorized by this subdivision. The attorney for the state shall determine the fair market value of property that is substantially similar to the property that was sold but that has not

been increased in value by notoriety and deduct that amount from the proceeds of the sale. After transferring income to the attorney general, the attorney for the state shall transfer the remainder of the proceeds of the sale to the owner of the property. The attorney for the state, the attorney general, or a person who may be entitled to claim money from the escrow account described by Subdivision (3) in satisfaction of a claim may at any time bring an action to enjoin the waste of income described by this subdivision.

(3) The attorney general shall deposit the money or proceeds from the sale of the property into an escrow account. The money in the account is available to satisfy a judgment against the person who committed the crime in favor of a victim of the crime if the judgment is for damages incurred by the victim caused by the commission of the crime. The attorney general shall transfer the money in the account that has not been ordered paid to a victim in satisfaction of a judgment to the compensation to victims of crime fund on the fifth anniversary of the date the account was established. In this subsection, "victim" has the meaning assigned by Article 56.32.

(*l*) A law enforcement agency that, or an attorney representing the state who, does not receive proceeds or property under this chapter during an annual period as described by Subsection (g) shall, not later than the 30th day after the date on which the annual period ends, report to the attorney general that the agency or attorney, as appropriate, did not receive proceeds or property under this chapter during the annual period.

(m) As a specific exception to Subdivisions (1)—(3) of Subsection (c), a law enforcement agency or attorney representing the state may use proceeds received under this chapter to contract with a person or entity to prepare an audit as required by Subsection (g).

(n) As a specific exception to Subsection (c)(2) or (3), a local law enforcement agency may transfer not more than a total of 10 percent of the gross amount credited to the agency's fund to a separate special fund in the treasury of the political subdivision. The agency shall administer the separate special fund, and expenditures from the fund are at the sole discretion of the agency and may be used only for financial assistance as described by Subsection (o).

(o) The governing body of a political subdivision or a local law enforcement agency may provide financial assistance under Subsection (h)(4) or (n) only to a person who is a Texas resident, who plans to enroll or is enrolled at an institution of higher education in an undergraduate degree or certificate program in a field related to law enforcement, and who plans to return to that locality to work for the political subdivision or the agency in a field related to law enforcement. To ensure the promotion of a law enforcement purpose of the political subdivision or the agency, the governing body of the political subdivision or the agency shall impose other reasonable criteria related to the provision of this financial assistance, including a requirement that a recipient of the financial assistance work for a certain period of time for the political subdivision or the agency in a field related to law enforcement and including a requirement that the recipient sign an agreement to perform that work for that period of time. In this subsection, "institution of higher education" has the meaning assigned by Section 61.003, Education Code.

(p) Notwithstanding Subsection (a), and to the extent necessary to protect the commission's ability to recover amounts wrongfully obtained by the owner of the property and associated damages and penalties to which the commission may otherwise be entitled by law, the attorney representing the state shall transfer to the Health and Human Services Commission all forfeited property defined as contraband under Article 59.01(2)(B)(vii). If the forfeited property consists of property other than money or negotiable instruments, the attorney representing the state may, if approved by the commission, sell the property and deliver to the commission the proceeds from the sale, minus costs attributable to the sale. The sale must be conducted in a manner that is reasonably expected to result in receiving the fair market value for the property.

(q) (1) Notwithstanding any other provision of this article, a multicounty drug task force, or a county or municipality participating in the task force, that is not established in accordance with Section 362.004, Local Government Code, or that fails to comply with the policies and procedures established by the Department of Public Safety under that section, and that participates in the seizure of contraband shall forward to the comptroller all proceeds received by the task force from the forfeiture of the contraband. The comptroller shall deposit the proceeds in the state treasury to the credit of the general revenue fund.

(2) The attorney general shall ensure the enforcement of Subdivision (1) by filing any

necessary legal proceedings in the county in which the contraband is forfeited or in Travis County.

(Enacted by Acts 1989, 71st Leg., 1st C.S., ch. 12 (H.B. 65), § 1, effective October 18, 1989; am. Acts 1991, 72nd Leg., ch. 312 (H.B. 1185), §§ 1, 2, effective September 1, 1991; am. Acts 1993, 73rd Leg., ch. 780 (H.B. 605), §§ 3, 4, effective September 1, 1993; am. Acts 1993, 73rd Leg., ch. 814 (H.B. 2766), § 1, effective August 30, 1993; am. Acts 1995, 74th Leg., ch. 76 (S.B. 959), § 5.95(112), effective September 1, 1995; am. Acts 1997, 75th Leg., ch. 975 (H.B. 2257), § 1, effective September 1, 1997; am. Acts 1999, 76th Leg., ch. 481 (S.B. 1486), §§ 1, 2, effective September 1, 1999; am. Acts 1999, 76th Leg., ch. 582 (S.B. 579), § 2, effective September 1, 1999; am. Acts 1999, 76th Leg., ch. 707 (H.B. 855), § 1, effective September 1, 1999; am. Acts 2001, 77th Leg., ch. 124 (S.B. 795), § 2, effective September 1, 2001; am. Acts 2001, 77th Leg., ch. 929 (S.B. 563), § 3, effective September 1, 2001; am. Acts 2003, 78th Leg., ch. 198 (H.B. 2292), § 2.142, effective September 1, 2003; am. Acts 2003, 78th Leg., ch. 257 (H.B. 1743), § 18, effective September 1, 2003; am. Acts 2003, 78th Leg., ch. 428 (H.B. 406), § 2, effective September 1, 2003; am. Acts 2005, 79th Leg., ch. 556 (H.B. 1239), § 4, effective September 1, 2005; am. Acts 2007, 80th Leg., ch. 120 (S.B. 1106), § 2, effective September 1, 2007; am. Acts 2007, 80th Leg., ch. 446 (H.B. 195), § 1, effective September 1, 2007; am. Acts 2009, 81st Leg., ch. 187 (H.B. 2062), § 1, effective May 27, 2009; am. Acts 2009, 81st Leg., ch. 941 (H.B. 3140), § 1, effective September 1, 2009; am. Acts 2011, 82nd Leg., ch. 508 (H.B. 1674), § 23, effective September 1, 2011; am. Acts 2011, 82nd Leg., ch. 1321 (S.B. 316), § 2, effective September 1, 2011.)

## Art. 59.061. Audits and Investigations.

(a) The state auditor may at any time perform an audit or conduct an investigation, in accordance with this article and Chapter 321, Government Code, related to the seizure, forfeiture, receipt, and specific expenditure of proceeds and property received under this chapter.

(b) The state auditor is entitled at any time to access any book, account, voucher, confidential or nonconfidential report, or other record of information, including electronic data, maintained under Article 59.06, except that if the release of the applicable information is restricted under state or federal law, the state auditor may access the information only with the approval of a court or federal administrative agency, as appropriate.

(c) If the results of an audit or investigation under this article indicate that a law enforcement agency or attorney representing the state has knowingly violated or is knowingly violating a provision of this chapter relating to the disposition of proceeds or property received under this chapter, the state auditor shall promptly notify the attorney general for the purpose of initiating appropriate enforcement proceedings under Article 59.062.

(d) The law enforcement agency or attorney representing the state shall reimburse the state auditor for costs incurred by the state auditor in performing an audit under this article.

(Enacted by Acts 2011, 82nd Leg., ch. 1321 (S.B. 316), § 3, effective September 1, 2011.)

## Art. 59.062. Enforcement.

(a) In the name of the state, the attorney general may institute in a district court in Travis County or in a county served by the law enforcement agency or attorney representing the state, as applicable, a suit for injunctive relief, to recover a civil penalty, or for both injunctive relief and a civil penalty if the results of an audit or investigation under Article 59.061 indicate that the law enforcement agency or attorney representing the state has knowingly violated or is knowingly violating a provision of this chapter relating to the disposition of proceeds or property received under this chapter.

(b) On application for injunctive relief and a finding that the law enforcement agency or attorney representing the state is knowingly violating a provision of this chapter relating to the disposition of proceeds or property received under this chapter, the district court shall grant the injunctive relief the facts may warrant, without requirement for bond.

(c) A law enforcement agency or attorney representing the state who knowingly commits a violation described by Subsection (a) is liable to the state for a civil penalty in an amount not to exceed $100,000 as determined by the district court to be appropriate for the nature and seriousness of the violation. In determining an appropriate penalty for the violation, the court shall consider:

(1) any previous violations committed by the agency or attorney;

(2) the seriousness of the violation, including the nature, circumstances, extent, and gravity of the violation;

(3) the demonstrated good faith of the agency or attorney; and

(4) the amount necessary to deter future violations.

(d) If the attorney general brings a suit under this article and an injunction is granted or a civil penalty is imposed, the attorney general may recover reasonable expenses, court costs, investigative costs, and attorney's fees.

(e) Notwithstanding any other provision of this article, a law enforcement agency or attorney representing the state ordered to pay a civil penalty, expense, cost, or fee under this article shall make the payment out of money available in any fund established by the agency or attorney, as applicable, for the purpose of administering proceeds or property received under this chapter. If sufficient money is not available to make payment in full at the time the court enters an order requiring payment, the agency or attorney shall continue to make payments out of money available in any fund described by this subsection until the payment is made in full.

(f) A civil penalty collected under this article shall be deposited to the credit of the drug court account in the general revenue fund to help fund drug court programs established under Chapter 469, Health and Safety Code.

(g) A law enforcement agency or attorney representing the state is immune from liability under this article if the agency or attorney reasonably relied on:

(1) the advice, consent, or approval of an entity that conducts an audit of the agency or attorney under this chapter; or

(2) a written opinion of the attorney general relating to:

(A) the statute or other provision of law the agency or attorney is alleged to have knowingly violated; or

(B) a fact situation that is substantially similar to the fact situation in which the agency or attorney is involved.

(Enacted by Acts 2011, 82nd Leg., ch. 1321 (S.B. 316), § 3, effective September 1, 2011.)

## Art. 59.07. Immunity.

This chapter does not impose any additional liability on any authorized state, county, or municipal officer engaged in the lawful performance of the officer's duties.

(Enacted by Acts 1989, 71st Leg., 1st C.S., ch. 12 (H.B. 65), § 1, effective October 18, 1989.)

## Art. 59.08. Deposit of Money Pending Disposition.

(a) If money that is contraband is seized, the attorney representing the state may deposit the money in an interest-bearing bank account in the jurisdiction of the attorney representing the state until a final judgment is rendered concerning the contraband.

(b) If a final judgment is rendered concerning contraband, money that has been placed in an interest-bearing bank account under Subsection (a) of this article shall be distributed in the same manner as proceeds are distributed under Article 59.06 of this code, with any interest being distributed in the same manner and used for the same purpose as the principal.

(Enacted by Acts 1989, 71st Leg., 1st C.S., ch. 12 (H.B. 65), § 1, effective October 18, 1989.)

## Art. 59.09. Right to Attorney Not to Be Abridged.

This chapter is not intended to abridge an accused person's right to counsel in a criminal case.

(Enacted by Acts 1989, 71st Leg., 1st C.S., ch. 12 (H.B. 65), § 1, effective October 18, 1989.)

## Art. 59.10. Election of Laws.

If property is subject to forfeiture under this chapter and under any other law of this state, the attorney representing the state may bring forfeiture proceedings under either law.

(Enacted by Acts 1989, 71st Leg., 1st C.S., ch. 12 (H.B. 65), § 1, effective October 18, 1989.)

## Art. 59.11. Report of Seized and Forfeited Aircraft.

Not later than the 10th day after the last day of each quarter of the fiscal year, the Department of Public Safety shall report to the State Aircraft Pooling Board:

(1) a description of each aircraft that the department has received by forfeiture under this chapter during the preceding quarter and the purposes for which the department intends to use the aircraft; and

(2) a description of each aircraft the department knows to have been seized under this chapter during the preceding quarter and the purposes for which the department would use the aircraft if it were forfeited to the department.

(Enacted by Acts 1991, 72nd Leg., ch. 14 (S.B. 404), § 283, effective September 1, 1991.)

## Art. 59.12. Seizure of Accounts and Assets at Regulated Financial Institution.

(a) This article applies to property consisting of a depository account or assets in a regulated financial institution.

(b) A regulated financial institution, at the time a seizure warrant issued under Chapter 18 is served on the institution, may either:

(1) pay an account or tender assets held as security for an obligation owed to the institution at the time of the service of the seizure warrant; or

(2) transfer the depository account or assets to a segregated interest-bearing account in the name of the attorney representing the state as trustee, to remain in the account until the time has expired for an appeal from a decision of the court relating to the forfeiture of accounts or assets under Article 59.05.

(c) Immediately on service of the seizure warrant, the regulated financial institution shall take action as necessary to segregate the account or assets and shall provide evidence, certified by an officer of the institution, of the terms and amount of the account or a detailed inventory of the assets to the peace officer serving the warrant. Except as otherwise provided by this article, a transaction involving an account or assets, other than the deposit or reinvestment of interest, dividends, or other normally recurring payments on the account or assets that do not involve distribution of proceeds to the owner, is not authorized unless approved by the court that issued the seizure warrant or, if a forfeiture action has been instituted, the court in which that action is pending.

(d) Any accrual to the value of the account or assets during the pendency of the forfeiture proceedings is subject to the procedures for the disbursement of interest under Article 59.08.

(e) If the regulated financial institution fails to release the depository account or assets to a peace officer pursuant to a seizure warrant or transfer the account or assets as required by Subsection (b), and as a result cannot comply with the court's forfeiture order, the court:

(1) shall order the regulated financial institution and its culpable officers, agents, or employees to pay actual damages, attorney's fees, and court costs incurred as a result of the institution's failure to comply; and

(2) may find the regulated financial institution and its culpable officers, agents, or employees in contempt.

(f) A regulated financial institution that complies with this article is not liable in damages because of the compliance.

(g) This article does not:

(1) impair the right of the state to obtain possession of physical evidence or to seize a depository account or other assets for purposes other than forfeiture under this chapter; or

(2) waive criminal or civil remedies available under other law.

(Enacted by Acts 2001, 77th Leg., ch. 438 (S.B. 626), § 5, effective September 1, 2001.)

## Art. 59.13. Disclosure of Information Relating to Accounts and Assets at Regulated Financial Institution.

(a) The attorney representing the state may disclose information to the primary state or federal financial institution regulator, including grand jury information or otherwise confidential information, relating to any action contemplated or brought under this chapter that involves property consisting of a depository account in a regulated financial institution or assets held by a regulated financial institution as security for an obligation owed to a regulated financial institution. An attorney representing the state who discloses information as permitted by this subsection is not subject to contempt under Article 20.02 for that disclosure.

(b) A primary state or federal financial institution regulator shall keep confidential any information provided by the attorney representing the state under Subsection (a). The sharing of information under Subsection (a) by a representative of the state is not considered a waiver by the state of any privilege or claim of confidentiality.

(c) A regulator described by Subsection (b) commits an offense if the regulator knowingly discloses information in violation of this article. An offense under this subsection is punishable by confinement in jail for a period not to exceed 30 days, a fine not to exceed $500, or both such confinement and fine.

(Enacted by Acts 2001, 77th Leg., ch. 438 (S.B. 626), § 5, effective September 1, 2001.)

## Art. 59.14. Notice to Primary State and Federal Financial Institution Regulators.

(a) Before taking any action under this chapter that implicates a potentially culpable officer or director of a regulated financial institution, the attorney representing the state shall notify the banking commissioner, who shall notify the appropriate state or federal financial institution regulator.

(b) A state or federal financial institution regulator shall keep confidential any information provided by the attorney representing the state under Subsection (a).

(c) A regulator described by Subsection (b) commits an offense if the regulator knowingly discloses information in violation of this article. An offense under this subsection is punishable by confinement in jail for a period not to exceed 30 days, a fine not to exceed $500, or both such confinement and fine.

(d) The provision of notice under Subsection (a) is not considered a waiver by the state of any privilege or claim of confidentiality.

(Enacted by Acts 2001, 77th Leg., ch. 438 (S.B. 626), § 5, effective September 1, 2001.)

# CHAPTER 60
# CRIMINAL HISTORY RECORD SYSTEM

## Art. 60.01. Definitions.

In this chapter:

(1) "Administration of criminal justice" means the performance of any of the following activities: detection, apprehension, detention, pretrial release, post-trial release, prosecution, adjudication, correctional supervision, or rehabilitation of an offender. The term includes criminal identification activities and the collection, storage, and dissemination of criminal history record information.

(2) "Appeal" means the review of a decision of a lower court by a superior court other than by collateral attack.

(3) "Computerized criminal history system" means the data base containing arrest, disposition, and other criminal history maintained by the Department of Public Safety.

(4) "Corrections tracking system" means the data base maintained by the Texas Department of Criminal Justice on all offenders under its supervision.

(5) "Council" means the Criminal Justice Policy Council.

(6) "Criminal justice agency" means a federal or state agency that is engaged in the administration of criminal justice under a statute or executive order and allocates a substantial part of its annual budget to the administration of criminal justice.

(7) "Criminal justice information system" means the computerized criminal history system and the corrections tracking system.

(8) "Disposition" means an action that results in the termination, transfer to another jurisdiction, or indeterminate suspension of the prosecution of a criminal charge.

(9) "Incident number" means a unique number assigned to a specific person during a specific arrest.

(10) "Offender" means any person who is assigned an incident number.

(11) "Offense code" means a numeric code for each offense category.

(12) "Rejected case" means:

(A) a charge that, after the arrest of the offender, the prosecutor declines to include in an information or present to a grand jury; or

(B) an information or indictment that, after the arrest of the offender, the prosecutor refuses to prosecute.

(13) "Release" means the termination of jurisdiction over an individual by the criminal justice system.

(14) "State identification number" means a unique number assigned by the Department of Public Safety to each person whose name appears in the criminal justice information system.

(15) "Uniform incident fingerprint card" means a multiple part form containing a unique incident number with space for infor-

mation relating to the charge or charges for which a person is being arrested, the person's fingerprints, and other information relevant to the arrest.

(16) "Electronic means" means the transmission of data between word processors, data processors, or similar automated information equipment over dedicated cables, commercial lines, or other similar methods of transmission. (Enacted by Acts 1989, 71st Leg., ch. 785 (H.B. 2335), § 6.01, effective September 1, 1989; am. Acts 1990, 71st Leg., 6th C.S., ch. 25 (S.B. 41), § 28, effective June 18, 1990; am. Acts 1993, 73rd Leg., ch. 790 (S.B. 510), § 37, effective September 1, 1993; am. Acts 1993, 73rd Leg., ch. 1025 (H.B. 2761), § 1, effective September 1, 1993.)

## Art. 60.02. Information Systems.

(a) The Texas Department of Criminal Justice is responsible for recording data and establishing and maintaining a data base for a corrections tracking system.

(b) The Department of Public Safety is responsible for recording data and maintaining a data base for a computerized criminal history system that serves as the record creation point for criminal history information maintained by the state.

(c) The criminal justice information system shall be established and maintained to supply the state with a system:

(1) that provides law enforcement officers with an accurate criminal history record depository;

(2) that provides criminal justice agencies with an accurate criminal history record depository for operational decision making;

(3) from which accurate criminal justice system modeling can be conducted;

(4) that improves the quality of data used to conduct impact analyses of proposed legislative changes in the criminal justice system; and

(5) that improves the ability of interested parties to analyze the functioning of the criminal justice system.

(d) The data bases must contain the information required by this chapter.

(e) The Department of Public Safety shall designate the offense codes and has the sole responsibility for designating the state identification number for each person whose name appears in the criminal justice information system.

(f) The Department of Public Safety and the Texas Department of Criminal Justice shall implement a system to link the computerized criminal history system and the corrections tracking system. Data received by the Texas Department of Criminal Justice that is required by the Department of Public Safety for the preparation of a criminal history record shall be made available to the computerized criminal history system not later than the seventh day after the date on which the Texas Department of Criminal Justice receives the request for the data from the Department of Public Safety.

(g) The Department of Public Safety is responsible for the operation of the computerized criminal history system and shall develop the necessary interfaces in the system to accommodate inquiries from a statewide automated fingerprint identification system, if such a system is implemented by the department.

(h) Whenever possible, the reporting of information relating to dispositions and subsequent offender processing data shall be conducted electronically.

(i) The Department of Public Safety and the Texas Department of Criminal Justice, with advice from the council and the Department of Information Resources, shall develop biennial plans to improve the reporting and accuracy of the criminal justice information system and to develop and maintain monitoring systems capable of identifying missing information.

(j) At least once during each five-year period the council shall coordinate an examination of the records and operations of the criminal justice information system to ensure the accuracy and completeness of information in the system and to ensure the promptness of information reporting. The state auditor, or other appropriate entity selected by the council, shall conduct the examination with the cooperation of the council, the Department of Public Safety, and the Texas Department of Criminal Justice. The Department of Public Safety, the council, and the Texas Department of Criminal Justice may examine the records of the agencies required to report information to the Department of Public Safety or the Texas Department of Criminal Justice. The examining entity shall submit to the legislature and the council a report that summarizes the findings of each examination and contains recommendations for improving the system. Not later than the first anniversary after the date the examining entity submits its report, the Department of Public Safety shall report to the Legislative Budget Board, the governor, the state auditor, and the council on the department's progress in implementing the examining entity's recommendations, including for each recommendation not implemented the reason for not implementing the recommendation. The Department of Public Safety shall submit a similar report each year following the submission of the first report until each of the examining entity's recommendations is implemented.

(k) The council, the Department of Public Safety, the criminal justice division of the governor's office, and the Department of Information Resources cooperatively shall develop and adopt a grant program, to be implemented by the criminal justice division at a time and in a manner determined by the division, to aid local law enforcement agencies, prosecutors, and court personnel in obtaining equipment and training necessary to operate a telecommunications network capable of:

(1) making inquiries to and receiving responses from the statewide automated fingerprint identification system and from the computerized criminal history system; and

(2) transmitting information to those systems.

(*l*) [Blank]

(m) Notwithstanding Subsection (j), work performed under this section by the state auditor is subject to approval by the legislative audit committee for inclusion in the audit plan under Section 321.013(c), Government Code.

(Enacted by Acts 1989, 71st Leg., ch. 785 (H.B. 2335), § 6.01, effective September 1, 1989; am. Acts 1990, 71st Leg., 6th C.S., ch. 25 (S.B. 41), § 28, effective June 18, 1990; am. Acts 1991, 72nd Leg., ch. 362 (H.B. 2841), § 1, effective August 26, 1991; am. Acts 2001, 77th Leg., ch. 474 (H.B. 776), § 1, effective September 1, 2001; am. Acts 2003, 78th Leg., ch. 785 (S.B. 19), § 72, effective September 1, 2003.)

### Art. 60.03. Interagency Cooperation; Confidentiality.

(a) Criminal justice agencies, the Legislative Budget Board, and the council are entitled to access to the data bases of the Department of Public Safety, the Texas Juvenile Probation Commission, the Texas Youth Commission, and the Texas Department of Criminal Justice in accordance with applicable state or federal law or regulations. The access granted by this subsection does not grant an agency, the Legislative Budget Board, or the council the right to add, delete, or alter data maintained by another agency.

(b) The council or the Legislative Budget Board may submit to the Department of Public Safety, the Texas Juvenile Probation Commission, the Texas Youth Commission, and the Texas Department of Criminal Justice an annual request for a data file containing data elements from the departments' systems. The Department of Public Safety, the Texas Juvenile Probation Commission, the Texas Youth Commission, and the Texas Department of Criminal Justice shall provide the council and the Legislative Budget Board with that data file for the period requested, in accordance with state and federal law and regulations. If the council submits data file requests other than the annual data file request, the director of the agency maintaining the requested records must approve the request. The Legislative Budget Board may submit data file requests other than the annual data file request without the approval of the director of the agency maintaining the requested records.

(c) Neither a criminal justice agency, the council, nor the Legislative Budget Board may disclose to the public information in an individual's criminal history record if the record is protected by state or federal law or regulation.

(Enacted by Acts 1989, 71st Leg., ch. 785 (H.B. 2335), § 6.01, effective September 1, 1989; am. Acts 1990, 71st Leg., 6th C.S., ch. 25 (S.B. 41), § 28, effective June 18, 1990; am. Acts 2005, 79th Leg., ch. 741 (H.B. 2753), § 1, effective June 17, 2005.)

### Art. 60.04. Compatibility of Data.

(a) Data supplied to the criminal justice information system must be compatible with the system and must contain both incident numbers and state identification numbers.

(b) A discrete submission of information under any article of this chapter must contain, in conjunction with information required, the defendant's name and state identification number.

(Enacted by Acts 1989, 71st Leg., ch. 785 (H.B. 2335), § 6.01, effective September 1, 1989; am. Acts 1990, 71st Leg., 6th C.S., ch. 25 (S.B. 41), § 28, effective June 18, 1990.)

### Art. 60.05. Types of Information Collected.

The criminal justice information system must contain but is not limited to the following types of information for each arrest for a felony or a misdemeanor not punishable by fine only:

(1) information relating to offenders;

(2) information relating to arrests;

(3) information relating to prosecutions;

(4) information relating to the disposition of cases by courts;

(5) information relating to sentencing; and

(6) information relating to the handling of offenders received by a correctional agency, facility, or other institution.

(Enacted by Acts 1989, 71st Leg., ch. 785 (H.B. 2335), § 6.01, effective September 1, 1989; am. Acts 1990, 71st Leg., 6th C.S., ch. 25 (S.B. 41), § 28, effective June 18, 1990.)

## Art. 60.051. Information in Computerized Criminal History System.

(a) Information in the computerized criminal history system relating to an offender must include:

(1) the offender's name, including other names by which the offender is known;

(2) the offender's date of birth;

(3) the offender's physical description, including sex, weight, height, race, ethnicity, eye color, hair color, scars, marks, and tattoos; and

(4) the offender's state identification number.

(b) Information in the computerized criminal history system relating to an arrest must include:

(1) the name of the offender;

(2) the offender's state identification number;

(3) the arresting agency;

(4) the arrest charge by offense code and incident number;

(5) whether the arrest charge is a misdemeanor or felony;

(6) the date of the arrest;

(7) the exact disposition of the case by a law enforcement agency following the arrest; and

(8) the date of disposition of the case by the law enforcement agency.

(c) Information in the computerized criminal history system relating to a prosecution must include:

(1) each charged offense by offense code and incident number;

(2) the level of the offense charged or the degree of the offense charged for each offense in Subdivision (1) of this subsection; and

(3) for a rejected case, the date of rejection, offense code, and incident number, and whether the rejection is a result of a successful pretrial diversion program.

(d) Information in the computerized criminal history system relating to the disposition of a case that was not rejected must include:

(1) the final pleading to each charged offense and the level of the offense;

(2) a listing of each charged offense disposed of by the court and:

(A) the date of disposition;

(B) the offense code for the disposed charge and incident number; and

(C) the type of disposition; and

(3) for a conviction that is appealed the final court decision and the final disposition of the offender on appeal.

(e) Information in the computerized criminal history system relating to sentencing must include for each sentence:

(1) the sentencing date;

(2) the sentence for each offense by offense code and incident number;

(3) if the offender was sentenced to confinement:

(A) the agency that receives custody of the offender;

(B) the length of sentence for each offense; and

(C) if multiple sentences were ordered, whether they were ordered to be served consecutively or concurrently;

(4) if the offender was sentenced to a fine, the amount of the fine;

(5) if a sentence to confinement or fine was ordered but was deferred, probated, suspended, or otherwise not imposed:

(A) the length of sentence or the amount of the fine that was deferred, probated, suspended, or otherwise not imposed; and

(B) the offender's name, offense code, and incident number; and

(6) if a sentence other than fine or confinement was ordered, a description of the sentence ordered.

(f) The department shall maintain in the computerized criminal history system any information the department maintains in the central database under Article 62.005.

(g) In addition to the information described by Subsections (a—f), information in the computerized criminal history system must include the age of the victim of the offense if the defendant was arrested for or charged with an offense under:

(1) Section 21.02 (Continuous sexual abuse of young child or children), Penal Code;

(2) Section 21.11 (Indecency with a child), Penal Code;

(3) Section 22.011 (Sexual assault) or 22.021 (Aggravated sexual assault), Penal Code;

Criminal Procedure

(4) Section 43.25 (Sexual performance by a child), Penal Code;

(5) Section 20.04(a)(4) (Aggravated kidnapping), Penal Code, if the defendant committed the offense with intent to violate or abuse the victim sexually;

(6) Section 30.02 (Burglary), Penal Code, if the offense is punishable under Subsection (d) of that section and the defendant committed the offense with intent to commit an offense described by Subdivision (2), (3), or (5);

(7) Section 20A.02 (Trafficking of persons), Penal Code, if the defendant:

(A) trafficked a person with the intent or knowledge that the person would engage in sexual conduct, as defined by Section 43.25, Penal Code; or

(B) benefited from participating in a venture that involved a trafficked person engaging in sexual conduct, as defined by Section 43.25, Penal Code; or

(8) Section 43.05(a)(2) (Compelling prostitution), Penal Code.

(Am. Acts 1990, 71st Leg., 6th C.S., ch. 25 (S.B. 41), § 28, effective June 18, 1990 (renumbered from art. 60.05(b) to (f)); am. Acts 1993, 73rd Leg., ch. 1025 (H.B. 2761), § 9, effective September 1, 1993; am. Acts 1995, 74th Leg., ch. 258 (S.B. 267), § 14, effective September 1, 1995; am. Acts 1997, 75th Leg., ch. 668 (S.B. 875), § 8, effective September 1, 1997; am. Acts 2005, 79th Leg., ch. 1008 (H.B. 867), § 2 (2.03), effective September 1, 2005; am. Acts 2011, 82nd Leg., ch. 515 (H.B. 2014), § 2.05, effective September 1, 2011.)

## Art. 60.052. Information in Corrections Tracking System.

(a) Information in the corrections tracking system relating to a sentence to be served under the jurisdiction of the Texas Department of Criminal Justice must include:

(1) the offender's name;

(2) the offender's state identification number;

(3) the sentencing date;

(4) the sentence for each offense by offense code and incident number;

(5) if the offender was sentenced to imprisonment:

(A) the unit of imprisonment;

(B) the length of sentence for each offense; and

(C) if multiple sentences were ordered, whether they were ordered to be served consecutively or concurrently; and

(6) if a sentence other than a fine or imprisonment was ordered, a description of the sentence ordered.

(b) Sentencing information in the corrections tracking system must also include the following information about each deferred adjudication, probation, or other alternative to imprisonment ordered:

(1) each conviction for which sentence was ordered but was deferred, probated, suspended, or otherwise not imposed, by offense code and incident number; and

(2) if a sentence or portion of a sentence of imprisonment was deferred, probated, suspended, or otherwise not imposed:

(A) the offense, the sentence, and the amount of the sentence deferred, probated, suspended, or otherwise not imposed;

(B) a statement of whether a return to confinement or other imprisonment was a condition of probation or an alternative sentence;

(C) the community supervision and corrections department exercising jurisdiction over the offender;

(D) the date the offender was received by a community supervision and corrections department;

(E) any program in which an offender is placed or has previously been placed and the level of supervision the offender is placed on while under the jurisdiction of a community supervision and corrections department;

(F) the date a program described by Paragraph (E) of this subdivision begins, the date the program ends, and whether the program was completed successfully;

(G) the date a level of supervision described by Paragraph (E) of this subdivision begins and the date the level of supervision ends;

(H) if the offender's probation is revoked:

(i) the reason for the revocation and the date of revocation by offense code and incident number; and

(ii) other current sentences of probation or other alternatives to confinement that have not been revoked, by offense code and incident number; and

(I) the date of the offender's release from the community supervision and corrections department.

(c) Information in the corrections tracking system relating to the handling of offenders must include the following information about each imprisonment, confinement, or execution of an offender:

    (1) the date of the imprisonment or confinement;

    (2) if the offender was sentenced to death:

      (A) the date of execution; and

      (B) if the death sentence was commuted, the sentence to which the sentence of death was commuted and the date of commutation;

    (3) the date the offender was released from imprisonment or confinement and whether the release was a discharge or a release on parole or mandatory supervision;

    (4) if the offender is released on parole or mandatory supervision:

      (A) the offense for which the offender was convicted by offense code and incident number;

      (B) the date the offender was received by an office of the parole division;

      (C) the county in which the offender resides while under supervision;

      (D) any program in which an offender is placed or has previously been placed and the level of supervision the offender is placed on while under the jurisdiction of the parole division;

      (E) the date a program described by Paragraph (D) begins, the date the program ends, and whether the program was completed successfully;

      (F) the date a level of supervision described by Paragraph (D) begins and the date the level of supervision ends;

      (G) if the offender's release status is revoked, the reason for the revocation and the date of revocation;

      (H) the expiration date of the sentence; and

      (I) the date of the offender's release from the parole division or the date on which the offender is granted clemency; and

    (5) if the offender is released under Section 6(a), Article 42.12, the date of the offender's release.

(Am. Acts 1990, 71st Leg., 6th C.S., ch. 25 (S.B. 41), § 28, effective June 18, 1990 (renumbered from art. 60.05(g) to (i)); am. Acts 2009, 81st Leg., ch. 87 (S.B. 1969), § 25.044, effective September 1, 2009.)

## Art. 60.06. Duties of Agencies.

  (a) Each criminal justice agency shall:

    (1) compile and maintain records needed for reporting data required by the Texas Department of Criminal Justice and the Department of Public Safety;

    (2) transmit to the Texas Department of Criminal Justice and the Department of Public Safety, when and in the manner the Texas Department of Criminal Justice and the Department of Public Safety direct, all data required by the Texas Department of Criminal Justice and the Department of Public Safety;

    (3) give the Department of Public Safety and the Texas Department of Criminal Justice or their accredited agents access to the agency for the purpose of inspection to determine the completeness and accuracy of data reported;

    (4) cooperate with the Department of Public Safety and the Texas Department of Criminal Justice so that the Department of Public Safety and the Texas Department of Criminal Justice may properly and efficiently perform their duties under this chapter; and

    (5) cooperate with the Department of Public Safety and the Texas Department of Criminal Justice to identify and eliminate redundant reporting of information to the criminal justice information system.

  (b) Information on an individual that consists of an identifiable description and notation of an arrest, detention, indictment, information, or other formal criminal charge and a disposition of the charge, including sentencing, correctional supervision, and release that is collected and compiled by the Department of Public Safety and the Texas Department of Criminal Justice from criminal justice agencies and maintained in a central location is not subject to public disclosure except as authorized by federal or state law or regulation.

  (c) Subsection (b) of this section does not apply to a document maintained by a criminal justice agency that is the source of information collected by the Department of Public Safety or the Texas Department of Criminal Justice. Each criminal justice agency shall retain documents described by this subsection.

  (d) An optical disk or other technology may be used instead of microfilm as a medium to store information if allowed by the applicable state laws or regulations relating to the archiving of state agency information.

  (e) An official of an agency may not intentionally conceal or destroy any record with intent to violate this section.

  (f) The duties imposed on a criminal justice agency under this article are also imposed on district court and county court clerks.

(Enacted by Acts 1989, 71st Leg., ch. 785 (H.B. 2335), § 6.01, effective September 1, 1989; am. Acts 1990, 71st Leg., 6th C.S., ch. 25 (S.B. 41), § 28, effective June 18, 1990; am. Acts 1995, 74th Leg., ch. 750 (H.B. 269), § 1, effective August 28, 1995.)

## Art. 60.061. Information on Persons Licensed by Certain Agencies.

(a) The Texas State Board of Medical Examiners, the Texas State Board of Podiatric Medical Examiners, the State Board of Dental Examiners, the Texas State Board of Pharmacy, the Texas State Board of Examiners of Psychologists, and the State Board of Veterinary Medical Examiners shall provide to the Department of Public Safety through electronic means, magnetic tape, or disk, as specified by the department, a list including the name, date of birth, and any other personal descriptive information required by the department for each person licensed by the respective agency. Each agency shall update this information and submit to the Department of Public Safety the updated information quarterly.

(b) The Department of Public Safety shall perform at least quarterly a computer match of the licensing list against the convictions maintained in the computerized criminal history system. The Department of Public Safety shall report to the appropriate licensing agency for verification and administrative action, as considered appropriate by the licensing agency, the name of any person found to have a record of conviction, except a defendant whose prosecution is deferred during a period of community supervision without an adjudication or plea of guilt. The Department of Public Safety may charge the licensing agency a fee not to exceed the actual direct cost incurred by the department in performing a computer match and reporting to the agency.

(c) The transmission of information by electronic means under Subsection (a) of this article does not affect whether the information is subject to disclosure under Chapter 552, Government Code.

(Enacted by Acts 1993, 73rd Leg., ch. 790 (S.B. 510), § 38, effective September 1, 1993; enacted by Acts 1993, 73rd Leg., ch. 1025 (H.B. 2761), § 2, effective September 1, 1993; am. Acts 1995, 74th Leg., ch. 76 (S.B. 959), §§ 3.21, 5.95(88), effective September 1, 1995; am. Acts 1995, 74th Leg., ch. 965 (S.B. 673), § 78, effective September 1, 1995; am. Acts 1999, 76th Leg., ch. 1189 (S.B. 370), § 43, effective September 1, 1999; am. Acts 2005,

79th Leg., ch. 143 (H.B. 1015), § 23, effective September 1, 2005.)

## Art. 60.07. Uniform Incident Fingerprint Card.

(a) The Department of Public Safety, in consultation with the council, shall design, print, and distribute to each law enforcement agency in the state a uniform incident fingerprint card.

(b) The incident card must:

(1) be serially numbered with an incident number in such a manner that the individual incident of arrest may be readily ascertained; and

(2) be a multiple part form that can be transmitted with the offender through the criminal justice process and that allows each agency to report required data to the Department of Public Safety or the Texas Department of Criminal Justice.

(c) Subject to available telecommunications capacity, the Department of Public Safety shall develop the capability to receive by electronic means from a law enforcement agency the information on the uniform incident fingerprint card. The information must be in a form that is compatible to the form required of data supplied to the criminal justice information system.

(Enacted by Acts 1989, 71st Leg., ch. 785 (H.B. 2335), § 6.01, effective September 1, 1989; am. Acts 1990, 71st Leg., 6th C.S., ch. 25 (S.B. 41), § 28, effective June 18, 1990; am. Acts 1993, 73rd Leg., ch. 790 (S.B. 510), § 39, effective September 1, 1993; am. Acts 1993, 73rd Leg., ch. 1025 (H.B. 2761), § 3, effective September 1, 1993.)

## Art. 60.08. Reporting.

(a) The Department of Public Safety and the Texas Department of Criminal Justice shall, by rule, develop reporting procedures that:

(1) ensure that the offender processing data is reported from the time an offender is arrested until the time an offender is released; and

(2) provide measures and policies designed to identify and eliminate redundant reporting of information to the criminal justice information system.

(b) The arresting agency shall prepare a uniform incident fingerprint card and initiate the reporting process for each offender charged with a felony or a misdemeanor not punishable by fine only.

(c) The clerk of the court exercising jurisdiction over a case shall report the disposition of the case to the Department of Public Safety.

(d) Except as otherwise required by applicable state laws or regulations, information or data required by this chapter to be reported to the Texas Department of Criminal Justice or the Department of Public Safety shall be reported promptly but not later than the 30th day after the date on which the information or data is received by the agency responsible for reporting it except in the case of an arrest. An offender's arrest shall be reported to the Department of Public Safety not later than the seventh day after the date of the arrest.

(e) A court that orders the release of an offender under Section 6(a), Article 42.12, at a time when the offender is under a bench warrant and not physically imprisoned in the Texas Department of Criminal Justice shall report the release to the department not later than the seventh day after the date of the release.

(Enacted by Acts 1989, 71st Leg., ch. 785 (H.B. 2335), § 6.01, effective September 1, 1989; am. Acts 1990, 71st Leg., 6th C.S., ch. 25 (S.B. 41), § 28, effective June 18, 1990; am. Acts 1995, 74th Leg., ch. 750 (H.B. 269), § 2, effective August 28, 1995; am. Acts 2009, 81st Leg., ch. 87 (S.B. 1969), § 25.045, effective September 1, 2009.)

## Art. 60.09. Local Data Advisory Boards.

(a) The commissioners court of each county may create local data advisory boards to, among other duties:

(1) analyze the structure of local automated and manual data systems to identify redundant data entry and data storage;

(2) develop recommendations for the commissioners to improve the local data systems;

(3) develop recommendations, when appropriate, for the effective electronic transfer of required data from local agencies to state agencies; and

(4) perform any related duties to be determined by the commissioners court.

(b) Local officials responsible for collecting, storing, reporting, and using data may be appointed to the local data advisory board.

(c) The council and the Department of Public Safety shall, to the extent that resources allow, provide technical assistance and advice on the request of the local data advisory board.

(Enacted by Acts 1989, 71st Leg., ch. 785 (H.B. 2335), § 6.01, effective September 1, 1989; am. Acts 1990, 71st Leg., 6th C.S., ch. 25 (S.B. 41), § 28, effective June 18, 1990.)

## Art. 60.10. [Expires September 1, 2013] Data Reporting Improvement Plan.

(a) In this article, "disposition completeness percentage" has the meaning assigned by Article 60.21(c).

(b) This article applies only to a county that has an average disposition completeness percentage, including both juvenile and adult dispositions, of less than 90 percent, as reflected in the first report the Department of Public Safety submits under Article 60.21(b)(2) on or after January 1, 2009.

(c) The commissioners court of a county described by Subsection (b) shall establish a local data advisory board as described by Article 60.09 not later than November 1, 2009. A local data advisory board established under this article may include any person described by Article 60.09(b) and must include:

(1) the sheriff of the county, or the sheriff's designee;

(2) an attorney who represents the state in the district courts of the county;

(3) an attorney who represents the state in the county courts of the county;

(4) the clerk for the district courts of the county, or the clerk's designee;

(5) the clerk for the county courts of the county, or the clerk's designee;

(6) the police chief of the municipality with the greatest population located in the county, or the chief's designee;

(7) a representative of the county's automated data processing services, if the county performs those services; and

(8) a representative of an entity with whom the county contracts for automated data processing services, if the county contracts for those services.

(d) In addition to the duties described by Article 60.09(a), a local data advisory board established under this article must prepare a data reporting improvement plan. The data reporting improvement plan must:

(1) describe the manner in which the county intends to improve the county's disposition completeness percentage;

(2) ensure that the county takes the steps necessary for the county's average disposition completeness percentage to be equal to or greater than 90 percent in the first report the Department of Public Safety submits under Article 60.21(b)(2) on or after January 1, 2013; and

(3) include a comprehensive strategy by which the county will permanently maintain the county's disposition completeness percentage at or above 90 percent.

(e) Not later than June 1, 2010, a local data advisory board established under this article shall submit to the Department of Public Safety the data reporting improvement plan prepared for the county. On receipt of a data reporting improvement plan under this article, the department shall post the plan on the Internet website maintained by the department.

(f) The public safety director of the Department of Public Safety may adopt rules concerning the contents and form of a data reporting improvement plan prepared under this article.

(g) This article expires September 1, 2013.
(Enacted by Acts 2009, 81st Leg., ch. 1146 (H.B. 2730), § 21.001, effective September 1, 2009.)

### Art. 60.11. Operation Date [Repealed].

Repealed by Acts 2005, 79th Leg., ch. 1218 (H.B. 967), § 6(2), effective September 1, 2005. (Enacted by Acts 1991, 72nd Leg., 2nd C.S., ch. 10 (H.B. 93), § 7.05, effective December 1, 1991.)

### Art. 60.12. Fingerprint and Arrest Information in Computerized System.

(a) The Department of Public Safety shall, when a jurisdiction transmits fingerprints and arrest information by a remote terminal accessing the statewide automated fingerprint identification system, use that transmission either to create a permanent record in the criminal justice information system or to create a temporary arrest record in the criminal justice information system to be maintained by the department until the department receives and processes the physical copy of the arrest information.

(b) The Department of Public Safety shall make available to a criminal justice agency making a background criminal inquiry any information contained in a temporary arrest record maintained by the department, including a statement that a physical copy of the arrest information was not available at the time the information was entered in the system.
(Enacted by Acts 1991, 72nd Leg., 2nd C.S., ch. 10 (H.B. 93), § 7.05, effective December 1, 1991; am. Acts 1993, 73rd Leg., ch. 790 (S.B. 510), § 40, effective September 1, 1993; am. Acts 1993, 73rd Leg., ch. 1025 (H.B. 2761), § 4, effective September 1, 1993.)

### Art. 60.13. Contracts for Software Development [Repealed].

Repealed by Acts 2005, 79th Leg., ch. 1218 (H.B. 967), § 6(3), effective September 1, 2005. (Enacted by Acts 1991, 72nd Leg., 2nd C.S., ch. 10 (H.B. 93), § 7.05, effective December 1, 1991.)

### Art. 60.14. Allocation of Grant Program Money for Criminal Justice Programs.

An agency of the state, before allocating money to a county from any federal or state grant program for the enhancement of criminal justice programs, shall certify that the county has taken or will take, using all or part of the allocated funds, all action necessary to provide the Texas Department of Criminal Justice and the Department of Public Safety any criminal history records maintained by the county in the manner specified for purposes of those departments.
(Enacted by Acts 1991, 72nd Leg., 2nd C.S., ch. 10 (H.B. 93), § 7.05, effective December 1, 1991.)

### Art. 60.15. Timetable for System Records [Repealed].

Repealed by Acts 2005, 79th Leg., ch. 1218 (H.B. 967), § 6(4), effective September 1, 2005. (Enacted by Acts 1991, 72nd Leg., 2nd C.S., ch. 10 (H.B. 93), § 7.05, effective December 1, 1991.)

### Art. 60.16. Report [Repealed].

Repealed by Acts 2005, 79th Leg., ch. 1218 (H.B. 967), § 6(5), effective September 1, 2005. (Enacted by Acts 1991, 72nd Leg., 2nd C.S., ch. 10 (H.B. 93), § 7.05, effective December 1, 1991.)

### Art. 60.17. Coordination of Implementation Process [Repealed].

Repealed by Acts 2005, 79th Leg., ch. 1218 (H.B. 967), § 6(6), effective September 1, 2005. (Enacted by Acts 1991, 72nd Leg., 2nd C.S., ch. 10 (H.B. 93), § 7.05, effective December 1, 1991.)

### Art. 60.18. Information on Subsequent Arrest of Certain Individuals.

The Texas Department of Criminal Justice and the Department of Public Safety shall develop the capability to send by electronic means information about the subsequent arrest of a person under supervision to, as applicable:

(1) the community supervision and corrections department serving the court of original jurisdiction; or

(2) the district parole office supervising the person.
(Enacted by Acts 1993, 73rd Leg., ch. 790 (S.B. 510), § 41, effective September 1, 1993; enacted

by Acts 1993, 73rd Leg., ch. 1025 (H.B. 2761), § 5, effective September 1, 1993; am. Acts 2005, 79th Leg., ch. 1218 (H.B. 967), § 2, effective September 1, 2005.)

## Art. 60.19. Information Related to Misused Identity.

(a) On receipt of information from a local law enforcement agency under Article 2.28, the department shall:

(1) provide the notice described by Subdivision (1) of that article to the person whose identity was misused, if the local law enforcement agency was unable to notify the person under that subdivision;

(2) take action to ensure that the information maintained in the computerized criminal history system reflects the use of the person's identity as a stolen alias; and

(3) notify the Texas Department of Criminal Justice that the person's identifying information may have been falsely used by an inmate in the custody of the department.

(b) On receipt of a declaration under Section 411.0421, Government Code, or on receipt of information similar to that contained in a declaration, the department shall separate information maintained in the computerized criminal history system regarding an individual whose identity has been misused from information maintained in that system regarding the person who misused the identity.

(Enacted by Acts 1999, 76th Leg., ch. 1334 (H.B. 153), § 2, effective September 1, 1999; am. Acts 2003, 78th Leg., ch. 339 (S.B. 566), § 5, effective September 1, 2003.)

## Art. 60.20. Information Related to Non-Fingerprint Supported Actions.

On receipt of a report of prosecution or court disposition information from a jurisdiction for which corresponding arrest data does not exist in the computerized criminal history system, the Department of Public Safety shall enter the report into a non-fingerprint supported file that is separate from the computerized criminal history system. The department shall grant access to records in the non-fingerprint supported file that include the subject's name or other identifier in the same manner as the department is required to grant access to criminal history record information under Subchapter F, Chapter 411, Government Code. On receipt of a report of arrest information that corresponds to a record in the non-fingerprint supported file, the department shall transfer the record from the non-fingerprint supported file to the computerized criminal history system.

(Enacted by Acts 2001, 77th Leg., ch. 474 (H.B. 776), § 2, effective September 1, 2001.)

## Art. 60.21. Monitoring Tracking; Information Submission.

(a) The Department of Information Resources shall monitor the development of the corrections tracking system by the Texas Department of Criminal Justice to ensure implementation of the system not later than June 1, 2005.

(b) The Department of Public Safety shall:

(1) monitor the submission of arrest and disposition information by local jurisdictions;

(2) annually submit to the Legislative Budget Board, the governor, the lieutenant governor, the state auditor, and the standing committees in the senate and house of representatives that have primary jurisdiction over criminal justice and the Department of Public Safety a report regarding the level of reporting by local jurisdictions;

(3) identify local jurisdictions that do not report arrest or disposition information or that partially report information; and

(4) for use in determining the status of outstanding dispositions, publish monthly on the Department of Public Safety's Internet website or on another electronic publication a report listing each arrest by local jurisdiction for which there is no corresponding final court disposition.

(c) The report described by Subsection (b)(2) must contain a disposition completeness percentage for each county in this state. For purposes of this subsection, "disposition completeness percentage" means the percentage of arrest charges a county reports to the Department of Public Safety to be entered in the computerized criminal history system under this chapter that were brought against a person in the county for which a disposition has been subsequently reported and entered into the computerized criminal history system.

(Enacted by Acts 2001, 77th Leg., ch. 474 (H.B. 776), § 2, effective September 1, 2001; am. Acts 2005, 79th Leg., ch. 1218 (H.B. 967), § 3, effective September 1, 2005; am. Acts 2009, 81st Leg., ch. 1146 (H.B. 2730), § 21.002, effective September 1, 2009.)

# CHAPTER 61
# COMPILATION OF INFORMATION PERTAINING TO CRIMINAL COMBINATIONS AND CRIMINAL STREET GANGS

## Art. 61.01. Definitions.

In this chapter:

(1) "Combination" and "criminal street gang" have the meanings assigned by Section 71.01, Penal Code.

(2) "Child" has the meaning assigned by Section 51.02, Family Code.

(3) "Criminal information" means facts, material, photograph, or data reasonably related to the investigation or prosecution of criminal activity.

(4) "Criminal activity" means conduct that is subject to prosecution.

(5) "Criminal justice agency" has the meaning assigned by Article 60.01 and also means a municipal or county agency, or school district law enforcement agency, that is engaged in the administration of criminal justice under a statute or executive order.

(6) "Administration of criminal justice" has the meaning assigned by Article 60.01.

(7) "Department" means the Department of Public Safety of the State of Texas.

(8) "Intelligence database" means a collection or compilation of data organized for search and retrieval to evaluate, analyze, disseminate, or use intelligence information relating to a criminal combination or a criminal street gang for the purpose of investigating or prosecuting criminal offenses.

(9) "Law enforcement agency" does not include the Texas Department of Criminal Justice, the Texas Juvenile Probation Commission, a local juvenile probation department, or the Texas Youth Commission.

(10) "Juvenile justice agency" has the meaning assigned by Section 58.101, Family Code. (Enacted by Acts 1995, 74th Leg., ch. 671 (H.B. 466), § 1, effective August 28, 1995; am. Acts 1999, 76th Leg., ch. 1154 (S.B. 8), § 2, effective September 1, 1999; am. Acts 2011, 82nd Leg., ch. 380 (S.B. 315), § 1, effective June 17, 2011.)

## Art. 61.02. Criminal Combination and Criminal Street Gang Intelligence Database; Submission Criteria.

(a) Subject to Subsection (b), a criminal justice agency or a juvenile justice agency shall compile criminal information into an intelligence database for the purpose of investigating or prosecuting the criminal activities of criminal combinations or criminal street gangs.

(b) A law enforcement agency in a municipality with a population of 50,000 or more or in a county with a population of 100,000 or more shall compile and maintain in a local or regional intelligence database criminal information relating to a criminal street gang as provided by Subsection (a). The information must be compiled and maintained in accordance with the criminal intelligence systems operating policies established under 28 C.F.R. Section 23.1 et seq. and the submission criteria established under Subsection (c).

(b-1) Information described by this article may be compiled on paper, by computer, or in any other useful manner by a criminal justice agency, juvenile justice agency, or law enforcement agency.

(c) Criminal information collected under this chapter relating to a criminal street gang must:

(1) be relevant to the identification of an organization that is reasonably suspected of involvement in criminal activity; and

(2) consist of:

(A) a judgment under any law that includes, as a finding or as an element of a criminal offense, participation in a criminal street gang;

(B) a self-admission by the individual of criminal street gang membership that is made during a judicial proceeding; or

(C) except as provided by Subsection (d), any two of the following:

(i) a self-admission by the individual of criminal street gang membership that is not made during a judicial proceeding, including the use of the Internet or other electronic format or medium to post photographs or other documentation identifying the individual as a member of a criminal street gang;

(ii) an identification of the individual as a criminal street gang member by a reliable informant or other individual;

(iii) a corroborated identification of the individual as a criminal street gang member by an informant or other individual of unknown reliability;

(iv) evidence that the individual frequents a documented area of a criminal street gang and associates with known criminal street gang members;

(v) evidence that the individual uses, in more than an incidental manner, criminal street gang dress, hand signals, tattoos, or symbols, including expressions of letters, numbers, words, or marks, regardless of how or the means by which the symbols are displayed, that are associated with a criminal street gang that operates in an area frequented by the individual and described by Subparagraph (iv);

(vi) evidence that the individual has been arrested or taken into custody with known criminal street gang members for an offense or conduct consistent with criminal street gang activity;

(vii) evidence that the individual has visited a known criminal street gang member, other than a family member of the individual, while the gang member is confined in or committed to a penal institution; or

(viii) evidence of the individual's use of technology, including the Internet, to recruit new criminal street gang members.

(d) Evidence described by Subsections (c)(2)(C)(iv) and (vii) is not sufficient to create the eligibility of a person's information to be included in an intelligence database described by this chapter unless the evidence is combined with information described by another subparagraph of Subsection (c)(2)(C).

(e) In this article:

(1) "Family member" means a person related to another person within the third degree by consanguinity or affinity, as described by Subchapter B, Chapter 573, Government Code,

except that the term does not include a person who is considered to be related to another person by affinity only as described by Section 573.024(b), Government Code.

(2) "Penal institution" means a confinement facility operated by or under a contract with any division of the Texas Department of Criminal Justice, a confinement facility operated by or under contract with the Texas Youth Commission, or a juvenile secure pre-adjudication or post-adjudication facility operated by or under a local juvenile probation department, or a county jail.

(Enacted by Acts 1995, 74th Leg., ch. 671 (H.B. 466), § 1, effective August 28, 1995; am. Acts 1999, 76th Leg., ch. 1154 (S.B. 8), § 3, effective September 1, 1999; Acts 2007, 80th Leg., ch. 258 (S.B. 11), § 18.05, effective September 1, 2007; am. Acts 2009, 81st Leg., ch. 736 (S.B. 418), § 1, effective September 1, 2009; am. Acts 2009, 81st Leg., ch. 1130 (H.B. 2086), § 36, effective September 1, 2009; am. Acts 2011, 82nd Leg., ch. 380 (S.B. 315), § 2, effective June 17, 2011.)

## Art. 61.03. Release of Information.

(a) A criminal justice agency may release on request information maintained under this chapter to:

(1) another criminal justice agency;

(2) a court; or

(3) a defendant in a criminal proceeding who is entitled to the discovery of the information under Chapter 39.

(b) A criminal justice agency or court may use information received under this article only for the administration of criminal justice. A defendant may use information received under this article only for a defense in a criminal proceeding.

(c) A local law enforcement agency described by Article 61.02(b) shall send to the department information compiled and maintained under this chapter.

(d) The department shall establish an intelligence database and shall maintain information received from an agency under Subsection (c) in the database in accordance with the policies established under 28 C.F.R. Section 23.1 et seq. and the submission criteria under Article 61.02(c).

(e) The department shall designate a code to distinguish criminal information contained in the intelligence database relating to a child from criminal information contained in the database relating to an adult offender.

(Enacted by Acts 1995, 74th Leg., ch. 671 (H.B. 466), § 1, effective August 28, 1995; am. Acts

1997, 75th Leg., ch. 898 (H.B. 2874), § 1, effective September 1, 1997; am. Acts 1999, 76th Leg., ch. 1154 (S.B. 8), § 4, effective September 1, 1999; am. Acts 2009, 81st Leg., ch. 736 (S.B. 418), § 2, effective September 1, 2009.)

## Art. 61.04. Criminal Information Relating to Child.

(a) Notwithstanding Chapter 58, Family Code, criminal information relating to a child associated with a combination or a criminal street gang may be compiled and released under this chapter regardless of the age of the child.

(b) A criminal justice agency or a juvenile justice agency may release information maintained under this chapter to an attorney representing a child who is a party to a proceeding under Title 3, Family Code, if the juvenile court determines the information:

(1) is material to the proceeding; and

(2) is not privileged under law.

(c) An attorney may use information received under this article only for a child's defense in a proceeding under Title 3, Family Code.

(d) The governing body of a county or municipality served by a law enforcement agency described by Article 61.02(b) may adopt a policy to notify the parent or guardian of a child of the agency's observations relating to the child's association with a criminal street gang.

(Enacted by Acts 1995, 74th Leg., ch. 671 (H.B. 466), § 1, effective August 28, 1995; am. Acts 1997, 75th Leg., ch. 165 (S.B. 898), § 7.05, effective September 1, 1997; am. Acts 1997, 75th Leg., ch. 898 (H.B. 2874), § 2, effective September 1, 1997; am. Acts 1999, 76th Leg., ch. 1154 (S.B. 8), § 5, effective September 1, 1999; am. Acts 2009, 81st Leg., ch. 736 (S.B. 418), § 3, effective September 1, 2009; am. Acts 2011, 82nd Leg., ch. 380 (S.B. 315), § 3, effective June 17, 2011.)

## Art. 61.05. Unauthorized Use or Release of Criminal Information.

(a) A person commits an offense if the person knowingly:

(1) uses criminal information obtained under this chapter for an unauthorized purpose; or

(2) releases the information to a person who is not entitled to the information.

(b) An offense under this article is a Class A misdemeanor.

(Enacted by Acts 1995, 74th Leg., ch. 671 (H.B. 466), § 1, effective August 28, 1995.)

## Art. 61.06. Removal of Records Relating to an Individual Other Than a Child.

(a) This article does not apply to information collected under this chapter by the Texas Department of Criminal Justice or the Texas Youth Commission.

(b) Subject to Subsection (c), information collected under this chapter relating to a criminal street gang must be removed from an intelligence database established under Article 61.02 and the intelligence database maintained by the department under Article 61.03 after five years if:

(1) the information relates to the investigation or prosecution of criminal activity engaged in by an individual other than a child; and

(2) the individual who is the subject of the information has not been arrested for criminal activity reported to the department under Chapter 60.

(c) In determining whether information is required to be removed from an intelligence database under Subsection (b), the five-year period does not include any period during which the individual who is the subject of the information is:

(1) confined in a correctional facility operated by or under contract with the Texas Department of Criminal Justice;

(2) committed to a secure correctional facility operated by or under contract with the Texas Youth Commission, as defined by Section 51.02, Family Code; or

(3) confined in a county jail or confined in or committed to a facility operated by a juvenile board in lieu of being confined in a correctional facility operated by or under contract with the Texas Department of Criminal Justice or being committed to a secure correctional facility operated by or under contract with the Texas Youth Commission.

(Enacted by Acts 1995, 74th Leg., ch. 671 (H.B. 466), § 1, effective August 28, 1995; am. Acts 1997, 75th Leg., ch. 898 (H.B. 2874), § 3, effective September 1, 1997; am. Acts 1999, 76th Leg., ch. 1154 (S.B. 8), § 6, effective September 1, 1999; am. Acts 2007, 80th Leg., ch. 258 (S.B. 11), § 18.06, effective September 1, 2007; am. Acts 2007, 80th Leg., ch. 263 (S.B. 103), § 2, effective June 8, 2007; am. Acts 2007, 80th Leg., ch. 1308 (S.B. 909), § 10, effective June 15, 2007; am. Acts 2009, 81st Leg., ch. 1130 (H.B. 2086), §§ 37, 38, effective September 1, 2009.)

## Art. 61.07. Removal of Records Relating to a Child.

(a) This article does not apply to information collected under this chapter by the Texas Department of Criminal Justice or the Texas Youth Commission.

(b) Subject to Subsection (c), information collected under this chapter relating to a criminal street gang must be removed from an intelligence database established under Article 61.02 and the intelligence database maintained by the department under Article 61.03 after two years if:

(1) the information relates to the investigation or prosecution of criminal activity engaged in by a child; and

(2) the child who is the subject of the information has not been:

(A) arrested for criminal activity reported to the department under Chapter 60; or

(B) taken into custody for delinquent conduct reported to the department under Chapter 58, Family Code.

(c) In determining whether information is required to be removed from an intelligence database under Subsection (b), the two-year period does not include any period during which the child who is the subject of the information is:

(1) committed to the Texas Youth Commission for conduct that violates a penal law of the grade of felony; or

(2) confined in the Texas Department of Criminal Justice.

(Enacted by Acts 1999, 76th Leg., ch. 1154 (S.B. 8), § 7, effective September 1, 1999; am. Acts 2009, 81st Leg., ch. 87 (S.B. 1969), § 25.046, effective September 1, 2009.)

## Art. 61.075. Right to Request Existence of Criminal Information.

(a) A person or the parent or guardian of a child may request a law enforcement agency to determine whether the agency has collected or is maintaining, under criteria established under Article 61.02(c), criminal information relating solely to the person or child. The law enforcement agency shall respond to the request not later than the 10th business day after the date the agency receives the request.

(b) Before responding to a request under Subsection (a), a law enforcement agency may require reasonable written verification of the identity of the person making the request and the relationship between the parent or guardian and the child, if applicable, including written verifi-

cation of an address, date of birth, driver's license number, state identification card number, or social security number.

(Enacted by Acts 2007, 80th Leg., ch. 258 (S.B. 11), § 18.07, effective September 1, 2007.)

## Art. 61.08. Right to Request Review of Criminal Information.

(a) On receipt of a written request of a person or the parent or guardian of a child that includes a showing by the person or the parent or guardian that a law enforcement agency may have collected criminal information under this chapter relating to the person or child that is inaccurate or that does not comply with the submission criteria under Article 61.02(c), the head of the agency or the designee of the agency head shall review criminal information collected by the agency under this chapter relating to the person or child to determine if:

(1) reasonable suspicion exists to believe that the information is accurate; and

(2) the information complies with the submission criteria established under Article 61.02(c).

(b) If, after conducting a review of criminal information under Subsection (a), the agency head or designee determines that:

(1) reasonable suspicion does not exist to believe that the information is accurate or the information does not comply with the submission criteria, the agency shall:

(A) destroy all records containing the information; and

(B) notify the department and the person who requested the review of the agency's determination and the destruction of the records; or

(2) reasonable suspicion does exist to believe that the information is accurate and the information complies with the submission criteria, the agency shall notify the person who requested the review of the agency's determination and that the person is entitled to seek judicial review of the agency's determination under Article 61.09.

(c) On receipt of notice under Subsection (b), the department shall immediately destroy all records containing the information that is the subject of the notice in the intelligence database maintained by the department under Article 61.03.

(d) A person who is committed to the Texas Youth Commission or confined in the Texas De-

**Criminal Procedure**

partment of Criminal Justice does not while committed or confined have the right to request review of criminal information under this article. (Enacted by Acts 1999, 76th Leg., ch. 1154 (S.B. 8), § 7, effective September 1, 1999; am. Acts 2009, 81st Leg., ch. 87 (S.B. 1969), § 25.047, effective September 1, 2009.)

## Art. 61.09. Judicial Review.

(a) A person who is entitled to seek judicial review of a determination made under Article 61.08(b)(2) may file a petition for review in district court in the county in which the person resides.

(b) On the filing of a petition for review under Subsection (a), the district court shall conduct an in camera review of the criminal information that is the subject of the determination to determine if:

(1) reasonable suspicion exists to believe that the information is accurate; and

(2) the information complies with the submission criteria under Article 61.02(c).

(c) If, after conducting an in camera review of criminal information under Subsection (b), the court finds that reasonable suspicion does not exist to believe that the information is accurate or that the information does not comply with the submission criteria, the court shall:

(1) order the law enforcement agency that collected the information to destroy all records containing the information; and

(2) notify the department of the court's determination and the destruction of the records.

(d) A petitioner may appeal a final judgment of a district court conducting an in camera review under this article.

(e) Information that is the subject of an in camera review under this article is confidential and may not be disclosed. (Enacted by Acts 1999, 76th Leg., ch. 1154 (S.B. 8), § 7, effective September 1, 1999.)

## Art. 61.10. Texas Violent Gang Task Force.

(a) In this article, "task force" means the Texas Violent Gang Task Force.

(b) The purpose of the task force is to form a strategic partnership among local, state, and federal criminal justice, juvenile justice, and correctional agencies to better enable those agencies to take a proactive stance towards tracking gang activity and the growth and spread of gangs statewide.

(c) The task force shall focus its efforts on:

(1) developing, through regional task force meetings, a statewide networking system that will provide timely access to gang information;

(2) establishing communication between different criminal justice, juvenile justice, and correctional agencies, combining independent agency resources, and joining agencies together in a cooperative effort to focus on gang membership, gang activity, and gang migration trends; and

(3) forming a working group of criminal justice, juvenile justice, and correctional representatives from throughout the state to discuss specific cases and investigations involving gangs and other related gang activities.

(d) The task force may take any other actions as necessary to accomplish the purposes of this article.

(e) The Department of Public Safety shall support the task force to assist in coordinating statewide antigang initiatives.

(f) The task force shall consist of:

(1) a representative of the Department of Public Safety designated by the director of that agency;

(2) two representatives of the Texas Department of Criminal Justice, including a representative of the parole division, designated by the executive director of that agency;

(3) a representative of the office of the inspector general of the Texas Department of Criminal Justice designated by the inspector general;

(4) a representative of the Texas Youth Commission designated by the executive director of that agency;

(5) a representative of the Texas Juvenile Probation Commission designated by the executive director of that agency;

(6) a representative of the office of the attorney general designated by the attorney general;

(7) six representatives who are local law enforcement officers or local community supervision personnel, including juvenile probation personnel, designated by the governor; and

(8) two representatives who are local prosecutors designated by the governor.

(g) If practicable, the task force shall consult with representatives from one or more United States Attorneys' Offices in this state and with representatives from the following federal agencies who are available and assigned to a duty station in this state:

(1) the Federal Bureau of Investigation;

(2) the Federal Bureau of Prisons;

(3) the United States Drug Enforcement Administration;

(4) United States Immigration and Customs Enforcement;

(5) United States Customs and Border Protection;

(6) the Bureau of Alcohol, Tobacco, Firearms and Explosives;

(7) the United States Marshals Service; and

(8) the United States Probation and Pretrial Services System.

(Enacted by Acts 1999, 76th Leg., ch. 492 (S.B. 1580), § 1, effective June 18, 1999; am. Acts 2001, 77th Leg., ch. 1420 (H.B. 2812), § 21.001(14), effective September 1, 2001 (renumbered from art. 61.07); am. Acts 2011, 82nd Leg., ch. 380 (S.B. 315), § 4, effective June 17, 2011.)

## Art. 61.11. Gang Resource System.

(a) The office of the attorney general shall establish an electronic gang resource system to provide criminal justice agencies and juvenile justice agencies with information about criminal street gangs in the state. The system may include the following information with regard to any gang:

(1) gang name;

(2) gang identifiers, such as colors used, tattoos, and clothing preferences;

(3) criminal activities;

(4) migration trends;

(5) recruitment activities; and

(6) a local law enforcement contact.

(b) Upon request by the office of the attorney general, criminal justice agencies and juvenile justice agencies shall make a reasonable attempt to provide gang information to the office of the attorney general for the purpose of maintaining an updated, comprehensive gang resource system.

(c) The office of the attorney general shall cooperate with criminal justice agencies and juvenile justice agencies in collecting and maintaining the accuracy of the information included in the gang resource system.

(d) Information relating to the identity of a specific offender or alleged offender may not be maintained in the gang resource system.

(e) Information in the gang resource system may be used in investigating gang-related crimes but may be included in affidavits or subpoenas or used in connection with any other legal or judicial proceeding only if the information from the system is corroborated by information not provided or maintained in the system.

(f) Access to the gang resource system shall be limited to criminal justice agency personnel and juvenile justice agency personnel.

(g) Information in the gang resource system shall be accessible by:

(1) municipality or county; and

(2) gang name.

(h) The office of the attorney general may coordinate with the Texas Department of Criminal Justice to include information in the gang resource system regarding groups which have been identified by the Security Threat Group Management Office of the Texas Department of Criminal Justice.

(Enacted by Acts 1999, 76th Leg., ch. 491 (S.B. 1578), § 1, effective August 30, 1999; am. Acts 2001, 77th Leg., ch. 1420 (H.B. 2812), § 21.001(15), effective September 1, 2001 (renumbered from art. 61.08).)

## Art. 61.12. Database User Training.

(a) The department shall enter into a memorandum of understanding with the United States Department of Justice or other appropriate federal department or agency to provide any person in this state who enters information into or retrieves information from an intelligence database described by this chapter with training regarding the operating principles described by 28 C.F.R. Part 23, as those principles relate to an intelligence database established or maintained under this chapter.

(b) A person in this state who enters information into or retrieves information from an intelligence database described by this chapter shall complete continuing education training on the material described by Subsection (a) at least once for each continuous two-year period the person has primary responsibility for performing a function described by this subsection.

(c) The department shall adopt the rules necessary to implement this article.

(Enacted by Acts 2009, 81st Leg., ch. 736 (S.B. 418), § 4, effective September 1, 2009.)

# CHAPTER 62
# SEX OFFENDER REGISTRATION PROGRAM

# SUBCHAPTER A
# GENERAL PROVISIONS

## Art. 62.001. Definitions.

In this chapter:

(1) "Department" means the Department of Public Safety.

(2) "Local law enforcement authority" means, as applicable, the office of the chief of police of a municipality, the office of the sheriff of a county in this state, or a centralized registration authority.

(3) "Penal institution" means a confinement facility operated by or under a contract with any division of the Texas Department of Criminal Justice, a confinement facility operated by or under contract with the Texas Youth Commission, or a juvenile secure pre-adjudication or post-adjudication facility operated by or un-

der a local juvenile probation department, or a county jail.

(4) "Released" means discharged, paroled, placed in a nonsecure community program for juvenile offenders, or placed on juvenile probation, community supervision, or mandatory supervision.

(5) "Reportable conviction or adjudication" means a conviction or adjudication, including an adjudication of delinquent conduct or a deferred adjudication, that, regardless of the pendency of an appeal, is a conviction for or an adjudication for or based on:

(A) a violation of Section 21.02 (Continuous sexual abuse of young child or children), 21.11 (Indecency with a child), 22.011 (Sexual assault), 22.021 (Aggravated sexual assault), or 25.02 (Prohibited sexual conduct), Penal Code;

(B) a violation of Section 43.05 (Compelling prostitution), 43.25 (Sexual performance by a child), or 43.26 (Possession or promotion of child pornography), Penal Code;

(C) a violation of Section 20.04(a)(4) (Aggravated kidnapping), Penal Code, if the actor committed the offense or engaged in the conduct with intent to violate or abuse the victim sexually;

(D) a violation of Section 30.02 (Burglary), Penal Code, if the offense or conduct is punishable under Subsection (d) of that section and the actor committed the offense or engaged in the conduct with intent to commit a felony listed in Paragraph (A) or (C);

(E) a violation of Section 20.02 (Unlawful restraint), 20.03 (Kidnapping), or 20.04 (Aggravated kidnapping), Penal Code, if, as applicable:

(i) the judgment in the case contains an affirmative finding under Article 42.015; or

(ii) the order in the hearing or the papers in the case contain an affirmative finding that the victim or intended victim was younger than 17 years of age;

(F) the second violation of Section 21.08 (Indecent exposure), Penal Code, but not if the second violation results in a deferred adjudication;

(G) an attempt, conspiracy, or solicitation, as defined by Chapter 15, Penal Code, to commit an offense or engage in conduct listed in Paragraph (A), (B), (C), (D), (E), or (K);

(H) a violation of the laws of another state, federal law, the laws of a foreign country, or the Uniform Code of Military Justice for or

based on the violation of an offense containing elements that are substantially similar to the elements of an offense listed under Paragraph (A), (B), (C), (D), (E), (G), (J), or (K), but not if the violation results in a deferred adjudication;

(I) the second violation of the laws of another state, federal law, the laws of a foreign country, or the Uniform Code of Military Justice for or based on the violation of an offense containing elements that are substantially similar to the elements of the offense of indecent exposure, but not if the second violation results in a deferred adjudication;

(J) a violation of Section 33.021 (Online solicitation of a minor), Penal Code; or

(K) a violation of Section 20A.02(a)(3), (4), (7), or (8) (Trafficking of persons), Penal Code.

(6) "Sexually violent offense" means any of the following offenses committed by a person 17 years of age or older:

(A) an offense under Section 21.02 (Continuous sexual abuse of young child or children), 21.11(a)(1) (Indecency with a child), 22.011 (Sexual assault), or 22.021 (Aggravated sexual assault), Penal Code;

(B) an offense under Section 43.25 (Sexual performance by a child), Penal Code;

(C) an offense under Section 20.04(a)(4) (Aggravated kidnapping), Penal Code, if the defendant committed the offense with intent to violate or abuse the victim sexually;

(D) an offense under Section 30.02 (Burglary), Penal Code, if the offense is punishable under Subsection (d) of that section and the defendant committed the offense with intent to commit a felony listed in Paragraph (A) or (C) of Subdivision (5); or

(E) an offense under the laws of another state, federal law, the laws of a foreign country, or the Uniform Code of Military Justice if the offense contains elements that are substantially similar to the elements of an offense listed under Paragraph (A), (B), (C), or (D).

(7) "Residence" includes a residence established in this state by a person described by Article 62.152(e).

(8) "Public or private institution of higher education" includes a college, university, community college, or technical or trade institute.

(9) "Authority for campus security" means the authority with primary law enforcement

jurisdiction over property under the control of a public or private institution of higher education, other than a local law enforcement authority.

(10) "Extrajurisdictional registrant" means a person who:

(A) is required to register as a sex offender under:

(i) the laws of another state with which the department has entered into a reciprocal registration agreement;

(ii) federal law or the Uniform Code of Military Justice; or

(iii) the laws of a foreign country; and

(B) is not otherwise required to register under this chapter because:

(i) the person does not have a reportable conviction for an offense under the laws of the other state, federal law, the laws of the foreign country, or the Uniform Code of Military Justice containing elements that are substantially similar to the elements of an offense requiring registration under this chapter; or

(ii) the person does not have a reportable adjudication of delinquent conduct based on a violation of an offense under the laws of the other state, federal law, or the laws of the foreign country containing elements that are substantially similar to the elements of an offense requiring registration under this chapter.

(11) "Centralized registration authority" means a mandatory countywide registration location designated under Article 62.0045.

(12) "Online identifier" means electronic mail address information or a name used by a person when sending or receiving an instant message, social networking communication, or similar Internet communication or when participating in an Internet chat. The term includes an assumed name, nickname, pseudonym, moniker, or user name established by a person for use in connection with an electronic mail address, chat or instant chat room platform, commercial social networking site, or online picture-sharing service.

(Am. Acts 2005, 79th Leg., ch. 1008 (H.B. 867), § 1.01, effective September 1, 2005 (renumbered from art. 62.01); am. Acts 2007, 80th Leg., ch. 593 (H.B. 8), §§ 3.22(a),(b), 3.23, effective September 1, 2007; am. Acts 2007, 80th Leg., ch. 921 (H.B. 3167), § 3.002(a), effective September 1, 2007; am. Acts 2009, 81st Leg., ch. 566 (S.B. 2048), § 1, effective June 19, 2009; am. Acts 2009, 81st Leg.,

ch. 755 (S.B. 689), § 2, effective September 1, 2009; am. Acts 2011, 82nd Leg., ch. 1 (S.B. 24), § 2.10, effective September 1, 2011; am. Acts 2011, 82nd Leg., ch. 91 (S.B. 1303), § 27.001(4), effective September 1, 2011; am. Acts 2011, 82nd Leg., ch. 233 (H.B. 530), § 1, effective June 17, 2011.)

## Art. 62.0015. Presumption Regarding Parentage [Renumbered].

Renumbered to Tex. Code of Crim. Proc. art. 63.0015 by Acts 2009, 81st Leg., ch. 87 (S.B. 1969), § 27.001(3), effective September 1, 2009.

## Art. 62.002. Applicability of Chapter.

(a) This chapter applies only to a reportable conviction or adjudication occurring on or after September 1, 1970.

(b) Except as provided by Subsection (c), the duties imposed on a person required to register under this chapter on the basis of a reportable conviction or adjudication, and the corresponding duties and powers of other entities in relation to the person required to register on the basis of that conviction or adjudication, are not affected by:

(1) an appeal of the conviction or adjudication; or

(2) a pardon of the conviction or adjudication.

(c) If a conviction or adjudication that is the basis of a duty to register under this chapter is set aside on appeal by a court or if the person required to register under this chapter on the basis of a conviction or adjudication receives a pardon on the basis of subsequent proof of innocence, the duties imposed on the person by this chapter and the corresponding duties and powers of other entities in relation to the person are terminated.

(Enacted by Acts 2005, 79th Leg., ch. 1008 (H.B. 867), § 1.01, effective September 1, 2005.)

## Art. 62.003. Determination Regarding Substantially Similar Elements of Offense.

(a) For the purposes of this chapter, the department is responsible for determining whether an offense under the laws of another state, federal law, the laws of a foreign country, or the Uniform Code of Military Justice contains elements that are substantially similar to the elements of an offense under the laws of this state.

(b) The department annually shall provide or make available to each prosecuting attorney's office in this state:

(1) the criteria used in making a determination under Subsection (a); and

(2) any existing record or compilation of offenses under the laws of another state, federal law, the laws of a foreign country, and the Uniform Code of Military Justice that the department has already determined to contain elements that are substantially similar to the elements of offenses under the laws of this state.

(c) An appeal of a determination made under this article shall be brought in a district court in Travis County.

(Am. Acts 2005, 79th Leg., ch. 1008 (H.B. 867), § 1.01, effective September 1, 2005 (renumbered from art. 62.0101).)

### Art. 62.004. Determination Regarding Primary Registration Authority.

(a) Except as provided by Subsection (a-1), for each person subject to registration under this chapter, the department shall determine which local law enforcement authority serves as the person's primary registration authority based on the municipality or county in which the person resides or, as provided by Article 62.152, the municipality or county in which the person works or attends school.

(a-1) Notwithstanding any other provision of this chapter, if a person resides or, as described by Article 62.152, works or attends school in a county with a centralized registration authority, the centralized registration authority serves as the person's primary registration authority under this chapter, regardless of whether the person resides, works, or attends school, as applicable, in any municipality located in that county.

(b) The department shall notify each person subject to registration under this chapter of the person's primary registration authority in a timely manner.

(Am. Acts 2005, 79th Leg., ch. 1008 (H.B. 867), § 1.01, effective September 1, 2005 (renumbered from art. 62.0102).)

### Art. 62.0045. Centralized Registration Authority.

(a) The commissioners court in a county with a population of 100,000 or more may designate the office of the sheriff of the county or may, through interlocal agreement, designate the office of a chief of police of a municipality in that county to serve as a mandatory countywide registration location for persons subject to this chapter.

(b) Notwithstanding any other provision of this chapter, a person who is subject to this chapter shall register under Article 62.051 or verify registration under Article 62.058 only with the centralized registration authority for the county, regardless of whether the person resides in any municipality located in that county. If the person resides in a municipality, and the local law enforcement authority in the municipality does not serve as the person's centralized registration authority, the centralized registration authority, not later than the third day after the date the person registers or verifies registration with that authority, shall provide to the local law enforcement authority in that municipality notice of the person's registration or verification of registration, as applicable, with the centralized registration authority.

(Enacted by Acts 2009, 81st Leg., ch. 566 (S.B. 2048), § 3, effective June 19, 2009.)

### Art. 62.005. Central Database; Public Information.

(a) The department shall maintain a computerized central database containing the information required for registration under this chapter. The department may include in the computerized central database the numeric risk level assigned to a person under this chapter.

(b) The information contained in the database, including the numeric risk level assigned to a person under this chapter, is public information, with the exception of any information:

(1) regarding the person's social security number or driver's license number, or any home, work, or cellular telephone number of the person;

(2) that is described by Article 62.051(c)(7) or required by the department under Article 62.051(c)(8); or

(3) that would identify the victim of the offense for which the person is subject to registration.

(c) Notwithstanding Chapter 730, Transportation Code, the department shall maintain in the database, and shall post on any department website related to the database, any photograph of the person that is available through the process for obtaining or renewing a personal identification certificate or driver's license under Section 521.103 or 521.272, Transportation Code. The department shall update the photograph in the database and on the website annually or as the photograph otherwise becomes available through the renewal process for the certificate or license.

(d) A local law enforcement authority shall release public information described under Subsection (b) to any person who requests the information from the authority. The authority may charge the person a fee not to exceed the amount reasonably necessary to cover the administrative costs associated with the authority's release of information to the person under this subsection.

(e) The department shall provide a licensing authority with notice of any person required to register under this chapter who holds or seeks a license that is issued by the authority. The department shall provide the notice required by this subsection as the applicable licensing information becomes available through the person's registration or verification of registration.

(f) On the written request of a licensing authority that identifies an individual and states that the individual is an applicant for or a holder of a license issued by the authority, the department shall release any information described by Subsection (a) to the licensing authority.

(g) For the purposes of Subsections (e) and (f):

(1) "License" means a license, certificate, registration, permit, or other authorization that:

(A) is issued by a licensing authority; and

(B) a person must obtain to practice or engage in a particular business, occupation, or profession.

(2) "Licensing authority" means a department, commission, board, office, or other agency of the state or a political subdivision of the state that issues a license.

(h) Not later than the third day after the date on which the applicable information becomes available through the person's registration or verification of registration or under Article 62.058, the department shall send notice of any person required to register under this chapter who is or will be employed, carrying on a vocation, or a student at a public or private institution of higher education in this state to:

(1) for an institution in this state:

(A) the authority for campus security for that institution; or

(B) if an authority for campus security for that institution does not exist, the local law enforcement authority of:

(i) the municipality in which the institution is located; or

(ii) the county in which the institution is located, if the institution is not located in a municipality; or

(2) for an institution in another state, any existing authority for campus security at that institution.

(i) On the written request of an institution of higher education described by Subsection (h) that identifies an individual and states that the individual has applied to work or study at the institution, the department shall release any information described by Subsection (a) to the institution.

(j) The department, for law enforcement purposes, shall release all relevant information described by Subsection (a), including information that is not public information under Subsection (b), to a peace officer, an employee of a local law enforcement authority, or the attorney general on the request of the applicable person or entity.
(Enacted by Acts 2005, 79th Leg., ch. 1008 (H.B. 867), § 1.01, effective September 1, 2005; am. Acts 2009, 81st Leg., ch. 755 (S.B. 689), § 3, effective September 1, 2009.)

## Art. 62.006. Information Provided to Peace Officer on Request.

The department shall establish a procedure by which a peace officer or employee of a law enforcement agency who provides the department with a driver's license number, personal identification certificate number, or license plate number is automatically provided information as to whether the person to whom the driver's license or personal identification certificate is issued is required to register under this chapter or whether the license plate number is entered in the computerized central database under Article 62.005 as assigned to a vehicle owned or driven by a person required to register under this chapter.
(Enacted by Acts 2005, 79th Leg., ch. 1008 (H.B. 867), § 1.01, effective September 1, 2005.)

## Art. 62.0061. Request for Online Identifiers by Social Networking Sites.

(a) On request by a commercial social networking site, the department may provide to the commercial social networking site:

(1) all public information that is contained in the database maintained under Article 62.005; and

(2) notwithstanding Article 62.005(b)(2), any online identifier established or used by a person who uses the site, is seeking to use the site, or is precluded from using the site.

(b) The department by rule shall establish a procedure through which a commercial social networking site may request information under Subsection (a), including rules regarding the eligibility of commercial social networking sites to request information under Subsection (a). The department shall consult with the attorney general, other appropriate state agencies, and other appropriate entities in adopting rules under this subsection.

(c) A commercial social networking site or the site's agent:

(1) may use information received under Subsection (a) only to:

(A) prescreen persons seeking to use the site; or

(B) preclude persons registered under this chapter from using the site; and

(2) may not use any information received under Subsection (a) that the networking site obtained solely under Subsection (a) in any manner not described by Subdivision (1).

(d) A commercial social networking site that uses information received under Subsection (a) in any manner not described by Subsection (c)(1) or that violates a rule adopted by the department under Subsection (b) is subject to a civil penalty of $1,000 for each misuse of information or rule violation. A commercial social networking site that is assessed a civil penalty under this article shall pay, in addition to the civil penalty, all court costs, investigative costs, and attorney's fees associated with the assessment of the penalty. A civil penalty assessed under this subsection shall be deposited to the compensation to victims of crime fund established under Subchapter B, Chapter 56.

(e) This article does not create a private cause of action against a commercial social networking site, including a cause of action that is based on the site:

(1) identifying, removing, disabling, blocking, or otherwise affecting the user of a commercial social networking site, based on a good faith belief that the person is required to register as a sex offender under this chapter or federal law; or

(2) failing to identify, remove, disable, block, or otherwise affect the user of a commercial social networking site who is required to register as a sex offender under this chapter or federal law.

(f) In this article, "commercial social networking site":

(1) means an Internet website that:

(A) allows users, through the creation of Internet web pages or profiles or other simi-

lar means, to provide personal information to the public or other users of the Internet website;

(B) offers a mechanism for communication with other users of the Internet website; and

(C) has the primary purpose of facilitating online social interactions; and

(2) does not include an Internet service provider, unless the Internet service provider separately operates and directly derives revenue from an Internet website described by Subdivision (1).

(Enacted by Acts 2009, 81st Leg., ch. 755 (S.B. 689), § 4, effective September 1, 2009.)

## Art. 62.007. Risk Assessment Review Committee; Sex Offender Screening Tool.

(a) The Texas Department of Criminal Justice shall establish a risk assessment review committee composed of at least seven members, each of whom serves on the review committee in addition to the member's other employment-related duties. The review committee, to the extent feasible, must include at least:

(1) one member having experience in law enforcement;

(2) one member having experience working with juvenile sex offenders;

(3) one member having experience as a sex offender treatment provider;

(4) one member having experience working with victims of sex offenses;

(5) the executive director of the Council on Sex Offender Treatment; and

(6) one sex offender treatment provider registered under Chapter 110, Occupations Code, and selected by the executive director of the Council on Sex Offender Treatment to serve on the review committee.

(b) The risk assessment review committee functions in an oversight capacity. The committee shall:

(1) develop or select, from among existing tools or from any tool recommended by the Council on Sex Offender Treatment, a sex offender screening tool to be used in determining the level of risk of a person subject to registration under this chapter;

(2) ensure that staff is trained on the use of the screening tool;

(3) monitor the use of the screening tool in the state; and

(4) analyze other screening tools as they become available and revise or replace the existing screening tool if warranted.

(c) The sex offender screening tool must use an objective point system under which a person is assigned a designated number of points for each of various factors. In developing or selecting the sex offender screening tool, the risk assessment review committee shall use or shall select a screening tool that may be adapted to use the following general guidelines:

(1) level one (low): a designated range of points on the sex offender screening tool indicating that the person poses a low danger to the community and will not likely engage in criminal sexual conduct;

(2) level two (moderate): a designated range of points on the sex offender screening tool indicating that the person poses a moderate danger to the community and might continue to engage in criminal sexual conduct; and

(3) level three (high): a designated range of points on the sex offender screening tool indicating that the person poses a serious danger to the community and will continue to engage in criminal sexual conduct.

(d) The risk assessment review committee, the Texas Department of Criminal Justice, the Texas Youth Commission, or a court may override a risk level only if the entity:

(1) believes that the risk level assessed is not an accurate prediction of the risk the offender poses to the community; and

(2) documents the reason for the override in the offender's case file.

(e) Notwithstanding Chapter 58, Family Code, records and files, including records that have been sealed under Section 58.003 of that code, relating to a person for whom a court, the Texas Department of Criminal Justice, or the Texas Youth Commission is required under this article to determine a level of risk shall be released to the court, department, or commission, as appropriate, for the purpose of determining the person's risk level.

(f) Chapter 551, Government Code, does not apply to a meeting of the risk assessment review committee.

(g) The numeric risk level assigned to a person using the sex offender screening tool described by this article is not confidential and is subject to disclosure under Chapter 552, Government Code. (Enacted by Acts 2005, 79th Leg., ch. 1008 (H.B. 867), § 1.01, effective September 1, 2005.)

### Art. 62.008. General Immunity.

The following persons are immune from liability for good faith conduct under this chapter:

(1) an employee or officer of the Texas Department of Criminal Justice, the Texas Youth Commission, the Texas Juvenile Probation Commission, the Department of Public Safety, the Board of Pardons and Paroles, or a local law enforcement authority;

(2) an employee or officer of a community supervision and corrections department or a juvenile probation department;

(3) a member of the judiciary; and

(4) a member of the risk assessment review committee established under Article 62.007. (Enacted by Acts 2005, 79th Leg., ch. 1008 (H.B. 867), § 1.01, effective September 1, 2005.)

### Art. 62.009. Immunity for Release of Public Information.

(a) The department, a penal institution, a local law enforcement authority, or an authority for campus security may release to the public information regarding a person required to register under this chapter only if the information is public information under this chapter.

(b) An individual, agency, entity, or authority is not liable under Chapter 101, Civil Practice and Remedies Code, or any other law for damages arising from conduct authorized by Subsection (a).

(c) For purposes of determining liability, the release or withholding of information by an appointed or elected officer of an agency, entity, or authority is a discretionary act.

(d) A private primary or secondary school, public or private institution of higher education, or administrator of a private primary or secondary school or public or private institution of higher education may release to the public information regarding a person required to register under this chapter only if the information is public information under this chapter and is released to the administrator under Article 62.005, 62.053, 62.054, 62.055, or 62.153. A private primary or secondary school, public or private institution of higher education, or administrator of a private primary or secondary school or public or private institution of higher education is not liable under any law for damages arising from conduct authorized by this subsection. (Enacted by Acts 2005, 79th Leg., ch. 1008 (H.B. 867), § 1.01, effective September 1, 2005.)

### Art. 62.010. Rulemaking Authority.

The Texas Department of Criminal Justice, the Texas Youth Commission, the Texas Juvenile Pro-

bation Commission, and the department may adopt any rule necessary to implement this chapter.
(Enacted by Acts 2005, 79th Leg., ch. 1008 (H.B. 867), § 1.01, effective September 1, 2005.)

## Art. 62.01. Definitions [Renumbered].

Renumbered to Tex. Code Crim. Proc. art. 62.001 by Acts 2005, 79th Leg., ch. 1008 (H.B. 867), § 1.01, effective September 1, 2005.

## Art. 62.0101. Determination Regarding Substantially Similar Elements of Offense [Renumbered].

Renumbered to Tex. Code Crim. Proc. art. 62.003 by Acts 2005, 79th Leg., ch. 1008 (H.B. 867), § 1.01, effective September 1, 2005.

## Art. 62.0102. Determination Regarding Primary Registration Authority [Renumbered].

Renumbered to Tex. Code Crim. Proc. art. 62.004 by Acts 2005, 79th Leg., ch. 1008 (H.B. 867), § 1.01, effective September 1, 2005.

## Art. 62.0105. Exemption from Registration for Certain Sex Offenders [Deleted].

Deleted by Acts 2005, 79th Leg., ch. 1008 (H.B. 867), § 1.01, effective September 1, 2005.
(Enacted by Acts 2001, 77th Leg., ch. 1159 (H.B. 2987), § 6, effective September 1, 2001.)

## Art. 62.011. Workers or Students [Deleted].

Deleted by Acts 2005, 79th Leg., ch. 1008 (H.B. 867), § 1.01, effective September 1, 2005.
(Enacted by Acts 1999, 76th Leg., ch. 1193 (S.B. 399), § 8, effective September 1, 1999; enacted by Acts 1999, 76th Leg., ch. 1415 (H.B. 2145), § 9, effective September 1, 1999; am. Acts 2003, 78th Leg., ch. 347 (S.B. 871), § 3, effective September 1, 2003.)

## Art. 62.012. Report of Inquiry [Renumbered].

Renumbered to Tex. Code Crim. Proc. art. 63.012 by Acts 1999, 76th Leg., ch. 62 (S.B. 1368), § 19.01(8)(A), effective September 1, 1999.

## Art. 62.013. Information to Clearinghouse [Renumbered].

Renumbered to Tex. Code Crim. Proc. art. 63.013 by Acts 1999, 76th Leg., ch. 62 (S.B. 1368), § 19.01(8)(A), effective September 1, 1999.

## Art. 62.014. Cross-Checking and Matching [Renumbered].

Renumbered to Tex. Code Crim. Proc. art. 63.014 by Acts 1999, 76th Leg., ch. 62 (S.B. 1368), § 19.01(8)(A), effective September 1, 1999.

## Art. 62.015. Availability of Information Through Other Agencies [Renumbered].

Renumbered to Tex. Code Crim. Proc. art. 63.015 by Acts 1999, 76th Leg., ch. 62 (S.B. 1368), § 19.01(8)(A), effective September 1, 1999.

## Art. 62.016. Donations [Renumbered].

Renumbered to Tex. Code Crim. Proc. art. 63.016 by Acts 1999, 76th Leg., ch. 62 (S.B. 1368), § 19.01(8)(A), effective September 1, 1999.

## Art. 62.017. Confidentiality of Certain Records [Renumbered].

Renumbered to Tex. Code Crim. Proc. art. 63.017 by Acts 1999, 76th Leg., ch. 62 (S.B. 1368), § 19.01(8)(A), effective September 1, 1999.

## Art. 62.018. Death Certificates [Renumbered].

Renumbered to Tex. Code Crim. Proc. art. 63.018 by Acts 1999, 76th Leg., ch. 62 (S.B. 1368), § 19.01(8)(A), effective September 1, 1999.

## Art. 62.02. Registration [Renumbered].

Renumbered to Tex. Code Crim. Proc. art. 62.051 by Acts 2005, 79th Leg., ch. 1008 (H.B. 867), § 1.01, effective September 1, 2005.

## Art. 62.021. Out of State Registrants [Renumbered].

Renumbered to Tex. Code Crim. Proc. art. 62.052 by Acts 2005, 79th Leg., ch. 1008 (H.B. 867), § 1.01, effective September 1, 2005.

## Art. 62.023. Receivership for Certain Missing Persons [Repealed].

Repealed by Acts 1999, 76th Leg., ch. 1081 (H.B. 3343), § 8, effective September 1, 1999.
(Enacted by Acts 1997, 75th Leg., ch. 1376 (H.B. 1317), § 5, effective September 1, 1997.)

## Art. 62.024. Notice and Citation for Receivership for Certain Missing Persons [Repealed].

Repealed by Acts 1999, 76th Leg., ch. 1081 (H.B. 3343), § 8, effective September 1, 1999.

(Enacted by Acts 1997, 75th Leg., ch. 1376 (H.B. 1317), § 5, effective September 1, 1997.)

### Art. 62.03. Prerelease Notification [Renumbered].

Renumbered to Tex. Code Crim. Proc. art. 62.053 by Acts 2005, 79th Leg., ch. 1008 (H.B. 867), § 1.01, effective September 1, 2005.

### Art. 62.031. Limitations on Newspaper Publication [Deleted].

Deleted by Acts 2005, 79th Leg., ch. 1008 (H.B. 867), § 1.01, effective September 1, 2005. (Enacted by Acts 2003, 78th Leg., ch. 347 (S.B. 871), § 6, effective September 1, 2003.)

### Art. 62.032. Circumstances Requiring Notice to Superintendent or School Administrator [Renumbered].

Renumbered to Tex. Code Crim. Proc. art. 62.054 by Acts 2005, 79th Leg., ch. 1008 (H.B. 867), § 1.01, effective September 1, 2005.

### Art. 62.035. Risk Assessment Review Committee; Sex Offender Screening Tool [Deleted].

Deleted by Acts 2005, 79th Leg., ch. 1008 (H.B. 867), § 1.01, effective September 1, 2005. (Enacted by Acts 1999, 76th Leg., ch. 1557 (S.B. 1650), § 2, effective August 30, 1999; am. Acts 2001, 77th Leg., ch. 177 (S.B. 1206), § 2, effective September 1, 2001.)

### Art. 62.04. Change of Address [Renumbered].

Renumbered to Tex. Code Crim. Proc. art. 62.055 by Acts 2005, 79th Leg., ch. 1008 (H.B. 867), § 1.01, effective September 1, 2005.

### Art. 62.041. Authority of Political Subdivision to Collect Costs of Certain Notice [Deleted].

Deleted by Acts 2005, 79th Leg., ch. 1008 (H.B. 867), § 1.01, effective September 1, 2005. (Enacted by Acts 2003, 78th Leg., ch. 1300 (S.B. 146), § 3, effective September 1, 2003.)

### Art. 62.045. Additional Public Notice for Certain Offenders [Renumbered].

Renumbered to Tex. Code Crim. Proc. art. 62.056 by Acts 2005, 79th Leg., ch. 1008 (H.B. 867), § 1.01, effective September 1, 2005.

### Art. 62.0451. Additional Public Notice for Individuals Subject to Civil Commitment [Deleted].

Deleted by Acts 2005, 79th Leg., ch. 1008 (H.B. 867), § 1.01, effective September 1, 2005. (Enacted by Acts 1999, 76th Leg., ch. 444 (S.B. 1224), § 5(a), effective September 1, 1999; am. Acts 2001, 77th Leg., ch. 211 (S.B. 1380), § 8, effective September 1, 2001.)

### Art. 62.05. Status Report by Supervising Officer or Local Law Enforcement Agency [Renumbered].

Renumbered to Tex. Code Crim. Proc. art. 62.057 by Acts 2005, 79th Leg., ch. 1008 (H.B. 867), § 1.01, effective September 1, 2005.

## SUBCHAPTER B
## REGISTRATION AND VERIFICATION REQUIREMENTS; RELATED NOTICE

### Art. 62.051. Registration: General.

(a) A person who has a reportable conviction or adjudication or who is required to register as a condition of parole, release to mandatory supervision, or community supervision shall register or, if the person is a person for whom registration is completed under this chapter, verify registration as provided by Subsection (f), with the local law enforcement authority in any municipality where the person resides or intends to reside for more than seven days. If the person does not reside or intend to reside in a municipality, the person shall register or verify registration in any county where the person resides or intends to reside for more than seven days. The person shall satisfy the requirements of this subsection not later than the later of:

(1) the seventh day after the person's arrival in the municipality or county; or

(2) the first date the local law enforcement authority of the municipality or county by policy allows the person to register or verify registration, as applicable.

(b) The department shall provide the Texas Department of Criminal Justice, the Texas Youth Commission, the Texas Juvenile Probation Commission, and each local law enforcement authority, authority for campus security, county jail, and court with a form for registering persons required by this chapter to register.

(c) The registration form shall require:

(1) the person's full name, date of birth, sex, race, height, weight, eye color, hair color, social security number, driver's license number, and shoe size;

(1-a) the address at which the person resides or intends to reside or, if the person does not reside or intend to reside at a physical address, a detailed description of each geographical location at which the person resides or intends to reside;

(1-b) each alias used by the person and any home, work, or cellular telephone number of the person;

(2) a recent color photograph or, if possible, an electronic digital image of the person and a complete set of the person's fingerprints;

(3) the type of offense the person was convicted of, the age of the victim, the date of conviction, and the punishment received;

(4) an indication as to whether the person is discharged, paroled, or released on juvenile probation, community supervision, or mandatory supervision;

(5) an indication of each license, as defined by Article 62.005(g), that is held or sought by the person;

(6) an indication as to whether the person is or will be employed, carrying on a vocation, or a student at a particular public or private institution of higher education in this state or another state, and the name and address of that institution;

(7) the identification of any online identifier established or used by the person; and

(8) any other information required by the department.

(d) The registration form must contain a statement and description of any registration duties the person has or may have under this chapter.

(e) Not later than the third day after a person's registering, the local law enforcement authority with whom the person registered shall send a copy of the registration form to the department and, if the person resides on the campus of a public or private institution of higher education, to any authority for campus security for that institution.

(f) Not later than the seventh day after the date on which the person is released, a person for whom registration is completed under this chapter shall report to the applicable local law enforcement authority to verify the information in the registration form received by the authority under this chapter. The authority shall require the person to produce proof of the person's identity and residence before the authority gives the registration form to the person for verification. If the information in the registration form is complete and accurate, the person shall verify registration by signing the form. If the information is not complete or not accurate, the person shall make any necessary additions or corrections before signing the form.

(g) A person who is required to register or verify registration under this chapter shall ensure that the person's registration form is complete and accurate with respect to each item of information required by the form in accordance with Subsection (c).

(h) If a person subject to registration under this chapter does not move to an intended residence by the end of the seventh day after the date on which the person is released or the date on which the person leaves a previous residence, the person shall:

(1) report to the juvenile probation officer, community supervision and corrections department officer, or parole officer supervising the person by not later than the seventh day after the date on which the person is released or the date on which the person leaves a previous residence, as applicable, and provide the officer with the address of the person's temporary residence; and

(2) continue to report to the person's supervising officer not less than weekly during any period of time in which the person has not moved to an intended residence and provide the officer with the address of the person's temporary residence.

(i) If the other state has a registration requirement for sex offenders, a person who has a reportable conviction or adjudication, who resides in this state, and who is employed, carries on a vocation, or is a student in another state shall, not later than the 10th day after the date on which the person begins to work or attend school in the other state, register with the law enforcement authority that is identified by the department as the authority designated by that state to receive registration information. If the person is employed, carries on a vocation, or is a student at a public or private institution of higher education in the other state and if an authority for campus security exists at the institution, the person shall also register with that authority not later than the 10th day after the date on which the person begins to work or attend school.

(j) If a person subject to registration under this chapter is released from a penal institution without being released to parole or placed on any other form of supervision and the person does not move to the address indicated on the registration form as the person's intended residence or does not indicate an address on the registration form, the person shall, not later than the seventh day after the date on which the person is released:

(1) report in person to the local law enforcement authority for the municipality or county, as applicable, in which the person is residing and provide that authority with the address at which the person is residing or, if the person's residence does not have a physical address, a detailed description of the geographical location of the person's residence; and

(2) until the person indicates the person's current address as the person's intended residence on the registration form or otherwise complies with the requirements of Article 62.055, as appropriate, continue to report, in the manner required by Subdivision (1), to that authority not less than once in each succeeding 30-day period and provide that authority with the address at which the person is residing or, if applicable, a detailed description of the geographical location of the person's residence.

(k) A person required to register under this chapter may not refuse or otherwise fail to provide any information required for the accurate completion of the registration form.

(Redesignated from V.A.C.S. Art. 6252-13.c1 § 2 and amended by Acts 1997, 75th Leg., ch. 668 (S.B. 875), § 1, effective September 1, 1997; Acts 1999, 76th Leg., ch. 444 (S.B. 1224), § 1, effective September 1, 1999; Acts 1999, 76th Leg., ch. 1193 (S.B. 399), § 5, effective September 1, 1999; Acts 1999, 76th Leg., ch. 1415 (H.B. 2145), § 10, effective September 1, 1999; Acts 2001, 77th Leg., ch. 932 (S.B. 654), § 1, effective September 1, 2001; Acts 2003, 78th Leg., ch. 347 (S.B. 871), § 4, effective September 1, 2003; Acts 2003, 78th Leg., ch. 1276 (H.B. 3507), § 5, effective September 1, 2003; am. Acts 2005, 79th Leg., ch. 1008 (H.B. 867), § 1.01, effective September 1, 2005 (renumbered from art. 62.02); am. Acts 2009, 81st Leg., ch. 661 (H.B. 2153), § 2, effective September 1, 2009; am. Acts 2009, 81st Leg., ch. 755 (S.B. 689), § 5, effective September 1, 2009; am. Acts 2011, 82nd Leg., ch. 91 (S.B. 1303), § 6.005, effective September 1, 2011.)

## Art. 62.052. Registration: Extrajurisdictional Registrants.

(a) An extrajurisdictional registrant is required to comply with the annual verification requirements of Article 62.058 in the same manner as a person who is required to verify registration on the basis of a reportable conviction or adjudication.

(b) The duty to register for an extrajurisdictional registrant expires on the date the person's duty to register would expire under the laws of the other state or foreign country had the person remained in that state or foreign country, under federal law, or under the Uniform Code of Military Justice, as applicable.

(c) The department may negotiate and enter into a reciprocal registration agreement with any other state to prevent residents of this state and residents of the other state from frustrating the public purpose of the registration of sex offenders by moving from one state to the other.

(Acts 1999, 76th Leg., ch. 444 (S.B. 1224), § 2, effective September 1, 1999; Acts 1999, 76th Leg., ch. 1415 (H.B. 2145), § 11, effective September 1, 1999; Acts 2001, 77th Leg., ch. 211 (S.B. 1380), § 3, effective September 1, 2001; Acts 2003, 78th Leg., ch. 1005 (H.B. 236), § 10, effective September 1, 2003; Am. Acts 2005, 79th Leg., ch. 1008 (H.B. 867), § 1.01, effective September 1, 2005 (renumbered from art. 62.021).)

## Art. 62.053. Prerelease Notification.

(a) Before a person who will be subject to registration under this chapter is due to be released from a penal institution, the Texas Department of Criminal Justice or the Texas Youth Commission shall determine the person's level of risk to the community using the sex offender screening tool developed or selected under Article 62.007 and assign to the person a numeric risk level of one, two, or three. Before releasing the person, an official of the penal institution shall:

(1) inform the person that:

(A) not later than the later of the seventh day after the date on which the person is released or after the date on which the person moves from a previous residence to a new residence in this state or not later than the first date the applicable local law enforcement authority by policy allows the person to register or verify registration, the person must register or verify registration with the local law enforcement authority in the municipality or county in which the person intends to reside;

(B) not later than the seventh day after the date on which the person is released or the date on which the person moves from a previous residence to a new residence in this state, the person must, if the person has not moved to an intended residence, report to the applicable entity or entities as required by Article 62.051(h) or (j) or 62.055(e);

(C) not later than the seventh day before the date on which the person moves to a new residence in this state or another state, the person must report in person to the local law enforcement authority designated as the person's primary registration authority by the department and to the juvenile probation officer, community supervision and corrections department officer, or parole officer supervising the person;

(D) not later than the 10th day after the date on which the person arrives in another state in which the person intends to reside, the person must register with the law enforcement agency that is identified by the department as the agency designated by that state to receive registration information, if the other state has a registration requirement for sex offenders;

(E) not later than the 30th day after the date on which the person is released, the person must apply to the department in person for the issuance of an original or renewal driver's license or personal identification certificate and a failure to apply to the department as required by this paragraph results in the automatic revocation of any driver's license or personal identification certificate issued by the department to the person; and

(F) the person must notify appropriate entities of any change in status as described by Article 62.057;

(2) require the person to sign a written statement that the person was informed of the person's duties as described by Subdivision (1) or Subsection (g) or, if the person refuses to sign the statement, certify that the person was so informed;

(3) obtain the address or, if applicable, a detailed description of each geographical location where the person expects to reside on the person's release and other registration information, including a photograph and complete set of fingerprints; and

(4) complete the registration form for the person.

(b) On the seventh day before the date on which a person who will be subject to registration under this chapter is due to be released from a penal institution, or on receipt of notice by a penal institution that a person who will be subject to registration under this chapter is due to be released in less than seven days, an official of the penal institution shall send the person's completed registration form and numeric risk level to the department and to:

(1) the applicable local law enforcement authority in the municipality or county in which the person expects to reside, if the person expects to reside in this state; or

(2) the law enforcement agency that is identified by the department as the agency designated by another state to receive registration information, if the person expects to reside in that other state and that other state has a registration requirement for sex offenders.

(c) If a person who is subject to registration under this chapter receives an order deferring adjudication, placing the person on community supervision or juvenile probation, or imposing only a fine, the court pronouncing the order or sentence shall make a determination of the person's numeric risk level using the sex offender screening tool developed or selected under Article 62.007, assign to the person a numeric risk level of one, two, or three, and ensure that the prerelease notification and registration requirements specified in this article are conducted on the day of entering the order or sentencing. If a community supervision and corrections department representative is available in court at the time a court pronounces a sentence of deferred adjudication or community supervision, the representative shall immediately obtain the person's numeric risk level from the court and conduct the prerelease notification and registration requirements specified in this article. In any other case in which the court pronounces a sentence under this subsection, the court shall designate another appropriate individual to obtain the person's numeric risk level from the court and conduct the prerelease notification and registration requirements specified in this article.

(d) If a person who has a reportable conviction described by Article 62.001(5)(H) or (I) is placed under the supervision of the parole division of the Texas Department of Criminal Justice or a community supervision and corrections department under Section 510.017, Government Code, the division or community supervision and corrections department shall conduct the prerelease notification and registration requirements specified in this article on the date the person is placed under the supervision of the division or community supervision and corrections department. If a person who has a reportable adjudication of delinquent conduct described by Article 62.001(5)(H) or (I) is, as permitted by Section 60.002, Family Code, placed under the supervision of the Texas Youth Commission, a public or private vendor operating under contract with the Texas Youth Commission, a local juvenile probation department, or a juvenile secure pre-adjudication or post-adjudication facility, the commission, vendor, probation department, or facility shall conduct the prerelease notification and registration requirements specified in this article on the date the person is placed under the supervision of the commission, vendor, probation department, or facility.

(e) Not later than the eighth day after receiving a registration form under Subsection (b), (c), or (d), the local law enforcement authority shall verify the age of the victim, the basis on which the person is subject to registration under this chapter, and the person's numeric risk level. The local law enforcement authority shall immediately provide notice to the superintendent of the public school district and to the administrator of any private primary or secondary school located in the public school district in which the person subject to registration intends to reside by mail to the office of the superintendent or administrator, as appropriate, in accordance with Article 62.054. On receipt of a notice under this subsection, the superintendent shall release the information contained in the notice to appropriate school district personnel, including peace officers and security personnel, principals, nurses, and counselors.

(f) The local law enforcement authority shall include in the notice to the superintendent of the public school district and to the administrator of any private primary or secondary school located in the public school district any information the authority determines is necessary to protect the public, except:

(1) the person's social security number or driver's license number, or any home, work, or cellular telephone number of the person; and

(2) any information that would identify the victim of the offense for which the person is subject to registration.

(g) Before a person who will be subject to registration under this chapter is due to be released from a penal institution in this state, an official of the penal institution shall inform the person that:

(1) if the person intends to reside in another state and to work or attend school in this state, the person must, not later than the later of the seventh day after the date on which the person begins to work or attend school or the first date the applicable local law enforcement authority by policy allows the person to register or verify registration, register or verify registration with the local law enforcement authority in the municipality or county in which the person intends to work or attend school;

(2) if the person intends to reside in this state and to work or attend school in another state and if the other state has a registration requirement for sex offenders, the person must:

(A) not later than the 10th day after the date on which the person begins to work or attend school in the other state, register with the law enforcement authority that is identified by the department as the authority designated by that state to receive registration information; and

(B) if the person intends to be employed, carry on a vocation, or be a student at a public or private institution of higher education in the other state and if an authority for campus security exists at the institution, register with that authority not later than the 10th day after the date on which the person begins to work or attend school; and

(3) regardless of the state in which the person intends to reside, if the person intends to be employed, carry on a vocation, or be a student at a public or private institution of higher education in this state, the person must:

(A) not later than the later of the seventh day after the date on which the person begins to work or attend school or the first date the applicable authority by policy allows the person to register, register with:

(i) the authority for campus security for that institution; or

(ii) except as provided by Article 62.153(e), if an authority for campus security for that institution does not exist, the local law enforcement authority of:

(a) the municipality in which the institution is located; or

(b) the county in which the institution is located, if the institution is not located in a municipality; and

(B) not later than the seventh day after the date the person stops working or attending school, notify the appropriate authority for campus security or local law enforcement authority of the termination of the person's status as a worker or student.

(Redesignated from V.A.C.S. Art. 6252-13.c1 § 3 and amended by Acts 1997, 75th Leg., ch. 668 (S.B. 875), § 1, effective September 1, 1997; Acts 1999, 76th Leg., ch. 444 (S.B. 1224), § 3, effective

September 1, 1999, Acts 1999, 76th Leg., ch. 1193 (S.B. 399), §§ 6, 7, effective September 1, 1999; Acts 1999, 76th Leg., ch. 1415 (H.B. 2145), § 12, effective September 1, 1999; Acts 1999, 76th Leg., ch. 1401 (H.B. 1939), § 2, effective September 1, 2000, Acts 1999, 76th Leg., ch. 1557 (S.B. 1650), § 1, effective August 30, 1999; am. Acts 2001, 77th Leg., ch. 177 (S.B. 1206), § 1, effective September 1, 2001; am. Acts 2001, 77th Leg., ch. 211 (S.B. 1380), § 4, effective September 1, 2001; am. Acts 2001, 77th Leg., ch. 1420 (H.B. 2812), § 3, effective September 1, 2001; am. Acts 2003, 78th Leg., ch. 347 (S.B. 871), § 5, effective September 1, 2003; am. Acts 2005, 79th Leg., ch. 1008 (H.B. 867), § 1.01, effective September 1, 2005 (renumbered from art. 62.03); am. Acts 2009, 81st Leg., ch. 87 (S.B. 1969), § 25.048, effective September 1, 2009; am. Acts 2009, 81st Leg., ch. 661 (H.B. 2153), § 3, effective September 1, 2009; am. Acts 2009, 81st Leg., ch. 755 (S.B. 689), § 6, effective September 1, 2009.)

## Art. 62.054. Circumstances Requiring Notice to Superintendent or School Administrator.

(a) A local law enforcement authority shall provide notice to the superintendent and each administrator under Article 62.053(e) or 62.055(f) only if:

(1) the victim was at the time of the offense a child younger than 17 years of age or a student enrolled in a public or private secondary school;

(2) the person subject to registration is a student enrolled in a public or private secondary school; or

(3) the basis on which the person is subject to registration is a conviction, a deferred adjudication, or an adjudication of delinquent conduct for an offense under Section 43.25 or 43.26, Penal Code, or an offense under the laws of another state, federal law, or the Uniform Code of Military Justice that contains elements substantially similar to the elements of an offense under either of those sections.

(b) A local law enforcement authority may not provide notice to the superintendent or any administrator under Article 62.053(e) or 62.055(f) if the basis on which the person is subject to registration is a conviction, a deferred adjudication, or an adjudication of delinquent conduct for an offense under Section 25.02, Penal Code, or an offense under the laws of another state, federal law, or the Uniform Code of Military Justice that

contains elements substantially similar to the elements of an offense under that section.

(Acts 2003, 78th Leg., ch. 347 (S.B. 871), § 6, effective September 1, 2003; am. Acts 2005, 79th Leg., ch. 1008 (H.B. 867), § 1.01, effective September 1, 2005 (renumbered from art. 62.032).)

## Art. 62.055. Change of Address; Lack of Address.

(a) If a person required to register under this chapter intends to change address, regardless of whether the person intends to move to another state, the person shall, not later than the seventh day before the intended change, report in person to the local law enforcement authority designated as the person's primary registration authority by the department and to the juvenile probation officer, community supervision and corrections department officer, or parole officer supervising the person and provide the authority and the officer with the person's anticipated move date and new address. If a person required to register changes address, the person shall, not later than the later of the seventh day after changing the address or the first date the applicable local law enforcement authority by policy allows the person to report, report in person to the local law enforcement authority in the municipality or county in which the person's new residence is located and provide the authority with proof of identity and proof of residence.

(b) Not later than the third day after receipt of notice under Subsection (a), the person's juvenile probation officer, community supervision and corrections department officer, or parole officer shall forward the information provided under Subsection (a) to the local law enforcement authority designated as the person's primary registration authority by the department and, if the person intends to move to another municipality or county in this state, to the applicable local law enforcement authority in that municipality or county.

(c) If the person moves to another state that has a registration requirement for sex offenders, the person shall, not later than the 10th day after the date on which the person arrives in the other state, register with the law enforcement agency that is identified by the department as the agency designated by that state to receive registration information.

(d) Not later than the third day after receipt of information under Subsection (a) or (b), whichever is earlier, the local law enforcement authority shall forward this information to the department and, if the person intends to move to another municipality or county in this state, to the applicable local law enforcement authority in that municipality or county.

(e) If a person who reports to a local law enforcement authority under Subsection (a) does not move on or before the anticipated move date or does not move to the new address provided to the authority, the person shall:

(1) not later than the seventh day after the anticipated move date, and not less than weekly after that seventh day, report to the local law enforcement authority designated as the person's primary registration authority by the department and provide an explanation to the authority regarding any changes in the anticipated move date and intended residence; and

(2) report to the juvenile probation officer, community supervision and corrections department officer, or parole officer supervising the person not less than weekly during any period in which the person has not moved to an intended residence.

(f) If the person moves to another municipality or county in this state, the department shall inform the applicable local law enforcement authority in the new area of the person's residence not later than the third day after the date on which the department receives information under Subsection (a). Not later than the eighth day after the date on which the local law enforcement authority is informed under Subsection (a) or under this subsection, the authority shall verify the age of the victim, the basis on which the person is subject to registration under this chapter, and the person's numeric risk level. The local law enforcement authority shall immediately provide notice to the superintendent of the public school district and to the administrator of any private primary or secondary school located in the public school district in which the person subject to registration intends to reside by mail to the office of the superintendent or administrator, as appropriate, in accordance with Article 62.054. On receipt of a notice under this subsection, the superintendent shall release the information contained in the notice to appropriate school district personnel, including peace officers and security personnel, principals, nurses, and counselors.

(g) The local law enforcement authority shall include in the notice to the superintendent of the public school district and the administrator of any private primary or secondary school located in the public school district any information the authority determines is necessary to protect the public, except:

(1) the person's social security number or driver's license number, or any home, work, or cellular telephone number of the person; and

(2) any information that would identify the victim of the offense for which the person is subject to registration.

(h) If the person moves to another state, the department shall, immediately on receiving information under Subsection (d):

(1) inform the agency that is designated by the other state to receive registration information, if that state has a registration requirement for sex offenders; and

(2) send to the Federal Bureau of Investigation a copy of the person's registration form, including the record of conviction and a complete set of fingerprints.

(i) If a person required to register under this chapter resides for more than seven days at a location or locations to which a physical address has not been assigned by a governmental entity, the person, not less than once in each 30-day period, shall confirm the person's location or locations by:

(1) reporting to the local law enforcement authority in the municipality where the person resides or, if the person does not reside in a municipality, the local law enforcement authority in the county in which the person resides; and

(2) providing a detailed description of the applicable location or locations.

(Redesignated from V.A.C.S. Art. 6252-13.c1 § 4 and amended by Acts 1997, 75th Leg., ch. 668 (S.B. 875), § 1, effective September 1, 1997; Acts 1999, 76th Leg., ch. 444 (S.B. 1224), § 4, effective September 1, 1999; Acts 1999, 76th Leg., ch. 1415 (H.B. 2145), § 13, effective September 1, 1999; Acts 1999, 76th Leg., ch. 1557 (S.B. 1650), § 3, effective August 30, 1999; Acts 2001, 77th Leg., ch. 177 (S.B. 1206), § 3, effective September 1, 2001; Acts 2001, 77th Leg., ch. 211 (S.B. 1380), § 5, effective September 1, 2001; Acts 2001, 77th Leg., ch. 1420 (H.B. 2812), § 3, effective September 1, 2001; Acts 2003, 78th Leg., ch. 347 (S.B. 871), § 7, effective September 1, 2003; am. Acts 2005, 79th Leg., ch. 1008 (H.B. 867), § 1.01, effective September 1, 2005 (renumbered from art. 62.04).)

## Art. 62.0551. Change in Online Identifiers.

(a) If a person required to register under this chapter changes any online identifier included on the person's registration form or establishes any new online identifier not already included on the person's registration form, the person, not later than the later of the seventh day after the change or establishment or the first date the applicable authority by policy allows the person to report, shall report the change or establishment to the person's primary registration authority in the manner prescribed by the authority.

(b) A primary registration authority that receives information under this article shall forward information in the same manner as information received by the authority under Article 62.055.

(Enacted by Acts 2009, 81st Leg., ch. 755 (S.B. 689), § 8, effective September 1, 2009.)

## Art. 62.056. Additional Public Notice for Certain Offenders.

(a) On receipt of notice under this chapter that a person subject to registration is due to be released from a penal institution, has been placed on community supervision or juvenile probation, or intends to move to a new residence in this state, the department shall verify the person's numeric risk level assigned under this chapter. If the person is assigned a numeric risk level of three, the department shall, not later than the seventh day after the date on which the person is released or the 10th day after the date on which the person moves, provide written notice mailed or delivered to at least each address, other than a post office box, within a one-mile radius, in an area that has not been subdivided, or a three-block area, in an area that has been subdivided, of the place where the person intends to reside. In providing written notice under this subsection, the department shall use employees of the department whose duties in providing the notice are in addition to the employees' regular duties.

(b) The department shall provide the notice in English and Spanish and shall include in the notice any information that is public information under this chapter. The department may not include any information that is not public information under this chapter.

(c) The department shall establish procedures for a person with respect to whom notice is provided under Subsection (a), other than a person subject to registration on the basis of an adjudication of delinquent conduct, to pay to the department all costs incurred by the department in providing the notice. The person shall pay those costs in accordance with the procedures established under this subsection.

(d) On receipt of notice under this chapter that a person subject to registration under this chapter is required to register or verify registration with a local law enforcement authority and has been assigned a numeric risk level of three, the local law enforcement authority may provide notice to the public in any manner determined appropriate by the local law enforcement authority, including publishing notice in a newspaper or other periodical or circular in circulation in the area where the person intends to reside, holding a neighborhood meeting, posting notices in the area where the person intends to reside, distributing printed notices to area residents, or establishing a specialized local website. The local law enforcement authority may include in the notice only information that is public information under this chapter.

(e) An owner, builder, seller, or lessor of a single-family residential real property or any improvement to residential real property or that person's broker, salesperson, or other agent or representative in a residential real estate transaction does not have a duty to make a disclosure to a prospective buyer or lessee about registrants under this chapter. To the extent of any conflict between this subsection and another law imposing a duty to disclose information about registered sex offenders, this subsection controls.

(Acts 1999, 76th Leg., ch. 1557 (S.B. 1650) § 4, effective August 30, 1999; Acts 2001, 77th Leg., ch. 177 (S.B. 1206), § 4, effective September 1, 2001; Acts 2001, 77th Leg., ch. 211 (S.B. 1380), § 6, effective September 1, 2001; am. Acts 2005, 79th Leg., ch. 1008 (H.B. 867), § 1.01, effective September 1, 2005 (renumbered from art. 62.045).)

## Art. 62.057. Status Report by Supervising Officer or Local Law Enforcement Authority.

(a) If the juvenile probation officer, community supervision and corrections department officer, or parole officer supervising a person subject to registration under this chapter receives information to the effect that the person's status has changed in any manner that affects proper supervision of the person, including a change in the person's name, online identifiers, physical health, job or educational status, including higher educational status, incarceration, or terms of release, the supervising officer shall promptly notify the appropriate local law enforcement authority or authorities of that change. If the person required to register intends to change address, the supervising officer shall notify the local law enforcement authorities designated by Article 62.055(b). Not later than the seventh day after the date the supervising officer receives the relevant information, the supervising officer shall notify the local law enforcement authority of any change in the person's job or educational status in which the person:

(1) becomes employed, begins to carry on a vocation, or becomes a student at a particular public or private institution of higher education; or

(2) terminates the person's status in that capacity.

(b) Not later than the later of the seventh day after the date of the change or the first date the applicable authority by policy allows the person to report, a person subject to registration under this chapter shall report to the local law enforcement authority designated as the person's primary registration authority by the department any change in the person's name, online identifiers, physical health, or job or educational status, including higher educational status.

(c) For purposes of Subsection (b):

(1) a person's job status changes if the person leaves employment for any reason, remains employed by an employer but changes the location at which the person works, or begins employment with a new employer;

(2) a person's health status changes if the person is hospitalized as a result of an illness;

(3) a change in a person's educational status includes the person's transfer from one educational facility to another; and

(4) regarding a change of name, notice of the proposed name provided to a local law enforcement authority as described by Sections 45.004 and 45.103, Family Code, is sufficient, except that the person shall promptly notify the authority of any denial of the person's petition for a change of name.

(d) Not later than the seventh day after the date the local law enforcement authority receives the relevant information, the local law enforcement authority shall notify the department of any change in the person's job or educational status in which the person:

(1) becomes employed, begins to carry on a vocation, or becomes a student at a particular

public or private institution of higher education; or

(2) terminates the person's status in that capacity.

(Added by Acts 1997, 75th Leg., ch. 668 (S.B. 875), § 1, effective September 1, 1997; Acts 1999, 76th Leg., ch. 444 (S.B. 1224), § 6, effective September 1, 1999; Acts 1999, 76th Leg., ch. 1415 (H.B. 2145), § 14, effective September 1, 1999; Acts 2001, 77th Leg., ch. 19 (H.B. 121), § 1, effective September 1, 2001; Acts 2003, 78th Leg., ch. 347 (S.B. 871), § 8, effective September 1, 2003; Acts 2003, 78th Leg., ch. 1300 (S.B. 146), § 4, effective September 1, 2003; am. Acts 2005, 79th Leg., ch. 1008 (H.B. 867), § 1.01, effective September 1, 2005 (renumbered from art. 62.05); am. Acts 2009, 81st Leg., ch. 755 (S.B. 689), § 9, effective September 1, 2009.)

### Art. 62.058. Law Enforcement Verification of Registration Information.

(a) A person subject to registration under this chapter who has for a sexually violent offense been convicted two or more times, received an order of deferred adjudication two or more times, or been convicted and received an order of deferred adjudication shall report to the local law enforcement authority designated as the person's primary registration authority by the department not less than once in each 90-day period following the date the person first registered under this chapter to verify the information in the registration form maintained by the authority for that person. A person subject to registration under this chapter who is not subject to the 90-day reporting requirement described by this subsection shall report to the local law enforcement authority designated as the person's primary registration authority by the department once each year not earlier than the 30th day before and not later than the 30th day after the anniversary of the person's date of birth to verify the information in the registration form maintained by the authority for that person. For purposes of this subsection, a person complies with a requirement that the person register within a 90-day period following a date if the person registers at any time on or after the 83rd day following that date but before the 98th day after that date.

(b) A local law enforcement authority designated as a person's primary registration authority by the department may direct the person to report to the authority to verify the information in the registration form maintained by the authority for that person. The authority may direct the person to report under this subsection once in each 90-day period following the date the person first registered under this chapter, if the person is required to report not less than once in each 90-day period under Subsection (a) or once in each year not earlier than the 30th day before and not later than the 30th day after the anniversary of the person's date of birth, if the person is required to report once each year under Subsection (a). A local law enforcement authority may not direct a person to report to the authority under this subsection if the person is required to report under Subsection (a) and is in compliance with the reporting requirements of that subsection.

(c) A local law enforcement authority with whom a person reports under this article shall require the person to produce proof of the person's identity and residence before the authority gives the registration form to the person for verification. If the information in the registration form is complete and accurate, the person shall verify registration by signing the form. If the information is not complete or not accurate, the person shall make any necessary additions or corrections before signing the form.

(d) A local law enforcement authority designated as a person's primary registration authority by the department may at any time mail a nonforwardable verification form to the last reported address of the person. Not later than the 21st day after receipt of a verification form under this subsection, the person shall:

(1) indicate on the form whether the person still resides at the last reported address and, if not, provide on the form the person's new address;

(2) complete any other information required by the form;

(3) sign the form; and

(4) return the form to the authority.

(e) For purposes of this article, a person receives multiple convictions or orders of deferred adjudication regardless of whether:

(1) the judgments or orders are entered on different dates; or

(2) the offenses for which the person was convicted or placed on deferred adjudication arose out of different criminal transactions.

(Added by Acts 1997, 75th Leg., ch. 668 (S.B. 875), § 1, effective September 1, 1997; Acts 1999,

76th Leg., ch. 444 (S.B. 1224), § 7, effective September 1, 1999; Acts 1999, 76th Leg., ch. 1415 (H.B. 2145), § 15, effective September 1, 1999; Acts 2001, 77th Leg., ch. 211 (S.B. 1380), § 9, effective September 1, 2001; am. Acts 2005, 79th Leg., ch. 1008 (H.B. 867), § 1.01, effective September 1, 2005 (renumbered from art. 62.06).)

### Art. 62.059. Registration of Persons Regularly Visiting Location.

(a) A person subject to this chapter who on at least three occasions during any month spends more than 48 consecutive hours in a municipality or county in this state, other than the municipality or county in which the person is registered under this chapter, before the last day of that month shall report that fact to:

(1) the local law enforcement authority of the municipality in which the person is a visitor; or

(2) if the person is a visitor in a location that is not a municipality, the local law enforcement authority of the county in which the person is a visitor.

(b) A person described by Subsection (a) shall provide the local law enforcement authority with:

(1) all information the person is required to provide under Article 62.051(c);

(2) the address of any location in the municipality or county, as appropriate, at which the person was lodged during the month; and

(3) a statement as to whether the person intends to return to the municipality or county during the succeeding month.

(c) This article does not impose on a local law enforcement authority requirements of public notification or notification to schools relating to a person about whom the authority is not otherwise required by this chapter to make notifications.
(Acts 1999, 76th Leg., ch. 444 (S.B. 1224), § 8, effective September 1, 1999; Acts 1999, 76th Leg., ch. 1415 (H.B. 2145), § 16, effective September 1, 1999; am. Acts 2005, 79th Leg., ch. 1008 (H.B. 867), § 1.01, effective September 1, 2005 (renumbered from art. 62.062).)

### Art. 62.06. Law Enforcement Verification of Registration Information [Renumbered].

Renumbered to Tex. Code Crim. Proc. art. 62.058 by Acts 2005, 79th Leg., ch. 1008 (H.B. 867), § 1.01, effective September 1, 2005.

Criminal Procedure

## Art. 62.060. Requirements Relating to Driver's License or Personal Identification Certificate.

(a) A person subject to registration under this chapter shall apply to the department in person for the issuance of, as applicable, an original or renewal driver's license under Section 521.272, Transportation Code, an original or renewal personal identification certificate under Section 521.103, Transportation Code, or an original or renewal commercial driver's license or commercial driver learner's permit under Section 522.033, Transportation Code, not later than the 30th day after the date:

(1) the person is released from a penal institution or is released by a court on community supervision or juvenile probation; or

(2) the department sends written notice to the person of the requirements of this article.

(b) The person shall annually renew in person each driver's license or personal identification certificate issued by the department to the person, including each renewal, duplicate, or corrected license or certificate, until the person's duty to register under this chapter expires.
(Acts 1999, 76th Leg., ch. 1401 (H.B. 1939), § 3, effective September 1, 2000; Acts 2001, 77th Leg., ch. 546 (H.B. 2663), § 1, effective September 1, 2001; am. Acts 2005, 79th Leg., ch. 1008 (H.B. 867), § 1.01, effective September 1, 2005 (renumbered from art. 62.065).)

## Art. 62.061. DNA Specimen.

A person required to register under this chapter shall comply with a request for a DNA specimen made by a law enforcement agency under Section 411.1473, Government Code.
(Enacted by Acts 2005, 79th Leg., ch. 1008 (H.B. 867), § 1.01, effective September 1, 2005.)

## Art. 62.062. Limitation on Newspaper Publication.

(a) Except as provided by Subsection (b), a local law enforcement authority may not publish notice in a newspaper or other periodical or circular concerning a person's registration under this chapter if the only basis on which the person is subject to registration is one or more adjudications of delinquent conduct.

(b) This article does not apply to a publication of notice under Article 62.056.
(Enacted Acts 2005, 79th Leg., ch. 1008 (H.B. 867), § 1.01, effective September 1, 2005.)

## Art. 62.063. Registration of Certain Workers or Students [Deleted].

Deleted by Acts 2005, 79th Leg., ch. 1008 (H.B. 867), § 1.01, effective September 1, 2005.
(Enacted by Acts 1999, 76th Leg., ch. 1193 (S.B. 399), § 8, effective September 1, 1999; enacted by Acts 1999, 76th Leg., ch. 1415 (H.B. 2145), § 16, effective September 1, 1999; am. Acts 2003, 78th Leg., ch. 1275 (H.B. 3506), § 2(10), effective September 1, 2003 (renumbered from art. 62.061).)

## Art. 62.064. Registration of Workers or Students at Instituions of Higher Education [Deleted].

Deleted by Acts 2005, 79th Leg., ch. 1008 (H.B. 867), § 1.01, effective September 1, 2005.
(Enacted by Acts 2003, 78th Leg., ch. 347 (S.B. 871), § 11, effective September 1, 2003.)

## Art. 62.065. Requirements Relating to Driver's License or Personal Identification Certificate [Renumbered].

Renumbered to Tex. Code Crim. Proc. art. 62.060 by Acts 2005, 79th Leg., ch. 1008 (H.B. 867), § 1.01, effective September 1, 2005.

## Art. 62.07. Remedies Related to Public Notice [Deleted].

Deleted by Acts 2005, 79th Leg., ch. 1008 (H.B. 867), § 1.01, effective September 1, 2005.
(Enacted by Acts 1997, 75th Leg., ch. 668 (S.B. 875), § 1, effective September 1, 1997 (renumbered from Rev. Civ. Stat. art. 6252-13c.1, § 4A).)

## Art. 62.08. Central Database; Public Information [Deleted].

Deleted by Acts 2005, 79th Leg., ch. 1008 (H.B. 867), § 1.01, effective September 1, 2005.
(Enacted by Acts 1997, 75th Leg., ch. 668 (S.B. 875), § 1, effective September 1, 1997 (renumbered from Rev. Civ. Stat. art. 6252-13c.1, § 5); am. Acts 1999, 76th Leg., ch. 1415 (H.B. 2145), § 17, effective September 1, 1999; am. Acts 2001, 77th Leg., ch. 211 (S.B. 1380), § 10, effective September 1, 2001; am. Acts 2001, 77th Leg., ch. 932 (S.B. 654), § 2, effective September 1, 2001; am. Acts 2003, 78th Leg., ch. 347 (S.B. 871), § 12, effective September 1, 2003; am. Acts 2003, 78th Leg., ch. 1276 (H.B. 3507), § 5.003(a), effective September 1, 2003.)

**Art. 62.085. Information Provided to Peace Officer [Deleted].**

Deleted by Acts 2005, 79th Leg., ch. 1008 (H.B. 867), § 1.01, effective September 1, 2005.
(Enacted by Acts 1999, 76th Leg., ch. 1401 (H.B. 1939), § 3, effective September 1, 2000.)

**Art. 62.09. Immunity for Release of Public Information [Deleted].**

Deleted by Acts 2005, 79th Leg., ch. 1008 (H.B. 867), § 1.01, effective September 1, 2005.
(Am. Acts 1997, 75th Leg., ch. 668 (S.B. 875), § 1, effective September 1, 1997 (renumbered from art. 6252-13c.1, § 5A); am. Acts 2003, 78th Leg., ch. 347 (S.B. 871), § 13, effective September 1, 2003.)

**Art. 62.091. General Immunity [Deleted].**

Deleted by Acts 2005, 79th Leg., ch. 1008 (H.B. 867), § 1.01, effective September 1, 2005.
(Enacted by Acts 2001, 77th Leg., ch. 177 (S.B. 1206), § 5, effective September 1, 2001.)

**Art. 62.10. Failure to Comply with Registration Requirements [Renumbered].**

Renumbered to Tex. Code Crim. Proc. art. 62.102 by Acts 2005, 79th Leg., ch. 1008 (H.B. 867), § 1.01, effective September 1, 2005.

## SUBCHAPTER C
## EXPIRATION OF DUTY TO REGISTER; GENERAL PENALTIES FOR NONCOMPLIANCE

**Art. 62.101. Expiration of Duty to Register.**

(a) Except as provided by Subsection (b) and Subchapter I, the duty to register for a person ends when the person dies if the person has a reportable conviction or adjudication, other than an adjudication of delinquent conduct, for:

(1) a sexually violent offense;

(2) an offense under Section 20A.02(a)(3), (4), (7), or (8), 25.02, 43.05(a)(2), or 43.26, Penal Code;

(3) an offense under Section 21.11(a)(2), Penal Code, if before or after the person is convicted or adjudicated for the offense under Section 21.11(a)(2), Penal Code, the person receives or has received another reportable conviction or adjudication, other than an adjudication of delinquent conduct, for an offense or

conduct that requires registration under this chapter;

(4) an offense under Section 20.02, 20.03, or 20.04, Penal Code, if:

(A) the judgment in the case contains an affirmative finding under Article 42.015 or, for a deferred adjudication, the papers in the case contain an affirmative finding that the victim or intended victim was younger than 17 years of age; and

(B) before or after the person is convicted or adjudicated for the offense under Section 20.02, 20.03, or 20.04, Penal Code, the person receives or has received another reportable conviction or adjudication, other than an adjudication of delinquent conduct, for an offense or conduct that requires registration under this chapter; or

(5) an offense under Section 43.23, Penal Code, that is punishable under Subsection (h) of that section.

(b) Except as provided by Subchapter I, the duty to register for a person otherwise subject to Subsection (a) ends on the 10th anniversary of the date on which the person is released from a penal institution or discharges community supervision or the court dismisses the criminal proceedings against the person and discharges the person, whichever date is later, if the person's duty to register is based on a conviction or an order of deferred adjudication in a cause that was transferred to a district court or criminal district court under Section 54.02, Family Code.

(c) Except as provided by Subchapter I, the duty to register for a person with a reportable conviction or adjudication for an offense other than an offense described by Subsection (a) ends:

(1) if the person's duty to register is based on an adjudication of delinquent conduct, on the 10th anniversary of the date on which the disposition is made or the person completes the terms of the disposition, whichever date is later; or

(2) if the person's duty to register is based on a conviction or on an order of deferred adjudication, on the 10th anniversary of the date on which the court dismisses the criminal proceedings against the person and discharges the person, the person is released from a penal institution, or the person discharges community supervision, whichever date is later.

(Enacted by Acts 2005, 79th Leg., ch. 1008 (H.B. 867), § 1.01, effective September 1, 2005; am. Acts 2011, 82nd Leg., ch. 1 (S.B. 24), § 2.11, effective September 1, 2011.)

## Art. 62.102. Failure to Comply with Registration Requirements.

(a) A person commits an offense if the person is required to register and fails to comply with any requirement of this chapter.

(b) An offense under this article is:

(1) a state jail felony if the actor is a person whose duty to register expires under Article 62.101(b) or (c);

(2) a felony of the third degree if the actor is a person whose duty to register expires under Article 62.101(a) and who is required to verify registration once each year under Article 62.058; and

(3) a felony of the second degree if the actor is a person whose duty to register expires under Article 62.101(a) and who is required to verify registration once each 90-day period under Article 62.058.

(c) If it is shown at the trial of a person for an offense or an attempt to commit an offense under this article that the person has previously been convicted of an offense or an attempt to commit an offense under this article, the punishment for the offense or the attempt to commit the offense is increased to the punishment for the next highest degree of felony.

(Redesignated from V.A.C.S. Art. 6252-13.c1 § 7 and amended by Acts 1997, 75th Leg., ch. 668 (S.B. 875), § 1, effective September 1, 1997; Acts 1999, 76th Leg., ch. 444 (S.B. 1224), § 9, effective September 1, 1999; Acts 1999, 76th Leg., ch. 1415 (H.B. 2145), § 18, effective September 1, 1999; am. Acts 2005, 79th Leg., ch. 1008 (H.B. 867), § 1.01, effective September 1, 2005 (renumbered from art. 62.10).)

## Art. 62.11. Applicability [Deleted].

Deleted by Acts 2005, 79th Leg., ch. 1008 (H.B. 867), § 1.01, effective September 1, 2005.
(Enacted by Acts 1997, 75th Leg., ch. 668 (S.B. 875), § 1, effective September 1, 1997 (renumbered from Rev. Civ. Stat. art. 6252-13c.1, § 8); am. Acts 2001, 77th Leg., ch. 211 (S.B. 1380), § 11, effective September 1, 2001.)

## Art. 62.12. Expiration of Duty to Register [Deleted].

Deleted by Acts 2005, 79th Leg., ch. 1008 (H.B. 867), § 1.01, effective September 1, 2005.
(Enacted by Acts 1997, 75th Leg., ch. 668 (S.B. 875), § 1, effective September 1, 1997 (renum-

bered from Rev. Civ. Stat. art. 6252-13c.1, § 9); am. Acts 1999, 76th Leg., ch. 1415 (H.B. 2145), § 25, effective September 1, 1999; am. Acts 2001, 77th Leg., ch. 211 (S.B. 1380), § 12, effective September 1, 2001; am. Acts 2001, 77th Leg., ch. 1297 (H.B. 1118), § 53, effective September 1, 2001; am. Acts 2003, 78th Leg., ch. 347 (S.B. 871), § 14, effective September 1, 2003.)

## Art. 62.13. Hearing to Determine Need for Registration of a Juvenile [Deleted].

Deleted by Acts 2005, 79th Leg., ch. 1008 (H.B. 867), § 1.01, effective September 1, 2005.
(Enacted by Acts 2001, 77th Leg., ch. 1297 (H.B. 1118), § 54, effective September 1, 2001; am. Acts 2003, 78th Leg., ch. 283 (H.B. 2319), § 36, effective September 1, 2003; am. Acts 2003, 78th Leg., ch. 347 (S.B. 871), § 15, effective September 1, 2003.)

## Art. 62.14. Removing Juvenile Registration Information When Duty to Register Expires [Renumbered].

Renumbered to Tex. Code Crim. Proc. art. 62.251 by Acts 2005, 79th Leg., ch. 1008 (H.B. 867), § 1.01, effective September 1, 2005.

## SUBCHAPTER D
## PROVISIONS APPLICABLE TO CERTAIN WORKERS AND STUDENTS

## Art. 62.151. Definitions.

For purposes of this subchapter, a person:

(1) is employed or carries on a vocation if the person works or volunteers on a full-time or part-time basis for a consecutive period exceeding 14 days or for an aggregate period exceeding 30 days in a calendar year;

(2) works regardless of whether the person works for compensation or for governmental or educational benefit; and

(3) is a student if the person enrolls on a full-time or part-time basis in any educational facility, including:

(A) a public or private primary or secondary school, including a high school or alternative learning center; or

(B) a public or private institution of higher education.

(Enacted by Acts 2005, 79th Leg., ch. 1008 (H.B. 867), § 1.01, effective September 1, 2005.)

## Art. 62.152. Registration of Certain Workers or Students.

(a) A person is subject to this subchapter and, except as otherwise provided by this article, to the other subchapters of this chapter if the person:

(1) has a reportable conviction or adjudication;

(2) resides in another state; and

(3) is employed, carries on a vocation, or is a student in this state.

(b) A person described by Subsection (a) is subject to the registration and verification requirements of Articles 62.051 and 62.058 and to the change of address requirements of Article 62.055, except that the registration and verification and the reporting of a change of address are based on the municipality or county in which the person works or attends school. The person is subject to the school notification requirements of Articles 62.053—62.055, except that notice provided to the superintendent and any administrator is based on the public school district in which the person works or attends school.

(c) A person described by Subsection (a) is not subject to Article 62.101.

(d) The duty to register for a person described by Subsection (a) ends when the person no longer works or studies in this state, provides notice of that fact to the local law enforcement authority in the municipality or county in which the person works or attends school, and receives notice of verification of that fact from the authority. The authority must verify that the person no longer works or studies in this state and must provide to the person notice of that verification within a reasonable time.

(e) Notwithstanding Subsection (a), this article does not apply to a person who has a reportable conviction or adjudication, who resides in another state, and who is employed, carries on a vocation, or is a student in this state if the person establishes another residence in this state to work or attend school in this state. However, that person remains subject to the other articles of this chapter based on that person's residence in this state.

(Enacted by Acts 2005, 79th Leg., ch. 1008 (H.B. 867), § 1.01, effective September 1, 2005.)

## Art. 62.153. Registration of Workers or Students at Institutions of Higher Education.

(a) Not later than the later of the seventh day after the date on which the person begins to work or attend school or the first date the applicable authority by policy allows the person to register, a person required to register under Article 62.152 or any other provision of this chapter who is employed, carries on a vocation, or is a student at a public or private institution of higher education in this state shall report that fact to:

(1) the authority for campus security for that institution; or

(2) if an authority for campus security for that institution does not exist, the local law enforcement authority of:

(A) the municipality in which the institution is located; or

(B) the county in which the institution is located, if the institution is not located in a municipality.

(b) A person described by Subsection (a) shall provide the authority for campus security or the local law enforcement authority with all information the person is required to provide under Article 62.051(c).

(c) A person described by Subsection (a) shall notify the authority for campus security or the local law enforcement authority not later than the seventh day after the date of termination of the person's status as a worker or student at the institution.

(d) The authority for campus security or the local law enforcement authority shall promptly forward to the administrative office of the institution any information received from the person under this article and any information received from the department under Article 62.005.

(e) Subsection (a)(2) does not require a person to register with a local law enforcement authority if the person is otherwise required by this chapter to register with that authority.

(f) This article does not impose the requirements of public notification or notification to public or private primary or secondary schools on:

(1) an authority for campus security; or

(2) a local law enforcement authority, if those requirements relate to a person about whom the authority is not otherwise required by this chapter to make notifications.

(g) Notwithstanding Article 62.059, the requirements of this article supersede those of Article 62.059 for a person required to register under both this article and Article 62.059.

(Enacted by Acts 2005, 79th Leg., ch. 1008 (H.B. 867), § 1.01, effective September 1, 2005.)

## SUBCHAPTER E
## PROVISIONS APPLICABLE TO PERSONS SUBJECT TO CIVIL COMMITMENT

### Art. 62.201. Additional Public Notice for Individuals Subject to Civil Commitment.

(a) On receipt of notice under this chapter that a person subject to registration who is civilly committed as a sexually violent predator is due to be released from a penal institution or intends to move to a new residence in this state, the department shall, not later than the seventh day after the date on which the person is released or the seventh day after the date on which the person moves, provide written notice mailed or delivered to at least each address, other than a post office box, within a one-mile radius, in an area that has not been subdivided, or a three-block area, in an area that has been subdivided, of the place where the person intends to reside.

(b) The department shall provide the notice in English and Spanish and shall include in the notice any information that is public information under this chapter. The department may not include any information that is not public information under this chapter.

(c) The department shall establish procedures for a person with respect to whom notice is provided under this article to pay to the department all costs incurred by the department in providing the notice. The person shall pay those costs in accordance with the procedures established under this subsection.

(d) The department's duty to provide notice under this article in regard to a particular person ends on the date on which a court releases the person from all requirements of the civil commitment process.

(Enacted by Acts 2005, 79th Leg., ch. 1008 (H.B. 867), § 1.01, effective September 1, 2005.)

### Art. 62.202. Verification of Individuals Subject to Commitment.

(a) Notwithstanding Article 62.058, if an individual subject to registration under this chapter is civilly committed as a sexually violent predator, the person shall report to the local law enforcement authority designated as the person's primary registration authority by the department not less than once in each 30-day period following the date the person first registered under this chapter to verify the information in the registration form maintained by the authority for that person. For purposes of this subsection, a person complies with a requirement that the person register within a 30-day period following a date if the person registers at any time on or after the 27th day following that date but before the 33rd day after that date.

(b) On the date a court releases a person described by Subsection (a) from all requirements of the civil commitment process:

(1) the person's duty to verify registration as a sex offender is no longer imposed by this article; and

(2) the person is required to verify registration as provided by Article 62.058.

(Enacted by Acts 2005, 79th Leg., ch. 1008 (H.B. 867), § 1.01, effective September 1, 2005.)

### Art. 62.203. Failure to Comply: Individuals Subject to Commitment.

(a) A person commits an offense if the person, after commitment as a sexually violent predator but before the person is released from all requirements of the civil commitment process, fails to comply with any requirement of this chapter.

(b) An offense under this article is a felony of the second degree.

(Acts 1999, 76th Leg., ch. 444 (S.B. 1224), § 5(c), effective January 1, 2000; am. Acts 2005, 79th Leg., ch. 1008 (H.B. 867), § 1.01, effective September 1, 2005 (renumbered from art. 62.101).)

## SUBCHAPTER F
## REMOVAL OF REGISTRATION INFORMATION

### Art. 62.251. Removing Registration Information When Duty to Register Expires.

(a) When a person is no longer required to register as a sex offender under this chapter, the department shall remove all information about the person from the sex offender registry.

(b) The duty to remove information under Subsection (a) arises if:

(1) the department has received notice from a local law enforcement authority under Subsection (c) or (d) that the person is no longer required to register or will no longer be required to renew registration and the department verifies the correctness of that information;

(2) the court having jurisdiction over the case for which registration is required requests

removal and the department determines that the duty to register has expired; or

(3) the person or the person's representative requests removal and the department determines that the duty to register has expired.

(c) When a person required to register under this chapter appears before a local law enforcement authority to renew or modify registration information, the authority shall determine whether the duty to register has expired. If the authority determines that the duty to register has expired, the authority shall remove all information about the person from the sex offender registry and notify the department that the person's duty to register has expired.

(d) When a person required to register under this chapter appears before a local law enforcement authority to renew registration information, the authority shall determine whether the renewal is the final annual renewal of registration required by law. If the authority determines that the person's duty to register will expire before the next annual renewal is scheduled, the authority shall automatically remove all information about the person from the sex offender registry on expiration of the duty to register and notify the department that the information about the person has been removed from the registry.

(e) When the department has removed information under Subsection (a), the department shall notify all local law enforcement authorities that have provided registration information to the department about the person of the removal. A local law enforcement authority that receives notice from the department under this subsection shall remove all registration information about the person from its registry.

(f) When the department has removed information under Subsection (a), the department shall notify all public and private agencies or organizations to which it has provided registration information about the person of the removal. On receiving notice, the public or private agency or organization shall remove all registration information about the person from any registry the agency or organization maintains that is accessible to the public with or without charge.

(Acts 2003, 78th Leg., ch. 283 (H.B. 2319), § 37, effective September 1, 2003; am. Acts 2005, 79th Leg., ch. 1008 (H.B. 867), § 1.01, effective September 1, 2005 (renumbered from art. 62.14).)

## SUBCHAPTER G
## EXEMPTION FROM REGISTRATION FOR CERTAIN YOUNG ADULT SEX OFFENDERS

### Art. 62.301. Exemption from Registration for Certain Young Adult Sex Offenders.

(a) If eligible under Subsection (b) or (c), a person required to register under this chapter may petition the court having jurisdiction over the case for an order exempting the person from registration under this chapter at any time on or after the date of the person's sentencing or the date the person is placed on deferred adjudication community supervision, as applicable.

(b) A person is eligible to petition the court as described by Subsection (a) if:

(1) the person is required to register only as a result of a single reportable conviction or adjudication, other than an adjudication of delinquent conduct; and

(2) the court has entered in the appropriate judgment or has filed with the appropriate papers a statement of an affirmative finding described by Article 42.017 or Section 5(g), Article 42.12.

(c) A defendant who before September 1, 2011, is convicted of or placed on deferred adjudication community supervision for an offense under Section 21.11 or 22.011, Penal Code, is eligible to petition the court as described by Subsection (a). The court may consider the petition only if the petition states and the court finds that the defendant would have been entitled to the entry of an affirmative finding under Article 42.017 or Section 5(g), Article 42.12, as appropriate, had the conviction or placement on deferred adjudication community supervision occurred after September 1, 2011.

(c-1) At a hearing on the petition described by Subsection (a), the court may consider:

(1) testimony from the victim or intended victim, or a member of the victim's or intended victim's family, concerning the requested exemption;

(2) the relationship between the victim or intended victim and the petitioner at the time of the hearing; and

(3) any other evidence that the court determines is relevant and admissible.

(d) After a hearing on the petition described by Subsection (a), the court may issue an order exempting the person from registration under this chapter if it appears by a preponderance of the evidence that:

(1) the exemption does not threaten public safety;

(2) the person's conduct did not occur without the consent of the victim or intended victim as described by Section 22.011(b), Penal Code;

(3) the exemption is in the best interest of the victim or intended victim; and

(4) the exemption is in the best interest of justice.

(e) An order exempting the person from registration under this chapter does not expire, but the court shall withdraw the order if after the order is issued the person receives a reportable conviction or adjudication under this chapter. (Enacted by Acts 2005, 79th Leg., ch. 1008 (H.B. 867), § 1.01, effective September 1, 2005; am. Acts 2011, 82nd Leg., ch. 134 (S.B. 198), § 3, effective September 1, 2011.)

## SUBCHAPTER H
## EXEMPTIONS FROM REGISTRATION FOR CERTAIN JUVENILES

### Art. 62.351. Motion and Hearing Generally.

(a) During or after disposition of a case under Section 54.04, Family Code, for adjudication of an offense for which registration is required under this chapter, the juvenile court on motion of the respondent shall conduct a hearing to determine whether the interests of the public require registration under this chapter. The motion may be filed and the hearing held regardless of whether the respondent is under 18 years of age. Notice of the motion and hearing shall be provided to the prosecuting attorney.

(b) The hearing is without a jury and the burden of persuasion is on the respondent to show by a preponderance of evidence that the criteria of Article 62.352(a) have been met. The court at the hearing may make its determination based on:

(1) the receipt of exhibits;

(2) the testimony of witnesses;

(3) representations of counsel for the parties; or

(4) the contents of a social history report prepared by the juvenile probation department that may include the results of testing and

examination of the respondent by a psychologist, psychiatrist, or counselor.

(c) All written matter considered by the court shall be disclosed to all parties as provided by Section 54.04(b), Family Code.

(d) If a respondent, as part of a plea agreement, promises not to file a motion seeking an order exempting the respondent from registration under this chapter, the court may not recognize a motion filed by a respondent under this article.
(Enacted by Acts 2005, 79th Leg., ch. 1008 (H.B. 867), § 1.01, effective September 1, 2005.)

### Art. 62.352. Order Generally.

(a) The court shall enter an order exempting a respondent from registration under this chapter if the court determines:

(1) that the protection of the public would not be increased by registration of the respondent under this chapter; or

(2) that any potential increase in protection of the public resulting from registration of the respondent is clearly outweighed by the anticipated substantial harm to the respondent and the respondent's family that would result from registration under this chapter.

(b) After a hearing under Article 62.351 or under a plea agreement described by Article 62.355(b), the juvenile court may enter an order:

(1) deferring decision on requiring registration under this chapter until the respondent has completed treatment for the respondent's sexual offense as a condition of probation or while committed to the Texas Youth Commission; or

(2) requiring the respondent to register as a sex offender but providing that the registration information is not public information and is restricted to use by law enforcement and criminal justice agencies, the Council on Sex Offender Treatment, and public or private institutions of higher education.

(c) If the court enters an order described by Subsection (b)(1), the court retains discretion and jurisdiction to require, or exempt the respondent from, registration under this chapter at any time during the treatment or on the successful or unsuccessful completion of treatment, except that during the period of deferral, registration may not be required. Following successful completion of treatment, the respondent is exempted from registration under this chapter unless a hearing under this subchapter is held on motion of the state, regardless of whether the respondent is 18 years of age or older, and the court determines the interests of the public require registration. Not later than the 10th day after the date of the respondent's successful completion of treatment, the treatment provider shall notify the juvenile court and prosecuting attorney of the completion.

(d) Information that is the subject of an order described by Subsection (b)(2) may not be posted on the Internet or released to the public.
(Enacted by Acts 2005, 79th Leg., ch. 1008 (H.B. 867), § 1.01, effective September 1, 2005.)

## Art. 62.353. Motion, Hearing, and Order Concerning Person Already Registered.

(a) A person who has registered as a sex offender for an adjudication of delinquent conduct, regardless of when the delinquent conduct or the adjudication for the conduct occurred, may file a motion in the adjudicating juvenile court for a hearing seeking:

(1) exemption from registration under this chapter as provided by Article 62.351; or

(2) an order under Article 62.352(b)(2) that the registration become nonpublic.

(b) The person may file a motion under Subsection (a) in the original juvenile case regardless of whether the person, at the time of filing the motion, is 18 years of age or older. Notice of the motion shall be provided to the prosecuting attorney. A hearing on the motion shall be provided as in other cases under this subchapter.

(c) Only one subsequent motion may be filed under Subsection (a) if a previous motion under this article has been filed concerning the case.

(d) To the extent feasible, the motion under Subsection (a) shall identify those public and private agencies and organizations, including public or private institutions of higher education, that possess sex offender registration information about the case.

(e) The juvenile court, after a hearing, may:

(1) deny a motion filed under Subsection (a);

(2) grant a motion described by Subsection (a)(1); or

(3) grant a motion described by Subsection (a)(2).

(f) If the court grants a motion filed under Subsection (a), the clerk of the court shall by certified mail, return receipt requested, send a copy of the order to the department, to each local law enforcement authority that the person has proved to the juvenile court has registration information about the person, and to each public or private agency or organization that the person has proved to the juvenile court has information about the person that is currently available to the public with or without payment of a fee. The clerk of the court shall by certified mail, return receipt requested, send a copy of the order to any other agency or organization designated by the person. The person shall identify the agency or organization and its address and pay a fee of $20 to the court for each agency or organization the person designates.

(g) In addition to disseminating the order under Subsection (f), at the request of the person, the clerk of the court shall by certified mail, return receipt requested, send a copy of the order to each public or private agency or organization that at any time following the initial dissemination of the order under Subsection (f) gains possession of sex offender registration information pertaining to that person, if the agency or organization did not otherwise receive a copy of the order under Subsection (f).

(h) An order under Subsection (f) must require the recipient to conform its records to the court's order either by deleting the sex offender registration information or changing its status to nonpublic, as applicable. A public or private institution of higher education may not be required to delete the sex offender registration information under this subsection.

(i) A private agency or organization that possesses sex offender registration information the agency or organization obtained from a state, county, or local governmental entity is required to conform the agency's or organization's records to the court's order on or before the 30th day after the date of the entry of the order. Unless the agency or organization is a public or private institution of higher education, failure to comply in that period automatically bars the agency or organization from obtaining sex offender registration information from any state, county, or local governmental entity in this state in the future.
(Enacted by Acts 2005, 79th Leg., ch. 1008 (H.B. 867), § 1.01, effective September 1, 2005.)

## Art. 62.354. Motion, Hearing, and Order Concerning Person Required to Register Because of Out-of-State Adjudication.

(a) A person required to register as a sex offender in this state because of an out-of-state adjudication of delinquent conduct may file in the juvenile court of the person's county of residence a petition under Article 62.351 for an order exempting the person from registration under this chapter.

(b) If the person is already registered as a sex offender in this state because of an out-of-state adjudication of delinquent conduct, the person may file in the juvenile court of the person's county of residence a petition under Article 62.353 for an order removing the person from sex offender registries in this state.

(c) On receipt of a petition under this article, the juvenile court shall conduct a hearing and make rulings as in other cases under this subchapter.

(d) An order entered under this article requiring removal of registration information applies only to registration information derived from registration in this state.
(Enacted by Acts 2005, 79th Leg., ch. 1008 (H.B. 867), § 1.01, effective September 1, 2005.)

## Art. 62.355. Waiver of Hearing.

(a) The prosecuting attorney may waive the state's right to a hearing under this subchapter and agree that registration under this chapter is not required. A waiver under this subsection must state whether the waiver is entered under a plea agreement.

(b) If the waiver is entered under a plea agreement, the court, without a hearing, shall:

(1) enter an order exempting the respondent from registration under this chapter; or

(2) under Section 54.03(j), Family Code, inform the respondent that the court believes a hearing under this article is required and give the respondent the opportunity to:

(A) withdraw the respondent's plea of guilty, nolo contendere, or true; or

(B) affirm the respondent's plea and participate in the hearing.

(c) If the waiver is entered other than under a plea agreement, the court, without a hearing, shall enter an order exempting the respondent from registration under this chapter.
(Enacted by Acts 2005, 79th Leg., ch. 1008 (H.B. 867), § 1.01, effective September 1, 2005.)

## Art. 62.356. Effect of Certain Orders.

(a) A person who has an adjudication of delinquent conduct that would otherwise be reportable under Article 62.001(5) does not have a reportable adjudication of delinquent conduct for pur-

poses of this chapter if the juvenile court enters an order under this subchapter exempting the person from the registration requirements of this chapter.

(b) If the juvenile court enters an order exempting a person from registration under this chapter, the respondent may not be required to register in this or any other state for the offense for which registration was exempted.
(Enacted by Acts 2005, 79th Leg., ch. 1008 (H.B. 867), § 1.01, effective September 1, 2005.)

## Art. 62.357. Appeal of Certain Orders.

(a) Notwithstanding Section 56.01, Family Code, on entry by a juvenile court of an order under Article 62.352(a) exempting a respondent from registration under this chapter, the prosecuting attorney may appeal that order by giving notice of appeal within the time required under Rule 26.2(b), Texas Rules of Appellate Procedure. The appeal is civil and the standard of review in the appellate court is whether the juvenile court committed procedural error or abused its discretion in exempting the respondent from registration under this chapter. The appeal is limited to review of the order exempting the respondent from registration under this chapter and may not include any other issues in the case.

(b) A respondent may under Section 56.01, Family Code, appeal a juvenile court's order under Article 62.352(a) requiring registration in the same manner as the appeal of any other legal issue in the case. The standard of review in the appellate court is whether the juvenile court committed procedural error or abused its discretion in requiring registration.
(Enacted by Acts 2005, 79th Leg., ch. 1008 (H.B. 867), § 1.01, effective September 1, 2005.)

## SUBCHAPTER I
## EARLY TERMINATION OF CERTAIN PERSONS' OBLIGATION TO REGISTER

## Art. 62.401. Definition.

In this subchapter, "council" means the Council on Sex Offender Treatment.
(Enacted by Acts 2005, 79th Leg., ch. 1008 (H.B. 867), § 1.01, effective September 1, 2005.)

## Art. 62.402. Determination of Minimum Required Registration Period.

(a) The department by rule shall determine the minimum required registration period under federal law for each reportable conviction or adjudication under this chapter.

(b) After determining the minimum required registration period for each reportable conviction or adjudication under Subsection (a), the department shall compile and publish a list of reportable convictions or adjudications for which a person must register under this chapter for a period that exceeds the minimum required registration period under federal law.

(c) To the extent possible, the department shall periodically verify with the United States Department of Justice's Office of Sex Offender Sentencing, Monitoring, Apprehending, Registering, and Tracking or another appropriate federal agency or office the accuracy of the list of reportable convictions or adjudications described by Subsection (b).

(Enacted by Acts 2005, 79th Leg., ch. 1008 (H.B. 867), § 1.01, effective September 1, 2005; am. Acts 2011, 82nd Leg., ch. 134 (S.B. 198), § 4, effective September 1, 2011.)

## Art. 62.403. Individual Risk Assessment.

(a) The council by rule shall establish, develop, or adopt an individual risk assessment tool or a group of individual risk assessment tools that:

(1) evaluates the criminal history of a person required to register under this chapter; and

(2) seeks to predict:

(A) the likelihood that the person will engage in criminal activity that may result in the person receiving a second or subsequent reportable adjudication or conviction; and

(B) the continuing danger, if any, that the person poses to the community.

(b) On the written request of a person with a single reportable adjudication or conviction that appears on the list published under Article 62.402(b), the council shall:

(1) evaluate the person using the individual risk assessment tool or group of individual risk assessment tools established, developed, or adopted under Subsection (a); and

(2) provide to the person a written report detailing the outcome of an evaluation conducted under Subdivision (1).

(c) An individual risk assessment provided to a person under this subchapter is confidential and is not subject to disclosure under Chapter 552, Government Code.

(Enacted by Acts 2005, 79th Leg., ch. 1008 (H.B. 867), § 1.01, effective September 1, 2005.)

## Art. 62.404. Motion for Early Termination.

(a) A person required to register under this chapter who has requested and received an individual risk assessment under Article 62.403 may file with the trial court that sentenced the person for the reportable conviction or adjudication a motion for early termination of the person's obligation to register under this chapter.

(b) A motion filed under this article must be accompanied by:

(1) a written explanation of how the reportable conviction or adjudication giving rise to the movant's registration under this chapter qualifies as a reportable conviction or adjudication that appears on the list published under Article 62.402(b); and

(2) a certified copy of a written report detailing the outcome of an individual risk assessment evaluation conducted under Article 62.403(b)(1).

(Enacted by Acts 2005, 79th Leg., ch. 1008 (H.B. 867), § 1.01, effective September 1, 2005.)

## Art. 62.405. Hearing on Petition.

(a) After reviewing a motion filed with the court under Article 62.404, the court may:

(1) deny without a hearing the movant's request for early termination; or

(2) hold a hearing on the motion to determine whether to grant or deny the motion.

(b) The court may not grant a motion filed under Article 62.404 if:

(1) the motion is not accompanied by the documents required under Article 62.404(b); or

(2) the court determines that the reportable conviction or adjudication for which the movant is required to register under this chapter is not a reportable conviction or adjudication for which the movant is required to register for a period that exceeds the minimum required registration period under federal law.

(Enacted by Acts 2005, 79th Leg., ch. 1008 (H.B. 867), § 1.01, effective September 1, 2005.)

## Art. 62.406. Costs of Individual Risk Assessment and of Court.

A person required to register under this chapter who files a motion for early termination of the person's registration obligation under this chapter is responsible for and shall remit to the council and to the court, as applicable, all costs associated with and incurred by the council in providing the individual risk assessment or by the court in holding a hearing under this subchapter.

(Enacted by Acts 2005, 79th Leg., ch. 1008 (H.B. 867), § 1.01, effective September 1, 2005.)

### Art. 62.407. Effect of Order Granting Early Termination.

(a) If, after notice to the person and to the prosecuting attorney and a hearing, the court grants a motion filed under Article 62.404 for the early termination of a person's obligation to register under this chapter, notwithstanding Article 62.101, the person's obligation to register under this chapter ends on the later of:

(1) the date the court enters the order of early termination; or

(2) the date the person has paid each cost described by Section 62.406.

(b) If the court grants a motion filed under Article 62.404 for the early termination of a person's obligation to register under this chapter, all conditions of the person's parole, release to mandatory supervision, or community supervision shall be modified in accordance with the court's order.

(Enacted by Acts 2005, 79th Leg., ch. 1008 (H.B. 867), § 1.01, effective September 1, 2005.)

### Art. 62.408. Nonapplicability.

This subchapter does not apply to a person without a reportable conviction or adjudication who is required to register as a condition of parole, release to mandatory supervision, or community supervision.

(Enacted by Acts 2005, 79th Leg., ch. 1008 (H.B. 867), § 1.01, effective September 1, 2005.)

## CHAPTER 63
## MISSING CHILDREN AND MISSING PERSONS

### Subchapter A. General Provisions

### Subchapter B. University of North Texas Health Science Center At Fort Worth Missing Persons DNA Database

## SUBCHAPTER A
## GENERAL PROVISIONS

### Art. 63.001. Definitions.

In this chapter:

(1) "Child" means a person under 18 years of age.

(2) "Missing person" means a person 18 years old or older whose disappearance is possibly not voluntary.

(3) "Missing child" means a child whose whereabouts are unknown to the child's legal custodian, the circumstances of whose absence indicate that:

(A) the child did not voluntarily leave the care and control of the custodian, and the taking of the child was not authorized by law;

(B) the child voluntarily left the care and control of the custodian without the custodian's consent and without intent to return;

(C) the child was taken or retained in violation of the terms of a court order for possession of or access to the child; or

(D) the child was taken or retained without the permission of the custodian and with the effect of depriving the custodian of possession of or access to the child unless the taking or retention of the child was prompted by the commission or attempted commission of family violence, as defined by Section 71.004, Family Code, against the child or the actor.

(4) "Missing child" or "missing person" also includes a person of any age who is missing and:

(A) is under proven physical or mental disability or is senile, and because of one or more of these conditions is subject to immediate danger or is a danger to others;

(B) is in the company of another person or is in a situation the circumstances of which indicate that the missing child's or missing person's safety is in doubt; or

(C) is unemancipated as defined by the law of this state.

(5) "Missing child or missing person report" or "report" means information that is:

(A) given to a law enforcement agency on a form used for sending information to the national crime information center; and

(B) about a child or missing person whose whereabouts are unknown to the reporter and who is alleged in the form by the reporter to be missing.

(6) "Legal custodian of a child" means a parent of a child if no managing conservator or guardian of the person of the child has been appointed, the managing conservator of a child or a guardian of a child if a managing conservator or guardian has been appointed for the child, a possessory conservator of a child if the child is absent from the possessory conservator of the child at a time when the possessory conservator is entitled to possession of the child and the child is not believed to be with the managing conservator, or any other person who has assumed temporary care and control of a child if at the time of disappearance the child was not living with his parent, guardian, managing conservator, or possessory conservator.

(7) "Clearinghouse" means the missing children and missing persons information clearinghouse.

(8) "Law enforcement agency" means a police department of a city in this state, a sheriff of a county in this state, or the Department of Public Safety.

(9) "Possible match" occurs if the similarities between an unidentified body and a missing child or person would lead one to believe they are the same person.

(10) "City or state agency" means an employment commission, the Texas Department of Human Services, the Texas Department of Transportation, and any other agency that is funded or supported by the state or a city government.

(11) "Birth certificate agency" means a municipal or county official that records and maintains birth certificates and the bureau of vital statistics.

(12) "Bureau of vital statistics" means the bureau of vital statistics of the Texas Department of Health.

(13) "School" means a public primary school or private primary school that charges a fee for tuition and has more than 25 students enrolled and attending courses at a single location.

(Enacted by Acts 1985, 69th Leg., ch. 132 (H.B. 248), § 1, effective May 22, 1985; am. Acts 1987, 70th Leg., ch. 167 (S.B. 892), § 5.01(a 26), effective September 1, 1987 (renumbered from Hum. Res. Code Sec. 74.001); am. Acts 1987, 70th Leg., ch. 657 (S.B. 223), § 1, effective June 18, 1987; am. Acts 1987, 70th Leg., ch. 1052 (S.B. 298), § 7.03, effective September 1, 1987; am. Acts 1995, 74th Leg., ch. 165 (S.B. 971), § 22(43), effective September 1, 1995; am. Acts 1995, 74th Leg., ch. 178 (H.B. 223), § 1, effective September 1, 1995; am. Acts 1997, 75th Leg., ch. 51 (H.B. 1092), § 1, effective May 7, 1997; am. Acts 1997, 75th Leg., ch. 1084 (H.B. 1516), § 1, effective September 1, 1997; am. Acts 1997, 75th Leg., ch. 1427 (H.B. 2899), § 1, effective September 1, 1997 (renumbered from Hum. Res. Code Sec. 79.001); am. Acts 1999, 76th Leg., ch. 7 (S.B. 351), § 1, effective September 1, 1999; am. Acts 1999, 76th Leg., ch. 62 (S.B. 1368), §§ 3.10, 19.01(8), effective September 1, 1999 (renumbered from art. 62.001); am. Acts 2011, 82nd Leg., ch. 840 (H.B. 3439), § 1, effective September 1, 2011; am. Acts 2011, 82nd Leg., ch. 1019 (H.B. 2662), § 1, effective September 1, 2011; am. Acts 2011, 82nd Leg., ch. 1100 (S.B. 1551), § 2, effective September 1, 2011.)

## Art. 63.0015. Presumption Regarding Parentage.

For purposes of this chapter, a person named as a child's mother or father in the child's birth certificate is presumed to be the child's parent.

(Enacted by Acts 1999, 76th Leg., ch. 685 (H.B. 668), effective September 1, 1999; am. Acts 2009, 81st Leg., ch. 87 (S.B. 1969), § 27.001(3), effective September 1, 2009 (renumbered from art. 62.0015).)

## Art. 63.002. Missing Children and Missing Persons Information Clearinghouse.

(a) The missing children and missing persons information clearinghouse is established within the Department of Public Safety.

(b) The clearinghouse is under the administrative direction of the director of the department.

(c) The clearinghouse shall be used by all law enforcement agencies of the state.

(Enacted by Acts 1985, 69th Leg., ch. 132 (H.B. 248), § 1, effective May 22, 1985; am. Acts 1987, 70th Leg., ch. 167 (S.B. 892), § 5.01(a)(26), effective September 1, 1987 (renumbered from Hum. Res. Code Sec. 74.002); am. Acts 1997, 75th Leg., ch. 1427 (H.B. 2899), § 1, effective September 1, 1997 (renumbered from Hum. Res. Code Sec. 79.002); am. Acts 1999, 76th Leg., ch. 62 (S.B. 1368), § 19.01(8)(A), effective September 1, 1999 (renumbered from art. 62.002).)

## Art. 63.003. Function of Clearinghouse.

(a) The clearinghouse is a central repository of information on missing children and missing persons.

(b) The clearinghouse shall:

(1) establish a system of intrastate communication of information relating to missing children and missing persons;

(2) provide a centralized file for the exchange of information on missing children, missing persons, and unidentified dead bodies within the state;

(3) communicate with the national crime information center for the exchange of information on missing children and missing persons suspected of interstate travel;

(4) collect, process, maintain, and disseminate accurate and complete information on missing children and missing persons;

(5) provide a statewide toll-free telephone line for the reporting of missing children and missing persons and for receiving information on missing children and missing persons; and

(6) provide and disseminate to legal custodians, law enforcement agencies, and the Texas Education Agency information that explains how to prevent child abduction and what to do if a child becomes missing.

(Enacted by Acts 1985, 69th Leg., ch. 132 (H.B. 248), § 1, effective May 22, 1985; am. Acts 1987, 70th Leg., ch. 167 (S.B. 892), § 5.01(a)(26), effective September 1, 1987 (renumbered from Hum. Res. Code Sec. 74.003); am. Acts 1997, 75th Leg., ch. 165 (S.B. 898), § 6.59, effective September 1, 1997; am. Acts 1997, 75th Leg., ch. 1427 (H.B. 2899), § 1, effective September 1, 1997 (renumbered from Hum. Res. Code Sec. 79.003); am. Acts 1999, 76th Leg., ch. 62 (S.B. 1368), § 19.01(8)(A), effective September 1, 1999 (renumbered from art. 62.003).)

## Art. 63.004. Report Forms.

(a) The Department of Public Safety shall distribute missing children and missing person report forms.

(b) A missing child or missing person report may be made to a law enforcement officer authorized by that department to receive reports in person or by telephone or other indirect method of communication and the officer may enter the information on the form for the reporting person. A report form may also be completed by the reporting person and delivered to a law enforcement officer.

(Enacted by Acts 1985, 69th Leg., ch. 132 (H.B. 248), § 1, effective May 22, 1985; am. Acts 1987, 70th Leg., ch. 167 (S.B. 892), § 5.01(a)(26), effective September 1, 1987 (renumbered from Hum. Res. Code Sec. 74.004); am. Acts 1997, 75th Leg., ch. 1427 (H.B. 2899), § 1, effective September 1, 1997 (renumbered from Hum. Res. Code Sec. 79.004); am. Acts 1999, 76th Leg., ch. 62 (S.B. 1368), § 19.01(8)(A), effective September 1, 1999 (renumbered from art. 62.004).)

## Art. 63.005. Distribution of Information.

(a) The clearinghouse shall print and distribute posters, flyers, and other forms of information containing descriptions of missing children.

(b) The clearinghouse shall also provide to the Texas Education Agency information about missing children who may be located in the school systems.

(c) The clearinghouse may also receive information about missing children from the Public Education Information Management System of the Texas Education Agency and from school districts.

(Enacted by Acts 1985, 69th Leg., ch. 132 (H.B. 248), § 1, effective May 22, 1985; am. Acts 1987,

70th Leg., ch. 167 (S.B. 892), § 5.01(a)(26), effective September 1, 1987 (renumbered from Hum. Res. Code Sec. 74.005); am. Acts 1989, 71st Leg., ch. 190 (S.B. 402), § 2, effective August 28, 1989; am. Acts 1997, 75th Leg., ch. 165 (S.B. 898), § 6.60, effective September 1, 1997; am. Acts 1997, 75th Leg., ch. 1427 (S.B. 2899), § 1, effective September 1, 1997 (renumbered from Hum. Res. Code Sec. 79.005); am. Acts 1999, 76th Leg., ch. 62 (S.B. 1368), § 19.01(8)(A), effective September 1, 1999 (renumbered from art. 62.005).)

## Art. 63.006. Release of Dental Records.

(a) At the time a report is made for a missing child, the person to whom the report is given shall give or mail to the reporter a dental record release form. The officer receiving the report shall endorse the form with the notation that a missing child report has been made in compliance with this chapter. When the form is properly completed by the reporter, and contains the endorsement, the form is sufficient to permit any dentist or physician in this state to release dental records relating to the child reported missing.

(b) At any time a report is made for a missing person the law enforcement officer taking the report shall complete a dental release form that states that the person is missing and that there is reason to believe that the person has not voluntarily relocated or removed himself from communications with others and that authorizes the bearer of the release to obtain dental information records from any dentist or physician in this state.

(c) Any person who obtains dental records through the use of the form authorized by this article shall send the records to the clearinghouse.

(d) The judge of any court of record of this state may for good cause shown authorize the release of dental records of a missing child or missing person.

(e) A dentist or physician who releases dental records to a person presenting a proper release executed or ordered under this article is immune from civil liability or criminal prosecution for the release of those records.

(Enacted by Acts 1985, 69th Leg., ch. 132 (H.B. 248), § 1, effective May 22, 1985; am. Acts 1987, 70th Leg., ch. 167 (S.B. 892), § 5.01(a)(26), effective September 1, 1987 (renumbered from Hum. Res. Code Sec. 74.006); am. Acts 1997, 75th Leg., ch. 1427 (S.B. 2899), § 1, effective September 1, 1997 (renumbered from Hum. Res. Code Sec. 79.006); am. Acts 1999, 76th Leg., ch. 62 (S.B. 1368), § 19.01(8)(A), effective September 1, 1999 (renumbered from art. 62.006); am. Acts 1999, 76th Leg., ch. 685 (H.B. 668), § 3, effective September 1, 1999.)

## Art. 63.007. Release of Medical Records.

(a) At the time a report is made for a missing child or adult, the law enforcement officer taking the report shall give a medical record release form to the parent, spouse, adult child, or legal guardian who is making the report. The officer receiving the report shall endorse the form with the notation that a missing child or missing adult report has been made in compliance with this chapter. When the form is properly completed by the parent, spouse, adult child, or legal guardian, and contains the endorsement, the form is sufficient to permit any physician, health care facility, or other licensed health care provider in this state to release to the law enforcement officer presenting the release dental records, blood type, height, weight, X rays, and information regarding scars, allergies, or any unusual illnesses suffered by the person who is reported missing. Except as provided by Subsection (d), a medical record of a missing child may be released only if the medical record release form is signed by a parent or legal guardian.

(b) At any time a report is made for an adult missing person, the law enforcement officer taking the report shall complete a medical release form that states that the person is missing and that there is reason to believe that the person has not voluntarily relocated or removed himself or herself from communications with others. A release under this subsection is not valid unless it is signed by the adult missing person's:

(1) spouse;

(2) adult child who is reasonably available;

(3) parent; or

(4) legal guardian.

(c) A law enforcement officer who obtains medical records under this article shall send a copy of the records to the clearinghouse. A law enforcement officer who obtains records under this article, a law enforcement agency using the records, and the clearinghouse are prohibited from disclosing the information contained in or obtained through the medical records unless permitted by law. Information contained in or obtained through medical records may be used only for purposes directly related to locating the missing person.

(d) The judge of any court of record of this state may for good cause shown authorize the release of pertinent medical records of a missing child or missing adult.

(e) A physician, health care facility, or other licensed health care provider releasing a medical record to a person presenting a proper release executed or ordered under this article is immune from civil liability or criminal prosecution for the release of the record.

(Enacted by Acts 1995, 74th Leg., ch. 438 (H.B. 76), § 1, effective August 28, 1995; am. Acts 1997, 75th Leg., ch. 1427 (H.B. 2899), § 1, effective September 1, 1997 (renumbered from Hum. Res. Code Sec. 79.0065); am. Acts 1999, 76th Leg., ch. 62 (S.B. 1368), § 19.01(8)(A), effective September 1, 1999 (renumbered from art. 62.007).)

### Art. 63.008. Missing Children Program.

(a) The Texas Education Agency shall develop and administer a program for the location of missing children who may be enrolled within the Texas school system, including nonpublic schools, and for the reporting of children who may be missing or who may be unlawfully removed from schools.

(b) The program shall include the use of information received from the missing children and missing persons information clearinghouse and shall be coordinated with the operations of that information clearinghouse.

(c) The State Board of Education may adopt rules for the operation of the program and shall require the participation of all school districts and accredited private schools in this state.

(Enacted by Acts 1985, 69th Leg., ch. 132 (H.B. 248), § 1, effective May 22, 1985; am. Acts 1987, 70th Leg., ch. 167 (S.B. 892), § 5.01(a)(26), effective September 1, 1987 (renumbered from Hum. Res. Code Sec. 74.007); am. Acts 1997, 75th Leg., ch. 165 (S.B. 898), § 6.61, effective September 1, 1997; am. Acts 1997, 75th Leg., ch. 1427 (S.B. 2899), § 1, effective September 1, 1997 (renumbered from Hum. Res. Code Sec. 79.007); am. Acts 1999, 76th Leg., ch. 62 (S.B. 1368), § 19.01(8)(A), effective September 1, 1999 (renumbered from art. 62.008).)

### Art. 63.009. Law Enforcement Requirements.

(a) Local law enforcement agencies, on receiving a report of a missing child or a missing person, shall:

(1) if the subject of the report is a child and the well-being of the child is in danger or if the subject of the report is a person who is known by the agency to have or is reported to have chronic dementia, including Alzheimer's dementia, whether caused by illness, brain defect, or brain injury, immediately start an investigation in order to determine the present location of the child or person;

(2) if the subject of the report is a child or person other than a child or person described by Subdivision (1), start an investigation with due diligence in order to determine the present location of the child or person;

(3) immediately, but not later than two hours after receiving the report, enter the name of the child or person into the clearinghouse, the national crime information center missing person file if the child or person meets the center's criteria, and the Alzheimer's Association Safe Return crisis number, if applicable, with all available identifying features such as dental records, fingerprints, other physical characteristics, and a description of the clothing worn when last seen, and all available information describing any person reasonably believed to have taken or retained the missing child or missing person; and

(4) inform the person who filed the report of the missing child or missing person that the information will be entered into the clearinghouse, the national crime information center missing person file, and the Alzheimer's Association Safe Return crisis number, if applicable.

(b) Information not immediately available shall be obtained by the agency and entered into the clearinghouse and the national crime information center file as a supplement to the original entry as soon as possible.

(c) All Texas law enforcement agencies are required to enter information about all unidentified bodies into the clearinghouse and the national crime information center unidentified person file. A law enforcement agency shall, not later than the 10th working day after the date the death is reported to the agency, enter all available identifying features of the unidentified body (fingerprints, dental records, any unusual physical characteristics, and a description of the clothing found on the body) into the clearinghouse and the national crime information center file. If an information entry into the national crime information center file results in an automatic entry of the information into the clearinghouse, the law enforcement agency is not required to make a direct entry of that information into the clearinghouse.

(d) If a local law enforcement agency investigating a report of a missing child or missing person obtains a warrant for the arrest of a person for taking or retaining the missing child or missing person, the local law enforcement agency shall immediately enter the name and other descriptive information of the person into the national crime information center wanted person file if the person meets the center's criteria. The local law enforcement agency shall also enter all available identifying features, including dental records, fingerprints, and other physical characteristics of the missing child or missing person. The information shall be cross-referenced with the information in the national crime information center missing person file.

(e) A local law enforcement agency that has access to the national crime information center database shall cooperate with other law enforcement agencies in entering or retrieving information from the national crime information center database.

(f) Immediately after the return of a missing child or missing person or the identification of an unidentified body, the local law enforcement agency having jurisdiction of the investigation shall cancel the entry in the national crime information center database.

(g) On determining the location of a child under Subsection (a)(1) or (2), other than a child who is subject to the continuing jurisdiction of a district court, an officer shall take possession of the child and shall deliver or arrange for the delivery of the child to a person entitled to possession of the child. If the person entitled to possession of the child is not immediately available, the law enforcement officer shall deliver the child to the Department of Protective and Regulatory Services.

(Enacted by Acts 1985, 69th Leg., ch. 132 (H.B. 248), § 1, effective May 22, 1985; am. Acts 1987, 70th Leg., ch. 167 (S.B. 892), § 5.01(a)(26), effective September 1, 1987 (renumbered from Hum. Res. Code Sec. 74.008); am. Acts 1987, 70th Leg, ch. 657 (S.B. 223), § 2, effective June 18, 1987; am. Acts 1989, 71st Leg., ch. 190 (S.B. 402), § 3, effective August 28, 1989; am. Acts 1997, 75th Leg., ch. 51 (H.B. 1092), § 2, effective May 7, 1997; am. Acts 1997, 75th Leg., ch. 771 (H.B. 1912), § 1, effective September 1, 1997; am. Acts 1997, 75th Leg., ch. 1427 (S.B. 2899), § 1, effective September 1, 1997 (renumbered from Hum. Res. Code Sec. 79.008); am. Acts 1999, 76th Leg.,

ch. 62 (S.B. 1368), §§ 3.11, 3.12, 19.01 (8)(A), effective September 1, 1999 (renumbered from art. 62.009); am. Acts 1999, 76th Leg., ch. 200 (H.B. 605), §§ 1, 2, effective September 1, 1999; am. Acts 1999, 76th Leg., ch. 685 (H.B. 668), §§ 4, 5, effective September 1, 1999; am. Acts 2001, 77th Leg., ch. 1420 (H.B. 2812), § 3.005, effective September 1, 2001; am. Acts 2011, 82nd Leg., ch. 1130 (H.B. 943), § 2, effective September 1, 2011.)

## Art. 63.010. Attorney General to Require Compliance.

The attorney general shall require each law enforcement agency to comply with this chapter and may seek writs of mandamus or other appropriate remedies to enforce this chapter.

(Enacted by Acts 1985, 69th Leg., ch. 132 (H.B. 248), § 1, effective May 22, 1985; am. Acts 1987, 70th Leg., ch. 167 (S.B. 892), § 5.01(a)(26), effective September 1, 1987 (renumbered from Hum. Res. Code Sec. 74.009); am. Acts 1997, 75th Leg., ch. 1427 (H.B. 2899), § 1, effective September 1, 1997 (renumbered from Hum. Res. Code Sec. 79.009); am. Acts 1999, 76th Leg., ch. 62 (S.B. 1368), § 19.01(8)(A), effective September 1, 1999 (renumbered from art. 62.010).)

## Art. 63.011. Missing Children Investigations.

On the written request made to a law enforcement agency by a parent, foster parent, managing or possessory conservator, guardian of the person or the estate, or other court-appointed custodian of a child whose whereabouts are unknown, the law enforcement agency shall request from the missing children and missing persons information clearinghouse information concerning the child that may aid the person making the request in the identification or location of the child.

(Enacted by Acts 1985, 69th Leg., ch. 132 (H.B. 248), § 1, effective May 22, 1985; am. Acts 1987, 70th Leg., ch. 167 (S.B. 892), § 5.01(a)(26), effective September 1, 1987 (renumbered from Hum. Res. Code Sec. 74.010); am. Acts 1997, 75th Leg., ch. 1427 (H.B. 2899), § 1, effective September 1, 1997 (renumbered from Hum. Res. Code Sec. 79.010); am. Acts 1999, 76th Leg., ch. 62 (S.B. 1368), § 19.01(8)(A), effective September 1, 1999 (renumbered from art. 62.011).)

## Art. 63.012. Report of Inquiry.

A law enforcement agency to which a request has been made under Article 63.011 of this code shall report to the parent on the results of its inquiry within 14 days after the day that the written request is filed with the law enforcement agency.

(Enacted by Acts 1985, 69th Leg., ch. 132 (H.B. 248), § 1, effective May 22, 1985; am. Acts 1987, 70th Leg., ch. 167 (S.B. 892), § 5.01(a)(26), (27), effective September 1, 1987 (renumbered from Hum. Res. Code Sec. 74.011); am. Acts 1997, 75th Leg., ch. 1427 (H.B. 2899), § 1, effective September 1, 1997 (renumbered from Hum. Res. Code Sec. 79.011); am. Acts 1999, 76th Leg., ch. 62 (S.B. 1368), §§ 19.01(8)(A), 19.02(1), effective September 1, 1999 (renumbered from art. 62.012).)

## Art. 63.013. Information to Clearinghouse.

Each law enforcement agency shall provide to the missing children and missing persons information clearinghouse any information that would assist in the location or identification of any missing child who has been reported to the agency as missing.

(Enacted by Acts 1985, 69th Leg., ch. 132 (H.B. 248), § 1, effective May 22, 1985; am. Acts 1987, 70th Leg., ch. 167 (S.B. 892), § 5.01(a)(26), effective September 1, 1987 (renumbered from Hum. Res. Code Sec. 74.012); am. Acts 1997, 75th Leg., ch. 1427 (H.B. 2899), § 1, effective September 1, 1997 (renumbered from Hum. Res. Code Sec. 79.012); am. Acts 1999, 76th Leg., ch. 62 (S.B. 1368), § 19.01(8)(A), effective September 1, 1999 (renumbered from art. 62.013).)

## Art. 63.014. Cross-Checking and Matching.

(a) The clearinghouse shall cross-check and attempt to match unidentified bodies with missing children or missing persons. When the clearinghouse discovers a possible match between an unidentified body and a missing child or missing person, the Department of Public Safety shall notify the appropriate law enforcement agencies.

(b) Those law enforcement agencies that receive notice of a possible match shall make arrangements for positive identification and complete and close out the investigation with notification to the clearinghouse.

(Enacted by Acts 1985, 69th Leg., ch. 132 (H.B. 248), § 1, effective May 22, 1985; am. Acts 1987, 70th Leg., ch. 167 (S.B. 892), § 5.01(a)(26), effective September 1, 1987 (renumbered from Hum. Res. Code Sec. 74.013); am. Acts 1997, 75th Leg.,

ch. 1427 (H.B. 2899), § 1, effective September 1, 1997 (renumbered from Hum. Res. Code Sec. 79.013); am. Acts 1999, 76th Leg., ch. 62 (S.B. 1368), § 19.01(8)(A), effective September 1, 1999 (renumbered from art. 62.014).)

## Art. 63.015. Availability of Information Through Other Agencies.

(a) On the request of any law enforcement agency, a city or state agency shall furnish the law enforcement agency with any information about a missing child or missing person that will assist in completing the investigation.

(b) The information given under Subsection (a) of this article is confidential and may not be released to any other person outside of the law enforcement agency.

(Enacted by Acts 1985, 69th Leg., ch. 132 (H.B. 248), § 1, effective May 22, 1985; am. Acts 1987, 70th Leg., ch. 167 (S.B. 892), § 5.01(a)(26), effective September 1, 1987 (renumbered from Hum. Res. Code Sec. 74.014); am. Acts 1997, 75th Leg., ch. 1427 (H.B. 2899), § 1, effective September 1, 1997 (renumbered from Hum. Res. Code Sec. 79.014); am. Acts 1999, 76th Leg., ch. 62 (S.B. 1368), § 19.01(8)(A), effective September 1, 1999 (renumbered from art. 62.015).)

## Art. 63.016. Donations.

The Department of Public Safety may accept money donated from any source to assist in financing the activities and purposes of the missing children and missing persons information clearinghouse.

(Enacted by Acts 1987, 70th Leg., ch. 894 (H.B. 1630), § 1, effective June 19, 1987; am. Acts 1997, 75th Leg., ch. 1427 (H.B. 2899), § 1, effective September 1, 1997 (renumbered from Hum. Res. Code Sec. 79.015); am. Acts 1999, 76th Leg., ch. 62 (S.B. 1368), § 19.01(8)(A), effective September 1, 1999 (renumbered from art. 62.016).)

## Art. 63.017. Confidentiality of Certain Records.

Clearinghouse records that relate to the investigation by a law enforcement agency of a missing child, a missing person, or an unidentified body and records or notations that the clearinghouse maintains for internal use in matters relating to missing children, missing persons, or unidentified bodies are confidential.

(Enacted by Acts 1989, 71st Leg., ch. 190 (S.B. 402), § 1, effective August 28, 1989; am. Acts 1997, 75th Leg., ch. 1427 (H.B. 2899), § 1, effective September 1, 1997 (renumbered from Hum. Res. Code Sec. 79.016); am. Acts 1999, 76th Leg., ch. 62 (S.B. 1368), § 19.01(8)(A), effective September 1, 1999 (renumbered from art. 62.017).)

### Art. 63.018. Death Certificates.

A physician who performs a postmortem examination on the body of an unidentified person shall complete and file a death certificate in accordance with Chapter 193, Health and Safety Code. The physician shall note on the certificate the name of the law enforcement agency that submitted the body for examination and shall send a copy of the certificate to the clearinghouse not later than the 10th working day after the date the physician files the certificate.

(Enacted by Acts 1997, 75th Leg., ch. 1427 (H.B. 2899), § 1, effective September 1, 1997; am. Acts 1999, 76th Leg., ch. 62 (S.B. 1368), § 19.01(8)(A), effective September 1, 1999 (renumbered from art. 62.018).)

### Art. 63.019. School Records System.

(a) On enrollment of a child under 11 years of age in a school for the first time at the school, the school shall:

(1) request from the person enrolling the child the name of each previous school attended by the child;

(2) request from each school identified in Subdivision (1), the school records for the child and, if the person enrolling the child provides copies of previous school records, request verification from the school of the child's name, address, birth date, and grades and dates attended; and

(3) notify the person enrolling the student that not later than the 30th day after enrollment, or the 90th day if the child was not born in the United States, the person must provide:

(A) a certified copy of the child's birth certificate; or

(B) other reliable proof of the child's identity and age and a signed statement explaining the person's inability to produce a copy of the child's birth certificate.

(b) If a person enrolls a child under 11 years of age in school and does not provide the valid prior school information or documentation required by this section, the school shall notify the appropriate law enforcement agency before the 31st day after the person fails to comply with this section. On receipt of notification, the law enforcement agency shall immediately check the clearing-

house to determine if the child has been reported missing. If the child has been reported missing, the law enforcement agency shall immediately notify other appropriate law enforcement agencies that the missing child has been located.

(Enacted by Acts 1997, 75th Leg., ch. 1084 (H.B. 1516), § 2, effective September 1, 1997; am. Acts 1999, 76th Leg., ch. 62 (S.B. 1368), § 19.01(8)(B), effective September 1, 1999 (renumbered from Human Resources Code Sec. 79.017).)

### Art. 63.020. Duty of Schools and Other Entities to Flag Missing Children's Records.

(a) When a report that a child under 11 years of age is missing is received by a law enforcement agency, the agency shall immediately notify each school and day care facility that the child attended or in which the child was enrolled as well as the bureau of vital statistics, if the child was born in the state, that the child is missing.

(b) On receipt of notice that a child under 11 years of age is missing, the bureau of vital statistics shall notify the appropriate municipal or county birth certificate agency that the child is missing.

(c) A school, day care facility, or birth certificate agency that receives notice concerning a child under this section shall flag the child's records that are maintained by the school, facility, or agency.

(d) The law enforcement agency shall notify the clearinghouse that the notification required under this section has been made. The clearinghouse shall provide the notice required under this section if the clearinghouse determines that the notification has not been made by the law enforcement agency.

(e) If a missing child under 11 years of age, who was the subject of a missing child report made in this state, was born in or attended a school or licensed day care facility in another state, the law enforcement agency shall notify law enforcement or the missing and exploited children clearinghouse in each appropriate state regarding the missing child and request the law enforcement agency or clearinghouse to contact the state birth certificate agency and each school or licensed day care facility the missing child attended to flag the missing child's records.

(Enacted by Acts 1997, 75th Leg., ch. 1084 (H.B. 1516), § 2, effective September 1, 1997; am. Acts 1999, 76th Leg., ch. 62 (S.B. 1368), § 19.01(8)(B), effective September 1, 1999 (renumbered from

**Criminal Procedure**

Human Resources Code Sec. 79.018) (renumbered from Human Resources Code Sec. 79.018).)

## Art. 63.021. System for Flagging Records.

(a) On receipt of notification by a law enforcement agency or the clearinghouse regarding a missing child under 11 years of age, the school, day care facility, or birth certificate agency shall maintain the child's records in its possession so that on receipt of a request regarding the child, the school, day care facility, or agency will be able to notify law enforcement or the clearinghouse that a request for a flagged record has been made.

(b) When a request concerning a flagged record is made in person, the school, day care facility, or agency may not advise the requesting party that the request concerns a missing child and shall:

(1) require the person requesting the flagged record to complete a form stating the person's name, address, telephone number, and relationship to the child for whom a request is made and the name, address, and birth date of the child;

(2) obtain a copy of the requesting party's driver's license or other photographic identification, if possible;

(3) if the request is for a birth certificate, inform the requesting party that a copy of a certificate will be sent by mail; and

(4) immediately notify the appropriate law enforcement agency that a request has been made concerning a flagged record and include a physical description of the requesting party, the identity and address of the requesting party, and a copy of the requesting party's driver's license or other photographic identification.

(c) After providing the notification required under Subsection (a)(4), the school, day care facility, or agency shall mail a copy of the requested record to the requesting party on or after the 21st day after the date of the request.

(d) When a request concerning a flagged record is made in writing, the school, day care facility, or agency may not advise the party that the request concerns a missing child and shall immediately notify the appropriate law enforcement agency that a request has been made concerning a flagged record and provide to the law enforcement agency a copy of the written request. After

providing the notification under this subsection, the school, day care facility, or agency shall mail a copy of the requested record to the requesting party on or after the 21st day after the date of the request.

(Enacted by Acts 1997, 75th Leg., ch. 1084 (H.B. 1516), § 2, effective September 1, 1997; am. Acts 1999, 76th Leg., ch. 62 (S.B. 1368), § 19.01(8)(B), effective September 1, 1999 (renumbered from Human Resources Code Sec. 79.019).)

## Art. 63.022. Removal of Flag From Records.

(a) On the return of a missing child under 11 years of age, the law enforcement agency shall notify each school or day care facility that has maintained flagged records for the child and the bureau of vital statistics that the child is no longer missing. The law enforcement agency shall notify the clearinghouse that notification under this section has been made. The bureau of vital statistics shall notify the appropriate municipal or county birth certificate agency. The clearinghouse shall notify the school, day care facility, or bureau of vital statistics that the missing child is no longer missing if the clearinghouse determines that the notification was not provided by the law enforcement agency.

(b) On notification by the law enforcement agency or the clearinghouse that a missing child has been recovered, the school, day care facility, or birth certificate agency that maintained flagged records shall remove the flag from the records.

(c) A school, day care facility, or birth certificate agency that has reason to believe a missing child has been recovered may request confirmation that the missing child has been recovered from the appropriate law enforcement agency or the clearinghouse. If a response is not received after the 45th day after the date of the request for confirmation, the school, day care facility, or birth certificate agency may remove the flag from the record and shall inform the law enforcement agency or the clearinghouse that the flag has been removed.

(Enacted by Acts 1997, 75th Leg., ch. 1084 (H.B. 1516), § 2, effective September 1, 1997; am. Acts 1999, 76th Leg., ch. 62 (S.B. 1368), § 19.01(8)(B), effective September 1, 1999 (renumbered from Human Resources Code Sec. 79.020).)

## SUBCHAPTER B
## UNIVERSITY OF NORTH TEXAS HEALTH SCIENCE CENTER AT FORT WORTH MISSING PERSONS DNA DATABASE

### Art. 63.051. Definitions.

In this subchapter:

(1) "Board" means the board of regents of the University of North Texas System.

(2) "Center" means the University of North Texas Health Science Center at Fort Worth.

(3) "DNA" means deoxyribonucleic acid.

(4) "DNA database" means the database containing forensic DNA analysis results, including any known name of the person who is the subject of the forensic DNA analysis, that is maintained by the center.

(5) "High-risk missing person" means:

(A) a person missing as a result of an abduction by a stranger;

(B) a person missing under suspicious or unknown circumstances; or

(C) a person who has been missing more than 30 days, or less than 30 days at the discretion of the investigating agency, if there is reason to believe that the person is in danger or deceased.

(6) "Law enforcement agency" means the law enforcement agency primarily responsible for investigating a report of a high-risk missing person.

(Acts 2001, 77th Leg., ch. 1496 (S.B. 1304), § 1, effective September 1, 2001; Acts 2003, 78th Leg., ch. 1275 (H.B. 3506), § 2(48), effective September 1, 2003 (renumbered from Education Code Sec. 105.111); am. Acts 2005, 79th Leg., ch. 319 (S.B. 651), § 2, effective June 17, 2005 (renumbered from Education Code Sec. 105.451).)

### Sec. 63.0515. Criminal Justice Agency.

For purposes of this subchapter, the center is a criminal justice agency that performs forensic DNA analyses on evidence, including evidence related to a case involving unidentified human remains or a high-risk missing person. The center shall comply with 42 U.S.C. Section 14132.

(Enacted by Acts 2011, 82nd Leg., ch. 320 (H.B. 2385), § 1, effective June 17, 2011.)

### Art. 63.052. Establishment of DNA Database for Missing or Unidentified Persons.

(a) The board shall develop at the University of North Texas Health Science Center at Fort Worth a DNA database for any case based on the report of unidentified human remains or a report of a high-risk missing person.

(b) The database may be used to identify unidentified human remains and high-risk missing persons.

(c) [Repealed by Acts 2011, 82nd Leg., ch. 320 (H.B. 2385), § 3, effective June 17, 2011.]

(Acts 2001, 77th Leg., ch. 1496 (S.B. 1304), § 1, effective September 1, 2001; Acts 2003, 78th Leg., ch. 1275 (H.B. 3506), § 2(48), effective September 1, 2003 (renumbered from Education Code Sec. 105.112); am. Acts 2005, 79th Leg., ch. 319 (S.B. 651), § 2, effective June 17, 2005 (renumbered from Education Code Sec. 105.452); am. Acts 2011, 82nd Leg., ch. 320 (H.B. 2385), §§ 2, 3, effective June 17, 2011.)

### Art. 63.053. Information Stored in Database.

(a) The database required in Article 63.052 may contain only DNA genetic markers that are commonly recognized as appropriate for human identification. Except to the extent that those markers are appropriate for human identification, the database may not contain DNA genetic markers that predict biological function. The center shall select the DNA genetic markers for inclusion in the DNA database based on existing technology for forensic DNA analysis.

(b) The results of the forensic DNA analysis must be compatible with the CODIS DNA database established by the Federal Bureau of Investigation and the center must make the results available for inclusion in that database.

(Acts 2001, 77th Leg., ch. 1496 (S.B. 1304), § 1, effective September 1, 2001; Acts 2003, 78th Leg., ch. 1275 (H.B. 3506), § 2(48), effective September 1, 2003 (renumbered from Education Code Sec. 105.113); am. Acts 2005, 79th Leg., ch. 319 (S.B. 651), § 2, effective June 17, 2005 (renumbered from Education Code Sec. 105.453).)

### Art. 63.054. Comparison of Samples.

The center shall compare DNA samples taken from unidentified human remains with DNA samples taken from personal articles belonging to high-risk missing persons or from parents of high-risk missing persons or other appropriate persons.

(Acts 2001, 77th Leg., ch. 1496 (S.B. 1304), § 1, effective September 1, 2001; Acts 2003, 78th Leg., ch. 1275 (H.B. 3506), § 2(48), effective September 1, 2003 (renumbered from Education Code Sec. 105.114); am. Acts 2005, 79th Leg., ch. 319 (S.B. 651), § 2, effective June 17, 2005 (renumbered from Education Code Sec. 105.454).)

### Art. 63.055. Standards Collection; Storage.

In consultation with the center, the board by rule shall develop standards and guidelines for the collection of DNA samples submitted to the center and the center's storage of DNA samples. (Acts 2001, 77th Leg., ch. 1496 (S.B. 1304), § 1, effective September 1, 2001; Acts 2003, 78th Leg., ch. 1275 (H.B. 3506), § 2(48), effective September 1, 2003 (renumbered from Education Code Sec. 105.115); am. Acts 2005, 79th Leg., ch. 319 (S.B. 651), § 2, effective June 17, 2005 (renumbered from Education Code Sec. 105.455).)

### Art. 63.056. Collection of Samples from Unidentified Human Remains.

(a) A physician acting on the request of a justice of the peace under Subchapter A, Chapter 49, a county coroner, a county medical examiner, or other law enforcement entity, as appropriate, shall collect samples from unidentified human remains. The justice of the peace, coroner, medical examiner, or other law enforcement entity shall submit those samples to the center for forensic DNA analysis and inclusion of the results in the DNA database.

(b) After the center has performed the forensic DNA analysis, the center shall return the remaining sample to the entity that submitted the sample under Subsection (a). (Acts 2001, 77th Leg., ch. 1496 (S.B. 1304), § 1, effective September 1, 2001; Acts 2003, 78th Leg., ch. 1275 (H.B. 3506), § 2(48), effective September 1, 2003 (renumbered from Education Code Sec. 105.116); am. Acts 2005, 79th Leg., ch. 319 (S.B. 651), § 2, effective June 17, 2005 (renumbered from Education Code Sec. 105.456).)

### Art. 63.057. Duty of Law Enforcement Agency to Notify Appropriate Persons Regarding Provision of Voluntary Sample.

Not later than the 30th day after the date a report of a high-risk missing person is filed, the law enforcement agency shall inform a parent or any other person considered appropriate by the agency that the person may provide:

(1) a DNA sample for forensic DNA analysis; or

(2) for purposes of DNA sampling, a personal article belonging to the high-risk missing person.

(Acts 2001, 77th Leg., ch. 1496 (S.B. 1304), § 1, effective September 1, 2001; Acts 2003, 78th Leg., ch. 1275 (H.B. 3506), § 2(48), effective September 1, 2003 (renumbered from Education Code Sec. 105.117); am. Acts 2005, 79th Leg., ch. 319 (S.B. 651), § 2, effective June 17, 2005 (renumbered from Education Code Sec. 105.457).)

### Art. 63.058. Release Form.

(a) The center shall develop a standard release form that authorizes a parent or other appropriate person to voluntarily provide under Article 63.057 a DNA sample or a personal article for purposes of DNA sampling. The release must explain that the DNA sample is to be used only to identify the high-risk missing person.

(b) A law enforcement agency may not use any form of incentive or coercion to compel the parent or other appropriate person to provide a sample or article under this subchapter. (Acts 2001, 77th Leg., ch. 1496 (S.B. 1304), § 1, effective September 1, 2001; Acts 2003, 78th Leg., ch. 1275 (H.B. 3506), § 2(48), effective September 1, 2003 (renumbered from Education Code Sec. 105.118); am. Acts 2005, 79th Leg., ch. 319 (S.B. 651), § 2, effective June 17, 2005 (renumbered from Education Code Sec. 105.458).)

### Art. 63.059. Protocol for Obtaining Samples Relating to High-Risk Missing Persons.

(a) The law enforcement agency shall take DNA samples from parents or other appropriate persons under Article 63.057 in any manner prescribed by the center.

(b) The center shall develop a model kit to be used by a law enforcement agency to take DNA samples from parents or other appropriate persons. (Acts 2001, 77th Leg., ch. 1496 (S.B. 1304), § 1, effective September 1, 2001; Acts 2003, 78th Leg., ch. 1275 (H.B. 3506), § 2(48), effective September 1, 2003 (renumbered from Education Code Sec. 105.119); am. Acts 2005, 79th Leg., ch. 319 (S.B. 651), § 2, effective June 17, 2005 (renumbered from Education Code Sec. 105.459).)

### Art. 63.060. Submission of Sample to Center.

(a) Before submitting to the center a DNA sample obtained under Article 63.057, the law

*Criminal Procedure*

enforcement agency shall reverify the status of a high-risk missing person.

(b) As soon as practicable after a DNA sample is obtained, the law enforcement agency shall submit the DNA sample, a copy of the missing person's report, and any supplemental information to the center.

(Acts 2001, 77th Leg., ch. 1496 (S.B. 1304), § 1, effective September 1, 2001; Acts 2003, 78th Leg., ch. 1275 (H.B. 3506), § 2(48), effective September 1, 2003 (renumbered from Education Code Sec. 105.120); am. Acts 2005, 79th Leg., ch. 319 (S.B. 651), § 2, effective June 17, 2005 (renumbered from Education Code Sec. 105.460).)

## Art. 63.061. Destruction of Samples.

All DNA samples extracted from a living person shall be destroyed after a positive identification is made and a report is issued.

(Acts 2001, 77th Leg., ch. 1496 (S.B. 1304), § 1, effective September 1, 2001; Acts 2003, 78th Leg., ch. 1275 (H.B. 3506), § 2(48), effective September 1, 2003 (renumbered from Education Code Sec. 105.121); am. Acts 2005, 79th Leg., ch. 319 (S.B. 651), § 2, effective June 17, 2005 (renumbered from Education Code Sec. 105.461).)

## Art. 63.062. Confidentiality.

(a) Except as provided by Subsection (b), the results of a forensic DNA analysis performed by the center are confidential.

(b) The center may disclose the results of a forensic DNA analysis only to:

(1) personnel of the center;

(2) law enforcement agencies;

(3) justices of the peace, coroners, medical examiners, or other law enforcement entities submitting a sample to the center under Article 63.056;

(4) attorneys representing the state; and

(5) a parent or other appropriate person voluntarily providing a DNA sample or an article under Article 63.057.

(Acts 2001, 77th Leg., ch. 1496 (S.B. 1304), § 1, effective September 1, 2001; Acts 2003, 78th Leg., ch. 1275 (H.B. 3506), § 2(48), effective September 1, 2003 (renumbered from Education Code Sec. 105.122); am. Acts 2005, 79th Leg., ch. 319 (S.B. 651), § 2, effective June 17, 2005 (renumbered from Education Code Sec. 105.462).)

## Art. 63.063. Criminal Penalty.

(a) A person who collects, processes, or stores a DNA sample from a living person for forensic

DNA analysis under this subchapter commits an offense if the person intentionally violates Article 63.061 or 63.062.

(b) An offense under this section is a Class B misdemeanor.

(Acts 2001, 77th Leg., ch. 1496 (S.B. 1304), § 1, effective September 1, 2001; Acts 2003, 78th Leg., ch. 1275 (H.B. 3506), § 2(48), effective September 1, 2003 (renumbered from Education Code Sec. 105.123); am. Acts 2005, 79th Leg., ch. 319 (S.B. 651), § 2, effective June 17, 2005 (renumbered from Education Code Sec. 105.463).)

## Art. 63.064. Civil Penalty.

A person who collects, processes, or stores a DNA sample from a living person for forensic DNA analysis under this subchapter and who intentionally violates Article 63.061 or 63.062 is liable in civil damages to the donor of the DNA in the amount of $5,000 for each violation, plus reasonable attorney's fees and court costs.

(Acts 2001, 77th Leg., ch. 1496 (S.B. 1304), § 1, effective September 1, 2001; Acts 2003, 78th Leg., ch. 1275 (H.B. 3506), § 2(48), effective September 1, 2003 (renumbered from Education Code Sec. 105.124); am. Acts 2005, 79th Leg., ch. 319 (S.B. 651), § 2, effective June 17, 2005 (renumbered from Education Code Sec. 105.464).)

## Art. 63.065. Missing Persons DNA Database Fund.

(a) The missing persons DNA database fund is a separate account in the general revenue fund.

(b) Notwithstanding Article 56.54(g), the legislature may appropriate money in the compensation to victims of crime fund and the compensation to victims of crime auxiliary fund to fund the University of North Texas Health Science Center at Fort Worth missing persons DNA database. Legislative appropriations under this subsection shall be deposited to the credit of the account created under Subsection (a).

(c) Money in the account may be used only for purposes of developing and maintaining the DNA database as described by this section.

(d) The center may use money in the account only to:

(1) establish and maintain center infrastructure;

(2) pay the costs of DNA sample storage, forensic DNA analysis, and labor costs for cases of high-risk missing persons and unidentified human remains;

(3) reimburse counties for the purposes of pathology and exhumation as considered necessary by the center;

(4) publicize the DNA database for the purpose of contacting parents and other appropriate persons so that they may provide a DNA sample or a personal article for DNA sampling;

(5) educate law enforcement officers about the DNA database and DNA sampling; and

(6) provide outreach programs related to the purposes of this chapter.

(e) Section 403.095(b), Government Code, does not apply to the account established under Subsection (a).

(Acts 2001, 77th Leg., ch. 1496 (S.B. 1304), § 1, effective September 1, 2001; Acts 2003, 78th Leg., ch. 1275 (H.B. 3506), § 2(48), effective September 1, 2003 (renumbered from Education Code Sec. 105.125); am. Acts 2005, 79th Leg., ch. 319 (S.B. 651), § 2, effective June 17, 2005 (renumbered from Education Code Sec. 105.465).)

## Art. 63.066. Backlog of Unidentified Human Remains: Advisory Committee and Outsourcing.

(a) The center shall create an advisory committee, consisting of medical examiners, law enforcement officials, and other interested persons as determined appropriate by the center, to impose priorities regarding the identification of the backlog of high-risk missing person cases and unidentified human remains.

(b) The center shall use any available federal funding to assist in reducing the backlog of high-risk missing person cases and unidentified human remains.

(c) The reduction of the backlog may be outsourced to other appropriate laboratories at the center's discretion.

(Acts 2001, 77th Leg., ch. 1496 (S.B. 1304), § 1, effective September 1, 2001; Acts 2003, 78th Leg., ch. 1275 (H.B. 3506), § 2(48), effective September 1, 2003 (renumbered from Education Code Sec. 105.126); am. Acts 2005, 79th Leg., ch. 319 (S.B. 651), § 2, effective June 17, 2005 (renumbered from Education Code Sec. 105.466).)

## Art. 63.067. Initial Operations [Expired].

Expired pursuant to Acts 2001, 77th Leg., ch. 1496 (S.B. 1304), § 1, effective January 1, 2006. (Enacted by Acts 2001, 77th Leg., ch. 1496 (S.B. 1304), § 1, effective September 1, 2001; am. Acts 2003, 78th Leg., ch. 1275 (H.B. 3506), § 2(48), effective September 1, 2003 (renumbered from Education Code Sec. 105.127); am. Acts 2005, 79th Leg., ch. 319 (S.B. 651), § 2, effective June

17, 2005 (renumbered from Education Code Sec. 105.467).)

# CHAPTER 64
# MOTION FOR FORENSIC DNA TESTING

## Art. 64.01. Motion.

(a) In this section, "biological material":

(1) means an item that is in possession of the state and that contains blood, semen, hair, saliva, skin tissue or cells, fingernail scrapings, bone, bodily fluids, or other identifiable biological evidence that may be suitable for forensic DNA testing; and

(2) includes the contents of a sexual assault evidence collection kit.

(a-1) A convicted person may submit to the convicting court a motion for forensic DNA testing of evidence containing biological material. The motion must be accompanied by an affidavit, sworn to by the convicted person, containing statements of fact in support of the motion.

(b) The motion may request forensic DNA testing only of evidence described by Subsection (a-1) that was secured in relation to the offense that is the basis of the challenged conviction and was in the possession of the state during the trial of the offense, but:

(1) was not previously subjected to DNA testing; or

(2) although previously subjected to DNA testing, can be subjected to testing with newer testing techniques that provide a reasonable likelihood of results that are more accurate and probative than the results of the previous test.

(c) A convicted person is entitled to counsel during a proceeding under this chapter. The convicting court shall appoint counsel for the convicted person if the person informs the court that the person wishes to submit a motion under this chapter, the court finds reasonable grounds for a motion to be filed, and the court determines that the person is indigent. Counsel must be appointed under this subsection not later than the 45th day after the date the court finds reasonable grounds or the date the court determines that the person is indigent, whichever is later. Compensation of counsel is provided in the same manner as is required by:

(1) Article 11.071 for the representation of a petitioner convicted of a capital felony; and

(2) Chapter 26 for the representation in a habeas corpus hearing of an indigent defendant convicted of a felony other than a capital felony. (Enacted by Acts 2001, 77th Leg., ch. 2 (S.B. 3), § 2, effective April 5, 2001; am. Acts 2003, 78th Leg., ch. 13 (H.B. 1011), § 1, effective September 1, 2003; am. Acts 2007, 80th Leg., ch. 1006 (H.B. 681), § 2, effective September 1, 2007; am. Acts 2011, 82nd Leg., ch. 278 (H.B. 1573), § 5, effective September 1, 2011; am. Acts 2011, 82nd Leg., ch. 366 (S.B. 122), § 1, effective September 1, 2011.)

## Art. 64.011. Guardians and Other Representatives.

(a) In this chapter, "guardian of a convicted person" means a person who is the legal guardian of the convicted person, whether the legal relationship between the guardian and convicted person exists because of the age of the convicted person or because of the physical or mental incompetency of the convicted person.

(b) A guardian of a convicted person may submit motions for the convicted person under this chapter and is entitled to counsel otherwise provided to a convicted person under this chapter. (Enacted by Acts 2003, 78th Leg., ch. 13 (H.B. 1011), § 2, effective September 1, 2003.)

## Art. 64.02. Notice to State; Response.

(a) On receipt of the motion, the convicting court shall:

(1) provide the attorney representing the state with a copy of the motion; and

(2) require the attorney representing the state to take one of the following actions in response to the motion not later than the 60th day after the date the motion is served on the attorney representing the state:

(A) deliver the evidence to the court, along with a description of the condition of the evidence; or

(B) explain in writing to the court why the state cannot deliver the evidence to the court.

(b) The convicting court may proceed under Article 64.03 after the response period described by Subsection (a)(2) has expired, regardless of whether the attorney representing the state submitted a response under that subsection.

(Enacted by Acts 2001, 77th Leg., ch. 2 (S.B. 3), § 2, effective April 5, 2001; am. Acts 2007, 80th Leg., ch. 1006 (H.B. 681), § 3, effective September 1, 2007.)

## Art. 64.03. Requirements; Testing.

(a) A convicting court may order forensic DNA testing under this chapter only if:

(1) the court finds that:

(A) the evidence:

(i) still exists and is in a condition making DNA testing possible; and

(ii) has been subjected to a chain of custody sufficient to establish that it has not been substituted, tampered with, replaced, or altered in any material respect; and

(B) identity was or is an issue in the case; and

(2) the convicted person establishes by a preponderance of the evidence that:

(A) the person would not have been convicted if exculpatory results had been obtained through DNA testing; and

(B) the request for the proposed DNA testing is not made to unreasonably delay the execution of sentence or administration of justice.

(b) A convicted person who pleaded guilty or nolo contendere or, whether before or after conviction, made a confession or similar admission in the case may submit a motion under this chapter, and the convicting court is prohibited from finding that identity was not an issue in the case solely on the basis of that plea, confession, or admission, as applicable.

(c) If the convicting court finds in the affirmative the issues listed in Subsection (a)(1) and the convicted person meets the requirements of Subsection (a)(2), the court shall order that the requested forensic DNA testing be conducted. The court may order the test to be conducted by:

(1) the Department of Public Safety;

(2) a laboratory operating under a contract with the department; or

(3) on the request of the convicted person, another laboratory if that laboratory is accredited under Section 411.0205, Government Code.

(d) If the convicting court orders that the forensic DNA testing be conducted by a laboratory other than a Department of Public Safety laboratory or a laboratory under contract with the department, the State of Texas is not liable for

**Criminal Procedure**

the cost of testing under this subsection unless good cause for payment of that cost has been shown. A political subdivision of the state is not liable for the cost of testing under this subsection, regardless of whether good cause for payment of that cost has been shown. If the court orders that the testing be conducted by a laboratory described by this subsection, the court shall include in the order requirements that:

(1) the DNA testing be conducted in a timely and efficient manner under reasonable conditions designed to protect the integrity of the evidence and the testing process;

(2) the DNA testing employ a scientific method sufficiently reliable and relevant to be admissible under Rule 702, Texas Rules of Evidence; and

(3) on completion of the DNA testing, the results of the testing and all data related to the testing required for an evaluation of the test results be immediately filed with the court and copies of the results and data be served on the convicted person and the attorney representing the state.

(e) The convicting court, not later than the 30th day after the conclusion of a proceeding under this chapter, shall forward the results to the Department of Public Safety.

(Enacted by Acts 2001, 77th Leg., ch. 2 (S.B. 3), § 2, effective April 5, 2001; am. Acts 2003, 78th Leg., ch. 13 (H.B. 1011), § 3, effective September 1, 2003; am. Acts 2007, 80th Leg., ch. 1006 (H.B. 681), § 4, effective September 1, 2007.)

## Sec. 64.035.   Unidentified DNA Profiles.

If an analyzed sample meets the applicable requirements of state or federal submission policies, on completion of the testing under Article 64.03, the convicting court shall order any unidentified DNA profile to be compared with the DNA profiles in:

(1) the DNA database established by the Federal Bureau of Investigation; and

(2) the DNA database maintained by the Department of Public Safety under Subchapter G, Chapter 411, Government Code.

(Enacted by Acts 2011, 82nd Leg., ch. 278 (H.B. 1573), § 6, effective September 1, 2011; Enacted by Acts 2011, 82nd Leg., ch. 366 (S.B. 122), § 2, effective September 1, 2011.)

## Art. 64.04.  Finding.

After examining the results of testing under Article 64.03 and any comparison of a DNA profile under Article 64.035, the convicting court shall hold a hearing and make a finding as to whether, had the results been available during the trial of the offense, it is reasonably probable that the person would not have been convicted.

(Enacted by Acts 2001, 77th Leg., ch. 2 (S.B. 3), § 2, effective April 5, 2001; am. Acts 2003, 78th Leg., ch. 13 (H.B. 1011), § 4, effective September 1, 2003; am. Acts 2011, 82nd Leg., ch. 278 (H.B. 1573), § 7, effective September 1, 2011; am. Acts 2011, 82nd Leg., ch. 366 (S.B. 122), § 3, effective September 1, 2011.)

## Art. 64.05.  Appeals.

An appeal under this chapter is to a court of appeals in the same manner as an appeal of any other criminal matter, except that if the convicted person was convicted in a capital case and was sentenced to death, the appeal is a direct appeal to the court of criminal appeals.

(Enacted by Acts 2001, 77th Leg., ch. 2 (S.B. 3), § 2, effective April 5, 2001; am. Acts 2003, 78th Leg., ch. 13 (H.B. 1011), § 5, effective September 1, 2003.)

# TITLE 2

# CODE OF CRIMINAL PROCEDURE

## CHAPTER 101
## GENERAL PROVISIONS

**Article**

## Art. 101.001.  Purpose of Title.

(a) This title is enacted as a part of the state's

continuing statutory revision program, begun by the Texas Legislative Council in 1963 as directed by the legislature in Chapter 448, Acts of the 58th Legislature, Regular Session, 1963 (Article 5429b-1, Vernon's Texas Civil Statutes). The program contemplates a topic-by-topic revision of the state's general and permanent statute law without substantive change.

(b) Consistent with the objectives of the statutory revision program, the purpose of this title is to make the law encompassed by this title more accessible and understandable by:

(1) rearranging the statutes into a more logical order;

(2) employing a format and numbering system designed to facilitate citation of the law and to accommodate future expansion of the law;

(3) eliminating repealed, duplicative, unconstitutional, expired, executed, and other ineffective provisions; and

(4) restating the law in modern American English to the greatest extent possible.

(Enacted by Acts 1985, 69th Leg., ch. 269 (S.B. 854), § 1, effective September 1, 1985.)

## Art. 101.002. Construction of Title.

The Code Construction Act (Article 5429b-2, Vernon's Texas Civil Statutes) applies to the construction of each provision in this title, except as otherwise expressly provided by this title.

(Enacted by Acts 1985, 69th Leg., ch. 269 (S.B. 854), § 1, effective September 1, 1985.)

## Art. 101.003. Internal References.

In this title:

(1) a reference to a chapter or article without further identification is a reference to a chapter or article of this title; and

(2) a reference to a subchapter, article, subsection, subdivision, paragraph, or other numbered or lettered unit without further identification is a reference to a unit of the next larger unit of this title in which the reference appears.

(Enacted by Acts 1985, 69th Leg., ch. 269 (S.B. 854), § 1, effective September 1, 1985.)

# CHAPTER 102
## COSTS PAID BY DEFENDANTS

### Subchapter A. General Costs

### Subchapter B. Criminal Justice Planning Fund

### Subchapter C. Court Costs and Fees

## SUBCHAPTER A
## GENERAL COSTS

## Art. 102.001. Fees for Services of Peace Officers.

(a) [Repealed by Acts 1989, 71st Leg., ch. 826 (S.B. 356), § 2, effective September 1, 1989.]

(b) In addition to fees provided by Subsection (a), a defendant required to pay fees under this article shall also pay 15 cents per mile for mileage required of an officer to perform a service listed in this subsection and to return from performing that service. If the service provided is the execution of a writ and the writ is directed to two or more persons or the officer executes more than one writ in a case, the defendant is required to pay only mileage actually and necessarily traveled. In calculating mileage, the officer must use the railroad or the most practical route by private conveyance. This subsection applies to:

(1) conveying a prisoner after conviction to the county jail;

(2) conveying a prisoner arrested on a warrant or capias issued in another county to the court or jail of the county in which the warrant or capias was issued; and

(3) traveling to execute criminal process, to summon or attach a witness, and to execute process not otherwise described by this article.

(c) to (e) [Repealed by Acts 1989, 71st Leg., ch. 826 (S.B. 356), § 2, effective September 1, 1989.]

(f) An officer who receives fees imposed under Subsection (a)(1) of this section in a municipal court shall keep separate records of the funds collected and shall deposit the funds in the municipal treasury. The officer collecting the fees under Subsection (a)(1) or (a)(2) of this article in a justice, county, or district court shall keep separate records of the funds collected and shall deposit the funds in the county treasury.

(g) [Repealed by Acts 1989, 71st Leg., ch. 826 (S.B. 356), § 2, effective September 1, 1989.]

(h) The custodian of a municipal or county treasury who receives fees under Subsection (a)(1) of this article for services performed by peace officers employed by the state shall remit all fees to the comptroller of public accounts in the manner directed by the comptroller. The custodian of a county treasury who receives fees under Subsection (a)(2) of this article for services performed by peace officers employed by the state may retain $2 of the fee for the county and shall forward the remainder to the comptroller in the manner directed by the comptroller. All custodians of municipal and county treasuries who receive fees under Subsection (a)(1) or (a)(2) of this article shall keep records of the amount of funds collected that are on deposit with them and, not later than the last day of the month following each calendar quarter, shall remit to the comptroller funds collected under Subsection (a)(1) or (a)(2) of this article during the preceding quarter in a manner directed by the comptroller. The municipality or county may retain all interest earned on those funds. The comptroller shall credit funds received under this subsection to the General Revenue Fund.

(Enacted by Acts 1985, 69th Leg., ch. 269 (S.B. 854), § 1, effective September 1, 1985; am. Acts 1987, 70th Leg., ch. 167 (S.B. 892), § 4.01(a), effective September 1, 1987; am. Acts 1987, 70th Leg., ch. 821 (H.B. 2107), § 1, effective September 1, 1987; am. Acts 1989, 71st Leg., ch. 2 (S.B. 221), § 16.01(12), effective August 28, 1989; am. Acts 1989, 71st Leg., ch. 347 (S.B. 1085), § 1, effective October 1, 1989.)

## Art. 102.002. Witness Fees.

(a) [Repealed by Acts 1999, 76th Leg., ch. 580 (S.B. 577), § 11(a), effective September 1, 1999.]

(b) The justices of the peace and municipal courts shall maintain a record of and the clerks of district and county courts and county courts at law shall keep a book and record in the book:

(1) the number and style of each criminal action before the court;

(2) the name of each witness subpoenaed, attached, or recognized to testify in the action; and

(3) whether the witness was a witness for the state or for the defendant.

(c) Except as otherwise provided by this subsection, a defendant is liable on conviction for the fees provided by this article for witnesses in the defendant's case. If a defendant convicted of a misdemeanor does not pay the defendant's fines and costs, the county or municipality, as appropriate, is liable for the fees provided by this article for witnesses in the defendant's case.

(d) If a person is subpoenaed as a witness in a criminal case and fails to appear, the person is liable for the costs of an attachment, unless he shows good cause to the court why he did not appear.

(Enacted by Acts 1985, 69th Leg., ch. 269 (S.B. 854), § 1, effective September 1, 1985; am. Acts 1999, 76th Leg., ch. 580 (S.B. 577), § 11(a), effective September 1, 1999; am. Acts 1999, 76th Leg., ch. 1545 (S.B. 1230), § 63, effective September 1, 1999.)

## Art. 102.003. Trial Fee [Repealed].

Repealed by Acts 1995, 74th Leg., ch. 122 (S.B. 1060), § 4, effective September 1, 1995.

(Enacted by Acts 1965, 59th Leg., ch. 722 (S.B. 107), § 1, effective January 1, 1966; am. Acts 1985, 69th Leg., ch. 269 (S.B. 854), § 1, effective September 1, 1985 (renumbered from art. 53.06); am. Acts 1989, 71st Leg., ch. 1080 (S.B. 49), § 2, effective September 1, 1989.)

## Art. 102.004. Jury Fee.

(a) A defendant convicted by a jury in a trial before a justice or municipal court shall pay a jury fee of $3. A defendant in a justice or municipal court who requests a trial by jury and who withdraws the request not earlier than 24 hours before the time of trial shall pay a jury fee of $3, if the defendant is convicted of the offense or final disposition of the defendant's case is deferred. A defendant convicted by a jury in a county court, a county court at law, or a district court shall pay a jury fee of $20.

(b) If two or more defendants are tried jointly in a justice or municipal court, only one jury fee of $3 may be imposed under this article. If the defendants sever and are tried separately, each defendant convicted shall pay a jury fee.

(c) In this article, "conviction" has the meaning assigned by Section 133.101, Local Government Code.

(Enacted by Acts 1985, 69th Leg., ch. 269 (S.B. 854), § 1, effective September 1, 1985; am. Acts 1989, 71st Leg., ch. 1080 (S.B. 49), § 3, effective September 1, 1989; am. Acts 1995, 74th Leg., ch. 122 (S.B. 1060), § 2, effective September 1, 1995; am. Acts 1999, 76th Leg., ch. 1545 (S.B. 1230), § 64, effective September 1, 1999; am. Acts 2003, 78th Leg., ch. 209 (H.B. 2424), § 67(a), effective January 1, 2004.)

## Art. 102.0045. Fee for Jury Reimbursement to Counties.

(a) A person convicted of any offense, other than an offense relating to a pedestrian or the parking of a motor vehicle, shall pay as a court cost, in addition to all other costs, a fee of $4 to be used to reimburse counties for the cost of juror services as provided by Section 61.0015, Government Code.

(b) The clerk of the court shall remit the fees collected under this article to the comptroller in the manner provided by Subchapter B, Chapter 133, Local Government Code. The comptroller shall deposit the fees in the jury service fund.

(c) The jury service fund is created in the state treasury. If, at any time, the unexpended balance of the jury service fund exceeds $10 million, the comptroller shall transfer the amount in excess of $10 million to the fair defense account.

(d) Fees deposited in the jury service fund under this article are exempt from the application of Section 403.095, Government Code.

(Enacted by Acts 2005, 79th Leg., ch. 1360 (S.B. 1704), § 5, effective September 1, 2005; am. Acts 2011, 82nd Leg., ch. 91 (S.B. 1303), § 6.006, effective September 1, 2011.)

## Art. 102.005. Fees to Clerks.

(a) A defendant convicted of an offense in a county court, a county court at law, or a district court shall pay for the services of the clerk of the court a fee of $40.

(b) In this article, a person is considered convicted if:

(1) a sentence is imposed on the person;

(2) the person receives community supervision, including deferred adjudication; or

(3) the court defers final disposition of the person's case.

(c) Except as provided by Subsection (d), the fee imposed under Subsection (a) is for all clerical duties performed by the clerk, including:

(1) filing a complaint or information;

(2) docketing the case;

(3) taxing costs against the defendant;

(4) issuing original writs and subpoenas;

(5) swearing in and impaneling a jury;

(6) receiving and recording the verdict;

(7) filing each paper entered in the case; and

(8) swearing in witnesses in the case.

(d) The fee imposed by law for issuing a certified or noncertified copy is in addition to the fee imposed by Subsection (a). The clerk may issue a copy only if a person requests the copy and pays the appropriate fee as required by Sections 118.011, 118.014, 118.0145, 118.052, 118.060, and 118.0605, Local Government Code, and Sections 51.318 and 51.319, Government Code.

(e) [Repealed by Acts 1999, 76th Leg., ch. 580 (S.B. 577), § 11(b), effective September 1, 1999.]

(f) A defendant convicted of an offense in a county court, a county court at law, or a district court shall pay a fee of $25 for records management and preservation services performed by the county as required by Chapter 203, Local Government Code. The fee shall be collected and distributed by the clerk of the court to the county treasurer, or to an official who discharges the duties commonly delegated to the county treasurer, for deposit as follows:

(1) $22.50 to the county records management and preservation fund for records management and preservation, including automation, in various county offices; and

(2) $2.50 to the records management and preservation fund of the clerk of the court for records management and preservation services performed by the clerk of the court.

(g) A fee deposited in accordance with Subsection (f) may be used only to provide funds for specific records management and preservation, including for automation purposes, on approval by the commissioners court of a budget as provided by Chapter 111, Local Government Code.

(h) An expenditure from a records management and preservation fund must comply with Subchapter C, Chapter 262, Local Government Code.

Criminal Procedure

(Enacted by Acts 1985, 69th Leg., ch. 269 (S.B. 854), § 1, effective September 1, 1985; am. Acts 1989, 71st Leg., ch. 1080 (S.B. 49), § 4, effective September 1, 1989; am. Acts 1993, 73rd Leg., ch. 675 (S.B. 1058), § 6, effective September 1, 1993; am. Acts 1995, 74th Leg., ch. 764 (S.B. 349), § 1, effective August 28, 1995; am. Acts 1999, 76th Leg., ch. 580 (S.B. 577), § 11(b), effective September 1, 1999; am. Acts 1999, 76th Leg., ch. 1031 (H.B. 2968), § 1, effective September 1, 1999; am. Acts 2005, 79th Leg., ch. 804 (S.B. 526), § 2, effective June 17, 2005.)

## Art. 102.006. Fees in Expunction Proceedings.

(a) In addition to any other fees required by other law and except as provided by Subsection (b), a petitioner seeking expunction of a criminal record shall pay the following fees:

(1) the fee charged for filing an ex parte petition in a civil action in district court;

(2) $1 plus postage for each certified mailing of notice of the hearing date; and

(3) $2 plus postage for each certified mailing of certified copies of an order of expunction.

(b) The fees under Subsection (a) shall be waived if:

(1) the petitioner seeks expunction of a criminal record that relates to an arrest for an offense of which the person was acquitted, other than an acquittal for an offense described by Article 55.01(c); and

(2) the petition for expunction is filed not later than the 30th day after the date of the acquittal.

(Enacted by Acts 1985, 69th Leg., ch. 269 (S.B. 854), § 1, effective September 1, 1985; am. Acts 2005, 79th Leg., ch. 886 (S.B. 1426), § 4, effective September 1, 2005; am. Acts 2009, 81st Leg., ch. 140 (S.B. 1224), § 1, effective September 1, 2009.)

## Art. 102.007. Fee for Collecting and Processing Sight Order.

(a) A county attorney, district attorney, or criminal district attorney may collect a fee if his office collects and processes a check or similar sight order if the check or similar sight order:

(1) has been issued or passed in a manner that makes the issuance or passing an offense under:

(A) Section 31.03, Penal Code;

(B) Section 31.04, Penal Code; or

(C) Section 32.41, Penal Code; or

(2) has been forged, as defined by Section 32.21, Penal Code.

(b) The county attorney, district attorney, or criminal district attorney may collect the fee from any person who is a party to the offense described in Subsection (a).

(c) The amount of the fee may not exceed:

(1) $10 if the face amount of the check or sight order does not exceed $10;

(2) $15 if the face amount of the check or sight order is greater than $10 but does not exceed $100;

(3) $30 if the face amount of the check or sight order is greater than $100 but does not exceed $300;

(4) $50 if the face amount of the check or sight order is greater than $300 but does not exceed $500; and

(5) $75 if the face amount of the check or sight order is greater than $500.

(d) If the person from whom the fee is collected was a party to the offense of forgery, as defined by Section 32.21, Penal Code, committed by altering the face amount of the check or sight order, the face amount as altered governs for the purposes of determining the amount of the fee.

(e) In addition to the collection fee specified in Subsection (c) of this article, the county attorney, district attorney, or criminal district attorney may collect the fee authorized by Section 3.506, Business & Commerce Code, for the benefit of the holder of a check or its assignee, agent, representative, or any other person retained by the holder to seek collection of the check.

(f) Fees collected under Subsection (c) of this article shall be deposited in the county treasury in a special fund to be administered by the county attorney, district attorney, or criminal district attorney. Expenditures from this fund shall be at the sole discretion of the attorney and may be used only to defray the salaries and expenses of the prosecutor's office, but in no event may the county attorney, district attorney, or criminal district attorney supplement his or her own salary from this fund.

(g) In addition to the collection fee specified in Subsections (b) and (c), the issuer of a check or similar sight order that has been issued or passed as described by Subsection (a)(1) is liable for a fee in an amount equal to the costs of delivering notification by registered or certified mail with return receipt requested. The fee under this subsection must be collected in all cases described by Subsection (a)(1), and on receipt of proof of the actual costs expended, the fee shall be remitted to the holder of the check or similar sight order.

(Enacted by Acts 1985, 69th Leg., ch. 269 (S.B. 854), § 1, effective September 1, 1985; am. Acts 1997, 75th Leg., ch. 256 (S.B. 174), § 1, effective September 1, 1997; am. Acts 1999, 76th Leg., ch. 49 (S.B. 284), § 1, effective September 1, 1999; am. Acts 2001, 77th Leg., ch. 1420 (H.B. 2812), § 2.001(b), effective September 1, 2001; am. Acts 2007, 80th Leg., ch. 976 (S.B. 548), § 3, effective September 1, 2007.)

### Art. 102.0071. Justice Court Dishonored Check.

On conviction in justice court of an offense under Section 32.41, Penal Code, or an offense under Section 31.03 or 31.04, Penal Code, in which it is shown that the defendant committed the offense by issuing or passing a check that was subsequently dishonored, the court may collect from the defendant and pay to the holder of the check the fee permitted by Section 3.506, Business & Commerce Code.
(Enacted by Acts 1991, 72nd Leg., ch. 396 (H.B. 703), § 2, effective September 1, 1991; am. Acts 2001, 77th Leg., ch. 1420 (H.B. 2812), § 2.001(c), effective September 1, 2001.)

### Art. 102.008. Fees for Services of Prosecutors.

(a) Except as provided by Subsection (b), a defendant convicted of a misdemeanor or a gambling offense shall pay a fee of $25 for the trying of the case by the district or county attorney. If the court appoints an attorney to represent the state in the absence of the district or county attorney, the appointed attorney is entitled to the fee otherwise due.

(b) No fee for the trying of a case may be charged against a defendant prosecuted in a justice court for violation of a penal statute or of the Uniform Act Regulating Traffic on Highways.

(c) If two or more defendants are tried jointly, only one fee may be charged under this article. If the defendants sever and are tried separately, each defendant shall pay the fee.

(d) A defendant is liable for fees imposed by Subsection (a) if the defendant is convicted of an offense and:

(1) the defendant does not appeal the conviction; or

(2) the conviction is affirmed on appeal.
(Enacted by Acts 1985, 69th Leg., ch. 269 (S.B. 854), § 1, effective September 1, 1985; am. Acts 1989, 71st Leg., ch. 1080 (S.B. 49), § 5, effective September 1, 1989.)

### Art. 102.009. Court Costs in Certain Counties.

In counties with a population of 3.3 million or more, the commissioners court may set court costs for persons convicted of a Class C misdemeanor in the justice courts. Court costs set as provided by this article may not exceed $7 for each conviction.
(Enacted by Acts 1985, 69th Leg., ch. 269 (S.B. 854), § 1, effective September 1, 1985; am. Acts 2001, 77th Leg., ch. 669 (H.B. 2810), § 9, effective September 1, 2001.)

### Art. 102.010. [Reserved for expansion].

### Art. 102.011. Fees for Services of Peace Officers.

(a) A defendant convicted of a felony or a misdemeanor shall pay the following fees for services performed in the case by a peace officer:

(1) $5 for issuing a written notice to appear in court following the defendant's violation of a traffic law, municipal ordinance, or penal law of this state, or for making an arrest without a warrant;

(2) $50 for executing or processing an issued arrest warrant, capias, or capias pro fine with the fee imposed for the services of:

(A) the law enforcement agency that executed the arrest warrant or capias, if the agency requests of the court, not later than the 15th day after the date of the execution of the arrest warrant or capias, the imposition of the fee on conviction; or

(B) the law enforcement agency that processed the arrest warrant or capias, if:

(i) the arrest warrant or capias was not executed; or

(ii) the executing law enforcement agency failed to request the fee within the period required by Paragraph (A) of this subdivision;

(3) $5 for summoning a witness;

(4) $35 for serving a writ not otherwise listed in this article;

(5) $10 for taking and approving a bond and, if necessary, returning the bond to the courthouse;

(6) $5 for commitment or release;

(7) $5 for summoning a jury, if a jury is summoned; and

(8) $8 for each day's attendance of a prisoner in a habeas corpus case if the prisoner has been remanded to custody or held to bail.

(b) In addition to fees provided by Subsection (a) of this article, a defendant required to pay fees under this article shall also pay 29 cents per mile for mileage required of an officer to perform a service listed in this subsection and to return from performing that service. If the service provided is the execution of a writ and the writ is directed to two or more persons or the officer executes more than one writ in a case, the defendant is required to pay only mileage actually and necessarily traveled. In calculating mileage, the officer must use the railroad or the most practical route by private conveyance. The defendant shall also pay all necessary and reasonable expenses for meals and lodging incurred by the officer in the performance of services under this subsection, to the extent such expenses meet the requirements of Section 611.001, Government Code. This subsection applies to:

(1) conveying a prisoner after conviction to the county jail;

(2) conveying a prisoner arrested on a warrant or capias issued in another county to the court or jail of the county; and

(3) traveling to execute criminal process, to summon or attach a witness, and to execute process not otherwise described by this article.

(c) If an officer attaches a witness on the order of a court outside the county, the defendant shall pay $10 per day or part of a day spent by the officer conveying the witness and actual necessary expenses for travel by the most practical public conveyance. In order to receive expenses under this subsection, the officer must make a sworn statement of the expenses and the judge issuing the attachment must approve the statement.

(d) A defendant shall pay for the services of a sheriff or constable who serves process and attends an examining trial in a felony or a misdemeanor case the same fees allowed for those services in the trial of a felony or a misdemeanor, not to exceed $5.

(e) A fee under Subsection (a)(1) or (a)(2) of this article shall be assessed on conviction, regardless of whether the defendant was also arrested at the same time for another offense, and shall be assessed for each arrest made of a defendant arising out of the offense for which the defendant has been convicted.

(f) to (h) [Repealed by Acts 2003, 78th Leg., ch. 209 (H.B. 2424), § 85(a)(5), effective January 1, 2004.]

(i) In addition to fees provided by Subsections (a) through (g) of this article, a defendant required to pay fees under this article shall also pay the costs of overtime paid to a peace officer for time spent testifying in the trial of the case or for traveling to or from testifying in the trial of the case.

(j) In this article, "conviction" has the meaning assigned by Section 133.101, Local Government Code.

(Enacted by Acts 1987, 70th Leg., ch. 821 (H.B. 2107), § 2, effective September 1, 1987; am. Acts 1989, 71st Leg., ch. 826 (S.B. 356), § 1, effective September 1, 1989; am. Acts 1991, 72nd Leg., ch. 575 (S.B. 355), § 1, effective September 1, 1991; am. Acts 1993, 73rd Leg., ch. 988 (S.B. 532), § 2.04(a), effective September 1, 1993; am. Acts 1995, 74th Leg., ch. 267 (S.B. 187), § 1, effective September 1, 1995; am. Acts 1995, 74th Leg., ch. 560 (S.B. 206), § 1, effective September 1, 1995; am. Acts 1999, 76th Leg., ch. 44 (S.B. 163), § 1, effective September 1, 1999; am. Acts 2003, 78th Leg., ch. 209 (H.B. 2424), §§ 68(a), 85(a)(5), effective January 1, 2004; am. Acts 2007, 80th Leg., ch. 1263 (H.B. 3060), §§ 20, 21, effective September 1, 2007; am. Acts 2009, 81st Leg., ch. 87 (S.B. 1969), § 6.008, effective September 1, 2009.)

### Art. 102.012. Fees for Pretrial Intervention Programs.

(a) A court that authorizes a defendant to participate in a pretrial intervention program established under Section 76.011, Government Code, may order the defendant to pay to the court a supervision fee in an amount not more than $60 per month as a condition of participating in the program.

(b) In addition to or in lieu of the supervision fee authorized by Subsection (a), the court may order the defendant to pay or reimburse a community supervision and corrections department for any other expense that is:

(1) incurred as a result of the defendant's participation in the pretrial intervention program, other than an expense described by Article 102.0121; or

(2) necessary to the defendant's successful completion of the program.

(Enacted by Acts 1990, 71st Leg., 6th C.S., ch. 28 (S.B 41), § 1, effective September 6, 1990; am. Acts 1995, 74th Leg., ch. 76 (S.B. 959), § 7.16, effective September 1, 1995; am. Acts 2005, 79th Leg., ch. 91 (S.B. 1006), § 2, effective September 1, 2005; am. Acts 2007, 80th Leg., ch. 1226 (H.B. 2385), § 1, effective September 1, 2007.)

## Art. 102.0121. Fees for Certain Expenses Related to Pretrial Intervention Programs.

(a) A district attorney, criminal district attorney, or county attorney may collect a fee in an amount not to exceed $500 to be used to reimburse a county for expenses, including expenses of the district attorney's, criminal district attorney's, or county attorney's office, related to a defendant's participation in a pretrial intervention program offered in that county.

(b) The district attorney, criminal district attorney, or county attorney may collect the fee from any defendant who participates in a pretrial intervention program administered in any part by the attorney's office.

(c) Fees collected under this article shall be deposited in the county treasury in a special fund to be used solely to administer the pretrial intervention program. An expenditure from the fund may be made only in accordance with a budget approved by the commissioners court.

(Enacted by Acts 2007, 80th Leg., ch. 1226 (H.B. 2385), § 2, effective September 1, 2007.)

## Art. 102.013. Court Costs; Crime Stoppers Assistance Account.

(a) The legislature shall appropriate funds from the crime stoppers assistance account to the Criminal Justice Division of the Governor's Office. The Criminal Justice Division may use 10 percent of the funds for the operation of the toll-free telephone service under Section 414.012, Government Code, and shall distribute the remainder of the funds only to crime stoppers organizations. The Criminal Justice Division may adopt a budget and rules to implement the distribution of these funds.

(b) All funds distributed by the Criminal Justice Division under Subsection (a) of this article are subject to audit by the state auditor. All funds collected or distributed are subject to audit by the Governor's Division of Planning Coordination.

(c) In this article, "crime stoppers organization" has the meaning assigned by Section 414.001, Government Code.

(Enacted by Acts 1990, 71st Leg., 6th C.S., ch. 28 (S.B 41), § 1, effective September 6, 1990; am. Acts 1991, 72nd Leg., ch. 16 (S.B. 232) § 19.01(7), effective August 26, 1991 (renumbered from art. 102.012); am. Acts 1991, 72nd Leg., ch. 727 (H.B. 2578), § 2, effective September 1, 1991; am. Acts 1993, 73rd Leg., ch. 807 (H.B. 2456), § 2, effective August 30, 1993; am. Acts 1997, 75th Leg., ch.

700 (S.B. 1546), § 13, effective September 1, 1997; am. Acts 1997, 75th Leg., ch. 1100 (H.B. 2272), § 1, effective September 1, 1997.)

## Art. 102.014. Court Costs for Child Safety Fund in Municipalities.

(a) The governing body of a municipality with a population greater than 850,000 according to the most recent federal decennial census that has adopted an ordinance, regulation, or order regulating the stopping, standing, or parking of vehicles as allowed by Section 542.202, Transportation Code, or Chapter 682, Transportation Code, shall by order assess a court cost on each parking violation not less than $2 and not to exceed $5. The court costs under this subsection shall be collected in the same manner that other fines in the case are collected.

(b) The governing body of a municipality with a population less than 850,000 according to the most recent federal decennial census that has adopted an ordinance, regulation, or order regulating the stopping, standing, or parking of vehicles as allowed by Section 542.202, Transportation Code, or Chapter 682, Transportation Code, may by order assess a court cost on each parking violation not to exceed $5. The additional court cost under this subsection shall be collected in the same manner that other fines in the case are collected.

(c) A person convicted of an offense under Subtitle C, Title 7, Transportation Code, when the offense occurs within a school crossing zone as defined by Section 541.302 of that code, shall pay as court costs $25 in addition to other taxable court costs. A person convicted of an offense under Section 545.066, Transportation Code, shall pay as court costs $25 in addition to other taxable court costs. The additional court costs under this subsection shall be collected in the same manner that other fines and taxable court costs in the case are collected and shall be assessed only in a municipality.

(d) A person convicted of an offense under Section 25.093 or 25.094, Education Code, shall pay as taxable court costs $20 in addition to other taxable court costs. The additional court costs under this subsection shall be collected in the same manner that other fines and taxable court costs in the case are collected.

(e) In this article, a person is considered to have been convicted in a case if the person would be considered to have been convicted under Section 133.101, Local Government Code.

(f) In a municipality with a population greater than 850,000 according to the most recent federal decennial census, the officer collecting the costs in a municipal court case shall deposit money collected under this article in the municipal child safety trust fund established as required by Chapter 106, Local Government Code.

(g) In a municipality with a population less than 850,000 according to the most recent federal decennial census, the money collected under this article in a municipal court case must be used for a school crossing guard program if the municipality operates one. If the municipality does not operate a school crossing guard program or if the money received from court costs from municipal court cases exceeds the amount necessary to fund the school crossing guard program, the municipality may:

(1) deposit the additional money in an interest-bearing account;

(2) expend the additional money for programs designed to enhance child safety, health, or nutrition, including child abuse prevention and intervention and drug and alcohol abuse prevention; or

(3) expend the additional money for programs designed to enhance public safety and security.

(h) Money collected under this article in a justice, county, or district court shall be used to fund school crossing guard programs in the county where they are collected. If the county does not operate a school crossing guard program, the county may:

(1) remit fee revenues to school districts in its jurisdiction for the purpose of providing school crossing guard services;

(2) fund programs the county is authorized by law to provide which are designed to enhance child safety, health, or nutrition, including child abuse prevention and intervention and drug and alcohol abuse prevention;

(3) provide funding to the sheriff's department for school-related activities;

(4) provide funding to the county juvenile probation department; or

(5) deposit the money in the general fund of the county.

(i) Each collecting officer shall keep separate records of money collected under this article. (Enacted by Acts 1991, 72nd Leg., ch. 830 (S.B. 460), § 2, effective July 1, 1991; am. Acts 1995, 74th Leg., ch. 76 (S.B. 959), § 10.03, effective September 1, 1995; am. Acts 1997, 75th Leg., ch. 50 (H.B. 1018), § 1, effective September 1, 1997;

am. Acts 1997, 75th Leg., ch. 165 (S.B. 898), § 6.05, effective September 1, 1997; am. Acts 1997, 75th Leg., ch. 1384 (H.B. 1553), § 1, effective September 1, 1997; am. Acts 2001, 77th Leg., ch. 983 ( H.B. 374), § 1, effective September 1, 2001; am. Acts 2001, 77th Leg., ch. 1514 (S.B. 1432), § 10, effective September 1, 2001; am. Acts 2003, 78th Leg., ch. 209 (H.B. 2424), § 69(a), effective January 1, 2004; am. Acts 2009, 81st Leg., ch. 162 (S.B. 446), § 1, effective May 26, 2009.)

### Art. 102.015. Misdemeanor Costs [Repealed].

Repealed by Acts 1997, 75th Leg., ch. 1100 (H.B. 2272), § 6(2), effective September 1, 1997. (Enacted by Acts 1991, 72nd Leg., 1st C.S., ch. 5 (H.B. 11), § 5.02(a), effective September 1, 1991.)

### Art. 102.016. Costs for Breath Alcohol Testing Program.

(a) The custodians of municipal and county treasuries may deposit funds collected under this article in interest-bearing accounts and retain for the municipality or county interest earned on the funds. The custodians shall keep records of funds received and disbursed under this article and shall provide a yearly report of all funds received and disbursed under this article to the comptroller, the Department of Public Safety, and to each agency in the county served by the court that participates in or maintains a certified breath alcohol testing program. The comptroller shall approve the form of the report.

(b) The custodian of a municipal or county treasury in a county that maintains a certified breath alcohol testing program but does not use the services of a certified technical supervisor employed by the department may, to defray the costs of maintaining and supporting a certified breath alcohol testing program, retain $22.50 of each court cost collected under Section 133.102, Local Government Code, on conviction of an offense under Chapter 49, Penal Code, other than an offense that is a Class C misdemeanor.

(c) The legislature may appropriate money deposited to the credit of the breath alcohol testing account in the general revenue fund under this subsection to the Department of Public Safety for use by the department in the implementation, administration, and maintenance of the statewide certified breath alcohol testing program.

(d) The Department of Public Safety shall maintain a list of counties that do not use the services of a certified technical supervisor employed by the department.

(Enacted by Acts 1991, 72nd Leg., 1st C.S., ch. 5 (H.B. 11), § 5.03(a), effective September 1, 1991; am. Acts 1993, 73rd Leg., ch. 900 (S.B. 1067), § 3.03, effective September 1, 1994; am. Acts 1997, 75th Leg., ch. 1100 (H.B. 2272), § 2, effective September 1, 1997; am. Acts 2009, 81st Leg., ch. 1204 (S.B. 333), § 1, effective September 1, 2009.)

## Art. 102.0169. Court Costs; County and District Court Technology Fund.

(a) A defendant convicted of a criminal offense in a county court, statutory county court, or district court shall pay a $4 county and district court technology fee as a cost of court.

(b) In this article, a person is considered convicted if:

(1) a sentence is imposed on the person;

(2) the person receives community supervision, including deferred adjudication; or

(3) the court defers final disposition of the person's case.

(c) The clerks of the courts described by Subsection (a) shall collect the costs and pay them to the county treasurer or to any other official who discharges the duties commonly delegated to the county treasurer, as appropriate, for deposit in a fund to be known as the county and district court technology fund.

(d) A fund designated by this article may be used only to finance:

(1) the cost of continuing education and training for county court, statutory county court, or district court judges and clerks regarding technological enhancements for those courts; and

(2) the purchase and maintenance of technological enhancements for a county court, statutory county court, or district court, including:

(A) computer systems;

(B) computer networks;

(C) computer hardware;

(D) computer software;

(E) imaging systems;

(F) electronic kiosks; and

(G) docket management systems.

(e) The county and district court technology fund shall be administered by or under the direction of the commissioners court of the county.

(Enacted by Acts 2009, 81st Leg., ch. 1183 (H.B. 3637), § 1, effective September 1, 2009.)

## Art. 102.017. Court Costs; Courthouse Security Fund; Municipal Court Building Security Fund; Justice Court Building Security Fund.

(a) A defendant convicted of a felony offense in a district court shall pay a $5 security fee as a cost of court.

(b) A defendant convicted of a misdemeanor offense in a county court, county court at law, or district court shall pay a $3 security fee as a cost of court. A defendant convicted of a misdemeanor offense in a justice court shall pay a $4 security fee as a cost of court. The governing body of a municipality by ordinance may create a municipal court building security fund and may require a defendant convicted of a misdemeanor offense in a municipal court to pay a $3 security fee as a cost of court.

(c) In this article, a person is considered convicted if:

(1) a sentence is imposed on the person;

(2) the person receives community supervision, including deferred adjudication; or

(3) the court defers final disposition of the person's case.

(d) Except as provided by Subsection (d-2), the clerks of the respective courts shall collect the costs and pay them to the county or municipal treasurer, as appropriate, or to any other official who discharges the duties commonly delegated to the county or municipal treasurer, as appropriate, for deposit in a fund to be known as the courthouse security fund or a fund to be known as the municipal court building security fund, as appropriate. Money deposited in a courthouse security fund may be used only for security personnel, services, and items related to buildings that house the operations of district, county, or justice courts, and money deposited in a municipal court building security fund may be used only for security personnel, services, and items related to buildings that house the operations of municipal courts. For purposes of this subsection, operations of a district, county, or justice court include the activities of associate judges, masters, magistrates, referees, hearing officers, criminal law magistrate court judges, and masters in chancery appointed under:

(1) Section 61.311, Alcoholic Beverage Code;

(2) Section 51.04(g) or Chapter 201, Family Code;

(3) Section 574.0085, Health and Safety Code;

(4) Section 33.71, Tax Code;

(5) **[2 Versions: Effective until January 1, 2012]** Chapter 54, Government Code; or

Criminal Procedure

(5) **[2 Versions: Effective January 1, 2012]** Chapter 54A, Government Code; or

(6) Rule 171, Texas Rules of Civil Procedure.

(d-1) **[2 Versions: As amended by Acts 2011, 82nd Leg., ch. 664]** For purposes of this article, the term "security personnel, services, and items" includes:

(1) the purchase or repair of X-ray machines and conveying systems;

(2) handheld metal detectors;

(3) walkthrough metal detectors;

(4) identification cards and systems;

(5) electronic locking and surveillance equipment;

(6) bailiffs, deputy sheriffs, deputy constables, or contract security personnel during times when they are providing appropriate security services;

(7) signage;

(8) confiscated weapon inventory and tracking systems;

(9) locks, chains, alarms, or similar security devices;

(10) the purchase or repair of bullet-proof glass;

(11) continuing education on security issues for court personnel and security personnel; and

(12) warrant officers and related equipment.

(d-1) **[2 Versions: As amended by Acts 2011, 82nd Leg., ch. 1031]** For purposes of this article, the term "security personnel, services, and items" includes:

(1) the purchase or repair of X-ray machines and conveying systems;

(2) handheld metal detectors;

(3) walkthrough metal detectors;

(4) identification cards and systems;

(5) electronic locking and surveillance equipment;

(6) video teleconferencing systems;

(7) bailiffs, deputy sheriffs, deputy constables, or contract security personnel during times when they are providing appropriate security services;

(8) signage;

(9) confiscated weapon inventory and tracking systems;

(10) locks, chains, alarms, or similar security devices;

(11) the purchase or repair of bullet-proof glass; and

(12) continuing education on security issues for court personnel and security personnel.

(d-2) (1) This subsection applies only to a justice court located in a county in which one or more justice courts are located in a building that is not the county courthouse.

(2) The county treasurer shall deposit one-fourth of the cost of court collected under Subsection (b) in a justice court described by Subdivision (1) into a fund to be known as the justice court building security fund. A fund designated by this subsection may be used only for the purpose of providing security personnel, services, and items for a justice court located in a building that is not the county courthouse.

(e) The courthouse security fund and the justice court building security fund shall be administered by or under the direction of the commissioners court. The municipal court building fund shall be administered by or under the direction of the governing body of the municipality.

(f) A local administrative judge shall provide to the Office of Court Administration of the Texas Judicial System a written report regarding any security incident involving court security that occurs in or around a building housing a court for which the judge serves as local administrative judge not later than the third business day after the date the incident occurred.

(Enacted by Acts 1993, 73rd Leg., ch. 818 (S.B. 243), § 1, effective September 1, 1993; enacted by Acts 1993, 73rd Leg., ch. 900 (S.B. 1067), § 1.07, effective September 1, 1994; am. Acts 1995, 74th Leg., ch. 764 (S.B. 349), § 2, effective August 28, 1995; am. Acts 1997, 75th Leg., ch. 12 (S.B. 182), § 1, effective September 1, 1997; am. Acts 1999, 76th Leg., ch. 110 (H.B. 1177), § 1, effective May 17, 1999; am. Acts 2005, 79th Leg., ch. 83 (S.B. 550), § 2, effective September 1, 2005; am. Acts 2005, 79th Leg., ch. 1087 (H.B. 1934), §§ 1, 2, effective September 1, 2005; am. Acts 2007, 80th Leg., ch. 221 (H.B. 1380), § 1, effective September 1, 2007; am. Acts 2011, 82nd Leg., ch. 664 (S.B. 1521), § 1, effective June 17, 2011; am. Acts 2011, 82nd Leg., ch. 1031 (H.B. 2847), § 7, effective September 1, 2011; am. Acts 2011, 82nd Leg., 1st C.S., (H.B. 79), § 6.07, effective January 1, 2012.)

## Art. 102.0171. Court Costs: Juvenile Delinquency Prevention Funds.

(a) A defendant convicted of an offense under Section 28.08, Penal Code, in a county court, county court at law, or district court shall pay a $50 juvenile delinquency prevention and graffiti eradication fee as a cost of court.

(b) In this article, a person is considered convicted if:

(1) a sentence is imposed on the person;

(2) the person receives community supervision, including deferred adjudication; or

(3) the court defers final disposition of the person's case.

(c) The clerks of the respective courts shall collect the costs and pay them to the county treasurer or to any other official who discharges the duties commonly delegated to the county treasurer for deposit in a fund to be known as the county juvenile delinquency prevention fund. A fund designated by this subsection may be used only to:

(1) repair damage caused by the commission of offenses under Section 28.08, Penal Code;

(2) provide educational and intervention programs and materials, including printed educational materials for distribution to primary and secondary school students, designed to prevent individuals from committing offenses under Section 28.08, Penal Code;

(3) provide to the public rewards for identifying and aiding in the apprehension and prosecution of offenders who commit offenses under Section 28.08, Penal Code;

(4) provide funding for teen recognition and teen recreation programs;

(5) provide funding for local teen court programs;

(6) provide funding for the local juvenile probation department; and

(7) provide educational and intervention programs designed to prevent juveniles from engaging in delinquent conduct.

(d) The county juvenile delinquency prevention fund shall be administered by or under the direction of the commissioners court.

(Enacted by Acts 1997, 75th Leg., ch. 593 (S.B. 758), § 2, effective September 1, 1997; am. Acts 2007, 80th Leg., ch. 1053 (H.B. 2151), § 3, effective September 1, 2007.)

## Art. 102.0172. Court Costs; Municipal Court Technology Fund.

(a) The governing body of a municipality by ordinance may create a municipal court technology fund and may require a defendant convicted of a misdemeanor offense in a municipal court or municipal court of record to pay a technology fee not to exceed $4 as a cost of court.

(b) In this article, a person is considered convicted if:

(1) a sentence is imposed on the person;

(2) the person is placed on community supervision, including deferred adjudication community supervision; or

(3) the court defers final disposition of the person's case.

(c) The municipal court clerk shall collect the costs and pay the funds to the municipal treasurer, or to any other official who discharges the duties commonly delegated to the municipal treasurer, for deposit in a fund to be known as the municipal court technology fund.

(d) A fund designated by this article may be used only to finance the purchase of or to maintain technological enhancements for a municipal court or municipal court of record, including:

(1) computer systems;

(2) computer networks;

(3) computer hardware;

(4) computer software;

(5) imaging systems;

(6) electronic kiosks;

(7) electronic ticket writers; and

(8) docket management systems.

(e) The municipal court technology fund shall be administered by or under the direction of the governing body of the municipality.

(f) [Repealed by Acts 2003, 78th Leg., ch. 502 (H.B. 1066), § 2, effective September 1, 2003.] (Enacted by Acts 1999, 76th Leg., ch. 285 (S.B. 601), § 1, effective September 1, 1999; am. Acts 2003, 78th Leg., ch. 502 (H.B. 1066), § 1, effective September 1, 2003; am. Acts 2003, 78th Leg., ch. 502 (H.B. 1066), § 2, effective September 1, 2003.)

## Art. 102.0173. Court Costs; Justice Court Technology Fund.

(a) The commissioners court of a county by order shall create a justice court technology fund. A defendant convicted of a misdemeanor offense in justice court shall pay a $4 justice court technology fee as a cost of court for deposit in the fund.

(b) In this article, a person is considered convicted if:

(1) a sentence is imposed on the person; or

(2) the court defers final disposition of the person's case.

(c) The justice court clerk shall collect the costs and pay the funds to the county treasurer, or to any other official who discharges the duties commonly delegated to the county treasurer, for deposit in a fund to be known as the justice court technology fund.

(d) A fund designated by this article may be used only to finance:

(1) the cost of continuing education and training for justice court judges and clerks

Criminal Procedure

regarding technological enhancements for justice courts; and

(2) the purchase and maintenance of technological enhancements for a justice court, including:

(A) computer systems;

(B) computer networks;

(C) computer hardware;

(D) computer software;

(E) imaging systems;

(F) electronic kiosks;

(G) electronic ticket writers; and

(H) docket management systems.

(e) The justice court technology fund shall be administered by or under the direction of the commissioners court of the county.

(f) [Repealed by Acts 2005, 79th Leg., ch. 240 (H.B. 1418), § 3, effective September 1, 2005.]
(Enacted by Acts 2001, 77th Leg., ch. 977 (H.B. 177), § 1, effective September 1, 2001; am. Acts 2005, 79th Leg., ch. 240 (H.B. 1418), § 1, effective September 1, 2005; am. Acts 2005, 79th Leg., ch. 240 (H.B. 1418), § 3, effective September 1, 2005.)

## Art. 102.0174. Court Costs; Juvenile Case Manager Fund.

(a) In this article, "fund" means a juvenile case manager fund.

(b) The governing body of a municipality by ordinance may create a juvenile case manager fund and may require a defendant convicted of a fine-only misdemeanor offense in a municipal court to pay a juvenile case manager fee not to exceed $5 as a cost of court.

(c) The commissioners court of a county by order may create a juvenile case manager fund and may require a defendant convicted of a fine-only misdemeanor offense in a justice court, county court, or county court at law to pay a juvenile case manager fee not to exceed $5 as a cost of court.

(d) The ordinance or order must authorize the judge or justice to waive the fee required by Subsection (b) or (c) in a case of financial hardship.

(e) In this article, a defendant is considered convicted if:

(1) a sentence is imposed on the defendant;

(2) the defendant receives deferred disposition, including deferred proceedings under Article 45.052 or 45.053; or

(3) the defendant receives deferred adjudication in county court.

(f) The clerks of the respective courts shall collect the costs and pay them to the county or municipal treasurer, as applicable, or to any other official who discharges the duties commonly delegated to the county or municipal treasurer for deposit in the fund.

(g) A fund created under this section may be used only to finance the salary and benefits of a juvenile case manager employed under Article 45.056.

(h) A fund must be administered by or under the direction of the commissioners court or under the direction of the governing body of the municipality.
(Enacted by Acts 2005, 79th Leg., ch. 949 (H.B. 1575), § 35, effective September 1, 2005; am. Acts 2011, 82nd Leg., ch. 868 (S.B. 61), § 3, effective June 17, 2011; am. Acts 2011, 82nd Leg., ch. 1098 (S.B. 1489), § 8, effective September 1, 2011.)

## Art. 102.0178. Costs Attendant to Certain Intoxication and Drug Convictions.

(a) In addition to other costs on conviction imposed by this chapter, a person shall pay $60 as a court cost on conviction of an offense punishable as a Class B misdemeanor or any higher category of offense under:

(1) Chapter 49, Penal Code; or

(2) Chapter 481, Health and Safety Code.

(b) For purposes of this article, a person is considered to have been convicted if:

(1) a sentence is imposed; or

(2) the defendant receives community supervision or deferred adjudication.

(c) Court costs under this article are collected in the same manner as other fines or costs. An officer collecting the costs shall keep separate records of the funds collected as costs under this article and shall deposit the funds in the county treasury, as appropriate.

(d) The custodian of a county treasury shall:

(1) keep records of the amount of funds on deposit collected under this article; and

(2) except as provided by Subsection (e), send to the comptroller before the last day of the first month following each calendar quarter the funds collected under this article during the preceding quarter.

(e) A county is entitled to:

(1) if the custodian of the county treasury complies with Subsection (d), retain 10 percent of the funds collected under this article by an officer of the county during the calendar quarter as a service fee; and

(2) if the county has established a drug court program or establishes a drug court program before the expiration of the calendar quarter, retain in addition to the 10 percent authorized by Subdivision (1) another 50 percent of the funds collected under this article by an officer of the county during the calendar quarter to be used exclusively for the development and maintenance of drug court programs operated within the county.

(f) If no funds due as costs under this article are deposited in a county treasury in a calendar quarter, the custodian of the treasury shall file the report required for the quarter in the regular manner and must state that no funds were collected.

(g) The comptroller shall deposit the funds received under this article to the credit of the drug court account in the general revenue fund to help fund drug court programs established under Chapter 469, Health and Safety Code. The legislature shall appropriate money from the account solely to the criminal justice division of the governor's office for distribution to drug court programs that apply for the money.

(h) Funds collected under this article are subject to audit by the comptroller.

(Enacted by Acts 2007, 80th Leg., ch. 625 (H.B. 530), § 8, effective June 15, 2007; am. Acts 2009, 81st Leg., ch. 902 (H.B. 666), § 1, effective September 1, 2009.)

## Art. 102.018. Costs Attendant to Intoxication Convictions.

(a) Except as provided by Subsection (d) of this article, on conviction of an offense relating to the driving or operating of a motor vehicle under Section 49.04, Penal Code, the court shall impose a cost of $15 on a defendant if, subsequent to the arrest of the defendant, a law enforcement agency visually recorded the defendant with an electronic device. Costs imposed under this subsection are in addition to other court costs and are due whether or not the defendant is granted probation in the case. The court shall collect the costs in the same manner as other costs are collected in the case.

(b) Except as provided by Subsection (d) of this article, on conviction of an offense relating to the driving or operating of a motor vehicle punishable under Section 49.04(b), Penal Code, the court shall impose as a cost of court on the defendant an amount that is equal to the cost of an evaluation of the defendant performed under

Section 13(a), Article 42.12, of this code. Costs imposed under this subsection are in addition to other court costs and are due whether or not the defendant is granted probation in the case, except that if the court determines that the defendant is indigent and unable to pay the cost, the court may waive the imposition of the cost.

(c) (1) Except as provided by Subsection (d) of this article, if a person commits an offense under Chapter 49, Penal Code, and as a direct result of the offense the person causes an incident resulting in an accident response by a public agency, the person is liable on conviction for the offense for the reasonable expense to the agency of the accident response. In this article, a person is considered to have been convicted in a case if:

(A) sentence is imposed;

(B) the defendant receives probation or deferred adjudication; or

(C) the court defers final disposition of the case.

(2) The liability authorized by this subsection may be established by civil suit; however, if a determination is made during a criminal trial that a person committed an offense under Chapter 49, Penal Code, and as a direct result of the offense the person caused an incident resulting in an accident response by a public agency, the court may include the obligation for the liability as part of the judgment. A judgment that includes such an obligation is enforceable as any other judgment.

(3) The liability is a debt of the person to the public agency, and the public agency may collect the debt in the same manner as the public agency collects an express or implied contractual obligation to the agency.

(4) A person's liability under this subsection for the reasonable expense of an accident response may not exceed $1,000 for a particular incident. For the purposes of this subdivision, a reasonable expense for an accident response includes only those costs to the public agency arising directly from an accident response to a particular incident, such as the cost of providing police, fire-fighting, rescue, ambulance, and emergency medical services at the scene of the incident and the salaries of the personnel of the public agency responding to the incident.

(5) A bill for the expense of an accident response sent to a person by a public agency under this subsection must contain an itemized accounting of the components of the total charge. A bill that complies with this subdivi-

sion is prima facie evidence of the reasonableness of the costs incurred in the accident response to which the bill applies.

(6) A policy of motor vehicle insurance delivered, issued for delivery, or renewed in this state may not cover payment of expenses charged to a person under this subsection.

(7) In this subsection, "public agency" means the state, a county, a municipality district, or a public authority located in whole or in part in this state that provides police, fire-fighting, rescue, ambulance, or emergency medical services.

(d) Subsections (a), (b), and (c) of this article do not apply to an offense under Section 49.02 or 49.03, Penal Code.

(Enacted by Acts 1993, 73rd Leg., ch. 900 (S.B. 1067), § 1.07, effective September 1, 1994; am. Acts 1995, 74th Leg., ch. 76 (S.B. 959), § 17.01(4), effective September 1, 1995 (renumbered from art. 102.017).)

## Art. 102.0185. Additional Costs Attendant to Intoxication Convictions: Emergency Medical Services, Trauma Facilities, and Trauma Care Systems.

(a) In addition to the costs on conviction imposed by Articles 102.016 and 102.018, a person convicted of an offense under Chapter 49, Penal Code, except for Sections 49.02 and 49.031, shall pay $100 on conviction of the offense.

(b) Costs imposed under this article are imposed without regard to whether the defendant is placed on community supervision after being convicted of the offense or receives deferred disposition or deferred adjudication for the offense.

(c) Costs imposed under this article are collected in the manner provided by Subchapter B, Chapter 133, Local Government Code.

(d) The officer collecting the costs under this article shall keep separate records of the money collected and shall pay the money to the custodian of the municipal or county treasury.

(e) The custodian of the municipal or county treasury shall:

(1) keep records of the amount of money collected under this article that is deposited with the treasury under this article; and

(2) not later than the last day of the first month following each calendar quarter:

(A) pay the money collected under this article during the preceding calendar quarter to the comptroller; or

(B) if, in the calendar quarter, the custodian of the municipal or county treasury did

not receive any money attributable to costs paid under this article, file a report with the comptroller stating that fact.

(f) The comptroller shall deposit the funds received under this article to the credit of the account established under Section 773.006, Health and Safety Code.

(Enacted by Acts 2003, 78th Leg., ch. 1213 (S.B. 1131), § 4, effective September 1, 2003; am. Acts 2011, 82nd Leg., ch. 91 (S.B. 1303), § 6.007, effective September 1, 2011.)

## Art. 102.0186. Additional Costs Attendant to Certain Child Sexual Assault and Related Convictions.

(a) A person convicted of an offense under Section 21.02, 21.11, 22.011(a)(2), 22.021(a)(1)(B), 43.25, 43.251, or 43.26, Penal Code, shall pay $100 on conviction of the offense.

(b) Costs imposed under this article are imposed without regard to whether the defendant is placed on community supervision after being convicted of the offense or receives deferred adjudication for the offense.

(c) The clerks of the respective courts shall collect the costs and pay them to the county treasurer or to any other official who discharges the duties commonly delegated to the county treasurer for deposit in a fund to be known as the county child abuse prevention fund. A fund designated by this subsection may be used only to fund child abuse prevention programs in the county where the court is located.

(d) The county child abuse prevention fund shall be administered by or under the direction of the commissioners court.

(Enacted by Acts 2005, 79th Leg., ch. 268 (S.B. 6), § 1.127, effective September 1, 2005; am. Acts 2007, 80th Leg., ch. 593 (H.B. 8), § 3.24, effective September 1, 2007.)

## Art. 102.019. Costs on Conviction for Fugitive Apprehension [Repealed].

Repealed by Acts 2003, 78th Leg., ch. 209 (H.B. 2424), § 85(6), effective January 1, 2004.

(Enacted by Acts 1997, 75th Leg., ch. 1100 (H.B. 2272), § 3, effective September 1, 1997.)

## Art. 102.020. Costs Related to DNA Testing.

(a) A person shall pay as a cost of court:

(1) $250 on conviction of an offense listed in Section 411.1471(a)(1), Government Code;

(2) $50 on conviction of an offense listed in Section 411.1471(a)(3) of that code; or

(3) $34 on placement of the person on community supervision, including deferred adjudication community supervision, if the person is required to submit a DNA sample under Section 11(j), Article 42.12.

(b) The court shall assess and make a reasonable effort to collect the cost due under this article whether or not any other court cost is assessed or collected.

(c) For purposes of this article, a person is considered to have been convicted if:

(1) a sentence is imposed; or

(2) the defendant receives community supervision or deferred adjudication.

(d) Court costs under this article are collected in the same manner as other fines or costs. An officer collecting the costs shall keep separate records of the funds collected as costs under this article and shall deposit the funds in the county treasury.

(e) The custodian of a county treasury shall:

(1) keep records of the amount of funds on deposit collected under this article; and

(2) send to the comptroller before the last day of the first month following each calendar quarter the funds collected under this article during the preceding quarter.

(f) A county may retain 10 percent of the funds collected under this article by an officer of the county as a collection fee if the custodian of the county treasury complies with Subsection (e).

(g) If no funds due as costs under this article are deposited in a county treasury in a calendar quarter, the custodian of the treasury shall file the report required for the quarter in the regular manner and must state that no funds were collected.

(h) Except as provided by Subsection (h-1), the comptroller shall deposit 35 percent of the funds received under this article in the state treasury to the credit of the state highway fund and 65 percent of the funds received under this article to the credit of the criminal justice planning account in the general revenue fund.

(h-1) The clerk of the court shall transfer to the comptroller any funds received under Subsection (a)(3). The comptroller shall credit the funds to the Department of Public Safety to help defray the cost of any analyses performed on DNA samples provided by defendants who are required to pay a court cost under this article.

(i) Funds collected under this article are subject to audit by the comptroller.

(j) The court may waive the imposition of a court cost under this article if the court determines that the defendant is indigent and unable to pay the cost.
(Enacted by Acts 2001, 77th Leg., ch. 1490 (S.B. 638), § 6, effective September 1, 2001; am. Acts 2009, 81st Leg., ch. 1209 (S.B. 727), §§ 1, 2, effective September 1, 2009.)

## Art. 102.021. [Blank].

## Art. 102.022. Costs on Conviction to Fund Statewide Repository for Data Related to Civil Justice.

(a) In this article, "moving violation" means an offense that:

(1) involves the operation of a motor vehicle; and

(2) is classified as a moving violation by the Department of Public Safety under Section 708.052, Transportation Code.

(b) A defendant convicted of a moving violation in a justice court, county court, county court at law, or municipal court shall pay a fee of 10 cents as a cost of court.

(c) In this article, a person is considered convicted if:

(1) a sentence is imposed on the person;

(2) the person receives community supervision, including deferred adjudication; or

(3) the court defers final disposition of the person's case.

(d) The clerks of the respective courts shall collect the costs described by this article. The clerk shall keep separate records of the funds collected as costs under this article and shall deposit the funds in the county or municipal treasury, as appropriate.

(e) The custodian of a county or municipal treasury shall:

(1) keep records of the amount of funds on deposit collected under this article; and

(2) send to the comptroller before the last day of the first month following each calendar quarter the funds collected under this article during the preceding quarter.

(f) A county or municipality may retain 10 percent of the funds collected under this article by an officer of the county or municipality as a collection fee if the custodian of the county or municipal treasury complies with Subsection (e).

(g) If no funds due as costs under this article are deposited in a county or municipal treasury in a calendar quarter, the custodian of the treasury shall file the report required for the quarter in the regular manner and must state that no funds were collected.

(h) The comptroller shall deposit the funds received under this article to the credit of the Civil Justice Data Repository fund in the general revenue fund, to be used only by the Commission on Law Enforcement Officer Standards and Education to implement duties under Section 1701.162, Occupations Code.

(i) Funds collected under this article are subject to audit by the comptroller.

(Enacted by Acts 2009, 81st Leg., ch. 1172 (H.B. 3389), § 30, effective September 1, 2009.)

## SUBCHAPTER B
## CRIMINAL JUSTICE PLANNING FUND

### Art. 102.051. Misdemeanor and Felony Costs [Repealed].

Repealed by Acts 1997, 75th Leg., ch. 1100 (H.B. 2272), § 6(3), effective September 1, 1997. (Enacted by Acts 1985, 69th Leg., ch. 269 (S.B. 854), § 1, effective September 1, 1985; am. Acts 1989, 71st Leg., ch. 347 (S.B. 1085), § 2, effective October 1, 1989; am. Acts 1991, 72nd Leg., ch. 108 (H.B. 407), § 5, effective September 1, 1991.)

### Art. 102.052. Record of Collection [Repealed].

Repealed by Acts 1997, 75th Leg., ch. 1100 (H.B. 2272), § 6(3), effective September 1, 1997. (Enacted by Acts 1985, 69th Leg., ch. 269 (S.B. 854), § 1, effective September 1, 1985.)

### Art. 102.053. Reports Required [Repealed].

Repealed by Acts 1997, 75th Leg., ch. 1100 (H.B. 2272), § 6(3), effective September 1, 1997. (Enacted by Acts 1985, 69th Leg., ch. 269 (S.B. 854), § 1, effective September 1, 1985.)

### Art. 102.054. Transfer of Funds to Comptroller [Repealed].

Repealed by Acts 1997, 75th Leg., ch. 1100 (H.B. 2272), § 6(3), effective September 1, 1997. (Enacted by Acts 1985, 69th Leg., ch. 269 (S.B. 854), § 1, effective September 1, 1985; am. Acts 1989, 71st Leg., ch. 347 (S.B. 1085), § 3, effective October 1, 1989.)

### Art. 102.055. Special Fund [Repealed].

Repealed by Acts 1997, 75th Leg., ch. 1100 (H.B. 2272), § 6(3), effective September 1, 1997. (Enacted by Acts 1985, 69th Leg., ch. 269 (S.B. 854), § 1, effective September 1, 1985.)

### Art. 102.056. Distribution of Funds.

(a) The legislature shall determine and appropriate the necessary amount from the criminal justice planning fund to the criminal justice division of the governor's office for expenditure for state and local criminal justice projects and for costs of administering the funds for the projects. The criminal justice division shall allocate not less than 20 percent of these funds to juvenile justice programs. The distribution of the funds to local units of government shall be in an amount equal at least to the same percentage as local expenditures for criminal justice activities are to total state and local expenditures for criminal justice activities for the preceding state fiscal year. Funds shall be allocated among combinations of local units of government taking into consideration the population of the combination of local units of government as compared to the population of the state and the incidence of crime in the jurisdiction of the combination of local units of government as compared to the incidence of crime in the state. All funds collected are subject to audit by the comptroller of public accounts. All funds expended are subject to audit by the State Auditor. All funds collected or expended are subject to audit by the governor's division of planning coordination.

(b) The legislature may appropriate any unobligated balance of the criminal justice planning fund for any court-related purpose.

(c) Notwithstanding any other provision of this article, the criminal justice division shall allocate to a local unit of government or combination of local units of government located in an impacted region occurring as the result of the establishment of a significant new naval military facility an amount that exceeds by 10 percent the amount it would otherwise receive under this article.

(d) In this article, "significant new naval military facility" and "impacted region" have the meanings assigned by Section 4, Article 1, National Defense Impacted Region Assistance Act of 1985.

(e) The legislature shall determine and appropriate the necessary amount from the criminal justice planning account to the criminal justice division of the governor's office for reimbursement in the form of grants to the Department of Public Safety of the State of Texas and other law enforcement agencies for expenses incurred in performing duties imposed on those agencies under Section 411.1471 or Subchapter B-1, Chapter 420, Government Code, as applicable. On the first day after the end of a calendar quarter, a law

enforcement agency incurring expenses described by this subsection in the previous calendar quarter shall send a certified statement of the costs incurred to the criminal justice division. The criminal justice division through a grant shall reimburse the law enforcement agency for the costs not later than the 30th day after the date the certified statement is received. If the criminal justice division does not reimburse the law enforcement agency before the 90th day after the date the certified statement is received, the agency is not required to perform duties imposed under Section 411.1471 or Subchapter B-1, Chapter 420, Government Code, as applicable, until the agency has been compensated for all costs for which the agency has submitted a certified statement under this subsection.
(Enacted by Acts 1985, 69th Leg., ch. 269 (S.B. 854), § 1, effective September 1, 1985; am. Acts 1986, 69th Leg., 2nd C.S., ch. 11 (H.B. 27), § 8, effective September 22, 1986; am. Acts 1991, 72nd Leg., ch. 16 (S.B. 232), § 4.07(a), effective August 26, 1991; am. Acts 2001, 77th Leg., ch. 1490 (S.B. 638), § 7, effective September 1, 2001; am. Acts 2011, 82nd Leg., ch. 91 (S.B. 1303), § 6.008, effective September 1, 2011; am. Acts 2011, 82nd Leg., ch. 1105 (S.B. 1636), § 13, effective September 1, 2011.)

## SUBCHAPTER C
## COURT COSTS AND FEES

### Art. 102.071. Collection, Allocation, and Administration.

The comptroller of public accounts may require state court costs and fees in criminal cases to be reported in lump-sum amounts. The comptroller shall allocate the amounts received to the appropriate fund, with each fund receiving the same amount of money the fund would have received if the costs and fees had been reported individually.
(Enacted by Acts 1989, 71st Leg., ch. 347 (S.B. 1085), § 4, effective October 1, 1989.)

### Art. 102.072. Administrative Fee.

An officer listed in Article 103.003 or a community supervision and corrections department may assess an administrative fee for each transaction made by the officer or department relating to the collection of fines, fees, restitution, or other costs imposed by a court. The fee may not exceed $2 for each transaction. This article does not apply to a

transaction relating to the collection of child support.
(Enacted by Acts 1995, 74th Leg., ch. 217 (H.B. 2265), § 2, effective May 23, 1995; am. Acts 1999, 76th Leg., ch. 1345 (H.B. 662), § 1, effective September 1, 1999.)

### Art. 102.075. Court Costs for Special Services [Repealed].

Repealed by Acts 2003, 78th Leg., ch. 209 (H.B. 2424), § 85(7), effective January 1, 2004.
(Enacted by Acts 1997, 75th Leg., ch. 1100 (H.B. 2272), § 4, effective September 1, 1997; am. Acts 1999, 76th Leg., ch. 1467 (H.B. 3211), § 2.01, effective October 1, 1999; am. Acts 2001, 77th Leg., ch. 368 (S.B. 1421), § 1, effective September 1, 2001; am. Acts 2001, 77th Leg., ch. 906 (S.B. 7), § 10, effective January 1, 2002.)

## SUBCHAPTER D
## COMPREHENSIVE REHABILITATION FUND
## [REPEALED]

### Art. 102.081. Traffic Conviction Costs [Repealed].

Repealed by Acts 1997, 75th Leg., ch. 1100 (H.B. 2272), § 6(4), effective September 1, 1997.
(Enacted by Acts 1991, 72nd Leg., ch. 101 (S.B. 195), § 1, effective September 1, 1991; am. Acts 1993, 73rd Leg., ch. 900 (S.B. 1067), § 3.04, effective September 1, 1994.)

### Art. 102.082. Record of Collection [Repealed].

Repealed by Acts 1997, 75th Leg., ch. 1100 (H.B. 2272), § 6(4), effective September 1, 1997.
(Enacted by Acts 1991, 72nd Leg., ch. 101 (S.B. 195), § 1, effective September 1, 1991.)

### Art. 102.083. Reports Required [Repealed].

Repealed by Acts 1997, 75th Leg., ch. 1100 (H.B. 2272), § 6(4), effective September 1, 1997.
(Enacted by Acts 1991, 72nd Leg., ch. 101 (S.B. 195), § 1, effective September 1, 1991.)

### Art. 102.084. Transfer of Funds to Comptroller [Repealed].

Repealed by Acts 1997, 75th Leg., ch. 1100 (H.B. 2272), § 6(4), effective September 1, 1997.
(Enacted by Acts 1991, 72nd Leg., ch. 101 (S.B. 195), § 1, effective September 1, 1991.)

## Art. 102.085. Special Fund [Repealed].

Repealed by Acts 1997, 75th Leg., ch. 1100 (H.B. 2272), § 6(4), effective September 1, 1997. (Enacted by Acts 1991, 72nd Leg., ch. 101 (S.B. 195), § 1, effective September 1, 1991.)

## CHAPTER 103
## COLLECTION AND
## RECORDKEEPING

## Art. 103.001. Costs Payable.

A cost is not payable by the person charged with the cost until a written bill is produced or is ready to be produced, containing the items of cost, signed by the officer who charged the cost or the officer who is entitled to receive payment for the cost.
(Enacted by Acts 1985, 69th Leg., ch. 269 (S.B. 854), § 1, effective September 1, 1985.)

## Art. 103.002. Certain Costs Barred.

An officer may not impose a cost for a service not performed or for a service for which a cost is not expressly provided by law.
(Enacted by Acts 1985, 69th Leg., ch. 269 (S.B. 854), § 1, effective September 1, 1985.)

## Art. 103.003. Collection.

(a) District and county attorneys, clerks of district and county courts, sheriffs, constables, and justices of the peace may collect money payable under this title.

(b) A community supervision and corrections department and a county treasurer may collect money payable under this title with the written approval of the clerk of the court or fee officer, and may collect money payable as otherwise provided by law.

(b-1) The commissioners court of a county that has implemented a collection improvement pro-gram under Article 103.0033 may collect money payable under this title or under other law.

(c) This article does not limit the authority of a commissioners court to contract with a private vendor or private attorney for the provision of collection services under Article 103.0031.
(Enacted by Acts 1985, 69th Leg., ch. 269 (S.B. 854), § 1, effective September 1, 1985; am. Acts 1995, 74th Leg., ch. 217 (H.B. 2265), § 3, effective May 23, 1995; am. Acts 2001, 77th Leg., ch. 1279 (S.B. 1778), § 1, effective June 15, 2001; am. Acts 2005, 79th Leg., ch. 1064 (H.B. 1470), § 1, effective June 18, 2005; am. Acts 2011, 82nd Leg., ch. 270 (H.B. 1426), § 1, effective June 17, 2011; am. Acts 2011, 82nd Leg., ch. 606 (S.B. 373), § 1, effective September 1, 2011.)

## Art. 103.0031. Collection Contracts.

(a) The commissioners court of a county or the governing body of a municipality may enter into a contract with a private attorney or a public or private vendor for the provision of collection services for one or more of the following items:

(1) debts and accounts receivable such as unpaid fines, fees, court costs, forfeited bonds, and restitution ordered paid by:

(A) a court serving the county or a court serving the municipality, as applicable; or

(B) a hearing officer serving the municipality under Chapter 682, Transportation Code;

(2) amounts in cases in which the accused has failed to appear:

(A) as promised under Subchapter A, Chapter 543, Transportation Code, or other law;

(B) in compliance with a lawful written notice to appear issued under Article 14.06(b) or other law;

(C) in compliance with a lawful summons issued under Article 15.03(b) or other law;

(D) in compliance with a lawful order of a court serving the county or municipality; or

(E) as specified in a citation, summons, or other notice authorized by Section 682.002, Transportation Code, that charges the accused with a parking or stopping offense; and

(3) false alarm penalties or fees imposed by a county under Chapter 118 or 233, Local Government Code, or by a municipality under a municipal ordinance.

(b) A commissioners court or governing body of a municipality that enters into a contract with a private attorney or private vendor under this article may authorize the addition of a collection fee in the amount of 30 percent on each item described in Subsection (a) that is more than 60 days past due and has been referred to the attorney or vendor for collection. The collection fee does not apply to a case that has been dismissed by a court of competent jurisdiction or to any amount that has been satisfied through time-served credit or community service. The collection fee may be applied to any balance remaining after a partial credit for time served or community service if the balance is more than 60 days past due. Unless the contract provides otherwise, the court shall calculate the amount of any collection fee due to the governmental entity or to the private attorney or private vendor performing the collection services and shall receive all fees, including the collection fee. With respect to cases described by Subsection (a)(2), the amount to which the 30 percent collection fee applies is:

(1) the amount to be paid that is communicated to the accused as acceptable to the court under its standard policy for resolution of the case, if the accused voluntarily agrees to pay that amount; or

(2) the amount ordered paid by the court after plea or trial.

(c) The governing body of a municipality with a population of more than 1.9 million may authorize the addition of collection fees under Subsection (b) for a collection program performed by employees of the governing body.

(d) A defendant is not liable for the collection fees authorized under Subsection (b) if the court of original jurisdiction has determined the defendant is indigent, or has insufficient resources or income, or is otherwise unable to pay all or part of the underlying fine or costs.

(e) If a county or municipality has entered into a contract under Subsection (a) and a person pays an amount that is less than the aggregate total to be collected under Subsections (a) and (b), the allocation to the comptroller, the county or municipality, and the private attorney or vendor shall be reduced proportionately.

(f) An item subject to collection services under Subsection (a) and to the additional collection fee authorized by Subsection (b) is considered more than 60 days past due under Subsection (b) if it remains unpaid on the 61st day after the following appropriate date:

(1) with respect to an item described by Subsection (a)(1), the date on which the debt, fine, fee, forfeited bond, or court cost must be

paid in full as determined by the court or hearing officer;

(2) with respect to an item described by Subsection (a)(2), the date by which the accused promised to appear or was notified, summoned, or ordered to appear; or

(3) with respect to an item described by Subsection (a)(3), the date on which a penalty or fee is due under a rule or order adopted under Chapter 233, Local Government Code, or an ordinance, policy, procedure, or rule of a municipality.

(g) A county or municipality that enters into a contract under Subsection (a) may not use the additional 30 percent collection fee authorized by Subsection (b) for any purpose other than compensating the private attorney or private vendor who earns the fee.

(h) This section does not apply to the collection of commercial bail bonds.

(i) The commissioners court of a county or the governing body of a municipality may enter into a contract as described in this article to collect a debt incurred as a result of the commission of a criminal or civil offense committed before the effective date of this subsection. The collection fee does not apply to a debt collected pursuant to a contract entered into under this subsection.

(j) A communication to the accused person regarding the amount of payment that is acceptable to the court under the court's standard policy for resolution of a case must include a notice of the person's right to enter a plea or go to trial on any offense charged.

(Enacted by Acts 1993, 73rd Leg., ch. 809 (H.B. 2535), § 3, effective August 30, 1993; am. Acts 2001, 77th Leg., ch. 1279 (S.B. 1778), § 2, effective June 15, 2001; am. Acts 2003, 78th Leg., ch. 346 (S.B. 782), § 1, effective June 18, 2003; am. Acts 2005, 79th Leg., ch. 1296 (H.B. 2626), § 4, effective June 18, 2005.)

## Art. 103.0032. Collection Improvement Plans.

Not later than January 1 of each even-numbered year, the Office of Court Administration of the Texas Judicial System may award grants to counties and municipalities to prepare a collection plan. The grants shall reimburse the county or municipality for the cost of preparing the plan. The plan shall provide methods to improve the collection of court costs, fees, and fines imposed in criminal cases. The Office of Court Administration of the Texas Judicial System may require that the county or municipality reimburse the state from the additional collections as a condition of the grant.

(Enacted by Acts 2001, 77th Leg., ch. 1469 (H.B. 3498), § 1, effective September 1, 2001.)

## Art. 103.0033. Collection Improvement Program.

(a) In this article:

(1) "Eligible case" means a criminal case in which the judgment has been entered by a trial court. The term does not include a criminal case in which a defendant has been placed on deferred disposition or has elected to take a driving safety course.

(2) "Office" means the Office of Court Administration of the Texas Judicial System.

(3) "Program" means the program to improve the collection of court costs, fees, and fines imposed in criminal cases, as developed and implemented under this article.

(b) **[2 Versions: Effective until September 28, 2011]** This article applies to each county in this state and to each municipality with a population of 100,000 or greater.

(b) **[2 Versions: Effective September 28, 2011]** This article applies only to:

(1) a county with a population of 50,000 or greater; and

(2) a municipality with a population of 100,000 or greater.

(c) **[2 Versions: Effective until September 28, 2011]** Unless granted a waiver under Subsection (h), each municipality shall develop and implement a program that complies with the prioritized implementation schedule under Subsection (h). A county may develop and implement a program that complies with the prioritized implementation schedule under Subsection (h). A county program must include district, county, and justice courts.

(c) **[2 Versions: Effective September 28, 2011]** Unless granted a waiver under Subsection (h), each county and municipality shall develop and implement a program that complies with the prioritized implementation schedule under Subsection (h). A county program must include district, county, and justice courts.

(d) The program must consist of:

(1) a component that conforms with a model developed by the office and designed to improve in-house collections for eligible cases through the application of best practices; and

(2) a component designed to improve the collection of balances for eligible cases more than 60 days past due, which may be implemented by entering into a contract with a private attorney or public or private vendor in accordance with Article 103.0031.

(e) **[2 Versions: Effective until September 28, 2011]** Not later than June 1 of each year, the office shall identify those counties and municipalities that:

(1) have not implemented a program; and

(2) are planning to implement a program before April 1 of the following year.

(e) **[2 Versions: Effective September 28, 2011]** Not later than June 1 of each year, the office shall identify those counties and municipalities that:

(1) have not implemented a program; and

(2) are able to implement a program before April 1 of the following year.

(f) The office shall develop a methodology for determining the collection rate of counties and municipalities described by Subsection (e) before implementation of a program. The office shall determine the rate for each county and municipality not later than the first anniversary of the county's or municipality's adoption of a program.

(g) The office shall:

(1) make available on the office's Internet website requirements for a program; and

(2) assist counties and municipalities in implementing a program by providing training and consultation, except that the office may not provide employees for implementation of a program.

(h) **[2 Versions: Effective until September 28, 2011]** The office may:

(1) use case dispositions, population, revenue data, or other appropriate measures to develop a prioritized implementation schedule for programs; and

(2) for a municipality, determine whether it is not actually cost-effective to implement a program in the municipality and grant a waiver to the municipality.

(h) **[2 Versions: Effective September 28, 2011]** The office may:

(1) use case dispositions, population, revenue data, or other appropriate measures to develop a prioritized implementation schedule for programs; and

(2) determine whether it is not cost-effective to implement a program in a county or municipality and grant a waiver to the county or municipality.

(i) **[2 Versions: Effective until September 28, 2011]** Each county that implements a program and each municipality shall at least annually submit to the office a written report that includes updated information regarding the program, as determined by the office. The report must be in a form approved by the office.

(i) **[2 Versions: Effective September 28, 2011]** Each county and municipality shall at least annually submit to the office a written report that includes updated information regarding the program, as determined by the office. The report must be in a form approved by the office.

(j) **[2 Versions: Effective until September 28, 2011]** The office shall periodically audit municipalities to verify information reported under Subsection (i) and confirm that the municipality is conforming with requirements relating to the program.

(j) **[2 Versions: Effective September 28, 2011]** The office shall periodically audit counties and municipalities to verify information reported under Subsection (i) and confirm that the county or municipality is conforming with requirements relating to the program.

(Enacted by Acts 2005, 79th Leg., ch. 899 (S.B. 1863), § 10.01, effective August 29, 2005; am. Acts 2011, 82nd Leg., ch. 1171 (H.B. 2949), § 1, effective September 1, 2011; am. Acts 2011, 82nd Leg., 1st C.S., (S.B. 1), § 41.01, effective September 28, 2011.)

### Art. 103.004. Disposition of Collected Money.

(a) Except as provided by Subsection (c), an officer who collects recognizances, bail bonds, fines, forfeitures, judgments, jury fees, and other obligations recovered in the name of the state under any provision of this title shall deposit the money in the county treasury not later than the next regular business day after the date that the money is collected. If it is not possible for the officer to deposit the money in the county treasury by that date, the officer shall deposit the money in the county treasury as soon as possible, but not later than the fifth regular business day after the date that the money is collected.

(b) [Repealed by Acts 2011, 82nd Leg., ch. 606 (S.B. 373), § 31(a), effective September 1, 2011.]

(c) The commissioners court of a county with a population of less than 50,000 may authorize an officer who is required to deposit money under Subsection (a) to deposit the money in the county treasury not later than the 15th day after the date that the money is collected.

(d) The custodian of the county treasury shall deposit money received from fees imposed under Article 102.012 in the special fund of the county treasury for the community supervision and corrections department serving the county.

(Enacted by Acts 1985, 69th Leg., ch. 269 (S.B. 854), § 1, effective September 1, 1985; am. Acts 1990, 71st Leg., 6th C.S., ch. 25 (S.B. 41), § 21, effective June 18, 1990; am. Acts 1999, 76th Leg., ch. 1462 (H.B. 3173), § 1, effective September 1, 1999; am. Acts 2011, 82nd Leg., ch. 606 (S.B. 373), §§ 2, 31(a), effective September 1, 2011.)

### Art. 103.005. Report Required.

(a) An officer listed in Article 103.003 who collects money other than taxes for a county shall report to the commissioners court of the county for which the money was collected during each term of the court.

(b) An officer listed in Article 103.003 who collects money other than taxes for the state shall report to the district court having jurisdiction in the county the officer serves on the first day of each term of the court.

(c) The report must state for the reporting period:

(1) the amount of money collected by the officer;

(2) when and from whom the money was collected;

(3) the process by which the money was collected; and

(4) the disposition of the money.

(d) The report must be in writing and under the oath of the officer.

(e) If an officer has not collected money since the last report required to be filed with the court or the commissioners court, the officer shall report that fact to the court or commissioners court.

(Enacted by Acts 1985, 69th Leg., ch. 269 (S.B. 854), § 1, effective September 1, 1985.)

### Art. 103.006. Transfer of Bill of Costs.

If a criminal action or proceeding is transferred from one court to another or is appealed, an officer of the court shall certify and sign a bill of costs stating the costs that have accrued and send the bill of costs to the court to which the action or proceeding is transferred or appealed.

(Enacted by Acts 1985, 69th Leg., ch. 269 (S.B. 854), § 1, effective September 1, 1985.)

### Art. 103.007. Additional Costs After Payment.

After a defendant has paid costs, no more costs may be charged against the defendant unless the

court rules on a motion presented to the court that additional costs are due.
(Enacted by Acts 1985, 69th Leg., ch. 269 (S.B. 854), § 1, effective September 1, 1985.)

### Art. 103.008. Correction of Costs.

(a) On the filing of a motion by a defendant not later than one year after the date of the final disposition of a case in which costs were imposed, the court in which the case is pending or was last pending shall correct any error in the costs.

(b) The defendant must notify each person affected by the correction of costs in the same manner as notice of a similar motion is given in a civil action.
(Enacted by Acts 1985, 69th Leg., ch. 269 (S.B. 854), § 1, effective September 1, 1985.)

### Art. 103.009. Fee Records.

(a) Each clerk of a court, county judge, justice of the peace, sheriff, constable, and marshal shall keep a fee record. The record must contain:

(1) a statement of each fee or item of cost charged for a service rendered in a criminal action or proceeding;

(2) the number and style of the action or proceeding; and

(3) the name of the officer or person who is entitled to receive the fee.

(b) Any person may inspect a fee record described by Subsection (a).

(c) A statement of an item of cost in a fee record is prima facie evidence of the correctness of the statement.

(d) The county shall provide to officers required to keep a fee record by this article equipment and supplies necessary to keep the record.
(Enacted by Acts 1985, 69th Leg., ch. 269 (S.B. 854), § 1, effective September 1, 1985; am. Acts 1993, 73rd Leg., ch. 988 (S.B. 532), § 2.05, effective September 1, 1993.)

### Art. 103.010. Receipt Book.

(a) Each county shall provide a receipt book to each officer collecting fines and fees in criminal cases for the county. The book must contain duplicate official receipts. Each receipt must bear a distinct number and a facsimile of the official seal of the county.

(b) An officer who collects fines or fees in a criminal case shall give the person paying the money a receipt from the receipt book. The receipt must show:

(1) the amount of money paid;

(2) the date the money was paid;

(3) the style and number of the case in which the costs were accrued;

(4) the item of costs;

(5) the name of the person paying the money; and

(6) the official signature of the officer receiving the money.

(c) Instead of a receipt book, each officer collecting fines or fees in criminal cases for the county may maintain the information listed in Subsections (b)(1)—(5) in a computer database. The officer shall provide a receipt to each person paying a fine or fee.
(Enacted by Acts 1985, 69th Leg., ch. 269 (S.B. 854), § 1, effective September 1, 1985; am. Acts 1999, 76th Leg., ch. 412 (S.B. 1023), § 1, effective June 18, 1999.)

### Art. 103.011. Audit.

An officer shall deliver the receipt book or a copy of any receipt records contained in a computer database to the county auditor at the end of each month's business or at the end of each month shall allow the county auditor electronic access to receipt records contained in the computer database. The county auditor shall examine the receipt book or computer records and determine whether the money collected has been properly disposed of. If each receipt in a receipt book has been used, the county auditor shall keep the book. If any receipt in the book has not been used, the auditor shall return the book to the officer. The county auditor may keep a copy of computer generated receipt records delivered to the county auditor. Any person may inspect a receipt book or a computer generated receipt record kept by the county auditor.
(Enacted by Acts 1985, 69th Leg., ch. 269 (S.B. 854), § 1, effective September 1, 1985; am. Acts 1999, 76th Leg., ch. 412 (S.B. 1023), § 2, effective June 18, 1999.)

### Art. 103.012. Penalty.

(a) An officer commits an offense if the officer violates a provision of Article 103.010 or Article 103.011.

(b) An offense under this article is a Class C misdemeanor.

(c) An officer who violates a provision of Article 103.010 or Article 103.011 or whose deputy violates a provision of those articles may be removed from office on the petition of the county or district attorney.

(Enacted by Acts 1985, 69th Leg., ch. 269 (S.B. 854), § 1, effective September 1, 1985.)

## Art. 103.013. Collection of Fees for Delinquent Traffic Fines [Repealed].

Repealed by Acts 2003, 78th Leg., ch. 1276 (H.B. 3507), § 5.004, effective September 1, 2003. (Enacted by Acts 2001, 77th Leg., ch. 1420 (H.B. 2812), § 3.006 (a), effective September 1, 2001.)

# CHAPTER 104
# CERTAIN EXPENSES PAID BY STATE OR COUNTY

## Art. 104.001. Jury Pay and Expenses for Jurors.

(a) The sheriff of a county shall, with the approval of the commissioners court, provide food and lodging for jurors impaneled in a felony case tried in the county. A juror may pay his own expenses and draw his script.

(b) A juror in a felony case is entitled to receive as jury pay the amount authorized by Article 2122, Revised Statutes.

(c) The county treasurer shall pay a juror the amount due the juror for expenses under this article after receiving a certificate from a clerk of a court or justice of the peace stating the amount due the juror.

(d) A draft or certificate issued under this article may be transferred by delivery and, without further action of any authority except registration by the county treasurer, may be used at par to pay county taxes owed by the holder of the draft or certificate.

(e) If a defendant is indicted in one county and tried in another county after a change of venue, the county in which the defendant was indicted is liable for jury pay and expenses paid to jurors by the county trying the case.

(f) At each regular meeting of the commissioners court of a county, the court shall determine whether, since the last regular meeting of the court, a defendant described by Subsection (e) has been tried in the county. The commissioners court shall prepare an account against another county liable for jury pay and expenses under this article. The account must show the number of days the jury was impaneled in the case and the

jury pay and expenses incurred by the county in the case.

(g) The county judge of the county in which the defendant was tried shall certify the correctness of the account and send the account to the county judge of the county in which the defendant was indicted. The county in which the defendant was indicted shall pay the account in the same manner required for payment of the expenses of transferred prisoners under Article 104.002. (Enacted by Acts 1985, 69th Leg., ch. 269 (S.B. 854), § 1, effective September 1, 1985.)

## Art. 104.002. Expenses for Prisoners.

(a) Except as otherwise provided by this article, a county is liable for all expenses incurred in the safekeeping of prisoners confined in the county jail or kept under guard by the county. If a prisoner is transferred to a county from another county on a change of venue, for safekeeping, or for a habeas corpus hearing, the county transferring the prisoner is liable for the expenses described by this article.

(b) If a county incurs expenses for the safekeeping of a prisoner from another county, the sheriff shall submit to the county judge an account of expenses incurred by the county for the prisoner. The county judge shall approve the amount he determines is a correct statement of the expenses and sign and date the account.

(c) The county judge shall submit to the commissioners court of the county for which the prisoner was kept, at a regular term of the court, his signed statement of the account described by Subsection (b). If the commissioners court determines that the account is in accordance with the law, it shall order the county treasurer to issue to the sheriff of the county submitting the statement a draft in an amount approved by the court.

(d) A person who is or was a prisoner in a county jail and received medical, dental, or health related services from a county or a hospital district shall be required to pay for such services when they are rendered. If such prisoner is an eligible county resident as defined in Section 61.002, Health and Safety Code, the county or hospital district providing the services has a right of subrogation to the prisoner's right of recovery from any source, limited to the cost of services provided. A prisoner, unless the prisoner fully pays for the cost of services received, shall remain obligated to reimburse the county or hospital district for any medical, dental, or health services provided, and the county or hospital district may apply for reimbursement in the manner provided by Chapter 61, Health and Safety Code. A county or hospital district shall have authority to recover the amount expended in a civil action.

(Enacted by Acts 1985, 69th Leg., ch. 269 (S.B. 854), § 1, effective September 1, 1985; am. Acts 1987, 70th Leg., ch. 1010 (H.B. 2308), § 1, effective June 19, 1987; am. Acts 1991, 72nd Leg., ch. 14 (S.B. 404), § 284(19), effective September 1, 1991; am. Acts 1991, 72nd Leg., ch. 434 (H.B. 1652), § 1, effective August 26, 1991; am. Acts 1995, 74th Leg., ch. 76 (S.B. 959), § 3.22, effective September 1, 1995.)

## Art. 104.003. State Payment of Certain Prosecution Costs.

(a) In a prosecution of a criminal offense or delinquent conduct committed on property owned or operated by or under contract with the Texas Department of Criminal Justice or the Texas Youth Commission, or committed by or against a person in the custody of the department or commission while the person is performing a duty away from department or commission property, the state shall reimburse the county for expenses incurred by the county, in an amount that the court determines to be reasonable, for payment of:

(1) salaries and expenses of foreign language interpreters and interpreters for deaf persons whose services are necessary to the prosecution;

(2) consultation fees of experts whose assistance is directly related to the prosecution;

(3) travel expenses for witnesses;

(4) expenses for the food, lodging, and compensation of jurors;

(5) compensation of witnesses;

(6) the cost of preparation of a statement of facts and a transcript of the trial for purposes of appeal;

(7) if the death of a person is an element of the offense, expenses of an inquest relating to the death;

(8) food, lodging, and travel expenses incurred by the prosecutor's staff during travel essential to the prosecution of the offense;

(9) court reporter's fees; and

(10) the cost of special security officers.

(b) If there is a change of venue, the court may, in its discretion, determine that a special prosecutor should be hired for the prosecution of an offense described in Section (a), and the state shall reimburse the county for the salary and expenses of the special prosecutor if the court determines that the hiring of the special prosecutor was reasonable and necessary for effective prosecution. The amount of reimbursement may not exceed an amount that the court determines to be reasonable.

(c) The court shall certify the amount of reimbursement for expenses under Sections (a) and (b) on presentation by the county of an itemized and verified receipt for those expenses.

(d) The state shall reimburse the county for expenses incurred by the county for the investigation of an offense described in Section (a), whether or not the investigation results in the prosecution of an offense, and shall reimburse the county for reasonable operational expenses of the special prison prosecution unit, including educational activities for the staff and general expenses relating to its investigative and prosecutorial duties.

(e) The court shall certify the amount of reimbursement for expenses under Sections (a) and (b) to the comptroller. The comptroller shall issue a warrant in that amount to the commissioners court of the county or, if the comptroller determines that the amount certified by the court is unreasonable, in an amount that the comptroller determines to be reasonable.

(f) The commissioners court of the county shall certify the amount of reimbursement for expenses under Section (d) to the comptroller. The comptroller shall issue a warrant in that amount to the commissioners court or, if the comptroller determines that the amount certified by the commissioners court is unreasonable, in an amount that the comptroller determines to be reasonable.

(g) Notwithstanding any other provision of this article, the expenses submitted by the county for reimbursement may not exceed the amount the county would pay for the same activity or service, if that activity or service was not reimbursed by the state. The county judge shall certify compliance with this section on request by the comptroller.

(Enacted by Acts 1989, 71st Leg., ch. 2 (S.B. 221), § 5.06(a), effective August 28, 1989; am. Acts 1989, 71st Leg., ch. 461 (H.B. 1879), § 1, effective June 14, 1989; am. Acts 1991, 72nd Leg., ch. 14 (S.B. 404), § 284(60), effective September 1, 1991; am. Acts 2007, 80th Leg., ch. 263 (S.B. 103), § 3, effective June 8, 2007.)

## Art. 104.004. Extraordinary Costs of Prosecution.

(a) The criminal justice division of the governor's office may distribute money appropriated by the legislature for the purposes of this article to a county for the reimbursement of expenses incurred by the county during the fiscal year during which application is made or the fiscal year preceding the year during which application is made for the investigation or prosecution of an offense under Section 19.03, Penal Code, or an offense under the Penal Code alleged by the attorney representing the state to have been committed for a purpose or reason described by Article 42.014.

(b) For each fiscal year, the division shall distribute at least 50 percent of the money distributed under this article during that year to counties with a population of less than 50,000, except that if the total distributions applied for by those counties is less than 50 percent of the money distributed during that year, the division is only required to distribute to those counties the amount of money for which applications have been made.

(c) The division may adopt a budget and rules for the distribution of money under this article.

(d) All money distributed to a county under this article and its expenditure by the county are subject to audit by the state auditor.

(Enacted by Acts 1999, 76th Leg., ch. 664 (H.B. 424), § 1, effective September 1, 1999; am. Acts 2001, 77th Leg., ch. 85 (H.B. 587), § 2.01, effective September 1, 2001.)

# TRANSPORTATION CODE

Transportation

# TITLE 3

# AVIATION

## CHAPTER 24
## OPERATION OF AIRCRAFT

## SUBCHAPTER B
## OTHER FEDERAL REQUIREMENTS REGARDING AIRCRAFT

### Sec. 24.011. Failure to Register Aircraft; Offense.

(a) A person commits an offense if the person operates or navigates an aircraft that the person knows is not properly registered under Federal Aviation Administration aircraft registration regulations, 14 C.F.R. Part 47, as those regulations existed on September 1, 1985.

(b) An offense under Subsection (a) is a felony of the third degree.

(Enacted by Acts 1995, 74th Leg., ch. 165 (S.B. 971), § 1, effective September 1, 1995.)

### Sec. 24.012. Aircraft Identification Numbers; Offense.

(a) The failure to have the aircraft identification numbers clearly displayed on an aircraft in compliance with federal aviation regulations is probable cause for a peace officer to further inspect the aircraft to determine the identity of the owner of the aircraft.

(b) A peace officer may inspect an aircraft under Subsection (a) if the aircraft is located on public property or on private property if the officer has the consent of the property owner.

(c) A person commits an offense if the person operates an aircraft that the person knows does not have aircraft identification numbers that comply with federal aviation regulations.

(d) An offense under Subsection (c) is a felony of the third degree.

(e) In this section, "federal aviation regulations" means the regulations adopted by the Federal Aviation Administration regarding identification and registration marking, 14 C.F.R. Part 45, as those regulations existed on September 1, 1985, except a regulation in existence on September 1, 1985, that is inconsistent with a regulation adopted after that date.

(Enacted by Acts 1995, 74th Leg., ch. 165 (S.B. 971), § 1, effective September 1, 1995.)

### Sec. 24.013. Aircraft Fuel Containers; Offense.

(a) A person commits an offense if the person operates or intends to operate an aircraft equipped with:

(1) a fuel container that the person knows does not conform to federal aviation regulations or that has not been approved by the Federal Aviation Administration by inspection or special permit; or

(2) a pipe, hose, or auxiliary pump that is used or intended for transferring fuel to the primary fuel system of an aircraft from a fuel container that the person knows does not conform to federal aviation regulations or that has not been approved by the Federal Aviation Administration by inspection or special permit.

(b) An offense under Subsection (a) is a felony of the third degree.

(c) A peace officer may seize an aircraft equipped with a fuel container that is the subject of an offense under Subsection (a).

(d) An aircraft seized under Subsection (c) may be forfeited to the Department of Public Safety in the same manner as property subject to forfeiture under Article 18.18, Code of Criminal Procedure.

(e) An aircraft forfeited under Subsection (d) is subject to Chapter 2205, Government Code.

(f) In this section:

(1) "Federal aviation regulations" means the following regulations adopted by the Federal Aviation Administration as those regulations existed on September 1, 1985, except a regulation in existence on September 1, 1985, that is inconsistent with a regulation adopted after that date:

(A) certification procedures for products and parts, 14 C.F.R. Part 21;

(B) maintenance, preventive maintenance, rebuilding, and alteration regulations, 14 C.F.R. Part 43; and

(C) general operating and flight rules, 14 C.F.R. Part 91.

(2) "Operate" means to use, cause to use, or authorize to use an aircraft for air navigation and includes:

(A) the piloting of an aircraft, with or without the right of legal control;

(B) the taxiing of an aircraft before takeoff or after landing; and

(C) the postflight or preflight inspection or starting of the engine of an aircraft.

(Enacted by Acts 1995, 74th Leg., ch. 165 (S.B. 971), § 1, effective September 1, 1995.)

### SUBCHAPTER C
### USE OF PUBLIC ROADS BY AIRCRAFT

### Sec. 24.021. Taking Off, Landing, or Maneuvering Aircraft on Highways, Roads, or Streets; Offense.

(a) A person commits an offense if the person takes off, lands, or maneuvers an aircraft, whether heavier or lighter than air, on a public highway, road, or street except:

(1) when necessary to prevent serious injury to a person or property;

(2) during or within a reasonable time after an emergency; or

(3) as provided by Section 24.022.

(b) An offense under Subsection (a) is a misdemeanor punishable by a fine of not less than $25 and not more than $200.

(c) The procedure prescribed by Section 543.003 applies to a violation of this section.

(Enacted by Acts 1995, 74th Leg., ch. 165 (S.B. 971), § 1, effective September 1, 1995; am. Acts 1997, 75th Leg., ch. 165 (S.B. 898), § 30.04, effective September 1, 1997.)

### Sec. 24.022.  Use of Aircraft on County Roads.

(a) A commissioners court of a county may enact ordinances to ensure the safe use of county roads by aircraft. An ordinance may:

(1) limit the kinds of aircraft that may use the roads;

(2) establish the procedure that a pilot shall follow before using a road, including requiring the pilot to furnish persons with flags at both ends of the road to be used; or

(3) establish other requirements considered necessary for the safe use of the roads by aircraft.

(b) A pilot who follows the ordinances adopted under Subsection (a):

(1) may land or take off in the aircraft on a county road; and

(2) is not subject to the traffic laws of this state during the landing or takeoff.

(Enacted by Acts 1995, 74th Leg., ch. 165 (S.B. 971), § 1, effective September 1, 1995.)

# TITLE 5
# RAILROADS

## SUBTITLE Z
## MISCELLANEOUS PROVISIONS

## CHAPTER 192
## ENGINEER'S OPERATOR PERMIT AND TRAIN OPERATOR PERMIT

### Sec. 192.001.  Issuance of Permit.

(a) A railroad company shall issue an engineer's operator permit to each person whom the company employs to operate or permits to operate a railroad locomotive in this state.

(b) A railroad company shall issue a train operator permit to each person:

(1) whom the company employs to operate or permits to operate a train in this state; and

(2) who has not been issued an engineer's operator permit.

(Enacted by Acts 2011, 82nd Leg., ch. 91 (S.B. 1303), § 24.101, effective September 1, 2011.)

### Sec. 192.002.  Permit Required.

(a) A person operating a railroad locomotive in this state shall have in the person's immediate possession an engineer's operator permit issued under this chapter.

(b) A person operating a train in this state, other than a person issued a permit under Section 192.001(a), shall have in the person's immediate possession a train operator permit issued under this chapter.

(Enacted by Acts 2011, 82nd Leg., ch. 91 (S.B. 1303), § 24.101, effective September 1, 2011.)

### Sec. 192.003.  Form of Permit.

A permit issued under this chapter must include the permit holder's name, address, physical description, photograph, and date of birth.

(Enacted by Acts 2011, 82nd Leg., ch. 91 (S.B. 1303), § 24.101, effective September 1, 2011.)

### Sec. 192.004.  Proof of Identification.

If a peace officer requires a person to show proof of identification in connection with the person's operation of a railroad locomotive or train, the person:

(1) shall display the person's permit issued under this chapter; and

(2) may not be required to display a driver's license issued under Chapter 521 or commercial driver's license issued under Chapter 522.

(Enacted by Acts 2011, 82nd Leg., ch. 91 (S.B. 1303), § 24.101, effective September 1, 2011.)

### Sec. 192.005.  Record of Accident or Violation.

If a person operating a railroad locomotive or train is involved in an accident with another train or a motor vehicle or is arrested for violation of a law relating to the person's operation of a railroad locomotive or train:

(1) the number of or other identifying information on the person's driver's license or com-

mercial driver's license may not be included in any report of the accident or violation; and

(2) the person's involvement in the accident or violation may not be recorded in the person's individual driving record maintained by the Department of Public Safety.

(Enacted by Acts 2011, 82nd Leg., ch. 91 (S.B. 1303), § 24.101, effective September 1, 2011.)

# TITLE 6
# ROADWAYS

## SUBTITLE A
## TEXAS DEPARTMENT OF TRANSPORTATION

## CHAPTER 201
## GENERAL PROVISIONS AND ADMINISTRATION

### Subchapter K. Road and Highway Use; Signs

## SUBCHAPTER K
## ROAD AND HIGHWAY USE; SIGNS

### Sec. 201.901. Prohibiting Use of Highway or Road.

(a) The commission may prohibit the use of any part of a highway or road under the control of the department by any vehicle that will unduly damage the highway or road when:

(1) because of wet weather or recent construction or repairs, the highway or road cannot be safely used without probable serious damage to it; or

(2) a bridge or culvert on the highway or road is unsafe.

(b) Before prohibiting the use of a highway or road under this section, the commission shall post notices that state the maximum load permitted and the time the use of the highway or road is prohibited. The notices must be posted at locations that enable drivers to detour to avoid the restricted highway or road.

(c) The commission may not prohibit the use of a highway or road under this section until a detour has been provided.

(d) If the owner or operator of a vehicle that is prohibited from using a highway or road under this section is aggrieved by the prohibition, the person may file with the county judge of the county in which the restricted highway or road is located a written complaint that sets forth the nature of the grievance. On the filing of the complaint the county judge immediately shall set the issue for a hearing to be held not later than the third day after the date on which the complaint is filed. The county judge shall give to the commission written notice of the day and purpose of each hearing.

(e) The county judge shall hear testimony offered by the parties. On conclusion of the hearing, the county judge shall sustain, revoke, or modify the commission's decision on the restriction. The county judge's judgment is final as to the issues raised.

(f) A person who violates a prohibition established under this section before or after it is approved by the county judge under Subsection (e) commits an offense. An offense under this section is a misdemeanor punishable by a fine not to exceed $200.

(Enacted by Acts 1995, 74th Leg., ch. 165 (S.B. 971), § 1, effective September 1, 1995.)

### Sec. 201.902. Road Use by Bicyclists.

(a) The department shall designate:

(1) a statewide bicycle coordinator; and

(2) a bicycle coordinator in each regional office.

(b) A bicycle coordinator shall assist the department in developing rules and plans to enhance the use of the state highway system by bicyclists.

(c) The commission shall adopt rules relating to use of roads in the state highway system by bicyclists, including provisions for:

(1) the specific duties of the statewide bicycle coordinator and the regional bicycle coordinators;

(2) obtaining comments from bicyclists on:

**Transportation**

(A) a highway project that might affect bicycle use;

(B) the use of a highway for bicycling events; and

(C) department policies affecting bicycle use of state highways;

(3) the consideration of acceptable national bicycle design, construction, and maintenance standards on a project in an area with significant bicycle use; and

(4) any other matter the commission determines necessary to enhance the use of the state highway system by bicyclists.

(d) A rule adopted under this section may not be inconsistent with Chapter 551.

(Enacted by Acts 1995, 74th Leg., ch. 165 (S.B. 971), § 1, effective September 1, 1995.)

### Sec. 201.903.  Classification, Designation, and Marking of Highways.

(a) The department may classify, designate, and mark state highways in this state.

(b) The department may provide a uniform system of marking and signing state highways under the control of the state. The system must correlate with and, to the extent possible, conform to the system adopted in other states.

(Enacted by Acts 1995, 74th Leg., ch. 165 (S.B. 971), § 1, effective September 1, 1995.)

### Sec. 201.904.  Speed Signs.

The department shall erect and maintain on the highways and roads of this state appropriate signs that show the maximum lawful speed for commercial motor vehicles, truck tractors, truck trailers, truck semitrailers, and motor vehicles engaged in the business of transporting passengers for compensation or hire (buses).

(Enacted by Acts 1995, 74th Leg., ch. 165 (S.B. 971), § 1, effective September 1, 1995.)

### SUBCHAPTER L
### ELECTRONIC ISSUANCE OF LICENSES

### Sec. 201.931.  Definitions.

In this subchapter:

(1) "Digital signature" means an electronic identifier intended by the person using it to have the same force and effect as the use of a manual signature.

(2) "License" includes:

(A) a permit issued by the department that authorizes the operation of a vehicle and its load or a combination of vehicles and load exceeding size or weight limitations; and

(B) a license or permit for outdoor advertising issued under Chapter 391 or 394.

(Enacted by Acts 1997, 75th Leg., ch. 1171 (S.B. 370), § 1.15, effective September 1, 1997; am. Acts 2003, 78th Leg., ch. 1276 (H.B. 3507), § 14A.819, effective September 1, 2003; am. Acts 2009, 81st Leg., ch. 933 (H.B. 3097), § 2A.02, effective September 1, 2009.)

### Sec. 201.932.  Application for and Issuance of License.

(a) The commission may by rule provide for the filing of a license application and the issuance of a license by electronic means.

(b) The commission may limit applicant eligibility under Subsection (a) if the rules include reasonable eligibility criteria.

(Enacted by Acts 1997, 75th Leg., ch. 1171 (S.B. 370), § 1.15, effective September 1, 1997.)

### Sec. 201.933.  Digital Signature.

(a) A license application received by the department is considered signed if a digital signature is transmitted with the application and intended by the applicant to authenticate the license in accordance with Subsection (b).

(b) The department may only accept a digital signature used to authenticate a license application under procedures that:

(1) comply with any applicable rules of another state agency having jurisdiction over department use or acceptance of a digital signature; and

(2) provide for consideration of factors that may affect a digital signature's reliability, including whether a digital signature is:

(A) unique to the person using it;

(B) capable of independent verification;

(C) under the sole control of the person using it; and

(D) transmitted in a manner that will make it infeasible to change the data in the communication or digital signature without invalidating the digital signature.

(Enacted by Acts 1997, 75th Leg., ch. 1171 (S.B. 370), § 1.15, effective September 1, 1997.)

### Sec. 201.934.  Payment of Fees.

The commission may adopt rules regarding the method of payment of a fee for a license issued under this subchapter. The rules may authorize the use of electronic funds transfer or a valid

credit card issued by a financial institution chartered by a state or the federal government or by a nationally recognized credit organization approved by the department. The rules may require the payment of a discount or service charge for a credit card payment in addition to the fee.
(Enacted by Acts 1997, 75th Leg., ch. 1171 (S.B. 370), § 1.15, effective September 1, 1997.)

## SUBTITLE B
## STATE HIGHWAY SYSTEM

## CHAPTER 224
## ACQUISITION, CONSTRUCTION, AND MAINTENANCE

### SUBCHAPTER F
### CONGESTION MITIGATION PROJECTS AND FACILITIES

### Sec. 224.155. Failure or Refusal to Pay Toll; Offense [Repealed].

Repealed by Acts 2005, 79th Leg., ch. 281 (H.B. 2702), § 2.101(3), effective June 14, 2005.
(Enacted by Acts 1997, 75th Leg., ch. 1171 (S.B. 370), § 1.24, effective September 1, 1997; am. Acts 2001, 77th Leg., ch. 1246 (S.B. 454), § 1, effective September 1, 2001.)

### Sec. 224.156. Collection Fee; Notice; Offense [Repealed].

Repealed by Acts 2005, 79th Leg., ch. 281 (H.B. 2702), § 2.101(3), effective June 14, 2005.
(Enacted by Acts 1997, 75th Leg., ch. 1171 (S.B. 370), § 1.24, effective September 1, 1997; am. Acts 2001, 77th Leg., ch. 1246 (S.B. 454), § 2, effective September 1, 2001; am. Acts 2003, 78th Leg., ch. 1049 (H.B. 1208), § 7, effective June 20, 2003.)

### Sec. 224.158. Use and Return of Transponders [Repealed].

Repealed by Acts 2005, 79th Leg., ch. 281 (H.B. 2702), § 2.101(3), effective June 14, 2005.
(Enacted by Acts 1997, 75th Leg., ch. 1171 (S.B. 370), § 1.24, effective September 1, 1997; am. Acts 2001, 77th Leg., ch. 1246 (S.B. 454), § 4, effective September 1, 2001; am. Acts 2003, 78th Leg., ch. 1049 (H.B. 1208), § 8, effective June 20, 2003.)

### Sec. 224.160. Automated Enforcement Technology [Repealed].

Repealed by Acts 2005, 79th Leg., ch. 281 (H.B. 2702), § 2.101(3), effective June 14, 2005.
(Enacted by Acts 2001, 77th Leg., ch. 1246 (S.B. 454), § 5, effective September 1, 2001.)

## CHAPTER 228
## STATE HIGHWAY TOLL PROJECTS

**Subchapter B. Use and Operation of Toll Projects or Systems.**

Section
228.054.   Failure or Refusal to Pay Toll; Offense.
228.0545. Alternative Tolling Methods.

### SUBCHAPTER B
### USE AND OPERATION OF TOLL PROJECTS OR SYSTEMS.

### Sec. 228.054. Failure or Refusal to Pay Toll; Offense.

(a) Except as provided by Subsection (e) or Section 228.0545, the operator of a vehicle, other than an authorized emergency vehicle, as defined by Section 541.201, that is driven or towed through a toll collection facility shall pay the proper toll. The exemption from payment of a toll for an authorized emergency vehicle applies regardless of whether the vehicle is:

(1) responding to an emergency;

(2) displaying a flashing light; or

(3) marked as an emergency vehicle.

(b) The operator of a vehicle who drives or tows a vehicle through a toll collection facility and does not pay the proper toll commits an offense.

(c) An offense under this section is a misdemeanor punishable by a fine not to exceed $250.

(d) In this section, "authorized emergency vehicle" has the meaning assigned by Section 541.201.

(e) Notwithstanding Subsection (a), the department may waive the requirement of the payment of a toll or may authorize the payment of a reduced toll for any vehicle or class of vehicles.
(Enacted by Acts 1995, 74th Leg., ch. 165 (S.B. 971), § 1, effective September 1, 1995; am. Acts 1995, 74th Leg., ch. 872 (S.B. 1360), § 2.15, effective September 1, 1995; am. Acts 2001, 77th Leg., ch. 1246 (S.B. 454), § 6, effective September 1, 2001; am. Acts 2005, 79th Leg., ch. 281 (H.B. 2702), § 2.41, effective June 14, 2005 (renumbered from Sec. 361.252); am. Acts 2005, 79th Leg., ch. 23 (S.B. 129), effective September 1, 2005; am. Acts 2007, 80th Leg., ch. 258 (S.B. 11), § 4.01, effective September 1, 2007; am. Acts

2011, 82nd Leg., ch. 641 (S.B. 959), § 2, effective June 17, 2011.)

### Sec. 228.0545. Alternative Tolling Methods.

(a) As an alternative to requiring payment of a toll at the time a vehicle is driven or towed through a toll collection facility, the department may use video billing or other tolling methods to permit the registered owner of the vehicle to pay the toll at a later date.

(b) The department may use automated enforcement technology authorized under Section 228.058 to identify the registered owner of the vehicle for purposes of billing, collection, and enforcement activities.

(c) The department shall send by first class mail to the registered owner of the vehicle a written notice of the total amount due. The notice must specify the date, which may not be earlier than the 30th day after the date the notice is mailed, by which the amount due must be paid. The registered owner shall pay the amount due on or before the date specified in the notice.

(d) The department shall send the notice required under Subsection (c) and subsequent notices to:

(1) the registered owner's address as shown in the vehicle registration records of the Texas Department of Motor Vehicles or the analogous department or agency of another state or country; or

(2) an alternate address provided by the owner or derived through other reliable means.
(Enacted by Acts 2011, 82nd Leg., ch. 641 (S.B. 959), § 3, effective June 17, 2011.)

## SUBTITLE C
## COUNTY ROADS AND BRIDGES

## CHAPTER 251
## GENERAL COUNTY AUTHORITY RELATING TO ROADS AND BRIDGES

## SUBCHAPTER A
## GENERAL PROVISIONS

### Sec. 251.011. Detour Roads.

(a) The commissioners court of a county shall establish detour roads for the convenience of the public when a county road that is not part of the state highway system must be closed to traffic for road construction. When a county detour road is in use, the county has the same authority over the road as over an established public road.

(b) The commissioners court shall:

(1) post all signs necessary for the convenience and guidance of the public at each end of a county detour road; and

(2) maintain a county detour road so that it is reasonably adequate for normal traffic requirements.
(Enacted by Acts 1995, 74th Leg., ch. 165 (S.B. 971), § 1, effective September 1, 1995.)

### Sec. 251.013. Road Names and Address Numbers.

(a) The commissioners court of a county by order may adopt uniform standards for naming public roads located wholly or partly in unincorporated areas of the county and for assigning address numbers to property located in unincorporated areas of the county. The standards apply to any new public road that is established.

(b) The commissioners court of a county by order may adopt a name for a public road located wholly or partly in an unincorporated area of the county and may assign address numbers to property located in an unincorporated area of the county for which there is no established address system.

(b-1) The commissioners court of a county by order may:

(1) adopt standards and specifications for the design and installation of address number signs to identify properties located in unincor-

porated areas of the county, including standards or specifications as to sign size, material, longevity, ability to be seen and to reflect light, and any other factor the commissioners court considers necessary or appropriate; and

(2) require the owners or occupants of properties in unincorporated areas of the county to:

(A) obtain address number signs that comply with the standards and specifications adopted under Subdivision (1); and

(B) install and maintain those signs at the locations and in the manner required by those standards and specifications.

(c) If an order adopted under this section conflicts with a municipal ordinance, the municipal ordinance prevails in the territory in which it is effective.

(d) A commissioners court may adopt an order under this section only after conducting a public hearing on the proposed order. The court shall give public notice of the hearing at least two weeks before the date of the hearing.

(e) A person who knowingly fails or refuses to comply with an order of a commissioners court under Subsection (b-1)(2) commits an offense. An offense under this subsection is a Class C misdemeanor.

(Enacted by Acts 1995, 74th Leg., ch. 165 (S.B. 971), § 1, effective September 1, 1995; am. Acts 2009, 81st Leg., ch. 688 (H.B. 2665), § 1, effective June 19, 2009.)

## Sec. 251.016.  General County Authority over Roads, Highways, and Bridges.

The commissioners court of a county may exercise general control over all roads, highways, and bridges in the county.

(Enacted by Acts 1999, 76th Leg., ch. 62 (S.B. 1368), § 13.11(b), effective September 1, 1999.)

## Sec. 251.0165.  Control of Access Within Certain Counties.

(a) Except as limited by Section 203.032, a county with a population of 3.3 million or more or a county adjacent to a county with a population of 3.3 million or more, by resolution or order, may:

(1) deny access to or from a controlled access highway within the county and outside the limits of a municipality, including a state highway, from or to adjoining public or private real property and from or to a public or private way intersecting the highway, except at specific locations designated by the county; and

(2) designate locations on a controlled access highway within the county and outside the limits of a municipality, including a state highway, at which access to or from the highway is permitted and determine the type and extent of access permitted at each location.

(b) This section does not apply to the placement of or access to a utility facility in or near a highway right-of-way.

(Enacted by Acts 2007, 80th Leg., ch. 1400 (H.B. 2991), § 1, effective June 15, 2007.)

## SUBCHAPTER E
## COUNTY TRAFFIC REGULATIONS

## Sec. 251.151.  Authority of Commissioners Court.

The commissioners court of a county may regulate traffic on a county road or on real property owned by the county that is under the jurisdiction of the commissioners court.

(Enacted by Acts 1995, 74th Leg., ch. 165 (S.B. 971), § 1, effective September 1, 1995.)

## Sec. 251.152.  Public Hearing Required.

(a) Except as provided by Section 251.159, before the commissioners court may issue a traffic regulation under this subchapter, the commissioners court must hold a public hearing on the proposed regulation.

(b) The commissioners court shall publish notice of the hearing in a newspaper of general circulation in the county. The notice must be published not later than the seventh or earlier than the 30th day before the date of the hearing.

(Enacted by Acts 1995, 74th Leg., ch. 165 (S.B. 971), § 1, effective September 1, 1995.)

## Sec. 251.153.  Load Limits on County Roads and Bridges.

(a) The commissioners court of a county may establish load limits for any county road or bridge in the manner prescribed by Section 621.301.

(b) The commissioners court may authorize a county traffic officer, sheriff, deputy sheriff, constable, or deputy constable to weigh a vehicle to ascertain whether the vehicle's load exceeds the limit prescribed by the commissioners court.

(Enacted by Acts 1995, 74th Leg., ch. 165 (S.B. 971), § 1, effective September 1, 1995; am. Acts 2001, 77th Leg., ch. 1227 (S.B. 220), § 1, effective September 1, 2001.)

Transportation

## Sec. 251.154. Maximum Reasonable and Prudent Speeds on County Roads.

(a) The commissioners court of a county, by order entered on the minutes of the court, may determine and set a maximum reasonable and prudent speed for a vehicle travelling on any segment of a county road, including a road or highway intersection, railroad grade crossing, curve, or hill.

(b) In determining the maximum reasonable and prudent speed, the commissioners court shall consider all circumstances on the affected segment of the road, including the width and condition of the road surface and the usual traffic on the road.

(c) The maximum reasonable and prudent speed set by the commissioners court under this section may be lower than the maximum speed set by law for a vehicle travelling on a public highway.

(d) A speed limit set by the commissioners court under this section is effective when appropriate signs giving notice of the speed limit are installed on the affected segment of the county road.

(Enacted by Acts 1995, 74th Leg., ch. 165 (S.B. 971), § 1, effective September 1, 1995.)

## Sec. 251.155. Restricted Traffic Zones.

(a) The commissioners court of a county may adopt regulations establishing a system of traffic control devices in restricted traffic zones on property described by Section 251.151.

(b) A system of traffic control devices adopted under this section must conform to the manual and specifications of the Texas Department of Transportation.

(c) The commissioners court by order entered on its minutes may install and maintain on property to which this section applies any traffic signal light, stop sign, or no-parking sign that the court considers necessary for public safety.

(Enacted by Acts 1995, 74th Leg., ch. 165 (S.B. 971), § 1, effective September 1, 1995.)

## Sec. 251.156. Parking Restrictions.

(a) The commissioners court of a county by order may have signs installed that prohibit or restrict the stopping, standing, or parking of a vehicle in a restricted traffic zone on property described by Section 251.151, if in the opinion of the court the stopping, standing, or parking:

(1) is dangerous to those using the road or property; or

(2) will unduly interfere with:

(A) the free movement of traffic; or

(B) the necessary control or use of the property.

(b) The commissioners court of a county by order may provide that in a prosecution for an offense involving the stopping, standing, or parking of an unattended motor vehicle in a restricted traffic zone on property described by Section 251.151 it is presumed that the registered owner of the vehicle is the person who stopped, stood, or parked the vehicle at the time and place the offense occurred.

(Enacted by Acts 1995, 74th Leg., ch. 165 (S.B. 971), § 1, effective September 1, 1995; am. Acts 2001, 77th Leg., ch. 1080 (H.B. 2173), § 1, effective September 1, 2001.)

## Sec. 251.157. Prohibiting Use of Road.

(a) In this section, "road supervisor" means a person authorized to supervise roads in a county or in a district or precinct of a county.

(b) A road supervisor may prohibit the use of a road or a section of a road under the supervisor's control by any vehicle that will unduly damage the road when:

(1) because of wet weather or recent construction or repairs, the road cannot be safely used without probable serious damage to it; or

(2) a bridge or culvert on the road is unsafe.

(c) Before prohibiting the use of a road under this section, the road supervisor shall post notices that state the maximum load permitted and the time the use of the road is prohibited. The notices must be posted at locations that enable drivers to detour to avoid the restricted road.

(d) The road supervisor may not prohibit the use of a road under this section until a detour has been provided.

(e) If the owner or operator of a vehicle that is prohibited from using a road under this section is aggrieved by the prohibition, the person may file with the county judge of the county in which the restricted road is located a written complaint that sets forth the nature of the grievance. On the filing of the complaint the county judge promptly shall set the issue for a hearing to be held not later than the third day after the date on which the complaint is filed. The county judge shall give to the road supervisor written notice of the date and purpose of each hearing.

(f) The county judge shall hear testimony offered by the parties. On conclusion of the hearing, the county judge shall sustain, revoke, or modify the road supervisor's decision on the restriction. The county judge's judgment is final as to the issues raised.

(Enacted by Acts 1995, 74th Leg., ch. 165 (S.B. 971), § 1, effective September 1, 1995.)

### Sec. 251.158. Temporary Use of County Road for Festival or Civic Event.

(a) The commissioners court of a county by order may permit the temporary use of a county road located in an unincorporated area of the county for a civic event, including a festival.

(b) The court by order shall establish procedures for the temporary diversion of traffic from the road being used for the event.

(Enacted by Acts 1995, 74th Leg., ch. 165 (S.B. 971), § 1, effective September 1, 1995.)

### Sec. 251.159. Delegation of Commissioners' Authority.

(a) This section applies only to a county with a population of more than 78,000.

(b) The commissioners court of a county may delegate to the county engineer or other county employee any function of the commissioners court under this subchapter, except as provided by Subsection (e). An action of the county engineer or other county employee under this section has the same effect as if the action were an action of the commissioners court.

(c) Before issuing a traffic regulation under this subchapter, the commissioners court, in lieu of publishing notice required by a law other than this subchapter, may give notice of the proposed regulation by posting a conspicuous sign in any location to be affected by the regulation.

(d) The commissioners court is not required to hold a public hearing on the proposed traffic regulation unless a resident of the county requests a public hearing. The request must be in writing and made before the eighth day after the later of:

(1) the date that the sign is posted; or

(2) the date that the notice under Section 251.152 is published.

(e) If a public hearing is requested, the commissioners court may not delegate the duty to hold the hearing.

(Enacted by Acts 1995, 74th Leg., ch. 165 (S.B. 971), § 1, effective September 1, 1995; am. Acts

1999, 76th Leg., ch. 885 (H.B. 2034), § 1, effective June 18, 1999; am. Acts 2007, 80th Leg., ch. 780 (H.B. 3955), § 1, effective September 1, 2007.)

### Sec. 251.160. Liability of Owner or Operator for Road Damage.

(a) A person who operates or moves a vehicle or other object on a public road or bridge and the owner of the vehicle or other object are jointly and severally liable for damage sustained by the road or bridge as a result of the negligent operation or moving of the vehicle or other object or as a result of the operation or movement of the vehicle at a time prohibited by the officials with authority over the road.

(b) The county judge by appropriate legal action may recover damages for which liability is provided by this section. The county attorney shall represent the county in an action under this subsection. Damages collected under this subsection are for the use of the county to benefit the damaged road or bridge.

(Enacted by Acts 1995, 74th Leg., ch. 165 (S.B. 971), § 1, effective September 1, 1995.)

### Sec. 251.161. Violations of Subchapter; Offense.

(a) A person commits a misdemeanor offense if the person:

(1) stops, stands, or parks a vehicle in violation of a restriction stated on a sign installed under Section 251.156;

(2) defaces, injures, knocks down, or removes a sign or traffic control device installed under an order of the commissioners court of a county issued under this subchapter;

(3) operates a motor vehicle in violation of an order of the commissioners court entered under this subchapter; or

(4) otherwise violates this subchapter.

(b) An offense under this section is punishable by a fine not to exceed $200.

(c) If conduct that constitutes an offense under this section also constitutes an offense under any other law, the actor may be prosecuted under this section or the other law.

(d) [Repealed by Acts 2007, 80th Leg., ch. 806 (S.B. 1127), § 2, effective September 1, 2007.]

(Enacted by Acts 1995, 74th Leg., ch. 165 (S.B. 971), § 1, effective September 1, 1995; am. Acts 2007, 80th Leg., ch. 806 (S.B. 1127), §§ 1, 2, effective September 1, 2007.)

Transportation

## SUBTITLE D
## ROAD LAWS RELATING TO PARTICULAR COUNTIES

## CHAPTER 284
## CAUSEWAYS, BRIDGES, TUNNELS, TURNPIKES, FERRIES, AND HIGHWAYS IN CERTAIN COUNTIES

### Subchapter C. Construction and Operation

### Subchapter D. Unauthorized Use of Toll Roads in Certain Counties

## SUBCHAPTER C
## CONSTRUCTION AND OPERATION

### Sec. 284.069. Tolls and Charges.

If bonds under this chapter are payable in whole or in part from project revenue, the county shall impose tolls and charges that are, together with other money or revenues available for the project, including ad valorem tax, sufficient to:

(1) pay the maintenance and operating expenses of the project;

(2) pay the principal of, premium of, if any, and interest on the bonds when due;

(3) establish a reserve for payment of bond principal, premium, and interest; and

(4) establish an adequate fund for project depreciation and replacement.

(Enacted by Acts 1995, 74th Leg., ch. 165 (S.B. 971), § 1, effective September 1, 1995.)

### Sec. 284.070. Nonpayment of Toll; Offense.

(a) A person commits an offense if the person:

(1) operates a vehicle on a county project; and

(2) fails or refuses to pay a toll imposed under Section 284.069.

(b) An offense under this section is a misdemeanor punishable by a fine not to exceed $100.

(c) The county may take and retain possession of a vehicle operated in violation of Subsection (a) until the amount of the toll and all charges in connection with the toll are paid.

(d) In a county with a population over 2.8 million, an offense under this section may be prosecuted in any precinct in the county in which the offense was committed.

(e) An authorized emergency vehicle, as defined by Section 541.201, is exempt from payment of a toll imposed under this chapter regardless of whether the vehicle is:

(1) responding to an emergency;

(2) displaying a flashing light; or

(3) marked as an emergency vehicle.

(Enacted by Acts 1995, 74th Leg., ch. 165 (S.B. 971), § 1, effective September 1, 1995; am. Acts 1997, 75th Leg., ch. 1107 (H.B. 2502), § 1, effective September 1, 1997; am. Acts 2007, 80th Leg., ch. 258 (S.B. 11), § 4.02, effective September 1, 2007.)

### Sec. 284.0701. Administrative Costs; Notice; Offense.

(a) In the event of an offense committed under Section 284.070, on issuance of a written notice of nonpayment, the registered owner of the nonpaying vehicle is liable for the payment of both the proper toll and an administrative cost.

(b) The county may impose and collect the administrative cost so as to recover the expense of collecting the unpaid toll, not to exceed $100. The county shall send a written notice of nonpayment to the registered owner of the vehicle at that owner's address as shown in the vehicle registration records of the Texas Department of Motor Vehicles by first-class mail not later than the 30th day after the date of the alleged failure to pay and may require payment not sooner than the 30th day after the date the notice was mailed. The registered owner shall pay a separate toll and administrative cost for each event of nonpayment under Section 284.070.

(c) The registered owner of a vehicle for which the proper toll was not paid who is mailed a written notice of nonpayment under Subsection (b) and fails to pay the proper toll and administrative cost within the time specified by the notice of nonpayment commits an offense. Each failure to pay a toll or administrative cost under this subsection is a separate offense.

(d) It is an exception to the application of Subsection (a) or (c) if the registered owner of the vehicle is a lessor of the vehicle and not later than the 30th day after the date the notice of nonpayment is mailed provides to the authority:

(1) a copy of the rental, lease, or other contract document covering the vehicle on the date of the nonpayment under Section 284.070, with the name and address of the lessee clearly legible; or

(2) electronic data, other than a photocopy or scan of a rental or lease contract, that contains the information required under Sections 521.460(c)(1), (2), and (3) covering the vehicle on the date of the nonpayment under Section 284.070.

(d-1) If the lessor provides the required information within the period prescribed under Subsection (d), the authority may send a notice of nonpayment to the lessee at the address provided under Subsection (d) by first class mail before the 30th day after the date of receipt of the required information from the lessor. The lessee of the vehicle for which the proper toll was not paid who is mailed a written notice of nonpayment under this subsection and fails to pay the proper toll and administrative cost within the time specified by the notice of nonpayment commits an offense. The lessee shall pay a separate toll and administrative cost for each event of nonpayment. Each failure to pay a toll or administrative cost under this subsection is a separate offense.

(e) It is an exception to the application of Subsection (a) or (c) if the registered owner of the vehicle transferred ownership of the vehicle to another person before the event of nonpayment under Section 284.070 occurred, submitted written notice of the transfer to the Texas Department of Motor Vehicles in accordance with Section 520.023, and before the 30th day after the date the notice of nonpayment is mailed, provides to the county the name and address of the person to whom the vehicle was transferred. If the former owner of the vehicle provides the required information within the period prescribed, the county may send a notice of nonpayment to the person to whom ownership of the vehicle was transferred at the address provided by the former owner by first-class mail before the 30th day after

the date of receipt of the required information from the former owner. The subsequent owner of the vehicle for which the proper toll was not paid who is mailed a written notice of nonpayment under this subsection and fails to pay the proper toll and administrative cost within the time specified by the notice of nonpayment commits an offense. The subsequent owner shall pay a separate toll and administrative cost for each event of nonpayment under Section 284.070. Each failure to pay a toll or administrative cost under this subsection is a separate offense.

(f) An offense under this section is a misdemeanor punishable by a fine not to exceed $250.

(g) The court in which a person is convicted of an offense under this section shall also collect the proper toll and administrative cost and forward the toll and cost to the county.

(h) In this section, "registered owner" means the owner of a vehicle as shown on the vehicle registration records of the Texas Department of Motor Vehicles or the analogous department or agency of another state or country.

(Enacted by Acts 2003, 78th Leg., ch. 372 (S.B. 1464), § 1, effective September 1, 2003; am. Acts 2009, 81st Leg., ch. 918 (H.B. 2983), § 3, effective September 1, 2009; am. Acts 2009, 81st Leg., ch. 933 (H.B. 3097), § 2C.01, effective September 1, 2009.)

### Sec. 284.0702. Prima Facie Evidence; Defense.

(a) In the prosecution of an offense under Section 284.070 or 284.0701, proof that the vehicle was driven or towed through the toll collection facility without payment of the proper toll may be shown by a video recording, photograph, electronic recording, or other appropriate evidence, including evidence obtained by automated enforcement technology.

(b) In the prosecution of an offense under Section 284.0701(c), (d-1), or (e):

(1) a computer record of the department of the registered owner of the vehicle is prima facie evidence of its contents and that the defendant was the registered owner of the vehicle when the underlying event of nonpayment under Section 284.070 occurred; and

(2) a copy of the rental, lease, or other contract document, or the electronic data provided to the authority under Section 284.0701(d), covering the vehicle on the date of the underlying event of nonpayment under Section 284.070 is prima facie evidence of its contents

Transportation

and that the defendant was the lessee of the vehicle when the underlying event of nonpayment under Section 284.070 occurred.

(c) It is a defense to prosecution under Section 284.0701(c), (d-1), or (e) that the vehicle in question was stolen before the failure to pay the proper toll occurred and had not been recovered before the failure to pay occurred, but only if the theft was reported to the appropriate law enforcement authority before the earlier of:

(1) the occurrence of the failure to pay; or

(2) eight hours after the discovery of the theft.

(Enacted by Acts 2003, 78th Leg., ch. 372 (S.B. 1464), § 1, effective September 1, 2003; am. Acts 2009, 81st Leg., ch. 918 (H.B. 2983), § 4, effective September 1, 2009.)

## SUBCHAPTER D
## UNAUTHORIZED USE OF TOLL ROADS IN CERTAIN COUNTIES

### Sec. 284.201.  Applicability of Subchapter.

This subchapter applies only to:

(1) a county with a population of more than 3.3 million; or

(2) a county adjacent to a county with a population of more than 3.3 million.

(Enacted by Acts 1997, 75th Leg., ch. 165 (S.B. 898), § 30.18(a), effective September 1, 1997; am. Acts 2001, 77th Leg., ch. 669 (H.B. 2810), § 131, effective September 1, 2001; am. Acts 2003, 78th Leg., ch. 670 (H.B. 2384), § 1, effective June 20, 2003.)

### Sec. 284.202.  Order Prohibiting Operation of Motor Vehicle on Toll Project.

(a) The commissioners court of a county by order may prohibit the operation of a motor vehicle on a county project described by Section 284.001(3) if:

(1) an operator of the vehicle has failed to pay a required toll or charge; and

(2) the county provides the registered owner of the vehicle with notice of the unpaid toll or charge.

(b) The notice required by Subsection (a)(2) must be mailed to the registered owner of the vehicle at least 10 days before the date the prohibition takes effect.

(c) If the registered owner of the vehicle fails to pay a toll or charge not later than the 10th day after the notice under Subsection (b) is mailed,

the commissioners court by order may impose a reasonable cost for expenses associated with collecting the unpaid toll or charge.

(Enacted by Acts 1997, 75th Leg., ch. 165 (S.B. 898), § 30.18(a), effective September 1, 1997; am. Acts 2003, 78th Leg., ch. 372 (S.B. 1464), § 2, effective September 1, 2003.)

### Sec. 284.203.  Violation of Order; Offense.

(a) A person commits an offense if the person operates a motor vehicle or causes or allows the operation of a motor vehicle in violation of an order adopted under Section 284.202(a).

(b) An offense under this section is a Class C misdemeanor.

(Enacted by Acts 1997, 75th Leg., ch. 165 (S.B. 898), § 30.18(a), effective September 1, 1997.)

### Sec. 284.2031.  Civil and Criminal Enforcement Cost.

(a) A county may impose, in addition to other costs, $1 as a court cost on conviction to a defendant convicted of an offense under Section 284.070, 284.0701, or 284.203 in an action brought by the county or district attorney.

(b) In this section, a person is considered convicted if:

(1) a sentence is imposed on the person; or

(2) the court defers final disposition of the person's case.

(c) In a county with a population of 3.3 million or more, money collected under Subsection (a) shall be deposited in the county treasury in a special fund to be administered by the county attorney or district attorney. Expenditures from this fund shall be at the sole discretion of the attorney and may be used only to defray the salaries and expenses of the prosecutor's office, but in no event may the county attorney or district attorney supplement his or her own salary from this fund.

(d) In a county with a population of less than 3.3 million, money collected under Subsection (a) shall be deposited in the general fund of the county.

(Enacted by Acts 2003, 78th Leg., ch. 372 (S.B. 1464), § 3, effective September 1, 2003; am. Acts 2005, 79th Leg., ch. 963 (H.B. 1672), § 1, effective June 18, 2005.)

### Sec. 284.2032.  Additional Administrative Cost in Certain Counties.

(a) A county with a population of 3.3 million or more may impose, in addition to other costs, $1 as an administrative cost associated with collecting a toll or charge for each event of nonpayment of a required toll or charge imposed under Section 284.069.

(b) Money collected under Subsection (a) shall be deposited in the county treasury in a special fund to be administered by the county attorney. Expenditures from the fund shall be at the sole discretion of the attorney and may be used only to defray the salaries and expenses of the attorney's office, but in no event may the county attorney supplement his or her own salary from the fund. (Enacted by Acts 2005, 79th Leg., ch. 963 (H.B. 1672), § 2(a), effective September 1, 2005.)

### Sec. 284.204. Administrative Adjudication Hearing Procedure.

(a) The commissioners court of a county may adopt an administrative adjudication hearing procedure for a person who is suspected of having violated an order adopted under Section 284.202(a) on at least two separate occasions within a 12-month period.

(b) A hearing procedure adopted under Subsection (a) must provide:

(1) a period for a person charged with violating the order:

(A) to pay the toll or charge plus administrative costs authorized by Sections 284.202 and 284.2031; or

(B) to request a hearing;

(2) for appointment of one or more hearing officers with authority to administer oaths and issue orders compelling the attendance of witnesses and the production of documents; and

(3) for the amount and disposition of civil fines, costs, and fees.

(c) An order issued under Subsection (b)(2) may be enforced by a justice of the peace. (Enacted by Acts 1997, 75th Leg., ch. 165 (S.B. 898), § 30.18(a), effective September 1, 1997; am. Acts 2003, 78th Leg., ch. 372 (S.B. 1464), § 4, effective September 1, 2003.)

### Sec. 284.205. Citation or Summons.

(a) A citation or summons issued under this subchapter must:

(1) inform the recipient of the time and place of the hearing; and

(2) notify the person charged with a violation that the person has the right of a hearing without delay.

(b) The original or any copy of the summons or citation is a record kept in the ordinary course of business of the county and is rebuttable proof of the facts it contains. (Enacted by Acts 1997, 75th Leg., ch. 165 (S.B. 898), § 30.18(a), effective September 1, 1997.)

### Sec. 284.206. Administrative Hearing: Presumption; Evidence of Ownership.

(a) In an administrative adjudication hearing under this subchapter it is presumed that the registered owner of the motor vehicle that is the subject of the hearing is the person who operated or allowed the operation of the motor vehicle in violation of the order.

(b) A computer record of the department of the registered vehicle owner is prima facie evidence of its contents and that the defendant was the registered owner of the vehicle at the time the violation occurred.

(c) Proof of the violation of the order may be shown by a video recording, photograph, electronic recording, or other appropriate evidence, including evidence obtained by automated enforcement technology.

(d) It is a defense to prosecution under this subchapter that the vehicle in question was stolen before the failure to pay the proper toll occurred and had not been recovered before the failure to pay occurred, but only if the theft was reported to the appropriate law enforcement authority before the earlier of:

(1) the occurrence of the failure to pay; or

(2) eight hours after the discovery of the theft.
(Enacted by Acts 1997, 75th Leg., ch. 165 (S.B. 898), § 30.18(a), effective September 1, 1997; am. Acts 2003, 78th Leg., ch. 372 (S.B. 1464), § 5, effective September 1, 2003.)

### Sec. 284.207. Attendance on Hearing.

(a) The peace officer or toll road agent who alleges a violation is not required to attend the hearing.

(b) The failure of a person charged with an offense to appear at the hearing is considered an admission of liability for the violation. (Enacted by Acts 1997, 75th Leg., ch. 165 (S.B. 898), § 30.18(a), effective September 1, 1997.)

### Sec. 284.208. Decision of Hearing Officer.

(a) The hearing officer shall issue a decision stating:

(1) whether the person charged is liable for a violation of the order; and

(2) the amount of the fine and costs to be assessed against the person.

(b) The hearing officer shall file the decision with the county clerk.

(c) A decision of a hearing officer filed under Subsection (b) must be kept in a separate index and file. The decision may be recorded using a computer printout, microfilm, microfiche, or a similar data processing technique.

(d), (e) [Repealed by Acts 2005, 79th Leg., ch. 963 (H.B. 1672), § 2(b), effective September 1, 2005.]

(Enacted by Acts 1997, 75th Leg., ch. 165 (S.B. 898), § 30.18(a), effective September 1, 1997; am. Acts 2003, 78th Leg., ch. 372 (S.B. 1464), § 6, effective September 1, 2003; am. Acts 2005, 79th Leg., ch. 963 (H.B. 1672), § 2(b), effective September 1, 2005.)

### Sec. 284.209.   Enforcement of Decision.

A decision issued under Section 284.208(a) may be enforced by:

(1) placing a device that prohibits movement of a motor vehicle on the vehicle that is the subject of the decision;

(2) imposing an additional fine if the fine for the offense is not paid within a specified time; or

(3) refusing to allow the registration of the vehicle.

(Enacted by Acts 1997, 75th Leg., ch. 165 (S.B. 898), § 30.18(a), effective September 1, 1997.)

### Sec. 284.210.   Appeal of Hearing Officer Decision.

(a) A person determined by a hearing officer to be in violation of an order may appeal the determination to a county court at law.

(b) To appeal, the person must file a petition with the court not later than the 30th day after the date the hearing officer's decision is filed with the county clerk. The petition must be accompanied by payment of the costs required by law for the court.

(Enacted by Acts 1997, 75th Leg., ch. 165 (S.B. 898), § 30.18(a), effective September 1, 1997.)

### Sec. 284.211.   Hearing on Appeal.

The court in which an appeal petition is filed shall:

(1) schedule a hearing; and

(2) notify all parties of the date, time, and place of the hearing.

(Enacted by Acts 1997, 75th Leg., ch. 165 (S.B. 898), § 30.18(a), effective September 1, 1997.)

### Sec. 284.212.   Effect of Appeal.

Service of notice of appeal does not stay the enforcement and collection of the decision of the hearing officer unless the person who files the appeal posts a bond with an agency designated by the county to accept payment for a violation.

(Enacted by Acts 1997, 75th Leg., ch. 165 (S.B. 898), § 30.18(a), effective September 1, 1997.)

### Sec. 284.213.   Seizure of Transponders.

(a) For purposes of this section, "transponder" means a device, placed on or within a motor vehicle, that is capable of transmitting information used to assess or to collect tolls. A transponder is insufficiently funded when there are no remaining funds in the account in connection with which the transponder was issued.

(b) Any peace officer of this state may seize a stolen or insufficiently funded transponder and return it to the county, except that an insufficiently funded transponder may not be seized sooner than the 30th day after the date the county has sent a notice of delinquency to the holder of the account.

(Enacted by Acts 2003, 78th Leg., ch. 372 (S.B. 1464), § 7, effective September 1, 2003.)

## CHAPTER 285
## COUNTY REGULATION OF ROADSIDE VENDOR AND SOLICITOR IN CERTAIN COUNTIES

Section

### Sec. 285.001.   Regulation of Roadside Vendor and Solicitor.

To promote the public safety, the commissioners court of a county with a population of more than 1.3 million by order may regulate the following in the unincorporated area of the county if they occur on a public highway or road, in the right-of-way of a public highway or road, or in a parking lot:

(1) the sale of items by a vendor of food or merchandise, including live animals;

Transportation

(2) the erection, maintenance, or placement of a structure by a vendor of food or merchandise, including live animals; and

(3) the solicitation of money.

(Enacted by Acts 1995, 74th Leg., ch. 165 (S.B. 971), § 1, effective September 1, 1995; am. Acts 2001, 77th Leg., ch. 669 (H.B. 2810), § 132, effective September 1, 2001; am. Acts 2007, 80th Leg., ch. 493 (S.B. 254), § 1, effective September 1, 2007.)

## Sec. 285.002. Permit; Removal of Structure.

The commissioners court may:

(1) require a vendor or a person soliciting money to obtain a permit to sell the food or merchandise or to solicit money;

(2) charge a reasonable fee for the permit; and

(3) provide for the removal of a structure that is in violation of the regulations.

(Enacted by Acts 1995, 74th Leg., ch. 165 (S.B. 971), § 1, effective September 1, 1995.)

## Sec. 285.003. Conflict with Statute or State Agency Rule.

If a regulation adopted under this chapter conflicts with a statute or state agency rule, the statute or rule prevails to the extent of the conflict.

(Enacted by Acts 1995, 74th Leg., ch. 165 (S.B. 971), § 1, effective September 1, 1995.)

## Sec. 285.004. Violation of Regulation; Offense.

(a) A person commits an offense if the person knowingly:

(1) violates a regulation adopted under this chapter; or

(2) obstructs or threatens to obstruct the removal of a structure that is in violation of a regulation adopted under this chapter.

(b) Each day a violation continues is a separate offense.

(c) An offense under this section is a Class C misdemeanor.

(Enacted by Acts 1995, 74th Leg., ch. 165 (S.B. 971), § 1, effective September 1, 1995.)

## SUBTITLE G
## TURNPIKES AND TOLL PROJECTS

## CHAPTER 370
## REGIONAL MOBILITY AUTHORITIES

### Subchapter E. Acquisition, Construction, and Operation of Transportation Projects

## SUBCHAPTER E
## ACQUISITION, CONSTRUCTION, AND OPERATION OF TRANSPORTATION PROJECTS

## Sec. 370.177. Failure or Refusal to Pay Turnpike Project Toll; Offense; Administrative Penalty.

(a) Except as provided by Subsection (a-1), the operator of a vehicle, other than an authorized emergency vehicle as defined by Section 541.201, that is driven or towed through a toll collection facility of a turnpike project shall pay the proper toll. The operator of a vehicle who drives or tows a vehicle through a toll collection facility and does not pay the proper toll commits an offense. An offense under this subsection is a misdemeanor punishable by a fine not to exceed $250. The exemption from payment of a toll for an authorized emergency vehicle applies regardless of whether the vehicle is:

(1) responding to an emergency;

(2) displaying a flashing light; or

(3) marked as an emergency vehicle.

(a-1) Notwithstanding Subsection (a), the board may waive the requirement of the payment of a toll or may authorize the payment of a reduced toll for any vehicle or class of vehicles.

(b) In the event of nonpayment of the proper toll as required by Subsection (a), on issuance of a written notice of nonpayment, the registered owner of the nonpaying vehicle is liable for the payment of both the proper toll and an administrative fee.

(c) The authority may impose and collect the administrative fee to recover the cost of collecting the unpaid toll, not to exceed $100. The authority shall send a written notice of nonpayment to the registered owner of the vehicle at that owner's address as shown in the vehicle registration records of the department by first class mail not later than the 30th day after the date of the alleged failure to pay and may require payment not sooner than the 30th day after the date the notice was mailed. The registered owner shall pay a separate toll and administrative fee for each event of nonpayment under Subsection (a).

(d) The registered owner of a vehicle for which the proper toll was not paid who is mailed a written notice of nonpayment under Subsection (c) and fails to pay the proper toll and administrative fee within the time specified by the notice of nonpayment commits an offense. Each failure to pay a toll or administrative fee under this subsection is a separate offense.

(e) It is an exception to the application of Subsection (b) or (d) that the registered owner of the vehicle is a lessor of the vehicle and not later than the 30th day after the date the notice of nonpayment is mailed provides to the authority:

(1) a copy of the rental, lease, or other contract document covering the vehicle on the date of the nonpayment under Subsection (a), with the name and address of the lessee clearly legible; or

(2) electronic data, other than a photocopy or scan of a rental or lease contract, that contains the information required under Sections 521.460(c)(1), (2), and (3) covering the vehicle on the date of the nonpayment under Subsection (a).

(e-1) If the lessor provides the required information within the period prescribed under Subsection (e), the authority may send a notice of nonpayment to the lessee at the address provided under Subsection (e) by first class mail before the 30th day after the date of receipt of the required information from the lessor. The lessee of the vehicle for which the proper toll was not paid who is mailed a written notice of nonpayment under this subsection and fails to pay the proper toll and administrative fee within the time specified by the notice of nonpayment commits an offense.

The lessee shall pay a separate toll and administrative fee for each event of nonpayment. Each failure to pay a toll or administrative fee under this subsection is a separate offense.

(f) It is an exception to the application of Subsection (b) or (d) that the registered owner of the vehicle transferred ownership of the vehicle to another person before the event of nonpayment under Subsection (a) occurred, submitted written notice of the transfer to the department in accordance with Section 520.023, and before the 30th day after the date the notice of nonpayment is mailed, provides to the authority the name and address of the person to whom the vehicle was transferred. If the former owner of the vehicle provides the required information within the period prescribed, the authority may send a notice of nonpayment to the person to whom ownership of the vehicle was transferred at the address provided by the former owner by first class mail before the 30th day after the date of receipt of the required information from the former owner. The subsequent owner of the vehicle for which the proper toll was not paid who is mailed a written notice of nonpayment under this subsection and fails to pay the proper toll and administrative fee within the time specified by the notice of nonpayment commits an offense. The subsequent owner shall pay a separate toll and administrative fee for each event of nonpayment under Subsection (a). Each failure to pay a toll or administrative fee under this subsection is a separate offense.

(g) An offense under Subsection (d), (e-1), or (f) is a misdemeanor punishable by a fine not to exceed $250.

(h) The court in which a person is convicted of an offense under this section shall also collect the proper toll and administrative fee and forward the toll and fee to the authority.

(i) In the prosecution of an offense under this section, proof that the vehicle passed through a toll collection facility without payment of the proper toll together with proof that the defendant was the registered owner or the driver of the vehicle when the failure to pay occurred, establishes the nonpayment of the registered owner. The proof may be by testimony of a peace officer or authority employee, video surveillance, or any other reasonable evidence, including:

(1) evidence obtained by automated enforcement technology that the authority determines is necessary, including automated enforcement

technology described by Sections 228.058(a) and (b); or

(2) a copy of the rental, lease, or other contract document or the electronic data provided to the authority under Subsection (e) that shows the defendant was the lessee of the vehicle when the underlying event of nonpayment occurred.

(j) It is a defense to prosecution under this section that the motor vehicle in question was stolen before the failure to pay the proper toll occurred and was not recovered by the time of the failure to pay, but only if the theft was reported to the appropriate law enforcement authority before the earlier of:

(1) the occurrence of the failure to pay; or

(2) eight hours after the discovery of the theft.

(k) In this section, "registered owner" means the owner of a vehicle as shown on the vehicle registration records of the department or the analogous department or agency of another state or country.

(*l*) In addition to the other powers and duties provided by this chapter, with regard to its toll collection and enforcement powers for its turnpike projects or other toll projects developed, financed, constructed, and operated under an agreement with the authority or another entity, an authority has the same powers and duties as the department under Chapter 228, a county under Chapter 284, and a regional tollway authority under Chapter 366.
(Enacted by Acts 2003, 78th Leg., ch. 1325 (H.B. 3588), § 2.01, effective June 21, 2003; am. Acts 2005, 79th Leg., ch. 23 (S.B. 129), § 2, effective September 1, 2005; am. Acts 2005, 79th Leg., ch. 281 (H.B. 2702), § 2.70, effective June 14, 2005; am. Acts 2007, 80th Leg., ch. 258 (S.B. 11), § 4.04, effective September 1, 2007; am. Acts 2009, 81st Leg., ch. 918 (H.B. 2983), § 6, effective September 1, 2009; am. Acts 2011, 82nd Leg., ch. 1279 (H.B. 1112), § 11, effective June 17, 2011.)

## Sec. 370.178. Use and Return of Transponders.

(a) For purposes of this section, "transponder" means a device placed on or within an automobile that is capable of transmitting or receiving information used to assess or collect tolls. A transponder is insufficiently funded if there is no money in the account for which the transponder was issued.

(b) Any law enforcement or peace officer of an entity with which an authority has contracted under Section 370.181(c) may seize a stolen or insufficiently funded transponder and return it to the authority that issued the transponder. An insufficiently funded transponder may not be seized before the 30th day after the date that an authority has sent a notice of delinquency to the holder of the account.

(c) The following entities shall consider offering motor vehicle operators the option of using a transponder to pay tolls without stopping, to mitigate congestion at toll locations, to enhance traffic flow, and to otherwise increase the efficiency of operations:

(1) the authority;

(2) an entity to which a project authorized by this chapter is transferred; or

(3) a third-party service provider under contract with an entity described by Subdivision (1) or (2).

(d) Transponder customer account information, including contact and payment information and trip data, is confidential and not subject to disclosure under Chapter 552, Government Code.
(Enacted by Acts 2003, 78th Leg., ch. 1325 (H.B. 3588), § 2.01, effective June 21, 2003; am. Acts 2005, 79th Leg., ch. 281 (H.B. 2702), § 2.71, effective June 14, 2005.)

## Sec. 370.179. Controlled Access to Turnpike Projects.

(a) An authority by order may designate a turnpike project or a portion of a project as a controlled-access toll road.

(b) An authority by order may:

(1) prohibit the use of or access to or from a turnpike project by a motor vehicle, bicycle, another classification or type of vehicle, or a pedestrian;

(2) deny access to or from:

(A) a turnpike project;

(B) real property adjacent to a turnpike project; or

(C) a street, road, alley, highway, or other public or private way intersecting a turnpike project;

(3) designate locations on a turnpike project at which access to or from the toll road is permitted;

(4) control, restrict, and determine the type and extent of access permitted at a designated location of access to a turnpike project; or

(5) erect appropriate protective devices to preserve the utility, integrity, and use of a turnpike project.

Transportation

(c) Denial of access to or from a segment of the state highway system is subject to the approval of the commission.

(Enacted by Acts 2003, 78th Leg., ch. 1325 (H.B. 3588), § 2.01, effective June 21, 2003.)

## Sec. 370.180. Promotion of Transportation Project.

An authority may promote the use of a transportation project, including a project that it operates on behalf of another entity, by appropriate means, including advertising or marketing as the authority determines appropriate.

(Enacted by Acts 2003, 78th Leg., ch. 1325 (H.B. 3588), § 2.01, effective June 21, 2003.)

## Sec. 370.181. Operation of Transportation Project.

(a) An authority shall operate a transportation project with employees of the authority or by using services contracted under Subsection (b) or (c).

(b) An authority may enter into an agreement with one or more persons to provide, on terms and conditions approved by the authority, personnel and services to design, construct, operate, maintain, expand, enlarge, or extend the transportation project of the authority.

(c) An authority may contract with any state or local government for the services of peace officers of that agency.

(d) An authority may not directly provide water, wastewater, natural gas, petroleum pipeline, electric transmission, electric distribution, telecommunications, information, or cable television services.

(e) Nothing in this chapter, or any contractual right obtained under a contract with an authority authorized by this chapter, supersedes or renders ineffective any provision of another law applicable to the owner or operator of a public utility facility, including any provision of the Utilities Code regarding licensing, certification, and regulatory jurisdiction of the Public Utility Commission of Texas or Railroad Commission of Texas.

(Enacted by Acts 2003, 78th Leg., ch. 1325 (H.B. 3588), § 2.01, effective June 21, 2003.)

## Sec. 370.186. Contracts with Governmental Entities.

(a) Except as provided by Subsection (c), an authority may not construct, maintain, or operate a turnpike or toll project in an area having a governmental entity established under Chapter 284 or 366 unless the governmental entity and the authority enter into a written agreement specifying the terms and conditions under which the project shall be undertaken. An authority may not construct, maintain, or operate a transportation project that another governmental entity has determined to be a project under Chapter 451, 452, or 460 unless the governmental entity and the authority enter into a written agreement specifying the terms and conditions under which the project shall be undertaken.

(b) An authority may not receive or be paid revenue derived by another governmental entity operating under Chapter 284, 366, 451, 452, or 460 unless the governmental entity and the authority enter into a written agreement specifying the terms and conditions under which the revenue shall be received by or paid to the authority.

(c) Subsection (a) does not apply to a turnpike or toll project located in a county in which a regional tollway authority has transferred under Section 366.036 or 366.172:

(1) all turnpike projects of the regional tollway authority that are located in the county; and

(2) all work product developed by the regional tollway authority in determining the feasibility of the construction, improvement, extension, or expansion of a turnpike project to be located in the county.

(d) An authority may not construct, maintain, or operate a passenger rail facility within the boundaries of an intermunicipal commuter rail district created under former Article 6550c-1, Vernon's Texas Civil Statutes, as those boundaries existed on September 1, 2005, unless the district and the authority enter into a written agreement specifying the terms and conditions under which the project will be undertaken.

(Enacted by Acts 2003, 78th Leg., ch. 1325 (H.B. 3588), § 2.01, effective June 21, 2003; am. Acts 2005, 79th Leg., ch. 281 (H.B. 2702), § 2.72, effective June 14, 2005; am. Acts 2009, 81st Leg., ch. 85 (S.B. 1540), § 4.09, effective April 1, 2011.)

## Sec. 370.187. Project Approval.

(a) An authority may not begin construction of a transportation project that will connect to the state highway system or to a department rail facility without the approval of the commission.

(b) The commission by rule shall establish procedures and criteria for an approval under this section. The rules must require the commission to consider a request for project approval not later than the 60th day after the date the department receives all information reasonably necessary to review the request.

(Enacted by Acts 2003, 78th Leg., ch. 1325 (H.B. 3588), § 2.01, effective June 21, 2003.)

### Sec. 370.191. Commercial Transportation Processing Systems.

(a) In this section, "port of entry" means a place designated by executive order of the president of the United States, by order of the United States secretary of the treasury, or by act of the United States Congress at which a customs officer is authorized to accept entries of merchandise, to collect duties, and to enforce the various provisions of the customs and navigation laws.

(b) This section applies only to a port of entry for land traffic from the United Mexican States and does not apply to a port of entry for marine traffic.

(c) To the extent an authority considers appropriate to expedite commerce and based on the Texas ITS/CVO Business Plan prepared by the department, the Department of Public Safety, and the comptroller, the authority shall provide for implementation by the appropriate agencies of the use of Intelligent Transportation Systems for Commercial Vehicle Operations (ITS/CVO) in any new commercial motor vehicle inspection facility constructed by the authority and in any existing facility located at a port of entry to which this section applies. The authority shall coordinate with other state and federal transportation officials to develop interoperability standards for the systems.

(d) If an authority constructs a facility at which commercial vehicle safety inspections are conducted, the facility may not be used solely for the purpose of conducting commercial motor vehicle inspections by the Department of Public Safety and the facility must include implementation of ITS/CVO technology by the appropriate agencies to support all commercial motor vehicle regulation and enforcement functions.

(e) As part of its implementation of technology under this section, an authority shall to the greatest extent possible as a requirement of the construction of the facility:

(1) enhance efficiency and reduce complexity for motor carriers by providing a single point of contact between carriers and regulating state and federal government officials and providing a single point of information, available to wireless access, about federal and state regulatory and enforcement requirements;

(2) prevent duplication of state and federal procedures and locations for regulatory and enforcement activities, including consolidation of collection of applicable fees;

(3) link information systems of the authority, the department, the Department of Public Safety, the comptroller, and, to the extent possible, the United States Department of Transportation and other appropriate regulatory and enforcement entities; and

(4) take other necessary action to:

(A) facilitate the flow of commerce;

(B) assist federal interdiction efforts;

(C) protect the environment by reducing idling time of commercial motor vehicles at the facilities;

(D) prevent highway damage caused by overweight commercial motor vehicles; and

(E) seek federal funds to assist in the implementation of this section.

(f) Construction of a facility to which this section applies is subject to the availability of federal funding for that purpose.

(Enacted by Acts 2003, 78th Leg., ch. 1325 (H.B. 3588), § 2.01, effective June 21, 2003.)

## SUBTITLE H
## HIGHWAY BEAUTIFICATION

## CHAPTER 391
## HIGHWAY BEAUTIFICATION ON INTERSTATE AND PRIMARY SYSTEMS AND CERTAIN ROADS

Transportation

## SUBCHAPTER A
## GENERAL PROVISIONS

### Sec. 391.001.   Definitions.

In this chapter:

(1) "Automobile graveyard" means an establishment that is maintained, used, or operated for storing, buying, or selling wrecked, scrapped, ruined, or dismantled motor vehicles or motor vehicle parts.

(2) "Eligible highway" means a highway along which an information logo sign may be located as determined by the commission under Section 391.092(d).

(3) [Repealed by Acts 2007, 80th Leg., ch. 935 (H.B. 3441), § 4, effective June 15, 2007.]

(4) "Information logo sign" means a specific information logo sign or a major shopping area guide sign.

(5) "Interstate system" means that portion of the national system of interstate and defense highways that is located in this state and is designated officially by the commission and approved under Title 23, United States Code.

(6) "Junk" means:

(A) old or scrap copper, brass, rope, rags, batteries, paper, trash, rubber, debris, or waste;

(B) junked, dismantled, or wrecked automobiles or automobile parts; or

(C) iron, steel, and other old or scrap ferrous or nonferrous material.

(7) "Junkyard" means:

(A) an automobile graveyard;

(B) an establishment maintained, used, or operated for storing, buying, or selling junk or processing scrap metal; or

(C) a garbage dump or sanitary fill.

(8) [Repealed by Acts 2007, 80th Leg., ch. 935 (H.B. 3441), § 4, effective June 15, 2007.]

(9) "Major shopping area guide sign" means a rectangular guide sign panel imprinted with the name of a major shopping area eligible to have its name displayed as determined by the commission under Section 391.0935 and containing directional information to the major shopping area.

(10) "Outdoor advertising" means an outdoor sign, display, light, device, figure, painting, drawing, message, plaque, poster, billboard, or other thing designed, intended, or used to advertise or inform if any part of the advertising or information content is visible from the main-traveled way of the interstate or primary system. The term does not include a sign or marker giving information about the location of an underground electric transmission line, telegraph or telephone property or facility, pipeline, public sewer, or waterline.

(11) "Primary system" means that portion of connected main highways located in this state that is designated officially by the commission and approved under Title 23, United States Code.

(12) "Specific information logo sign" means a rectangular sign imprinted with the words "GAS," "FOOD," "LODGING," "CAMPING," or "24 HOUR Rx," or with a combination of those words, and the specific brand names of commercial establishments offering those services.

(13) "Urban area" means an area defined by the commission in cooperation with local officials, subject to approval by the secretary of the United States Department of Transportation, that as a minimum includes an urban place as designated by the United States Bureau of the Census having a population of 5,000 or more and not located within an urbanized area.

(14) "Urbanized area" means an area defined by the commission in cooperation with local officials, subject to approval by the secretary of the United States Department of Transportation, that as a minimum includes an urbanized area as defined by the United States Bureau of the Census or that part of a multistate urbanized area located in this state.

(Enacted by Acts 1995, 74th Leg., ch. 165 (S.B. 971), § 1, effective September 1, 1995; am. Acts 1997, 75th Leg., ch. 165 (S.B. 898), § 30.22(a), effective September 1, 1997; am. Acts 2003, 78th Leg., ch. 602 (H.B. 1831), § 1, effective September 1, 2003; am. Acts 2003, 78th Leg., ch. 743 (H.B. 3330), § 1, effective September 1, 2003; am. Acts 2007, 80th Leg., ch. 935 (H.B. 3441), §§ 1, 4, effective June 15, 2007.)

### Sec. 391.003.   Violation of Rule; Offense.

(a) A person commits an offense if the person wilfully violates a rule adopted by the commission under this chapter.

(b) An offense under this section is a misdemeanor punishable by a fine of not less than $500 or more than $1,000.

(c) Each day of a rule violation is a separate offense.

(Enacted by Acts 1995, 74th Leg., ch. 165 (S.B. 971), § 1, effective September 1, 1995.)

## SUBCHAPTER E
## REGULATION OF JUNKYARDS AND AUTOMOBILE GRAVEYARDS

### Sec. 391.121. Prohibited Junkyard; Offense.

(a) A person commits an offense if:

(1) the person wilfully establishes, operates, or maintains a junkyard any portion of which is within 1,000 feet of the nearest edge of a right-of-way of a highway in the interstate or primary system; and

(2) the junkyard is not:

(A) screened by appropriate means, including natural objects, plantings, or fences, so that it is not visible from the main-traveled way of the interstate or primary highway; or

(B) located in an area that is a zoned or unzoned industrial area.

(b) The determination of whether an area is industrial must be made under criteria established by commission rule and according to actual land use.

(c) An offense under this section is a misdemeanor punishable by a fine of not less than $500 or more than $1,000. Each day of the proscribed conduct is a separate offense.

(Enacted by Acts 1995, 74th Leg., ch. 165 (S.B. 971), § 1, effective September 1, 1995.)

### Sec. 391.122. Authority of Commission to Screen Junkyard.

(a) The commission may screen with appropriate means, including natural objects, plantings, or fences, a lawfully existing junkyard that is within 1,000 feet of the nearest edge of a right-of-way of a highway in the interstate or primary system.

(b) The commission may acquire an area outside of a highway right-of-way so that a junkyard may be screened from the main-traveled way of a highway in the interstate or primary system.

(Enacted by Acts 1995, 74th Leg., ch. 165 (S.B. 971), § 1, effective September 1, 1995.)

### Sec. 391.123. Rules Relating to Screening of Junkyards.

The commission may adopt rules governing the location, planting, construction, and maintenance of the materials used in screening junkyards.

(Enacted by Acts 1995, 74th Leg., ch. 165 (S.B. 971), § 1, effective September 1, 1995.)

### Sec. 391.124. Compensation to Owner of Junkyard.

If the commission determines that the screening of a lawfully existing junkyard that is within 1,000 feet of the nearest edge of a right-of-way of a highway in the interstate or primary system is not feasible, the commission shall pay just compensation to:

(1) the owner of the junkyard for its relocation, removal, or disposal; and

(2) the owner or, if appropriate, the lessee of the real property on which the junkyard is located for the taking of the right to erect and maintain a junkyard.

(Enacted by Acts 1995, 74th Leg., ch. 165 (S.B. 971), § 1, effective September 1, 1995.)

### Sec. 391.125. Injunction to Require Screening.

(a) On written notice by certified mail from the department, an owner of a junkyard that is established, operated, or maintained in violation of this subchapter or a rule adopted under this subchapter shall screen the junkyard in accordance with Section 391.121. If the owner does not screen the junkyard within 45 days of the date of the notice, the department may request the attorney general to apply for an injunction to require the screening of the junkyard.

(b) Under an action brought under Subsection (a), the state is entitled to recover from the owner of a junkyard all administrative and legal costs and expenses incurred to require the screening of the junkyard, including court costs and reasonable attorney's fees.

(Enacted by Acts 1999, 76th Leg., ch. 442 (S.B. 1220), § 2, effective June 18, 1999.)

### Sec. 391.126. Civil Penalty.

(a) In addition to being subject to a criminal penalty or injunctive action, a person who intentionally violates this subchapter is liable to the state for a civil penalty. The attorney general may sue to collect the penalty.

(b) The amount of a civil penalty under this section is not less than $500 or more than $1,000 for each violation, depending on the seriousness of the violation. A separate penalty may be collected for each day a continuing violation occurs.

Transportation

(Enacted by Acts 1999, 76th Leg., ch. 442 (S.B. 1220), § 2, effective June 18, 1999.)

### Sec. 391.127.  Salvage Vehicle Dealer License.

The commission may revoke or suspend a license issued under Chapter 2302, Occupations Code, or place on probation a license holder whose license is suspended, if the license holder violates this chapter or a rule adopted under this chapter.

(Enacted by Acts 1999, 76th Leg., ch. 442 (S.B. 1220), § 2, effective June 18, 1999; am. Acts 2003, 78th Leg., ch. 1276 (H.B. 3507), § 14A.820, effective September 1, 2003.)

## SUBCHAPTER I
## PROHIBITION OF SIGNS ON
## CERTAIN HIGHWAYS

### Sec. 391.251.  Definitions.

In this subchapter:

(1) "Off-premise sign" means an outdoor sign displaying advertising that pertains to a business, person, organization, activity, event, place, service, or product not principally located or primarily manufactured or sold on the premises on which the sign is located.

(2) "Advertising" means a message seeking to attract the public or to direct the attention of the public to any goods, services, or merchandise.

(Enacted by Acts 2001, 77th Leg., ch. 1264 (S.B. 1128), § 3, effective September 1, 2001.)

### Sec. 391.252.  Off-Premise Signs Prohibited.

(a) A person may not erect an off-premise sign that is adjacent to and visible from:

(1) U.S. Highway 290 between the western city limits of the city of Austin and the eastern city limits of the city of Fredericksburg;

(2) State Highway 317 between the northern city limits of the city of Belton to the southern city limits of the city of Valley Mills;

(3) State Highway 16 between the northern city limits of the city of Kerrville and Interstate Highway 20;

(4) U.S. Highway 77 between State Highway 186 and State Highway 44;

(5) U.S. Highway 281 between:

(A) State Highway 186 and Interstate Highway 37, exclusive of the segment of U.S.

Highway 281 located in the city limits of Three Rivers; and

(B) the southern boundary line of Comal County and State Highway 306;

(6) State Highway 17 between State Highway 118 and U.S. Highway 90;

(7) State Highway 67 between U.S. Highway 90 and Farm-to-Market Road 170;

(8) Farm-to-Market Road 170 between State Highway 67 and State Highway 118;

(9) State Highway 118 between Farm-to-Market Road 170 and State Highway 17;

(10) State Highway 105 between the western city limits of the city of Sour Lake to the eastern city limits of the city of Cleveland;

(11) State Highway 73 between the eastern city limits of the city of Winnie to the western city limits of the city of Port Arthur;

(12) State Highway 21 between the southern city limits of the city of College Station and U.S. Highway 290;

(13) a highway located in:

(A) the Sabine National Forest;

(B) the Davy Crockett National Forest; or

(C) the Sam Houston National Forest;

(14) Segments 1 through 4 of State Highway 130;

(15) a highway in Bandera County that is part of the state highway system;

(16) Farm-to-Market Road 3238 beginning at State Highway 71 and any extension of that road through Hays and Blanco Counties;

(17) Farm-to-Market Road 2978 between Farm-to-Market Road 1488 and the boundary line between Harris and Montgomery Counties;

(18) U.S. Highway 90 between the western city limits of the city of San Antonio and the eastern city limits of the city of Hondo; or

(19) **[Effective upon satisfaction of terms provided in Acts 2007, 80th Leg., ch. 1020 (H.B. 1521), § 3 — See Note]** the following highways in Austin County:

(A) State Highway 159;

(B) Farm-to-Market Road 331;

(C) Farm-to-Market Road 529;

(D) Farm-to-Market Road 1094; and

(E) Farm-to-Market Road 2502.

(b) This section does not affect the ability of a municipality to regulate a sign located on the portion of a roadway listed in Subsection (a) that is within the corporate limits or extraterritorial jurisdiction of the municipality in accordance with Chapter 216, Local Government Code.

(c) This section does not prohibit a person from erecting an off-premise sign permitted by other law, rule, or regulation that is adjacent to and visible from a roadway not listed in this section and is visible from a roadway listed under this section if the intended purpose of the sign is to be visible only from the roadway not listed under this section.

(Enacted by Acts 2001, 77th Leg., ch. 1264 (S.B. 1128), § 3, effective September 1, 2001; am. Acts 2005, 79th Leg., ch. 281 (H.B. 2702), § 2.78, effective June 14, 2005; am. Acts 2005, 79th Leg., ch. 352 (S.B. 1206), § 1, effective September 1, 2005; am. Acts 2005, 79th Leg., ch. 405 (S.B. 1579), § 1, effective September 1, 2005; am. Acts 2005, 79th Leg., ch. 796 (S.B. 369), § 1, effective September 1, 2005; am. Acts 2005, 79th Leg., ch. 903 (H.B. 34), § 1, effective September 1, 2005; am. Acts 2005, 79th Leg., ch. 983 (H.B. 1851), § 1, effective September 1, 2005; am. Acts 2005, 79th Leg., ch. 1046 (H.B. 1248), § 1, effective September 1, 2005; am. Acts 2005, 79th Leg., ch. 1353 (S.B. 1204), § 1, effective September 1, 2005; am. Acts 2007, 80th Leg., ch. 1020 (H.B. 1521), § 1, effective September 1, 2007.)

### STATUTORY NOTES

**Editor's notes.** — Acts 2007, 80th Leg., ch. 1020 (H.B. 1521), § 3 provides:

"(a) Except as otherwise provided by this section, this Act takes effect September 1, 2007.

(b) Before Section 391.252(a)(19), Transportation Code, as added by this Act can become effective, notice shall be published in a newspaper of general circulation in the county or counties in which a segment of public road affected by Section 391.252(a)(19), Transportation Code, as added by this Act is located. The notice shall identify the segment of public road affected by Section 391.252(a)(19), Transportation Code, as added by this Act and state that the landowner's future right to lease the landowner's property for the purpose of erecting an off-premise sign will be terminated unless the landowner notifies the Texas Department of Transportation that the landowner plans to exclude the landowner's property from the application of Section 391.252(a)(19), Transportation Code, as added by this Act. The notice must be published by the appropriate county clerk or clerks in accordance with this subsection within 45 days of the effective date of this Act. The appropriate county clerk or clerks shall notify the Texas Department of Transportation in writing, by certified mail, when the notice is published in accordance with this subsection. The notice provided to the Texas Department of Transportation by the county clerk is public information for the purposes of Chapter 552, Government Code, and must include the affidavit of the publisher of the newspaper notice indicating the date the notice was pub-

lished, accompanied by a printed copy of the notice as published.

(c) Section 391.252(a)(19), Transportation Code, as added by this Act takes effect on the 91st day after the Texas Department of Transportation receives notification from all appropriate county clerks as provided in Subsection (b)."

## Sec. 391.253. Reerection, Reconstruction, Repair, or Rebuilding of Off-Premise Signs.

(a) An off-premise sign that is adjacent to and visible from a highway listed in Section 391.252 that is blown down, destroyed, taken down, or removed for a purpose other than maintenance or to change a letter, symbol, or other matter on the sign may be reerected, reconstructed, repaired, or rebuilt only if the cost of reerecting, reconstructing, repairing, or rebuilding the sign is not more than 60 percent of the cost of erecting a new off-premise sign of the same size, type, and construction at the same location.

(b) The department shall permit the relocation of an off-premise sign adjacent to and visible from a highway listed in Section 391.252 to another location that is adjacent to and visible from the same highway if:

(1) the construction, reconstruction, or expansion of a highway requires the removal of the sign;

(2) the sign is not modified to increase the above-grade height, the area of each sign face, the dimensions of the sign face, the number of sign faces, or the illumination of the sign; and

(3) the department identifies an alternate site for the relocation of the sign adjacent to and visible from the highway listed in Section 391.252.

(c) For purposes of this section, the department shall specify, within 30 days of receipt of a request for a relocation site, a minimum of three alternate sites that meet permitting requirements for an off-premise sign to be reerected, reconstructed, repaired, or rebuilt adjacent to and visible from a highway listed in Section 391.252.

(d) The owner of an off-premise sign that is reerected, reconstructed, repaired, or rebuilt according to Subsection (a) or relocated according to Subsection (b) may alter the materials and design of the sign to reduce the number of upright supports, subject to other restrictions in this section, in a manner that meets or exceeds the pre-existing structural specifications of the sign.

(Enacted by Acts 2001, 77th Leg., ch. 1264 (S.B. 1128), § 3, effective September 1, 2001.)

## Sec. 391.254.  Civil Penalty.

(a) A person who violates Section 391.252 is liable to the state for a civil penalty of not less than $500 or more than $1,000 for each violation, depending on the seriousness of the violation. A separate penalty may be imposed for each day a continuing violation occurs.

(b) The attorney general, the district or county attorney for the county, or the municipal attorney of the municipality in which the violation is alleged to have occurred may bring suit to collect the penalty.

(c) A civil penalty collected by the attorney general under this section shall be deposited to the credit of the state highway fund.

(d) Before a suit may be brought for a violation of Section 391.252, the attorney general, the district or county attorney for the county, or the municipal attorney of the municipality in which the violation is alleged to have occurred shall give the owner of the off-premise sign a written notice that:

(1) describes the violation and specific location of the sign found to be in violation;

(2) states the amount of the proposed penalty for the violation; and

(3) gives the owner 30 days from receipt to remove the sign and cure the violation to avoid the penalty unless the sign owner was given notice and opportunity to cure a similar violation within the preceding 12 months.

(Enacted by Acts 2001, 77th Leg., ch. 1264 (S.B. 1128), § 3, effective September 1, 2001.)

## Sec. 391.255.  Applicability of Subchapter.

The restrictions imposed by this subchapter are in addition to those imposed by the remainder of this chapter.

(Enacted by Acts 2001, 77th Leg., ch. 1264 (S.B. 1128), § 3, effective September 1, 2001.)

## Sec. 391.256.  Scenic Byways Program [Expired].

Expired pursuant to Acts 2001, 77th Leg., ch. 1264 (S.B. 1128), § 3, effective January 2, 2003.

(Enacted by Acts 2001, 77th Leg., ch. 1264 (S.B. 1128), § 3, effective September 1, 2001.)

# CHAPTER 392
# HIGHWAY BEAUTIFICATION ON STATE HIGHWAY RIGHT-OF-WAY

**Subchapter B. Signs on State Highway Right-Of-Way**

## SUBCHAPTER B
## SIGNS ON STATE HIGHWAY RIGHT-OF-WAY

## Sec. 392.032.  Offense.

(a) A person may not place or maintain a sign on a state highway right-of-way unless authorized by state law.

(b) A person commits an offense if the person violates this section.

(c) An offense under this section is a Class C misdemeanor.

(Enacted by Acts 1995, 74th Leg., ch. 165 (S.B. 971), § 1, effective September 1, 1995.)

## Sec. 392.0325.  Exception.

(a) A person may submit a request to the department for an exception to this subchapter for a sign that is attached to a building located on property other than a state highway right-of-way and that refers to a commercial activity or business located in the building if the sign:

(1) consists solely of the name of the establishment;

(2) identifies the establishment's principal product or services; or

(3) advertises the sale or lease of the property on which the sign is located.

(b) The department shall approve a request submitted under Subsection (a) if the department:

(1) determines that the sign will not constitute a safety hazard;

(2) determines that the sign will not interfere with the construction, reconstruction, op-

eration, or maintenance of the highway facility; and

(3) obtains the approval of the Federal Highway Administration if approval is required under federal law.

(c) This subchapter does not apply to a temporary directional sign or kiosk erected by a political subdivision as part of a program approved by the department and administered by the political subdivision on a highway within the boundaries of the political subdivision.

(d) This subchapter does not apply to a sign placed in the right-of-way by a public utility or its contractor for purposes of the utility.

(Enacted by Acts 1999, 76th Leg., ch. 442 (S.B. 1220), § 3, effective June 18, 1999; am. Acts 2007, 80th Leg., ch. 612 (H.B. 413), § 1, effective September 1, 2007.)

### Sec. 392.036. Defense.

It is a defense to prosecution or suit for a violation under this chapter if at the time of the alleged violation the defendant is a candidate for elective public office and the sign is placed:

(1) by a person other than the defendant; and

(2) in connection with a campaign for an elective public office by the defendant.

(Enacted by Acts 1995, 74th Leg., ch. 165 (S.B. 971), § 1, effective September 1, 1995; am. Acts 2007, 80th Leg., ch. 612 (H.B. 413), § 3, effective September 1, 2007.)

# SUBTITLE K
# MASS TRANSPORTATION

# CHAPTER 451
# METROPOLITAN RAPID TRANSIT AUTHORITIES

## SUBCHAPTER B
## POWERS OF AUTHORITIES

### Sec. 451.0612. Fare Enforcement Officers in Certain Authorities.

(a) An authority confirmed before July 1, 1985, in which the principal municipality has a population of less than 850,000 may employ persons to serve as fare enforcement officers to enforce the payment of fares for use of the public transportation system by:

(1) requesting and inspecting evidence showing payment of the appropriate fare from a person using the public transportation system; and

(2) issuing a citation to a person described by Section 451.0611(d)(1).

(b) Before commencing duties as a fare enforcement officer, a person must complete a 40-hour training course approved by the authority that is appropriate to the duties required of a fare enforcement officer.

(c) While performing duties, a fare enforcement officer shall:

(1) wear a distinctive uniform that identifies the officer as a fare enforcement officer; and

(2) work under the direction of the authority's manager of safety and security.

(d) A fare enforcement officer may:

(1) request evidence showing payment of the appropriate fare from passengers of the public transportation system;

(2) request personal identification from a passenger who does not produce evidence showing payment of the appropriate fare on request by the officer;

(3) request that a passenger leave the public transportation system if the passenger does not possess evidence of payment of the appropriate fare; and

(4) file a complaint in the appropriate court that charges the person with an offense under Section 451.0611(d).

(e) A fare enforcement officer may not carry a weapon while performing duties under this section.

(f) A fare enforcement officer is not a peace officer and has no authority to enforce a criminal law, other than the authority possessed by any other person who is not a peace officer.

(Enacted by Acts 2009, 81st Leg., ch. 1221 (S.B. 1263), § 2, effective September 1, 2009; am. Acts 2011, 82nd Leg., ch. 1163 (H.B. 2702), § 138, effective September 1, 2011.)

Transportation

## SUBTITLE Z
## MISCELLANEOUS ROADWAY PROVISIONS

## CHAPTER 471
## RAILROAD AND ROADWAY CROSSINGS

## Sec. 471.001.  Duty to Maintain Crossings.

(a) A railway company shall maintain the part of its roadbed and right-of-way that is crossed by a public street of a Type B general-law municipality in proper condition for use by travelers.

(b) A railway company that does not make needed repairs before the 31st day after the date the municipal marshal gives written notice to the section boss of the section where repairs are needed is liable to the municipality for a penalty of $25 for each week the railway company does not make needed repairs. The municipality may sue to recover the penalty.

(Enacted by Acts 1995, 74th Leg., ch. 165 (S.B. 971), § 1, effective September 1, 1995.)

## Sec. 471.002.  Signs at Crossings.

(a) A railway company shall place at each place where its railroad crosses a first or second class public road a sign with large and distinct letters giving notice that the railroad is near and warning persons to watch for railroad cars. The sign must be high enough above the road to permit the free passage of vehicles.

(b) A railway company that does not erect a sign required by Subsection (a) is liable for a resulting injury to a person or resulting damage to property.

(Enacted by Acts 1995, 74th Leg., ch. 165 (S.B. 971), § 1, effective September 1, 1995.)

## Sec. 471.003.  Telephone Service to Report Malfunctions of Mechanical Safety Devices at Crossings.

(a) The Department of Public Safety shall maintain a statewide toll-free telephone service to receive a report of a malfunction of a device, including a signal or crossbar, placed at an intersection of a railroad track and a public road to promote safety.

(b) At each intersection of a railroad track and a public road that is maintained by the state or a municipality and at which a mechanical safety device is placed, the Texas Department of Transportation shall affix on the crossbars of the device the telephone number, an explanation of its purpose, and the crossing number. At each intersection of a railroad track and a public road that is maintained by a political subdivision other than a municipality and at which a mechanical safety device is placed, the political subdivision shall affix on the crossbars of the device the telephone number, an explanation of its purpose, and the crossing number. The Texas Department of Transportation shall provide to the political subdivision the sign or label displaying the telephone number. A railway company shall permit personnel to affix the telephone number on the company's property as required by this subsection.

(c) The Department of Public Safety shall notify the identified railway company of each report of a malfunction received under Subsection (a).

(d) The Department of Public Safety shall maintain a computerized list of each intersection of a railroad track and a public road and of the railroad crossing safety equipment located at each intersection, using crossing numbers compiled by the Texas Department of Transportation.

(e) Not later than the fifth day after the date it places railroad crossing safety equipment in operation at an intersection subject to this section, a state agency or a political subdivision of the state other than a municipality shall notify the Department of Public Safety of:

(1) the location and type of the equipment installed; and

(2) the date it was placed in operation.

(f) The state, an agency or political subdivision of the state, or a railway company is not liable for damages caused by an action taken under this section or failure to perform a duty imposed by this section. Evidence may not be introduced in a judicial proceeding that the telephone service required by this section exists or that the state or railway company relies on the service.

(g) Except as provided by Subsection (d), a state agency is not required to make or retain a permanent record of information obtained in implementing this section.
(Enacted by Acts 1995, 74th Leg., ch. 165 (S.B. 971), § 1, effective September 1, 1995.)

## Sec. 471.004. Warning Sign Visibility at Railroad Grade Crossings.

(a) The department shall develop guidelines and specifications for the installation and maintenance of reflecting material at each unsignaled crossing. The material shall be affixed to the back and support post of each crossbuck in a manner that reflects light from vehicle headlights to focus attention on the presence of the unsignaled crossing.

(b) The department shall pay the cost of initial installation of reflecting material from money appropriated to the department to maintain grade crossing warning devices. The department or the local jurisdiction responsible for maintaining the roadway at each grade crossing shall pay the maintenance costs of the material.

(c) The state, an agency or political subdivision of the state, or a railway company is not liable for damages caused by an action taken under this section or failure to perform a duty imposed by this section. Evidence may not be introduced in a judicial proceeding that reflecting material exists or that the state or railway company relies on the material.

(d) The department shall adopt rules governing the installation and maintenance of reflecting material at grade crossings.

(e) A railway company shall permit department personnel to affix the reflecting material on the company's property.

(f) In this section:
(1) "Active warning device" means an automatically activated warning device, including a bell, flashing light, gate, or wigwag.
(2) "Crossbuck" means a standard grade crossing warning sign designated as Number R 15-1 and described in the Manual of Uniform Traffic Control Devices issued by the United States Department of Transportation, Federal Highway Administration.
(3) "Department" means the Texas Department of Transportation.
(4) "Grade crossing" means the intersection at grade of a railroad and a roadway constructed and maintained with public money.
(5) "Reflecting material" means material that reflects light so that the paths of the reflected light rays are parallel to those of the incident rays.
(6) "Unsignaled crossing" means a grade crossing not protected by active warning devices.
(7) "Warning device" means a traffic control sign, including an active warning device or crossbuck, the purpose of which is to alert motorists of a grade crossing.
(Enacted by Acts 1995, 74th Leg., ch. 165 (S.B. 971), § 1, effective September 1, 1995.)

## Sec. 471.005. Dismantling of Warning Signals at Railroad Grade Crossings; Offense.

(a) A person may not dismantle a warning signal at a grade crossing on an active rail line, as defined by rule of the Texas Department of Transportation, if the cost of the warning signal was originally paid entirely or partly from public money unless the person:
(1) obtains a permit from the governmental entity that maintains the road or highway that intersects the rail line at the grade crossing; and
(2) pays that governmental entity an amount equal to the present salvage value of the warning signal, as determined by the governmental entity.

(b) The governmental entity shall grant the permit if:
(1) payment is received; and
(2) the entity finds that removal of the warning signal will not adversely affect public safety.

(c) Money received under Subsection (a)(2) shall be deposited in the state treasury.

(d) This section does not apply to a Class I or Class II railroad, as defined by Interstate Commerce Commission regulations.

(e) A person commits an offense if the person violates this section. An offense under this section is a Class C misdemeanor.

(f) The Texas Department of Transportation may adopt rules necessary to administer this section.

(g) In this section:
(1) "Grade crossing" has the meaning assigned by Section 472.004(f).
(2) "Warning signal" means a traffic control device that is activated by the approach or presence of a train, including a flashing light signal, an automatic gate, or a similar device that displays to motorists a warning of the approach or presence of a train.

(Enacted by Acts 1995, 74th Leg., ch. 165 (S.B. 971), § 1, effective September 1, 1995.)

## Sec. 471.006.  Use of Bell and Whistle or Siren at Crossings; Offense.

(a) A railway company shall place on each locomotive:

(1) a bell weighing at least 30 pounds; and

(2) a steam whistle, air whistle, or air siren.

(b) The engineer in charge of the locomotive shall ring the bell and blow the whistle or siren at least one-quarter mile from the place where the railroad crosses a public road or street. The engineer shall continue to ring the bell until the locomotive has crossed the road or stopped.

(c) The railway company is liable for any damages sustained by a person because of a violation of Subsection (a) or (b).

(d) The engineer in charge of the locomotive commits an offense if the engineer violates Subsection (b). An offense under this subsection is a misdemeanor punishable by a fine of not less than $5 or more than $100.

(e) Notwithstanding Subsections (a) and (b), the governing body of a municipality having a population of at least 5,000 may regulate by ordinance the ringing of bells and blowing of whistles and sirens within its limits. Compliance with the ordinance is compliance with those subsections and a sufficient warning to the public at a crossing the ordinance affects.

(Enacted by Acts 1995, 74th Leg., ch. 165 (S.B. 971), § 1, effective September 1, 1995.)

## Sec. 471.007.  Obstructing Railroad Crossings; Offense.

(a) A railway company commits an offense if a train of the railway company obstructs for more than 10 minutes a street, railroad crossing, or public highway.

(b) An offense under this section is a misdemeanor punishable by a fine of not less than $100 or more than $300.

(c) An officer charging a railway company for an offense under this section shall prepare in duplicate a citation to appear in court and attach one copy of the citation to the train or deliver the copy to an employee or other agent of the railway company. The citation must show:

(1) the name of the railway company;

(2) the offense charged; and

(3) the time and place that a representative of the railway company is to appear in court.

(d) It is a defense to prosecution under this section that the train obstructs the street, rail-road crossing, or public highway because of an act of God or breakdown of the train.

(e) The hearing must be before a magistrate who has jurisdiction of the offense in the municipality or county in which the offense is alleged to have been committed.

(f) An appearance by counsel complies with the written promise to appear in court.

(Enacted by Acts 1995, 74th Leg., ch. 165 (S.B. 971), § 1, effective September 1, 1995; am. Acts 1999, 76th Leg., ch. 1023 (H.B. 2922), § 1, effective September 1, 1999.)

## Sec. 471.008.  Franchise to Obstruct Street Crossing.

(a) The governing body of a municipality by ordinance may grant a franchise to a railway company to obstruct a street crossing, other than a crossing of a designated state highway, by a passenger train for the purpose of receiving or discharging passengers, mail, express, or freight for a longer period than specified by Section 472.007.

(b) Section 471.007 does not apply to a street crossing named in an ordinance granting a franchise under this section.

(c) This section does not apply to a municipality having a special charter unless it amends its charter to adopt this section.

(Enacted by Acts 1995, 74th Leg., ch. 165 (S.B. 971), § 1, effective September 1, 1995.)

## Sec. 471.009.  Enhanced Pavement Marking Visibility at Certain Grade Crossings.

(a) In this section:

(1) "Grade crossing" and "reflecting material" have the meanings assigned by Section 471.004.

(2) "Pavement markings" means markings applied or attached to the surface of a roadway to regulate, warn, or guide traffic.

(3) "Stop bar" means the marking that is applied or attached to the surface of a roadway on either side of a grade crossing and that indicates that a vehicle must stop at the grade crossing.

(b) A county or municipality shall use standards developed by the department in applying pavement markings or a stop bar at a grade crossing if the cost of the markings or stop bar is paid either entirely or partly from state or federal funds. In developing its standards, the department shall follow the standards in the Manual on

Uniform Traffic Control Devices issued by the United States Department of Transportation Federal Highway Administration and, where appropriate, require the use of reflecting materials. (Enacted by Acts 2009, 81st Leg., ch. 85 (S.B. 1540), § 2.06, effective April 1, 2011.)

# CHAPTER 472
## MISCELLANEOUS PROVISIONS

### Subchapter B. Department Authority to Remove Property from State Highways

### Subchapter C. Criminal Offenses and Penalties Regarding Warning Signs and Barricades

# SUBCHAPTER B
# DEPARTMENT AUTHORITY TO REMOVE PROPERTY FROM STATE HIGHWAYS

## Sec. 472.011.　Definition.

In this subchapter, "personal property" includes personal property of any kind or character, including:

(1) a vehicle, as defined by Section 502.001, that is damaged or disabled;

(2) spilled cargo;

(3) a hazardous material as defined by 49 U.S.C. App. Section 1802; and

(4) a hazardous substance as defined by Section 26.263, Water Code.

(Enacted by Acts 1995, 74th Leg., ch. 165 (S.B. 971), § 1, effective September 1, 1995; am. Acts 1997, 75th Leg., ch. 1171 (S.B. 370), § 1.43(a), effective September 1, 1997.)

## Sec. 472.012.　Department Authority Generally.

(a) The department may remove personal property from the right-of-way or roadway of the state highway system if the department deter-

mines the property blocks the roadway or endangers public safety.

(b) The department may remove the personal property without the consent of the owner or carrier of the property.

(Enacted by Acts 1995, 74th Leg., ch. 165 (S.B. 971), § 1, effective September 1, 1995.)

## Sec. 472.013.　Owner and Carrier Responsible for Costs of Removal and Disposition.

The owner and the carrier of personal property removed under this subchapter shall reimburse the department for the costs of removal and disposition.

(Enacted by Acts 1995, 74th Leg., ch. 165 (S.B. 971), § 1, effective September 1, 1995.)

## Sec. 472.014.　Department Not Liable for Damages.

Notwithstanding any other provision of law, the department and its officers and employees are not liable for:

(1) any damage to personal property resulting from its removal or disposal by the department unless the removal or disposal is carried out recklessly or in a grossly negligent manner; or

(2) any damage resulting from the failure to exercise authority granted under this subchapter.

(Enacted by Acts 1995, 74th Leg., ch. 165 (S.B. 971), § 1, effective September 1, 1995; am. Acts 1997, 75th Leg., ch. 1171 (S.B. 370), § 1.43(b), effective September 1, 1997.)

## Sec. 472.015.　Contracts for Removal of Property.

In contracting with a private business or businesses for the removal of personal property from the right-of-way or roadway of the state highway system, the department may:

(1) use a purchasing method described in Chapter 2156, Government Code;

(2) include the removal work in a contract entered into under Chapter 223; or

(3) select a business or businesses based on an evaluation of the experience of the business and the price and quality of the business's equipment and services.

Transportation

(Enacted by Acts 2001, 77th Leg., ch. 1272 (S.B. 1458), § 9.01, effective June 15, 2001.)

## SUBCHAPTER C
## CRIMINAL OFFENSES AND PENALTIES REGARDING WARNING SIGNS AND BARRICADES

### Sec. 472.021. Tampering with Warning Devices.

(a) A person commits an offense if the person tampers with, damages, or removes a barricade, flare pot, sign, flasher signal, or other device warning of construction, repair, or detour on or adjacent to a highway set out by the state, a political subdivision, a contractor, or a public utility.

(b) This section does not apply to a person acting within the scope and duty of employment if the person is:

(1) an officer, agent, independent contractor, employee, or trustee of the state or a political subdivision;

(2) a contractor; or

(3) a public utility.

(c) An offense under this section is a misdemeanor punishable by:

(1) a fine of not less than $25 or more than $1,000;

(2) confinement in a county jail for a term not to exceed two years; or

(3) both the fine and the confinement.

(d) In this section:

(1) "Contractor" means a person engaged in highway construction or repair under contract with this state or a political subdivision of this state.

(2) "Highway" means the entire width between the boundary lines of a publicly maintained way, any part of which is open to the public for vehicular travel or any part of which is under construction or repair and intended for public vehicular travel on completion. The term includes the space above or below the highway surface.

(3) "Person" means an individual, firm, association, or corporation and includes an officer, agent, independent contractor, employee, or trustee of that individual or entity.

(4) "Political subdivision" includes a county, municipality, local board, or other body of this state having authority to authorize highway construction or repair.

(5) "Public utility" means:

(A) a telegraph, telephone, water, gas, light, or sewage company or cooperative;

(B) a contractor of a company or cooperative described by Subdivision (A); or

(C) another business recognized by the legislature as a public utility.

(Enacted by Acts 1995, 74th Leg., ch. 165 (S.B. 971), § 1, effective September 1, 1995.)

### Sec. 472.022. Obeying Warning Signs and Barricades.

(a) A person commits an offense if the person:

(1) disobeys the instructions, signals, warnings, or markings of a warning sign; or

(2) drives around a barricade.

(b) This section does not apply to:

(1) a person who is following the directions of a police officer; or

(2) a person, including an employee of the department, a political subdivision of this state, or a contractor or subcontractor, whose duties require the person to go beyond or around a barricade.

(c) Each violation of this section is a separate offense.

(d) An offense under this section is a misdemeanor punishable by a fine of not less than $1 or more than $200, except that:

(1) if the offense is committed in a construction or maintenance work zone when workers are present and any written notice to appear issued for the offense states on its face that workers were present when the offense was committed, the offense is a misdemeanor punishable by a fine of not less than $2 or more than $400; or

(2) if a person commits an offense under Subsection (a) where a warning sign or barricade has been placed because water is over any portion of a road, street, or highway, the offense is a Class B misdemeanor.

(e) In this section:

(1) "Barricade" means an obstruction:

(A) placed on or across a road, street, or highway of this state by the department, a political subdivision of this state, or a contractor or subcontractor constructing or repairing the road, street, or highway under authorization of the department or a political subdivision of this state; and

(B) placed to prevent the passage of motor vehicles over the road, street, or highway during construction, repair, or dangerous conditions.

(2) "Construction or maintenance work zone" means a portion of a highway or street:

(A) where highway construction or maintenance is being undertaken, other than mobile operations as defined by the Texas Manual on Uniform Traffic Control Devices; and

(B) that is marked by signs:

(i) indicating that it is a construction or maintenance work zone;

(ii) indicating where the zone begins and ends; and

(iii) stating: "Fines double when workers present."

(3) "Warning sign" means a signal, marking, or device placed on a barricade or on a road, street, or highway during construction, repair, or dangerous conditions by the department, a political subdivision of this state, or a contractor or subcontractor to warn or regulate motor vehicular traffic. The term includes a flagger deployed on a road, street, or highway by the department, a political subdivision of this state, or a contractor or subcontractor to direct traffic around or on the road, street, or highway during construction, repair, or dangerous conditions.

(f) Articles 45.051 and 45.0511, Code of Criminal Procedure, do not apply to an offense under this section committed in a construction or maintenance work zone when workers are present.

(Enacted by Acts 1995, 74th Leg., ch. 165 (S.B. 971), § 1, effective September 1, 1995; am. Acts 1997, 75th Leg., ch. 674 (H.B. 981), § 1, effective January 1, 1998; am. Acts 1999, 76th Leg., ch. 789 (H.B. 1425), §§ 1, 2, effective September 1, 1999; am. Acts 1999, 76th Leg., ch. 965 (H.B. 2541), § 1, effective September 1, 1999; am. Acts 1999, 76th Leg., ch. 1088 (H.B. 3433), § 1, effective September 1, 1999; am. Acts 2001, 77th Leg., ch. 1420 (H.B. 2812), § 19.005, effective September 1, 2001; am. Acts 2003, 78th Leg., ch. 991 (S.B. 1904), § 1, effective September 1, 2003; am. Acts 2003, 78th Leg., ch. 1182 (S.B. 631), § 3, effective September 1, 2003; am. Acts 2005, 79th Leg., ch. 576 (H.B. 1481), §§ 1, 2, effective September 1, 2005.)

# TITLE 7
# VEHICLES AND TRAFFIC

## SUBTITLE A
## CERTIFICATES OF TITLE AND REGISTRATION OF VEHICLES

## CHAPTER 501
## CERTIFICATE OF TITLE ACT

### Subchapter A. General Provisions

### Subchapter B. Certificate of Title Requirements

Transportation

## SUBCHAPTER A
## GENERAL PROVISIONS

### Sec. 501.001.   Short Title.

This chapter may be cited as the Certificate of
Title Act.

(Enacted by Acts 1995, 74th Leg., ch. 165 (S.B.
971), § 1, effective September 1, 1995.)

### Sec. 501.002.   [2 Versions: Effective until January 1, 2012] Definitions.

In this chapter:

(1) "Certificate of title" means an instrument
issued under Section 501.021.

(2) "Dealer" means a person who purchases
motor vehicles for sale at retail.

(3) "Department" means the Texas Department of Motor Vehicles.

(4) "Distributor" means a person engaged in
the business of selling to a dealer motor vehicles purchased from a manufacturer.

(5) "First sale" means:

(A) the bargain, sale, transfer, or delivery
of a motor vehicle that has not been previously registered or licensed, with intent to
pass an interest in the motor vehicle, other
than a lien, regardless of where the bargain,
sale, transfer, or delivery occurred; and

(B) the registration or licensing of that
vehicle.

(6) "House trailer" means a trailer designed
for human habitation. The term does not include manufactured housing.

(7) "Importer" means a person, other than a
manufacturer, that brings a used motor vehicle
into this state for sale in this state.

(8) "Importer's certificate" means a certificate for a used motor vehicle brought into this
state for sale in this state.

(9) "Lien" means:

(A) a lien provided for by the constitution
or statute in a motor vehicle;

(B) a security interest, as defined by Section 1.201, Business & Commerce Code, in a
motor vehicle, other than an absolute title,
created by any written security agreement,
as defined by Section 9.102, Business & Commerce Code, including a lease, conditional
sales contract, deed of trust, chattel mortgage, trust receipt, or reservation of title; or

(C) a child support lien under Chapter
157, Family Code.

(10) "Manufactured housing" has the meaning assigned by Chapter 1201, Occupations
Code.

(11) "Manufacturer" means a person regularly engaged in the business of manufacturing
or assembling new motor vehicles.

(12) "Manufacturer's permanent vehicle
identification number" means the number affixed by the manufacturer to a motor vehicle in
a manner and place easily accessible for physical examination and die-stamped or otherwise
permanently affixed on one or more removable
parts of the vehicle.

(13) "Motorcycle" means a motor vehicle,
other than a tractor, designed to propel itself
with not more than three wheels in contact
with the ground.

(14) "Motor vehicle" means:

(A) any motor driven or propelled vehicle
required to be registered under the laws of
this state;

(B) a trailer or semitrailer, other than
manufactured housing, that has a gross vehicle weight that exceeds 4,000 pounds;

(C) a house trailer;

(D) an all-terrain vehicle or a recreational
off-highway vehicle, as those terms are defined by Section 502.001, designed by the
manufacturer for off-highway use that is not
required to be registered under the laws of
this state; or

(E) a motorcycle, motor-driven cycle, or
moped that is not required to be registered

under the laws of this state, other than a motorcycle, motor-driven cycle, or moped designed for and used exclusively on a golf course.

(15) "New motor vehicle" means a motor vehicle that has not been the subject of a first sale.

(16) "Owner" includes a person, other than a manufacturer, importer, distributor, or dealer, claiming title to or having a right to operate under a lien a motor vehicle that has been subject to a first sale.

(17) "Semitrailer" means a vehicle that is designed or used with a motor vehicle so that part of the weight of the vehicle and its load rests on or is carried by another vehicle.

(18) "Serial number" means a vehicle identification number that is affixed to a part of a motor vehicle and that is:

(A) the manufacturer's permanent vehicle identification number;

(B) a derivative number of the manufacturer's permanent vehicle identification number;

(C) the motor number; or

(D) the vehicle identification number assigned by the department.

(19) "Steal" has the meaning assigned by Section 31.01, Penal Code.

(20) "Subsequent sale" means:

(A) the bargain, sale, transfer, or delivery of a motor vehicle that has been previously registered or licensed in this state or elsewhere, with intent to pass an interest in the vehicle, other than a lien, regardless of where the bargain, sale, transfer, or delivery occurs; and

(B) the registration of the vehicle if registration is required under the laws of this state.

(21) "Title receipt" means an instrument issued under Section 501.024.

(22) "Trailer" means a vehicle that:

(A) is designed or used to carry a load wholly on the trailer's own structure; and

(B) is drawn or designed to be drawn by a motor vehicle.

(23) "Used motor vehicle" means a motor vehicle that has been the subject of a first sale. (Enacted by Acts 1995, 74th Leg., ch. 165 (S.B. 971), § 1, effective September 1, 1995; am. Acts 1999, 76th Leg., ch. 414 (S.B. 1058), § 2.42, effective July 1, 2001; am. Acts 2003, 78th Leg., ch. 1276 (H.B. 3507), § 14A.821, effective September 1, 2003; am. Acts 2005, 79th Leg., ch. 586

(H.B. 1646), § 1, effective September 1, 2005; am. Acts 2007, 80th Leg., ch. 972 (S.B. 228), § 64, effective September 1, 2007; am. Acts 2009, 81st Leg., ch. 933 (H.B. 3097), § 2D.01, effective September 1, 2009; am. Acts 2009, 81st Leg., ch. 1136 (H.B. 2553), § 4, effective September 1, 2009.)

## Sec. 501.002. [2 Versions: Effective January 1, 2012] Definitions.

In this chapter:

(1) "Certificate of title" means a printed record of title issued under Section 501.021.

(2) "Credit card" means a card, plate, or similar device used to make a purchase or to borrow money.

(3) "Dealer" has the meaning assigned by Section 503.001.

(4) "Debit card" means a card that enables the holder to withdraw money or to have the cost of a purchase charged directly to the holder's bank account.

(5) "Department" means the Texas Department of Motor Vehicles.

(6) "Distributor" has the meaning assigned by Section 2301.002, Occupations Code

(7) "Electric bicycle" has the meaning assigned by Section 541.201.

(8) "First sale" means:

(A) the bargain, sale, transfer, or delivery of a motor vehicle that has not been previously registered or titled, with intent to pass an interest in the motor vehicle, other than a lien, regardless of where the bargain, sale, transfer, or delivery occurred; and

(B) the registration or titling of that vehicle.

(9) "House trailer" means a trailer designed for human habitation. The term does not include manufactured housing.

(10) "Importer" means a person, other than a manufacturer, that brings a used motor vehicle into this state for sale in this state.

(11) "Importer's certificate" means a certificate for a used motor vehicle brought into this state for sale in this state.

(12) "Lien" means:

(A) a lien provided for by the constitution or statute in a motor vehicle;

(B) a security interest, as defined by Section 1.201, Business & Commerce Code, in a motor vehicle, other than an absolute title, created by any written security agreement, as defined by Section 9.102, Business & Commerce Code, including a lease, conditional sales contract, deed of trust, chattel mortgage, trust receipt, or reservation of title; or

(C) a child support lien under Chapter 157, Family Code.

(13) "Manufactured housing" has the meaning assigned by Chapter 1201, Occupations Code.

(14) "Manufacturer" has the meaning assigned by Section 503.001.

(15) "Manufacturer's permanent vehicle identification number" means the number affixed by the manufacturer to a motor vehicle in a manner and place easily accessible for physical examination and die-stamped or otherwise permanently affixed on one or more removable parts of the vehicle.

(16) "Motorcycle" has the meaning assigned by Section 521.001 or 541.201, as applicable.

(17) "Motor vehicle" means:

(A) any motor driven or propelled vehicle required to be registered under the laws of this state;

(B) a trailer or semitrailer, other than manufactured housing, that has a gross vehicle weight that exceeds 4,000 pounds;

(C) a travel trailer;

(D) an all-terrain vehicle or a recreational off-highway vehicle, as those terms are defined by Section 502.001, designed by the manufacturer for off-highway use that is not required to be registered under the laws of this state; or

(E) a motorcycle, motor-driven cycle, or moped that is not required to be registered under the laws of this state.

(18) "New motor vehicle" has the meaning assigned by Section 2301.002, Occupations Code.

(19) "Owner" means a person, other than a manufacturer, importer, distributor, or dealer, claiming title to or having a right to operate under a lien a motor vehicle that has been subject to a first sale.

(20) "Purchaser" means a person or entity to which a motor vehicle is donated, given, sold, or otherwise transferred.

(21) "Record of title" means an electronic record of motor vehicle ownership in the department's motor vehicle database that is created under Subchapter I.

(22) "Seller" means a person or entity that donates, gives, sells, or otherwise transfers ownership of a motor vehicle.

(23) "Semitrailer" means a vehicle that is designed or used with a motor vehicle so that

part of the weight of the vehicle and its load rests on or is carried by another vehicle.

(24) "Serial number" means a vehicle identification number that is affixed to a part of a motor vehicle and that is:

(A) the manufacturer's permanent vehicle identification number;

(B) a derivative number of the manufacturer's permanent vehicle identification number;

(C) the motor number; or

(D) the vehicle identification number assigned by the department.

(25) "Steal" has the meaning assigned by Section 31.01, Penal Code.

(26) "Subsequent sale" means:

(A) the bargain, sale, transfer, or delivery of a used motor vehicle, with intent to pass an interest in the vehicle, other than a lien; and

(B) the registration of the vehicle if registration is required under the laws of this state.

(27) "Title" means a certificate or record of title that is issued under Section 501.021.

(28) "Title receipt" means a document issued under Section 501.024.

(29) "Trailer" means a vehicle that:

(A) is designed or used to carry a load wholly on the trailer's own structure; and

(B) is drawn or designed to be drawn by a motor vehicle.

(30) "Travel trailer" means a house trailer-type vehicle or a camper trailer:

(A) that is a recreational vehicle defined under 24 C.F.R. Section 3282.8(g); or

(B) that:

(i) is less than eight feet in width or 40 feet in length, exclusive of any hitch installed on the vehicle;

(ii) is designed primarily for use as temporary living quarters in connection with recreational, camping, travel, or seasonal use;

(iii) is not used as a permanent dwelling; and

(iv) is not a utility trailer, enclosed trailer, or other trailer that does not have human habitation as its primary function.

(31) "Used motor vehicle" means a motor vehicle that has been the subject of a first sale.

(32) "Vehicle identification number" means:

(A) the manufacturer's permanent vehicle identification number affixed by the manufacturer to the motor vehicle that is easily accessible for physical examination and permanently affixed on one or more removable parts of the vehicle; or

(B) a serial number affixed to a part of a motor vehicle that is:

(i) a derivative number of the manufacturer's permanent vehicle identification number;

(ii) the motor number; or

(iii) a vehicle identification number assigned by the department.

(Enacted by Acts 1995, 74th Leg., ch. 165 (S.B. 971), § 1, effective September 1, 1995; am. Acts 1999, 76th Leg., ch. 414 (S.B. 1058), § 2.42, effective July 1, 2001; am. Acts 2003, 78th Leg., ch. 1276 (H.B. 3507), § 14A.821, effective September 1, 2003; am. Acts 2005, 79th Leg., ch. 586 (H.B. 1646), § 1, effective September 1, 2005; am. Acts 2007, 80th Leg., ch. 972 (S.B. 228), § 64, effective September 1, 2007; am. Acts 2009, 81st Leg., ch. 933 (H.B. 3097), § 2D.01, effective September 1, 2009; am. Acts 2009, 81st Leg., ch. 1136 (H.B. 2553), § 4, effective September 1, 2009; am. Acts 2011, 82nd Leg., ch. 1296 (H.B. 2357), § 1, effective January 1, 2012.)

## Sec. 501.003. [2 Versions: Effective until January 1, 2012] Construction.

This chapter shall be liberally construed to lessen and prevent:

(1) the theft of motor vehicles;

(2) the importation into this state of and traffic in motor vehicles that are stolen; and

(3) the sale of an encumbered motor vehicle without the enforced disclosure to the purchaser of a lien secured by the vehicle.

(Enacted by Acts 1995, 74th Leg., ch. 165 (S.B. 971), § 1, effective September 1, 1995.)

## Sec. 501.003. [2 Versions: Effective January 1, 2012] Purpose.

This chapter shall be liberally construed to lessen and prevent:

(1) the theft of motor vehicles;

(2) the importation into this state of and traffic in motor vehicles that are stolen; and

(3) the sale of an encumbered motor vehicle without the enforced disclosure to the purchaser of a lien secured by the vehicle.

(Enacted by Acts 1995, 74th Leg., ch. 165 (S.B. 971), § 1, effective September 1, 1995; am. Acts 2011, 82nd Leg., ch. 1296 (H.B. 2357), § 2, effective January 1, 2012.)

## Sec. 501.004. Applicability.

(a) [2 Versions: Effective until January 1, 2012] This chapter applies to a motor vehicle owned by the state or a political subdivision of the state.

(a) [2 Versions: Effective January 1, 2012] Except as provided by this section, this chapter applies to all motor vehicles, including a motor vehicle owned by the state or a political subdivision of the state.

(b) This chapter does not apply to:

(1) a trailer or semitrailer used only for the transportation of farm products if the products are not transported for hire;

(2) the filing or recording of a lien that is created only on an automobile accessory, including a tire, radio, or heater;

(3) a motor vehicle while it is owned or operated by the United States; or

(4) a new motor vehicle on loan to a political subdivision of the state for use only in a driver education course approved by the Central Education Agency.

(Enacted by Acts 1995, 74th Leg., ch. 165 (S.B. 971), § 1, effective September 1, 1995; am. Acts 2011, 82nd Leg., ch. 1296 (H.B. 2357), § 3, effective January 1, 2012.)

## Sec. 501.0041. [Effective January 1, 2012] Rules; Forms.

(a) The department may adopt rules to administer this chapter.

(b) The department shall post forms on the Internet and provide each county assessor-collector with a sufficient supply of any necessary forms on request.

(Enacted by Acts 1995, 74th Leg., ch. 165 (S.B. 971), § 1, effective September 1, 1995; am. Acts 2011, 82nd Leg., ch. 1296 (H.B. 2357), § 4, effective January 1, 2012, (renumbered from Sec. 501.131).)

## Sec. 501.005. Conflicts with Business & Commerce Code.

Chapters 1—9, Business & Commerce Code, control over a conflicting provision of this chapter. (Enacted by Acts 1995, 74th Leg., ch. 165 (S.B. 971), § 1, effective September 1, 1995.)

## Sec. 501.006. [Effective January 1, 2012] Alias Title.

On receipt of a verified request approved by the executive administrator of a law enforcement

Transportation

agency, the department may issue a title in the form requested by the executive administrator for a vehicle in an alias for the law enforcement agency's use in a covert criminal investigation. (Enacted by Acts 1995, 74th Leg., ch. 165 (S.B. 971), § 1, effective September 1, 1995; am. Acts 2011, 82nd Leg., ch. 1296 (H.B. 2357), § 5, effective January 1, 2012, (renumbered from Sec. 501.159).)

**Secs. 501.007 to 501.020 [Reserved for expansion].**

## SUBCHAPTER B
## CERTIFICATE OF TITLE
## REQUIREMENTS

**Sec. 501.021. [2 Versions: Effective until January 1, 2012] Certificate of Title.**

(a) A motor vehicle certificate of title is an instrument issued by the department that includes:

(1) the name and address of the purchaser and seller at the first sale or the transferee and transferor at a subsequent sale;

(2) the make of the motor vehicle;

(3) the body type of the vehicle;

(4) the manufacturer's permanent vehicle identification number of the vehicle or the vehicle's motor number if the vehicle was manufactured before the date that stamping a permanent identification number on a motor vehicle was universally adopted;

(5) the serial number for the vehicle;

(6) the number on the vehicle's current Texas license plates, if any;

(7) a statement:

(A) that no lien on the vehicle is recorded; or

(B) of the name and address of each lienholder and the date of each lien on the vehicle, listed in the chronological order in which the lien was recorded;

(8) a space for the signature of the owner of the vehicle;

(9) a statement indicating rights of survivorship under Section 501.031;

(10) if the vehicle has an odometer, the odometer reading indicated by the application for the certificate of title; and

(11) any other information required by the department.

(b) A certificate of title must bear the following statement on its face:

"UNLESS OTHERWISE AUTHORIZED BY LAW, IT IS A VIOLATION OF STATE LAW TO SIGN THE NAME OF ANOTHER PERSON ON A CERTIFICATE OF TITLE OR OTHERWISE GIVE FALSE INFORMATION ON A CERTIFICATE OF TITLE."

(c) A certificate of title for a motor vehicle that has been the subject of an ordered repurchase or replacement under Chapter 2301, Occupations Code, must contain on its face a notice sufficient to inform a purchaser that the motor vehicle has been the subject of an ordered repurchase or replacement. (Enacted by Acts 1995, 74th Leg., ch. 165 (S.B. 971), § 1, effective September 1, 1995; am. Acts 1999, 76th Leg., ch. 1423 (H.B. 2409), § 1, effective September 1, 1999; am. Acts 2009, 81st Leg., ch. 542 (S.B. 1617), § 1, effective September 1, 2009.)

**Sec. 501.021. [2 Versions: Effective January 1, 2012] Title for Motor Vehicle.**

(a) A motor vehicle title issued by the department must include:

(1) the name and address of each purchaser and seller at the first sale or a subsequent sale;

(2) the make of the motor vehicle;

(3) the body type of the vehicle;

(4) the manufacturer's permanent vehicle identification number of the vehicle or the vehicle's motor number if the vehicle was manufactured before the date that stamping a permanent identification number on a motor vehicle was universally adopted;

(5) the serial number for the vehicle;

(6) the name and address of each lienholder and the date of each lien on the vehicle, listed in the chronological order in which the lien was recorded;

(7) a statement indicating rights of survivorship under Section 501.031;

(8) if the vehicle has an odometer, the odometer reading at the time of application for the title; and

(9) any other information required by the department.

(b) A printed certificate of title must bear the following statement on its face:

"UNLESS OTHERWISE AUTHORIZED BY LAW, IT IS A VIOLATION OF STATE LAW TO SIGN THE NAME OF ANOTHER PERSON ON

A CERTIFICATE OF TITLE OR OTHERWISE GIVE FALSE INFORMATION ON A CERTIFICATE OF TITLE."

(c) A title for a motor vehicle that has been the subject of an ordered repurchase or replacement under Chapter 2301, Occupations Code, must contain on its face a notice sufficient to inform a purchaser that the motor vehicle has been the subject of an ordered repurchase or replacement. (Enacted by Acts 1995, 74th Leg., ch. 165 (S.B. 971), § 1, effective September 1, 1995; am. Acts 1999, 76th Leg., ch. 1423 (H.B. 2409), § 1, effective September 1, 1999; am. Acts 2009, 81st Leg., ch. 542 (S.B. 1617), § 1, effective September 1, 2009; am. Acts 2011, 82nd Leg., ch. 1296 (H.B. 2357), § 6, effective January 1, 2012.)

### Sec. 501.022. [2 Versions: Effective until January 1, 2012] Certificate of Title Required.

(a) The owner of a motor vehicle registered in this state may not operate or permit the operation of the vehicle on a public highway until the owner obtains a certificate of title for the vehicle or until the owner obtains registration for the vehicle if a receipt evidencing title to the vehicle is issued under Section 501.029(b).

(b) A person may not operate a motor vehicle registered in this state on a public highway if the person knows or has reason to believe that the owner has not obtained a certificate of title for the vehicle.

(c) The owner of a motor vehicle that is required to be registered in this state must apply for a certificate of title of the vehicle before selling or disposing of the vehicle.

(d) Subsection (c) does not apply to a motor vehicle operated on a public highway in this state with a metal dealer's license plate or a dealer's or buyer's temporary tag attached to the vehicle as provided by Chapter 503. (Enacted by Acts 1995, 74th Leg., ch. 165 (S.B. 971), § 1, effective September 1, 1995; am. Acts 2001, 77th Leg., ch. 67 (H.B. 642), § 1, effective September 1, 2001; am. Acts 2009, 81st Leg., ch. 793 (S.B. 1235), § 1, effective September 1, 2009.)

### Sec. 501.022. [2 Versions: Effective January 1, 2012] Motor Vehicle Title Required.

(a) The owner of a motor vehicle registered in this state:

(1) except as provided by Section 501.029, shall apply for title to the vehicle; and

(2) may not operate or permit the operation of the vehicle on a public highway until the owner obtains:

(A) title and registration for the vehicle; or

(B) a receipt evidencing title for registration purposes only under Section 501.029.

(b) A person may not operate a motor vehicle registered in this state on a public highway if the person knows or has reason to believe that the owner has not obtained a title for the vehicle.

(c) The owner of a motor vehicle that is required to be titled and registered in this state must obtain a title to the vehicle before selling or disposing of the vehicle.

(d) Subsection (c) does not apply to a motor vehicle operated on a public highway in this state with a metal dealer's license plate or a dealer's or buyer's temporary tag attached to the vehicle as provided by Chapter 503. (Enacted by Acts 1995, 74th Leg., ch. 165 (S.B. 971), § 1, effective September 1, 1995; am. Acts 2001, 77th Leg., ch. 67 (H.B. 642), § 1, effective September 1, 2001; am. Acts 2009, 81st Leg., ch. 793 (S.B. 1235), § 1, effective September 1, 2009; am. Acts 2011, 82nd Leg., ch. 1296 (H.B. 2357), §§ 7, 8, effective January 1, 2012.)

### Sec. 501.023. [2 Versions: Effective Until January 1, 2012] Application for Certificate of Title.

(a) The owner of a motor vehicle must present identification and apply for a title as prescribed by the department, unless otherwise exempted by law. To obtain a title, the owner must apply:

(1) to the county assessor-collector in the county in which:

(A) the owner is domiciled; or

(B) the motor vehicle is purchased or encumbered; or

(2) if the county in which the owner resides has been declared by the governor as a disaster area, to the county assessor-collector in one of the closest unaffected counties to a county that asks for assistance and:

(A) continues to be declared by the governor as a disaster area because the county has been rendered inoperable by the disaster; and

(B) is inoperable for a protracted period of time.

(b) The assessor-collector shall send the application to the department or enter it into the department's titling system within 72 hours after receipt of the application.

Transportation

(c) The owner or a lessee of a commercial motor vehicle operating under the International Registration Plan or other agreement described by Section 502.054 that is applying for a title for purposes of registration only may apply directly to the department. Notwithstanding Section 501.138(a), an applicant for registration under this subsection shall pay the fee imposed by that section. The fee shall be distributed to the appropriate county assessor-collector in the manner provided by Section 501.138.

(d) An application filed by the owner or lessee of a foreign commercial motor vehicle, as defined by Section 648.001, must be accompanied by a copy of the applicable federal declaration form required by the Federal Motor Carrier Safety Administration or its successor in connection with the importation of a motor vehicle or motor vehicle equipment subject to the federal motor vehicle safety, bumper, and theft prevention standards.

(e) Applications submitted to the department electronically must request the purchaser's choice of county as stated in Subsection (a) as the recipient of all taxes, fees, and other revenue collected as a result of the transaction.
(Enacted by Acts 1995, 74th Leg., ch. 165 (S.B. 971), § 1, effective September 1, 1995; am. Acts 1999, 76th Leg., ch. 1423 (H.B. 2409), § 2, effective September 1, 1999; am. Acts 2009, 81st Leg., ch. 919 (H.B. 2985), § 1, effective September 1, 2009; am. Acts 2011, 82nd Leg., ch. 1290 (H.B. 2017), § 22, effective September 1, 2011.)

## Sec. 501.023. [2 Versions: Effective January 1, 2012] Application for Title.

(a) The owner of a motor vehicle must present identification and apply for a title as prescribed by the department, unless otherwise exempted by law. To obtain a title, the owner must apply:

(1) to the county assessor-collector in the county in which:

(A) the owner is domiciled; or

(B) the motor vehicle is purchased or encumbered; or

(2) if the county in which the owner resides has been declared by the governor as a disaster area, to the county assessor-collector in one of the closest unaffected counties to a county that asks for assistance and:

(A) continues to be declared by the governor as a disaster area because the county has been rendered inoperable by the disaster; and

(B) is inoperable for a protracted period of time.

(b) The assessor-collector shall send the application to the department or enter it into the department's titling system within 72 hours after receipt of the application.

(c) The owner or a lessee of a commercial motor vehicle operating under the International Registration Plan or other agreement described by Section 502.091 that is applying for a title for purposes of registration only may apply directly to the department. Notwithstanding Section 501.138(a), an applicant for registration under this subsection shall pay the fee imposed by that section. The fee shall be distributed to the appropriate county assessor-collector in the manner provided by Section 501.138.

(d) An application filed by the owner or lessee of a foreign commercial motor vehicle, as defined by Section 648.001, must be accompanied by a copy of the applicable federal declaration form required by the Federal Motor Carrier Safety Administration or its successor in connection with the importation of a motor vehicle or motor vehicle equipment subject to the federal motor vehicle safety, bumper, and theft prevention standards.

(e) Applications submitted to the department electronically must request the purchaser's choice of county as stated in Subsection (a) as the recipient of all taxes, fees, and other revenue collected as a result of the transaction.
(Enacted by Acts 1995, 74th Leg., ch. 165 (S.B. 971), § 1, effective September 1, 1995; am. Acts 1999, 76th Leg., ch. 1423 (H.B. 2409), § 2, effective September 1, 1999; am. Acts 2009, 81st Leg., ch. 919 (H.B. 2985), § 1, effective September 1, 2009; am. Acts 2011, 82nd Leg., ch. 1296 (H.B. 2357), § 10, effective September 1, 2011; am. Acts 2012, 82nd Leg., ch. 1296 (H.B. 2357), §§ 9, 10, effective January 1, 2012.)

## Sec. 501.0234. [2 Versions: Effective until January 1, 2012] Duty of Vehicle Dealer on Sale of Certain Vehicles.

(a) A person who sells at the first or a subsequent sale a motor vehicle and who holds a general distinguishing number issued under Chapter 503 of this code or Chapter 2301, Occupations Code, shall:

(1) except as provided by this section, in the time and manner provided by law, apply, in the name of the purchaser of the vehicle, for the registration of the vehicle, if the vehicle is to be

registered, and a certificate of title for the vehicle and file with the appropriate designated agent each document necessary to transfer title to or register the vehicle; and at the same time

(2) remit any required motor vehicle sales tax.

(b) This section does not apply to a motor vehicle:

(1) that has been declared a total loss by an insurance company in the settlement or adjustment of a claim;

(2) for which the certificate of title has been surrendered in exchange for:

(A) a salvage vehicle title issued under this chapter;

(B) a nonrepairable vehicle title issued under this chapter;

(C) a certificate of authority issued under Subchapter D, Chapter 683; or

(D) an ownership document issued by another state that is comparable to a document described by Paragraphs (A)—(C);

(3) with a gross weight in excess of 11,000 pounds; or

(4) purchased by a commercial fleet buyer who is a full-service deputy under Section 502.114 and who utilizes the dealer title application process developed to provide a method to submit title transactions to the county in which the commercial fleet buyer is a full-service deputy.

(c) Each duty imposed by this section on the seller of a motor vehicle is solely that of the seller.

(d) A seller who applies for the registration or a certificate of title for a motor vehicle under Subsection (a)(1) shall apply in the county as directed by the purchaser from the counties set forth in Section 501.023 of this code.

(e) The department shall promulgate a form on which the purchaser of a motor vehicle shall designate the purchaser's choice as set out in Section 501.023 as the recipient of all taxes, fees, and other revenue collected as a result of the transaction, which the tax assessor-collector is authorized by law to retain. A seller shall make that form available to the purchaser of a vehicle at the time of purchase.

(f) A seller has a reasonable time to comply with the terms of Subsection (a)(1) and is not in violation of that provision during the time the seller is making a good faith effort to comply. Notwithstanding compliance with this chapter, equitable title to a vehicle passes to the purchaser of the vehicle at the time the vehicle is the

subject of a sale that is enforceable by either party.

(Enacted by Acts 1997, 75th Leg., ch. 165 (S.B. 898), § 30.37(a), effective September 1, 1997; am. Acts 1999, 76th Leg., ch. 1423 (H.B. 2409), § 3, effective September 1, 1999; am. Acts 2001, 77th Leg., ch. 76 (H.B. 1664), § 1, effective May 14, 2001; am. Acts 2003, 78th Leg., ch. 1276 (H.B. 3507), § 14A.822, effective September 1, 2003; am. Acts 2003, 78th Leg., ch. 1325 (H.B. 3588), § 17.01, effective September 1, 2003; am. Acts 2005, 79th Leg., ch. 1023 (H.B. 988), § 1, effective September 1, 2005; am. Acts 2009, 81st Leg., ch. 1173 (H.B. 3433), § 3, effective September 1, 2009; am. Acts 2009, 81st Leg., ch. 1232 (S.B. 1759), § 3, effective September 1, 2009.)

### Sec. 501.0234. [2 Versions: Effective January 1, 2012] Duty of Vehicle Dealer on Sale of Certain Vehicles.

(a) A person who sells at the first or a subsequent sale a motor vehicle and who holds a general distinguishing number issued under Chapter 503 of this code or Chapter 2301, Occupations Code, shall:

(1) except as provided by this section, in the time and manner provided by law, apply, in the name of the purchaser of the vehicle, for the registration of the vehicle, if the vehicle is to be registered, and a title for the vehicle and file with the appropriate designated agent each document necessary to transfer title to or register the vehicle; and at the same time

(2) remit any required motor vehicle sales tax.

(b) This section does not apply to a motor vehicle:

(1) that has been declared a total loss by an insurance company in the settlement or adjustment of a claim;

(2) for which the title has been surrendered in exchange for:

(A) a salvage vehicle title or salvage record of title issued under this chapter;

(B) a nonrepairable vehicle title or nonrepairable vehicle record of title issued under this chapter or Subchapter D, Chapter 683; or

(C) an ownership document issued by another state that is comparable to a document described by Paragraph (A) or (B);

(3) with a gross weight in excess of 11,000 pounds; or

(4) purchased by a commercial fleet buyer who is a full-service deputy under Section

520.008 and who utilizes the dealer title application process developed to provide a method to submit title transactions to the county in which the commercial fleet buyer is a full-service deputy.

(c) Each duty imposed by this section on the seller of a motor vehicle is solely that of the seller.

(d) A seller who applies for the registration or a title for a motor vehicle under Subsection (a)(1) shall apply in the county as directed by the purchaser from the counties set forth in Section 501.023.

(e) The department shall develop a form or electronic process in which the purchaser of a motor vehicle shall designate the purchaser's choice as set out in Section 501.023 as the recipient of all taxes, fees, and other revenue collected as a result of the transaction, which the tax assessor-collector is authorized by law to retain. A seller shall make that form or electronic process available to the purchaser of a vehicle at the time of purchase.

(f) A seller has a reasonable time to comply with the terms of Subsection (a)(1) and is not in violation of that provision during the time the seller is making a good faith effort to comply. Notwithstanding compliance with this chapter, equitable title to a vehicle passes to the purchaser of the vehicle at the time the vehicle is the subject of a sale that is enforceable by either party.

(Enacted by Acts 1997, 75th Leg., ch. 165 (S.B. 898), § 30.37(a), effective September 1, 1997; am. Acts 1999, 76th Leg., ch. 1423 (H.B. 2409), § 3, effective September 1, 1999; am. Acts 2001, 77th Leg., ch. 76 (H.B. 1664), § 1, effective May 14, 2001; am. Acts 2003, 78th Leg., ch. 1276 (H.B. 3507), § 14A.822, effective September 1, 2003; am. Acts 2003, 78th Leg., ch. 1325 (H.B. 3588), § 17.01, effective September 1, 2003; am. Acts 2005, 79th Leg., ch. 1023 (H.B. 988), § 1, effective September 1, 2005; am. Acts 2009, 81st Leg., ch. 1173 (H.B. 3433), § 3, effective September 1, 2009; am. Acts 2009, 81st Leg., ch. 1232 (S.B. 1759), § 3, effective September 1, 2009; am. Acts 2011, 82nd Leg., ch. 1296 (H.B. 2357), § 11, effective January 1, 2012.)

## Sec. 501.0235.  [Effective January 1, 2012] Personal Identification Information for Obtaining Title.

(a) The department may require an applicant for a title to provide current personal identification as determined by department rule.

(b) Any identification number required by the department under this section may be entered in the department's electronic titling system but may not be printed on the title.

(Am. Acts 2011, 82nd Leg., ch. 1296 (H.B. 2357), § 12, effective January 1, 2012.)

## Sec. 501.024.  [2 Versions: Effective until January 1, 2012] Title Receipt.

(a) A county assessor-collector who receives an application for a certificate of title shall, after the requirements of this chapter are met, including the payment of the fees required under Section 501.138, issue a title receipt on which is noted information concerning the motor vehicle required for the certificate of title under Section 501.021, including a statement of the existence of each lien as disclosed on the application or a statement that no lien is disclosed.

(b) If a lien is not disclosed on the application for a certificate of title, the assessor-collector shall mark the title receipt "original" and deliver it to the applicant.

(c) If a lien is disclosed on the application for a certificate of title, the assessor-collector shall issue duplicate title receipts. The assessor-collector shall:

(1) mark one receipt "original" and mail or deliver it to the first lienholder disclosed on the application; and

(2) mark the second receipt "duplicate original" and mail or deliver it to the address of the applicant provided on the application.

(d) A title receipt authorizes the operation of the motor vehicle on a public highway in this state for 10 days or until the certificate of title is issued, whichever period is shorter.

(Enacted by Acts 1995, 74th Leg., ch. 165 (S.B. 971), § 1, effective September 1, 1995; am. Acts 2001, 77th Leg., ch. 67 (H.B. 642), § 2, effective September 1, 2001.)

## Sec. 501.024.  [2 Versions: Effective January 1, 2012] Title Receipt.

(a) A county assessor-collector who receives an application for a title shall issue a title receipt to the applicant containing the information concerning the motor vehicle required for issuance of a title under Section 501.021 or Subchapter I after:

(1) the requirements of this chapter are met, including the payment of the fees required under Section 501.138; and

(2) the information is entered into the department's titling system.

(b) If a lien is not disclosed on the application for a title, the assessor-collector shall issue a title receipt to the applicant.

(c) If a lien is disclosed on the application for a title, the assessor-collector shall issue a duplicate title receipt to the lienholder.

(d) A title receipt with registration or permit authorizes the operation of the motor vehicle on a public highway in this state for 10 days or until the title is issued, whichever period is shorter. (Enacted by Acts 1995, 74th Leg., ch. 165 (S.B. 971), § 1, effective September 1, 1995; am. Acts 2001, 77th Leg., ch. 67 (H.B. 642), § 2, effective September 1, 2001; am. Acts 2011, 82nd Leg., ch. 1296 (H.B. 2357), § 13, effective January 1, 2012.)

### Sec. 501.025. [2 Versions: Effective until January 1, 2012] Title Receipt Required on First Sale; Manufacturer's Certificate.

A county assessor-collector may not issue a title receipt on the first sale of a motor vehicle unless the applicant for the certificate of title provides to the assessor-collector the application for a certificate of title and a manufacturer's certificate, on a form prescribed by the department, that:

(1) is assigned to the applicant by the manufacturer, distributor, or dealer shown on the manufacturer's certificate as the last transferee; and

(2) shows the transfer of the vehicle from its manufacturer to the purchaser, whether a distributor, dealer, or owner, and each subsequent transfer from distributor to dealer, dealer to dealer, and dealer to applicant.

(Enacted by Acts 1995, 74th Leg., ch. 165 (S.B. 971), § 1, effective September 1, 1995.)

### Sec. 501.025. [2 Versions: Effective January 1, 2012] Manufacturer's Certificate Required on First Sale.

A county assessor-collector may not issue a title receipt on the first sale of a motor vehicle unless the applicant for the title provides the application for a title and a manufacturer's certificate in a manner prescribed by the department.

(Enacted by Acts 1995, 74th Leg., ch. 165 (S.B. 971), § 1, effective September 1, 1995; am. Acts 2011, 82nd Leg., ch. 1296 (H.B. 2357), § 14, effective January 1, 2012.)

### Sec. 501.026. [Repealed January 1, 2012] Importer's Certificate.

(a) A county assessor-collector may not issue a title receipt for a used motor vehicle imported into this state for the purpose of sale in this state unless the applicant for the certificate of title provides the assessor-collector with an importer's certificate properly assigned by the importer.

(b) An importer's certificate must be accompanied by evidence required by the department showing good title to the motor vehicle and the name and address of any lienholder on the vehicle.

(Enacted by Acts 1995, 74th Leg., ch. 165 (S.B. 971), § 1, effective September 1, 1995.)

### Sec. 501.027. [2 Versions: Effective until January 1, 2012] Issuance of Certificate of Title.

(a) On the day that a county assessor-collector issues a title receipt, the assessor-collector shall mail to the department:

(1) a copy of the receipt; and

(2) the evidence of title delivered to the assessor-collector by the applicant.

(b) Not later than the fifth day after the date the department receives an application for a certificate of title and the department determines the requirements of this chapter are met, the department shall issue the certificate of title. If a lien is not disclosed on the application, the department shall send the certificate by first class mail to the applicant at the address provided on the application. If a lien is disclosed on the application, the department shall send the certificate by first class mail to the first lienholder as disclosed on the application.

(Enacted by Acts 1995, 74th Leg., ch. 165 (S.B. 971), § 1, effective September 1, 1995; am. Acts 2001, 77th Leg., ch. 67 (H.B. 642), § 3, effective September 1, 2001.)

### Sec. 501.027. [2 Versions: Effective January 1, 2012] Issuance of Title.

(a) On the day that a county assessor-collector issues a title receipt, a copy of the title receipt and all evidence of title shall be submitted to the department in the period specified in Section 501.023(b).

(b) Not later than the fifth day after the date the department receives an application for a title and the department determines the requirements of this chapter are met:

(1) the title shall be issued to the first lienholder or to the applicant if a lien is not disclosed on the application; or

(2) the department shall notify the applicant that the department's titling system has estab-

Transportation

lished a record of title of the motor vehicle in the applicant's name if a lien is not disclosed. If a lien is disclosed on the application, the department shall notify the lienholder that the lien has been recorded.

(Enacted by Acts 1995, 74th Leg., ch. 165 (S.B. 971), § 1, effective September 1, 1995; am. Acts 2001, 77th Leg., ch. 67 (H.B. 642), § 3, effective September 1, 2001; am. Acts 2011, 82nd Leg., ch. 1296 (H.B. 2357), § 15, effective January 1, 2012.)

## Sec. 501.0275.   [2 Versions: Effective until January 1, 2012] Issuance of Title for Unregistered Vehicle.

(a) The department shall issue a certificate of title for a motor vehicle that complies with the other requirements for issuance of a certificate of title under this chapter except that:

   (1) the vehicle is not registered for a reason other than a reason provided by Section 501.051(6); and

   (2) the applicant does not provide evidence of financial responsibility that complies with Section 502.153.

(b) On application for a certificate of title under this section, the applicant must surrender any license plates issued for the motor vehicle and any registration insignia for validation of those plates to the department.

(Enacted by Acts 1999, 76th Leg., ch. 1423 (H.B. 2409), § 4, effective September 1, 1999.)

## Sec. 501.0275.   [2 Versions: Effective January 1, 2012] Issuance of Title for Unregistered Vehicle.

(a) The department shall issue a title for a motor vehicle that complies with the other requirements under this chapter unless:

   (1) the vehicle is not registered for a reason other than a reason provided by Section 501.051(a)(6); and

   (2) the applicant does not provide evidence of financial responsibility that complies with Section 502.046.

(b) On application for a title under this section, the applicant must surrender any license plates issued for the motor vehicle if the plates are not being transferred to another vehicle and any registration insignia for validation of those plates to the department.

(Enacted by Acts 1999, 76th Leg., ch. 1423 (H.B. 2409), § 4, effective September 1, 1999; am. Acts 2011, 82nd Leg., ch. 1296 (H.B. 2357), § 16, effective January 1, 2012.)

## Sec. 501.0276.   [2 Versions: Effective until January 1, 2012] Denial of Title Receipt or Certificate of Title for Failure to Provide Proof of Emissions Testing.

A county assessor-collector may not issue a title receipt and the department may not issue a certificate of title for a vehicle subject to Section 548.3011 unless proof that the vehicle has passed a vehicle emissions test as required by that section, in a form authorized by that section, is presented to the county assessor-collector with the application for certificate of title.

(Enacted by Acts 2001, 77th Leg., ch. 1075 (H.B. 2134), § 3, effective September 1, 2001.)

## Sec. 501.0276.   [2 Versions: Effective January 1, 2012] Denial of Title Receipt, Title, or Record of Title for Failure to Provide Proof of Emissions Testing.

A county assessor-collector may not issue a title receipt and the department may not issue a certificate of title for a vehicle subject to Section 548.3011 unless proof that the vehicle has passed a vehicle emissions test as required by that section, in a manner authorized by that section, is presented to the county assessor-collector with the application for a title.

(Enacted by Acts 2001, 77th Leg., ch. 1075 (H.B. 2134), § 3, effective September 1, 2001; am. Acts 2011, 82nd Leg., ch. 1296 (H.B. 2357), § 17, effective January 1, 2012.)

## Sec. 501.028.   Owner's Signature.

On receipt of a certificate of title, the owner of a motor vehicle shall write the owner's name in ink in the space provided on the certificate.

(Enacted by Acts 1995, 74th Leg., ch. 165 (S.B. 971), § 1, effective September 1, 1995.)

## Sec. 501.029.   [2 Versions: Effective until January 1, 2012] Use of Registration Receipt or Title Receipt to Evidence Title.

(a) A person may use a registration receipt issued under Chapter 502 or a title receipt to evidence title to a motor vehicle and not to transfer an interest in or establish a lien on the vehicle.

(b) The department by rule may provide for the issuance of a receipt that evidences title to a motor vehicle for registration purposes only. The fee for application for the receipt is the fee applicable to application for a certificate of title.

(Enacted by Acts 1995, 74th Leg., ch. 165 (S.B. 971), § 1, effective September 1, 1995; am. Acts 2001, 77th Leg., ch. 67 (H.B. 642), § 4, effective September 1, 2001.)

## Sec. 501.029. [2 Versions: Effective January 1, 2012] Acceptable Proof of Ownership.

The board by rule may provide a list of the documents required for the issuance of a receipt that evidences title to a motor vehicle for registration purposes only. The fee for application for the receipt is the fee applicable to application for a title. The title receipt may not be used to transfer an interest in or establish a lien on the vehicle.

(Enacted by Acts 1995, 74th Leg., ch. 165 (S.B. 971), § 1, effective September 1, 1995; am. Acts 2001, 77th Leg., ch. 67 (H.B. 642), § 4, effective September 1, 2001; am. Acts 2011, 82nd Leg., ch. 1296 (H.B. 2357), § 18, effective January 1, 2012.)

## Sec. 501.030. [2 Versions: Effective until January 1, 2012] Motor Vehicles Brought into State.

(a) Before a motor vehicle that was last registered or titled in another state or country may be titled in this state, the applicant must furnish the county assessor-collector with a verification form under Section 548.256.

(b) Before a motor vehicle that was not manufactured for sale or distribution in the United States may be titled in this state, the applicant must:

(1) provide to the assessor-collector:

(A) a bond release letter, with all attachments, issued by the United States Department of Transportation acknowledging:

(i) receipt of a statement of compliance submitted by the importer of the vehicle; and

(ii) that the statement meets the safety requirements of 19 C.F.R. 12.80(e);

(B) a bond release letter, with all attachments, issued by the United States Environmental Protection Agency stating that the vehicle has been tested and shown to conform to federal emission requirements; and

(C) a receipt or certificate issued by the United States Department of the Treasury showing that all gas guzzler taxes due on the vehicle under 26 U.S.C. Section 4064(a) have been paid; or

(2) provide to the assessor-collector proof satisfactory to the assessor-collector that the vehicle was not brought into the United States from outside of the country.

(c) Subsections (a) and (b) do not apply to a motor vehicle lawfully imported into the United States by a distributor or dealer from the vehicle's manufacturer.

(d) If a motor vehicle has not been titled or registered in the United States, the application for certificate of title must be accompanied by:

(1) a manufacturer's certificate of origin written in English issued by the vehicle manufacturer;

(2) the original documents that constitute valid proof of ownership in the country where the vehicle was originally purchased, with an English translation of the documents verified as to the accuracy of the translation by an affidavit of the translator; or

(3) if the vehicle was imported from a country that cancels the vehicle registration and title for export, the documents assigned to the vehicle after the registration and title were canceled, with an English translation of the documents verified as to the accuracy of the translation by an affidavit of the translator.

(e) Before a motor vehicle that is required to be registered in this state and that is brought into this state by a person other than a manufacturer or importer may be bargained, sold, transferred, or delivered with an intent to pass an interest in the vehicle or encumbered by a lien, the owner must apply for a certificate of title on a form prescribed by the department to the county assessor-collector for the county in which the transaction is to take place. The assessor-collector may not issue a title receipt unless the applicant delivers to the assessor-collector satisfactory evidence of title showing that the applicant is the owner of the vehicle and that the vehicle is free of any undisclosed liens.

(f) A county assessor-collector may not be held liable for civil damages arising out of the assessor-collector's failure to reflect on the title receipt a lien or encumbrance on a motor vehicle to which Subsection (e) applies unless the assessor-collector's failure constitutes wilful or wanton negligence.

(g) Until an applicant has complied with this section:

(1) a county assessor-collector may not accept an application for certificate of title; and

(2) the applicant is not entitled to an appeal as provided by Sections 501.052 and 501.053.

(Enacted by Acts 1995, 74th Leg., ch. 165 (S.B. 971), § 1, effective September 1, 1995.)

## Sec. 501.030.    [2 Versions: Effective January 1, 2012] Motor Vehicles Brought into State.

(a) Before a motor vehicle that was last registered or titled in another state or country may be titled in this state, the applicant must furnish the county assessor-collector with a verification form under Section 548.256.

(b) Before a motor vehicle that was not manufactured for sale or distribution in the United States may be titled in this state, the applicant must:

(1) provide to the assessor-collector:

(A) a bond release letter, with all attachments, issued by the United States Department of Transportation acknowledging:

(i) receipt of a statement of compliance submitted by the importer of the vehicle; and

(ii) that the statement meets the safety requirements of 19 C.F.R. 12.80(e);

(B) a bond release letter, with all attachments, issued by the United States Environmental Protection Agency stating that the vehicle has been tested and shown to conform to federal emission requirements; and

(C) a receipt or certificate issued by the United States Department of the Treasury showing that all gas guzzler taxes due on the vehicle under 26 U.S.C. Section 4064(a) have been paid; or

(2) provide to the assessor-collector proof, satisfactory to the department that the vehicle was not brought into the United States from outside the country.

(c) Subsections (a) and (b) do not apply to a motor vehicle lawfully imported into the United States by a distributor or dealer from the vehicle's manufacturer.

(d) If a motor vehicle has not been titled or registered in the United States, the application for title must be accompanied by:

(1) a manufacturer's certificate of origin written in English issued by the vehicle manufacturer;

(2) the original documents that constitute valid proof of ownership in the country where the vehicle was originally purchased, with an English translation of the documents verified as to the accuracy of the translation by an affidavit of the translator; or

(3) if the vehicle was imported from a country that cancels the vehicle registration and title for export, the documents assigned to the vehicle after the registration and title were canceled, with an English translation of the documents verified as to the accuracy of the translation by an affidavit of the translator.

(e) Before a motor vehicle that is required to be registered in this state and that is brought into this state by a person other than a manufacturer or importer may be bargained, sold, transferred, or delivered with an intent to pass an interest in the vehicle or encumbered by a lien, the owner must apply for a title in a manner prescribed by the department to the county assessor-collector for the county in which the transaction is to take place. The assessor-collector may not issue a title receipt unless the applicant delivers to the assessor-collector satisfactory evidence showing that the applicant is the owner of the vehicle and that the vehicle is free of any undisclosed liens.

(f) A county assessor-collector may not be held liable for civil damages arising out of the assessor-collector's failure to reflect on the title receipt a lien or encumbrance on a motor vehicle to which Subsection (e) applies unless the failure constitutes wilful or wanton negligence.

(g) Until an applicant has complied with this section:

(1) a county assessor-collector may not accept an application for title; and

(2) the applicant is not entitled to an appeal as provided by Sections 501.052 and 501.053. (Enacted by Acts 1995, 74th Leg., ch. 165 (S.B. 971), § 1, effective September 1, 1995; am. Acts 2011, 82nd Leg., ch. 1296 (H.B. 2357), § 19, effective January 1, 2012.)

## Sec. 501.031.    [2 Versions: Effective until January 1, 2012] Rights of Survivorship Agreement.

(a) The department shall include on each certificate of title a rights of survivorship agreement form. The form must:

(1) provide that if the agreement is signed by two or more eligible persons, the motor vehicle is held jointly by those persons with the interest of a person who dies to survive to the surviving person or persons; and

(2) provide blanks for the signatures of the persons.

(b) If the vehicle is registered in the name of one or more of the persons who signed the agreement, the certificate of title may contain a:

(1) rights of survivorship agreement signed by all the persons; or

(2) remark if a rights of survivorship agreement is surrendered with the application for certificate of title or otherwise on file with the department.

(c) Except as provided in Subsection (g), ownership of the vehicle may be transferred only:

(1) by all the persons acting jointly, if all the persons are alive; and

(2) on the death of one of the persons by the surviving person or persons by transferring the certificate of title, in the manner otherwise required by law for transfer of ownership of the vehicle, with a copy of the death certificate of the deceased person attached to the certificate of title application.

(d) A rights of survivorship agreement under this section may be revoked only by surrender of the certificate of title to the department and joint application by the persons who signed the agreement for a new title in the name of the person or persons designated in the application.

(e) A person is eligible to sign a rights of survivorship agreement under this section if the person:

(1) is married and the spouse of the signing person is the only other party to the agreement;

(2) is unmarried and attests to that unmarried status by affidavit; or

(3) is married and provides the department with an affidavit from the signing person's spouse that attests that the signing person's interest in the vehicle is the signing person's separate property.

(f) If the title is being issued in connection with the sale of the vehicle, the seller is not eligible to sign a rights of survivorship agreement under this section unless the seller is the child, grandchild, parent, grandparent, brother, or sister of each other person signing the agreement. A family relationship required by this subsection may be a relationship established by adoption.

(g) If an agreement, other than the agreement provided for in Subsection (a), providing for right of survivorship is signed by two or more persons, the department shall issue a new certificate of title to the surviving person or persons upon application accompanied by a copy of the death certificate of the deceased person. The department may develop for public use under this subsection an optional rights of survivorship agreement form.

(Enacted by Acts 1995, 74th Leg., ch. 165 (S.B. 971), § 1, effective September 1, 1995; am. Acts 1997, 75th Leg., ch. 165 (S.B. 898), § 30.39(a), effective September 1, 1997; am. Acts 1999, 76th Leg., ch. 62 (S.B. 1368), § 17.05, effective September 1, 1999; am. Acts 1999, 76th Leg., ch. 241 (H.B. 381), § 1, effective September 1, 1999.)

## Sec. 501.031. [2 Versions: Effective January 1, 2012] Rights of Survivorship Agreement.

(a) The department shall include on each title an optional rights of survivorship agreement that:

(1) provides that if the agreement is between two or more eligible persons, the motor vehicle is held jointly by those persons with the interest of a person who dies to transfer to the surviving person or persons; and

(2) provides for the acknowledgment by signature, either electronically or by hand, of the persons.

(b) If the vehicle is registered in the name of one or more of the persons who acknowledged the agreement, the title may contain a:

(1) rights of survivorship agreement acknowledged by all the persons; or

(2) remark if a rights of survivorship agreement is on file with the department.

(c) Ownership of the vehicle may be transferred only:

(1) by all the persons acting jointly, if all the persons are alive; and

(2) on the death of one of the persons by the surviving person or persons by transferring ownership of the vehicle, in the manner otherwise required by law, with a copy of the death certificate of the deceased person.

(d) A rights of survivorship agreement under this section may be revoked only if the persons named in the agreement file a joint application for a new title in the name of the person or persons designated in the application.

(e) A person is eligible to file a rights of survivorship agreement under this section if the person:

(1) is married and the spouse of the person is the only other party to the agreement;

(2) is unmarried and attests to that unmarried status by affidavit; or

(3) is married and provides the department with an affidavit from the person's spouse that attests that the person's interest in the vehicle is the person's separate property.

(f) The department may develop an optional electronic rights of survivorship agreement for public use.

Transportation

(Enacted by Acts 1995, 74th Leg., ch. 165 (S.B. 971), § 1, effective September 1, 1995; am. Acts 1997, 75th Leg., ch. 165 (S.B. 898), § 30.39(a), effective September 1, 1997; am. Acts 1999, 76th Leg., ch. 62 (S.B. 1368), § 17.05, effective September 1, 1999; am. Acts 1999, 76th Leg., ch. 241 (H.B. 381), § 1, effective September 1, 1999; am. Acts 2011, 82nd Leg., ch. 1296 (H.B. 2357), § 20, effective January 1, 2012.)

### Sec. 501.032.  [2 Versions: Effective until January 1, 2012] Assignment of Serial Number by Department.

(a) On proper application, the department shall assign a serial number to a house trailer, a trailer or semitrailer that has a gross vehicle weight that exceeds 4,000 pounds, or an item of equipment, including a tractor, farm implement, unit of special mobile equipment, or unit of off-road construction equipment on which:

(1) a serial number was not die-stamped by the manufacturer; or

(2) the serial number die-stamped by the manufacturer has been lost, removed, or obliterated.

(b) The applicant shall die-stamp the assigned serial number at the place designated by the department on the house trailer, trailer, semi-trailer, or equipment.

(c) The manufacturer's serial number or the serial number assigned by the department shall be affixed on the carriage or axle part of the house trailer, trailer, or semitrailer. The department shall use the number as the major identification of the vehicle in the issuance of a certificate of title.

(Enacted by Acts 1995, 74th Leg., ch. 165 (S.B. 971), § 1, effective September 1, 1995.)

### Sec. 501.032.  [2 Versions: Effective January 1, 2012] Assignment of Vehicle Identification Number by Department.

(a) On proper application, the department shall assign a vehicle identification number to a travel trailer, a trailer or semitrailer that has a gross vehicle weight that exceeds 4,000 pounds, or an item of equipment, including a tractor, farm implement, unit of special mobile equipment, or unit of off-road construction equipment on which:

(1) a vehicle identification number was not die-stamped by the manufacturer; or

(2) a vehicle identification number die-stamped by the manufacturer has been lost, removed, or obliterated.

(b) The applicant shall die-stamp the assigned vehicle identification number at the place designated by the department on the travel trailer, trailer, semitrailer, or equipment.

(c) The manufacturer's vehicle identification number or the vehicle identification number assigned by the department shall be affixed on the carriage or axle part of the travel trailer, trailer, or semitrailer. The department shall use the number as the major identification of the vehicle in the issuance of a title.

(Enacted by Acts 1995, 74th Leg., ch. 165 (S.B. 971), § 1, effective September 1, 1995; am. Acts 2011, 82nd Leg., ch. 1296 (H.B. 2357), § 21, effective January 1, 2012.)

### Sec. 501.033.  [2 Versions: Effective until January 1, 2012] Assignment of Identification Number by Department.

(a) A person determined by the department or a court to be the owner of a motor vehicle, a part of a motor vehicle, or an item of equipment including a tractor, farm implement, unit of special mobile equipment, or unit of off-road construction equipment that has had the serial number removed, altered, or obliterated may apply to the department for an assigned vehicle identification number.

(b) An application under this section must be on a form prescribed and furnished by the department and accompanied by the certificate of title for the vehicle or other valid evidence of ownership as required by the department if there is no certificate of title.

(c) A fee of $2 must accompany each application under this section to be deposited in the state highway fund.

(d) The assigned number shall be die-stamped or otherwise affixed to the motor vehicle, part, or item of equipment at the location and in the manner designated by the department.

(e) If the auto theft unit of a county or municipal law enforcement agency conducts an inspection required by the department under this section, the agency may impose a fee of $40. The county or municipal treasurer shall credit the fee to the general fund of the county or municipality, as applicable, to defray the agency's cost associated with the inspection. The fee shall be waived by the department or agency imposing the fee if the person applying under this section is the current registered owner.

(Enacted by Acts 1995, 74th Leg., ch. 165 (S.B. 971), § 1, effective September 1, 1995; am. Acts

2009, 81st Leg., ch. 223 (S.B. 1356), § 1, effective September 1, 2009.)

## Sec. 501.033. [2 Versions: Effective January 1, 2012] Assignment of Identification Number by Department.

(a) A person determined by law enforcement or a court to be the owner of a motor vehicle, a part of a motor vehicle, or an item of equipment including a tractor, farm implement, unit of special mobile equipment, or unit of off-road construction equipment may apply to the department for an assigned vehicle identification number that has been removed, altered, or obliterated.

(b) An application under this section must be in a manner prescribed by the department and accompanied by valid evidence of ownership as required by the department.

(c) A fee of $2 must accompany each application under this section to be deposited in the state highway fund.

(d) The assigned vehicle identification number shall be die-stamped or otherwise affixed in the manner designated by the department.

(e) If the auto theft unit of a county or municipal law enforcement agency conducts an inspection required by the department under this section, the agency may impose a fee of $40. The county or municipal treasurer shall credit the fee to the general fund of the county or municipality, as applicable, to defray the agency's cost associated with the inspection. The fee shall be waived by the department or agency imposing the fee if the person applying under this section is the current registered owner.

(Enacted by Acts 1995, 74th Leg., ch. 165 (S.B. 971), § 1, effective September 1, 1995; am. Acts 2009, 81st Leg., ch. 223 (S.B. 1356), § 1, effective September 1, 2009; am. Acts 2011, 82nd Leg., ch. 1296 (H.B. 2357), § 22, effective January 1, 2012.)

## Sec. 501.0331. [Effective January 1, 2012] Motor Number Required for Registration.

A person may not apply to the county assessor-collector for the registration of a motor vehicle from which the original motor number has been removed, erased, or destroyed until the motor vehicle bears the motor number assigned by the department.

(Enacted by Acts 1995, 74th Leg., ch. 165 (S.B. 971), § 1, effective September 1, 1995; am. Acts

2011, 82nd Leg., ch. 1296 (H.B. 2357), § 23, effective January 1, 2012, (renumbered from Sec. 520.011).)

## Sec. 501.0332. [Effective January 1, 2012] Application for Motor Number Record.

(a) To obtain a motor number assigned by the department, the owner of a motor vehicle that has had the original motor number removed, erased, or destroyed must file a sworn application with the department.

(b) The department shall maintain a record of each motor number assigned by the department that includes:

(1) the motor number assigned by the department;

(2) the name and address of the owner of the motor vehicle; and

(3) the make, model, and year of manufacture of the motor vehicle.

(Enacted by Acts 1995, 74th Leg., ch. 165 (S.B. 971), § 1, effective September 1, 1995; am. Acts 2011, 82nd Leg., ch. 1296 (H.B. 2357), § 24, effective January 1, 2012, (renumbered from Sec. 520.012).)

## Sec. 501.034. [2 Versions: Effective until January 1, 2012] Issuance of Title to Government Agency.

The department may issue a certificate of title to a government agency if a vehicle or part of a vehicle is:

(1) forfeited to the government agency;

(2) delivered by court order under the Code of Criminal Procedure to a government agency for official purposes; or

(3) sold as abandoned or unclaimed property under the Code of Criminal Procedure.

(Enacted by Acts 1995, 74th Leg., ch. 165 (S.B. 971), § 1, effective September 1, 1995.)

## Sec. 501.034. [2 Versions: Effective January 1, 2012] Issuance of Title to Government Agency.

The department may issue a title to a government agency if a vehicle or part of a vehicle is:

(1) forfeited to the government agency;

(2) delivered by court order under the Code of Criminal Procedure to a government agency for official purposes; or

(3) sold as abandoned or unclaimed property under the Code of Criminal Procedure.

(Enacted by Acts 1995, 74th Leg., ch. 165 (S.B. 971), § 1, effective September 1, 1995; am. Acts

2011, 82nd Leg., ch. 1296 (H.B. 2357), § 25, effective January 1, 2012.)

### Sec. 501.035.  [2 Versions: Effective until January 1, 2012] Certificate of Title for Former Military Vehicle.

(a) Notwithstanding any other law, the department shall issue a certificate of title for a former military vehicle that is not registered under the laws of this state if all other requirements for issuance of a certificate of title are met.

(b) In this section, "former military vehicle" has the meaning assigned by Section 504.502(i). (Enacted by Acts 1997, 75th Leg., ch. 165 (S.B. 898), § 30.40(a), effective September 1, 1997; am. Acts 2011, 82nd Leg., ch. 91 (S.B. 1303), § 24.006, effective September 1, 2011.)

### Sec. 501.035.  [2 Versions: Effective January 1, 2012] Title for Former Military Vehicle.

(a) Notwithstanding any other law, the department shall issue a title for a former military vehicle if all requirements for issuance of a title are met.

(b) In this section, "former military vehicle" has the meaning assigned by Section 504.502(i) (Enacted by Acts 1997, 75th Leg., ch. 165 (S.B. 898), § 30.40(a), effective September 1, 1997; am. Acts 2011, 82nd Leg., ch. 1296 (H.B. 2357), § 26, effective January 1, 2012.)

### Sec. 501.036.  [2 Versions: Effective until January 1, 2012] Certificate of Title for Farm Semitrailer.

(a) Notwithstanding any other provision of this chapter, the department may issue a certificate of title for a farm semitrailer with a gross weight of more than 4,000 pounds if:

(1) the farm semitrailer is eligible for registration under Section 504.504; and

(2) all other requirements for issuance of a certificate of title are met.

(b) To obtain a certificate of title under this section, the owner of the farm semitrailer must:

(1) apply for the certificate of title in the manner required by Section 501.023; and

(2) pay the fee required by Section 501.138.

(c) The department shall adopt rules and forms to implement and administer this section.

(Enacted by Acts 2001, 77th Leg., ch. 422 (H.B. 2217), § 1, effective September 1, 2001; am. Acts 2007, 80th Leg., ch. 280 (H.B. 505), § 1, effective June 15, 2007.)

### Sec. 501.036.  [2 Versions: Effective January 1, 2012] Title for Farm Semitrailer.

(a) Notwithstanding any other provision of this chapter, the department may issue a title for a farm semitrailer with a gross weight of more than 4,000 pounds if:

(1) the farm semitrailer is eligible for registration under Section 502.146; and

(2) all other requirements for issuance of a title are met.

(b) To obtain a title under this section, the owner of the farm semitrailer must:

(1) apply for the title in the manner required by Section 501.023; and

(2) pay the fee required by Section 501.138.

(c) The department shall adopt rules to implement and administer this section.

(Enacted by Acts 2001, 77th Leg., ch. 422 (H.B. 2217), § 1, effective September 1, 2001; am. Acts 2007, 80th Leg., ch. 280 (H.B. 505), § 1, effective June 15, 2007; am. Acts 2011, 82nd Leg., ch. 1296 (H.B. 2357), § 27, effective January 1, 2012.)

### Sec. 501.037. [Reserved for expansion].

### Sec. 501.038.  Certificate of Title for Custom Vehicle or Street Rod.

(a) In this section, "custom vehicle" and "street rod" have the meanings assigned by Section 504.501.

(b) Notwithstanding any other provision of this chapter, if the department issues a certificate of title for a custom vehicle or street rod, the model year and make of the vehicle must be listed on the certificate of title and must be the model year and make that the body of the vehicle resembles. The certificate of title must also include the word "replica."

(c) The owner of the custom vehicle or street rod shall provide the department with documentation identifying the model year and make that the body of the vehicle resembles.

(Enacted by Acts 2011, 82nd Leg., ch. 729 (H.B. 890), § 1, effective September 1, 2011.)

**Secs. 501.039 to 501.050 [Reserved for expansion].**

**Sec. 501.051. [2 Versions: Effective Until January 1, 2012] Grounds for Refusal to Issue or for Revocation or Suspension of Certificate.**

The department shall refuse to issue a certificate of title or shall suspend or revoke a certificate of title if:

(1) the application for the certificate contains a false or fraudulent statement;

(2) the applicant failed to furnish required information requested by the department;

(3) the applicant is not entitled to a certificate of title;

(4) the department has reason to believe that the motor vehicle is stolen;

(5) the department has reason to believe that the issuance of a certificate of title would defraud the owner or a lienholder of the motor vehicle;

(6) the registration for the motor vehicle is suspended or revoked; or

(7) the required fee has not been paid.

(Enacted by Acts 1995, 74th Leg., ch. 165 (S.B. 971), § 1, effective September 1, 1995.)

**Sec. 501.051. [2 Versions: Effective January 1, 2012] Grounds for Refusal to Issue or for Revocation or Suspension of Title.**

(a) A title may be refused, canceled, suspended, or revoked by the department if:

(1) the application contains a false or fraudulent statement;

(2) the applicant failed to furnish required information requested by the department;

(3) the applicant is not entitled to a title;

(4) the department has reason to believe that the motor vehicle is stolen;

(5) the department has reason to believe that the issuance of a title would defraud the owner or a lienholder of the motor vehicle;

(6) the registration for the motor vehicle is suspended or revoked; or

(7) the required fee has not been paid.

(b) The department may rescind, cancel, or revoke an application for a title if a notarized affidavit is presented containing:

(1) a statement that the vehicle involved was a new motor vehicle in the process of a first sale;

(2) a statement that the dealer, the applicant, and any lienholder have canceled the sale;

(3) a statement that the vehicle:

(A) was never in the possession of the title applicant; or

(B) was in the possession of the title applicant; and

(4) the signatures of the dealer, the applicant, and any lienholder.

(c) A rescission, cancellation, or revocation containing the statement authorized under Subsection (b)(3)(B) does not negate the fact that the vehicle has been the subject of a previous retail sale.

(Enacted by Acts 1995, 74th Leg., ch. 165 (S.B. 971), § 1, effective September 1, 1995; am. Acts 2011, 82nd Leg., ch. 1296 (H.B. 2357), § 28, effective January 1, 2012.)

**Sec. 501.052. [2 Versions: Effective until January 1, 2012] Hearing on Refusal to Issue or Revocation or Suspension of Certificate of Title; Appeal.**

(a) An interested person aggrieved by a refusal, suspension, or revocation under Section 501.051 may apply for a hearing to the county assessor-collector for the county in which the person is domiciled. On the day an assessor-collector receives the application, the assessor-collector shall notify the department of the date of the hearing.

(b) The assessor-collector shall hold the hearing not earlier than the 11th day and not later than the 15th day after the date the assessor-collector receives the application for a hearing.

(c) At the hearing, the applicant and the department may submit evidence.

(d) A determination of the assessor-collector is binding on the applicant and the department as to whether the department correctly refused to issue or correctly revoked or suspended the certificate of title.

(e) An applicant aggrieved by the determination under Subsection (d) may appeal to the county court of the county of the applicant's residence. An applicant must file an appeal not later than the fifth day after the date of the assessor-collector's determination. The county court judge shall try the appeal in the manner of other civil cases. All rights and immunities granted in the trial of a civil case are available to the interested parties. If the department's action is not sustained, the department shall promptly issue a certificate of title for the vehicle.

(Enacted by Acts 1995, 74th Leg., ch. 165 (S.B. 971), § 1, effective September 1, 1995.)

### Sec. 501.052.  [2 Versions: Effective January 1, 2012] Hearing on Refusal to Issue or Revocation or Suspension of Title; Appeal.

(a) An interested person aggrieved by a refusal, recission, cancellation, suspension, or revocation under Section 501.051 may apply for a hearing to the county assessor-collector for the county in which the person is a resident. On the day an assessor-collector receives the application, the assessor-collector shall notify the department of the date of the hearing.

(b) The assessor-collector shall hold the hearing not earlier than the 11th day and not later than the 15th day after the date the assessor-collector receives the application for a hearing.

(c) At the hearing, the applicant and the department may submit evidence.

(d) A determination of the assessor-collector is binding on the applicant and the department as to whether the department correctly rescinded, canceled, revoked, or suspended the title.

(e) An applicant aggrieved by the determination under Subsection (d) may appeal to the county court of the county of the applicant's residence. An applicant must file an appeal not later than the fifth day after the date of the assessor-collector's determination. The county court judge shall try the appeal in the manner of other civil cases. All rights and immunities granted in the trial of a civil case are available to the interested parties. If the department's action is not sustained, the department shall promptly issue a title for the vehicle.

(Enacted by Acts 1995, 74th Leg., ch. 165 (S.B. 971), § 1, effective September 1, 1995; am. Acts 2011, 82nd Leg., ch. 1296 (H.B. 2357), §§ 29, 30, effective January 1, 2012.)

### Sec. 501.053.  [2 Versions: Effective until January 1, 2012] Filing of Bond As Alternative to Hearing.

(a) As an alternative to the procedure provided by Section 501.052, the person may file a bond with the department. On the filing of the bond the department may issue the certificate of title.

(b) The bond must be:

(1) in the form prescribed by the department;

(2) executed by the applicant;

(3) issued by a person authorized to conduct a surety business in this state;

(4) in an amount equal to one and one-half times the value of the vehicle as determined by the department; and

(5) conditioned to indemnify all prior owners and lienholders and all subsequent purchasers of the vehicle or persons who acquire a security interest in the vehicle, and their successors in interest, against any expense, loss, or damage, including reasonable attorney's fees, occurring because of the issuance of the certificate of title for the vehicle or for a defect in or undisclosed security interest on the right, title, or interest of the applicant to the vehicle.

(c) An interested person has a right of action to recover on the bond for a breach of the bond's condition. The aggregate liability of the surety to all persons may not exceed the amount of the bond.

(d) A bond under this section expires on the third anniversary of the date the bond became effective. The department shall return an expired bond to the person who filed the bond unless the department has been notified of a pending action to recover on the bond.

(Enacted by Acts 1995, 74th Leg., ch. 165 (S.B. 971), § 1, effective September 1, 1995.)

### Sec. 501.053.  [2 Versions: Effective January 1, 2012] Filing of Bond As Alternative to Hearing.

(a) As an alternative to the procedure provided by Section 501.052, the person may file a bond with the department. On the filing of the bond the person may obtain a title.

(b) The bond must be:

(1) in the manner prescribed by the department;

(2) executed by the applicant;

(3) issued by a person authorized to conduct a surety business in this state;

(4) in an amount equal to one and one-half times the value of the vehicle as determined by the department; which may set an appraisal system by rule if it is unable to determine that value; and

(5) conditioned to indemnify all prior owners and lienholders and all subsequent purchasers of the vehicle or persons who acquire a security interest in the vehicle, and their successors in

interest, against any expense, loss, or damage, including reasonable attorney's fees, occurring because of the issuance of the title for the vehicle or for a defect in or undisclosed security interest on the right, title, or interest of the applicant to the vehicle.

(c) An interested person has a right of action to recover on the bond for a breach of the bond's condition. The aggregate liability of the surety to all persons may not exceed the amount of the bond.

(d) A bond under this section expires on the third anniversary of the date the bond became effective.

(e) The board by rule may establish a fee to cover the cost of administering this section.
(Enacted by Acts 2011, 82nd Leg., ch. 1296 (H.B. 2357), § 31, effective January 1, 2012.)

**Secs. 501.054 to 501.070 [Reserved for expansion].**

## SUBCHAPTER D
## SALES OF MOTOR VEHICLES AND TRANSFERS OF TITLE

**Sec. 501.071. [2 Versions: Effective until January 1, 2012] Sale of Vehicle; Transfer of Title.**

(a) Except as provided in Section 503.039, a motor vehicle may not be the subject of a subsequent sale unless the owner designated in the certificate of title transfers the certificate of title at the time of the sale.

(b) The transfer of the certificate of title must be on a form prescribed by the department that includes a statement that:

(1) the signer is the owner of the vehicle; and

(2) there are no liens on the vehicle except as shown on the certificate of title or as fully described in the statement.
(Enacted by Acts 1995, 74th Leg., ch. 165 (S.B. 971), § 1, effective September 1, 1995; am. Acts 2005, 79th Leg., ch. 1127 (H.B. 2495), § 1, effective September 1, 2005.)

**Sec. 501.071. [2 Versions: Effective January 1, 2012] Sale of Vehicle; Transfer of Title.**

(a) Except as provided in Section 503.039, a motor vehicle may not be the subject of a subsequent sale unless the owner designated on the title submits a transfer of ownership of the title.

(b) The transfer of the title must be in a manner prescribed by the department that:

(1) certifies the purchaser is the owner of the vehicle; and

(2) certifies there are no liens on the vehicle or provides a release of each lien on the vehicle.
(Enacted by Acts 1995, 74th Leg., ch. 165 (S.B. 971), § 1, effective September 1, 1995; am. Acts 2005, 79th Leg., ch. 1127 (H.B. 2495), § 1, effective September 1, 2005; am. Acts 2011, 82nd Leg., ch. 1296 (H.B. 2357), § 32, effective January 1, 2012.)

**Sec. 501.072. Odometer Disclosure Statement.**

(a) Except as provided by Subsection (c), the seller of a motor vehicle sold in this state shall provide to the buyer, on a form prescribed by the department, a written disclosure of the vehicle's odometer reading at the time of the sale. The form must include space for the signature and printed name of both the seller and buyer.

(b) When application for a certificate of title is made, the owner shall record the current odometer reading on the application. The written disclosure required by Subsection (a) must accompany the application.

(c) An odometer disclosure statement is not required for the sale of a motor vehicle that:

(1) has a manufacturer's rated carrying capacity of more than two tons;

(2) is not self-propelled;

(3) is 10 or more years old;

(4) is sold directly by the manufacturer to an agency of the United States government in conformity with contractual specifications; or

(5) is a new motor vehicle.
(Enacted by Acts 1995, 74th Leg., ch. 165 (S.B. 971), § 1, effective September 1, 1995.)

**Sec. 501.0721. [Effective January 1, 2012] Delivery of Receipt and Title to Purchaser of Used Motor Vehicle.**

A person, whether acting for that person or another, who sells, trades, or otherwise transfers a used motor vehicle shall deliver to the purchaser at the time of delivery of the vehicle a properly assigned title or other evidence of title as required under this chapter.
(Enacted by Acts 1995, 74th Leg., ch. 165 (S.B. 971), § 1, effective September 1, 1995; am. Acts 1999, 76th Leg., ch. 1423 (H.B. 2409), § 5, effective September 1, 1999; am. Acts 2011, 82nd Leg., ch. 1296 (H.B. 2357), § 33, effective January 1, 2012, (renumbered from Sec. 520.022).)

Transportation

## Sec. 501.073.  Sales in Violation of Chapter.

A sale made in violation of this chapter is void and title may not pass until the requirements of this chapter are satisfied.

(Enacted by Acts 1995, 74th Leg., ch. 165 (S.B. 971), § 1, effective September 1, 1995.)

## Sec. 501.074.  [2 Versions: Effective until January 1, 2012] Transfer of Vehicle by Operation of Law.

(a) The department shall issue a new certificate of title for a motor vehicle registered in this state for which the ownership is transferred by operation of law, including by inheritance, devise or bequest, bankruptcy, receivership, judicial sale, or other involuntary divestiture of ownership after receiving:

(1) a certified copy of the order appointing a temporary administrator or of the probate proceedings;

(2) letters testamentary or letters of administration;

(3) if administration of an estate is not necessary, an affidavit showing that administration is not necessary, identifying all heirs, and including a statement by the heirs of the name in which the certificate shall be issued;

(4) a court order; or

(5) the bill of sale from an officer making a judicial sale.

(b) If a lien is foreclosed by nonjudicial means, the department may issue a new certificate of title in the name of the purchaser at the foreclosure sale on receiving the affidavit of the lienholder of the fact of the nonjudicial foreclosure.

(c) If a constitutional or statutory lien is foreclosed, the department may issue a new certificate of title in the name of the purchaser at the foreclosure sale on receiving:

(1) the affidavit of the lienholder of the fact of the creation of the lien and of the divestiture of title according to law; and

(2) proof of notice as required by Sections 70.004 and 70.006, Property Code, or by Section 59.0445, Property Code.

(d) Notwithstanding the terms of Section 501.005, in the event of a conflict between this section and other law, this section controls.

(Enacted by Acts 1995, 74th Leg., ch. 165 (S.B. 971), § 1, effective September 1, 1995; am. Acts 1997, 75th Leg., ch. 165 (S.B. 898), § 30.41, effective September 1, 1997; am. Acts 2001, 77th Leg., ch. 76 (H.B. 1664), § 2, effective May 14, 2001; am. Acts 2011, 82nd Leg., ch. 405 (S.B. 690), § 8, effective January 1, 2012.)

## Sec. 501.074.  [2 Versions: Effective January 1, 2012] Transfer of Vehicle by Operation of Law.

(a) The department shall issue a new title for a motor vehicle registered in this state for which the ownership is transferred by operation of law or other involuntary divestiture of ownership after receiving:

(1) a certified copy of an order appointing a temporary administrator or of the probate proceedings;

(2) letters testamentary or letters of administration;

(3) if administration of an estate is not necessary, an affidavit showing that administration is not necessary, identifying all heirs, and including a statement by the heirs of the name in which the certificate shall be issued;

(4) a court order; or

(5) the bill of sale from an officer making a judicial sale.

(b) If a lien is foreclosed by nonjudicial means, the department may issue a new title in the name of the purchaser at the foreclosure sale on receiving the affidavit of the lienholder of the fact of the nonjudicial foreclosure.

(c) If a constitutional or statutory lien is foreclosed, the department may issue a new title in the name of the purchaser at the foreclosure sale on receiving:

(1) the affidavit of the lienholder of the fact of the creation of the lien and of the divestiture of title according to law; and

(2) proof of notice as required by Sections 70.004 and 70.006, Property Code, or by Section 59.0445, Property Code.

(d) Notwithstanding the terms of Section 501.005, in the event of a conflict between this section and other law, this section controls.

(Enacted by Acts 1995, 74th Leg., ch. 165 (S.B. 971), § 1, effective September 1, 1995; am. Acts 1997, 75th Leg., ch. 165 (S.B. 898), § 30.41, effective September 1, 1997; am. Acts 2001, 77th Leg., ch. 76 (H.B. 1664), § 2, effective May 14, 2001; am. Acts 2011, 82nd Leg., ch. 1296 (H.B. 2357), § 34, effective January 1, 2012.)

## Sec. 501.075.  [Repealed January 1, 2012] Validity of Documents Not Notarized.

A document necessary to transfer ownership of a motor vehicle is valid without regard to whether the document is executed before a notary public.

(Enacted by Acts 1995, 74th Leg., ch. 165 (S.B. 971), § 1, effective September 1, 1995.)

### Sec. 501.076. Limited Power of Attorney.

(a) An owner who has a contractual option to transfer ownership of a vehicle in full or partial satisfaction of the balance owed on the vehicle, as provided in Section 348.123(b)(5), Finance Code, may execute a written limited power of attorney that authorizes an agent to complete and sign for the owner, and provide to the transferee, the form to transfer the title under Section 501.071 and the odometer disclosure under Section 501.072, and the other documents necessary to transfer title.

(b) The owner may execute the limited power of attorney at the time the owner enters the contract giving the owner the option to transfer the vehicle or at any time after that date. The limited power of attorney may only be used if an owner elects to transfer the vehicle in full or partial satisfaction of the contract and may not be used by the holder of the contract as part of the holder's exercise of a remedy for a default by the owner under the contract.

(c) **[2 Versions: Effective until January 1, 2012]** The person named as the agent in the limited power of attorney must meet the following requirements:

(1) the person may be a person who has been appointed by the commissioner's court as a deputy to perform vehicle registration functions under Section 502.112, a license vehicle auction company holding a wholesale general distinguishing number under Section 503.022, a person who has a permit similar to one of the foregoing that is issued by the state in which the owner is located, or another person authorized by law to execute title documents in the state in which the owner executes the documents; and

(2) the person may not be the transferee or an employee of the transferee. The person may not act as the agent of both the transferor and transferee in the transaction. For the purposes of this section, a person is not the agent of both the transferor and transferee in a transaction unless the person has the authority to sign the documents pertaining to the transfer of title on behalf of both the transferor and the transferee.

(c) **[2 Versions: Effective January 1, 2012]** The person named as the agent in the limited power of attorney must meet the following requirements:

(1) the person may be a person who has been appointed by the commissioners court as a deputy to perform vehicle registration functions under Section 520.0091, a licensed vehicle auction company holding a wholesale general distinguishing number under Section 503.022, a person who has a permit similar to one of the foregoing that is issued by the state in which the owner is located, or another person authorized by law to execute title documents in the state in which the owner executes the documents; and

(2) the person may not be the transferee or an employee of the transferee. The person may not act as the agent of both the transferor and transferee in the transaction. For the purposes of this section, a person is not the agent of both the transferor and transferee in a transaction unless the person has the authority to sign the documents pertaining to the transfer of title on behalf of both the transferor and the transferee.

(d) If a limited power of attorney is used under Subsection (a), the holder of the contract shall accompany the power of attorney with a written statement that the vehicle was returned at the election of the owner in full or partial satisfaction of the owner's obligations under the contract and not as the result of the exercise by the holder of the contract of its remedies for default.

(e) A signed and dated written odometer disclosure containing the information described in this subsection may be included on or with the power of attorney if the power of attorney is executed within 120 days before the date of the transfer and is accompanied by the conspicuous written notification described in this subsection. If an odometer disclosure is not obtained in that manner, the transferee or agent or the person to whom the vehicle is delivered at the time of the transfer shall request an odometer disclosure as provided in this subsection. Not more than 120 days before the transfer of the vehicle by the owner, the transferee or agent under the power of attorney or person receiving delivery of the vehicle shall in writing request the owner to provide a signed and dated written statement stating the odometer reading (not to include tenths of a mile) as of the date of the statement, and further stating words to the effect that either: (i) to the best of the owner's knowledge, the odometer reading reflects the actual mileage of the vehicle; (ii) the actual mileage has gone over the odometer's mechanical limits and the odometer reading reflects the amount of mileage in excess of the mechanical limits of the odometer, if the owner knows that to be the case; or (iii) the odometer reading is not the actual mileage, if the owner knows that to be the case. The statement may consist of a form in which the agent or transferee or person receiving the vehicle includes the identification of the vehicle and owner and which allows the owner to fill in the odometer reading and mark an applicable box to indicate which of condition (i), (ii), or (iii) is applicable and to date and sign the statement. With the request for the owner's statement, the transferee or agent or person receiving the vehicle shall provide a written notification to the owner to the effect that the owner has a duty under law to state the odometer reading, state which of conditions (i), (ii), or (iii) is applicable, and sign, date, and return the statement and that failing to do so or providing false information may result in fines or imprisonment. Unless the written notification is delivered to the owner at substantially the same time that the owner is delivering the signed and dated owner's statement, the written notification must also state a date by which the owner must provide this information and an address to which it may be delivered. This written notification to the owner must be in bold letters, underlined, or otherwise conspicuous and may be in a separate document or included as part of a form to be used for the owner's statement or in another document relating to the potential transfer. The transferee or agent or the person receiving delivery of the vehicle may mail the request and notification to the last known address of the owner or may otherwise send or deliver it to the owner. If there are multiple owners of the same vehicle, the request and notification may be sent to one or more of them and it shall be sufficient for one owner to sign the statement. The owner has a duty to return the signed and dated statement as directed in the notification. In completing the odometer disclosure on the owner's behalf, the agent shall identify the same condition (i), (ii), or (iii) provided in the owner's statement, unless the agent knows that the condition identified in the owner's statement is not correct. The agent will not indicate in the odometer disclosure it completes on the owner's behalf that the odometer reading is not the actual mileage unless either the owner has so indicated in the owner's statement or the agent knows that the owner's state-

ment is not correct. The agent shall transmit the owner's statement it receives to the transferee after the title transfer is completed. The owner's statement received by the transferee under this subsection need not be filed with the filing office for the other title documents, but the transferee shall retain the owner's statement for a time period and in a similar manner to the retention methods used by a lessor to retain statements under 49 C.F.R. Section 580.8(b), as it may from time to time be amended. The transferee may rely upon the agent's odometer disclosure and the owner's statement unless it knows that they are not correct. A failure by an owner to comply with an obligation under this subsection subjects the owner to the penalties and enforcement provisions of Subchapter H but does not affect the validity of the transfer of title.

(f) This section does not in any way impair or impede any transfers made through use of a power of attorney prior to the effective date of this section, and such transfers shall continue to be valid if they comply with the provisions of this section or would otherwise comply with the law in effect prior to the effective date of this section. This section does not apply to powers of attorney authorized under federal law or regulation that authorize a transferee to act as the agent of the transferor under certain circumstances or to powers of attorney otherwise authorized by the law of this state. This section does not affect the use of powers of attorney to sign, complete, and deliver the form to transfer title and other documents necessary to transfer title, including the odometer disclosure, in title transfers other than those described in Subsection (a).

(g) The power of attorney created in this section shall be limited for the purposes and duration specified in this section.
(Enacted by Acts 2003, 78th Leg., ch. 958 (S.B. 1507), § 1, effective September 1, 2003; am. Acts 2011, 82nd Leg., ch. 1296 (H.B. 2357), § 35, effective January 1, 2012.)

**Secs. 501.077 to 501.090 [Reserved for expansion].**

### SUBCHAPTER E
### NONREPAIRABLE AND SALVAGE MOTOR VEHICLES

**Sec. 501.091.     [2 Versions: Effective until January 1, 2012] Definitions.**
     In this subchapter:

(1) "Actual cash value" means the market value of a motor vehicle.

(2) "Casual sale" means the sale by a salvage vehicle dealer or an insurance company of not more than five nonrepairable motor vehicles or salvage motor vehicles to the same person during a calendar year. The term does not include:

(A) a sale at auction to a salvage vehicle dealer; or

(B) the sale of an export-only motor vehicle to a person who is not a resident of the United States.

(3) "Damage" means sudden damage to a motor vehicle caused by the motor vehicle being wrecked, burned, flooded, or stripped of major component parts. The term does not include gradual damage from any cause, sudden damage caused by hail, or any damage caused only to the exterior paint of the motor vehicle.

(4) "Export-only motor vehicle" means a motor vehicle described by Section 501.099.

(5) "Insurance company" means:

(A) a person authorized to write automobile insurance in this state; or

(B) an out-of-state insurance company that pays a loss claim for a motor vehicle in this state.

(6) "Major component part" means one of the following parts of a motor vehicle:

(A) the engine;

(B) the transmission;

(C) the frame;

(D) a fender;

(E) the hood;

(F) a door allowing entrance to or egress from the passenger compartment of the motor vehicle;

(G) a bumper;

(H) a quarter panel;

(I) a deck lid, tailgate, or hatchback;

(J) the cargo box of a one-ton or smaller truck, including a pickup truck;

(K) the cab of a truck;

(L) the body of a passenger motor vehicle;

(M) the roof or floor pan of a passenger motor vehicle, if separate from the body of the motor vehicle.

(7) "Metal recycler" means a person who:

(A) is predominately engaged in the business of obtaining ferrous or nonferrous metal that has served its original economic purpose to convert the metal, or sell the metal for conversion, into raw material products consisting of prepared grades and having an existing or potential economic value;

(B) has a facility to convert ferrous or nonferrous metal into raw material products consisting of prepared grades and having an existing or potential economic value, by method other than the exclusive use of hand tools, including the processing, sorting, cutting, classifying, cleaning, baling, wrapping, shredding, shearing, or changing the physical form or chemical content of the metal; and

(C) sells or purchases the ferrous or nonferrous metal solely for use as raw material in the production of new products.

(8) "Motor vehicle" has the meaning assigned by Section 501.002(14).

(9) "Nonrepairable motor vehicle" means a motor vehicle that:

(A) is damaged, wrecked, or burned to the extent that the only residual value of the vehicle is as a source of parts or scrap metal; or

(B) comes into this state under a title or other ownership document that indicates that the vehicle is nonrepairable, junked, or for parts or dismantling only.

(10) "Nonrepairable vehicle title" means a document issued by the department that evidences ownership of a nonrepairable motor vehicle.

(11) "Out-of-state buyer" means a person licensed in an automotive business by another state or jurisdiction if the department has listed the holders of such a license as permitted purchasers of salvage motor vehicles or nonrepairable motor vehicles based on substantially similar licensing requirements and on whether salvage vehicle dealers licensed in Texas are permitted to purchase salvage motor vehicles or nonrepairable motor vehicles in the other state or jurisdiction.

(12) "Out-of-state ownership document" means a negotiable document issued by another state or jurisdiction that the department considers sufficient to prove ownership of a nonrepairable motor vehicle or salvage motor vehicle and to support the issuance of a comparable Texas certificate of title for the motor vehicle. The term does not include a title issued by the department, including a regular certificate of title, a nonrepairable vehicle title, a salvage vehicle title, a Texas Salvage Certificate, Certificate of Authority to Demolish a

Motor Vehicle, or another ownership document issued by the department.

(13) "Public highway" has the meaning assigned by Section 502.001.

(14) "Rebuilder" means a person who acquires and repairs, rebuilds, or reconstructs for operation on a public highway, three or more salvage motor vehicles in a calendar year.

(15) "Salvage motor vehicle":

(A) means a motor vehicle that:

(i) has damage to or is missing a major component part to the extent that the cost of repairs, including parts and labor other than the cost of materials and labor for repainting the motor vehicle and excluding sales tax on the total cost of repairs, exceeds the actual cash value of the motor vehicle immediately before the damage; or

(ii) is damaged and that comes into this state under an out-of-state salvage motor vehicle certificate of title or similar out-of-state ownership document that states on its face "accident damage," "flood damage," "inoperable," "rebuildable," "salvageable," or similar notation; and

(B) does not include an out-of-state motor vehicle with a "rebuilt," "prior salvage," "salvaged," or similar notation, a nonrepairable motor vehicle, or a motor vehicle for which an insurance company has paid a claim for:

(i) the cost of repairing hail damage; or

(ii) theft, unless the motor vehicle was damaged during the theft and before recovery to the extent described by Paragraph (A)(i).

(16) "Salvage vehicle title" means a document issued by the department that evidences ownership of a salvage motor vehicle.

(17) "Salvage vehicle dealer" means a person engaged in this state in the business of acquiring, selling, repairing, rebuilding, reconstructing, or otherwise dealing in nonrepairable motor vehicles, salvage motor vehicles, or, if incidental to a salvage motor vehicle dealer's primary business, used automotive parts. The term does not include a person who casually repairs, rebuilds, or reconstructs fewer than five salvage motor vehicles in the same calendar year or, except as provided by Paragraph (C), a used automotive parts recycler. The term includes a person engaged in the business of:

(A) a salvage vehicle dealer, regardless of whether the person holds a license issued by the department to engage in that business;

(B) dealing in nonrepairable motor vehicles or salvage motor vehicles; or

(C) a used automotive parts recycler if the sale of repaired, rebuilt, or reconstructed nonrepairable motor vehicles or salvage motor vehicles is more than an incidental part of the used automotive parts recycler's business.

(18) "Self-insured motor vehicle" means a motor vehicle for which the evidence of ownership is a manufacturer's certificate of origin or for which the department or another state or jurisdiction has issued a regular certificate of title, is self-insured by the owner, and is owned by an individual, a business, or a governmental entity, without regard to the number of motor vehicles they own or operate. The term does not include a motor vehicle that is insured by an insurance company.

(19) "Used part" means a part that is salvaged, dismantled, or removed from a motor vehicle for resale as is or as repaired. The term includes a major component part but does not include a rebuildable or rebuilt core, including an engine, block, crankshaft, transmission, or other core part that is acquired, possessed, or transferred in the ordinary course of business.

(20) "Used parts dealer" and "used automotive parts recycler" have the meaning assigned to "used automotive parts recycler" by Section 2309.002, Occupations Code.

(Enacted by Acts 1997, 75th Leg., ch. 165 (S.B. 898), § 30.43(a), effective September 1, 1997; am. Acts 2003, 78th Leg., ch. 1325 (H.B. 3588), § 17.02, effective September 1, 2003 (renumbered from Sec. 501.0911); am. Acts 2005, 79th Leg., ch. 567 (H.B. 1350), § 1, effective September 1, 2005; am. Acts 2009, 81st Leg., ch. 783 (S.B. 1095), § 8, effective September 1, 2009; am. Acts 2009, 81st Leg., ch. 933 (H.B. 3097), § 4.08, effective September 1, 2009.)

## Sec. 501.091. [2 Versions: Effective January 1, 2012] Definitions.

In this subchapter:

(1) "Actual cash value" means the market value of a motor vehicle.

(2) "Casual sale" means the sale by a salvage vehicle dealer or an insurance company of five or fewer nonrepairable motor vehicles or salvage motor vehicles to the same person during a calendar year, but does not include:

(A) a sale at auction to a salvage vehicle dealer;

(B) a sale to an insurance company, out-of-state buyer, or governmental entity; or

(C) the sale of an export-only motor vehicle to a person who is not a resident of the United States.

(3) "Damage" means sudden damage to a motor vehicle caused by the motor vehicle being wrecked, burned, flooded, or stripped of major component parts. The term does not include:

(A) gradual damage from any cause;

(B) sudden damage caused by hail;

(C) any damage caused only to the exterior paint of the motor vehicle; or

(D) theft, unless the motor vehicle was damaged during the theft and before recovery.

(4) "Export-only motor vehicle" means a motor vehicle described by Section 501.099.

(5) "Insurance company" means:

(A) a person authorized to write automobile insurance in this state; or

(B) an out-of-state insurance company that pays a loss claim for a motor vehicle in this state.

(6) "Major component part" means one of the following parts of a motor vehicle:

(A) the engine;

(B) the transmission;

(C) the frame;

(D) a fender;

(E) the hood;

(F) a door allowing entrance to or egress from the passenger compartment of the motor vehicle;

(G) a bumper;

(H) a quarter panel;

(I) a deck lid, tailgate, or hatchback;

(J) the cargo box of a vehicle with a gross vehicle weight of 10,000 pounds or less, including a pickup truck;

(K) the cab of a truck;

(L) the body of a passenger motor vehicle;

(M) the roof or floor pan of a passenger motor vehicle, if separate from the body of the motor vehicle.

(7) "Metal recycler" means a person who:

(A) is engaged in the business of obtaining, converting, or selling ferrous or nonferrous metal for conversion into raw material products consisting of prepared grades and having an existing or potential economic value;

(B) has a facility to convert ferrous or nonferrous metal into raw material products by method other than the exclusive use of hand tools, including the processing, sorting, cutting, classifying, cleaning, baling, wrapping, shredding, shearing, or changing the physical form or chemical content of the metal; and

(C) sells or purchases the ferrous or nonferrous metal solely for use as raw material in the production of new products.

(8) "Motor vehicle" has the meaning assigned by Section 501.002.

(9) "Nonrepairable motor vehicle" means a motor vehicle that:

(A) is damaged, wrecked, or burned to the extent that the only residual value of the vehicle is as a source of parts or scrap metal; or

(B) comes into this state under a comparable ownership document that indicates that the vehicle is nonrepairable.

(10) "Nonrepairable vehicle title" means a printed document issued by the department that evidences ownership of a nonrepairable motor vehicle.

(10-a) "Nonrepairable record of title" means an electronic record of ownership of a nonrepairable motor vehicle.

(11) "Out-of-state buyer" means a person licensed in an automotive business by another state or jurisdiction if the department has listed the holders of such a license as permitted purchasers of salvage motor vehicles or nonrepairable motor vehicles based on substantially similar licensing requirements and on whether salvage vehicle dealers licensed in Texas are permitted to purchase salvage motor vehicles or nonrepairable motor vehicles in the other state or jurisdiction.

(12) "Out-of-state ownership document" means a negotiable document issued by another state or jurisdiction that the department considers sufficient to prove ownership of a nonrepairable motor vehicle or salvage motor vehicle and to support the issuance of a comparable Texas title for the motor vehicle. The term does not include any title or certificate issued by the department.

(13) "Public highway" has the meaning assigned by Section 502.001.

(14) "Rebuilder" means a person who acquires and repairs, rebuilds, or reconstructs for operation on a public highway, more than five salvage motor vehicles in a calendar year.

(15) "Salvage motor vehicle" means a motor vehicle that:

Transportation

(A) has damage to or is missing a major component part to the extent that the cost of repairs, including parts and labor other than the cost of materials and labor for repainting the motor vehicle and excluding sales tax on the total cost of repairs, exceeds the actual cash value of the motor vehicle immediately before the damage; or

(B) comes into this state under an out-of-state salvage motor vehicle title or similar out-of-state ownership document.

(16) "Salvage vehicle title" means a printed document issued by the department that evidences ownership of a salvage motor vehicle.

(16-a) "Salvage record of title" means an electronic record of ownership of a salvage motor vehicle.

(17) "Salvage vehicle dealer" means a person engaged in this state in the business of acquiring, selling, repairing, rebuilding, reconstructing, or otherwise dealing in nonrepairable motor vehicles, salvage motor vehicles, or, if incidental to a salvage motor vehicle dealer's primary business, used automotive parts regardless of whether the person holds a license issued by the department to engage in that business. The term does not include an unlicensed person who:

(A) casually repairs, rebuilds, or reconstructs not more than five nonrepairable motor vehicles or salvage motor vehicles in the same calendar year;

(B) buys not more than five nonrepairable motor vehicles or salvage motor vehicles in the same calendar year; or

(C) is a licensed used automotive parts recycler if the sale of repaired, rebuilt, or reconstructed nonrepairable motor vehicles or salvage motor vehicles is more than an incidental part of the used automotive parts recycler's business.

(18) "Self-insured motor vehicle" means a motor vehicle for which the owner or a governmental entity assumes full financial responsibility for motor vehicle loss claims without regard to the number of motor vehicles they own or operate. The term does not include a motor vehicle that is insured by an insurance company.

(19) "Used part" means a part that is salvaged, dismantled, or removed from a motor vehicle for resale as is or as repaired. The term includes a major component part but does not include a rebuildable or rebuilt core, including an engine, block, crankshaft, transmission, or other core part that is acquired, possessed, or transferred in the ordinary course of business.

(20) "Used parts dealer" and "used automotive parts recycler" have the meaning assigned to "used automotive parts recycler" by Section 2309.002, Occupations Code.

(Enacted by Acts 1997, 75th Leg., ch. 165 (S.B. 898), § 30.43(a), effective September 1, 1997; am. Acts 2003, 78th Leg., ch. 1325 (H.B. 3588), § 17.02, effective September 1, 2003 (renumbered from Sec. 501.0911); am. Acts 2005, 79th Leg., ch. 567 (H.B. 1350), § 1, effective September 1, 2005; am. Acts 2009, 81st Leg., ch. 783 (S.B. 1095), § 8, effective September 1, 2009; am. Acts 2009, 81st Leg., ch. 933 (H.B. 3097), § 4.08, effective September 1, 2009; am. Acts 2011, 82nd Leg., ch. 1296 (H.B. 2357), § 36, effective January 1, 2012.)

## Sec. 501.0911.  Definitions [Renumbered].

Renumbered to Tex. Transp. Code § 501.091 by Acts 2003, 78th Leg., ch. 1325 (H.B. 3588), § 17.02, effective September 1, 2003.

## Sec. 501.09111.  [Effective January 1, 2012] Rights and Limitations of Nonrepairable Vehicle Title, Nonrepairable Record of Title, Salvage Vehicle Title, or Salvage Record of Title.

(a) A person who owns a nonrepairable motor vehicle:

(1) is entitled to possess, transport, dismantle, scrap, destroy, record a lien as provided for in Section 501.097(a)(3)(A), and sell, transfer, or release ownership of the motor vehicle or a used part from the motor vehicle; and

(2) may not:

(A) operate or permit the operation of the motor vehicle on a public highway, in addition to any other requirement of law;

(B) repair, rebuild, or reconstruct the motor vehicle; or

(C) register the motor vehicle.

(b) A person who holds a nonrepairable certificate of title issued prior to September 1, 2003 is entitled to the same rights listed in Subsection (a) and may repair, rebuild, or reconstruct the motor vehicle.

(c) A person who owns a salvage motor vehicle:

(1) is entitled to possess, transport, dismantle, scrap, destroy, repair, rebuild, reconstruct, record a lien on, and sell, transfer, or release

ownership of the motor vehicle or a used part from the motor vehicle; and

(2) may not operate, register, or permit the operation of the motor vehicle on a public highway, in addition to any other requirement of law.

(Enacted by Acts 1997, 75th Leg., ch. 165 (S.B. 898), § 30.43(a), effective September 1, 1997; am. Acts 2003, 78th Leg., ch. 1325 (H.B. 3588), § 17.02, effective September 1, 2003 (renumbered from Sec. 501.0921); am. Acts 2011, 82nd Leg., ch. 1296 (H.B. 2357), § 37, effective January 1, 2012, (renumbered from Sec. 501.098).)

### Sec. 501.09112. [Effective January 1, 2012] Appearance of Nonrepairable Vehicle Title or Salvage Vehicle Title.

(a) The department's printed nonrepairable vehicle title must clearly indicate that it is the negotiable ownership document for a nonrepairable motor vehicle.

(b) A nonrepairable vehicle title must clearly indicate that the motor vehicle:

(1) may not be:

(A) issued a regular title;

(B) registered in this state; or

(C) repaired, rebuilt, or reconstructed; and

(2) may be used only as a source for used parts or scrap metal.

(c) The department's printed salvage vehicle title must clearly show that it is the ownership document for a salvage motor vehicle.

(d) A salvage vehicle title or a salvage record of title for a vehicle that is a salvage motor vehicle because of damage caused exclusively by flood must bear a notation that the department considers appropriate. If the title for a motor vehicle reflects the notation required by this subsection, the owner may sell, transfer, or release the motor vehicle only as provided by this subchapter.

(e) An electronic application for a nonrepairable vehicle title, nonrepairable record of title, salvage vehicle title, or salvage record of title must clearly advise the applicant of the same provisions required on a printed title.

(f) A nonrepairable vehicle title, nonrepairable record of title, salvage vehicle title, or salvage record of title in the department's electronic database must include appropriate remarks so that the vehicle record clearly shows the status of the vehicle.

(Enacted by Acts 1997, 75th Leg., ch. 165 (S.B. 898), § 30.43(a), effective September 1, 1997; am.

Acts 2003, 78th Leg., ch. 1325 (H.B. 3588), § 17.02, effective September 1, 2003 (renumbered from Sec. 501.0928); am. Acts 2011, 82nd Leg., ch. 1296 (H.B. 2357), § 38, effective January 1, 2012, (renumbered from Sec. 501.103).)

### Sec. 501.09113. [Effective January 1, 2012] Out-of-State Salvage or Rebuilt Salvage Vehicle.

(a) This section applies only to a motor vehicle brought into this state from another state or jurisdiction that has on any title or comparable out-of-state ownership document issued by the other state or jurisdiction:

(1) a "rebuilt," "salvage," or similar notation; or

(2) a "nonrepairable," "dismantle only," "parts only," "junked," "scrapped," or similar notation.

(b) On receipt of a complete application from the owner of the motor vehicle, the department shall issue the applicant the appropriate title for the motor vehicle.

(Enacted by Acts 1997, 75th Leg., ch. 165 (S.B. 898), § 30.43(a), effective September 1, 1997; am. Acts 2003, 78th Leg., ch. 1325 (H.B. 3588), § 17.02, effective September 1, 2003 (renumbered from Sec. 501.0924); am. Acts 2011, 82nd Leg., ch. 1296 (H.B. 2357), § 39, effective January 1, 2012, (renumbered from Sec. 501.101).)

### Sec. 501.0912. Insurance Company to Surrender Certificates of Title to Certain Late Model Salvage Motor Vehicles [Renumbered].

Renumbered to Tex. Transp. Code § 501.092 by Acts 2003, 78th Leg., ch. 1325 (H.B. 3588), § 17.02, effective September 1, 2003.

### Sec. 501.0913. Insurance Company to Deliver Certificates of Title to Certain Motor Vehicles [Repealed].

Repealed by Acts 2003, 78th Leg., ch. 1325 (H.B. 3588), § 17.09(1), effective September 1, 2003.

(Enacted by Acts 1997, 75th Leg., ch. 165 (S.B. 898), § 30.43(a), effective September 1, 1997.)

### Sec. 501.0914. Nonapplicability [Repealed].

Repealed by Acts 2003, 78th Leg., ch. 1325 (H.B. 3588), § 17.09(1), effective September 1, 2003.

(Enacted by Acts 1997, 75th Leg., ch. 165 (S.B. 898), § 30.43(a), effective September 1, 1997.)

Transportation

### Sec. 501.0915.  Insurance Company to Submit Report to Department [Renumbered].

Renumbered to Tex. Transp. Code § 501.093 by Acts 2003, 78th Leg., ch. 1325 (H.B. 3588), § 17.02, effective September 1, 2003.

### Sec. 501.0916.  Sale, Transfer, or Release of Late Model Salvage or Nonrepairable Motor Vehicle [Renumbered].

Renumbered to Tex. Transp. Code § 501.095 by Acts 2003, 78th Leg., ch. 1325 (H.B. 3588), § 17.02, effective September 1, 2003.

### Sec. 501.0917.  Salvage Vehicle Dealer to Submit Report to Department [Renumbered].

Renumbered to Tex. Transp. Code § 501.096 by Acts 2003, 78th Leg., ch. 1325 (H.B. 3588), § 17.02, effective September 1, 2003.

### Sec. 501.0918.  Person Acquiring Late Model Salvage Motor Vehicle to Surrender Certificate of Title [Repealed].

Repealed by Acts 2003, 78th Leg., ch. 1325 (H.B. 3588), § 17.09(1), effective September 1, 2003.

(Enacted by Acts 1997, 75th Leg., ch. 165 (S.B. 898), § 30.43(a), effective September 1, 1997.)

### Sec. 501.0919.  Sale of Certain Late Model Salvage Motor Vehicles [Repealed].

Repealed by Acts 2003, 78th Leg., ch. 1325 (H.B. 3588), § 17.09(1), effective September 1, 2003.

(Enacted by Acts 1997, 75th Leg., ch. 165 (S.B. 898), § 30.43(a), effective September 1, 1997.)

### Sec. 501.092.  [Renumbered January 1, 2012] Insurance Company to Surrender Certificates of Title to Certain Salvage Motor Vehicles or Nonrepairable Motor Vehicles.

(a) Except as provided by Section 501.0925, an insurance company that is licensed to conduct business in this state and that acquires, through payment of a claim, ownership or possession of a salvage motor vehicle or nonrepairable motor vehicle covered by a certificate of title issued by this state or a manufacturer's certificate of origin shall surrender a properly assigned title or manufacturer's certificate of origin to the department, on a form prescribed by the department.

(b) For a salvage motor vehicle, the insurance company shall apply for a salvage vehicle title. For a nonrepairable motor vehicle, the insurance company shall apply for a nonrepairable vehicle title.

(c) An insurance company may not sell a salvage motor vehicle or nonrepairable motor vehicle unless the department has issued a salvage vehicle title or a nonrepairable vehicle title, as appropriate, for the motor vehicle or a comparable ownership document has been issued by another state or jurisdiction for the motor vehicle.

(d) An insurance company may sell a salvage motor vehicle or nonrepairable motor vehicle, or assign a salvage vehicle title or a nonrepairable vehicle title for a motor vehicle, only to a salvage vehicle dealer, an out-of-state buyer, a buyer in a casual sale at auction, a metal recycler, or a used automotive parts recycler. If a motor vehicle is not a salvage motor vehicle or a nonrepairable motor vehicle, the insurance company is not required to surrender the regular certificate of title for the vehicle or to be issued a salvage vehicle title or a nonrepairable vehicle title for the motor vehicle.

(e) An insurance company or other person who acquires ownership of a motor vehicle other than a nonrepairable or salvage motor vehicle may voluntarily and on proper application obtain a salvage vehicle title or a nonrepairable vehicle title for the vehicle.

(Enacted by Acts 1997, 75th Leg., ch. 165 (S.B. 898), § 30.43(a), effective September 1, 1997; am. Acts 2003, 78th Leg., ch. 1325 (H.B. 3588), § 17.02, effective September 1, 2003 (renumbered from Sec. 501.0912); am. Acts 2009, 81st Leg., ch. 783 (S.B. 1095), § 9, effective September 1, 2009; am. Acts 2009, 81st Leg., ch. 933 (H.B. 3097), § 4.09, effective September 1, 2009; am. Acts 2011, 82nd Leg., ch. 1136 (H.B. 1422), § 1, effective September 1, 2011.)

STATUTORY NOTES

**Editor's notes.** — This section is renumbered to Transportation. Code § 501.1001 pursuant to Acts 2011, 82nd Leg., ch. 1296 (H.B. 2357), § 44, effective January 1, 2012.

### Sec. 501.0920.  Application for Salvage Motor Vehicle Certificate of Title [Renumbered].

Renumbered to Tex. Transp. Code § 501.097 by Acts 2003, 78th Leg., ch. 1325 (H.B. 3588), § 17.02, effective September 1, 2003.

## Sec. 501.0921. Possession and Operation of Salvage Motor Vehicle [Renumbered].

Renumbered to Tex. Transp. Code § 501.098 by Acts 2003, 78th Leg., ch. 1325 (H.B. 3588), § 17.02, effective September 1, 2003.

## Sec. 501.0922. Application for Regular Certificate of Title for Salvage Motor Vehicle [Renumbered].

Renumbered to Tex. Transp. Code § 501.100(a) by Acts 2003, 78th Leg., ch. 1325 (H.B. 3588), § 17.02, effective September 1, 2003.

## Sec. 501.0923. Issuance of Certificate of Title for Rebuilt Salvage Motor Vehicle [Renumbered].

Renumbered to Tex. Transp. Code § 501.100(b) and (c) by Acts 2003, 78th Leg., ch. 1325 (H.B. 3588), § 17.02, effective September 1, 2003.

## Sec. 501.0924. Issuance of Certificate of Title to Certain Vehicles Brought into State [Renumbered].

Renumbered to Tex. Transp. Code § 501.101 by Acts 2003, 78th Leg., ch. 1325 (H.B. 3588), § 17.02, effective September 1, 2003.

## Sec. 501.0925. Insurance Company Not Required to Surrender Certificates of Title in Certain Situations.

(a) An insurance company that acquires, through payment of a claim, ownership or possession of a motor vehicle covered by a certificate of title that the company is unable to obtain may obtain from the department not earlier than the 30th day after the date of payment of the claim:

(1) a salvage vehicle title for a salvage motor vehicle;

(2) a nonrepairable vehicle title for a nonrepairable motor vehicle; or

(3) a regular certificate of title for a motor vehicle other than a salvage motor vehicle or a nonrepairable motor vehicle.

(b) An application for a title under Subsection (a) must be submitted to the department on a form prescribed by the department and include:

(1) a statement that the insurance company has provided at least two written notices attempting to obtain the certificate of title for the motor vehicle; and

(2) evidence acceptable to the department that the insurance company has made payment of a claim involving the motor vehicle.

(c) An insurance company that acquires, through payment of a claim, ownership or possession of a motor vehicle covered by a certificate of title for which the company is unable to obtain proper assignment of the certificate may obtain from the department not earlier than the 30th day after the date of payment of the claim:

(1) a salvage vehicle title for a salvage motor vehicle;

(2) a nonrepairable vehicle title for a nonrepairable motor vehicle; or

(3) a regular certificate of title for a motor vehicle other than a salvage motor vehicle or a nonrepairable motor vehicle.

(d) An application for a title under Subsection (c) must be submitted to the department on a form prescribed by the department and include:

(1) a statement that the insurance company has provided at least two written notices attempting to obtain a proper assignment of the certificate of title; and

(2) the certificate of title.

(e) A title issued under Subsection (a) or (c) must be issued in the name of the insurance company.

(f) An insurance company that acquires, through payment of a claim, ownership or possession of a salvage motor vehicle or nonrepairable motor vehicle covered by an out-of-state ownership document may obtain from the department a salvage vehicle title or nonrepairable vehicle title if:

(1) the motor vehicle was damaged, stolen, or recovered in this state;

(2) the motor vehicle owner from whom the company acquired ownership resides in this state; or

(3) otherwise allowed by department rule.

(g) A title may be issued under Subsection (f) if the insurance company:

(1) surrenders a properly assigned title on a form prescribed by the department; or

(2) complies with the application process for a title issued under Subsection (a) or (c).

(h) The department shall issue the appropriate title to a person authorized to apply for the title under this section if the department determines that the application is complete and complies with applicable law.

(i) The department by rule may provide that a person required by this section to provide notice may provide the notice electronically, including through the use of e-mail or an interactive website established by the department for that purpose.

(j) Sections 501.092(c), (d), and (e) apply to a motor vehicle acquired by an insurance company as described in Subsection (a), (c), or (f).

(k) The department may adopt rules to implement this section.
(Enacted by Acts 2011, 82nd Leg., ch. 1136 (H.B. 1422), § 2, effective September 1, 2011.)

## Sec. 501.0926.    Offense [Renumbered].

Renumbered to Tex. Transp. Code § 501.102 by Acts 2003, 78th Leg., ch. 1325 (H.B. 3588), § 17.02, effective September 1, 2003.

## Sec. 501.0927.    Application for Certificate of Title by Rebuilder of Nonrepairable Motor Vehicle [Repealed].

Repealed by Acts 2003, 78th Leg., ch. 1325 (H.B. 3588), § 17.09(1), effective September 1, 2003.
(Enacted by Acts 1997, 75th Leg., ch. 165 (S.B. 898), § 30.43(a), effective September 1, 1997.)

## Sec. 501.0928.    Department to Print Salvage and Nonrepairable Motor Vehicle Certificates of Title [Renumbered].

Renumbered to Tex. Transp. Code § 501.103 by Acts 2003, 78th Leg., ch. 1325 (H.B. 3588), § 17.02, effective September 1, 2003.

## Sec. 501.0929.    Rebuilder to Possess Certificate of Title [Renumbered].

Renumbered to Tex. Transp. Code § 501.104 by Acts 2003, 78th Leg., ch. 1325 (H.B. 3588), § 17.02, effective September 1, 2003.

## Sec. 501.093.    [Renumbered January 1, 2012] Insurance Company Report on Certain Vehicles.

(a) If an insurance company pays a claim on a nonrepairable motor vehicle or salvage motor vehicle and the insurance company does not acquire ownership of the motor vehicle, the insurance company shall:

(1) submit to the department, before the 31st day after the date of the payment of the claim, on the form prescribed by the department, a report stating that the insurance company:

(A) has paid a claim on the motor vehicle; and

(B) has not acquired ownership of the motor vehicle; and

(2) provide notice to the owner of the motor vehicle of:

(A) the report required under Subdivision (1); and

(B) the requirements for operation or transfer of ownership of the motor vehicle under Subsection (b).

(b) The owner of a motor vehicle to which this section applies may not operate or permit operation of the motor vehicle on a public highway or transfer ownership of the motor vehicle by sale or otherwise unless the department has issued a salvage vehicle title or a nonrepairable vehicle title for the motor vehicle or a comparable ownership document has been issued by another state or jurisdiction for the motor vehicle.

(c) Subsection (b) does not apply if:

(1) the department has issued a nonrepairable vehicle title or salvage vehicle title for the motor vehicle; or

(2) another state or jurisdiction has issued a comparable out-of-state ownership document for the motor vehicle.
(Enacted by Acts 1997, 75th Leg., ch. 165 (S.B. 898), § 30.43(a), effective September 1, 1997; am. Acts 2003, 78th Leg., ch. 1325 (H.B. 3588), § 17.02, effective September 1, 2003 (renumbered from Sec. 501.0915); am. Acts 2011, 82nd Leg., ch. 1136 (H.B. 1422), § 3, effective September 1, 2011.)

STATUTORY NOTES

**Editor's notes.** — This section is renumbered to Tex. Transp. Code § 501.1002 by Acts 2011, 82nd Leg., ch. 1296 (H.B. 2357), § 45, effective January 1, 2012.

## Sec. 501.0930.    Enforcement of Subchapter [Renumbered].

Renumbered to Tex. Transp. Code § 501.106 by Acts 2003, 78th Leg., ch. 1325 (H.B. 3588), § 17.02, effective September 1, 2003.

## Sec. 501.0931.    Applicability of Subchapter [Renumbered].

Renumbered to Tex. Transp. Code § 501.107 by Acts 2003, 78th Leg., ch. 1325 (H.B. 3588), § 17.02, effective September 1, 2003.

## Sec. 501.0935.    Issuance of Title to Salvage Pool Operator.

(a) In this section, "salvage pool operator" has the meaning assigned by Section 2302.001, Occupations Code.

(b) This section applies only to a salvage pool operator who, on request of an insurance company, takes possession of a motor vehicle that is the subject of an insurance claim and the insurance company subsequently:

(1) denies coverage with respect to the motor vehicle; or

(2) does not otherwise take ownership of the motor vehicle.

(b-1) An insurance company described by Subsection (b) shall notify the salvage pool operator of the denial of the claim regarding the motor vehicle or other disposition of the motor vehicle. The insurance company must include in the notice the name and address of the owner of the motor vehicle and the lienholder, if any.

(c) Before the 31st day after receiving notice under Subsection (b-1), a salvage pool operator shall notify the owner of the motor vehicle and any lienholder that:

(1) the owner or lienholder must remove the motor vehicle from the salvage pool operator's possession at the location specified in the notice to the owner and any lienholder not later than the 30th day after the date the notice is mailed; and

(2) if the motor vehicle is not removed within the time specified in the notice, the salvage pool operator will sell the motor vehicle and retain from the proceeds any costs actually incurred by the operator in obtaining, handling, and disposing of the motor vehicle as described by Subsection (d).

(d) The salvage pool operator may include in the costs described by Subsection (c)(2) only costs actually incurred by the salvage pool operator that have not been reimbursed by a third party or are not subject to being reimbursed by a third party, such as costs of notices, title searches, and towing and other costs incurred with respect to the motor vehicle. The costs described by Subsection (c)(2):

(1) may not include charges for storage or impoundment of the motor vehicle; and

(2) may be deducted only from the proceeds of a sale of the motor vehicle.

(e) The notice required of a salvage pool operator under this section must be sent by registered or certified mail, return receipt requested.

(f) If a motor vehicle is not removed from a salvage pool operator's possession before the 31st day after the date notice is mailed to the motor vehicle's owner and any lienholder under Subsection (c), the salvage pool operator may obtain from the department:

(1) a salvage vehicle title for a salvage motor vehicle; or

(2) a nonrepairable vehicle title for a nonrepairable motor vehicle.

(g) An application for a title under Subsection (f) must:

(1) be submitted to the department on a form prescribed by the department; and

(2) include evidence that the notice was mailed as required by Subsection (c) to the motor vehicle owner and any lienholder.

(h) A title issued under this section must be issued in the name of the salvage pool operator.

(i) The department shall issue the appropriate title to a person authorized to apply for the title under this section if the department determines that the application is complete and complies with applicable law.

(j) On receipt of a title under this section, the salvage pool operator shall sell the motor vehicle and retain from the proceeds of the sale the costs incurred by the salvage pool operator as permitted by Subsection (d) along with the cost of titling and selling the motor vehicle. The salvage pool operator shall pay any excess proceeds from the sale to the previous owner of the motor vehicle and the lienholder, if any. The excess proceeds must be mailed to the lienholder.

(k) If the previous owner of the motor vehicle and the lienholder, if any, cannot be identified or located, any excess proceeds from the sale of the motor vehicle under Subsection (j) shall escheat to the State of Texas. The proceeds shall be administered by the comptroller and shall be disposed of in the manner provided by Chapter 74, Property Code.

(Enacted by Acts 2011, 82nd Leg., ch. 1136 (H.B. 1422), § 2, effective September 1, 2011.)

## Sec. 501.094. [Repealed January 1, 2012] Self-Insured Motor Vehicle.

(a) This section applies only to a motor vehicle in this state that is:

(1) a self-insured motor vehicle;

(2) damaged to the extent it becomes a nonrepairable or salvage motor vehicle; and

(3) removed from normal operation by the owner.

(b) The owner of a motor vehicle to which this section applies shall submit to the department before the 31st day after the date of the damage, on the form prescribed by the department, a report stating that the motor vehicle was self-insured, damaged, and was removed from normal operation.

(c) When the owner submits a report under Subsection (b), the owner shall:

Transportation

(1) surrender the regular certificate of title or manufacturer's certificate of origin for the motor vehicle; and

(2) apply for a nonrepairable vehicle title or salvage vehicle title under this subchapter. (Enacted by Acts 2003, 78th Leg., ch. 1325 (H.B. 3588), § 17.02, effective September 1, 2003.)

## Sec. 501.095. [2 Versions: Effective until January 1, 2012] Sale, Transfer, or Release of Nonrepairable Motor Vehicle or Salvage Motor Vehicle.

(a) If the department has not issued a nonrepairable vehicle title or salvage vehicle title for the motor vehicle and an out-of-state ownership document for the motor vehicle has not been issued by another state or jurisdiction, a business or governmental entity described by Subdivisions (1)-(3) may sell, transfer, or release a nonrepairable motor vehicle or salvage motor vehicle only to a person who is:

(1) a licensed salvage vehicle dealer, a used automotive parts recycler under Chapter 2309, Occupations Code, or a metal recycler under Chapter 2302, Occupations Code;

(2) an insurance company that has paid a claim on the nonrepairable or salvage motor vehicle;

(3) a governmental entity; or

(4) an out-of-state buyer.

(b) A person, other than a salvage vehicle dealer, a used automotive parts recycler, or an insurance company licensed to do business in this state, who acquired ownership of a nonrepairable or salvage motor vehicle that has not been issued a nonrepairable vehicle title, salvage vehicle title, or a comparable ownership document issued by another state or jurisdiction shall, before selling the motor vehicle, surrender the properly assigned certificate of title for the motor vehicle to the department and apply to the department for:

(1) a nonrepairable vehicle title if the vehicle is a nonrepairable motor vehicle; or

(2) a salvage vehicle title if the vehicle is a salvage motor vehicle.

(c) If the department has issued a nonrepairable vehicle title or salvage vehicle title for the motor vehicle or another state or jurisdiction has issued a comparable out-of-state ownership document for the motor vehicle, a person may sell, transfer, or release a nonrepairable motor vehicle or salvage motor vehicle to any person.

(Enacted by Acts 1997, 75th Leg., ch. 165 (S.B. 898), § 30.43(a), effective September 1, 1997; am.

Acts 2001, 77th Leg., ch. 1421 (H.B. 2813), § 10, effective June 1, 2003; am. Acts 2003, 78th Leg., ch. 1325 (H.B. 3588), § 17.02, effective September 1, 2003 (renumbered from Sec. 501.0916); am. Acts 2009, 81st Leg., ch. 783 (S.B. 1095), § 10, effective September 1, 2009; am. Acts 2009, 81st Leg., ch. 933 (H.B. 3097), § 4.10, effective September 1, 2009.)

## Sec. 501.095. [2 Versions: Effective January 1, 2012] Sale, Transfer, or Release.

(a) If the department has not issued a nonrepairable vehicle title, nonrepairable record of title, salvage vehicle title, or salvage record of title for the motor vehicle and a comparable out-of-state ownership document for the motor vehicle has not been issued by another state or jurisdiction, a business or governmental entity described by Subdivisions (1)-(3) may sell, transfer, or release a nonrepairable motor vehicle or salvage motor vehicle only to a person who is:

(1) a licensed salvage vehicle dealer, a used automotive parts recycler under Chapter 2309, Occupations Code, or a metal recycler under Chapter 2302, Occupations Code;

(2) an insurance company that has paid a claim on the nonrepairable or salvage motor vehicle; or

(3) a governmental entity.

(b) An owner, other than a salvage vehicle dealer, a used automotive parts recycler, or an insurance company licensed to do business in this state, who acquired ownership of a nonrepairable or salvage motor vehicle that has not been issued a nonrepairable vehicle title, nonrepairable record of title, salvage vehicle title, salvage record of title, or a comparable ownership document issued by another state or jurisdiction shall, before selling the motor vehicle, surrender the properly assigned title for the motor vehicle to the department and apply to the department for the appropriate ownership document.

(c) If the department has issued a nonrepairable vehicle title or salvage vehicle title for the motor vehicle or another state or jurisdiction has issued a comparable out-of-state ownership document for the motor vehicle, a person may sell, transfer, or release a nonrepairable motor vehicle or salvage motor vehicle to any person.

(Enacted by Acts 1997, 75th Leg., ch. 165 (S.B. 898), § 30.43(a), effective September 1, 1997; am. Acts 2001, 77th Leg., ch. 1421 (H.B. 2813), § 10,

Transportation

effective June 1, 2003; am. Acts 2003, 78th Leg., ch. 1325 (H.B. 3588), § 17.02, effective September 1, 2003 (renumbered from Sec. 501.0916); am. Acts 2009, 81st Leg., ch. 783 (S.B. 1095), § 10, effective September 1, 2009; am. Acts 2009, 81st Leg., ch. 933 (H.B. 3097), § 4.10, effective September 1, 2009; am. Acts 2011, 82nd Leg., ch. 1296 (H.B. 2357), §§ 40, 41, effective January 1, 2012.)

### Sec. 501.096. [Renumbered January 1, 2012] Nonrepairable Motor Vehicle or Salvage Motor Vehicle Dismantled, Scrapped, or Destroyed.

(a) If a salvage vehicle dealer acquires ownership of a nonrepairable motor vehicle or salvage motor vehicle for the purpose of dismantling, scrapping, or destroying the motor vehicle, the dealer shall, before the 31st day after the date the dealer acquires the motor vehicle, submit to the department a report stating that the motor vehicle will be dismantled, scrapped, or destroyed. The dealer shall:

(1) make the report on a form prescribed by the department; and

(2) submit with the report a properly assigned manufacturer's certificate of origin, regular certificate of title, nonrepairable vehicle title, salvage vehicle title, or comparable out-of-state ownership document for the motor vehicle.

(b) After receiving the report and title or document, the department shall issue the salvage vehicle dealer a receipt for the manufacturer's certificate of origin, regular certificate of title, nonrepairable vehicle title, salvage vehicle title, or comparable out-of-state ownership document.

(c) The salvage vehicle dealer shall:

(1) keep on the business premises of the dealer, until the third anniversary of the date the report on the motor vehicle is submitted to the department, a record of the vehicle, its ownership, and its condition as dismantled, scrapped, or destroyed; and

(2) present to the department, on the form prescribed by the department, evidence that the motor vehicle was dismantled, scrapped, or destroyed before the 61st day after the date the dealer completed the dismantling, scrapping, or destruction of the motor vehicle.

(Enacted by Acts 1997, 75th Leg., ch. 165 (S.B. 898), § 30.43(a), effective September 1, 1997; am. Acts 2001, 77th Leg., ch. 1421 (H.B. 2813), § 11, effective June 1, 2003; am. Acts 2003, 78th Leg.,

ch. 1325 (H.B. 3588), § 17.02, effective September 1, 2003 (renumbered from Sec. 501.0917).)

STATUTORY NOTES

**Editor's notes.** — This section is renumbered to Transportation Code § 501.1003 pursuant to Acts 2011, 82nd Leg., ch. 1296 (H.B. 2357), § 46, effective January 1 2012.

### Sec. 501.097. [2 Versions: Effective until January 1, 2012] Application for Nonrepairable Vehicle Title or Salvage Vehicle Title.

(a) An application for a nonrepairable vehicle title or salvage vehicle title must:

(1) be made on a form prescribed by the department and accompanied by a $8 application fee;

(2) include, in addition to any other information required by the department:

(A) the name and current address of the owner;

(B) a description of the motor vehicle, including the make, style of body, model year, and vehicle identification number; and

(C) a statement describing whether the motor vehicle:

(i) was the subject of a total loss claim paid by an insurance company under Section 501.092, 501.0925, or 501.093;

(ii) is a self-insured motor vehicle under Section 501.094;

(iii) is an export-only motor vehicle under Section 501.099;

(iv) was sold, transferred, or released to the owner or former owner of the motor vehicle or a buyer at a casual sale; or

(v) is a motor vehicle for which an insurance company does not take ownership under Section 501.0935; and

(3) include the name and address of:

(A) any currently recorded lienholder, if the motor vehicle is a nonrepairable motor vehicle; or

(B) any currently recorded lienholder or a new lienholder, if the motor vehicle is a salvage motor vehicle.

(b) Except as provided by Sections 501.0925 and 501.0935, on receipt of a complete application, the properly assigned title or manufacturer's certificate of origin, and the application fee, the department shall, before the sixth business day after the date the department receives the application, issue the applicant the appropriate title for the motor vehicle.

(c) A nonrepairable vehicle title must state on its face that the motor vehicle:

(1) may not:

(A) be repaired, rebuilt, or reconstructed;

(B) be issued a regular certificate of title or registered in this state;

(C) be operated on a public highway, in addition to any other requirement of law; and

(2) may only be used as a source for used parts or scrap metal.

(d) The fee collected under Subsection (a)(1) shall be credited to the state highway fund to defray the costs of administering this subchapter and the costs to the department for issuing the title.

(Enacted by Acts 1997, 75th Leg., ch. 165 (S.B. 898), § 30.43(a), effective September 1, 1997; am. Acts 2003, 78th Leg., ch. 1325 (H.B. 3588), § 17.02, effective September 1, 2003 (renumbered from Sec. 501.0920); am. Acts 2011, 82nd Leg., ch. 1136 (H.B. 1422), § 4, effective September 1, 2011.)

## Sec. 501.097. [2 Versions: Effective January 1, 2012] Application for Nonrepairable Vehicle Title or Salvage Vehicle Title.

(a) An application for a nonrepairable vehicle title, nonrepairable record of title, salvage vehicle title, or salvage record of title must:

(1) be made in a manner prescribed by the department and accompanied by a $8 application fee;

(2) **[2 versions: As amended by Acts 2011, 82nd Leg., ch. 1136]** include, in addition to any other information required by the department:

(A) the name and current address of the owner;

(B) a description of the motor vehicle, including the make, style of body, model year, and vehicle identification number; and

(C) a statement describing whether the motor vehicle:

(i) was the subject of a total loss claim paid by an insurance company under Section 501.092, 501.0925, or 501.093;

(ii) is a self-insured motor vehicle under Section 501.094;

(iii) is an export-only motor vehicle under Section 501.099;

(iv) was sold, transferred, or released to the owner or former owner of the motor vehicle or a buyer at a casual sale; or

(v) is a motor vehicle for which an insurance company does not take ownership under Section 501.0935; and

(2) **[2 versions: As amended by Acts 2011, 82nd Leg., ch. 1296]** include, in addition to any other information required by the department:

(A) the name and current address of the owner; and

(B) a description of the motor vehicle, including the make, style of body, model year, and vehicle identification number; and

(3) include the name and address of:

(A) any currently recorded lienholder, if the motor vehicle is a nonrepairable motor vehicle; or

(B) any currently recorded lienholder or a new lienholder, if the motor vehicle is a salvage motor vehicle.

(b) Except as provided by Sections 501.0925 and 501.0935, on receipt of a complete application, the properly assigned title or manufacturer's certificate of origin, and the application fee, the department shall, before the sixth business day after the date the department receives the application, issue the applicant the appropriate title for the motor vehicle.

(c) A printed nonrepairable vehicle title must state on its face that the motor vehicle:

(1) may not:

(A) be repaired, rebuilt, or reconstructed;

(B) be issued a title or registered in this state;

(C) be operated on a public highway, in addition to any other requirement of law; and

(2) may only be used as a source for used parts or scrap metal.

(c-1) The department's titling system must include a remark that clearly identifies the vehicle as a salvage or nonrepairable motor vehicle.

(d) The fee collected under Subsection (a)(1) shall be credited to the state highway fund to defray the costs of administering this subchapter and the costs to the department for issuing the title.

(Enacted by Acts 1997, 75th Leg., ch. 165 (S.B. 898), § 30.43(a), effective September 1, 1997; am. Acts 2003, 78th Leg., ch. 1325 (H.B. 3588), § 17.02, effective September 1, 2003 (renumbered from Sec. 501.0920); am. Acts 2011, 82nd Leg., ch. 1136 (H.B. 1422), § 4, effective September 1, 2011; am. Acts 2011, 82nd Leg., ch. 1296 (H.B. 2357), § 42, effective January 1, 2012.)

## Sec. 501.098. [Renumbered January 1, 2012] Rights of Holder of Nonrepairable Vehicle Title or Salvage Vehicle Title.

(a) A person who holds a nonrepairable vehicle title for a motor vehicle:

(1) is entitled to possess, transport, dismantle, scrap, destroy, record a lien as provided for in Section 501.097(a)(3)(A), and sell, transfer, or release ownership of the motor vehicle or a used part from the motor vehicle;

(2) may not:

(A) operate or permit the operation of the motor vehicle on a public highway, in addition to any other requirement of law;

(B) repair, rebuild, or reconstruct the motor vehicle; or

(C) register the motor vehicle.

(b) A person who holds a nonrepairable certificate of title issued prior to September 1, 2003:

(1) is entitled to:

(A) repair, rebuild, or reconstruct the motor vehicle;

(B) possess, transport, dismantle, scrap, or destroy the motor vehicle; and

(C) sell, transfer, or release ownership of the vehicle or a used part from the motor vehicle; and

(2) may not:

(A) operate or permit the operation of the motor vehicle on a public highway, in addition to any other requirement of law; or

(B) register the motor vehicle.

(c) A person who holds a salvage vehicle title for a motor vehicle:

(1) is entitled to possess, transport, dismantle, scrap, destroy, repair, rebuild, reconstruct, record a lien on, and sell, transfer, or release ownership of the motor vehicle or a used part from the motor vehicle; and

(2) may not operate or permit the operation of the motor vehicle on a public highway, in addition to any other requirement of law.

(Enacted by Acts 1997, 75th Leg., ch. 165 (S.B. 898), § 30.43(a), effective September 1, 1997; am. Acts 2003, 78th Leg., ch. 1325 (H.B. 3588), § 17.02, effective September 1, 2003 (renumbered from Sec. 501.0921).)

### STATUTORY NOTES

**Editor's notes.** — This section is renumbered to Transportation Code § 501.09111 pursuant to Acts 2011, 82nd Leg., ch. 1296 (H.B. 2357), § 37, effective January 1, 2012.

## Sec. 501.099. Sale of Export-Only Motor Vehicles.

(a) This section applies to a nonrepairable motor vehicle or a salvage motor vehicle that is offered for sale in this state to a person who resides in a jurisdiction outside the United States.

(b) A person may purchase a nonrepairable motor vehicle or a salvage motor vehicle only if:

(1) the person purchases the motor vehicle from a licensed salvage vehicle dealer or a governmental entity;

(2) the motor vehicle has been issued a nonrepairable vehicle title or a salvage vehicle title; and

(3) the purchaser certifies to the seller on a form provided by the department that the purchaser will:

(A) remove the motor vehicle from the United States; and

(B) not return the motor vehicle to any state of the United States as a motor vehicle titled or registered under its manufacturer's vehicle identification number.

(c) A salvage vehicle dealer or a governmental entity that sells a nonrepairable motor vehicle or a salvage motor vehicle to a person who is not a resident of the United States shall, before the sale of the motor vehicle, obtain a copy, photocopy, or other accurate reproduction of a valid identification card, identification certificate, or an equivalent document issued to the purchaser by the appropriate authority of the jurisdiction in which the purchaser resides that bears a photograph of the purchaser and is capable of being verified using identification standards adopted by the United States or the international community.

(d) The department by rule shall establish a list of identification documents that are valid under Subsection (c) and provide a copy of the list to each holder of a salvage vehicle dealer license and to each appropriate governmental entity.

(e) A salvage vehicle dealer or a governmental entity that sells a nonrepairable motor vehicle or a salvage motor vehicle to a person who is not a resident of the United States shall:

(1) stamp on the face of the title so as not to obscure any name, date, or mileage statement on the title the words "FOR EXPORT ONLY" in capital letters that are black; and

(2) stamp in each unused reassignment space on the back of the title the words "FOR EXPORT ONLY" and print the number of the

Transportation

dealer's salvage vehicle license or the name of the governmental entity, as applicable.

(f) The words "FOR EXPORT ONLY" required by Subsection (e) must be at least two inches wide and clearly legible.

(g) A salvage vehicle dealer or governmental entity who sells a nonrepairable motor vehicle or a salvage motor vehicle under this section to a person who is not a resident of the United States shall keep on the business premises of the dealer or entity until the third anniversary of the date of the sale:

(1) a copy of each document related to the sale of the vehicle; and

(2) a list of all vehicles sold under this section that contains:

(A) the date of the sale;

(B) the name of the purchaser;

(C) the name of the country that issued the identification document provided by the purchaser, as shown on the document; and

(D) the vehicle identification number.

(h) This section does not prevent a person from exporting or importing a used part obtained from an export-only motor vehicle.
(Enacted by Acts 2003, 78th Leg., ch. 1325 (H.B. 3588), § 17.02, effective September 1, 2003.)

### Sec. 501.100. [2 Versions: Effective until January 1, 2012] Application for Regular Certificate of Title for Salvage Vehicle.

(a) A vehicle for which a nonrepairable certificate of title issued prior to September 1, 2003 or a salvage vehicle title has been issued may be issued a regular certificate of title after the motor vehicle has been repaired, rebuilt, or reconstructed by a person described by Section 501.104(a) and, in addition to any other requirement of law, only if the application is accompanied by a separate form that:

(1) describes each major component part used to repair the motor vehicle; and

(2) shows the identification number required by federal law to be affixed to or inscribed on the part.

(b) On receipt of a complete application under this section accompanied by the $13 fee for the certificate of title, the department shall issue the applicant a regular certificate of title for the motor vehicle.

(c) A regular certificate of title issued under this section must:

(1) describe or disclose the motor vehicle's former condition in a manner reasonably un-

derstandable to a potential purchaser of the motor vehicle; and

(2) bear on its face the words "REBUILT SALVAGE" in capital letters that:

(A) are red;

(B) are centered on and occupy at least 15 percent of the face of the certificate of title; and

(C) do not prevent any other words on the title from being read or copied.

(d) In addition to the fee described by Subsection (b), the applicant shall pay a $65 rebuilder fee.

(e) On or after the 31st day after the date the department receives a rebuilder fee under Subsection (d), the department shall deposit $50 of the fee to the credit of the state highway fund to be used only by the Department of Public Safety to enforce this chapter and $15 to the credit of the general revenue fund.

(f) The department may not issue a regular certificate of title for a motor vehicle based on a:

(1) nonrepairable vehicle title or comparable out-of-state ownership document;

(2) receipt issued under Section 501.096(b); or

(3) certificate of authority.
(Enacted by Acts 1997, 75th Leg., ch. 165 (S.B. 898), § 30.43(a), effective September 1, 1997; am. Acts 2003, 78th Leg., ch. 1325 (H.B. 3588), § 17.02, effective September 1, 2003 (renumbered from Secs. 501.0922, 501.0923).)

### Sec. 501.100. [2 Versions: Effective January 1, 2012] Application for Regular Certificate of Title for Salvage Vehicle.

(a) A vehicle for which a nonrepairable certificate of title issued prior to September 1, 2003, or for which a salvage vehicle title or salvage record of title has been issued may obtain a title after the motor vehicle has been repaired, rebuilt, or reconstructed and, in addition to any other requirement of law, only if the application:

(1) describes each major component part used to repair the motor vehicle;

(2) states the name of each person from whom the parts used in assembling the vehicle were obtained; and

(3) shows the identification number required by federal law to be affixed to or inscribed on the part.

(b) On receipt of a complete application under this section accompanied by the fee for the title, the department shall issue the applicant a title.

(c) A title issued under this section must describe or disclose the motor vehicle's former condition in a manner reasonably understandable to a potential purchaser of the motor vehicle.

(d) In addition to the fee described by Subsection (b), the applicant shall pay a $65 rebuilder fee.

(e) On or after the 31st day after the date the department receives a rebuilder fee under Subsection (d), the department shall deposit $50 of the fee to the credit of the state highway fund to be used only by the Department of Public Safety to enforce this chapter and $15 to the credit of the general revenue fund.

(f) The department may not issue a regular title for a motor vehicle based on a:

(1) nonrepairable vehicle title or comparable out-of-state ownership document;

(2) receipt issued under Section 501.1003(b); or

(3) certificate of authority.

(Enacted by Acts 1997, 75th Leg., ch. 165 (S.B. 898), § 30.43(a), effective September 1, 1997; am. Acts 2003, 78th Leg., ch. 1325 (H.B. 3588), § 17.02, effective September 1, 2003 (renumbered from Secs. 501.0922, 501.0923); am. Acts 2011, 82nd Leg., ch. 1296 (H.B. 2357), § 43, effective January 1, 2012.)

### Sec. 501.1001. [2 Versions: As amended by Acts 2011, 82nd Leg., ch. 1136] Salvage Motor Vehicles or Nonrepairable Motor Vehicles for Insurance Companies or Self-Insured Persons.

(a) Except as provided by Section 501.0925, an insurance company that is licensed to conduct business in this state and that acquires, through payment of a claim, ownership or possession of a salvage motor vehicle or nonrepairable motor vehicle covered by a certificate of title issued by this state or a manufacturer's certificate of origin shall surrender a properly assigned title or manufacturer's certificate of origin to the department, on a form prescribed by the department.

(b) For a salvage motor vehicle, the insurance company shall apply for a salvage vehicle title. For a nonrepairable motor vehicle, the insurance company shall apply for a nonrepairable vehicle title.

(c) An insurance company may not sell a salvage motor vehicle or nonrepairable motor vehicle unless the department has issued a salvage vehicle title or a nonrepairable vehicle title, as appropriate, for the motor vehicle or a comparable ownership document has been issued by another state or jurisdiction for the motor vehicle.

(d) An insurance company may sell a salvage motor vehicle or nonrepairable motor vehicle, or assign a salvage vehicle title or a nonrepairable vehicle title for a motor vehicle, only to a salvage vehicle dealer, an out-of-state buyer, a buyer in a casual sale at auction, a metal recycler, or a used automotive parts recycler. If a motor vehicle is not a salvage motor vehicle or a nonrepairable motor vehicle, the insurance company is not required to surrender the regular certificate of title for the vehicle or to be issued a salvage vehicle title or a nonrepairable vehicle title for the motor vehicle.

(e) An insurance company or other person who acquires ownership of a motor vehicle other than a nonrepairable or salvage motor vehicle may voluntarily and on proper application obtain a salvage vehicle title or a nonrepairable vehicle title for the vehicle.

(Enacted by Acts 1997, 75th Leg., ch. 165 (S.B. 898), § 30.43(a), effective September 1, 1997; am. Acts 2003, 78th Leg., ch. 1325 (H.B. 3588), § 17.02, effective September 1, 2003 (renumbered from Sec. 501.0912); am. Acts 2009, 81st Leg., ch. 783 (S.B. 1095), § 9, effective September 1, 2009; am. Acts 2009, 81st Leg., ch. 933 (H.B. 3097), § 4.09, effective September 1, 2009; am. Acts 2011, 82nd Leg., ch. 1136 (H.B. 1422), § 1, effective September 1, 2011; am. Acts 2011, 82nd Leg., ch. 1296 (H.B. 2357), § 44, effective January 1, 2012 (renumbered from Sec. 501.092).)

### Sec. 501.1001. [2 Versions: As amended by Acts 2011, 82nd Leg., ch. 1296, Effective January 1, 2012] Salvage Motor Vehicles or Nonrepairable Motor Vehicles for Insurance Companies or Self-Insured Persons.

(a) An insurance company that is licensed to conduct business in this state and that acquires, through payment of a claim, ownership or possession of a salvage motor vehicle or nonrepairable motor vehicle covered by a title issued by this state or a manufacturer's certificate of origin shall surrender a properly assigned title or manufacturer's certificate of origin to the department, in a manner prescribed by the department, except that not earlier than the 31st day after the date of payment of the claim the insurance company may surrender a title, in a manner prescribed by the department, and receive a salvage vehicle title or a nonrepairable vehicle title without obtaining a properly assigned title if the insurance company:

(1) has obtained the release of all liens on the motor vehicle;

(2) is unable to locate one or more owners of the motor vehicle; and

(3) has provided notice to the last known address in the department's records to each owner that has not been located:

(A) by registered or certified mail, return receipt requested; or

(B) if a notice sent under Paragraph (A) is returned unclaimed, by publication in a newspaper of general circulation in the area where the unclaimed mail notice was sent.

(b) For a salvage motor vehicle, the insurance company shall apply for a salvage vehicle title or salvage record of title. For a nonrepairable motor vehicle, the insurance company shall apply for a nonrepairable vehicle title or nonrepairable record of title.

(c) An insurance company or other person who acquires ownership of a motor vehicle other than a nonrepairable or salvage motor vehicle may voluntarily and on proper application obtain a salvage vehicle title, salvage record of title, nonrepairable vehicle title, or nonrepairable record of title for the vehicle.

(d) This subsection applies only to a motor vehicle in this state that is a self-insured motor vehicle and that is damaged to the extent it becomes a nonrepairable or salvage motor vehicle. The owner of a motor vehicle to which this subsection applies shall submit to the department before the 31st business day after the date of the damage, in a manner prescribed by the department, a statement that the motor vehicle was self-insured and damaged. When the owner submits a report, the owner shall surrender the ownership document and apply for a nonrepairable vehicle title, nonrepairable record of title, salvage vehicle title, or salvage record of title.

(Enacted by Acts 1997, 75th Leg., ch. 165 (S.B. 898), § 30.43(a), effective September 1, 1997; am. Acts 2003, 78th Leg., ch. 1325 (H.B. 3588), § 17.02, effective September 1, 2003 (renumbered from Sec. 501.0912); am. Acts 2009, 81st Leg., ch. 783 (S.B. 1095), § 9, effective September 1, 2009; am. Acts 2009, 81st Leg., ch. 933 (H.B. 3097), § 4.09, effective September 1, 2009; am. Acts 2011, 82nd Leg., ch. 1296 (H.B. 2357), § 44, effective January 1, 2012 (renumbered from Sec. 501.092).)

## Sec. 501.1002. [2 Versions: As amended by Acts 2011, 82nd Leg., ch. 1136] Owner-Retained Vehicles.

(a) If an insurance company pays a claim on a nonrepairable motor vehicle or salvage motor vehicle and the insurance company does not acquire ownership of the motor vehicle, the insurance company shall:

(1) submit to the department, before the 31st day after the date of the payment of the claim, on the form prescribed by the department, a report stating that the insurance company:

(A) has paid a claim on the motor vehicle; and

(B) has not acquired ownership of the motor vehicle; and

(2) provide notice to the owner of the motor vehicle of:

(A) the report required under Subdivision (1); and

(B) the requirements for operation or transfer of ownership of the motor vehicle under Subsection (b).

(b) The owner of a motor vehicle to which this section applies may not operate or permit operation of the motor vehicle on a public highway or transfer ownership of the motor vehicle by sale or otherwise unless the department has issued a salvage vehicle title or a nonrepairable vehicle title for the motor vehicle or a comparable ownership document has been issued by another state or jurisdiction for the motor vehicle.

(c) Subsection (b) does not apply if:

(1) the department has issued a nonrepairable vehicle title or salvage vehicle title for the motor vehicle; or

(2) another state or jurisdiction has issued a comparable out-of-state ownership document for the motor vehicle.

(Enacted by Acts 1997, 75th Leg., ch. 165 (S.B. 898), § 30.43(a), effective September 1, 1997; am. Acts 2003, 78th Leg., ch. 1325 (H.B. 3588), § 17.02, effective September 1, 2003 (renumbered from Sec. 501.0915); am. Acts 2011, 82nd Leg., ch. 1136 (H.B. 1422), § 3, effective September 1, 2011; am. Acts 2011, 82nd Leg., ch. 1296 (H.B. 2357), § 45, effective January 1, 2012 (renumbered from Sec. 501.093).)

## Sec. 501.1002. [2 Versions: As amended by Acts 2011, 82nd Leg., ch. 1296, Effective January 1, 2012] Owner-Retained Vehicles.

(a) If an insurance company pays a claim on a nonrepairable motor vehicle or salvage motor vehicle and the insurance company does not acquire ownership of the motor vehicle, the insurance company shall:

(1) apply on behalf of the owner for a nonrepairable vehicle title, nonrepairable record of title, salvage vehicle title, or salvage record of title; or

(2) notify the owner of the information contained in:

(A) Subsection (b); or

(B) Section 501.09111; and

(3) submit to the department, before the 31st day after the date of the payment of the claim, in a manner prescribed by the department, a report stating that the insurance company:

(A) has paid a claim on the motor vehicle; and

(B) has not acquired ownership of the motor vehicle; and

(b) The owner of a motor vehicle to which this section applies may not operate or permit operation of the motor vehicle on a public highway or transfer ownership of the motor vehicle by sale or otherwise unless the department has issued a salvage vehicle title, salvage record of title, nonrepairable vehicle title, or nonrepairable record of title for the motor vehicle or a comparable ownership document has been issued by another state or jurisdiction for the motor vehicle. (Enacted by Acts 1997, 75th Leg., ch. 165 (S.B. 898), § 30.43(a), effective September 1, 1997; am. Acts 2003, 78th Leg., ch. 1325 (H.B. 3588), § 17.02, effective September 1, 2003 (renumbered from Sec. 501.0915); am. Acts 2011, 82nd Leg., ch. 1296 (H.B. 2357), § 45, effective January 1, 2012 (renumbered from Sec. 501.093).)

### Sec. 501.1003. [Effective January 1, 2012] Salvage Dealer Responsibilities.

(a) If a salvage vehicle dealer acquires ownership of a nonrepairable motor vehicle or salvage motor vehicle for the purpose of dismantling, scrapping, or destroying the motor vehicle, the dealer shall, before the 31st day after the date the dealer acquires the motor vehicle, submit to the department a report stating that the motor vehicle will be dismantled, scrapped, or destroyed. The dealer shall:

(1) make the report in a manner prescribed by the department; and

(2) submit with the report a properly assigned manufacturer's certificate of origin, regular certificate of title, nonrepairable vehicle title, salvage vehicle title, or comparable out-of-state ownership document for the motor vehicle.

(b) After receiving the report and title or document, the department shall issue the salvage vehicle dealer a receipt for the manufacturer's certificate of origin, regular certificate of title, nonrepairable vehicle title, salvage vehicle title, or comparable out-of-state ownership document.

(c) The department shall adopt rules to notify the salvage dealer if the vehicle was not issued a printed title, but has a record of title in the department's titling system. (Enacted by Acts 1997, 75th Leg., ch. 165 (S.B. 898), § 30.43(a), effective September 1, 1997; am. Acts 2001, 77th Leg., ch. 1421 (H.B. 2813), § 11, effective June 1, 2003; am. Acts 2003, 78th Leg., ch. 1325 (H.B. 3588), § 17.02, effective September 1, 2003 (renumbered from Sec. 501.0917); am. Acts 2011, 82nd Leg., ch. 1296 (H.B. 2357), § 46, effective January 1, 2012, (renumbered from Sec. 501.096).)

### Sec. 501.101. [Renumbered January 1, 2012] Issuance of Title to Motor Vehicle Brought into State.

(a) This section applies only to a motor vehicle brought into this state from another state or jurisdiction that has on any certificate of title or comparable out-of-state ownership document issued by the other state or jurisdiction:

(1) a "rebuilt," "salvage," or similar notation; or

(2) a "nonrepairable," "dismantle only," "parts only," "junked," "scrapped," or similar notation.

(b) On receipt of a complete application from the owner of the motor vehicle, the department shall issue the applicant the appropriate certificate of title for the motor vehicle.

(c) A certificate of title issued under this section must show on its face:

(1) the date of issuance;

(2) the name and address of the owner;

(3) any registration number assigned to the motor vehicle; and

(4) a description of the motor vehicle or other notation the department considers necessary or appropriate. (Enacted by Acts 1997, 75th Leg., ch. 165 (S.B. 898), § 30.43(a), effective September 1, 1997; am. Acts 2003, 78th Leg., ch. 1325 (H.B. 3588), § 17.02, effective September 1, 2003 (renumbered from Sec. 501.0924).)

STATUTORY NOTES

**Editor's notes.** — This section is renumbered to Transportation Code § 501.09113 pursuant to Acts 2011, 82nd Leg., ch. 1296 (H.B. 2357), § 39, effective January 1, 2012.

## Sec. 501.102. [Renumbered January 1, 2012] Offenses.

(a) A person commits an offense if the person:

(1) applies to the department for a regular certificate of title for a motor vehicle; and

(2) knows or reasonably should know that:

(A) the vehicle is a nonrepairable motor vehicle that has been repaired, rebuilt, or reconstructed;

(B) the vehicle identification number assigned to the motor vehicle belongs to a nonrepairable motor vehicle that has been repaired, rebuilt, or reconstructed;

(C) the title issued to the motor vehicle belongs to a nonrepairable motor vehicle that has been repaired, rebuilt, or reconstructed;

(D) the vehicle identification number assigned to the motor vehicle belongs to an export-only motor vehicle;

(E) the motor vehicle is an export-only motor vehicle; or

(F) the motor vehicle is a nonrepairable motor vehicle or salvage motor vehicle for which a nonrepairable vehicle title, salvage vehicle title, or comparable ownership document issued by another state or jurisdiction has not been issued.

(b) A person commits an offense if the person knowingly sells, transfers, or releases a salvage motor vehicle in violation of this subchapter.

(c) A person commits an offense if the person knowingly fails or refuses to surrender a regular certificate of title after the person:

(1) receives a notice from an insurance company that the motor vehicle is a nonrepairable or salvage motor vehicle; or

(2) knows the vehicle has become a nonrepairable motor vehicle or salvage motor vehicle under Section 501.094.

(d) Except as provided by Subsection (e), an offense under this section is a Class C misdemeanor.

(e) If it is shown on the trial of an offense under this section that the defendant has been previously convicted of:

(1) one offense under this section, the offense is a Class B misdemeanor; or

(2) two or more offenses under this section, the offense is a state jail felony.

(f) Subsection (c) does not apply to an applicant for a title under Sections 501.0925 and 501.0935.

(Enacted by Acts 1997, 75th Leg., ch. 165 (S.B. 898), § 30.43(a), effective September 1, 1997; am. Acts 2003, 78th Leg., ch. 1325 (H.B. 3588), § 17.02, effective September 1, 2003 (renumbered from Sec. 501.0926); am. Acts 2011, 82nd Leg., ch. 1136 (H.B. 1422), § 5, effective September 1, 2011.)

STATUTORY NOTES

**Editor's notes.** — This section is renumbered to Transportation Code § 501.109 pursuant to Acts 2011, 82nd Leg., ch. 1296 (H.B. 2357), § 49, effective January 1, 2012.

## Sec. 501.103. [Renumbered January 1, 2012] Color of Nonrepairable Vehicle Title or Salvage Vehicle Title.

(a) The department shall print a nonrepairable vehicle title:

(1) in a color that distinguishes it from a regular certificate of title or salvage vehicle title; and

(2) so that it clearly shows that it is the negotiable ownership document for a nonrepairable motor vehicle.

(b) A nonrepairable vehicle title must state on its face that the motor vehicle:

(1) may not be:

(A) issued a regular certificate of title;

(B) registered in this state; or

(C) repaired, rebuilt, or reconstructed; and

(2) may be used only as a source for used parts or scrap metal.

(c) The department shall print a salvage vehicle title:

(A) in a color that distinguishes it from a regular certificate of title or nonrepairable vehicle title; and

(B) so that each document clearly shows that it is the ownership document for a salvage motor vehicle.

(d) A salvage vehicle title for a vehicle that is a salvage motor vehicle because of damage caused exclusively by flood must bear a notation on its face that the department considers appropriate. If the title for a motor vehicle reflects the notation required by this subsection, the owner may sell, transfer, or release the motor vehicle only as provided by this subchapter.

(e) The department may provide a stamp to a person who is a licensed salvage vehicle dealer

under Chapter 2302, Occupations Code, to mark the face of a title under this subchapter. The department shall provide the stamp to the person for a fee in the amount determined by the department to be necessary for the department to recover the cost of providing the stamp.
(Enacted by Acts 1997, 75th Leg., ch. 165 (S.B. 898), § 30.43(a), effective September 1, 1997; am. Acts 2003, 78th Leg., ch. 1325 (H.B. 3588), § 17.02, effective September 1, 2003 (renumbered from Sec. 501.0928).)

### STATUTORY NOTES

**Editor's notes.** — This section is renumbered to Transportation. Code § 501.09112 pursuant to Acts 2011, 82nd Leg., ch. 1296 (H.B. 2357), § 38, effective January 1, 2012.

## Sec. 501.104. [2 Versions: Effective until January 1, 2012] Rebuilder to Possess Title or Other Documentation.

(a) This section applies only to:
(1) a rebuilder licensed as a salvage vehicle dealer;
(2) a person engaged in the business of a rebuilder, regardless of whether the person is licensed to engage in that business; or
(3) a person engaged in the casual repair, rebuilding, or reconstruction of fewer than three motor vehicles in the same 12-month period.
(b) A person described by Subsection (a) must possess:
(1) a regular certificate of title, nonrepairable vehicle title, salvage vehicle title, or comparable out-of-state ownership document for any motor vehicle that is:
(A) owned by the person;
(B) in the person's inventory; and
(C) being offered for resale; or
(2) a contract entered into with the owner, a work order, or another document that shows the authority for the person to possess any motor vehicle that is:
(A) owned by another person;
(B) on the person's business or casual premises; and
(C) being repaired, rebuilt, or reconstructed for the other person.
(Enacted by Acts 1997, 75th Leg., ch. 165 (S.B. 898), § 30.43(a), effective September 1, 1997; am. Acts 2003, 78th Leg., ch. 1325 (H.B. 3588), § 17.02, effective September 1, 2003 (renumbered from Sec. 501.0929).)

## Sec. 501.104. [2 Versions: Effective January 1, 2012] Rebuilder to Possess Title or Other Documentation.

(a) This section applies to a person engaged in repairing, rebuilding, or reconstructing more than five motor vehicles, regardless of whether the person is licensed to engage in that business.
(b) A person described by Subsection (a) must possess:
(1) an acceptable ownership document or proof of ownership for any motor vehicle that is:
(A) owned by the person;
(B) in the person's inventory; and
(C) being offered for resale; or
(2) a contract entered into with the owner, a work order, or another document that shows the authority for the person to possess any motor vehicle that is:
(A) owned by another person;
(B) on the person's business or casual premises; and
(C) being repaired, rebuilt, or reconstructed for the other person.
(Enacted by Acts 1997, 75th Leg., ch. 165 (S.B. 898), § 30.43(a), effective September 1, 1997; am. Acts 2003, 78th Leg., ch. 1325 (H.B. 3588), § 17.02, effective September 1, 2003 (renumbered from Sec. 501.0929); am. Acts 2011, 82nd Leg., ch. 1296 (H.B. 2357), § 47, effective January 1, 2012.)

## Sec. 501.105. [Renumbered January 1, 2012] Retention of Records Relating to Certain Casual Sales.

Each licensed salvage vehicle dealer, used automotive parts recycler, or insurance company that sells a nonrepairable motor vehicle or a salvage motor vehicle at a casual sale shall keep on the business premises of the dealer or the insurance company a list of all casual sales made during the preceding 36-month period that contains:
(1) the date of the sale;
(2) the name of the purchaser;
(3) the name of the jurisdiction that issued the identification document provided by the purchaser, as shown on the document; and
(4) the vehicle identification number.
(Enacted by Acts 2003, 78th Leg., ch. 1325 (H.B. 3588), § 17.02, effective September 1, 2003; am. Acts 2009, 81st Leg., ch. 783 (S.B. 1095), § 11, effective September 1, 2009; am. Acts 2009, 81st Leg., ch. 933 (H.B. 3097), § 4.11, effective September 1, 2009.)

**Transportation**

STATUTORY NOTES

**Editor's notes.** — This section is renumbered to Transportation Code § 501.108 pursuant to Acts 2011, 82nd Leg., ch. 1296 (H.B. 2357), § 48, effective January 1, 2012.

## Sec. 501.106. [Renumbered January 1, 2012] Enforcement of Subchapter.

(a) This subchapter shall be enforced by the department and any other governmental or law enforcement entity, including the Department of Public Safety, and the personnel of the entity as provided by this subchapter.

(b) The department, an agent, officer, or employee of the department, or another person enforcing this subchapter is not liable to a person damaged or injured by an act or omission relating to the issuance of a regular certificate of title, nonrepairable vehicle title, or salvage vehicle title under this subchapter.

(Enacted by Acts 1997, 75th Leg., ch. 165 (S.B. 898), § 30.43(a), effective September 1, 1997; am. Acts 2003, 78th Leg., ch. 1325 (H.B. 3588), § 17.02, effective September 1, 2003 (renumbered from Sec. 501.0930).)

STATUTORY NOTES

**Editor's notes.** — This section is renumbered to Transportation Code § 501.110 pursuant to Acts 2011, 82nd Leg., ch. 1296 (H.B. 2357), § 50, effective January 1, 2012.

## Sec. 501.107. Applicability of Subchapter to Recycler.

(a) This subchapter does not apply to a sale to, purchase by, or other transaction by or with, a metal recycler except as provided by Subsections (b) and (c).

(b) A metal recycler shall submit to the department the properly assigned manufacturer's certificate of origin, regular certificate of title, nonrepairable vehicle title, salvage vehicle title, or comparable out-of-state ownership document that the person receives in conjunction with the purchase of a motor vehicle not later than the 60th day after the date the metal recycler receives the title or out-of-state ownership document.

(c) This subchapter applies to a transaction with a metal recycler in which a motor vehicle:

(1) is sold or delivered to the metal recycler for the purpose of reuse or resale as a motor vehicle or as a source of used parts; and

(2) is used for that purpose.

(Enacted by Acts 1997, 75th Leg., ch. 165 (S.B. 898), § 30.43(a), effective September 1, 1997; am.

Acts 2003, 78th Leg., ch. 1325 (H.B. 3588), § 17.02, effective September 1, 2003 (renumbered from Sec. 501.0931).)

## Sec. 501.108. [Effective January 1, 2012] Record Retention.

(a) Each licensed salvage vehicle dealer, used automotive parts recycler, or insurance company that sells a nonrepairable motor vehicle or a salvage motor vehicle at a casual sale shall keep on the business premises of the dealer or the insurance company a list of all casual sales made during the preceding 36-month period that contains:

(1) the date of the sale;

(2) the name of the purchaser;

(3) the name of the jurisdiction that issued the identification document provided by the purchaser, as shown on the document; and

(4) the vehicle identification number.

(b) A salvage vehicle dealer or used automotive parts recycler shall keep on the business premises of the dealer or recycler, until the third anniversary of the date the report on the motor vehicle is submitted to the department, a record of the vehicle, its ownership, and its condition as dismantled, scrapped, or destroyed as required by Section 501.1003.

(Enacted by Acts 2003, 78th Leg., ch. 1325 (H.B. 3588), § 17.02, effective September 1, 2003; am. Acts 2009, 81st Leg., ch. 783 (S.B. 1095), § 11, effective September 1, 2009; am. Acts 2009, 81st Leg., ch. 933 (H.B. 3097), § 4.11, effective September 1, 2009; am. Acts 2011, 82nd Leg., ch. 1296 (H.B. 2357), § 48, effective January 1, 2012 (renumbered from Sec. 501.105).)

## Sec. 501.109. [Effective January 1, 2012] Offenses.

(a) A person commits an offense if the person:

(1) applies to the department for a title for a motor vehicle; and

(2) knows or reasonably should know that:

(A) the vehicle is a nonrepairable motor vehicle that has been repaired, rebuilt, or reconstructed;

(B) the vehicle identification number assigned to the motor vehicle belongs to a nonrepairable motor vehicle that has been repaired, rebuilt, or reconstructed;

(C) the title issued to the motor vehicle belongs to a nonrepairable motor vehicle that has been repaired, rebuilt, or reconstructed;

(D) the vehicle identification number assigned to the motor vehicle belongs to an export-only motor vehicle;

(E) the motor vehicle is an export-only motor vehicle; or

(F) the motor vehicle is a nonrepairable motor vehicle or salvage motor vehicle for which a nonrepairable vehicle title, salvage vehicle title, or comparable ownership document issued by another state or jurisdiction has not been issued.

(b) A person commits an offense if the person knowingly sells, transfers, or releases a salvage motor vehicle in violation of this subchapter.

(c) A person commits an offense if the person knowingly fails or refuses to surrender a regular certificate of title after the person:

(1) receives a notice from an insurance company that the motor vehicle is a nonrepairable or salvage motor vehicle; or

(2) knows the vehicle has become a nonrepairable motor vehicle or salvage motor vehicle under Section 501.1001.

(d) Except as provided by Subsection (e), an offense under this section is a Class C misdemeanor.

(e) If it is shown on the trial of an offense under this section that the defendant has been previously convicted of:

(1) one offense under this section, the offense is a Class B misdemeanor; or

(2) two or more offenses under this section, the offense is a state jail felony.

(f) Subsection (c) does not apply to an applicant for a title under Sections 501.0925 and 501.0935.

(Enacted by Acts 1997, 75th Leg., ch. 165 (S.B. 898), § 30.43(a), effective September 1, 1997; am. Acts 2003, 78th Leg., ch. 1325 (H.B. 3588), § 17.02, effective September 1, 2003 (renumbered from Sec. 501.0926); am. Acts 2011, 82nd Leg., ch. 1136 (H.B. 1422), § 5, effective September 1, 2011; am. Acts 2011, 82nd Leg., ch. 1296 (H.B. 2357), § 49, effective January 1, 2012 (renumbered from Sec. 501.102).)

## Sec. 501.110. [Effective January 1, 2012] Enforcement of Subchapter.

(a) This subchapter shall be enforced by the department and any other governmental or law enforcement entity, including the Department of Public Safety, and the personnel of the entity as provided by this subchapter.

(b) The department, an agent, officer, or employee of the department, or another person enforcing this subchapter is not liable to a person damaged or injured by an act or omission relating to the issuance or revocation of a title, nonrepairable vehicle title, nonrepairable record of title, or salvage vehicle title, or salvage record of title under this subchapter.

(Enacted by Acts 1997, 75th Leg., ch. 165 (S.B. 898), § 30.43(a), effective September 1, 1997; am. Acts 2003, 78th Leg., ch. 1325 (H.B. 3588), § 17.02, effective September 1, 2003 (renumbered from Sec. 501.0930); am. Acts 2011, 82nd Leg., ch. 1296 (H.B. 2357), § 50, effective January 1, 2012, (renumbered from Sec. 501.106).)

## SUBCHAPTER F
## SECURITY INTERESTS

### Sec. 501.111. Perfection of Security Interest.

(a) **[2 Versions: Effective until January 1, 2012]** Except as provided by Subsection (b), a person may perfect a security interest in a motor vehicle that is the subject of a first or subsequent sale only by recording the security interest on the certificate of title as provided by this chapter.

(a) **[2 Versions: Effective January 1, 2012]** Except as provided by Subsection (b), a person may perfect a security interest in a motor vehicle that is the subject of a first or subsequent sale only by recording the security interest on the title as provided by this chapter.

(b) A person may perfect a security interest in a motor vehicle held as inventory by a person in the business of selling motor vehicles only by complying with Chapter 9, Business & Commerce Code.

(Enacted by Acts 1995, 74th Leg., ch. 165 (S.B. 971), § 1, effective September 1, 1995; am. Acts 2011, 82nd Leg., ch. 1296 (H.B. 2357), § 51, effective January 1, 2012.)

### Sec. 501.112. Sale or Security Interest Not Created by Certain Vehicle Leases.

Notwithstanding any other law, an agreement for the lease of a motor vehicle does not create a sale or security interest by merely providing that the rental price is permitted or required to be adjusted under the agreement as determined by the amount realized on the sale or other disposition of the vehicle.

(Enacted by Acts 1995, 74th Leg., ch. 165 (S.B. 971), § 1, effective September 1, 1995.)

### Sec. 501.113.  [2 Versions: Effective until January 1 2012] Recordation of Security Interest.

(a) Recordation of a lien under this chapter is considered to occur when the county assessor-collector:

(1) is presented with an application for a certificate of title that discloses the lien with tender of the filing fee; or

(2) accepts the application.

(b) For purposes of Chapter 9, Business & Commerce Code, the time of recording a lien under this chapter is considered to be the time of filing the security interest, and on such recordation, the recorded lienholder and assignees under Section 501.114 obtain priority over the rights of a lien creditor, as defined by Section 9.102, Business & Commerce Code, for so long as the lien is recorded on the certificate of title.

(Enacted by Acts 1995, 74th Leg., ch. 165 (S.B. 971), § 1, effective September 1, 1995; am. Acts 2009, 81st Leg., ch. 814 (S.B. 1592), § 4, effective June 19, 2009.)

### Sec. 501.113.  [2 Versions: Effective January 1, 2012] Recordation of Security Interest.

(a) Recordation of a lien under this chapter is considered to occur when:

(1) the department's titling system is updated; or

(2) the county assessor-collector accepts the application of title that discloses the lien with the filing fee.

(b) For purposes of Chapter 9, Business & Commerce Code, the time of recording a lien under this chapter is considered to be the time of filing the security interest, and on such recordation, the recorded lienholder and assignees under Section 501.114 obtain priority over the rights of a lien creditor, as defined by Section 9.102, Business & Commerce Code, for so long as the lien is recorded on the title.

(Enacted by Acts 1995, 74th Leg., ch. 165 (S.B. 971), § 1, effective September 1, 1995; am. Acts 2009, 81st Leg., ch. 814 (S.B. 1592), § 4, effective June 19, 2009; am. Acts 2011, 82nd Leg., ch. 1296 (H.B. 2357), § 52, effective January 1, 2012.)

### Sec. 501.114.  Assignment of Lien.

(a) A lienholder may assign a lien recorded under Section 501.113 without making any filing or giving any notice under this chapter. The lien assigned remains valid and perfected and retains its priority, securing the obligation assigned to the assignee, against transferees from and creditors of the debtor, including lien creditors, as defined by Section 9.102, Business & Commerce Code.

(b) **[2 Versions: Effective until January 1, 2012]** An assignee or assignor may, but need not to retain the validity, perfection, and priority of the lien assigned, as evidence of the assignment of a lien recorded under Section 501.113:

(1) apply to the county assessor-collector for the assignee to be named as lienholder on the certificate of title; and

(2) notify the debtor of the assignment.

(b) **[2 Versions: Effective January 1, 2012]** An assignee or assignor may, but need not to retain the validity, perfection, and priority of the lien assigned, as evidence of the assignment of a lien recorded under Section 501.113:

(1) apply to the county assessor-collector for the assignee to be named as lienholder on the title; and

(2) notify the debtor of the assignment.

(c) Failure to make application under Subsection (b) or notify a debtor of an assignment does not create a cause of action against the recorded lienholder, the assignor, or the assignee or affect the continuation of the perfected status of the assigned lien in favor of the assignee against transferees from and creditors of the debtor, including lien creditors, as defined by Section 9.102, Business & Commerce Code.

(d) **[2 Versions: Effective until January 1, 2012]** An application under Subsection (b) must be:

(1) signed by the assignee; and

(2) accompanied by:

(A) the applicable fee;

(B) a copy of the assignment agreement executed by the parties; and

(C) the certificate of title on which the lien to be assigned is recorded.

(d) **[2 Versions: Effective January 1, 2012]** An application under Subsection (b) must be acknowledged by the assignee.

(e) **[2 Versions: Effective until January 1, 2012]** On receipt of the completed application and fee, the department:

(1) may amend the department's records to substitute the assignee for the recorded lienholder; and

(2) shall issue a new certificate of title as provided by Section 501.027.

(e) **[2 Versions: Effective January 1, 2012]** On receipt of the completed application and fee, the department may:

(1) amend the department's records to substitute the assignee for the recorded lienholder; and

(2) issue a new title as provided by this chapter.

(f) **[2 Versions: Effective until January 1, 2012]** The issuance of a certificate of title under Subsection (e) is recordation of the assignment.

(f) **[2 Versions: Effective January 1, 2012]** The issuance of a title under Subsection (e) is recordation of the assignment.

(g) **[2 Versions: Effective until January 1, 2012]** Regardless of whether application is made for the assignee to be named as lienholder on the certificate of title, the time of the recordation of a lien assigned under this section is considered to be the time the lien was initially recorded under Section 501.113.

(g) **[2 Versions: Effective January 1, 2012]** Regardless of whether application is made for the assignee to be named as lienholder on the title, the time of the recordation of a lien assigned under this section is considered to be the time the lien was initially recorded under Section 501.113.

(h) Notwithstanding Subsections (a)-(g) and procedures that may be conducted under those subsections, the assignment of a lien does not affect the procedures applicable to the foreclosure of a worker's lien under Chapter 70, Property Code, or the rights of the holder of a worker's lien. Notice given to the last known lienholder of record, as provided by that chapter, is adequate to allow foreclosure under that chapter.

(i) Notwithstanding Subsections (a)-(g) and the procedures that may be conducted under those subsections, the assignment of a lien does not affect the procedures applicable to the release of a holder's lien under Section 348.408, Finance Code.

(Enacted by Acts 1995, 74th Leg., ch. 165 (S.B. 971), § 1, effective September 1, 1995; am. Acts 2009, 81st Leg., ch. 814 (S.B. 1592), § 5, effective June 19, 2009; am. Acts 2011, 82nd Leg., ch. 1296 (H.B. 2357), § 53, effective January 1, 2012.)

## Sec. 501.115. [2 Versions: Effective until January 1, 2012] Discharge of Lien.

(a) When a debt or claim secured by a lien has been satisfied, the lienholder shall, within a reasonable time not to exceed the maximum time allowed by Section 348.408 or 353.405(b), Finance Code, as applicable, execute and deliver to the owner, or the owner's designee, a discharge of the lien on a form prescribed by the department.

(b) The owner may present the discharge and certificate of title to the county assessor-collector with an application for a new certificate of title and the department shall issue a new certificate of title.

(Enacted by Acts 1995, 74th Leg., ch. 165 (S.B. 971), § 1, effective September 1, 1995; am. Acts 1997, 75th Leg., ch. 296 (H.B. 1137), § 1, effective September 1, 1997; am. Acts 1999, 76th Leg., ch. 268 (H.B. 2176), § 1, effective May 28, 1999; am. Acts 2011, 82nd Leg., ch. 117 (H.B. 2559), § 24, effective September 1, 2011.)

## Sec. 501.115. [2 Versions: Effective January 1, 2012] Discharge of Lien.

(a) **[2 Versions: As amended by Acts 2011, 82nd Leg., ch. 117]** When a debt or claim secured by a lien has been satisfied, the lienholder shall, within a reasonable time not to exceed the maximum time allowed by Section 348.408 or 353.405(b), Finance Code, as applicable, execute and deliver to the owner, or the owner's designee, a discharge of the lien on a form prescribed by the department.

(a) **[2 Versions: As amended by Acts 2011, 82nd Leg., ch. 1296, effective January 1, 2012]** When a debt or claim secured by a lien has been satisfied, the lienholder shall, within a reasonable time not to exceed the maximum time allowed by Section 348.408, Finance Code, execute and deliver to the owner, or the owner's designee, a discharge of the lien in a manner prescribed by the department.

(b) The owner may submit the discharge and title to the department for a new title.

(Enacted by Acts 1995, 74th Leg., ch. 165 (S.B. 971), § 1, effective September 1, 1995; am. Acts 1997, 75th Leg., ch. 296 (H.B. 1137), § 1, effective September 1, 1997; am. Acts 1999, 76th Leg., ch. 268 (H.B. 2176), § 1, effective May 28, 1999; am. Acts 2011, 82nd Leg., ch. 117 (H.B. 2559), § 24, effective September 1, 2011; am. Acts 2011, 82nd Leg., ch. 1296 (H.B. 2357), § 54, effective January 1, 2012.)

## Sec. 501.116. [2 Versions: Effective until January 1, 2012] Cancellation of Discharged Lien.

The department may cancel a discharged lien that has been recorded on a certificate of title for six years or more if the recorded lienholder:

(1) does not exist; or

(2) cannot be located for the owner to obtain a release of the lien.

(Enacted by Acts 1995, 74th Leg., ch. 165 (S.B. 971), § 1, effective September 1, 1995.)

### Sec. 501.116.  [2 Versions: Effective January 1, 2012] Cancellation of Discharged Lien.

The department may cancel a discharged lien that has been recorded on a title for 10 years or more if the recorded lienholder:

(1) does not exist; or

(2) cannot be located for the owner to obtain a release of the lien.

(Enacted by Acts 1995, 74th Leg., ch. 165 (S.B. 971), § 1, effective September 1, 1995; am. Acts 2011, 82nd Leg., ch. 1296 (H.B. 2357), § 55, effective January 1, 2012.)

### Sec. 501.117.  Electronic Lien System.

(a) The department by rule shall develop a system under which a security interest in a motor vehicle may be perfected, assigned, discharged, and canceled electronically instead of by record maintained on a certificate of title. The department may establish categories of lienholders that may participate in the system and, except as provided by this section, may require a lienholder to participate in the system.

(b) The department shall publish and distribute procedures for using the system to county assessor-collectors and to financial institutions and other potential motor vehicle lienholders.

(c) The provisions of this chapter relating to perfecting, assigning, discharging, and canceling a security interest in a motor vehicle by record maintained on a certificate of title do not apply to the extent the security interest is governed by rules adopted under this section.

(d) The department may not require a depository institution, as defined by Section 180.002, Finance Code, to participate in the system if the department has issued fewer than 100 notifications of security interests in motor vehicles to the depository institution during a calendar year.

(d-1) **[Expires January 1, 2013]** The department may not require a depository institution, as defined by Section 180.002, Finance Code, to participate in the system:

(1) during 2011, if the department issues fewer than 200 notifications of security interests in motor vehicles to the depository institution between September 1, 2011, and December 31, 2011; and

(2) during 2012, if the depository institution was exempt under Subdivision (1) and the department issues fewer than 200 notifications of security interests in motor vehicles to the depository institution in 2012.

(d-2) **[Expires January 1, 2013]** This subsection and Subsection (d-1) expire January 1, 2013.

(e) The department by rule shall establish a reasonable schedule for compliance with the requirements of Subsection (a) for each category of lienholder that the department requires to participate in the system.

(f) The department may not:

(1) prohibit a lienholder from using an intermediary to access the system; or

(2) require a lienholder to use an intermediary to access the system.

(Enacted by Acts 2001, 77th Leg., ch. 505 (H.B. 1535), § 1, effective September 1, 2001; am. Acts 2011, 82nd Leg., ch. 813 (H.B. 2575), § 1, effective September 1, 2011.)

### Secs. 501.118 to 501.130 [Reserved for expansion].

## SUBCHAPTER G
## ADMINISTRATIVE PROVISIONS

### Sec. 501.131.  [Renumbered January 1, 2012] Rules; Forms.

(a) The department may adopt rules to administer this chapter.

(b) The department shall:

(1) in addition to the forms required by this chapter, prescribe forms for a title receipt, manufacturer's certificate, and importer's certificate, and other forms the department determines necessary; and

(2) provide each county assessor-collector with a sufficient supply of the forms.

(Enacted by Acts 1995, 74th Leg., ch. 165 (S.B. 971), § 1, effective September 1, 1995.)

STATUTORY NOTES

**Editor's notes.** — This section is renumbered to Transportation Code § 501.0041 pursuant to Acts 2011, 82nd Leg., ch. 1296 (H.B. 2357), § 4, effective January 1, 2012.

### Sec. 501.132.  Duplicate Title Receipt.

Except as otherwise provided by department rule, the department may not issue a duplicate title receipt unless the original title receipt or certificate of title is surrendered.

(Enacted by Acts 1995, 74th Leg., ch. 165 (S.B. 971), § 1, effective September 1, 1995; am. Acts 2001, 77th Leg., ch. 67 (H.B. 642), § 5, effective September 1, 2001.)

## Sec. 501.133. [Repealed January 1, 2012] Issuance of New Certificate of Title Because of Subsequent Sales.

(a) If all of the forms of transfer on a certificate of title have been used because of subsequent sales, the certificate may be delivered to a county assessor-collector, who shall:

(1) provide a title receipt in the manner required for a first sale; and

(2) send the certificate of title to the department on the same day the certificate is received.

(b) On receipt of the certificate of title, the department shall issue a new certificate of title. (Enacted by Acts 1995, 74th Leg., ch. 165 (S.B. 971), § 1, effective September 1, 1995.)

## Sec. 501.134. [2 Versions: Effective until January 1, 2012] Lost or Destroyed Certificate of Title.

(a) If a certificate of title is lost or destroyed, the owner or lienholder disclosed on the certificate may obtain, in the manner provided by this section and department rule, a certified copy of the lost or destroyed certificate of title directly from the department by applying on a form prescribed by the department and paying a fee of $2. A fee collected under this subsection shall be deposited to the credit of the state highway fund and may be spent only as provided by Section 501.138.

(b) If a lien is disclosed on a certificate of title, the department may issue a certified copy of the original certificate of title only to the first lienholder.

(c) The department must plainly mark "certified copy" on the face of a certified copy issued under this section, and each subsequent certificate issued for the motor vehicle until the vehicle is transferred. A subsequent purchaser or lienholder of the vehicle only acquires the rights, title, or interest in the vehicle held by the holder of the certified copy.

(d) A purchaser or lienholder of a motor vehicle having a certified copy issued under this section may at the time of the purchase or establishment of the lien require that the seller or owner indemnify the purchaser or lienholder and all subsequent purchasers of the vehicle against any loss

the person may suffer because of a claim presented on the original certificate of title.

(e) If the certificate of title is recovered, the owner of the vehicle shall promptly surrender the certificate of title to the department for cancellation, and the department shall eliminate the words "certified copy" from any certificate of title issued for that vehicle after that date.

(f) Except as provided by Subsection (g), the department may not issue a certified copy of a certificate of title before the fourth business day after the date application is made.

(g) The department may issue a certified copy of a certificate of title before the fourth business day after the date application is made only if the applicant:

(1) is the registered owner of the vehicle, the holder of a recorded lien against the vehicle, or a verified agent of the owner or lienholder; and

(2) submits personal identification, including a photograph, issued by an agency of this state or the United States.

(h) If the applicant is the agent of the owner or lienholder of the vehicle and is applying on behalf of the owner or lienholder, the applicant must submit verifiable proof that the person is the agent of the owner or lienholder.

(i) If an applicant for a certified copy of a certificate of title is a person other than a person described by Subsection (g)(1), the department may issue a certified copy of the certificate of title only by mail.
(Enacted by Acts 1995, 74th Leg., ch. 165 (S.B. 971), § 1, effective September 1, 1995; am. Acts 1997, 75th Leg., ch. 165 (S.B. 898), § 30.42(a), effective September 1, 1997; am. Acts 2001, 77th Leg., ch. 67 (H.B. 642), § 6, effective September 1, 2001.)

## Sec. 501.134. [2 Versions: Effective January 1, 2012] Lost or Destroyed Certificate of Title.

(a) If a printed title is lost or destroyed, the owner or lienholder disclosed on the title may obtain, in the manner provided by this section and department rule, a certified copy of the lost or destroyed title directly from the department by applying in a manner prescribed by the department and paying a fee of $2. A fee collected under this subsection shall be deposited to the credit of the state highway fund and may be spent only as provided by Section 501.138.

(b) If a lien is disclosed on a title, the department may issue a certified copy of the original title only to the first lienholder or the lienholder's verified agent.

(c) The department must plainly mark "certified copy" on the face of a certified copy issued under this section. A subsequent purchaser or lienholder of the vehicle only acquires the rights, title, or interest in the vehicle held by the holder of the certified copy.

(d) A purchaser or lienholder of a motor vehicle having a certified copy issued under this section may at the time of the purchase or establishment of the lien require that the seller or owner indemnify the purchaser or lienholder and all subsequent purchasers of the vehicle against any loss the person may suffer because of a claim presented on the original title.

(e) Repealed by Acts 2011, 82nd Leg., ch. 1296 (H.B. 2357), § 247(3), effective January 1, 2012].

(f) Repealed by Acts 2011, 82nd Leg., ch. 1296 (H.B. 2357), § 247(3), effective January 1, 2012].

(g) The department may issue a certified copy of a title only if the applicant:

(1) is the registered owner of the vehicle, the holder of a recorded lien against the vehicle, or a verified agent of the owner or lienholder; and

(2) submits personal identification as required by department rule.

(h) If the applicant is the agent of the owner or lienholder of the vehicle and is applying on behalf of the owner or lienholder, the applicant must submit verifiable proof that the person is the agent of the owner or lienholder.

(i) Repealed by Acts 2011, 82nd Leg., ch. 1296 (H.B. 2357), § 247(3), effective January 1, 2012].
(Enacted by Acts 1995, 74th Leg., ch. 165 (S.B. 971), § 1, effective September 1, 1995; am. Acts 1997, 75th Leg., ch. 165 (S.B. 898), § 30.42(a), effective September 1, 1997; am. Acts 2001, 77th Leg., ch. 67 (H.B. 642), § 6, effective September 1, 2001; am. Acts 2011, 82nd Leg., ch. 1296 (H.B. 2357), §§ 56, 247(3), effective January 1, 2012.)

### Sec. 501.135.   Record of Stolen or Concealed Motor Vehicle.

(a) **[2 Versions: Effective until January 1, 2012]** The department shall:

(1) make a record of each report to the department that a motor vehicle registered in this state has been stolen or concealed in violation of Section 32.33, Penal Code; and

(2) note the fact of the report in the department's records of the vehicle's certificate of title.

(a) **[2 Versions: Effective January 1, 2012]** The department shall:

(1) make a record of each report to the department that a motor vehicle registered in this state has been stolen or concealed in violation of Section 32.33, Penal Code; and

(2) note the fact of the report in the department's records.

(b) A person who reports a motor vehicle as stolen or concealed under Subsection (a) shall notify the department promptly if the vehicle is recovered, and the department shall change its records accordingly.
(Enacted by Acts 1995, 74th Leg., ch. 165 (S.B. 971), § 1, effective September 1, 1995; am. Acts 2011, 82nd Leg., ch. 1296 (H.B. 2357), § 57, effective January 1, 2012.)

### Sec. 501.136.   [Renumbered January 1, 2012] Acts by Deputy County Assessor-Collector.

A deputy county assessor-collector, other than a limited service deputy appointed under Section 502.112, may perform the duties of an assessor-collector under this chapter.
(Enacted by Acts 1995, 74th Leg., ch. 165 (S.B. 971), § 1, effective September 1, 1995.)

STATUTORY NOTES

**Editor's notes.** — This section is renumbered to Transportation Code § 520.0092 pursuant to Acts 2011, 82nd Leg., ch. 1296 (H.B. 2357), § 231, effective January 1, 2012.

### Sec. 501.137.   Duty of County Assessor-Collector [Renumbered].

Renumbered to Tex. Transp. Code § 520.005 by Acts 2011, 82nd Leg., ch. 1290 (H.B. 2017), § 31, effective September 1, 2011 and by Acts 2011, 82nd Leg., ch. 1296 (H.B. 2237), § 225, effective January 1, 2012.

### Sec. 501.138.   Collection and Disposition of Fees.

(a) **[2 Versions: Effective until January 1, 2012]** An applicant for a certificate of title, other than the state or a political subdivision of the state, must pay the county assessor-collector a fee of:

(1) $33 if the applicant's residence is a county located within a nonattainment area as defined under Section 107(d) of the federal Clean Air Act (42 U.S.C. Section 7407), as amended, or is an affected county, as defined by Section 386.001, Health and Safety Code; or

(2) $28 if the applicant's residence is any other county.

(a) **[2 Versions: Effective January 1, 2012]** An applicant for a title, other than the state or a political subdivision of the state, must pay a fee of:

(1) $33 if the applicant's residence is a county located within a nonattainment area as defined under Section 107(d) of the federal Clean Air Act (42 U.S.C. Section 7407), as amended, or is an affected county, as defined by Section 386.001, Health and Safety Code; or

(2) $28 if the applicant's residence is any other county.

(b) **[2 Versions: Effective until January 1, 2012]** The county assessor-collector shall send:

(1) $5 of the fee to the county treasurer for deposit in the officers' salary fund;

(2) $8 of the fee to the department:

(A) together with the application within the time prescribed by Section 501.023; or

(B) if the fee is deposited in an interest-bearing account or certificate in the county depository or invested in an investment authorized by Subchapter A, Chapter 2256, Government Code, not later than the 35th day after the date on which the fee is received; and

(3) the following amount to the comptroller at the time and in the manner prescribed by the comptroller:

(A) $20 of the fee if the applicant's residence is a county located within a nonattainment area as defined under Section 107(d) of the federal Clean Air Act (42 U.S.C. Section 7407), as amended, or is an affected county, as defined by Section 386.001, Health and Safety Code; or

(B) $15 of the fee if the applicant's residence is any other county.

(b) **[2 Versions: Effective January 1, 2012]** The fees shall be distributed as follows:

(1) $5 of the fee to the county treasurer for deposit in the officers' salary fund;

(2) $8 of the fee to the department:

(A) together with the application within the time prescribed by Section 501.023; or

(B) if the fee is deposited in an interest-bearing account or certificate in the county depository or invested in an investment authorized by Subchapter A, Chapter 2256, Government Code, not later than the 35th day after the date on which the fee is received; and

(3) the following amount to the comptroller at the time and in the manner prescribed by the comptroller:

(A) $20 of the fee if the applicant's residence is a county located within a nonattainment area as defined under Section 107(d) of the federal Clean Air Act (42 U.S.C. Section 7407), as amended, or is an affected county, as defined by Section 386.001, Health and Safety Code; or

(B) $15 of the fee if the applicant's residence is any other county.

(b-1) **[2 Versions: Effective until January 1, 2012]** Fees collected under Subsection (b) to be sent to the comptroller shall be deposited as follows:

(1) before September 1, 2008, to the credit of the Texas emissions reduction plan fund; and

(2) on or after September 1, 2008, to the credit of the Texas Mobility Fund, except that $5 of each fee imposed under Subsection (a)(1) and deposited on or after September 1, 2008, and before September 1, 2015, shall be deposited to the credit of the Texas emissions reduction plan fund.

(b-1) **[2 Versions: Effective January 1, 2012]** Fees collected under Subsection (b) to be sent to the comptroller shall be deposited to the credit of the Texas Mobility Fund, except that $5 of each fee imposed under Subsection (a)(1) and deposited on or after September 1, 2008, and before September 1, 2015, shall be deposited to the credit of the Texas emissions reduction plan fund.

(b-2) **[Expires August 31, 2019]** The comptroller shall establish a record of the amount of the fees deposited to the credit of the Texas Mobility Fund under Subsection (b-1). On or before the fifth workday of each month, the department shall remit to the comptroller for deposit to the credit of the Texas emissions reduction plan fund an amount of money equal to the amount of the fees deposited by the comptroller to the credit of the Texas Mobility Fund under Subsection (b-1) in the preceding month. The department shall use for remittance to the comptroller as required by this subsection money in the state highway fund that is not required to be used for a purpose specified by Section 7-a, Article VIII, Texas Constitution, and may not use for that remittance money received by this state under the congestion mitigation and air quality improvement program established under 23 U.S.C. Section 149.

(b-3) **[Expires August 31, 2019]** This subsection and Subsection (b-2) expire August 31, 2019.

(c) Of the amount received under Subsection (b)(2), the department shall deposit:

(1) $5 in the general revenue fund; and

(2) $3 to the credit of the state highway fund to recover the expenses necessary to administer this chapter.

(d) The county owns all interest earned on fees deposited or invested under Subsection (b)(2)(B). The county treasurer shall credit that interest to the county general fund.

(Enacted by Acts 1995, 74th Leg., ch. 165 (S.B. 971), § 1, effective September 1, 1995; am. Acts 2003, 78th Leg., ch. 1331 (H.B. 1365), § 24, effective June 20, 2003; am. Acts 2005, 79th Leg., ch. 1125 (H.B. 2481), § 19, effective September 1, 2005; am. Acts 2007, 80th Leg., ch. 262 (S.B. 12), §§ 2.15, 2.16, effective June 8, 2007; am. Acts 2009, 81st Leg., ch. 1125 (H.B. 1796), § 20, effective September 1, 2009; am. Acts 2011, 82nd Leg., ch. 1296 (H.B. 2357), § 58, effective January 1, 2012.)

**Secs. 501.139 to 501.144 [Reserved for expansion].**

## SUBCHAPTER H
## PENALTIES AND OTHER
## ENFORCEMENT PROVISIONS

**Sec. 501.145.  [Effective January 1, 2012] Filing by Purchaser; Application for Transfer of Titile.**

(a) Not later than the later of the 30th day after the date of assignment on the documents or the date provided by Section 152.069, Tax Code, the purchaser of the used motor vehicle shall file with the county assessor-collector:

(1) the certificate of title or other evidence of title; or

(2) if appropriate, a document described by Section 502.457 and the title or other evidence of ownership.

(b) The filing under Subsection (a) is an application for transfer of title as required under this chapter and an application for transfer of the registration of the motor vehicle.

(c) Notwithstanding Subsection (a), if the purchaser is a member of the armed forces of the United States, a member of the Texas National Guard or of the National Guard of another state serving on active duty under an order of the president of the United States, or a member of a reserve component of the armed forces of the United States serving on active duty under an order of the president of the United States, the documents described by Subsection (a) must be filed with the county assessor-collector not later than the 60th day after the date of assignment of ownership.

(Enacted by Acts 1995, 74th Leg., ch. 165 (S.B. 971), § 1, effective September 1, 1995; am. Acts 1999, 76th Leg., ch. 836 (H.B. 1743), § 3, effective September 1, 1999; am. Acts 1999, 76th Leg., ch. 1423 (H.B. 2409), § 6, effective September 1, 1999; am. Acts 2007, 80th Leg., ch. 75 (H.B. 481), § 2, effective January 1, 2008; am. Acts 2011, 82nd Leg., ch. 1296 (H.B. 2357), § 59, effective January 1, 2012 (renumbered from Sec. 520.031).)

**Sec. 501.146.  [Effective January 1, 2012] Title Transfer; Late Fee.**

(a) If the application for the transfer of title is not filed during the period provided by Section 501.145, the late fee is to be paid to the county assessor-collector when the application is filed. If the seller holds a general distinguishing number issued under Chapter 503 of this code or Chapter 2301, Occupations Code, the seller is liable for the late fee in the amount of $10. If the seller does not hold a general distinguishing number, subject to Subsection (b) the applicant's late fee is $25.

(b) If the application is filed after the 60th day after the date the purchaser was assigned ownership of the documents under Section 501.0721, the late fee imposed under Subsection (a) accrues an additional penalty in the amount of $25 for each subsequent 30-day period, or portion of a 30-day period, in which the application is not filed.

(c) Subsections (a) and (b) do not apply if the motor vehicle is eligible to be issued:

(1) classic vehicle license plates under Section 504.501; or

(2) antique vehicle license plates under Section 504.502.

(Enacted by Acts 1995, 74th Leg., ch. 165 (S.B. 971), § 1, effective September 1, 1995; am. Acts 2007, 80th Leg., ch. 75 (H.B. 481), § 3, effective January 1, 2008; am. Acts 2011, 82nd Leg., ch. 1296 (H.B. 2357), § 60, effective January 1, 2012, (renumbered from Sec. 520.032).)

**Sec. 501.147.  [Effective January 1, 2012] Vehicle Transfer Notification.**

(a) On receipt of a written notice of transfer from the seller of a motor vehicle, the department shall indicate the transfer on the motor vehicle records maintained by the department. As an alternative to a written notice of transfer, the department shall establish procedures that permit the seller of a motor vehicle to electronically submit a notice of transfer to the department through the department's Internet website. A notice of transfer provided through the department's Internet website is not required to bear the signature of the seller or include the date of signing.

(b) The notice of transfer shall be provided by the department and must include a place for the seller to state:

(1) a complete description of the vehicle as prescribed by the department;

(2) the full name and address of the seller;

(3) the full name and address of the purchaser;

(4) the date the seller delivered possession of the vehicle to the purchaser;

(5) the signature of the seller; and

(6) the date the seller signed the form.

(c) This subsection applies only if the department receives notice under Subsection (a) before the 30th day after the date the seller delivered possession of the vehicle to the purchaser or in accordance with Section 152.069, Tax Code. After the date of the transfer of the vehicle shown on the records of the department, the purchaser of the vehicle shown on the records is rebuttably presumed to be:

(1) the owner of the vehicle; and

(2) subject to civil and criminal liability arising out of the use, operation, or abandonment of the vehicle, to the extent that ownership of the vehicle subjects the owner of the vehicle to criminal or civil liability under another provision of law.

(d) The department may adopt rules to implement this section.

(e) This section does not impose or establish civil or criminal liability on the owner of a motor vehicle who transfers ownership of the vehicle but does not disclose the transfer to the department.

(f) The department may not issue a title or register the vehicle until the purchaser applies for a title to the county assessor-collector as provided by this chapter.

(g) A transferor who files the appropriate form with the department as provided by, and in accordance with, this section, whether that form is a part of a title or a form otherwise promulgated by the department to comply with the terms of this section, has no vicarious civil or criminal liability arising out of the use, operation, or abandonment of the vehicle by another person. Proof by the transferor that the transferor filed a form under this section is a complete defense to an action brought against the transferor for an act or omission, civil or criminal, arising out of the use, operation, or abandonment of the vehicle by another person after the transferor filed the form. A copy of the form filed under this section is proof of the filing of the form.

(Enacted by Acts 1995, 74th Leg., ch. 165 (S.B. 971), § 1, effective September 1, 1995; am. Acts 1997, 75th Leg., ch. 165 (S.B. 898), § 30.71(a), effective September 1, 1997; am. Acts 2007, 80th Leg., ch. 75 (H.B. 481), § 1, effective January 1, 2008; am. Acts 2009, 81st Leg., ch. 542 (S.B. 1617), § 2, effective September 1, 2009; am. Acts 2011, 82nd Leg., ch. 1296 (H.B. 2357), § 61, effective January 1, 2012, (renumbered from Sec. 520.023).)

## Sec. 501.148. [Effective January 1, 2012] Allocation of Fees.

(a) The county assessor-collector may retain as commission for services provided under this subchapter half of each late fee.

(b) The county assessor-collector shall report and remit the balance of the fees collected to the department on Monday of each week as other fees are required to be reported and remitted.

(c) Of each late fee collected from a person who does not hold a general distinguishing number by the department under Subsection (b), $10 may be used only to fund a statewide public awareness campaign designed to inform and educate the public about the provisions of this chapter.

(Enacted by Acts 1995, 74th Leg., ch. 165 (S.B. 971), § 1, effective September 1, 1995; am. Acts 2007, 80th Leg., ch. 75 (H.B. 481), § 4, effective January 1, 2008; am. Acts 2011, 82nd Leg., ch. 1296 (H.B. 2357), § 62, effective January 1, 2012, (renumbered from Sec. 520.033).)

## Secs. 501.149 to 501.150 [Reserved for expansion].

## Sec. 501.151. Placement of Serial Number with Intent to Change Identity.

(a) A person commits an offense if the person stamps or places a serial number on a vehicle or part of a vehicle with the intent of changing the identity of the vehicle.

(b) It is an affirmative defense to prosecution of an offense under this section that the person acted with respect to a number assigned by:

(1) a vehicle manufacturer and the person was an employee of the manufacturer acting within the course and scope of employment; or

(2) the department, and the person was:

(A) discharging official duties as an agent of the department; or

(B) complying with department rule as an applicant for a serial number assigned by the department.

(c) An offense under this section is a felony of the third degree.

(Enacted by Acts 1995, 74th Leg., ch. 165 (S.B. 971), § 1, effective September 1, 1995.)

### Sec. 501.152.   Sale or Offer Without Title Receipt or Title.

(a) Except as provided by this section, a person commits an offense if the person:

(1) sells, offers to sell, or offers as security for an obligation a motor vehicle registered in this state; and

(2) does not possess the title receipt or certificate of title for the vehicle.

(b) **[2 Versions: Effective until January 1, 2012]** It is not a violation of this section for the beneficial owner of a vehicle to sell or offer to sell a vehicle without having possession of the certificate of title to the vehicle if the sole reason he or she does not have possession of the certificate of title is that the title is in the possession of a lienholder who has not complied with the terms of Section 501.115(a) of this code.

(b) **[2 Versions: Effective January 1, 2012]** It is not a violation of this section for the beneficial owner of a vehicle to sell or offer to sell a vehicle without having possession of the title to the vehicle if the sole reason he or she does not have possession of the title is that the title is in the possession of a lienholder who has not complied with the terms of Section 501.115(a).

(Enacted by Acts 1995, 74th Leg., ch. 165 (S.B. 971), § 1, effective September 1, 1995; am. Acts 1997, 75th Leg., ch. 296 (H.B. 1137), § 2, effective September 1, 1997; am. Acts 2011, 82nd Leg., ch. 1296 (H.B. 2357), § 63, effective January 1, 2012.)

### Sec. 501.153.   [2 Versions: Effective until January 1, 2012] Application for Title for Stolen or Concealed Vehicle.

A person commits an offense if the person applies for a certificate of title for a motor vehicle that the person knows is stolen or concealed in violation of Section 32.33, Penal Code.

(Enacted by Acts 1995, 74th Leg., ch. 165 (S.B. 971), § 1, effective September 1, 1995.)

### Sec. 501.153.   [2 Versions: Effective January 1, 2012] Application for Title for Stolen or Concealed Vehicle.

A person commits an offense if the person applies for a title for a motor vehicle that the person knows is stolen or concealed in violation of Section 32.33, Penal Code.

(Enacted by Acts 1995, 74th Leg., ch. 165 (S.B. 971), § 1, effective September 1, 1995; am. Acts 2011, 82nd Leg., ch. 1296 (H.B. 2357), § 64, effective January 1, 2012.)

### Sec. 501.154.   [2 Versions: Effective until January 1, 2012] Alteration of Certificate or Receipt.

A person commits an offense if the person alters a manufacturer's or importer's certificate, a title receipt, or a certificate of title.

(Enacted by Acts 1995, 74th Leg., ch. 165 (S.B. 971), § 1, effective September 1, 1995.)

### Sec. 501.154.   [2 Versions: Effective January 1, 2012] Alteration of Certificate or Receipt.

A person commits an offense if the person alters a manufacturer's certificate, a title receipt, or a title.

(Enacted by Acts 1995, 74th Leg., ch. 165 (S.B. 971), § 1, effective September 1, 1995; am. Acts 2011, 82nd Leg., ch. 1296 (H.B. 2357), § 65, effective January 1, 2012.)

### Sec. 501.155.   False Name, False Information, and Forgery.

(a) A person commits an offense if the person knowingly provides false or incorrect information or without legal authority signs the name of another person on:

(1) **[2 Versions: Effective until January 1, 2012]** an application for a certificate of title;

(1) **[2 Versions: Effective January 1, 2012]** an application for a title;

(2) **[2 Versions: Effective until January 1, 2012]** an application for a certified copy of an original certificate of title;

(2) **[2 Versions: Effective January 1, 2012]** an application for a certified copy of an original title;

(3) an assignment of title for a motor vehicle;

(4) a discharge of a lien on a title for a motor vehicle; or

(5) any other document required by the department or necessary to the transfer of ownership of a motor vehicle.

(b) An offense under this section is a felony of the third degree.

(Enacted by Acts 1995, 74th Leg., ch. 165 (S.B. 971), § 1, effective September 1, 1995; am. Acts 2011, 82nd Leg., ch. 1296 (H.B. 2357), § 66, effective January 1, 2012.)

## Sec. 501.156. Duty of Transporters to Determine Right of Possession; Offense.

(a) The master or captain of a ship or airplane or a person who owns or controls the operation of a ship or airplane, in whole or part:

(1) may not take on board or allow to be taken on board the ship or airplane in this state for transport a motor vehicle without inquiring of the motor vehicle titles and registration division of the department as to the recorded ownership of the motor vehicle; and

(2) must make a reasonable inquiry as to the right of possession of a motor vehicle by the person delivering the vehicle for transport if the recorded owner of the vehicle is a person other than the person delivering the vehicle for transport.

(b) A person who violates this section commits an offense. An offense under this section is a misdemeanor punishable by a fine of not less than $50 or more than $500 for a first offense and, at the jury's discretion, not less than $100 or more than $1,000 for a subsequent offense.

(Enacted by Acts 1995, 74th Leg., ch. 165 (S.B. 971), § 1, effective September 1, 1995.)

## Sec. 501.157. Penalties.

(a) Unless otherwise provided by this chapter, an offense under this chapter is a misdemeanor punishable by a fine of not less than $1 or more than $100 for the first offense. If a person is subsequently convicted of the same offense, at the jury's discretion, a person may be fined not less than $2 or more than $200.

(b) A person commits an offense if the person violates Subchapter E or a rule adopted under that subchapter. An offense under this subsection is a Class A misdemeanor.

(Enacted by Acts 1995, 74th Leg., ch. 165 (S.B. 971), § 1, effective September 1, 1995; am. Acts 1997, 75th Leg., ch. 165 (S.B. 898), § 30.43(b), effective September 1, 1997.)

## Sec. 501.158. [2 Versions: Effective until January 1, 2012] Seizure of Stolen Vehicle or Vehicle with Altered Serial Number.

(a) A peace officer may seize a vehicle or part of a vehicle without a warrant if the officer has probable cause to believe that the vehicle or part:

(1) is stolen; or

(2) has had the serial number removed, altered, or obliterated.

(b) A vehicle or part seized under this section may be treated as stolen property for purposes of custody and disposition of the vehicle or part.

(Enacted by Acts 1995, 74th Leg., ch. 165 (S.B. 971), § 1, effective September 1, 1995.)

## Sec. 501.158. [2 Versions: Effective January 1, 2012] Seizure of Stolen Vehicle or Vehicle with Altered Vehicle Identification Number.

(a) A peace officer may seize a vehicle or part of a vehicle without a warrant if the officer has probable cause to believe that the vehicle or part:

(1) is stolen; or

(2) has had the serial number removed, altered, or obliterated.

(b) A vehicle or part seized under this section may be treated as stolen property for purposes of custody and disposition of the vehicle or part.

(Enacted by Acts 1995, 74th Leg., ch. 165 (S.B. 971), § 1, effective September 1, 1995; am. Acts 2011, 82nd Leg., ch. 1296 (H.B. 2357), § 67, effective January 1, 2012.)

## Sec. 501.159. [Renumbered January 1, 2012] Alias Certificate of Title.

On receipt of a written request approved by the executive administrator of a law enforcement agency, the department may issue a certificate of title for a vehicle in an alias for the law enforcement agency's use in a covert criminal investigation.

(Enacted by Acts 1995, 74th Leg., ch. 165 (S.B. 971), § 1, effective September 1, 1995.)

STATUTORY NOTES

**Editor's notes.** — This section is renumbered to Transportation Code § 501.006 pursuant to Acts 2011, 82nd Leg., ch. 1296 (H.B. 2357), § 5, effective January 1, 2012.

## Sec. 501.160. [Reserved for expansion].

## Sec. 501.161. [Effective January 1, 2012] Execution of Transfer Docu-

**ments; Penalty.**

(a) A person who transfers a motor vehicle in this state shall complete in full and date as of the date of the transfer all documents relating to the transfer of registration or title. A person who transfers a vehicle commits an offense if the person fails to execute the documents in full.

(b) A person commits an offense if the person:

(1) accepts a document described by Subsection (a) that does not contain all of the required information; or

(2) alters or mutilates such a document.

(c) An offense under this section is a misdemeanor punishable by a fine of not less than $50 and not more than $200.

(Enacted by Acts 1995, 74th Leg., ch. 165 (S.B. 971), § 1, effective September 1, 1995; am. Acts 2011, 82nd Leg., ch. 1296 (H.B. 2357), § 68, effective January 1, 2012, (renumbered from Sec. 520.035).)

### Sec. 501.162.   [Effective January 1, 2012] Motor Number Required for Registration; Penalty.

A person commits an offense if the person violates Section 501.0331. An offense under this section is a misdemeanor punishable by a fine of not less than $50 and not more than $100.

(Enacted by Acts 2011, 82nd Leg., ch. 1296 (H.B. 2357), § 69, effective January 1, 2012.)

### Sec. 501.163.   [Effective January 1, 2012] Application for Motor Number Record; Penalty.

A person who fails to comply with Section 501.0332 commits an offense. An offense under this section is a misdemeanor punishable by a fine of not less than $10 and not more than $100.

(Enacted by Acts 2011, 82nd Leg., ch. 1296 (H.B. 2357), § 69, effective January 1, 2012.)

### Secs. 501.164 to 501.170 [Reserved for expansion].

## SUBCHAPTER I
## ELECTRONIC TITLING SYSTEM

### Sec. 501.171.   Application of Subchapter.

This subchapter applies only if the department implements a titling system under Section 501.173.

(Enacted by Acts 2011, 82nd Leg., ch. 1290 (H.B. 2017), § 23, effective September 1, 2011; Enacted

by Acts 2011, 82nd Leg., ch. 1296 (H.B. 2357), § 70, effective January 1, 2012.)

### Sec. 501.172.   Definitions.

In this subchapter:

(1) "Document" means information that is inscribed on a tangible medium or that is stored in an electronic or other medium and is retrievable in perceivable form.

(2) "Electronic" means relating to technology having electrical, digital, magnetic, wireless, optical, electromagnetic, or similar capabilities.

(3) "Electronic document" means a document that is in an electronic form.

(4) "Electronic signature" means an electronic sound, symbol, or process attached to or logically associated with a document and executed or adopted by a person with the intent to sign the document.

(5) "Paper document" means a document that is in printed form.

(Enacted by Acts 2011, 82nd Leg., ch. 1290 (H.B. 2017), § 23, effective September 1, 2011; Enacted by Acts 2011, 82nd Leg., ch. 1296 (H.B. 2357), § 70, effective January 1, 2012.)

### Sec. 501.173.   Electronic Titling System.

(a) The board by rule may implement an electronic titling system.

(b) A record of title maintained electronically by the department in the titling system is the official record of vehicle ownership unless the owner requests that the department issue a printed title.

(Enacted by Acts 2011, 82nd Leg., ch. 1290 (H.B. 2017), § 23, effective September 1, 2011; Enacted by Acts 2011, 82nd Leg., ch. 1296 (H.B. 2357), § 70, effective January 1, 2012.)

### Sec. 501.174.   Validity of Electronic Documents.

(a) If this chapter requires that a document be an original, be on paper or another tangible medium, or be in writing, the requirement is met by an electronic document that complies with this subchapter.

(b) If a law requires that a document be signed, the requirement is satisfied by an electronic signature.

(c) A requirement that a document or a signature associated with a document be notarized, acknowledged, verified, witnessed, or made under oath is satisfied if the electronic signature of the person authorized to perform that act, and all other information required to be included, is attached to or logically associated with the document or signature. A physical or electronic image of a stamp, impression, or seal is not required to accompany an electronic signature.

(Enacted by Acts 2011, 82nd Leg., ch. 1290 (H.B. 2017), § 23, effective September 1, 2011; Enacted by Acts 2011, 82nd Leg., ch. 1296 (H.B. 2357), § 70, effective January 1, 2012.)

### Sec. 501.175. Recording of Documents.

(a) Under the titling system, the department may:

(1) receive, index, store, archive, and transmit electronic documents;

(2) provide for access to, and for search and retrieval of, documents and information by electronic means; and

(3) convert into electronic form:

(A) paper documents that it accepts for the titling of a motor vehicle; and

(B) information recorded and documents that were accepted for the titling of a motor vehicle before the titling system was implemented.

(b) The department shall continue to accept paper documents after the titling system is implemented.

(Enacted by Acts 2011, 82nd Leg., ch. 1290 (H.B. 2017), § 23, effective September 1, 2011; Enacted by Acts 2011, 82nd Leg., ch. 1296 (H.B. 2357), § 70, effective January 1, 2012.)

### Sec. 501.176. [2 Versions: As added by Acts 2011, 82nd Leg., ch. 1290] Payment of Fees by Electronic Funds Transfer or Credit Card.

(a) The department may accept payment by electronic funds transfer, credit card, or debit card of any title or registration fee that the department is required or authorized to collect under this chapter.

(b) The department may collect a fee for processing a title or registration payment by electronic funds transfer, credit card, or debit card. The amount of the fee must not exceed the charges incurred by the state because of the use of the electronic funds transfer, credit card, or debit card.

(c) For online transactions the department may collect from a person making payment by electronic funds transfer, credit card, or debit card an amount equal to any fee charged in accordance with Section 2054.2591, Government Code.

(Enacted by Acts 2011, 82nd Leg., ch. 1290 (H.B. 2017), § 23, effective September 1, 2011.)

### Sec. 501.176. [2 Versions: As added by Acts 2011, 82nd Leg., ch. 1296, Effective January 1, 2012] Payment of Fees by Electronic Funds Transfer or Credit Card.

(a) The department may accept payment by electronic funds transfer, credit card, or debit card of any title or registration fee that the department is required or authorized to collect under this chapter.

(b) The department may collect a fee for processing a title or registration payment by electronic funds transfer, credit card, or debit card in an amount not to exceed the amount of the charges incurred by the department to process the payment.

(c) The department may collect the fee set under Section 2054.2591, Government Code, from a person making a payment by electronic funds transfer, credit card, or debit card through the online project implemented under Section 2054.252, Government Code.

(Enacted by Acts 2011, 82nd Leg., ch. 1296 (H.B. 2357), § 70, effective January 1, 2012.)

### Sec. 501.177. Service Charge.

If, for any reason, the payment of a fee under this chapter by electronic funds transfer, credit card, or debit card is not honored by the funding institution, or by the electronic funds transfer, credit card, or debit card company on which the funds are drawn, the department may collect from the person who owes the fee being collected a service charge that is for the collection of that original amount and is in addition to the original fee. The amount of the service charge must be reasonably related to the expense incurred by the department in collecting the original amount.

(Enacted by Acts 2011, 82nd Leg., ch. 1290 (H.B. 2017), § 23, effective September 1, 2011; Enacted by Acts 2011, 82nd Leg., ch. 1296 (H.B. 2357), § 70, effective January 1, 2012.)

### Sec. 501.178. Disposition of Fees.

All fees collected under this subchapter shall be deposited to the credit of the state highway fund.

(Enacted by Acts 2011, 82nd Leg., ch. 1290 (H.B. 2017), § 23, effective September 1, 2011; Enacted

Transportation

by Acts 2011, 82nd Leg., ch. 1296 (H.B. 2357), § 70, effective January 1, 2012.)

### Sec. 501.179. Relation to Electronic Signatures in Global and National Commerce Act.

This subchapter modifies, limits, and supersedes the federal Electronic Signatures in Global and National Commerce Act (15 U.S.C. Section 7001 et seq.) but does not modify, limit, or supersede Section 101(c) of that Act (15 U.S.C. Section 7001(c)) or authorize electronic delivery of any of the notices described in Section 103(b) of that Act (15 U.S.C. Section 7003(b)).

(Enacted by Acts 2011, 82nd Leg., ch. 1290 (H.B. 2017), § 23, effective September 1, 2011; Enacted by Acts 2011, 82nd Leg., ch. 1296 (H.B. 2357), § 70, effective January 1, 2012.)

# CHAPTER 502
# REGISTRATION OF VEHICLES

### Subchapter A. General Provisions

**Transportation**

## SUBCHAPTER A
## GENERAL PROVISIONS

**Sec. 502.001.   [2 Versions: Effective until January 1, 2012] Definitions.**

In this chapter:

(1) "All-terrain vehicle" means a motor vehicle that is:

(A) equipped with a saddle for the use of:

(i) the rider; and

(ii) a passenger, if the motor vehicle is designed by the manufacturer to transport a passenger;

(B) designed to propel itself with three or more tires in contact with the ground;

(C) designed by the manufacturer for off-highway use; and

(D) not designed by the manufacturer primarily for farming or lawn care.

(1-a) **[2 Versions: As amended by Acts 2009, 81st Leg., ch. 933]** "Board" means the board of the Texas Department of Motor Vehicles.

(1-a) **[2 Versions: As amended by Acts 2009, 81st Leg., chs. 1173 and 1232]** "Commercial fleet" means a group of at least 25 nonapportioned motor vehicles, semitrailers, or trailers owned, operated, or leased by a corporation, limited or general partnership, limited liability company, or other business entity and used for the business purposes of that entity.

(2) "Commercial motor vehicle" means a motor vehicle, other than a motorcycle, designed or used primarily to transport property. The term includes a passenger car reconstructed and used primarily for delivery purposes. The term does not include a passenger car used to deliver the United States mail.

(3) "Department" means the Texas Department of Motor Vehicles.

(4) "Farm semitrailer" means a semitrailer designed and used primarily as a farm vehicle.

(5) "Farm tractor" has the meaning assigned by Section 541.201.

(6) "Farm trailer" means a trailer designed and used primarily as a farm vehicle.

(7) "Golf cart" means a motor vehicle designed by the manufacturer primarily for transporting persons on a golf course.

(8) "Implements of husbandry" means farm implements, machinery, and tools as used in tilling the soil, including self-propelled machinery specifically designed or adapted for applying plant food materials or agricultural chemicals but not specifically designed or adapted for the sole purpose of transporting the materials or chemicals. The term does not include a passenger car or truck.

(9) "Light truck" means a commercial motor vehicle that has a manufacturer's rated carrying capacity of one ton or less.

(10) "Moped" has the meaning assigned by Section 541.201.

(11) "Motor bus" includes every vehicle used to transport persons on the public highways for compensation, other than:

(A) a vehicle operated by muscular power; or

(B) a municipal bus.

(12) "Motorcycle" means a motor vehicle designed to propel itself with not more than three wheels in contact with the ground. The term does not include a tractor.

(13) "Motor vehicle" means a vehicle that is self-propelled.

(14) "Municipal bus" includes every vehicle, other than a passenger car, used to transport persons for compensation exclusively within the limits of a municipality or a suburban addition to the municipality.

(28) "Net carrying capacity" means the heaviest net load that is able to be carried on a vehicle, but not less than the manufacturer's rated carrying capacity.

(15) "Operate temporarily on the highways" means to travel between:

(A) different farms;

(B) a place of supply or storage and a farm; or

(C) an owner's farm and the place at which the owner's farm produce is prepared for market or is marketed.

(16) "Owner" means a person who:

(A) holds the legal title of a vehicle;

(B) has the legal right of possession of a vehicle; or

(C) has the legal right of control of a vehicle.

(17) "Passenger car" means a motor vehicle, other than a motorcycle, golf cart, light truck, or bus, designed or used primarily for the transportation of persons.

(18) "Public highway" includes a road, street, way, thoroughfare, or bridge:

(A) that is in this state;

(B) that is for the use of vehicles;

(C) that is not privately owned or controlled; and

(D) over which the state has legislative jurisdiction under its police power.

(19) "Public property" means property owned or leased by this state or a political subdivision of this state.

(19-a) "Recreational off-highway vehicle" means a motor vehicle that is:

(A) equipped with a non-straddle seat for the use of:

(i) the rider; and

(ii) a passenger, if the vehicle is designed by the manufacturer to transport a passenger;

(B) designed to propel itself with four or more tires in contact with the ground;

(C) designed by the manufacturer for off-highway use by the operator only; and

(D) not designed by the manufacturer primarily for farming or lawn care.

(38) "Road tractor" means a vehicle designed for the purpose of mowing the right-of-way of a public highway or a motor vehicle designed or used for drawing another vehicle or a load and not constructed to carry:

(A) an independent load; or

(B) a part of the weight of the vehicle and load to be drawn.

(21) "Semitrailer" means a vehicle designed or used with a motor vehicle so that part of the weight of the vehicle and its load rests on or is carried by another vehicle.

(22) "Trailer" means a vehicle that:

(A) is designed or used to carry a load wholly on its own structure; and

(B) is drawn or designed to be drawn by a motor vehicle.

(23) "Truck-tractor" means a motor vehicle:

(A) designed and used primarily for drawing another vehicle; and

(B) not constructed to carry a load other than a part of the weight of the vehicle and load to be drawn.

(24) "Vehicle" means a device in or by which a person or property is or may be transported or drawn on a public highway, other than a device used exclusively on stationary rails or tracks.

(Enacted by Acts 1995, 74th Leg., ch. 165 (S.B. 971), § 1, effective September 1, 1995; am. Acts 1997, 75th Leg., ch. 625 (S.B. 1630), § 1, effective September 1, 1997; am. Acts 2005, 79th Leg., ch. 586 (H.B. 1646), § 2, effective September 1, 2005; am. Acts 2007, 80th Leg., ch. 1280 (H.B. 3849), § 1, effective June 15, 2007; am. Acts 2009, 81st Leg., ch. 933 (H.B. 3097), § 2E.01, effective Sep-

tember 1, 2009; am. Acts 2009, 81st Leg., ch. 1136 (H.B. 2553), § 5, effective September 1, 2009; am. Acts 2009, 81st Leg., ch. 1173 (H.B. 3433), § 1, effective September 1, 2009; am. Acts 2009, 81st Leg., ch. 1232 (S.B. 1759), § 1, effective September 1, 2009.)

## Sec. 502.001. [2 Versions: Effective January 1, 2012] Definitions.

In this chapter:

(1) "All-terrain vehicle" means a motor vehicle that is:

(A) equipped with a saddle for the use of:

(i) the rider; and

(ii) a passenger, if the motor vehicle is designed by the manufacturer to transport a passenger;

(B) designed to propel itself with three or more tires in contact with the ground;

(C) designed by the manufacturer for off-highway use; and

(D) not designed by the manufacturer primarily for farming or lawn care.

(2) "Apportioned license plate" means a license plate issued in lieu of a truck license plate or combination license plate to a motor carrier in this state who proportionally registers a vehicle owned or leased by the carrier in one or more other states.

(3) "Board" means the board of the Texas Department of Motor Vehicles.

(4) "Combination license plate" means a license plate issued for a truck or truck-tractor that is used or intended to be used in combination with a semitrailer that has a gross weight of more than 6,000 pounds.

(5) "Combined gross weight" means the empty weight of the truck-tractor or commercial motor vehicle combined with the empty weight of the heaviest semitrailer used or to be used in combination with the truck-tractor or commercial motor vehicle plus the heaviest net load to be carried on the combination during the registration year.

(6) "Commercial fleet" means a group of at least 25 nonapportioned motor vehicles, semitrailers, or trailers owned, operated, or leased by a corporation, limited or general partnership, limited liability company, or other business entity and used for the business purposes of that entity.

(7) "Commercial motor vehicle" means a commercial motor vehicle as defined by Section 644.001.

(8) "Construction machinery" means a vehicle that:

(A) is used for construction;

(B) is built from the ground up;

(C) is not mounted or affixed to another vehicle such as a trailer;

(D) was originally and permanently designed as machinery;

(E) was not in any way originally designed to transport persons or property; and

(F) does not carry a load, including fuel.

(9) "Credit card" has the meaning assigned by Section 501.002.

(10) "Debit card" has the meaning assigned by Section 501.002.

(11) "Department" means the Texas Department of Motor Vehicles.

(12) "Electric bicycle" has the meaning assigned by Section 541.201.

(13) "Electric personal assistive mobility device" has the meaning assigned by Section 551.201.

(14) "Empty weight" means the unladen weight of a truck-tractor or commercial motor vehicle and semitrailer combination fully equipped, as certified by a public weigher or license and weight inspector of the Department of Public Safety.

(15) "Farm semitrailer" or "farm trailer" means a vehicle designed and used primarily as a farm vehicle.

(16) "Farm tractor" has the meaning assigned by Section 541.201.

(17) "Forestry vehicle" means a vehicle designed and used exclusively for transporting forest products in their natural state, including logs, debarked logs, untreated ties, stave bolts, plywood bolts, pulpwood billets, wood chips, stumps, sawdust, moss, bark, and wood shavings, and property used in production of those products.

(18) "Golf cart" means a motor vehicle designed by the manufacturer primarily for use on a golf course.

(19) "Gross vehicle weight" has the meaning assigned by Section 541.401.

(20) "Implements of husbandry" has the meaning assigned by Section 541.201.

(21) "Light truck" has the meaning assigned by Section 541.201.

(22) "Moped" has the meaning assigned by Section 541.201.

(23) "Motor bus" includes every vehicle used to transport persons on the public highways for compensation, other than:

(A) a vehicle operated by muscular power; or

(B) a municipal bus.

(24) "Motorcycle" has the meaning assigned by Section 521.001 or 541.201, as applicable.

(25) "Motor vehicle" means a vehicle that is self-propelled.

(26) "Motorized mobility device" has the meaning assigned by Section 542.009.

(27) "Municipal bus" includes every vehicle, other than a passenger car, used to transport persons for compensation exclusively within the limits of a municipality or a suburban addition to the municipality.

(28) "Net carrying capacity" means the heaviest net load that is able to be carried on a vehicle, but not less than the manufacturer's rated carrying capacity.

(29) "Oil well servicing, cleanout, or drilling machinery":

(A) has the meaning assigned by Section 623.149; or

(B) means a mobile crane:

(i) that is an unladen, self-propelled vehicle constructed as a machine and used solely to raise, shift, or lower heavy weights by means of a projecting, swinging mast with an engine for power on a chassis permanently constructed or assembled for that purpose; and

(ii) for which the owner has secured a permit from the department under Section 623.142.

(30) "Operate temporarily on the highways" means to travel between:

(A) different farms;

(B) a place of supply or storage and a farm; or

(C) an owner's farm and the place at which the owner's farm produce is prepared for market or is marketed.

(31) "Owner" means a person who:

(A) holds the legal title of a vehicle;

(B) has the legal right of possession of a vehicle; or

(C) has the legal right of control of a vehicle.

(32) "Passenger car" has the meaning assigned by Section 541.201.

(33) "Power sweeper" means an implement, with or without motive power, designed for the removal by a broom, vacuum, or regenerative air system of debris, dirt, gravel, litter, or sand from asphaltic concrete or cement concrete surfaces, including surfaces of parking lots, roads,

streets, highways, and warehouse floors. The term includes a vehicle on which the implement is permanently mounted if the vehicle is used only as a power sweeper.

(34) "Private bus" means a bus that:

(A) is not operated for hire; and

(B) is not a municipal bus or a motor bus.

(35) "Public highway" includes a road, street, way, thoroughfare, or bridge:

(A) that is in this state;

(B) that is for the use of vehicles;

(C) that is not privately owned or controlled; and

(D) over which the state has legislative jurisdiction under its police power.

(36) "Public property" means property owned or leased by this state or a political subdivision of this state.

(37) "Recreational off-highway vehicle" means a motor vehicle that is:

(A) equipped with a non-straddle seat for the use of:

(i) the rider; and

(ii) a passenger, if the vehicle is designed by the manufacturer to transport a passenger;

(B) designed to propel itself with four or more tires in contact with the ground;

(C) designed by the manufacturer for off-highway use by the operator only; and

(D) not designed by the manufacturer primarily for farming or lawn care.

(38) "Road tractor" means a vehicle designed for the purpose of mowing the right-of-way of a public highway or a motor vehicle designed or used for drawing another vehicle or a load and not constructed to carry:

(A) an independent load; or

(B) a part of the weight of the vehicle and load to be drawn.

(39) "Semitrailer" means a vehicle designed or used with a motor vehicle so that part of the weight of the vehicle and its load rests on or is carried by another vehicle.

(40) "Token trailer" means a semitrailer that:

(A) has a gross weight of more than 6,000 pounds; and

(B) is operated in combination with a truck or a truck-tractor that has been issued:

(i) an apportioned license plate;

(ii) a combination license plate; or

(iii) a forestry vehicle license plate.

(41) "Tow truck" means a motor vehicle adapted or used to tow, winch, or otherwise move another motor vehicle.

(42) "Trailer" means a vehicle that:

(A) is designed or used to carry a load wholly on its own structure; and

(B) is drawn or designed to be drawn by a motor vehicle.

(43) "Travel trailer" has the meaning assigned by Section 501.002.

(44) "Truck-tractor" means a motor vehicle:

(A) designed and used primarily for drawing another vehicle; and

(B) not constructed to carry a load other than a part of the weight of the vehicle and load to be drawn.

(45) "Vehicle" means a device in or by which a person or property is or may be transported or drawn on a public highway, other than a device used exclusively on stationary rails or tracks.

(Enacted by Acts 1995, 74th Leg., ch. 165 (S.B. 971), § 1, effective September 1, 1995; am. Acts 1997, 75th Leg., ch. 625 (S.B. 1630), § 1, effective September 1, 1997; am. Acts 2005, 79th Leg., ch. 586 (H.B. 1646), § 2, effective September 1, 2005; am. Acts 2007, 80th Leg., ch. 1280 (H.B. 3849), § 1, effective June 15, 2007; am. Acts 2009, 81st Leg., ch. 933 (H.B. 3097), § 2E.01, effective September 1, 2009; am. Acts 2009, 81st Leg., ch. 1136 (H.B. 2553), § 5, effective September 1, 2009; am. Acts 2009, 81st Leg., ch. 1173 (H.B. 3433), § 1, effective September 1, 2009; am. Acts 2009, 81st Leg., ch. 1232 (S.B. 1759), § 1, effective September 1, 2009; am. Acts 2011, 82nd Leg., ch. 1296 (H.B. 2357), § 71, effective January 1, 2012.)

## Sec. 502.002. [Renumbered January 1, 2012] Registration Required; General Rule.

(a) Not more than 30 days after purchasing a vehicle or becoming a resident of this state, the owner of a motor vehicle, trailer, or semitrailer shall apply for the registration of the vehicle for:

(1) each registration year in which the vehicle is used or to be used on a public highway; and

(2) if the vehicle is unregistered for a registration year that has begun and that applies to the vehicle and if the vehicle is used or to be used on a public highway, the remaining portion of that registration year.

(b) The application must be accompanied by personal identification as determined by department rule and made in a manner prescribed by the department:

(1) through the county assessor-collector of the county in which the owner resides; or

(2) if the county in which the owner resides has been declared by the governor as a disaster area, through the county assessor-collector of a county that is one of the closest unaffected counties to a county that asks for assistance and:

(A) continues to be declared by the governor as a disaster area because the county has been rendered inoperable by the disaster; and

(B) is inoperable for a protracted period of time.

(c) A provision of this chapter that conflicts with this section prevails over this section to the extent of the conflict.

(d) A county assessor-collector, a deputy county assessor-collector, or a person acting on behalf of a county assessor-collector is not liable to any person for:

(1) refusing to register a motor vehicle because of the person's failure to submit evidence of residency that complies with the department's rules; or

(2) registering a motor vehicle under this section.

(Enacted by Acts 1995, 74th Leg., ch. 165 (S.B. 971), § 1, effective September 1, 1995; am. Acts 1997, 75th Leg., ch. 165 (S.B. 898), § 30.44(a), effective September 1, 1997; am. Acts 2011, 82nd Leg., ch. 1290 (H.B. 2017), § 24, effective September 1, 2011.)

### STATUTORY NOTES

**Editor's notes.** — This section is renumbered to Transportation Code Section 502.040 pursuant to Acts 2011, 82nd Leg., ch. 1296 (H.B. 2357), § 78, effective January 1, 2012.

### Sec. 502.0021. [2 Versions: Effective until January 1, 2012] Rules and Forms.

(a) The department may adopt rules to administer this chapter.

(b) The department shall:

(1) prescribe forms determined by the department to be necessary for the administration of this chapter; and

(2) provide each county assessor-collector with an adequate supply of each form necessary for the performance of a duty under this chapter by the assessor-collector.

(Enacted by Acts 1997, 75th Leg., ch. 625 (S.B. 1630), § 2, effective September 1, 1997; am. Acts 1999, 76th Leg., ch. 62 (S.B. 1368), § 19.01(100), effective September 1, 1999 (renumbered from Sec. 502.009).)

### Sec. 502.0021. [2 Versions: Effective January 1, 2012] Rules and Forms.

(a) The department may adopt rules to administer this chapter.

(b) The department shall post forms on the Internet and provide each county assessor-collector with a sufficient supply of any necessary forms on request.

(Enacted by Acts 1997, 75th Leg., ch. 625 (S.B. 1630), § 2, effective September 1, 1997; am. Acts 1999, 76th Leg., ch. 62 (S.B. 1368), § 19.01(100), effective September 1, 1999 (renumbered from Sec. 502.009); am. Acts 2011, 82nd Leg., ch. 1296 (H.B. 2357), § 72, effective January 1, 2012.)

### Sec. 502.00211. [Effective January 1, 2012] Design of Registration Insignia.

The department shall prepare the designs and specifications to be used as the registration insignia.

(Enacted by Acts 1995, 74th Leg., ch. 165 (S.B. 971), § 1, effective September 1, 1995; am. Acts 2007, 80th Leg., ch. 937 (H.B. 3560), § 1.113, effective September 1, 2007; am. Acts 2009, 81st Leg., ch. 933 (H.B. 3097), § 2E.03, effective September 1, 2009; am. Acts 2011, 82nd Leg., ch. 1296 (H.B. 2357), § 73, effective January 1, 2012 (renumbered from Sec. 502.052).)

### Sec. 502.0022. Consolidated Registration of Fleet Vehicles [Repealed].

Repealed by Acts 2009, 81st Leg., ch. 1173 (H.B. 3433), § 4, effective September 1, 2009 and Acts 2009, 81st Leg., ch. 1232 (S.B. 1759), § 7, effective September 1, 2009.

(Enacted by Acts 2001, 77th Leg., ch. 638 (H.B. 1368), § 1, effective September 1, 2001; enacted by Acts 2001, 77th Leg., ch. 645 (H.B. 2124), § 1, effective September 1, 2001.)

### Sec. 502.0023. [Effective until January 1, 2012] Extended Registration of Commercial Fleet Motor Vehicles; [Effective January 1, 2012] Extended Registration of Commercial Fleet Vehicles.

(a) **[Effective until January 1, 2012]** Notwithstanding Section 502.158(c), the department shall develop and implement a system of registration to allow an owner of a commercial fleet to register the motor vehicles in the commercial fleet for an extended registration period of not less than one year or more than eight years. The owner may select the number of years for registration under this section within that range and register the commercial fleet for that period. Payment for all registration fees for the entire registration period selected is due at the time of registration.

(a) **[Effective January 1, 2012]** Notwithstanding Section 502.044(c), the department shall develop and implement a system of registration to allow an owner of a commercial fleet to register the motor vehicles, semitrailers, and trailers in the commercial fleet for an extended registration period of not less than one year or more than eight years. The owner may select the number of years for registration under this section within that range and register the commercial fleet for that period. Payment for all registration fees for the entire registration period selected is due at the time of registration.

(b) A system of extended registration under this section must allow the owner of a commercial fleet to register:

(1) an entire commercial fleet in the county of the owner's residence or principal place of business; or

(2) the motor vehicles in a commercial fleet that are operated most regularly in the same county.

(c) **[Effective until January 1, 2012]** In addition to the registration fees prescribed by Subchapter D, an owner registering a commercial fleet under this section shall pay:

(1) an annual commercial fleet registration fee of $10 per motor vehicle in the fleet; and

(2) except as provided by Subsection (e), a one-time license plate manufacturing fee of $1.50 for each fleet motor vehicle license plate.

(c) **[Effective January 1, 2012]** In addition to the registration fees prescribed by this chapter, an owner registering a commercial fleet under this section shall pay:

(1) an annual commercial fleet registration fee of $10 per motor vehicle, semitrailer, or trailer in the fleet; and

(2) except as provided by Subsection (e), a one-time license plate manufacturing fee of $1.50 for each fleet motor vehicle, semitrailer, or trailer license plate.

(d) A license plate issued under this section:

(1) may, on request of the owner, include the name or logo of the business entity that owns the vehicle;

(2) must include the expiration date of the registration period; and

(3) does not require an annual registration insignia to be valid.

(e) In addition to all other applicable registration fees, an owner registering a commercial fleet under this section shall pay a one-time license plate manufacturing fee of $8 for each set of plates issued that includes on the legend the name or logo of the business entity that owns the vehicle instead of the fee imposed by Subsection (c)(2).

(f) If a motor vehicle registered under this section has a gross weight in excess of 10,000 pounds, the department shall also issue a registration card for the vehicle that is valid for the selected registration period.

(g) The department shall adopt rules to implement this section, including rules on suspension from the commercial fleet program for failure to comply with this section or rules adopted under this section.

(h) The department and the counties in their budgeting processes shall consider any temporary increases and resulting decreases in revenue that will result from the use of the process provided under this section.

(i) **[Effective January 1, 2012]** The department may provide for credits for fleet registration.

(Enacted by Acts 2009, 81st Leg., ch. 1173 (H.B. 3433), § 2, effective September 1, 2009; enacted by Acts 2009, 81st Leg., ch. 1232 (S.B. 1759), § 2, effective September 1, 2009; am. Acts 2011, 82nd Leg., ch. 1296 (H.B. 2357), §§ 74, 75, effective January 1, 2012.)

## Sec. 502.0025. [Renumbered January 1, 2012] Effect of Certain Military Service on Registration Requirement.

(a) This section applies only to a motor vehicle that is owned by a person who:

(1) is a resident of this state;

(2) is on active duty in the armed forces of the United States;

(3) is stationed in or has been assigned to another nation under military orders; and

(4) has registered the vehicle or been issued a license for the vehicle under the applicable status of forces agreement by:

(A) the appropriate branch of the armed forces of the United States; or

(B) the nation in which the person is stationed or to which the person has been assigned.

(b) Unless the registration or license issued for a vehicle described by Subsection (a) is suspended, canceled, or revoked by this state as provided by law:

Transportation

(1) Section 502.002(a) does not apply; and

(2) the registration or license issued by the armed forces or host nation remains valid and the motor vehicle may be operated in this state under that registration or license for a period of not more than 90 days after the date on which the vehicle returns to this state.

(Enacted by Acts 1999, 76th Leg., ch. 836 (H.B. 1743), § 1, effective September 1, 1999.)

### STATUTORY NOTES

**Editor's notes.** — This section is renumbered to Transportation Code Section 502.090 pursuant to Acts 2011, 82nd Leg., ch. 1296 (H.B. 2357), § 93, effective January 1, 2012.

### Sec. 502.003. Registration by Political Subdivision Prohibited.

(a) Except as provided by Subsection (b), a political subdivision of this state may not require an owner of a motor vehicle to:

(1) register the vehicle;

(2) pay a motor vehicle registration fee; or

(3) pay an occupation tax or license fee in connection with a motor vehicle.

(b) This section does not affect the authority of a municipality to:

(1) license and regulate the use of motor vehicles for compensation within the municipal limits; and

(2) impose a permit fee or street rental charge for the operation of each motor vehicle used to transport passengers for compensation, other than a motor vehicle operating under a registration certificate from the department or a permit from the federal Surface Transportation Board.

(c) A fee or charge under Subsection (b) may not exceed two percent of the annual gross receipts from the vehicle.

(d) This section does not impair the payment provisions of an agreement or franchise between a municipality and the owners or operators of motor vehicles used to transport passengers for compensation.

(Enacted by Acts 1995, 74th Leg., ch. 165 (S.B. 971), § 1, effective September 1, 1995; am. Acts 1997, 75th Leg., ch. 165 (S.B. 898), § 30.45, effective September 1, 1997.)

### Sec. 502.004. [Renumbered January 1, 2012] Collection of Fees.

A person may not collect a registration fee under this chapter unless the person is:

(1) an officer or employee of the department; or

(2) a county assessor-collector or a deputy county assessor-collector.

(Enacted by Acts 1995, 74th Leg., ch. 165 (S.B. 971), § 1, effective September 1, 1995.)

### STATUTORY NOTES

**Editor's notes.** — This section is renumbered to Transportation Code Section 502.191 pursuant to Acts 2011, 82nd Leg., ch. 1296 (H.B. 2357), § 108, effective January 1, 2012.

### Sec. 502.005. [Renumbered January 1, 2012] Refusal to Register Unsafe Vehicle.

(a) The department may refuse to register a motor vehicle and may revoke a registration if the department determines that a motor vehicle is unsafe, improperly equipped, or otherwise unfit to be operated on a public highway.

(b) The department may refuse to register a motorcycle and may suspend or revoke the registration of a motorcycle if the department determines that the motorcycle's braking system does not comply with Section 547.408.

(Enacted by Acts 1995, 74th Leg., ch. 165 (S.B. 971), § 1, effective September 1, 1995.)

### STATUTORY NOTES

**Editor's notes.** — This section is renumbered to Transportation Code Section 502.048 pursuant to Acts 2011, 82nd Leg., ch. 1296 (H.B. 2357), § 86, effective January 1, 2012.

### Sec. 502.006. [Renumbered January 1, 2012] Certain Off-Highway Vehicles.

(a) Except as provided by Subsection (b), a person may not register an all-terrain vehicle or a recreational off-highway vehicle, with or without design alterations, for operation on a public highway.

(b) The state, a county, or a municipality may register an all-terrain vehicle or a recreational off-highway vehicle for operation on a public beach or highway to maintain public safety and welfare.

(c) A recreational off-highway vehicle registered as provided by Subsection (b) may be operated on a public or private beach in the same manner as a golf cart may be operated on a public or private beach under Section 502.0071. The operator must hold and have in the operator's possession a driver's license issued under Chapter 521 or a commercial driver's license issued under Chapter 522.

(d) Section 502.172 does not apply to an all-terrain vehicle or a recreational off-highway vehicle.

(Enacted by Acts 1995, 74th Leg., ch. 165 (S.B. 971), § 1, effective September 1, 1995; am. Acts 1999, 76th Leg., ch. 311 (H.B. 523), § 1, effective May 29, 1999; am. Acts 2007, 80th Leg., ch. 1280 (H.B. 3849), § 6, effective June 15, 2007; am. Acts 2009, 81st Leg., ch. 1136 (H.B. 2553), § 6, effective September 1, 2009.)

### STATUTORY NOTES

**Editor's notes.** — This section is renumbered to Transportation Code Section 502.140 pursuant to Acts 2011, 82nd Leg., ch. 1296 (H.B. 2357), § 100, effective January 1, 2012.

## Sec. 502.007. [Repealed September 1, 2011] Mopeds.

(a) For the registration purposes of this chapter, a moped is treated as if it were a motorcycle.

(b) A license plate issued for a moped must have a distinctive lettering designation and include the word "moped."

(Enacted by Acts 1995, 74th Leg., ch. 165 (S.B. 971), § 1, effective September 1, 1995.)

## Sec. 502.0071. Golf Carts [Repealed].

Repealed by Acts 2009, 81st Leg., ch. 1136 (H.B. 2553), § 12(1), effective September 1, 2009. (Enacted by Acts 2003, 78th Leg., ch. 1320 (H.B. 2971), § 1, effective September 1, 2003.)

## Sec. 502.0072. [Renumbered January 1, 2012] Manufactured Housing.

Manufactured housing, as defined by Section 1201.003, Occupations Code, is not a vehicle subject to this chapter.

(Enacted by Acts 2003, 78th Leg., ch. 1320 (H.B. 2971), § 1, effective September 1, 2003.)

### STATUTORY NOTES

**Editor's notes.** — This section is renumbered to Transportation Code Section 502.142 pursuant to Acts 2011, 82nd Leg., ch. 1296 (H.B. 2357), § 101, effective January 1, 2012.

## Sec. 502.0073. [Renumbered January 1, 2012] Power Sweepers.

(a) An owner of a power sweeper is not required to register the power sweeper.

(b) In this section, "power sweeper" means an implement, with or without motive power, designed for the removal by broom, vacuum, or regenerative air system of debris, dirt, gravel, litter, or sand from asphaltic concrete or cement concrete surfaces, including surfaces of parking lots, roads, streets, highways, and warehouse floors. The term includes a vehicle on which the

implement is permanently mounted if the vehicle is used only as a power sweeper.

(Enacted by Acts 2003, 78th Leg., ch. 1320 (H.B. 2971), § 1, effective September 1, 2003.)

### STATUTORY NOTES

**Editor's notes.** — This section is renumbered to Transportation Code Section 502.143 pursuant to Acts 2011, 82nd Leg., ch. 1296 (H.B. 2357), § 102, effective January 1, 2012.

## Sec. 502.0074. [Repealed January 1, 2012] Motorized Mobility Device.

The owner of a motorized mobility device, as defined by Section 542.008, as amended by Chapter 497, Acts of the 77th Legislature, Regular Session, 2001, is not required to register the motorized mobility device.

(Enacted by Acts 2003, 78th Leg., ch. 1320 (H.B. 2971), § 1, effective September 1, 2003.)

## Sec. 502.0075. [Repealed January 1, 2012] Electric Bicycles.

(a) In this section, "electric bicycle" has the meaning assigned by Section 541.201.

(b) This chapter does not require the owner of an electric bicycle to register the electric bicycle.

(Enacted by Acts 2001, 77th Leg., ch. 1085 (H.B. 2204), § 4, effective September 1, 2001.)

## Sec. 502.0078. [Renumbered January 1, 2012] Vehicles Operated on Public Highway Separating Real Property Under Vehicle Owner's Control.

Where a public highway separates real property under the control of the owner of a motor vehicle, the operation of the motor vehicle by the owner or the owner's agent or employee across the highway is not a use of the motor vehicle on the public highway.

(Enacted by Acts 2003, 78th Leg., ch. 1320 (H.B. 2971), § 1, effective September 1, 2003.)

### STATUTORY NOTES

**Editor's notes.** — This section is renumbered to Transportation Code Section 502.144 pursuant to Acts 2011, 82nd Leg., ch. 1296 (H.B. 2357), § 103, effective January 1, 2012.

## Sec. 502.0079. [Renumbered January 1, 2012] Vehicles Operated by Certain Nonresidents.

(a) A nonresident owner of a motor vehicle, trailer, or semitrailer that is registered in the state or country in which the person resides may operate the vehicle to transport persons or property for compensation without being registered in this state, if the person does not exceed two trips in a calendar month and each trip does not exceed four days.

(b) A nonresident owner of a privately owned vehicle that is not registered in this state may not make more than five occasional trips in any calendar month into this state using the vehicle. Each occasional trip into this state may not exceed five days.

(c) A nonresident owner of a privately owned passenger car that is registered in the state or country in which the person resides and that is not operated for compensation may operate the car in this state for the period in which the car's license plates are valid. In this subsection, "nonresident" means a resident of a state or country other than this state whose presence in this state is as a visitor and who does not engage in gainful employment or enter into business or an occupation, except as may otherwise be provided by any reciprocal agreement with another state or country.

(d) This section does not prevent:

(1) a nonresident owner of a motor vehicle from operating the vehicle in this state for the sole purpose of marketing farm products raised exclusively by the person; or

(2) a resident of an adjoining state or country from operating in this state a privately owned and registered vehicle to go to and from the person's place of regular employment and to make trips to purchase merchandise, if the vehicle is not operated for compensation.

(e) The privileges provided by this section may be allowed only if, under the laws of the appropriate state or country, similar privileges are granted to vehicles registered under the laws of this state and owned by residents of this state.

(f) This section does not affect the right or status of a vehicle owner under any reciprocal agreement between this state and another state or country.

(Enacted by Acts 2003, 78th Leg., ch. 1320 (H.B. 2971), § 1, effective September 1, 2003.)

STATUTORY NOTES

**Editor's notes.** — This section is renumbered to Transportation Code Section 502.145 pursuant to Acts 2011, 82nd Leg., ch. 1296 (H.B. 2357), § 104, effective January 1, 2012.

## Sec. 502.008. [Repealed January 1, 2012] Release of Information in Vehicle Registration Records.

(a) The department or a county may not release to any person information contained in vehicle registration records in response to a telephone inquiry by license number. The department or a county may release information only if the person:

(1) submits in writing a request that:

(A) provides the person's name and address; and

(B) states that the use of the information is for a lawful and legitimate purpose; or

(2) enters into a written service agreement with the department or county to receive the information.

(b) This section does not apply to the release of information to:

(1) a peace officer, as defined in Article 2.12, Code of Criminal Procedure, acting in an official capacity; or

(2) an official of this state or a political subdivision of this state if the official is requesting the information for:

(A) tax purposes; or

(B) the purpose of determining eligibility for a state public assistance program.

(c) The department shall provide a dedicated line to its vehicle registration record database for use by other state agencies. The access to or transmission of information under this subsection does not affect whether the information is subject to disclosure under Chapter 552, Government Code.

(d) This section does not authorize the release of information that is prohibited from disclosure under Chapter 730.

(Enacted by Acts 1995, 74th Leg., ch. 165 (S.B. 971), § 1, effective September 1, 1995; am. Acts 1997, 75th Leg., ch. 165 (S.B. 898), § 30.46(a), effective September 1, 1997; am. Acts 1997, 75th Leg., ch. 1187 (S.B. 1069), § 6, effective September 1, 1997.)

## Sec. 502.009. [Renumbered January 1, 2012] Motor Vehicle Emissions Inspection and Maintenance Requirements.

(a) The Department of Public Safety shall ensure compliance with the motor vehicle emissions inspection and maintenance program through a vehicle inspection sticker-based enforcement system except as provided by this section or Section 548.3011. Subsections (b)—(e) apply only if the United States Environmental Protection Agency determines that the state has not demonstrated, as required by 40 C.F.R. Section 51.361, that sticker-based enforcement of the program is more effective than registration-based enforcement and gives the Texas Natural Resource Conservation Commission or the governor written notification that the reregistration-based enforcement of the program, as described by those subsections, will be required. If Subsections (b)—(e) are made applicable as provided by this subsection, the department shall terminate reregistration-based enforcement of the program under those subsections on the date the United States Environmental Protection Agency gives the Texas Natural Resource Conservation Commission or a person the commission designates written notification that reregistration-based enforcement is not required for the state implementation plan.

(b) The department may not register a motor vehicle if the department receives from the Texas Natural Resource Conservation Commission or the Department of Public Safety notification that the registered owner of the vehicle has not complied with Subchapter F, Chapter 548.

(c) The county tax assessor-collector may not register a vehicle denied registration under Subsection (b) unless the tax assessor-collector has verification that the registered vehicle owner is in compliance with Subchapter F, Chapter 548.

(d) The department, the Texas Natural Resource Conservation Commission, and the Department of Public Safety shall enter an agreement regarding the responsibilities for costs associated with implementing this section.

(e) A county tax assessor-collector is not liable to any person for refusing to register a motor vehicle because of the person's failure to provide verification of the person's compliance with Subchapter F, Chapter 548.

(Enacted by Acts 1997, 75th Leg., ch. 1069 (S.B. 1856), § 3, effective June 19, 1997; am. Acts 2001, 77th Leg., ch. 1075 (H.B. 2134), § 4, effective September 1, 2001.)

STATUTORY NOTES

**Editor's notes.** — This section is renumbered to Transportation Code Section 502.047 pursuant to Acts 2011, 82nd Leg., ch. 1296 (H.B. 2357), § 85, effective January 1, 2012.

## Sec. 502.010. [Effective January 1, 2012] County Scofflaw.

(a) A county assessor-collector or the department may refuse to register a motor vehicle if the assessor-collector or the department receives information that the owner of the vehicle:

(1) owes the county money for a fine, fee, or tax that is past due; or

(2) failed to appear in connection with a complaint, citation, information, or indictment in a court in the county in which a criminal proceeding is pending against the owner.

(b) A county may contract with the department to provide information to the department necessary to make a determination under Subsection (a).

(c) A county that has a contract under Subsection (b) shall notify the department regarding a person for whom the county assessor-collector or the department has refused to register a motor vehicle on:

(1) the person's payment or other means of discharge of the past due fine, fee, or tax; or

(2) perfection of an appeal of the case contesting payment of the fine, fee, or tax.

(d) After notice is received under Subsection (c), the county assessor-collector or the department may not refuse to register the motor vehicle under Subsection (a).

(e) A contract under Subsection (b) must be entered into in accordance with Chapter 791, Government Code, and is subject to the ability of the parties to provide or pay for the services required under the contract.

(f) **[2 Versions: As amended by Acts 2011, 82nd Leg., ch. 1094]** A county that has a contract under Subsection (b) may impose an additional fee of $20 to:

(1) a person who fails to pay a fine, fee, or tax to the county by the date on which the fine, fee, or tax is due; or

(2) a person who fails to appear in connection with a complaint, citation, information, or indictment in a court in which a criminal proceeding is pending against the owner.

(f) **[2 Versions: As amended by Acts 2011, 82nd Leg., ch. 1296]** A county that has a contract under Subsection (b) may impose an additional fee to a person paying a fine, fee, or tax to the county after it is past due. The additional fee may be used only to reimburse the department or the county for its expenses for providing services under the contract.

(f-1) The additional fee may be used only to reimburse the department or the county assessor-collector for its expenses for providing services under the contract, or another county department for expenses related to services under the contract.

(g) In this section:

(1) a fine, fee, or tax is considered past due if it is unpaid 90 or more days after the date it is due; and

(2) registration of a motor vehicle includes renewal of the registration of the vehicle.

(h) This section does not apply to the registration of a motor vehicle under Section 501.0234, unless the vehicle is titled and registered in the name of a person who holds a general distinguishing number.

(Enacted by Acts 1997, 75th Leg., ch. 192 (H.B. 1532), § 1, effective September 1, 1997; am. Acts 1999, 76th Leg., ch. 97 (S.B. 401), § 1, effective May 17, 1999; am. Acts 2011, 82nd Leg., ch. 1094 (S.B. 1386), § 1, effective September 1, 2011; am. Acts 2011, 82nd Leg., ch. 1296 (H.B. 2357), § 76, effective January 1, 2012 (renumbered from Sec. 502.185).)

**Secs. 502.011 to 502.039 [Reserved for expansion].**

## SUBCHAPTER B
## [EFFECTIVE UNTIL JANUARY 1, 2012] STATE ADMINISTRATION; [EFFECTIVE JANUARY 1, 2012] REGISTRATION REQUIREMENTS

**Sec. 502.040. [Effective January 1, 2012] Registration Required; General Rule.**

(a) Not more than 30 days after purchasing a vehicle or becoming a resident of this state, the owner of a motor vehicle, trailer, or semitrailer shall apply for the registration of the vehicle for:

(1) each registration year in which the vehicle is used or to be used on a public highway; and

(2) if the vehicle is unregistered for a registration year that has begun and that applies to the vehicle and if the vehicle is used or to be used on a public highway, the remaining portion of that registration year.

(b) The application must be accompanied by personal identification as determined by department rule and made in a manner prescribed by the department:

(1) through the county assessor-collector of the county in which the owner resides; or

(2) if the county in which the owner resides has been declared by the governor as a disaster area, through the county assessor-collector of a county that is one of the closest unaffected counties to a county that asks for assistance and:

(A) continues to be declared by the governor as a disaster area because the county has

been rendered inoperable by the disaster; and

(B) is inoperable for a protracted period of time.

(c) A provision of this chapter that conflicts with this section prevails over this section to the extent of the conflict.

(d) A county assessor-collector, a deputy county assessor-collector, or a person acting on behalf of a county assessor-collector is not liable to any person for:

(1) refusing to register a motor vehicle because of the person's failure to submit evidence of residency that complies with the department's rules; or

(2) registering a motor vehicle under this section.

(Enacted by Acts 1995, 74th Leg., ch. 165 (S.B. 971), § 1, effective September 1, 1995; am. Acts 1997, 75th Leg., ch. 165 (S.B. 898), § 30.44(a), effective September 1, 1997; am. Acts 2011, 82nd Leg., ch. 1290 (H.B. 2017), § 24, effective September 1, 2011; am. Acts 2011, 82nd Leg., ch. 1296 (H.B. 2357), § 78, effective January 1, 2012 (renumbered from Sec. 502.002).)

**Sec. 502.041. [Effective January 1, 2012] Initial Registration.**

(a) Notwithstanding Section 502.040, the owner of a vehicle may concurrently apply for a title and for registration through the county assessor-collector of the county in which:

(1) the owner resides; or

(2) the vehicle is purchased or encumbered.

(b) The first time an owner applies for registration of a vehicle, the owner may demonstrate compliance with Section 502.046(a) as to the vehicle by showing proof of financial responsibility in any manner specified in Section 502.046(c) as to:

(1) any vehicle of the owner; or

(2) any vehicle used as part of the consideration for the purchase of the vehicle the owner applies to register.

(Enacted by Acts 1995, 74th Leg., ch. 165 (S.B. 971), § 1, effective September 1, 1995; am. Acts 2011, 82nd Leg., ch. 1296 (H.B. 2357), § 79, effective January 1, 2012 (renumbered from Sec. 502.157).)

**Sec. 502.042. [Effective January 1, 2012] Title Required for Registration.**

The department may not register or renew the registration of a motor vehicle for which a title is required under Chapter 501 unless the owner:

(1) obtains a title for the vehicle; or

(2) presents satisfactory evidence that a title was previously issued to the owner by the department or another jurisdiction.

(Enacted by Acts 1995, 74th Leg., ch. 165 (S.B. 971), § 1, effective September 1, 1995; am. Acts 2001, 77th Leg., ch. 67 (H.B. 642), § 7, effective September 1, 2001; am. Acts 2011, 82nd Leg., ch. 1296 (H.B. 2357), § 80, effective January 1, 2012 (renumbered from Sec. 502.152).)

### Sec. 502.043. [Effective January 1, 2012] Application for Registration.

(a) An application for vehicle registration must:

(1) be made in a manner prescribed and include the information required by the department by rule; and

(2) contain a full description of the vehicle as required by department rule.

(b) The department shall deny the registration of a commercial motor vehicle, truck-tractor, trailer, or semitrailer if the applicant:

(1) has a business operated, managed, or otherwise controlled or affiliated with a person who is ineligible for registration or whose privilege to operate has been suspended, including the applicant entity, a relative, a family member, a corporate officer, or a shareholder;

(2) has a vehicle that has been prohibited from operating by the Federal Motor Carrier Safety Administration for safety-related reasons;

(3) is a carrier whose business is operated, managed, or otherwise controlled or affiliated with a person who is ineligible for registration, including the owner, a relative, a family member, a corporate officer, or a shareholder; or

(4) fails to deliver to the county assessor-collector proof of the weight of the vehicle, the maximum load to be carried on the vehicle, and the gross weight for which the vehicle is to be registered.

(c) In lieu of filing an application during a year as provided by Subsection (a), the owner of a vehicle registered in any state for that year or the preceding year may present the registration receipt and transfer receipt, if any. The county assessor-collector shall accept the receipt as an application for renewal of the registration if the receipt indicates the applicant owns the vehicle. This section allows issuance for registration purposes only but does not authorize the department to issue a title.

(d) The department may require an applicant for registration to provide current personal identification as determined by department rule. Any identification number required by the department under this subsection may be entered into the department's electronic titling system but may not be printed on the title.

(Enacted by Acts 1995, 74th Leg., ch. 165 (S.B. 971), § 1, effective September 1, 1995; am. Acts 2011, 82nd Leg., ch. 1290 (H.B. 2017), § 25, effective September 1, 2011; am. Acts 2011, 82nd Leg., ch. 1296 (H.B. 2357), § 81, effective January 1, 2012 (renumbered from Sec. 502.151).)

### Sec. 502.044. [Effective January 1, 2012] Registration Period.

(a) The department shall designate a vehicle registration year of 12 consecutive months to begin on the first day of a calendar month and end on the last day of the 12th calendar month.

(b) The department shall designate vehicle registration years so as to distribute the work of the department and the county assessor-collectors as uniformly as possible throughout the year. The department may establish separate registration years for any vehicle or classification of vehicle and may adopt rules to administer the year-round registration system.

(c) The department may designate a registration period of less than 12 months to be computed at a rate of one-twelfth the annual registration fee multiplied by the number of months in the registration period. The board by rule may allow payment of registration fees for a designated period not to exceed the amount of time determined by department rule.

(d) The department shall issue a registration receipt and registration insignia that are valid until the expiration of the designated period.

(Enacted by Acts 1995, 74th Leg., ch. 165 (S.B. 971), § 1, effective September 1, 1995; am. Acts 1997, 75th Leg., ch. 433 (H.B. 1306), § 1, effective September 1, 1997; am. Acts 1999, 76th Leg., ch. 641 (H.B. 89), § 2, effective September 1, 1999; am. Acts 2001, 77th Leg., ch. 638 (H.B. 1368), § 2, effective September 1, 2001; am. Acts 2011, 82nd Leg., ch. 1296 (H.B. 2357), § 82, effective January 1, 2012 (renumbered from Sec. 502.158).)

### Sec. 502.045. [Effective January 1, 2012] Delinquent Registration.

(a) A registration fee for a vehicle becomes delinquent immediately if the vehicle is used on a

Transportation

public highway without the fee having been paid in accordance with this chapter.

(b) An applicant for registration who provides evidence to establish good reason for delinquent registration and who complies with the other requirements for registration under this chapter may register the vehicle for a 12-month period that ends on the last day of the 11th month after the month in which the registration occurs under this subsection.

(c) An applicant for registration who is delinquent and has not provided evidence acceptable to establish good reason for delinquent registration but who complies with the other requirements for registration under this chapter shall register the vehicle for a 12-month period without changing the initial month of registration.

(d) A person who has been arrested or received a citation for a violation of Section 502.472 may register the vehicle being operated at the time of the offense for a 12-month period without change to the initial month of registration only if the person:

(1) meets the other requirements for registration under this chapter; and

(2) pays an additional charge equal to 20 percent of the prescribed fee.

(e) The board by rule shall adopt a list of evidentiary items sufficient to establish good reason for delinquent registration under Subsection (b) and provide for the evidence that may be used to establish good reason under that subsection.

(f) The board by rule shall adopt procedures to implement this section in connection with the delinquent registration of a vehicle registered directly with the department or through other means.

(Enacted by Acts 1995, 74th Leg., ch. 165 (S.B. 971), § 1, effective September 1, 1995; am. Acts 1999, 76th Leg., ch. 641 (H.B. 89), § 1, effective September 1, 1999; am. Acts 2011, 82nd Leg., ch. 1296 (H.B. 2357), § 83, effective January 1, 2012 (renumbered from Sec. 502.176).)

## Sec. 502.046. [Effective January 1, 2012] Evidence of Financial Responsibility.

(a) Evidence of financial responsibility as required by Section 601.051 other than for a trailer or semitrailer shall be submitted with the application for registration under Section 502.043. A county assessor-collector may not register the motor vehicle unless the owner or the owner's representative submits the evidence of financial responsibility.

(b) The county assessor-collector shall examine the evidence of financial responsibility to determine whether it complies with Subsection (c). After examination, the evidence shall be returned unless it is in the form of a photocopy or an electronic submission.

(c) In this section, evidence of financial responsibility may be:

(1) a document listed under Section 601.053(a) or verified in compliance with Section 601.452;

(2) a liability self-insurance or pool coverage document issued by a political subdivision or governmental pool under the authority of Chapter 791, Government Code, Chapter 119, Local Government Code, or other applicable law in at least the minimum amounts required by Chapter 601;

(3) a photocopy of a document described by Subdivision (1) or (2); or

(4) an electronic submission of a document or the information contained in a document described by Subdivision (1) or (2).

(d) A personal automobile policy used as evidence of financial responsibility under this section must comply with Section 1952.052 et seq. and Sections 2301.051 through 2301.055, Insurance Code.

(e) At the time of registration, the county assessor-collector shall provide to a person registering a motor vehicle a statement that the motor vehicle may not be operated in this state unless:

(1) liability insurance coverage for the motor vehicle in at least the minimum amounts required by law remains in effect to insure against potential losses; or

(2) the motor vehicle is exempt from the insurance requirement because the person has established financial responsibility in a manner described by Sections 601.051(2)—(5) or is exempt under Section 601.052.

(f) A county assessor-collector is not liable to any person for refusing to register a motor vehicle to which this section applies because of the person's failure to submit evidence of financial responsibility that complies with Subsection (c).

(g) A county, a county assessor-collector, a deputy county assessor-collector, a person acting for or on behalf of a county or a county assessor-collector, or a person acting on behalf of an owner for purposes of registering a motor vehicle is not liable to any person for registering a motor vehicle under this section.

(h) This section does not prevent a person from registering a motor vehicle by mail or through an electronic submission.

(i) To be valid under this section, an electronic submission must be in a format that is:

(1) submitted by electronic means, including a telephone, facsimile machine, or computer;

(2) approved by the department; and

(3) authorized by the commissioners court for use in the county.

(j) This section does not apply to a vehicle registered pursuant to Section 501.0234.

(Enacted by Acts 1995, 74th Leg., ch. 165 (S.B. 971), § 1, effective September 1, 1995; am. Acts 1997, 75th Leg., ch. 148 (S.B. 655), § 8, effective September 1, 1997; am. Acts 1999, 76th Leg., ch. 260 (H.B. 1707), § 1, effective May 28, 1999; am. Acts 2003, 78th Leg., ch. 206 (S.B. 14), § 21.45, effective June 11, 2003; am. Acts 2011, 82nd Leg., ch. 1296 (H.B. 2357), § 84, effective January 1, 2012 (renumbered from Sec. 502.153).)

### Sec. 502.047. [Effective January 1, 2012] Motor Vehicle Emissions Inspection and Maintenance Requirements.

(a) The Department of Public Safety shall ensure compliance with the motor vehicle emissions inspection and maintenance program through a vehicle inspection sticker-based enforcement system except as provided by this section or Section 548.3011. Subsections (b)—(e) apply only if the United States Environmental Protection Agency determines that the state has not demonstrated, as required by 40 C.F.R. Section 51.361, that sticker-based enforcement of the program is more effective than registration-based enforcement and gives the Texas Commission on Environmental Quality or the governor written notification that the reregistration-based enforcement of the program, as described by those subsections, will be required. If Subsections (b)—(e) are made applicable as provided by this subsection, the department shall terminate reregistration-based enforcement of the program under those subsections on the date the United States Environmental Protection Agency gives the Texas Commission on Environmental Quality or a person the commission designates written notification that reregistration-based enforcement is not required for the state implementation plan.

(b) A motor vehicle may not be registered if the department receives from the Texas Commission on Environmental Quality or the Department of Public Safety notification that the registered owner of the vehicle has not complied with Subchapter F, Chapter 548.

(c) A motor vehicle may not be registered if the vehicle was denied registration under Subsection

(b) unless verification is received that the registered vehicle owner is in compliance with Subchapter F, Chapter 548.

(d) The department, the Texas Commission on Environmental Quality, and the Department of Public Safety shall enter an agreement regarding the responsibilities for costs associated with implementing this section.

(e) A county tax assessor-collector is not liable to any person for refusing to register a motor vehicle because of the person's failure to provide verification of the person's compliance with Subchapter F, Chapter 548.

(Enacted by Acts 1997, 75th Leg., ch. 1069 (S.B. 1856), § 3, effective June 19, 1997; am. Acts 2001, 77th Leg., ch. 1075 (H.B. 2134), § 4, effective September 1, 2001; am. Acts 2011, 82nd Leg., ch. 1296 (H.B. 2357), § 85, effective January 1, 2012 (renumbered from Sec. 502.009).)

### Sec. 502.048. [Effective January 1, 2012] Refusal to Register Unsafe Vehicle.

The department may refuse to register a motor vehicle and may cancel, suspend, or revoke a registration if the department determines that a motor vehicle is unsafe, improperly equipped, or otherwise unfit to be operated on a public highway.

(Enacted by Acts 1995, 74th Leg., ch. 165 (S.B. 971), § 1, effective September 1, 1995; am. Acts 2011, 82nd Leg., ch. 1296 (H.B. 2357), § 86, effective January 1, 2012 (renumbered from Sec. 502.005).)

### Sec. 502.051. [Renumbered January 1, 2012] Deposit of Registration Fees in State Highway Fund.

Except as otherwise provided by this chapter, the board and the department shall deposit all money received from registration fees in the state treasury to the credit of the state highway fund.

(Enacted by Acts 1995, 74th Leg., ch. 165 (S.B. 971), § 1, effective September 1, 1995; am. Acts 2009, 81st Leg., ch. 933 (H.B. 3097), § 2E.02, effective September 1, 2009.)

#### STATUTORY NOTES

**Editor's notes.** — This section is renumbered to Transportation Code Section 502.196 pursuant to Acts 2011, 82nd Leg., ch. 1296 (H.B. 2357), § 113, effective January 1, 2012.

### Sec. 502.052. [Renumbered January 1, 2012] License Plates and Registration Insignia; Reflectorized Material.

(a) The department shall prepare the designs and specifications of license plates and devices selected by the board to be used as the registration insignia.

(b) The department shall design each license plate to include a design at least one-half inch wide that represents in silhouette the shape of Texas and that appears between letters and numerals. The department may omit the silhouette of Texas from specially designed license plates.

(c) To promote highway safety, each license plate shall be made with a reflectorized material that provides effective and dependable brightness for the period for which the plate is issued. The purchase of reflectorized material shall be submitted to the comptroller for approval.
(Enacted by Acts 1995, 74th Leg., ch. 165 (S.B. 971), § 1, effective September 1, 1995; am. Acts 2007, 80th Leg., ch. 937 (H.B. 3560), § 1.113, effective September 1, 2007; am. Acts 2009, 81st Leg., ch. 933 (H.B. 3097), § 2E.03, effective September 1, 2009.)

### STATUTORY NOTES

**Editor's notes.** — This section is renumbered to Transportation Code Section 502.00211 pursuant to Acts 2011, 82nd Leg., ch. 1296 (H.B. 2357), § 73, effective January 1, 2012.

### Sec. 502.053. [Renumbered January 1, 2012] Cost of Manufacturing License Plates or Registration Insignia.

(a) The department shall reimburse the Texas Department of Criminal Justice for the cost of manufacturing license plates or registration insignia as the license plates or insignia and the invoice for the license plates or insignia are delivered to the department.

(b) When manufacturing is started, the Texas Department of Criminal Justice, the department, and the comptroller, after negotiation, shall set the price to be paid for each license plate or insignia. The price must be determined from:

(1) the cost of metal, paint, and other materials purchased;

(2) the inmate maintenance cost per day;

(3) overhead expenses;

(4) miscellaneous charges; and

(5) a previously approved amount of profit for the work.

(c) The annual profit received by the Texas Department of Criminal Justice from all contracts for the manufacturing of license plates or related manufacturing may not be less than the profit received by the Texas Department of Corrections for manufacturing license plates for use in 1974.

(Enacted by Acts 1995, 74th Leg., ch. 165 (S.B. 971), § 1, effective September 1, 1995; am. Acts 2003, 78th Leg., ch. 1056 (H.B. 1372), § 7, effective September 1, 2003; am. Acts 2007, 80th Leg., ch. 937 (H.B. 3560), § 1.114, effective September 1, 2007; am. Acts 2009, 81st Leg., ch. 933 (H.B. 3097), § 2E.04, effective September 1, 2009.)

### STATUTORY NOTES

**Editor's notes.** — This section is renumbered to Transportation Code Section 504.006 pursuant to Acts 2011, 82nd Leg., ch. 1296 (H.B. 2357), § 171, effective January 1, 2012.

### Sec. 502.054. [Renumbered January 1, 2012] Agreements with Other Jurisdictions; Offense.

(a) The department, through its director, may enter into an agreement with an authorized officer of another jurisdiction, including another state of the United States, a foreign country or a state, province, territory, or possession of a foreign country, to provide for:

(1) the registration of vehicles by residents of this state and nonresidents on an allocation or mileage apportionment plan, as under the International Registration Plan; and

(2) the exemption from payment of registration fees by nonresidents if residents of this state are granted reciprocal exemptions.

(b) The department may adopt and enforce rules to carry out the International Registration Plan or other agreement under this section.

(c) To carry out the International Registration Plan or other agreement under this section, the department shall direct that fees collected for other jurisdictions under the agreement be deposited to the credit of the proportional registration distributive fund in the state treasury and distributed to the appropriate jurisdiction through that fund.

(d) This section prevails to the extent of conflict with another law relating to the subject of this section.

(e) A person commits an offense if the person owns or operates a vehicle not registered in this state in violation of:

(1) an agreement under this section; or

(2) the applicable registration laws of this state, in the absence of an agreement under this section.

(f) An offense under Subsection (e) is a misdemeanor punishable by a fine not to exceed $200.
(Enacted by Acts 1995, 74th Leg., ch. 165 (S.B. 971), § 1, effective September 1, 1995; am. Acts

2005, 79th Leg., ch. 1215 (H.B. 925), § 5, effective September 1, 2005.)

## Sec. 502.055. Determination of Weight.

(a) The weight, net weight, or gross weight of a vehicle, as determined by the department, is the correct weight for registration purposes, regardless of any other purported weight of the vehicle.

(b) **[2 Versions: Effective until January 1, 2012]** The department may require an applicant for registration under this chapter to provide the department with evidence of:

(1) the manufacturer's rated carrying capacity for the vehicle;

(2) the nominal tonnage rating of the vehicle;

(3) the gross weight rating of the vehicle; or

(4) any combination of information described in Subdivisions (1)-(3).

(b) **[2 Versions: Effective January 1, 2012]** The department may require an applicant for registration under this chapter to provide the department with evidence of:

(1) the manufacturer's rated carrying capacity for the vehicle; or

(2) the gross vehicle weight rating.

(Enacted by Acts 1995, 74th Leg., ch. 165 (S.B. 971), § 1, effective September 1, 1995; am. Acts 1997, 75th Leg., ch. 625 (S.B. 1630), § 3, effective September 1, 1997; am. Acts 2011, 82nd Leg., ch. 1296 (H.B. 2357), § 87, effective January 1, 2012.)

## Sec. 502.056. Disputed Classification of Vehicle.

In a disputed case, the department may determine:

(1) the classification to which a vehicle belongs; and

(2) the amount of the registration fee for the vehicle.

(Enacted by Acts 1995, 74th Leg., ch. 165 (S.B. 971), § 1, effective September 1, 1995.)

## Sec. 502.057. [Effective January 1, 2012] Registration Receipt.

The department shall issue or require to be issued to the owner of a vehicle registered under this chapter a registration receipt showing the information required by rule.

(Enacted by Acts 1995, 74th Leg., ch. 165 (S.B. 971), § 1, effective September 1, 1995; am. Acts 2011, 82nd Leg., ch. 1296 (H.B. 2357), § 88, effective January 1, 2012 (renumbered from Sec. 502.178).)

## Sec. 502.058. [Effective January 1, 2012] Duplicate Registration Receipt.

(a) The owner of a vehicle for which the registration receipt has been lost or destroyed may obtain a duplicate receipt from the department or the county assessor-collector who issued the original receipt by paying a fee of $2.

(b) The office issuing a duplicate receipt shall retain the fee received.

(Enacted by Acts 1995, 74th Leg., ch. 165 (S.B. 971), § 1, effective September 1, 1995; am. Acts 2011, 82nd Leg., ch. 1296 (H.B. 2357), § 89, effective January 1, 2012 (renumbered from Sec. 502.179).)

## Sec. 502.059. [Effective January 1, 2012] Issuance of Registration Insignia.

(a) On payment of the prescribed fee an applicant for motor vehicle registration shall be issued a registration insignia.

(b) On application and payment of the prescribed fee for a renewal of the registration of a vehicle through the period set by rule, the department shall issue a registration insignia for the validation of the license plate or plates to be attached as provided by Subsection (c).

(c) Except as provided by Subsection (f), the registration insignia for validation of a license plate shall be attached to the inside of the vehicle's windshield, if the vehicle has a windshield, within six inches of the place where the motor vehicle inspection sticker is required to be placed. If the vehicle does not have a windshield, the owner, when applying for registration or renewal of registration, shall notify the department, and the department shall issue a distinctive device for attachment to the rear license plate of the vehicle.

(d) Department rules may provide for the use of an automated registration process, including:

(1) the automated on-site production of registration insignia; and

(2) automated on-premises and off-premises self-service registration.

(e) Subsection (c) does not apply to:

(1) the issuance of specialized license plates as designated by the department, including state official license plates, exempt plates for governmental entities, and temporary registration plates; or

(2) the issuance or validation of replacement license plates, except as provided by Chapter 504.

(f) The registration insignia shall be attached to the rear license plate of the vehicle, if the vehicle is:

(1) a motorcycle;

(2) machinery used exclusively to drill water wells or construction machinery for which a distinguishing license plate has been issued under Section 502.146; or

(3) oil well servicing, oil clean out, or oil well drilling machinery or equipment for which a distinguishing license plate has been issued under Subchapter G, Chapter 623.

(Enacted by Acts 1995, 74th Leg., ch. 165 (S.B. 971), § 1, effective September 1, 1995; am. Acts 1997, 75th Leg., ch. 165 (S.B. 898), § 30.49(a), effective September 1, 1997; am. Acts 1999, 76th Leg., ch. 1455 (H.B. 3014), § 2, effective September 1, 1999; am. Acts 2007, 80th Leg., ch. 101 (H.B. 310), § 1, effective January 1, 2008; am. Acts 2007, 80th Leg., ch. 280 (H.B. 505), § 3, effective June 15, 2007; am. Acts 2011, 82nd Leg., ch. 1296 (H.B. 2357), § 90, effective January 1, 2012 (renumbered from Sec. 502.180).)

## Sec. 502.060. [Effective January 1, 2012] Replacement of Registration.

(a) The owner of a registered motor vehicle may obtain a replacement registration insignia by:

(1) certifying that the replacement registration insignia will not be used on any other vehicle owned or operated by the person making the statement;

(2) paying a fee of $6 plus the fees required by Section 502.356(a) for each replacement registration insignia, except as provided by other law; and

(3) returning each replaced registration insignia in the owner's possession.

(b) No fee is required under this section if the replacement fee for a license plate has been paid under Section 504.007.

(c) A county assessor-collector may not issue a replacement registration insignia without complying with this section.

(d) A county assessor-collector shall retain $2.50 of each fee collected under this section and

shall report and send the remainder to the department.

(Enacted by Acts 1995, 74th Leg., ch. 165 (S.B. 971), § 1, effective September 1, 1995; am. Acts 1997, 75th Leg., ch. 165 (S.B. 898), § 30.49(b), (c), effective September 1, 1997; am. Acts 1999, 76th Leg., ch. 1455 (H.B. 3014), § 3, effective September 1, 1999; am. Acts 2005, 79th Leg., ch. 728 (H.B. 2018), § 20.003(a), effective September 1, 2005; am. Acts 2007, 80th Leg., ch. 1166 (H.B. 191), § 1, effective September 1, 2007; am. Acts 2009, 81st Leg. ch. 1136 (H.B. 2553), §§ 28, 29, effective September 1, 2011; am. Acts 2011, 82nd Leg., ch. 1296 (H.B. 2357), § 91, effective January 1, 2012 (renumbered from Sec. 502.184).)

## Secs. 502.061 to 502.089 [Reserved for expansion].

## SUBCHAPTER C
### [EFFECTIVE UNTIL JANUARY 1, 2012] COUNTY ADMINISTRATION; [EFFECTIVE JANUARY 1, 2012] SPECIAL REGISTRATIONS

## Sec. 502.090. [Effective January 1, 2012] Effect of Certain Military Service on Registration Requirement.

(a) This section applies only to a motor vehicle that is owned by a person who:

(1) is a resident of this state;

(2) is on active duty in the armed forces of the United States;

(3) is stationed in or has been assigned to another nation under military orders; and

(4) has registered the vehicle or been issued a license for the vehicle under the applicable status of forces agreement by:

(A) the appropriate branch of the armed forces of the United States; or

(B) the nation in which the person is stationed or to which the person has been assigned.

(b) Unless the registration or license issued for a vehicle described by Subsection (a) is suspended, canceled, or revoked by this state as provided by law:

(1) Section 502.040(a) does not apply; and

(2) the registration or license issued by the armed forces or host nation remains valid and the motor vehicle may be operated in this state under that registration or license for a period of not more than 90 days after the date on which the vehicle returns to this state.

(Enacted by Acts 1999, 76th Leg., ch. 836 (H.B. 1743), § 1, effective September 1, 1999; am. Acts 2011, 82nd Leg., ch. 1296 (H.B. 2357), § 93, effective January 1, 2012 (renumbered from Sec. 502.0025).)

### Sec. 502.091. [Effective January 1, 2012] International Registration Plan.

(a) The department, through its director, may enter into an agreement with an authorized officer of another jurisdiction, including another state of the United States, a foreign country or a state, province, territory, or possession of a foreign country, to provide for:

(1) the registration of vehicles by residents of this state and nonresidents on an allocation or mileage apportionment plan, as under the International Registration Plan; and

(2) the exemption from payment of registration fees by nonresidents if residents of this state are granted reciprocal exemptions.

(b) The department may adopt and enforce rules to carry out the International Registration Plan or other agreement under this section.

(c) To carry out the International Registration Plan or other agreement under this section, the department shall direct that fees collected for other jurisdictions under the agreement be deposited to the credit of the proportional registration distributive fund in the state treasury and distributed to the appropriate jurisdiction through that fund. The department is not required to refund any amount less than $10 unless required by the plan.

(d) This section prevails to the extent of conflict with another law relating to the subject of this section.

(e) A person commits an offense if the person owns or operates a vehicle not registered in this state in violation of:

(1) an agreement under this section; or

(2) the applicable registration laws of this state, in the absence of an agreement under this section.

(f) An offense under Subsection (e) is a misdemeanor punishable by a fine not to exceed $200. (Enacted by Acts 1995, 74th Leg., ch. 165 (S.B. 971), § 1, effective September 1, 1995; am. Acts 2005, 79th Leg., ch. 1215 (H.B. 925), § 5, effective September 1, 2005; am. Acts 2011, 82nd Leg., ch. 1296 (H.B. 2357), § 94, effective January 1, 2012 (renumbered from Sec. 502.054).)

### Sec. 502.092. [Effective January 1, 2012] Nonresident-Owned Vehicles Used to Transport Farm Products.

(a) The department may issue to a nonresident owner a permit for a truck, truck-tractor, trailer, or semitrailer that:

(1) is registered in the owner's home state or country; and

(2) will be used to transport:

(A) farm products produced in this state from the place of production to a place of market or storage or a railhead that is not more than 75 miles from the place of production;

(B) machinery used to harvest farm products produced in this state; or

(C) farm products produced outside this state from the point of entry into this state to a place of market, storage, or processing or a railhead or seaport that is not more than 80 miles from the point of entry.

(b) The department shall issue a distinguishing insignia for a vehicle issued a permit under this section. The insignia must be attached to the vehicle in lieu of regular license plates and must show the permit expiration date. A permit issued under this section is valid until the earlier of:

(1) the date the vehicle's registration in the owner's home state or country expires; or

(2) the 30th day after the date the permit is issued.

(c) A person may obtain a permit under this section by:

(1) applying to the department in a manner prescribed by the department;

(2) paying a fee equal to $\frac{1}{12}$ the registration fee prescribed by this chapter for the vehicle;

(3) furnishing satisfactory evidence that the motor vehicle is insured under an insurance policy that complies with Section 601.072 and that is written by:

(A) an insurance company or surety company authorized to write motor vehicle liability insurance in this state; or

(B) with the department's approval, a surplus lines insurer that meets the requirements of Chapter 981, Insurance Code, and rules adopted by the commissioner of insurance under that chapter, if the applicant is unable to obtain insurance from an insurer described by Paragraph (A); and

(4) furnishing evidence that the vehicle has been inspected as required under Chapter 548.

(d) A nonresident owner may not obtain more than three permits under this section during a registration year.

(e) A vehicle for which a permit is issued under this section may not be operated in this state after the permit expires unless the owner:

(1) obtains another temporary permit; or

(2) registers the vehicle under Section 502.253, 502.254, 502.255, or 502.256, as appropriate, for the remainder of the registration year.

(f) A vehicle for which a permit is issued under this section may not be registered under Section 502.433.

(g) A mileage referred to in this section is a state highway mileage.

(Enacted by Acts 1995, 74th Leg., ch. 165 (S.B. 971), § 1, effective September 1, 1995; am. Acts 2003, 78th Leg., ch. 1276 (H.B. 3507), § 10A.553, effective September 1, 2003; am. Acts 2009, 81st Leg., ch. 933 (H.B. 3097), § 2E.07, effective September 1, 2009; am. Acts 2011, 82nd Leg., ch. 1296 (H.B. 2357), § 95, effective January 1, 2012 (renumbered from Sec. 502.355).)

### Sec. 502.093.  [Effective January 1, 2012] Annual Permits.

(a) The department may issue an annual permit in lieu of registration to a foreign commercial motor vehicle, trailer, or semitrailer that is subject to registration in this state and is not authorized to travel on a public highway because of the lack of registration in this state or the lack of reciprocity with the state or country in which the vehicle is registered.

(b) A permit issued under this section is valid for a vehicle registration year to begin on the first day of a calendar month designated by the department and end on the last day of the last calendar month of the registration year.

(c) A permit may not be issued under this section for the importation of citrus fruit into this state from a foreign country except for foreign export or processing for foreign export.

(d) A person may obtain a permit under this section by:

(1) applying in the manner prescribed by the department;

(2) paying a fee in the amount required by Subsection (e) in the manner prescribed by the department, including a service charge for a credit card payment or escrow account; and

(3) furnishing evidence of financial responsibility for the motor vehicle that complies with

Sections 502.046(c) and 601.168(a), the policies to be written by an insurance company or surety company authorized to write motor vehicle liability insurance in this state.

(e) The fee for a permit under this section is the fee that would be required for registering the vehicle under Section 502.253 or 502.255, except as provided by Subsection (f).

(f) A vehicle registered under this section is exempt from the token fee and is not required to display the associated distinguishing license plate if the vehicle:

(1) is a semitrailer that has a gross weight of more than 6,000 pounds; and

(2) is used or intended to be used in combination with a truck tractor or commercial motor vehicle with a gross vehicle weight of more than 10,000 pounds.

(g) A vehicle registered under this section is not subject to the fee required by Section 502.401 or 502.403.

(Enacted by Acts 1995, 74th Leg., ch. 165 (S.B. 971), § 1, effective September 1, 1995; am. Acts 1997, 75th Leg., ch. 165 (S.B. 898), § 30.63(a), effective September 1, 1997; am. Acts 2011, 82nd Leg., ch. 1296 (H.B. 2357), § 96, effective January 1, 2012 (renumbered from Sec. 502.353).)

### Sec. 502.094.  [Effective January 1, 2012] 72- or 144-Hour Permits.

(a) The department may issue a temporary registration permit in lieu of registration for a commercial motor vehicle, trailer, semitrailer, or motor bus that:

(1) is owned by a resident of the United States, Canada, or the United Mexican States;

(2) is subject to registration in this state; and

(3) is not authorized to travel on a public highway because of the lack of registration in this state or the lack of reciprocity with the state or province in which the vehicle is registered.

(b) A permit issued under this section is valid for the period stated on the permit, effective from the date and time shown on the receipt issued as evidence of registration under this section.

(c) A person may obtain a permit under this section by:

(1) applying to the county assessor-collector, the department, or the department's wire service agent, if the department has a wire service agent;

(2) paying a fee of $25 for a 72-hour permit or $50 for a 144-hour permit in the manner

prescribed by the department that may include a service charge for a credit card payment or escrow account;

(3) furnishing to the county assessor-collector, the department, or the department's wire service agent, evidence of financial responsibility for the vehicle that complies with Sections 502.046(c) and 601.168(a); and

(4) submitting a copy of the applicable federal declaration form required by the Federal Motor Carrier Safety Administration or its successor in connection with the importation of a motor vehicle or motor vehicle equipment subject to the federal motor vehicle safety, bumper, and theft prevention standards.

(d) A county assessor-collector shall report and send a fee collected under this section in the manner provided by Section 502.198. Each week, a wire service agent shall send to the department a report of all permits issued by the agent during the previous week. The board by rule shall prescribe the format and content of a report required by this subsection.

(e) A vehicle issued a permit under this section is subject to Subchapters B and F, Chapter 548, unless the vehicle:

(1) is registered in another state of the United States, in a province of Canada, or in a state of the United Mexican States; or

(2) is mobile drilling or servicing equipment used in the production of gas, crude petroleum, or oil, including a mobile crane or hoisting equipment, mobile lift equipment, forklift, or tug.

(f) A commercial motor vehicle, trailer, semitrailer, or motor bus apprehended for violating a registration law of this state:

(1) may not be issued a permit under this section; and

(2) is immediately subject to registration in this state.

(g) A person who operates a commercial motor vehicle, trailer, or semitrailer with an expired permit issued under this section is considered to be operating an unregistered vehicle subject to each penalty prescribed by law.

(h) The department may establish one or more escrow accounts in the state highway fund for the prepayment of a 72-hour permit or a 144-hour permit. Any fee established by the department for the administration of this subsection shall be administered as required by an agreement entered into by the department.

(Enacted by Acts 1995, 74th Leg., ch. 165 (S.B. 971), § 1, effective September 1, 1995; am. Acts 1997, 75th Leg., ch. 165 (S.B. 898), § 30.61(a), effective September 1, 1997; am. Acts 1997, 75th Leg., ch. 625 (S.B. 1630), § 11, effective September 1, 1997; am. Acts 2009, 81st Leg., ch. 919 (H.B. 2985), § 2, effective September 1, 2009; am. Acts 2009, 81st Leg., ch. 933 (H.B. 3097), § 2E.06, effective September 1, 2009; am. Acts 2011, 82nd Leg., ch. 1296 (H.B. 2357), § 97, effective January 1, 2012 (renumbered from Sec. 502.352).)

### Sec. 502.095. [Effective January 1, 2012] One-Trip or 30-Day Trip Permits.

(a) The department may issue a temporary permit in lieu of registration for a vehicle subject to registration in this state that is not authorized to travel on a public highway because of the lack of registration in this state or the lack of reciprocity with the state or country in which the vehicle is registered.

(b) A permit issued under this section is valid for:

(1) one trip, as provided by Subsection (c); or

(2) 30 days, as provided by Subsection (d).

(c) A one-trip permit is valid for one trip between the points of origin and destination and those intermediate points specified in the application and registration receipt. Unless the vehicle is a bus operating under charter that is not covered by a reciprocity agreement with the state or country in which the bus is registered, a one-trip permit is for the transit of the vehicle only, and the vehicle may not be used for the transportation of any passenger or property. A one-trip permit may not be valid for longer than 15 days from the effective date of registration.

(d) A 30-day permit may be issued only to a passenger vehicle, a private bus, a trailer or semitrailer with a gross weight of not more than 10,000 pounds, a light truck, or a light commercial vehicle with a gross vehicle weight of more than 10,000 pounds that will operate unladen. A person may obtain multiple 30-day permits. The department may issue a single registration receipt to apply to all of the periods for which the vehicle is registered.

(e) A person may obtain a permit under this section by:

(1) applying as provided by the department to:

(A) the county assessor-collector of the county in which the vehicle will first be operated on a public highway; or

(B) the department in Austin or at one of the department's vehicle title and registration regional offices;

(2) paying a fee, in the manner prescribed by the department including a registration service charge for a credit card payment or escrow account of:

    (A) $5 for a one-trip permit; or

    (B) $25 for each 30-day period; and

(3) furnishing evidence of financial responsibility for the vehicle in a form listed under Section 504.046(c).

(f) A registration receipt shall be carried in the vehicle at all times during the period in which it is valid. The temporary tag must contain all pertinent information required by this section and must be displayed in the rear window of the vehicle so that the tag is clearly visible and legible when viewed from the rear of the vehicle. If the vehicle does not have a rear window, the temporary tag must be attached on or carried in the vehicle to allow ready inspection. The registration receipt must be carried in the vehicle at all times during the period in which it is valid.

(g) The department may refuse and may instruct a county assessor-collector to refuse to issue a temporary registration for any vehicle if, in the department's opinion, the vehicle or the owner of the vehicle has been involved in operations that constitute an abuse of the privilege granted by this section. A registration issued after notice to a county assessor-collector under this subsection is void.

(Enacted by Acts 1995, 74th Leg., ch. 165 (S.B. 971), § 1, effective September 1, 1995; am. Acts 1997, 75th Leg., ch. 1092 (H.B. 2067), § 1, effective June 19, 1997; am. Acts 2011, 82nd Leg., ch. 1296 (H.B. 2357), § 98, effective January 1, 2012 (renumbered from Sec. 502.354).)

## Secs. 502.096 to 502.100 [Reserved for expansion].

## Sec. 502.101. [Renumbered January 1, 2012] Registration by Mail or Electronic Means; Service Charge.

(a) A county assessor-collector may collect a service charge of $1 from each applicant registering a vehicle by mail. The service charge shall be used to pay the costs of handling and postage to mail the registration receipt and insignia to the applicant.

(b) With the approval of the commissioners court of a county, a county assessor-collector may contract with a private entity to enable an applicant for registration to use an electronic off-premises location. A private entity may charge an applicant not more than $1 for the service provided.

(c) The department may adopt rules to cover the timely application for and issuance of registration receipts and insignia by mail or through an electronic off-premises location.

(Enacted by Acts 1995, 74th Leg., ch. 165 (S.B. 971), § 1, effective September 1, 1995.)

### STATUTORY NOTES

**Editor's notes.** — This section is renumbered to Transportation Code Section 502.197 pursuant to Acts 2011, 82nd Leg., ch. 1296 (H.B. 2357), § 114, effective January 1, 2012.

## Sec. 502.102. [Renumbered January 1, 2012] Disposition of Fees Generally.

(a) Except as provided by Sections 502.103 and 502.104, this section applies to all fees collected by a county assessor-collector under this chapter.

(b) Each Monday, a county assessor-collector shall credit to the county road and bridge fund an amount equal to the net collections made during the preceding week until the amount so credited for the calendar year equals the total of:

    (1) $60,000;

    (2) $350 for each mile of county road maintained by the county, according to the most recent information available from the department, not to exceed 500 miles; and

    (3) an additional amount of fees equal to the amount calculated under Section 502.1025.

(c) After the credits to the county road and bridge fund equal the total computed under Subsection (b), each Monday the county assessor-collector shall:

    (1) credit to the county road and bridge fund an amount equal to 50 percent of the net collections made during the preceding week, until the amount so credited for the calendar year equals $125,000; and

    (2) send to the department an amount equal to 50 percent of those collections.

(d) After the credits to the county road and bridge fund equal the total amounts computed under Subsections (b) and (c)(1), each Monday the county assessor-collector shall send to the department all collections made during the preceding week.

(e) Each Monday the county assessor-collector shall send to the department a copy of each receipt issued the previous week for a registration fee under this chapter.

(Enacted by Acts 1995, 74th Leg., ch. 165 (S.B. 971), § 1, effective September 1, 1995; am. Acts

2003, 78th Leg., ch. 1325 (H.B. 3588), § 9.02, effective September 1, 2005.)

STATUTORY NOTES

**Editor's notes.** — This section is renumbered to Transportation Code Section 502.198 pursuant to Acts 2011, 82nd Leg., ch. 1296 (H.B. 2357), § 115, effective January 1, 2012.

## Sec. 502.1025. [Renumbered January 1, 2012] Calculation of Additional Fee Amounts Retained by a County.

(a) The county tax assessor-collector each calendar year shall calculate five percent of the tax and penalties collected by the county tax assessor-collector under Chapter 152, Tax Code, in the preceding calendar year. In addition, the county tax assessor-collector shall calculate each calendar year an amount equal to five percent of the tax and penalties that the comptroller:

(1) collected under Section 152.047, Tax Code, in the preceding calendar year; and

(2) determines are attributable to sales in the county.

(b) A county tax assessor-collector shall retain under Section 502.102(b) fees based on the following percentage of the amounts calculated under subsection (a) during each of the following fiscal years:

(1) in fiscal year 2006, 90 percent;

(2) in fiscal year 2007, 80 percent;

(3) in fiscal year 2008, 70 percent;

(4) in fiscal year 2009, 60 percent;

(5) in fiscal year 2010, 50 percent;

(6) in fiscal year 2011, 40 percent;

(7) in fiscal year 2012, 30 percent;

(8) in fiscal year 2013, 20 percent;

(9) in fiscal year 2014, 10 percent;

(10) in fiscal year 2015 and succeeding years, 0 percent.

(c) The county shall credit the amounts retained under Subsection (b) to the county road and bridge fund. Money credited to the fund under this section may only be used for:

(1) county road construction, maintenance, and repair;

(2) bridge construction, maintenance, and repair;

(3) the purchase of right-of-way for road or highway purposes; or

(4) the relocation of utilities for road or highway purposes.

(Enacted by Acts 2003, 78th Leg., ch. 1325 (H.B. 3588), § 9.03, effective September 1, 2005.)

STATUTORY NOTES

**Editor's notes.** — This section is renumbered to Transportation Code Section 502.1981 pursuant to Acts 2011, 82nd Leg., ch. 1296 (H.B. 2357), § 116, effective January 1, 2012.

## Sec. 502.103. [Renumbered January 1, 2012] Disposition of Optional County Road and Bridge Fee.

Each Monday a county assessor-collector shall apportion the collections for the preceding week for a fee imposed under Section 502.172 by:

(1) crediting an amount equal to 97 percent of the collections to the county road and bridge fund; and

(2) sending to the department an amount equal to three percent of the collections to defray the department's costs of administering Section 502.172.

(Enacted by Acts 1995, 74th Leg., ch. 165 (S.B. 971), § 1, effective September 1, 1995.)

STATUTORY NOTES

**Editor's notes.** — This section is renumbered to Transportation Code Section 502.1982 pursuant to Acts 2011, 82nd Leg., ch. 1296 (H.B. 2357), § 117, effective January 1, 2012.

## Sec. 502.104. [Repealed January 1, 2012] Disposition of Certain Special Fees.

Each Monday a county assessor-collector shall send to the department an amount equal to collections for the preceding week for:

(1) each transfer fee collected under Section 502.175; and

(2) each fee collected under Section 502.169(b), 502.1715, or 502.279.

(Enacted by Acts 1995, 74th Leg., ch. 165 (S.B. 971), § 1, effective September 1, 1995; am. Acts 2003, 78th Leg., ch. 1325 (H.B. 3588), § 19B.02, effective September 1, 2003.)

## Sec. 502.105. [Repealed January 1, 2012] Report of Fees Collected.

Together with each remittance of fees under Sections 502.102, 502.103, and 502.104, a county assessor-collector shall send to the department a complete report of the fees collected and the disposition of those fees. The department shall prescribe the form and the content requirements of the report.

(Enacted by Acts 1995, 74th Leg., ch. 165 (S.B. 971), § 1, effective September 1, 1995.)

Transportation

## Sec. 502.106. [Renumbered January 1, 2012] Deposit of Fees in Interest-Bearing Account.

(a) Except as provided by Sections 502.103 and 502.104, a county assessor-collector may:

(1) deposit the fees in an interest-bearing account or certificate in the county depository; and

(2) send the fees to the department not later than the 34th day after the date the fees are due under Section 502.104.

(b) The county owns all interest earned on fees deposited under this section. The county treasurer shall credit the interest to the county general fund.

(Enacted by Acts 1995, 74th Leg., ch. 165 (S.B. 971), § 1, effective September 1, 1995.)

### STATUTORY NOTES

**Editor's notes.** — This section is renumbered to Transportation Code Section 502.1983 pursuant to Acts 2011, 82nd Leg., ch. 1296 (H.B. 2357), § 118, effective January 1, 2012.

## Sec. 502.107. [Renumbered January 1, 2012] Interest on Fees.

(a) A fee required to be sent to the department under this chapter bears interest for the benefit of the state highway fund at an annual rate of 10 percent beginning on the 60th day after the date the county assessor-collector collects the fee.

(b) The department shall audit the registration and transfer fees collected and disbursed by each county assessor-collector and shall determine the exact amount of interest due on any fee not sent to the department.

(c) The state has a claim against a county assessor-collector and the sureties on the assessor-collector's official bond for the amount of interest due on a fee.

(Enacted by Acts 1995, 74th Leg., ch. 165 (S.B. 971), § 1, effective September 1, 1995.)

### STATUTORY NOTES

**Editor's notes.** — This section is renumbered to Transportation Code Section 502.1984 pursuant to Acts 2011, 82nd Leg., ch. 1296 (H.B. 2357), § 119, effective January 1, 2012.

## Sec. 502.108. [Renumbered January 1, 2012] Use of Registration Fees Retained by County.

(a) Money credited to the county road and bridge fund under Section 502.102 or 502.103 may not be used to pay the compensation of the county judge or a county commissioner. The money may be used only for the construction and maintenance of lateral roads in the county, under the supervision of the county engineer.

(b) If there is not a county engineer, the commissioners court of the county may require the services of the department's district engineer or resident engineer to supervise the construction and surveying of lateral roads in the county.

(c) A county may use money allocated to it under this chapter to:

(1) pay obligations issued in the construction or improvement of any roads, including state highways in the county;

(2) improve the roads in the county road system; or

(3) construct new roads.

(d) To the maximum extent possible, contracts for roads constructed by a county using funds provided under this chapter should be awarded by competitive bids.

(e) [Repealed by Acts 2003, 78th Leg., ch. 1325 (H.B. 3588), § 9.04, effective September 1, 2005.]

(f) [Repealed by Acts 1997, 75th Leg., ch. 165 (S.B. 898), § 30.47(a), effective September 1, 1997.]

(Enacted by Acts 1995, 74th Leg., ch. 165 (S.B. 971), § 1, effective September 1, 1995; am. Acts 1997, 75th Leg., ch. 165 (S.B. 898), § 30.47(a), effective September 1, 1997; am. Acts 2003, 78th Leg., ch. 1325 (H.B. 3588), § 9.04, effective September 1, 2005.)

### STATUTORY NOTES

**Editor's notes.** — This section is renumbered to Transportation Code Section 502.1985 pursuant to Acts 2011, 82nd Leg., ch. 1296 (H.B. 2357), § 120, effective January 1, 2012.

## Sec. 502.109. Compensation of Assessor-Collector [Renumbered].

Renumbered to Transportation Code § 520.006 by Acts 2011, 82nd Leg., ch. 1290 (H.B. 2017), § 32, effective September 1, 2011 and Acts 2011, 82nd Leg., ch. 1296 (H.B. 2357), § 226, effective January 1, 2012.

## Sec. 502.110. [Renumbered January 1, 2012] Contingent Provision for Distribution of Fees Between State and Counties.

If the method of distributing vehicle registration fees collected under this chapter between the state and counties is declared invalid because of inequality of collection or distribution of those fees, 60 percent of each fee shall be distributed to the county collecting the fee and 40 percent shall be sent to the state in the manner provided by this chapter.

(Enacted by Acts 1995, 74th Leg., ch. 165 (S.B. 971), § 1, effective September 1, 1995.)

STATUTORY NOTES

Editor's notes. — This section is renumbered to Transportation Code Section 502.1986 pursuant to Acts 2011, 82nd Leg., ch. 1296 (H.B. 2357), § 121, effective January 1, 2012.

## Sec. 502.111. [Renumbered January 1, 2012] Branch Offices.

(a) The commissioners court of a county may authorize the county assessor-collector to:

(1) establish a suboffice or branch office for vehicle registration at one or more locations in the county other than the county courthouse; or

(2) appoint a deputy to register vehicles in the same manner and with the same authority as though done in the office of the assessor-collector.

(b) The report of vehicles registered through a suboffice or branch office shall be made through the office of the county assessor-collector.

(Enacted by Acts 1995, 74th Leg., ch. 165 (S.B. 971), § 1, effective September 1, 1995.)

STATUTORY NOTES

Editor's notes. — This section is renumbered to Transportation Code Section 520.007 pursuant to Acts 2011, 82nd Leg., ch. 1296 (H.B. 2357), § 227, effective January 1, 2012.

## Sec. 502.112. [Renumbered January 1, 2012] Deputy Assessor-Collectors.

(a) A county assessor-collector, with the approval of the commissioners court of the county, may deputize an individual or business entity to:

(1) issue motor vehicle registration receipts as a limited-service deputy; or

(2) issue motor vehicle registration receipts and prepare or accept applications for title transfers as a full-service deputy.

(b) An individual or business entity is eligible to be deputized as a limited-service deputy if the person:

(1) is trained to issue registration receipts by the county assessor-collector; and

(2) posts a bond payable to the county assessor-collector:

(A) in an amount determined by the assessor-collector; and

(B) conditioned on the person's proper accounting and remittance of all fees the person collects.

(c) An individual or business entity is eligible to be deputized as a full-service deputy if the person:

(1) meets the requirements of Subsection (b); and

(2) has experience in title transfers.

(d) A person deputized under this section shall keep a separate account of the fees collected and a record of daily receipts.

(Enacted by Acts 1995, 74th Leg., ch. 165 (S.B. 971), § 1, effective September 1, 1995.)

STATUTORY NOTES

Editor's notes. — This section is renumbered to Transportation Code Section 520.0091 pursuant to Acts 2011, 82nd Leg., ch. 1296 (H.B. 2357), § 230, effective January 1, 2012.

## Sec. 502.113. [Renumbered January 1, 2012] Limited-Service Deputies.

(a) A limited-service deputy appointed under Section 502.112 may only accept registration renewal cards provided by the department and may not prepare or accept an application for title transfer.

(b) The county assessor-collector may pay a limited-service deputy an amount not to exceed the fee the assessor-collector could collect under Section 502.109(a) for each registration receipt issued. The commissioners court of the county may permit a limited-service deputy to charge and retain an additional fee not to exceed $1 for each registration receipt issued.

(Enacted by Acts 1995, 74th Leg., ch. 165 (S.B. 971), § 1, effective September 1, 1995.)

STATUTORY NOTES

Editor's notes. — This section is renumbered to Transportation Code Section 520.009 pursuant to Acts 2011, 82nd Leg., ch. 1296 (H.B. 2357), § 229, effective January 1, 2012.

## Sec. 502.114. [Renumbered January 1, 2012] Full-Service Deputies.

(a) A full-service deputy appointed under Section 502.112 shall accept any application for registration, registration renewal, or title transfer that the county assessor-collector may accept.

(b) A full-service deputy may charge and retain an additional motor vehicle registration fee not to exceed $5 for each motor vehicle registration issued.

(c) A county assessor-collector may delegate to a full-service deputy, in the manner selected by the assessor-collector, the authority to use data processing equipment and software provided by

Transportation

the department for use in the titling and registration of motor vehicles. The department may not limit a county assessor-collector's ability to delegate the assessor-collector's functions regarding the titling and registration of motor vehicles to a qualified full-service deputy in the manner the assessor-collector considers appropriate.
(Enacted by Acts 1995, 74th Leg., ch. 165 (S.B. 971), § 1, effective September 1, 1995.)

STATUTORY NOTES

**Editor's notes.** — This section is renumbered to Transportation Code Section 520.008 pursuant to Acts 2011, 82nd Leg., ch. 1296 (H.B. 2357), § 228, effective January 1, 2012.

## Secs. 502.115 to 502.139 [Reserved for expansion].

## SUBCHAPTER D
### [EFFECTIVE UNTIL JANUARY 1, 2012] REGISTRATION PROCEDURES AND FEES; [EFFECTIVE JANUARY 1, 2012] VEHICLES NOT ISSUED REGISTRATION

### Sec. 502.140.   [Effective January 1, 2012] Certain Off-Highway Vehicles.

(a) Except as provided by Subsection (b), a person may not register an all-terrain vehicle or a recreational off-highway vehicle, with or without design alterations, for operation on a public highway.

(b) The state, a county, or a municipality may register an all-terrain vehicle or a recreational off-highway vehicle for operation on a public beach or highway to maintain public safety and welfare.

(c) A recreational off-highway vehicle registered as provided by Subsection (b) may be operated on a public or private beach in the same manner as a golf cart may be operated on a public or private beach under Section 551.403. The operator must hold and have in the operator's possession a driver's license issued under Chapter 521 or a commercial driver's license issued under Chapter 522.

(d) Section 504.401 does not apply to an all-terrain vehicle or a recreational off-highway vehicle.

(e) Operation of an all-terrain vehicle or recreational off-highway vehicle in compliance with Section 663.037 does not require registration under Subsection (b).

(Enacted by Acts 1995, 74th Leg., ch. 165 (S.B. 971), § 1, effective September 1, 1995; am. Acts 1999, 76th Leg., ch. 311 (H.B. 523), § 1, effective May 29, 1999; am. Acts 2007, 80th Leg., ch. 1280 (H.B. 3849), § 6, effective June 15, 2007; am. Acts 2009, 81st Leg., ch. 1136 (H.B. 2553), § 6, effective September 1, 2009; am. Acts 2011, 82nd Leg., ch. 1296 (H.B. 2357), § 100, effective January 1, 2012 (renumbered from Sec. 502.006).)

### Sec. 502.142.   [Effective January 1, 2012] Manufactured Housing.

Manufactured housing, as defined by Section 1201.003, Occupations Code, is not a vehicle subject to this chapter.
(Enacted by Acts 2003, 78th Leg., ch. 1320 (H.B. 2971), § 1, effective September 1, 2003; am. Acts 2011, 82nd Leg., ch. 1296 (H.B. 2357), § 101, effective January 1, 2012 (renumbered from Sec. 502.0072).)

### Sec. 502.143.   [Effective January 1, 2012] Other Vehicles.

An owner may not register the following vehicles for operation on a public highway:

(1) power sweepers;

(2) motorized mobility devices;

(3) electric personal assistive mobility devices; and

(4) electric bicycles.

(Enacted by Acts 2003, 78th Leg., ch. 1320 (H.B. 2971), § 1, effective September 1, 2003; am. Acts 2011, 82nd Leg., ch. 1296 (H.B. 2357), § 102, effective January 1, 2012 (renumbered from Sec. 502.0073).)

### Sec. 502.144.   [Effective January 1, 2012] Vehicles Operated on Public Highway Separating Real Property Under Vehicle Owner's Control.

Where a public highway separates real property under the control of the owner of a motor vehicle, the operation of the motor vehicle by the owner or the owner's agent or employee across the highway is not a use of the motor vehicle on the public highway.
(Enacted by Acts 2003, 78th Leg., ch. 1320 (H.B. 2971), § 1, effective September 1, 2003; am. Acts 2011, 82nd Leg., ch. 1296 (H.B. 2357), § 103, effective January 1, 2012 (renumbered from Sec. 502.0078).)

### Sec. 502.145.   [Effective January 1, 2012] Vehicles Operated by Certain Nonresidents.

(a) A nonresident owner of a privately owned passenger car that is registered in the state or country in which the person resides and that is not operated for compensation may operate the car in this state for the period in which the car's license plates are valid. In this subsection, "nonresident" means a resident of a state or country other than this state whose presence in this state is as a visitor and who does not engage in gainful employment or enter into business or an occupation, except as may otherwise be provided by any reciprocal agreement with another state or country.

(b) This section does not prevent:

(1) a nonresident owner of a motor vehicle from operating the vehicle in this state for the sole purpose of marketing farm products raised exclusively by the person; or

(2) a resident of an adjoining state or country from operating in this state a privately owned and registered vehicle to go to and from the person's place of regular employment and to make trips to purchase merchandise, if the vehicle is not operated for compensation.

(c) The privileges provided by this section may be allowed only if, under the laws of the appropriate state or country, similar privileges are granted to vehicles registered under the laws of this state and owned by residents of this state.

(d) This section does not affect the right or status of a vehicle owner under any reciprocal agreement between this state and another state or country.

(Enacted by Acts 2003, 78th Leg., ch. 1320 (H.B. 2971), § 1, effective September 1, 2003; am. Acts 2011, 82nd Leg., ch. 1296 (H.B. 2357), § 104, effective January 1, 2012 (renumbered from Sec. 502.0079).)

## Sec. 502.146. [Effective January 1, 2012] Certain Farm Vehicles and Drilling and Construction Equipment.

(a) The department shall issue specialty license plates to a vehicle described by Subsection (b) or (c). The fee for the license plates is $5.

(b) **[2 Versions: As amended by Acts 2011, 82nd Leg., ch. 1035]** An owner is not required to register a vehicle that is used only temporarily on the highways if the vehicle is:

(1) a farm trailer or farm semitrailer with a gross weight of more than 4,000 pounds but not more than 34,000 pounds that is used exclusively:

(A) to transport seasonally harvested agricultural products or livestock from the place of production to the place of processing, market, or storage;

(B) to transport farm supplies from the place of loading to the farm; or

(C) for the purpose of participating in equine activities or attending livestock shows, as defined by Section 87.001, Civil Practice and Remedies Code;

(2) machinery used exclusively for the purpose of drilling water wells; or

(3) construction machinery that is not designed to transport persons or property on a public highway.

(b) **[2 Versions: As amended by Acts 2011, 82nd Leg., ch. 1296]** An owner is not required to register a vehicle that is used only temporarily on the highways if the vehicle is:

(1) a farm trailer or farm semitrailer with a gross weight of more than 4,000 pounds but not more than 34,000 pounds that is used exclusively to transport:

(A) seasonally harvested agricultural products or livestock from the place of production to the place of processing, market, or storage; or

(B) farm supplies from the place of loading to the farm;

(2) machinery used exclusively for the purpose of drilling water wells;

(3) oil well servicing or drilling machinery and if at the time of obtaining the license plates, the applicant submits proof that the applicant has a permit under Section 623.142; or

(4) construction machinery.

(c) An owner is not required to register a vehicle that is:

(1) a farm trailer or farm semitrailer owned by a cotton gin and used exclusively to transport agricultural products without charge from the place of production to the place of processing, market, or storage;

(2) a trailer used exclusively to transport fertilizer without charge from a place of supply or storage to a farm; or

(3) a trailer used exclusively to transport cottonseed without charge from a place of supply or storage to a farm or place of processing.

(d) A vehicle described by Subsection (b) is exempt from the inspection requirements of Subchapters B and F, Chapter 548.

(e) This section does not apply to a farm trailer or farm semitrailer that:

(1) is used for hire;

(2) has metal tires operating in contact with the highway;

(3) is not equipped with an adequate hitch pinned or locked so that it will remain securely engaged to the towing vehicle while in motion; or

(4) is not operated and equipped in compliance with all other law.

(f) A vehicle to which this section applies that is operated on a public highway in violation of this section is considered to be operated while unregistered and is immediately subject to the applicable registration fees and penalties prescribed by this chapter.

(g) In this section, the gross weight of a trailer or semitrailer is the combined weight of the vehicle and the load carried on the highway.

(Enacted by Acts 2003, 78th Leg., ch. 1320 (H.B. 2971), § 6, effective September 1, 2003; am. Acts 2011, 82nd Leg., ch. 1035 (H.B. 2960), § 2, effective June 17, 2011; am. Acts 2011, 82nd Leg., ch. 1296 (H.B. 2357), § 105, effective January 1, 2012 (renumbered from Sec. 504.504).)

## Secs. 502.147 to 502.150 [Reserved for expansion].

## Sec. 502.151.   [Renumbered January 1, 2012] Application for Registration.

(a) An application for vehicle registration must:

(1) be made in a manner prescribed and include the information required by the department by rule; and

(2) contain a full description of the vehicle as required by department rule.

(b) The department shall deny the registration of a commercial motor vehicle, truck-tractor, trailer, or semitrailer if the applicant:

(1) has a business operated, managed, or otherwise controlled or affiliated with a person who is ineligible for registration or whose privilege to operate has been suspended, including the applicant entity, a relative, a family member, a corporate officer, or a shareholder;

(2) has a vehicle that has been prohibited from operating by the Federal Motor Carrier Safety Administration for safety-related reasons;

(3) is a carrier whose business is operated, managed, or otherwise controlled or affiliated with a person who is ineligible for registration, including the owner, a relative, a family member, a corporate officer, or a shareholder; or

(4) fails to deliver to the county assessor-collector proof of the weight of the vehicle, the maximum load to be carried on the vehicle, and the gross weight for which the vehicle is to be registered.

(c) In lieu of filing an application during a year as provided by Subsection (a), the owner of a vehicle registered in any state for that year or the preceding year may present the registration receipt and transfer receipt, if any. The county assessor-collector shall accept the receipt as an application for renewal of the registration if the receipt indicates the applicant owns the vehicle. This section allows issuance for registration purposes only but does not authorize the department to issue a title.

(d) The department may require an applicant for registration to provide current personal identification as determined by department rule. Any identification number required by the department under this subsection may be entered into the department's electronic titling system but may not be printed on the title.

(Enacted by Acts 1995, 74th Leg., ch. 165 (S.B. 971), § 1, effective September 1, 1995; am. Acts 2011, 82nd Leg., ch. 1290 (H.B. 2017), § 25, effective September 1, 2011.)

### STATUTORY NOTES

**Editor's notes.** — This section is renumbered to Transportation Code Section 502.043 pursuant to Acts 2011, 82nd Leg., ch. 1296 (H.B. 2357), § 81, effective January 1, 2012.

## Sec. 502.1515.   Outsourcing Production of Renewal Notices; Paid Advertising.

The board may authorize the department to enter into a contract with a private vendor to produce and distribute motor vehicle registration renewal notices. The contract may provide for the inclusion of paid advertising in the registration renewal notice packet.

(Enacted by Acts 2005, 79th Leg., ch. 281 (H.B. 2702), § 2.85, effective June 14, 2005; am. Acts 2009, 81st Leg., ch. 933 (H.B. 3097), § 2E.05, effective September 1, 2009.)

## Sec. 502.152.   [Renumbered January 1, 2012] Certificate of Title Required for Registration.

(a) The department may not register or renew the registration of a motor vehicle for which a certificate of title is required under Chapter 501 unless the owner:

(1) obtains a certificate of title for the vehicle; or

(2) presents satisfactory evidence that a certificate of title was previously issued to the owner by the department or another jurisdiction.

(b) This section does not apply to an automobile that was purchased new before January 1, 1936.

(Enacted by Acts 1995, 74th Leg., ch. 165 (S.B. 971), § 1, effective September 1, 1995; am. Acts 2001, 77th Leg., ch. 67 (H.B. 642), § 7, effective September 1, 2001.)

### STATUTORY NOTES

**Editor's notes.** — This section is renumbered to Transportation Code Section 502.042 pursuant to Acts 2011, 82nd Leg., ch. 1296 (H.B. 2357), § 80, effective January 1, 2012.

## Sec. 502.153. [Renumbered January 1, 2012] Evidence of Financial Responsibility.

(a) Except as provided by Subsection (j), the owner of a motor vehicle, other than a trailer or semitrailer, for which evidence of financial responsibility is required by Section 601.051 or a person who represents the owner for purposes of registering a motor vehicle shall submit evidence of financial responsibility with the application for registration under Section 502.151. A county assessor-collector may not register the motor vehicle unless the owner or the owner's representative submits the evidence of financial responsibility.

(b) The county assessor-collector shall examine the evidence of financial responsibility to determine whether it complies with Subsection (c). After examining the evidence, the assessor-collector shall return the evidence unless it is in the form of a photocopy or an electronic submission.

(c) In this section, evidence of financial responsibility may be:

(1) a document listed under Section 601.053(a);

(2) a liability self-insurance or pool coverage document issued by a political subdivision or governmental pool under the authority of Chapter 791, Government Code, Chapter 119, Local Government Code, or other applicable law in at least the minimum amounts required by Chapter 601;

(3) a photocopy of a document described by Subdivision (1) or (2); or

(4) an electronic submission of a document or the information contained in a document described by Subdivision (1) or (2).

(d) A personal automobile policy used as evidence of financial responsibility under this section must comply with Article 5.06 or 5.145, Insurance Code.

(e) At the time of registration, the county assessor-collector shall provide to a person registering a motor vehicle a separate statement that the motor vehicle being registered may not be operated in this state unless:

(1) liability insurance coverage for the motor vehicle in at least the minimum amounts required by law remains in effect to insure against potential losses; or

(2) the motor vehicle is exempt from the insurance requirement because the person has established financial responsibility in a manner described by Section 601.051(2)—(5) or is exempt under Section 601.052.

(f) A county assessor-collector is not liable to any person for refusing to register a motor vehicle to which this section applies because of the person's failure to submit evidence of financial responsibility that complies with Subsection (c).

(g) A county, a county assessor-collector, a deputy county assessor-collector, a person acting for or on behalf of a county or a county assessor-collector, or a person acting on behalf of an owner for purposes of registering a motor vehicle is not liable to any person for registering a motor vehicle under this section.

(h) This section does not prevent a person from registering a motor vehicle by mail or through an electronic submission.

(i) To be valid under this section, an electronic submission must be in a format that is:

(1) submitted by electronic means, including a telephone, facsimile machine, or computer;

(2) approved by the department; and

(3) authorized by the commissioners court for use in the county.

(j) This section does not apply to a vehicle registered pursuant to Section 501.0234.

(Enacted by Acts 1995, 74th Leg., ch. 165 (S.B. 971), § 1, effective September 1, 1995; am. Acts 1997, 75th Leg., ch. 148 (S.B. 655), § 8, effective September 1, 1997; am. Acts 1999, 76th Leg., ch. 260 (H.B. 1707), § 1, effective May 28, 1999; am. Acts 2003, 78th Leg., ch. 206 (S.B. 14), § 21.45, effective June 11, 2003.)

### STATUTORY NOTES

**Editor's notes.** — This section is renumbered to Transportation. Code § 502.046 pursuant to Acts 2011, 82nd Leg., ch. 1296 (H.B. 2357), § 84, effective January 1, 2012.

## Sec. 502.1535. [Repealed January 1, 2012] Evidence of Vehicle Emissions Inspection.

A county assessor-collector may not register a motor vehicle subject to Section 548.3011 unless proof that the vehicle has passed a vehicle emissions test as required by that section, in a form authorized by that section, is presented to the county assessor-collector with the application for registration.

(Enacted by Acts 2001, 77th Leg., ch. 1075 (H.B. 2134), § 5, effective September 1, 2001.)

## Sec. 502.154. [Repealed January 1, 2012] Report by County Assessor-Collector.

A county assessor-collector shall submit an annual report to the Texas Natural Resource Conservation Commission and the department that shows:

(1) the number of registrations denied because of the applicant's failure to provide an original emissions inspection certificate or a valid waiver;

(2) the number of registrations denied because of the failure to provide proof of residency; and

(3) an itemized accounting of the costs to the county of administering Sections 502.002 and 502.006(a), (b), and (c).

(Enacted by Acts 1995, 74th Leg., ch. 165 (S.B. 971), § 1, effective September 1, 1995; am. Acts 1997, 75th Leg., ch. 165 (S.B. 898), § 30.44(c), effective September 1, 1997.)

## Sec. 502.155. Proof of Residency Required in Certain Counties [Repealed].

Repealed by Acts 1997, 75th Leg., ch. 165 (S.B. 898), § 30.44(d), effective September 1, 1997.

(Enacted by Acts 1995, 74th Leg., ch. 165 (S.B. 971), § 1, effective September 1, 1995.)

## Sec. 502.156. Statement Required for Rebuilt Vehicles.

A county assessor-collector shall require an applicant for registration of a rebuilt vehicle to provide a statement that the vehicle is rebuilt and that states the name of each person from whom the parts used in assembling the vehicle were obtained.

(Enacted by Acts 1995, 74th Leg., ch. 165 (S.B. 971), § 1, effective September 1, 1995.)

## Sec. 502.157. [Renumbered January 1, 2012] Initial Registration.

(a) Notwithstanding Section 502.002, when a motor vehicle must be registered before an application for a certificate of title will be accepted, the owner of the vehicle may concurrently apply for a certificate of title and for registration through the county assessor-collector of the county in which:

(1) the owner resides; or

(2) the vehicle is purchased or encumbered.

(b) The first time an owner applies for registration of a vehicle, the owner may demonstrate compliance with Section 502.153(a) as to the vehicle by showing proof of financial responsibility in any manner specified in Section 502.153(c) as to:

(1) any vehicle of the owner; or

(2) any vehicle used as part of the consideration for the purchase of the vehicle the owner applies to register.

(Enacted by Acts 1995, 74th Leg., ch. 165 (S.B. 971), § 1, effective September 1, 1995.)

### STATUTORY NOTES

**Editor's notes.** — This section is renumbered to Transportation Code Section 502.041 pursuant to Acts 2011, 82nd Leg., ch. 1296 (H.B. 2357), § 79, effective January 1, 2012.

## Sec. 502.158. [Renumbered January 1, 2012] Registration Year.

(a) The department shall designate a vehicle registration year of 12 consecutive months to begin on the first day of a calendar month and end on the last day of the 12th calendar month.

(b) The department shall designate vehicle registration years so as to distribute the work of the department and the county assessor-collectors as uniformly as possible throughout the year. The department may establish separate registration years for any vehicle or classification of vehicle and may adopt rules to administer the year-round registration system.

(c) The department may designate a registration period of less than 12 months. The registration fee for a registration period of less than 12 months is computed at a rate of one-twelfth the annual registration fee multiplied by the number of months in the registration period. The department may not designate a registration period of more than 12 months, but:

(1) with the consent of the department, an owner may pay registration fees for a designated period of more than 12 months; and

(2) an owner of a vehicle may pay registration fees for a designated period of 12, 24, or 36 months.

(d) An application for registration shall be made during the two months preceding the date on which the registration expires.

(e) The fee to be paid for renewing a registration is the fee that will be in effect on the first day of the vehicle registration year.

(f) [Repealed by Acts 1999, 76th Leg., ch. 641 (H.B. 89), § 2, effective September 1, 1999.]

(g) The department shall issue the applicant for registration who pays registration fees for a designated period of 24 or 36 months a registration receipt and registration insignia that are valid until the expiration of the designated period.

(Enacted by Acts 1995, 74th Leg., ch. 165 (S.B. 971), § 1, effective September 1, 1995; am. Acts 1997, 75th Leg., ch. 433 (H.B. 1306), § 1, effective September 1, 1997; am. Acts 1999, 76th Leg., ch. 641 (H.B. 89), § 2, effective September 1, 1999; am. Acts 2001, 77th Leg., ch. 638 (H.B. 1368), § 2, effective September 1, 2001.)

STATUTORY NOTES

**Editor's notes.** — This section is renumbered to Transportation Code Section 502.044 pursuant to Acts 2011, 82nd Leg., ch. 1296 (H.B. 2357), § 82, effective January 1, 2012.

## Sec. 502.1585. Designation of Registration Period by Owner.

(a) This section applies only to a person who owns more than one motor vehicle or trailer that is subject to registration under this chapter.

(b) Notwithstanding Section 502.158, the owner of a motor vehicle or a trailer may designate an initial or a renewal registration period for that vehicle so that the registration period for the vehicle or trailer expires on the same date as the registration period for another vehicle or trailer previously registered by that owner.

(c) A registration period designated under this section must begin on the first day of a calendar month and end on the last day of a calendar month and may not be for less than 12 months.

(d) The registration fee for a registration period designated under this section is computed at a rate of one-twelfth the annual registration fee multiplied by the number of months in the designated registration period.

(e) The department shall issue an applicant for registration who pays registration fees for a designated period under this section a registration receipt and registration insignia that are valid until the expiration of the designated period.

(Enacted by Acts 1999, 76th Leg., ch. 1197 (S.B. 432), § 1, effective September 1, 1999.)

## Sec. 502.1586. [Renumbered January 1, 2012] Registration Period for Truck-Tractor or Commercial Motor Vehicle Transporting Seasonal Agricultural Products.

(a) The department shall provide for a monthly registration period for a truck-tractor or a commercial motor vehicle that:

(1) is used exclusively to transport a seasonal agricultural product; and

(2) would otherwise be registered for a vehicle registration year.

(b) The department shall adopt forms for registration under this section. An applicant must indicate the number of months registration is applied for.

(c) The department shall design, prescribe, and furnish a registration receipt that is valid until the expiration of the designated registration period.

(d) The registration fee for a registration under this section is computed at a rate of one-twelfth the annual registration fee under Section 502.162, 502.163, or 502.167, as applicable, multiplied by the number of months in the registration period specified in the application for the registration.

(e) A person issued a registration under this section commits an offense if the person, during the registration period for the truck-tractor or commercial motor vehicle, uses the truck-tractor or commercial motor vehicle for a purpose other than to transport a seasonal agricultural product.

(f) A truck-tractor or commercial motor vehicle may not be registered under this section for a registration period that is less than one month or longer than six months.

(g) For purposes of this section, "to transport a seasonal agricultural product" includes any transportation activity necessary for the production, harvest, or delivery of an agricultural product that is produced seasonally.

(Enacted by Acts 1999, 76th Leg., ch. 732 (H.B. 1041), § 1, effective September 1, 1999; am. Acts 2001, 77th Leg., ch. 832 (H.B. 1128), §§ 1, 2, effective September 1, 2001 (renumbered from Sec. 502.1585); am. Acts 2001, 77th Leg., ch. 1420 (H.B. 2812), § 21.001(105), effective September 1, 2001 (renumbered from Sec. 502.1585).)

STATUTORY NOTES

**Editor's notes.** — This section is renumbered to Transportation Code Section 502.432 pursuant to Acts

Transportation

2011, 82nd Leg., ch. 1296 (H.B. 2357), § 142, effective January 1, 2012.

## Sec. 502.159. [Renumbered January 1, 2012] Schedule of Fees.

The department shall compile and furnish to each county assessor-collector a complete schedule of registration fees to be collected on the various makes, models, and types of vehicles. (Enacted by Acts 1995, 74th Leg., ch. 165 (S.B. 971), § 1, effective September 1, 1995.)

### STATUTORY NOTES

**Editor's notes.** — This section is renumbered to Transportation Code Section 502.190 pursuant to Acts 2011, 82nd Leg., ch. 1296 (H.B. 2357), § 107, effective January 1, 2012.

## Sec. 502.160. [Renumbered January 1, 2012] Fee: Motorcycle or Moped.

The fee for a registration year for registration of a motorcycle or moped is $30. (Enacted by Acts 1995, 74th Leg., ch. 165 (S.B. 971), § 1, effective September 1, 1995; am. Acts 2009, 81st Leg. ch. 1136 (H.B. 2553), § 17, effective September 1, 2011.)

### STATUTORY NOTES

**Editor's notes.** — This section is renumbered to Transportation Code Section 502.251 pursuant to Acts 2011, 82nd Leg., ch. 1296 (H.B. 2357), § 123, effective January 1, 2012.

## Sec. 502.161. [Renumbered January 1, 2012] Fee: Vehicles That Weigh 6,000 Pounds or Less.

(a) The fee for a registration year for registration of a vehicle with a gross weight of 6,000 pounds or less is $50.75, unless otherwise provided in this chapter.

(b) [Repealed by Acts 2009, 81st Leg., ch. 1136 (H.B. 2553), § 39(2), effective September 1, 2011.]

(c) For registration purposes, the weight of a passenger car, a municipal bus, or a private bus is the weight generally accepted as its correct shipping weight plus 100 pounds.

(d) In this section, "private bus" has the meaning assigned by Section 502.294. (Enacted by Acts 1995, 74th Leg., ch. 165 (S.B. 971), § 1, effective September 1, 1995; am. Acts 1997, 75th Leg., ch. 625 (S.B. 1630), § 4, effective September 1, 1997; am. Acts 2009, 81st Leg. ch. 1136 (H.B. 2553), § 18, effective September 1, 2011.)

### STATUTORY NOTES

**Editor's notes.** — This section is renumbered to Transportation Code Section 502.252 pursuant to Acts

2011, 82nd Leg., ch. 1296 (H.B. 2357), § 124, effective January 1, 2012.

## Sec. 502.162. [Renumbered January 1, 2012] Fee: Vehicles That Weigh More Than 6,000 pounds.

(a) The fee for a registration year for registration of a commercial motor vehicle or truck-tractor is $25 plus an amount determined according to the vehicle's gross weight and tire equipment, as follows:

| Weight Classification in pounds | Fee Schedule |
|---|---|
| 6,001—10,000 | $54.00 |
| 10,001—18,000 | $110.00 |
| 18,001—25,999 | $205.00 |
| 26,000—40,000 | $340.00 |
| 40,001—54,999 | $535.00 |
| 55,000—70,000 | $740.00 |
| 70,001—80,000 | $840.00 |

(b) The gross weight of a vehicle is the actual weight of the vehicle, fully equipped with a body and other equipment, as certified by a public weigher or a license and weight inspector of the Department of Public Safety, plus its net carrying capacity.

(c) The net carrying capacity of a vehicle other than a bus is the heaviest net load to be carried on the vehicle, but not less than the manufacturer's rated carrying capacity.

(d) The net carrying capacity of a bus is computed by multiplying its seating capacity by 150 pounds. The seating capacity of a bus is:

(1) the manufacturer's rated seating capacity, excluding the operator's seat; or

(2) if the manufacturer has not rated the vehicle for seating capacity, a number computed by allowing one passenger for each 16 inches of seating on the bus, excluding the operator's seat. (Enacted by Acts 1995, 74th Leg., ch. 165 (S.B. 971), § 1, effective September 1, 1995; am. Acts 2009, 81st Leg. ch. 1136 (H.B. 2553), § 20, effective September 1, 2011.)

### STATUTORY NOTES

**Editor's notes.** — This section is renumbered to Transportation Code Section 502.253 pursuant to Acts 2011, 82nd Leg., ch. 1296 (H.B. 2357), § 125, effective January 1, 2012.

## Sec. 502.163. [Renumbered January 1, 2012] Fee: Commercial Motor Vehicle Used Primarily for Farm Purposes; Offense.

(a) The registration fee for a commercial motor vehicle as a farm vehicle is 50 percent of the applicable fee under Section 502.162 if the vehicle's owner will use the vehicle for commercial purposes only to transport:

(1) the person's own poultry, dairy, livestock, livestock products, timber in its natural state, or farm products to market or another place for sale or processing;

(2) laborers from their place of residence to the owner's farm or ranch; or

(3) without charge, materials, tools, equipment, or supplies from the place of purchase or storage to the owner's farm or ranch exclusively for the owner's use or for use on the farm or ranch.

(b) A commercial motor vehicle may be registered under this section despite its use for transporting without charge the owner or a member of the owner's family:

(1) to attend church or school;

(2) to visit a doctor for medical treatment or supplies;

(3) for other necessities of the home or family; or

(4) for the purpose of participating in equine activities or attending livestock shows, as defined by Section 87.001, Civil Practice and Remedies Code.

(c) Subsection (b) does not permit the use of a vehicle registered under this section in connection with gainful employment other than farming or ranching.

(d) The department shall provide distinguishing license plates for a vehicle registered under this section.

(e) The owner of a commercial motor vehicle registered under this section commits an offense if the person uses or permits to be used the vehicle for a purpose other than one permitted by this section. Each use or permission for use in violation of this section is a separate offense.

(f) An offense under this section is a misdemeanor punishable by a fine of not less than $25 or more than $200.

(Enacted by Acts 1995, 74th Leg., ch. 165 (S.B. 971), § 1, effective September 1, 1995; am. Acts 2011, 82nd Leg., ch. 1035 (H.B. 2960), § 1, effective June 17, 2011.)

STATUTORY NOTES

**Editor's notes.** — This section is renumbered to Transportation Code Section 502.433 pursuant to Acts 2011, 82nd Leg., ch. 1296 (H.B. 2357), § 143, effective January 1, 2012.

### Sec. 502.164. [Renumbered January 1, 2012] Fee: Motor Vehicle Used Exclusively to Transport and Spread Fertilizer.

The fee for a registration year for registration of a motor vehicle designed or modified and used exclusively to transport to the field and spread fertilizer, including agricultural limestone, is $75.

(Enacted by Acts 1995, 74th Leg., ch. 165 (S.B. 971), § 1, effective September 1, 1995.)

STATUTORY NOTES

**Editor's notes.** — This section is renumbered to Transportation Code Section 502.431 pursuant to Acts 2011, 82nd Leg., ch. 1296 (H.B. 2357), § 141, effective January 1, 2012.

### Sec. 502.165. [Renumbered January 1, 2012] Fee: Road Tractor.

The fee for a registration year for registration of a road tractor is the fee prescribed by weight as certified by a public weigher or a license and weight inspector of the Department of Public Safety under Section 502.161 or 502.162, as applicable.

(Enacted by Acts 1995, 74th Leg., ch. 165 (S.B. 971), § 1, effective September 1, 1995; am. Acts 2009, 81st Leg. ch. 1136 (H.B. 2553), § 22, effective September 1, 2011.)

STATUTORY NOTES

**Editor's notes.** — This section is renumbered to Transportation Code Section 502.256 pursuant to Acts 2011, 82nd Leg., ch. 1296 (H.B. 2357), § 128, effective January 1, 2012.

### Sec. 502.166. [Renumbered January 1, 2012] Fee: Trailer, Travel Trailer, or Semitrailer.

(a) The fee for a registration year for registration of a trailer, travel trailer, or semitrailer with a gross weight of 6,000 pounds or less is $45.00.

(a-1) The fee for a registration year for registration of a trailer, travel trailer, or semitrailer with a gross weight of more than 6,000 pounds is calculated by gross weight according to Section 502.162.

(b) The gross weight of a trailer or semitrailer is the actual weight of the vehicle, as certified by a public weigher or a license and weight inspector of the Department of Public Safety, plus its net carrying capacity.

(c) The net carrying capacity of a vehicle is the heaviest net load to be carried on the vehicle, but not less than the manufacturer's rated carrying capacity.

(d) The department may issue specially designed license plates for rental trailers and travel trailers that include, as appropriate, the words "rental trailer" or "travel trailer."

(e) In this section:

(1) "Rental fleet" means five or more vehicles that are:

(A) owned by the same owner;

(B) offered for rent or rented without drivers; and

(C) designated by the owner in the manner prescribed by the department as a rental fleet.

(2) "Rental trailer" means a utility trailer that:

(A) has a gross weight of 4,000 pounds or less; and

(B) is part of a rental fleet.

(3) "Travel trailer" means a house trailer-type vehicle or a camper trailer that is:

(A) less than eight feet in width or 40 feet in length, exclusive of any hitch installed on the vehicle; and

(B) designed primarily for use as temporary living quarters in connection with recreational, camping, travel, or seasonal use and not as a permanent dwelling; provided that "travel trailer" shall not include a utility trailer, enclosed trailer, or other trailer not having human habitation as its primary purpose.

(Enacted by Acts 1995, 74th Leg., ch. 165 (S.B. 971), § 1, effective September 1, 1995; am. Acts 1997, 75th Leg., ch. 625 (S.B. 1630), § 5, effective September 1, 1997; am. Acts 2009, 81st Leg., ch. 1136 (H.B. 2553), §§ 23, 24, effective September 1, 2011.)

## STATUTORY NOTES

**Editor's notes.** — This section is renumbered to Transportation Code Section 502.254 pursuant to Acts 2011, 82nd Leg., ch. 1296 (H.B. 2357), § 126, effective January 1, 2012.

## Sec. 502.167. [Renumbered January 1, 2012] Truck-Tractor or Commercial Motor Vehicle Combination Fee; Semitrailer Token Fee.

(a) This section applies only to a truck-tractor or commercial motor vehicle with a gross weight of more than 10,000 pounds that is used or is to be used in combination with a semitrailer that has a gross weight of more than 6,000 pounds.

(b) The fee for a registration year for registration of a truck-tractor or commercial motor vehicle is calculated by gross weight according to Section 502.162.

(c) The fee for registration of a semitrailer used in the manner described by Subsection (a), regardless of the date the semitrailer is registered, is $15 for a registration year.

(d) A registration made under Subsection (c) is valid only when the semitrailer is used in the manner described by Subsection (a).

(e) For registration purposes, a semitrailer converted to a trailer by means of an auxiliary axle assembly retains its status as a semitrailer.

(f) A combination of vehicles may not be registered under this section for a combined gross weight of less than 18,000 pounds.

(g) This section does not apply to:

(1) a combination of vehicles that includes a vehicle that has a distinguishing license plate under Section 504.504;

(2) a truck-tractor or commercial motor vehicle registered or to be registered with $5 distinguishing license plates for which the vehicle is eligible under this chapter;

(3) a truck-tractor or commercial motor vehicle used exclusively in combination with a semitrailer of the housetrailer type; or

(4) a vehicle registered or to be registered:

(A) with a temporary registration permit;

(B) under Section 502.163; or

(C) under Section 502.188.

(h) The department may adopt rules to administer this section.

(i) The department may issue specially designed license plates for token trailers.

(j) A person may register a semitrailer under this section for a registration period of five consecutive years if the person:

(1) applies to the department for the five-year registration;

(2) provides proof of the person's eligibility to register the vehicle under this subsection as required by the department; and

(3) pays a fee of $15, plus any applicable fee under Section 502.172, for each year included in the registration period.

(k) If during the five-year registration period for a vehicle registered under Subsection (j) the amount of a fee imposed under that subsection is increased, the owner of the vehicle is liable to the department for the amount of the increase. If the amount of a fee is decreased, the owner of the vehicle is not entitled to a refund.

(*l*) In this section:

(1) "Combined gross weight" means the empty weight of the truck-tractor or commercial motor vehicle combined with the empty weight of the heaviest semitrailer used or to be used in combination with the truck-tractor or commercial motor vehicle plus the heaviest net load to be carried on the combination during the registration year.

(2) "Empty weight" means the unladen weight of the truck-tractor or commercial motor vehicle and semitrailer combination fully equipped, as certified by a public weigher or license and weight inspector of the Department of Public Safety.

(3) "Token trailer" means a semitrailer that:

(A) has a gross weight of more than 6,000 pounds; and

(B) is operated in combination with a truck or a truck-tractor that has been issued:

(i) an apportioned license plate;

(ii) a combination license plate; or

(iii) a forestry vehicle license plate.

(4) "Apportioned license plate" means a license plate issued in lieu of truck license plates or combination license plates to a motor carrier in this state who proportionally registers a vehicle owned by the carrier in one or more other states.

(5) "Combination license plate" means a license plate issued for a truck or truck-tractor that:

(A) has a manufacturer's rated carrying capacity of more than one ton; and

(B) is used or intended to be used in combination with a semitrailer that has a gross weight of more than 6,000 pounds.

(Enacted by Acts 1995, 74th Leg., ch. 165 (S.B. 971), § 1, effective September 1, 1995; am. Acts 1997, 75th Leg., ch. 625 (S.B. 1630), § 6, effective September 1, 1997; am. Acts 2007, 80th Leg., ch. 280 (H.B. 505), § 2, effective June 15, 2007; am. Acts 2007, 80th Leg., ch. 744 (H.B. 2992), § 1, effective September 1, 2007; am. Acts 2009, 81st Leg., ch. 1136 (H.B. 2553), § 25, effective September 1, 2011; am. Acts 2011, 82nd Leg., ch. 700 (H.B. 441), § 1, effective September 1, 2011.)

STATUTORY NOTES

**Editor's notes.** — This section is renumbered to Transportation Code Section 502.255 pursuant to Acts 2011, 82nd Leg., ch. 1296 (H.B. 2357), § 127, effective January 1, 2012.

## Sec. 502.1675. [Renumbered January 1, 2012] Texas Emissions Reduction Plan Surcharge.

(a) In addition to the registration fees charged under Section 502.167, a surcharge is imposed on the registration of a truck-tractor or commercial motor vehicle under that section in an amount equal to 10 percent of the total fees due for the registration of the truck-tractor or commercial motor vehicle under that section.

(b) The county tax assessor-collector shall remit the surcharge collected under this section to the comptroller at the time and in the manner prescribed by the comptroller for deposit in the Texas emissions reduction plan fund.

(c) This section expires August 31, 2019.

(Enacted by Acts 2001, 77th Leg., ch. 967 (S.B. 5), § 7, effective September 1, 2001; am. Acts 2005, 79th Leg., ch. 1125 (H.B. 2481), § 20, effective September 1, 2005; am. Acts 2007, 80th Leg., ch. 262 (S.B. 12), § 2.17, effective June 8, 2007; am. Acts 2009, 81st Leg., ch. 1125 (H.B. 1796), § 21, effective September 1, 2009.)

STATUTORY NOTES

**Editor's notes.** — This section is renumbered to Transportation Code Section 502.358 pursuant to Acts 2011, 82nd Leg., ch. 1296 (H.B. 2357), § 132, effective January 1, 2012.

## Sec. 502.168. Fee: Motor Bus.

The fee for a registration year for registration of a motor bus is the fee prescribed by Section 502.161 or 502.162, as applicable.

(Enacted by Acts 1995, 74th Leg., ch. 165 (S.B. 971), § 1, effective September 1, 1995; am. Acts 2009, 81st Leg. ch. 1136 (H.B. 2553), § 26, effective September 1, 2011.)

## Sec. 502.169. Fee: All-Terrain Vehicle [Repealed].

Repealed by Acts 2007, 80th Leg., ch. 1280 (H.B. 3849), § 6, effective June 15, 2007.

(Enacted by Acts 1995, 74th Leg., ch. 165 (S.B. 971), § 1, effective September 1, 1995.)

## Sec. 502.170. Additional Fee for Reflectorized License Plates [Repealed].

Repealed by Acts 2009, 81st Leg., ch. 1136 (H.B. 2553), § 39(3), effective September 1, 2011.

(Enacted by Acts 1995, 74th Leg., ch. 165 (S.B. 971), § 1, effective September 1, 1995.)

## Sec. 502.1705. [Renumbered January 1, 2012] Additional Fee for Automated Registration and Title System.

(a) In addition to other registration fees for a license plate or set of license plates or other device used as the registration insignia, a fee of $1 shall be collected.

(b) The department may use money collected under this section to provide for or enhance:

(1) automated on-premises and off-premises registration; and

(2) services related to the titling of vehicles.

(c) [Repealed by Acts 2009, 81st Leg., ch. 1136 (H.B. 2553), § 39(4), effective September 1, 2011.]

(Enacted by Acts 1999, 76th Leg., ch. 1455 (H.B. 3014), § 1, effective September 1, 1999; am. Acts 2009, 81st Leg., ch. 1136 (H.B. 2553), §§ 27, 39(4), effective September 1, 2011.)

### STATUTORY NOTES

**Editor's notes.** — This section is renumbered to Transportation Code Section 502.356 pursuant to Acts 2011, 82nd Leg., ch. 1296 (H.B. 2357), § 130, effective January 1, 2012.

## Sec. 502.171. [Renumbered January 1, 2012] Additional Fee for Certain Vehicles Using Diesel Motor.

(a) The registration fee under this chapter for a motor vehicle other than a passenger car, a truck with a manufacturer's rated carrying capacity of two tons or less, or a vehicle registered in combination under Section 502.167 is increased by 11 percent if the vehicle has a diesel motor.

(b) A county assessor-collector shall show on the registration receipt for a motor vehicle, other than a passenger car or a truck with a manufacturer's rated carrying capacity of two tons or less, that the vehicle has a diesel motor.

(c) The department may adopt rules to administer this section.

(Enacted by Acts 1995, 74th Leg., ch. 165 (S.B. 971), § 1, effective September 1, 1995.)

### STATUTORY NOTES

**Editor's notes.** — This section is renumbered to Transportation Code Section 502.359 pursuant to Acts 2011, 82nd Leg., ch. 1296 (H.B. 2357), § 133, effective January 1, 2012.

## Sec. 502.1715. [Renumbered January 1, 2012] Additional Fee for Certain Department Programs.

(a) In addition to other fees imposed for registration of a motor vehicle, at the time of application for registration or renewal of registration of a motor vehicle for which the owner is required to submit evidence of financial responsibility under Section 502.153, the applicant shall pay a fee of

$1. In addition to other fees imposed for registration of a motor vehicle, at the time of application for registration of a motor vehicle that is subject to Section 501.0234, the applicant shall pay a fee of $1.

(b) Fees collected under this section shall be deposited to the credit of the state highway fund. Subject to appropriations, the money shall be used by the Department of Public Safety to:

(1) support the Department of Public Safety's reengineering of the driver's license system to provide for the issuance by the Department of Public Safety of a driver's license or personal identification certificate, to include use of image comparison technology;

(2) establish and maintain a system to support the driver responsibility program under Chapter 708; and

(3) make lease payments to the master lease purchase program for the financing of the driver's license reengineering project.

(c) Fees collected under this section shall be deposited to the credit of the state highway fund. Subject to appropriation, the money may be used by the Department of Public Safety, the Texas Department of Insurance, the Department of Information Resources, and the department to carry out Subchapter N, Chapter 601.

(d) The Department of Public Safety, the Texas Department of Insurance, the Department of Information Resources, and the department shall jointly adopt rules and develop forms necessary to administer this section.

(Enacted by Acts 2003, 78th Leg., ch. 1325 (H.B. 3588), § 19B.03, effective September 1, 2003; am. Acts 2003, 78th Leg., 3rd C.S., ch. 8 (H.B. 2), § 5.08, effective January 11, 2004; am. Acts 2005, 79th Leg., ch. 892 (S.B. 1670), §§ 2, 3, effective September 1, 2005; am. Acts 2005, 79th Leg., ch. 1108 (H.B. 2337), §§ 1, 2, effective September 1, 2005; am. Acts 2011, 82nd Leg., ch. 91 (S.B. 1303), § 24.007, effective September 1, 2011.)

### STATUTORY NOTES

**Editor's notes.** — This section is renumbered to Transportation Code Section 502.357 pursuant to Acts 2011, 82nd Leg., ch. 1296 (H.B. 2357), § 131, effective January 1, 2012.

## Sec. 502.172. [Renumbered January 1, 2012] Optional County Fee for Road and Bridge Fund.

(a) The commissioners court of a county by order may impose an additional fee, not to exceed $10, for registering a vehicle in the county.

(b) A vehicle that may be registered under this chapter without payment of a registration fee may be registered in a county imposing a fee under this section without payment of the additional fee.

(c) A fee imposed under this section may take effect only on January 1 of a year. The county must adopt the order and notify the department not later than September 1 of the year preceding the year in which the fee takes effect.

(d) A fee imposed under this section may be removed. The removal may take effect only on January 1 of a year. A county may remove the fee only by:

(1) rescinding the order imposing the fee; and

(2) notifying the department not later than September 1 of the year preceding the year in which the removal takes effect.

(e) The county assessor-collector of a county imposing a fee under this section shall collect the additional fee for a vehicle when other fees imposed under this chapter are collected.

(f) The department shall collect the additional fee on a vehicle that is owned by a resident of a county imposing a fee under this section and that, under this chapter, must be registered directly with the department. The department shall send all fees collected for a county under this subsection to the county treasurer to be credited to the county road and bridge fund.

(g) The department shall adopt rules and develop forms necessary to administer registration by mail for a vehicle being registered in a county imposing a fee under this section.

(Enacted by Acts 1995, 74th Leg., ch. 165 (S.B. 971), § 1, effective September 1, 1995.)

### STATUTORY NOTES

**Editor's notes.** — This section is renumbered to Transportation Code Section 502.401 pursuant to Acts 2011, 82nd Leg., ch. 1296 (H.B. 2357), § 135, effective January 1, 2012.

## Sec. 502.1725. [Renumbered January 1, 2012] Optional County Fee for Transportation Projects.

(a) This section applies only to a county:

(1) that borders the United Mexican States;

(2) that has a population of more than 300,000; and

(3) in which the largest municipality has a population of less than 300,000.

(b) The commissioners court of a county by order may impose an additional fee, not to exceed $10, for registering a vehicle in the county.

(c) A vehicle that may be registered under this chapter without payment of a registration fee may be registered in a county imposing a fee under this section without payment of the additional fee.

(d) A fee imposed under this section may take effect only on January 1 of a year. The county must adopt the order and notify the department not later than September 1 of the year preceding the year in which the fee takes effect.

(e) A fee imposed under this section may be removed. The removal may take effect only on January 1 of a year. A county may remove the fee only by:

(1) rescinding the order imposing the fee; and

(2) notifying the department not later than September 1 of the year preceding the year in which the removal takes effect.

(f) The county assessor-collector of a county imposing a fee under this section shall collect the additional fee for a vehicle when other fees imposed under this chapter are collected. The county shall send the fee revenue to the regional mobility authority of the county to fund long-term transportation projects in the county.

(g) The department shall collect the additional fee on a vehicle that is owned by a resident of a county imposing a fee under this section and that, under this chapter, must be registered directly with the department. The department shall send all fees collected for a county under this subsection to the regional mobility authority of the county to fund long-term transportation projects in the county.

(h) The department shall adopt rules and develop forms necessary to administer registration by mail for a vehicle being registered in a county imposing a fee under this section.

(Enacted by Acts 2007, 80th Leg., ch. 249 (H.B. 3437), § 1, effective May 25, 2007.)

### STATUTORY NOTES

**Editor's notes.** — This section is renumbered to Transportation Code Section 502.402 pursuant to Acts 2011, 82nd Leg., ch. 1296 (H.B. 2357), § 136, effective January 1, 2012.

## Sec. 502.173. [Renumbered January 1, 2012] Optional County Fee for Child Safety.

(a) The commissioners court of a county that has a population greater than 1.3 million and in which a municipality with a population of more than one million is primarily located may impose by order an additional fee of not less than 50 cents or more than $1.50 for registering a vehicle in the county. The commissioners court of any other county may impose by order an additional fee of not more than $1.50 for registering a vehicle in the county.

(b) A vehicle that may be registered under this chapter without payment of a registration fee may be registered in a county imposing a fee under this section without payment of the additional fee.

(c) A fee imposed under this section may take effect only on January 1 of a year. The county must adopt the order and notify the department not later than September 10 of the year preceding the year in which the fee takes effect.

(d) A fee imposed under this section may be removed. The removal may take effect only on January 1 of a year. A county may remove the fee only by:

(1) rescinding the order imposing the fee; and

(2) notifying the department not later than September 1 of the year preceding the year in which the removal takes effect.

(e) The county assessor-collector of a county imposing a fee under this section shall collect the additional fee for a vehicle when other fees imposed under this chapter are collected.

(f) A county imposing a fee under this section may deduct for administrative costs an amount of not more than 10 percent of the revenue it receives from the fee. The county may also deduct from the fee revenue an amount proportional to the percentage of county residents who live in unincorporated areas of the county. After making the deductions provided for by this subsection, the county shall send the remainder of the fee revenue to the municipalities in the county according to their population.

(g) A municipality with a population greater than 850,000 shall deposit revenue from a fee imposed under this subsection to the credit of the child safety trust fund created under Section 106.001, Local Government Code. A municipality with a population less than 850,000 shall use revenue from a fee imposed under this section in accordance with Article 102.014(g), Code of Criminal Procedure.

(h) After deducting administrative costs, a county may use revenue from a fee imposed under this section only for a purpose permitted by Subsection (g), Article 102.014, Code of Criminal Procedure.

(Enacted by Acts 1995, 74th Leg., ch. 165 (S.B. 971), § 1, effective September 1, 1995; am. Acts 1997, 75th Leg., ch. 165 (S.B. 898), § 30.48, effective September 1, 1997; am. Acts 2001, 77th Leg., ch. 669 (H.B. 2810), § 141, effective September 1, 2001; am. Acts 2009, 81st Leg., ch. 162 (S.B. 446), § 2, effective May 26, 2009.)

### STATUTORY NOTES

**Editor's notes.** — This section is renumbered to Transportation Code Section 502.403 pursuant to Acts 2011, 82nd Leg., ch. 1296 (H.B. 2357), § 137, effective January 1, 2012.

### Sec. 502.174. [Renumbered January 1, 2012] Voluntary Assessment for Young Farmer Loan Guarantees.

(a) When a person registers a commercial motor vehicle under Section 502.163, the person shall pay a voluntary assessment of $5.

(b) The county assessor-collector shall send an assessment collected under this section to the comptroller, at the time and in the manner prescribed by the Texas Agricultural Finance Authority, for deposit in the Texas agricultural fund.

(c) The Texas Agricultural Finance Authority shall prescribe procedures under which an assessment collected under this section may be refunded. The county assessor-collector of the county in which an assessment is collected shall:

(1) implement the refund procedures; and

(2) provide notice of those procedures to a person paying an assessment at the time of payment.

(Enacted by Acts 1995, 74th Leg., ch. 165 (S.B. 971), § 1, effective September 1, 1995; am. Acts 1997, 75th Leg., ch. 1423 (H.B. 2841), § 18.04, effective September 1, 1997; am. Acts 1999, 76th Leg., ch. 1459 (H.B. 3050), § 15, effective June 19, 1999; am. Acts 2009, 81st Leg., ch. 506 (S.B. 1016), § 1.20, effective September 1, 2009.)

### STATUTORY NOTES

**Editor's notes.** — This section is renumbered to Transportation Code Section 502.404 pursuant to Acts 2011, 82nd Leg., ch. 1296 (H.B. 2357), § 138, effective January 1, 2012.

### Sec. 502.1745. [Renumbered January 1, 2012] Voluntary Fee.

(a) The department shall provide to each county assessor-collector the educational materials for prospective donors provided as required by the Donor Education, Awareness, and Registry Program of Texas under Chapter 49, Health and Safety Code. A county assessor-collector shall make the educational materials available in each office authorized to accept applications for registration of motor vehicles.

(b) **[2 Versions: Effective until January 1, 2012]** A county assessor-collector shall collect an additional fee of $1 for the registration or renewal of registration of a motor vehicle to pay the costs of the Donor Education, Awareness, and Registry Program of Texas, established under Chapter 49, Health and Safety Code, and of the Texas Organ, Tissue, and Eye Donor Council, established under Chapter 113, Health and Safety Code, if the person registering or renewing the registration of a motor vehicle opts to pay the additional fee. Notwithstanding any other provision of this chapter, the county assessor-collector shall remit all fees collected under this subsection to the comptroller, who shall maintain the identity of the source of the fees.

(b) **[2 Versions: Effective January 1, 2012]** A county assessor-collector shall collect an additional fee of $1 for the registration or renewal of registration of a motor vehicle to pay the costs of the Glenda Dawson Donate Life-Texas Registry established under Chapter 692A, Health and Safety Code, if the person registering or renewing the registration of a motor vehicle opts to pay the additional fee. Notwithstanding any other provision of this chapter, the county assessor-collector shall remit all fees collected under this subsection to the comptroller, who shall maintain the identity of the source of the fees.

(c) Three percent of all money collected under this section may be appropriated only to the department to administer this section.

(Enacted by Acts 2005, 79th Leg., ch. 1186 (H.B. 120), § 8, effective September 1, 2005; am. Acts 2011, 82nd Leg., ch. 554 (H.B. 2904), § 2, effective January 1, 2012.)

### STATUTORY NOTES

**Editor's notes.** — This section is renumbered to Transportation Code Section 502.405 pursuant to Acts 2011, 82nd Leg., ch. 1296 (H.B. 2357), § 139, effective January 1, 2012.

## Sec. 502.1746. Voluntary Contribution to Veterans' Assistance Fund.

(a) When a person registers a motor vehicle under this chapter, the person is entitled to make a voluntary contribution in any amount to the fund for veterans' assistance established by Section 434.017, Government Code, as redesignated and amended by Chapter 1418 (H.B. 3107), Acts of the 80th Legislature, Regular Session, 2007.

(b) The county assessor-collector shall send any contribution made under this section to the comptroller for deposit in the state treasury to the credit of the fund for veterans' assistance before the 31st day after the date the contribution is made. A contribution made under this section may be used only for the purposes of the fund for veterans' assistance.

(c) The department shall:

(1) include space on each motor vehicle registration renewal notice, on the page that states the total fee for registration renewal, that allows a person renewing a registration to indicate the amount that the person is voluntarily contributing to the fund for veterans' assistance;

(2) provide an opportunity to contribute to the fund for veterans' assistance similar to the opportunity described by Subsection (a) and in the manner described by Subdivision (1) in any registration renewal system that succeeds the system in place on September 1, 2011; and

(3) provide an opportunity for a person to contribute to the fund for veterans' assistance during the registration renewal process on the department's Internet website.

(d) If a person makes a contribution under this section and does not pay the full amount of a registration fee, the county assessor-collector may credit all or a portion of the contribution to the person's registration fee.

(e) The department shall consult with the Texas Veterans Commission in performing the department's duties under this section.

(Enacted by Acts 2009, 81st Leg., ch. 840 (S.B. 1940), § 3, effective June 19, 2009; am. Acts 2011, 82nd Leg., ch. 669 (S.B. 1635), § 2, effective June 17, 2011.)

## Sec. 502.1747. Voluntary Contribution to Parks and Wildlife Department.

(a) When a person registers or renews the registration of a motor vehicle under this chapter, the person may contribute $5 or more to the Parks and Wildlife Department.

(b) The department shall:

(1) include space on each motor vehicle registration renewal notice, on the page that states the total fee for registration renewal, that allows a person renewing a registration to indicate the amount that the person is voluntarily contributing to the state parks account;

(2) provide an opportunity to contribute to the state parks account similar to the opportu-

nity described by Subsection (a) and in the manner described by Subdivision (1) in any registration renewal system that succeeds the system in place on September 1, 2011; and

(3) provide an opportunity for a person to contribute to the state parks account during the registration renewal process on the department's Internet website.

(c) If a person makes a contribution under this section and does not pay the full amount of a registration fee, the county assessor-collector may credit all or a portion of the contribution to the person's registration fee.

(d) The county assessor-collector shall send any contribution made under this section to the comptroller for deposit to the credit of the state parks account under Section 11.035, Parks and Wildlife Code. Money received by the Parks and Wildlife Department under this section may be used only for the operation and maintenance of state parks, historic sites, or natural areas under the jurisdiction of the Parks and Wildlife Department.

(e) The department shall consult with the Parks and Wildlife Department in performing the department's duties under this section.
(Enacted by Acts 2011, 82nd Leg., ch. 749 (H.B. 1301), § 1, effective June 17, 2011.)

## Sec. 502.1748.   Disposition of Certain Voluntary Contributions.

If a person makes a voluntary contribution under Section 502.1746 or 502.1747 at the time the person registers or renews the registration of a motor vehicle under this chapter but the person does not clearly specify the entity to which the person intends to contribute, the county assessor-collector shall divide the contribution between the entities authorized to receive contributions under those sections.
(Enacted by Acts 2011, 82nd Leg., ch. 749 (H.B. 1301), § 1, effective June 17, 2011.)

## Sec. 502.175.   [Repealed January 1, 2012] Transfer Fee.

(a) A person other than a dealer who sells a vehicle subject to registration under this chapter shall indorse on the certificate of registration a written transfer of the vehicle.

(b) The purchaser of a motor vehicle to which Subsection (a) applies shall:

(1) pay a transfer fee of $1 to the county assessor-collector of the county in which the person resides; and

(2) provide the person's full name and address to the assessor-collector.

(c) On compliance with Subsection (b), a person is considered to be the owner of the vehicle and is subject to this chapter.
(Enacted by Acts 1995, 74th Leg., ch. 165 (S.B. 971), § 1, effective September 1, 1995.)

## Sec. 502.176.   [Renumbered January 1, 2012] Delinquent Registration.

(a) A registration fee prescribed by this chapter for a vehicle becomes delinquent immediately if the vehicle is used on a public highway without the fee having been paid in accordance with this chapter.

(b) A county assessor-collector that determines that an applicant for registration for which payment of the registration fee is delinquent has provided evidence acceptable to the assessor-collector sufficient to establish good reason for delinquent registration and that the application complies with the other requirements for registration under this chapter shall register the vehicle for a 12-month period that ends on the last day of the 11th month after the month in which the registration occurs under this subsection. The registration period for vehicles registered in accordance with Sections 502.164, 502.167, 502.203, 502.255, 502.267, 502.277, 502.278, 502.293, as added by Chapter 1222, Acts of the 75th Legislature, Regular Session, 1997, and 502.295, as added by Chapter 625, Acts of the 75th Legislature, Regular Session, 1997, will end on the annual registration date, and the registration fees will be prorated.

(c) A county assessor-collector that determines that an applicant for registration that is delinquent has not provided evidence acceptable to the assessor-collector sufficient to establish good reason for delinquent registration but that the application complies with the other requirements for registration under this chapter shall register the vehicle for a 12-month period without changing the initial month of registration.

(d) A person who has been arrested or received a citation for a violation of Section 502.402 may register the vehicle being operated at the time of the offense with the county assessor-collector for a 12-month period without change to the initial month of registration only if the person:

(1) meets the other requirements for registration under this chapter; and

(2) pays an additional charge equal to 20 percent of the prescribed fee.

(e) The county assessor-collector shall adopt a list of evidentiary items sufficient to establish good reason for delinquent registration under Subsection (b) and provide for the forms of evidence that may be used to establish good reason under that subsection. The list of evidentiary items adopted under this section must allow for delinquent registration under Subsection (b) because of:

(1) extensive repairs on the vehicle;

(2) the absence of the owner of the vehicle from this country;

(3) seasonal use of the vehicle; or

(4) any other reason determined by the assessor-collector to be a valid explanation for the delinquent registration.

(f) The department by rule shall adopt procedures to implement this section in connection with the delinquent registration of a vehicle registered directly with the department.

(Enacted by Acts 1995, 74th Leg., ch. 165 (S.B. 971), § 1, effective September 1, 1995; am. Acts 1999, 76th Leg., ch. 641 (H.B. 89), § 1, effective September 1, 1999.)

STATUTORY NOTES

**Editor's notes.** — This section is renumbered to Transportation Code Section 502.045 pursuant to Acts 2011, 82nd Leg., ch. 1296 (H.B. 2357), § 83, effective January 1, 2012.

## Sec. 502.177. [Repealed January 1, 2012] Minimum Registration Fee.

Notwithstanding any other provision of this chapter and without regard to the month in which the application for registration is filed, the minimum registration fee for any vehicle may not be less than $5.

(Enacted by Acts 1995, 74th Leg., ch. 165 (S.B. 971), § 1, effective September 1, 1995.)

## Sec. 502.178. [Renumbered January 1, 2012] Registration Receipt.

(a) The department shall issue or require to be issued to the owner of a vehicle registered under this chapter a registration receipt showing:

(1) the date of issuance;

(2) the license number assigned to the vehicle;

(3) the name and address of the owner; and

(4) other information as determined by the department.

(b) The registration receipt issued for a commercial motor vehicle, truck-tractor, trailer, or semitrailer must show the gross weight for which the vehicle is registered.

(Enacted by Acts 1995, 74th Leg., ch. 165 (S.B. 971), § 1, effective September 1, 1995.)

STATUTORY NOTES

**Editor's notes.** — This section is renumbered to Transportation Code Section 502.057 pursuant to Acts 2011, 82nd Leg., ch. 1296 (H.B. 2357), § 88, effective January 1, 2012.

## Sec. 502.179. [Renumbered January 1, 2012] Duplicate Registration Receipt.

(a) The owner of a vehicle for which the registration receipt has been lost or destroyed may obtain a duplicate receipt from the department or the county assessor-collector who issued the original receipt by paying a fee of $2.

(b) The office issuing a duplicate receipt shall retain the fee received as a fee of office.

(Enacted by Acts 1995, 74th Leg., ch. 165 (S.B. 971), § 1, effective September 1, 1995.)

STATUTORY NOTES

**Editor's notes.** — This section is renumbered to Transportation Code Section 502.058 pursuant to Acts 2011, 82nd Leg., ch. 1296 (H.B. 2357), § 89, effective January 1, 2012.

## Sec. 502.180. [Renumbered January 1, 2012] Issuance of License Plate or Registration Insignia.

(a) On payment of the prescribed fee, the department shall issue to an applicant for motor vehicle registration a license plate or set of plates or a device that, when attached to the vehicle as prescribed by the department, is the registration insignia for the period for which it was issued.

(b) Subject to Subchapter I, the department shall issue only one license plate or set of plates for a vehicle during a five-year period.

(c) On application and payment of the prescribed fee for a renewal of the registration of a vehicle for the first, second, third, or fourth registration year after the issuance of a license plate or set of plates for the vehicle, the department shall issue a registration insignia for the validation of the license plate or plates to be attached as provided by Subsection (d).

(d) Except as provided by Subsection (h), the registration insignia for validation of a license plate shall be attached to the inside of the vehicle's windshield, if the vehicle has a windshield, within six inches of the place where the motor vehicle inspection sticker is required to be placed. If the vehicle does not have a windshield, the owner, when applying for registration or renewal of registration, shall notify the department, and the department shall issue a distinctive device for attachment to the rear license plate of the vehicle.

(e) The department shall adopt rules for the issuance and use of license plates and registration insignia issued under this chapter. The rules may provide for the use of an automated registration process, including:

(1) the automated on-site production of registration insignia; and

(2) automated on-premises and off-premises self-service registration.

(f) Subsections (b)—(d) do not apply to:

(1) the issuance of specialized license plates as designated by the department, including state official license plates, exempt plates for governmental entities, and temporary registration plates; or

(2) the issuance or validation of replacement license plates, except as provided by Section 502.184.

(g) The department shall provide a separate and distinctive tab to be affixed to the license plate of an automobile, pickup, or recreational vehicle that is offered for rent, as a business, to any part of the public.

(h) The registration insignia for validation of a license plate shall be attached to the rear license plate of the vehicle, if the vehicle is:

(1) a motorcycle;

(2) machinery used exclusively to drill water wells or construction machinery for which a distinguishing license plate has been issued under Section 504.504; or

(3) oil well servicing, oil clean out, or oil well drilling machinery or equipment for which a distinguishing license plate has been issued under Subchapter G, Chapter 623.

(Enacted by Acts 1995, 74th Leg., ch. 165 (S.B. 971), § 1, effective September 1, 1995; am. Acts 1997, 75th Leg., ch. 165 (S.B. 898), § 30.49(a), effective September 1, 1997; am. Acts 1999, 76th Leg., ch. 1455 (H.B. 3014), § 2, effective September 1, 1999; am. Acts 2007, 80th Leg., ch. 101 (H.B. 310), § 1, effective January 1, 2008; am. Acts 2007, 80th Leg., ch. 280 (H.B. 505), § 3, effective June 15, 2007.)

### STATUTORY NOTES

**Editor's notes.** — This section is renumbered to Transportation Code Section 502.059 pursuant to Acts 2011, 82nd Leg., ch. 1296 (H.B. 2357), § 90, effective January 1, 2012.

## Sec. 502.181.  [Renumbered January 1, 2012] Payment of Registration Fee by Check Drawn Against Insufficient Funds.

(a) A county assessor-collector who receives from any person a check or draft drawn on a bank or trust company in payment of a registration fee for a registration year that has not ended on a motor vehicle, trailer, or motorcycle sidecar that is returned unpaid because of insufficient funds or no funds in the bank or trust company to the credit of the drawer of the check or draft shall certify the fact to the sheriff or a constable or highway patrol officer in the county after attempts to contact the person fail to result in the collection of payment. The certification must be made before the 30th day after the date the check or draft is returned unpaid and:

(1) be under the assessor-collector's official seal;

(2) include the name and address of the person who gave the assessor-collector the check or draft;

(3) include the license plate number and make of the vehicle;

(4) be accompanied by the check or draft; and

(5) be accompanied by documentation of any attempt to contact the person and collect payment.

(b) On receiving a complaint under Subsection (a) from the county assessor-collector, the sheriff, constable, or highway patrol officer shall find the person who gave the assessor-collector the check or draft, if the person is in the county, and demand immediate redemption of the check or draft from the person. If the person fails or refuses to redeem the check or draft, the sheriff, constable, or highway patrol officer shall:

(1) seize and remove the license plates from the vehicle; and

(2) return the license plates to the county assessor-collector.

(Enacted by Acts 1995, 74th Leg., ch. 165 (S.B. 971), § 1, effective September 1, 1995; am. Acts 2009, 81st Leg., ch. 434 (H.B. 2186), § 1, effective September 1, 2009.)

### STATUTORY NOTES

**Editor's notes.** — This section is renumbered to Transportation Code Section 502.193 pursuant to Acts 2011, 82nd Leg., ch. 1296 (H.B. 2357), § 110, effective January 1, 2012.

## Sec. 502.182. [Renumbered January 1, 2012] Credit for Registration Fee Paid on Motor Vehicle Subsequently Destroyed.

(a) The owner of a motor vehicle that is destroyed to the extent that it cannot afterwards be operated on a public highway is entitled to a registration fee credit if the prorated portion of the registration fee for the remainder of the registration year is more than $15. The owner must claim the credit by:

(1) sending the registration fee receipt and the license plates for the vehicle to the department; and

(2) executing a statement on a form provided by the department showing that the license plates have been surrendered to the department.

(b) The department, on satisfactory proof that the vehicle is destroyed, shall issue a registration fee credit slip to the owner in an amount equal to the prorated portion of the registration fee for the remainder of the registration year. The owner, during the same or the next registration year, may use the registration fee credit slip as payment or part payment for the registration of another vehicle to the extent of the credit.

(c) A statement executed under Subsection (a)(2) shall be delivered to a purchaser of the destroyed vehicle. The purchaser may surrender the statement to the department in lieu of the vehicle license plates.

(d) The department shall adopt rules to administer this section.

(Enacted by Acts 1995, 74th Leg., ch. 165 (S.B. 971), § 1, effective September 1, 1995.)

STATUTORY NOTES

**Editor's notes.** — This section is renumbered to Transportation Code Section 502.194 pursuant to Acts 2011, 82nd Leg., ch. 1296 (H.B. 2357), § 111, effective January 1, 2012.

## Sec. 502.183. [Renumbered January 1, 2012] Refund of Overcharged Registration Fee.

(a) The owner of a motor vehicle that is required to be registered who pays an annual registration fee in excess of the statutory amount is entitled to a refund of the overcharge.

(b) The county assessor-collector who collects the excessive fee shall refund an overcharge on presentation to the assessor-collector of satisfactory evidence of the overcharge. The owner must make a claim for a refund of an overcharge not later than the fifth anniversary of the date the excessive registration fee was paid.

(c) A refund shall be paid from the fund in which the county's share of registration fees is deposited.

(Enacted by Acts 1995, 74th Leg., ch. 165 (S.B. 971), § 1, effective September 1, 1995.)

STATUTORY NOTES

**Editor's notes.** — This section is renumbered to Transportation Code Section 502.195 pursuant to Acts 2011, 82nd Leg., ch. 1296 (H.B. 2357), § 112, effective January 1, 2012.

## Sec. 502.184. [Renumbered January 1, 2012] Replacement of Registration Insignia.

(a) The owner of a registered motor vehicle may obtain a replacement registration insignia by:

(1) certifying that the replacement registration insignia will not be used on any other vehicle owned or operated by the person making the statement;

(2) paying a fee of $6 plus the fees required by Section 502.1705(a) for each replacement registration insignia, except as provided by other law; and

(3) returning each replaced registration insignia in the owner's possession.

(b) No fee is required under this section if the replacement fee for a license plate has been paid under Section 502.1841.

(c) The fee for replacement of license plates issued under Section 504.507 is the amount prescribed by the department as necessary to recover the cost of providing the replacement plates.

(d) If license plates approved under Section 504.501(b) or 504.502(c) are lost, stolen, or mutilated, the owner of the vehicle may obtain approval of another set of license plates as provided by Section 504.501 or 504.502, respectively. The fee for approval of replacement license plates is $5.

(e) A county assessor-collector may not issue a replacement registration insignia without complying with this section.

(f) A county assessor-collector shall retain $2.50 of each fee collected under this section and shall report and send the remainder to the department.

(g) Replacement license plates may be used in the registration year in which the plates are issued and during each succeeding year of the five-year period as prescribed by Section

*Transportation*

502.180(b) if the registration insignia is properly attached.

(h) Subsection (g) does not apply to the issuance of specialized license plates as designated by the department, including state official license plates, exempt plates for governmental entities, and temporary registration plates.

(i) The owner of a vehicle listed in Section 502.180(h) may obtain replacement plates and a replacement registration insignia by paying a fee of $5 plus the fees required by Sections 502.170(a) and 502.1705(a).

(Enacted by Acts 1995, 74th Leg., ch. 165 (S.B. 971), § 1, effective September 1, 1995; am. Acts 1997, 75th Leg., ch. 165 (S.B. 898), § 30.49(b), (c), effective September 1, 1997; am. Acts 1999, 76th Leg., ch. 1455 (H.B. 3014), § 3, effective September 1, 1999; am. Acts 2005, 79th Leg., ch. 728 (H.B. 2018), § 20.003(a), effective September 1, 2005; am. Acts 2007, 80th Leg., ch. 1166 (H.B. 191), § 1, effective September 1, 2007; am. Acts 2009, 81st Leg. ch. 1136 (H.B. 2553), §§ 28, 29, effective September 1, 2011.)

STATUTORY NOTES

**Editor's notes.** — This section is renumbered to Transportation Code Section 502.060 pursuant to Acts 2011, 82nd Leg., ch. 1296 (H.B. 2357), § 91, effective January 1, 2012.

## Sec. 502.1841. [Renumbered January 1, 2012] Replacement License Plates.

(a) The owner of a registered motor vehicle may obtain replacement license plates for the vehicle by:

(1) certifying that the replacement plates will not be used on any other vehicle owned or operated by the person making the statement;

(2) paying a fee of $6 plus the fee required by Section 502.1705(a) for each set of replacement license plates, unless otherwise specified by law; and

(3) returning to the department each license plate in the owner's possession for which a replacement license plate is obtained.

(b) Replacement license plates may not be issued except as provided by this section.

(c) A county assessor-collector shall retain $2.50 of each fee collected under this section and forward the remainder of the fee to the department.

(d) The fee required by this section applies to the issuance of license plates for a transferred used vehicle for which the registration and license plates were not transferred under Subchapter I.

(Enacted by Acts 2009, 81st Leg., ch. 1136 (H.B. 2553), § 30, effective September 1, 2011.)

STATUTORY NOTES

**Editor's notes.** — This section is renumbered to Transportation Code Section 504.007 pursuant to Acts 2011, 82nd Leg., ch. 1296 (H.B. 2357), § 172, effective January 1, 2012.

## Sec. 502.185. [Renumbered January 1, 2012] Refusal to Register Vehicle in Certain Counties.

(a) A county assessor-collector or the department may refuse to register a motor vehicle if the assessor-collector or the department receives information that the owner of the vehicle:

(1) owes the county money for a fine, fee, or tax that is past due; or

(2) failed to appear in connection with a complaint, citation, information, or indictment in a court in the county in which a criminal proceeding is pending against the owner.

(b) A county may contract with the department to provide information to the department necessary to make a determination under Subsection (a).

(c) A county that has a contract under Subsection (b) shall notify the department regarding a person for whom the county assessor-collector or the department has refused to register a motor vehicle on:

(1) the person's payment or other means of discharge of the past due fine, fee, or tax; or

(2) perfection of an appeal of the case contesting payment of the fine, fee, or tax.

(d) After notice is received under Subsection (c), the county assessor-collector or the department may not refuse to register the motor vehicle under Subsection (a).

(e) A contract under Subsection (b) must be entered into in accordance with Chapter 791, Government Code, and is subject to the ability of the parties to provide or pay for the services required under the contract.

(f) A county that has a contract under Subsection (b) may impose an additional fee of $20 to:

(1) a person who fails to pay a fine, fee, or tax to the county by the date on which the fine, fee, or tax is due; or

(2) a person who fails to appear in connection with a complaint, citation, information, or indictment in a court in which a criminal proceeding is pending against the owner.

(f-1) The additional fee may be used only to reimburse the department or the county assessor-collector for its expenses for providing services under the contract, or another county department for expenses related to services under the contract.

(g) In this section:

(1) a fine, fee, or tax is considered past due if it is unpaid 90 or more days after the date it is due; and

(2) registration of a motor vehicle includes renewal of the registration of the vehicle.

(h) This section does not apply to the registration of a motor vehicle under Section 501.0234.
(Enacted by Acts 1997, 75th Leg., ch. 192 (H.B. 1532), § 1, effective September 1, 1997; am. Acts 1999, 76th Leg., ch. 97 (S.B. 401), § 1, effective May 17, 1999; am. Acts 2011, 82nd Leg., ch. 1094 (S.B. 1386), § 1, effective September 1, 2011.)

STATUTORY NOTES

**Editor's notes.** — This section is renumbered to Transportation Code Section 502.010 pursuant to Acts 2011, 82nd Leg., ch. 1296 (H.B. 2357), § 76, effective January 1, 2012.

## Sec. 502.186. "Low-Emissions Vehicle" Insignia for Certain Motor Vehicles [Expired].

Expired pursuant to Acts 2001, 77th Leg., ch. 967 (S.B. 5), § 8, effective August 31, 2008.
(Enacted by Acts 2001, 77th Leg., ch. 967 (S.B. 5), § 8, effective September 1, 2001.)

## Sec. 502.187. [Repealed September 1, 2011] Parade Vehicles Owned by Nonprofit Service Organizations.

(a) A motor vehicle owned and operated by a nonprofit service organization and designed, constructed, and used primarily for parade purposes is subject to registration as provided by this chapter but is exempt from the fee otherwise prescribed by this chapter.

(b) Subsection (a) does not apply to a vehicle for which a registration fee has been paid under other law.
(Enacted by Acts 2003, 78th Leg., ch. 1320 (H.B. 2971), § 2, effective September 1, 2003.)

## Sec. 502.188. [Renumbered January 1, 2012] Certain Soil Conservation Equipment.

(a) The owner of a truck-tractor, semitrailer, or low-boy trailer used on a highway exclusively to transport the owner's soil conservation machinery or equipment used in clearing real property, terracing, or building farm ponds, levees, or

ditches may register the vehicle for a fee equal to 50 percent of the fee otherwise prescribed by this chapter for the vehicle.

(b) An owner may register only one truck-tractor and only one semitrailer or low-boy trailer under this section.

(c) An owner applying for registration under this section must submit a statement that the vehicle is to be used only as provided by Subsection (a).

(d) The registration receipt issued for a vehicle registered under this section shall state the nature of the operation for which the vehicle may be used. The receipt must be carried at all times in or on the vehicle to permit ready inspection.

(e) A vehicle to which this section applies that is operated on a public highway in violation of this section is considered to be operated while unregistered and is immediately subject to the applicable registration fees and penalties prescribed by this chapter.
(Enacted by Acts 2003, 78th Leg., ch. 1320 (H.B. 2971), § 2, effective September 1, 2003.)

STATUTORY NOTES

**Editor's notes.** — This section is renumbered to Transportation Code Section 502.435 pursuant to Acts 2011, 82nd Leg., ch. 1296 (H.B. 2357), § 145, effective January 1, 2012.

## Sec. 502.189. Donor Registry Information.

(a) **[2 Versions: Effective until January 1, 2012]** The department, with expert input and support from the Texas Organ, Tissue, and Eye Donor Council, shall:

(1) add a link from the department's Internet website to the Donor Education, Awareness, and Registry Program of Texas established under Chapter 49, Health and Safety Code; and

(2) provide a method to distribute donor registry information to interested individuals in each office authorized to issue motor vehicle registrations.

(a) **[2 Versions: Effective January 1, 2012]** The department, with expert input and support from the nonprofit organization administering the Glenda Dawson Donate Life-Texas Registry under Chapter 692A, Health and Safety Code, shall:

(1) add a link from the department's Internet website to the Glenda Dawson Donate Life-Texas Registry operated under Chapter 692A, Health and Safety Code; and

**Transportation**

(2) provide a method to distribute donor registry information to interested individuals in each office authorized to issue motor vehicle registrations.

(b) The department shall make available for distribution to each office authorized to issue motor vehicle registrations Donate Life brochures that provide basic donor information in English and Spanish and a contact phone number and e-mail address. The department shall ensure that the question provided in Section 521.401(c)(1)(B) and information on the donor registry Internet website is included with registration renewal notices.

(Enacted by Acts 2009, 81st Leg., ch. 831 (S.B. 1803), § 3, effective September 1, 2009; am. Acts 2011, 82nd Leg., ch. 554 (H.B. 2904), § 3, effective January 1, 2012.)

## SUBCHAPTER E
## [EFFECTIVE UNTIL JANUARY 1, 2012] SPECIALLY DESIGNATED LICENSE PLATES; EXEMPTIONS FOR GOVERNMENTAL AND QUASI-GOVERNMENTAL VEHICLES; [EFFECTIVE JANUARY 1, 2012] ADMINISTRATION OF FEES

### Sec. 502.190. [Effective January 1, 2012] Schedule of Registration Fees.

The department shall post a complete schedule of registration fees on the Internet.

(Enacted by Acts 1995, 74th Leg., ch. 165 (S.B. 971), § 1, effective September 1, 1995; am. Acts 2011, 82nd Leg., ch. 1296 (H.B. 2357), § 107, effective January 1, 2012 (renumbered from Sec. 502.159).)

### Sec. 502.191. [Effective January 1, 2012] Collection of Fees.

(a) A person may not collect a registration fee under this chapter unless the person is:

(1) an officer or employee of the department; or

(2) a county assessor-collector or a deputy county assessor-collector.

(b) The department may accept electronic payment by electronic funds transfer, credit card, or debit card of any fee that the department is authorized to collect under this chapter.

(c) The department may collect a fee for processing a payment by electronic funds transfer, credit card, or debit card in an amount not to exceed the amount of the charges incurred by the department to process the payment.

(d) The department may collect the fee set under Section 2054.2591, Government Code, from a person making a payment by electronic funds transfer, credit card, or debit card through the online project implemented under Section 2054.252, Government Code.

(e) If, for any reason, the payment of a fee under this chapter by electronic funds transfer, credit card, or debit card is not honored by the funding institution or by the electronic funds transfer, credit card, or debit card company on which the funds are drawn, the department may collect from the person who owes the fee being collected a service charge that is for the collection of that original amount and is in addition to the original fee. The amount of the service charge must be reasonably related to the expense incurred by the department in collecting the original amount.

(Enacted by Acts 1995, 74th Leg., ch. 165 (S.B. 971), § 1, effective September 1, 1995; am. Acts 2011, 82nd Leg., ch. 1296 (H.B. 2357), § 108, effective January 1, 2012 (renumbered from Sec. 502.004).)

### Sec. 502.192. [Effective January 1, 2012] Transfer Fee.

The purchaser of a used motor vehicle shall pay, in addition to any fee required under Chapter 501 for the transfer of title, a transfer fee of $2.50 for the transfer of the registration of the motor vehicle. The county assessor-collector may retain as commission for services provided under this subchapter half of each transfer fee collected.

(Enacted by Acts 2011, 82nd Leg., ch. 1296 (H.B. 2357), § 109, effective January 1, 2012.)

### Sec. 502.193. [Effective January 1, 2012] Payment by Check Drawn Against Insufficient Funds.

(a) A county assessor-collector who receives from any person a check or draft for payment of a registration fee for a registration year that has not ended that is returned unpaid because of insufficient funds or no funds in the bank or trust company to the credit of the drawer of the check or draft shall certify the fact to the sheriff or a constable or highway patrol officer in the county after attempts to contact the person fail to result in the collection of payment. The certification must be made before the 30th day after the date the check or draft is returned unpaid and:

(1) be under the assessor-collector's official seal;

(2) include the name and address of the person who gave the check or draft;

(3) include the license plate number and make of the vehicle;

(4) be accompanied by the check or draft; and

(5) be accompanied by documentation of any attempt to contact the person and collect payment.

(b) On receiving a complaint under Subsection (a) from the county assessor-collector, the sheriff, constable, or highway patrol officer shall find the person who gave the check or draft, if the person is in the county, and demand immediate redemption of the check or draft from the person. If the person fails or refuses to redeem the check or draft, the sheriff, constable, or highway patrol officer shall:

(1) seize and remove the license plates and registration insignia from the vehicle; and

(2) return the license plates and registration insignia to the county assessor-collector.

(Enacted by Acts 1995, 74th Leg., ch. 165 (S.B. 971), § 1, effective September 1, 1995; am. Acts 2009, 81st Leg., ch. 434 (H.B. 2186), § 1, effective September 1, 2009; am. Acts 2011, 82nd Leg., ch. 1296 (H.B. 2357), § 110, effective January 1, 2012 (renumbered from Sec. 502.181).)

### Sec. 502.194. [Effective January 1, 2012] Credit for Registration Fee Paid on Motor Vehicle Subsequently Destroyed.

(a) The owner of a motor vehicle that is destroyed to the extent that it cannot afterwards be operated on a public highway is entitled to a registration fee credit if the prorated portion of the registration fee for the remainder of the registration year is more than $15. The owner must claim the credit by sending the registration fee receipt for the vehicle to the department.

(b) The department, on satisfactory proof that the vehicle is destroyed, shall issue a registration fee credit slip to the owner in an amount equal to the prorated portion of the registration fee for the remainder of the registration year. The owner, during the same or the next registration year, may use the registration fee credit slip as payment or part payment for the registration of another vehicle to the extent of the credit.

(Enacted by Acts 1995, 74th Leg., ch. 165 (S.B. 971), § 1, effective September 1, 1995; am. Acts

2011, 82nd Leg., ch. 1296 (H.B. 2357), § 111, effective January 1, 2012 (renumbered from Sec. 502.182).)

### Sec. 502.195. [Effective January 1, 2012] Refund of Overcharged Registration Fee.

(a) The owner of a motor vehicle who pays an annual registration fee in excess of the statutory amount is entitled to a refund of the overcharge.

(b) The county assessor-collector who collects the excessive fee shall refund an overcharge on presentation to the assessor-collector of satisfactory evidence of the overcharge not later than the first anniversary of the date the excessive registration fee was paid.

(c) A refund shall be paid from the fund in which the county's share of registration fees is deposited.

(Enacted by Acts 1995, 74th Leg., ch. 165 (S.B. 971), § 1, effective September 1, 1995; am. Acts 2011, 82nd Leg., ch. 1296 (H.B. 2357), § 112, effective January 1, 2012 (renumbered from Sec. 502.183).)

### Sec. 502.196. [Effective January 1, 2012] Deposit of Registration Fees in State Highway Fund.

Except as otherwise provided by this chapter, the board and the department shall deposit all money received from registration fees in the state treasury to the credit of the state highway fund.

(Enacted by Acts 1995, 74th Leg., ch. 165 (S.B. 971), § 1, effective September 1, 1995; am. Acts 2009, 81st Leg., ch. 933 (H.B. 3097), § 2E.02, effective September 1, 2009; am. Acts 2011, 82nd Leg., ch. 1296 (H.B. 2357), § 113, effective January 1, 2012 (renumbered from Sec. 502.051).)

### Sec. 502.197. [Effective January 1, 2012] Registration by Mail or Electronic Means; Service Charge.

(a) A county assessor-collector may collect a service charge of $1 from each applicant registering a vehicle by mail. The service charge shall be used to pay the costs of handling and postage to mail the registration receipt and insignia to the applicant.

(b) With the approval of the commissioners court of a county, a county assessor-collector may contract with a private entity to enable an applicant for registration to use an electronic off-premises location. A private entity may charge an applicant not more than $1 for the service provided.

Transportation

(c) The department may adopt rules to cover the timely application for and issuance of registration receipts and insignia by mail or through an electronic off-premises location.

(Enacted by Acts 1995, 74th Leg., ch. 165 (S.B. 971), § 1, effective September 1, 1995; am. Acts 2011, 82nd Leg., ch. 1296 (H.B. 2357), § 114, effective January 1, 2012 (renumbered from Sec. 502.101).)

## Sec. 502.198. [Effective January 1, 2012] Disposition of Fees Generally.

(a) Except as provided by Sections 502.1982 and 502.357, this section applies to all fees collected by a county assessor-collector under this chapter.

(b) Each Monday, a county assessor-collector shall credit to the county road and bridge fund an amount equal to the net collections made during the preceding week until the amount so credited for the calendar year equals the total of:

(1) $60,000;

(2) $350 for each mile of county road maintained by the county, according to the most recent information available from the department, not to exceed 500 miles; and

(3) an additional amount of fees equal to the amount calculated under Section 502.1981.

(c) After the credits to the county road and bridge fund equal the total computed under Subsection (b), each Monday the county assessor-collector shall:

(1) credit to the county road and bridge fund an amount equal to 50 percent of the net collections made during the preceding week, until the amount so credited for the calendar year equals $125,000; and

(2) send to the department an amount equal to 50 percent of those collections.

(d) After the credits to the county road and bridge fund equal the total amounts computed under Subsections (b) and (c)(1), each Monday the county assessor-collector shall send to the department all collections made during the preceding week.

(Enacted by Acts 1995, 74th Leg., ch. 165 (S.B. 971), § 1, effective September 1, 1995; am. Acts 2003, 78th Leg., ch. 1325 (H.B. 3588), § 9.02, effective September 1, 2005; am. Acts 2011, 82nd Leg., ch. 1296 (H.B. 2357), § 115, effective January 1, 2012 (renumbered from Sec. 502.102).)

## Sec. 502.1981. [Effective January 1, 2012] Calculation of Additional Fee Amounts Retained by a County.

(a) The county tax assessor-collector each calendar year shall calculate five percent of the tax and penalties collected by the county tax assessor-collector under Chapter 152, Tax Code, in the preceding calendar year. In addition, the county tax assessor-collector shall calculate each calendar year an amount equal to five percent of the tax and penalties that the comptroller:

(1) collected under Section 152.047, Tax Code, in the preceding calendar year; and

(2) determines are attributable to sales in the county.

(b) A county tax assessor-collector shall retain under Section 502.198(b) fees based on the following percentage of the amounts calculated under Subsection (a) during each of the following fiscal years:

(1) in fiscal year 2012, 30 percent;

(2) in fiscal year 2013, 20 percent;

(3) in fiscal year 2014, 10 percent;

(4) in fiscal year 2015 and succeeding years, 0 percent.

(c) The county shall credit the amounts retained under Subsection (b) to the county road and bridge fund. Money credited to the fund under this section may only be used for:

(1) county road construction, maintenance, and repair;

(2) bridge construction, maintenance, and repair;

(3) the purchase of right-of-way for road or highway purposes; or

(4) the relocation of utilities for road or highway purposes.

(Enacted by Acts 2003, 78th Leg., ch. 1325 (H.B. 3588), § 9.03, effective September 1, 2005; am. Acts 2011, 82nd Leg., ch. 1296 (H.B. 2357), § 116, effective January 1, 2012 (renumbered from Sec. 502.1025).)

## Sec. 502.1982. [Effective January 1, 2012] Disposition of Optional County Road and Bridge Fee.

Each Monday a county assessor-collector shall apportion the collections for the preceding week for a fee imposed under Section 502.401 by:

(1) crediting an amount equal to 97 percent of the collections to the county road and bridge fund; and

(2) sending to the department an amount equal to three percent of the collections to defray the department's costs of administering Section 502.401.

(Enacted by Acts 1995, 74th Leg., ch. 165 (S.B. 971), § 1, effective September 1, 1995; am. Acts 2011, 82nd Leg., ch. 1296 (H.B. 2357), § 117, effective January 1, 2012 (renumbered from Sec. 502.103).)

## Sec. 502.1983. [Effective January 1, 2012] Deposit of Fees in Interest-Bearing Account.

(a) Except as provided by Sections 502.1982 and 502.357, a county assessor-collector may:

(1) deposit the fees in an interest-bearing account or certificate in the county depository; and

(2) send the fees to the department not later than the 34th day after the date the fees are due under Section 502.357.

(b) The county owns all interest earned on fees deposited under this section. The county treasurer shall credit the interest to the county general fund.

(Enacted by Acts 1995, 74th Leg., ch. 165 (S.B. 971), § 1, effective September 1, 1995; am. Acts 2011, 82nd Leg., ch. 1296 (H.B. 2357), § 118, effective January 1, 2012 (renumbered from Sec. 502.106).)

## Sec. 502.1984. [Effective January 1, 2012] Interest on Fees.

(a) A fee required to be sent to the department under this chapter bears interest for the benefit of the state highway fund at an annual rate of 10 percent beginning on the 60th day after the date the county assessor-collector collects the fee.

(b) The department shall audit the registration and transfer fees collected and disbursed by each county assessor-collector and shall determine the exact amount of interest due on any fee not sent to the department.

(c) The state has a claim against a county assessor-collector and the sureties on the assessor-collector's official bond for the amount of interest due on a fee.

(Enacted by Acts 1995, 74th Leg., ch. 165 (S.B. 971), § 1, effective September 1, 1995; am. Acts 2011, 82nd Leg., ch. 1296 (H.B. 2357), § 119, effective January 1, 2012 (renumbered from Sec. 502.107).)

## Sec. 502.1985. [Effective January 1, 2012] Use of Registration Fees Retained by County.

(a) Money credited to the county road and bridge fund under Section 502.198 or 502.1982 may not be used to pay the compensation of the county judge or a county commissioner. The money may be used only for the construction and maintenance of lateral roads in the county, under the supervision of the county engineer.

(b) If there is not a county engineer, the commissioners court of the county may require the services of the department's district engineer or resident engineer to supervise the construction and surveying of lateral roads in the county.

(c) A county may use money allocated to it under this chapter to:

(1) pay obligations issued in the construction or improvement of any roads, including state highways in the county;

(2) improve the roads in the county road system; or

(3) construct new roads.

(d) To the maximum extent possible, contracts for roads constructed by a county using funds provided under this chapter should be awarded by competitive bids.

(Enacted by Acts 1995, 74th Leg., ch. 165 (S.B. 971), § 1, effective September 1, 1995; am. Acts 1997, 75th Leg., ch. 165 (S.B. 898), § 30.47(a), effective September 1, 1997; am. Acts 2003, 78th Leg., ch. 1325 (H.B. 3588), § 9.04, effective September 1, 2005; am. Acts 2011, 82nd Leg., ch. 1296 (H.B. 2357), § 120, effective January 1, 2012 (renumbered from Sec. 502.108).)

## Sec. 502.1986. [Effective January 1, 2012] Contingent Provision for Distribution of Fees Between State and Counties.

If the method of distributing vehicle registration fees collected under this chapter between the state and counties is declared invalid because of inequality of collection or distribution of those fees, 60 percent of each fee shall be distributed to the county collecting the fee and 40 percent shall be sent to the state in the manner provided by this chapter.

(Enacted by Acts 1995, 74th Leg., ch. 165 (S.B. 971), § 1, effective September 1, 1995; am. Acts 2011, 82nd Leg., ch. 1296 (H.B. 2357), § 121, effective January 1, 2012 (renumbered from Sec. 502.110).)

Transportation

## Sec. 502.200. [Reserved for expansion].

## Sec. 502.201. [Renumbered January 1, 2012] License Plates for Exempt Vehicles.

(a) Before license plates are issued or delivered to the owner of a vehicle that is exempt by law from payment of registration fees, the department must approve the application for registration. The department may not approve an application if there is the appearance that:

(1) the vehicle was transferred to the owner or purported owner:

(A) for the sole purpose of evading the payment of registration fees; or

(B) in bad faith; or

(2) the vehicle is not being used in accordance with the exemption requirements.

(b) The department shall revoke the registration of a vehicle issued license plates under this section and may recall the plates if the vehicle is no longer:

(1) owned and operated by the person whose ownership of the vehicle qualified the vehicle for the exemption; or

(2) used in accordance with the exemption requirements.

(c) [Repealed September 1, 2011] The owner of a vehicle described by Subsection (b) shall return the license plates and registration receipt to the department for cancellation.

(d) The department shall provide by rule for the issuance of specially designated license plates for vehicles that are exempt by law. Except as provided by Subsection (g), the license plates must bear the word "exempt."

(e) A license plate under Subsection (d) is not issued annually, but remains on the vehicle until:

(1) the registration is revoked as provided by Subsection (b); or

(2) the plate is lost, stolen, or mutilated.

(f) A person who operates on a public highway a vehicle after the registration has been revoked is liable for the penalties for failing to register a vehicle.

(g) The department shall provide by rule for the issuance of regularly designed license plates not bearing the word "exempt" for a vehicle that is exempt by law and that is:

(1) a law enforcement vehicle, if the agency certifies to the department that the vehicle will be dedicated to law enforcement activities;

(2) a vehicle exempt from inscription requirements under a rule adopted as provided by Section 721.003; or

(3) a vehicle exempt from inscription requirements under an order or ordinance adopted by a governing body of a municipality or commissioners court of a county as provided by Section 721.005, if the applicant presents a copy of the order or ordinance.

(Enacted by Acts 1995, 74th Leg., ch. 165 (S.B. 971), § 1, effective September 1, 1995; am. Acts 1997, 75th Leg., ch. 485 (S.B. 557), § 1, effective September 1, 1997; am. Acts 2009, 81st Leg., ch. 1136 (H.B. 2553), § 39(6), effective September 1, 2011.)

### STATUTORY NOTES

**Editor's notes.** — This section is renumbered to Transportation Code Section 502.451 pursuant to Acts 2011, 82nd Leg., ch. 1296 (H.B. 2357), § 147, effective January 1, 2012.

## Sec. 502.2015. [Renumbered January 1, 2012] Limitation on Issuance of Exempt License Plates; Seizure of Certain Vehicles.

(a) The department may not issue exempt license plates for a vehicle owned by the United States, this state, or a political subdivision of this state unless when application is made for registration of the vehicle, the person who under Section 502.202 has authority to certify to the department that the vehicle qualifies for registration under that section also certifies in writing to the department that there is printed on each side of the vehicle, in letters that are at least two inches high or in an emblem that is at least 100 square inches in size, the name of the agency, department, bureau, board, commission, or officer of the United States, this state, or the political subdivision of this state that has custody of the vehicle. The letters or emblem must be of a color sufficiently different from the body of the vehicle to be clearly legible from a distance of 100 feet.

(b) The department may not issue exempt license plates for a vehicle owned by a person other than the United States, this state, or a political subdivision of this state unless, when application is made for registration of the vehicle, the person who under Section 502.202 has authority to certify to the department that the vehicle qualifies for registration under that section also certifies in writing to the department that the name of the owner of the vehicle is printed on the vehicle in the manner prescribed by Subsection (a).

(c) A peace officer listed in Article 2.12, Code of Criminal Procedure, may seize a motor vehicle displaying exempt license plates if the vehicle is:

(1) operated on a public highway; and

(2) not identified in the manner prescribed by Subsection (a) or (b), unless the vehicle is covered by Subsection (f).

(d) A peace officer who seizes a motor vehicle under Subsection (c) may require that the vehicle be:

(1) moved to the nearest place of safety off the main-traveled part of the highway; or

(2) removed and placed in the nearest vehicle storage facility designated or maintained by the law enforcement agency that employs the peace officer.

(e) To obtain the release of the vehicle, in addition to any other requirement of law, the owner of a vehicle seized under Subsection (c) must:

(1) remedy the defect by identifying the vehicle as required by Subsection (a) or (b); or

(2) agree in writing with the law enforcement agency to provide evidence to that agency, before the 10th day after the date the vehicle is released, that the defect has been remedied by identifying the vehicle as required by Subsection (a) or (b).

(f) Subsections (a) and (b) do not apply to a vehicle to which Section 502.201(g) or 502.206 applies.

(g) For purposes of this section, an exempt license plate is a license plate issued by the department that is plainly marked with the word "exempt."

(Enacted by Acts 1997, 75th Leg., ch. 165 (S.B. 898), § 30.50(a), effective September 1, 1997; enacted by Acts 1997, 75th Leg., ch. 485 (S.B. 557), § 2, effective September 1, 1997.)

### STATUTORY NOTES

**Editor's notes.** — This section is renumbered to Transportation Code Section 502.452 pursuant to Acts 2011, 82nd Leg., ch. 1296 (H.B. 2357), § 148, effective January 1, 2012.

## Sec. 502.202. [Renumbered January 1, 2012] Government-Owned Vehicles; Public School Buses; Fire-Fighting Vehicles; County Marine Law Enforcement Vehicles.

(a) The owner of a motor vehicle, trailer, or semitrailer may annually apply for registration under Section 502.201 and is exempt from the payment of a registration fee under this chapter if the vehicle is:

(1) owned by and used exclusively in the service of:

(A) the United States;

(B) this state; or

(C) a county, municipality, or school district in this state;

(2) owned by a commercial transportation company and used exclusively to provide public school transportation services to a school district under Section 34.008, Education Code;

(3) designed and used exclusively for fire fighting;

(4) owned by a volunteer fire department and used exclusively in the conduct of department business; or

(5) privately owned and used by a volunteer exclusively in county marine law enforcement activities, including rescue operations, under the direction of the sheriff's department.

(b) An application for registration under this section must be made by a person having the authority to certify that the vehicle meets the exemption requirements prescribed by Subsection (a). An application for registration under this section of a fire-fighting vehicle described by Subsection (a)(3) must include a reasonable description of the vehicle and of any fire-fighting equipment mounted on the vehicle. An application for registration under this section of a vehicle described by Subsection (a)(5) must include a statement signed by a person having the authority to act for a sheriff's department that the vehicle is used exclusively in marine law enforcement activities under the direction of the sheriff's department.

(Enacted by Acts 1995, 74th Leg., ch. 165 (S.B. 971), § 1, effective September 1, 1995; am. Acts 1999, 76th Leg., ch. 62 (S.B. 1368), § 17.06, effective September 1, 1999.)

### STATUTORY NOTES

**Editor's notes.** — This section is renumbered to Transportation Code Section 502.453 pursuant to Acts 2011, 82nd Leg., ch. 1296 (H.B. 2357), § 149, effective January 1, 2012.

## Sec. 502.203. [Renumbered January 1, 2012] Vehicles Used by Nonprofit Disaster Relief Organizations.

(a) The owner of a commercial motor vehicle, trailer, or semitrailer may apply for registration under Section 502.201 and is exempt from the payment of the registration fee that would otherwise be required by this chapter if the vehicle is owned and used exclusively for emergencies by a nonprofit disaster relief organization.

(b) An application for registration under this section must include:

(1) a statement by the owner of the vehicle that the vehicle is used exclusively for emergencies and has not been used for any other purpose;

(2) a statement signed by an officer of the nonprofit disaster relief organization that the vehicle has not been used for any purpose other than emergencies and qualifies for registration under this section; and

(3) a reasonable description of the vehicle and the emergency equipment included in the vehicle.

(c) An applicant for registration under this section must pay a fee of $5.

(d) A commercial motor vehicle registered under this section must display the name of the organization that owns it on each front door.

(e) A vehicle registered under this section must display at all times an appropriate license plate showing the vehicle's status.

(f) A vehicle registered under this section that is used for any purpose other than an emergency may not again be registered under this section. (Enacted by Acts 1995, 74th Leg., ch. 165 (S.B. 971), § 1, effective September 1, 1995; am. Acts 2001, 77th Leg., ch. 638 (H.B. 1368), § 3, effective September 1, 2001.)

### STATUTORY NOTES

**Editor's notes.** — This section is renumbered to Transportation Code Section 502.454 pursuant to Acts 2011, 82nd Leg., ch. 1296 (H.B. 2357), § 150, effective January 1, 2012.

## Sec. 502.2035. [Renumbered January 1, 2012] Trailers and Semitrailers Owned by Religious Organizations.

(a) A trailer or semitrailer may be registered without payment if the trailer or semitrailer is:

(1) owned by an organization that qualifies as a religious organization under Section 11.20, Tax Code; and

(2) used primarily for the purpose of transporting property in connection with the charitable activities and functions of the organization.

(b) An application for registration under this section must include a statement signed by an officer of the religious organization stating that the trailer or semitrailer qualifies for registration under this section. (Enacted by Acts 1999, 76th Leg., ch. 1194 (S.B. 408), § 1, effective September 1, 1999.)

### STATUTORY NOTES

**Editor's notes.** — This section is renumbered to Transportation Code Section 502.455 pursuant to Acts 2011, 82nd Leg., ch. 1296 (H.B. 2357), § 151, effective January 1, 2012.

## Sec. 502.204. [Renumbered January 1, 2012] Emergency Services Vehicles.

(a) A vehicle may be registered without payment if:

(1) the vehicle is owned or leased by an emergency medical services provider that:

(A) is a nonprofit entity; or

(B) is created and operated by:

(i) a county;

(ii) a municipality; or

(iii) any combination of counties and municipalities through a contract, joint agreement, or other method provided by Chapter 791, Government Code, or other law authorizing counties and municipalities to provide joint programs; and

(2) the vehicle:

(A) is authorized under an emergency medical services provider license issued by the Texas Board of Health under Chapter 773, Health and Safety Code, and is used exclusively as an emergency medical services vehicle; or

(B) is an emergency medical services chief or supervisor vehicle and is used exclusively as an emergency services vehicle.

(b) A vehicle may be registered without payment of a registration fee if the vehicle:

(1) is owned by the Civil Air Patrol, Texas Wing; and

(2) is used exclusively as an emergency services vehicle by members of the Civil Air Patrol, Texas Wing.

(c) An application for registration under Subsection (a) must be accompanied by a copy of the license issued by the Texas Board of Health. An application for registration of an emergency medical services vehicle must include a statement signed by an officer of the emergency medical services provider that the vehicle is used exclusively as an emergency response vehicle and qualifies for registration under this section. An application for registration of an emergency medical services chief or supervisor vehicle must include a statement signed by an officer of the emergency medical services provider stating that the vehicle qualifies for registration under this section.

(d) An application for registration under Subsection (b) must include a statement signed by an officer of the Civil Air Patrol, Texas Wing, that the vehicle is used exclusively as an emergency services vehicle by members of the Civil Air Patrol, Texas Wing.

(e) The department must approve an application for registration under this section as provided by Section 502.201.

(Enacted by Acts 1995, 74th Leg., ch. 165 (S.B. 971), § 1, effective September 1, 1995.)

## Sec. 502.205.  All-Terrain Vehicles [Repealed].

Repealed by Acts 2007, 80th Leg., ch. 1280 (H.B. 3849), § 6, effective June 15, 2007.

(Enacted by Acts 1995, 74th Leg., ch. 165 (S.B. 971), § 1, effective September 1, 1995.)

## Sec. 502.206.  [Repealed January 1, 2012] Registration of Certain Law Enforcement Vehicles Under Alias.

On receipt of a written request approved by the executive administrator of a law enforcement agency, the department may issue exempt license plates for a vehicle and register the vehicle under an alias for the law enforcement agency's use in covert criminal investigations.

(Enacted by Acts 1995, 74th Leg., ch. 165 (S.B. 971), § 1, effective September 1, 1995.)

## Secs. 502.207 to 502.250 [Reserved for expansion].

## SUBCHAPTER F
### [EFFECTIVE UNTIL JANUARY 1, 2012] SPECIALIZED LICENSE PLATES; EXEMPTIONS FOR PRIVATELY OWNED VEHICLES; [EFFECTIVE JANUARY 1, 2012] REGULAR REGISTRATION FEES

## Sec. 502.251.  [Effective January 1, 2012] Fee: Motorcycle or Moped.

The fee for a registration year for registration of a motorcycle or moped is $30.

(Enacted by Acts 1995, 74th Leg., ch. 165 (S.B. 971), § 1, effective September 1, 1995; am. Acts 2009, 81st Leg. ch. 1136 (H.B. 2553), § 17, effective September 1, 2011; am. Acts 2011, 82nd Leg., ch. 1296 (H.B. 2357), § 123, effective January 1, 2012 (renumbered from Sec. 502.160).)

## Sec. 502.252.  [Effective January 1, 2012] Fee: Vehicles that Weigh 6,000 Pounds or Less.

(a) The fee for a registration year for registration of a vehicle with a gross weight of 6,000 pounds or less is $50.75, unless otherwise provided in this chapter.

(b) For registration purposes, the weight of a passenger car, a municipal bus, or a private bus is the weight generally accepted as its correct shipping weight plus 100 pounds.

(Enacted by Acts 1995, 74th Leg., ch. 165 (S.B. 971), § 1, effective September 1, 1995; am. Acts 1997, 75th Leg., ch. 625 (S.B. 1630), § 4, effective September 1, 1997; am. Acts 2009, 81st Leg. ch. 1136 (H.B. 2553), § 18, effective September 1, 2011; am. Acts 2011, 82nd Leg., ch. 1296 (H.B. 2357), § 124, effective January 1, 2012 (renumbered from Sec. 502.161).)

## Sec. 502.2525.  Discontinuance of Certain Specialized License Plates [Repealed].

Repealed by Acts 2003, 78th Leg., ch. 1320 (H.B. 2971), § 10(a), effective September 1, 2003. (Enacted by Acts 1999, 76th Leg., ch. 951 (H.B. 2461), § 1, effective August 30, 1999.)

## Sec. 502.2526.  Specialized License Plates Authorized After January 1, 1999 [Repealed].

Repealed by Acts 2003, 78th Leg., ch. 1320 (H.B. 2971), § 10(a), effective September 1, 2003. (Enacted by Acts 1999, 76th Leg., ch. 951 (H.B. 2461), § 1, effective August 30, 1999.)

## Sec. 502.253.  [Effective January 1, 2012] Fee: Vehicles that Weigh More than 6,000 Pounds.

The fee for a registration year for registration of a commercial motor vehicle or truck-tractor is $25 plus an amount determined according to the vehicle's gross weight and tire equipment, as follows:

| Weight Classification in pounds | Fee Schedule |
|---|---|
| 6,001—10,000 | $54.00 |
| 10,001—18,000 | $110.00 |
| 18,001—25,999 | $205.00 |
| 26,000—40,000 | $340.00 |
| 40,001—54,999 | $535.00 |
| 55,000—70,000 | $740.00 |
| 70,001—80,000 | $840.00 |

(Enacted by Acts 1995, 74th Leg., ch. 165 (S.B. 971), § 1, effective September 1, 1995; am. Acts

Transportation

2009, 81st Leg. ch. 1136 (H.B. 2553), § 20, effective September 1, 2011; am. Acts 2011, 82nd Leg., ch. 1296 (H.B. 2357), § 125, effective January 1, 2012 (renumbered from Sec. 502.162).)

### Sec. 502.2531.   Issuance of Disabled Plates to Certain Institutions [Repealed].

Repealed by Acts 2003, 78th Leg., ch. 1320 (H.B. 2971), § 10(a), effective September 1, 2003. (Enacted by Acts 1999, 76th Leg., ch. 513 (S.B. 21), § 1, effective September 1, 1999; am. Acts 2001, 77th Leg., ch. 777 (H.B. 15), § 1, effective September 1, 2001.)

### Sec. 502.254.   [Effective January 1, 2012] Fee: Trailer, Travel Trailer, or Semitrailer.

(a) The fee for a registration year for registration of a trailer, travel trailer, or semitrailer with a gross weight of 6,000 pounds or less is $45.00.

(b) The fee for a registration year for registration of a trailer, travel trailer, or semitrailer with a gross weight of more than 6,000 pounds is calculated by gross weight according to Section 502.253.

(Enacted by Acts 1995, 74th Leg., ch. 165 (S.B. 971), § 1, effective September 1, 1995; am. Acts 1997, 75th Leg., ch. 625 (S.B. 1630), § 5, effective September 1, 1997; am. Acts 2009, 81st Leg., ch. 1136 (H.B. 2553), §§ 23, 24, effective September 1, 2011; am. Acts 2011, 82nd Leg., ch. 1296 (H.B. 2357), § 126, effective January 1, 2012 (renumbered from Sec. 502.166).)

### Sec. 502.255.   [Effective January 1, 2012] Truck-Tractor or Commercial Motor Vehicle Combination Fee; Semitrailer Token Fee.

(a) This section applies only to a truck-tractor or commercial motor vehicle with a gross weight of more than 10,000 pounds that is used or is to be used in combination with a semitrailer that has a gross weight of more than 6,000 pounds.

(b) The fee for a registration year for registration of a truck-tractor or commercial motor vehicle is calculated by gross weight according to Section 502.253.

(c) The fee for registration of a semitrailer used in the manner described by Subsection (a), regardless of the date the semitrailer is registered, is $15 for a registration year.

(d) A registration made under Subsection (c) is valid only when the semitrailer is used in the manner described by Subsection (a).

(e) For registration purposes, a semitrailer converted to a trailer by means of an auxiliary axle assembly retains its status as a semitrailer.

(f) A combination of vehicles may not be registered under this section for a combined gross weight of less than 18,000 pounds.

(g) This section does not apply to:

(1) a combination of vehicles that includes a vehicle that has a distinguishing license plate under Section 502.146;

(2) a truck-tractor or commercial motor vehicle registered or to be registered with $5 distinguishing license plates for which the vehicle is eligible under this chapter;

(3) a truck-tractor or commercial motor vehicle used exclusively in combination with a semitrailer of the travel trailer type; or

(4) a vehicle registered or to be registered:

(A) with a temporary registration permit;

(B) under Section 502.433; or

(C) under Section 502.435.

(h) The department may adopt rules to administer this section.

(i) The department may issue specially designed license plates for token trailers.

(j) A person may register a semitrailer under this section if the person:

(1) applies to the department for registration;

(2) provides proof of the person's eligibility to register the vehicle under this subsection as required by the department; and

(3) pays a fee of $15, plus any applicable fee under Section 502.401, for each year included in the registration period.

(Enacted by Acts 1995, 74th Leg., ch. 165 (S.B. 971), § 1, effective September 1, 1995; am. Acts 1997, 75th Leg., ch. 625 (S.B. 1630), § 6, effective September 1, 1997; am. Acts 2007, 80th Leg., ch. 280 (H.B. 505), § 2, effective June 15, 2007; am. Acts 2007, 80th Leg., ch. 744 (H.B. 2992), § 1, effective September 1, 2007; am. Acts 2009, 81st Leg., ch. 1136 (H.B. 2553), § 25, effective September 1, 2011; am. Acts 2011, 82nd Leg., ch. 700 (H.B. 441), § 1, effective September 1, 2011; am. Acts 2011, 82nd Leg., ch. 1296 (H.B. 2357), § 127, effective January 1, 2012 (renumbered from Sec. 502.167).)

### Sec. 502.2555.   Air Force Cross or Distinguished Service Cross, Army Distinguished Service Cross, Navy Cross, or Medal of Honor Recipients [Repealed].

Repealed by Acts 2003, 78th Leg., ch. 1320 (H.B. 2971), § 10(a), effective September 1, 2003.

(Enacted by Acts 1997, 75th Leg., ch. 165 (S.B. 898), § 30.53(a), effective September 1, 1997; am. Acts 2001, 77th Leg., ch. 758 (S.B. 1353), § 1, effective September 1, 2001.)

## Sec. 502.256. [Effective January 1, 2012] Fee: Road Tractor.

The fee for a registration year for registration of a road tractor is the fee prescribed by weight as certified by a public weigher or a license and weight inspector of the Department of Public Safety under Section 502.252 or 502.253, as applicable.

(Enacted by Acts 1995, 74th Leg., ch. 165 (S.B. 971), § 1, effective September 1, 1995; am. Acts 2009, 81st Leg. ch. 1136 (H.B. 2553), § 22, effective September 1, 2011; am. Acts 2011, 82nd Leg., ch. 1296 (H.B. 2357), § 128, effective January 1, 2012 (renumbered from Sec. 502.165).)

## Sec. 502.257. Former Prisoners of War [Repealed].

Repealed by Acts 2003, 78th Leg., ch. 1320 (H.B. 2971), § 10(a), effective September 1, 2003. (Enacted by Acts 1995, 74th Leg., ch. 165 (S.B. 971), § 1, effective September 1, 1995; am. Acts 2001, 77th Leg., ch. 758 (S.B. 1353), § 2, effective September 1, 2001.)

## Sec. 502.258. Members or Former Members of United States Armed Forces [Repealed].

Repealed by Acts 2003, 78th Leg., ch. 1320 (H.B. 2971), § 10(a), effective September 1, 2003. (Enacted by Acts 1995, 74th Leg., ch. 165 (S.B. 971), § 1, effective September 1, 1995; am. Acts 1997, 75th Leg., ch. 165 (S.B. 898), § 30.54(a), (b), effective September 1, 1997.)

## Sec. 502.2585. Persons Retired from Service in Merchant Marine of the United States [Repealed].

Repealed by Acts 2003, 78th Leg., ch. 1320 (H.B. 2971), § 10(a), effective September 1, 2003. (Enacted by Acts 1999, 76th Leg., ch. 991 (H.B. 2760), § 1, effective September 1, 1999.)

## Sec. 502.259. Pearl Harbor Survivors [Repealed].

Repealed by Acts 2003, 78th Leg., ch. 1320 (H.B. 2971), § 10(a), effective September 1, 2003. (Enacted by Acts 1995, 74th Leg., ch. 165 (S.B. 971), § 1, effective September 1, 1995; am. Acts 1997, 75th Leg., ch. 165 (S.B. 898), § 30.54(c), effective September 1, 1997.)

## Sec. 502.260. Purple Heart Recipients [Repealed].

Repealed by Acts 2003, 78th Leg., ch. 1320 (H.B. 2971), § 10(a), effective September 1, 2003. (Enacted by Acts 1995, 74th Leg., ch. 165 (S.B. 971), § 1, effective September 1, 1995; am. Acts 1997, 75th Leg., ch. 165 (S.B. 898), § 30.54(d), effective September 1, 1997; am. Acts 1997, 75th Leg., ch. 625 (S.B. 1630), § 8, effective September 1, 1997.)

## Sec. 502.261. Members of United States Armed Forces Auxiliaries [Repealed].

Repealed by Acts 2003, 78th Leg., ch. 1320 (H.B. 2971), § 10(a), effective September 1, 2003. (Enacted by Acts 1995, 74th Leg., ch. 165 (S.B. 971), § 1, effective September 1, 1995; am. Acts 1997, 75th Leg., ch. 165 (S.B. 898), § 30.54(e), effective September 1, 1997.)

## Sec. 502.262. World War II Veterans [Repealed].

Repealed by Acts 2003, 78th Leg., ch. 1320 (H.B. 2971), § 10(a), effective September 1, 2003. (Enacted by Acts 1995, 74th Leg., ch. 165 (S.B. 971), § 1, effective September 1, 1995; am. Acts 1997, 75th Leg., ch. 165 (S.B. 898), § 30.54(f), effective September 1, 1997; am. Acts 1999, 76th Leg., ch. 1249 (S.B. 997), § 1, effective September 1, 1999.)

## Sec. 502.263. Korean Conflict Veterans [Repealed].

Repealed by Acts 2003, 78th Leg., ch. 1320 (H.B. 2971), § 10(a), effective September 1, 2003. (Enacted by Acts 1995, 74th Leg., ch. 165 (S.B. 971), § 1, effective September 1, 1995; am. Acts 1997, 75th Leg., ch. 165 (S.B. 898), § 30.54(g), effective September 1, 1997; am. Acts 1999, 76th Leg., ch. 590 (S.B. 641), § 1, effective June 18, 1999; am. Acts 1999, 76th Leg., ch. 1249 (S.B. 997), § 1, effective September 1, 1999.)

## Sec. 502.264. Vietnam Veterans [Repealed].

Repealed by Acts 2003, 78th Leg., ch. 1320 (H.B. 2971), § 10(a), effective September 1, 2003. (Enacted by Acts 1995, 74th Leg., ch. 165 (S.B. 971), § 1, effective September 1, 1995; am. Acts 1997, 75th Leg., ch. 165 (S.B. 898), § 30.54(h), effective September 1, 1997; am. Acts 1999, 76th Leg., ch. 1249 (S.B. 997), § 1, effective September 1, 1999; am. Acts 2001, 77th Leg., ch. 266 (S.B. 1089), § 1, effective September 1, 2001.)

Transportation

### Sec. 502.265. Desert Shield or Desert Storm Veterans [Repealed].

Repealed by Acts 2003, 78th Leg., ch. 1320 (H.B. 2971), § 10(a), effective September 1, 2003. (Enacted by Acts 1995, 74th Leg., ch. 165 (S.B. 971), § 1, effective September 1, 1995; am. Acts 1997, 75th Leg., ch. 165 (S.B. 898), § 30.54(i), effective September 1, 1997; am. Acts 1999, 76th Leg., ch. 1249 (S.B. 997), § 1, effective September 1, 1999.)

### Sec. 502.266. Surviving Spouses of Certain Military Veterans [Repealed].

Repealed by Acts 2003, 78th Leg., ch. 1320 (H.B. 2971), § 10(a), effective September 1, 2003. (Enacted by Acts 1995, 74th Leg., ch. 165 (S.B. 971), § 1, effective September 1, 1995; am. Acts 1997, 75th Leg., ch. 165 (S.B. 898), § 30.54(j), effective September 1, 1997; am. Acts 1997, 75th Leg., ch. 625 (S.B. 1630), § 9, effective September 1, 1997; am. Acts 1999, 76th Leg., ch. 530 (S.B. 171), § 1, effective September 1, 1999.)

### Sec. 502.2661. Gold Star Mothers [Repealed].

Repealed by Acts 2003, 78th Leg., ch. 1320 (H.B. 2971), § 10(a), effective September 1, 2003. (Enacted by Acts 1997, 75th Leg., ch. 1312 (S.B. 745), § 1, effective Septbember 1, 1997; am. Acts 1999, 76th Leg., ch. 62 (S.B. 1368), § 19.01(103), effective September 1, 1999 (renumbered from Sec. 502.292).)

### Sec. 502.2663. New Millenium License Plates [Repealed].

Repealed by Acts 2003, 78th Leg., ch. 1320 (H.B. 2971), § 10(a), effective September 1, 2003. (Enacted by Acts 1999, 76th Leg., ch. 763 (H.B. 1227), § 1, effective September 1, 1999.)

### Sec. 502.267. Honorary Consuls [Repealed].

Repealed by Acts 2003, 78th Leg., ch. 1320 (H.B. 2971), § 10(a), effective September 1, 2003. (Enacted by Acts 1995, 74th Leg., ch. 165 (S.B. 971), § 1, effective September 1, 1995.)

### Sec. 502.268. Volunteer Firefighters [Repealed].

Repealed by Acts 2003, 78th Leg., ch. 1320 (H.B. 2971), § 10(a), effective September 1, 2003. (Enacted by Acts 1995, 74th Leg., ch. 165 (S.B. 971), § 1, effective September 1, 1995; am. Acts 1999, 76th Leg., ch. 818 (H.B. 1616), § 1, effective September 1, 1999.)

### Sec. 502.269. Texas Capitol License Plates [Repealed].

Repealed by Acts 2003, 78th Leg., ch. 1320 (H.B. 2971), § 10(a), effective September 1, 2003. (Enacted by Acts 1995, 74th Leg., ch. 165 (S.B. 971), § 1, effective September 1, 1995.)

### Sec. 502.270. Collegiate License Plates [Repealed].

Repealed by Acts 2003, 78th Leg., ch. 1320 (H.B. 2971), § 10(a), effective September 1, 2003. (Enacted by Acts 1995, 74th Leg., ch. 165 (S.B. 971), § 1, effective September 1, 1995; am. Acts 1997, 75th Leg., ch. 165 (S.B. 898), § 30.55, effective September 1, 1997.)

### Sec. 502.2703. Professional Sports Team License Plates [Repealed].

Repealed by Acts 2003, 78th Leg., ch. 1320 (H.B. 2971), § 10(a), effective September 1, 2003. (Enacted by Acts 1997, 75th Leg., ch. 1171 (S.B. 370), § 1.44, effective September 1, 1997.)

### Sec. 502.2704. United States Olympic Committee License Plates [Repealed].

Repealed by Acts 2003, 78th Leg., ch. 1320 (H.B. 2971), § 10(a), effective September 1, 2003. (Enacted by Acts 1997, 75th Leg., ch. 61 (S.B. 460), § 1, effective Septbember 1, 1997; am. Acts 1999, 76th Leg., ch. 62 (S.B. 1368), § 19.01(101), effective September 1, 1999 (renumbered from Sec. 502.291).)

### Sec. 502.271. [Repealed January 1, 2012] Texas Aerospace and Aviation License Plates.

(a) The department shall issue specially designed Texas Aerospace and Aviation license plates for passenger cars and light trucks.

(b) The license plates must include the name "Texas Aerospace and Aviation" and be of a color, quality, and design approved by the Texas Economic Development and Tourism Office.

(c) [Repealed by Acts 2003, 78th Leg., ch. 149 (S.B. 652), § 25, effective May 28, 2003 and Acts 2003, 78th Leg., ch. 1320 (H.B. 2971), § 10(a), effective September 1, 2003.]

(d) Of each fee collected under this section, the department shall deposit $25 under this section in the general revenue fund to the credit of the Texas Economic Development and Tourism Office account, which may be used only to support the activities of the aerospace and aviation office established by the Texas Economic Development and Tourism Office, and $5 to the credit of the state highway fund.

(e) [Repealed by Acts 2003, 78th Leg., ch. 149 (S.B. 652), § 25, effective May 28, 2003 and Acts 2003, 78th Leg., ch. 1320 (H.B. 2971), § 10(a), effective September 1, 2003.]

(Enacted by Acts 1995, 74th Leg., ch. 165 (S.B. 971), § 1, effective September 1, 1995; am. Acts 2003, 78th Leg., ch. 149 (S.B. 652), § 25, effective May 28, 2003; am. Acts 2003, 78th Leg., ch. 814 (S.B. 275), §§ 1.63, 1.64, effective September 1, 2003; am. Acts 2003, 78th Leg., ch. 1320 (H.B. 2971), § 10(a), effective September 1, 2003.)

### Sec. 502.272. Texas Commission on the Arts License Plates [Repealed].

Repealed by Acts 2003, 78th Leg., ch. 1320 (H.B. 2971), § 10(a), effective September 1, 2003. (Enacted by Acts 1995, 74th Leg., ch. 165 (S.B. 971), § 1, effective September 1, 1995.)

### Sec. 502.2721. Texas Commission on Alcohol and Drug Abuse License Plates [Repealed].

Repealed by Acts 2003, 78th Leg., ch. 1320 (H.B. 2971), § 10(a), effective September 1, 2003. (Enacted by Acts 1997, 75th Leg., ch. 1222 (H.B. 344), § 5, effective September 1, 1997; enacted by Acts 1997, 75th Leg., ch. 1247 (H.B. 2198), § 1, effective September 1, 1997; am. Acts 1999, 76th Leg., ch. 62 (S.B. 1368), § 19.01(105), effective September 1, 1999 (renumbered from Secs. 502.293, 502.294).)

### Sec. 502.2722. Texas Commission for the Deaf and Hard of Hearing License Plates [Repealed].

Repealed by Acts 2003, 78th Leg., ch. 1320 (H.B. 2971), § 10(a), effective September 1, 2003. (Enacted by Acts 2001, 77th Leg., ch. 621 (S.B. 1563), § 1, effective September 1, 2001; am. Acts 2003, 78th Leg., ch. 1275 (H.B. 3506), § 2(134), effective September 1, 2003 (renumbered from Sec. 502.2735).)

### Sec. 502.273. Private Nonprofit Organizations [Repealed].

Repealed by Acts 2003, 78th Leg., ch. 1320 (H.B. 2971), § 10(a), effective September 1, 2003. (Enacted by Acts 1995, 74th Leg., ch. 165 (S.B. 971), § 1, effective September 1, 1995.)

### Sec. 502.2731. Keep Texas Beautiful License Plates [Repealed].

Repealed by Acts 2003, 78th Leg., ch. 1320 (H.B. 2971), § 10(a), effective September 1, 2003. (Enacted by Acts 1997, 75th Leg., ch. 1258 (H.B. 2681), § 1, effective September 1, 1997; am. Acts 1999, 76th Leg., ch. 951 (H.B. 2461), § 2, effective August 30, 1999.)

### Sec. 502.2732. Big Bend National Park License Plates [Repealed].

Repealed by Acts 2003, 78th Leg., ch. 1320 (H.B. 2971), § 10(a), effective September 1, 2003. (Enacted by Acts 1997, 75th Leg., ch. 581 (H.B. 2519), § 1, effective September 1, 1997; am. Acts 1999, 76th Leg., ch. 62 (S.B. 1368), § 19.01(106), effective September 1, 1999 (renumbered from Sec. 502.295).)

### Sec. 502.2733. Texas. It's Like a Whole Other Country License Plates [Repealed].

Repealed by Acts 2003, 78th Leg., ch. 1320 (H.B. 2971), § 10(a), effective September 1, 2003. (Enacted by Acts 1999, 76th Leg., ch. 1220 (S.B. 639), § 1, effective September 1, 1999.)

### Sec. 502.2734. Conservation License Plates [Repealed].

Repealed by Acts 2003, 78th Leg., ch. 1320 (H.B. 2971), § 10(a), effective September 1, 2003. (Enacted by Acts 1999, 76th Leg., ch. 862 (H.B. 1906), § 1, effective September 1, 1999; am. Acts 2001, 77th Leg., ch. 1420 (H.B. 2812), § 21.001(106), effective September 1, 2001 (renumbered from Sec. 502.298).)

### Sec. 502.2735. Texans Conquer Cancer License Plates [Repealed].

Repealed by Acts 2003, 78th Leg., ch. 1320 (H.B. 2971), § 10(a), effective September 1, 2003. (Enacted by Acts 2001, 77th Leg., ch. 869 (H.B. 1831), § 3(a), effective June 14, 2001.)

### Sec. 502.274. Classic Motor Vehicles [Repealed].

Repealed by Acts 2003, 78th Leg., ch. 1320 (H.B. 2971), § 10(a), effective September 1, 2003. (Enacted by Acts 1995, 74th Leg., ch. 165 (S.B. 971), § 1, effective September 1, 1995; am. Acts 1997, 75th Leg., ch. 1222 (H.B. 344), § 1, effective September 1, 1997.)

### Sec. 502.275.  Certain Exhibition Vehicles; Offense [Repealed].

Repealed by Acts 2003, 78th Leg., ch. 1320 (H.B. 2971), § 10(a), effective September 1, 2003. (Enacted by Acts 1995, 74th Leg., ch. 165 (S.B. 971), § 1, effective September 1, 1995; am. Acts 1997, 75th Leg., ch. 165 (S.B. 898), § 30.56(a), effective September 1, 1997; am. Acts 1997, 75th Leg., ch. 1222 (H.B. 344), § 2, effective September 1, 1997.)

### Sec. 502.276.  Certain Farm Vehicles and Drilling and Construction Equipment [Repealed].

Repealed by Acts 2003, 78th Leg., ch. 1320 (H.B. 2971), § 10(a), effective September 1, 2003. (Enacted by Acts 1995, 74th Leg., ch. 165 (S.B. 971), § 1, effective September 1, 1995; am. Acts 1997, 75th Leg., ch. 165 (S.B. 898), § 30.57, effective September 1, 1997; am. Acts 1999, 76th Leg., ch. 572 (S.B. 518), § 1, effective September 1, 1999.)

### Sec. 502.2761.  Texas Agricultural Products License Plates [Repealed].

Repealed by Acts 2003, 78th Leg., ch. 1320 (H.B. 2971), § 10(a), effective September 1, 2003. (Enacted by Acts 1999, 76th Leg., ch. 186 (H.B. 2719), § 3, effective September 1, 1999; am. Acts 2001, 77th Leg., ch. 208 (S.B. 571), § 8, effective May 21, 2001.)

### Sec. 502.277.  Cotton Vehicles [Repealed].

Repealed by Acts 2003, 78th Leg., ch. 1320 (H.B. 2971), § 10(a), effective September 1, 2003. (Enacted by Acts 1995, 74th Leg., ch. 165 (S.B. 971), § 1, effective September 1, 1995; am. Acts 1997, 75th Leg., ch. 848 (H.B. 920), § 1, effective June 18, 1997.)

### Sec. 502.278.  Certain Soil Conservation Equipment [Repealed].

Repealed by Acts 2003, 78th Leg., ch. 1320 (H.B. 2971), § 10(a), effective September 1, 2003. (Enacted by Acts 1995, 74th Leg., ch. 165 (S.B. 971), § 1, effective September 1, 1995.)

### Sec. 502.279.  Certain Log-Loader Vehicles [Repealed].

Repealed by Acts 2003, 78th Leg., ch. 1320 (H.B. 2971), § 10(a), effective September 1, 2003. (Enacted by Acts 1995, 74th Leg., ch. 165 (S.B. 971), § 1, effective September 1, 1995.)

### Sec. 502.280.  Forestry Vehicles [Repealed].

Repealed by Acts 2003, 78th Leg., ch. 1320 (H.B. 2971), § 10(a), effective September 1, 2003. (Enacted by Acts 1995, 74th Leg., ch. 165 (S.B. 971), § 1, effective September 1, 1995; am. Acts 1997, 75th Leg., ch. 165 (S.B. 898), § 30.58(a), effective September 1, 1997.)

### Sec. 502.281.  Tow Trucks [Repealed].

Repealed by Acts 2003, 78th Leg., ch. 1320 (H.B. 2971), § 10(a), effective September 1, 2003. (Enacted by Acts 1995, 74th Leg., ch. 165 (S.B. 971), § 1, effective September 1, 1995; am. Acts 1997, 75th Leg., ch. 165 (S.B. 898), § 30.59, effective September 1, 1997.)

### Sec. 502.282.  Vehicles Carrying Mobile Amateur Radio Equipment [Repealed].

Repealed by Acts 2003, 78th Leg., ch. 1320 (H.B. 2971), § 10(a), effective September 1, 2003. (Enacted by Acts 1995, 74th Leg., ch. 165 (S.B. 971), § 1, effective September 1, 1995.)

### Sec. 502.283.  Parade Vehicles Owned by Nonprofit Service Organizations [Repealed].

Repealed by Acts 2003, 78th Leg., ch. 1320 (H.B. 2971), § 10(a), effective September 1, 2003. (Enacted by Acts 1995, 74th Leg., ch. 165 (S.B. 971), § 1, effective September 1, 1995.)

### Sec. 502.284.  Golf Carts [Repealed].

Repealed by Acts 2003, 78th Leg., ch. 1320 (H.B. 2971), § 10(a), effective September 1, 2003. (Enacted by Acts 1995, 74th Leg., ch. 165 (S.B. 971), § 1, effective September 1, 1995; am. Acts 1997, 75th Leg., ch. 896 (H.B. 2733), § 1, effective September 1, 1997; am. Acts 1997, 75th Leg., ch. 1128 (H.B. 3063), § 1, effective June 19, 1997; am. Acts 1999, 76th Leg., ch. 780 (H.B. 1359), § 1, effective September 1, 1999; am. Acts 2001, 77th Leg., ch. 669 (H.B. 2810), § 142, effective September 1, 2001.)

### Sec. 502.285.  Manufactured Housing [Repealed].

Repealed by Acts 2003, 78th Leg., ch. 1320 (H.B. 2971), § 10(a), effective September 1, 2003. (Enacted by Acts 1995, 74th Leg., ch. 165 (S.B. 971), § 1, effective September 1, 1995.)

Transportation

### Sec. 502.286. Power Sweepers [Repealed].

Repealed by Acts 2003, 78th Leg., ch. 1320 (H.B. 2971), § 10(a), effective September 1, 2003. (Enacted by Acts 1995, 74th Leg., ch. 165 (S.B. 971), § 1, effective September 1, 1995.)

### Sec. 502.2861. [Motorized Mobility Device] [Repealed].

Repealed by Acts 2003, 78th Leg., ch. 1320 (H.B. 2971), § 10(a), effective September 1, 2003. (Enacted by Acts 2001, 77th Leg., ch. 497 (H.B. 1378), § 1, effective June 11, 2001.)

### Sec. 502.2862. [Repealed January 1, 2012] Electric Personal Assistive Mobility Devices.

The owner of an electric personal assistive mobility device, as defined by Section 551.201, is not required to register the electric personal assistive mobility device.
(Enacted by Acts 2003, 78th Leg., ch. 1318 (H.B. 1997), § 1, effective September 1, 2003.)

### Sec. 502.287. Vehicles Operated on Public Highway Separating Real Property Under Vehicle Owner's Control [Repealed].

Repealed by Acts 2003, 78th Leg., ch. 1320 (H.B. 2971), § 10(a), effective September 1, 2003. (Enacted by Acts 1995, 74th Leg., ch. 165 (S.B. 971), § 1, effective September 1, 1995.)

### Sec. 502.288. Vehicles Operated by Certain Nonresidents [Repealed].

Repealed by Acts 2003, 78th Leg., ch. 1320 (H.B. 2971), § 10(a), effective September 1, 2003. (Enacted by Acts 1995, 74th Leg., ch. 165 (S.B. 971), § 1, effective September 1, 1995.)

### Sec. 502.289. Peace Officers Wounded or Killed in Line of Duty [Repealed].

Repealed by Acts 2003, 78th Leg., ch. 1320 (H.B. 2971), § 10(a), effective September 1, 2003. (Enacted by Acts 1997, 75th Leg., ch. 165 (S.B. 898), § 30.51(b), effective September 1, 1997; am. Acts 2001, 77th Leg., ch. 785 (H.B. 149), § 1, effective September 1, 2001.)

### Sec. 502.290. Foreign Organization Vehicles [Repealed].

Repealed by Acts 2003, 78th Leg., ch. 1320 (H.B. 2971), § 10(a), effective September 1, 2003.

(Enacted by Acts 1997, 75th Leg., ch. 165 (S.B. 898), § 30.60(a), effective September 1, 1997.)

### Sec. 502.291. Animal Friendly License Plates [Repealed].

Repealed by Acts 2003, 78th Leg., ch. 1320 (H.B. 2971), § 10(a), effective September 1, 2003. (Enacted by Acts 1997, 75th Leg., ch. 657 (H.B. 3250), § 2, effective September 1, 1997.)

### Sec. 502.292. Read to Succeed [Repealed].

Repealed by Acts 2003, 78th Leg., ch. 1320 (H.B. 2971), § 10(a), effective September 1, 2003. (Enacted by Acts 1997, 75th Leg., ch. 397 (H.B. 107), § 1, effective September 1, 1997.)

### Sec. 502.2921. Volunteer Advocate Program License Plates [Repealed].

Repealed by Acts 2003, 78th Leg., ch. 1320 (H.B. 2971), § 10(a), effective September 1, 2003. (Enacted by Acts 1997, 75th Leg., ch. 61 (S.B. 460), § 1, effective September 1, 1997; am. Acts 1999, 76th Leg., ch. 62 (S.B. 1368), § 19.01(102), effective September 1, 1999 (renumbered from Sec. 502.292).)

### Sec. 502.2922. Special Olympics Texas License Plates [Repealed].

Repealed by Acts 2003, 78th Leg., ch. 1320 (H.B. 2971), § 10(a), effective September 1, 2003. (Enacted by Acts 2001, 77th Leg., ch. 475 (H.B. 811), § 2, effective September 1, 2001.)

### Sec. 502.293. Houston Livestock Show and Rodeo License Plates [Repealed].

Repealed by Acts 2003, 78th Leg., ch. 1320 (H.B. 2971), § 10(a), effective September 1, 2003. (Enacted by Acts 1997, 75th Leg., ch. 511 (S.B. 1506), § 1, effective September 1, 1997.)

### Sec. 502.2931. Girl Scout License Plates [Repealed].

Repealed by Acts 2003, 78th Leg., ch. 1320 (H.B. 2971), § 10(a), effective September 1, 2003. (Enacted by Acts 1999, 76th Leg., ch. 550 (S.B. 322), § 1, effective September 1, 1999.)

### Sec. 502.2932. Texas YMCA [Repealed].

Repealed by Acts 2003, 78th Leg., ch. 1320 (H.B. 2971), § 10(a), effective September 1, 2003.

Transportation

(Enacted by Acts 1999, 76th Leg., ch. 433 (S.B. 1176), § 1, effective September 1, 1999; am. Acts 2001, 77th Leg., ch. 869 (H.B. 1831), § 2(a), effective June 14, 2001; am. Acts 2001, 77th Leg., ch. 1420 (H.B. 2812), § 21.001(107), effective September 1, 2001 (renumbered from Sec. 502.299).)

### Sec. 502.2933.  Texas Young Lawyers Association License Plates [Repealed].

Repealed by Acts 2003, 78th Leg., ch. 1320 (H.B. 2971), § 10(a), effective September 1, 2003. (Enacted by Acts 1999, 76th Leg., ch. 634 (S.B. 987), § 1, effective September 1, 1999; am. Acts 2001, 77th Leg., ch. 1420 (H.B. 2812 ), § 21.001(108), effective September 1, 2001 (renumbered from Sec. 502.299).)

### Sec. 502.294.  Municipal and Private Buses [Repealed].

Repealed by Acts 2003, 78th Leg., ch. 1320 (H.B. 2971), § 10(a), effective September 1, 2003. (Enacted by Acts 1997, 75th Leg., ch. 625 (S.B. 1630), § 10, effective September 1, 1997.)

### Sec. 502.295.  State Officials [Repealed].

Repealed by Acts 2003, 78th Leg., ch. 1320 (H.B. 2971), § 10(a), effective September 1, 2003. (Enacted by Acts 1997, 75th Leg., ch. 625 (S.B. 1630), § 10, effective September 1, 1997.)

### Sec. 502.2951.  County Judges [Repealed].

Repealed by Acts 2003, 78th Leg., ch. 1320 (H.B. 2971), § 10(a), effective September 1, 2003. (Enacted by Acts 1997, 75th Leg., ch. 1222 (H.B. 344), § 3, effective September 1, 1997; am. Acts 1999, 76th Leg., ch. 62 (S.B. 1368), § 19.01(104), effective September 1, 1999 (renumbered from Sec. 502.293).)

### Sec. 502.296.  Members of Congress [Repealed].

Repealed by Acts 2003, 78th Leg., ch. 1320 (H.B. 2971), § 10(a), effective September 1, 2003. (Enacted by Acts 1997, 75th Leg., ch. 625 (S.B. 1630), § 10, effective September 1, 1997.)

### Sec. 502.297.  State and Federal Judges [Repealed].

Repealed by Acts 2003, 78th Leg., ch. 1320 (H.B. 2971), § 10(a), effective September 1, 2003.

(Enacted by Acts 1997, 75th Leg., ch. 625 (S.B. 1630), § 10, effective September 1, 1997.)

### Sec. 502.2971.  [Repealed January 1, 2012] Federal Administrative Law Judges.

(a) The department shall issue specially designed license plates for a passenger car or light truck owned by a federal administrative law judge.

(b) License plates issued under this section must include the words "Fed. A.L. Judge."

(c) The department shall issue license plates under this section to a person who:

(1) applies to the department on a form prescribed by the department;

(2) furnishes evidence acceptable to the department that the person is eligible to register the vehicle under this section; and

(3) pays the fee prescribed by Section 502.161.

(d) A person may be issued three sets of license plates under this section.

(e) A registration under this section is for a registration period of 12 consecutive months or until March 31, whichever period is shorter.

(f) If the owner of a vehicle registered under this section disposes of the vehicle during the registration period, the owner shall surrender the special license plates to the department.
(Enacted by Acts 2003, 78th Leg., ch. 223 (H.B. 510), § 1, effective September 1, 2003.)

### Sec. 502.298.  100th Football Season of Stephen F. Austin High School [Repealed].

Repealed by Acts 2003, 78th Leg., ch. 1320 (H.B. 2971), § 10(a), effective September 1, 2003. (Enacted by Acts 1999, 76th Leg., ch. 951 (H.B. 2461), § 4, effective August 30, 1999.)

### Sec. 502.299.  Texas Citrus Industry [Repealed].

Repealed by Acts 2003, 78th Leg., ch. 1320 (H.B. 2971), § 10(a), effective September 1, 2003. (Enacted by Acts 1999, 76th Leg., ch. 1230 (S.B. 754), § 1, effective September 1, 1999.)

### Secs. 502.300 to 502.302 [Reserved for expansion].

### Sec. 502.303.  Waterfowl and Wetland

**Conservation License Plates [Re-pealed].**

Repealed by Acts 2003, 78th Leg., ch. 1320 (H.B. 2971), § 10(a), effective September 1, 2003. (Enacted by Acts 1999, 76th Leg., ch. 951 (H.B. 2461), § 3, effective August 30, 1999.)

**Secs. 502.304 to 502.350 [Reserved for expansion].**

*SUBCHAPTER G*
*[EFFECTIVE UNTIL JANUARY 1, 2012] TEMPORARY REGISTRATION; [EFFECTIVE JANUARY 1, 2012] ADDITIONAL FEES*

**Sec. 502.351. [Renumbered January 1, 2012] Farm Vehicles: Excess Weight.**

(a) The owner of a registered commercial motor vehicle, truck-tractor, trailer, or semitrailer may obtain a short-term permit to haul loads of a weight more than that for which the vehicle is registered by paying an additional fee before the additional weight is hauled to transport:

(1) the person's own seasonal agricultural products to market or another point for sale or processing;

(2) seasonal laborers from their place of residence to a farm or ranch; or

(3) materials, tools, equipment, or supplies, without charge, from the place of purchase or storage to a farm or ranch exclusively for use on the farm or ranch.

(b) A permit may not be issued under this section for a period that is less than one month or that:

(1) is greater than one year; or

(2) extends beyond the expiration of the registration year for the vehicle.

(c) A permit issued under this section for a quarter must be for a calendar quarter.

(d) The fee for a permit under this section is a percentage of the difference between the registration fee otherwise prescribed by this chapter for the vehicle and the annual fee for the desired weight, as follows:

| | |
|---|---|
| One month (30 consecutive days) | 10 percent |
| One quarter | 30 percent |
| Two quarters | 60 percent |
| Three quarters | 90 percent |

(e) The department shall design, prescribe, and furnish a sticker, plate, or other means of indicating the additional weight and the registra-tion period for each vehicle registered under this section.

(Enacted by Acts 1995, 74th Leg., ch. 165 (S.B. 971), § 1, effective September 1, 1995.)

STATUTORY NOTES

**Editor's notes.** — This section is renumbered to Transportation Code Section 502.434 pursuant to Acts 2011, 82nd Leg., ch. 1296 (H.B. 2357), § 144, effective January 1, 2012.

**Sec. 502.352. [Renumbered January 1, 2012] Foreign Commercial Vehicles.**

(a) The department may issue a temporary permit for a commercial motor vehicle, trailer, semitrailer, or motor bus that:

(1) is owned by a resident of the United States, Canada, or the United Mexican States;

(2) is subject to registration in this state; and

(3) is not authorized to travel on a public highway because of the lack of registration in this state or the lack of reciprocity with the state or province in which the vehicle is registered.

(b) A permit issued under this section:

(1) is in lieu of registration; and

(2) is valid for the period stated on the permit, effective from the date and time shown on the receipt issued as evidence of registration under this section.

(c) [2 Versions: As amended by Acts 2009, 81st Leg., ch. 919] A person may obtain a permit under this section by:

(1) applying to the county assessor-collector, the department, or the department's wire service agent, if the department has a wire service agent;

(2) paying a fee of $25 for a 72-hour permit or $50 for a 144-hour permit:

(A) in cash;

(B) by postal money order;

(C) by certified check;

(D) by wire transfer through the department's wire service agent, if any;

(E) by an escrow account; or

(F) where the service is provided, by a credit card issued by:

(i) a financial institution chartered by a state or the United States; or

(ii) a nationally recognized credit organization approved by the Texas Transportation Commission;

(3) paying a discount or service charge for a credit card payment or escrow account, in addition to the fee;

(4) furnishing to the county assessor-collector, the department, or the department's wire service agent, evidence of financial responsibility for the vehicle that complies with Sections 502.153(c) and 601.168(a) and is written by an insurance company or surety company authorized to write motor vehicle liability insurance in this state; and

(5) submitting a copy of the applicable federal declaration form required by the Federal Motor Carrier Safety Administration or its successor in connection with the importation of a motor vehicle or motor vehicle equipment subject to the federal motor vehicle safety, bumper, and theft prevention standards.

(c) **[2 Versions: As amended by Acts 2009, 81st Leg., ch. 933]** A person may obtain a permit under this section by:

(1) applying to the county assessor-collector, the department, or the department's wire service agent, if the department has a wire service agent;

(2) paying a fee of $25 for a 72-hour permit or $50 for a 144-hour permit:

(A) in cash;

(B) by postal money order;

(C) by certified check;

(D) by wire transfer through the department's wire service agent, if any;

(E) by an escrow account; or

(F) where the service is provided, by a credit card issued by:

(i) a financial institution chartered by a state or the United States; or

(ii) a nationally recognized credit organization approved by the board;

(3) paying a discount or service charge for a credit card payment or escrow account, in addition to the fee; and

(4) furnishing to the county assessor-collector, the department, or the department's wire service agent, evidence of financial responsibility for the vehicle that complies with Sections 502.153(c) and 601.168(a) and is written by an insurance company or surety company authorized to write motor vehicle liability insurance in this state.

(d) A county assessor-collector shall report and send a fee collected under this section in the manner provided by Sections 502.102 and 502.105. Each week, a wire service agent shall send to the department a report of all permits issued by the agent during the previous week. The department by rule shall prescribe the form and content of a report required by this subsection.

(e) The department may:

(1) adopt rules to administer this section; and

(2) prescribe an application for a permit and other forms under this section.

(f) A vehicle issued a permit under this section is subject to Subchapters B and F, Chapter 548, unless the vehicle:

(1) is registered in another state of the United States, in a province of Canada, or in a state of the United Mexican States; or

(2) is mobile drilling or servicing equipment used in the production of gas, crude petroleum, or oil, including a mobile crane or hoisting equipment, mobile lift equipment, forklift, or tug.

(g) A commercial motor vehicle, trailer, semitrailer, or motor bus apprehended for violating a registration law of this state:

(1) may not be issued a permit under this section; and

(2) is immediately subject to registration in this state.

(h) A person who operates a commercial motor vehicle, trailer, or semitrailer with an expired permit issued under this section is considered to be operating an unregistered vehicle subject to each penalty prescribed by law.

(i) The department may establish one or more escrow accounts in the state highway fund for the prepayment of a 72-hour permit or a 144-hour permit. Any fee established by the department for the administration of this subsection shall be administered as required by an agreement entered into by the department.

(Enacted by Acts 1995, 74th Leg., ch. 165 (S.B. 971), § 1, effective September 1, 1995; am. Acts 1997, 75th Leg., ch. 165 (S.B. 898), § 30.61(a), effective September 1, 1997; am. Acts 1997, 75th Leg., ch. 625 (S.B. 1630), § 11, effective September 1, 1997; am. Acts 2009, 81st Leg., ch. 919 (H.B. 2985), § 2, effective September 1, 2009; am. Acts 2009, 81st Leg., ch. 933 (H.B. 3097), § 2E.06, effective September 1, 2009.)

### STATUTORY NOTES

**Editor's notes.** — This section is renumbered to Transportation Code Section 502.094 pursuant to Acts

2011, 82nd Leg., ch. 1296 (H.B. 2357), § 97, effective January 1, 2012.

### Sec. 502.353. [Renumbered January 1, 2012] Foreign Commercial Vehicles; Annual Permits; Offense.

(a) The department may issue an annual permit to a foreign commercial motor vehicle, trailer, or semitrailer that:

(1) is subject to registration in this state; and

(2) is not authorized to travel on a public highway because of the lack of registration in this state or the lack of reciprocity with the state or country in which the vehicle is registered.

(b) A permit issued under this section:

(1) is in lieu of registration; and

(2) is valid for a vehicle registration year to begin on the first day of a calendar month designated by the department and end on the last day of the last calendar month of the registration year.

(c) A permit may not be issued under this section for the importation of citrus fruit into this state from a foreign country except for foreign export or processing for foreign export.

(d) A person may obtain a permit under this section by:

(1) applying to the department;

(2) paying a fee in the amount required by Subsection (e) in cash or by postal money order or certified check; and

(3) furnishing evidence of financial responsibility for the motor vehicle that complies with Sections 502.153(c) and 601.168(a), the policies to be written by an insurance company or surety company authorized to write motor vehicle liability insurance in this state.

(e) The fee for a permit under this section is the fee that would be required for registering the vehicle under Section 502.162 or 502.167, except as provided by Subsection (f).

(f) A vehicle registered under this section is exempt from the token fee and is not required to display the associated distinguishing license plate if the vehicle:

(1) is a semitrailer that has a gross weight of more than 6,000 pounds; and

(2) is used or intended to be used in combination with a truck tractor or commercial motor vehicle with a manufacturer's rated carrying capacity of more than one ton.

(g) A vehicle registered under this section is not subject to the fee required by Section 502.172 or 502.173.

(h) The department may:

(1) adopt rules to administer this section; and

(2) prescribe an application for a permit and other forms under this section.

(i) A person who violates this section commits an offense. An offense under this section is a misdemeanor punishable by a fine not to exceed $200.

(Enacted by Acts 1995, 74th Leg., ch. 165 (S.B. 971), § 1, effective September 1, 1995; am. Acts 1997, 75th Leg., ch. 165 (S.B. 898), § 30.63(a), effective September 1, 1997.)

#### STATUTORY NOTES

**Editor's notes.** — This section is renumbered to Transportation Code Section 502.093 pursuant to Acts 2011, 82nd Leg., ch. 1296 (H.B. 2357), § 96, effective January 1, 2012.

### Sec. 502.354. [Renumbered January 1, 2012] Single or 30-Day Trip Permits; Offense.

(a) The department may issue a temporary permit for a vehicle that:

(1) is subject to registration in this state; and

(2) is not authorized to travel on a public highway because of the lack of registration in this state or the lack of reciprocity with the state or country in which the vehicle is registered.

(b) A permit issued under this section:

(1) is in lieu of registration; and

(2) is valid for:

(A) one trip, as provided by Subsection (c); or

(B) 30 days, as provided by Subsection (d).

(c) A one-trip permit is valid for one trip between the points of origin and destination and those intermediate points specified in the application and registration receipt. Unless the vehicle is a bus operating under charter that is not covered by a reciprocity agreement with the state or country in which the bus is registered, a one-trip permit is for the transit of the vehicle only, and the vehicle may not be used for the transportation of any passenger or property. A one-trip permit may not be valid for longer than 15 days from the effective date of registration.

(d) A 30-day permit may be issued only to a passenger vehicle, a private bus, a trailer or semitrailer with a gross weight of not more than 10,000 pounds, a light truck, or a light commercial vehicle with a manufacturer's rated carrying capacity of more than one ton that will operate unladen. A person may obtain multiple 30-day permits. The department may issue a single registration receipt to apply to all of the periods for which the vehicle is registered.

(e) A person may obtain a permit under this section by:

(1) applying on a form provided by the department to:

(A) the county assessor-collector of the county in which the vehicle will first be operated on a public highway; or

(B) the department in Austin or at one of the department's vehicle title and registration regional offices;

(2) paying a fee, in cash or by postal money order or certified check, of:

(A) $5 for a one-trip permit; or

(B) $25 for each 30-day period; and

(3) furnishing evidence of financial responsibility for the vehicle in a form listed under Section 502.153(c).

(f) A registration receipt and temporary tag shall be issued on forms provided by the department. The temporary tag must contain all pertinent information required by this section and must be displayed in the rear window of the vehicle so that the tag is clearly visible and legible when viewed from the rear of the vehicle. If the vehicle does not have a rear window, the temporary tag must be attached on or carried in the vehicle to allow ready inspection. The registration receipt must be carried in the vehicle at all times during the period in which it is valid.

(g) The department may refuse and may instruct a county assessor-collector to refuse to issue a temporary registration for any vehicle if, in the department's opinion, the vehicle or the owner of the vehicle has been involved in operations that constitute an abuse of the privilege granted by this section. A registration issued after notice to a county assessor-collector under this subsection is void.

(h) A person issued a temporary registration under this section who operates a vehicle in violation of Subsection (f) commits an offense. An offense under this subsection is a Class C misdemeanor.

(i) The department may:

(1) adopt rules to administer this section; and

(2) prescribe an application for a permit and other forms under this section.

(Enacted by Acts 1995, 74th Leg., ch. 165 (S.B. 971), § 1, effective September 1, 1995; am. Acts 1997, 75th Leg., ch. 1092 (H.B. 2067), § 1, effective June 19, 1997.)

STATUTORY NOTES

**Editor's notes.** — This section is renumbered to Transportation Code Section 502.095 pursuant to Acts 2011, 82nd Leg., ch. 1296 (H.B. 2357), § 98, effective January 1, 2012.

## Sec. 502.355. [Renumbered January 1, 2012] Nonresident-Owned Vehicles Used to Transport Farm Products; Offense.

(a) The department may issue to a nonresident owner a permit for a truck, truck-tractor, trailer, or semitrailer that:

(1) is registered in the owner's home state or country; and

(2) will be used to transport:

(A) farm products produced in this state from the place of production to a place of market or storage or a railhead that is not more than 75 miles from the place of production;

(B) machinery used to harvest farm products produced in this state; or

(C) farm products produced outside this state from the point of entry into this state to a place of market, storage, or processing or a railhead or seaport that is not more than 80 miles from the point of entry.

(b) The department shall issue a distinguishing insignia for a vehicle issued a permit under this section. The insignia must be attached to the vehicle in lieu of regular license plates and must show the permit expiration date. A permit issued under this section is valid until the earlier of:

(1) the date the vehicle's registration in the owner's home state or country expires; or

(2) the 30th day after the date the permit is issued.

(c) A person may obtain a permit under this section by:

(1) applying to the department on a form prescribed by the department;

(2) paying a fee equal to $\frac{1}{12}$ the registration fee prescribed by this chapter for the vehicle;

(3) furnishing satisfactory evidence that the motor vehicle is insured under an insurance policy that complies with Section 601.072 and that is written by:

(A) an insurance company or surety company authorized to write motor vehicle liability insurance in this state; or

(B) with the department's approval, a surplus lines insurer that meets the requirements of Chapter 981, Insurance Code, and rules adopted by the commissioner of insurance under that chapter, if the applicant is unable to obtain insurance from an insurer described by Paragraph (A); and

(4) furnishing evidence that the vehicle has been inspected as required under Chapter 548.

(d) A nonresident owner may not obtain more than three permits under this section during a registration year.

(e) A vehicle for which a permit is issued under this section may not be operated in this state after the permit expires unless the owner:

(1) obtains another temporary permit; or

(2) registers the vehicle under Section 502.162, 502.165, 502.166, or 502.167, as appropriate, for the remainder of the registration year.

(f) A vehicle for which a permit is issued under this section may not be registered under Section 502.163.

(g) A mileage referred to in this section is a state highway mileage.

(h) A person operating a vehicle under a permit issued under this section commits an offense if the person:

(1) transports farm products to a place of market, storage, or processing or a railhead or seaport that is farther from the place of production or point of entry, as appropriate, than the distance provided for in the permit; or

(2) follows a route other than that prescribed by the board.

(i) An offense under Subsection (h) is a misdemeanor punishable by a fine of not less than $25 or more than $200. (Enacted by Acts 1995, 74th Leg., ch. 165 (S.B. 971), § 1, effective September 1, 1995; am. Acts 2003, 78th Leg., ch. 1276 (H.B. 3507), § 10A.553, effective September 1, 2003; am. Acts 2009, 81st Leg., ch. 933 (H.B. 3097), § 2E.07, effective September 1, 2009.)

STATUTORY NOTES

**Editor's notes.** — This section is renumbered to Transportation Code Section 502.092 pursuant to Acts 2011, 82nd Leg., ch. 1296 (H.B. 2357), § 95, effective January 1, 2012.

## Sec. 502.356. [Effective January 1, 2012] Automated Registration and Titling System.

(a) In addition to other registration fees for a license plate or set of license plates or other device used as the registration insignia, a fee of $1 shall be collected.

(b) The department may use money collected under this section to provide for or enhance:

(1) automated on-premises and off-premises registration; and

(2) services related to the titling of vehicles. (Enacted by Acts 1999, 76th Leg., ch. 1455 (H.B. 3014), § 1, effective September 1, 1999; am. Acts 2009, 81st Leg., ch. 1136 (H.B. 2553), §§ 27, 39(4), effective September 1, 2011; am. Acts 2011, 82nd Leg., ch. 1296 (H.B. 2357), § 130, effective September 1, 2011 (renumbered from Sec. 502.1705).)

## Sec. 502.357. [Effective January 1, 2012] Financial Responsibility Programs.

(a) In addition to other fees imposed for registration of a motor vehicle, at the time of application for registration or renewal of registration of a motor vehicle for which the owner is required to submit evidence of financial responsibility under Section 502.046, the applicant shall pay a fee of $1. In addition to other fees imposed for registration of a motor vehicle, at the time of application for registration of a motor vehicle that is subject to Section 501.0234, the applicant shall pay a fee of $1. Fees collected under this section shall be remitted weekly to the department.

(b) Fees collected under this section shall be deposited to the credit of the state highway fund. Subject to appropriations, the money shall be used by the Department of Public Safety to:

(1) support the Department of Public Safety's reengineering of the driver's license system to provide for the issuance by the Department of Public Safety of a driver's license or personal identification certificate, to include use of image comparison technology;

(2) establish and maintain a system to support the driver responsibility program under Chapter 708; and

(3) make lease payments to the master lease purchase program for the financing of the driver's license reengineering project.

(c) Fees collected under this section shall be deposited to the credit of the state highway fund. Subject to appropriation, the money may be used by the Department of Public Safety, the Texas Department of Insurance, the Department of Information Resources, and the department to carry out Subchapter N, Chapter 601.

(d) The Department of Public Safety, the Texas Department of Insurance, the Department of Information Resources, and the department shall jointly adopt rules and develop forms necessary to administer this section.

(Enacted by Acts 2003, 78th Leg., ch. 1325 (H.B. 3588), § 19B.03, effective September 1, 2003; am. Acts 2003, 78th Leg., 3rd C.S., ch. 8 (H.B. 2), § 5.08, effective January 11, 2004; am. Acts 2005, 79th Leg., ch. 892 (S.B. 1670), §§ 2, 3, effective September 1, 2005; am. Acts 2005, 79th Leg., ch. 1108 (H.B. 2337), §§ 1, 2, effective September 1, 2005; am. Acts 2011, 82nd Leg., ch. 91 (S.B. 1303), § 24.007, effective September 1, 2011; am. Acts 2011, 82nd Leg., ch. 1296 (H.B. 2357), § 131, effective January 1, 2012 (renumbered from Sec. 502.1715).)

## Sec. 502.358.　[Effective January 1, 2012, Expires August 31, 2019] Texas Emissions Reduction Plan Surcharge.

(a) In addition to the registration fees charged under Section 502.255, a surcharge is imposed on the registration of a truck-tractor or commercial motor vehicle under that section in an amount equal to 10 percent of the total fees due for the registration of the truck-tractor or commercial motor vehicle under that section.

(b) The county tax assessor-collector shall remit the surcharge collected under this section to the comptroller at the time and in the manner prescribed by the comptroller for deposit in the Texas emissions reduction plan fund.

(c) This section expires August 31, 2019.

(Enacted by Acts 2001, 77th Leg., ch. 967 (S.B. 5), § 7, effective September 1, 2001; am. Acts 2005, 79th Leg., ch. 1125 (H.B. 2481), § 20, effective September 1, 2005; am. Acts 2007, 80th Leg., ch. 262 (S.B. 12), § 2.17, effective June 8, 2007; am. Acts 2009, 81st Leg., ch. 1125 (H.B. 1796), § 21, effective September 1, 2009; am. Acts 2011, 82nd Leg., ch. 1296 (H.B. 2357), § 132, effective January 1, 2012 (renumbered from Sec. 502.1675).)

## Sec. 502.359.　[Effective January 1, 2012] Additional Fee for Certain Vehicles Using Diesel Motor.

(a) The registration fee under this chapter for a motor vehicle other than a passenger car, a truck with a gross vehicle weight of 18,000 pounds or less, or a vehicle registered in combination under Section 502.255 is increased by 11 percent if the vehicle has a diesel motor.

(b) The registration receipt for a motor vehicle, other than a passenger car or a truck with a gross vehicle weight of 18,000 pounds or less, must show that the vehicle has a diesel motor.

(c) The department may adopt rules to administer this section.

(Enacted by Acts 1995, 74th Leg., ch. 165 (S.B. 971), § 1, effective September 1, 1995; am. Acts 2011, 82nd Leg., ch. 1296 (H.B. 2357), § 133, effective January 1, 2012 (renumbered from Sec. 502.171).)

## Secs. 502.360 to 502.400 [Reserved for expansion].

### SUBCHAPTER H
### [EFFECTIVE UNTIL JANUARY 1, 2012] OFFENSES AND PENALTIES; [EFFECTIVE JANUARY 1, 2012] OPTIONAL FEES

## Sec. 502.401.　[2 Versions: Renumbered January 1, 2012] General Penalty.

(a) A person commits an offense if the person violates a provision of this chapter and no other penalty is prescribed for the violation.

(b) This section does not apply to a violation of Section 502.003, 502.101, 502.109, 502.112, 502.113, 502.114, 502.152, 502.164, or 502.282.

(c) An offense under this section is a misdemeanor punishable by a fine not to exceed $200.

(Enacted by Acts 1995, 74th Leg., ch. 165 (S.B. 971), § 1, effective September 1, 1995.)

### STATUTORY NOTES

**Editor's notes.** — This section is renumbered to Transportation Code Section 502.471 pursuant to Acts 2011, 82nd Leg., ch. 1296 (H.B. 2357), § 155, effective January 1, 2012.

## Sec. 502.401.　[2 Versions: Effective January 1, 2012] Optional County Fee for Road and Bridge Fund.

(a) The commissioners court of a county by order may impose an additional fee, not to exceed $10, for registering a vehicle in the county.

(b) A vehicle that may be registered under this chapter without payment of a registration fee may be registered in a county imposing a fee under this section without payment of the additional fee.

(c) A fee imposed under this section may take effect only on January 1 of a year. The county must adopt the order and notify the department not later than September 1 of the year preceding the year in which the fee takes effect.

(d) A fee imposed under this section may be removed. The removal may take effect only on

January 1 of a year. A county may remove the fee only by:

(1) rescinding the order imposing the fee; and

(2) notifying the department not later than September 1 of the year preceding the year in which the removal takes effect.

(e) The county assessor-collector of a county imposing a fee under this section shall collect the additional fee for a vehicle when other fees imposed under this chapter are collected.

(f) The department shall collect the additional fee on a vehicle that is owned by a resident of a county imposing a fee under this section that must be registered directly with the department. The department shall send all fees collected for a county under this subsection to the county treasurer to be credited to the county road and bridge fund.

(g) The department shall adopt rules necessary to administer registration for a vehicle being registered in a county imposing a fee under this section.

(Enacted by Acts 1995, 74th Leg., ch. 165 (S.B. 971), § 1, effective September 1, 1995; am. Acts 2011, 82nd Leg., ch. 1296 (H.B. 2357), § 135, effective January 1, 2012 (renumbered from Sec. 502.172).)

## Sec. 502.402. [2 Versions: Renumbered January 1, 2012] Operation of Unregistered Motor Vehicle.

(a) A person commits an offense if the person operates a motor vehicle that has not been registered as required by law. An offense under this subsection is a misdemeanor punishable by a fine not to exceed $200.

(b), (c) [Repealed by Acts 1997, 75th Leg., ch. 165 (S.B. 898), § 30.64, effective September 1, 1997.]

(Enacted by Acts 1995, 74th Leg., ch. 165 (S.B. 971), § 1, effective September 1, 1995; am. Acts 1997, 75th Leg., ch. 165 (S.B. 898), § 30.64, effective September 1, 1997.)

### STATUTORY NOTES

**Editor's notes.** — This section is renumbered to Transportation Code Section 502.472 pursuant to Acts 2011, 82nd Leg., ch. 1296 (H.B. 2357), § 156, effective January 1, 2012.

## Sec. 502.402. [2 Versions: Effective January 1, 2012] Optional County Fee for Transportation Projects.

(a) This section applies only to a county:

(1) that borders the United Mexican States;

(2) that has a population of more than 300,000; and

(3) in which the largest municipality has a population of less than 300,000.

(b) The commissioners court of a county by order may impose an additional fee, not to exceed $10, for a vehicle registered in the county.

(c) A vehicle that may be registered under this chapter without payment of a registration fee may be registered under this section without payment of the additional fee.

(d) A fee imposed under this section may take effect and be removed in accordance with the requirements of Section 502.401.

(e) The additional fee shall be collected for a vehicle when other fees imposed under this chapter are collected. The fee revenue collected shall be sent to the regional mobility authority of the county to fund long-term transportation projects in the county.

(f) The department shall adopt rules necessary to administer registration for a vehicle being registered in a county imposing a fee under this section.

(Enacted by Acts 2007, 80th Leg., ch. 249 (H.B. 3437), § 1, effective May 25, 2007; am. Acts 2011, 82nd Leg., ch. 1296 (H.B. 2357), § 136, effective January 1, 2012 (renumbered from Sec. 502.1725).)

## Sec. 502.403. [2 Versions: Repealed January 1, 2012] Operation of Vehicle Under Improper Registration.

(a) A person commits an offense if the person operates on a public highway a motor vehicle registered for a class other than that to which the vehicle belongs.

(b) An offense under this section is a misdemeanor punishable by a fine not to exceed $200.

(Enacted by Acts 1995, 74th Leg., ch. 165 (S.B. 971), § 1, effective September 1, 1995.)

## Sec. 502.403. [2 Versions: Effective January 1, 2012] Optional County Fee for Child Safety.

(a) The commissioners court of a county that has a population greater than 1.3 million and in which a municipality with a population of more than one million is primarily located may impose by order an additional fee of not less than 50 cents or more than $1.50 for a vehicle registered in the county. The commissioners court of any other county may impose by order an additional fee of not more than $1.50 for registering a vehicle in the county.

(b) A vehicle that may be registered under this chapter without payment of a registration fee may be registered without payment of the additional fee.

(c) A fee imposed under this section may take effect and be removed in accordance with the provisions of Section 502.401.

(d) The additional fee shall be collected for a vehicle when other fees imposed under this chapter are collected.

(e) A county imposing a fee under this section may deduct for administrative costs an amount of not more than 10 percent of the revenue it receives from the fee. The county may also deduct from the fee revenue an amount proportional to the percentage of county residents who live in unincorporated areas of the county. After making the deductions provided for by this subsection, the county shall send the remainder of the fee revenue to the municipalities in the county according to their population.

(f) A municipality with a population greater than 850,000 shall deposit revenue from a fee imposed under this subsection to the credit of the child safety trust fund created under Section 106.001, Local Government Code. A municipality with a population less than 850,000 shall use revenue from a fee imposed under this section in accordance with Article 102.014(g), Code of Criminal Procedure.

(g) After deducting administrative costs, a county may use revenue from a fee imposed under this section only for a purpose permitted by Article 102.014(g), Code of Criminal Procedure. (Enacted by Acts 1995, 74th Leg., ch. 165 (S.B. 971), § 1, effective September 1, 1995; am. Acts 1997, 75th Leg., ch. 165 (S.B. 898), § 30.48, effective September 1, 1997; am. Acts 2001, 77th Leg., ch. 669 (H.B. 2810), § 141, effective September 1, 2001; am. Acts 2009, 81st Leg., ch. 162 (S.B. 446), § 2, effective May 26, 2009; am. Acts 2011, 82nd Leg., ch. 1296 (H.B. 2357), § 137, effective January 1, 2012 (renumbered from Sec. 502.173).)

### Sec. 502.404. [2 Versions: Renumbered January 1, 2012] Operation of Vehicle Without License Plate or Registration Insignia.

(a) A person commits an offense if the person operates on a public highway during a registration period a passenger car or commercial motor vehicle that does not display two license plates, at the front and rear of the vehicle, that have been:

(1) assigned by the department for the period; or

(2) validated by a registration insignia issued by the department that establishes that the vehicle is registered for the period.

(b) A person commits an offense if the person operates on a public highway during a registration period a passenger car or commercial motor vehicle, other than a vehicle assigned license plates for the registration period, that does not properly display the registration insignia issued by the department that establishes that the license plates have been validated for the period.

(c) A person commits an offense if the person operates on a public highway during a registration period a road tractor, motorcycle, trailer, or semitrailer that does not display a license plate, attached to the rear of the vehicle, that has been:

(1) assigned by the department for the period; or

(2) validated by a registration insignia issued by the department that establishes that the vehicle is registered for the period.

(d) Subsections (a) and (b) do not apply to a dealer operating a vehicle as provided by law.

(e) An offense under this section is a misdemeanor punishable by a fine not to exceed $200.

(f) A court may dismiss a charge brought under Subsection (a) if the defendant:

(1) remedies the defect before the defendant's first court appearance; and

(2) pays an administrative fee not to exceed $10.

(g) A court may dismiss a charge brought under Subsection (b) if the defendant:

(1) shows that:

(A) the passenger car or commercial motor vehicle was issued a registration insignia by the department that establishes that the vehicle was registered for the period during which the offense was committed; and

(B) the registration insignia described in Paragraph (A) was attached to the passenger car or commercial motor vehicle before the defendant's first court appearance; and

(2) pays an administrative fee not to exceed $10.

(Enacted by Acts 1995, 74th Leg., ch. 165 (S.B. 971), § 1, effective September 1, 1995; am. Acts 2007, 80th Leg., ch. 1027 (H.B. 1623), § 1, effective September 1, 2007.)

### STATUTORY NOTES

**Editor's notes.** — This section is renumbered to Transportation Code Section 502.473 pursuant to Acts

2011, 82nd Leg., ch. 1296 (H.B. 2357), § 157, effective January 1, 2012.

## Sec. 502.404. [2 Versions: Effective January 1, 2012] Voluntary Assessment for Young Farmer Loan Guarantees.

(a) When a person registers a commercial motor vehicle under Section 502.433, the person shall pay a voluntary assessment of $5.

(b) The county assessor-collector shall send an assessment collected under this section to the comptroller, at the time and in the manner prescribed by the Texas Agricultural Finance Authority, for deposit in the Texas agricultural fund.

(c) The Texas Agricultural Finance Authority shall prescribe procedures under which an assessment collected under this section may be refunded. The county assessor-collector of the county in which an assessment is collected shall:

    (1) implement the refund procedures; and

    (2) provide notice of those procedures to a person paying an assessment at the time of payment.

(Enacted by Acts 1995, 74th Leg., ch. 165 (S.B. 971), § 1, effective September 1, 1995; am. Acts 1997, 75th Leg., ch. 1423 (H.B. 2841), § 18.04, effective September 1, 1997; am. Acts 1999, 76th Leg., ch. 1459 (H.B. 3050), § 15, effective June 19, 1999; am. Acts 2009, 81st Leg., ch. 506 (S.B. 1016), § 1.20, effective September 1, 2009; am. Acts 2011, 82nd Leg., ch. 1296 (H.B. 2357), § 138, effective January 1, 2012 (renumbered from Sec. 502.174).)

## Sec. 502.405. [2 Versions: Repealed January 1, 2012] Operation of Motorcycle Without Seal.

(a) A person commits an offense if the person operates, or as the owner permits another to operate, on a public highway during a registration period a motorcycle that does not have attached a registration seal for the period.

(b) An offense under this section is a misdemeanor punishable by a fine not to exceed $200.
(Enacted by Acts 1995, 74th Leg., ch. 165 (S.B. 971), § 1, effective September 1, 1995.)

## Sec. 502.405. [2 Versions: Effective January 1, 2012] Donor Education, Awareness, and Registry Program.

(a) The department shall provide to each county assessor-collector the educational materials for prospective donors provided as required by the Donor Education, Awareness, and Registry Program of Texas under Chapter 49, Health and Safety Code. The educational materials shall be made available in each office authorized to accept applications for registration of motor vehicles.

(b) [3 Versions: Effective until January 1, 2012] A county assessor-collector shall collect an additional fee of $1 for the registration or renewal of registration of a motor vehicle to pay the costs of the Donor Education, Awareness, and Registry Program of Texas, established under Chapter 49, Health and Safety Code, and of the Texas Organ, Tissue, and Eye Donor Council, established under Chapter 113, Health and Safety Code, if the person registering or renewing the registration of a motor vehicle opts to pay the additional fee. Notwithstanding any other provision of this chapter, the county assessor-collector shall remit all fees collected under this subsection to the comptroller, who shall maintain the identity of the source of the fees.

(b) [3 Versions, effective January 1, 2012: As amended by Acts 2011, 82nd Leg., ch. 554] A county assessor-collector shall collect an additional fee of $1 for the registration or renewal of registration of a motor vehicle to pay the costs of the Glenda Dawson Donate Life-Texas Registry established under Chapter 692A, Health and Safety Code, if the person registering or renewing the registration of a motor vehicle opts to pay the additional fee. Notwithstanding any other provision of this chapter, the county assessor-collector shall remit all fees collected under this subsection to the comptroller, who shall maintain the identity of the source of the fees.

(b) [3 Versions, effective January 1, 2012: As amended by Acts 2011, 82nd Leg., ch. 1296] A person may elect to pay an additional fee of $1 for the registration or renewal of registration of a motor vehicle to pay the costs of the Donor Education, Awareness, and Registry Program of Texas, established under Chapter 49, Health and Safety Code, and of the Texas Organ, Tissue, and Eye Donor Council, established under Chapter 113, Health and Safety Code. Notwithstanding any other provision of this chapter, all fees collected under this subsection shall be remitted to the comptroller, who shall maintain the identity of the source of the fees.

(c) Three percent of all money collected under this section may be appropriated only to the department to administer this section.
(Enacted by Acts 2005, 79th Leg., ch. 1186 (H.B. 120), § 8, effective September 1, 2005; am. Acts 2011, 82nd Leg., ch. 554 (H.B. 2904), § 2, effective January 1, 2012; am. Acts 2011, 82nd Leg.,

ch. 1296 (H.B. 2357), § 139, effective January 1, 2012 (renumbered from Sec. 502.1745).)

### Sec. 502.406. Operation of All-Terrain Vehicle Without Sticker [Repealed].

Repealed by Acts 2007, 80th Leg., ch. 1280 (H.B. 3849), § 6, effective June 15, 2007.

(Enacted by Acts 1995, 74th Leg., ch. 165 (S.B. 971), § 1, effective September 1, 1995.)

### Sec. 502.407. Operation of Vehicle with Expired License Plate.

(a) A person commits an offense if, after the fifth working day after the date the registration for the vehicle expires:

(1) the person operates on a public highway during a registration period a motor vehicle, trailer, or semitrailer that has attached to it a license plate for the preceding period; and

(2) the license plate has not been validated by the attachment of a registration insignia for the registration period in effect.

(b) A justice of the peace or municipal court judge having jurisdiction of the offense may:

(1) dismiss a charge of driving with an expired motor vehicle registration if the defendant:

(A) remedies the defect not later than the 20th working day after the date of the offense or before the defendant's first court appearance date, whichever is later; and

(B) establishes that the fee prescribed by Section 502.176 has been paid; and

(2) assess an administrative fee not to exceed $20 when the charge is dismissed.

(c) **[Repealed January 1, 2012]** An offense under this section is a misdemeanor punishable by a fine not to exceed $200.

(Enacted by Acts 1995, 74th Leg., ch. 165 (S.B. 971), § 1, effective September 1, 1995; am. Acts 1999, 76th Leg., ch. 207 (H.B. 924), § 1, effective September 1, 1999; am. Acts 2007, 80th Leg., ch. 1027 (H.B. 1623), § 2, effective September 1, 2007; am. Acts 2011, 82nd Leg., ch. 1296 (H.B. 2357), § 247(6), effective January 1, 2012.)

### Sec. 502.408. [Renumbered January 1, 2012] Operation of Vehicle with Wrong License Plate.

(a) A person commits an offense if the person operates, or as the owner permits another to operate, on a public highway a motor vehicle that has attached to it a number plate or registration insignia issued for a different vehicle. An offense under this subsection is a misdemeanor punishable by a fine not to exceed $200.

(b) to (d) [Repealed by Acts 1997, 75th Leg., ch. 165 (S.B. 898), § 30.65, effective September 1, 1997.]

(Enacted by Acts 1995, 74th Leg., ch. 165 (S.B. 971), § 1, effective September 1, 1995; am. Acts 1997, 75th Leg., ch. 165 (S.B. 898), § 30.65, effective September 1, 1997.)

STATUTORY NOTES

**Editor's notes.** — This section is renumbered to Transportation Code Section 504.944 pursuant to Acts 2011, 82nd Leg., ch. 1296 (H.B. 2357), § 222, effective January 1, 2012.

### Sec. 502.409. [Renumbered January 1, 2012] Wrong, Fictitious, Altered, or Obscured License Plate.

(a) A person commits an offense if the person attaches to or displays on a motor vehicle a number plate or registration insignia that:

(1) is assigned to a different motor vehicle;

(2) is assigned to the vehicle under any other motor vehicle law other than by the department;

(3) is assigned for a registration period other than the registration period in effect;

(4) is fictitious;

(5) has blurring or reflective matter that significantly impairs the readability of the name of the state in which the vehicle is registered or the letters or numbers of the license plate number at any time;

(6) has an attached illuminated device or sticker, decal, emblem, or other insignia that is not authorized by law and that interferes with the readability of the letters or numbers of the license plate number or the name of the state in which the vehicle is registered; or

(7) has a coating, covering, protective material, or other apparatus that:

(A) distorts angular visibility or detectability;

(B) alters or obscures one-half or more of the name of the state in which the vehicle is registered; or

(C) alters or obscures the letters or numbers of the license plate number or the color of the plate.

(b) Except as provided by Subsection (f), an offense under Subsection (a) is a misdemeanor punishable by a fine of not more than $200, unless it is shown at the trial of the offense that the owner knowingly altered or made illegible the letters, numbers, and other identification marks, in which case the offense is a Class B misdemeanor.

(c) Subsection (a)(7) may not be construed to apply to:

(1) a trailer hitch installed on a vehicle in a normal or customary manner;

(2) a transponder, as defined by Section 228.057, that is attached to a vehicle in the manner required by the issuing authority;

(3) a wheelchair lift or wheelchair carrier that is attached to a vehicle in a normal or customary manner;

(4) a trailer being towed by a vehicle; or

(5) a bicycle rack that is attached to a vehicle in a normal or customary manner.

(d) A court may dismiss a charge brought under Subsection (a)(3), (5), (6), or (7) if the defendant:

(1) remedies the defect before the defendant's first court appearance; and

(2) pays an administrative fee not to exceed $10.

(e) [Repealed by Acts 1997, 75th Leg., ch. 165 (S.B. 898), § 30.66, effective September 1, 1997.]

(f) An offense under Subsection (a)(4) is a Class B misdemeanor.
(Enacted by Acts 1995, 74th Leg., ch. 165 (S.B. 971), § 1, effective September 1, 1995; am. Acts 1997, 75th Leg., ch. 165 (S.B. 898), § 30.66, effective September 1, 1997; am. Acts 1997, 75th Leg., ch. 851 (H.B. 1048), § 1, effective September 1, 1997; am. Acts 1999, 76th Leg., ch. 1189 (S.B. 370), § 17, effective September 1, 1999; am. Acts 2003, 78th Leg., ch. 837 (S.B. 439), §§ 1, 2, effective September 1, 2003; am. Acts 2007, 80th Leg., ch. 30 (S.B. 369), § 1, effective September 1, 2007; am. Acts 2007, 80th Leg., ch. 1027 (H.B. 1623), § 3, effective September 1, 2007; am. Acts 2009, 81st Leg., ch. 87 (S.B. 1969), § 27.001(102), effective September 1, 2009.)

### STATUTORY NOTES

**Editor's notes.** — This section is renumbered to Transportation Code Section 502.475 pursuant to Acts 2011, 82nd Leg., ch. 1296 (H.B. 2357), § 159, effective January 1, 2012.

## Sec. 502.410.  Falsification or Forgery.

(a) A person commits an offense if the person knowingly provides false or incorrect information or without legal authority signs the name of another person on a statement or application filed or given as required by this chapter.

(b) Subsection (a) does not apply to a statement or application filed or given under Section 502.184, 502.352, 502.353, 502.354, 502.355, 504.201, 504.411, or 504.508.

(c) An offense under this section is a felony of the third degree.
(Enacted by Acts 1995, 74th Leg., ch. 165 (S.B. 971), § 1, effective September 1, 1995; am. Acts 1997, 75th Leg., ch. 165 (S.B. 898), § 30.67(a), effective September 1, 1997; am. Acts 2005, 79th Leg., ch. 728 (H.B. 2018), § 20.003(b), effective September 1, 2005.)

## Sec. 502.411.  Bribery of County Officer or Agent.

(a) A person commits an offense if the person directly or indirectly agrees with the commissioners court of a county or an officer or agent of the commissioners court or county that the person will register or cause to be registered a motor vehicle, trailer, or semitrailer in that county in consideration of:

(1) the use by the county of the funds derived from the registration in the purchase of property; or

(2) an act to be performed by the commissioners court or an agent or officer of the commissioners court or the county.

(b) The registration of each separate vehicle in violation of Subsection (a) is a separate offense. The agreement or conspiracy to register is a separate offense.

(c) A person who makes or seeks to make an agreement prohibited by Subsection (a) shall be restrained by injunction on application by the district or county attorney of the county in which the vehicle is registered or the attorney general.

(d) An offense under this section is punishable in the same manner as an offense under Section 36.02, Penal Code.
(Enacted by Acts 1995, 74th Leg., ch. 165 (S.B. 971), § 1, effective September 1, 1995.)

## Sec. 502.412.  Operation of Vehicle at Weight Greater Than Stated in Registration Application.

(a) A person commits an offense if the person operates, or permits to be operated, a motor vehicle registered under this chapter that has a weight greater than that stated in the person's application for registration. Each use of the vehicle is a separate offense.

(b) Venue for a prosecution under this section is in any county in which the motor vehicle is operated with a gross weight greater than that stated in the person's application for registration.

Transportation

(c) [Repealed January 1, 2012] An offense under this section is a misdemeanor punishable by a fine not to exceed $200.

(Enacted by Acts 1995, 74th Leg., ch. 165 (S.B. 971), § 1, effective September 1, 1995; am. Acts 2011, 82nd Leg., ch. 1296 (H.B. 2357), § 247(7), effective January 1, 2012).

**Secs. 502.413 to 502.430 [Reserved for expansion].**

## SUBCHAPTER I
### [EFFECTIVE UNTIL JANUARY 1, 2012] REGISTRATION TRANSFER AND REMOVAL OF LICENSE PLATES FOR THE SALE OR TRANSFER OF USED VEHICLES; [EFFECTIVE JANUARY 1, 2012] ALTERNATE REGISTRATION FEES

**Sec. 502.431.  [Effective January 1, 2012] Fee: Motor Vehicle Used Exclusively to Transport and Spread Fertilizer.**

The fee for a registration year for registration of a motor vehicle designed or modified and used exclusively to transport to the field and spread fertilizer, including agricultural limestone, is $75.

(Enacted by Acts 1995, 74th Leg., ch. 165 (S.B. 971), § 1, effective September 1, 1995; am. Acts 2011, 82nd Leg., ch. 1296 (H.B. 2357), § 141, effective January 1, 2012 (renumbered from Sec. 502.164).)

**Sec. 502.432.  [Effective January 1, 2012] Vehicle Transporting Seasonal Agricultural Products.**

(a) The department shall provide for a monthly registration period for a truck-tractor or a commercial motor vehicle:

(1) that is used exclusively to transport a seasonal agricultural product;

(2) that would otherwise be registered for a vehicle registration year; and

(3) for which the owner can show proof of payment of the heavy vehicle use tax or exemption.

(b) The department shall prescribe a registration receipt that is valid until the expiration of the designated registration period.

(c) The registration fee for a registration under this section is computed at a rate of one-twelfth the annual registration fee under Section 502.253, 502.255, or 502.433, as applicable, multiplied by the number of months in the registration period specified in the application for the registration, which may not be less than one month or longer than six months.

(d) For purposes of this section, "to transport a seasonal agricultural product" includes any transportation activity necessary for the production, harvest, or delivery of an agricultural product that is produced seasonally.

(Enacted by Acts 1999, 76th Leg., ch. 732 (H.B. 1041), § 1, effective September 1, 1999; am. Acts 2001, 77th Leg., ch. 832 (H.B. 1128), §§ 1, 2, effective September 1, 2001 (renumbered from Sec. 502.1585); am. Acts 2001, 77th Leg., ch. 1420 (H.B. 2812), § 21.001(105), effective September 1, 2001 (renumbered from Sec. 502.1585); am. Acts 2011, 82nd Leg., ch. 1296 (H.B. 2357), § 142, effective January 1, 2012 (renumbered from Sec. 502.1586).)

**Sec. 502.433.  [Effective January 1, 2012] Fee: Commercial Farm Motor Vehicle.**

(a) The registration fee for a commercial motor vehicle as a farm vehicle is 50 percent of the applicable fee under Section 502.253 if the vehicle's owner will use the vehicle for commercial purposes only to transport:

(1) the person's own poultry, dairy, livestock, livestock products, timber in its natural state, or farm products to market or another place for sale or processing;

(2) laborers from their place of residence to the owner's farm or ranch; or

(3) without charge, materials, tools, equipment, or supplies from the place of purchase or storage to the owner's farm or ranch exclusively for the owner's use or for use on the farm or ranch.

(b) A commercial motor vehicle may be registered under this section despite its use for transporting without charge the owner or a member of the owner's family:

(1) to attend church or school;

(2) to visit a doctor for medical treatment or supplies;

(3) for other necessities of the home or family; or

(4) for the purpose of participating in equine activities or attending livestock shows, as defined by Section 87.001, Civil Practice and Remedies Code.

(c) Subsection (b) does not permit the use of a vehicle registered under this section in connection with gainful employment other than farming or ranching.

(d) The department shall provide distinguishing license plates for a vehicle registered under this section.
(Enacted by Acts 1995, 74th Leg., ch. 165 (S.B. 971), § 1, effective September 1, 1995; am. Acts 2011, 82nd Leg., ch. 1035 (H.B. 2960), § 1, effective June 17, 2011; am. Acts 2011, 82nd Leg., ch. 1296 (H.B. 2357), § 143, effective January 1, 2012 (renumbered from Sec. 502.163).)

### Sec. 502.434. [Effective January 1, 2012] Farm Vehicles: Excess Weight.

(a) The owner of a registered commercial motor vehicle, truck-tractor, trailer, or semitrailer may obtain a short-term permit to haul loads of a weight more than that for which the vehicle is registered by paying an additional fee before the additional weight is hauled to transport:

(1) the person's own seasonal agricultural products to market or another point for sale or processing;

(2) seasonal laborers from their place of residence to a farm or ranch; or

(3) materials, tools, equipment, or supplies, without charge, from the place of purchase or storage to a farm or ranch exclusively for use on the farm or ranch.

(b) A permit may not be issued under this section for a period that is less than one month or that:

(1) is greater than one year; or

(2) extends beyond the expiration of the registration year for the vehicle.

(c) A permit issued under this section for a quarter must be for a calendar quarter.

(d) The fee for a permit under this section is a percentage of the difference between the registration fee otherwise prescribed for the vehicle and the annual fee for the desired weight, as follows:

| | |
|---|---|
| One month (30 consecutive days) | 10 percent |
| One quarter | 30 percent |
| Two quarters | 60 percent |
| Three quarters | 90 percent |

(e) The department shall design, prescribe, and furnish a sticker, plate, or other means of indicating the additional weight and the registration period for each vehicle registered under this section.
(Enacted by Acts 1995, 74th Leg., ch. 165 (S.B. 971), § 1, effective September 1, 1995; am. Acts 2011, 82nd Leg., ch. 1296 (H.B. 2357), § 144, effective January 1, 2012 (renumbered from Sec. 502.351).)

### Sec. 502.435. [Effective January 1, 2012] Certain Soil Conservation Equipment.

(a) The owner of a truck-tractor, semitrailer, or low-boy trailer used on a highway exclusively to transport the owner's soil conservation machinery or equipment used in clearing real property, terracing, or building farm ponds, levees, or ditches may register the vehicle for a fee equal to 50 percent of the fee otherwise prescribed by this chapter for the vehicle.

(b) An owner may register only one truck-tractor and only one semitrailer or low-boy trailer under this section.

(c) An owner must certify that the vehicle is to be used only as provided by Subsection (a).

(d) The registration receipt issued for a vehicle registered under this section must be carried in or on the vehicle and state the nature of the operation for which the vehicle may be used.

(e) A vehicle to which this section applies that is operated on a public highway in violation of this section is considered to be operated while unregistered and is immediately subject to the applicable registration fees and penalties prescribed by this chapter.
(Enacted by Acts 2003, 78th Leg., ch. 1320 (H.B. 2971), § 2, effective September 1, 2003; am. Acts 2011, 82nd Leg., ch. 1296 (H.B. 2357), § 145, effective January 1, 2012 (renumbered from Sec. 502.188).)

### Secs. 502.436 to 502.450 [Reserved for expansion].

### SUBCHAPTER J
### [EFFECTIVE JANUARY 1, 2012]
### REGISTRATIONS EXEMPT
### FROM FEES

### Sec. 502.451. [2 Versions: Renumbered January 1, 2012] Transfer of Vehicle Registration.

(a) On the sale or transfer of a motor vehicle to a dealer, as defined by Section 503.001, who holds a general distinguishing number issued under Chapter 503, the dealer shall remove each license plate and the registration insignia issued for the motor vehicle. The registration period remaining at the time of sale or transfer expires at the time of sale or transfer.

(a-1) On the sale of a used motor vehicle by a dealer, the dealer shall issue to the buyer new registration documents for an entire registration year.

(a-2) On a sale or transfer of a motor vehicle to a person that does not hold a general distinguishing number issued under Chapter 503, the seller or transferor may remove each license plate and the registration insignia issued for the motor vehicle.

(b) A license plate removed from a motor vehicle under Subsection (a) or (a-1) must be:

(1) disposed of in the manner specified by the department; or

(2) transferred to another vehicle owned by the seller or transferor as provided by Section 502.452.

(c) On a sale or transfer of a motor vehicle in which neither party holds a general distinguishing number issued under Chapter 503, the part of the registration period remaining at the time of the sale or transfer shall continue with the vehicle being sold or transferred and does not transfer with the license plates or registration validation insignia. To continue the remainder of the registration period, the purchaser or transferee must file the documents required under Section 520.031.

(Enacted by Acts 2007, 80th Leg., ch. 101 (H.B. 310), § 2, effective January 1, 2008; am. Acts 2011, 82nd Leg., ch. 432 (S.B. 1057), § 1, effective September 1, 2011.)

### STATUTORY NOTES

**Editor's notes.** — This section is renumbered to Transportation Code Section 502.491 pursuant to Acts 2011, 82nd Leg., ch. 1296 (H.B. 2357), § 163, effective January 1, 2012.

## Sec. 502.451.  [2 Versions: Effective January 1, 2012] Exempt Vehicles.

(a) Before license plates are issued or delivered to the owner of a vehicle that is exempt by law from payment of registration fees, the department must approve the application for registration. The department may not approve an application if there is the appearance that:

(1) the vehicle was transferred to the owner or purported owner:

(A) for the sole purpose of evading the payment of registration fees; or

(B) in bad faith; or

(2) the vehicle is not being used in accordance with the exemption requirements.

(b) The department shall revoke the registration of a vehicle issued license plates under this section and may recall the plates if the vehicle is no longer:

(1) owned and operated by the person whose ownership of the vehicle qualified the vehicle for the exemption; or

(2) used in accordance with the exemption requirements.

(c) The department shall provide by rule for the issuance of specially designated license plates for vehicles that are exempt by law. Except as provided by Subsection (f), the license plates must bear the word "exempt."

(d) A license plate under Subsection (c) is not issued annually, but remains on the vehicle until:

(1) the registration is revoked as provided by Subsection (b); or

(2) the plate is lost, stolen, or mutilated.

(e) A person who operates on a public highway a vehicle after the registration has been revoked is liable for the penalties for failing to register a vehicle.

(f) The department shall provide by rule for the issuance of regularly designed license plates not bearing the word "exempt" for a vehicle that is exempt by law and that is:

(1) a law enforcement vehicle, if the agency certifies to the department that the vehicle will be dedicated to law enforcement activities;

(2) a vehicle exempt from inscription requirements under a rule adopted as provided by Section 721.003; or

(3) a vehicle exempt from inscription requirements under an order or ordinance adopted by a governing body of a municipality or commissioners court of a county as provided by Section 721.005, if the applicant presents a copy of the order or ordinance.

(Enacted by Acts 1995, 74th Leg., ch. 165 (S.B. 971), § 1, effective September 1, 1995; am. Acts 1997, 75th Leg., ch. 485 (S.B. 557), § 1, effective September 1, 1997; am. Acts 2009, 81st Leg., ch. 1136 (H.B. 2553), § 39(6), effective September 1, 2011; am. Acts 2011, 82nd Leg., ch. 1296 (H.B. 2357), § 147, effective January 1, 2012 (renumbered from Sec. 502.201).)

## Sec. 502.452.  [2 Versions: Repealed January 1, 2012] Transfer of Removed Plates.

(a) A person may use license plates removed from a vehicle under Section 502.451 on another motor vehicle that is titled in the person's name after the person:

(1) obtains:

    (A) the department's approval of an application to transfer the license plates; and

    (B) a new registration insignia for the motor vehicle; and

(2) pays the appropriate fees required under Section 502.453.

(b) A person may use the license plates removed from a motor vehicle under Section 502.451 on a new motor vehicle purchased from a dealer licensed under Chapter 503 after the person:

    (1) obtains the department's approval of a title and registration application; and

    (2) pays the applicable title and vehicle registration fees and the transfer fee required under Section 502.453.

(Enacted by Acts 2007, 80th Leg., ch. 101 (H.B. 310), § 2, effective January 1, 2008.)

## Sec. 502.452. [2 Versions: Effective January 1, 2012] Limitation on Issuance of Exempt License Plates; Seizure of Certain Vehicles.

(a) The department may not issue exempt license plates for a vehicle owned by the United States, this state, or a political subdivision of this state unless when application is made for registration of the vehicle, the person who under Section 502.453 has authority to certify to the department that the vehicle qualifies for registration under that section also certifies in writing to the department that there is printed on each side of the vehicle, in letters that are at least two inches high or in an emblem that is at least 100 square inches in size, the name of the agency, department, bureau, board, commission, or officer of the United States, this state, or the political subdivision of this state that has custody of the vehicle. The letters or emblem must be of a color sufficiently different from the body of the vehicle to be clearly legible from a distance of 100 feet.

(b) The department may not issue exempt license plates for a vehicle owned by a person other than the United States, this state, or a political subdivision of this state unless, when application is made for registration of the vehicle, the person who under Section 502.453 has authority to certify to the department that the vehicle qualifies for registration under that section also certifies in writing to the department that the name of the owner of the vehicle is printed on the vehicle in the manner prescribed by Subsection (a).

(c) A peace officer listed in Article 2.12, Code of Criminal Procedure, may seize a motor vehicle displaying exempt license plates if the vehicle is:

    (1) operated on a public highway; and

    (2) not identified in the manner prescribed by Subsection (a) or (b), unless the vehicle is covered by Subsection (f).

(d) A peace officer who seizes a motor vehicle under Subsection (c) may require that the vehicle be:

    (1) moved to the nearest place of safety off the main-traveled part of the highway; or

    (2) removed and placed in the nearest vehicle storage facility designated or maintained by the law enforcement agency that employs the peace officer.

(e) To obtain the release of the vehicle, in addition to any other requirement of law, the owner of a vehicle seized under Subsection (c) must:

    (1) remedy the defect by identifying the vehicle as required by Subsection (a) or (b); or

    (2) agree in writing with the law enforcement agency to provide evidence to that agency, before the 10th day after the date the vehicle is released, that the defect has been remedied by identifying the vehicle as required by Subsection (a) or (b).

(f) Subsections (a) and (b) do not apply to a vehicle to which Section 502.451(f) ] applies.

(g) For purposes of this section, an exempt license plate is a license plate issued by the department that is plainly marked with the word "exempt."

(Enacted by Acts 1997, 75th Leg., ch. 165 (S.B. 898), § 30.50(a), effective September 1, 1997; enacted by Acts 1997, 75th Leg., ch. 485 (S.B. 557), § 2, effective September 1, 1997; am. Acts 2011, 82nd Leg., ch. 1296 (H.B. 2357), § 148, effective January 1, 2012 (renumbered from Sec. 502.2015).)

## Sec. 502.453. [Effective January 1, 2012] Government-Owned Vehicles; Public School Buses; Fire-Fighting Vehicles; County Marine Law Enforcement Vehicles.

(a) The owner of a motor vehicle, trailer, or semitrailer may annually apply for registration under Section 502.451 and is exempt from the payment of a registration fee under this chapter if the vehicle is:

    (1) owned by and used exclusively in the service of:

        (A) the United States;

        (B) this state; or

        (C) a county, municipality, or school district in this state;

(2) owned by a commercial transportation company and used exclusively to provide public school transportation services to a school district under Section 34.008, Education Code;

(3) designed and used exclusively for fire fighting;

(4) owned by a volunteer fire department and used exclusively in the conduct of department business;

(5) privately owned and used by a volunteer exclusively in county marine law enforcement activities, including rescue operations, under the direction of the sheriff's department; or

(6) used by law enforcement under an alias for covert criminal investigations.

(b) An application for registration under this section must be made by a person having the authority to certify that the vehicle meets the exemption requirements prescribed by Subsection (a). An application for registration under this section of a fire-fighting vehicle described by Subsection (a)(3) must include a reasonable description of the vehicle and of any fire-fighting equipment mounted on the vehicle. An application for registration under this section of a vehicle described by Subsection (a)(5) must include a statement signed by a person having the authority to act for a sheriff's department that the vehicle is used exclusively in marine law enforcement activities under the direction of the sheriff's department.

(Enacted by Acts 1995, 74th Leg., ch. 165 (S.B. 971), § 1, effective September 1, 1995; am. Acts 1999, 76th Leg., ch. 62 (S.B. 1368), § 17.06, effective September 1, 1999; am. Acts 2011, 82nd Leg., ch. 1296 (H.B. 2357), § 149, effective January 1, 2012 (renumbered from Sec. 502.202).)

## Sec. 502.454. [2 Versions: Renumbered January 1, 2012] Temporary Permit for a Vehicle Purchased in a Private Party Transaction.

(a) A purchaser or transferee may obtain from the department a temporary single-trip permit to operate a motor vehicle:

(1) that is subject to registration in this state;

(2) from which the license plates and the registration insignia have been removed as authorized by Section 502.451(a-1); and

(3) that is not authorized to travel on a public roadway because the required license plates and the registration insignia are not attached to the vehicle.

(b) The department may issue the permit in accordance with this section.

(c) A permit issued under this section is valid for one trip between the point of origin and the destination and those intermediate points specified in the permit.

(d) A permit issued under this section may not be valid for longer than a five-day period.

(e) A person may obtain a permit under this section by applying, on a form provided by the department, to the department. Application may be made using the department's Internet website.

(f) A person is eligible to receive only one permit under this section for a motor vehicle.

(g) A permit receipt issued under this section must be on a form provided by the department. The receipt must contain the information required by this section and shall be carried in the vehicle at all times during which it is valid.

(h) The department may refuse to issue a permit under this section for any vehicle if in the department's opinion the applicant has been involved in operations that constitute an abuse of the privilege granted under this section.

(Enacted by Acts 2007, 80th Leg., ch. 101 (H.B. 310), § 2, effective January 1, 2008.)

### STATUTORY NOTES

**Editor's notes.** — This section is renumbered to Transportation Code Section 502.492 pursuant to Acts 2011, 82nd Leg., ch. 1296 (H.B. 2357), § 164, effective January 1, 2012.

## Sec. 502.454. [2 Versions: Effective January 1, 2012] Vehicles Used by Nonprofit Disaster Relief Organizations.

(a) The owner of a commercial motor vehicle, trailer, or semitrailer may apply for registration under Section 502.451 and is exempt from the payment of the registration fee that would otherwise be required by this chapter if the vehicle is owned and used exclusively for emergencies by a nonprofit disaster relief organization.

(b) An application for registration under this section must include:

(1) a statement by the owner of the vehicle that the vehicle is used exclusively for emergencies and has not been used for any other purpose;

(2) a statement signed by an officer of the nonprofit disaster relief organization that the vehicle has not been used for any purpose other than emergencies and qualifies for registration under this section; and

(3) a reasonable description of the vehicle and the emergency equipment included in the vehicle.

(c) An applicant for registration under this section must pay a fee of $5.

(d) A commercial motor vehicle registered under this section must display the name of the organization that owns it on each front door.

(e) A vehicle registered under this section must display at all times an appropriate license plate showing the vehicle's status.

(f) A vehicle registered under this section that is used for any purpose other than an emergency may not again be registered under this section. (Enacted by Acts 1995, 74th Leg., ch. 165 (S.B. 971), § 1, effective September 1, 1995; am. Acts 2001, 77th Leg., ch. 638 (H.B. 1368), § 3, effective September 1, 2001; am. Acts 2011, 82nd Leg., ch. 1296 (H.B. 2357), § 150, effective January 1, 2012 (renumbered from Sec. 502.203).)

## Sec. 502.455. [Effective January 1, 2012] Trailers and Semitrailers Owned by Religious Organizations.

(a) A trailer or semitrailer may be registered without payment if the trailer or semitrailer is:

(1) owned by an organization that qualifies as a religious organization under Section 11.20, Tax Code; and

(2) used primarily for the purpose of transporting property in connection with the charitable activities and functions of the organization.

(b) An application for registration under this section must include a statement signed by an officer of the religious organization stating that the trailer or semitrailer qualifies for registration under this section. (Enacted by Acts 1999, 76th Leg., ch. 1194 (S.B. 408), § 1, effective September 1, 1999; am. Acts 2011, 82nd Leg., ch. 1296 (H.B. 2357), § 151, effective January 1, 2012 (renumbered from Sec. 502.2035).)

## Sec. 502.456. [2 Versions: Repealed January 1, 2012] Department Support.

(a) The department may enter into a system design contract to determine the feasibility and benefits of an electronic registration and title system to facilitate the registration and titling of motor vehicles under this subchapter.

(b) Subsection (a) may not be construed to authorize the department to implement a system or enter into a contract for the implementation of a system that affects the issuance of temporary license tags under Chapter 503. (Enacted by Acts 2007, 80th Leg., ch. 101 (H.B. 310), § 2, effective January 1, 2008.)

## Sec. 502.456. [2 Versions: Effective January 1, 2012] Emergency Services Vehicles.

(a) A vehicle may be registered without payment if:

(1) the vehicle is owned or leased by an emergency medical services provider that:

(A) is a nonprofit entity; or

(B) is created and operated by:

(i) a county;

(ii) a municipality; or

(iii) any combination of counties and municipalities through a contract, joint agreement, or other method provided by Chapter 791, Government Code, or other law authorizing counties and municipalities to provide joint programs; and

(2) the vehicle:

(A) is authorized under an emergency medical services provider license issued by the Department of State Health Services under Chapter 773, Health and Safety Code, and is used exclusively as an emergency medical services vehicle; or

(B) is an emergency medical services chief or supervisor vehicle and is used exclusively as an emergency services vehicle.

(b) A vehicle may be registered without payment of a registration fee if the vehicle:

(1) is owned by the Civil Air Patrol, Texas Wing; and

(2) is used exclusively as an emergency services vehicle by members of the Civil Air Patrol, Texas Wing.

(c) An application for registration under Subsection (a) must be accompanied by a copy of the license issued by the Department of State Health Services. An application for registration of an emergency medical services vehicle must include a statement signed by an officer of the emergency medical services provider that the vehicle is used exclusively as an emergency response vehicle and qualifies for registration under this section. An application for registration of an emergency medical services chief or supervisor vehicle must include a statement signed by an officer of the emergency medical services provider stating that the vehicle qualifies for registration under this section.

Transportation

(d) An application for registration under Subsection (b) must include a statement signed by an officer of the Civil Air Patrol, Texas Wing, that the vehicle is used exclusively as an emergency services vehicle by members of the Civil Air Patrol, Texas Wing.

(e) The department must approve an application for registration under this section as provided by Section 502.451.

(Enacted by Acts 1995, 74th Leg., ch. 165 (S.B. 971), § 1, effective September 1, 1995; am. Acts 2011, 82nd Leg., ch. 1296 (H.B. 2357), § 152, effective January 1, 2012 (renumbered from Sec. 502.204).)

### Sec. 502.457.  [Effective January 1, 2012] Persons on Active Duty in Armed Forces of United States.

(a) This section applies only to a used motor vehicle that is owned by a person who:

(1) is on active duty in the armed forces of the United States;

(2) is stationed in or has been assigned to another nation under military orders; and

(3) has registered the vehicle or been issued a license for the vehicle under the applicable status of forces agreement by:

(A) the appropriate branch of the armed forces of the United States; or

(B) the nation in which the person is stationed or to which the person has been assigned.

(b) The requirement that a used vehicle be registered under the law of this state does not apply to a vehicle described by Subsection (a). In lieu of delivering the license receipt to the transferee of the vehicle, as required by Section 501.0721, the person selling, trading, or otherwise transferring a used motor vehicle described by Subsection (a) shall deliver to the transferee:

(1) a letter written on official letterhead by the owner's unit commander attesting to the registration of the vehicle under Subsection (a)(3); or

(2) the registration receipt issued by the appropriate branch of the armed forces or host nation.

(c) A registration receipt issued by a host nation that is not written in the English language must be accompanied by:

(1) a written translation of the registration receipt in English; and

(2) an affidavit, in English and signed by the person translating the registration receipt, attesting to the person's ability to translate the registration receipt into English.

(Enacted by Acts 1999, 76th Leg., ch. 836 (H.B. 1743), § 2, effective September 1, 1999; am. Acts 2011, 82nd Leg., ch. 1296 (H.B. 2357), § 153, effective January 1, 2012 (renumbered from Sec. 520.0225).)

## SUBCHAPTER K
## [EFFECTIVE JANUARY 1, 2012]
## OFFENSES AND PENALTIES

### Sec. 502.471.  [Effective January 1, 2012] General Penalty.

(a) A person commits an offense if the person violates a provision of this chapter and no other penalty is prescribed for the violation.

(b) This section does not apply to a violation of Section 502.003, 502.042, 502.197, or 502.431.

(c) Unless otherwise specified, an offense under this section is a misdemeanor punishable by a fine not to exceed $200.

(Enacted by Acts 1995, 74th Leg., ch. 165 (S.B. 971), § 1, effective September 1, 1995; am. Acts 2011, 82nd Leg., ch. 1296 (H.B. 2357), § 155, effective January 1, 2012 (renumbered from Sec. 502.401).)

### Sec. 502.472.  [Effective January 1, 2012] Operation of Vehicle Under Improper Registration.

A person commits an offense if the person operates a motor vehicle that has not been registered or registered for a class other than that to which the vehicle belongs as required by law.

(Enacted by Acts 1995, 74th Leg., ch. 165 (S.B. 971), § 1, effective September 1, 1995; am. Acts 1997, 75th Leg., ch. 165 (S.B. 898), § 30.64, effective September 1, 1997; am. Acts 2011, 82nd Leg., ch. 1296 (H.B. 2357), § 156, effective January 1, 2012 (renumbered from Sec. 502.402).)

### Sec. 502.473.  [Effective January 1, 2012] Operation of Vehicle Without Registration Insignia.

(a) A person commits an offense if the person operates on a public highway during a registration period a motor vehicle that does not properly display the registration insignia issued by the department that establishes that the license plates have been validated for the period.

(b) A person commits an offense if the person operates on a public highway during a registration period a road tractor, motorcycle, trailer, or semitrailer that does not display a registration insignia issued by the department that establishes that the vehicle is registered for the period.

(c) This section does not apply to a dealer operating a vehicle as provided by law.

(d) A court may dismiss a charge brought under Subsection (a) if the defendant:

(1) shows that the motor vehicle was issued a registration insignia by the department that was attached to the motor vehicle, establishing that the vehicle was registered for the period during which the offense was committed; and

(2) pays an administrative fee not to exceed $10.

(Enacted by Acts 1995, 74th Leg., ch. 165 (S.B. 971), § 1, effective September 1, 1995; am. Acts 2007, 80th Leg., ch. 1027 (H.B. 1623), § 1, effective September 1, 2007; am. Acts 2011, 82nd Leg., ch. 1296 (H.B. 2357), § 157, effective January 1, 2012 (renumbered from Sec. 502.404).)

### Sec. 502.474. [Effective January 1, 2012] Operation of One-Trip Permit Vehicle.

A person commits an offense if the person operates a vehicle for which a one-trip permit is required without the registration receipt and properly displayed temporary tag.

(Enacted by Acts 2011, 82nd Leg., ch. 1296 (H.B. 2357), § 158, effective January 1, 2012.)

### Sec. 502.475. [Effective January 1, 2012] Wrong, Fictitious, Altered, or Obscured Insignia.

(a) A person commits an offense if the person attaches to or displays on a motor vehicle a registration insignia that:

(1) is assigned to a different motor vehicle;

(2) is assigned to the vehicle under any other motor vehicle law other than by the department;

(3) is assigned for a registration period other than the registration period in effect; or

(4) is fictitious.

(b) Except as provided by Subsection (d), an offense under Subsection (a) is a misdemeanor punishable by a fine of not more than $200, unless it is shown at the trial of the offense that the owner knowingly altered or made illegible the letters, numbers, and other identification marks, in which case the offense is a Class B misdemeanor.

(c) A court may dismiss a charge brought under Subsection (a)(3) if the defendant:

(1) remedies the defect before the defendant's first court appearance; and

(2) pays an administrative fee not to exceed $10.

(d) An offense under Subsection (a)(4) is a Class B misdemeanor.

(Enacted by Acts 1995, 74th Leg., ch. 165 (S.B. 971), § 1, effective September 1, 1995; am. Acts 1997, 75th Leg., ch. 165 (S.B. 898), § 30.66, effective September 1, 1997; am. Acts 1997, 75th Leg., ch. 851 (H.B. 1048), § 1, effective September 1, 1997; am. Acts 1999, 76th Leg., ch. 1189 (S.B. 370), § 17, effective September 1, 1999; am. Acts 2003, 78th Leg., ch. 837 (S.B. 439), §§ 1, 2, effective September 1, 2003; am. Acts 2007, 80th Leg., ch. 30 (S.B. 369), § 1, effective September 1, 2007; am. Acts 2007, 80th Leg., ch. 1027 (H.B. 1623), § 3, effective September 1, 2007; am. Acts 2009, 81st Leg., ch. 87 (S.B. 1969), § 27.001(102), effective September 1, 2009; am. Acts 2011, 82nd Leg., ch. 1296 (H.B. 2357), § 159, effective January 1, 2012 (renumbered from Sec. 502.409).)

### Sec. 502.476. [Effective January 1, 2012] Annual Permits; Offense.

A person who violates Section 502.093 commits an offense.

(Enacted by Acts 2011, 82nd Leg., ch. 1296 (H.B. 2357), § 160, effective January 1, 2012.)

### Sec. 502.477. [Effective January 1, 2012] Nonresident-Owned Vehicles Used to Transport Agricultural Product; Offense.

(a) A person operating a vehicle under a permit issued under Section 502.092 commits an offense if the person transports farm products to a place of market, storage, or processing or a railhead or seaport that is farther from the place of production or point of entry, as appropriate, than the distance provided for in the permit.

(b) An offense under this section is a misdemeanor punishable by a fine of not less than $25 or more than $200.

(Enacted by Acts 2011, 82nd Leg., ch. 1296 (H.B. 2357), § 160, effective January 1, 2012.)

### Sec. 502.478. [Effective January 1, 2012] Commercial Motor Vehicle Used Primarily for Agricultural Purposes; Offense.

(a) The owner of a commercial motor vehicle

registered under Section 502.433 commits an offense if the person uses or permits the use of the vehicle for a purpose other than one allowed under Section 502.433. Each use or permission of use in violation of this section is a separate offense.

(b) An offense under this section is a misdemeanor punishable by a fine of not less than $25 or more than $200.

(Enacted by Acts 2011, 82nd Leg., ch. 1296 (H.B. 2357), § 160, effective January 1, 2012.)

### Sec. 502.479. [Effective January 1, 2012] Seasonal Agricultural Vehicle; Offense.

A person issued a registration under Section 502.432 commits an offense if the person, during the registration period, uses the truck-tractor or commercial motor vehicle for a purpose other than to transport a seasonal agricultural product.

(Enacted by Acts 2011, 82nd Leg., ch. 1296 (H.B. 2357), § 160, effective January 1, 2012.)

### Sec. 502.480. [Effective January 1, 2012] Violation by County Assessor-Collector; Penalty.

(a) A county assessor-collector commits an offense if the county assessor-collector knowingly accepts an application for the registration of a motor vehicle that:

(1) has had the original motor number or vehicle identification number removed, erased, or destroyed; and

(2) does not bear a motor number or vehicle identification number assigned by the department.

(b) An offense under this section is a misdemeanor punishable by a fine of not less than $10 and not more than $50.

(Enacted by Acts 1995, 74th Leg., ch. 165 (S.B. 971), § 1, effective September 1, 1995; am. Acts 2011, 82nd Leg., ch. 1296 (H.B. 2357), § 161, effective January 1, 2012 (renumbered from Sec. 520.014).)

### SUBCHAPTER L
### [EFFECTIVE JANUARY 1, 2012]
### REGISTRATION AND TRANSFER OF USED VEHICLES

### Sec. 502.491. [Effective January 1, 2012] Transfer of Vehicle Registration.

(a) [2 Versions: As amended by Acts 2011, 82nd Leg., ch. 432] On the sale or transfer of a motor vehicle to a dealer, as defined by Section 503.001, who holds a general distinguishing number issued under Chapter 503, the dealer shall remove each license plate and the registration insignia issued for the motor vehicle. The registration period remaining at the time of sale or transfer expires at the time of sale or transfer.

(a) [2 Versions: As amended by Acts 2011, 82nd Leg., ch. 1296] On the sale or transfer of a motor vehicle, the registration insignia issued for the motor vehicle shall be removed.

(a-2) On a sale or transfer of a motor vehicle to a person that does not hold a general distinguishing number issued under Chapter 503, the seller or transferor may remove each license plate and the registration insignia issued for the motor vehicle.

(b) On a sale or transfer of a motor vehicle in which neither party holds a general distinguishing number issued under Chapter 503, the part of the registration period remaining at the time of the sale or transfer shall continue with the vehicle being sold or transferred and does not transfer with the license plates or registration validation insignia. To continue the remainder of the registration period, the purchaser or transferee must file the documents required under Section 501.145.

(c) [2 Versions: As amended by Acts 2011, 82nd Leg., ch. 432] On a sale or transfer of a motor vehicle in which neither party holds a general distinguishing number issued under Chapter 503, the part of the registration period remaining at the time of the sale or transfer shall continue with the vehicle being sold or transferred and does not transfer with the license plates or registration validation insignia. To continue the remainder of the registration period, the purchaser or transferee must file the documents required under Section 520.031.

(c) [2 Versions: As amended by Acts 2011, 82nd Leg., ch. 1296] On the sale or transfer of a motor vehicle to a dealer, as defined by Section 503.001, who holds a general distinguishing number issued under Chapter 503, the registration period remaining at the time of the sale or transfer expires at the time of the sale or transfer. On the sale of a used motor vehicle by a dealer, the dealer shall issue to the buyer new registration documents for an entire registration year.

(Enacted by Acts 2007, 80th Leg., ch. 101 (H.B. 310), § 2, effective January 1, 2008; am. Acts

2011, 82nd Leg., ch. 432 (S.B. 1057), § 1, effective September 1, 2011; am. Acts 2011, 82nd Leg., ch. 1296 (H.B. 2357), § 163, effective January 1, 2012 (renumbered from Sec. 502.451).)

## Sec. 502.492. [Effective January 1, 2012] Temporary Transit Permit for a Vehicle Purchased.

(a) A purchaser may obtain from the department a temporary transit permit to operate a motor vehicle:

(1) that is subject to registration in this state;

(2) from which the license plates and the registration insignia have been removed as authorized by Section 502.491 or 504.901; and

(3) that is not authorized to travel on a public roadway because the required license plates and the registration insignia are not attached to the vehicle.

(b) The department may issue the permit in accordance with this section.

(c) A permit issued under this section is valid for one trip between the point of origin and the destination and those intermediate points specified in the permit.

(d) A permit issued under this section may not be valid for longer than a five-day period.

(e) A person may obtain a permit under this section by applying, as provided by the department, to the department. Application may be made using the department's Internet website.

(f) A person is eligible to receive only one permit under this section for a motor vehicle.

(g) A permit receipt issued under this section must be in a manner provided by the department. The receipt must contain the information required by this section and shall be carried in the vehicle at all times during which it is valid.

(h) The department may refuse to issue a permit under this section for any vehicle if in the department's opinion the applicant has been involved in operations that constitute an abuse of the privilege granted under this section.

(Enacted by Acts 2007, 80th Leg., ch. 101 (H.B. 310), § 2, effective January 1, 2008; am. Acts 2011, 82nd Leg., ch. 1296 (H.B. 2357), § 164, effective January 1, 2012 (renumbered from Sec. 502.454).)

# CHAPTER 503
# DEALER'S AND MANUFACTURER'S VEHICLE LICENSE PLATES

## Subchapter A. General Provisions

## Subchapter B. General Distinguishing Number

Transportation

## SUBCHAPTER A
## GENERAL PROVISIONS

## Sec. 503.001.   Definitions.

In this chapter:

(1) "Board" has the meaning assigned by Chapter 2301, Occupations Code.

(2) "Commission" means the board of the Texas Department of Motor Vehicles.

(3) "Converter" has the meaning assigned by Chapter 2301, Occupations Code.

(4) "Dealer" means a person who regularly and actively buys, sells, or exchanges vehicles at an established and permanent location. The term includes a franchised motor vehicle dealer, an independent motor vehicle dealer, an independent mobility motor vehicle dealer, and a wholesale motor vehicle dealer.

(5) "Department" means the Texas Department of Motor Vehicles.

(6) "Drive-a-way operator" means a person who transports and delivers a vehicle in this state from the manufacturer or another point of origin to a location in this state using the vehicle's own power or using the full-mount method, the saddle-mount method, the tow-bar method, or a combination of those methods.

(7) "Franchise" has the meaning assigned by Chapter 2301, Occupations Code.

(8) "Franchised motor vehicle dealer" means a person engaged in the business of buying, selling, or exchanging new motor vehicles at an established and permanent place of business under a franchise in effect with a motor vehicle manufacturer or distributor.

(8-a) "Independent mobility motor vehicle dealer" has the meaning assigned by Section 2301.002, Occupations Code.

(9) "Independent motor vehicle dealer" means a dealer other than a franchised motor vehicle dealer, an independent mobility motor vehicle dealer, or a wholesale motor vehicle dealer.

(10) "Manufacturer" means a person who manufactures, distributes, or assembles new vehicles.

(11) "Motorcycle" has the meaning assigned by Section 502.001.

(12) "Motor vehicle" has the meaning assigned by Section 502.001.

(13) "Semitrailer" has the meaning assigned by Section 502.001.

(14) "Trailer" has the meaning assigned by Section 502.001.

(15) "Vehicle" means a motor vehicle, motorcycle, house trailer, trailer, or semitrailer.

(16) "Wholesale motor vehicle auction" means the offering of a motor vehicle for sale to the highest bidder during a transaction that is one of a series of regular periodic transactions that occur at a permanent location.

(17) "Wholesale motor vehicle dealer" means a dealer who sells motor vehicles only to a person who is:

(A) the holder of a dealer's general distinguishing number; or

(B) a foreign dealer authorized by a law of this state or interstate reciprocity agreement to purchase a vehicle in this state without remitting the motor vehicle sales tax.

(Enacted by Acts 1995, 74th Leg., ch. 165 (S.B. 971), § 1, effective September 1, 1995; am. Acts 1997, 75th Leg., ch. 165 (S.B. 898), § 30.69(a), effective September 1, 1997; am. Acts 2001, 77th Leg., ch. 76 (H.B. 1664), § 3, effective May 14, 2001; am. Acts 2003, 78th Leg., ch. 1276 (H.B. 3507), § 14A.828, effective September 1, 2003;

am. Acts 2007, 80th Leg., ch. 710 (H.B. 2216), § 3, effective June 15, 2007; am. Acts 2009, 81st Leg., ch. 933 (H.B. 3097), § 2F.01, effective September 1, 2009.)

## Sec. 503.002. Rules.

The board may adopt rules for the administration of this chapter.
(Enacted by Acts 1995, 74th Leg., ch. 165 (S.B. 971), § 1, effective September 1, 1995; am. Acts 2001, 77th Leg., ch. 76 (H.B. 1664), § 4, effective May 14, 2001.)

## Sec. 503.003. Display or Sale of Non-motorized Vehicle or Trailer.

This chapter does not prohibit the display or sale of a nonmotorized vehicle or trailer at a regularly scheduled vehicle or boat show involving multiple dealers conducted in accordance with board rules.
(Enacted by Acts 1995, 74th Leg., ch. 165 (S.B. 971), § 1, effective September 1, 1995; am. Acts 2001, 77th Leg., ch. 76 (H.B. 1664), § 5, effective May 14, 2001.)

## Sec. 503.004. Buying, Selling, Exchanging, or Manufacturing Vehicles.

This chapter does not prohibit a person from entering into the business of buying, selling, or exchanging new or used vehicles at wholesale or retail or from manufacturing vehicles.
(Enacted by Acts 1995, 74th Leg., ch. 165 (S.B. 971), § 1, effective September 1, 1995.)

## Sec. 503.005. Notice of Sale or Transfer.

(a) A manufacturer or dealer shall immediately notify the department if the manufacturer or dealer transfers, including by sale or lease, a motor vehicle, trailer, or semitrailer to a person other than a manufacturer or dealer.

(b) The notice must be in writing using the form provided by the department and must include:

(1) the date of the transfer;

(2) the names and addresses of the transferrer and transferee; and

(3) a description of the vehicle.

(c) A dealer who submits information to the database under Section 503.0631 satisfies the requirement for the dealer to notify the department of the sale or transfer of a motor vehicle, trailer, or semitrailer under this section.

(d) The notice required under this section is in addition to the application for vehicle registration and certificate of title a dealer is required to submit under Section 501.0234.
(Enacted by Acts 1995, 74th Leg., ch. 165 (S.B. 971), § 1, effective September 1, 1995; am. Acts 2007, 80th Leg., ch. 258 (S.B. 11), § 8.01, effective September 1, 2007; am. Acts 2007, 80th Leg., ch. 1336 (S.B. 1786), § 1, effective September 1, 2007.)

## Sec. 503.006. Notice of Change of Address.

A dealer or manufacturer who has been issued dealer's, converter's, or manufacturer's license plates shall notify the department of a change to the dealer's, converter's, or manufacturer's address not later than the 10th day after the date the change occurs.
(Enacted by Acts 1995, 74th Leg., ch. 165 (S.B. 971), § 1, effective September 1, 1995; am. Acts 2001, 77th Leg., ch. 76 (H.B. 1664), § 6, effective May 14, 2001.)

## Sec. 503.007. Fees for General Distinguishing Number.

(a) The fee for an original general distinguishing number is $500 for the first year and $200 for each subsequent year for which the number is valid.

(b) The fee for the renewal of a general distinguishing number is $200 a year.

(c) The registration fee for a drive-a-way in-transit license is $50 a year.

(d) A fee collected under this section shall be deposited to the credit of the state highway fund.
(Enacted by Acts 1995, 74th Leg., ch. 165 (S.B. 971), § 1, effective September 1, 1995; am. Acts 1997, 75th Leg., ch. 165 (S.B. 898), § 30.69(b), effective September 1, 1997; am. Acts 2007, 80th Leg., ch. 732 (H.B. 2651), § 6, effective September 1, 2007.)

## Sec. 503.008. Fees for License Plates.

(a) The fee for a metal dealer's license plate is $20 a year.

(b) The fee for a manufacturer's license plate is $40 a year.

(c) The fee for an additional set of drive-a-way in-transit license plates is $5 a year.

(d) A fee collected under this section shall be deposited to the credit of the state highway fund.
(Enacted by Acts 1995, 74th Leg., ch. 165 (S.B. 971), § 1, effective September 1, 1995; am. Acts 1997, 75th Leg., ch. 165 (S.B. 898), § 30.69(c), effective September 1, 1997; am. Acts 2007, 80th

Leg., ch. 732 (H.B. 2651), § 7, effective September 1, 2007.)

### Sec. 503.009. Procedure for Certain Contested Cases.

(a) The department's Motor Vehicle Board may conduct hearings in contested cases brought under and as provided by this chapter.

(b) The procedures applicable to a hearing conducted under this section are those applicable to a hearing conducted as provided by Section 2301.606(a), Occupations Code.

(c) A decision or final order issued under this section is final and may not be appealed, as a matter of right, to the commission.

(d) The department's Motor Vehicle Board may adopt rules for the procedure, a hearing, or an enforcement proceeding for an action brought under this section.

(Enacted by Acts 2001, 77th Leg., ch. 1421 (H.B. 2813), § 12, effective June 1, 2003.)

### Sec. 503.010. Term of General Distinguishing Number, License, or License Plate.

Each general distinguishing number, license, or license plate issued under this chapter is valid for the period prescribed by the commission.

(Enacted by Acts 2007, 80th Leg., ch. 732 (H.B. 2651), § 8, effective September 1, 2007.)

### Sec. 503.011. Prorating Fees.

If the board prescribes the term of a general distinguishing number, license, or license plate under this chapter for a period other than one year, the board shall prorate the applicable annual fee required under this chapter as necessary to reflect the term of the number, license, or license plate.

(Enacted by Acts 2007, 80th Leg., ch. 732 (H.B. 2651), § 8, effective September 1, 2007; am. Acts 2011, 82nd Leg., ch. 1290 (H.B. 2017), § 26, effective September 1, 2011.)

### Sec. 503.012. Collected Money.

Section 403.095, Government Code, does not apply to money received by the department and deposited to the credit of the state highway fund in accordance with this chapter.

(Enacted by Acts 2007, 80th Leg., ch. 732 (H.B. 2651), § 8, effective September 1, 2007.)

### Secs. 503.013 to 503.020 [Reserved for expansion].

## SUBCHAPTER B
## GENERAL DISTINGUISHING NUMBER

### Sec. 503.021. Dealer General Distinguishing Number.

A person may not engage in business as a dealer, directly or indirectly, including by consignment, without a dealer general distinguishing number in one of the categories described by Section 503.029(a)(6) for each location from which the person conducts business as a dealer.

(Enacted by Acts 1995, 74th Leg., ch. 165 (S.B. 971), § 1, effective September 1, 1995; am. Acts 1997, 75th Leg., ch. 165 (S.B. 898), § 30.69(d), effective September 1, 1997; am. Acts 2007, 80th Leg., ch. 710 (H.B. 2216), § 4, effective June 15, 2007.)

### Sec. 503.022. Wholesale Motor Vehicle Auction General Distinguishing Number.

A person may not engage in the business of conducting a wholesale motor vehicle auction without a wholesale motor vehicle auction general distinguishing number for each location from which the person conducts business.

(Enacted by Acts 1995, 74th Leg., ch. 165 (S.B. 971), § 1, effective September 1, 1995.)

### Sec. 503.023. Drive-a-Way Operator License.

A person may not engage in business as a drive-a-way operator without a drive-a-way in-transit license.

(Enacted by Acts 1995, 74th Leg., ch. 165 (S.B. 971), § 1, effective September 1, 1995.)

### Sec. 503.024. Exclusions for Dealer.

(a) A person is not required to obtain a dealer general distinguishing number if the person:

(1) sells or offers to sell during a calendar year fewer than five vehicles of the same type that are owned and registered in that person's name; or

(2) is a federal, state, or local governmental agency.

(b) For the purposes of Section 503.021, a person is not engaging in business as a dealer by:

(1) selling or offering to sell a vehicle the person acquired for personal or business use to a person other than a retail buyer if the sale or offer is not made to avoid a requirement of this chapter;

(2) selling, in a manner provided by law for the forced sale of vehicles, a vehicle in which the person holds a security interest;

(3) acting under a court order as a receiver, trustee, administrator, executor, guardian, or other appointed person;

(4) selling a vehicle the person acquired from the vehicle's owner as a result of paying an insurance claim if the person is an insurance company;

(5) selling an antique passenger car or truck that is at least 25 years of age; or

(6) selling a special interest vehicle that is at least 12 years of age if the person is a collector.

(c) For the purposes of Section 503.021, a domiciliary of another state who holds a dealer license and bond, if applicable, issued by the other state is not engaging in business as a dealer by buying a vehicle from, selling a vehicle to, or exchanging a vehicle with a person who:

(1) holds a general distinguishing number issued by the department, if the transaction is not intended to avoid a requirement of this chapter; or

(2) is a domiciliary of another state who holds a dealer license and bond, if applicable, issued by the other state and the transaction is not intended to avoid a requirement of this chapter.

(d) For the purposes of Section 503.021, a licensed auctioneer is not engaging in business as a dealer by, as a bid caller, selling or offering to sell property to the highest bidder at a bona fide auction if:

(1) legal or equitable title does not pass to the auctioneer;

(2) the auction is not held to avoid a requirement of this chapter; and

(3) for an auction of vehicles owned legally or equitably by a person who holds a general distinguishing number, the auction is conducted at the location for which the general distinguishing number was issued.

(e) In this section, "special interest vehicle" has the meaning assigned by Section 683.077(b).
(Enacted by Acts 1995, 74th Leg., ch. 165 (S.B. 971), § 1, effective September 1, 1995.)

## Sec. 503.025. Wholesale Motor Vehicle Auction Exception.

A person exempt under Section 503.024(d) is not required to obtain a wholesale motor vehicle auction general distinguishing number.
(Enacted by Acts 1995, 74th Leg., ch. 165 (S.B. 971), § 1, effective September 1, 1995.)

## Sec. 503.026. Requirement for Each Type of Dealer Vehicle.

A person must obtain a dealer general distinguishing number for each type of vehicle the person intends to sell.
(Enacted by Acts 1995, 74th Leg., ch. 165 (S.B. 971), § 1, effective September 1, 1995; am. Acts 1997, 75th Leg., ch. 871 (H.B. 1790), § 1, effective September 1, 1997.)

## Sec. 503.027. Requirements Relating to Dealer Location.

(a) If a dealer consigns for sale more than five vehicles in a calendar year from a location other than the location for which the dealer holds a general distinguishing number, the dealer must also hold a general distinguishing number for the consignment location unless the consignment location is a wholesale motor vehicle auction.

(b) If a person is not otherwise prohibited from doing business as a dealer at more than one location in the territory of a municipality, a person may buy, sell, or exchange a vehicle of the type for which the person holds a dealer general distinguishing number from more than one location in the territory of the municipality without obtaining an additional dealer general distinguishing number. Each location must comply with the requirements prescribed by this chapter and board rules relating to an established and permanent place of business.
(Enacted by Acts 1995, 74th Leg., ch. 165 (S.B. 971), § 1, effective September 1, 1995; am. Acts 2001, 77th Leg., ch. 76 (H.B. 1664), § 7, effective May 14, 2001; am. Acts 2011, 82nd Leg., ch. 1290 (H.B. 2017), § 27, effective September 1, 2011.)

## Sec. 503.028. Requirements Relating to Wholesale Motor Vehicle Auction Location.

(a) Except as provided by Subsection (b), the department may not issue more than one general distinguishing number for a location for which the wholesale motor vehicle auction general distinguishing number has been issued.

(b) The department may issue to a person who holds a wholesale motor vehicle auction general distinguishing number a dealer general distinguishing number for the location for which the wholesale motor vehicle auction general distinguishing number is issued. The provisions of this subchapter relating to the application for and issuance of a dealer general distinguishing number apply to an application for and issuance of a dealer general distinguishing number issued under this subsection.

(Enacted by Acts 1995, 74th Leg., ch. 165 (S.B. 971), § 1, effective September 1, 1995.)

## Sec. 503.029. Application for Dealer General Distinguishing Number.

(a) An applicant for an original or renewal dealer general distinguishing number must submit to the department a written application on a form that:

(1) is provided by the department;

(2) contains the information required by the department;

(3) contains information that demonstrates the person meets the requirements prescribed by Section 503.032;

(4) contains information that demonstrates the applicant has complied with all applicable state laws and municipal ordinances;

(5) states that the applicant agrees to allow the department to examine during working hours the ownership papers for each registered or unregistered vehicle in the applicant's possession or control; and

(6) specifies whether the applicant proposes to be a:

(A) franchised motor vehicle dealer;

(B) independent motor vehicle dealer;

(C) wholesale motor vehicle dealer;

(D) motorcycle dealer;

(E) house trailer dealer;

(F) trailer or semitrailer dealer; or

(G) independent mobility motor vehicle dealer.

(b) The applicant must swear to the truth of the information contained in the application before an officer authorized to administer oaths.

(c) A renewal application must be:

(1) submitted before the date the general distinguishing number expires; and

(2) accompanied by the appropriate fee prescribed by Section 503.007.

(Enacted by Acts 1995, 74th Leg., ch. 165 (S.B. 971), § 1, effective September 1, 1995; am. Acts 1997, 75th Leg., ch. 165 (S.B. 898), § 30.69(e), effective September 1, 1997; am. Acts 1997, 75th Leg., ch. 871 (H.B. 1790), § 2, effective September 1, 1997; am. Acts 2007, 80th Leg., ch. 710 (H.B. 2216), § 5, effective June 15, 2007.)

## Sec. 503.0295. Independent Mobility Motor Vehicle Dealers.

A person who seeks to act as an independent mobility motor vehicle dealer shall provide with each application for a general distinguishing number and each renewal application:

(1) a written statement that the dealer:

(A) shall maintain written records until at least the third anniversary of the date that adaptive work is performed; and

(B) agrees to comply with Chapter 469, Government Code; and

(2) proof that the person:

(A) maintains a garagekeeper's insurance policy in an amount of at least $50,000 and a products-completed operations insurance policy in an amount of at least $1 million per occurrence and in the aggregate;

(B) holds a welder's certification, or that the person's approved subcontractor holds a certificate, that complies with the standards of the American Welding Society Sections D1.1 and D1.3, if the person or subcontractor will perform any structural modifications; and

(C) is registered with the National Highway Traffic and Safety Administration.

(Enacted by Acts 2007, 80th Leg., ch. 710 (H.B. 2216), § 6, effective June 15, 2007.)

## Sec. 503.030. Application for Wholesale Motor Vehicle Auction General Distinguishing Number.

(a) An applicant for an original or renewal wholesale motor vehicle auction general distinguishing number must submit to the department an application that contains:

(1) the information required by the department;

(2) information that demonstrates the person meets the requirements prescribed by Section 503.032; and

(3) information that demonstrates the applicant has complied with all applicable state laws and municipal ordinances.

(b) The applicant must swear to the truth of the information contained in the application.

(Enacted by Acts 1995, 74th Leg., ch. 165 (S.B. 971), § 1, effective September 1, 1995.)

## Sec. 503.031. Application for Drive-a-Way In-Transit License.

(a) An applicant for a drive-a-way in-transit license must submit to the commission an application containing the information required by the commission.

(b) The license application must be accompanied by the registration fee prescribed by Section 503.007(c).

(Enacted by Acts 1995, 74th Leg., ch. 165 (S.B. 971), § 1, effective September 1, 1995.)

### Sec. 503.032. Established and Permanent Place of Business.

(a) An applicant for a dealer general distinguishing number or wholesale motor vehicle auction general distinguishing number must demonstrate that the location for which the applicant requests the number is an established and permanent place of business. A location is considered to be an established and permanent place of business if the applicant:

(1) owns the real property on which the business is situated or has a written lease for the property that has a term of not less than the term of the general distinguishing number;

(2) maintains on the location:

(A) a permanent furnished office that is equipped as required by the department for the sale of the vehicles of the type specified in the application; and

(B) a conspicuous sign with letters at least six inches high showing the name of the applicant's business; and

(3) has sufficient space on the location to display at least five vehicles of the type specified in the application.

(b) An applicant for a general distinguishing number as a wholesale motor vehicle dealer is not required to maintain display space in accordance with Subsection (a)(3).

(c) The applicant must demonstrate that:

(1) the applicant intends to remain regularly and actively engaged in the business specified in the application for a time equal to at least the term of the general distinguishing number at the location specified in the application; and

(2) the applicant or a bona fide employee of the applicant will be:

(A) at the location to buy, sell, lease, or exchange vehicles; and

(B) available to the public or the department at that location during reasonable and lawful business hours.

(Enacted by Acts 1995, 74th Leg., ch. 165 (S.B. 971), § 1, effective September 1, 1995; am. Acts 1997, 75th Leg., ch. 165 (S.B. 898), § 30.69(f), effective September 1, 1997; am. Acts 2007, 80th Leg., ch. 732 (H.B. 2651), § 9, effective September 1, 2007.)

### Sec. 503.033. Security Requirement.

(a) The department may not issue or renew a motor vehicle dealer general distinguishing number or a wholesale motor vehicle auction general distinguishing number unless the applicant provides to the department:

(1) satisfactory proof that the applicant has purchased a properly executed surety bond in the amount of $25,000 with a good and sufficient surety approved by the department; or

(2) other security under Subsection (c).

(b) The surety bond must be:

(1) in a form approved by the attorney general;

(2) conditioned on:

(A) the payment by the applicant of all valid bank drafts, including checks, drawn by the applicant to buy motor vehicles; and

(B) the transfer by the applicant of good title to each motor vehicle the applicant offers for sale.

(c) [Repealed by Acts 2011, 82nd Leg., ch. 1290 (H.B. 2017), § 44(a)(3), effective September 1, 2011.]

(d) A person may recover against a surety bond or other security if the person obtains against a person issued a motor vehicle dealer general distinguishing number or a wholesale motor vehicle auction general distinguishing number a judgment assessing damages and reasonable attorney's fees based on an act or omission on which the bond is conditioned that occurred during the term for which the general distinguishing number was valid.

(e) The liability imposed on a surety is limited to:

(1) the amount:

(A) of the valid bank drafts, including checks, drawn by the applicant to buy motor vehicles; or

(B) paid to the applicant for a motor vehicle for which the applicant did not deliver good title; and

(2) attorney's fees that are incurred in the recovery of the judgment and that are reasonable in relation to the work performed.

(f) The liability of a surety may not exceed the face value of the surety bond. A surety is not liable for successive claims in excess of the bond amount regardless of the number of claims made against the bond or the number of years the bond remains in force.

(g) This section does not apply to a person licensed as a franchised motor vehicle dealer by the department.

(Enacted by Acts 1995, 74th Leg., ch. 165 (S.B. 971), § 1, effective September 1, 1995; am. Acts 1997, 75th Leg., ch. 755 (H.B. 1473), § 1, effective

September 1, 1997; am. Acts 2011, 82nd Leg., ch. 1290 (H.B. 2017), §§ 28, 44(a)(3), effective September 1, 2011.)

### Sec. 503.034. Issuance and Renewal or Denial of Dealer or Wholesale Motor Vehicle Auction General Distinguishing Number.

(a) The department shall deny an application for the issuance or renewal of a dealer general distinguishing number or a wholesale motor vehicle auction general distinguishing number if the department is satisfied from the application or from other information before it that:

(1) information in the application is not true; or

(2) the applicant is guilty of conduct that would result in the cancellation of the general distinguishing number under Section 503.038.

(b) The department may not issue a dealer general distinguishing number until the applicant complies with the requirements of this chapter.

(c) [Repealed by Acts 2001, 77th Leg., ch. 76 (H.B. 1664), § 8, effective May 14, 2001.]

(Enacted by Acts 1995, 74th Leg., ch. 165 (S.B. 971), § 1, effective September 1, 1995; am. Acts 1997, 75th Leg., ch. 165 (S.B. 898), § 30.69(g), effective September 1, 1997; am. Acts 2001, 77th Leg., ch. 76 (H.B. 1664), § 8, effective May 14, 2001.)

### Sec. 503.035. Issuance and Renewal of Drive-a-Way In-Transit License.

The department shall issue to an applicant on the filing of the application and the payment of the fee a drive-a-way in-transit license and in-transit license plates.

(Enacted by Acts 1995, 74th Leg., ch. 165 (S.B. 971), § 1, effective September 1, 1995; am. Acts 1997, 75th Leg., ch. 871 (H.B. 1790), § 3, effective September 1, 1997; am. Acts 2007, 80th Leg., ch. 732 (H.B. 2651), § 10, effective September 1, 2007.)

### Sec. 503.036. Reassignment of Evidence of Ownership; Dealer Categories.

(a) The holder of a franchised motor vehicle dealer's general distinguishing number may buy, sell, or exchange new or used motor vehicles and reassign a manufacturer's certificate of origin, certificate of title, or other basic evidence of ownership of any type of vehicle owned by the

dealer that the dealer is not otherwise prohibited by law from selling or offering for sale.

(b) The holder of an independent motor vehicle dealer's general distinguishing number or an independent mobility motor vehicle dealer's general distinguishing number may reassign a certificate of title or other basic evidence of ownership of any type of vehicle owned by the dealer that the dealer is not otherwise prohibited by law from selling or offering for sale.

(c) The holder of a wholesale motor vehicle dealer's general distinguishing number may sell or offer to sell motor vehicles to no person except:

(1) a person who holds a general distinguishing number; or

(2) a person who is legally recognized as and duly licensed or otherwise qualified as a dealer under the laws of another state or foreign jurisdiction.

(Enacted by Acts 1995, 74th Leg., ch. 165 (S.B. 971), § 1, effective September 1, 1995; am. Acts 1997, 75th Leg., ch. 165 (S.B. 898), § 30.69(h), effective September 1, 1997; am. Acts 1997, 75th Leg., ch. 755 (H.B. 1473), § 2, effective September 1, 1997; am. Acts 2007, 80th Leg., ch. 710 (H.B. 2216), § 7, effective June 15, 2007.)

### Sec. 503.037. Rights of Wholesale Motor Vehicle Auction.

(a) A person who holds a wholesale motor vehicle auction general distinguishing number may accept on consignment one or more motor vehicles to auction. The person may offer a motor vehicle for sale only at the location for which the general distinguishing number is issued and only by bid to the highest bidder. The title to a motor vehicle may be in the name in which the general distinguishing number is issued.

(b) Except as provided by Subsection (d), a person who holds a wholesale motor vehicle auction general distinguishing number may not sell a motor vehicle to a person other than a person who:

(1) is a dealer; or

(2) has a license and, if applicable, a bond issued by the appropriate authority of another state or nation.

(c) A person who holds a wholesale motor vehicle auction general distinguishing number may not allow another person to use the auction's facilities or general distinguishing number to sell or auction a motor vehicle.

(d) Subsection (b) does not prohibit a person who holds a wholesale motor vehicle auction general distinguishing number from offering for sale a motor vehicle to a person who is not a dealer or who does not have a license issued by the appropriate authority of another state, if the motor vehicle is owned by:

(1) this state or a department, agency, or subdivision of this state; or

(2) the United States.

(Enacted by Acts 1995, 74th Leg., ch. 165 (S.B. 971), § 1, effective September 1, 1995; am. Acts 1997, 75th Leg., ch. 165 (S.B. 898), § 30.70(a), effective September 1, 1997.)

## Sec. 503.038. Cancellation of General Distinguishing Number.

(a) The department may cancel a dealer's general distinguishing number if the dealer:

(1) falsifies or forges a title document, including an affidavit making application for a certified copy of a title;

(2) files a false or forged tax document, including a sales tax affidavit;

(3) fails to take assignment of any basic evidence of ownership, including a certificate of title or manufacturer's certificate, for a vehicle the dealer acquires;

(4) fails to assign any basic evidence of ownership, including a certificate of title or manufacturer's certificate, for a vehicle the dealer sells;

(5) uses or permits the use of a metal dealer's license plate or a dealer's temporary tag on a vehicle that the dealer does not own or control or that is not in stock and offered for sale;

(6) makes a material misrepresentation in an application or other information filed with the department;

(7) fails to maintain the qualifications for a general distinguishing number;

(8) fails to provide to the department within 30 days after the date of demand by the department satisfactory and reasonable evidence that the person is regularly and actively engaged in business as a wholesale or retail dealer;

(9) has been licensed for at least 12 months and has not assigned at least five vehicles during the previous 12-month period;

(10) has failed to demonstrate compliance with Sections 23.12, 23.121, and 23.122, Tax Code;

(11) uses or allows the use of the dealer's general distinguishing number or the location for which the general distinguishing number is issued to avoid the requirements of this chapter;

(12) misuses or allows the misuse of a temporary tag authorized under this chapter;

(13) refuses to show on a buyer's temporary tag the date of sale or other reasonable information required by the department; or

(14) otherwise violates this chapter or a rule adopted under this chapter.

(b) The department shall cancel a dealer's general distinguishing number if the dealer obtains the number by submitting false or misleading information.

(c) A person whose general distinguishing number is canceled under this chapter shall surrender to a representative of the department each license, license plate, temporary tag, sticker, and receipt issued under this chapter not later than the 10th day after the date the general distinguishing number is canceled. The department shall direct any peace officer to secure and return to the department any plate, tag, sticker, or receipt of a person who does not comply with this subsection.

(d) A person whose general distinguishing number is canceled automatically loses any benefits and privileges afforded under Chapter 501 to the person as a dealer.

(Enacted by Acts 1995, 74th Leg., ch. 165 (S.B. 971), § 1, effective September 1, 1995; am. Acts 1997, 75th Leg., ch. 165 (S.B. 898), § 30.69(i), effective September 1, 1997; am. Acts 1997, 75th Leg., ch. 871 (H.B. 1790), §§ 4, 11(a), effective September 1, 1997; am. Acts 2003, 78th Leg., ch. 1320 (H.B. 2971), § 3, effective September 1, 2003; am. Acts 2009, 81st Leg., ch. 793 (S.B. 1235), § 2, effective September 1, 2009.)

## Sec. 503.039. Public Motor Vehicle Auctions.

(a) A motor vehicle may not be the subject of a subsequent sale at a public auction by a holder of a dealer's general distinguishing number unless equitable or legal title has passed to the selling dealer before the transfer of title to the subsequent buyer.

(b) The holder of a dealer's general distinguishing number who sells a motor vehicle at a public auction must transfer the certificate of title for that vehicle to the buyer before the 21st day after the date of the sale.

(Enacted by Acts 2005, 79th Leg., ch. 1127 (H.B. 2495), § 2, effective September 1, 2005; am. Acts

2011, 82nd Leg., ch. 1290 (H.B. 2017), § 29, effective September 1, 2011.)

## Sec. 503.040. Sales of Certain Used Motor Vehicles Constitute Private Disposition.

(a) This section applies only to the sale of a used motor vehicle that constitutes collateral by a secured party acting under Chapter 9, Business & Commerce Code, and occurs at an auction conducted by an independent motor vehicle dealer:

(1) at which neither the debtor nor the secured party is permitted to bid; and

(2) for which there has been no advertisement or public notice before the sale that specifically describes the collateral to be sold, other than the inclusion of the motor vehicle in a list of the vehicles to be offered at the auction made available to potential bidders at the auction.

(b) The sale of the used motor vehicle constitutes a private disposition for purposes of Chapter 9, Business & Commerce Code.
(Enacted by Acts 2009, 81st Leg., ch. 836 (S.B. 1827), § 1, effective September 1, 2009.)

## Secs. 503.041 to 503.060 [Reserved for expansion].

## SUBCHAPTER C
## LICENSE PLATES AND TAGS

## Sec. 503.061. Dealer's License Plates.

(a) Instead of registering under Chapter 502 a vehicle that the dealer owns, operates, or permits to be operated on a public street or highway, the dealer may apply for, receive, and attach metal dealer's license plates to the vehicle if it is the type of vehicle:

(1) that the dealer sells; and

(2) for which the dealer has been issued a general distinguishing number.

(b) The board may adopt rules regulating the issuance and use of a license plate issued pursuant to the terms of this section.
(Enacted by Acts 1995, 74th Leg., ch. 165 (S.B. 971), § 1, effective September 1, 1995; am. Acts 2003, 78th Leg., ch. 1320 (H.B. 2971), § 4, effective September 1, 2003.)

## Sec. 503.0615. Personalized Prestige Dealer's License Plates.

(a) The department shall establish and issue personalized prestige dealer's license plates. The department may not issue identically lettered or numbered dealer's plates to more than one dealer.

(b) The department shall establish procedures for continuous application for and issuance of personalized prestige dealer's license plates. A dealer must make a new application and pay a new fee for each registration period for which the dealer seeks to obtain personalized prestige dealer's license plates. A dealer who obtains personalized prestige dealer's license plates has first priority on those plates for each subsequent registration period for which the dealer applies.

(c) The annual fee for personalized prestige dealer's license plates is $40, in addition to any fee otherwise prescribed by this chapter.

(d) The department may issue to an applicant only one set of personalized prestige dealer's license plates for a vehicle for a six-year period. The department may issue a new set of personalized prestige dealer's license plates within the six-year period if the applicant pays a fee of $50 in addition to the fees required by Subsection (c).

(e) On application and payment of the required fee for a registration period following the issuance of the plates, the department shall issue a registration insignia.

(f) Of each fee collected by the department under this section:

(1) $1.25 shall be deposited to the credit of the state highway fund to defray the cost of administering this section; and

(2) the remainder shall be deposited to the credit of the general revenue fund.
(Enacted by Acts 1997, 75th Leg., ch. 871 (H.B. 1790), § 5, effective September 1, 1997.)

## Sec. 503.0618. Converter's License Plates.

(a) In this section, "converter" means a person who holds a converter's license issued under Chapter 2301, Occupations Code.

(b) Instead of registering under Chapter 502 a vehicle that a converter operates or permits to be operated on a public street or highway, the converter may apply for, receive, and attach metal converter's license plates to the vehicle if it is the type of vehicle that the converter is engaged in the business of assembling or modifying.

(c) The fee for a metal converter's license plate is $20 a year.

(d) The department shall prescribe the form of an application under this section.
(Enacted by Acts 1999, 76th Leg., ch. 964 (H.B. 2539), § 1, effective September 1, 1999; am. Acts

2003, 78th Leg., ch. 1276 (H.B. 3507), § 14A.829, effective September 1, 2003; am. Acts 2007, 80th Leg., ch. 732 (H.B. 2651), § 11, effective September 1, 2007.)

### Sec. 503.062. Dealer's Temporary Tags.

(a) A dealer may issue a temporary tag for use on an unregistered vehicle by the dealer or the dealer's employees only to:

(1) demonstrate or cause to be demonstrated to a prospective buyer the vehicle for sale purposes only;

(2) convey or cause to be conveyed the vehicle:

(A) from one of the dealer's places of business in this state to another of the dealer's places of business in this state;

(B) from the dealer's place of business to a place the vehicle is to be repaired, reconditioned, or serviced;

(C) from the state line or a location in this state where the vehicle is unloaded to the dealer's place of business;

(D) from the dealer's place of business to a place of business of another dealer;

(E) from the point of purchase by the dealer to the dealer's place of business; or

(F) to road test the vehicle; or

(3) use the vehicle for or allow its use by a charitable organization.

(b) Subsection (a) (1) does not prohibit a dealer from permitting:

(1) a prospective buyer to operate a vehicle while the vehicle is being demonstrated; or

(2) a customer to operate a vehicle temporarily while the customer's vehicle is being repaired.

(c) A vehicle being conveyed under this section is exempt from the inspection requirements of Chapter 548.

(d) The department may not issue a dealer temporary tag or contract for the issuance of a dealer temporary tag but shall prescribe:

(1) the specifications, form, and color of a dealer temporary tag;

(2) procedures for a dealer to generate a vehicle-specific number using the database developed under Section 503.0626 and assign it to each tag;

(3) procedures to clearly display the vehicle-specific number on the tag; and

(4) the period for which a tag may be used for or by a charitable organization.

(e) For purposes of this section, "charitable organization" means an organization organized to relieve poverty, to advance education, religion, or science, to promote health, governmental, or municipal purposes, or for other purposes beneficial to the community without financial gain.
(Enacted by Acts 1995, 74th Leg., ch. 165 (S.B. 971), § 1, effective September 1, 1995; am. Acts 1997, 75th Leg., ch. 871 (H.B. 1790), § 6, effective September 1, 1997; am. Acts 2007, 80th Leg., ch. 258 (S.B. 11), § 8.02, effective September 1, 2007; am. Acts 2007, 80th Leg., ch. 1336 (S.B. 1786), § 2, effective September 1, 2007; am. Acts 2009, 81st Leg., ch. 793 (S.B. 1235), §§ 3, 4, effective September 1, 2009.)

### Sec. 503.0625. Converter's Temporary Tags.

(a) In this section, "converter" means a person who holds a converter's license issued under Chapter 2301, Occupations Code.

(b) A converter may issue a temporary tag for use on an unregistered vehicle by the converter or the converter's employees only to:

(1) demonstrate or cause to be demonstrated to a prospective buyer who is an employee of a franchised motor vehicle dealer the vehicle; or

(2) convey or cause to be conveyed the vehicle:

(A) from one of the converter's places of business in this state to another of the converter's places of business in this state;

(B) from the converter's place of business to a place the vehicle is to be assembled, repaired, reconditioned, modified, or serviced;

(C) from the state line or a location in this state where the vehicle is unloaded to the converter's place of business;

(D) from the converter's place of business to a place of business of a franchised motor vehicle dealer; or

(E) to road test the vehicle.

(c) Subsection (b)(1) does not prohibit a converter from permitting a prospective buyer who is an employee of a franchised motor vehicle dealer to operate a vehicle while the vehicle is being demonstrated.

(d) A vehicle being conveyed while displaying a temporary tag issued under this section is exempt from the inspection requirements of Chapter 548.

(e) The department may not issue a converter temporary tag or contract for the issuance of a converter temporary tag but shall prescribe:

(1) the specifications, form, and color of a converter temporary tag;

(2) procedures for a converter to generate a vehicle-specific number using the database developed under Section 503.0626 and assign it to each tag; and

(3) procedures to clearly display the vehicle-specific number on the tag.

(f) A converter or employee of a converter may not use a temporary tag issued under this section as authorization to operate a vehicle for the converter's or the employee's personal use.

(Enacted by Acts 1999, 76th Leg., ch. 964 (H.B. 2539), § 2, effective September 1, 1999; am. Acts 2003, 78th Leg., ch. 1276 (H.B. 3507), § 14A.830, effective September 1, 2003; am. Acts 2007, 80th Leg., ch. 258 (S.B. 11), § 8.03, effective September 1, 2007; am. Acts 2007, 80th Leg., ch. 1336 (S.B. 1786), § 3, effective September 1, 2007; am. Acts 2009, 81st Leg., ch. 793 (S.B. 1235), §§ 5, 6, effective September 1, 2009.)

## Sec. 503.0626.   Dealer's and Converter's Temporary Tag Database.

(a) The department shall develop and maintain a secure, real-time database of information on vehicles to which dealers and converters have affixed temporary tags. The database shall be managed by the vehicle titles and registration division of the department.

(b) The database must allow law enforcement agencies to use the vehicle-specific number assigned to and displayed on the tag as required by Section 503.062(d) or Section 503.0625(e) to obtain information about the dealer or converter that owns the vehicle.

(c) Before a dealer's or converter's temporary tag may be displayed on a vehicle, the dealer or converter must enter into the database through the Internet information on the vehicle and information about the dealer or converter as prescribed by the department. The department may not deny access to the database to any dealer who holds a general distinguishing number issued under this chapter or who is licensed under Chapter 2301, Occupations Code, or to any converter licensed under Chapter 2301, Occupations Code.

(d) The department shall adopt rules and prescribe procedures as necessary to implement this section.

(Enacted by Acts 2007, 80th Leg., ch. 258 (S.B. 11), § 8.04, effective September 1, 2007; enacted by Acts 2007, 80th Leg., ch. 1336 (S.B. 1786), § 4, effective September 1, 2007; am. Acts 2009, 81st Leg., ch. 793 (S.B. 1235), § 7, effective September 1, 2009.)

## Sec. 503.063.   Buyer's Temporary Tags.

(a) Except as provided by this section, a dealer shall issue to a person who buys a vehicle one temporary buyer's tag for the vehicle.

(b) Except as provided by this section, the buyer's tag is valid for the operation of the vehicle until the earlier of:

(1) the date on which the vehicle is registered; or

(2) the 60th day after the date of purchase.

(c) The dealer:

(1) must show in ink on the buyer's tag the actual date of sale and any other required information; and

(2) is responsible for displaying the tag.

(d) The dealer is responsible for the safekeeping and distribution of each buyer's tag the dealer obtains.

(e) The department may not issue a buyer's tag or contract for the issuance of a buyer's tag but shall prescribe:

(1) the specifications, color, and form of a buyer's tag; and

(2) procedures for a dealer to:

(A) generate a vehicle-specific number using the database developed under Section 503.0631 and assign it to each tag;

(B) generate a vehicle-specific number using the database developed under Section 503.0631 for future use for when a dealer is unable to access the Internet at the time of sale; and

(C) clearly display the vehicle-specific number on the tag.

(f) The department shall ensure that a dealer may generate in advance a sufficient amount of vehicle-specific numbers under Subsection (e)(2)(B) in order to continue selling vehicles for a period of up to one week in which a dealer is unable to access the Internet due to an emergency. The department shall establish an expedited procedure to allow affected dealers to apply for additional vehicle-specific numbers so they may remain in business during an emergency.

(g) For each buyer's temporary tag, a dealer shall charge the buyer a registration fee of not more than $5 as prescribed by the department to be sent to the comptroller for deposit to the credit of the state highway fund.

(Enacted by Acts 1995, 74th Leg., ch. 165 (S.B. 971), § 1, effective September 1, 1995; am. Acts 1997, 75th Leg., ch. 296 (H.B. 1137), § 3, effective September 1, 1997; am. Acts 1997, 75th Leg., ch. 871 (H.B. 1790), § 7, effective September 1, 1997; am. Acts 2007, 80th Leg., ch. 258 (S.B. 11), § 8.05, effective September 1, 2007; am. Acts 2007, 80th Leg., ch. 1336 (S.B. 1786), § 5, effective September 1, 2007; am. Acts 2009, 81st Leg., ch. 793 (S.B. 1235), §§ 8, 9, effective September 1, 2009.)

### Sec. 503.0631. Buyer's Temporary Tag Database.

(a) The department shall develop and maintain a secure, real-time database of information on persons to whom temporary buyer's tags are issued that may be used by a law enforcement agency in the same manner that the agency uses vehicle registration information. The database shall be managed by the vehicle titles and registration division of the department.

(b) The database must allow law enforcement agencies to use a vehicle-specific number assigned to and displayed on the tag as required by Section 503.063(e)(2) to obtain information about the person to whom the tag was issued.

(c) Except as provided by Subsection (d), before a buyer's temporary tag may be displayed on a vehicle, a dealer must enter into the database through the Internet information about the buyer of the vehicle for which the tag was issued as prescribed by the department and generate a vehicle-specific number for the tag as required by Section 503.063(e). The department may not deny access to the database to any dealer who holds a general distinguishing number issued under this chapter or who is licensed under Chapter 2301, Occupations Code.

(d) A dealer shall obtain 24-hour Internet access at its place of business, but if the dealer is unable to access the Internet at the time of the sale of a vehicle, the dealer shall complete and sign a form, as prescribed by the department, that states the dealer has Internet access, but was unable to access the Internet at the time of sale. The buyer shall keep the original copy of the form in the vehicle until the vehicle is registered to the buyer. Not later than the next business day after the time of sale, the dealer shall submit the information required under Subsection (c).

(e) The department shall adopt rules and prescribe procedures as necessary to implement this section.

(f) The dealer may charge a reasonable fee not to exceed $20 for costs associated with complying with this section.

(Enacted by Acts 2007, 80th Leg., ch. 258 (S.B. 11), § 8.06, effective September 1, 2007; enacted by Acts 2007, 80th Leg., ch. 1336 (S.B. 1786), § 6, effective September 1, 2007; am. Acts 2009, 81st Leg., ch. 793 (S.B. 1235), § 10, effective September 1, 2009.)

### Sec. 503.0632. Notice to Buyer [Repealed].

Repealed by Acts 2009, 81st Leg., ch. 793 (S.B. 1235), § 17, effective September 1, 2009.

(Enacted by Acts 2007, 80th Leg., ch. 258 (S.B. 11), § 8.06, effective September 1, 2007; enacted by Acts 2007, 80th Leg., ch. 1336 (S.B. 1786), § 6, effective September 1, 2007.)

### Sec. 503.064. Manufacturer's License Plates.

(a) Instead of registering a new vehicle that a manufacturer intends to test on a public street or highway or to loan to a consumer for the purpose described by Section 2301.605, Occupations Code, the manufacturer may apply for, receive, and attach manufacturer's license plates to the vehicle.

(b) If the vehicle to which the manufacturer's license plates are attached is a commercial motor vehicle, the vehicle may not carry a load.

(Enacted by Acts 1995, 74th Leg., ch. 165 (S.B. 971), § 1, effective September 1, 1995; am. Acts 2003, 78th Leg., ch. 1276 (H.B. 3507), § 14A.831, effective September 1, 2003.)

### Sec. 503.065. Buyer's Out-of-State License Plates.

(a) The department may issue or cause to be issued to a person a temporary license plate authorizing the person to operate a new unregistered vehicle on a public highway of this state if the person:

(1) buys the vehicle from a dealer outside this state and intends to drive the vehicle from the dealer's place of business; or

(2) buys the vehicle from a dealer in this state but intends to drive the vehicle from the manufacturer's place of business outside this state.

(b) The department may not issue a temporary license plate under this section to a manufacturer or dealer of a motor vehicle, trailer, or semitrailer or to a representative of such a dealer.

(c) A person may not use a temporary license plate issued under this section on a vehicle transporting property.

(d) A temporary license plate issued under this section expires not later than the 30th day after the date on which it is issued. The department shall place or cause to be placed on the license plate at the time of issuance the date of expiration and the type of vehicle for which the license plate is issued.

(e) The fee for a temporary license plate issued under this section is $3. Only one license plate may be issued for each vehicle.

(Enacted by Acts 1995, 74th Leg., ch. 165 (S.B. 971), § 1, effective September 1, 1995; am. Acts 2009, 81st Leg., ch. 793 (S.B. 1235), § 11, effective September 1, 2009.)

## Sec. 503.066. Application for Dealer's or Manufacturer's License Plates.

(a) An applicant for one or more original or renewal dealer's or manufacturer's license plates must submit to the department a written application on a form that:

(1) is provided by the department; and

(2) contains a statement that the applicant agrees to allow the department to examine during working hours the ownership papers for each registered or unregistered vehicle in the applicant's possession or control.

(b) The applicant must swear to the truth of the information contained in the application before an officer authorized to administer oaths.

(c) An application must be:

(1) submitted before the date the plate expires; and

(2) accompanied by the appropriate fee prescribed by Section 503.008.

(d) A metal license plate issued under this chapter expires on the same date as the expiration of the license under which it is issued.

(Enacted by Acts 1995, 74th Leg., ch. 165 (S.B. 971), § 1, effective September 1, 1995; am. Acts 1997, 75th Leg., ch. 165 (S.B. 898), § 30.69(j), effective September 1, 1997; am. Acts 1997, 75th Leg., ch. 871 (H.B. 1790), § 8, effective September 1, 1997; am. Acts 2001, 77th Leg., ch. 76 (H.B. 1664), § 9, effective May 14, 2001; am. Acts 2003, 78th Leg., ch. 1320 (H.B. 2971), § 5, effective September 1, 2003; am. Acts 2007, 80th Leg., ch. 732 (H.B. 2651), § 12, effective September 1, 2007.)

## Sec. 503.067. Unauthorized Reproduction, Purchase, Use, or Sale of Temporary Tags.

(a) A person may not produce or reproduce a temporary tag or an item represented to be a temporary tag for the purpose of distributing the tag to someone other than a dealer or converter.

(b) A person may not operate a vehicle that displays an unauthorized temporary tag.

(c) A person other than a dealer or converter may not purchase a temporary tag.

(d) A person may not sell or distribute a temporary tag or an item represented to be a temporary tag unless the person is:

(1) a dealer issuing the tag in connection with the sale of a vehicle; or

(2) a printer or distributor engaged in the business of selling temporary tags solely for uses authorized under this chapter.

(Enacted by Acts 1995, 74th Leg., ch. 165 (S.B. 971), § 1, effective September 1, 1995; am. Acts 2007, 80th Leg., ch. 258 (S.B. 11), §§ 8.07, 8.08, effective September 1, 2007; am. Acts 2007, 80th Leg., ch. 1336 (S.B. 1786), §§ 7, 8, effective September 1, 2007; am. Acts 2009, 81st Leg., ch. 793 (S.B. 1235), § 12, effective September 1, 2009.)

## Sec. 503.068. Limitation on Use of Dealer's License Plates and Tags.

(a) A dealer or an employee of a dealer may not use a dealer's temporary tag as authorization to operate a vehicle for the dealer's or the employee's personal use.

(b) A person may not use a metal dealer's license plate or dealer's temporary tag on:

(1) a service or work vehicle; or

(2) a commercial vehicle that is carrying a load.

(c) For purposes of this section, a boat trailer carrying a boat is not a commercial vehicle carrying a load. A dealer complying with this chapter may affix to the rear of a boat trailer the dealer owns or sells a metal dealer's license plate or temporary tag issued under Section 503.061, 503.062, or 503.063.

(d) This section does not prohibit the operation or conveyance of an unregistered vehicle using the full-mount method, saddle-mount method, tow-bar method, or a combination of those methods in accordance with Section 503.062 or 503.063.

(Enacted by Acts 1995, 74th Leg., ch. 165 (S.B. 971), § 1, effective September 1, 1995; am. Acts

2009, 81st Leg., ch. 793 (S.B. 1235), § 13, effective September 1, 2009.)

## Sec. 503.069. Display of License Plates and Tags.

(a) A license plate, other than an in-transit license plate, or a temporary tag issued under this chapter shall be displayed in accordance with commission rules.

(b) A drive-a-way operator who has been issued a drive-a-way in-transit license shall display the operator's in-transit license plates on each transported motor vehicle from the vehicle's point of origin to its point of destination in this state in accordance with the laws relating to the operation of a vehicle on a public highway.
(Enacted by Acts 1995, 74th Leg., ch. 165 (S.B. 971), § 1, effective September 1, 1995; am. Acts 2001, 77th Leg., ch. 76 (H.B. 1664), § 10, effective May 14, 2001; am. Acts 2009, 81st Leg., ch. 793 (S.B. 1235), § 14, effective September 1, 2009.)

## Sec. 503.070. Removal of Out-of-State License Plates.

(a) A dealer who purchases a vehicle that displays an out-of-state license plate must remove the plate within a reasonable time.

(b) A dealer who purchases a vehicle for resale may not operate the vehicle on a public street or highway in this state while the vehicle displays an out-of-state license plate.
(Enacted by Acts 1995, 74th Leg., ch. 165 (S.B. 971), § 1, effective September 1, 1995.)

## Sec. 503.071. Notice of Driving or Towing from Out of State.

(a) A motor vehicle that is manufactured outside this state and is driven or towed from the place of manufacture to this state for sale in this state must have affixed to it a sticker stating that the vehicle is being driven or towed from the place it was manufactured.

(b) The sticker must be at least three inches in diameter and must be affixed to the windshield or front of the motor vehicle in plain view.

(c) The sticker must remain on the motor vehicle until the vehicle is sold by a dealer.
(Enacted by Acts 1995, 74th Leg., ch. 165 (S.B. 971), § 1, effective September 1, 1995.)

## Secs. 503.072 to 503.090 [Reserved for expansion].

## SUBCHAPTER D
## ENFORCEMENT

## Sec. 503.091. Enforcement Agreement.

The department may agree with an authorized official of another jurisdiction to regulate activities and exchange information relating to the wholesale operations of nonresident vehicle dealers.
(Enacted by Acts 1995, 74th Leg., ch. 165 (S.B. 971), § 1, effective September 1, 1995.)

## Sec. 503.092. Action to Enforce Chapter.

(a) The attorney general or a district, county, or city attorney may enforce this chapter and bring an enforcement action in the county in which a violation of this chapter is alleged to have occurred.

(b) A justice or municipal court has concurrent original jurisdiction with the county court or a county court at law over an action to enforce this chapter.
(Enacted by Acts 1995, 74th Leg., ch. 165 (S.B. 971), § 1, effective September 1, 1995; am. Acts 2005, 79th Leg., ch. 1128 (H.B. 2509), § 1, effective June 18, 2005.)

## Sec. 503.093. Action to Enforce Subchapter.

(a) The department or any interested person may bring an action, including an action for an injunction, to:

(1) enforce a provision of Subchapter B; or

(2) prohibit a person from operating in violation of the person's application for a general distinguishing number.

(b) A plaintiff other than the department may recover the plaintiff's attorney's fees.
(Enacted by Acts 1995, 74th Leg., ch. 165 (S.B. 971), § 1, effective September 1, 1995; am. Acts 1997, 75th Leg., ch. 871 (H.B. 1790), § 9, effective September 1, 1997.)

## Sec. 503.094. Criminal Penalty.

(a) A person commits an offense if the person violates this chapter.

(b) Except as otherwise provided by this section, an offense under this section is a misdemeanor punishable by a fine of not less than $50 or more than $5,000.

(c) If the trier of fact finds that the person committed the violation wilfully or with conscious indifference to law, the court may treble the fine otherwise due as a penalty for the violation.

(d) An offense involving a violation of:

(1) Section 503.067(b) or (c) is a Class C misdemeanor;

(2) Section 503.067(d) is a Class A misdemeanor;

(3) Section 503.067(a) is a state jail felony; and

(4) Section 503.067(b), (c), or (d) is a state jail felony if the person who committed the offense criminally conspired to engage in organized criminal activity.

(Enacted by Acts 1995, 74th Leg., ch. 165 (S.B. 971), § 1, effective September 1, 1995; am. Acts 2007, 80th Leg., ch. 258 (S.B. 11), § 8.09, effective September 1, 2007; am. Acts 2007, 80th Leg., ch. 1336 (S.B. 1786), § 9, effective September 1, 2007.)

### Sec. 503.095.  Civil Penalty.

(a) In addition to any other penalty prescribed by this chapter, a person who violates this chapter or a rule adopted under this chapter is subject to a civil penalty of not less than $50 or more than $1,000.

(b) For purposes of this section, each act in violation of this chapter and each day of a continuing violation is a separate violation.

(Enacted by Acts 1995, 74th Leg., ch. 165 (S.B. 971), § 1, effective September 1, 1995.)

# CHAPTER 504
## [EFFECTIVE UNTIL JANUARY 1, 2012] SPECIALTY LICENSE PLATES [EFFECTIVE JANUARY 1, 2012] LICENSE PLATES

### Subchapter A. General Provisions

### Subchapter B. Personalized License Plates

### Subchapter C. License Plates for Vehicles Used by Persons with Disabilities

### Subchapter D. Specialty License Plates for the Military

Transportation

## SUBCHAPTER A
## GENERAL PROVISIONS

### Sec. 504.001.  Definitions.

(a) In this chapter:

(1) "Board" means the board of the Texas Department of Motor Vehicles.

(2) "Department" means the Texas Department of Motor Vehicles.

(3) **[Effective January 1, 2012]** "Purchaser" and "seller" have the meanings assigned by Section 501.002.

(b) A word or phrase that is not defined by this chapter but is defined by Section 502.001 has the meaning in this chapter that is assigned by that section.

(Enacted by Acts 2003, 78th Leg., ch. 1320 (H.B. 2971), § 6, effective September 1, 2003; am. Acts 2009, 81st Leg., ch. 933 (H.B. 3097), § 2G.01, effective September 1, 2009; am. Acts 2011, 82nd Leg., ch. 1296 (H.B. 2357), § 166, effective January 1, 2012.)

### Sec. 504.0011. [Effective January 1, 2012] Rules.

The board may adopt rules to implement and administer this chapter.

(Enacted by Acts 2003, 78th Leg., ch. 1320 (H.B. 2971), § 6, effective September 1, 2003; am. Acts 2009, 81st Leg., ch. 933 (H.B. 3097), § 2G.02, effective September 1, 2009; am. Acts 2011, 82nd Leg., ch. 1296 (H.B. 2357), § 167, effective January 1, 2012 (renumbered from Sec. 504.004).)

### Sec. 504.002. [2 Versions: Effective until January 1, 2012] Provisions of General Applicability.

Unless expressly provided by this chapter or by department rule:

(1) any vehicle is eligible to be issued specialty license plates, provided that the department may vary the design of a license plate to accommodate or reflect its use on a motor vehicle other than a passenger car or light truck;

(2) an application for specialty license plates must be submitted in the manner specified by the department, provided that if issuance of a specialty license plate is limited to particular persons or motor vehicles, the application must be accompanied by evidence satisfactory to the department that the applicant or the applicant's vehicle is eligible;

(3) the fee for issuance of a specialty license plate is in addition to each other fee that is paid for or at the time of the registration of the motor vehicle and shall be deposited to the credit of the state highway fund;

(4) each fee described by this chapter is an annual fee, provided that the department may prorate the fee for a specialty license plate fee on a monthly basis to align the license plate fee to the registration period for the motor vehicle for which the license plate was issued, and if a fee is prorated the allocation of the fee by this chapter to an account or fund shall be prorated in proportion;

(5) the department is the exclusive owner of the design of each specialty license plate;

(6) the director may refuse to issue a specialty license plate with a design or alphanu-

meric pattern that the director considers potentially objectionable to one or more members of the public and the director's refusal may not be overturned in the absence of an abuse of discretion;

(7) for each specialty license plate that is issued through a county tax assessor-collector and for which the department is allocated a portion of a fee for administrative costs, the department shall credit 50 cents from its administrative costs to the county treasurer of the applicable county, who shall credit the money to the general fund of the county to defray the costs to the county of administering this chapter;

(8) if a specialty license plate is lost, stolen, or mutilated, an application for a replacement plate must be accompanied by the fee prescribed by Section 502.184(a)(2);

(9) if the owner of a motor vehicle for which a specialty license plate is issued disposes of the vehicle or for any reason ceases to be eligible for that specialty license plate, the owner shall return the specialty license plate to the department; and

(10) a person who is issued a specialty license plate may not transfer it to another person or vehicle without first receiving approval from the department.

(Enacted by Acts 2003, 78th Leg., ch. 1320 (H.B. 2971), § 6, effective September 1, 2003.)

### Sec. 504.002. [2 Versions: Effective January 1, 2012] General Provisions.

Unless expressly provided by this chapter or by department rule:

(1) except for license plates specified as exempt, the fee for issuance of a license plate, including replacement plates, is in addition to each other fee that is paid for at the time of the registration of the motor vehicle and shall be deposited to the credit of the state highway fund;

(2) if the registration period is greater than 12 months, the expiration date of a specialty license plate, symbol, tab, or other device shall be aligned with the registration period, and the specialty plate fee shall be adjusted pro rata, except that if the statutory annual fee for a specialty license plate is $5 or less, it may not be prorated;

(3) the department is the exclusive owner of the design of each license plate;

(4) if a license plate is lost, stolen, or mutilated, an application for a replacement plate

must be accompanied by the fee prescribed by Section 502.060; and

(5) the department shall prepare the designs and specifications of license plates.

(Enacted by Acts 2003, 78th Leg., ch. 1320 (H.B. 2971), § 6, effective September 1, 2003; am. Acts 2011, 82nd Leg., ch. 1296 (H.B. 2357), § 168, effective January 1, 2012.)

### Sec. 504.003. [Renumbered January 1, 2012] Souvenir License Plates.

(a) The department may issue a souvenir version of any specialty license plate for any vehicle, including a motorcycle.

(b) The fee for a single souvenir license plate is $20. The fee shall be deposited to the credit of the state highway fund unless the souvenir license plate is a replica of a specialty license plate issued under Subchapter G or I for which the fee is deposited to an account other than the state highway fund, in which case:

(1) $10 of the fee for the souvenir license plate shall be deposited to the credit of the designated account; and

(2) $10 of the fee for the souvenir license plate shall be deposited to the credit of the state highway fund.

(c) If a souvenir license plate issued before September 1, 2009, is personalized, the fee for the plate is $40. Of the fee:

(1) $20 shall be deposited to the credit of the state highway fund;

(2) $10 shall be deposited to the credit of the designated account if the souvenir license plate is a replica of a specialty license plate issued under Subchapter G or I for which the fee is deposited to a designated account other than the state highway fund; and

(3) the remainder shall be deposited to the credit of the general revenue fund.

(c-1) The fee for a souvenir license plate issued on or after September 1, 2009, is the amount established under Section 504.851(c).

(d) A souvenir license plate may not be used on a motor vehicle, including a motorcycle, and is not an insignia of registration for a motor vehicle. Each souvenir license plate must be identified by the department in a way that identifies it to law enforcement officers and others as a souvenir license plate.

(e) A beneficiary of a specialty license plate issued under Subchapter G or I, as designated by the applicable section of those subchapters, may purchase the specialty license plates, in boxes of

25, for use or resale by the beneficiary. The beneficiary shall pay the required fee per plate, less the amount of the fee that would be deposited to the credit of the designated account.

(Enacted by Acts 2003, 78th Leg., ch. 1320 (H.B. 2971), § 6, effective September 1, 2003; am. Acts 2005, 79th Leg., ch. 279 (H.B. 1735), § 1, effective June 14, 2005; am. Acts 2009, 81st Leg., ch. 1381 (S.B. 1616), § 1, effective September 1, 2009.)

#### STATUTORY NOTES

**Editor's notes.** — This section is renumbered to Transportation Code Section 504.009 pursuant to Acts 2011, 82nd Leg., ch. 1296 (H.B. 2357), § 174, effective January 1, 2012.

### Sec. 504.004. [Renumbered January 1, 2012] Rules and Forms.

The board may adopt rules and the department may issue forms to implement and administer this chapter.

(Enacted by Acts 2003, 78th Leg., ch. 1320 (H.B. 2971), § 6, effective September 1, 2003; am. Acts 2009, 81st Leg., ch. 933 (H.B. 3097), § 2G.02, effective September 1, 2009.)

#### STATUTORY NOTES

**Editor's notes.** — This section is renumbered to Transportation Code Section 504.0011 pursuant to Acts 2011, 82nd Leg., ch. 1296 (H.B. 2357), § 167, effective January 1, 2012.

### Sec. 504.005. [Effective January 1, 2012] Design and Alphanumeric Pattern.

(a) The department has sole control over the design, typeface, color, and alphanumeric pattern for all license plates.

(b) The department shall prepare the designs and specifications of license plates and devices selected by the board to be used as a unique identifier.

(c) The department shall design each license plate to include a design at least one-half inch wide that represents in silhouette the shape of Texas and that appears between letters and numerals. The department may omit the silhouette of Texas from specially designed license plates.

(d) To promote highway safety, each license plate shall be made with a reflectorized material that provides effective and dependable brightness for the period for which the plate is issued.

(Enacted by Acts 2003, 78th Leg., ch. 1320 (H.B. 2971), § 6, effective September 1, 2003; am. Acts 2011, 82nd Leg., ch. 1296 (H.B. 2357), § 169, effective January 1, 2012 (renumbered from Sec. 504.103).)

### Sec. 504.0051. [Effective January 1, 2012] Personalized License Plates.

(a) The department shall issue personalized license plates, including those issued in accordance with the marketing vendor as provided in Subchapter J. The department may not issue more than one set of license plates with the same alphanumeric pattern.

(b) The department may not issue a replacement set of personalized plates to the same person before the period set by rule unless the applicant for issuance of replacement plates pays the fee required by Section 504.007.

(Enacted by Acts 2011, 82nd Leg., ch. 1296 (H.B. 2357), § 170, effective January 1, 2012.)

### Sec. 504.006. [Effective January 1, 2012] Cost of Manufacturing.

(a) The department shall reimburse the Texas Department of Criminal Justice for the cost of manufacturing license plates as the invoices for the license plates are delivered to the department.

(b) When manufacturing is started, the Texas Department of Criminal Justice and the department, after negotiation, shall set the price to be paid for each license plate. The price must be determined from:

(1) the cost of metal, paint, and other materials purchased;

(2) the inmate maintenance cost per shift;

(3) overhead expenses;

(4) miscellaneous charges; and

(5) a previously agreed upon amount of profit for the work.

(Enacted by Acts 1995, 74th Leg., ch. 165 (S.B. 971), § 1, effective September 1, 1995; am. Acts 2003, 78th Leg., ch. 1056 (H.B. 1372), § 7, effective September 1, 2003; am. Acts 2007, 80th Leg., ch. 937 (H.B. 3560), § 1.114, effective September 1, 2007; am. Acts 2009, 81st Leg., ch. 933 (H.B. 3097), § 2E.04, effective September 1, 2009; am. Acts 2011, 82nd Leg., ch. 1296 (H.B. 2357), § 171, effective January 1, 2012 (renumbered from Sec. 502.053).)

### Sec. 504.007. [Effective January 1, 2012] Replacement License Plates.

(a) The owner of a registered motor vehicle may obtain replacement license plates for the vehicle by:

(1) certifying that the replacement plates will not be used on any other vehicle owned or operated by the person making the statement;

(2) paying a fee of $6 plus the fee required by Section 502.356(a) for each set of replacement license plates, unless otherwise specified by law; and

(3) returning to the department each license plate in the owner's possession for which a replacement license plate is obtained.

(b) Replacement license plates may not be issued except as provided by this section.

(c) A county assessor-collector shall retain $2.50 of each fee collected under this section and forward the remainder of the fee to the department.

(d) The fee required by this section applies to the issuance of license plates for a transferred used vehicle for which the registration and license plates were not transferred under Section 504.901.

(e) Replacement license plates may be used in the registration year in which the plates are issued and during each succeeding year of the registration period as set by rule if the registration insignia is properly displayed on the vehicle.

(f) Subsection (e) does not apply to the issuance of specialized license plates for limited distribution, including exempt plates for governmental entities and temporary registration plates.

(Enacted by Acts 2009, 81st Leg., ch. 1136 (H.B. 2553), § 30, effective September 1, 2011; am. Acts 2011, 82nd Leg., ch. 1296 (H.B. 2357), § 172, effective January 1, 2012 (renumbered from Sec. 502.1841).)

### Sec. 504.008. [Effective January 1, 2012] Specialty License Plates.

(a) The department shall prepare the designs and specifications of specialty license plates.

(b) Any motor vehicle other than a vehicle manufactured for off-highway use only is eligible to be issued specialty license plates, provided that the department may vary the design of a license plate to accommodate or reflect its use on a motor vehicle other than a passenger car or light truck.

(c) An application for specialty license plates must be submitted in the manner specified by the department, provided that if issuance of a specialty license plate is limited to particular persons or motor vehicles, the application must be accompanied by evidence satisfactory to the de-

**Transportation**

partment that the applicant or the applicant's vehicle is eligible.

(d) Each fee described by this chapter is an annual fee, provided that the department may prorate the fee for a specialty license plate fee on a monthly basis to align the license plate fee to the registration month for the motor vehicle for which the license plate was issued, and if a fee is prorated the allocation of the fee by this chapter to an account or fund shall be prorated in proportion.

(e) The director or the director's designee may refuse to issue a specialty license plate with a design or alphanumeric pattern that the director or designee considers potentially objectionable to one or more members of the public and the director or designee's refusal may not be overturned in the absence of an abuse of discretion.

(f) For each specialty license plate that is issued by a county assessor-collector and for which the department is allocated a portion of the fee for administrative costs, the department shall credit 50 cents from its administrative costs to the county treasurer of the applicable county, who shall credit the money to the general fund of the county to defray the costs to the county of administering this chapter.

(g) If the owner of a motor vehicle for which a specialty license plate is issued disposes of the vehicle or for any reason ceases to be eligible for that specialty license plate, the owner shall return the specialty license plate to the department.

(h) A person who is issued a specialty license plate may not transfer the plate to another person or vehicle unless the department approves the transfer.

(Enacted by Acts 2011, 82nd Leg., ch. 1296 (H.B. 2357), § 173, effective January 1, 2012.)

### Sec. 504.009. [Effective January 1, 2012] Souvenir License Plates.

(a) The department may issue a souvenir version of any specialty license plate for any vehicle.

(b) The fee for a single souvenir license plate is $20. The fee shall be deposited to the credit of the state highway fund unless the souvenir license plate is a replica of a specialty license plate issued under Subchapter G or I for which the fee is deposited to an account other than the state highway fund, in which case:

(1) $10 of the fee for the souvenir license plate shall be deposited to the credit of the designated account; and

(2) $10 of the fee for the souvenir license plate shall be deposited to the credit of the state highway fund.

(c) If a souvenir license plate issued before November 19, 2009, is personalized, the fee for the plate is $40. Of the fee:

(1) $20 shall be deposited to the credit of the state highway fund;

(2) $10 shall be deposited to the credit of the designated account if the souvenir license plate is a replica of a specialty license plate issued under Subchapter G or I for which the fee is deposited to a designated account other than the state highway fund; and

(3) the remainder shall be deposited to the credit of the general revenue fund.

(c-1) The fee for a souvenir license plate issued on or after November 19, 2009, is the amount established under Section 504.851(c).

(d) A souvenir license plate may not be used on a motor vehicle and is not an insignia of registration for a motor vehicle. Each souvenir license plate must be identified by the department in a way that identifies it to law enforcement officers and others as a souvenir license plate.

(e) A beneficiary of a specialty license plate issued under Subchapter G or I, as designated by the applicable section of those subchapters, may purchase the specialty license plates, in minimum amounts determined by the department, for use or resale by the beneficiary. The beneficiary shall pay the required fee per plate, less the amount of the fee that would be deposited to the credit of the designated account.

(Enacted by Acts 2003, 78th Leg., ch. 1320 (H.B. 2971), § 6, effective September 1, 2003; am. Acts 2005, 79th Leg., ch. 279 (H.B. 1735), § 1, effective June 14, 2005; am. Acts 2009, 81st Leg., ch. 1381 (S.B. 1616), § 1, effective September 1, 2009; am. Acts 2011, 82nd Leg., ch. 1296 (H.B. 2357), § 174, effective January 1, 2012 (renumbered from Sec. 504.003).)

### Sec. 504.010. [Effective January 1, 2012] Issuance and Placement of License Plate.

(a) On payment of the prescribed fee, an applicant for motor vehicle registration shall be issued a license plate or set of plates.

(b) Subject to Section 504.901, the department shall issue only one license plate or set of plates for a vehicle during the registration period set by rule.

(c) The board may adopt rules regarding the placement of license plates for a motor vehicle, road tractor, motorcycle, trailer, or semitrailer.

(Enacted by Acts 2011, 82nd Leg., ch. 1296 (H.B. 2357), § 175, effective January 1, 2012.)

## Secs. 504.011 to 504.100 [Reserved for expansion].

### SUBCHAPTER B
### PERSONALIZED LICENSE PLATES

### Sec. 504.101. [Effective January 1, 2012] Personalized License Plates.

The department shall issue personalized license plates, including those sold by the private vendor under a contract with the department as provided by Section 504.851.

(Enacted by Acts 2011, 82nd Leg., ch. 1296 (H.B. 2357), § 176, effective January 1, 2012.)

### Sec. 504.102. Personalization of Specialty License Plate.

Unless expressly prohibited by this chapter or department rule, any specialty license plate issued under this chapter may be personalized. If a specialty license plate is personalized, the fee for personalization of the specialty license plate shall be added to the fee for issuance of that specialty license plate.

(Enacted by Acts 2003, 78th Leg., ch. 1320 (H.B. 2971), § 6, effective September 1, 2003; am. Acts 2009, 81st Leg., ch. 1381 (S.B. 1616), § 2, effective September 1, 2009.)

### Sec. 504.103. [Renumbered January 1, 2012] Design and Alphanumeric Pattern.

The department has sole control over the design, typeface, color, and alphanumeric pattern for a personalized license plate.

(Enacted by Acts 2003, 78th Leg., ch. 1320 (H.B. 2971), § 6, effective September 1, 2003.)

#### STATUTORY NOTES

**Editor's notes.** — This section is renumbered to Transportation Code Section 504.005 pursuant to Acts 2011, 82nd Leg., ch. 1296 (H.B. 2357), § 169, effective January 1, 2012.

## Secs. 504.104 to 504.200 [Reserved for expansion].

### SUBCHAPTER C
### LICENSE PLATES FOR VEHICLES
### USED BY PERSONS WITH
### DISABILITIES

### Sec. 504.201. Persons with Disabilities.

(a) In this section:

(1) "Disability" and "mobility problem that substantially impairs a person's ability to ambulate" have the meanings assigned by Section 681.001.

(2) "Legally blind" means a condition described by Section 681.001(2)(B) or (C).

(3) "Practice of optometry" and "practice of therapeutic optometry" have the meanings assigned by Section 351.002, Occupations Code.

(b) **[2 Versions: Effective until January 1, 2012]** The department shall issue specialty license plates for a motor vehicle that:

(1) has a manufacturer's rated carrying capacity of two tons or less; and

(2) is regularly operated for noncommercial use by or for the transportation of a person with a permanent disability.

(b) **[2 Versions: Effective January 1, 2012]** The department shall issue specialty license plates for a motor vehicle that:

(1) has a gross vehicle weight of 18,000 pounds or less; and

(2) is regularly operated for noncommercial use by or for the transportation of a person with a permanent disability.

(c) An owner of a motor vehicle regularly operated by or for the transportation of a person described by Subsection (a) may apply to the department for registration under this section.

(d) **[2 Versions: Effective until January 1, 2012]** Except as provided by Subsection (d-1), the initial application for specialty license plates under this section must be accompanied by a written statement from a physician who is licensed to practice medicine in this state or in a state adjacent to this state or who is authorized by applicable law to practice medicine in a hospital or other health facility of the Department of Veterans Affairs. If the applicant has a mobility problem caused by a disorder of the foot, the written statement may be issued by a person licensed to practice podiatry in this state or a state adjacent to this state. In this subsection, "podiatry" has the meaning assigned by Section 681.001. The statement must certify that the person making the application or on whose behalf the application is made is legally blind or has a mobility problem that substantially impairs the person's ability to ambulate. The statement must also certify whether a mobility problem is temporary or permanent. A written statement is not required as acceptable medical proof if:

(1) the person with a disability:

(A) has had a limb, hand, or foot amputated; or

(B) must use a wheelchair; and

(2) the applicant and the county assessor-collector processing the application execute an affidavit attesting to the person's disability.

(d) **[2 Versions: Effective January 1, 2012]** Except as provided by Subsection (d-1), the initial application for specialty license plates under this section must be accompanied by a written statement from a physician who is licensed to practice medicine in this state or in a state adjacent to this state or who is authorized by applicable law to practice medicine in a hospital or other health facility of the Department of Veterans Affairs. If the applicant has a mobility problem caused by a disorder of the foot, the written statement may be issued by a person licensed to practice podiatry in this state or a state adjacent to this state. In this subsection, "podiatry" has the meaning assigned by Section 681.001. The statement must certify that the person making the application or on whose behalf the application is made is legally blind or has a mobility problem that substantially impairs the person's ability to ambulate. The statement must also certify whether a mobility problem is temporary or permanent. A written statement is not required as acceptable medical proof if:

(1) the person with a disability:

(A) has had a limb, hand, or foot amputated; or

(B) must use a wheelchair; and

(2) the applicant executes a statement attesting to the person's disability before the county assessor-collector.

(d-1) If the initial application for specialty license plates under this section is made by or on behalf of a person who is legally blind, the written statement required by Subsection (d) may be issued by a person licensed to engage in the practice of optometry or the practice of therapeutic optometry in this state or a state adjacent to this state.

(e) A person with a disability may receive:

(1) one disabled parking placard under Section 681.002 if the person receives a set of license plates under this section; or

(2) two disabled parking placards under Section 681.002 if the person does not receive a set of license plates under this section.

(f) A license plate issued under this section must include the symbol of access adopted by Rehabilitation International in 1969 at its Eleventh World Congress on Rehabilitation of the Disabled. The symbol must be the same size as the numbers on the license plate.

(g) **[2 Versions: Effective until January 1, 2012]** In addition to a license plate issued under this section, an eligible person is entitled to be issued a set of the license plates for each motor vehicle owned by the person that has a carrying capacity of two tons or less and is equipped with special equipment that:

(1) is designed to allow a person who has lost the use of one or both of the person's legs to operate the vehicle; and

(2) is not standard equipment on that type of vehicle for use by a person who has use of both legs.

(g) **[2 Versions: Effective January 1, 2012]** In addition to a license plate issued under this section, an eligible person is entitled to be issued a set of the license plates for each motor vehicle owned by the person that has a gross vehicle weight of 18,000 pounds or less and is equipped with special equipment that:

(1) is designed to allow a person who has lost the use of one or both of the person's legs to operate the vehicle; and

(2) is not standard equipment on that type of vehicle for use by a person who has use of both legs.

(h) **[Repealed January 1, 2012]** The department shall include the international symbol of access, as defined by Section 681.001, on a specialty license plate issued under this chapter to a person who is eligible for a license plate issued under this section.

(Enacted by Acts 2003, 78th Leg., ch. 1320 (H.B. 2971), § 6, effective September 1, 2003; am. Acts 2007, 80th Leg., ch. 153 (S.B. 959), § 1, effective September 1, 2007; am. Acts 2009, 81st Leg., ch. 531 (S.B. 1367), §§ 1, 2, effective September 1, 2009; am. Acts 2011, 82nd Leg., ch. 1296 (H.B. 2357), §§ 177, 247(9), effective January 1, 2012.)

## Sec. 504.202.   Veterans with Disabilities.

(a) A person entitled to specialty license plates under this section may register, for the person's own use, one vehicle without payment of any fee paid for or at the time of registration except the fee for the license plates. Registration under this section is valid for one year.

(b) **[2 Versions: Effective until January 1, 2012]** A veteran of the United States armed forces is entitled to register, for the person's own use, motor vehicles under this section if:

(1) the person has suffered, as a result of military service:

(A) at least a 50 percent service-connected disability; or

(B) a 40 percent service-connected disability because of the amputation of a lower extremity;

(2) the person receives compensation from the United States because of the disability; and

(3) the motor vehicle:

(A) is owned by the person; and

(B) has a manufacturer's rated carrying capacity of two tons or less.

(b) **[2 Versions: Effective January 1, 2012]** A veteran of the United States armed forces is entitled to register, for the person's own use, motor vehicles under this section if:

(1) the person has suffered, as a result of military service:

(A) at least a 50 percent service-connected disability; or

(B) a 40 percent service-connected disability because of the amputation of a lower extremity;

(2) the person receives compensation from the United States because of the disability; and

(3) the motor vehicle:

(A) is owned by the person; and

(B) has a gross vehicle weight of 18,000 pounds or less.

(c) An organization may register a motor vehicle under this section if:

(1) the vehicle is used exclusively to transport veterans of the United States armed forces who have suffered, as a result of military service, a service-connected disability; and

(2) the veterans are not charged for the transportation.

(d) A statement by the veterans county service officer of the county in which a vehicle described by Subsection (c) is registered or by the Department of Veterans Affairs that a vehicle is used exclusively to transport veterans with disabilities without charge is satisfactory proof of eligibility for an organization.

(e) Other than license plates issued under Subsection (h), license plates issued under this section must include:

(1) the letters "DV" as a prefix or suffix to any numeral on the plate; and

(2) the words "Disabled Veteran" and "U.S. Armed Forces" at the bottom of each license plate.

(e-1) Other than license plates issued under Subsection (h), license plates issued under this section to a person also entitled to license plates issued under Section 504.308, 504.315, or

504.316 may, at the request of the person, include one emblem from the other license plates to which the person is entitled.

(f) **[2 Versions: Effective until January 1, 2012]** The fee for the first set of license plates is $3. There is no fee for each additional set of license plates. If a license plate is lost, stolen, or mutilated, on payment of a $1 fee the department shall issue a set of replacement plates.

(f) **[2 Versions: Effective January 1, 2012]** The fee for the first set of license plates is $3. There is no fee for each additional set of license plates.

(g) A person who receives license plates under this section may receive a disabled parking placard under Section 681.004 for each set of license plates without providing additional documentation.

(h) A person entitled to license plates under this section may elect to receive license plates issued under Chapter 502 under the same conditions for the issuance of license plates under this section.

(i) **[Effective January 1, 2012]** A license plate with the letters "DV" may be personalized with up to four characters.

(Enacted by Acts 2003, 78th Leg., ch. 1320 (H.B. 2971), § 6, effective September 1, 2003; am. Acts 2003, 78th Leg., 3rd C.S., ch. 8 (H.B. 2), § 5.09, effective January 11, 2004; am. Acts 2007, 80th Leg., ch. 98 (H.B. 2105), § 1, effective May 15, 2007; am. Acts 2009, 81st Leg., ch. 617 (H.B. 965), § 1, effective June 19, 2009; am. Acts 2009, 81st Leg., ch. 965 (H.B. 3593), § 1, effective September 1, 2009; am. Acts 2011, 82nd Leg., ch. 460 (S.B. 1755), § 1, effective September 1, 2011; am. Acts 2011, 82nd Leg., ch. 1296 (H.B. 2357), § 178, effective January 1, 2012.)

## Sec. 504.203. Issuance of Disabled License Plates to Certain Institutions.

(a) The department shall issue specialty license plates under this subchapter for a van or bus operated by an institution, facility, or residential retirement community for the elderly or for veterans in which an eligible person resides, including:

(1) an institution that holds a license issued under Chapter 242, Health and Safety Code; or

(2) a facility that holds a license issued under Chapter 246 or 247 of that code.

(b) **[2 Versions: Effective until January 1, 2012]** An application for license plates under this section must be accompanied by a written state-

Transportation

ment signed by the administrator or manager of the institution, facility, or retirement community certifying that the institution, facility, or retirement community regularly transports, as a part of the services that the institution, facility, or retirement community provides, one or more eligible persons who reside in the institution, facility, or retirement community. The department shall determine the eligibility of the institution, facility, or retirement community on the evidence the applicant provides.

(b) **[2 Versions: Effective January 1, 2012]** An application for license plates under this section must be accompanied by a written statement acknowledged by the administrator or manager of the institution, facility, or retirement community certifying that the institution, facility, or retirement community regularly transports, as a part of the services that the institution, facility, or retirement community provides, one or more eligible persons who reside in the institution, facility, or retirement community. The department shall determine the eligibility of the institution, facility, or retirement community on the evidence the applicant provides.

(c) The application and eligibility requirements for a license plate under this section are the same as those provided by Sections 504.201 and 504.202, as applicable.

(Enacted by Acts 2003, 78th Leg., ch. 1320 (H.B. 2971), § 6, effective September 1, 2003; am. Acts 2011, 82nd Leg., ch. 1296 (H.B. 2357), § 179, effective January 1, 2012.)

**Secs. 504.204 to 504.300 [Reserved for expansion].**

## SUBCHAPTER D
## SPECIALTY LICENSE PLATES FOR THE MILITARY

**Sec. 504.301.  [2 Versions: Effective until January 1, 2012] Provisions Generally Applicable to Military Specialty License Plates.**

Unless expressly provided by this subchapter or department rule:

(1) the department shall design specialty license plates for the military; and

(2) a person is not eligible to be issued a specialty license plate under this subchapter if the person was discharged from the armed forces under conditions less than honorable.

(Enacted by Acts 2003, 78th Leg., ch. 1320 (H.B. 2971), § 6, effective September 1, 2003.)

**Sec. 504.301.  [2 Versions: Effective January 1, 2012] Provisions Generally Applicable to Military Specialty License Plates.**

(a) Unless expressly provided by this subchapter or department rule:

(1) the department shall design specialty license plates for the military; and

(2) a person is not eligible to be issued a specialty license plate under this subchapter if the person was discharged from the armed forces under conditions less than honorable.

(b) Notwithstanding any other provision of this subchapter, the department may design the wording on a specialty license plate authorized by this subchapter to enhance the legibility and reflectivity of the license plate.

(Enacted by Acts 2003, 78th Leg., ch. 1320 (H.B. 2971), § 6, effective September 1, 2003; am. Acts 2011, 82nd Leg., ch. 1296 (H.B. 2357), § 180, effective January 1, 2012.)

**Sec. 504.3011.  [2 Versions: Effective until January 1, 2012] Design of Certain License Plates for the Military.**

(a) License plates issued under Section 504.303 must at a minimum bear a color depiction of the emblem of the appropriate branch of the United States armed forces.

(b) License plates issued under Section 504.308(a) or 504.315(e), (f), or (g) must at a minimum bear a color depiction of the appropriate medal.

(c) The department shall design license plates to which this section applies in consultation with veterans organizations.

(Enacted by Acts 2007, 80th Leg., ch. 258 (S.B. 11), § 11.01, effective September 1, 2007.)

**Sec. 504.3011.  [2 Versions: Effective January 1, 2012] Design of Certain License Plates for the Military.**

The department shall design military license plates that:

(1) bear a color depiction of the emblem of the appropriate branch of the United States armed forces or a color depiction of the appropriate medal as provided by the United States Department of Defense; and

(2) include the words "Honorably Discharged" for license plates issued to former members of the United States armed forces.

(Enacted by Acts 2007, 80th Leg., ch. 258 (S.B. 11), § 11.01, effective September 1, 2007; am. Acts 2011, 82nd Leg., ch. 1296 (H.B. 2357), § 181, effective January 1, 2012.)

### Sec. 504.3015. Fees for Military Specialty License Plates.

(a) A person applying for a set of license plates under this subchapter shall pay the registration fee required under Chapter 502 and the applicable special plate fee required under this section, except that one set of license plates shall be issued under Section 504.308 or 504.315 without the payment of the registration fee.

(b) The fee for the issuance of one set of specialty license plates issued under Section 504.315(c), (d), or (g) is $3. There is no additional fee for a specialty license plate issued under another provision of this subchapter.

(c) A surviving spouse applying for a set of license plates under Section 504.302 shall pay the fees required for the type of license plate for which the surviving spouse is eligible.
(Enacted by Acts 2007, 80th Leg., ch. 1166 (H.B. 191), § 2, effective September 1, 2007.)

### Sec. 504.302. Surviving Spouses of Certain Military Veterans.

(a) The surviving spouse of a person who would be eligible for a specialty license plate under this subchapter is entitled to continue to register one vehicle under the applicable section as long as the spouse remains unmarried.

(b) An applicant for registration under this section must submit proof of the eligibility of the applicant's deceased spouse for the applicable specialty license plate.

(c) A surviving spouse applying for specialty license plates under this section must submit a written statement that the spouse is unmarried. If the surviving spouse is applying for Former Prisoner of War, Pearl Harbor Survivor, or Purple Heart specialty license plates, the statement must be sworn to by the surviving spouse.
(Enacted by Acts 2003, 78th Leg., ch. 1320 (H.B. 2971), § 6, effective September 1, 2003.)

### Sec. 504.303. Members or Former Members of United States Armed Forces.

(a) The department shall issue specialty license plates for active or former members of the United States armed forces. The license plates must designate the appropriate branch of the United States armed forces.

(b) [Repealed by Acts 2007, 80th Leg., ch. 1166 (H.B. 191), § 13, effective September 1, 2007.]
(Enacted by Acts 2003, 78th Leg., ch. 1320 (H.B. 2971), § 6, effective September 1, 2003; am. Acts 2007, 80th Leg., ch. 1166 (H.B. 191), § 13, effective September 1, 2007.)

### Sec. 504.304. Members of United States Armed Forces Auxiliaries.

(a) The department shall issue specialty license plates for members of:

    (1) the United States Air Force Auxiliary, Civil Air Patrol;

    (2) the United States Coast Guard Auxiliary; and

    (3) the Marine Corps League or its auxiliary.

(b) The license plates must include the words "Texas Wing Civil Air Patrol," the words "Coast Guard Auxiliary," or the emblem of the Marine Corps League and the words "Marine Corps League," as applicable.

(c) [Repealed by Acts 2007, 80th Leg., ch. 1166 (H.B. 191), § 13, effective September 1, 2007.]
(Enacted by Acts 2003, 78th Leg., ch. 1320 (H.B. 2971), § 6, effective September 1, 2003; am. Acts 2007, 80th Leg., ch. 1166 (H.B. 191), § 13, effective September 1, 2007.)

### Sec. 504.305. Members of Texas National Guard, State Guard, or United States Armed Forces Reserves.

(a) The department shall issue specialty license plates for:

    (1) active members of the Texas National Guard or Texas State Guard;

    (2) retired members of the Texas National Guard or Texas State Guard who have completed 20 or more years of satisfactory federal service; and

    (3) members of a reserve component of the United States armed forces.

(b) The department shall design the license plates in consultation with the adjutant general. The license plates must include the words "Texas Guard" or "Armed Forces Reserve," as applicable.

(c) A letter from the United States Department of Defense, the Department of the Army, or the Department of the Air Force stating that a retired guard member has 20 or more years of satisfactory federal service is satisfactory proof of eligibility.
(Enacted by Acts 2003, 78th Leg., ch. 1320 (H.B. 2971), § 6, effective September 1, 2003; am. Acts 2007, 80th Leg., ch. 1166 (H.B. 191), § 3, effective September 1, 2007.)

## Sec. 504.306. Persons Retired from Service in Merchant Marine of the United States.

The department shall issue specialty license plates for persons retired from service in the merchant marine of the United States. The license plates must include the words "Merchant Marine."
(Enacted by Acts 2003, 78th Leg., ch. 1320 (H.B. 2971), § 6, effective September 1, 2003; am. Acts 2007, 80th Leg., ch. 1166 (H.B. 191), § 4, effective September 1, 2007.)

## Sec. 504.307. United States Paratroopers.

(a) The department shall issue specialty license plates for active and former members of the United States armed services who have:
(1) satisfactorily completed the prescribed proficiency tests while assigned or attached to an airborne unit or the Airborne Department of the United States Army Infantry School; or
(2) participated in at least one combat parachute jump.
(b) The license plates must include:
(1) a likeness of the parachutist badge authorized by the Department of the Army; and
(2) the words "U.S. Paratrooper. "
(Enacted by Acts 2003, 78th Leg., ch. 1320 (H.B. 2971), § 6, effective September 1, 2003; am. Acts 2007, 80th Leg., ch. 1166 (H.B. 191), § 13, effective September 1, 2007; am. Acts 2011, 82nd Leg., ch. 1215 (S.B. 461), § 1, effective September 1, 2011.)

## Sec. 504.308. Distinguished Flying Cross Medal Recipients.

(a) The department shall issue specialty license plates for persons who have received the Distinguished Flying Cross medal. The license plates must bear a depiction of the Distinguished Flying Cross medal and the words "Distinguished Flying Cross" at the bottom of each license plate.
(b) [Repealed by Acts 2007, 80th Leg., ch. 1166 (H.B. 191), § 13, effective September 1, 2007.]
(Enacted by Acts 2003, 78th Leg., ch. 1320 (H.B. 2971), § 6, effective September 1, 2003; am. Acts 2007, 80th Leg., ch. 1166 (H.B. 191), § 13, effective September 1, 2007.)

## Sec. 504.309. Military Academy License Plates.

The department shall issue specialty license plates for persons who:

(1) are graduates of the United States Military Academy, the United States Naval Academy, or the United States Air Force Academy; and
(2) are current or former commissioned officers of the United States armed forces.
(Enacted by Acts 2003, 78th Leg., ch. 1320 (H.B. 2971), § 6, effective September 1, 2003; am. Acts 2007, 80th Leg., ch. 1166 (H.B. 191), § 5, effective September 1, 2007.)

## Sec. 504.310. World War II Veterans.

The department shall issue specialty license plates for persons who served in the United States or Allied armed forces during World War II. The license plates must include the words "WWII Veteran."
(Enacted by Acts 2003, 78th Leg., ch. 1320 (H.B. 2971), § 6, effective September 1, 2003; am. Acts 2007, 80th Leg., ch. 1166 (H.B. 191), § 6, effective September 1, 2007.)

## Sec. 504.311. Korean War Veterans.

The department shall issue specialty license plates for persons who served in the United States armed forces after June 26, 1950, and before February 1, 1955. License plates issued under this section must include the words "Korea Veteran."
(Enacted by Acts 2003, 78th Leg., ch. 1320 (H.B. 2971), § 6, effective September 1, 2003; am. Acts 2007, 80th Leg., ch. 1166 (H.B. 191), § 7, effective September 1, 2007.)

## Sec. 504.312. Vietnam Veterans.

(a) The department shall issue specialty license plates for persons who served in the United States armed forces during:
(1) the period beginning on February 28, 1961, and ending on May 7, 1975, in the case of a veteran who served in the Republic of Vietnam during that period; or
(2) the period beginning on August 5, 1964, and ending on May 7, 1975, in all other cases.
(b) License plates issued under this section must include the words "Vietnam Veteran."
(Enacted by Acts 2003, 78th Leg., ch. 1320 (H.B. 2971), § 6, effective September 1, 2003; am. Acts 2007, 80th Leg., ch. 1166 (H.B. 191), § 8, effective September 1, 2007.)

## Sec. 504.313. Desert Shield or Desert Storm Veterans.

The department shall issue specialty license plates for persons who served in the United

States armed forces after August 1, 1990, and before April 12, 1991. License plates issued under this section must include the words "Desert Storm."

(Enacted by Acts 2003, 78th Leg., ch. 1320 (H.B. 2971), § 6, effective September 1, 2003; am. Acts 2007, 80th Leg., ch. 1166 (H.B. 191), § 9, effective September 1, 2007.)

### Sec. 504.3135. Operation Iraqi Freedom.

The department shall issue specialty license plates for persons who served in the United States armed forces and participated in Operation Iraqi Freedom. License plates issued under this section must include the words "Operation Iraqi Freedom."

(Enacted by Acts 2003, 78th Leg., ch. 1320 (H.B. 2971), § 6, effective September 1, 2003; am. Acts 2005, 79th Leg., ch. 575 (H.B. 1480), § 1(a), effective September 1, 2005; am. Acts 2007, 80th Leg., ch. 1166 (H.B. 191), § 10, effective September 1, 2007.)

### Sec. 504.314. Enduring Freedom Veterans.

The department shall issue specialty license plates for persons who served in the United States armed services and participated in Operation Enduring Freedom. The license plates must include the words "Enduring Freedom."

(Enacted by Acts 2003, 78th Leg., ch. 1320 (H.B. 2971), § 6, effective September 1, 2003; am. Acts 2007, 80th Leg., ch. 1166 (H.B. 191), § 11, effective September 1, 2007.)

### Sec. 504.315. Military Specialty License Plates for Extraordinary Service.

(a) **[2 Versions: As added by Acts 2011, 82nd Leg., ch. 460]** The department shall issue specialty license plates for recipients of the Distinguished Service Medal. License plates issued under this subsection must include the Distinguished Service Medal emblem and the words "Distinguished Service Medal" at the bottom of each plate. Section 504.702 does not apply to license plates authorized by this subsection.

(a) **[2 Versions: As added by Acts 2011, 82nd Leg., ch. 709]** The department shall issue specialty license plates for recipients of the Bronze Star Medal and Bronze Star Medal with Valor. License plates issued under this subsection must include the Bronze Star Medal emblem and

must include the words "Bronze Star Medal" at the bottom of each plate. License plates issued under this subsection to recipients of the Bronze Star Medal with Valor that are not personalized must also include the letter "V" as a prefix or suffix to the numerals on each plate. Section 504.702 does not apply to license plates authorized by this subsection.

(b) [Repealed by Acts 2007, 80th Leg., ch. 1166 (H.B. 191), § 13, effective September 1, 2007.]

(c) The department shall issue specialty license plates for a person who was captured and incarcerated by an enemy of the United States during a period of conflict with the United States. The license plates must show that the recipient is a former prisoner of war.

(d) **[2 Versions: Effective until January 1, 2012]** The department shall issue specialty license plates for survivors of the attack on Pearl Harbor on December 7, 1941. The license plates must include the words "Pearl Harbor Survivor" and must be consecutively numbered. A person is eligible if the person:

(1) served in the United States armed forces;

(2) was stationed in the Hawaiian Islands on December 7, 1941; and

(3) survived the attack on Pearl Harbor on December 7, 1941.

(d) **[2 Versions: Effective January 1, 2012]** The department shall issue specialty license plates for survivors of the attack on Pearl Harbor on December 7, 1941. The license plates must include the words "Pearl Harbor Survivor." A person is eligible if the person:

(1) served in the United States armed forces;

(2) was stationed in the Hawaiian Islands on December 7, 1941; and

(3) survived the attack on Pearl Harbor on December 7, 1941.

(e) The department shall issue specialty license plates to a recipient of a Congressional Medal of Honor awarded under Title 10, United States Code. The department shall assign the license plate number, and the plates may not be personalized.

(f) The department shall issue specialty license plates for recipients of the Air Force Cross or Distinguished Service Cross, the Army Distinguished Service Cross, the Navy Cross, or the Medal of Honor. The license plates must include the words "Legion of Valor."

(g) The department shall issue specialty license plates for recipients of the Purple Heart. License plates issued under this subsection must include:

Transportation

(1) the Purple Heart emblem;

(2) the words "Purple Heart" at the bottom of each plate; and

(3) the letters "PH" as a prefix or suffix to the numerals on the plate if the plate is not personalized.

(h) The department shall issue special license plates for recipients of the Silver Star Medal. License plates issued under this subsection must include the Silver Star Medal emblem and must include the words "Silver Star Medal" at the bottom of each plate. Section 504.702 does not apply to license plates authorized by this subsection.

(i) A vehicle registered under this section must be for the use of the applicant who qualifies under this section.

(Enacted by Acts 2003, 78th Leg., ch. 1320 (H.B. 2971), § 6, effective September 1, 2003; am. Acts 2007, 80th Leg., ch. 358 (S.B. 274), § 1, effective September 1, 2007; am. Acts 2007, 80th Leg., ch. 1166 (H.B. 191), §§ 12, 13, effective September 1, 2007; am. Acts 2009, 81st Leg., ch. 87 (S.B. 1969), § 27.001(103), effective September 1, 2009; am. Acts 2011, 82nd Leg., ch. 460 (S.B. 1755), § 2, effective September 1, 2011; am. Acts 2011, 82nd Leg., ch. 709 (H.B. 559), § 1, effective September 1, 2011; am. Acts 2011, 82nd Leg., ch. 1296 (H.B. 2357), § 182, effective January 1, 2012.)

### Sec. 504.316.　Legion of Merit Medal Recipients.

(a) The department shall issue specialty license plates for persons who have received the Legion of Merit medal. The license plates must include the words "Legion of Merit."

(b) [Repealed January 1, 2012] The fee for issuance of the license plates is:

(1) $10 for the first set of license plates; and

(2) $15 for each additional set of license plates.

(Enacted by Acts 2007, 80th Leg., ch. 317 (H.B. 2282), § 1, effective September 1, 2007; am. Acts 2011, 82nd Leg., ch. 1296 (H.B. 2357), § 247(10), effective January 1, 2012.)

### Sec. 504.317.　[2 Versions: As added by Acts 2011, 82nd Leg., chs. 845 and 1296] Surviving Spouses of Disabled Veterans Specialty License Plates.

(a) In this section, "surviving spouse" means the individual married to a disabled veteran at the time of the veteran's death.

(b) The department shall issue specialty license plates for surviving spouses of disabled veterans of the United States armed forces.

(Enacted by Acts 2011, 82nd Leg., ch. 845 (H.B. 3580), § 1, effective September 1, 2011; Enacted by Acts 2011, 82nd Leg., ch. 1296 (H.B. 2357), § 183, effective January 1, 2012.)

### Sec. 504.317.　[2 Versions: As added by Acts 2011, 82nd Leg., ch. 1281] Women Veterans.

The department shall issue specialty license plates for female active or former members of the United States armed forces, Texas National Guard, or Texas State Guard. The license plates must include the words "Woman Veteran" in red. (Enacted by Acts 2011, 82nd Leg., ch. 1281 (H.B. 1178), § 4, effective June 17, 2011.)

### Secs. 504.318 to 504.399 [Reserved for expansion].

## SUBCHAPTER E
## SPECIALTY LICENSE PLATES WITH RESTRICTED DISTRIBUTION

### Sec. 504.400.　[Effective January 1, 2012] Fees for Certain Restricted Plates.

The department shall issue, without charge, not more than three sets of specialty license plates under this subchapter.

(Enacted by Acts 2011, 82nd Leg., ch. 1296 (H.B. 2357), § 184, effective January 1, 2012.)

### Sec. 504.401.　State Officials.

(a) [2 Versions: Effective until January 1, 2012] The department shall issue without charge specialty license plates to a state official. The license plates must include the words "State Official."

(a) [2 Versions: Effective January 1, 2012] The department shall issue specialty license plates that include the words "State Official" to a state official.

(b) [Repealed January 1, 2012] A state official may be issued three sets of license plates under this section.

(c) [2 Versions: Effective until January 1, 2012] The license plates remain valid until December 31 of each year.

(c) [2 Versions: Effective January 1, 2012] The registration remains valid until December 31 of each year.

(d) In this section, "state official" means:

(1) a member of the legislature;

(2) the governor;

(3) the lieutenant governor;

(4) a justice of the supreme court;

(5) a judge of the court of criminal appeals;

(6) the attorney general;

(7) the commissioner of the General Land Office;

(8) the comptroller;

(9) a member of the Railroad Commission of Texas;

(10) the commissioner of agriculture;

(11) the secretary of state; or

(12) a member of the State Board of Education.

(Enacted by Acts 2003, 78th Leg., ch. 1320 (H.B. 2971), § 6, effective September 1, 2003; am. Acts 2011, 82nd Leg., ch. 1296 (H.B. 2357), §§ 185, 247(11), effective January 1, 2012.)

## Sec. 504.402. Members of Congress.

(a) **[2 Versions: Effective until January 1, 2012]** The department shall issue without charge specialty license plates for members of congress. License plates issued under this section must include the words "U.S. Congress."

(a) **[2 Versions: Effective January 1, 2012]** The department shall issue specialty license plates to members of congress, which must include the words "U.S. Congress."

(b) **[Repealed January 1, 2012]** A person may be issued three sets of license plates under this section.

(c) The license plates remain valid until December 31 of each year.

(Enacted by Acts 2003, 78th Leg., ch. 1320 (H.B. 2971), § 6, effective September 1, 2003; am. Acts 2011, 82nd Leg., ch. 1296 (H.B. 2357), §§ 186, 247(12), effective January 1, 2012.)

## Sec. 504.403. State and Federal Judges.

(a) **[Effective January 1, 2012]** The department shall issue specialty license plates for a current or visiting state or federal judge. The license plates must include the words "State Judge" or "U.S. Judge," as appropriate.

(b) [Repealed by Acts 2011, 82nd Leg., ch. 1290 (H.B. 2017), § 44(4), effective September 1, 2011 and by Acts 2011, 82nd Leg., ch. 1296 (H.B. 2357), § 247(13), effective January 1, 2012.]

(c) [Repealed by Acts 2011, 82nd Leg., ch. 1290 (H.B. 2017), § 44(4), effective September 1, 2011.

(d) [Repealed by Acts 2011, 82nd Leg., ch. 1290 (H.B. 2017), § 44(4), effective September 1, 2011].

(1) [Repealed by Acts 2011, 82nd Leg., ch. 1290 (H.B. 2017), § 44(4), effective September 1, 2011].

(2) **[Effective January 1, 2012]** "State judge" means:

(A) a justice of the supreme court;

(B) a judge of the court of criminal appeals;

(C) a judge of a court of appeals of this state;

(D) a district court judge;

(E) a presiding judge of an administrative judicial district; or

(F) a statutory county court judge.

(Enacted by Acts 2003, 78th Leg., ch. 1320 (H.B. 2971), § 6, effective September 1, 2003; am. Acts 2011, 82nd Leg., ch. 1296 (H.B. 2357), §§ 187, 188, 247(13), effective January 1, 2012.)

### STATUTORY NOTES

**Editor's notes.** — Without referencing the amendment of this section by Acts 2011, 82nd Leg., ch. 1296 (H.B. 2357), §§ 187 and 188, Acts 2011, 82nd Leg., ch. 1290 (H.B. 2017), § 44(4), repealed the section, effective September 1, 2011.

## Sec. 504.404. Federal Administrative Law Judges.

(a) **[Effective January 1, 2012]** The department shall issue specialty license plates to current federal administrative law judges that bear the words "U.S. A. L. Judge."

(b) [Repealed by Acts 2011, 82nd Leg., ch. 1290 (H.B. 2017), § 44(4), effective September 1, 2011.]

(Enacted by Acts 2003, 78th Leg., ch. 1320 (H.B. 2971), § 6, effective September 1, 2003; am. Acts 2011, 82nd Leg., ch. 1296 (H.B. 2357), § 189, effective January 1, 2012.)

### STATUTORY NOTES

**Editor's notes.** — Without referencing the amendment of this section by Acts 2011, 82nd Leg., ch. 1296 (H.B. 2357), § 189, Acts 2011, 82nd Leg., ch. 1290 (H.B. 2017), § 44(4) repealed the section, effective September 1, 2011.

## Sec. 504.405. County Judges.

(a) **[2 Versions: Effective until January 1, 2012]** The department shall issue without charge specialty license plates for current county judges of this state. The license plates shall bear the words "County Judge."

(a) **[2 Versions: Effective January 1, 2012]** The department shall issue specialty license plates for current county judges of this state that bear the words "County Judge."

(b) **[Repealed January 1, 2012]** A person may be issued three sets of license plates under this section.

(c) In this section, "county judge" means the judge of the county court established by Section 15, Article V, Texas Constitution.

(Enacted by Acts 2003, 78th Leg., ch. 1320 (H.B. 2971), § 6, effective September 1, 2003; am. Acts 2011, 82nd Leg., ch. 1296 (H.B. 2357), §§ 190, 247(15), effective January 1, 2012.)

### Sec. 504.406. [Effective January 1, 2012] Texas Constables.

The department shall issue specialty license plates for Texas constables that bear the words "Texas Constable."

(Enacted by Acts 2003, 78th Leg., ch. 1320 (H.B. 2971), § 6, effective September 1, 2003; am. Acts 2011, 82nd Leg., ch. 1296 (H.B. 2357), § 191, effective January 1, 2012.)

STATUTORY NOTES

**Editor's notes.** — Without referencing the amendment of this section by Acts 2011, 82nd Leg., ch. 1296 (H.B. 2357), § 191, Acts 2011, 82nd Leg., ch. 1290 (H.B. 2017), § 44(4), repealed the section, effective September 1, 2011.

### Sec. 504.4061. [Effective January 1, 2012] Foreign Organization Vehcles.

(a) The department shall issue specialty license plates for an instrumentality established by a foreign government recognized by the United States before January 1, 1979, that is without official representation or diplomatic relations with the United States. The license plates must include the words "Foreign Organization" and shall remain valid for seven years.

(b) A person entitled to specialty license plates under this section may register the vehicle without payment of any fee paid for or at the time of registration.

(Enacted by Acts 2003, 78th Leg., ch. 1320 (H.B. 2971), § 6, effective September 1, 2003; am. Acts 2011, 82nd Leg., ch. 1296 (H.B. 2357), § 192, effective January 1, 2012 (renumbered from Sec. 504.412).)

### Sec. 504.407. [Renumbered January 1, 2012] Peace Officers Wounded or Killed in Line of Duty.

(a) The department shall issue specialty license plates for:

(1) a person wounded in the line of duty as a peace officer; or

(2) a surviving spouse, parent, brother, sister, or adult child, including an adopted child or stepchild, of a person killed in the line of duty as a peace officer.

(b) License plates issued under this section must include the words "To Protect and Serve" above an insignia depicting a yellow rose superimposed over the outline of a badge.

(c) The fee for issuance of the license plates is $20.

(d) In this section, "peace officer" has the meaning assigned by Section 1.07, Penal Code.

(Enacted by Acts 2003, 78th Leg., ch. 1320 (H.B. 2971), § 6, effective September 1, 2003.)

STATUTORY NOTES

**Editor's notes.** — This section is renumbered to Transportation Code Section 504.511 pursuant to Acts 2011, 82nd Leg., ch. 1296 (H.B. 2357), § 199, effective January 1, 2012.

### Sec. 504.408. [Renumbered January 1, 2012] Gold Star Mother, Father, Spouse, or Family Member.

(a) The department shall issue a specialty license plate for the mother, father, or surviving spouse or an immediate family member of a person who died while serving in the United States armed forces. License plates issued under this section must include the words "Gold Star Mother," "Gold Star Father," "Gold Star Spouse," or "Gold Star Family" and a gold star. A person may not be issued more than one set of the license plates at a time.

(a-1) In this section "immediate family member" means the parent, child, or sibling of a person who died while serving in the United States armed forces.

(b) The fee for issuance of the license plates is $10.

(Enacted by Acts 2003, 78th Leg., ch. 1320 (H.B. 2971), § 6, effective September 1, 2003; am. Acts 2007, 80th Leg., ch. 721 (H.B. 2398), §§ 1, 2, effective June 15, 2007; am. Acts 2011, 82nd Leg., ch. 423 (S.B. 896), §§ 1, 2, effective September 1, 2011.)

STATUTORY NOTES

**Editor's notes.** — This section is renumbered to Transportation Code Section 504.512 pursuant to Acts 2011, 82nd Leg., ch. 1296 (H.B. 2357), § 199, effective January 1, 2012.

### Sec. 504.409. [Renumbered January 1, 2012] Firefighters.

(a) The department shall issue specialty license plates for:

(1) volunteer firefighters certified by:

(A) the Texas Commission on Fire Protection; or

(B) the State Firemen's and Fire Marshals' Association of Texas; and

(2) fire protection personnel as that term is defined by Section 419.021, Government Code.

(b) [Repealed by Acts 2009, 81st Leg, ch. 1136 (H.B. 2553), § 39(8), effective September 1, 2011.]

(c) A person may be issued not more than three sets of license plates.

(Enacted by Acts 2003, 78th Leg., ch. 1320 (H.B. 2971), § 6, effective September 1, 2003; am. Acts 2009, 81st Leg, ch. 1136 (H.B. 2553), § 39(8), effective September 1, 2011; am. Acts 2009, 81st Leg., ch. 1381 (S.B. 1616), § 3, effective September 1, 2009.)

STATUTORY NOTES

**Editor's notes.** — This section is renumbered to Transportation Code Section 504.513 pursuant to Acts 2011, 82nd Leg., ch. 1296 (H.B. 2357), § 200, effective January 1, 2012.

## Sec. 504.410. [Renumbered January 1, 2012] Emergency Medical Services Personnel.

(a) The department shall issue specialty license plates for emergency medical services personnel certified by the Texas Department of Health under Subchapter C, Chapter 773, Health and Safety Code.

(b) The fee for issuance of the license plates is $8.

(c) A person may be issued only one set of the license plates.

(Enacted by Acts 2003, 78th Leg., ch. 1320 (H.B. 2971), § 6, effective September 1, 2003.)

STATUTORY NOTES

**Editor's notes.** — This section is renumbered to Transportation Code Section 504.514 pursuant to Acts 2011, 82nd Leg., ch. 1296 (H.B. 2357), § 201, effective January 1, 2012.

## Sec. 504.411. [Renumbered January 1, 2012] Honorary Consuls.

(a) The department shall issue specialty license plates for a person who is an honorary consul authorized by the United States to perform consular duties. License plates issued under this section must include the words "Honorary Consul."

(b) The fee for issuance of the license plates is $40.

(Enacted by Acts 2003, 78th Leg., ch. 1320 (H.B. 2971), § 6, effective September 1, 2003.)

STATUTORY NOTES

**Editor's notes.** — This section is renumbered to Transportation Code Section 504.515 pursuant to Acts 2011, 82nd Leg., ch. 1296 (H.B. 2357), § 201, effective January 1, 2012.

## Sec. 504.412. [Renumbered January 1, 2012] Foreign Organization Vehicles.

(a) The department shall issue specialty license plates for an instrumentality established by a foreign government recognized by the United States before January 1, 1979, that is without official representation or diplomatic relations with the United States. The license plates must include the words "Foreign Organization" and shall remain valid for five years.

(b) A person entitled to specialty license plates under this section may register the vehicle without payment of any fee paid for or at the time of registration.

(Enacted by Acts 2003, 78th Leg., ch. 1320 (H.B. 2971), § 6, effective September 1, 2003.)

STATUTORY NOTES

**Editor's notes.** — This section is renumbered to Transportation Code Section 504.4061 pursuant to Acts 2011, 82nd Leg., ch. 1296 (H.B. 2357), § 192, effective January 1, 2012.

## Sec. 504.413. [Renumbered January 1, 2012] Members of American Legion.

(a) The department shall issue specialty license plates for members of the American Legion. The license plates shall include the words "Still Serving America" and the emblem of the American Legion. The department shall design the license plates in consultation with the American Legion.

(b) The fee for the license plates is $30.

(c) After deduction of $8 to reimburse the department for its administrative costs, the remainder of the fee for issuance of the license plates shall be deposited to the credit of the American Legion, Department of Texas account in the state treasury. Money in the account may be used only by the Texas Veterans Commission in making grants to the American Legion Endowment Fund for scholarships and youth programs sponsored by the American Legion, Department of Texas.

(Enacted by Acts 2003, 78th Leg., ch. 1320 (H.B. 2971), § 6, effective September 1, 2003.)

STATUTORY NOTES

**Editor's notes.** — This section is renumbered to Transportation Code Section 504.659 pursuant to Acts

Transportation

2011, 82nd Leg., ch. 1296 (H.B. 2357), § 210, effective January 1, 2012.

### Sec. 504.414.   Professional Firefighter Plates.

(a) The professional firefighter plate may be issued to qualified firefighters. The sponsor of the plate may nominate a state agency for receipt of funds under Section 504.801(e)(2)(A).

(b) After deduction of the department's administrative costs in accordance with Section 504.801, the remainder of the fees from the sale of professional firefighter plates shall be deposited to the credit of an account in the state treasury to be used by the nominated state agency for the purpose of making grants to support the activities of an organization of professional firefighters located in this state that provides emergency relief and college scholarship funds to the professional firefighters and their dependents.
(Enacted by Acts 2009, 81st Leg., ch. 712 (H.B. 2854), § 1, effective June 19, 2009.)

### Sec. 504.415.   [Effective January 1, 2012] Vehicles Carrying Mobile Amateur Radio Equipment.

The department shall issue specialty license plates for a person who holds an amateur radio station license issued by the Federal Communications Commission and who operates receiving and transmitting mobile amateur radio equipment. The license plates shall include the person's amateur call letters as assigned by the Federal Communications Commission. A person may register more than one vehicle equipped with mobile amateur radio equipment under this section, and the department shall issue license plates that include the same amateur call letters for each vehicle.
(Enacted by Acts 2003, 78th Leg., ch. 1320 (H.B. 2971), § 6, effective September 1, 2003; am. Acts 2009, 81st Leg., ch. 1136 (H.B. 2553), § 36, effective September 1, 2011; am. Acts 2011, 82nd Leg., ch. 1296 (H.B. 2357), § 193, effective January 1, 2012 (renumbered from Sec. 504.509).)

### Secs. 504.416 to 504.500 [Reserved for expansion].

### SUBCHAPTER F
### [EFFECTIVE UNTIL JANUARY 1, 2012] SPECIALTY LICENSE PLATES FOR CERTAIN VEHICLES [EFFECTIVE JANUARY 1, 2012] SPECIALTY LICENSE PLATES WITH RESTRICTED DISTRIBUTION AND REGULAR LICENSE PLATE FEES

### Sec. 504.501.   Classic Motor Vehicles and Travel Trailers; Custom Vehicles; Street Rods.

(a) The department shall issue specialty license plates for a motor vehicle that is at least 25 years old or is a custom vehicle or street rod. The license plates must include the word or words "Classic," "Custom Vehicle," or "Street Rod," or a similar designation, as appropriate.

(b) A person eligible for the license plates may instead use license plates that were issued by this state in the same year as the model year of the vehicle and are approved by the department. The department may require the attachment of a registration insignia to the license plate in a manner that does not affect the display of information originally on the license plate.

(c) There is no fee for issuance or approval of license plates under this section.

(d) Notwithstanding Chapter 547, a custom vehicle or street rod eligible to receive license plates under this section is not required to be equipped with a specific piece of equipment unless the specific piece of equipment was required by statute as a condition of sale during the year listed as the model year on the certificate of title.

(e) On initial registration of a custom vehicle or street rod, the owner must provide proof, acceptable to the department, that the custom vehicle or street rod passed a safety inspection that has been approved by the department. The department shall create a safety inspection process for inspecting custom vehicles and street rods.

(f) In this section:
   (1) "Custom vehicle" means a vehicle:
      (A) that is:
         (i) at least 25 years old and of a model year after 1948; or

Transportation

(ii) manufactured to resemble a vehicle that is at least 25 years old and of a model year after 1948; and

(B) that:

(i) has been altered from the manufacturer's original design; or

(ii) has a body constructed from materials not original to the vehicle.

(2) "Street rod" means a vehicle:

(A) that was manufactured:

(i) before 1949; or

(ii) after 1948 to resemble a vehicle manufactured before 1949; and

(B) that:

(i) has been altered from the manufacturer's original design; or

(ii) has a body constructed from materials not original to the vehicle.

(Enacted by Acts 2003, 78th Leg., ch. 1320 (H.B. 2971), § 6, effective September 1, 2003; am. Acts 2009, 81st Leg., ch. 1136 (H.B. 2553), § 32, effective September 1, 2011; am. Acts 2011, 82nd Leg., ch. 729 (H.B. 890), §§ 2, 3, effective September 1, 2011; am. Acts 2011, 82nd Leg., ch. 1296 (H.B. 2357), § 195, effective September 1, 2011.)

## Sec. 504.5011. [Repealed September 1, 2011] Classic Travel Trailers.

(a) In this section, "travel trailer" has the meaning assigned by Section 502.166.

(b) The department shall issue specialty license plates for a travel trailer that is at least 25 years old. The license plates must include the words "Classic Travel Trailer" or a similar designation.

(c) A person eligible for the license plates may instead use license plates that were issued by this state in the same year as the model year of the travel trailer and are approved by the department. The department may require the attachment of a registration insignia to the license plate in a manner that does not affect the display of information originally on the license plate.

(d) The fee for issuance or approval of license plates under this section is $15.

(Enacted by Acts 2005, 79th Leg., ch. 1045 (H.B. 1244), § 1, effective September 1, 2005.)

## Sec. 504.502. Certain Exhibition Vehicles; Offense.

(a) The department shall issue specialty license plates for a passenger car, truck, motorcycle, or former military vehicle that:

(1) is at least 25 years old, if the vehicle is a passenger car, truck, or motorcycle;

(2) is a collector's item;

(3) is used exclusively for exhibitions, club activities, parades, and other functions of public interest and is not used for regular transportation; and

(4) does not carry advertising.

(b) The license plates must include the words "Antique Auto," "Antique Truck," "Antique Motorcycle," or "Military Vehicle," as appropriate.

(c) A person eligible for the license plates may instead use license plates issued by this state in the same year as the model year of the vehicle and approved by the department, provided that a passenger car must bear passenger car or truck license plates and a truck must bear passenger car or truck license plates. The department may require attachment of a registration insignia to the license plate in a manner that does not affect the display of information originally on the license plate.

(d) License plates issued or approved under this section expire on the fifth anniversary of the date of issuance or approval.

(e) The fee for issuance or approval of license plates under this section is:

(1) $10 for each year or portion of a year remaining in the five-year registration period if the vehicle was manufactured in 1921 or later; or

(2) $8 for each year or portion of a year remaining in the five-year registration period if the vehicle was manufactured before 1921.

(f) The department may exempt a former military vehicle from the requirement to display a license plate or registration insignia if the exemption is necessary to maintain the vehicle's accurate military markings. The department may approve an alternative registration insignia that is compatible with the vehicle's original markings.

(g) [2 Versions: Effective until January 1, 2012] A person entitled to specialty license plates or to department approval under this section may register the vehicle without payment of any fees paid for or at the time of registration except the fee for the license plate. An owner of a vehicle registered under this subsection who violates this section commits an offense. An offense under this section is a misdemeanor punishable by a fine of not less than $5 or more than $200.

(g) [2 Versions: Effective January 1, 2012] A person entitled to specialty license plates or to department approval under this section may register the vehicle without payment of any fees paid for or at the time of registration except the fee for the license plate.

(h) Notwithstanding any other provision of law, a vehicle issued license plates under Subsection (a) shall be required to attach and display only one license plate on the rear of the vehicle.

(i) In this section, "former military vehicle" means a vehicle, including a trailer, regardless of the vehicle's size, weight, or year of manufacture, that:

(1) was manufactured for use in any country's military forces; and

(2) is maintained to represent its military design and markings accurately.

(j) **[Repealed January 1, 2012]** It is an affirmative defense to prosecution of an offense under this section that at the time of the offense the vehicle was en route to or from a location for the purpose of routine maintenance of the vehicle.
(Enacted by Acts 2003, 78th Leg., ch. 1320 (H.B. 2971), § 6, effective September 1, 2003; am. Acts 2005, 79th Leg., ch. 1318 (H.B. 3425), § 1, effective September 1, 2005; am. Acts 2011, 82nd Leg., ch. 1296 (H.B. 2357), §§ 196, 247(16), effective January 1, 2012.)

### Sec. 504.503. [2 Versions: Effective until January 1, 2012] Municipal and Private Buses.

(a) The department shall issue without charge specialty license plates for municipal buses and private buses. The license plates must include the words "City Bus " or "Private Bus, " as appropriate.

(b) In this section, "private bus " means a bus that:

(1) is not operated for hire; and

(2) is not classified as a municipal bus or a motor bus.
(Enacted by Acts 2003, 78th Leg., ch. 1320 (H.B. 2971), § 6, effective September 1, 2003.)

### Sec. 504.503. [2 Versions: Effective January 1, 2012] Municipal, Motor, and Private Buses.

The department shall issue without charge specialty license plates for municipal buses, motor buses, and private buses The license plates must include the words "City Bus, " "Motor Bus," or "Private Bus," as appropriate.
(Enacted by Acts 2003, 78th Leg., ch. 1320 (H.B. 2971), § 6, effective September 1, 2003; am. Acts 2011, 82nd Leg., ch. 1296 (H.B. 2357), § 197, effective January 1, 2012.)

### Sec. 504.504. [Renumbered January 1, 2012] Certain Farm Vehicles and Drilling and Construction Equipment.

(a) The department shall issue specialty license plates to a vehicle described by Subsection (b) or (c). The fee for the license plates is $5.

(b) An owner is not required to register a vehicle that is used only temporarily on the highways if the vehicle is:

(1) a farm trailer or farm semitrailer with a gross weight of more than 4,000 pounds but not more than 34,000 pounds that is used exclusively:

(A) to transport seasonally harvested agricultural products or livestock from the place of production to the place of processing, market, or storage;

(B) to transport farm supplies from the place of loading to the farm; or

(C) for the purpose of participating in equine activities or attending livestock shows, as defined by Section 87.001, Civil Practice and Remedies Code;

(2) machinery used exclusively for the purpose of drilling water wells; or

(3) construction machinery that is not designed to transport persons or property on a public highway.

(c) An owner is not required to register a vehicle that is:

(1) a farm trailer or farm semitrailer owned by a cotton gin and used exclusively to transport agricultural products without charge from the place of production to the place of processing, market, or storage;

(2) a trailer used exclusively to transport fertilizer without charge from a place of supply or storage to a farm; or

(3) a trailer used exclusively to transport cottonseed without charge from a place of supply or storage to a farm or place of processing.

(d) A vehicle described by Subsection (b) is exempt from the inspection requirements of Subchapters B and F, Chapter 548.

(e) This section does not apply to a farm trailer or farm semitrailer that:

(1) is used for hire;

(2) has metal tires operating in contact with the highway;

(3) is not equipped with an adequate hitch pinned or locked so that it will remain securely engaged to the towing vehicle while in motion; or

(4) is not operated and equipped in compliance with all other law.

(f) A vehicle to which this section applies that is operated on a public highway in violation of this section is considered to be operated while unregistered and is immediately subject to the applicable registration fees and penalties prescribed by Chapter 502.

(g) In this section, the gross weight of a trailer or semitrailer is the combined weight of the vehicle and the load carried on the highway.
(Enacted by Acts 2003, 78th Leg., ch. 1320 (H.B. 2971), § 6, effective September 1, 2003; am. Acts 2011, 82nd Leg., ch. 1035 (H.B. 2960), § 2, effective June 17, 2011.)

### STATUTORY NOTES

**Editor's notes.** — This section is renumbered to Transportation Code Section 502.146 pursuant to Acts 2011, 82nd Leg., ch. 1296 (H.B. 2357), § 105, effective January 1, 2012.

## Sec. 504.505. Cotton Vehicles.

(a) The department shall issue specialty license plates for a single motor vehicle that is:

(1) used only to transport chile pepper modules, seed cotton, cotton, cotton burrs, or equipment used in transporting or processing chile peppers or cotton; and

(2) not more than 10 feet in width.

(b) The license plates must include the words "Cotton Vehicle."

(c) There is no fee for issuance of the license plates. The license plates may be renewed without payment of a fee.
(Enacted by Acts 2003, 78th Leg., ch. 1320 (H.B. 2971), § 6, effective September 1, 2003; am. Acts 2005, 79th Leg., ch. 247 (H.B. 749), § 1, effective September 1, 2005; am. Acts 2009, 81st Leg., ch. 1136 (H.B. 2553), § 33, effective September 1, 2011.)

## Sec. 504.506. [2 Versions: Effective until January 1, 2012] Certain Log Loader Vehicles.

(a) The department shall issue specialty license plates for a vehicle that is temporarily operated on public highways, during daylight hours only, and on which machinery is mounted solely to load logs on other vehicles.

(b) The fee for issuance of the license plates is $62.50.

(c) A person entitled to specialty license plates under this section may register the vehicle without payment of any fee paid for or at the time of registration other than the fee for the license plates.

(d) A vehicle having a license plate issued under this section is exempt from the inspection requirements of Chapter 548.

(e) This section does not apply to a vehicle used to haul logs.

(f) A vehicle to which this section applies that is operated on a public highway in violation of this section is considered to be operated or moved while unregistered and is immediately subject to the applicable fees and penalties prescribed by Chapter 502.
(Enacted by Acts 2003, 78th Leg., ch. 1320 (H.B. 2971), § 6, effective September 1, 2003.)

## Sec. 504.506. [2 Versions: Effective January 1, 2012] Log Loader Vehicles.

(a) The department shall issue specialty license plates for a vehicle that is temporarily operated on public highways, during daylight hours only, and on which machinery is mounted solely to load logs on other vehicles.

(b) The fee for issuance of the license plates is $62.50.

(c) A person entitled to specialty license plates under this section may register the vehicle without payment of any fee paid for or at the time of registration other than the fee for the license plates.

(d) A vehicle having a license plate issued under this section is exempt from the inspection requirements of Chapter 548.

(e) This section does not apply to a vehicle used to haul logs.

(f) [Repealed by Acts 2011, 82nd Leg., ch. 1296 (H.B. 2357), § 247(17), effective January 1, 2012.]
(Enacted by Acts 2003, 78th Leg., ch. 1320 (H.B. 2971), § 6, effective September 1, 2003; am. Acts 2011, 82nd Leg., ch. 1296 (H.B. 2357), §§ 198, 247(17), effective January 1, 2012.)

## Sec. 504.507. Forestry Vehicles.

(a) The department shall issue specialty license plates for forestry vehicles. License plates issued under this section must include the words "Forestry Vehicle."

(b) There is no fee for issuance of the license plates. The department shall:

(1) collect any fee that a county imposes under this chapter for registration of a forestry vehicle; and

(2) send the fee to the appropriate county for disposition.

(c) **[Repealed January 1, 2012]** In this section, "forestry vehicle" means a vehicle used ex-

Transportation

clusively for transporting forest products in their natural state, including logs, debarked logs, untreated ties, stave bolts, plywood bolts, pulpwood billets, wood chips, stumps, sawdust, moss, bark, wood shavings, and property used in production of those products.

(Enacted by Acts 2003, 78th Leg., ch. 1320 (H.B. 2971), § 6, effective September 1, 2003; am. Acts 2009, 81st Leg., ch. 1136 (H.B. 2553), § 34, effective September 1, 2011; am. Acts 2011, 82nd Leg., ch. 1296 (H.B. 2357), § 247(18), effective January 1, 2012.)

### Sec. 504.508.   Tow Trucks.

(a) The department shall issue specialty license plates for a commercial motor vehicle used as a tow truck. The license plates must include the words "Tow Truck." A vehicle used commercially as a tow truck shall display license plates issued under this section.

(b) There is no fee for issuance of the license plates.

(c) Proof of eligibility for license plates under this section must include a copy of the permit certificate issued by the Texas Department of Licensing and Regulation for the tow truck.

(d) **[Repealed January 1, 2012]** In this section, "tow truck" means a motor vehicle adapted or used to tow, winch, or otherwise move another motor vehicle.

(Enacted by Acts 2003, 78th Leg., ch. 1320 (H.B. 2971), § 6, effective September 1, 2003; am. Acts 2007, 80th Leg., ch. 1046 (H.B. 2094), § 3.05, effective September 1, 2007; am. Acts 2009, 81st Leg., ch. 1136 (H.B. 2553), § 35, effective September 1, 2011; am. Acts 2011, 82nd Leg., ch. 1296 (H.B. 2357), § 247(19), effective January 1, 2012.)

### Sec. 504.509.   [Renumbered January 1, 2012] Vehicles Carrying Mobile Amateur Radio Equipment.

The department shall issue specialty license plates for a person who holds an amateur radio station license issued by the Federal Communications Commission and who operates receiving and transmitting mobile amateur radio equipment. The license plates shall include the person's amateur call letters as assigned by the Federal Communications Commission. A person may register more than one vehicle equipped with mobile amateur radio equipment under this section, and the department shall issue license plates that include the same amateur call letters for each vehicle.

(Enacted by Acts 2003, 78th Leg., ch. 1320 (H.B. 2971), § 6, effective September 1, 2003; am. Acts 2009, 81st Leg., ch. 1136 (H.B. 2553), § 36, effective September 1, 2011.)

STATUTORY NOTES

**Editor's notes.** — This section is renumbered to Transportation Code Section 504.415 pursuant to Acts 2011, 82nd Leg., ch. 1296 (H.B. 2357), § 193, effective January 1, 2012.

### Sec. 504.510.   Golf Cart License Plates.

(a) The department shall issue specialty license plates for an eligible golf cart.

(b) The fee for issuance of the license plates is $6.

(c) A person entitled to specialty license plates under this section may register the golf cart without payment of any fees paid for or at the time of registration other than the fee for the license plates. This section does not authorize the operation of a golf cart on a public road where it is otherwise prohibited by law.

(d) **[2 Versions: As amended by Acts 2011, 82nd Leg., ch. 1163]** This section applies only to an owner of a golf cart who resides:

(1) on real property that is owned or under the control of the United States Corps of Engineers and is required by that agency to register the owner's golf cart under this chapter; and

(2) in a county that borders another state and has a population of more than 120,750 but less than 121,000.

(d) **[2 Versions: As amended by Acts 2011, 82nd Leg., 1st C.S., (S.B. 1), effective September 28, 2011]** This section applies only to an owner of a golf cart who resides on real property that is owned or under the control of the United States Corps of Engineers and is required by that agency to register the owner's golf cart under this chapter.

(Enacted by Acts 2003, 78th Leg., ch. 1320 (H.B. 2971), § 6, effective September 1, 2003; am. Acts 2009, 81st Leg., ch. 1136 (H.B. 2553), § 37, effective September 1, 2011; am. Acts 2011, 82nd Leg., ch. 1163 (H.B. 2702), § 174, effective September 1, 2011; am. Acts 2011, 82nd Leg., 1st C.S., (S.B. 1), § 68.01, effective September 28, 2011.)

### Sec. 504.511.   [Effective January 1, 2012] Peace Officers Wounded or Killed in Line of Duty.

(a) The department shall issue specialty license plates for:

(1) a person wounded in the line of duty as a peace officer; or

(2) a surviving spouse, parent, brother, sister, or adult child, including an adopted child or stepchild, of a person killed in the line of duty as a peace officer.

(b) License plates issued under this section must include the words "To Protect and Serve" above an insignia depicting a yellow rose superimposed over the outline of a badge.

(c) The fee for issuance of the license plates is $20.

(d) In this section, "peace officer" has the meaning assigned by Section 1.07, Penal Code.

(Enacted by Acts 2003, 78th Leg., ch. 1320 (H.B. 2971), § 6, effective September 1, 2003; am. Acts 2011, 82nd Leg., ch. 1296 (H.B. 2357), § 199, effective January 1, 2012 (renumbered from Sec. 504.407).)

## Sec. 504.512. [Effective January 1, 2012] Gold Star Mother, Father, Spouse, or Family Member.

(a) The department shall issue a specialty license plate for the mother, father, or surviving spouse or an immediate family member of a person who died while serving in the United States armed forces. License plates issued under this section must include the words "Gold Star Mother," "Gold Star Father," "Gold Star Spouse," or "Gold Star Family" and a gold star. A person may not be issued more than one set of the license plates at a time.

(a-1) In this section "immediate family member" means the parent, child, or sibling of a person who died while serving in the United States armed forces.

(b) The fee for issuance of the license plates is $10.

(Enacted by Acts 2003, 78th Leg., ch. 1320 (H.B. 2971), § 6, effective September 1, 2003; am. Acts 2007, 80th Leg., ch. 721 (H.B. 2398), §§ 1, 2, effective June 15, 2007; am. Acts 2011, 82nd Leg., ch. 423 (S.B. 896), §§ 1, 2, effective September 1, 2011; am. Acts 2011, 82nd Leg., ch. 1296 (H.B. 2357), § 199, effective January 1, 2012 (renumbered from Sec. 504.408).)

## Sec. 504.513. [Effective January 1, 2012] Firefighters.

(a) The department shall issue specialty license plates for:

(1) volunteer firefighters certified by:

(A) the Texas Commission on Fire Protection; or

(B) the State Firemen's and Fire Marshals' Association of Texas; and

(2) fire protection personnel as that term is defined by Section 419.021, Government Code.

(b) A person may be issued not more than three sets of license plates.

(Enacted by Acts 2003, 78th Leg., ch. 1320 (H.B. 2971), § 6, effective September 1, 2003; am. Acts 2009, 81st Leg, ch. 1136 (H.B. 2553), § 39(8), effective September 1, 2011; am. Acts 2009, 81st Leg., ch. 1381 (S.B. 1616), § 3, effective September 1, 2009; am. Acts 2011, 82nd Leg., ch. 1296 (H.B. 2357), § 200, effective January 1, 2012 (renumbered from Sec. 504.409).)

## Sec. 504.514. [Effective January 1, 2012] Emergency Medical Services Personnel.

(a) The department shall issue specialty license plates for emergency medical services personnel certified by the Department of State Health Services under Subchapter C, Chapter 773, Health and Safety Code.

(b) The fee for issuance of the license plates is $8.

(c) A person may be issued only one set of license plates.

(Enacted by Acts 2003, 78th Leg., ch. 1320 (H.B. 2971), § 6, effective September 1, 2003; am. Acts 2011, 82nd Leg., ch. 1296 (H.B. 2357), § 201, effective January 1, 2012 (renumbered from Sec. 504.410).)

## Sec. 504.515. [Effective January 1, 2012] Honorary Consuls.

(a) The department shall issue specialty license plates for a person who is an honorary consul authorized by the United States to perform consular duties. License plates issued under this section must include the words "Honorary Consul."

(b) The fee for issuance of the license plates is $40.

(Enacted by Acts 2003, 78th Leg., ch. 1320 (H.B. 2971), § 6, effective September 1, 2003; am. Acts 2011, 82nd Leg., ch. 1296 (H.B. 2357), § 201, effective January 1, 2012 (renumbered from Sec. 504.411).)

## Sec. 504.516. [Effective January 1, 2012] Rental Trailer or Travel Trailer Fee: Trailer or Semitrailer.

(a) The department may issue specially designed license plates for rental trailers and travel

Transportation

trailers that include, as appropriate, the words "rental trailer" or "travel trailer."

(b) In this section:

(1) "Rental fleet" means vehicles that are designated in the manner prescribed by the department as a rental fleet.

(2) "Rental trailer" means a utility trailer.

(3) "Travel trailer" has the meaning assigned by Section 501.002.

(Enacted by Acts 2011, 82nd Leg., ch. 1296 (H.B. 2357), § 202, effective January 1, 2012.)

**Secs. 504.517 to 504.600 [Reserved for expansion].**

## SUBCHAPTER G
## SPECIALTY LICENSE PLATES FOR GENERAL DISTRIBUTION

### Sec. 504.601.   General Provisions Applicable to Specialty License Plates for General Distribution.

(a) Unless expressly provided by this subchapter or department rule:

(1) the fee for issuance of a license plate under this subchapter is $30; and

(2) of each fee received under this subchapter, the department shall use $8 to defray its administrative costs in complying with this subchapter.

(b) This section does not apply to a specialty license plate marketed and sold by a private vendor at the request of the specialty license plate sponsor under Section 504.6011.

(Enacted by Acts 2003, 78th Leg., ch. 1320 (H.B. 2971), § 6, effective September 1, 2003; am. Acts 2009, 81st Leg., ch. 1381 (S.B. 1616), § 4, effective September 1, 2009.)

### Sec. 504.6011.   General Provisions Applicable to Specialty License Plates for General Distribution Sold Through Private Vendor.

(a) **[2 Versions: Effective until January 1, 2012]** The sponsor of a specialty license plate authorized to be issued under this subchapter before September 1, 2009, may contract with the private vendor authorized under Subchapter J for the marketing and sale of the specialty license plate.

(a) **[2 Versions: Effective January 1, 2012]** The sponsor of a specialty license plate may contract with the private vendor authorized un-

der Subchapter J for the marketing and sale of the specialty license plate.

(b) The fee for issuance of a specialty license plate described by Subsection (a) is the amount established under Section 504.851.

(c) Notwithstanding any other law, from each fee received for the issuance of a specialty license plate described by Subsection (a), the department shall:

(1) deduct the administrative costs described by Section 504.601(a)(2);

(2) deposit to the credit of the account designated by the law authorizing the specialty license plate the portion of the fee for the sale of the plate that the state would ordinarily receive under the contract described by Section 504.851(a); and

(3) pay to the private vendor the remainder of the fee.

(d) **[Effective January 1, 2012]** A sponsor of a specialty license plate authorized to be issued under this subchapter before November 19, 2009, may reestablish its specialty license plate under Sections 504.601 and 504.702 and be credited its previous deposit with the department if a contract entered into by the sponsor under Subsection (a) terminates.

(Enacted by Acts 2009, 81st Leg., ch. 1381 (S.B. 1616), § 5, effective September 1, 2009; am. Acts 2011, 82nd Leg., ch. 1296 (H.B. 2357), § 203, effective January 1, 2012.)

### Sec. 504.602.   Keep Texas Beautiful License Plates.

(a) The department shall issue specialty license plates including the words "Keep Texas Beautiful." The department shall design the license plates in consultation with Keep Texas Beautiful, Inc.

(b) After deduction of the department's administrative costs, the remainder of the fee for issuance of the license plates shall be used in connection with the department's litter prevention and community beautification programs.

(Enacted by Acts 2003, 78th Leg., ch. 1320 (H.B. 2971), § 6, effective September 1, 2003.)

### Sec. 504.603.   Texas Capitol License Plates.

(a) The department shall issue specialty license plates depicting the State Capitol.

(b) After deduction of the department's administrative costs, the remainder of the fee for issuance of the license plates shall be deposited to the credit of the general revenue fund.

(Enacted by Acts 2003, 78th Leg., ch. 1320 (H.B. 2971), § 6, effective September 1, 2003.)

## Sec. 504.604. Texas Commission on the Arts License Plates.

(a) The department shall issue specialty license plates including the words "State of the Arts." The department shall design the license plates in consultation with the Texas Commission on the Arts.

(b) After deduction of the department's administrative costs, the remainder of the fee for issuance of the license plates shall be deposited to the credit of the Texas Commission on the Arts operating fund established under Section 444.027, Government Code.

(Enacted by Acts 2003, 78th Leg., ch. 1320 (H.B. 2971), § 6, effective September 1, 2003.)

## Sec. 504.605. Animal Friendly License Plates.

(a) The department shall issue specialty license plates including the words "Animal Friendly." The department shall design the license plates.

(b) After deduction of the department's administrative costs, the remainder of the fee for issuance of the license plates shall be deposited to the credit of the animal friendly account established by Section 828.014, Health and Safety Code.

(Enacted by Acts 2003, 78th Leg., ch. 1320 (H.B. 2971), § 6, effective September 1, 2003.)

## Sec. 504.606. Big Bend National Park License Plates.

(a) The department shall issue specialty license plates that include one or more graphic images of a significant feature of Big Bend National Park. The department shall design the license plates in consultation with the Parks and Wildlife Department and any organization designated by it.

(b) After deduction of the department's administrative costs, the remainder of the fee for issuance of the license plates shall be deposited to the credit of the Big Bend National Park account in the state treasury. Money in the account may be used only by the Parks and Wildlife Department to support the activities of a designated nonprofit organization whose primary purpose is the improvement or preservation of Big Bend National Park.

(Enacted by Acts 2003, 78th Leg., ch. 1320 (H.B. 2971), § 6, effective September 1, 2003.)

## Sec. 504.607. Read to Succeed.

(a) The department shall issue specialty license plates including the words "Read to Succeed." The department shall design the license plates.

(b) After deduction of the department's administrative costs, the remainder of the fee shall be deposited to the credit of the "Read to Succeed" account in the general revenue fund. Money in the account may be used only to provide educational materials for public school libraries. The account is composed of:

(1) money required to be deposited to the credit of the account under this subsection; and

(2) donations made to the account.

(Enacted by Acts 2003, 78th Leg., ch. 1320 (H.B. 2971), § 6, effective September 1, 2003.)

## Sec. 504.608. Mothers Against Drunk Driving License Plates.

(a) The department shall issue specialty license plates that include the words "Mothers Against Drunk Driving." The department shall design the license plates in consultation with Mothers Against Drunk Driving.

(b) After deduction of the department's administrative costs, the remainder of the fee for issuance of the license plates shall be deposited to the credit of the general revenue fund and may be appropriated only to the Texas Higher Education Coordinating Board in making grants to benefit drug-abuse prevention and education programs sponsored by Mothers Against Drunk Driving.

(Enacted by Acts 2003, 78th Leg., ch. 1320 (H.B. 2971), § 6, effective September 1, 2003; am. Acts 2005, 79th Leg., ch. 575 (H.B. 1480), § 2, effective September 1, 2005.)

## Sec. 504.609. United States Olympic Committee License Plates.

The department shall issue specialty license plates including the words "United States Olympic Committee." The department shall design the license plates in consultation with the United States Olympic Committee.

(Enacted by Acts 2003, 78th Leg., ch. 1320 (H.B. 2971), § 6, effective September 1, 2003.)

## Sec. 504.610. Texas Aerospace Commission License Plates.

(a) The department shall issue specialty license plates including the words "Texas Aerospace Commission." The department shall design the license plates in consultation with the Texas Aerospace Commission.

(b) After deduction of the department's administrative costs, the remainder of the fee for issuance of the license plates shall be deposited to the credit of the general revenue fund.
(Enacted by Acts 2003, 78th Leg., ch. 1320 (H.B. 2971), § 6, effective September 1, 2003.)

### Sec. 504.611.  Volunteer Advocate Program License Plates.

(a) The department shall issue specialty license plates in recognition of children. The department shall design the license plates in consultation with the attorney general.

(b) After deduction of the department's administrative costs, the remainder of the fee for issuance of the license plates shall be deposited to the credit of the attorney general volunteer advocate program account in the general revenue fund. Money deposited to the credit of the volunteer advocate program account may be used only by the attorney general to fund a contract entered into by the attorney general under Section 264.602, Family Code.
(Enacted by Acts 2003, 78th Leg., ch. 1320 (H.B. 2971), § 6, effective September 1, 2003.)

### Sec. 504.612.  Texas Young Lawyers Association License Plates.

(a) The department shall issue specialty license plates including the words "And Justice for All." The department shall design the license plates in consultation with the Texas Young Lawyers Association.

(b) After deduction of the department's administrative costs, the remainder of the fee for issuance of the license plates shall be deposited to the credit of the basic civil legal services account established by Section 51.943, Government Code.
(Enacted by Acts 2003, 78th Leg., ch. 1320 (H.B. 2971), § 6, effective September 1, 2003.)

### Sec. 504.613.  Houston Livestock Show and Rodeo License Plates.

(a) The department shall issue specialty license plates including the words "Houston Livestock Show and Rodeo." The department shall design the license plates in consultation with the Houston Livestock Show and Rodeo.

(b) After deduction of the department's administrative costs, the remainder of the fee for issuance of the license plates shall be deposited to the credit of the Houston Livestock Show and Rodeo scholarship account in the state treasury. Money in the account may be used only by the Texas

Higher Education Coordinating Board in making grants to benefit the Houston Livestock Show and Rodeo.
(Enacted by Acts 2003, 78th Leg., ch. 1320 (H.B. 2971), § 6, effective September 1, 2003.)

### Sec. 504.614.  Professional Sports Team License Plates.

(a) [Effective until January 1, 2012] The department may issue specialty license plates that include the name and insignia of a professional sports team located in this state. The department shall design the license plates in consultation with the professional sports team and may enter a trademark license with the professional sports team or its league to implement this section. A license plate may be issued under this section only for a professional sports team that:

(1) certifies to the department that it has determined that at least 3,500 persons will apply for the plates; and

(2) plays its home games in a facility constructed or operated, in whole or in part, with public funds.

(a) [Effective January 1, 2012] The department may issue specialty license plates that include the name and insignia of a professional sports team located in this state. The department shall design the license plates in consultation with the professional sports team and may enter a trademark license with the professional sports team or its league to implement this section. A license plate may be issued under this section only for a professional sports team that:

(1) certifies to the department that the requirements of Section 504.702 are met; and

(2) plays its home games in a facility constructed or operated, in whole or in part, with public funds.

(b) After deduction of the department's administrative costs, the remainder of the fee for issuance of the license plates shall be sent to the public entity that provided public funds for the construction or renovation of the facility in which the professional sports team plays its home games or that provides public funds for the operation of that facility. The funds shall be deposited to the credit of the venue project fund, if the public entity has created a venue project fund under Section 334.042 or 335.072, Local Government Code. If the public entity has not created a venue project fund, funds distributed to a public entity under this section must first be used to retire any public debt incurred by the public entity in the construction or acquisition of the facility in which the professional sports team plays its home games. After that debt is retired, funds distributed to the public entity may be spent only for maintenance or improvement of the facility.

(b-1) [**Effective January 1, 2012**] A public entity that receives money under Subsection (b) may contract with the private vendor under Section 504.6011 to distribute the entity's portion of the money in a manner other than that described by Subsection (b).

(c) In this section:

(1) "Public entity" includes a municipality, county, industrial development corporation, or special district that is authorized to plan, acquire, establish, develop, construct, or renovate a facility in which a professional sports team plays its home games.

(2) "Professional sports team" means a sports team that is a member or an affiliate of a member of the National Football League, National Basketball Association, or National Hockey League or a major league baseball team.

(Enacted by Acts 2003, 78th Leg., ch. 1320 (H.B. 2971), § 6, effective September 1, 2003; am. Acts 2011, 82nd Leg., ch. 1296 (H.B. 2357), § 204, effective January 1, 2012.)

## Sec. 504.615. Collegiate License Plates.

(a) [**2 Versions: Effective until January 1, 2012**] The department shall issue specialty license plates that include the name and insignia of a college. The department shall design the license plates in consultation with the applicable college. The department may issue a license plate under this section only for a college that certifies to the department that it has determined that at least 1,500 persons will apply for the plates.

(a) [**2 Versions: Effective January 1, 2012**] The department shall issue specialty license plates that include the name and insignia of a college. The department shall design the license plates in consultation with the applicable college. The department may issue a license plate under this section only for a college that certifies to the department that the requirements of Section 504.702 are met.

(b) After deduction of the department's administrative costs, the remainder of the fee for issuance of the license plates shall be deposited to the credit of the general revenue fund. The money may be used only for:

(1) scholarships to students who demonstrate a need for financial assistance under Texas Higher Education Coordinating Board rule; or

(2) Texas Public Educational Grants awarded under Subchapter C, Chapter 56, Education Code, if the fee is for the issuance of a license plate for a college described by Subsection (e)(1).

(c) If the fee is for the issuance of license plates for a college described by Subsection (e)(1), the money:

(1) shall be deposited to the credit of the institution of higher education designated on the license plates; and

(2) is supplementary and is not income for purposes of reducing general revenue appropriations to that institution of higher education.

(d) If the fee is for the issuance of license plates for a college described by Subsection (e)(2), the money shall be deposited to the credit of the Texas Higher Education Coordinating Board. The money:

(1) shall be allocated to students at the college designated on the plates; and

(2) is in addition to other money that the board may allocate to that college.

(d-1) [**Effective January 1, 2012**] If the fee is for the issuance of license plates for a college described by Subsection (e)(3), the money:

(1) shall be deposited to the credit of the Texas Higher Education Coordinating Board; and

(2) is supplementary and is not income for purposes of reducing general revenue appropriations to that board.

(e) [**2 Versions: Effective until January 1, 2012**] In this section, "college" means:

(1) an institution of higher education as defined by Section 61.003, Education Code; or

(2) a private college or university described by Section 61.222, Education Code.

(e) [**2 Versions: Effective January 1, 2012**] In this section, 'college' means:

(1) an institution of higher education as defined by Section 61.003, Education Code;

(2) a private college or university described by Section 61.222, Education Code; or

(3) a college or university that is not located in this state.

(Enacted by Acts 2003, 78th Leg., ch. 1320 (H.B. 2971), § 6, effective September 1, 2003; am. Acts 2005, 79th Leg., ch. 1181 (S.B. 1227), § 53, effective September 1, 2005; am. Acts 2011, 82nd Leg., ch. 1296 (H.B. 2357), § 205, effective January 1, 2012.)

### Sec. 504.616.   Texas Reads License Plates.

(a) **[2 Versions: Effective until January 1, 2012]** The department shall issue specialty license plates including the words "Texas Reads." The department shall design the license plates to incorporate one or more submissions from middle school students in a competition conducted by the department.

(a) **[2 Versions: Effective January 1, 2012]** The department shall issue specialty license plates including the words "Texas Reads" that incorporate one or more submissions from middle school students in a competition conducted by the department.

(b) After deduction of the department's administrative costs, the remainder of the fee shall be deposited to the credit of the Texas Reads account in the general revenue fund. Money from the account may be used only to make grants under Section 441.0092, Government Code. The account is composed of:

(1) money required to be deposited to the credit of the account under this subsection; and

(2) donations made to the account.

(Enacted by Acts 2003, 78th Leg., ch. 1320 (H.B. 2971), § 6, effective September 1, 2003; am. Acts 2011, 82nd Leg., ch. 1296 (H.B. 2357), § 206, effective January 1, 2012.)

### Sec. 504.617.   Texas. It's Like a Whole Other Country License Plates.

(a) The department shall issue specialty license plates that include the trademarked Texas patch and the words "Texas. It's Like A Whole Other Country." The department shall design the license plates in consultation with the Texas Department of Economic Development.

(b) After deduction of the department's administrative costs, the remainder of the fee for issuance of the license plates shall be deposited to the credit of the tourism account in the general revenue fund to finance the Texas Department of Economic Development's tourism activities.

(Enacted by Acts 2003, 78th Leg., ch. 1320 (H.B. 2971), § 6, effective September 1, 2003.)

### Sec. 504.618.   Conservation License Plates.

(a) The department shall issue specialty license plates to support Parks and Wildlife De-

partment activities. The department shall design the license plates in consultation with the Parks and Wildlife Department.

(b) After deduction of the department's administrative costs, the remainder of the fee for issuance of the license plates shall be deposited to the credit of the Texas parks and wildlife conservation and capital account established by Section 11.043, Parks and Wildlife Code. Money deposited in the Texas parks and wildlife conservation and capital account under this section is supplementary and is not income for the purposes of reducing general revenue appropriations to the Parks and Wildlife Department.

(Enacted by Acts 2003, 78th Leg., ch. 1320 (H.B. 2971), § 6, effective September 1, 2003.)

### Sec. 504.619.   Texas Commission for the Deaf and Hard of Hearing License Plates.

(a) The department shall issue specialty license plates in support of the Texas Commission for the Deaf and Hard of Hearing. The department shall design the license plates in consultation with the Texas Commission for the Deaf and Hard of Hearing.

(b) After deduction of the department's administrative costs, the remainder of the fee for issuance of the license plates:

(1) shall be deposited to the credit of the general revenue fund; and

(2) may be appropriated only to the Texas Commission for the Deaf and Hard of Hearing for direct services programs, training, and education.

(Enacted by Acts 2003, 78th Leg., ch. 1320 (H.B. 2971), § 6, effective September 1, 2003.)

### Sec. 504.620.   Texans Conquer Cancer License Plates.

(a) The department shall issue specialty license plates that include the words "Texans Conquer Cancer." The department shall design the license plates in consultation with the Cancer Prevention and Research Institute of Texas.

(b) After deduction of the department's administrative costs, the remainder of the fee for issuance of the license plates shall be deposited to the credit of the cancer prevention and research fund established by Section 102.201, Health and Safety Code.

(Enacted by Acts 2003, 78th Leg., ch. 1320 (H.B. 2971), § 6, effective September 1, 2003; am. Acts 2007, 80th Leg., ch. 266 (H.B. 14), § 6, effective November 6, 2007.)

### Sec. 504.6201. Cancer of Unknown Primary Origin Awareness License Plates.

(a) The department shall issue specialty license plates to raise awareness of cancer of unknown primary origin. The license plates must include the words "A Fine Cause for Unknown Cancer." The department shall design the license plates in consultation with the Orange Grove Family Career and Community Leaders of America.

(b) After deduction of the department's administrative costs, the remainder of the fee for issuance of the license plates shall be deposited to the credit of the cancer prevention and research fund established by Section 102.201, Health and Safety Code.

(Enacted by Acts 2009, 81st Leg., ch. 1005 (H.B. 4064), § 1, effective September 1, 2009.)

### Sec. 504.621. Special Olympics Texas License Plates.

(a) The department shall issue specialty license plates that include the words "Special Olympics Texas." The department shall design the license plates in consultation with Special Olympics Texas.

(b) After deduction of the department's administrative costs, the remainder of the fee for issuance of the license plates shall be deposited to the credit of the Special Olympics Texas account established by Section 533.018, Health and Safety Code.

(Enacted by Acts 2003, 78th Leg., ch. 1320 (H.B. 2971), § 6, effective September 1, 2003.)

### Sec. 504.622. Girl Scout License Plates.

(a) The department shall issue specialty license plates that include the words "Girl Scouts." The department shall design the license plates in consultation with the Girl Scout Councils of Texas.

(b) After deduction of the department's administrative costs, the remainder of the fee for issuance of the license plates shall be deposited to the credit of the Girl Scout account in the state treasury. Money in the account may be used by the Texas Higher Education Coordinating Board in making grants to benefit educational projects sponsored by the Girl Scout Councils of Texas.

(Enacted by Acts 2003, 78th Leg., ch. 1320 (H.B. 2971), § 6, effective September 1, 2003.)

### Sec. 504.623. Texas YMCA.

(a) The department shall issue specialty license plates in honor of the Young Men's Christian Association. The department shall design the license plates.

(b) After deduction of the department's administrative costs, the remainder of the fee for issuance of the license plates shall be deposited to the credit of the YMCA account established by Section 7.025, Education Code, as added by Chapter 869, Acts of the 77th Legislature, Regular Session, 2001.

(Enacted by Acts 2003, 78th Leg., ch. 1320 (H.B. 2971), § 6, effective September 1, 2003.)

### Sec. 504.624. [Repealed January 1, 2012] 100th Football Season of Stephen F. Austin High School.

(a) The department shall issue specialty license plates in honor of the 100th football season of Stephen F. Austin High School in Austin. The department shall design the license plates in consultation with the principal of Stephen F. Austin High School.

(b) After deduction of the department's administrative costs, the remainder of the fee for issuance of the license plates shall be sent to the Texas Education Agency for distribution to the Austin Independent School District to be used only for the benefit of the Austin High School Athletic Department.

(Enacted by Acts 2003, 78th Leg., ch. 1320 (H.B. 2971), § 6, effective September 1, 2003.)

### Sec. 504.625. Texas Agricultural Products License Plates.

(a) The department shall issue specialty license plates that include the words "Go Texan" and the "Go Texan" logo of the Department of Agriculture. The department shall design the license plates in consultation with the commissioner of agriculture.

(b) After deduction of the department's administrative costs, the department shall deposit the remainder of the proceeds to the credit of the "Go Texan" partner program account established by Section 46.008, Agriculture Code.

(Enacted by Acts 2003, 78th Leg., ch. 1320 (H.B. 2971), § 6, effective September 1, 2003.)

### Sec. 504.626. Texas Citrus Industry.

(a) The department shall issue specialty license plates in honor of the citrus industry in this

Transportation

state. The department shall design the license plates.

(b) After deduction of the department's administrative costs, the remainder of the fee for issuance of the license plates shall be deposited to the credit of an account in the general revenue fund that may be appropriated only to Texas A&M University--Kingsville to provide financial assistance to graduate students in the College of Agriculture and Human Sciences.

(Enacted by Acts 2003, 78th Leg., ch. 1320 (H.B. 2971), § 6, effective September 1, 2003.)

### Sec. 504.627.  Waterfowl and Wetland Conservation License Plates.

(a) The department shall issue specialty license plates including one or more graphic images supplied by the Parks and Wildlife Department. The department shall design the license plates in consultation with the Parks and Wildlife Department and any organization designated by it.

(b) After deducting the department's administrative costs, the remainder of the fee for issuance of the license plates shall be deposited to the credit of an account in the state treasury. Money in the account may be used only by the Parks and Wildlife Department to support the activities of a designated nonprofit organization whose primary purpose is the conservation of waterfowl and wetland.

(Enacted by Acts 2003, 78th Leg., ch. 1320 (H.B. 2971), § 6, effective September 1, 2003.)

### Sec. 504.6275.  Save Our Beaches License Plates.

(a) The department shall issue specialty license plates to support the coastal protection and improvement program.

(b) After deduction of the department's administrative costs, the remainder of the fee for issuance of the license plates shall be deposited to the credit of the coastal protection and improvement fund established by Section 33.653, Natural Resources Code, to fund the cleaning, maintaining, nourishing, and protecting of state beaches.

(Enacted by Acts 2009, 81st Leg., ch. 625 (H.B. 1286), § 1, effective September 1, 2009.)

### Sec. 504.628.  United We Stand License Plates.

(a) The department shall issue specialty license plates that include the words "United We Stand" and include only the colors red, white, blue, and black.

(b) After deduction of the department's administrative costs, the remainder of the fee for issuance of the license plates shall be deposited to the credit of the Texas mobility fund.

(Enacted by Acts 2003, 78th Leg., ch. 1320 (H.B. 2971), § 6, effective September 1, 2003.)

### Sec. 504.629.  [Repealed January 1, 2012] Texas PGA Junior Golf License Plates.

(a) The department shall issue specialty license plates in honor of Texas PGA Junior Golf. The department shall design the license plates in consultation with Texas PGA Junior Golf.

(b) After deduction of the department's administrative costs, the remainder of the fee shall be deposited to the credit of the general revenue fund for use only by the Parks and Wildlife Department in making grants to benefit Texas PGA Junior Golf to provide scholarships to students.

(Enacted by Acts 2003, 78th Leg., ch. 1320 (H.B. 2971), § 6, effective September 1, 2003.)

### Sec. 504.630.  Air Force Association License Plates.

(a) The department shall issue specialty license plates that include the words "Air Force Association." The department shall design the license plates in consultation with the Air Force Association of Texas.

(b) After deduction of the department's administrative costs, the remainder of the fee shall be deposited to the credit of the Air Force Association of Texas account in the state treasury. Money in the account may be used by the Texas Veterans Commission in making grants to benefit projects sponsored by the Air Force Association of Texas.

(Enacted by Acts 2003, 78th Leg., ch. 1320 (H.B. 2971), § 6, effective September 1, 2003.)

### Sec. 504.631.  Texas State Rifle Association License Plates.

(a) The department shall issue specialty license plates to honor the Texas State Rifle Association.

(b) After deduction of the department's administrative costs, the remainder of the fee shall be deposited to the credit of an account in the general revenue fund that may be appropriated only to the Texas Cooperative Extension of The Texas A&M University System as follows:

(1) 50 percent to supplement existing and future scholarship programs supported by the Texas State Rifle Association; and

Transportation

(2) 50 percent to support the 4-H Shooting Sports Program for youth.

(Enacted by Acts 2003, 78th Leg., ch. 1320 (H.B. 2971), § 6, effective September 1, 2003; am. Acts 2007, 80th Leg., ch. 311 (H.B. 2045), § 1, effective September 1, 2007.)

### Sec. 504.632.   Urban Forestry License Plates.

(a) The department shall issue specialty license plates to benefit urban forestry. The department shall design the license plates in consultation with an organization described in Subsection (b).

(b) After deduction of the department's administrative costs, the remainder of the fee shall be deposited to the credit of the urban forestry account in the state treasury. Money in the account may be used by the Texas Forest Service in making grants to support the activities of a nonprofit organization located in Texas whose primary purpose is to sponsor projects involving urban and community:

(1) tree planting;

(2) tree preservation; and

(3) tree education programs.

(Enacted by Acts 2003, 78th Leg., ch. 1320 (H.B. 2971), § 6, effective September 1, 2003.)

### Sec. 504.633.   Share the Road License Plates.

(a) The department shall issue specialty license plates that include the words "Share the Road" and the image of a bicycle or a bicycle with a rider. The department shall design the plates in consultation with the Texas Bicycle Coalition Education Fund.

(b) After deduction of the department's administrative costs, the remainder of the fee shall be deposited to the credit of the share the road account in the state treasury to be used only by the Texas Education Agency to support the activities of a designated nonprofit organization whose primary purpose is to promote bicyclist safety, education, and access through:

(1) education and awareness programs; and

(2) training, workshops, educational materials, and media events.

(c) Up to 25 percent of the amount in Subsection (b) may be used to support the activities of the nonprofit organization in marketing and promoting the share the road concept and license plates.

(Enacted by Acts 2003, 78th Leg., ch. 1320 (H.B. 2971), § 6, effective September 1, 2003.)

### Sec. 504.634.   [Repealed January 1, 2012] San Antonio Missions National Historical Park License Plates.

(a) The department shall issue San Antonio Missions National Historical Park specialty license plates. The department shall design the license plates in consultation with Los Compadres de San Antonio Missions National Historical Park.

(b) After deduction of the department's administrative costs, the remainder of the fee shall be deposited to the credit of Los Compadres de San Antonio Missions National Historical Park account in the state treasury. Money in the account may be used only by the Texas Historical Commission in making grants to Los Compadres de San Antonio Missions National Historical Park to be used for the purpose of the preservation and rehabilitation of the San Antonio Missions National Historical Park.

(Enacted by Acts 2003, 78th Leg., ch. 1320 (H.B. 2971), § 6, effective September 1, 2003.)

### Sec. 504.635.   El Paso Mission Valley License Plates.

(a) The department shall issue El Paso Mission Valley specialty license plates. The department shall design the license plates in consultation with the Socorro Mission Restoration Effort.

(b) After deduction of the department's administrative costs, the remainder of the fee shall be deposited to the credit of the El Paso Mission Restoration account in the state treasury. Money in the account may be used only by the Texas Historical Commission in making grants to the Socorro Mission Restoration Effort to be used for the purpose of the preservation and rehabilitation of the Socorro Mission.

(Enacted by Acts 2003, 78th Leg., ch. 1320 (H.B. 2971), § 6, effective September 1, 2003.)

### Sec. 504.636.   Cotton Boll License Plates.

(a) The department shall issue specialty license plates depicting a graphic image of a cotton boll. The department shall design the license plates in consultation with Texas Cotton Producers, Inc.

(b) After deduction of the department's administrative costs, the remainder of the fee shall be deposited to the credit of the general revenue fund for use only by the Texas Higher Education Coordinating Board in making grants to benefit Texas Cotton Producers, Inc., for the sole purpose of providing scholarships to students who are pursuing a degree in an agricultural field related to the cotton industry while enrolled in an institution of higher education, as defined by Section 61.003, Education Code.

(Enacted by Acts 2003, 78th Leg., ch. 1320 (H.B. 2971), § 6, effective September 1, 2003.)

### Sec. 504.637. Daughters of the Republic of Texas License Plates.

(a) The department shall issue specialty license plates that include the words "Native Texan." The department shall design the license plates in consultation with the Daughters of the Republic of Texas.

(b) After deduction of the department's administrative costs, the remainder of the fee shall be deposited to the credit of the Daughters of the Republic of Texas account in the state treasury. Money in the account may be used only by the Texas Department of Economic Development or its successor agency in making grants to the Daughters of the Republic of Texas to be used only for the purpose of:

(1) preserving Texas historic sites; or

(2) funding educational programs that teach Texas history.

(Enacted by Acts 2003, 78th Leg., ch. 1320 (H.B. 2971), § 6, effective September 1, 2003.)

### Sec. 504.638. Knights of Columbus License Plates.

(a) The department shall issue specialty license plates that include the words "Knights of Columbus" and the emblem of the Order of the Knights of Columbus. The department shall design the license plates in consultation with the Knights of Columbus.

(b) After deduction of the department's administrative costs, the remainder of the fee for issuance of the license plates shall be deposited to the credit of the State Council Charities account in the general revenue fund. Money in the account may be used only by the Texas Education Agency to make grants to State Council Charities to carry out the purposes of that organization.

(Enacted by Acts 2003, 78th Leg., ch. 1320 (H.B. 2971), § 6, effective September 1, 2003.)

### Sec. 504.639. Texas Music License Plates.

(a) The department shall issue specialty license plates that include the words "Texas Music." The department shall design the license plates in consultation with the governor's office.

(b) After deduction of the department's administrative costs, the remainder of the fee for issuance of the license plates shall be deposited to the credit of the Texas Music Foundation account established by Section 7.027, Education Code.

(Enacted by Acts 2003, 78th Leg., ch. 1320 (H.B. 2971), § 6, effective September 1, 2003.)

### Sec. 504.640. Space Shuttle Columbia License Plates.

(a) The department shall issue Space Shuttle Columbia specialty license plates. The department shall design the license plates in consultation with the Aviation and Space Foundation of Texas.

(b) After deduction of the department's administrative costs, the remainder of the fee for issuance of the license plates shall be deposited to the credit of the general revenue fund and may be used only by the Texas Aerospace Commission or its successor agency in making grants to benefit the Aviation and Space Foundation of Texas for the purposes of furthering aviation and space activities in Texas and providing Columbia Crew memorial scholarships to students.

(Enacted by Acts 2003, 78th Leg., ch. 1320 (H.B. 2971), § 6, effective September 1, 2003.)

### Sec. 504.641. Be a Blood Donor License Plates.

(a) The department shall issue Be a Blood Donor specialty license plates. The department shall design the license plates in consultation with the Gulf Coast Regional Blood Center in Houston.

(b) After deduction of the department's administrative costs, the remainder of the fee for issuance of the license plates shall be deposited to the credit of the be a blood donor account under Section 162.016, Health and Safety Code.

(Enacted by Acts 2003, 78th Leg., ch. 1320 (H.B. 2971), § 6, effective September 1, 2003.)

### Sec. 504.642. [2 Versions: Effective Until January 1, 2012] Texas County Child Welfare Board License Plates.

(a) The department shall issue Texas County Child Welfare Boards specialty license plates. The department shall design the license plates in consultation with the Texas Council of Child Welfare Boards, Inc.

(b) After deduction of the department's administrative costs, the remainder of the fee for issuance of the license plates shall be deposited to the

credit of a special account for abused and neglected children established at the Department of Protective and Regulatory Services. Money in the account may be used only by the Department of Protective and Regulatory Services to fund programs and services supporting abused and neglected children under Section 264.004, Family Code.
(Enacted by Acts 2003, 78th Leg., ch. 1320 (H.B. 2971), § 6, effective September 1, 2003.)

### Sec. 504.642. [2 Versions: Effective January 1, 2012] Texas Council of Child Welfare Boards License Plates.

(a) The department shall issue Texas Council of Child Welfare Boards specialty license plates. The department shall design the license plates in consultation with the Texas Council of Child Welfare Boards, Inc.

(b) After deduction of the department's administrative costs, the remainder of the fee for issuance of the license plates shall be deposited to the credit of a special account for abused and neglected children established at the Department of Protective and Regulatory Services. Money in the account may be used only by the Department of Protective and Regulatory Services to fund programs and services supporting abused and neglected children under Section 264.004, Family Code.
(Enacted by Acts 2003, 78th Leg., ch. 1320 (H.B. 2971), § 6, effective September 1, 2003; am. Acts 2011, 82nd Leg., ch. 1296 (H.B. 2357), §§ 207, 208, effective January 1, 2012.)

### Sec. 504.643. [Repealed January 1, 2012] STAR Day School Library Readers Are Leaders License Plates.

(a) The department shall issue specialty license plates that include the words "STAR Day School Library Readers Are Leaders." The department shall design the license plates in consultation with the State of Texas Anniversary Remembrance (STAR) Day Foundation.

(b) After deduction of the department's administrative costs, the remainder of the fee for issuance of the license plates shall be deposited to the credit of the general revenue fund and used only by the Texas Education Agency in making grants to benefit the State of Texas Anniversary Remembrance (STAR) Day Foundation to be used only for the purpose of providing supplementary reading and service programs in partnership with public schools in this state for seventh and eighth grade public school students.

(Enacted by Acts 2003, 78th Leg., ch. 1320 (H.B. 2971), § 6, effective September 1, 2003.)

### Sec. 504.644. Marine Mammal Recovery License Plates.

(a) The department shall issue Marine Mammal Recovery specialty license plates. The department shall design the license plates in consultation with the Parks and Wildlife Department and the Texas Marine Mammal Stranding Network.

(b) After deduction of the department's administrative costs, the remainder of the fee for issuance of the license plates shall be deposited to the credit of an account in the state treasury. Money in the account may be used only by the Parks and Wildlife Department to support the activities of the Texas Marine Mammal Stranding Network in the recovery, rehabilitation, and release of stranded marine mammals. The Parks and Wildlife Department shall establish reporting and other mechanisms necessary to ensure that the money is spent for purposes for which it is dedicated.
(Enacted by Acts 2003, 78th Leg., ch. 1320 (H.B. 2971), § 6, effective September 1, 2003.)

### Sec. 504.645. 4-H License Plates.

(a) The department shall issue specialty license plates that include the words "To Make the Best Better," the words "Texas 4-H," and the 4-H symbol of the four-leaf clover. The department shall design the license plates in consultation with the Texas 4-H and Youth Development Program.

(b) After deduction of the department's administrative costs, the remainder of the fee for issuance of the license plates shall be deposited to the credit of the general revenue fund and shall be used only by the Texas Cooperative Extension of the Texas A&M University System for 4-H and Youth Development Programs and to support the Texas Cooperative Extension's activities related to 4-H and Youth Development Programs.
(Enacted by Acts 2003, 78th Leg., ch. 1320 (H.B. 2971), § 6, effective September 1, 2003.)

### Sec. 504.646. Smile Texas Style License Plates.

(a) The department shall issue specialty license plates that include the words "Smile Texas Style." The department shall design the license plates in consultation with the Texas Dental Association.

Transportation

(b) After deduction of the department's administrative costs, the remainder of the fee for issuance of the license plates shall be deposited to the credit of the general revenue fund to be used only by the Texas Department of Health in making grants to benefit the Texas Dental Association Financial Services for the sole use of providing charitable dental care.

(Enacted by Acts 2003, 78th Leg., ch. 1320 (H.B. 2971), § 6, effective September 1, 2003.)

## Sec. 504.647.  Fight Terrorism License Plates.

(a) **[2 Versions: Effective until January 1, 2012]** The department shall issue Fight Terrorism specialty license plates. The license plates shall include a pentagon-shaped border surrounding:

(1) the date "9-11-01" with the likeness of the World Trade Center towers forming the "11";

(2) the likeness of the United States flag; and

(3) the words "Fight Terrorism."

(a) **[2 Versions: Effective January 1, 2012]** The department shall issue Fight Terrorism specialty license plates that include a pentagon-shaped border surrounding:

(1) the date "9-11-01" with the likeness of the World Trade Center towers forming the "11";

(2) the likeness of the United States flag; and

(3) the words "Fight Terrorism."

(b) The fee shall be deposited to the credit of the state highway fund.

(Enacted by Acts 2003, 78th Leg., ch. 1320 (H.B. 2971), § 6, effective September 1, 2003; am. Acts 2011, 82nd Leg., ch. 1296 (H.B. 2357), § 209, effective January 1, 2012.)

## Sec. 504.648.  God Bless Texas and God Bless America License Plates.

(a) The department shall issue specialty license plates that include the words "God Bless Texas" and "God Bless America."

(b) After deduction of the department's administrative costs, the remainder of the fee shall be deposited to the credit of the share the road account in the state treasury and may only be used by the Texas Education Agency to support the Safe Routes to School Program of a designated statewide nonprofit organization whose primary purpose is to promote bicyclist safety, education, and access through:

(1) education and awareness programs; and

(2) training, workshops, educational materials, and media events.

(c) The fee for the license plates is $40.

(d) Up to 25 percent of the amount in Subsection (b) may be used to support the activities of the nonprofit organization in marketing and promoting the Safe Routes to School Program and the God Bless Texas and God Bless America license plates.

(e) The Texas Education Agency may use money received under this section to secure funds available under federal matching programs for safe routes to school and obesity prevention.

(Enacted by Acts 2003, 78th Leg., ch. 1320 (H.B. 2971), § 6, effective September 1, 2003; am. Acts 2009, 81st Leg., ch. 201 (S.B. 161), § 1, effective May 27, 2009.)

## Sec. 504.649.  [Repealed January 1, 2012] Texas Juneteenth License Plates.

(a) The department shall issue Texas Juneteenth specialty license plates. The department shall design the license plates in consultation with the Texas Emancipation Juneteenth Cultural and Historical Commission.

(b) After deduction of the department's administrative costs, the remainder of the fee for issuance of the license plates shall be deposited to the credit of the Texas Emancipation Juneteenth Cultural and Historical Commission in a special account in the state treasury. Money in the account may be used only by the Texas Emancipation Juneteenth Cultural and Historical Commission for grants to Juneteenth USA to erect a Juneteenth Memorial Monument on the south grounds of the State Capitol, place Juneteenth monuments and markers in various historical parts of Texas, develop a Juneteenth Museum, Cultural, and Educational Institute, Recreation Center, and Park, and otherwise support the activities and projects of Juneteenth USA and its affiliates.

(Enacted by Acts 2003, 78th Leg., ch. 1320 (H.B. 2971), § 6, effective September 1, 2003.)

## Sec. 504.650.  [Repealed January 1, 2012] Keeping Texas Strong License Plates.

(a) The department shall issue Keeping Texas Strong specialty license plates. The department shall design the license plates in consultation with the Texas Alliance of Energy Producers.

(b) After deduction of the department's administrative costs, the remainder of the fee for issuance of the license plates shall be deposited to the credit of the Texas Alliance Education Program account in the general revenue fund. Money in the account may be used only by the Texas Education Agency to finance the education programs of the Texas Alliance of Energy Producers. (Enacted by Acts 2003, 78th Leg., ch. 1320 (H.B. 2971), § 6, effective September 1, 2003.)

## Sec. 504.651. March of Dimes License Plates.

(a) The department shall issue specialty license plates that include the words "March of Dimes." The department shall design the license plates in consultation with the March of Dimes Texas Chapter.

(b) After deduction of the department's administrative costs, the remainder of the fee for issuance of the license plates shall be deposited to the credit of the Texas Department of Health for use in the Birth Defects Registry.

(Enacted by Acts 2003, 78th Leg., ch. 1320 (H.B. 2971), § 6, effective September 1, 2003.)

## Sec. 504.652. Master Gardener License Plates.

(a) The department shall issue specialty license plates that include the seal of the Texas Master Gardener program of Texas Cooperative Extension.

(b) After deduction of the department's administrative costs, the remainder of the fee for issuance of the license plates shall be deposited to the credit of an account in the general revenue fund. Money in the account may be used only by Texas Cooperative Extension for graduate student assistantships within the Texas Master Gardener program and to support Texas Cooperative Extension's activities related to the Texas Master Gardener program.

(Enacted by Acts 2003, 78th Leg., ch. 1320 (H.B. 2971), § 6, effective September 1, 2003.)

## Sec. 504.653. [Repealed January 1, 2012] Mother-Child Survivors Educational Scholarship Fund License Plates.

(a) The department shall issue mother-child survivors educational scholarship fund specialty license plates. The department shall design the license plates in consultation with Texans for Equal Justice.

(b) After deduction of the department's administrative costs, the remainder of the fee for issu-

ance of the license plates shall be deposited to the credit of the general revenue fund and may only be used by the attorney general to support the Texans for Equal Justice mother-child survivors educational scholarship fund for educational scholarships to:

(1) surviving spouses of homicide victims who have one or more minor children and who need further education to adequately support the family; and

(2) surviving children of homicide victims entering an institution of higher education or vocational school for the first time.

(Enacted by Acts 2003, 78th Leg., ch. 1320 (H.B. 2971), § 6, effective September 1, 2003.)

## Sec. 504.654. Eagle Scout License Plates.

(a) The department shall issue specialty license plates that bear a depiction of the Eagle Scout medal.

(b) After deduction of the department's administrative costs, the remainder of the fee for issuance of the license plates shall be deposited to the credit of the Eagle Scout account in the general revenue fund. Money in the account may be used only by the Texas Higher Education Coordinating Board in making grants to support projects sponsored by Boy Scout councils in this state. The Texas Higher Education Coordinating Board shall distribute grants under this section geographically as nearly as possible in proportion to the number of license plates issued under this section in each region of the state.

(Enacted by Acts 2003, 78th Leg., ch. 1320 (H.B. 2971), § 6, effective September 1, 2003.)

## Sec. 504.6545. Boy Scout License Plates.

(a) The department shall issue specialty license plates that include the words "Boy Scouts of America." The department shall design the license plates in consultation with the Boy Scouts of America.

(b) After deduction of the department's administrative costs, the remainder of the fee for issuance of the license plates shall be deposited to the credit of the Boy Scout account in the general revenue fund. Money in the account may be used only by the Texas Higher Education Coordinating Board in making grants to benefit educational projects sponsored by Boy Scout councils in this state.

(Enacted by Acts 2005, 79th Leg., ch. 575 (H.B. 1480), § 3, effective September 1, 2005.)

**Sec. 504.655. [Repealed January 1, 2012] Tejano Monument License Plates.**

(a) The department shall issue Tejano Monument specialty license plates. The department shall design the license plates in consultation with The Tejano Monument, Inc.

(b) After deduction of the department's administrative costs, the remainder of the fee for issuance of the license plates shall be deposited to the credit of the Tejano Monument account in the general revenue fund. Money in the account may be used only by the State Preservation Board to design and erect a Tejano Monument for placement on the Capitol grounds or related educational programs.

(Enacted by Acts 2003, 78th Leg., ch. 1320 (H.B. 2971), § 6, effective September 1, 2003.)

**Sec. 504.656. Texas Lions Camp License Plates.**

(a) The department shall issue Texas Lions Camp specialty license plates. The department shall design the license plates in consultation with the Texas Lions League for Crippled Children.

(b) After deduction of the department's administrative costs, the remainder of the fee for issuance of the license plates shall be deposited to the credit of the Texas Lions Camp account in the state treasury. Money in the account may be used only by the Parks and Wildlife Department to support the activities of a designated nonprofit organization that is accredited by the American Camping Association and is licensed by the Texas Department of Health and whose primary purpose is to provide, without charge, a camp for physically disabled, hearing or vision impaired, and diabetic children who reside in this state, regardless of race, religion, or national origin. The Parks and Wildlife Department shall establish reporting and other mechanisms necessary to ensure that the money is spent only for the purposes for which it is dedicated.

(Enacted by Acts 2003, 78th Leg., ch. 1320 (H.B. 2971), § 6, effective September 1, 2003.)

**Sec. 504.657. Higher Education Coordinating Board License Plates.**

(a) The department shall issue specialty license plates for the Texas Higher Education Coordinating Board. The department shall design the license plates in consultation with the coordinating board.

(b) After deduction of the department's administrative costs, the remainder of the fee shall be deposited to the credit of the "College For Texans" campaign account in the general revenue fund for use only by the Texas Higher Education Coordinating Board for purposes of the campaign.

(Enacted by Acts 2005, 79th Leg., ch. 1181 (S.B. 1227), § 54, effective September 1, 2005.)

**Sec. 504.658. Insure Texas Kids License Plates.**

(a) The department shall issue specialty license plates that include the words "Insure Texas Kids."

(b) After deduction of the department's administrative costs, the remainder of the fee for issuance of the license plates shall be deposited to the credit of the general revenue fund and may be appropriated only to the Health and Human Services Commission to fund outreach efforts for public and private health benefit plans available for children.

(Enacted by Acts 2007, 80th Leg., ch. 1313 (S.B. 1032), § 1, effective September 1, 2007.)

**Sec. 504.659. [Effective January 1, 2012] Members of American Legion.**

(a) The department shall issue specialty license plates for members of the American Legion. The license plates shall include the words "Still Serving America" and the emblem of the American Legion. The department shall design the license plates in consultation with the American Legion.

(b) The fee for the license plates is $30.

(c) After deduction of $8 to reimburse the department for its administrative costs, the remainder of the fee for issuance of the license plates shall be deposited to the credit of the American Legion, Department of Texas account in the state treasury. Money in the account may be used only by the Texas Veterans Commission in making grants to the American Legion Endowment Fund for scholarships and youth programs sponsored by the American Legion, Department of Texas.

(Enacted by Acts 2003, 78th Leg., ch. 1320 (H.B. 2971), § 6, effective September 1, 2003; am. Acts 2011, 82nd Leg., ch. 1296 (H.B. 2357), § 210, effective January 1, 2012 (renumbered from Sec. 504.413).)

**Sec. 504.660. [2 Versions: As added by Acts 2009, 81st Leg., ch. 397] Marine Conservation License Plates.**

(a) After deduction of the department's administrative costs in accordance with Section

*Transportation*

504.801, the remainder of the fees allocated under Section 504.801(e)(2)(A) from the sale of Marine Conservation plates shall be deposited to the credit of an account in the state treasury to be used by the Texas Parks and Wildlife Department to support the activities of Coastal Conservation Association Texas in the conservation of marine resources.

(b) The Texas Parks and Wildlife Department shall establish reporting and other mechanisms necessary to ensure that the money is spent for the purpose for which it is dedicated.

(Enacted by Acts 2009, 81st Leg., ch. 397 (H.B. 1749), § 1, effective September 1, 2009.)

### Sec. 504.660. [2 Versions: As added by Acts 2009, 81st Leg., ch. 1381] Sexual Assault Awareness License Plates.

(a) The department shall design and issue specialty license plates to support victims of sexual assault.

(b) The license plates must include the words "Speak up. Speak out." and an image of a blue ribbon.

(c) After deduction of the department's administrative costs, the remainder of the fee for issuance of the license plates shall be deposited to the credit of the sexual assault program fund established by Section 420.008, Government Code.

(Enacted by Acts 2009, 81st Leg., ch. 1381 (S.B. 1616), § 6, effective September 1, 2009.)

### Sec. 504.661. [Reserved].

### Sec. 504.662. Choose Life License Plates.

(a) The department shall issue specially designed license plates that include the words "Choose Life." The department shall design the license plates in consultation with the attorney general.

(b) After deduction of the department's administrative costs, the department shall deposit the remainder of the fee for issuance of license plates under this section in the state treasury to the credit of the Choose Life account established by Section 402.036, Government Code.

(Enacted by Acts 2011, 82nd Leg., ch. 63 (S.B. 257), § 1, effective September 1, 2011.)

### Secs. 504.663 to 504.700 [Reserved for expansion].

## SUBCHAPTER H
## ADMINISTRATIVE PROVISIONS RELATING TO SPECIALTY LICENSE PLATES FOR GENERAL DISTRIBUTION

### Sec. 504.701. [Repealed January 1, 2012] Discontinuance of Certain Specialty License Plates.

(a) This section applies only to license plates authorized by:

(1) Section 504.602;

(2) Section 504.603;

(3) Section 504.604;

(4) Section 504.605;

(5) Section 504.606;

(6) Section 504.607;

(7) Section 504.608;

(8) Section 504.609;

(9) Section 504.610;

(10) Section 504.611;

(11) Section 504.612;

(12) Section 504.613;

(13) Section 504.614; or

(14) Section 504.615.

(b) Except as provided by Subsections (d) and (e), on or after September 1, 2004, the department may continue to issue license plates to which this section applies only if before that date at least:

(1) 3,500 sets of the license plates authorized by the applicable section of this chapter have been issued or presold;

(2) $15,000 has been received by the department from the issuance of license plates under that section; or

(3) $15,000 has been deposited with the department for the continued issuance of those license plates.

(c) If before September 1, 2004, one of the conditions described by Subsection (b) is not met for the license plate, the section that authorizes the issuance of that license plate expires on that date.

(d) On or after September 1, 2004, the department may continue to issue license plates under:

(1) Section 504.615 for a particular institution of higher education or private college or university only if before that date:

(A) 800 sets of license plates for the particular institution, college, or university have been issued or presold;

(B) $8,000 has been received by the department from the issuance of the license plates for that institution, college, or university; or

(C) $8,000 has been deposited with the department for the continued issuance of the license plates for that institution, college, or university; or

(2) Section 504.614 for a particular professional sports team only if before that date:

(A) 1,900 sets of the license plates for that sports team have been issued or presold;

(B) $8,000 has been received by the department from the issuance of license plates for that sports team; or

(C) $8,000 has been deposited with the department for the continued issuance of license plates for that sports team.

(e) Money deposited with the department under Subsection (b)(3), (d)(1)(C), or (d)(2)(C) shall be returned by the department to the person who made the deposit only after the requisite number of license plates under those subsections are issued or presold.

(Enacted by Acts 2003, 78th Leg., ch. 1320 (H.B. 2971), § 6, effective September 1, 2003; am. Acts 2007, 80th Leg., ch. 729 (H.B. 2627), § 1, effective September 1, 2007.)

### Sec. 504.702. Specialty License Plates Authorized After January 1, 1999.

(a) This section applies only to specialty license plates that are authorized to be issued by a law that takes effect on or after January 1, 1999.

(b) **[2 Versions: Effective until January 1, 2012]** The department may manufacture the specialty license plates only if a request for manufacture of the license plates is filed with the department. The request must be:

(1) made on a form adopted by the department;

(2) filed before the fifth anniversary of the effective date of the law that authorizes the issuance of the specialty license plates; and

(3) accompanied by:

(A) a deposit of $8,000; or

(B) applications for issuance of at least 1,900 sets of the license plates plus the fees for issuance of that number of sets.

(b) **[2 Versions: Effective January 1, 2012]** The department may manufacture the specialty license plates only if a request for manufacture of the license plates is filed with the department. The request must be:

(1) made in a manner prescribed by the department;

(2) filed before the fifth anniversary of the effective date of the law that authorizes the issuance of the specialty license plates; and

(3) accompanied by a deposit of $8,000.

(c) **[Repealed January 1, 2012]** Money deposited with the department under Subsection (b)(3)(A) shall be returned to the person who made the deposit only if 1,900 sets of the applicable license plates are issued or presold.

(d) If a request is not filed with the department before the date specified by Subsection (b)(2), the law that authorizes the issuance of the specialty license plates expires on that date.

(e) **[Effective January 1, 2012]** The department may issue license plates under:

(1) Section 504.614 for a particular professional sports team only if $8,000 has been deposited with the department for that sports team; or

(2) Section 504.615 for a particular institution of higher education or private college or university only if $8,000 has been deposited with the department for that institution, college, or university.

(f) **[Effective January 1, 2012]** Money deposited with the department under Subsection (b)(3) or (e) shall be returned by the department to the person who made the deposit after 800 sets of plates have been issued.

(Enacted by Acts 2003, 78th Leg., ch. 1320 (H.B. 2971), § 6, effective September 1, 2003; am. Acts 2007, 80th Leg., ch. 729 (H.B. 2627), § 2, effective September 1, 2007; am. Acts 2011, 82nd Leg., ch. 1296 (H.B. 2357), §§ 211, 247(21), effective January 1, 2012.)

### Secs. 504.703 to 504.800 [Reserved for expansion].

## SUBCHAPTER I
## DEVELOPMENT OF NEW SPECIALTY LICENSE PLATES

### Sec. 504.801. Creation of New Specialty License Plates by the Department.

(a) **[2 Versions: Effective until January 1, 2012]** The department may create new specialty license plates on its own initiative or on receipt of an application from a potential sponsor. A new specialty license plate created under this section must comply with each requirement of Section

504.702 unless the license is created by the department on its own initiative. The department may permit a specialty license plate created under this section to be personalized. The redesign of an existing specialty license plate at the request of a sponsor shall be treated like the issuance of a new specialty license plate, except that the department may require a nonrefundable design fee.

(a) **[2 Versions: Effective January 1, 2012]** The department may create new specialty license plates on its own initiative or on receipt of an application from a potential sponsor. A new specialty license plate created under this section must comply with each requirement of Section 504.702 unless the license is created by the department on its own initiative. The department may permit a specialty license plate created under this section to be personalized. The redesign of an existing specialty license plate at the request of a sponsor shall be treated like the issuance of a new specialty license plate.

(b) **[2 Versions: Effective until January 1, 2012]** Any person may sponsor a new specialty license plate by submitting an application to the department. An application may nominate a state agency to receive funds derived from the issuance of the license plates. The application may also identify uses to which those funds should be appropriated.

(b) **[2 Versions: Effective January 1, 2012]** Any nonprofit entity may submit an application to the department to sponsor a new specialty license plate. An application may nominate a state agency to receive funds derived from the issuance of the license plates. The application may also identify uses to which those funds should be appropriated.

(c) The department shall design each new specialty license plate in consultation with the sponsor, if any, that applied for creation of that specialty license plate. The department may refuse to create a new specialty license plate if the design might be offensive to any member of the public, if the nominated state agency does not consent to receipt of the funds derived from issuance of the license plate, if the uses identified for those funds might violate a statute or constitutional provision, or for any other reason established by rule. At the request of the sponsor, distribution of the license plate may be limited by the department.

(d) **[2 Versions: Effective until January 1, 2012]** The fee for issuance of license plates created under this subchapter before September 1,

2009, is $30 unless the department sets a higher fee. This subsection does not apply to a specialty license plate marketed and sold by a private vendor at the request of the specialty license plate sponsor.

(d) **[2 Versions: Effective January 1, 2012]** The fee for issuance of license plates created under this subchapter before November 19, 2009, is $30 unless the department sets a higher fee. This subsection does not apply to a specialty license plate marketed and sold by a private vendor at the request of the specialty license plate sponsor.

(d-1) **[2 Versions: Effective until January 1, 2012]** The fee for issuance of license plates created under this subchapter on or after September 1, 2009, is the amount established under Section 504.851.

(d-1) **[2 Versions: Effective January 1, 2012]** The fee for issuance of license plates created under this subchapter on or after November 19, 2009, is the amount established under Section 504.851.

(e) For each fee collected for a license plate issued by the department under this section:

(1) $8 shall be used to reimburse the department for its administrative costs; and

(2) the remainder shall be deposited to the credit of:

(A) the specialty license plate fund, which is an account in the general revenue fund, if the sponsor nominated a state agency to receive the funds; or

(B) the state highway fund if the sponsor did not nominate a state agency to receive the funds or if there is no sponsor.

(f) Subchapter D, Chapter 316, Government Code, and Section 403.095, Government Code, do not apply to fees collected under this subchapter.

(g) The department may report to the legislature at any time concerning implementation of this section. The report may include recommendations concerning the appropriations, by amount, state agency, and uses, that are necessary to implement the requests of sponsors.

(h) The department may vary the design of a license plate created under this section to accommodate or reflect its use on a motor vehicle other than a passenger car or light truck.

(i) The sponsor of a new specialty plate may not be a for-profit enterprise.

(Enacted by Acts 2003, 78th Leg., ch. 1320 (H.B. 2971), § 6, effective September 1, 2003; am. Acts 2009, 81st Leg., ch. 1136 (H.B. 2553), § 38, effective September 1, 2011; am. Acts 2009, 81st Leg., ch. 1381 (S.B. 1616), § 7, effective September 1, 2009; am. Acts 2011, 82nd Leg., ch. 1296 (H.B. 2357), § 212, effective January 1, 2012.)

### Sec. 504.802. [2 Versions: Effective until January 1, 2012] Marketing and Sale by Private Vendor of Specialty License Plates Created Before September 1, 2009.

(a) A sponsor of a specialty license plate created under this subchapter before September 1, 2009, may contract with the private vendor authorized under Subchapter J for the marketing and sale of the specialty license plate.

(b) The fee for issuance of a specialty license plate described by Subsection (a) is the amount established under Section 504.851(c).

(c) Notwithstanding any other law, from each fee received from the issuance of a specialty license plate marketed and sold by the private vendor under this section, the department shall:

(1) deduct the administrative costs described by Section 504.801(e)(1);

(2) deposit the portion of the fee for the sale of the plate that the state would ordinarily receive under the contract described by Section 504.851(a) to the credit of:

(A) the specialty license plate fund, if the sponsor nominated a state agency to receive the funds; or

(B) the general revenue fund, if the sponsor did not nominate a state agency to receive the funds or if there is no sponsor; and

(3) pay to the private vendor the remainder of the fee.

(Enacted by Acts 2009, 81st Leg., ch. 1381 (S.B. 1616), § 8, effective September 1, 2009.)

### Sec. 504.802. [2 Versions: Effective January 1, 2012] Marketing and Sale by Private Vendor of Specialty License Plates.

(a) A sponsor of a specialty license plate created under this subchapter may contract with the private vendor authorized under Subchapter J for the marketing and sale of the specialty license plate.

(b) The fee for issuance of a specialty license plate described by Subsection (a) is the amount established under Section 504.851(c).

(c) Notwithstanding any other law, from each fee received from the issuance of a specialty license plate marketed and sold by the private vendor under this section, the department shall:

(1) deduct the administrative costs described by Section 504.801(e)(1);

(2) deposit the portion of the fee for the sale of the plate that the state would ordinarily receive under the contract described by Section 504.851(a) to the credit of:

(A) the specialty license plate fund, if the sponsor nominated a state agency to receive the funds;

(B) the general revenue fund, if the sponsor did not nominate a state agency to receive the funds or if there is no sponsor; or

(C) for a license plate issued under Section 504.614, the public entity that provides or provided funds for the professional sports team's facility; and

(3) pay to the private vendor the remainder of the fee.

(d) A sponsor of a specialty license plate may reestablish its specialty license plate under Sections 504.601 and 504.702 and be credited its previous deposit with the department if a contract entered into by the sponsor under Subsection (a) terminates.

(Enacted by Acts 2009, 81st Leg., ch. 1381 (S.B. 1616), § 8, effective September 1, 2009; am. Acts 2011, 82nd Leg., ch. 1296 (H.B. 2357), §§ 213, 214, effective January 1, 2012.)

### Secs. 504.803 to 504.850 [Reserved for expansion].

## SUBCHAPTER J
## MARKETING OF SPECIALTY PLATES THROUGH PRIVATE VENDOR

### Sec. 504.851. Contract with Private Vendor.

(a) [2 Versions: Effective until January 1, 2014] The department shall enter into a contract with the private vendor whose proposal is most advantageous to the state, as determined from competitive sealed proposals that satisfy the requirements of this section, for the marketing and sale of:

(1) personalized license plates; or

(2) with the agreement of the private vendor, other specialty license plates authorized by Subchapters G and I.

(a) [2 Versions: Effective January 1, 2014] The department may enter into a contract with the private vendor whose proposal is most advantageous to the state, as determined from competitive sealed proposals that satisfy the requirements of this section, for the marketing and sale of:

(1) personalized license plates; or

(2) with the agreement of the private vendor, other specialty license plates authorized by Subchapters G and I.

(a-1) The department may not issue specialty, personalized, or souvenir license plates with background colors other than white, unless the plates are marketed and sold by the private vendor.

(a-2) **[2 Versions: Effective until January 1, 2012]** Specialty license plates authorized for marketing and sale under Subsection (a) must include:

(1) specialty license plates created under Subchapters G and I on or after September 1, 2009; and

(2) at the request of the specialty license plate sponsor, an existing specialty license plate created under Subchapters G and I before September 1, 2009.

(a-2) **[2 Versions: Effective January 1, 2012]** Specialty license plates authorized for marketing and sale under Subsection (a) may be personalized and must include:

(1) specialty license plates created under Subchapters G and I on or after November 19, 2009; and

(2) at the request of the specialty license plate sponsor, an existing specialty license plate created under Subchapters G and I before November 19, 2009.

(a-3) **[Effective January 1, 2012]** The department may contract with the private vendor for the vendor to:

(1) host all or some of the specialty license plates on the vendor's website;

(2) process the purchase of specialty license plates hosted on the vendor's website and pay any additional transaction cost; and

(3) share in the personalization fee for the license plates hosted on the vendor's website.

(b) **[2 Versions: As amended by Acts 2009, 81st Leg., ch. 933]** Instead of the fees established by Section 504.101(c), the board by rule shall establish fees for the issuance or renewal of personalized license plates that are marketed and sold by the private vendor. Fees must be reasonable and not less than the greater of:

(1) the amounts necessary to allow the department to recover all reasonable costs to the department associated with the evaluation of the competitive sealed proposals received by the department and with the implementation

and enforcement of the contract, including direct, indirect, and administrative costs; or

(2) the amount established by Section 504.101(c).

(b) **[2 Versions: As amended by Acts 2009, 81st Leg., ch. 1381]** The commission by rule shall establish fees for the issuance or renewal of personalized license plates that are marketed and sold by the private vendor. Fees must be reasonable and not less than the greater of:

(1) the amounts necessary to allow the department to recover all reasonable costs to the department associated with the evaluation of the competitive sealed proposals received by the department and with the implementation and enforcement of the contract, including direct, indirect, and administrative costs; or

(2) the amount established by Section 504.853(b).

(c) **[2 Versions: Effective until January 1, 2012]** The board by rule shall establish the fees for the issuance or renewal of souvenir license plates, specialty license plates, or souvenir or specialty license plates that are personalized that are marketed and sold by the private vendor. Fees must be reasonable and not less than the amounts necessary to allow the department to recover all reasonable costs to the department associated with the evaluation of the competitive sealed proposals received by the department and with the implementation and enforcement of the contract, including direct, indirect, and administrative costs. A fee established under this subsection is in addition to:

(1) the registration fee and any optional registration fee prescribed by this chapter for the vehicle for which specialty license plates are issued;

(2) any additional fee prescribed by this subchapter for the issuance of specialty license plates for that vehicle; and

(3) any additional fee prescribed by this subchapter for the issuance of personalized license plates for that vehicle.

(c) **[2 Versions: Effective January 1, 2012]** The board by rule shall establish the fees for the issuance or renewal of souvenir license plates, specialty license plates, or souvenir or specialty license plates that are personalized that are marketed and sold by the private vendor or hosted on the private vendor's website. The state's portion of the personalization fee may not be less than $40 for each year issued. Other fees must be reasonable and not less than the amounts necessary to allow the department to recover all reasonable costs to the department associated with the evaluation of the competitive sealed proposals received by the department and with the implementation and enforcement of the contract, including direct, indirect, and administrative costs. A fee established under this subsection is in addition to:

(1) the registration fee and any optional registration fee prescribed by this chapter for the vehicle for which specialty license plates are issued;

(2) any additional fee prescribed by this subchapter for the issuance of specialty license plates for that vehicle; and

(3) any additional fee prescribed by this subchapter for the issuance of personalized license plates for that vehicle.

(c-1) Subsections (b) and (c) do not apply to the sale at auction of a specialty plate or personalized specialty plate that is not used on a motor vehicle.

(d) At any time as necessary to comply with Subsection (b) or (c), the board may increase or decrease the amount of a fee established under the applicable subsection.

(e) **[2 Versions: Effective until January 1, 2012]** The portion of a contract with a private vendor regarding the marketing and sale of personalized license plates is payable only from amounts derived from the collection of the fee established under Subsection (b). The portion of a contract with a private vendor regarding the marketing and sale of souvenir license plates, specialty license plates, or souvenir or specialty license plates that are personalized under Section 504.102 is payable only from amounts derived from the collection of the fee established under Subsection (c).

(e) **[2 Versions: Effective January 1, 2012]** The portion of a contract with a private vendor regarding the marketing and sale of personalized license plates is payable only from amounts derived from the collection of the fee established under Subsection (b). The portion of a contract with a private vendor regarding the marketing, hosting, and sale of souvenir license plates, specialty license plates, or souvenir or specialty license plates that are personalized under Section 504.102 is payable only from amounts derived from the collection of the fee established under Subsection (c).

(f) **[2 Versions: Effective until January 1, 2012]** The department may approve new design and color combinations for personalized license plates that are marketed and sold by a private vendor under a contract entered into with the

private vendor. Each approved license plate design and color combination remains the property of the department.

(f) **[2 Versions: Effective January 1, 2012]** The department may approve new design and color combinations for personalized or specialty license plates that are marketed and sold by a private vendor under a contract entered into with the private vendor. Each approved license plate design and color combination remains the property of the department.

(g) The department may approve new design and color combinations for specialty license plates authorized by this chapter, including specialty license plates that may be personalized, that are marketed and sold by a private vendor under a contract entered into with the private vendor. Each approved license plate design and color combination remains the property of the department. Except as otherwise provided by this chapter, this subsection does not authorize:

(1) the department to approve a design or color combination for a specialty license plate that is inconsistent with the design or color combination specified for the license plate by the section of this chapter that authorizes the issuance of the specialty license plate; or

(2) the private vendor to market and sell a specialty license plate with a design or color combination that is inconsistent with the design or color combination specified by that section.

(g-1) The department may not:

(1) publish a proposed design or color combination for a specialty license plate for public comment in the Texas Register or otherwise, except on the department's website for a period not to exceed 10 days; or

(2) restrict the background color, color combinations, or color alphanumeric license plate numbers of a specialty license plate, except as determined by the Department of Public Safety as necessary for law enforcement purposes.

(h) **[2 Versions: Effective until January 1, 2012]** Subject to the limitations provided by Subsections (g) and (g-1), the department may cancel a license plate or require the discontinuation of a license plate design or color combination that is marketed and sold by a private vendor under contract at any time if the department determines that the cancellation or discontinuation is in the best interest of this state or the motoring public.

(h) **[2 Versions: Effective January 1, 2012]** Subject to the limitations provided by Subsections (g) and (g-1), the department may disapprove a design, cancel a license plate, or require the discontinuation of a license plate design or color combination that is marketed, hosted, or sold by a private vendor under contract at any time if the department determines that the disapproval, cancellation, or discontinuation is in the best interest of this state or the motoring public.

(i) A contract entered into by the department with a private vendor under this section:

    (1) must comply with any law generally applicable to a contract for services entered into by the department;

    (2) must require the private vendor to render at least quarterly to the department periodic accounts that accurately detail all material transactions, including information reasonably required by the department to support fees that are collected by the vendor, and to regularly remit all money payable to the department under the contract; and

    (3) may allow or require the private vendor to establish an electronic infrastructure coordinated and compatible with the department's registration system, by which motor vehicle owners may electronically send and receive applications, other documents, or required payments, and that, when secure access is necessary, can be electronically validated by the department.

(j) From amounts received by the department under the contract described by Subsection (a), the department shall deposit to the credit of the state highway fund an amount sufficient to enable the department to recover its administrative costs for all license plates issued under this section, any payments to the vendor under the contract, and any other amounts allocated by law to the state highway fund. To the extent that the disposition of other amounts received by the department is governed by another law, those amounts shall be deposited in accordance with the other law. Any additional amount received by the department under the contract shall be deposited to the credit of the general revenue fund.

(k) **[Repealed January 1, 2012]** The department shall certify to the comptroller the estimate, with a detailed explanation of the basis on which the estimate is calculated, of all reasonable costs to the department associated with the evaluation of competitive sealed proposals received by the department under this section and associated with the implementation and enforcement of a contract entered into under this section, including direct, indirect, and administrative costs for the issuance or renewal of personalized license plates or specialty license plates.

(*l*) A contract entered into with the private vendor shall provide for the department to recover all costs incurred by the department in implementing this section. Under the contract, the department may require the private vendor to reimburse the department in advance for:

    (1) not more than one-half of the department's anticipated costs in connection with the contract; and

    (2) the department's anticipated costs in connection with the introduction of a new specialty license plate.

(m) **[Effective January 1, 2012]** If the private vendor ceases operation:

    (1) the program may be operated temporarily by the department under new agreements with the license plate sponsors until another vendor is selected and begins operation; and

    (2) the private vendor's share of the revenue is deposited to the credit of the general revenue fund.

(Enacted by Acts 2003, 78th Leg., ch. 1320 (H.B. 2971), § 6, effective September 1, 2003; am. Acts 2005, 79th Leg., ch. 754 (H.B. 2894), § 1, effective June 17, 2005; am. Acts 2009, 81st Leg., ch. 933 (H.B. 3097), § 2G.03, effective September 1, 2009; am. Acts 2009, 81st Leg., ch. 1381 (S.B. 1616), §§ 9, 11(2), effective September 1, 2009; am. Acts 2011, 82nd Leg., ch. 1296 (H.B. 2357), §§ 215, 216, 247(22), effective January 1, 2012.)

### Sec. 504.852. Contract Limitations.

(a) In a contract under Section 504.851, the department may not:

    (1) unreasonably disapprove or limit any aspect of a private vendor's marketing and sales plan;

    (2) unreasonably interfere with the selection, assignment, or management by the private vendor of the private vendor's employees, agents, or subcontractors; or

    (3) require a private vendor to market and sell souvenir license plates, specialty license plates, or souvenir or specialty license plates personalized under Section 504.102.

(b) If a private vendor contracts to market and sell souvenir license plates, specialty license plates, or souvenir or specialty license plates personalized under Section 504.102, the initial term of the contract shall be for at least five years from the effective date of the contract. The contract may provide, with the agreement of the department and the private vendor, a second term at least equal in length to the initial term of the contract.

(c) Notwithstanding Subsection (b), a private vendor may not market and sell souvenir license plates, specialty license plates, or souvenir or specialty license plates personalized under Section 504.102 that compete directly for sales with another specialty license plate issued under this chapter unless the department and the sponsoring agency or organization of the other license plate approve.

(Enacted by Acts 2005, 79th Leg., ch. 754 (H.B. 2894), § 2, effective June 17, 2005.)

### Sec. 504.853.  [2 Versions: Effective until January 1, 2012] Personalized License Plates Issued Before September 1, 2009.

(a) A personalized license plate issued before September 1, 2009, may be issued for a subsequent registration period only if the applicant submits an application and pays the required fee for the applicable registration period. A person who is issued a personalized license plate has first priority on that license plate for each subsequent registration period for which the person submits a new application for that plate.

(b) The fee for issuance of a personalized license plate issued before September 1, 2009, is $40, unless the director adopts by rule a higher fee.

(c) A person who is issued a personalized license plate by the department before September 1, 2009, may:

(1) submit an application for the plate under Subsection (a) and pay the required fee for each subsequent registration period under Subsection (b); or

(2) purchase through the private vendor a license to display the alphanumeric pattern on a license plate for any term allowed by law.

(d) The department may not issue a replacement set of personalized license plates to the same person before the sixth anniversary of the date of issuance unless the applicant for issuance of replacement plates pays an additional fee of $30.

(e) Of each fee collected by the department under this section:

(1) $1.25 shall be used to defray the cost of administering this section; and

(2) the remainder shall be deposited to the credit of the general revenue fund.

(Enacted by Acts 2009, 81st Leg., ch. 1381 (S.B. 1616), § 10, effective September 1, 2009; am. Acts 2011, 82nd Leg., ch. 1296 (H.B. 2357), § 217, effective January 1, 2012.)

### Sec. 504.853.  [2 Versions: Effective January 1, 2012] Specialty and Personalized License Plates Issued Before November 19, 2009.

(a) A specialty or personalized license plate issued before November 19, 2009, may be issued for a subsequent registration period only if the applicant submits an application and pays the required fee for the applicable registration period. A person who is issued a personalized license plate has first priority on that license plate for each subsequent registration period for which the person submits a new application for that plate.

(b) Unless the board by rule adopts a higher fee or the license plate is not renewed annually, the fee for issuance of a license plate issued before November 19, 2009, is:

(1) the fee provided for in Section 504.601 for a specialty license plate; and

(2) $40 for a personalized license plate.

(c) A person who is issued a specialty or personalized license plate by the department before November 19, 2009, may:

(1) submit an application for the plate under Subsection (a) and pay the required fee for each subsequent registration period under Subsection (b); or

(2) purchase through the private vendor a license to display the alphanumeric pattern on a license plate for any term allowed by law.

(d) The department may not issue a replacement set of personalized license plates to the same person before the period set by rule unless the applicant for issuance of replacement plates pays an additional fee of $30.

(e) Of each fee collected by the department under Subsection (b)(2):

(1) $1.25 shall be used by the department to defray the cost of administering this section; and

(2) the remainder shall be deposited to the credit of the general revenue fund.

(Enacted by Acts 2009, 81st Leg., ch. 1381 (S.B. 1616), § 10, effective September 1, 2009; am. Acts 2011, 82nd Leg., ch. 1296 (H.B. 2357), § 217, effective January 1, 2012.)

**Sec. 504.854. [2 Versions: Effective until January 1, 2012] Auction.**

(a) The private vendor may sell at auction a license to display a unique alphanumeric pattern on a license plate.

(b) Only a license to display an alphanumeric pattern purchased under this section or a license to display an alphanumeric pattern sold by the private vendor under Section 504.853 may be transferred to another person. The transferee is entitled to the same rights and privileges as the transferor.

(c) The transferee shall file a form prescribed by the department to notify the department of the transfer. The department may set a fee to be paid by the transferee to the department for the transfer.

(Enacted by Acts 2009, 81st Leg., ch. 1381 (S.B. 1616), § 10, effective September 1, 2009; am. Acts 2011, 82nd Leg., ch. 1296 (H.B. 2357), § 247(23), effective January 1, 2012.)

**Sec. 504.854. [2 Versions: Effective January 1, 2012] Auction.**

(a) The board by rule may provide for the private vendor to:

(1) sell at auction a license to display a unique alphanumeric pattern on a license plate for a period set by board rule;

(2) reserve an unissued alphanumeric pattern from the department for purposes of auctioning a license to display the pattern for a period set by board rule; and

(3) purchase from a customer an unexpired license to display an alphanumeric pattern for purposes of auction by the vendor.

(b) A license to display an alphanumeric pattern purchased under this section may be transferred to another person without payment of the fee provided by Section 504.855.

(c) [Repealed by Acts 2011, 82nd Leg., ch. 1296 (H.B. 2357), § 247(23), effective January 1, 2012].

(Enacted by Acts 2009, 81st Leg., ch. 1381 (S.B. 1616), § 10, effective September 1, 2009; am. Acts 2011, 82nd Leg., ch. 1296 (H.B. 2357), § 247(23), effective January 1, 2012.)

**Sec. 504.855. [Effective January 1, 2012] Transferability of Certain Patterns.**

The board by rule may:

(1) authorize a person who purchases a license to display an alphanumeric pattern for a period of five years or more to transfer the license; and

(2) establish a transfer fee to be distributed in accordance with the contract with the private vendor.

(Enacted by Acts 2011, 82nd Leg., ch. 1296 (H.B. 2357), § 219, effective January 1, 2012.)

**SUBCHAPTER K
[EFFECTIVE JANUARY 1, 2012]
TRANSFER AND REMOVAL OF
LICENSE PLATES**

**Sec. 504.901. [Effective January 1, 2012] Transfer and Removal of License Plates.**

(a) On the sale or transfer of a motor vehicle to a dealer who holds a general distinguishing number issued under Chapter 503, the dealer shall remove each license plate issued for the motor vehicle. A person may use the license plates removed from a motor vehicle on a new motor vehicle purchased from a dealer after the person obtains the department's approval of a title and registration application.

(b) On the sale or transfer of a motor vehicle to a person who does not hold a general distinguishing number issued under Chapter 503, the seller may remove each license plate issued for the motor vehicle. The license plates may be transferred to another vehicle titled in the seller's name if the seller obtains:

(1) the department's approval of an application to transfer the license plates; and

(2) a new registration insignia for the motor vehicle.

(c) A license plate removed from a motor vehicle that is not transferred to another motor vehicle must be disposed of in a manner specified by the department.

(d) To be eligible for transfer, license plates must be appropriate for the class of vehicle to which the plates are being transferred.

(Enacted by Acts 2011, 82nd Leg., ch. 1296 (H.B. 2357), § 220, effective January 1, 2012.)

**SUBCHAPTER L
[EFFECTIVE JANUARY 1, 2012]
OFFENSES AND PENALTIES**

**Sec. 504.941. [Effective January 1, 2012] Antique Vehicles; Offense.**

(a) A person who violates Section 504.502 commits an offense. An offense under this section is a

Transportation

misdemeanor punishable by a fine of not less than $5 or more than $200.

(b) It is an affirmative defense to prosecution under this section that at the time of the offense the vehicle was en route to or from a location for the purpose of routine maintenance of the vehicle.

(Enacted by Acts 2011, 82nd Leg., ch. 1296 (H.B. 2357), § 221, effective January 1, 2012.)

### Sec. 504.942. [Effective January 1, 2012] Log Loader Vehicles; Penalties.

A vehicle operated in violation of Section 504.506 is considered to be operated or moved while unregistered and is immediately subject to the applicable fees and penalties prescribed by this chapter.

(Enacted by Acts 2011, 82nd Leg., ch. 1296 (H.B. 2357), § 221, effective January 1, 2012.)

### Sec. 504.943. [Effective January 1, 2012] Operation of Vehicle Without License Plate.

(a) Except as provided by Subsection (b), a person commits an offense if the person operates on a public highway, during a registration period, a motor vehicle that does not display two license plates that:

(1) have been assigned by the department for the period; and

(2) comply with department rules regarding the placement of license plates.

(b) A person commits an offense if the person operates on a public highway during a registration period a road tractor, motorcycle, trailer, or semitrailer that does not display a license plate that:

(1) has been assigned by the department for the period; and

(2) complies with department rules regarding the placement of license plates.

(c) This section does not apply to a dealer operating a vehicle as provided by law.

(d) A court may dismiss a charge brought under Subsection (a)(1) if the defendant:

(1) remedies the defect before the defendant's first court appearance; and

(2) pays an administrative fee not to exceed $10.

(Enacted by Acts 2011, 82nd Leg., ch. 1296 (H.B. 2357), § 221, effective January 1, 2012.)

### Sec. 504.944. [Effective January 1, 2012] Operation of Vehicle with Wrong License Plate.

A person commits an offense if the person operates, or as the owner permits another to operate, on a public highway a motor vehicle that has attached to it a number plate or registration insignia issued for a different vehicle. An offense under this section is a misdemeanor punishable by a fine not to exceed $200.

(Enacted by Acts 1995, 74th Leg., ch. 165 (S.B. 971), § 1, effective September 1, 1995; am. Acts 1997, 75th Leg., ch. 165 (S.B. 898), § 30.65, effective September 1, 1997; am. Acts 2011, 82nd Leg., ch. 1296 (H.B. 2357), § 222, effective January 1, 2012 (renumbered from Sec. 502.408).)

### Sec. 504.945. [Effective January 1, 2012] Wrong, Fictitious, Altered, or Obscured License Plate.

(a) A person commits an offense if the person attaches to or displays on a motor vehicle a license plate that:

(1) is issued for a different motor vehicle;

(2) is issued for the vehicle under any other motor vehicle law other than by the department;

(3) is assigned for a registration period other than the registration period in effect;

(4) is fictitious;

(5) has blurring or reflective matter that significantly impairs the readability of the name of the state in which the vehicle is registered or the letters or numbers of the license plate number at any time;

(6) has an attached illuminated device or sticker, decal, emblem, or other insignia that is not authorized by law and that interferes with the readability of the letters or numbers of the license plate number or the name of the state in which the vehicle is registered; or

(7) has a coating, covering, protective substance, or other material that:

(A) distorts angular visibility or detectability;

(B) alters or obscures one-half or more of the name of the state in which the vehicle is registered; or

(C) alters or obscures the letters or numbers of the license plate number or the color of the plate.

(b) Except as provided by Subsection (e), an offense under Subsection (a) is a misdemeanor punishable by a fine of not more than $200, unless it is shown at the trial of the offense that the owner knowingly altered or made illegible the letters, numbers, and other identification marks, in which case the offense is a Class B misdemeanor.

(c) Subsection (a)(7) may not be construed to apply to:

(1) a trailer hitch installed on a vehicle in a normal or customary manner;

(2) a transponder, as defined by Section 228.057, that is attached to a vehicle in the manner required by the issuing authority;

(3) a wheelchair lift or wheelchair carrier that is attached to a vehicle in a normal or customary manner;

(4) a trailer being towed by a vehicle; or

(5) a bicycle or motorcycle rack that is attached to a vehicle in a normal or customary manner.

(d) A court may dismiss a charge brought under Subsection (a)(3), (5), (6), or (7) if the defendant:

(1) remedies the defect before the defendant's first court appearance; and

(2) pays an administrative fee not to exceed $10.

(e) An offense under Subsection (a)(4) is a Class B misdemeanor.

(Enacted by Acts 2011, 82nd Leg., ch. 1296 (H.B. 2357), § 223, effective January 1, 2012.)

# CHAPTERS 505 TO 519
## [RESERVED FOR EXPANSION]

# CHAPTER 520
## MISCELLANEOUS PROVISIONS

### Subchapter A. General Provisions

### Subchapter B. [Effective Until January 1, 2012] Motor Number Record Requirements [Effective January 1, 2012] Administrative Provisions

### Subchapter C. [Repealed January 1, 2012] General Requirements Relating to Transfers of Used Motor Vehicles

### Subchapter D. [Repealed January 1, 2012] Transfer of Title and Registration of Used Vehicle

### Subchapter E. Motor Vehicle Title Services

Transportation

## SUBCHAPTER A
## GENERAL PROVISIONS

### Sec. 520.001.   Definition.

In this chapter, "department" means the Texas Department of Motor Vehicles.

(Enacted by Acts 1995, 74th Leg., ch. 165 (S.B. 971), § 1, effective September 1, 1995; am. Acts 2009, 81st Leg., ch. 933 (H.B. 3097), § 2H.01, effective September 1, 2009.)

### Sec. 520.002.   [Renumbered January 1, 2012] Lease of Additional Computer Equipment.

(a) This section applies only to the lease of equipment to a county for the operation of the automated registration and title system in addition to the equipment provided by the department at no cost to the county under a formula prescribed by the department.

(b) On the request of the tax assessor-collector of a county, the department may enter into an agreement with the commissioners court of that county under which the department leases additional equipment to the county for the use of the tax assessor-collector in operating the automated registration and title system in that county.

(c) A county may install equipment leased under this section at offices of the county or of an agent of the county.

(d) Equipment leased under this section:

(1) remains the property of the department; and

(2) must be used primarily for the automated registration and title system.

(e) Under the agreement, the department shall charge the county an amount not less than the amount of the cost to the department to provide the additional equipment and any related services under the lease. All money collected under the lease shall be deposited to the credit of the state highway fund.

(Enacted by Acts 1999, 76th Leg., ch. 876 (H.B. 2004), § 1, effective June 18, 1999.)

#### STATUTORY NOTES

**Editor's notes.** — This section is renumbered to Transportation Code Section 520.0093 pursuant to Acts 2011, 82nd Leg., ch. 1296 (H.B. 2357), § 232, effective January 1, 2012.

### Sec. 520.003.   Rules; Waiver of Fees.

The department may adopt rules to administer this chapter, including rules that waive the payment of fees if a dealer has gone out of business and the applicant can show that fees were paid to the dealer.

(Enacted by Acts 2011, 82nd Leg., ch. 1290 (H.B. 2017), § 30, effective September 1, 2011; Enacted by Acts 2011, 82nd Leg., ch. 1296 (H.B. 2357), § 224, effective January 1, 2012.)

### Sec. 520.004.   Department Responsibilities.

The department has jurisdiction over the registration and titling of, and the issuance of license plates to, motor vehicles in compliance with the applicable statutes. The department by rule:

(1) shall provide services that are reasonable, adequate, and efficient;

(2) shall establish standards for uniformity and service quality for counties and dealers licensed under Section 520.005; and

(3) may conduct public service education campaigns related to the department's functions.

(Enacted by Acts 2011, 82nd Leg., ch. 1290 (H.B. 2017), § 30, effective September 1, 2011; Enacted by Acts 2011, 82nd Leg., ch. 1296 (H.B. 2357), § 224, effective January 1, 2012.)

### Sec. 520.005.   Duty and Responsibilities of County Assessor-Collector.

(a) Each county assessor-collector shall comply with Chapter 501.

(b) An assessor-collector who fails or refuses to comply with Chapter 501 is liable on the assessor-collector's official bond for resulting damages suffered by any person.

(c) **[2 Versions: As added by Acts 2011, 82nd Leg., ch. 1290]** The assessor-collector may license franchised and nonfranchised motor vehicle dealers to title and register motor vehicles in accordance with rules adopted under Section 520.004. The county assessor-collector may pay a fee to a motor vehicle dealer independent of or as part of the portion of the fees that would be collected by the county for each title and registration receipt issued.

(c) **[2 Versions: As added by Acts 2011, 82nd Leg., ch. 1296; Effective January 1, 2012]** Notwithstanding the requirements of Sections 520.008 and 520.0091, the assessor-collector may license franchised and non-franchised motor vehicle dealers to title and register motor vehicles in accordance with rules adopted under Section 520.004. The county assessor-collector may pay a fee to a motor vehicle dealer independent of or as part of the portion of the fees that would be collected by the county for each title and registration receipt issued.

(Enacted by Acts 1995, 74th Leg., ch. 165 (S.B. 971), § 1, effective September 1, 1995;am. Acts 2011, 82nd Leg., ch. 1290 (H.B. 2017), § 31, effective September 1, 2011 (renumbered from Sec. 501.137); am. Acts 2011, 82nd Leg., ch. 1296 (H.B. 2357), § 225, effective January 1, 2012 (renumbered from Sec. 501.137).)

## Sec. 520.006. Compensation of Assessor-Collector.

(a) A county assessor-collector shall receive a fee of $1.90 for each receipt issued under Chapter 502.

(a-1) **[2 Versions: As added by Acts 2011, 82nd Leg., ch. 1290]** A county assessor-collector collecting fees on behalf of a county that has been declared as a disaster area for purposes of Section 501.023 or 502.002 may retain the commission for fees collected, but shall allocate the fees to the county declared as a disaster area.

(a-1) **[2 Versions: As added by Acts 2011, 82nd Leg., ch. 1296, Effective January 1, 2012]** A county collecting fees on behalf of a county that has been declared as a disaster area for purposes of Section 501.023 or 502.040 may retain the commission for fees collected, but shall allocate the fees to the county declared as a disaster area.

(b) A county assessor-collector who is compensated under this section shall pay the entire expense of issuing registration receipts and license plates under Chapter 501 or 502 from the compensation allowed under this section.

(Enacted by Acts 1995, 74th Leg., ch. 165 (S.B. 971), § 1, effective September 1, 1995; am. Acts 1997, 75th Leg., ch. 165 (S.B. 898), § 30.44(b), effective September 1, 1997; am. Acts 2011, 82nd Leg., ch. 1290 (H.B. 2017), § 32, effective September 1, 2011 (renumbered from Sec. 502.109); am. Acts 2011, 82nd Leg., ch. 1296 (H.B. 2357), § 226, effective January 1, 2012 (renumbered from Sec. 502.109).)

## Sec. 520.007. [Effective January 1, 2012] County Branch Offices.

(a) The commissioners court of a county may authorize the county assessor-collector to:

(1) establish a suboffice or branch office for vehicle registration at one or more locations in the county other than the county courthouse; or

(2) appoint a deputy to register vehicles in the same manner and with the same authority as though done in the office of the assessor-collector.

(b) The report of vehicles registered through a suboffice or branch office shall be made through the office of the county assessor-collector.

(Enacted by Acts 1995, 74th Leg., ch. 165 (S.B. 971), § 1, effective September 1, 1995; am. Acts 2011, 82nd Leg., ch. 1296 (H.B. 2357), § 227, effective January 1, 2012 (renumbered from Sec. 502.111).)

## Sec. 520.008. [Effective January 1, 2012] Full-Service Deputies.

(a) A full-service deputy appointed under Section 520.0091 shall accept any application for registration, registration renewal, or title transfer that the county assessor-collector may accept.

(b) A full-service deputy may charge and retain an additional motor vehicle registration fee not to exceed $5 for each motor vehicle registration issued.

(c) A county assessor-collector may delegate to a full-service deputy, in the manner selected by the assessor-collector, the authority to use data processing equipment and software provided by the department for use in the titling and registration of motor vehicles. The department may not limit a county assessor-collector's ability to delegate the assessor-collector's functions regarding the titling and registration of motor vehicles to a qualified full-service deputy in the manner the assessor-collector considers appropriate.

(Enacted by Acts 1995, 74th Leg., ch. 165 (S.B. 971), § 1, effective September 1, 1995; am. Acts 2011, 82nd Leg., ch. 1296 (H.B. 2357), § 228, effective January 1, 2012 (renumbered from Sec. 502.114).)

## Sec. 520.009. [Effective January 1, 2012] Limited-Service Deputies.

(a) A limited-service deputy appointed under Section 520.0091 may only accept registration renewals provided by the department and may not prepare or accept an application for title transfer.

(b) The county assessor-collector may pay a limited-service deputy an amount not to exceed the fee the assessor-collector could collect under Section 520.006(a) for each registration receipt issued. The commissioners court of the county may permit a limited-service deputy to charge and retain an additional fee not to exceed $1 for each registration receipt issued by the deputy.

(Enacted by Acts 1995, 74th Leg., ch. 165 (S.B. 971), § 1, effective September 1, 1995; am. Acts 2011, 82nd Leg., ch. 1296 (H.B. 2357), § 229, effective January 1, 2012 (renumbered from Sec. 502.113).)

### Sec. 520.0091. [Effective January 1, 2012] Deputy Assessor-Collectors.

(a) A county assessor-collector, with the approval of the commissioners court of the county, may deputize an individual or business entity to:

(1) issue motor vehicle registration receipts as a limited-service deputy; or

(2) issue motor vehicle registration receipts and prepare or accept applications for title transfers as a full-service deputy.

(b) An individual or business entity is eligible to be deputized as a limited-service deputy if the person:

(1) is trained to issue registration receipts by the county assessor-collector; and

(2) posts a bond payable to the county assessor-collector:

(A) in an amount determined by the assessor-collector; and

(B) conditioned on the person's proper accounting and remittance of all fees the person collects.

(c) An individual or business entity is eligible to be deputized as a full-service deputy if the person:

(1) meets the requirements of Subsection (b); and

(2) has experience in title transfers.

(d) A person deputized under this section shall keep a separate account of the fees collected and a record of daily receipts.

(Enacted by Acts 1995, 74th Leg., ch. 165 (S.B. 971), § 1, effective September 1, 1995; am. Acts 2011, 82nd Leg., ch. 1296 (H.B. 2357), § 230, effective January 1, 2012 (renumbered from Sec. 502.112).)

### Sec. 520.0092. [Effective January 1, 2012] Acts by Deputy County Assessor-Collector.

A deputy county assessor-collector, other than a limited service deputy appointed under Section 520.0091, may perform the duties of an assessor-collector under Chapter 501.

(Enacted by Acts 1995, 74th Leg., ch. 165 (S.B. 971), § 1, effective September 1, 1995; am. Acts 2011, 82nd Leg., ch. 1296 (H.B. 2357), § 231, effective January 1, 2012 (renumbered from Sec. 501.136).)

### Sec. 520.0093. [Effective January 1, 2012] Lease of Additional Computer Equipment.

(a) This section applies only to the lease of equipment to a county for the operation of the automated registration and titling system in addition to the equipment provided by the department at no cost to the county under a formula prescribed by the department.

(b) On the request of the tax assessor-collector of a county, the department may enter into an agreement with the commissioners court of that county under which the department leases additional equipment to the county for the use of the tax assessor-collector in operating the automated registration and titling system in that county.

(c) A county may install equipment leased under this section at offices of the county or of an agent of the county.

(d) Equipment leased under this section:

(1) remains the property of the department; and

(2) must be used primarily for the automated registration and titling system.

(e) Under the agreement, the department shall charge an amount not less than the amount of the cost to the department to provide the additional equipment and any related services under the lease. All money collected under the lease shall be deposited to the credit of the state highway fund.

(Enacted by Acts 2011, 82nd Leg., ch. 1296 (H.B. 2357), § 232, effective January 1, 2012, (renumbered from Sec. 520.002).)

## SUBCHAPTER B
### [EFFECTIVE UNTIL JANUARY 1, 2012] MOTOR NUMBER RECORD REQUIREMENTS [EFFECTIVE JANUARY 1, 2012] ADMINISTRATIVE PROVISIONS

### Sec. 520.011. [Renumbered January 1, 2012] Motor Number Required for Vehicle Registration; Penalty.

(a) A person may not apply to the county assessor-collector for the registration of a motor vehicle from which the original motor number has been removed, erased, or destroyed until the motor vehicle bears the motor number assigned by the department.

(b) A person commits an offense if the person violates this section. An offense under this subsection is a misdemeanor punishable by a fine of not less than $50 and not more than $100.

(Enacted by Acts 1995, 74th Leg., ch. 165 (S.B. 971), § 1, effective September 1, 1995.)

**Editor's notes.** — This section is renumbered to Transportation Code Section 501.0331 pursuant to Acts 2011, 82nd Leg., ch. 1296 (H.B. 2357), § 23, effective January 1, 2012.

## Sec. 520.012. [Renumbered January 1, 2012] Application for Motor Number Record; Record; Penalty.

(a) To obtain a motor number assigned by the department, the owner of a motor vehicle that has had the original motor number removed, erased, or destroyed must file a sworn application with the department.

(b) The department shall maintain a separate register for recording each motor number assigned by the department. For each motor number assigned by the department, the record must indicate:

(1) the motor number assigned by the department;

(2) the name and address of the owner of the motor vehicle; and

(3) the make, model, and year of manufacture of the motor vehicle.

(c) A person who fails to comply with this section commits an offense. An offense under this subsection is a misdemeanor punishable by a fine of not less than $10 and not more than $100.

(Enacted by Acts 1995, 74th Leg., ch. 165 (S.B. 971), § 1, effective September 1, 1995.)

**Editor's notes.** — This section is renumbered to Transportation Code Section 501.0332 pursuant to Acts 2011, 82nd Leg., ch. 1296 (H.B. 2357), § 24, effective January 1, 2012.

## Sec. 520.013. [Repealed January 1, 2012] Presentation of Motor Number Receipt Required; Penalty.

(a) A person who receives a motor number from the department shall present the receipt received from the department for the assignment of the motor number to the county assessor-collector when the person applies for the registration of the motor vehicle.

(b) A person commits an offense if the person violates this section. An offense under this subsection is a misdemeanor punishable by a fine of not less than $10 and not more than $50.

(Enacted by Acts 1995, 74th Leg., ch. 165 (S.B. 971), § 1, effective September 1, 1995.)

## Sec. 520.014. [Renumbered January 1, 2012] Violation by County Assessor-Collector; Penalty.

(a) A county assessor-collector commits an offense if the county assessor-collector knowingly accepts an application for the registration of a motor vehicle that:

(1) has had the original motor number removed, erased, or destroyed; and

(2) does not bear a motor number assigned by the department.

(b) An offense under this section is a misdemeanor punishable by a fine of not less than $10 and not more than $50.

(Enacted by Acts 1995, 74th Leg., ch. 165 (S.B. 971), § 1, effective September 1, 1995.)

**Editor's notes.** — This section is renumbered to Transportation Code Section 502.480 pursuant to Acts 2011, 82nd Leg., ch. 1296 (H.B. 2357), § 161, effective January 1, 2012.

## Sec. 520.015. Information Consolidation Study.

(a) In consultation with the Department of Public Safety, the department shall conduct a study on the consolidation of similar information that is collected separately by each agency. The study should include recommendations that sufficiently protect the privacy of the public and the security and integrity of information provided.

(b) The study must be completed not later than September 1, 2012.

(Enacted by Acts 2011, 82nd Leg., ch. 1296 (H.B. 2357), § 234, effective January 1, 2012.)

## Sec. 520.016. [Effective January 1, 2012] General Penalty.

(a) A person commits an offense if the person violates this subchapter in a manner for which a specific penalty is not provided.

(b) An offense under this section is a misdemeanor punishable by a fine of not less than $50 and not more than $200.

(c) This section does not apply to a violation of Section 520.006, 520.008, 520.009, 520.0091, or 520.0092.

(Enacted by Acts 2011, 82nd Leg., ch. 1296 (H.B. 2357), § 235, effective January 1, 2012, (renumbered from Sec. 520.036).)

Transportation

Secs. 520.017 to 520.020. [Reserved].

## SUBCHAPTER C
## [REPEALED JANUARY 1, 2012]
## GENERAL REQUIREMENTS
## RELATING TO TRANSFERS OF USED
## MOTOR VEHICLES

### Sec. 520.021.   Current Registration Required [Repealed].

Repealed by Acts 2007, 80th Leg., ch. 101 (H.B. 310), § 3, effective January 1, 2008.

(Enacted by Acts 1995, 74th Leg., ch. 165 (S.B. 971), § 1, effective September 1, 1995.)

### Sec. 520.022.   [Renumbered January 1, 2012] Delivery of Receipt and Title to Transferee; Penalty.

(a) A person, whether acting for that person or another, who sells, trades, or otherwise transfers a used motor vehicle shall deliver to the transferee at the time of delivery of the vehicle:

(1) the license receipt issued by the department for registration of the vehicle, if the vehicle was required to be registered at the time of the delivery; and

(2) a properly assigned certificate of title or other evidence of title as required under Chapter 501.

(b) A person commits an offense if the person violates this section. An offense under this subsection is a misdemeanor punishable by a fine not to exceed $200.

(Enacted by Acts 1995, 74th Leg., ch. 165 (S.B. 971), § 1, effective September 1, 1995; am. Acts 1999, 76th Leg., ch. 1423 (H.B. 2409), § 5, effective September 1, 1999.)

STATUTORY NOTES

**Editor's notes.** — This section is renumbered to Transportation Code Section 501.0721 pursuant to Acts 2011, 82nd Leg., ch. 1296 (H.B. 2357), § 33, effective January 1, 2012.

### Sec. 520.0225.   [Renumbered January 1, 2012] Persons on Active Duty in Armed Forces of United States.

(a) This section applies only to a used motor vehicle that is owned by a person who:

(1) is on active duty in the armed forces of the United States;

(2) is stationed in or has been assigned to another nation under military orders; and

(3) has registered the vehicle or been issued a license for the vehicle under the applicable status of forces agreement by:

(A) the appropriate branch of the armed forces of the United States; or

(B) the nation in which the person is stationed or to which the person has been assigned.

(b) The requirement in Section 520.021 that a used vehicle be registered under the law of this state does not apply to a vehicle described by Subsection (a). In lieu of delivering the license receipt to the transferee of the vehicle, as required by Section 520.022, the person selling, trading, or otherwise transferring a used motor vehicle described by Subsection (a) shall deliver to the transferee:

(1) a letter written on official letterhead by the owner's unit commander attesting to the registration of the vehicle under Subsection (a)(3); or

(2) the registration receipt issued by the appropriate branch of the armed forces or host nation.

(c) A registration receipt issued by a host nation that is not written in the English language must be accompanied by:

(1) a written translation of the registration receipt in English; and

(2) an affidavit, in English and signed by the person translating the registration receipt, attesting to the person's ability to translate the registration receipt into English.

(Enacted by Acts 1999, 76th Leg., ch. 836 (H.B. 1743), § 2, effective September 1, 1999.)

STATUTORY NOTES

**Editor's notes.** — This section is renumbered to Transportation Code Section 502.457 pursuant to Acts 2011, 82nd Leg., ch. 1296 (H.B. 2357), § 153, effective January 1, 2012.

### Sec. 520.023.   [Renumbered January 1, 2012] Powers and Duties of Department on Transfer of Used Vehicle.

(a) On receipt of a written notice of transfer from the transferor of a motor vehicle, the department shall indicate the transfer on the motor vehicle records maintained by the department. As an alternative to a written notice of transfer, the department shall establish procedures that permit the transferor of a motor vehicle to electronically submit a notice of transfer to the department through the department's Internet website. A notice of transfer provided through the department's Internet website is not required to bear the signature of the transferor or include the date of signing.

(b) The department may design the written notice of transfer to be part of the certificate of title for the vehicle. The form shall be provided by the department and must include a place for the transferor to state:

(1) the vehicle identification number of the vehicle;

(2) the number of the license plate issued to the vehicle, if any;

(3) the full name and address of the transferor;

(4) the full name and address of the transferee;

(5) the date the transferor delivered possession of the vehicle to the transferee;

(6) the signature of the transferor; and

(7) the date the transferor signed the form.

(c) This subsection applies only if the department receives notice under Subsection (a) before the 30th day after the date the transferor delivered possession of the vehicle to the transferee. After the date of the transfer of the vehicle shown on the records of the department, the transferee of the vehicle shown on the records is rebuttably presumed to be:

(1) the owner of the vehicle; and

(2) subject to civil and criminal liability arising out of the use, operation, or abandonment of the vehicle, to the extent that ownership of the vehicle subjects the owner of the vehicle to criminal or civil liability under another provision of law.

(d) The department may adopt:

(1) rules to implement this section; and

(2) a fee for filing a notice of transfer under this section in an amount not to exceed the lesser of the actual cost to the department of implementing this section or $5.

(e) This section does not impose or establish civil or criminal liability on the owner of a motor vehicle who transfers ownership of the vehicle but does not disclose the transfer to the department.

(f) This section does not require the department to issue a certificate of title to a person shown on a notice of transfer as the transferee of a motor vehicle. The department may not issue a certificate of title for the vehicle until the transferee applies to the county assessor-collector as provided by Chapter 501.

(g) A transferor who files the appropriate form with the department as provided by, and in accordance with, this section, whether that form is a part of a certificate of title or a form otherwise promulgated by the department to comply with the terms of this section, has no vicarious civil or criminal liability arising out of the use, operation, or abandonment of the vehicle by another person. Proof by the transferor that the transferor filed a form under this section is a complete defense to an action brought against the transferor for an act or omission, civil or criminal, arising out of the use, operation, or abandonment of the vehicle by another person after the transferor filed the form. A copy of the form filed under this section is proof of the filing of the form.

(Enacted by Acts 1995, 74th Leg., ch. 165 (S.B. 971), § 1, effective September 1, 1995; am. Acts 1997, 75th Leg., ch. 165 (S.B. 898), § 30.71(a), effective September 1, 1997; am. Acts 2007, 80th Leg., ch. 75 (H.B. 481), § 1, effective January 1, 2008; am. Acts 2009, 81st Leg., ch. 542 (S.B. 1617), § 2, effective September 1, 2009.)

### STATUTORY NOTES

**Editor's notes.** — This section is renumbered to Tex. Trnsp. Code § 501.147 pursuant to Acts 2011, 82nd Leg., ch. 1296 (H.B. 2357), § 61, effective January 1, 2012.

## Secs. 520.024 to 520.030 [Reserved for expansion].

## SUBCHAPTER D
## [REPEALED JANUARY 1, 2012]
## TRANSFER OF TITLE AND
## REGISTRATION OF USED VEHICLE

### Sec. 520.031.  [Renumbered January 1, 2012] Filing by Transferee; Application for Transfer of Title and Registration.

(a) **[2 Versions: As amended by Acts 1999, 76th Leg., ch. 836]** Not later than the 20th working day after the date of receiving the documents under Section 520.022 or 520.0225, the transferee of the used motor vehicle shall file with the county assessor-collector:

(1) the license receipt and the certificate of title or other evidence of title; or

(2) if appropriate, a document described by Section 520.0225(b)(1) or (2) and the certificate of title or other evidence of title.

(a) **[2 Versions: As amended by Acts 1999, 76th Leg., ch. 1423]** Not later than the 20th working day after the date of receiving the documents under Section 520.022, the transferee of the used motor vehicle shall file with the county assessor-collector each document received under that section.

(b) The filing under Subsection (a) is an application for transfer of title as required under Chapter 501 and, if the license receipt is filed, an application for transfer of the registration of the motor vehicle.

(c) In this section, "working day" means any day other than a Saturday, a Sunday, or a holiday on which county offices are closed.

(d) Notwithstanding Subsection (a), if the transferee is a member of the armed forces of the United States, a member of the Texas National Guard or of the National Guard of another state serving on active duty under an order of the president of the United States, or a member of a reserve component of the armed forces of the United States serving on active duty under an order of the president of the United States, the documents described by Subsection (a) must be filed with the county assessor-collector not later than the 60th working day after the date of their receipt by the transferee.

(Enacted by Acts 1995, 74th Leg., ch. 165 (S.B. 971), § 1, effective September 1, 1995; am. Acts 1999, 76th Leg., ch. 836 (H.B. 1743), § 3, effective September 1, 1999; am. Acts 1999, 76th Leg., ch. 1423 (H.B. 2409), § 6, effective September 1, 1999; am. Acts 2007, 80th Leg., ch. 75 (H.B. 481), § 2, effective January 1, 2008.)

### STATUTORY NOTES

**Editor's notes.** — This section is renumbered to Tex. Trnsp. Code § 501.145 pursuant to Acts 2011, 82nd Leg., ch. 1296 (H.B. 2357), § 59, effective January 1, 2012.

## Sec. 520.032. [Renumbered January 1, 2012] Transfer Fee; Late Fee.

(a) The transferee of a used motor vehicle shall pay, in addition to any fee required under Chapter 501 for the transfer of title, a transfer fee of $2.50 for the transfer of the registration of the motor vehicle.

(b) If the transferee does not file the application during the period provided by Section 520.031, the transferee is liable for a late fee to be paid to the county assessor-collector when the application is filed. If the transferee holds a general distinguishing number issued under Chapter 503 of this code or Chapter 2301, Occupations Code, the amount of the late fee is $10. If the transferee does not hold a general distinguishing number, subject to Subsection (b-1) the amount of the late fee is $25.

(b-1) If the application is filed after the 31st working day after the date the transferee re-ceived the documents under Section 520.022, the late fee imposed under Subsection (b) accrues an additional penalty in the amount of $25 for each subsequent 30-day period, or portion of a 30-day period, in which the application is not filed.

(c) The county assessor-collector and the surety on the county assessor-collector's bond are liable for the late fee if the county assessor-collector does not collect the late fee.

(d) Subsections (b) and (b-1) do not apply if the motor vehicle is eligible to be issued:

(1) classic vehicle license plates under Section 504.501; or

(2) antique vehicle license plates under Section 504.502.

(Enacted by Acts 1995, 74th Leg., ch. 165 (S.B. 971), § 1, effective September 1, 1995; am. Acts 2007, 80th Leg., ch. 75 (H.B. 481), § 3, effective January 1, 2008.)

### STATUTORY NOTES

**Editor's notes.** — This section is renumbered to Tex. Trnsp. Code § 501.146 pursuant to Acts 2011, 82nd Leg., ch. 1296 (H.B. 2357), § 60, effective January 1, 2012.

## Sec. 520.033. [Renumbered January 1, 2012] Allocation of Fees.

(a) The county assessor-collector may retain as commission for services provided under this subchapter half of each transfer fee collected, half of each late fee, and half of each additional penalty collected under Section 520.032.

(b) The county assessor-collector shall report and remit the balance of the fees collected to the department on Monday of each week as other registration fees are required to be reported and remitted.

(c) Of each late fee collected from a person who does not hold a general distinguishing number that the department receives under Subsection (b), $10 may be used only to fund a statewide public awareness campaign designed to inform and educate the public about the provisions of this chapter.

(Enacted by Acts 1995, 74th Leg., ch. 165 (S.B. 971), § 1, effective September 1, 1995; am. Acts 2007, 80th Leg., ch. 75 (H.B. 481), § 4, effective January 1, 2008.)

### STATUTORY NOTES

**Editor's notes.** — This section is renumbered to Tex. Trnsp. Code § 501.148 pursuant to Acts 2011, 82nd Leg., ch. 1296 (H.B. 2357), § 62, effective January 1, 2012.

### Sec. 520.034. [Repealed January 1, 2012] Processing of Application; Rules.

(a) On receipt of an application for the transfer of a certificate of title and registration, the county assessor-collector shall process the application for transfer of title as provided under Chapter 501, and the department shall issue a transfer of registration receipt when the department receives the application for transfer of registration.

(b) The department may adopt rules and prescribe forms to implement this subchapter.
(Enacted by Acts 1995, 74th Leg., ch. 165 (S.B. 971), § 1, effective September 1, 1995.)

### Sec. 520.035. [Renumbered January 1, 2012] Execution of Transfer Documents; Penalty.

(a) A person who transfers a motor vehicle in this state shall execute in full and date as of the date of the transfer all documents relating to the transfer of registration or certificate of title. A person who transfers a vehicle commits an offense if the person fails to execute the documents in full.

(b) A person commits an offense if the person:
  (1) accepts a document described by Subsection (a) that does not contain all of the required information; or
  (2) alters or mutilates such a document.

(c) An offense under this section is a misdemeanor punishable by a fine of not less than $50 and not more than $200.
(Enacted by Acts 1995, 74th Leg., ch. 165 (S.B. 971), § 1, effective September 1, 1995.)

#### STATUTORY NOTES

**Editor's notes.** — This section is renumbered to Tex. Trnsp. code § 501.161 pursuant to Acts 2011, 82nd Leg., ch. 1296 (H.B. 2357), § 68, effective January 1, 2012.

### Sec. 520.036. [Renumbered January 1, 2012] General Penalty.

(a) A person commits an offense if the person violates this subchapter in a manner for which a specific penalty is not provided.

(b) An offense under this section is a misdemeanor punishable by a fine of not less than $50 and not more than $200.
(Enacted by Acts 1995, 74th Leg., ch. 165 (S.B. 971), § 1, effective September 1, 1995.)

#### STATUTORY NOTES

**Editor's notes.** — This section is renumbered to Transportation Code Section 520.016 pursuant to Acts

2011, 82nd Leg., ch. 1296 (H.B. 2357), § 235, effective January 1, 2012.

### Secs. 520.037 to 520.050 [Reserved for expansion].

## SUBCHAPTER E
## MOTOR VEHICLE TITLE SERVICES

### Sec. 520.051. Definitions.

In this subchapter:
  (1) "Motor vehicle" has the meaning assigned by Section 501.002.
  (2) "Motor vehicle title service" means any person that for compensation directly or indirectly assists other persons in obtaining title documents by submitting, transmitting, or sending applications for title documents to the appropriate government agencies.
  (3) "Title documents" means motor vehicle title applications, motor vehicle registration renewal applications, motor vehicle mechanic's lien title applications, motor vehicle storage lien title applications, motor vehicle temporary registration permits, motor vehicle title application transfers occasioned by the death of the title holder, or notifications under Chapter 683 of this code or Chapter 70, Property Code.
  (4) "Title service license holder" means a person who holds a motor vehicle title service license or a title service runner's license.
  (5) [2 Versions: Effective until January 1, 2012] "Title service record" means the written record for each transaction in which a motor vehicle title service receives compensation.
  (5) [2 Versions: Effective January 1, 2012] "Title service record" means the written or electronic record for each transaction in which a motor vehicle title service receives compensation.
  (6) "Title service runner" means any person employed by a licensed motor vehicle title service to submit or present title documents to the county tax assessor-collector.
(Enacted by Acts 1999, 76th Leg., ch. 1478 (H.B. 3521), § 2, effective September 1, 1999; am. Acts 2011, 82nd Leg., ch. 1296 (H.B. 2357), § 236, effective January 1, 2012.)

### Sec. 520.052. Applicability.

This subchapter applies to any motor vehicle title service operating in a county:
  (1) that has a population of more than 500,000; or

(2) in which the commissioners court by order has adopted this subchapter.

(Enacted by Acts 1999, 76th Leg., ch. 1478 (H.B. 3521), § 2, effective September 1, 1999; am. Acts 2003, 78th Leg., ch. 448 (H.B. 623), § 1, effective September 1, 2003.)

### Sec. 520.053.  License Required.

A person may not act as a motor vehicle title service or act as an agent for that business unless that person holds a license issued under this subchapter.

(Enacted by Acts 1999, 76th Leg., ch. 1478 (H.B. 3521), § 2, effective September 1, 1999.)

### Sec. 520.054.  General License Application Requirements.

(a) An applicant for a motor vehicle title service license must apply on a form prescribed by the county tax assessor-collector. The application form must be signed by the applicant and accompanied by the application fee.

(b) An application must include:

(1) the applicant's name, business address, and business telephone number;

(2) the name under which the applicant will do business;

(3) the physical address of each office from which the applicant will conduct business;

(4) a statement indicating whether the applicant has previously applied for a license under this subchapter, the result of the previous application, and whether the applicant has ever been the holder of a license under this subchapter that was revoked or suspended;

(5) information from the applicant as required by the county tax assessor-collector to establish the business reputation and character of the applicant;

(6) the applicant's federal tax identification number;

(7) the applicant's state sales tax number; and

(8) any other information required by rules adopted under this subchapter.

(Enacted by Acts 1999, 76th Leg., ch. 1478 (H.B. 3521), § 2, effective September 1, 1999.)

### Sec. 520.055.  Application Requirements: Corporation.

In addition to the information required in Section 520.054, an applicant for a motor vehicle title service license that intends to engage in business as a corporation shall submit the following information:

(1) the state of incorporation;

(2) the name, address, date of birth, and social security number of each of the principal owners and directors of the corporation;

(3) information about each officer and director as required by the county tax assessor-collector to establish the business reputation and character of the applicant; and

(4) a statement indicating whether an employee, officer, or director has been refused a motor vehicle title service license or a title service runner's license or has been the holder of a license that was revoked or suspended.

(Enacted by Acts 1999, 76th Leg., ch. 1478 (H.B. 3521), § 2, effective September 1, 1999.)

### Sec. 520.056.  Application Requirements: Partnership.

In addition to the information required in Section 520.054, a motor vehicle title service license applicant that intends to engage in business as a partnership shall submit an application that includes the following information:

(1) the name, address, date of birth, and social security number of each partner;

(2) information about each partner as required by the county tax assessor-collector to establish the business reputation and character of the applicant; and

(3) a statement indicating whether a partner or employee has been refused a motor vehicle title service license or a title service runner's license or has been the holder of a license that was revoked or suspended.

(Enacted by Acts 1999, 76th Leg., ch. 1478 (H.B. 3521), § 2, effective September 1, 1999.)

### Sec. 520.057.  Records.

(a) A holder of a motor vehicle title service license shall maintain records as required by this section on a form prescribed and made available by the county tax assessor-collector for each transaction in which the license holder receives compensation. The records shall include:

(1) the date of the transaction;

(2) the name, age, address, sex, driver's license number, and a legible photocopy of the driver's license for each customer; and

(3) the license plate number, vehicle identification number, and a legible photocopy of proof of financial responsibility for the motor vehicle involved.

(b) A motor vehicle title service shall keep:

(1) two copies of all records required under this section for at least two years after the date of the transaction;

(2) legible photocopies of any documents submitted by a customer; and

(3) legible photocopies of any documents submitted to the county tax assessor-collector. (Enacted by Acts 1999, 76th Leg., ch. 1478 (H.B. 3521), § 2, effective September 1, 1999.)

### Sec. 520.058. Inspection of Records.

A motor vehicle title service license holder or any of its employees shall allow an inspection of records required under Section 520.057 by a peace officer on the premises of the motor vehicle title service at any reasonable time to verify, check, or audit the records.
(Enacted by Acts 1999, 76th Leg., ch. 1478 (H.B. 3521), § 2, effective September 1, 1999.)

### Sec. 520.059. Denial, Suspension, or Revocation of License.

(a) The county tax assessor-collector may deny, suspend, revoke, or reinstate a license issued under this subchapter.

(b) The county tax assessor-collector shall adopt rules that establish grounds for the denial, suspension, revocation, or reinstatement of a license and rules that establish procedures for disciplinary action. Procedures issued under this subchapter are subject to Chapter 2001, Government Code.

(c) A person whose license is revoked may not apply for a new license before the first anniversary of the date of the revocation.

(d) A license may not be issued under a fictitious name that is similar to or may be confused with the name of a governmental entity or that is deceptive or misleading to the public.
(Enacted by Acts 1999, 76th Leg., ch. 1478 (H.B. 3521), § 2, effective September 1, 1999.)

### Sec. 520.060. License Renewal.

(a) A license issued under this subchapter expires on the first anniversary of the date of issuance and may be renewed annually on or before the expiration date on payment of the required renewal fee.

(b) A person who is otherwise eligible to renew a license may renew an unexpired license by paying to the county tax assessor-collector before the expiration date of the license the required renewal fee. A person whose license has expired may not engage in activities that require a license until the license has been renewed under this section.

(c) If a person's license has been expired for 90 days or less, the person may renew the license by paying to the county tax assessor-collector 1-½ times the required renewal fee.

(d) If a person's license has been expired for longer than 90 days but less than one year, the person may renew the license by paying to the county tax assessor-collector two times the required renewal fee.

(e) If a person's license has been expired for one year or longer, the person may not renew the license. The person may obtain a new license by complying with the requirements and procedures for obtaining an original license.

(f) Notwithstanding Subsection (e), if a person was licensed in this state, moved to another state, and has been doing business in the other state for the two years preceding application, the person may renew an expired license. The person must pay to the county tax assessor-collector a fee that is equal to two times the required renewal fee for the license.

(g) Before the 30th day preceding the date on which a person's license expires, the county tax assessor-collector shall notify the person of the impending expiration. The notice must be in writing and sent to the person's last known address according to the records of the county tax assessor-collector.
(Enacted by Acts 1999, 76th Leg., ch. 1478 (H.B. 3521), § 2, effective September 1, 1999.)

### Sec. 520.061. Criminal Penalty.

(a) A person commits an offense if the person violates this subchapter or a rule adopted by the county tax assessor-collector under this subchapter.

(b) An offense under this section is a Class A misdemeanor.
(Enacted by Acts 1999, 76th Leg., ch. 1478 (H.B. 3521), § 2, effective September 1, 1999.)

### Sec. 520.062. Injunction.

(a) A district attorney of the county in which the motor vehicle title service is located may bring an action to enjoin the operation of a motor vehicle title service if the motor vehicle title service license holder or a runner of the motor vehicle title service while in the scope of the runner's employment is convicted of more than one offense under this subchapter.

(b) If the court grants relief under Subsection (a), the court may:

(1) enjoin the person from maintaining or participating in the business of a motor vehicle title service for a period of time as determined by the court; or

Transportation

(2) declare the place where the person's business is located to be closed for any use relating to the business of the motor vehicle title service for as long as the person is enjoined from participating in that business.
(Enacted by Acts 1999, 76th Leg., ch. 1478 (H.B. 3521), § 2, effective September 1, 1999.)

## Sec. 520.063. Exemptions.

The following persons and their agents are exempt from the licensing and other requirements established by this subchapter:

(1) a franchised motor vehicle dealer or independent motor vehicle dealer who holds a general distinguishing number issued by the department under Chapter 503;

(2) a vehicle lessor holding a license issued by the Motor Vehicle Board under Chapter 2301, Occupations Code, or a trust or other entity that is specifically not required to obtain a lessor license under Section 2301.254(a) of that code; and

(3) a vehicle lease facilitator holding a license issued by the Motor Vehicle Board under Chapter 2301, Occupations Code.
(Enacted by Acts 1999, 76th Leg., ch. 1478 (H.B. 3521), § 2, effective September 1, 1999; am. Acts 2003, 78th Leg., ch. 1276 (H.B. 3507), § 14A.832, effective September 1, 2003.)

## SUBTITLE B
## DRIVER'S LICENSES AND PERSONAL IDENTIFICATION CARDS

## CHAPTER 521
## DRIVER'S LICENSES AND CERTIFICATES

### Subchapter A. General Provisions

Transportation

## SUBCHAPTER A
## GENERAL PROVISIONS

### Sec. 521.001. Definitions.

(a) In this chapter:

(1) "Correctional facility" means:

(A) a place described by Section 1.07(a)(14), Penal Code; or

(B) a secure correctional facility or secure detention facility, as defined by Section 51.02, Family Code.

(1-a) "Department" means the Department of Public Safety.

(2) "Director" means the public safety director.

(3) "Driver's license" means an authorization issued by the department for the operation of a motor vehicle. The term includes:

(A) a temporary license or instruction permit; and

(B) an occupational license.

(3-a) "Federal judge" means:

(A) a judge of a United States court of appeals;

(B) a judge of a United States district court;

(C) a judge of a United States bankruptcy court; or

(D) a magistrate judge of a United States district court.

(4) "Gross combination weight rating" has the meaning assigned by Section 522.003.

(5) "Gross vehicle weight rating" has the meaning assigned by Section 522.003.

(6) "License" means an authorization to operate a motor vehicle that is issued under or granted by the laws of this state. The term includes:

(A) a driver's license;

(B) the privilege of a person to operate a motor vehicle regardless of whether the person holds a driver's license; and

(C) a nonresident's operating privilege.

(6-a) "Motorcycle" includes an enclosed three-wheeled passenger vehicle that:

(A) is designed to operate with three wheels in contact with the ground;

(B) has a minimum unladen weight of 900 lbs.;

(C) has a single, completely enclosed, occupant compartment;

(D) at a minimum, is equipped with:

(i) seats that are certified by the vehicle manufacturer to meet the requirements of Federal Motor Vehicle Safety Standard No. 207, 49 C.F.R. Section 571.207;

(ii) a steering wheel used to maneuver the vehicle;

(iii) a propulsion unit located in front of or behind the enclosed occupant compartment;

(iv) a seat belt for each vehicle occupant certified by the manufacturer to meet the requirements of Federal Motor Vehicle Safety Standard No. 209, 49 C.F.R. Section 571.209;

(v) a windshield and one or more windshield wipers certified by the manufacturer to meet the requirements of Federal Motor Vehicle Safety Standard No. 205, 49 C.F.R. Section 571.205, and Federal Motor Vehicle Safety Standard No. 104, 49 C.F.R. Section 571.104; and

(vi) a vehicle structure certified by the vehicle manufacturer to meet the requirements of Federal Motor Vehicle Safety Standard No. 216, 49 C.F.R. Section 571.216; and

(E) is produced by its manufacturer in a minimum quantity of 300 in any calendar year.

(7) "Nonresident" means a person who is not a resident of this state.

(7-a) "Parole facility" means a place described by Section 508.118 or 508.119, Government Code.

(8) "State" means a state, territory, or possession of the United States, the District of Columbia, or the Commonwealth of Puerto Rico.

(8-a) "State judge" means:

(A) the judge of an appellate court, a district court, or a county court at law of this state; or

(B) an associate judge appointed under Chapter 201, Family Code.

(9) "Image comparison technology" means any technology that is used to compare facial images, thumbprints, or fingerprints.

(b) A word or phrase that is not defined by this chapter but is defined by Subtitle C has the meaning in this chapter that is assigned by that subtitle.

(Enacted by Acts 1995, 74th Leg., ch. 165 (S.B. 971), § 1, effective September 1, 1995; am. Acts 2005, 79th Leg., ch. 1108 (H.B. 2337), § 3, effective September 1, 2005; am. Acts 2009, 81st Leg., ch. 316 (H.B. 598), § 1, effective September 1, 2009; am. Acts 2009, 81st Leg., ch. 722 (S.B. 129), § 3, effective September 1, 2009; am. Acts 2009, 81st Leg., ch. 967 (H.B. 3599), § 1, effective September 1, 2009; am. Acts 2009, 81st Leg., ch. 1146 (H.B. 2730), § 13A.01, effective September 1, 2009; am. Acts 2009, 81st Leg., ch. 1288 (H.B. 2161), § 3, effective September 1, 2009; am. Acts 2009, 81st Leg., ch. 1391 (S.B. 1967), § 2, effective September 1, 2009.)

## Sec. 521.002. Convenience to Public.

The department shall implement its duties under this chapter in the manner that provides the greatest convenience to the public.

(Enacted by Acts 1995, 74th Leg., ch. 165 (S.B. 971), § 1, effective September 1, 1995.)

### Sec. 521.003.   Enrollment and Attendance Verification.

The Texas Education Agency shall design a standard form for use by public and private schools to verify a student's enrollment and attendance for purposes of this chapter. The form must be approved by the department.

(Enacted by Acts 1995, 74th Leg., ch. 165 (S.B. 971), § 1, effective September 1, 1995; am. Acts 2003, 78th Leg., ch. 1276 (H.B. 3507), § 16.003, effective September 1, 2003.)

### Sec. 521.004.   Penal Code References.

In this chapter:

(1) a reference to an offense under Section 49.04, Penal Code, includes an offense under Article 6701*l*-1, Revised Statutes, as that law existed immediately before September 1, 1994;

(2) a reference to an offense under Section 49.07, Penal Code:

(A) means only an offense under that section involving the operation of a motor vehicle; and

(B) includes an offense under Section 6701*l*-1, Revised Statutes, as that law existed immediately before September 1, 1994; and

(3) a reference to an offense under Section 49.08, Penal Code:

(A) means only an offense under that section involving the operation of a motor vehicle; and

(B) includes an offense under Section 19.05(a)(2), Penal Code, as that law existed immediately before September 1, 1994.

(Enacted by Acts 1995, 74th Leg., ch. 165 (S.B. 971), § 1, effective September 1, 1995.)

### Sec. 521.005.   Rulemaking Authority.

The department may adopt rules necessary to administer this chapter.

(Enacted by Acts 1997, 75th Leg., ch. 165 (S.B. 898), § 30.72, effective September 1, 1997.)

### Sec. 521.006.   Advertising in Driver's Handbook and Driver's License Mailings.

(a) Except as provided by Subsection (c), the department may sell advertising for inclusion in:

(1) any driver's handbook that the department publishes; and

(2) any mailing the department makes in connection with a driver's license.

(b) The department shall deposit the proceeds from the advertising to the credit of the driver's license administration advertising account. The driver's license administration advertising account is an account in the general revenue fund that may be appropriated only for the purpose of administration of this chapter.

(c) The department may not include in the driver's handbook or a driver's license mailing advertising for an alcoholic beverage or a product promoting alcoholic beverages.

(Enacted by Acts 1999, 76th Leg., ch. 1258 (S.B. 1169), § 1, effective August 30, 1999; am. Acts 2007, 80th Leg., ch. 154 (S.B. 1084), § 1, effective May 21, 2007.)

### Sec. 521.007.   [Effective September 28, 2011] Temporary Visitor Stations.

(a) The department shall designate as temporary visitor stations certain driver's license offices.

(b) A driver's license office designated as a temporary visitor station under this section must have at least two staff members who have completed specialized training on the temporary visitor issuance guide published by the department.

(c) A driver's license office designated as a temporary visitor station shall provide information and assistance to other driver's license offices in the state.

(Enacted by Acts 2011, 82nd Leg., 1st C.S., (S.B. 1), § 72.01, effective September 28, 2011.)

### Secs. 521.008 to 521.020 [Reserved for expansion].

### SUBCHAPTER B
### GENERAL LICENSE REQUIREMENTS

### Sec. 521.021.   License Required.

A person, other than a person expressly exempted under this chapter, may not operate a motor vehicle on a highway in this state unless the person holds a driver's license issued under this chapter.

(Enacted by Acts 1995, 74th Leg., ch. 165 (S.B. 971), § 1, effective September 1, 1995.)

### Sec. 521.022.   Restrictions on Operators of Certain School Buses.

(a) A person under 18 years of age may not operate a school bus for the transportation of students.

(b) A person who is 18 years of age or older may not operate a school bus unless the person holds an appropriate class of driver's license for the vehicle being operated.

(c) A person may not operate a school bus for the transportation of students unless the person meets the mental and physical capability requirements the department establishes by rule and has passed an examination approved by the department to determine the person's mental and physical capabilities to operate a school bus safely. A physician, advanced practice nurse, or physician assistant may conduct the examination. An ophthalmologist, optometrist, or therapeutic optometrist may conduct the part of the examination relating to the person's vision. Each school bus operator must pass the examination annually.

(d) A person may not operate a school bus for the transportation of students unless the person's driving record is acceptable according to minimum standards adopted by the department. A check of the person's driving record shall be made with the department annually. The minimum standards adopted by the department must provide that a person's driving record is not acceptable if the person has been convicted of an offense under Section 49.04, 49.045, 49.07, or 49.08, Penal Code, within the 10-year period preceding the date of the check of the person's driving record.

(e) A person may not operate a school bus for the transportation of students unless the person is certified in school bus safety education or has enrolled in a school bus safety education class under provisions adopted by the department. Effective on the date and under provisions determined by the department, a school bus operator must hold a card that states that the operator is enrolled in or has completed a driver training course approved by the department in school bus safety education. The card is valid for three years.

(f) Before a person is employed to operate a school bus to transport students, the employer must obtain a criminal history record check. A school district, school, service center, or shared services arrangement, or a commercial transportation company under contract with a school district, that obtains information that a person has been convicted of a felony or misdemeanor involving moral turpitude may not employ the person to drive a school bus on which students are transported unless the employment is ap-

proved by the board of trustees of the school district or the board's designee.

(g) This section does not affect the right of an otherwise qualified person with a hearing disability to be licensed, certified, and employed as a bus operator for vehicles used to transport hearing-impaired students.

(h) This section does not apply to the operation of a vehicle owned by a public institution of higher education to transport students of a school district that operates within that institution if:

    (1) the person operating the vehicle is approved by the institution to operate the vehicle; and

    (2) the transportation is for a special event, including a field trip.

(i) For purposes of this section, "school bus" includes a school activity bus as defined by Section 541.201.

(Enacted by Acts 1995, 74th Leg., ch. 165 (S.B. 971), § 1, effective September 1, 1995; am. Acts 1997, 75th Leg., ch. 165 (S.B. 898), § 30.73(a), (b), effective September 1, 1997; am. Acts 1997, 75th Leg., ch. 1438 (H.B. 3249), § 7, effective September 1, 1997; am. Acts 1999, 76th Leg., ch. 663 (H.B. 385), § 3, effective June 18, 1999; am. Acts 1999, 76th Leg., ch. 786 (H.B. 1409), § 1, effective June 18, 1999; am. Acts 2007, 80th Leg., ch. 923 (H.B. 3190), § 1, effective September 1, 2007.)

### Sec. 521.023. Junior College Buses.

(a) A person who is 18 years of age or older and who is licensed by the department to operate a motor vehicle as a school bus may operate the motor vehicle for the transportation of junior college students and employees to and from school or official school activities.

(b) A school bus operated by a junior college may also be used to transport public school students if it is convenient. If students of a local public school district are transported to and from school on a bus operated by a junior college and the operator is under 21 years of age, the selection of the operator must be approved by the principal of the public school whose students are transported on that bus.

(c) This section does not apply to the operator of a vehicle operated under a registration certificate issued under Chapter 643.

(Enacted by Acts 1995, 74th Leg., ch. 165 (S.B. 971), § 1, effective September 1, 1995; am. Acts 1997, 75th Leg., ch. 165 (S.B. 898), § 30.74, effective September 1, 1997.)

Transportation

## Sec. 521.024. Restrictions on Certain Common Carriers.

(a) A person under 18 years of age may not operate a motor vehicle while that vehicle is in use as a public or common carrier of persons unless the person is licensed to operate the vehicle.

(b) A person may not operate a taxicab unless the person is at least 18 years of age.

(Enacted by Acts 1995, 74th Leg., ch. 165 (S.B. 971), § 1, effective September 1, 1995.)

## Sec. 521.025. License to Be Carried and Exhibited on Demand; Criminal Penalty.

(a) A person required to hold a license under Section 521.021 shall:

(1) have in the person's possession while operating a motor vehicle the class of driver's license appropriate for the type of vehicle operated; and

(2) display the license on the demand of a magistrate, court officer, or peace officer.

(b) A peace officer may stop and detain a person operating a motor vehicle to determine if the person has a driver's license as required by this section.

(c) A person who violates this section commits an offense. An offense under this subsection is a misdemeanor punishable by a fine not to exceed $200, except that:

(1) for a second conviction within one year after the date of the first conviction, the offense is a misdemeanor punishable by a fine of not less than $25 or more than $200;

(2) for a third or subsequent conviction within one year after the date of the second conviction the offense is a misdemeanor punishable by:

(A) a fine of not less than $25 or more than $500;

(B) confinement in the county jail for not less than 72 hours or more than six months; or

(C) both the fine and confinement; and

(3) if it is shown on the trial of the offense that at the time of the offense the person was operating the motor vehicle in violation of Section 601.191 and caused or was at fault in a motor vehicle accident that resulted in serious bodily injury to or the death of another person, an offense under this section is a Class A misdemeanor.

(d) It is a defense to prosecution under this section if the person charged produces in court a driver's license:

(1) issued to that person;

(2) appropriate for the type of vehicle operated; and

(3) valid at the time of the arrest for the offense.

(e) The judge of each court shall report promptly to the department each conviction obtained in the court under this section.

(f) The court may assess a defendant an administrative fee not to exceed $10 if a charge under this section is dismissed because of the defense listed under Subsection (d).

(Enacted by Acts 1995, 74th Leg., ch. 165 (S.B. 971), § 1, effective September 1, 1995; am. Acts 2007, 80th Leg., ch. 1027 (H.B. 1623), § 4, effective September 1, 2007; am. Acts 2011, 82nd Leg., ch. 195 (S.B. 1608), § 1, effective September 1, 2011.)

## Sec. 521.026. Dismissal of Expired License Charge.

(a) A judge may dismiss a charge of driving with an expired license if the defendant remedies this defect within 20 working days or before the defendant's first court appearance date, whichever is later.

(b) The judge may assess the defendant an administrative fee not to exceed $20 when the charge of driving with an expired driver's license is dismissed under Subsection (a).

(Enacted by Acts 1995, 74th Leg., ch. 165 (S.B. 971), § 1, effective September 1, 1995; am. Acts 2007, 80th Leg., ch. 1027 (H.B. 1623), § 5, effective September 1, 2007.)

## Sec. 521.027. Persons Exempt from License Requirement.

The following persons are exempt from the license requirement imposed under this chapter:

(1) a person in the service of the state military forces or the United States while the person is operating an official motor vehicle in the scope of that service;

(2) a person while the person is operating a road machine, farm tractor, or implement of husbandry on a highway, unless the vehicle is a commercial motor vehicle under Section 522.003;

(3) a nonresident on active duty in the armed forces of the United States who holds a license issued by the person's state or Canadian province of residence; and

(4) a person who is the spouse or dependent child of a nonresident exempt under Subdivi-

sion (3) and who holds a license issued by the person's state or Canadian province of residence.

(Enacted by Acts 1995, 74th Leg., ch. 165 (S.B. 971), § 1, effective September 1, 1995.)

### Sec. 521.028. Effect of Military Service on License Requirement.

(a) Unless the license is suspended, canceled, or revoked as provided by law, a driver's license issued by this state that is held by a person who is on active duty in the armed forces of the United States and is absent from this state, notwithstanding the expiration date of the license, remains valid while the person is absent from this state. If the person is honorably discharged from active duty, the license remains valid until the earlier of:

(1) the 91st day after the date of the discharge; or

(2) the date on which the person returns to this state.

(b) A person on active duty in the armed forces of the United States who has in the person's possession a license issued in a foreign country by the armed forces of the United States may operate a motor vehicle in this state for a period of not more than 90 days after the date on which the person returns to the United States.

(Enacted by Acts 1995, 74th Leg., ch. 165 (S.B. 971), § 1, effective September 1, 1995.)

### Sec. 521.029. Operation of Motor Vehicle by New State Residents.

(a) A person who enters this state as a new resident may operate a motor vehicle in this state for no more than 90 days after the date on which the person enters this state if the person:

(1) is 16 years of age or older; and

(2) has in the person's possession a driver's license issued to the person by the person's state or country of previous residence.

(b) If a person subject to this section is prosecuted for operating a motor vehicle without a driver's license, the prosecution alleges that the person has resided in this state for more than 90 days, and the person claims to have been covered by Subsection (a), the person must prove by the preponderance of the evidence that the person has not resided in this state for more than 90 days.

(Enacted by Acts 1995, 74th Leg., ch. 165 (S.B. 971), § 1, effective September 1, 1995; am. Acts 2009, 81st Leg., ch. 1146 (H.B. 2730), § 13.01, effective June 19, 2009.)

### Sec. 521.030. Reciprocal License.

(a) A nonresident who is 18 years of age or older and who has in the person's possession a license issued to the person by the person's state or country of residence that is similar to a Class A or Class B driver's license issued under this chapter is not required to hold a Class A or Class B driver's license issued under this chapter if that state or country of residence recognizes such a license issued by this state and exempts the holder from securing a license issued by the state or foreign country.

(b) A nonresident who is 16 years of age or older and who has in the person's possession a driver's license issued to the person by the person's state or Canadian province of residence may operate a type of motor vehicle that is permitted to be operated with a Class C or Class M driver's license in this state if the license held by the nonresident permits operation of that type of vehicle in the person's state or province of residence.

(Enacted by Acts 1995, 74th Leg., ch. 165 (S.B. 971), § 1, effective September 1, 1995.)

### Sec. 521.0305. Agreements with Foreign Countries.

(a) The department may enter into an agreement with a foreign country under which:

(1) a person who is 18 years of age or older and who has in the person's possession a license issued to the person by that country that is similar to a Class C driver's license issued under this chapter may receive a Class C driver's license issued in a priority manner under this chapter; and

(2) a person who is 18 years of age or older and who has in the person's possession a Class C driver's license issued under this chapter may receive a license similar to a Class C driver's license issued in a priority manner from the foreign country.

(b) The department may only enter into an agreement with a country under Subsection (a) if:

(1) the foreign country and this state are both parties to a reciprocity agreement in driver licensing; and

(2) the foreign country's motor vehicle laws, ordinances, and administrative rules and regulations are similar to those of this state, as determined by the department.

(c) A person who is not a citizen of the United States must present to the department documentation issued by the United States agency responsible for citizenship and immigration authorizing the person to be in the United States before the person may be issued a driver's license under an agreement under this section.

(Enacted by Acts 2005, 79th Leg., ch. 1228 (H.B. 1137), § 1, effective June 18, 2005.)

### Sec. 521.031.   License from Other Authority.

A person holding a driver's license under this chapter is not required to obtain a license for the operation of a motor vehicle from another state authority or department.

(Enacted by Acts 1995, 74th Leg., ch. 165 (S.B. 971), § 1, effective September 1, 1995.)

### Sec. 521.032.   Enhanced Driver's License or Personal Identification Certificate.

(a) The department may issue an enhanced driver's license or personal identification certificate for the purposes of crossing the border between this state and Mexico to an applicant who provides the department with proof of United States citizenship, identity, and state residency. If the department issues an enhanced driver's license or personal identification certificate, the department shall continue to issue a standard driver's license and personal identification certificate and offer each applicant the option of receiving the standard or enhanced driver's license or personal identification certificate.

(b) The department shall implement a one-to-many biometric matching system for the enhanced driver's license or personal identification certificate. An applicant for an enhanced driver's license or personal identification certificate must submit a biometric identifier as designated by the department, which, notwithstanding any other law, may be used only to verify the identity of the applicant for purposes relating to implementation of the border crossing initiative established by this section. An applicant must sign a declaration acknowledging the applicant's understanding of the one-to-many biometric match.

(c) The enhanced driver's license or personal identification certificate must include reasonable security measures to protect the privacy of the license or certificate holders, including reasonable safeguards to protect against the unautho-

rized disclosure of information about the holders. If the enhanced driver's license or personal identification certificate includes a radio frequency identification chip or similar technology, the department shall ensure that the technology is encrypted or otherwise secure from unauthorized information access.

(d) The requirements of this section are in addition to any other requirements imposed on applicants for a driver's license or personal identification certificate. The department shall adopt rules necessary to implement this section. The department shall periodically review technological innovations related to the security of driver's licenses and personal identification certificates and amend the rules as appropriate, consistent with this section, to protect the privacy of driver's license and personal identification certificate holders.

(e) The department may set a fee for issuance of an enhanced driver's license or personal identification certificate in a reasonable amount necessary to implement and administer this section.

(f) The department may enter into a memorandum of understanding with any federal agency for the purposes of facilitating the crossing of the border between this state and Mexico. The department may enter into an agreement with Mexico, to the extent permitted by federal law, to implement a border crossing initiative authorized by this section. The department shall implement a statewide education campaign to educate residents of this state about the border crossing initiative. The campaign must include information on:

(1) the forms of travel for which the existing and enhanced driver's license and personal identification certificate can be used; and

(2) relevant dates for implementation of laws that affect identification requirements at the border with Mexico.

(g) A person may not sell or otherwise disclose biometric information accessed from an enhanced driver's license or any information from an enhanced driver's license radio frequency identification chip or similar technology to another person or an affiliate of the person. This subsection does not apply to a financial institution described by Section 521.126(e).

(Enacted by Acts 2007, 80th Leg., ch. 258 (S.B. 11), § 21.01, effective September 1, 2007.)

**Secs. 521.033 to 521.040 [Reserved for expansion].**

## SUBCHAPTER C
## DEPARTMENT LICENSE RECORDS

### Sec. 521.041. Application Records; Records of Denial, Suspension, Cancellation, or Revocation.

(a) The department shall record each driver's license application received by the department.

(b) **[2 Versions: Effective until September 28, 2011]** The department shall maintain suitable indexes, in alphabetical or numerical order, that contain:

(1) each denied application and the reasons for the denial;

(2) each application that is granted; and

(3) the name of each license holder whose license has been suspended, canceled, or revoked and the reasons for that action.

(b) **[2 Versions: Effective September 28, 2011]** The department shall maintain suitable indexes, in alphabetical or numerical order, that contain:

(1) each denied application and the reasons for the denial;

(2) each application that is granted;

(3) the name of each license holder whose license has been suspended, canceled, or revoked and the reasons for that action; and

(4) the citizenship status of each holder of a license or personal identification certificate.

(c) The department shall maintain the application records for personal identification certificates in the manner required for license applications under this section.

(Enacted by Acts 1995, 74th Leg., ch. 165 (S.B. 971), § 1, effective September 1, 1995; am. Acts 2011, 82nd Leg., 1st C.S., (S.B. 1), § 72.02, effective September 28, 2011.)

### Sec. 521.042. Accident and Conviction Reports; Individual Records.

(a) Except as provided by this section, the department shall record each accident report and abstract of the court record of a conviction received by the department under a law of this state.

(b) The records must enable the department to consider, on receipt of a renewal application and at other suitable times, the record of each license holder that shows any:

(1) conviction of that license holder; and

(2) traffic accident in which the license holder has been involved.

(c) The record of a license holder who is employed as a peace officer, fire fighter, or emergency medical services employee of this state, a political subdivision of this state, or a special purpose district may not include information relating to a traffic accident that occurs while the peace officer, fire fighter, or emergency medical services employee is driving an official vehicle in the course and scope of the license holder's official duties if:

(1) the traffic accident resulted in damages to property of less than $1,000; or

(2) an investigation of the accident by a peace officer, other than a peace officer involved in the accident, determines that the peace officer, fire fighter, or emergency medical services employee involved in the accident was not at fault.

(d) Before issuing or renewing a license, the department shall examine the record of the applicant for information relating to a conviction of a traffic violation or involvement in a traffic accident. The department may not issue or renew a license if the department determines that the issuance or renewal of the license would be inimical to the public safety.

(e) The director may maintain records required under this subchapter on microfilm or computer.

(Enacted by Acts 1995, 74th Leg., ch. 165 (S.B. 971), § 1, effective September 1, 1995; am. Acts 2011, 82nd Leg., ch. 689 (H.B. 343), § 1, effective September 1, 2011.)

### Sec. 521.043. Elimination of Certain Unnecessary Records.

The department is not required to maintain records relating to a person if the director decides that the records are no longer necessary, except that the department shall maintain a record of a conviction as long as the record may be used:

(1) as grounds for a license cancellation, suspension, revocation, or denial; or

(2) in conjunction with other records of convictions, to establish that a person is a frequent violator of traffic laws.

(Enacted by Acts 1995, 74th Leg., ch. 165 (S.B. 971), § 1, effective September 1, 1995.)

### Sec. 521.044. Use or Disclosure of Social Security Number Information.

(a) Information provided on a driver's license application that relates to the applicant's social security number may be used only by the department or disclosed only to:

(1) the child support enforcement division of the attorney general's office;

(2) another state entity responsible for enforcing the payment of child support;

(3) the United States Selective Service System as provided by Section 521.147; or

(4) the unclaimed property division of the comptroller's office.

(b) The department shall enter an applicant's social security number in the department's electronic database but may not print the number on the applicant's driver's license.

(c) On the request of a state entity responsible for investigating or enforcing the payment of child support, the department shall disclose information regarding an applicant's social security number.

(d) Information disclosed under this section may be used by a state entity responsible for enforcing the payment of child support only to implement the duties of the state entity.

(e) The department shall include in the department's legislative appropriations requests and budgets, in quarterly performance reports, and in audits of the department's local offices performance measures on the percentage of complete and correct social security numbers on driver's licenses.

(f) This section does not prohibit the department from requiring an applicant for a driver's license to provide the applicant's social security number.

(Enacted by Acts 1995, 74th Leg., ch. 165 (S.B. 971), § 1, effective September 1, 1995; am. Acts 1997, 75th Leg., ch. 420 (H.B. 3281), § 28, effective September 1, 1997; am. Acts 1999, 76th Leg., ch. 556 (S.B. 368), § 77(a), effective September 1, 1999; am. Acts 2001, 77th Leg., ch. 973 (H.B. 116), § 1, effective September 1, 2001; am. Acts 2009, 81st Leg., ch. 232 (S.B. 1589), §§ 9, 10, effective September 1, 2009.)

## Sec. 521.0445.  Notice Regarding Suspension of License for Nonpayment of Child Support.

The department shall include in each notice sent to a driver's license holder a statement advising a holder who is delinquent in the payment of child support to make satisfactory arrangements with the office of the attorney general to correct the delinquency and that failure to contact the attorney general or to make satisfac-

tory arrangements may result in the commencement by the attorney general of procedures to suspend the holder's driver's license.

(Enacted by Acts 1997, 75th Leg., ch. 420 (H.B. 3281), § 29, effective September 1, 1997.)

## Sec. 521.045.  Disclosure of Certain Information Relating to Individual Operator.

On receipt of a written request and payment of a $4 fee, the department may disclose information relating to an individual's date of birth, current license status, and most recent address, as shown in the department's records, to a person who:

(1) is eligible to receive the information under Chapter 730; and

(2) submits to the department the individual's driver's license number or the individual's full name and date of birth.

(Enacted by Acts 1995, 74th Leg., ch. 165 (S.B. 971), § 1, effective September 1, 1995; am. Acts 1997, 75th Leg., ch. 1187 (S.B. 1069), § 7, effective September 1, 1997.)

## Sec. 521.046.  Disclosure of Accident and Conviction Information.

(a) In addition to the information authorized to be released under Section 521.045, on receipt of a written request and payment of a $6 fee, the department may disclose that information and information regarding each reported motor vehicle moving violation, as defined by department rule, resulting in a traffic law conviction and each motor vehicle accident in which the individual received a citation, by date and location, within the three years preceding the date of the request, to a person who:

(1) is eligible to receive the information under Chapter 730; and

(2) submits to the department the individual's driver's license number or the individual's full name and date of birth.

(b) If the department receives requests for information under this section in quantities of 100 or more from a single person at one time and on data processing request forms acceptable to the department, the department may reduce the fee to $5 for each individual request.

(Enacted by Acts 1995, 74th Leg., ch. 165 (S.B. 971), § 1, effective September 1, 1995; am. Acts 1997, 75th Leg., ch. 356 (S.B. 1268), § 1, effective September 1, 1997; am. Acts 1997, 75th Leg., ch. 1187 (S.B. 1069), § 8, effective September 1, 1997.)

## Sec. 521.047. Disclosure of Information to License Holder.

(a) The department may disclose information relating to a license holder to that license holder on receipt of a written request that includes the individual's driver's license number or the individual's full name and date of birth, and payment of a $7 fee.

(b) The department may disclose information as recorded in department records that relates to:

(1) the individual's date of birth;

(2) the current license status of the individual;

(3) the individual's most recent address;

(4) the completion of an approved driver education course by the individual;

(5) the fact of, but not the reason for, completion of a driver safety course by the individual; and

(6) each of the individual's reported traffic law violations and motor vehicle accidents, by date and location.

(Enacted by Acts 1995, 74th Leg., ch. 165 (S.B. 971), § 1, effective September 1, 1995.)

## Sec. 521.0475. Disclosure of Abstract Record.

(a) Except as provided by Subsection (b) or (c), the department shall provide a certified abstract of a complete driving record of a license holder, for a fee of $20, to the license holder or a person eligible to receive the information under Sections 730.007(a)(2)(A), (D), and (I).

(b) If an abstract of a complete driving record does not exist for a license holder, the department shall provide a person making a request under Subsection (a) a certified statement to that effect.

(c) If the department provides information under Subsection (a) or (b) through the system described by Section 521.055, the information may not be marked as certified.

(Enacted by Acts 2003, 78th Leg., ch. 991 (S.B. 1904), § 2, effective September 1, 2003.)

## Sec. 521.048. Certified Information.

The department may disclose information under Section 521.046 or 521.047 that is certified by the custodian of records on payment of a $10 fee for each individual request.

(Enacted by Acts 1995, 74th Leg., ch. 165 (S.B. 971), § 1, effective September 1, 1995.)

## Sec. 521.0485. Requests for Information by Mail or Electronic Means.

(a) The department by rule may provide that the holder of a driver's license issued by the department may submit a request for information under Sections 521.045—521.048 by mail, by telephone, over the Internet, or by other electronic means.

(b) A rule adopted under Subsection (a):

(1) may prescribe eligibility standards for release of the requested information; and

(2) may not conflict with any provision of this chapter or another law that relates to the release of the information by the department.

(Enacted by Acts 2001, 77th Leg., ch. 866 (H.B. 1762), § 1, effective September 1, 2001.)

## Sec. 521.049. Information Supplied to Certain Governmental Entities.

(a) The department shall disclose information relating to the name, date of birth, and most recent address as shown in department records to the Texas Department of Health during an emergency or epidemic declared by the commissioner of health to notify individuals of the need to receive certain immunizations.

(b) The department may not charge a fee for information disclosed to a law enforcement agency or other governmental agency for an official purpose, except that the department may charge its regular fees for information provided to those governmental agencies in bulk for research projects.

(c) The department may make information from driver's license record files, including class-type listings, available to an official of the United States, the state, or a political subdivision of this state for government purposes only.

(d) To assist chief appraisers in determining the eligibility of individuals for residence homestead exemptions from ad valorem taxation under Section 11.13, Tax Code, the department shall provide, without charge, to the chief appraiser of each appraisal district in this state:

(1) a copy of each driver's license record or personal identification certificate record held by the department; or

(2) information relating to the name, date of birth, driver's license or personal identification certificate number, and most recent address as shown in the records of individuals included in the department's driver's license or personal identification certificate records.

(e) A driver's license record or personal identification certificate record provided under Subsection (d)(1) may not include information relating to an individual's social security number or any accident or conviction information about an individual.

Transportation

(f) The department shall respond to a request for a driving record check received from another state under 49 C.F.R. Section 384.206 within 30 days of the date of the request.

(Enacted by Acts 1995, 74th Leg., ch. 165 (S.B. 971), § 1, effective September 1, 1995; am. Acts 2007, 80th Leg., ch. 424 (S.B. 1372), § 1, effective January 1, 2008; am. Acts 2007, 80th Leg., ch. 766 (H.B. 3514), § 1, effective June 15, 2007; am. Acts 2009, 81st Leg., ch. 87 (S.B. 1969), § 27.001(104), effective September 1, 2009.)

### Sec. 521.050. Sale of License Information.

(a) In addition to the provisions of this subchapter relating to the disclosure of driver's license information on an individual, the department may provide a purchaser with a magnetic tape of the names, addresses, and dates of birth of all license holders that are contained in the department's basic driver's license record file if the purchaser certifies in writing that the purchaser is eligible to receive the information under Chapter 730.

(b) The department may also periodically provide to the purchaser of the information any addition to that file.

(c) The department shall impose and collect a fee of:

(1) $2,000 for each magnetic tape provided under Subsection (a); and

(2) if the department provides a weekly update of the information on the tape, $75 for each update.

(Enacted by Acts 1995, 74th Leg., ch. 165 (S.B. 971), § 1, effective September 1, 1995; am. Acts 1997, 75th Leg., ch. 1187 (S.B. 1069), § 9, effective September 1, 1997; am. Acts 2001, 77th Leg., ch. 1032 (H.B. 1544), § 2, effective September 1, 2001.)

### Sec. 521.051. Disclosure of Certain Information Prohibited.

The department may not disclose class-type listings from the basic driver's license record file to any person except as provided by Section 521.049(c), regardless of whether the requestor is eligible to receive the information under Chapter 730.

(Enacted by Acts 1995, 74th Leg., ch. 165 (S.B. 971), § 1, effective September 1, 1995; am. Acts 1997, 75th Leg., ch. 1187 (S.B. 1069), § 10, effective September 1, 1997.)

### Sec. 521.052. Disclosure of Individual Information Prohibited.

Except as provided by Sections 521.045, 521.046, 521.0475, 521.049(c), and 521.050, and by Chapter 730, the department may not disclose information from the department's files that relates to personal information, as that term is defined by Section 730.003.

(Enacted by Acts 1995, 74th Leg., ch. 165 (S.B. 971), § 1, effective September 1, 1995; am. Acts 1997, 75th Leg., ch. 1187 (S.B. 1069), § 11, effective September 1, 1997; am. Acts 2001, 77th Leg., ch. 1032 (H.B. 1544), § 3, effective September 1, 2001; am. Acts 2003, 78th Leg., ch. 991 (S.B. 1904), § 3, effective September 1, 2003.)

### Sec. 521.053. Commercial Driver's License Information.

(a) The department may provide to any person the information specified by Section 521.045, 521.046, 521.0475, or 521.047, for the fee required by those sections, that relate to the holder of or applicant for a commercial driver's license under Chapter 522 if the person is eligible to receive the information under Chapter 730.

(b) If the information is provided through the commercial driver license information system, the fee for this service is the fee specified in the applicable section plus $2.

(c) The department may provide information under Subsection (a) through the system described by Section 521.055.

(d) The department may provide information maintained under Section 644.252 that relates to a holder of a commercial driver's license under Chapter 522 to the holder, the holder's current employer, or a person acting on behalf of the employer if the department receives the holder's specific written consent to the release of information.

(Enacted by Acts 1995, 74th Leg., ch. 165 (S.B. 971), § 1, effective September 1, 1995; am. Acts 1997, 75th Leg., ch. 1187 (S.B. 1069), § 12, effective September 1, 1997; am. Acts 2003, 78th Leg., ch. 991 (S.B. 1904), § 4, effective September 1, 2003; am. Acts 2005, 79th Leg., ch. 9 (S.B. 217), § 1, effective September 1, 2005.)

### Sec. 521.054. Notice of Change of Address or Name.

(a) This section applies to a person who:

(1) after applying for or being issued a license or certificate moves to a new residence address;

(2) has used the procedure under Section 521.121(c) and whose status as a federal judge, a state judge, or the spouse of a federal or state judge becomes inapplicable; or

(3) changes the person's name by marriage or otherwise.

(b) A person subject to this section shall notify the department of the change not later than the 30th day after the date on which the change takes effect and apply for a duplicate license or certificate as provided by Section 521.146. The duplicate license must include the person's current residence address.

(c) A person changing the person's address shall notify the department of the old and new addresses and the number of the license or certificate held by the person. A person changing the person's name shall notify the department of the former and new names and the number of the license or certificate held by the person.

(d) A court may dismiss a charge for a violation of this section if the defendant remedies the defect not later than the 20th working day after the date of the offense and pays an administrative fee not to exceed $20. The court may waive the administrative fee if the waiver is in the interest of justice.

(e), (f) [Repealed by Acts 2005, 79th Leg., ch. 1249 (H.B. 1789), § 3(1), effective September 1, 2005.]

(Enacted by Acts 1995, 74th Leg., ch. 165 (S.B. 971), § 1, effective September 1, 1995; am. Acts 2005, 79th Leg., ch. 1249 (H.B. 1789), §§ 1, 3(1), effective September 1, 2005; am. Acts 2007, 80th Leg., ch. 1027 (H.B. 1623), § 6, effective September 1, 2007; am. Acts 2009, 81st Leg., ch. 316 (H.B. 598), § 2, effective September 1, 2009; am. Acts 2009, 81st Leg., ch. 1146 (H.B. 2730), § 13A.02, effective September 1, 2009; am. Acts 2011, 82nd Leg., ch. 91 (S.B. 1303), § 24.008, effective September 1, 2011.)

### Sec. 521.055. Establishment of Interactive System.

(a) The department may establish a system, separate from the department's mainframe computer, that will allow interactive access to certain driver's license record information.

(b) The system may provide for the release of driving records described in:

(1) Section 521.045;

(2) Section 521.046;

(3) Section 521.047; and

(4) Section 521.0475.

(c) The fee for a driving record under Subsection (b)(1) is $2.50. The fee for a driving record under Subsection (b)(2) is $4.50. The fee for a driving record under Subsection (b)(3) is $5.50. The fee for a driving record under Subsection (b)(4) is $20.

(d) [Repealed by Acts 2003, 78th Leg., ch. 1325 (H.B. 3588), § 11.10, effective September 1, 2003.]

(e) The department may contract with private vendors as necessary to implement this section.

(f) The department may adopt rules as necessary to administer this section.

(g) For purposes of this section, a release of information to persons eligible to receive the information under Chapter 730 occurs each time a query is made of the system.

(Enacted by Acts 1997, 75th Leg., ch. 1365 (H.B. 972), § 1, effective June 20, 1997; am. Acts 2001, 77th Leg., ch. 1032 (H.B. 1544), § 4, effective September 1, 2001; am. Acts 2003, 78th Leg., ch. 991 (S.B. 1904), § 5, effective September 1, 2003; am. Acts 2003, 78th Leg., ch. 1325 (H.B. 3588), § 11.10, effective September 1, 2003.)

### Sec. 521.056. National Driver Register.

(a) The department may process file check requests under the National Driver Register on behalf of current or prospective employers of individuals employed or seeking employment as operators of motor vehicles or railway locomotive operators if the individual:

(1) has given written consent to the release of the information; and

(2) has a license in this state.

(b) The fee for a request under Subsection (a) is $4.

(c) The department shall forward a request made under Subsection (a) directly to the current or prospective employer.

(d) The department shall assist and provide procedures for an individual to obtain information from the National Driver Register on the individual's own driving record. The department may by rule establish a reasonable fee for this service, in conformity with the policies of the National Driver Register.

(e) The department may adopt forms and rules as necessary to carry out the purposes of this section and comply with the policies of the National Driver Register.

(Enacted by Acts 1997, 75th Leg., ch. 1365 (H.B. 972), § 1, effective June 20, 1997.)

Transportation

### Sec. 521.057. Information Regarding Certain Sex Offenders.

(a) On receipt of a court order issued under Article 42.016, Code of Criminal Procedure, the department shall ensure that any driver's license record or personal identification certificate record maintained by the department for the person includes an indication that the person is subject to the registration requirements of Chapter 62, Code of Criminal Procedure, as added by Chapter 668, Acts of the 75th Legislature, Regular Session, 1997.

(b) The department shall include the indication required by Subsection (a) in any driver's license record or personal identification certificate record maintained by the department for the person until the expiration of the person's duty to register under Chapter 62, Code of Criminal Procedure, as added by Chapter 668, Acts of the 75th Legislature, Regular Session, 1997.

(Enacted by Acts 1999, 76th Leg., ch. 1401 (H.B. 1939), § 4, effective September 1, 2000.)

### Sec. 521.058. Disposition of Fees.

Each fee collected under this subchapter shall be deposited to the credit of the Texas mobility fund.

(Enacted by Acts 2003, 78th Leg., ch. 1325 (H.B. 3588), § 11.01, effective September 1, 2003.)

### Sec. 521.059. Image Verification System.

(a) The department shall establish an image verification system based on the following identifiers collected by the department:

(1) an applicant's facial image; and

(2) an applicant's thumbprints or fingerprints.

(b) The department shall authenticate the facial image and thumbprints or fingerprints provided by an applicant for a personal identification certificate, driver's license, or commercial driver's license or permit using image comparison technology to ensure that the applicant:

(1) is issued only one original license, permit, or certificate;

(2) does not fraudulently obtain a duplicate license, permit, or certificate; and

(3) does not commit other fraud in connection with the application for a license, permit, or certificate.

(c) The department shall use the image verification system established under this section only to the extent allowed by Chapter 730, Transportation Code, to aid other law enforcement agencies in:

(1) establishing the identity of a victim of a disaster or crime that a local law enforcement agency is unable to establish; or

(2) conducting an investigation of criminal conduct.

(d) [Expired pursuant to Acts 2005, 79th Leg., ch. 1108 (H.B. 2337), § 4, effective September 1, 2010.]

(Enacted by Acts 2005, 79th Leg., ch. 1108 (H.B. 2337), § 4, effective September 1, 2005.)

### Sec. 521.060. Emergency Contact and Medical Information Databases.

(a) The department shall maintain in its files a record of the name, address, and telephone number of each individual identified by the holder of a driver's license or personal identification certificate as an individual the holder authorizes to be contacted in the event that the holder is injured or dies in or as a result of a vehicular accident or another emergency situation. In addition, the department shall maintain in its files a record of any medical information described by Section 521.125(a) that is provided to the department under Subsection (c) or any health condition information that is voluntarily provided to the department under Section 521.142(h).

(b) A record maintained by the department under Subsection (a) is confidential and, on request, may be disclosed:

(1) only to a peace officer in this or another state;

(2) only if the peace officer is otherwise authorized to obtain information in the driver's license or personal identification certificate files of the department; and

(3) only for the purpose, as applicable, of making contact with a named individual to report the injury to or death of the holder of the driver's license or personal identification certificate, learning the nature of any medical information reported by the person who holds the driver's license or identification certificate, or learning whether the person who holds the driver's license or identification certificate has a health condition that may impede communications with the peace officer.

(c) An application for an original, renewal, or duplicate driver's license or personal identification certificate must:

(1) be designed to allow, but not require, the applicant to provide:

(A) the name, address, and telephone number of not more than two individuals to be contacted if the applicant is injured or dies in a circumstance described by Subsection (a); and

(B) in addition to health condition information voluntarily provided under Section 521.142(h), medical information described by Section 521.125(a); and

(2) include a statement that:

(A) describes the confidential nature of the information; and

(B) states that by providing the department with the information, the applicant consents to the limited disclosure and use of the information.

(d) The department shall establish and maintain on the department's Internet website forms and procedures by which the holder of a driver's license or personal identification certificate may request that the department:

(1) add specific emergency contact or medical information described by Subsection (a) to the appropriate file maintained by the department; or

(2) amend or delete emergency contact or medical information the holder previously provided to the department.

(e) The forms and procedures maintained under Subsection (d) must comply with Subsection (c).

(f) Subsection (b) does not prohibit the department from disclosing information to the holder of a driver's license or personal identification certificate who provided the information or to an authorized agent of the holder.

(Enacted by Acts 2009, 81st Leg., ch. 1362 (S.B. 652), § 1, effective September 1, 2009.)

## Sec. 521.061. Internal Verification System.

(a) The department by rule shall establish a system for identifying unique addresses that are submitted in license or certificate applications under this chapter or Chapter 522 in a frequency or number that, in the department's determination, casts doubt on whether the addresses are the actual addresses where the applicants reside.

(b) The department may contract with a third-party personal data verification service to assist the department in implementing this section.

(c) The department shall investigate the validity of addresses identified under Subsection (a).

(d) The department may disclose the results of an investigation under Subsection (c) to a criminal justice agency for the purposes of enforcing Section 521.4565 or other provisions of this chapter or Chapter 522.

(e) In this section, "criminal justice agency" has the meaning assigned by Article 60.01, Code of Criminal Procedure.

(Enacted by Acts 2009, 81st Leg., ch. 1146 (H.B. 2730), § 13.02, effective June 19, 2009; am. Acts 2011, 82nd Leg., ch. 91 (S.B. 1303), § 27.001(62), effective September 1, 2011 (renumbered from Sec. 521.060).)

## Sec. 521.062. Driver Record Monitoring Pilot Program.

(a) The department by rule may establish a driver record monitoring pilot program. The term of the pilot program may not exceed one year.

(b) Under the pilot program, the department may enter into a contract with a person to provide driver record monitoring services, as described by Subsection (c), and certain information from the department's driver's license records to the person, if the person:

(1) is an employer, an insurer, an insurance support organization, an employer support organization, or an entity that self-insures its motor vehicles; and

(2) is eligible to receive the information under Chapter 730.

(c) A contract entered into by the department must require:

(1) the department, during the term of the contract, to:

(A) monitor the driver record of each holder of a driver's license issued by the department that is requested by the person with whom the department has contracted;

(B) identify any change in the status of a driver's license or any conviction for a traffic offense reported to the department during the monitoring period; and

(C) periodically, as specified in the contract, provide reports of those individuals identified as having a change in status or convictions to the person with whom the department has contracted; and

(2) the person with whom the department has contracted:

(A) to purchase under Section 521.046 a copy of the driver record of each individual identified in a report provided under Subdivision (1)(C);

(B) to warrant that:

(i) the person will not directly or indirectly disclose information received from

*Transportation*

the department under the contract to a third party without the express written consent of the department, except as required by law or legal process; and

(ii) if a disclosure is required by law or legal process, the person will immediately notify the department so that the department may seek to oppose, limit, or restrict the required disclosure; and

(C) if the person is an insurance support organization, to warrant that the person will not seek to obtain information about a holder of a driver's license under the contract unless the license holder is insured by a client of the organization, and that the person will provide the department with the name of each client to whom the insurance support organization provides information received from the department under the contract.

(d) The attorney general may file a suit against a person with whom the department has contracted under this section for:

(1) injunctive relief to prevent or restrain the person from violating a term of the contract or from directly or indirectly disclosing information received from the department under the contract in a manner that violates the terms of the contract; or

(2) a civil penalty in an amount not to exceed $2,000 for each disclosure in violation of those terms.

(e) If the attorney general brings an action against a person under Subsection (d) and an injunction is granted against the person or the person is found liable for a civil penalty, the attorney general may recover reasonable expenses, court costs, investigative costs, and attorney's fees. Each day a violation continues or occurs is a separate violation for purposes of imposing a penalty under Subsection (d).

(f) A violation of the terms of a contract entered into with the department by the person with whom the department has contracted is a false, misleading, or deceptive act or practice under Subchapter E, Chapter 17, Business & Commerce Code.

(g) A civil action brought under this section shall be filed in a district court:

(1) in Travis County; or

(2) in any county in which the violation occurred.

(h) A person with whom the department has contracted under this section commits an offense if the person directly or indirectly discloses information received from the department under the

contract in a manner that violates the terms of the contract. An offense under this subsection is a Class B misdemeanor. If conduct constituting an offense under this subsection also constitutes an offense under another law, the actor may be prosecuted under this subsection, the other law, or both.

(i) The department shall impose a fee on each person with whom the department contracts under this section for the services provided by the department under the contract. The fee must be reasonable and be not less than the amount necessary to allow the department to recover all reasonable costs to the department associated with entering into the contract and providing services to the person under the contract, including direct, indirect, and administrative costs and costs related to the development and deployment of the pilot program.

(j) The department may establish a reasonable deadline by which a person must apply to enter into a contract with the department under this section and may not enter into a contract with a person who fails to apply before that deadline.

(k) To the fullest extent practicable, the services of the department under a contract entered into under this section shall be provided by, through, or in conjunction with the interactive system established under Section 521.055.

(*l*) At the conclusion of the term of the pilot program, and on the recommendation of the department, the commission may authorize the department to implement the pilot program as a permanent program.

(m) Before the department recommends that the pilot program be implemented as a permanent program, the department shall submit to the lieutenant governor, the speaker of the house of representatives, and each member of the legislature a report that contains an analysis of the scope, effectiveness, and cost benefits of the pilot program. The report must include:

(1) a list of each insurance support organization with which the department has contracted under this section; and

(2) a list of each client to whom the insurance support organization has provided information received from the department under this section.

(Enacted by Acts 2009, 81st Leg., ch. 1146 (H.B. 2730), § 6.07, effective September 1, 2009; am. Acts 2011, 82nd Leg., ch. 91 (S.B. 1303), § 27.001(63), effective September 1, 2011 (renumbered from Sec. 521.060).)

### Sec. 521.063. Mailing Address Verification System.

The department by rule shall establish a system to ensure that addresses of driver's license holders are verified and matched to United States Postal Service delivery addresses by use of address-matching software. The software must meet certification standards under the Coding Accuracy Support System adopted by the United States Postal Service or a subsequent standard adopted by the United States Postal Service to replace Coding Accuracy Support System standards for preparation of bulk mailings. If the department contracts with a provider for bulk mailing services, the contract must require that the provider use address-matching software that meets or exceeds certification standards under the Coding Accuracy Support System or subsequent standards adopted by the United States Postal Service.

(Enacted by Acts 2011, 82nd Leg., ch. 468 (H.B. 266), § 2, effective September 1, 2011.)

### Secs. 521.064 to 521.080 [Reserved for expansion].

## SUBCHAPTER D
## CLASSIFICATION OF DRIVER'S LICENSES

### Sec. 521.081. Class A License.

A Class A driver's license authorizes the holder of the license to operate:

(1) a vehicle with a gross vehicle weight rating of 26,001 pounds or more; or

(2) a combination of vehicles that has a gross combination weight rating of 26,001 pounds or more, if the gross vehicle weight rating of any vehicle or vehicles in tow is more than 10,000 pounds.

(Enacted by Acts 1995, 74th Leg., ch. 165 (S.B. 971), § 1, effective September 1, 1995.)

### Sec. 521.082. Class B License.

(a) A Class B driver's license authorizes the holder of the license to operate:

(1) a vehicle with a gross vehicle weight rating that is more than 26,000 pounds;

(2) a vehicle with a gross vehicle weight rating of 26,000 pounds or more towing:

(A) a vehicle, other than a farm trailer, with a gross vehicle weight rating that is not more than 10,000 pounds; or

(B) a farm trailer with a gross vehicle weight rating that is not more than 20,000 pounds; and

(3) a bus with a seating capacity of 24 passengers or more.

(b) For the purposes of Subsection (a)(3), seating capacity is computed in accordance with Section 502.162, except that the operator's seat is included in the computation.

(Enacted by Acts 1995, 74th Leg., ch. 165 (S.B. 971), § 1, effective September 1, 1995.)

### Sec. 521.083. Class C License.

A Class C driver's license authorizes the holder of the license to operate:

(1) a vehicle or combination of vehicles not described by Section 521.081 or 521.082; and

(2) a vehicle with a gross vehicle weight rating of less than 26,001 pounds towing a farm trailer with a gross vehicle weight rating that is not more than 20,000 pounds.

(Enacted by Acts 1995, 74th Leg., ch. 165 (S.B. 971), § 1, effective September 1, 1995.)

### Sec. 521.084. Class M License.

A Class M driver's license authorizes the holder of the license to operate a motorcycle or moped.

(Enacted by Acts 1995, 74th Leg., ch. 165 (S.B. 971), § 1, effective September 1, 1995.)

### Sec. 521.085. Type of Vehicle Authorized.

(a) Unless prohibited by Chapter 522, and except as provided by Subsection (b), the license holder may operate any vehicle of the type for which that class of license is issued and any lesser type of vehicle other than a motorcycle or moped.

(b) Subsection (a) does not prohibit a license holder from operating a lesser type of vehicle that is a motorcycle described by Section 521.001(a)(6-a).

(Enacted by Acts 1995, 74th Leg., ch. 165 (S.B. 971), § 1, effective September 1, 1995; am. Acts 2009, 81st Leg., ch. 722 (S.B. 129), § 4, effective September 1, 2009; am. Acts 2009, 81st Leg., ch. 967 (H.B. 3599), § 2, effective September 1, 2009; am. Acts 2009, 81st Leg., ch. 1391 (S.B. 1967), § 3, effective September 1, 2009.)

Transportation

**Secs. 521.086 to 521.100 [Reserved for expansion].**

## SUBCHAPTER E
## CLASSIFICATION OF CERTIFICATES

### Sec. 521.101.  Personal Identification Certificate.

(a) The department shall issue personal identification certificates.

(b) A personal identification certificate must be similar in form to, but distinguishable in color from, a driver's license.

(c) The department shall indicate "UNDER 21" on the face of a personal identification certificate issued to a person under 21 years of age.

(d) The department may require each applicant for an original, renewal, or duplicate personal identification certificate to furnish to the department the information required by Section 521.142.

(d-1) **[Effective September 28, 2011]** Unless the information has been previously provided to the department, the department shall require each applicant for an original, renewal, or duplicate personal identification certificate to furnish to the department:

(1) proof of the applicant's United States citizenship; or

(2) documentation described by Subsection (f-2).

(e) The department may cancel and require surrender of a personal identification certificate after determining that the holder was not entitled to the certificate or gave incorrect or incomplete information in the application for the certificate.

(f) **[2 Versions: Effective until September 28, 2011]** A certificate expires on a date specified by the department, except that a certificate issued to a person 60 years of age or older does not expire.

(f) **[2 Versions: Effective September 28, 2011]** A personal identification certificate:

(1) for an applicant who is a citizen, national, or legal permanent resident of the United States or a refugee or asylee lawfully admitted into the United States:

(A) expires on a date specified by the department if the applicant is younger than 60 years of age; or

(B) does not expire if the applicant is 60 years of age or older; or

(2) for an applicant not described by Subdivision (1), expires on:

(A) the earlier of:

(i) a date specified by the department; or

(ii) the expiration date of the applicant's authorized stay in the United States; or

(B) the first anniversary of the date of issuance, if there is no definite expiration date for the applicant's authorized stay in the United States.

(f-1) A personal identification certificate issued to a person whose residence or domicile is a correctional facility or a parole facility expires on the first birthday of the license holder occurring after the first anniversary of the date of issuance.

(f-2) **[Effective September 28, 2011]** An applicant who is not a citizen of the United States must present to the department documentation issued by the appropriate United States agency that authorizes the applicant to be in the United States.

(f-3) **[Effective September 28, 2011]** The department may not issue a personal identification certificate to an applicant who fails or refuses to comply with Subsection (f-2).

(f-4) **[Effective September 28, 2011]** The department may not deny a personal identification certificate to an applicant who complies with Subsection (f-2) based on the duration of the person's authorized stay in the United States, as indicated by the documentation presented under Subsection (f-2).

(g) An individual, corporation, or association may not deny the holder of a personal identification certificate access to goods, services, or facilities, except as provided by Section 521.460 or in regard to the operation of a motor vehicle, because the holder has a personal identification certificate rather than a driver's license.

(h) The department shall automatically revoke each personal identification certificate issued by the department to a person who:

(1) is subject to the registration requirements of Chapter 62, Code of Criminal Procedure; and

(2) fails to apply to the department for renewal of the personal identification certificate as required by Article 62.060, Code of Criminal Procedure.

(i) The department may issue a personal identification certificate to a person whose certificate is revoked under Subsection (h) only if the person applies for an original or renewal certificate under Section 521.103.

(j) The department may not issue a personal identification certificate to a person who has not established a domicile in this state.

(k) **[Effective September 28, 2011]** Except as provided by this section, a personal identification certificate issued under this chapter:

(1) must:

(A) be in the same format;

(B) have the same appearance and orientation; and

(C) contain the same type of information; and

(2) may not include any information that this chapter does not reference or require.

(Enacted by Acts 1995, 74th Leg., ch. 165 (S.B. 971), § 1, effective September 1, 1995; am. Acts 1997, 75th Leg., ch. 165 (S.B. 898), § 30.75(a), effective September 1, 1997; am. Acts 1997, 75th Leg., ch. 1372 (H.B. 1200), § 1, effective September 1, 1997; am. Acts 1999, 76th Leg., ch. 1401 (H.B. 1939), § 5, effective September 1, 2000; am. Acts 2005, 79th Leg., ch. 1008 (H.B. 867), § 2.12, effective September 1, 2005; am. Acts 2009, 81st Leg., ch. 1146 (H.B. 2730), § 13.03, effective June 19, 2009; am. Acts 2009, 81st Leg., ch. 1288 (H.B. 2161), § 4, effective September 1, 2009; am. Acts 2011, 82nd Leg., 1st C.S., (S.B. 1), § 72.03, effective September 28, 2011.)

### Sec. 521.102. Disability or Health Condition Certificate [Repealed].

Repealed by Acts 2005, 79th Leg., ch. 1249 (H.B. 1789), § 3(2), effective September 1, 2005. (Enacted by Acts 1995, 74th Leg., ch. 165 (S.B. 971), § 1, effective September 1, 1995.)

### Sec. 521.103. Expiration and Renewal Requirements for Certain Sex Offenders.

(a) The department may issue an original or renewal personal identification certificate to a person whose driver's license or personal identification certificate record indicates that the person is subject to the registration requirements of Chapter 62, Code of Criminal Procedure, only if the person:

(1) applies in person for the issuance of a certificate under this section; and

(2) pays a fee of $20.

(b) A personal identification certificate issued under this section, including a renewal, duplicate, or corrected certificate, expires on the first birthday of the certificate holder occurring after the date of application, except that the initial certificate issued under this section expires on the second birthday of the certificate holder occurring after the date of application.

(c) **[Effective September 28, 2011]** Sections 521.101(f-2), (f-3), and (f-4) apply to a personal identification certificate for which application is made under this section.

(Enacted by Acts 1999, 76th Leg., ch. 1401 (H.B. 1939), § 6, effective September 1, 2000; am. Acts 2005, 79th Leg., ch. 1008 (H.B. 867), § 2.13, effective September 1, 2005; am. Acts 2011, 82nd Leg., 1st C.S., (S.B. 1), § 72.04, effective September 28, 2011.)

### Sec. 521.104. Renewal by Mail or Electronic Means.

The department by rule may provide that the holder of a personal identification certificate may renew the certificate by mail, by telephone, over the Internet, or by other electronic means. A rule adopted under this section may prescribe eligibility standards for renewal under this section.

(Enacted by Acts 1999, 76th Leg., ch. 1189 (S.B. 370), § 19, effective September 1, 1999; am. Acts 2001, 77th Leg., ch. 1420 (H.B. 2812), § 21.001(109), effective September 1, 2001 (renumbered from Sec. 521.103).)

### Secs. 521.105 to 521.120 [Reserved for expansion].

### *SUBCHAPTER F*
### *APPEARANCE OF DRIVER'S LICENSE*

### Sec. 521.121. General Information on Driver's License.

(a) The driver's license must include:

(1) a distinguishing number assigned by the department to the license holder;

(2) a color photograph of the entire face of the holder;

(3) the full name and date of birth of the holder;

(4) a brief description of the holder; and

(5) the license holder's residence address or, for a license holder using the procedure under Subsection (c), the street address of the courthouse in which the license holder or license holder's spouse serves as a federal judge or state judge.

(b) The driver's license must include a facsimile of the license holder's signature or a space on which the holder shall write the holder's usual signature in ink immediately on receipt of the license. A license is not valid until it complies with this subsection.

(c) The department shall establish a procedure for a federal judge, a state judge, or the spouse of a federal or state judge to omit the license holder's residence address on the license and to include, in lieu of that address, the street address of the courthouse in which the license holder or license holder's spouse serves as a federal judge or state judge. In establishing the procedure, the department shall require sufficient documentary evidence to establish the license holder's status as a federal judge, a state judge, or the spouse of a federal or state judge.

(d) [Repealed by Acts 2011, 82nd Leg., ch. 91 (S.B. 1303), § 24.010, effective September 1, 2011.]

(e) **[Effective September 28, 2011]** Except as provided by this section, a driver's license issued under this chapter:

(1) must:

(A) be in the same format;

(B) have the same appearance and orientation; and

(C) contain the same type of information; and

(2) may not include any information that this chapter does not reference or require.

(Enacted by Acts 1995, 74th Leg., ch. 165 (S.B. 971), § 1, effective September 1, 1995; am. Acts 2001, 77th Leg., ch. 448 (S.B. 1213), § 1, effective September 1, 2001; am. Acts 2009, 81st Leg., ch. 316 (H.B. 598), § 3, effective September 1, 2009; am. Acts 2009, 81st Leg., ch. 1146 (H.B. 2730), § 13A.03, effective September 1, 2009; am. Acts 2011, 82nd Leg., ch. 91 (S.B. 1303), §§ 24.009, 24.010, effective September 1, 2011; am. Acts 2011, 82nd Leg., 1st C.S., (S.B. 1), § 72.05, effective September 28, 2011.)

## Sec. 521.1211.   Driver's License for Peace Officer.

(a) In this section, "peace officer" has the meaning assigned by Article 2.12, Code of Criminal Procedure.

(b) Notwithstanding Section 521.121(a), the department by rule shall adopt procedures for the issuance of a driver's license to a peace officer that omits the license holder's actual residence address and includes, as an alternative, an address that is in the municipality or county of the peace officer's residence and is acceptable to the department.

(c) To be issued a driver's license under this section, a peace officer must apply to the department and provide sufficient evidence acceptable to the department to establish the applicant's status as a peace officer. On issuance of the license, the license holder shall surrender any other driver's license issued to the holder by the department.

(d) If the holder of a driver's license that includes an alternative address moves to a new residence or if the name of the person is changed by marriage or otherwise, the license holder shall, not later than the 30th day after the date of the address or name change, notify the department and provide the department with the number of the person's driver's license and, as applicable, the person's:

(1) former and new addresses; or

(2) former and new names.

(e) If the holder of a driver's license that includes an alternative address ceases to be a peace officer, the license holder shall, not later than the 30th day after the date of the status change, apply to the department for issuance of a duplicate license. The duplicate license must include the person's actual current residence address.

(Acts 2011, 82nd Leg., ch. 441 (S.B. 1292), § 1, effective September 1, 2011.)

## Sec. 521.122.   Type of Vehicle Required to Be Indicated on License.

(a) The department shall show on each driver's license the general type of vehicle that the license holder is authorized to operate.

(b) The department may include on the driver's license an authorization to operate a motorcycle or moped if the license holder has met all requirements for a Class M license.

(Enacted by Acts 1995, 74th Leg., ch. 165 (S.B. 971), § 1, effective September 1, 1995.)

## Sec. 521.123.   Designator on License Issued to Person Under 21 Years of Age.

The department shall:

(1) designate and clearly mark as a provisional license each original driver's license issued by the department to a person who is under 18 years of age; and

(2) for each original, renewed, or duplicate license issued to a person who is under 21 years of age:

(A) indicate "UNDER 21" on the face of the license; and

(B) orient the information on the license to clearly distinguish the license from a license that is issued to a person who is 21 years of age or older.

(Enacted by Acts 1995, 74th Leg., ch. 165 (S.B. 971), § 1, effective September 1, 1995; am. Acts 2001, 77th Leg., ch. 448 (S.B. 1213), § 2, effective September 1, 2001.)

## Sec. 521.1235. Designator on License Issued to Veteran.

(a) In this section, "veteran" means a person who:

   (1) has served in:

      (A) the army, navy, air force, coast guard, or marine corps of the United States; or

      (B) the Texas National Guard as defined by Section 431.001, Government Code; and

   (2) has been honorably discharged from the branch of the service in which the person served.

(b) The department shall include the designation "VETERAN" on a driver's license issued to a veteran in an available space either on the face of the driver's license or on the reverse side of the driver's license if:

   (1) the veteran requests the designation; and

   (2) the veteran provides proof of the veteran's military service and honorable discharge.

(Enacted by Acts 2011, 82nd Leg., ch. 273 (H.B. 1514), § 1, effective September 1, 2011.)

## Sec. 521.124. Temporary License; Issued Without Photograph.

(a) The department may issue a temporary license without a photograph of the license holder:

   (1) to an applicant who is out of state or a member of the armed forces of the United States; or

   (2) if the department otherwise determines that a temporary license is necessary.

(b) A temporary license is valid only until the applicant has time to appear and be photographed and a license with a photograph is issued.

(Enacted by Acts 1995, 74th Leg., ch. 165 (S.B. 971), § 1, effective September 1, 1995.)

## Sec. 521.125. Medical and Emergency Information on License.

(a) On the reverse side of a driver's license, the department shall:

   (1) print:

      (A) "Allergic Reaction to Drugs: _____";

      (B) "Directive to physician has been filed at tel. #";

      (C) "Emergency contact tel. #"; and

      (D) if space allows, any medical information provided by the license holder under Section 521.142(h);

   (2) include to the right of the statements under Subdivisions (1)(B) and (C) a surface on which the license holder may write the appropriate telephone number; and

   (3) include to the left of each of the statements under Subdivisions (1)(B) and (C) a box that the license holder may use to indicate for what purpose the telephone number applies.

(b) In addition to the requirements of Subsection (a)(1)(D), if space allows, the department shall indicate any medical information by a uniform symbol or code on the face of the license in the space where the department indicates a restriction or endorsement.

(Enacted by Acts 1995, 74th Leg., ch. 165 (S.B. 971), § 1, effective September 1, 1995; am. Acts 1999, 76th Leg., ch. 1189 (S.B. 370), § 20, effective September 1, 1999; am. Acts 2003, 78th Leg., ch. 1335 (H.B. 1330), § 1, effective January 1, 2004.)

## Sec. 521.126. Electronically Readable Information.

(a) The department may not include any information on a driver's license, commercial driver's license, or personal identification certificate in an electronically readable form other than the information printed on the license and a physical description of the licensee.

(b) Except as provided by Subsections (d), (e), (g), (i), and (j), a person commits an offense if the person:

   (1) accesses or uses electronically readable information derived from a driver's license, commercial driver's license, or personal identification certificate; or

   (2) compiles or maintains a database of electronically readable information derived from driver's licenses, commercial driver's licenses, or personal identification certificates.

(c) An offense under Subsection (b) is a Class A misdemeanor.

(d) The prohibition provided by Subsection (b) does not apply to a person who accesses, uses, compiles, or maintains a database of the information for a law enforcement or governmental purpose, including:

   (1) an officer or employee of the department carrying out law enforcement or government purposes;

*Transportation*

(2) a peace officer, as defined by Article 2.12, Code of Criminal Procedure, acting in the officer's official capacity;

(3) a license deputy, as defined by Section 12.702, Parks and Wildlife Code, issuing a license, stamp, tag, permit, or other similar item through use of a point-of-sale system under Section 12.703, Parks and Wildlife Code;

(4) a person acting as authorized by Section 109.61, Alcoholic Beverage Code;

(5) a person establishing the identity of a voter under Chapter 63, Election Code;

(6) a person acting as authorized by Section 161.0825, Health and Safety Code; or

(7) a person screening an individual who will work with or have access to children if the person is an employee or an agent of an employee of a public school district or an organization exempt from federal income tax under Section 501(c)(3), Internal Revenue Code of 1986, as amended, that sponsors a program for youth.

(e) The prohibition provided by Subsection (b)(1) does not apply to a financial institution or a business if the information is accessed and used only for purposes of identification verification of an individual or check verification at the point of sale for a purchase of a good or service by check. The prohibition provided by Subsection (b)(2) does not apply to a financial institution if each license or certificate holder whose information is included in the compilation or database consents to the inclusion of the person's information in the compilation or database. Consent under this subsection must be on a separate document, signed by the license or certificate holder, that explains in at least 14-point bold type the information that will be included in the compilation or database. For the purposes of this subsection, "financial institution" has the meaning assigned by 31 U.S.C. Section 5312(a)(2), as amended.

(f) A person may not use information derived from electronically readable information from a driver's license, commercial driver's license, or personal identification certificate to engage in telephone solicitation to encourage the purchase or rental of, or investment in, goods, other property, or services.

(g) If authorized by the executive or administrative head of a maritime facility as defined in the Maritime Transportation Security Act of 2002 (46 U.S.C. Section 70101 et seq.), or of a port, port authority, or navigation district created or operating under Section 52, Article III, or Section 59, Article XVI, Texas Constitution, a person may access, use, compile, or maintain in a database electronically readable information derived from a driver's license, commercial driver's license, or personal identification certificate to secure the facility or port. The information may be used only to:

(1) identify an individual;

(2) provide official credentials for an individual;

(3) track or limit the movement of an individual on facility property;

(4) establish a secure database of visitors to the facility;

(5) access the information at terminal and gate operations of the facility; or

(6) conduct other security or operational activities as determined by the executive or administrative head.

(h) Except as provided by Section 418.183, Government Code, the electronically readable information derived from a driver's license, commercial driver's license, or personal identification certificate for the purposes of Subsection (g) is confidential and not subject to disclosure, inspection, or copying under Chapter 552, Government Code.

(i) The prohibition provided by Subsection (b) does not apply to a hospital that accesses, uses, compiles, or maintains a database of the information to provide health care services to the individual who holds the driver's license, commercial driver's license, or personal identification certificate.

(j) Except as otherwise provided by this subsection, a hospital may not sell, transfer, or otherwise disseminate the information described by Subsection (i) to a third party for any purpose, including any marketing, advertising, or promotional activities. A hospital that obtains information described by Subsection (i) may transfer the information only in accordance with the rules implementing the federal Health Insurance Portability and Accountability Act of 1996 (Pub. L. No. 104-191). A business associate, and any subcontractor of the business associate who receives the transferred information, may use the information only to service or maintain the hospital's database of the information.

(k) If an individual objects to the hospital collecting the individual's information from the individual's driver's license as described by Subsection (i), the hospital must use an alternative method for collecting the individual's information.

(Enacted by Acts 1999, 76th Leg., ch. 1340 (H.B. 571), § 1, effective September 1, 1999; am. Acts 2003, 78th Leg., ch. 1233 (S.B. 1445), § 1, effective September 1, 2003; am. Acts 2005, 79th Leg., ch. 250 (H.B. 1009), § 1, effective May 30, 2005; am. Acts 2005, 79th Leg., ch. 391 (S.B. 1465), § 2, effective September 1, 2005; am. Acts 2005, 79th Leg., ch. 1189 (H.B. 178), § 2, effective September 1, 2005; am. Acts 2007, 80th Leg., ch. 102 (H.B. 320), § 1, effective September 1, 2007; am. Acts 2007, 80th Leg., ch. 533 (S.B. 955), § 1, effective June 16, 2007; am. Acts 2007, 80th Leg., ch. 1012 (H.B. 1060), § 1, effective September 1, 2007.)

**Secs. 521.127 to 521.140 [Reserved for expansion].**

## SUBCHAPTER G
## LICENSE APPLICATION
## REQUIREMENTS

### Sec. 521.141. General Application Requirements.

(a) An applicant for an original or renewal of a driver's license must apply in a manner prescribed by the department.

(b) An application for an original license must be verified by the applicant before a person authorized to administer oaths. An officer or employee of the department may administer the oath. An officer or employee of this state may not charge for the administration of the oath.

(c) The application must be accompanied by the required fee and must be submitted to the department before the department may administer an examination.

(Enacted by Acts 1995, 74th Leg., ch. 165 (S.B. 971), § 1, effective September 1, 1995; am. Acts 1999, 76th Leg., ch. 1189 (S.B. 370), § 21, effective September 1, 1999.)

### Sec. 521.142. Application for Original License.

(a) **[2 Versions: Effective until September 28, 2011]** An application for an original license must state the applicant's full name and place and date of birth. This information must be verified by presentation of proof of identity satisfactory to the department. An applicant who is not a citizen of the United States must present to the department documentation issued by the appropriate United States agency that authorizes the applicant to be in the United States before the

applicant may be issued a driver's license. The department must accept as satisfactory proof of identity under this subsection an offender identification card or similar form of identification issued to an inmate by the Texas Department of Criminal Justice if the applicant also provides supplemental verifiable records or documents that aid in establishing identity.

(a) **[2 Versions: Effective September 28, 2011]** An application for an original license must state the applicant's full name and place and date of birth. This information must be verified by presentation of proof of identity satisfactory to the department. An applicant who is not a citizen of the United States must present to the department documentation issued by the appropriate United States agency that authorizes the applicant to be in the United States before the applicant may be issued a driver's license. The department must accept as satisfactory proof of identity under this subsection an offender identification card or similar form of identification issued to an inmate by the Texas Department of Criminal Justice if the applicant also provides supplemental verifiable records or documents that aid in establishing identity.

(b) The application must include:

(1) the thumbprints of the applicant or, if thumbprints cannot be taken, the index fingerprints of the applicant;

(2) a photograph of the applicant;

(3) the signature of the applicant; and

(4) a brief description of the applicant.

(c) The application must state:

(1) the sex of the applicant;

(2) the residence address of the applicant, or if the applicant is a federal judge, a state judge, or the spouse of a federal or state judge using the procedure developed under Section 521.121(c), the street address of the courthouse in which the applicant or the applicant's spouse serves as a federal judge or a state judge;

(3) whether the applicant has been licensed to drive a motor vehicle before;

(4) if previously licensed, when and by what state or country;

(5) whether that license has been suspended or revoked or a license application denied;

(6) the date and reason for the suspension, revocation, or denial;

(7) whether the applicant is a citizen of the United States; and

(8) the county of residence of the applicant.

(d) **[2 Versions: As amended by Acts 2009, 81st Leg., ch. 1253]** If the applicant is under 21 years of age, the application must state whether the applicant has completed a driver education course required by Section 521.1601.

(d) **[2 Versions: As amended by Acts 2009, 81st Leg., ch, 1413]** If the applicant is under 25 years of age, the application must state whether the applicant has completed a driver education course required by Section 521.1601.

(e) **[2 Versions: Effective until September 28, 2011]** The application must include any other information the department requires to determine the applicant's identity, competency, and eligibility.

(e) **[2 Versions: Effective September 28, 2011]** The application must include any other information the department requires to determine the applicant's identity, residency, competency, and eligibility as required by the department or state law.

(f) Information supplied to the department relating to an applicant's medical history is for the confidential use of the department and may not be disclosed to any person or used as evidence in a legal proceeding other than a proceeding under Subchapter N. This subsection does not apply to information provided by an applicant under Subsection (h).

(g) The department may require an applicant to provide the applicant's social security number only for a purpose permitted by Section 521.044.

(h) The application must provide space for the applicant to voluntarily list any health condition that may impede communication with a peace officer as evidenced by a written statement from a licensed physician.

(i) The application must provide space for the applicant:

(1) to voluntarily list any military service that may qualify the applicant to receive a license with a veteran's designation under Section 521.1235; and

(2) to include proof required by the department to determine the applicant's eligibility to receive that designation.

(Enacted by Acts 1995, 74th Leg., ch. 165 (S.B. 971), § 1, effective September 1, 1995; am. Acts 1999, 76th Leg., ch. 556 (S.B. 368), § 78(a), effective September 1, 1999; am. Acts 1999, 76th Leg., ch. 640 (H.B. 82), § 3, effective September 1, 1999; am. Acts 2003, 78th Leg., ch. 1335 (H.B. 1330), § 2, effective January 1, 2004; am. Acts 2005, 79th Leg., ch. 1108 (H.B. 2337), § 5, effective September 1, 2005; am. Acts 2005, 79th Leg., ch. 1218 (H.B. 967), § 4, effective September 1, 2005; am. Acts 2009, 81st Leg., ch. 316 (H.B. 598),

§ 4, effective September 1, 2009; am. Acts 2009, 81st Leg., ch. 1146 (H.B. 2730), §§ 13A.04, 14.01, effective September 1, 2009; am. Acts 2009, 81st Leg., ch. 1253 (H.B. 339), § 9, effective September 1, 2009; am. Acts 2009, 81st Leg., ch. 1413 (S.B. 1317), § 1, effective March 1, 2010; am. Acts 2011, 82nd Leg., ch. 91 (S.B. 1303), § 24.011, effective September 1, 2011; am. Acts 2011, 82nd Leg., ch. 273 (H.B. 1514), § 2, effective September 1, 2011; am. Acts 2011, 82nd Leg., 1st C.S., (S.B. 1), § 72.06, effective September 28, 2011.)

## Sec. 521.1421.  Inmate Identification Verification Pilot Program.

(a) The department shall participate in an inmate identification verification pilot program for the purpose of issuing driver's licenses and personal identification certificates to inmates of the Texas Department of Criminal Justice.

(b) Under the pilot program, the department may:

(1) enter into a contract with the Texas Department of Criminal Justice and the Department of State Health Services to establish an identification verification process for inmates of the Texas Department of Criminal Justice; and

(2) issue a driver's license or a personal identification certificate to an inmate whose identity has been confirmed through the verification process and who otherwise meets the requirements for the issuance of the driver's license or personal identification certificate.

(c) At the conclusion of the pilot program the governing bodies of the participating agencies may agree to continue the pilot program on a permanent basis.

(d) Not later than December 1, 2010, the department and the Texas Department of Criminal Justice shall jointly issue a report to the standing committees of the legislature with jurisdiction over issues related to criminal justice and homeland security addressing:

(1) the status of the pilot program;

(2) the effectiveness of the pilot program; and

(3) an analysis of the feasibility of implementing a statewide program based on the pilot program.

(Enacted by Acts 2009, 81st Leg., ch. 1146 (H.B. 2730), § 14.02, effective September 1, 2009.)

## Sec. 521.1425.  Information Required to Be Furnished to Department.

(a) **[2 Versions: Effective until September 28, 2011]** Except as provided by Subsection (b), the department may require each applicant for an original, renewal, or duplicate driver's license to furnish to the department the information required by Section 521.142.

(a) **[2 Versions: Effective September 28, 2011]** Except as provided by Subsections (b) and (c), the department may require each applicant for an original, renewal, or duplicate driver's license to furnish to the department the information required by Section 521.142.

(b) The department shall require each applicant for an original, renewal, or duplicate driver's license to furnish to the department the information required by Sections 521.142(c)(7) and (8).

(c) **[Effective September 28, 2011]** Unless the information has been previously provided to the department, the department shall require each applicant for an original, renewal, or duplicate driver's license to furnish to the department:

(1) proof of the applicant's United States citizenship; or

(2) documentation described by Section 521.142(a).

(d) **[Effective September 28, 2011]** The department may not deny a driver's license to an applicant who provides documentation described by Section 521.142(a) based on the duration of the person's authorized stay in the United States, as indicated by the documentation presented under Section 521.142(a).

(Enacted by Acts 1997, 75th Leg., ch. 165 (S.B. 898), § 30.76(a), effective September 1, 1997; am. Acts 1999, 76th Leg., ch. 640 (H.B. 82), § 4, effective September 1, 1999; am. Acts 2011, 82nd Leg., 1st C.S., (S.B. 1), § 72.07, effective September 28, 2011.)

## Sec. 521.1426. Domicile Requirement; Verification.

(a) The department may not issue a driver's license or a personal identification certificate to a person who has not established a domicile in this state.

(b) The department shall adopt rules for determining whether a domicile has been established, including rules prescribing the types of documentation the department may require from the applicant to verify the validity of the claimed domicile.

(c) The department may contract with a third-party personal data verification service to assist the department in verifying a claim of domicile, including whether the physical address provided by the applicant is the applicant's actual residence.

(Enacted by Acts 2009, 81st Leg., ch. 1146 (H.B. 2730), § 13.04, effective June 19, 2009.)

## Sec. 521.1427. Post Office Box Not Valid As Address.

(a) In this section, "post office box address" means a United States Postal Service post office box address or a private mailbox address.

(b) Unless an exception exists under state or federal law, an applicant may receive delivery of a license or a personal identification certificate at a post office box address only if the applicant has provided the department the physical address where the applicant resides.

(c) The department may require the applicant to provide documentation that the department determines necessary to verify the validity of the physical address provided under Subsection (b).

(d) The department may contract with a third-party personal data verification service to assist the department in verifying whether the physical address provided by the applicant is the applicant's actual residence.

(Enacted by Acts 2009, 81st Leg., ch. 1146 (H.B. 2730), § 13.04, effective June 19, 2009.)

## Sec. 521.143. Evidence of Financial Responsibility Required.

(a) An application for an original driver's license must be accompanied by evidence of financial responsibility or a statement that the applicant does not own a motor vehicle for which evidence of financial responsibility is required under Chapter 601. The department may require an application for a renewal of a driver's license to be accompanied by evidence of financial responsibility or a statement that the applicant does not own a motor vehicle for which evidence of financial responsibility is required under Chapter 601.

(b) Evidence of financial responsibility presented under this section must be in at least the minimum amounts required by Section 601.072 and must cover each motor vehicle owned by the applicant for which the applicant is required to maintain evidence of financial responsibility. The evidence may be shown in the manner provided by Section 601.053(a).

(c) A personal automobile insurance policy used as evidence of financial responsibility under this section must comply with Article 5.06 or 5.145, Insurance Code.

(d) A statement that an applicant does not own a motor vehicle to which the evidence of financial

Transportation

responsibility requirement applies must be sworn to and signed by the applicant.

(Enacted by Acts 1995, 74th Leg., ch. 165 (S.B. 971), § 1, effective September 1, 1995; am. Acts 1999, 76th Leg., ch. 1189 (S.B. 370), § 23, effective September 1, 1999; am. Acts 2003, 78th Leg., ch. 206 (S.B. 14), § 21.46, effective June 11, 2003.)

### Sec. 521.144.  Application by New State Resident.

(a) A new resident of this state who applies for a driver's license must submit with the application:

(1) evidence that each motor vehicle owned by the person is registered under Chapter 502; or

(2) an affidavit that the applicant does not own a motor vehicle required to be registered under Chapter 502.

(b) The department may not issue a driver's license to a new resident who fails to comply with Subsection (a).

(c) A registration receipt issued by the county assessor-collector of the county in which the new resident resides is satisfactory evidence that a motor vehicle is registered under Chapter 502.

(Enacted by Acts 1995, 74th Leg., ch. 165 (S.B. 971), § 1, effective September 1, 1995.)

### Sec. 521.145.  Application by Person Under 18 Years of Age.

(a) The application of an applicant under 18 years of age must be signed by:

(1) the parent or guardian who has custody of the applicant; or

(2) if the applicant has no parent or guardian:

(A) the applicant's employer; or

(B) the county judge of the county in which the applicant resides.

(b) The department shall provide the applicant and the cosigner with information concerning state laws relating to driving while intoxicated, driving by a minor with alcohol in the minor's system, and implied consent. The applicant and cosigner must acknowledge receipt of this information.

(Enacted by Acts 1995, 74th Leg., ch. 165 (S.B. 971), § 1, effective September 1, 1995; am. Acts 1997, 75th Leg., ch. 1013 (S.B. 35), § 19, effective September 1, 1997.)

### Sec. 521.146.  Application for Duplicate License or Certificate.

(a) If a driver's license or certificate issued under this chapter is lost or destroyed, or there is a change in pertinent information, the person to whom the license or certificate was issued may obtain a duplicate or corrected version.

(b) An applicant for a corrected driver's license or certificate must submit to the department the required fee, accompanied by the required information that has changed with proof satisfactory to the department that supports the change.

(c) The department by rule may provide that the holder of a driver's license or identification certificate issued by the department may apply for the issuance of a duplicate license or certificate by mail, by telephone, over the Internet, or by other electronic means.

(d) A rule adopted under Subsection (c) may prescribe eligibility standards for issuance of a duplicate driver's license or identification certificate under this section.

(Enacted by Acts 1995, 74th Leg., ch. 165 (S.B. 971), § 1, effective September 1, 1995; am. Acts 2001, 77th Leg., ch. 866 (H.B. 1762), § 2, effective September 1, 2001.)

### Sec. 521.147.  Registration with Selective Service System.

(a) After an application for an original, renewal, or duplicate driver's license or personal identification certificate is submitted by a male applicant who on the date of the application is at least 18 years of age but younger than 26 years of age, the department shall send in an electronic format to the United States Selective Service System the information from the application necessary to register the applicant under the Military Selective Service Act (50 U.S.C. App. Section 451 et seq.).

(b) An application under this section must give written notice to an applicant that the application also constitutes registration with the United States Selective Service System for persons who are subject to registration and have not previously registered. The notice must be conspicuous on the application and state: "By submitting this application, I am consenting to registration with the United States Selective Service System if my registration is required by federal law."

(c) An application under this section must give written notice to an applicant that information regarding alternative service options for applicants who object to conventional military service for religious or other conscientious reasons is available from the department upon request.

(d) The applicant's submission of the application following this notification constitutes the applicant's consent to the sending of the information and the registration.

(e) In addition to the notifications required by Subsections (b) and (c), the department may conspicuously post at each location where applications for driver's licenses and personal identification certificates are accepted one or more signs, in English and Spanish, providing the information contained in the notifications.

(f) Subsections (a) and (d) do not apply to an applicant concerning whom the department has previously sent information to the Selective Service System.

(Enacted by Acts 2001, 77th Leg., ch. 973 (H.B. 116), § 2, effective September 1, 2001; am. Acts 2011, 82nd Leg., ch. 167 (S.B. 132), § 1, effective September 1, 2011.)

### Sec. 521.148. Application for Class M License or Authorization to Operate Motorcycle.

(a) An applicant for an original Class M license or Class A, B, or C driver's license that includes an authorization to operate a motorcycle must furnish to the department evidence satisfactory to the department that the applicant has successfully completed a basic motorcycle operator training course approved by the department under Chapter 662.

(b) The department may not issue an original Class M license or Class A, B, or C driver's license that includes an authorization to operate a motorcycle to an applicant who fails to comply with Subsection (a).

(c) **[2 Versions: Effective until January 1, 2012]** When the department issues a license to which this section applies, the department shall provide the person to whom the license is issued with written information about the Glenda Dawson Donate Life-Texas Registry program established under Chapter 49, Health and Safety Code.

(c) **[2 Versions: Effective January 1, 2012]** When the department issues a license to which this section applies, the department shall provide the person to whom the license is issued with written information about the Glenda Dawson Donate Life-Texas Registry operated under Chapter 692A, Health and Safety Code.

(Enacted by Acts 2009, 81st Leg., ch. 1391 (S.B. 1967), § 4, effective September 1, 2009; am. Acts 2011, 82nd Leg., ch. 554 (H.B. 2904), § 4, effective January 1, 2012.)

### Secs. 521.149 to 521.160 [Reserved for expansion].

## SUBCHAPTER H
## EDUCATION AND EXAMINATION REQUIREMENTS

### Sec. 521.1601. [2 Versions: As added by Acts 2009, 81st Leg., ch. 1253] Driver Education Required.

The department may not issue a driver's license to a person who is younger than 21 years of age unless the person submits to the department a driver education certificate issued under Chapter 1001, Education Code, that states that the person has completed and passed:

(1) a driver education and traffic safety course approved by the Texas Education Agency under Section 29.902, Education Code, or a driver education course approved by that agency under Section 1001.101 of that code or approved by the department under Section 521.205; or

(2) if the person is 18 years of age or older, a driver education course approved by the Texas Education Agency under Section 1001.101 or 1001.1015, Education Code.

(Enacted by Acts 2009, 81st Leg., ch. 1253 (H.B. 339), § 11, effective September 1, 2009.)

### Sec. 521.1601. [2 Versions: As added by Acts 2009, 81st Leg., ch. 1413] Driver Education Required.

The department may not issue a driver's license to a person who is younger than 25 years of age unless the person submits to the department a driver education certificate issued under Chapter 1001, Education Code, that states that the person has completed and passed:

(1) a driver education and traffic safety course approved by the Texas Education Agency under Section 29.902, Education Code, or a driver education course approved by that agency under Section 1001.101(a)(1) of that code or approved by the department under Section 521.205; or

(2) if the person is 18 years of age or older, a driver education course approved by the Texas

Education Agency under Section 1001.101(a)(1) or (2), Education Code.
(Enacted by Acts 2009, 81st Leg., ch. 1413 (S.B. 1317), § 3, effective March 1, 2010.)

## Sec. 521.161.  Examination of License Applicants.

(a) Except as otherwise provided by this subchapter, the department shall examine each applicant for a driver's license. The examination shall be held in the county in which the applicant resides or applies not later than the 10th day after the date on which the application is made.

(b) The examination must include:

(1) a test of the applicant's:

(A) vision;

(B) ability to identify and understand highway signs in English that regulate, warn, or direct traffic;

(C) knowledge of the traffic laws of this state; and

(D) knowledge of motorists' rights and responsibilities in relation to bicyclists;

(2) a demonstration of the applicant's ability to exercise ordinary and reasonable control in the operation of a motor vehicle of the type that the applicant will be licensed to operate; and

(3) any additional examination the department finds necessary to determine the applicant's fitness to operate a motor vehicle safely.

(c) The department shall give each applicant the option of taking the parts of the examination under Subsections (b)(1)(B), (C), and (D) in writing in addition to or instead of through a mechanical, electronic, or other testing method. If the applicant takes that part of the examination in writing in addition to another testing method, the applicant is considered to have passed that part of the examination if the applicant passes either version of the examination. The department shall inform each person taking the examination of the person's rights under this subsection.

(d) On payment of the required fee, an applicant is entitled to three examinations of each element under Subsection (b) for each application to qualify for a driver's license. If the applicant has not qualified after the third examination, the applicant must submit a new application accompanied by the required fee.

(e) The department may not issue a driver's license to a person who has not passed each examination required under this chapter.
(Enacted by Acts 1995, 74th Leg., ch. 165 (S.B. 971), § 1, effective September 1, 1995; am. Acts

1997, 75th Leg., ch. 165 (S.B. 898), § 30.77(a), effective September 1, 1997; am. Acts 2009, 81st Leg., ch. 565 (S.B. 2041), § 1, effective September 1, 2009.)

## Sec. 521.162.  Alternate Examination in Spanish.

(a) The department shall design and administer in each county of this state an alternate examination for Spanish-speaking applicants who are unable to take the regular examination in English.

(b) The alternate examination must be identical to the examination administered to other applicants under Section 521.161 except that all directions and written material, other than the text of highway signs, must be in Spanish. The text of highway signs must be in English.
(Enacted by Acts 1995, 74th Leg., ch. 165 (S.B. 971), § 1, effective September 1, 1995.)

## Sec. 521.163.  Reexamination.

(a) The director may require the holder of a license to be reexamined if the director determines that the holder is incapable of safely operating a motor vehicle.

(b) The reexamination shall be conducted in the license holder's county of residence unless the holder and the director agree to a different location.
(Enacted by Acts 1995, 74th Leg., ch. 165 (S.B. 971), § 1, effective September 1, 1995.)

## Sec. 521.164.  Exemption from Certain Examination Requirements for Licensed Nonresidents.

(a) The department by rule may provide that a holder of a driver's license issued to the person by another state or Canadian province and who is otherwise qualified may, after passing the vision test and paying the required fees, be issued a driver's license without the complete examination required under Section 521.161.

(b) A license issued under this section must be of the class of license equivalent to the license issued by the other jurisdiction.
(Enacted by Acts 1995, 74th Leg., ch. 165 (S.B. 971), § 1, effective September 1, 1995.)

## Sec. 521.165.  Testing by Other Entities.

(a) The director may certify and set standards for the certification of certain employers, government agencies, and other appropriate organizations to allow those persons to train and test for the ability to operate certain types of vehicles.

(b) The department shall set the standards for the training and testing of driver's license applicants under Subsection (a).

(c) Except as provided by Subsection (d), in issuing a driver's license for certain types of vehicles, the director may waive a driving test for an applicant who has successfully completed and passed the training and testing conducted by a person certified under Subsection (a).

(d) The director may not waive the driving test required by Section 521.161 for an applicant who is under 18 years of age.

(Enacted by Acts 1995, 74th Leg., ch. 165 (S.B. 971), § 1, effective September 1, 1995; am. Acts 2009, 81st Leg., ch. 1146 (H.B. 2730), § 12.05, effective September 1, 2009; am. Acts 2009, 81st Leg., ch. 1253 (H.B. 339), § 12, effective September 1, 2009.)

## Sec. 521.1655.　Testing by Driver Education School.

(a) A driver education school licensed under the Texas Driver and Traffic Safety Education Act (Article 4413(29c), Vernon's Texas Civil Statutes) may administer to a student of that school the vision, highway sign, and traffic law parts of the examination required by Section 521.161.

(b) An examination administered under this section complies with the examination requirements of this subchapter as to the parts of the examination administered.

(Enacted by Acts 1997, 75th Leg., ch. 165 (S.B. 898), § 30.77(a), effective September 1, 1997.)

## Sec. 521.166.　Motorcycle Road Test Requirements.

(a) An applicant required to submit to a motorcycle road test must provide a passenger vehicle and a licensed driver to convey the license examiner during the road test.

(b) The department may refuse to administer any part of the road test to an applicant who fails to comply with Subsection (a).

(Enacted by Acts 1995, 74th Leg., ch. 165 (S.B. 971), § 1, effective September 1, 1995.)

## Sec. 521.167.　[2 Versions: As added by Acts 2009, 81st Leg., ch. 1253] Waiver of Certain Education and Examination Requirements.

A person who has completed and passed a driver education course approved by the Texas Education Agency under Section 1001.1015, Education Code, is not required to take the highway sign and traffic law parts of the examination required under Section 521.161 if those parts have been successfully completed as determined by a licensed driver education instructor.

(Enacted by Acts 2009, 81st Leg., ch. 1253 (H.B. 339), § 11, effective September 1, 2009.)

## Sec. 521.167.　[2 Versions: As added by Acts 2009, 81st Leg., ch. 1413] Waiver of Certain Education and Examination Requirements.

A person who has completed and passed a driver education course approved by the Texas Education Agency under Section 1001.101(a)(2), Education Code, is not required to take the highway sign and traffic law parts of the examination required under Section 521.161 if those parts have been successfully completed as determined by a licensed driver education instructor.

(Enacted by Acts 2009, 81st Leg., ch. 1413 (S.B. 1317), § 3, effective March 1, 2010.)

## Secs. 521.168 to 521.180 [Reserved for expansion].

## SUBCHAPTER I
## ISSUANCE OF DRIVER'S LICENSE

## Sec. 521.181.　Issuance of Driver's License.

On payment of the required fee, the department shall issue to each qualifying applicant a driver's license of the class for which the applicant has applied.

(Enacted by Acts 1995, 74th Leg., ch. 165 (S.B. 971), § 1, effective September 1, 1995.)

## Sec. 521.1811.　Waiver of Fees for Foster Care Youth.

A person is exempt from the payment of any fee for the issuance of a driver's license, as provided under this chapter, if that person is:

(1) younger than 18 years of age and in the managing conservatorship of the Department of Family and Protective Services; or

(2) at least 18 years of age, but younger than 21 years of age, and resides in a foster care placement, the cost of which is paid by the Department of Family and Protective Services.

(Enacted by Acts 2011, 82nd Leg., ch. 598 (S.B. 218), § 10, effective September 1, 2011.)

Transportation

## Sec. 521.182. Surrender of License Issued by Other Jurisdiction.

(a) A person is not entitled to receive a driver's license until the person surrenders to the department each driver's license in the person's possession that was issued by this state or another state or Canadian province.

(b) The department shall send to the state or province that issued the license:

(1) the surrendered license or a notification that the license has been surrendered; and

(2) a statement that the person holds a driver's license issued by this state.

(Enacted by Acts 1995, 74th Leg., ch. 165 (S.B. 971), § 1, effective September 1, 1995.)

## Secs. 521.183 to 521.200 [Reserved for expansion].

## SUBCHAPTER J
## PERSONS INELIGIBLE FOR LICENSE

## Sec. 521.201. License Ineligibility in General.

The department may not issue any license to a person who:

(1) is under 15 years of age;

(2) is under 18 years of age unless the person complies with the requirements imposed by Section 521.204;

(3) is shown to be addicted to the use of alcohol, a controlled substance, or another drug that renders a person incapable of driving;

(4) holds a driver's license issued by this state or another state or country that is revoked, canceled, or under suspension;

(5) has been determined by a judgment of a court to be totally incapacitated or incapacitated to act as the operator of a motor vehicle unless the person has, by the date of the license application, been:

(A) restored to capacity by judicial decree; or

(B) released from a hospital for the mentally incapacitated on a certificate by the superintendent or administrator of the hospital that the person has regained capacity;

(6) the department determines to be afflicted with a mental or physical disability or disease that prevents the person from exercising reasonable and ordinary control over a motor vehicle while operating the vehicle on a highway, except that a person may not be refused a license because of a physical defect if common experience shows that the defect does not incapacitate a person from safely operating a motor vehicle;

(7) has been reported by a court under Section 521.3452 for failure to appear unless the court has filed an additional report on final disposition of the case; or

(8) has been reported by a court for failure to appear or default in payment of a fine for a misdemeanor that is not covered under Subdivision (7) and that is punishable by a fine only, including a misdemeanor under a municipal ordinance, committed by a person who was under 17 years of age at the time of the alleged offense, unless the court has filed an additional report on final disposition of the case.

(Enacted by Acts 1995, 74th Leg., ch. 165 (S.B. 971), § 1, effective September 1, 1995; am. Acts 1997, 75th Leg., ch. 560 (H.B. 1055), § 1, effective September 1, 1997; am. Acts 1999, 76th Leg., ch. 1080 (H.B. 3342), § 1, effective September 1, 1999; am. Acts 2003, 78th Leg., ch. 283 (H.B. 2319), § 54, effective September 1, 2003; am. Acts 2005, 79th Leg., ch. 949 (H.B. 1575), § 50, effective September 1, 2005.)

## Sec. 521.202. Ineligibility for License Based on Certain Convictions.

(a) Unless the period of suspension that would have applied if the person held a license at the time of the conviction has expired, the department may not issue a license to a person convicted of an offense:

(1) described by Section 49.04, 49.07, or 49.08, Penal Code; or

(2) to which Section 521.342(a) applies.

(b) Until the period specified in the juvenile court order has expired, the department may not issue a license to a person if the department has been ordered by a juvenile court under Section 54.042, Family Code, to deny the person a license.

(c) A person does not have a privilege to operate a vehicle in this state during a period of suspension under Subsection (a) or (b) if the department is prohibited from issuing a license to that person.

(Enacted by Acts 1995, 74th Leg., ch. 165 (S.B. 971), § 1, effective September 1, 1995.)

## Sec. 521.203. Restrictions on Class A and B Licenses.

The department may not issue a Class A or Class B driver's license to a person who:

(1) is under 17 years of age;

(2) is under 18 years of age unless the person has completed a driver training course approved by the Central Education Agency; or

(3) has not provided the department with an affidavit, on a form prescribed by the department, that states that no vehicle that the person will drive that requires a Class A or Class B license is a commercial motor vehicle as defined by Section 522.003.

(Enacted by Acts 1995, 74th Leg., ch. 165 (S.B. 971), § 1, effective September 1, 1995.)

## Sec. 521.204. Restrictions on Minor.

(a) The department may issue a Class C driver's license to an applicant under 18 years of age only if the applicant:

(1) is 16 years of age or older;

(2) has submitted to the department a driver education certificate issued under Section 1001.055, Education Code, that states that the person has completed and passed a driver education course approved by the department under Section 521.205 or by the Texas Education Agency;

(3) has obtained a high school diploma or its equivalent or is a student:

(A) enrolled in a public school, home school, or private school who attended school for at least 80 days in the fall or spring semester preceding the date of the driver's license application; or

(B) who has been enrolled for at least 45 days, and is enrolled as of the date of the application, in a program to prepare persons to pass the high school equivalency exam;

(4) has submitted to the department written parental or guardian permission:

(A) for the department to access the applicant's school enrollment records maintained by the Texas Education Agency; and

(B) for a school administrator or law enforcement officer to notify the department in the event that the person has been absent from school for at least 20 consecutive instructional days; and

(5) has passed the examination required by Section 521.161.

(b) The department may not issue a Class A, B, or C driver's license other than a hardship license to an applicant under 18 years of age unless the applicant has held an instruction permit or hardship license for at least six months preceding the date of the application.

(Enacted by Acts 1995, 74th Leg., ch. 165 (S.B. 971), § 1, effective September 1, 1995; am. Acts

1997, 75th Leg., ch. 165 (S.B. 898), § 30.78(a), effective September 1, 1997; am. Acts 2001, 77th Leg., ch. 1251 (S.B. 577), § 1, effective January 1, 2002; am. Acts 2009, 81st Leg., ch. 1146 (H.B. 2730), § 12.06, effective September 1, 2009; am. Acts 2009, 81st Leg., ch. 1253 (H.B. 339), § 13, effective September 1, 2009; am. Acts 2011, 82nd Leg., ch. 1160 (H.B. 2466), § 1, effective September 1, 2011.)

## Sec. 521.205. Department-Approved Courses.

(a) The department by rule shall provide for approval of a driver education course conducted by the parent, stepparent, foster parent, legal guardian, step-grandparent, or grandparent of a person who is required to complete a driver education course to obtain a Class C license. The rules must provide that:

(1) the person conducting the course possess a valid license for the preceding three years that has not been suspended, revoked, or forfeited in the past three years for an offense that involves the operation of a motor vehicle;

(2) the student driver spend a minimum number of hours in:

(A) classroom instruction; and

(B) behind-the-wheel instruction;

(3) the person conducting the course not be convicted of:

(A) criminally negligent homicide; or

(B) driving while intoxicated;

(4) the person conducting the course not be disabled because of mental illness; and

(5) the person conducting the course not have six or more points assigned to the person's driver's license under Subchapter B, Chapter 708, at the time the person begins conducting the course.

(b) The department may not approve a course unless it determines that the course materials are at least equal to those required in a course approved by the Texas Education Agency, except that the department may not require that:

(1) the classroom instruction be provided in a room with particular characteristics or equipment; or

(2) the vehicle used for the behind-the-wheel instruction have equipment other than the equipment otherwise required by law for operation of the vehicle on a highway while the vehicle is not being used for driver training.

(c) The rules must provide a method by which:

(1) approval of a course is obtained;

**Transportation**

(2) an applicant submits proof of completion of the course; and

(3) approval for delivering course materials by an alternative method, including electronic means, is obtained.

(d) Completion of a driver education course approved under this section has the same effect under this chapter as completion of a driver education course approved by the Texas Education Agency.

(Enacted by Acts 1997, 75th Leg., ch. 165 (S.B. 898), § 30.79(a), effective September 1, 1997; am. Acts 1999, 76th Leg., ch. 721 (H.B. 953), § 1, effective September 1, 1999; am. Acts 2003, 78th Leg., ch. 1196 (S.B. 895), § 1, effective September 1, 2003; am. Acts 2009, 81st Leg., ch. 1146 (H.B. 2730), § 12.07, effective September 1, 2009; am. Acts 2009, 81st Leg., ch. 1253 (H.B. 339), § 14, effective September 1, 2009.)

## Sec. 521.206. Collision Rate Statistics Publication.

(a) The department shall collect data regarding collisions of students taught by public schools, driver education schools licensed under Chapter 1001, Education Code, and other entities that offer driver education courses to students for which a uniform certificate of course completion is issued. The collision rate is computed by determining the number of an entity's students who complete a driver education course during a state fiscal year, dividing that number by the number of collisions that involved students who completed such a course and that occurred in the 12-month period following their licensure, and expressing the quotient as a percentage.

(b) The department shall collect data regarding the collision rate of students taught by course instructors approved under Section 521.205. The collision rate is computed by determining the number of students who completed a course approved under Section 521.205 during a state fiscal year, dividing that number by the number of collisions that involved students who completed such a course and that occurred in the 12-month period following their licensure, and expressing the quotient as a percentage.

(c) Not later than October 1 of each year, the department shall issue a publication listing the collision rate for students taught by each driver education entity and the collision rate for students taught by a course instructor approved under Section 521.205, noting the severity of collisions involving students of each entity and each type of course.

(Enacted by Acts 2009, 81st Leg., ch. 1146 (H.B. 2730), § 12.08, effective September 1, 2009; enacted by Acts 2009, 81st Leg., ch. 1253 (H.B. 339), § 15, effective September 1, 2009.)

## Secs. 521.207 to 521.220 [Reserved for expansion].

## SUBCHAPTER K
## RESTRICTED LICENSES

## Sec. 521.221. Imposition of Special Restrictions and Endorsements.

(a) For good cause the department may impose a restriction or require an endorsement suitable to the driver's license holder's driving ability. The restriction or endorsement may relate to:

(1) the type of motor vehicle that the holder may operate;

(2) a special mechanical control device required on a motor vehicle that the holder may operate;

(3) mechanical attachments, including glasses or an artificial limb, required on the person of the holder;

(4) an area, location, road, or highway in this state on which the holder is permitted to drive a motor vehicle;

(5) the time of day that the holder is permitted to operate a motor vehicle; and

(6) any other condition the department determines to be appropriate to ensure the safe operation of a motor vehicle by the holder.

(b) The department may issue a special restricted license or state the applicable restriction on the regular license.

(c) A person commits an offense if the person operates a motor vehicle in violation of a restriction imposed or without the endorsement required on the license issued to that person. An offense under this subsection is a misdemeanor punishable under Section 521.461.

(d) A court may dismiss a charge for a violation of this section if:

(1) the restriction or endorsement was imposed:

(A) because of a physical condition that was surgically or otherwise medically corrected before the date of the offense; or

(B) in error and that fact is established by the defendant;

(2) the department removes the restriction or endorsement before the defendant's first court appearance; and

(3) the defendant pays an administrative fee not to exceed $10.

(Enacted by Acts 1995, 74th Leg., ch. 165 (S.B. 971), § 1, effective September 1, 1995; am. Acts 2007, 80th Leg., ch. 1027 (H.B. 1623), § 7, effective September 1, 2007.)

### Sec. 521.222. Instruction Permit.

(a) The department or a driver education school licensed under the Texas Driver and Traffic Safety Education Act (Article 4413(29c), Vernon's Texas Civil Statutes) may issue an instruction permit, including a Class A or Class B driver's license instruction permit, to a person who:

(1) is 15 years of age or older but under 18 years of age;

(2) has satisfactorily completed and passed the classroom phase of an approved driver education course, which may be a course approved under Section 521.205;

(3) meets the requirements imposed under Section 521.204(3); and

(4) has passed each examination required under Section 521.161 other than the driving test.

(b) The department may issue an instruction permit to a person 18 years of age or older who has successfully passed all parts of the driver's examination required under Section 521.161 other than the driving test.

(c) A driver education school may issue an instruction permit to a person 18 years of age or older who has successfully passed:

(1) a six-hour adult classroom driver education course approved by the Texas Education Agency; and

(2) each part of the driver's examination required by Section 521.161 other than the driving test.

(d) An instruction permit entitles the holder to operate a type of motor vehicle on a highway while:

(1) the permit is in the holder's possession; and

(2) the holder is accompanied by a person occupying the seat by the operator who:

(A) holds a license that qualifies the operator to operate that type of vehicle;

(B) is 21 years of age or older; and

(C) has at least one year of driving experience.

(e) Except as provided by Subsection (f), an instruction permit is not required to include a photograph.

(f) The department may issue an instruction permit under this section to a person who is subject to the registration requirements under Chapter 62, Code of Criminal Procedure, and is otherwise eligible for the permit. An instruction permit issued under this subsection must include a photograph of the person.

(g) A person who occupies the seat in a vehicle by a holder of an instruction permit commits an offense if, while the holder is operating the vehicle, the person:

(1) sleeps;

(2) is intoxicated, as defined by Section 49.01, Penal Code; or

(3) is engaged in an activity that prevents the person from observing and responding to the actions of the operator.

(h) It is a defense to prosecution of a violation under Subsection (g) that at the time of the violation another person in addition to the defendant:

(1) occupied the seat by the operator;

(2) complied with the requirements of Subsections (d)(2)(A)—(C); and

(3) was not in violation of Subsection (g).

(Enacted by Acts 1995, 74th Leg., ch. 165 (S.B. 971), § 1, effective September 1, 1995; am. Acts 1997, 75th Leg., ch. 165 (S.B. 898), § 30.80(a), effective September 1, 1997; am. Acts 2001, 77th Leg., ch. 546 (H.B. 2663), § 2, effective September 1, 2001; am. Acts 2001, 77th Leg., ch. 1251 (S.B. 577), § 2, effective January 1, 2002; am. Acts 2007, 80th Leg., ch. 347 (S.B. 153), § 1, effective September 1, 2007.)

### Sec. 521.223. Hardship License.

(a) The department may issue a license to a person who complies with the requirements of Subsection (b) if the department finds that:

(1) the failure to issue the license will result in an unusual economic hardship for the family of the applicant;

(2) the license is necessary because of the illness of a member of the applicant's family; or

(3) the license is necessary because the applicant is enrolled in a vocational education program and requires a driver's license to participate in the program.

(b) An applicant for a license under Subsection (a) must be 15 years of age or older and must:

(1) have passed a driver education course approved by the department, which may be a course approved under Section 521.205; and

(2) pass the examination required by Section 521.161.

(c) To be eligible to take the driver training course, the person must be at least 14 years of age.

(d) [Repealed by Acts 2011, ch. 1121 (H.B. 90), § 3, effective September 1, 2011]

(e) A person who is refused a driver's license under this section may appeal to the county court of the county in which the person resides. The court may try the matter on the request of the petitioner or respondent.

(f) In the manner provided by Subchapter N, the department shall suspend a license issued under this section if the holder of the license is convicted of two or more moving violations committed within a 12-month period.

(g) The department may issue a hardship license to a person who is subject to the registration requirements under Chapter 62, Code of Criminal Procedure, and is otherwise eligible for the license. A hardship license issued under this section must include a photograph of the person.
(Enacted by Acts 1995, 74th Leg., ch. 165 (S.B. 971), § 1, effective September 1, 1995; am. Acts 1997, 75th Leg., ch. 165 (S.B. 898), §§ 30.81(a), 30.82, effective September 1, 1997; am. Acts 2001, 77th Leg., ch. 546 (H.B. 2663), § 3, effective September 1, 2001; am. Acts 2011, 82nd Leg., ch. 1121 (H.B. 90), §§ 2, 3, effective September 1, 2011.)

## Sec. 521.224.  Restricted Class M License.

(a) In this section, "motorcycle" includes a motor driven cycle.

(b) The department may issue a special restricted Class M license that authorizes the holder to operate only a motorcycle that has not more than a 250 cubic centimeter piston displacement.

(c) A person is eligible for a restricted motorcycle license if the person:

(1) is 15 years of age or older but under 18 years of age;

(2) has completed and passed a motorcycle operator training course approved by the department; and

(3) has met the requirements imposed under Section 521.145.

(d) The department shall make the motorcycle operator training course available.

(e) On the 16th birthday of a holder of a special restricted Class M license, the department shall remove the 250 cubic centimeter restriction from the license without completion by the holder of an additional motorcycle operator training course.

(f) An applicant for the special restricted license must apply in accordance with Subchapter G. The applicant is subject to the requirements of Section 521.161 and to other provisions of this chapter in the same manner as an applicant for another license. The department shall prescribe the form of the license.
(Enacted by Acts 1995, 74th Leg., ch. 165 (S.B. 971), § 1, effective September 1, 1995; am. Acts 1999, 76th Leg., ch. 797 (H.B. 1492), § 1, effective September 1, 1999.)

## Sec. 521.225.  Moped License.

(a) A person may not operate a moped unless the person holds a driver's license. An applicant for a moped license must be 15 years of age or older.

(b) The department shall administer to an applicant for a moped license a written examination relating to the traffic laws applicable to the operation of mopeds. A test involving the operation of the vehicle is not required.

(c) An applicable provision of this chapter relating to a restricted Class M license applies also to a moped license, including a provision relating to the application, issuance, duration, suspension, cancellation, or revocation of that license.

(d) The department shall certify whether a vehicle alleged to be a moped is a moped. The department shall:

(1) by rule establish the procedure for determining whether a vehicle is a moped;

(2) compile a list of mopeds certified by the department; and

(3) make the list available to the public on request.
(Enacted by Acts 1995, 74th Leg., ch. 165 (S.B. 971), § 1, effective September 1, 1995; am. Acts 1999, 76th Leg., ch. 797 (H.B. 1492), § 2, effective September 1, 1999.)

## Sec. 521.226.  Certification [Repealed].

Repealed by Acts 1999, 76th Leg., ch. 797 (H.B. 1492), § 4, effective September 1, 1999.
(Enacted by Acts 1995, 74th Leg., ch. 165 (S.B. 971), § 1, effective September 1, 1995.)

## Sec. 521.227.  Inspection by Peace Officer.

Any peace officer may stop and detain a motorcycle, motor driven cycle, or moped to determine if the vehicle is of a model and make certified by the department.

(Enacted by Acts 1995, 74th Leg., ch. 165 (S.B. 971), § 1, effective September 1, 1995.)

**Secs. 521.228 to 521.240 [Reserved for expansion].**

## SUBCHAPTER L
## OCCUPATIONAL LICENSE

### Sec. 521.241. Definitions.

In this subchapter:

(1) "Essential need" means a need of a person for the operation of a motor vehicle:

(A) in the performance of an occupation or trade or for transportation to and from the place at which the person practices the person's occupation or trade;

(B) for transportation to and from an educational facility in which the person is enrolled; or

(C) in the performance of essential household duties.

(2) "Ignition interlock device" means a device that uses a deep-lung breath analysis mechanism to make impractical the operation of a motor vehicle if ethyl alcohol is detected in the breath of the operator of the vehicle.

(Enacted by Acts 1995, 74th Leg., ch. 165 (S.B. 971), § 1, effective September 1, 1995.)

### Sec. 521.242. Petition.

(a) A person whose license has been suspended for a cause other than a physical or mental disability or impairment or a conviction under Section 49.04, Penal Code, may apply for an occupational license by filing a verified petition with the clerk of the county court or district court with jurisdiction in the county in which:

(1) the person resides; or

(2) the offense occurred for which the license was suspended.

(b) A person may apply for an occupational license by filing a verified petition only with the clerk of the county court or district court in which the person was convicted if:

(1) the person's license has been automatically suspended or canceled under this chapter for a conviction of an offense under the laws of this state; and

(2) the person has not been issued, in the 10 years preceding the date of the filing of the petition, more than one occupational license after a conviction under the laws of this state.

(c) A petition filed under this section must set forth in detail the person's essential need.

(d) A petition filed under Subsection (b) must state that the petitioner was convicted in that court for an offense under the laws of this state.

(e) The clerk of the court shall file the petition as in any other civil matter.

(f) A court may not grant an occupational license for the operation of a commercial motor vehicle to which Chapter 522 applies.

(Enacted by Acts 1995, 74th Leg., ch. 165 (S.B. 971), § 1, effective September 1, 1995; am. Acts 1997, 75th Leg., ch. 165 (S.B. 898), § 30.83(a), effective September 1, 1997; am. Acts 1997, 75th Leg., ch. 1289 (S.B. 322), §§ 1, 2, effective September 1, 1997; am. Acts 2001, 77th Leg., ch. 941 (S.B. 886), § 1, effective September 1, 2001.)

### Sec. 521.243. Notice to State; Presentation of Evidence.

(a) The clerk of the court shall send by certified mail to the attorney representing the state a copy of the petition and notice of the hearing if the petitioner's license was suspended following a conviction for:

(1) an offense under Section 19.05, 49.04, 49.07, or 49.08, Penal Code; or

(2) an offense to which Section 521.342 applies.

(b) A person who receives a copy of a petition under Subsection (a) may attend the hearing and may present evidence at the hearing against granting the petition.

(Enacted by Acts 1995, 74th Leg., ch. 165 (S.B. 971), § 1, effective September 1, 1995.)

### Sec. 521.244. Hearing; Order; Determination of Essential Need.

(a) The judge who hears the petition shall sign an order finding whether an essential need exists.

(b) In determining whether an essential need exists, the judge shall consider:

(1) the petitioner's driving record; and

(2) any evidence presented by a person under Section 521.243(b).

(c) If the judge finds that there is an essential need, the judge also, as part of the order, shall:

(1) determine the actual need of the petitioner to operate a motor vehicle; and

(2) require the petitioner to provide evidence of financial responsibility in accordance with Chapter 601.

(d) Except as provided by Section 521.243(b), the hearing on the petition may be ex parte.

(Enacted by Acts 1995, 74th Leg., ch. 165 (S.B. 971), § 1, effective September 1, 1995.)

## Sec. 521.245.  Required Counseling.

(a) If the petitioner's license has been suspended under Chapter 524 or 724, the court shall require the petitioner to attend a program approved by the court that is designed to provide counseling and rehabilitation services to persons for alcohol dependence. This requirement shall be stated in the order granting the occupational license.

(b) The program required under Subsection (a) may not be the program provided by Section 521.344 or by Section 13, Article 42.12, Code of Criminal Procedure.

(c) The court may require the person to report periodically to the court to verify that the person is attending the required program.

(d) On finding that the person is not attending the program as required, the court may revoke the order granting the occupational license. The court shall send a certified copy of the order revoking the license to the department.

(e) On receipt of the copy under Subsection (d), the department shall suspend the person's occupational license for:

(1) 60 days, if the original driver's license suspension was under Chapter 524; or

(2) 120 days, if the original driver's license suspension was under Chapter 724.

(f) A suspension under Subsection (e):

(1) takes effect on the date on which the court signs the order revoking the occupational license; and

(2) is cumulative of the original suspension.

(g) A person is not eligible for an occupational license during a period of suspension under Subsection (e).

(Enacted by Acts 1995, 74th Leg., ch. 165 (S.B. 971), § 1, effective September 1, 1995.)

## Sec. 521.246.  Ignition Interlock Device Requirement.

(a) If the person's license has been suspended after a conviction under Section 49.04, 49.07, or 49.08, Penal Code, the judge, before signing an order, shall determine from the criminal history record information maintained by the department whether the person has any previous conviction under those laws.

(b) As part of the order the judge may restrict the person to the operation of a motor vehicle equipped with an ignition interlock device if the judge determines that the person's license has been suspended following a conviction under Section 49.04, 49.07, or 49.08, Penal Code. As part of the order, the judge shall restrict the person to the operation of a motor vehicle equipped with an ignition interlock device if the judge determines that:

(1) the person has two or more convictions under any combination of Section 49.04, 49.07, or 49.08, Penal Code; or

(2) the person's license has been suspended after a conviction under Section 49.04, Penal Code, for which the person has been punished under Section 49.09, Penal Code.

(c) The person shall obtain the ignition interlock device at the person's own expense unless the court finds that to do so is not in the best interest of justice and enters that finding in the record. If the court determines that the person is unable to pay for the device, the court may impose a reasonable payment schedule for a term not to exceed twice the period of the court's order.

(d) The court shall order the ignition interlock device to remain installed for at least half of the period of supervision.

(e) A person to whom this section applies may operate a motor vehicle without the installation of an approved ignition interlock device if:

(1) the person is required to operate a motor vehicle in the course and scope of the person's employment;

(2) the vehicle is owned by the person's employer;

(3) the employer is not owned or controlled by the person whose driving privilege is restricted;

(4) the employer is notified of the driving privilege restriction; and

(5) proof of that notification is with the vehicle.

(f) A previous conviction may not be used for purposes of restricting a person to the operation of a motor vehicle equipped with an interlock ignition device under this section if:

(1) the previous conviction was a final conviction under Section 49.04, 49.07, or 49.08, Penal Code, and was for an offense committed more than 10 years before the instant offense for which the person was convicted; and

(2) the person has not been convicted of an offense under Section 49.04, 49.07, or 49.08 of that code committed within 10 years before the date on which the instant offense for which the person was convicted.

(Enacted by Acts 1995, 74th Leg., ch. 165 (S.B. 971), § 1, effective September 1, 1995; am. Acts 1997, 75th Leg., ch. 165 (S.B. 898), § 30.84(a), effective September 1, 1997; am. Acts 1999, 76th Leg., ch. 1105 (H.B. 3492), § 1, effective September 1, 1999.)

### Sec. 521.2461. Testing for Alcohol or Controlled Substances.

The court granting an occupational license under this subchapter may require as a condition of the license that the person submit to periodic testing for alcohol or controlled substances, to be conducted by an entity specified by the court, if the person's license has been suspended under Chapter 524 or 724 or as a result of the person's conviction of an offense involving the operation of a motor vehicle while intoxicated.
(Enacted by Acts 2011, 82nd Leg., ch. 426 (S.B. 953), § 1, effective September 1, 2011.)

### Sec. 521.2462. Supervision of Person Issued Occupational Driver's License.

(a) The court granting an occupational license under this subchapter may order the person receiving the license to:

(1) submit to supervision by the local community supervision and corrections department to verify compliance with the conditions specified by the order granting the license, including the conditions specified in accordance with Section 521.248; and

(2) pay a monthly administrative fee under Section 76.015, Government Code.

(b) The court may order the supervision to continue until the end of the period of suspension of the person's driver's license, including any extensions of that period.

(c) The court for good cause may modify or terminate supervision before the end of the period of license suspension.
(Enacted by Acts 2011, 82nd Leg., ch. 426 (S.B. 953), § 1, effective September 1, 2011.)

### Sec. 521.2465. Restricted License.

(a) On receipt of notice that a person has been restricted to the use of a motor vehicle equipped with an ignition interlock device, the department shall notify that person that the person's driver's license expires on the 30th day after the date of the notice. On application by the person and payment of a fee of $10, the department shall issue a special restricted license that authorizes the person to operate only a motor vehicle equipped with an ignition interlock device.

(b) On receipt of a copy of a court order removing the restriction, the department shall issue the person a driver's license without the restriction.
(Enacted by Acts 1997, 75th Leg., ch. 165 (S.B. 898), § 30.85(a), effective September 1, 1997.)

### Sec. 521.247. Approval of Ignition Interlock Devices by Department.

(a) The department shall adopt rules for the approval of ignition interlock devices used under this subchapter.

(b) The department by rule shall establish general standards for the calibration and maintenance of the devices. The manufacturer or an authorized representative of the manufacturer is responsible for calibrating and maintaining the device.

(c) If the department approves a device, the department shall notify the manufacturer of that approval in writing. Written notice from the department to a manufacturer is admissible in a civil or criminal proceeding in this state. The manufacturer shall reimburse the department for any cost incurred by the department in approving the device.

(d) The department is not liable in a civil or criminal proceeding that arises from the use of an approved device.
(Enacted by Acts 1995, 74th Leg., ch. 165 (S.B. 971), § 1, effective September 1, 1995; am. Acts 1997, 75th Leg., ch. 165 (S.B. 898), § 30.84(b), effective September 1, 1997;.)

### Sec. 521.2475. Ignition Interlock Device Evaluation.

(a) On January 1 of each year, the department shall issue an evaluation of each ignition interlock device approved under Section 521.247 using guidelines established by the National Highway Traffic Safety Administration, including:

(1) whether the device provides accurate detection of alveolar air;

(2) the moving retest abilities of the device;

(3) the use of tamper-proof blood alcohol content level software by the device;

(4) the anticircumvention design of the device;

(5) the recalibration requirements of the device; and

(6) the breath action required by the operator.

(b) The department shall assess the cost of preparing the evaluation equally against each manufacturer of an approved device.

Transportation

(Enacted by Acts 1997, 75th Leg., ch. 165 (S.B. 898), § 30.86(a), effective September 1, 1997.)

### Sec. 521.2476. Minimum Standards for Vendors of Ignition Interlock Devices.

(a) The department by rule shall establish:

(1) minimum standards for vendors of ignition interlock devices who conduct business in this state; and

(2) procedures to ensure compliance with those standards, including procedures for the inspection of a vendor's facilities.

(b) The minimum standards shall require each vendor to:

(1) be authorized by the department to do business in this state;

(2) install a device only if the device is approved under Section 521.247;

(3) obtain liability insurance providing coverage for damages arising out of the operation or use of devices in amounts and under the terms specified by the department;

(4) install the device and activate any anticircumvention feature of the device within a reasonable time after the vendor receives notice that installation is ordered by a court;

(5) install and inspect the device in accordance with any applicable court order;

(6) repair or replace a device not later than 48 hours after receiving notice of a complaint regarding the operation of the device;

(7) submit a written report of any violation of a court order to that court and to the person's supervising officer, if any, not later than 48 hours after the vendor discovers the violation;

(8) maintain a record of each action taken by the vendor with respect to each device installed by the vendor, including each action taken as a result of an attempt to circumvent the device, until at least the fifth anniversary after the date of installation;

(9) make a copy of the record available for inspection by or send a copy of the record to any court, supervising officer, or the department on request; and

(10) annually provide to the department a written report of each service and ignition interlock device feature made available by the vendor.

(c) The department may revoke the department's authorization for a vendor to do business in this state if the vendor or an officer or employee of the vendor violates:

(1) any law of this state that applies to the vendor; or

(2) any rule adopted by the department under this section or another law that applies to the vendor.

(d) A vendor shall reimburse the department for the reasonable cost of conducting each inspection of the vendor's facilities under this section.

(e) In this section, "offense relating to the operating of a motor vehicle while intoxicated" has the meaning assigned by Section 49.09, Penal Code.

(Enacted by Acts 1999, 76th Leg., ch. 1105 (H.B. 3492), § 2, effective September 1, 1999.)

### Sec. 521.248. Order Requirements.

(a) An order granting an occupational license must specify:

(1) the hours of the day and days of the week during which the person may operate a motor vehicle;

(2) the reasons for which the person may operate a motor vehicle;

(3) areas or routes of travel permitted;

(4) that the person is restricted to the operation of a motor vehicle equipped with an ignition interlock device, if applicable; and

(5) that the person must submit to periodic testing for alcohol or controlled substances, if applicable.

(b) The person may not operate a motor vehicle for more than four hours in any 24-hour period, except that on a showing of necessity the court may allow the person to drive for any period determined by the court that does not exceed 12 hours in any 24-hour period.

(c) An order granting an occupational license remains valid until the end of the period of suspension of the person's regular driver's license.

(Enacted by Acts 1995, 74th Leg., ch. 165 (S.B. 971), § 1, effective September 1, 1995; am. Acts 2011, 82nd Leg., ch. 426 (S.B. 953), § 2, effective September 1, 2011.)

### Sec. 521.249. Notice to Department; Issuance of Occupational License.

(a) The court shall send a certified copy of the petition and the court order setting out the judge's findings and restrictions to the department. The person may use a copy of the order as a restricted license until the 31st day after the date on which the order takes effect.

(b) On receipt of the copy under this section and after compliance with Chapter 601, the de-

partment shall issue an occupational license to the person. The license must refer on its face to the court order.
(Enacted by Acts 1995, 74th Leg., ch. 165 (S.B. 971), § 1, effective September 1, 1995.)

### Sec. 521.250. Court Order in Operator's Possession.

A person who is issued an occupational license shall have in the person's possession a certified copy of the court order granting the license while operating a motor vehicle. The person shall allow a peace officer to examine the order on request.
(Enacted by Acts 1995, 74th Leg., ch. 165 (S.B. 971), § 1, effective September 1, 1995.)

### Sec. 521.251. Effective Date of Occupational License.

(a) If a person's license is suspended under Chapter 524 or 724 and the person has not had a prior suspension arising from an alcohol-related or drug-related enforcement contact in the five years preceding the date of the person's arrest, an order under this subchapter granting the person an occupational license takes effect immediately. However, the court shall order the person to comply with the counseling and rehabilitation program required under Section 521.245.

(b) If the person's driver's license has been suspended as a result of an alcohol-related or drug-related enforcement contact during the five years preceding the date of the person's arrest, the order may not take effect before the 91st day after the effective date of the suspension.

(c) If the person's driver's license has been suspended as a result of a conviction under Section 49.04, 49.07, or 49.08, Penal Code, during the five years preceding the date of the person's arrest, the order may not take effect before the 181st day after the effective date of the suspension.

(d) Notwithstanding any other provision in this section, if the person's driver's license has been suspended as a result of a second or subsequent conviction under Section 49.04, 49.07, or 49.08, Penal Code, committed within five years of the date on which the most recent preceding offense was committed, an order granting the person an occupational license may not take effect before the first anniversary of the effective date of the suspension.

(e) For the purposes of this section, "alcohol-related or drug-related enforcement contact" has the meaning assigned by Section 524.001.

(Enacted by Acts 1995, 74th Leg., ch. 165 (S.B. 971), § 1, effective September 1, 1995; am. Acts 2001, 77th Leg., ch. 969 (H.B. 5), § 5, effective September 1, 2001.)

### Sec. 521.252. License Revocation.

(a) The court that signs an order granting an occupational license may issue at any time an order revoking the license for good cause.

(b) The court shall send a certified copy of the order to the department.
(Enacted by Acts 1995, 74th Leg., ch. 165 (S.B. 971), § 1, effective September 1, 1995.)

### Sec. 521.253. Criminal Penalty.

(a) A person who holds an occupational license commits an offense if the person:

(1) operates a motor vehicle in violation of a restriction imposed on the license; or

(2) fails to have in the person's possession a certified copy of the court order as required under Section 521.250.

(b) An offense under this section is a Class B misdemeanor.

(c) On conviction of an offense under this section, the occupational license and the order granting that license are revoked.
(Enacted by Acts 1995, 74th Leg., ch. 165 (S.B. 971), § 1, effective September 1, 1995.)

### Secs. 521.254 to 521.270 [Reserved for expansion].

## SUBCHAPTER M
## LICENSE EXPIRATION, RENEWAL, AND NUMBER CHANGE

### Sec. 521.271. [2 Versions: Effective until September 28, 2011] License Expiration.

(a) Each original driver's license and provisional license expires as follows:

(1) except as provided by Section 521.2711, a driver's license expires on the first birthday of the license holder occurring after the sixth anniversary of the date of the application;

(2) a provisional license expires on the 18th birthday of the license holder;

(3) an instruction permit expires on the 18th birthday of the license holder;

(4) an occupational license expires on the first anniversary of the court order granting the license; and

(5) unless an earlier date is otherwise provided, a driver's license issued to a person whose residence or domicile is a correctional facility or a parole facility expires on the first birthday of the license holder occurring after the first anniversary of the date of issuance.

(a-1) [Repealed by Acts 2011, ch. 1160 (H.B. 2466), § 5, effective September 1, 2011].

(b) Except as provided by Section 521.2711, a driver's license that is renewed expires on the earlier of:

(1) the sixth anniversary of the expiration date before renewal; or

(2) for a renewal driver's license issued to a person whose residence or domicile is a correctional facility or a parole facility, the first birthday of the license holder occurring after the first anniversary of the date of issuance unless an earlier date is otherwise provided.

(Enacted by Acts 1995, 74th Leg., ch. 165 (S.B. 971), § 1, effective September 1, 1995; am. Acts 1997, 75th Leg., ch. 1372 (H.B. 1200), § 2, effective September 1, 1997; am. Acts 2003, 78th Leg., ch. 497 (H.B. 1032), § 1, effective September 1, 2003; am. Acts 2007, 80th Leg., ch. 37 (H.B. 84), § 2, effective September 1, 2007; am. Acts 2009, 81st Leg., ch. 1146 (H.B. 2730), § 12.09, effective September 1, 2009; am. Acts 2009, 81st Leg., ch. 1253 (H.B. 339), § 16, effective September 1, 2009; am. Acts 2009, 81st Leg., ch. 1288 (H.B. 2161), § 5, effective September 1, 2009; am. Acts 2011, 82nd Leg., ch. 1160 (H.B. 2466), § 5, effective September 1, 2011; am. Acts 2011, 82nd Leg., 1st C.S., ch. xxx (S.B. 1), § 72.08, effective September 28, 2011.)

## Sec. 521.271. [2 Versions: Effective September 28, 2011] License Expiration.

(a) Each original driver's license, provisional license, instruction permit, or occupational driver's license issued to an applicant who is a citizen, national, or legal permanent resident of the United States or a refugee or asylee lawfully admitted into the United States expires as follows:

(1) except as provided by Section 521.2711, a driver's license expires on the first birthday of the license holder occurring after the sixth anniversary of the date of the application;

(2) a provisional license expires on the 18th birthday of the license holder;

(3) an instruction permit expires on the 18th birthday of the license holder;

(4) an occupational driver's license expires on the first anniversary of the court order granting the license; and

(5) unless an earlier date is otherwise provided, a driver's license issued to a person whose residence or domicile is a correctional facility or a parole facility expires on the first birthday of the license holder occurring after the first anniversary of the date of issuance.

(a-1) [Repealed by Acts 2011, ch. 1160 (H.B. 2466), § 5, effective September 1, 2011].

(a-2) Each original driver's license issued to an applicant who is not a citizen, national, or legal permanent resident of the United States or a refugee or asylee lawfully admitted into the United States expires on:

(1) the earlier of:

(A) the first birthday of the license holder occurring after the sixth anniversary of the date of the application; or

(B) the expiration date of the license holder's lawful presence in the United States as determined by the appropriate United States agency in compliance with federal law; or

(2) the first anniversary of the date of issuance, if there is no definite expiration date for the applicant's authorized stay in the United States.

(a-3) Each original provisional license or instruction permit issued to an applicant who is not a citizen, national, or legal permanent resident of the United States or a refugee or asylee lawfully admitted into the United States expires on the earliest of:

(1) the 18th birthday of the license holder;

(2) the first birthday of the license holder occurring after the date of the application; or

(3) the expiration of the license holder's lawful presence in the United States as determined by the United States agency responsible for citizenship and immigration in compliance with federal law.

(a-4) Each original occupational driver's license issued to an applicant who is not a citizen, national, or legal permanent resident of the United States or a refugee or asylee lawfully admitted into the United States expires on the earlier of:

(1) the first anniversary of the date of issuance; or

(2) the expiration of the license holder's lawful presence in the United States as determined by the appropriate United States agency in compliance with federal law.

(b) Except as provided by Section 521.2711, a driver's license that is renewed expires on the earlier of:

(1) the sixth anniversary of the expiration date before renewal if the applicant is a citizen, national, or legal permanent resident of the United States or a refugee or asylee lawfully admitted into the United States;

(1-a) for an applicant not described by Subdivision (1):

(A) the earlier of:

(i) the sixth anniversary of the expiration date before renewal; or

(ii) the expiration date of the applicant's authorized stay in the United States; or

(B) the first anniversary of the date of issuance, if there is no definite expiration date for the applicant's authorized stay in the United States; or

(2) for a renewal driver's license issued to a person whose residence or domicile is a correctional facility or a parole facility, the first birthday of the license holder occurring after the first anniversary of the date of issuance unless an earlier date is otherwise provided.

(Enacted by Acts 1995, 74th Leg., ch. 165 (S.B. 971), § 1, effective September 1, 1995; am. Acts 1997, 75th Leg., ch. 1372 (H.B. 1200), § 2, effective September 1, 1997; am. Acts 2003, 78th Leg., ch. 497 (H.B. 1032), § 1, effective September 1, 2003; am. Acts 2007, 80th Leg., ch. 37 (H.B. 84), § 2, effective September 1, 2007; am. Acts 2009, 81st Leg., ch. 1146 (H.B. 2730), § 12.09, effective September 1, 2009; am. Acts 2009, 81st Leg., ch. 1253 (H.B. 339), § 16, effective September 1, 2009; am. Acts 2009, 81st Leg., ch. 1288 (H.B. 2161), § 5, effective September 1, 2009; am. Acts 2011, 82nd Leg., ch. 1160 (H.B. 2466), § 5, effective September 1, 2011; am. Acts 2011, 82nd Leg., 1st C.S., (S.B. 1), § 72.08, effective September 28, 2011.)

### Sec. 521.2711.  License Expiration: Person at Least 85 Years of Age.

(a) Each original driver's license of a person 85 years of age or older expires on the license holder's second birthday after the date of the license application.

(b) A driver's license of a person 85 years of age or older that is renewed expires on the second anniversary of the expiration date before renewal.

(c) **[Effective September 28, 2011]** Notwithstanding Subsections (a) and (b), an original or

renewal driver's license issued to an applicant who is 85 years of age or older and not a citizen, national, or legal permanent resident of the United States or a refugee or asylee lawfully admitted into the United States expires on:

(1) the earlier of:

(A) the second anniversary of the expiration date before renewal; or

(B) the expiration date of the applicant's authorized stay in the United States; or

(2) the first anniversary of the date of issuance if there is no definite expiration date for the applicant's authorized stay in the United States.

(Enacted by Acts 2007, 80th Leg., ch. 37 (H.B. 84), § 3, effective September 1, 2007; am. Acts 2011, 82nd Leg., 1st C.S., (S.B. 1), § 72.09, effective September 28, 2011.)

### Sec. 521.272.  Renewal of License Issued to Certain Sex Offenders.

(a) The department may issue an original or renewal driver's license to a person whose driver's license or personal identification certificate record indicates that the person is subject to the registration requirements of Chapter 62, Code of Criminal Procedure, only if the person:

(1) applies in person for the issuance of a license under this section; and

(2) pays the fee required by Section 521.421(h).

(b) Notwithstanding Section 521.143, a person is not required to provide proof of financial responsibility to receive the person's initial driver's license under this section.

(c) **[2 Versions: Effective until September 28, 2011]** Notwithstanding Section 521.271, a driver's license issued under this section, including a renewal, duplicate, or corrected license, expires on the first birthday of the license holder occurring after the date of application, except that the initial license issued under this section expires on the second birthday of the license holder occurring after the date of application. This subsection does not apply to:

(1) a provisional license;

(2) an instruction permit issued under Section 521.222; or

(3) a hardship license issued under Section 521.223.

(c) **[2 Versions: Effective September 28, 2011]** Notwithstanding Sections 521.271 and 521.2711, a driver's license issued under this section, including a renewal, duplicate, or corrected license, expires:

(1) if the license holder is a citizen, national, or legal permanent resident of the United States or a refugee or asylee lawfully admitted into the United States, on the first birthday of the license holder occurring after the date of application, except that the initial license issued under this section expires on the second birthday of the license holder occurring after the date of application; or

(2) if the applicant is not described by Subdivision (1), on the earlier of:

(A) the expiration date of the applicant's authorized stay in the United States; or

(B) the first birthday of the license holder occurring after the date of application, except that the initial license issued under this section expires on the second birthday of the license holder occurring after the date of application.

(d) **[Effective September 28, 2011]** Subsection (c) does not apply to:

(1) a provisional license;

(2) an instruction permit issued under Section 521.222; or

(3) a hardship license issued under Section 521.223.

(Enacted by Acts 1999, 76th Leg., ch. 1401 (H.B. 1939), § 7, effective September 1, 2000; am. Acts 2001, 77th Leg., ch. 546 (H.B. 2663), § 4, effective September 1, 2001; am. Acts 2011, 82nd Leg., 1st C.S., (S.B. 1), § 72.10, effective September 28, 2011.)

### Sec. 521.273. Renewal Examinations.

(a) The department may require and prescribe the procedure and standards for an examination for the renewal of a driver's license.

(b) A license holder who fails to obtain a renewal license as provided by this subchapter may be required to take any examination required for the original license.

(Enacted by Acts 1995, 74th Leg., ch. 165 (S.B. 971), § 1, effective September 1, 1995.)

### Sec. 521.274. Renewal by Mail or Electronic Means.

(a) The department by rule may provide that the holder of a driver's license may renew the license by mail, by telephone, over the Internet, or by other electronic means.

(b) A rule adopted under this section:

(1) may prescribe eligibility standards for renewal under this section;

(2) may not permit a person subject to the registration requirements under Chapter 62,

Code of Criminal Procedure, to register by mail or electronic means; and

(3) may not permit renewal by mail or electronic means of a driver's license of a person who is 79 years of age or older.

(Enacted by Acts 1995, 74th Leg., ch. 165 (S.B. 971), § 1, effective September 1, 1995; am. Acts 1999, 76th Leg., ch. 1189 (S.B. 370), § 24, effective September 1, 1999; am. Acts 1999, 76th Leg., ch. 1401 (H.B. 1939), § 8, effective September 1, 2000; am. Acts 2001, 77th Leg., ch. 546 (H.B. 2663), § 5, effective September 1, 2001; am. Acts 2007, 80th Leg., ch. 37 (H.B. 84), § 4, effective September 1, 2007.)

### Sec. 521.275. Change of Driver's License or Personal Identification Certificate Number.

(a) The department shall issue to a person a new driver's license number or personal identification certificate number on the person's showing a court order stating that the person has been the victim of domestic violence.

(b) The department may require each applicant to furnish the information required by Section 521.142. If the applicant's name has changed, the department may require evidence identifying the applicant by both the former and new name.

(c) Except as provided by Sections 521.049(c), 730.005, and 730.006, the department may not disclose:

(1) the changed license or certificate number; or

(2) the person's name or any former name.

(Enacted by Acts 1999, 76th Leg., ch. 709 (H.B. 865), § 2, effective September 1, 1999; enacted by Acts 1999, 76th Leg., ch. 1189 (S.B. 370), § 26, effective September 1, 1999.)

### Secs. 521.276 to 521.290 [Reserved for expansion].

### SUBCHAPTER N
### GENERAL PROVISIONS RELATING TO LICENSE DENIAL, SUSPENSION, OR REVOCATION

### Sec. 521.291. Rules.

The department shall adopt rules to administer this subchapter.

(Enacted by Acts 1999, 76th Leg., ch. 1117 (H.B. 3641), § 1, effective September 1, 2000.)

## Sec. 521.292. Department's Determination for License Suspension.

(a) The department shall suspend the person's license if the department determines that the person:

(1) has operated a motor vehicle on a highway while the person's license was suspended, canceled, disqualified, or revoked, or without a license after an application for a license was denied;

(2) is a habitually reckless or negligent operator of a motor vehicle;

(3) is a habitual violator of the traffic laws;

(4) has permitted the unlawful or fraudulent use of the person's license;

(5) has committed an offense in another state or Canadian province that, if committed in this state, would be grounds for suspension;

(6) has been convicted of two or more separate offenses of a violation of a restriction imposed on the use of the license;

(7) has been responsible as a driver for any accident resulting in serious personal injury or serious property damage;

(8) is the holder of a provisional license issued under Section 521.123 and has been convicted of two or more moving violations committed within a 12-month period; or

(9) has committed an offense under Section 545.421.

(b) For purposes of Subsection (a)(3), a person is a "habitual violator" if the person has four or more convictions that arise out of different transactions in 12 consecutive months, or seven or more convictions that arise out of different transactions in 24 months, if the convictions are for moving violations of the traffic laws of any state, Canadian province, or political subdivision, other than a violation under:

(1) Section 621.101, 621.201, or 621.203—621.207;

(2) Subchapter B or C, Chapter 623; or

(3) Section 545.413.

(Enacted by Acts 1999, 76th Leg., ch. 1117 (H.B. 3641), § 1, effective September 1, 2000; am. Acts 2005, 79th Leg., ch. 357 (S.B. 1257), § 1, effective September 1, 2005.)

## Sec. 521.293. Period of Suspension Under Section 521.292.

(a) Except as provided by Subsection (b), if the person does not request a hearing, the period of license suspension under Section 521.292 is 90 days.

(b) If the department determines that the person engaged in conduct described by Section 521.292(a)(1), the period of license suspension is extended for an additional period of the lesser of:

(1) the term of the original suspension; or

(2) one year.

(Enacted by Acts 1999, 76th Leg., ch. 1117 (H.B. 3641), § 1, effective September 1, 2000.)

## Sec. 521.294. Department's Determination for License Revocation.

The department shall revoke the person's license if the department determines that the person:

(1) is incapable of safely operating a motor vehicle;

(2) has not complied with the terms of a citation issued by a jurisdiction that is a party to the Nonresident Violator Compact of 1977 for a traffic violation to which that compact applies;

(3) has failed to provide medical records or has failed to undergo medical or other examinations as required by a panel of the medical advisory board;

(4) has failed to pass an examination required by the director under this chapter;

(5) has been reported by a court under Section 521.3452 for failure to appear unless the court files an additional report on final disposition of the case;

(6) has been reported within the preceding two years by a justice or municipal court for failure to appear or for a default in payment of a fine for a misdemeanor punishable only by fine, other than a failure reported under Section 521.3452, committed by a person who is at least 14 years of age but younger than 17 years of age when the offense was committed, unless the court files an additional report on final disposition of the case; or

(7) has committed an offense in another state or Canadian province that, if committed in this state, would be grounds for revocation.

(Enacted by Acts 1999, 76th Leg., ch. 1117 (H.B. 3641), § 1, effective September 1, 2000; am. Acts 2003, 78th Leg., ch. 283 (H.B. 2319), § 55, effective September 1, 2003; am. Acts 2005, 79th Leg., ch. 949 (H.B. 1575), § 51, effective September 1, 2005.)

## Sec. 521.295. Notice of Department's Determination.

(a) If the department suspends a person's license under Section 521.292 or revokes a person's

Transportation

license under Section 521.294 or 521.2965, the department shall send a notice of suspension or revocation by first class mail to the person's address in the records of the department.

(b) Notice is considered received on the fifth day after the date the notice is mailed.
(Enacted by Acts 1999, 76th Leg., ch. 1117 (H.B. 3641), § 1, effective September 1, 2000; am. Acts 2011, 82nd Leg., ch. 1160 (H.B. 2466), § 2, effective September 1, 2011.)

## Sec. 521.296.  Notice of Suspension or Revocation.

A notice of suspension under Section 521.292 or revocation under Section 521.294 must state:

(1) the reason and statutory grounds for the suspension or revocation;

(2) the effective date of the suspension or revocation;

(3) the right of the person to a hearing;

(4) how to request a hearing; and

(5) the period in which the person must request a hearing.
(Enacted by Acts 1999, 76th Leg., ch. 1117 (H.B. 3641), § 1, effective September 1, 2000; am. Acts 2011, 82nd Leg., ch. 1160 (H.B. 2466), § 3, effective September 1, 2011.)

## Sec. 521.297.  Suspension, Revocation, or Disqualification Effective Date.

(a) A license suspension under Section 521.292 or revocation under Section 521.294 takes effect on the 40th day after the date the person is considered to have received notice of the suspension or revocation under Section 521.295(b).

(b) A license disqualification under Section 522.081(a) takes effect on the 40th day after the date the person is considered to have received notice of the disqualification under Section 521.295(b), unless a disqualification is currently in effect. If a disqualification is currently in effect, the periods of disqualifications run consecutively.
(Enacted by Acts 1999, 76th Leg., ch. 1117 (H.B. 3641), § 1, effective September 1, 2000; am. Acts 2007, 80th Leg., ch. 424 (S.B. 1372), § 2, effective January 1, 2008.)

## Sec. 521.298.  Hearing Request.

If, not later than the 15th day after the date on which the person is considered to have received notice of the suspension or revocation under Section 521.295(b), the department receives at its headquarters in Austin, in writing, including a facsimile transmission, or by another manner

prescribed by the department, a request that a hearing be held, a hearing shall be held as provided by Sections 521.295—521.303.
(Enacted by Acts 1999, 76th Leg., ch. 1117 (H.B. 3641), § 1, effective September 1, 2000.)

## Sec. 521.299.  Hearing Date; Rescheduling.

(a) A hearing requested under Section 521.298 shall be held not earlier than the 11th day after the date on which the person requesting the hearing is notified of the hearing. The hearing shall be set for the earliest practical date.

(b) A hearing may be continued on a motion of the person, the department, both parties, or as necessary to accommodate the docket of the presiding officer.

(c) A request for a hearing stays suspension or revocation of a person's license until the date of the final decision of the presiding officer.
(Enacted by Acts 1999, 76th Leg., ch. 1117 (H.B. 3641), § 1, effective September 1, 2000.)

## Sec. 521.300.  Hearing: Location; Presiding Officer.

(a) A hearing under this subchapter shall be conducted in a municipal court or a justice court in the county in which the person resides. The judge of the municipal court or the justice is designated as the presiding officer.

(b) The presiding officer is entitled to receive a fee for hearing the case if a fee is approved and set by the commissioners court of the county in which the person resides. The fee may not exceed $5 and shall be paid from the general revenue fund of the county.

(c) The presiding officer may administer oaths and issue subpoenas to compel the attendance of witnesses and the production of relevant books and documents.
(Enacted by Acts 1999, 76th Leg., ch. 1117 (H.B. 3641), § 1, effective September 1, 2000.)

## Sec. 521.301.  Issue at Hearing.

(a) The issue that must be proved at the hearing by a preponderance of the evidence is whether the grounds for suspension or revocation stated in the notice are true.

(b) If the presiding officer finds in the affirmative on that issue, the suspension or revocation is sustained.

(c) If the presiding officer sustains a suspension, the department shall suspend the person's license for the period specified by the presiding officer, which may not be less than 30 days or more than one year.

(d) If the presiding officer does not find in the affirmative on that issue, the department may not suspend or revoke the person's license.

(e) The decision of the presiding officer is final when issued and signed.

(Enacted by Acts 1999, 76th Leg., ch. 1117 (H.B. 3641), § 1, effective September 1, 2000.)

## Sec. 521.302. Failure to Appear.

A person who requests a hearing under this subchapter and fails to appear without just cause waives the right to a hearing and the department's determination is final.

(Enacted by Acts 1999, 76th Leg., ch. 1117 (H.B. 3641), § 1, effective September 1, 2000.)

## Sec. 521.303. Continuance.

A continuance under Section 521.299 stays the suspension or revocation of a license until the date of the final decision of the presiding officer.

(Enacted by Acts 1999, 76th Leg., ch. 1117 (H.B. 3641), § 1, effective September 1, 2000.)

## Sec. 521.304. Cancellation of Minor's License on Cosigner's Request; Release from Liability.

(a) The person who cosigned a minor's application for a driver's license under Section 521.145 may file with the department a request that the department cancel the license. The request must be in writing and acknowledged.

(b) On receipt of a request under Subsection (a), the department shall cancel the minor's license. On cancellation, the person who cosigned the application is released from liability based on the person's signing of the application for any subsequent negligence or wilful misconduct of the minor in operating a motor vehicle.

(Enacted by Acts 1995, 74th Leg., ch. 165 (S.B. 971), § 1, effective September 1, 1995; am. Acts 1999, 76th Leg., ch. 1117 (H.B. 3641), § 1, effective September 1, 2000 (renumbered from Sec. 521.296).)

## Sec. 521.305. Cancellation of Minor's License on Death of Cosigner.

On receipt of information satisfactory to the department of the death of a person who cosigned a minor's application for a driver's license under Section 521.145, the department shall cancel the license if the license holder is under 18 years of age and the department may not issue a new license until the minor files a new application that complies with this chapter.

(Enacted by Acts 1995, 74th Leg., ch. 165 (S.B. 971), § 1, effective September 1, 1995; am. Acts 1999, 76th Leg., ch. 1117 (H.B. 3641), § 1, effective September 1, 2000 (renumbered from Sec. 521.297).)

## Sec. 521.306. Effect of Conduct in Other Jurisdiction; Suspension Under Driver's License Compact.

(a) The department may suspend or revoke the license of a resident or the operating privilege of a nonresident to operate a motor vehicle in this state on receipt of notice of a conviction of the individual in another state or a Canadian province of an offense that, if committed in this state, would be grounds for the suspension or revocation of a driver's license.

(b) The department may give the same effect to the conduct of a resident of this state that occurs in another state or Canadian province that the department may give to conduct that occurs in this state under state law.

(c) The department may seek the suspension of the license of a person who has failed to comply with the terms of a citation to which Chapter 523 applies.

(Enacted by Acts 1995, 74th Leg., ch. 165 (S.B. 971), § 1, effective September 1, 1995; am. Acts 1999, 76th Leg., ch. 1117 (H.B. 3641), § 1, effective September 1, 2000 (renumbered from Sec. 521.299).)

## Sec. 521.307. Suspension of Certain Provisional Licenses.

(a) On the recommendation of a juvenile court with jurisdiction over the holder of a provisional license, the department shall suspend a provisional license if it is found by the juvenile court that the provisional license holder has committed:

(1) an offense that would be classified as a felony if the license holder were an adult; or

(2) a misdemeanor in which a motor vehicle was used to travel to or from the scene of the offense, other than an offense specified by Chapter 729.

(b) The department shall suspend the license for the period set by the juvenile court but not to exceed one year.

(c) The court shall report its recommendation promptly to the department in the manner and form prescribed by the department.

Transportation

(Enacted by Acts 1995, 74th Leg., ch. 165 (S.B. 971), § 1, effective September 1, 1995; am. Acts 1999, 76th Leg., ch. 1117 (H.B. 3641), § 1, effective September 1, 2000 (renumbered from Sec. 521.300).)

### Sec. 521.308. Appeal; Judicial Review.

(a) A person whose driver's license suspension or revocation has been sustained by a presiding officer under this subchapter may appeal the decision of the presiding officer.

(b) To appeal the decision of the presiding officer, the person must file a petition not later than the 30th day after the date on which the department order was entered in the county court at law of the county in which the person resides, or, if there is no county court at law, in the county court. The person must send a file-stamped copy of the petition, certified by the clerk of the court in which the petition is filed, to the department by certified mail.

(c) The court shall notify the department of the hearing not later than the 31st day before the date the court sets for the hearing.

(d) The court shall take testimony, examine the facts of the case, and determine whether the petitioner is subject to the suspension or revocation of a license under this subchapter.

(e) A trial on appeal is a trial de novo, and the person has the right to trial by jury.

(f) The filing of a petition of appeal as provided by this section stays an order of suspension, probated suspension, or revocation until the earlier of the 91st day after the date the appeal petition is filed or the date the trial is completed and final judgment is rendered.

(g) On expiration of the stay, the department shall impose the suspension, probated suspension, or revocation. The stay may not be extended, and an additional stay may not be granted.
(Enacted by Acts 1995, 74th Leg., ch. 165 (S.B. 971), § 1, effective September 1, 1995; am. Acts 1999, 76th Leg., ch. 1117 (H.B. 3641), § 1, effective September 1, 2000 (renumbered from Sec. 521.302).)

### Sec. 521.309. Probation of Suspension.

(a) On determining that a license shall be suspended, the presiding officer who conducts a hearing under this subchapter, or the court that tries an appeal under this subchapter, may recommend that the suspension be probated on any terms and conditions considered necessary or proper by the presiding officer or court, if it appears that justice and the best interests of the public and the person will be served by the probation.

(b) The revocation of a license may not be probated.

(c) The report to the department of the results of the hearing must include any terms and conditions of the probation.

(d) If probation is recommended, the department shall probate the suspension.

(e) If a presiding officer or a court probates a suspension of a license under this section, the probationary period shall be for a term of not less than 90 days or more than two years.
(Enacted by Acts 1995, 74th Leg., ch. 165 (S.B. 971), § 1, effective September 1, 1995; am. Acts 1999, 76th Leg., ch. 1117 (H.B. 3641), § 1, effective September 1, 2000 (renumbered from Sec. 521.303).)

### Sec. 521.310. Probation Violation.

(a) If the director believes that a person who has been placed on probation under Section 521.309 has violated a term or condition of the probation, the director shall notify the person and summon the person to appear at a hearing in the court or before the presiding officer or judge who recommended that the person be placed on probation after notice as provided by Sections 521.295 and 521.296.

(b) The issue at the hearing under this section is whether a term or condition of the probation has been violated. The presiding officer or judge presiding at the hearing shall report the finding to the department. If the finding is that a term or condition of the probation has been violated, the department shall take the action as determined in the original hearing.
(Enacted by Acts 1995, 74th Leg., ch. 165 (S.B. 971), § 1, effective September 1, 1995; am. Acts 1999, 76th Leg., ch. 1117 (H.B. 3641), § 1, effective September 1, 2000 (renumbered from Sec. 521.304).)

### Sec. 521.311. Effective Date of Order.

Except as provided by another section of this subchapter to the contrary, a decision under this subchapter takes effect on the 11th day after the date on which an order is rendered.
(Enacted by Acts 1995, 74th Leg., ch. 165 (S.B. 971), § 1, effective September 1, 1995; am. Acts 1999, 76th Leg., ch. 1117 (H.B. 3641), § 1, effec-

tive September 1, 2000 (renumbered from Sec. 521.305).)

### Sec. 521.312. Period of Suspension or Revocation; Reinstatement of License.

(a) Revocation of a license is for an indefinite period.

(b) Except as provided by Subsection (c), Section 521.293(b), or Subchapter O, the department may not suspend a license for a period that exceeds one year.

(c) The department may not reinstate a license revoked under Section 521.294(5) until the court that filed the report for which the license was revoked files an additional report on final disposition of the case.

(Enacted by Acts 1995, 74th Leg., ch. 165 (S.B. 971), § 1, effective September 1, 1995; am. Acts 1997, 75th Leg., ch. 165 (S.B. 898), § 30.90, effective September 1, 1997; am. Acts 1999, 76th Leg., ch. 1117 (H.B. 3641), § 1, effective September 1, 2000 (renumbered from Sec. 521.306).)

### Sec. 521.313. Reinstatement and Reissuance; Fee.

(a) A license suspended or revoked under this subchapter may not be reinstated or another license issued to the person until the person pays the department a fee of $100 in addition to any other fee required by law.

(b) The payment of a reinstatement fee is not required if a suspension or revocation under this subchapter is:

(1) rescinded by the department; or

(2) not sustained by a presiding officer or a court.

(c) Each fee collected under this section shall be deposited to the credit of the Texas mobility fund.

(Enacted by Acts 1999, 76th Leg., ch. 1117 (H.B. 3641), § 1, effective September 1, 2000; am. Acts 2003, 78th Leg., ch. 1325 (H.B. 3588), § 11.02, effective September 1, 2003.)

### Sec. 521.314. Cancellation Authority.

The department may cancel a license or certificate if it determines that the holder:

(1) was not entitled to the license or certificate; or

(2) failed to give required information in the application for the license or certificate.

(Enacted by Acts 1995, 74th Leg., ch. 165 (S.B. 971), § 1, effective September 1, 1995; am. Acts 1999, 76th Leg., ch. 1117 (H.B. 3641), § 1, effec-

tive September 1, 2000 (renumbered from Sec. 521.307).)

### Sec. 521.315. Surrender of License; Return.

(a) On the suspension, cancellation, disqualification, or revocation of a license by the department, the department may require the holder to surrender the license to the department.

(b) The department shall return a suspended license to the holder on the expiration of the suspension period.

(c) A person commits an offense if the person's license has been demanded in accordance with Subsection (a) and the person fails or refuses to surrender the license to the department.

(d) An offense under this section is a Class B misdemeanor.

(Enacted by Acts 1995, 74th Leg., ch. 165 (S.B. 971), § 1, effective September 1, 1995; am. Acts 1999, 76th Leg., ch. 884 (H.B. 2032), § 1, effective September 1, 1999; am. Acts 1999, 76th Leg., ch. 1117 (H.B. 3641), § 1, effective September 1, 2000 (renumbered from Sec. 521.308); am. Acts 2001, 77th Leg., ch. 933 (S.B. 671), § 1, effective September 1, 2001.)

### Sec. 521.316. Suspended Foreign License.

A person whose driver's license or privilege to operate a vehicle in this state is suspended or revoked under this chapter may not operate a motor vehicle in this state under a license, permit, or registration certificate issued by any other state or Canadian province during the suspension period or after the revocation until a new license is obtained as provided by this chapter.

(Enacted by Acts 1995, 74th Leg., ch. 165 (S.B. 971), § 1, effective September 1, 1995; am. Acts 1999, 76th Leg., ch. 1117 (H.B. 3641), § 1, effective September 1, 2000 (renumbered from Sec. 521.309).)

### Sec. 521.317. Denial of License Renewal After Warning.

The department may deny the renewal of the driver's license of a person about whom the department has received information under Section 706.004 until the date the department receives a notification from the political subdivision under Section 706.005 that there is no cause to deny the renewal based on the person's previous failure to appear for a complaint, citation, or court order to pay a fine involving a violation of a traffic law.

(Enacted by Acts 1995, 74th Leg., ch. 165 (S.B. 971), § 1, effective September 1, 1995; am. Acts 1997, 75th Leg., ch. 165 (S.B. 898), § 30.91(a), effective September 1, 1997; am. Acts 1999, 76th Leg., ch. 1117 (H.B. 3641), § 1, effective September 1, 2000 (renumbered from Sec. 521.310).)

### Sec. 521.318. Nonresidents.

(a) The department may suspend or revoke a nonresident's operating privilege in the same manner and for the same causes as a driver's license issued under this chapter.

(b) On receipt of a record of conviction of a nonresident in this state under the motor vehicle laws of this state, the department may forward a certified copy of the record to the motor vehicle administrator of the state or Canadian province of which the convicted person is a resident.

(Enacted by Acts 1995, 74th Leg., ch. 165 (S.B. 971), § 1, effective September 1, 1995; am. Acts 1999, 76th Leg., ch. 1117 (H.B. 3641), § 1, effective September 1, 2000 (renumbered from Sec. 521.311).)

### Sec. 521.319. Revocation for Medical Reasons.

(a) A person may not operate a motor vehicle if the person:

(1) is a chemically dependent person who:

(A) is likely to cause serious harm to the person or to others; or

(B) will, if not treated, continue to suffer abnormal mental, emotional, or physical distress, or to deteriorate in ability to function independently; or

(2) has been determined by a judgment of a court to be totally incapacitated or incapacitated to act as the operator of a motor vehicle.

(b) The driver's license of a person is revoked on:

(1) the judgment of a court that the person is totally incapacitated or incapacitated to act as the operator of a motor vehicle; or

(2) the order of a court of involuntary treatment of the person under Subchapter D, Chapter 462, Health and Safety Code.

(c) If the person has not been issued a driver's license, the judgment or order of a court under Subsection (b) automatically prohibits the department from issuing a driver's license to the person.

(d) The clerk of the court that renders a judgment or enters an order under Subsection (b) shall notify the department of the court's judgment or order before the 10th day after the date the court renders the judgment or enters the order.

(e) The revocation of a driver's license under Subsection (b) or the prohibition against the issuance of a driver's license under Subsection (c) expires on the date on which:

(1) the person is:

(A) restored to capacity by judicial decree; or

(B) released from a hospital for the mentally incapacitated on a certificate of the superintendent or administrator that the person has regained capacity; or

(2) the order of involuntary treatment of the chemically dependent person expires.

(f) Before the 10th day after the date under Subsection (e)(1)(A) or (2), the clerk of the appropriate court shall notify the department that:

(1) the person has been restored to capacity by judicial decree; or

(2) the order of involuntary treatment has expired or has been terminated under Section 462.080(d), Health and Safety Code.

(g) Before the 10th day after the date under Subsection (e)(1)(B), the superintendent or administrator of the hospital shall notify the department that the person has been released from the hospital on a certificate that the person has regained capacity.

(h) In this section:

(1) "Chemically dependent person" means a person with chemical dependency.

(2) "Chemical dependency" and "treatment" have the meanings assigned by Section 462.001, Health and Safety Code.

(Enacted by Acts 1995, 74th Leg., ch. 165 (S.B. 971), § 1, effective September 1, 1995; am. Acts 1997, 75th Leg., ch. 165 (S.B. 898), § 30.92(a), effective September 1, 1997; am. Acts 1999, 76th Leg., ch. 1117 (H.B. 3641), § 1, effective September 1, 2000 (renumbered from Sec. 521.312).)

### Sec. 521.320. Suspension for Certain Criminal Mischief; License Denial.

(a) A court may order the department to suspend a person's driver's license on conviction of an offense under Section 28.08, Penal Code.

(b) A court may order the department to deny an application for reinstatement or issuance of a driver's license to a person convicted of an offense under Section 28.08, Penal Code, who, on the date of the conviction, did not hold a driver's license.

(c) The period of suspension under this section is one year after the date of a final conviction. The period of license denial is one year after the date the person applies to the department for reinstatement or issuance of a driver's license.

(d) The department may not reinstate a driver's license suspended under Subsection (a) unless the person whose license was suspended applies to the department for reinstatement.

(e) A person whose license is suspended under Subsection (a) remains eligible to receive an occupational license under Subchapter L.

(f) For the purposes of this section, a person is convicted of an offense regardless of whether sentence is imposed or the person is placed on community supervision for the offense under Article 42.12, Code of Criminal Procedure.
(Enacted by Acts 1997, 75th Leg., ch. 593 (S.B. 758), § 5, effective September 1, 1997; am. Acts 1999, 76th Leg., ch. 1117 (H.B. 3641), § 1, effective September 1, 2000 (renumbered from Sec. 521.314).)

**Secs. 521.321 to 521.340 [Reserved for expansion].**

## SUBCHAPTER O
## AUTOMATIC SUSPENSION

### Sec. 521.341. Requirements for Automatic License Suspension.

Except as provided by Sections 521.344(d)—(i), a license is automatically suspended on final conviction of the license holder of:

(1) an offense under Section 19.05, Penal Code, committed as a result of the holder's criminally negligent operation of a motor vehicle;

(2) an offense under Section 38.04, Penal Code, if the holder used a motor vehicle in the commission of the offense;

(3) an offense under Section 49.04, 49.045, or 49.08, Penal Code;

(4) an offense under Section 49.07, Penal Code, if the holder used a motor vehicle in the commission of the offense;

(5) an offense punishable as a felony under the motor vehicle laws of this state;

(6) an offense under Section 550.021;

(7) an offense under Section 521.451 or 521.453; or

(8) an offense under Section 19.04, Penal Code, if the holder used a motor vehicle in the commission of the offense.

(Enacted by Acts 1995, 74th Leg., ch. 165 (S.B. 971), § 1, effective September 1, 1995; am. Acts 1997, 75th Leg., ch. 165 (S.B. 898), § 30.93(a), effective September 1, 1997; am. Acts 2005, 79th Leg., ch. 728 (H.B. 2018), § 20.004, effective September 1, 2005; am. Acts 2007, 80th Leg., ch. 652 (H.B. 1049), § 1, effective September 1, 2007; am. Acts 2009, 81st Leg., ch. 1146 (H.B. 2730), § 16.01, effective September 1, 2009; am. Acts 2009, 81st Leg., ch. 1348 (S.B. 328), § 7, effective September 1, 2009.)

### Sec. 521.342. Person Under 21 Years of Age.

(a) Except as provided by Section 521.344, the license of a person who was under 21 years of age at the time of the offense, other than an offense classified as a misdemeanor punishable by fine only, is automatically suspended on conviction of:

(1) an offense under Section 49.04, 49.045, or 49.07, Penal Code, committed as a result of the introduction of alcohol into the body;

(2) an offense under the Alcoholic Beverage Code, other than an offense to which Section 106.071 of that code applies, involving the manufacture, delivery, possession, transportation, or use of an alcoholic beverage;

(3) a misdemeanor offense under Chapter 481, Health and Safety Code, for which Subchapter P does not require the automatic suspension of the license;

(4) an offense under Chapter 483, Health and Safety Code, involving the manufacture, delivery, possession, transportation, or use of a dangerous drug; or

(5) an offense under Chapter 485, Health and Safety Code, involving the manufacture, delivery, possession, transportation, or use of an abusable volatile chemical.

(b) The department shall suspend for one year the license of a person who is under 21 years of age and is convicted of an offense under Section 49.04, 49.045, 49.07, or 49.08, Penal Code, regardless of whether the person is required to attend an educational program under Section 13(h), Article 42.12, Code of Criminal Procedure, that is designed to rehabilitate persons who have operated motor vehicles while intoxicated, unless the person is placed under community supervision under that article and is required as a condition of the community supervision to not operate a motor vehicle unless the vehicle is equipped with the device described by Section 13(i) of that article. If the person is required to

**Transportation**

attend such a program and does not complete the program before the end of the person's suspension, the department shall suspend the person's license or continue the suspension, as appropriate, until the department receives proof that the person has successfully completed the program. On the person's successful completion of the program, the person's instructor shall give notice to the department and to the community supervision and corrections department in the manner provided by Section 13(h), Article 42.12, Code of Criminal Procedure.

(c) A person whose license is suspended under Subsection (a) remains eligible to receive an occupational license under Subchapter L. Suspension under Subsection (a) is not a suspension for physical or mental disability or impairment for purposes of eligibility to apply for an occupational license under Subchapter L.

(Enacted by Acts 1995, 74th Leg., ch. 165 (S.B. 971), § 1, effective September 1, 1995; am. Acts 1997, 75th Leg., ch. 165 (S.B. 898), §§ 30.94(a), 30.95(a), effective September 1, 1997; am. Acts 1997, 75th Leg., ch. 1013 (S.B. 35), § 20, effective September 1, 1997; am. Acts 1999, 76th Leg., ch. 580 (S.B. 577), § 9, effective September 1, 1999; am. Acts 2003, 78th Leg., ch. 861 (S.B. 613), § 1, effective September 1, 2003am. Acts 2009, 81st Leg., ch. 1146 (H.B. 2730), § 16.02, effective September 1, 2009; am. Acts 2009, 81st Leg., ch. 1348 (S.B. 328), § 8, effective September 1, 2009.)

## Sec. 521.343. Period of Suspension; Extension.

(a) Except as provided by Sections 521.342(b), 521.344(a), (b), (d), (e), (f), (g), (h), and (i), 521.345, 521.346, 521.3465, and 521.351, a suspension under this subchapter is for one year.

(b) If a license is suspended under this subchapter for a subsequent period, the subsequent suspension is for 18 months except as otherwise provided by a section listed in Subsection (a).

(c) If the license holder is convicted of operating a motor vehicle while the license to operate a motor vehicle is cancelled, disqualified, suspended, revoked, or denied, the period is extended for the same term as the original suspension or disqualification, in addition to any penalty assessed under this chapter or Chapter 522.

(Enacted by Acts 1995, 74th Leg., ch. 165 (S.B. 971), § 1, effective September 1, 1995; am. Acts 1997, 75th Leg., ch. 851 (H.B. 1048), § 3, effective September 1, 1997; am. Acts 2005, 79th Leg., ch. 1056 (H.B. 1357), § 2, effective September 1, 2005.)

## Sec. 521.344. Suspension for Offenses Involving Intoxication.

(a) Except as provided by Sections 521.342(b) and 521.345, and by Subsections (d)—(i), if a person is convicted of an offense under Section 49.04, 49.045, or 49.07, Penal Code, the license suspension:

(1) begins on a date set by the court that is not earlier than the date of the conviction or later than the 30th day after the date of the conviction, as determined by the court; and

(2) continues for a period set by the court according to the following schedule:

(A) not less than 90 days or more than one year, if the person is punished under Section 49.04, 49.045, or 49.07, Penal Code, except that if the person's license is suspended for a second or subsequent offense under Section 49.07 committed within five years of the date on which the most recent preceding offense was committed, the suspension continues for a period of one year;

(B) not less than 180 days or more than two years, if the person is punished under Section 49.09(a) or (b), Penal Code; or

(C) not less than one year or more than two years, if the person is punished under Section 49.09(a) or (b), Penal Code, and is subject to Section 49.09(h) of that code.

(b) Except as provided by Section 521.342(b), if a person is convicted of an offense under Section 49.08, Penal Code, the license suspension:

(1) begins on a date set by the court that is not earlier than the date of the conviction or later than the 30th day after the date of the conviction, as determined by the court; and

(2) continues for a period set by the court of not less than 180 days or more than two years, except that if the person's license is suspended for a second or subsequent offense under Section 49.08, Penal Code, committed within 10 years of the date on which the most recent preceding offense was committed, the suspension continues for a period set by the court of not less than one year or more than two years.

(c) The court shall credit toward the period of suspension a suspension imposed on the person for refusal to give a specimen under Chapter 724 if the refusal followed an arrest for the same offense for which the court is suspending the person's license under this chapter. The court may not extend the credit to a person:

(1) who has been previously convicted of an offense under Section 49.04, 49.045, 49.07, or 49.08, Penal Code; or

(2) whose period of suspension is governed by Section 521.342(b).

(d) Except as provided by Subsection (e) and Section 521.342(b), during a period of probation the department may not revoke the person's license if the person is required under Section 13(h) or (j), Article 42.12, Code of Criminal Procedure, to successfully complete an educational program designed to rehabilitate persons who have operated motor vehicles while intoxicated, unless the person was punished under Section 49.09(a) or (b), Penal Code, and was subject to Section 49.09(h) of that code. The department may not revoke the license of a person:

(1) for whom the jury has recommended that the license not be revoked under Section 13(g), Article 42.12, Code of Criminal Procedure; or

(2) who is placed under community supervision under that article and is required as a condition of community supervision to not operate a motor vehicle unless the vehicle is equipped with the device described by Section 13(i) of that article, unless the person was punished under Section 49.09(a) or (b), Penal Code, and was subject to Section 49.09(h) of that code.

(e) After the date has passed, according to department records, for successful completion of the educational program designed to rehabilitate persons who operated motor vehicles while intoxicated, the director shall revoke the license of a person who does not successfully complete the program or, if the person is a resident without a license to operate a motor vehicle in this state, shall issue an order prohibiting the person from obtaining a license.

(f) After the date has passed, according to department records, for successful completion of an educational program for repeat offenders as required by Section 13, Article 42.12, Code of Criminal Procedure, the director shall suspend the license of a person who does not successfully complete the program or, if the person is a resident without a license, shall issue an order prohibiting the person from obtaining a license.

(g) A revocation, suspension, or prohibition order under Subsection (e) or (f) remains in effect until the department receives notice of successful completion of the educational program. The director shall promptly send notice of a revocation or prohibition order issued under Subsection (e) or (f) by first class mail to the person at the person's most recent address as shown in the records of the department. The notice must include the date of the revocation or prohibition order, the reason

for the revocation or prohibition, and a statement that the person has the right to request in writing that a hearing be held on the revocation or prohibition. Notice is considered received on the fifth day after the date the notice is mailed. A revocation or prohibition under Subsection (e) or (f) takes effect on the 30th day after the date the notice is mailed. The person may request a hearing not later than the 20th day after the date the notice is mailed. If the department receives a request under this subsection, the department shall set the hearing for the earliest practical time and the revocation or prohibition does not take effect until resolution of the hearing.

(h) The hearing shall be held in a municipal or justice court in the county of the person's residence in the manner provided for a suspension hearing under Subchapter N. The issues to be determined at the hearing are whether the person has successfully completed a required educational program and whether the period for completion of the program has passed. If the presiding officer determines that the educational program has not been completed and the period for completion has passed, the officer shall confirm the revocation or prohibition and shall notify the department of that fact. The director may not revoke or prohibit the license if the officer finds that the program has been completed, that, before the hearing, the court that originally imposed the requirement to attend an educational program has granted an extension that has not expired, or that the period for completion has not passed. If the person or the person's agent fails to appear at the hearing, the department shall revoke the person's license until the department receives notice of successful completion of the educational program.

(i) On the date that a suspension order under Section 521.343(c) is to expire, the period of suspension or the corresponding period in which the department is prohibited from issuing a license is automatically increased to two years unless the department receives notice of successful completion of the educational program as required by Section 13, Article 42.12, Code of Criminal Procedure. At the time a person is convicted of an offense under Section 49.04 or 49.045, Penal Code, the court shall warn the person of the effect of this subsection. On the person's successful completion of the program, the person's instructor shall give notice to the department and to the community supervision and corrections department in the manner required by Section 13, Article 42.12, Code of Criminal Procedure. If the department receives proof of completion after a period has been extended under this subsection, the department shall immediately end the suspension or prohibition.

(Enacted by Acts 1995, 74th Leg., ch. 165 (S.B. 971), § 1, effective September 1, 1995; am. Acts 1997, 75th Leg., ch. 165 (S.B. 898), § 30.96(a), effective September 1, 1997; am. Acts 1999, 76th Leg., ch. 580 (S.B. 577), § 10, effective September 1, 1999; am. Acts 1999, 76th Leg., ch. 1117 (H.B. 3641), § 2, effective September 1, 2000; am. Acts 1999, 76th Leg., ch. 1409 (H.B. 2031), § 2, effective September 1, 1999; am. Acts 2001, 77th Leg., ch. 969 (H.B. 5), §§ 6, 7, effective September 1, 2001; am. Acts 2003, 78th Leg., ch. 1275 (H.B. 3506), § 3(41), effective September 1, 2003; am. Acts 2009, 81st Leg., ch. 1146 (H.B. 2730), § 16.03, effective September 1, 2009; am. Acts 2009, 81st Leg., ch. 1348 (S.B. 328), § 9, effective September 1, 2009.)

### Sec. 521.345. Suspension on Order of Juvenile Court or on Order of Court Based on Alcoholic Beverage Violation by Minor.

(a) The department shall suspend the license of a person on receipt of an order to suspend the license that is issued by:

(1) a juvenile court under Section 54.042, Family Code; or

(2) a court under Section 106.115, Alcoholic Beverage Code.

(b) The period of suspension is for the period specified in the order.

(Enacted by Acts 1995, 74th Leg., ch. 165 (S.B. 971), § 1, effective September 1, 1995; am. Acts 1997, 75th Leg., ch. 165 (S.B. 898), § 30.97(a), effective September 1, 1997.)

### Sec. 521.3451. Suspension or Denial on Order of Justice or Municipal Court for Contempt of Court; Reinstatement.

(a) The department shall suspend or deny the issuance of a license or instruction permit on receipt of an order to suspend or deny the issuance of the license or permit from a justice or municipal court under Article 45.050, Code of Criminal Procedure.

(b) The department shall reinstate a license or permit suspended or reconsider a license or permit denied under Subsection (a) on receiving notice from the justice or municipal court that

ordered the suspension or denial that the contemnor has fully complied with the court's order. (Enacted by Acts 2003, 78th Leg., ch. 283 (H.B. 2319), § 56, effective September 1, 2003.)

### Sec. 521.3452. Procedure in Cases Involving Minors.

(a) A court shall report to the department a person charged with a traffic offense under this chapter who does not appear before the court as required by law.

(b) In addition to any other action or remedy provided by law, the department may deny renewal of the person's driver's license under Section 521.317 or Chapter 706.

(c) The court shall also report to the department on final disposition of the case.

(Enacted by Acts 2005, 79th Leg., ch. 949 (H.B. 1575), § 49, effective September 1, 2005.)

### Sec. 521.346. Suspension on Conviction of Certain Fraudulent Activities.

(a) If an individual is convicted of an offense under Section 521.451 or 521.453, the period of suspension shall be for the period set by the court of not less than 90 days or more than one year.

(b) If the court does not set the period, the department shall suspend the license for one year.

(Enacted by Acts 1995, 74th Leg., ch. 165 (S.B. 971), § 1, effective September 1, 1995.)

### Sec. 521.3465. Automatic Suspension on Conviction of Certain Offenses Involving Fictitious Motor Vehicle License Plates, Registration Insignia, or Safety Inspection Certificates.

(a) A license is automatically suspended on final conviction of the license holder of:

(1) an offense under Section 502.409(a)(4); or

(2) an offense under Section 548.603(a)(1) that involves a fictitious safety inspection certificate.

(b) A suspension under this section is for 180 days.

(c) If the person is a resident of this state without a driver's license to operate a motor vehicle, the director shall issue an order prohibiting the person from being issued a driver's license before the 181st day after the date of the conviction.

(Enacted by Acts 1997, 75th Leg., ch. 851 (H.B. 1048), § 4, effective September 1, 1997.)

### Sec. 521.3466. Automatic Revocation for Offense Involving Certain Fraudulent Governmental Records.

(a) A license is automatically revoked on final conviction of the license holder of an offense under Section 37.10, Penal Code, if the governmental record was a motor vehicle license plate or registration insignia, within the meaning of Chapter 502, or a safety inspection certificate, within the meaning of Chapter 548.

(b) If the person is a resident of this state without a driver's license to operate a motor vehicle, the director shall issue an order prohibiting the person from being issued a driver's license until the second anniversary of the date of the conviction.

(c) Section 521.347 applies to a conviction under Section 37.10, Penal Code, in the same manner that section applies to a conviction of an offense that requires automatic suspension of a person's driver's license.

(d) The department may not issue a driver's license to the person before the second anniversary of the date of the conviction. The department may issue a driver's license to the person only if the person:

    (1) applies to the department for the license;

    (2) is otherwise qualified for the license; and

    (3) pays, in addition to the fee required by Section 521.421, a fee of $100.

(e) Each fee collected under this section shall be deposited to the credit of the Texas mobility fund.

(Enacted by Acts 1997, 75th Leg., ch. 851 (H.B. 1048), § 4, effective September 1, 1997; am. Acts 2003, 78th Leg., ch. 1325 (H.B. 3588), § 11.03, effective September 1, 2003.)

### Sec. 521.347. Reports; Recommended Suspension.

(a) The court in which a person is convicted of an offense for which this chapter or Chapter 522 requires automatic suspension of the person's driver's license may require the person to surrender to the court each driver's license held by the person. Not later than the 10th day after the date on which the license is surrendered to the court, the clerk of the court shall send to the department:

    (1) the license; and

    (2) a record of the conviction that states whether the vehicle involved in the offense was a commercial motor vehicle as defined by Chapter 522 or was involved in the transport of hazardous materials.

(b) Each court with jurisdiction of an offense under this chapter or another law of this state regulating the operation of a motor vehicle on a highway shall send to the department a record of conviction of any person convicted in the court of such a violation. The court may recommend the suspension of the person's driver's license as provided by Subchapter N.

(c) For purposes of this section, "conviction" means a final conviction. A conviction is a final conviction regardless of whether any portion of the sentence for the conviction was suspended or probated but is not a final conviction if the defendant receives a deferred adjudication in the case or if the court defers final disposition of the case, unless the court subsequently proceeds with an adjudication of guilt and imposes a sentence on the defendant. For purposes of this section, a final judgment of forfeiture of bail or collateral deposited to secure a defendant's appearance in court is a conviction if the forfeiture is not vacated.

(Enacted by Acts 1995, 74th Leg., ch. 165 (S.B. 971), § 1, effective September 1, 1995; am. Acts 1999, 76th Leg., ch. 581 (S.B. 578), § 1, effective June 18, 1999; am. Acts 1999, 76th Leg., ch. 884 (H.B. 2032), § 2, effective September 1, 1999.)

### Sec. 521.348. Automatic Revocation for Certain Sex Offenders.

(a) A driver's license is automatically revoked if the holder of the license:

    (1) is subject to the registration requirements of Chapter 62, Code of Criminal Procedure; and

    (2) fails to apply to the department for renewal of the license as required by Article 62.060, Code of Criminal Procedure.

(b) The department may issue a driver's license to a person whose license is revoked under this section only if the person:

    (1) applies for an original or renewal license under Section 521.272; and

    (2) is otherwise qualified for the license.

(Enacted by Acts 1999, 76th Leg., ch. 1401 (H.B. 1939), § 9, effective September 1, 2000; am. Acts

2005, 79th Leg., ch. 1008 (H.B. 867), § 2.14, effective September 1, 2005.)

### Sec. 521.349. Acquiring Motor Fuel Without Payment: Automatic Suspension; License Denial.

(a) A person's driver's license is automatically suspended on final conviction of an offense under Section 31.03, Penal Code, if the judgment in the case contains a special affirmative finding under Article 42.019, Code of Criminal Procedure.

(b) The department may not issue a driver's license to a person convicted of an offense specified in Subsection (a) who, on the date of the conviction, did not hold a driver's license.

(c) The period of suspension under this section is the 180 days after the date of a final conviction, and the period of license denial is the 180 days after the date the person applies to the department for reinstatement or issuance of a driver's license, unless the person has previously been denied a license under this section or had a license suspended, in which event the period of suspension is one year after the date of a final conviction, and the period of license denial is one year after the date the person applies to the department for reinstatement or issuance of a driver's license.

(Enacted by Acts 2001, 77th Leg., ch. 359 (S.B. 968), § 2, effective September 1, 2001.)

### Sec. 521.350. Suspension for Offense Relating to Racing of Motor Vehicle on Public Highway or Street.

(a) A license is automatically suspended on conviction of an offense under Section 545.420(a).

(b) A suspension under this section is for one year, except as provided by this section.

(c) A person whose license is suspended under Subsection (a) remains eligible to receive an occupational license under Subchapter L, except that an occupational license issued to a person younger than 18 years of age whose license is suspended under this section may permit the operation of a motor vehicle only for transportation to and from an educational facility in which the person is enrolled and the place where the person resides.

(d) A person whose license is suspended under Subsection (a) shall be required by the court in which the person was convicted to perform at least 10 hours of community service as ordered by the court. If the person is a resident of this state without a driver's license to operate a motor

vehicle, the court shall issue an order prohibiting the department from issuing the person a driver's license before the person completes the community service. Community service required under this subsection is in addition to any community service required of the person as a condition of community supervision under Section 16, Article 42.12, Code of Criminal Procedure.

(e) If a person who is required to perform community service under Subsection (d) completes that community service before the end of the person's license suspension, the person may apply to the department for reinstatement of the person's license or the issuance of a new license. The application must include proof satisfactory to the department that the person has performed the community service.

(f) If a person whose license is suspended under this section is subsequently convicted of an offense under Section 521.457(a) during the period of license suspension, in addition to the penalties provided by Section 521.457, the department shall revoke the person's license until the first anniversary of the date of conviction and may not reinstate the person's license or issue the person a new license before that date.

(Enacted by Acts 2003, 78th Leg., ch. 535 (H.B. 1326), § 2, effective September 1, 2003.)

### Sec. 521.351. Purchase of Alcohol for Minor or Furnishing Alcohol to Minor: Automatic Suspension; License Denial.

(a) A person's driver's license is automatically suspended on final conviction of an offense under Section 106.06, Alcoholic Beverage Code.

(b) The department may not issue a driver's license to a person convicted of an offense under Section 106.06, Alcoholic Beverage Code, who, on the date of the conviction, did not hold a driver's license.

(c) The period of suspension under this section is the 180 days after the date of a final conviction, and the period of license denial is the 180 days after the date the person applies to the department for reinstatement or issuance of a driver's license, unless the person has previously been denied a license under this section or had a license suspended, in which event the period of suspension is one year after the date of a final conviction, and the period of license denial is one year after the date the person applies to the department for reinstatement or issuance of a driver's license.

(Enacted by Acts 2005, 79th Leg., ch. 1056 (H.B. 1357), § 3, effective September 1, 2005.)

Transportation

**Secs. 521.352 to 521.370 [Reserved for expansion].**

## SUBCHAPTER P
## AUTOMATIC SUSPENSION FOR CERTAIN DRUG OFFENSES.

### Sec. 521.371. Definitions.

In this subchapter:

(1) "Controlled Substances Act" means the federal Controlled Substances Act (21 U.S.C. Sec. 801 et seq.).

(2) "Convicted" includes an adjudication under juvenile proceedings.

(3) "Drug offense" has the meaning assigned under 23 U.S.C. Section 159(c) and includes an offense under Section 49.04, 49.07, or 49.08, Penal Code, that is committed as a result of the introduction into the body of any substance the possession of which is prohibited under the Controlled Substances Act.

(Enacted by Acts 1995, 74th Leg., ch. 165 (S.B. 971), § 1, effective September 1, 1995.)

### Sec. 521.372. Automatic Suspension; License Denial.

(a) A person's driver's license is automatically suspended on final conviction of:

(1) an offense under the Controlled Substances Act;

(2) a drug offense; or

(3) a felony under Chapter 481, Health and Safety Code, that is not a drug offense.

(b) The department may not issue a driver's license to a person convicted of an offense specified in Subsection (a) who, on the date of the conviction, did not hold a driver's license.

(c) Except as provided by Section 521.374(b), the period of suspension under this section is the 180 days after the date of a final conviction, and the period of license denial is the 180 days after the date the person applies to the department for reinstatement or issuance of a driver's license.

(Enacted by Acts 1995, 74th Leg., ch. 165 (S.B. 971), § 1, effective September 1, 1995.)

### Sec. 521.373. Reinstatement Requirements.

(a) The department may not reinstate a driver's license suspended under Section 521.372 unless the person whose license was suspended applies to the department for reinstatement.

(b) The department may not reinstate the driver's license of a person convicted of an offense

specified by Section 521.372(a) if the driver's license was under suspension on the date of the conviction.

(Enacted by Acts 1995, 74th Leg., ch. 165 (S.B. 971), § 1, effective September 1, 1995.)

### Sec. 521.374. Educational Program.

(a) A person whose license is suspended under Section 521.372 may attend an educational program, approved by the Texas Commission on Alcohol and Drug Abuse under rules adopted by the commission and the department, that is designed to educate persons on the dangers of drug abuse.

(b) The period of suspension or prohibition under Section 521.372(c) continues for an indefinite period until the individual successfully completes the educational program.

(Enacted by Acts 1995, 74th Leg., ch. 165 (S.B. 971), § 1, effective September 1, 1995.)

### Sec. 521.375. Joint Adoption of Rules.

(a) The Texas Commission on Alcohol and Drug Abuse and the department shall jointly adopt rules for the qualification and approval of providers of educational programs under Section 521.374.

(b) The Texas Commission on Alcohol and Drug Abuse shall publish the jointly adopted rules.

(Enacted by Acts 1995, 74th Leg., ch. 165 (S.B. 971), § 1, effective September 1, 1995.)

### Sec. 521.376. Duties of Texas Commission on Alcohol and Drug Abuse; Application and Renewal Fees.

The Texas Commission on Alcohol and Drug Abuse:

(1) shall monitor, coordinate, and provide training to persons who provide educational programs under Section 521.374;

(2) shall administer the approval of those educational programs; and

(3) may charge a nonrefundable application fee for:

(A) initial certification of approval; and

(B) renewal of the certification.

(Enacted by Acts 1995, 74th Leg., ch. 165 (S.B. 971), § 1, effective September 1, 1995; am. Acts 1997, 75th Leg., ch. 577 (H.B. 2119), § 19, effective September 1, 1997.)

### Sec. 521.377. License Reinstatement.

(a) The department, on payment of the applicable fee, shall reinstate a person's license or, if the person otherwise qualifies for a license, issue the license, if:

(1) the department receives notification from the clerk of the court in which the person was convicted that the person has successfully completed an educational program under this subchapter; and

(2) the person's driver's license has been suspended or license application denied for at least the period provided by Section 521.372(c).

(b) A person whose license is suspended under Section 521.372 remains eligible to receive an occupational license under Subchapter L. Suspension under Section 521.372 is not a suspension for physical or mental disability or impairment for purposes of eligibility to apply for an occupational license under Subchapter L.
(Enacted by Acts 1995, 74th Leg., ch. 165 (S.B. 971), § 1, effective September 1, 1995.)

**Secs. 521.378 to 521.400 [Reserved for expansion].**

## SUBCHAPTER Q
## ANATOMICAL GIFTS

### Sec. 521.401.   Statement of Gift.

(a) A person who wishes to be an eye, tissue, or organ donor may execute a statement of gift.

(b) The statement of gift may be shown on a donor's driver's license or personal identification certificate or by a card designed to be carried by the donor to evidence the donor's intentions with respect to organ, tissue, and eye donation. A donor card signed by the donor shall be given effect as if executed pursuant to Section 692A.005, Health and Safety Code.

(c) **[3 Versions: As amended by Acts 2009, 81st Leg., ch. 186, Effective until January 1, 2012]** Donor cards shall be provided to the department by organ procurement organizations, tissue banks, or eye banks, as those terms are defined in Section 692A.002, Health and Safety Code, or by the Glenda Dawson Donate Life-Texas Registry established under Chapter 692A, Health and Safety Code. The department shall:

(1) provide to each applicant for the issuance of an original, renewal, corrected, or duplicate driver's license or personal identification certificate who applies in person, by mail, over the Internet, or by other electronic means:

(A) the opportunity to indicate on the person's driver's license or personal identification certificate that the person is willing to

make an anatomical gift, in the event of death, in accordance with Section 692A.005, Health and Safety Code; and

(B) an opportunity for the person to consent in writing to the department's provision of the person's name, date of birth, driver's license number, most recent address, and other information needed for identification purposes at the time of donation to the organization selected by the commissioner of state health services under Section 692A.020, Health and Safety Code, for inclusion in the statewide Internet-based registry of organ, tissue, and eye donors and for release to procurement organizations; and

(2) provide a means to distribute donor cards to interested individuals in each office authorized to issue driver's licenses or personal identification certificates.

(c) **[3 Versions: As amended by Acts 2009, 81st Leg., ch. 831, Effective until January 1, 2012]** Donor registry information shall be provided to the department and the Texas Department of Transportation by qualified organ or tissue procurement organizations or eye banks, as those terms are defined in Section 692.002, Health and Safety Code, or by the Donor Education, Awareness, and Registry Program of Texas established under Chapter 49, Health and Safety Code. The department, with expert input and support from the Texas Organ, Tissue, and Eye Donor Council, shall:

(1) provide to each applicant for the issuance of an original, renewal, corrected, or duplicate driver's license or personal identification certificate who applies in person, by mail, over the Internet, or by other electronic means:

(A) the opportunity to indicate on the person's driver's license or personal identification certificate that the person is willing to make an anatomical gift, in the event of death, in accordance with Section 692.003, Health and Safety Code; and

(B) an opportunity for the person to consent in writing to the department's provision of the person's name, date of birth, driver's license number, most recent address, and other information needed for identification purposes at the time of donation to the organization selected by the commissioner of state health services under Chapter 49, Health and Safety Code, for inclusion in the statewide Internet-based registry of organ, tissue, and eye donors and for release to qualified organ, tissue, and eye bank organizations by specifically asking each applicant only the question, "Would you like to register as an organ donor?"; and

(2) provide a means to distribute donor registry information to interested individuals in each office authorized to issue driver's licenses or personal identification certificates.

(c) **[3 Versions: Effective January 1, 2012]** Donor registry information shall be provided to the department and the Texas Department of Transportation by organ procurement organizations, tissue banks, or eye banks, as those terms are defined in Section 692A.002, Health and Safety Code, or by the Glenda Dawson Donate Life-Texas Registry operated under Chapter 692A, Health and Safety Code. The department, with expert input and support from the nonprofit organization administering the Glenda Dawson Donate Life-Texas Registry, shall:

(1) provide to each applicant for the issuance of an original, renewal, corrected, or duplicate driver's license or personal identification certificate who applies in person, by mail, over the Internet, or by other electronic means:

(A) the opportunity to indicate on the person's driver's license or personal identification certificate that the person is willing to make an anatomical gift, in the event of death, in accordance with Section 692A.005, Health and Safety Code; and

(B) an opportunity for the person to consent to inclusion in the statewide Internet-based registry of organ, tissue, and eye donors and release to procurement organizations in the manner provided by Subsection (c-1); and

(2) provide a means to distribute donor registry information to interested individuals in each office authorized to issue driver's licenses or personal identification certificates.

(c-1) **[Effective January 1, 2012]** The department shall:

(1) specifically ask each applicant only the question, "Would you like to register as an organ donor?"; and

(2) if the applicant responds affirmatively to the question asked under Subdivision (1), provide the person's name, date of birth, driver's license number, most recent address, and other information needed for identification purposes at the time of donation to the nonprofit organization contracted to maintain the statewide donor registry under Section 692A.020, Health and Safety Code, for inclusion in the registry.

(d) An affirmative statement of gift on a person's driver's license or personal identification certificate executed after August 31, 2005, shall be conclusive evidence of a decedent's status as a donor and serve as consent for organ, tissue, and eye removal.

(e) The department shall distribute at all field offices Donate Life brochures that provide basic donation information in English and Spanish and include a contact phone number and e-mail address. The department shall include the question required under Subsection (c)(1)(B) and information on the donor registry Internet website in renewal notices.

(Enacted by Acts 1995, 74th Leg., ch. 165 (S.B. 971), § 1, effective September 1, 1995; am. Acts 1997, 75th Leg., ch. 225 (S.B. 952), § 1, effective September 1, 1997; am. Acts 2005, 79th Leg., ch. 1186 (H.B. 120), § 1, effective June 18, 2005; am. Acts 2009, 81st Leg., ch. 186 (H.B. 2027), § 9, effective September 1, 2009; am. Acts 2009, 81st Leg., ch. 831 (S.B. 1803), § 4, effective September 1, 2009; am. Acts 2011, 82nd Leg., ch. 554 (H.B. 2904), § 5, effective January 1, 2012.)

### Sec. 521.402. Revocation of Statement of Gift.

(a) To revoke an affirmative statement of gift on a person's driver's license or personal identification certificate, a person must apply to the department for an amendment to the license or certificate.

(b) The fee for an amendment is the same as the fee for a duplicate license.

(c) **[2 Versions: Effective until January 1, 2012]** To have a person's name deleted from the statewide Internet-based registry of organ, tissue, and eye donors maintained as provided by Chapter 49, Health and Safety Code, a person must provide written notice to the organization selected by the commissioner of state health services under that chapter to maintain the registry directing the deletion of the person's name from the registry. On receipt of a written notice under this subsection, the organization shall promptly remove the person's name and information from the registry.

(c) **[2 Versions: Effective January 1, 2012]** To have a person's name deleted from the statewide Internet-based registry of organ, tissue, and eye donors maintained as provided by Chapter 692A, Health and Safety Code, a person must provide written notice to the nonprofit organization selected under that chapter to maintain the

registry directing the deletion of the person's name from the registry. On receipt of a written notice under this subsection, the organization shall promptly remove the person's name and information from the registry.
(Enacted by Acts 1995, 74th Leg., ch. 165 (S.B. 971), § 1, effective September 1, 1995; am. Acts 1997, 75th Leg., ch. 225 (S.B. 952), § 1, effective September 1, 1997; am. Acts 2005, 79th Leg., ch. 1186 (H.B. 120), § 2, effective June 18, 2005; am. Acts 2011, 82nd Leg., ch. 554 (H.B. 2904), § 6, effective January 1, 2012.)

### Sec. 521.403.  Information Provided to Hospital [Repealed].

Repealed by Acts 2009, 81st Leg., ch. 186 (H.B. 2027), § 11(4), effective September 1, 2009.
(Enacted by Acts 1995, 74th Leg., ch. 165 (S.B. 971), § 1, effective September 1, 1995; am. Acts 1997, 75th Leg., ch. 225 (S.B. 952), § 1, effective September 1, 1997; am. Acts 2005, 79th Leg., ch. 1186 (H.B. 120), § 3, effective June 17, 2005.)

### Sec. 521.404.  Notification to Procurement Organization [Repealed].

Repealed by Acts 2009, 81st Leg., ch. 186 (H.B. 2027), § 11(5), effective September 1, 2009.
(Enacted by Acts 1995, 74th Leg., ch. 165 (S.B. 971), § 1, effective September 1, 1995.)

### Sec. 521.405.  Determination; Request; Removal of Certain Organs [Repealed].

Repealed by Acts 2005, 79th Leg., ch. 1069 (H.B. 1544), § 3, effective September 1, 2005.
(Enacted by Acts 1995, 74th Leg., ch. 165 (S.B. 971), § 1, effective September 1, 1995.)

### Secs.  521.406 to 521.420 [Reserved for expansion].

## SUBCHAPTER R
## FEES

### Sec. 521.421.  License Fees; Examination Fees.

(a) The fee for issuance or renewal of a license not otherwise provided for by this section is $24.
(a-1) The fee for a personal identification certificate issued under Section 501.0165, Government Code, is $5.
(a-2) Except as provided by Subsection (a-1), the department by rule shall establish the fee for a personal identification certificate or driver's license issued to a person whose residence or domicile is a correctional facility or a parole facility.
(a-3) **[Effective September 28, 2011]** Except as provided by Subsections (a-1) and (a-2), the fee for a driver's license or personal identification certificate that is issued to a person who is not a citizen, national, or legal permanent resident of the United States or a refugee or asylee lawfully admitted into the United States and that is valid for not more than one year is $24.
(b) The fee for renewal of a Class M license or for renewal of a license that includes authorization to operate a motorcycle is $32.
(c) The fee for issuance of a provisional license or instruction permit is $15.
(d) The fee for issuance or renewal of an occupational license is $10.
(e) An applicant who changes from a lower to a higher class of license or who adds a type of vehicle other than a motorcycle to the license shall pay a $10 fee for the required examination.
(f) **[2 Versions: As added by Acts 1997, 75th Leg., ch. 1156]** An applicant applying for additional authorization to operate a motorcycle shall pay a $15 fee for the required application.
(f) **[2 Versions: As added by Acts 1997, 75th Leg., ch. 1372]** If a Class A, B, or C driver's license includes an authorization to operate a motorcycle or moped, the fee for the driver's license is increased by $8.
(g) **[2 Versions: Effective until January 1, 2012]** The department shall collect an additional fee of $1 for the issuance or renewal of a license, including a duplicate license, a license issued to reflect an additional authorization or a change in classification, or a license issued or renewed over the Internet or by other electronic means, to pay the costs of the Donor Education, Awareness, and Registry Program of Texas, established under Chapter 49, Health and Safety Code, and, subject to Section 113.104, Health and Safety Code, of the Texas Organ, Tissue, and Eye Donor Council, established under Chapter 113, Health and Safety Code, if the person applying for, renewing, or changing a license opts to pay the additional fee. The department shall remit fees collected under this subsection to the comptroller, who shall maintain the identity of the source of the fees. Subject to appropriation, the department may retain three percent of the money collected under this subsection to cover the costs in administering this subsection.
(g) **[2 Versions: Effective January 1, 2012]** The department shall collect an additional fee of

$1 for the issuance or renewal of a license, including a duplicate license, a license issued to reflect an additional authorization or a change in classification, or a license issued or renewed over the Internet or by other electronic means, to pay the costs of the Glenda Dawson Donate Life-Texas Registry operated under Chapter 692A, Health and Safety Code, if the person applying for, renewing, or changing a license opts to pay the additional fee. The department shall remit fees collected under this subsection to the comptroller, who shall maintain the identity of the source of the fees. Subject to appropriation, the department may retain three percent of the money collected under this subsection to cover the costs in administering this subsection.

(h) The fee for issuance or renewal of a driver's license, a provisional license, an instruction permit, or a hardship license issued to a person subject to the registration requirements under Chapter 62, Code of Criminal Procedure, is $20.

(i) The fee for issuance or renewal of a driver's license is $8 for a license with an expiration date established under Section 521.2711.

(j) The department shall collect an additional fee of $1 for the issuance or renewal of a license to fund the Blindness Education, Screening, and Treatment Program established under Section 91.027, Human Resources Code, if the person applying for or renewing a license opts to pay the additional fee.

(Enacted by Acts 1995, 74th Leg., ch. 165 (S.B. 971), § 1, effective September 1, 1995; am. Acts 1997, 75th Leg., ch. 510 (S.B. 1403), § 2, effective September 1, 1997; am. Acts 1997, 75th Leg., ch. 1156 (S.B. 99), § 1, effective September 1, 1997; am. Acts 1997, 75th Leg., ch. 1372 (H.B. 1200), § 3, effective September 1, 1997; am. Acts 1999, 76th Leg., ch. 1516 (S.B. 673), § 2, effective September 1, 1999; am. Acts 2001, 77th Leg., ch. 546 (H.B. 2663), § 6, effective September 1, 2001; am. Acts 2001, 77th Leg., ch. 1420 (H.B. 2812), § 21.002(20), effective September 1, 2001; am. Acts 2005, 79th Leg., ch. 1186 (H.B. 120), § 6, effective June 18, 2005; am. Acts 2007, 80th Leg., ch. 37 (H.B. 84), § 5, effective September 1, 2007; am. Acts 2009, 81st Leg., ch. 87 (S.B. 1969), § 27.001(105), effective September 1, 2009; am. Acts 2009, 81st Leg., ch. 1146 (H.B. 2730), § 12.10, effective September 1, 2009; am. Acts 2009, 81st Leg., ch. 1253 (H.B. 339), § 17, effective September 1, 2009; am. Acts 2009, 81st Leg., ch. 1288 (H.B. 2161), § 6, effective September 1, 2009; am. Acts 2011, 82nd Leg., ch. 554 (H.B. 2904), § 7, effective January 1, 2012; am. Acts

2011, 82nd Leg., 1st C.S., (S.B. 1), § 72.11, effective September 28, 2011.)

### Sec. 521.422. Personal Identification Certificate Fee.

(a) The fee for a personal identification certificate is:

(1) $15 for a person under 60 years of age;

(2) $5 for a person 60 years of age or older; and

(3) $20 for a person subject to the registration requirements under Chapter 62, Code of Criminal Procedure.

(b) The department shall collect an additional fee of $1 for the issuance or renewal of a personal identification card to fund the Blindness Education, Screening, and Treatment Program established under Section 91.027, Human Resources Code, if the person applying for or renewing a personal identification card opts to pay the additional fee.

(c) [2 Versions: Effective until January 1, 2012] The department shall collect an additional fee of $1 for the issuance or renewal of a personal identification card, including a duplicate personal identification card or a personal identification card issued or renewed over the Internet or by other electronic means, to pay the costs of the Donor Education, Awareness, and Registry Program of Texas, established under Chapter 49, Health and Safety Code, and, subject to Section 113.104, Health and Safety Code, of the Texas Organ, Tissue, and Eye Donor Council, established under Chapter 113, Health and Safety Code, if the person applying for or renewing a personal identification card opts to pay the additional fee. The department shall remit fees collected under this subsection to the comptroller, who shall maintain the identity of the source of the fees. Subject to appropriation, the department may retain three percent of the money collected under this subsection to cover the costs in administering this subsection.

(c) [2 Versions: Effective January 1, 2012] The department shall collect an additional fee of $1 for the issuance or renewal of a personal identification card, including a duplicate personal identification card or a personal identification card issued or renewed over the Internet or by other electronic means, to pay the costs of the Glenda Dawson Donate Life-Texas Registry established under Chapter 692A, Health and Safety Code, if the person applying for or renewing a personal identification card opts to pay the

Transportation

additional fee. The department shall remit fees collected under this subsection to the comptroller, who shall maintain the identity of the source of the fees. Subject to appropriation, the department may retain three percent of the money collected under this subsection to cover the costs in administering this subsection.
(Enacted by Acts 1995, 74th Leg., ch. 165 (S.B. 971), § 1, effective September 1, 1995; am. Acts 1997, 75th Leg., ch. 510 (S.B. 1403), § 3, effective September 1, 1997; am. Acts 1997, 75th Leg., ch. 1372 (H.B. 1200), § 4, effective September 1, 1997; am. Acts 1999, 76th Leg., ch. 1516 (S.B. 673), § 3, effective September 1, 1999; am. Acts 2001, 77th Leg., ch. 546 (H.B. 2663), § 7, effective September 1, 2001; am. Acts 2001, 77th Leg., ch. 1420 (H.B. 2812), § 21.002(21), effective September 1, 2001; am. Acts 2005, 79th Leg., ch. 1186 (H.B. 120), § 7, effective June 18, 2005; am. Acts 2011, 82nd Leg., ch. 554 (H.B. 2904), § 8, effective January 1, 2012.)

### Sec. 521.423.  Fee for Disability Certificate or Health Condition Certificate [Repealed].

Repealed by Acts 2005, 79th Leg., ch. 1249 (H.B. 1789), § 3(3), effective September 1, 2005. (Enacted by Acts 1995, 74th Leg., ch. 165 (S.B. 971), § 1, effective September 1, 1995.)

### Sec. 521.424.  Duplicate License or Certificate Fee.

The fee for a duplicate driver's license or duplicate personal identification certificate is $10.
(Enacted by Acts 1995, 74th Leg., ch. 165 (S.B. 971), § 1, effective September 1, 1995; am. Acts 2005, 79th Leg., ch. 1249 (H.B. 1789), § 2, effective September 1, 2005.)

### Sec. 521.425.  Remittance of Fees and Charges.

Each fee or charge required by this chapter and collected by an officer or agent of the department shall be sent without deduction to the department in Austin.
(Enacted by Acts 1995, 74th Leg., ch. 165 (S.B. 971), § 1, effective September 1, 1995.)

### Sec. 521.426.  Disabled Veteran Exemption.

(a) Except as provided by Subsection (c), a veteran of service in the armed forces of the United States is exempt from the payment of fees under this chapter for the issuance of a driver's license or personal identification certificate if the veteran:
   (1) was honorably discharged;
   (2) has a service-related disability of at least 60 percent; and
   (3) receives compensation from the United States because of the disability.
(b) The department shall adopt rules relating to the proof of entitlement to this exemption.
(c) Subsection (a) does not apply to a person subject to the registration requirements of Chapter 62, Code of Criminal Procedure.
(Enacted by Acts 1995, 74th Leg., ch. 165 (S.B. 971), § 1, effective September 1, 1995; am. Acts 2001, 77th Leg., ch. 546 (H.B. 2663), § 8, effective September 1, 2001; am. Acts 2011, 82nd Leg., ch. 1133 (H.B. 1148), § 1, effective September 1, 2011.)

### Sec. 521.427.  Disposition of Fees.

(a) Except as provided by Subsections (b) and (c), each fee collected under this subchapter shall be deposited to the credit of the Texas mobility fund.
(b) Subsection (a) does not apply to:
   (1) the portion of a fee collected under Section 521.421(b) or Section 521.421(f), as added by Chapter 1156, Acts of the 75th Legislature, Regular Session, 1997, that is required by Section 662.011 to be deposited to the credit of the motorcycle education fund account;
   (2) a fee collected under Section 521.421(j);
   (3) a fee collected under Section 521.421(g); or
   (4) a fee collected under Section 521.422(b) or (c).
(c) [Repealed by Acts 2003, 78th Leg., 3rd C.S., ch. 8 (H.B. 2), § 6.02(1), effective January 11, 2004.]
(Enacted by Acts 2003, 78th Leg., ch. 1325 (H.B. 3588), § 11.04, effective September 1, 2003; am. Acts 2003, 78th Leg., 3rd C.S., ch. 8 (H.B. 2), § 6.02(1), effective January 11, 2004; am. Acts 2009, 81st Leg., ch. 87 (S.B. 1969), § 27.002(34), effective September 1, 2009.)

### Secs. 521.428 to 521.450 [Reserved for expansion].

## SUBCHAPTER S
## MISCELLANEOUS OFFENSES

### Sec. 521.451.  General Violation.

(a) Except as provided by Section 521.452, a person may not:

(1) display, cause or permit to be displayed, or have in the person's possession a driver's license or certificate that the person knows is fictitious or has been altered;

(2) lend the person's driver's license or certificate to another person or knowingly permit another person to use the person's driver's license or certificate;

(3) display or represent as the person's own a driver's license or certificate not issued to the person;

(4) possess more than one currently valid driver's license or more than one currently valid certificate; or

(5) in an application for an original, renewal, or duplicate driver's license or certificate:

(A) provide a false name, false address, or a counterfeit document; or

(B) knowingly make a false statement, conceal a material fact, or otherwise commit fraud.

(b) An offense under this section is a Class A misdemeanor.

(c) If conduct that constitutes an offense under Subsection (a) also constitutes an offense under Section 106.07, Alcoholic Beverage Code, the actor may be prosecuted only under Section 106.07, Alcoholic Beverage Code.

(Enacted by Acts 1995, 74th Leg., ch. 165 (S.B. 971), § 1, effective September 1, 1995; am. Acts 1999, 76th Leg., ch. 659 (H.B. 319), § 3, effective September 1, 1999; am. Acts 2001, 77th Leg., ch. 933 (S.B. 671), § 2, effective September 1, 2001; am. Acts 2005, 79th Leg., ch. 1208 (H.B. 699), § 1, effective September 1, 2005.)

## Sec. 521.452. Alias Driver's License for Law Enforcement Purposes.

(a) After written approval by the director, the department may issue to a law enforcement officer an alias driver's license to be used in supervised activities involving a criminal investigation.

(b) An application for, or possession or use of, an alias driver's license for a purpose described by this section by the officer to whom the license is issued is not a violation of this subchapter unless the department has canceled, suspended, or revoked the license.

(Enacted by Acts 1995, 74th Leg., ch. 165 (S.B. 971), § 1, effective September 1, 1995.)

## Sec. 521.453. Fictitious License or Certificate.

(a) Except as provided by Subsection (f), a person under the age of 21 years commits an offense if the person possesses, with the intent to represent that the person is 21 years of age or older, a document that is deceptively similar to a driver's license or a personal identification certificate unless the document displays the statement "NOT A GOVERNMENT DOCUMENT" diagonally printed clearly and indelibly on both the front and back of the document in solid red capital letters at least one-fourth inch in height.

(b) For purposes of this section, a document is deceptively similar to a driver's license or personal identification certificate if a reasonable person would assume that it was issued by the department, another agency of this state, another state, or the United States.

(c) A peace officer listed in Article 2.12, Code of Criminal Procedure, may confiscate a document that:

(1) is deceptively similar to a driver's license or personal identification certificate; and

(2) does not display the statement required under Subsection (a).

(d) For purposes of this section, an offense under Subsection (a) is a Class C misdemeanor.

(e) The attorney general, district attorney, or prosecuting attorney performing the duties of the district attorney may bring an action to enjoin a violation or threatened violation of this section. The action must be brought in a court in the county in which the violation or threatened violation occurs.

(f) Subsection (a) does not apply to:

(1) a government agency, office, or political subdivision that is authorized to produce or sell personal identification certificates; or

(2) a person that provides a document similar to a personal identification certificate to an employee of the person for a business purpose.

(g) In this section:

(1) "Driver's license" includes a driver's license issued by another state or by the United States.

(2) "Personal identification certificate" means a personal identification certificate issued by the department, by another agency of this state, by another state, or by the United States.

(h) In addition to the punishment provided by Subsection (d), a court, if the court is located in a municipality or county that has established a community service program, may order a person younger than 21 years of age who commits an offense under this section to perform eight hours of community service unless the person is shown to have previously committed an offense under this section, in which case the court may order the person to perform 12 hours of community service.

(i) If the person ordered to perform community service under Subsection (h) is younger than 17 years of age, the community service shall be performed as if ordered by a juvenile court under Section 54.044(a), Family Code, as a condition of probation under Section 54.04(d), Family Code. (Enacted by Acts 1995, 74th Leg., ch. 165 (S.B. 971), § 1, effective September 1, 1995; am. Acts 1997, 75th Leg., ch. 823 (S.B. 89), § 1, effective September 1, 1997; am. Acts 1997, 75th Leg., ch. 1358 (H.B. 677), § 1, effective September 1, 1997.)

### Sec. 521.454.   False Application.

(a) A person commits an offense if the person knowingly swears to or affirms falsely before a person authorized to take statements under oath any matter, information, or statement required by the department in an application for an original, renewal, or duplicate driver's license or certificate issued under this chapter.

(b) An information or indictment for a violation of Subsection (a) that alleges that the declarant has made inconsistent statements under oath, both of which cannot be true, need not allege which statement is false and the prosecution is not required to prove which statement is false.

(c) An offense under this section is a Class A misdemeanor.

(d) If conduct constituting an offense under this section also constitutes an offense under another law, the actor may be prosecuted under this section, the other law, or both. (Enacted by Acts 1995, 74th Leg., ch. 165 (S.B. 971), § 1, effective September 1, 1995; am. Acts 1999, 76th Leg., ch. 658 (H.B. 318), § 1, effective September 1, 1999; am. Acts 2009, 81st Leg., ch. 1130 (H.B. 2086), § 32, effective September 1, 2009.)

### Sec. 521.455.   Use of Illegal License or Certificate.

(a) A person commits an offense if the person intentionally or knowingly uses a driver's license or certificate obtained in violation of Section 521.451 or 521.454 to harm or defraud another.

(b) An offense under this section is a Class A misdemeanor.

(c) If conduct constituting an offense under this section also constitutes an offense under

another law, the actor may be prosecuted under this section, the other law, or both. (Enacted by Acts 1995, 74th Leg., ch. 165 (S.B. 971), § 1, effective September 1, 1995; am. Acts 2009, 81st Leg., ch. 1130 (H.B. 2086), § 33, effective September 1, 2009.)

### Sec. 521.456.   Delivery or Manufacture of Counterfeit Instrument.

(a) A person commits an offense if the person possesses with the intent to sell, distribute, or deliver a forged or counterfeit instrument that is not printed, manufactured, or made by or under the direction of, or issued, sold, or circulated by or under the direction of, a person, board, agency, or authority authorized to do so under this chapter or under the laws of the United States, another state, or a Canadian province. An offense under this subsection is a Class A misdemeanor.

(b) A person commits an offense if the person manufactures or produces with the intent to sell, distribute, or deliver a forged or counterfeit instrument that the person knows is not printed, manufactured, or made by or under the direction of, or issued, sold, or circulated by or under the direction of, a person, board, agency, or authority authorized to do so under this chapter or under the laws of the United States, another state, or a Canadian province. An offense under this subsection is a felony of the third degree.

(c) A person commits an offense if the person possesses with the intent to use, circulate, or pass a forged or counterfeit instrument that is not printed, manufactured, or made by or under the direction of, or issued, sold, or circulated by or under the direction of, a person, board, agency, or authority authorized to do so under this chapter or under the laws of the United States, another state, or a Canadian province. An offense under this subsection is a Class C misdemeanor.

(d) For purposes of this section, "instrument" means a driver's license, driver's license form, personal identification certificate, stamp, permit, license, official signature, certificate, evidence of fee payment, or any other instrument.

(e) If conduct constituting an offense under this section also constitutes an offense under another law, the actor may be prosecuted under this section, the other law, or both. (Enacted by Acts 1995, 74th Leg., ch. 165 (S.B. 971), § 1, effective September 1, 1995; am. Acts 1997, 75th Leg., ch. 165 (S.B. 898), § 30.99, effective September 1, 1997; am. Acts 1997, 75th Leg., ch. 823 (S.B. 89), § 2, effective September 1,

*Transportation*

1997; am. Acts 2009, 81st Leg., ch. 1130 (H.B. 2086), § 34, effective September 1, 2009.)

## Sec. 521.4565. Conspiring to Manufacture Counterfeit License or Certificate.

(a) In this section:

(1) "Combination," "conspires to commit," "profits," and "criminal street gang" have the meanings assigned by Section 71.01, Penal Code.

(2) "Conspires to manufacture or produce" means that:

(A) a person agrees with one or more other persons to engage in the manufacture or production of a forged or counterfeit instrument; and

(B) the person and one or more of the other persons perform an overt act in pursuance of the agreement.

(3) "Instrument" means a driver's license, commercial driver's license, or personal identification certificate.

(4) "Public servant" has the meaning assigned by Section 1.07, Penal Code.

(b) [2 Versions: As added by Acts 2009, 81st Leg., ch. 1146, § 6.08] A person commits an offense if the person establishes, maintains, or participates in or conspires to establish, maintain, or participate in a combination or criminal street gang, or participates in the profits of a combination or criminal street gang, with the intent to manufacture or produce a forged or counterfeit instrument for the purpose of selling, distributing, or delivering the instrument. An agreement that constitutes conspiring to manufacture or produce may be inferred from the acts of the parties.

(b) [2 Versions: As added by Acts 2009, 81st Leg., ch. 1146, § 13.06] A person commits an offense if the person establishes, maintains, or participates in or conspires to establish, maintain, or participate in a combination or criminal street gang, or participates in the profits of a combination or criminal street gang, with the intent to manufacture or produce a forged or counterfeit instrument for the purpose of selling, distributing, or delivering such instrument. An agreement constituting conspiring to manufacture or produce may be inferred from the acts of the parties.

(c) An offense under this section is a state jail felony, except that an offense committed by a public servant is a felony of the third degree.

(Enacted by Acts 2009, 81st Leg., ch. 1146 (H.B. 2730), § 6.08, effective September 1, 2009; enacted by Acts 2009, 81st Leg., ch. 1146 (H.B. 2730), § 13.06, effective June 19, 2009).

## Sec. 521.457. Driving While License Invalid.

(a) A person commits an offense if the person operates a motor vehicle on a highway:

(1) after the person's driver's license has been canceled under this chapter if the person does not have a license that was subsequently issued under this chapter;

(2) during a period that the person's driver's license or privilege is suspended or revoked under any law of this state;

(3) while the person's driver's license is expired if the license expired during a period of suspension; or

(4) after renewal of the person's driver's license has been denied under any law of this state, if the person does not have a driver's license subsequently issued under this chapter.

(b) A person commits an offense if the person is the subject of an order issued under any law of this state that prohibits the person from obtaining a driver's license and the person operates a motor vehicle on a highway.

(c) It is not a defense to prosecution under this section that the person did not receive actual notice of a suspension imposed as a result of a conviction for an offense under Section 521.341.

(d) Except as provided by Subsection (c), it is an affirmative defense to prosecution of an offense, other than an offense under Section 521.341, that the person did not receive actual notice of a cancellation, suspension, revocation, or prohibition order relating to the person's license. For purposes of this section, actual notice is presumed if the notice was mailed in accordance with law.

(e) Except as provided by Subsections (f), (f-1), and (f-2), an offense under this section is a Class C misdemeanor.

(f) An offense under this section is a Class B misdemeanor if it is shown on the trial of the offense that the person:

(1) has previously been convicted of an offense under this section or an offense under Section 601.371(a), as that law existed before September 1, 2003; or

(2) at the time of the offense, was operating the motor vehicle in violation of Section 601.191.

(f-1) If it is shown on the trial of an offense under this section that the license of the person has previously been suspended as the result of an offense involving the operation of a motor vehicle while intoxicated, the offense is a Class B misdemeanor.

(f-2) An offense under this section is a Class A misdemeanor if it is shown on the trial of the offense that at the time of the offense the person was operating the motor vehicle in violation of Section 601.191 and caused or was at fault in a motor vehicle accident that resulted in serious bodily injury to or the death of another person.

(g) For purposes of this section, a conviction for an offense that involves operation of a motor vehicle after August 31, 1987, is a final conviction, regardless of whether the sentence for the conviction is probated.

(Enacted by Acts 1995, 74th Leg., ch. 165 (S.B. 971), § 1, effective September 1, 1995; am. Acts 1997, 75th Leg., ch. 165 (S.B. 898), § 30.98(a), effective September 1, 1997; am. Acts 1999, 76th Leg., ch. 1207 (S.B. 528), § 6, effective September 1, 1999; am. Acts 2003, 78th Leg., ch. 855 (S.B. 582), § 1, effective September 1, 2003; am. Acts 2007, 80th Leg., ch. 1027 (H.B. 1623), § 8, effective September 1, 2007; am. Acts 2009, 81st Leg., ch. 1284 (H.B. 2012), § 2, effective September 1, 2009.)

### Sec. 521.458.   Permitting Unauthorized Person to Drive.

(a) A person may not knowingly permit or cause the person's child or ward who is under 18 years of age to operate a motor vehicle on a highway in violation of this chapter.

(b) A person may not authorize or knowingly permit a motor vehicle owned by or under the control of the person to be operated on a highway by any person in violation of this chapter.

(Enacted by Acts 1995, 74th Leg., ch. 165 (S.B. 971), § 1, effective September 1, 1995.)

### Sec. 521.459.   Employment of Unlicensed Driver.

(a) Before employing a person as an operator of a motor vehicle used to transport persons or property, an employer shall request from the department:

(1) a list of convictions for traffic violations contained in the department records on the potential employee; and

(2) a verification that the person has a license.

(b) A person may not employ a person as an operator of a motor vehicle used to transport persons or property who does not hold the appropriate driver's license to operate the vehicle as provided by this chapter.

(Enacted by Acts 1995, 74th Leg., ch. 165 (S.B. 971), § 1, effective September 1, 1995.)

### Sec. 521.460.   Motor Vehicle Rentals.

(a) A person may not rent a motor vehicle to any other person unless the other person holds a driver's license under this chapter or, if a nonresident, holds a license issued under the laws of the state or Canadian province in which the person resides, unless that state or province does not require that the operator of a motor vehicle hold a license.

(b) A person may not rent a motor vehicle to another person until inspecting the driver's license of the renter and comparing and verifying the signature on the renter's driver's license with the renter's signature written in the person's presence.

(c) Each person who rents a motor vehicle to another shall maintain a record of:

(1) the number of the license plate issued for the motor vehicle;

(2) the name and address of the person to whom the vehicle is rented;

(3) the license number of the person to whom the vehicle is rented;

(4) the date the license was issued; and

(5) the place where the license was issued.

(d) The record maintained under Subsection (c) may be inspected by any police officer or officer or employee of the department.

(Enacted by Acts 1995, 74th Leg., ch. 165 (S.B. 971), § 1, effective September 1, 1995.)

### Sec. 521.461.   General Criminal Penalty.

(a) A person who violates a provision of this chapter for which a specific penalty is not provided commits an offense.

(b) An offense under this section is a misdemeanor punishable by a fine not to exceed $200.

(Enacted by Acts 1995, 74th Leg., ch. 165 (S.B. 971), § 1, effective September 1, 1995.)

# CHAPTER 521A
## ELECTION IDENTIFICATION CERTIFICATE

**Sec. 521A.001. [Effective January 1, 2012] Election Identification Certificate.**

(a) The department shall issue an election identification certificate to a person who states that the person is obtaining the certificate for the purpose of satisfying Section 63.001(b), Election Code, and does not have another form of identification described by Section 63.0101, Election Code, and:

　(1) who is a registered voter in this state and presents a valid voter registration certificate; or

　(2) who is eligible for registration under Section 13.001, Election Code, and submits a registration application to the department.

(b) The department may not collect a fee for an election identification certificate or a duplicate election identification certificate issued under this section.

(c) An election identification certificate may not be used or accepted as a personal identification certificate.

(d) An election officer may not deny the holder of an election identification certificate the ability to vote because the holder has an election identification certificate rather than a driver's license or personal identification certificate issued under this subtitle.

(e) An election identification certificate must be similar in form to, but distinguishable in color from, a driver's license and a personal identification certificate. The department may cooperate with the secretary of state in developing the form and appearance of an election identification certificate.

(f) The department may require each applicant for an original or renewal election identification certificate to furnish to the department the information required by Section 521.142.

(g) The department may cancel and require surrender of an election identification certificate after determining that the holder was not entitled to the certificate or gave incorrect or incomplete information in the application for the certificate.

(h) A certificate expires on a date specified by the department, except that a certificate issued to a person 70 years of age or older does not expire. (Enacted by Acts 2011, 82nd Leg., ch. 123 (S.B. 14), § 20, effective January 1, 2012.)

# CHAPTER 522
## COMMERCIAL DRIVER'S LICENSES

### Subchapter A. General Provisions

Transportation

## SUBCHAPTER A
## GENERAL PROVISIONS

### Sec. 522.001.   Short Title.

This chapter may be cited as the Texas Commercial Driver's License Act.

(Enacted by Acts 1995, 74th Leg., ch. 165 (S.B. 971), § 1, effective September 1, 1995.)

### Sec. 522.002.   Construction.

This chapter is a remedial law that shall be liberally construed to promote the public health, safety, and welfare.

(Enacted by Acts 1995, 74th Leg., ch. 165 (S.B. 971), § 1, effective September 1, 1995.)

### Sec. 522.003.   Definitions.

In this chapter:

(1) "Alcohol" means:

(A) beer, ale, port, stout, sake, or any other similar fermented beverages or products containing one-half of one percent or more of alcohol by volume, brewed or produced wholly or in part from malt or a malt substitute;

(B) wine containing one-half of one percent or more of alcohol by volume; or

(C) distilled spirits, including ethyl alcohol, ethanol, and spirits of wine in any form, and all dilutions and mixtures of distilled spirits from whatever source or by whatever process produced.

(2) "Alcohol concentration" means the number of grams of alcohol for each:

(A) 100 milliliters of blood;

(B) 210 liters of breath; or

(C) 67 milliliters of urine.

(3) "Commercial driver's license" means a license issued to an individual that authorizes the individual to drive a class of commercial motor vehicle.

(4) "Commercial driver learner's permit" means a commercial driver's license that restricts the holder to driving a commercial motor vehicle as provided by Section 522.011(a)(2)(B).

(5) "Commercial motor vehicle" means a motor vehicle or combination of motor vehicles used to transport passengers or property that:

(A) has a gross combination weight or a gross combination weight rating of 26,001 or more pounds, including a towed unit with a gross vehicle weight or a gross vehicle weight rating of more than 10,000 pounds;

(B) has a gross vehicle weight or a gross vehicle weight rating of 26,001 or more pounds;

(C) is designed to transport 16 or more passengers, including the driver; or

(D) is transporting hazardous materials and is required to be placarded under 49 C.F.R. Part 172, Subpart F.

(6) "Controlled substance" means a substance classified as a controlled substance under:

(A) Section 102(6), Controlled Substances Act (21 U.S.C. Section 802(6)), including Schedules I—V of 21 C.F.R. Part 1308; or

(B) Chapter 481, Health and Safety Code.

(7) "Conviction" means:

(A) an adjudication of guilt, an unvacated forfeiture of bail or collateral deposited to secure the person's appearance in court, a plea of guilty or nolo contendere accepted by the court, the payment of a fine or court costs, or the violation of a condition of release without bail, in a court, regardless of whether the penalty is suspended, probated, or rebated; or

(B) a determination by a court, an authorized administrative tribunal or officer, or the department as authorized by this chapter that:

(i) the person has refused to give a specimen to determine the person's alcohol concentration or the presence in the person's body of a controlled substance or drug while driving a commercial motor vehicle; or

(ii) the person has driven a commercial motor vehicle while the person's alcohol concentration was 0.04 or more.

(8) "Department" means the Department of Public Safety.

(9) "Disqualify" means to withdraw the privilege to drive a commercial motor vehicle, including to suspend, cancel, or revoke that privilege under a state or federal law.

(10) "Domicile" means the place where a person has the person's true, fixed, and permanent home and principal residence and to which the person intends to return whenever absent.

(11) "Drive" means to operate or be in physical control of a motor vehicle.

(12) "Driver's license" has the meaning assigned by Section 521.001.

(13) "Drug" has the meaning assigned by Section 481.002, Health and Safety Code.

(14) "Employer" means a person who owns or leases a commercial motor vehicle or assigns a person to drive a commercial motor vehicle.

(15) "Federal act" means the Commercial Motor Vehicle Safety Act of 1986 (49 U.S.C. App. Section 2701 et seq.).

(16) "Foreign jurisdiction" means a jurisdiction other than a state.

(17) "Gross combination weight rating" means the value specified by the manufacturer as the loaded weight of a combination or artic-

ulated vehicle or, if the manufacturer has not specified a value, the sum of the gross vehicle weight rating of the power unit and the total weight of the towed unit or units and any load on a towed unit.

(18) "Gross vehicle weight rating" means the value specified by the manufacturer as the loaded weight of a single vehicle.

(19) "Hazardous materials" has the meaning assigned by 49 C.F.R. Section 383.5.

(20) [Repealed by Acts 2001, 77th Leg., ch. 941 (S.B. 866), § 43, effective September 1, 2001.]

(21) "Motor vehicle" means a vehicle, machine, tractor, trailer, or semitrailer propelled or drawn by mechanical power and used on a highway. The term does not include a vehicle, machine, tractor, trailer, or semitrailer operated exclusively on a rail.

(22) "Nonresident commercial driver's license" means a commercial driver's license issued by a state to an individual who resides in a foreign jurisdiction.

(23) "Out-of-service order" means:

(A) a temporary prohibition against driving a commercial motor vehicle issued under Section 522.101, the law of another state, or 49 C.F.R. Section 383.5; or

(B) a declaration by the Federal Motor Carrier Safety Administration or an authorized enforcement officer of a state or local jurisdiction that a driver, commercial motor vehicle, or motor carrier operation is out of service under 49 C.F.R. Section 383.5.

(24) "Secretary" means the United States secretary of transportation.

(24-a) "Seed cotton module" means compacted seed cotton in any form.

(25) "Serious traffic violation" means:

(A) a conviction arising from the driving of a motor vehicle, other than a parking, vehicle weight, or vehicle defect violation, for:

(i) excessive speeding, involving a single charge of driving 15 miles per hour or more above the posted speed limit;

(ii) reckless driving, as defined by state or local law;

(iii) a violation of a state or local law related to motor vehicle traffic control, including a law regulating the operation of vehicles on highways, arising in connection with a fatal accident;

(iv) improper or erratic traffic lane change;

(v) following the vehicle ahead too closely; or

(vi) a violation of Sections 522.011 or 522.042; or

(B) a violation of Section 522.015.

(26) "State" means a state of the United States or the District of Columbia.

(Enacted by Acts 1995, 74th Leg., ch. 165 (S.B. 971), § 1, effective September 1, 1995; am. Acts 2001, 77th Leg., ch. 941 (S.B. 886), §§ 2, 43, effective September 1, 2001; am. Acts 2003, 78th Leg., ch. 991 (S.B. 1904), § 6, effective June 1, 2005; am. Acts 2003, 78th Leg., ch. 1325 (H.B. 3588), § 8.01, effective June 1, 2005; am. Acts 2005, 79th Leg., ch. 247 (H.B. 749), § 2, effective September 1, 2005; am. Acts 2007, 80th Leg., ch. 424 (S.B. 1372), § 3, effective January 1, 2008; am. Acts 2009, 81st Leg., ch. 782 (S.B. 1093), § 1, effective September 1, 2009.)

## Sec. 522.004.  Applicability.

(a) This chapter does not apply to:

(1) a vehicle that is controlled and operated by a farmer and:

(A) used to transport agricultural products, farm machinery, or farm supplies to or from a farm;

(B) used within 150 miles of the person's farm; and

(C) not used in the operations of a common or contract motor carrier;

(2) a fire-fighting or emergency vehicle necessary to the preservation of life or property or the execution of emergency governmental functions, whether operated by an employee of a political subdivision or by a volunteer fire fighter;

(3) a military vehicle or a commercial motor vehicle, when operated for military purposes by military personnel, including:

(A) active duty military personnel, including personnel serving in the United States Coast Guard; and

(B) members of the reserves and national guard on active duty, including personnel on full-time national guard duty, personnel engaged in part-time training, and national guard military technicians;

(4) a recreational vehicle that is driven for personal use;

(5) a vehicle that is owned, leased, or controlled by an air carrier, as defined by Section 21.155, and that is driven or operated exclusively by an employee of the air carrier only on the premises of an airport, as defined by Section 22.001, on service roads to which the public does not have access; or

(6) a vehicle used exclusively to transport seed cotton modules or cotton burrs.

(b) In this section, "recreational vehicle" means a motor vehicle primarily designed as temporary living quarters for recreational camping or travel use. The term includes a travel trailer, camping trailer, truck camper, and motor home.

(Enacted by Acts 1995, 74th Leg., ch. 165 (S.B. 971), § 1, effective September 1, 1995; am. Acts 1997, 75th Leg., ch. 1061 (S.B. 1486), § 13, effective September 1, 1997; am. Acts 2005, 79th Leg., ch. 357 (S.B. 1257), § 2, effective September 1, 2005; am. Acts 2007, 80th Leg., ch. 424 (S.B. 1372), § 4, effective January 1, 2008.)

## Sec. 522.005.  [2 Versions: Effective until September 28, 2011] Rulemaking Authority.

The department may adopt rules necessary to carry out this chapter and the federal act.

(Enacted by Acts 1995, 74th Leg., ch. 165 (S.B. 971), § 1, effective September 1, 1995; am. Acts 2011, 82nd Leg., 1st C.S., ch. xxx (S.B. 1), § 72.12, effective September 28, 2011.)

## Sec. 522.005.  [2 Versions: Effective September 28, 2011] Rulemaking Authority.

The department may adopt rules necessary to carry out this chapter and the federal act and to maintain compliance with 49 C.F.R. Parts 383 and 384.

(Enacted by Acts 1995, 74th Leg., ch. 165 (S.B. 971), § 1, effective September 1, 1995; am. Acts 2011, 82nd Leg., 1st C.S., (S.B. 1), § 72.12, effective September 28, 2011.)

## Sec. 522.006.  Contracting Authority.

The department may enter into a contract to carry out this chapter, including a contract with an agency of another state or with another organization.

(Enacted by Acts 1995, 74th Leg., ch. 165 (S.B. 971), § 1, effective September 1, 1995.)

## Sec. 522.007.  Exemption for Neighboring States.

(a) The public safety director shall enter negotiations with an appropriate person or entity of a state bordering this state for the purpose of applying the exemption contained in Section 522.004(a)(1) to residents of that state.

(b) The public safety director may enter an agreement to apply the exemption contained in Section 522.004(a)(1) to residents of a bordering state only if that state extends a similar exemption to residents of this state.

(Enacted by Acts 1997, 75th Leg., ch. 1061 (S.B. 1486), § 14, effective September 1, 1997.)

### Secs. 522.008 to 522.010 [Reserved for expansion].

## SUBCHAPTER B
## LICENSE OR PERMIT REQUIRED

### Sec. 522.011. License or Permit Required; Offense.

(a) A person may not drive a commercial motor vehicle unless:

(1) the person:

(A) has in the person's immediate possession a commercial driver's license issued by the department appropriate for the class of vehicle being driven; and

(B) is not disqualified or subject to an out-of-service order;

(2) the person:

(A) has in the person's immediate possession a commercial driver learner's permit issued by the department; and

(B) is accompanied by the holder of a commercial driver's license issued by the department appropriate for the class of vehicle being driven, and the license holder:

(i) occupies a seat beside the permit holder for the purpose of giving instruction in driving the vehicle; and

(ii) is not disqualified or subject to an out-of-service order; or

(3) the person is authorized to drive the vehicle under Section 522.015.

(b) A person commits an offense if the person violates Subsection (a).

(c) An offense under this section is a Class C misdemeanor.

(d) It is a defense to prosecution under Subsection (a)(1)(A) if the person charged produces in court a commercial driver's license that:

(1) was issued to the person;

(2) is appropriate for the class of vehicle being driven; and

(3) was valid when the offense was committed.

(Enacted by Acts 1995, 74th Leg., ch. 165 (S.B. 971), § 1, effective September 1, 1995; am. Acts 2001, 77th Leg., ch. 941 (S.B. 886), § 3, effective September 1, 2001.)

### Sec. 522.012. Restricted License.

(a) If the department is authorized under the federal act to grant the waiver, the department by rule may waive the knowledge and skills tests required by Section 522.022 and issue a restricted commercial driver's license to an employee of a farm-related service industry.

(b) In granting a waiver under this section, the department is subject to any condition or requirement established for the waiver by the secretary or the Federal Motor Carrier Safety Administration.

(c) In addition to any restriction or limitation imposed by this chapter or the department, a restricted commercial driver's license issued under this section is subject to any restriction or limitation imposed by the secretary or the Federal Motor Carrier Safety Administration.

(d) In this section, "farm-related service industry" has the meaning assigned by the secretary or the Federal Motor Carrier Safety Administration under the federal act.

(Enacted by Acts 1995, 74th Leg., ch. 165 (S.B. 971), § 1, effective September 1, 1995; am. Acts 2001, 77th Leg., ch. 941 (S.B. 886), § 4, effective September 1, 2001.)

### Sec. 522.013. Nonresident License.

(a) The department may issue a nonresident commercial driver's license to a resident of a foreign jurisdiction if the secretary has determined that the commercial motor vehicle testing and licensing standards in the foreign jurisdiction do not meet the testing standards established by 49 C.F.R. Part 383.

(b) An applicant must surrender any nonresident commercial driver's license issued by another state.

(c) Before issuing a nonresident commercial driver's license, the department must establish the practical capability of disqualifying the person under the conditions applicable to a commercial driver's license issued to a resident of this state.

(d) "Nonresident" must appear on the face of a license issued under this section.

(e) The department may issue a temporary nonresident commercial driver's license to a person who does not present a social security card as

Transportation

required by Section 522.021(a-1)(1) but who otherwise meets the requirements for a nonresident commercial driver's license, including the requirement that the commercial motor vehicle testing and licensing standards of the country of which the applicant is a resident not meet the testing and licensing standards established by 49 C.F.R. Part 383. A license issued under this subsection:

    (1) expires on the earlier of:

      (A) the 60th day after the date the license is issued;

      (B) the expiration date of the visa presented under Section 522.021(a-1)(2)(B); or

      (C) the expiration date of the Form I-94 Arrival/Departure record, or a successor document, presented under Section 522.021(a-1)(2)(C); and

    (2) may not be renewed.

  (f) The department may not issue more than one temporary nonresident commercial driver's license to a person.

(Enacted by Acts 1995, 74th Leg., ch. 165 (S.B. 971), § 1, effective September 1, 1995; am. Acts 2007, 80th Leg., ch. 1319 (S.B. 1260), § 1, effective September 1, 2007.)

### Sec. 522.014.   Permit.

The department may issue a commercial driver learner's permit to an individual who has passed the vision and written tests required for a Texas driver's license appropriate for the class of vehicle to be driven.

(Enacted by Acts 1995, 74th Leg., ch. 165 (S.B. 971), § 1, effective September 1, 1995.)

### Sec. 522.015.   License or Permit Issued by Other Jurisdiction.

A person may drive a commercial motor vehicle in this state if:

    (1) the person has a commercial driver's license or commercial driver learner's permit issued by:

      (A) another state in accordance with the minimum federal standards for the issuance of a commercial motor vehicle driver's license; or

      (B) a foreign jurisdiction the testing and licensing standards of which the United States Department of Transportation has determined meet the requirements of the federal act;

    (2) the person's license or permit is appropriate for the class of vehicle being driven;

    (3) the person is not disqualified from driving a commercial motor vehicle and is not subject to an out-of-service order; and

    (4) the person has not had a domicile in this state for more than 30 days.

(Enacted by Acts 1995, 74th Leg., ch. 165 (S.B. 971), § 1, effective September 1, 1995.)

### Secs. 522.016 to 522.020 [Reserved for expansion].

## SUBCHAPTER C
## LICENSE OR PERMIT APPLICATION AND ISSUANCE

### Sec. 522.021.   Application; Offense.

  (a) An application for a commercial driver's license or commercial driver learner's permit must include:

    (1) the full name and current residence and mailing address of the applicant;

    (2) a physical description of the applicant, including sex, height, and eye color;

    (3) the applicant's date of birth;

    (4) the applicant's social security number, unless the application is for a nonresident commercial driver's license and the applicant is a resident of a foreign jurisdiction;

    (5) certifications, including those required by 49 C.F.R. Section 383.71(a); and

    (6) any other information required by the department.

  (a-1) If the application is for a nonresident commercial driver's license and the applicant is a resident of a foreign jurisdiction that does not meet the testing and licensing standards established by 49 C.F.R. Part 383, the applicant must present:

    (1) a social security card issued to the applicant; and

    (2) each of the following:

      (A) a passport issued to the applicant by the country of which the applicant is a resident;

      (B) a Temporary Worker visa; and

      (C) a Form I-94 Arrival/Departure record or a successor document.

  (b) The application must be sworn to and signed by the applicant. An officer or employee of the department may administer the oath. An officer or employee of this state may not charge for administering the oath.

  (c) The application must meet the requirements of an application under Section 521.141

and must be accompanied by the fee required under Section 522.029. The department may require documentary evidence to verify the information required by Subsection (a).

(c-1) If the department requires proof of an applicant's identity as part of an application under this section, the department must accept as satisfactory proof of identity an offender identification card or similar form of identification issued to an inmate by the Texas Department of Criminal Justice if the applicant also provides supplemental verifiable records or documents that aid in establishing identity.

(d) A person who knowingly falsifies information or a certification required by Subsection (a) commits an offense and is subject to a 60-day cancellation of the person's commercial driver's license, commercial driver learner's permit, or application. An offense under this subsection is a Class C misdemeanor.

(Enacted by Acts 1995, 74th Leg., ch. 165 (S.B. 971), § 1, effective September 1, 1995; am. Acts 2001, 77th Leg., ch. 941 (S.B. 886), § 5, effective September 1, 2001; am. Acts 2005, 79th Leg., ch. 1218 (H.B. 967), § 5, effective September 1, 2005; am. Acts 2007, 80th Leg., ch. 1319 (S.B. 1260), § 2, effective September 1, 2007; am. Acts 2009, 81st Leg., ch. 1146 (H.B. 2730), § 14.03, effective September 1, 2009.)

### Sec. 522.022. License Requirements.

The department may not issue a commercial driver's license other than a nonresident license to a person unless the person:

(1) has a domicile in this state;

(2) has passed knowledge and skills tests for driving a commercial motor vehicle that comply with minimal federal standards established by 49 C.F.R. Part 383, Subparts G and H; and

(3) has satisfied the requirements imposed by the federal act, federal regulation, or state law.

(Enacted by Acts 1995, 74th Leg., ch. 165 (S.B. 971), § 1, effective September 1, 1995.)

### Sec. 522.0225. Verification of Domicile.

(a) The department shall adopt rules for determining whether a domicile has been established under Section 522.022, including rules prescribing the types of documentation the department may require from the applicant to determine the validity of the claimed domicile.

(b) The department may contract with a third-party personal data verification service to assist

the department in verifying a claim of domicile, including whether the physical address provided by the applicant is the applicant's actual residence.

(Enacted by Acts 2009, 81st Leg., ch. 1146 (H.B. 2730), § 13.05, effective June 19, 2009.)

### Sec. 522.0226. Post Office Box Not Valid As Address.

(a) In this section, "post office box address" means a United States Postal Service post office box address or a private mailbox address.

(b) Unless an exception exists under state or federal law, an applicant may receive delivery of a commercial driver's license at a post office box address only if the applicant has provided the department the physical address where the applicant resides.

(c) The department may require the applicant to provide documentation that the department determines necessary to verify the validity of the physical address provided under Subsection (b).

(d) The department may contract with a third-party personal data verification service to assist the department in verifying whether the physical address provided by the applicant is the applicant's actual residence.

(Enacted by Acts 2009, 81st Leg., ch. 1146 (H.B. 2730), § 13.05, effective June 19, 2009.)

### Sec. 522.023. Tests.

(a) The tests required by Section 522.022 must be prescribed by the department.

(b) The knowledge test must be conducted by the department. The department shall provide each applicant who has a reading impairment an opportunity to take the knowledge test orally or, at the applicant's option, the applicant may have the questions read to the applicant and may answer in writing.

(c) Except as provided by Subsection (d), the department must conduct the skills test.

(d) The department may authorize a person, including an agency of this or another state, an employer, a private driver training facility or other private institution, or a department, agency, or instrumentality of local government, to administer the skills test specified by this section if:

(1) the test is the same that would be administered by the department; and

(2) the person has entered into an agreement with the department that complies with 49 C.F.R. Section 383.75.

Transportation

(e) The skills test must be taken in a commercial motor vehicle that is representative of the type of vehicle the person drives or expects to drive.

(f) The department may waive the skills test for an applicant who meets the requirements of 49 C.F.R. Section 383.77.

(g) The department shall test the applicant's ability to understand highway traffic signs and signals that are written in English.

(h) An applicant who pays the applicable fee required by Section 522.029 is entitled to three examinations of each element under Section 522.022. If the applicant has not qualified after the third examination, the applicant must submit a new application accompanied by the required fee.

(i) The department may not issue a commercial driver's license to a person who has not passed each examination required under this chapter.

(Enacted by Acts 1995, 74th Leg., ch. 165 (S.B. 971), § 1, effective September 1, 1995; am. Acts 2007, 80th Leg., ch. 424 (S.B. 1372), § 5, effective January 1, 2008.)

### Sec. 522.0235.  Waiver of Visual Standards for Intrastate Driver.

(a) Except as provided by Subsection (b), the department by rule may provide for a waiver of the visual standards for a commercial driver's license in 49 C.F.R. Part 391, Subpart E, if the person who is applying for a commercial driver's license or who has been issued a commercial driver's license is a person who drives a commercial motor vehicle only in this state.

(b) Subsection (a) does not apply to standards for distant binocular acuity.

(Enacted by Acts 1997, 75th Leg., ch. 165 (S.B. 898), § 30.100(a), effective September 1, 1997.)

### Sec. 522.024.  Additional Testing.

To ensure compliance with the federal act and to promote the systematic conversion to commercial driver's licenses, the department may require the commercial driver's license testing of a person to whom the department has previously issued a driver's license that authorizes the driving of a vehicle that may be subject to this chapter. The testing may be required before the expiration of an existing license.

(Enacted by Acts 1995, 74th Leg., ch. 165 (S.B. 971), § 1, effective September 1, 1995.)

### Sec. 522.025.  Limitations on Issuance of License or Permit.

(a) The department may not issue a commercial driver's license or commercial driver learner's permit to a person who is disqualified from driving a commercial motor vehicle or while the person's driver's license or driving privilege is suspended, revoked, or canceled in any state.

(b) The department may not issue a commercial driver's license to a person who has a driver's license, commercial driver's license, or commercial driver learner's permit issued by another state unless the person surrenders the license or permit. The department shall return a surrendered license or permit to the issuing state for cancellation.

(Enacted by Acts 1995, 74th Leg., ch. 165 (S.B. 971), § 1, effective September 1, 1995.)

### Sec. 522.026.  Limitation on Number of Driver's Licenses; Offense.

(a) A person commits an offense if the person drives a commercial motor vehicle and has more than one driver's license.

(b) It is an affirmative defense to prosecution of an offense under this section that the offense occurred during the 10-day period beginning on the date the person was issued a driver's license.

(c) An offense under this section is a Class C misdemeanor.

(Enacted by Acts 1995, 74th Leg., ch. 165 (S.B. 971), § 1, effective September 1, 1995.)

### Sec. 522.027.  Minimum Age.

The department may not issue a commercial driver's license or a commercial driver learner's permit to a person who is younger than 18 years of age.

(Enacted by Acts 1995, 74th Leg., ch. 165 (S.B. 971), § 1, effective September 1, 1995.)

### Sec. 522.028.  Check of Driving Record.

Before issuing a commercial driver's license, the department shall check the applicant's driving record as required by 49 C.F.R. Section 383.73.

(Enacted by Acts 1995, 74th Leg., ch. 165 (S.B. 971), § 1, effective September 1, 1995.)

### Sec. 522.029.  Fees.

(a) The fee for a commercial driver's license or commercial driver learner's permit issued by the department is $60, except as provided by Subsections (f), (h), (j), and (k).

(b) The fee for a commercial driver's license or commercial driver learner's permit shall be reduced by $4 for each remaining year of validity of a driver's license, other than a commercial driver's license or commercial driver learner's permit issued by the department to the applicant.

(c) The fee for a duplicate commercial driver's license or commercial driver learner's permit is $10.

(d) An applicant who is changing a class of license, endorsement, or restriction or who is adding a class of vehicle other than a motorcycle to the license must pay a fee of $10 for the examination, except for a renewal or original issuance of a commercial driver's license.

(e) The fees required by this chapter and collected by an officer or agent of the department shall be remitted without deduction to the department.

(f) **[2 Versions: As added by Acts 1997, 75th Leg., ch. 1156]** The fee for renewal of a commercial driver's license or a commercial driver learner's permit that includes authorization to operate a motorcycle is $45.

(f) **[2 Versions: As added by Acts 1997, 75th Leg., ch. 1372]** If a commercial driver's license or commercial driver learner's permit includes an authorization to operate a motorcycle or moped, the fee for the driver's license or permit is increased by $8.

(g) An applicant who is applying for additional authorization to operate a motorcycle shall pay a fee of $15 for the examination.

(h) The fee for a commercial driver's license or commercial driver learner's permit issued under Section 522.033 is $20.

(i) Except as provided by Section 662.011, each fee collected under this section shall be deposited to the credit of the Texas mobility fund.

(j) The fee for issuance or renewal of a commercial driver's license or commercial driver learner's permit is $25 for a license with an expiration date established under Section 522.054.

(k) The fee for a nonresident commercial driver's license is $120. The fee for a temporary nonresident commercial driver's license is $20.
(Enacted by Acts 1995, 74th Leg., ch. 165 (S.B. 971), § 1, effective September 1, 1995; am. Acts 1997, 75th Leg., ch. 1156 (S.B. 99), § 2, effective September 1, 1997; am. Acts 1997, 75th Leg., ch. 1372 (H.B. 1200), § 5, effective September 1, 1997; am. Acts 2001, 77th Leg., ch. 546 (H.B. 2663), § 9, effective September 1, 2001; am. Acts

2003, 78th Leg., ch. 1325 (H.B. 3588), § 11.05, effective September 1, 2003; am. Acts 2007, 80th Leg., ch. 37 (H.B. 84), § 6, effective September 1, 2007; am. Acts 2007, 80th Leg., ch. 1319 (S.B. 1260), § 3, effective September 1, 2007; am. Acts 2009, 81st Leg., ch. 87 (S.B. 1969), §§ 27.001(106), 27.002(35), effective September 1, 2009.)

## Sec. 522.030. [2 Versions: Effective until September 28, 2011] Content of License.

A commercial driver's license must:

(1) be marked "Commercial Driver License" or "CDL";

(2) be, to the extent practicable, tamperproof; and

(3) include:

(A) the name and mailing address of the person to whom it is issued;

(B) the person's color photograph;

(C) a physical description of the person, including sex, height, and eye color;

(D) the person's date of birth;

(E) a number or identifier the department considers appropriate;

(F) the person's signature;

(G) each class of commercial motor vehicle that the person is authorized to drive, with any endorsements or restrictions;

(H) the name of this state; and

(I) the dates between which the license is valid.
(Enacted by Acts 1995, 74th Leg., ch. 165 (S.B. 971), § 1, effective September 1, 1995.)

## Sec. 522.030. [2 Versions: Effective September 28, 2011] Content of License.

(a) A commercial driver's license must:

(1) be marked "Commercial Driver License" or "CDL";

(2) be, to the extent practicable, tamperproof; and

(3) include:

(A) the name and mailing address of the person to whom it is issued;

(B) the person's color photograph;

(C) a physical description of the person, including sex, height, and eye color;

(D) the person's date of birth;

(E) a number or identifier the department considers appropriate;

(F) the person's signature;

(G) each class of commercial motor vehicle that the person is authorized to drive, with any endorsements or restrictions;

(H) the name of this state; and

(I) the dates between which the license is valid.

(b) Except as provided by this section, a commercial driver's license issued under this chapter:

(1) must:

(A) be in the same format;

(B) have the same appearance and orientation; and

(C) contain the same type of information; and

(2) may not include any information that this chapter does not reference or require.

(c) To the extent of a conflict or inconsistency between this section and Section 522.013 or 522.051, Section 522.013 or 522.051 controls.

(Enacted by Acts 1995, 74th Leg., ch. 165 (S.B. 971), § 1, effective September 1, 1995; am. Acts 2011, 82nd Leg., 1st C.S., (S.B. 1), § 72.13, effective September 28, 2011.)

## Sec. 522.031. Notification of License Issuance.

(a) After issuing a commercial driver's license, the department shall notify the commercial driver's license information system of that fact and provide the information required to ensure identification of the person.

(b) In this section, "commercial driver's license information system" means the information system established under the federal act as a clearinghouse for locating information related to the licensing and identification of commercial motor vehicle drivers.

(Enacted by Acts 1995, 74th Leg., ch. 165 (S.B. 971), § 1, effective September 1, 1995.)

## Sec. 522.032. Change of Name or Address of License or Permit Holder; Offense.

(a) The holder of a commercial driver's license or commercial driver learner's permit who changes the holder's name or mailing address must apply for a duplicate license or permit not later than the 30th day after the date of the change in the manner provided by Section 521.054.

(b) The holder of a commercial driver's license or commercial driver learner's permit who changes the holder's residence address shall notify the department not later than the 30th day after the date of the change.

(c) A person commits an offense if the person violates this section. An offense under this section is a Class C misdemeanor.

(Enacted by Acts 1995, 74th Leg., ch. 165 (S.B. 971), § 1, effective September 1, 1995.)

## Sec. 522.033. Commercial Driver's License Issued to Certain Sex Offenders.

(a) The department may issue an original or renewal commercial driver's license or commercial driver learner's permit to a person whose driver's license or personal identification certificate record indicates that the person is subject to the registration requirements of Chapter 62, Code of Criminal Procedure, only if the person is otherwise eligible for the commercial driver's license or commercial driver learner's permit and:

(1) applies in person for the issuance of a license or permit under this section; and

(2) pays a fee of $20.

(b) [2 Versions: Effective until September 28, 2011] Notwithstanding Section 522.051, a commercial driver's license or commercial driver learner's permit issued under this section, including a renewal, duplicate, or corrected license, expires on the first birthday of the license holder occurring after the date of application, except that the initial license issued under this section expires on the second birthday of the license holder occurring after the date of application.

(b) [2 Versions: Effective September 28, 2011] Notwithstanding Section 522.051, a commercial driver's license or commercial driver learner's permit issued under this section, including a renewal, duplicate, or corrected license, expires:

(1) if the license or permit holder is a citizen, national, or legal permanent resident of the United States or a refugee or asylee lawfully admitted into the United States, on the first birthday of the license holder occurring after the date of application, except that the initial license issued under this section expires on the second birthday of the license holder occurring after the date of application; or

(2) if the applicant is not described by Subdivision (1), on the earlier of:

(A) the expiration date of the applicant's authorized stay in the United States; or

(B) the first birthday of the license holder occurring after the date of application, except that the initial license issued under this section expires on the second birthday of the license holder occurring after the date of application.

(Enacted by Acts 2001, 77th Leg., ch. 546 (H.B. 2663), § 10, effective September 1, 2001; am. Acts 2011, 82nd Leg., 1st C.S., (S.B. 1), § 72.14, effective September 28, 2011.)

### Sec. 522.034. Application for Authorization to Operate Motorcycle.

(a) An applicant for an original commercial driver's license or commercial driver learner's permit that includes an authorization to operate a motorcycle must furnish to the department evidence satisfactory to the department that the applicant has successfully completed a basic motorcycle operator training course approved by the department under Chapter 662.

(b) The department may not issue an original commercial driver's license or commercial driver learner's permit that includes an authorization to operate a motorcycle to an applicant who fails to comply with Subsection (a).

(c) **[2 Versions: Effective until January 1, 2012]** When the department issues a license or permit to which this section applies, the department shall provide the person to whom the license is issued with written information about the Glenda Dawson Donate Life-Texas Registry program established under Chapter 49, Health and Safety Code.

(c) **[2 Versions: Effective January 1, 2012]** When the department issues a license or permit to which this section applies, the department shall provide the person to whom the license is issued with written information about the Glenda Dawson Donate Life-Texas Registry program established under Chapter 692A, Health and Safety Code.

(Enacted by Acts 2009, 81st Leg., ch. 1391 (S.B. 1967), § 5, effective September 1, 2009; am. Acts 2011, 82nd Leg., ch. 554 (H.B. 2904), § 9, effective January 1, 2012.)

### Secs. 522.035 to 522.040 [Reserved for expansion].

## SUBCHAPTER D
## CLASSIFICATION, ENDORSEMENT, OR RESTRICTION OF LICENSE

### Sec. 522.041. Classifications.

(a) The department may issue a Class A, Class B, or Class C commercial driver's license.

(b) Class A covers a combination of vehicles with a gross combination weight rating of 26,001 pounds or more, if the gross vehicle weight rating of the towed vehicle or vehicles exceeds 10,000 pounds.

(c) Class B covers:

(1) a single vehicle with a gross vehicle weight rating of 26,001 pounds or more;

(2) a single vehicle with a gross vehicle weight rating of 26,001 pounds or more towing a vehicle with a gross vehicle weight rating of 10,000 pounds or less; and

(3) a vehicle designed to transport 24 passengers or more, including the driver.

(d) Class C covers a single vehicle or combination of vehicles not described by Subsection (b) or (c) that is:

(1) designed to transport 16—23 passengers, including the driver; or

(2) used in the transportation of hazardous materials that require the vehicle to be placarded under 49 C.F.R. Part 172, Subpart F.

(e) The holder of a commercial driver's license may drive any vehicle in the class for which the license is issued and lesser classes of vehicles except a motorcycle or moped. The holder may drive a motorcycle only if authorization to drive a motorcycle is shown on the commercial driver's license and the requirements for issuance of a motorcycle license have been met.

(Enacted by Acts 1995, 74th Leg., ch. 165 (S.B. 971), § 1, effective September 1, 1995.)

### Sec. 522.042. Endorsements; Offense.

(a) The department may issue a commercial driver's license with endorsements:

(1) authorizing the driving of a vehicle transporting hazardous materials, subject to the requirements of Title 49 C.F.R. Part 1572;

(2) authorizing the towing of a double or triple trailer or a trailer over a specified weight;

(3) authorizing the driving of a vehicle carrying passengers;

(4) authorizing the driving of a tank vehicle;

(5) representing a combination of hazardous materials and tank vehicle endorsements; or

(6) authorizing the driving of a school bus, as defined by Section 541.201.

(b) The holder of a commercial driver's license may not drive a vehicle that requires an endorsement unless the proper endorsement appears on the license.

(c) A person commits an offense if the person violates Subsection (b). An offense under this section is a Class C misdemeanor.

Transportation

(Enacted by Acts 1995, 74th Leg., ch. 165 (S.B. 971), § 1, effective September 1, 1995; am. Acts 2001, 77th Leg., ch. 941 (S.B. 886), § 6, effective September 1, 2001; am. Acts 2005, 79th Leg., ch. 358 (S.B. 1258), § 1, effective September 1, 2005.)

### Sec. 522.0425. Hazardous Materials Endorsement; Cancellation.

(a) The department shall cancel or deny the issuance of a hazardous materials endorsement of a person's commercial driver's license within 15 days of the date the department receives notification from a federal agency authorized to make a final determination of threat assessment under 49 C.F.R. Section 1572.13.

(b) On receipt of a notification from a federal agency authorized to make an initial determination of threat assessment under 49 C.F.R. Section 1572.13, the department shall immediately cancel or deny the person the issuance of a hazardous materials endorsement of a commercial driver's license.

(c) The cancellation or denial of a hazardous materials endorsement under this section shall be reported to the commercial driver's license information system before the 16th day after the date of cancellation or denial.

(Enacted by Acts 2007, 80th Leg., ch. 424 (S.B. 1372), § 6, effective January 1, 2008.)

### Sec. 522.043. Restrictions; Offense.

(a) On issuing a commercial driver's license, the department for good cause may impose one or more restrictions suitable to the license holder's driving ability and limitations, including restrictions:

    (1) prohibiting the license holder from driving a vehicle equipped with air brakes; and

    (2) as provided by 49 C.F.R. Part 391, prohibiting driving a commercial vehicle in interstate commerce by a person who:

      (A) is under 21 years of age;

      (B) does not meet applicable physical guidelines; or

      (C) cannot sufficiently read and speak the English language.

(b) For purposes of this section, the department may not administer examinations or tests relating to the applicant's proficiency in the English language, but if an applicant cannot speak English sufficiently to communicate to department personnel the applicant's need for a commercial driver's license, the department may issue to the person a commercial driver's license restricted to operation in intrastate commerce.

(c) A person commits an offense if the person drives a commercial motor vehicle in violation of a restriction. An offense under this section is a Class C misdemeanor.

(Enacted by Acts 1995, 74th Leg., ch. 165 (S.B. 971), § 1, effective September 1, 1995.)

### Secs. 522.044 to 522.050 [Reserved for expansion].

## SUBCHAPTER E
## EXPIRATION AND RENEWAL OF LICENSE OR PERMIT

### Sec. 522.051. Expiration of License or Permit.

(a) Except as provided by Subsection (f) and Sections 522.013(e), 522.033, and 522.054, an original commercial driver's license or commercial driver learner's permit expires five years after the applicant's next birthday.

(b) Except as provided by Section 522.054, a commercial driver's license or commercial driver learner's permit issued to a person holding a Texas Class A, B, C, or M license that would expire one year or more after the date of issuance of the commercial driver's license or commercial driver learner's permit expires five years after the applicant's next birthday.

(c) Except as provided by Section 522.054, a commercial driver's license or commercial driver learner's permit issued to a person holding a Texas Class A, B, C, or M license that would expire less than one year after the date of issuance of the commercial driver's license or commercial driver learner's permit or that has been expired for less than one year expires five years after the expiration date shown on the Class A, B, C, or M license.

(d) Except as provided by Section 522.054, a commercial driver's license or commercial driver learner's permit issued to a person holding a Texas Class A, B, C, or M license that has been expired for at least one year but not more than two years expires five years after the applicant's last birthday.

(e) For purposes of this section, a person's "last birthday" is the birthday that occurs on or before the date of issuance, and a person's "next birthday" is the birthday that occurs on or after the date of issuance.

(f) Except as provided by Section 522.013, a nonresident commercial driver's license other than a temporary nonresident commercial driver's license under Section 522.013(e) expires on the earlier of:

(1) the expiration date of the visa presented under Section 522.021(a-1)(2)(B); or

(2) the expiration date of the Form I-94 Arrival/Departure record, or a successor document, presented under Section 522.021(a-1)(2)(C).

(g) A commercial driver's license issued to a person whose residence or domicile is a correctional facility or a parole facility expires on the first birthday of the license holder occurring after the first anniversary of the date of issuance. The department by rule shall establish the fee for a commercial driver's license issued to a person whose residence or domicile is a correctional facility or a parole facility.

(Enacted by Acts 1995, 74th Leg., ch. 165 (S.B. 971), § 1, effective September 1, 1995; am. Acts 1997, 75th Leg., ch. 1372 (H.B. 1200), § 6, effective September 1, 1997; am. Acts 2001, 77th Leg., ch. 546 (H.B. 2663), § 11, effective September 1, 2001; am. Acts 2005, 79th Leg., ch. 358 (S.B. 1258), § 2, effective September 1, 2005; am. Acts 2007, 80th Leg., ch. 37 (H.B. 84), § 7, effective September 1, 2007; am. Acts 2007, 80th Leg., ch. 1319 (S.B. 1260), § 4, effective September 1, 2007; am. Acts 2009, 81st Leg., ch. 87 (S.B. 1969), § 23.006, effective September 1, 2009; am. Acts 2009, 81st Leg., ch. 1288 (H.B. 2161), § 7, effective September 1, 2009.)

## Sec. 522.052. Renewal of License.

(a) Except as provided by Subsection (g), a commercial driver's license issued by the department may be renewed in the year preceding the expiration date.

(b) Except as provided by Section 522.054, a renewal of a commercial driver's license that has been expired for less than one year expires five years after the expiration date shown on the commercial driver's license.

(c) Except as provided by Section 522.054, a renewal of a commercial driver's license that has been expired for at least one year but not more than two years expires six years after the applicant's last birthday.

(d) If a commercial driver's license has been expired for more than two years, the person must make an application and meet the requirements for original issuance of a commercial driver's license.

(e) A commercial driver learner's permit may not be renewed.

(f) For purposes of this section, a person's "last birthday" is the birthday that occurs on or before the date of issuance.

(g) A commercial driver's license issued under Section 522.033 or to which Section 522.054 applies may not be renewed before the 60th day preceding the expiration date.

(h) A renewal commercial driver's license issued to a person whose residence or domicile is a correctional facility or a parole facility expires on the first birthday of the license holder occurring after the first anniversary of the date of issuance.

(i) **[Effective September 28, 2011]** Unless the information has been previously provided to the department, the department shall require each applicant for a renewal or duplicate commercial driver's license to furnish to the department:

(1) proof of the applicant's United States citizenship; or

(2) documentation described by Section 521.142(a).

(j) **[Effective September 28, 2011]** The department may not deny a renewal or duplicate commercial driver's license to an applicant who provides documentation described by Section 521.142(a) based on the duration of the person's authorized stay in the United States, as indicated by the documentation presented under Section 521.142(a).

(Enacted by Acts 1995, 74th Leg., ch. 165 (S.B. 971), § 1, effective September 1, 1995; am. Acts 1997, 75th Leg., ch. 1372 (H.B. 1200), § 7, effective September 1, 1997; am. Acts 2001, 77th Leg., ch. 546 (H.B. 2663), § 12, effective September 1, 2001; am. Acts 2005, 79th Leg., ch. 358 (S.B. 1258), § 3, effective September 1, 2005; am. Acts 2007, 80th Leg., ch. 37 (H.B. 84), § 8, effective September 1, 2007; am. Acts 2009, 81st Leg., ch. 1288 (H.B. 2161), § 8, effective September 1, 2009; am. Acts 2011, 82nd Leg., 1st C.S., (S.B. 1), § 72.15, effective September 28, 2011.)

## Sec. 522.053. License Renewal Procedures.

(a) A person applying for renewal of a commercial driver's license must complete the application form required by the department, including updated information and required certifications.

(b) To retain a hazardous materials endorsement, an applicant must pass the written test for that endorsement.

(c) The department may require an examination, including a vision test, for the renewal of a commercial driver's license.

Transportation

(d) Before renewing a commercial driver's license, the department shall check the applicant's driving record as required by 49 C.F.R. Section 383.73.

(Enacted by Acts 1995, 74th Leg., ch. 165 (S.B. 971), § 1, effective September 1, 1995.)

### Sec. 522.054. License Expiration: Person at Least 85 Years of Age.

(a) Each original commercial driver's license and commercial driver learner's permit of a person 85 years of age or older expires on the license holder's second birthday after the date of the license application.

(b) A commercial driver's license of a person 85 years of age or older that is renewed expires on the second anniversary of the expiration date before renewal.

(Enacted by Acts 2007, 80th Leg., ch. 37 (H.B. 84), § 9, effective September 1, 2007.)

### Sec. 522.0541. Denial of Renewal of Commercial Driver License.

(a) In the manner ordered by a court in another state in connection with a matter involving the violation of a state law or local ordinance relating to motor vehicle traffic control and on receipt of the necessary information from the other state, the department may deny renewal of the commercial driver's license issued to a person by the department for the person's:

(1) failure to appear in connection with a complaint or citation; or

(2) failure to pay or satisfy a judgment ordering the payment of a fine and costs.

(b) The information necessary under Subsection (a) may be transmitted through the commercial driver's license information system and must include:

(1) the name, date of birth, and the commercial driver's license number of the license held by the person;

(2) notice that the person failed to appear as required by law or failed to satisfy a judgment that ordered the payment of a fine and costs in the manner ordered by the court;

(3) the nature of the violation; and

(4) any other information required by the department.

(Enacted by Acts 2007, 80th Leg., ch. 424 (S.B. 1372), § 7, effective January 1, 2008; am. Acts 2009, 81st Leg., ch. 87 (S.B. 1969), § 27.001(107), effective September 1, 2009 (renumbered from Sec. 522.054).)

### Sec. 522.055. Clearance Notice to Department.

On receipt of notice from the other state that the grounds for denial of the renewal of the commercial driver's license based on the license holder's previous failure to appear or failure to pay a fine and costs previously reported by that state under Section 522.0541 have ceased to exist, the department shall renew the person's commercial driver's license.

(Enacted by Acts 2007, 80th Leg., ch. 424 (S.B. 1372), § 7, effective January 1, 2008; am. Acts 2009, 81st Leg., ch. 87 (S.B. 1969), § 27.002(36), effective September 1, 2009.)

### Secs. 522.056 to 522.060 [Reserved for expansion].

## SUBCHAPTER F
## NOTIFICATION OF CONVICTION, ADMINISTRATIVE ACTION, OR PREVIOUS EMPLOYMENT

### Sec. 522.061. Notification of Conviction to Department or Employer.

(a) A person who holds or is required to hold a commercial driver's license under this chapter and who is convicted in another state of violating a state law or local ordinance relating to motor vehicle traffic control shall notify the department in the manner specified by the department not later than the seventh day after the date of conviction.

(b) A person who holds or is required to hold a commercial driver's license under this chapter and who is convicted in this state or another state of violating a state law or local ordinance relating to motor vehicle traffic control, including a law regulating the operation of vehicles on highways, shall notify the person's employer in writing of the conviction not later than the seventh day after the date of conviction.

(c) A notification to the department or an employer must be in writing and must contain:

(1) the driver's full name;

(2) the driver's license number;

(3) the date of conviction;

(4) the nature of the violation;

(5) a notation of whether the violation was committed in a commercial motor vehicle;

(6) the location where the offense was committed; and

(7) the driver's signature.

(d) This section does not apply to a parking violation.

(Enacted by Acts 1995, 74th Leg., ch. 165 (S.B. 971), § 1, effective September 1, 1995; am. Acts 2009, 81st Leg., ch. 1146 (H.B. 2730), § 17.01, effective September 1, 2009.)

### Sec. 522.062. Notification of Conviction to Licensing Authority in Other State.

(a) If a person holds a commercial driver's license issued by another state and is finally convicted of a violation of a state traffic law or local traffic ordinance that was committed in a commercial motor vehicle, the department shall notify the driver's licensing authority in the issuing state of that conviction, in the time and manner required by 49 U.S.C. Section 31311.

(b) This section does not apply to a parking violation.

(Enacted by Acts 1995, 74th Leg., ch. 165 (S.B. 971), § 1, effective September 1, 1995; am. Acts 2001, 77th Leg., ch. 941 (S.B. 886), § 7, effective September 1, 2001.)

### Sec. 522.063. Notification of Disqualification.

A person who is denied the privilege of driving a commercial motor vehicle in a state for any period, who is disqualified from driving a commercial motor vehicle, or who is subject to an out-of-service order shall notify the person's employer of that fact before the end of the first business day after the date the person receives notice of that fact.

(Enacted by Acts 1995, 74th Leg., ch. 165 (S.B. 971), § 1, effective September 1, 1995.)

### Sec. 522.064. Notification of Previous Employment and Offenses.

(a) A person who applies for employment as a commercial motor vehicle driver shall provide the employer, at the time of the application, with the following information for the 10 years preceding the date of application:

(1) a list of the names and addresses of the applicant's previous employers for which the applicant drove a commercial motor vehicle;

(2) the dates between which the applicant drove for each employer;

(3) the reason for leaving the employment of each employer; and

(4) each specific criminal offense or serious traffic violation of which the applicant has been convicted and each suspension, revocation, or cancellation of driving privileges that resulted from the conviction.

(b) The applicant must certify that the information furnished is true and complete. An employer may require an applicant to provide additional information. Before an application is submitted, the employer shall inform the applicant that the information provided by the applicant under this section may be used, and the applicant's previous employers may be contacted, to investigate the applicant's work history.

(c) An employer shall require each applicant to provide the information specified by Subsections (a) and (b).

(Enacted by Acts 1995, 74th Leg., ch. 165 (S.B. 971), § 1, effective September 1, 1995.)

### Secs. 522.065 to 522.070 [Reserved for expansion].

## SUBCHAPTER G
## UNAUTHORIZED DRIVING

### Sec. 522.071. Driving While Disqualified Prohibited.

(a) A person commits an offense if the person drives a commercial motor vehicle on a highway:

(1) after the person has been denied the issuance of a license, unless the person has a driver's license appropriate for the class of vehicle being driven that was subsequently issued;

(2) during a period that a disqualification of the person's driver's license or privilege is in effect;

(3) while the person's driver's license is expired, if the license expired during a period of disqualification;

(4) during a period that the person was subject to an order prohibiting the person from obtaining a driver's license; or

(5) **[2 Versions: As amended by Acts 2007, 80th Leg., ch. 424]** during a period in which the person, the person's employer, or the vehicle being operated is subject to an out-of-service order.

(5) **[2 Versions: As amended by Acts 2007, 80th Leg., ch. 499]** in violation of an out-of-service order.

(b) It is not a defense to prosecution that the person had not received notice of a disqualification imposed as a result of a conviction that results in an automatic disqualification of the person's driver's license or privilege.

(c) Except as provided by Subsection (b), it is an affirmative defense to prosecution of an offense under this section that the person had not received notice of a denial, disqualification, prohibition order, or out-of-service order concerning the person's driver's license, permit, or privilege to operate a motor vehicle. For purposes of this subsection, notice is presumed if the notice was sent by first class mail to the last known address of the person as shown by the records of the department or licensing authority of another state.

(d) An offense under this section is a misdemeanor punishable as provided for an offense under Section 521.457.

(e) For the purposes of Subsection (a)(5), "commercial motor vehicle" has the meaning assigned by Section 644.001.

(Enacted by Acts 1995, 74th Leg., ch. 165 (S.B. 971), § 1, effective September 1, 1995; am. Acts 1999, 76th Leg., ch. 1409 (H.B. 2031), § 3, effective September 1, 1999; am. Acts 2007, 80th Leg., ch. 424 (S.B. 1372), § 8, effective January 1, 2008; am. Acts 2007, 80th Leg., ch. 499 (S.B. 333), § 1, effective September 1, 2007.)

### Sec. 522.072.  Employer Responsibilities.

(a) An employer may not knowingly permit a person to drive a commercial motor vehicle during a period in which:

(1) the person has been denied the privilege of driving a commercial motor vehicle;

(2) the person is disqualified from driving a commercial motor vehicle;

(3) the person, the person's employer, or the vehicle being operated is subject to an out-of-service order in a state; or

(4) the person has more than one commercial driver's license, except during the 10-day period beginning on the date the person is issued a driver's license.

(b) An employer may not knowingly require a driver to operate a commercial motor vehicle in violation of a federal, state, or local law that regulates the operation of a motor vehicle at a railroad grade crossing.

(b-1) An employer who violates Subsection (a) or (b) commits an offense. An offense under this subsection is a Class B misdemeanor.

(c) In addition to any penalty imposed under this chapter, an employer who violates this section may be penalized or disqualified under 49 C.F.R. Part 383.

(d) For purposes of Subsections (a)(1)(C) and (a)(2), "commercial motor vehicle" has the meaning assigned by Section 644.001.

(Enacted by Acts 1995, 74th Leg., ch. 165 (S.B. 971), § 1, effective September 1, 1995; am. Acts 2001, 77th Leg., ch. 941 (S.B. 886), §§ 8, 9, effective September 1, 2001; am. Acts 2007, 80th Leg., ch. 13 (S.B. 332), § 1, effective September 1, 2007; am. Acts 2007, 80th Leg., ch. 424 (S.B. 1372), § 9, effective January 1, 2008; am. Acts 2009, 81st Leg., ch. 782 (S.B. 1093), § 2, effective September 1, 2009.)

### Secs. 522.073 to 522.080 [Reserved for expansion].

## SUBCHAPTER H
## DISQUALIFICATION FROM DRIVING COMMERCIAL MOTOR VEHICLE

### Sec. 522.081.  Disqualification.

(a) This subsection applies to a violation committed while operating any motor vehicle, including a commercial motor vehicle. A person who holds a commercial driver's license is disqualified from driving a commercial motor vehicle for:

(1) 60 days if convicted of:

(A) two serious traffic violations that occur within a three-year period; or

(B) one violation of a law that regulates the operation of a motor vehicle at a railroad grade crossing; or

(2) 120 days if convicted of:

(A) three serious traffic violations arising from separate incidents occurring within a three-year period; or

(B) two violations of a law that regulates the operation of a motor vehicle at a railroad grade crossing that occur within a three-year period.

(b) This subsection applies to a violation committed while operating any motor vehicle, including a commercial motor vehicle, except as provided by this subsection. A person who holds a commercial driver's license is disqualified from driving a commercial motor vehicle for one year:

(1) if convicted of three violations of a law that regulates the operation of a motor vehicle at a railroad grade crossing that occur within a three-year period;

(2) on first conviction of:

(A) driving a motor vehicle under the influence of alcohol or a controlled substance, including a violation of Section 49.04 or 49.07, Penal Code;

(B) leaving the scene of an accident involving a motor vehicle driven by the person;

(C) using a motor vehicle in the commission of a felony, other than a felony described by Subsection (d)(2);

(D) causing the death of another person through the negligent or criminal operation of a motor vehicle; or

(E) driving a commercial motor vehicle while the person's commercial driver's license is revoked, suspended, or canceled, or while the person is disqualified from driving a commercial motor vehicle, for an action or conduct that occurred while operating a commercial motor vehicle;

(3) for refusing to submit to a test under Chapter 724 to determine the person's alcohol concentration or the presence in the person's body of a controlled substance or drug while operating a motor vehicle in a public place; or

(4) if an analysis of the person's blood, breath, or urine under Chapter 522, 524, or 724 determines that the person:

(A) had an alcohol concentration of 0.04 or more, or that a controlled substance or drug was present in the person's body, while operating a commercial motor vehicle in a public place; or

(B) had an alcohol concentration of 0.08 or more while operating a motor vehicle, other than a commercial motor vehicle, in a public place.

(c) A person who holds a commercial driver's license is disqualified from operating a commercial motor vehicle for three years if:

(1) the person:

(A) is convicted of an offense listed in Subsection (b)(2) and the vehicle being operated by the person was transporting a hazardous material required to be placarded; or

(B) refuses to submit to a test under Chapter 724 to determine the person's alcohol concentration or the presence in the person's body of a controlled substance or drug while operating a motor vehicle in a public place and the vehicle being operated by the person was transporting a hazardous material required to be placarded; or

(2) an analysis of the person's blood, breath, or urine under Chapter 522, 524, or 724 determines that while transporting a hazardous material required to be placarded the person:

(A) while operating a commercial motor vehicle in a public place had an alcohol concentration of 0.04 or more, or a controlled substance or drug present in the person's body; or

(B) while operating a motor vehicle, other than a commercial motor vehicle, in a public place had an alcohol concentration of 0.08 or more.

(d) A person is disqualified from driving a commercial motor vehicle for life:

(1) if the person is convicted two or more times of an offense specified by Subsection (b)(2), or a combination of those offenses, arising from two or more separate incidents;

(2) if the person uses a motor vehicle in the commission of a felony involving:

(A) the manufacture, distribution, or dispensing of a controlled substance; or

(B) possession with intent to manufacture, distribute, or dispense a controlled substance;

(3) for any combination of two or more of the following, arising from two or more separate incidents:

(A) a conviction of the person for an offense described by Subsection (b)(2);

(B) a refusal by the person described by Subsection (b)(3); and

(C) an analysis of the person's blood, breath, or urine described by Subsection (b)(4); or

(4) if the person uses a motor vehicle in the commission of an offense under 8 U.S.C. Section 1324 that involves the transportation, concealment, or harboring of an alien.

(e) A person may not be issued a commercial driver's license and is disqualified from operating a commercial motor vehicle if, in connection with the person's operation of a commercial motor vehicle, the person commits an offense or engages in conduct that would disqualify the holder of a commercial driver's license from operating a commercial motor vehicle, or is determined to have had an alcohol concentration of 0.04 or more or to have had a controlled substance or drug present in the person's body. The period of prohibition under this subsection is equal to the appropriate period of disqualification required by Subsections (a)—(d).

(f) In this section, "felony" means an offense under state or federal law that is punishable by death or imprisonment for a term of more than one year.

(g) A person who holds a commercial driver's license is disqualified from operating a commercial motor vehicle if the person's driving is determined to constitute an imminent hazard under 49 C.F.R. Section 383.52. The disqualification is for the disqualification period imposed under that section and shall be noted on the person's driving record.

(h) A disqualification imposed under Subsection (g) must run concurrently with any imminent hazard disqualification that is then currently in effect.

(Enacted by Acts 1995, 74th Leg., ch. 165 (S.B. 971), § 1, effective September 1, 1995; am. Acts 2001, 77th Leg., ch. 941 (S.B. 886), § 10, effective September 1, 2001; am. Acts 2003, 78th Leg., ch. 991 (S.B. 1904), § 7, effective June 1, 2005; am. Acts 2003, 78th Leg., ch. 1325 (H.B. 3588), § 8.02, effective June 1, 2005; am. Acts 2005, 79th Leg., ch. 357 (S.B. 1257), § 3, effective September 1, 2005; am. Acts 2007, 80th Leg., ch. 424 (S.B. 1372), § 10, effective January 1, 2008; am. Acts 2009, 81st Leg., ch. 1146 (H.B. 2730), § 18.01, effective September 1, 2009.)

### Sec. 522.082.   Reinstatement Following Disqualification for Life.

(a) The department may adopt rules establishing guidelines, including conditions, under which a person disqualified for life under Section 522.081(d)(1) may apply to the department for reinstatement of the person's commercial driver's license, if authorized under federal law.

(b) A person is not eligible for reinstatement unless the person has been disqualified for at least 10 years and meets the department's conditions for reinstatement.

(c) If a reinstated driver is subsequently convicted of another disqualifying offense as specified by Section 522.081(b), the person is permanently disqualified and is not eligible for reinstatement.

(Enacted by Acts 1995, 74th Leg., ch. 165 (S.B. 971), § 1, effective September 1, 1995.)

### Sec. 522.083.   Update of Records.

After disqualifying a person, the department shall update its records to reflect that action.

(Enacted by Acts 1995, 74th Leg., ch. 165 (S.B. 971), § 1, effective September 1, 1995.)

### Sec. 522.084.   Notification to Other Jurisdiction.

After disqualifying a person who has a domicile in another state or in a foreign jurisdiction, the department shall give notice of that fact to the licensing authority of the state that issued the person's commercial driver's license or commercial driver learner's permit.

(Enacted by Acts 1995, 74th Leg., ch. 165 (S.B. 971), § 1, effective September 1, 1995.)

### Sec. 522.085.   Probation of Disqualification Prohibited.

Notwithstanding Section 521.303, if a person is disqualified under this chapter, the disqualification may not be probated.

(Enacted by Acts 1995, 74th Leg., ch. 165 (S.B. 971), § 1, effective September 1, 1995.)

### Sec. 522.086.   Issuance of Essential Need or Occupational Driver's License Prohibited.

A person who is disqualified from operating a commercial motor vehicle may not be granted an essential need or occupational driver's license that would authorize operation of a commercial motor vehicle.

(Enacted by Acts 1995, 74th Leg., ch. 165 (S.B. 971), § 1, effective September 1, 1995.)

### Sec. 522.087.   Procedures Applicable to Disqualification.

(a) A person is automatically disqualified under Section 522.081(a)(1)(B), Section 522.081(b)(2), or Section 522.081(d)(2). An appeal may not be taken from the disqualification.

(b) Disqualifying a person under Section 522.081(a), other than under Subdivision (1)(B) of that subsection, Section 522.081(b)(1), or Section 522.081(d)(1) or (3) is subject to the notice and hearing procedures of Sections 521.295—521.303. An appeal of the disqualification is subject to Section 521.308.

(c) A disqualification imposed under Section 522.081(a) must run consecutively to any other disqualification that is then currently in effect.

(Enacted by Acts 1995, 74th Leg., ch. 165 (S.B. 971), § 1, effective September 1, 1995; am. Acts 1999, 76th Leg., ch. 1117 (H.B. 3641), § 3, effective September 1, 2000; am. Acts 2001, 77th Leg., ch. 941 (S.B. 886), § 11, effective September 1, 2001; am. Acts 2003, 78th Leg., ch. 991 (S.B. 1904), § 8, effective June 1, 2005; am. Acts 2003, 78th Leg., ch. 1325 (H.B. 3588), § 8.03, effective June 1, 2005; am. Acts 2007, 80th Leg., ch. 424 (S.B. 1372), § 11, effective January 1, 2008.)

Transportation

## Sec. 522.088. Applicability of Other Law.

Section 521.344 of this code and Section 13, Article 42.12, Code of Criminal Procedure, do not apply to a person disqualified under this chapter. (Enacted by Acts 1995, 74th Leg., ch. 165 (S.B. 971), § 1, effective September 1, 1995.)

## Sec. 522.089. Effect of Suspension, Revocation, Cancellation, or Denial of License Under Other Law.

(a) A suspension, revocation, cancellation, or denial of a driver's license or privilege under Chapter 521 or another law of this state disqualifies the person under this chapter.

(b) If this chapter disqualifies a person for a longer period than the other law, the person is disqualified for the longer period. (Enacted by Acts 1995, 74th Leg., ch. 165 (S.B. 971), § 1, effective September 1, 1995.)

## Sec. 522.090. Additional Penalty.

In addition to any penalty imposed under this chapter, a person convicted of an offense under Section 522.071(a)(5) may be penalized or disqualified under 49 C.F.R. Part 383. (Enacted by Acts 1995, 74th Leg., ch. 165 (S.B. 971), § 1, effective September 1, 1995.)

## Sec. 522.091. Recognition of Action Taken by Other State.

(a) The department shall give an out-of-state conviction, disqualification, or denial full faith and credit and treat it for sanctioning purposes under this chapter as if it occurred in this state.

(b) The department may include the conviction, disqualification, or denial on the person's driving record. (Enacted by Acts 1995, 74th Leg., ch. 165 (S.B. 971), § 1, effective September 1, 1995.)

## Sec. 522.092. Suspension, Revocation, Cancellation, or Denial of Driver's License Under Other Laws.

A person subject to disqualification under this chapter may also have the person's driver's license suspended, revoked, canceled, or denied under one or more of the following, if the conduct that is a ground for disqualification is also a ground for the suspension, revocation, cancellation, or denial of a driver's license suspension under:

(1) Chapter 521;

(2) Chapter 524;

(3) Chapter 601; or

(4) Chapter 724. (Enacted by Acts 1995, 74th Leg., ch. 165 (S.B. 971), § 1, effective September 1, 1995.)

## Secs. 522.093 to 522.100 [Reserved for expansion].

## SUBCHAPTER I
## DRIVING WHILE HAVING ALCOHOL, CONTROLLED SUBSTANCE, OR DRUG IN SYSTEM

## Sec. 522.101. Driving While Having Alcohol in System Prohibited.

(a) Notwithstanding any other law of this state, a person may not drive a commercial motor vehicle in this state while having a measurable or detectable amount of alcohol in the person's system.

(b) A person who violates Subsection (a) or who refuses to submit to an alcohol test under Section 522.102 shall be placed out of service for 24 hours.

(c) A peace officer may issue an out-of-service order based on probable cause that the person has violated this section. The order must be on a form approved by the department. The peace officer shall submit the order to the department. (Enacted by Acts 1995, 74th Leg., ch. 165 (S.B. 971), § 1, effective September 1, 1995.)

## Sec. 522.102. Implied Consent to Taking of Specimen.

(a) A person who drives a commercial motor vehicle in this state is considered to have consented, subject to Chapter 724, to the taking of one or more specimens of the person's breath, blood, or urine for the purpose of analysis to determine the person's alcohol concentration or the presence in the person's body of a controlled substance or drug.

(b) Notwithstanding Chapter 724, one or more specimens may be taken at the request of a peace officer who, after stopping or detaining a person driving a commercial motor vehicle, has probable cause to believe that the person was driving the vehicle while having alcohol, a controlled substance, or a drug in the person's system.

(c) This section and Section 522.103 apply only to a person who is stopped or detained while driving a commercial motor vehicle. (Enacted by Acts 1995, 74th Leg., ch. 165 (S.B. 971), § 1, effective September 1, 1995; am. Acts

2001, 77th Leg., ch. 941 (S.B. 886), § 12, effective September 1, 2001.)

### Sec. 522.103.  Warning by Peace Officer.

(a) A peace officer requesting a person to submit a specimen under Section 522.102 shall warn the person that a refusal to submit a specimen will result in the person's being immediately placed out of service for 24 hours and being disqualified from driving a commercial motor vehicle for at least one year under Section 522.081.

(b) A peace officer requesting a person to submit a specimen under Section 522.102 is not required to comply with Section 724.015.

(Enacted by Acts 1995, 74th Leg., ch. 165 (S.B. 971), § 1, effective September 1, 1995; am. Acts 2001, 77th Leg., ch. 941 (S.B. 886), § 13, effective September 1, 2001.)

### Sec. 522.104.  Submission of Report to Department.

If a person driving a commercial motor vehicle refuses to give a specimen or submits a specimen that discloses an alcohol concentration of 0.04 or more, the peace officer shall submit to the department a sworn report, on a form approved by the department, certifying that the specimen was requested under Section 522.102 and that the person refused to submit a specimen or submitted a specimen that disclosed an alcohol concentration of 0.04 or more.

(Enacted by Acts 1995, 74th Leg., ch. 165 (S.B. 971), § 1, effective September 1, 1995.)

### Sec. 522.105.  Disqualification of Driver.

(a) On receipt of a report under Section 522.104, the department shall disqualify the person from driving a commercial motor vehicle under Section 522.081.

(b) Except as provided by Subsection (c), the procedure for notice and disqualification under this section is that specified by Subchapters C and D, Chapter 724, or Chapter 524.

(c) The department shall disqualify the person from driving a commercial motor vehicle for the period authorized by this chapter if, in a hearing held under this section, the court finds that:

(1) probable cause existed that the person was driving a commercial motor vehicle while having alcohol, a controlled substance, or a drug in the person's system;

(2) the person was offered an opportunity to give a specimen under this chapter; and

(3) the person submitted a specimen that disclosed an alcohol concentration of 0.04 or more or refused to submit a specimen.

(d) An appeal of a disqualification under this section is subject to Sections 524.041—524.044.

(Enacted by Acts 1995, 74th Leg., ch. 165 (S.B. 971), § 1, effective September 1, 1995.)

### Sec. 522.106.  Affidavit by Certified Breath Test Technical Supervisor.

(a) In a proceeding under this chapter, the certified breath test technical supervisor responsible for maintaining and directing the operation of the breath test instruments in compliance with department rules, in lieu of appearing in court, may attest by affidavit to:

(1) the reliability of the instrument used to take or analyze a specimen of a person's breath to determine alcohol concentration; and

(2) the validity of the results of the analysis.

(b) An affidavit submitted under this section must contain statements regarding:

(1) the reliability of the instrument and the analytical results; and

(2) compliance with state law in the administration of the program.

(c) A certified copy of an affidavit prepared in accordance with this section is admissible only if the department serves a copy of the affidavit on the person or the person's attorney not later than the seventh day before the date on which the hearing begins.

(Enacted by Acts 1995, 74th Leg., ch. 165 (S.B. 971), § 1, effective September 1, 1995.)

## CHAPTER 523
## DRIVER'S LICENSE COMPACT OF 1993

### Sec. 523.001.  Enactment.

The Driver's License Compact of 1993 is enacted and entered into.

(Enacted by Acts 1995, 74th Leg., ch. 165 (S.B. 971), § 1, effective September 1, 1995.)

## Sec. 523.002. Findings and Declaration of Policy.

(a) The states find that:

(1) the safety of their streets and highways is materially affected by the degree of compliance with state laws and local ordinances relating to the operation of motor vehicles;

(2) violation of such a law or ordinance is evidence that the violator engages in conduct which is likely to endanger the safety of persons and property; and

(3) the continuance in force of a license to drive is predicated on compliance with laws and ordinances relating to the operation of motor vehicles in whichever jurisdiction the vehicle is operated.

(b) It is the policy of each of the states to:

(1) promote compliance with the laws, ordinances, and administrative rules and regulations relating to the operation of motor vehicles by their operators in each of the jurisdictions where the operators drive motor vehicles; and

(2) make the reciprocal recognition of licenses to drive and eligibility therefor more just and equitable by considering the overall compliance with motor vehicle laws, ordinances, and administrative rules and regulations as a condition precedent to the continuance or issuance of any license by reason of which the licensee is authorized or permitted to operate a motor vehicle in any of the states.

(Enacted by Acts 1995, 74th Leg., ch. 165 (S.B. 971), § 1, effective September 1, 1995.)

## Sec. 523.003. Definitions.

In this compact:

(1) "Conviction" has the same meaning as provided in Section 522.003.

(2) "Executive director" means the director of the Department of Public Safety or the equivalent officer of another state.

(3) "Home state" means the state which has issued a license or permit and has the power to suspend or revoke use of the license or permit to operate a motor vehicle.

(4) "License" means a license or permit to operate a motor vehicle issued by a state.

(5) "Licensing authority" means the Department of Public Safety or the equivalent agency of another state.

(6) "State" means a state, territory, or possession of the United States, the District of Columbia, or the commonwealth of Puerto Rico.

(7) "Violation" means the commission of an offense related to the use or operation of a motor vehicle, even if there has been no conviction. A suspension by reason of a violation includes a suspension for failure to appear in court or comply with a court order or suspension for violating an implied consent law.

(Enacted by Acts 1995, 74th Leg., ch. 165 (S.B. 971), § 1, effective September 1, 1995.)

## Sec. 523.004. Reports of Convictions.

The licensing authority of a state shall report each conviction of a person from another state occurring within its jurisdiction to the licensing authority of the home state of the licensee. Such report shall clearly identify the person convicted; describe the violation specifying the section of the statute, code, or ordinance violated; identify the court in which action was taken; indicate whether a plea of guilty or not guilty was entered or the conviction was a result of the forfeiture of bail, bond, or other security; and include any special findings made in connection with the conviction. A conviction or judicial or administrative action of a federal or military court or tribunal may be reported to this state subject to this chapter.

(Enacted by Acts 1995, 74th Leg., ch. 165 (S.B. 971), § 1, effective September 1, 1995; am. Acts 1999, 76th Leg., ch. 1257 (S.B. 1157), § 1, effective September 1, 1999.)

## Sec. 523.005. Effect of Conviction.

(a) The licensing authority in the home state, for the purpose of suspension, revocation, cancellation, denial, disqualification, or limitation of the privilege to operate a motor vehicle, shall give the same effect to the conduct reported pursuant to Section 523.004 as it would if such conduct had occurred in the home state in the case of conviction for:

(1) manslaughter or negligent homicide resulting from the operation of a motor vehicle;

(2) driving a motor vehicle while under the influence of alcoholic beverages or a narcotic to a degree which renders the driver incapable of safely driving a motor vehicle;

(3) any felony in the commission of which a motor vehicle is used; or

(4) failure to stop and render aid or information in the event of a motor vehicle accident resulting in the death or personal injury of another.

(b) As to other convictions reported pursuant to this compact, the licensing authority in the home state shall give such effect to the conduct as is provided by the laws of the home state.

(c) If the laws of a state do not provide for offenses or violations denominated or described in precisely the words employed in Subsection (a), those offenses or violations of a substantially similar nature and the laws of that state shall be understood to contain such provisions as may be necessary to ensure that full force and effect is given to this compact.

(Enacted by Acts 1995, 74th Leg., ch. 165 (S.B. 971), § 1, effective September 1, 1995.)

## Sec. 523.006.  Applications for New Licenses.

On receiving an application for a license to drive, the licensing authority in a state shall ascertain whether the applicant has ever held or is the holder of a license to drive issued by any other state. The licensing authority in the state where application is made shall not issue a license to the applicant if the applicant:

(1) has held a license but the license has been suspended by reason, in whole or in part, of a violation and the suspension period has not terminated;

(2) has held a license but the license has been revoked by reason, in whole or in part, of a violation and the revocation has not terminated, except that after the expiration of one year from the date the license was revoked the person may apply for a new license if permitted by law; the licensing authority may refuse to issue a license to any such applicant if, after investigation, the licensing authority determines that it will not be safe to grant the person the privilege of driving a motor vehicle on the public highways; or

(3) is the holder of a license issued by another state currently in force unless the applicant surrenders such license or provides an affidavit prescribed by the licensing authority that such license is no longer in the person's possession.

(Enacted by Acts 1995, 74th Leg., ch. 165 (S.B. 971), § 1, effective September 1, 1995.)

## Sec. 523.007.  Applicability of Other Laws.

Except as expressly required by provisions of this compact, nothing contained herein shall be construed to affect the right of any state to apply any of its other laws relating to licenses to drive to any person or circumstance nor to invalidate or prevent any driver's license agreement or other cooperative arrangement between a member state and a nonmember state.

(Enacted by Acts 1995, 74th Leg., ch. 165 (S.B. 971), § 1, effective September 1, 1995.)

## Sec. 523.008.  Compact Administrator and Interchange of Information and Compensation of Expenses.

(a) The compact administrator shall be appointed by the executive director of the licensing authority. A compact administrator may provide for the discharge of his duties and the performance of his position by an alternate. The administrators, acting jointly, shall have the power to formulate all necessary and proper procedures for the exchange of information under this compact.

(b) The administrator of each state shall furnish to the administrator of each other state any information or documents reasonably necessary to facilitate the administration of this compact.

(c) The compact administrator provided for in this compact shall not be entitled to any additional compensation on account of his service as such administrator but shall be entitled to expenses incurred in connection with his duties and responsibilities as such administrator in the same manner as for expenses incurred in connection with any other duties or responsibilities of his office or employment.

(Enacted by Acts 1995, 74th Leg., ch. 165 (S.B. 971), § 1, effective September 1, 1995.)

## Sec. 523.009.  Effective Date; Withdrawal from Compact.

(a) This compact shall enter into force and become effective as to any state when it has enacted the compact into law.

(b) Any member state may withdraw from this compact by enacting a statute repealing the compact, but no such withdrawal shall take effect until six months after the executive director of the withdrawing state has given notice of the withdrawal to the executive directors of all other member states. No withdrawal shall affect the validity or applicability by the licensing authorities of states remaining party to the compact of any report of conviction occurring prior to the withdrawal.

(Enacted by Acts 1995, 74th Leg., ch. 165 (S.B. 971), § 1, effective September 1, 1995.)

## Sec. 523.010. Rulemaking Authority.

The licensing authority may adopt any rules and regulations deemed necessary by the executive director to administer and enforce the provisions of this compact.

(Enacted by Acts 1995, 74th Leg., ch. 165 (S.B. 971), § 1, effective September 1, 1995.)

## Sec. 523.011. Construction and Severability.

This compact shall be liberally construed so as to effectuate the purposes thereof. The provisions of this compact shall be severable; if any phrase, clause, sentence, or provision of this compact is declared to be contrary to the constitution of any state or of the United States or the applicability thereof to any government, agency, person, or circumstance is held invalid, the validity of the remainder of this compact and the applicability thereof to any government, agency, person, or circumstance shall not be affected thereby. If this compact is held contrary to the constitution of any state party thereto, the compact shall remain in full force and effect in the remaining states and in full force and effect in the state affected with regard to all severable matters.

(Enacted by Acts 1995, 74th Leg., ch. 165 (S.B. 971), § 1, effective September 1, 1995.)

## CHAPTER 524
## ADMINISTRATIVE SUSPENSION OF DRIVER'S LICENSE FOR FAILURE TO PASS TEST FOR INTOXICATION

## SUBCHAPTER A
## GENERAL PROVISIONS

### Sec. 524.001. Definitions.

In this chapter:

(1) "Adult" means an individual 21 years of age or older.

(2) "Alcohol concentration" has the meaning assigned by Section 49.01, Penal Code.

(3) "Alcohol-related or drug-related enforcement contact" means a driver's license suspension, disqualification, or prohibition order under the laws of this state or another state resulting from:

(A) a conviction of an offense prohibiting the operation of a motor vehicle or watercraft while:

(i) intoxicated;

(ii) under the influence of alcohol; or

(iii) under the influence of a controlled substance;

(B) a refusal to submit to the taking of a breath or blood specimen following an arrest for an offense prohibiting the operation of a motor vehicle or an offense prohibiting the operation of a watercraft, if the watercraft was powered with an engine having a manufacturer's rating of 50 horsepower or more, while:

(i) intoxicated;

(ii) under the influence of alcohol; or

(iii) under the influence of a controlled substance; or

(C) an analysis of a breath or blood specimen showing an alcohol concentration of a level specified by Section 49.01, Penal Code, following an arrest for an offense prohibiting the operation of a motor vehicle or watercraft while intoxicated.

(4) "Arrest" includes the taking into custody of a child, as defined by Section 51.02, Family Code.

(5) "Conviction" includes an adjudication under Title 3, Family Code.

(6) "Criminal charge" includes a charge that may result in a proceeding under Title 3, Family Code.

(7) "Criminal prosecution" includes a proceeding under Title 3, Family Code.

(8) "Department" means the Department of Public Safety.

(9) "Director" means the public safety director of the department.

(10) "Driver's license" has the meaning assigned by Section 521.001. The term includes a commercial driver's license or a commercial driver learner's permit issued under Chapter 522.

(11) "Minor" means an individual under 21 years of age.

(12) "Public place" has the meaning assigned by Section 1.07(a), Penal Code.

(Enacted by Acts 1995, 74th Leg., ch. 165 (S.B. 971), § 1, effective September 1, 1995; am. Acts 1997, 75th Leg., ch. 1013 (S.B. 35), § 21, effective September 1, 1997; am. Acts 2001, 77th Leg., ch. 444 (H.B. 63), § 1, effective September 1, 2001; am. Acts 2009, 81st Leg., ch. 1348 (S.B. 328), § 10, effective September 1, 2009.)

## Sec. 524.002. Rules; Application of Administrative Procedure Act.

(a) The department and the State Office of Administrative Hearings shall adopt rules to administer this chapter.

(b) Chapter 2001, Government Code, applies to a proceeding under this chapter to the extent consistent with this chapter.

(c) The State Office of Administrative Hearings may adopt a rule that conflicts with Chapter 2001, Government Code, if a conflict is necessary to expedite the hearings process within the time required by this chapter and applicable federal funding guidelines.

(Enacted by Acts 1995, 74th Leg., ch. 165 (S.B. 971), § 1, effective September 1, 1995.)

**Secs. 524.003 to 524.010 [Reserved for expansion].**

## SUBCHAPTER B
## SUSPENSION DETERMINATION AND NOTICE

## Sec. 524.011. Officer's Duties for Driver's License Suspension.

(a) An officer arresting a person shall comply with Subsection (b) if:

(1) the person is arrested for an offense under Section 49.04, 49.045, or 49.06, Penal Code, or an offense under Section 49.07 or 49.08 of that code involving the operation of a motor vehicle or watercraft, submits to the taking of a specimen of breath or blood and an analysis of the specimen shows the person had an alcohol concentration of a level specified by Section 49.01(2)(B), Penal Code; or

(2) the person is a minor arrested for an offense under Section 106.041, Alcoholic Beverage Code, or Section 49.04, 49.045, or 49.06, Penal Code, or an offense under Section 49.07 or 49.08, Penal Code, involving the operation of a motor vehicle or watercraft and:

(A) the minor is not requested to submit to the taking of a specimen; or

(B) the minor submits to the taking of a specimen and an analysis of the specimen shows that the minor had an alcohol concentration of greater than .00 but less than the level specified by Section 49.01(2)(B), Penal Code.

(b) A peace officer shall:

(1) serve or, if a specimen is taken and the analysis of the specimen is not returned to the arresting officer before the person is admitted to bail, released from custody, delivered as provided by Title 3, Family Code, or committed to jail, attempt to serve notice of driver's license suspension by delivering the notice to the arrested person;

(2) take possession of any driver's license issued by this state and held by the person arrested;

(3) issue a temporary driving permit to the person unless department records show or the officer otherwise determines that the person does not hold a driver's license to operate a motor vehicle in this state; and

(4) send to the department not later than the fifth business day after the date of the arrest:

(A) a copy of the driver's license suspension notice;

(B) any driver's license taken by the officer under this subsection;

(C) a copy of any temporary driving permit issued under this subsection; and

(D) a sworn report of information relevant to the arrest.

(c) The report required under Subsection (b)(4)(D) must:

(1) identify the arrested person;

(2) state the arresting officer's grounds for believing the person committed the offense;

(3) give the analysis of the specimen if any; and

(4) include a copy of the criminal complaint filed in the case, if any.

(d) A peace officer shall make the report on a form approved by the department and in the manner specified by the department.

(e) The department shall develop forms for the notice of driver's license suspension and temporary driving permits to be used by all state and local law enforcement agencies.

(f) A temporary driving permit issued under this section expires on the 41st day after the date of issuance. If the person was driving a commercial motor vehicle, as defined by Section 522.003, a temporary driving permit that authorizes the person to drive a commercial motor vehicle is not effective until 24 hours after the time of arrest. (Enacted by Acts 1995, 74th Leg., ch. 165 (S.B. 971), § 1, effective September 1, 1995; am. Acts 1997, 75th Leg., ch. 609 (S.B. 531), § 1, effective September 1, 1997; am. Acts 1997, 75th Leg., ch. 1013 (S.B. 35), § 22, effective September 1, 1997; am. Acts 2001, 77th Leg., ch. 444 (H.B. 63), § 2, effective September 1, 2001; am. Acts 2005, 79th Leg., ch. 728 (H.B. 2018), § 20.0045, effective September 1, 2005; am. Acts 2009, 81st Leg., ch. 1348 (S.B. 328), § 11, effective September 1, 2009.)

## Sec. 524.012. Department's Determination for Driver's License Suspension.

(a) On receipt of a report under Section 524.011, if the officer did not serve a notice of suspension of driver's license at the time the results of the analysis of a breath or blood specimen were obtained, the department shall determine from the information in the report whether to suspend the person's driver's license.

(b) The department shall suspend the person's driver's license if the department determines that:

(1) the person had an alcohol concentration of a level specified by Section 49.01(2)(B), Penal Code, while operating a motor vehicle in a public place or while operating a watercraft; or

(2) the person was a minor on the date that the breath or blood specimen was obtained and had any detectable amount of alcohol in the minor's system while operating a motor vehicle in a public place or while operating a watercraft.

(c) The department may not suspend a person's driver's license if:

(1) the person is an adult and the analysis of the person's breath or blood specimen determined that the person had an alcohol concentration of a level below that specified by Section 49.01(2)(B), Penal Code, at the time the specimen was taken; or

(2) the person is a minor and the department does not determine that the minor had any detectable amount of alcohol in the minor's system when the minor was arrested.

(d) A determination under this section is final unless a hearing is requested under Section 524.031.

(e) A determination under this section:

(1) is a civil matter;

(2) is independent of and is not an estoppel to any matter in issue in an adjudication of a criminal charge arising from the occurrence that is the basis for the suspension; and

(3) does not preclude litigation of the same or similar facts in a criminal prosecution. (Enacted by Acts 1995, 74th Leg., ch. 165 (S.B. 971), § 1, effective September 1, 1995; am. Acts 1997, 75th Leg., ch. 165 (S.B. 898), § 30.102, effective September 1, 1997; am. Acts 1997, 75th Leg., ch. 1013 (S.B. 35), § 23, effective September 1, 1997; am. Acts 2009, 81st Leg., ch. 1348 (S.B. 328), § 12, effective September 1, 2009.)

## Sec. 524.013. Notice of Department's Determination.

(a) If the department suspends a person's driver's license, the department shall send a notice of suspension by first class mail to the person's address:

(1) in the records of the department; or

(2) in the peace officer's report if it is different from the address in the department's records.

(b) Notice is considered received on the fifth day after the date the notice is mailed.

(c) If the department determines not to suspend a person's driver's license, the department

Transportation

shall notify the person of that determination and shall rescind any notice of driver's license suspension served on the person.

(Enacted by Acts 1995, 74th Leg., ch. 165 (S.B. 971), § 1, effective September 1, 1995; am. Acts 1999, 76th Leg., ch. 1409 (H.B. 2031), § 4, effective September 1, 1999.)

### Sec. 524.014. Notice of Suspension.

A notice of suspension under Section 524.013 must state:

(1) the reason and statutory grounds for the suspension;

(2) the effective date of the suspension;

(3) the right of the person to a hearing;

(4) how to request a hearing; and

(5) the period in which the person must request a hearing.

(Enacted by Acts 1995, 74th Leg., ch. 165 (S.B. 971), § 1, effective September 1, 1995.)

### Sec. 524.015. Effect of Disposition of Criminal Charge on Driver's License Suspension.

(a) Except as provided by Subsection (b), the disposition of a criminal charge does not affect a driver's license suspension under this chapter and does not bar any matter in issue in a driver's license suspension proceeding under this chapter.

(b) A suspension may not be imposed under this chapter on a person who is acquitted of a criminal charge under Section 49.04, 49.045, 49.06, 49.07, or 49.08, Penal Code, or Section 106.041, Alcoholic Beverage Code, arising from the occurrence that was the basis for the suspension. If a suspension was imposed before the acquittal, the department shall rescind the suspension and shall remove any reference to the suspension from the person's computerized driving record.

(Enacted by Acts 1995, 74th Leg., ch. 165 (S.B. 971), § 1, effective September 1, 1995; am. Acts 1997, 75th Leg., ch. 1013 (S.B. 35), § 24, effective September 1, 1997; am. Acts 2009, 81st Leg., ch. 1348 (S.B. 328), § 13, effective September 1, 2009.)

### Secs. 524.016 to 524.020 [Reserved for expansion].

## SUBCHAPTER C
## SUSPENSION PROVISIONS

### Sec. 524.021. Suspension Effective Date.

(a) A driver's license suspension under this chapter takes effect on the 40th day after the date the person:

(1) receives a notice of suspension under Section 524.011; or

(2) is presumed to have received notice of suspension under Section 524.013.

(b) A suspension under this chapter may not be probated.

(Enacted by Acts 1995, 74th Leg., ch. 165 (S.B. 971), § 1, effective September 1, 1995.)

### Sec. 524.022. Period of Suspension.

(a) A period of suspension under this chapter for an adult is:

(1) 90 days if the person's driving record shows no alcohol-related or drug-related enforcement contact during the 10 years preceding the date of the person's arrest; or

(2) one year if the person's driving record shows one or more alcohol-related or drug-related enforcement contacts during the 10 years preceding the date of the person's arrest.

(b) A period of suspension under this chapter for a minor is:

(1) 60 days if the minor has not been previously convicted of an offense under Section 106.041, Alcoholic Beverage Code, or Section 49.04, 49.045, or 49.06, Penal Code, or an offense under Section 49.07 or 49.08, Penal Code, involving the operation of a motor vehicle or a watercraft;

(2) 120 days if the minor has been previously convicted once of an offense listed by Subdivision (1); or

(3) 180 days if the minor has been previously convicted twice or more of an offense listed by Subdivision (1).

(c) For the purposes of determining whether a minor has been previously convicted of an offense described by Subsection (b)(1):

(1) an adjudication under Title 3, Family Code, that the minor engaged in conduct described by Subsection (b)(1) is considered a conviction under that provision; and

(2) an order of deferred adjudication for an offense alleged under a provision described by Subsection (b)(1) is considered a conviction of an offense under that provision.

(d) A minor whose driver's license is suspended under this chapter is not eligible for an occupational license under Subchapter L, Chapter 521, for:

(1) the first 30 days of a suspension under Subsection (b)(1);

(2) the first 90 days of a suspension under Subsection (b)(2); or

(3) the entire period of a suspension under Subsection (b)(3).

(Enacted by Acts 1995, 74th Leg., ch. 165 (S.B. 971), § 1, effective September 1, 1995; am. Acts 1997, 75th Leg., ch. 1013 (S.B. 35), § 25, effective September 1, 1997; am. Acts 2001, 77th Leg., ch. 444 (H.B. 63), § 3, effective September 1, 2001; am. Acts 2009, 81st Leg., ch. 1348 (S.B. 328), § 14, effective September 1, 2009.)

### Sec. 524.023. Application of Suspension Under Other Laws.

(a) If a person is convicted of an offense under Section 106.041, Alcoholic Beverage Code, or Section 49.04, 49.045, 49.06, 49.07, or 49.08, Penal Code, and if any conduct on which that conviction is based is a ground for a driver's license suspension under this chapter and Section 106.041, Alcoholic Beverage Code, Subchapter O, Chapter 521, or Subchapter H, Chapter 522, each of the suspensions shall be imposed.

(b) The court imposing a driver's license suspension under Section 106.041, Alcoholic Beverage Code, or Chapter 521 or 522 as required by Subsection (a) shall credit a period of suspension imposed under this chapter toward the period of suspension required under Section 106.041, Alcoholic Beverage Code, or Subchapter O, Chapter 521, or Subchapter H, Chapter 522, unless the person was convicted of an offense under Article 6701*l*-1, Revised Statutes, as that law existed before September 1, 1994, Section 19.05(a)(2), Penal Code, as that law existed before September 1, 1994, Section 49.04, 49.045, 49.06, 49.07, or 49.08, Penal Code, or Section 106.041, Alcoholic Beverage Code, before the date of the conviction on which the suspension is based, in which event credit may not be given.

(Enacted by Acts 1995, 74th Leg., ch. 165 (S.B. 971), § 1, effective September 1, 1995; am. Acts 1997, 75th Leg., ch. 1013 (S.B. 35), § 26, effective September 1, 1997; am. Acts 2009, 81st Leg., ch.

1348 (S.B. 328), § 15, effective September 1, 2009.)

### Secs. 524.024 to 524.030 [Reserved for expansion].

## SUBCHAPTER D
## HEARING AND APPEAL

### Sec. 524.031. Hearing Request.

If, not later than the 15th day after the date on which the person receives notice of suspension under Section 524.011 or is presumed to have received notice under Section 524.013, the department receives at its headquarters in Austin, in writing, including a facsimile transmission, or by another manner prescribed by the department, a request that a hearing be held, a hearing shall be held as provided by this subchapter.

(Enacted by Acts 1995, 74th Leg., ch. 165 (S.B. 971), § 1, effective September 1, 1995.)

### Sec. 524.032. Hearing Date; Rescheduling.

(a) A hearing requested under this subchapter shall be held not earlier than the 11th day after the date on which the person requesting the hearing is notified of the hearing unless the parties agree to waive this requirement. The hearing shall be held before the effective date of the suspension.

(b) A hearing shall be rescheduled if, before the fifth day before the date scheduled for the hearing, the department receives a request for a continuance from the person who requested the hearing. Unless both parties agree otherwise, the hearing shall be rescheduled for a date not earlier than the fifth day after the date the department receives the request for the continuance.

(c) A person who requests a hearing under this chapter may obtain only one continuance under this section unless the person shows that a medical condition prevents the person from attending the rescheduled hearing, in which event one additional continuance may be granted for a period not to exceed 10 days.

(d) A request for a hearing stays suspension of a person's driver's license until the date of the final decision of the administrative law judge. If the person's driver's license was taken by a peace officer under Section 524.011(b), the department shall notify the person of the effect of the request on the suspension of the person's license before the expiration of any temporary driving permit

issued to the person, if the person is otherwise eligible, in a manner that will permit the person to establish to a peace officer that the person's driver's license is not suspended.
(Enacted by Acts 1995, 74th Leg., ch. 165 (S.B. 971), § 1, effective September 1, 1995; am. Acts 2001, 77th Leg., ch. 444 (H.B. 63), § 4, effective September 1, 2001.)

## Sec. 524.033.  State Office of Administrative Hearings.

(a) A hearing under this subchapter shall be heard by an administrative law judge employed by the State Office of Administrative Hearings.

(b) The State Office of Administrative Hearings shall provide for the stenographic or electronic recording of the hearing.
(Enacted by Acts 1995, 74th Leg., ch. 165 (S.B. 971), § 1, effective September 1, 1995.)

## Sec. 524.034.  Hearing Location.

A hearing under this subchapter shall be held:
(1) at a location designated by the State Office of Administrative Hearings:
(A) in the county of arrest if the arrest occurred in a county with a population of 300,000 or more; or
(B) in the county in which the person is alleged to have committed the offense for which the person was arrested or not more than 75 miles from the county seat of the county in which the person was arrested; or
(2) with the consent of the person and the department, by telephone conference call.
(Enacted by Acts 1995, 74th Leg., ch. 165 (S.B. 971), § 1, effective September 1, 1995.)

## Sec. 524.035.  Hearing.

(a) The issues that must be proved at a hearing by a preponderance of the evidence are:
(1) whether:
(A) the person had an alcohol concentration of a level specified by Section 49.01(2)(B), Penal Code, while operating a motor vehicle in a public place or while operating a watercraft; or
(B) the person was a minor on the date that the breath or blood specimen was obtained and had any detectable amount of alcohol in the minor's system while operating a motor vehicle in a public place or while operating a watercraft; and
(2) whether reasonable suspicion to stop or probable cause to arrest the person existed.

(b) If the administrative law judge finds in the affirmative on each issue in Subsection (a), the suspension is sustained.

(c) If the administrative law judge does not find in the affirmative on each issue in Subsection (a), the department shall:
(1) return the person's driver's license to the person, if the license was taken by a peace officer under Section 524.011(b);
(2) reinstate the person's driver's license; and
(3) rescind an order prohibiting the issuance of a driver's license to the person.

(d) An administrative law judge may not find in the affirmative on the issue in Subsection (a)(1) if:
(1) the person is an adult and the analysis of the person's breath or blood determined that the person had an alcohol concentration of a level below that specified by Section 49.01, Penal Code, at the time the specimen was taken; or
(2) the person was a minor on the date that the breath or blood specimen was obtained and the administrative law judge does not find that the minor had any detectable amount of alcohol in the minor's system when the minor was arrested.

(e) The decision of the administrative law judge is final when issued and signed.
(Enacted by Acts 1995, 74th Leg., ch. 165 (S.B. 971), § 1, effective September 1, 1995; am. Acts 1997, 75th Leg., ch. 1013 (S.B. 35), § 27, effective September 1, 1997; am. Acts 2001, 77th Leg., ch. 444 (H.B. 63), § 5, effective September 1, 2001; am. Acts 2009, 81st Leg., ch. 1348 (S.B. 328), § 16, effective September 1, 2009.)

## Sec. 524.036.  Failure to Appear.

A person who requests a hearing and fails to appear without just cause waives the right to a hearing and the department's determination is final.
(Enacted by Acts 1995, 74th Leg., ch. 165 (S.B. 971), § 1, effective September 1, 1995.)

## Sec. 524.037.  Continuance.

(a) A continuance under Section 524.032 stays the suspension of a driver's license until the date of the final decision of the administrative law judge.

(b) A suspension order may not go into effect pending a final decision of the administrative law judge as a result of a continuance granted under Section 524.039.

(c) If the person's driver's license was taken by a peace officer under Section 524.011(b), the department shall notify the person of the effect of the continuance on the suspension of the person's license before the expiration of any temporary driving permit issued to the person, if the person is otherwise eligible, in a manner that will permit the person to establish to a peace officer that the person's driver's license is not suspended.
(Enacted by Acts 1995, 74th Leg., ch. 165 (S.B. 971), § 1, effective September 1, 1995; am. Acts 2001, 77th Leg., ch. 444 (H.B. 63), § 6, effective September 1, 2001.)

## Sec. 524.038. Instrument Reliability and Analysis Validity.

(a) The reliability of an instrument used to take or analyze a specimen of a person's breath to determine alcohol concentration and the validity of the results of the analysis may be attested to in a proceeding under this subchapter by affidavit from the certified breath test technical supervisor responsible for maintaining and directing the operation of breath test instruments in compliance with department rule.
(b) An affidavit submitted under Subsection (a) must contain statements on:
   (1) the reliability of the instrument and the analytical results; and
   (2) compliance with state law in the administration of the program.
(c) An affidavit of an expert witness contesting the reliability of the instrument or the results is admissible.
(d) An affidavit from a person whose presence is timely requested under this section is inadmissible if the person fails to appear at a hearing without a showing of good cause. Otherwise, an affidavit under this section may be submitted in lieu of an appearance at the hearing by the breath test operator, breath test technical supervisor, or expert witness.
(Enacted by Acts 1995, 74th Leg., ch. 165 (S.B. 971), § 1, effective September 1, 1995.)

## Sec. 524.039. Appearance of Technicians at Hearing.

(a) Not later than the fifth day before the date of a scheduled hearing, the person who requested a hearing may apply to the State Office of Administrative Hearings to issue a subpoena for the attendance of the breath test operator who took the specimen of the person's breath to determine alcohol concentration or the certified breath test

technical supervisor responsible for maintaining and directing the operation of the breath test instrument used to analyze the specimen of the person's breath, or both. The State Office of Administrative Hearings shall issue the subpoena only on a showing of good cause.
(b) The department may reschedule a hearing once not less than 48 hours before the hearing if a person subpoenaed under Subsection (a) is unavailable. The department may also reschedule the hearing on showing good cause that a person subpoenaed under Subsection (a) is not available at the time of the hearing.
(Enacted by Acts 1995, 74th Leg., ch. 165 (S.B. 971), § 1, effective September 1, 1995; am. Acts 2009, 81st Leg., ch. 1146 (H.B. 2730), § 3.01, effective September 1, 2009.)

## Sec. 524.040. Notice Requirements.

(a) Notice required to be provided by the department under this subchapter may be given by telephone or other electronic means. If notice is given by telephone or other electronic means, written notice must also be provided.
(b) Notice by mail is considered received on the fifth day after the date the notice is deposited with the United States Postal Service.
(Enacted by Acts 1995, 74th Leg., ch. 165 (S.B. 971), § 1, effective September 1, 1995.)

## Sec. 524.041. Appeal from Administrative Hearing.

(a) A person whose driver's license suspension is sustained may appeal the decision by filing a petition not later than the 30th day after the date the administrative law judge's decision is final. The administrative law judge's final decision is immediately appealable without the requirement of a motion for rehearing.
(b) A petition under Subsection (a) must be filed in a county court at law in the county in which the person was arrested or, if there is not a county court at law in the county, in the county court. If the county judge is not a licensed attorney, the county judge shall transfer the case to a district court for the county on the motion of either party or of the judge.
(c) A person who files an appeal under this section shall send a copy of the petition by certified mail to the department and to the State Office of Administrative Hearings at each agency's headquarters in Austin. The copy must be certified by the clerk of the court in which the petition is filed.

(d) The department's right to appeal is limited to issues of law.

(e) A district or county attorney may represent the department in an appeal.

(Enacted by Acts 1995, 74th Leg., ch. 165 (S.B. 971), § 1, effective September 1, 1995.)

### Sec. 524.042.  Stay of Suspension on Appeal.

(a) A suspension of a driver's license under this chapter is stayed on the filing of an appeal petition only if:

(1) the person's driver's license has not been suspended as a result of an alcohol-related or drug-related enforcement contact during the five years preceding the date of the person's arrest; and

(2) the person has not been convicted during the 10 years preceding the date of the person's arrest of an offense under:

(A) Article 6701*l*-1, Revised Statutes, as that law existed before September 1, 1994;

(B) Section 19.05(a)(2), Penal Code, as that law existed before September 1, 1994;

(C) Section 49.04, 49.045, or 49.06, Penal Code;

(D) Section 49.07 or 49.08, Penal Code, if the offense involved the operation of a motor vehicle or a watercraft; or

(E) Section 106.041, Alcoholic Beverage Code.

(b) A stay under this section is effective for not more than 90 days after the date the appeal petition is filed. On the expiration of the stay, the department shall impose the suspension. The department or court may not grant an extension of the stay or an additional stay.

(Enacted by Acts 1995, 74th Leg., ch. 165 (S.B. 971), § 1, effective September 1, 1995; am. Acts 1997, 75th Leg., ch. 1013 (S.B. 35), § 28, effective September 1, 1997; am. Acts 2009, 81st Leg., ch. 1348 (S.B. 328), § 17, effective September 1, 2009.)

### Sec. 524.043.  Review; Additional Evidence.

(a) Review on appeal is on the record certified by the State Office of Administrative Hearings with no additional testimony.

(b) On appeal, a party may apply to the court to present additional evidence. If the court is satisfied that the additional evidence is material and that there were good reasons for the failure to present it in the proceeding before the admin-istrative law judge, the court may order that the additional evidence be taken before an adminis-trative law judge on conditions determined by the court.

(c) There is no right to a jury trial in an appeal under this section.

(d) An administrative law judge may change a finding or decision as to whether the person had an alcohol concentration of a level specified in Section 49.01, Penal Code, or whether a minor had any detectable amount of alcohol in the minor's system because of the additional evidence and shall file the additional evidence and any changes, new findings, or decisions with the re-viewing court.

(e) A remand under this section does not stay the suspension of a driver's license.

(Enacted by Acts 1995, 74th Leg., ch. 165 (S.B. 971), § 1, effective September 1, 1995; am. Acts 1997, 75th Leg., ch. 1013 (S.B. 35), § 29, effective September 1, 1997.)

### Sec. 524.044.  Transcript of Administrative Hearing.

(a) To obtain a transcript of an administrative hearing, the party who appeals the administra-tive law judge's decision must apply to the State Office of Administrative Hearings.

(b) On payment of a fee not to exceed the actual cost of preparing the transcript, the State Office of Administrative Hearings shall promptly furnish both parties with a transcript of the administrative hearing.

(Enacted by Acts 1995, 74th Leg., ch. 165 (S.B. 971), § 1, effective September 1, 1995.)

### Secs. 524.045 to 524.050 [Reserved for expansion].

## SUBCHAPTER E
## REINSTATEMENT AND REISSUANCE OF DRIVER'S LICENSE

### Sec. 524.051.  Reinstatement and Reissuance.

(a) A driver's license suspended under this chapter may not be reinstated or another driver's license issued to the person until the person pays the department a fee of $125 in addition to any other fee required by law.

(b) The payment of a reinstatement fee is not required if a suspension under this chapter is:

(1) rescinded by the department; or

(2) not sustained by an administrative law judge, or a court.

(c) Each fee collected under this section shall be deposited to the credit of the Texas mobility fund.

(Enacted by Acts 1995, 74th Leg., ch. 165 (S.B. 971), § 1, effective September 1, 1995; am. Acts 2001, 77th Leg., ch. 444 (H.B. 63), § 14, effective September 1, 2001; am. Acts 2003, 78th Leg., ch. 1325 (H.B. 3588), § 11.06, effective September 1, 2003.)

# CHAPTER 525
# MOTORCYCLE AND BICYCLE AWARENESS

## Sec. 525.001.  Motorcycle and Bicycle Awareness.

(a) In this section, "motorcycle" has the meaning assigned that term by Section 502.001, and includes a motorcycle equipped with a sidecar.

(b) The Department of Public Safety shall include motorcycle and bicycle awareness information in any edition of the Texas driver's handbook published after the department exhausts the supply of the handbook that the department had on September 1, 1993.

(Enacted by Acts 1995, 74th Leg., ch. 165 (S.B. 971), § 1, effective September 1, 1995.)

# CHAPTERS 526 TO 540
# [RESERVED FOR EXPANSION]

# SUBTITLE C
# RULES OF THE ROAD

# CHAPTER 541
# DEFINITIONS

# SUBCHAPTER A
# PERSONS AND GOVERNMENTAL AUTHORITIES

## Sec. 541.001.  Persons.

In this subtitle:

(1) "Operator" means, as used in reference to a vehicle, a person who drives or has physical control of a vehicle.

(2) "Owner" means, as used in reference to a vehicle, a person who has a property interest in or title to a vehicle. The term:

(A) includes a person entitled to use and possess a vehicle subject to a security interest; and

(B) excludes a lienholder and a lessee whose lease is not intended as security.

(3) "Pedestrian" means a person on foot.

(4) "Person" means an individual, firm, partnership, association, or corporation.

(5) "School crossing guard" means a responsible person who is at least 18 years of age and is designated by a local authority to direct traffic in a school crossing zone for the protection of children going to or leaving a school.

(Enacted by Acts 1995, 74th Leg., ch. 165 (S.B. 971), § 1, effective September 1, 1995; am. Acts 1997, 75th Leg., ch. 165 (S.B. 898), § 30.103, effective September 1, 1997.)

## Sec. 541.002.  Governmental Authorities.

In this subtitle:

(1) "Department" means the Department of Public Safety acting directly or through its authorized officers and agents.

(2) "Director" means the public safety director.

(3) "Local authority" means:

(A) a county, municipality, or other local entity authorized to enact traffic laws under the laws of this state; or

(B) a school district created under the laws of this state only when it is designating

Transportation

school crossing guards for schools operated by the district.

(4) "Police officer" means an officer authorized to direct traffic or arrest persons who violate traffic regulations.

(5) "State" has the meaning assigned by Section 311.005, Government Code, and includes a province of Canada.

(Enacted by Acts 1995, 74th Leg., ch. 165 (S.B. 971), § 1, effective September 1, 1995.)

## Secs. 541.003 to 541.100 [Reserved for expansion].

## SUBCHAPTER B
## PROPERTY AREAS

### Sec. 541.101. Metropolitan Area.

In this subtitle, "metropolitan area" means an area that:

(1) contains at least one municipality with a population of at least 100,000; and

(2) includes the adjacent municipalities and unincorporated urban districts.

(Enacted by Acts 1995, 74th Leg., ch. 165 (S.B. 971), § 1, effective September 1, 1995.)

### Sec. 541.102. Restricted Districts.

In this subtitle:

(1) "Business district" means the territory adjacent to and including a highway if buildings used for business or industrial purposes, including a building used as a hotel, bank, office building, public building, or railroad station:

(A) are located within a 600-foot segment along the highway; and

(B) within that segment the buildings occupy at least 300 feet of frontage:

(i) on one side of the highway; or

(ii) collectively on both sides of the highway.

(2) "Residence district" means the territory, other than a business district, adjacent to and including a highway, if at least 300 feet of the highway frontage is primarily improved with:

(A) residences; or

(B) buildings used for business purposes and residences.

(3) "Urban district" means the territory adjacent to and including a highway, if the territory:

(A) is not in a municipality; and

(B) is improved with structures that are used for business, industry, or dwelling houses and located at intervals of less than 100 feet for a distance of at least one-quarter mile on either side of the highway.

(Enacted by Acts 1995, 74th Leg., ch. 165 (S.B. 971), § 1, effective September 1, 1995.)

## Secs. 541.103 to 541.200 [Reserved for expansion].

## SUBCHAPTER C
## VEHICLES, RAIL TRANSPORTATION, AND EQUIPMENT

### Sec. 541.201. Vehicles.

In this subtitle:

(1) "Authorized emergency vehicle" means:

(A) a fire department or police vehicle;

(B) a public or private ambulance operated by a person who has been issued a license by the Texas Department of Health;

(C) a municipal department or public service corporation emergency vehicle that has been designated or authorized by the governing body of a municipality;

(D) a private vehicle of a volunteer firefighter or a certified emergency medical services employee or volunteer when responding to a fire alarm or medical emergency;

(E) an industrial emergency response vehicle, including an industrial ambulance, when responding to an emergency, but only if the vehicle is operated in compliance with criteria in effect September 1, 1989, and established by the predecessor of the Texas Industrial Emergency Services Board of the State Firemen's and Fire Marshals' Association of Texas;

(F) a vehicle of a blood bank or tissue bank, accredited or approved under the laws of this state or the United States, when making emergency deliveries of blood, drugs, medicines, or organs; or

(G) a vehicle used for law enforcement purposes that is owned or leased by a federal governmental entity.

(2) "Bicycle" means a device that a person may ride and that is propelled by human power and has two tandem wheels at least one of which is more than 14 inches in diameter.

(3) "Bus" means:

(A) a motor vehicle used to transport persons and designed to accommodate more than 10 passengers, including the operator; or

(B) a motor vehicle, other than a taxicab, designed and used to transport persons for compensation.

(4) "Farm tractor" means a motor vehicle designed and used primarily as a farm implement to draw an implement of husbandry, including a plow or a mowing machine.

(5) "House trailer" means a trailer or semitrailer, other than a towable recreational vehicle, that:

(A) is transportable on a highway in one or more sections;

(B) is less than 40 feet in length, excluding tow bar, while in the traveling mode;

(C) is built on a permanent chassis;

(D) is desig[...] for commerci[...] quired utiliti[...]

(E) include[...] tioning, and e[...]

(6) "Impleme[...] cle, other than [...] designed and ad[...] ment, machiner[...]

(7) "Light tru[...] pickup truck, p[...] truck, that has [...] capacity of 2,00[...]

(8) "Moped" [...] cannot attain a[...] 30 miles per ho[...]

(A) cannot [...] horsepower; a[...]

(B) if an intern[...] piston displacement of 50 cubic centimeters or less and connects to a power drive system that does not require the operator to shift gears.

(9) "Motorcycle" means a motor vehicle, other than a tractor, that is equipped with a rider's saddle and designed to have when propelled not more than three wheels on the ground.

(10) "Motor-driven cycle" means a motorcycle equipped with a motor that has an engine piston displacement of 250 cubic centimeters or less. The term does not include an electric bicycle.

(11) "Motor vehicle" means a self-propelled vehicle or a vehicle that is propelled by electric power from overhead trolley wires. The term does not include an electric bicycle or an elec-

tric personal assistive mobility device, as defined by Section 551.201.

(11-a) "Multifunction school activity bus" means a motor vehicle that was manufactured in compliance with the federal motor vehicle safety standards for school buses in effect on the date of manufacture other than the standards requiring the bus to display alternately flashing red lights and to be equipped with movable stop arms, and that is used to transport preprimary, primary, or secondary students on a school-related activity trip other than on routes to and from school. The term does not include a school bus, a school activity bus, a school-chartered bus, or a bus operated by a mass transit authority.

(12) "Passenger car" means a motor vehicle, other than a motorcycle, used to transport [...] signed to accommodate 10 or [...]s, including the operator.

[...]iler" means a vehicle without [...]

[...]d to be drawn by another vehi- [...]ed to the other vehicle by pole, [...]r other security device; and [...]ily used to transport a long or [...]haped load, including poles, [...]ctural members, generally ca- [...]taining themselves as beams [...]upporting connections.

[...] vehicle" means a vehicle used [...]er, as defined by Article 2.12, [...]al Procedure, for law enforce- [...]hat:

[...]d or leased by a governmental

[...]d or leased by the police department of a private institution of higher education that commissions peace officers under Section 51.212, Education Code; or

(C) is:

(i) a private vehicle owned or leased by the peace officer; and

(ii) approved for use for law enforcement purposes by the head of the law enforcement agency that employs the peace officer, or by that person's designee, provided that use of the private vehicle must, if applicable, comply with any rule adopted by the commissioners court of a county under Section 170.001, Local Government Code, and that the private vehicle may not be considered an authorized emergency vehicle for exemption purposes under Section 228.054, 284.070, 366.178, or

Transportation

370.177, Transportation Code, unless the vehicle is marked.

(14) "Road tractor" means a motor vehicle designed and used to draw another vehicle but not constructed to carry a load independently or a part of the weight of the other vehicle or its load.

(15) "School activity bus" means a bus designed to accommodate more than 15 passengers, including the operator, that is owned, operated, rented, or leased by a school district, county school, open-enrollment charter school, regional education service center, or shared services arrangement and that is used to transport public school students on a school-related activity trip, other than on routes to and from school. The term does not include a chartered bus, a bus operated by a mass transit authority, a school bus, or a multifunction school activity bus.

(16) "School bus" means a motor vehicle that was manufactured in compliance with the federal motor vehicle safety standards for school buses in effect on the date of manufacture and that is used to transport pre-primary, primary, or secondary students on a route to or from school or on a school-related activity trip other than on routes to and from school. The term does not include a school-chartered bus or a bus operated by a mass transit authority.

(17) "Semitrailer" means a vehicle with or without motive power, other than a pole trailer:

(A) designed to be drawn by a motor vehicle and to transport persons or property; and

(B) constructed so that part of the vehicle's weight and load rests on or is carried by another vehicle.

(18) "Special mobile equipment" means a vehicle that is not designed or used primarily to transport persons or property and that is only incidentally operated on a highway. The term:

(A) includes ditchdigging apparatus, well boring apparatus, and road construction and maintenance machinery, including an asphalt spreader, bituminous mixer, bucket loader, tractor other than a truck tractor, ditcher, levelling grader, finishing machine, motor grader, road roller, scarifier, earthmoving carryall and scraper, power shovel or dragline, or self-propelled crane and earthmoving equipment; and

(B) excludes a vehicle that is designed to transport persons or property and that has machinery attached, including a house

trailer, dump truck, truck-mounted transit mixer, crane, and shovel.

(19) "Towable recreational vehicle" means a nonmotorized vehicle that:

(A) is designed:

(i) to be towable by a motor vehicle; and

(ii) for temporary human habitation for uses including recreational camping or seasonal use;

(B) is permanently built on a single chassis;

(C) may contain one or more life-support systems; and

(D) may be used permanently or temporarily for advertising, selling, displaying, or promoting merchandise or services, but is not used for transporting property for hire or for distribution by a private carrier.

(20) "Trailer" means a vehicle, other than a pole trailer, with or without motive power:

(A) designed to be drawn by a motor vehicle and to transport persons or property; and

(B) constructed so that no part of the vehicle's weight and load rests on the motor vehicle.

(21) "Truck" means a motor vehicle designed, used, or maintained primarily to transport property.

(22) "Truck tractor" means a motor vehicle designed and used primarily to draw another vehicle but not constructed to carry a load other than a part of the weight of the other vehicle and its load.

(23) "Vehicle" means a device that can be used to transport or draw persons or property on a highway. The term does not include:

(A) a device exclusively used on stationary rails or tracks; or

(B) manufactured housing as that term is defined by Chapter 1201, Occupations Code.

(24) "Electric bicycle" means a bicycle that:

(A) is designed to be propelled by an electric motor, exclusively or in combination with the application of human power;

(B) cannot attain a speed of more than 20 miles per hour without the application of human power; and

(C) does not exceed a weight of 100 pounds.

(Enacted by Acts 1995, 74th Leg., ch. 165 (S.B. 971), § 1, effective September 1, 1995; am. Acts 1997, 75th Leg., ch. 1020 (S.B. 343), § 1, effective September 1, 1997; am. Acts 1997, 75th Leg., ch. 1438 (H.B. 3249), § 8, effective September 1, 1997; am. Acts 1999, 76th Leg., ch. 663 (H.B.

385), § 1, effective June 18, 1999; am. Acts 1999, 76th Leg., ch. 797 (H.B. 1492), § 3, effective September 1, 1999; am. Acts 2001, 77th Leg., ch. 1085 (H.B. 2204), § 5, effective September 1, 2001; am. Acts 2003, 78th Leg., ch. 1276 (H.B. 3507), § 14A.833, effective September 1, 2003; am. Acts 2003, 78th Leg., ch. 1318 (H.B. 1997), § 2, effective September 1, 2003; am. Acts 2005, 79th Leg., ch. 558 (H.B. 1267), § 3, effective September 1, 2005; am. Acts 2007, 80th Leg., ch. 258 (S.B. 11), § 4.06, effective September 1, 2007; am. Acts 2007, 80th Leg., ch. 923 (H.B. 3190), § 2, effective September 1, 2007; am. Acts 2009, 81st Leg., ch. 1280 (H.B. 1831), § 1.20, effective September 1, 2009.)

### Sec. 541.202.  Rail Transportation.

In this subtitle:

(1) "Railroad" means a carrier that operates cars, other than streetcars, on stationary rails to transport persons or property.

(2) "Railroad train" means a steam engine or electric or other motor with or without an attached car operated on rails, other than a streetcar.

(3) "Streetcar" means a car, other than a railroad train, used to transport persons or property and operated on rails located primarily within a municipality.

(Enacted by Acts 1995, 74th Leg., ch. 165 (S.B. 971), § 1, effective September 1, 1995.)

### Sec. 541.203.  Equipment.

In this subtitle:

(1) "Exhaust emission system" means a motor vehicle engine modification designed to control or reduce the emission of substances from a motor vehicle or motor vehicle engine, of a model year of 1968 or later, and installed on or incorporated in a motor vehicle or motor vehicle engine in compliance with requirements imposed by the Motor Vehicle Air Pollution Control Act (42 U.S.C. Section 1857 et seq.) or other applicable law.

(2) "Metal tire" includes a tire the surface of which in contact with the highway is wholly or partly made of metal or other hard, nonresilient material.

(3) "Muffler" means a device that reduces noise using:

(A) a mechanical design, including a series of chambers or baffle plates, to receive exhaust gas from an internal combustion engine; or

(B) turbine wheels to receive exhaust gas from a diesel engine.

(4) "Solid tire" includes only a tire that:

(A) is made of rubber or another resilient material; and

(B) does not use compressed air to support its load.

(Enacted by Acts 1995, 74th Leg., ch. 165 (S.B. 971), § 1, effective September 1, 1995.)

### Secs. 541.204 to 541.300 [Reserved for expansion].

## SUBCHAPTER D
## TRAFFIC, TRAFFIC AREAS, AND TRAFFIC CONTROL

### Sec. 541.301.  Traffic.

In this subtitle "traffic" means pedestrians, ridden or herded animals, and conveyances, including vehicles and streetcars, singly or together while using a highway for the purposes of travel.

(Enacted by Acts 1995, 74th Leg., ch. 165 (S.B. 971), § 1, effective September 1, 1995.)

### Sec. 541.302.  Traffic Areas.

In this subtitle:

(1) "Alley" means a street that:

(A) is not used primarily for through traffic; and

(B) provides access to rear entrances of buildings or lots along a street.

(2) "Crosswalk" means:

(A) the portion of a roadway, including an intersection, designated as a pedestrian crossing by surface markings, including lines; or

(B) the portion of a roadway at an intersection that is within the connections of the lateral lines of the sidewalks on opposite sides of the highway measured from the curbs or, in the absence of curbs, from the edges of the traversable roadway.

(3) "Freeway" means a divided, controlled-access highway for through traffic.

(4) "Freeway main lane" means a freeway lane having an uninterrupted flow of through traffic.

(5) "Highway or street" means the width between the boundary lines of a publicly maintained way any part of which is open to the public for vehicular travel.

(6) "Improved shoulder" means a paved shoulder.

(7) "Laned roadway" means a roadway that is divided into at least two clearly marked lanes for vehicular travel.

(8) "Limited-access or controlled-access highway" means a highway or roadway to which:

(A) persons, including owners or occupants of abutting real property, have no right of access; and

(B) access by persons to enter or exit the highway or roadway is restricted under law except at a place and in the manner determined by the authority that has jurisdiction over the highway or roadway.

(9) "Private road or driveway" means a privately owned way or place used for vehicular travel and used only by the owner and persons who have the owner's express or implied permission.

(10) "Ramp" means an interconnecting roadway of a traffic interchange, or a connecting roadway between highways at different levels or between parallel highways, that allows a vehicle to enter or exit a roadway.

(11) "Roadway" means the portion of a highway, other than the berm or shoulder, that is improved, designed, or ordinarily used for vehicular travel. If a highway includes at least two separate roadways, the term applies to each roadway separately.

(12) "Safety zone" means the area in a roadway officially designated for exclusive pedestrian use and that is protected or so marked or indicated by adequate signs as to be plainly visible at all times while so designated.

(13) "School crossing zone" means a reduced-speed zone designated on a street by a local authority to facilitate safe crossing of the street by children going to or leaving a public or private elementary or secondary school during the time the reduced speed limit applies.

(14) "School crosswalk" means a crosswalk designated on a street by a local authority to facilitate safe crossing of the street by children going to or leaving a public or private elementary or secondary school.

(15) "Shoulder" means the portion of a highway that is:

(A) adjacent to the roadway;

(B) designed or ordinarily used for parking;

(C) distinguished from the roadway by different design, construction, or marking; and

(D) not intended for normal vehicular travel.

(16) "Sidewalk" means the portion of a street that is:

(A) between a curb or lateral line of a roadway and the adjacent property line; and

(B) intended for pedestrian use.

(Enacted by Acts 1995, 74th Leg., ch. 165 (S.B. 971), § 1, effective September 1, 1995.)

## Sec. 541.303. Intersection.

(a) In this subtitle, "intersection" means the common area at the junction of two highways, other than the junction of an alley and a highway.

(b) The dimensions of an intersection include only the common area:

(1) within the connection of the lateral curb lines or, in the absence of curb lines, the lateral boundary lines of the roadways of intersecting highways that join at approximate right angles; or

(2) at the place where vehicles could collide if traveling on roadways of intersecting highways that join at any angle other than an approximate right angle.

(c) Each junction of each roadway of a highway that includes two roadways at least 30 feet apart with the roadway of an intersecting highway, including each roadway of an intersecting highway that includes two roadways at least 30 feet apart, is a separate intersection.

(Enacted by Acts 1995, 74th Leg., ch. 165 (S.B. 971), § 1, effective September 1, 1995.)

## Sec. 541.304. Traffic Control.

In this subtitle:

(1) "Official traffic-control device" means a sign, signal, marking, or device that is:

(A) consistent with this subtitle;

(B) placed or erected by a public body or officer having jurisdiction; and

(C) used to regulate, warn, or guide traffic.

(2) "Railroad sign or signal" means a sign, signal, or device erected by a railroad, public body, or public officer to notify traffic of railroad tracks or an approaching railroad train.

(3) "Traffic-control signal" means a manual, electric, or mechanical device that alternately directs traffic to stop and to proceed.

(Enacted by Acts 1995, 74th Leg., ch. 165 (S.B. 971), § 1, effective September 1, 1995.)

**Secs. 541.305 to 541.400 [Reserved for expansion].**

## SUBCHAPTER E .
## MISCELLANEOUS TERMS

### Sec. 541.401.  Miscellaneous Terms.

In this subtitle:

(1) "Daytime" means the period beginning one-half hour before sunrise and ending one-half hour after sunset.

(2) "Explosive" means a chemical compound or mechanical mixture that:

(A) is commonly intended for use or used to produce an explosion; and

(B) contains ingredients, which may include oxidizing or combustive units, in packing, proportions, or quantities that, if ignited by fire, friction, concussion, percussion, or detonator, could suddenly generate highly heated gases that could damage surrounding objects or destroy life or limb.

(3) "Flammable liquid" means a liquid that has a flash point of not more than 70 degrees Fahrenheit as determined by a tagliabue or equivalent closed-cup test device.

(4) "Gross vehicle weight" means the weight of a vehicle and the weight of its load.

(5) "Nighttime" means the period beginning one-half hour after sunset and ending one-half hour before sunrise.

(6) "Park" or "parking" means to stand an occupied or unoccupied vehicle, other than temporarily while loading or unloading merchandise or passengers.

(7) "Personal injury" means an injury to any part of the human body and that requires treatment.

(8) "Right-of-way" means the right of one vehicle or pedestrian to proceed in a lawful manner in preference to another vehicle or pedestrian that is approaching from a direction, at a speed, and within a proximity that could cause a collision unless one grants precedence to the other.

(9) "Stand" or "standing" means to halt an occupied or unoccupied vehicle, other than temporarily while receiving or discharging passengers.

(10) "Stop" or "stopping" means:

(A) when required, to completely cease movement; and

(B) when prohibited, to halt, including momentarily halting, an occupied or unoccupied vehicle, unless necessary to avoid conflict with other traffic or to comply with the directions of a police officer or a traffic-control sign or signal.

(Enacted by Acts 1995, 74th Leg., ch. 165 (S.B. 971), § 1, effective September 1, 1995.)

## CHAPTER 542
## GENERAL PROVISIONS

Transportation

## SUBCHAPTER A
## APPLICABILITY

### Sec. 542.001.   Vehicles on Highways.

A provision of this subtitle relating to the operation of a vehicle applies only to the operation of a vehicle on a highway unless the provision specifically applies to a different place.
(Enacted by Acts 1995, 74th Leg., ch. 165 (S.B. 971), § 1, effective September 1, 1995.)

### Sec. 542.002.   Government Vehicles.

A provision of this subtitle applicable to an operator of a vehicle applies to the operator of a vehicle owned or operated by the United States, this state, or a political subdivision of this state, except as specifically provided otherwise by this subtitle for an authorized emergency vehicle.
(Enacted by Acts 1995, 74th Leg., ch. 165 (S.B. 971), § 1, effective September 1, 1995.)

### Sec. 542.003.   Animals and Animal-Drawn Vehicles.

A person riding an animal on a roadway or operating a vehicle drawn by an animal on a roadway has the rights and duties applicable to the operator of a vehicle under this subtitle, except a right or duty that by its nature cannot apply to a person riding an animal or operating a vehicle drawn by an animal.
(Enacted by Acts 1995, 74th Leg., ch. 165 (S.B. 971), § 1, effective September 1, 1995.)

### Sec. 542.004.   Persons and Equipment Engaged in Work on Highway Surface.

This subtitle does not apply to a person, team, motor vehicle, or other equipment engaged in work on a highway unless the provision is specifically made applicable, but does apply to those persons and vehicles while traveling to or from that work.
(Enacted by Acts 1995, 74th Leg., ch. 165 (S.B. 971), § 1, effective September 1, 1995.)

### Sec. 542.005.   Rules on Private Property.

This subtitle does not prevent an owner of private property that is a private road from:
(1)  regulating or prohibiting use of the property by the public for vehicular travel; or
(2)  requiring conditions different from or in addition to those specified by this subtitle.
(Enacted by Acts 1995, 74th Leg., ch. 165 (S.B. 971), § 1, effective September 1, 1995.)

### Sec. 542.006.   Speed Restrictions on Private Roads.

(a)  The owners of a majority of the parcels of real property abutting a private road may petition the Texas Transportation Commission to extend the speed restrictions of this subtitle to the portion of the road in a subdivision or across adjacent subdivisions if:
(1)  the road is not in a municipality;
(2)  the total number of residents in the subdivision and subdivisions adjacent to the subdivision is at least 400; and
(3)  a plat for the subdivision and each adjacent subdivision included to determine the number of residents under Subdivision (2) has been filed in the deed records of the county.
(b)  After the commission receives a petition and verifies the property ownership of its signers, the commission may issue an order extending the speed restrictions to the private road if the commission finds the order is in the interests of the area residents and the public generally.
(c)  If the commission rejects the petition, the commission shall hold a public hearing on the advisability of making the speed restrictions applicable. The hearing must be held in the county in which the portion of the road that is the subject of the petition is located. The commission shall publish notice of the hearing in a newspaper of general circulation in that county at least 10 days before the date of the hearing.
(d)  At the hearing, if the commission finds that it would be in the interests of the area residents and the public generally, the commission shall issue an order extending the speed restrictions to the private road.
(e)  After the commission issues an order under this section, the private road is a public highway for purposes of setting and enforcing speed restrictions under this subtitle, and the commission shall post speed limit signs on property abutting the private road with the consent of the owner of the property on which a sign is placed.
(Enacted by Acts 1995, 74th Leg., ch. 165 (S.B. 971), § 1, effective September 1, 1995; am. Acts 1999, 76th Leg., ch. 308 (H.B. 434), § 1, effective May 29, 1999.)

### Sec. 542.007.   Traffic Regulations: Private Subdivision in Certain Counties.

(a)  This section applies only to a subdivision that is located in the unincorporated area of a county with a population of 500,000 or less.
(b)  On petition of 25 percent of the property owners residing in a subdivision in which the

roads are privately maintained or on the request of the governing body of the entity that maintains those roads, the commissioners court of the county by order may extend any traffic rules that apply to a county road to the roads of the subdivision if the commissioners court finds the order in the interest of the county generally. The petition must specify the traffic rules that are sought to be extended. The court order may extend any or all of the requested traffic rules.

(c) As a condition of extending a traffic rule under Subsection (b), the commissioners court may require that owners of the property in the subdivision pay all or part of the cost of extending and enforcing the traffic rules in the subdivision. The commissioners court shall consult with the sheriff to determine the cost of enforcing traffic rules in the subdivision.

(d) On issuance of an order under this section, the private roads in the subdivision are considered to be county roads for purposes of the application and enforcement of the specified traffic rules. The commissioners court may place official traffic control devices on property abutting the private roads if:

   (1) those devices relate to the specified traffic rule; and

   (2) the consent of the owner of that property is obtained.

(Enacted by Acts 1999, 76th Leg., ch. 1393 (H.B. 1703), § 1, effective September 1, 1999; am. Acts 2001, 77th Leg., ch. 913 (S.B. 217), § 2, effective September 1, 2001; am. Acts 2003, 78th Leg., ch. 243 (H.B. 1439), § 1, effective September 1, 2003.)

### Sec. 542.008. Traffic Regulations: Private Subdivisions in Certain Municipalities.

(a) This section applies only to a subdivision in which the roads are privately owned or maintained that is located in a municipality with a population of 300 or more.

(b) On petition of 25 percent of the property owners residing in the subdivision or on the request of the governing body of the entity that maintains the roads, the governing body of the municipality may extend by ordinance any traffic rules that apply to a road owned by the municipality, or by the county in which the municipality is located, to the roads in the subdivision so that the roads of the subdivision are under the same traffic rules, if the governing body of the municipality finds the ordinance in the interest of the

municipality generally. A petition under this subsection must specify the traffic rules that are sought to be extended. The ordinance may extend any or all of the requested rules.

(c) As a condition of extending a traffic rule under Subsection (b), the governing body of the municipality may require that owners of property in the subdivision pay all or part of the cost of extending and enforcing the traffic rules in the subdivision, including the costs associated with the placement of necessary official traffic control devices. The governing body of the municipality shall consult with the appropriate law enforcement entity to determine the cost of enforcing traffic rules in the subdivision.

(d) On issuance of an order under this section, the private roads in the subdivision are considered to be public highways or streets for purposes of the application and enforcement of the specified traffic rules. The governing body of the municipality may place official traffic control devices on property abutting the private roads if:

   (1) those devices relate to the specified traffic rule; and

   (2) the consent of the owner of that property is obtained or an easement is available for the placement.

(Enacted by Acts 2001, 77th Leg., ch. 913 (S.B. 217), § 1, effective September 1, 2001.)

### Sec. 542.0081. Traffic Regulations: Special District in Certain Counties.

(a) This section applies only to a road owned or maintained by a special district that is located in the unincorporated area of a county with a population of less than one million.

(b) The residents of all or any portion of a special district may file a petition with the commissioners court of the county in which the roads are located requesting that county enforcement of traffic rules on county roads be extended to the roads of the district. The petition must:

   (1) specify the roads over which county enforcement is sought;

   (2) specify the traffic rules for which county enforcement is sought; and

   (3) be signed by 50 percent of the property owners residing in the area that is served by the roads of the district over which county enforcement is sought.

(c) If the commissioners court finds that granting the request is in the interest of the county generally, the commissioners court shall by order extend the enforcement of traffic rules by the county to the roads of the district specified in the petition. The order may grant enforcement of some or all traffic rules requested in the petition.

(d) As a condition of extending a traffic rule under Subsection (c), the commissioners court may require the special district to pay for all or a part of the costs of extending enforcement to the roads of the district. The commissioners court shall consult with the sheriff to determine the cost of extending enforcement.

(e) On issuance of an order under this section, the roads specified in the order are considered to be county roads for the purposes of the application and enforcement of the specified traffic rules. The commissioners court may place official traffic control devices on the right-of-way of the roads of the district if those devices relate to the specified traffic rules.
(Enacted by Acts 2011, 82nd Leg., ch. 812 (H.B. 2541), § 1, effective June 17, 2011.)

## Sec. 542.009.  Operators of Certain Mobility Devices.

(a) In this section, "motorized mobility device" means a device designed for transportation of persons with physical disabilities that:

(1) has three or more wheels;

(2) is propelled by a battery-powered motor;

(3) has not more than one forward gear; and

(4) is not capable of speeds exceeding eight miles per hour.

(b) For the purposes of this subtitle, a person operating a nonmotorized wheelchair or motorized mobility device is considered to be a pedestrian.
(Enacted by Acts 2001, 77th Leg., ch. 497 (H.B. 1378), § 2, effective June 11, 2001; am. Acts 2003, 78th Leg., ch. 1275 (H.B. 3506), § 2(135), effective September 1, 2003 (renumbered from Sec. 542.008).)

## Secs. 542.010 to 542.200 [Reserved for expansion].

### SUBCHAPTER B
### UNIFORMITY AND INTERPRETATION OF TRAFFIC LAWS

## Sec. 542.201.  General Rule of Uniformity.

This subtitle applies uniformly throughout this state. A local authority may not enact or enforce an ordinance or rule that conflicts with this subtitle unless expressly authorized by this subtitle. However, a local authority may regulate traffic in a manner that does not conflict with this subtitle.
(Enacted by Acts 1995, 74th Leg., ch. 165 (S.B. 971), § 1, effective September 1, 1995.)

## Sec. 542.202.  Powers of Local Authorities.

(a) This subtitle does not prevent a local authority, with respect to a highway under its jurisdiction and in the reasonable exercise of the police power, from:

(1) regulating traffic by police officers or traffic-control devices;

(2) regulating the stopping, standing, or parking of a vehicle;

(3) regulating or prohibiting a procession or assemblage on a highway;

(4) regulating the operation and requiring registration and licensing of a bicycle or electric bicycle, including payment of a registration fee, except as provided by Section 551.106;

(5) regulating the time, place, and manner in which a roller skater may use a highway;

(6) regulating the speed of a vehicle in a public park;

(7) regulating or prohibiting the turning of a vehicle or specified type of vehicle at an intersection;

(8) designating an intersection as a stop intersection or a yield intersection and requiring each vehicle to stop or yield at one or more entrances to the intersection;

(9) designating a highway as a through highway;

(10) designating a highway as a one-way highway and requiring each vehicle on the highway to move in one specific direction;

(11) designating school crossing guards and school crossing zones;

(12) altering a speed limit as authorized by this subtitle; or

(13) adopting other traffic rules specifically authorized by this subtitle.

(b) In this section:

(1) "Roller skater" means a person wearing footwear with a set of wheels attached.

(2) "Through highway" means a highway or a portion of a highway on which:

(A) vehicular traffic is given preferential right-of-way; and

(B) vehicular traffic entering from an intersecting highway is required by law to yield right-of-way in compliance with an official traffic-control device.

(3) "Regulating" means criminal, civil, and administrative enforcement against a person, including the owner or operator of a motor vehicle, in accordance with a state law or a municipal ordinance.

(Enacted by Acts 1995, 74th Leg., ch. 165 (S.B. 971), § 1, effective September 1, 1995; am. Acts 2001, 77th Leg., ch. 1085 (H.B. 2204), § 6, effective September 1, 2001; am. Acts 2003, 78th Leg., ch. 359 (S.B. 1184), § 1, effective September 1, 2003.)

## Sec. 542.203. Limitation on Local Authorities.

(a) A local authority may not erect or maintain a traffic-control device to direct the traffic on a state highway, including a farm-to-market or ranch-to-market road, to stop or yield before entering or crossing an intersecting highway unless permitted by agreement between the local authority and the Texas Department of Transportation under Section 221.002.

(b) An ordinance or rule of a local authority is not effective until signs giving notice are posted on or at the entrance to the highway or part of the highway, as may be most appropriate. This subsection applies only to an ordinance or rule that:

(1) regulates the speed of a vehicle in a public park;

(2) alters a speed limit as authorized by this subtitle;

(3) designates an intersection as a stop intersection or a yield intersection; or

(4) designates a highway as a one-way highway or a through highway.

(c) An ordinance or rule of a local authority regulating the time, place, and manner in which a roller skater may use a highway may not alter the local authority's standard of care or liability with regard to construction, design, or maintenance of a highway.

(Enacted by Acts 1995, 74th Leg., ch. 165 (S.B. 971), § 1, effective September 1, 1995.)

## Sec. 542.2035. Limitation on Municipalities.

(a) A municipality may not implement or operate an automated traffic control system with respect to a highway or street under its jurisdiction for the purpose of enforcing compliance with posted speed limits. The attorney general shall enforce this subsection.

(b) In this section, "automated traffic control system" means a photographic device, radar device, laser device, or other electrical or mechanical device designed to:

(1) record the speed of a motor vehicle; and

(2) obtain one or more photographs or other recorded images of:

(A) the vehicle;

(B) the license plate attached to the vehicle; or

(C) the operator of the vehicle.

(Enacted by Acts 2007, 80th Leg., ch. 646 (H.B. 922), § 1, effective June 15, 2007.)

## Sec. 542.204. Powers Related to Intersections.

The Texas Transportation Commission and a local authority may, in a matter of highway or traffic engineering design, consider the separate intersections of divided highways with medians at least 30 feet apart as components of a single intersection.

(Enacted by Acts 1995, 74th Leg., ch. 165 (S.B. 971), § 1, effective September 1, 1995.)

## Sec. 542.205. Conflict Between This Subtitle and an Order, Rule, or Regulation of Certain Agencies.

(a) If this subtitle conflicts with an order, rule, regulation, or requirement of the federal Surface Transportation Board or the department relating to a vehicle safety requirement, including a requirement relating to vehicle equipment, compliance by the owner or operator of the vehicle with the order, rule, regulation, or requirement of the federal Surface Transportation Board or the department is compliance with this subtitle.

(b) The owner or operator of a vehicle shall comply with any requirement of this subtitle that is in addition to, but not in conflict with, a requirement of the federal Surface Transportation Board or the department.

(Enacted by Acts 1995, 74th Leg., ch. 165 (S.B. 971), § 1, effective September 1, 1995; am. Acts 1997, 75th Leg., ch. 165 (S.B. 898), § 30.104, effective September 1, 1997.)

## Sec. 542.206. Effect of Speed Limits in a Civil Action.

A provision of this subtitle declaring a maximum or minimum speed limit does not relieve the plaintiff in a civil action from the burden of proving negligence of the defendant as the proximate cause of an accident.

Transportation

(Enacted by Acts 1995, 74th Leg., ch. 165 (S.B. 971), § 1, effective September 1, 1995.)

**Secs. 542.207 to 542.300 [Reserved for expansion].**

## SUBCHAPTER C
## OFFENSES

### Sec. 542.301. General Offense.

(a) A person commits an offense if the person performs an act prohibited or fails to perform an act required by this subtitle.

(b) Except as otherwise provided, an offense under this subtitle is a misdemeanor.
(Enacted by Acts 1995, 74th Leg., ch. 165 (S.B. 971), § 1, effective September 1, 1995.)

### Sec. 542.302. Offense by Person Owning or Controlling Vehicle.

A person who owns a vehicle or employs or otherwise directs the operator of a vehicle commits an offense if the person requires or knowingly permits the operator of the vehicle to operate the vehicle in a manner that violates law.
(Enacted by Acts 1995, 74th Leg., ch. 165 (S.B. 971), § 1, effective September 1, 1995.)

### Sec. 542.303. Inchoate Offense.

(a) A person who attempts to commit or conspires to commit an act declared by this subtitle to be an offense is guilty of the offense.

(b) A person who falsely, fraudulently, or wilfully permits another to violate this subtitle is guilty of the violation.
(Enacted by Acts 1995, 74th Leg., ch. 165 (S.B. 971), § 1, effective September 1, 1995.)

**Secs. 542.304 to 542.400 [Reserved for expansion].**

## SUBCHAPTER D
## PENALTIES AND COSTS OF COURT

### Sec. 542.401. General Penalty.

A person convicted of an offense that is a misdemeanor under this subtitle for which another penalty is not provided shall be punished by a fine of not less than $1 or more than $200.
(Enacted by Acts 1995, 74th Leg., ch. 165 (S.B. 971), § 1, effective September 1, 1995.)

### Sec. 542.402. Disposition of Fines.

(a) Except as provided by Subsection (b-1), a municipality or county shall use a fine collected for a violation of a highway law in this title to:

(1) construct and maintain roads, bridges, and culverts in the municipality or county;

(2) enforce laws regulating the use of highways by motor vehicles; and

(3) defray the expense of county traffic officers.

(b) In each fiscal year, a municipality having a population of less than 5,000 may retain, from fines collected for violations of this title and from special expenses collected under Article 45.051, Code of Criminal Procedure, in cases in which a violation of this title is alleged, an amount equal to 30 percent of the municipality's revenue for the preceding fiscal year from all sources, other than federal funds and bond proceeds, as shown by the audit performed under Section 103.001, Local Government Code. After a municipality has retained that amount, the municipality shall send to the comptroller any portion of a fine or a special expense collected that exceeds $1.

(b-1) Subject to Subsection (b-2), a county may use a fine collected for a violation of a highway law as the county determines appropriate if:

(1) the county has a population of less than 5,000; and

(2) the commissioners court of the county by resolution elects to spend the revenue in a manner other than as provided by Subsection (a).

(b-2) In each fiscal year, a county described by Subsection may retain, from fines collected for violations of this title and from special expenses collected under Article 45.051, Code of Criminal Procedure, in cases in which a violation of this title is alleged, an amount equal to 30 percent of the county's revenue for the preceding fiscal year from all sources, other than federal funds and bond proceeds, as shown by an audit performed under Chapter 115, Local Government Code. After a county has retained that amount, the county shall send to the comptroller any portion of a fine or a special expense collected that exceeds $1.

(c) The comptroller shall enforce Subsections (b) and (b-2).

(d) In a fiscal year in which a municipality retains from fines and special expenses collected for violations of this title an amount equal to at least 20 percent of the municipality's revenue for the preceding fiscal year from all sources other than federal funds and bond proceeds, not later than the 120th day after the last day of the municipality's fiscal year, the municipality shall send to the comptroller:

(1) a copy of the municipality's financial statement for that fiscal year filed under Chapter 103, Local Government Code; and

(2) a report that shows the total amount collected for that fiscal year from fines and special expenses under Subsection (b).

(d-1) In a fiscal year in which a county retains from fines and special expenses collected for violations of this title an amount equal to at least 20 percent of the county's revenue for the preceding fiscal year from all sources other than federal funds and bond proceeds, not later than the 120th day after the last day of the county's fiscal year, the county shall send to the comptroller:

(1) a copy of the county's financial statement; and

(2) a report that shows the total amount collected for that fiscal year from fines and special expenses under Subsection

(e) If an audit is conducted by the comptroller under Subsection (c) and it is determined that the municipality or county is retaining more than 20 percent of the amounts under Subsection (b) or (b-2), as applicable, and has not complied with Subsection (d) or (d-1), as applicable, the municipality or county shall pay the costs incurred by the comptroller in conducting the audit.

(f) **[Expires September 1, 2021]** A municipality may include the revenue generated from services provided in the municipality by a utility company operating within the municipality as municipal revenue for a fiscal year under Subsection (b) if:

(1) the municipality has a population of more than 1,000 but less than 1,200; and

(2) part of the municipality's boundary is a river that forms part of the boundary between two counties.

(g) **[Expires September 1, 2021]** This subsection and Subsection (f) expire on September 1, 2021.

(Enacted by Acts 1995, 74th Leg., ch. 165 (S.B. 971), § 1, effective September 1, 1995; am. Acts 1997, 75th Leg., ch. 165 (S.B. 898), § 30.105(a), effective September 1, 1997; am. Acts 1999, 76th Leg., ch. 1336 (H.B. 352), § 1, effective September 1, 1999; am. Acts 1999, 76th Leg., ch. 1545 (S.B. 1230), § 72, effective September 1, 1999; am. Acts 2011, 82nd Leg., ch. 1286 (H.B. 1517), § 1, effective September 1, 2011.)

## Sec. 542.403. Court Costs.

(a) In addition to other costs, a person convicted of a misdemeanor under this subtitle shall pay $3 as a cost of court.

(b) The officer who collects a cost under this section shall:

(1) deposit in the municipal treasury a cost collected in a municipal court case; and

(2) deposit in the county treasury a cost collected in a justice court case or in a county court case, including a case appealed from a justice or municipal court.

(c) In this section, "conviction" has the meaning assigned by Section 133.101, Local Government Code.

(Enacted by Acts 1995, 74th Leg., ch. 165 (S.B. 971), § 1, effective September 1, 1995; am. Acts 2003, 78th Leg., ch. 209 (H.B. 2424), § 77(a), effective January 1, 2004.)

## Sec. 542.4031. State Traffic Fine.

(a) In addition to the fine prescribed by Section 542.401 or another section of this subtitle, as applicable, a person who enters a plea of guilty or nolo contendere to or is convicted of an offense under this subtitle shall pay $30 as a state traffic fine. The person shall pay the state traffic fine when the person enters the person's plea of guilty or nolo contendere, or on the date of conviction, whichever is earlier. The state traffic fine shall be paid regardless of whether:

(1) a sentence is imposed on the person;

(2) the court defers final disposition of the person's case; or

(3) the person is placed on community supervision, including deferred adjudication community supervision.

(b) An officer collecting a state traffic fine under this section in a case in municipal court shall keep separate records of the money collected and shall deposit the money in the municipal treasury.

(c) An officer collecting a state traffic fine under this section in a justice, county, or district court shall keep separate records of the money collected and shall deposit the money in the county treasury.

(d) Each calendar quarter, an officer collecting a state traffic fine under this section shall submit a report to the comptroller. The report must comply with Articles 103.005(c) and (d), Code of Criminal Procedure.

(e) The custodian of money in a municipal or county treasury may deposit money collected under this section in an interest-bearing account. The custodian shall:

(1) keep records of the amount of money collected under this section that is on deposit in the treasury; and

(2) not later than the last day of the month following each calendar quarter, remit to the

comptroller money collected under this section during the preceding quarter, as required by the comptroller.

(f) A municipality or county may retain five percent of the money collected under this section as a service fee for the collection if the municipality or county remits the funds to the comptroller within the period prescribed in Subsection (e). The municipality or county may retain any interest accrued on the money if the custodian of the money deposited in the treasury keeps records of the amount of money collected under this section that is on deposit in the treasury and remits the funds to the comptroller within the period prescribed in Subsection (e).

(g) Of the money received by the comptroller under this section, the comptroller shall deposit:

(1) 67 percent to the credit of the undedicated portion of the general revenue fund; and

(2) 33 percent to the credit of the designated trauma facility and emergency medical services account under Section 780.003, Health and Safety Code.

(h) Notwithstanding Subsection (g)(1), in any state fiscal year the comptroller shall deposit 67 percent of the money received under Subsection (e)(2) to the credit of the general revenue fund only until the total amount of the money deposited to the credit of the general revenue fund under Subsection (g)(1) and Section 780.002(b), Health and Safety Code, equals $250 million for that year. If in any state fiscal year the amount received by the comptroller under those laws for deposit to the credit of the general revenue fund exceeds $250 million, the comptroller shall deposit the additional amount to the credit of the Texas mobility fund.

(i) Money collected under this section is subject to audit by the comptroller. Money spent is subject to audit by the state auditor.

(j) [Repealed by Acts 2003, 78th Leg., 3rd C.S., ch. 8 (H.B. 2), § 6.02(2), effective January 11, 2004.]

(k) [Repealed by Acts 2005, 79th Leg., ch. 1123 (H.B. 2470), § 6(2), effective September 1, 2005.] (Enacted by Acts 2003, 78th Leg., ch. 1325 (H.B. 3588), § 12.01(a), effective September 1, 2003; am. Acts 2003, 78th Leg., 3rd C.S., ch. 8 (H.B. 2), §§ 2.01, 2.02, 6.02(2), effective January 11, 2004; am. Acts 2005, 79th Leg., ch. 1123 (H.B. 2470), § 6(2), effective September 1, 2005.)

## Sec. 542.404. Fine for Offense in Construction or Maintenance Work Zone.

(a) If an offense under this subtitle, other than an offense under Chapter 548 or 552 or Section 545.412 or 545.413, is committed in a construction or maintenance work zone when workers are present and any written notice to appear issued for the offense states on its face that workers were present when the offense was committed:

(1) the minimum fine applicable to the offense is twice the minimum fine that would be applicable to the offense if it were committed outside a construction or maintenance work zone; and

(2) the maximum fine applicable to the offense is twice the maximum fine that would be applicable to the offense if it were committed outside a construction or maintenance work zone.

(b) In this section, "construction or maintenance work zone" has the meaning assigned by Section 472.022.

(Enacted by Acts 1997, 75th Leg., ch. 674 (H.B. 981), § 2, effective January 1, 1998; am. Acts 1999, 76th Leg., ch. 789 (H.B. 1425), § 3, effective September 1, 1999.)

## Sec. 542.4045. Penalties for Failure to Yield Right-of-Way Offense Resulting in Accident.

If it is shown on the trial of an offense under this subtitle in which an element is the failure by the operator of a vehicle to yield the right-of-way to another vehicle that an accident resulted from the operator's failure to yield the right-of-way:

(1) the offense is punishable by a fine of not less than $500 or more than $2,000, if a person other than the operator of the vehicle suffered bodily injury, as defined by Section 1.07, Penal Code, in the accident; and

(2) the offense is punishable by a fine of not less than $1,000 or more than $4,000, if a person other than the operator of the vehicle suffered serious bodily injury, as defined by Section 1.07, Penal Code, in the accident.

(Enacted by Acts 2009, 81st Leg., ch. 1391 (S.B. 1967), § 6, effective September 1, 2009.)

## Sec. 542.405. Amount of Civil Penalty; Late Payment Penalty.

If a local authority enacts an ordinance to enforce compliance with the instructions of a traffic-control signal by the imposition of a civil or administrative penalty, the amount of:

(1) the civil or administrative penalty may not exceed $75; and

(2) a late payment penalty may not exceed $25.

(Enacted by Acts 2007, 80th Leg., ch. 1027 (H.B. 1623), § 9, effective September 1, 2007.)

## Sec. 542.406.  Deposit of Revenue from Certain Traffic Penalties.

(a) In this section, "photographic traffic signal enforcement system" means a system that:

(1) consists of a camera system and vehicle sensor installed to exclusively work in conjunction with an electrically operated traffic-control signal;

(2) is capable of producing one or more recorded photographic or digital images that depict the license plate attached to the front or the rear of a motor vehicle that is not operated in compliance with the instructions of the traffic-control signal; and

(3) is designed to enforce compliance with the instructions of the traffic-control signal by imposition of a civil or administrative penalty against the owner of the motor vehicle.

(b) This section applies only to a civil or administrative penalty imposed on the owner of a motor vehicle by a local authority that operates or contracts for the operation of a photographic traffic signal enforcement system with respect to a highway under its jurisdiction or that operates or contracts for the operation of any other type of electronic traffic law enforcement system consisting of a camera system that automatically produces one or more recorded photographs or digital images of the license plate on a motor vehicle or the operator of a motor vehicle.

(c) Not later than the 60th day after the end of a local authority's fiscal year, after deducting amounts the local authority is authorized by Subsection (d) to retain, the local authority shall:

(1) send 50 percent of the revenue derived from civil or administrative penalties collected by the local authority under this section to the comptroller for deposit to the credit of the regional trauma account established under Section 782.002, Health and Safety Code; and

(2) deposit the remainder of the revenue in a special account in the local authority's treasury that may be used only to fund traffic safety programs, including pedestrian safety programs, public safety programs, intersection improvements, and traffic enforcement.

(d) A local authority may retain an amount necessary to cover the costs of:

(1) purchasing or leasing equipment that is part of or used in connection with the photographic traffic signal enforcement system in the local authority;

(2) installing the photographic traffic signal enforcement system at sites in the local authority, including the costs of installing cameras, flashes, computer equipment, loop sensors, detectors, utility lines, data lines, poles and mounts, networking equipment, and associated labor costs;

(3) operating the photographic traffic signal enforcement system in the local authority, including the costs of creating, distributing, and delivering violation notices, review of violations conducted by employees of the local authority, the processing of fine payments and collections, and the costs associated with administrative adjudications and appeals; and

(4) maintaining the general upkeep and functioning of the photographic traffic signal enforcement system.

(e) Chapter 133, Local Government Code, applies to fee revenue described by Subsection (c)(1).

(f) If under Section 133.059, Local Government Code, the comptroller conducts an audit of a local authority and determines that the local authority retained more than the amounts authorized by this section or failed to deposit amounts as required by this section, the comptroller may impose a penalty on the local authority equal to twice the amount the local authority:

(1) retained in excess of the amount authorized by this section; or

(2) failed to deposit as required by this section.

(Enacted by Acts 2007, 80th Leg., ch. 1027 (H.B. 1623), § 9, effective September 1, 2007.)

## Secs. 542.407 to 542.500 [Reserved for expansion].

### SUBCHAPTER E
### MISCELLANEOUS

## Sec. 542.501.  Obedience Required to Police Officers and to School Crossing Guards.

A person may not wilfully fail or refuse to comply with a lawful order or direction of:

(1) a police officer; or

(2) a school crossing guard who:

(A) is performing crossing guard duties in a school crosswalk to stop and yield to a pedestrian; or

(B) has been trained under Section 600.004 and is directing traffic in a school crossing zone.

(Enacted by Acts 1995, 74th Leg., ch. 165 (S.B. 971), § 1, effective September 1, 1995; am. Acts 1999, 76th Leg., ch. 724 (H.B. 964), § 1, effective August 30, 1999.)

# CHAPTER 543
## ARREST AND PROSECUTION OF VIOLATORS

**Subchapter A. Arrest and Charging Procedures; Notices and Promises to Appear**

## SUBCHAPTER A
### ARREST AND CHARGING PROCEDURES; NOTICES AND PROMISES TO APPEAR

### Sec. 543.001.  Arrest Without Warrant Authorized.

Any peace officer may arrest without warrant a person found committing a violation of this subtitle.

(Enacted by Acts 1995, 74th Leg., ch. 165 (S.B. 971), § 1, effective September 1, 1995.)

### Sec. 543.002.  Person Arrested to Be Taken Before Magistrate.

(a) A person arrested for a violation of this subtitle punishable as a misdemeanor shall be immediately taken before a magistrate if:

(1) the person is arrested on a charge of failure to stop in the event of an accident causing damage to property; or

(2) the person demands an immediate appearance before a magistrate or refuses to make a written promise to appear in court as provided by this subchapter.

(b) The person must be taken before a magistrate who:

(1) has jurisdiction of the offense;

(2) is in the county in which the offense charged is alleged to have been committed; and

(3) is nearest or most accessible to the place of arrest.

(Enacted by Acts 1995, 74th Leg., ch. 165 (S.B. 971), § 1, effective September 1, 1995.)

### Sec. 543.003.  Notice to Appear Required: Person Not Taken Before Magistrate.

An officer who arrests a person for a violation of this subtitle punishable as a misdemeanor and who does not take the person before a magistrate shall issue a written notice to appear in court showing the time and place the person is to appear, the offense charged, the name and address of the person charged, and, if applicable, the license number of the person's vehicle.

(Enacted by Acts 1995, 74th Leg., ch. 165 (S.B. 971), § 1, effective September 1, 1995; am. Acts 1999, 76th Leg., ch. 701 (H.B. 806), § 3, effective August 30, 1999.)

### Sec. 543.004.  Notice to Appear Required: Certain Offenses.

(a) An officer shall issue a written notice to appear if:

    (1) the offense charged is speeding or a violation of the open container law, Section 49.03, Penal Code; and

    (2) the person makes a written promise to appear in court as provided by Section 543.005.

    (b) If the person is a resident of or is operating a vehicle licensed in a state or country other than this state, Subsection (a) applies only as provided by Chapter 703.

    (c) The offenses specified by Subsection (a) are the only offenses for which issuance of a written notice to appear is mandatory.

(Enacted by Acts 1995, 74th Leg., ch. 165 (S.B. 971), § 1, effective September 1, 1995; am. Acts 1999, 76th Leg., ch. 62 (S.B. 1368), § 17.07, effective September 1, 1999.)

### Sec. 543.005. Promise to Appear; Release.

    To secure release, the person arrested must make a written promise to appear in court by signing the written notice prepared by the arresting officer. The signature may be obtained on a duplicate form or on an electronic device capable of creating a copy of the signed notice. The arresting officer shall retain the paper or electronic original of the notice and deliver the copy of the notice to the person arrested. The officer shall then promptly release the person from custody.

(Enacted by Acts 1995, 74th Leg., ch. 165 (S.B. 971), § 1, effective September 1, 1995; am. Acts 1999, 76th Leg., ch. 701 (H.B. 806), § 4, effective August 30, 1999.)

### Sec. 543.006. Time and Place of Appearance.

    (a) The time specified in the notice to appear must be at least 10 days after the date of arrest unless the person arrested demands an earlier hearing.

    (b) The place specified in the notice to appear must be before a magistrate having jurisdiction of the offense who is in the municipality or county in which the offense is alleged to have been committed.

(Enacted by Acts 1995, 74th Leg., ch. 165 (S.B. 971), § 1, effective September 1, 1995.)

### Sec. 543.007. Notice to Appear: Commercial Vehicle or License.

    A notice to appear issued to the operator of a commercial motor vehicle or holder of a commercial driver's license or commercial driver learner's permit, for the violation of a law regulating the operation of vehicles on highways, must contain the information required by department rule, to comply with Chapter 522 and the federal Commercial Motor Vehicle Safety Act of 1986 (Title 49, U.S.C. Section 2701 et seq.).

(Enacted by Acts 1995, 74th Leg., ch. 165 (S.B. 971), § 1, effective September 1, 1995; am. Acts 1999, 76th Leg., ch. 701 (H.B. 806), § 5, effective August 30, 1999.)

### Sec. 543.008. Violation by Officer.

    A violation by an officer of a provision of Sections 543.003—543.007 is misconduct in office and the officer is subject to removal from the officer's position.

(Enacted by Acts 1995, 74th Leg., ch. 165 (S.B. 971), § 1, effective September 1, 1995.)

### Sec. 543.009. Compliance with or Violation of Promise to Appear.

    (a) A person may comply with a written promise to appear in court by an appearance by counsel.

    (b) A person who wilfully violates a written promise to appear in court, given as provided by this subchapter, commits a misdemeanor regardless of the disposition of the charge on which the person was arrested.

(Enacted by Acts 1995, 74th Leg., ch. 165 (S.B. 971), § 1, effective September 1, 1995.)

### Sec. 543.010. Specifications of Speeding Charge.

    The complaint and the summons or notice to appear on a charge of speeding under this subtitle must specify:

    (1) the maximum or minimum speed limit applicable in the district or at the location; and

    (2) the speed at which the defendant is alleged to have driven.

(Enacted by Acts 1995, 74th Leg., ch. 165 (S.B. 971), § 1, effective September 1, 1995.)

*Defensive Driving not available → 25 mph over limit*

### Sec. 543.011. Persons Licensed by State Department or Claiming Diplomatic or Consular Immunity.

    (a) This section applies to a person who:

    (1) is stopped or issued a notice to appear by a peace officer in connection with a violation of:

      (A) this subtitle;

      (B) Section 49.03 or 49.04, Penal Code; or

      (C) Section 49.07 or 49.08, Penal Code, involving operation of a motor vehicle; and

(2) presents to the peace officer a driver's license issued by the United States Department of State or claims immunities or privileges under 22 U.S.C. Chapter 6.

(b) A peace officer who stops or issues a notice to appear to a person to whom this section applies shall record all relevant information from any driver's license or identification card presented by the person or any statement made by the person relating to immunities or privileges and promptly deliver the record to the law enforcement agency that employs the peace officer.

(c) The law enforcement agency shall:

(1) as soon as practicable contact the United States Department of State to verify the person's status and immunity, if any; and

(2) not later than the fifth working day after the date of the stop or issuance of the notice to appear, send to the Bureau of Diplomatic Security Office of Foreign Missions of the United States Department of State the following:

(A) a copy of any notice to appear issued to the person and any accident report prepared; or

(B) if a notice to appear was not issued and an accident report was not prepared, a written report of the incident.

(d) This section does not affect application of a law described by Subsection (a)(1) to a person to whom this section applies.
(Enacted by Acts 2001, 77th Leg., ch. 446 (S.B. 148), § 1, effective September 1, 2001.)

**Secs. 543.012 to 543.100 [Reserved for expansion].**

## SUBCHAPTER B
## DISMISSAL OF CERTAIN MISDEMEANOR CHARGES ON COMPLETING DRIVING SAFETY COURSE

### Sec. 543.101. Statement of Right Provided on Notice to Appear [Repealed].
Repealed by Acts 2003, 78th Leg., ch. 991 (S.B. 1904), § 14(1), effective September 1, 2003 and Acts 2003, 78th Leg., ch. 1182 (S.B. 631), § 4(1), effective September 1, 2003.
(Enacted by Acts 1995, 74th Leg., ch. 165 (S.B. 971), § 1, effective September 1, 1995.)

### Sec. 543.102. Notice of Right to Complete Course [Repealed].
Repealed by Acts 1999, 76th Leg., ch. 1387

(H.B. 1603), § 3, effective September 1, 1999 and Acts 1999, 76th Leg., ch. 1545 (S.B. 1230), § 75(b), effective September 1, 1999.
(Enacted by Acts 1995, 74th Leg., ch. 165 (S.B. 971), § 1, effective September 1, 1995; am. Acts 1997, 75th Leg., ch. 165 (S.B. 898), § 30.106(a), effective September 1, 1997.)

### Sec. 543.103. Mandatory Deferral [Repealed].
Repealed by Acts 1999, 76th Leg., ch. 1387 (H.B. 1603), § 3, effective September 1, 1999 and Acts 1999, 76th Leg., ch. 1545 (S.B. 1230), § 75(b), effective September 1, 1999.
(Enacted by Acts 1995, 74th Leg., ch. 165 (S.B. 971), § 1, effective September 1, 1995; am. Acts 1997, 75th Leg., ch. 165 (S.B. 898), § 30.106(b), effective September 1, 1997.)

### Sec. 543.104. Permissive Deferral [Repealed].
Repealed by Acts 1999, 76th Leg., ch. 1387 (H.B. 1603), § 3, effective September 1, 1999 and Acts 1999, 76th Leg., ch. 1545 (S.B. 1230), § 75(b), effective September 1, 1999.
(Enacted by Acts 1995, 74th Leg., ch. 165 (S.B. 971), § 1, effective September 1, 1995; am. Acts 1997, 75th Leg., ch. 165 (S.B. 898), § 30.106(c), effective September 1, 1997.)

### Sec. 543.105. Timely Request Constitutes Appearance [Repealed].
Repealed by Acts 1999, 76th Leg., ch. 1387 (H.B. 1603), § 3, effective September 1, 1999 and Acts 1999, 76th Leg., ch. 1545 (S.B. 1230), § 75(b), effective September 1, 1999.
(Enacted by Acts 1995, 74th Leg., ch. 165 (S.B. 971), § 1, effective September 1, 1995.)

### Sec. 543.106. Fee for Request [Repealed].
Repealed by Acts 1999, 76th Leg., ch. 1387 (H.B. 1603), § 3, effective September 1, 1999 and Acts 1999, 76th Leg., ch. 1545 (S.B. 1230), § 75(b), effective September 1, 1999.
(Enacted by Acts 1995, 74th Leg., ch. 165 (S.B. 971), § 1, effective September 1, 1995.)

### Sec. 543.107. Failure to Present Evidence of Course Completion [Repealed].
Repealed by Acts 1999, 76th Leg., ch. 1387 (H.B. 1603), § 3, effective September 1, 1999 and

Acts 1999, 76th Leg., ch. 1545 (S.B. 1230), § 75(b), effective September 1, 1999.
(Enacted by Acts 1995, 74th Leg., ch. 165 (S.B. 971), § 1, effective September 1, 1995.)

### Sec. 543.108. Court Procedures on Successful Course Completion [Repealed].

Repealed by Acts 1999, 76th Leg., ch. 1387 (H.B. 1603), § 3, effective September 1, 1999 and Acts 1999, 76th Leg., ch. 1545 (S.B. 1230), § 75(b), effective September 1, 1999.
(Enacted by Acts 1995, 74th Leg., ch. 165 (S.B. 971), § 1, effective September 1, 1995.)

### Sec. 543.109. Dismissal Limited to One Charge [Repealed].

Repealed by Acts 1999, 76th Leg., ch. 1387 (H.B. 1603), § 3, effective September 1, 1999 and Acts 1999, 76th Leg., ch. 1545 (S.B. 1230), § 75(b), effective September 1, 1999.
(Enacted by Acts 1995, 74th Leg., ch. 165 (S.B. 971), § 1, effective September 1, 1995.)

### Sec. 543.110. Use of Information Regarding Dismissed Charge on Completed Course [Repealed].

Repealed by Acts 1999, 76th Leg., ch. 1387 (H.B. 1603), § 3, effective September 1, 1999 and Acts 1999, 76th Leg., ch. 1545 (S.B. 1230), § 75(b), effective September 1, 1999.
(Enacted by Acts 1995, 74th Leg., ch. 165 (S.B. 971), § 1, effective September 1, 1995.)

### Sec. 543.111. Regulation by Certain State Agencies.

(a) The State Board of Education shall enter into a memorandum of understanding with the Texas Department of Insurance for the interagency development of a curriculum for driving safety courses.

(b) The Texas Education Agency shall:

(1) adopt and administer comprehensive rules governing driving safety courses; and

(2) investigate options to develop and implement procedures to electronically transmit information pertaining to driving safety courses to municipal and justice courts.
(Enacted by Acts 1995, 74th Leg., ch. 165 (S.B. 971), § 1, effective September 1, 1995; am. Acts 1997, 75th Leg., ch. 165 (S.B. 898), § 30.106(d), effective September 1, 1997.)

### Sec. 543.112. Standards for Uniform Certificate of Course Completion.

(a) The Texas Education Agency by rule shall provide for the design and distribution of uniform certificates of course completion so as to prevent to the greatest extent possible the unauthorized production or misuse of the certificates.

(b) The uniform certificate of course completion must include an identifying number by which the Texas Education Agency, the court, or the department may verify its authenticity with the course provider and must be in a form adopted by the Texas Education Agency.

(c) The Texas Education Agency shall issue duplicate uniform certificates of course completion. The State Board of Education by rule shall determine the amount of the fee to be charged for issuance of a duplicate certificate.

(d) A driving safety course provider shall electronically submit data identified by the Texas Education Agency pertaining to issued uniform certificates of course completion to the agency as directed by the agency.
(Enacted by Acts 1995, 74th Leg., ch. 165 (S.B. 971), § 1, effective September 1, 1995; am. Acts 1997, 75th Leg., ch. 165 (S.B. 898), § 30.106(e), effective September 1, 1997.)

### Sec. 543.113. Fees for Printing and Supplying Certificate.

(a) The Texas Education Agency shall print the uniform certificates and supply them to persons who are licensed providers of courses approved under the Texas Driver and Traffic Safety Education Act (Article 4413(29c), Vernon's Texas Civil Statutes). The agency may charge a fee for each certificate. The fee may not exceed $4.

(b) A course provider shall charge an operator a fee equal to the fee paid to the agency for a certificate.

(c) Money collected by the Texas Education Agency under this section may be used only to pay monetary awards for information relating to abuse of uniform certificates that leads to the conviction or removal of an approval, license, or authorization.
(Enacted by Acts 1995, 74th Leg., ch. 165 (S.B. 971), § 1, effective September 1, 1995; am. Acts 1997, 75th Leg., ch. 165 (S.B. 898), § 30.106(f), effective September 1, 1997.)

### Sec. 543.114. Distribution of Written Information on Provider.

(a) A person may not distribute written information to advertise a provider of a driving safety course within 500 feet of a court having jurisdiction over an offense to which this subchapter applies. A violation of this section by a provider or a provider's agent, employee, or representative results in loss of the provider's status as a provider of a course approved under the Texas Driver and Safety Education Act (Article 4413(29c), Vernon's Texas Civil Statutes).

(b) This section does not apply to distribution of information:

(1) by a court;

(2) to a court to obtain approval of the course; or

(3) to a court to advise the court of the availability of the course.

(Enacted by Acts 1995, 74th Leg., ch. 165 (S.B. 971), § 1, effective September 1, 1995.)

## Sec. 543.115. Fees for Driving Safety Course.

(a) A driving safety course may not be provided to a student for less than $25.

(b) A course provider shall charge each student a fee for course materials and for overseeing and administering the course. The fee may not be less than $3.

(Enacted by Acts 1997, 75th Leg., ch. 165 (S.B. 898), § 30.106(g), effective September 1, 1997.)

## Sec. 543.116. Delivery of Uniform Certificate of Course Completion.

(a) A driving safety course provider shall mail an issued uniform certificate of course completion to a person who successfully completes the course.

(b) The certificate must be mailed not later than the 15th working day after the date a person successfully completes the course.

(Enacted by Acts 1997, 75th Leg., ch. 165 (S.B. 898), § 30.106(g), effective September 1, 1997.)

## Sec. 543.117. Offense in Construction or Maintenance Work Zone [Repealed].

Repealed by Acts 2003, 78th Leg., ch. 991 (S.B. 1904), § 14(2), effective September 1, 2003 and Acts 2003, 78th Leg., ch. 1182 (S.B. 631), § 4(2), effective September 1, 2003.

(Enacted by Acts 1999, 76th Leg., ch. 1088 (H.B. 3433), § 2, effective September 1, 1999.)

## Secs. 543.118 to 543.200 [Reserved for expansion].

## SUBCHAPTER C
## RECORDS AND INFORMATION
## MAINTAINED BY DEPARTMENT

## Sec. 543.201. Conviction Reported to Department.

Each magistrate or judge of a court not of record and each clerk of a court of record shall keep a record of each case in which a person is charged with a violation of law regulating the operation of vehicles on highways.

(Enacted by Acts 1995, 74th Leg., ch. 165 (S.B. 971), § 1, effective September 1, 1995.)

## Sec. 543.202. Form of Record.

(a) In this section, "race or ethnicity" means of a particular descent, including Caucasian, African, Hispanic, Asian, or Native American descent.

(b) The record must be made on a form or by a data processing method acceptable to the department and must include:

(1) the name, address, physical description, including race or ethnicity, date of birth, and driver's license number of the person charged;

(2) the registration number of the vehicle involved;

(3) whether the vehicle was a commercial motor vehicle as defined by Chapter 522 or was involved in transporting hazardous materials;

(4) the person's social security number, if the person was operating a commercial motor vehicle or was the holder of a commercial driver's license or commercial driver learner's permit;

(5) the date and nature of the offense, including whether the offense was a serious traffic violation as defined by Chapter 522;

(6) whether a search of the vehicle was conducted and whether consent for the search was obtained;

(7) the plea, the judgment, whether the individual was adjudicated under Article 45.0511, Code of Criminal Procedure, and whether bail was forfeited;

(8) the date of conviction; and

(9) the amount of the fine or forfeiture.

(Enacted by Acts 1995, 74th Leg., ch. 165 (S.B. 971), § 1, effective September 1, 1995; am. Acts 2001, 77th Leg., ch. 947 (S.B. 1074), § 6, effective

September 1, 2001; am. Acts 2003, 78th Leg., ch. 1325 (H.B. 3588), § 8.04, effective June 1, 2005.)

### Sec. 543.203. Submitting Record to Department.

Not later than the seventh day after the date of conviction or forfeiture of bail of a person on a charge of violating a law regulating the operation of a vehicle on a highway or conviction of a person of negligent homicide or a felony in the commission of which a vehicle was used, the magistrate, judge, or clerk of the court in which the conviction was had or bail was forfeited shall immediately submit to the department a written record of the case containing the information required by Section 543.202.

(Enacted by Acts 1995, 74th Leg., ch. 165 (S.B. 971), § 1, effective September 1, 1995; am. Acts 2009, 81st Leg., ch. 1146 (H.B. 2730), § 17.02, effective September 1, 2009.)

### Sec. 543.204. Submission of Record Prohibited.

(a) A justice of the peace or municipal judge who defers further proceedings, suspends all or part of the imposition of the fine, and places a defendant on probation under Article 45.051, Code of Criminal Procedure, or a county court judge who follows that procedure under Article 42.111, Code of Criminal Procedure, may not submit a written record to the department, except that if the justice or judge subsequently adjudicates the defendant's guilt, the justice or judge shall submit the record not later than the seventh day after the date on which the justice or judge adjudicates guilt.

(b) The department may not keep a record for which submission is prohibited by this section.

(c) The department may receive a record prepared by a department employee from court records.

(Enacted by Acts 1995, 74th Leg., ch. 165 (S.B. 971), § 1, effective September 1, 1995; am. Acts 1999, 76th Leg., ch. 1545 (S.B. 1230), § 73, effective September 1, 1999; am. Acts 2009, 81st Leg., ch. 1146 (H.B. 2730), § 17.03, effective September 1, 2009.)

### Sec. 543.205. Record Received at Main Office.

The department shall receive all records under Section 543.204(a) at its main office.

(Enacted by Acts 1995, 74th Leg., ch. 165 (S.B. 971), § 1, effective September 1, 1995.)

### Sec. 543.206. Violation.

A violation by a judicial officer of this subchapter may constitute misconduct in office and may be grounds for removal from the officer's position. (Enacted by Acts 1995, 74th Leg., ch. 165 (S.B. 971), § 1, effective September 1, 1995.)

# CHAPTER 544
# TRAFFIC SIGNS, SIGNALS, AND MARKINGS

### Sec. 544.001. Adoption of Sign Manual for State Highways.

The Texas Transportation Commission shall adopt a manual and specifications for a uniform system of traffic-control devices consistent with this chapter that correlates with and to the extent possible conforms to the system approved by the American Association of State Highway and Transportation Officials.

(Enacted by Acts 1995, 74th Leg., ch. 165 (S.B. 971), § 1, effective September 1, 1995.)

### Sec. 544.002. Placing and Maintaining Traffic-Control Device.

(a) To implement this subtitle, the Texas Department of Transportation may place and maintain a traffic-control device on a state highway as provided by the manual and specifications adopted under Section 544.001. The Texas Department of Transportation may provide for the placement and maintenance of the device under Section 221.002.

(b) To implement this subtitle or a local traffic ordinance, a local authority may place and maintain a traffic-control device on a highway under the authority's jurisdiction. The traffic-control device must conform to the manual and specifications adopted under Section 544.001.

(c) A local authority may not place or maintain a traffic-control device on a highway under the jurisdiction of the Texas Department of Transportation without that department's permission, except as authorized under Section 545.3561.

(Enacted by Acts 1995, 74th Leg., ch. 165 (S.B. 971), § 1, effective September 1, 1995; am. Acts 2011, 82nd Leg., ch. 216 (H.B. 109), § 1, effective September 1, 2011.)

## Sec. 544.003. Authority to Designate Through Highway and Stop and Yield Intersections.

(a) The Texas Transportation Commission may:

(1) designate a state or county highway as a through highway and place a stop or yield sign at a specified entrance; or

(2) designate an intersection on a state or county highway as a stop intersection or a yield intersection and place a sign at one or more entrances to the intersection.

(b) A local authority may:

(1) designate a highway under its jurisdiction as a through highway and place a stop or yield sign at a specified entrance; or

(2) designate an intersection on a highway under its jurisdiction as a stop intersection or a yield intersection and place a sign at one or more entrances to the intersection.

(c) The stop or yield sign indicating the preferential right-of-way must:

(1) conform to the manual and specifications adopted under Section 544.001; and

(2) be located:

(A) as near as practicable to the nearest line of the crosswalk; or

(B) in the absence of a crosswalk, at the nearest line of the roadway.

(Enacted by Acts 1995, 74th Leg., ch. 165 (S.B. 971), § 1, effective September 1, 1995.)

## Sec. 544.004. Compliance with Traffic-Control Device.

(a) The operator of a vehicle or streetcar shall comply with an applicable official traffic-control device placed as provided by this subtitle unless the person is:

(1) otherwise directed by a traffic or police officer; or

(2) operating an authorized emergency vehicle and is subject to exceptions under this subtitle.

(b) A provision of this subtitle requiring an official traffic-control device may not be enforced against an alleged violator if at the time and place of the alleged violation the device is not in proper position and sufficiently legible to an ordinarily observant person. A provision of this subtitle that does not require an official traffic-control device is effective regardless of whether a device is in place.

(Enacted by Acts 1995, 74th Leg., ch. 165 (S.B. 971), § 1, effective September 1, 1995.)

## Sec. 544.005. Interference with Traffic-Control Device or Railroad Sign or Signal.

A person may not, without lawful authority, alter, injure, knock down, or remove or attempt to alter, injure, knock down, or remove:

(1) an official traffic-control device or railroad sign or signal;

(2) an inscription, shield, or insignia on an official traffic-control device or railroad sign or signal; or

(3) another part of an official traffic-control device or railroad sign or signal.

(Enacted by Acts 1995, 74th Leg., ch. 165 (S.B. 971), § 1, effective September 1, 1995.)

## Sec. 544.0055. Traffic-Control Signal Preemption Device; Offense.

(a) In this section, "traffic-control signal preemption device" means a device designed, intended, or used to interfere with or alter the operation of a traffic-control signal.

(b) Except as provided by Subsection (e), a person commits an offense if the person uses, sells, offers for sale, purchases, or possesses for use or sale a traffic-control signal preemption device.

(c) The possession of a traffic-control signal preemption device creates the presumption that the person possessed the device for use or sale.

(d) An offense under this section is a Class C misdemeanor.

(e) This section does not apply to:

(1) a person who provides fire-fighting, law enforcement, ambulance, medical, or other emergency services in the course of providing those services;

(2) a manufacturer, wholesaler, or retailer of traffic-control signal preemption devices in the course of manufacturing, selling, providing, or transporting a traffic-control signal preemption device to a person described by Subdivision (1); or

(3) a transit vehicle operated by an authority under Chapter 451 or 452 or a transit department under Chapter 453.

(Enacted by Acts 2005, 79th Leg., ch. 244 (H.B. 364), § 1, effective May 30, 2005.)

## Sec. 544.006. Display of Unauthorized Signs, Signals, or Markings.

(a) A person may not place, maintain, or display on or in view of a highway an unauthorized sign, signal, marking, or device that:

(1) imitates or resembles an official traffic-control device or railroad sign or signal;

(2) attempts to direct the movement of traffic; or

(3) hides from view or hinders the effectiveness of an official traffic-control device or railroad sign or signal.

(b) A person may not place or maintain on a highway, and a public authority may not permit on a highway, a traffic sign or signal bearing commercial advertising.

(c) A person may not place or maintain a flashing light or flashing electric sign within 1,000 feet of an intersection except under a permit issued by the Texas Transportation Commission.

(d) This section does not prohibit a person from placing on private property adjacent to a highway a sign that gives useful directional information and that cannot be mistaken for an official sign.

(e) A sign, signal, light, or marking prohibited under this section is a public nuisance. The authority with jurisdiction over the highway may remove that sign, signal, light, or marking without notice.

(Enacted by Acts 1995, 74th Leg., ch. 165 (S.B. 971), § 1, effective September 1, 1995.)

## Sec. 544.007. Traffic-Control Signals in General.

(a) A traffic-control signal displaying different colored lights or colored lighted arrows successively or in combination may display only green, yellow, or red and applies to operators of vehicles as provided by this section.

(b) An operator of a vehicle facing a circular green signal may proceed straight or turn right or left unless a sign prohibits the turn. The operator shall yield the right-of-way to other vehicles and to pedestrians lawfully in the intersection or an adjacent crosswalk when the signal is exhibited.

(c) An operator of a vehicle facing a green arrow signal, displayed alone or with another signal, may cautiously enter the intersection to move in the direction permitted by the arrow or other indication shown simultaneously. The operator shall yield the right-of-way to a pedestrian lawfully in an adjacent crosswalk and other traffic lawfully using the intersection.

(d) An operator of a vehicle facing only a steady red signal shall stop at a clearly marked stop line. In the absence of a stop line, the operator shall stop before entering the crosswalk on the near side of the intersection. A vehicle that is not turning shall remain standing until an indication to proceed is shown. After stopping, standing until the intersection may be entered safely, and yielding right-of-way to pedestrians lawfully in an adjacent crosswalk and other traffic lawfully using the intersection, the operator may:

(1) turn right; or

(2) turn left, if the intersecting streets are both one-way streets and a left turn is permissible.

(e) An operator of a vehicle facing a steady yellow signal is warned by that signal that:

(1) movement authorized by a green signal is being terminated; or

(2) a red signal is to be given.

(f) The Texas Transportation Commission, a municipal authority, or the commissioners court of a county may prohibit within the entity's jurisdiction a turn by an operator of a vehicle facing a steady red signal by posting notice at the intersection that the turn is prohibited.

(g) This section applies to an official traffic-control signal placed and maintained at a place other than an intersection, except for a provision that by its nature cannot apply. A required stop shall be made at a sign or marking on the pavement indicating where the stop shall be made. In the absence of such a sign or marking, the stop shall be made at the signal.

(h) The obligations imposed by this section apply to an operator of a streetcar in the same manner they apply to the operator of a vehicle.

(i) An operator of a vehicle facing a traffic-control signal, other than a freeway entrance ramp control signal or a pedestrian hybrid beacon, that does not display an indication in any of the signal heads shall stop as provided by Section 544.010 as if the intersection had a stop sign.

(j) In this section:

(1) "Freeway entrance ramp control signal" means a traffic-control signal that controls the flow of traffic entering a freeway.

(2) "Pedestrian hybrid beacon" means a pedestrian-controlled traffic-control signal that displays different colored lights successively only when activated by a pedestrian.

(Enacted by Acts 1995, 74th Leg., ch. 165 (S.B. 971), § 1, effective September 1, 1995; am. Acts 2003, 78th Leg., ch. 1325 (H.B. 3588), § 19.04, effective September 1, 2003; am. Acts 2011, 82nd Leg., ch. 485 (H.B. 885), § 1, effective June 17, 2011.)

### Sec. 544.0075.  Certain Traffic-Actuated Electric Traffic-Control Signals.

(a) This section applies only to a traffic-actuated electric traffic-control signal that consists of a traffic-control signal for which the intervals vary according to the demands of vehicular traffic as registered by a detector and that is installed and operating at an intersection.

(b) In addition to any other type of vehicle the presence of which the detector for the traffic-actuated electric traffic-control signal may register, the detector for a traffic-actuated electric traffic-control device to which this section applies must be capable of registering the presence of a motorcycle.

(Enacted by Acts 2007, 80th Leg., ch. 219 (H.B. 1279), § 1, effective September 1, 2007.)

### Sec. 544.008.  Flashing Signals.

(a) The operator of a vehicle facing a flashing red signal shall stop at a clearly marked stop line. In the absence of a stop line, the operator shall stop before entering the crosswalk on the near side of the intersection. In the absence of a crosswalk, the operator shall stop at the place nearest the intersecting roadway where the operator has a view of approaching traffic on the intersecting roadway. The right to proceed is subject to the rules applicable after stopping at a stop sign.

(b) The operator of a vehicle facing a flashing yellow signal may proceed through an intersection or past the signal only with caution.

(c) This section does not apply at a railroad crossing.

(Enacted by Acts 1995, 74th Leg., ch. 165 (S.B. 971), § 1, effective September 1, 1995.)

### Sec. 544.009.  Lane-Direction-Control Signals.

If a lane-direction-control signal is placed over an individual lane of a highway, a vehicle may travel in a lane over which a green signal is shown but may not enter or travel in a lane over which a red signal is shown.

(Enacted by Acts 1995, 74th Leg., ch. 165 (S.B. 971), § 1, effective September 1, 1995.)

### Sec. 544.010.  Stop Signs and Yield Signs.

(a) Unless directed to proceed by a police officer or traffic-control signal, the operator of a vehicle or streetcar approaching an intersection with a stop sign shall stop as provided by Subsection (c).

(b) If safety requires, the operator of a vehicle approaching a yield sign shall stop as provided by Subsection (c).

(c) An operator required to stop by this section shall stop before entering the crosswalk on the near side of the intersection. In the absence of a crosswalk, the operator shall stop at a clearly marked stop line. In the absence of a stop line, the operator shall stop at the place nearest the intersecting roadway where the operator has a view of approaching traffic on the intersecting roadway.

(Enacted by Acts 1995, 74th Leg., ch. 165 (S.B. 971), § 1, effective September 1, 1995.)

### Sec. 544.011.  Lane Use Signs.

If, on a highway having more than one lane with vehicles traveling in the same direction, the Texas Department of Transportation or a local authority places a sign that directs slower traffic to travel in a lane other than the farthest left lane, the sign must read "left lane for passing only."

(Enacted by Acts 1997, 75th Leg., ch. 628 (H.B. 297), § 1, effective September 1, 1997; am. Acts 1999, 76th Leg., ch. 62 (S.B. 1368), § 17.08, effective September 1, 1999.)

### Sec. 544.012.  Notification of Photographic Traffic Monitoring System.

(a) In this section:

(1) "Photographic traffic monitoring system" means a system that:

(A) consists of a camera and vehicle sensor installed to work in conjunction with an electrically operated traffic-control signal; and

(B) is capable of producing one or more recorded images that depict the license plate attached to a motor vehicle that is not operated in compliance with the instructions of the traffic-control signal.

(2) "Recorded image" means an image that:

(A) depicts a motor vehicle; and

(B) is automatically recorded on a photograph or digital image.

(b) This section applies only to a municipality that pursuant to an ordinance of the municipality employs a photographic traffic monitoring system to enforce compliance with the instructions of traffic-control signals in the municipality.

(c) The municipality shall install signs along each roadway that leads to an intersection at which a photographic traffic monitoring system is in active use. The signs must be at least 100 feet from the intersection or located according to standards established in the manual adopted by the Texas Transportation Commission under Section 544.001, be easily readable to any operator approaching the intersection, and clearly indicate the presence of a photographic monitoring system that records violations that may result in the issuance of a notice of violation and the imposition of a monetary penalty.

(d) A municipality that fails to comply with Subsection (c) may not impose or attempt to impose a civil or administrative penalty against a person, including the owner of a motor vehicle or an operator, for a failure to comply with the instructions of a traffic-control signal located at the applicable intersection.

(e) Subsection (d) does not prohibit a peace officer from arresting or issuing a citation and notice to appear to a person whom the officer observes to have failed to comply with the instructions of a traffic-control signal located at the intersection.

(Enacted by Acts 2007, 80th Leg., ch. 653 (H.B. 1052), § 1, effective September 1, 2007.)

## Sec. 544.013. Changeable Message Sign System.

(a) In this section, "changeable message sign" means a sign that conforms to the manual and specifications adopted under Section 544.001. The term includes a dynamic message sign.

(b) The Texas Department of Transportation in cooperation with local governments shall actively manage a system of changeable message signs located on highways under the jurisdiction of the department to mitigate traffic congestion by providing current information to the traveling public, including information about traffic incidents, weather conditions, road construction, and alternative routes when applicable.

(Enacted by Acts 2011, 82nd Leg., ch. 1345 (S.B. 1420), § 53, effective September 1, 2011.)

# CHAPTER 545
# OPERATION AND MOVEMENT OF VEHICLES

### Subchapter A. General Provisions

**Transportation**

Transportation

## SUBCHAPTER A
## GENERAL PROVISIONS

### Sec. 545.001.  Definitions.

In this chapter:

(1) "Pass" or "passing" used in reference to a vehicle means to overtake and proceed past another vehicle moving in the same direction as the passing vehicle or to attempt that maneuver.

(2) "School bus" includes a multifunction school activity bus.

(Enacted by Acts 1995, 74th Leg., ch. 165 (S.B. 971), § 1, effective September 1, 1995; am. Acts 2007, 80th Leg., ch. 923 (H.B. 3190), § 3, effective September 1, 2007.)

### Sec. 545.002.  Operator.

In this chapter, a reference to an operator includes a reference to the vehicle operated by the operator if the reference imposes a duty or provides a limitation on the movement or other operation of that vehicle.

(Enacted by Acts 1995, 74th Leg., ch. 165 (S.B. 971), § 1, effective September 1, 1995.)

### Secs. 545.003 to 545.050 [Reserved for expansion].

## SUBCHAPTER B
## DRIVING ON RIGHT SIDE OF
## ROADWAY AND PASSING

### Sec. 545.051.  Driving on Right Side of Roadway.

(a) An operator on a roadway of sufficient width shall drive on the right half of the roadway, unless:

(1) the operator is passing another vehicle;

(2) an obstruction necessitates moving the vehicle left of the center of the roadway and the operator yields the right-of-way to a vehicle that:

(A) is moving in the proper direction on the unobstructed portion of the roadway; and

(B) is an immediate hazard;

(3) the operator is on a roadway divided into three marked lanes for traffic; or

(4) the operator is on a roadway restricted to one-way traffic.

(b) An operator of a vehicle on a roadway moving more slowly than the normal speed of other vehicles at the time and place under the existing conditions shall drive in the right-hand lane available for vehicles, or as close as practicable to the right-hand curb or edge of the roadway, unless the operator is:

(1) passing another vehicle; or

(2) preparing for a left turn at an intersection or into a private road or driveway.

(c) An operator on a roadway having four or more lanes for moving vehicles and providing for two-way movement of vehicles may not drive left of the center line of the roadway except:

(1) as authorized by an official traffic-control device designating a specified lane to the left side of the center of the roadway for use by a vehicle not otherwise permitted to use the lane;

(2) under the conditions described by Subsection (a)(2); or

(3) in crossing the center line to make a left turn into or out of an alley, private road, or driveway.

(Enacted by Acts 1995, 74th Leg., ch. 165 (S.B. 971), § 1, effective September 1, 1995.)

### Sec. 545.052.  Driving Past Vehicle Moving in Opposite Direction.

An operator moving in the opposite direction of the movement of another operator shall:

(1) move to or remain to the right; and

(2) on a roadway wide enough for not more than one line of vehicle movement in each direction, give the other operator:

(A) at least one-half of the main traveled portion of the roadway; or

(B) if complying with Paragraph (A) is not possible, as much of the roadway as possible.

(Enacted by Acts 1995, 74th Leg., ch. 165 (S.B. 971), § 1, effective September 1, 1995.)

### Sec. 545.053.  Passing to the Left; Return; Being Passed.

(a) An operator passing another vehicle:

(1) shall pass to the left of the other vehicle at a safe distance; and

(2) may not move back to the right side of the roadway until safely clear of the passed vehicle.

(b) An operator being passed by another vehicle:

(1) shall, on audible signal, move or remain to the right in favor of the passing vehicle; and

(2) may not accelerate until completely passed by the passing vehicle.

(c) Subsection (b) does not apply when passing to the right is permitted.

(Enacted by Acts 1995, 74th Leg., ch. 165 (S.B. 971), § 1, effective September 1, 1995.)

## Sec. 545.054. Passing to the Left: Safe Distance.

(a) An operator may not drive on the left side of the center of the roadway in passing another vehicle unless:

(1) driving on the left side of the center of the roadway is authorized by this subtitle; and

(2) the left side is clearly visible and free of approaching traffic for a distance sufficient to permit passing without interfering with the operation of the passed vehicle or a vehicle approaching from the opposite direction.

(b) An operator passing another vehicle shall return to an authorized lane of travel:

(1) before coming within 200 feet of an approaching vehicle, if a lane authorized for vehicles approaching from the opposite direction is used in passing; or otherwise

(2) as soon as practicable.

(Enacted by Acts 1995, 74th Leg., ch. 165 (S.B. 971), § 1, effective September 1, 1995.)

## Sec. 545.055. Passing to the Left: Passing Zones.

(a) An operator shall obey the directions of a sign or marking in Subsection (c) or (d) if the sign or marking is in place and clearly visible to an ordinarily observant person.

(b) An operator may not drive on the left side of the roadway in a no-passing zone or on the left side of any pavement striping designed to mark a no-passing zone. This subsection does not prohibit a driver from crossing pavement striping, or the center line in a no-passing zone marked by signs only, to make a left turn into or out of an alley or private road or driveway.

(c) The Texas Transportation Commission, on a state highway under the jurisdiction of the commission, may:

(1) determine those portions of the highway where passing or driving to the left of the roadway would be especially hazardous; and

(2) show the beginning and end of each no-passing zone by appropriate signs or markings on the roadway.

(d) A local authority, on a highway under the jurisdiction of the local authority, may:

(1) determine those portions of the highway where passing or driving to the left of the roadway would be especially hazardous; and

(2) show the beginning and end of each no-passing zone by appropriate signs or markings on the roadway.

(Enacted by Acts 1995, 74th Leg., ch. 165 (S.B. 971), § 1, effective September 1, 1995.)

## Sec. 545.056. Driving to Left of Center of Roadway: Limitations Other Than Passing.

(a) An operator may not drive to the left side of the roadway if the operator is:

(1) approaching within 100 feet of an intersection or railroad grade crossing in a municipality;

(2) approaching within 100 feet of an intersection or railroad grade crossing outside a municipality and the intersection or crossing is shown by a sign or marking in accordance with Section 545.055;

(3) approaching within 100 feet of a bridge, viaduct, or tunnel; or

(4) awaiting access to a ferry operated by the Texas Transportation Commission.

(b) The limitations in Subsection (a) do not apply:

(1) on a one-way roadway; or

(2) to an operator turning left into or from an alley or private road or driveway.

(c) The Texas Transportation Commission shall post signs along the approach to a ferry operated by the commission notifying operators that passing is prohibited if there is a standing line of vehicles awaiting access to the ferry.

(Enacted by Acts 1995, 74th Leg., ch. 165 (S.B. 971), § 1, effective September 1, 1995.)

## Sec. 545.057. Passing to the Right.

(a) An operator may pass to the right of another vehicle only if conditions permit safely passing to the right and:

(1) the vehicle being passed is making or about to make a left turn; and

(2) the operator is:

(A) on a highway having unobstructed pavement not occupied by parked vehicles and sufficient width for two or more lines of moving vehicles in each direction; or

(B) on a one-way street or on a roadway having traffic restricted to one direction of movement and the roadway is free from obstructions and wide enough for two or more lines of moving vehicles.

(b) An operator may not pass to the right by leaving the main traveled portion of a roadway except as provided by Section 545.058.

(Enacted by Acts 1995, 74th Leg., ch. 165 (S.B. 971), § 1, effective September 1, 1995.)

## Sec. 545.058. Driving on Improved Shoulder.

(a) An operator may drive on an improved shoulder to the right of the main traveled portion of a roadway if that operation is necessary and may be done safely, but only:

    (1) to stop, stand, or park;

    (2) to accelerate before entering the main traveled lane of traffic;

    (3) to decelerate before making a right turn;

    (4) to pass another vehicle that is slowing or stopped on the main traveled portion of the highway, disabled, or preparing to make a left turn;

    (5) to allow another vehicle traveling faster to pass;

    (6) as permitted or required by an official traffic-control device; or

    (7) to avoid a collision.

(b) An operator may drive on an improved shoulder to the left of the main traveled portion of a divided or limited-access or controlled-access highway if that operation may be done safely, but only:

    (1) to slow or stop when the vehicle is disabled and traffic or other circumstances prohibit the safe movement of the vehicle to the shoulder to the right of the main traveled portion of the roadway;

    (2) as permitted or required by an official traffic-control device; or

    (3) to avoid a collision.

(c) A limitation in this section on driving on an improved shoulder does not apply to:

    (1) an authorized emergency vehicle responding to a call;

    (2) a police patrol; or

    (3) a bicycle.

(Enacted by Acts 1995, 74th Leg., ch. 165 (S.B. 971), § 1, effective September 1, 1995.)

### Sec. 545.059. One-Way Roadways and Rotary Traffic Islands.

(a) The Texas Transportation Commission may designate a highway or separate roadway under the jurisdiction of the commission for one-way traffic and shall erect appropriate signs giving notice of the designation.

(b) On a roadway that is designated and on which signs are erected for one-way traffic, an operator shall drive only in the direction indicated.

(c) An operator moving around a rotary traffic island shall drive only to the right of the island.

(Enacted by Acts 1995, 74th Leg., ch. 165 (S.B. 971), § 1, effective September 1, 1995.)

### Sec. 545.060. Driving on Roadway Laned for Traffic.

(a) An operator on a roadway divided into two or more clearly marked lanes for traffic:

    (1) shall drive as nearly as practical entirely within a single lane; and

    (2) may not move from the lane unless that movement can be made safely.

(b) If a roadway is divided into three lanes and provides for two-way movement of traffic, an operator on the roadway may not drive in the center lane except:

    (1) if passing another vehicle and the center lane is clear of traffic within a safe distance;

    (2) in preparing to make a left turn; or

    (3) where the center lane is designated by an official traffic-control device for movement in the direction in which the operator is moving.

(c) Without regard to the center of the roadway, an official traffic-control device may be erected directing slow-moving traffic to use a designated lane or designating lanes to be used by traffic moving in a particular direction.

(d) Official traffic-control devices prohibiting the changing of lanes on sections of roadway may be installed.

(Enacted by Acts 1995, 74th Leg., ch. 165 (S.B. 971), § 1, effective September 1, 1995.)

### Sec. 545.061. Driving on Multiple-Lane Roadway.

On a roadway divided into three or more lanes and providing for one-way movement of traffic, an operator entering a lane of traffic from a lane to the right shall yield the right-of-way to a vehicle entering the same lane of traffic from a lane to the left.

(Enacted by Acts 1995, 74th Leg., ch. 165 (S.B. 971), § 1, effective September 1, 1995.)

### Sec. 545.062. Following Distance.

(a) An operator shall, if following another vehicle, maintain an assured clear distance between the two vehicles so that, considering the speed of the vehicles, traffic, and the conditions of the highway, the operator can safely stop without colliding with the preceding vehicle or veering into another vehicle, object, or person on or near the highway.

(b) An operator of a truck or of a motor vehicle drawing another vehicle who is on a roadway outside a business or residential district and who is following another truck or motor vehicle drawing another vehicle shall, if conditions permit, leave sufficient space between the vehicles so that a vehicle passing the operator can safely enter and occupy the space. This subsection does not prohibit a truck or a motor vehicle drawing another vehicle from passing another vehicle.

(c) An operator on a roadway outside a business or residential district driving in a caravan of other vehicles or a motorcade shall allow sufficient space between the operator and the vehicle preceding the operator so that another vehicle can safely enter and occupy the space. This subsection does not apply to a funeral procession.
(Enacted by Acts 1995, 74th Leg., ch. 165 (S.B. 971), § 1, effective September 1, 1995.)

## Sec. 545.063.   Driving on Divided Highway.

(a) On a highway having two or more roadways separated by a space, physical barrier, or clearly indicated dividing section constructed to impede vehicular traffic, an operator shall drive on the right roadway unless directed or permitted to use another roadway by an official traffic-control device or police officer.

(b) An operator may not drive over, across, or in a dividing space, physical barrier, or section constructed to impede vehicular traffic except:

(1) through an opening in the physical barrier or dividing section or space; or

(2) at a crossover or intersection established by a public authority.
(Enacted by Acts 1995, 74th Leg., ch. 165 (S.B. 971), § 1, effective September 1, 1995.)

## Sec. 545.064.   Restricted Access.

An operator may not drive on or from a limited-access or controlled-access roadway except at an entrance or exit that is established by a public authority.
(Enacted by Acts 1995, 74th Leg., ch. 165 (S.B. 971), § 1, effective September 1, 1995.)

## Sec. 545.065.   State and Local Regulation of Limited-Access or Controlled-Access Highways.

(a) The Texas Transportation Commission by resolution or order recorded in its minutes may prohibit the use of a limited-access or controlled-access highway under the jurisdiction of the commission by a parade, funeral procession, pedestrian, bicycle, electric bicycle, motor-driven cycle, or nonmotorized traffic.

(b) If the commission adopts a rule under Subsection (a), the commission shall erect and maintain official traffic-control devices on the portions of the limited-access or controlled-access highway to which the rule applies.

(c) A local authority by ordinance may prohibit the use of a limited-access or controlled-access roadway under the jurisdiction of the authority by a parade, funeral procession, pedestrian, bicycle, electric bicycle, motor-driven cycle, or nonmotorized traffic.

(d) If a local authority adopts an ordinance under Subsection (c), the authority shall erect and maintain official traffic-control devices on the portions of the limited-access or controlled-access roadway to which the ordinance applies.
(Enacted by Acts 1995, 74th Leg., ch. 165 (S.B. 971), § 1, effective September 1, 1995; am. Acts 2001, 77th Leg., ch. 1085 (H.B. 2204), § 7, effective September 1, 2001.)

## Sec. 545.0651.   Restriction on Use of Highway.

(a) In this section:

(1) "Commission" means the Texas Transportation Commission.

(1-a) "Department" means the Texas Department of Transportation.

(2) "Highway" means a public highway that:

(A) is in the designated state highway system;

(B) is designated a controlled access facility; and

(C) has a minimum of three travel lanes, excluding access or frontage roads, in each direction of traffic that may be part of a single roadway or may be separate roadways that are constructed as an upper and lower deck.

(b) The commission by order may restrict, by class of vehicle, through traffic to two or more designated lanes of a highway. If the lanes to be restricted by the commission are located within a municipality, the commission shall consult with the municipality before adopting an order under this section. A municipality by ordinance may restrict, by class of vehicle, through traffic to two or more designated lanes of a highway in the municipality.

(c) An order or ordinance under Subsection (b) must allow a restricted vehicle to use any lane of the highway to pass another vehicle and to enter and exit the highway.

(d) Before adopting an ordinance, a municipality shall submit to the department a description of the proposed restriction. The municipality may not enforce the restrictions unless the department's executive director or the executive director's designee has approved the restrictions.

(e) Department approval under Subsection (d) must:

(1) be based on a traffic study performed by the department to evaluate the effect of the proposed restriction; and

(2) to the greatest extent practicable, ensure a systems approach to preclude the designation of inconsistent lane restrictions among adjacent municipalities.

(f) The department's executive director or the executive director's designee may suspend or rescind approval of any restrictions approved under Subsection (d) for one or more of the following reasons:

(1) a change in pavement conditions;

(2) a change in traffic conditions;

(3) a geometric change in roadway configuration;

(4) construction or maintenance activity; or

(5) emergency or incident management.

(g) The department shall erect and maintain official traffic control devices necessary to implement and enforce an order adopted or an ordinance adopted and approved under this section. A restriction approved under this section may not be enforced until the appropriate traffic control devices are in place.

(Enacted by Acts 1997, 75th Leg., ch. 384 (S.B. 773), § 1, effective May 28, 1997; am. Acts 2003, 78th Leg., ch. 1049 (H.B. 1208), § 9, effective June 20, 2003.)

## Sec. 545.0652. County Restriction on Use of Highway.

(a) In this section:

(1) "Department" means the Texas Department of Transportation.

(2) "Highway" means a public roadway that:

(A) is in the designated state highway system;

(B) is designated a controlled access facility; and

(C) has a minimum of three travel lanes, excluding access or frontage roads, in each direction of traffic.

(b) A county commissioners court by order may restrict, by class of vehicle, through traffic to two or more designated lanes of a highway located in the county and outside the jurisdiction of a municipality.

(c) An order under Subsection (b) must allow a restricted vehicle to use any lane of the highway to pass another vehicle and to enter and exit the highway.

(d) Before issuing an order under this section, the commissioners court shall submit to the department a description of the proposed restriction. The commissioners court may not enforce the restrictions unless:

(1) the department's executive director or the executive director's designee has approved the restrictions; and

(2) the appropriate traffic-control devices are in place.

(e) Department approval under Subsection (d) must to the greatest extent practicable ensure a systems approach to preclude the designation of inconsistent lane restrictions among adjacent counties or municipalities.

(f) The department's executive director or the executive director's designee may suspend or rescind approval under this section for one or more of the following reasons:

(1) a change in pavement conditions;

(2) a change in traffic conditions;

(3) a geometric change in roadway configuration;

(4) construction or maintenance activity; or

(5) emergency or incident management.

(g) The department shall erect and maintain official traffic-control devices necessary to implement and enforce an order issued and approved under this section.

(Enacted by Acts 2003, 78th Leg., ch. 846 (S.B. 514), § 1, effective September 1, 2003.)

## Sec. 545.066. Passing a School Bus; Offense.

(a) An operator on a highway, when approaching from either direction a school bus stopped on the highway to receive or discharge a student:

(1) shall stop before reaching the school bus when the bus is operating a visual signal as required by Section 547.701; and

(2) may not proceed until:

(A) the school bus resumes motion;

(B) the operator is signaled by the bus driver to proceed; or

(C) the visual signal is no longer actuated.

(b) An operator on a highway having separate roadways is not required to stop:

(1) for a school bus that is on a different roadway; or

(2) if on a controlled-access highway, for a school bus that is stopped:

**Transportation**

Transportation

(A) in a loading zone that is a part of or adjacent to the highway; and

(B) where pedestrians are not permitted to cross the roadway.

(c) An offense under this section is a misdemeanor punishable by a fine of not less than $200 or more than $1,000, except that the offense is:

(1) a Class A misdemeanor if the person causes serious bodily injury to another; or

(2) a state jail felony if the person has been previously convicted under Subdivision (1).

(d) The court may order that the driver's license of a person convicted of a second or subsequent offense under this section be suspended for not longer than six months beginning on the date of conviction. In this subsection, "driver's license" has the meaning assigned by Chapter 521.

(e) If a person does not pay the previously assessed fine or costs on a conviction under this section, or is determined by the court to have insufficient resources or income to pay a fine or costs on a conviction under this section, the court may order the person to perform community service. The court shall set the number of hours of service under this subsection.

(f) For the purposes of this section:

(1) a highway is considered to have separate roadways only if the highway has roadways separated by an intervening space on which operation of vehicles is not permitted, a physical barrier, or a clearly indicated dividing section constructed to impede vehicular traffic; and

(2) a highway is not considered to have separate roadways if the highway has roadways separated only by a left turn lane.

(Enacted by Acts 1995, 74th Leg., ch. 165 (S.B. 971), § 1, effective September 1, 1995; am. Acts 1997, 75th Leg., ch. 1438 (H.B. 3249), § 9, effective September 1, 1997; am. Acts 2003, 78th Leg., ch. 1325 (H.B. 3588), § 19.06(a), effective September 1, 2003.)

**Secs. 545.067 to 545.100 [Reserved for expansion].**

## SUBCHAPTER C
## TURNING AND SIGNALS FOR STOPPING AND TURNING

### Sec. 545.101.   Turning at Intersection.

(a) To make a right turn at an intersection, an operator shall make both the approach and the turn as closely as practicable to the right-hand curb or edge of the roadway.

(b) To make a left turn at an intersection, an operator shall:

(1) approach the intersection in the extreme left-hand lane lawfully available to a vehicle moving in the direction of the vehicle; and

(2) after entering the intersection, turn left, leaving the intersection so as to arrive in a lane lawfully available to traffic moving in the direction of the vehicle on the roadway being entered.

(c) On a street or roadway designated for two-way traffic, the operator turning left shall, to the extent practicable, turn in the portion of the intersection to the left of the center of the intersection.

(d) To turn left, an operator who is approaching an intersection having a roadway designated for one-way traffic and for which signs are posted from a roadway designated for one-way traffic and for which signs are posted shall make the turn as closely as practicable to the left-hand curb or edge of the roadway.

(e) The Texas Transportation Commission or a local authority, with respect to a highway in its jurisdiction, may:

(1) authorize the placement of an official traffic-control device in or adjacent to an intersection; and

(2) require a course different from that specified in this section for movement by vehicles turning at an intersection.

(Enacted by Acts 1995, 74th Leg., ch. 165 (S.B. 971), § 1, effective September 1, 1995.)

### Sec. 545.102.   Turning on Curve or Crest of Grade.

An operator may not turn the vehicle to move in the opposite direction when approaching a curve or the crest of a grade if the vehicle is not visible to the operator of another vehicle approaching from either direction within 500 feet.

(Enacted by Acts 1995, 74th Leg., ch. 165 (S.B. 971), § 1, effective September 1, 1995.)

### Sec. 545.103.   Safely Turning.

An operator may not turn the vehicle to enter a private road or driveway, otherwise turn the vehicle from a direct course, or move right or left on a roadway unless movement can be made safely.

(Enacted by Acts 1995, 74th Leg., ch. 165 (S.B. 971), § 1, effective September 1, 1995.)

## Sec. 545.104. Signaling Turns; Use of Turn Signals.

(a) An operator shall use the signal authorized by Section 545.106 to indicate an intention to turn, change lanes, or start from a parked position.

(b) An operator intending to turn a vehicle right or left shall signal continuously for not less than the last 100 feet of movement of the vehicle before the turn.

(c) An operator may not light the signals on only one side of the vehicle on a parked or disabled vehicle or use the signals as a courtesy or "do pass" signal to the operator of another vehicle approaching from the rear.
(Enacted by Acts 1995, 74th Leg., ch. 165 (S.B. 971), § 1, effective September 1, 1995.)

## Sec. 545.105. Signaling Stops.

An operator may not stop or suddenly decrease the speed of the vehicle without first giving a stop signal as provided by this subchapter to the operator of a vehicle immediately to the rear when there is an opportunity to give the signal.
(Enacted by Acts 1995, 74th Leg., ch. 165 (S.B. 971), § 1, effective September 1, 1995.)

## Sec. 545.106. Signals by Hand and Arm or by Signal Lamp.

(a) Except as provided by Subsection (b), an operator required to give a stop or turn signal shall do so by:

(1) using the hand and arm; or

(2) lighting signal lamps approved by the department.

(b) A motor vehicle in use on a highway shall be equipped with signal lamps, and the required signal shall be given by lighting the lamps, if:

(1) the distance from the center of the top of the steering post to the left outside limit of the body, cab, or load of the motor vehicle is more than two feet; or

(2) the distance from the center of the top of the steering post to the rear limit of the body or load, including the body or load of a combination of vehicles, is more than 14 feet.
(Enacted by Acts 1995, 74th Leg., ch. 165 (S.B. 971), § 1, effective September 1, 1995.)

## Sec. 545.107. Method of Giving Hand and Arm Signals.

An operator who is permitted to give a hand and arm signal shall give the signal from the left side of the vehicle as follows:

(1) to make a left turn signal, extend hand and arm horizontally;

(2) to make a right turn signal, extend hand and arm upward, except that a bicycle operator may signal from the right side of the vehicle with the hand and arm extended horizontally; and

(3) to stop or decrease speed, extend hand and arm downward.
(Enacted by Acts 1995, 74th Leg., ch. 165 (S.B. 971), § 1, effective September 1, 1995.)

## Secs. 545.108 to 545.150 [Reserved for expansion].

### SUBCHAPTER D
### RIGHT-OF-WAY

## Sec. 545.151. Vehicle Approaching or Entering Intersection.

(a) An operator approaching an intersection:

(1) shall stop, yield, and grant immediate use of the intersection:

(A) in obedience to an official traffic-control device, including a stop sign or yield right-of-way sign; or

(B) if a traffic-control signal is present but does not display an indication in any of the signal heads; and

(2) after stopping, may proceed when the intersection can be safely entered without interference or collision with traffic using a different street or roadway.

(b) An operator on a single-lane or two-lane street or roadway who approaches an intersection that is not controlled by an official traffic-control device and that is located on a divided highway or on a street or roadway divided into three or more marked traffic lanes:

(1) shall stop, yield, and grant immediate use of the intersection to a vehicle on the other street or roadway that is within the intersection or approaching the intersection in such proximity as to be a hazard; and

(2) after stopping, may proceed when the intersection can be safely entered without interference or collision with traffic using a different street or roadway.

(c) An operator on an unpaved street or roadway approaching an intersection of a paved street or roadway:

(1) shall stop, yield, and grant immediate use of the intersection to a vehicle on the paved street or roadway that is within the intersec-

tion or approaching the intersection in such proximity as to be a hazard; and

(2) after stopping, may proceed when the intersection can be safely entered without interference or collision with traffic using the paved street or roadway.

(d) Except as provided in Subsection (e), an operator approaching an intersection of a street or roadway that is not controlled by an official traffic-control device:

(1) shall stop, yield, and grant immediate use of the intersection to a vehicle that has entered the intersection from the operator's right or is approaching the intersection from the operator's right in a proximity that is a hazard; and

(2) after stopping, may proceed when the intersection can be safely entered without interference or collision with traffic using a different street or roadway.

(e) An operator approaching an intersection of a street or roadway from a street or roadway that terminates at the intersection and that is not controlled by an official traffic-control device or controlled as provided by Subsection (b) or (c):

(1) shall stop, yield, and grant immediate use of the intersection to another vehicle that has entered the intersection from the other street or roadway or is approaching the intersection on the other street or roadway in a proximity that is a hazard; and

(2) after stopping, may proceed when the intersection can be safely entered without interference or collision with the traffic using the other street or roadway.

(f) An operator who is required by this section to stop and yield the right-of-way at an intersection to another vehicle and who is involved in a collision or interferes with other traffic at the intersection to whom right-of-way is to be given is presumed not to have yielded the right-of-way.
(Enacted by Acts 1995, 74th Leg., ch. 165 (S.B. 971), § 1, effective September 1, 1995; am. Acts 2003, 78th Leg., ch. 1325 (H.B. 3588), § 19.05, effective September 1, 2003.)

### Sec. 545.152.  Vehicle Turning Left.

To turn left at an intersection or into an alley or private road or driveway, an operator shall yield the right-of-way to a vehicle that is approaching from the opposite direction and that is in the intersection or in such proximity to the intersection as to be an immediate hazard.

(Enacted by Acts 1995, 74th Leg., ch. 165 (S.B. 971), § 1, effective September 1, 1995.)

### Sec. 545.153.  Vehicle Entering Stop or Yield Intersection.

(a) Preferential right-of-way at an intersection may be indicated by a stop sign or yield sign as authorized in Section 544.003.

(b) Unless directed to proceed by a police officer or official traffic-control device, an operator approaching an intersection on a roadway controlled by a stop sign, after stopping as required by Section 544.010, shall yield the right-of-way to a vehicle that has entered the intersection from another highway or that is approaching so closely as to be an immediate hazard to the operator's movement in or across the intersection.

(c) An operator approaching an intersection on a roadway controlled by a yield sign shall:

(1) slow to a speed that is reasonable under the existing conditions; and

(2) yield the right-of-way to a vehicle in the intersection or approaching on another highway so closely as to be an immediate hazard to the operator's movement in or across the intersection.

(d) If an operator is required by Subsection (c) to yield and is involved in a collision with a vehicle in an intersection after the operator drove past a yield sign without stopping, the collision is prima facie evidence that the operator failed to yield the right-of-way.
(Enacted by Acts 1995, 74th Leg., ch. 165 (S.B. 971), § 1, effective September 1, 1995.)

### Sec. 545.154.  Vehicle Entering or Leaving Limited-Access or Controlled-Access Highway.

An operator on an access or feeder road of a limited-access or controlled-access highway shall yield the right-of-way to a vehicle entering or about to enter the access or feeder road from the highway or leaving or about to leave the access or feeder road to enter the highway.
(Enacted by Acts 1995, 74th Leg., ch. 165 (S.B. 971), § 1, effective September 1, 1995.)

### Sec. 545.155.  Vehicle Entering Highway from Private Road or Driveway.

An operator about to enter or cross a highway from an alley, building, or private road or driveway shall yield the right-of-way to a vehicle approaching on the highway to be entered.

(Enacted by Acts 1995, 74th Leg., ch. 165 (S.B. 971), § 1, effective September 1, 1995.)

### Sec. 545.156. Vehicle Approached by Authorized Emergency Vehicle.

(a) On the immediate approach of an authorized emergency vehicle using audible and visual signals that meet the requirements of Sections 547.305 and 547.702, or of a police vehicle lawfully using only an audible signal, an operator, unless otherwise directed by a police officer, shall:

(1) yield the right-of-way;

(2) immediately drive to a position parallel to and as close as possible to the right-hand edge or curb of the roadway clear of any intersection; and

(3) stop and remain standing until the authorized emergency vehicle has passed.

(b) This section does not exempt the operator of an authorized emergency vehicle from the duty to drive with due regard for the safety of all persons using the highway.

(Enacted by Acts 1995, 74th Leg., ch. 165 (S.B. 971), § 1, effective September 1, 1995.)

### Sec. 545.157. Passing Authorized Emergency Vehicle.

(a) On approaching a stationary authorized emergency vehicle using visual signals that meet the requirements of Sections 547.305 and 547.702, or a stationary tow truck using equipment authorized by Section 547.305(d), an operator, unless otherwise directed by a police officer, shall:

(1) vacate the lane closest to the emergency vehicle or tow truck when driving on a highway with two or more lanes traveling in the direction of the emergency vehicle or tow truck; or

(2) slow to a speed not to exceed:

(A) 20 miles per hour less than the posted speed limit when the posted speed limit is 25 miles per hour or more; or

(B) five miles per hour when the posted speed limit is less than 25 miles per hour.

(b) A violation of this section is:

(1) a misdemeanor punishable under Section 542.401;

(2) a misdemeanor punishable by a fine of $500 if the violation results in property damage; or

(3) a Class B misdemeanor if the violation results in bodily injury.

(c) If conduct constituting an offense under this section also constitutes an offense under another section of this code or the Penal Code, the actor may be prosecuted under either section or under both sections.

(d) In this section, "tow truck" means a vehicle that:

(1) has been issued a permit under Subchapter C, Chapter 2308, Occupations Code; and

(2) is operated by a person licensed under Subchapter D, Chapter 2308, Occupations Code.

(Enacted by Acts 2003, 78th Leg., ch. 327 (S.B. 193), § 2, effective September 1, 2003; am. Acts 2011, 82nd Leg., ch. 229 (H.B. 378), § 1, effective September 1, 2011.)

### Secs. 545.158 to 545.200 [Reserved for expansion].

## SUBCHAPTER E
## STREETCARS

### Sec. 545.201. Passing Streetcar to Left.

(a) An operator may not pass to the left or drive on the left side of a streetcar moving in the same direction, even if the streetcar is temporarily at rest, unless the operator:

(1) is directed to do so by a police officer;

(2) is on a one-way street; or

(3) is on a street on which the location of the tracks prevents compliance with this section.

(b) An operator when lawfully passing to the left of a streetcar that has stopped to receive or discharge a passenger:

(1) shall reduce speed;

(2) may proceed only on exercising due caution for pedestrians; and

(3) shall accord a pedestrian the right-of-way as required by this subtitle.

(Enacted by Acts 1995, 74th Leg., ch. 165 (S.B. 971), § 1, effective September 1, 1995.)

### Sec. 545.202. Passing Streetcar to Right.

(a) An operator passing to the right of a streetcar stopped or about to stop to receive or discharge a passenger shall:

(1) stop the vehicle at least five feet to the rear of the nearest running board or door of the streetcar; and

(2) remain standing until all passengers have entered the streetcar or, on leaving, have reached a place of safety.

Transportation

(b) An operator is not required to stop before passing a streetcar to the right if a safety zone has been established and may proceed past the streetcar at a reasonable speed and with due caution for the safety of pedestrians.
(Enacted by Acts 1995, 74th Leg., ch. 165 (S.B. 971), § 1, effective September 1, 1995.)

### Sec. 545.203. Driving on Streetcar Tracks.

(a) An operator on a streetcar track in front of a streetcar shall move the operator's vehicle off the track as soon as possible after a signal from the operator of the streetcar.

(b) An operator may not drive on or cross a streetcar track in an intersection in front of a streetcar crossing the intersection.

(c) An operator who is passing a streetcar may not turn in front of the streetcar so as to interfere with or impede its movement.
(Enacted by Acts 1995, 74th Leg., ch. 165 (S.B. 971), § 1, effective September 1, 1995.)

### Sec. 545.204. Streetcar Approached by Authorized Emergency Vehicle.

(a) On the immediate approach of an authorized emergency vehicle using audible and visual signals that meet the requirements of Sections 547.305 and 547.702, or of a police vehicle lawfully using only an audible signal, the operator of a streetcar shall immediately stop the streetcar clear of any intersection and remain there until the authorized emergency vehicle has passed, unless otherwise directed by a police officer.

(b) This section does not exempt the operator of an authorized emergency vehicle from the duty to drive with due regard for the safety of all persons using the highway.
(Enacted by Acts 1995, 74th Leg., ch. 165 (S.B. 971), § 1, effective September 1, 1995.)

### Sec. 545.205. Crossing Fire Hose.

An operator of a streetcar may not, without the consent of the fire department official in command, drive over an unprotected hose of a fire department when the hose is on a streetcar track and intended for use at a fire or alarm of fire.
(Enacted by Acts 1995, 74th Leg., ch. 165 (S.B. 971), § 1, effective September 1, 1995.)

### Sec. 545.206. Obstruction of Operator's View or Driving Mechanism.

A passenger in a streetcar may not ride in a position that interferes with the operator's view

ahead or to the side or with control over the driving mechanism of the streetcar.
(Enacted by Acts 1995, 74th Leg., ch. 165 (S.B. 971), § 1, effective September 1, 1995.)

### Secs. 545.207 to 545.250 [Reserved for expansion].

## SUBCHAPTER F
## SPECIAL STOPS AND SPEED RESTRICTIONS

### Sec. 545.251. Obedience to Signal Indicating Approach of Train.

(a) An operator approaching a railroad grade crossing shall stop not closer than 15 feet or farther than 50 feet from the nearest rail if:

(1) a clearly visible railroad signal warns of the approach of a railroad train;

(2) a crossing gate is lowered, or a flagger warns of the approach or passage of a train;

(3) a railroad engine approaching within approximately 1,500 feet of the highway crossing emits a signal audible from that distance and the engine is an immediate hazard because of its speed or proximity to the crossing;

(4) an approaching railroad train is plainly visible to the operator and is in hazardous proximity to the crossing; or

(5) the operator is required to stop by:

(A) other law;

(B) a rule adopted under a statute;

(C) an official traffic-control device; or

(D) a traffic-control signal.

(b) An operator of a vehicle required by Subsection (a) to stop shall remain stopped until permitted to proceed and it is safe to proceed.

(c) An operator of a vehicle who approaches a railroad grade crossing equipped with railroad crossbuck signs without automatic, electric, or mechanical signal devices, crossing gates, or a flagger warning of the approach or passage of a train shall yield the right-of-way to a train in hazardous proximity to the crossing, and proceed at a speed that is reasonable for the existing conditions. If required for safety, the operator shall stop at a clearly marked stop line before the grade crossing or, if no stop line exists, not closer than 15 feet or farther than 50 feet from the nearest rail.

(d) An operator commits an offense if the operator drives around, under, or through a crossing gate or a barrier at a railroad crossing while the gate or barrier is closed, being closed, or being opened.

(e) In a prosecution under this section, proof that at the time of the offense a train was in hazardous proximity to the crossing and that the train was plainly visible to the operator is prima facie evidence that it was not safe for the operator to proceed.

(f) An offense under this section is punishable by a fine of not less than $50 or more than $200. (Enacted by Acts 1995, 74th Leg., ch. 165 (S.B. 971), § 1, effective September 1, 1995; am. Acts 1997, 75th Leg., ch. 165 (S.B. 898), § 30.107(a), effective September 1, 1997; am. Acts 1997, 75th Leg., ch. 1097 (H.B. 2101), § 1, effective September 1, 1997.)

## Sec. 545.252. All Vehicles to Stop at Certain Railroad Grade Crossings.

(a) The Texas Department of Transportation or a local authority, with respect to a highway in its jurisdiction, may:

(1) designate a railroad grade crossing as particularly dangerous; and

(2) erect a stop sign or other official traffic-control device at the grade crossing.

(b) An operator approaching a stop sign or other official traffic-control device that requires a stop and that is erected under Subsection (a) shall stop not closer than 15 feet or farther than 50 feet from the nearest rail of the railroad and may proceed only with due care.

(c) The costs of installing and maintaining a mechanically operated grade crossing safety device, gate, sign, or signal erected under this section shall be apportioned and paid on the same percentage ratio and in the same proportionate amounts by this state and all participating political subdivisions of this state as costs are apportioned and paid between the state and the United States.

(d) An offense under this section is punishable by a fine of not less than $50 or more than $200. (Enacted by Acts 1995, 74th Leg., ch. 165 (S.B. 971), § 1, effective September 1, 1995; am. Acts 1997, 75th Leg., ch. 165 (S.B. 898), § 30.107(b), effective September 1, 1997.)

## Sec. 545.253. Buses to Stop at All Railroad Grade Crossings.

(a) Except as provided by Subsection (c), the operator of a motor bus carrying passengers for hire, before crossing a railroad grade crossing:

(1) shall stop the vehicle not closer than 15 feet or farther than 50 feet from the nearest rail of the railroad;

(2) while stopped, shall listen and look in both directions along the track for an approaching train and signals indicating the approach of a train; and

(3) may not proceed until it is safe to do so.

(b) After stopping as required by Subsection (a), an operator described by Subsection (a) shall proceed without manually shifting gears while crossing the track.

(c) A vehicle is not required to stop at the crossing if a police officer or a traffic-control signal directs traffic to proceed.

(d) This section does not apply at a railway grade crossing in a business or residence district.

(e) An offense under this section is punishable by a fine of not less than $50 or more than $200. (Enacted by Acts 1995, 74th Leg., ch. 165 (S.B. 971), § 1, effective September 1, 1995; am. Acts 1997, 75th Leg., ch. 165 (S.B. 898), § 30.107(c), effective September 1, 1997; am. Acts 1997, 75th Leg., ch. 1061 (S.B. 1486), § 15, effective September 1, 1997; am. Acts 1997, 75th Leg., ch. 1438 (H.B. 3249), § 10, effective September 1, 1997.)

## Sec. 545.2535. School Buses to Stop at All Railroad Grade Crossings.

(a) Except as provided by Subsection (c), the operator of a school bus, before crossing a track at a railroad grade crossing:

(1) shall stop the vehicle not closer than 15 feet or farther than 50 feet from the track;

(2) while stopped, shall listen and look in both directions along the track for an approaching train and signals indicating the approach of a train; and

(3) may not proceed until it is safe to do so.

(b) After stopping as required by Subsection (a), the operator may proceed in a gear that permits the vehicle to complete the crossing without a change of gears. The operator may not shift gears while crossing the track.

(c) An operator is not required to stop at:

(1) an abandoned railroad grade crossing that is marked with a sign reading "tracks out of service"; or

(2) an industrial or spur line railroad grade crossing that is marked with a sign reading "exempt."

(d) A sign under Subsection (c) may be erected only by or with the consent of the appropriate state or local governmental official. (Enacted by Acts 1997, 75th Leg., ch. 1061 (S.B. 1486), § 16, effective September 1, 1997; enacted by Acts 1997, 75th Leg., ch. 1438 (H.B. 3249), § 11, effective September 1, 1997.)

Transportation

## Sec. 545.254. Vehicles Carrying Explosive Substances or Flammable Liquids.

(a) Before crossing a railroad grade crossing, an operator of a vehicle that has an explosive substance or flammable liquid as the vehicle's principal cargo and that is moving at a speed of more than 20 miles per hour:

(1) shall reduce the speed of the vehicle to 20 miles per hour or less before coming within 200 feet of the nearest rail of the railroad;

(2) shall listen and look in both directions along the track for an approaching train and for signals indicating the approach of a train; and

(3) may not proceed until the operator determines that the course is clear.

(b) The operator of a vehicle that has an explosive substance or flammable liquid as the vehicle's principal cargo, before crossing a railroad grade crossing on a highway in a municipality:

(1) shall stop the vehicle not closer than 15 feet or farther than 50 feet from the nearest rail of the railroad;

(2) while stopped, shall listen and look in both directions along the track for an approaching train and for signals indicating the approach of a train; and

(3) may not proceed until the operator determines that the course is clear.

(c) Subsections (a) and (b) do not apply:

(1) if a police officer, crossing flagger, or traffic-control signal directs traffic to proceed;

(2) where a railroad flashing signal is installed and does not indicate an approaching train;

(3) to an abandoned or exempted grade crossing that is clearly marked by or with the consent of the state, if the markings can be read from the operator's location;

(4) at a streetcar crossing in a business or residential district of a municipality; or

(5) to a railroad track used exclusively for industrial switching purposes in a business district.

(d) This section does not exempt the operator from compliance with Section 545.251 or 545.252.

(e) An offense under this section is punishable by a fine of not less than $50 or more than $200. (Enacted by Acts 1995, 74th Leg., ch. 165 (S.B. 971), § 1, effective September 1, 1995; am. Acts 1997, 75th Leg., ch. 165 (S.B. 898), § 30.107(d), effective September 1, 1997.)

## Sec. 545.255. Moving Heavy Equipment at Railroad Grade Crossings.

(a) This section applies only to:

(1) a crawler-type tractor, steam shovel, derrick, or roller; and

(2) any other equipment or structure with:

(A) a normal operating speed of 10 miles per hour or less; or

(B) a vertical body or load clearance of less than one-half inch per foot of the distance between two adjacent axles or less than nine inches measured above the level surface of a roadway.

(b) An operator of a vehicle or equipment may not move on or across a track at a railroad grade crossing unless the operator has given notice to a station agent of the railroad and given the railroad reasonable time to provide proper protection at the crossing.

(c) To move a vehicle or equipment on or across a track at a railroad grade crossing, the operator:

(1) shall stop the vehicle or equipment not closer than 15 feet or farther than 50 feet from the nearest rail of the railroad;

(2) while stopped, shall listen and look in both directions along the track for an approaching train and for signals indicating the approach of a train; and

(3) may not proceed until it is safe to cross the track.

(d) An operator of a vehicle or equipment may not cross a railroad grade crossing when warning of the immediate approach of a railroad car or train is given by automatic signal, crossing gates, a flagger, or otherwise. If a flagger is provided by the railroad, the operator shall move the vehicle or equipment over the crossing at the flagger's direction.

(e) An offense under this section is punishable by a fine of not less than $50 or more than $200. (Enacted by Acts 1995, 74th Leg., ch. 165 (S.B. 971), § 1, effective September 1, 1995; am. Acts 1997, 75th Leg., ch. 165 (S.B. 898), § 30.107(e), effective September 1, 1997.)

## Sec. 545.2555. Report and Investigation of Certain Railroad Crossing Violations.

(a) A person who on site observes a violation of Section 545.251, 545.252, 545.253, 545.254, or 545.255 may file a report of the violation if the person:

(1) is an on-engine employee of a railroad; and

(2) observes the violation while on a moving engine.

(b) A report under this section must:

(1) be made:

(A) on a form approved by the department; and

(B) not later than 72 hours after the violation;

(2) be filed with:

(A) an office of the department located in the county in which the violation occurred;

(B) the sheriff of the county in which the violation occurred, if the violation occurred in the unincorporated area of the county; or

(C) the police department of a municipality, if the violation occurred in the municipality; and

(3) contain, in addition, to any other required information:

(A) the date, time, and location of the violation;

(B) the license plate number and a description of the vehicle involved in the violation;

(C) a description of the operator of the vehicle involved in the violation; and

(D) the name, address, and telephone number of the person filing the report.

(c) A peace officer may:

(1) before the seventh day after the date a report under this section is filed, initiate an investigation of the alleged violation; and

(2) request the owner of the reported vehicle, as shown by the vehicle registration records of the Texas Department of Transportation, to disclose the name and address of the individual operating that vehicle at the time of the violation alleged in the report.

(d) Unless the owner of the reported vehicle believes that to provide the peace officer with the name and address of the individual operating the vehicle at the time of the violation alleged would incriminate the owner, the owner shall, to the best of the owner's ability, disclose that individual's name and address.

(e) An investigating peace officer who has probable cause to believe that a charge against an individual for a violation of Section 545.251, 545.252, 545.253, 545.254, or 545.255 is justified may:

(1) prepare a written notice to appear in court that complies with Sections 543.003, 543.006, and 543.007; and

(2) deliver the notice to the individual named in the notice in person or by certified mail.

(Enacted by Acts 1997, 75th Leg., ch. 165 (S.B. 898), § 30.108(a), effective September 1, 1997.)

### Sec. 545.256. Emerging from an Alley, Driveway, or Building.

An operator emerging from an alley, driveway, or building in a business or residence district shall:

(1) stop the vehicle before moving on a sidewalk or the sidewalk area extending across an alley or driveway;

(2) yield the right-of-way to a pedestrian to avoid collision; and

(3) on entering the roadway, yield the right-of-way to an approaching vehicle.

(Enacted by Acts 1995, 74th Leg., ch. 165 (S.B. 971), § 1, effective September 1, 1995.)

### Secs. 545.257 to 545.300 [Reserved for expansion].

## SUBCHAPTER G
## STOPPING, STANDING, AND PARKING

### Sec. 545.301. Stopping, Standing, or Parking Outside a Business or Residence District.

(a) An operator may not stop, park, or leave standing an attended or unattended vehicle on the main traveled part of a highway outside a business or residence district unless:

(1) stopping, parking, or leaving the vehicle off the main traveled part of the highway is not practicable;

(2) a width of highway beside the vehicle is unobstructed and open for the passage of other vehicles; and

(3) the vehicle is in clear view for at least 200 feet in each direction on the highway.

(b) This section does not apply to an operator of:

(1) a vehicle that is disabled while on the paved or main traveled part of a highway if it is impossible to avoid stopping and temporarily leaving the vehicle on the highway;

(2) a vehicle used exclusively to transport solid, semisolid, or liquid waste operated at the time in connection with the removal or transportation of solid, semisolid, or liquid waste from a location adjacent to the highway; or

(3) a tow truck, as defined by Section 545.157(d), that is performing towing duties under Chapter 2308, Occupations Code.

(Enacted by Acts 1995, 74th Leg., ch. 165 (S.B. 971), § 1, effective September 1, 1995; am. Acts 2009, 81st Leg., ch. 782 (S.B. 1093), § 3, effective September 1, 2009; am. Acts 2011, 82nd Leg., ch. 229 (H.B. 378), § 2, effective September 1, 2011.)

## Sec. 545.302.  Stopping, Standing, or Parking Prohibited in Certain Places.

(a) An operator may not stop, stand, or park a vehicle:

(1) on the roadway side of a vehicle stopped or parked at the edge or curb of a street;

(2) on a sidewalk;

(3) in an intersection;

(4) on a crosswalk;

(5) between a safety zone and the adjacent curb or within 30 feet of a place on the curb immediately opposite the ends of a safety zone, unless the governing body of a municipality designates a different length by signs or markings;

(6) alongside or opposite a street excavation or obstruction if stopping, standing, or parking the vehicle would obstruct traffic;

(7) on a bridge or other elevated structure on a highway or in a highway tunnel;

(8) on a railroad track; or

(9) where an official sign prohibits stopping.

(b) An operator may not, except momentarily to pick up or discharge a passenger, stand or park an occupied or unoccupied vehicle:

(1) in front of a public or private driveway;

(2) within 15 feet of a fire hydrant;

(3) within 20 feet of a crosswalk at an intersection;

(4) within 30 feet on the approach to a flashing signal, stop sign, yield sign, or traffic-control signal located at the side of a roadway;

(5) within 20 feet of the driveway entrance to a fire station and on the side of a street opposite the entrance to a fire station within 75 feet of the entrance, if the entrance is properly marked with a sign; or

(6) where an official sign prohibits standing.

(c) An operator may not, except temporarily to load or unload merchandise or passengers, park an occupied or unoccupied vehicle:

(1) within 50 feet of the nearest rail of a railroad crossing; or

(2) where an official sign prohibits parking.

(d) A person may stop, stand, or park a bicycle on a sidewalk if the bicycle does not impede the normal and reasonable movement of pedestrian or other traffic on the sidewalk.

(e) A municipality may adopt an ordinance exempting a private vehicle operated by an elevator constructor responding to an elevator emergency from Subsections (a)(1), (a)(5), (a)(6), (a)(9), (b), and (c).

(f) Subsections (a), (b), and (c) do not apply if the avoidance of conflict with other traffic is necessary or if the operator is complying with the law or the directions of a police officer or official traffic-control device.

(g) If the governing body of a municipality determines that it is necessary to improve the economic development of the municipality's central business district and that it will not adversely affect public safety, the governing body may adopt an ordinance regulating the standing, stopping, or parking of a vehicle at a place described by Subsection (a)(1), other than a road or highway in the state highway system, in the central business district of the municipality as defined in the ordinance. To the extent of any conflict between the ordinance and Subsection (a)(1), the ordinance controls.

(Enacted by Acts 1995, 74th Leg., ch. 165 (S.B. 971), § 1, effective September 1, 1995; am. Acts 1999, 76th Leg., ch. 814 (H.B. 1575), § 1, effective June 18, 1999.)

## Sec. 545.303.  Additional Parking Regulations.

(a) An operator who stops or parks on a two-way roadway shall do so with the right-hand wheels of the vehicle parallel to and within 18 inches of the right-hand curb or edge of the roadway.

(b) An operator who stops or parks on a one-way roadway shall stop or park the vehicle parallel to the curb or edge of the roadway in the direction of authorized traffic movement with the right-hand wheels within 18 inches of the right-hand curb or edge of the roadway or the left-hand wheels within 18 inches of the left-hand curb or edge of the roadway. This subsection does not apply where a local ordinance otherwise regulates stopping or parking on the one-way roadway.

(c) A local authority by ordinance may permit angle parking on a roadway. This subsection does not apply to a federal-aid or state highway unless the director of the Texas Department of Transportation determines that the roadway is wide enough to permit angle parking without interfering with the free movement of traffic.

(d) The Texas Department of Transportation, on a highway under the jurisdiction of that department, may place signs prohibiting or restricting the stopping, standing, or parking of a vehicle on the highway where the director of the Texas Department of Transportation determines that stopping, standing, or parking is dangerous to, or would unduly interfere with, the free movement of traffic on the highway.

(e) To the extent of any conflict between Subsection (a) or (b) and a municipal ordinance adopted under Section 545.302(g), the ordinance controls.

(Enacted by Acts 1995, 74th Leg., ch. 165 (S.B. 971), § 1, effective September 1, 1995; am. Acts 1999, 76th Leg., ch. 814 (H.B. 1575), § 2, effective June 18, 1999.)

### Sec. 545.304. Moving the Vehicle of Another; Unlawful Parking.

A person may not move a vehicle that is not lawfully under the person's control:

(1) into an area where a vehicle is prohibited under Section 545.302; or

(2) away from a curb a distance that is unlawful under Section 545.303.

(Enacted by Acts 1995, 74th Leg., ch. 165 (S.B. 971), § 1, effective September 1, 1995.)

### Sec. 545.305. Removal of Unlawfully Stopped Vehicle.

(a) A peace officer listed under Article 2.12, Code of Criminal Procedure, or a license and weight inspector of the department may remove or require the operator or a person in charge of a vehicle to move a vehicle from a highway if the vehicle:

(1) is unattended on a bridge, viaduct, or causeway or in a tube or tunnel and the vehicle is obstructing traffic;

(2) is unlawfully parked and blocking the entrance to a private driveway;

(3) has been reported as stolen;

(4) is identified as having been stolen in a warrant issued on the filing of a complaint;

(5) is unattended and the officer has reasonable grounds to believe that the vehicle has been abandoned for longer than 48 hours;

(6) is disabled so that normal operation is impossible or impractical and the owner or person in charge of the vehicle is:

(A) incapacitated and unable to provide for the vehicle's removal or custody; or

(B) not in the immediate vicinity of the vehicle;

(7) is disabled so that normal operation is impossible or impractical and the owner or

person in charge of the vehicle does not designate a particular towing or storage company;

(8) is operated by a person an officer arrests for an alleged offense and the officer is required by law to take the person into custody; or

(9) is, in the opinion of the officer, a hazard, interferes with a normal function of a governmental agency, or because of a catastrophe, emergency, or unusual circumstance is imperiled.

(b) An officer acting under Subsection (a) may require that the vehicle be taken to:

(1) the nearest garage or other place of safety;

(2) a garage designated or maintained by the governmental agency that employs the officer; or

(3) a position off the paved or main traveled part of the highway.

(c) A law enforcement agency other than the department that removes an abandoned vehicle in an unincorporated area shall notify the sheriff.

(d) The owner of a vehicle that is removed or stored under this section is liable for all reasonable towing and storage fees incurred.

(e) In this section:

(1) "Towing company" means an individual, corporation, partnership, or other association engaged in the business of towing vehicles on a highway for compensation or with the expectation of compensation for the towing or storage of the vehicles and includes the owner, operator, employee, or agent of a towing company.

(2) "Storage company" means an individual, corporation, partnership, or other association engaged in the business of storing or repairing vehicles for compensation or with the expectation of compensation for the storage or repair of vehicles and includes the owner, operator, employee, or agent of a storage company.

(Enacted by Acts 1995, 74th Leg., ch. 165 (S.B. 971), § 1, effective September 1, 1995.)

### Sec. 545.3051. Removal of Personal Property from Roadway or Right-of-Way.

(a) In this section:

(1) "Authority" means:

(A) a metropolitan rapid transit authority operating under Chapter 451; or

(B) a regional transportation authority operating under Chapter 452.

(2) "Law enforcement agency" means:

(A) the department;

Transportation

(B) the police department of a municipality;

(C) the sheriff's office of a county; or

(D) a constable's office of a county.

(3) "Personal property" means:

(A) a vehicle described by Section 545.305;

(B) spilled cargo;

(C) a hazardous material as defined by 49 U.S.C. Section 5102 and its subsequent amendments; or

(D) a hazardous substance as defined by Section 26.263, Water Code.

(b) An authority or a law enforcement agency may remove personal property from a roadway or right-of-way if the authority or law enforcement agency determines that the property blocks the roadway or endangers public safety.

(c) Personal property may be removed under this section without the consent of the owner or carrier of the property.

(d) The owner and any carrier of personal property removed under this section shall reimburse the authority or law enforcement agency for any reasonable cost of removal and disposition of the property.

(e) Notwithstanding any other provision of law, an authority or a law enforcement agency is not liable for:

(1) any damage to personal property removed from a roadway or right-of-way under this section, unless the removal is carried out recklessly or in a grossly negligent manner; or

(2) any damage resulting from the failure to exercise the authority granted by this section.

(Enacted by Acts 2003, 78th Leg., ch. 803 (S.B. 165), § 1, effective June 20, 2003.)

## Sec. 545.306. Regulation of Towing Companies in Certain Counties.

(a) The commissioners court of a county with a population of 3.3 million or more shall by ordinance provide for the licensing of or the granting of a permit to a person to remove or store a vehicle authorized by Section 545.305 to be removed in an unincorporated area of the county. The ordinance must include rules to ensure the protection of the public and the safe and efficient operation of towing and storage services in the county and may not regulate or restrict the use of lighting equipment more than the extent allowed by state and federal law. The sheriff shall determine the rules included in the ordinance with the review and consent of the commissioners court.

(b) The commissioners court shall set the fee for the license or permit in an amount that reasonably offsets the costs of enforcing the ordinance. The commissioners court shall use each license or permit fee to pay salaries and expenses of the sheriff's office for conducting inspections to determine compliance with the ordinance and laws relating to dealers in scrap metal and salvage.

(Enacted by Acts 1995, 74th Leg., ch. 165 (S.B. 971), § 1, effective September 1, 1995; am. Acts 2001, 77th Leg., ch. 669 (H.B. 2810), § 143, effective September 1, 2001; am. Acts 2003, 78th Leg., ch. 1034 (H.B. 849), § 3, effective September 1, 2003.)

## Sec. 545.307. Overnight Parking of Commercial Motor Vehicle in or Near Residential Subdivision.

(a) In this section:

(1) "Commercial motor vehicle" means:

(A) a commercial motor vehicle, as defined by Section 522.003, and includes a vehicle meeting that definition regardless of whether the vehicle is used for a commercial purpose; or

(B) a road tractor, truck tractor, pole trailer, or semitrailer, as those terms are defined by Section 541.201.

(2) "Residential subdivision" means a subdivision in a county with a population greater than 220,000:

(A) for which a plat is recorded in the county real property records; and

(B) in which the majority of lots are subject to deed restrictions limiting the lots to residential use.

(b) Except as provided by Subsection (b-1), after 10 p.m. and before 6 a.m., a person may not park a commercial motor vehicle or leave the vehicle parked on a street that is maintained by a county or municipality and for which signs are posted as provided by Subsection (c) if the street:

(1) is located within a residential subdivision; or

(2) is adjacent to a residential subdivision and within 1,000 feet of the property line of a residence, school, place of worship, or park.

(b-1) A person may park a commercial motor vehicle or leave the vehicle parked on a street for which signs are posted as provided by Subsection (c) if the commercial motor vehicle:

(1) is transporting persons or property to or from the residential subdivision or performing work in the subdivision; and

(2) remains parked in or adjacent to the subdivision only for the period necessary to complete the transportation or work.

(c) The residents of a residential subdivision may petition a county or municipality in which the subdivision is located for the posting of signs prohibiting the overnight parking of a commercial motor vehicle in the subdivision or on a street adjacent to the subdivision and within 1,000 feet of the property line of a residence, school, place of worship, or park. The petition must be signed by at least 25 percent of the owners or tenants of residences in the subdivision. Not more than one person for each residence may sign the petition, and each person signing must be at least 18 years of age. Promptly after the filing of a petition meeting the requirements of this subsection and subject to Subsection (d), the county or municipality receiving the petition shall post the signs. The signs must:

    (1) be posted:

      (A) at each entrance of the subdivision through which a commercial motor vehicle may enter the subdivision or within the subdivision if there is not defined entrance to the subdivision; or

      (B) on a street adjacent to the subdivision; and

    (2) state, in letters at least two inches in height, that overnight parking of a commercial motor vehicle is prohibited in the subdivision or on a street adjacent to the subdivision.

(d) A county or municipality receiving a petition under Subsection (c) may condition the posting of the signs on payment by the residents of the residential subdivision of the cost of providing the signs.

(e) A person commits an offense if the person parks a commercial motor vehicle in violation of Subsection (b).

(f) This section does not limit the power of a municipality to regulate the parking of commercial motor vehicles.

(g) For the purposes of this section, contiguous subdivisions that are developed by the same entity or a successor to that entity and that are given the same public name or a variation of the same public name are considered one subdivision. Separation of one of the subdivisions from another by a road, stream, greenbelt, or similar barrier does not make the subdivisions noncontiguous.

(h) This section does not apply to:

    (1) a vehicle owned by a utility that an employee of the utility who is on call 24 hours a day parks at the employee's residence; or

    (2) a vehicle owned by a commercial establishment that is parked on the street adjacent to where the establishment is located.

(Enacted by Acts 1997, 75th Leg., ch. 173 (H.B. 327), § 1, effective September 1, 1997; am. Acts 1999, 76th Leg., ch. 731 (H.B. 1024), § 1, effective September 1, 1999; am. Acts 1999, 76th Leg., ch. 1419 (H.B. 2207), § 1, effective June 19, 1999; am. Acts 2007, 80th Leg., ch. 1021 (H.B. 1522), §§ 1, 2, effective September 1, 2007.)

### Sec. 545.308. Presumption.

The governing body of a local authority, by ordinance, order, or other official action, may provide that in a prosecution for an offense under this subchapter involving the stopping, standing, or parking of an unattended motor vehicle it is presumed that the registered owner of the vehicle is the person who stopped, stood, or parked the vehicle at the time and place the offense occurred. (Enacted by Acts 2001, 77th Leg., ch. 1080 (H.B. 2173), § 2, effective September 1, 2001.)

### Secs. 545.309 to 545.350 [Reserved for expansion].

## SUBCHAPTER H
## SPEED RESTRICTIONS

### Sec. 545.351. Maximum Speed Requirement.

(a) An operator may not drive at a speed greater than is reasonable and prudent under the circumstances then existing.

(b) An operator:

    (1) may not drive a vehicle at a speed greater than is reasonable and prudent under the conditions and having regard for actual and potential hazards then existing; and

    (2) shall control the speed of the vehicle as necessary to avoid colliding with another person or vehicle that is on or entering the highway in compliance with law and the duty of each person to use due care.

(c) An operator shall, consistent with Subsections (a) and (b), drive at an appropriate reduced speed if:

    (1) the operator is approaching and crossing an intersection or railroad grade crossing;

    (2) the operator is approaching and going around a curve;

    (3) the operator is approaching a hill crest;

    (4) the operator is traveling on a narrow or winding roadway; and

    (5) a special hazard exists with regard to traffic, including pedestrians, or weather or highway conditions.

CAN'T DRIVE FASTER THAN THE POSTED SPEED LIMIT

(Enacted by Acts 1995, 74th Leg., ch. 165 (S.B. 971), § 1, effective September 1, 1995; am. Acts 1997, 75th Leg., ch. 165 (S.B. 898), § 30.109, effective September 1, 1997.)

### Sec. 545.352. Prima Facie Speed Limits.

(a) A speed in excess of the limits established by Subsection (b) or under another provision of this subchapter is prima facie evidence that the speed is not reasonable and prudent and that the speed is unlawful.

(b) Unless a special hazard exists that requires a slower speed for compliance with Section 545.351(b), the following speeds are lawful:

(1) 30 miles per hour in an urban district on a street other than an alley and 15 miles per hour in an alley;

(2) except as provided by Subdivision (4), 70 miles per hour on a highway numbered by this state or the United States outside an urban district, including a farm-to-market or ranch-to-market road;

(3) except as provided by Subdivision (4), 60 miles per hour on a highway that is outside an urban district and not a highway numbered by this state or the United States;

(4) outside an urban district:

(A) 60 miles per hour if the vehicle is a school bus that has passed a commercial motor vehicle inspection under Section 548.201 and is on a highway numbered by the United States or this state, including a farm-to-market road; or

(B) 50 miles per hour if the vehicle is a school bus that:

(i) has not passed a commercial motor vehicle inspection under Section 548.201; or

(ii) is traveling on a highway not numbered by the United States or this state;

(5) on a beach, 15 miles per hour; or

(6) on a county road adjacent to a public beach, 15 miles per hour, if declared by the commissioners court of the county.

(c) The speed limits for a bus or other vehicle engaged in the business of transporting passengers for compensation or hire, for a commercial vehicle used as a highway post office vehicle for highway post office service in the transportation of United States mail, for a light truck, and for a school activity bus are the same as required for a passenger car at the same time and location.

(d) In this section:

(1) "Interstate highway" means a segment of the national system of interstate and defense highways that is:

(A) located in this state;

(B) officially designated by the Texas Transportation Commission; and

(C) approved under Title 23, United States Code.

(2) "Light truck" means a truck with a manufacturer's rated carrying capacity of not more than 2,000 pounds, including a pick-up truck, panel delivery truck, and carry-all truck.

(3) "Urban district" means the territory adjacent to and including a highway, if the territory is improved with structures that are used for business, industry, or dwelling houses and are located at intervals of less than 100 feet for a distance of at least one-quarter mile on either side of the highway.

(e) An entity that establishes or alters a speed limit under this subchapter shall establish the same speed limit for daytime and nighttime.

(Enacted by Acts 1995, 74th Leg., ch. 165 (S.B. 971), § 1, effective September 1, 1995; am. Acts 1997, 75th Leg., ch. 165 (S.B. 898), § 30.110(a), effective September 1, 1997; am. Acts 1997, 75th Leg., ch. 1020 (S.B. 343), § 2, effective September 1, 1997; am. Acts 1999, 76th Leg., ch. 663 (H.B. 385), § 2, effective June 18, 1999; am. Acts 1999, 76th Leg., ch. 739 (H.B. 1075), § 1, effective September 1, 1999; am. Acts 1999, 76th Leg., ch. 1346 (H.B. 676), § 1, effective September 1, 1999; am. Acts 2011, 82nd Leg., ch. 265 (H.B. 1353), §§ 1, 2, effective September 1, 2011.)

### Sec. 545.353. Authority of Texas Transportation Commission to Alter Speed Limits.

(a) If the Texas Transportation Commission determines from the results of an engineering and traffic investigation that a prima facie speed limit in this subchapter is unreasonable or unsafe on a part of the highway system, the commission, by order recorded in its minutes, and except as provided in Subsection (d), may determine and declare:

(1) a reasonable and safe prima facie speed limit; and

(2) another reasonable and safe speed because of wet or inclement weather.

(b) In determining whether a prima facie speed limit on a part of the highway system is reasonable and safe, the commission shall consider the width and condition of the pavement, the usual traffic at the affected area, and other circumstances.

(c) A prima facie speed limit that is declared by the commission under this section is effective when the commission erects signs giving notice of the new limit. A new limit that is enacted for a highway under this section is effective at all times or at other times as determined.

(d) Except as provided by Subsection (h-1), the commission may not:

(1) modify the rules established by Section 545.351(b);

(2) establish a speed limit of more than 75 miles per hour; or

(3) increase the speed limit for a vehicle described by Section 545.352(b)(4).

(e) The commission, in conducting the engineering and traffic investigation specified by Subsection (a), shall follow the "Procedure for Establishing Speed Zones" as adopted by the commission. The commission may revise the procedure to accommodate technological advancement in traffic operation, the design and construction of highways and motor vehicles, and the safety of the motoring public.

(f) The commission's authority to alter speed limits applies:

(1) to any part of a highway officially designated or marked by the commission as part of the state highway system; and

(2) both inside and outside the limits of a municipality, including a home-rule municipality, for a limited-access or controlled-access highway.

(g) For purposes of this section, "wet or inclement weather" means a condition of the roadway that makes driving on the roadway unsafe and hazardous and that is caused by precipitation, including water, ice, and snow.

(h) Notwithstanding Section 545.352(b), the commission may establish a speed limit of 75 miles per hour on a part of the highway system if the commission determines that 75 miles per hour is a reasonable and safe speed for that part of the highway system.

(h-1) Notwithstanding Section 545.352(b), the commission may establish a speed limit of 80 miles per hour on a part of Interstate Highway 10 or Interstate Highway 20 in Crockett, Culberson, Hudspeth, Jeff Davis, Kerr, Kimble, Pecos, Reeves, Sutton, or Ward County if the commission determines that 80 miles per hour is a reasonable and safe speed for that part of the highway.

(h-2) Notwithstanding Section 545.352(b), as amended by Chapters 663 (H.B. 385) and 739 (H.B. 1075), Acts of the 76th Legislature, Regular Session, 1999, the commission may establish a speed limit not to exceed 85 miles per hour on a part of the state highway system if:

(1) that part of the highway system is designed to accommodate travel at that established speed or a higher speed; and

(2) the commission determines, after an engineering and traffic investigation, that the established speed limit is reasonable and safe for that part of the highway system.

(i) [Repealed by Acts 2011, 82nd Leg., ch. 265 (H.B. 1353), § 9, effective September 1, 2011]

(j) The commission may not determine or declare, or agree to determine or declare, a prima facie speed limit for environmental purposes on a part of the highway system.

(Enacted by Acts 1995, 74th Leg., ch. 165 (S.B. 971), § 1, effective September 1, 1995; am Acts 1997, 75th Leg., ch. 165 (S.B. 898), § 30.111, effective September 1, 1997; am. Acts 2001, 77th Leg., ch. 1518 (H.B. 299), § 1, effective June 17, 2001; am. Acts 2003, 78th Leg., ch. 1331 (H.B. 1365), § 25, effective June 20, 2003; am. Acts 2005, 79th Leg., ch. 730 (H.B. 2257), § 1, effective June 17, 2005; am. Acts 2011, 82nd Leg., ch. 259 (H.B. 1201), § 11, effective September 1, 2011; am. Acts 2011, 82nd Leg., ch. 265 (H.B. 1353), §§ 3, 9, effective September 1, 2011.)

## Sec. 545.3531. Authority of Texas Transportation Commission to Establish Speed Limits on Trans-Texas Corridor [Repealed].

Repealed by Acts 2011, 82nd Leg., ch. 259 (H.B. 1201), § 14(6), effective June 17, 2011.
(Enacted by Acts 2003, 78th Leg., ch. 1325 (H.B. 3588), § 1.02, effective June 21, 2003.)

## Sec. 545.3535. Authority of Texas Transportation Commission to Alter Speed Limits on Certain Roads.

(a) The commissioners court of a county by resolution may request the Texas Transportation Commission to determine and declare a reasonable and safe prima facie speed limit that is lower than a speed limit established by Section 545.352 on any part of a farm-to-market or a ranch-to-market road of the highway system that is located in that county and is without improved shoulders.

(b) The commission shall give consideration to local public opinion and may determine and declare a lower speed limit on any part of the road without an engineering and traffic investigation, but the commission must use sound and generally accepted traffic engineering practices in determining and declaring the lower speed limit.

(c) The commission by rule shall establish standards for determining lower speed limits within a set range.

(Enacted by Acts 1997, 75th Leg., ch. 1171 (S.B. 370), § 1.45, effective September 1, 1997; am. Acts 1999, 76th Leg., ch. 1346 (H.B. 676), § 2, effective September 1, 1999.)

## Sec. 545.354. Authority of Regional Tollway Authorities to Alter Speed Limits on Turnpike Projects.

(a) (1) In this section, "authority" means a regional tollway authority governed by Chapter 366.

(2) If an authority determines from the results of an engineering and traffic investigation that a prima facie speed limit described in this subchapter is unreasonable or unsafe on a part of a turnpike constructed and maintained by the authority, the authority by order recorded in its minutes shall determine and declare a reasonable and safe prima facie speed limit for vehicles or classes of vehicles on the turnpike.

(b) In determining whether a prima facie speed limit on a part of a turnpike constructed and maintained by the authority is reasonable or safe, the authority shall consider the width and condition of the pavement, the usual traffic on the turnpike, and other circumstances.

(c) A prima facie speed limit that is declared by the authority in accordance with this section is effective when the authority erects signs giving notice of the new limit. A new limit that is adopted for a turnpike project constructed and maintained by the authority in accordance with this section is effective at all times or at other times as determined.

(d) The authority's power to alter prima facie speed limits is effective and exclusive on any part of a turnpike project constructed and maintained by the authority inside and outside the limits of a municipality, including a home-rule municipality.

(e) The authority may not:

(1) alter the general rule established by Section 545.351(a); or

(2) establish a speed limit of more than 75 miles per hour.

(f) The authority, in conducting the engineering and traffic investigation specified by Subsec-

tion (a), shall follow the procedure for establishing speed zones adopted by the Texas Department of Transportation.

(Enacted by Acts 1995, 74th Leg., ch. 165 (S.B. 971), § 1, effective September 1, 1995; am. Acts 1999, 76th Leg., ch. 576 (S.B. 537), § 3, effective September 1, 1999; am. Acts 2001, 77th Leg., ch. 920 (S.B. 409), § 18, effective June 14, 2001; am. Acts 2003, 78th Leg., ch. 312 (H.B. 3184), §§ 74, 75, effective June 18, 2003; am. Acts 2003, 78th Leg., ch. 1325 (H.B. 3588), §§ 15.71, 15.72, effective June 21, 2003; am. Acts 2011, 82nd Leg., ch. 265 (H.B. 1353), § 4, effective September 1, 2011.)

## Sec. 545.355. Authority of County Commissioners Court to Alter Speed Limits.

(a) The commissioners court of a county, for a county road or highway outside the limits of the right-of-way of an officially designated or marked highway or road of the state highway system and outside a municipality, has the same authority to increase prima facie speed limits from the results of an engineering and traffic investigation as the Texas Transportation Commission on an officially designated or marked highway of the state highway system.

(b) The commissioners court of a county may declare a lower speed limit of not less than:

(1) 30 miles per hour on a county road or highway to which this section applies, if the commissioners court determines that the prima facie speed limit on the road or highway is unreasonable or unsafe; or

(2) 20 miles per hour in a residence district, unless the roadway has been designated as a major thoroughfare by a city planning commission.

(c) The commissioners court may not modify the rule established by Section 545.351(a) or establish a speed limit of more than 60 miles per hour.

(d) The commissioners court may modify a prima facie speed limit in accordance with this section only by an order entered on its records.

(e) The commissioners court of a county with a population of more than 2.8 million may establish from the results of an engineering and traffic investigation a speed limit of not more than 75 miles per hour on any part of a highway of that county that is a limited-access or controlled-access highway, regardless of the location of the part of the highway.

(Enacted by Acts 1995, 74th Leg., ch. 165 (S.B. 971), § 1, effective September 1, 1995; am. Acts 1997, 75th Leg., ch. 58 (S.B. 161), § 1, effective May 9, 1997; am. Acts 1997, 75th Leg., ch. 833 (H.B. 130), § 1, effective June 18, 1997; am. Acts 2003, 78th Leg., ch. 852 (S.B. 540), § 1, effective June 20, 2003; am. Acts 2011, 82nd Leg., ch. 265 (H.B. 1353), § 5, effective September 1, 2011.)

## Sec. 545.356. Authority of Municipality to Alter Speed Limits.

(a) The governing body of a municipality, for a highway or part of a highway in the municipality, including a highway of the state highway system, has the same authority to alter by ordinance prima facie speed limits from the results of an engineering and traffic investigation as the Texas Transportation Commission on an officially designated or marked highway of the state highway system. The governing body of a municipality may not modify the rule established by Section 545.351(a) or establish a speed limit of more than 75 miles per hour.

(b) The governing body of a municipality, for a highway or part of a highway in the municipality, including a highway of the state highway system, has the same authority to alter prima facie speed limits from the results of an engineering and traffic investigation as the commission for an officially designated or marked highway of the state highway system, when the highway or part of the highway is under repair, construction, or maintenance. A municipality may not modify the rule established by Section 545.351(a) or establish a speed limit of more than 75 miles per hour.

(b-1) Except as provided by Subsection (b-3), the governing body of a municipality, for a highway or a part of a highway in the municipality that is not an officially designated or marked highway or road of the state highway system, may declare a lower speed limit of not less than 25 miles per hour, if the governing body determines that the prima facie speed limit on the highway is unreasonable or unsafe.

(b-2) Subsection (b-1) applies only to a two-lane, undivided highway or part of a highway.

(b-3) The governing body of a municipality with a population of 2,000 or less, for a highway or a part of a highway in the municipality that is a one-lane highway used for two-way access and that is not an officially designated or marked highway or road of the state highway system, may declare a lower speed limit of not less than 10 miles per hour, if the governing body determines that the prima facie speed limit on the highway is unreasonable or unsafe.

(c) A prima facie speed limit that is altered by the governing body of a municipality under Subsection (b), (b-1), or (b-3) is effective when the governing body erects signs giving notice of the new limit and at all times or at other times as determined.

(d) The governing body of a municipality that declares a lower speed limit on a highway or part of a highway under Subsection (b-1) or (b-3), not later than February 1 of each year, shall publish on its Internet website and submit to the department a report that compares for each of the two previous calendar years:

(1) the number of traffic citations issued by peace officers of the municipality and the alleged speed of the vehicles, for speed limit violations on the highway or part of the highway;

(2) the number of warning citations issued by peace officers of the municipality on the highway or part of the highway; and

(3) the number of vehicular accidents that resulted in injury or death and were attributable to speed limit violations on the highway or part of the highway.

(Enacted by Acts 1995, 74th Leg., ch. 165 (S.B. 971), § 1, effective September 1, 1995; am. Acts 2005, 79th Leg., ch. 166 (H.B. 87), § 1, effective May 27, 2005; am. Acts 2009, 81st Leg., ch. 1144 (H.B. 2682), § 1, effective June 19, 2009; am. Acts 2011, 82nd Leg., ch. 265 (H.B. 1353), § 6, effective June 17, 2011; am. Acts 2011, 82nd Leg., ch. 1016 (H.B. 2596), § 1, effective June 17, 2011.)

## Sec. 545.3561. Authority of Municipality or County to Temporarily Lower Speed Limit at Vehicular Accident Reconstruction Site.

(a) The governing body of a municipality by ordinance may give a designated official with transportation engineering experience establishing speed limits discretion to temporarily lower a prima facie speed limit for a highway or part of a highway in the municipality, including a highway of the state highway system, at the site of an investigation using vehicular accident reconstruction.

(b) A county commissioners court by order may give a designated official with transportation engineering experience establishing speed limits discretion to temporarily lower prima facie speed limits for a county road or highway outside the

Transportation

boundaries of a municipality at the site of an investigation using vehicular accident reconstruction. The authority granted under this subsection does not include a road or highway in the state highway system.

(c) The Texas Department of Transportation shall develop safety guidelines for the use of vehicular accident reconstruction in investigations. A municipality, county, or designated official shall comply with the guidelines.

(d) A designated official may temporarily lower prima facie speed limits without the approval of or permission from the Texas Department of Transportation. A designated official who intends to temporarily lower a prima facie speed limit at the site of an investigation using vehicular accident reconstruction shall, at least 48 hours before temporary speed limit signs are posted for the vehicular accident reconstruction site, provide to the Texas Department of Transportation notice that includes:

(1) the date and time of the accident reconstruction;

(2) the location of the accident reconstruction site;

(3) the entities involved at the site;

(4) the general size of the area affected by the site; and

(5) an estimate of how long the site will be used for the accident reconstruction.

(e) A temporary speed limit established under this section:

(1) is a prima facie prudent and reasonable speed limit enforceable in the same manner as other prima facie speed limits established under other provisions of this subchapter; and

(2) supersedes any other established speed limit that would permit a person to operate a motor vehicle at a higher rate of speed.

(f) A designated official who temporarily lowers a speed limit shall:

(1) place and maintain at the vehicular accident reconstruction site temporary speed limit signs that conform to the manual and specifications adopted under Section 544.001;

(2) temporarily conceal all other signs on the highway segment affected by the vehicular accident reconstruction site that give notice of a speed limit that would permit a person to operate a motor vehicle at a higher rate of speed; and

(3) remove all temporary speed limit signs placed under Subdivision (1) and concealments of other signs placed under Subdivision (2) when the official finds that the vehicular acci-

dent reconstruction is complete and all equipment is removed from the vehicular accident reconstruction site.

(g) A temporary speed limit established under this section is effective when a designated official places temporary speed limit signs and conceals other signs that would permit a person to operate a motor vehicle at a higher rate of speed as required under Subsection (f).

(h) A temporary speed limit established under this section is effective until the designated official under Subsection (a) or (b):

(1) finds that the vehicular accident reconstruction is complete; and

(2) removes all temporary signs, concealments, and equipment used at the vehicular accident reconstruction site.

(i) If a designated official does not comply with the requirements of Subsection (f)(3) for a vehicular accident reconstruction on a state highway associated with the reconstruction, the Texas Department of Transportation may remove signs and concealments.

(Enacted by Acts 2011, 82nd Leg., ch. 216 (H.B. 109), § 2, effective September 1, 2011.)

### Sec. 545.357. Public Hearing to Consider Speed Limits Where Certain Schools Are Located.

(a) The governing body of a municipality in which a public or private elementary or secondary school or an institution of higher education as defined by Section 61.003(8) or (15), Education Code, is located shall on request hold a public hearing at least once each calendar year to consider prima facie speed limits on a highway in the municipality, including a highway of the state highway system, near the school or institution of higher education.

(b) If a county road outside the state highway system is located within 500 feet of a public or private elementary or secondary school or an institution of higher education that is not in a municipality, the commissioners court of the county on request shall hold a public hearing at least once each calendar year to consider the prima facie speed limit on the road near the school or institution of higher education.

(c) A municipal governing body or commissioners court on request may hold one public hearing for all public and private elementary and secondary schools and institutions of higher education in its jurisdiction.

(d) The Texas Transportation Commission, on request, shall hold a public hearing at least once each calendar year to consider prima facie speed limits on highways in the state highway system that are near public or private elementary or secondary schools or institutions of higher education.

(Enacted by Acts 1995, 74th Leg., ch. 165 (S.B. 971), § 1, effective September 1, 1995; am. Acts 1997, 75th Leg., ch. 350 (S.B. 1016), § 1, effective September 1, 1997.)

## Sec. 545.358. Authority of Commanding Officer of United States Military Reservation to Alter Speed Limits.

The commanding officer of a United States military reservation, for a highway or part of a highway in the military reservation, including a highway of the state highway system, has the same authority by order to alter prima facie speed limits from the results of an engineering and traffic investigation as the Texas Transportation Commission for an officially designated or marked highway of the state highway system. A commanding officer may not modify the rule established by Section 545.351(a) or establish a speed limit of more than 75 miles per hour.

(Enacted by Acts 1995, 74th Leg., ch. 165 (S.B. 971), § 1, effective September 1, 1995; am. Acts 2011, 82nd Leg., ch. 265 (H.B. 1353), § 7, effective September 1, 2011.)

## Sec. 545.359. Conflicting Designated Speed Limits.

An order of the Texas Transportation Commission declaring a speed limit on a part of a designated or marked route of the state highway system made under Section 545.353 or 545.362 supersedes any conflicting designated speed established under Sections 545.356 and 545.358.

(Enacted by Acts 1995, 74th Leg., ch. 165 (S.B. 971), § 1, effective September 1, 1995.)

## Sec. 545.360. Duty of Texas Transportation Commission and State Board of Education to Provide Information and Assistance.

The chairman of the Texas Transportation Commission and the chairman of the State Board of Education shall provide assistance and information relevant to consideration of speed limits to commissioners courts, municipal governing bodies, and other interested persons.

(Enacted by Acts 1995, 74th Leg., ch. 165 (S.B. 971), § 1, effective September 1, 1995.)

## Sec. 545.361. Special Speed Limitations.

(a) An operator of a motor-driven cycle may not drive at a speed of more than 35 miles per hour during the time specified by Section 547.302(a) unless the cycle is equipped with a headlamp or lamps that reveal a person or vehicle 300 feet ahead.

(b) An operator of a vehicle equipped with solid rubber or cushion tires may not drive at a speed of more than 10 miles per hour.

(c) An operator driving over a bridge or other elevated structure that is a part of a highway may not drive at a speed of more than the maximum speed that can be maintained with safety to the bridge or structure, when signs are posted as provided by this section.

(d) An operator of self-propelled machinery designed or adapted for applying plant food materials or agricultural chemicals and not designed or adapted for the sole purpose of transporting the materials or chemicals may not drive at a speed of more than 30 miles per hour unless the machinery is registered under Chapter 502.

(e) The Texas Transportation Commission, for a state highway, the Texas Turnpike Authority, for any part of a turnpike constructed and maintained by the authority, and a local authority for a highway under the jurisdiction of the local authority, may investigate a bridge or other elevated structure that is a part of a highway. If after conducting the investigation the commission, turnpike authority, or local authority finds that the structure cannot safely withstand vehicles traveling at a speed otherwise permissible under this subtitle, the commission, turnpike authority, or local authority shall:

(1) determine and declare the maximum speed of vehicles that the structure can safely withstand; and

(2) post and maintain signs before each end of the structure stating the maximum speed.

(Enacted by Acts 1995, 74th Leg., ch. 165 (S.B. 971), § 1, effective September 1, 1995.)

## Sec. 545.362. Temporary Speed Limits.

(a) Subject to Subsection (c), the Texas Transportation Commission may enter an order establishing prima facie speed limits of not more than 75 miles per hour applicable to all highways, including a turnpike under the authority of the Texas Turnpike Authority or a highway under the control of a municipality or county. An order entered under this section does not have the effect of increasing a speed limit on any highway.

(b) The limits established under this section:

(1) are prima facie prudent and reasonable speed limits enforceable in the same manner as prima facie limits established under other provisions of this subchapter; and

(2) supersede any other established speed limit that would permit a person to operate a motor vehicle at a higher rate of speed.

(c) An order may be issued under Subsection (a) only if the commission finds and states in the order that:

(1) a severe shortage of motor fuel or other petroleum product exists, the shortage was caused by war, national emergency, or other circumstances, and a reduction of speed limits will foster conservation and safety; or

(2) the failure to alter state speed limits will prevent the state from receiving money from the United States for highway purposes.

(d) Unless a specific speed limit is required by federal law or directive under threat of loss of highway money of the United States, the commission may not set prima facie speed limits under this section of all vehicles at less than 60 miles per hour, except on a divided highway of at least four lanes, for which the commission may not set prima facie speed limits of all vehicles at less than 65 miles per hour.

(e) Before the commission may enter an order establishing a prima facie speed limit, it must hold a public hearing preceded by the publication in at least three newspapers of general circulation in the state of a notice of the date, time, and place of the hearing and of the action proposed to be taken. The notice must be published at least 12 days before the date of the hearing. At the hearing, all interested persons may present oral or written testimony regarding the proposed order.

(f) If the commission enters an order under this section, it shall file the order in the office of the governor. The governor shall then make an independent finding of fact and determine the existence of the facts in Subsection (c). Before the 13th day after the date the order is filed in the governor's office, the governor shall conclude the finding of fact, issue a proclamation stating whether the necessary facts exist to support the issuance of the commission's order, and file copies of the order and the proclamation in the office of the secretary of state.

(g) If the governor's proclamation states that the facts necessary to support the issuance of the commission's order exist, the order takes effect according to Subsection (h). Otherwise, the order has no effect.

(h) In an order issued under this section, the commission may specify the date the order takes effect, but that date may not be sooner than the eighth day after the date the order is filed with the governor. If the order does not have an effective date, it takes effect on the 21st day after the date it is filed with the governor. Unless the order by its own terms expires earlier, it remains in effect until a subsequent order adopted by the procedure prescribed by this section amends or repeals it, except that an order adopted under this section expires when this section expires. The procedure for repealing an order is the same as for adopting an order, except that the commission and the governor must find that the facts required to support the issuance of an order under Subsection (c) no longer exist.

(i) If an order is adopted in accordance with this section, the commission and all governmental authorities responsible for the maintenance of highway speed limit signs shall take appropriate action to conceal or remove all signs that give notice of a speed limit of more than the one contained in the order and to erect appropriate signs. All governmental entities responsible for administering traffic safety programs and enforcing traffic laws shall use all available resources to notify the public of the effect of the order. To accomplish this purpose, the governmental entities shall request the cooperation of all news media in the state.

(j) A change in speed limits under this section is effective until the commission makes a finding that the conditions in Subsection (c) require or authorize an additional change in those speed limits or in the highway or sections of highway to which those speed limits apply.

(k) This section expires when the national maximum speed limits are repealed.
(Enacted by Acts 1995, 74th Leg., ch. 165 (S.B. 971), § 1, effective September 1, 1995; am. Acts 2011, 82nd Leg., ch. 265 (H.B. 1353), § 8, effective September 1, 2011.)

## Sec. 545.3625. Confidentiality of Violation Information: Fuel Conservation Speed Limit.

(a) If a person violates a maximum prima facie speed limit imposed under Section 545.362, as that law existed immediately before December 8, 1995, and the person was not traveling at a speed, as alleged in the citation, if not contested by the person, or, if contested by the person, as alleged in the complaint and found by the court, that is greater than the maximum prima facie speed limit for the location that has been established under this chapter, other than under Section 545.362, information in the custody of the department concerning the violation is confidential.

(b) The department may not release the information to any person or to another state governmental entity.

(Enacted by Acts 1997, 75th Leg., ch. 165 (S.B. 898), § 30.112(a), effective September 1, 1997.)

### Sec. 545.363. Minimum Speed Regulations.

(a) An operator may not drive so slowly as to impede the normal and reasonable movement of traffic, except when reduced speed is necessary for safe operation or in compliance with law.

(b) When the Texas Transportation Commission, the Texas Turnpike Authority, the commissioners court of a county, or the governing body of a municipality, within the jurisdiction of each, as applicable, as specified in Sections 545.353—545.357, determines from the results of an engineering and traffic investigation that slow speeds on a part of a highway consistently impede the normal and reasonable movement of traffic, the commission, authority, county commissioners court, or governing body may determine and declare a minimum speed limit on the highway.

(c) If appropriate signs are erected giving notice of a minimum speed limit adopted under this section, an operator may not drive a vehicle more slowly than that limit except as necessary for safe operation or in compliance with law.

(Enacted by Acts 1995, 74th Leg., ch. 165 (S.B. 971), § 1, effective September 1, 1995.)

### Sec. 545.364. Speed Limits on Beaches [Repealed].

Repealed by Acts 1999, 76th Leg., ch. 1346 (H.B. 676), § 3, effective September 1, 1999. (Enacted by Acts 1995, 74th Leg., ch. 165 (S.B. 971), § 1, effective September 1, 1995.)

### Sec. 545.365. Speed Limit Exception for Emergencies; Municipal Regulation.

(a) The regulation of the speed of a vehicle under this subchapter does not apply to:

(1) an authorized emergency vehicle responding to a call;

(2) a police patrol; or

(3) a physician or ambulance responding to an emergency call.

(b) A municipality by ordinance may regulate the speed of:

(1) an ambulance;

(2) an emergency medical services vehicle; or

(3) an authorized vehicle operated by a blood or tissue bank.

(Enacted by Acts 1995, 74th Leg., ch. 165 (S.B. 971), § 1, effective September 1, 1995.)

### Secs. 545.366 to 545.400 [Reserved for expansion].

## SUBCHAPTER I
## MISCELLANEOUS RULES

### Sec. 545.401. Reckless Driving; Offense.

(a) A person commits an offense if the person drives a vehicle in wilful or wanton disregard for the safety of persons or property.

(b) An offense under this section is a misdemeanor punishable by:

(1) a fine not to exceed $200;

(2) confinement in county jail for not more than 30 days; or

(3) both the fine and the confinement.

(c) Notwithstanding Section 542.001, this section applies to:

(1) a private access way or parking area provided for a client or patron by a business, other than a private residential property or the property of a garage or parking lot for which a charge is made for the storing or parking of motor vehicles; and

(2) a highway or other public place.

(d) Notwithstanding Section 542.004, this section applies to a person, a team, or motor vehicles and other equipment engaged in work on a highway surface.

(Enacted by Acts 1995, 74th Leg., ch. 165 (S.B. 971), § 1, effective September 1, 1995.)

### Sec. 545.402. Moving a Parked Vehicle.

An operator may not begin movement of a stopped, standing, or parked vehicle unless the movement can be made safely.

(Enacted by Acts 1995, 74th Leg., ch. 165 (S.B. 971), § 1, effective September 1, 1995.)

## Sec. 545.403. Driving Through Safety Zone.

An operator may not drive through or in a safety zone.

(Enacted by Acts 1995, 74th Leg., ch. 165 (S.B. 971), § 1, effective September 1, 1995.)

## Sec. 545.404. Unattended Motor Vehicle.

An operator may not leave the vehicle unattended without:

(1) stopping the engine;

(2) locking the ignition;

(3) removing the key from the ignition;

(4) setting the parking brake effectively; and

(5) if standing on a grade, turning the front wheels to the curb or side of the highway.

(Enacted by Acts 1995, 74th Leg., ch. 165 (S.B. 971), § 1, effective September 1, 1995.)

## Sec. 545.405. Driving on Mountain Highway.

An operator moving through a defile or canyon or on a mountain highway shall:

(1) hold the vehicle under control and as near the right-hand edge of the highway as possible; and

(2) on approaching a curve that obstructs the view of the highway for 200 feet, give warning with the horn of the motor vehicle.

(Enacted by Acts 1995, 74th Leg., ch. 165 (S.B. 971), § 1, effective September 1, 1995.)

## Sec. 545.406. Coasting.

(a) An operator moving on a downgrade may not coast with the gears or transmission of the vehicle in neutral.

(b) An operator of a truck, tractor, or bus moving on a downgrade may not coast with the clutch disengaged.

(Enacted by Acts 1995, 74th Leg., ch. 165 (S.B. 971), § 1, effective September 1, 1995.)

## Sec. 545.407. Following or Obstructing Fire Apparatus or Ambulance.

(a) An operator, unless on official business, may not follow closer than 500 feet a fire apparatus responding to a fire alarm or drive into or park the vehicle in the block where the fire apparatus has stopped to answer a fire alarm.

(b) An operator may not:

(1) follow closer than 500 feet an ambulance that is flashing red lights unless the operator is on official business; or

(2) drive or park the vehicle where an ambulance has been summoned for an emergency call in a manner intended to interfere with the arrival or departure of the ambulance.

(Enacted by Acts 1995, 74th Leg., ch. 165 (S.B. 971), § 1, effective September 1, 1995.)

## Sec. 545.408. Crossing Fire Hose.

An operator may not, without the consent of the fire department official in command, drive over an unprotected hose of a fire department if the hose is on a street or private driveway and is intended for use at a fire or alarm of fire.

(Enacted by Acts 1995, 74th Leg., ch. 165 (S.B. 971), § 1, effective September 1, 1995.)

## Sec. 545.409. Drawbars and Trailer Hitches; Saddle-Mount Towing.

(a) The drawbar or other connection between a vehicle drawing another vehicle and the drawn vehicle:

(1) must be strong enough to pull all weight drawn; and

(2) may not exceed 15 feet between the vehicles except for a connection between two vehicles transporting poles, pipe, machinery, or other objects of structural nature that cannot readily be dismembered.

(b) An operator drawing another vehicle and using a chain, rope, or cable to connect the vehicles shall display on the connection a white flag or cloth not less than 12 inches square.

(c) A motor vehicle may not draw more than three motor vehicles attached to it by the triple saddle-mount method. In this subsection, "triple saddle-mount method" means the mounting of the front wheels of trailing vehicles on the bed of another vehicle while leaving the rear wheels only of the trailing vehicles in contact with the roadway.

(Enacted by Acts 1995, 74th Leg., ch. 165 (S.B. 971), § 1, effective September 1, 1995.)

## Sec. 545.410. Towing Safety Chains.

(a) An operator of a passenger car or light truck may not draw a trailer, semitrailer, house trailer, or another motor vehicle unless safety chains of a type approved by the department are attached in a manner approved by the department from the trailer, semitrailer, house trailer, or drawn motor vehicle to the drawing vehicle. This subsection does not apply to the drawing of a trailer or semitrailer used for agricultural purposes.

(b) The department shall adopt rules prescribing the type of safety chains required to be used according to the weight of the trailer, semitrailer, house trailer, or motor vehicle being drawn. The rules shall:

(1) require safety chains to be strong enough to maintain the connection between the trailer, semitrailer, house trailer, or drawn motor vehicle and the drawing vehicle; and

(2) show the proper method to attach safety chains between the trailer, semitrailer, house trailer, or drawn motor vehicle and the drawing vehicle.

(c) Subsection (b) does not apply to trailers, semitrailers, or house trailers that are equipped with safety chains installed by the original manufacturer before the effective date of the rules.

(d) This section does not apply to a trailer, semitrailer, house trailer, or drawn motor vehicle that is operated in compliance with the federal motor carrier safety regulations.

(e) In this section, "safety chains" means flexible tension members connected from the front of a drawn vehicle to the rear of the drawing vehicle to maintain connection between the vehicles if the primary connecting system fails. (Enacted by Acts 1995, 74th Leg., ch. 165 (S.B. 971), § 1, effective September 1, 1995; am. Acts 1997, 75th Leg., ch. 165 (S.B. 898), § 30.113(a), effective September 1, 1997; am. Acts 1999, 76th Leg., ch. 1357 (H.B. 932), § 1, effective September 1, 1999.)

### Sec. 545.411. Use of Rest Area: Offense.

(a) A person commits an offense if the person remains at a rest area for longer than 24 hours or erects a tent, shelter, booth, or structure at the rest area and the person:

(1) has notice while conducting the activity that the activity is prohibited; or

(2) receives notice that the activity is prohibited but does not depart or remove the structure within eight hours after receiving notice.

(b) For purposes of this section, a person:

(1) has notice if a sign stating the prohibited activity and penalty is posted on the premises; or

(2) receives notice if a peace officer orally communicates to the person the prohibited activity and penalty for the offense.

(c) It is an exception to Subsection (a) if a nonprofit organization erects a temporary structure at a rest area to provide food services, food,

or beverages to travelers and the Texas Department of Transportation:

(1) finds that the services would constitute a public service for the benefit of the traveling public; and

(2) issues a permit to the organization.

(d) In this section, "rest area" means public real property designated as a rest area, comfort station, picnic area, roadside park, or scenic overlook by the Texas Department of Transportation. (Enacted by Acts 1995, 74th Leg., ch. 165 (S.B. 971), § 1, effective September 1, 1995.)

### Sec. 545.412. Child Passenger Safety Seat Systems; Offense.

(a) A person commits an offense if the person operates a passenger vehicle, transports a child who is younger than eight years of age, unless the child is taller than four feet, nine inches, and does not keep the child secured during the operation of the vehicle in a child passenger safety seat system according to the instructions of the manufacturer of the safety seat system.

(b) An offense under this section is a misdemeanor punishable by a fine of not more than $25 for the first offense and not more than $250 for a second or subsequent offense.

(b-1) **[2 Versions: Effective until September 28, 2011]** In addition to all other fees and court costs, a person shall pay 15 cents as a court cost on conviction of an offense under this section. Court costs due under this section shall be collected in the same manner as other fees, fines, or costs are collected in the case. The clerk at least monthly shall send the court costs collected under this section to the comptroller for deposit in a separate account in the general revenue fund that may be appropriated only to the Texas Department of Transportation and used to purchase child passenger safety seat systems and distribute them to low-income families.

(b-1) **[2 Versions: Effective September 28, 2011]** [Repealed by Acts 2011, 82nd Leg., 1st C.S, ch. xxx (S.B. 1), § 69.01(1), effective September 28, 2011.]

(c) It is a defense to prosecution under this section that the person was operating the vehicle in an emergency or for a law enforcement purpose.

(d) [Repealed by Acts 2003, 78th Leg., ch. 204 (H.B. 4), § 8.01, effective September 1, 2003.]

(e) This section does not apply to a person:

(1) operating a vehicle transporting passengers for hire, excluding third-party transport

service providers when transporting clients pursuant to a contract to provide nonemergency Medicaid transportation; or

(2) transporting a child in a vehicle in which all seating positions equipped with child passenger safety seat systems or safety belts are occupied.

(f) In this section:

(1) "Child passenger safety seat system" means an infant or child passenger restraint system that meets the federal standards for crash-tested restraint systems as set by the National Highway Traffic Safety Administration.

(2) "Passenger vehicle" means a passenger car, light truck, sport utility vehicle, passenger van designed to transport 15 or fewer passengers, including the driver, truck, or truck tractor.

(3) "Safety belt" means a lap belt and any shoulder straps included as original equipment on or added to a vehicle.

(4) "Secured," in connection with use of a safety belt, means using the lap belt and any shoulder straps according to the instructions of:

(A) the manufacturer of the vehicle, if the safety belt is original equipment; or

(B) the manufacturer of the safety belt, if the safety belt has been added to the vehicle.

(g) A judge, acting under Article 45.0511, Code of Criminal Procedure, who elects to defer further proceedings and to place a defendant accused of a violation of this section on probation under that article, in lieu of requiring the defendant to complete a driving safety course approved by the Texas Education Agency, shall require the defendant to attend and present proof that the defendant has successfully completed a specialized driving safety course approved by the Texas Education Agency under the Texas Driver and Traffic Safety Education Act (Article 4413(29c), Vernon's Texas Civil Statutes) that includes four hours of instruction that encourages the use of child passenger safety seat systems and the wearing of seat belts and emphasizes:

(1) the effectiveness of child passenger safety seat systems and seat belts in reducing the harm to children being transported in motor vehicles; and

(2) the requirements of this section and the penalty for noncompliance.

(h) Notwithstanding Section 542.402(a), a municipality or county, at the end of the municipality's or county's fiscal year, shall send to the comptroller an amount equal to 50 percent of the fines collected by the municipality or the county for violations of this section. The comptroller shall deposit the amount received to the credit of the tertiary care fund for use by trauma centers. (Enacted by Acts 1995, 74th Leg., ch. 165 (S.B. 971), § 1, effective September 1, 1995; am. Acts 1997, 75th Leg., ch. 165 (S.B. 898), § 30.114(a), effective September 1, 1997; am. Acts 2001, 77th Leg., ch. 618 (S.B. 1367), § 1, effective September 1, 2001; am. Acts 2001, 77th Leg., ch. 910 (S.B. 113), § 1, effective September 1, 2001; am. Acts 2001, 77th Leg., ch. 1042 (H.B. 1739), § 1, effective September 1, 2001; am. Acts 2003, 78th Leg., ch. 204 (H.B. 4), § 8.01, effective September 1, 2003; am. Acts 2005, 79th Leg., ch. 913 (H.B. 183), §§ 1, 2, effective September 1, 2005; am. Acts 2009, 81st Leg., ch. 255 (S.B. 61), § 1, effective September 1, 2009; am. Acts 2009, 81st Leg., ch. 1257 (H.B. 537), § 1, effective September 1, 2009; am. Acts 2011, 82nd Leg., 1st C.S., ch. xxx (S.B. 1), § 69.01, effective September 28, 2011.)

## Sec. 545.4121.   Defense; Possession of Child Passenger Safety Seat System.

(a) This section applies to an offense committed under Section 545.412.

(b) It is a defense to prosecution of an offense to which this section applies that the defendant provides to the court evidence satisfactory to the court that the defendant possesses an appropriate child passenger safety seat system for each child required to be secured in a child passenger safety seat system under Section 545.412(a). (Enacted by Acts 2005, 79th Leg., ch. 913 (H.B. 183), § 3, effective September 1, 2005.)

## Sec. 545.413.   Safety Belts; Offense.

(a) A person commits an offense if:

(1) the person:

(A) is at least 15 years of age;

(B) is riding in a passenger vehicle while the vehicle is being operated;

(C) is occupying a seat that is equipped with a safety belt; and

(D) is not secured by a safety belt; or

(2) as the operator of a school bus equipped with a safety belt for the operator's seat, the person is not secured by the safety belt.

(b) A person commits an offense if the person:

(1) operates a passenger vehicle that is equipped with safety belts; and

(2) allows a child who is younger than 17 years of age and who is not required to be

secured in a child passenger safety seat system under Section 545.412(a) to ride in the vehicle without requiring the child to be secured by a safety belt, provided the child is occupying a seat that is equipped with a safety belt.

(b-1) A person commits an offense if the person allows a child who is younger than 17 years of age and who is not required to be secured in a child passenger safety seat system under Section 545.412(a) to ride in a passenger van designed to transport 15 or fewer passengers, including the driver, without securing the child individually by a safety belt, if the child is occupying a seat that is equipped with a safety belt.

(c) A passenger vehicle or a seat in a passenger vehicle is considered to be equipped with a safety belt if the vehicle is required under Section 547.601 to be equipped with safety belts.

(d) An offense under Subsection (a) is a misdemeanor punishable by a fine of not less than $25 or more than $50. An offense under Subsection (b) is a misdemeanor punishable by a fine of not less than $100 or more than $200.

(e) It is a defense to prosecution under this section that:

(1) the person possesses a written statement from a licensed physician stating that for a medical reason the person should not wear a safety belt;

(2) the person presents to the court, not later than the 10th day after the date of the offense, a statement from a licensed physician stating that for a medical reason the person should not wear a safety belt;

(3) the person is employed by the United States Postal Service and performing a duty for that agency that requires the operator to service postal boxes from a vehicle or that requires frequent entry into and exit from a vehicle;

(4) the person is engaged in the actual delivery of newspapers from a vehicle or is performing newspaper delivery duties that require frequent entry into and exit from a vehicle;

(5) the person is employed by a public or private utility company and is engaged in the reading of meters or performing a similar duty for that company requiring the operator to frequently enter into and exit from a vehicle;

(6) the person is operating a commercial vehicle registered as a farm vehicle under the provisions of Section 502.163 that does not have a gross weight, registered weight, or gross weight rating of 48,000 pounds or more; or

(7) the person is the operator of or a passenger in a vehicle used exclusively to transport solid waste and performing duties that require frequent entry into and exit from the vehicle.

(f) The department shall develop and implement an educational program to encourage the wearing of safety belts and to emphasize:

(1) the effectiveness of safety belts and other restraint devices in reducing the risk of harm to passengers in motor vehicles; and

(2) the requirements of this section and the penalty for noncompliance.

(g) [Repealed by Acts 2003, 78th Leg., ch. 204 (H.B. 4), § 8.01, effective September 1, 2003.]

(h) In this section, "passenger vehicle," "safety belt," and "secured" have the meanings assigned by Section 545.412.

(i) A judge, acting under Article 45.0511, Code of Criminal Procedure, who elects to defer further proceedings and to place a defendant accused of a violation of Subsection (b) on probation under that article, in lieu of requiring the defendant to complete a driving safety course approved by the Texas Education Agency, shall require the defendant to attend and present proof that the defendant has successfully completed a specialized driving safety course approved by the Texas Education Agency under the Texas Driver and Traffic Safety Education Act (Article 4413(29c), Vernon's Texas Civil Statutes) that includes four hours of instruction that encourages the use of child passenger safety seat systems and the wearing of seat belts and emphasizes:

(1) the effectiveness of child passenger safety seat systems and seat belts in reducing the harm to children being transported in motor vehicles; and

(2) the requirements of this section and the penalty for noncompliance.

(j) Notwithstanding Section 542.402(a), a municipality or county, at the end of the municipality's or county's fiscal year, shall send to the comptroller an amount equal to 50 percent of the fines collected by the municipality or the county for violations of Subsection (b) of this section. The comptroller shall deposit the amount received to the credit of the tertiary care fund for use by trauma centers.

(Enacted by Acts 1995, 74th Leg., ch. 165 (S.B. 971), § 1, effective September 1, 1995; am. Acts 1997, 75th Leg., ch. 165 (S.B. 898), § 30.115(a), effective September 1, 1997; am. Acts 1999, 76th Leg., ch. 316 (H.B. 856), § 1, effective September 1, 1999; am. Acts 1999, 76th Leg., ch. 515 (S.B. 60), § 1, effective September 1, 1999; am. Acts 2001, 77th Leg., ch. 618 (S.B. 1367), § 2, effective September 1, 2001; am. Acts 2001, 77th Leg., ch.

Transportation

910 (S.B. 113), § 2, effective September 1, 2001; am. Acts 2001, 77th Leg., ch. 1042 (H.B. 1739), § 2, effective September 1, 2001; am. Acts 2003, 78th Leg., ch. 204 (H.B. 4), § 8.01, effective September 1, 2003; am. Acts 2003, 78th Leg., ch. 431 (H.B. 418), § 1, effective September 1, 2003; am. Acts 2005, 79th Leg., ch. 913 (H.B. 183), § 4, effective September 1, 2005; am. Acts 2007, 80th Leg., ch. 923 (H.B. 3190), § 4, effective September 1, 2007; am. Acts 2009, 81st Leg., ch. 974 (H.B. 3638), § 1, effective September 1, 2009; am. Acts 2009, 81st Leg., ch. 1257 (H.B. 537), § 2, effective September 1, 2009.)

### Sec. 545.414.  Riding in Open Beds; Offense.

(a) A person commits an offense if the person operates an open-bed pickup truck or an open flatbed truck or draws an open flatbed trailer when a child younger than 18 years of age is occupying the bed of the truck or trailer.

(b) An offense under this section is a misdemeanor punishable by a fine of not less than $25 or more than $200.

(c) It is a defense to prosecution under this section that the person was:

(1) operating or towing the vehicle in a parade or in an emergency;

(2) operating the vehicle to transport farmworkers from one field to another field on a farm-to-market road, ranch-to-market road, or county road outside a municipality;

(3) operating the vehicle on a beach;

(4) operating a vehicle that is the only vehicle owned or operated by the members of a household; or

(5) operating the vehicle in a hayride permitted by the governing body of or a law enforcement agency of each county or municipality in which the hayride will occur.

(d) Compliance or noncompliance with Subsection (a) is not admissible evidence in a civil trial.

(e) In this section, "household" has the meaning assigned by Section 71.005, Family Code.
(Enacted by Acts 1995, 74th Leg., ch. 165 (S.B. 971), § 1, effective September 1, 1995; am. Acts 2001, 77th Leg., ch. 79 (S.B. 399), § 1, effective September 1, 2001.)

### Sec. 545.4145.  Riding in or on Boat or Personal Watercraft Drawn by Vehicle; Offense.

(a) A person commits an offense if the person operates a motor vehicle on a highway or street when a child younger than 18 years of age is occupying a boat or personal watercraft being drawn by the motor vehicle.

(b) It is a defense to prosecution under this section that the person was:

(1) operating the motor vehicle in a parade or in an emergency; or

(2) operating the motor vehicle on a beach.

(c) In this section, "boat" and "personal watercraft" have the meanings assigned by Section 31.003, Parks and Wildlife Code.
(Enacted by Acts 2011, 82nd Leg., ch. 1172 (H.B. 2981), § 1, effective September 1, 2011.)

### Sec. 545.415.  Backing a Vehicle.

(a) An operator may not back the vehicle unless the movement can be made safely and without interference with other traffic.

(b) An operator may not back the vehicle on a shoulder or roadway of a limited-access or controlled-access highway.
(Enacted by Acts 1995, 74th Leg., ch. 165 (S.B. 971), § 1, effective September 1, 1995.)

### Sec. 545.416.  Riding on Motorcycle.

(a) An operator of a motorcycle shall ride on the permanent and regular seat attached to the motorcycle.

(b) An operator may not carry another person on the motorcycle, and a person who is not operating the motorcycle may not ride on the motorcycle, unless the motorcycle is designed to carry more than one person.

(c) If the motorcycle is designed to carry more than one person, a passenger may ride only on the permanent and regular seat, if designed for two persons, or on another seat firmly attached to the motorcycle behind or to the side of the operator.

(d) Except as provided by Subsection (e), an operator may not carry another person on a motorcycle unless the other person is at least five years of age. An offense under this subsection is a misdemeanor punishable by a fine of not less than $100 or more than $200. It is a defense to prosecution under this subsection that the operator was operating the motorcycle in an emergency or for a law enforcement purpose.

(e) Subsection (d) does not prohibit an operator from carrying on a motorcycle a person younger than five years of age who is seated in a sidecar attached to the motorcycle.
(Enacted by Acts 1995, 74th Leg., ch. 165 (S.B. 971), § 1, effective September 1, 1995; am. Acts

2009, 81st Leg., ch. 1257 (H.B. 537), § 3, effective September 1, 2009.)

### Sec. 545.417. Obstruction of Operator's View or Driving Mechanism.

(a) An operator may not drive a vehicle when it is loaded so that, or when the front seat has a number of persons, exceeding three, so that:

(1) the view of the operator to the front or sides of the vehicle is obstructed; or

(2) there is interference with the operator's control over the driving mechanism of the vehicle.

(b) A passenger in a vehicle may not ride in a position that interferes with the operator's view to the front or sides or control over the driving mechanism of the vehicle.

(Enacted by Acts 1995, 74th Leg., ch. 165 (S.B. 971), § 1, effective September 1, 1995.)

### Sec. 545.418. Opening Vehicle Doors.

A person may not:

(1) open the door of a motor vehicle on the side available to moving traffic, unless the door may be opened in reasonable safety without interfering with the movement of other traffic; or

(2) leave a door on the side of a vehicle next to moving traffic open for longer than is necessary to load or unload a passenger.

(Enacted by Acts 1995, 74th Leg., ch. 165 (S.B. 971), § 1, effective September 1, 1995.)

### Sec. 545.419. Riding in House Trailer.

A person may not occupy a house trailer while it is being moved.

(Enacted by Acts 1995, 74th Leg., ch. 165 (S.B. 971), § 1, effective September 1, 1995.)

### Sec. 545.4191. Person Riding in Trailer or Semitrailer Drawn by Truck, Road Tractor, or Truck Tractor.

(a) A person may not operate a truck, road tractor, or truck tractor when another person occupies a trailer or semitrailer being drawn by the truck, road tractor, or truck tractor.

(b) It is a defense to prosecution under this section that:

(1) the person was operating or towing the vehicle:

(A) in a parade or in an emergency;

(B) to transport farmworkers from one field to another field on a farm-to-market road, ranch-to-market road, or county road outside a municipality; or

(C) in a hayride permitted by the governing body of or a law enforcement agency of each county or municipality in which the hayride will occur;

(2) the person operating or towing the vehicle did not know that another person occupied the trailer or semitrailer; or

(3) the person occupying the trailer or semitrailer was in a part of the trailer or semitrailer designed for human habitation.

(c) An offense under this section is a Class B misdemeanor.

(Enacted by Acts 2003, 78th Leg., ch. 641 (H.B. 2096), § 1, effective September 1, 2003.)

### Sec. 545.420. Racing on Highway.

(a) A person may not participate in any manner in:

(1) a race;

(2) a vehicle speed competition or contest;

(3) a drag race or acceleration contest;

(4) a test of physical endurance of the operator of a vehicle; or

(5) in connection with a drag race, an exhibition of vehicle speed or acceleration or to make a vehicle speed record.

(b) In this section:

(1) "Drag race" means the operation of:

(A) two or more vehicles from a point side by side at accelerating speeds in a competitive attempt to outdistance each other; or

(B) one or more vehicles over a common selected course, from the same place to the same place, for the purpose of comparing the relative speeds or power of acceleration of the vehicle or vehicles in a specified distance or time.

(2) "Race" means the use of one or more vehicles in an attempt to:

(A) outgain or outdistance another vehicle or prevent another vehicle from passing;

(B) arrive at a given destination ahead of another vehicle or vehicles; or

(C) test the physical stamina or endurance of an operator over a long-distance driving route.

(c) [Blank]

(d) Except as provided by Subsections (e)—(h), an offense under Subsection (a) is a Class B misdemeanor.

(e) An offense under Subsection (a) is a Class A misdemeanor if it is shown on the trial of the offense that:

(1) the person has previously been convicted one time of an offense under that subsection; or

(2) the person, at the time of the offense:

(A) was operating the vehicle while intoxicated, as defined by Section 49.01, Penal Code; or

(B) was in possession of an open container, as defined by Section 49.031, Penal Code.

(f) An offense under Subsection (a) is a state jail felony if it is shown on the trial of the offense that the person has previously been convicted two times of an offense under that subsection.

(g) An offense under Subsection (a) is a felony of the third degree if it is shown on the trial of the offense that as a result of the offense, an individual suffered bodily injury.

(h) An offense under Subsection (a) is a felony of the second degree if it is shown on the trial of the offense that as a result of the offense, an individual suffered serious bodily injury or death.

(i) This subsection applies only to a motor vehicle used in the commission of an offense under this section that results in an accident with property damage or personal injury. A peace officer shall require the vehicle to be taken to the nearest licensed vehicle storage facility unless the vehicle is seized as evidence, in which case the vehicle may be taken to a storage facility as designated by the peace officer involved. Notwithstanding Article 18.23, Code of Criminal Procedure, the owner of a motor vehicle that is removed or stored under this subsection is liable for all removal and storage fees incurred and is not entitled to take possession of the vehicle until those fees are paid.

(Enacted by Acts 1995, 74th Leg., ch. 165 (S.B. 971), § 1, effective September 1, 1995; am. Acts 2003, 78th Leg., ch. 535 (H.B. 1326), § 1, effective September 1, 2003; am. Acts 2009, 81st Leg., ch. 1258 (H.B. 548), § 1, effective September 1, 2009.)

### Sec. 545.421. Fleeing or Attempting to Elude Police Officer; Offense.

(a) A person commits an offense if the person operates a motor vehicle and wilfully fails or refuses to bring the vehicle to a stop or flees, or attempts to elude, a pursuing police vehicle when given a visual or audible signal to bring the vehicle to a stop.

(b) A signal under this section that is given by a police officer pursuing a vehicle may be by hand, voice, emergency light, or siren. The officer giving the signal must be in uniform and prominently display the officer's badge of office. The officer's vehicle must bear the insignia of a law enforcement agency, regardless of whether the vehicle displays an emergency light.

(c) Except as provided by Subsection (d), an offense under this section is a Class B misdemeanor.

(d) An offense under this section is a Class A misdemeanor if the person, during the commission of the offense, recklessly engages in conduct that places another in imminent danger of serious bodily injury.

(e) A person is presumed to have recklessly engaged in conduct placing another in imminent danger of serious bodily injury under Subsection (d) if the person while intoxicated knowingly operated a motor vehicle during the commission of the offense. In this subsection, "intoxicated" has the meaning assigned by Section 49.01, Penal Code.

(Enacted by Acts 1995, 74th Leg., ch. 165 (S.B. 971), § 1, effective September 1, 1995; am. Acts 2009, 81st Leg., ch. 1280 (H.B. 1831), § 1.21, effective September 1, 2009.)

### Sec. 545.422. Crossing Sidewalk or Hike and Bike Trail.

(a) A person may not drive a motor vehicle on a sidewalk, sidewalk area, or hike and bike trail except on a permanent or authorized temporary driveway.

(b) Subsection (a) does not prohibit the operation of a motor vehicle on a hike and bike trail in connection with maintenance of the trail.

(c) In this section, "hike and bike trail" means a trail designed for the exclusive use of pedestrians, bicyclists, or both.

(Enacted by Acts 1995, 74th Leg., ch. 165 (S.B. 971), § 1, effective September 1, 1995; am. Acts 1997, 75th Leg., ch. 165 (S.B. 898), § 30.116(a), effective September 1, 1997.)

### Sec. 545.423. Crossing Property.

(a) An operator may not cross a sidewalk or drive through a driveway, parking lot, or business or residential entrance without stopping the vehicle.

(b) An operator may not cross or drive in or on a sidewalk, driveway, parking lot, or business or residential entrance at an intersection to turn right or left from one highway to another highway.

(Enacted by Acts 1995, 74th Leg., ch. 165 (S.B. 971), § 1, effective September 1, 1995.)

## Sec. 545.424. Operation of Vehicle by Person Under 18 Years of Age.

(a) A person under 18 years of age may not operate a motor vehicle while using a wireless communications device, except in case of emergency.

(a-1) A person under 18 years of age may not operate a motor vehicle during the 12-month period following issuance of an original Class A, B, or C driver's license to the person:

(1) after midnight and before 5 a.m. unless the operation of the vehicle is necessary for the operator to attend or participate in employment or a school-related activity or because of a medical emergency; or

(2) with more than one passenger in the vehicle under 21 years of age who is not a family member.

(b) A person under 17 years of age who holds a restricted motorcycle license or moped license may not operate a motorcycle or moped while using a wireless communications device, except in case of emergency.

(b-1) A person under 17 years of age who holds a restricted motorcycle license or moped license, during the 12-month period following the issuance of an original motorcycle license or moped license to the person, may not operate a motorcycle or moped after midnight and before 5 a.m. unless:

(1) the person is in sight of the person's parent or guardian; or

(2) the operation of the vehicle is necessary for the operator to attend or participate in employment or a school-related activity or because of a medical emergency.

(c) This section does not apply to:

(1) the holder of a hardship license;

(2) a person operating a motor vehicle while accompanied in the manner required by Section 521.222(d)(2) for the holder of an instruction permit; or

(3) a person licensed by the Federal Communications Commission to operate a wireless communication device or a radio frequency device.

(d) For the purposes of this section, employment includes work on a family farm by a member of the family that owns or operates the farm.

(e) A peace officer may not stop a vehicle or detain the operator of a vehicle for the sole purpose of determining whether the operator of the vehicle has violated this section.

(f) In this section, "wireless communication device" means a handheld or hands-free device that uses commercial mobile service, as defined by 47 U.S.C. Section 332.

(Enacted by Acts 2001, 77th Leg., ch. 1251 (S.B. 577), § 3, effective January 1, 2002; am. Acts 2005, 79th Leg., ch. 357 (S.B. 1257), § 4, effective September 1, 2005; am. Acts 2009, 81st Leg., ch. 1146 (H.B. 2730), § 12.11, effective September 1, 2009; am. Acts 2009, 81st Leg., ch. 1253 (H.B. 339), § 18, effective September 1, 2009; am. Acts 2011, 82nd Leg., ch. 1160 (H.B. 2466), § 4, effective September 1, 2011.)

## Sec. 545.425. Use of Wireless Communication Device; Offense.

(a) In this section:

(1) "Hands-free device" means speakerphone capability or a telephone attachment or other piece of equipment, regardless of whether permanently installed in the motor vehicle, that allows use of the wireless communication device without use of either of the operator's hands.

(2) "Wireless communication device" means a device that uses a commercial mobile service, as defined by 47 U.S.C. Section 332.

(b) Except as provided by Subsection (c), an operator may not use a wireless communication device while operating a motor vehicle within a school crossing zone, as defined by Section 541.302, Transportation Code, unless:

(1) the vehicle is stopped; or

(2) the wireless communication device is used with a hands-free device.

(b-1) Except as provided by Subsection (b-2), a municipality, county, or other political subdivision that enforces this section shall post a sign that complies with the standards described by this subsection at the entrance to each school crossing zone in the municipality, county, or other political subdivision. The department shall adopt standards that:

(1) allow for a sign required to be posted under this subsection to be attached to an existing sign at a minimal cost; and

(2) require that a sign required to be posted under this subsection inform an operator that:

(A) the use of a wireless communication device is prohibited in the school crossing zone; and

(B) the operator is subject to a fine if the operator uses a wireless communication device in the school crossing zone.

(b-2) A municipality, county, or other political subdivision that by ordinance or rule prohibits the use of a wireless communication device while operating a motor vehicle throughout the jurisdiction of the political subdivision is not required to post a sign as required by Subsection (b-1) if the political subdivision:

(1) posts signs that are located at each point at which a state highway, U.S. highway, or interstate highway enters the political subdivision and that state:

(A) that an operator is prohibited from using a wireless communication device while operating a motor vehicle in the political subdivision; and

(B) that the operator is subject to a fine if the operator uses a wireless communication device while operating a motor vehicle in the political subdivision; and

(2) subject to all applicable United States Department of Transportation Federal Highway Administration rules, posts a message that complies with Subdivision (1) on any dynamic message sign operated by the political subdivision located on a state highway, U.S. highway, or interstate highway in the political subdivision.

(b-3) A sign posted under Subsection (b-2)(1) must be readable to an operator traveling at the applicable speed limit.

(b-4) The political subdivision shall pay the costs associated with the posting of signs under Subsection (b-2).

(c) An operator may not use a wireless communication device while operating a passenger bus with a minor passenger on the bus unless the passenger bus is stopped.

(d) It is an affirmative defense to prosecution of an offense under this section that:

(1) the wireless communication device was used to make an emergency call to:

(A) an emergency response service, including a rescue, emergency medical, or hazardous material response service;

(B) a hospital;

(C) a fire department;

(D) a health clinic;

(E) a medical doctor's office;

(F) an individual to administer first aid treatment; or

(G) a police department; or

(2) a sign required by Subsection (b-1) was not posted at the entrance to the school crossing zone at the time of an offense committed in the school crossing zone.

(d-1) The affirmative defense available in Subsection (d)(2) is not available for an offense under

Subsection (b) committed in a school crossing zone located in a municipality, county, or other political subdivision that is in compliance with Subsection (b-2).

(e) This section does not apply to:

(1) an operator of an authorized emergency vehicle using a wireless communication device while acting in an official capacity; or

(2) an operator who is licensed by the Federal Communications Commission while operating a radio frequency device other than a wireless communication device.

(f) Except as provided by Subsection (b-2), this section preempts all local ordinances, rules, or regulations that are inconsistent with specific provisions of this section adopted by a political subdivision of this state relating to the use of a wireless communication device by the operator of a motor vehicle.

(Enacted by Acts 2005, 79th Leg., ch. 357 (S.B. 1257), § 5, effective September 1, 2005; am. Acts 2009, 81st Leg., ch. 1105 (H.B. 55), § 1, effective September 1, 2009; am. Acts 2011, 82nd Leg., ch. 774 (H.B. 1899), § 1, effective September 1, 2011.)

## Sec. 545.426.  Operation of School Bus.

(a) A person may not operate a school bus if:

(1) the door of the school bus is open; or

(2) the number of passengers on the bus is greater than the manufacturer's design capacity for the bus.

(b) An operator of a school bus, while operating the bus, shall prohibit a passenger from:

(1) standing in the bus; or

(2) sitting:

(A) on the floor of the bus; or

(B) in any location on the bus that is not designed as a seat.

(c) The department may adopt rules necessary to administer and enforce this section.

(Enacted by Acts 2007, 80th Leg., ch. 923 (H.B. 3190), § 5, effective September 1, 2007.)

## Sec. 545.427.  Operation of Vehicle with Insufficient Undercarriage Clearance.

(a) An operator may not drive on or cross a railroad grade crossing unless the vehicle being operated has sufficient undercarriage clearance.

(b) An offense under this section is a misdemeanor punishable by a fine of not less than $50 or more than $200.

(Enacted by Acts 2007, 80th Leg., ch. 424 (S.B. 1372), § 12, effective January 1, 2008; am. Acts 2009, 81st Leg., ch. 87 (S.B. 1969), § 27.001(108), effective September 1, 2009 (renumbered from Sec. 545.426).)

# CHAPTER 546
## OPERATION OF AUTHORIZED EMERGENCY VEHICLES AND CERTAIN OTHER VEHICLES

**Subchapter A. Authorized Emergency Vehicles**

## SUBCHAPTER A
## AUTHORIZED EMERGENCY VEHICLES

### Sec. 546.001. Permissible Conduct.

In operating an authorized emergency vehicle the operator may:

(1) park or stand, irrespective of another provision of this subtitle;

(2) proceed past a red or stop signal or stop sign, after slowing as necessary for safe operation;

(3) exceed a maximum speed limit, except as provided by an ordinance adopted under Section 545.365, as long as the operator does not endanger life or property; and

(4) disregard a regulation governing the direction of movement or turning in specified directions.

(Enacted by Acts 1995, 74th Leg., ch. 165 (S.B. 971), § 1, effective September 1, 1995.)

### Sec. 546.002. When Conduct Permissible.

(a) In this section, "police escort" means facilitating the movement of a funeral, oversized or hazardous load, or other traffic disruption for public safety purposes by a peace officer described by Articles 2.12(1)—(4), (8), and (22), Code of Criminal Procedure.

(b) Section 546.001 applies only when the operator is:

(1) responding to an emergency call;

(2) pursuing an actual or suspected violator of the law;

(3) responding to but not returning from a fire alarm;

(4) directing or diverting traffic for public safety purposes; or

(5) conducting a police escort.

(Enacted by Acts 1995, 74th Leg., ch. 165 (S.B. 971), § 1, effective September 1, 1995; am. Acts 2003, 78th Leg., ch. 66 (S.B. 461), § 1, effective May 16, 2003; am. Acts 2005, 79th Leg., ch. 834 (S.B. 866), § 1, effective June 17, 2005.)

### Sec. 546.003. Audible or Visual Signals Required.

Except as provided by Section 546.004, the operator of an authorized emergency vehicle engaging in conduct permitted by Section 546.001 shall use, at the discretion of the operator in accordance with policies of the department or the local government that employs the operator, audible or visual signals that meet the pertinent requirements of Sections 547.305 and 547.702. (Enacted by Acts 1995, 74th Leg., ch. 165 (S.B. 971), § 1, effective September 1, 1995.)

### Sec. 546.004. Exceptions to Signal Requirement.

(a) A volunteer fire fighter who operates a private vehicle as an authorized emergency vehicle may engage in conduct permitted by Section 546.001 only when the fire fighter is using visual signals meeting the pertinent requirements of Sections 547.305 and 547.702.

(b) An authorized emergency vehicle that is operated as a police vehicle is not required to be equipped with or display a red light visible from the front of the vehicle.

(c) A police officer may operate an authorized emergency vehicle for a law enforcement purpose without using the audible or visual signals required by Section 546.003 if the officer is:

(1) responding to an emergency call or pursuing a suspected violator of the law with probable cause to believe that:

(A) knowledge of the presence of the officer will cause the suspect to:

(i) destroy or lose evidence of a suspected felony;

(ii) end a suspected continuing felony before the officer has obtained sufficient evidence to establish grounds for arrest; or

(iii) evade apprehension or identification of the suspect or the suspect's vehicle; or

(B) because of traffic conditions on a multilaned roadway, vehicles moving in response to the audible or visual signals may:

(i) increase the potential for a collision; or

(ii) unreasonably extend the duration of the pursuit; or

(2) complying with a written regulation relating to the use of audible or visible signals adopted by the local government that employs the officer or by the department.

(Enacted by Acts 1995, 74th Leg., ch. 165 (S.B. 971), § 1, effective September 1, 1995.)

### Sec. 546.005.   Duty of Care.

This chapter does not relieve the operator of an authorized emergency vehicle from:

(1) the duty to operate the vehicle with appropriate regard for the safety of all persons; or

(2) the consequences of reckless disregard for the safety of others.

(Enacted by Acts 1995, 74th Leg., ch. 165 (S.B. 971), § 1, effective September 1, 1995.)

### Sec. 546.006.   Designated Emergency Vehicle During Declared Disasters.

(a) From recommendations made under Section 418.013(c), Government Code, the department shall designate which vehicles may be operated by which designated organizations as emergency vehicles during declared disasters.

(b) A vehicle designated under Subsection (a) may be operated by a designated organization as if the vehicle were an authorized emergency vehicle under this subtitle if:

(1) the governor declares a state of disaster under Section 418.014, Government Code;

(2) the department requests assistance from the designated organization; and

(3) the vehicle is operated by the designated organization or a member of the designated organization in response to the state of disaster.

(c) The department shall adopt rules as necessary to implement this section.

(Enacted by Acts 2007, 80th Leg., ch. 258 (S.B. 11), § 5.02, effective September 1, 2007.)

### Sec. 546.007.   Closure of Road or Highway by Firefighter.

(a) This section applies only to a firefighter who is employed by or a member of:

(1) a fire department operated by an emergency services district;

(2) a volunteer fire department; or

(3) a fire department of a general-law municipality.

(b) A firefighter, when performing the firefighter's official duties, may close one or more lanes of a road or highway to protect the safety of persons or property.

(c) The closure shall be limited to the affected lane or lanes and one additional lane unless the safety of emergency personnel operating on the road or highway requires more lanes to be closed.

(d) In making a closure under this section, the firefighter shall deploy one or more authorized emergency vehicles with audible and visual signals that meet the requirements of Sections 547.305 and 547.702.

(Enacted by Acts 2011, 82nd Leg., ch. 490 (H.B. 993), § 1, effective September 1, 2011.)

### Secs. 546.008 to 546.020. [Reserved for expansion].

### SUBCHAPTER B
### OPERATION OF CERTAIN FIRE-FIGHTING EQUIPMENT

### Sec. 546.021.   Mutual Aid Organizations.

(a) Two or more businesses whose activities require the maintenance of fire-fighting equipment may form a mutual aid organization in which the member businesses agree to assist each other during an emergency by supplying fire-fighting equipment or services.

(b) The presiding officer or director of an organization formed under this section shall deliver a list to the county fire marshal, or to the commissioners court of a county if the county does not have a fire marshal, in each county in which a member business is located. The list must contain the name of the registered owner and license plate number of each motor vehicle that each member intends to use in supplying fire-fighting equipment or services.

(c) If the county fire marshal or commissioners court determines that the operation of the vehicles on the list is in the public interest and not a threat to public safety, the marshal or court shall approve the list.

(d) On approval of the list by the county fire marshal or commissioners court, a person operating a listed motor vehicle in response to a call for emergency fire-fighting assistance from a member has the rights and restrictions placed by this subtitle on the operator of an authorized emergency vehicle.

(e) A county is not liable for damage to a person or property caused by a person approved by the county under this section to operate a motor vehicle for emergency fire-fighting assistance.

(Enacted by Acts 1995, 74th Leg., ch. 165 (S.B. 971), § 1, effective September 1, 1995.)

# CHAPTER 547
# VEHICLE EQUIPMENT

### Subchapter A. General Provisions

### Subchapter B. Adoption of Rules and Standards

### Subchapter C. Provisions Relating to the Offer, Distribution, and Sale of Vehicle Equipment

### Subchapter D. General Provisions Regarding Lighting Requirements

### Subchapter E. General Lighting Requirements for Vehicles

### Subchapter F. Additional Lighting Requirements for Certain Large Vehicles

### Subchapter G. Alternative Lighting Requirements for Farm Tractors, Farm Equipment, and Implements of Husbandry

### Subchapter H. Lighting Requirements in Special Circumstances

### Subchapter I. Provisions Relating to Brake Requirements on Vehicles

### Subchapter J. Provisions Relating to Warning Device Requirements on Vehicles

## SUBCHAPTER A
## GENERAL PROVISIONS

### Sec. 547.001.　Definitions.

In this chapter:

(1) "Air-conditioning equipment" means mechanical vapor compression refrigeration equipment used to cool a motor vehicle passenger or operator compartment.

(2) "Explosive cargo vehicle" means a motor vehicle used to transport explosives or a cargo tank truck used to transport a flammable liquid or compressed gas.

(2-a) "Golf cart" has the meaning assigned by Section 502.001.

(3) "Light transmission" means the ratio of the amount of light that passes through a material to the amount of light that falls on the material and the glazing.

(4) "Luminous reflectance" means the ratio of the amount of light that is reflected by a material to the amount of light that falls on the material.

(5) "Multipurpose vehicle" means a motor vehicle that is:

(A) designed to carry 10 or fewer persons; and

(B) constructed on a truck chassis or with special features for occasional off-road use.

(6) "Safety glazing material" includes only a glazing material that is constructed, treated, or combined with another material to reduce substantially, as compared to ordinary sheet or plate glass, the likelihood of injury to persons by an external object or by cracked or broken glazing material.

(7) "Slow-moving vehicle" means:

(A) a motor vehicle designed to operate at a maximum speed of 25 miles per hour or less, not including an electric personal assistive mobility device, as defined by Section 551.201; or

(B) a vehicle, implement of husbandry, or machinery, including road construction machinery, that is towed by:

(i) an animal; or

(ii) a motor vehicle designed to operate at a maximum speed of 25 miles per hour or less.

(8) "Slow-moving-vehicle emblem" means a triangular emblem that conforms to standards and specifications adopted by the director under Section 547.104.

(9) "Sunscreening device" means a film, material, or device that meets the department's standards for reducing effects of the sun.

(10) "Vehicle equipment" means:

(A) a system, part, or device that is manufactured or sold as original or replacement equipment or as a vehicle accessory; or

(B) a device or apparel manufactured or sold to protect a vehicle operator or passenger.

(Enacted by Acts 1995, 74th Leg., ch. 165 (S.B. 971), § 1, effective September 1, 1995; am. Acts 2003, 78th Leg., ch. 1318 (H.B. 1997), § 3, effective September 1, 2003; am. Acts 2009, 81st Leg., ch. 1136 (H.B. 2553), § 7, effective September 1, 2009.)

## Sec. 547.002. Applicability.

Unless a provision is specifically made applicable, this chapter and the rules of the department adopted under this chapter do not apply to:

(1) an implement of husbandry;

(2) road machinery;

(3) a road roller;

(4) a farm tractor;

(5) a bicycle, a bicyclist, or bicycle equipment;

(6) an electric bicycle, an electric bicyclist, or electric bicycle equipment; or

(7) a golf cart that is operated only as authorized by Section 551.403.

(Enacted by Acts 1995, 74th Leg., ch. 165 (S.B. 971), § 1, effective September 1, 1995; am. Acts 1997, 75th Leg., ch. 896 (H.B. 2733), § 2, effective September 1, 1997; am. Acts 2001, 77th Leg., ch. 1085 (H.B. 2204), § 8, effective September 1, 2001; am. Acts 2009, 81st Leg., ch. 1136 (H.B. 2553), § 8, effective September 1, 2009.)

## Sec. 547.003. Equipment Not Affected.

This chapter does not prohibit and the department by rule may not prohibit the use of:

(1) equipment required by an agency of the United States; or

(2) a part or accessory not inconsistent with this chapter or a rule adopted under this chapter.

(Enacted by Acts 1995, 74th Leg., ch. 165 (S.B. 971), § 1, effective September 1, 1995.)

## Sec. 547.004. General Offenses.

(a) A person commits an offense that is a misdemeanor if the person operates or moves or, as an owner, knowingly permits another to operate or move, a vehicle that:

(1) is unsafe so as to endanger a person;

(2) is not equipped in a manner that complies with the vehicle equipment standards and requirements established by this chapter; or

(3) is equipped in a manner prohibited by this chapter.

(b) A person commits an offense that is a misdemeanor if the person operates a vehicle equipped with an item of vehicle equipment that the person knows has been determined in a compliance proceeding under Section 547.206 to not comply with a department standard.

(c) A court may dismiss a charge brought under this section if the defendant:

(1) remedies the defect before the defendant's first court appearance; and

(2) pays an administrative fee not to exceed $10.

(d) Subsection (c) does not apply to an offense involving a commercial motor vehicle.

(Enacted by Acts 1995, 74th Leg., ch. 165 (S.B. 971), § 1, effective September 1, 1995; am. Acts 2007, 80th Leg., ch. 1027 (H.B. 1623), § 10, effective September 1, 2007.)

## Sec. 547.005. Offense Relating to Violation of Special-Use Provisions.

(a) A person may not use a slow-moving-vehicle emblem on a stationary object or a vehicle other than a slow-moving vehicle.

(b) A person may not operate a motor vehicle bearing the words "school bus" unless the vehicle is used primarily to transport persons to or from school or a school-related activity. In this subsection, "school" means a privately or publicly supported elementary or secondary school, day-care center, preschool, or institution of higher education and includes a church if the church is engaged in providing formal education.

(Enacted by Acts 1995, 74th Leg., ch. 165 (S.B. 971), § 1, effective September 1, 1995.)

## Secs. 547.006 to 547.100 [Reserved for expansion].

## SUBCHAPTER B
## ADOPTION OF RULES AND STANDARDS

## Sec. 547.101. Rules and Standards in General.

(a) The department may adopt rules necessary to administer this chapter.

(b) The department may adopt standards for vehicle equipment to:

(1) protect the public from unreasonable risk of death or injury; and

(2) enforce safety standards of the United States as permitted under the federal motor vehicle act.

(c) A department standard must:

(1) duplicate a standard of the United States that applies to the same aspect of vehicle equipment performance as the department standard; or

(2) if there is no standard of the United States for the same aspect of vehicle equipment performance as the department standard, conform as closely as possible to a relevant standard of the United States, similar standards

established by other states, and a standard issued or endorsed by recognized national standard-setting organizations or agencies.

(d) The department may not adopt a vehicle equipment standard inconsistent with a standard provided by this chapter.

(Enacted by Acts 1995, 74th Leg., ch. 165 (S.B. 971), § 1, effective September 1, 1995.)

### Sec. 547.102.    School Bus Equipment Standards.

The department may adopt standards and specifications that:

(1) supplement the standards and specifications provided by this chapter;

(2) apply to lighting and warning device equipment required for a school bus; and

(3) at the time adopted, correlate with and conform as closely as possible to specifications approved by the Society of Automotive Engineers.

(Enacted by Acts 1995, 74th Leg., ch. 165 (S.B. 971), § 1, effective September 1, 1995.)

### Sec. 547.103.    Air-Conditioning Equipment Standards.

The department may adopt safety requirements, rules, and specifications that:

(1) apply to air-conditioning equipment; and

(2) correlate with and conform as closely as possible to recommended practices or standards approved by the Society of Automotive Engineers.

(Enacted by Acts 1995, 74th Leg., ch. 165 (S.B. 971), § 1, effective September 1, 1995.)

### Sec. 547.104.    Slow-Moving-Vehicle Emblem Standards.

The director shall adopt standards and specifications that:

(1) apply to the color, size, and mounting position of a slow-moving-vehicle emblem; and

(2) at the time adopted, correlate with and conform as closely as practicable to the standards and specifications adopted or approved by the American Society of Agricultural Engineers for a uniform emblem to identify a slow-moving vehicle.

(Enacted by Acts 1995, 74th Leg., ch. 165 (S.B. 971), § 1, effective September 1, 1995.)

### Sec. 547.105.    Maintenance and Service Equipment Lighting Standards.

(a) The Texas Department of Transportation shall adopt standards and specifications that:

(1) apply to lamps on highway maintenance and service equipment, including snow-removal equipment; and

(2) correlate with and conform as closely as possible to standards and specifications approved by the American Association of State Highway and Transportation Officials.

(b) The Texas Department of Transportation may adopt standards and specifications for lighting that permit the use of flashing lights for identification purposes on highway maintenance and service equipment, including snow-removal equipment.

(c) The standards and specifications adopted under this section are in lieu of the standards and specifications otherwise provided by this chapter for lamps on vehicles.

(Enacted by Acts 1995, 74th Leg., ch. 165 (S.B. 971), § 1, effective September 1, 1995.)

### Secs. 547.106 to 547.200 [Reserved for expansion].

## SUBCHAPTER C
## PROVISIONS RELATING TO THE OFFER, DISTRIBUTION, AND SALE OF VEHICLE EQUIPMENT

### Sec. 547.201.    Offenses Relating to the Offer, Distribution, and Sale of Vehicle Equipment.

(a) A person may not offer or distribute for sale or sell an item of vehicle equipment for which a standard is prescribed by this chapter or the department and that does not comply with the standard. It is an affirmative defense to prosecution under this subsection that the person did not have reason to know in the exercise of due care that the item did not comply with the applicable standard.

(b) A person may not offer or distribute for sale or sell an item of vehicle equipment for which a standard is prescribed by this chapter or the department, unless the item or its package:

(1) bears the manufacturer's trademark or brand name; or

(2) complies with each applicable identification requirement established by an agency of the United States or the department.

(Enacted by Acts 1995, 74th Leg., ch. 165 (S.B. 971), § 1, effective September 1, 1995.)

## Sec. 547.202. Department Certification or Approval of Vehicle Equipment.

(a) When or after an item of vehicle equipment is sold in this state, the department shall determine whether a department standard is prescribed for the item. If a department standard is prescribed, the department shall determine whether the item complies with the standard.

(b) If a standard of an agency of the United States or of the department is not prescribed, the department by rule may require departmental approval before the sale of the item.

(Enacted by Acts 1995, 74th Leg., ch. 165 (S.B. 971), § 1, effective September 1, 1995.)

## Sec. 547.203. Vehicle Equipment Testing: Department Standards.

(a) The department shall prescribe standards for and approve testing facilities to:

(1) review test data submitted by a manufacturer to show compliance with a department standard; and

(2) test an item of vehicle equipment independently in connection with a proceeding to determine compliance with a department standard.

(b) The department may not impose a product certification or approval fee, including a fee for testing facility approval.

(c) The department may:

(1) by rule, require a manufacturer of an item of vehicle equipment sold in this state to submit adequate test data to show that the item complies with department standards;

(2) periodically require a manufacturer to submit revised test data to demonstrate continuing compliance;

(3) purchase an item of vehicle equipment at retail for the purpose of review and testing under Subsection (a); and

(4) enter into cooperative arrangements with other states and interstate agencies to reduce duplication of testing and to facilitate compliance with rules under Subsection (c)(1).

(Enacted by Acts 1995, 74th Leg., ch. 165 (S.B. 971), § 1, effective September 1, 1995.)

## Sec. 547.204. Vehicle Equipment Testing: Federal Standards.

(a) For a vehicle or item of vehicle equipment subject to a motor vehicle safety standard of the United States, the department may, on or after the first sale of the vehicle or item of vehicle equipment:

(1) require the manufacturer to submit adequate test data to show that the vehicle or item of vehicle equipment complies with standards of the United States;

(2) review the manufacturer's laboratory test data and the qualifications of the laboratory; and

(3) independently test the vehicle or item of vehicle equipment.

(b) The department may not require certification or approval of an item of vehicle equipment subject to a motor vehicle safety standard of the United States.

(c) The department may not require a manufacturer of a vehicle or of an item of vehicle equipment subject to a motor vehicle safety standard of the United States to use an outside laboratory or a specified laboratory.

(Enacted by Acts 1995, 74th Leg., ch. 165 (S.B. 971), § 1, effective September 1, 1995.)

## Sec. 547.205. Initiation of Compliance Proceeding.

(a) The department may initiate a proceeding to determine whether an item of vehicle equipment complies with a department standard if the department reasonably believes that the item is being offered or distributed for sale or sold in violation of the standard.

(b) The department shall send written notice of the proceeding to the manufacturer of the item by certified mail, return receipt requested.

(c) The notice required by Subsection (b) must:

(1) cite the standard that the item allegedly violates; and

(2) state that the manufacturer must file a written request with the department for a hearing not later than the 30th day after the date the notice is received to obtain a hearing on the issue of compliance.

(d) When the department sends notice under Subsection (b), the department shall require the manufacturer to submit to the department, not later than the 30th day after the date the notice is received, the names and addresses of the persons the manufacturer knows to be offering the item for sale to retail merchants.

(e) On receipt under Subsection (d) of the names and addresses, the department shall send by certified mail, return receipt requested, written notice of the compliance proceeding to those persons.

(f) The notice must:

(1) cite the standard that the item allegedly violates;

(2) state that the manufacturer of the item has been notified and may request a hearing on the issue of compliance before a stated date;

(3) state that if the manufacturer or another person requests a hearing, the person may appear at the hearing;

(4) state that if the manufacturer does not request a hearing, the person may request a hearing by filing a written request with the department not later than the 30th day after the date notice is received; and

(5) state that the person may determine from the department whether a hearing will be held and the time and place of the hearing.

(Enacted by Acts 1995, 74th Leg., ch. 165 (S.B. 971), § 1, effective September 1, 1995.)

## Sec. 547.206.  Compliance Proceeding Hearing.

The department shall conduct a hearing on the issue of compliance if a person required by Section 547.205 to be notified requests a hearing in the manner and within the time specified by that section.

(Enacted by Acts 1995, 74th Leg., ch. 165 (S.B. 971), § 1, effective September 1, 1995.)

## Sec. 547.207.  Compliance Proceeding Issues.

(a) In a hearing under Section 547.206 or in the absence of a request for a hearing, the department may make a determination of the following issues only:

(1) whether an item of vehicle equipment has been offered, distributed, or sold in violation of a department standard;

(2) whether the manufacturer did not submit test data required by the department under Section 547.203; and

(3) whether an item of vehicle equipment has been offered, distributed, or sold without the identification required by Section 547.201.

(b) The department by order shall prohibit the manufacture, offer for sale, distribution for sale, or sale of the item if the department finds affirmatively on at least one of the issues.

(c) After entering its order, the department shall send written notice by certified mail, return receipt requested, to each person the department notified under Section 547.205.

(Enacted by Acts 1995, 74th Leg., ch. 165 (S.B. 971), § 1, effective September 1, 1995.)

## Sec. 547.208.  Judicial Review and Judicial Enforcement.

(a) A person may appeal an order entered under Section 547.207 to a district court in Travis County only if a hearing was held by the department and the person:

(1) is aggrieved by the order; and

(2) appeared at the hearing on compliance.

(b) The department may bring suit in a district court of Travis County for an injunction to prohibit the manufacture, offer, distribution, or sale of an item of vehicle equipment that is the subject of a department order entered under Section 547.207. The attorney general shall represent the department in the suit.

(Enacted by Acts 1995, 74th Leg., ch. 165 (S.B. 971), § 1, effective September 1, 1995.)

## Secs. 547.209 to 547.300 [Reserved for expansion].

## SUBCHAPTER D
## GENERAL PROVISIONS REGARDING LIGHTING REQUIREMENTS

## Sec. 547.301.  General Provisions Relating to Measurements.

(a) Unless expressly stated otherwise, a visibility distance requirement imposed by this chapter for a lamp or device applies when a lighted lamp or device is required and is measured as if the vehicle were unloaded and on a straight, level, unlighted highway under normal atmospheric conditions.

(b) A mounted height requirement imposed by this chapter for a lamp or device is measured as if the vehicle were unloaded and on level ground and is measured from the center of the lamp or device to the ground.

(Enacted by Acts 1995, 74th Leg., ch. 165 (S.B. 971), § 1, effective September 1, 1995.)

## Sec. 547.302.  Duty to Display Lights.

(a) A vehicle shall display each lighted lamp and illuminating device required by this chapter to be on the vehicle:

(1) at nighttime; and

(2) when light is insufficient or atmospheric conditions are unfavorable so that a person or vehicle on the highway is not clearly discernible at a distance of 1,000 feet ahead.

(b) A signaling device, including a stoplamp or a turn signal lamp, shall be lighted as prescribed by this chapter.

(c) At least one lighted lamp shall be displayed on each side of the front of a motor vehicle.

(d) Not more than four of the following may be lighted at one time on the front of a motor vehicle:

(1) a headlamp required by this chapter; or

(2) a lamp, including an auxiliary lamp or spotlamp, that projects a beam with an intensity brighter than 300 candlepower.

(Enacted by Acts 1995, 74th Leg., ch. 165 (S.B. 971), § 1, effective September 1, 1995.)

## Sec. 547.303. Color Requirements.

(a) Unless expressly provided otherwise, a lighting device or reflector mounted on the rear of a vehicle must be or reflect red.

(b) A signaling device mounted on the rear of a vehicle may be red, amber, or yellow.

(Enacted by Acts 1995, 74th Leg., ch. 165 (S.B. 971), § 1, effective September 1, 1995.)

## Sec. 547.304. Applicability.

(a) A provision of this chapter that requires a vehicle to be equipped with fixed electric lights does not apply to a farm trailer or fertilizer trailer registered under Section 504.504 or a boat trailer with a gross weight of 3,000 pounds or less if the trailer is not operated at a time or under a condition specified by Section 547.302(a).

(b) Except for Sections 547.323 and 547.324, a provision of this chapter that requires a vehicle to be equipped with fixed electric lights does not apply to a boat trailer with a gross weight of less than 4,500 pounds if the trailer is not operated at a time or under a condition specified by Section 547.302(a).

(c) Except for Sections 547.323 and 547.324, a provision of this chapter that requires a vehicle to be equipped with lamps, reflectors, and lighting equipment does not apply to a mobile home if the mobile home:

(1) is moved under a permit issued by the Texas Department of Motor Vehicles under Subchapter D, Chapter 623; and

(2) is not moved at a time or under a condition specified by Section 547.302(a).

(d) A mobile home lighted as provided by this section may be moved only during daytime.

(Enacted by Acts 1995, 74th Leg., ch. 165 (S.B. 971), § 1, effective September 1, 1995; am. Acts 2007, 80th Leg., ch. 280 (H.B. 505), § 4, effective June 15, 2007; am. Acts 2011, 82nd Leg., ch. 1345 (S.B. 1420), § 96, effective September 1, 2011.)

## Sec. 547.305. Restrictions on Use of Lights.

(a) A motor vehicle lamp or illuminating device, other than a headlamp, spotlamp, auxiliary lamp, turn signal lamp, or emergency vehicle, tow truck, or school bus warning lamp, that projects a beam with an intensity brighter than 300 candlepower shall be directed so that no part of the high-intensity portion of the beam strikes the roadway at a distance of more than 75 feet from the vehicle.

(b) Except as expressly authorized by law, a person may not operate or move equipment or a vehicle, other than a police vehicle, with a lamp or device that displays a red light visible from directly in front of the center of the equipment or vehicle.

(c) A person may not operate a motor vehicle equipped with a red, white, or blue beacon, flashing, or alternating light unless the equipment is:

(1) used as specifically authorized by this chapter; or

(2) a running lamp, headlamp, taillamp, backup lamp, or turn signal lamp that is used as authorized by law.

(d) A vehicle may be equipped with alternately flashing lighting equipment described by Section 547.701 or 547.702 only if the vehicle is:

(1) a school bus;

(2) an authorized emergency vehicle;

(3) a church bus that has the words "church bus" printed on the front and rear of the bus so as to be clearly discernable to other vehicle operators;

(4) a tow truck while under the direction of a law enforcement officer at the scene of an accident or while hooking up to a disabled vehicle on a roadway; or

(5) a tow truck with a mounted light bar which has turn signals and stop lamps in addition to those required by Sections 547.322, 547.323, and 547.324, Transportation Code.

(e) A person may not operate highway maintenance or service equipment, including snow-removal equipment, that is not equipped with lamps or that does not display lighted lamps as required by the standards and specifications adopted by the Texas Department of Transportation.

(f) In this section "tow truck" means a motor vehicle or mechanical device that is adapted or used to tow, winch, or move a disabled vehicle.

(Enacted by Acts 1995, 74th Leg., ch. 165 (S.B. 971), § 1, effective September 1, 1995; am. Acts 1999, 76th Leg., ch. 380 (H.B. 3366), § 1, effective July 1, 1999; am. Acts 2011, 82nd Leg., ch. 229 (H.B. 378), § 3, effective September 1, 2011.)

**Secs. 547.306 to 547.320 [Reserved for expansion].**

## SUBCHAPTER E
## GENERAL LIGHTING REQUIREMENTS FOR VEHICLES

### Sec. 547.321. Headlamps Required.

(a) A motor vehicle shall be equipped with at least two headlamps.

(b) At least one headlamp shall be mounted on each side of the front of the vehicle.

(c) Each headlamp shall be mounted at a height from 24 to 54 inches.
(Enacted by Acts 1995, 74th Leg., ch. 165 (S.B. 971), § 1, effective September 1, 1995.)

### Sec. 547.3215. Use of Federal Standard.

Unless specifically prohibited by this chapter, lighting, reflective devices, and associated equipment on a vehicle or motor vehicle must comply with:

(1) the current federal standards in 49 C.F.R. Section 571.108; or

(2) the federal standards in that section in effect, if any, at the time the vehicle or motor vehicle was manufactured.
(Enacted by Acts 1997, 75th Leg., ch. 324 (H.B. 2138), § 1, effective September 1, 1997.)

### Sec. 547.322. Taillamps Required.

(a) Except as provided by Subsection (b), a motor vehicle, trailer, semitrailer, pole trailer, or vehicle that is towed at the end of a combination of vehicles shall be equipped with at least two taillamps.

(b) A passenger car or truck that was manufactured or assembled before the model year 1960 shall be equipped with at least one taillamp.

(c) Taillamps shall be mounted on the rear of the vehicle:

(1) at a height from 15 to 72 inches; and

(2) at the same level and spaced as widely apart as practicable if a vehicle is equipped with more than one lamp.

(d) A taillamp shall emit a red light plainly visible at a distance of 1,000 feet from the rear of the vehicle.

(e) If vehicles are traveling in combination, only the taillamps on the rearmost vehicle are required to emit a light for the distance specified in Subsection (d).

(f) A taillamp or a separate lamp shall be constructed and mounted to emit a white light that:

(1) illuminates the rear license plate; and

(2) makes the plate clearly legible at a distance of 50 feet from the rear.

(g) A taillamp, including a separate lamp used to illuminate a rear license plate, must emit a light when a headlamp or auxiliary driving lamp is lighted.
(Enacted by Acts 1995, 74th Leg., ch. 165 (S.B. 971), § 1, effective September 1, 1995.)

### Sec. 547.323. Stoplamps Required.

(a) Except as provided by Subsection (b), a motor vehicle, trailer, semitrailer, or pole trailer shall be equipped with at least two stoplamps.

(b) A passenger car manufactured or assembled before the model year 1960 shall be equipped with at least one stoplamp.

(c) A stoplamp shall be mounted on the rear of the vehicle.

(d) A stoplamp shall emit a red or amber light, or a color between red and amber, that is:

(1) visible in normal sunlight at a distance of at least 300 feet from the rear of the vehicle; and

(2) displayed when the vehicle service brake is applied.

(e) If vehicles are traveling in combination, only the stoplamps on the rearmost vehicle are required to emit a light for the distance specified in Subsection (d).

(f) A stoplamp may be included as a part of another rear lamp.
(Enacted by Acts 1995, 74th Leg., ch. 165 (S.B. 971), § 1, effective September 1, 1995.)

### Sec. 547.324. Turn Signal Lamps Required.

(a) Except as provided by Subsection (b), a motor vehicle, trailer, semitrailer, or pole trailer shall be equipped with electric turn signal lamps that indicate the operator's intent to turn by displaying flashing lights to the front and rear of a vehicle or combination of vehicles and on that side of the vehicle or combination toward which the turn is to be made.

(b) Subsection (a) does not apply to a passenger car or truck less than 80 inches wide manufactured or assembled before the model year 1960.

(c) Turn signal lamps:

(1) shall be mounted at the same level and spaced as widely apart as practicable on the front and on the rear of the vehicle; and

(2) may be included as a part of another lamp on the vehicle.

(d) A turn signal lamp shall emit:

(1) a white or amber light, or a color between white and amber, if the lamp is mounted on the front of the vehicle; or

(2) a red or amber light, or a color between red and amber, if the lamp is mounted on the rear of the vehicle.

(e) A turn signal lamp must be visible in normal sunlight at a distance of:

(1) at least 500 feet from the front and rear of the vehicle if the vehicle is at least 80 inches wide; and

(2) at least 300 feet from the front and rear of the vehicle if the vehicle is less than 80 inches wide.

(Enacted by Acts 1995, 74th Leg., ch. 165 (S.B. 971), § 1, effective September 1, 1995.)

## Sec. 547.325. Reflectors Required.

(a) Except as provided by Subchapter F, a motor vehicle, trailer, semitrailer, or pole trailer shall be equipped with at least two red reflectors on the rear of the vehicle. A red reflector may be included as a part of a taillamp.

(b) A reflector shall be:

(1) mounted at a height from 15 to 60 inches; and

(2) visible at night at all distances:

(A) from 100 to 600 feet when directly in front of lawful lower beams of headlamps; or

(B) from 100 to 350 feet when directly in front of lawful upper beams of headlamps if the vehicle was manufactured or assembled before January 1, 1972.

(Enacted by Acts 1995, 74th Leg., ch. 165 (S.B. 971), § 1, effective September 1, 1995.)

## Sec. 547.326. Minimum Lighting Equipment Required.

(a) A vehicle that is not specifically required to be equipped with lamps or other lighting devices shall be equipped at the times specified in Section 547.302(a) with at least one lamp that emits a white light visible at a distance of at least 1,000 feet from the front and:

(1) two lamps that emit a red light visible at a distance of at least 1,000 feet from the rear; or

(2) one lamp that emits a red light visible at a distance of at least 1,000 feet from the rear and two red reflectors visible when illuminated by the lawful lower beams of headlamps at all distances from 100 to 600 feet to the rear.

(b) This section also applies to an animal-drawn vehicle and a vehicle exempted from this chapter by Section 547.002.

(Enacted by Acts 1995, 74th Leg., ch. 165 (S.B. 971), § 1, effective September 1, 1995.)

## Sec. 547.327. Spotlamps Permitted.

(a) A motor vehicle may be equipped with not more than two spotlamps.

(b) A spotlamp shall be aimed so that no part of the high-intensity portion of the beam strikes the windshield, window, mirror, or occupant of another vehicle in use.

(Enacted by Acts 1995, 74th Leg., ch. 165 (S.B. 971), § 1, effective September 1, 1995.)

## Sec. 547.328. Fog Lamps Permitted.

(a) A motor vehicle may be equipped with not more than two fog lamps.

(b) A fog lamp shall be:

(1) mounted on the front of the vehicle at a height from 12 to 30 inches; and

(2) aimed so that no part of the high-intensity portion of the beam from a lamp mounted to the left of center on a vehicle projects a beam of light at a distance of 25 feet that is higher than four inches below the level of the center of the lamp.

(c) Lighted fog lamps may be used with lower headlamp beams as specified by Section 547.333.

(Enacted by Acts 1995, 74th Leg., ch. 165 (S.B. 971), § 1, effective September 1, 1995.)

## Sec. 547.329. Auxiliary Passing Lamps Permitted.

(a) A motor vehicle may be equipped with no more than two auxiliary passing lamps.

(b) An auxiliary passing lamp shall be mounted on the front of the vehicle at a height from 24 to 42 inches.

(c) An auxiliary passing lamp may be used with headlamps as specified by Section 547.333.

(Enacted by Acts 1995, 74th Leg., ch. 165 (S.B. 971), § 1, effective September 1, 1995.)

## Sec. 547.330. Auxiliary Driving Lamps Permitted.

(a) A motor vehicle may be equipped with no more than two auxiliary driving lamps.

(b) An auxiliary driving lamp shall be mounted on the front of the vehicle at a height from 16 to 42 inches.

(c) Auxiliary driving lamps may be used with headlamps as specified by Section 547.333.

(Enacted by Acts 1995, 74th Leg., ch. 165 (S.B. 971), § 1, effective September 1, 1995.)

### Sec. 547.331. Hazard Lamps Permitted.

(a) A vehicle may be equipped with lamps to warn other vehicle operators of a vehicular traffic hazard that requires unusual care in approaching, overtaking, or passing.

(b) The lamps shall be:

(1) mounted at the same level and spaced as widely apart as practicable on the front and on the rear of the vehicle; and

(2) visible at a distance of at least 500 feet in normal sunlight.

(c) The lamps shall display simultaneously flashing lights that emit:

(1) a white or amber light, or a color between white and amber, if the lamp is mounted on the front of the vehicle; or

(2) a red or amber light, or a color between red and amber, if the lamp is mounted on the rear of the vehicle.

(Enacted by Acts 1995, 74th Leg., ch. 165 (S.B. 971), § 1, effective September 1, 1995.)

### Sec. 547.332. Other Lamps Permitted.

A motor vehicle may be equipped with:

(1) not more than two side cowl or fender lamps that emit an amber or white light without glare;

(2) not more than two running board courtesy lamps, one on each side of the vehicle, that emit an amber or white light without glare; and

(3) one or more backup lamps that:

(A) emit an amber or white light only when the vehicle is not moving forward; and

(B) may be displayed separately or in combination with another lamp.

(Enacted by Acts 1995, 74th Leg., ch. 165 (S.B. 971), § 1, effective September 1, 1995.)

### Sec. 547.333. Multiple-Beam Lighting Equipment Required.

(a) Unless provided otherwise, a headlamp, auxiliary driving lamp, auxiliary passing lamp, or combination of those lamps mounted on a motor vehicle, other than a motorcycle or motor-driven cycle:

(1) shall be arranged so that the operator can select at will between distributions of light projected at different elevations; and

(2) may be arranged so that the operator can select the distribution automatically.

(b) A lamp identified by Subsection (a) shall produce:

(1) an uppermost distribution of light or composite beam that is aimed and emits light sufficient to reveal a person or vehicle at a distance of at least 450 feet ahead during all conditions of loading; and

(2) a lowermost distribution of light or composite beam that:

(A) is aimed and emits light sufficient to reveal a person or vehicle at a distance of at least 150 feet ahead; and

(B) is aimed so that no part of the high-intensity portion of the beam on a vehicle that is operated on a straight, level road under any condition of loading projects into the eyes of an approaching vehicle operator.

(c) A person who operates a vehicle on a roadway or shoulder shall select a distribution of light or composite beam that is aimed and emits light sufficient to reveal a person or vehicle at a safe distance ahead of the vehicle, except that:

(1) an operator approaching an oncoming vehicle within 500 feet shall select:

(A) the lowermost distribution of light or composite beam, regardless of road contour or condition of loading; or

(B) a distribution aimed so that no part of the high-intensity portion of the lamp projects into the eyes of an approaching vehicle operator; and

(2) an operator approaching a vehicle from the rear within 300 feet may not select the uppermost distribution of light.

(d) A motor vehicle of a model year of 1948 or later, other than a motorcycle or motor-driven cycle, that has multiple-beam lighting equipment shall be equipped with a beam indicator that is:

(1) designed and located so that the lighted indicator is visible without glare to the vehicle operator; and

(2) lighted only when the uppermost distribution of light is in use.

(Enacted by Acts 1995, 74th Leg., ch. 165 (S.B. 971), § 1, effective September 1, 1995.)

### Sec. 547.334. Single-Beam Lighting Equipment Permitted.

(a) In lieu of the multiple-beam lighting equipment required by Section 547.333, a headlamp system that provides a single distribution of light and meets the requirements of Subsection (b) is permitted for:

(1) a farm tractor; or

(2) a motor vehicle manufactured and sold before September 4, 1948.

(b) The headlamp system specified by Subsection (a) shall:

(1) emit a light sufficient to reveal a person or vehicle at a distance of at least 200 feet; and

(2) be aimed so that no part of the high-intensity portion of the lamp projects a beam:

(A) higher than five inches below the level of the center of the lamp at a distance of 25 feet ahead; or

(B) higher than 42 inches above the ground at a distance of 75 feet ahead.

(Enacted by Acts 1995, 74th Leg., ch. 165 (S.B. 971), § 1, effective September 1, 1995.)

## Sec. 547.335. Alternative Road Lighting Equipment Permitted.

In lieu of the multiple-beam or single-beam lighting equipment otherwise required by this subchapter, a motor vehicle that is operated at a speed of not more than 20 miles per hour under the conditions specified in Section 547.302(a) may be equipped with two lighted lamps:

(1) mounted on the front of the vehicle; and

(2) capable of revealing a person or vehicle 100 feet ahead.

(Enacted by Acts 1995, 74th Leg., ch. 165 (S.B. 971), § 1, effective September 1, 1995.)

## Secs. 547.336 to 547.350 [Reserved for expansion].

## SUBCHAPTER F
## ADDITIONAL LIGHTING REQUIREMENTS FOR CERTAIN LARGE VEHICLES

## Sec. 547.351. Applicability.

The color, mounting, and visibility requirements in this subchapter apply only to equipment on a vehicle described by Section 547.352.

(Enacted by Acts 1995, 74th Leg., ch. 165 (S.B. 971), § 1, effective September 1, 1995.)

## Sec. 547.352. Additional Lighting Equipment Requirements.

In addition to other equipment required by this chapter:

(1) a bus, truck, trailer, or semitrailer that is at least 80 inches wide shall be equipped with:

(A) two clearance lamps on the front, one at each side;

(B) two clearance lamps on the rear, one at each side;

(C) four side marker lamps, one on each side at or near the front and one on each side at or near the rear;

(D) four reflectors, one on each side at or near the front and one on each side at or near the rear; and

(E) hazard lamps that meet the requirements of Section 547.331;

(2) a bus or truck that is at least 30 feet long shall be equipped with hazard lamps that meet the requirements of Section 547.331;

(3) a trailer or semitrailer that is at least 30 feet long shall be equipped with:

(A) two side marker lamps, one centrally mounted on each side with respect to the length of the vehicle;

(B) two reflectors, one centrally mounted on each side with respect to the length of the vehicle; and

(C) hazard lamps that meet the requirements of Section 547.331;

(4) a pole trailer shall be equipped with:

(A) two side marker lamps, one at each side at or near the front of the load;

(B) one reflector at or near the front of the load;

(C) one combination marker lamp that:

(i) emits an amber light to the front and a red light to the rear and side; and

(ii) is mounted on the rearmost support for the load to indicate the maximum width of the trailer; and

(D) hazard lamps that meet the requirements of Section 547.331, if the pole trailer is at least 30 feet long or at least 80 inches wide;

(5) a truck-tractor shall be equipped with:

(A) two clearance lamps, one at each side on the front of the cab; and

(B) hazard lamps that meet the requirements of Section 547.331, if the truck-tractor is at least 30 feet long or at least 80 inches wide; and

(6) a vehicle at least 80 inches wide may be equipped with:

(A) not more than three front identification lamps without glare; and

(B) not more than three rear identification lamps without glare.

Transportation

(Enacted by Acts 1995, 74th Leg., ch. 165 (S.B. 971), § 1, effective September 1, 1995.)

### Sec. 547.353.   Color Requirements.

(a) A clearance lamp, identification lamp, side marker lamp, or reflector mounted on the front, on the side near the front, or in the center of the vehicle must be or reflect amber.

(b) A clearance lamp, identification lamp, side marker lamp, or reflector mounted on the rear or the side near the rear of the vehicle must be or reflect red.

(Enacted by Acts 1995, 74th Leg., ch. 165 (S.B. 971), § 1, effective September 1, 1995.)

### Sec. 547.354.   Mounting Requirements.

(a) A reflector shall be mounted:

(1) at a height from 24 to 60 inches; or

(2) as high as practicable on the permanent structure of the vehicle if the highest part of the permanent structure is less than 24 inches.

(b) A rear reflector may be:

(1) included as a part of a taillamp if the reflector meets each other requirement of this subchapter; and

(2) mounted on each side of the bolster or load, if the vehicle is a pole trailer.

(c) A clearance lamp shall be mounted, if practicable, on the permanent structure of the vehicle to indicate the extreme height and width of the vehicle, except that:

(1) a clearance lamp on a truck-tractor shall be mounted to indicate the extreme width of the cab; and

(2) a front clearance lamp may be mounted at a height that indicates, as near as practicable, the extreme width of the trailer if mounting of the lamp as otherwise provided by this section would not indicate the extreme width of the trailer.

(d) A clearance lamp and side marker lamp may be mounted in combination if each lamp complies with the visibility requirements of Section 547.355.

(Enacted by Acts 1995, 74th Leg., ch. 165 (S.B. 971), § 1, effective September 1, 1995.)

### Sec. 547.355.   Visibility Requirements.

(a) A clearance lamp, identification lamp, or side marker lamp shall be visible and recognizable under normal atmospheric conditions at all distances from 50 to 500 feet from the vehicle on the side, front, or rear where the lamp is mounted.

(b) A reflector required by this chapter mounted on a vehicle subject to this subchapter shall be visible from the rear, if a rear reflector, or from the applicable side, if a side reflector, at nighttime at all distances from 100 to 600 feet from the vehicle when the reflector is directly in front of:

(1) lawful lower beams of headlamps; or

(2) lawful upper beams of headlamps on a vehicle manufactured or assembled before January 1, 1972.

(Enacted by Acts 1995, 74th Leg., ch. 165 (S.B. 971), § 1, effective September 1, 1995.)

### Secs. 547.356 to 547.370 [Reserved for expansion].

### SUBCHAPTER G
### ALTERNATIVE LIGHTING REQUIREMENTS FOR FARM TRACTORS, FARM EQUIPMENT, AND IMPLEMENTS OF HUSBANDRY

### Sec. 547.371.   General Lighting Equipment Requirements.

(a) Except as provided by Subsection (b), a farm tractor, self-propelled unit of farm equipment, or implement of husbandry shall be equipped with:

(1) at least two headlamps that comply with Section 547.333, 547.334, or 547.335;

(2) at least one red lamp visible at a distance of at least 1,000 feet from the rear and mounted as far to the left of the center of the vehicle as practicable;

(3) at least two red reflectors visible at all distances from 100 to 600 feet from the rear when directly in front of lawful lower beams of headlamps; and

(4) hazard lamps as described in Section 547.331, which shall be lighted and visible in normal sunlight at a distance of at least 1,000 feet from the front and rear.

(b) A farm tractor, self-propelled unit of farm equipment, or implement of husbandry manufactured or assembled on or before January 1, 1972, is required to be equipped as provided by Subsection (a) only at the times specified by Section 547.302(a), and hazard lamps are not required.

(Enacted by Acts 1995, 74th Leg., ch. 165 (S.B. 971), § 1, effective September 1, 1995.)

### Sec. 547.372.   Lighting Requirements for Combination Vehicles.

(a) If a unit of farm equipment or implement of husbandry is towed by a farm tractor and the towed object or its load extends more than four feet to the rear of the tractor or obscures a light on the tractor, the towed object shall be equipped at the times specified by Section 547.302(a) with at least two rear red reflectors that are:

(1) visible at all distances from 100 to 600 feet when directly in front of lawful lower beams of headlamps; and

(2) mounted to indicate, as nearly as practicable, the extreme width of the vehicle or combination of vehicles.

(b) If a unit of farm equipment or implement of husbandry is towed by a farm tractor and extends more than four feet to the left of the centerline of the tractor, the towed object shall be equipped at the times specified by Section 547.302(a) with a front amber reflector that is:

(1) visible at all distances from 100 to 600 feet when directly in front of lawful lower beams of headlamps; and

(2) mounted to indicate, as nearly as practicable, the extreme left projection of the towed object.

(c) Reflective tape or paint may be used as an alternative to the reflectors required by this section if the alternative complies with the other requirements of this section.

(Enacted by Acts 1995, 74th Leg., ch. 165 (S.B. 971), § 1, effective September 1, 1995.)

**Secs. 547.373 to 547.380 [Reserved for expansion].**

## SUBCHAPTER H
## LIGHTING REQUIREMENTS IN SPECIAL CIRCUMSTANCES

### Sec. 547.381. Obstructed Lights on Combination Vehicles.

(a) A motor vehicle when operated in combination with another vehicle is not required to display a lighted lamp, other than a taillamp, if the lamp is obscured because of its location by another vehicle in the combination of vehicles.

(b) Subsection (a) is not an exception for the lighting as provided by this chapter of:

(1) front clearance lamps on the frontmost vehicle in the combination; or

(2) rear lamps on the rearmost vehicle in the combination.

(Enacted by Acts 1995, 74th Leg., ch. 165 (S.B. 971), § 1, effective September 1, 1995.)

### Sec. 547.382. Lighting Equipment on Projecting Loads.

(a) A vehicle transporting a load that extends to the rear at least four feet beyond the bed or body of the vehicle shall display on the extreme end of the load at the times specified in Section 547.302(a):

(1) two red lamps visible at a distance of at least 500 feet from the rear;

(2) two red reflectors that indicate the maximum width and are visible at nighttime at all distances from 100 to 600 feet from the rear when directly in front of lawful lower beams of headlamps; and

(3) two red lamps, one on each side, that indicate the maximum overhang and are visible at a distance of at least 500 feet from the side.

(b) At all other times, a vehicle transporting a load that extends beyond the vehicle's sides or more than four feet beyond the vehicle's rear shall display red flags that:

(1) are at least 12 inches square;

(2) mark the extremities of the load; and

(3) are placed where a lamp is required by this section.

(Enacted by Acts 1995, 74th Leg., ch. 165 (S.B. 971), § 1, effective September 1, 1995.)

### Sec. 547.383. Lighting Requirements on Parked Vehicles.

(a) A vehicle, other than a motor-driven cycle, shall be equipped with at least one lamp, or a combination of lamps, that:

(1) emits a white or amber light visible at a distance of 1,000 feet from the front and a red light visible at a distance of 1,000 feet from the rear; and

(2) is mounted so that at least one lamp is installed as near as practicable to the side of the vehicle that is closest to passing traffic.

(b) A vehicle, other than a motor-driven cycle, that is parked or stopped on a roadway or shoulder at a time specified in Section 547.302(a) shall display a lamp that complies with Subsection (a).

(c) A vehicle that is lawfully parked on a highway is not required to display lights at night-time if there is sufficient light to reveal a person or vehicle on the highway at a distance of 1,000 feet.

(d) A lighted headlamp on a parked vehicle shall be dimmed.

(Enacted by Acts 1995, 74th Leg., ch. 165 (S.B. 971), § 1, effective September 1, 1995.)

Transportation

**Secs. 547.384 to 547.400 [Reserved for expansion].**

## SUBCHAPTER I
## PROVISIONS RELATING TO BRAKE REQUIREMENTS ON VEHICLES

### Sec. 547.401.  Brakes Required.

(a) Except as provided by Subsection (b), a motor vehicle, trailer, semitrailer, pole trailer, or combination of those vehicles shall be equipped with brakes that comply with this chapter.

(b) A trailer, semitrailer, or pole trailer is not required to have brakes if:

　　(1) its gross weight is 4,500 pounds or less; or

　　(2) its gross weight is heavier than 4,500 pounds but not heavier than 15,000 pounds, and it is drawn at a speed of not more than 30 miles per hour.

(Enacted by Acts 1995, 74th Leg., ch. 165 (S.B. 971), § 1, effective September 1, 1995.)

### Sec. 547.402.  Operation and Maintenance of Brakes.

(a) Required brakes shall operate on each wheel of a vehicle except:

　　(1) special mobile equipment;

　　(2) a vehicle that is towed as a commodity when at least one set of the towed vehicle's wheels is on the roadway, if the combination of vehicles complies with the performance requirements of this chapter; and

　　(3) a trailer, semitrailer, or pole trailer with a gross weight heavier than 4,500 pounds but not heavier than 15,000 pounds drawn at a speed of more than 30 miles per hour, if the brakes operate on both wheels of the rear axle.

(b) A truck or truck-tractor that has at least three axles is not required to have brakes on the front wheels, but must have brakes that:

　　(1) operate on the wheels of one steerable axle if the vehicle is equipped with at least two steerable axles; and

　　(2) comply with the performance requirements of this chapter.

(c) A trailer or semitrailer that has a gross weight of 15,000 pounds or less may use surge or inertia brake systems to satisfy the requirements of Subsection (a).

(d) Brakes shall be maintained in good working order and adjusted to operate on wheels on each side of the vehicle as equally as practicable.

(Enacted by Acts 1995, 74th Leg., ch. 165 (S.B. 971), § 1, effective September 1, 1995.)

### Sec. 547.403.  Service Brakes Required.

(a) A vehicle required to have brakes by this subchapter, other than special mobile equipment, shall be equipped with service brakes that:

　　(1) comply with the performance requirements of this subchapter; and

　　(2) are adequate to control the movement of the vehicle, including stopping and holding, under all loading conditions and when on any grade on which the vehicle is operated.

(b) A vehicle required to have brakes by this subchapter shall be equipped so that one control device operates the service brakes. This subsection does not prohibit an additional control device that may be used to operate brakes on a towed vehicle. A vehicle that tows another vehicle as a commodity when at least one set of the towed vehicle's wheels is on the roadway is not required to comply with this requirement unless the brakes on the towing and towed vehicles are designed to be operated by a single control on the towing vehicle.

(Enacted by Acts 1995, 74th Leg., ch. 165 (S.B. 971), § 1, effective September 1, 1995.)

### Sec. 547.404.  Parking Brakes Required.

(a) A vehicle required to have brakes by this subchapter, other than a motorcycle or motor-driven cycle, shall be equipped with parking brakes adequate to hold the vehicle:

　　(1) on any grade on which the vehicle is operated;

　　(2) under all loading conditions; and

　　(3) on a surface free from snow, ice, or loose material.

(b) The parking brakes shall be:

　　(1) designed to operate continuously as required once applied, despite a leakage or an exhaustion of power source; and

　　(2) activated by the vehicle operator's muscular effort, by spring action, or by equivalent means.

(c) The parking brakes may be assisted by the service brakes or by another power source, unless a failure in the power source would prevent the parking brakes from operating as required by this section.

(d) The same brake drums, brake shoes and lining assemblies, brake shoe anchors, and mechanical brake shoe actuation mechanism normally associated with wheel brake assemblies may be used for the parking brakes and service brakes.

(e) If the means of applying the parking brakes and service brakes are connected, the brake system shall be constructed so that the failure of one part will not cause the vehicle to be without operative brakes.

(Enacted by Acts 1995, 74th Leg., ch. 165 (S.B. 971), § 1, effective September 1, 1995.)

## Sec. 547.405. Emergency Brakes Required.

(a) A vehicle used to tow another vehicle equipped with air-controlled brakes shall be equipped with the following means, together or separate, for applying the trailer brakes in an emergency:

(1) an automatic device that applies the brakes to a fixed pressure from 20 to 45 pounds per square inch if the towing vehicle's air supply is reduced; and

(2) a manual device to apply and release the brakes that is readily operable by a person seated in the operator's seat and arranged so that:

(A) its emergency position or method of operation is clearly indicated; and

(B) its use does not prevent operation of the automatic brakes.

(b) In addition to the single control device required by Section 547.403, a vehicle used to tow another vehicle equipped with vacuum brakes shall be equipped with a second control device that:

(1) is used to operate the brakes on a towed vehicle in an emergency;

(2) is independent of brake air, hydraulic, or other pressure and independent of other controls, unless the braking system is arranged to automatically apply the towed vehicle's brakes if the pressure for the second control device on the towing vehicle fails; and

(3) is not required to provide modulated braking.

(c) Subsections (a) and (b) do not apply to a vehicle that tows another vehicle as a commodity when at least one set of wheels of the towed vehicle is on the roadway.

(d) A trailer, semitrailer, or pole trailer that is equipped with air or vacuum brakes or that has a gross weight heavier than 3,000 pounds shall be equipped with brakes that:

(1) operate on all wheels; and

(2) are promptly applied automatically and remain applied for at least 15 minutes in case of a breakaway from the towing vehicle.

(e) A motor vehicle used to tow a trailer, semitrailer, or pole trailer equipped with brakes shall be equipped with service brakes arranged so that, in case of a breakaway of the towed vehicle, the towing vehicle is capable of stopping by use of its service brakes.

(Enacted by Acts 1995, 74th Leg., ch. 165 (S.B. 971), § 1, effective September 1, 1995.)

## Sec. 547.406. Brake Reservoir or Reserve Capacity Required.

(a) A bus, truck, or truck-tractor equipped with air brakes shall be equipped with at least one reservoir that:

(1) is sufficient to ensure that the service brakes can be fully applied without lowering the reservoir pressure, if fully charged to the maximum pressure as regulated by the air compressor governor cut-out setting, by more than 20 percent; and

(2) has a means for readily draining accumulated oil or water.

(b) A truck with at least three axles that is equipped with vacuum brakes or a truck-tractor or truck used to tow a vehicle equipped with vacuum brakes shall be equipped with a reserve capacity or a vacuum reservoir sufficient to ensure that, with the reserve capacity or vacuum reservoir fully charged and with the engine stopped, the service brakes can be fully applied without depleting the vacuum supply by more than 40 percent.

(c) A motor vehicle, trailer, semitrailer, or pole trailer that is equipped with an air or vacuum reservoir or reserve capacity shall be equipped with a check valve or equivalent device to prevent depletion of the air or vacuum supply by failure or leakage.

(d) An air brake system installed on a trailer shall be designed to prevent a backflow of air from the supply reservoir through the supply line.

(Enacted by Acts 1995, 74th Leg., ch. 165 (S.B. 971), § 1, effective September 1, 1995.)

## Sec. 547.407. Brake Warning Devices Required.

(a) A bus, truck, or truck-tractor that uses air to operate its brakes or the brakes of a towed vehicle shall be equipped with:

(1) a warning signal, other than a pressure gauge, that is readily audible or visible to the vehicle operator and that shows when the air reservoir pressure is below 50 percent of the air compressor governor cut-out pressure; and

(2) a pressure gauge visible to the vehicle operator that shows in pounds per square inch the pressure available for braking.

(b) A truck-tractor or truck used to tow a vehicle equipped with vacuum brakes, or a truck with at least three axles that is equipped with vacuum brakes, shall be equipped with a warning signal, other than a gauge showing vacuum, that is readily audible or visible to the vehicle operator and that shows when the vacuum in the reservoir or reserve capacity is less than eight inches of mercury. This subsection does not apply to an operation in which a motor vehicle, trailer, or semitrailer is transported as a commodity when at least one set of the vehicle's wheels is on the roadway.

(c) If a vehicle required to be equipped with a warning device is equipped with air and vacuum power to operate its brakes or the brakes on a towed vehicle, the warning devices required may be combined into a single device that is not a pressure or vacuum gauge.

(Enacted by Acts 1995, 74th Leg., ch. 165 (S.B. 971), § 1, effective September 1, 1995.)

## Sec. 547.408. Performance Requirements for Brakes.

(a) A motor vehicle or combination of vehicles shall be equipped with service brakes capable of:

(1) developing a braking force that is not less than:

(A) 52.8 percent of the gross weight of the vehicle for a passenger vehicle; or

(B) 43.5 percent of the gross weight of the vehicle for a vehicle other than a passenger vehicle;

(2) decelerating to a stop from 20 miles per hour or less at not less than:

(A) 17 feet per second per second for a passenger vehicle; or

(B) 14 feet per second per second for other vehicles; and

(3) stopping from a speed of 20 miles per hour in a distance, measured from the location where the service brake pedal or control is activated, of not more than:

(A) 25 feet for a passenger vehicle;

(B) 30 feet for a motorcycle, motor-driven cycle, or single unit vehicle with a manufac-

turer's gross vehicle weight rating of 10,000 pounds or less;

(C) 40 feet for:

(i) a single unit vehicle with a manufacturer's gross weight rating of more than 10,000 pounds;

(ii) a two-axle towing vehicle and trailer combination with a weight of 3,000 pounds or less;

(iii) a bus that does not have a manufacturer's gross weight rating; and

(iv) the combination of vehicles in an operation exempted by Section 547.407(b); and

(D) 50 feet for other vehicles.

(b) A test for deceleration or stopping distance shall be performed on a dry, smooth, hard surface that:

(1) is free of loose material; and

(2) does not exceed plus or minus one percent grade.

(c) In this section, "passenger vehicle" means a vehicle that has a maximum seating capacity of 10 persons, including the operator, and that does not have a manufacturer's gross vehicle weight rating.

(Enacted by Acts 1995, 74th Leg., ch. 165 (S.B. 971), § 1, effective September 1, 1995.)

## Secs. 547.409 to 547.500 [Reserved for expansion].

## SUBCHAPTER J
## PROVISIONS RELATING TO WARNING DEVICE REQUIREMENTS ON VEHICLES

## Sec. 547.501. Audible Warning Devices.

(a) A motor vehicle shall be equipped with a horn in good working condition that emits a sound audible under normal conditions at a distance of at least 200 feet.

(b) A vehicle may not be equipped with and a person may not use on a vehicle a siren, whistle, or bell unless the vehicle is:

(1) a commercial vehicle that is equipped with a theft alarm signal device arranged so that the device cannot be used as an ordinary warning signal; or

(2) an authorized emergency vehicle that is equipped with a siren, whistle, or bell that complies with Section 547.702.

(c) A motor vehicle operator shall use a horn to provide audible warning only when necessary to insure safe operation.

(d) A warning device, including a horn, may not emit an unreasonably loud or harsh sound or a whistle.

(Enacted by Acts 1995, 74th Leg., ch. 165 (S.B. 971), § 1, effective September 1, 1995.)

### Sec. 547.502. Visible Warning Devices Required.

(a) Except as provided by Subsection (b), a person who operates, outside an urban district or on a divided highway, a truck, bus, or truck-tractor or a motor vehicle towing a house trailer shall carry in the vehicle:

(1) at daytime:

(A) at least two red flags at least 12 inches square; and

(B) standards to support the flags; and

(2) at nighttime:

(A) at least three flares and at least three red-burning fusees;

(B) at least three red electric lanterns; or

(C) at least three portable red emergency reflectors.

(b) A person who operates an explosive cargo vehicle at nighttime:

(1) shall carry in the vehicle three red electric lanterns or three portable red emergency reflectors; and

(2) may not carry in the vehicle a flare, fusee, or signal produced by flame.

(c) A flare, electric lantern, or portable reflector must be visible and distinguishable at a distance of at least 600 feet at night under normal atmospheric conditions.

(d) A portable reflector unit must be designed and constructed to reflect a red light clearly visible at all distances from 100 to 600 feet under normal atmospheric conditions at night when directly in front of lawful lower beams of headlamps.

(e) A flare, fusee, electric lantern, portable reflector, or warning flag must be a type approved by the department.

(Enacted by Acts 1995, 74th Leg., ch. 165 (S.B. 971), § 1, effective September 1, 1995.)

### Sec. 547.503. Display of Hazard Lamps.

(a) The operator of a vehicle that is described by Subsection (b) and that is stopped on a roadway or shoulder shall immediately display vehic-

ular hazard warning lamps that comply with Section 547.331, unless the vehicle:

(1) is parked lawfully in an urban district;

(2) is stopped lawfully to receive or discharge a passenger;

(3) is stopped to avoid conflict with other traffic;

(4) is stopped to comply with a direction of a police officer or an official traffic-control device; or

(5) displays other warning devices as required by Sections 547.504—547.507.

(b) This section applies to a truck, bus, truck-tractor, trailer, semitrailer, or pole trailer at least 80 inches wide or at least 30 feet long.

(Enacted by Acts 1995, 74th Leg., ch. 165 (S.B. 971), § 1, effective September 1, 1995.)

### Sec. 547.504. Display of Devices When Lighted Lamps Required.

(a) Unless sufficient light exists to reveal a person or vehicle at a distance of 1,000 feet, the operator of a vehicle described by Section 547.503(b) or an explosive cargo vehicle shall display warning devices that comply with the requirements of Section 547.502:

(1) when lighted lamps are required; and

(2) under the conditions stated in this section.

(b) Except as provided by Section 547.506 and Subsection (d), the operator of a vehicle described by Section 547.503(b) or an explosive cargo vehicle that is disabled, or stopped for more than 10 minutes, on a roadway outside an urban district shall:

(1) immediately place a lighted red electric lantern or a portable red emergency reflector at the traffic side of the vehicle in the direction of the nearest approaching traffic; and

(2) place in the following order and as soon as practicable within 15 minutes one lighted red electric lamp or portable red emergency reflector:

(A) in the center of the lane occupied by the vehicle toward approaching traffic approximately 100 feet from the vehicle; and

(B) in the center of the lane occupied by the vehicle in the opposite direction approximately 100 feet from the vehicle.

(c) Except as provided by Section 547.506 and Subsection (d), the operator of a vehicle described by Section 547.503(b) or an explosive cargo vehicle that is disabled, or stopped for more than 10 minutes, on a roadway of a divided highway shall place the warning devices described by Subsection (b):

(1) in the center of the lane occupied by the vehicle toward approaching traffic approximately 200 feet from the vehicle;

(2) in the center of the lane occupied by the vehicle toward approaching traffic approximately 100 feet from the vehicle; and

(3) at the traffic side approximately 10 feet from the vehicle in the direction of the nearest approaching traffic.

(d) As an alternative to the use of electric lamps or red reflectors and except as provided by Subsection (e), the operator of a vehicle described by Section 547.503(b) may display a lighted fusee to comply with the requirements of Subsection (b)(1) or liquid-burning flares to comply with the requirements of Subsections (b)(2) and (c). If the operator uses liquid-burning flares to comply with Subsection (b)(2), the operator shall also, after complying with Subsection (b)(2)(B), place a liquid-burning flare at the traffic side of the vehicle at least 10 feet in the direction of the nearest approaching traffic. If a fusee is used to comply with Subsection (b)(1), the operator shall comply with Subsection (b)(2) within the burning period of the fusee.

(e) The operator of an explosive cargo vehicle may not display as a warning device a flare, fusee, or signal produced by flame.
(Enacted by Acts 1995, 74th Leg., ch. 165 (S.B. 971), § 1, effective September 1, 1995.)

### Sec. 547.505.  Display of Devices When Lighted Lamps Are Not Required.

(a) The operator of a vehicle described by Section 547.503(b) or an explosive cargo vehicle that is disabled, or stopped for more than 10 minutes, on a roadway outside an urban district or on a roadway of a divided highway when lighted lamps are not required shall display two red flags that comply with Section 547.502.

(b) If traffic on the roadway moves in two directions, one flag shall be placed approximately 100 feet to the rear and one approximately 100 feet ahead of the vehicle in the center of the lane occupied by the vehicle.

(c) If traffic on the roadway moves in one direction, one flag shall be placed approximately 100 feet and one approximately 200 feet to the rear of the vehicle in the center of the lane occupied by the vehicle.
(Enacted by Acts 1995, 74th Leg., ch. 165 (S.B. 971), § 1, effective September 1, 1995.)

### Sec. 547.506.  Display of Devices: Vehicles Off Roadway.

The operator of a vehicle described by Section 547.503(b) or an explosive cargo vehicle that is stopped entirely on the shoulder at a time and in a place referred to in this subchapter shall place required warning devices on the shoulder as close as practicable to the edge of the roadway.
(Enacted by Acts 1995, 74th Leg., ch. 165 (S.B. 971), § 1, effective September 1, 1995.)

### Sec. 547.507.  Display of Devices When View of Vehicle Obstructed.

Unless sufficient light exists to reveal a person or vehicle at a distance of 1,000 feet, the operator of a vehicle described by Section 547.503(b) or an explosive cargo vehicle that is disabled, or stopped for more than 10 minutes, within 500 feet of a curve, hillcrest, or other obstruction to view shall place the required warning device for the direction of the obstruction from 100 to 500 feet from the vehicle so as to provide ample warning to other traffic.
(Enacted by Acts 1995, 74th Leg., ch. 165 (S.B. 971), § 1, effective September 1, 1995.)

### Sec. 547.508.  Offense Relating to Warning Devices.

(a) Except as provided by Subsection (b), a person may not remove, damage, destroy, misplace, or extinguish a warning device required under Sections 547.502—547.507 when the device is being displayed or used as required.

(b) This section does not apply to:

(1) an owner of a vehicle or the owner's authorized agent or employee; or

(2) a peace officer acting in an official capacity.
(Enacted by Acts 1995, 74th Leg., ch. 165 (S.B. 971), § 1, effective September 1, 1995.)

### Secs. 547.509 to 547.600 [Reserved for expansion].

## SUBCHAPTER K
## PROVISIONS RELATING TO OTHER VEHICLE EQUIPMENT

### Sec. 547.601.  Safety Belts Required.

A motor vehicle required by Chapter 548 to be inspected shall be equipped with front safety belts if safety belt anchorages were part of the manufacturer's original equipment on the vehicle.

(Enacted by Acts 1995, 74th Leg., ch. 165 (S.B. 971), § 1, effective September 1, 1995.)

## Sec. 547.602. Mirrors Required.

A motor vehicle, including a motor vehicle used to tow another vehicle, shall be equipped with a mirror located to reflect to the operator a view of the highway for a distance of at least 200 feet from the rear of the vehicle.
(Enacted by Acts 1995, 74th Leg., ch. 165 (S.B. 971), § 1, effective September 1, 1995.)

## Sec. 547.603. Windshield Wipers Required.

A motor vehicle shall be equipped with a device that is operated or controlled by the operator of the vehicle and that cleans moisture from the windshield. The device shall be maintained in good working condition.
(Enacted by Acts 1995, 74th Leg., ch. 165 (S.B. 971), § 1, effective September 1, 1995.)

## Sec. 547.604. Muffler Required.

(a) A motor vehicle shall be equipped with a muffler in good working condition that continually operates to prevent excessive or unusual noise.

(b) A person may not use a muffler cutout, bypass, or similar device on a motor vehicle.
(Enacted by Acts 1995, 74th Leg., ch. 165 (S.B. 971), § 1, effective September 1, 1995.)

## Sec. 547.605. Emission Systems Required.

(a) The engine and power mechanism of a motor vehicle shall be equipped and adjusted to prevent the escape of excessive smoke or fumes.

(b) A motor vehicle or motor vehicle engine, of a model year after 1967, shall be equipped to prevent the discharge of crankcase emissions into the ambient atmosphere.

(c) The owner or operator of a motor vehicle or motor vehicle engine, of a model year after 1967, that is equipped with an exhaust emission system:

(1) shall maintain the system in good working condition;

(2) shall use the system when the motor vehicle or motor vehicle engine is operated; and

(3) may not remove the system or a part of the system or intentionally make the system inoperable in this state, unless the owner or operator removes the system or part to install another system or part intended to be equally effective in reducing atmospheric emissions.

(d) Except when travel conditions require the downshifting or use of lower gears to maintain reasonable momentum, a person commits an offense if the person operates, or as an owner knowingly permits another person to operate, a vehicle that emits:

(1) visible smoke for 10 seconds or longer; or

(2) visible smoke that remains suspended in the air for 10 seconds or longer before fully dissipating.

(e) An offense under this section is a misdemeanor punishable by a fine of not less than $1 and not more than $350 for each violation. If a person has previously been convicted of an offense under this section, an offense under this section is a misdemeanor punishable by a fine of not less than $200 and not more than $1,000 for each violation.
(Enacted by Acts 1995, 74th Leg., ch. 165 (S.B. 971), § 1, effective September 1, 1995; am. Acts 2001, 77th Leg., ch. 1075 (H.B. 2134), § 6, effective September 1, 2001.)

## Sec. 547.606. Safety Guards or Flaps Required.

(a) A road tractor, truck, trailer, truck-tractor in combination with a semitrailer, or semitrailer in combination with a towing vehicle that has at least four tires or at least two super single tires on the rearmost axle of the vehicle or the rearmost vehicle in the combination shall be equipped with safety guards or flaps that:

(1) are of a type prescribed by the department; and

(2) are located and suspended behind the rearmost wheels of the vehicle or the rearmost vehicle in the combination within eight inches of the surface of the highway.

(b) This section does not apply to a truck-tractor operated alone or a pole trailer.

(c) In this section, "super single tire" means a wide-base, single tire that may be used in place of two standard tires on the same axle.
(Enacted by Acts 1995, 74th Leg., ch. 165 (S.B. 971), § 1, effective September 1, 1995; am. Acts 2011, 82nd Leg., ch. 752 (H.B. 1330), § 1, effective September 1, 2011.)

## Sec. 547.607. Fire Extinguisher Required.

A school bus or a motor vehicle that transports passengers for hire or lease shall be equipped with at least one quart of chemical-type fire extinguisher in good condition and located for immediate use.

(Enacted by Acts 1995, 74th Leg., ch. 165 (S.B. 971), § 1, effective September 1, 1995.)

## Sec. 547.608. Safety Glazing Material Required.

(a) Except as provided by Subsection (b), a person who sells or registers a new passenger-type motor vehicle, including a passenger bus and school bus, shall equip the vehicle doors, windows, and windshield with safety glazing material of a type approved by the department.

(b) The requirements of Subsection (a) do not apply to a glazing material in a compartment of a truck, including a truck-tractor, that is not designed and equipped for a person to ride in.

(c) A person may not replace or require the replacement of glass in a door, window, or windshield of any motor vehicle if the replacement is not made with safety glazing material.

(d) A person who sells or attaches to a motor vehicle a camper manufactured or assembled after January 1, 1972, shall equip the camper doors and windows with safety glazing material of a type approved by the department. In this subsection "camper" means a structure designed to:

    (1) be loaded on or attached to a motor vehicle; and

    (2) provide temporary living quarters for recreation, travel, or other use.

(e) A person who sells imperfect safety glass for a door, window, or windshield of a motor vehicle shall:

    (1) label the glass "second," "imperfect," or by a similar term in red letters at least one inch in size to indicate to the consumer the quality of the glass;

    (2) orally notify the consumer of each imperfection and the possible result of using imperfect glass; and

    (3) deliver written notice at the time of purchase notifying the consumer of each imperfection and the possible result of using imperfect glass.

(Enacted by Acts 1995, 74th Leg., ch. 165 (S.B. 971), § 1, effective September 1, 1995.)

## Sec. 547.609. Required Label for Sunscreening Devices.

A sunscreening device must have a label that:

    (1) is legible;

    (2) contains information required by the department on light transmission and luminous reflectance of the device;

    (3) if the device is placed on or attached to a windshield or a side or rear window, states that the light transmission of the device is consistent with Section 547.613(b)(1) or (2), as applicable; and

    (4) is permanently installed between the material and the surface to which the material is applied.

(Enacted by Acts 1995, 74th Leg., ch. 165 (S.B. 971), § 1, effective September 1, 1995; am. Acts 2009, 81st Leg., ch. 750 (S.B. 589), § 1, effective September 1, 2009.)

## Sec. 547.610. Safe Air-Conditioning Equipment Required; Sale of Noncomplying Vehicle.

(a) Air-conditioning equipment:

    (1) shall be manufactured, installed, and maintained to ensure the safety of the vehicle occupants and the public; and

    (2) may not contain any refrigerant that is flammable or is toxic to persons unless the refrigerant is included in the list published by the United States Environmental Protection Agency as a safe alternative motor vehicle air conditioning substitute for chlorofluorocarbon-12, pursuant to 42 U.S.C. Section 7671k(c).

(b) A person may not possess or offer for sale, sell, or equip a motor vehicle with air-conditioning equipment that does not comply with the requirements of this section and Section 547.103.

(Enacted by Acts 1995, 74th Leg., ch. 165 (S.B. 971), § 1, effective September 1, 1995; am. Acts 2009, 81st Leg., ch. 282 (S.B. 2019), § 1, effective May 30, 2009.)

## Sec. 547.611. Use of Certain Video Equipment and Television Receivers.

(a) A motor vehicle may be equipped with video receiving equipment, including a television, a digital video disc player, a videocassette player, or similar equipment, only if the equipment is located so that the video display is not visible from the operator's seat unless the vehicle's transmission is in park or the vehicle's parking brake is applied.

(b) A motor vehicle specially designed as a mobile unit used by a licensed television station may have video receiving equipment located so that the video display is visible from the operator's side, but the receiver may be used only when the vehicle is stopped.

(c) This section does not prohibit the use of:

    (1) equipment used:

(A) exclusively for receiving digital information for commercial purposes;

(B) exclusively for a safety or law enforcement purpose, if each installation is approved by the department;

(C) in a remote television transmission truck; or

(D) exclusively for monitoring the performance of equipment installed on a vehicle used for safety purposes in connection with the operations of a natural gas, water, or electric utility; or

(2) a monitoring device that:

(A) produces an electronic display; and

(B) is used exclusively in conjunction with a mobile navigation system installed in the vehicle.

(Enacted by Acts 1995, 74th Leg., ch. 165 (S.B. 971), § 1, effective September 1, 1995; am. Acts 1997, 75th Leg., ch. 165 (S.B. 898), § 30.117(a), effective September 1, 1997; am. Acts 2003, 78th Leg., ch. 20 (S.B. 209), §§ 1, 2, effective September 1, 2003; am. Acts 2007, 80th Leg., ch. 942 (H.B. 3832), § 1, effective June 15, 2007.)

## Sec. 547.612. Restrictions on Use and Sale of Tires.

(a) A solid rubber tire used on a vehicle must have rubber on the traction surface that extends above the edge of the flange of the periphery.

(b) A person may not operate or move a motor vehicle, trailer, or semitrailer that has a metal tire in contact with the roadway, unless:

(1) the vehicle is a farm wagon or farm trailer that has a gross weight of less than 5,000 pounds; and

(2) the owner is transporting farm products to market, for processing, or from farm to farm.

(c) A tire used on a moving vehicle may not have on its periphery a block, stud, flange, cleat, or spike or other protuberance of a material other than rubber that projects beyond the tread of the traction surface, unless the protuberance:

(1) does not injure the highway; or

(2) is a tire chain of reasonable proportion that is used as required for safety because of a condition that might cause the vehicle to skid.

(d) The Texas Transportation Commission and a local authority within its jurisdiction may issue a special permit that authorizes a person to operate a tractor or traction engine that has movable tracks with transverse corrugations on the periphery or a farm tractor or other farm machinery.

(e) A person commits an offense if the person offers for sale or sells a private passenger automobile tire that is regrooved. An offense under this section is a misdemeanor punishable by a fine of not less than $500 or more than $2,000. (Enacted by Acts 1995, 74th Leg., ch. 165 (S.B. 971), § 1, effective September 1, 1995.)

## Sec. 547.613. Restrictions on Windows.

(a) Except as provided by Subsection (b), a person commits an offense that is a misdemeanor:

(1) if the person operates a motor vehicle that has an object or material that is placed on or attached to the windshield or side or rear window and that obstructs or reduces the operator's clear view; or

(2) if a person, including an installer or manufacturer, places on or attaches to the windshield or side or rear window of a motor vehicle a transparent material that alters the color or reduces the light transmission.

(a-1) A person in the business of placing or attaching transparent material that alters the color or reduces the light transmission to the windshield or side or rear window of a motor vehicle commits a misdemeanor punishable by a fine not to exceed $1,000 if the person:

(1) places or attaches such transparent material to the windshield or side or rear window of a motor vehicle; and

(2) does not install a label that complies with Section 547.609 between the transparent material and the windshield or side or rear window of the vehicle, as applicable.

(b) Subsection (a) does not apply to:

(1) a windshield that has a sunscreening device that:

(A) in combination with the windshield has a light transmission of 25 percent or more;

(B) in combination with the windshield has a luminous reflectance of 25 percent or less;

(C) is not red, blue, or amber; and

(D) does not extend downward beyond the AS-1 line or more than five inches from the top of the windshield, whichever is closer to the top of the windshield;

(2) a wing vent or a window that is to the left or right of the vehicle operator if the vent or window has a sunscreening device that in combination with the vent or window has:

(A) a light transmission of 25 percent or more; and

(B) a luminous reflectance of 25 percent or less;

(2-a) a side window that is to the rear of the vehicle operator;

(3) a rear window, if the motor vehicle is equipped with an outside mirror on each side of the vehicle that reflects to the vehicle operator a view of the highway for a distance of at least 200 feet from the rear;

(4) a rearview mirror;

(5) an adjustable nontransparent sun visor that is mounted in front of a side window and not attached to the glass;

(6) a direction, destination, or termination sign on a passenger common carrier motor vehicle, if the sign does not interfere with the vehicle operator's view of approaching traffic;

(7) a rear window wiper motor;

(8) a rear trunk lid handle or hinge;

(9) a luggage rack attached to the rear trunk;

(10) a side window that is to the rear of the vehicle operator on a multipurpose vehicle;

(11) a window that has a United States, state, or local certificate placed on or attached to it as required by law;

(12) a motor vehicle that is not registered in this state;

(13) a window that complies with federal standards for window materials, including a factory-tinted or a pretinted window installed by the vehicle manufacturer, or a replacement window meeting the specifications required by the vehicle manufacturer;

(14) a vehicle that is:

(A) used regularly to transport passengers for a fee; and

(B) authorized to operate under license or permit by a local authority;

(15) a vehicle that is maintained by a law enforcement agency and used for law enforcement purposes; or

(16) a commercial motor vehicle as defined by Section 644.001.

(c) A manufacturer shall certify to the department that the sunscreening device made or assembled by the manufacturer complies with the light transmission and luminous reflectance specifications established by Subsection (b) for sunscreening devices in combination with a window.

(d) The department may determine that a window that has a sunscreening device is exempt under Subsection (b)(2) if the light transmission

or luminous reflectance varies by no more than three percent from the standard established in that subsection.

(e) It is a defense to prosecution under Subsection (a) that the defendant or a passenger in the vehicle at the time of the violation is required for a medical reason to be shielded from direct rays of the sun.

(f) It is not an offense under this section for a person to offer for sale or sell a motor vehicle with a windshield or window that does not comply with this section.

(g) In this section:

(1) "Installer" means a person who fabricates, laminates, or tempers a safety glazing material to incorporate, during the installation process, the capacity to reflect light or reduce light transmission.

(2) "Manufacturer" means a person who:

(A) manufactures or assembles a sunscreening device; or

(B) fabricates, laminates, or tempers safety glazing material to incorporate, during the manufacturing process, the capacity to reflect light or reduce light transmission.

(Enacted by Acts 1995, 74th Leg., ch. 165 (S.B. 971), § 1, effective September 1, 1995; am. Acts 1997, 75th Leg., ch. 165 (S.B. 898), § 30.118(a), effective September 1, 1997; am. Acts 2003, 78th Leg., ch. 136 (S.B. 345), § 1, effective September 1, 2003; am. Acts 2007, 80th Leg., ch. 368 (S.B. 329), § 1, effective June 15, 2007; am. Acts 2009, 81st Leg., ch. 750 (S.B. 589), § 2, effective September 1, 2009.)

## Sec. 547.614. Restrictions on Airbags.

(a) In this section, "counterfeit airbag" means an airbag that does not meet all applicable federal safety regulations for an airbag designed to be installed in a vehicle of a particular make, model, and year.

(a-1) A person commits an offense if the person knowingly:

(1) installs or purports to install an airbag in a vehicle; and

(2) does not install an airbag or installs a counterfeit airbag.

(a-2) A person commits an offense if the person:

(1) makes or sells a counterfeit airbag to be installed in a motor vehicle;

(2) intentionally alters an airbag that is not counterfeit in a manner that causes the airbag to not meet all applicable federal safety regu-

lations for an airbag designed to be installed in a vehicle of a particular make, model, and year;

(3) represents to another person that a counterfeit airbag installed in a motor vehicle is not counterfeit; or

(4) causes another person to violate Subsection (a-1) or Subdivision (1), (2), or (3) or assists a person in violating Subsection (a-1) or Subdivision (1), (2), or (3).

(b) Except as provided by Subsections (c) and (d), an offense under this section is a Class A misdemeanor.

(c) An offense under this section is a felony of the third degree if it is shown on the trial of the offense that the defendant has been previously convicted of an offense under this section.

(d) An offense under this section is a felony of the second degree if it is shown on the trial of the offense that as a result of the offense an individual suffered bodily injury.

(Enacted by Acts 2001, 77th Leg., ch. 910 (S.B. 113), § 3, effective September 1, 2001; am. Acts 2007, 80th Leg., ch. 269 (H.B. 71), § 1, effective September 1, 2007.)

## Sec. 547.615. Recording Devices.

(a) In this section:

(1) "Owner" means a person who:

(A) has all the incidents of ownership of a motor vehicle, including legal title, regardless of whether the person lends, rents, or creates a security interest in the vehicle;

(B) is entitled to possession of a motor vehicle as a purchaser under a security agreement; or

(C) is entitled to possession of a motor vehicle as a lessee under a written lease agreement if the agreement is for a period of not less than three months.

(2) "Recording device" means a feature that is installed by the manufacturer in a motor vehicle and that does any of the following for the purpose of retrieving information from the vehicle after an accident in which the vehicle has been involved:

(A) records the speed and direction the vehicle is traveling;

(B) records vehicle location data;

(C) records steering performance;

(D) records brake performance, including information on whether brakes were applied before an accident;

(E) records the driver's safety belt status; or

(F) transmits information concerning the accident to a central communications system when the accident occurs.

(b) A manufacturer of a new motor vehicle that is sold or leased in this state and that is equipped with a recording device shall disclose that fact in the owner's manual of the vehicle.

(c) Information recorded or transmitted by a recording device may not be retrieved by a person other than the owner of the motor vehicle in which the recording device is installed except:

(1) on court order;

(2) with the consent of the owner for any purpose, including for the purpose of diagnosing, servicing, or repairing the motor vehicle;

(3) for the purpose of improving motor vehicle safety, including for medical research on the human body's reaction to motor vehicle accidents, if the identity of the owner or driver of the vehicle is not disclosed in connection with the retrieved information; or

(4) for the purpose of determining the need for or facilitating emergency medical response in the event of a motor vehicle accident.

(d) For information recorded or transmitted by a recording device described by Subsection (a)(2)(B), a court order may be obtained only after a showing that:

(1) retrieval of the information is necessary to protect the public safety; or

(2) the information is evidence of an offense or constitutes evidence that a particular person committed an offense.

(e) For the purposes of Subsection (c)(3):

(1) disclosure of a motor vehicle's vehicle identification number with the last six digits deleted or redacted is not disclosure of the identity of the owner or driver; and

(2) retrieved information may be disclosed only:

(A) for the purposes of motor vehicle safety and medical research communities to advance the purposes described in Subsection (c)(3); or

(B) to a data processor solely for the purposes described in Subsection (c)(3).

(f) If a recording device is used as part of a subscription service, the subscription service agreement must disclose that the device may record or transmit information as described by Subsection (a)(2). Subsection (c) does not apply to a subscription service under this subsection.

(Enacted by Acts 2005, 79th Leg., ch. 910 (H.B. 160), § 1, effective September 1, 2006.)

**Transportation**

## Sec. 547.616. Radar Interference Devices; Offense.

(a) In this section, "radar interference device" means a device, a mechanism, an instrument, or equipment that is designed, manufactured, used, or intended to be used to interfere with, scramble, disrupt, or otherwise cause to malfunction a radar or laser device used to measure the speed of a motor vehicle by a law enforcement agency of this state or a political subdivision of this state, including a "radar jamming device," "jammer," "scrambler," or "diffuser." The term does not include a ham radio, band radio, or similar electronic device.

(b) A person, other than a law enforcement officer in the discharge of the officer's official duties, may not use, attempt to use, install, operate, or attempt to operate a radar interference device in a motor vehicle operated by the person.

(c) A person may not purchase, sell, or offer for sale a radar interference device to be used in a manner described by Subsection (b).

(d) A person who violates this section commits an offense. An offense under this subsection is a Class C misdemeanor.

(Enacted by Acts 2011, 82nd Leg., ch. 739 (H.B. 1116), § 1, effective September 1, 2011.)

## Secs. 547.617 to 547.700 [Reserved for expansion].

## SUBCHAPTER L
## ADDITIONAL EQUIPMENT REQUIREMENTS FOR SCHOOL BUSES, AUTHORIZED EMERGENCY VEHICLES, AND SLOW-MOVING VEHICLES

## Sec. 547.701. Additional Equipment Requirements for School Buses and Other Buses Used to Transport Schoolchildren.

(a) A school bus shall be equipped with:

(1) a convex mirror or other device that reflects to the school bus operator a clear view of the area immediately in front of the vehicle that would otherwise be hidden from view; and

(2) signal lamps that:

(A) are mounted as high and as widely spaced laterally as practicable;

(B) display four alternately flashing red lights, two located on the front at the same level and two located on the rear at the same level; and

(C) emit a light visible at a distance of 500 feet in normal sunlight.

(b) A school bus may be equipped with:

(1) rooftop warning lamps:

(A) that conform to and are placed on the bus in accordance with specifications adopted under Section 34.002, Education Code; and

(B) that are operated under rules adopted by the school district; and

(2) movable stop arms:

(A) that conform to regulations adopted under Section 34.002, Education Code; and

(B) that may be operated only when the bus is stopped to load or unload students.

(c) When a school bus is being stopped or is stopped on a highway to permit students to board or exit the bus, the operator of the bus shall activate all flashing warning signal lights and other equipment on the bus designed to warn other drivers that the bus is stopping to load or unload children. A person may not operate such a light or other equipment except when the bus is being stopped or is stopped on a highway to permit students to board or exit the bus.

(d) The exterior of a school bus may not bear advertising or another paid announcement directed at the public if the advertising or announcement distracts from the effectiveness of required safety warning equipment. The department shall adopt rules to implement this subsection. A school bus that violates this section or rules adopted under this section shall be placed out of service until it complies.

(e) In this subsection, "bus" includes a school bus and a school activity bus. A bus operated by or contracted for use by a school district for the transportation of schoolchildren shall be equipped with a three-point seat belt for each passenger, including the operator. This subsection applies to:

(1) each bus purchased by a school district on or after September 1, 2010, for the transportation of schoolchildren; and

(2) each school-chartered bus contracted for use by a school district on or after September 1, 2011, for the transportation of schoolchildren.

(f) A school district is required to comply with Subsection (e) only to the extent that the legislature has appropriated money for the purpose of reimbursing school districts for expenses incurred in complying with Subsection (e).

(Enacted by Acts 1995, 74th Leg., ch. 165 (S.B. 971), § 1, effective September 1, 1995; am. Acts

1997, 75th Leg., ch. 1438 (H.B. 3249), § 12, effective September 1, 1997; am. Acts 1999, 76th Leg., ch. 183 (H.B. 1744), § 1, effective September 1, 1999; am. Acts 2007, 80th Leg., ch. 259 (H.B. 323), § 1, effective September 1, 2007; am. Acts 2007, 80th Leg., ch. 259 (H.B. 323), § 2, effective September 1, 2007; am. Acts 2009, 81st Leg., ch. 1328 (H.B. 3646), § 90(b), (c), effective September 1, 2009; am. Acts 2011, 82nd Leg., ch. 451 (S.B. 1610), § 1, effective September 1, 2011.)

### Sec. 547.7011. Additional Equipment Requirements for Other Buses.

(a) A bus, other than a school bus, that provides public transportation and that was acquired on or after September 1, 1997, shall be equipped with two or more hazard lamps that:

(1) are mounted at the same level on the rear of the bus;

(2) are visible at a distance of 500 feet in normal sunlight;

(3) flash; and

(4) emit amber light.

(b) An operator of a bus to which this section applies shall activate the hazard lamps if the bus stops to load or unload a person under 18 years of age.

(c) A bus to which this section applies must bear a sign on the rear of the bus stating: "Caution—children may be exiting".
(Enacted by Acts 1997, 75th Leg., ch. 1131 (H.B. 3092), § 1, effective September 1, 1997.)

### Sec. 547.7012. Requirements for Multifunction School Activity Buses.

A multifunction school activity bus may not be painted National School Bus Glossy Yellow.
(Enacted by Acts 2007, 80th Leg., ch. 923 (H.B. 3190), § 6, effective September 1, 2007.)

### Sec. 547.7015. Rules Relating to School Buses.

(a) The department shall adopt and enforce rules governing the design, color, lighting and other equipment, construction, and operation of a school bus for the transportation of schoolchildren that is:

(1) owned and operated by a school district in this state; or

(2) privately owned and operated under a contract with a school district in this state.

(b) In adopting rules under this section, the department shall emphasize:

(1) safety features; and

(2) long-range, maintenance-free factors.

(c) Rules adopted under this section:

(1) apply to each school district, the officers and employees of a district, and each person employed under contract by a school district; and

(2) shall by reference be made a part of any contract that is entered into by a school district in this state for the transportation of schoolchildren on a privately owned school bus.
(Enacted by Acts 1997, 75th Leg., ch. 165 (S.B. 898), § 30.119(a), effective September 1, 1997; am. Acts 2003, 78th Leg., ch. 309 (H.B. 3042), § 9.02, effective June 18, 2003.)

### Sec. 547.702. Additional Equipment Requirements for Authorized Emergency Vehicles.

(a) An authorized emergency vehicle may be equipped with a siren, exhaust whistle, or bell:

(1) of a type approved by the department; and

(2) that emits a sound audible under normal conditions at a distance of at least 500 feet.

(b) The operator of an authorized emergency vehicle shall use the siren, whistle, or bell when necessary to warn other vehicle operators or pedestrians of the approach of the emergency vehicle.

(c) Except as provided by this section, an authorized emergency vehicle shall be equipped with signal lamps that:

(1) are mounted as high and as widely spaced laterally as practicable;

(2) display four alternately flashing red lights, two located on the front at the same level and two located on the rear at the same level; and

(3) emit a light visible at a distance of 500 feet in normal sunlight.

(d) A private vehicle operated by a volunteer firefighter responding to a fire alarm or a medical emergency may, but is not required to, be equipped with signal lamps that comply with the requirements of Subsection (c).

(e) A private vehicle operated by a volunteer firefighter responding to a fire alarm or a medical emergency may be equipped with a signal lamp that is temporarily attached to the vehicle roof and flashes a red light visible at a distance of at least 500 feet in normal sunlight.

(f) A police vehicle may, but is not required to, be equipped with signal lamps that comply with Subsection (c).

Transportation

(Enacted by Acts 1995, 74th Leg., ch. 165 (S.B. 971), § 1, effective September 1, 1995.)

### Sec. 547.703. Additional Equipment Requirements for Slow-Moving Vehicles.

(a) Except as provided by Subsection (b), a slow-moving vehicle shall display a slow-moving-vehicle emblem that:

(1) has a reflective surface designed to be clearly visible in daylight or at night from the light of standard automobile headlamps at a distance of at least 500 feet;

(2) is mounted base down on the rear of the vehicle at a height from three to five feet above the road surface; and

(3) is maintained in a clean, reflective condition.

(b) Subsection (a) does not apply to a vehicle that is used in construction or maintenance work and is traveling in a construction area that is marked as required by the Texas Transportation Commission.

(c) If a motor vehicle displaying a slow-moving-vehicle emblem tows machinery, including an implement of husbandry, and the visibility of the emblem is not obstructed, the towed unit is not required to display a slow-moving-vehicle emblem.

(d) A golf cart that is operated at a speed of not more than 25 miles per hour is required to display a slow-moving-vehicle emblem when it is operated on a public highway, as defined by Section 502.001, under Section 551.403 or 551.404.

(e) [Repealed by Acts 2009, 81st Leg., ch. 1136 (H.B. 2553), § 12(2), effective September 1, 2009.]

(Enacted by Acts 1995, 74th Leg., ch. 165 (S.B. 971), § 1, effective September 1, 1995; am. Acts 2009, 81st Leg., ch. 1136 (H.B. 2553), §§ 9, 12(2), effective September 1, 2009.)

### Secs. 547.704 to 547.800 [Reserved for expansion].

## SUBCHAPTER M
## ADDITIONAL OR ALTERNATIVE EQUIPMENT REQUIREMENTS FOR MOTORCYCLES AND MOTOR-DRIVEN CYCLES

### Sec. 547.801. Lighting Equipment.

(a) A motorcycle, including a motor-driven cycle, shall be equipped with:

(1) not more than two headlamps mounted at a height from 24 to 54 inches;

(2) at least one taillamp mounted at a height from 20 to 72 inches;

(3) a taillamp or separate lamp to illuminate the rear license plate that complies with the requirements of Sections 547.322(f) and (g);

(4) at least one stoplamp that complies with the requirements of Section 547.323(d); and

(5) at least one rear red reflector that complies with the requirements of Section 547.325(b) and may be included as a part of the taillamp.

(b) A motorcycle, other than a motor-driven cycle, shall be equipped with multiple-beam lighting equipment that produces:

(1) an uppermost distribution of light that reveals a person or vehicle at a distance of at least 300 feet ahead; and

(2) a lowermost distribution of light that:

(A) reveals a person or vehicle at a distance of at least 150 feet ahead; and

(B) is aimed so that no part of the high-intensity portion of the beam on the motorcycle that is on a straight and level road under any condition of loading projects into the eyes of an approaching vehicle operator.

(c) A motor-driven cycle shall be equipped with:

(1) multiple-beam lighting equipment that complies with the requirements of Subsection (b); or

(2) single-beam lighting equipment that:

(A) emits light sufficient to reveal a person or vehicle:

(i) at a distance of at least 100 feet when the cycle is operated at a speed less than 25 miles per hour;

(ii) at a distance of at least 200 feet when the cycle is operated at a speed of 25 miles per hour or more; and

(iii) at a distance of at least 300 feet when the cycle is operated at a speed of 35 miles per hour or more; and

(B) is aimed so that no part of the high-intensity portion of the beam from the lamp on a loaded cycle projects a beam higher than the level center of the lamp for a distance of 25 feet ahead.

(d) A motorcycle may not be operated at any time unless at least one headlamp on the motorcycle is illuminated. This subsection does not apply to a motorcycle manufactured before the model year 1975.

(Enacted by Acts 1995, 74th Leg., ch. 165 (S.B. 971), § 1, effective September 1, 1995; am. Acts 1997, 75th Leg., ch. 782 (H.B. 2522), § 1, effective September 1, 1997; am. Acts 1999, 76th Leg., ch. 1022 (H.B. 2920), § 1, effective September 1, 1999.)

## Sec. 547.802. Brake Equipment.

(a) If a motorcycle, including a motor-driven cycle, complies with the performance requirements of Section 547.408, brakes are not required on the wheel of a sidecar attached to the cycle.

(b) If a motor-driven cycle complies with the performance standards of Section 547.408, brakes are not required on the front wheel of the cycle.

(c) The director may require an inspection of a motor-driven cycle braking system and may disapprove a system that:

(1) does not comply with the brake performance requirements in Section 547.408; or

(2) is not designed or constructed to ensure reasonable and reliable performance during actual use.

(Enacted by Acts 1995, 74th Leg., ch. 165 (S.B. 971), § 1, effective September 1, 1995.)

## CHAPTER 548
## COMPULSORY INSPECTION OF VEHICLES

### Subchapter A. General Provisions

### Subchapter B. Vehicles and Equipment Subject to Inspection and Reinspection

### Subchapter C. Periods of Inspection; Prerequisites to Issuance of Inspection Certificate

### Subchapter D. Inspection of Commercial Motor Vehicles

### Subchapter E. Issuance, Recording, and Proof of Inspection Certificates and Verification Forms

### Subchapter F. Motor Vehicle Emissions Inspection and Maintenance

### Subchapter G. Certification of Inspection Station or Inspector

## SUBCHAPTER A
## GENERAL PROVISIONS

### Sec. 548.001. Definitions.

In this chapter:

(1) "Commercial motor vehicle" means a self-propelled or towed vehicle, other than a farm vehicle with a gross weight, registered weight, or gross weight rating of less than 48,000 pounds, that is used on a public highway to transport passengers or cargo if:

(A) the vehicle, including a school activity bus as defined in Section 541.201, or combination of vehicles has a gross weight, registered weight, or gross weight rating of more than 26,000 pounds;

(B) the vehicle, including a school activity bus as defined in Section 541.201, is designed or used to transport more than 15 passengers, including the driver; or

(C) the vehicle is used to transport hazardous materials in a quantity requiring placarding by a regulation issued under the Hazardous Materials Transportation Act (49 U.S.C. Section 5101 et seq.).

(2) "Commission" means the Public Safety Commission.

(3) "Conservation commission" means the Texas Commission on Environmental Quality.

(4) "Department" means the Department of Public Safety.

(5) "Farm vehicle" has the meaning assigned by the federal motor carrier safety regulations.

(6) "Federal motor carrier safety regulation" has the meaning assigned by Section 644.001.

(7) "Inspection station" means a facility certified to conduct inspections of vehicles under this chapter.

(8) "Inspector" means an individual certified to conduct inspections of vehicles under this chapter.

(9) "Nonattainment area" means an area so designated within the meaning of Section 107(d) of the Clean Air Act (42 U.S.C. Section 7407).

(Enacted by Acts 1995, 74th Leg., ch. 165 (S.B. 971), § 1, effective September 1, 1995; am. Acts 1997, 75th Leg., ch. 165 (S.B. 898), §§ 30.120, 30.122(a), effective September 1, 1997; am. Acts 1997, 75th Leg., ch. 1061 (S.B. 1486), § 17, effective September 1, 1997; am. Acts 1997, 75th Leg., ch. 1069 (S.B. 1856), § 4, effective June 19, 1997; am. Acts 1999, 76th Leg., ch. 663 (H.B. 385), § 4, effective June 18, 1999; am. Acts 2003, 78th Leg., ch. 359 (S.B. 1184), § 2, effective September 1, 2003; am. Acts 2003, 78th Leg., ch. 1325 (H.B. 3588), § 16.01, effective September 1, 2003; am. Acts 2007, 80th Leg., ch. 323 (H.B. 2565), § 1, effective September 1, 2007.)

### Sec. 548.002. Department Rules.

The department may adopt rules to administer and enforce this chapter.

(Enacted by Acts 1995, 74th Leg., ch. 165 (S.B. 971), § 1, effective September 1, 1995.)

### Sec. 548.003. Department Certification and Supervision of Inspection Stations.

(a) The department may certify inspection stations to carry out this chapter and may instruct and supervise the inspection stations and mechanics for the inspection of vehicles and equipment subject to this chapter.

(b) The department shall certify at least one inspection station for each county.

(Enacted by Acts 1995, 74th Leg., ch. 165 (S.B. 971), § 1, effective September 1, 1995.)

### Sec. 548.004. Department Certification of Inspection Stations for Political Subdivisions and State Agencies.

(a) The department may certify a vehicle maintenance facility owned and operated by a political subdivision or agency of this state as an inspection station.

(b) An inspection station certified under this section is subject to the requirements of this chapter applicable to another inspection station, except as otherwise provided by this chapter.

(c) The facility may inspect only a vehicle owned by the political subdivision or state agency. An officer, employee, or inspector of the subdivision or agency may not place an inspection certificate received from the department under this section on a vehicle not owned by the subdivision or agency.

(Enacted by Acts 1995, 74th Leg., ch. 165 (S.B. 971), § 1, effective September 1, 1995.)

### Sec. 548.005. Inspection Only by State-Certified and Supervised Inspection Station.

A compulsory inspection under this chapter may be made only by an inspection station, except that the department may:

(1) permit inspection to be made by an inspector under terms and conditions the department prescribes;

(2) authorize the acceptance in this state of a certificate of inspection and approval issued in another state having a similar inspection law; and

(3) authorize the acceptance in this state of a certificate of inspection and approval issued in compliance with 49 C.F.R. Part 396 to a motor bus, as defined by Section 502.001, that is registered in this state but is not domiciled in this state.

(Enacted by Acts 1995, 74th Leg., ch. 165 (S.B. 971), § 1, effective September 1, 1995; am. Acts 2009, 81st Leg., ch. 1146 (H.B. 2730), § 6.09, effective September 1, 2009.)

### Sec. 548.006. Advisory Committee.

(a) An advisory committee consisting of nine members shall:

(1) advise the conservation commission and the department on the conservation commission's and department's rules relating to the operation of the vehicle inspection program under this chapter;

(2) make recommendations to the conservation commission and the department relating to the content of rules involving the operation of the vehicle inspection program; and

(3) perform any other advisory function requested by the conservation commission or the department in administering this chapter and Chapter 382, Health and Safety Code.

(b) The members of the commission shall appoint seven members of the committee as follows:

(1) four persons to represent inspection station owners and operators, with two of those persons from counties conducting vehicle emissions testing under Subchapter F and two of those persons from counties conducting safety only inspections;

(2) one person to represent manufacturers of motor vehicle emissions inspection devices;

(3) one person to represent independent vehicle equipment repair technicians; and

(4) one person to represent the public interest.

(c) The presiding officer of the conservation commission and the presiding officer of the commission shall each appoint one member of the committee who will alternate serving as the presiding officer of the committee.

(d) Committee members serve staggered three-year terms.

(e) A vacancy on the committee is filled in the same manner as other appointments to the committee.

(f) A member of the committee is not entitled to compensation, but is entitled to reimbursement of the member's travel expenses as provided in the General Appropriations Act for state employees.

(g) The committee may elect an assistant presiding officer and a secretary from among its members and may adopt rules for the conduct of its own activities.

(h) The committee is entitled to review and comment on rules to be considered for adoption by the conservation commission, the commission, or the department under this chapter or Chapter 382, Health and Safety Code, before the rules are adopted.

(i) The committee shall hold a meeting at least once each quarter.

(j) Chapter 2110, Government Code, does not apply to the committee.

(Enacted by Acts 2001, 77th Leg., ch. 1075 (H.B. 2134), § 7, effective September 1, 2001; am. Acts 2007, 80th Leg., ch. 323 (H.B. 2565), § 2, effective September 1, 2007; am. Acts 2009, 81st Leg., ch. 1146 (H.B. 2730), § 1.01, effective September 1, 2009.)

Transportation

## Sec. 548.007. Contracts and Instruments to Implement Certain Inspection and Maintenance Programs.

The department may execute any contract or instrument that is necessary or convenient to exercise its powers or perform its duties in implementing a motor vehicle emissions inspection and maintenance program under Section 382.302, Health and Safety Code.

(Enacted by Acts 2003, 78th Leg., ch. 203 (S.B. 1159), § 3, effective June 10, 2003.)

## Sec. 548.008. Vehicle Inspection Program Director.

(a) The vehicle inspection program is managed by a program director. The program director may not be a commissioned officer.

(b) The office of the vehicle inspection program director must be located in Austin, Texas.

(c) The duties of the program director include:

(1) responsibility for the quality of the vehicle inspection program;

(2) coordination of the regional offices;

(3) compilation of regional and statewide performance data;

(4) the establishment of best practices and distribution of those practices to the regional offices;

(5) setting goals for the entire program, in consultation with the public safety director or the public safety director's designee, and setting goals for each regional office in consultation with the regional managers;

(6) monitoring the progress toward the goals set in Subdivision (5) and evaluating the program based on that progress; and

(7) coordination with the Texas Highway Patrol to enforce provisions related to vehicle inspection.

(d) The regional offices shall make reports as requested by the program director.

(Enacted by Acts 2009, 81st Leg., ch. 1146 (H.B. 2730), § 1.02, effective September 1, 2009.)

## Secs. 548.009 to 548.050 [Reserved for expansion].

## SUBCHAPTER B
## VEHICLES AND EQUIPMENT SUBJECT TO INSPECTION AND REINSPECTION

## Sec. 548.051. Vehicles and Equipment Subject to Inspection.

(a) A motor vehicle, trailer, semitrailer, pole trailer, or mobile home, registered in this state, must have the following items inspected at an inspection station or by an inspector:

(1) tires;

(2) wheel assembly;

(3) safety guards or flaps, if required by Section 547.606;

(4) brake system, including power brake unit;

(5) steering system, including power steering;

(6) lighting equipment;

(7) horns and warning devices;

(8) mirrors;

(9) windshield wipers;

(10) sunscreening devices, unless the vehicle is exempt from sunscreen device restrictions under Section 547.613;

(11) front seat belts in vehicles on which seat belt anchorages were part of the manufacturer's original equipment;

(12) tax decal, if required by Section 548.104(d)(1);

(13) exhaust system;

(14) exhaust emission system;

(15) fuel tank cap, using pressurized testing equipment approved by department rule; and

(16) emissions control equipment as designated by department rule.

(b) A moped is subject to inspection in the same manner as a motorcycle, except that the only items of equipment required to be inspected are the brakes, headlamps, rear lamps, and reflectors, which must comply with the standards prescribed by Sections 547.408 and 547.801.

(Enacted by Acts 1995, 74th Leg., ch. 165 (S.B. 971), § 1, effective September 1, 1995; am. Acts 1999, 76th Leg., ch. 1189 (S.B. 370), § 29, effective September 1, 1999.)

## Sec. 548.052. Vehicles Not Subject to Inspection.

This chapter does not apply to:

(1) a trailer, semitrailer, pole trailer, or mobile home moving under or bearing a current factory-delivery license plate or current in-transit license plate;

(2) [2 Versions: Effective until January 1, 2012] a vehicle moving under or bearing a paper dealer in-transit tag, machinery license, disaster license, parade license, prorate tab, one-trip permit, antique license, custom vehicle license, street rod license, temporary 24-hour permit, or permit license;

(2) [2 Versions: Effective January 1, 2012] a vehicle moving under or bearing a

paper dealer in-transit tag, machinery license, disaster license, parade license, prorate tab, one-trip permit, vehicle temporary transit permit, antique license, custom vehicle license, street rod license, temporary 24-hour permit, or permit license;

(3) a trailer, semitrailer, pole trailer, or mobile home having an actual gross weight or registered gross weight of 4,500 pounds or less;

(4) farm machinery, road-building equipment, a farm trailer, or a vehicle required to display a slow-moving-vehicle emblem under Section 547.703;

(5) a former military vehicle, as defined by Section 504.502;

(6) a vehicle qualified for a tax exemption under Section 152.092, Tax Code; or

(7) a vehicle for which a certificate of title has been issued but that is not required to be registered.

(Enacted by Acts 1995, 74th Leg., ch. 165 (S.B. 971), § 1, effective September 1, 1995; am. Acts 1997, 75th Leg., ch. 165 (S.B. 898), § 30.121(a), effective September 1, 1997; am. Acts 1999, 76th Leg., ch. 963 (H.B. 2538), § 1, effective June 18, 1999; am. Acts 1999, 76th Leg., ch. 1423 (H.B. 2409), § 7, effective September 1, 1999; am. Acts 2001, 77th Leg., ch. 1420 (H.B. 2812), § 19.006, effective September 1, 2001; am. Acts 2011, 82nd Leg., ch. 91 (S.B. 1303), § 24.012, effective September 1, 2011; am. Acts 2011, 82nd Leg., ch. 729 (H.B. 890), § 4, effective September 1, 2011; am. Acts 2011, 82nd Leg., ch. 1296 (H.B. 2357), § 237, effective January 1, 2012.)

## Sec. 548.053. Reinspection of Vehicle Requiring Adjustment, Correction, or Repair.

(a) If an inspection discloses the necessity for adjustment, correction, or repair, an inspection station or inspector may not issue an inspection certificate until the adjustment, correction, or repair is made. The owner of the vehicle may have the adjustment, correction, or repair made by a qualified person of the owner's choice, subject to reinspection. The vehicle shall be reinspected once free of charge within 15 days after the date of the original inspection, not including the date the original inspection is made, at the same inspection station after the adjustment, correction, or repair is made.

(b) A vehicle that is inspected and is subsequently involved in an accident affecting the safe operation of an item of inspection must be rein-spected following repair. The reinspection must be at an inspection station and shall be treated and charged as an initial inspection.

(c) If a vehicle subject to this chapter is damaged to the apparent extent that it would require repair before passing inspection, the investigating officer shall remove the inspection certificate from the vehicle windshield and give the operator of the vehicle a dated receipt. The vehicle must be reinspected not later than the 30th day after the date shown on the receipt.

(Enacted by Acts 1995, 74th Leg., ch. 165 (S.B. 971), § 1, effective September 1, 1995.)

## Secs. 548.054 to 548.100 [Reserved for expansion].

## SUBCHAPTER C
## PERIODS OF INSPECTION; PREREQUISITES TO ISSUANCE OF INSPECTION CERTIFICATE

## Sec. 548.101. General One-Year Inspection Period.

Except as provided by Section 548.102, the department shall require an annual inspection. The department shall set the periods of inspection and may make rules with respect to those periods.

(Enacted by Acts 1995, 74th Leg., ch. 165 (S.B. 971), § 1, effective September 1, 1995.)

## Sec. 548.102. Two-Year Initial Inspection Period for Passenger Car or Light Truck.

(a) The initial inspection period is two years for a passenger car or light truck that:

(1) is sold in this state;

(2) has not been previously registered in this or another state; and

(3) on the date of sale is of the current or preceding model year.

(b) This section does not affect a requirement that a motor vehicle emission inspection be conducted during an initial inspection period in a county covered by an inspection and maintenance program approved by the United States Environmental Protection Agency under Section 548.301 and the Clean Air Act (42 U.S.C. Section 7401 et seq.).

(Enacted by Acts 1995, 74th Leg., ch. 165 (S.B. 971), § 1, effective September 1, 1995.)

Transportation

### Sec. 548.103. Extended Inspection Period for Certain Vehicles.

The department may extend the time within which the resident owner of a vehicle that is not in this state when an inspection is required must obtain an inspection certificate in this state.

(Enacted by Acts 1995, 74th Leg., ch. 165 (S.B. 971), § 1, effective September 1, 1995.)

### Sec. 548.104. Equipment-Related Prerequisites to Issuance of Inspection Certificate.

(a) The commission shall adopt uniform standards of safety applicable to each item required to be inspected by Section 548.051. The standards and the list of items to be inspected shall be posted in each inspection station.

(b) An inspection station or inspector may issue an inspection certificate only if the vehicle is inspected and found to be in proper and safe condition and to comply with this chapter and the rules adopted under this chapter.

(c) An inspection station or inspector may inspect only the equipment required to be inspected by Section 548.051 and may not:

(1) falsely and fraudulently represent to an applicant that equipment required to be inspected must be repaired, adjusted, or replaced before the vehicle will pass inspection; or

(2) require an applicant to have another part of the vehicle or other equipment inspected as a prerequisite for issuance of an inspection certificate.

(d) An inspection station or inspector may not issue an inspection certificate for a vehicle equipped with:

(1) a carburetion device permitting the use of liquefied gas alone or interchangeably with another fuel, unless a valid liquefied gas tax decal issued by the comptroller is attached to the lower right-hand corner of the front windshield of the vehicle on the passenger side; or

(2) a sunscreening device prohibited by Section 547.613, except that the department by rule shall provide procedures for issuance of an inspection certificate for a vehicle exempt under Section 547.613(c).

(e) The department shall adopt rules relating to inspection of and issuance of an inspection certificate for a moped.

(Enacted by Acts 1995, 74th Leg., ch. 165 (S.B. 971), § 1, effective September 1, 1995.)

### Sec. 548.105. Evidence of Financial Responsibility As Prerequisite to Issuance of Inspection Certificate.

(a) An inspection station or inspector may not issue an inspection certificate for a vehicle unless the owner or operator furnishes evidence of financial responsibility at the time of inspection. Evidence of financial responsibility may be shown in the manner specified under Section 601.053(a). A personal automobile insurance policy used as evidence of financial responsibility must be written for a term of 30 days or more as required by Article 5.06, Insurance Code.

(b) An inspection station is not liable to a person, including a third party, for issuing an inspection certificate in reliance on evidence of financial responsibility furnished to the station. An inspection station that is the seller of a motor vehicle may rely on an oral insurance binder.

(Enacted by Acts 1995, 74th Leg., ch. 165 (S.B. 971), § 1, effective September 1, 1995.)

### Secs. 548.106 to 548.200 [Reserved for expansion].

## SUBCHAPTER D
## INSPECTION OF COMMERCIAL MOTOR VEHICLES

### Sec. 548.201. Commercial Motor Vehicle Inspection Program.

(a) The commission shall establish an inspection program for commercial motor vehicles that:

(1) meets the requirements of federal motor carrier safety regulations; and

(2) requires a commercial motor vehicle registered in this state to pass an annual inspection of all safety equipment required by the federal motor carrier safety regulations.

(b) A program under this section also applies to any:

(1) vehicle or combination of vehicles with a gross weight rating of more than 10,000 pounds that is operated in interstate commerce and registered in this state;

(2) school activity bus, as defined in Section 541.201, that has a gross weight, registered weight, or gross weight rating of more than 26,000 pounds, or is designed to transport more than 15 passengers, including the driver; and

(3) school bus that will operate at a speed authorized by Section 545.352(b)(5)(A).

(Enacted by Acts 1995, 74th Leg., ch. 165 (S.B. 971), § 1, effective September 1, 1995; am. Acts 1997, 75th Leg., ch. 1061 (S.B. 1486), § 18, effective September 1, 1997; am. Acts 1999, 76th Leg., ch. 663 (H.B. 385), § 5, effective June 18, 1999.)

### Sec. 548.202. General Applicability of Chapter to Commercial Motor Vehicles.

This chapter applies to a commercial motor vehicle inspection program established under Section 548.201 except as otherwise provided. (Enacted by Acts 1995, 74th Leg., ch. 165 (S.B. 971), § 1, effective September 1, 1995.)

### Sec. 548.203. Exemptions.

The commission by rule may exempt a type of commercial motor vehicle from the application of this subchapter if the vehicle:

(1) was manufactured before September 1, 1995;

(2) is operated only temporarily on a highway of this state and at a speed of less than 30 miles per hour; and

(3) complies with Section 548.051 and each applicable provision in Title 49, Code of Federal Regulations. (Enacted by Acts 1997, 75th Leg., ch. 165 (S.B. 898), § 30.122(b), effective September 1, 1997.)

### Secs. 548.204 to 548.250 [Reserved for expansion].

### SUBCHAPTER E
### ISSUANCE, RECORDING, AND PROOF OF INSPECTION CERTIFICATES AND VERIFICATION FORMS

### Sec. 548.251. Department to Provide Inspection Certificates and Verification Forms.

The department shall provide serially numbered inspection certificates and verification forms to inspection stations. The department may issue a unique inspection certificate for:

(1) a commercial motor vehicle inspected under Section 548.201; or

(2) a vehicle inspected under Subchapter F. (Enacted by Acts 1995, 74th Leg., ch. 165 (S.B. 971), § 1, effective September 1, 1995; am. Acts 1997, 75th Leg., ch. 165 (S.B. 898), § 30.123(c), effective September 1, 1997; am. Acts 1997, 75th

Leg., ch. 1069 (S.B. 1856), § 5, effective June 19, 1997.)

### Sec. 548.252. Safekeeping and Control of Inspection Certificates and Verification Forms.

On being licensed, an inspector or owner of an inspection station shall:

(1) provide for the safekeeping of inspection certificates and verification forms;

(2) safeguard the certificates and forms against theft, loss, or damage;

(3) control the sequence of issuance of the certificates and forms; and

(4) ensure that the certificates and forms are issued in accordance with department rules. (Enacted by Acts 1995, 74th Leg., ch. 165 (S.B. 971), § 1, effective September 1, 1995.)

### Sec. 548.253. Information to Be Recorded on Issuance of Inspection Certificate and Verification Form.

An inspection station or inspector, on issuing an inspection certificate and verification form, shall:

(1) make a record and report as prescribed by the department of the inspection and certificate issued; and

(2) include in the inspection certificate and verification form the information required by the department for the type of vehicle inspected. (Enacted by Acts 1995, 74th Leg., ch. 165 (S.B. 971), § 1, effective September 1, 1995.)

### Sec. 548.254. Validity of Inspection Certificate.

An inspection certificate is invalid after the end of the 12th month following the month in which the certificate is issued. An unused inspection certificate representing a previous inspection period may not be issued after the beginning of the next period. (Enacted by Acts 1995, 74th Leg., ch. 165 (S.B. 971), § 1, effective September 1, 1995.)

### Sec. 548.255. Attachment or Production of Inspection Certificate.

(a) An inspection certificate shall be attached to or produced for a vehicle in the manner required by department rule.

(b) The department shall:

(1) require that a certificate for a motorcycle be attached to the rear of the motorcycle near the license plate; and

(2) adopt rules with respect to display of an inspection certificate for a moped.

(Enacted by Acts 1995, 74th Leg., ch. 165 (S.B. 971), § 1, effective September 1, 1995.)

### Sec. 548.256. Verification Form Required to Register Vehicle.

(a) Before a vehicle that is brought into this state by a person other than a manufacturer or importer may be registered, the owner must have the vehicle inspected and have the inspection station record the following information on a verification form prescribed and provided by the department:

(1) the vehicle identification number;

(2) the number appearing on the odometer of the vehicle at the time of the inspection, if the vehicle has an odometer; and

(3) other information the department requires.

(b) An inspection station may not issue the verification form unless the vehicle complies with the inspection requirements of this chapter.

(c), (d) [Repealed by Acts 2005, 79th Leg., ch. 1125 (H.B. 2481), § 22, effective September 1, 2005.]

(Enacted by Acts 1995, 74th Leg., ch. 165 (S.B. 971), § 1, effective September 1, 1995; am. Acts 1997, 75th Leg., ch. 165 (S.B. 898), § 30.123(a), effective September 1, 1997; am. Acts 1997, 75th Leg., ch. 1069 (S.B. 1856), § 19(2), effective June 19, 1997; am. Acts 1999, 76th Leg., ch. 1423 (H.B. 2409), §§ 8, 9, effective September 1, 1999; am. Acts 2001, 77th Leg., ch. 967 (S.B. 5), § 9, effective September 1, 2001; am. Acts 2005, 79th Leg., ch. 1125 (H.B. 2481), § 22, effective September 1, 2005.)

### Sec. 548.257. Lost, Stolen, or Destroyed Certificate.

(a) If an inspection certificate is lost, stolen, or destroyed during the period during which the certificate is valid, the vehicle must be reinspected and any applicable fee paid before a new certificate is issued, except that the vehicle is not subject to any emissions inspection. The replacement certificate is valid for the remaining period of validity of the original certificate.

(b) The department by rule shall specify the method for establishing that:

(1) the certificate has been lost, stolen, or destroyed; and

(2) the reinspection is within the period of validity of the lost, stolen, or destroyed certificate.

(c) As part of its rules under Subsection (b), the department shall adopt measures to ensure that the reinspection procedure provided by this section is not used fraudulently to avoid any required inspection.

(Enacted by Acts 2003, 78th Leg., ch. 1325 (H.B. 3588), § 19.03, effective September 1, 2003.)

### Sec. 548.258. Use of State Electronic Internet Portal.

(a) In this section, "state electronic Internet portal" has the meaning assigned by Section 2054.003, Government Code.

(b) The department may adopt rules to require an inspection station to use the state electronic Internet portal to:

(1) purchase inspection certificates; or

(2) send to the department a record, report, or other information required by the department.

(Enacted by Acts 2005, 79th Leg., ch. 1260 (H.B. 2048), § 22, effective June 18, 2005; enacted by Acts 2005, 79th Leg., ch. 1292 (H.B. 2593), § 11, effective June 18, 2005; am. Acts 2011, 82nd Leg., ch. 973 (H.B. 1504), § 31, effective June 17, 2011.)

### Secs. 548.259 to 548.300 [Reserved for expansion].

### SUBCHAPTER F
### MOTOR VEHICLE EMISSIONS INSPECTION AND MAINTENANCE

### Sec. 548.301. Commission to Establish Program.

(a) The commission shall establish a motor vehicle emissions inspection and maintenance program for vehicles as required by any law of the United States or the state's air quality state implementation plan.

(b) The commission by rule may establish a motor vehicle emissions inspection and maintenance program for vehicles specified by the conservation commission in a county for which the conservation commission has adopted a resolution requesting the commission to establish such a program and for which the county and the municipality with the largest population in the county by resolution have formally requested a proactive air quality plan consisting of such a program.

(b-1) The commission by rule may establish a motor vehicle emissions inspection and maintenance program for vehicles subject to an early action compact as defined by Section 382.301, Health and Safety Code, that is consistent with the early action compact.

(c) A program established under Subsection (b) or (b-1) may include reregistration-based enforcement.

(d) A vehicle emissions inspection under this section may be performed by the same facility that performs a safety inspection if the facility is authorized and certified by the department to perform the vehicle emissions inspection and certified by the department to perform the safety inspection.

(Enacted by Acts 1995, 74th Leg., ch. 165 (S.B. 971), § 1, effective September 1, 1995; am. Acts 1997, 75th Leg., ch. 165 (S.B. 898), § 30.123(d), effective September 1, 1997; am. Acts 1997, 75th Leg., ch. 1069 (S.B. 1856), § 6, effective June 19, 1997; am. Acts 2001, 77th Leg., ch. 1075 (H.B. 2134 ), § 8, effective September 1, 2001; am. Acts 2003, 78th Leg., ch. 203 (S.B. 1159), § 4, effective June 10, 2003.)

## Sec. 548.3011. Emissions Test on Resale.

(a) This section applies only to a vehicle:

(1) the most recent certificate of title for which or registration of which was issued in a county without a motor vehicle emissions inspection and maintenance program; and

(2) the ownership of which has changed and which has been the subject of a retail sale as defined by Section 2301.002, Occupations Code.

(b) Notwithstanding Subsection (a), this section does not apply to a vehicle that is a 1996 or newer model that has less than 50,000 miles.

(c) A vehicle subject to this section is not eligible for a title receipt under Section 501.024, a certificate of title under Section 501.027, or registration under Chapter 502 in a county with a motor vehicle emissions inspection and maintenance program unless proof is presented with the application for certificate of title or registration, as appropriate, that the vehicle, not earlier than the 90th day before the date on which the new owner's application for certificate of title or registration is filed with the county clerk or county assessor-collector, as appropriate, has passed an approved vehicle emissions test in the county in which it is to be titled or registered.

(d) The proof required by Subsection (c) may be in the form of a Vehicle Inspection Report (VIR) or other proof of program compliance as authorized by the department.

(Enacted by Acts 2001, 77th Leg., ch. 1075 (H.B. 2134), § 9, effective September 1, 2001; am. Acts 2003, 78th Leg., ch. 1276 (H.B. 3507), § 14A.834, effective September 1, 2003.)

## Sec. 548.3012. Exemption: Vehicle Not Used Primarily in County of Registration.

(a) This section applies only to a vehicle that:

(1) is to be registered in a county with a motor vehicle emissions inspection and maintenance program; and

(2) will be used in that county for fewer than 60 days during the registration period for which registration is sought.

(b) The owner of a vehicle described by Subsection (a) may obtain for that vehicle an exemption from the vehicle emissions test requirements of this subchapter by submitting to the county assessor-collector an affidavit stating that the named vehicle will be used in the county of registration for fewer than 60 calendar days during the registration period for which registration is sought.

(Enacted by Acts 2001, 77th Leg., ch. 1075 (H.B. 2134), § 9, effective September 1, 2001.)

## Sec. 548.302. Commission to Adopt Standards and Requirements.

The commission shall:

(1) adopt standards for emissions-related inspection criteria consistent with requirements of the United States and the conservation commission applicable to a county in which a program is established under this subchapter; and

(2) develop and impose requirements necessary to ensure that an inspection certificate is not issued to a vehicle subject to a program established under this subchapter unless the vehicle has passed a motor vehicle emissions inspection at a facility authorized and certified by the department.

(Enacted by Acts 1995, 74th Leg., ch. 165 (S.B. 971), § 1, effective September 1, 1995; am. Acts 1997, 75th Leg., ch. 165 (S.B. 898), § 30.123(e), effective September 1, 1997; am. Acts 1997, 75th Leg., ch. 1069 (S.B. 1856), § 7, effective June 19, 1997.)

## Sec. 548.303. Program Administration.

The commission shall administer the motor vehicle emissions inspection and maintenance program under this subchapter.

Transportation

(Enacted by Acts 1995, 74th Leg., ch. 165 (S.B. 971), § 1, effective September 1, 1995; am. Acts 1997, 75th Leg., ch. 165 (S.B. 898), § 30.123(f), effective September 1, 1997; am. Acts 1997, 75th Leg., ch. 1069 (S.B. 1856), § 8, effective June 19, 1997.)

## Sec. 548.304. Stations Licensed to Conduct Emissions Inspections.

(a) The department may authorize and certify inspection stations as necessary to implement the emissions-related inspection requirements of the motor vehicle emissions inspection and maintenance program established under this subchapter if the station meets the department's certification requirements.

(b) The department shall provide inspection certificates for distribution and issuance at inspection stations certified by the department. (Enacted by Acts 1995, 74th Leg., ch. 165 (S.B. 971), § 1, effective September 1, 1995; am. Acts 1997, 75th Leg., ch. 165 (S.B. 898), § 30.123(g), effective September 1, 1997; am. Acts 1997, 75th Leg., ch. 1069 (S.B. 1856), § 9, effective June 19, 1997.)

## Sec. 548.3045. Appointment of Decentralized Facility.

(a) The department may issue an inspection station certificate to a decentralized facility authorized and licensed by the department under Section 548.304 if the facility meets the certification requirements of that section and the department.

(b) A decentralized facility issued a certificate under Subsection (a) is authorized to perform an inspection under this subchapter or Subchapter B. (Enacted by Acts 1997, 75th Leg., ch. 165 (S.B. 898), § 30.123(h), effective September 1, 1997.)

## Sec. 548.305. Dealer Authority Regarding Emissions-Related Inspections [Repealed].

Repealed by Acts 1997, 75th Leg., ch. 1069 (S.B. 1856), § 19(2), effective June 19, 1997. (Enacted by Acts 1995, 74th Leg., ch. 165 (S.B. 971), § 1, effective September 1, 1995.)

## Sec. 548.306. Excessive Motor Vehicle Emissions.

(a) This section applies to a motor vehicle registered or operated for more than 60 days per calendar year in:

(1) a county or a portion of a county designated by department rule in accordance with Section 548.301; or

(2) a county adjacent to a county described in Subdivision (1).

(b) The registered owner of a motor vehicle commits an offense if the vehicle, in an area described by Subsection (a), emits:

(1) hydrocarbons, carbon monoxide, or nitrogen oxide in an amount that is excessive under United States Environmental Protection Agency standards or standards provided by department rule; or

(2) another vehicle-related pollutant that is listed by a department rule adopted to comply with Part A, National Emission Standards Act (42 U.S.C. Sections 7602-7619), or rules of the United States Environmental Protection Agency in an amount identified as excessive under that rule.

(c) The department shall provide a notice of violation to the registered owner of a vehicle that is detected violating Subsection (b). The notice of violation must be made by personal delivery to the registered owner or by mailing the notice to the registered owner at the last known address of the owner. The department shall include in the notice the date and location of the violation detected and instructions for the registered owner explaining how the owner must proceed to obtain and pass a verification emissions inspection and to make any repair to the vehicle necessary to pass the inspection and explaining any extension or assistance that may be available to the owner for making any necessary repair. Notice by mail is presumed delivered on the 10th day after the date the notice is deposited in the mail.

(d) A registered owner of a vehicle commits an offense if:

(1) notice is delivered to the owner under Subsection (c); and

(2) the owner fails to comply with any provision of the notice before the 31st day after the date the notice is delivered.

(e) An offense under this section is a misdemeanor punishable by a fine of not less than $1 and not more than $350. If a person has previously been convicted of an offense under this section, an offense under this section is a misdemeanor punishable by a fine of not less than $200 and not more than $1,000.

(f) It is an affirmative defense to an offense under this section that the registered owner of the vehicle, before the 31st day after the date the owner receives a notice of violation:

(1) after a verification emissions inspection indicated that the vehicle did not comply with applicable emissions standards, repaired the vehicle as necessary and passed another verification emissions inspection; and

(2) has complied with rules of the department concerning a violation under this section.

(g) The department may contract with a private person to implement this section. The person must comply with terms, policies, rules, and procedures the department adopts to administer this section.

(h) The Texas Department of Transportation may deny reregistration of a vehicle if the registered owner of the vehicle has received notification under Subsection (c) and the vehicle has not passed a verification emissions inspection.

(i) A hearing for a citation issued under this section shall be heard by a justice of the peace of any precinct in the county in which the vehicle is registered.

(j) Enforcement of the remote sensing component of the vehicle emissions inspection and maintenance program may not involve any method of screening in which the registered owner of a vehicle found to have allowable emissions by remote sensing technology is charged a fee.

(k) The department by rule may require that a vehicle determined by on-road testing to have excessive emissions be assessed an on-road emissions testing fee not to exceed the emissions testing fee charged by a certified emissions testing facility.

(*l*) The department by rule may establish procedures for reimbursing a fee for a verification test required by Subsection (c) if the owner demonstrates to the department's satisfaction that:

(1) the vehicle passed the verification emissions test not later than the 30th day after the date the vehicle owner received notice that the vehicle was detected as having excessive emissions; and

(2) the vehicle did not receive any repair, modification, alteration, or additive to the fuel, fuel tank, fuel delivery system, engine, exhaust system, or any attached emissions control components that would have, or could have, caused the vehicle to experience improved emissions performance between the date of detection and the date of the verification emissions test.

(Enacted by Acts 1997, 75th Leg., ch. 1069 (S.B. 1856), § 10, effective June 19, 1997; am. Acts

1999, 76th Leg., ch. 1189 (S.B. 370), § 30, effective September 1, 1999; am. Acts 2001, 77th Leg., ch. 1075 (H.B. 2134), § 10, effective September 1, 2001.)

## Sec. 548.3065. Administrative Penalty.

(a) In lieu of criminal proceedings for a violation of Section 548.306, the department may impose an administrative penalty against a person who knowingly violates this chapter or a rule adopted by the commission under this chapter.

(b) The amount of the administrative penalty may not exceed $1,000 for each violation. The aggregate penalty for multiple violations may not exceed $10,000. Each day a violation continues or occurs is a separate violation for purposes of imposing a penalty.

(c) For purposes of Subsection (a), the procedures for determining and administering an administrative penalty against a person charged with violating this chapter are the same as those prescribed by Section 643.251 for determining and administering an administrative penalty against a motor carrier under that section.

(c-1) The conservation commission may impose an administrative penalty on a person in the amount of not more than $500 for each violation of this subchapter or a rule adopted by the conservation commission under this subchapter.

(d) An administrative penalty collected under this section shall be deposited in a special account in the general revenue fund and may be used only by the department.

(Enacted by Acts 2001, 77th Leg., ch. 1075 (H.B. 2134), § 11, effective September 1, 2001; am. Acts 2011, 82nd Leg., ch. 1202 (S.B. 197), § 1, effective September 1, 2011.)

## Sec. 548.307. Alternative Testing Methodology for Certain Counties.

The commission by rule may establish procedures for testing and enforcing vehicle emissions standards by use of alternative testing methodology that meets or exceeds United States Environmental Protection Agency requirements in a county participating in an early action compact under Subchapter H, Chapter 382, Health and Safety Code.

(Enacted by Acts 2003, 78th Leg., ch. 203 (S.B. 1159), § 5, effective June 10, 2003.)

## Sec. 548.3075. Limited Emissions Inspection.

(a) In this section, "limited emissions inspection" means an emissions inspection of a motor vehicle conducted only by using the onboard diagnostic system of the vehicle.

(b) A department rule that allows a qualified inspection station to perform a limited emissions inspection of a motor vehicle may not restrict the station to fewer than 150 inspections per month. (Enacted by Acts 2009, 81st Leg., ch. 1110 (H.B. 715), § 1, effective December 31, 2010.)

### Secs. 548.308 to 548.400 [Reserved for expansion].

## SUBCHAPTER G
## CERTIFICATION OF INSPECTION STATION OR INSPECTOR

### Sec. 548.401.   Certification Generally.

A person may perform an inspection or issue an inspection certificate only if certified to do so by the department under rules adopted by the department. (Enacted by Acts 1995, 74th Leg., ch. 165 (S.B. 971), § 1, effective September 1, 1995.)

### Sec. 548.402.   Application for Certification As Inspection Station.

(a) To operate as an inspection station, a person must apply to the department for certification. The application must:

(1) be filed with the department on a form prescribed and provided by the department; and

(2) state:

(A) the name of the applicant;

(B) if the applicant is an association, the names and addresses of the persons constituting the association;

(C) if the applicant is a corporation, the names and addresses of its principal officers;

(D) the name under which the applicant transacts or intends to transact business;

(E) the location of the applicant's place of business in the state; and

(F) other information required by the department, including information required by the department for identification.

(b) The application must be signed and sworn or affirmed by:

(1) if the applicant is an individual, the owner; or

(2) if the applicant is a corporation, an executive officer or person specifically authorized by the corporation to sign the application, to which shall be attached written evidence of the person's authority.

(c) An applicant who has or intends to have more than one place of business in this state must file a separate application for each place of business. (Enacted by Acts 1995, 74th Leg., ch. 165 (S.B. 971), § 1, effective September 1, 1995.)

### Sec. 548.403.   Approval and Certification As Inspection Station.

(a) The department may approve an application for certification as an inspection station only if:

(1) the location complies with department requirements; and

(2) the applicant complies with department rules.

(b) On approval of an application, the department shall issue to the applicant an inspection station certificate. The certificate is valid for each person in whose name the certificate is issued and for the transaction of business at the location designated in the certificate. A certificate is not assignable.

(c) An inspection station certificate shall be conspicuously displayed at the station for which the certificate was issued. (Enacted by Acts 1995, 74th Leg., ch. 165 (S.B. 971), § 1, effective September 1, 1995.)

### Sec. 548.4035.   Entry onto Premises.

(a) A member, employee, or agent of the department may enter an inspection station during normal business hours to conduct an investigation, inspection, or audit of the inspection station or an inspector to determine whether the inspection station or inspector is in compliance with:

(1) this chapter;

(2) department rules under this chapter; or

(3) Chapter 382, Health and Safety Code.

(b) A member, employee, or agent of the department who enters an inspection station for a purpose described by Subsection (a):

(1) shall notify the manager or person in charge of the inspection station of the presence of the member, employee, or agent;

(2) shall present the manager or person in charge of the inspection station with proper credentials identifying the member, employee, or agent as a member, employee, or agent of the department; and

(3) is entitled to have access to emissions testing equipment, inspection records, and any

required inspection station certificate or inspector certificate.

(c) A member, employee, or agent of the department who enters an inspection station to conduct an investigation, inspection, or audit under Subsection (a) must observe the inspection station's rules relating to safety, security, and fire protection.

(d) Subsection (b) does not prohibit the department from conducting an undercover investigation or a covert audit of an inspection station. (Enacted by Acts 2001, 77th Leg., ch. 1169 (H.B. 3071), § 1, effective September 1, 2001.)

## Sec. 548.404. Application for Certification As Inspector.

An application for certification as an inspector shall:

(1) be made on a form prescribed and provided by the department; and

(2) state:

(A) the name of the applicant;

(B) the address of the applicant's residence and place of employment;

(C) the applicant's driver's license number; and

(D) other information required by the department.

(Enacted by Acts 1995, 74th Leg., ch. 165 (S.B. 971), § 1, effective September 1, 1995.)

## Sec. 548.4045. Bond Required for Certain Inspection Stations.

(a) This section applies only to an inspection station that:

(1) is located in a county in which the conservation commission has established a motor vehicle emissions inspection and maintenance program under Subchapter F; and

(2) has been convicted of a violation of this chapter relating to an emissions inspection.

(b) An application for certification as an inspection station must be accompanied by a surety bond in the amount of $5,000, payable to this state and conditioned on the future compliance with this chapter and rules adopted by the department or the conservation commission under this chapter.

(c) The attorney general or the district or county attorney for the county in which the inspection station is located or in which the inspection station that employs the inspector is located may bring suit in the name of this state to recover on the bond.

(Enacted by Acts 2011, 82nd Leg., ch. 1202 (S.B. 197), § 2, effective September 1, 2011.)

## Sec. 548.405. Denial, Revocation, or Suspension of Certificate.

(a) The department may deny a person's application for a certificate, revoke or suspend the certificate of a person, inspection station, or inspector, place on probation a person who holds a suspended certificate, or reprimand a person who holds a certificate if:

(1) the station or inspector conducts an inspection, fails to conduct an inspection, or issues a certificate:

(A) in violation of this chapter or a rule adopted under this chapter; or

(B) without complying with the requirements of this chapter or a rule adopted under this chapter;

(2) the person, station, or inspector commits an offense under this chapter or violates this chapter or a rule adopted under this chapter;

(3) the applicant or certificate holder does not meet the standards for certification under this chapter or a rule adopted under this chapter;

(4) the station or inspector does not maintain the qualifications for certification or does not comply with a certification requirement under Subchapter G;

(5) the certificate holder or the certificate holder's agent, employee, or representative commits an act or omission that would cause denial, revocation, or suspension of a certificate to an individual applicant or certificate holder;

(6) the station or inspector does not pay a fee required by Subchapter H; or

(7) the inspector or owner of an inspection station is convicted of a:

(A) felony or Class A or Class B misdemeanor;

(B) similar crime under the jurisdiction of another state or the federal government that is punishable to the same extent as a felony or a Class A or Class B misdemeanor in this state; or

(C) crime under the jurisdiction of another state or the federal government that would be a felony or a Class A or Class B misdemeanor if the crime were committed in this state.

(b) For purposes of Subsection (a)(7), a person is convicted of an offense if a court enters against the person an adjudication of the person's guilt, including an order of probation or deferred adjudication.

(c) If the department suspends a certificate because of a violation of Subchapter F, the suspension must be for a period of not less than six months. The suspension may not be probated or deferred.

(d) Until an inspector or inspection station whose certificate is suspended or revoked receives a new certificate, has the certificate reinstated, or has the suspension expire, the inspector or station may not be directly or indirectly involved in an inspection operation.

(e) An immediate family member of an inspector or owner of an inspection station whose certificate is suspended or revoked may not be granted a certificate under this subchapter if the location of the family member's place of business is the same as that of the inspector or owner whose certificate is suspended or revoked unless the family member proves that the inspector or owner whose certificate is suspended or revoked has no involvement with the family member's place of business.

(f) Subsection (a) applies to:

(1) each member of a partnership or association issued a certificate under this subchapter;

(2) each director or officer of a corporation issued a certificate under this subchapter; and

(3) a shareholder who receives compensation from the day-to-day operation of the corporation in the form of a salary.

(g) The department may not suspend, revoke, or deny all certificates of a person who holds more than one inspection station certificate based on a suspension, revocation, or denial of one of that person's inspection station certificates without proof of culpability related to a prior action under this subsection.

(h) The department shall develop, by September 1, 2002, a penalty schedule consisting of warnings, re-education, suspensions, and revocations based on the severity and frequency of offenses committed under Chapter 548, Transportation Code, and rules adopted by the department under this chapter.

(i) The department shall develop, by September 1, 2002, a penalty schedule consisting of suspensions and revocations based on the severity and frequency of offenses committed in the emissions testing of motor vehicles under Section 382.202, Health and Safety Code, and Chapter 548, Subchapter F, of this code.

(Enacted by Acts 1995, 74th Leg., ch. 165 (S.B. 971), § 1, effective September 1, 1995; am. Acts 1997, 75th Leg., ch. 1069 (S.B. 1856), § 11, effective June 19, 1997; am. Acts 1999, 76th Leg., ch. 1189 (S.B. 370), § 31, effective September 1, 1999; am. Acts 2001, 77th Leg., ch. 1169 (H.B. 3071), § 2, effective September 1, 2001; am. Acts 2003, 78th Leg., ch. 1276 (H.B. 3507), § 10.008(d), effective September 1, 2003.)

## Sec. 548.406. Certificate Holder on Probation May Be Required to Report.

The director may require the holder of a suspended certificate who is placed on probation to report regularly to the department on a matter that is the basis of the probation.
(Enacted by Acts 1995, 74th Leg., ch. 165 (S.B. 971), § 1, effective September 1, 1995.)

## Sec. 548.407. Hearing on Denial, Revocation, or Suspension of Certificate.

(a) Before an application for certification as an inspection station or inspector is denied, the director or a person the director designates shall give the person written notification of:

(1) the proposed denial;

(2) each reason for the proposed denial; and

(3) the person's right to an administrative hearing to determine whether the evidence warrants the denial.

(b) Before a certificate of appointment as an inspector or inspection station is revoked or suspended, the director or a person the director designates shall give written notification to the inspector or inspection station of the revocation or the period of suspension. The notice shall include:

(1) the effective date of the revocation or the period of the suspension, as applicable;

(2) each reason for the revocation or suspension; and

(3) a statement explaining the person's right to an administrative hearing to determine whether the evidence warrants the revocation or suspension.

(c) Notice under Subsection (a) or (b) must be made by personal delivery or by mail to the last address given to the department by the person.

(d) The department may provide that a revocation or suspension takes effect on receipt of notice under Subsection (b) if the department finds that the action is necessary to prevent or remedy a threat to public health, safety, or welfare. Violations that present a threat to public health, safety, or welfare include:

(1) issuing an inspection certificate with knowledge that the issuance is in violation of this chapter or rules adopted under this chapter;

(2) falsely or fraudulently representing to the owner or operator of a vehicle that equipment inspected or required to be inspected must be repaired, adjusted, or replaced for the vehicle to pass an inspection;

(3) issuing an inspection certificate:

    (A) without authorization to issue the certificate; or

    (B) without inspecting the vehicle;

(4) issuing an inspection certificate for a vehicle with knowledge that the vehicle has not been repaired, adjusted, or corrected after an inspection has shown a repair, adjustment, or correction to be necessary;

(5) knowingly issuing an inspection certificate:

    (A) for a vehicle without conducting an inspection of each item required to be inspected; or

    (B) for a vehicle that is missing an item required to be inspected or that has an item required to be inspected that is not in compliance with state law or department rules;

(6) refusing to allow a vehicle's owner to have a qualified person of the owner's choice make a required repair, adjustment, or correction;

(7) charging for an inspection an amount greater than the authorized fee;

(8) a violation of Subchapter F;

(9) a violation of Section 548.603; or

(10) a conviction of a felony or a Class A or B misdemeanor that directly relates to or affects the duties or responsibilities of a vehicle inspection station or inspector or a conviction of a similar crime under the jurisdiction of another state or the federal government.

(e) For purposes of Subsection (d)(10), a person is convicted of an offense if a court enters against the person an adjudication of the person's guilt, including an order of probation or deferred adjudication.

(f) To obtain an administrative hearing on a denial, suspension, or revocation under this section, a person must submit a written request for a hearing to the director not later than the 20th day after the date notice is delivered personally or is mailed.

(g) If the director receives a timely request under Subsection (f), the director shall provide the person with an opportunity for a hearing as soon as practicable. A hearing on a revocation or suspension under Subsection (d) that takes effect on receipt of the notice must be held not later than 14 days after the department receives the request for hearing. The revocation or suspension continues in effect until the hearing is completed if the hearing is continued beyond the 14-day period:

    (1) at the request of the inspector or inspection station; or

    (2) on a finding of good cause by a judge, administrative law judge, or hearing officer.

(h) If the director does not receive a timely request under Subsection (f), the director may deny the application, revoke or suspend a certificate, or sustain the revocation or suspension of a certificate without a hearing.

(i) Except as provided by Subsection (g), the hearing must be held not earlier than the 11th day after the date written notice of the hearing and a copy of the charges is given to the person by personal service or by certified mail to the last address given to the department by the person.

(j) The director or a person designated by the director shall conduct the hearing and may administer oaths and issue subpoenas for the attendance of witnesses and the production of relevant books, papers, or documents. If the hearing is conducted by a person designated by the director, the director may take action under this section on a recommendation of the designated person.

(k) On the basis of the evidence submitted at the hearing, the director may deny the application or revoke or suspend the certificate.

(*l*) If an administrative law judge of the State Office of Administrative Hearings conducts a hearing under this section and the proposal for decision supports the position of the department, the proposal for decision may recommend a denial of an application or a revocation or suspension of a certificate only. The proposal may not recommend a reprimand or a probated or otherwise deferred disposition of the denial, revocation, or suspension. If the administrative law judge makes a proposal for a decision to deny an application or to suspend or revoke a certificate, the administrative law judge shall include in the proposal a finding of the costs, fees, expenses, and reasonable and necessary attorney's fees the state incurred in bringing the proceeding. The director may adopt the finding for costs, fees, and expenses and make the finding a part of the final order entered in the proceeding. Proceeds collected from a finding made under this subsection shall be paid to the department.

(Enacted by Acts 1995, 74th Leg., ch. 165 (S.B. 971), § 1, effective September 1, 1995; am. Acts 1997, 75th Leg., ch. 1069 (S.B. 1856), § 12, effective June 19, 1997; am. Acts 1999, 76th Leg., ch. 1189 (S.B. 370), § 32, effective September 1, 1999.)

### Sec. 548.408. Judicial Review of Administrative Action.

(a) A person dissatisfied with the final decision of the director may appeal the decision by filing a petition as provided by Subchapter G, Chapter 2001, Government Code.

(b) The district or county attorney or the attorney general shall represent the director in the appeal, except that an attorney who is a full-time employee of the department may represent the director in the appeal with the approval of the attorney general.

(c) The court in which the appeal is filed shall:

(1) set the matter for hearing after 10 days' written notice to the director and the attorney representing the director; and

(2) determine whether an enforcement action of the director shall be suspended pending hearing and enter an order for the suspension.

(d) The court order takes effect when served on the director.

(e) The director shall provide a copy of the petition and court order to the attorney representing the director.

(f) A stay under this section may not be effective for more than 90 days after the date the petition for appeal is filed. On the expiration of the stay, the director's enforcement action shall be reinstated or imposed. The department or court may not extend the stay or grant an additional stay.

(g) Judicial review of the final decision of the director is under the substantial evidence rule. (Enacted by Acts 1995, 74th Leg., ch. 165 (S.B. 971), § 1, effective September 1, 1995; am. Acts 1999, 76th Leg., ch. 1189 (S.B. 370), § 33, effective September 1, 1999; am. Acts 2001, 77th Leg., ch. 1169 (H.B. 3071), § 3, effective September 1, 2001.)

### Sec. 548.409. Complaints.

(a) The department shall adopt rules regarding the efficient handling and investigation of complaints by citizens, applicants, inspectors, and inspection stations against an employee or agent of the department who may investigate the compliance of an inspection station or inspector

regarding Subchapter F or rules adopted under Subchapter F or this subchapter.

(b) The rules must provide for a fair, expeditious, and equitable investigation and resolution to complaints received by the department. (Enacted by Acts 2001, 77th Leg., ch. 1169 (H.B. 3071), § 4, effective September 1, 2001.)

### Secs. 548.410 to 548.500 [Reserved for expansion].

### SUBCHAPTER H
### INSPECTION AND CERTIFICATION FEES

### Sec. 548.501. Inspection Fees Generally.

(a) Except as provided by Sections 548.503 and 548.504, the fee for inspection of a motor vehicle other than a moped is $12.50. The fee for inspection of a moped is $5.75. The fee for a verification form issued as required by Section 548.256 is $1.

(b) An inspection station shall pay to the department $5.50 of each fee for an inspection. The department may require the station to make an advance payment of $5.50 for each inspection certificate provided to the station. If advance payment is made:

(1) no further payment may be required on issuance of a certificate;

(2) the inspection station may waive the fee due from the owner of an inspected vehicle who is issued a certificate to which the advance payment applies;

(3) the department shall refund to the inspection station $5.50 for each unissued certificate that the station returns to the department in accordance with department rules; and

(4) the conservation commission shall pay to the department $2 for each unissued certificate that the station returns to the department. (Enacted by Acts 1995, 74th Leg., ch. 165 (S.B. 971), § 1, effective September 1, 1995; am. Acts 1999, 76th Leg., ch. 1189 (S.B. 370), § 34, effective September 1, 1999.)

### Sec. 548.502. Inspection by Political Subdivision or State Agency.

A political subdivision or state agency for which the department certifies an inspection station under Section 548.004:

(1) shall pay to the department an advance payment of $5.50 for each inspection certificate provided to it; and

(2) may not be required to pay the compulsory inspection fee.

(Enacted by Acts 1995, 74th Leg., ch. 165 (S.B. 971), § 1, effective September 1, 1995.)

### Sec. 548.503. Initial Two-Year Inspection of Passenger Car or Light Truck.

(a) The fee for inspection of a passenger car or light truck under Section 548.102 shall be set by the department by rule on or before September 1 of each year. A fee set by the department under this subsection must be based on the costs of producing certificates, providing inspections, and administering the program, but may not be less than $21.75.

(b) The department shall require an inspection station to make an advance payment of $14.75 for a certificate to be issued under this section. Additional payment may not be required of the station for the certificate. The inspection station may waive the fee due from the owner of the vehicle inspected. A refund for an unissued certificate shall be made in the same manner as provided for other certificate refunds.

(Enacted by Acts 1995, 74th Leg., ch. 165 (S.B. 971), § 1, effective September 1, 1995; am. Acts 1999, 76th Leg., ch. 1189 (S.B. 370), § 35, effective September 1, 1999.)

### Sec. 548.504. Inspection of Commercial Motor Vehicle.

(a) The fee for inspection of a commercial motor vehicle under the program established under Section 548.201 is $50.

(b) The inspection station shall pay to the department $10 of each fee for inspection of a commercial motor vehicle. The department may require the station to make an advance payment of $10 for a certificate to be issued under this section. If advance payment is made:

(1) no additional payment may be required of the station for the certificate; and

(2) a refund for an unissued certificate shall be made in the same manner as provided for other certificate refunds.

(Enacted by Acts 1995, 74th Leg., ch. 165 (S.B. 971), § 1, effective September 1, 1995.)

### Sec. 548.505. Emissions-Related Inspection Fee.

(a) The department by rule may impose an inspection fee for a vehicle inspected under Section 548.301(a) in addition to the fee provided by Section 548.501, 548.502, 548.503, or 548.504. A fee imposed under this subsection must be based on the costs of:

(1) producing certificates;

(2) providing inspections; and

(3) administering the program.

(b) The department may provide a maximum fee for an inspection under this subchapter. The department may not set a minimum fee for an inspection under this subchapter.

(Enacted by Acts 1995, 74th Leg., ch. 165 (S.B. 971), § 1, effective September 1, 1995; am. Acts 1997, 75th Leg., ch. 165 (S.B. 898), § 30.123(i), effective September 1, 1997; am. Acts 1997, 75th Leg., ch. 1069 (S.B. 1856), § 13, effective June 19, 1997.)

### Sec. 548.5055. [Expires August 31, 2019] Texas Emission Reduction Plan Fee.

(a) In addition to other fees required by this subchapter, to fund the Texas emissions reduction plan established under Chapter 386, Health and Safety Code, the department shall collect for every commercial motor vehicle required to be inspected under Subchapter D, a fee of $10.

(b) The department shall remit fees collected under this section to the comptroller at the time and in the manner prescribed by the comptroller for deposit in the Texas emission reduction plan fund.

(c) This section expires August 31, 2019.

(Enacted by Acts 2001, 77th Leg., ch. 967 (S.B. 5), § 10, effective September 1, 2001; am. Acts 2005, 79th Leg., ch. 1125 (H.B. 2481), § 21, effective September 1, 2005; am. Acts 2007, 80th Leg., ch. 262 (S.B. 12), § 2.18, effective June 8, 2007; am. Acts 2009, 81st Leg., ch. 1125 (H.B. 1796), § 22, effective September 1, 2009.)

### Sec. 548.506. Fee for Certification As Inspector.

An applicant for certification as an inspector must submit with the applicant's first application a fee of $25 for certification until August 31 of the even-numbered year following the date of certification. To be certified after August 31 of that year, the applicant must pay $25 as a certificate fee for each subsequent two-year period.

Transportation

(Enacted by Acts 1995, 74th Leg., ch. 165 (S.B. 971), § 1, effective September 1, 1995; am. Acts 2011, 82nd Leg., ch. 1202 (S.B. 197), § 3, effective September 1, 2011.)

### Sec. 548.507.  Fee for Certification As Inspection Station.

(a) Except as provided by Subsection (b) or (c), after an applicant for certification as an inspection station is notified that the application will be approved, the applicant must pay a fee of $100 for certification until August 31 of the odd-numbered year after the date of appointment. To be certified after August 31 of that year, the applicant must pay a fee of $100 for certification for each subsequent two-year period.

(b) If an applicant for certification as an inspection station has been convicted of a violation of this chapter relating to an emissions inspection under Subchapter F, after notification that the application will be approved, the applicant must pay a fee of $500 for certification until August 31 of the odd-numbered year after the date of appointment. To be certified after August 31 of that year, the applicant must pay a fee of $100 for certification for each subsequent two-year period.

(c) If an applicant for certification as an inspection station has been convicted of two or more violations of this chapter relating to an emissions inspection under Subchapter F, after notification that the application will be approved, the applicant must pay a fee of $1,500 for certification until August 31 of the odd-numbered year after the date of appointment. To be certified after August 31 of that year, the applicant must pay a fee of $100 for certification for each subsequent two-year period.

(Enacted by Acts 1995, 74th Leg., ch. 165 (S.B. 971), § 1, effective September 1, 1995; am. Acts 2011, 82nd Leg., ch. 1202 (S.B. 197), § 4, effective September 1, 2011.)

### Sec. 548.508.  Disposition of Fees.

Except as provided by Sections 382.0622 and 382.202, Health and Safety Code, and Section 548.5055, each fee collected by the department under this subchapter shall be deposited to the credit of the Texas mobility fund.

(Enacted by Acts 2003, 78th Leg., ch. 1325 (H.B. 3588), § 11.07, effective September 1, 2003; am. Acts 2011, 82nd Leg., ch. 91 (S.B. 1303), § 24.013, effective September 1, 2011.)

**Secs. 548.509 to 548.600 [Reserved for expansion].**

### SUBCHAPTER I
### VIOLATIONS AND OFFENSES

### Sec. 548.601.  Offense Generally.

(a) A person, including an inspector or an inspection station, commits an offense if the person:

(1) issues an inspection certificate with knowledge that the issuance is in violation of this chapter or rules adopted under this chapter;

(2) falsely or fraudulently represents to the owner or operator of a vehicle that equipment inspected or required to be inspected must be repaired, adjusted, or replaced for the vehicle to pass an inspection;

(3) misrepresents:

(A) material information in an application in violation of Section 548.402 or 548.403; or

(B) information filed with the department under this chapter or as required by department rule;

(4) issues an inspection certificate:

(A) without authorization to issue the certificate; or

(B) without inspecting the vehicle;

(5) issues an inspection certificate for a vehicle with knowledge that the vehicle has not been repaired, adjusted, or corrected after an inspection has shown a repair, adjustment, or correction to be necessary;

(6) knowingly issues an inspection certificate:

(A) for a vehicle without conducting an inspection of each item required to be inspected; or

(B) for a vehicle that is missing an item required to be inspected or that has an item required to be inspected that is not in compliance with state law or department rules;

(7) refuses to allow a vehicle's owner to have a qualified person of the owner's choice make a required repair, adjustment, or correction;

(8) charges for an inspection an amount greater than the authorized fee; or

(9) performs an act prohibited by or fails to perform an act required by this chapter or a rule adopted under this chapter.

(b) Unless otherwise specified in this chapter, an offense under this section is a Class C misdemeanor.

(c) A designated representative of the depart-

ment may issue a notice of an offense or a notice to appear to a person, including an inspector or inspection station, who violates this chapter or a rule adopted under this chapter.
(Enacted by Acts 1995, 74th Leg., ch. 165 (S.B. 971), § 1, effective September 1, 1995; am. Acts 1997, 75th Leg., ch. 1069 (S.B. 1856), § 14, effective June 19, 1997; am. Acts 1999, 76th Leg., ch. 1189 (S.B. 370), § 36, effective September 1, 1999.)

## Sec. 548.6015. Civil Penalties.

(a) An inspection station that violates a provision of this chapter relating to an emissions inspection under Subchapter F is liable for a civil penalty of not less than $250 or more than $500 for each violation. The district or county attorney for the county in which the inspection station is located or the attorney general may bring suit in the name of this state to collect the penalty.

(b) An inspector who violates a provision of this chapter relating to an emissions inspection under Subchapter F is liable for a civil penalty of not less than $50 or more than $150 for each violation. The district or county attorney for the county in which the inspection station that employs the inspector is located or the attorney general may bring suit in the name of this state to collect the penalty.

(c) A penalty imposed under this section is in lieu of a civil or administrative penalty imposed under another provision of this chapter for the same violation.
(Enacted by Acts 2011, 82nd Leg., ch. 1202 (S.B. 197), § 5, effective September 1, 2011.)

## Sec. 548.602. Failure to Display Inspection Certificate.

(a) After the fifth day after the date of expiration of the period designated for inspection, a person may not operate:

(1) a motor vehicle registered in this state unless a current and appropriate inspection certificate is displayed on the vehicle; or

(2) a commercial motor vehicle registered in this state unless it is equipped as required by federal motor carrier safety regulations and displays an inspection certificate issued under the program established under Section 548.201.

(b) A peace officer who exhibits a badge or other sign of authority may stop a vehicle not displaying an inspection certificate on the windshield and require the owner or operator to produce an inspection certificate for the vehicle.

(c) It is a defense to prosecution under Subsection (a)(1) that an inspection certificate for the vehicle is in effect at the time of the arrest.
(Enacted by Acts 1995, 74th Leg., ch. 165 (S.B. 971), § 1, effective September 1, 1995; am. Acts 1997, 75th Leg., ch. 1069 (S.B. 1856), § 15, effective June 19, 1997; am. Acts 1999, 76th Leg., ch. 1189 (S.B. 370), § 37, effective September 1, 1999.)

## Sec. 548.603. Fictitious or Counterfeit Inspection Certificate or Insurance Document.

(a) A person commits an offense if the person:

(1) displays or causes or permits to be displayed an inspection certificate or insurance document knowing that the certificate or document is counterfeit, tampered with, altered, fictitious, issued for another vehicle, issued for a vehicle failing to meet all emissions inspection requirements, or issued in violation of:

(A) this chapter, rules adopted under this chapter, or other law of this state; or

(B) a law of another state, the United States, the United Mexican States, a state of the United Mexican States, Canada, or a province of Canada;

(2) transfers an inspection certificate from a windshield or location to another windshield or location;

(3) with intent to circumvent the emissions inspection requirements seeks an inspection of a vehicle at a station not certified to perform an emissions inspection if the person knows that the vehicle is required to be inspected under Section 548.301;

(4) knowingly does not comply with an emissions inspection requirement for a vehicle; or

(5) displays on a vehicle an inspection certificate that was obtained knowing that the vehicle does not meet all emissions inspection requirements for the vehicle.

(b) A person commits an offense if the person:

(1) makes or possesses, with the intent to sell, circulate, or pass, a counterfeit inspection certificate or insurance document; or

(2) possesses any part of a stamp, dye, plate, negative, machine, or other device that is used or designated for use in making a counterfeit inspection certificate or insurance document.

(c) The owner of a vehicle commits an offense if the owner knowingly allows the vehicle to be registered or operated while the vehicle displays an inspection certificate in violation of Subsection (a).

Transportation

(d) An offense under Subsection (a) or (c) is a Class B misdemeanor. An offense under Subsection (b) is a third degree felony unless the person acts with the intent to defraud or harm another person, in which event the offense is a second degree felony.

(e) In this section:

(1) "Counterfeit" means an imitation of a document that is printed, engraved, copied, photographed, forged, or manufactured by a person not authorized to take that action under:

(A) this chapter, rules adopted under this chapter, or other law of this state; or

(B) a law of another state, the United States, the United Mexican States, a state of the United Mexican States, Canada, or a province of Canada.

(2) "Inspection certificate" means a document that is printed, manufactured, or made by the department or an authorized agent of the department for issuance after a vehicle passes an inspection performed under this chapter.

(3) "Insurance document" means a standard proof of motor vehicle insurance coverage that is:

(A) in a form prescribed by the Texas Department of Insurance or by a similarly authorized board, agency, or authority of another state; and

(B) issued by an insurer or insurer's agent who is authorized to write motor vehicle insurance coverage.

(4) "Person" includes an inspection station or inspector.

(f) **[2 Versions: As added by Acts 1997, 75th Leg., ch. 851]** Notwithstanding Subsection (c), an offense under Subsection (a)(1) that involves a fictitious inspection certificate is a Class B misdemeanor.

(f) **[2 Versions: As added by Acts 1997, 75th Leg., ch. 1069]** A motor vehicle on which a vehicle emissions inspection certificate is displayed in violation of Subsection (a) and that is operated or parked on a public roadway may be impounded by a peace officer or other authorized employee of this state or a political subdivision of this state in which the vehicle is operated or parked.

(Enacted by Acts 1995, 74th Leg., ch. 165 (S.B. 971), § 1, effective September 1, 1995; am. Acts 1997, 75th Leg., ch. 165 (S.B. 898), §§ 30.123(j), (k), effective September 1, 1997; am. Acts 1997, 75th Leg., ch. 851 (H.B. 1048), § 2, effective

September 1, 1997; am. Acts 1997, 75th Leg., ch. 1069 (S.B. 1856), § 16, effective June 19, 1997.)

### Sec. 548.6035.   Fraudulent Emissions Inspection of Motor Vehicle.

(a) A person commits an offense if, in connection with a required emissions inspection of a motor vehicle, the person knowingly:

(1) places or causes to be placed on a motor vehicle an inspection certificate, if:

(A) the vehicle does not meet the emissions requirements established by the department; or

(B) the person has not inspected the vehicle;

(2) manipulates an emissions test result;

(3) uses or causes to be used emissions data from another motor vehicle as a substitute for the motor vehicle being inspected; or

(4) bypasses or circumvents a fuel cap test.

(b) A first offense under Subsections (a)(1)-(3) is a Class B misdemeanor.

(c) Except as provided by Subsection (d), a second or subsequent offense under Subsections (a)(1)-(3) is a Class A misdemeanor.

(d) If it is found on trial of an offense under Subsections (a)(1)-(3) that the person committing the offense acted with the intent to defraud or harm another person, the offense is a state jail felony.

(e) An offense under Subsection (a)(4) is a Class C misdemeanor.

(f) It is a defense to prosecution under Subsection (a)(4) that the analyzer used by the person developed a functional problem during the emissions inspection of the fuel cap that prevented the person from properly conducting the fuel cap test portion of the emissions inspection.

(Enacted by Acts 2011, 82nd Leg., ch. 1202 (S.B. 197), § 6, effective September 1, 2011.)

### Sec. 548.6036.   Actions of Employee.

(a) Except as provided by Subsection (b), an inspection station is not subject to an administrative or civil penalty or criminal prosecution under this subchapter for an act of an employee of the inspection station if the inspection station requires the employee to sign a written agreement to abide by the provisions of:

(1) this chapter;

(2) Chapter 382, Health and Safety Code; and

(3) all rules adopted under those chapters.

(b) An inspection station is subject to prosecution under this subchapter for an act of an employee of the inspection station if the inspection station:

(1)  has received written notification from the department or another agency that the employee has committed an offense under this chapter; and

(2)  continues to allow the employee to perform inspections under this chapter.

(Enacted by Acts 2011, 82nd Leg., ch. 1202 (S.B. 197), § 6, effective September 1, 2011.)

## Sec. 548.604.  Penalty for Certain Violations.

(a)  A person commits an offense if the person operates or moves a motor vehicle, trailer, semitrailer, pole trailer, or mobile home, or a combination of those vehicles, that is:

(1)  equipped in violation of this chapter or a rule adopted under this chapter; or

(2)  in a mechanical condition that endangers a person, including the operator or an occupant, or property.

(b)  An offense under this section is a misdemeanor punishable by a fine not to exceed $200.

(Enacted by Acts 1995, 74th Leg., ch. 165 (S.B. 971), § 1, effective September 1, 1995.)

## Sec. 548.605.  Dismissal of Charge; Administrative Fee.

(a)  In this section, "working day" means any day other than a Saturday, a Sunday, or a holiday on which county offices are closed.

(b)  The court shall:

(1)  dismiss a charge of driving with an expired inspection certificate if:

(A)  the defendant remedies the defect within 20 working days or before the defendant's first court appearance date, whichever is later; and

(B)  the inspection certificate has not been expired for more than 60 days; and

(2)  assess an administrative fee not to exceed $20 when the charge of driving with an expired inspection certificate has been remedied.

(c)  Notwithstanding Subsection (b)(1)(B), the court may dismiss a charge of driving with an expired inspection certificate that has been expired for more than 60 days.

(Enacted by Acts 1995, 74th Leg., ch. 165 (S.B. 971), § 1, effective September 1, 1995; am. Acts 1999, 76th Leg., ch. 688 (H.B. 707), § 1, effective September 1, 1999; am. Acts 2007, 80th Leg., ch. 1027 (H.B. 1623), § 11, effective September 1, 2007.)

# CHAPTER 549
## MOTOR CARRIER SAFETY STANDARDS
## [REPEALED]

## SUBCHAPTER A
## GENERAL PROVISIONS

## Sec. 549.001.  Definitions [Repealed].

Repealed by Acts 1997, 75th Leg., ch. 165 (S.B. 898), § 30.124, effective September 1, 1997. (Enacted by Acts 1995, 74th Leg., ch. 165 (S.B. 971), § 1, effective September 1, 1995.)

## Sec. 549.002.  Conflicts of Law [Repealed].

Repealed by Acts 1997, 75th Leg., ch. 165 (S.B. 898), § 30.124, effective September 1, 1997. (Enacted by Acts 1995, 74th Leg., ch. 165 (S.B. 971), § 1, effective September 1, 1995.)

## SUBCHAPTER B
## ADOPTION OF RULES

## Sec. 549.101.  Authority to Adopt Rules [Repealed].

Repealed by Acts 1997, 75th Leg., ch. 165 (S.B. 898), § 30.124, effective September 1, 1997. (Enacted by Acts 1995, 74th Leg., ch. 165 (S.B. 971), § 1, effective September 1, 1995.)

## Sec. 549.102.  Purpose of Rules; Consistency with Federal Regulations [Repealed].

Repealed by Acts 1997, 75th Leg., ch. 165 (S.B. 898), § 30.124, effective September 1, 1997. (Enacted by Acts 1995, 74th Leg., ch. 165 (S.B. 971), § 1, effective September 1, 1995.)

## Sec. 549.103.  Applicability of Rules [Repealed].

Repealed by Acts 1997, 75th Leg., ch. 165 (S.B. 898), § 30.124, effective September 1, 1997. (Enacted by Acts 1995, 74th Leg., ch. 165 (S.B. 971), § 1, effective September 1, 1995.)

## Sec. 549.104.  Limitations of Rules [Repealed].

Repealed by Acts 1997, 75th Leg., ch. 165 (S.B. 898), § 30.124, effective September 1, 1997. (Enacted by Acts 1995, 74th Leg., ch. 165 (S.B. 971), § 1, effective September 1, 1995.)

Transportation

## SUBCHAPTER C
## OTHER REQUIREMENTS

### Sec. 549.201.  Insurance [Repealed].
Repealed by Acts 1997, 75th Leg., ch. 165 (S.B. 898), § 30.124, effective September 1, 1997. (Enacted by Acts 1995, 74th Leg., ch. 165 (S.B. 971), § 1, effective September 1, 1995.)

### Sec. 549.202.  Registration [Repealed].
Repealed by Acts 1997, 75th Leg., ch. 165 (S.B. 898), § 30.124, effective September 1, 1997. (Enacted by Acts 1995, 74th Leg., ch. 165 (S.B. 971), § 1, effective September 1, 1995.)

## SUBCHAPTER D
## ADMINISTRATIVE ENFORCEMENT

### Sec. 549.301.  Certification of Municipal Peace Officers [Repealed].
Repealed by Acts 1997, 75th Leg., ch. 165 (S.B. 898), § 30.124, effective September 1, 1997. (Enacted by Acts 1995, 74th Leg., ch. 165 (S.B. 971), § 1, effective September 1, 1995.)

### Sec. 549.302.  Municipal Enforcement Requirements [Repealed].
Repealed by Acts 1997, 75th Leg., ch. 165 (S.B. 898), § 30.124, effective September 1, 1997. (Enacted by Acts 1995, 74th Leg., ch. 165 (S.B. 971), § 1, effective September 1, 1995.)

### Sec. 549.303.  Detention of Vehicles [Repealed].
Repealed by Acts 1997, 75th Leg., ch. 165 (S.B. 898), § 30.124, effective September 1, 1997. (Enacted by Acts 1995, 74th Leg., ch. 165 (S.B. 971), § 1, effective September 1, 1995.)

### Sec. 549.304.  Inspection of Premises [Repealed].
Repealed by Acts 1997, 75th Leg., ch. 165 (S.B. 898), § 30.124, effective September 1, 1997. (Enacted by Acts 1995, 74th Leg., ch. 165 (S.B. 971), § 1, effective September 1, 1995.)

## SUBCHAPTER E
## OFFENSES, PENALTIES, AND JUDICIAL ENFORCEMENT

### Sec. 549.401.  Offenses [Repealed].
Repealed by Acts 1997, 75th Leg., ch. 165 (S.B. 898), § 30.124, effective September 1, 1997.

(Enacted by Acts 1995, 74th Leg., ch. 165 (S.B. 971), § 1, effective September 1, 1995.)

### Sec. 549.402.  Civil Penalty [Repealed].
Repealed by Acts 1997, 75th Leg., ch. 165 (S.B. 898), § 30.124, effective September 1, 1997. (Enacted by Acts 1995, 74th Leg., ch. 165 (S.B. 971), § 1, effective September 1, 1995.)

### Sec. 549.403.  Administrative Penalty [Repealed].
Repealed by Acts 1997, 75th Leg., ch. 165 (S.B. 898), § 30.124, effective September 1, 1997. (Enacted by Acts 1995, 74th Leg., ch. 165 (S.B. 971), § 1, effective September 1, 1995.)

### Sec. 549.404.  Suit for Injunction [Repealed].
Repealed by Acts 1997, 75th Leg., ch. 165 (S.B. 898), § 30.124, effective September 1, 1997. (Enacted by Acts 1995, 74th Leg., ch. 165 (S.B. 971), § 1, effective September 1, 1995.)

# CHAPTER 550
# ACCIDENTS AND ACCIDENT REPORTS

## SUBCHAPTER A
## GENERAL PROVISIONS

### Sec. 550.001. Applicability of Chapter.

This chapter applies only to:

(1) a road owned and controlled by a water control and improvement district;

(2) a private access way or parking area provided for a client or patron by a business, other than a private residential property, or the property of a garage or parking lot for which a charge is made for storing or parking a motor vehicle; and

(3) a highway or other public place.

(Enacted by Acts 1995, 74th Leg., ch. 165 (S.B. 971), § 1, effective September 1, 1995.)

### Secs. 550.002 to 550.020 [Reserved for expansion].

## SUBCHAPTER B
## DUTIES FOLLOWING ACCIDENT

### Sec. 550.021. Accident Involving Personal Injury or Death.

(a) The operator of a vehicle involved in an accident resulting in injury to or death of a person shall:

(1) immediately stop the vehicle at the scene of the accident or as close to the scene as possible;

(2) immediately return to the scene of the accident if the vehicle is not stopped at the scene of the accident; and

(3) remain at the scene of the accident until the operator complies with the requirements of Section 550.023.

(b) An operator of a vehicle required to stop the vehicle by Subsection (a) shall do so without obstructing traffic more than is necessary.

(c) A person commits an offense if the person does not stop or does not comply with the requirements of this section. An offense under this section:

(1) involving an accident resulting in death of or serious bodily injury, as defined by Section 1.07, Penal Code, to a person is a felony of the third degree; and

(2) involving an accident resulting in injury to which Subdivision (1) does not apply is punishable by:

(A) imprisonment in the Texas Department of Criminal Justice for not more than five years or confinement in the county jail for not more than one year;

(B) a fine not to exceed $5,000; or

(C) both the fine and the imprisonment or confinement.

(Enacted by Acts 1995, 74th Leg., ch. 165 (S.B. 971), § 1, effective September 1, 1995; am. Acts 2007, 80th Leg., ch. 97 (H.B. 1840), § 2, effective September 1, 2007.)

### Sec. 550.022. Accident Involving Damage to Vehicle.

(a) Except as provided by Subsection (b), the operator of a vehicle involved in an accident resulting only in damage to a vehicle that is driven or attended by a person shall:

(1) immediately stop the vehicle at the scene of the accident or as close as possible to the scene of the accident without obstructing traffic more than is necessary;

(2) immediately return to the scene of the accident if the vehicle is not stopped at the scene of the accident; and

(3) remain at the scene of the accident until the operator complies with the requirements of Section 550.023.

(b) If an accident occurs on a main lane, ramp, shoulder, median, or adjacent area of a freeway in a metropolitan area and each vehicle involved can be normally and safely driven, each operator shall move the operator's vehicle as soon as possible to a designated accident investigation site, if available, a location on the frontage road, the nearest suitable cross street, or other suitable location to complete the requirements of Section 550.023 and minimize interference with freeway traffic.

(c) A person commits an offense if the person does not stop or does not comply with the requirements of Subsection (a). An offense under this subsection is:

(1) a Class C misdemeanor, if the damage to all vehicles is less than $200; or

(2) a Class B misdemeanor, if the damage to all vehicles is $200 or more.

(c-1) A person commits an offense if the person does not comply with the requirements of Subsection (b). An offense under this subsection is a Class C misdemeanor.

Transportation

(d) In this section, a vehicle can be normally and safely driven only if the vehicle:

(1) does not require towing; and

(2) can be operated under its own power and in its usual manner, without additional damage or hazard to the vehicle, other traffic, or the roadway.

(Enacted by Acts 1995, 74th Leg., ch. 165 (S.B. 971), § 1, effective September 1, 1995; am. Acts 2005, 79th Leg., ch. 1066 (H.B. 1484), § 1, effective September 1, 2005.)

### Sec. 550.023.  Duty to Give Information and Render Aid.

The operator of a vehicle involved in an accident resulting in the injury or death of a person or damage to a vehicle that is driven or attended by a person shall:

(1) give the operator's name and address, the registration number of the vehicle the operator was driving, and the name of the operator's motor vehicle liability insurer to any person injured or the operator or occupant of or person attending a vehicle involved in the collision;

(2) if requested and available, show the operator's driver's license to a person described by Subdivision (1); and

(3) provide any person injured in the accident reasonable assistance, including transporting or making arrangements for transporting the person to a physician or hospital for medical treatment if it is apparent that treatment is necessary, or if the injured person requests the transportation.

(Enacted by Acts 1995, 74th Leg., ch. 165 (S.B. 971), § 1, effective September 1, 1995.)

### Sec. 550.024.  Duty on Striking Unattended Vehicle.

(a) The operator of a vehicle that collides with and damages an unattended vehicle shall immediately stop and:

(1) locate the operator or owner of the unattended vehicle and give that person the name and address of the operator and the owner of the vehicle that struck the unattended vehicle; or

(2) leave in a conspicuous place in, or securely attach in a plainly visible way to, the unattended vehicle a written notice giving the name and address of the operator and the owner of the vehicle that struck the unattended vehicle and a statement of the circumstances of the collision.

(b) A person commits an offense if the person violates Subsection (a). An offense under this section is:

(1) a Class C misdemeanor, if the damage to all vehicles involved is less than $200; or

(2) a Class B misdemeanor, if the damage to all vehicles involved is $200 or more.

(Enacted by Acts 1995, 74th Leg., ch. 165 (S.B. 971), § 1, effective September 1, 1995.)

### Sec. 550.025.  Duty on Striking Structure, Fixture, or Highway Landscaping.

(a) The operator of a vehicle involved in an accident resulting only in damage to a structure adjacent to a highway or a fixture or landscaping legally on or adjacent to a highway shall:

(1) take reasonable steps to locate and notify the owner or person in charge of the property of the accident and of the operator's name and address and the registration number of the vehicle the operator was driving;

(2) if requested and available, show the operator's driver's license to the owner or person in charge of the property; and

(3) report the accident if required by Section 550.061.

(b) A person commits an offense if the person violates Subsection (a). An offense under this section is:

(1) a Class C misdemeanor, if the damage to all fixtures and landscaping is less than $200; or

(2) a Class B misdemeanor, if the damage to all fixtures and landscaping is $200 or more.

(Enacted by Acts 1995, 74th Leg., ch. 165 (S.B. 971), § 1, effective September 1, 1995; am. Acts 2011, 82nd Leg., ch. 680 (H.B. 42), §§ 1, 2, effective September 1, 2011.)

### Sec. 550.026.  Immediate Report of Accident.

(a) The operator of a vehicle involved in an accident resulting in injury to or death of a person or damage to a vehicle to the extent that it cannot be normally and safely driven shall immediately by the quickest means of communication give notice of the accident to the:

(1) local police department if the accident occurred in a municipality;

(2) local police department or the sheriff's office if the accident occurred not more than 100 feet outside the limits of a municipality; or

(3) sheriff's office or the nearest office of the department if the accident is not required to be reported under Subdivision (1) or (2).

(b) If a section of road is within 100 feet of the limits of more than one municipality, the municipalities may agree regarding the maintenance of reports made under Subsection (a)(2). A county may agree with municipalities in the county regarding the maintenance of reports made under Subsection (a)(2). An agreement under this subsection does not affect the duty to report an accident under Subsection (a).

(Enacted by Acts 1995, 74th Leg., ch. 165 (S.B. 971), § 1, effective September 1, 1995.)

## Secs. 550.027 to 550.040 [Reserved for expansion].

## SUBCHAPTER C
## INVESTIGATION OF ACCIDENT

### Sec. 550.041.  Investigation by Peace Officer.

(a) A peace officer who is notified of a motor vehicle accident resulting in injury to or death of a person or property damage to an apparent extent of at least $1,000 may investigate the accident and file justifiable charges relating to the accident without regard to whether the accident occurred on property to which this chapter applies.

(b) This section does not apply to:

(1) a privately owned residential parking area; or

(2) a privately owned parking lot where a fee is charged for parking or storing a vehicle.

(Enacted by Acts 1995, 74th Leg., ch. 165 (S.B. 971), § 1, effective September 1, 1995; am. Acts 2001, 77th Leg., ch. 531 (H.B. 2230), § 1, effective September 1, 2001.)

## Secs. 550.042 to 550.060 [Reserved for expansion].

## SUBCHAPTER D
## WRITTEN ACCIDENT REPORT

### Sec. 550.0601.  Definition.

In this subchapter, "department" means the Texas Department of Transportation.

(Enacted by Acts 2007, 80th Leg., ch. 1407 (S.B. 766), § 2, effective September 1, 2007.)

### Sec. 550.061.  Operator's Accident Report.

(a) The operator of a vehicle involved in an accident shall make a written report of the acci-

dent if the accident is not investigated by a law enforcement officer and the accident resulted in injury to or the death of a person or damage to the property of any one person to an apparent extent of $1,000 or more.

(b) The report required by Subsection (a) must be filed with the department not later than the 10th day after the date of the accident.

(c) A person commits an offense if the person does not file the report with the department as required by this section.

(d) Venue for the prosecution of an offense under this section is in the county in which the accident occurred.

(e) The department may require:

(1) the operator of a vehicle involved in an accident in which a report is required by this section to file a supplemental report if the department considers the original report insufficient; and

(2) a witness of an accident to make a report with the department.

(Enacted by Acts 1995, 74th Leg., ch. 165 (S.B. 971), § 1, effective September 1, 1995; am. Acts 2001, 77th Leg., ch. 531 (H.B. 2230), § 2, effective September 1, 2001.)

### Sec. 550.062.  Officer's Accident Report.

(a) A law enforcement officer who in the regular course of duty investigates a motor vehicle accident shall make a written report of the accident if the accident resulted in injury to or the death of a person or damage to the property of any one person to the apparent extent of $1,000 or more.

(b) The report required by Subsection (a) must be filed with the department not later than the 10th day after the date of the accident.

(c) This section applies without regard to whether the officer investigates the accident at the location of the accident and immediately after the accident or afterwards by interviewing those involved in the accident or witnesses to the accident.

(Enacted by Acts 1995, 74th Leg., ch. 165 (S.B. 971), § 1, effective September 1, 1995; am. Acts 2001, 77th Leg., ch. 531 (H.B. 2230), § 3, effective September 1, 2001.)

### Sec. 550.063.  Report on Appropriate Form.

The form of all written accident reports must be approved by the department and the Depart-

Transportation

ment of Public Safety. A person who is required to file a written accident report shall report on the appropriate form and shall disclose all information required by the form unless the information is not available.

(Enacted by Acts 1995, 74th Leg., ch. 165 (S.B. 971), § 1, effective September 1, 1995; am. Acts 2007, 80th Leg., ch. 1407 (S.B. 766), § 3, effective September 1, 2007.)

*ONLY USE BLACK INK, WHEN FILLING OUT FORMS*

### Sec. 550.064.  Accident Report Forms.

(a) The department shall prepare and when requested supply to police departments, coroners, sheriffs, garages, and other suitable agencies or individuals the accident report forms appropriate for the persons required to make a report and appropriate for the purposes to be served by those reports.

(b) An accident report form prepared by the department must:

(1) require sufficiently detailed information to disclose the cause and conditions of and the persons and vehicles involved in an accident if the form is for the report to be made by a person involved in or investigating the accident;

(2) include a way to designate and identify a peace officer, firefighter, or emergency medical services employee who is involved in an accident while driving a law enforcement vehicle, fire department vehicle, or emergency medical services vehicle while performing the person's duties;

(3) require a statement by a person described by Subdivision (2) as to the nature of the accident; and

(4) include a way to designate whether an individual involved in an accident wants to be contacted by a person seeking to obtain employment as a professional described by Section 38.01(12), Penal Code.

(Enacted by Acts 1995, 74th Leg., ch. 165 (S.B. 971), § 1, effective September 1, 1995; am. Acts 1997, 75th Leg., ch. 750 (H.B. 1327), § 3, effective September 1, 1997; am. Acts 2011, 82nd Leg., ch. 689 (H.B. 343), § 2, effective September 1, 2011.)

### Sec. 550.065.  Release of Certain Information Relating to Accidents.

(a) This section applies only to information that is held by the department or another governmental entity and relates to a motor vehicle accident reported under this chapter or Section 601.004, including accident report information

compiled under Section 201.805, as added by Chapter 1407 (S.B. 766), Acts of the 80th Legislature, Regular Session, 2007.

(b) Except as provided by Subsection (c) or (e), the information is privileged and for the confidential use of:

(1) the department; and

(2) an agency of the United States, this state, or a local government of this state that has use for the information for accident prevention purposes.

(c) On written request and payment of any required fee, the department or the governmental entity shall release the information to:

(1) an entity described by Subsection (b);

(2) the law enforcement agency that employs the peace officer who investigated the accident and sent the information to the department;

(3) the court in which a case involving a person involved in the accident is pending if the report is subpoenaed; or

(4) a person who provides the department or governmental entity with two or more of the following:

(A) the date of the accident;

(B) the specific address or the highway or street where the accident occurred; or

(C) the name of any person involved in the accident.

(d) The fee for a copy of the accident report is $6. The copy may be certified by the department or the governmental entity for an additional fee of $2. The department or the governmental entity may issue a certification that no report or information is on file for a fee of $6.

(e) In addition to the information required to be released under Subsection (c), the department may release:

(1) information relating to motor vehicle accidents that the department compiles under Section 201.805, as added by Chapter 1407 (S.B. 766), Acts of the 80th Legislature, Regular Session, 2007; or

(2) a vehicle identification number and specific accident information relating to that vehicle.

(f) The department:

(1) may not release under Subsection (e) information that:

(A) is personal information, as defined by Section 730.003; or

(B) would allow a person to satisfy the requirements of Subsection (c)(4) for the release of information for a specific motor vehicle accident; and

(2) shall withhold or redact the following items of information:

(A) the first, middle, and last name of any person listed in an accident report, including a vehicle driver, occupant, owner, or lessee, a bicyclist, a pedestrian, or a property owner;

(B) the number of any driver's license, commercial driver's license, or personal identification certificate issued to any person listed in an accident report;

(C) the date of birth, other than the year, of any person listed in an accident report;

(D) the address, other than zip code, and telephone number of any person listed in an accident report;

(E) the license plate number of any vehicle listed in an accident report;

(F) the date of any accident, other than the year;

(G) the name of any insurance company listed as a provider of financial responsibility for a vehicle listed in an accident report;

(H) the number of any insurance policy issued by an insurance company listed as a provider of financial responsibility;

(I) the date the peace officer who investigated the accident was notified of the accident;

(J) the date the investigating peace officer arrived at the accident site;

(K) the date the investigating officer's report was prepared;

(L) the badge number or identification number of the investigating officer;

(M) the date on which any person who died as a result of the accident died;

(N) the date of any commercial motor vehicle report; and

(O) the place where any person injured or killed in an accident was taken and the person or entity that provided the transportation.

(g) The amount that may be charged for information provided under Subsection (e) shall be calculated in the manner specified by Chapter 552, Government Code, for public information provided by a governmental body under that chapter.

(Enacted by Acts 1995, 74th Leg., ch. 165 (S.B. 971), § 1, effective September 1, 1995; am. Acts 1997, 75th Leg., ch. 165 (S.B. 898), § 30.125(a), effective September 1, 1997; am. Acts 1997, 75th Leg., ch. 1187 (S.B. 1069), § 13, effective September 1, 1997; am. Acts 2001, 77th Leg., ch. 1032 (H.B. 1544), § 5, effective September 1, 2001; am.

Acts 2009, 81st Leg., ch. 470 (S.B. 375), § 1, effective June 19, 2009.)

### Sec. 550.066. Admissibility of Certain Accident Report Information.

An individual's response to the information requested on an accident report form as provided by Section 550.064(b)(4) is not admissible evidence in a civil trial.

(Enacted by Acts 1995, 74th Leg., ch. 165 (S.B. 971), § 1, effective September 1, 1995.)

### Sec. 550.067. Municipal Authority to Require Accident Reports.

(a) A municipality by ordinance may require the operator of a vehicle involved in an accident to file with a designated municipal department:

(1) a report of the accident, if the accident results in injury to or the death of a person or the apparent total property damage is $25 or more; or

(2) a copy of a report required by this chapter to be filed with the department.

(b) A report filed under Subsection (a) is for the confidential use of the municipal department and subject to the provisions of Section 550.065.

(c) A municipality by ordinance may require the person in charge of a garage or repair shop where a motor vehicle is brought if the vehicle shows evidence of having been involved in an accident requiring a report to be filed under Section 550.061 or 550.062 or shows evidence of having been struck by a bullet to report to a department of the municipality within 24 hours after the garage or repair shop receives the motor vehicle, giving the engine number, registration number, and the name and address of the owner or operator of the vehicle.

(Enacted by Acts 1995, 74th Leg., ch. 165 (S.B. 971), § 1, effective September 1, 1995.)

### Sec. 550.068. Changing Accident Report.

(a) Except as provided by Subsection (b), a change in or a modification of a written report of a motor vehicle accident prepared by a peace officer or the operator of a vehicle involved in an accident that alters a material fact in the report may be made only by the peace officer or person who prepared the report.

(b) A change in or a modification of the written report of the accident may be made by a person other than the peace officer or the operator of the vehicle if:

(1) the change is made by a written supplement to the report; and

(2) the written supplement clearly indicates the name of the person who originated the change.

(Enacted by Acts 1997, 75th Leg., ch. 214 (S.B. 526), § 1, effective September 1, 1997.)

**Secs. 550.069 to 550.080 [Reserved for expansion].**

## SUBCHAPTER E
## OTHER REPORTS

### Sec. 550.081.  Report of Medical Examiner or Justice of the Peace.

(a) In this section:

(1) "Department" means the Texas Department of Transportation.

(2) "Bridge collapse" means the abrupt failure of the basic structure of a bridge that impairs the ability of the bridge to serve its intended purpose and that damages a highway located on or under the structure.

(b) A medical examiner or justice of the peace acting as coroner in a county that does not have a medical examiner's office or that is not part of a medical examiner's district shall submit a report in writing to the department of the death of a person that was the result of a traffic accident or bridge collapse:

(1) to which this chapter applies; and

(2) that occurred within the jurisdiction of the medical examiner or justice of the peace in the preceding calendar quarter.

(c) The report must be submitted before the 11th day of each calendar month and include:

(1) the name of the deceased and a statement as to whether the deceased was:

(A) the operator of or a passenger in a vehicle involved in the accident; or

(B) a pedestrian or other nonoccupant of a vehicle;

(2) the date of the accident and the name of the county in which the accident occurred, and, if a bridge collapse, the location of the bridge in that county;

(3) the name of any laboratory, medical examiner's office, or other facility that conducted toxicological testing relative to the deceased; and

(4) the results of any toxicological testing that was conducted.

(d) A report required by this section shall be sent to:

(1) the crash records bureau of the department at its headquarters in Austin; or

(2) any other office or bureau of the department that the department designates.

(e) If toxicological test results are not available to the medical examiner or justice of the peace on the date a report must be submitted, the medical examiner or justice shall:

(1) submit a report that includes the statement "toxicological test results unavailable"; and

(2) submit a supplement to the report that contains the information required by Subsections (c)(3) and (4) as soon as practicable after the toxicological test results become available.

(f) The department shall prepare and when requested supply to medical examiners' offices and justices of the peace the forms necessary to make the reports required by this section.

(Enacted by Acts 1995, 74th Leg., ch. 165 (S.B. 971), § 1, effective September 1, 1995; am. Acts 2007, 80th Leg., ch. 74 (H.B. 423), § 1, effective September 1, 2007; am. Acts 2007, 80th Leg., ch. 1407 (S.B. 766), § 4, effective September 1, 2007; am. Acts 2009, 81st Leg., ch. 522 (S.B. 1218), § 2, effective September 1, 2009.)

## CHAPTER 551
## OPERATION OF BICYCLES, MOPEDS, AND PLAY VEHICLES

Transportation

## SUBCHAPTER A
## APPLICATION OF CHAPTER

### Sec. 551.001. Persons Affected.

Except as provided by Subchapter C, this chapter applies only to a person operating a bicycle on:

(1) a highway; or

(2) a path set aside for the exclusive operation of bicycles.

(Enacted by Acts 1995, 74th Leg., ch. 165 (S.B. 971), § 1, effective September 1, 1995; am. Acts 2003, 78th Leg., ch. 1318 (H.B. 1997), § 4, effective September 1, 2003.)

### Sec. 551.002. Moped and Electric Bicycle Included.

A provision of this subtitle applicable to a bicycle also applies to:

(1) a moped, other than a provision that by its nature cannot apply to a moped; and

(2) an electric bicycle, other than a provision that by its nature cannot apply to an electric bicycle.

(Enacted by Acts 1995, 74th Leg., ch. 165 (S.B. 971), § 1, effective September 1, 1995; am. Acts 2001, 77th Leg., ch. 1085 (H.B. 2204), § 9, effective September 1, 2001.)

### Secs. 551.003 to 551.100 [Reserved for expansion].

## SUBCHAPTER B
## REGULATION OF OPERATION

### Sec. 551.101. Rights and Duties.

(a) A person operating a bicycle has the rights and duties applicable to a driver operating a vehicle under this subtitle, unless:

(1) a provision of this chapter alters a right or duty; or

(2) a right or duty applicable to a driver operating a vehicle cannot by its nature apply to a person operating a bicycle.

(b) A parent of a child or a guardian of a ward may not knowingly permit the child or ward to violate this subtitle.

(Enacted by Acts 1995, 74th Leg., ch. 165 (S.B. 971), § 1, effective September 1, 1995.)

### Sec. 551.102. General Operation.

(a) A person operating a bicycle shall ride only on or astride a permanent and regular seat attached to the bicycle.

(b) A person may not use a bicycle to carry more persons than the bicycle is designed or equipped to carry.

(c) A person operating a bicycle may not use the bicycle to carry an object that prevents the person from operating the bicycle with at least one hand on the handlebars of the bicycle.

(d) A person operating a bicycle, coaster, sled, or toy vehicle or using roller skates may not attach either the person or the bicycle, coaster, sled, toy vehicle, or roller skates to a streetcar or vehicle on a roadway.

(Enacted by Acts 1995, 74th Leg., ch. 165 (S.B. 971), § 1, effective September 1, 1995.)

### Sec. 551.103. Operation on Roadway.

(a) Except as provided by Subsection (b), a person operating a bicycle on a roadway who is moving slower than the other traffic on the roadway shall ride as near as practicable to the right curb or edge of the roadway, unless:

(1) the person is passing another vehicle moving in the same direction;

(2) the person is preparing to turn left at an intersection or onto a private road or driveway;

(3) a condition on or of the roadway, including a fixed or moving object, parked or moving vehicle, pedestrian, animal, or surface hazard prevents the person from safely riding next to the right curb or edge of the roadway; or

(4) the person is operating a bicycle in an outside lane that is:

(A) less than 14 feet in width and does not have a designated bicycle lane adjacent to that lane; or

(B) too narrow for a bicycle and a motor vehicle to safely travel side by side.

(b) A person operating a bicycle on a one-way roadway with two or more marked traffic lanes may ride as near as practicable to the left curb or edge of the roadway.

(c) Persons operating bicycles on a roadway may ride two abreast. Persons riding two abreast on a laned roadway shall ride in a single lane.

Transportation

Persons riding two abreast may not impede the normal and reasonable flow of traffic on the roadway. Persons may not ride more than two abreast unless they are riding on a part of a roadway set aside for the exclusive operation of bicycles.

(d) [Repealed by Acts 2001, 77th Leg., ch. 1085 (H.B. 2204), § 13, effective September 1, 2001.] (Enacted by Acts 1995, 74th Leg., ch. 165 (S.B. 971), § 1, effective September 1, 1995; am. Acts 2001, 77th Leg., ch. 1085 (H.B. 2204), §§ 10, 13, effective September 1, 2001.)

### Sec. 551.104. Safety Equipment.

(a) A person may not operate a bicycle unless the bicycle is equipped with a brake capable of making a braked wheel skid on dry, level, clean pavement.

(b) A person may not operate a bicycle at nighttime unless the bicycle is equipped with:

(1) a lamp on the front of the bicycle that emits a white light visible from a distance of at least 500 feet in front of the bicycle; and

(2) on the rear of the bicycle:

(A) a red reflector that is:

(i) of a type approved by the department; and

(ii) visible when directly in front of lawful upper beams of motor vehicle headlamps from all distances from 50 to 300 feet to the rear of the bicycle; or

(B) a lamp that emits a red light visible from a distance of 500 feet to the rear of the bicycle.

(Enacted by Acts 1995, 74th Leg., ch. 165 (S.B. 971), § 1, effective September 1, 1995; am. Acts 2001, 77th Leg., ch. 1085 (H.B. 2204), § 11, effective September 1, 2001.)

### Sec. 551.105. Competitive Racing.

(a) In this section, "bicycle" means a nonmotorized vehicle propelled by human power.

(b) A sponsoring organization may hold a competitive bicycle race on a public road only with the approval of the appropriate local law enforcement agencies.

(c) The local law enforcement agencies and the sponsoring organization may agree on safety regulations governing the movement of bicycles during a competitive race or during training for a competitive race, including the permission for bicycle operators to ride abreast.

(Enacted by Acts 1995, 74th Leg., ch. 165 (S.B. 971), § 1, effective September 1, 1995.)

### Sec. 551.106. Regulation of Electric Bicycles.

(a) The department or a local authority may not prohibit the use of an electric bicycle on a highway that is used primarily by motor vehicles. The department or a local authority may prohibit the use of an electric bicycle on a highway used primarily by pedestrians.

(b) The department shall establish rules for the administration of this section.

(Enacted by Acts 2001, 77th Leg., ch. 1085 (H.B. 2204), § 12, effective September 1, 2001.)

### Secs. 551.107 to 551.200 [Reserved for expansion].

## SUBCHAPTER C
## ELECTRIC PERSONAL ASSISTIVE MOBILITY DEVICES

### Sec. 551.201. Definition.

In this subchapter, "electric personal assistive mobility device" means a two non-tandem wheeled device designed for transporting one person that is:

(1) self-balancing; and

(2) propelled by an electric propulsion system with an average power of 750 watts or one horsepower.

(Enacted by Acts 2003, 78th Leg., ch. 1318 (H.B. 1997), § 5, effective September 1, 2003.)

### Sec. 551.202. Operation on Roadway.

(a) A person may operate an electric personal assistive mobility device on a residential street, roadway, or public highway with a speed limit of 30 miles per hour or less only:

(1) while making a direct crossing of a highway in a marked or unmarked crosswalk;

(2) where no sidewalk is available; or

(3) when so directed by a traffic control device or by a law enforcement officer.

(b) A person may operate an electric personal assistive mobility device on a path set aside for the exclusive operation of bicycles.

(c) Any person operating an electric personal assistive mobility device on a residential street, roadway, or public highway shall ride as close as practicable to the right-hand edge.

(d) Except as otherwise provided by this section, provisions of this title applicable to the operation of bicycles apply to the operation of electric personal assistive mobility devices.

(Enacted by Acts 2003, 78th Leg., ch. 1318 (H.B. 1997), § 5, effective September 1, 2003.)

### Sec. 551.203. Sidewalks.

A person may operate an electric personal assistive mobility device on a sidewalk.
(Enacted by Acts 2003, 78th Leg., ch. 1318 (H.B. 1997), § 5, effective September 1, 2003.)

### Secs. 551.204 to 551.300 [Reserved for expansion].

## SUBCHAPTER D
## NEIGHBORHOOD ELECTRIC VEHICLES

### Sec. 551.301. Definition.

In this subchapter, "neighborhood electric vehicle" means a vehicle that can attain a maximum speed of 35 miles per hour on a paved level surface and otherwise complies with Federal Motor Vehicle Safety Standard 500 (49 C.F.R. Section 571.500).
(Enacted by Acts 2003, 78th Leg., ch. 1320 (H.B. 2971), § 7, effective September 1, 2003; enacted by Acts 2003, 78th Leg., ch. 1325 (H.B. 3588), § 19.07, effective September 1, 2003; am. Acts 2005, 79th Leg., ch. 281 (H.B. 2702), § 2.86, effective June 14, 2005; am. Acts 2005, 79th Leg., ch. 1242 (H.B. 1596), § 2, effective June 18, 2005; am. Acts 2009, 81st Leg., ch. 722 (S.B. 129), § 1, effective September 1, 2009; am. Acts 2011, 82nd Leg., ch. 91 (S.B. 1303), § 24.014, effective September 1, 2011.)

### Sec. 551.302. Registration.

The Texas Department of Motor Vehicles may adopt rules relating to the registration and issuance of license plates to neighborhood electric vehicles.
(Enacted by Acts 2003, 78th Leg., ch. 1320 (H.B. 2971), § 7, effective September 1, 2003; am. Acts 2009, 81st Leg., ch. 933 (H.B. 3097), § 2I.01, effective September 1, 2009.)

### Sec. 551.303. Operation on Roadways.

(a) A neighborhood electric vehicle may be operated only on a street or highway for which the posted speed limit is 45 miles per hour or less. A neighborhood electric vehicle may cross a road or street at an intersection where the road or street has a posted speed limit of more than 45 miles per hour. A neighborhood electric vehicle may not be operated on a street or highway at a speed that exceeds the lesser of:
(1) the posted speed limit; or
(2) 35 miles per hour.
(b) A county or municipality may prohibit the operation of a neighborhood electric vehicle on a street or highway if the governing body of the county or municipality determines that the prohibition is necessary in the interest of safety.
(c) The Texas Department of Transportation may prohibit the operation of a neighborhood electric vehicle on a highway if that department determines that the prohibition is necessary in the interest of safety.
(Enacted by Acts 2003, 78th Leg., ch. 1320 (H.B. 2971), § 7, effective September 1, 2003; am. Acts 2009, 81st Leg., ch. 722 (S.B. 129), § 2, effective September 1, 2009.)

### Sec. 551.304. Application of Subchapter to Pocket Bike or Minimotorbike [Renumbered].

Renumbered to Sec. 551.353 by Acts 2011, 82nd Leg., ch. 91 (S.B. 1303), § 27.001(64), effective September 1, 2011.

### Secs. 551.305 to 551.350 [Reserved for expansion].

## SUBCHAPTER E
## MOTOR-ASSISTED SCOOTERS

### Sec. 551.351. Definitions.

In this subchapter:
(1) "Motor-assisted scooter":
(A) means a self-propelled device with:
(i) at least two wheels in contact with the ground during operation;
(ii) a braking system capable of stopping the device under typical operating conditions;
(iii) a gas or electric motor not exceeding 40 cubic centimeters;
(iv) a deck designed to allow a person to stand or sit while operating the device; and
(v) the ability to be propelled by human power alone; and
(B) does not include a pocket bike or a minimotorbike.
(2) "Pocket bike or minimotorbike" means a self-propelled vehicle that is equipped with an electric motor or internal combustion engine having a piston displacement of less than 50 cubic centimeters, is designed to propel itself

with not more than two wheels in contact with the ground, has a seat or saddle for the use of the operator, is not designed for use on a highway, and is ineligible for a certificate of title under Chapter 501. The term does not include:

(A) a moped or motorcycle;

(B) an electric bicycle or motor-driven cycle, as defined by Section 541.201;

(C) a motorized mobility device, as defined by Section 542.009;

(D) an electric personal assistive mobility device, as defined by Section 551.201; or

(E) a neighborhood electric vehicle, as defined by Section 551.301.

(Enacted by Acts 2005, 79th Leg., ch. 1242 (H.B. 1596), § 3, effective June 18, 2005; am. Acts 2011, 82nd Leg., ch. 91 (S.B. 1303), § 24.015, effective September 1, 2011.)

### Sec. 551.352.  Operation on Roadways or Sidewalks.

(a) A motor-assisted scooter may be operated only on a street or highway for which the posted speed limit is 35 miles per hour or less. The motor-assisted scooter may cross a road or street at an intersection where the road or street has a posted speed limit of more than 35 miles per hour.

(b) A county or municipality may prohibit the operation of a motor-assisted scooter on a street, highway, or sidewalk if the governing body of the county or municipality determines that the prohibition is necessary in the interest of safety.

(c) The department may prohibit the operation of a motor-assisted scooter on a highway if it determines that the prohibition is necessary in the interest of safety.

(d) A person may operate a motor-assisted scooter on a path set aside for the exclusive operation of bicycles or on a sidewalk. Except as otherwise provided by this section, a provision of this title applicable to the operation of a bicycle applies to the operation of a motor-assisted scooter.

(e) A provision of this title applicable to a motor vehicle does not apply to a motor-assisted scooter.

(Enacted by Acts 2005, 79th Leg., ch. 1242 (H.B. 1596), § 3, effective June 18, 2005.)

### Sec. 551.353.  Application of Subchapter to Pocket Bike or Minimotorbike.

This subchapter may not be construed to authorize the operation of a pocket bike or minimotorbike on any:

(1) highway, road, or street;

(2) path set aside for the exclusive operation of bicycles; or

(3) sidewalk.

(Enacted by Acts 2005, 79th Leg., ch. 281 (H.B. 2702), § 2.87, effective June 14, 2005, am. Acts 2011, 82nd Leg., ch.91 (S.B. 1303), § 27.001(64), effective September 1, 2011 (renumbered from Sec. 551.304).)

### Secs. 551.354 to 551.400 [Reserved for expansion].

## SUBCHAPTER F
## GOLF CARTS AND UTILITY VEHICLES

### Sec. 551.401.  [Effective until January 1, 2012] Definitions.

In this subchapter, "golf cart " and "public highway " have the meanings assigned by Section 502.001.

(Enacted by Acts 2009, 81st Leg., ch. 1136 (H.B. 2553), § 10, effective September 1, 2009.)

### Sec. 551.401.  [Effective January 1, 2012] Definitions.

In this subchapter:

(1) "Golf cart" and "public highway" have the meanings assigned by Section 502.001.

(2) "Utility vehicle" means a motor vehicle that is not a golf cart or lawn mower and is:

(A) equipped with side-by-side seating for the use of the operator and a passenger;

(B) designed to propel itself with at least four tires in contact with the ground;

(C) designed by the manufacturer for off-highway use only; and

(D) designed by the manufacturer primarily for utility work and not for recreational purposes.

(Enacted by Acts 2009, 81st Leg., ch. 1136 (H.B. 2553), § 10, effective September 1, 2009; am. Acts 2011, 82nd Leg., ch. 1296 (H.B. 2357), § 239, effective January 1, 2012.)

### Sec. 551.402.  Registration Not Authorized.

(a) The Texas Department of Transportation may not register a golf cart for operation on a public highway regardless of whether any alteration has been made to the golf cart.

(b) The department may issue license plates for a golf cart only as authorized by Section 504.510.

(Enacted by Acts 2009, 81st Leg., ch. 1136 (H.B. 2553), § 10, effective September 1, 2009.)

## Sec. 551.403. Limited Operation.

(a) An operator may operate a golf cart:

(1) in a master planned community:

(A) that has in place a uniform set of restrictive covenants; and

(B) for which a county or municipality has approved a plat;

(2) on a public or private beach; or

(3) on a public highway for which the posted speed limit is not more than 35 miles per hour, if the golf cart is operated:

(A) during the daytime; and

(B) not more than two miles from the location where the golf cart is usually parked and for transportation to or from a golf course.

(b) The Texas Department of Transportation or a county or municipality may prohibit the operation of a golf cart on a public highway if the department or the governing body of the county or municipality determines that the prohibition is necessary in the interest of safety.

(Enacted by Acts 2009, 81st Leg., ch. 1136 (H.B. 2553), § 10, effective September 1, 2009.)

## Sec. 551.404. [Effective until January 1, 2012] Operation in Municipalities.

(a) In addition to the operation authorized by Section 551.403, the governing body of a municipality may allow an operator to operate a golf cart on all or part of a public highway that:

(1) is in the corporate boundaries of the municipality; and

(2) has a posted speed limit of not more than 35 miles per hour.

(b) A golf cart operated under Subsection (a) must have the following equipment:

(1) headlamps;

(2) taillamps;

(3) reflectors;

(4) parking brake; and

(5) mirrors.

(Enacted by Acts 2009, 81st Leg., ch. 1136 (H.B. 2553), § 10, effective September 1, 2009.)

## Sec. 551.404. [Effective January 1, 2012] Operation in Municipalities and Certain Counties.

(a) In addition to the operation authorized by Section 551.403, the governing body of a municipality may allow an operator to operate a golf cart on all or part of a public highway that:

(1) is in the corporate boundaries of the municipality; and

(2) has a posted speed limit of not more than 35 miles per hour.

(a-1) In addition to the operation authorized by Section 551.403, the commissioners court of a county that borders or contains a portion of the Guadalupe River and contains a part of a barrier island that borders the Gulf of Mexico may allow an operator to operate a golf cart or utility vehicle on all or part of a public highway that:

(1) is located in the unincorporated area of the county; and

(2) has a speed limit of not more than 35 miles per hour.

(b) A golf cart or utility vehicle operated under this section must have the following equipment:

(1) headlamps;

(2) taillamps;

(3) reflectors;

(4) parking brake; and

(5) mirrors.

(Enacted by Acts 2009, 81st Leg., ch. 1136 (H.B. 2553), § 10, effective September 1, 2009; am. Acts 2011, 82nd Leg., ch. 1296 (H.B. 2357), §§ 240, 241, effective January 1, 2012.)

## Sec. 551.405. Crossing Certain Roadways.

A golf cart may cross intersections, including a road or street that has a posted speed limit of more than 35 miles per hour.

(Enacted by Acts 2009, 81st Leg., ch. 1136 (H.B. 2553), § 10, effective September 1, 2009.)

# CHAPTER 552
# PEDESTRIANS

## Sec. 552.001. Traffic Control Signals.

(a) A traffic control signal displaying green, red, and yellow lights or lighted arrows applies to a pedestrian as provided by this section unless the pedestrian is otherwise directed by a special pedestrian control signal.

(b) A pedestrian facing a green signal may proceed across a roadway within a marked or unmarked crosswalk unless the sole green signal is a turn arrow.

(c) A pedestrian facing a steady red signal alone or a steady yellow signal may not enter a roadway.
(Enacted by Acts 1995, 74th Leg., ch. 165 (S.B. 971), § 1, effective September 1, 1995.)

### Sec. 552.002. Pedestrian Right-of-Way If Control Signal Present.

(a) A pedestrian control signal displaying "Walk," "Don't Walk," or "Wait" applies to a pedestrian as provided by this section.

(b) A pedestrian facing a "Walk" signal may proceed across a roadway in the direction of the signal, and the operator of a vehicle shall yield the right-of-way to the pedestrian.

(c) A pedestrian may not start to cross a roadway in the direction of a "Don't Walk" signal or a "Wait" signal. A pedestrian who has partially crossed while the "Walk" signal is displayed shall proceed to a sidewalk or safety island while the "Don't Walk" signal or "Wait" signal is displayed.
(Enacted by Acts 1995, 74th Leg., ch. 165 (S.B. 971), § 1, effective September 1, 1995.)

### Sec. 552.003. Pedestrian Right-of-Way at Crosswalk.

(a) The operator of a vehicle shall yield the right-of-way to a pedestrian crossing a roadway in a crosswalk if:

(1) no traffic control signal is in place or in operation; and

(2) the pedestrian is:

(A) on the half of the roadway in which the vehicle is traveling; or

(B) approaching so closely from the opposite half of the roadway as to be in danger.

(b) Notwithstanding Subsection (a), a pedestrian may not suddenly leave a curb or other place of safety and proceed into a crosswalk in the path of a vehicle so close that it is impossible for the vehicle operator to yield.

(c) The operator of a vehicle approaching from the rear of a vehicle that is stopped at a crosswalk to permit a pedestrian to cross a roadway may not pass the stopped vehicle.

(d) If it is shown on the trial of an offense under Subsection (a) that as a result of the commission of the offense a collision occurred

causing serious bodily injury or death to a visually impaired or disabled person, the offense is a misdemeanor punishable by:

(1) a fine of not more than $500; and

(2) 30 hours of community service to an organization or agency that primarily serves visually impaired or disabled persons, to be completed in not less than six months and not more than one year.

(d-1) A portion of the community service required under Subsection (d)(2) shall include sensitivity training.

(e) For the purposes of this section:

(1) "Visually impaired" has the meaning assigned by Section 91.002, Human Resources Code.

(2) "Disabled" means a person who cannot walk without the use or assistance of:

(A) a device, including a brace, cane, crutch, prosthesis, or wheelchair; or

(B) another person.

(f) If conduct constituting an offense under this section also constitutes an offense under another section of this code or the Penal Code, the actor may be prosecuted under either section or both sections.
(Enacted by Acts 1995, 74th Leg., ch. 165 (S.B. 971), § 1, effective September 1, 1995; am. Acts 2009, 81st Leg., ch. 1272 (H.B. 1343), § 2, effective September 1, 2009.)

### Sec. 552.004. Pedestrian to Keep to Right.

A pedestrian shall proceed on the right half of a crosswalk if possible.
(Enacted by Acts 1995, 74th Leg., ch. 165 (S.B. 971), § 1, effective September 1, 1995.)

### Sec. 552.005. Crossing at Point Other Than Crosswalk.

(a) A pedestrian shall yield the right-of-way to a vehicle on the highway if crossing a roadway at a place:

(1) other than in a marked crosswalk or in an unmarked crosswalk at an intersection; or

(2) where a pedestrian tunnel or overhead pedestrian crossing has been provided.

(b) Between adjacent intersections at which traffic control signals are in operation, a pedestrian may cross only in a marked crosswalk.

(c) A pedestrian may cross a roadway intersection diagonally only if and in the manner authorized by a traffic control device.
(Enacted by Acts 1995, 74th Leg., ch. 165 (S.B. 971), § 1, effective September 1, 1995.)

## Sec. 552.006. Use of Sidewalk.

(a) A pedestrian may not walk along and on a roadway if an adjacent sidewalk is provided and is accessible to the pedestrian.

(b) If a sidewalk is not provided, a pedestrian walking along and on a highway shall if possible walk on:

(1) the left side of the roadway; or

(2) the shoulder of the highway facing oncoming traffic.

(c) The operator of a vehicle emerging from or entering an alley, building, or private road or driveway shall yield the right-of-way to a pedestrian approaching on a sidewalk extending across the alley, building entrance or exit, road, or driveway.

(Enacted by Acts 1995, 74th Leg., ch. 165 (S.B. 971), § 1, effective September 1, 1995; am. Acts 2001, 77th Leg., ch. 497 (H.B. 1378), § 3, effective June 11, 2001.)

## Sec. 552.007. Solicitation by Pedestrians.

(a) A person may not stand in a roadway to solicit a ride, contribution, employment, or business from an occupant of a vehicle, except that a person may stand in a roadway to solicit a charitable contribution if authorized to do so by the local authority having jurisdiction over the roadway.

(b) A person may not stand on or near a highway to solicit the watching or guarding of a vehicle parked or to be parked on the highway.

(c) In this section, "charitable contribution" means a contribution to an organization defined as charitable by the standards of the United States Internal Revenue Service.

(Enacted by Acts 1995, 74th Leg., ch. 165 (S.B. 971), § 1, effective September 1, 1995.)

## Sec. 552.0071. Local Authorization for Solicitation by Pedestrian.

(a) A local authority shall grant authorization for a person to stand in a roadway to solicit a charitable contribution as provided by Section 552.007(a) if the persons to be engaged in the solicitation are employees or agents of the local authority and the other requirements of this section are met.

(b) A person seeking authorization under this section shall file a written application with the local authority not later than the 11th day before the date the solicitation is to begin. The application must include:

(1) the date or dates and times when the solicitation is to occur;

(2) each location at which solicitation is to occur; and

(3) the number of solicitors to be involved in solicitation at each location.

(c) This section does not prohibit a local authority from requiring a permit or the payment of reasonable fees to the local authority.

(d) The applicant shall also furnish to the local authority advance proof of liability insurance in the amount of at least $1 million to cover damages that may arise from the solicitation. The insurance must provide coverage against claims against the applicant and claims against the local authority.

(e) A local authority, by acting under this section or Section 552.007, does not waive or limit any immunity from liability applicable under law to the local authority. The issuance of an authorization under this section and the conducting of the solicitation authorized is a governmental function of the local authority.

(f) Notwithstanding any provision of this section, the existing rights of individuals or organizations under Section 552.007 are not impaired.

(g) For purposes of a solicitation under Subsection (a), a roadway is defined to include the roadbed, shoulder, median, curbs, safety zones, sidewalks, and utility easements located adjacent to or near the roadway.

(Enacted by Acts 2005, 79th Leg., ch. 12 (S.B. 245), § 2, effective May 3, 2005; am. Acts 2007, 80th Leg., ch. 333 (H.B. 3089), § 1, effective June 15, 2007.)

## Sec. 552.008. Drivers to Exercise Due Care.

Notwithstanding another provision of this chapter, the operator of a vehicle shall:

(1) exercise due care to avoid colliding with a pedestrian on a roadway;

(2) give warning by sounding the horn when necessary; and

(3) exercise proper precaution on observing a child or an obviously confused or incapacitated person on a roadway.

(Enacted by Acts 1995, 74th Leg., ch. 165 (S.B. 971), § 1, effective September 1, 1995.)

## Sec. 552.009. Ordinances Relating to Pedestrians.

A local authority may by ordinance:

(1) require pedestrians to comply strictly with the directions of an official traffic control signal; and

(2) prohibit pedestrians from crossing a roadway in a business district or a designated highway except in a crosswalk.

(Enacted by Acts 1995, 74th Leg., ch. 165 (S.B. 971), § 1, effective September 1, 1995.)

### Sec. 552.010.   Blind Pedestrians.

(a) No person may carry a white cane on a public street or highway unless the person is totally or partially blind.

(b) The driver of a vehicle approaching an intersection or crosswalk where a pedestrian guided by an assistance animal or carrying a white cane is crossing or attempting to cross shall take necessary precautions to avoid injuring or endangering the pedestrian. The driver shall bring the vehicle to a full stop if injury or danger can be avoided only by that action.

(c) If it is shown on the trial of an offense under this section that as a result of the commission of the offense a collision occurred causing serious bodily injury or death to a blind person, the offense is a misdemeanor punishable by:

(1) a fine of not more than $500; and

(2) 30 hours of community service to an organization or agency that primarily serves visually impaired or disabled persons, to be completed in not less than six months and not more than one year.

(c-1) A portion of the community service required under Subsection (c)(2) shall include sensitivity training.

(d) For the purposes of this section:

(1) "Assistance animal" has the meaning assigned by Section 121.002, Human Resources Code.

(2) "White cane" has the meaning assigned by Section 121.002, Human Resources Code.

(e) If conduct constituting an offense under this section also constitutes an offense under another section of this code or the Penal Code, the actor may be prosecuted under either section or both sections.

(Enacted by Acts 1979, 66th Leg., ch. 842 (H.B. 1834), art. 1, § 1, effective September 1, 1979; am. Acts 1985, 69th Leg., ch. 278 (H.B. 2086), § 5, effective June 5, 1985; am. Acts 1997, 75th Leg., ch. 649 (H.B. 2525), § 8, effective September 1, 1997; am. Acts 2009, 81st Leg., ch. 1272 (H.B. 1343), § 1, effective September 1, 2009 (renumbered from Human Resources Code Sec. 121.007).)

## CHAPTER 553
## ENACTMENT AND ENFORCEMENT OF CERTAIN TRAFFIC LAWS IN CERTAIN MUNICIPALITIES

### Sec. 553.001.   Applicability.

This chapter applies only to a municipality with a population of less than 2,500 in a county with a population of 250,000 or more.

(Enacted by Acts 1995, 74th Leg., ch. 165 (S.B. 971), § 1, effective September 1, 1995.)

### Sec. 553.002.   Traffic Signals or Signs in Municipality.

(a) A municipality may not enact an ordinance governing the erection or operation of a traffic signal or sign in the municipality on a state highway funded in whole or in part by the state without prior approval by the Texas Department of Transportation.

(b) A municipality intending to erect or operate a traffic signal or sign described by Subsection (a) must apply in writing to the Texas Department of Transportation. After the application is filed, the Texas Department of Transportation shall designate an employee to investigate the application and shall grant or refuse the application not later than the 90th day after the date of the designation.

(c) In granting an application, the Texas Department of Transportation:

(1) may prescribe the conditions under which the municipality may erect and operate the signal or sign and all other aspects of the signal or sign; and

(2) shall consider the convenience of the traveling public in raising speed limits in noncongested areas and the control of traffic for the protection of schoolchildren and other inhabitants of small communities where there are areas of congestion and cross-traffic.

(d) This section does not apply to an ordinance enacted or a temporary speed limit sign erected or operated under Section 545.3561.

(Enacted by Acts 1995, 74th Leg., ch. 165 (S.B. 971), § 1, effective September 1, 1995; am. Acts

2011, 82nd Leg., ch. 216 (H.B. 109), § 3, effective September 1, 2011.)

### Sec. 553.003. Injunction Against Unauthorized Signal or Sign.

(a) If a municipality erects or maintains a traffic signal or sign without meeting the requirements of this chapter, the district or county attorney of the county where the signal or sign is located shall bring a suit to enjoin the erection and maintenance of the signal or sign.

(b) If the district or county attorney does not institute a suit under Subsection (a) within 15 days after the date a request to do so is received from a resident of the state, any state resident may institute and prosecute the suit.

(Enacted by Acts 1995, 74th Leg., ch. 165 (S.B. 971), § 1, effective September 1, 1995.)

### CHAPTERS 554 TO 599
### [RESERVED FOR EXPANSION]

### CHAPTER 600
### MISCELLANEOUS PROVISIONS

### Sec. 600.001. Removing Material from Highway.

(a) A person who drops or permits to be dropped or thrown on a highway destructive or injurious material shall immediately remove the material or cause it to be removed.

(b) A person who removes a wrecked or damaged vehicle from a highway shall remove glass or another injurious substance dropped on the highway from the vehicle.

(Enacted by Acts 1995, 74th Leg., ch. 165 (S.B. 971), § 1, effective September 1, 1995.)

### Sec. 600.002. Identification Required for Vehicle Near Mexican Border.

On demand of a peace officer within 250 feet of the Mexican border at a checkpoint authorized by Section 411.0095, Government Code, as added by Chapter 497, Acts of the 73rd Legislature, Regular Session, 1993, the driver of a vehicle shall produce a driver's license and proof of compliance with Chapter 601.

(Enacted by Acts 1995, 74th Leg., ch. 165 (S.B. 971), § 1, effective September 1, 1995.)

### Sec. 600.003. Enforcement of Certain Traffic Laws by Private Institutions of Higher Education.

(a) In this section, "private or independent institution of higher education" has the meaning assigned by Section 61.003(15), Education Code.

(b) A private or independent institution of higher education may enforce a traffic law of this state under Chapter 545 restricting or prohibiting the operation or movement of vehicles on a road of the institution if:

(1) the road of the institution is open to the public at the time the traffic law is enforced;

(2) the governing body of the institution adopts a regulation to enforce the traffic law; and

(3) the restriction or prohibition on the operation and movement of vehicles adopted by the institution:

(A) is posted by means of a sign, marking, signal, or other device visible to and, if it contains writing, able to be read by an operator of a vehicle to whom the restriction or prohibition applies in the same manner as a similar restriction or prohibition on the operation and movement of vehicles would be posted by a municipality; and

(B) has been approved by:

(i) the commissioners court of the county in which the applicable road of the institution is located, if the road is located in the unincorporated area of a county; or

(ii) the governing body of the municipality in which the applicable road of the institution is located, if the road is located in a municipality.

(c) Campus security personnel of the institution commissioned under Section 51.212, Education Code, are authorized to enforce the provisions of this section and have the authority to issue and use traffic tickets and summons in a form prescribed by the Texas Department of Public Safety to enforce this chapter only on the property of the institution that commissioned the campus security personnel under Section 51.212, Education Code.

(d) The same procedures that apply to a traffic ticket or summons by a commissioned peace officer of an institution of higher education under Sections 51.206 and 51.210, Education Code, also apply to a ticket or summons issued under this section.

(e) The governing body of the municipality or the commissioners court of the county that approves the enforcement of traffic laws under Subsection (b) shall also determine the disposition of funds collected under this section from any fees or fines from the enforcement of a traffic law of this state.

(Enacted by Acts 1997, 75th Leg., ch. 620 (S.B. 1368), § 1, effective September 1, 1997.)

## Sec. 600.004.　Training of School Crossing Guard.

(a) A local authority may authorize a school crossing guard to direct traffic in a school crossing zone if the guard successfully completes a training program in traffic direction as defined by the basic peace officer course curriculum established by the Commission on Law Enforcement Standards and Education.

(b) A school crossing guard trained under this section:

(1) is not a peace officer; and

(2) may not carry a weapon while directing traffic in a school crossing zone.

(Enacted by Acts 1999, 76th Leg., ch. 724 (H.B. 964), § 2, effective August 30, 1999.)

# SUBTITLE D
# MOTOR VEHICLE SAFETY RESPONSIBILITY

# CHAPTER 601
# MOTOR VEHICLE SAFETY RESPONSIBILITY ACT

### Subchapter A. General Provisions

**Transportation**

## SUBCHAPTER A
## GENERAL PROVISIONS

# Sec. 601.001. Short Title.

This chapter may be cited as the Texas Motor Vehicle Safety Responsibility Act.

(Enacted by Acts 1995, 74th Leg., ch. 165 (S.B. 971), § 1, effective September 1, 1995.)

## Sec. 601.002.  Definitions.

In this chapter:

(1) "Department" means the Department of Public Safety.

(2) "Driver's license" has the meaning assigned by Section 521.001.

(3) "Financial responsibility" means the ability to respond in damages for liability for an accident that:

(A) occurs after the effective date of the document evidencing the establishment of the financial responsibility; and

(B) arises out of the ownership, maintenance, or use of a motor vehicle.

(4) "Highway" means the entire width between property lines of a road, street, or way in this state that is not privately owned or controlled and:

(A) some part of which is open to the public for vehicular traffic; and

(B) over which the state has legislative jurisdiction under its police power.

(5) "Motor vehicle" means a self-propelled vehicle designed for use on a highway, a trailer or semitrailer designed for use with a self-propelled vehicle, or a vehicle propelled by electric power from overhead wires and not operated on rails. The term does not include:

(A) a traction engine;

(B) a road roller or grader;

(C) a tractor crane;

(D) a power shovel;

(E) a well driller;

(F) an implement of husbandry; or

(G) an electric personal assistive mobility device, as defined by Section 551.201.

(6) "Nonresident" means a person who is not a resident of this state.

(7) "Nonresident's operating privilege" means the privilege conferred on a nonresident by the laws of this state relating to the operation of a motor vehicle in this state by the nonresident or the use in this state of a motor vehicle owned by the nonresident.

(8) "Operator" means the person in actual physical control of a motor vehicle.

(9) "Owner" means:

(A) the person who holds legal title to a motor vehicle;

(B) the purchaser or lessee of a motor vehicle subject to an agreement for the con-

ditional sale or lease of the vehicle, if the person has:

(i) the right to purchase the vehicle on performing conditions stated in the agreement; and

(ii) an immediate right to possess the vehicle; or

(C) a mortgagor of a motor vehicle who is entitled to possession of the vehicle.

(10) "Person" means an individual, firm, partnership, association, or corporation.

(11) "State" means:

(A) a state, territory, or possession of the United States; or

(B) the District of Columbia.

(12) "Vehicle registration" means:

(A) a registration certificate, registration receipt, or number plate issued under Chapter 502; or

(B) a dealer's license plate or temporary tag issued under Chapter 503.

(Enacted by Acts 1995, 74th Leg., ch. 165 (S.B. 971), § 1, effective September 1, 1995; am. Acts 2003, 78th Leg., ch. 1318 (H.B. 1997), § 6, effective September 1, 2003; am. Acts 2009, 81st Leg., ch. 793 (S.B. 1235), § 15, effective September 1, 2009.)

## Sec. 601.003.  Judgment; Satisfied Judgment.

(a) For purposes of this chapter, judgment refers only to a final judgment that is no longer appealable or has been finally affirmed on appeal and that was rendered by a court of any state, a province of Canada, or the United States on a cause of action:

(1) for damages for bodily injury, death, or damage to or destruction of property arising out of the ownership, maintenance, or use of a motor vehicle; or

(2) on an agreement of settlement for damages for bodily injury, death, or damage to or destruction of property arising out of the ownership, maintenance, or use of a motor vehicle.

(b) For purposes of this chapter, a judgment is considered to be satisfied as to the appropriate part of the judgment set out by this subsection if:

(1) the total amount credited on one or more judgments for bodily injury to or death of one person resulting from one accident equals or exceeds the amount required under Section 601.072(a)(1) to establish financial responsibility;

(2) the total amount credited on one or more judgments for bodily injury to or death of two or

more persons resulting from one accident equals or exceeds the amount required under Section 601.072(a)(2) to establish financial responsibility; or

(3) the total amount credited on one or more judgments for damage to or destruction of property of another resulting from one accident equals or exceeds the amount required under Section 601.072(a)(3) to establish financial responsibility.

(c) In determining whether a judgment is satisfied under Subsection (b), a payment made in settlement of a claim for damages for bodily injury, death, or damage to or destruction of property is considered to be an amount credited on a judgment.

(d) For purposes of this section:

(1) damages for bodily injury or death include damages for care and loss of services; and

(2) damages for damage to or destruction of property include damages for loss of use.

(Enacted by Acts 1995, 74th Leg., ch. 165 (S.B. 971), § 1, effective September 1, 1995.)

## Sec. 601.004. Accident Report.

(a) The operator of a motor vehicle that is involved in an accident in this state shall report the accident to the Texas Department of Transportation not later than the 10th day after the date of the accident if:

(1) the accident is not investigated by a law enforcement officer; and

(2) at least one person, including the operator, sustained:

(A) bodily injury or death; or

(B) property damage to an apparent extent of at least $1,000.

(b) If the operator is physically incapable of making the report, the owner of the motor vehicle shall make the report not later than the 10th day after the date the owner learns of the accident.

(c) The report must be made in writing in the form prescribed by the Texas Department of Transportation and the department and must contain information as necessary to enable the department to determine if the requirements for the deposit of security under Subchapter F do not apply because of the existence of insurance or an exception specified in this chapter. The operator or owner shall provide additional information as required by the department.

(d) A written report of an accident made to the Texas Department of Transportation under Section 550.061 or 550.062 complies with this section

if that report contains the information required by this section.

(e) The department may rely on the accuracy of information contained in the report unless the department has reason to believe that the information is erroneous.

(f) An accident report that is released for insurance purposes, other than investigation of a specific accident, may show only an accident for which the insured was issued a citation for a violation of Subtitle C.

(g) The department shall suspend the driver's license or nonresident's operating privilege of a person who fails to make a report as required by this section if another person sustained bodily injury, death, or property damage to the extent described by Subsection (a)(2)(B). The suspension continues until a date set by the department that is not earlier than the date the report is filed and not later than the 30th day after the date the report is filed.

(h) A person commits an offense if the person fails to report an accident as required by this section. An offense under this subsection is a misdemeanor punishable by a fine not to exceed $25.

(i) A person commits an offense if the person provides information under this section that the person knows or has reason to believe is false. An offense under this subsection is a misdemeanor punishable by:

(1) a fine not to exceed $1,000;

(2) confinement in county jail for a term not to exceed one year; or

(3) both the fine and the confinement.

(Enacted by Acts 1995, 74th Leg., ch. 165 (S.B. 971), § 1, effective September 1, 1995; am. Acts 2001, 77th Leg., ch. 531 (H.B. 2230), § 4, effective September 1, 2001; am. Acts 2007, 80th Leg., ch. 1407 (S.B. 766), § 5, effective September 1, 2007.)

## Sec. 601.005. Evidence in Civil Suit.

On the filing of a report under Section 601.004, a person at a trial for damages may not refer to or offer as evidence of the negligence or due care of a party:

(1) an action taken by the department under this chapter;

(2) the findings on which that action is based; or

(3) the security or evidence of financial responsibility filed under this chapter.

(Enacted by Acts 1995, 74th Leg., ch. 165 (S.B. 971), § 1, effective September 1, 1995.)

Transportation

## Sec. 601.006. Applicability to Certain Owners and Operators.

If an owner or operator of a motor vehicle involved in an accident in this state does not have a driver's license or vehicle registration or is a nonresident, the person may not be issued a driver's license or registration until the person has complied with this chapter to the same extent that would be necessary if, at the time of the accident, the person had a driver's license or registration.

(Enacted by Acts 1995, 74th Leg., ch. 165 (S.B. 971), § 1, effective September 1, 1995.)

## Sec. 601.007. Applicability of Chapter to Government Vehicles.

(a) This chapter does not apply to a government vehicle.

(b) The provisions of this chapter, other than Section 601.004, do not apply to an officer, agent, or employee of the United States, this state, or a political subdivision of this state while operating a government vehicle in the course of that person's employment.

(c) The provisions of this chapter, other than Sections 601.004 and 601.054, do not apply to a motor vehicle that is subject to Chapter 643.

(d) In this section, "government vehicle" means a motor vehicle owned by the United States, this state, or a political subdivision of this state.

(Enacted by Acts 1995, 74th Leg., ch. 165 (S.B. 971), § 1, effective September 1, 1995; am. Acts 1997, 75th Leg., ch. 165 (S.B. 898), § 30.126(a), effective September 1, 1997.)

## Sec. 601.008. Violation of Chapter; Offense.

(a) A person commits an offense if the person violates a provision of this chapter for which a penalty is not otherwise provided.

(b) An offense under this section is a misdemeanor punishable by:

(1) a fine not to exceed $500;

(2) confinement in county jail for a term not to exceed 90 days; or

(3) both the fine and the confinement.

(Enacted by Acts 1995, 74th Leg., ch. 165 (S.B. 971), § 1, effective September 1, 1995.)

## Sec. 601.009. Report from Other State or Canada.

(a) On receipt of a certification by the department that the operating privilege of a resident of this state has been suspended or revoked in another state or a province of Canada under a financial responsibility law, the department shall contact the official who issued the certification to request information relating to the specific nature of the resident's failure to comply.

(b) Except as provided by Subsection (c), the department shall suspend the resident's driver's license and vehicle registrations if the evidence shows that the resident's operating privilege was suspended in the other state or the province for violation of a financial responsibility law under circumstances that would require the department to suspend a nonresident's operating privilege had the accident occurred in this state.

(c) The department may not suspend the resident's driver's license and registration if the alleged failure to comply is based on the failure of the resident's insurance company or surety company to:

(1) obtain authorization to write motor vehicle liability insurance in the other state or the province; or

(2) execute a power of attorney directing the appropriate official in the other state or the province to accept on the company's behalf service of notice or process in an action under the policy arising out of an accident.

(d) Suspension of a driver's license and vehicle registrations under this section continues until the resident furnishes evidence of compliance with the financial responsibility law of the other state or the province.

(e) In this section, "financial responsibility law" means a law authorizing suspension or revocation of an operating privilege for failure to:

(1) deposit security for the payment of a judgment;

(2) satisfy a judgment; or

(3) file evidence of financial responsibility.

(Enacted by Acts 1995, 74th Leg., ch. 165 (S.B. 971), § 1, effective September 1, 1995.)

## Secs. 601.010 to 601.020 [Reserved for expansion].

### SUBCHAPTER B
### ADMINISTRATION BY DEPARTMENT

## Sec. 601.021. Department Powers and Duties; Rules.

The department shall:

(1) administer and enforce this chapter; and

(2) provide for hearings on the request of a person aggrieved by an act of the department under this chapter.

(Enacted by Acts 1995, 74th Leg., ch. 165 (S.B. 971), § 1, effective September 1, 1995.)

### Sec. 601.022. Department to Provide Operating Record [Repealed].

Repealed by Acts 2003, 78th Leg., ch. 991 (S.B. 1904), § 14(3), effective September 1, 2003.
(Enacted by Acts 1995, 74th Leg., ch. 165 (S.B. 971), § 1, effective September 1, 1995; am. Acts 1997, 75th Leg., ch. 1187 (S.B. 1069), § 14, effective September 1, 1997.)

### Sec. 601.023. Payment of Statutory Fees.

The department may pay:

(1) a statutory fee required by the Texas Department of Motor Vehicles for a certified abstract or in connection with suspension of a vehicle registration; or

(2) a statutory fee payable to the comptroller for issuance of a certificate of deposit required by Section 601.122.

(Enacted by Acts 1995, 74th Leg., ch. 165 (S.B. 971), § 1, effective September 1, 1995; am. Acts 1997, 75th Leg., ch. 1423 (H.B. 2841), § 18.05, effective September 1, 1997; am. Acts 2009, 81st Leg., ch. 933 (H.B. 3097), § 2J.01, effective September 1, 2009.)

### Secs. 601.024 to 601.050 [Reserved for expansion].

### SUBCHAPTER C
### FINANCIAL RESPONSIBILITY; REQUIREMENTS

### Sec. 601.051. Requirement of Financial Responsibility.

A person may not operate a motor vehicle in this state unless financial responsibility is established for that vehicle through:

(1) a motor vehicle liability insurance policy that complies with Subchapter D;

(2) a surety bond filed under Section 601.121;

(3) a deposit under Section 601.122;

(4) a deposit under Section 601.123; or

(5) self-insurance under Section 601.124.

(Enacted by Acts 1995, 74th Leg., ch. 165 (S.B. 971), § 1, effective September 1, 1995.)

### Sec. 601.052. Exceptions to Financial Responsibility Requirement.

(a) Section 601.051 does not apply to:

(1) the operation of a motor vehicle that:

(A) is a former military vehicle or is at least 25 years old;

(B) is used only for exhibitions, club activities, parades, and other functions of public interest and not for regular transportation; and

(C) for which the owner files with the department an affidavit, signed by the owner, stating that the vehicle is a collector's item and used only as described by Paragraph (B);

(2) the operation of a golf cart that is operated only as authorized by Section 551.403; or

(3) a volunteer fire department for the operation of a motor vehicle the title of which is held in the name of a volunteer fire department.

(b) Subsection (a)(3) does not exempt from the requirement of Section 601.051 a person who is operating a vehicle described by that subsection.

(c) In this section:

(1) "Former military vehicle" has the meaning assigned by Section 504.502(i).

(2) "Volunteer fire department" means a company, department, or association that is:

(A) organized in an unincorporated area to answer fire alarms and extinguish fires or to answer fire alarms, extinguish fires, and provide emergency medical services; and

(B) composed of members who:

(i) do not receive compensation; or

(ii) receive only nominal compensation.

(Enacted by Acts 1995, 74th Leg., ch. 165 (S.B. 971), § 1, effective September 1, 1995; am. Acts 1997, 75th Leg., ch. 165 (S.B. 898), § 30.127(a), effective September 1, 1997; am. Acts 1997, 75th Leg., ch. 896 (H.B. 2733), § 3, effective September 1, 1997; am. Acts 2009, 81st Leg., ch. 1136 (H.B. 2553), § 11, effective September 1, 2009; am. Acts 2011, 82nd Leg., ch. 91 (S.B. 1303), § 24.016, effective September 1, 2011.)

### Sec. 601.053. Evidence of Financial Responsibility.

(a) As a condition of operating in this state a motor vehicle to which Section 601.051 applies, the operator of the vehicle on request shall provide to a peace officer, as defined by Article 2.12, Code of Criminal Procedure, or a person involved in an accident with the operator evidence of financial responsibility by exhibiting:

(1) a motor vehicle liability insurance policy covering the vehicle that satisfies Subchapter D or a photocopy of the policy;

(2) a standard proof of motor vehicle liability insurance form prescribed by the Texas Depart-

ment of Insurance under Section 601.081 and issued by a liability insurer for the motor vehicle;

(3) an insurance binder that confirms the operator is in compliance with this chapter;

(4) a surety bond certificate issued under Section 601.121;

(5) a certificate of a deposit with the comptroller covering the vehicle issued under Section 601.122;

(6) a copy of a certificate of a deposit with the appropriate county judge covering the vehicle issued under Section 601.123; or

(7) a certificate of self-insurance covering the vehicle issued under Section 601.124 or a photocopy of the certificate.

(b) Except as provided by Subsection (c), an operator who does not exhibit evidence of financial responsibility under Subsection (a) is presumed to have operated the vehicle in violation of Section 601.051.

(c) Subsection (b) does not apply if the peace officer determines through use of the verification program established under Subchapter N that financial responsibility has been established for the vehicle.

(Enacted by Acts 1995, 74th Leg., ch. 165 (S.B. 971), § 1, effective September 1, 1995; am. Acts 1997, 75th Leg., ch. 1423 (H.B. 2841), § 18.06, effective September 1, 1997; am. Acts 2009, 81st Leg., ch. 1146 (H.B. 2730), § 15A.01, effective September 1, 2009.)

### Sec. 601.054. Owner May Provide Evidence of Financial Responsibility for Others.

(a) The department shall accept evidence of financial responsibility from an owner for another person required to establish evidence of financial responsibility if the other person is:

(1) an operator employed by the owner; or

(2) a member of the owner's immediate family or household.

(b) The evidence of financial responsibility applies to a person who becomes subject to Subsection (a)(1) or (2) after the effective date of that evidence.

(c) Evidence of financial responsibility accepted by the department under Subsection (a) is a substitute for evidence by the other person and permits the other person to operate a motor vehicle for which the owner has provided evidence of financial responsibility.

(d) The department shall designate the restrictions imposed by this section on the face of the other person's driver's license.

(Enacted by Acts 1995, 74th Leg., ch. 165 (S.B. 971), § 1, effective September 1, 1995.)

### Sec. 601.055. Substitution of Evidence of Financial Responsibility.

(a) If a person who has filed evidence of financial responsibility substitutes other evidence of financial responsibility that complies with this chapter, and the department accepts the other evidence, the department shall:

(1) consent to the cancellation of a bond or certificate of insurance filed as evidence of financial responsibility; or

(2) direct the comptroller to return money or securities deposited with the comptroller as evidence of financial responsibility to the person entitled to the return of the money or securities.

(b) The comptroller shall return money or securities deposited with the comptroller in accordance with the direction of the department under Subsection (a)(2).

(Enacted by Acts 1995, 74th Leg., ch. 165 (S.B. 971), § 1, effective September 1, 1995; am. Acts 1997, 75th Leg., ch. 1423 (H.B. 2841), § 18.07, effective September 1, 1997.)

### Sec. 601.056. Cancellation, Return, or Waiver of Evidence of Financial Responsibility.

(a) As provided by this section, the department, on request, shall:

(1) consent to the cancellation of a bond or certificate of insurance filed as evidence of financial responsibility;

(2) direct the comptroller to return money or securities deposited with the comptroller as evidence of financial responsibility to the person entitled to the return of the money or securities; or

(3) waive the requirement of filing evidence of financial responsibility.

(b) Evidence of financial responsibility may be canceled, returned, or waived under Subsection (a) if:

(1) the department, during the two years preceding the request, has not received a record of a conviction or a forfeiture of bail that would require or permit the suspension or revocation of the driver's license, vehicle registration, or nonresident's operating privilege of the person by or for whom the evidence was provided;

(2) the person for whom the evidence of financial responsibility was provided dies or

has a permanent incapacity to operate a motor vehicle; or

(3) the person for whom the evidence of financial responsibility was provided surrenders the person's license and vehicle registration to the department.

(c) A cancellation, return, or waiver under Subsection (b)(1) may be made only after the second anniversary of the date the evidence of financial responsibility was required.

(d) The comptroller shall return the money or securities as directed by the department under Subsection (a)(2).

(e) The department may not act under Subsection (a)(1) or (2) if:

(1) an action for damages on a liability covered by the evidence of financial responsibility is pending;

(2) a judgment for damages on a liability covered by the evidence of financial responsibility is not satisfied; or

(3) the person for whom the bond has been filed or for whom money or securities have been deposited has, within the two years preceding the request for cancellation or return of the evidence of financial responsibility, been involved as an operator or owner in a motor vehicle accident resulting in bodily injury to, or property damage to the property of, another person.

(f) In the absence of evidence to the contrary in the records of the department, the department shall accept as sufficient an affidavit of the person requesting action under Subsection (a) stating that:

(1) the facts described by Subsection (e) do not exist; or

(2) the person has been released from the liability or has been finally adjudicated as not liable for bodily injury or property damage described by Subsection (e)(3).

(g) A person whose evidence of financial responsibility has been canceled or returned under Subsection (b)(3) may not be issued a new driver's license or vehicle registration unless the person establishes financial responsibility for the remainder of the two-year period beginning on the date the evidence of financial responsibility was required.

(Enacted by Acts 1995, 74th Leg., ch. 165 (S.B. 971), § 1, effective September 1, 1995; am. Acts 1997, 75th Leg., ch. 1423 (H.B. 2841), § 18.08, effective September 1, 1997.)

### Sec. 601.057. Evidence That Does Not Fulfill Requirements; Suspension.

If evidence filed with the department does not continue to fulfill the purpose for which it was required, the department shall suspend the driver's license and all vehicle registrations or nonresident's operating privilege of the person who filed the evidence pending the filing of other evidence of financial responsibility.

(Enacted by Acts 1995, 74th Leg., ch. 165 (S.B. 971), § 1, effective September 1, 1995.)

### Secs. 601.058 to 601.070 [Reserved for expansion].

## SUBCHAPTER D
## ESTABLISHMENT OF FINANCIAL RESPONSIBILITY THROUGH MOTOR VEHICLE LIABILITY INSURANCE

### Sec. 601.071. Motor Vehicle Liability Insurance; Requirements.

For purposes of this chapter, a motor vehicle liability insurance policy must be an owner's or operator's policy that:

(1) except as provided by Section 601.083, is issued by an insurance company authorized to write motor vehicle liability insurance in this state;

(2) is written to or for the benefit of the person named in the policy as the insured; and

(3) meets the requirements of this subchapter.

(Enacted by Acts 1995, 74th Leg., ch. 165 (S.B. 971), § 1, effective September 1, 1995.)

### Sec. 601.072. Minimum Coverage Amounts; Exclusions.

(a) [Expired pursuant to Acts 2007, 80th Leg., ch. 1298 (S.B. 502), § 1, effective December 31, 2010.]

(a-1) Effective January 1, 2011, the minimum amounts of motor vehicle liability insurance coverage required to establish financial responsibility under this chapter are:

(1) $30,000 for bodily injury to or death of one person in one accident;

(2) $60,000 for bodily injury to or death of two or more persons in one accident, subject to the amount provided by Subdivision (1) for bodily injury to or death of one of the persons; and

Transportation

Transportation

(3) $25,000 for damage to or destruction of property of others in one accident.

(b) The coverage required under this section may exclude, with respect to one accident:

(1) the first $250 of liability for bodily injury to or death of one person;

(2) the first $500 of liability for bodily injury to or death of two or more persons, subject to the amount provided by Subdivision (1) for bodily injury to or death of one of the persons; and

(3) the first $250 of liability for property damage to or destruction of property of others.

(c) The Texas Department of Insurance shall establish an outreach program to inform persons of the requirements of this chapter and the ability to comply with the financial responsibility requirements of this chapter through motor vehicle liability insurance coverage. The commissioner, by rule, shall establish the requirements for the program. The program must be designed to encourage compliance with the financial responsibility requirements, and must be made available in English and Spanish.

(d) [Expired pursuant to Acts 2007, 80th Leg., ch. 1298 (S.B. 502), § 1, effective December 31, 2010.]

(Enacted by Acts 1995, 74th Leg., ch. 165 (S.B. 971), § 1, effective September 1, 1995; am. Acts 2007, 80th Leg., ch. 1298 (S.B. 502), § 1, effective September 1, 2007.)

## Sec. 601.073.  Required Policy Terms.

(a) A motor vehicle liability insurance policy must state:

(1) the name and address of the named insured;

(2) the coverage provided under the policy;

(3) the premium charged for the policy;

(4) the policy period; and

(5) the limits of liability.

(b) The policy must contain an agreement or endorsement that the insurance coverage provided under the policy is:

(1) provided in accordance with the coverage required by this chapter for bodily injury, death, and property damage; and

(2) subject to this chapter.

(c) The liability of the insurance company for the insurance required by this chapter becomes absolute at the time bodily injury, death, or damage covered by the policy occurs. The policy may not be canceled as to this liability by an agreement between the insurance company and the insured that is entered into after the occurrence of the injury or damage. A statement made by or on behalf of the insured or a violation of the policy does not void the policy.

(d) The policy may not require the insured to satisfy a judgment for bodily injury, death, or property damage as a condition precedent under the policy to the right or duty of the insurance company to make payment for the injury, death, or damage.

(e) The insurance company may settle a claim covered by the policy. If the settlement is made in good faith, the amount of the settlement is deductible from the amounts specified in Section 601.072.

(f) The policy, any written application for the policy, and any rider or endorsement that does not conflict with this chapter constitute the entire contract between the parties.

(g) Subsections (c)—(f) apply to the policy without regard to whether those provisions are stated in the policy.

(Enacted by Acts 1995, 74th Leg., ch. 165 (S.B. 971), § 1, effective September 1, 1995.)

## Sec. 601.074.  Optional Terms.

(a) A motor vehicle liability insurance policy may provide that the insured shall reimburse the insurance company for a payment that, in the absence of this chapter, the insurance company would not have been obligated to make under the terms of the policy.

(b) A policy may allow prorating of the insurance provided under the policy with other collectible insurance.

(Enacted by Acts 1995, 74th Leg., ch. 165 (S.B. 971), § 1, effective September 1, 1995.)

## Sec. 601.075.  Prohibited Terms.

A motor vehicle liability insurance policy may not insure against liability:

(1) for which the insured or the insured's insurer may be held liable under a workers' compensation law;

(2) for bodily injury to or death of an employee of the insured while engaged in the employment, other than domestic, of the insured, or in domestic employment if benefits for the injury are payable or required to be provided under a workers' compensation law; or

(3) for injury to or destruction of property owned by, rented to, in the care of, or transported by the insured.

(Enacted by Acts 1995, 74th Leg., ch. 165 (S.B. 971), § 1, effective September 1, 1995.)

### Sec. 601.076. Required Terms: Owner's Policy.

An owner's motor vehicle liability insurance policy must:

(1) cover each motor vehicle for which coverage is to be granted under the policy; and

(2) pay, on behalf of the named insured or another person who, as insured, uses a covered motor vehicle with the express or implied permission of the named insured, amounts the insured becomes obligated to pay as damages arising out of the ownership, maintenance, or use of the motor vehicle in the United States or Canada, subject to the amounts, excluding interest and costs, and exclusions of Section 601.072.

(Enacted by Acts 1995, 74th Leg., ch. 165 (S.B. 971), § 1, effective September 1, 1995.)

### Sec. 601.077. Required Terms: Operator's Policy.

An operator's motor vehicle liability insurance policy must pay, on behalf of the named insured, amounts the insured becomes obligated to pay as damages arising out of the use by the insured of a motor vehicle the insured does not own, subject to the same territorial limits, payment limits, and exclusions as for an owner's policy under Section 601.076.

(Enacted by Acts 1995, 74th Leg., ch. 165 (S.B. 971), § 1, effective September 1, 1995.)

### Sec. 601.078. Additional Coverage.

(a) An insurance policy that provides the coverage required for a motor vehicle liability insurance policy may also provide lawful coverage in excess of or in addition to the required coverage.

(b) The excess or additional coverage is not subject to this chapter.

(c) In the case of a policy that provides excess or additional coverage, the term "motor vehicle liability insurance policy" applies only to that part of the coverage that is required under this subchapter.

(Enacted by Acts 1995, 74th Leg., ch. 165 (S.B. 971), § 1, effective September 1, 1995.)

### Sec. 601.079. Multiple Policies.

The requirements for a motor vehicle liability insurance policy may be satisfied by a combination of policies of one or more insurance companies if the policies in combination meet the requirements.

(Enacted by Acts 1995, 74th Leg., ch. 165 (S.B. 971), § 1, effective September 1, 1995.)

### Sec. 601.080. Insurance Binder.

A binder issued pending the issuance of a motor vehicle liability insurance policy satisfies the requirements for such a policy.

(Enacted by Acts 1995, 74th Leg., ch. 165 (S.B. 971), § 1, effective September 1, 1995.)

### Sec. 601.081. Standard Proof of Motor Vehicle Liability Insurance Form.

A standard proof of motor vehicle liability insurance form prescribed by the Texas Department of Insurance must include:

(1) the name of the insurer;

(2) the insurance policy number;

(3) the policy period;

(4) the name and address of each insured;

(5) the policy limits or a statement that the coverage of the policy complies with the minimum amounts of motor vehicle liability insurance required by this chapter; and

(6) the make and model of each covered vehicle.

(Enacted by Acts 1995, 74th Leg., ch. 165 (S.B. 971), § 1, effective September 1, 1995.)

### Sec. 601.082. Motor Vehicle Liability Insurance; Certification.

If evidence of financial responsibility is required to be filed with the department under this chapter, a motor vehicle liability insurance policy that is to be used as evidence must be certified under Section 601.083 or 601.084.

(Enacted by Acts 1995, 74th Leg., ch. 165 (S.B. 971), § 1, effective September 1, 1995.)

### Sec. 601.083. Certificate of Motor Vehicle Liability Insurance.

(a) A person may provide evidence of financial responsibility by filing with the department the certificate of an insurance company authorized to write motor vehicle liability insurance in this state certifying that a motor vehicle liability insurance policy for the benefit of the person required to provide evidence of financial responsibility is in effect.

(b) The certificate must state the effective date of the policy, which must be the same date as the effective date of the certificate.

(c) The certificate must cover each motor vehicle owned by the person required to provide the evidence of financial responsibility, unless the policy is issued to a person who does not own a motor vehicle.

(d) A motor vehicle may not be registered in the name of a person required to provide evidence of financial responsibility unless the vehicle is covered by a certificate.

(e) If a person files a certificate of insurance to establish financial responsibility under Section 601.153, the certificate must state that the requirements of Section 601.153(b) are satisfied. (Enacted by Acts 1995, 74th Leg., ch. 165 (S.B. 971), § 1, effective September 1, 1995; am. Acts 1997, 75th Leg., ch. 178 (H.B. 627), § 1, effective September 1, 1997.)

### Sec. 601.084. Nonresident Certificate.

(a) Subject to Subsection (c), a nonresident owner of a motor vehicle that is not registered in this state may provide evidence of financial responsibility by filing with the department the certificate of an insurance company authorized to transact business in the state in which the vehicle is registered certifying that a motor vehicle liability insurance policy for the benefit of the person required to provide evidence of financial responsibility is in effect.

(b) Subject to Subsection (c), a nonresident who does not own a motor vehicle may provide evidence of financial responsibility by filing with the department the certificate of an insurance company authorized to transact business in the state in which the nonresident resides.

(c) The department shall accept the certificate of an insurer not authorized to transact business in this state if the certificate otherwise complies with this chapter and the insurance company:

(1) executes a power of attorney authorizing the department to accept on its behalf service of notice or process in an action arising out of a motor vehicle accident in this state; and

(2) agrees in writing that its policies will be treated as conforming to the laws of this state relating to the terms of a motor vehicle liability insurance policy.

(d) The department may not accept a certificate of an insurance company not authorized to transact business in this state during the period that the company is in default in any undertaking or agreement under this section. (Enacted by Acts 1995, 74th Leg., ch. 165 (S.B. 971), § 1, effective September 1, 1995.)

### Sec. 601.085. Termination of Certified Policy.

(a) If an insurer has certified a policy under Section 601.083 or 601.084, the policy may not be terminated before the sixth day after the date a notice of the termination is received by the department except as provided by Subsection (b).

(b) A policy that is obtained and certified terminates a previously certified policy on the effective date of the certification of a subsequent policy. (Enacted by Acts 1995, 74th Leg., ch. 165 (S.B. 971), § 1, effective September 1, 1995.)

### Sec. 601.086. Response of Insurance Company If Policy Not in Effect.

An insurance company that is notified by the department of an accident in connection with which an owner or operator has reported a motor vehicle liability insurance policy with the company shall advise the department if a policy is not in effect as reported. (Enacted by Acts 1995, 74th Leg., ch. 165 (S.B. 971), § 1, effective September 1, 1995.)

### Sec. 601.087. Governmental Record: Unauthorized Certificate or Form [Repealed].

Repealed by Acts 1999, 76th Leg., ch. 659 (H.B. 319), § 4, effective September 1, 1999. (Enacted by Acts 1995, 74th Leg., ch. 165 (S.B. 971), § 1, effective September 1, 1995; am. Acts 1997, 75th Leg., ch. 148 (S.B. 655), § 9, effective September 1, 1997.)

### Sec. 601.088. Effect on Certain Other Policies.

(a) This chapter does not apply to or affect a policy of motor vehicle liability insurance required by another law of this state. If that policy contains an agreement or is endorsed to conform to the requirements of this chapter, the policy may be certified as evidence of financial responsibility under this chapter.

(b) This chapter does not apply to or affect a policy that insures only the named insured against liability resulting from the maintenance or use of a motor vehicle that is not owned by the insured by persons who are:

(1) employed by the insured; or

(2) acting on the insured's behalf. (Enacted by Acts 1995, 74th Leg., ch. 165 (S.B. 971), § 1, effective September 1, 1995.)

Transportation

**Secs. 601.089 to 601.120 [Reserved for expansion].**

## SUBCHAPTER E
## ALTERNATIVE METHODS OF ESTABLISHING FINANCIAL RESPONSIBILITY

### Sec. 601.121.    Surety Bond.

(a) A person may establish financial responsibility by filing with the department a bond:

(1) with at least two individual sureties, each of whom owns real property in this state that is not exempt from execution under the constitution or laws of this state;

(2) conditioned for payment in the amounts and under the same circumstances as required under a motor vehicle liability insurance policy;

(3) that is not cancelable before the sixth day after the date the department receives written notice of the cancellation;

(4) accompanied by the fee required by Subsection (e); and

(5) approved by the department.

(b) The real property required by Subsection (a)(1) must be described in the bond approved by a judge of a court of record. The assessor-collector of the county in which the property is located must certify the property as free of any tax lien. The sureties in combination must have equity in the property in an amount equal to at least twice the amount of the bond.

(c) The bond is a lien in favor of the state on the real property described in the bond. The lien exists in favor of a person who holds a final judgment against the person who filed the bond.

(d) On filing of a bond, the department shall issue to the person who filed the bond a certificate of compliance with this section.

(e) The department shall file notice of the bond in the office of the county clerk of the county in which the real property is located. The notice must include a description of the property described in the bond. The county clerk or the county clerk's deputy, on receipt of the notice, shall acknowledge the notice and record it in the lien records. The recording of the notice is notice in accordance with statutes governing the recordation of a lien on real property.

(f) If a judgment rendered against the person who files a bond under this section is not satisfied before the 61st day after the date the judgment becomes final, the judgment creditor, for the judgment creditor's own use and benefit and at the judgment creditor's expense, may bring an action in the name of the state against the sureties on the bond, including an action to foreclose a lien on the real property of a surety. The foreclosure action must be brought in the same manner as, and is subject to the law applicable to, an action to foreclose a mortgage on real property.

(g) Cancellation of a bond filed under this section does not prevent recovery for a right or cause of action arising before the date of the cancellation.

(Enacted by Acts 1995, 74th Leg., ch. 165 (S.B. 971), § 1, effective September 1, 1995.)

### Sec. 601.122.    Deposit of Cash or Securities with Comptroller.

(a) A person may establish financial responsibility by depositing $55,000 with the comptroller in:

(1) cash; or

(2) securities that:

(A) are of the type that may legally be purchased by savings banks or trust funds; and

(B) have a market value equal to the required amount.

(b) On receipt of the deposit, the comptroller shall issue to the person making the deposit a certificate stating that a deposit complying with this section has been made.

(c) The comptroller may not accept the deposit and the department may not accept the certificate unless the deposit or certificate is accompanied by evidence that an unsatisfied judgment of any character against the person making the deposit does not exist in the county in which the person making the deposit resides.

(d) The comptroller shall hold a deposit made under this section to satisfy, in accordance with this chapter, an execution on a judgment issued against the person making the deposit for damages that:

(1) result from the ownership, maintenance, use, or operation of a motor vehicle after the date the deposit was made; and

(2) are for:

(A) bodily injury to or death of any person, including damages for care and loss of services; or

(B) damage to or destruction of property, including the loss of use of the property.

(e) Money or securities deposited under this section are not subject to attachment or execution

unless the attachment or execution arises out of a suit for damages described by Subsection (d).
(Enacted by Acts 1995, 74th Leg., ch. 165 (S.B. 971), § 1, effective September 1, 1995; am. Acts 1997, 75th Leg., ch. 1423 (H.B. 2841), § 18.09, effective September 1, 1997.)

### Sec. 601.123. Deposit of Cash or Cashier's Check with County Judge.

(a) A person may establish financial responsibility by making a deposit with the county judge of the county in which the motor vehicle is registered.

(b) The deposit must be made in cash or a cashier's check in the amount of at least $55,000.

(c) On receipt of the deposit, the county judge shall issue to the person making the deposit a certificate stating that a deposit complying with this section has been made. The certificate must be acknowledged by the sheriff of that county and filed with the department.
(Enacted by Acts 1995, 74th Leg., ch. 165 (S.B. 971), § 1, effective September 1, 1995.)

### Sec. 601.124. Self-Insurance.

(a) A person in whose name more than 25 motor vehicles are registered may qualify as a self-insurer by obtaining a certificate of self-insurance issued by the department as provided by this section.

(b) The department may issue a certificate of self-insurance to a person if:

(1) the person applies for the certificate; and

(2) the department is satisfied that the person has and will continue to have the ability to pay judgments obtained against the person.

(c) The self-insurer must supplement the certificate with an agreement that, for accidents occurring while the certificate is in force, the self-insurer will pay the same judgments in the same amounts as an insurer would be obligated to pay under an owner's motor vehicle liability insurance policy issued to the self-insurer if such policy were issued.

(d) The department for cause may cancel a certificate of self-insurance after a hearing. The self-insurer must receive at least five days' notice of the hearing. Cause includes failure to pay a judgment before the 31st day after the date the judgment becomes final.
(Enacted by Acts 1995, 74th Leg., ch. 165 (S.B. 971), § 1, effective September 1, 1995.)

### Secs. 601.125 to 601.150 [Reserved for expansion].

## SUBCHAPTER F
## SECURITY FOLLOWING ACCIDENT

### Sec. 601.151. Applicability of Subchapter.

(a) This subchapter applies only to a motor vehicle accident in this state that results in bodily injury or death or in damage to the property of one person of at least $1,000.

(b) This subchapter does not apply to:

(1) an owner or operator who has in effect at the time of the accident a motor vehicle liability insurance policy that covers the motor vehicle involved in the accident;

(2) an operator who is not the owner of the motor vehicle, if a motor vehicle liability insurance policy or bond for the operation of a motor vehicle the person does not own is in effect at the time of the accident;

(3) an owner or operator whose liability for damages resulting from the accident, in the judgment of the department, is covered by another liability insurance policy or bond;

(4) an owner or operator, if there was not bodily injury to or damage of the property of a person other than the owner or operator;

(5) the owner or operator of a motor vehicle that at the time of the accident was legally parked or legally stopped at a traffic signal;

(6) the owner of a motor vehicle that at the time of the accident was being operated without the owner's express or implied permission or was parked by a person who had been operating the vehicle without that permission; or

(7) a person qualifying as a self-insurer under Section 601.124 or a person operating a motor vehicle for a self-insurer.
(Enacted by Acts 1995, 74th Leg., ch. 165 (S.B. 971), § 1, effective September 1, 1995.)

### Sec. 601.152. Suspension of Driver's License and Vehicle Registration or Privilege.

(a) Subject to Section 601.153, the department shall suspend the driver's license and vehicle registrations of the owner and operator of a motor vehicle if:

(1) the vehicle is involved in any manner in an accident; and

(2) the department finds that there is a

reasonable probability that a judgment will be rendered against the person as a result of the accident.

(b) If the owner or operator is a nonresident, the department shall suspend the person's non-resident operating privilege and the privilege of use of any motor vehicle owned by the nonresident.

(Enacted by Acts 1995, 74th Leg., ch. 165 (S.B. 971), § 1, effective September 1, 1995.)

## Sec. 601.153. Deposit of Security; Evidence of Financial Responsibility.

(a) The department may not suspend a driver's license, vehicle registration, or nonresident's privilege under this subchapter if the owner or operator:

(1) deposits with the department security in an amount determined to be sufficient under Section 601.154 or 601.157 as appropriate; and

(2) files evidence of financial responsibility as required by this chapter.

(b) If the owner or operator chooses to establish financial responsibility under Subsection (a)(2) by filing evidence of motor vehicle liability insurance, the owner or operator must file a certificate of insurance for a policy that has a policy period of at least six months and for which the premium for the entire policy period is paid in full.

(c) Notwithstanding Section 601.085, coverage for a motor vehicle under a motor vehicle liability policy for which a person files with the department a certificate of insurance under Subsection (b) may not be canceled unless:

(1) the person no longer owns the motor vehicle;

(2) the person dies;

(3) the person has a permanent incapacity that renders the person unable to drive the motor vehicle; or

(4) the person surrenders to the department the person's driver's license and the vehicle registration for the motor vehicle.

(Enacted by Acts 1995, 74th Leg., ch. 165 (S.B. 971), § 1, effective September 1, 1995; am. Acts 1997, 75th Leg., ch. 178 (H.B. 627), § 2, effective September 1, 1997.)

## Sec. 601.154. Department Determination of Probability of Liability.

(a) Subject to Subsection (d), if the department finds that there is a reasonable probability that a judgment will be rendered against an owner or

operator as a result of an accident, the department shall determine the amount of security sufficient to satisfy any judgment for damages resulting from the accident that may be recovered from the owner or operator.

(b) The department may not require security in an amount:

(1) less than $1,000; or

(2) more than the limits prescribed by Section 601.072.

(c) In determining whether there is a reasonable probability that a judgment will be rendered against the person as a result of an accident and the amount of security that is sufficient under Subsection (a), the department may consider:

(1) a report of an investigating officer;

(2) an accident report of a party involved; and

(3) an affidavit of a person who has knowledge of the facts.

(d) The department shall make the determination required by Subsection (a) only if the department has not received, before the 21st day after the date the department receives a report of a motor vehicle accident, satisfactory evidence that the owner or operator has:

(1) been released from liability;

(2) been finally adjudicated not to be liable; or

(3) executed an acknowledged written agreement providing for the payment of an agreed amount in installments for all claims for injuries or damages resulting from the accident.

(Enacted by Acts 1995, 74th Leg., ch. 165 (S.B. 971), § 1, effective September 1, 1995.)

## Sec. 601.155. Notice of Determination.

(a) The department shall notify the affected person of a determination made under Section 601.154.

(b) The notice must state that:

(1) the person's driver's license and vehicle registration or the person's nonresident's operating privilege will be suspended unless the person, not later than the 20th day after the date the notice was personally served or mailed, establishes that:

(A) this subchapter does not apply to the person, and the person has previously provided this information to the department; or

(B) there is no reasonable probability that a judgment will be rendered against the person as a result of the accident; and

Transportation

(2) the person is entitled to a hearing under this subchapter if a written request for a hearing is delivered or mailed to the department not later than the 20th day after the date the notice was personally served or mailed.

(c) Notice under this section that is mailed must be mailed to the person's last known address, as shown by the department's records.

(d) For purposes of this section, notice is presumed to be received if the notice was mailed to the person's last known address, as shown by the department's records.

(Enacted by Acts 1995, 74th Leg., ch. 165 (S.B. 971), § 1, effective September 1, 1995; am. Acts 1997, 75th Leg., ch. 1395 (H.B. 1937), § 1, effective September 1, 1997.)

### Sec. 601.156.  Setting of Hearing.

(a) A hearing under this subchapter is subject to the notice and hearing procedures of Sections 521.295—521.303 and shall be heard by a judge of a municipal court or a justice of the peace of the county in which the person requesting the hearing resides. A party is not entitled to a jury.

(b) The court shall set a date for the hearing. The hearing must be held at the earliest practical time after notice is given to the person requesting the hearing.

(c) The department shall summon the person requesting the hearing to appear at the hearing. Notice under this subsection shall be delivered through personal service or mailed by first class mail to the person's last known address, as shown by the department's records. The notice must include written charges issued by the department.

(Enacted by Acts 1995, 74th Leg., ch. 165 (S.B. 971), § 1, effective September 1, 1995; am. Acts 1999, 76th Leg., ch. 1117 (H.B. 3641), § 4, effective September 1, 2000; am. Acts 1999, 76th Leg., ch. 1409 (H.B. 2031), § 6, effective September 1, 1999.)

### Sec. 601.157.  Hearing Procedures.

(a) The judge may administer oaths and issue subpoenas for the attendance of witnesses and the production of relevant books and papers.

(b) The judge at the hearing shall determine:

(1) whether there is a reasonable probability that a judgment will be rendered against the person requesting the hearing as a result of the accident; and

(2) if there is a reasonable probability that a judgment will be rendered, the amount of secu-

rity sufficient to satisfy any judgment for damages resulting from the accident.

(c) The amount of security under Subsection (b)(2) may not be less than the amount specified as a minimum by Section 601.154.

(d) The judge shall report the judge's determination to the department.

(e) The judge may receive a fee to be paid from the general revenue fund of the county for holding a hearing under this subchapter. The fee must be approved by the commissioners court of the county and may not be more than $5 for each hearing.

(Enacted by Acts 1995, 74th Leg., ch. 165 (S.B. 971), § 1, effective September 1, 1995.)

### Sec. 601.158.  Appeal.

(a) If, after a hearing under this subchapter, the judge determines that there is a reasonable probability that a judgment will be rendered against the person requesting the hearing as a result of the accident, the person may appeal the determination.

(b) To appeal a determination under Subsection (a), the person must file a petition not later than the 30th day after the date of the determination in the county court at law of the county in which the person resides, or, if there is no county court at law, in the county court of the county.

(c) A person who files an appeal under this section shall send a file-stamped copy of the petition by certified mail to the department at the department's headquarters in Austin. The copy must be certified by the clerk of the court in which the petition is filed.

(d) The filing of a petition of appeal as provided by this section stays an order of suspension until the earlier of the 91st day after the date the appeal petition is filed or the date the trial is completed and final judgment is rendered.

(e) On expiration of the stay, the department shall impose the suspension. The stay may not be extended, and an additional stay may not be granted.

(f) A trial on appeal is de novo.

(Enacted by Acts 1995, 74th Leg., ch. 165 (S.B. 971), § 1, effective September 1, 1995; am. Acts 1999, 76th Leg., ch. 1117 (H.B. 3641), § 5, effective September 1, 2000.)

### Sec. 601.159.  Procedures for Suspension of Driver's License and Vehicle Registration or Privilege.

The department shall suspend the driver's license and each vehicle registration of an owner or operator or the nonresident's operating privilege of an owner or operator unless:

(1) if a hearing is not requested, the person, not later than the 20th day after the date the notice under Section 601.155 was personally served or mailed:

(A) delivers or mails to the department a written request for a hearing;

(B) shows that this subchapter does not apply to the person; or

(C) complies with Section 601.153; or

(2) the person complies with Section 601.153 not later than the 20th day after:

(A) the date of the expiration of the period in which an appeal may be brought, if the determination at a hearing is rendered against the owner or operator and the owner or operator does not appeal; or

(B) the date of a decision against the person following the appeal.

(Enacted by Acts 1995, 74th Leg., ch. 165 (S.B. 971), § 1, effective September 1, 1995.)

### Sec. 601.160. Suspension Stayed Pending Hearing or Appeal.

The department may not suspend a driver's license, vehicle registration, or nonresident's operating privilege pending the outcome of a hearing and any appeal under this subchapter.

(Enacted by Acts 1995, 74th Leg., ch. 165 (S.B. 971), § 1, effective September 1, 1995.)

### Sec. 601.161. Notice of Suspension.

Not later than the 11th day before the effective date of a suspension under Section 601.159, the department shall send notice of the suspension to each affected owner or operator. The notice must state the amount required as security under Section 601.153 and the necessity for the owner or operator to file evidence of financial responsibility with the department.

(Enacted by Acts 1995, 74th Leg., ch. 165 (S.B. 971), § 1, effective September 1, 1995.)

### Sec. 601.162. Duration of Suspension.

(a) The suspension of a driver's license, vehicle registration, or nonresident's operating privilege under this subchapter remains in effect, the license, registration, or privilege may not be renewed, and a license or vehicle registration may not be issued to the holder of the suspended license, registration, or privilege, until:

(1) the date the person, or a person acting on the person's behalf, deposits security and files

evidence of financial responsibility under Section 601.153;

(2) the second anniversary of the date of the accident, if evidence satisfactory to the department is filed with the department that, during the two-year period, an action for damages arising out of the accident has not been instituted; or

(3) the date evidence satisfactory to the department is filed with the department of:

(A) a release from liability for claims arising out of the accident;

(B) a final adjudication that the person is not liable for claims arising out of the accident; or

(C) an installment agreement described by Section 601.154(d)(3).

(b) If a suspension is terminated under Subsection (a)(3)(C), on notice of a default in the payment of an installment under the agreement, the department shall promptly suspend the driver's license and vehicle registration or nonresident's operating privilege of the person defaulting. A suspension under this subsection continues until:

(1) the person deposits and maintains security in accordance with Section 601.153 in an amount determined by the department at the time of suspension under this subsection and files evidence of financial responsibility in accordance with Section 601.153; or

(2) the second anniversary of the date security was required under Subdivision (1) if, during that period, an action on the agreement has not been instituted in a court in this state.

(Enacted by Acts 1995, 74th Leg., ch. 165 (S.B. 971), § 1, effective September 1, 1995; am. Acts 2005, 79th Leg., ch. 728 (H.B. 2018), § 20.005, effective September 1, 2005.)

### Sec. 601.163. Form of Security.

(a) The security required under this subchapter shall be made:

(1) by cash deposit;

(2) through a bond that complies with Section 601.168; or

(3) in another form as required by the department.

(b) A person depositing security shall specify in writing the person on whose behalf the deposit is made. A single deposit of security is applicable only on behalf of persons required to provide security because of the same accident and the same motor vehicle.

(c) The person depositing the security may amend in writing the specification of the person on whose behalf the deposit is made to include an additional person. This amendment may be made at any time the deposit is in the custody of the department or the comptroller.

(Enacted by Acts 1995, 74th Leg., ch. 165 (S.B. 971), § 1, effective September 1, 1995; am. Acts 1997, 75th Leg., ch. 1423 (H.B. 2841), § 18.10, effective September 1, 1997.)

### Sec. 601.164.  Reduction in Security.

(a) The department may reduce the amount of security ordered in a case within six months after the date of the accident if, in the department's judgment, the amount is excessive.

(b) The amount of security originally deposited that exceeds the reduced amount shall be returned promptly to the depositor or the depositor's personal representative.

(Enacted by Acts 1995, 74th Leg., ch. 165 (S.B. 971), § 1, effective September 1, 1995.)

### Sec. 601.165.  Custody of Cash Security.

The department shall place cash deposited in compliance with this subchapter in the custody of the comptroller.

(Enacted by Acts 1995, 74th Leg., ch. 165 (S.B. 971), § 1, effective September 1, 1995; am. Acts 1997, 75th Leg., ch. 1423 (H.B. 2841), § 18.11, effective September 1, 1997.)

### Sec. 601.166.  Payment of Cash Security.

(a) Cash security may be applied only to the payment of:

(1) a judgment rendered against the person on whose behalf the deposit is made for damages arising out of the accident; or

(2) a settlement, agreed to by the depositor, of a claim arising out of the accident.

(b) For payment under Subsection (a), the action under which the judgment was rendered must have been instituted before the second anniversary of the later of:

(1) the date of the accident; or

(2) the date of the deposit, in the case of a deposit of security under Section 601.162(b).

(Enacted by Acts 1995, 74th Leg., ch. 165 (S.B. 971), § 1, effective September 1, 1995.)

### Sec. 601.167.  Return of Cash Security.

Cash security or any balance of the security shall be returned to the depositor or the depositor's personal representative when:

(1) evidence satisfactory to the department is filed with the department that there has been:

(A) a release of liability;

(B) a final adjudication that the person on whose behalf the deposit is made is not liable; or

(C) an agreement as described by Section 601.154(d)(3);

(2) reasonable evidence is provided to the department after the second anniversary of the date of the accident that no action arising out of the accident is pending and no judgment rendered in such an action is unpaid; or

(3) in the case of a deposit of security under Section 601.162(b), reasonable evidence is provided to the department after the second anniversary of the date of the deposit that no action arising out of the accident is pending and no unpaid judgment rendered in such an action is unpaid.

(Enacted by Acts 1995, 74th Leg., ch. 165 (S.B. 971), § 1, effective September 1, 1995.)

### Sec. 601.168.  Insurance Policy or Bond; Limits.

(a) A bond or motor vehicle liability insurance policy under this subchapter must:

(1) be issued by a surety company or insurance company:

(A) authorized to write motor vehicle liability insurance in this state; or

(B) that complies with Subsection (b); and

(2) cover the amounts, excluding interest and costs, required to establish financial responsibility under Section 601.072.

(b) A bond or motor vehicle liability insurance policy issued by a surety company or insurance company that is not authorized to do business in this state is effective under this subchapter only if:

(1) the bond or policy is issued for a motor vehicle that:

(A) is not registered in this state; or

(B) was not registered in this state on the effective date of the most recent renewal of the policy; and

(2) the surety company or insurance company executes a power of attorney authorizing the department to accept on the company's behalf service of notice or process in an action arising out of the accident on the bond or policy.

(c) The bond must be filed with and approved by the department.

(Enacted by Acts 1995, 74th Leg., ch. 165 (S.B. 971), § 1, effective September 1, 1995.)

### Sec. 601.169. Reasonable Probability Not Admissible in Civil Suit.

A determination under Section 601.154 or 601.157 that there is a reasonable probability that a judgment will be rendered against a person as a result of an accident may not be introduced in evidence in a suit for damages arising from that accident.

(Enacted by Acts 1995, 74th Leg., ch. 165 (S.B. 971), § 1, effective September 1, 1995.)

### Sec. 601.170. Department Acting on Erroneous Information.

If the department is given erroneous information relating to a matter covered by Section 601.151(b)(1) or (b)(2) or to a person's status as an employee of the United States acting within the scope of the person's employment, the department shall take appropriate action as provided by this subchapter not later than the 60th day after the date the department receives correct information.

(Enacted by Acts 1995, 74th Leg., ch. 165 (S.B. 971), § 1, effective September 1, 1995.)

### Secs. 601.171 to 601.190 [Reserved for expansion].

### SUBCHAPTER G
### FAILURE TO MAINTAIN MOTOR VEHICLE LIABILITY INSURANCE OR OTHERWISE ESTABLISH FINANCIAL RESPONSIBILITY; CRIMINAL PENALTIES

### Sec. 601.191. Operation of Motor Vehicle in Violation of Motor Vehicle Liability Insurance Requirement; Offense.

(a) A person commits an offense if the person operates a motor vehicle in violation of Section 601.051.

(b) Except as provided by Subsections (c) and (d), an offense under this section is a misdemeanor punishable by a fine of not less than $175 or more than $350.

(c) If a person has been previously convicted of an offense under this section, an offense under this section is a misdemeanor punishable by a fine of not less than $350 or more than $1,000.

(d) If the court determines that a person who has not been previously convicted of an offense

under this section is economically unable to pay the fine, the court may reduce the fine to less than $175.

(Enacted by Acts 1995, 74th Leg., ch. 165 (S.B. 971), § 1, effective September 1, 1995.)

### Sec. 601.192. Court Costs [Repealed].

Repealed by Acts 1997, 75th Leg., ch. 1100 (H.B. 2272), § 6(5), effective September 1, 1997.

(Enacted by Acts 1995, 74th Leg., ch. 165 (S.B. 971), § 1, effective September 1, 1995.)

### Sec. 601.193. Defense: Financial Responsibility in Effect at Time of Alleged Offense.

(a) It is a defense to prosecution under Section 601.191 or 601.195 that the person charged produces to the court one of the documents listed in Section 601.053(a) that was valid at the time that the offense is alleged to have occurred.

(b) After the court verifies a document produced under Subsection (a), the court shall dismiss the charge.

(Enacted by Acts 1995, 74th Leg., ch. 165 (S.B. 971), § 1, effective September 1, 1995; am. Acts 1997, 75th Leg., ch. 844 (H.B. 853), § 1, effective September 1, 1997; am. Acts 1999, 76th Leg., ch. 961 (H.B. 2535), § 1, effective September 1, 1999.)

### Sec. 601.194. Defense: Possession of Motor Vehicle for Maintenance or Repair.

It is a defense to prosecution of an offense under Section 601.191 that the motor vehicle operated by the person charged:

(1) was in the possession of that person for the sole purpose of maintenance or repair; and

(2) was not owned in whole or in part by that person.

(Enacted by Acts 1995, 74th Leg., ch. 165 (S.B. 971), § 1, effective September 1, 1995.)

### Sec. 601.195. Operation of Motor Vehicle in Violation of Requirement to Establish Financial Responsibility; Offense.

(a) A person commits an offense if the person:

(1) is required to establish financial responsibility under Subchapter F or K;

(2) does not maintain evidence of financial responsibility; and

(3) during the period evidence of financial responsibility must be maintained:

(A) operates on a highway a motor vehicle owned by the person; or

(B) knowingly permits another person, who is not otherwise permitted to operate a vehicle under this chapter, to operate on a highway a motor vehicle owned by the person.

(b) An offense under this section is a misdemeanor punishable by:

(1) a fine not to exceed $500;

(2) confinement in county jail for a term not to exceed six months; or

(3) both the fine and the confinement.

(Enacted by Acts 1995, 74th Leg., ch. 165 (S.B. 971), § 1, effective September 1, 1995.)

### Sec. 601.196.  Evidence Forged or Signed Without Authority; Offense [Repealed].

Repealed by Acts 1999, 76th Leg., ch. 659 (H.B. 319), § 4, effective September 1, 1999.

(Enacted by Acts 1995, 74th Leg., ch. 165 (S.B. 971), § 1, effective September 1, 1995; am. Acts 1997, 75th Leg., ch. 148 (S.B. 655), § 10, effective September 1, 1997.)

### Secs. 601.197 to 601.230 [Reserved for expansion].

## SUBCHAPTER H
## FAILURE TO MAINTAIN EVIDENCE OF FINANCIAL RESPONSIBILITY; SUSPENSION OF DRIVER'S LICENSE AND MOTOR VEHICLE REGISTRATION

### Sec. 601.231.  Suspension of Driver's License and Vehicle Registration.

(a) If a person is convicted of an offense under Section 601.191 and a prior conviction of that person under that section has been reported to the department by a magistrate or the judge or clerk of a court, the department shall suspend the driver's license and vehicle registrations of the person unless the person files and maintains evidence of financial responsibility with the department until the second anniversary of the date of the subsequent conviction.

(b) The department may waive the requirement of maintaining evidence of financial responsibility under Subsection (a) if satisfactory evidence is filed with the department showing that at the time of arrest the person was in compliance with the financial responsibility requirement of Section 601.051 or was exempt from that section under Section 601.007 or 601.052(a)(3).

(Enacted by Acts 1995, 74th Leg., ch. 165 (S.B. 971), § 1, effective September 1, 1995.)

### Sec. 601.232.  Notice of Suspension.

(a) The department shall mail in a timely manner a notice to each person whose driver's license and vehicle registrations are suspended under Section 601.231.

(b) The notice must state that the person's driver's license and registration are suspended and that the person may apply for reinstatement of the license and vehicle registration or issuance of a new license and registration as provided by Sections 601.162 and 601.376.

(Enacted by Acts 1995, 74th Leg., ch. 165 (S.B. 971), § 1, effective September 1, 1995.)

### Sec. 601.233.  Notice of Potential Suspension.

(a) A citation for an offense under Section 601.191 issued as a result of Section 601.053 must include, in type larger than other type on the citation, except for the type of the statement required by Section 708.105, the following statement:

"A second or subsequent conviction of an offense under the Texas Motor Vehicle Safety Responsibility Act will result in the suspension of your driver's license and motor vehicle registration unless you file and maintain evidence of financial responsibility with the Department of Public Safety for two years from the date of conviction. The department may waive the requirement to file evidence of financial responsibility if you file satisfactory evidence with the department showing that at the time this citation was issued, the vehicle was covered by a motor vehicle liability insurance policy or that you were otherwise exempt from the requirements to provide evidence of financial responsibility."

(b) A judge presiding at a trial at which a person is convicted of an offense under Section 601.191 shall notify the person that the person's driver's license is subject to suspension if the person fails to provide to the department evidence of financial responsibility as required by Section 601.231.

(Enacted by Acts 1995, 74th Leg., ch. 165 (S.B. 971), § 1, effective September 1, 1995; am. Acts 2005, 79th Leg., ch. 1123 (H.B. 2470), § 3, effective September 1, 2005.)

### Sec. 601.234. Issuance or Continuation of Vehicle Registration.

A motor vehicle may not be registered in the name of a person required to file evidence of financial responsibility unless evidence of financial responsibility is furnished for the vehicle.
(Enacted by Acts 1995, 74th Leg., ch. 165 (S.B. 971), § 1, effective September 1, 1995.)

### Secs. 601.235 to 601.260 [Reserved for expansion].

## SUBCHAPTER I
## FAILURE TO MAINTAIN EVIDENCE OF FINANCIAL RESPONSIBILITY; IMPOUNDMENT OF MOTOR VEHICLE

### Sec. 601.261. Impoundment of Motor Vehicle.

On a second or subsequent conviction for an offense under Section 601.191, the court shall order the sheriff of the county in which the court has jurisdiction to impound the motor vehicle operated by the defendant at the time of the offense if the defendant:

(1) was an owner of the motor vehicle at the time of the offense; and

(2) is an owner on the date of that conviction.
(Enacted by Acts 1995, 74th Leg., ch. 165 (S.B. 971), § 1, effective September 1, 1995.)

### Sec. 601.262. Duration of Impoundment.

(a) The duration of an impoundment under Section 601.261 is 180 days.

(b) The court may not order the release of the vehicle unless the defendant applies to the court for the vehicle's release and provides evidence of financial responsibility that complies with Section 601.053 and this section.

(c) The evidence of financial responsibility must cover the two-year period immediately following the date the defendant applies for release of the impounded vehicle. The court, by order, shall permit a defendant to provide evidence of insurability in increments of a period of not less than six months.

(d) If an insurance binder is offered as evidence of financial responsibility under this section, the binder must confirm to the court's satisfaction that the defendant is in compliance with this chapter for the period required by Subsection (c).

(Enacted by Acts 1995, 74th Leg., ch. 165 (S.B. 971), § 1, effective September 1, 1995; am. Acts 2009, 81st Leg., ch. 313 (H.B. 586), § 1, effective September 1, 2009.)

### Sec. 601.263. Cost for Impoundment.

The court shall impose against the defendant a cost of $15 a day for each day of impoundment of the defendant's vehicle.
(Enacted by Acts 1995, 74th Leg., ch. 165 (S.B. 971), § 1, effective September 1, 1995.)

### Sec. 601.264. Penalties Cumulative.

Impoundment of a motor vehicle under this subchapter is in addition to any other punishment imposed under this chapter.
(Enacted by Acts 1995, 74th Leg., ch. 165 (S.B. 971), § 1, effective September 1, 1995.)

### Sec. 601.265. Transfer of Title of Impounded Motor Vehicle.

(a) To transfer title to a motor vehicle impounded under Section 601.261, the owner must apply to the court for permission.

(b) If the court finds that the transfer is being made in good faith and is not being made to circumvent this chapter, the court shall approve the transfer.
(Enacted by Acts 1995, 74th Leg., ch. 165 (S.B. 971), § 1, effective September 1, 1995.)

### Sec. 601.266. Release on Involuntary Transfer of Title of Impounded Motor Vehicle.

(a) Notwithstanding Section 601.262, the court shall order the release of a motor vehicle impounded under Section 601.261 if, while the vehicle is impounded, title to the vehicle is transferred by:

(1) foreclosure;

(2) sale on execution;

(3) cancellation of a conditional sales contract; or

(4) judicial order.
(Enacted by Acts 1995, 74th Leg., ch. 165 (S.B. 971), § 1, effective September 1, 1995.)

### Sec. 601.267. Release of Impounded Motor Vehicle by Sheriff.

A sheriff who impounds a motor vehicle shall release the vehicle:

(1) on presentation of an order of release from the court and payment of the fee for the impoundment by the defendant or a person authorized by the owner; or

(2) to a person who is shown as a lienholder on the vehicle's certificate of title on presentation of the certificate of title and an accompanying affidavit from an officer of the lienholder establishing that the debt secured by the vehicle is in default or has matured.

(Enacted by Acts 1995, 74th Leg., ch. 165 (S.B. 971), § 1, effective September 1, 1995.)

**Secs. 601.268 to 601.290 [Reserved for expansion].**

## SUBCHAPTER J
## IMPOUNDMENT OF MOTOR VEHICLE NOT REGISTERED IN THIS STATE

### Sec. 601.291.    Applicability of Subchapter.

This subchapter applies only to the owner or operator of a motor vehicle that:

(1) is not registered in this state; and

(2) is involved in a motor vehicle accident in this state that results in bodily injury, death, or damage to the property of one person to an apparent extent of at least $500.

(Enacted by Acts 1995, 74th Leg., ch. 165 (S.B. 971), § 1, effective September 1, 1995.)

### Sec. 601.292.    Duty to Provide Evidence of Financial Responsibility to Investigating Officer.

A person to whom this subchapter applies shall provide evidence of financial responsibility to a law enforcement officer of this state or a political subdivision of this state who is conducting an investigation of the accident.

(Enacted by Acts 1995, 74th Leg., ch. 165 (S.B. 971), § 1, effective September 1, 1995.)

### Sec. 601.293.    Failure to Provide Evidence of Financial Responsibility; Magistrate's Inquiry and Order.

(a) A person to whom this subchapter applies who fails to provide evidence under Section 601.292 shall be taken before a magistrate as soon as practicable.

(b) The magistrate shall conduct an inquiry on the issues of negligence and liability for bodily injury, death, or property damage sustained in the accident.

(c) If the magistrate determines that there is a reasonable possibility that a judgment will be rendered against the person for bodily injury, death, or property damage sustained in the acci-

dent, the magistrate shall order the person to provide:

(1) evidence of financial responsibility for the bodily injury, death, or property damage; or

(2) evidence that the person is exempt from the requirement of Section 601.051.

(d) A determination of negligence or liability under Subsection (c) does not act as collateral estoppel on an issue in a criminal or civil adjudication arising from the accident.

(Enacted by Acts 1995, 74th Leg., ch. 165 (S.B. 971), § 1, effective September 1, 1995.)

### Sec. 601.294.    Impoundment of Motor Vehicle.

If a person to whom this subchapter applies does not provide evidence required under Section 601.293(c), the magistrate shall enter an order directing the sheriff of the county or the chief of police of the municipality to impound the motor vehicle owned or operated by the person that was involved in the accident.

(Enacted by Acts 1995, 74th Leg., ch. 165 (S.B. 971), § 1, effective September 1, 1995.)

### Sec. 601.295.    Duration of Impoundment; Release.

(a) A motor vehicle impounded under Section 601.294 remains impounded until the owner, operator, or person authorized by the owner presents to the person authorized to release the vehicle:

(1) a certificate of release obtained from the department; and

(2) payment for the cost of impoundment.

(b) On presentation of the items described by Subsection (a), the person authorized to release an impounded motor vehicle shall release the vehicle.

(Enacted by Acts 1995, 74th Leg., ch. 165 (S.B. 971), § 1, effective September 1, 1995.)

### Sec. 601.296.    Certificate of Release.

(a) The department shall issue a certificate of release of an impounded motor vehicle to the owner, operator, or person authorized by the owner on submission to the department of:

(1) evidence of financial responsibility under Section 601.053 that shows that at the time of the accident the vehicle was in compliance with Section 601.051 or was exempt from the requirement of Section 601.051;

(2) a release executed by each person damaged in the accident other than the operator of

the vehicle for which the certificate of release is requested; or

(3) security in a form and amount determined by the department to secure the payment of damages for which the operator may be liable.

(b) A person may satisfy the requirement of Subsection (a)(1) or (2) by submitting a photocopy of the item required.

(c) The department shall adopt the form, content, and procedures for issuance of a certificate of release.

(d) Security provided under this section is subject to Sections 601.163—601.167.
(Enacted by Acts 1995, 74th Leg., ch. 165 (S.B. 971), § 1, effective September 1, 1995.)

### Sec. 601.297. Liability for Cost of Impoundment.

The owner of an impounded vehicle is liable for the costs of the impoundment.
(Enacted by Acts 1995, 74th Leg., ch. 165 (S.B. 971), § 1, effective September 1, 1995.)

### Secs. 601.298 to 601.330 [Reserved for expansion].

### SUBCHAPTER K
### EVIDENCE OF FINANCIAL RESPONSIBILITY FOLLOWING JUDGMENT, CONVICTION, PLEA, OR FORFEITURE OR FOLLOWING SUSPENSION OR REVOCATION

### Sec. 601.331. Report of Unsatisfied Judgment or Conviction, Plea, or Forfeiture of Bail; Nonresident.

(a) If a person does not satisfy a judgment before the 61st day after the date of the judgment, the clerk of the court, on the written request of a judgment creditor or a judgment creditor's attorney, immediately shall send a certified copy of the judgment to the department.

(b) The clerk of the court immediately shall send to the department a certified copy of the action of the court in relation to:

(1) a conviction for a violation of a motor vehicle law; or

(2) a guilty plea or forfeiture of bail by a person charged with violation of a motor vehicle law.

(c) A certified copy sent to the department under Subsection (b) is prima facie evidence of the conviction, plea, forfeiture, or other action.

(d) If the court does not have a clerk, the judge of the court shall send the certified copy required by this section.

(e) If the defendant named in a judgment reported to the department is a nonresident, the department shall send a certified copy of the judgment to the official in charge of issuing driver's licenses and vehicle registrations of the state, province of Canada, or state of Mexico in which the defendant resides.
(Enacted by Acts 1995, 74th Leg., ch. 165 (S.B. 971), § 1, effective September 1, 1995; am. Acts 1997, 75th Leg., ch. 75 (H.B. 1049), § 1, effective September 1, 1997.)

### Sec. 601.332. Suspension of Driver's License and Vehicle Registration or Nonresident's Operating Privilege for Unsatisfied Judgment.

(a) Except as provided by Sections 601.333, 601.334, and 601.336, on receipt of a certified copy of a judgment under Section 601.331, the department shall suspend the judgment debtor's:

(1) driver's license and vehicle registrations; or

(2) nonresident's operating privilege.

(b) Subject to Sections 601.333, 601.334, and 601.336, the suspension continues, and the person's driver's license, vehicle registrations, or nonresident's operating privilege may not be renewed or the person issued a driver's license or registration in the person's name, until:

(1) the judgment is stayed or satisfied; and

(2) the person provides evidence of financial responsibility.
(Enacted by Acts 1995, 74th Leg., ch. 165 (S.B. 971), § 1, effective September 1, 1995.)

### Sec. 601.333. Relief from Suspension: Motor Vehicle Liability Insurance.

(a) A person whose driver's license, vehicle registrations, or nonresident's operating privilege has been suspended or is subject to suspension under Section 601.332 may file with the department:

(1) evidence that there was a motor vehicle liability insurance policy covering the motor vehicle involved in the accident out of which the judgment arose in effect at the time of the accident;

(2) an affidavit stating that the person was insured at the time of the accident, that the insurance company is liable to pay the judgment, and the reason, if known, that the insurance company has not paid the judgment;

(3) the original policy of insurance or a certified copy of the policy, if available; and

(4) any other documents required by the department to show that the loss, injury, or damage for which the judgment was rendered was covered by the insurance.

(b) The department may not suspend the driver's license, vehicle registrations, or nonresident's operating privilege, and shall reinstate a license, registration, or privilege that has been suspended, if it is satisfied from the documents filed under Subsection (a) that:

(1) there was a motor vehicle liability insurance policy in effect for the vehicle at the time of the accident;

(2) the insurance company that issued the policy was authorized to issue the policy in this state at the time the policy was issued; and

(3) the insurance company is liable to pay the judgment to the extent and for the amounts required by this chapter.

(Enacted by Acts 1995, 74th Leg., ch. 165 (S.B. 971), § 1, effective September 1, 1995.)

### Sec. 601.334. Relief from Suspension: Consent of Judgment Creditor.

(a) The department may allow a judgment debtor's driver's license and vehicle registrations or nonresident's operating privilege to continue, notwithstanding Section 601.332, if:

(1) the judgment creditor consents to the continuation in writing in the form prescribed by the department; and

(2) the judgment debtor provides evidence of financial responsibility to the department.

(b) Continuation of a judgment debtor's driver's license and vehicle registrations or nonresident's operating privilege expires on the later of:

(1) the date the consent of the judgment creditor is revoked in writing; or

(2) the expiration of six months after the effective date of the consent.

(c) Subsection (b) applies notwithstanding default in the payment of the judgment or any installments to be made under Section 601.335.

(Enacted by Acts 1995, 74th Leg., ch. 165 (S.B. 971), § 1, effective September 1, 1995.)

### Sec. 601.335. Installment Payments Authorized.

(a) A judgment debtor, on notice to the judgment creditor, may apply to the court in which judgment was rendered to pay the judgment in installments.

(b) The court may order payment in installments and may establish the amounts and times of the payments.

(c) An order issued under this section is issued without prejudice to any other legal remedy that the judgment creditor has.

(Enacted by Acts 1995, 74th Leg., ch. 165 (S.B. 971), § 1, effective September 1, 1995.)

### Sec. 601.336. Relief from Suspension: Installment Payments; Default.

(a) Subject to Subsection (c), the department may not suspend a judgment debtor's driver's license, vehicle registration, or nonresident's operating privilege under Section 601.332 if the judgment debtor:

(1) files evidence of financial responsibility with the department; and

(2) obtains an order under Section 601.335 permitting the payment of the judgment in installments.

(b) Subject to Subsection (c), the department shall restore a judgment debtor's driver's license, vehicle registrations, or nonresident's operating privilege that was suspended following nonpayment of a judgment if the judgment debtor complies with Subsections (a)(1) and (2).

(c) On notice that a judgment debtor has failed to pay an installment as specified in an order issued under Section 601.335, the department shall suspend the judgment debtor's driver's license, vehicle registrations, or nonresident's operating privilege. The suspensions continue until the judgment is satisfied as provided by this chapter.

(Enacted by Acts 1995, 74th Leg., ch. 165 (S.B. 971), § 1, effective September 1, 1995.)

### Sec. 601.337. Effect of Bankruptcy.

A discharge in bankruptcy after a judgment is rendered relieves the judgment debtor from the requirements of this chapter, except for financial responsibility requirements arising after the date of the discharge.

(Enacted by Acts 1995, 74th Leg., ch. 165 (S.B. 971), § 1, effective September 1, 1995.)

### Sec. 601.338. Evidence of Financial Responsibility or Suspension of Driver's License and Vehicle Registration of Owner of Motor Vehicle.

(a) The department shall suspend the driver's license and vehicle registrations of the owner of a motor vehicle that was used with the owner's consent by another person at the time of an offense resulting in conviction or a plea of guilty, if under state law the department:

(1) suspends or revokes the driver's license of the other person on receipt of a record of a conviction; or

(2) suspends the vehicle registration of the other person on receipt of a record of a plea of guilty.

(b) The department may not suspend the driver's license and vehicle registration of an owner under this section if the owner files and maintains evidence of financial responsibility with the department for each motor vehicle registered in the name of the owner.

(Enacted by Acts 1995, 74th Leg., ch. 165 (S.B. 971), § 1, effective September 1, 1995.)

## Sec. 601.339. Evidence of Financial Responsibility Following Conviction, Plea, or Forfeiture.

(a) Except as provided by Subsection (c), the department may not issue a driver's license to a person who does not hold a driver's license and who:

(1) enters a plea of guilty to an offense or is convicted by a final order or a judgment that:

(A) requires the suspension or revocation of a driver's license;

(B) is imposed for operating a motor vehicle on a highway without a driver's license; or

(C) is imposed for operating an unregistered motor vehicle on a highway; or

(2) forfeits bail or collateral deposited to secure an appearance for trial for an offense described by Subdivision (1).

(b) Except as described by Subsection (c), a motor vehicle may not be registered in the name of a person described by Subsection (a).

(c) Notwithstanding Subsections (a) and (b), a driver's license may be issued or a motor vehicle may be registered if the person files and maintains evidence of financial responsibility with the department.

(Enacted by Acts 1995, 74th Leg., ch. 165 (S.B. 971), § 1, effective September 1, 1995.)

## Sec. 601.340. Evidence of Financial Responsibility or Suspension of Vehicle Registration Following Suspension or Revocation of Driver's License.

(a) Except as provided by Subsection (b) or (c), the department shall suspend the registration of each motor vehicle registered in the name of a person if the department:

(1) under any state law, other than Section 521.341(7), suspends or revokes the person's driver's license on receipt of a record of a conviction or a forfeiture of bail; or

(2) receives a record of a guilty plea of the person entered for an offense for which the department would be required to suspend the driver's license of a person convicted of the offense.

(b) The department, unless otherwise required by law, may not suspend a registration under Subsection (a) if the person files and maintains evidence of financial responsibility with the department for each motor vehicle registered in the name of the person.

(c) This section does not apply to a suspension of a driver's license for an offense under Chapter 106, Alcoholic Beverage Code, other than an offense that includes confinement as an authorized sanction.

(Enacted by Acts 1995, 74th Leg., ch. 165 (S.B. 971), § 1, effective September 1, 1995; am. Acts 1997, 75th Leg., ch. 165 (S.B. 898), § 30.128, effective September 1, 1997; am. Acts 1997, 75th Leg., ch. 1013 (S.B. 35), § 30, effective September 1, 1997; am. Acts 2005, 79th Leg., ch. 728 (H.B. 2018), § 20.006, effective September 1, 2005.)

## Sec. 601.341. Evidence of Financial Responsibility; Termination of Penalty.

Unless a person whose driver's license or vehicle registration has been suspended or revoked under this subchapter files and maintains evidence of financial responsibility with the department:

(1) the suspension or revocation may not be terminated;

(2) the driver's license or registration may not be renewed;

(3) a new driver's license may not be issued to the person; or

(4) a motor vehicle may not be registered in the name of the person.

(Enacted by Acts 1995, 74th Leg., ch. 165 (S.B. 971), § 1, effective September 1, 1995; am. Acts 1997, 75th Leg., ch. 165 (S.B. 898), § 30.129, effective September 1, 1997.)

## Sec. 601.342. Evidence of Financial Responsibility Following Suspension or Revocation of Nonresident's Operating Privilege.

The department may not terminate the suspension or revocation of a nonresident's operating privilege suspended or revoked under this sub-chapter because of a conviction, forfeiture of bail, or guilty plea unless the person files and maintains evidence of financial responsibility with the department.

(Enacted by Acts 1995, 74th Leg., ch. 165 (S.B. 971), § 1, effective September 1, 1995; am. Acts 1997, 75th Leg., ch. 165 (S.B. 898), § 30.129, effective September 1, 1997.)

**Secs. 601.343 to 601.370 [Reserved for expansion].**

## SUBCHAPTER L
## EFFECT OF SUSPENSION

### Sec. 601.371.   Operation of Motor Vehicle in Violation of Suspension; Offense.

(a) A person commits an offense if the person, during a period that a suspension of the person's vehicle registration is in effect under this chapter, knowingly permits a motor vehicle owned by the person to be operated on a highway.

(b) It is an affirmative defense to prosecution under this section that the person had not received notice of a suspension order concerning the person's vehicle registration. For purposes of this subsection, notice is presumed to be received if the notice was mailed in accordance with this chapter to the last known address of the person as shown by department records.

(c) Except as provided by Subsection (d), an offense under this section is a misdemeanor punishable by:

(1) a fine of not less than $100 or more than $500; and

(2) confinement in county jail for a term of not less than 72 hours or more than six months.

(d) If it is shown on the trial of an offense under this section that the person has previously been convicted of an offense under this section, the offense is punishable as a Class A misdemeanor.

(e) In this section, a conviction for an offense that involves operation of a motor vehicle after August 31, 1987, is a final conviction, whether the sentence for the conviction is imposed or probated.

(Enacted by Acts 1995, 74th Leg., ch. 165 (S.B. 971), § 1, effective September 1, 1995; am. Acts 2003, 78th Leg., ch. 855 (S.B. 582), § 2, effective September 1, 2003.)

### Sec. 601.372.   Return of Driver's License and Vehicle Registration to Department.

(a) The department shall give written notice of a suspension of a driver's license and vehicle registration to a person who is required to maintain a motor vehicle liability insurance policy or bond under this chapter and whose policy or bond is canceled or terminated or who does not provide other evidence of financial responsibility on the request of the department.

(b) The notice must be by personal delivery to the person or by deposit in the United States mail addressed to the person at the last address supplied to the department by the person. Notice by mail is presumed to be received on the 10th day after the date the notice is mailed.

(c) The department by rule may require the person to send the person's driver's license and vehicle registrations not later than the 10th day after the date the person receives written notice from the department.

(d) Proof of the notice may be made by the certificate of a department employee stating that:

(1) the notice was prepared in the regular course of business and placed in the United States mail as part of the regular organized activity of the department; or

(2) the employee delivered the notice in person.

(e) A certificate under Subsection (d)(2) must specify the name of the person to whom the notice was given and the time, place, and manner of the delivery of the notice.

(Enacted by Acts 1995, 74th Leg., ch. 165 (S.B. 971), § 1, effective September 1, 1995; am. Acts 1999, 76th Leg., ch. 884 (H.B. 2032), § 3, effective September 1, 1999.)

### Sec. 601.373.   Failure to Return Driver's License or Vehicle Registration; Offense.

(a) A person commits an offense if the person wilfully fails to send a driver's license or vehicle registration as required by Section 601.372. An offense under this subsection is a misdemeanor punishable by a fine not to exceed $200.

(b) The department may direct a department employee to obtain and send to the department the driver's license and vehicle registration of a person who fails to send the person's license or registration in accordance with Section 601.372. The director of the department or the person designated by the director may file a complaint against a person for an offense under Subsection (a).

(Enacted by Acts 1995, 74th Leg., ch. 165 (S.B. 971), § 1, effective September 1, 1995; am. Acts 1999, 76th Leg., ch. 884 (H.B. 2032), § 4, effective September 1, 1999.)

### Sec. 601.374. Transfer of Vehicle Registration Prohibited.

(a) An owner whose vehicle registration has been suspended under this chapter may not:

(1) transfer the registration unless the transfer is authorized under Subsection (b); or

(2) register in another name the motor vehicle to which the registration applies.

(b) The department may authorize the transfer of vehicle registration if the department is satisfied that the transfer is proposed in good faith and not to defeat the purposes of this chapter.

(c) This section does not affect the rights of a conditional vendor or lessor of, or person with a security interest in, a motor vehicle owned by a person who is subject to this section if the vendor, lessor, or secured party is not the registered owner of the vehicle.

(Enacted by Acts 1995, 74th Leg., ch. 165 (S.B. 971), § 1, effective September 1, 1995.)

### Sec. 601.375. Cooperation with Other State or Canada.

(a) The department shall send a certified copy of the record of the department's action suspending a nonresident's operating privilege under Subchapter F or under Sections 601.332, 601.333, and 601.334 to the official in charge of issuing driver's licenses and vehicle registrations of the state or province of Canada in which the nonresident resides.

(b) Subsection (a) applies only if the law of the other state or the province provides for action similar to the action required by Section 601.009.

(Enacted by Acts 1995, 74th Leg., ch. 165 (S.B. 971), § 1, effective September 1, 1995.)

### Sec. 601.376. Reinstatement Fee.

(a) A driver's license, vehicle registration, or nonresident's operating privilege that has been suspended under this chapter may not be reinstated and a new license or registration may not be issued to the holder of the suspended license, registration, or privilege until the person:

(1) pays to the department a fee of $100; and

(2) complies with the other requirements of this chapter.

(b) The fee imposed by this section is in addition to other fees imposed by law.

(c) A person is required to pay only one fee under this section, without regard to the number of driver's licenses and vehicle registrations to be reinstated for or issued to the person in connection with the payment.

(Enacted by Acts 1995, 74th Leg., ch. 165 (S.B. 971), § 1, effective September 1, 1995; am. Acts 1999, 76th Leg., ch. 1189 (S.B. 370), § 38, effective September 1, 1999.)

### Secs. 601.377 to 601.400 [Reserved for expansion].

## SUBCHAPTER M
## APPEAL OF DEPARTMENT ACTION

### Sec. 601.401. Department Actions Subject to Review.

(a) An action of the department under this chapter may be appealed, unless:

(1) an order of suspension by the department is based on an existing unsatisfied final judgment rendered against a person by a court in this state arising out of the use of a motor vehicle in this state; or

(2) the suspension is automatic under Section 601.231(a).

(b) To appeal an action of the department, the person must file a petition not later than the 30th day after the date of the action in the county court at law in the county in which the person resides or the county court of the county in which the person resides, if the county does not have a county court at law.

(c) A person who files an appeal under this section shall send a file-stamped copy of the petition by certified mail to the department at the department's headquarters in Austin. The copy must be certified by the clerk of the court in which the petition is filed.

(d) The filing of a petition of appeal as provided by this section stays an order of suspension until the earlier of the 91st day after the date the appeal petition is filed or the date the trial is completed and final judgment is rendered.

(e) On expiration of the stay, the department shall impose the suspension. The stay may not be extended, and an additional stay may not be granted.

(f) A trial on appeal is de novo.

(Enacted by Acts 1995, 74th Leg., ch. 165 (S.B. 971), § 1, effective September 1, 1995; am. Acts

1999, 76th Leg., ch. 1117 (H.B. 3641), § 6, effective September 1, 2000.)

### Sec. 601.402. Time for Appeal [Repealed].

Repealed by Acts 1999, 76th Leg., ch. 1117 (H.B. 3641), § 9, effective September 1, 2000. (Enacted by Acts 1995, 74th Leg., ch. 165 (S.B. 971), § 1, effective September 1, 1995.)

### Sec. 601.403. Trial [Repealed].

Repealed by Acts 1999, 76th Leg., ch. 1117 (H.B. 3641), § 9, effective September 1, 2000. (Enacted by Acts 1995, 74th Leg., ch. 165 (S.B. 971), § 1, effective September 1, 1995.)

### Sec. 601.404. Stay of Act on Appeal [Repealed].

Repealed by Acts 1999, 76th Leg., ch. 1117 (H.B. 3641), § 9, effective September 1, 2000. (Enacted by Acts 1995, 74th Leg., ch. 165 (S.B. 971), § 1, effective September 1, 1995.)

### Sec. 601.405. Filing of Evidence of Financial Responsibility; Effect on Appeal [Repealed].

Repealed by Acts 1999, 76th Leg., ch. 1117 (H.B. 3641), § 9, effective September 1, 2000. (Enacted by Acts 1995, 74th Leg., ch. 165 (S.B. 971), § 1, effective September 1, 1995.)

### Sec. 601.406. Temporary Stay of Departments Order on Filing of Affidavit [Repealed].

Repealed by Acts 1999, 76th Leg., ch. 1117 (H.B. 3641), § 9, effective September 1, 2000. (Enacted by Acts 1995, 74th Leg., ch. 165 (S.B. 971), § 1, effective September 1, 1995.)

### Sec. 601.407. Stay After Plea or Conviction [Repealed].

Repealed by Acts 1999, 76th Leg., ch. 1117 (H.B. 3641), § 9, effective September 1, 2000. (Enacted by Acts 1995, 74th Leg., ch. 165 (S.B. 971), § 1, effective September 1, 1995.)

### Sec. 601.408. Stay After Acquittal or Dismissal [Repealed].

Repealed by Acts 1999, 76th Leg., ch. 1117 (H.B. 3641), § 9, effective September 1, 2000. (Enacted by Acts 1995, 74th Leg., ch. 165 (S.B. 971), § 1, effective September 1, 1995.)

### Sec. 601.409. Maintenance of Evidence of Financial Responsibility [Repealed].

Repealed by Acts 1999, 76th Leg., ch. 1117 (H.B. 3641), § 9, effective September 1, 2000. (Enacted by Acts 1995, 74th Leg., ch. 165 (S.B. 971), § 1, effective September 1, 1995.)

### Sec. 601.410. Limit on Courts [Repealed].

Repealed by Acts 1999, 76th Leg., ch. 1117 (H.B. 3641), § 9, effective September 1, 2000. (Enacted by Acts 1995, 74th Leg., ch. 165 (S.B. 971), § 1, effective September 1, 1995.)

### Secs. 601.411 to 601.449 [Reserved for expansion].

## SUBCHAPTER N
## FINANCIAL RESPONSIBILITY VERIFICATION PROGRAM

### Sec. 601.450. Feasibility Study [Repealed].

Repealed by Acts 2009, 81st Leg., ch. 933 (H.B. 3097), § 2J.03, effective September 1, 2009 and by Acts 2009, 81st Leg., ch. 1146 (H.B. 2730), § 15A.02, effective September 1, 2009. (Enacted by Acts 2003, 78th Leg., ch. 1325 (H.B. 3588), § 19B.01, effective September 1, 2003.)

### Sec. 601.451. Definition.

In this subchapter, "implementing agencies" means:

(1) the department;

(2) the Texas Department of Motor Vehicles;

(3) the Texas Department of Insurance; and

(4) the Department of Information Resources.

(Enacted by Acts 2005, 79th Leg., ch. 892 (S.B. 1670), § 1, effective September 1, 2005; am. Acts 2009, 81st Leg., ch. 933 (H.B. 3097), § 2J.02, effective September 1, 2009.)

### Sec. 601.452. Implementation of Program; Rules.

(a) The Texas Department of Insurance in consultation with the other implementing agencies shall establish a program for verification of whether owners of motor vehicles have established financial responsibility. The program established must be:

(1) the program most likely to:

(A) reduce the number of uninsured motorists in this state;

(B) operate reliably;

(C) be cost-effective;

(D) sufficiently protect the privacy of the motor vehicle owners;

(E) sufficiently safeguard the security and integrity of information provided by insurance companies;

(F) identify and employ a method of compliance that improves public convenience; and

(G) provide information that is accurate and current; and

(2) capable of being audited by an independent auditor.

(b) The implementing agencies shall jointly adopt rules to administer this subchapter.

(c) The implementing agencies shall convene a working group to facilitate the implementation of the program, assist in the development of rules, and coordinate a testing phase and necessary changes identified in the testing phase. The working group must consist of representatives of the implementing agencies and the insurance industry and technical experts with the skills and knowledge, including knowledge of privacy laws, required to create and maintain the program.

(Enacted by Acts 2005, 79th Leg., ch. 892 (S.B. 1670), § 1, effective September 1, 2005.)

## Sec. 601.453. Agent.

(a) The Texas Department of Insurance in consultation with the other implementing agencies, under a competitive bidding procedure, shall select an agent to develop, implement, operate, and maintain the program.

(b) The implementing agencies shall jointly enter into a contract with the selected agent.

(c) A contract under this section may not have a term of more than five years.

(Enacted by Acts 2005, 79th Leg., ch. 892 (S.B. 1670), § 1, effective September 1, 2005.)

## Sec. 601.454. Information Provided by Insurance Company; Privacy.

(a) Each insurance company providing motor vehicle liability insurance policies in this state shall provide necessary information for those policies to allow the agent to carry out this subchapter, subject to the agent's contract with the implementing agencies and rules adopted under this subchapter.

(b) The agent is entitled only to information that is at that time available from the insurance company and that is determined by the implementing agencies to be necessary to carry out this subchapter.

(c) Information obtained under this subchapter is confidential. The agent:

(1) may use the information only for a purpose authorized under this subchapter;

(2) may not use the information for a commercial purpose; and

(3) on request, and subject to appropriate safeguards to protect the privacy of motor vehicle owners developed by the implementing agencies and the attorney general, may provide the information to the attorney general for the purpose of enforcing child support obligations.

(d) A person commits an offense if the person knowingly uses information obtained under this subchapter for any purpose not authorized under this subchapter. An offense under this subsection is a Class B misdemeanor.

(Enacted by Acts 2005, 79th Leg., ch. 892 (S.B. 1670), § 1, effective September 1, 2005; am. Acts 2009, 81st Leg., ch. 767 (S.B. 865), § 36, effective June 19, 2009.)

## CHAPTERS 602 TO 620 [RESERVED FOR EXPANSION]

## SUBTITLE E VEHICLE SIZE AND WEIGHT

## CHAPTER 621 GENERAL PROVISIONS RELATING TO VEHICLE SIZE AND WEIGHT

### Subchapter A. General Provisions

**Transportation**

## SUBCHAPTER A
## GENERAL PROVISIONS

### Sec. 621.001.  Definitions.

In this chapter:

(1) "Commercial motor vehicle" means a motor vehicle, other than a motorcycle, designed or used for:

(A) the transportation of property; or

(B) delivery purposes.

(2) "Commission" means the Texas Transportation Commission.

(3) "Department" means the Texas Department of Motor Vehicles.

(4) "Director" means the executive director of the Texas Department of Motor Vehicles.

(5) "Motor vehicle" means a vehicle that is self-propelled.

(6) "Semitrailer" means a vehicle without motive power that is designed, or used with a motor vehicle, so that some of its weight and the weight of its load rests on or is carried by the motor vehicle.

(7) "Trailer" means a vehicle without motive power that is:

(A) designed or used to carry property or passengers on its own structure exclusively; and

(B) drawn by a motor vehicle.

(8) "Truck-tractor" means a motor vehicle designed or used primarily for drawing another vehicle:

(A) that is not constructed to carry a load other than a part of the weight of the vehicle and load being drawn; or

(B) that is engaged with a semitrailer in the transportation of automobiles or boats and that transports the automobiles or boats on part of the truck-tractor.

(9) "Vehicle" means a mechanical device, other than a device moved by human power or used exclusively upon stationary rails or tracks, in, on, or by which a person or property can be transported on a public highway. The term includes a motor vehicle, commercial motor vehicle, truck-tractor, trailer, or semitrailer but does not include manufactured housing as defined by Chapter 1201, Occupations Code.

(10) "Single axle weight" means the total weight transmitted to the road by all wheels whose centers may be included between two parallel transverse vertical planes 40 inches apart, extending across the full width of the vehicle.

(11) "Tandem axle weight" means the total weight transmitted to the road by two or more consecutive axles whose centers may be included between parallel transverse vertical planes spaced more than 40 inches and not

more than 96 inches apart, extending across the full width of the vehicle.

(12) "Port of entry" means a place designated by executive order of the president of the United States, by order of the United States secretary of the treasury, or by act of the United States Congress at which a customs officer is authorized to accept entries of merchandise, collect duties, and enforce customs and navigation laws. The term includes a publicly owned or privately owned international port of entry between this state and the United Mexican States.

(13) "Board" means the board of the Texas Department of Motor Vehicles.

(Enacted by Acts 1995, 74th Leg., ch. 165 (S.B. 971), § 1, effective September 1, 1995; am. Acts 2001, 77th Leg., ch. 941 (S.B. 886), § 14, effective September 1, 2001; am. Acts 2001, 77th Leg., ch. 1227 (S.B. 220), § 2, effective September 1, 2001; am. Acts 2003, 78th Leg., ch. 1276 (H.B. 3507), § 14A.835, effective September 1, 2003; am. Acts 2005, 79th Leg., ch. 313 (S.B. 619), § 1, effective September 1, 2005; am. Acts 2011, 82nd Leg., ch. 1345 (S.B. 1420), § 54, effective September 1, 2011.)

### Sec. 621.002. Vehicle Registration Receipt for Certain Heavy Vehicles.

(a) A copy of the registration receipt issued under Section 502.178 for a commercial motor vehicle, truck-tractor, trailer, or semitrailer shall be:

(1) carried on the vehicle when the vehicle is on a public highway; and

(2) presented to an officer authorized to enforce this chapter on request of the officer.

(b) A copy of the registration receipt is:

(1) admissible in evidence in any cause in which the gross registered weight of the vehicle is an issue; and

(2) prima facie evidence of the gross weight for which the vehicle is registered.

(Enacted by Acts 1995, 74th Leg., ch. 165 (S.B. 971), § 1, effective September 1, 1995.)

### Sec. 621.003. Reciprocal Agreement with Another State for Issuance of Permits.

(a) The board by rule may authorize the director to enter into with the proper authority of another state an agreement that authorizes:

(1) the authority of the other state to issue on behalf of the department to the owner or operator of a vehicle, or combination of vehicles, that exceeds the weight or size limits allowed by this state a permit that authorizes the operation or transportation on a highway in this state of the vehicle or combination of vehicles; and

(2) the department to issue on behalf of the authority of the other state to the owner or operator of a vehicle, or combination of vehicles, that exceeds the weight or size limits allowed by that state a permit that authorizes the operation or transportation on a highway of that state of the vehicle or combination of vehicles.

(b) A permit issued by the authority of another state under an agreement entered into under this section has the same validity in this state as a permit issued by the department.

(c) The holder of a permit issued by the authority of another state under an agreement entered into under this section is subject to all applicable laws of this state and rules of the department.

(d) The department may contract with a third party to act as the department's agent in the processing of a permit application and the distribution of a permit issued by the department under this section.

(e) An agreement entered into under this section may provide for a third party to act as the agent of each state in the processing of a permit application and the distribution of a permit issued by a state under this section.

(Enacted by Acts 1995, 74th Leg., ch. 165 (S.B. 971), § 1, effective September 1, 1995; am. Acts 1997, 75th Leg., ch. 515 (S.B. 1631), § 1, effective September 1, 1997; am. Acts 2011, 82nd Leg., ch. 1345 (S.B. 1420), § 55, effective September 1, 2011.)

### Sec. 621.004. Admissibility of Certificate of Vertical Clearance.

In each civil or criminal proceeding in which a violation of this chapter may be an issue, a certificate of the vertical clearance of a structure, including a bridge or underpass, signed by the executive director of the Texas Department of Transportation is admissible in evidence for all purposes.

(Enacted by Acts 1995, 74th Leg., ch. 165 (S.B. 971), § 1, effective September 1, 1995; am. Acts

Transportation

2011, 82nd Leg., ch. 1345 (S.B. 1420), § 56, effective September 1, 2011.)

### Sec. 621.005. Effect of Increased Limits by United States.

If the United States prescribes or adopts vehicle size or weight limits greater than those prescribed by 23 U.S.C. Section 127 on March 18, 1975, for the national system of interstate and defense highways, the increased limits apply to the national system of interstate and defense highways in this state.

(Enacted by Acts 1995, 74th Leg., ch. 165 (S.B. 971), § 1, effective September 1, 1995.)

### Sec. 621.006. Restricted Operation on Certain Holidays.

The commission by rule may impose restrictions on the weight and size of vehicles to be operated on state highways on the following holidays only:

(1) New Year's Day;

(2) Memorial Day;

(3) Independence Day;

(4) Labor Day;

(5) Thanksgiving Day; and

(6) Christmas Day.

(Enacted by Acts 1995, 74th Leg., ch. 165 (S.B. 971), § 1, effective September 1, 1995; am. Acts 2011, 82nd Leg., ch. 1345 (S.B. 1420), § 57, effective September 1, 2011.)

### Sec. 621.007. Evidence of Violation.

(a) In a proceeding in which a violation of a weight restriction under this subtitle may be an issue, a document is admissible as relevant evidence of the violation if:

(1) the document is:

(A) a record kept under Section 621.410; or

(B) a bill of lading, freight bill, weight certification, or similar document that is issued by a person consigning cargo for shipment or engaged in the business of transporting or forwarding cargo; and

(2) the document states:

(A) a gross weight of the vehicle or combination of vehicles and cargo that exceeds a weight restriction under this subtitle; or

(B) a gross weight of the cargo that combined with the empty weight of the vehicle or combination of vehicles exceeds a weight restriction under this subtitle.

(b) This section does not limit the admissibility of any other evidence relating to the violation.

(Enacted by Acts 2001, 77th Leg., ch. 1227 (S.B. 220), § 3, effective September 1, 2001.)

### Sec. 621.008. Rulemaking Authority.

The board may adopt rules necessary to implement and enforce this chapter.

(Enacted by Acts 2011, 82nd Leg., ch. 1345 (S.B. 1420), § 58, effective September 1, 2011.)

### Secs. 621.009 to 621.100 [Reserved for expansion].

## SUBCHAPTER B
## WEIGHT LIMITATIONS

### Sec. 621.101. Maximum Weight of Vehicle or Combination.

(a) A vehicle or combination of vehicles may not be operated over or on a public highway or at a port-of-entry between Texas and the United Mexican States if the vehicle or combination has:

(1) a single axle weight heavier than 20,000 pounds, including all enforcement tolerances;

(2) a tandem axle weight heavier than 34,000 pounds, including all enforcement tolerances;

(3) an overall gross weight on a group of two or more consecutive axles heavier than the weight computed using the following formula and rounding the result to the nearest 500 pounds:

$$W = 500((LN/(N - 1)) + 12N + 36)$$

where:

"W" is maximum overall gross weight on the group;

"L" is distance in feet between the axles of the group that are the farthest apart; and

"N" is number of axles in the group; or

(4) tires that carry a weight heavier than the weight specified and marked on the sidewall of the tire, unless the vehicle is being operated under the terms of a special permit.

(b) Notwithstanding Subsection (a)(3), two consecutive sets of tandem axles may carry a gross load of not more than 34,000 pounds each if the overall distance between the first and last axles of the consecutive sets is 36 feet or more. The overall gross weight on a group of two or more consecutive axles may not be heavier than 80,000 pounds, including all enforcement tolerances, regardless of tire ratings, axle spacing (bridge), and number of axles.

(c) This section does not:

(1) authorize size or weight limits on the national system of interstate and defense highways in this state greater than those permitted under 23 U.S.C. Section 127, as amended;

(2) prohibit the operation of a vehicle or combination of vehicles that could be lawfully operated on a highway or road of this state on December 16, 1974; or

(3) apply to a vehicle or combination of vehicles that operates exclusively:

(A) at a private port of entry;

(B) on private roads associated with the port of entry; and

(C) across a public highway between private roads associated with the port of entry under a contract under Section 623.052.

(Enacted by Acts 1995, 74th Leg., ch. 165 (S.B. 971), § 1, effective September 1, 1995; am. Acts 1999, 76th Leg., ch. 601 (S.B. 749), § 1, effective September 1, 1999; am. Acts 2001, 77th Leg., ch. 941 (S.B. 886), § 15, effective September 1, 2001; am. Acts 2001, 77th Leg., ch. 1227 (S.B. 220), § 4, effective September 1, 2001; am. Acts 2005, 79th Leg., ch. 313 (S.B. 619), § 2, effective September 1, 2005.)

## Sec. 621.102. [2 Versions: As amended by Acts 2011, 82nd Leg., ch. 571] Authority to Set Maximum Weights.

(a) The director may set the maximum single axle weight, tandem axle weight, or gross weight of a vehicle, or maximum single axle weight, tandem axle weight, or gross weight of a combination of vehicles and loads, that may be moved over a state highway or a farm or ranch road if the director finds that heavier maximum weight would rapidly deteriorate or destroy the road or a bridge or culvert along the road. A maximum weight set under this subsection may not exceed the maximum set by statute for that weight.

(b) The director must make the finding under this section on an engineering and traffic investigation and in making the finding shall consider the width, condition, and type of pavement structures and other circumstances on the road.

(c) A maximum weight or load set under this section becomes effective on a highway or road when appropriate signs giving notice of the maximum weight or load are erected on the highway or road.

(d) A vehicle operating under a permit issued under Section 623.011, 623.071, 623.094, 623.121, 623.142, 623.181, 623.192, or 623.212 may operate under the conditions authorized by the permit over a road for which the director has set a maximum weight under this section.

(e) For the purpose of this section, a farm or ranch road is a state highway that is shown in the records of the commission to be a farm-to-market or ranch-to-market road.

(f) This section does not apply to a vehicle delivering groceries, farm products, or liquefied petroleum gas.

(Enacted by Acts 1995, 74th Leg., ch. 165 (S.B. 971), § 1, effective September 1, 1995; am. Acts 1997, 75th Leg., ch. 165 (S.B. 898), § 30.131, effective September 1, 1997; am. Acts 2001, 77th Leg., ch. 920 (S.B. 409), § 19, effective June 14, 2001; am. Acts 2001, 77th Leg., ch. 941 (S.B. 886), § 16, effective September 1, 2001; am. Acts 2003, 78th Leg., ch. 312 (H.B. 3184), §§ 76, 77, effective June 18, 2003; am. Acts 2003, 78th Leg., ch. 1325 (H.B. 3588), §§ 15.73, 15.74, effective June 21, 2003; am. Acts 2011, 82nd Leg., ch. 571 (H.B. 3309), § 1, effective June 17, 2011.)

## Sec. 621.102. [2 Versions: As amended by Acts 2011, 82nd Leg., ch. 1345] Authority to Set Maximum Weights.

(a) The executive director of the Texas Department of Transportation may set the maximum single axle weight, tandem axle weight, or gross weight of a vehicle, or maximum single axle weight, tandem axle weight, or gross weight of a combination of vehicles and loads, that may be moved over a state highway or a farm or ranch road if the executive director finds that heavier maximum weight would rapidly deteriorate or destroy the road or a bridge or culvert along the road. A maximum weight set under this subsection may not exceed the maximum set by statute for that weight.

(b) The executive director of the Texas Department of Transportation must make the finding under this section on an engineering and traffic investigation and in making the finding shall consider the width, condition, and type of pavement structures and other circumstances on the road.

(c) A maximum weight or load set under this section becomes effective on a highway or road when appropriate signs giving notice of the maximum weight or load are erected on the highway or road by the Texas Department of Transportation under order of the commission.

(d) A vehicle operating under a permit issued under Section 623.011, 623.071, 623.094, 623.121, 623.142, 623.181, 623.192, or 623.212

**Transportation**

may operate under the conditions authorized by the permit over a road for which the executive director of the Texas Department of Transportation has set a maximum weight under this section.

(e) For the purpose of this section, a farm or ranch road is a state highway that is shown in the records of the commission to be a farm-to-market or ranch-to-market road.

(f) This section does not apply to a vehicle delivering groceries, farm products, or liquefied petroleum gas.

(Enacted by Acts 1995, 74th Leg., ch. 165 (S.B. 971), § 1, effective September 1, 1995; am. Acts 1997, 75th Leg., ch. 165 (S.B. 898), § 30.131, effective September 1, 1997; am. Acts 2001, 77th Leg., ch. 920 (S.B. 409), § 19, effective June 14, 2001; am. Acts 2001, 77th Leg., ch. 941 (S.B. 886), § 16, effective September 1, 2001; am. Acts 2003, 78th Leg., ch. 312 (H.B. 3184), §§ 76, 77, effective June 18, 2003; am. Acts 2003, 78th Leg., ch. 1325 (H.B. 3588), §§ 15.73, 15.74, effective June 21, 2003; am. Acts 2011, 82nd Leg., ch. 1345 (S.B. 1420), § 59, effective September 1, 2011.)

**Secs. 621.103 to 621.200 [Reserved for expansion].**

## SUBCHAPTER C
## SIZE LIMITATIONS

### Sec. 621.201.    Maximum Width.

(a) The total width of a vehicle operated on a public highway other than a vehicle to which Subsection (b) applies, including a load on the vehicle but excluding any safety device determined by the United States Department of Transportation or the Texas Department of Public Safety to be necessary for the safe and efficient operation of motor vehicles of that type, may not be greater than 102 inches.

(b) The total width of a passenger vehicle and its load may not be greater than eight feet. This subsection does not apply to a motor bus or trolley bus operated exclusively in the territory of a municipality, in suburbs contiguous to the municipality, or in the county in which the municipality is located.

(c) A passenger vehicle may not carry a load extending more than three inches beyond the left side line of its fenders or more than six inches beyond the right side line of its fenders.

(Enacted by Acts 1995, 74th Leg., ch. 165 (S.B. 971), § 1, effective September 1, 1995.)

### Sec. 621.202.    Commission's Authority to Set Maximum Width.

(a) To comply with safety and operational requirements of federal law, the commission by order may set the maximum width of a vehicle, including the load on the vehicle, at eight feet for a designated highway or segment of a highway if the results of an engineering and traffic study, conducted by the Texas Department of Transportation, that includes an analysis of structural capacity of bridges and pavements, traffic volume, unique climatic conditions, and width of traffic lanes support the change.

(b) An order under this section becomes effective on the designated highway or segment when appropriate signs giving notice of the limitations are erected by the Texas Department of Transportation.

(c) This section is intended to comply with the Surface Transportation Assistance Act of 1982 (23 U.S.C.A. Section 101 et seq.) and is conditioned on that Act and federal regulations implementing that Act.

(Enacted by Acts 1995, 74th Leg., ch. 165 (S.B. 971), § 1, effective September 1, 1995; am. Acts 2011, 82nd Leg., ch. 1345 (S.B. 1420), § 60, effective September 1, 2011.)

### Sec. 621.203.    Maximum Length of Motor Vehicle.

(a) A motor vehicle, other than a truck-tractor, may not be longer than 45 feet.

(b) A motor bus as defined by Section 502.001 that is longer than 35 feet but not longer than 45 feet may be operated on a highway if the motor bus is equipped with air brakes and has either three or more axles or a minimum of four tires on the rear axle.

(c) The limitation prescribed by Subsection (a) does not apply to a house trailer or towable recreational vehicle or a combination of a house trailer or towable recreational vehicle and a motor vehicle. A house trailer or towable recreational vehicle and motor vehicle combination may not be longer than 65 feet.

(d) In this section, "house trailer" and "towable recreational vehicle" have the meanings assigned by Section 541.201.

(Enacted by Acts 1995, 74th Leg., ch. 165 (S.B. 971), § 1, effective September 1, 1995; am. Acts

1997, 75th Leg., ch. 1020 (S.B. 343), § 3, effective September 1, 1997.)

### Sec. 621.204. Maximum Length of Semitrailer or Trailer.

(a) A semitrailer that is operated in a truck-tractor and semitrailer combination may not be longer than 59 feet, excluding the length of the towing device.

(b) A semitrailer or trailer that is operated in a truck-tractor, semitrailer, and trailer combination may not be longer than 28-½ feet, excluding the length of the towing device.

(c) The limitations prescribed by this section do not include any safety device determined by regulation of the United States Department of Transportation or by rule of the Department of Public Safety to be necessary for the safe and efficient operation of motor vehicles.

(d) The limitations prescribed by this section do not apply to a semitrailer or trailer that has the dimensions of a semitrailer or trailer, as appropriate, that was being operated lawfully in this state on December 1, 1982.

(Enacted by Acts 1995, 74th Leg., ch. 165 (S.B. 971), § 1, effective September 1, 1995; am. Acts 2001, 77th Leg., ch. 941 (S.B. 886), § 17, effective September 1, 2001.)

### Sec. 621.205. Maximum Length of Vehicle Combinations.

(a) Except as provided by this section, a combination of not more than three vehicles, including a truck and semitrailer, truck and trailer, truck-tractor and semitrailer and trailer, or a truck-tractor and two trailers, may be coupled together if the combination of vehicles, other than a truck-tractor combination, is not longer than 65 feet.

(b) A passenger car or another motor vehicle that has an unloaded weight of less than 2,500 pounds may not be coupled with more than one other vehicle or towing device at one time. This subsection does not apply to the towing of a disabled vehicle to the nearest intake place for repair.

(c) A motor vehicle, including a passenger car, that has an unloaded weight of 2,500 pounds or more may be coupled with a towing device and one other vehicle.

(d) In this section:

(1) "Passenger car" means a motor vehicle designed to transport 10 or fewer persons simultaneously.

(2) "Towing device" means a device used to tow a vehicle behind a motor vehicle by supporting one end of the towed vehicle above the surface of the road and permitting the wheels at the other end of the towed vehicle to remain in contact with the road.

(Enacted by Acts 1995, 74th Leg., ch. 165 (S.B. 971), § 1, effective September 1, 1995.)

### Sec. 621.206. Maximum Extended Length of Load.

(a) A vehicle or combination of vehicles may not carry a load that extends more than three feet beyond its front or, except as permitted by other law, more than four feet beyond its rear.

(b) Subsection (a) does not apply to vehicles collecting garbage, rubbish, refuse, or recyclable materials which are equipped with front-end loading attachments and containers provided that the vehicle is actively engaged in the collection of garbage, rubbish, refuse, or recyclable materials.

(Enacted by Acts 1995, 74th Leg., ch. 165 (S.B. 971), § 1, effective September 1, 1995; am. Acts 1997, 75th Leg., ch. 25 (S.B. 977), § 1, effective September 1, 1997; am. Acts 1997, 75th Leg., ch. 165 (S.B. 898), § 30.132, effective September 1, 1997; am. Acts 2001, 77th Leg., ch. 941 (S.B. 886), § 18, effective September 1, 2001; am. Acts 2001, 77th Leg., ch. 1420 (H.B. 2812), § 19.0065, effective September 1, 2001.)

### Sec. 621.2061. Exception to Maximum Extended Length of Load: Certain Motor Vehicles.

Notwithstanding Section 621.206, a trailer may carry a load that extends more than four feet beyond the rear of the trailer if the load consists of a motor vehicle that:

(1) is designed and intended to be carried at the rear of the trailer;

(2) is used or intended to be used to load or unload a commodity on or off the trailer;

(3) does not extend more than seven feet beyond the rear of the trailer; and

(4) complies with each applicable federal motor carrier safety regulation.

(Enacted by Acts 1997, 75th Leg., ch. 25 (S.B. 977), § 2, effective September 1, 1997.)

### Sec. 621.207. Maximum Height.

(a) A vehicle and its load may not be higher than 14 feet.

(b) The operator of a vehicle that is higher than 13 feet 6 inches shall ensure that the vehicle will pass through each vertical clearance of a structure in its path without touching the structure.

(c) Any damage to a bridge, underpass, or similar structure that is caused by the height of a vehicle is the responsibility of the owner of the vehicle.

(Enacted by Acts 1995, 74th Leg., ch. 165 (S.B. 971), § 1, effective September 1, 1995.)

**Secs. 621.208 to 621.300 [Reserved for expansion].**

### SUBCHAPTER D
### LOCAL REGULATIONS

### Sec. 621.301. County's Authority to Set Maximum Weights.

(a) The commissioners court of a county may establish load limits for any county road or bridge only with the concurrence of the Texas Department of Transportation. A load limit shall be deemed concurred with by the Texas Department of Transportation 30 days after the county submits to the Texas Department of Transportation the load limit accompanied by supporting documentation and calculations reviewed and sealed by an engineer licensed in this state, though the Texas Department of Transportation may review the load limit and withdraw concurrence at any time after the 30-day period.

(b) The commissioners court may limit the maximum weights to be moved on or over a county road, bridge, or culvert by exercising its authority under this subsection in the same manner and under the same conditions provided by Section 621.102 for the commission to limit maximum weights on highways and roads to which that section applies.

(c) The commissioners court shall record an action under Subsection (b) in its minutes.

(d) A maximum weight set under this section becomes effective on a road when appropriate signs giving notice of the maximum weight are erected by the Texas Department of Transportation on the road under order of the commissioners court.

(e) A vehicle operating under a permit issued under Section 623.011, 623.071, 623.094, 623.121, 623.142, 623.181, 623.192, or 623.212 may operate under the conditions authorized by the permit over a road for which the commissioners court has set a maximum weight under this section.

(Enacted by Acts 1995, 74th Leg., ch. 165 (S.B. 971), § 1, effective September 1, 1995; am. Acts 2001, 77th Leg., ch. 941 (S.B. 886), § 19, effective September 1, 2001; am. Acts 2001, 77th Leg., ch. 1227 (S.B. 220), § 5, effective September 1, 2001; am. Acts 2011, 82nd Leg., ch. 1345 (S.B. 1420), § 61, effective September 1, 2011.)

### Sec. 621.302. Exception to County's Weight Limitations.

A maximum weight set under Section 621.301 does not apply to a vehicle delivering groceries or farm products to a destination requiring travel over a road for which the maximum is set.

(Enacted by Acts 1995, 74th Leg., ch. 165 (S.B. 971), § 1, effective September 1, 1995.)

### Sec. 621.303. Municipal Regulation of Loads and Equipment.

The governing body of any municipality may regulate the movement and operation on a public road, other than a state highway in the territory of the municipality, of:

(1) an overweight, oversize, or overlength commodity that cannot reasonably be dismantled; and

(2) superheavy or oversize equipment for the transportation of an overweight, oversize, or overlength commodity that cannot be reasonably dismantled.

(Enacted by Acts 1995, 74th Leg., ch. 165 (S.B. 971), § 1, effective September 1, 1995.)

**Secs. 621.304 to 621.350 [Reserved for expansion].**

### SUBCHAPTER E
### FEES

### Sec. 621.351. Escrow Account for Prepayment of Permit Fees.

(a) The department may establish one or more escrow accounts in the state highway fund for the prepayment of a fee for a permit issued by the department that authorizes the operation of a vehicle and its load or a combination of vehicles and load exceeding size or weight limitations.

(b) The fees and any fees established by the department for the administration of this section shall be administered in accordance with an agreement containing terms and conditions agreeable to the department.

(c) The department shall deposit each fee established under this section to the credit of the

state highway fund. The fees may be appropriated only to the department for purposes of administering this section.
(Enacted by Acts 1995, 74th Leg., ch. 165 (S.B. 971), § 1, effective September 1, 1995.)

## Sec. 621.352. Fees for Permits Issued Under Reciprocal Agreement.

(a) The board by rule may establish fees for the administration of Section 621.003 in an amount that, when added to the other fees collected by the department, does not exceed the amount sufficient to recover the actual cost to the department of administering that section. An administrative fee collected under this section shall be sent to the comptroller for deposit to the credit of the state highway fund and may be appropriated only to the department for the administration of Section 621.003.

(b) A permit fee collected by the department under Section 621.003 for another state shall be sent to the comptroller for deposit to the credit of the permit distributive account in the general revenue fund. The comptroller shall distribute money in the permit distributive account only to the proper authorities of other states and only as directed by the department.
(Enacted by Acts 1995, 74th Leg., ch. 165 (S.B. 971), § 1, effective September 1, 1995; am. Acts 1997, 75th Leg., ch. 1423 (H.B. 2841), § 18.12, effective September 1, 1997; am. Acts 2011, 82nd Leg., ch. 1345 (S.B. 1420), § 62, effective September 1, 2011.)

## Sec. 621.353. Distribution of Fee for Permit for Excess Weight.

(a) The comptroller shall send $50 of each base fee collected under Section 623.011 for an excess weight permit to the counties of the state, with each county receiving an amount determined according to the ratio of the total number of miles of county roads maintained by the county to the total number of miles of county roads maintained by all of the counties of this state. The comptroller shall deposit $40 of each base fee, plus each fee collected under Section 623.0112, to the credit of the state highway fund. Money deposited to the credit of that fund under this subsection may be appropriated only to the department to administer this section and Sections 623.011, 623.0111, and 623.0112.

(b) The comptroller shall send the amount due each county under Subsection (a) to the county treasurer or officer performing the function of that office at least twice each fiscal year.

(c) The comptroller shall send each fee collected under Section 623.0111 for an excess weight permit to the counties designated on the application for the permit, with each county shown on the application receiving an amount determined according to the ratio of the total number of miles of county roads maintained by the county to the total number of miles of county roads maintained by all of the counties designated on the application.

(d) The county treasurer or officer shall deposit amounts received under this section to the credit of the county road and bridge fund. Money deposited to the credit of that fund under this subsection may be used only for a purpose authorized by Section 256.001(a).
(Enacted by Acts 1995, 74th Leg., ch. 165 (S.B. 971), § 1, effective September 1, 1995; am. Acts 1997, 75th Leg., ch. 165 (S.B. 898), § 30.133(a), effective September 1, 1997; am. Acts 1997, 75th Leg., ch. 1423 (H.B. 2841), § 18.13, effective September 1, 1997; am. Acts 2007, 80th Leg., ch. 1396 (H.B. 2093), § 2, effective September 1, 2007; am. Acts 2011, 82nd Leg., ch. 700 (H.B. 441), § 3, effective September 1, 2011.)

## Sec. 621.354. Disposition of Fees for Permit for Movement of Cylindrical Hay Bales.

The department shall deposit each fee collected under Section 623.017 in the state treasury to the credit of the state highway fund.
(Enacted by Acts 1995, 74th Leg., ch. 165 (S.B. 971), § 1, effective September 1, 1995.)

## Sec. 621.355. Distribution of Fees for Registration of Additional Weight.

(a) If an operator or owner is required to pay for registration of additional weight under Section 621.406 in a county other than the county in which the owner resides, the assessor-collector of the county in which the payment is made shall send the amount collected to the department for deposit to the credit of the state highway fund.

(b) The department shall send the county's share of the amount collected under Section 621.406 to the county in which the owner resides.
(Enacted by Acts 1995, 74th Leg., ch. 165 (S.B. 971), § 1, effective September 1, 1995.)

## Sec. 621.356. Form of Payment.

The board may adopt rules prescribing the method for payment of a fee for a permit issued by the department that authorizes the operation

Transportation

of a vehicle and its load or a combination of vehicles and load exceeding size or weight limitations. The rules may:

(1) authorize the use of electronic funds transfer or a credit card issued by:

(A) a financial institution chartered by a state or the federal government; or

(B) a nationally recognized credit organization approved by the board; and

(2) require the payment of a discount or service charge for a credit card payment in addition to the fee.

(Enacted by Acts 1997, 75th Leg., ch. 515 (S.B. 1631), § 2, effective September 1, 1997; am. Acts 2011, 82nd Leg., ch. 1345 (S.B. 1420), § 63, effective September 1, 2011.)

**Secs. 621.357 to 621.400 [Reserved for expansion].**

## SUBCHAPTER F
## ENFORCEMENT

### Sec. 621.401. Definition.

In this subchapter, "weight enforcement officer" means:

(1) a license and weight inspector of the Department of Public Safety;

(2) a highway patrol officer;

(3) a sheriff or sheriff's deputy;

(4) a municipal police officer in a municipality with a population of:

(A) 100,000 or more; or

(B) 74,000 or more in a county with a population of more than 1.5 million;

(5) a police officer certified under Section 644.101; or

(6) a constable or deputy constable designated under Section 621.4015.

(Enacted by Acts 1995, 74th Leg., ch. 165 (S.B. 971), § 1, effective September 1, 1995; am. Acts 1997, 75th Leg., ch. 364 (S.B. 1828), § 3, effective May 27, 1997; am. Acts 1999, 76th Leg., ch. 62 (S.B. 1368), § 17.09, effective September 1, 1999; am. Acts 1999, 76th Leg., ch. 1523 (S.B. 844), § 1, effective September 1, 1999; am. Acts 2005, 79th Leg., ch. 931 (H.B. 602), § 1, effective June 18, 2005.)

### Sec. 621.4015. Designation by Commissioners Court.

(a) A county commissioners court may designate a constable or deputy constable of the county as a weight enforcement officer in a county:

(1) that is a county with a population of 1.5 million or more and is within 200 miles of an international border; or

(2) that is adjacent to a county with a population of 3.3 million or more; and

(3) in which a planned community is located that has 20,000 or more acres of land, that was originally established under the Urban Growth and New Community Development Act of 1970 (42 U.S.C. Section 4501 et seq.), and that is subject to restrictive covenants containing ad valorem or annual variable budget based assessments on real property.

(b) A constable or deputy constable designated under this section shall be subject to the requirements of Subchapter C, Chapter 644, Transportation Code.

(Enacted by Acts 2005, 79th Leg., ch. 931 (H.B. 602), § 2, effective June 18, 2005; am. Acts 2011, 82nd Leg., ch. 1163 (H.B. 2702), § 175, effective September 1, 2011.)

### Sec. 621.402. Weighing Loaded Vehicle.

(a) A weight enforcement officer who has reason to believe that the single axle weight, tandem axle weight, or gross weight of a loaded motor vehicle is unlawful may:

(1) weigh the vehicle using portable or stationary scales furnished or approved by the Department of Public Safety; or

(2) require the vehicle to be weighed by a public weigher.

(b) The officer may require that the vehicle be driven to the nearest available scales.

(c) A noncommissioned employee of the Department of Public Safety who is certified for the purpose by the public safety director and who is supervised by an officer of the Department of Public Safety may, in a port of entry or at a commercial motor vehicle inspection site, weigh a vehicle, require the vehicle to be weighed, or require a vehicle to be driven to the nearest scale under Subsections (a) and (b).

(d) Prior to assessment of a penalty for weight which exceeds the maximum allowable axle weights, the owner or operator is authorized to shift the load to reduce or eliminate such excess axle weight penalties as long as no part of the shipment is removed.

(Enacted by Acts 1995, 74th Leg., ch. 165 (S.B. 971), § 1, effective September 1, 1995; am. Acts 2001, 77th Leg., ch. 737 (S.B. 888), § 1, effective September 1, 2001; am. Acts 2001, 77th Leg., ch.

941 (S.B. 886), § 20, effective September 1, 2001; am. Acts 2003, 78th Leg., ch. 1275 (H.B. 3506), § 2(136), effective September 1, 2003; am. Acts 2007, 80th Leg., ch. 12 (S.B. 330), § 1, effective April 23, 2007.)

### Sec. 621.403. Unloading Vehicle If Gross Weight Exceeded.

(a) If the gross weight of a motor vehicle weighed under Section 621.402 is heavier than the weight equal to the maximum gross weight authorized by law for that vehicle plus a tolerance allowance equal to five percent of that maximum weight, the weight enforcement officer shall require the operator or owner of the vehicle to unload a part of the load necessary to decrease the gross weight of the vehicle to a gross weight that is not heavier than the weight equal to the vehicle's maximum gross weight plus the applicable tolerance allowance.

(b) The operator or owner of the vehicle immediately shall unload the vehicle to the extent necessary to reduce the gross weight as required by Subsection (a), and the vehicle may not be operated further over a public highway or road of this state until the gross weight has been reduced as required by Subsection (a).

(Enacted by Acts 1995, 74th Leg., ch. 165 (S.B. 971), § 1, effective September 1, 1995.)

### Sec. 621.404. Unloading Vehicle If Axle Load Exceeded.

(a) If the axle weight of a motor vehicle weighed under Section 621.402 is heavier than the maximum axle weight authorized by law for the vehicle plus a tolerance allowance equal to five percent of that maximum weight, the weight enforcement officer shall require the operator or owner of the vehicle to rearrange the vehicle's cargo, if possible, to bring the vehicle's axles within the maximum axle weight allowed by law for that vehicle. If the requirement cannot be satisfied by rearrangement of cargo, a part of the vehicle's load shall be unloaded to decrease the axle weight to a weight that is not heavier than the maximum axle weight allowed by law for the vehicle plus the applicable tolerance allowance.

(b) The vehicle may not be operated further over the public highways or roads of the state until the axle weight of the vehicle has been reduced as required by Subsection (a).

(Enacted by Acts 1995, 74th Leg., ch. 165 (S.B. 971), § 1, effective September 1, 1995; am. Acts 2001, 77th Leg., ch. 941 (S.B. 886), § 21, effective September 1, 2001.)

### Sec. 621.405. Unloading Exceptions.

(a) The operator or owner of a vehicle is not required to unload any part of the vehicle's load under Section 621.403 or 621.404 if the vehicle is:

(1) a motor vehicle loaded with timber, pulp wood, or agricultural products in their natural state being transported from the place of production to the place of marketing or first processing; or

(2) a vehicle crossing a highway as provided by Subchapter C, Chapter 623.

(b) The operator of a motor vehicle may proceed to the vehicle's destination without unloading the vehicle as required by Section 621.403 or 621.404 if the vehicle is loaded with livestock.

(Enacted by Acts 1995, 74th Leg., ch. 165 (S.B. 971), § 1, effective September 1, 1995; am. Acts 2001, 77th Leg., ch. 941 (S.B. 886), § 22, effective September 1, 2001.)

### Sec. 621.406. Additional Gross Weight Registration.

(a) If the gross weight of the motor vehicle is not heavier than the maximum gross weight allowed for the vehicle but is heavier than the registered gross weight for the vehicle, the weight enforcement officer shall require the operator or owner of the vehicle to apply to the nearest available county assessor-collector to increase the gross weight for which the vehicle is registered to a weight equal to or heavier than the gross weight of the vehicle before the operator or owner may proceed.

(b) The vehicle may not be operated further over the public highways or roads of the state until the registered gross weight of the vehicle has been increased as required by Subsection (a) unless the load consists of livestock or perishable merchandise, in which event the operator or owner may proceed with the vehicle in the direction of the vehicle's destination to the nearest practical location at which the vehicle's load can be protected from damage or destruction before increasing the registered weight.

(c) If an operator or owner is found to be carrying a load that is heavier than the load allowed for the registered gross weight of the vehicle, the operator or owner shall pay for the registration of the additional weight for the entire period for which the vehicle is registered without regard to whether the owner or operator has been carrying similar loads from the date of purchase of the vehicle's current license registration for that registration period.

(Enacted by Acts 1995, 74th Leg., ch. 165 (S.B. 971), § 1, effective September 1, 1995.)

### Sec. 621.407.  Forms; Accounting Procedures.

The department shall prescribe all forms and accounting procedures necessary to carry out Sections 621.401—621.406.

(Enacted by Acts 1995, 74th Leg., ch. 165 (S.B. 971), § 1, effective September 1, 1995.)

### Sec. 621.408.  Powers of Weight Enforcement Officers.

(a) Except for the authority granted to a port-of-entry supervisor or inspector by Section 621.409, weight enforcement officers have exclusive authority to enforce this subchapter in any area of this state, including all ports of entry between Texas and the United Mexican States.

(b) If a noncommissioned employee weighs a vehicle under Section 621.402 and determines that an enforcement action, such as the issuance of a citation, is warranted, the employee may take enforcement action only if the employee is under the supervision of an officer of the Department of Public Safety.

(Enacted by Acts 1995, 74th Leg., ch. 165 (S.B. 971), § 1, effective September 1, 1995; am. Acts 1999, 76th Leg., ch. 601 (S.B. 749), § 2, effective September 1, 1999; am. Acts 1999, 76th Leg., ch. 1523 (S.B. 844), § 2, effective September 1, 1999; am. Acts 2001, 77th Leg., ch. 737 (S.B. 888), § 2, effective September 1, 2001; am. Acts 2005, 79th Leg., ch. 313 (S.B. 619), § 3, effective September 1, 2005.)

### Sec. 621.409.  Weighing of Loaded Vehicles by Port-of-Entry Supervisors, Inspectors, or Weight Enforcement Officers.

(a) A port-of-entry supervisor, an inspector employed by the Alcoholic Beverage Commission, or a weight enforcement officer who has reason to believe that the axle or gross weight of a loaded motor vehicle is unlawful may weigh the vehicle using portable or stationary scales furnished or approved by the Department of Public Safety.

(b) If the vehicle exceeds the maximum gross weight authorized by law, plus the tolerance allowance provided by Section 621.403, the supervisor, inspector, or weight enforcement officer may prohibit the vehicle from proceeding farther into the state.

(Enacted by Acts 1995, 74th Leg., ch. 165 (S.B. 971), § 1, effective September 1, 1995; am. Acts 1997, 75th Leg., ch. 364 (S.B. 1828), § 4, effective May 27, 1997; am. Acts 2001, 77th Leg., ch. 941 (S.B. 886), § 23, effective September 1, 2001.)

### Sec. 621.410.  Weight Record.

(a) This section applies only to cargo other than timber or another agricultural product in its natural state transported by a commercial motor vehicle.

(b) A person who weighs cargo before or after unloading shall keep a written record, in the form prescribed by the department, containing the information required by Subsection (c).

(c) A record under this section must state:

(1) the origin, weight, and composition of the cargo;

(2) the date of loading or unloading, as applicable;

(3) the name and address of the shipper;

(4) the total number of axles on the vehicle or combination of vehicles transporting the cargo;

(5) an identification number of the vehicle or other identification of the vehicle required by department rules; and

(6) any other information required by the department.

(d) A person required to keep a record under this section shall keep the record for not less than 180 days after the date it is created. The person shall make the record available to inspection and copying by a weight enforcement officer on demand.

(e) This section does not apply to a vehicle that:

(1) transports material regulated under Section 623.161;

(2) is weighed by a weight enforcement officer;

(3) is weighed on scales owned by the state or a political subdivision of the state; or

(4) is weighed on scales owned by an enterprise principally engaged in the retail sale of motor fuels to the general public.

(Enacted by Acts 2001, 77th Leg., ch. 1227 (S.B. 220), § 6, effective September 1, 2001; am. Acts 2003, 78th Leg., ch. 256 (H.B. 1733), § 1, effective June 18, 2003.)

Secs. 621.411 to 621.500 [Reserved for expansion].

## SUBCHAPTER G
## OFFENSES AND PENALTIES

### Sec. 621.501. Failure to Carry or Present Vehicle License Receipt.

(a) A person commits an offense if the person fails in violation of Section 621.002 to carry or present a vehicle registration receipt.

(b) An offense under this section is a misdemeanor punishable by a fine not to exceed $200. (Enacted by Acts 1995, 74th Leg., ch. 165 (S.B. 971), § 1, effective September 1, 1995.)

### Sec. 621.502. Prohibitions on Size and Weight; Restrictions on Construction and Equipment.

(a) A person may not operate or move a vehicle on a highway if:

(1) the vehicle's size is larger than the applicable maximum size authorized for that vehicle by this subtitle;

(2) the vehicle's single axle weight, tandem axle weight, or gross weight is greater than the applicable weight authorized for that vehicle by this subtitle; or

(3) the vehicle is not constructed or equipped as required by this subtitle.

(b) The owner of a vehicle the size of which or the weight, axle load, or wheel load of which is greater than the applicable maximum size, weight, or load authorized for that vehicle by this subtitle or a vehicle that is not constructed or equipped as required by this chapter may not cause or allow the vehicle to be operated or moved on a highway.

(c) A person may not transport on a vehicle a load the size or weight of which is more than the applicable maximum size, weight, or load authorized for that vehicle by this subtitle.

(d) Intent to operate a vehicle at a weight that is heavier than the weight authorized by a permit issued under Section 623.011 is presumed if:

(1) the vehicle is operated at a weight that is heavier than the applicable weight plus the tolerance allowance provided by Section 623.011(a); and

(2) a permit to operate at that weight has not been issued for the vehicle.

(Enacted by Acts 1995, 74th Leg., ch. 165 (S.B. 971), § 1, effective September 1, 1995; am. Acts 2001, 77th Leg., ch. 941 (S.B. 886), § 24, effective September 1, 2001.)

### Sec. 621.503. Prohibition of Loading More Than Weight Limitation.

(a) A person may not load, or cause to be loaded, a vehicle for operation on a public highway of this state that exceeds the weight limitations for operation of that vehicle provided by Section 621.101.

(b) Intent to violate a limitation is presumed if the weight of the loaded vehicle is heavier than the applicable axle or gross weight limit by 15 percent or more.

(c) This section does not apply to the loading of an agricultural or a forestry commodity before the commodity is changed in processing from its natural state.

(Enacted by Acts 1995, 74th Leg., ch. 165 (S.B. 971), § 1, effective September 1, 1995; am. Acts 1997, 75th Leg., ch. 364 (S.B. 1828), § 5, effective May 27, 1997; am. Acts 2001, 77th Leg., ch. 941 (S.B. 886), § 25, effective September 1, 2001.)

### Sec. 621.504. Bridge or Underpass Clearance.

A person may not operate or attempt to operate a vehicle over or on a bridge or through an underpass or similar structure unless the height of the vehicle, including load, is less than the vertical clearance of the structure as shown by the records of the Texas Department of Transportation.

(Enacted by Acts 1995, 74th Leg., ch. 165 (S.B. 971), § 1, effective September 1, 1995; am. Acts 2011, 82nd Leg., ch. 1345 (S.B. 1420), § 64, effective September 1, 2011.)

### Sec. 621.505. Maximum Size and Weight of Containers [Repealed].

Repealed by Acts 2001, 77th Leg., ch. 941 (S.B. 886), § 44, effective September 1, 2001.
(Enacted by Acts 1995, 74th Leg., ch. 165 (S.B. 971), § 1, effective September 1, 1995.)

### Sec. 621.506. Offense of Operating or Loading Overweight Vehicle; Penalty; Defense.

(a) A person commits an offense if the person:

(1) operates a vehicle or combination of vehicles in violation of Section 621.101, 622.012, 622.031, 622.133, 622.953, or 623.162; or

(2) loads a vehicle or causes a vehicle to be loaded in violation of Section 621.503.

(b) An offense under this section is a misdemeanor punishable:

(1) by a fine of not less than $100 and not more than $150;

(2) on conviction of an offense involving a vehicle having a single axle weight, tandem axle weight, or gross weight that is more than 5,000 but not more than 10,000 pounds heavier than the vehicle's allowable weight, by a fine of not less than $300 or more than $500;

(3) on conviction of an offense involving a vehicle having a single axle weight, tandem axle weight, or gross weight that is more than 10,000 pounds heavier than the vehicle's allowable weight, by a fine of not less than $500 or more than $1,000; or

(4) on conviction before the first anniversary of the date of a previous conviction under this section, by a fine in an amount that is twice the amount specified by Subdivision (1), (2), or (3).

(c) On conviction of a violation of an axle weight limitation, the court may assess a fine less than the applicable minimum amount prescribed by Subsection (b) if the court finds that when the violation occurred:

(1) the vehicle was registered to carry the maximum gross weight authorized for that vehicle under Section 621.101; and

(2) the gross weight of the vehicle did not exceed that maximum gross weight.

(d) A judge or justice shall promptly report to the Department of Public Safety each conviction obtained in the judge's or the justice's court under this section. The Department of Public Safety shall keep a record of each conviction reported to it under this subsection.

(e) If a corporation fails to pay the fine assessed on conviction of an offense under this section, the district or county attorney in the county in which the conviction occurs may file suit against the corporation to collect the fine.

(f) A justice or municipal court has jurisdiction of an offense under this section.

(g) Except as provided by Subsection (h), a governmental entity that collects a fine under this section for an offense involving a vehicle having a single axle weight, tandem axle weight, or gross weight that is more than 5,000 pounds heavier than the vehicle's allowable weight shall send an amount equal to 50 percent of the fine to the comptroller in the manner provided by Subchapter B, Chapter 133, Local Government Code.

(h) If the offense described by Subsection (g) occurred within 20 miles of an international border, the entire amount of the fine shall be deposited for the purposes of road maintenance in:

(1) the municipal treasury, if the fine was imposed by a municipal court; or

(2) the county treasury, if the fine was imposed by a justice court.

(Enacted by Acts 1995, 74th Leg., ch. 165 (S.B. 971), § 1, effective September 1, 1995; am. Acts 1997, 75th Leg., ch. 165 (S.B. 898), § 30.133(b), effective September 1, 1997; am. Acts 1999, 76th Leg., ch. 1101 (H.B. 3467), § 1, effective September 1, 1999; am. Acts 2001, 77th Leg., ch. 941 (S.B. 886), § 26, effective September 1, 2001; am. Acts 2003, 78th Leg., ch. 209 (H.B. 2424), § 78(a), effective January 1, 2004; am. Acts 2005, 79th Leg., ch. 332 (S.B. 737), § 1, effective June 17, 2005.)

### Sec. 621.507. General Offense; Penalty.

(a) A person commits an offense if the person violates a provision of this subtitle for which an offense is not specified by another section of this subtitle.

(b) An offense under this section is a misdemeanor punishable:

(1) by a fine not to exceed $200;

(2) on conviction before the first anniversary of the date of a previous conviction under this section:

(A) by a fine not to exceed $500, by confinement in a county jail for not more than 60 days, or by both the fine and confinement; or

(B) if the convicted person is a corporation, by a fine not to exceed $1,000; or

(3) on a conviction before the first anniversary of the date of a previous conviction under this section that was punishable under Subdivision (2) or this subdivision:

(A) by a fine not to exceed $1,000, by confinement in the county jail for not more than six months, or by both the fine and confinement; or

(B) if the convicted person is a corporation, by a fine not to exceed $2,000.

(Enacted by Acts 1995, 74th Leg., ch. 165 (S.B. 971), § 1, effective September 1, 1995; am. Acts 2001, 77th Leg., ch. 941 (S.B. 886), § 27, effective September 1, 2001.)

### Sec. 621.508. Affirmative Defense for Operating Vehicle over Maximum Allowable Axle Weight.

It is an affirmative defense to prosecution of, or an action under Subchapter F for, the offense of operating a vehicle with a single axle weight or tandem axle weight heavier than the axle weight authorized by law that at the time of the offense the vehicle:

(1) had a single axle weight or tandem axle weight that was not heavier than the axle weight authorized by law plus 12 percent;

(2) was loaded with timber, pulp wood, wood chips, or cotton, livestock, or other agricultural products that are:

(A) in their natural state; and

(B) being transported from the place of production to the place of first marketing or first processing; and

(3) was not being operated on a portion of the national system of interstate and defense highways.

(Enacted by Acts 1995, 74th Leg., ch. 165 (S.B. 971), § 1, effective September 1, 1995; am. Acts 2001, 77th Leg., ch. 941 (S.B. 886), § 28, effective September 1, 2001.)

## Sec. 621.509. Failure to Maintain Weight Record.

(a) A person commits an offense if the person fails to keep a weight record in violation of Section 621.410.

(b) An offense under this section is a Class C misdemeanor.

(Enacted by Acts 2001, 77th Leg., ch. 1227 (S.B. 220), § 7, effective October 1, 2001.)

# CHAPTER 622
# SPECIAL PROVISIONS AND EXCEPTIONS FOR OVERSIZE OR OVERWEIGHT VEHICLES

### Subchapter A. General Provisions

## SUBCHAPTER A
## GENERAL PROVISIONS

## Sec. 622.001. Definitions.

In this chapter:

(1) "Commission" means the Texas Transportation Commission.

(2) "Department" means the Texas Department of Motor Vehicles.

(Enacted by Acts 1995, 74th Leg., ch. 165 (S.B. 971), § 1, effective September 1, 1995; am. Acts 2011, 82nd Leg., ch. 1345 (S.B. 1420), § 65, effective September 1, 2011.)

### Sec. 622.002. Rulemaking Authority.

The board of the department may adopt rules necessary to implement and enforce this chapter. (Enacted by Acts 2011, 82nd Leg., ch. 1345 (S.B. 1420), § 66, effective September 1, 2011.)

### Secs. 622.003 to 622.010 [Reserved for expansion].

## SUBCHAPTER B
## VEHICLES TRANSPORTING READY-MIXED CONCRETE

### Sec. 622.011. Definition; Designation As Perishable.

(a) In this subchapter, "ready-mixed concrete truck" means:

(1) a vehicle designed exclusively to transport or manufacture ready-mixed concrete and includes a vehicle designed exclusively to transport and manufacture ready-mixed concrete; or

(2) a concrete pump truck.

(b) Ready-mixed concrete is a perishable product.

(Enacted by Acts 1995, 74th Leg., ch. 165 (S.B. 971), § 1, effective September 1, 1995; am. Acts 1997, 75th Leg., ch. 165 (S.B. 898), § 30.134(a), effective September 1, 1997.)

### Sec. 622.012. Axle Weight Restrictions.

(a) A ready-mixed concrete truck may be operated on a public highway of this state only if the tandem axle weight is not heavier than 46,000 pounds and the single axle weight is not heavier than 23,000 pounds.

(b) A truck may be operated at a weight that exceeds the maximum single axle or tandem axle weight limitation by not more than 10 percent if the gross weight is not heavier than 69,000 pounds.

(Enacted by Acts 1995, 74th Leg., ch. 165 (S.B. 971), § 1, effective September 1, 1995; am. Acts 1997, 75th Leg., ch. 165 (S.B. 898), § 30.135,

effective September 1, 1997; am. Acts 2001, 77th Leg., ch. 941 (S.B. 886), § 29, effective September 1, 2001.)

### Sec. 622.013. Surety Bond.

(a) The owner of a ready-mixed concrete truck with a tandem axle weight heavier than 34,000 pounds shall before operating the vehicle on a public highway of this state file with the department a surety bond subject to the approval of the Texas Department of Transportation in the principal amount set by the Texas Department of Transportation not to exceed $15,000 for each truck.

(b) The bond must be conditioned that the owner of the truck will pay to the Texas Department of Transportation, within the limit of the bond, any damage to a highway caused by the operation of the truck.

(c) A copy of the bond shall be:

(1) carried on the vehicle when the vehicle is on a public highway; and

(2) presented to an officer authorized to enforce this chapter on request of the officer.

(Enacted by Acts 1995, 74th Leg., ch. 165 (S.B. 971), § 1, effective September 1, 1995; am. Acts 2001, 77th Leg., ch. 941 (S.B. 886), § 30, effective September 1, 2001; am. Acts 2001, 77th Leg., ch. 942 (S.B. 889), § 1, effective September 1, 2001; am. Acts 2011, 82nd Leg., ch. 1345 (S.B. 1420), § 67, effective September 1, 2011.)

### Sec. 622.014. Local Regulation.

(a) The governing body of a county or municipality that determines a public highway under its jurisdiction is insufficient to carry a load authorized by Section 622.012 may prescribe, by order or ordinance, rules governing the operation of a ready-mixed concrete truck over a public highway maintained by the county or municipality.

(b) The rules may include weight limitations on a truck with:

(1) a tandem axle weight that is heavier than 36,000 pounds;

(2) a single axle weight that is heavier than 12,000 pounds; or

(3) a gross weight that is heavier than 48,000 pounds.

(Enacted by Acts 1995, 74th Leg., ch. 165 (S.B. 971), § 1, effective September 1, 1995; am. Acts 2001, 77th Leg., ch. 941 (S.B. 886), § 31, effective September 1, 2001.)

### Sec. 622.015. Local Surety Bond.

The governing body of a county or municipality may require the owner of a ready-mixed concrete truck to file a surety bond in an amount not to exceed $15,000 and conditioned that the owner of the truck will pay to the county or municipality any damage to a highway caused by the operation of the truck with a tandem axle weight that is heavier than 34,000 pounds.

(Enacted by Acts 1995, 74th Leg., ch. 165 (S.B. 971), § 1, effective September 1, 1995; am. Acts 2001, 77th Leg., ch. 941 (S.B. 886), § 32, effective September 1, 2001.)

## Sec. 622.016. Interstate and Defense Highways.

(a) This subchapter does not authorize the operation on the national system of interstate and defense highways in this state of a vehicle of a size or weight greater than that authorized by 23 U.S.C. Section 127, as amended.

(b) If the United States authorizes the operation on the national system of interstate and defense highways of a vehicle of a size or weight greater than that authorized on January 1, 1977, the new limit automatically takes effect on the national system of interstate and defense highways in this state.

(Enacted by Acts 1995, 74th Leg., ch. 165 (S.B. 971), § 1, effective September 1, 1995.)

## Sec. 622.017. Penalties.

(a) [Repealed by Acts 2001, 77th Leg., ch. 941 (S.B. 886), § 44, effective September 1, 2001.]

(b) Except as provided by Subsections (c) and (d), an offense under this section is a misdemeanor punishable:

(1) by a fine of not more than $200;

(2) on conviction within one year after the date of a prior conviction under this section that was punishable under Subdivision (1), by a fine of not more than $500, by confinement in the county jail for not more than 60 days, or by both the fine and the confinement; or

(3) on conviction within one year after the date of a prior conviction under this section that was punishable under Subdivision (2) or this subdivision, by a fine of not more than $1,000, by confinement in the county jail for not more than six months, or by both the fine and the confinement.

(c) [Repealed by Acts 2001, 77th Leg., ch. 941 (S.B. 886), § 44, effective September 1, 2001.]

(d) A person commits an offense if the person fails in violation of Section 622.013(c) to carry or present the copy of the bond filed with the department. An offense under this subsection is a misdemeanor punishable by a fine not to exceed $200.

(Enacted by Acts 1995, 74th Leg., ch. 165 (S.B. 971), § 1, effective September 1, 1995; am. Acts 2001, 77th Leg., ch. 941 (S.B. 886), § 44, effective September 1, 2001; am. Acts 2001, 77th Leg., ch. 942 (S.B. 889), § 2, effective September 1, 2001.)

## Sec. 622.018. Defense to Prosecution: Bond in Effect.

(a) It is a defense to prosecution under Section 622.017 that the person charged produces a surety bond that complies with Section 622.013 that was valid at the time the offense is alleged to have occurred.

(b) If the court verifies the bond produced by the person, the court shall dismiss the charge.

(Enacted by Acts 2001, 77th Leg., ch. 942 (S.B. 889), § 3, effective September 1, 2001.)

## Secs. 622.019 to 622.030 [Reserved for expansion].

## SUBCHAPTER C
## VEHICLES TRANSPORTING MILK

## Sec. 622.031. Length and Axle-Load Restrictions.

A vehicle used exclusively to transport milk may be operated on a public highway of this state only if:

(1) the distance between the front wheel of the forward tandem axle and the rear wheel of the rear tandem axle, measured longitudinally, is 28 feet or more; and

(2) the weight carried on any group of axles is not heavier than 68,000 pounds.

(Enacted by Acts 1995, 74th Leg., ch. 165 (S.B. 971), § 1, effective September 1, 1995; am. Acts 2001, 77th Leg., ch. 941 (S.B. 886), § 33, effective September 1, 2001.)

## Sec. 622.032. Interstate and Defense Highways.

(a) This subchapter does not authorize the operation on the national system of interstate and defense highways in this state of a vehicle of a size or weight greater than that authorized by 23 U.S.C. Section 127, as amended.

(b) If the United States authorizes the operation on the national system of interstate and defense highways of a vehicle of a size or weight greater than that authorized by 23 U.S.C. Section 127 on August 29, 1977, the new limit takes effect

on the national system of interstate and defense highways in this state.
(Enacted by Acts 1995, 74th Leg., ch. 165 (S.B. 971), § 1, effective September 1, 1995.)

## Sec. 622.033.   Penalties [Repealed].

Repealed by Acts 2001, 77th Leg., ch. 941 (S.B. 886), § 44, effective September 1, 2001.
(Enacted by Acts 1995, 74th Leg., ch. 165 (S.B. 971), § 1, effective September 1, 1995.)

## Secs. 622.034 to 622.040 [Reserved for expansion].

## SUBCHAPTER D
## VEHICLES TRANSPORTING TIMBER OR TIMBER PRODUCTS

## Sec. 622.041.   Length Limitation.

(a) A person may operate over a highway or road of this state a vehicle or combination of vehicles that is used exclusively for transporting poles, piling, or unrefined timber from the point of origin of the timber (the forest where the timber is felled) to a wood processing mill if:

(1) the vehicle, or combination of vehicles, is not longer than 90 feet, including the load; and

(2) the distance from the point of origin to the destination or delivery point does not exceed 125 miles.

(b) Subsection (a)(1) does not apply to a truck-tractor or truck-tractor combination transporting poles, piling, or unrefined timber.
(Enacted by Acts 1995, 74th Leg., ch. 165 (S.B. 971), § 1, effective September 1, 1995; am. Acts 2001, 77th Leg., ch. 941 (S.B. 886), § 34, effective September 1, 2001.)

## Sec. 622.042.   Time of Operation; Display of Flag, Cloth, or Strobe Light.

(a) A vehicle subject to this subchapter may be operated only during daytime.

(b) In this section, "daytime" has the meaning assigned by Section 541.401.

(c) A red flag or cloth not less than 12 inches square or a strobe light must be displayed at the rear of the load carried on the vehicle so that the light or the entire area of the flag or cloth is visible to the driver of a vehicle approaching from the rear.
(Enacted by Acts 1995, 74th Leg., ch. 165 (S.B. 971), § 1, effective September 1, 1995; am. Acts 1997, 75th Leg., ch. 165 (S.B. 898), § 30.134(b), effective September 1, 1997; am. Acts 1999, 76th

Leg., ch. 749 (H.B. 1147), § 1, effective September 1, 1999.)

## Sec. 622.043.   Conformity with General Provisions Relating to Vehicle Size and Weight.

The width, height, and gross weight of a vehicle or combination of vehicles subject to this subchapter shall conform to Chapter 621.
(Enacted by Acts 1995, 74th Leg., ch. 165 (S.B. 971), § 1, effective September 1, 1995.)

## Sec. 622.0435.   Vehicles Transporting Raw Wood Products.

(a) The width, height, and gross weight of a vehicle or combination of vehicles subject to this subchapter that is transporting raw wood products shall conform to Chapters 621 and 623, except that a vehicle or combination of vehicles transporting raw wood products that has an outer bridge of 39 feet or more may have a maximum gross weight of 80,000 pounds.

(b) Notwithstanding any other provision of law, Subsection (a) does not authorize the operation of a vehicle or combination of vehicles subject to this subchapter that is transporting raw wood products on a bridge with a load limitation at a weight that exceeds that limitation.
(Enacted by Acts 1997, 75th Leg., ch. 1106 (H.B. 2469), § 1, effective September 1, 1997; am. Acts 2001, 77th Leg., ch. 941 (S.B. 886), § 35, effective September 1, 2001.)

## Sec. 622.044.   Extension of Load Beyond Rear of Vehicle.

Section 621.206(a) does not apply to a vehicle to which this subchapter applies to the extent that section prescribes a limit on the extension of the load beyond the rear of the vehicle.
(Enacted by Acts 1995, 74th Leg., ch. 165 (S.B. 971), § 1, effective September 1, 1995.)

## Sec. 622.045.   Interstate and Defense Highways.

(a) This subchapter does not authorize the operation on the national system of interstate and defense highways in this state of a vehicle of a size or weight greater than those permitted under 23 U.S.C. Section 127, as amended.

(b) If the United States authorizes the operation on the national system of interstate and defense highways of a vehicle of a size or weight greater than those permitted under 23 U.S.C. Section 127 on August 29, 1997, the new limit automatically takes effect on the national system of interstate and defense highways in this state. (Enacted by Acts 2001, 77th Leg., ch. 941 (S.B. 886), § 36, effective September 1, 2001.)

**Secs. 622.046 to 622.050 [Reserved for expansion].**

## SUBCHAPTER E
## VEHICLES TRANSPORTING ELECTRIC POWER TRANSMISSION POLES

### Sec. 622.051.  Length Limitation; Fee.

(a) A person may operate over a highway or road of this state a vehicle or combination of vehicles that is used exclusively for transporting poles required for the maintenance of electric power transmission and distribution lines if:

(1) the vehicle, or combination of vehicles, is not longer than 75 feet, including the load; and

(2) the operator of the vehicle, or combination of vehicles, pays to the department $120 each calendar year.

(b) Subsection (a)(1) does not apply to a truck-tractor or truck-tractor combination transporting poles for the maintenance of electric power transmission or distribution lines.

(Enacted by Acts 1995, 74th Leg., ch. 165 (S.B. 971), § 1, effective September 1, 1995; am. Acts 2001, 77th Leg., ch. 941 (S.B. 886), § 37, effective September 1, 2001.)

### Sec. 622.052.  Time of Operation; Speed; Lighting Requirements.

(a) A vehicle to which this subchapter applies may be operated only:

(1) between sunrise and sunset as defined by law; and

(2) at a speed not to exceed 50 miles per hour.

(b) A vehicle to which this subchapter applies shall display on the extreme end of the load:

(1) two red lamps visible at a distance of at least 500 feet from the rear;

(2) two red reflectors that indicate the maximum width and are visible, when light is insufficient or atmospheric conditions are unfavorable, at all distances from 100 to 600 feet from the rear when directly in front of lawful lower beams of headlamps; and

(3) two red lamps, one on each side, that indicate the maximum overhang and are vis-

ible at a distance of at least 500 feet from the side.

(c) The limitation in Subsection (a)(1) does not apply to a vehicle being operated to prevent interruption or impairment of electric service or to restore electric service that has been interrupted.

(Enacted by Acts 1995, 74th Leg., ch. 165 (S.B. 971), § 1, effective September 1, 1995; am. Acts 1999, 76th Leg., ch. 749 (H.B. 1147), §§ 2, 3, effective September 1, 1999.)

### Sec. 622.053.  Conformity with General Provisions Relating to Vehicle Size and Weight.

The width, height, and gross weight of a vehicle or combination of vehicles to which this subchapter applies shall conform to Chapter 621.

(Enacted by Acts 1995, 74th Leg., ch. 165 (S.B. 971), § 1, effective September 1, 1995.)

**Secs. 622.054 to 622.060 [Reserved for expansion].**

## SUBCHAPTER F
## VEHICLES TRANSPORTING POLES OR PIPE

### Sec. 622.061.  Length Limitation.

(a) A person may operate over a highway or road of this state a vehicle or combination of vehicles exclusively for the transportation of poles or pipe if the vehicle or combination of vehicles is not longer than 65 feet, including the load.

(b) Subsection (a) does not apply to a truck-tractor or truck-tractor combination transporting poles or pipe.

(Enacted by Acts 1995, 74th Leg., ch. 165 (S.B. 971), § 1, effective September 1, 1995; am. Acts 2001, 77th Leg., ch. 941 (S.B. 886), § 38, effective September 1, 2001.)

### Sec. 622.062.  Time of Operation; Lighting Requirements.

(a) A vehicle to which this subchapter applies may be operated only during daytime.

(b) A vehicle to which this subchapter applies shall display on the extreme end of the load:

(1) two red lamps visible at a distance of at least 500 feet from the rear;

(2) two red reflectors that indicate the maximum width and are visible, when light is insufficient or atmospheric conditions are un-

favorable, at all distances from 100 to 600 feet from the rear when directly in front of lawful lower beams of headlamps; and

(3) two red lamps, one on each side, that indicate the maximum overhang and are visible at a distance of at least 500 feet from the side.

(c) In this section, "daytime" has the meaning assigned by Section 541.401.

(Enacted by Acts 1995, 74th Leg., ch. 165 (S.B. 971), § 1, effective September 1, 1995; am. Acts 1997, 75th Leg., ch. 165 (S.B. 898), § 30.134(c), effective September 1, 1997; am. Acts 1997, 75th Leg., ch. 1106 (H.B. 2469), § 2, effective September 1, 1997; am. Acts 1999, 76th Leg., ch. 749 (H.B. 1147), §§ 4, 5, effective September 1, 1999.)

### Sec. 622.063. Conformity with General Provisions Relating to Vehicle Size and Weight.

A vehicle or combination of vehicles to which this subchapter applies shall conform to the length, width, height, and weight requirements of Chapter 621.

(Enacted by Acts 1995, 74th Leg., ch. 165 (S.B. 971), § 1, effective September 1, 1995.)

### Secs. 622.064 to 622.070 [Reserved for expansion].

## SUBCHAPTER G
## SPECIAL MOBILE EQUIPMENT

### Sec. 622.071. Definition.

In this subchapter, "special mobile equipment" has the meaning assigned by Section 541.201.

(Enacted by Acts 1995, 74th Leg., ch. 165 (S.B. 971), § 1, effective September 1, 1995.)

### Sec. 622.072. Identification Markings on Special Mobile Equipment; Offense.

(a) Before the 31st day after the date a person becomes the owner of a unit of special mobile equipment, the person shall mark in a conspicuous place on the main chassis the manufacturer's serial number, an operation identification number recognized by law enforcement agencies, or a company identification number in a manner that is visible from not less than 50 feet.

(b) A person commits an offense if the person:

(1) owns a unit of special mobile equipment; and

(2) fails to mark the unit as provided by this section.

(c) An offense under this section is a misdemeanor punishable by a fine of not less than $10 or more than $100 for each unit.

(Enacted by Acts 1995, 74th Leg., ch. 165 (S.B. 971), § 1, effective September 1, 1995.)

### Sec. 622.073. Transportation of Special Mobile Equipment; Offense.

(a) A person commits an offense if the person transports on a public road or highway a unit of special mobile equipment that is not marked as required by Section 622.072.

(b) Except as provided by Subsection (c), an offense under this section is a misdemeanor punishable by a fine of not less than $25 or more than $200.

(c) An offense under this section is a misdemeanor punishable by a fine of not less than $200 or more than $500, confinement in the county jail for a term of not less than 60 days or more than 180 days, or both the fine and the confinement if:

(1) the person committing the offense fails or refuses to exhibit, on demand of a peace officer, a document that contains:

(A) the name, address, and telephone number of the owner of the unit of special mobile equipment;

(B) the place of origin of the unit, including the address of and telephone number at that point and the date the unit was picked up;

(C) the destination of the unit, including the address or telephone number;

(D) a description of the unit being transported, including the manufacturer's serial number and other identification numbers;

(E) a description of the motor vehicle transporting the unit; and

(F) the name, address, and telephone number of the person operating the motor vehicle transporting the unit;

(2) the person committing the offense exhibits a false or forged document purporting to contain the information described by Subdivision (1); or

(3) on inspection by the peace officer, the peace officer determines that the identification number of the unit of special mobile equipment has been removed, covered, or altered.

(d) For purposes of Subsection (c)(3), a peace officer has probable cause to inspect a unit of special mobile equipment to determine the identification numbers of the unit if:

(1) the person operating the motor vehicle transporting the unit fails or refuses to exhibit

on demand a document described by Subsection (c)(1); or

(2) the unit is not marked as required by Section 622.072.

(Enacted by Acts 1995, 74th Leg., ch. 165 (S.B. 971), § 1, effective September 1, 1995.)

### Sec. 622.074. Nonapplicability of Subchapter.

This subchapter does not apply to:

(1) farm equipment used for a purpose other than construction;

(2) special mobile equipment owned by a dealer or distributor;

(3) a vehicle used to propel special mobile equipment that is registered as a farm vehicle as defined by Section 502.163; or

(4) equipment while being used by a commercial hauler to transport special mobile equipment under hire of a person who derives $500 in gross receipts annually from a farming or ranching enterprise.

(Enacted by Acts 1995, 74th Leg., ch. 165 (S.B. 971), § 1, effective September 1, 1995.)

### Secs. 622.075 to 622.080 [Reserved for expansion].

## SUBCHAPTER H
## VEHICLES TRANSPORTING LUMBER

### Sec. 622.081. Weight of Lumber [Repealed].

Repealed by Acts 2001, 77th Leg., ch. 941 (S.B. 886), § 44, effective September 1, 2001.

(Enacted by Acts 1995, 74th Leg., ch. 165 (S.B. 971), § 1, effective September 1, 1995.)

### Secs. 622.082 to 622.100 [Reserved for expansion].

## SUBCHAPTER I
## VEHICLES TRANSPORTING CERTAIN AGRICULTURAL PRODUCTS OR EQUIPMENT

### Sec. 622.101. Vehicle Transporting Certain Agricultural Products or Processing Equipment.

(a) A single motor vehicle used exclusively to transport chile pepper modules, seed cotton, cotton, cotton burrs, or equipment used to transport or process chile pepper modules or cotton, includ-

ing a motor vehicle or burr spreader, may not be operated on a highway or road if the vehicle is:

(1) wider than 10 feet and the highway has not been designated by the commission under Section 621.202;

(2) longer than 48 feet; or

(3) higher than 14 feet 6 inches.

(b) A motor vehicle that transports agricultural products under this section must be registered under Section 504.505.

(Enacted by Acts 1995, 74th Leg., ch. 165 (S.B. 971), § 1, effective September 1, 1995; am. Acts 1997, 75th Leg., ch. 848 (H.B. 920), § 2, effective June 18, 1997; am. Acts 2005, 79th Leg., ch. 247 (H.B. 749), § 3, effective September 1, 2005.)

### Secs. 622.102 to 622.130 [Reserved for expansion].

## SUBCHAPTER J
## CERTAIN VEHICLES TRANSPORTING RECYCLABLE MATERIALS

### Sec. 622.131. Definition.

In this subchapter, "recyclable material" has the meaning assigned by Section 361.421, Health and Safety Code.

(Enacted by Acts 1997, 75th Leg., ch. 165 (S.B. 898), § 30.136(a), effective September 1, 1997; enacted by Acts 1997, 75th Leg., ch. 436 (H.B. 1524), § 1, effective July 15, 1997.)

### Sec. 622.132. Applicability of Subchapter.

This subchapter applies only to a vehicle other than a tractor-trailer combination, only if equipped with a container roll-off unit or a front-end loader.

(Enacted by Acts 1997, 75th Leg., ch. 165 (S.B. 898), § 30.136(a), effective September 1, 1997; enacted by Acts 1997, 75th Leg., ch. 436 (H.B. 1524), § 1, effective July 15, 1997.)

### Sec. 622.133. Axle-Weight Restrictions.

A single motor vehicle used exclusively to transport recyclable materials may be operated on a public highway only if the tandem axle weight is not heavier than 44,000 pounds, a single axle load is not heavier than 21,000 pounds, and the gross load is not heavier than 64,000 pounds.

(Enacted by Acts 1997, 75th Leg., ch. 165 (S.B. 898), § 30.136(a), effective September 1, 1997;

enacted by Acts 1997, 75th Leg., ch. 436 (H.B. 1524), § 1, effective July 15, 1997; am. Acts 2001, 77th Leg., ch. 941 (S.B. 886), § 39, effective September 1, 2001; am. Acts 2001, 77th Leg., ch. 942 (S.B. 889 ), § 4, effective September 1, 2001.)

## Sec. 622.134.  Surety Bond.

(a) Except as provided by Subsection (c), the owner of a vehicle covered by this subchapter with a tandem axle weight heavier than 34,000 pounds shall before operating the vehicle on a public highway of this state file with the department a surety bond subject to the approval of the Texas Department of Transportation in the principal amount set by the Texas Department of Transportation not to exceed $15,000 for each vehicle.

(b) The bond must be conditioned that the owner of the vehicle will pay, within the limits of the bond, to the Texas Department of Transportation any damage to a highway, to a county any damage to a county road, and to a municipality any damage to a municipal street caused by the operation of the vehicle.

(c) Subsection (a) does not apply to a vehicle owned by a municipality or a county.

(d) A copy of the bond shall be:

(1) carried on the vehicle when the vehicle is on a public highway; and

(2) presented to an officer authorized to enforce this chapter on request of the officer.

(Enacted by Acts 1997, 75th Leg., ch. 165 (S.B. 898), § 30.136(a), effective September 1, 1997; enacted by Acts 1997, 75th Leg., ch. 436 (H.B. 1524), § 1, effective July 15, 1997; am. Acts 2001, 77th Leg., ch. 941 (S.B. 886), § 40, effective September 1, 2001; am. Acts 2001, 77th Leg., ch. 942 (S.B. 889 ), § 5, effective September 1, 2001; am. Acts 2011, 82nd Leg., ch. 1345 (S.B. 1420), § 68, effective September 1, 2011.)

## Sec. 622.135.  Interstate and Defense Highways.

(a) This subchapter does not authorize the operation on the national system of interstate and defense highways in this state of a vehicle of a size or weight greater than authorized in 23 U.S.C. Section 127, as amended.

(b) If the United States government authorizes the operation on the national system of interstate and defense highways of vehicles of a size or weight greater than those authorized on January 1, 1983, the new limit automatically takes effect on the national system of interstate and defense highways in this state.

(Enacted by Acts 1997, 75th Leg., ch. 165 (S.B. 898), § 30.136(a), effective September 1, 1997; enacted by Acts 1997, 75th Leg., ch. 436 (H.B. 1524), § 1, effective July 15, 1997.)

## Sec. 622.136.  Penalty.

A person commits an offense if the person fails in violation of Section 622.134(d) to carry or present the copy of the bond filed with the department. An offense under this section is a misdemeanor punishable by a fine not to exceed $200. (Enacted by Acts 1997, 75th Leg., ch. 165 (S.B. 898), § 30.136(a), effective September 1, 1997; enacted by Acts 1997, 75th Leg., ch. 436 (H.B. 1524), § 1, effective July 15, 1997; am. Acts 2001, 77th Leg., ch. 942 (S.B. 889), § 6, effective September 1, 2001; am. Acts 2003, 78th Leg., ch. 1276 (H.B. 3507), § 16.004, effective September 1, 2003.)

## Sec. 622.137.  Defense to Prosecution: Bond in Effect.

(a) It is a defense to prosecution under Section 622.136 that the person charged produces a surety bond that complies with Section 622.134 that was valid at the time the offense is alleged to have occurred.

(b) If the court verifies the bond produced by the person, the court shall dismiss the charge. (Enacted by Acts 2001, 77th Leg., ch. 942 (S.B. 889), § 7, effective September 1, 2001.)

## Secs. 622.138 to 622.900 [Reserved for expansion].

### SUBCHAPTER Y
### MISCELLANEOUS SIZE EXCEPTIONS

## Sec. 622.901.  Width Exceptions.

The width limitation provided by Section 621.201 does not apply to:

(1) highway building or maintenance machinery that is traveling:

(A) during daylight on a public highway other than a highway that is part of the national system of interstate and defense highways; or

(B) for not more than 50 miles on a highway that is part of the national system of interstate and defense highways;

(2) a vehicle traveling during daylight on a public highway other than a highway that is part of the national system of interstate and defense highways or traveling for not more

than 50 miles on a highway that is part of the national system of interstate and defense highways if the vehicle is:

    (A) a farm tractor or implement of husbandry; or

    (B) a vehicle on which a farm tractor or implement of husbandry, other than a tractor or implement being transported from one dealer to another, is being moved by the owner of the tractor or implement or by an agent or employee of the owner:

      (i) to deliver the tractor or implement to a new owner;

      (ii) to transport the tractor or implement to or from a mechanic for maintenance or repair; or

      (iii) in the course of an agricultural operation;

  (3) machinery that is used solely for drilling water wells, including machinery that is a unit or a unit mounted on a conventional vehicle or chassis, and that is traveling:

    (A) during daylight on a public highway other than a highway that is part of the national system of interstate and defense highways; or

    (B) for not more than 50 miles on a highway that is part of the national system of interstate and defense highways;

  (4) a vehicle owned or operated by a public, private, or volunteer fire department;

  (5) a vehicle registered under Section 502.164; or

  (6) a recreational vehicle to which Section 622.903 applies.

(Enacted by Acts 1995, 74th Leg., ch. 165 (S.B. 971), § 1, effective September 1, 1995; am. Acts 2003, 78th Leg., ch. 491 (H.B. 946), § 1, effective September 1, 2003.)

## Sec. 622.902. Length Exceptions.

The length limitations provided by Sections 621.203 to 621.205 do not apply to:

  (1) machinery used exclusively for drilling water wells, including machinery that is itself a unit or that is a unit mounted on a conventional vehicle or chassis;

  (2) a vehicle owned or operated by a public, private, or volunteer fire department;

  (3) a vehicle or combination of vehicles operated exclusively in the territory of a municipality or to a combination of vehicles operated by a municipality in a suburb adjoining the municipality in which the municipality has been

using the equipment or similar equipment in connection with an established service to the suburb;

  (4) a truck-tractor, truck-tractor combination, or truck-trailer combination exclusively transporting machinery, materials, and equipment used in the construction, operation, and maintenance of facilities, including pipelines, that are used for the discovery, production, and processing of natural gas or petroleum;

  (5) a drive-away saddlemount vehicle transporter combination or a drive-away saddlemount with fullmount vehicle transporter combination, as defined by 23 C.F.R. Part 658 or its successor, if:

    (A) the overall length of the combination is not longer than 97 feet; and

    (B) the combination does not have more than three saddlemounted vehicles if the combination does not include more than one fullmount vehicle;

  (6) the combination of a tow truck and another vehicle or vehicle combination if:

    (A) the other vehicle or vehicle combination cannot be normally or safely driven or was abandoned on a highway; and

    (B) the tow truck is towing the other vehicle or vehicle combination directly to the nearest authorized place of repair, terminal, or destination of unloading; or

  (7) a vehicle or combination of vehicles used to transport a combine that is used in farm custom harvesting operations on a farm if the overall length of the vehicle or combination is not longer than:

    (A) 75 feet if the vehicle is traveling on a highway that is part of the national system of interstate and defense highways or the federal aid primary highway system; or

    (B) 81-½ feet if the vehicle is not traveling on a highway that is part of the national system of interstate and defense highways or the federal aid primary highway system.

(Enacted by Acts 1995, 74th Leg., ch. 165 (S.B. 971), § 1, effective September 1, 1995; am. Acts 1997, 75th Leg., ch. 165 (S.B. 898), § 30.137(a), effective September 1, 1997; am. Acts 1997, 75th Leg., ch. 1144 (H.B. 3570), § 1, effective June 19, 1997; am. Acts 2007, 80th Leg., ch. 83 (S.B. 331), § 1, effective May 14, 2007; am. Acts 2009, 81st Leg., ch. 212 (S.B. 969), § 1, effective September 1, 2009.)

## Sec. 622.903. Width Limitation on Certain Recreational Vehicles.

  (a) In this section:

Transportation

(1) "Appurtenance" includes an awning, a grab handle, lighting equipment, or a vent. The term does not include a load-carrying device.

(2) "Recreational vehicle" has the meaning assigned by Section 522.004.

(b) A recreational vehicle may exceed a width limitation established by Section 621.201 or 621.202 if the excess width is attributable to an appurtenance that extends six inches or less beyond a fender on one or both sides of the vehicle.

(Enacted by Acts 2003, 78th Leg., ch. 491 (H.B. 946), § 1, effective September 1, 2003.)

**Secs. 622.904 to 622.950 [Reserved for expansion].**

## SUBCHAPTER Z
## MISCELLANEOUS WEIGHT EXCEPTIONS

### Sec. 622.951. Oil Field Service Equipment [Repealed].

Repealed by Acts 2001, 77th Leg., ch. 941 (S.B. 886), § 44, effective September 1, 2001.

(Enacted by Acts 1995, 74th Leg., ch. 165 (S.B. 971), § 1, effective September 1, 1995.)

### Sec. 622.952. Fire Department Vehicle.

(a) The weight limitations of Section 621.101 do not apply to a vehicle owned or operated by a public, private, or volunteer fire department.

(b) The weight of a fire department's vehicle may not be heavier than the manufacturer's gross vehicle weight capacity or axle design rating.

(Enacted by Acts 1995, 74th Leg., ch. 165 (S.B. 971), § 1, effective September 1, 1995.)

### Sec. 622.953. Vehicle Transporting Seed Cotton or Chile Pepper Modules.

(a) The weight limitations of Section 621.101 do not apply to a single motor vehicle used exclusively to transport chile pepper modules, seed cotton, or equipment, including a motor vehicle, used to transport or process chile pepper modules or seed cotton.

(b) The overall gross weight of a single motor vehicle used to transport seed cotton or equipment used to transport or process seed cotton may not be heavier than 64,000 pounds.

(c) The overall gross weight of a single motor vehicle used to transport chile pepper modules or equipment used to transport or process chile pepper modules may not be heavier than 54,000 pounds.

(d) The owner of a single motor vehicle to which this section applies that has a gross weight above the gross weight authorized by this section that is applicable to the vehicle is liable to the state, county, or municipality for any damage to a highway, street, road, or bridge caused by the weight of the load.

(e) A vehicle to which this section applies may not be operated on the national system of interstate and defense highways if the vehicle exceeds the maximum weight authorized by 23 U.S.C. Section 127, as amended.

(Enacted by Acts 1995, 74th Leg., ch. 165 (S.B. 971), § 1, effective September 1, 1995; am. Acts 2001, 77th Leg., ch. 941 (S.B. 886), § 41, effective September 1, 2001; am. Acts 2005, 79th Leg., ch. 247 (H.B. 749), § 4, effective September 1, 2005; am. Acts 2007, 80th Leg., ch. 1396 (H.B. 2093), § 3, effective September 1, 2007.)

### Sec. 622.954. Tow Trucks.

(a) A permit is not required to exceed the weight limitations of Section 621.101 by a combination of a tow truck and another vehicle or vehicle combination if:

(1) the nature of the service provided by the tow truck is needed to remove disabled, abandoned, or accident-damaged vehicles; and

(2) the tow truck is towing the other vehicle or vehicle combination directly to the nearest authorized place of repair, terminal, or vehicle storage facility.

(b) This section does not authorize the operation on the national system of interstate and defense highways in this state of vehicles with a weight greater than authorized by federal law.

(Enacted by Acts 2001, 77th Leg., ch. 135 (H.B. 1679), § 1, effective May 16, 2001.)

### Sec. 622.955. Increase of Maximum Weight for Vehicles with Idle Reduction Systems.

(a) For purposes of this section, "idle reduction system" means a system that provides heating, cooling, or electrical service to a commercial vehicle's sleeper berth for the purpose of reducing the idling of a motor vehicle.

(b) Notwithstanding any provision to the contrary, the maximum gross vehicle weight limit and axle weight limit for any vehicle or combination of vehicles equipped with an idle reduction system shall be increased by an amount necessary to compensate for the additional weight of the idle reduction system.

(c) The weight increase under Subsection (b) may not be greater than 400 pounds.

(d) On request by an appropriate law enforcement officer or an official of an appropriate regulatory agency, the vehicle operator shall provide proof that:

(1) the idle reduction technology is fully functional at all times; and

(2) the weight increase is not used for any purpose other than the use of an idle reduction system.

(Enacted by Acts 2011, 82nd Leg., ch. 390 (S.B. 493), § 2, effective June 17, 2011.)

# CHAPTER 623
# PERMITS FOR OVERSIZE OR OVERWEIGHT VEHICLES

## Subchapter A. General Provisions

**Transportation**

## SUBCHAPTER A
## GENERAL PROVISIONS

### Sec. 623.001.  Definitions.

In this chapter:

(1) "Department" means the Texas Department of Motor Vehicles.

(2) "Shipper" means a person who consigns the movement of a shipment.

(3) "Shipper's certificate of weight" means a document described by Section 623.274.

(4) "Board" means the board of the Texas Department of Motor Vehicles.

(5) "Commission" means the Texas Transportation Commission.

(Enacted by Acts 1995, 74th Leg., ch. 165 (S.B. 971), § 1, effective September 1, 1995; am. Acts 2007, 80th Leg., ch. 1396 (H.B. 2093), § 14, effective September 1, 2007; am. Acts 2011, 82nd Leg., ch. 1345 (S.B. 1420), § 69, effective September 1, 2011.)

### Sec. 623.002.  Rulemaking Authority.

The board may adopt rules necessary to implement and enforce this chapter.

(Enacted by Acts 2011, 82nd Leg., ch. 1345 (S.B. 1420), § 70, effective September 1, 2011.)

### Sec. 623.003.  Route Determination.

(a) To the extent the department is required to determine a route under this chapter, the department shall base the department's routing decision on information provided by the Texas Department of Transportation.

(b) The Texas Department of Transportation shall provide the department with all routing information necessary to complete a permit issued under Section 623.071, 623.121, 623.142, or 623.192.

(Enacted by Acts 2011, 82nd Leg., ch. 1345 (S.B. 1420), § 70, effective September 1, 2011.)

## Secs. 623.004 to 623.010 [Reserved for expansion].

## SUBCHAPTER B
## GENERAL PERMITS

## Sec. 623.011. Permit for Excess Axle or Gross Weight.

(a) The department may issue a permit that authorizes the operation of a commercial motor vehicle, trailer, semitrailer, or combination of those vehicles, or a truck-tractor or combination of a truck-tractor and one or more other vehicles:

(1) at an axle weight that is not heavier than the weight equal to the maximum allowable axle weight for the vehicle or combination plus a tolerance allowance of 10 percent of that allowable weight; and

(2) at a gross weight that is not heavier than the weight equal to the maximum allowable gross weight for the vehicle or combination plus a tolerance allowance of five percent.

(b) To qualify for a permit under this section:

(1) the vehicle must be registered under Chapter 502 for the maximum gross weight applicable to the vehicle under Section 621.101, not to exceed 80,000 pounds;

(2) the security requirement of Section 623.012 must be satisfied; and

(3) a base permit fee of $90, any additional fee required by Section 623.0111, and any additional fee set by the department under Section 623.0112 must be paid.

(c) A permit issued under this section:

(1) is valid for one year; and

(2) must be carried in the vehicle for which it is issued.

(d) When the department issues a permit under this section, the department shall issue a sticker to be placed on the front windshield of the vehicle above the inspection certificate issued to the vehicle. The department shall design the form of the sticker to aid in the enforcement of weight limits for vehicles.

(e) The sticker must:

(1) indicate the expiration date of the permit; and

(2) be removed from the vehicle when:

(A) the permit for operation of the vehicle expires;

(B) a lease of the vehicle expires; or

(C) the vehicle is sold.

(f) A person commits an offense if the person fails to display the sticker in the manner required by Subsection (d). An offense under this subsection is a Class C misdemeanor. Section 623.019(g) applies to an offense under this subsection.

(g) A vehicle operating under a permit issued under this section may exceed the maximum allowable gross weight tolerance allowance by not more than five percent, regardless of the weight of any one axle or tandem axle, if no axle or tandem axle exceeds the tolerance permitted by Subsection (a).

(Enacted by Acts 1995, 74th Leg., ch. 165 (S.B. 971), § 1, effective September 1, 1995; am. Acts 1997, 75th Leg., ch. 165 (S.B. 898), § 30.138(a), effective September 1, 1997; am. Acts 2001, 77th Leg., ch. 1227 (S.B. 220), § 8, effective September 1, 2001; am. Acts 2011, 82nd Leg., ch. 700 (H.B. 441), § 2, effective September 1, 2011.)

## Sec. 623.0111. Additional Fee for Operation of Vehicle Under Permit.

(a) When a person applies for a permit under Section 623.011, the person must:

(1) designate in the application each county in which the vehicle will be operated; and

(2) pay in addition to other fees an annual fee in an amount determined according to the following table:

| Number of Counties Designated | Fee |
|---|---|
| 1—5 | $175 |
| 6—20 | $250 |
| 21—40 | $450 |
| 41—60 | $625 |
| 61—80 | $800 |
| 81—100 | $900 |
| 101—254 | $1,000 |

(b) A permit issued under Section 623.011 does not authorize the operation of the vehicle in a county that is not designated in the application.

(c) Of the fees collected under Subsection (a) the following amounts shall be deposited to the general revenue fund and the remainder shall be deposited to the credit of the state highway fund:

| Number of Counties | Amount Allocated to |
|---|---|

| Designated | General Revenue Fund |
|---|---|
| 1—5 | $125 |
| 6—20 | $125 |
| 21—40 | $345 |
| 41—60 | $565 |
| 61—80 | $785 |
| 81—100 | $900 |
| 101—254 | $1,000 |

(Enacted by Acts 1997, 75th Leg., ch. 165 (S.B. 898), § 30.138(b), effective September 1, 1997; am. Acts 2007, 80th Leg., ch. 1396 (H.B. 2093), § 4, effective September 1, 2007.)

### Sec. 623.0112.  Additional Administrative Fee.

When a person applies for a permit under Section 623.011, the person must pay in addition to other fees an administrative fee adopted by board rule in an amount not to exceed the direct and indirect cost to the department of:

(1) issuing a sticker under Section 623.011(d);

(2) distributing fees under Section 621.353; and

(3) notifying counties under Section 623.013.

(Enacted by Acts 1997, 75th Leg., ch. 165 (S.B. 898), § 30.138(b), effective September 1, 1997; am. Acts 2011, 82nd Leg., ch. 1345 (S.B. 1420), § 71, effective September 1, 2011.)

### Sec. 623.0113.  Route Restrictions.

(a) Except as provided by Subsection (b), a permit issued under Section 623.011 does not authorize the operation of a vehicle on:

(1) the national system of interstate and defense highways in this state if the weight of the vehicle is greater than authorized by federal law; or

(2) a bridge for which a maximum weight and load limit has been established and posted by the Texas Transportation Commission under Section 621.102 or the commissioners court of a county under Section 621.301, if the gross weight of the vehicle and load or the axles and wheel loads are greater than the limits established and posted under those sections.

(b) The restrictions under Subsection (a)(2) do not apply if a bridge described by Subsection (a)(2) provides the only public vehicular access from an origin or to a destination by a holder of a permit issued under Section 623.011.

(Enacted by Acts 2001, 77th Leg., ch. 1227 (S.B. 220), § 9, effective September 1, 2001.)

### Sec. 623.012.  Security for Permit.

(a) An applicant for a permit under Section 623.011, other than a permit to operate a vehicle loaded with timber or pulp wood, wood chips, cotton, or agricultural products in their natural state, shall file with the department:

(1) a blanket bond; or

(2) an irrevocable letter of credit issued by a financial institution the deposits of which are guaranteed by the Federal Deposit Insurance Corporation.

(b) The bond or letter of credit must:

(1) be in the amount of $15,000 payable to the Texas Department of Transportation and the counties of this state;

(2) be conditioned that the applicant will pay the Texas Department of Transportation for any damage to a state highway, and a county for any damage to a road or bridge of the county, caused by the operation of the vehicle for which the permit is issued at a heavier weight than the maximum weights authorized by Subchapter B of Chapter 621 or Section 621.301; and

(3) provide that the issuer is to notify the Texas Department of Transportation and the applicant in writing promptly after a payment is made by the issuer on the bond or letter of credit.

(c) If an issuer of a bond or letter of credit pays under the bond or letter of credit, the permit holder shall file with the department before the 31st day after the date on which the payment is made:

(1) a replacement bond or letter of credit in the amount prescribed by Subsection (b) for the original bond or letter of credit; or

(2) a notification from the issuer of the existing bond or letter of credit that the bond or letter of credit has been restored to the amount prescribed by Subsection (b).

(d) If the filing is not made as required by Subsection (c), each permit held by the permit holder under Section 623.011 automatically expires on the 31st day after the date on which the payment is made on the bond or letter of credit.

(Enacted by Acts 1995, 74th Leg., ch. 165 (S.B. 971), § 1, effective September 1, 1995; am. Acts 2011, 82nd Leg., ch. 1345 (S.B. 1420), § 72, effective September 1, 2011.)

### Sec. 623.013.  Department's Notice to County.

(a) Not later than the 14th day after the date the department issues a permit under Section

623.011, the department shall notify the county clerk of each county listed in the application for the permit. The notice must include:

(1) the name and address of the person for whom a permit was issued; and

(2) the vehicle identification number and license plate number of the vehicle.

(b) The department shall send a copy of the permit and the bond or letter of credit required for the permit with the notice required by this section.

(Enacted by Acts 1995, 74th Leg., ch. 165 (S.B. 971), § 1, effective September 1, 1995; am. Acts 1997, 75th Leg., ch. 165 (S.B. 898), § 30.138(c), effective September 1, 1997.)

## Sec. 623.014. Transfer of Permit.

(a) A permit issued under Section 623.011 may not be transferred.

(b) If the vehicle for which a permit was issued is destroyed or permanently inoperable, a person may apply to the department for a credit for the remainder of the permit period.

(c) The department shall issue the prorated credit if the person:

(1) pays the fee adopted by the department; and

(2) provides the department with:

(A) the original permit; or

(B) if the original permit does not exist, written evidence in a form approved by the department that the vehicle has been destroyed or is permanently inoperable.

(d) The fee adopted by the department under Subsection (c)(1) may not exceed the cost of issuing the credit.

(e) A credit issued under Subsection (c) may be used only toward the payment of a permit fee under this subchapter.

(Enacted by Acts 1995, 74th Leg., ch. 165 (S.B. 971), § 1, effective September 1, 1995; am. Acts 1997, 75th Leg., ch. 165 (S.B. 898), § 30.138(d), effective September 1, 1997.)

## Sec. 623.015. Liability for Damage.

(a) The liability of a holder of a permit issued under Section 623.011 for damage to a state road or highway or a county road is not limited to the amount of the bond or letter of credit required for the issuance of the permit.

(b) The holder of a permit issued under Section 623.011 who has filed the bond or letter of credit required for the permit and who has filed the notice required by Section 623.013 is liable to the county only for the actual damage to a county road, bridge, or culvert with a load limitation established under Subchapter B of Chapter 621 or Section 621.301 caused by the operation of the vehicle in excess of the limitation. If a county judge, county commissioner, county road supervisor, or county traffic officer requires the vehicle to travel over a designated route, it is presumed that the designated route, including a bridge or culvert on the route, is of sufficient strength and design to carry and withstand the weight of the vehicle traveling over the designated route.

(Enacted by Acts 1995, 74th Leg., ch. 165 (S.B. 971), § 1, effective September 1, 1995.)

## Sec. 623.0155. Indemnification from Motor Carrier Prohibited.

(a) A person may not require indemnification from a motor carrier as a condition to:

(1) the transportation of property for compensation or hire by the carrier;

(2) entrance on property by the carrier for the purpose of loading, unloading, or transporting property for compensation or hire; or

(3) a service incidental to an activity described by Subdivision (1) or (2), including storage of property.

(b) Subsection (a) does not apply to:

(1) a claim arising from damage or loss from a wrongful or negligent act or omission of the carrier; or

(2) services or goods other than those described by Subsection (a).

(c) In this section, "motor carrier" means a common carrier, specialized carrier, or contract carrier that transports property for hire. The term does not include a person who transports property as an incidental activity of a nontransportation business activity regardless of whether the person imposes a separate charge for the transportation.

(d) A provision that is contrary to Subsection (a) is not enforceable.

(Enacted by Acts 1997, 75th Leg., ch. 1061 (S.B. 1486), § 19, effective September 1, 1997.)

## Sec. 623.016. Recovery on Permit Security.

(a) The Texas Department of Transportation or a county may recover on the bond or letter of credit required for a permit issued under Section 623.011 only by a suit against the permit holder and the issuer of the bond or letter of credit.

(b) Venue for a suit by the Texas Department of Transportation is in a district court in:

(1) the county in which the defendant resides;

(2) the county in which the defendant has its principal place of business in this state if the defendant is a corporation or partnership; or

(3) Travis County if the defendant is a corporation or partnership that does not have a principal place of business in this state.

(c) Venue for a suit by a county is in district court in:

(1) the county in which the defendant resides;

(2) the county in which the defendant has its principal place of business in this state; or

(3) the county in which the damage occurred.

(Enacted by Acts 1995, 74th Leg., ch. 165 (S.B. 971), § 1, effective September 1, 1995; am. Acts 2001, 77th Leg., ch. 455 (S.B. 545), § 1, effective September 1, 2001; am. Acts 2011, 82nd Leg., ch. 1345 (S.B. 1420), § 73, effective September 1, 2011.)

## Sec. 623.017.  Permit for Movement of Cylindrical Hay Bales.

(a) The department may issue an annual permit to authorize the movement of a vehicle that is used to carry cylindrical bales of hay and that is wider than the maximum allowable vehicle width but not wider than 12 feet.

(b) A $10 permit fee must accompany an application for a permit under this section.

(Enacted by Acts 1995, 74th Leg., ch. 165 (S.B. 971), § 1, effective September 1, 1995.)

## Sec. 623.018.  County Permit.

(a) The commissioners court of a county, through the county judge, may issue a permit for:

(1) the transportation over highways of that county, other than state highways and public roads in the territory of a municipality, of an overweight, oversize, or overlength commodity that cannot be reasonably dismantled; or

(2) the operation over a highway of that county other than a state highway or public road in the territory of a municipality of:

(A) superheavy or oversize equipment for the transportation of an overweight, oversize, or overlength commodity that cannot be reasonably dismantled; or

(B) vehicles or combinations of vehicles that exceed the weights authorized under Subchapter B, Chapter 621, or Section 621.301.

(b) A permit under Subsection (a) may not be issued for longer than 90 days.

(c) The commissioners court of a county, through the county judge, may issue an annual permit to a dealer in implements of husbandry to allow the dealer to use vehicles that exceed the width limitations provided by this chapter to transport an implement on a highway. The county judge may exercise authority under this subsection independently of the commissioners court until the commissioners court takes action on the request.

(d) If a vehicle has a permit issued under Section 623.011, a commissioners court may not:

(1) issue a permit under this section or charge an additional fee for or otherwise regulate or restrict the operation of the vehicle because of weight; or

(2) require the owner or operator to execute or comply with a road use agreement or indemnity agreement, to make a filing or application, or to provide a bond or letter of credit other than the bond or letter of credit prescribed by Section 623.012.

(e) The commissioners court may require a bond to be executed by an applicant in an amount sufficient to guarantee the payment of any damage to a road or bridge sustained as a consequence of the transportation authorized by the permit.

(Enacted by Acts 1995, 74th Leg., ch. 165 (S.B. 971), § 1, effective September 1, 1995.)

## Sec. 623.0181.  Permits for Auxiliary Power Units.

The department may issue a permit that authorizes the operation of a commercial motor vehicle, trailer, semitrailer, or combination of those vehicles, or a truck-tractor or combination of a truck-tractor and one or more other vehicles, that exceeds the maximum weight limit as set by the department due to the presence of an auxiliary power unit that allows the vehicle to operate on electricity or battery power if the department finds that such an exemption would reduce nitrogen oxide emissions.

(Enacted by Acts 2011, 82nd Leg., ch. 941 (H.B. 422), § 1, effective June 17, 2011.)

## Sec. 623.019.  Violations of Subchapter; Offenses.

(a) A person who holds a permit issued under Section 623.011 commits an offense if:

(1) the person:

(A) operates or directs the operation of the vehicle for which the permit was issued on a public highway or road; and

(B) is criminally negligent with regard to the operation of the vehicle at a weight heavier than the weight limit authorized by Section 623.011; or

(2) the person operates or directs the operation of the vehicle for which the permit was issued:

(A) in a county not designated in the person's application under Section 623.0111; and

(B) at a weight heavier than a weight limit established under:

(i) Subchapter E, Chapter 251;

(ii) Chapter 621 or 622; or

(iii) this chapter.

(b) Except as provided by Subsections (c) and (d), an offense under Subsection (a) is a misdemeanor punishable by a fine of not less than $100 or more than $150.

(c) An offense under Subsection (a) is a misdemeanor and, except as provided by Subsection (d), is punishable by a fine of:

(1) not less than $300 or more than $500 if the offense involves a vehicle having a gross weight that is heavier than 5,000 but not heavier than 10,000 pounds over the vehicle's allowable gross weight; or

(2) not less than $500 or more than $1,000 if the offense involves a vehicle having a gross weight that is at least 10,000 pounds heavier than the vehicle's allowable gross weight.

(d) On conviction before the first anniversary of the date of a previous conviction under Subsection (a), an offense is punishable by a fine in an amount that is twice the amount specified by Subsection (c).

(e) A governmental entity collecting a fine under Subsection (c) shall send an amount equal to 50 percent of the fine to the comptroller.

(f) A justice of the peace has jurisdiction of any offense under this section. A municipal court has jurisdiction of an offense under this section in which the fine does not exceed $500.

(g) A justice or judge who renders a conviction under this section shall report the conviction to the Department of Public Safety. The Department of Public Safety shall keep a record of each conviction reported under this subsection.

(Enacted by Acts 1997, 75th Leg., ch. 165 (S.B. 898), § 30.139(c), effective September 1, 1997.)

**Secs. 623.020 to 623.050 [Reserved for expansion].**

## SUBCHAPTER C
## CONTRACTS FOR CROSSING ROADS

### Sec. 623.051. Contract Allowing Oversize or Overweight Vehicle to Cross Road; Surety Bond.

(a) A person may operate a vehicle that cannot comply with one or more of the restrictions of Subchapter C of Chapter 621 or Section 621.101 to cross the width of any road or highway under the jurisdiction of the Texas Department of Transportation, other than a controlled access highway as defined by Section 203.001, from private property to other private property if the person contracts with the commission to indemnify the Texas Department of Transportation for the cost of maintenance and repair of the part of the highway crossed by the vehicle.

(b) The commission shall adopt rules relating to the forms and procedures to be used under this section and other matters that the commission considers necessary to carry out this section.

(c) To protect the safety of the traveling public, minimize any delays and inconveniences to the operators of vehicles in regular operation, and assure payment for the added wear on the highways in proportion to the reduction of service life, the commission, in adopting rules under this section, shall consider:

(1) the safety and convenience of the general traveling public;

(2) the suitability of the roadway and subgrade on the road or highway to be crossed, variation in soil grade prevalent in the different regions of the state, and the seasonal effects on highway load capacity, the highway shoulder design, and other highway geometrics; and

(3) the state's investment in its highway system.

(d) Before exercising any right under a contract under this section, a person must execute with a corporate surety authorized to do business in this state a surety bond in an amount determined by the commission to compensate for the cost of maintenance and repairs as provided by this section. The bond must be approved by the comptroller and the attorney general and must be conditioned on the person fulfilling the obligations of the contract.

(e) [Repealed by Acts 1997, 75th Leg., ch. 165

(S.B. 898), § 30.140, effective September 1, 1997.]

(Enacted by Acts 1995, 74th Leg., ch. 165 (S.B. 971), § 1, effective September 1, 1995; am. Acts 1997, 75th Leg., ch. 165 (S.B. 898), § 30.140, effective September 1, 1997; am. Acts 1997, 75th Leg., ch. 1423 (H.B. 2841), § 18.14, effective September 1, 1997; am. Acts 2011, 82nd Leg., ch. 1345 (S.B. 1420), § 74, effective September 1, 2011.)

### Sec. 623.052. Contract Allowing Overweight Vehicle with Commodities or Products to Cross Highway; Surety Bond.

(a) A person may operate a vehicle that exceeds the overall gross weight limits provided by Section 621.101 to cross the width of a highway from private property to other private property if:

(1) the vehicle is transporting grain, sand, or another commodity or product and the vehicle's overall gross weight is not heavier than 110,000 pounds; or

(2) the vehicle is an unlicensed vehicle that is transporting sand, gravel, stones, rock, caliche, or a similar commodity.

(b) Before a person may operate a vehicle under this section, the person must:

(1) contract with the Texas Department of Transportation to indemnify the Texas Department of Transportation for the cost of the maintenance and repair for damage caused by a vehicle crossing that part of the highway; and

(2) execute an adequate surety bond to compensate for the cost of maintenance and repair, approved by the comptroller and the attorney general, with a corporate surety authorized to do business in this state, conditioned on the person fulfilling each obligation of the agreement.

(Enacted by Acts 1995, 74th Leg., ch. 165 (S.B. 971), § 1, effective September 1, 1995; am. Acts 1997, 75th Leg., ch. 1423 (H.B. 2841), § 18.15, effective September 1, 1997; am. Acts 2011, 82nd Leg., ch. 1345 (S.B. 1420), § 75, effective September 1, 2011.)

### Secs. 623.053 to 623.070 [Reserved for expansion].

### SUBCHAPTER D
### HEAVY EQUIPMENT

### Sec. 623.071. Permit to Move Certain Heavy Equipment.

(a) The department may issue a permit to a person to operate over a state highway superheavy or oversize equipment that:

(1) is used to transport cylindrically shaped bales of hay or a commodity that cannot reasonably be dismantled; and

(2) has a gross weight or size that exceeds the limits allowed by law to be transported over a state highway.

(b) The department may issue a permit to a person to operate over a farm-to-market or ranch-to-market road superheavy or oversize equipment that:

(1) is used to transport oilfield drill pipe or drill collars stored in a pipe box; and

(2) has a gross weight or size that exceeds the limits allowed by law to be transported over a state highway.

(c) The department may issue an annual permit to allow the operation on a state highway of equipment that exceeds weight and size limits provided by law for the movement of:

(1) an implement of husbandry by a dealer;

(2) water well drilling machinery and equipment or harvesting equipment being moved as part of an agricultural operation; or

(3) superheavy or oversize equipment that:

(A) cannot reasonably be dismantled; and

(B) does not exceed:

(i) 12 feet in width;

(ii) 14 feet in height;

(iii) 110 feet in length; or

(iv) 120,000 pounds gross weight.

(d) The department may issue an annual permit to a motor carrier, as defined by Section 643.001, that allows the motor carrier to operate on a state highway two or more vehicles for the movement of superheavy or oversize equipment described by Subsection (c)(3). An application under this subsection must be on the form prescribed by the department and include a description of each vehicle to be operated by the motor carrier under the permit. A permit issued under this subsection:

(1) may not authorize the operation of more than one vehicle at the same time; and

(2) must be carried in the vehicle that is being operated to move the superheavy or oversize equipment under the permit.

(e) The department may not issue a permit under this section unless the equipment may be operated without material damage to the highway.

(f) In this section, "pipe box" means a container specifically constructed to safely transport and handle oilfield drill pipe and drill collars.

(g) A single trip permit that increases the height or width limits established in Subsection (c)(3)(B)(i) or (ii) may be issued by the department and used in conjunction with an annual permit issued under Subsection (c).

(h) If on completion of a route and engineering study the department determines that the additional length can be transported safely, the department may issue to a person a single trip permit that allows the person to operate over a highway in this state superheavy or oversize equipment exceeding the length limitation established by Subsection (c) and that may be used in conjunction with an annual permit issued under that subsection.

(Enacted by Acts 1995, 74th Leg., ch. 165 (S.B. 971), § 1, effective September 1, 1995; am. Acts 1997, 75th Leg., ch. 568 (H.B. 1345), § 1, effective June 2, 1997; am. Acts 1999, 76th Leg., ch. 807 (H.B. 1538), § 1, effective September 1, 1999; am. Acts 2011, 82nd Leg., ch. 941 (H.B. 422), § 3, effective June 17, 2011.)

### Sec. 623.0711. Permits Authorized by Commission.

(a) The commission by rule may authorize the department to issue a permit to a motor carrier, as defined by Section 643.001, to transport multiple loads of the same commodity over a state highway if all of the loads are traveling between the same general locations.

(b) The commission may not authorize the issuance of a permit that would allow a vehicle to:

(1) violate federal regulations on size and weight requirements; or

(2) transport equipment that could reasonably be dismantled for transportation as separate loads.

(c) The commission rules must require that, before the department issues a permit under this section, the department:

(1) determine that the state will benefit from the consolidated permitting process; and

(2) complete a route and engineering study that considers:

(A) the estimated number of loads to be transported by the motor carrier under the permit;

(B) the size and weight of the commodity;

(C) available routes that can accommodate the size and weight of the vehicle and load to be transported;

(D) the potential roadway damage caused by repeated use of the road by the permitted vehicle;

(E) any disruption caused by the movement of the permitted vehicle; and

(F) the safety of the traveling public.

(d) The commission rules may authorize the department to impose on the motor carrier any condition regarding routing, time of travel, axle weight, and escort vehicles necessary to ensure safe operation and minimal damage to the roadway.

(e) A permit issued under this section may provide multiple routes to minimize damage to the roadways.

(f) The commission shall require the motor carrier to file a bond in an amount set by the commission, payable to the department and conditioned on the motor carrier paying to the department any damage that is sustained to a state highway because of the operation of a vehicle under a permit issued under this section.

(g) An application for a permit under this section must be accompanied by the permit fee established by the commission for the permit, not to exceed $9,000. The department shall send each fee to the comptroller for deposit to the credit of the state highway fund.

(h) In addition to the fee established under Subsection (g), the commission rules must authorize the department to collect a consolidated permit payment for a permit under this section in an amount not to exceed 15 percent of the fee established under Subsection (g), to be deposited to the credit of the state highway fund.

(i) The executive director of the department or the executive director's designee may suspend a permit issued under this section or alter a designated route because of:

(1) a change in pavement conditions;

(2) a change in traffic conditions;

(3) a geometric change in roadway configuration;

(4) construction or maintenance activity; or

(5) emergency or incident management.

(j) A violation of a permit issued under this section is subject to the administrative sanctions of Subchapter N.

(k) In this section, "commission" means the Texas Transportation Commission.

(Enacted by Acts 2011, 82nd Leg., ch. 941 (H.B. 422), § 2, effective June 17, 2011.)

### Sec. 623.072. Designated Route in Municipality.

(a) A municipality having a state highway in its territory shall designate to the department the route in the municipality to be used by equipment described by Section 623.071 operating over the state highway. The department shall show the designated route on each map routing the equipment.

(b) If a municipality does not designate a route, the department shall determine the route of the equipment and the commodity on each state highway in the municipality.

(c) A municipality may not require a fee, permit, or license for movement of superheavy or oversize equipment on the route of a state highway designated by the municipality or department.

(Enacted by Acts 1995, 74th Leg., ch. 165 (S.B. 971), § 1, effective September 1, 1995.)

### Sec. 623.073.   Agent [Repealed].

Repealed by Acts 1997, 75th Leg., ch. 515 (S.B. 1631), § 3, effective September 1, 1997.
(Enacted by Acts 1995, 74th Leg., ch. 165 (S.B. 971), § 1, effective September 1, 1995.)

### Sec. 623.074.   Application.

(a) The department may issue a permit under this subchapter on the receipt of an application for the permit.

(b) The application must:

(1) be in writing;

(2) state the kind of equipment to be operated;

(3) describe the equipment;

(4) give the weight and dimensions of the equipment;

(5) give the width, height, and length of the equipment;

(6) state the kind of commodity to be transported and the weight of the total load; and

(7) be dated and signed by the applicant.

(c) An application for a permit under Section 623.071(a) or (b) must also also state:

(1) each highway over which the equipment is to be operated, if the permit is for a single trip; or

(2) the region or area, as required by rule, over which the equipment is to be operated, if the permit is for other than a single trip.

(d) The department may by rule authorize an applicant to submit an application electronically. An electronically submitted application shall be considered signed if a digital signature is transmitted with the application and intended by the applicant to authenticate the application. For purposes of this subsection, "digital signature" means an electronic identifier intended by the person using it to have the same force and effect as the use of a manual signature.

(Enacted by Acts 1995, 74th Leg., ch. 165 (S.B. 971), § 1, effective September 1, 1995; am. Acts 1997, 75th Leg., ch. 515 (S.B. 1631), § 4, effective September 1, 1997; am. Acts 1997, 75th Leg., ch. 568 (H.B. 1345), § 2, effective June 2, 1997; am. Acts 1997, 75th Leg., ch. 1171 (S.B. 370), § 1.30, effective September 1, 1997.)

### Sec. 623.075.   Bond.

(a) Before the department may issue a permit under this subchapter, the applicant shall file with the department a bond in an amount set by the Texas Department of Transportation, payable to the Texas Department of Transportation, and conditioned that the applicant will pay to the Texas Department of Transportation any damage that might be sustained to the highway because of the operation of the equipment for which a permit is issued.

(b) Venue of a suit for recovery on the bond is in Travis County.

(c) This section applies to the delivery of farm equipment to a farm equipment dealer. This section does not apply to:

(1) the driving or transporting of farm equipment that is being used for an agricultural purpose and is driven or transported by or under the authority of the owner of the equipment; or

(2) a vehicle or equipment operated by a motor carrier registered under Chapter 643 or Chapter 645.

(Enacted by Acts 1995, 74th Leg., ch. 165 (S.B. 971), § 1, effective September 1, 1995; am. Acts 1997, 75th Leg., ch. 165 (S.B. 898), § 30.141(a), effective September 1, 1997; am. Acts 2011, 82nd Leg., ch. 1345 (S.B. 1420), § 76, effective September 1, 2011.)

### Sec. 623.076.   Permit Fee.

(a) An application for a permit under this subchapter must be accompanied by a permit fee of:

(1) $60 for a single-trip permit;

(2) $120 for a permit that is valid for a period not exceeding 30 days;

(3) $180 for a permit that is valid for a period of 31 days or more but not exceeding 60 days;

(4) $240 for a permit that is valid for a period of 61 days or more but not exceeding 90 days; or

(5) $270 for a permit issued under Section 623.071(c)(1) or (2).

(a-1) The following amounts collected under Subsection (a) shall be deposited to the general revenue fund and the remainder deposited to the credit of the state highway fund:

| Amount of Fee | Amount Allocated to General Revenue Fund |
|---|---|
| $60 (single-trip permit) | $30 |
| $120 (30-day permit) | $60 |
| $180 | $90 |
| $240 | $120 |
| $270 | $135 |

(b) The board may adopt rules for the payment of a fee under Subsection (a). The rules may:

(1) authorize the use of electronic funds transfer;

(2) authorize the use of a credit card issued by:

(A) a financial institution chartered by a state or the United States; or

(B) a nationally recognized credit organization approved by the board; and

(3) require the payment of a discount or service charge for a credit card payment in addition to the fee prescribed by Subsection (a).

(c) An application for a permit under Section 623.071(c)(3) or (d) must be accompanied by the permit fee established by the board, in consultation with the commission, for the permit, not to exceed $7,000. Of each fee collected under this subsection, the department shall send:

(1) the first $1,000 to the comptroller for deposit to the credit of the general revenue fund; and

(2) any amount in excess of $1,000 to the comptroller for deposit to the credit of the state highway fund.

(Enacted by Acts 1995, 74th Leg., ch. 165 (S.B. 971), § 1, effective September 1, 1995; am. Acts 1997, 75th Leg., ch. 515 (S.B. 1631), § 5, effective September 1, 1997; am. Acts 1997, 75th Leg., ch. 568 (H.B. 1345), § 3, effective June 2, 1997; am. Acts 1999, 76th Leg., ch. 807 (H.B. 1538), § 2, effective September 1, 1999; am. Acts 2007, 80th Leg., ch. 1396 (H.B. 2093), § 5, effective September 1, 2007; am. Acts 2011, 82nd Leg., ch. 1345 (S.B. 1420), § 77, effective September 1, 2011.)

## Sec. 623.077. Highway Maintenance Fee.

(a) An applicant for a permit under this subchapter, other than a permit under Section 623.071(c)(3), must also pay a highway maintenance fee in an amount determined according to the following table:

| Vehicle Weight in Pounds | Fee |
|---|---|
| 80,001 to 120,000 | $150 |
| 120,001 to 160,000 | $225 |
| 160,001 to 200,000 | $300 |
| 200,001 and above | $375 |

(b) The department shall send each fee collected under Subsection (a) to the comptroller for deposit to the credit of the state highway fund.

(Enacted by Acts 1995, 74th Leg., ch. 165 (S.B. 971), § 1, effective September 1, 1995; am. Acts 1997, 75th Leg., ch. 568 (H.B. 1345), § 4, effective June 2, 1997; am. Acts 1997, 75th Leg., ch. 1423 (H.B. 2841), § 18.16, effective September 1, 1997; am. Acts 2007, 80th Leg., ch. 1396 (H.B. 2093), § 6, effective September 1, 2007.)

## Sec. 623.078. Vehicle Supervision Fee.

(a) Each applicant for a permit under this subchapter for a vehicle that is heavier than 200,000 pounds must also pay a vehicle supervision fee in an amount determined by the Texas Department of Transportation and designed to recover the direct cost of providing safe transportation of the vehicle over the state highway system, including the cost of:

(1) bridge structural analysis;

(2) the monitoring of the trip process; and

(3) moving traffic control devices.

(b) The board shall send each fee collected under Subsection (a) to the comptroller for deposit to the credit of the state highway fund.

(Enacted by Acts 1995, 74th Leg., ch. 165 (S.B. 971), § 1, effective September 1, 1995; am. Acts 1997, 75th Leg., ch. 1423 (H.B. 2841), § 18.17, effective September 1, 1997; am. Acts 2011, 82nd Leg., ch. 1345 (S.B. 1420), § 78, effective September 1, 2011.)

## Sec. 623.079. Registration of Equipment.

A permit under this subchapter may be issued only if the equipment to be operated under the permit is registered under Chapter 502 for maximum gross weight applicable to the vehicle under Section 621.101 that is not heavier than 80,000 pounds overall gross weight.

(Enacted by Acts 1995, 74th Leg., ch. 165 (S.B. 971), § 1, effective September 1, 1995.)

## Sec. 623.080. Contents of Permit.

(a) Except as provided by Subsection (b), a permit under this subchapter must include:

Transportation

(1) the name of the applicant;

(2) the date of issuance;

(3) the signature of the director of the department;

(4) a statement of the kind of equipment to be transported over the highway, the weight and dimensions of the equipment, and the kind and weight of each commodity to be transported; and

(5) a statement of any condition on which the permit is issued.

(b) A permit issued under Section 623.071(a) or (b) must also state:

(1) each highway over which the equipment is to be transported, if the permit is for a single trip; or

(2) the region or area, as required by rule, over which the equipment is to be operated, if the permit is for other than a single trip.

(Enacted by Acts 1995, 74th Leg., ch. 165 (S.B. 971), § 1, effective September 1, 1995; am. Acts 1997, 75th Leg., ch. 515 (S.B. 1631), § 6, effective September 1, 1997; am. Acts 2011, 82nd Leg., ch. 1345 (S.B. 1420), § 79, effective September 1, 2011.)

## Sec. 623.081.  Permit Issued by Telephone.

(a) The department shall provide for issuing a permit by telephone for the operation of an overweight or oversize motor vehicle over a state highway.

(b) The department shall issue a permit under this section for a period and at the rate provided by Section 623.076(a).

(c) An applicant for a permit under this section must provide by telephone to the department:

(1) the information required for a permit issued under Section 623.071(a) or (b), other than the applicant's signature; and

(2) the account number of a credit card approved by the department.

(d) On granting a permit under this section, the agent shall:

(1) issue to the applicant an approval number; and

(2) provide to the applicant the agent's name, designation, and office address.

(e) After receiving an approval number, the applicant shall prepare, on a form provided by the department, a permit with the information provided to the agent under Subsection (c) and the information received under Subsection (d).

(f) The applicant shall keep the permit in the vehicle for which the permit was issued until the day after the date the permit expires.

(Enacted by Acts 1995, 74th Leg., ch. 165 (S.B. 971), § 1, effective September 1, 1995; am. Acts 1997, 75th Leg., ch. 515 (S.B. 1631), § 7, effective September 1, 1997.)

## Sec. 623.082.  Penalties.

(a) A person commits an offense if the person violates this subchapter.

(b) Except as provided by Subsection (c), an offense under this section is a misdemeanor punishable:

(1) by a fine of not more than $200;

(2) on conviction within one year after the date of a prior conviction under this section that was punishable under Subdivision (1), by a fine of not more than $500, by confinement in the county jail for not more than 60 days, or by both the fine and the confinement; or

(3) on conviction within one year after the date of a prior conviction under this section that was punishable under Subdivision (2) or this subdivision, by a fine of not more than $1,000, by confinement in the county jail for not more than six months, or by both the fine and the confinement.

(c) A corporation is not subject to confinement for an offense under this section, but two times the maximum fine provided for in the applicable subdivision of Subsection (b) may be imposed against the corporation.

(d) The judge shall report a conviction under this section to the Department of Public Safety. The Department of Public Safety shall keep a record of each conviction.

(e) If a corporation does not pay a fine assessed under this section, the district or county attorney for the county in which the conviction was obtained may file suit to collect the fine.

(Enacted by Acts 1995, 74th Leg., ch. 165 (S.B. 971), § 1, effective September 1, 1995.)

## Secs. 623.083 to 623.090 [Reserved for expansion].

### SUBCHAPTER E
### MANUFACTURED AND
### INDUSTRIALIZED HOUSING

## Sec. 623.091.  Definition.

In this subchapter, "manufactured house" means "industrialized building" as defined by Chapter 1202, Occupations Code, "industrialized housing" as defined by Chapter 1202, Occupations Code, or "manufactured home" as defined by

Chapter 1201, Occupations Code. The term includes a temporary chassis system or returnable undercarriage used for the transportation of a manufactured house and a transportable section of a manufactured house that is transported on a chassis system or returnable undercarriage and that is constructed so that it cannot, without dismantling or destruction, be transported within the legal size limits for a motor vehicle.
(Enacted by Acts 1995, 74th Leg., ch. 165 (S.B. 971), § 1, effective September 1, 1995; am. Acts 2003, 78th Leg., ch. 1276 (H.B. 3507), § 14A.836, effective September 1, 2003.)

### Sec. 623.092.   Permit Requirement.

(a) A manufactured house in excess of legal size limits for a motor vehicle may not be moved over a highway, road, or street in this state except in accordance with a permit issued by the department.

(b) A county or municipality may not require a permit, bond, fee, or license, in addition to that required by state law, for the movement of a manufactured house.
(Enacted by Acts 1995, 74th Leg., ch. 165 (S.B. 971), § 1, effective September 1, 1995.)

### Sec. 623.093.   Contents of Application and Permit.

(a) The application for a permit and the permit must be in the form prescribed by the department. The permit must show:

(1)  the length, width, and height of the manufactured house and the towing vehicle in combination;

(2)  the complete identification or serial number, the Department of Housing and Urban Development label number, or the state seal number of the house;

(3)  the name of the owner of the house;

(4)  the location from which the house is being transported;

(5)  the location to which the house is being transported; and

(6)  the route for the transportation of the house.

(b) The length of the manufactured house and the towing vehicle in combination includes the length of the hitch or towing device. The height is measured from the roadbed to the highest elevation of the manufactured house. The width of the house or section includes any roof or eave extension or overhang on either side.

(c) The route must be the shortest distance from the place where the transportation begins in

this state to the place where the transportation ends in this state and include divided and interstate systems, except where construction is in progress or bridge or overpass width or height creates a safety hazard. A county or municipality may designate to the department the route to be used inside the territory of the county or municipality.

(d) [Repealed by Acts 2005, 79th Leg., ch. 1284 (H.B. 2438), § 34(3), effective June 18, 2005.]

(e) Each quarter the department shall send a copy of each permit for the transportation of a manufactured house that begins or ends in this state, or provide the essential information in the permit, to the chief appraiser of the appraisal district in each county in which the transportation begins or ends.

(f) If an application for a permit to move a manufactured house is accompanied by a copy of a writ of possession issued by a court of competent jurisdiction, the applicant is not required to submit the written statement from the chief appraiser.
(Enacted by Acts 1995, 74th Leg., ch. 165 (S.B. 971), § 1, effective September 1, 1995; am. Acts 1997, 75th Leg., ch. 165 (S.B. 898), § 30.142(a), effective September 1, 1997; am. Acts 1997, 75th Leg., ch. 791 (H.B. 2703), § 19, effective September 1, 1997; am. Acts 1999, 76th Leg., ch. 62 (S.B. 1368), § 19.01(107), effective September 1, 1999; am. Acts 2001, 77th Leg., ch. 988 (H.B. 468), § 4, effective September 1, 2001; am. Acts 2003, 78th Leg., ch. 1276 (H.B. 3507), § 14A.837, effective September 1, 2003; am. Acts 2005, 79th Leg., ch. 1284 (H.B. 2438), § 34(3), effective June 18, 2005; am. Acts 2011, 82nd Leg., ch. 1345 (S.B. 1420), § 80, effective September 1, 2011.)

### Sec. 623.094.   Permit Issuance.

(a) Except as authorized by Section 623.095, the department may issue a permit only to:

(1)  a person licensed by the Texas Department of Housing and Community Affairs as a manufacturer, retailer, or installer; or

(2)  motor carriers registered with the department.

(b) The license or registration number of the person to whom the permit is issued shall be affixed to the rear of the manufactured house during transportation and have letters and numbers that are at least eight inches high.
(Enacted by Acts 1995, 74th Leg., ch. 165 (S.B. 971), § 1, effective September 1, 1995; am. Acts 1997, 75th Leg., ch. 165 (S.B. 898), § 30.143(a),

effective September 1, 1997; am. Acts 1997, 75th Leg., ch. 791 (H.B. 2703), § 20, effective September 1, 1997.)

## Sec. 623.095.  Permit Types.

(a) The department may issue a single-trip permit for the transportation of a manufactured house to:

 (1) the owner of a manufactured house if:

  (A) the title to the manufactured house and the title to the towing vehicle show that the owner of the manufactured house and the owner of the towing vehicle are the same person; or

  (B) a lease shows that the owner of the manufactured house and the lessee of the towing vehicle are the same person;

 (2) a person authorized to be issued permits by Section 623.094.

(b) A person or owner must have proof of the insurance coverage required by Section 623.103.

(c) In lieu of a single-trip permit, the department may issue an annual permit to any person authorized to be issued permits by Section 623.094 for the transportation of new manufactured homes from a manufacturing facility to a temporary storage location not to exceed 20 miles from the point of manufacture. A copy of the permit must be carried in the vehicle transporting a manufactured home from the manufacturer to temporary storage. The department may adopt rules concerning requirements for a permit issued under this subsection.

(Enacted by Acts 1995, 74th Leg., ch. 165 (S.B. 971), § 1, effective September 1, 1995; am. Acts 1997, 75th Leg., ch. 165 (S.B. 898), § 30.143(b), effective September 1, 1997; am. Acts 1997, 75th Leg., ch. 791 (H.B. 2703), § 21, effective September 1, 1997.)

## Sec. 623.096.  Permit Fee.

(a) The department shall collect a fee of $40 for each permit issued under this subchapter. Of each fee, $19.70 shall be deposited to the credit of the general revenue fund and the remainder deposited to the credit of the state highway fund.

(b) The board, in consultation with the Texas Department of Transportation, shall adopt rules concerning fees for each annual permit issued under Section 623.095(c) at a cost not to exceed $3,000.

(c) The department may establish an escrow account for the payment of permit fees.

(Enacted by Acts 1995, 74th Leg., ch. 165 (S.B. 971), § 1, effective September 1, 1995; am. Acts

1997, 75th Leg., ch. 165 (S.B. 898), § 30.144(a), effective September 1, 1997; am. Acts 1997, 75th Leg., ch. 791 (H.B. 2703), § 22, effective September 1, 1997; am. Acts 2007, 80th Leg., ch. 1396 (H.B. 2093), § 7, effective September 1, 2007; am. Acts 2011, 82nd Leg., ch. 1345 (S.B. 1420), § 81, effective September 1, 2011.)

## Sec. 623.097.  Duration of Permit.

A permit is valid for a five-day period.
(Enacted by Acts 1995, 74th Leg., ch. 165 (S.B. 971), § 1, effective September 1, 1995.)

## Sec. 623.098.  Caution Lights.

(a) A manufactured house that is wider than 12 feet must have one rotating amber beacon of not less than eight inches mounted at the rear of the manufactured house on the roof or one flashing amber light mounted at each rear corner of the manufactured house approximately six feet above ground level. In addition, the towing vehicle must have one rotating amber beacon of not less than eight inches mounted on top of the cab.

(b) Each beacon shall be operated during a move under a permit and while on a highway, road, or street in this state.

(Enacted by Acts 1995, 74th Leg., ch. 165 (S.B. 971), § 1, effective September 1, 1995; am. Acts 1997, 75th Leg., ch. 165 (S.B. 898), § 30.145(a), effective September 1, 1997.)

## Sec. 623.099.  Escort Flag Vehicle.

(a) A manufactured house that is wider than 16 feet, but is not wider than 18 feet, must have one escort flag vehicle that must:

 (1) precede the house on a two-lane roadway; or

 (2) follow the house on a roadway of four or more lanes.

(b) A manufactured house that is wider than 18 feet must be preceded and followed by escort flag vehicles while moving over a highway, road, or street in this state.

(c) An escort flag vehicle must have:

 (1) on top of the vehicle and visible from the front and rear:

  (A) two lights flashing simultaneously; or

  (B) one rotating amber beacon of not less than eight inches;

 (2) four red 16-inch square flags mounted on the four corners of the vehicle so that one flag is on each corner; and

 (3) signs that:

  (A) are mounted on the front and rear of the vehicle; and

(B) have a yellow background and black letters at least eight inches high stating "wide load."

(d) Two transportable sections of a multisection manufactured house or two single-section manufactured houses towed in convoy are considered one house for purposes of the escort flag vehicle requirements of this section if the distance between the two does not exceed 1,000 feet.

(e) The Texas Department of Transportation shall publish and annually revise a map or list of the bridges or overpasses that because of height or width require an escort flag vehicle to stop oncoming traffic while a manufactured house crosses the bridge or overpass.

(f) An escort flag vehicle may not be required under this subchapter except as expressly provided by this section.

(Enacted by Acts 1995, 74th Leg., ch. 165 (S.B. 971), § 1, effective September 1, 1995; am. Acts 1997, 75th Leg., ch. 487 (S.B. 605), § 1, effective September 1, 1997; am. Acts 2011, 82nd Leg., ch. 1345 (S.B. 1420), § 82, effective September 1, 2011.)

### Sec. 623.100. Times and Days of Movement.

(a) Movement authorized by a permit issued under this subchapter may be made on any day, except a national holiday, but shall be made only during daylight hours.

(b) The Texas Department of Transportation may limit the hours for travel on certain routes because of heavy traffic conditions.

(c) The Texas Department of Transportation shall publish the limitation on movements prescribed by this section and the limitations adopted under Subsection (b) and shall make the publications available to the public. Each limitation adopted by the Texas Department of Transportation must be made available to the public before it takes effect.

(Enacted by Acts 1995, 74th Leg., ch. 165 (S.B. 971), § 1, effective September 1, 1995; am. Acts 2011, 82nd Leg., ch. 1345 (S.B. 1420), § 83, effective September 1, 2011.)

### Sec. 623.101. Speed Limit.

(a) A manufactured house or house trailer may not be towed in excess of the posted speed limit or 55 miles per hour, whichever is less.

(b) In this section, "house trailer" has the meaning assigned by Section 541.201.

(Enacted by Acts 1995, 74th Leg., ch. 165 (S.B. 971), § 1, effective September 1, 1995; am. Acts 1997, 75th Leg., ch. 1020 (S.B. 343), § 4, effective September 1, 1997.)

### Sec. 623.102. Equipment.

(a) The brakes on a towing vehicle and a manufactured house must be capable of stopping the vehicle and house from an initial velocity of 20 miles per hour in not more than 40 feet.

(b) Each manufactured house must be equipped with a wiring harness during transportation over a roadway to provide on the rear of the house:

    (1) right-turn and left-turn signal lights;

    (2) braking or stopping lights; and

    (3) parking lights.

(Enacted by Acts 1995, 74th Leg., ch. 165 (S.B. 971), § 1, effective September 1, 1995.)

### Sec. 623.103. Liability Insurance.

A vehicle towing a manufactured house shall be covered by liability insurance of not less than $300,000 combined single limit.

(Enacted by Acts 1995, 74th Leg., ch. 165 (S.B. 971), § 1, effective September 1, 1995.)

### Sec. 623.104. Civil and Criminal Penalties.

(a) A person commits an offense if the person violates this subchapter. An offense under this subsection is a Class C misdemeanor, except as provided by Subsection (d).

(b) A person convicted of an offense under Subsection (a) may also be assessed a civil penalty of not less than $200 or more than $500 for failure to:

    (1) obtain a permit;

    (2) have a required rotating amber beacon on the manufactured house or towing vehicle;

    (3) provide a required escort flag vehicle; or

    (4) have the required insurance.

(c) The civil penalty:

    (1) may be awarded by a court having jurisdiction over a Class C misdemeanor; and

    (2) shall be paid to the county in which the person was convicted.

(d) Except as provided by Subsection (e), if the offense involves the movement of a manufactured house over a highway, road, or street in this state without a permit issued by the department, the offense is a misdemeanor punishable by a fine of $1,000.

(e) If it is shown on the trial of an offense punishable under Subsection (d) that the defendant has previously been punished under Subsection (d):

(1) one time, the offense is punishable by a fine of $2,000; or

(2) two or more times, the offense is punishable by a fine of $4,000.

(Enacted by Acts 1995, 74th Leg., ch. 165 (S.B. 971), § 1, effective September 1, 1995; am. Acts 2001, 77th Leg., ch. 988 (H.B. 468), § 5, effective September 1, 2001; am. Acts 2003, 78th Leg., ch. 338 (S.B. 521), § 48, effective June 18, 2003.)

## Sec. 623.105. Penalty for Compensating Certain Unlawful Actions.

(a) A person commits an offense if the person:

(1) provides compensation to another for the movement of a manufactured home over a highway, road, or street in this state; and

(2) knows the other person is not authorized by law to move the home.

(b) An offense under this section is a misdemeanor punishable by a fine of $1,000.

(Enacted by Acts 2003, 78th Leg., ch. 338 (S.B. 521), § 49, effective June 18, 2003.)

## Secs. 623.106 to 623.120 [Reserved for expansion].

## SUBCHAPTER F
## PORTABLE BUILDING UNITS

## Sec. 623.121. Permit to Move Portable Building Unit.

(a) The department may issue a permit to a person to operate equipment to move over a state highway one or more portable building units that in combination with the towing vehicle are in excess of the length or width limitations provided by law but less than 80 feet in length.

(b) The length limitation in this section does not apply to a truck-tractor or truck-tractor combination towing or carrying the portable building units.

(c) In this section, "portable building unit" means the prefabricated structural and other components incorporated and delivered by the manufacturer as a complete inspected unit with a distinct serial number. The term includes a fully assembled configuration, a partially assembled configuration, or a kit or unassembled configuration, when loaded for transport.

(Enacted by Acts 1995, 74th Leg., ch. 165 (S.B. 971), § 1, effective September 1, 1995; am. Acts 1997, 75th Leg., ch. 165 (S.B. 898), § 30.146(a), effective September 1, 1997.)

## Sec. 623.122. Designated Route in Municipality.

(a) A municipality having a state highway in its territory shall designate to the department the route in the municipality to be used by equipment described by Section 623.121 moving over the state highway. The department shall show the designated route on each map routing the equipment.

(b) If a municipality does not designate a route, the department shall determine the route to be used by the equipment on the state highway within the municipality.

(c) A municipality may not require a fee or license for movement of a portable building unit on the route of a state highway designated by the department or the municipality.

(Enacted by Acts 1995, 74th Leg., ch. 165 (S.B. 971), § 1, effective September 1, 1995.)

## Sec. 623.123. Application.

The application for a permit under Section 623.121 must:

(1) be in writing;

(2) state the make and model of the portable building unit or units;

(3) state the length and width of the portable building unit or units;

(4) state the make and model of the towing vehicle;

(5) state the length and width of the towing vehicle;

(6) state the length and width of the combined portable building unit or units and towing vehicle;

(7) state each highway over which the portable building unit or units are to be moved;

(8) indicate the point of origin and destination; and

(9) be dated and signed by the applicant.

(Enacted by Acts 1995, 74th Leg., ch. 165 (S.B. 971), § 1, effective September 1, 1995.)

## Sec. 623.124. Fee.

(a) An application for a permit must be accompanied by a fee of $15.

(b) The department shall send each fee collected under this section to the comptroller. Of each fee received from the department, the comptroller shall deposit $7.50 to the credit of the general revenue fund and $7.50 to the credit of the state highway fund.

(Enacted by Acts 1995, 74th Leg., ch. 165 (S.B. 971), § 1, effective September 1, 1995; am. Acts 2007, 80th Leg., ch. 1396 (H.B. 2093), § 8, effective September 1, 2007.)

### Sec. 623.125. Agent [Repealed].

Repealed by Acts 1997, 75th Leg., ch. 515 (S.B. 1631), § 8, effective September 1, 1997.

(Enacted by Acts 1995, 74th Leg., ch. 165 (S.B. 971), § 1, effective September 1, 1995.)

### Sec. 623.126. Form of Permit.

(a) A permit issued under this subchapter must:

(1) contain the name of the applicant;

(2) be dated and signed by the director of the department or a designated agent;

(3) state the make and model of the portable building unit or units to be transported over the highways;

(4) state the make and model of the towing vehicle;

(5) state the combined length and width of the portable building unit or units and towing vehicle; and

(6) state each highway over which the portable building unit or units are to be moved.

(b) A permit is valid if it is substantially in the form provided by this section.

(Enacted by Acts 1995, 74th Leg., ch. 165 (S.B. 971), § 1, effective September 1, 1995; am. Acts 2011, 82nd Leg., ch. 1345 (S.B. 1420), § 84, effective September 1, 2011.)

### Sec. 623.127. Duration of Permit.

A permit issued under this subchapter is effective for a 10-day period and valid only for a single continuous movement.

(Enacted by Acts 1995, 74th Leg., ch. 165 (S.B. 971), § 1, effective September 1, 1995.)

### Sec. 623.128. Time of Movement.

Movement authorized by a permit issued under this subchapter shall be made only during daylight hours.

(Enacted by Acts 1995, 74th Leg., ch. 165 (S.B. 971), § 1, effective September 1, 1995.)

### Sec. 623.129. Escort Flag Vehicle.

The escort flag vehicle requirements provided by Section 623.099 apply to the movement of portable building units and compatible cargo under this subchapter as if such building units and cargo were a manufactured house.

(Enacted by Acts 1997, 75th Leg., ch. 487 (S.B. 605), § 2, effective September 1, 1997.)

### Sec. 623.130. Compatible Cargo.

(a) A permit issued under this subchapter may authorize the movement of cargo, other than a portable building unit, manufactured, assembled, or distributed by a portable building unit manufacturer, as an authorized distributor if:

(1) the movement is conducted by employees of the manufacturer or by independent drivers and equipment under exclusive contract to the manufacturer during the movement;

(2) the movement is to or from a location where the manufacturer's building units may be legally stored, sold, or delivered; and

(3) the cargo is compatible with the movement of portable building units in that:

(A) the cargo does not cause the load to exceed applicable height or weight limits; and

(B) the cargo is loaded to properly distribute weight, width, and height to maximize safety and economy without exceeding size or weight limits authorized for movement of portable building units.

(b) If cargo moved under this section exceeds any width limit that would apply to the cargo if it were moved in a manner not governed by this section, the department shall collect an amount equal to any fee that would apply to movement of the cargo if the cargo were moved in a manner not governed by this section in addition to the fee required under this subchapter.

(Enacted by Acts 1997, 75th Leg., ch. 487 (S.B. 605), § 2, effective September 1, 1997.)

### Secs. 623.131 to 623.140 [Reserved for expansion].

## SUBCHAPTER G
## OIL WELL SERVICING AND DRILLING MACHINERY

### Sec. 623.141. Optional Procedure.

This subchapter provides an optional procedure for the issuance of a permit for the movement of oversize or overweight oil well servicing or oil well drilling machinery and equipment.

(Enacted by Acts 1995, 74th Leg., ch. 165 (S.B. 971), § 1, effective September 1, 1995.)

### Sec. 623.142. Permit to Move Oil Well Servicing or Drilling Machinery.

(a) The department may, on application, issue a permit for the movement over a road or highway under the jurisdiction of the Texas Department of Transportation of a vehicle that:

(1) is a piece of fixed-load mobile machinery or equipment used to service, clean out, or drill an oil well; and

(2) cannot comply with the restrictions set out in Subchapter C of Chapter 621 and Section 621.101.

(b) The department may not issue a permit under this section unless the vehicle may be moved without material damage to the highway or serious inconvenience to highway traffic.

(Enacted by Acts 1995, 74th Leg., ch. 165 (S.B. 971), § 1, effective September 1, 1995; am. Acts 2011, 82nd Leg., ch. 1345 (S.B. 1420), § 85, effective September 1, 2011.)

## Sec. 623.143. Designated Route in Municipality.

(a) A municipality having a state highway in its territory may designate to the department the route in the municipality to be used by a vehicle described by Section 623.142 operating over the state highway. When the route is designated, the department shall show the route on each map routing the vehicles.

(b) If a municipality does not designate a route, the department shall determine the route to be used by a vehicle on a state highway in the municipality.

(c) A municipality may not require a fee, permit, or license for movement of vehicles on the route of a state highway designated by the municipality or department.

(Enacted by Acts 1995, 74th Leg., ch. 165 (S.B. 971), § 1, effective September 1, 1995.)

## Sec. 623.144. Registration of Vehicle.

A permit under this subchapter may be issued only if the vehicle is registered under Chapter 502 for the maximum gross weight applicable to the vehicle under Section 621.101 or has the distinguishing license plates as provided by Section 504.504 if applicable to the vehicle.

(Enacted by Acts 1995, 74th Leg., ch. 165 (S.B. 971), § 1, effective September 1, 1995; am. Acts 2007, 80th Leg., ch. 280 (H.B. 505), § 5, effective June 15, 2007; am. Acts 2007, 80th Leg., ch. 1396 (H.B. 2093), § 9, effective September 1, 2007.)

## Sec. 623.145. Rules; Forms and Procedures; Fees.

(a) The board, in consultation with the commission, by rule shall provide for the issuance of permits under this subchapter. The rules must include each matter the board and commission determine necessary to implement this subchapter and:

(1) requirements for forms and procedures used in applying for a permit;

(2) conditions with regard to route and time of movement;

(3) requirements for flags, flaggers, and warning devices;

(4) the fee for a permit; and

(5) standards to determine whether a permit is to be issued for one trip only or for a period established by the commission.

(b) In adopting a rule or establishing a fee, the board and commission shall consider and be guided by:

(1) the state's investment in its highway system;

(2) the safety and convenience of the general traveling public;

(3) the registration or license fee paid on the vehicle for which the permit is requested;

(4) the fees paid by vehicles operating within legal limits;

(5) the suitability of roadways and subgrades on the various classes of highways of the system;

(6) the variation in soil grade prevalent in the different regions of the state;

(7) the seasonal effects on highway load capacity;

(8) the highway shoulder design and other highway geometrics;

(9) the load capacity of the highway bridges;

(10) administrative costs;

(11) added wear on highways; and

(12) compensation for inconvenience and necessary delays to highway users.

(Enacted by Acts 1995, 74th Leg., ch. 165 (S.B. 971), § 1, effective September 1, 1995; am. Acts 2011, 82nd Leg., ch. 1345 (S.B. 1420), § 86, effective September 1, 2011.)

## Sec. 623.146. Violation of Rule.

A permit under this subchapter is void on the failure of an owner or the owner's representative to comply with a rule of the board or with a condition placed on the permit, and immediately on the violation, further movement over the highway of an oversize or overweight vehicle violates the law regulating the size or weight of a vehicle on a public highway.

(Enacted by Acts 1995, 74th Leg., ch. 165 (S.B. 971), § 1, effective September 1, 1995; am. Acts

2011, 82nd Leg., ch. 1345 (S.B. 1420), § 86, effective September 1, 2011.)

### Sec. 623.147. Deposit of Fee in State Highway Fund.

A fee collected under this subchapter shall be deposited to the credit of the state highway fund. (Enacted by Acts 1995, 74th Leg., ch. 165 (S.B. 971), § 1, effective September 1, 1995.)

### Sec. 623.148. Liability for Damage to Highways.

(a) By issuing a permit under this subchapter, the department does not guarantee that a highway can safely accommodate the movement.

(b) The owner of a vehicle involved in the movement of an oversize or overweight vehicle, even if a permit has been issued for the movement, is strictly liable for any damage the movement causes the highway system or any of its structures or appurtenances.

(Enacted by Acts 1995, 74th Leg., ch. 165 (S.B. 971), § 1, effective September 1, 1995.)

### Sec. 623.149. Determination Whether Vehicle Subject to Registration or Eligible for Distinguishing License Plate.

(a) The department may establish criteria to determine whether oil well servicing, oil well clean out, or oil well drilling machinery or equipment is subject to registration under Chapter 502 or eligible for the distinguishing license plate provided by Section 504.504.

(b) Notwithstanding Subsection (a), a vehicle authorized by the department before August 22, 1963, to operate without registration under Chapter 502 may not be required to register under that chapter.

(c) In this section, "oil well servicing, oil well clean out, or oil well drilling machinery or equipment" means a vehicle constructed as a machine used solely for servicing, cleaning out, or drilling an oil well and consisting in general of a mast, an engine for power, a draw works, and a chassis permanently constructed or assembled for one or more of those purposes.

(Enacted by Acts 1995, 74th Leg., ch. 165 (S.B. 971), § 1, effective September 1, 1995; am. Acts 2007, 80th Leg., ch. 280 (H.B. 505), § 6, effective June 15, 2007; am. Acts 2007, 80th Leg., ch. 1396 (H.B. 2093), § 10, effective September 1, 2007.)

### Sec. 623.150. Nonapplicability of Subchapter.

This subchapter does not apply to a person issued a registration certificate under Chapter

643, even if not all the operations of the person are performed under that certificate.

(Enacted by Acts 1995, 74th Leg., ch. 165 (S.B. 971), § 1, effective September 1, 1995; am. Acts 1997, 75th Leg., ch. 165 (S.B. 898), § 30.147, effective September 1, 1997.)

### Secs. 623.151 to 623.160 [Reserved for expansion].

## SUBCHAPTER H
## VEHICLES TRANSPORTING SOLID WASTE

### Sec. 623.161. Definition.

In this subchapter, "solid waste" has the meaning assigned by Chapter 361, Health and Safety Code, except that it does not include hazardous waste.

(Enacted by Acts 1995, 74th Leg., ch. 165 (S.B. 971), § 1, effective September 1, 1995.)

### Sec. 623.162. Axle Weight Restrictions.

A single vehicle used exclusively to transport solid waste may be operated on a public highway of this state only if the tandem axle weight is not heavier than 44,000 pounds, the single axle weight is not heavier than 21,000 pounds, and the gross weight is not heavier than 64,000 pounds.

(Enacted by Acts 1995, 74th Leg., ch. 165 (S.B. 971), § 1, effective September 1, 1995; am. Acts 2001, 77th Leg., ch. 941 (S.B. 886), § 42, effective September 1, 2001.)

### Sec. 623.163. Surety Bond.

(a) The owner of a vehicle used exclusively to transport solid waste with a tandem axle load heavier than 34,000 pounds shall before operating the vehicle on a public highway of this state file with the department a surety bond subject to the approval of the Texas Department of Transportation in the principal amount set by the Texas Department of Transportation not to exceed $15,000 for each vehicle.

(b) The bond must be conditioned that the owner of the vehicle will pay to the Texas Department of Transportation and to any municipality in which the vehicle is operated on a municipal street, within the limit of the bond, any damages to a highway or municipal street caused by the operation of the vehicle.

Transportation

(c) This section does not apply to a vehicle owned by a municipality.

(d) A copy of the bond shall be:

(1) carried on the vehicle when the vehicle is on a public highway; and

(2) presented to an officer authorized to enforce this chapter on request of the officer.

(Enacted by Acts 1995, 74th Leg., ch. 165 (S.B. 971), § 1, effective September 1, 1995; am. Acts 2001, 77th Leg., ch. 942 (S.B. 889), § 8, effective September 1, 2001; am. Acts 2011, 82nd Leg., ch. 1345 (S.B. 1420), § 87, effective September 1, 2011.)

### Sec. 623.164.  Interstate and Defense Highways.

(a) This subchapter does not authorize the operation on the national system of interstate and defense highways in this state of a vehicle of a size or weight greater than that authorized by 23 U.S.C. Section 127, as amended.

(b) If the United States authorizes the operation on the national system of interstate and defense highways of a vehicle of a size or weight greater than that authorized on January 1, 1983, the new limit automatically takes effect on the national system of interstate and defense highways in this state.

(Enacted by Acts 1995, 74th Leg., ch. 165 (S.B. 971), § 1, effective September 1, 1995.)

### Sec. 623.165.  Penalty.

A person commits an offense if the person fails in violation of Section 623.163(d) to carry or present the copy of the bond filed with the department. An offense under this section is a misdemeanor punishable by a fine not to exceed $200.

(Enacted by Acts 1995, 74th Leg., ch. 165 (S.B. 971), § 1, effective September 1, 1995; am. Acts 2001, 77th Leg., ch. 942 (S.B. 889), § 9, effective September 1, 2001; am. Acts 2003, 78th Leg., ch. 1276 (H.B. 3507), § 16.004, effective September 1, 2003.)

### Sec. 623.166.  Defense to Prosecution: Bond in Effect.

(a) It is a defense to prosecution under Section 623.165 that the person charged produces a surety bond that complies with Section 623.163 that was valid at the time the offense is alleged to have occurred.

(b) If the court verifies the bond produced by the person, the court shall dismiss the charge.

(Enacted by Acts 2001, 77th Leg., ch. 942 (S.B. 889), § 10, effective September 1, 2001.)

### Secs. 623.167 to 623.180 [Reserved for expansion].

## SUBCHAPTER I
## UNLADEN LIFT EQUIPMENT MOTOR VEHICLES; ANNUAL PERMIT

### Sec. 623.181.  Annual Permit.

(a) The department may issue an annual permit for the movement over a highway or road of this state of an unladen lift equipment motor vehicle that because of its design for use as lift equipment exceeds the maximum weight or width limitations prescribed by statute.

(b) The department may issue a permit on receipt of an application for the permit.

(Enacted by Acts 1995, 74th Leg., ch. 165 (S.B. 971), § 1, effective September 1, 1995.)

### Sec. 623.182.  Permit Fee.

(a) The fee for a permit under this subchapter is $100.

(b) The department shall send each fee collected under this subchapter to the comptroller. Of each fee received from the department, the comptroller shall deposit $50 to the credit of the general revenue fund and $50 to the credit of the state highway fund.

(Enacted by Acts 1995, 74th Leg., ch. 165 (S.B. 971), § 1, effective September 1, 1995; am. Acts 2007, 80th Leg., ch. 1396 (H.B. 2093), § 11, effective September 1, 2007.)

### Secs. 623.183 to 623.190 [Reserved for expansion].

## SUBCHAPTER J
## UNLADEN LIFT EQUIPMENT MOTOR VEHICLES; TRIP PERMITS

### Sec. 623.191.  Optional Procedure.

This subchapter provides an optional procedure for the issuance of a permit for the movement of an unladen lift equipment motor vehicle that because of its design for use as lift equipment exceeds the maximum weight and width limitations prescribed by statute.

(Enacted by Acts 1995, 74th Leg., ch. 165 (S.B. 971), § 1, effective September 1, 1995.)

### Sec. 623.192.  Permit to Move Unladen Lift Equipment Motor Vehicles.

(a) The department may, on application, issue a permit to a person to move over a road or highway under the jurisdiction of the Texas Department of Transportation an unladen lift equipment motor vehicle that cannot comply with the restrictions set out in Subchapter C of Chapter 621 and Section 621.101.

(b) The department may not issue a permit under this section unless the vehicle may be moved without material damage to the highway or serious inconvenience to highway traffic.

(Enacted by Acts 1995, 74th Leg., ch. 165 (S.B. 971), § 1, effective September 1, 1995; am. Acts 2011, 82nd Leg., ch. 1345 (S.B. 1420), § 88, effective September 1, 2011.)

### Sec. 623.193. Designated Route in Municipality.

(a) A municipality having a state highway in its territory may designate to the department the route in the municipality to be used by a vehicle described by Section 623.192 operating over the state highway. The department shall show the designated route on each map routing the vehicle.

(b) If a municipality does not designate a route, the department shall determine the route of the vehicle on each state highway in the municipality.

(c) A municipality may not require a fee, permit, or license for movement of the vehicles on the route of a state highway designated by the municipality or department.

(Enacted by Acts 1995, 74th Leg., ch. 165 (S.B. 971), § 1, effective September 1, 1995.)

### Sec. 623.194. Registration of Vehicle.

A permit under this subchapter may be issued only if the vehicle to be moved is registered under Chapter 502 for the maximum gross weight applicable to the vehicle under Section 621.101 or has the distinguishing license plates as provided by Section 504.504 if applicable to the vehicle.

(Enacted by Acts 1995, 74th Leg., ch. 165 (S.B. 971), § 1, effective September 1, 1995; am. Acts 2007, 80th Leg., ch. 280 (H.B. 505), § 7, effective June 15, 2007; am. Acts 2007, 80th Leg., ch. 1396 (H.B. 2093), § 12, effective September 1, 2007.)

### Sec. 623.195. Rules; Forms and Procedures; Fees.

(a) The board, in consultation with the commission, by rule shall provide for the issuance of a permit under this subchapter. The rules must include each matter the board and the commission determine necessary to implement this subchapter and:

(1) requirements for forms and procedures used in applying for a permit;

(2) conditions with regard to route and time of movement;

(3) requirements for flags, flaggers, and warning devices;

(4) the fee for a permit; and

(5) standards to determine whether a permit is to be issued for one trip only or for a period established by the commission.

(b) In adopting a rule or establishing a fee, the board and the commission shall consider and be guided by:

(1) the state's investment in its highway system;

(2) the safety and convenience of the general traveling public;

(3) the registration or license fee paid on the vehicle for which the permit is requested;

(4) the fees paid by vehicles operating within legal limits;

(5) the suitability of roadways and subgrades on the various classes of highways of the system;

(6) the variation in soil grade prevalent in the different regions of the state;

(7) the seasonal effects on highway load capacity;

(8) the highway shoulder design and other highway geometrics;

(9) the load capacity of highway bridges;

(10) administrative costs;

(11) added wear on highways; and

(12) compensation for inconvenience and necessary delays to highway users.

(Enacted by Acts 1995, 74th Leg., ch. 165 (S.B. 971), § 1, effective September 1, 1995; am. Acts 2011, 82nd Leg., ch. 1345 (S.B. 1420), § 89, effective September 1, 2011.)

### Sec. 623.196. Violation of Rule.

A permit under this subchapter is void on the failure of an owner or the owner's representative to comply with a rule of the board or with a condition placed on the permit, and immediately on the violation, further movement over a highway of an oversize or overweight vehicle violates the law regulating the size or weight of a vehicle on a public highway.

(Enacted by Acts 1995, 74th Leg., ch. 165 (S.B. 971), § 1, effective September 1, 1995; am. Acts 2011, 82nd Leg., ch. 1345 (S.B. 1420), § 89, effective September 1, 2011.)

Transportation

## Sec. 623.197.   Deposit of Fee in State Highway Fund.

A fee collected under this subchapter shall be deposited to the credit of the state highway fund. (Enacted by Acts 1995, 74th Leg., ch. 165 (S.B. 971), § 1, effective September 1, 1995.)

## Sec. 623.198.   Liability for Damage to Highways.

(a) By issuing a permit under this subchapter, the department does not guarantee that a highway can safely accommodate the movement.

(b) The owner of a vehicle involved in the movement of an oversize or overweight vehicle, even if a permit has been issued for the movement, is strictly liable for any damage the movement causes the highway system or any of its structures or appurtenances.

(Enacted by Acts 1995, 74th Leg., ch. 165 (S.B. 971), § 1, effective September 1, 1995.)

## Sec. 623.199.   Determination Whether Vehicle Subject to Registration or Eligible for Distinguishing License Plate.

(a) The department may establish criteria to determine whether an unladen lift equipment motor vehicle that because of its design for use as lift equipment exceeds the maximum weight and width limitations prescribed by statute is subject to registration under Chapter 502 or eligible for the distinguishing license plate provided by Section 504.504.

(b) Notwithstanding Subsection (a), a vehicle authorized by the department before June 11, 1985, to operate without registration under Chapter 502 may not be required to register under that chapter.

(Enacted by Acts 1995, 74th Leg., ch. 165 (S.B. 971), § 1, effective September 1, 1995; am. Acts 2007, 80th Leg., ch. 280 (H.B. 505), § 8, effective June 15, 2007; am. Acts 2007, 80th Leg., ch. 1396 (H.B. 2093), § 13, effective September 1, 2007.)

## Sec. 623.200.   Nonapplicability of Subchapter.

This subchapter does not apply to a person issued a registration certificate under Chapter 643, even if not all the operations of the person are performed under that certificate.

(Enacted by Acts 1995, 74th Leg., ch. 165 (S.B. 971), § 1, effective September 1, 1995; am. Acts 1997, 75th Leg., ch. 165 (S.B. 898), § 30.147, effective September 1, 1997.)

## Secs. 623.201 to 623.209 [Reserved for expansion].

## SUBCHAPTER K
## PORT AUTHORITY PERMITS

## Sec. 623.210.   Optional Procedure.

This subchapter provides an optional procedure for the issuance of a permit for the movement of oversize or overweight vehicles carrying cargo on state highways located in counties contiguous to the Gulf of Mexico or a bay or inlet opening into the gulf:

(1) adjacent to at least two counties with a population of 550,000 or more; or

(2) bordering the United Mexican States.

(Enacted by Acts 1997, 75th Leg., ch. 1194 (S.B. 1276), § 1, effective September 1, 1997; am. Acts 2011, 82nd Leg., ch. 967 (H.B. 1305), § 1, effective June 17, 2011.)

## Sec. 623.211.   Definition.

In this subchapter, "port authority" means a port authority or navigation district created or operating under Section 52, Article III, or Section 59, Article XVI, Texas Constitution.

(Enacted by Acts 1997, 75th Leg., ch. 1194 (S.B. 1276), § 1, effective September 1, 1997; am. Acts 2011, 82nd Leg., ch. 967 (H.B. 1305), § 2, effective June 17, 2011.)

## Sec. 623.212.   [2 Versions: As amended by Acts 2011, 82nd Leg., ch. 967] Permits by Port Authority.

The department may authorize a port authority to issue permits for the movement of oversize or overweight vehicles carrying cargo on state highways located in counties contiguous to the Gulf of Mexico or a bay or inlet opening into the gulf and:

(1) adjacent to at least two counties with a population of 550,000 or more; or

(2) bordering the United Mexican States.

(Enacted by Acts 1997, 75th Leg., ch. 1194 (S.B. 1276), § 1, effective September 1, 1997; am. Acts 2011, 82nd Leg., ch. 967 (H.B. 1305), § 3, effective September 1, 2011.)

## Sec. 623.212.   [2 Versions: As amended by Acts 2011, 82nd Leg., ch. 1345] Permits by Port Authority.

The commission may authorize a port authority to issue permits for the movement of oversize or overweight vehicles carrying cargo on state highways located in counties contiguous to the Gulf of Mexico or a bay or inlet opening into the gulf and bordering the United Mexican States.

Transportation

(Enacted by Acts 1997, 75th Leg., ch. 1194 (S.B. 1276), § 1, effective September 1, 1997; am. Acts 2011, 82nd Leg., ch. 1345 (S.B. 1420), § 90, effective September 1, 2011.)

### Sec. 623.213. Maintenance Contracts [Repealed].

Repealed by Acts 2009, 81st Leg., ch. 61 (S.B. 1373), § 1.04, effective May 19, 2009.

(Enacted by Acts 1997, 75th Leg., ch. 1194 (S.B. 1276), § 1, effective September 1, 1997.)

### Sec. 623.214. Permit Fees.

(a) A port authority may collect a fee for permits issued under this subchapter. Such fees shall not exceed $80 per trip.

(b) Fees collected under Subsection (a), less administrative costs, shall be used solely to provide funds for the maintenance and improvement of state highways subject to this subchapter. The administrative costs, which may not exceed 15 percent of the fees collected, may be retained by the port authority. The fees, less administrative costs, shall be deposited in the State Highway Fund.

(Enacted by Acts 1997, 75th Leg., ch. 1194 (S.B. 1276), § 1, effective September 1, 1997; am. Acts 1999, 76th Leg., ch. 624 (S.B. 934), § 1, effective June 18, 1999; am. Acts 2009, 81st Leg., ch. 61 (S.B. 1373), §§ 1.01, 2.01, effective May 19, 2009.)

### Sec. 623.215. Permit Requirements.

(a) A permit issued under this subchapter must include:

(1) the name of the applicant;

(2) the date of issuance;

(3) the signature of the director of the port authority;

(4) a statement of the kind of cargo being transported under the permit, the maximum weight and dimensions of the equipment, and the kind and weight of each commodity to be transported provided the gross weight of such equipment and commodities shall not exceed 125,000 pounds;

(5) a statement of any condition on which the permit is issued;

(6) a statement of the route designated under Section 623.219;

(7) the name of the driver of the vehicle in which the cargo is to be transported; and

(8) the location where the cargo was loaded.

(b) A port authority shall report to the Texas Department of Transportation all permits issued under this subchapter.

(Enacted by Acts 1997, 75th Leg., ch. 1194 (S.B. 1276), § 1, effective September 1, 1997; am. Acts 1999, 76th Leg., ch. 624 (S.B. 934), § 2, effective June 18, 1999; am. Acts 2009, 81st Leg., ch. 61 (S.B. 1373), §§ 1.02, 2.01, effective May 19, 2009; am. Acts 2011, 82nd Leg., ch. 1345 (S.B. 1420), § 91, effective September 1, 2011.)

### Sec. 623.216. Time of Movement.

A permit issued under this subchapter shall specify the time in which movement authorized by the permit is allowed.

(Enacted by Acts 1997, 75th Leg., ch. 1194 (S.B. 1276), § 1, effective September 1, 1997.)

### Sec. 623.217. Speed Limit.

Movement authorized by a permit issued under this subchapter shall not exceed the posted speed limit or 55 miles per hour, whichever is less. Violation of this provision shall constitute a moving violation.

(Enacted by Acts 1997, 75th Leg., ch. 1194 (S.B. 1276), § 1, effective September 1, 1997.)

### Sec. 623.218. Enforcement.

The Department of Public Safety shall have authority to enforce the provisions of this subchapter.

(Enacted by Acts 1997, 75th Leg., ch. 1194 (S.B. 1276), § 1, effective September 1, 1997.)

### Sec. 623.219. Route Designation.

(a) For a permit issued by a port authority located in a county that borders the United Mexican States, the commission shall, with the consent of the port authority, designate the most direct route from the Gateway International Bridge or the Veterans International Bridge at Los Tomates to the entrance of the Port of Brownsville using State Highways 48 and 4 or United States Highways 77 and 83 or using United States Highway 77 and United States Highway 83, East Loop Corridor, and State Highway 4.

(b) For a permit issued by a port authority located in a county that is adjacent to at least two counties with a population of 550,000 or more, the commission shall, with the consent of the port authority, designate the most direct route from:

(1) the intersection of Farm-to-Market Road 523 and Moller Road to the entrance of Port Freeport using Farm-to-Market Roads 523 and 1495;

(2) the intersection of State Highway 288 and Chlorine Road to the entrance of Port Freeport using State Highway 288; and

Transportation

(3) the intersection of State Highway 288 and Chlorine Road to the entrance of Port Freeport using State Highways 288 and 332 and Farm-to-Market Roads 523 and 1495.

(c) If the commission designates a route or changes the route designated under this section, the commission shall notify the port authority of the route not later than the 60th day before the date that the designation takes effect.

(Enacted by Acts 2009, 81st Leg., ch. 61 (S.B. 1373), § 1.03, effective May 19, 2009; am. Acts 2011, 82nd Leg., ch. 967 (H.B. 1305), § 4, effective June 17, 2011.)

**Secs. 623.220 to 623.229 [Reserved for expansion].**

## SUBCHAPTER L
## VICTORIA COUNTY NAVIGATION DISTRICT PERMITS

### Sec. 623.230.  Optional Procedure.

This subchapter provides an optional procedure for the issuance of a permit by the Victoria County Navigation District for the movement of oversize or overweight vehicles carrying cargo in Victoria County.

(Enacted by Acts 2003, 78th Leg., ch. 786 (S.B. 20), § 1, effective September 1, 2003; am. Acts 2011, 82nd Leg., ch. 613 (S.B. 524), § 1, effective September 1, 2011.)

### Sec. 623.231.  Definition.

In this subchapter, "district" means the Victoria County Navigation District.

(Enacted by Acts 2003, 78th Leg., ch. 786 (S.B. 20), § 1, effective September 1, 2003.)

### Sec. 623.232.  Issuance of Permits.

The Texas Transportation Commission may authorize the district to issue permits for the movement of oversize or overweight vehicles carrying cargo only on the following highways and roads located in Victoria County:

(1) Farm-to-Market Road 1432 between the Port of Victoria and State Highway 185;

(2) State Highway 185 between U.S. Highway 59 and McCoy Road;

(3) U.S. Highway 59, including a frontage road of U.S. Highway 59, between State Highway 185 and Loop 463; and

(4) Loop 463 between U.S. Highway 59 and North Lone Tree Road.

(Enacted by Acts 2003, 78th Leg., ch. 786 (S.B. 20), § 1, effective September 1, 2003; am. Acts 2011, 82nd Leg., ch. 613 (S.B. 524), § 2, effective September 1, 2011.)

### Sec. 623.233.  Maintenance Contracts.

The district shall make payments to the Texas Department of Transportation to provide funds for the maintenance of state highways subject to this subchapter.

(Enacted by Acts 2003, 78th Leg., ch. 786 (S.B. 20), § 1, effective September 1, 2003; am. Acts 2011, 82nd Leg., ch. 1345 (S.B. 1420), § 92, effective September 1, 2011.)

### Sec. 623.234.  Permit Fees.

(a) The district may collect a fee for permits issued under this subchapter. The fees shall not exceed $100 per trip.

(b) Fees collected under Subsection (a) shall be used solely to provide funds for the payments provided for under Section 623.233 less administrative costs, which shall not exceed 15 percent of the fees collected. The fees shall be deposited in the state highway fund. Fees deposited in the state highway fund under this section are exempt from the application of Section 403.095, Government Code.

(Enacted by Acts 2003, 78th Leg., ch. 786 (S.B. 20), § 1, effective September 1, 2003; am. Acts 2011, 82nd Leg., ch. 613 (S.B. 524), § 3, effective September 1, 2011.)

### Sec. 623.235.  Permit Requirements.

(a) A permit issued under this subchapter must include:

(1) the name of the applicant;

(2) the date of issuance;

(3) the signature of the director of the district or the director's designee;

(4) a statement of the kind of cargo being transported, the maximum weight and dimensions of the equipment, and the kind and weight of each commodity to be transported, provided that the gross weight of such equipment and commodities shall not exceed 140,000 pounds;

(5) a statement of any condition on which the permit is issued;

(6) a statement that the cargo shall only be transported on a road designated under Section 623.232;

(7) the name of the driver of the vehicle in which the cargo is to be transported; and

(8) the location where the cargo was loaded.

(b) The district shall report to the Texas Department of Transportation all permits issued under this subchapter.

(Enacted by Acts 2003, 78th Leg., ch. 786 (S.B. 20), § 1, effective September 1, 2003; am. Acts 2011, 82nd Leg., ch. 613 (S.B. 524), § 4, effective September 1, 2011; am. Acts 2011, 82nd Leg., ch. 1345 (S.B. 1420), § 93, effective September 1, 2011.)

### Sec. 623.236. Time of Movement.

A permit issued under this subchapter shall specify the time in which movement authorized by the permit is allowed.

(Enacted by Acts 2003, 78th Leg., ch. 786 (S.B. 20), § 1, effective September 1, 2003.)

### Sec. 623.237. Speed Limit.

Movement authorized by a permit issued under this subchapter shall not exceed the posted speed limit or 55 miles per hour, whichever is less. Violation of this provision shall constitute a moving violation.

(Enacted by Acts 2003, 78th Leg., ch. 786 (S.B. 20), § 1, effective September 1, 2003.)

### Sec. 623.238. Enforcement.

The Department of Public Safety shall have authority to enforce the provisions of this subchapter.

(Enacted by Acts 2003, 78th Leg., ch. 786 (S.B. 20), § 1, effective September 1, 2003.)

### Sec. 623.239. Rules.

The Texas Transportation Commission may adopt rules necessary to implement this subchapter.

(Enacted by Acts 2003, 78th Leg., ch. 786 (S.B. 20), § 1, effective September 1, 2003.)

### Secs. 623.240 to 623.249 [Reserved for expansion].

## SUBCHAPTER M
## CHAMBERS COUNTY PERMITS

### Sec. 623.250. Optional Procedure.

This subchapter provides an optional procedure for the issuance of a permit by Chambers County for the movement of oversize or overweight vehicles carrying cargo on certain state highways located in Chambers County.

(Enacted by Acts 2005, 79th Leg., ch. 538 (H.B. 1044), § 1, effective June 17, 2005.)

### Sec. 623.251. Definition.

In this subchapter, "county" means Chambers County.

(Enacted by Acts 2005, 79th Leg., ch. 538 (H.B. 1044), § 1, effective June 17, 2005.)

### Sec. 623.252. Issuance of Permits.

(a) The Texas Transportation Commission may authorize the county to issue permits for the movement of oversize or overweight vehicles carrying cargo on state highways located in Chambers County.

(b) A permit issued under this subchapter may authorize:

(1) the transport of cargo only on the following roads in Chambers County:

(A) Farm-to-Market Road 1405 between its intersection with Farm-to-Market Road 2354 and its intersection with Farm-to-Market Road 565;

(B) the frontage road of State Highway 99 located in the Cedar Crossing Business Park;

(C) Farm-to-Market Road 565 from its intersection with Farm-to-Market Road 1405 east approximately 6,200 linear feet to the western edge of the 10-foot pipeline easement recorded at volume 351, page 760, of the Chambers County deed records; and

(D) Farm-to-Market Road 2354 from its intersection with Farm-to-Market Road 1405 northwest approximately 300 linear feet to the termination of the state-maintained portion of the road; and

(2) the movement of equipment and commodities weighing 100,000 pounds or less.

(Enacted by Acts 2005, 79th Leg., ch. 538 (H.B. 1044), § 1, effective June 17, 2005; am. Acts 2009, 81st Leg., ch. 1053 (H.B. 4594), § 1, effective June 19, 2009.)

### Sec. 623.253. Maintenance Contracts.

The county shall make payments to the Texas Department of Transportation to provide funds for the maintenance of state highways subject to this subchapter.

(Enacted by Acts 2005, 79th Leg., ch. 538 (H.B. 1044), § 1, effective June 17, 2005; am. Acts 2011, 82nd Leg., ch. 1345 (S.B. 1420), § 94, effective September 1, 2011.)

### Sec. 623.254. Permit Fees.

(a) The county may collect a fee for permits issued under this subchapter. The fee may not exceed $80 per trip.

(b) Fees collected under Subsection (a) may be used only to provide funds for the payments under Section 623.253 and for the county's administrative costs, which may not exceed 15 percent of the fees collected. The fees shall be deposited in the state highway fund. Fees deposited in the state highway fund under this section are exempt from the application of Section 403.095, Government Code.
(Enacted by Acts 2005, 79th Leg., ch. 538 (H.B. 1044), § 1, effective June 17, 2005.)

### Sec. 623.255.  Permit Requirements.

(a) A permit issued under this subchapter must include:

(1) the name of the applicant;

(2) the date of issuance;

(3) the signature of the designated agent for the county;

(4) a statement of the kind of cargo being transported, the maximum weight and dimensions of the equipment, and the kind and weight of each commodity to be transported;

(5) a statement of any condition on which the permit is issued;

(6) a statement that the cargo may be transported in Chambers County only over the roads described by Section 623.252(b)(1); and

(7) the location where the cargo was loaded.

(b) The county shall report to the department all permits issued under this subchapter.
(Enacted by Acts 2005, 79th Leg., ch. 538 (H.B. 1044), § 1, effective June 17, 2005; am. Acts 2009, 81st Leg., ch. 1053 (H.B. 4594), § 2, effective June 19, 2009.)

### Sec. 623.256.  Time of Movement.

A permit issued under this subchapter must specify the time during which movement authorized by the permit is allowed.
(Enacted by Acts 2005, 79th Leg., ch. 538 (H.B. 1044), § 1, effective June 17, 2005.)

### Sec. 623.257.  Speed Limit.

Movement authorized by a permit issued under this subchapter may not exceed the posted speed limit or 55 miles per hour, whichever is less. A violation of this provision constitutes a moving violation.
(Enacted by Acts 2005, 79th Leg., ch. 538 (H.B. 1044), § 1, effective June 17, 2005.)

### Sec. 623.258.  Enforcement.

The Department of Public Safety has authority to enforce this subchapter.

(Enacted by Acts 2005, 79th Leg., ch. 538 (H.B. 1044), § 1, effective June 17, 2005.)

### Sec. 623.259.  Rules.

The Texas Transportation Commission may adopt rules necessary to implement this subchapter.
(Enacted by Acts 2005, 79th Leg., ch. 538 (H.B. 1044), § 1, effective June 17, 2005.)

### Secs. 623.260 to 623.270 [Reserved for expansion].

## SUBCHAPTER N
## ADMINISTRATIVE SANCTIONS

### Sec. 623.271.  Administrative Enforcement.

(a) The department may investigate and, except as provided by Subsection (f), may impose an administrative penalty or revoke an oversize or overweight permit issued under this chapter if the person or the holder of the permit, as applicable:

(1) provides false information on the permit application or another form required by the department for the issuance of an oversize or overweight permit;

(2) violates this chapter, Chapter 621, or Chapter 622;

(3) violates a rule or order adopted under this chapter, Chapter 621, or Chapter 622; or

(4) fails to obtain an oversize or overweight permit if a permit is required.

(b) The notice and hearing requirements of Section 643.2525 apply to the imposition of an administrative penalty or the revocation of a permit under this section as if the action were being taken under that section.

(c) It is an affirmative defense to administrative enforcement under this section that the person or holder of the permit relied on the shipper's certificate of weight.

(d) The amount of an administrative penalty imposed under this section is calculated in the same manner as the amount of an administrative penalty imposed under Section 643.251.

(e) A person who has been ordered to pay an administrative penalty under this section and the vehicle that is the subject of the enforcement order may not be issued a permit under this chapter until the amount of the penalty has been paid to the department.

(f) This subsection applies only to a vehicle or combination that is used to transport agricultural products or timber products from the place of production to the place of first marketing or first processing. In connection with a violation of a vehicle or combination weight restriction or limitation in this chapter, Chapter 621, or Chapter 622, the department may not impose an administrative penalty against a person or the holder of an overweight permit if the weight of the vehicle or combination involved in the violation did not exceed the allowable weight by more than three percent.

(Enacted by Acts 2007, 80th Leg., ch. 1396 (H.B. 2093), § 15, effective September 1, 2007.)

### Sec. 623.272. Administrative Penalty for False Information on Certificate.

(a) The department may investigate and impose an administrative penalty on a shipper who provides false information on a shipper's certificate of weight that the shipper delivers to a person transporting a shipment.

(b) The notice and hearing requirements of Section 643.2525 apply to the imposition of an administrative penalty under this section as if the action were being taken under that section.

(c) The amount of an administrative penalty imposed under this section is calculated in the same manner as the amount of an administrative penalty imposed under Section 643.251.

(Enacted by Acts 2007, 80th Leg., ch. 1396 (H.B. 2093), § 15, effective September 1, 2007.)

### Sec. 623.273. Injunctive Relief.

(a) The attorney general, at the request of the department, may petition a district court for appropriate injunctive relief to prevent or abate a violation of this chapter or a rule or order adopted under this chapter.

(b) Venue in a suit for injunctive relief under this section is in Travis County.

(c) On application for injunctive relief and a finding that a person is violating or has violated this chapter or a rule or order adopted under this chapter, the court shall grant the appropriate relief without bond.

(d) The attorney general and the department may recover reasonable expenses incurred in obtaining injunctive relief under this section, including court costs, reasonable attorney's fees, investigative costs, witness fees, and deposition expenses.

(Enacted by Acts 2007, 80th Leg., ch. 1396 (H.B. 2093), § 15, effective September 1, 2007.)

### Sec. 623.274. Shipper's Certificate of Weight.

(a) The department shall prescribe a form to be used for a shipper's certificate of weight. The form must provide space for the maximum weight of the shipment being transported.

(b) For a shipper's certificate of weight to be valid, the shipper must:

(1) certify that the information contained on the form is accurate; and

(2) deliver the certificate to the motor carrier or other person transporting the shipment before the motor carrier or other person applies for an overweight permit under this chapter.

(Enacted by Acts 2007, 80th Leg., ch. 1396 (H.B. 2093), § 15, effective September 1, 2007.)

### Secs. 623.275 to 623.279 [Reserved for expansion].

## SUBCHAPTER O
## PORT OF CORPUS CHRISTI
## AUTHORITY ROADWAY PERMITS

### Sec. 623.280. Optional Procedure.

This subchapter provides an optional procedure for the issuance of a permit by the Port of Corpus Christi Authority for the movement of oversize or overweight vehicles carrying cargo on a roadway owned and maintained by the Port of Corpus Christi Authority that is located in San Patricio County or Nueces County.

(Enacted by Acts 2009, 81st Leg., ch. 812 (S.B. 1571), § 1, effective September 1, 2009.)

### Sec. 623.281. Definition.

In this subchapter, "port authority" means the Port of Corpus Christi Authority.

(Enacted by Acts 2009, 81st Leg., ch. 812 (S.B. 1571), § 1, effective September 1, 2009.)

### Sec. 623.282. Issuance of Permits.

The port authority may issue permits for the movement of oversize or overweight vehicles carrying cargo on a roadway owned and maintained by the port authority that is located in San Patricio County or Nueces County. A permit issued under this subchapter is in addition to other permits required by law.

(Enacted by Acts 2009, 81st Leg., ch. 812 (S.B. 1571), § 1, effective September 1, 2009.)

### Sec. 623.283. Permit Fees.

(a) The port authority may collect a fee for permits issued under this subchapter. The fees may not exceed $80 per trip.

(b) Fees collected under Subsection (a) shall be used solely for the construction and maintenance of port authority roadways.
(Enacted by Acts 2009, 81st Leg., ch. 812 (S.B. 1571), § 1, effective September 1, 2009.)

### Sec. 623.284. Permit Requirements.

A permit issued under this subchapter must include:

(1) the name of the applicant;

(2) the date of issuance;

(3) the signature of the manager of transportation of the port authority;

(4) a statement of the kind of cargo being transported, the maximum weight and dimensions of the equipment, and the kind and weight of each commodity to be transported;

(5) a statement of any condition on which the permit is issued;

(6) a statement that the cargo may only be transported on roadways that are owned and maintained by the port authority and located in San Patricio County or Nueces County; and

(7) the location where the cargo was loaded.
(Enacted by Acts 2009, 81st Leg., ch. 812 (S.B. 1571), § 1, effective September 1, 2009.)

### Sec. 623.285. Time of Movement.

A permit issued under this subchapter must specify the time in which movement authorized by the permit is allowed.
(Enacted by Acts 2009, 81st Leg., ch. 812 (S.B. 1571), § 1, effective September 1, 2009.)

### Sec. 623.286. Speed Limit.

Movement authorized by a permit issued under this subchapter may not exceed the posted speed limit or 55 miles per hour, whichever is less. Violation of this provision shall constitute a moving violation.
(Enacted by Acts 2009, 81st Leg., ch. 812 (S.B. 1571), § 1, effective September 1, 2009.)

### Sec. 623.287. Enforcement.

The Department of Public Safety shall have authority to enforce the provisions of this subchapter.
(Enacted by Acts 2009, 81st Leg., ch. 812 (S.B. 1571), § 1, effective September 1, 2009.)

### Sec. 623.288. Rules.

The Texas Transportation Commission may adopt rules necessary to implement this subchapter.

(Enacted by Acts 2009, 81st Leg., ch. 812 (S.B. 1571), § 1, effective September 1, 2009.)

### Secs. 623.289 to 623.300 [Reserved for expansion].

## SUBCHAPTER P
## PORT OF CORPUS CHRISTI AUTHORITY SPECIAL FREIGHT CORRIDOR PERMITS

### Sec. 623.301. Optional Procedure.

This subchapter provides an optional procedure for the issuance of a permit by the Port of Corpus Christi Authority for the movement of oversize or overweight vehicles carrying cargo on a state highway special freight corridor located in San Patricio County.
(Enacted by Acts 2009, 81st Leg., ch. 812 (S.B. 1571), § 1, effective September 1, 2009.)

### Sec. 623.302. Definitions.

In this subchapter:

(1) "Port authority" means the Port of Corpus Christi Authority; and

(2) "Special freight corridor" means a highway built by this state specifically for the movement of oversize or overweight vehicles carrying cargo in San Patricio County to and from the port authority's La Quinta terminal.
(Enacted by Acts 2009, 81st Leg., ch. 812 (S.B. 1571), § 1, effective September 1, 2009.)

### Sec. 623.303. Issuance of Permits.

The Texas Transportation Commission may authorize the port authority to issue permits for the movement of oversize or overweight vehicles carrying cargo on state highway special freight corridors located in San Patricio County. The port authority may issue a permit under this subchapter only if the cargo being transported weighs 125,000 pounds or less.
(Enacted by Acts 2009, 81st Leg., ch. 812 (S.B. 1571), § 1, effective September 1, 2009.)

### Sec. 623.304. Maintenance Contracts.

The port authority shall make payments to the Texas Department of Transportation to provide funds for the maintenance of state highways subject to this subchapter.
(Enacted by Acts 2009, 81st Leg., ch. 812 (S.B. 1571), § 1, effective September 1, 2009; am. Acts 2011, 82nd Leg., ch. 1345 (S.B. 1420), § 95, effective September 1, 2011.)

## Sec. 623.305.  Permit Fees.

(a) The port authority may collect a fee for permits issued under this subchapter. The fees may not exceed $80 per trip.

(b) Fees collected under Subsection (a) shall be used solely to provide funds for the payments provided for under Section 623.304 and for the port authority's administrative costs, which may not exceed 15 percent of the fees collected. The fees shall be deposited in the state highway fund. Fees deposited in the state highway fund under this section are exempt from the application of Section 403.095, Government Code.

(Enacted by Acts 2009, 81st Leg., ch. 812 (S.B. 1571), § 1, effective September 1, 2009.)

## Sec. 623.306.  Permit Requirements.

(a) A permit issued under this subchapter must include:

(1) the name of the applicant;

(2) the date of issuance;

(3) the signature of the manager of transportation of the port authority;

(4) a statement of the kind of cargo being transported, the maximum weight and dimensions of the equipment, and the kind and weight of each commodity to be transported;

(5) a statement of any condition on which the permit is issued;

(6) a statement that the cargo may only be transported to and from the port authority's La Quinta terminal in San Patricio County using a state highway special freight corridor in San Patricio County; and

(7) the location where the cargo was loaded.

(b) The port authority shall report to the department all permits issued under this subchapter.

(Enacted by Acts 2009, 81st Leg., ch. 812 (S.B. 1571), § 1, effective September 1, 2009.)

## Sec. 623.307.  Time of Movement.

A permit issued under this subchapter must specify the time in which movement authorized by the permit is allowed.

(Enacted by Acts 2009, 81st Leg., ch. 812 (S.B. 1571), § 1, effective September 1, 2009.)

## Sec. 623.308.  Speed Limit.

Movement authorized by a permit issued under this subchapter may not exceed the posted speed limit or 55 miles per hour, whichever is less. Violation of this provision shall constitute a moving violation.

(Enacted by Acts 2009, 81st Leg., ch. 812 (S.B. 1571), § 1, effective September 1, 2009.)

## Sec. 623.309.  Enforcement.

The Department of Public Safety may enforce the provisions of this subchapter.

(Enacted by Acts 2009, 81st Leg., ch. 812 (S.B. 1571), § 1, effective September 1, 2009.)

## Sec. 623.310.  Rules.

The Texas Transportation Commission may adopt rules necessary to implement this subchapter.

(Enacted by Acts 2009, 81st Leg., ch. 812 (S.B. 1571), § 1, effective September 1, 2009.)

# CHAPTERS 624 TO 640
# [RESERVED FOR EXPANSION]

# SUBTITLE F
# COMMERCIAL MOTOR VEHICLES

# CHAPTER 641
# OPERATION OF LEASED
# COMMERCIAL MOTOR VEHICLES
# AND TRUCK-TRACTORS
# [REPEALED]

## SUBCHAPTER A
## GENERAL PROVISIONS

## Sec. 641.001.  Definitions [Repealed].

Repealed by Acts 1997, 75th Leg., ch. 165 (S.B. 898), § 30.148, effective September 1, 1997.

(Enacted by Acts 1995, 74th Leg., ch. 165 (S.B. 971), § 1, effective September 1, 1995.)

## Sec. 641.002.  Effect of Compliance with Chapter [Repealed].

Repealed by Acts 1997, 75th Leg., ch. 165 (S.B. 898), § 30.148, effective September 1, 1997.

(Enacted by Acts 1995, 74th Leg., ch. 165 (S.B. 971), § 1, effective September 1, 1995.)

## SUBCHAPTER B
## VEHICLE OPERATED UNDER LEASE

## Sec. 641.021.  Filing of Lease Required [Repealed].

Repealed by Acts 1997, 75th Leg., ch. 165 (S.B. 898), § 30.148, effective September 1, 1997.

(Enacted by Acts 1995, 74th Leg., ch. 165 (S.B. 971), § 1, effective September 1, 1995.)

### Sec. 641.022.    Contents of Lease [Repealed].

Repealed by Acts 1997, 75th Leg., ch. 165 (S.B. 898), § 30.148, effective September 1, 1997. (Enacted by Acts 1995, 74th Leg., ch. 165 (S.B. 971), § 1, effective September 1, 1995.)

### Sec. 641.023.    Manner of Filing; Fee [Repealed].

Repealed by Acts 1997, 75th Leg., ch. 165 (S.B. 898), § 30.148, effective September 1, 1997. (Enacted by Acts 1995, 74th Leg., ch. 165 (S.B. 971), § 1, effective September 1, 1995.)

### Sec. 641.024.    Acknowledgment [Repealed].

Repealed by Acts 1997, 75th Leg., ch. 165 (S.B. 898), § 30.148, effective September 1, 1997. (Enacted by Acts 1995, 74th Leg., ch. 165 (S.B. 971), § 1, effective September 1, 1995.)

### Sec. 641.025.    Maintenance and Display of Lease or Acknowledgment [Repealed].

Repealed by Acts 1997, 75th Leg., ch. 165 (S.B. 898), § 30.148, effective September 1, 1997. (Enacted by Acts 1995, 74th Leg., ch. 165 (S.B. 971), § 1, effective September 1, 1995.)

### Sec. 641.026.    Subsequent Lease; Fee [Repealed].

Repealed by Acts 1997, 75th Leg., ch. 165 (S.B. 898), § 30.148, effective September 1, 1997. (Enacted by Acts 1995, 74th Leg., ch. 165 (S.B. 971), § 1, effective September 1, 1995.)

### Sec. 641.027.    Lease Confidential [Repealed].

Repealed by Acts 1997, 75th Leg., ch. 165 (S.B. 898), § 30.148, effective September 1, 1997. (Enacted by Acts 1995, 74th Leg., ch. 165 (S.B. 971), § 1, effective September 1, 1995.)

### SUBCHAPTER C
### SIGNS

### Sec. 641.041.    Signs Required [Repealed].

Repealed by Acts 1997, 75th Leg., ch. 165 (S.B.

898), § 30.148, effective September 1, 1997. (Enacted by Acts 1995, 74th Leg., ch. 165 (S.B. 971), § 1, effective September 1, 1995.)

### Sec. 641.042.    Placement and Content of Signs [Repealed].

Repealed by Acts 1997, 75th Leg., ch. 165 (S.B. 898), § 30.148, effective September 1, 1997. (Enacted by Acts 1995, 74th Leg., ch. 165 (S.B. 971), § 1, effective September 1, 1995.)

### SUBCHAPTER D
### EXCEPTIONS

### Sec. 641.061.    Operation by Agent [Repealed].

Repealed by Acts 1997, 75th Leg., ch. 165 (S.B. 898), § 30.148, effective September 1, 1997. (Enacted by Acts 1995, 74th Leg., ch. 165 (S.B. 971), § 1, effective September 1, 1995.)

### Sec. 641.062.    Farm Vehicles [Repealed].

Repealed by Acts 1997, 75th Leg., ch. 165 (S.B. 898), § 30.148, effective September 1, 1997. (Enacted by Acts 1995, 74th Leg., ch. 165 (S.B. 971), § 1, effective September 1, 1995.)

### Sec. 641.063.    Vehicles Used to Transport Earth and Road-Building Materials [Repealed].

Repealed by Acts 1997, 75th Leg., ch. 165 (S.B. 898), § 30.148, effective September 1, 1997. (Enacted by Acts 1995, 74th Leg., ch. 165 (S.B. 971), § 1, effective September 1, 1995.)

### Sec. 641.064.    Passenger Car Used to Deliver Mail [Repealed].

Repealed by Acts 1997, 75th Leg., ch. 165 (S.B. 898), § 30.148, effective September 1, 1997. (Enacted by Acts 1995, 74th Leg., ch. 165 (S.B. 971), § 1, effective September 1, 1995.)

### Sec. 641.065.    Vehicles Used to Transport Liquefied Petroleum Gas [Repealed].

Repealed by Acts 1997, 75th Leg., ch. 165 (S.B. 898), § 30.148, effective September 1, 1997. (Enacted by Acts 1995, 74th Leg., ch. 165 (S.B. 971), § 1, effective September 1, 1995.)

### Sec. 641.066. Vehicles Used to Transport Household and Office Goods [Repealed].

Repealed by Acts 1997, 75th Leg., ch. 165 (S.B. 898), § 30.148, effective September 1, 1997. (Enacted by Acts 1995, 74th Leg., ch. 165 (S.B. 971), § 1, effective September 1, 1995.)

### Sec. 641.067. Vehicles Leased from Certain Leasing Companies [Repealed].

Repealed by Acts 1997, 75th Leg., ch. 165 (S.B. 898), § 30.148, effective September 1, 1997. (Enacted by Acts 1995, 74th Leg., ch. 165 (S.B. 971), § 1, effective September 1, 1995.)

## SUBCHAPTER E
## VIOLATION; PENALTIES

### Sec. 641.081. Offense [Repealed].

Repealed by Acts 1997, 75th Leg., ch. 165 (S.B. 898), § 30.148, effective September 1, 1997. (Enacted by Acts 1995, 74th Leg., ch. 165 (S.B. 971), § 1, effective September 1, 1995.)

### Sec. 641.082. Defense: Loan of Vehicle Without Compensation [Repealed].

Repealed by Acts 1997, 75th Leg., ch. 165 (S.B. 898), § 30.148, effective September 1, 1997. (Enacted by Acts 1995, 74th Leg., ch. 165 (S.B. 971), § 1, effective September 1, 1995.)

## CHAPTER 642
## IDENTIFYING MARKINGS ON COMMERCIAL MOTOR VEHICLES

**Section**
642.001. Definitions.
642.002. Identifying Markings on Certain Vehicles Required; Offense; Penalty.
642.003. Nonapplicability.

### Sec. 642.001. Definitions.

In this chapter:

(1) "Motor vehicle" means a motor vehicle, other than a motorcycle, that is designed or used primarily for the transportation of persons or property.

(2) "Operator" means the person who is in actual physical control of a motor vehicle.

(3) "Owner" means a person who has:

(A) legal title to a motor vehicle; or

(B) the right to possess or control the vehicle.

(4) "Road-tractor" means a motor vehicle that is:

(A) used for towing manufactured housing; or

(B) designed and used for drawing other vehicles and not constructed so as to carry any load independently or as a part of the weight of a vehicle or load it is drawing.

(5) "Truck-tractor" means a motor vehicle that:

(A) transports passenger cars loaded on the vehicle while the vehicle is engaged with a semitrailer transporting passenger cars; or

(B) is designed or used primarily for pulling other vehicles and constructed to carry only a part of the weight of a vehicle it is pulling.

(6) "Tow truck" has the meaning assigned that term by Section 2308.002, Occupations Code.

(Enacted by Acts 1995, 74th Leg., ch. 165 (S.B. 971), § 1, effective September 1, 1995; am. Acts 1997, 75th Leg., ch. 1171 (S.B. 370), § 4.12(a), effective September 1, 1997; am. Acts 2009, 81st Leg., ch. 87 (S.B. 1969), § 23.008, effective September 1, 2009.)

### Sec. 642.002. Identifying Markings on Certain Vehicles Required; Offense; Penalty.

(a) A person commits an offense if:

(1) the person operates on a public street, road, or highway:

(A) a commercial motor vehicle that has three or more axles;

(B) a truck-tractor;

(C) a road-tractor; or

(D) a tow truck; and

(2) the vehicle does not have on each side of the power unit identifying markings that comply with the identifying marking requirements specified by 49 C.F.R. Section 390.21 or that:

(A) show the name of the owner or operator of the vehicle;

(B) have clearly legible letters and numbers of a height of at least two inches; and

(C) show the motor carrier registration number in clearly legible letters and numbers, if the vehicle is required to be registered under this chapter.

(b) A person commits an offense if the person operates on a public street, road, or highway a tow truck that does not show on each side of the power unit, in addition to the markings required by Subsection (a)(2), the city in which the owner or operator maintains its place of business and the telephone number, including area code, at that place of business in clearly legible letters and numbers.

(c) The owner of a vehicle commits an offense if the owner or operator permits another to operate a vehicle in violation of Subsection (a) or (b).

(d) The Texas Department of Motor Vehicles by rule may prescribe additional requirements regarding the form of the markings required by Subsection (a)(2) that are not inconsistent with that subsection.

(e) An offense under this section is a Class C misdemeanor.

(Enacted by Acts 1995, 74th Leg., ch. 165 (S.B. 971), § 1, effective September 1, 1995; am. Acts 1997, 75th Leg., ch. 1171 (S.B. 370), § 4.12(b), effective September 1, 1997; am. Acts 1999, 76th Leg., ch. 566 (S.B. 450), § 1, effective June 18, 1999; am. Acts 2009, 81st Leg., ch. 933 (H.B. 3097), § 2K.01, effective September 1, 2009.)

### Sec. 642.003.  Nonapplicability.

Section 642.002 does not apply to a commercial motor vehicle, road-tractor, or truck-tractor that is:

(1) registered under Section 502.163;

(2) required to be registered under Section 113.131, Natural Resources Code;

(3) operated in private carriage that is subject to Title 49, Code of Federal Regulations, Part 397.21;

(4) operated under the direct control, supervision, or authority of a public utility, as recognized by the legislature, that is otherwise visibly marked; or

(5) transporting timber products in their natural state from first point of production or harvest to first point of processing.

(Enacted by Acts 1995, 74th Leg., ch. 165 (S.B. 971), § 1, effective September 1, 1995; am. Acts 1997, 75th Leg., ch. 165 (S.B. 898), § 30.149(a), effective September 1, 1997.)

## CHAPTER 643
## MOTOR CARRIER REGISTRATION

### Subchapter A. General Provisions

### Subchapter B. Registration

### Subchapter C. Insurance

### Subchapter D. Economic Regulation

### Subchapter F. Enforcement

## SUBCHAPTER A
## GENERAL PROVISIONS

### Sec. 643.001.  Definitions.

In this chapter:

(1) "Department" means the Texas Department of Motor Vehicles.

(2) "Director" means:

(A) the executive director of the department; or

(B) an employee of the department who:

(i) is a division or special office director or holds a higher rank; and

(ii) is designated by the director.

(3) "Hazardous material" has the meaning assigned by 49 U.S.C. Section 5102.

(4) "Household goods" has the meaning assigned by 49 U.S.C. Section 13102.

(5) "Insurer" means a person, including a surety, authorized in this state to write lines of insurance coverage required by this chapter.

(6) "Motor carrier" means an individual, association, corporation, or other legal entity that controls, operates, or directs the operation of one or more vehicles that transport persons or cargo over a road or highway in this state.

(7) [Repealed by Acts 2007, 80th Leg., ch. 1046 (H.B. 2094), § 5.01(a)(1), effective September 1, 2007.]

(7-a) "Unified carrier registration system" means a motor vehicle registration system established under 49 U.S.C. Section 14504a or a similar federal registration program that replaces that system.

(8) "Vehicle requiring registration" means a vehicle described by Section 643.051.

(Enacted by Acts 1997, 75th Leg., ch. 165 (S.B. 898), § 30.150(a), effective September 1, 1997; am. Acts 2007, 80th Leg., ch. 1046 (H.B. 2094), § 5.01(a)(1), effective September 1, 2007; am. Acts 2007, 80th Leg., ch. 1396 (H.B. 2093), § 16, effective September 1, 2007; am. Acts 2009, 81st Leg., ch. 933 (H.B. 3097), § 2L.01, effective September 1, 2009.)

## Sec. 643.002. Exemptions.

This chapter does not apply to:

(1) motor carrier operations exempt from registration by the Unified Carrier Registration Act of 2005 (49 U.S.C. Section 14504a) or a motor vehicle registered under the single state registration system established under 49 U.S.C. Section 14504(c) when operating exclusively in interstate or international commerce;

(2) a motor vehicle registered as a cotton vehicle under Section 504.505;

(3) a motor vehicle the department by rule exempts because the vehicle is subject to comparable registration and a comparable safety program administered by another governmental entity;

(4) a motor vehicle used to transport passengers operated by an entity whose primary function is not the transportation of passengers, such as a vehicle operated by a hotel, day-care center, public or private school, nursing home, or similar organization;

(5) a vehicle operating under a private carrier permit issued under Chapter 42, Alcoholic Beverage Code;

(6) a vehicle operated by a governmental entity; or

(7) a tow truck, as defined by Section 2308.002, Occupations Code.

(Enacted by Acts 1997, 75th Leg., ch. 165 (S.B. 898), § 30.150(a), effective September 1, 1997; am. Acts 1999, 76th Leg., ch. 62 (S.B. 1368), § 17.10(a), effective September 1, 1999; am. Acts 1999, 76th Leg., ch. 603 (S.B. 775), § 1, effective August 30, 1999; am. Acts 2007, 80th Leg., ch. 1046 (H.B. 2094), § 3.06, effective September 1, 2007; am. Acts 2007, 80th Leg., ch. 1396 (H.B. 2093), § 17, effective September 1, 2007.)

## Sec. 643.003. Rules.

The department may adopt rules to administer this chapter.

(Enacted by Acts 1997, 75th Leg., ch. 165 (S.B. 898), § 30.150(a), effective September 1, 1997.)

## Sec. 643.004. Payment of Fees.

(a) The department may adopt rules on the method of payment of a fee under this chapter, including:

(1) authorizing the use of:

(A) escrow accounts described by Subsection (b); and

(B) electronic funds transfer or a credit card issued by a financial institution chartered by a state or the United States or by a nationally recognized credit organization approved by the department; and

(2) requiring the payment of a discount or service charge for a credit card payment in addition to the fee.

(b) The department may establish one or more escrow accounts in the state highway fund for the prepayment of a fee under this chapter. Prepaid fees and any fees established by the department for the administration of this section shall be:

(1) administered under an agreement approved by the department; and

(2) deposited to the credit of the state highway fund to be appropriated only to the department for the purposes of administering this chapter.

(Enacted by Acts 1997, 75th Leg., ch. 165 (S.B. 898), § 30.150(a), effective September 1, 1997; am. Acts 1999, 76th Leg., ch. 62 (S.B. 1368), § 17.11(a), effective September 1, 1999.)

Transportation

**Secs. 643.005 to 643.050 [Reserved for expansion].**

## SUBCHAPTER B
## REGISTRATION

### Sec. 643.051.   Registration Required.

(a) A motor carrier may not operate a commercial motor vehicle, as defined by Section 548.001, on a road or highway of this state unless the carrier registers with the department under this subchapter.

(b) A motor carrier may not operate a vehicle, regardless of size of the vehicle, to transport household goods for compensation unless the carrier registers with the department under this subchapter.
(Enacted by Acts 1997, 75th Leg., ch. 165 (S.B. 898), § 30.150(a), effective September 1, 1997; am. Acts 2005, 79th Leg., ch. 281 (H.B. 2702), § 6.01, effective June 14, 2005; am. Acts 2007, 80th Leg., ch. 1046 (H.B. 2094), § 3.07, effective September 1, 2007.)

### Sec. 643.052.   Application.

To register under this subchapter a motor carrier must submit to the department an application on a form prescribed by the department. The application must include:

(1) the name of the owner and the principal business address of the motor carrier;

(2) the name and address of the legal agent for service of process on the carrier in this state, if different;

(3) a description of each vehicle requiring registration the carrier proposes to operate, including the motor vehicle identification number, make, and unit number;

(4) a statement as to whether the carrier proposes to transport household goods or a hazardous material;

(5) a declaration that the applicant has knowledge of all laws and rules relating to motor carrier safety, including this chapter, Chapter 644, and Subtitle C;

(6) a certification that the carrier is in compliance with the drug testing requirements of 49 C.F.R. Part 382, and if the carrier belongs to a consortium, as defined by 49 C.F.R. Part 382, the names of the persons operating the consortium;

(7) a valid identification number issued to the motor carrier by or under the authority of the Federal Motor Carrier Safety Administration or its successor; and

(8) any other information the department by rule determines is necessary for the safe operation of a motor carrier under this chapter.
(Enacted by Acts 1997, 75th Leg., ch. 165 (S.B. 898), § 30.150(a), effective September 1, 1997; am. Acts 2003, 78th Leg., ch. 991 (S.B. 1904), § 9, effective September 1, 2003; am. Acts 2009, 81st Leg., ch. 919 (H.B. 2985), § 3, effective September 1, 2009.)

### Sec. 643.053.   Filing of Application.

An application under Section 643.052 must be filed with the department and accompanied by:

(1) an application fee of $100 plus a $10 fee for each vehicle requiring registration;

(2) evidence of insurance or financial responsibility as required by Section 643.103(a); and

(3) any insurance filing fee required under Section 643.103(c).
(Enacted by Acts 1997, 75th Leg., ch. 165 (S.B. 898), § 30.150(a), effective September 1, 1997; am. Acts 2003, 78th Leg., ch. 1034 (H.B. 849), § 4, effective September 1, 2003; am. Acts 2007, 80th Leg., ch. 1046 (H.B. 2094), § 3.08, effective September 1, 2007.)

### Sec. 643.054.   Department Approval; Issuance of Certificate.

(a) The department shall register a motor carrier under this subchapter if the carrier complies with Sections 643.052 and 643.053. The department may deny a registration if the applicant has had a registration revoked under Section 643.252.

(b) The department shall issue a certificate containing a single registration number to a motor carrier, regardless of the number of vehicles requiring registration the carrier operates.

(c) To avoid multiple registrations of a single motor carrier, the department shall adopt simplified procedures for the registration of motor carriers transporting household goods as agents for carriers required to register under this chapter.
(Enacted by Acts 1997, 75th Leg., ch. 165 (S.B. 898), § 30.150(a), effective September 1, 1997; am. Acts 1999, 76th Leg., ch. 62 (S.B. 1368), § 17.12(a), effective September 1, 1999.)

### Sec. 643.055.   Conditional Acceptance.

(a) The department may conditionally accept an incomplete application for registration under this subchapter if the motor carrier complies with Section 643.053.

(b) The department shall notify a motor carrier that an application is incomplete and inform the

carrier of the information required for completion. If the motor carrier fails to provide the information before the 46th day after the date the department provides the notice, the application is considered withdrawn, and the department shall retain each fee required by Section 643.053(1).
(Enacted by Acts 1997, 75th Leg., ch. 165 (S.B. 898), § 30.150(a), effective September 1, 1997.)

## Sec. 643.056. Supplemental Registration.

(a) A motor carrier required to register under this subchapter shall supplement the carrier's application for registration before:

(1) the carrier transports a hazardous material or household goods if the carrier has not provided notice of the transportation to the department in the carrier's initial or a supplemental application for registration;

(2) the carrier operates a vehicle requiring registration that is not described on the carrier's initial or a supplemental application for registration; or

(3) the carrier changes the carrier's principal business address, legal agent, ownership, consortium, as defined by 49 C.F.R. Part 382, or name.

(b) The department shall prescribe the form of a supplemental application for registration under Subsection (a).
(Enacted by Acts 1997, 75th Leg., ch. 165 (S.B. 898), § 30.150(a), effective September 1, 1997; am. Acts 2003, 78th Leg., ch. 991 (S.B. 1904), § 10, effective September 1, 2003.)

## Sec. 643.057. Additional Vehicles and Fees.

(a) A motor carrier may not operate an additional vehicle requiring registration unless the carrier pays a registration fee of $10 for each additional vehicle and shows the department evidence of insurance or financial responsibility for the vehicle in an amount at least equal to the amount set by the department under Section 643.101.

(b) A motor carrier is not required to pay the applicable registration fee under Subsection (a) for a vehicle for which the same fee is required and that replaces a vehicle for which the fee has been paid.

(c) A registered motor carrier may not transport household goods or a hazardous material unless the carrier shows the department evidence of insurance or financial responsibility in an

amount at least equal to the amount set by the department under Section 643.101 for a vehicle carrying household goods or a hazardous material.

(d) The department may not collect more than $10 in equipment registration fees for a vehicle registered under both this subchapter and Chapter 645.
(Enacted by Acts 1997, 75th Leg., ch. 165 (S.B. 898), § 30.150(a), effective September 1, 1997; am. Acts 2003, 78th Leg., ch. 1034 (H.B. 849), § 5, effective September 1, 2003; am. Acts 2007, 80th Leg., ch. 1046 (H.B. 2094), § 3.09, effective September 1, 2007.)

## Sec. 643.058. Renewal of Registration.

(a) Except as provided in Section 643.061, a registration issued under this subchapter is valid for one year. The department may adopt a system under which registrations expire at different times during the year.

(b) At least 30 days before the date on which a motor carrier's registration expires, the department shall notify the carrier of the impending expiration. The notice must be in writing and sent to the motor carrier's last known address according to the records of the department.

(c) A motor carrier may renew a registration under this subchapter by:

(1) supplementing the application with any new information required under Section 643.056;

(2) paying a $10 fee for each vehicle requiring registration; and

(3) providing the department evidence of continuing insurance or financial responsibility in an amount at least equal to the amount set by the department under Section 643.101.
(Enacted by Acts 1997, 75th Leg., ch. 165 (S.B. 898), § 30.150(a), effective September 1, 1997; am. Acts 1999, 76th Leg., ch. 62 (S.B. 1368), § 17.13(a), effective September 1, 1999; am. Acts 1999, 76th Leg., ch. 603 (S.B. 775), § 2, effective August 30, 1999; am. Acts 2003, 78th Leg., ch. 1034 (H.B. 849), § 6, effective September 1, 2003; am. Acts 2007, 80th Leg., ch. 1046 (H.B. 2094), § 3.10, effective September 1, 2007.)

## Sec. 643.059. Cab Cards.

(a) The department shall issue a cab card for each vehicle requiring registration. A cab card must:

(1) show the registration number of the certificate issued under Section 643.054(b);

(2) show the vehicle unit number;

(3) show the vehicle identification number; and

(4) contain a statement that the vehicle is registered to operate under this subchapter.

(b) The department shall issue cab cards at the time a motor carrier pays a registration fee under this subchapter. The department may charge a fee of $1 for each cab card.

(c) A motor carrier required to register under this subchapter must keep the cab card in the cab of each vehicle requiring registration the carrier operates.

(d) The department may order a motor carrier to surrender a cab card if the carrier's registration is suspended or revoked under Section 643.252.

(e) If the department determines that the cab card system described by Subsections (a)—(c) is not an efficient means of enforcing this subchapter, the department by rule may adopt an alternative method that is accessible by law enforcement personnel in the field and provides for the enforcement of the registration requirements of this subchapter.

(f) A cab card or a vehicle registration issued under the alternative method described in Subsection (e) must be valid for the same duration of time as a motor carrier's certificate issued under Section 643.054(b) or Section 643.061(c)(1).

(Enacted by Acts 1997, 75th Leg., ch. 165 (S.B. 898), § 30.150(a), effective September 1, 1997; am. Acts 1999, 76th Leg., ch. 603 (S.B. 775), § 3, effective August 30, 1999.)

### Sec. 643.060.  Temporary Registration of International Motor Carrier.

The department by rule may provide for the temporary registration of an international motor carrier that provides evidence of insurance as required for a domestic motor carrier. The department may charge a fee for a temporary registration in an amount not to exceed the cost of administering this section.

(Enacted by Acts 1997, 75th Leg., ch. 165 (S.B. 898), § 30.150(a), effective September 1, 1997.)

### Sec. 643.061.  Optional Registration Periods.

(a) The department may vary the registration period under this subchapter by adopting rules that provide for:

(1) an optional two-year registration; and

(2) an optional temporary registration that is valid for less than one year.

(b) A motor carrier applying for registration under this section must pay:

(1) a $20 fee for each vehicle registered under Subsection (a)(1);

(2) a $10 fee for each vehicle registered under Subsection (a)(2); and

(3) application and insurance filing fees the department by rule adopts in an amount not to exceed $100 each.

(c) The department shall issue to a motor carrier registering under this section:

(1) a motor carrier's certificate, in the manner provided by Section 643.054; and

(2) a cab card or the equivalent of a cab card, in the manner provided by Section 643.059.

(Enacted by Acts 1999, 76th Leg., ch. 603 (S.B. 775), § 4, effective August 30, 1999; am. Acts 2003, 78th Leg., ch. 1034 (H.B. 849), § 7, effective September 1, 2003; am. Acts 2007, 80th Leg., ch. 1046 (H.B. 2094), § 3.11, effective September 1, 2007.)

### Sec. 643.062.  Limitation on International Motor Carrier.

(a) A foreign-based international motor carrier required to register under this chapter or registered under Chapter 645 may not transport persons or cargo in intrastate commerce in this state.

(b) A person may not assist a foreign-based international motor carrier in violating Subsection (a).

(Enacted by Acts 1999, 76th Leg., ch. 62 (S.B. 1368), § 17.14(a), effective September 1, 1999; enacted by Acts 1999, 76th Leg., ch. 603 (S.B. 775), § 4, effective August 30, 1999.)

### Sec. 643.063.  Vehicles Operated Under Short-Term Lease and Substitute Vehicles.

(a) In this section:

(1) "Leasing business" means a person that leases vehicles requiring registration.

(2) "Short-term lease" means a lease of 30 days or less.

(b) A vehicle requiring registration operated under a short-term lease is exempt from the registration requirements of Sections 643.052—643.059. The department shall adopt rules providing for the operation of these vehicles under flexible procedures. A vehicle requiring registration operated under a short-term lease is not required to carry a cab card or other proof of registration if a copy of the lease agreement is carried in the cab of the vehicle.

(c) A motor carrier may operate a substitute vehicle without notifying the department in advance if the substitute is a temporary replacement because of maintenance, repair, or other unavailability of the vehicle originally leased. A substitute vehicle is not required to carry a cab card or other proof of registration if a copy of the lease agreement for the vehicle originally leased is carried in the cab of the substitute.

(d) Instead of the registration procedures described by Sections 643.052—643.059, the department shall adopt rules that allow a leasing business to report annually to the department on the number of vehicles requiring registration that the leasing business actually operated in the previous 12 months. The rules may not require the vehicles operated to be described with particularity. The registration fee for each vehicle operated may be paid at the time the report is filed.

(e) A leasing business that registers its vehicles under Subsection (d) may comply with the liability insurance requirements of Subchapter C by filing evidence of a contingency liability policy satisfactory to the department.

(f) Rules adopted by the department under this section:

(1) must be designed to avoid requiring a vehicle to be registered more than once in a calendar year; and

(2) may allow a leasing business to register a vehicle on behalf of a lessee.

(Enacted by Acts 1999, 76th Leg., ch. 62 (S.B. 1368), § 17.15(a), effective September 1, 1999.)

### Sec. 643.064. Issuance of United States Department of Transportation Numbers.

The department by rule shall provide for the issuance to a motor carrier of an identification number authorized by the Federal Motor Carrier Safety Administration. A rule must conform to rules of the Federal Motor Carrier Safety Administration or its successor.

(Enacted by Acts 2009, 81st Leg., ch. 919 (H.B. 2985), § 4, effective September 1, 2009.)

### Secs. 643.065 to 643.100 [Reserved for expansion].

### SUBCHAPTER C
### INSURANCE

### Sec. 643.101. Amount Required.

(a) A motor carrier required to register under Subchapter B shall maintain liability insurance in an amount set by the department for each vehicle requiring registration the carrier operates.

(b) Except as provided by Section 643.1015, the department by rule may set the amount of liability insurance required at an amount that does not exceed the amount required for a motor carrier under a federal regulation adopted under 49 U.S.C. Section 13906(a)(1). In setting the amount the department shall consider:

(1) the class and size of the vehicle; and

(2) the persons or cargo being transported.

(c) A motor carrier required to register under Subchapter B that transports household goods shall maintain cargo insurance in the amount required for a motor carrier transporting household goods under federal law.

(d) [Repealed by Acts 2007, 80th Leg., ch. 1046 (H.B. 2094), § 5.01(a)(2), effective September 1, 2007.]

(e) Unless state law permits a commercial motor vehicle to be self-insured, any insurance required for a commercial motor vehicle must be obtained from:

(1) an insurer authorized to do business in this state whose aggregate net risk, after reinsurance, under any one insurance policy is not in excess of 10 percent of the insurer's policyholders' surplus, and credit for such reinsurance is permitted by law; or

(2) an insurer that meets the eligibility requirements of a surplus lines insurer pursuant to Chapter 981, Insurance Code. Notwithstanding any other provision in law, an insurer in compliance with this subsection shall be deemed to be in compliance with any rating or financial criteria established for motor carriers by any political subdivision of the state.

(Enacted by Acts 1997, 75th Leg., ch. 165 (S.B. 898), § 30.150(a), effective September 1, 1997; am. Acts 2003, 78th Leg., ch. 1034 (H.B. 849), § 8, effective September 1, 2003; am. Acts 2005, 79th Leg., ch. 144 (H.B. 1018), § 1, effective May 24, 2005; am. Acts 2005, 79th Leg., ch. 728 (H.B. 2018), § 11.163, effective September 1, 2005; am. Acts 2007, 80th Leg., ch. 1046 (H.B. 2094), § 5.01(a)(2), effective September 1, 2007.)

### Sec. 643.1015. Amount Required for Certain School Buses.

(a) This section applies only to a school bus that:

(1) is owned by a motor carrier required to be registered under Subchapter B;

(2) is in compliance with the requirements of Chapter 548; and

(3) is operated exclusively within the boundaries of a municipality by a person who:

(A) holds a driver's license or commercial driver's license of the appropriate class required for the operation of the school bus; and

(B) meets the requirements of Section 521.022.

(b) The owner of a school bus shall maintain liability insurance in the amount of at least $500,000 combined single limit.

(c) In this section, "school bus" means a motor vehicle that is operated by a motor carrier and used to transport preprimary, primary, or secondary school students on a route between the students' residences and a public, private, or parochial school or day-care facility.
(Enacted by Acts 2005, 79th Leg., ch. 144 (H.B. 1018), § 2, effective May 24, 2005.)

### Sec. 643.102.   Self-Insurance.

A motor carrier may comply with Section 643.101 through self-insurance if the carrier demonstrates to the department that it can satisfy its obligations for liability for bodily injury or property damage. In the interest of public safety, the department by rule shall provide for a responsible system of self-insurance for a motor carrier.
(Enacted by Acts 1997, 75th Leg., ch. 165 (S.B. 898), § 30.150(a), effective September 1, 1997.)

### Sec. 643.103.   Filing; Evidence of Insurance; Fees.

(a) A motor carrier that is required to register under Subchapter B must file with the department evidence of insurance in the amounts required by Section 643.101 or 643.1015, or evidence of financial responsibility as described by Section 643.102, in a form prescribed by the department. The form must be filed:

(1) at the time of the initial registration;

(2) at the time of a subsequent registration if the motor carrier was required to be continuously registered under Subchapter B and the carrier failed to maintain continuous registration;

(3) at the time a motor carrier changes insurers; and

(4) at the time a motor carrier changes ownership, as determined by rules adopted by the department.

(b) A motor carrier shall keep evidence of insurance in a form approved by the department in the cab of each vehicle requiring registration the carrier operates.

(c) The department may charge a fee of $100 for a filing under Subsection (a).
(Enacted by Acts 1997, 75th Leg., ch. 165 (S.B. 898), § 30.150(a), effective September 1, 1997; am. Acts 2005, 79th Leg., ch. 144 (H.B. 1018), § 3, effective May 24, 2005.)

### Sec. 643.104.   Termination of Insurance Coverage.

(a) An insurer may not terminate coverage provided to a motor carrier registered under Subchapter B unless the insurer provides the department with notice at least 30 days before the date the termination takes effect.

(b) Notice under Subsection (a) must be in a form approved by the department and the Texas Department of Insurance. The department shall notify the Department of Public Safety and other law enforcement agencies of each motor carrier whose certificate of registration has been revoked for failing to maintain liability insurance coverage.

(c) The Department of Public Safety or a local law enforcement agency shall confirm that no operations are being performed by a motor carrier if notice has been received under Subsection (b) that the certificate of registration for that carrier has been revoked.

(d) A law enforcement officer may detain or impound any commercial vehicle operating without liability insurance until such coverage is properly filed with the department.
(Enacted by Acts 1997, 75th Leg., ch. 165 (S.B. 898), § 30.150(a), effective September 1, 1997; am. Acts 2003, 78th Leg., ch. 163 (S.B. 1063), § 1, effective September 1, 2003.)

### Sec. 643.105.   Insolvency of Insurer.

If an insurer for a motor carrier becomes insolvent, is placed in receivership, or has its certificate of authority suspended or revoked and if the carrier no longer has insurance coverage as required by this subchapter, the carrier shall file with the department, not later than the 10th day after the date the coverage lapses:

(1) evidence of insurance as required by Section 643.103; and

(2) an affidavit that:

(A) indicates that an accident from which the carrier may incur liability did not occur while the coverage was not in effect; or

(B) contains a plan acceptable to the department indicating how the carrier will satisfy claims of liability against the carrier for an accident that occurred while the coverage was not in effect.

(Enacted by Acts 1997, 75th Leg., ch. 165 (S.B. 898), § 30.150(a), effective September 1, 1997.)

### Sec. 643.106. Insurance for Employees.

(a) Notwithstanding any provision of any law or regulation, a motor carrier that is required to register under Subchapter B and whose primary business is transportation for compensation or hire between two or more municipalities shall protect its employees by obtaining:

(1) workers' compensation insurance coverage as defined under Subtitle A, Title 5, Labor Code; or

(2) accidental insurance coverage approved by the department from:

(A) a reliable insurance company authorized to write accidental insurance policies in this state; or

(B) a surplus lines insurer under Chapter 981, Insurance Code.

(b) The department shall determine the amount of insurance coverage under Subsection (a)(2). The amount may not be less than:

(1) $300,000 for medical expenses for at least 104 weeks;

(2) $100,000 for accidental death and dismemberment;

(3) 70 percent of an employee's pre-injury income for at least 104 weeks when compensating for loss of income; and

(4) $500 for the maximum weekly benefit.

(Enacted by Acts 1997, 75th Leg., ch. 165 (S.B. 898), § 30.150(a), effective September 1, 1997; am. Acts 1999, 76th Leg., ch. 62 (S.B. 1368), § 17.17(a), effective September 1, 1999; am. Acts 1999, 76th Leg., ch. 886 (H.B. 2035), § 1, effective August 30, 1999; am. Acts 2003, 78th Leg., ch. 1276 (H.B. 3507), § 10A.554, effective September 1, 2003.)

### Secs. 643.107 to 643.150 [Reserved for expansion].

## SUBCHAPTER D
## ECONOMIC REGULATION

### Sec. 643.151. Prohibition.

Except as provided by this subchapter, the department may not regulate the prices, routes, or services provided by a motor carrier.

(Enacted by Acts 1997, 75th Leg., ch. 165 (S.B. 898), § 30.150(a), effective September 1, 1997.)

### Sec. 643.152. Voluntary Standards.

The department may establish voluntary standards for uniform cargo liability, uniform bills of lading or receipts for cargo being transported, and uniform cargo credit. A standard adopted under this section must be consistent with Subtitle IV, Title 49, United States Code, or a regulation adopted under that law.

(Enacted by Acts 1997, 75th Leg., ch. 165 (S.B. 898), § 30.150(a), effective September 1, 1997.)

### Sec. 643.153. Motor Carrier Transporting Household Goods.

(a) The department shall adopt rules to protect a consumer using the service of a motor carrier who is transporting household goods for compensation.

(b) The department may adopt rules necessary to ensure that a customer of a motor carrier transporting household goods is protected from deceptive or unfair practices and unreasonably hazardous activities. The rules must:

(1) establish a formal process for resolving a dispute over a fee or damage;

(2) require a motor carrier to indicate clearly to a customer whether an estimate is binding or nonbinding and disclose the maximum price a customer could be required to pay;

(3) create a centralized process for making complaints about a motor carrier that also allows a customer to inquire about a carrier's complaint record; and

(4) require a motor carrier transporting household goods to list a place of business with a street address in this state and the carrier's registration number issued under this article in any print advertising published in this state.

(c) [Repealed by Acts 2005, 79th Leg., ch. 281 (H.B. 2702), § 6.06, effective June 14, 2005.]

(d) A motor carrier that is required to register under Subchapter B and that transports household goods shall file a tariff with the department that establishes maximum charges for transportation between two or more municipalities. A motor carrier may comply with this requirement by filing a copy of the carrier's tariff governing interstate transportation services on a highway between two or more municipalities. The department shall make tariffs filed under this subsection available for public inspection at the department.

(e) The department may not adopt rules regulating the rates, except as provided by this section, or routes of a motor carrier transporting household goods.

(f) The unauthorized practice of the insurance business under Chapter 101, Insurance Code, does not include the offer of insurance by a household goods motor carrier, or its agent, that transports goods for up to the full value of a customer's property transported or stored, if the offer is authorized by a rule adopted under Subsection (b).

(g) A motor carrier may designate an association or an agent of an association as its collective maximum ratemaking association for the purpose of the filing of a tariff under Subsection (d). (Enacted by Acts 1997, 75th Leg., ch. 165 (S.B. 898), § 30.150(a), effective September 1, 1997; am. Acts 1999, 76th Leg., ch. 62 (S.B. 1368), § 17.19(a), effective September 1, 1999; am. Acts 1999, 76th Leg., ch. 603 (S.B. 775), § 5, effective August 30, 1999; am. Acts 2003, 78th Leg., ch. 1276 (H.B. 3507), § 10A.555, effective September 1, 2003; am. Acts 2005, 79th Leg., ch. 281 (H.B. 2702), § 6.02, effective June 14, 2005; am. Acts 2005, 79th Leg., ch. 281 (H.B. 2702), § 6.06, effective June 14, 2005.)

## Sec. 643.154. Antitrust Exemption.

(a) Chapter 15, Business & Commerce Code, does not apply to a discussion or agreement between a motor carrier that is required to register under Subchapter B and that transports household goods and an agent of the carrier involving:

(1) the following matters if they occur under the authority of the principal carrier:

(A) a rate for the transportation of household goods;

(B) an access, terminal, storage, or other charge incidental to the transportation of household goods; or

(C) an allowance relating to the transportation of household goods; or

(2) ownership of the carrier by the agent or membership on the board of directors of the carrier by the agent.

(b) An agent under Subsection (a) may itself be a motor carrier required to register under Subchapter B.

(c) The department by rule may exempt a motor carrier required to register under Subchapter B from Chapter 15, Business & Commerce Code, for an activity relating to the establishment of a joint line rate, route, classification, or mileage guide.

(d) A motor carrier that is required to register under Subchapter B and that transports household goods, or an agent of the carrier, may enter into a collective ratemaking agreement with another motor carrier of household goods or an agent of that carrier concerning the establishment and filing of maximum rates, classifications, rules, or procedures. The agreement must be submitted to the department for approval.

(e) The department shall approve an agreement submitted under Subsection (d) if the agreement provides that each meeting of parties to the agreement is open to the public and that notice of each meeting must be given to customers who are multiple users of the services of a motor carrier that is a party to the agreement. The department may withhold approval of the agreement if it determines, after notice and hearing, that the agreement fails to comply with this subsection.

(f) Unless disapproved by the department, an agreement made under Subsection (d) is valid, and Chapter 15, Business & Commerce Code, does not apply to a motor carrier that is a party to the agreement.
(Enacted by Acts 1997, 75th Leg., ch. 165 (S.B. 898), § 30.150(a), effective September 1, 1997.)

## Sec. 643.155. Rules Advisory Committee.

(a) The department shall appoint a rules advisory committee consisting of representatives of motor carriers transporting household goods using small, medium, and large equipment, the public, and the department.

(b) Members of the committee serve at the pleasure of the department and are not entitled to compensation or reimbursement of expenses for serving on the committee. The department may adopt rules to govern the operations of the advisory committee.

(c) The committee shall examine the rules adopted by the department under Sections 643.153(a) and (b) and make recommendations to the department on modernizing and streamlining the rules.
(Enacted by Acts 1997, 75th Leg., ch. 165 (S.B. 898), § 30.150(a), effective September 1, 1997; am. Acts 1999, 76th Leg., ch. 62 (S.B. 1368), § 17.19(b), effective September 1, 1999; am. Acts 2005, 79th Leg., ch. 281 (H.B. 2702), § 6.03, effective June 14, 2005.)

## Sec. 643.156. Regulation of Advertising.

(a) The department may not by rule restrict competitive bidding or advertising by a motor carrier except to prohibit false, misleading, or deceptive practices.

(b) A rule to prohibit false, misleading, or deceptive practices may not:

(1) restrict the use of:

(A) any medium for an advertisement;

(B) a motor carrier's advertisement under a trade name; or

(C) a motor carrier's personal appearance or voice in an advertisement, if the motor carrier is an individual; or

(2) relate to the size or duration of an advertisement by a motor carrier.

(Enacted by Acts 1999, 76th Leg., ch. 62 (S.B. 1368), § 17.20(a), effective September 1, 1999.)

## Secs. 643.157 to 643.200 [Reserved for expansion].

### SUBCHAPTER E
### TOW TRUCKS

## Sec. 643.201. Tow Truck Regulation by Political Subdivisions [Renumbered].

Renumbered to Tex. Occ. Code § 2308.201 by Acts 2007, 80th Leg., ch. 1046 (H.B. 2094), § 2.01, effective September 1, 2007.

## Sec. 643.202. Rules Advisory Committee [Repealed].

Repealed by Acts 2007, 80th Leg., ch. 1046 (H.B. 2094), § 5.01(a)(3), effective September 1, 2007.

(Enacted by Acts 1997, 75th Leg., ch. 165 (S.B. 898), § 30.150(a), effective September 1, 1997; am. Acts 2003, 78th Leg., ch. 1276 (H.B. 3507), § 14A.838, effective September 1, 2003.)

## Sec. 643.203. Regulation by Political Subdivisions of Fees for Nonconsent Tows [Renumbered].

Renumbered to Tex. Occ. Code § 2308.202 by Acts 2007, 80th Leg., ch. 1046 (H.B. 2094), § 2.01, effective September 1, 2007.

## Sec. 643.204. Towing Fee Studies [Renumbered].

Renumbered to Tex. Occ. Code § 2308.203 by Acts 2007, 80th Leg., ch. 1046 (H.B. 2094), § 2.01, effective September 1, 2007.

## Sec. 643.205. Fees for Nonconsent Tows in Other Areas [Renumbered].

Renumbered to Tex. Occ. Code § 2308.204 by Acts 2007, 80th Leg., ch. 1046 (H.B. 2094), § 2.01, effective September 1, 2007.

## Sec. 643.206. Storage of Towed Vehicles [Renumbered].

Renumbered to Tex. Occ. Code § 2308.205 by Acts 2007, 80th Leg., ch. 1046 (H.B. 2094), § 2.01, effective September 1, 2007.

## Sec. 643.207. Required Filing [Renumbered].

Renumbered to Tex. Occ. Code § 2308.206 by Acts 2007, 80th Leg., ch. 1046 (H.B. 2094), § 2.01, effective September 1, 2007.

## Sec. 643.208. Required Posting [Renumbered].

Renumbered to Tex. Occ. Code § 2308.207 by Acts 2007, 80th Leg., ch. 1046 (H.B. 2094), § 2.01, effective September 1, 2007.

## Sec. 643.209. Tow Rotation List in Certain Counties [Renumbered].

Renumbered to Tex. Occ. Code § 2308.209 by Acts 2009, 81st Leg., ch. 87 (S.B. 1969), § 27.001(109), effective September 1, 2009.

## Secs. 643.210 to 643.250 [Reserved for expansion].

### SUBCHAPTER F
### ENFORCEMENT

## Sec. 643.251. Administrative Penalty.

(a) The department may impose an administrative penalty against a motor carrier required to register under Subchapter B that violates this chapter or a rule or order adopted under this chapter.

(b) Except as provided by this section, the amount of an administrative penalty may not exceed $5,000. If it is found that the motor carrier knowingly committed the violation, the penalty may not exceed $15,000. If it is found that the motor carrier knowingly committed multiple violations, the aggregate penalty for the multiple violations may not exceed $30,000. Each day a violation continues or occurs is a separate violation for purposes of imposing a penalty.

(c) The amount of the penalty shall be based on:

(1) the seriousness of the violation, including the nature, circumstances, extent, and gravity of any prohibited act, and the hazard or potential hazard created to the health, safety, or economic welfare of the public;

(2) the economic harm to property or the environment caused by the violation;

(3) the history of previous violations;

(4) the amount necessary to deter future violations;

(5) efforts to correct the violation; and

(6) any other matter that justice may require.

(d) to (r) [Repealed by Acts 2007, 80th Leg., ch. 1396 (H.B. 2093), § 26(1), effective September 1, 2007.]

(Enacted by Acts 1997, 75th Leg., ch. 165 (S.B. 898), § 30.150(a), effective September 1, 1997; am. Acts 2007, 80th Leg., ch. 1396 (H.B. 2093), §§ 18, 26(1), effective September 1, 2007.)

## Sec. 643.252. Administrative Sanctions.

(a) The department may suspend, revoke, or deny a registration issued under this chapter or place on probation a motor carrier whose registration is suspended if a motor carrier:

(1) fails to maintain insurance or evidence of financial responsibility as required by Section 643.101(a), (b), (c), or (d);

(2) fails to keep evidence of insurance in the cab of each vehicle as required by Section 643.103(b);

(3) fails to register a vehicle requiring registration;

(4) violates any other provision of this chapter;

(5) knowingly provides false information on any form filed with the department under this chapter; or

(6) violates a rule or order adopted under this chapter.

(b) The Department of Public Safety may request that the department suspend or revoke a registration issued under this chapter or place on probation a motor carrier whose registration is suspended if a motor carrier has:

(1) an unsatisfactory safety rating under 49 C.F.R. Part 385; or

(2) multiple violations of Chapter 644, a rule adopted under that chapter, or Subtitle C.

(c) The department shall revoke or deny a registration issued under this chapter to a for-hire motor carrier of passengers if the motor carrier is required to register with the Federal Motor Carrier Safety Administration and the federal registration is denied, revoked, suspended, or otherwise terminated.

(d), (e) [Repealed by Acts 2007, 80th Leg., ch. 1396 (H.B. 2093), § 26(2), effective September 1, 2007.]

(Enacted by Acts 1997, 75th Leg., ch. 165 (S.B. 898), § 30.150(a), effective September 1, 1997; am. Acts 1999, 76th Leg., ch. 62 (S.B. 1368), § 17.21(a), effective September 1, 1999; am. Acts 2003, 78th Leg., ch. 1034 (H.B. 849), § 11, effective September 1, 2003; am. Acts 2005, 79th Leg., ch. 281 (H.B. 2702), § 6.04, effective June 14, 2005; am. Acts 2007, 80th Leg., ch. 1396 (H.B. 2093), §§ 19, 20, 26(2), effective September 1, 2007; am. Acts 2009, 81st Leg., ch. 919 (H.B. 2985), § 5, effective September 1, 2009.)

## Sec. 643.2525. Administrative Hearing Process.

(a) If the department determines that a violation has occurred for which an enforcement action is being taken under Section 643.251 or 643.252, the department shall give written notice to the motor carrier by first class mail to the carrier's address as shown in the records of the department.

(b) A notice required by Subsection (a) must include:

(1) a brief summary of the alleged violation;

(2) a statement of each administrative sanction being taken;

(3) the effective date of each sanction;

(4) a statement informing the carrier of the carrier's right to request a hearing; and

(5) a statement as to the procedure for requesting a hearing, including the period during which a request must be made.

(c) If not later than the 26th day after the date the notice is mailed the department receives a written request for a hearing, the department shall set a hearing and give notice of the hearing to the carrier. The hearing shall be conducted by an administrative law judge of the State Office of Administrative Hearings.

(d) If the motor carrier does not timely request a hearing under Subsection (c), the department's decision becomes final on the expiration of the period described by Subsection (c).

(e) The administrative law judge shall make findings of fact and conclusions of law and promptly issue to the director a proposal for a decision as to the occurrence of the violation and the administrative penalties or sanctions.

(f) In addition to a penalty or sanction proposed under Subsection (e), the administrative law judge shall include in the proposal for a decision a finding setting out costs, fees, expenses, and reasonable and necessary attorney's fees incurred by the state in bringing the proceeding. The director may adopt the finding and make it a part of a final order entered in the proceeding.

(g) Based on the findings of fact, conclusions of law, and proposal for a decision, the director by order may find that a violation has occurred and impose the sanctions or may find that a violation has not occurred.

(h) The director shall provide written notice to the motor carrier of a finding made under Subsection (g) and shall include in the notice a statement of the right of the carrier to judicial review of the order.

(i) Before the 31st day after the date the director's order under Subsection (g) becomes final as provided by Section 2001.144, Government Code, the motor carrier may appeal the order by filing a petition for judicial review contesting the order. Judicial review is under the substantial evidence rule.

(j) A petition filed under Subsection (i) stays the enforcement of the administrative action until the earlier of the 550th day after the date the petition was filed or the date a final judgment is rendered by the court.

(k) If the motor carrier is required to pay a penalty or cost under Subsection (f), failure to pay the penalty or cost before the 61st day after the date the requirement becomes final is a violation of this chapter and may result in an additional penalty, revocation or suspension of a motor carrier registration, or denial of renewal of a motor carrier registration.

(*l*) A motor carrier that is required to pay a penalty, cost, fee, or expense under this section or Section 643.251 is not eligible for a reinstatement or renewal of a registration under this chapter until all required amounts have been paid to the department.

(m) If the suspension of a motor carrier's registration is probated, the department may require the carrier to report regularly to the department on any matter that is the basis of the probation. Any violation of the probation may result in the imposition of an administrative penalty or the revocation of the registration.

(n) All proceedings under this section are subject to Chapter 2001, Government Code.
(Enacted by Acts 2007, 80th Leg., ch. 1396 (H.B. 2093), § 21, effective September 1, 2007.)

## Sec. 643.253. Offenses and Penalties.

(a) A person commits an offense if the person fails to:

(1) register as required by Subchapter B;

(2) maintain insurance or evidence of financial responsibility as required by Subchapter C; or

(3) keep a cab card in the cab of a vehicle as required by Section 643.059.

(b) A person commits an offense if the person engages in or solicits the transportation of household goods for compensation and is not registered as required by Subchapter B.

(c) Except as provided by Subsection (e), an offense under this section is a Class C misdemeanor.

(d) [Renumbered to Tex. Occ. Code § 2308.505 by Acts 2007, 80th Leg., ch. 1046 (H.B. 2094), § 2.10, effective September 1, 2007.]

(e) An offense under Subsection (b) is a Class C misdemeanor, except that the offense is:

(1) a Class B misdemeanor if the person has previously been convicted one time of an offense under Subsection (b); and

(2) a Class A misdemeanor if the person has previously been convicted two or more times of an offense under Subsection (b).

(f) A peace officer may issue a citation for a violation under this section.
(Enacted by Acts 1997, 75th Leg., ch. 165 (S.B. 898), § 30.150(a), effective September 1, 1997; am. Acts 1999, 76th Leg., ch. 62 (S.B. 1368), § 17.22(a), effective September 1, 1999; am. Acts 2003, 78th Leg., ch. 1034 (H.B. 849), §§ 12, 13, effective September 1, 2003; am. Acts 2005, 79th Leg., ch. 281 (H.B. 2702), § 6.05, effective June 14, 2005; am. Acts 2007, 80th Leg., ch. 1046 (H.B. 2094), §§ 2.10, 3.12, effective September 1, 2007; am. Acts 2011, 82nd Leg., ch. 274 (H.B. 1523), § 1, effective September 1, 2011.)

## Sec. 643.254. Inspection of Documents.

(a) To investigate an alleged violation of this chapter or a rule or order adopted under this chapter, an officer or employee of the department who has been certified for the purpose by the director may enter a motor carrier's premises to inspect, copy, or verify the correctness of a document, including an operation log or insurance certificate.

(b) The officer or employee may conduct the inspection:

(1) at a reasonable time;

(2) after stating the purpose of the inspection; and

(3) by presenting to the motor carrier:

(A) appropriate credentials; and

(B) a written statement from the department to the motor carrier indicating the officer's or employee's authority to inspect.

(c) A motor carrier domiciled outside this state must:

(1) designate a location in the state for inspection of records concerning the alleged violation; or

(2) request that an officer or employee of the department conduct the inspection at an office of the motor carrier located outside this state.

(d) A motor carrier requesting an out-of-state inspection will be responsible for payment of actual expenses incurred by the department in conducting the inspection.

(Enacted by Acts 1997, 75th Leg., ch. 165 (S.B. 898), § 30.150(a), effective September 1, 1997; am. Acts 1999, 76th Leg., ch. 603 (S.B. 775), § 6, effective August 30, 1999; am. Acts 2007, 80th Leg., ch. 1396 (H.B. 2093), § 22, effective September 1, 2007.)

### Sec. 643.255. Injunctive Relief.

(a) The attorney general, at the request of the department, may petition a district court for appropriate injunctive relief to prevent or abate a violation of this chapter or a rule or order adopted under this chapter.

(b) Venue in a suit for injunctive relief under this section is in Travis County.

(c) On application for injunctive relief and a finding that a person is violating or has violated this chapter or a rule or order adopted under this chapter, the court shall grant the appropriate relief without bond.

(d) The attorney general and the department may recover reasonable expenses incurred in obtaining injunctive relief under this section, including court costs, reasonable attorney's fees, investigative costs, witness fees, and deposition expenses.

(Enacted by Acts 2007, 80th Leg., ch. 1396 (H.B. 2093), § 23, effective September 1, 2007.)

### Sec. 643.256. Cease and Desist Order.

The department may issue a cease and desist order if the department determines that the action is necessary to:

(1) prevent a violation of this chapter; and

(2) protect the public health and safety.

(Enacted by Acts 2009, 81st Leg., ch. 919 (H.B. 2985), § 6, effective September 1, 2009.)

# CHAPTER 644
# COMMERCIAL MOTOR VEHICLE SAFETY STANDARDS

## SUBCHAPTER A
## GENERAL PROVISIONS

### Sec. 644.001. Definitions.

In this chapter:

(1) "Commercial motor vehicle" means:

(A) a commercial motor vehicle as defined by 49 C.F.R. Section 390.5, if operated interstate; or

(B) a commercial motor vehicle as defined by Section 548.001, if operated intrastate.

(2) "Department" means the Department of Public Safety.

(3) "Director" means the public safety director.

(4) "Federal hazardous material regulation" means a federal regulation in 49 C.F.R. Parts 101-199.

(5) "Federal motor carrier safety regulation" means a federal regulation in Subtitle A, Title 49, or Subchapter B, Chapter III, Subtitle B, Title 49, Code of Federal Regulations.

(6) "Federal safety regulation" means a federal hazardous material regulation or a federal motor carrier safety regulation.

(7) "Port of entry" has the meaning assigned by Section 621.001.

(Enacted by Acts 1997, 75th Leg., ch. 165 (S.B. 898), § 30.151(a), effective September 1, 1997; am. Acts 1999, 76th Leg., ch. 62 (S.B. 1368), §§ 17.24(a), 17.25(a), effective September 1, 1999; am. Acts 2003, 78th Leg., ch. 359 (S.B. 1184), § 3, effective September 1, 2003; am. Acts 2003, 78th Leg., ch. 1325 (H.B. 3588), § 16.02, effective September 1, 2003; am. Acts 2005, 79th Leg., ch. 313 (S.B. 619), § 4, effective September 1, 2005.)

### Sec. 644.002. Conflicts of Law.

(a) A federal motor carrier safety regulation prevails over a conflicting provision of this title applicable to a commercial vehicle operated in interstate commerce. A rule adopted by the director under this chapter prevails over a conflicting provision of a federal motor carrier safety regulation applicable to a commercial vehicle operated in intrastate commerce.

(b) A safety rule adopted under this chapter prevails over a conflicting rule adopted by a local government, authority, or state agency or officer, other than a conflicting rule adopted by the Railroad Commission of Texas under Chapter 113, Natural Resources Code.

(Enacted by Acts 1997, 75th Leg., ch. 165 (S.B. 898), § 30.151(a), effective September 1, 1997; am. Acts 2005, 79th Leg., ch. 872 (S.B. 1074), § 1, effective September 1, 2005.)

### Sec. 644.003. Rules.

The department may adopt rules to administer this chapter.

(Enacted by Acts 1997, 75th Leg., ch. 165 (S.B. 898), § 30.151(a), effective September 1, 1997.)

### Sec. 644.004. Applicability to Foreign Commercial Motor Vehicles.

Except as otherwise provided by law, this chapter also applies to a foreign commercial motor vehicle, as defined by Section 648.001.

(Enacted by Acts 1999, 76th Leg., ch. 62 (S.B. 1368), § 17.26(a), effective September 1, 1999.)

### Sec. 644.005. Department Database.

The department shall develop and maintain a database on roadside vehicle inspection reports for defects on any intermodal equipment. The database shall include all citations involving intermodal equipment issued by officers certified under Section 644.101. The database shall be used to identify violations discovered on intermodal equipment during a roadside inspection.

(Enacted by Acts 2001, 77th Leg., ch. 1227 (S.B. 220), § 10, effective September 1, 2001.)

### Secs. 644.006 to 644.050 [Reserved for expansion].

## SUBCHAPTER B
## ADOPTION OF RULES

### Sec. 644.051. Authority to Adopt Rules.

(a) The director shall, after notice and a public hearing, adopt rules regulating:

(1) the safe transportation of hazardous materials; and

(2) the safe operation of commercial motor vehicles.

(b) A rule adopted under this chapter must be consistent with federal regulations, including federal safety regulations.

(c) The director may adopt all or part of the federal safety regulations by reference.

(d) Rules adopted under this chapter must ensure that:

(1) a commercial motor vehicle is safely maintained, equipped, loaded, and operated;

(2) the responsibilities imposed on a commercial motor vehicle's operator do not impair the operator's ability to operate the vehicle safely; and

(3) the physical condition of a commercial motor vehicle's operator enables the operator to operate the vehicle safely.

Transportation

(e) A motor carrier safety rule adopted by a local government, authority, or state agency or officer must be consistent with corresponding federal regulations.
(Enacted by Acts 1997, 75th Leg., ch. 165 (S.B. 898), § 30.151(a), effective September 1, 1997.)

## Sec. 644.052. Applicability of Rules.

(a) Notwithstanding an exemption provided in the federal safety regulations, other than an exemption relating to intracity or commercial zone operations provided in 49 C.F.R. Part 395, a rule adopted by the director under this chapter applies uniformly throughout this state.

(b) A rule adopted under this chapter applies to a vehicle that requires a hazardous material placard.

(c) A rule adopted under this chapter may not apply to a vehicle that is operated intrastate and that is:

(1) a machine generally consisting of a mast, engine, draw works, and chassis permanently constructed or assembled to be used and used in oil or water well servicing or drilling;

(2) a mobile crane that is an unladen, self-propelled vehicle constructed as a machine to raise, shift, or lower weight; or

(3) a vehicle transporting seed cotton.
(Enacted by Acts 1997, 75th Leg., ch. 165 (S.B. 898), § 30.151(a), effective September 1, 1997; am. Acts 2005, 79th Leg., ch. 247 (H.B. 749), § 5, effective September 1, 2005.)

## Sec. 644.053. Limitations of Rules.

(a) A rule adopted under this chapter may not:

(1) prevent an intrastate operator from operating a vehicle up to 12 hours following eight consecutive hours off;

(2) require a person to meet the medical standards provided in the federal motor carrier safety regulations if the person:

(A) was regularly employed in this state as a commercial motor vehicle operator in intrastate commerce before August 28, 1989; and

(B) is not transporting property that requires a hazardous material placard;

(3) require a person who returns to the work-reporting location, is released from work within 12 consecutive hours, has at least eight consecutive hours off between each 12-hour period the person is on duty, and operates within a 150-air-mile radius of the normal work-reporting location to maintain a driver's record of duty status as described by 49 C.F.R. Section 395.8, provided that the person maintains time records in compliance with 49 C.F.R. Section 395.1(e)(5) and documents that verify the truth and accuracy of the time records such as:

(A) business records maintained by the owner that provide the date, time, and location of the delivery of a product or service; or

(B) documents required to be maintained by law, including delivery tickets or sales invoices, that provide the date of delivery and the quantity of merchandise delivered; or

(4) impose during a planting or harvesting season maximum driving and on-duty times on an operator of a vehicle transporting an agricultural commodity in intrastate commerce for agricultural purposes from the source of the commodity to the first place of processing or storage or the distribution point for the commodity, if the place is located within 150 air miles of the source.

(b) For purposes of Subsection (a)(3)(A), an owner's time records must at a minimum include:

(1) the time an operator reports for duty each day;

(2) the number of hours an operator is on duty each day;

(3) the time an operator is released from duty each day; and

(4) an operator's signed statement in compliance with 49 C.F.R. Section 395.8(j)(2).

(c) In this section, "agricultural commodity" means an agricultural, horticultural, viticultural, silvicultural, or vegetable product, bees or honey, planting seed, cottonseed, rice, livestock or a livestock product, or poultry or a poultry product that is produced in this state, either in its natural form or as processed by the producer, including woodchips.

(d) A rule adopted by the director under this chapter that relates to hours of service, an operator's record of duty status, or an operator's daily log, for operations outside a 150-mile radius of the normal work-reporting location, also applies to and must be complied with by a motor carrier of household goods not using a commercial motor vehicle. In this subsection:

(1) "commercial motor vehicle" has the meaning assigned by Section 548.001; and

(2) "motor carrier" has the meaning assigned by Section 643.001.
(Enacted by Acts 1997, 75th Leg., ch. 165 (S.B. 898), § 30.151(a), effective September 1, 1997;

am. Acts 1999, 76th Leg., ch. 62 (S.B. 1368), §§ 17.27(a), 17.27(b), effective September 1, 1999; am. Acts 2005, 79th Leg., ch. 872 (S.B. 1074), § 2, effective September 1, 2005.)

### Sec. 644.054. Regulation of Contract Carriers of Certain Passengers.

(a) This section applies only to a contract carrier that transports an operating employee of a railroad on a road or highway of this state in a vehicle designed to carry 15 or fewer passengers.

(b) The department shall adopt rules regulating the operation of a contract carrier to which this section applies. The rules must:

(1) prohibit a person from operating a vehicle for more than 12 hours in a day;

(2) require a person who operates a vehicle for the number of consecutive hours or days the department determines is excessive to rest for a period determined by the department;

(3) require a contract carrier to keep a record of all hours a vehicle subject to regulation under this section is operated;

(4) require a contract carrier to perform alcohol and drug testing of vehicle operators on employment, on suspicion of alcohol or drug abuse, and periodically as determined by the department;

(5) require a contract carrier, at a minimum, to maintain liability insurance in the amount of $1.5 million for each vehicle; and

(6) be determined by the department to be necessary to protect the safety of a passenger being transported or the general public.

(c) The department shall inform contract carriers and railroad companies that employ contract carriers of the requirements of state statutes applicable to contract carriers.

(Enacted by Acts 1999, 76th Leg., ch. 62 (S.B. 1368), § 17.28(a), effective September 1, 1999; am. Acts 2009, 81st Leg., ch. 126 (S.B. 481), § 1, effective September 1, 2009.)

### Secs. 644.055 to 644.100 [Reserved for expansion].

## SUBCHAPTER C
## ADMINISTRATIVE ENFORCEMENT

### Sec. 644.101. Certification of Certain Peace Officers.

(a) The department shall establish procedures, including training, for the certification of municipal police officers, sheriffs, and deputy sheriffs to enforce this chapter.

(b) A police officer of any of the following municipalities is eligible to apply for certification under this section:

(1) a municipality with a population of 50,000 or more;

(2) municipality with a population of 25,000 or more any part of which is located in a county with a population of 500,000 or more;

(3) a municipality with a population of less than 25,000:

(A) any part of which is located in a county with a population of 3.3 million; and

(B) that contains or is adjacent to an international port;

(4) a municipality with a population of at least 34,000 that is located in a county that borders two or more states;

(5) a municipality any part of which is located in a county bordering the United Mexican States;

(6) a municipality with a population of less than 5,000 that is located:

(A) adjacent to a bay connected to the Gulf of Mexico; and

(B) in a county adjacent to a county with a population greater than 3.3 million;

(7) a municipality that is located:

(A) within 25 miles of an international port; and

(B) in a county that does not contain a highway that is part of the national system of interstate and defense highways and is adjacent to a county with a population greater than 3.3 million; or

(8) a municipality with a population of less than 8,500 that:

(A) is the county seat; and

(B) contains a highway that is part of the national system of interstate and defense highways.

(c) A sheriff or a deputy sheriff of a county bordering the United Mexican States or of a county with a population of 2.2 million or more is eligible to apply for certification under this section.

(d) A sheriff, a deputy sheriff, or any peace officer that does not attend continuing education courses on the enforcement of traffic and highway laws and on the use of radar equipment as prescribed by Subchapter F, Chapter 1701, Occupations Code, shall not enforce traffic and highway laws.

(e) The department by rule shall establish reasonable fees sufficient to recover from a municipality or a county the cost of certifying its peace officers under this section.

(Enacted by Acts 1997, 75th Leg., ch. 165 (S.B. 898), § 30.151(a), effective September 1, 1997; am. Acts 1999, 76th Leg., ch. 62 (S.B. 1368), § 17.29(a), effective September 1, 1999; am. Acts 1999, 76th Leg., ch. 1189 (S.B. 370), § 39, effective September 1, 1999; am. Acts 2001, 77th Leg., ch. 1227 (S.B. 220), § 11, effective September 1, 2001; am. Acts 2007, 80th Leg., ch. 508 (S.B. 545), § 2, effective September 1, 2007; am. Acts 2007, 80th Leg., ch. 702 (H.B. 2077), § 1, effective June 15, 2007; am. Acts 2007, 80th Leg., ch. 1030 (H.B. 1638), § 1, effective September 1, 2007; am. Acts 2009, 81st Leg., ch. 87 (S.B. 1969), § 23.009, effective September 1, 2009; am. Acts 2011, 82nd Leg., ch. 249 (H.B. 1010), § 1, effective September 1, 2011; am. Acts 2011, 82nd Leg., ch. 1163 (H.B. 2702), § 176, effective September 1, 2011.)

## Sec. 644.102. Municipal Enforcement Requirements.

(a) The department by rule shall establish uniform standards for municipal or county enforcement of this chapter.

(b) A municipality or county that engages in enforcement under this chapter:

(1) shall pay all costs relating to the municipality's or county's enforcement;

(2) may not be considered, in the context of a federal grant related to this chapter:

(A) a party to a federal grant agreement, except as provided by Subsection (b-1); or

(B) a grantee under a federal grant to the department; and

(3) must comply with the standards established under Subsection (a).

(b-1) Subsection (b) does not prohibit a municipality or county from receiving High Priority Activity Funds provided under the federal Motor Carrier Safety Assistance Program.

(c) Municipal or county enforcement under Section 644.103(b) is not considered departmental enforcement for purposes of maintaining levels of effort required by a federal grant.

(d) In each fiscal year, a municipality may retain fines from the enforcement of this chapter in an amount not to exceed 110 percent of the municipality's actual expenses for enforcement of this chapter in the preceding fiscal year, as determined by the comptroller after reviewing the most recent municipal audit conducted under Section 103.001, Local Government Code. If there are no actual expenses for enforcement of this chapter in the most recent municipal audit, a municipality may retain fines in an amount not to exceed 110 percent of the amount the comptroller estimates would be the municipality's actual expenses for enforcement of this chapter during the year.

(e) In each fiscal year, a county may retain fines from the enforcement of this chapter in an amount not to exceed 110 percent of the county's actual expenses for enforcement of this chapter in the preceding fiscal year, as determined by the comptroller after reviewing the most recent county audit conducted under Chapter 115, Local Government Code. If there are no actual expenses for enforcement of this chapter in the most recent county audit, a county may retain fines in an amount not to exceed 110 percent of the amount the comptroller estimates would be the county's actual expenses for enforcement of this chapter during the year.

(f) A municipality or county shall send to the comptroller the proceeds of all fines that exceed the limit imposed by Subsection (d) or (e). The comptroller shall then deposit the remaining funds to the credit of the Texas Department of Transportation.

(g) The department shall revoke or rescind the certification of any peace officer who fails to comply with any standard established under Subsection (a).

(Enacted by Acts 1997, 75th Leg., ch. 165 (S.B. 898), § 30.151(a), effective September 1, 1997; am. Acts 1999, 76th Leg., ch. 292 (S.B. 1019), § 1, effective September 1, 1999; am. Acts 2001, 77th Leg., ch. 1227 (S.B. 220), § 12, effective September 1, 2001; am. Acts 2007, 80th Leg., ch. 258 (S.B. 11), § 13.01, effective September 1, 2007.)

## Sec. 644.103. Detention of Vehicles.

(a) An officer of the department may stop, enter, or detain on a highway or at a port of entry a motor vehicle that is subject to this chapter.

(b) A municipal police officer who is certified under Section 644.101 may stop, enter, or detain on a highway or at a port of entry within the territory of the municipality a motor vehicle that is subject to this chapter. A sheriff or deputy sheriff who is certified under Section 644.101 may stop, enter, or detain on a highway or at a port of entry within the territory of the county a motor vehicle that is subject to this chapter.

(c) A person who detains a vehicle under this section may prohibit the further operation of the vehicle on a highway if the vehicle or operator of the vehicle is in violation of a federal safety regulation or a rule adopted under this chapter.

(d) A noncommissioned employee of the department who is certified for the purpose by the director and who is supervised by an officer of the department may, at a commercial motor vehicle inspection site, stop, enter, or detain a motor vehicle that is subject to this chapter. If the employee's inspection shows that an enforcement action, such as the issuance of a citation, is warranted for a violation of this title or a rule adopted under this title, including a federal safety regulation adopted under this chapter, the noncommissioned employee may take enforcement action only if the employee is under the supervision of an officer of the department.

(e) The department's training and other requirements for certification of a noncommissioned employee of the department under this section must be the same as the training and requirements, other than the training and requirements for becoming and remaining a peace officer, for officers who enforce this chapter.

(Enacted by Acts 1997, 75th Leg., ch. 165 (S.B. 898), § 30.151(a), effective September 1, 1997; am. Acts 1999, 76th Leg., ch. 62 (S.B. 1368), § 17.31(a), effective September 1, 1999; am. Acts 1999, 76th Leg., ch. 1189 (S.B. 370), § 40, effective September 1, 1999; am. Acts 2001, 77th Leg., ch. 1227 (S.B. 220), § 13, effective September 1, 2001; am. Acts 2003, 78th Leg., ch. 359 (S.B. 1184), § 4, effective September 1, 2003; am. Acts 2003, 78th Leg., ch. 1325 (H.B. 3588), § 16.03, effective September 1, 2003; am. Acts 2005, 79th Leg., ch. 313 (S.B. 619), § 5, effective September 1, 2005; am. Acts 2007, 80th Leg., ch. 12 (S.B. 330), § 2, effective April 23, 2007.)

### Sec. 644.104. Inspection of Premises.

(a) An officer or employee of the department who has been certified for the purpose by the director may enter a motor carrier's premises to:

   (1) inspect real property, including a building, or equipment; or

   (2) copy or verify the correctness of documents, including records or reports, required to be kept or made by rules adopted under this chapter.

(b) The officer or employee may conduct the inspection:

   (1) at a reasonable time;

   (2) after stating the purpose of the inspection; and

   (3) by presenting to the motor carrier:

     (A) appropriate credentials; and

     (B) a written statement from the department to the motor carrier indicating the officer's or employee's authority to inspect.

(c) The department may use an officer to conduct an inspection under this section if the inspection involves a situation that the department determines to reasonably require the use or presence of an officer to accomplish the inspection.

(d) The department's training and other requirements for certification of a noncommissioned employee of the department under this section must be the same as the training and requirements, other than the training and requirements for becoming and remaining a peace officer, for officers who enforce this chapter.

(e) A municipal police officer who is certified under Section 644.101 may enter a motor carrier's premises to inspect equipment on a per unit basis or in a manner agreeable between the motor carrier and the enforcement entity:

   (1) at a reasonable time;

   (2) after stating the purpose of the inspection; and

   (3) by presenting to the motor carrier appropriate credentials.

(Enacted by Acts 1997, 75th Leg., ch. 165 (S.B. 898), § 30.151(a), effective September 1, 1997; am. Acts 1999, 76th Leg., ch. 1189 (S.B. 370), § 41, effective September 1, 1999; am. Acts 2001, 77th Leg., ch. 642 (H.B. 2058), § 1, effective June 13, 2001.)

### Secs. 644.105 to 644.150 [Reserved for expansion].

## SUBCHAPTER D
## OFFENSES, PENALTIES, AND JUDICIAL ENFORCEMENT

### Sec. 644.151. Criminal Offense.

(a) A person commits an offense if the person:

   (1) violates a rule adopted under this chapter; or

   (2) does not permit an inspection authorized under Section 644.104.

(b) An offense under this section is a Class C misdemeanor.

(c) Each day a violation continues under Subsection (a)(1) or each day a person refuses to allow an inspection described under Subsection (a)(2) is a separate offense.

(Enacted by Acts 1997, 75th Leg., ch. 165 (S.B. 898), § 30.151(a), effective September 1, 1997.)

## Sec. 644.152.   Civil Penalty.

(a) A person who does not permit an inspection authorized by Section 644.104 is liable to the state for a civil penalty in an amount not to exceed $1,000.

(b) The attorney general may sue to collect the penalty in:

(1) the county in which the violation is alleged to have occurred; or

(2) Travis County.

(c) The penalty provided by this section is in addition to the penalty provided by Section 644.151.

(d) Each day a person refuses to permit an inspection described by Subsection (a) is a separate violation for purposes of imposing a penalty. (Enacted by Acts 1997, 75th Leg., ch. 165 (S.B. 898), § 30.151(a), effective September 1, 1997.)

## Sec. 644.153.   Administrative Penalty.

(a) The department may impose an administrative penalty against a person who violates:

(1) a rule adopted under this chapter; or

(2) a provision of Subchapter C that the department by rule subjects to administrative penalties.

(b) To be designated as subject to an administrative penalty under Subsection (a)(2), a provision must relate to the safe operation of a commercial motor vehicle.

(c) The department shall:

(1) designate one or more employees to investigate violations and conduct audits of persons subject to this chapter; and

(2) impose an administrative penalty if the department discovers a violation that is covered by Subsection (a) or (b).

(d) A penalty under this section may not exceed the maximum penalty provided for a violation of a similar federal safety regulation.

(e) If the department determines to impose a penalty, the department shall issue a notice of claim. The department shall send the notice of claim by certified mail, registered mail, personal delivery, or another manner of delivery that records the receipt of the notice by the person responsible. The notice of claim must include a brief summary of the alleged violation and a statement of the amount of the recommended penalty and inform the person that the person is entitled to a hearing on the occurrence of the violation, the amount of the penalty, or both the occurrence of the violation and the amount of the penalty. A person who is subject to an administrative penalty imposed by the department under this section is required to pay the penalty or respond to the department within 20 days of receipt of the department's notice of claim.

(f) Before the 21st day after the date the person receives the notice of claim, the person may:

(1) accept the determination and pay the recommended penalty; or

(2) make a written request for an informal hearing or an administrative hearing on the occurrence of the violation, the amount of the penalty, or both the occurrence of the violation and the amount of the penalty.

(g) At the conclusion of an informal hearing requested under Subsection (f), the department may modify the recommendation for a penalty.

(h) If the person requests an administrative hearing, the department shall set a hearing and give notice of the hearing to the person. The hearing shall be held by an administrative law judge of the State Office of Administrative Hearings. The administrative law judge shall make findings of fact and conclusions of law and promptly issue to the director a proposal for a decision as to the occurrence of the violation and the amount of a proposed penalty.

(i) If a penalty is proposed under Subsection (h), the administrative law judge shall include in the proposal for a decision a finding setting out costs, fees, expenses, and reasonable and necessary attorney's fees incurred by the state in bringing the proceeding. The director may adopt the finding and make it a part of a final order entered in the proceeding.

(j) Based on the findings of fact, conclusions of law, and proposal for a decision, the director by order may find that a violation has occurred and impose a penalty or may find that no violation occurred. The director may, pursuant to Section 2001.058(e), Government Code, increase or decrease the amount of the penalty recommended by the administrative law judge within the limits prescribed by this chapter.

(k) Notice of the director's order shall be given to the affected person in the manner required by Chapter 2001, Government Code, and must include a statement that the person is entitled to seek a judicial review of the order.

(l) Before the 31st day after the date the director's order becomes final as provided by Section 2001.144, Government Code, the person must:

(1) pay the amount of the penalty;

(2) pay the amount of the penalty and file a petition for judicial review contesting:

   (A) the occurrence of the violation;

   (B) the amount of the penalty; or

   (C) both the occurrence of the violation and the amount of the penalty; or

(3) without paying the amount of the penalty, file a petition for judicial review contesting:

   (A) the occurrence of the violation;

   (B) the amount of the penalty; or

   (C) both the occurrence of the violation and the amount of the penalty.

(m) Within the 30-day period under Subsection (l), a person who acts under Subsection (l) may:

   (1) stay enforcement of the penalty by:

     (A) paying the amount of the penalty to the court for placement in an escrow account; or

     (B) filing with the court a supersedeas bond approved by the court for the amount of the penalty that is effective until all judicial review of the director's order is final; or

   (2) request the court to stay enforcement of the penalty by:

     (A) filing with the court an affidavit of the person stating that the person is financially unable to pay the amount of the penalty and is financially unable to give the supersedeas bond; and

     (B) sending a copy of the affidavit to the director by certified mail.

(n) Before the sixth day after the date the director receives a copy of an affidavit filed under Subsection (m)(2), the department may file with the court a contest to the affidavit. The court shall hold a hearing on the facts alleged in the affidavit as soon as practicable and shall stay the enforcement of the penalty if the court finds that the alleged facts are true. The person who files an affidavit under Subsection (m)(2) has the burden of proving that the person is financially unable to:

   (1) pay the amount of the penalty; and

   (2) file the supersedeas bond.

(o) If the person does not pay the amount of the penalty and the enforcement of the penalty is not stayed, the director may:

   (1) refer the matter to the attorney general for collection of the amount of the penalty;

   (2) initiate an impoundment proceeding under Subsection (q); or

   (3) refer the matter to the attorney general and initiate the impoundment proceeding.

(p) A person who fails to pay, or becomes delinquent in the payment of an administrative penalty imposed by the department under this subchapter may not operate or direct the operation of a commercial motor vehicle on the highways of this state until the administrative penalty has been remitted to the department.

(q) The department shall impound any commercial motor vehicle owned or operated by a person in violation of Subsection (p) after the department has first served the person with a notice of claim. Service of the notice may be by certified mail, registered mail, personal delivery, or any other manner of delivery showing receipt of the notice.

(r) A commercial motor vehicle impounded by the department under Subsection (q) shall remain impounded until the administrative penalties imposed against the person are remitted to the department, except that an impounded commercial motor vehicle left at a vehicle storage facility controlled by the department or any other person shall be considered an abandoned motor vehicle on the 11th day after the date of impoundment if the delinquent administrative penalty is not remitted to the department before that day. Chapter 683 applies to the commercial motor vehicle, except that the department is entitled to receive from the proceeds of the sale the amount of the delinquent administrative penalty and costs.

(s) All costs associated with the towing and storage of the commercial motor vehicle and load shall be the responsibility of the person and not the department or the State of Texas.

(t) A proceeding under this section is subject to Chapter 2001, Government Code.

(u) Each penalty collected under this section shall be deposited to the credit of the Texas mobility fund.

(Enacted by Acts 1997, 75th Leg., ch. 165 (S.B. 898), § 30.151(a), effective September 1, 1997; am. Acts 1999, 76th Leg., ch. 292 (S.B. 1019), § 2, effective September 1, 1999; am. Acts 2003, 78th Leg., ch. 359 (S.B. 1184), § 5, effective September 1, 2003; am. Acts 2003, 78th Leg., ch. 1325 (H.B. 3588), §§ 11.08, 16.04, effective September 1, 2003; am. Acts 2005, 79th Leg., ch. 728 (H.B. 2018), § 23.001(85), effective September 1, 2005.)

## Sec. 644.154. Suit for Injunction.

(a) The attorney general shall sue to enjoin a violation or a threatened violation of a rule adopted under this chapter on request of the director.

(b) The suit must be brought in the county in which the violation or threat is alleged to have occurred.

(c) The court may grant the director, without bond or other undertaking:

(1) a prohibitory or mandatory injunction, including a temporary restraining order; or

(2) after notice and hearing, a temporary or permanent injunction.

(Enacted by Acts 1997, 75th Leg., ch. 165 (S.B. 898), § 30.151(a), effective September 1, 1997.)

## Sec. 644.155.  Compliance Review and Safety Audit Program.

The department shall implement and enforce a compliance review and safety audit program similar to the federal program established under 49 C.F.R. Part 385 for any person who owns or operates a commercial motor vehicle that is domiciled in this state.

(Enacted by Acts 1997, 75th Leg., ch. 165 (S.B. 898), § 30.151(a), effective September 1, 1997; am. Acts 1999, 76th Leg., ch. 292 (S.B. 1019), § 3, effective September 1, 1999; am. Acts 2003, 78th Leg., ch. 359 (S.B. 1184), § 6, effective September 1, 2003; am. Acts 2003, 78th Leg., ch. 1325 (H.B. 3588), § 16.05, effective September 1, 2003.)

## Secs. 644.156 to 644.200 [Reserved for expansion].

## SUBCHAPTER E
## ROUTING OF HAZARDOUS MATERIALS

## Sec. 644.201.  Adoption of Rules.

(a) The Texas Transportation Commission shall adopt rules under this subchapter consistent with 49 C.F.R. Part 397 for the routing of nonradioactive hazardous materials.

(b) Rules concerning signage, public participation, and procedural requirements may impose more stringent requirements than provided by 49 C.F.R. Part 397.

(c) The rules must provide for consultation with a political subdivision when a route is being proposed within the jurisdiction of the political subdivision.

(Enacted by Acts 1999, 76th Leg., ch. 62 (S.B. 1368), § 17.32(a), effective September 1, 1999.)

## Sec. 644.202.  Designation of Route.

(a) A political subdivision of this state or a state agency may designate a route for the transportation of nonradioactive hazardous materials over a public road or highway in this state only if the Texas Department of Transportation approves the route.

(b) A municipality with a population of more than 850,000 shall develop a route for commercial motor vehicles carrying hazardous materials on a road or highway in the municipality and submit the route to the Texas Department of Transportation for approval. If the Texas Department of Transportation determines that the route complies with all applicable federal and state regulations regarding the transportation of hazardous materials, the Texas Department of Transportation shall approve the route and notify the municipality of the approved route.

(c) The Texas Transportation Commission may designate a route for the transportation of nonradioactive hazardous materials over any public road or highway in this state. The designation may include a road or highway that is not a part of the state highway system only on the approval of the governing body of the political subdivision that maintains the road or highway.

(Enacted by Acts 1999, 76th Leg., ch. 62 (S.B. 1368), § 17.32(a), effective September 1, 1999; am. Acts 2011, 82nd Leg., ch. 1163 (H.B. 2702), § 177, effective September 1, 2011.)

## Sec. 644.203.  Signs.

(a) The Texas Department of Transportation shall provide signs for a designated route under Section 644.202(c) over a road or highway that is not part of the state highway system. Notwithstanding Section 222.001, the Texas Department of Transportation may use money in the state highway fund to pay for the signs.

(b) The political subdivision that maintains the road or highway shall bear the costs for installation and maintenance of the signs.

(Enacted by Acts 1999, 76th Leg., ch. 62 (S.B. 1368), § 17.32(a), effective September 1, 1999.)

## Secs. 644.204 to 644.250 [Reserved for expansion].

## SUBCHAPTER F
## REPORT ON ALCOHOL AND DRUG TESTING

## Sec. 644.251.  Definitions.

In this subchapter:

(1) "Employee" has the meaning assigned by 49 C.F.R. Section 40.3.

(2) "Valid positive result" means:

(A) an alcohol concentration of 0.04 or greater on an alcohol confirmation test; or

(B) a result at or above the cutoff concentration levels listed in 49 C.F.R. Section 40.87 on a confirmation drug test.

(Enacted by Acts 2005, 79th Leg., ch. 9 (S.B. 217), § 2, effective September 1, 2005.)

## Sec. 644.252. Report of Refusal and Certain Results.

(a) An employer required to conduct alcohol and drug testing of an employee who holds a commercial driver's license under Chapter 522 under federal safety regulations as part of the employer's drug testing program or consortium, as defined by 49 C.F.R. Part 382, shall report to the department:

(1) a valid positive result on an alcohol or drug test performed and whether the specimen producing the result was a dilute specimen, as defined by 49 C.F.R. Section 40.3;

(2) a refusal to provide a specimen for an alcohol or drug test; or

(3) an adulterated specimen or substituted specimen, as those terms are defined by 49 C.F.R. Section 40.3, on an alcohol or drug test performed.

(b) The department shall maintain the information provided under this section.

(c) Information maintained under this section is confidential and only subject to release as provided by Section 521.053.

(Enacted by Acts 2005, 79th Leg., ch. 9 (S.B. 217), § 2, effective September 1, 2005; am. Acts 2007, 80th Leg., ch. 367 (S.B. 328), § 1, effective September 1, 2007.)

## CHAPTER 645
## SINGLE STATE REGISTRATION

## Sec. 645.001. Federal Motor Carrier Registration.

The Texas Department of Motor Vehicles may, to the fullest extent practicable, participate in a federal motor carrier registration program under the unified carrier registration system as defined by Section 643.001 or a single state registration system established under federal law.

(Enacted by Acts 1997, 75th Leg., ch. 165 (S.B. 898), § 30.152(a), effective September 1, 1997; am. Acts 2007, 80th Leg., ch. 1396 (H.B. 2093), § 24, effective September 1, 2007; am. Acts 2009, 81st Leg., ch. 933 (H.B. 3097), § 2M.01, effective September 1, 2009.)

## Sec. 645.002. Fees.

(a) The department may charge a motor carrier holding a permit issued under Subtitle IV, Title 49, United States Code, a fee for filing proof of insurance consistent with 49 U.S.C. Section 14504 not to exceed the maximum fee established under federal law.

(b) The department may adopt rules regarding the method of payment of a fee under this chapter. The rules may:

(1) authorize the use of an escrow account described by Subsection (c), an electronic funds transfer, or a valid credit card issued by a financial institution chartered by a state or the United States or by a nationally recognized credit organization approved by the department; and

(2) require the payment of a discount or service charge for a credit card payment in addition to the fee.

(c) The department may establish one or more escrow accounts in the state highway fund for the prepayment of a fee under this chapter. A prepaid fee or any fee established by the department for the administration of this section shall be:

(1) administered under an agreement approved by the department; and

(2) deposited to the credit of the state highway fund to be appropriated only to the department for the purposes of administering this chapter.

(Enacted by Acts 1997, 75th Leg., ch. 165 (S.B. 898), § 30.152(a), effective September 1, 1997; am. Acts 1999, 76th Leg., ch. 62 (S.B. 1368), § 17.33(a), effective September 1, 1999.)

## Sec. 645.003. Enforcement Rules.

The department shall adopt rules that are consistent with federal law providing for administrative penalties and sanctions for a failure to register as required by the unified carrier registration system or single state registration system or for a violation of this chapter or a rule adopted under this chapter in the same manner as Subchapter F, Chapter 643.

(Enacted by Acts 1997, 75th Leg., ch. 165 (S.B. 898), § 30.152(a), effective September 1, 1997; am. Acts 2007, 80th Leg., ch. 1396 (H.B. 2093), § 25, effective September 1, 2007.)

## Sec. 645.004.   Criminal Offense.

(a) A person commits an offense if the person:

(1) violates a rule adopted under this chapter; or

(2) fails to register a vehicle required to be registered under this chapter.

(b) An offense under this section is a Class C misdemeanor.

(c) Each day a violation of a rule occurs is a separate offense under this section.

(Enacted by Acts 1997, 75th Leg., ch. 165 (S.B. 898), § 30.152(a), effective September 1, 1997.)

# CHAPTER 646
# MOTOR TRANSPORTATION BROKERS

## Sec. 646.001.   Definition.

In this chapter, "motor transportation broker" means a person who:

(1) sells, offers for sale, provides, or negotiates for the transportation of cargo by a motor carrier operated by another person; or

(2) aids or abets a person in performing an act described by Subdivision (1).

(Enacted by Acts 1997, 75th Leg., ch. 165 (S.B. 898), § 30.153(a), effective September 1, 1997.)

## Sec. 646.002.   Exception.

This chapter does not apply to a motor transportation broker who:

(1) is registered as a motor carrier under Chapter 643; or

(2) holds a permit issued under Subtitle IV, Title 49, United States Code.

(Enacted by Acts 1997, 75th Leg., ch. 165 (S.B. 898), § 30.153(a), effective September 1, 1997.)

## Sec. 646.003.   Bond Required.

(a) A person may not act as a motor transportation broker unless the person provides a bond to the Texas Department of Motor Vehicles.

(b) The bond must be in an amount of at least $10,000 and must be:

(1) executed by a bonding company authorized to do business in this state;

(2) payable to this state or a person to whom the motor transportation broker provides services; and

(3) conditioned on the performance of the contract for transportation services between the broker and the person for whom services are provided.

(c) The department may charge the broker a bond review fee in an amount not to exceed the cost of reviewing the bond.

(d) The department may adopt rules regarding the method of payment of a fee under this chapter. The rules may:

(1) authorize the use of electronic funds transfer or a credit card issued by a financial institution chartered by a state or the United States or by a nationally recognized credit organization approved by the department; and

(2) require the payment of a discount or service charge for a credit card payment in addition to the fee.

(Enacted by Acts 1997, 75th Leg., ch. 165 (S.B. 898), § 30.153(a), effective September 1, 1997; am. Acts 2009, 81st Leg., ch. 933 (H.B. 3097), § 2N.01, effective September 1, 2009.)

## Sec. 646.004.   Criminal Offense.

(a) A person commits an offense if the person fails to provide the bond required by Section 646.003.

(b) An offense under this section is a Class C misdemeanor.

(Enacted by Acts 1997, 75th Leg., ch. 165 (S.B. 898), § 30.153(a), effective September 1, 1997.)

# CHAPTER 647
# MOTOR TRANSPORTATION OF MIGRANT AGRICULTURAL WORKERS

Transportation

## Sec. 647.001. Definitions.

In this chapter:

(1) "Bus" means a motor vehicle that is designed, constructed, and used to transport passengers. The term does not include a passenger automobile or a station wagon other than a taxicab.

(2) "Highway" has the meaning assigned by Section 541.302.

(3) "Migrant agricultural worker" means a person who:

(A) performs or seeks to perform farm labor of a seasonal nature, including labor necessary to process an agricultural food product; and

(B) occupies living quarters other than the individual's permanent home during the period of employment.

(4) "Motor vehicle" means any vehicle, machine, tractor, trailer, or semitrailer propelled or drawn by mechanical power and used on a highway to transport passengers or property or both. The term does not include:

(A) a vehicle, locomotive, or car that operates exclusively on one or more rails; or

(B) a trolley bus that operates on electricity generated from a fixed overhead wire and that provides local passenger transportation in street-railway service.

(5) "Operator" means a person who operates a motor vehicle.

(6) "Semitrailer" has the meaning assigned by Section 541.201.

(7) "Truck" has the meaning assigned by Section 541.201.

(8) "Truck tractor" has the meaning assigned by Section 541.201.

(Enacted by Acts 1999, 76th Leg., ch. 62 (S.B. 1368), § 17.34(a), effective September 1, 1999.)

## Sec. 647.002. Application of Chapter.

(a) This chapter applies to any carrier, including a carrier under contract, who at any time uses a motor vehicle to transport to or from a place of employment in this state at least five migrant agricultural workers for a total distance of more than 50 miles.

(b) This chapter does not apply if:

(1) the carrier is a common carrier;

(2) the motor vehicle used is a station wagon or passenger automobile; or

(3) the carrier is a migrant agricultural worker transporting the worker or a member of the worker's immediate family.

(Enacted by Acts 1999, 76th Leg., ch. 62 (S.B. 1368), § 17.34(a), effective September 1, 1999.)

## Sec. 647.003. Type of Vehicle Allowed.

(a) A carrier may transport migrant agricultural workers only in a:

(1) bus;

(2) truck to which a trailer is not attached; or

(3) semitrailer attached to a truck tractor.

(b) A carrier may not:

(1) attach a trailer to a semitrailer described by Subsection (a)(3); or

(2) use a closed van that does not have windows or a method to ensure ventilation.

(Enacted by Acts 1999, 76th Leg., ch. 62 (S.B. 1368), § 17.34(a), effective September 1, 1999.)

## Sec. 647.004. Compliance with Requirements of Chapter.

(a) A carrier shall comply with the requirements and specifications of this chapter.

(b) An officer, agent, representative, or employee of a carrier who operates a motor vehicle used to transport migrant agricultural workers or who hires, supervises, trains, assigns, or dispatches operators of those motor vehicles shall comply with the requirements of Sections 647.006, 647.007, and 647.008.

(c) An officer, agent, representative, operator, or employee of a carrier who is directly involved in the management, maintenance, or operation of a motor vehicle used to transport migrant agricultural workers shall comply with the requirements of Sections 647.003, 647.005, 647.009, 647.010, 647.011, 647.012, 647.014, 647.016, and 647.017. The carrier shall instruct its officers, agents, representatives, and operators with the requirements of those sections and shall take necessary measures to ensure compliance with those requirements.

(d) An officer, agent, representative, operator, or employee of a carrier who is directly involved with the installation or maintenance of equipment and accessories of a motor vehicle used to transport migrant agricultural workers shall comply with the requirements and specifications of Sections 647.012, 647.013, 647.014, 647.015, and 647.016. A carrier may not operate a motor vehicle transporting migrant agricultural workers or cause or permit the vehicle to be operated unless the vehicle is equipped as required by those sections.

(e) A carrier shall systematically inspect and maintain each motor vehicle used to transport migrant agricultural workers and their accessories subject to its control to ensure that the vehicle and its accessories are in safe and proper operating condition.
(Enacted by Acts 1999, 76th Leg., ch. 62 (S.B. 1368), § 17.34(a), effective September 1, 1999.)

## Sec. 647.005. Operation in Accordance with Law.

If this chapter imposes a greater affirmative obligation or restraint on the operation of a motor vehicle transporting migrant agricultural workers than the laws, ordinances, and regulations of the jurisdiction in which the vehicle is operated, the operator shall comply with this chapter.
(Enacted by Acts 1999, 76th Leg., ch. 62 (S.B. 1368), § 17.34(a), effective September 1, 1999.)

## Sec. 647.006. Operator Age and Experience Requirements.

A person may not operate a motor vehicle transporting migrant agricultural workers and a carrier may not permit or require a person to operate the motor vehicle unless the person:

(1) is at least 18 years of age;

(2) has at least one year of experience in operating any type of motor vehicle, including a private automobile, during the different seasons;

(3) is familiar with the law relating to operating a motor vehicle; and

(4) is authorized by law to operate that type of motor vehicle.
(Enacted by Acts 1999, 76th Leg., ch. 62 (S.B. 1368), § 17.34(a), effective September 1, 1999.)

## Sec. 647.007. Operator Physical Requirements.

(a) A person may not operate a motor vehicle transporting migrant agricultural workers and a carrier may not permit or require a person to operate the motor vehicle if the person:

(1) is missing a foot, leg, hand, or arm;

(2) has a mental, nervous, organic, or functional disorder that is likely to interfere with the person's ability to safely operate the motor vehicle;

(3) is missing fingers, has impaired use of a foot, leg, finger, hand, or arm, or has another structural defect or limitation likely to inter-

fere with the person's ability to safely operate the motor vehicle;

(4) has a visual acuity of less than 20/40 (Snellen) in each eye either without glasses or with corrective lenses;

(5) has a form field of vision in the horizontal median of less than a total of 140 degrees;

(6) cannot distinguish the colors red, green, and yellow;

(7) has hearing ability of less than 10/20 in the better ear for conversational tones without the use of a hearing aid; or

(8) is addicted to alcohol, narcotics, or habit-forming drugs.

(b) An operator who requires corrective lenses for vision shall use properly prescribed corrective lenses when operating the motor vehicle.
(Enacted by Acts 1999, 76th Leg., ch. 62 (S.B. 1368), § 17.34(a), effective September 1, 1999.)

## Sec. 647.008. Physical Examination Requirement.

(a) A person may not operate a motor vehicle transporting migrant agricultural workers and a carrier may not permit or require a person to operate the motor vehicle unless:

(1) the person has been physically examined by a licensed doctor of medicine or osteopathy during the preceding 36 months; and

(2) the doctor certifies that the person is physically qualified in accordance with Section 647.007.

(b) The doctor's certificate must state:

"Doctor's Certificate

(Operator of Migrant Agricultural Workers)

This is to certify that I have this day examined _____ in accordance with the Texas law governing physical qualifications of operators of migrant agricultural workers and that I find

_____

Qualified under that law

Qualified only when wearing glasses or corrective lenses

_____          _____
(Date)                         (Place)

_____
(Signature of Examining Doctor)

_____
(Address of Doctor)

Signature of Operator: _____
Address of Operator: _____ "

(c) A carrier shall keep in its files at the carrier's principal place of business a legible doctor's certificate or a legible photographically reproduced copy of the doctor's certificate for each operator it employs or uses.

(d) An operator shall carry the operator's legible doctor's certificate or a legible photographically reproduced copy of the doctor's certificate when operating the motor vehicle.

(Enacted by Acts 1999, 76th Leg., ch. 62 (S.B. 1368), § 17.34(a), effective September 1, 1999.)

### Sec. 647.009. Limitation on Operation of Motor Vehicle.

(a) Except in an emergency, a person assigned to operate a motor vehicle transporting migrant workers may not allow another person to operate the motor vehicle without the carrier's authorization.

(b) A person may not operate a motor vehicle if the person's alertness or ability to operate the vehicle is impaired for any reason, including fatigue or illness, to the extent that it is not safe for the person to begin or to continue. This subsection does not apply if there is a grave emergency in which failure to operate a motor vehicle would result in a greater hazard to passengers. However, the person may operate the motor vehicle only to the nearest location at which the passengers' safety is ensured.

(c) A carrier may not permit or require a person to operate a motor vehicle from one location to another in a period that would necessitate the operation of the vehicle at a speed in excess of the applicable speed limit.

(d) An operator shall make a meal stop of not less than 30 minutes at least every six hours. The carrier shall provide for reasonable rest stops at least once between each meal stop.

(e) The operator of a truck transporting migrant agricultural workers for more than 500 miles shall stop for at least eight hours to provide rest for the operator and passengers either before or at the completion of each 500 miles.

(f) A person may not operate and a carrier may not permit or require the person to operate a motor vehicle for more than 10 hours in the aggregate, excluding meal and rest stops, during any 24-hour period unless the person rests for at least eight consecutive hours at the end of the 10-hour period. For purposes of this subsection, the 24-hour period begins at the time the operator reports for duty.

(Enacted by Acts 1999, 76th Leg., ch. 62 (S.B. 1368), § 17.34(a), effective September 1, 1999.)

### Sec. 647.010. Required Stop at Railroad Crossing.

(a) An operator transporting migrant agricultural workers who approaches a railroad grade crossing:

(1) shall stop the motor vehicle not less than 15 feet or more than 50 feet from the nearest rail of the crossing; and

(2) may proceed only after the operator determines that the course is clear.

(b) An operator is not required to stop at:

(1) a streetcar crossing that is in a municipal business or residential district;

(2) a railroad grade crossing at which a police officer or traffic-control signal other than a railroad flashing signal directs traffic to proceed; or

(3) a grade crossing that the proper state authority has clearly marked as being abandoned or exempted if the marking can be read from the operator's position.

(c) The motor vehicle must display a sign on the rear of the vehicle that states: "This Vehicle Stops at Railroad Crossings."

(Enacted by Acts 1999, 76th Leg., ch. 62 (S.B. 1368), § 17.34(a), effective September 1, 1999.)

### Sec. 647.011. Fuel Restrictions.

(a) An operator or carrier employee fueling a motor vehicle used to transport migrant agricultural workers may not:

(1) fuel the motor vehicle while the engine is running unless running the engine is required to fuel the vehicle;

(2) smoke or expose any open flame in the vicinity of the motor vehicle;

(3) fuel the motor vehicle when the nozzle of the fuel hose is not in continuous contact with the intake pipe of the fuel tank; or

(4) permit any other person to engage in an activity that would likely result in a fire or explosion.

(b) A person may carry fuel on the motor vehicle for use in the motor vehicle or an accessory only in a properly mounted fuel tank.

(Enacted by Acts 1999, 76th Leg., ch. 62 (S.B. 1368), § 17.34(a), effective September 1, 1999.)

### Sec. 647.012. Required Vehicle Equipment; Use of Required Equipment.

(a) A motor vehicle used to transport migrant agricultural workers must be equipped with:

(1) at least one properly mounted fire extinguisher;

(2) road warning devices, including at least one red-burning fusee and at least three red flares, red electric lanterns, or red emergency reflectors;

(3) coupling devices as prescribed by Subsection (c), if the vehicle is a truck tractor or dolly; and

(4) tires as prescribed by Subsection (d).

(b) A person may not operate a motor vehicle unless the person is satisfied that the equipment required under Subsection (a) and the following equipment is in good working order:

(1) the brakes, including service brakes, trailer brake connections, and hand parking brakes;

(2) lighting devices and reflectors;

(3) the steering mechanism;

(4) the horn;

(5) each windshield wiper; and

(6) each rearview mirror.

(c) Adequate means must be provided positively to prevent the shifting of the lower half of each fifth wheel attached to the frame of a truck tractor or dolly. The lower half of each fifth wheel must be securely fastened to the frame by U-bolts that are of adequate size and are securely tightened. Another method may be used if the method provides equivalent security. A U-bolt may not be of welded construction and must be installed so as not to crack, warp, or deform the frame. The upper half of each fifth wheel must be fastened with at least the security required for the lower half. A locking means must be provided in each fifth wheel mechanism, including adapters when used, so that the upper and lower half will not separate without the use of a positive manual release, such as a release mechanism that the operator uses from the cab. If the fifth wheel is designed and constructed to be readily separable, the requirement for a fifth wheel coupling device applies to a vehicle manufactured after December 31, 1952.

(d) Vehicle tires must be of adequate capacity to support the vehicle's gross weight. Each tire must have a tread configuration on the part of the tire that is in contact with the road and may not be so smooth as to expose any tread fabric. A tire may not have a defect likely to cause failure. A front tire may not be regrooved, recapped, or retreaded.

(e) An operator shall use required equipment as necessary.

(Enacted by Acts 1999, 76th Leg., ch. 62 (S.B. 1368), § 17.34(a), effective September 1, 1999.)

## Sec. 647.013.  Passenger Safety Provisions on Motor Vehicle Other Than Bus.

(a) A motor vehicle other than a bus transporting migrant agricultural workers must have a passenger compartment in accordance with this section.

(b) The floor of the passenger compartment must be substantially smooth and without cracks or holes. Except as necessary to secure the seats or other devices attached to the floor, the floor may not have any object that protrudes more than two inches in height.

(c) The side walls and ends of the passenger compartment must extend at least 60 inches from the floor. If necessary, sideboards may be attached to the body of the motor vehicle. Stake body construction meets the requirements of this subsection only if the space six inches or larger between any two stakes is suitably closed to prevent the passengers from falling off the vehicle.

(d) The floor and interior of the sides and ends of the passenger compartment must be free of protruding nails, screws, splinters, or any other protruding object that is likely to injure a passenger or the passenger's clothes.

(e) The motor vehicle must have an adequate means of exiting and entering the passenger compartment from the rear or from the right side of the vehicle. Each exit and entrance must have a gate or door that has at least one latch or fastening device that will keep the gate or door securely closed during transportation. The latch or fastening device must be readily operative without the use of tools. An exit or entrance must:

(1) be at least 18 inches wide;

(2) have a top and clear opening of at least 60 inches or as high as the passenger compartment side wall if the side wall is less than 60 inches high; and

(3) have a bottom that is at the floor of the passenger compartment.

(f) If the motor vehicle has a permanently attached roof, the vehicle must have at least one emergency exit on a side or rear of the vehicle that does not have a regular exit or entrance. The exit must have a gate or door and a latch and hold as prescribed by Subsection (e).

(g) If necessary, a ladder or steps shall be used to enter and exit the passenger compartment. The maximum vertical spacing of footholds may not exceed 12 inches and the lowest step may not be more than 18 inches above the ground when the vehicle is empty.

(h) The motor vehicle must include handholds or other devices that will enable passengers to enter and exit the vehicle without hazard.

(i) The motor vehicle must have a way for passengers to communicate with the operator, including a telephone, speaker tube, buzzer, pull cord, or other mechanical or electrical device. (Enacted by Acts 1999, 76th Leg., ch. 62 (S.B. 1368), § 17.34(a), effective September 1, 1999.)

### Sec. 647.014. Passenger Seating.

One seat must be provided for each passenger. Passengers shall remain seated while the vehicle is in motion. (Enacted by Acts 1999, 76th Leg., ch. 62 (S.B. 1368), § 17.34(a), effective September 1, 1999.)

### Sec. 647.015. Passenger Seating Requirements for Certain Trips.

(a) A motor vehicle transporting migrant agricultural workers for a total distance of 100 miles or more must have a passenger compartment in accordance with this section.

(b) Each passenger seat must:

(1) be securely attached to the vehicle during use;

(2) be not less than 16 or more than 19 inches above the floor;

(3) be at least 13 inches deep;

(4) be equipped with backrests that extend at least 36 inches above the floor;

(5) have at least 24 inches of space between the backrests or the edges of the opposite seats when positioned face to face;

(6) provide at least 18 inches of seat area for each passenger;

(7) not have any cracks that are more than one-fourth inch wide;

(8) not have any cracks in the backrests, if slatted, that are more than two inches wide; and

(9) have any exposed wood surfaces planed or sanded smooth and free of splinters. (Enacted by Acts 1999, 76th Leg., ch. 62 (S.B. 1368), § 17.34(a), effective September 1, 1999.)

### Sec. 647.016. Passenger Protection from Weather.

(a) If necessary to protect passengers from inclement weather, including rain, snow, or sleet, the passenger compartment must be equipped with a top that is at least 80 inches above the floor and with a means of closing the sides and ends. A tarpaulin or other removable protective device may be used if secured in place.

(b) The motor vehicle must have a safe method of protecting the passengers from cold or undue exposure. A motor vehicle may not have a heater that:

(1) conducts engine exhaust gases or engine compartment air into or through a space occupied by an individual;

(2) uses a flame that is not completely enclosed;

(3) might spill or leak fuel if the vehicle is tilted or overturned;

(4) uses heated or unheated air that comes from or through the engine compartment or from direct contact with any part of the exhaust system unless the heater ducts prevent contamination of the air from the exhaust or engine compartment gases; or

(5) is not securely fastened to the motor vehicle. (Enacted by Acts 1999, 76th Leg., ch. 62 (S.B. 1368), § 17.34(a), effective September 1, 1999.)

### Sec. 647.017. Operational Requirements.

(a) A person may not operate a motor vehicle transporting migrant agricultural workers that is loaded or that has a load that is distributed or secured in a manner that prevents the vehicle's safe operation.

(b) A person may not operate a motor vehicle if:

(1) a tailgate, tailboard, tarpaulin, door, fastening device, or equipment or rigging is not securely in place;

(2) an object:

(A) obscures the operator's view in any direction;

(B) interferes with the free movement of the operator's arms or legs;

(C) obstructs the operator's access to emergency accessories; or

(D) obstructs a person's entrance or exit from the cab or operator's compartment; or

(3) property on the vehicle is stowed so that it:

(A) restricts the operator's freedom of motion in properly operating the vehicle;

(B) obstructs a person's exit from the vehicle; or

(C) does not provide adequate protection to passengers and others from injury resulting from a falling or displaced article.

(c) An operator who leaves a motor vehicle unattended shall securely set the parking brake, chock the wheels, and take all reasonable precautions to prevent the vehicle from moving.

Transportation

(Enacted by Acts 1999, 76th Leg., ch. 62 (S.B. 1368), § 17.34(a), effective September 1, 1999.)

### Sec. 647.018.    Certificate of Compliance.

A carrier is considered to be in compliance with this chapter if the carrier holds a certificate of compliance with the United States Department of Transportation regulations governing transportation of migrant agricultural workers in interstate commerce.

(Enacted by Acts 1999, 76th Leg., ch. 62 (S.B. 1368), § 17.34(a), effective September 1, 1999.)

### Sec. 647.019.    Penalty.

(a) A carrier who violates this chapter commits an offense.

(b) An offense under this section is a misdemeanor punishable by a fine of not less than $5 or more than $50.

(Enacted by Acts 1999, 76th Leg., ch. 62 (S.B. 1368), § 17.34(a), effective September 1, 1999.)

## CHAPTER 648
## FOREIGN COMMERCIAL MOTOR TRANSPORTATION

### Subchapter A. General Provisions

## SUBCHAPTER A
## GENERAL PROVISIONS

### Sec. 648.001.    Definitions.

In this chapter:

(1) "Border" means the border between this state and the United Mexican States.

(2) "Border commercial zone" means a commercial zone established under 49 C.F.R. Part 372, Subpart B, any portion of which is contiguous to the border in this state.

(3) "Commercial motor vehicle" includes a foreign commercial motor vehicle.

(4) "Foreign commercial motor vehicle" means a commercial motor vehicle, as defined by 49 C.F.R. Section 390.5, that is owned by a person or entity that is domiciled in or a citizen of a country other than the United States.

(5) "Motor carrier" includes a foreign motor carrier and a foreign motor private carrier, as defined in 49 U.S.C. Sections 13102(6) and (7).

(Enacted by Acts 1999, 76th Leg., ch. 62 (S.B. 1368), § 17.35(a), effective September 1, 1999; am. Acts 2009, 81st Leg., ch. 39 (H.B. 782), § 1, effective September 1, 2009.)

### Sec. 648.002.    Rules.

In addition to rules required by this chapter, the Texas Department of Motor Vehicles, the Department of Public Safety, and the Texas Department of Insurance may adopt other rules to carry out this chapter.

(Enacted by Acts 1999, 76th Leg., ch. 62 (S.B. 1368), § 17.35(a), effective September 1, 1999; am. Acts 2009, 81st Leg., ch. 933 (H.B. 3097), § 20.01, effective September 1, 2009.)

### Sec. 648.003.    Reference to Federal Statute or Regulation.

A reference in this chapter to a federal statute or regulation includes any subsequent amendment or redesignation of the statute or regulation.

(Enacted by Acts 1999, 76th Leg., ch. 62 (S.B. 1368), § 17.35(a), effective September 1, 1999.)

### Secs. 648.004 to 648.050 [Reserved for expansion].

## SUBCHAPTER B
## BORDER COMMERCIAL ZONE

### Sec. 648.051.    Border Commercial Zone Exclusive; Boundaries.

(a) A law or agreement of less than statewide application that is adopted by an agency or political subdivision of this state and that regulates motor carriers or commercial motor vehicles or the operation of those carriers or vehicles in the transportation of cargo across the border or within an area adjacent to the border by foreign commercial motor vehicles has no effect unless the law or agreement applies uniformly to an entire border commercial zone and only in a border commercial zone.

(b) This subchapter supersedes that portion of any paired city, paired state, or similar understanding governing foreign commercial motor vehicles or motor carriers entered into under Section 502.054 or any other law.

(Enacted by Acts 1999, 76th Leg., ch. 62 (S.B. 1368), § 17.35(a), effective September 1, 1999.)

### Sec. 648.052. Modification of Zone Boundaries.

The boundaries of a border commercial zone may be modified or established only as provided by federal law.

(Enacted by Acts 1999, 76th Leg., ch. 62 (S.B. 1368), § 17.35(a), effective September 1, 1999.)

### Secs. 648.053 to 648.100 [Reserved for expansion].

## SUBCHAPTER C
## REGULATION OF OPERATION OF FOREIGN COMMERCIAL MOTOR VEHICLES

### Sec. 648.101. Registration Exemption in Border Commercial Zone.

(a) A foreign commercial motor vehicle is exempt from Chapter 502 and any other law of this state requiring the vehicle to be registered in this state, including a law providing for a temporary registration permit, if:

(1) the vehicle is engaged solely in transportation of cargo across the border into or from a border commercial zone;

(2) for each load of cargo transported the vehicle remains in this state:

(A) not more than 24 hours; or

(B) not more than 48 hours, if:

(i) the vehicle is unable to leave this state within 24 hours because of circumstances beyond the control of the motor carrier operating the vehicle; and

(ii) all financial responsibility requirements applying to the vehicle are satisfied;

(3) the vehicle is registered and licensed as required by the country in which the person that owns the vehicle is domiciled or is a citizen as evidenced by a valid metal license plate attached to the front or rear of the exterior of the vehicle; and

(4) the country in which the person that owns the vehicle is domiciled or is a citizen provides a reciprocal exemption for commercial motor vehicles owned by residents of this state.

(b) A foreign commercial motor vehicle operating under the exemption provided by this section and the vehicle's driver may be considered unregistered if the vehicle is operated in this state outside a border commercial zone or in violation of United States law.

(c) A valid reciprocity agreement between this state and another state of the United States or a Canadian province that exempts currently registered vehicles owned by nonresidents is effective in a border commercial zone.

(d) A foreign commercial motor vehicle that engages primarily in transportation of cargo across the border into or from a border commercial zone must be:

(1) registered in this state; or

(2) operated under the exemption provided by this section.

(e) A vehicle located in a border commercial zone must display a valid Texas registration if the vehicle is owned by a person who:

(1) owns a leasing facility or a leasing terminal located in this state; and

(2) leases the vehicle to a foreign motor carrier.

(Enacted by Acts 1999, 76th Leg., ch. 62 (S.B. 1368), § 17.35(a), effective September 1, 1999; am. Acts 2007, 80th Leg., ch. 72 (H.B. 313), § 1, effective September 1, 2007; am. Acts 2009, 81st Leg., ch. 39 (H.B. 782), § 2, effective September 1, 2009.)

### Sec. 648.102. Financial Responsibility.

(a) The Texas Department of Transportation shall adopt rules that conform with 49 C.F.R. Part 387 requiring motor carriers operating foreign commercial motor vehicles in this state to maintain financial responsibility.

(b) This chapter prevails over any other requirement of state law relating to financial responsibility for operation of foreign commercial motor vehicles in this state.

(Enacted by Acts 1999, 76th Leg., ch. 62 (S.B. 1368), § 17.35(a), effective September 1, 1999.)

### Sec. 648.103. Domestic Transportation.

A foreign motor carrier or foreign motor private carrier may not transport persons or cargo in intrastate commerce in this state unless the carrier is authorized to conduct operations in interstate and foreign commerce domestically between points in the United States under federal law or international agreement.

(Enacted by Acts 1999, 76th Leg., ch. 62 (S.B. 1368), § 17.35(a), effective September 1, 1999.)

# CHAPTERS 649 TO 660
## [RESERVED FOR EXPANSION]

## SUBTITLE G
## MOTORCYCLES AND OFF-HIGHWAY VEHICLES

## CHAPTER 661
## PROTECTIVE HEADGEAR FOR MOTORCYCLE OPERATORS AND PASSENGERS

## Sec. 661.001.  Definitions.
In this chapter:
(1) "Motorcycle" means a motor vehicle designed to propel itself with not more than three wheels in contact with the ground, and having a saddle for the use of the rider. The term does not include a tractor or a three-wheeled vehicle equipped with a cab or occupant compartment, seat, and seat belt and designed to contain the operator in the cab or occupant compartment.
(2) "Department" means the Department of Public Safety.
(Enacted by Acts 1995, 74th Leg., ch. 165 (S.B. 971), § 1, effective September 1, 1995; am. Acts 2009, 81st Leg., ch. 722 (S.B. 129), § 5, effective September 1, 2009; am. Acts 2009, 81st Leg., ch. 967 (H.B. 3599), § 3, effective September 1, 2009; am. Acts 2009, 81st Leg., ch. 1391 (S.B. 1967), § 7, effective September 1, 2009.)

## Sec. 661.002.  Department to Prescribe Minimum Safety Standards for Protective Headgear.
(a) To provide for the safety and welfare of motorcycle operators and passengers, the department shall prescribe minimum safety standards for protective headgear used by motorcyclists in this state.
(b) The department may adopt any part or all of the American National Standards Institute's standards for protective headgear for vehicular users.
(c) On request of a manufacturer of protective headgear, the department shall make the safety standards prescribed by the department available to the manufacturer.
(Enacted by Acts 1995, 74th Leg., ch. 165 (S.B. 971), § 1, effective September 1, 1995.)

## Sec. 661.003.  Offenses Relating to Not Wearing Protective Headgear.
(a) A person commits an offense if the person:
(1) operates or rides as a passenger on a motorcycle on a public street or highway; and
(2) is not wearing protective headgear that meets safety standards adopted by the department.
(b) A person commits an offense if the person carries on a motorcycle on a public street or highway a passenger who is not wearing protective headgear that meets safety standards adopted by the department.
(c) It is an exception to the application of Subsection (a) or (b) that at the time the offense was committed, the person required to wear protective headgear was at least 21 years old and had successfully completed a motorcycle operator training and safety course under Chapter 662 or was covered by a health insurance plan providing the person with medical benefits for injuries incurred as a result of an accident while operating or riding on a motorcycle. A peace officer may not arrest a person or issue a citation to a person for a violation of Subsection (a) or (b) if the person required to wear protective headgear is at least 21 years of age and presents evidence sufficient to show that the person required to wear protective headgear has successfully completed a motorcycle operator training and safety course or is covered by a health insurance plan as described by this subsection.
(c-1) A peace officer may not stop or detain a person who is the operator of or a passenger on a motorcycle for the sole purpose of determining whether the person has successfully completed the motorcycle operator training and safety course or is covered by a health insurance plan.
(c-2) The Texas Department of Insurance shall prescribe a standard proof of health insurance for issuance to persons who are at least 21 years of age and covered by a health insurance plan described by Subsection (c).
(d) to (g) [Repealed by Acts 2009, 81st Leg., ch. 1391 (S.B. 1967), § 12, effective September 1, 2009.]

(h) An offense under this section is a misdemeanor punishable by a fine of not less than $10 or more than $50.

(i) In this section, "health insurance plan" means an individual, group, blanket, or franchise insurance policy, insurance agreement, evidence of coverage, group hospital services contract, health maintenance organization membership, or employee benefit plan that provides benefits for health care services or for medical or surgical expenses incurred as a result of an accident.
(Enacted by Acts 1995, 74th Leg., ch. 165 (S.B. 971), § 1, effective September 1, 1995; am. Acts 1997, 75th Leg., ch. 165 (S.B. 898), § 30.154(a), effective September 1, 1997; am. Acts 1997, 75th Leg., ch. 1156 (S.B. 99), § 3, effective September 1, 1997; am. Acts 1999, 76th Leg., ch. 62 (S.B. 1368), § 17.36, effective September 1, 1999; am. Acts 2001, 77th Leg., ch. 657 (H.B. 2585), § 1, effective September 1, 2001; am. Acts 2009, 81st Leg., ch. 1391 (S.B. 1967), §§ 8, 12, effective September 1, 2009.)

## Sec. 661.004. Authority of Peace Officer to Inspect Protective Headgear.

Any peace officer may stop and detain a person who is a motorcycle operator or passenger to inspect the person's protective headgear for compliance with the safety standards prescribed by the department.
(Enacted by Acts 1995, 74th Leg., ch. 165 (S.B. 971), § 1, effective September 1, 1995.)

## CHAPTER 662
## MOTORCYCLE OPERATOR TRAINING AND SAFETY

**Section**
662.001. Designated State Agency.
662.002. Purpose of Program; Curriculum.
662.003. Program Director.
662.004. Motorcycle Safety Coordinator.
662.005. Contracts.
662.006. Unauthorized Training Prohibited.
662.007. Fee for Course.
662.008. Denial, Suspension, or Cancellation of Approval.
662.009. Rules.
662.010. Nonapplicability of Certain Other Law.
662.011. Motorcycle Education Fund Account.
662.012. Reports.

## Sec. 662.001. Designated State Agency.

The governor shall designate a state agency to establish and administer a motorcycle operator training and safety program.

(Enacted by Acts 1995, 74th Leg., ch. 165 (S.B. 971), § 1, effective September 1, 1995.)

## Sec. 662.002. Purpose of Program; Curriculum.

(a) The purpose of the motorcycle operator training and safety program is:
(1) to make available to motorcycle operators:
(A) information relating to the operation of motorcycles; and
(B) courses in knowledge, skills, and safety relating to the operation of motorcycles; and
(2) to provide information to the public on sharing roadways with motorcycles.
(b) The program shall include curricula developed by the Motorcycle Safety Foundation.
(Enacted by Acts 1995, 74th Leg., ch. 165 (S.B. 971), § 1, effective September 1, 1995.)

## Sec. 662.003. Program Director.

The designated state agency shall employ as program director a person who is certified as a chief instructor by the Motorcycle Safety Foundation.
(Enacted by Acts 1995, 74th Leg., ch. 165 (S.B. 971), § 1, effective September 1, 1995.)

## Sec. 662.004. Motorcycle Safety Coordinator.

(a) The designated state agency shall employ a motorcycle safety coordinator.
(b) The coordinator shall supervise the motorcycle operator training and safety program and shall determine:
(1) locations at which courses will be provided;
(2) fees for the courses;
(3) qualifications for instructors;
(4) instructor certification requirements; and
(5) eligibility requirements for program sponsors.
(c) The program must include instructor certification requirements developed by the Motorcycle Safety Foundation.
(Enacted by Acts 1995, 74th Leg., ch. 165 (S.B. 971), § 1, effective September 1, 1995.)

## Sec. 662.005. Contracts.

The designated state agency may license or contract with qualified persons to administer or operate the motorcycle operator training and safety program.

Transportation

(Enacted by Acts 1995, 74th Leg., ch. 165 (S.B. 971), § 1, effective September 1, 1995.)

### Sec. 662.006.  Unauthorized Training Prohibited.

A person may not offer training in motorcycle operation for a consideration unless the person is licensed by or contracts with the designated state agency.

(Enacted by Acts 1995, 74th Leg., ch. 165 (S.B. 971), § 1, effective September 1, 1995.)

### Sec. 662.007.  Fee for Course.

A person may charge, for a course under the motorcycle operator training and safety program, a fee that is reasonably related to the costs of administering the course.

(Enacted by Acts 1995, 74th Leg., ch. 165 (S.B. 971), § 1, effective September 1, 1995.)

### Sec. 662.008.  Denial, Suspension, or Cancellation of Approval.

(a) The designated state agency may deny, suspend, or cancel its approval for a program sponsor to conduct or for an instructor to teach a course offered under this chapter if the applicant, instructor, or sponsor:

(1) does not satisfy the requirements established under this chapter to receive or retain approval;

(2) permits fraud or engages in a fraudulent practice with reference to an application to the agency;

(3) induces or countenances fraud or a fraudulent practice by a person applying for a driver's license or permit;

(4) permits fraud or engages in a fraudulent practice in an action between the applicant or license holder and the public; or

(5) fails to comply with rules of the state agency.

(b) Before the designated state agency may deny, suspend, or cancel the approval of a program sponsor or an instructor, notice and opportunity for a hearing must be given as provided by:

(1) Chapter 2001, Government Code; and

(2) Chapter 53, Occupations Code.

(Enacted by Acts 1995, 74th Leg., ch. 165 (S.B. 971), § 1, effective September 1, 1995; am. Acts 2001, 77th Leg., ch. 1420 (H.B. 2812), § 14.838, effective September 1, 2001.)

### Sec. 662.009.  Rules.

The designated state agency may adopt rules to administer this chapter.

(Enacted by Acts 1995, 74th Leg., ch. 165 (S.B. 971), § 1, effective September 1, 1995.)

### Sec. 662.010.  Nonapplicability of Certain Other Law.

Chapter 332, Acts of the 60th Legislature, Regular Session, 1967 (Article 4413(29c), Vernon's Texas Civil Statutes), does not apply to training offered under this chapter.

(Enacted by Acts 1995, 74th Leg., ch. 165 (S.B. 971), § 1, effective September 1, 1995.)

### Sec. 662.011.  Motorcycle Education Fund Account.

(a) Of each fee collected under Sections 521.421(b) and (f) and Sections 522.029(f) and (g), the Department of Public Safety shall send $5 to the comptroller for deposit to the credit of the motorcycle education fund account.

(b) Money deposited to the credit of the motorcycle education fund account may be used only to defray the cost of administering the motorcycle operator training and safety program.

(c) The comptroller shall report to the governor and legislature not later than the first Monday in November of each even-numbered year on the condition of the account. The report must contain:

(1) a statement of the amount of money deposited to the credit of the account for the year;

(2) a statement of the amount of money disbursed by the comptroller from the account for the year;

(3) a statement of the balance of money in the account;

(4) a list of persons and entities that have received money from the account, including information for each person or entity that shows the amount of money received; and

(5) a statement of any significant problems encountered in administering the account, with recommendations for their solution.

(Enacted by Acts 1997, 75th Leg., ch. 165 (S.B. 898), § 30.155, effective September 1, 1997; enacted by Acts 1997, 75th Leg., ch. 1156 (S.B. 99), § 4, effective September 1, 1997; am. Acts 2001, 77th Leg., ch. 657 (H.B. 2585), § 2, effective September 1, 2001; am. Acts 2009, 81st Leg., ch. 1391 (S.B. 1967), § 9, effective September 1, 2009.)

### Sec. 662.012.  Reports.

(a) The designated state agency shall require each provider of a motorcycle operator training and safety program to compile and forward to the agency each month a report on the provider's programs. The report must include:

(1) the number and types of courses provided in the reporting period;

(2) the number of persons who took each course in the reporting period;

(3) the number of instructors available to provide training under the provider's program in the reporting period;

(4) information collected by surveying persons taking each course as to the length of any waiting period the person experienced before being able to enroll in the course;

(5) the number of persons on a waiting list for a course at the end of the reporting period; and

(6) any other information the agency reasonably requires.

(b) The designated state agency shall maintain a compilation of the reports submitted under Subsection (a) on a by-site basis. The agency shall update the compilation as soon as practicable after the beginning of each month.

(c) The designated state agency shall provide without charge a copy of the most recent compilation under Subsection (b) to any member of the legislature on request.

(Enacted by Acts 2001, 77th Leg., ch. 657 (H.B. 2585), § 3, effective September 1, 2001.)

# CHAPTER 663
## CERTAIN OFF-HIGHWAY VEHICLES

### Subchapter A. General Provisions

## SUBCHAPTER A
## GENERAL PROVISIONS

### Sec. 663.001. Definitions.

In this chapter:

(1) "All-terrain vehicle" means a motor vehicle that is:

(A) equipped with a saddle for the use of:

(i) the rider; and

(ii) a passenger, if the motor vehicle is designed by the manufacturer to transport a passenger;

(B) designed to propel itself with three or four tires in contact with the ground;

(C) designed by the manufacturer for off-highway use by the operator only; and

(D) not designed by the manufacturer for farming or lawn care.

(2) "Public property" means property owned or leased by the state or a political subdivision of the state.

(3) "Recreational off-highway vehicle" has the meaning assigned by Section 502.001.

(Enacted by Acts 1995, 74th Leg., ch. 165 (S.B. 971), § 1, effective September 1, 1995; am. Acts 2003, 78th Leg., ch. 115 (S.B. 1635), § 1, effective September 1, 2003; am. Acts 2009, 81st Leg., ch. 1136 (H.B. 2553), § 15, effective September 1, 2009.)

### Sec. 663.002. Nonapplicability of Certain Other Laws.

(a) Except as provided by Section 663.037, Chapter 521 does not apply to the operation or ownership of an all-terrain vehicle registered for off-highway operation.

(b) Chapter 332, Acts of the 60th Legislature, Regular Session, 1967 (Article 4413(29c), Vernon's Texas Civil Statutes), does not apply to instruction in the operation of an all-terrain vehicle provided under the operator education and certification program established by this chapter.

(Enacted by Acts 1995, 74th Leg., ch. 165 (S.B. 971), § 1, effective September 1, 1995; am. Acts 2001, 77th Leg., ch. 472 (H.B. 651), § 1, effective September 1, 2001.)

Transportation

### Sec. 663.003. Recreational Off-Highway Vehicles.

This chapter applies to the operator and operation of a recreational off-highway vehicle in the same manner as if the recreational off-highway vehicle were an all-terrain vehicle.
(Enacted by Acts 2009, 81st Leg., ch. 1136 (H.B. 2553), § 16, effective September 1, 2009.)

### Secs. 663.004 to 663.010 [Reserved for expansion].

## SUBCHAPTER B
## ALL-TERRAIN VEHICLE OPERATOR EDUCATION AND CERTIFICATION

### Sec. 663.011. Designated Division or State Agency.

The governor shall designate a division of the governor's office or a state agency to establish and administer an all-terrain vehicle operator education and certification program.
(Enacted by Acts 1995, 74th Leg., ch. 165 (S.B. 971), § 1, effective September 1, 1995.)

### Sec. 663.012. Purpose of Program.

The purpose of the all-terrain vehicle operator education and certification program is to make available courses in basic training and safety skills relating to the operation of all-terrain vehicles and to issue safety certificates to operators who successfully complete the educational program requirements or pass a test established under the program.
(Enacted by Acts 1995, 74th Leg., ch. 165 (S.B. 971), § 1, effective September 1, 1995.)

### Sec. 663.013. All-Terrain Vehicle Safety Coordinator.

(a) The designated division or state agency shall employ an all-terrain vehicle safety coordinator.

(b) The coordinator shall supervise the all-terrain vehicle operator education and certification program and shall determine:

(1) locations at which courses will be offered;

(2) fees for the courses;

(3) qualifications of instructors;

(4) course curriculum; and

(5) standards for operator safety certification.

(c) In establishing standards for instructors, curriculum, and operator certification, the coordinator shall consult and be guided by standards established by recognized all-terrain vehicle safety organizations.
(Enacted by Acts 1995, 74th Leg., ch. 165 (S.B. 971), § 1, effective September 1, 1995.)

### Sec. 663.014. Contracts.

To administer the education program and certify all-terrain vehicle operators, the designated division or state agency may contract with non-profit safety organizations, nonprofit educational organizations, or agencies of local governments.
(Enacted by Acts 1995, 74th Leg., ch. 165 (S.B. 971), § 1, effective September 1, 1995.)

### Sec. 663.015. Teaching and Testing Methods.

(a) If the all-terrain vehicle safety coordinator determines that vehicle operation is not feasible in a program component or at a particular program location, the operator education and certification program for persons who are at least 14 years of age may use teaching or testing methods that do not involve the actual operation of an all-terrain vehicle.

(b) An operator safety certificate may not be issued to a person younger than 14 years of age unless the person has successfully completed a training course that involves the actual operation of an all-terrain vehicle.
(Enacted by Acts 1995, 74th Leg., ch. 165 (S.B. 971), § 1, effective September 1, 1995.)

### Sec. 663.016. Fee for Course.

A person may charge, for a course under the all-terrain vehicle operator education and certification program, a fee that is reasonably related to the costs of administering the course.
(Enacted by Acts 1995, 74th Leg., ch. 165 (S.B. 971), § 1, effective September 1, 1995.)

### Sec. 663.017. Denial, Suspension, or Cancellation of Approval.

(a) The designated division or state agency may deny, suspend, or cancel its approval for a program sponsor to conduct or for an instructor to teach a course offered under this chapter if the applicant, sponsor, or instructor:

(1) does not satisfy the requirements established under this chapter to receive or retain approval;

(2) permits fraud or engages in fraudulent practices with reference to an application to the division or agency;

(3) induces or countenances fraud or fraudulent practices by a person applying for a driver's license or permit;

*Transportation*

(4) permits or engages in a fraudulent practice in an action between the applicant or license holder and the public; or

(5) fails to comply with rules of the division or agency.

(b) Before the designated division or agency may deny, suspend, or cancel the approval of a program sponsor or an instructor, notice and opportunity for a hearing must be given as provided by:

(1) Chapter 2001, Government Code; and

(2) Chapter 53, Occupations Code.

(Enacted by Acts 1995, 74th Leg., ch. 165 (S.B. 971), § 1, effective September 1, 1995; am. Acts 2001, 77th Leg., ch. 1420 (H.B. 2812), § 14.839, effective September 1, 2001.)

## Sec. 663.018. Rules.

The designated division or state agency may adopt rules to administer this chapter.

(Enacted by Acts 1995, 74th Leg., ch. 165 (S.B. 971), § 1, effective September 1, 1995.)

## Sec. 663.019. Exemptions.

The designated division or state agency by rule may temporarily exempt the residents of any county from Section 663.015 or from Section 663.031(a)(1) until the appropriate education and certification program is established at a location that is reasonably accessible to the residents of that county.

(Enacted by Acts 1995, 74th Leg., ch. 165 (S.B. 971), § 1, effective September 1, 1995.)

**Secs. 663.020 to 663.030 [Reserved for expansion].**

## SUBCHAPTER C
## OPERATION OF ALL-TERRAIN VEHICLES

## Sec. 663.031. Safety Certificate Required.

(a) A person may not operate an all-terrain vehicle on public property unless the person:

(1) holds a safety certificate issued under this chapter or under the authority of another state;

(2) is taking a safety training course under the direct supervision of a certified all-terrain vehicle safety instructor; or

(3) is under the direct supervision of an adult who holds a safety certificate issued un-

der this chapter or under the authority of another state.

(b) A person to whom a safety certificate required by Subsection (a) has been issued shall:

(1) carry the certificate when the person operates an all-terrain vehicle on public property; and

(2) display the certificate at the request of any law enforcement officer.

(Enacted by Acts 1995, 74th Leg., ch. 165 (S.B. 971), § 1, effective September 1, 1995.)

## Sec. 663.032. Operation by Person Younger Than 14.

A person younger than 14 years of age who is operating an all-terrain vehicle must be accompanied by and be under the direct supervision of:

(1) the person's parent or guardian; or

(2) an adult who is authorized by the person's parent or guardian.

(Enacted by Acts 1995, 74th Leg., ch. 165 (S.B. 971), § 1, effective September 1, 1995.)

## Sec. 663.033. Required Equipment; Display of Lights.

(a) An all-terrain vehicle that is operated on public property must be equipped with:

(1) a brake system maintained in good operating condition;

(2) an adequate muffler system in good working condition; and

(3) a United States Forest Service qualified spark arrester.

(b) An all-terrain vehicle that is operated on public property must display a lighted headlight and taillight:

(1) during the period from one-half hour after sunset to one-half hour before sunrise; and

(2) at any time when visibility is reduced because of insufficient light or atmospheric conditions.

(c) A person may not operate an all-terrain vehicle on public property if:

(1) the vehicle has an exhaust system that has been modified with a cutout, bypass, or similar device; or

(2) the spark arrester has been removed or modified, unless the vehicle is being operated in a closed-course competition event.

(d) The coordinator may exempt all-terrain vehicles that are participating in certain competitive events from the requirements of this section.

(Enacted by Acts 1995, 74th Leg., ch. 165 (S.B. 971), § 1, effective September 1, 1995.)

Transportation

### Sec. 663.034.  Safety Apparel Required.

A person may not operate, ride, or be carried on an all-terrain vehicle on public property unless the person wears:

(1) a safety helmet that complies with United States Department of Transportation standards; and

(2) eye protection.

(Enacted by Acts 1995, 74th Leg., ch. 165 (S.B. 971), § 1, effective September 1, 1995.)

### Sec. 663.035.  Reckless or Careless Operation Prohibited.

A person may not operate an all-terrain vehicle on public property in a careless or reckless manner that endangers, injures, or damages any person or property.

(Enacted by Acts 1995, 74th Leg., ch. 165 (S.B. 971), § 1, effective September 1, 1995.)

### Sec. 663.036.  Carrying Passengers.

A person may not carry a passenger on an all-terrain vehicle operated on public property unless the all-terrain vehicle is designed by the manufacturer to transport a passenger.

(Enacted by Acts 1995, 74th Leg., ch. 165 (S.B. 971), § 1, effective September 1, 1995; am. Acts 2003, 78th Leg., ch. 115 (S.B. 1635), § 2, effective September 1, 2003.)

### Sec. 663.037.  Operation on Public Roadway Prohibited.

(a) A person may not operate an all-terrain vehicle on a public street, road, or highway except as provided by this section.

(b) The operator of an all-terrain vehicle may drive the vehicle across a public street, road, or highway that is not an interstate or limited-access highway, if the operator:

(1) brings the vehicle to a complete stop before crossing the shoulder or main traveled way of the roadway;

(2) yields the right-of-way to oncoming traffic that is an immediate hazard; and

(3) makes the crossing:

(A) at an angle of approximately 90 degrees to the roadway;

(B) at a place where no obstruction prevents a quick and safe crossing; and

(C) with the vehicle's headlights and taillights lighted.

(c) The operator of an all-terrain vehicle may drive the vehicle across a divided highway other than an interstate or limited access highway only at an intersection of the highway with another public street, road, or highway.

(d) The operator of an all-terrain vehicle may drive the vehicle on a public street, road, or highway that is not an interstate or limited-access highway if:

(1) the transportation is in connection with:

(A) the production, cultivation, care, harvesting, preserving, drying, processing, canning, storing, handling, shipping, marketing, selling, or use of agricultural products, as defined by Section 52.002, Agriculture Code; or

(B) utility work performed by a utility;

(2) the operator attaches to the back of the vehicle on top of an eight-foot-long pole a triangular orange flag;

(3) the vehicle's headlights and taillights are illuminated;

(4) the operator holds a driver's license, as defined by Section 521.001;

(5) the operation of the all-terrain vehicle occurs in the daytime; and

(6) the operation of the all-terrain vehicle does not exceed a distance of 25 miles from the point of origin to the destination.

(d-1) Provisions of this code regarding helmet and eye protection use, safety certification, and other vehicular restrictions do not apply to Subsection (d).

(e) The director of the Department of Public Safety shall adopt standards and specifications that apply to the color, size, and mounting position of the flag required under Subsections (d)(2) and (g)(2).

(f) Except as provided by Subsection (g), this section does not apply to the operation of an all-terrain vehicle that is owned by the state, a county, or a municipality by a person who is an authorized operator of the vehicle.

(g) A peace officer may operate an all-terrain vehicle on a public street, road, or highway that is not an interstate or limited-access highway only if:

(1) the transportation is in connection with the performance of the officer's official duty;

(2) the officer attaches to the back of the vehicle on top of an eight-foot-long pole a triangular orange flag;

(3) the vehicle's headlights and taillights are illuminated;

(4) the officer holds a driver's license, as defined by Section 521.001; and

(5) the operation of the all-terrain vehicle does not exceed a distance of 25 miles from the point of origin to the destination.

(Enacted by Acts 1995, 74th Leg., ch. 165 (S.B. 971), § 1, effective September 1, 1995; am. Acts 2001, 77th Leg., ch. 472 (H.B. 651), § 2, effective September 1, 2001; am. Acts 2003, 78th Leg., ch. 483 (H.B. 900), § 1, effective September 1, 2003; am. Acts 2007, 80th Leg., ch. 242 (H.B. 2127), § 1, effective September 1, 2007.)

### Sec. 663.038. Violation of Chapter; Offense.

(a) A person commits an offense if the person violates a provision of this chapter.

(b) Except as otherwise provided by Title 6 or this title, an offense under this section is a Class C misdemeanor.

(Enacted by Acts 1995, 74th Leg., ch. 165 (S.B. 971), § 1, effective September 1, 1995.)

## CHAPTERS 664 TO 679 [RESERVED FOR EXPANSION]

## CHAPTER 680 MISCELLANEOUS PROVISIONS

## SUBCHAPTER A
## SALE OF MOTORCYCLE WITHOUT SERIAL NUMBERS

### Sec. 680.001. Definitions.

In this subchapter:

(1) "Department" means the Department of Public Safety.

(2) "Motorcycle" has the meaning assigned that term by Section 661.001.

(3) "Person" means an individual, partnership, firm, corporation, association, or other private entity.

(Enacted by Acts 1995, 74th Leg., ch. 165 (S.B. 971), § 1, effective September 1, 1995.)

### Sec. 680.002. Sale of Motorcycle Without Serial Numbers.

A person may not sell a motorcycle manufactured after January 1, 1976, unless:

(1) the serial number of the frame and the serial number of the engine are affixed so that they may not be removed without defacing the frame or engine; and

(2) the manufacturer has filed with the department a statement that:

(A) identifies the part to which each number is affixed;

(B) gives the exact dimensions of the part; and

(C) gives the location on the part to which the number is affixed.

(Enacted by Acts 1995, 74th Leg., ch. 165 (S.B. 971), § 1, effective September 1, 1995.)

### Sec. 680.003. Offense; Penalty.

(a) An individual who violates Section 680.002 commits an offense.

(b) An offense under this section is a misdemeanor punishable by:

(1) a fine not to exceed $200;

(2) confinement in county jail for a term not to exceed 30 days; or

(3) both the fine and confinement.

(c) Each sale of a motorcycle in violation of this subchapter is a separate offense.

(Enacted by Acts 1995, 74th Leg., ch. 165 (S.B. 971), § 1, effective September 1, 1995.)

### Sec. 680.004. Civil Penalty.

A partnership, firm, corporation, or association that violates Section 680.002 is liable to the state for a civil penalty of not more than $500 for each offense.

(Enacted by Acts 1995, 74th Leg., ch. 165 (S.B. 971), § 1, effective September 1, 1995.)

### Sec. 680.005. Director to Adopt Rules and Develop Forms.

The director of the department shall adopt rules and develop forms to administer this subchapter.

(Enacted by Acts 1995, 74th Leg., ch. 165 (S.B. 971), § 1, effective September 1, 1995.)

Transportation

**Secs. 680.006 to 680.010 [Reserved for expansion].**

## SUBCHAPTER B

### TOLLS FOR MOTORCYCLE; USE OF PREFERENTIAL LANE BY MOTORCYCLE

### Sec. 680.011.  Definitions.

In this subchapter:

(1) "Motorcycle" has the meaning assigned by Section 502.001 and includes a motorcycle equipped with a sidecar.

(2) "Preferential lane" means a traffic lane on a street or highway where motor vehicle usage is limited to:

(A) buses;

(B) vehicles occupied by a minimum number of persons; or

(C) car pool vehicles.

(Enacted by Acts 1995, 74th Leg., ch. 165 (S.B. 971), § 1, effective September 1, 1995.)

### Sec. 680.012.  Toll for Motorcycle.

A person who operates a toll road, toll bridge, or turnpike may not impose a toll for the operation of a motorcycle on the road, bridge, or turnpike that is greater than the toll imposed for the operation of a passenger car on the road, bridge, or turnpike.

(Enacted by Acts 1995, 74th Leg., ch. 165 (S.B. 971), § 1, effective September 1, 1995.)

### Sec. 680.013.  Use of Preferential Lane by Motorcycle.

A motorcycle, including a motorcycle described by Section 521.001(a)(6-a), may be operated in a preferential lane that is not closed to all vehicular traffic.

(Enacted by Acts 1995, 74th Leg., ch. 165 (S.B. 971), § 1, effective September 1, 1995; am. Acts 2009, 81st Leg., ch. 722 (S.B. 129), § 6, effective September 1, 2009; am. Acts 2009, 81st Leg., ch. 967 (H.B. 3599), § 4, effective September 1, 2009; am. Acts 2009, 81st Leg., ch. 1391 (S.B. 1967), § 10, effective September 1, 2009.)

## SUBTITLE H
## PARKING, TOWING, AND STORAGE OF VEHICLES

## CHAPTER 681
## PRIVILEGED PARKING

### Sec. 681.001.  Definitions.

In this chapter:

(1) "Department" means the Texas Department of Motor Vehicles.

(2) "Disability" means a condition in which a person has:

(A) mobility problems that substantially impair the person's ability to ambulate;

(B) visual acuity of $20/200$ or less in the better eye with correcting lenses; or

(C) visual acuity of more than $20/200$ but with a limited field of vision in which the widest diameter of the visual field subtends an angle of 20 degrees or less.

(3) "Disabled parking placard" means a placard issued under Section 681.002.

(4) "International symbol of access" means the symbol adopted by Rehabilitation International in 1969 at its Eleventh World Congress on Rehabilitation of the Disabled.

(5) "Mobility problem that substantially impairs a person's ability to ambulate" means that the person:

(A) cannot walk 200 feet without stopping to rest;

(B) cannot walk without the use of or assistance from an assistance device, including a brace, a cane, a crutch, another person, or a prosthetic device;

(C) cannot ambulate without a wheelchair or similar device;

(D) is restricted by lung disease to the extent that the person's forced respiratory expiratory volume for one second, measured by spirometry, is less than one liter, or the arterial oxygen tension is less than 60 millimeters of mercury on room air at rest;

(E) uses portable oxygen;

(F) has a cardiac condition to the extent that the person's functional limitations are classified in severity as Class III or Class IV according to standards set by the American Heart Association;

(G) is severely limited in the ability to walk because of an arthritic, neurological, or orthopedic condition;

(H) has a disorder of the foot that, in the opinion of a person licensed to practice podiatry in this state or in a state adjacent to this state, limits or impairs the person's ability to walk; or

(I) has another debilitating condition that, in the opinion of a physician licensed to practice medicine in this state or a state adjacent to this state, or authorized by applicable law to practice medicine in a hospital or other health facility of the Veterans Administration, limits or impairs the person's ability to walk.

(6) "Podiatry" has the meaning assigned by Section 202.001, Occupations Code.

(7) "Stand" or "standing" means to halt an occupied or unoccupied vehicle, other than temporarily while receiving or discharging passengers.

(Enacted by Acts 1995, 74th Leg., ch. 165 (S.B. 971), § 1, effective September 1, 1995; am. Acts 1997, 75th Leg., ch. 165 (S.B. 898), § 30.156(a), effective September 1, 1997; am. Acts 1999, 76th Leg., ch. 1172 (S.B. 132), § 2, effective June 19, 1999; am. Acts 2001, 77th Leg., ch. 105 (S.B. 777),

§ 2, effective September 1, 2001; am. Acts 2003, 78th Leg., ch. 1325 (H.B. 3588), § 19.08(a), effective September 1, 2003; am. Acts 2009, 81st Leg., ch. 933 (H.B. 3097), § 2P.01, effective September 1, 2009.)

## Sec. 681.002. Disabled Parking Placard.

(a) The department shall provide for the issuance of a disabled parking placard to a person with a disability.

(b) A disabled parking placard must be two-sided and hooked and include on each side:

(1) the international symbol of access, which must be at least three inches in height, be centered on the placard, and be:

(A) white on a blue shield for a placard issued to a person with a permanent disability; or

(B) white on a red shield for a placard issued to a person with a temporary disability;

(2) an identification number;

(3) an expiration date at least three inches in height; and

(4) the seal or other identification of the department.

(c) The department shall furnish the disabled parking placards to each county assessor-collector.

(d) A disabled parking placard must bear a hologram designed to prevent the reproduction of the placard or the production of a counterfeit placard.

(e) In addition to the expiration date included on a disabled parking placard under Subsection (b), the expiration date must be indicated on the placard by a month and year hole-punch system. (Enacted by Acts 1995, 74th Leg., ch. 165 (S.B. 971), § 1, effective September 1, 1995; am. Acts 1997, 75th Leg., ch. 1353 (H.B. 580), § 1, effective September 1, 1997; am. Acts 1999, 76th Leg., ch. 1362 (H.B. 1032), § 1, effective September 1, 1999; am. Acts 2009, 81st Leg., ch. 1160 (H.B. 3095), § 1, effective September 1, 2009.)

## Sec. 681.003. Parking Placard Application.

(a) An owner of a motor vehicle regularly operated by or for the transportation of a person with a disability may apply for a disabled parking placard.

(b) An application for a disabled parking placard must be:

Transportation

(1) on a form furnished by the department;

(2) submitted to the county assessor-collector of the county in which the person with the disability resides; and

(3) accompanied by a fee of $5 if the application is for a temporary placard.

(c) Subject to Subsections (e) and (f), the first application must be accompanied by a notarized written statement or written prescription of a physician licensed to practice medicine in this state or a state adjacent to this state, or authorized by applicable law to practice medicine in a hospital or other health facility of the United States Department of Veterans Affairs, certifying and providing evidence acceptable to the department that the person making the application or on whose behalf the application is made is legally blind or has a mobility problem that substantially impairs the person's ability to ambulate. The statement or prescription must include a certification of whether the disability is temporary or permanent and information acceptable to the department to determine the type of disabled parking placard for which the applicant is eligible. The department shall determine a person's eligibility based on evidence provided by the applicant establishing legal blindness or mobility impairment.

(d) Information concerning the name or address of a person to whom a disabled parking placard is issued or in whose behalf a disabled parking placard is issued is confidential and not subject to disclosure under Chapter 552, Government Code.

(e) If a first application for a disabled parking placard under this section is made by or on behalf of a person with:

(1) a mobility problem caused by a disorder of the foot, the notarized written statement or written prescription required by Subsection (c) may be issued by a person licensed to practice podiatry in this state or a state adjacent to this state; or

(2) a disability caused by an impairment of vision as provided by Section 681.001(2), the notarized written statement or written prescription required by Subsection (c) may be issued by a person licensed to engage in the practice of optometry or the practice of therapeutic optometry in this state or a state adjacent to this state.

(f) This subsection applies only to the first application for a disabled parking placard submitted by a person. The notarized written statement or prescription may be issued by:

(1) a person acting under the delegation and supervision of a licensed physician in conformance with Subchapter B, Chapter 157, Occupations Code; or

(2) a physician assistant licensed to practice in this state acting as the agent of a licensed physician under Section 204.202(e), Occupations Code.

(g) In this section, "practice of optometry" and "practice of therapeutic optometry" have the meanings assigned by Section 351.002, Occupations Code.

(Enacted by Acts 1995, 74th Leg., ch. 165 (S.B. 971), § 1, effective September 1, 1995; am. Acts 1997, 75th Leg., ch. 165 (S.B. 898), § 30.156(b), effective September 1, 1997; am. Acts 1997, 75th Leg., ch. 1353 (H.B. 580), § 2, effective September 1, 1997; am. Acts 1999, 76th Leg., ch. 1172 (S.B. 132), § 3, effective June 19, 1999; am. Acts 1999, 76th Leg., ch. 1362 (H.B. 1032), § 2, effective September 1, 1999; am. Acts 2001, 77th Leg., ch. 105 (S.B. 777), § 3, effective September 1, 2001; am. Acts 2009, 81st Leg., ch. 531 (S.B. 1367), § 3, effective September 1, 2009; am. Acts 2009, 81st Leg., ch. 842 (S.B. 1984), § 1, effective June 19, 2009; am. Acts 2009, 81st Leg., ch. 1160 (H.B. 3095), § 2, effective September 1, 2009; am. Acts 2011, 82nd Leg., ch. 91 (S.B. 1303), § 27.001(65), effective September 1, 2011; am. Acts 2011, 82nd Leg., ch. 1291 (H.B. 2080), § 1, effective June 17, 2011.)

## Sec. 681.0031. Applicant's Driver's License or Personal Identification Card Number.

(a) The applicant shall include on the application the applicant's driver's license number or the number of a personal identification card issued to the applicant under Chapter 521. The department shall provide for this information in prescribing the application form.

(b) The county assessor-collector shall record on any disabled parking placard issued to the applicant the following information in the following order:

(1) the county number assigned by the comptroller to the county issuing the placard;

(2) the first four digits of the applicant's driver's license number; and

(3) the applicant's initials.

(Enacted by Acts 1997, 75th Leg., ch. 1353 (H.B. 580), § 3, effective September 1, 1997; am. Acts 2003, 78th Leg., ch. 473 (H.B. 874), § 1, effective June 20, 2003; am. Acts 2007, 80th Leg., ch. 231 (H.B. 1781), § 1, effective September 1, 2007.)

## Sec. 681.0032.  Issuance of Disabled Parking Placards to Certain Institutions.

(a) The department shall provide for the issuance of disabled parking placards described by Section 681.002 for a van or bus operated by an institution, facility, or residential retirement community for the elderly in which a person described by Section 504.201(a) resides, including an institution licensed under Chapter 242, Health and Safety Code, and a facility licensed under Chapter 246 or 247 of that code.

(b) The application for a disabled parking placard must be made in the manner provided by Section 681.003(b) and be accompanied by a written statement signed by the administrator or manager of the institution, facility, or retirement community certifying to the department that the institution, facility, or retirement community regularly transports, as a part of the services that the institution, facility, or retirement community provides, one or more persons described by Section 504.201(a) who reside in the institution, facility, or retirement community. The department shall determine the eligibility of the institution, facility, or retirement community on the evidence the applicant provides.

(Enacted by Acts 1999, 76th Leg., ch. 513 (S.B. 21), § 2, effective September 1, 1999; am. Acts 2005, 79th Leg., ch. 728 (H.B. 2018), § 20.003(c), effective September 1, 2005.)

## Sec. 681.004.  Issuance of Parking Placard; Expiration.

(a) A person with a permanent disability may receive:

(1) two disabled parking placards, if the person does not receive a set of special license plates under Section 504.201;

(2) one disabled parking placard, if the person receives a set of special license plates under Section 504.201; or

(3) two disabled parking placards, if the person receives two sets of special license plates under Section 504.202.

(b) A person with a temporary disability may receive two disabled parking placards.

(c) A disabled parking placard issued to a person with a permanent disability is valid for a period of four years and shall be replaced or renewed on request of the person to whom the initial card was issued without presentation of evidence of eligibility.

(d) A disabled parking placard issued to a person with a temporary disability expires after the period set by the department and may be renewed at the end of that period if the disability remains as evidenced by a physician's statement or prescription submitted as required for a first application under Section 681.003(c).

(Enacted by Acts 1995, 74th Leg., ch. 165 (S.B. 971), § 1, effective September 1, 1995; am. Acts 1997, 75th Leg., ch. 1353 (H.B. 580), § 4, effective September 1, 1997; am. Acts 2005, 79th Leg., ch. 728 (H.B. 2018), § 20.003(d), effective September 1, 2005; am. Acts 2007, 80th Leg., ch. 98 (H.B. 2105), § 2, effective May 15, 2007.)

## Sec. 681.005.  [2 Versions: Effective until January 1, 2012] Duties of County Assessor-Collector.

Each county assessor-collector shall send to the department:

(1) each fee collected under Section 681.003, to be deposited in the state highway fund to defray the cost of providing the disabled parking placard; and

(2) a copy of each application for a disabled parking placard.

(Enacted by Acts 1995, 74th Leg., ch. 165 (S.B. 971), § 1, effective September 1, 1995.)

## Sec. 681.005.  [2 Versions: Effective January 1, 2012] Duties of County Assessor-Collector.

Each county assessor-collector shall send to the department each fee collected under Section 681.003, to be deposited in the state highway fund to defray the cost of providing the disabled parking placard.

(Enacted by Acts 1995, 74th Leg., ch. 165 (S.B. 971), § 1, effective September 1, 1995; am. Acts 2011, 82nd Leg., ch. 1296 (H.B. 2357), § 242, effective January 1, 2012.)

## Sec. 681.006.  Parking Privileges: Persons with Disabilities.

(a) Subject to Section 681.009(e), a vehicle may be parked for an unlimited period in a parking space or area that is designated specifically for persons with physical disabilities if:

(1) the vehicle is being operated by or for the transportation of a person with a disability; and

(2) there are:

(A) displayed on the vehicle special license plates issued under Section 504.201; or

(B) placed on the rearview mirror of the vehicle's front windshield a disabled parking placard.

Transportation

(b) The owner of a vehicle is exempt from the payment of a fee or penalty imposed by a governmental unit for parking at a meter if:

(1) the vehicle is being operated by or for the transportation of a person with a disability; and

(2) there are:

(A) displayed on the vehicle special license plates issued under Section 504.201; or

(B) placed on the rearview mirror of the vehicle's front windshield a disabled parking placard.

(c) The exemption provided by Subsection (b) or (e) does not apply to a fee or penalty:

(1) imposed by a branch of the United States government; or

(2) imposed by a governmental unit for parking at a meter, in a parking garage or lot, or in a space located within the boundaries of a municipal airport.

(d) This section does not permit a vehicle to be parked at a time when or a place where parking is prohibited.

(e) A governmental unit may provide by ordinance or order that the exemption provided by Subsection (b) also applies to payment of a fee or penalty imposed by the governmental unit for parking in a parking garage or lot or in a space with a limitation on the length of time for parking.

(Enacted by Acts 1995, 74th Leg., ch. 165 (S.B. 971), § 1, effective September 1, 1995; am. Acts 1997, 75th Leg., ch. 165 (S.B. 898), § 30.156(c), effective September 1, 1997; am. Acts 1997, 75th Leg., ch. 804 (H.B. 3025), § 1, effective September 1, 1997; am. Acts 1997, 75th Leg., ch. 1353 (H.B. 580), § 5, effective September 1, 1997; am. Acts 1999, 76th Leg., ch. 1362 (H.B. 1032), § 3, effective September 1, 1999; am. Acts 2005, 79th Leg., ch. 728 (H.B. 2018), § 20.003(e), effective September 1, 2005.)

### Sec. 681.007. Parking Privileges: Vehicles Displaying International Symbol of Access.

A vehicle may be parked and is exempt from the payment of a fee or penalty in the same manner as a vehicle that has displayed on the vehicle special license plates issued under Section 504.201 or a disabled parking placard as provided by Section 681.006 if there is displayed on the vehicle a license plate or placard that:

(1) bears the international symbol of access; and

(2) is issued by a state or by a state or province of a foreign country to the owner or operator of the vehicle for the transportation of a person with a disability.

(Enacted by Acts 1995, 74th Leg., ch. 165 (S.B. 971), § 1, effective September 1, 1995; am. Acts 2005, 79th Leg., ch. 728 (H.B. 2018), § 20.003(f), effective September 1, 2005.)

### Sec. 681.008. Parking Privileges: Certain Veterans and Military Award Recipients.

(a) A vehicle may be parked for an unlimited period in a parking space or area that is designated specifically for persons with physical disabilities if the vehicle:

(1) is being operated by or for the transportation of:

(A) the person who registered the vehicle under Section 504.202(a) or a person described by Section 504.202(b) if the vehicle is registered under that subsection; and

(B) displays special license plates issued under Section 504.202; or

(2) displays license plates issued by another state of the United States that indicate on the face of the license plates that the owner or operator of the vehicle is a disabled veteran of the United States armed forces.

(b) A vehicle on which license plates described by Subsection (a)(2) or issued under Section 504.202, Section 504.315(a), (c), (d), (e), (f), (g), or (h), or Section 504.316 are displayed is exempt from the payment of a parking fee collected through a parking meter charged by a governmental authority other than a branch of the federal government, when being operated by or for the transportation of:

(1) the person who registered the vehicle under Section 504.202(a), Section 504.315(a), (c), (d), (e), (f), (g), or (h), or Section 504.316;

(2) a person described in Section 504.202(b) if the vehicle is registered under that subsection; or

(3) the owner or operator of a vehicle displaying license plates described by Subsection (a)(2).

(c) This section does not permit a vehicle to be parked at a time when or a place where parking is prohibited.

(d) A governmental unit may provide by ordinance or order that the exemption provided by Subsection (b) also applies to payment of a fee or penalty imposed by the governmental unit for parking in a parking garage or lot or in a space with a limitation on the length of time for parking.

(Enacted by Acts 1995, 74th Leg., ch. 165 (S.B. 971), § 1, effective September 1, 1995; am. Acts 1999, 76th Leg., ch. 738 (H.B. 1070), § 1, effective September 1, 1999; am. Acts 1999, 76th Leg., ch. 1195 (S.B. 416), § 1, effective June 18, 1999; am. Acts 1999, 76th Leg., ch. 1362 (H.B. 1032), § 4, effective September 1, 1999; am. Acts 2001, 77th Leg., ch. 1420 (H.B. 2812), § 19.007, effective September 1, 2001; am. Acts 2005, 79th Leg., ch. 728 (H.B. 2018), § 20.003(g), effective September 1, 2005; am. Acts 2009, 81st Leg., ch. 115 (H.B. 2020), § 1, effective September 1, 2009; am. Acts 2009, 81st Leg., ch. 319 (H.B. 618), §§ 1, 2, effective June 19, 2009; am. Acts 2011, 82nd Leg., ch. 91 (S.B. 1303), § 24.017, effective September 1, 2011; am. Acts 2011, 82nd Leg., ch. 339 (H.B. 2928), § 1, effective September 1, 2011; am. Acts 2011, 82nd Leg., ch. 709 (H.B. 559), § 2, effective September 1, 2011.)

### Sec. 681.009. Designation of Parking Spaces by Political Subdivision or Private Property Owner.

(a) A political subdivision or a person who owns or controls property used for parking may designate one or more parking spaces or a parking area for the exclusive use of vehicles transporting persons with disabilities.

(b) A political subdivision must designate a parking space or area by conforming to the standards and specifications adopted by the Texas Commission of Licensing and Regulation under Section 5(i), Article 9102, Revised Statutes, relating to the identification and dimensions of parking spaces for persons with disabilities. A person who owns or controls private property used for parking may designate a parking space or area without conforming to those standards and specifications, unless required to conform by law.

(c) A political subdivision may require a private property owner or a person who controls property used for parking:

    (1) to designate one or more parking spaces or a parking area for the exclusive use of vehicles transporting persons with disabilities; or

    (2) to conform to the standards and specifications referred to in Subsection (b) when designating a parking space or area for persons with disabilities.

(d) The department shall provide at cost a design and stencil for use by a political subdivision or person who owns or controls property used for parking to designate spaces as provided by this section.

(e) Parking spaces or areas designated for the exclusive use of vehicles transporting persons with disabilities may be used by vehicles displaying a white on blue shield disabled parking placard, license plates issued under Section 504.201 or 504.202, or a white on red shield disabled parking placard.

(Enacted by Acts 1995, 74th Leg., ch. 165 (S.B. 971), § 1, effective September 1, 1995; am. Acts 1999, 76th Leg., ch. 1246 (S.B. 959), § 9, effective September 1, 1999; am. Acts 1999, 76th Leg., ch. 1362 (H.B. 1032), § 5, effective September 1, 1999; am. Acts 2005, 79th Leg., ch. 728 (H.B. 2018), § 20.003(h), effective September 1, 2005; am. Acts 2007, 80th Leg., ch. 357 (S.B. 251), § 1, effective September 1, 2007; am. Acts 2009, 81st Leg., ch. 1160 (H.B. 3095), § 3, effective September 1, 2009.)

### Sec. 681.010. Enforcement.

(a) A peace officer or a person designated by a political subdivision to enforce parking regulations may file a charge against a person who commits an offense under this chapter at a parking space or area designated as provided by Section 681.009.

(b) A security officer commissioned under Chapter 1702, Occupations Code, and employed by the owner of private property may file a charge against a person who commits an offense under this chapter at a parking space or area designated by the owner of the property as provided by Section 681.009.

(Enacted by Acts 1995, 74th Leg., ch. 165 (S.B. 971), § 1, effective September 1, 1995; am. Acts 2001, 77th Leg., ch. 1420 (H.B. 2812), § 14.840, effective September 1, 2001.)

### Sec. 681.0101. Enforcement by Certain Appointed Persons.

(a) A political subdivision may appoint a person to have authority to file a charge against a person who commits an offense under this chapter.

(b) A person appointed under this section must:

    (1) be a United States citizen of good moral character who has not been convicted of a felony;

    (2) take and subscribe to an oath of office that the political subdivision prescribes; and

Transportation

(3) successfully complete a training program of at least four hours in length developed by the political subdivision.

(c) A person appointed under this section:

(1) is not a peace officer;

(2) has no authority other than the authority applicable to a citizen to enforce a law other than this chapter; and

(3) may not carry a weapon while performing duties under this section.

(d) A person appointed under this section is not entitled to compensation for performing duties under this section or to indemnification from the political subdivision or the state for injury or property damage the person sustains or liability the person incurs in performing duties under this section.

(e) The political subdivision and the state are not liable for any damage arising from an act or omission of a person appointed under Subsection (a) in performing duties under this section.
(Enacted by Acts 1997, 75th Leg., ch. 165 (S.B. 898), § 30.156(d), effective September 1, 1997; enacted by Acts 1997, 75th Leg., ch. 1353 (H.B. 580), § 6, effective September 1, 1997.)

### Sec. 681.011.   Offenses; Presumption.

(a) A person commits an offense if:

(1) the person stands a vehicle on which are displayed license plates issued under Section 504.201 or 504.202 or a disabled parking placard in a parking space or area designated specifically for persons with disabilities by:

(A) a political subdivision; or

(B) a person who owns or controls private property used for parking as to which a political subdivision has provided for the application of this section under Subsection (f); and

(2) the standing of the vehicle in that parking space or area is not authorized by Section 681.006, 681.007, or 681.008.

(b) A person commits an offense if the person stands a vehicle on which license plates issued under Section 504.201 or 504.202 are not displayed and a disabled parking placard is not displayed in a parking space or area designated specifically for individuals with disabilities by:

(1) a political subdivision; or

(2) a person who owns or controls private property used for parking as to which a political subdivision has provided for the application of this section under Subsection (f).

(c) A person commits an offense if the person stands a vehicle so that the vehicle blocks an architectural improvement designed to aid persons with disabilities, including an access aisle or curb ramp.

(d) A person commits an offense if the person lends a disabled parking placard issued to the person to a person who uses the placard in violation of this section.

(e) In a prosecution under this section, it is presumed that the registered owner of the motor vehicle is the person who left the vehicle standing at the time and place the offense occurred.

(f) A political subdivision may provide that this section applies to a parking space or area for persons with disabilities on private property that is designated in compliance with the identification requirements referred to in Section 681.009(b).

(g) Except as provided by Subsections (h)—(k), an offense under this section is a misdemeanor punishable by a fine of not less than $500 or more than $750.

(h) If it is shown on the trial of an offense under this section that the person has been previously convicted one time of an offense under this section, the offense is punishable by:

(1) **[2 Versions: As added by Acts 2009, 81st Leg., ch. 1160]** a fine of not less than $550 or more than $800; and

(1) **[2 Versions: As added by Acts 2009, 81st Leg., ch. 1336]** a fine of not less than $500 or more than $800; and

(2) 10 hours of community service.

(i) If it is shown on the trial of an offense under this section that the person has been previously convicted two times of an offense under this section, the offense is punishable by:

(1) a fine of not less than $550 or more than $800; and

(2) **[2 Versions: As amended by Acts 2009, 81st Leg., ch. 1160]** not less than 20 or more than 30 hours of community service.

(2) **[2 Versions: As amended by Acts 2009, 81st Leg., ch. 1336]** 20 hours of community service.

(j) If it is shown on the trial of an offense under this section that the person has been previously convicted three times of an offense under this section, the offense is punishable by:

(1) a fine of not less than $800 or more than $1,100; and

(2) **[2 Versions: As amended by Acts 2009, 81st Leg., ch. 1160]** 50 hours of community service.

(2) **[2 Versions: As amended by Acts 2009, 81st Leg., ch. 1336]** 30 hours of community service.

(k) If it is shown on the trial of an offense under this section that the person has been previously convicted four times of an offense under this section, the offense is punishable by a fine of $1,250 and 50 hours of community service.

(*l*) A person commits an offense if the person:

(1) stands a vehicle on which are displayed license plates issued under Section 504.201 or a disabled parking placard in a parking space or area for which this chapter creates an exemption from payment of a fee or penalty imposed by a governmental unit;

(2) does not have a disability;

(3) is not transporting a person with disability; and

(4) does not pay any applicable fee related to standing in the space or area imposed by a governmental unit or exceeds a limitation on the length of time for standing in the space or area.

(Enacted by Acts 1995, 74th Leg., ch. 165 (S.B. 971), § 1, effective September 1, 1995; am. Acts 1997, 75th Leg., ch. 165 (S.B. 898), § 30.156(e), effective September 1, 1997; am. Acts 1999, 76th Leg., ch. 738 (H.B. 1070), § 2, effective September 1, 1999; am. Acts 1999, 76th Leg., ch. 1362 (H.B. 1032), §§ 6, 7, effective September 1, 1999; am. Acts 2003, 78th Leg., ch. 595 (H.B. 1784), § 1, effective September 1, 2003; am. Acts 2003, 78th Leg., ch. 1325 (H.B. 3588), § 19.08(b), effective September 1, 2003; am. Acts 2005, 79th Leg., ch. 728 (H.B. 2018), § 20.003(i), effective September 1, 2005; am. Acts 2007, 80th Leg., ch. 357 (S.B. 251), § 2, effective September 1, 2007; am. Acts 2009, 81st Leg., ch. 1160 (H.B. 3095), § 4, effective September 1, 2009; am. Acts 2009, 81st Leg., ch. 1336 (S.B. 52), § 1, effective September 1, 2009.)

### Sec. 681.0111. Manufacture, Sale, Possession, or Use of Counterfeit or Altered Placard.

(a) A person commits an offense if, without the department's authorization, the person:

(1) manufactures, sells, or possesses a placard that is deceptively similar to a disabled parking placard; or

(2) alters a genuine disabled parking placard.

(b) A person commits an offense if the person knowingly parks a vehicle displaying a counterfeit or altered placard in a parking space or area designated specifically for persons with disabilities.

(c) An offense under Subsection (a) is a Class A misdemeanor. An offense under Subsection (b) is a Class C misdemeanor.

(d) For purposes of this section, a placard is deceptively similar to a disabled parking placard if the placard is not a genuine disabled parking placard but a reasonable person would presume that it is a genuine disabled parking placard. (Enacted by Acts 2003, 78th Leg., ch. 400 (H.B. 148), § 1, effective September 1, 2003; am. Acts 2011, 82nd Leg., ch. 756 (H.B. 1473), §§ 1, 2, effective September 1, 2011.)

### Sec. 681.012. Seizure and Revocation of Placard.

(a) A law enforcement officer who believes that an offense under Section 681.011(a) or (d) has occurred in the officer's presence shall seize any disabled parking placard involved in the offense. Not later than 48 hours after the seizure, the officer shall determine whether probable cause existed to believe that the offense was committed. If the officer does not find that probable cause existed, the officer shall promptly return each placard to the person from whom it was seized. If the officer finds that probable cause existed, the officer, not later than the fifth day after the date of the seizure, shall submit each seized placard to the department.

(a-1) [2 Versions: Effective until January 1, 2012] A peace officer may seize a disabled parking placard from a person who operates a vehicle on which a disabled parking placard is displayed if the peace officer determines by inspecting the person's driver's license or personal identification certificate that the disabled parking placard does not contain the first four digits of the driver's license number or personal identification certificate number and the initials of:

(1) the person operating the vehicle; or

(2) a person being transported by the vehicle.

(a-1) [2 Versions: Effective January 1, 2012] A peace officer may seize a disabled parking placard from a person who operates a vehicle on which a disabled parking placard is displayed if the peace officer determines by inspecting the person's driver's license or personal identification certificate that the disabled parking placard does not contain the first four digits of the driver's license number or personal identification certificate number and the initials of:

(1) the person operating the vehicle;

(2) the applicant on behalf of a person being transported by the vehicle; or

Transportation

(3) a person being transported by the vehicle.

(a-2) A peace officer shall submit each seized parking placard to the department not later than the fifth day after the seizure.

(b) On submission to the department under Subsection (a) or (a-2), a placard is revoked. On request of the person from whom the placard was seized, the department shall conduct a hearing and determine whether the revocation should continue or the placard should be returned to the person and the revocation rescinded.

(Enacted by Acts 1997, 75th Leg., ch. 1353 (H.B. 580), § 7, effective September 1, 1997; am. Acts 2009, 81st Leg., ch. 1336 (S.B. 52), § 2, effective September 1, 2009; am. Acts 2011, 82nd Leg., ch. 1296 (H.B. 2357), § 243, effective January 1, 2012.)

### Sec. 681.013.  Dismissal of Charge; Administrative Fee.

(a) In this section, "working day" means any day other than a Saturday, a Sunday, or a holiday on which county offices are closed.

(b) The court shall:

(1) dismiss a charge for an offense under Section 681.011(b)(1) if:

(A) the vehicle displayed a disabled parking placard that was not valid as expired;

(B) the defendant remedies the defect by renewing the expired disabled parking placard within 20 working days from the date of the offense or before the defendant's first court appearance date, whichever is later; and

(C) the disabled parking placard has not been expired for more than 60 days; and

(2) assess an administrative fee not to exceed $20 when the charge has been remedied.

(c) Notwithstanding Subsection (b)(1)(C), the court may dismiss a charge of unlawfully parking a vehicle in a space designated specifically for persons with disabilities, if at the time of the offense the defendant's vehicle displays a disabled parking placard that has been expired for more than 60 days.

(Enacted by Acts 2009, 81st Leg., ch. 298 (H.B. 400), § 1, effective September 1, 2009.)

## CHAPTER 682
## ADMINISTRATIVE ADJUDICATION OF VEHICLE PARKING AND STOPPING OFFENSES

### Sec. 682.001.  [2 Versions: As amended by Acts 1999, 76th Leg., ch. 156] Applicability.

This chapter applies only to:

(1) a municipality that:

(A) has a population greater than 30,000 and operates under a council-manager form of government; or

(B) has a population of 500,000 or more; and

(2) an airport operated by a joint board to which Section 22.074(d) applies.

(Enacted by Acts 1995, 74th Leg., ch. 165 (S.B. 971), § 1, effective September 1, 1995; am. Acts 1999, 76th Leg., ch. 156 (S.B. 787), § 2, effective May 21, 1999.)

### Sec. 682.001.  [2 Versions: As amended by Acts 1999, 76th Leg., ch. 310] Applicability.

This chapter applies only to a municipality that has a population greater than 30,000.

(Enacted by Acts 1995, 74th Leg., ch. 165 (S.B. 971), § 1, effective September 1, 1995; am. Acts 1999, 76th Leg., ch. 310 (H.B. 516), § 1, effective May 29, 1999.)

### Sec. 682.002.  Civil Offense.

(a) A municipality may declare the violation of a municipal ordinance relating to parking or stopping a vehicle to be a civil offense.

(b) A joint board to which Section 22.074(d) applies may declare the violation of a resolution, rule, or order of the joint board relating to parking or stopping a vehicle to be a civil offense.
(Enacted by Acts 1995, 74th Leg., ch. 165 (S.B. 971), § 1, effective September 1, 1995; am. Acts 1999, 76th Leg., ch. 156 (S.B. 787), § 2, effective May 21, 1999.)

### Sec. 682.003. Adoption of Hearing Procedure.

A municipality may by ordinance or a joint board may by resolution, rule, or order establish an administrative adjudication hearing procedure under which a civil fine may be imposed.
(Enacted by Acts 1995, 74th Leg., ch. 165 (S.B. 971), § 1, effective September 1, 1995; am. Acts 1999, 76th Leg., ch. 156 (S.B. 787), § 2, effective May 21, 1999.)

### Sec. 682.004. Content of Ordinance.

An ordinance, resolution, rule, or order adopted under this chapter must provide that a person charged with violating a parking or stopping ordinance, resolution, rule, or order is entitled to a hearing and provide for:

(1) the period during which a hearing must be held;

(2) the appointment of a hearing officer with authority to administer oaths and issue orders compelling the attendance of witnesses and the production of documents; and

(3) the amount and disposition of civil fines, costs, and fees.
(Enacted by Acts 1995, 74th Leg., ch. 165 (S.B. 971), § 1, effective September 1, 1995; am. Acts 1999, 76th Leg., ch. 156 (S.B. 787), § 2, effective May 21, 1999.)

### Sec. 682.005. Enforcement of Order Concerning Witnesses and Documents.

A municipal court may enforce an order of the hearing officer compelling the attendance of a witness or the production of a document.
(Enacted by Acts 1995, 74th Leg., ch. 165 (S.B. 971), § 1, effective September 1, 1995.)

### Sec. 682.006. Citation or Summons.

(a) A citation or summons issued for a vehicle parking or stopping civil offense under this chapter must:

(1) provide information as to the time and place of an administrative adjudication hearing; and

(2) contain a notification that the person charged with the civil offense has the right to an instanter hearing.

(b) The original or any copy of the summons or citation shall be kept as a record in the ordinary course of business of the municipality and is rebuttable proof of the facts it contains.
(Enacted by Acts 1995, 74th Leg., ch. 165 (S.B. 971), § 1, effective September 1, 1995.)

### Sec. 682.007. Appearance at Hearing.

(a) A person charged with a civil offense who fails to appear at an administrative adjudication hearing authorized under this chapter is considered to admit liability for the offense charged.

(b) The person who issued the citation or summons is not required to attend an instanter hearing.
(Enacted by Acts 1995, 74th Leg., ch. 165 (S.B. 971), § 1, effective September 1, 1995.)

### Sec. 682.008. Presumptions.

In an administrative adjudication hearing under this chapter:

(1) it is presumed that the registered owner of the motor vehicle is the person who parked or stopped the vehicle at the time and place of the offense charged; and

(2) the Texas Department of Motor Vehicles' computer-generated record of the registered vehicle owner is prima facie evidence of the contents of the record.
(Enacted by Acts 1995, 74th Leg., ch. 165 (S.B. 971), § 1, effective September 1, 1995; am. Acts 2009, 81st Leg., ch. 933 (H.B. 3097), § 2Q.01, effective September 1, 2009.)

### Sec. 682.009. Order.

(a) The hearing officer at an administrative adjudication hearing under this chapter shall issue an order stating:

(1) whether the person charged with the violation is liable for the violation; and

(2) the amount of any fine, cost, or fee assessed against the person.

(b) The order issued under Subsection (a) may be filed with the clerk or secretary of the municipality or a person designated by the joint board. The clerk, secretary, or designated person shall keep the order in a separate index and file. The order may be recorded using microfilm, microfiche, or data processing techniques.
(Enacted by Acts 1995, 74th Leg., ch. 165 (S.B. 971), § 1, effective September 1, 1995; am. Acts

**Transportation**

1999, 76th Leg., ch. 156 (S.B. 787), § 3, effective May 21, 1999.)

### Sec. 682.010. Enforcement.

(a) An order filed under Section 682.009, or a fine, cost, or fee imposed under this chapter following a failure by the person charged to appear within the time specified by a municipality's ordinance, resolution, rule, or order, may be enforced by:

(1) impounding the vehicle if the offender has committed three or more vehicle parking or stopping offenses in a calendar year;

(2) placing a device on the vehicle that prohibits movement of the motor vehicle;

(3) imposing an additional fine if the original fine is not paid within a specified time;

(4) denying issuance of or revoking a parking or operating permit, as applicable; or

(5) filing an action to collect the fine, cost, or fee in a court of competent jurisdiction.

(b) An action to collect a fine, cost, or fee under Subsection (a)(5) must be brought:

(1) in the name of the municipality served by the hearing officer; and

(2) in a county in which all or part of that municipality is located.

(Enacted by Acts 1995, 74th Leg., ch. 165 (S.B. 971), § 1, effective September 1, 1995; am. Acts 1999, 76th Leg., ch. 156 (S.B. 787), § 4, effective May 21, 1999; am. Acts 2003, 78th Leg., ch. 346 (S.B. 782), § 2, effective June 18, 2003.)

### Sec. 682.011. Appeal.

(a) A person whom the hearing officer determines to be in violation of a vehicle parking or stopping ordinance may appeal the determination by filing a petition with the clerk of a municipal court and paying the costs required by law for municipal court not later than the 30th day after the date on which the order is filed.

(b) The municipal court clerk shall schedule a hearing and notify each party of the date, time, and place of the hearing.

(c) An appeal does not stay enforcement and collection of the judgment unless the person, before appealing, posts bond with, as applicable:

(1) the agency of the municipality designated by ordinance to accept payment for a violation of a parking or stopping ordinance; or

(2) the agency of the joint board designated by the resolution, rule, or order to accept payment for a violation of a parking or stopping resolution, rule, or order.

(Enacted by Acts 1995, 74th Leg., ch. 165 (S.B. 971), § 1, effective September 1, 1995; am. Acts 1999, 76th Leg., ch. 156 (S.B. 787), § 5, effective May 21, 1999.)

# CHAPTER 683
# ABANDONED MOTOR VEHICLES

### Subchapter A. General Provisions

Transportation

## SUBCHAPTER A
## GENERAL PROVISIONS

### Sec. 683.001. Definitions.

In this chapter:

(1) "Department" means the Texas Department of Motor Vehicles.

(2) "Garagekeeper" means an owner or operator of a storage facility.

(3) "Law enforcement agency" means:

(A) the Department of Public Safety;

(B) the police department of a municipality;

(C) the police department of an institution of higher education; or

(D) a sheriff or a constable.

(4) "Motor vehicle" means a vehicle that is subject to registration under Chapter 501.

(5) "Motor vehicle demolisher" means a person in the business of:

(A) converting motor vehicles into processed scrap or scrap metal; or

(B) wrecking or dismantling motor vehicles.

(6) "Outboard motor" means an outboard motor subject to registration under Chapter 31, Parks and Wildlife Code.

(7) "Storage facility" includes a garage, parking lot, or establishment for the servicing, repairing, or parking of motor vehicles.

(8) "Watercraft" means a vessel subject to registration under Chapter 31, Parks and Wildlife Code.

(9) "Abandoned nuisance vehicle" means a motor vehicle that is at least 10 years old and is of a condition only to be junked, crushed, or dismantled.

(10) "Vehicle storage facility" means a vehicle storage facility, as defined by Section 2303.002, Occupations Code, that is operated by a person who holds a license issued under Chapter 2303 of that code to operate that vehicle storage facility.

(11) "Aircraft" has the meaning assigned by Section 24.001.

(Enacted by Acts 1995, 74th Leg., ch. 165 (S.B. 971), § 1, effective September 1, 1995; am. Acts 2003, 78th Leg., ch. 1034 (H.B. 849), § 14, effective September 1, 2003; am. Acts 2009, 81st Leg., ch. 933 (H.B. 3097), § 2R.01, effective September 1, 2009; am. Acts 2011, 82nd Leg., ch. 720 (H.B. 787), § 3, effective September 1, 2011.)

### Sec. 683.002. Abandoned Motor Vehicle.

(a) For the purposes of this chapter, a motor vehicle is abandoned if the motor vehicle:

(1) is inoperable, is more than five years old, and has been left unattended on public property for more than 48 hours;

(2) has remained illegally on public property for more than 48 hours;

(3) has remained on private property without the consent of the owner or person in charge of the property for more than 48 hours;

(4) has been left unattended on the right-of-way of a designated county, state, or federal highway for more than 48 hours;

(5) has been left unattended for more than 24 hours on the right-of-way of a turnpike project constructed and maintained by the Texas Turnpike Authority division of the Texas Department of Transportation or a controlled access highway; or

(6) is considered an abandoned motor vehicle under Section 644.153(r).

(b) In this section, "controlled access highway" has the meaning assigned by Section 541.302.

(Enacted by Acts 1995, 74th Leg., ch. 165 (S.B. 971), § 1, effective September 1, 1995; am. Acts 1997, 75th Leg., ch. 165 (S.B. 898), § 30.157(a), effective September 1, 1997; am. Acts 2003, 78th Leg., ch. 359 (S.B. 1184), § 7, effective September 1, 2003; am. Acts 2003, 78th Leg., ch. 1325 (H.B. 3588), § 16.06, effective September 1, 2003.)

### Sec. 683.003. Conflict of Laws; Effect on Other Laws.

(a) Sections 683.051—683.055 may not be read as conflicting with Sections 683.074—683.078.

(b) This chapter does not affect a law authorizing the immediate removal of a vehicle left on public property that is an obstruction to traffic.

(Enacted by Acts 1995, 74th Leg., ch. 165 (S.B. 971), § 1, effective September 1, 1995.)

### Secs. 683.004 to 683.010 [Reserved for expansion].

## SUBCHAPTER B
## ABANDONED MOTOR VEHICLES:
## SEIZURE AND AUCTION

### Sec. 683.011. Authority to Take Abandoned Motor Vehicle into Custody.

(a) A law enforcement agency may take into custody an abandoned motor vehicle, aircraft,

Transportation

watercraft, or outboard motor found on public or private property.

(b) A law enforcement agency may use agency personnel, equipment, and facilities or contract for other personnel, equipment, and facilities to remove, preserve, store, send notice regarding, and dispose of an abandoned motor vehicle, aircraft, watercraft, or outboard motor taken into custody by the agency under this subchapter.
(Enacted by Acts 1995, 74th Leg., ch. 165 (S.B. 971), § 1, effective September 1, 1995; am. Acts 2005, 79th Leg., ch. 737 (H.B. 2630), § 1, effective September 1, 2005; am. Acts 2011, 82nd Leg., ch. 720 (H.B. 787), § 4, effective September 1, 2011.)

### Sec. 683.012.  Taking Abandoned Motor Vehicle into Custody: Notice.

(a) A law enforcement agency shall send notice of abandonment to:

(1) the last known registered owner of each motor vehicle, aircraft, watercraft, or outboard motor taken into custody by the agency or for which a report is received under Section 683.031; and

(2) each lienholder recorded:

(A) under Chapter 501 for the motor vehicle;

(B) with the Federal Aviation Administration or the secretary of state for the aircraft; or

(C) under Chapter 31, Parks and Wildlife Code, for the watercraft or outboard motor.

(a-1) A law enforcement agency that takes into custody an aircraft shall contact the Federal Aviation Administration in the manner described by Section 22.901 to attempt to identify the owner of the aircraft before sending the notice required by Subsection (a).

(b) The notice under Subsection (a) must:

(1) be sent by certified mail not later than the 10th day after the date the agency:

(A) takes the abandoned motor vehicle, aircraft, watercraft, or outboard motor into custody; or

(B) receives the report under Section 683.031;

(2) specify the year, make, model, and identification number of the item;

(3) give the location of the facility where the item is being held;

(4) inform the owner and lienholder of the right to claim the item not later than the 20th day after the date of the notice on payment of:

(A) towing, preservation, and storage charges; or

(B) garagekeeper's charges and fees under Section 683.032 and, if the vehicle is a commercial motor vehicle impounded under Section 644.153(q), the delinquent administrative penalty and costs; and

(5) state that failure of the owner or lienholder to claim the item during the period specified by Subdivision (4) is:

(A) a waiver by that person of all right, title, and interest in the item; and

(B) consent to the sale of the item at a public auction.

(c) Notice by publication in one newspaper of general circulation in the area where the motor vehicle, aircraft, watercraft, or outboard motor was abandoned is sufficient notice under this section if:

(1) the identity of the last registered owner cannot be determined;

(2) the registration has no address for the owner; or

(3) the determination with reasonable certainty of the identity and address of all lienholders is impossible.

(d) Notice by publication:

(1) must be published in the same period that is required by Subsection (b) for notice by certified mail and contain all of the information required by that subsection; and

(2) may contain a list of more than one abandoned motor vehicle, aircraft, watercraft, or outboard motor.

(e) A law enforcement agency is not required to send a notice, as otherwise required by Subsection (a), if the agency has received notice from a vehicle storage facility that an application has or will be submitted to the department for the disposal of the vehicle.

(f) In addition to the notice required under Subsection (a), if a law enforcement agency takes an abandoned motor vehicle into custody, the agency shall notify a person that files a theft report or similar report prepared by any law enforcement agency for the vehicle of that fact. The notice must be sent by regular mail on the next business day after the agency takes the vehicle into custody. The law enforcement agency shall also provide the name and address of the person that filed the theft report or similar report to the vehicle storage facility or governmental vehicle storage facility that is storing the vehicle.
(Enacted by Acts 1995, 74th Leg., ch. 165 (S.B. 971), § 1, effective September 1, 1995; am. Acts 2003, 78th Leg., ch. 359 (S.B. 1184), § 8, effective September 1, 2003; am. Acts 2003, 78th Leg., ch.

1034 (H.B. 849), § 15, effective September 1, 2003; am. Acts 2003, 78th Leg., ch. 1325 (H.B. 3588), § 16.07, effective September 1, 2003; am. Acts 2007, 80th Leg., ch. 1046 (H.B. 2094), § 4.01, effective September 1, 2007; am. Acts 2011, 82nd Leg., ch. 720 (H.B. 787), § 5, effective September 1, 2011.)

## Sec. 683.013. Storage Fees.

A law enforcement agency or the agent of a law enforcement agency that takes into custody an abandoned motor vehicle, aircraft, watercraft, or outboard motor is entitled to reasonable storage fees:

    (1) for not more than 10 days, beginning on the day the item is taken into custody and ending on the day the required notice is mailed; and

    (2) beginning on the day after the day the agency mails notice and ending on the day accrued charges are paid and the vehicle, aircraft, watercraft, or outboard motor is removed.

(Enacted by Acts 1995, 74th Leg., ch. 165 (S.B. 971), § 1, effective September 1, 1995; am. Acts 2011, 82nd Leg., ch. 720 (H.B. 787), § 6, effective September 1, 2011.)

## Sec. 683.014. Auction or Use of Abandoned Items; Waiver of Rights.

(a) If an abandoned motor vehicle, aircraft, watercraft, or outboard motor is not claimed under Section 683.012:

    (1) the owner or lienholder:

        (A) waives all rights and interests in the item; and

        (B) consents to the sale of the item by public auction or the transfer of the item, if a watercraft, as provided by Subsection (d); and

    (2) the law enforcement agency may sell the item at a public auction, transfer the item, if a watercraft, as provided by Subsection (d), or use the item as provided by Section 683.016.

(b) Proper notice of the auction shall be given. A garagekeeper who has a garagekeeper's lien shall be notified of the time and place of the auction.

(c) The purchaser of a motor vehicle, aircraft, watercraft, or outboard motor:

    (1) takes title free and clear of all liens and claims of ownership;

    (2) shall receive a sales receipt from the law enforcement agency; and

    (3) is entitled to register the motor vehicle, aircraft, watercraft, or outboard motor with

and receive a certificate of title from the appropriate authority.

(d) On consent of the Parks and Wildlife Department, the law enforcement agency may transfer a watercraft that is not claimed under Section 683.012 to the Parks and Wildlife Department for use as part of an artificial reef under Chapter 89, Parks and Wildlife Code, or for other use by the Parks and Wildlife Department permitted under the Parks and Wildlife Code. On transfer of the watercraft, the Parks and Wildlife Department:

    (1) takes title free and clear of all liens and claims of ownership; and

    (2) is entitled to register the watercraft and receive a certificate of title.

(Enacted by Acts 1995, 74th Leg., ch. 165 (S.B. 971), § 1, effective September 1, 1995; am. Acts 2005, 79th Leg., ch. 190 (H.B. 883), § 2, effective May 27, 2005; am. Acts 2011, 82nd Leg., ch. 720 (H.B. 787), § 7, effective September 1, 2011.)

## Sec. 683.015. Auction Proceeds.

(a) A law enforcement agency is entitled to reimbursement from the proceeds of the sale of an abandoned motor vehicle, aircraft, watercraft, or outboard motor for:

    (1) the cost of the auction;

    (2) towing, preservation, and storage fees resulting from the taking into custody; and

    (3) the cost of notice or publication as required by Section 683.012.

(b) After deducting the reimbursement allowed under Subsection (a), the proceeds of the sale shall be held for 90 days for the owner or lienholder of the vehicle.

(c) After the period provided by Subsection (b), proceeds unclaimed by the owner or lienholder shall be deposited in an account that may be used for the payment of auction, towing, preservation, storage, and notice and publication fees resulting from taking other vehicles, aircraft, watercraft, or outboard motors into custody if the proceeds from the sale of the other items are insufficient to meet those fees.

(d) A municipality or county may transfer funds in excess of $1,000 from the account to the municipality's or county's general revenue account to be used by the law enforcement agency.

(e) If the vehicle is a commercial motor vehicle impounded under Section 644.153(q), the Department of Public Safety is entitled from the proceeds of the sale to an amount equal to the amount of the delinquent administrative penalty and costs.

(f) A law enforcement agency may use funds transferred under Subsection (d) to compensate property owners whose property was damaged as a result of a pursuit involving the law enforcement agency, regardless of whether the agency would be liable under Chapter 101, Civil Practice and Remedies Code.

(g) Before a law enforcement agency may compensate a property owner under Subsection (f) using funds transferred to a county under Subsection (d), the sheriff or constable must submit the proposed payment for compensation for consideration, and the commissioners court shall consider the proposed payment for compensation, at the next regularly scheduled meeting of the commissioners court.

(Enacted by Acts 1995, 74th Leg., ch. 165 (S.B. 971), § 1, effective September 1, 1995; am. Acts 2003, 78th Leg., ch. 359 (S.B. 1184), § 9, effective September 1, 2003; am. Acts 2003, 78th Leg., ch. 1325 (H.B. 3588), § 16.08, effective September 1, 2003; am. Acts 2009, 81st Leg., ch. 304 (H.B. 453), § 1, effective June 19, 2009; am. Acts 2011, 82nd Leg., ch. 720 (H.B. 787), § 8, effective September 1, 2011; am. Acts 2011, 82nd Leg., ch. 1181 (H.B. 3422), § 1, effective June 17, 2011.)

### Sec. 683.016. Law Enforcement Agency Use of Certain Abandoned Motor Vehicles.

(a) The law enforcement agency that takes an abandoned motor vehicle into custody that is not claimed under Section 683.012 may:

(1) use the vehicle for agency purposes; or

(2) transfer the vehicle to any other municipal or county agency, a groundwater conservation district governed by Chapter 36, Water Code, or a school district for the use of that agency or district.

(b) The law enforcement agency shall auction the vehicle as provided by this subchapter if the law enforcement agency or the municipal or county agency, groundwater conservation district, or school district to which the vehicle was transferred under Subsection (a) discontinues use of the vehicle.

(c) This section does not apply to an abandoned vehicle on which there is a garagekeeper's lien.

(d) This section does not apply to a vehicle that is:

(1) taken into custody by a law enforcement agency located in a county with a population of 3.3 million or more; and

(2) removed to a privately owned storage facility.

(e) A law enforcement agency must comply with the notice requirements of Section 683.012 before the law enforcement agency may transfer a vehicle under Subsection (a)(2).

(Enacted by Acts 1995, 74th Leg., ch. 165 (S.B. 971), § 1, effective September 1, 1995; am. Acts 2007, 80th Leg., ch. 446 (H.B. 195), § 2, effective September 1, 2007; am. Acts 2009, 81st Leg., ch. 941 (H.B. 3140), § 2, effective September 1, 2009; am. Acts 2011, 82nd Leg., ch. 1163 (H.B. 2702), § 178, effective September 1, 2011.)

### Secs. 683.017 to 683.030 [Reserved for expansion].

## SUBCHAPTER C
## VEHICLE ABANDONED IN STORAGE FACILITY

### Sec. 683.031. Garagekeeper's Duty: Abandoned Motor Vehicles.

(a) A motor vehicle is abandoned if the vehicle is left in a storage facility operated for commercial purposes after the 10th day after the date on which:

(1) the garagekeeper gives notice by registered or certified mail, return receipt requested, to the last known registered owner of the vehicle and to each lienholder of record of the vehicle under Chapter 501 to remove the vehicle;

(2) a contract for the vehicle to remain on the premises of the facility expires; or

(3) the vehicle was left in the facility, if the vehicle was left by a person other than the registered owner or a person authorized to have possession of the vehicle under a contract of use, service, storage, or repair.

(b) If notice sent under Subsection (a)(1) is returned unclaimed by the post office, substituted notice is sufficient if published in one newspaper of general circulation in the area where the vehicle was left.

(c) The garagekeeper shall report the abandonment of the motor vehicle to a law enforcement agency with jurisdiction where the vehicle is located and shall pay a $10 fee to be used by the law enforcement agency for the cost of the notice required by this subchapter or other cost incurred in disposing of the vehicle.

(d) The garagekeeper shall retain custody of an abandoned motor vehicle until the law enforcement agency takes the vehicle into custody under Section 683.034.

(Enacted by Acts 1995, 74th Leg., ch. 165 (S.B. 971), § 1, effective September 1, 1995; am. Acts 2005, 79th Leg., ch. 737 (H.B. 2630), § 2, effective September 1, 2005; am. Acts 2007, 80th Leg., ch. 216 (H.B. 864), § 1, effective September 1, 2007.)

### Sec. 683.032. Garagekeeper's Fees and Charges.

(a) A garagekeeper who acquires custody of a motor vehicle for a purpose other than repair is entitled to towing, preservation, and notification charges and reasonable storage fees, in addition to storage fees earned under a contract, for each day:

    (1) not to exceed five days, until the notice described by Section 683.031(a) is mailed; and

    (2) after notice is mailed, until the vehicle is removed and all accrued charges are paid.

(b) A garagekeeper who fails to report an abandoned motor vehicle to a law enforcement agency within seven days after the date it is abandoned may not claim reimbursement for storage of the vehicle.

(c) This subchapter does not impair any lien that a garagekeeper has on a vehicle except for the termination or limitation of claim for storage for the failure to report the vehicle to the law enforcement agency.

(Enacted by Acts 1995, 74th Leg., ch. 165 (S.B. 971), § 1, effective September 1, 1995; am. Acts 1997, 75th Leg., ch. 165 (S.B. 898), § 30.158(a), effective September 1, 1997.)

### Sec. 683.033. Unauthorized Storage Fee; Offense.

(a) A person commits an offense if the person charges a storage fee for a period for which the fee is not authorized by Section 683.032.

(b) An offense under this subsection is a misdemeanor punishable by a fine of not less than $200 or more than $1,000.

(Enacted by Acts 1995, 74th Leg., ch. 165 (S.B. 971), § 1, effective September 1, 1995.)

### Sec. 683.034. Disposal of Vehicle Abandoned in Storage Facility.

(a) A law enforcement agency shall take into custody an abandoned vehicle left in a storage facility that has not been claimed in the period provided by the notice under Section 683.012. In this section, a law enforcement agency has custody if the agency:

    (1) has physical custody of the vehicle;

    (2) has given notice to the storage facility that the law enforcement agency intends to dispose of the vehicle under this section; or

    (3) has received a report under Section 683.031(c) and the garagekeeper has met all of the requirements of that subsection.

(b) The law enforcement agency may use the vehicle as authorized by Section 683.016 or sell the vehicle at auction as provided by Section 683.014. If a vehicle is sold, the proceeds of the sale shall first be applied to a garagekeeper's charges for providing notice regarding the vehicle and for service, towing, impoundment, storage, and repair of the vehicle.

(c) As compensation for expenses incurred in taking the vehicle into custody and selling it, the law enforcement agency shall retain:

    (1) two percent of the gross proceeds of the sale of the vehicle; or

    (2) all the proceeds if the gross proceeds of the sale are less than $10.

(d) Surplus proceeds shall be distributed as provided by Section 683.015.

(e) If the law enforcement agency does not take the vehicle into custody before the 31st day after the date the vehicle was reported abandoned under Section 683.031:

    (1) the law enforcement agency may not take the vehicle into custody; and

    (2) the storage facility may dispose of the vehicle under:

        (A) Chapter 70, Property Code, except that notice under Section 683.012 satisfies the notice requirements of that chapter; or

        (B) Chapter 2303, Occupations Code, if the storage facility is a vehicle storage facility.

(Enacted by Acts 1995, 74th Leg., ch. 165 (S.B. 971), § 1, effective September 1, 1995; am. Acts 1997, 75th Leg., ch. 165 (S.B. 898), § 30.158(b), effective September 1, 1997; am. Acts 2003, 78th Leg., ch. 1034 (H.B. 849), § 16, effective September 1, 2003; am. Acts 2005, 79th Leg., ch. 737 (H.B. 2630), § 3, effective September 1, 2005.)

**Secs. 683.035 to 683.050 [Reserved for expansion].**

### SUBCHAPTER D
### DEMOLITION OF ABANDONED MOTOR VEHICLES

### Sec. 683.051. Application for Authorization to Dispose of Certain Motor Vehicles.

A person may apply to the department for authority:

*Transportation*

(1) to sell, give away, or dispose of a motor vehicle to a motor vehicle demolisher if:

(A) the person owns the motor vehicle and the certificate of title to the vehicle is lost, destroyed, or faulty; or

(B) the vehicle is an abandoned motor vehicle and is:

(i) in the possession of the person; or

(ii) located on property owned by the person; or

(2) to dispose of a motor vehicle to a motor vehicle demolisher for demolition, wrecking, or dismantling if:

(A) the abandoned motor vehicle:

(i) is in the possession of the person;

(ii) is more than eight years old;

(iii) either has no motor or is otherwise totally inoperable or does not comply with all applicable air pollution emissions control related requirements included in: (aa) the vehicle inspection requirements under Chapter 548, as evidenced by a current inspection certificate affixed to the vehicle windshield; or (bb) the vehicle emissions inspection and maintenance requirements contained in the Public Safety Commission's motor vehicle emissions inspection and maintenance program under Subchapter F, Chapter 548, or the state's air quality state implementation plan; and

(iv) was authorized to be towed by a law enforcement agency; and

(B) the law enforcement agency approves the application.

(Enacted by Acts 1995, 74th Leg., ch. 165 (S.B. 971), § 1, effective September 1, 1995; am. Acts 1999, 76th Leg., ch. 612 (S.B. 845), § 1, effective September 1, 1999.)

### Sec. 683.052.　Contents of Application; Application Fee.

(a) An application under Section 683.051 must:

(1) contain the name and address of the applicant;

(2) state the year, make, model, and vehicle identification number of the vehicle, if ascertainable, and any other identifying feature of the vehicle; and

(3) include:

(A) a concise statement of facts about the abandonment;

(B) a statement that the certificate of title is lost or destroyed; or

(C) a statement of the reasons for the defect in the owner's certificate of title for the vehicle.

(b) An application under Section 683.051(2) must also include an affidavit containing a statement of the facts that make that subdivision applicable.

(c) The applicant shall make an affidavit stating that:

(1) the facts stated in the application are true; and

(2) no material fact has been withheld.

(d) The application must be accompanied by a fee of $2, unless the application is made by a unit of government. Fees collected under this subsection shall be deposited to the credit of the state highway fund.

(Enacted by Acts 1995, 74th Leg., ch. 165 (S.B. 971), § 1, effective September 1, 1995.)

### Sec. 683.053.　Department to Provide Notice.

Except as provided by Section 683.054(b), the department shall give notice as provided by Section 683.012 if it determines that an application under Section 683.051 is:

(1) executed in proper form; and

(2) shows that:

(A) the abandoned motor vehicle is in the possession of the applicant or has been abandoned on the applicant's property; or

(B) the vehicle is not an abandoned motor vehicle and the applicant appears to be the owner of the vehicle.

(Enacted by Acts 1995, 74th Leg., ch. 165 (S.B. 971), § 1, effective September 1, 1995.)

### Sec. 683.054.　Certificate of Authority to Dispose of Vehicle.

(a) The department shall issue the applicant a certificate of authority to dispose of the vehicle to a motor vehicle demolisher for demolition, wrecking, or dismantling if notice under Section 683.053 was given and the vehicle was not claimed as provided by the notice.

(b) Without giving the notice required by Section 683.053, the department may issue to an applicant under Section 683.051(2) a certificate of authority to dispose of the motor vehicle to a demolisher if the vehicle meets the requirements of Sections 683.051(2)(A)(ii) and (iii).

(c) A motor vehicle demolisher shall accept the certificate of authority in lieu of a certificate of title for the vehicle.

(Enacted by Acts 1995, 74th Leg., ch. 165 (S.B. 971), § 1, effective September 1, 1995; am. Acts 1999, 76th Leg., ch. 612 (S.B. 845), § 2, effective September 1, 1999.)

### Sec. 683.055.  Rules and Forms.

The department may adopt rules and prescribe forms to implement Sections 683.051—683.054. (Enacted by Acts 1995, 74th Leg., ch. 165 (S.B. 971), § 1, effective September 1, 1995.)

### Sec. 683.056.  Demolisher's Duty.

(a) A motor vehicle demolisher who acquires a motor vehicle for dismantling or demolishing shall obtain from the person delivering the vehicle:

(1) the motor vehicle's certificate of title;

(2) a sales receipt for the motor vehicle;

(3) a transfer document for the vehicle as provided by Subchapter B or Subchapter E; or

(4) a certificate of authority for the disposal of the motor vehicle.

(b) A demolisher is not required to obtain a certificate of title for the vehicle in the demolisher's name.

(c) On the department's demand, the demolisher shall surrender for cancellation the certificate of title or certificate of authority.

(d) The department shall adopt rules and forms necessary to regulate the surrender of auction sales receipts and certificates of title. (Enacted by Acts 1995, 74th Leg., ch. 165 (S.B. 971), § 1, effective September 1, 1995.)

### Sec. 683.057.  Demolisher's Records; Offense.

(a) A motor vehicle demolisher shall keep a record of a motor vehicle that is acquired in the course of business.

(b) The record must contain:

(1) the name and address of the person from whom the vehicle was acquired; and

(2) the date of acquisition of the vehicle.

(c) The demolisher shall keep the record until the first anniversary of the date of acquisition of the vehicle.

(d) The record shall be open to inspection by the department or any law enforcement agency at any time during normal business hours.

(e) A motor vehicle demolisher commits an offense if the demolisher fails to keep a record as provided by this section.

(f) An offense under Subsection (e) is a misdemeanor punishable by:

(1) a fine of not less than $100 or more than $1,000;

(2) confinement in the county jail for a term of not less than 10 days or more than six months; or

(3) both the fine and confinement.

(Enacted by Acts 1995, 74th Leg., ch. 165 (S.B. 971), § 1, effective September 1, 1995.)

### Secs. 683.058 to 683.070 [Reserved for expansion].

## SUBCHAPTER E
## JUNKED VEHICLES: PUBLIC NUISANCE; ABATEMENT

### Sec. 683.071.  [2 Versions: As amended by Acts 2011, 82nd Leg., ch. 720] Definition and Applicability.

(a) In this subchapter, "junked vehicle" means a vehicle that:

(1) is self-propelled; and

(2) is:

(A) wrecked, dismantled or partially dismantled, or discarded; or

(B) inoperable and has remained inoperable for more than:

(i) 72 consecutive hours, if the vehicle is on public property; or

(ii) 30 consecutive days, if the vehicle is on private property.

(b) For purposes of this subchapter, "junked vehicle" includes a motor vehicle, aircraft, or watercraft. This subchapter applies only to:

(1) a motor vehicle that does not have lawfully attached to it:

(A) an unexpired license plate; and

(B) a valid motor vehicle inspection certificate;

(2) an aircraft that does not have lawfully printed on the aircraft an unexpired federal aircraft identification number registered under Federal Aviation Administration aircraft registration regulations in 14 C.F.R. Part 47; or

(3) a watercraft that:

(A) does not have lawfully on board an unexpired certificate of number; and

(B) is not a watercraft described by Section 31.055, Parks and Wildlife Code.

(Enacted by Acts 1995, 74th Leg., ch. 165 (S.B. 971), § 1, effective September 1, 1995; am. Acts 1999, 76th Leg., ch. 746 (H.B. 1103), § 1, effective September 1, 1999; am. Acts 2001, 77th Leg., ch. 798 (H.B. 489), § 1, effective September 1, 2001;

am. Acts 2007, 80th Leg., ch. 500 (S.B. 350), § 1, effective September 1, 2007; am. Acts 2011, 82nd Leg., ch. 720 (H.B. 787), § 9, effective September 1, 2011.)

### Sec. 683.071. [2 Versions: As amended by Acts 2011, 82nd Leg., ch. 753] Definition.

In this subchapter, "junked vehicle" means a vehicle that is self-propelled and:

(1) displays an expired license plate or invalid motor vehicle inspection certificate or does not display a license plate or motor vehicle inspection certificate; and

(2) is:

(A) wrecked, dismantled or partially dismantled, or discarded; or

(B) inoperable and has remained inoperable for more than:

(i) 72 consecutive hours, if the vehicle is on public property; or

(ii) 30 consecutive days, if the vehicle is on private property.

(Enacted by Acts 1995, 74th Leg., ch. 165 (S.B. 971), § 1, effective September 1, 1995; am. Acts 1999, 76th Leg., ch. 746 (H.B. 1103), § 1, effective September 1, 1999; am. Acts 2001, 77th Leg., ch. 798 (H.B. 489), § 1, effective September 1, 2001; am. Acts 2007, 80th Leg., ch. 500 (S.B. 350), § 1, effective September 1, 2007; am. Acts 2011, 82nd Leg., ch. 753 (H.B. 1376), § 1, effective September 1, 2011.)

### Sec. 683.0711. Municipal Requirements.

An ordinance adopted by a governing body of a municipality may provide for a more inclusive definition of a junked vehicle subject to regulation under this subchapter.

(Enacted by Acts 2003, 78th Leg., ch. 1073 (H.B. 1773), § 1, effective September 1, 2003.)

### Sec. 683.072. Junked Vehicle Declared to Be Public Nuisance.

A junked vehicle, including a part of a junked vehicle, that is visible at any time of the year from a public place or public right-of-way:

(1) is detrimental to the safety and welfare of the public;

(2) tends to reduce the value of private property;

(3) invites vandalism;

(4) creates a fire hazard;

(5) is an attractive nuisance creating a hazard to the health and safety of minors;

(6) produces urban blight adverse to the maintenance and continuing development of municipalities; and

(7) is a public nuisance.

(Enacted by Acts 1995, 74th Leg., ch. 165 (S.B. 971), § 1, effective September 1, 1995; am. Acts 2003, 78th Leg., ch. 1073 (H.B. 1773), § 2, effective September 1, 2003.)

### Sec. 683.073. Offense.

(a) A person commits an offense if the person maintains a public nuisance described by Section 683.072.

(b) An offense under this section is a misdemeanor punishable by a fine not to exceed $200.

(c) The court shall order abatement and removal of the nuisance on conviction.

(Enacted by Acts 1995, 74th Leg., ch. 165 (S.B. 971), § 1, effective September 1, 1995.)

### Sec. 683.074. Authority to Abate Nuisance; Procedures.

(a) A municipality or county may adopt procedures that conform to this subchapter for the abatement and removal from private or public property or a public right-of-way of a junked vehicle or part of a junked vehicle as a public nuisance.

(b) The procedures must:

(1) prohibit a vehicle from being reconstructed or made operable after removal;

(2) require a public hearing on request of a person who receives notice as provided by Section 683.075 if the request is made not later than the date by which the nuisance must be abated and removed; and

(3) require that notice identifying the vehicle or part of the vehicle be given to the department not later than the fifth day after the date of removal.

(c) An appropriate court of the municipality or county may issue necessary orders to enforce the procedures.

(d) Procedures for abatement and removal of a public nuisance must be administered by regularly salaried, full-time employees of the municipality or county, except that any authorized person may remove the nuisance.

(e) A person authorized to administer the procedures may enter private property to examine a public nuisance, to obtain information to identify the nuisance, and to remove or direct the removal of the nuisance.

(f) On receipt of notice of removal of a motor vehicle under Subsection (b)(3), the department shall immediately cancel the certificate of title issued for the vehicle.

(g) The procedures may provide that the relocation of a junked vehicle that is a public nuisance to another location in the same municipality or county after a proceeding for the abatement and removal of the public nuisance has commenced has no effect on the proceeding if the junked vehicle constitutes a public nuisance at the new location.

(h) On receipt of notice of removal of a watercraft under Subsection (b)(3), the department shall notify the Parks and Wildlife Department of the removal. On receipt of the notice from the department, the Parks and Wildlife Department shall immediately cancel the certificate of title issued for the watercraft.
(Enacted by Acts 1995, 74th Leg., ch. 165 (S.B. 971), § 1, effective September 1, 1995; am. Acts 1999, 76th Leg., ch. 1226 (S.B. 688), § 1, effective June 18, 1999; am. Acts 2007, 80th Leg., ch. 500 (S.B. 350), § 2, effective September 1, 2007; am. Acts 2011, 82nd Leg., ch. 720 (H.B. 787), § 10, effective September 1, 2011.)

### Sec. 683.075. Notice.

(a) The procedures for the abatement and removal of a public nuisance under this subchapter must provide not less than 10 days' notice of the nature of the nuisance. The notice must be personally delivered, sent by certified mail with a five-day return requested, or delivered by the United States Postal Service with signature confirmation service to:

(1) the last known registered owner of the nuisance;

(2) each lienholder of record of the nuisance; and

(3) the owner or occupant of:

(A) the property on which the nuisance is located; or

(B) if the nuisance is located on a public right-of-way, the property adjacent to the right-of-way.

(b) The notice must state that:

(1) the nuisance must be abated and removed not later than the 10th day after the date on which the notice was personally delivered or mailed; and

(2) any request for a hearing must be made before that 10-day period expires.

(c) If the post office address of the last known registered owner of the nuisance is unknown, notice may be placed on the nuisance or, if the owner is located, personally delivered.

(d) If notice is returned undelivered, action to abate the nuisance shall be continued to a date not earlier than the 11th day after the date of the return.
(Enacted by Acts 1995, 74th Leg., ch. 165 (S.B. 971), § 1, effective September 1, 1995; am. Acts 2001, 77th Leg., ch. 413 (H.B. 1833), § 13, effective September 1, 2001; am. Acts 2007, 80th Leg., ch. 369 (S.B. 351), § 1, effective June 15, 2007.)

### Sec. 683.076. Hearing.

(a) The governing body of the municipality or county or a board, commission, or official designated by the governing body shall conduct hearings under the procedures adopted under this subchapter.

(b) If a hearing is requested by a person for whom notice is required under Section 683.075(a)(3), the hearing shall be held not earlier than the 11th day after the date of the service of notice.

(c) At the hearing, the junked motor vehicle is presumed, unless demonstrated otherwise by the owner, to be inoperable.

(d) If the information is available at the location of the nuisance, a resolution or order requiring removal of the nuisance must include:

(1) for a motor vehicle, the vehicle's:

(A) description;

(B) vehicle identification number; and

(C) license plate number;

(2) for an aircraft, the aircraft's:

(A) description; and

(B) federal aircraft identification number as described by Federal Aviation Administration aircraft registration regulations in 14 C.F.R. Part 47; and

(3) for a watercraft, the watercraft's:

(A) description; and

(B) identification number as set forth in the watercraft's certificate of number.
(Enacted by Acts 1995, 74th Leg., ch. 165 (S.B. 971), § 1, effective September 1, 1995; am. Acts 2011, 82nd Leg., ch. 720 (H.B. 787), § 11, effective September 1, 2011.)

### Sec. 683.0765. Alternative Procedure for Administrative Hearing.

A municipality by ordinance may provide for an administrative adjudication process under which an administrative penalty may be imposed for the enforcement of an ordinance adopted under this subchapter. If a municipality provides for an administrative adjudication process under this

Transportation

section, the municipality shall use the procedure described by Section 54.044, Local Government Code.

(Enacted by Acts 2001, 77th Leg., ch. 413 (H.B. 1833), § 14, effective September 1, 2001.)

## Sec. 683.077. Inapplicability of Subchapter.

(a) Procedures adopted under Section 683.074 or 683.0765 may not apply to a vehicle or vehicle part:

(1) that is completely enclosed in a building in a lawful manner and is not visible from the street or other public or private property; or

(2) that is stored or parked in a lawful manner on private property in connection with the business of a licensed vehicle dealer or junkyard, or that is an antique or special interest vehicle stored by a motor vehicle collector on the collector's property, if the vehicle or part and the outdoor storage area, if any, are:

(A) maintained in an orderly manner;

(B) not a health hazard; and

(C) screened from ordinary public view by appropriate means, including a fence, rapidly growing trees, or shrubbery.

(b) In this section:

(1) "Antique vehicle" means a passenger car or truck that is at least 25 years old.

(2) "Motor vehicle collector" means a person who:

(A) owns one or more antique or special interest vehicles; and

(B) acquires, collects, or disposes of an antique or special interest vehicle or part of an antique or special interest vehicle for personal use to restore and preserve an antique or special interest vehicle for historic interest.

(3) "Special interest vehicle" means a motor vehicle of any age that has not been changed from original manufacturer's specifications and, because of its historic interest, is being preserved by a hobbyist.

(Enacted by Acts 1995, 74th Leg., ch. 165 (S.B. 971), § 1, effective September 1, 1995; am. Acts 2001, 77th Leg., ch. 413 (H.B. 1833), § 15, effective September 1, 2001; am. Acts 2001, 77th Leg., ch. 1431 (H.B. 495), § 1, effective September 1, 2001.)

## Sec. 683.078. Junked Vehicle Disposal.

(a) A junked vehicle, including a part of a junked vehicle, may be removed to a scrapyard, a motor vehicle demolisher, or a suitable site operated by a municipality or county.

(b) A municipality or county may operate a disposal site if its governing body determines that commercial disposition of junked vehicles is not available or is inadequate. A municipality or county may:

(1) finally dispose of a junked vehicle or vehicle part; or

(2) transfer it to another disposal site if the disposal is scrap or salvage only.

(Enacted by Acts 1995, 74th Leg., ch. 165 (S.B. 971), § 1, effective September 1, 1995.)

# CHAPTER 684
# REMOVAL OF UNAUTHORIZED VEHICLES FROM PARKING FACILITY OR PUBLIC ROADWAY [REPEALED]

## SUBCHAPTER A
## GENERAL PROVISIONS

## Sec. 684.001. Definitions [Repealed].

Repealed by Acts 2007, 80th Leg., ch. 1046 (H.B. 2094), § 5.01(a)(4), effective September 1, 2007.

(Enacted by Acts 1995, 74th Leg., ch. 165 (S.B. 971), § 1, effective September 1, 1995; am. Acts 2001, 77th Leg., ch. 1420 (H.B. 2812), § 19.008, effective September 1, 2001; am. Acts 2003, 78th Leg., ch. 1276 (H.B. 3507), § 14A.839, effective September 1, 2003.)

## SUBCHAPTER B
## UNAUTHORIZED VEHICLES

## Sec. 684.011. Prohibition Against Unattended Vehicles in Certain Areas [Renumbered].

Renumbered to Tex. Occ. Code § 2308.251 by Acts 2007, 80th Leg., ch. 1046 (H.B. 2094), § 2.03, effective September 1, 2007.

## Sec. 684.012. Removal and Storage of Unauthorized Vehicle [Renumbered].

Renumbered to Tex. Occ. Code § 2308.252 by Acts 2007, 80th Leg., ch. 1046 (H.B. 2094), § 2.03, effective September 1, 2007.

## Sec. 684.0125. Unattended Vehicles on Parking Facility of Apartment Complex; Removal and Storage of Ve-

hicles [Renumbered].

Renumbered to Tex. Occ. Code § 2308.253 by Acts 2007, 80th Leg., ch. 1046 (H.B. 2094), § 2.03, effective September 1, 2007.

**Sec. 684.013. Limitation on Parking Facility Owner's Authority to Remove Unauthorized Vehicle [Renumbered].**

Renumbered to Tex. Occ. Code § 2308.254 by Acts 2007, 80th Leg., ch. 1046 (H.B. 2094), § 2.03, effective September 1, 2007.

**Sec. 684.014. Towing Company's Authority to Remove and Store Unauthorized Vehicle [Renumbered].**

Renumbered to Tex. Occ. Code § 2308.255 by Acts 2007, 80th Leg., ch. 1046 (H.B. 2094), § 2.03, effective September 1, 2007.

**Sec. 684.015. Vehicle Storage Facility's Duty to Report After Accepting Unauthorized Vehicle [Renumbered].**

Renumbered to Tex. Occ. Code § 2308.256 by Acts 2007, 80th Leg., ch. 1046 (H.B. 2094), § 2.03, effective September 1, 2007.

## SUBCHAPTER C
## SIGNS PROHIBITING UNAUTHORIZED VEHICLES AND DESIGNATING RESTRICTED AREAS

**Sec. 684.031. General Requirements for Sign Prohibiting Unauthorized Vehicles [Renumbered].**

Renumbered to Tex. Occ. Code § 2308.301 by Acts 2007, 80th Leg., ch. 1046 (H.B. 2094), § 2.04, effective September 1, 2007.

**Sec. 684.032. Color, Layout, and Lettering Height Requirements [Renumbered].**

Renumbered to Tex. Occ. Code § 2308.302 by Acts 2007, 80th Leg., ch. 1046 (H.B. 2094), § 2.04, effective September 1, 2007.

**Sec. 684.033. Telephone Number for Locating Towed Vehicle Required [Renumbered].**

Renumbered to Tex. Occ. Code § 2308.303 by Acts 2007, 80th Leg., ch. 1046 (H.B. 2094), § 2.04, effective September 1, 2007.

**Sec. 684.034. Designation of Restricted Parking Spaces on Otherwise**

Unrestricted Parking Facility [Renumbered].

Renumbered to Tex. Occ. Code § 2308.304 by Acts 2007, 80th Leg., ch. 1046 (H.B. 2094), § 2.04, effective September 1, 2007.

**Sec. 684.035. Individual Parking Restrictions in Restricted Area [Renumbered].**

Renumbered to Tex. Occ. Code § 2308.305 by Acts 2007, 80th Leg., ch. 1046 (H.B. 2094), § 2.04, effective September 1, 2007.

## SUBCHAPTER D
## REGULATION OF PARKING ON CERTAIN PUBLIC ROADWAY AREAS

**Sec. 684.051. Removal of Unauthorized Vehicle from Leased Right-of-Way [Renumbered].**

Renumbered to Tex. Occ. Code § 2308.351 by Acts 2007, 80th Leg., ch. 1046 (H.B. 2094), § 2.05, effective September 1, 2007.

**Sec. 684.052. Removal of Unauthorized Vehicle from Area Between Parking Facility and Public Roadway [Renumbered].**

Renumbered to Tex. Occ. Code § 2308.352 by Acts 2007, 80th Leg., ch. 1046 (H.B. 2094), § 2.05, effective September 1, 2007.

**Sec. 684.053. Removal Under Governmental Entity's Authority of Unauthorized Vehicle Parked in Right-of-Way [Renumbered].**

Renumbered to Tex. Occ. Code § 2308.353 by Acts 2007, 80th Leg., ch. 1046 (H.B. 2094), § 2.05, effective September 1, 2007.

**Sec. 684.054. Authority for Removal of Vehicle from Public Roadway [Renumbered].**

Renumbered to Tex. Occ. Code § 2308.354 by Acts 2007, 80th Leg., ch. 1046 (H.B. 2094), § 2.05, effective September 1, 2007.

## SUBCHAPTER E
## REGULATION OF TOWING COMPANIES AND PARKING FACILITY OWNERS

**Sec. 684.081. Parking Facility Owner Prohibited from Receiving Financial**

Transportation

**Gain from Towing Company [Renumbered].**

Renumbered to Tex. Occ. Code § 2308.401 by Acts 2007, 80th Leg., ch. 1046 (H.B. 2094), § 2.06, effective September 1, 2007.

**Sec. 684.082. Towing Company Prohibited from Financial Involvement with Parking Facility Owner [Renumbered].**

Renumbered to Tex. Occ. Code § 2308.402 by Acts 2007, 80th Leg., ch. 1046 (H.B. 2094), § 2.06, effective September 1, 2007.

**Sec. 684.083. Limitation on Liability of Parking Facility Owner for Removal or Storage of Unauthorized Vehicle [Renumbered].**

Renumbered to Tex. Occ. Code § 2308.403 by Acts 2007, 80th Leg., ch. 1046 (H.B. 2094), § 2.06, effective September 1, 2007.

**Sec. 684.084. Civil Liability of Towing Company or Parking Facility Owner for Violation of Chapter [Renumbered].**

Renumbered to Tex. Occ. Code § 2308.404 by Acts 2007, 80th Leg., ch. 1046 (H.B. 2094), § 2.06, effective September 1, 2007.

**Sec. 684.085. Violation of Chapter; Fine [Renumbered].**

Renumbered to Tex. Occ. Code § 2308.405 by Acts 2007, 80th Leg., ch. 1046 (H.B. 2094), § 2.06, effective September 1, 2007.

**Sec. 684.086. Violation of Chapter; Injunction [Renumbered].**

Renumbered to Tex. Occ. Code § 2308.406 by Acts 2007, 80th Leg., ch. 1046 (H.B. 2094), § 2.06, effective September 1, 2007.

**Sec. 684.087. Minor Sign or Lettering Height Variations [Renumbered].**

Renumbered to Tex. Occ. Code § 2308.407 by Acts 2007, 80th Leg., ch. 1046 (H.B. 2094), § 2.06, effective September 1, 2007.

## SUBCHAPTER F
## MISCELLANEOUS PROVISIONS

**Sec. 684.101. Municipal Ordinance Regulating Unauthorized Vehicles [Re-**

**numbered].**

Renumbered to Tex. Occ. Code § 2308.208 by Acts 2007, 80th Leg., ch. 1046 (H.B. 2094), § 2.02, effective September 1, 2007.

# CHAPTER 685
# RIGHTS OF OWNERS AND OPERATORS OF STORED VEHICLES [REPEALED]

**Sec. 685.001. Definitions [Repealed].**

Repealed by Acts 2007, 80th Leg., ch. 1046 (H.B. 2094), § 5.01(a)(5), effective September 1, 2007.

(Enacted by Acts 1995, 74th Leg., ch. 165 (S.B. 971), § 1, effective September 1, 1995; am. Acts 1997, 75th Leg., ch. 165 (S.B. 898), § 30.159(a), effective September 1, 1997; am. Acts 2003, 78th Leg., ch. 1276 (H.B. 3507), § 14A.840, effective September 1, 2003.)

**Sec. 685.002. Payment of Cost of Removal and Storage of Vehicle [Renumbered].**

Renumbered to Tex. Occ. Code § 2308.451 by Acts 2007, 80th Leg., ch. 1046 (H.B. 2094), § 2.07, effective September 1, 2007.

**Sec. 685.003. Right of Owner or Operator of Vehicle to Hearing [Renumbered].**

Renumbered to Tex. Occ. Code § 2308.452 by Acts 2007, 80th Leg., ch. 1046 (H.B. 2094), § 2.07, effective September 1, 2007.

**Sec. 685.004. Jurisdiction [Renumbered].**

Renumbered to Tex. Occ. Code § 2308.453 by Acts 2007, 80th Leg., ch. 1046 (H.B. 2094), § 2.07, effective September 1, 2007.

**Sec. 685.005. Notice to Vehicle Owner or Operator [Renumbered].**

Renumbered to Tex. Occ. Code § 2308.454 by Acts 2007, 80th Leg., ch. 1046 (H.B. 2094), § 2.07, effective September 1, 2007.

**Sec. 685.006. Contents of Notice [Renumbered].**

Renumbered to Tex. Occ. Code § 2308.455 by Acts 2007, 80th Leg., ch. 1046 (H.B. 2094), § 2.07, effective September 1, 2007.

## Sec. 685.007. Request for Hearing [Renumbered].

Renumbered to Tex. Occ. Code § 2308.456 by Acts 2007, 80th Leg., ch. 1046 (H.B. 2094), § 2.07, effective September 1, 2007.

## Sec. 685.008. Filing Fee Authorized [Renumbered].

Renumbered to Tex. Occ. Code § 2308.457 by Acts 2007, 80th Leg., ch. 1046 (H.B. 2094), § 2.07, effective September 1, 2007.

## Sec. 685.009. Hearing [Renumbered].

Renumbered to Tex. Occ. Code § 2308.458 by Acts 2007, 80th Leg., ch. 1046 (H.B. 2094), § 2.07, effective September 1, 2007.

## Sec. 685.010. Appeal [Renumbered].

Renumbered to Tex. Occ. Code § 2308.459 by Acts 2007, 80th Leg., ch. 1046 (H.B. 2094), § 2.07, effective September 1, 2007.

## CHAPTER 686
## VALET PARKING SERVICES

Section
686.001. Definitions.
686.002. Requirement of Financial Responsibility for Valet Parking Services.
686.003. Evidence of Financial Responsibility.
686.004. Minimum Coverage Amounts.
686.005. Common Law Defenses.
686.006. Operation of Motor Vehicle in Violation of Financial Responsibility Requirement; Offense.
686.007. Defense: Financial Responsibility in Effect at Time of Alleged Offense.

## Sec. 686.001. Definitions.

In this chapter:

(1) "Financial responsibility" means the ability to respond in damages for liability for an accident that:

(A) occurs after the effective date of the document evidencing the establishment of the financial responsibility; and

(B) arises out of the operation of a motor vehicle by an employee of a valet parking service.

(2) "Public accommodation" means any:

(A) inn, hotel, or motel;

(B) restaurant, cafeteria, or other facility principally engaged in selling food for consumption on the premises;

(C) bar, nightclub, or other facility engaged in selling alcoholic beverages for consumption on the premises;

(D) motion picture house, theater, concert hall, stadium, or other place of exhibition or entertainment; or

(E) other facility used by or open to members of the public.

(3) "Valet parking service" means a parking service through which the motor vehicles of patrons of a public accommodation are parked for a fee by a third party who is not an employee of the public accommodation.

(Enacted by Acts 2003, 78th Leg., ch. 816 (S.B. 279), § 23.002, effective March 1, 2004.)

## Sec. 686.002. Requirement of Financial Responsibility for Valet Parking Services.

A person may not operate a valet parking service unless financial responsibility for each employee who operates a motor vehicle for the service is established through:

(1) a motor vehicle liability or comprehensive general liability and garage insurance policy in an amount established by Section 686.004;

(2) a surety bond filed under Section 601.121; or

(3) a deposit in the amount of $450,000 under Section 601.122, notwithstanding any other amount prescribed by that section.

(Enacted by Acts 2003, 78th Leg., ch. 816 (S.B. 279), § 23.002, effective March 1, 2004.)

## Sec. 686.003. Evidence of Financial Responsibility.

(a) The owner or operator of a valet parking service shall provide evidence of financial responsibility in the same manner as required under Section 601.053.

(b) In addition to complying with Subsection (a), an owner or operator of a valet parking service shall exhibit, for public inspection, evidence of financial responsibility at a public accommodation whose patrons use the service.

(Enacted by Acts 2003, 78th Leg., ch. 816 (S.B. 279), § 23.002, effective March 1, 2004.)

## Sec. 686.004. Minimum Coverage Amounts.

(a) The minimum amounts of motor vehicle liability insurance coverage required to establish financial responsibility under this chapter are:

(1) $100,000 for bodily injury to or death of one person in one accident;

(2) $300,000 for bodily injury to or death of two or more persons in one accident, subject to

the amount provided by Subdivision (1) for bodily injury to or death of one of the persons; and

    (3) $50,000 for damage to or destruction of property of others in one accident.

(b) The comprehensive general liability insurance must be on a broad form and provide limits of liability for bodily injury and property damage of not less than $300,000 combined single limit or the equivalent.

(c) The garage insurance must provide limits of liability for bodily injury and property damage of not less than $300,000 combined single limit, or the equivalent, and must provide the following coverages:

    (1) comprehensive and collision coverage for physical damage;

    (2) coverage for vehicle storage; and

    (3) coverage for a vehicle driven by or at the direction of the valet parking service.

(Enacted by Acts 2003, 78th Leg., ch. 816 (S.B. 279), § 23.002, effective March 1, 2004.)

### Sec. 686.005.   Common Law Defenses.

In an action against an owner or operator of a valet parking service that has not established financial responsibility as required by this chapter to recover damages for personal injuries, death, or property damage sustained in a motor vehicle accident arising out of the operation of a valet parking service, it is not a defense that the party who brings the action:

    (1) was guilty of contributory negligence; or

    (2) assumed the risk of injury, death, or property damage.

(Enacted by Acts 2003, 78th Leg., ch. 816 (S.B. 279), § 23.002, effective March 1, 2004.)

### Sec. 686.006.   Operation of Motor Vehicle in Violation of Financial Responsibility Requirement; Offense.

(a) A person commits an offense if the person, while in the course and scope of the person's employment with a valet parking service, operates a motor vehicle of a patron of the service without the financial responsibility required by this chapter.

(b) Except as provided by Subsections (c) and (d), an offense under this section is a misdemeanor punishable by a fine of not less than $175 or more than $350.

(c) If a person has been previously convicted of an offense under this section, an offense under this section is a misdemeanor punishable by a fine of not less than $350 or more than $1,000.

(d) If the court determines that a person who has not been previously convicted of an offense under this section is economically unable to pay the fine, the court may reduce the fine to not less than $175.

(Enacted by Acts 2003, 78th Leg., ch. 816 (S.B. 279), § 23.002, effective March 1, 2004.)

### Sec. 686.007.   Defense: Financial Responsibility in Effect at Time of Alleged Offense.

It is a defense to prosecution under Section 686.002 that the person charged produces one of the documents listed in Section 601.053 that was valid at the time the offense is alleged to have occurred.

(Enacted by Acts 2003, 78th Leg., ch. 816 (S.B. 279), § 23.002, effective March 1, 2004.)

## CHAPTERS 687 TO 700
## [RESERVED FOR EXPANSION]

## SUBTITLE I
## ENFORCEMENT OF TRAFFIC LAWS

## CHAPTER 701
## COUNTY TRAFFIC OFFICERS

**Section**
701.001.   Authorization.
701.002.   Power to Act; Guidance.
701.003.   Duties.
701.004.   Compensation.
701.005.   Fees.
701.006.   Dismissal.

### Sec. 701.001.   Authorization.

(a) Except as provided by Subsection (c), acting in conjunction with the sheriff of the county, the commissioners court of a county may employ not more than five regular deputies as county traffic officers.

(b) Except as provided by Subsection (c), the commissioners court may employ not more than two additional deputies as county traffic officers to aid the regular officers in special emergencies.

(c) The limitation on the number of deputies that may be employed under Subsections (a) and (b) does not apply to a county with a population of more than two million.

(Enacted by Acts 1995, 74th Leg., ch. 165 (S.B. 971), § 1, effective September 1, 1995; am. Acts 2005, 79th Leg., ch. 548 (H.B. 1165), § 1, effective June 17, 2005.)

## Sec. 701.002.   Power to Act; Guidance.

(a) A county traffic officer:

(1) must be deputized by the sheriff or a constable of the county in which the officer is employed;

(2) must give a bond and take an oath of office as other deputy sheriffs;

(3) must work under the direction of the sheriff; and

(4) has the same right and duty as a deputy sheriff to arrest a person who violates a law.

(b) [Repealed by Acts 2009, 81st Leg., ch. 471 (S.B. 376), § 2, effective June 19, 2009.]

(Enacted by Acts 1995, 74th Leg., ch. 165 (S.B. 971), § 1, effective September 1, 1995; am. Acts 2009, 81st Leg., ch. 471 (S.B. 376), § 2, effective June 19, 2009.)

## Sec. 701.003.   Duties.

(a) A county traffic officer shall:

(1) be a motorcycle rider when practicable;

(2) cooperate with the police department of each municipality in the county to enforce state traffic laws in that municipality and in the county;

(3) enforce state laws that regulate the operation of a motor vehicle on a highway, street, or alley; and

(4) remain on and patrol the highway at all times when performing the officer's duties.

(b) An officer may leave a highway only in pursuit of an offender the officer is unable to apprehend on the highway.

(Enacted by Acts 1995, 74th Leg., ch. 165 (S.B. 971), § 1, effective September 1, 1995.)

## Sec. 701.004.   Compensation.

(a) The compensation to be paid a county traffic officer shall be set before the officer is employed.

(b) Salary paid to the officer is independent of a salary paid to the sheriff and sheriff's deputies who do not act as highway officers. Compensation for an officer may not be included in the sheriff's settlement in accounting for a fee of office or as salary paid to the sheriff or a sheriff's deputy.

(c) The commissioners court may provide necessary equipment for the officer at the county's expense. An officer's equipment may include a motorcycle and maintenance of that motorcycle.

(Enacted by Acts 1995, 74th Leg., ch. 165 (S.B. 971), § 1, effective September 1, 1995.)

## Sec. 701.005.   Fees.

A fee may not be charged for a service of a county traffic officer.

(Enacted by Acts 1995, 74th Leg., ch. 165 (S.B. 971), § 1, effective September 1, 1995.)

## Sec. 701.006.   Dismissal.

The commissioners court on its own initiative, or on recommendation of the sheriff, may dismiss a county traffic officer if the officer is no longer needed or if the officer's service is unsatisfactory.

(Enacted by Acts 1995, 74th Leg., ch. 165 (S.B. 971), § 1, effective September 1, 1995; am. Acts 2009, 81st Leg., ch. 471 (S.B. 376), § 1, effective June 19, 2009.)

# CHAPTER 702
# CONTRACTS FOR ENFORCEMENT OF CERTAIN ARREST WARRANTS

**Section**

702.001.   Definitions.
702.003.   Refusal to Register Vehicle.
702.004.   Warning; Citation.

## Sec. 702.001.   Definitions.

In this chapter:

(1) "Department" means the Texas Department of Motor Vehicles.

(2) "Registration" of a motor vehicle includes a renewal of the registration of that vehicle.

(3) "Traffic law" means a statute or ordinance, a violation of which is a misdemeanor punishable by a fine not to exceed $200, that regulates, on a street, road, or highway of this state:

(A) the conduct or condition of a person while operating a motor vehicle; or

(B) the condition of a motor vehicle being operated.

(Enacted by Acts 1995, 74th Leg., ch. 165 (S.B. 971), § 1, effective September 1, 1995; am. Acts 1997, 75th Leg., ch. 165 (S.B. 898), § 30.160(a), effective September 1, 1997; am. Acts 2009, 81st Leg., ch. 933 (H.B. 3097), § 2S.01, effective September 1, 2009.)

## Sec. 702.002.   Application [Repealed].

Repealed by Acts 2011, 82nd Leg., ch. 871 (S.B. 86), § 1, effective June 17, 2011.

(Enacted by Acts 1995, 74th Leg., ch. 165 (S.B. 971), § 1, effective September 1, 1995; am. Acts 1999, 76th Leg., ch. 744 (H.B. 1100), § 1, effective June 18, 1999.)

## Sec. 702.003.   Refusal to Register Vehicle.

(a) A county assessor-collector or the department may refuse to register a motor vehicle if the

Transportation

assessor-collector or the department receives under a contract information from a municipality that the owner of the vehicle has an outstanding warrant from that municipality for failure to appear or failure to pay a fine on a complaint that involves the violation of a traffic law.

(b) A municipality may contract with a county in which the municipality is located or the department to provide information to the county assessor-collector or department necessary to make a determination under Subsection (a).

(c) A municipality that has a contract under Subsection (b) shall notify the county assessor-collector or the department regarding a person for whom the county assessor-collector or the department has refused to register a motor vehicle on:

(1) entry of a judgment against the person and the person's payment to the court of the fine for the violation and of all court costs;

(2) perfection of an appeal of the case for which the arrest warrant was issued; or

(3) dismissal of the charge for which the arrest warrant was issued.

(d) After notice is received under Subsection (c), the county assessor-collector or the department may not refuse to register the motor vehicle under Subsection (a).

(e) A contract under Subsection (b) must be entered into in accordance with Chapter 791, Government Code, and is subject to the ability of the parties to provide or pay for the services required under the contract.

(e-1) A municipality that has a contract under Subsection (b) may impose an additional $20 fee to a person who has an outstanding warrant from the municipality for failure to appear or failure to pay a fine on a complaint that involves the violation of a traffic law. The additional fee may be used only to reimburse the department or the county assessor-collector for its expenses for providing services under the contract, or another county department for expenses related to services under the contract.

(f) This section does not apply to the registration of a motor vehicle under Section 501.0234.
(Enacted by Acts 1995, 74th Leg., ch. 165 (S.B. 971), § 1, effective September 1, 1995; am. Acts 1997, 75th Leg., ch. 165 (S.B. 898), § 30.160(b), effective September 1, 1997; am. Acts 2009, 81st Leg., ch. 542 (S.B. 1617), § 3, effective September 1, 2009; am. Acts 2011, 82nd Leg., ch. 1094 (S.B. 1386), § 2, effective September 1, 2011.)

## Sec. 702.004. Warning; Citation.

(a) A peace officer authorized to issue citations in a municipality that has a contract under Section 702.003 shall issue a written warning to each person to whom the officer issues a citation for a violation of a traffic law in the municipality.

(b) The warning must state that if the person fails to appear in court as provided by law for the prosecution of the offense or fails to pay a fine for the violation, the person might not be permitted to register a motor vehicle in this state.

(c) The warning required by this section may be printed on the citation.
(Enacted by Acts 1995, 74th Leg., ch. 165 (S.B. 971), § 1, effective September 1, 1995; am. Acts 1997, 75th Leg., ch. 165 (S.B. 898), § 30.160(d), effective September 1, 1997 (renumbered from Sec. 702.005).)

## Sec. 702.005. Warning; Citation [Renumbered].

Renumbered to Tex. Transp. Code § 702.004 by Acts 1997, 75th Leg., ch. 165 (S.B. 898), § 30.160(d), effective September 1, 1997.

# CHAPTER 703
# NONRESIDENT VIOLATOR
# COMPACT OF 1977

**Section**
703.001.   Definitions.
703.002.   Enactment; Terms of Compact.
703.003.   Nonresident Violator Compact Administrator.
703.004.   Reports of Failure to Comply with Citation.

## Sec. 703.001. Definitions.

In this chapter:

(1) "Citation" and "motorist" have the meanings assigned by Article II, Section (b), Nonresident Violator Compact of 1977.

(2) "Department" and "licensing authority" mean the Department of Public Safety.
(Enacted by Acts 1995, 74th Leg., ch. 165 (S.B. 971), § 1, effective September 1, 1995.)

## Sec. 703.002. Enactment; Terms of Compact.

The Nonresident Violator Compact of 1977 is enacted and entered into as follows:

*NONRESIDENT VIOLATOR COMPACT OF 1977*

## Art. I. FINDINGS, DECLARATION OF POLICY, AND PURPOSE

(a) The party jurisdictions find that:

(1) In most instances, a motorist who is cited for a traffic violation in a jurisdiction other than his home jurisdiction:

(i) Must post collateral or bond to secure appearance for trial at a later date; or

(ii) If unable to post collateral or bond, is taken into custody until the collateral or bond is posted; or

(iii) Is taken directly to court for his trial to be held.

(2) In some instances, the motorist's driver's license may be deposited as collateral to be returned after he has complied with the terms of the citation.

(3) The purpose of the practices described in paragraphs (1) and (2) above is to ensure compliance with the terms of a traffic citation by the motorist who, if permitted to continue on his way after receiving the traffic citation, could return to his home jurisdiction and disregard his duty under the terms of the traffic citation.

(4) A motorist receiving a traffic citation in his home jurisdiction is permitted, except for certain violations, to accept the citation from the officer at the scene of the violation and to immediately continue on his way after promising or being instructed to comply with the terms of the citation.

(5) The practice described in paragraph (1) above causes unnecessary inconvenience and, at times, a hardship for the motorist who is unable at the time to post collateral, furnish a bond, stand trial, or pay the fine, and thus is compelled to remain in custody until some arrangement can be made.

(6) The deposit of a driver's license as a bail bond, as described in paragraph (2) above, is viewed with disfavor.

(7) The practices described herein consume an undue amount of law enforcement time.

(b) It is the policy of the party jurisdictions to:

(1) Seek compliance with the laws, ordinances, and administrative rules and regulations relating to the operation of motor vehicles in each of the jurisdictions.

(2) Allow motorists to accept a traffic citation for certain violations and proceed on their way without delay whether or not the motorist is a resident of the jurisdiction in which the citation was issued.

(3) Extend cooperation to its fullest extent among the jurisdictions for obtaining compliance with the terms of a traffic citation issued in one jurisdiction to a resident of another jurisdiction.

(4) Maximize effective utilization of law enforcement personnel and assist court systems in the efficient disposition of traffic violations.

(c) The purpose of this compact is to:

(1) Provide a means through which the party jurisdictions may participate in a reciprocal program to effectuate the policies enumerated in paragraph (b) above in a uniform and orderly manner.

(2) Provide for the fair and impartial treatment of traffic violators operating within party jurisdictions in recognition of the motorist's right of due process and the sovereign status of a party jurisdiction.

## Art. II. DEFINITIONS

(a) In the Nonresident Violator Compact, the following words have the meaning indicated, unless the context requires otherwise.

(b) (1) "Citation" means any summons, ticket, or other official document issued by a police officer for a traffic violation containing an order which requires the motorist to respond.

(2) "Collateral" means any cash or other security deposited to secure an appearance for trial, following the issuance by a police officer of a citation for a traffic violation.

(3) "Court" means a court of law or traffic tribunal.

(4) "Driver's license" means any license or privilege to operate a motor vehicle issued under the laws of the home jurisdiction.

(5) "Home jurisdiction" means the jurisdiction that issued the driver's license of the traffic violator.

(6) "Issuing jurisdiction" means the jurisdiction in which the traffic citation was issued to the motorist.

(7) "Jurisdiction" means a state, territory, or possession of the United States, the District of Columbia, or the Commonwealth of Puerto Rico.

(8) "Motorist" means a driver of a motor vehicle operating in a party jurisdiction other than the home jurisdiction.

(9) "Personal recognizance" means an agreement by a motorist made at the time of issuance of the traffic citation that he will comply with the terms of that traffic citation.

Transportation

(10) "Police officer" means any individual authorized by the party jurisdiction to issue a citation for a traffic violation.

(11) "Terms of the citation" means those options expressly stated upon the citation.

## Art. III. PROCEDURE FOR ISSUING JURISDICTION

(a) When issuing a citation for a traffic violation, a police officer shall issue the citation to a motorist who possesses a driver's license issued by a party jurisdiction and shall not, subject to the exceptions noted in paragraph (b) of this article, require the motorist to post collateral to secure appearance, if the officer receives the motorist's personal recognizance that he or she will comply with the terms of the citation.

(b) Personal recognizance is acceptable only if not prohibited by law. If mandatory appearance is required, it must take place immediately following issuance of the citation.

(c) Upon failure of a motorist to comply with the terms of a traffic citation, the appropriate official shall report the failure to comply to the licensing authority of the jurisdiction in which the traffic citation was issued. The report shall be made in accordance with procedures specified by the issuing jurisdiction and shall contain information as specified in the Compact Manual as minimum requirements for effective processing by the home jurisdiction.

(d) Upon receipt of the report, the licensing authority of the issuing jurisdiction shall transmit to the licensing authority in the home jurisdiction of the motorist the information in a form and content as contained in the Compact Manual.

(e) The licensing authority of the issuing jurisdiction may not suspend the privilege of a motorist for whom a report has been transmitted.

(f) The licensing authority of the issuing jurisdiction shall not transmit a report on any violation if the date of transmission is more than six months after the date on which the traffic citation was issued.

(g) The licensing authority of the issuing jurisdiction shall not transmit a report on any violation where the date of issuance of the citation predates the most recent of the effective dates of entry for the two jurisdictions affected.

## Art. IV. PROCEDURE FOR HOME JURISDICTION

(a) Upon receipt of a report of a failure to comply from the licensing authority of the issuing jurisdiction, the licensing authority of the home jurisdiction shall notify the motorist and initiate a suspension action, in accordance with the home jurisdiction's procedures, to suspend the motorist's driver's license until satisfactory evidence of compliance with the terms of the traffic citation has been furnished to the home jurisdiction licensing authority. Due process safeguards will be accorded.

(b) The licensing authority of the home jurisdiction shall maintain a record of actions taken and make reports to issuing jurisdictions as provided in the Compact Manual.

## Art. V. APPLICABILITY OF OTHER LAWS

Except as expressly required by provisions of this compact, nothing contained herein shall be construed to affect the right of any party jurisdiction to apply any of its other laws relating to licenses to drive to any person or circumstance, or to invalidate or prevent any driver license agreement or other cooperative arrangement between a party jurisdiction and a nonparty jurisdiction.

## Art. VI. COMPACT ADMINISTRATOR PROCEDURES

(a) For the purpose of administering the provisions of this compact and to serve as a governing body for the resolution of all matters relating to the operation of this compact, a Board of Compact Administrators is established. The board shall be composed of one representative from each party jurisdiction to be known as the compact administrator. The compact administrator shall be appointed by the jurisdiction executive and will serve and be subject to removal in accordance with the laws of the jurisdiction he represents. A compact administrator may provide for the discharge of his duties and the performance of his functions as a board member by an alternate. An alternate may not be entitled to serve unless written notification of his identity has been given to the board.

(b) Each member of the Board of Compact Administrators shall be entitled to one vote. No action of the board shall be binding unless taken at a meeting at which a majority of the total number of votes on the board are cast in favor. Action by the board shall be only at a meeting at which a majority of the party jurisdictions are represented.

(c) The board shall elect annually, from its membership, a chairman and a vice chairman.

(d) The board shall adopt bylaws, not inconsistent with the provisions of this compact or the laws of a party jurisdiction, for the conduct of its business and shall have the power to amend and rescind its bylaws.

(e) The board may accept for any of its purposes and functions under this compact any and all donations, and grants of money, equipment, supplies, materials, and services, conditional or otherwise, from any jurisdiction, the United States, or any other governmental agency, and may receive, utilize, and dispose of the same.

(f) The board may contract with, or accept services or personnel from, any governmental or intergovernmental agency, person, firm, or corporation, or any private nonprofit organization or institution.

(g) The board shall formulate all necessary procedures and develop uniform forms and documents for administering the provisions of this compact. All procedures and forms adopted pursuant to board action shall be contained in the Compact Manual.

## Art. VII. ENTRY INTO COMPACT AND WITHDRAWAL

(a) This compact shall become effective when it has been adopted by at least two jurisdictions.

(b) (1) Entry into the compact shall be made by a Resolution of Ratification executed by the authorized officials of the applying jurisdiction and submitted to the chairman of the board.

(2) The resolution shall be in a form and content as provided in the Compact Manual and shall include statements that in substance are as follows:

(i) A citation of the authority by which the jurisdiction is empowered to become a party to this compact.

(ii) Agreement to comply with the terms and provisions of the compact.

(iii) That compact entry is with all jurisdictions then party to the compact and with any jurisdiction that legally becomes a party to the compact.

(3) The effective date of entry shall be specified by the applying jurisdiction, but it shall not be less than 60 days after notice has been given by the chairman of the Board of Compact Administrators or by the secretariat of the board to each party jurisdiction that the resolution from the applying jurisdiction has been received.

(c) A party jurisdiction may withdraw from this compact by official written notice to the other party jurisdictions, but a withdrawal shall not take effect until 90 days after notice of withdrawal is given. The notice shall be directed to the compact administrator of each member jurisdiction. No withdrawal shall affect the validity of this compact as to the remaining party jurisdictions.

## Art. VIII. EXCEPTIONS

The provisions of this compact shall not apply to offenses which mandate personal appearance, moving traffic violations which alone carry a suspension, equipment violations, inspection violations, parking or standing violations, size and weight limit violations, violations of law governing the transportation of hazardous materials, motor carrier violations, lease law violations, and registration law violations.

## Art. IX. AMENDMENTS TO THE COMPACT

(a) This compact may be amended from time to time. Amendments shall be presented in resolution form to the chairman of the Board of Compact Administrators and may be initiated by one or more party jurisdictions.

(b) Adoption of an amendment shall require endorsement of all party jurisdictions and shall become effective 30 days after the date of the last endorsement.

(c) Failure of a party jurisdiction to respond to the compact chairman within 120 days after receipt of the proposed amendment shall constitute endorsement.

## Art. X. CONSTRUCTION AND SEVERABILITY

This compact shall be liberally construed so as to effectuate the purposes stated herein. The provisions of this compact shall be severable and if any phrase, clause, sentence, or provision of this compact is declared to be contrary to the constitution of any party jurisdiction or of the United States or the applicability thereof to any government, agency, person, or circumstance, the compact shall not be affected thereby. If this compact shall be held contrary to the constitution of any jurisdiction party thereto, the compact shall remain in full force and effect as to the remaining jurisdictions and in full force and effect as to the jurisdiction affected as to all severable matters.

## Art. XI. TITLE

This compact shall be known as the Nonresident Violator Compact of 1977.
(Enacted by Acts 1995, 74th Leg., ch. 165 (S.B. 971), § 1, effective September 1, 1995.)

### Sec. 703.003.　Nonresident Violator Compact Administrator.

(a) The office of nonresident violator compact administrator is created.

(b) The governor shall appoint the compact administrator with the advice and consent of the senate to a two-year term that expires on February 1 of each odd-numbered year.

(c) The compact administrator is entitled to compensation and reimbursement for expenses as provided by legislative appropriation.
(Enacted by Acts 1995, 74th Leg., ch. 165 (S.B. 971), § 1, effective September 1, 1995.)

### Sec. 703.004.　Reports of Failure to Comply with Citation.

(a) The department shall report the failure of a motorist to comply with the terms of a citation.

(b) The department shall establish procedures for making the reports required by Subsection (a).
(Enacted by Acts 1995, 74th Leg., ch. 165 (S.B. 971), § 1, effective September 1, 1995.)

## CHAPTER 704
## FORFEITURE OF CERTAIN MOTOR VEHICLES

### Sec. 704.001.　Grounds for Forfeiture; Notice [Repealed].

Repealed by Acts 2005, 79th Leg., ch. 617 (H.B. 2275), § 2, effective September 1, 2005.
(Enacted by Acts 1995, 74th Leg., ch. 165 (S.B. 971), § 1, effective September 1, 1995.)

### Sec. 704.002.　Temporary Restraining Order Prohibiting Disposition of Vehicle Pending Trial of Offense [Repealed].

Repealed by Acts 2005, 79th Leg., ch. 617 (H.B. 2275), § 2, effective September 1, 2005.
(Enacted by Acts 1995, 74th Leg., ch. 165 (S.B. 971), § 1, effective September 1, 1995.)

### Sec. 704.003.　Forfeiture of Vehicle Following Conviction [Repealed].

Repealed by Acts 2005, 79th Leg., ch. 617 (H.B. 2275), § 2, effective September 1, 2005.
(Enacted by Acts 1995, 74th Leg., ch. 165 (S.B. 971), § 1, effective September 1, 1995.)

### Sec. 704.004.　Sale of Forfeited Vehicle; Certificate of Title [Repealed].

Repealed by Acts 2005, 79th Leg., ch. 617 (H.B. 2275), § 2, effective September 1, 2005.
(Enacted by Acts 1995, 74th Leg., ch. 165 (S.B. 971), § 1, effective September 1, 1995.)

## CHAPTER 705
## ALLOWING DANGEROUS DRIVER TO BORROW MOTOR VEHICLE

### Sec. 705.001.　Allowing Dangerous Driver to Borrow Motor Vehicle; Offense.

(a) A person commits an offense if the person:

(1) knowingly permits another to operate a motor vehicle owned by the person; and

(2) knows that at the time permission is given the other person's license has been suspended as a result of a:

(A) conviction of an offense under:

(i) Section 49.04, Penal Code;

(ii) Section 49.07, Penal Code, if the offense involved operation of a motor vehicle; or

(iii) Article 6701*l*-1, Revised Statutes, as that law existed before September 1, 1994; or

(B) failure to give a specimen under:

(i) Chapter 724; or

(ii) Chapter 434, Acts of the 61st Legislature, Regular Session, 1969 (Article 6701*l*-5, Vernon's Texas Civil Statutes), as that law existed before September 1, 1995.

(b) An offense under this section is a Class C misdemeanor.
(Enacted by Acts 1995, 74th Leg., ch. 165 (S.B. 971), § 1, effective September 1, 1995.)

# CHAPTER 706
# DENIAL OF RENEWAL OF LICENSE FOR FAILURE TO APPEAR

## Sec. 706.001. Definitions.

In this chapter:

(1) "Complaint" means a notice of an offense as described by Article 27.14(d) or 45.019, Code of Criminal Procedure.

(2) "Department" means the Department of Public Safety.

(3) "Driver's license" has the meaning assigned by Section 521.001.

(4) "Highway or street" has the meaning assigned by Section 541.302.

(5) "Motor vehicle" has the meaning assigned by Section 541.201.

(6) "Operator" has the meaning assigned by Section 541.001.

(7) "Political subdivision" means a municipality or county.

(8) "Public place" has the meaning assigned by Section 1.07, Penal Code.

(9) "Traffic law" means a statute or ordinance, a violation of which is a misdemeanor punishable by a fine in an amount not to exceed $1,000, that:

(A) regulates an operator's conduct or condition while operating a motor vehicle on a highway or street or in a public place;

(B) regulates the condition of a motor vehicle while it is being operated on a highway or street;

(C) relates to the driver's license status of an operator while operating a motor vehicle on a highway or street; or

(D) relates to the registration status of a motor vehicle while it is being operated on a highway or street.

(Enacted by Acts 1997, 75th Leg., ch. 165 (S.B. 898), § 30.161(a), effective September 1, 1997;

am. Acts 1999, 76th Leg., ch. 62 (S.B. 1368), § 17.37(a), effective September 1, 1999; am. Acts 1999, 76th Leg., ch. 1545 (S.B. 1230), § 74, effective September 1, 1999.)

## Sec. 706.002. Contract with Department.

(a) A political subdivision may contract with the department to provide information necessary for the department to deny renewal of the driver's license of a person who fails to appear for a complaint or citation or fails to pay or satisfy a judgment ordering payment of a fine and cost in the manner ordered by the court in a matter involving any offense that a court has jurisdiction of under Chapter 4, Code of Criminal Procedure.

(b) A contract under this section:

(1) must be made in accordance with Chapter 791, Government Code; and

(2) is subject to the ability of the parties to provide or pay for the services required under the contract.

(Enacted by Acts 1997, 75th Leg., ch. 165 (S.B. 898), § 30.161(a), effective September 1, 1997; am. Acts 1999, 76th Leg., ch. 62 (S.B. 1368), § 17.37(b), effective September 1, 1999; am. Acts 1999, 76th Leg., ch. 999 (H.B. 2802), § 1, effective September 1, 1999; am. Acts 2001, 77th Leg., ch. 1498 (S.B. 1371), § 1, effective September 1, 2001; am. Acts 2003, 78th Leg., ch. 346 (S.B. 782), § 3, effective June 18, 2003.)

## Sec. 706.003. Warning; Citation.

(a) If a political subdivision has contracted with the department, a peace officer authorized to issue a citation in the jurisdiction of the political subdivision shall issue a written warning to each person to whom the officer issues a citation for a violation of a traffic law in the jurisdiction of the political subdivision.

(b) The warning under Subsection (a):

(1) is in addition to any other warning required by law;

(2) must state in substance that if the person fails to appear in court as provided by law for the prosecution of the offense or if the person fails to pay or satisfy a judgment ordering the payment of a fine and cost in the manner ordered by the court, the person may be denied renewal of the person's driver's license; and

(3) may be printed on the same instrument as the citation.

(Enacted by Acts 1997, 75th Leg., ch. 165 (S.B. 898), § 30.161(a), effective September 1, 1997;

am. Acts 2001, 77th Leg., ch. 1498 (S.B. 1371), § 2, effective September 1, 2001.)

## Sec. 706.004. Denial of Renewal of Driver's License.

(a) If a political subdivision has contracted with the department, on receiving the necessary information from the political subdivision the department may deny renewal of the person's driver's license for failure to appear based on a complaint or citation or failure to pay or satisfy a judgment ordering the payment of a fine and cost in the manner ordered by the court in a matter involving an offense described by Section 706.002(a).

(b) The information must include:

   (1) the name, date of birth, and driver's license number of the person;

   (2) the nature and date of the alleged violation;

   (3) a statement that the person failed to appear as required by law or failed to satisfy a judgment ordering the payment of a fine and cost in the manner ordered by the court in a matter involving an offense described by Section 706.002(a); and

   (4) any other information required by the department.

(Enacted by Acts 1997, 75th Leg., ch. 165 (S.B. 898), § 30.161(a), effective September 1, 1997; am. Acts 1999, 76th Leg., ch. 62 (S.B. 1368), § 17.37(c), effective September 1, 1999; am. Acts 1999, 76th Leg., ch. 999 (H.B. 2802), § 2, effective September 1, 1999; am. Acts 2001, 77th Leg., ch. 1498 (S.B. 1371), § 3, effective September 1, 2001.)

## Sec. 706.005. Clearance Notice to Department.

(a) A political subdivision shall immediately notify the department that there is no cause to continue to deny renewal of a person's driver's license based on the person's previous failure to appear or failure to pay or satisfy a judgment ordering the payment of a fine and cost in the manner ordered by the court in a matter involving an offense described by Section 706.002(a), on payment of a fee as provided by Section 706.006 and:

   (1) the perfection of an appeal of the case for which the warrant of arrest was issued or judgment arose;

   (2) the dismissal of the charge for which the warrant of arrest was issued or judgment arose;

   (3) the posting of bond or the giving of other security to reinstate the charge for which the warrant was issued;

   (4) the payment or discharge of the fine and cost owed on an outstanding judgment of the court; or

   (5) other suitable arrangement to pay the fine and cost within the court's discretion.

(b) The department may not continue to deny the renewal of the person's driver's license under this chapter after the department receives notice:

   (1) under Subsection (a);

   (2) that the person was acquitted of the charge on which the person failed to appear; or

   (3) from the political subdivision that the failure to appear report or court order to pay a fine or cost relating to the person:

      (A) was sent to the department in error; or

      (B) has been destroyed in accordance with the political subdivision's records retention policy.

(Enacted by Acts 1997, 75th Leg., ch. 165 (S.B. 898), § 30.161(a), effective September 1, 1997; am. Acts 1999, 76th Leg., ch. 62 (S.B. 1368), § 17.37(c), effective September 1, 1999; am. Acts 1999, 76th Leg., ch. 999 (H.B. 2802), § 2, effective September 1, 1999; am. Acts 2001, 77th Leg., ch. 1498 (S.B. 1371), § 4, effective September 1, 2001; am. Acts 2011, 82nd Leg., ch. 1171 (H.B. 2949), § 4, effective September 1, 2011.)

## Sec. 706.006. Payment of Administrative Fee.

(a) A person who fails to appear for a complaint or citation for an offense described by Section 706.002(a) shall be required to pay an administrative fee of $30 for each complaint or citation reported to the department under this chapter, unless the person is acquitted of the charges for which the person failed to appear. The person shall pay the fee when:

   (1) the court enters judgment on the underlying offense reported to the department;

   (2) the underlying offense is dismissed; or

   (3) bond or other security is posted to reinstate the charge for which the warrant was issued.

(b) A person who fails to pay or satisfy a judgment ordering the payment of a fine and cost in the manner the court orders shall be required to pay an administrative fee of $30.

(c) The department may deny renewal of the driver's license of a person who does not pay a fee due under this section until the fee is paid. The fee required by this section is in addition to any other fee required by law.

(Enacted by Acts 1997, 75th Leg., ch. 165 (S.B. 898), § 30.161(a), effective September 1, 1997; am. Acts 1999, 76th Leg., ch. 62 (S.B. 1368), § 17.37(d), effective September 1, 1999; am. Acts 1999, 76th Leg., ch. 999 (H.B. 2802), § 3, effective September 1, 1999; am. Acts 2001, 77th Leg., ch. 1498 (S.B. 1371), § 5, effective September 1, 2001; am. Acts 2003, 78th Leg., ch. 209 (H.B. 2424), § 79(a), effective January 1, 2004.)

### Sec. 706.007. Records Relating to Fees; Disposition of Fees.

(a) An officer collecting a fee under Section 706.006 shall keep records and deposit the money as provided by Subchapter B, Chapter 133, Local Government Code.

(b) The custodian of the municipal or county treasury may deposit each fee collected under Section 706.006 as provided by Subchapter B, Chapter 133, Local Government Code.

(c) The custodian shall keep records of money received and disbursed under this section as provided by Subchapter B, Chapter 133, Local Government Code, and shall provide an annual report, in the form approved by the comptroller, of all money received and disbursed under this section to:

(1) the comptroller;

(2) the department; and

(3) another entity as provided by interlocal contract.

(d) Of each fee collected under Section 706.006, the custodian of a municipal or county treasury shall:

(1) send $20 to the comptroller on or before the last day of each calendar quarter; and

(2) deposit the remainder to the credit of the general fund of the municipality or county.

(e) Of each $20 received by the comptroller, the comptroller shall deposit $10 to the credit of the department to implement this chapter.

(Enacted by Acts 1997, 75th Leg., ch. 165 (S.B. 898), § 30.161(a), effective September 1, 1997; am. Acts 2003, 78th Leg., ch. 209 (H.B. 2424), § 80(a), effective January 1, 2004.)

### Sec. 706.008. Contract with Private Vendor; Compensation.

(a) The department may contract with a private vendor to implement this chapter.

(b) The vendor performing the contract may be compensated by each political subdivision that has contracted with the department.

(c) Except for an action based on a citation issued by a peace officer employed by the department, the vendor may not be compensated with state money.

(Enacted by Acts 1997, 75th Leg., ch. 165 (S.B. 898), § 30.161(a), effective September 1, 1997.)

### Sec. 706.009. Vendor to Provide Customer Support Services.

(a) A vendor must establish and maintain customer support services as directed by the department, including a toll-free telephone service line to answer and resolve questions from persons who are denied renewal of a driver's license under this chapter.

(b) The vendor shall comply with terms, policies, and rules adopted by the department to administer this chapter.

(Enacted by Acts 1997, 75th Leg., ch. 165 (S.B. 898), § 30.161(a), effective September 1, 1997.)

### Sec. 706.010. Use of Information Collected by Vendor.

Information collected under this chapter by a vendor may not be used by a person other than the department, the political subdivision, or a vendor as provided by this chapter.

(Enacted by Acts 1997, 75th Leg., ch. 165 (S.B. 898), § 30.161(a), effective September 1, 1997.)

### Sec. 706.011. Liability of State or Political Subdivision.

(a) An action for damages may not be brought against the state or a political subdivision based on an act or omission under this chapter, including the denial of renewal of a driver's license.

(b) The state or a political subdivision may not be held liable in damages based on an act or omission under this chapter, including the denial of renewal of a driver's license.

(Enacted by Acts 1997, 75th Leg., ch. 165 (S.B. 898), § 30.161(a), effective September 1, 1997.)

### Sec. 706.012. Rules.

The department may adopt rules to implement this chapter.

(Enacted by Acts 1997, 75th Leg., ch. 165 (S.B. 898), § 30.161(a), effective September 1, 1997.)

Transportation

# CHAPTER 707
# PHOTOGRAPHIC TRAFFIC SIGNAL ENFORCEMENT SYSTEM

## Sec. 707.001.   Definitions.

In this chapter:

(1) "Local authority" has the meaning assigned by Section 541.002.

(2) "Owner of a motor vehicle" means the owner of a motor vehicle as shown on the motor vehicle registration records of the Texas Department of Motor Vehicles or the analogous department or agency of another state or country.

(3) "Photographic traffic signal enforcement system" means a system that:

(A) consists of a camera system and vehicle sensor installed to exclusively work in conjunction with an electrically operated traffic-control signal; and

(B) is capable of producing at least two recorded images that depict the license plate attached to the front or the rear of a motor vehicle that is not operated in compliance with the instructions of the traffic-control signal.

(4) "Recorded image" means a photographic or digital image that depicts the front or the rear of a motor vehicle.

(5) "Traffic-control signal" has the meaning assigned by Section 541.304.

(Enacted by Acts 2007, 80th Leg., ch. 1149 (S.B. 1119), § 1, effective September 1, 2007; am. Acts 2009, 81st Leg., ch. 933 (H.B. 3097), § 2T.01, effective September 1, 2009.)

## Sec. 707.002.   Authority to Provide for Civil Penalty.

The governing body of a local authority by ordinance may implement a photographic traffic signal enforcement system and provide that the owner of a motor vehicle is liable to the local authority for a civil penalty if, while facing only a steady red signal displayed by an electrically operated traffic-control signal located in the local authority, the vehicle is operated in violation of the instructions of that traffic-control signal, as specified by Section 544.007(d).

(Enacted by Acts 2007, 80th Leg., ch. 1149 (S.B. 1119), § 1, effective September 1, 2007.)

## Sec. 707.0021.   Imposition of Civil Penalty on Owner of Authorized Emergency Vehicle.

(a) In this section, "authorized emergency vehicle" has the meaning assigned by Section 541.201.

(b) A local authority may not impose or attempt to impose a civil penalty under this chapter on the owner of an authorized emergency vehicle.

(c) This section does not prohibit an employer from taking disciplinary action against an employee who as the operator of an authorized emergency vehicle operated the vehicle in violation of a rule or policy of the employer.

(Enacted by Acts 2009, 81st Leg., ch. 502 (S.B. 926), § 1, effective September 1, 2009.)

## Sec. 707.003.   Installation and Operation of Photographic Traffic Signal Enforcement System.

(a) A local authority that implements a photographic traffic signal enforcement system under this chapter may:

(1) contract for the administration and enforcement of the system; and

(2) install and operate the system or contract for the installation or operation of the system.

(b) A local authority that contracts for the administration and enforcement of a photographic traffic signal enforcement system may not agree to pay the contractor a specified percentage of, or dollar amount from, each civil penalty collected.

(c) Before installing a photographic traffic signal enforcement system at an intersection approach, the local authority shall conduct a traffic engineering study of the approach to determine whether, in addition to or as an alternative to the system, a design change to the approach or a change in the signalization of the intersection is likely to reduce the number of red light violations at the intersection.

(d) An intersection approach must be selected for the installation of a photographic traffic signal enforcement system based on traffic volume, the history of accidents at the approach, the number or frequency of red light violations at the intersection, and similar traffic engineering and safety criteria, without regard to the ethnic or socioeconomic characteristics of the area in which the approach is located.

(e) A local authority shall report results of the traffic engineering study required by Subsection (c) to a citizen advisory committee consisting of one person appointed by each member of the governing body of the local authority. The committee shall advise the local authority on the installation and operation of a photographic traffic signal enforcement system established under this chapter.

(f) A local authority may not impose a civil penalty under this chapter on the owner of a motor vehicle if the local authority violates Subsection (b) or (c).

(g) The local authority shall install signs along each roadway that leads to an intersection at which a photographic traffic signal enforcement system is in active use. The signs must be at least 100 feet from the intersection or located according to standards established in the manual adopted by the Texas Transportation Commission under Section 544.001, be easily readable to any operator approaching the intersection, and clearly indicate the presence of a photographic monitoring system that records violations that may result in the issuance of a notice of violation and the imposition of a monetary penalty.

(h) A local authority or the person with which the local authority contracts for the administration and enforcement of a photographic traffic signal enforcement system may not provide information about a civil penalty imposed under this chapter to a credit bureau, as defined by Section 392.001, Finance Code.
(Enacted by Acts 2007, 80th Leg., ch. 1149 (S.B. 1119), § 1, effective September 1, 2007.)

## Sec. 707.004.  Report of Accidents.

(a) In this section, "department" means the Texas Department of Transportation.

(b) Before installing a photographic traffic signal enforcement system at an intersection approach, the local authority shall compile a written report of the number and type of traffic accidents that have occurred at the intersection for a period of at least 18 months before the date of the report.

(c) Not later than six months after the date of the installation of the photographic traffic signal enforcement system at the intersection, the local authority shall provide the department a copy of the report required by Subsection (b).

(d) After installing a photographic traffic signal enforcement system at an intersection approach, the local authority shall monitor and annually report to the department the number and type of traffic accidents at the intersection to determine whether the system results in a reduction in accidents or a reduction in the severity of accidents.

(e) The report must be in writing in the form prescribed by the department.

(f) Not later than December 1 of each year, the department shall publish the information submitted by a local authority under Subsection (d).
(Enacted by Acts 2007, 80th Leg., ch. 1149 (S.B. 1119), § 1, effective September 1, 2007.)

## Sec. 707.005.  Minimum Change Interval.

At an intersection at which a photographic traffic monitoring system is in use, the minimum change interval for a steady yellow signal must be established in accordance with the Texas Manual on Uniform Traffic Control Devices.
(Enacted by Acts 2007, 80th Leg., ch. 1149 (S.B. 1119), § 1, effective September 1, 2007.)

## Sec. 707.006.  General Surveillance Prohibited; Offense.

(a) A local authority shall operate a photographic traffic control signal enforcement system only for the purpose of detecting a violation or suspected violation of a traffic-control signal.

(b) A person commits an offense if the person uses a photographic traffic signal enforcement system to produce a recorded image other than in the manner and for the purpose specified by this chapter.

(c) An offense under this section is a Class A misdemeanor.

Transportation

Transportation

(Enacted by Acts 2007, 80th Leg., ch. 1149 (S.B. 1119), § 1, effective September 1, 2007.)

### Sec. 707.007. Amount of Civil Penalty; Late Payment Penalty.

If a local authority enacts an ordinance to enforce compliance with the instructions of a traffic-control signal by the imposition of a civil or administrative penalty, the amount of:

(1) the civil or administrative penalty may not exceed $75; and

(2) a late payment penalty may not exceed $25.

(Enacted by Acts 2007, 80th Leg., ch. 1149 (S.B. 1119), § 1, effective September 1, 2007.)

### Sec. 707.008. Deposit of Revenue from Certain Traffic Penalties.

(a) Not later than the 60th day after the end of a local authority's fiscal year, after deducting amounts the local authority is authorized by Subsection (b) to retain, the local authority shall:

(1) send 50 percent of the revenue derived from civil or administrative penalties collected by the local authority under this section to the comptroller for deposit to the credit of the regional trauma account established under Section 782.002, Health and Safety Code; and

(2) deposit the remainder of the revenue in a special account in the local authority's treasury that may be used only to fund traffic safety programs, including pedestrian safety programs, public safety programs, intersection improvements, and traffic enforcement.

(b) A local authority may retain an amount necessary to cover the costs of:

(1) purchasing or leasing equipment that is part of or used in connection with the photographic traffic signal enforcement system in the local authority;

(2) installing the photographic traffic signal enforcement system at sites in the local authority, including the costs of installing cameras, flashes, computer equipment, loop sensors, detectors, utility lines, data lines, poles and mounts, networking equipment, and associated labor costs;

(3) operating the photographic traffic signal enforcement system in the local authority, including the costs of creating, distributing, and delivering violation notices, review of violations conducted by employees of the local authority, the processing of fine payments and collections, and the costs associated with administrative adjudications and appeals; and

(4) maintaining the general upkeep and functioning of the photographic traffic signal enforcement system.

(c) Chapter 133, Local Government Code, applies to fee revenue described by Subsection (a)(1).

(d) If under Section 133.059, Local Government Code, the comptroller conducts an audit of a local authority and determines that the local authority retained more than the amounts authorized by this section or failed to deposit amounts as required by this section, the comptroller may impose a penalty on the local authority equal to twice the amount the local authority:

(1) retained in excess of the amount authorized by this section; or

(2) failed to deposit as required by this section.

(Enacted by Acts 2007, 80th Leg., ch. 1149 (S.B. 1119), § 1, effective September 1, 2007.)

### Sec. 707.009. Required Ordinance Provisions.

An ordinance adopted under Section 707.002 must provide that a person against whom the local authority seeks to impose a civil penalty is entitled to a hearing and shall:

(1) provide for the period in which the hearing must be held;

(2) provide for the appointment of a hearing officer with authority to administer oaths and issue orders compelling the attendance of witnesses and the production of documents; and

(3) designate the department, agency, or office of the local authority responsible for the enforcement and administration of the ordinance or provide that the entity with which the local authority contracts under Section 707.003(a)(1) is responsible for the enforcement and administration of the ordinance.

(Enacted by Acts 2007, 80th Leg., ch. 1149 (S.B. 1119), § 1, effective September 1, 2007.)

### Sec. 707.010. Effect on Other Enforcement.

(a) The implementation of a photographic traffic signal enforcement system by a local authority under this chapter does not:

(1) preclude the application or enforcement in the local authority of Section 544.007(d) in the manner prescribed by Chapter 543; or

(2) prohibit a peace officer from arresting a violator of Section 544.007(d) as provided by Chapter 543, if the peace officer personally

witnesses the violation, or from issuing the violator a citation and notice to appear as provided by that chapter.

(b) A local authority may not impose a civil penalty under this chapter on the owner of a motor vehicle if the operator of the vehicle was arrested or issued a citation and notice to appear by a peace officer for the same violation of Section 544.007(d) recorded by the photographic traffic signal enforcement system.

(Enacted by Acts 2007, 80th Leg., ch. 1149 (S.B. 1119), § 1, effective September 1, 2007.)

## Sec. 707.011. Notice of Violation; Contents.

(a) The imposition of a civil penalty under this chapter is initiated by the mailing of a notice of violation to the owner of the motor vehicle against whom the local authority seeks to impose the civil penalty.

(b) Not later than the 30th day after the date the violation is alleged to have occurred, the designated department, agency, or office of the local authority or the entity with which the local authority contracts under Section 707.003(a)(1) shall mail the notice of violation to the owner at:

(1) the owner's address as shown on the registration records of the Texas Department of Motor Vehicles; or

(2) if the vehicle is registered in another state or country, the owner's address as shown on the motor vehicle registration records of the department or agency of the other state or country analogous to the Texas Department of Motor Vehicles.

(c) The notice of violation must contain:

(1) a description of the violation alleged;

(2) the location of the intersection where the violation occurred;

(3) the date and time of the violation;

(4) the name and address of the owner of the vehicle involved in the violation;

(5) the registration number displayed on the license plate of the vehicle involved in the violation;

(6) a copy of a recorded image of the violation limited solely to a depiction of the area of the registration number displayed on the license plate of the vehicle involved in the violation;

(7) the amount of the civil penalty for which the owner is liable;

(8) the number of days the person has in which to pay or contest the imposition of the

civil penalty and a statement that the person incurs a late payment penalty if the civil penalty is not paid or imposition of the penalty is not contested within that period;

(9) a statement that the owner of the vehicle in the notice of violation may elect to pay the civil penalty by mail sent to a specified address instead of appearing at the time and place of the administrative adjudication hearing; and

(10) information that informs the owner of the vehicle named in the notice of violation:

(A) of the owner's right to contest the imposition of the civil penalty against the person in an administrative adjudication hearing;

(B) that imposition of the civil penalty may be contested by submitting a written request for an administrative adjudication hearing before the expiration of the period specified under Subdivision (8); and

(C) that failure to pay the civil penalty or to contest liability for the penalty in a timely manner is an admission of liability and a waiver of the owner's right to appeal the imposition of the civil penalty.

(d) A notice of violation is presumed to have been received on the fifth day after the date the notice is mailed.

(Enacted by Acts 2007, 80th Leg., ch. 1149 (S.B. 1119), § 1, effective September 1, 2007; am. Acts 2009, 81st Leg., ch. 933 (H.B. 3097), § 2T.02, effective September 1, 2009.)

## Sec. 707.012. Admission of Liability.

A person who fails to pay the civil penalty or to contest liability for the penalty in a timely manner or who requests an administrative adjudication hearing to contest the imposition of the civil penalty against the person and fails to appear at that hearing is considered to:

(1) admit liability for the full amount of the civil penalty stated in the notice of violation mailed to the person; and

(2) waive the person's right to appeal the imposition of the civil penalty.

(Enacted by Acts 2007, 80th Leg., ch. 1149 (S.B. 1119), § 1, effective September 1, 2007.)

## Sec. 707.013. Presumption.

(a) It is presumed that the owner of the motor vehicle committed the violation alleged in the notice of violation mailed to the person if the motor vehicle depicted in a photograph or digital image taken by a photographic traffic signal enforcement system belongs to the owner of the motor vehicle.

(b) If, at the time of the violation alleged in the notice of violation, the motor vehicle depicted in a photograph or digital image taken by a photographic traffic signal enforcement system was owned by a person in the business of selling, renting, or leasing motor vehicles or by a person who was not the person named in the notice of violation, the presumption under Subsection (a) is rebutted on the presentation of evidence establishing that the vehicle was at that time:

(1) being test driven by another person;

(2) being rented or leased by the vehicle's owner to another person; or

(3) owned by a person who was not the person named in the notice of violation.

(c) Notwithstanding Section 707.014, the presentation of evidence under Subsection (b) by a person who is in the business of selling, renting, or leasing motor vehicles or did not own the vehicle at the time of the violation must be made by affidavit, through testimony at the administrative adjudication hearing under Section 707.014, or by a written declaration under penalty of perjury. The affidavit or written declaration may be submitted by mail to the local authority or the entity with which the local authority contracts under Section 707.003(a)(1).

(d) If the presumption established by Subsection (a) is rebutted under Subsection (b), a civil penalty may not be imposed on the owner of the vehicle or the person named in the notice of violation, as applicable.

(e) If, at the time of the violation alleged in the notice of violation, the motor vehicle depicted in the photograph or digital image taken by the photographic traffic signal enforcement system was owned by a person in the business of renting or leasing motor vehicles and the vehicle was being rented or leased to an individual, the owner of the motor vehicle shall provide to the local authority or the entity with which the local authority contracts under Section 707.003(a)(1) the name and address of the individual who was renting or leasing the motor vehicle depicted in the photograph or digital image and a statement of the period during which that individual was renting or leasing the vehicle. The owner shall provide the information required by this subsection not later than the 30th day after the date the notice of violation is received. If the owner provides the required information, it is presumed that the individual renting or leasing the motor vehicle committed the violation alleged in the

notice of violation and the local authority or contractor may send a notice of violation to that individual at the address provided by the owner of the motor vehicle.

(Enacted by Acts 2007, 80th Leg., ch. 1149 (S.B. 1119), § 1, effective September 1, 2007.)

## Sec. 707.014. Administrative Adjudication Hearing.

(a) A person who receives a notice of violation under this chapter may contest the imposition of the civil penalty specified in the notice of violation by filing a written request for an administrative adjudication hearing. The request for a hearing must be filed on or before the date specified in the notice of violation, which may not be earlier than the 30th day after the date the notice of violation was mailed.

(b) On receipt of a timely request for an administrative adjudication hearing, the local authority shall notify the person of the date and time of the hearing.

(c) A hearing officer designated by the governing body of the local authority shall conduct the administrative adjudication hearing.

(d) In an administrative adjudication hearing, the issues must be proven by a preponderance of the evidence.

(e) The reliability of the photographic traffic signal enforcement system used to produce the recorded image of the motor vehicle involved in the violation may be attested to by affidavit of an officer or employee of the local authority or of the entity with which the local authority contracts under Section 707.003(a)(1) who is responsible for inspecting and maintaining the system.

(f) An affidavit of an officer or employee of the local authority or entity that alleges a violation based on an inspection of the applicable recorded image is:

(1) admissible in the administrative adjudication hearing and in an appeal under Section 707.016; and

(2) evidence of the facts contained in the affidavit.

(g) At the conclusion of the administrative adjudication hearing, the hearing officer shall enter a finding of liability for the civil penalty or a finding of no liability for the civil penalty. A finding under this subsection must be in writing and be signed and dated by the hearing officer.

(h) A finding of liability for a civil penalty must specify the amount of the civil penalty for which the person is liable. If the hearing officer enters a finding of no liability, a civil penalty for the violation may not be imposed against the person.

(i) A finding of liability or a finding of no liability entered under this section may:

(1) be filed with the clerk or secretary of the local authority or with a person designated by the governing body of the local authority; and

(2) be recorded on microfilm or microfiche or using data processing techniques.

(Enacted by Acts 2007, 80th Leg., ch. 1149 (S.B. 1119), § 1, effective September 1, 2007.)

### Sec. 707.015. Untimely Request for Administrative Adjudication Hearing.

Notwithstanding any other provision of this chapter, a person who receives a notice of violation under this chapter and who fails to timely pay the amount of the civil penalty or fails to timely request an administrative adjudication hearing is entitled to an administrative adjudication hearing if:

(1) the person submits a written request for the hearing to the designated hearing officer, accompanied by an affidavit that attests to the date on which the person received the notice of violation; and

(2) the written request and affidavit are submitted to the hearing officer within the same number of days after the date the person received the notice of violation as specified under Section 707.011(c)(8).

(Enacted by Acts 2007, 80th Leg., ch. 1149 (S.B. 1119), § 1, effective September 1, 2007.)

### Sec. 707.016. Appeal.

(a) The owner of a motor vehicle determined by a hearing officer to be liable for a civil penalty may appeal that determination to a judge by filing an appeal petition with the clerk of the court. The petition must be filed with:

(1) a justice court of the county in which the local authority is located; or

(2) if the local authority is a municipality, the municipal court of the municipality.

(b) The petition must be:

(1) filed before the 31st day after the date on which the administrative adjudication hearing officer entered the finding of liability for the civil penalty; and

(2) accompanied by payment of the costs required by law for the court.

(c) The court clerk shall schedule a hearing and notify the owner of the motor vehicle and the appropriate department, agency, or office of the local authority of the date, time, and place of the hearing.

(d) An appeal stays enforcement and collection of the civil penalty imposed against the owner of the motor vehicle. The owner shall file a notarized statement of personal financial obligation to perfect the owner's appeal.

(e) An appeal under this section shall be determined by the court by trial de novo.

(Enacted by Acts 2007, 80th Leg., ch. 1149 (S.B. 1119), § 1, effective September 1, 2007.)

### Sec. 707.017. Enforcement.

(a) If the owner of a motor vehicle is delinquent in the payment of a civil penalty imposed under this chapter, the county assessor-collector or the Texas Department of Motor Vehicles may refuse to register a motor vehicle alleged to have been involved in the violation.

(b) This section does not apply to the registration of a motor vehicle under Section 501.0234.

(Enacted by Acts 2007, 80th Leg., ch. 1149 (S.B. 1119), § 1, effective September 1, 2007; am. Acts 2009, 81st Leg., ch. 266 (H.B. 2530), § 1, effective May 30, 2009; am. Acts 2009, 81st Leg., ch. 542 (S.B. 1617), § 4, effective September 1, 2009; am. Acts 2009, 81st Leg., ch. 933 (H.B. 3097), § 2T.03, effective September 1, 2009; am. Acts 2011, 82nd Leg., ch. 91 (S.B. 1303), § 24.018, effective September 1, 2011.)

### Sec. 707.018. Imposition of Civil Penalty Not a Conviction.

The imposition of a civil penalty under this chapter is not a conviction and may not be considered a conviction for any purpose.

(Enacted by Acts 2007, 80th Leg., ch. 1149 (S.B. 1119), § 1, effective September 1, 2007.)

### Sec. 707.019. Failure to Pay Civil Penalty.

(a) If the owner of the motor vehicle fails to timely pay the amount of the civil penalty imposed against the owner:

(1) an arrest warrant may not be issued for the owner; and

(2) the imposition of the civil penalty may not be recorded on the owner's driving record.

(b) Notice of Subsection (a) must be included in the notice of violation required by Section 707.011(c).

(Enacted by Acts 2007, 80th Leg., ch. 1149 (S.B. 1119), § 1, effective September 1, 2007.)

# CHAPTER 708
# DRIVER RESPONSIBILITY PROGRAM

# SUBCHAPTER A
# GENERAL PROVISIONS

## Sec. 708.001.　Definitions.

In this chapter, "department" and "license" have the meanings assigned by Section 521.001. (Enacted by Acts 2003, 78th Leg., ch. 1325 (H.B. 3588), § 10.01, effective September 1, 2003.)

## Sec. 708.002.　Rules.

The department shall adopt and enforce rules to implement and enforce this chapter.

(Enacted by Acts 2003, 78th Leg., ch. 1325 (H.B. 3588), § 10.01, effective September 1, 2003.)

## Sec. 708.003.　Final Convictions.

For purposes of this chapter, a conviction for an offense to which this chapter applies is a final conviction, regardless of whether the sentence is probated.

(Enacted by Acts 2003, 78th Leg., ch. 1325 (H.B. 3588), § 10.01, effective September 1, 2003.)

## Secs. 708.004 to 708.050 [Reserved for expansion].

# SUBCHAPTER B
# DRIVER'S LICENSE POINTS SURCHARGE

## Sec. 708.051.　Nonapplicability.

This subchapter does not apply to:

(1) an offense committed before September 1, 2003; or

(2) an offense covered by Subchapter C.

(Enacted by Acts 2003, 78th Leg., ch. 1325 (H.B. 3588), § 10.01, effective September 1, 2003; am. Acts 2003, 78th Leg., 3rd C.S., ch. 8 (H.B. 2), § 2.03(a), effective January 11, 2004.)

## Sec. 708.052.　Assignment of Points for Certain Convictions.

(a) The driver's license of a person accumulates a point under this subchapter as of the date the department records a conviction of the person under Section 521.042 or other applicable law.

(b) For each conviction arising out of a separate transaction, the department shall assign points to a person's license as follows:

(1) two points for a moving violation of the traffic law of this state or another state that is not described by Subdivision (2); and

(2) three points for a moving violation of the traffic law of this state, another state, or a political subdivision of this or another state that resulted in an accident.

(c) The department by rule shall designate the offenses that constitute a moving violation of the traffic law under this section.

(d) Notwithstanding Subsection (b), the department may not assign points to a person's driver's license if the offense of which the person was convicted is the offense of speeding and the person was at the time of the offense driving less than 10 percent faster than the posted speed limit. This subsection does not apply to an offense committed in a school crossing zone as defined by Section 541.302.

(e) Notwithstanding Subsection (b), the department may not assign points to a person's license if the offense committed by the person was adjudicated under Article 45.051 or 45.0511, Code of Criminal Procedure.

(f) For the purposes of this section, an offense under Section 545.412 is a moving violation of a traffic law.

(Enacted by Acts 2003, 78th Leg., ch. 1325 (H.B. 3588), § 10.01, effective September 1, 2003; am. Acts 2005, 79th Leg., ch. 913 (H.B. 183), § 5, effective September 1, 2005.)

### Sec. 708.053. Annual Surcharge for Points.

Each year, the department shall assess a surcharge on the license of a person who has accumulated six or more points under this subchapter during the preceding 36-month period.

(Enacted by Acts 2003, 78th Leg., ch. 1325 (H.B. 3588), § 10.01, effective September 1, 2003.)

### Sec. 708.054. Amount of Points Surcharge.

The amount of a surcharge under this chapter is $100 for the first six points and $25 for each additional point.

(Enacted by Acts 2003, 78th Leg., ch. 1325 (H.B. 3588), § 10.01, effective September 1, 2003.)

### Sec. 708.055. Notice of Assignment of Fifth Point.

The department shall notify the holder of a driver's license of the assignment of a fifth point on that license by first class mail sent to the person's most recent address as shown on the records of the department.

(Enacted by Acts 2003, 78th Leg., ch. 1325 (H.B. 3588), § 10.01, effective September 1, 2003.)

### Sec. 708.056. [Effective September 1, 2011] Deduction of Points.

The department by rule shall establish a procedure to provide for the deduction of one point accumulated by a person under this subchapter to account for each year that the person has not accumulated points under this subchapter.

(Enacted by Acts 2009, 81st Leg., ch. 1146 (H.B. 2730), § 15.06, effective September 1, 2011.)

### Secs. 708.057 to 708.100 [Reserved for expansion].

## SUBCHAPTER C
## SURCHARGES FOR CERTAIN CONVICTIONS AND LICENSE SUSPENSIONS

### Sec. 708.101. Nonapplicability.

This subchapter does not apply to an offense committed before September 1, 2003.

(Enacted by Acts 2003, 78th Leg., ch. 1325 (H.B. 3588), § 10.01, effective September 1, 2003; am. Acts 2003, 78th Leg., 3rd C.S., ch. 8 (H.B. 2), § 2.03(a), effective January 11, 2004.)

### Sec. 708.102. Surcharge for Conviction of Certain Intoxicated Driver Offenses.

(a) In this section, "offense relating to the operating of a motor vehicle while intoxicated" has the meaning assigned by Section 49.09, Penal Code.

(b) Each year the department shall assess a surcharge on the license of each person who during the preceding 36-month period has been finally convicted of an offense relating to the operating of a motor vehicle while intoxicated.

(c) The amount of a surcharge under this section is $1,000 per year, except that the amount of the surcharge is:

(1) $1,500 per year for a second or subsequent conviction within a 36-month period; and

(2) $2,000 for a first or subsequent conviction if it is shown on the trial of the offense that an analysis of a specimen of the person's blood, breath, or urine showed an alcohol concentration level of 0.16 or more at the time the analysis was performed.

(d) A surcharge under this section for the same conviction may not be assessed in more than three years.

(Enacted by Acts 2003, 78th Leg., ch. 1325 (H.B. 3588), § 10.01, effective September 1, 2003.)

### Sec. 708.103. Surcharge for Conviction of Driving While License Invalid or Without Financial Responsibility.

(a) Each year the department shall assess a surcharge on the license of each person who during the preceding 36-month period has been convicted of an offense under Section 521.457, 601.191, or 601.371.

Transportation

(b) The amount of a surcharge under this section is $250 per year.
(Enacted by Acts 2003, 78th Leg., ch. 1325 (H.B. 3588), § 10.01, effective September 1, 2003.)

### Sec. 708.104. Surcharge for Conviction of Driving Without Valid License.

(a) Each year the department shall assess a surcharge on the license of a person who during the preceding 36-month period has been convicted of an offense under Section 521.021.

(b) The amount of a surcharge under this section is $100 per year.

(c) A surcharge under this section for the same conviction may not be assessed in more than three years.
(Enacted by Acts 2003, 78th Leg., ch. 1325 (H.B. 3588), § 10.01, effective September 1, 2003.)

### Sec. 708.105. Notice of Potential Surcharge.

(a) A citation issued for an offense under a traffic law of this state or a political subdivision of this state must include, in type larger than any other type on the citation, the following statement:

"A conviction of an offense under a traffic law of this state or a political subdivision of this state may result in the assessment on your driver's license of a surcharge under the Driver Responsibility Program."

(b) The warning required by Subsection (a) is in addition to any other warning required by law.
(Enacted by Acts 2005, 79th Leg., ch. 1123 (H.B. 2470), § 4, effective September 1, 2005.)

### Sec. 708.106. Deferral of Surcharges for Deployed Military Personnel.

The department by rule shall establish a deferral program for surcharges assessed under Section 708.103 or 708.104 against a person who is a member of the United States armed forces on active duty deployed outside of the continental United States. The program must:

　(1) toll the 36-month period while the person is deployed; and

　(2) defer assessment of surcharges against the person until the date the person is no longer deployed for an offense committed:

　　(A) before the person was deployed; or

　　(B) while the person is deployed.
(Enacted by Acts 2011, 82nd Leg., ch. 551 (H.B. 2851), § 1, effective September 1, 2011.)

### Secs. 708.107 to 708.150 [Reserved for expansion].

## SUBCHAPTER D
## COLLECTION OF SURCHARGES

### Sec. 708.151. Notice of Surcharge.

(a) The department shall send notices as required by Subsection (b) to the holder of a driver's license when a surcharge is assessed on that license. Each notice must:

　(1) be sent by first class mail to the person's most recent address as shown on the records of the department or to the person's most recent forwarding address on record with the United States Postal Service if it is different;

　(2) specify the date by which the surcharge must be paid;

　(3) state the total dollar amount of the surcharge that must be paid, the number of monthly payments required under an installment payment plan, and the minimum monthly payment required for a person to enter and maintain an installment payment plan with the department; and

　(4) state the consequences of a failure to pay the surcharge.

(b) The department shall send a first notice not later than the fifth day after the date the surcharge is assessed.

(c) If on or before the 45th day after the date the first notice was sent the person fails to pay the amount of the surcharge or fails to enter into an installment payment agreement with the department, the department shall send a second notice. If on or before the 60th day after the date the second notice was sent the person fails to pay the amount of the surcharge or fails to enter into an installment payment agreement with the department, the department shall send a third notice that advises the person that the person's driving privileges are suspended.
(Enacted by Acts 2003, 78th Leg., ch. 1325 (H.B. 3588), § 10.01, effective September 1, 2003; am. Acts 2009, 81st Leg., ch. 1146 (H.B. 2730), § 15.01, effective September 1, 2011.)

### Sec. 708.152. Failure to Pay Surcharge.

(a) If on the 60th day after the date the department sends a second notice under Section 708.151 the person fails to pay the amount of a surcharge on the person's license or fails to enter into an installment payment agreement with the department, the license of the person is automatically suspended. A person's license may not be suspended under this section before the 105th day after the date the surcharge was assessed by the department.

(b) A license suspended under this section remains suspended until the person pays the amount of the surcharge and any related costs. (Enacted by Acts 2003, 78th Leg., ch. 1325 (H.B. 3588), § 10.01, effective September 1, 2003; am. Acts 2009, 81st Leg., ch. 1146 (H.B. 2730), § 15.02, effective September 1, 2011.)

### Sec. 708.153. Installment Payment of Surcharge.

(a) The department by rule shall provide for the payment of a surcharge in installments.

(b) A rule under this section:

(1) may not require a person to:

(A) pay surcharges that total $500 or more over a period of less than 36 consecutive months;

(B) pay surcharges that total more than $250 but not more than $499 over a period of less than 24 consecutive months; or

(C) pay surcharges that total $249 or less over a period of less than 12 consecutive months; and

(2) may provide that if the person fails to make any required monthly installment payment, the department may reestablish the installment plan on receipt of a payment in the amount equal to at least a required monthly installment payment.

(Enacted by Acts 2003, 78th Leg., ch. 1325 (H.B. 3588), § 10.01, effective September 1, 2003; am. Acts 2005, 79th Leg., ch. 1123 (H.B. 2470), § 5, effective September 1, 2005; am. Acts 2007, 80th Leg., ch. 573 (S.B. 1723), § 1, effective September 1, 2007; am. Acts 2009, 81st Leg., ch. 1146 (H.B. 2730), § 15.03, effective September 1, 2011.)

### Sec. 708.154. Credit Card Payment of Surcharge.

(a) The department by rule may authorize the payment of a surcharge by use of a credit card. The rules shall require the person to pay all costs incurred by the department in connection with the acceptance of the credit card.

(b) If a surcharge or a related cost is paid by credit card and the amount is subsequently reversed by the issuer of the credit card, the license of the person is automatically suspended.

(c) A license suspended under this section remains suspended until the person pays the amount of the surcharge and any related costs.

(Enacted by Acts 2003, 78th Leg., ch. 1325 (H.B. 3588), § 10.01, effective September 1, 2003.)

### Sec. 708.155. Contracts for Collection of Surcharges.

(a) The department may enter into a contract with a private attorney or a public or private vendor for the provision of services for the collection of surcharges receivable and related costs under this chapter.

(b) To provide for alternative or additional collection methods for surcharges receivable, the department may amend a contract entered into under Subsection (a) and enter into additional contracts under Subsection (a).

(c) The total amount of compensation under a contract entered into under this section may not exceed 30 percent of the amount of the surcharges and related costs collected.

(Enacted by Acts 2003, 78th Leg., ch. 1325 (H.B. 3588), § 10.01, effective September 1, 2003; am. Acts 2003, 78th Leg., 3rd C.S., ch. 8 (H.B. 2), § 2.04, effective January 11, 2004; am. Acts 2007, 80th Leg., ch. 573 (S.B. 1723), § 2, effective September 1, 2007.)

### Sec. 708.156. Remittance of Surcharges Collected to Comptroller.

Each surcharge collected by the department under this chapter shall be remitted to the comptroller as required by Section 780.002, Health and Safety Code.

(Enacted by Acts 2003, 78th Leg., ch. 1325 (H.B. 3588), § 10.01, effective September 1, 2003.)

### Sec. 708.157. Amnesty and Incentives.

(a) The department by rule may establish a periodic amnesty program for holders of a driver's license on which a surcharge has been assessed for certain offenses, as determined by the department.

(b) The department by rule shall offer a holder of a driver's license on which a surcharge has been assessed an incentive for compliance with the law and efforts at rehabilitation, including a reduction of a surcharge or a decrease in the length of an installment plan.

(c) The department by rule shall establish an indigency program for holders of a driver's license on which a surcharge has been assessed for certain offenses, as determined by the department.

(Enacted by Acts 2007, 80th Leg., ch. 573 (S.B. 1723), § 3, effective September 1, 2007; am. Acts 2009, 81st Leg., ch. 1146 (H.B. 2730), § 6.10, effective September 1, 2009; am. Acts 2009 81st

Transportation

Leg., ch. 1146 (H.B. 2730), § 15.05, effective September 1, 2011; am. Acts 2011, 82nd Leg., ch. 711 (H.B. 588), § 1, effective September 1, 2011.)

### Sec. 708.158. Indigent Status and Reduction of Surcharges.

(a) The department shall waive all surcharges assessed under this chapter for a person who is indigent. For the purposes of this section, a person is considered to be indigent if the person provides the evidence described by Subsection (b) to the court.

(b) A person must provide information to the court in which the person is convicted of the offense that is the basis for the surcharge to establish that the person is indigent. The following documentation may be used as proof:

(1) a copy of the person's most recent federal income tax return that shows that the person's income or the person's household income does not exceed 125 percent of the applicable income level established by the federal poverty guidelines;

(2) a copy of the person's most recent statement of wages that shows that the person's income or the person's household income does not exceed 125 percent of the applicable income level established by the federal poverty guidelines; or

(3) documentation from a federal agency, state agency, or school district that indicates that the person or, if the person is a dependent as defined by Section 152, Internal Revenue Code of 1986, the taxpayer claiming the person as a dependent, receives assistance from:

(A) the food stamp program or the financial assistance program established under Chapter 31, Human Resources Code;

(B) the federal special supplemental nutrition program for women, infants, and children authorized by 42 U.S.C. Section 1786;

(C) the medical assistance program under Chapter 32, Human Resources Code;

(D) the child health plan program under Chapter 62, Health and Safety Code; or

(E) the national free or reduced-price lunch program established under 42 U.S.C. Section 1751 et seq.

(Enacted by Acts 2009, 81st Leg., ch. 1146 (H.B. 2730), § 15.04, effective September 1, 2011.)

### Sec. 708.159. Advance Payment of Surcharges.

(a) The department shall offer an option for a single up-front payment to a person who is as-

sessed an annual surcharge under this chapter to allow the person to pay in advance the total amount that will be owed for the 36-month period for which the surcharge will be assessed.

(b) Notice under Section 708.151 of an initial surcharge imposed under this chapter must notify the driver's license holder of:

(1) the total amount the person will owe for the 36-month period for which the surcharge will be assessed; and

(2) the availability of the advance payment option under this section.

(c) If a person makes a single up-front payment under this section in the amount specified in the notice under Subsection (b)(1) and the person is not, in the 36-month period for which the person made the up-front payment, subsequently convicted of an offense requiring a surcharge or an increase in the amount due to the department, the department is not required to:

(1) take any further action under Section 708.053, 708.102, 708.103, or 708.104, as applicable; or

(2) annually notify the person of the assessment of the surcharge under Section 708.151.

(Enacted by Acts 2011, 82nd Leg., ch. 711 (H.B. 588), § 2, effective September 1, 2011.)

## CHAPTERS 709 TO 719 [RESERVED FOR EXPANSION]

## CHAPTER 720 MISCELLANEOUS PROVISIONS

**Section**
720.001.   Badge of Sheriff, Constable, or Deputy.
720.002.   Prohibition on Traffic-Offense Quotas.

### Sec. 720.001. Badge of Sheriff, Constable, or Deputy.

(a) A sheriff, constable, or deputy sheriff or deputy constable may not arrest or accost a person for driving a motor vehicle on a highway in violation of a law relating to motor vehicles unless the sheriff, constable, or deputy displays a badge showing the sheriff's, constable's, or deputy's title.

(b) A person commits an offense if the person violates this section. An offense under this section is a misdemeanor punishable in the same manner as an offense under Section 86.011, Local Government Code.

(c) An officer charged by law to take or prosecute a complaint under this section shall be removed from office if the officer refuses to do so.

(Enacted by Acts 1995, 74th Leg., ch. 165 (S.B. 971), § 1, effective September 1, 1995.)

### Sec. 720.002. Prohibition on Traffic-Offense Quotas.

(a) A political subdivision or an agency of this state may not establish or maintain, formally or informally, a plan to evaluate, promote, compensate, or discipline:

(1) a peace officer according to the officer's issuance of a predetermined or specified number of any type or combination of types of traffic citations; or

(2) a justice of the peace or a judge of a county court, statutory county court, municipal court, or municipal court of record according to the amount of money the justice or judge collects from persons convicted of a traffic offense.

(b) A political subdivision or an agency of this state may not require or suggest to a peace officer, a justice of the peace, or a judge of a county court, statutory county court, municipal court, or municipal court of record:

(1) that the peace officer is required or expected to issue a predetermined or specified number of any type or combination of types of traffic citations within a specified period; or

(2) that the justice or judge is required or expected to collect a predetermined amount of money from persons convicted of a traffic offense within a specified period.

(c) [Repealed by Acts 2009, 81st Leg., ch. 737 (S.B. 420), § 1, effective June 19, 2009.]

(d) This section does not prohibit a municipality from obtaining budgetary information from a municipal court or a municipal court of record, including an estimate of the amount of money the court anticipates will be collected in a budget year.

(e) A violation of this section by an elected official is misconduct and a ground for removal from office. A violation of this section by a person who is not an elected official is a ground for removal from the person's position.

(f) In this section:

(1) "Conviction" means the rendition of an order by a court imposing a punishment of incarceration or a fine.

(2) "Traffic offense" means an offense under:

(A) Chapter 521; or

(B) Subtitle C.

(Enacted by Acts 1995, 74th Leg., ch. 165 (S.B. 971), § 1, effective September 1, 1995; am. Acts 2009, 81st Leg., ch. 737 (S.B. 420), § 1, effective June 19, 2009.)

### SUBTITLE J
### MISCELLANEOUS PROVISIONS

### CHAPTER 721
### INSCRIPTION REQUIRED ON STATE, MUNICIPAL, AND COUNTY MOTOR VEHICLES

### Sec. 721.001. Definition.

In this chapter, "state agency" means a department, bureau, board, commission, or office of state government.

(Enacted by Acts 1995, 74th Leg., ch. 165 (S.B. 971), § 1, effective September 1, 1995.)

### Sec. 721.002. Inscription Required on State-Owned Motor Vehicles.

(a) The official having control of a state-owned motor vehicle shall have printed on each side of the vehicle the word "Texas," followed by the title of the state agency having custody of the vehicle.

(b) The inscription must be in a color sufficiently different from the body of the motor vehicle so that the lettering is plainly legible at a distance of not less than 100 feet.

(c) The title of the state agency must be in letters not less than two inches high.

(Enacted by Acts 1995, 74th Leg., ch. 165 (S.B. 971), § 1, effective September 1, 1995.)

### Sec. 721.003. Exemption from Inscription Requirement for Certain State-Owned Motor Vehicles.

(a) The governing bodies of the following state agencies or divisions by rule may exempt from the requirements of Section 721.002 a motor vehicle that is under the control and custody of the agency or division:

(1) Texas Commission on Fire Protection;

(2) Texas State Board of Pharmacy;

(3) Department of State Health Services and Department of Aging and Disability Services;

Transportation

(4) Department of Public Safety of the State of Texas;

(5) Texas Department of Criminal Justice;

(6) Board of Pardons and Paroles;

(7) Parks and Wildlife Department;

(8) Railroad Commission of Texas;

(9) Texas Alcoholic Beverage Commission;

(10) Texas Department of Banking;

(11) Department of Savings and Mortgage Lending;

(12) Texas Juvenile Probation Commission;

(13) Texas Commission on Environmental Quality;

(14) Texas Youth Commission;

(15) Texas Lottery Commission;

(16) the office of the attorney general;

(17) Texas Department of Insurance; and

(18) an agency that receives an appropriation under an article of the General Appropriations Act that appropriates money to the legislature.

(b) [Repealed by Acts 2001, 77th Leg., ch. 81 (S.B. 817), § 2, effective September 1, 2001.]

(c) A rule adopted under this section must specify:

(1) the purpose served by not printing on the motor vehicle the inscription required by Section 721.002; and

(2) the primary use of the motor vehicle.

(d) A rule adopted under this section is not effective until the rule is filed with the secretary of state.

(e) A rule adopted by the Texas Lottery Commission under Subsection (a) may exempt from the requirements of Section 721.002 only a motor vehicle used exclusively for surveillance purposes.

(Enacted by Acts 1995, 74th Leg., ch. 165 (S.B. 971), § 1, effective September 1, 1995; am. Acts 2001, 77th Leg., ch. 81 (S.B. 817), §§ 1, 2, effective September 1, 2001; am. Acts 2001, 77th Leg., ch. 81 (S.B. 817), § 2, effective September 1, 2001; am. Acts 2007, 80th Leg., ch. 921 (H.B. 3167), § 6.066, effective September 1, 2007; am. Acts 2007, 80th Leg., ch. 1308 (S.B. 909), § 48, effective June 15, 2007.)

## Sec. 721.004. Inscription Required on Municipal and County-Owned Motor Vehicles and Heavy Equipment.

(a) The office having control of a motor vehicle or piece of heavy equipment owned by a municipality or county shall have printed on each side of the vehicle or equipment the name of the munic-ipality or county, followed by the title of the department or office having custody of the vehicle or equipment.

(b) The inscription must be in a color sufficiently different from the body of the vehicle or equipment so that the lettering is plainly legible.

(c) The title of the department or office must be in letters plainly legible at a distance of not less than 100 feet.

(Enacted by Acts 1995, 74th Leg., ch. 165 (S.B. 971), § 1, effective September 1, 1995.)

## Sec. 721.005. Exemption from Inscription Requirement for Certain Municipal and County-Owned Motor Vehicles.

(a) The governing body of a municipality may exempt from the requirements of Section 721.004:

(1) an automobile when used to perform an official duty by a:

(A) police department;

(B) magistrate as defined by Article 2.09, Code of Criminal Procedure;

(C) medical examiner;

(D) municipal code enforcement officer designated to enforce environmental criminal laws; or

(E) municipal fire marshal or arson investigator; or

(2) an automobile used by a municipal employee only when conducting an investigation involving suspected fraud or other mismanagement within the municipality.

(b) The commissioners court of a county may exempt from the requirements of Section 721.004:

(1) an automobile when used to perform an official duty by a:

(A) police department;

(B) sheriff's office;

(C) constable's office;

(D) criminal district attorney's office;

(E) district attorney's office;

(F) county attorney's office;

(G) magistrate as defined by Article 2.09, Code of Criminal Procedure;

(H) county fire marshal's office; or

(I) medical examiner; or

(2) a juvenile probation department vehicle used to transport children, when used to perform an official duty.

(c) An exemption provided under this section does not apply to a contract deputy.

(Enacted by Acts 1995, 74th Leg., ch. 165 (S.B. 971), § 1, effective September 1, 1995; am. Acts 1997, 75th Leg., ch. 355 (S.B. 1233), § 1, effective May 27, 1997; am. Acts 1997, 75th Leg., ch. 46 (H.B. 649), § 1, effective September 1, 1997; am. Acts 1999, 76th Leg., ch. 62 (S.B. 1368), § 17.38, effective September 1, 1999; am. Acts 2001, 77th Leg., ch. 66 (H.B. 630), § 1, effective May 14, 2001; am. Acts 2001, 77th Leg., ch. 140 (H.B. 2220), § 1, effective September 1, 2001; am. Acts 2007, 80th Leg., ch. 45 (S.B. 526), § 1, effective May 8, 2007.)

### Sec. 721.006.  Operation of Vehicle in Violation of Chapter; Offense.

(a) A person commits an offense if the person:

(1) operates on a municipal street or on a highway a motor vehicle or piece of equipment that does not have the inscription required by this chapter; or

(2) uses a motor vehicle that is exempt by rule under Section 721.003, and that use is not expressly specified by the rule.

(b) An offense under this section is a misdemeanor punishable by a fine of not less than $25 or more than $100.

(Enacted by Acts 1995, 74th Leg., ch. 165 (S.B. 971), § 1, effective September 1, 1995.)

# CHAPTER 722
# AUTOMOBILE CLUB SERVICES

### Sec. 722.001.  Short Title.

This chapter may be cited as the Automobile Club Services Act.

(Enacted by Acts 1995, 74th Leg., ch. 165 (S.B. 971), § 1, effective September 1, 1995.)

### Sec. 722.002.  Definitions.

In this chapter:

(1) "Agent" means a salesman or other individual appointed by an automobile club to sell memberships in the club to the public.

(2) "Automobile club" means a person who, for consideration, promises the membership assistance in matters relating to travel, and to the operation, use, or maintenance of a motor vehicle, by supplying services such as services related to:

(A) community traffic safety;

(B) travel and touring;

(C) theft prevention or rewards;

(D) maps;

(E) towing;

(F) emergency road assistance;

(G) bail bonds and legal fee reimbursement in the defense of traffic offenses; and

(H) purchase of accidental injury and death benefits insurance coverage from an authorized insurance company.

(Enacted by Acts 1995, 74th Leg., ch. 165 (S.B. 971), § 1, effective September 1, 1995.)

### Sec. 722.003.  Certificate of Authority Required.

(a) A person may not engage in business as an automobile club unless the person meets the requirements of this chapter and obtains an automobile club certificate of authority from the secretary of state.

(b) A person may not solicit or aid in the solicitation of another person to purchase a service contract or membership issued by an automobile club that does not hold an automobile club certificate of authority.

(Enacted by Acts 1995, 74th Leg., ch. 165 (S.B. 971), § 1, effective September 1, 1995.)

### Sec. 722.004.  Application.

(a) Each applicant for an automobile club certificate of authority must file an application with the secretary of state in the form and manner prescribed by the secretary. The secretary shall adopt the forms necessary for an applicant to comply with this chapter and shall furnish those forms on request to an applicant for a certificate of authority.

(b) An application must be executed under oath by the club president or other principal club officer and must be accompanied by:

(1) the first year's annual fee for the certificate of authority;

(2) a certificate by the secretary of state stating that the applicant has complied with the corporation laws of this state, if the applicant is a corporation;

(3) a list of each person who holds an ownership interest in the applicant and each officer

of the applicant, if the applicant is not incorporated;

(4) a copy of any operating agreement or management agreement affecting the club and a list of each party to the agreement if the applicant is not incorporated; and

(5) proof of security in a manner that complies with Section 722.005.

(c) The secretary of state shall issue the automobile club certificate of authority or deny the application not later than the 15th day after the day the secretary receives the application, certificate, or security. Failure to issue the certificate of authority within the prescribed time entitles the applicant to a refund of all money and security deposited with the application.

(Enacted by Acts 1995, 74th Leg., ch. 165 (S.B. 971), § 1, effective September 1, 1995.)

### Sec. 722.005. Security Requirements.

(a) An applicant for an automobile club certificate of authority may provide the security required for that certificate by depositing with the state or pledging in the form prescribed by the secretary of state:

(1) $25,000 in securities approved by the secretary;

(2) $25,000 in cash; or

(3) a $25,000 bond in the form prescribed by the secretary that is:

(A) payable to the state;

(B) executed by a corporate surety licensed to do business in this state; and

(C) conditioned on the faithful performance of the automobile club in selling or providing club services and the payment of any fines or penalties levied against the club for failure to comply with this chapter.

(b) The aggregate liability of the surety for all breaches of the bond conditions and for payment of all fines and penalties may not exceed the amount of the bond.

(c) The required security shall be maintained as long as the automobile club has any liability or obligation in this state. On showing to the satisfaction of the secretary of state that the club has ceased to do business and that all liabilities and obligations of the club have been satisfied, the secretary may return the security to the club or deliver the security in accordance with a court order.

(Enacted by Acts 1995, 74th Leg., ch. 165 (S.B. 971), § 1, effective September 1, 1995.)

### Sec. 722.006. Renewal.

(a) An automobile club certificate of authority expires annually on August 31. The certificate may be renewed by filing a renewal application in the manner prescribed by the secretary of state and paying the annual fee.

(b) The secretary of state may adopt forms for the renewal application.

(Enacted by Acts 1995, 74th Leg., ch. 165 (S.B. 971), § 1, effective September 1, 1995.)

### Sec. 722.007. Annual Fee.

The annual fee for an automobile club certificate of authority is $150.

(Enacted by Acts 1995, 74th Leg., ch. 165 (S.B. 971), § 1, effective September 1, 1995.)

### Sec. 722.008. Certificate Revocation or Suspension.

(a) After a public hearing, the secretary of state shall revoke or suspend an automobile club's certificate of authority if the secretary determines, for good cause shown, that:

(1) the club:

(A) has violated this chapter;

(B) is not acting as an automobile club;

(C) is insolvent or has assets valued at less than its liabilities;

(D) has refused to submit to an examination by the secretary; or

(E) is transacting business in a fraudulent manner; or

(2) an owner, officer, or manager of the club is not of good moral character.

(b) The secretary of state shall give public notice of the suspension or revocation in the manner the secretary considers appropriate.

(Enacted by Acts 1995, 74th Leg., ch. 165 (S.B. 971), § 1, effective September 1, 1995.)

### Sec. 722.009. Service Contract; Membership Information.

(a) Each automobile club operating under this chapter shall furnish to the membership a service contract or membership card that includes the following information:

(1) the club's name;

(2) the street address of the club's home office and of its usual place of business in this state; and

(3) a description of the services or benefits to which the members are entitled.

(b) For purposes of this chapter, the completed application for an automobile club certificate of

Transportation

authority and the description of services listed under Subsection (a) constitute the service contract.

(Enacted by Acts 1995, 74th Leg., ch. 165 (S.B. 971), § 1, effective September 1, 1995.)

### Sec. 722.010. Filing of Information.

(a) Each automobile club shall file a certified copy of its service contract with the secretary of state.

(b) If an automobile club provides participation in a group accidental injury or death policy, the club shall file with the service contract a copy of the certificate of participation.

(c) An automobile club shall file with the secretary of state any change to the service contract.

(Enacted by Acts 1995, 74th Leg., ch. 165 (S.B. 971), § 1, effective September 1, 1995.)

### Sec. 722.011. Agent Registration.

(a) An automobile club that operates in this state under an automobile club certificate of authority shall file with the secretary of state a notice of appointment of each agent not later than the 30th day after the date on which that agent is employed by the club.

(b) The notice of appointment must be in the form prescribed by the secretary of state and must contain:

(1) the name, address, age, sex, and social security number of the agent; and

(2) proof satisfactory to the secretary that the agent is of good moral character.

(c) Registration under this section is valid for one year from the date of the initial registration and may be renewed on each anniversary of that date. The annual registration fee is $10.

(d) Each automobile club shall notify the secretary of state of the termination of an agent's employment by the club not later than the 30th day after the date of the termination.

(Enacted by Acts 1995, 74th Leg., ch. 165 (S.B. 971), § 1, effective September 1, 1995.)

### Sec. 722.012. Advertising Restrictions.

An automobile club operating under this chapter may not:

(1) refer to its certificate of authority or to approval by the secretary of state in any advertising, contract, or membership card; or

(2) advertise or describe its services in a manner that would lead the public to believe that the services include automobile insurance.

(Enacted by Acts 1995, 74th Leg., ch. 165 (S.B. 971), § 1, effective September 1, 1995.)

### Sec. 722.013. Exemption from Certain Insurance Laws; Group Policy Requirements [Repealed].

Repealed by Acts 1999, 76th Leg., ch. 1530 (S.B. 957), § 5.02, effective September 1, 1999. (Enacted by Acts 1995, 74th Leg., ch. 165 (S.B. 971), § 1, effective September 1, 1995.)

### Sec. 722.014. Criminal Penalty.

(a) A person commits an offense if the person violates this chapter.

(b) An offense under this section is a misdemeanor punishable by:

(1) a fine not to exceed $500; and

(2) confinement in the county jail for a term not to exceed six months.

(Enacted by Acts 1995, 74th Leg., ch. 165 (S.B. 971), § 1, effective September 1, 1995.)

## CHAPTER 723
## TEXAS TRAFFIC SAFETY ACT

### Subchapter A. General Provisions

## SUBCHAPTER A
## GENERAL PROVISIONS

### Sec. 723.001. Short Title.

This chapter may be cited as the Texas Traffic Safety Act.

(Enacted by Acts 1995, 74th Leg., ch. 165 (S.B. 971), § 1, effective September 1, 1995.)

### Sec. 723.002. Governmental Purpose.

The establishment, development, and maintenance of a traffic safety program is a vital gov-

ernmental purpose and function of the state and its legal and political subdivisions.
(Enacted by Acts 1995, 74th Leg., ch. 165 (S.B. 971), § 1, effective September 1, 1995.)

### Sec. 723.003.　Traffic Safety Fund Account.

(a) The traffic safety fund account is an account in the general revenue fund. Money received from any source to implement this chapter shall be:

(1) deposited to the credit of the traffic safety fund account; and

(2) spent with other state money spent to implement this chapter in the manner in which the other state money is spent.

(b) A payment from the traffic safety fund account shall be made in compliance with this chapter and rules adopted by the governor.
(Enacted by Acts 1997, 75th Leg., ch. 165 (S.B. 898), § 30.162(a), effective September 1, 1997.)

### Secs. 723.004 to 723.010 [Reserved for expansion].

## SUBCHAPTER B
## PREPARATION AND ADMINISTRATION OF TRAFFIC SAFETY PROGRAM

### Sec. 723.011.　Governor's Responsibility for Program.

(a) The governor shall:

(1) prepare and administer a statewide traffic safety program designed to reduce traffic accidents and the death, injury, and property damage that result from traffic accidents;

(2) adopt rules for the administration of this chapter, including rules, procedures, and policy statements governing grants-in-aid and contractual relations;

(3) receive on the state's behalf for the implementation of this chapter money made available by the United States under federal law; and

(4) allocate money appropriated by the legislature in the General Appropriations Act to implement this chapter.

(b) In preparing and administering the traffic safety program, the governor may:

(1) cooperate with the United States or a legal or political subdivision of the state in research designed to aid in traffic safety;

(2) accept federal money available for research relating to traffic safety; and

(3) employ personnel necessary to administer this chapter.
(Enacted by Acts 1995, 74th Leg., ch. 165 (S.B. 971), § 1, effective September 1, 1995.)

### Sec. 723.012.　Traffic Safety Program.

The statewide traffic safety program must include:

(1) a driver education and training program administered by the governor through appropriate agencies that complies with Section 723.013;

(2) plans for improving:

(A) driver licensing;

(B) accident records;

(C) vehicle inspection, registration, and titling;

(D) traffic engineering;

(E) personnel;

(F) police traffic supervision;

(G) traffic courts;

(H) highway design; and

(I) uniform traffic laws; and

(3) plans for local traffic safety programs by legal and political subdivisions of this state that may be implemented if the programs:

(A) are approved by the governor; and

(B) conform with uniform standards adopted under the Highway Safety Act of 1966 (23 U.S.C. Sec. 401 et seq.).
(Enacted by Acts 1995, 74th Leg., ch. 165 (S.B. 971), § 1, effective September 1, 1995.)

### Sec. 723.013.　Driver Education and Training Program.

(a) The statewide driver education and training program required by Section 723.012 shall provide for:

(1) rules that permit controlled innovation and experimentation and that set minimum standards for:

(A) classroom instruction;

(B) driving skills training;

(C) instructor qualifications;

(D) program content; and

(E) supplementary materials and equipment;

(2) a method for continuing evaluation of approved driver education and training programs to identify the practices most effective in preventing traffic accidents; and

(3) contracts between the governing bodies of centrally located independent school dis-

tricts or other appropriate public or private agencies and the state to provide approved driver education and training programs.

(b) Instruction offered under a contract authorized by this section must be offered to any applicant who is over 15 years of age.

(Enacted by Acts 1995, 74th Leg., ch. 165 (S.B. 971), § 1, effective September 1, 1995.)

## Sec. 723.014. Cooperation of State Agencies, Officers, and Employees.

On the governor's request, a state agency or institution, state officer, or state employee shall cooperate in an activity of the state that is consistent with:

(1) this chapter; and

(2) the agency's, institution's, officer's, or employee's official functions.

(Enacted by Acts 1995, 74th Leg., ch. 165 (S.B. 971), § 1, effective September 1, 1995.)

## Sec. 723.015. Participation in Program by Legal or Political Subdivision.

A legal or political subdivision of this state may:

(1) cooperate and contract with the state, another legal or political subdivision of this state, or a private person in establishing, developing, and maintaining a statewide traffic safety program;

(2) spend money from any source for an activity related to performing a part of the traffic safety program; and

(3) contract and pay for a personal service or property to be used in the traffic safety program or for an activity related to the program.

(Enacted by Acts 1995, 74th Leg., ch. 165 (S.B. 971), § 1, effective September 1, 1995.)

## Secs. 723.016 to 723.030 [Reserved for expansion].

## SUBCHAPTER C
## GIFTS, GRANTS, DONATIONS, GRANTS-IN-AID, AND PAYMENTS

## Sec. 723.031. Gifts, Grants, and Donations.

To implement this chapter, the state may accept and spend a gift, grant, or donation of money or other property from a private source.

(Enacted by Acts 1995, 74th Leg., ch. 165 (S.B. 971), § 1, effective September 1, 1995.)

## Sec. 723.032. Grants-in-Aid and Contractual Payments.

(a) A grant-in-aid for a governmental purpose or a contractual payment may be made to a legal or political subdivision of this state to carry out a duty or activity that is part of the statewide traffic safety program.

(b) To implement this chapter, a contractual payment may be made from money in the traffic safety fund account for a service rendered or property furnished by a private person or an agency that is not a legal or political subdivision of this state.

(Enacted by Acts 1995, 74th Leg., ch. 165 (S.B. 971), § 1, effective September 1, 1995; am. Acts 1997, 75th Leg., ch. 165 (S.B. 898), § 30.162(b), effective September 1, 1997.)

## CHAPTER 724
## IMPLIED CONSENT

### Subchapter A. General Provisions

### Subchapter B. Taking and Analysis of Specimen

### Subchapter C. Suspension or Denial of License on Refusal of Specimen

### Subchapter D. Hearing

## SUBCHAPTER A
## GENERAL PROVISIONS

### Sec. 724.001.   Definitions.

In this chapter:

(1) "Alcohol concentration" has the meaning assigned by Section 49.01, Penal Code.

(2) "Arrest" includes the taking into custody of a child, as defined by Section 51.02, Family Code.

(3) "Controlled substance" has the meaning assigned by Section 481.002, Health and Safety Code.

(4) "Criminal charge" includes a charge that may result in a proceeding under Title 3, Family Code.

(5) "Criminal proceeding" includes a proceeding under Title 3, Family Code.

(6) "Dangerous drug" has the meaning assigned by Section 483.001, Health and Safety Code.

(7) "Department" means the Department of Public Safety.

(8) "Drug" has the meaning assigned by Section 481.002, Health and Safety Code.

(9) "Intoxicated" has the meaning assigned by Section 49.01, Penal Code.

(10) "License" has the meaning assigned by Section 521.001.

(11) "Operate" means to drive or be in actual control of a motor vehicle or watercraft.

(12) "Public place" has the meaning assigned by Section 1.07, Penal Code.

(Enacted by Acts 1995, 74th Leg., ch. 165 (S.B. 971), § 1, effective September 1, 1995; am. Acts 1997, 75th Leg., ch. 1013 (S.B. 35), § 31, effective September 1, 1997.)

### Sec. 724.002.   Applicability.

The provisions of this chapter that apply to suspension of a license for refusal to submit to the taking of a specimen (Sections 724.013, 724.015, and 724.048 and Subchapters C and D) apply only to a person arrested for an offense involving the operation of a motor vehicle or watercraft powered with an engine having a manufacturer's rating of 50 horsepower or above.

(Enacted by Acts 1995, 74th Leg., ch. 165 (S.B. 971), § 1, effective September 1, 1995; am. Acts 2001, 77th Leg., ch. 444 (H.B. 63), § 7, effective September 1, 2001.)

### Sec. 724.003.   Rulemaking.

The department and the State Office of Administrative Hearings shall adopt rules to administer this chapter.

(Enacted by Acts 1995, 74th Leg., ch. 165 (S.B. 971), § 1, effective September 1, 1995.)

### Secs. 724.004 to 724.010 [Reserved for expansion].

## SUBCHAPTER B
## TAKING AND ANALYSIS OF SPECIMEN

### Sec. 724.011.   Consent to Taking of Specimen.

(a) If a person is arrested for an offense arising out of acts alleged to have been committed while the person was operating a motor vehicle in a public place, or a watercraft, while intoxicated, or an offense under Section 106.041, Alcoholic Beverage Code, the person is deemed to have consented, subject to this chapter, to submit to the taking of one or more specimens of the person's breath or blood for analysis to determine the alcohol concentration or the presence in the person's body of a controlled substance, drug, dangerous drug, or other substance.

(b) A person arrested for an offense described by Subsection (a) may consent to submit to the taking of any other type of specimen to determine the person's alcohol concentration.

(Enacted by Acts 1995, 74th Leg., ch. 165 (S.B. 971), § 1, effective September 1, 1995; am. Acts 1997, 75th Leg., ch. 1013 (S.B. 35), § 32, effective September 1, 1997.)

### Sec. 724.012.   Taking of Specimen.

(a) One or more specimens of a person's breath or blood may be taken if the person is arrested and at the request of a peace officer having reasonable grounds to believe the person:

(1) while intoxicated was operating a motor vehicle in a public place, or a watercraft; or

(2) was in violation of Section 106.041, Alcoholic Beverage Code.

(b) A peace officer shall require the taking of a specimen of the person's breath or blood under any of the following circumstances if the officer arrests the person for an offense under Chapter 49, Penal Code, involving the operation of a motor vehicle or a watercraft and the person refuses the officer's request to submit to the taking of a specimen voluntarily:

(1) the person was the operator of a motor vehicle or a watercraft involved in an accident that the officer reasonably believes occurred as a result of the offense and, at the time of the arrest, the officer reasonably believes that as a direct result of the accident:

(A) any individual has died or will die;

(B) an individual other than the person has suffered serious bodily injury; or

(C) an individual other than the person has suffered bodily injury and been transported to a hospital or other medical facility for medical treatment;

(2) the offense for which the officer arrests the person is an offense under Section 49.045, Penal Code; or

(3) at the time of the arrest, the officer possesses or receives reliable information from a credible source that the person:

(A) has been previously convicted of or placed on community supervision for an offense under Section 49.045, 49.07, or 49.08, Penal Code, or an offense under the laws of another state containing elements substantially similar to the elements of an offense under those sections; or

(B) on two or more occasions, has been previously convicted of or placed on community supervision for an offense under Section 49.04, 49.05, 49.06, or 49.065, Penal Code, or an offense under the laws of another state containing elements substantially similar to the elements of an offense under those sections.

(c) The peace officer shall designate the type of specimen to be taken.

(d) In this section, "bodily injury" and "serious bodily injury" have the meanings assigned by Section 1.07, Penal Code.

(Enacted by Acts 1995, 74th Leg., ch. 165 (S.B. 971), § 1, effective September 1, 1995; am. Acts 1997, 75th Leg., ch. 1013 (S.B. 35), § 33, effective September 1, 1997; am. Acts 2003, 78th Leg., ch.

422 (H.B. 292), § 1, effective September 1, 2003; am. Acts 2009, 81st Leg., ch. 1348 (S.B. 328), § 18, effective September 1, 2009.)

## Sec. 724.013.  Prohibition on Taking Specimen If Person Refuses; Exception.

Except as provided by Section 724.012(b), a specimen may not be taken if a person refuses to submit to the taking of a specimen designated by a peace officer.

(Enacted by Acts 1995, 74th Leg., ch. 165 (S.B. 971), § 1, effective September 1, 1995.)

## Sec. 724.014.  Person Incapable of Refusal.

(a) A person who is dead, unconscious, or otherwise incapable of refusal is considered not to have withdrawn the consent provided by Section 724.011.

(b) If the person is dead, a specimen may be taken by:

(1) the county medical examiner or the examiner's designated agent; or

(2) a licensed mortician or a person authorized under Section 724.016 or 724.017 if there is not a county medical examiner for the county.

(c) If the person is alive but is incapable of refusal, a specimen may be taken by a person authorized under Section 724.016 or 724.017.

(Enacted by Acts 1995, 74th Leg., ch. 165 (S.B. 971), § 1, effective September 1, 1995.)

## Sec. 724.015.  Information Provided by Officer Before Requesting Specimen.

Before requesting a person to submit to the taking of a specimen, the officer shall inform the person orally and in writing that:

(1) if the person refuses to submit to the taking of the specimen, that refusal may be admissible in a subsequent prosecution;

(2) if the person refuses to submit to the taking of the specimen, the person's license to operate a motor vehicle will be automatically suspended, whether or not the person is subsequently prosecuted as a result of the arrest, for not less than 180 days;

(3) if the person refuses to submit to the taking of a specimen, the officer may apply for a warrant authorizing a specimen to be taken from the person;

(4) if the person is 21 years of age or older and submits to the taking of a specimen desig-

nated by the officer and an analysis of the specimen shows the person had an alcohol concentration of a level specified by Chapter 49, Penal Code, the person's license to operate a motor vehicle will be automatically suspended for not less than 90 days, whether or not the person is subsequently prosecuted as a result of the arrest;

(5) if the person is younger than 21 years of age and has any detectable amount of alcohol in the person's system, the person's license to operate a motor vehicle will be automatically suspended for not less than 60 days even if the person submits to the taking of the specimen, but that if the person submits to the taking of the specimen and an analysis of the specimen shows that the person had an alcohol concentration less than the level specified by Chapter 49, Penal Code, the person may be subject to criminal penalties less severe than those provided under that chapter;

(6) if the officer determines that the person is a resident without a license to operate a motor vehicle in this state, the department will deny to the person the issuance of a license, whether or not the person is subsequently prosecuted as a result of the arrest, under the same conditions and for the same periods that would have applied to a revocation of the person's driver's license if the person had held a driver's license issued by this state; and

(7) the person has a right to a hearing on the suspension or denial if, not later than the 15th day after the date on which the person receives the notice of suspension or denial or on which the person is considered to have received the notice by mail as provided by law, the department receives, at its headquarters in Austin, a written demand, including a facsimile transmission, or a request in another form prescribed by the department for the hearing. (Enacted by Acts 1995, 74th Leg., ch. 165 (S.B. 971), § 1, effective September 1, 1995; am. Acts 1997, 75th Leg., ch. 1013 (S.B. 35), § 34, effective September 1, 1997; am. Acts 2001, 77th Leg., ch. 444 (H.B. 63), § 8, effective September 1, 2001; am. Acts 2011, 82nd Leg., ch. 674 (S.B. 1787), § 1, effective September 1, 2011.)

### Sec. 724.016. Breath Specimen.

(a) A breath specimen taken at the request or order of a peace officer must be taken and analyzed under rules of the department by an individual possessing a certificate issued by the de-

partment certifying that the individual is qualified to perform the analysis.

(b) The department may:

(1) adopt rules approving satisfactory analytical methods; and

(2) ascertain the qualifications of an individual to perform the analysis.

(c) The department may revoke a certificate for cause.
(Enacted by Acts 1995, 74th Leg., ch. 165 (S.B. 971), § 1, effective September 1, 1995.)

### Sec. 724.017. Blood Specimen.

(a) Only a physician, qualified technician, chemist, registered professional nurse, or licensed vocational nurse may take a blood specimen at the request or order of a peace officer under this chapter. The blood specimen must be taken in a sanitary place.

(b) If the blood specimen was taken according to recognized medical procedures, the person who takes the blood specimen under this chapter, the facility that employs the person who takes the blood specimen, or the hospital where the blood specimen is taken is immune from civil liability for damages arising from the taking of the blood specimen at the request or order of the peace officer or pursuant to a search warrant as provided by this chapter and is not subject to discipline by any licensing or accrediting agency or body. This subsection does not relieve a person from liability for negligence in the taking of a blood specimen. The taking of a specimen from a person who objects to the taking of the specimen or who is resisting the taking of the specimen does not in itself constitute negligence and may not be considered evidence of negligence.

(c) In this section, "qualified technician" does not include emergency medical services personnel.

(d) A person whose blood specimen is taken under this chapter in a hospital is not considered to be present in the hospital for medical screening or treatment unless the appropriate hospital personnel determine that medical screening or treatment is required for proper medical care of the person.
(Enacted by Acts 1995, 74th Leg., ch. 165 (S.B. 971), § 1, effective September 1, 1995; am. Acts 2009, 81st Leg., ch. 1348 (S.B. 328), § 19, effective September 1, 2009.)

### Sec. 724.018. Furnishing Information Concerning Test Results.

On the request of a person who has given a specimen at the request of a peace officer, full

information concerning the analysis of the specimen shall be made available to the person or the person's attorney.
(Enacted by Acts 1995, 74th Leg., ch. 165 (S.B. 971), § 1, effective September 1, 1995.)

## Sec. 724.019. Additional Analysis by Request.

(a) A person who submits to the taking of a specimen of breath, blood, urine, or another bodily substance at the request or order of a peace officer may, on request and within a reasonable time not to exceed two hours after the arrest, have a physician, qualified technician, chemist, or registered professional nurse selected by the person take for analysis an additional specimen of the person's blood.

(b) The person shall be allowed a reasonable opportunity to contact a person specified by Subsection (a).

(c) A peace officer or law enforcement agency is not required to transport for testing a person who requests that a blood specimen be taken under this section.

(d) The failure or inability to obtain an additional specimen or analysis under this section does not preclude the admission of evidence relating to the analysis of the specimen taken at the request or order of the peace officer.

(e) A peace officer, another person acting for or on behalf of the state, or a law enforcement agency is not liable for damages arising from a person's request to have a blood specimen taken.
(Enacted by Acts 1995, 74th Leg., ch. 165 (S.B. 971), § 1, effective September 1, 1995.)

## Secs. 724.020 to 724.030 [Reserved for expansion].

## SUBCHAPTER C
## SUSPENSION OR DENIAL OF LICENSE ON REFUSAL OF SPECIMEN

## Sec. 724.031. Statement Requested on Refusal.

If a person refuses the request of a peace officer to submit to the taking of a specimen, the peace officer shall request the person to sign a statement that:

(1) the officer requested that the person submit to the taking of a specimen;

(2) the person was informed of the consequences of not submitting to the taking of a specimen; and

(3) the person refused to submit to the taking of a specimen.
(Enacted by Acts 1995, 74th Leg., ch. 165 (S.B. 971), § 1, effective September 1, 1995.)

## Sec. 724.032. Officer's Duties for License Suspension; Written Refusal Report.

(a) If a person refuses to submit to the taking of a specimen, whether expressly or because of an intentional failure of the person to give the specimen, the peace officer shall:

(1) serve notice of license suspension or denial on the person;

(2) take possession of any license issued by this state and held by the person arrested;

(3) issue a temporary driving permit to the person unless department records show or the officer otherwise determines that the person does not hold a license to operate a motor vehicle in this state; and

(4) make a written report of the refusal to the director of the department.

(b) The director must approve the form of the refusal report. The report must:

(1) show the grounds for the officer's belief that the person had been operating a motor vehicle or watercraft powered with an engine having a manufacturer's rating of 50 horsepower or above while intoxicated; and

(2) contain a copy of:

(A) the refusal statement requested under Section 724.031; or

(B) a statement signed by the officer that the person refused to:

(i) submit to the taking of the requested specimen; and

(ii) sign the requested statement under Section 724.031.

(c) The officer shall forward to the department not later than the fifth business day after the date of the arrest:

(1) a copy of the notice of suspension or denial;

(2) any license taken by the officer under Subsection (a);

(3) a copy of any temporary driving permit issued under Subsection (a); and

(4) a copy of the refusal report.

(d) The department shall develop forms for notices of suspension or denial and temporary driving permits to be used by all state and local law enforcement agencies.

(e) A temporary driving permit issued under this section expires on the 41st day after the date

**Transportation**

of issuance. If the person was driving a commercial motor vehicle, as defined by Section 522.003, a temporary driving permit that authorizes the person to drive a commercial motor vehicle is not effective until 24 hours after the time of arrest. (Enacted by Acts 1995, 74th Leg., ch. 165 (S.B. 971), § 1, effective September 1, 1995; am. Acts 2001, 77th Leg., ch. 444 (H.B. 63), § 9, effective September 1, 2001.)

### Sec. 724.033. Issuance by Department of Notice of Suspension or Denial of License.

(a) On receipt of a report of a peace officer under Section 724.032, if the officer did not serve notice of suspension or denial of a license at the time of refusal to submit to the taking of a specimen, the department shall mail notice of suspension or denial, by first class mail, to the address of the person shown by the records of the department or to the address given in the peace officer's report, if different.

(b) Notice is considered received on the fifth day after the date it is mailed. (Enacted by Acts 1995, 74th Leg., ch. 165 (S.B. 971), § 1, effective September 1, 1995; am. Acts 1999, 76th Leg., ch. 1409 (H.B. 2031), § 5, effective September 1, 1999.)

### Sec. 724.034. Contents of Notice of Suspension or Denial of License.

A notice of suspension or denial of a license must state:

(1) the reason and statutory grounds for the action;

(2) the effective date of the suspension or denial;

(3) the right of the person to a hearing;

(4) how to request a hearing; and

(5) the period in which a request for a hearing must be received by the department. (Enacted by Acts 1995, 74th Leg., ch. 165 (S.B. 971), § 1, effective September 1, 1995.)

### Sec. 724.035. Suspension or Denial of License.

(a) If a person refuses the request of a peace officer to submit to the taking of a specimen, the department shall:

(1) suspend the person's license to operate a motor vehicle on a public highway for 180 days; or

(2) if the person is a resident without a license, issue an order denying the issuance of a license to the person for 180 days.

(b) The period of suspension or denial is two years if the person's driving record shows one or more alcohol-related or drug-related enforcement contacts, as defined by Section 524.001(3), during the 10 years preceding the date of the person's arrest.

(c) A suspension or denial takes effect on the 40th day after the date on which the person:

(1) receives notice of suspension or denial under Section 724.032(a); or

(2) is considered to have received notice of suspension or denial under Section 724.033. (Enacted by Acts 1995, 74th Leg., ch. 165 (S.B. 971), § 1, effective September 1, 1995; am. Acts 1997, 75th Leg., ch. 165 (S.B. 898), § 30.163, effective September 1, 1997; am. Acts 1997, 75th Leg., ch. 1013 (S.B. 35), § 35, effective September 1, 1997; am. Acts 2001, 77th Leg., ch. 444 (H.B. 63), § 10, effective September 1, 2001.)

### Secs. 724.036 to 724.040 [Reserved for expansion].

### SUBCHAPTER D
### HEARING

### Sec. 724.041. Hearing on Suspension or Denial.

(a) If, not later than the 15th day after the date on which the person receives notice of suspension or denial under Section 724.032(a) or is considered to have received notice under Section 724.033, the department receives at its headquarters in Austin, in writing, including a facsimile transmission, or by another manner prescribed by the department, a request that a hearing be held, the State Office of Administrative Hearings shall hold a hearing.

(b) A hearing shall be held not earlier than the 11th day after the date the person is notified, unless the parties agree to waive this requirement, but before the effective date of the notice of suspension or denial.

(c) A request for a hearing stays the suspension or denial until the date of the final decision of the administrative law judge. If the person's license was taken by a peace officer under Section 724.032(a), the department shall notify the person of the effect of the request on the suspension of the person's license before the expiration of any temporary driving permit issued to the person, if the person is otherwise eligible, in a manner that will permit the person to establish to a peace officer that the person's license is not suspended.

(d) A hearing shall be held by an administrative law judge employed by the State Office of Administrative Hearings.

(e) A hearing shall be held:

(1) at a location designated by the State Office of Administrative Hearings:

(A) in the county of arrest if the county has a population of 300,000 or more; or

(B) in the county in which the person was alleged to have committed the offense for which the person was arrested or not more than 75 miles from the county seat of the county of arrest if the population of the county of arrest is less than 300,000; or

(2) with the consent of the person requesting the hearing and the department, by telephone conference call.

(f) The State Office of Administrative Hearings shall provide for the stenographic or electronic recording of a hearing under this subchapter.

(g) An administrative hearing under this section is governed by Sections 524.032(b) and (c), 524.035(e), 524.037(a), and 524.040.

(Enacted by Acts 1995, 74th Leg., ch. 165 (S.B. 971), § 1, effective September 1, 1995; am. Acts 1997, 75th Leg., ch. 165 (S.B. 898), § 30.164, effective September 1, 1997; am. Acts 2001, 77th Leg., ch. 444 (H.B. 63), § 11, effective September 1, 2001.)

## Sec. 724.042. Issues at Hearing.

The issues at a hearing under this subchapter are whether:

(1) reasonable suspicion or probable cause existed to stop or arrest the person;

(2) probable cause existed to believe that the person was:

(A) operating a motor vehicle in a public place while intoxicated; or

(B) operating a watercraft powered with an engine having a manufacturer's rating of 50 horsepower or above while intoxicated;

(3) the person was placed under arrest by the officer and was requested to submit to the taking of a specimen; and

(4) the person refused to submit to the taking of a specimen on request of the officer.

(Enacted by Acts 1995, 74th Leg., ch. 165 (S.B. 971), § 1, effective September 1, 1995; am. Acts 2001, 77th Leg., ch. 444 (H.B. 63), § 12, effective September 1, 2001.)

## Sec. 724.043. Findings of Administrative Law Judge.

(a) If the administrative law judge finds in the affirmative on each issue under Section 724.042,

the suspension order is sustained. If the person is a resident without a license, the department shall continue to deny to the person the issuance of a license for the applicable period provided by Section 724.035.

(b) If the administrative law judge does not find in the affirmative on each issue under Section 724.042, the department shall return the person's license to the person, if the license was taken by a peace officer under Section 724.032(a), and reinstate the person's license or rescind any order denying the issuance of a license because of the person's refusal to submit to the taking of a specimen under Section 724.032(a).

(Enacted by Acts 1995, 74th Leg., ch. 165 (S.B. 971), § 1, effective September 1, 1995; am. Acts 2001, 77th Leg., ch. 444 (H.B. 63), § 13, effective September 1, 2001.)

## Sec. 724.044. Waiver of Right to Hearing.

A person waives the right to a hearing under this subchapter and the department's suspension or denial is final and may not be appealed if the person:

(1) fails to request a hearing under Section 724.041; or

(2) requests a hearing and fails to appear, without good cause.

(Enacted by Acts 1995, 74th Leg., ch. 165 (S.B. 971), § 1, effective September 1, 1995.)

## Sec. 724.045. Prohibition on Probation of Suspension.

A suspension under this chapter may not be probated.

(Enacted by Acts 1995, 74th Leg., ch. 165 (S.B. 971), § 1, effective September 1, 1995.)

## Sec. 724.046. Reinstatement of License or Issuance of New License.

(a) A license suspended under this chapter may not be reinstated or a new license issued until the person whose license has been suspended pays to the department a fee of $125 in addition to any other fee required by law. A person subject to a denial order issued under this chapter may not obtain a license after the period of denial has ended until the person pays to the department a fee of $125 in addition to any other fee required by law.

(b) If a suspension or denial under this chapter is rescinded by the department, an administrative law judge, or a court, payment of the fee under this section is not required for reinstatement or issuance of a license.

(c) Each fee collected under this section shall be deposited to the credit of the Texas mobility fund.

(Enacted by Acts 1995, 74th Leg., ch. 165 (S.B. 971), § 1, effective September 1, 1995; am. Acts 2001, 77th Leg., ch. 444 (H.B. 63), § 14(b), effective September 1, 2001; am. Acts 2003, 78th Leg., ch. 1325 (H.B. 3588), § 11.09, effective September 1, 2003.)

### Sec. 724.047.  Appeal.

Chapter 524 governs an appeal from an action of the department, following an administrative hearing under this chapter, in suspending or denying the issuance of a license.

(Enacted by Acts 1995, 74th Leg., ch. 165 (S.B. 971), § 1, effective September 1, 1995.)

### Sec. 724.048.  Relationship of Administrative Proceeding to Criminal Proceeding.

(a) The determination of the department or administrative law judge:

(1) is a civil matter;

(2) is independent of and is not an estoppel as to any matter in issue in an adjudication of a criminal charge arising from the occurrence that is the basis for the suspension or denial; and

(3) does not preclude litigation of the same or similar facts in a criminal prosecution.

(b) Except as provided by Subsection (c), the disposition of a criminal charge does not affect a license suspension or denial under this chapter and is not an estoppel as to any matter in issue in a suspension or denial proceeding under this chapter.

(c) If a criminal charge arising from the same arrest as a suspension under this chapter results in an acquittal, the suspension under this chapter may not be imposed. If a suspension under this chapter has already been imposed, the department shall rescind the suspension and remove references to the suspension from the computerized driving record of the individual.

(Enacted by Acts 1995, 74th Leg., ch. 165 (S.B. 971), § 1, effective September 1, 1995; am. Acts 1997, 75th Leg., ch. 1013 (S.B. 35), § 36, effective September 1, 1997.)

Secs. 724.049 to 724.060 [Reserved for expansion].

### SUBCHAPTER E
### ADMISSIBILITY OF EVIDENCE

### Sec. 724.061.  Admissibility of Refusal of Person to Submit to Taking of Specimen.

A person's refusal of a request by an officer to submit to the taking of a specimen of breath or blood, whether the refusal was express or the result of an intentional failure to give the specimen, may be introduced into evidence at the person's trial.

(Enacted by Acts 1995, 74th Leg., ch. 165 (S.B. 971), § 1, effective September 1, 1995.)

### Sec. 724.062.  Admissibility of Refusal of Request for Additional Test.

The fact that a person's request to have an additional analysis under Section 724.019 is refused by the officer or another person acting for or on behalf of the state, that the person was not provided a reasonable opportunity to contact a person specified by Section 724.019(a) to take the specimen, or that reasonable access was not allowed to the arrested person may be introduced into evidence at the person's trial.

(Enacted by Acts 1995, 74th Leg., ch. 165 (S.B. 971), § 1, effective September 1, 1995.)

### Sec. 724.063.  Admissibility of Alcohol Concentration or Presence of Substance.

Evidence of alcohol concentration or the presence of a controlled substance, drug, dangerous drug, or other substance obtained by an analysis authorized by Section 724.014 is admissible in a civil or criminal action.

(Enacted by Acts 1995, 74th Leg., ch. 165 (S.B. 971), § 1, effective September 1, 1995; am. Acts 1997, 75th Leg., ch. 165 (S.B. 898), § 30.165, effective September 1, 1997.)

### Sec. 724.064.  Admissibility in Criminal Proceeding of Specimen Analysis.

On the trial of a criminal proceeding arising out of an offense under Chapter 49, Penal Code, involving the operation of a motor vehicle or a watercraft, or an offense under Section 106.041, Alcoholic Beverage Code, evidence of the alcohol concentration or presence of a controlled substance, drug, dangerous drug, or other substance as shown by analysis of a specimen of the person's blood, breath, or urine or any other bodily substance taken at the request or order of a peace officer is admissible.

(Enacted by Acts 1995, 74th Leg., ch. 165 (S.B. 971), § 1, effective September 1, 1995; am. Acts 1997, 75th Leg., ch. 1013 (S.B. 35), § 37, effective September 1, 1997.)

# CHAPTER 725
# TRANSPORTATION OF LOOSE MATERIALS

### Subchapter A. General Provisions

## SUBCHAPTER A
## GENERAL PROVISIONS

## Sec. 725.001.  Definitions.

In this chapter:

(1) "Load" means a load of loose material.

(2) "Loose material" means material that can be blown or spilled from a vehicle because of movement or exposure to air, wind currents, or other weather. The term includes dirt, sand, gravel, refuse, and wood chips but excludes an agricultural product in its natural state.

(3) "Motor vehicle" has the meaning assigned by Section 621.001.

(4) "Public highway" includes a public road or street.

(4-a) "Refuse" means trash, rubbish, garbage, or any other discarded material.

(5) "Semitrailer" has the meaning assigned by Section 621.001.

(6) "Trailer" has the meaning assigned by Section 621.001.

(7) "Vehicle" has the meaning assigned by Section 621.001.

(Enacted by Acts 1995, 74th Leg., ch. 165 (S.B. 971), § 1, effective September 1, 1995; am. Acts 2007, 80th Leg., ch. 800 (S.B. 387), § 1, effective September 1, 2007.)

## Sec. 725.002.  Applicability.

This chapter applies to any motor vehicle, trailer, or semitrailer operated on a public high-

way except a vehicle or construction or mining equipment that is:

(1) moving between construction barricades on a public works project; or

(2) crossing a public highway.

(Enacted by Acts 1995, 74th Leg., ch. 165 (S.B. 971), § 1, effective September 1, 1995; am. Acts 2007, 80th Leg., ch. 800 (S.B. 387), § 2, effective September 1, 2007.)

## Sec. 725.003.  Offense; Penalty.

(a) A person or the person's agent or employee may not transport loose material in violation of this chapter.

(b) A person, excluding this state or a political subdivision of this state but including an agent or employee of this state or a political subdivision of this state, commits an offense if the person violates Subsection (a).

(c) An offense under this section is a misdemeanor punishable by a fine of not less than $25 or more than $500.

(Enacted by Acts 1995, 74th Leg., ch. 165 (S.B. 971), § 1, effective September 1, 1995; am. Acts 2005, 79th Leg., ch. 938 (H.B. 754), § 1, effective September 1, 2005; am. Acts 2007, 80th Leg., ch. 800 (S.B. 387), § 3, effective September 1, 2007.)

## Secs. 725.004 to 725.020 [Reserved for expansion].

## SUBCHAPTER B
## REQUIREMENTS FOR
## TRANSPORTING LOOSE MATERIALS

## Sec. 725.021.  Containing Loose Materials.

(a) A vehicle subject to this chapter shall be equipped and maintained as required by this section to prevent loose material from escaping by blowing or spilling.

(b) A vehicle bed carrying a load:

(1) may not have a hole, crack, or other opening through which loose material can escape; and

(2) shall be enclosed:

(A) on both sides by side panels;

(B) on the front by a panel or the vehicle cab; and

(C) on the rear by a tailgate or panel.

(c) Except as provided by Subsection (e), the load shall be covered and the covering firmly secured at the front and back, unless the load:

(1) is completely enclosed by the load-carrying compartment; or

(2) does not blow from or spill over the top of the load-carrying compartment.

(d) The tailgate of the vehicle shall be securely closed to prevent spillage during transportation.

(e) If the vehicle is a commercial motor vehicle transporting loose material, the load shall be covered and the covering firmly secured at the front and back or shall be completely enclosed by the load-carrying compartment. For purposes of this section, "commercial motor vehicle" means a motor vehicle, trailer, or semitrailer used primarily in the business of transporting property.
(Enacted by Acts 1995, 74th Leg., ch. 165 (S.B. 971), § 1, effective September 1, 1995; am. Acts 2005, 79th Leg., ch. 938 (H.B. 754), § 2, effective September 1, 2005; am. Acts 2007, 80th Leg., ch. 800 (S.B. 387), § 4, effective September 1, 2007.)

### Sec. 725.022. Maintaining Non-Load-Carrying Vehicle Parts.

(a) Loose material that is spilled because of loading on a vehicle part that does not carry the load shall be removed before the vehicle is operated on a public highway.

(b) After the vehicle is unloaded and before the vehicle is operated on a public highway, residue of transported loose material on a vehicle part that does not carry the load shall be removed from the vehicle part.
(Enacted by Acts 1995, 74th Leg., ch. 165 (S.B. 971), § 1, effective September 1, 1995.)

## CHAPTER 726
## TESTING AND INSPECTION OF MOTOR VEHICLES BY CERTAIN MUNICIPALITIES

### Sec. 726.001. Applicability.

(a) This chapter applies only to a municipality with a population of more than 290,000.

(b) This section or an ordinance adopted under this section does not apply to a motor vehicle, trailer, or semitrailer operated under a registration certificate issued under Chapter 643.
(Enacted by Acts 1995, 74th Leg., ch. 165 (S.B. 971), § 1, effective September 1, 1995; am. Acts

1997, 75th Leg., ch. 165 (S.B. 898), § 30.166, effective September 1, 1997.)

### Sec. 726.002. Testing and Inspection of Motor Vehicles.

A municipality may adopt an ordinance:

(1) requiring each resident of the municipality, including a corporation having its principal office or place of business in the municipality, who owns a motor vehicle used for the transportation of persons or property and each person operating a motor vehicle on the public thoroughfares of the municipality to have each motor vehicle owned or operated, as appropriate, tested and inspected not more than four times in each calendar year;

(2) requiring each motor vehicle involved in an accident to be tested and inspected before it may be operated on the public thoroughfares of the municipality; or

(3) requiring that a motor vehicle operated on the public thoroughfares of the municipality be tested, inspected, and approved by the testing and inspecting authority.
(Enacted by Acts 1995, 74th Leg., ch. 165 (S.B. 971), § 1, effective September 1, 1995.)

### Sec. 726.003. Motor Vehicle Testing Stations; Testing and Inspection Fee.

(a) A municipality may acquire, establish, improve, operate, and maintain motor vehicle testing stations and pay for the stations from fees charged for testing and inspecting motor vehicles.

(b) A municipality may impose a fee for the testing and inspecting of a motor vehicle. The fee may not exceed $1 a year. Fees collected under this subsection shall be placed in a separate fund from which may be paid the costs in connection with automotive and safety education programs and the acquisition, establishment, improvement, operation, and maintenance of the testing stations.
(Enacted by Acts 1995, 74th Leg., ch. 165 (S.B. 971), § 1, effective September 1, 1995.)

### Sec. 726.004. Financing of Motor Vehicle Testing Stations.

(a) A municipality may borrow money to finance all or part of the cost of the acquisition, establishment, improvement, or repair of motor vehicle testing stations and may pledge all or part of the fees or other receipts derived from the operation of the stations for payment of principal and interest on the loan.

(b) A municipality may encumber a testing station, including things acquired pertaining to the station, to secure the payment of funds to construct all or part of the station or to improve, operate, or maintain the station. An encumbrance is not a debt of the municipality but is solely a charge on the property encumbered and may not be considered in determining the power of the municipality to issue bonds.

(Enacted by Acts 1995, 74th Leg., ch. 165 (S.B. 971), § 1, effective September 1, 1995.)

# CHAPTER 727
# MODIFICATION OF, TAMPERING WITH, AND EQUIPMENT OF MOTOR VEHICLES

## Sec. 727.001. Minimum Road Clearance of Certain Vehicles; Offense.

(a) A person commits an offense if the person operates on a public roadway a passenger or commercial vehicle that has been modified from its original design or weighted so that the clearance between any part of the vehicle other than the wheels and the surface of the level roadway is less than the clearance between the roadway and the lowest part of the rim of any wheel in contact with the roadway.

(b) An offense under this section is a misdemeanor punishable by a fine not to exceed $50.

(Enacted by Acts 1995, 74th Leg., ch. 165 (S.B. 971), § 1, effective September 1, 1995.)

## Sec. 727.002. Tampering with Odometer; Offense.

(a) A person commits an offense if the person, with intent to defraud, disconnects or resets an odometer to reduce the number of miles indicated on the odometer.

(b) Except as provided by Subsection (c), an offense under this section is punishable by:

(1) confinement in the county jail for not more than two years;

(2) a fine not to exceed $1,000; or

(3) both the confinement and fine.

(c) If it is shown on the trial of an offense under this section that the person has previously been convicted of an offense under this section, the offense is punishable by:

(1) confinement in the county jail for not less than 30 days or more than two years; and

(2) a fine not to exceed $2,000.

(d) In this section, "odometer" means an instrument for measuring and recording the distance a motor vehicle travels while in operation but does not include an auxiliary odometer designed to be reset by the operator to record mileage on trips.

(Enacted by Acts 1995, 74th Leg., ch. 165 (S.B. 971), § 1, effective September 1, 1995.)

## Sec. 727.003. Tire Equipment of Motor Vehicle, Trailer, or Tractor; Offense.

(a) A person commits an offense if the person operates or permits to be operated on a public highway a motor vehicle, trailer, semitrailer, or tractor equipped with:

(1) solid rubber tires less than one inch in thickness at any point from the surface to the rim; or

(2) pneumatic tires, one or more of which has been removed.

(b) An offense under this section is a misdemeanor punishable by a fine not to exceed $200.

(Enacted by Acts 1995, 74th Leg., ch. 165 (S.B. 971), § 1, effective September 1, 1995.)

## Sec. 727.004. Rim or Tire Width; Offense.

(a) A person commits an offense if the person sells or offers for sale a road vehicle, including a wagon, that has a rim or tire width less than:

(1) three inches, if the vehicle has an intended carrying capacity of more than 2,000 pounds and not more than 4,500 pounds; or

(2) four inches, if the vehicle has an intended carrying capacity of more than 4,500 pounds.

(b) This section does not apply to an individual who sells or offers for sale a road vehicle purchased for the individual's use.

(c) An offense under this section is punishable by a fine of not less than $100 or more than $1,000.

(Enacted by Acts 1995, 74th Leg., ch. 165 (S.B. 971), § 1, effective September 1, 1995.)

Transportation

# CHAPTER 728
## SALE OR TRANSFER OF MOTOR VEHICLES AND MASTER KEYS

## SUBCHAPTER A
## SALE OF MOTOR VEHICLES ON CONSECUTIVE SATURDAY AND SUNDAY

### Sec. 728.001.   Definitions.

In this subchapter:

(1) "Employer" means a person who:

(A) owns a facility that sells or offers for sale motor vehicles; or

(B) has the authority to determine the hours of operation of the facility.

(2) "Motor vehicle" means a self-propelled vehicle of two or more wheels designed to transport a person or property.

(Enacted by Acts 1995, 74th Leg., ch. 165 (S.B. 971), § 1, effective September 1, 1995.)

### Sec. 728.002.   Sale of Motor Vehicles on Consecutive Saturday and Sunday Prohibited.

(a) A person may not, on consecutive days of Saturday and Sunday:

(1) sell or offer for sale a motor vehicle; or

(2) compel an employee to sell or offer for sale a motor vehicle.

(b) Each day a motor vehicle is offered for sale is a separate violation. Each sale of a motor vehicle is a separate violation.

(c) This section does not prohibit the occasional sale of a motor vehicle by a person not in a business that includes the sale of motor vehicles.

(d) This section does not prohibit the quoting of a price for a motor home, tow truck, or towable recreational vehicle at a show or exhibition described by Section 2301.358, Occupations Code. (Enacted by Acts 1995, 74th Leg., ch. 165 (S.B. 971), § 1, effective September 1, 1995; am. Acts 2011, 82nd Leg., ch. 553 (H.B. 2872), § 1, effective June 17, 2011.)

### Sec. 728.003.   Civil Penalty.

(a) A person who violates Section 728.002 is subject to a civil penalty of:

(1) not more than $500 for a first violation;

(2) not less than $500 or more than $1,000 for a second violation; or

(3) not less than $1,000 or more than $5,000 for a third or subsequent violation.

(b) On a finding by the trier of fact that a person wilfully or with conscious indifference violated Section 728.002, the court may triple the penalty due under Subsection (a). (Enacted by Acts 1995, 74th Leg., ch. 165 (S.B. 971), § 1, effective September 1, 1995.)

### Sec. 728.004.   Enforcement; Injunction.

(a) The attorney general or a district, county, or municipal attorney may enforce this subchapter and may bring an action in the county in which a violation is alleged.

(b) The operation of a business in violation of this subchapter is a public nuisance. Any person, including a district, county, or municipal attorney, may obtain an injunction restraining a violation of this subchapter. A person who obtains an injunction under this subsection may recover the person's costs, including court costs and reasonable attorney's fees.

(c) An employer is a necessary party to an action brought against its employee under this section. An employer is strictly liable for all amounts, including civil penalties, damages, costs, and attorney's fees, resulting from a violation of Section 728.002 by its employee. (Enacted by Acts 1995, 74th Leg., ch. 165 (S.B. 971), § 1, effective September 1, 1995.)

Secs. 728.005 to 728.010 [Reserved for expansion].

## SUBCHAPTER B
## SALE OF MASTER KEY FOR MOTOR VEHICLE IGNITIONS

### Sec. 728.011. Sale of Master Key for Motor Vehicle Ignitions.

(a) A person commits an offense if the person sells or offers to sell a master key knowingly designed to fit the ignition switch on more than one motor vehicle.

(b) An offense under this section is a misdemeanor punishable by a fine of not less than $25 or more than $200.

(Enacted by Acts 1995, 74th Leg., ch. 165 (S.B. 971), § 1, effective September 1, 1995.)

Secs. 728.012 to 728.020 [Reserved for expansion].

## SUBCHAPTER C
## TRANSFER OF OWNERSHIP OF CERTAIN EMERGENCY VEHICLES

### Sec. 728.021. Transfer of Ownership of Certain Emergency Vehicles; Offense.

(a) The owner of an authorized emergency vehicle that is used to transport sick or injured persons commits an offense if the owner transfers ownership of the vehicle without:

(1) removing from the vehicle any vehicle equipment, including a light, siren, or device, that under Subtitle C only an authorized emergency vehicle may be equipped with; and

(2) removing or obliterating any emblem or marking on the vehicle that identifies the vehicle as an authorized emergency vehicle.

(b) Subsection (a) does not apply if the owner of the vehicle transfers ownership of the vehicle to a person:

(1) who holds a license as an emergency medical services provider under Chapter 773, Health and Safety Code;

(2) who is in the business of buying and selling used vehicles in this state and who specializes in authorized emergency vehicles; or

(3) described by Section 541.201 or a similar person operating in a foreign country.

(c) An offense under this section is a Class C misdemeanor.

(d) In this section:

(1) "Authorized emergency vehicle" has the meaning assigned by Section 541.201.

(2) "Vehicle equipment" has the meaning assigned by Section 547.001.

(Enacted by Acts 1995, 74th Leg., ch. 165 (S.B. 971), § 1, effective September 1, 1995.)

## CHAPTER 729
## OPERATION OF MOTOR VEHICLE BY MINOR

**Section**
729.001. Operation of Motor Vehicle by Minor in Violation of Traffic Laws; Offense.
729.002. Operation of Motor Vehicle by Minor Without License.

### Sec. 729.001. Operation of Motor Vehicle by Minor in Violation of Traffic Laws; Offense.

(a) A person who is younger than 17 years of age commits an offense if the person operates a motor vehicle on a public road or highway, a street or alley in a municipality, or a public beach in violation of any traffic law of this state, including:

(1) Chapter 502, other than Section 502.282 or 502.412;

(2) Chapter 521, other than an offense under Section 521.457;

(3) Subtitle C, other than an offense punishable by imprisonment or by confinement in jail under Section 550.021, 550.022, 550.024, or 550.025;

(4) Chapter 601;

(5) Chapter 621;

(6) Chapter 661; and

(7) Chapter 681.

(b) In this section, "beach" means a beach bordering on the Gulf of Mexico that extends inland from the line of mean low tide to the natural line of vegetation bordering on the seaward shore of the Gulf of Mexico, or the larger contiguous area to which the public has acquired a right of use or easement to or over by prescription, dedication, or estoppel, or has retained a right by virtue of continuous right in the public since time immemorial as recognized by law or custom.

(c) An offense under this section is punishable by the fine or other sanction, other than confinement or imprisonment, authorized by statute for violation of the traffic law listed under Subsection (a) that is the basis of the prosecution under this section.

(Enacted by Acts 1995, 74th Leg., ch. 165 (S.B. 971), § 1, effective September 1, 1995; am. Acts 1997, 75th Leg., ch. 165 (S.B. 898), § 30.167, effective September 1, 1997; am. Acts 1997, 75th Leg., ch. 822 (S.B. 81), § 1, effective September 1, 1997; am. Acts 1997, 75th Leg., ch. 1086 (H.B. 1550), § 40, effective September 1, 1997; am. Acts 1999, 76th Leg., ch. 1477 (H.B. 3517), § 36, effective September 1, 1999; am. Acts 2003, 78th Leg., ch. 283 (H.B. 2319), § 58, effective September 1, 2003.)

### Sec. 729.002.  Operation of Motor Vehicle by Minor Without License.

(a) A person who is younger than 17 years of age commits an offense if the person operates a motor vehicle without a driver's license authorizing the operation of a motor vehicle on a:

(1)  public road or highway;

(2)  street or alley in a municipality; or

(3)  public beach as defined by Section 729.001.

(b) An offense under this section is punishable in the same manner as if the person was 17 years of age or older and operated a motor vehicle without a license as described by Subsection (a), except that an offense under this section is not punishable by confinement or imprisonment.

(Enacted by Acts 1995, 74th Leg., ch. 165 (S.B. 971), § 1, effective September 1, 1995; am. Acts 1997, 75th Leg., ch. 1086 (H.B. 1550), § 43, effective September 1, 1997; am. Acts 1999, 76th Leg., ch. 1477 (H.B. 3517), § 37, effective September 1, 1999.)

### Sec. 729.003.  Procedure in Cases Involving Minors [Repealed].

Repealed by Acts 2005, 79th Leg., ch. 949 (H.B. 1575), § 52(2), effective September 1, 2005.

(Enacted by Acts 1995, 74th Leg., ch. 165 (S.B. 971), § 1, effective September 1, 1995; am. Acts 1997, 75th Leg., ch. 165 (S.B. 898), § 30.168(a), effective September 1, 1997; am. Acts 1997, 75th Leg., ch. 1086 (H.B. 1550), § 44, effective September 1, 1997; am. Acts 2003, 78th Leg., ch. 283 (H.B. 2319), §§ 59, 60, 61(2), effective September 1, 2003.)

### Sec. 729.004.  Fine for Offense in Construction or Maintenance Work Zone [Repealed].

Repealed by Acts 2003, 78th Leg., ch. 283 (H.B. 2319), § 61(2), effective September 1, 2003.

(Enacted by Acts 1997, 75th Leg., ch. 674 (H.B. 981), § 3, effective January 1, 1998; am. Acts

1999, 76th Leg., ch. 789 (H.B. 1425), § 4, effective September 1, 1999.)

## CHAPTER 730
## MOTOR VEHICLE RECORDS DISCLOSURE ACT

### Sec. 730.001.   Short Title.

This chapter may be cited as the Motor Vehicle Records Disclosure Act.

(Enacted by Acts 1997, 75th Leg., ch. 1187 (S.B. 1069), § 1, effective September 1, 1997.)

### Sec. 730.002.   Purpose.

The purpose of this chapter is to implement 18 U.S.C. Chapter 123 and to protect the interest of an individual in the individual's personal privacy by prohibiting the disclosure and use of personal information contained in motor vehicle records, except as authorized by the individual or by law.

(Enacted by Acts 1997, 75th Leg., ch. 1187 (S.B. 1069), § 1, effective September 1, 1997.)

### Sec. 730.003.   Definitions.

In this chapter:

(1) "Agency" includes any agency or political subdivision of this state, or an authorized agent or contractor of an agency or political subdivision of this state, that compiles or maintains motor vehicle records.

(2) "Disclose" means to make available or make known personal information contained in a motor vehicle record about a person to another person, by any means of communication.

(3) "Individual record" means a motor vehicle record obtained by an agency containing personal information about an individual who

is the subject of the record as identified in a request.

(4) "Motor vehicle record" means a record that pertains to a motor vehicle operator's or driver's license or permit, motor vehicle registration, motor vehicle title, or identification document issued by an agency of this state or a local agency authorized to issue an identification document. The term does not include:

(A) a record that pertains to a motor carrier; or

(B) an accident report prepared under Chapter 550 or 601.

(5) "Person" means an individual, organization, or entity but does not include this state or an agency of this state.

(6) "Personal information" means information that identifies a person, including an individual's photograph or computerized image, social security number, driver identification number, name, address, but not the zip code, telephone number, and medical or disability information. The term does not include:

(A) information on vehicle accidents, driving or equipment-related violations, or driver's license or registration status; or

(B) information contained in an accident report prepared under Chapter 550 or 601.

(7) "Record" includes any book, paper, photograph, photostat, card, film, tape, recording, electronic data, printout, or other documentary material regardless of physical form or characteristics.

(Enacted by Acts 1997, 75th Leg., ch. 1187 (S.B. 1069), § 1, effective September 1, 1997; am. Acts 2001, 77th Leg., ch. 1032 (H.B. 1544), § 6, effective September 1, 2001.)

### Sec. 730.004. Prohibition on Disclosure and Use of Personal Information from Motor Vehicle Records.

Notwithstanding any other provision of law to the contrary, including Chapter 552, Government Code, except as provided by Sections 730.005—730.007, an agency may not disclose personal information about any person obtained by the agency in connection with a motor vehicle record. (Enacted by Acts 1997, 75th Leg., ch. 1187 (S.B. 1069), § 1, effective September 1, 1997; am. Acts 2001, 77th Leg., ch. 1032 (H.B. 1544), § 7, effective September 1, 2001.)

### Sec. 730.005. Required Disclosure.

Personal information obtained by an agency in connection with a motor vehicle record shall be disclosed for use in connection with any matter of:

(1) motor vehicle or motor vehicle operator safety;

(2) motor vehicle theft;

(3) motor vehicle emissions;

(4) motor vehicle product alterations, recalls, or advisories;

(5) performance monitoring of motor vehicles or motor vehicle dealers by a motor vehicle manufacturer;

(6) removal of nonowner records from the original owner records of a motor vehicle manufacturer to carry out the purposes of:

(A) the Automobile Information Disclosure Act, 15 U.S.C. Section 1231 et seq.;

(B) 49 U.S.C. Chapters 301, 305, 323, 325, 327, 329, and 331;

(C) the Anti Car Theft Act of 1992, 18 U.S.C. Sections 553, 981, 982, 2119, 2312, 2313, and 2322, 19 U.S.C. Sections 1646b and 1646c, and 42 U.S.C. Section 3750a et seq., all as amended;

(D) the Clean Air Act, 42 U.S.C. Section 7401 et seq., as amended; and

(E) any other statute or regulation enacted or adopted under or in relation to a law included in Paragraphs (A)—(D);

(7) child support enforcement under Chapter 231, Family Code; or

(8) enforcement by the Texas Workforce Commission under Title 4, Labor Code.

(Enacted by Acts 1997, 75th Leg., ch. 1187 (S.B. 1069), § 1, effective September 1, 1997; am. Acts 2001, 77th Leg., ch. 1023 (H.B. 1365), § 72, effective September 1, 2001; am. Acts 2011, 82nd Leg., ch. 869 (S.B. 76), § 6, effective September 1, 2011.)

### Sec. 730.006. Required Disclosure with Consent.

Personal information obtained by an agency in connection with a motor vehicle record shall be disclosed to a requestor who demonstrates, in such form and manner as the agency requires, that the requestor has obtained the written consent of the person who is the subject of the information.

(Enacted by Acts 1997, 75th Leg., ch. 1187 (S.B. 1069), § 1, effective September 1, 1997.)

### Sec. 730.007. Permitted Disclosures.

(a) Personal information obtained by an agency in connection with a motor vehicle record may be disclosed to any requestor by an agency if the requestor:

(1) provides the requestor's name and address and any proof of that information required by the agency; and

(2) represents that the use of the personal information will be strictly limited to:

(A) use by:

(i) a government agency, including any court or law enforcement agency, in carrying out its functions; or

(ii) a private person or entity acting on behalf of a government agency in carrying out the functions of the agency;

(B) use in connection with a matter of:

(i) motor vehicle or motor vehicle operator safety;

(ii) motor vehicle theft;

(iii) motor vehicle product alterations, recalls, or advisories;

(iv) performance monitoring of motor vehicles, motor vehicle parts, or motor vehicle dealers;

(v) motor vehicle market research activities, including survey research; or

(vi) removal of nonowner records from the original owner records of motor vehicle manufacturers;

(C) use in the normal course of business by a legitimate business or an authorized agent of the business, but only:

(i) to verify the accuracy of personal information submitted by the individual to the business or the agent of the business; and

(ii) if the information is not correct, to obtain the correct information, for the sole purpose of preventing fraud by, pursuing a legal remedy against, or recovering on a debt or security interest against the individual;

(D) use in conjunction with a civil, criminal, administrative, or arbitral proceeding in any court or government agency or before any self-regulatory body, including service of process, investigation in anticipation of litigation, execution or enforcement of a judgment or order, or under an order of any court;

(E) use in research or in producing statistical reports, but only if the personal information is not published, redisclosed, or used to contact any individual;

(F) use by an insurer or insurance support organization, or by a self-insured entity, or an authorized agent of the entity, in connection with claims investigation activities, antifraud activities, rating, or underwriting;

(G) use in providing notice to an owner of a towed or impounded vehicle;

(H) use by a licensed private investigator agency or licensed security service for a purpose permitted under this section;

(I) use by an employer or an agent or insurer of the employer to obtain or verify information relating to a holder of a commercial driver's license that is required under 49 U.S.C. Chapter 313;

(J) use in connection with the operation of a private toll transportation facility;

(K) use by a consumer reporting agency, as defined by the Fair Credit Reporting Act (15 U.S.C. Section 1681 et seq.), for a purpose permitted under that Act; or

(L) use for any other purpose specifically authorized by law that relates to the operation of a motor vehicle or to public safety.

(b) The only personal information an agency may release under this section is the individual's:

(1) name and address;

(2) date of birth; and

(3) driver's license number.

(c) This section does not:

(1) prohibit the disclosure of a person's photographic image to:

(A) a law enforcement agency or a criminal justice agency for an official purpose;

(B) an agency of this state investigating an alleged violation of a state or federal law relating to the obtaining, selling, or purchasing of a benefit authorized by Chapter 31 or 33, Human Resources Code; or

(C) an agency of this state investigating an alleged violation of a state or federal law under authority provided by Title 4, Labor Code; or

(2) prevent a court from compelling by subpoena the production of a person's photographic image.

(d) Personal information obtained by an agency in connection with a motor vehicle record shall be disclosed to a requestor by an agency if the requestor:

(1) provides the requestor's name and address and any proof of that information required by the agency; and

(2) represents that the intent of the requestor is to use personal information in the motor vehicle record only for the purpose of preventing, detecting, or protecting against personal identity theft or other acts of fraud

and provides any proof of the requestor's intent required by the agency.

(e) If the agency determines that the requestor intends to use personal information requested under Subsection (d) only for the represented purpose, the agency shall release to the requestor any requested personal information in the motor vehicle record.

(f) Personal information obtained by an agency under Section 411.0845, Government Code, in connection with a motor vehicle record may be disclosed as provided by that section.

(Enacted by Acts 1997, 75th Leg., ch. 1187 (S.B. 1069), § 1, effective September 1, 1997; am. Acts 2001, 77th Leg., ch. 1032 (H.B. 1544), § 7, effective September 1, 2001; am. Acts 2007, 80th Leg., ch. 1372 (S.B. 9), § 26, effective June 15, 2007; am. Acts 2011, 82nd Leg., ch. 869 (S.B. 76), § 7, effective September 1, 2011.)

## Sec. 730.008. Disclosure of Individual Record [Repealed].

Repealed by Acts 2001, 77th Leg., ch. 1032 (H.B. 1544), § 9(1), effective September 1, 2001. (Enacted by Acts 1997, 75th Leg., ch. 1187 (S.B. 1069), § 1, effective September 1, 1997.)

## Sec. 730.009. Requests to Prohibit Disclosure [Repealed].

Repealed by Acts 2001, 77th Leg., ch. 1032 (H.B. 1544), § 9(1), effective September 1, 2001. (Enacted by Acts 1997, 75th Leg., ch. 1187 (S.B. 1069), § 1, effective September 1, 1997.)

## Sec. 730.010. Disclosure of Thumb or Finger Images Prohibited.

Notwithstanding any other provision of this chapter, if an agency obtains an image of an individual's thumb or finger in connection with the issuance of a license, permit, or certificate to the individual, the agency may:

(1) use the image only:

(A) in connection with the issuance of the license, permit, or certificate; or

(B) to verify the identity of an individual as provided by Section 521.059; and

(2) disclose the image only if disclosure is expressly authorized by law.

(Enacted by Acts 1997, 75th Leg., ch. 1187 (S.B. 1069), § 1, effective September 1, 1997; am. Acts 2005, 79th Leg., ch. 1108 (H.B. 2337), § 6, effective September 1, 2005.)

## Sec. 730.011. Fees.

Unless a fee is imposed by law, an agency that has obtained information in connection with a motor vehicle may adopt reasonable fees for disclosure of that personal information under this chapter.

(Enacted by Acts 1997, 75th Leg., ch. 1187 (S.B. 1069), § 1, effective September 1, 1997.)

## Sec. 730.012. Additional Conditions.

(a) In addition to the payment of a fee adopted under Section 730.011, an agency may require a requestor to provide reasonable assurance:

(1) as to the identity of the requestor; and

(2) that use of the personal information will be only as authorized or that the consent of the person who is the subject of the information has been obtained.

(b) An agency may require the requestor to make or file a written application in the form and containing any certification requirement the agency may prescribe.

(Enacted by Acts 1997, 75th Leg., ch. 1187 (S.B. 1069), § 1, effective September 1, 1997.)

## Sec. 730.013. Resale or Redisclosure.

(a) An authorized recipient of personal information may not resell or redisclose the personal information in the identical or a substantially identical format the personal information was disclosed to the recipient by the applicable agency.

(b) An authorized recipient of personal information may resell or redisclose the information only for a use permitted under Section 730.007.

(c) Any authorized recipient who resells or rediscloses personal information obtained from an agency shall be required by that agency to:

(1) maintain for a period of not less than five years records as to any person or entity receiving that information and the permitted use for which it was obtained; and

(2) provide copies of those records to the agency on request.

(d) A person commits an offense if the person violates this section. An offense under this subsection is a misdemeanor punishable by a fine not to exceed $25,000.

(Enacted by Acts 1997, 75th Leg., ch. 1187 (S.B. 1069), § 1, effective September 1, 1997; am. Acts 2001, 77th Leg., ch. 1032 (H.B. 1544), § 7, effective September 1, 2001.)

## Sec. 730.014. Agency Rules; Organization of Records.

(a) Each agency may adopt rules to implement and administer this chapter.

(b) An agency that maintains motor vehicle records in relation to motor vehicles is not required to also maintain those records in relation to the individuals named in those records.
(Enacted by Acts 1997, 75th Leg., ch. 1187 (S.B. 1069), § 1, effective September 1, 1997.)

## Sec. 730.015. Penalty for False Representation.

(a) A person who requests the disclosure of personal information from an agency's records under this chapter and misrepresents the person's identity or who makes a false statement to the agency on an application required by the agency under this chapter commits an offense.
(b) An offense under Subsection (a) is a Class A misdemeanor.
(Enacted by Acts 1997, 75th Leg., ch. 1187 (S.B. 1069), § 1, effective September 1, 1997.)

## Sec. 730.016. Ineligibility of Certain Persons to Receive Personal Information.

(a) A person who is convicted of an offense under this chapter, or who violates a rule adopted by an agency relating to the terms or conditions for a release of personal information to the person, is ineligible to receive personal information under Section 730.007.
(b) For purposes of Subsection (a), a person is considered to have been convicted in a case if:
(1) a sentence is imposed;
(2) the defendant receives probation or deferred adjudication; or
(3) the court defers final disposition of the case.
(Enacted by Acts 2001, 77th Leg., ch. 1032 ( H.B. 1544), § 8, effective September 1, 2001.)

# CHAPTER 731
## DISCLOSURE OF PERSONAL INFORMATION FROM MOTOR VEHICLE RECORDS [REPEALED]

## Sec. 731.001. Definitions [Repealed].
Repealed by Acts 2001, 77th Leg., ch. 1032 (H.B. 1544), § 9(2), effective September 1, 2001. (Enacted by Acts 1997, 75th Leg., ch. 1187 (S.B. 1069), § 2, effective September 1, 1997.)

## Sec. 731.002. Release of Personal Information by Agency [Repealed].
Repealed by Acts 2001, 77th Leg., ch. 1032

(H.B. 1544), § 9(2), effective September 1, 2001. (Enacted by Acts 1997, 75th Leg., ch. 1187 (S.B. 1069), § 2, effective September 1, 1997.)

## Sec. 731.003. Publication or Disclosure of Personal Information on Internet [Repealed].
Repealed by Acts 2001, 77th Leg., ch. 1032 (H.B. 1544), § 9(2), effective September 1, 2001. (Enacted by Acts 1997, 75th Leg., ch. 1187 (S.B. 1069), § 2, effective September 1, 1997.)

## Sec. 731.004. Civil Enforcement [Repealed].
Repealed by Acts 2001, 77th Leg., ch. 1032 (H.B. 1544), § 9(2), effective September 1, 2001. (Enacted by Acts 1997, 75th Leg., ch. 1187 (S.B. 1069), § 2, effective September 1, 1997.)

## Sec. 731.005. Civil Cause of Action [Repealed].
Repealed by Acts 2001, 77th Leg., ch. 1032 (H.B. 1544), § 9(2), effective September 1, 2001. (Enacted by Acts 1997, 75th Leg., ch. 1187 (S.B. 1069), § 2, effective September 1, 1997.)

## Sec. 731.006. False Statement to Agency; Penalty [Repealed].
Repealed by Acts 2001, 77th Leg., ch. 1032 (H.B. 1544), § 9(2), effective September 1, 2001. (Enacted by Acts 1997, 75th Leg., ch. 1187 (S.B. 1069), § 2, effective September 1, 1997.)

## Sec. 731.007. Dissemination or Publication of Personal Information on Internet Prohibited; Penalty [Repealed].
Repealed by Acts 2001, 77th Leg., ch. 1032 (H.B. 1544), § 9(2), effective September 1, 2001. (Enacted by Acts 1997, 75th Leg., ch. 1187 (S.B. 1069), § 2, effective September 1, 1997.)

## Sec. 731.008. Affirmative Defense to Civil Action or Prosecution [Repealed].
Repealed by Acts 2001, 77th Leg., ch. 1032 (H.B. 1544), § 9(2), effective September 1, 2001. (Enacted by Acts 1997, 75th Leg., ch. 1187 (S.B. 1069), § 2, effective September 1, 1997.)

## Sec. 731.009. Rules [Repealed].
Repealed by Acts 2001, 77th Leg., ch. 1032 (H.B. 1544), § 9(2), effective September 1, 2001.

(Enacted by Acts 1997, 75th Leg., ch. 1187 (S.B. 1069), § 2, effective September 1, 1997.)

## CHAPTERS 732 TO 749
### [RESERVED FOR EXPANSION]

## CHAPTER 750
### MISCELLANEOUS PROVISIONS

### Sec. 750.001.  Children Standing in School Bus [Repealed].

Repealed by Acts 1997, 75th Leg., ch. 165 (S.B. 898), § 30.169, effective September 1, 1997. (Enacted by Acts 1995, 74th Leg., ch. 165 (S.B. 971), § 1, effective September 1, 1995.)

### Sec. 750.002.  Speed of Vehicle in Park in County Bordering Gulf of Mexico.

(a) A person commits an offense if the person drives a vehicle at a speed greater than 30 miles per hour within the boundaries of a county park located in a county that borders on the Gulf of Mexico, other than on a beach as that term is defined by Section 61.012, Natural Resources Code, in the park.

(b) An offense under this section is a misdemeanor punishable by a fine of not less than $1 or more than $200.

(Enacted by Acts 1995, 74th Leg., ch. 165 (S.B. 971), § 1, effective September 1, 1995.)

### Sec. 750.003.  Operation of Vehicle on Dune Seaward of Dune Protection Line Prohibited.

(a) In this section, "vehicle" means a device that is designed to transport persons or property and is self-propelled or propelled by external means.

(b) A person commits an offense if the person operates a vehicle on a sand dune seaward of the dune protection line as defined in Section 63.012, Natural Resources Code, except on a roadway designated by a subdivision of the state.

(c) An offense under this section is a Class C misdemeanor.

(Enacted by Acts 2001, 77th Leg., ch. 176 (S.B. 1162), § 1, effective September 1, 2001.)

## CHAPTERS 751 TO 1000
### [RESERVED FOR EXPANSION]

Transportation

# Alcoholic Beverage Code

## TITLE 1
## GENERAL PROVISIONS

### CHAPTER 1
### GENERAL PROVISIONS

## Sec. 1.03.  Public Policy.

This code is an exercise of the police power of the state for the protection of the welfare, health, peace, temperance, and safety of the people of the state. It shall be liberally construed to accomplish this purpose.

(Enacted by Acts 1977, 65th Leg., ch. 194 (H.B. 815), § 1, effective September 1, 1977.)

## Sec. 1.04.  Definitions.

In this code:

(1) "Alcoholic beverage" means alcohol, or any beverage containing more than one-half of one percent of alcohol by volume, which is capable of use for beverage purposes, either alone or when diluted.

(2) "Consignment sale" means:

(A) the delivery of alcoholic beverages under an agreement, arrangement, condition, or system by which the person receiving the beverages has the right at any time to relinquish possession to them or to return them to the shipper and in which title to the beverages remains in the shipper;

(B) the delivery of alcoholic beverages under an agreement, arrangement, condition, or system by which the person designated as the receiver merely acts as an intermediary for the shipper or seller and the actual receiver;

(C) the delivery of alcoholic beverages to a factor or broker;

(D) any method employed by a shipper or seller by which a person designated as the purchaser of alcoholic beverages does not in fact purchase the beverages;

(E) any method employed by a shipper or seller by which a person is placed in actual or constructive possession of an alcoholic beverage without acquiring title to the beverage; or

(F) any other type of transaction which may legally be construed as a consignment sale.

(3) "Distilled spirits" means alcohol, spirits of wine, whiskey, rum, brandy, gin, or any liquor produced in whole or in part by the process of distillation, including all dilutions or mixtures of them, and includes spirit coolers that may have an alcoholic content as low as four percent alcohol by volume and that contain plain, sparkling, or carbonated water and may also contain one or more natural or artificial blending or flavoring ingredients.

(4) "Illicit beverage" means an alcoholic beverage:

(A) manufactured, distributed, bought, sold, bottled, rectified, blended, treated, fortified, mixed, processed, warehoused, stored, possessed, imported, or transported in violation of this code;

(B) on which a tax imposed by the laws of this state has not been paid and to which the tax stamp, if required, has not been affixed; or

(C) possessed, kept, stored, owned, or imported with intent to manufacture, sell, distribute, bottle, rectify, blend, treat, fortify, mix, process, warehouse, store, or transport in violation of this code.

(5) "Liquor" means any alcoholic beverage containing alcohol in excess of four percent by

ABC

weight, unless otherwise indicated. Proof that an alcoholic beverage is alcohol, spirits of wine, whiskey, liquor, wine, brandy, gin, rum, ale, malt liquor, tequila, mescal, habanero, or barreteago, is prima facie evidence that it is liquor.

(6) "Person" means a natural person or association of natural persons, trustee, receiver, partnership, corporation, organization, or the manager, agent, servant, or employee of any of them.

(7) "Wine and vinous liquor" means the product obtained from the alcoholic fermentation of juice of sound ripe grapes, fruits, berries, or honey, and includes wine coolers.

(8) "Hotel" means the premises of an establishment:

(A) where, in consideration of payment, travelers are furnished food and lodging;

(B) in which are located:

(i) at least 10 adequately furnished completely separate rooms with adequate facilities so comfortably disposed that persons usually apply for and receive overnight accommodations in the establishment, either in the course of usual and regular travel or as a residence; or

(ii) at least five rooms described by Subparagraph (i) if the building being used as a hotel is a historic structure as defined by Section 442.001, Government Code; and

(C) which operates a regular dining room constantly frequented by customers each day.

(9) "Applicant" means a person who submits or files an original or renewal application with the county judge, commission, or administrator for a license or permit.

(10) "Commission" means the Texas Alcoholic Beverage Commission.

(11) "Permittee" means a person who is the holder of a permit provided for in this code, or an agent, servant, or employee of that person.

(12) "Ale" or "malt liquor" means a malt beverage containing more than four percent of alcohol by weight.

(13) "Mixed beverage" means one or more servings of a beverage composed in whole or part of an alcoholic beverage in a sealed or unsealed container of any legal size for consumption on the premises where served or sold by the holder of a mixed beverage permit, the holder of a daily temporary mixed beverage permit, the holder of a caterer's permit, the holder of a mixed beverage late hours permit, the holder of a private club registration permit,

or the holder of a private club late hours permit.

(14) "Barrel" means, as a standard of measure, a quantity of beer equal to 31 standard gallons.

(15) "Beer" means a malt beverage containing one-half of one percent or more of alcohol by volume and not more than four percent of alcohol by weight, and does not include a beverage designated by label or otherwise by a name other than beer.

(16) "Licensee" means a person who is the holder of a license provided in this code, or any agent, servant, or employee of that person.

(17) "Manufacturer" means a person engaged in the manufacture or brewing of beer, whether located inside or outside the state.

(18) "Original package," as applied to beer, means a container holding beer in bulk, or any box, crate, carton, or other device used in packing beer that is contained in bottles or other containers.

(19) "Premises" has the meaning given it in Section 11.49 of this code.

(20) "Citizen of Texas" and "citizen of this state" mean a person who is a citizen of both the United States and Texas.

(21) "Minibar" means a closed container in a hotel guestroom with access to the interior of the container restricted by a locking device which requires the use of a key, magnetic card, or similar device.

(22) "Minibar key" means the key, magnetic card, or similar device which permits access to the interior of a minibar.

(23) "Guestroom" means a sleeping room, including any adjacent private living area, in a hotel which is rented to guests for their use as an overnight accommodation.

(24) "Wine cooler" means an alcoholic beverage consisting of vinous liquor plus plain, sparkling, or carbonated water and which may also contain one or more natural or artificial blending or flavoring ingredients. A wine cooler may have an alcohol content as low as one-half of one percent by volume.

(25) "Executive management" includes the administrator, the assistant administrator, individuals who report directly to the administrator, and the head of each division of the commission.

(Enacted by Acts 1977, 65th Leg., ch. 194 (H.B. 815), § 1, effective September 1, 1977; am. Acts 1989, 71st Leg., ch. 532 (H.B. 2840), § 1, effective August 28, 1989; am. Acts 1989, 71st Leg., ch. 692

(S.B. 1325), § 1, effective June 14, 1989; am. Acts 1993, 73rd Leg., ch. 934 (H.B. 1445), § 1, effective September 1, 1993; am. Acts 2005, 79th Leg., ch. 1182 (S.B. 1255), § 1, effective June 18, 2005; am. Acts 2007, 80th Leg., ch. 68 (S.B. 904), § 1, effective September 1, 2007; am. Acts 2007, 80th Leg., ch. 420 (S.B. 1257), § 1, effective September 1, 2007.)

### Sec. 1.05. General Penalty.

(a) A person who violates a provision of this code for which a specific penalty is not provided is guilty of a misdemeanor and on conviction is punishable by a fine of not less than $100 nor more than $1,000 or by confinement in the county jail for not more than one year or by both.

(b) The term "specific penalty," as used in this section, means a penalty which might be imposed as a result of a criminal prosecution.

(Enacted by Acts 1977, 65th Leg., ch. 194 (H.B. 815), § 1, effective September 1, 1977.)

# TITLE 2
# ADMINISTRATION OF CODE

## CHAPTER 5
## ALCOHOLIC BEVERAGE COMMISSION

### Subchapter B. Powers and Duties

## SUBCHAPTER B
## POWERS AND DUTIES

### Sec. 5.361. Enforcement.

(a) The commission shall develop a risk-based approach to conducting its enforcement activities that focuses on:

(1) detecting serious violations that impact public safety;

(2) monitoring entities that have a history of complaints and violations of this code; and

(3) any other factors the commission considers important.

(b) The commission shall develop benchmarks and goals to track key enforcement activities and the results of those activities. For each type of enforcement activity, the commission shall track the number of violations detected by the enforcement activity, the amount of time spent on the enforcement activity, and any other information the commission considers necessary. The commission shall use the information collected under this subsection and other information to compare the enforcement performance of each region and to determine the most effective enforcement activities.

(c) The commission shall track, on a statewide and regional basis, the type of violations detected, the disposition of the violations, and the entities that committed the most serious violations.

(d) The commission shall compile detailed statistics and analyze trends related to its enforcement activities. The commission shall:

(1) summarize the statistics and trends for executive management on a monthly basis and for the members of the commission on a quarterly basis; and

(2) make summary information available to the public, including by posting the information on the commission's Internet website.

(Acts 2007, 80th Leg., ch. 68 (S.B. 904), § 10, effective September 1, 2007.)

### Sec. 5.362. Schedule of Sanctions.

(a) The commission by rule shall adopt a schedule of sanctions that may be imposed on a license or permit holder for violations of this code or rules adopted under this code. In adopting the schedule of sanctions, the commission shall ensure that the severity of the sanction imposed is appropriate to the type of violation that is the basis for disciplinary action.

(b) For each violation for which a license or permit may be suspended, the schedule of sanctions must include the number of days a permit or license would be suspended and the corresponding civil penalty under Section 11.64.

(c) In determining the appropriate sanction for a violation under the schedule, the commission or administrator shall consider:

(1) the type of license or permit held by the person who committed the violation;

(2) the type of violation;

(3) any aggravating or ameliorating circumstances concerning the violation; and

(4) the license or permit holder's previous violations of this code.

(d) The schedule must:

(1) allow deviations from the schedule for clearly established mitigating circumstances, including circumstances listed in Section 11.64(c), or aggravating circumstances; and

(2) include a list of the most common violations by members of the manufacturing, wholesaling, and retailing tiers of the alcoholic beverage industry and the sanctions assessed for those violations.

(e) The commission shall develop policies to guide commission staff in determining the circumstances when it is appropriate to deviate from the schedule of sanctions. The policies must identify the circumstances when approval is required in order to deviate from the schedule.

(f) The commission shall make the schedule of sanctions available to the public, including by posting the schedule on the commission's Internet website.

(Acts 2007, 80th Leg., ch. 68 (S.B. 904), § 10, effective September 1, 2007.)

# TITLE 3
# LICENSES AND PERMITS

## SUBTITLE A
## PERMITS

## CHAPTER 26
## WINE AND BEER RETAILER'S OFF-PREMISE PERMIT

**Sec. 26.05. Warning Sign Required.**

(a) Each holder of a wine and beer retailer's off-premise permit shall display in a prominent place on his premises a sign stating in letters at least two inches high: IT IS A CRIME (MISDEMEANOR) TO CONSUME LIQUOR OR BEER ON THESE PREMISES. The commission or administrator may require the holder of the permit to also display the sign in a language other than English if it can be observed or determined that a substantial portion of the expected customers speak the other language as their familiar language.

(b) A permittee who fails to comply with this section commits a misdemeanor punishable by a fine of not more than $25.

(Enacted by Acts 1983, 68th Leg., ch. 414 (H.B. 877), § 2, effective September 1, 1983; am. Acts 1985, 69th Leg., ch. 689 (H.B. 167), § 1, effective September 1, 1985.)

## CHAPTER 28
## MIXED BEVERAGE PERMIT

**Sec. 28.13. Issuance of Permit for Certain Boats.**

(a) A mixed beverage permit may be issued for a boat if:

(1) the boat:

(A) carries at least 350 passengers;

(B) weighs at least 90 gross tons; and

(C) is at least 80 feet long; and

(2) the home port of the boat is in an area where the sale of mixed beverages is legal.

(a-1) A mixed beverage permit may be issued for a regularly scheduled excursion boat that is licensed by the United States Coast Guard to carry passengers on the navigable waters of the state if:

(1) the boat:

(A) carries at least 45 passengers;

(B) weighs at least 35 gross tons; and

(C) is at least 55 feet long;

(2) the home port of the boat is in an area where the sale of mixed beverages is legal; and

(3) the owner or operator of the boat is the sole permit holder for the boat.

(b) For purposes of Section 11.38 of this code, the home port of the boat is treated as the location of the licensed premises.

(c) [Repealed by Acts 2003, 78th Leg., 3rd C.S., ch. 3 (H.B. 7), § 21.05, effective January 11, 2004.]

(d) A mixed beverage permit may be issued under this section to a boat regularly used for voyages in international waters regardless of whether the sale of mixed beverages is lawful in the area of the home port. A person having authority to deliver alcoholic beverages to a mixed beverage permit holder in the county where the licensed premises is located may deliver alcoholic beverages purchased by the permit holder. Subsections (a)(2) and (a-1)(2) do not apply to this subsection.

(e) The provisions of Section 109.53 that relate to residency requirements and compliance with Texas laws of incorporation:

(1) do not apply to the holders of a mixed beverage permit under Subsection (a); and

(2) do apply to the holder of a mixed beverage permit under Subsection (a-1).

(f) A permit for an excursion boat issued under Subsection (a-1) is inoperative in a dry area. (Enacted by Acts 1985, 69th Leg., ch. 540 (H.B. 1132), § 1, effective June 12, 1985; am. Acts 2003, 78th Leg., 3rd C.S., ch. 3 (H.B. 7), §§ 21.02, 21.05, effective January 11, 2004; am. Acts 2007, 80th Leg., ch. 294 (H.B. 1248), § 1, effective September 1, 2007.)

# CHAPTER 30
## DAILY TEMPORARY MIXED BEVERAGE PERMIT

### Sec. 30.01. Authorized Activities.
The holder of a daily temporary mixed beverage permit may sell mixed beverages for consumption on the premises for which the permit is issued.
(Enacted by Acts 1977, 65th Leg., ch. 194 (H.B. 815), § 1, effective September 1, 1977.)

# TITLE 4
# REGULATORY AND PENAL PROVISIONS

## CHAPTER 101
## GENERAL CRIMINAL PROVISIONS

### Subchapter A. Procedural Provisions

## SUBCHAPTER A
## PROCEDURAL PROVISIONS

### Sec. 101.01. Restraining Orders and Injunctions.
(a) If a credible person by affidavit informs the attorney general or a county or district attorney that a person is violating or is about to violate a provision of this code, or that a permit or license was wrongfully issued, the attorney general or county or district attorney shall begin proceedings in district court to restrain the person from violating the code or operating under the permit or license.

(b) The court may issue a restraining order without a hearing, and on notice and hearing may grant an injunction, to prevent the threatened or further violation or operation. The court may require the complaining party to file a bond in an amount and with the conditions the court finds necessary.

(c) If the court finds that a person has violated a restraining order or injunction issued under this section, it shall enter a judgment to that effect. The judgment operates to cancel without further proceedings any license or permit held by the person. The district clerk shall notify the county judge of the county where the premises covered by the permit or license are located and shall notify the commission when a judgment is entered that operates to cancel a license or permit.

(d) No license or permit may be issued to a person whose license or permit is cancelled under

ABC

Subsection (c) of this section for one year after the cancellation.
(Enacted by Acts 1977, 65th Leg., ch. 194 (H.B. 815), § 1, effective September 1, 1977.)

### Sec. 101.02.    Arrest Without Warrant.

A peace officer may arrest without a warrant any person he observes violating any provision of this code or any rule or regulation of the commission. The officer shall take possession of all illicit beverages the person has in his possession or on his premises as provided in Chapter 103 of this code.
(Enacted by Acts 1977, 65th Leg., ch. 194 (H.B. 815), § 1, effective September 1, 1977.)

### Sec. 101.03.    Search and Seizure.

(a) A search warrant may issue under Chapter 18, Code of Criminal Procedure, 1965, as amended, to search for, seize, and destroy or otherwise dispose of in accordance with this code:

(1) an illicit beverage;

(2) any equipment or instrumentality used, or capable or designed to be used, to manufacture an illicit beverage;

(3) a vehicle or instrumentality used or to be used for the illegal transportation of an illicit beverage;

(4) unlawful equipment or materials used or to be used in the illegal manufacturing of an illicit beverage;

(5) a forged or counterfeit stamp, die, plate, official signature, certificate, evidence of tax payment, license, permit, or other instrument pertaining to this code; or

(6) any instrumentality or equipment, or parts of either of them, used or to be used, or designed or capable of use, to manufacture, print, etch, indite, or otherwise make a forged or counterfeit instrument covered by Subdivision (5) of this subsection.

(b) Any magistrate may issue a search warrant on the affidavit of a credible person, setting forth the name or description of the owner or person in charge of the premises (or stating that the name and description are unknown), the address or description of the premises, and showing that the described premises is a place where this code has been or is being violated. If the place to be searched is a private dwelling occupied as such and no part of it is used as a store, shop, hotel, boarding house, or for any other purpose except as a private residence, the affidavit must be made by two credible persons.

(c) All provisions of Chapter 18, Code of Criminal Procedure, 1965, as amended, apply to the application, issuance, and execution of the warrant except those that conflict with this section.

(d) The officer executing the warrant shall seize all items described in Subsection (a) of this section, and those items may not be taken from his custody by a writ of replevin or any other process. The officer shall retain the items pending final judgment in the proceedings.

(e) This section does not require a peace officer to obtain a search warrant to search premises covered by a license or permit.
(Enacted by Acts 1977, 65th Leg., ch. 194 (H.B. 815), § 1, effective September 1, 1977.)

### Sec. 101.04.    Consent to Inspection; Penalty.

(a) By accepting a license or permit, the holder consents to the commission, an authorized representative of the commission, or a peace officer entering the licensed premises at any time to conduct an investigation or inspect the premises for the purpose of performing any duty imposed by this code.

(b) A person commits an offense if the person refuses to allow the commission, an authorized representative of the commission, or a peace officer to enter a licensed or permitted premises as required by Subsection (a). An offense under this section is a Class A misdemeanor.
(Enacted by Acts 1977, 65th Leg., ch. 194 (H.B. 815), § 1, effective September 1, 1977; am. Acts 2007, 80th Leg., ch. 68 (S.B. 904), § 19, effective September 1, 2007.)

### Sec. 101.07.    Duty of Peace Officers.

All peace officers in the state, including those of cities, counties, and state, shall enforce the provisions of this code and cooperate with and assist the commission in detecting violations and apprehending offenders.
(Enacted by Acts 1977, 65th Leg., ch. 194 (H.B. 815), § 1, effective September 1, 1977.)

### SUBCHAPTER B
### OFFENSES RELATING TO DRY AREAS

### Sec. 101.31.    Alcoholic Beverages in Dry Areas.

(a) Except as otherwise provided in this code, no person in a dry area may manufacture, distill, brew, sell, import into the state, export from the state, transport, distribute, warehouse, store, solicit or take orders for, or possess with intent to sell an alcoholic beverage.

(b) An offense under this section is a Class B misdemeanor.

(c) If it is shown on the trial of an offense under this section that the person has previously been convicted two or more times of an offense under this section, the offense is a state jail felony.

(Enacted by Acts 1977, 65th Leg., ch. 194 (H.B. 815), § 1, effective September 1, 1977; am. Acts 2001, 77th Leg., ch. 462 (H.B. 269), § 1, effective September 1, 2001.)

### Sec. 101.32. Prima Facie Evidence of Intent to Sell.

(a) Possession of more than one quart of liquor in a dry area is prima facie evidence that it is possessed with intent to sell.

(b) Possession in a dry area of more than 24 twelve-ounce bottles of beer, or an equivalent amount, is prima facie evidence of possession with intent to sell.

(Enacted by Acts 1977, 65th Leg., ch. 194 (H.B. 815), § 1, effective September 1, 1977.)

## SUBCHAPTER D
## MISCELLANEOUS OFFENSES

### Sec. 101.61. Violation of Code or Rule.

A person who fails or refuses to comply with a requirement of this code or a valid rule of the commission violates this code.

(Enacted by Acts 1977, 65th Leg., ch. 194 (H.B. 815), § 1, effective September 1, 1977.)

### Sec. 101.62. Offensive Noise on Premises.

No licensee or permittee, on premises under his control, may maintain or permit a radio, television, amplifier, piano, phonograph, music machine, orchestra, band, singer, speaker, entertainer, or other device or person that produces, amplifies, or projects music or other sound that is loud, vociferous, vulgar, indecent, lewd, or otherwise offensive to persons on or near the licensed premises.

(Enacted by Acts 1977, 65th Leg., ch. 194 (H.B. 815), § 1, effective September 1, 1977.)

### Sec. 101.63. Sale to Certain Persons.

(a) A person commits an offense if the person with criminal negligence sells an alcoholic beverage to an habitual drunkard or an intoxicated or insane person.

(b) Except as provided in Subsection (c) of this section, a violation of this section is a misdemeanor punishable by a fine of not less than $100 nor more than $500, by confinement in jail for not more than one year, or by both.

(c) If a person has been previously convicted of a violation of this section or of Section 106.03 of this code, a violation is a misdemeanor punishable by a fine of not less than $500 nor more than $1,000, by confinement in jail for not more than one year, or by both.

(Enacted by Acts 1977, 65th Leg., ch. 194 (H.B. 815), § 1, effective September 1, 1977; am. Acts 2003, 78th Leg., ch. 508 (H.B. 1114), § 1, effective September 1, 2003.)

### Sec. 101.64. Indecent Graphic Material.

No holder of a license or permit may possess or display on the licensed premises a card, calendar, placard, picture, or handbill that is immoral, indecent, lewd, or profane.

(Enacted by Acts 1977, 65th Leg., ch. 194 (H.B. 815), § 1, effective September 1, 1977.)

### Sec. 101.65. Beverages Made from Certain Materials Prohibited.

No person may manufacture, import, sell, or possess for the purpose of sale an alcoholic beverage made from:

(1) any compound made from synthetic materials;

(2) substandard wines;

(3) imitation wines; or

(4) must concentrated at any time to more than 80 degrees Balling.

(Enacted by Acts 1977, 65th Leg., ch. 194 (H.B. 815), § 1, effective September 1, 1977; am. Acts 1999, 76th Leg., ch. 1297 (S.B. 1676), § 1, effective September 1, 1999.)

### Sec. 101.66. Beverages of Certain Alcohol Content Prohibited.

No person may manufacture, sell, barter, or exchange a beverage that contains alcohol in excess of one-half of one percent by volume and not more than four percent of alcohol by weight, except beer, wine coolers, and spirit coolers.

(Enacted by Acts 1977, 65th Leg., ch. 194 (H.B. 815), § 1, effective September 1, 1977; am. Acts 1993, 73rd Leg., ch. 934 (H.B. 1445), § 60, effective September 1, 1993.)

ABC

## Sec. 101.67.　Prior Approval of Malt Beverages.

(a) No person may ship or cause to be shipped into the state, import into the state, manufacture and offer for sale in the state, or distribute, sell, or store in the state any beer, ale, or malt liquor unless:

(1) a sample of the beverage or a sample of the same type and quality of beverage has been first submitted to an independent, reputable laboratory or the commission for analysis to verify the alcohol content of the beverage; and

(2) the label of the beverage has been first submitted to the commission or its representative and found to comply with all provisions of this code relating to the labeling of the particular type of beverage.

(b) Only a brewer's or nonresident brewer's permittee or a manufacturer's or nonresident manufacturer's licensee may apply for and receive label approval on beer, ale, or malt liquor.

(c) This section does not apply to the importation of beer for personal consumption and not for sale.

(d) If the commission determines that the product analysis provided by the independent laboratory or the sample, and the label, required by Subsection (a) comply with the provisions of this code and the rules of the commission, the commission shall issue a certificate of approval upon receipt of a fee in an amount that is sufficient to cover the cost of administering this section. A copy of the certificate shall be kept on file in the office of the commission.

(e) The commission by rule shall establish the procedures for accepting analysis of beer, ale, or malt liquor by an independent laboratory under Subsection (a)(1).

(Enacted by Acts 1977, 65th Leg., ch. 194 (H.B. 815), § 1, effective September 1, 1977; am. Acts 1987, 70th Leg., ch. 495 (H.B. 1978), § 4, effective August 31, 1987; am. Acts 2007, 80th Leg., ch. 68 (S.B. 904), § 20, effective September 1, 2007.)

## Sec. 101.671.　Prior Approval of Distilled Spirits and Wine.

(a) Before an authorized permittee may ship distilled spirits or wine into the state or sell distilled spirits or wine within the state, the permittee must register the distilled spirits or wine with the commission. The registration application must include a certificate of label approval issued by the United States Alcohol and Tobacco Tax and Trade Bureau for the product.

(b) On registration of a certificate of label approval issued by the United States Alcohol and Tobacco Tax and Trade Bureau, the commission shall approve the product under this section and issue a letter to that effect to the permittee. The commission may not require additional approval for the product unless there is a change to the label or product that requires reissuance of the federal certificate of label approval. The commission shall accept the certificate of label approval as constituting full compliance with any applicable standards adopted under Section 5.38 regarding quality, purity, and identity of distilled spirits or wine.

(c) The commission may not register a product unless the application is accompanied by a fee set by the commission in an amount that is sufficient to cover the cost of administering this section. A copy of the registration shall be kept on file in the office of the commission.

(d) The commission by rule shall establish procedures for accepting federal certificates of label approval for registration under this section. (Acts 2007, 80th Leg., ch. 68 (S.B. 904), § 21, effective September 1, 2007.)

## Sec. 101.68.　Consignment Sale Prohibited.

A person commits an offense if he is a party to, or directly or indirectly interested in or connected with, a consignment sale of an alcoholic beverage. (Enacted by Acts 1977, 65th Leg., ch. 194 (H.B. 815), § 1, effective September 1, 1977.)

## Sec. 101.69.　False Statement.

Except as provided in Section 103.05(d), a person who makes a false statement or false representation in an application for a permit or license or in a statement, report, or other instrument to be filed with the commission and required to be sworn commits an offense punishable by imprisonment in the Texas Department of Criminal Justice for not less than 2 nor more than 10 years. (Enacted by Acts 1977, 65th Leg., ch. 194 (H.B. 815), § 1, effective September 1, 1977; am. Acts 2009, 81st Leg., ch. 87 (S.B. 1969), § 25.007, effective September 1, 2009.)

## Sec. 101.70.　Common Nuisance.

(a) A room, building, boat, structure, or other place where alcoholic beverages are sold, bartered, manufactured, stored, possessed, or consumed in violation of this code or under circumstances contrary to the purposes of this code, the

ABC

beverages themselves, and all property kept or used in the place, are a common nuisance. A person who maintains or assists in maintaining the nuisance commits an offense.

(b) The county or district attorney in the county where the nuisance exists or the attorney general may sue in the name of the state for an injunction to abate and temporarily and permanently enjoin it. Except as otherwise provided in this section, the proceeding is conducted as other similar proceedings.

(c) The plaintiff is not required to give a bond. The final judgment is a judgment in rem against the property and a judgment against the defendant. If the court finds against the defendant, on final judgment it shall order that the place where the nuisance exists be closed for one year or less and until the owner, lessee, tenant, or occupant gives bond with sufficient surety as approved by the court in the penal sum of at least $1,000. The bond must be payable to the state and conditioned:

(1) that this code will not be violated;

(2) that no person will be permitted to resort to the place to drink alcoholic beverages in violation of this code; and

(3) that the defendant will pay all fines, costs, and damages assessed against him for any violation of this code.

(d) On appeal, the judgment may not be superseded except on filing an appeal bond in the penal sum of not more than $500, in addition to the bond for costs of the appeal. That bond must be approved by the trial court and must be posted before the judgment of the court may be superseded on appeal. The bond must be conditioned that if the judgment of the trial court is finally affirmed it may be forfeited in the same manner and for any cause for which a bond required on final judgment may be forfeited for an act committed during the pendency of an appeal.
(Enacted by Acts 1977, 65th Leg., ch. 194 (H.B. 815), § 1, effective September 1, 1977.)

### Sec. 101.71. Inspection of Vehicle.

No holder of a permit issued under Title 3, Subtitle A, of this code, may refuse to allow the commission or its authorized representative or a peace officer, on request, to make a full inspection, investigation, or search of any vehicle.
(Enacted by Acts 1977, 65th Leg., ch. 194 (H.B. 815), § 1, effective September 1, 1977.)

### Sec. 101.72. Consumption of Alcoholic Beverage on Premises Licensed for Off-Premises Consumption.

(a) A person commits an offense if the person knowingly consumes liquor or beer on the premises of a holder of a wine and beer retailer's off-premise permit or a retail dealer's off-premise license.

(b) A person is presumed to have knowingly violated Subsection (a) of this section if the warning sign required by either Section 26.05 or 71.10 of this code is displayed on the premises.

(c) Except as provided in Subsection (d) of this section, a violation of this section is a misdemeanor punishable by a fine of not less than $25 nor more than $200.

(d) If a person has been convicted of a violation of this section occurring within a year of a subsequent violation, the subsequent violation is a misdemeanor punishable by a fine of not less than $100 nor more than $200.
(Enacted by Acts 1983, 68th Leg., ch. 414 (H.B. 877), § 5, effective September 1, 1983.)

### Sec. 101.73. Expungement of Conviction for Consumption on Premises Licensed for Off-Premises Consumption.

(a) A person convicted of not more than one violation of Section 101.72 of this code within 12 months, after the first anniversary of the conviction, may apply to the court in which he was convicted to have the conviction expunged.

(b) The application shall contain the applicant's sworn statement that he was not convicted of an additional violation of Section 101.72 of this code during the previous 12 months.

(c) If the court finds that the applicant was not convicted of another violation of Section 101.72 of this code during the preceding 12 months, the court shall order the conviction, together with all complaints, verdicts, fines, and other documents relating to the offense, to be expunged from the applicant's record. After entry of the order, the applicant is released from all disabilities resulting from the conviction, and the conviction may not be shown or made known for any purpose.
(Enacted by Acts 1983, 68th Leg., ch. 414 (H.B. 877), § 5, effective September 1, 1983.)

### Sec. 101.74. Offenses Relating to Bingo.

(a) An organization licensed to conduct bingo under Chapter 2001, Occupations Code, may not

ABC

offer an alcoholic beverage as a bingo prize or as a door prize at a bingo occasion.

(b) A person who holds a permit or license at the manufacturing or wholesale levels of the alcoholic beverage industry or a person who holds a package store permit may not participate in advertising any bingo game or pay or contribute toward payment of the printing of bingo cards or of the supplying of any novelties of any sort to be used during or in connection with the conduct of a bingo game.

(Enacted by Acts 1989, 71st Leg., ch. 238 (H.B. 2260), § 41, effective January 1, 1990; am. Acts 2001, 77th Leg., ch. 1420 (H.B. 2812), § 14.727, effective September 1, 2001.)

### Sec. 101.75.  Consumption of Alcoholic Beverages Near Schools.

(a) A person commits an offense if the person possesses an open container or consumes an alcoholic beverage on a public street, public alley, or public sidewalk within 1,000 feet of the property line of a facility that is a public or private school, including a parochial school, that provides all or any part of prekindergarten through twelfth grade.

(b) This section does not apply to the possession of an open container or the consumption at an event duly authorized by appropriate authorities and held in compliance with all other applicable provisions of this code.

(c) An offense under this section is a Class C misdemeanor.

(d) In this section, "open container" has the meaning assigned in Section 109.35.

(Enacted by Acts 1993, 73rd Leg., ch. 934 (H.B. 1445), § 63, effective September 1, 1993; am. Acts 1995, 74th Leg., ch. 260 (S.B. 1), § 6, effective May 30, 1995; am. Acts 2001, 77th Leg., ch. 388 (H.B. 688), § 1, effective May 28, 2001.)

## CHAPTER 103
## ILLICIT BEVERAGES

### Sec. 103.01.  Illicit Beverages Prohibited.

No person may possess, manufacture, transport, or sell an illicit beverage.

(Enacted by Acts 1977, 65th Leg., ch. 194 (H.B. 815), § 1, effective September 1, 1977.)

### Sec. 103.02.  Equipment or Material for Manufacture of Illicit Beverages.

No person may possess equipment or material designed for, capable of use for, or used in manufacturing an illicit beverage.

(Enacted by Acts 1977, 65th Leg., ch. 194 (H.B. 815), § 1, effective September 1, 1977.)

### Sec. 103.03.  Seizure of Illicit Beverages, Etc.

A peace officer may seize without a warrant:

(1) any illicit beverage, its container, and its packaging;

(2) any vehicle, including an aircraft or watercraft, used to transport an illicit beverage;

(3) any equipment designed for use in or used in manufacturing an illicit beverage; or

(4) any material to be used in manufacturing an illicit beverage.

(Enacted by Acts 1977, 65th Leg., ch. 194 (H.B. 815), § 1, effective September 1, 1977.)

### Sec. 103.04.  Arrest of Person in Possession.

A peace officer may arrest without a warrant any person found in possession of:

(1) an illicit beverage;

(2) any equipment designed for use in or used in manufacturing an illicit beverage; or

(3) any material to be used in manufacturing an illicit beverage.

(Enacted by Acts 1977, 65th Leg., ch. 194 (H.B. 815), § 1, effective September 1, 1977.)

### Sec. 103.05.  Report of Seizure.

(a) A peace officer who makes a seizure under Section 103.03 of this code shall make a report in triplicate which lists each item seized and the place and name of the owner, operator, or other person from whom it is seized. One copy of the report shall be verified by oath.

(b) The verified copy shall be retained in the permanent files of the commission or other agency making the seizure. The copy is subject to inspection by any member of the legislature or by any authorized law enforcement agency of the state.

(c) One copy of the report shall be delivered to the person from whom the seizure is made.

(d) A peace officer who makes a false report of the property seized commits a felony punishable by confinement in the Texas Department of Criminal Justice for not less than two years and not more than five years.

(e) A peace officer who fails to file the reports of a seizure as required by this section commits a misdemeanor punishable by a fine of not less than $50 nor more than $100 or by confinement in jail for not less than 10 nor more than 90 days or by both. The commission shall insure that the reports are made by peace officers.

(Enacted by Acts 1977, 65th Leg., ch. 194 (H.B. 815), § 1, effective September 1, 1977; am. Acts 1983, 68th Leg., ch. 954 (H.B. 1875), § 1, effective August 29, 1983; am. Acts 2009, 81st Leg., ch. 87 (S.B. 1969), § 25.008, effective September 1, 2009.)

### Sec. 103.07.  Beverage of Illicit Manufacture or Unfit for Consumption.

(a) The commission may not sell alcoholic beverages seized by a peace officer, as provided in Section 103.03, that are unfit for public consumption or are of illicit manufacture.

(b) Alcoholic beverages are unfit for public consumption if:

(1) the manufacturer or wholesaler of the beverages determines that the beverages are inappropriate for sale to a consumer;

(2) the beverages are damaged; or

(3) the code date affixed by the manufacturer to the beverages has expired.

(c) If the commission determines that seized alcoholic beverages are unfit for public consumption or are of illicit manufacture, the commission shall destroy the alcoholic beverages.

(Enacted by Acts 1977, 65th Leg., ch. 194 (H.B. 815), § 1, effective September 1, 1977; am. Acts 2005, 79th Leg., ch. 1182 (S.B. 1255), § 8, effective June 18, 2005.)

### CHAPTER 105
### HOURS OF SALE AND CONSUMPTION

### Sec. 105.01.  Hours of Sale: Liquor.

(a) Except as provided in Sections 105.02, 105.03, 105.04, and 105.08, no person may sell, offer for sale, or deliver any liquor:

(1) on New Year's Day, Thanksgiving Day, or Christmas Day;

(2) on Sunday; or

(3) before 10 a.m. or after 9 p.m. on any other day.

(b) When Christmas Day or New Year's Day falls on a Sunday, Subsection (a) of this section applies to the following Monday.

(Enacted by Acts 1977, 65th Leg., ch. 194 (H.B. 815), § 1, effective September 1, 1977; am. Acts 1979, 66th Leg., ch. 777 (H.B. 1740), § 23, effective August 27, 1979; am. Acts 2005, 79th Leg., ch. 84 (S.B. 571), § 1, effective May 17, 2005.)

### Sec. 105.03.  Hours of Sale: Mixed Beverages.

(a) No person may sell or offer for sale mixed beverages at any time not permitted by this section.

(b) A mixed beverage permittee may sell and offer for sale mixed beverages between 7 a.m. and midnight on any day except Sunday. On Sunday he may sell mixed beverages between midnight and 1:00 a.m. and between 10 a.m. and midnight, except that an alcoholic beverage served to a customer between 10 a.m. and 12 noon on Sunday must be provided during the service of food to the customer.

(c) In a city or county having a population of 800,000 or more, according to the last preceding federal census, or 500,000 or more, according to the 22nd Decennial Census of the United States, as released by the Bureau of the Census on March 12, 2001, a holder of a mixed beverage late hours permit may also sell and offer for sale mixed beverages between midnight and 2 a.m. on any day.

(d) In a city or county other than a city or county described by Subsection (c), the extended hours prescribed in Subsection (c) of this section are effective for the sale of mixed beverages and the offer to sell them by a holder of a mixed beverages late hours permit:

(1) in the unincorporated areas of the county if the extended hours are adopted by an order of the commissioners court; and

(2) in an incorporated city or town if the extended hours are adopted by an ordinance of the governing body of the city or town.

(e) A violation of a city ordinance or order of a commissioners court adopted pursuant to Subsection (d) of this section is a violation of this code.

(Enacted by Acts 1977, 65th Leg., ch. 194 (H.B. 815), § 1, effective September 1, 1977; am. Acts

**ABC**

1993, 73rd Leg., ch. 923 (H.B. 908), § 2, effective September 1, 1993; am. Acts 1993, 73rd Leg., ch. 934 (H.B. 1445), § 70, effective September 1, 1993; am. Acts 2003, 78th Leg., ch. 685 (H.B. 2579), § 1, effective September 1, 2003; am. Acts 2005, 79th Leg., ch. 521 (H.B. 833), § 1, effective June 17, 2005.)

### Sec. 105.05.  Hours of Sale: Beer.

(a) No person may sell, offer for sale, or deliver beer at any time not permitted by this section.

(b) A person may sell, offer for sale, or deliver beer between 7 a.m. and midnight on any day except Sunday. On Sunday he may sell beer between midnight and 1:00 a.m. and between noon and midnight, except that permittees or licensees authorized to sell for on-premise consumption may sell beer between 10:00 a.m. and noon if the beer is served to a customer during the service of food to the customer.

(c) In a city or county having a population of 800,000 or more, according to the last preceding federal census, or 500,000 or more, according to the 22nd Decennial Census of the United States, as released by the Bureau of the Census on March 12, 2001, a holder of a retail dealer's on-premise late hours license may also sell, offer for sale, and deliver beer between midnight and 2 a.m. on any day.

(d) In a city or county other than a city or county described by Subsection (c), the extended hours prescribed in Subsection (c) of this section, or any part of the extended hours prescribed in Subsection (c) of this section are effective for the sale, offer to sell, and delivery of beer by a holder of a retail dealer's on-premise late hours license:

(1) in the unincorporated areas of the county if the extended hours are adopted by an order of the commissioners court; and

(2) in an incorporated city or town if the extended hours are adopted by an ordinance of the governing body of the city or town.

(e) A violation of a city ordinance or order of a commissioners court adopted pursuant to Subsection (d) of this section is a violation of this code.
(Enacted by Acts 1977, 65th Leg., ch. 194 (H.B. 815), § 1, effective September 1, 1977; am. Acts 1979, 66th Leg., ch. 777 (H.B. 1740), § 13, effective August 27, 1979; am. Acts 1993, 73rd Leg., ch. 923 (H.B. 908), § 1, effective September 1, 1993; am. Acts 1993, 73rd Leg., ch. 934 (H.B. 1445), §§ 72, 73, effective September 1, 1993; am. Acts 2003, 78th Leg., ch. 685 (H.B. 2579), § 2, effective September 1, 2003; am. Acts 2005, 79th

Leg., ch. 521 (H.B. 833), § 2, effective June 17, 2005.)

### Sec. 105.051.  Sale of Beer by Distributor's Licensee.

The holder of a general, local, or branch distributor's license may sell, offer for sale, or deliver beer 24 hours a day Monday through Saturday and between midnight and 1 a.m. and between noon and midnight on Sunday.
(Enacted by Acts 1993, 73rd Leg., ch. 934 (H.B. 1445), § 74, effective September 1, 1993; am. Acts 2009, 81st Leg., ch. 7 (H.B. 2594), § 2, effective May 5, 2009.)

### Sec. 105.052.  Sale of Beer by Distributor's Licensee in Certain Metropolitan Areas [Repealed].

Repealed by Acts 2009, 81st Leg., ch. 7 (H.B. 2594), § 3, effective May 5, 2009.
(Acts 2007, 80th Leg., ch. 1074 (H.B. 2724), § 1, effective June 15, 2007.)

### Sec. 105.06.  Hours of Consumption.

(a) In this section:

(1) "Extended hours area" means an area subject to the extended hours of sale provided in Section 105.03 or 105.05 of this code.

(2) "Standard hours area" means an area which is not an extended hours area.

(a-1) For the purposes of this section, a licensed or permitted premises is a public place.

(b) In a standard hours area, a person commits an offense if he consumes or possesses with intent to consume an alcoholic beverage in a public place at any time on Sunday between 1:15 a.m. and 12 noon or on any other day between 12:15 a.m. and 7 a.m.

(c) In an extended hours area, a person commits an offense if he consumes or possesses with intent to consume an alcoholic beverage in a public place at any time on Sunday between 2:15 a.m. and 12 noon and on any other day between 2:15 a.m. and 7 a.m.

(d) Proof that an alcoholic beverage was possessed with intent to consume in violation of this section requires evidence that the person consumed an alcoholic beverage on that day in violation of this section.

(e) An offense under this section is a Class C misdemeanor.
(Enacted by Acts 1977, 65th Leg., ch. 194 (H.B. 815), § 1, effective September 1, 1977; am. Acts 1993, 73rd Leg., ch. 923 (H.B. 908), § 3, effective

September 1, 1993; am. Acts 2005, 79th Leg., ch. 628 (H.B. 2451), § 2, effective September 1, 2005; am. Acts 2007, 80th Leg., ch. 68 (S.B. 904), § 23, effective September 1, 2007.)

## Sec. 105.08. Hours of Sale and Consumption: Winery.

The holder of a winery permit may sell, offer for sale, and deliver wine, and a person may consume wine on the premises of a winery:

(1) between 8 a.m. and midnight on any day except Sunday; and

(2) between 10 a.m. and midnight on Sunday.

(Enacted by Acts 2005, 79th Leg., ch. 84 (S.B. 571), § 2, effective May 17, 2005.)

## Sec. 105.09. Hours of Sale and Consumption: Certain Events.

Notwithstanding any other provision of this code, in addition to any other period during which the sale and consumption of alcohol is authorized under this code:

(1) a licensed or permitted premises located at a festival, fair, or concert may sell alcoholic beverages between 10 a.m. and noon; and

(2) a person may consume alcoholic beverages at a festival, fair, or concert between 10 a.m. and noon.

(Enacted by Acts 2005, 79th Leg., ch. 239 (H.B. 168), § 1, effective September 1, 2005; am. Acts 2007, 80th Leg., ch. 921 (H.B. 3167), § 17.001(5), effective September 1, 2007 (renumbered from Sec. 105.08).)

## Sec. 105.10. Penalty.

(a) A person commits an offense if the person, in violation of this chapter or Section 32.17(a)(7):

(1) sells or offers for sale an alcoholic beverage during prohibited hours; or

(2) consumes or permits the consumption of an alcoholic beverage on the person's licensed or permitted premises during prohibited hours.

(b) An offense under this section is a Class A misdemeanor.

(Acts 2007, 80th Leg., ch. 68 (S.B. 904), § 24, effective September 1, 2007.)

# CHAPTER 106
# PROVISIONS RELATING TO AGE

## Sec. 106.01. Definition.

In this code, "minor" means a person under 21 years of age.

(Enacted by Acts 1977, 65th Leg., ch. 194 (H.B. 815), § 1, effective September 1, 1977; am. Acts 1981, 67th Leg., ch. 107 (S.B. 306), § 8, effective September 1, 1981; am. Acts 1985, 69th Leg., ch. 285 (S.B. 21), § 8, effective September 1, 1986; am. Acts 1985, 69th Leg., ch. 285 (S.B. 21), § 15(c)(1); am. Acts 1985, 69th Leg., ch. 462 (H.B. 1819), § 9, effective September 1, 1986; am. Acts 1985, 69th Leg., ch. 462 (H.B. 1819), § 16(c)(1).)

## Sec. 106.02. Purchase of Alcohol by a Minor.

(a) A minor commits an offense if the minor purchases an alcoholic beverage. A minor does not commit an offense if the minor purchases an alcoholic beverage under the immediate supervision of a commissioned peace officer engaged in enforcing the provisions of this code.

ABC

(b) An offense under this section is punishable as provided by Section 106.071.

(Enacted by Acts 1977, 65th Leg., ch. 194 (H.B. 815), § 1, effective September 1, 1977; am. Acts 1991, 72nd Leg., ch. 163 (H.B. 2183), § 1, effective September 1, 1991; am. Acts 1993, 73rd Leg., ch. 934 (H.B. 1445), § 75, effective September 1, 1993; am. Acts 1997, 75th Leg., ch. 1013 (S.B. 35), § 1, effective September 1, 1997; am. Acts 1997, 75th Leg., ch. 1139 (H.B. 3441), § 1, effective June 19, 1997.)

### Sec. 106.025.  Attempt to Purchase Alcohol by a Minor.

(a) A minor commits an offense if, with specific intent to commit an offense under Section 106.02 of this code, the minor does an act amounting to more than mere preparation that tends but fails to effect the commission of the offense intended.

(b) An offense under this section is punishable as provided by Section 106.071.

(Enacted by Acts 1993, 73rd Leg., ch. 934 (H.B. 1445), § 76, effective September 1, 1993; am. Acts 1997, 75th Leg., ch. 1013 (S.B. 35), § 2, effective September 1, 1997.)

### Sec. 106.03.  Sale to Minors.

(a) A person commits an offense if with criminal negligence he sells an alcoholic beverage to a minor.

(b) A person who sells a minor an alcoholic beverage does not commit an offense if the minor falsely represents himself to be 21 years old or older by displaying an apparently valid proof of identification that contains a physical description and photograph consistent with the minor's appearance, purports to establish that the minor is 21 years of age or older, and was issued by a governmental agency. The proof of identification may include a driver's license or identification card issued by the Department of Public Safety, a passport, or a military identification card.

(c) An offense under this section is a Class A misdemeanor.

(d) Subsection (b) does not apply to a person who accesses electronically readable information under Section 109.61 that identifies a driver's license or identification certificate as invalid.

(Enacted by Acts 1977, 65th Leg., ch. 194 (H.B. 815), § 1, effective September 1, 1977; am. Acts 1981, 67th Leg., ch. 107 (S.B. 306), § 9, effective September 1, 1981; am. Acts 1983, 68th Leg., ch. 456 (S.B. 21), § 1, effective September 1, 1983; am. Acts 1985, 69th Leg., ch. 285 (S.B. 21), § 9,

effective September 1, 1986; am. Acts 1985, 69th Leg., ch. 285 (S.B. 21), § 15(c)(2); am. Acts 1985, 69th Leg., ch. 462 (H.B. 1819), § 10, effective September 1, 1986; am. Acts 1985, 69th Leg., ch. 462 (H.B. 1819), § 16(c)(2); am. Acts 1987, 70th Leg., ch. 582 (H.B. 1963), § 1, effective January 1, 1988; am. Acts 1997, 75th Leg., ch. 1013 (S.B. 35), § 3, effective September 1, 1997; am. Acts 2005, 79th Leg., ch. 391 (S.B. 1465), § 3, effective September 1, 2005; am. Acts 2009, 81st Leg., ch. 488 (S.B. 693), § 1, effective June 19, 2009.)

### Sec. 106.04.  Consumption of Alcohol by a Minor.

(a) A minor commits an offense if he consumes an alcoholic beverage.

(b) It is an affirmative defense to prosecution under this section that the alcoholic beverage was consumed in the visible presence of the minor's adult parent, guardian, or spouse.

(c) An offense under this section is punishable as provided by Section 106.071.

(d) A minor who commits an offense under this section and who has been previously convicted twice or more of offenses under this section is not eligible for deferred disposition. For the purposes of this subsection:

(1) an adjudication under Title 3, Family Code, that the minor engaged in conduct described by this section is considered a conviction of an offense under this section; and

(2) an order of deferred disposition for an offense alleged under this section is considered a conviction of an offense under this section.

(e) Subsection (a) does not apply to a minor who:

(1) requested emergency medical assistance in response to the possible alcohol overdose of the minor or another person;

(2) was the first person to make a request for medical assistance under Subdivision (1); and

(3) if the minor requested emergency medical assistance for the possible alcohol overdose of another person:

(A) remained on the scene until the medical assistance arrived; and

(B) cooperated with medical assistance and law enforcement personnel.

(Enacted by Acts 1977, 65th Leg., ch. 194 (H.B. 815), § 1, effective September 1, 1977; am. Acts 1991, 72nd Leg., ch. 163 (H.B. 2183), § 2, effective September 1, 1991; am. Acts 1993, 73rd Leg., ch. 934 (H.B. 1445), § 77, effective September 1, 1993; am. Acts 1997, 75th Leg., ch. 1013 (S.B. 35),

§ 4, effective September 1, 1997; am. Acts 1999, 76th Leg., ch. 1207 (S.B. 528), § 1, effective September 1, 1999; am. Acts 2011, 82nd Leg., ch. 842 (H.B. 3474), § 1, effective September 1, 2011; am. Acts 2011, 82nd Leg., ch. 1243 (S.B. 1331), § 1, effective September 1, 2011.)

## Sec. 106.041. Driving or Operating Watercraft Under the Influence of Alcohol by Minor.

(a) A minor commits an offense if the minor operates a motor vehicle in a public place, or a watercraft, while having any detectable amount of alcohol in the minor's system.

(b) Except as provided by Subsection (c), an offense under this section is a Class C misdemeanor.

(c) If it is shown at the trial of the defendant that the defendant is a minor who is not a child and who has been previously convicted at least twice of an offense under this section, the offense is punishable by:

(1) a fine of not less than $500 or more than $2,000;

(2) confinement in jail for a term not to exceed 180 days; or

(3) both the fine and confinement.

(d) In addition to any fine and any order issued under Section 106.115, the court shall order a minor convicted of an offense under this section to perform community service for:

(1) not less than 20 or more than 40 hours, if the minor has not been previously convicted of an offense under this section; or

(2) not less than 40 or more than 60 hours, if the minor has been previously convicted of an offense under this section.

(e) Community service ordered under this section must be related to education about or prevention of misuse of alcohol.

(f) A minor who commits an offense under this section and who has been previously convicted twice or more of offenses under this section is not eligible for deferred disposition or deferred adjudication.

(g) An offense under this section is not a lesser included offense under Section 49.04, 49.045, or 49.06, Penal Code.

(h) For the purpose of determining whether a minor has been previously convicted of an offense under this section:

(1) an adjudication under Title 3, Family Code, that the minor engaged in conduct described by this section is considered a conviction under this section; and

(2) an order of deferred disposition for an offense alleged under this section is considered a conviction of an offense under this section.

(i) A peace officer who is charging a minor with committing an offense under this section is not required to take the minor into custody but may issue a citation to the minor that contains written notice of the time and place the minor must appear before a magistrate, the name and address of the minor charged, and the offense charged.

(j) In this section:

(1) "Child" has the meaning assigned by Section 51.02, Family Code.

(2) "Motor vehicle" has the meaning assigned by Section 32.34(a), Penal Code.

(3) "Public place" has the meaning assigned by Section 1.07, Penal Code.

(4) "Watercraft" has the meaning assigned by Section 49.01, Penal Code.

(Enacted by Acts 1997, 75th Leg., ch. 1013 (S.B. 35), § 5, effective September 1, 1997; am. Acts 1999, 76th Leg., ch. 1207 (S.B. 528), § 2, effective September 1, 1999; am. Acts 2005, 79th Leg., ch. 949 (H.B. 1575), § 29, effective September 1, 2005; am. Acts 2009, 81st Leg., ch. 1348 (S.B. 328), §§ 2-4, effective September 1, 2009.)

## Sec. 106.05. Possession of Alcohol by a Minor.

(a) Except as provided in Subsection (b) of this section, a minor commits an offense if he possesses an alcoholic beverage.

(b) A minor may possess an alcoholic beverage:

(1) while in the course and scope of the minor's employment if the minor is an employee of a licensee or permittee and the employment is not prohibited by this code;

(2) if the minor is in the visible presence of his adult parent, guardian, or spouse, or other adult to whom the minor has been committed by a court; or

(3) if the minor is under the immediate supervision of a commissioned peace officer engaged in enforcing the provisions of this code.

(c) An offense under this section is punishable as provided by Section 106.071.

(d) Subsection (a) does not apply to a minor who:

(1) requested emergency medical assistance in response to the possible alcohol overdose of the minor or another person;

(2) was the first person to make a request for medical assistance under Subdivision (1); and

ABC

(3) if the minor requested emergency medical assistance for the possible alcohol overdose of another person:

(A) remained on the scene until the medical assistance arrived; and

(B) cooperated with medical assistance and law enforcement personnel.

(Enacted by Acts 1977, 65th Leg., ch. 194 (H.B. 815), § 1, effective September 1, 1977; am. Acts 1979, 66th Leg., ch. 777 (H.B. 1740), § 21, effective August 27, 1979; am. Acts 1991, 72nd Leg., ch. 163 (H.B. 2183), § 3, effective September 1, 1991; am. Acts 1993, 73rd Leg., ch. 934 (H.B. 1445), § 78, effective September 1, 1993; am. Acts 1997, 75th Leg., ch. 1013 (S.B. 35), § 6, effective September 1, 1997; am. Acts 1997, 75th Leg., ch. 1139 (H.B. 3441), § 2, effective June 19, 1997; am. Acts 2011, 82nd Leg., ch. 842 (H.B. 3474), § 2, effective September 1, 2011; am. Acts 2011, 82nd Leg., ch. 1243 (S.B. 1331), § 2, effective September 1, 2011.)

### Sec. 106.06.  Purchase of Alcohol for a Minor; Furnishing Alcohol to a Minor.

(a) **[2 versions: As amended by Acts 1993, 73rd Leg., ch. 437]** Except as provided in Subsection (b) of this section, a person commits an offense if he purchases an alcoholic beverage for or gives or makes available an alcoholic beverage to a minor with criminal negligence.

(a) **[2 versions: As amended by Acts 1993, 73rd Leg., ch. 934]** Except as provided in Subsection (b) of this section, a person commits an offense if he purchases an alcoholic beverage for or gives or with criminal negligence makes available an alcoholic beverage to a minor.

(b) A person may purchase an alcoholic beverage for or give an alcoholic beverage to a minor if he is the minor's adult parent, guardian, or spouse, or an adult in whose custody the minor has been committed by a court, and he is visibly present when the minor possesses or consumes the alcoholic beverage.

(c) An offense under this section is a Class A misdemeanor.

(d) A judge, acting under Article 42.12, Code of Criminal Procedure, who places a defendant charged with an offense under this section on community supervision under that article shall, if the defendant committed the offense at a gathering where participants were involved in the abuse of alcohol, including binge drinking or forcing or coercing individuals to consume alcohol, in addition to any other condition imposed by the judge:

(1) require the defendant to:

(A) perform community service for not less than 20 or more than 40 hours; and

(B) attend an alcohol awareness program approved under Section 106.115; and

(2) order the Department of Public Safety to suspend the driver's license or permit of the defendant or, if the defendant does not have a driver's license or permit, to deny the issuance of a driver's license or permit to the defendant for 180 days.

(e) Community service ordered under Subsection (d) is in addition to any community service ordered by the judge under Section 16, Article 42.12, Code of Criminal Procedure, and must be related to education about or prevention of misuse of alcohol if programs or services providing that education are available in the community in which the court is located. If programs or services providing that education are not available, the court may order community service that the court considers appropriate for rehabilitative purposes.

(Enacted by Acts 1977, 65th Leg., ch. 194 (H.B. 815), § 1, effective September 1, 1977; am. Acts 1993, 73rd Leg., ch. 437 (S.B. 55), § 4, effective September 1, 1993; am. Acts 1993, 73rd Leg., ch. 934 (H.B. 1445), § 79, effective September 1, 1993; am. Acts 1997, 75th Leg., ch. 1013 (S.B. 35), § 7, effective September 1, 1997; am. Acts 2001, 77th Leg., ch. 1097 (H.B. 2331), § 2, effective September 1, 2001; am. Acts 2011, 82nd Leg., ch. 842 (H.B. 3474), § 3, effective September 1, 2011; am. Acts 2011, 82nd Leg., ch. 1243 (S.B. 1331), § 3, effective September 1, 2011.)

### Sec. 106.07.  Misrepresentation of Age by a Minor.

(a) A minor commits an offense if he falsely states that he is 21 years of age or older or presents any document that indicates he is 21 years of age or older to a person engaged in selling or serving alcoholic beverages.

(b) An offense under this section is punishable as provided by Section 106.071.

(Enacted by Acts 1977, 65th Leg., ch. 194 (H.B. 815), § 1, effective September 1, 1977; am. Acts 1981, 67th Leg., ch. 107 (S.B. 306), § 10, effective September 1, 1981; am. Acts 1985, 69th Leg., ch. 285 (S.B. 21), § 10, effective September 1, 1986; am. Acts 1985, 69th Leg., ch. 285 (S.B. 21), § 15(c)(3); am. Acts 1985, 69th Leg., ch. 462 (H.B. 1819), § 11, effective September 1, 1986; am. Acts 1985, 69th Leg., ch. 462 (H.B. 1819), § 16(c)(3); am. Acts 1997, 75th Leg., ch. 1013 (S.B. 35), § 8, effective September 1, 1997.)

## Sec. 106.071. Punishment for Alcohol-Related Offense by Minor.

(a) This section applies to an offense under Section 106.02, 106.025, 106.04, 106.05, or 106.07.

(b) Except as provided by Subsection (c), an offense to which this section applies is a Class C misdemeanor.

(c) If it is shown at the trial of the defendant that the defendant is a minor who is not a child and who has been previously convicted at least twice of an offense to which this section applies, the offense is punishable by:

(1) a fine of not less than $250 or more than $2,000;

(2) confinement in jail for a term not to exceed 180 days; or

(3) both the fine and confinement.

(d) In addition to any fine and any order issued under Section 106.115:

(1) the court shall order a minor placed on deferred disposition for or convicted of an offense to which this section applies to perform community service for:

(A) not less than eight or more than 12 hours, if the minor has not been previously convicted of an offense to which this section applies; or

(B) not less than 20 or more than 40 hours, if the minor has been previously convicted once of an offense to which this section applies; and

(2) the court shall order the Department of Public Safety to suspend the driver's license or permit of a minor convicted of an offense to which this section applies or, if the minor does not have a driver's license or permit, to deny the issuance of a driver's license or permit for:

(A) 30 days, if the minor has not been previously convicted of an offense to which this section applies;

(B) 60 days, if the minor has been previously convicted once of an offense to which this section applies; or

(C) 180 days, if the minor has been previously convicted twice or more of an offense to which this section applies.

(e) Community service ordered under this section must be related to education about or prevention of misuse of alcohol if programs or services providing that education are available in the community in which the court is located. If programs or services providing that education are not available, the court may order community service that it considers appropriate for rehabilitative purposes.

(f) In this section:

(1) a prior adjudication under Title 3, Family Code, that the minor engaged in conduct described by this section is considered a conviction; and

(2) a prior order of deferred disposition for an offense alleged under this section is considered a conviction.

(g) In this section, "child" has the meaning assigned by Section 51.02, Family Code.

(h) A driver's license suspension under this section takes effect on the 11th day after the date the minor is convicted.

(i) A defendant who is not a child and who has been previously convicted at least twice of an offense to which this section applies is not eligible to receive a deferred disposition or deferred adjudication.

(Enacted by Acts 1997, 75th Leg., ch. 1013 (S.B. 35), § 9, effective September 1, 1997; am. Acts 1999, 76th Leg., ch. 76 (H.B. 688), § 4, effective September 1, 1999; am. Acts 1999, 76th Leg., ch. 1207 (S.B. 528), § 3, effective September 1, 1999; am. Acts 2005, 79th Leg., ch. 949 (H.B. 1575), § 30, effective September 1, 2005.)

## Sec. 106.08. Importation by a Minor.

No minor may import into this state or possess with intent to import into this state any alcoholic beverage.

(Enacted by Acts 1977, 65th Leg., ch. 194 (H.B. 815), § 1, effective September 1, 1977.)

## Sec. 106.09. Employment of Minors.

(a) Except as provided in Subsections (b), (c), and (e) of this section, no person may employ a person under 18 years of age to sell, prepare, serve, or otherwise handle liquor, or to assist in doing so.

(b) A holder of a wine only package store permit may employ a person 16 years old or older to work in any capacity.

(c) A holder of a permit or license providing for the on-premises consumption of alcoholic beverages may employ a person under 18 years of age to work in any capacity other than the actual selling, preparing, or serving of alcoholic beverages.

(d) The fact that a person is 18, 19, or 20 years of age is not a ground for refusal of an original or renewal permit or license issued under Chapter 35 or 73 of this code, provided that such a person to whom a permit or license is issued may carry out the activities authorized by those chapters only while in the actual course and scope of the person's employment.

(e) The holder of a permit or license providing for the on-premises consumption of alcoholic beverages who also holds a food and beverage certificate may employ a person under 18 years of age to work as a cashier for transactions involving the sale of alcoholic beverages if the alcoholic beverages are served by a person 18 years of age or older.

(Enacted by Acts 1977, 65th Leg., ch. 194 (H.B. 815), § 1, effective September 1, 1977; am. Acts 1981, 67th Leg., ch. 107 (S.B. 306), §§ 11, 12 effective September 1, 1981; am. Acts 1987, 70th Leg., ch. 754 (H.B. 258), § 1, effective August 31, 1987; am. Acts 2003, 78th Leg., ch. 499 (H.B. 1056), § 1, effective September 1, 2003.)

### Sec. 106.10.   Plea of Guilty by Minor.

No minor may plead guilty to an offense under this chapter except in open court before a judge. (Enacted by Acts 1977, 65th Leg., ch. 194 (H.B. 815), § 1, effective September 1, 1977.)

### Sec. 106.11.   Parent or Guardian at Trial [Repealed].

Repealed by Acts 2005, 79th Leg., ch. 949 (H.B. 1575), § 52(1), effective September 1, 2005. (Enacted by Acts 1977, 65th Leg., ch. 194 (H.B. 815), § 1, effective September 1, 1977; am. Acts 1987, 70th Leg., ch. 754 (H.B. 258), § 2, effective August 31, 1987.)

### Sec. 106.115.   Attendance at Alcohol Awareness Course; License Suspension.

(a) On the placement of a minor on deferred disposition for an offense under Section 49.02, Penal Code, or under Section 106.02, 106.025, 106.04, 106.041, 106.05, or 106.07, the court shall require the defendant to attend an alcohol awareness program approved by the Texas Commission on Alcohol and Drug Abuse. On conviction of a minor of an offense under one or more of those sections, the court, in addition to assessing a fine as provided by those sections, shall require a defendant who has not been previously convicted of an offense under one of those sections to attend the alcohol awareness program. If the defendant has been previously convicted once or more of an offense under one or more of those sections, the court may require the defendant to attend the

alcohol awareness program. If the defendant is younger than 18 years of age, the court may require the parent or guardian of the defendant to attend the program with the defendant. The Texas Commission on Alcohol and Drug Abuse:

(1) is responsible for the administration of the certification of approved alcohol awareness programs;

(2) may charge a nonrefundable application fee for:

(A) initial certification of the approval; or

(B) renewal of the certification;

(3) shall adopt rules regarding alcohol awareness programs approved under this section; and

(4) shall monitor, coordinate, and provide training to a person who provides an alcohol awareness program.

(b) When requested, an alcohol awareness program may be taught in languages other than English.

(c) The court shall require the defendant to present to the court, within 90 days of the date of final conviction, evidence in the form prescribed by the court that the defendant, as ordered by the court, has satisfactorily completed an alcohol awareness program or performed the required hours of community service. For good cause the court may extend this period by not more than 90 days. If the defendant presents the required evidence within the prescribed period, the court may reduce the assessed fine to an amount equal to no less than one-half of the amount of the initial fine.

(d) If the defendant does not present the required evidence within the prescribed period, the court:

(1) shall order the Department of Public Safety to:

(A) suspend the defendant's driver's license or permit for a period not to exceed six months or, if the defendant does not have a license or permit, to deny the issuance of a license or permit to the defendant for that period; or

(B) if the defendant has been previously convicted of an offense under one or more of the sections listed in Subsection (a), suspend the defendant's driver's license or permit for a period not to exceed one year or, if the defendant does not have a license or permit, to deny the issuance of a license or permit to the defendant for that period; and

(2) may order the defendant or the parent, managing conservator, or guardian of the de-

fendant to do any act or refrain from doing any act if the court determines that doing the act or refraining from doing the act will increase the likelihood that the defendant will present evidence to the court that the defendant has satisfactorily completed an alcohol awareness program or performed the required hours of community service.

(e) The Department of Public Safety shall send notice of the suspension or prohibition order issued under Subsection (d) by first class mail to the defendant. The notice must include the date of the suspension or prohibition order, the reason for the suspension or prohibition, and the period covered by the suspension or prohibition.

(Enacted by Acts 1991, 72nd Leg., ch. 163 (H.B. 2183), § 4, effective September 1, 1991; am. Acts 1993, 73rd Leg., ch. 934 (H.B. 1445), § 80, effective September 1, 1993; am. Acts 1995, 74th Leg., ch. 615 (H.B. 1375), § 1, effective September 1, 1995; am. Acts 1997, 75th Leg., ch. 577 (H.B. 2119), § 17, effective September 1, 1997; am. Acts 1997, 75th Leg., ch. 1013 (S.B. 35), § 10, effective September 1, 1997; am. Acts 1999, 76th Leg., ch. 62 (S.B. 1368), § 2.01, effective September 1, 1999; am. Acts 1999, 76th Leg., ch. 76 (H.B. 688), § 5, effective September 1, 1999; am. Acts 1999, 76th Leg., ch. 1207 (S.B. 528), § 4, effective September 1, 1999; am. Acts 1999, 76th Leg., ch. 1409 (H.B. 2031), § 7, effective September 1, 1999; am. Acts 2005, 79th Leg., ch. 1056 (H.B. 1357), § 1, effective September 1, 2005.)

## Sec. 106.116. Reports of Court to Commission.

Unless the clerk is otherwise required to include the information in a report submitted under Section 101.09, the clerk of a court, including a justice court, municipal court, or juvenile court, shall furnish to the commission on request a notice of a conviction of an offense under this chapter or an adjudication under Title 3, Family Code, for conduct that constitutes an offense under this chapter. The report must be in the form prescribed by the commission.

(Enacted by Acts 1997, 75th Leg., ch. 1013 (S.B. 35), § 11, effective September 1, 1997.)

## Sec. 106.117. Report of Court to Department of Public Safety.

(a) Each court, including a justice court, municipal court, or juvenile court, shall furnish to the Department of Public Safety a notice of each:

(1) adjudication under Title 3, Family Code, for conduct that constitutes an offense under this chapter;

(2) conviction of an offense under this chapter;

(3) order of deferred disposition for an offense alleged under this chapter; and

(4) acquittal of an offense under Section 106.041.

(b) The notice must be in a form prescribed by the Department of Public Safety and must contain the driver's license number of the defendant, if the defendant holds a driver's license.

(c) The Department of Public Safety shall maintain appropriate records of information in the notices and shall provide the information to law enforcement agencies and courts as necessary to enable those agencies and courts to carry out their official duties. The information is admissible in any action in which it is relevant. A person who holds a driver's license having the same number that is contained in a record maintained under this section is presumed to be the person to whom the record relates. The presumption may be rebutted only by evidence presented under oath.

(d) The information maintained under this section is confidential and may not be disclosed except as provided by this section. A provision of Chapter 58, Family Code, or other law limiting collection or reporting of information on a juvenile or other minor or requiring destruction of that information does not apply to information reported and maintained under this section.

(Enacted by Acts 1997, 75th Leg., ch. 1013 (S.B. 35), § 11, effective September 1, 1997; am. Acts 1999, 76th Leg., ch. 1207 (S.B. 528), § 5, effective September 1, 1999.)

## Sec. 106.12. Expungement of Conviction of a Minor.

(a) Any person convicted of not more than one violation of this code while a minor, on attaining the age of 21 years, may apply to the court in which he was convicted to have the conviction expunged.

(b) The application shall contain the applicant's sworn statement that he was not convicted of any violation of this code while a minor other than the one he seeks to have expunged.

(c) If the court finds that the applicant was not convicted of any other violation of this code while he was a minor, the court shall order the conviction, together with all complaints, verdicts, sentences, and other documents relating to the offense, to be expunged from the applicant's record. After entry of the order, the applicant shall be

ABC

released from all disabilities resulting from the conviction, and the conviction may not be shown or made known for any purpose.

(d) The court shall charge an applicant a fee in the amount of $30 for each application for expungement filed under this section to defray the cost of notifying state agencies of orders of expungement under this section.

(Enacted by Acts 1977, 65th Leg., ch. 194 (H.B. 815), § 1, effective September 1, 1977; am. Acts 1981, 67th Leg., ch. 107 (S.B. 306), § 13, effective September 1, 1981; am. Acts 1985, 69th Leg., ch. 285 (S.B. 21), § 11, effective September 1, 1986; am. Acts 1985, 69th Leg., ch. 285 (S.B. 21), § 15(c)(4); am. Acts 1985, 69th Leg., ch. 462 (H.B. 1819), § 12, effective September 1, 1986; am. Acts 1985, 69th Leg., ch. 462 (H.B. 1819), § 16(c)(4); am. Acts 2005, 79th Leg., ch. 886 (S.B. 1426), § 1, effective September 1, 2005.)

### Sec. 106.13. Sanctions Against Retailer.

(a) Except as provided in Subsections (b) and (c) of this section, the commission or administrator may cancel or suspend for not more than 90 days a retail license or permit or a private club registration permit if it is found, on notice and hearing, that the licensee or permittee with criminal negligence sold, served, dispensed, or delivered an alcoholic beverage to a minor or with criminal negligence permitted a minor to violate Section 106.04 or 106.05 of this code on the licensed premises.

(b) For a second offense the commission or administrator may cancel the license or permit or suspend it for not more than six months. For a third offense within a period of 36 consecutive months the commission or administrator may cancel the permit or suspend it for not more than 12 months.

(c) The commission or administrator may relax the provisions of this section concerning suspension and cancellation and assess a sanction the commission or administrator finds just under the circumstances if, at a hearing, the licensee or permittee establishes to the satisfaction of the commission or administrator:

(1) that the violation could not reasonably have been prevented by the permittee or licensee by the exercise of due diligence;

(2) that the permittee or licensee was entrapped; or

(3) that an agent, servant, or employee of the permittee or licensee violated this code without the knowledge of the permittee or licensee.

(Enacted by Acts 1977, 65th Leg., ch. 194 (H.B. 815), § 1, effective September 1, 1977; am. Acts 1993, 73rd Leg., ch. 437 (S.B. 55), § 5, effective September 1, 1993; am. Acts 1993, 73rd Leg., ch. 934 (H.B. 1445), § 81, effective September 1, 1993; am. Acts 1997, 75th Leg., ch. 798 (H.B. 2861), § 1, effective September 1, 1997; am. Acts 2001, 77th Leg., ch. 1097 (H.B. 2331), § 1, effective September 1, 2001.)

### Sec. 106.14. Actions of Employee.

(a) For purposes of this chapter and any other provision of this code relating to the sales, service, dispensing, or delivery of alcoholic beverages to a person who is not a member of a private club on the club premises, a minor, or an intoxicated person or the consumption of alcoholic beverages by a person who is not a member of a private club on the club premises, a minor, or an intoxicated person, the actions of an employee shall not be attributable to the employer if:

(1) the employer requires its employees to attend a commission-approved seller training program;

(2) the employee has actually attended such a training program; and

(3) the employer has not directly or indirectly encouraged the employee to violate such law.

(b) The commission shall adopt rules or policies establishing the minimum requirements for approved seller training programs. Upon application, the commission shall approve seller training programs meeting such requirements that are sponsored either privately, by public community colleges, or by public or private institutions of higher education that offer a four-year undergraduate program and a degree or certificate in hotel or motel management, restaurant management, or travel or tourism management. The commission may charge an application fee to be set by the commission in such amount as is necessary to defray the expense of processing the application.

(c) The commission may approve under this section a seller training program sponsored by a licensee or permittee for the purpose of training its employees whether or not such employees are located at the same premises. This subsection shall only apply to licensees or permittees who employ at least 150 persons at any one time during the license or permit year who sell, serve, or prepare alcoholic beverages.

(d) The commission may approve under this section a seller training program conducted by a hotel management company or a hotel operating company for the employees of five or more hotels operated or managed by the company if:

(1) the seller training program is administered through the corporate offices of the company; and

(2) the hotels employ a total of at least 200 persons at one time during the license or permit year who sell, serve, or prepare alcoholic beverages.

(e) After notice and hearing, the commission may cancel or suspend the commission's approval of a seller training program, the commission's certification of a trainer to teach a seller training program, or the commission's certification of a seller-server if the program, trainer, or seller-server violates this code or a commission rule. The commission may give a program, trainer, or seller-server the opportunity to pay a civil penalty rather than be subject to suspension under this subsection. Sections 11.62 through 11.67 apply to the program approval or certification as if the program approval or certification were a license or permit under this code.

(Enacted by Acts 1987, 70th Leg., ch. 582 (H.B. 1963), § 3, effective September 1, 1987; am. Acts 1989, 71st Leg., ch. 477 (H.B. 1978), § 1, effective August 28, 1989; am. Acts 1993, 73rd Leg., ch. 934 (H.B. 1445), § 82, effective September 1, 1993; am. Acts 1995, 74th Leg., ch. 270 (S.B. 258), § 1, effective September 1, 1995; am. Acts 2003, 78th Leg., ch. 643 (H.B. 2112), § 1, effective September 1, 2003; am. Acts 2011, 82nd Leg., ch. 158 (H.B. 1952), § 1, effective May 28, 2011.)

## Sec. 106.15. Prohibited Activities by Persons Younger Than 18.

(a) A permittee or licensee commits an offense if he employs, authorizes, permits, or induces a person younger than 18 years of age to dance with another person in exchange for a benefit, as defined by Section 1.07, Penal Code, on the premises covered by the permit or license.

(b) An offense under Subsection (a) is a Class A misdemeanor.

(c) In addition to a penalty imposed under Subsection (b), the commission or administrator shall:

(1) suspend for a period of five days the license or permit of a person convicted of a first offense under Subsection (a);

(2) suspend for a period of 60 days the license or permit of a person convicted of a second offense under Subsection (a); and

(3) cancel the license or permit of a person convicted of a third offense under Subsection (a).

(d) This section does not apply to a gift or benefit given for a dance at a wedding, anniversary, or similar event.

(e) A person does not commit an offense under Subsection (a) if the person younger than 18 years of age falsely represents the person's age to be at least 18 years of age by displaying an apparently valid Texas driver's license or an identification card issued by the Department of Public Safety containing a physical description consistent with the person's appearance.

(Enacted by Acts 1999, 76th Leg., ch. 80 (S.B. 222), § 2, effective September 1, 1999.)

# CHAPTER 107
# TRANSPORTATION AND
# IMPORTATION

Section

## Sec. 107.01. Transportation of Liquor: Statement Required.

(a) No person may transport liquor into this state or on a public highway, street, or alley in this state unless the person accompanying or in charge of the shipment has with him, available for exhibition and inspection, a written statement furnished and signed by the shipper showing the name and address of the consignor and the consignee, the origin and destination of the shipment, and any other information required by rule or regulation of the commission.

(b) The person in charge of the shipment while it is being transported shall exhibit the statement to the commission, an authorized representative of the commission, or a peace officer on demand, and it is a violation of this code to fail or refuse to do so. The representative or officer shall accept the written statement as prima facie evidence of the legal right to transport the liquor.

(Enacted by Acts 1977, 65th Leg., ch. 194 (H.B. 815), § 1, effective September 1, 1977.)

## Sec. 107.02. Transportation of Beer: Statement Required.

(a) It is lawful for a person to transport beer from any place where its sale, manufacture, or distribution is authorized to another place in the

ABC

state where its sale, manufacture, or distribution is authorized, or from the state boundary to a place where its sale, manufacture, or distribution is authorized, even though the route of transportation may cross a dry area.

(a-1) A person transporting beer to the premises of a distributor, including to a location from which the distributor is temporarily conducting business under Section 109.62, shall provide to the consignee a shipping invoice that clearly states:

(1) the name and address of the consignor and consignee;

(2) the origin and destination of the shipment; and

(3) any other information required by this code or commission rule, including the brands, sizes of containers, and quantities of beer contained in the shipment.

(b) A shipment of beer must be accompanied by a written statement furnished and signed by the shipper showing:

(1) the name and address of the consignor and consignee;

(2) the origin and destination of the shipment; and

(3) any other information required by the commission or administrator.

(c) The person in charge of the shipment while it is being transported shall exhibit the written statement to any representative of the commission or peace officer who demands to see it. The statement shall be accepted by the representative or peace officer as prima facie evidence of the legal right to transport the beer.

(d) A person who transports beer not accompanied by the required statement, or who fails to exhibit the statement after a lawful demand, violates this code.

(Enacted by Acts 1977, 65th Leg., ch. 194 (H.B. 815), § 1, effective September 1, 1977; am. Acts 2011, 82nd Leg., ch. 517 (H.B. 2035), § 2, effective June 17, 2011.)

## Sec. 107.08. Transportation of Beverages for Personal Consumption.

A person who purchases an alcoholic beverage for his own consumption may transport it from a place where its sale is legal to a place where its possession is legal without holding a license or permit.

(Enacted by Acts 1977, 65th Leg., ch. 194 (H.B. 815), § 1, effective September 1, 1977.)

ABC

# Constitution of the State of Texas

## 1876

## ARTICLE I

## Bill of Rights

### Preamble

That the general, great and essential principles of liberty and free government may be recognized and established, we declare:

### § 9.   Searches and Seizures.

The people shall be secure in their persons, houses, papers and possessions, from all unreasonable seizures or searches, and no warrant to search any place, or to seize any person or thing, shall issue without describing them as near as may be, nor without probable cause, supported by oath or affirmation.

### § 10.   Rights of Accused in Criminal Prosecutions.

In all criminal prosecutions the accused shall have a speedy public trial by an impartial jury. He shall have the right to demand the nature and cause of the accusation against him, and to have a copy thereof. He shall not be compelled to give evidence against himself, and shall have the right of being heard by himself or counsel, or both, shall be confronted by the witnesses against him and shall have compulsory process for obtaining witnesses in his favor, except that when the witness resides out of the State and the offense charged is a violation of any of the anti-trust laws of this State, the defendant and the State shall have the right to produce and have the evidence admitted by deposition, under such rules and laws as the Legislature may hereafter provide; and no person shall be held to answer for a criminal offense, unless on an indictment of a grand jury, except in cases in which the punish-

ment is by fine or imprisonment, otherwise than in the penitentiary, in cases of impeachment, and in cases arising in the army or navy, or in the militia, when in actual service in time of war or public danger.

### § 11.   Bail.

All prisoners shall be bailable by sufficient sureties, unless for capital offenses, when the proof is evident; but this provision shall not be so construed as to prevent bail after indictment found upon examination of the evidence, in such manner as may be prescribed by law.

### § 11a.   Multiple Convictions; Denial of Bail.

(a) Any person (1) accused of a felony less than capital in this State, who has been theretofore twice convicted of a felony, the second conviction being subsequent to the first, both in point of time of commission of the offense and conviction therefor, (2) accused of a felony less than capital in this State, committed while on bail for a prior felony for which he has been indicted, (3) accused of a felony less than capital in this State involving the use of a deadly weapon after being convicted of a prior felony, or (4) accused of a violent or sexual offense committed while under the supervision of a criminal justice agency of the State or a political subdivision of the State for a prior felony, after a hearing, and upon evidence substantially showing the guilt of the accused of the offense in (1) or (3) above, of the offense committed while on bail in (2) above, or of the offense in (4) above committed while under the supervision of a criminal justice agency of the State or a political subdivision of the State for a prior felony, may be denied bail pending trial, by a district judge in this State, if said order denying bail pending trial is issued within seven calendar days subsequent to the time of incarceration of the accused; provided, however, that if the accused is not accorded a trial upon the accusation under (1) or (3) above, the accusation and indictment used under (2) above, or the accusation or indictment used under (4) above within sixty (60) days from the time of his incarceration upon the accusation, the order denying bail shall be automatically set aside, unless a continuance is obtained upon the motion or request of the accused; provided, further, that the right of appeal to the Court of Criminal Appeals of this State is expressly accorded the accused for a review of any judgment or order made hereunder, and said appeal shall be given preference by the Court of Criminal Appeals.

   (b) In this section:

    (1) "Violent offense" means:

     (A) murder;

     (B) aggravated assault, if the accused used or exhibited a deadly weapon during the commission of the assault;

     (C) aggravated kidnapping; or

     (D) aggravated robbery.

    (2) "Sexual offense" means:

     (A) aggravated sexual assault;

     (B) sexual assault; or

     (C) indecency with a child.

# ARTICLE III

## Legislative Department

### § 14. Privilege from Arrest.

   Senators and Representatives shall, except in cases of treason, felony, or breach of the peace, be privileged from arrest during the session of the Legislature, and in going to and returning from the same.

(Amendment proposed by 1999 76th Leg., H.J.R. No. 62, approved by electorate (Prop. 3) at the November 2, 1999 election).

# ARTICLE VI

## Suffrage

### § 5. Privilege of Voters from Arrest.

   Voters shall, in all cases, except treason, felony or breach of the peace, be privileged from arrest during their attendance at elections, and in going to and returning therefrom.

# ARTICLE XVII

## Mode of Amending the Constitution of This State

### § 1. Proposed Amendments; Publication; Submission to Voters; Adoption.

   (a) The Legislature, at any regular session, or at any special session when the matter is included within the purposes for which the session is convened, may propose amendments revising the Constitution, to be voted upon by the qualified voters for statewide offices and propositions, as defined in the Constitution and statutes of this State. The date of the elections shall be specified by the Legislature. The proposal for submission must be approved by a vote of two-thirds of all the members elected to each House, entered by yeas and nays on the journals.

   (b) A brief explanatory statement of the nature of a proposed amendment, together with the date of the election and the wording of the proposition as it is to appear on the ballot, shall be published twice in each newspaper in the State which meets requirements set by the Legislature for the publication of official notices of officers and departments of the state government. The explanatory statement shall be prepared by the Secretary of State and shall be approved by the Attorney General. The Secretary of State shall send a full and complete copy of the proposed amendment or amendments to each county clerk who shall post the same in a public place in the courthouse at least 30 days prior to the election on said amendment. The first notice shall be published not more than 60 days nor less than 50 days before the date of the election, and the second notice shall be published on the same day in the succeeding week. The Legislature shall fix the standards for the rate of charge for the publication, which may not be higher than the newspaper's published national rate for advertising per column inch.

   (c) The election shall be held in accordance with procedures prescribed by the Legislature, and the returning officer in each county shall make returns to the Secretary of State of the number of legal votes cast at the election for and against each amendment. If it appears from the returns that a majority of the votes cast have been cast in favor of an amendment, it shall become a part of this Constitution, and proclamation thereof shall be made by the Governor.

(Amendment proposed by 1999 76th Leg., H.J.R. No. 62, approved by electorate (Prop. 3) at the November 2, 1999 constitutional amendment election).

# Agriculture Code

## TITLE 5
## PRODUCTION, PROCESSING, AND SALE OF HORTICULTURAL PRODUCTS

### SUBTITLE D
### HANDLING AND MARKETING OF HORTICULTURAL PRODUCTS

### CHAPTER 102
### HANDLING AND MARKETING OF CITRUS FRUIT

**Subchapter B. Transportation of Citrus Fruit**

### SUBCHAPTER B
### TRANSPORTATION OF CITRUS FRUIT

### Sec. 102.101.   Identification Signs.

(a) A motor vehicle, including a truck or tractor, that hauls citrus fruit in bulk or in open containers for commercial purposes on the highways of this state must be identified by signs showing:

(1) the name of the person who owns the vehicle; or

(2) the name of the person who leases or operates the vehicle.

(b) If a person licensed under Subchapter A of this chapter is the owner or operator of the vehicle, each identification sign must also show "Licensed Citrus Fruit Dealer" under the name of the person.

(c) The lettering on each identification sign must be at least three inches in height.

(d) An identification sign must appear on both sides of the vehicle or on both the front and the rear and must be affixed permanently or in another manner in which it may not easily be removed. If both a tractor and a trailer or two units are used in hauling the citrus fruit, both the tractor and the trailer or both units must be labeled with identification signs in the manner required by this subsection.

(Enacted by Acts 1981, 67th Leg., ch. 388 (H.B. 1436), § 1, effective September 1, 1981.)

### Sec. 102.102.   Certificate.

A person who operates a motor vehicle, including a truck or tractor, or a motor vehicle and a trailer for hauling citrus fruit in bulk or in open containers for commercial purposes on the highways of this state shall, when operating the vehicle, have on his or her person a certificate or other document showing:

(1) the approximate amount of citrus fruit being hauled;

(2) the name of the owner of the citrus fruit; and

(3) the origin of the citrus fruit.

(Enacted by Acts 1981, 67th Leg., ch. 388 (H.B. 1436), § 1, effective September 1, 1981.)

### Sec. 102.103.   Exception.

This subchapter does not apply to citrus fruit being hauled from the farm or grove to market or the place of first processing by the producer of the citrus fruit operating the producer's vehicle or by an employee of the producer operating a vehicle owned by the producer.

(Enacted by Acts 1981, 67th Leg., ch. 388 (H.B. 1436), § 1, effective September 1, 1981.)

### Sec. 102.104.   Penalty.

(a) A person commits an offense if the person:

(1) operates a motor vehicle or a motor vehi-

cle and trailer not identified in accordance with Section 102.101 of this code; or

(2) operates a motor vehicle or motor vehicle and trailer without a certificate or document required by Section 102.102 of this code.

(b) An offense under this section is a Class B misdemeanor.

(Enacted by Acts 1981, 67th Leg., ch. 388 (H.B. 1436), § 1, effective September 1, 1981; am. Acts 1989, 71st Leg., ch. 230 (S.B. 489), § 118, effective September 1, 1989.)

# TITLE 6

# PRODUCTION, PROCESSING, AND SALE OF ANIMAL PRODUCTS

## SUBTITLE B
## LIVESTOCK

## CHAPTER 143
## FENCES; RANGE RESTRICTIONS

## SUBCHAPTER D
## LOCAL OPTION TO PREVENT CATTLE OR DOMESTIC TURKEYS FROM RUNNING AT LARGE

### Sec. 143.082.   Penalty.

(a) A person commits an offense if the person knowingly permits a head of cattle or a domestic turkey to run at large in a county or area that has adopted this subchapter.

(b) An offense under this section is a Class C misdemeanor.

(Enacted by Acts 1981, 67th Leg., ch. 388 (H.B. 1436), § 1, effective September 1, 1981; am. Acts 1987, 70th Leg., ch. 51 (S.B. 20), § 3, effective September 1, 1987.)

## SUBCHAPTER E
## ANIMALS RUNNING AT LARGE ON HIGHWAYS

### Sec. 143.101.   Definition.

In this subchapter, "highway" means a U.S. highway or a state highway in this state, but does not include a numbered farm-to-market road. The term includes the portion of Recreation Road Number 255 that is located in Newton County between State Highway Number 87 and the boundary line with Jasper County.

(Enacted by Acts 1981, 67th Leg., ch. 388 (H.B. 1436), § 1, effective September 1, 1981; am. Acts 1987, 70th Leg., ch. 380 (H.B. 2404), § 1, effective August 31, 1987.)

### Sec. 143.102.   Running at Large on Highway Prohibited.

A person who owns or has responsibility for the control of a horse, mule, donkey, cow, bull, steer, hog, sheep, or goat may not knowingly permit the animal to traverse or roam at large, unattended, on the right-of-way of a highway.

(Enacted by Acts 1981, 67th Leg., ch. 388 (H.B. 1436), § 1, effective September 1, 1981.)

### Sec. 143.103.   Immunity from Liability.

A person whose vehicle strikes, kills, injures, or damages an unattended animal running at large on a highway is not liable for damages to the animal except on a finding of:

(1) gross negligence in the operation of the vehicle; or

(2) wilful intent to strike, kill, injure, or damage the animal.

(Enacted by Acts 1981, 67th Leg., ch. 388 (H.B. 1436), § 1, effective September 1, 1981.)

### Sec. 143.104. Herding of Livestock Along Highway.

This subchapter does not prevent the movement of livestock from one location to another by herding, leading, or driving the livestock on, along, or across a highway.
(Enacted by Acts 1981, 67th Leg., ch. 388 (H.B. 1436), § 1, effective September 1, 1981.)

### Sec. 143.105. Impounding of Livestock [Repealed].

Repealed by Acts 1987, 70th Leg., ch. 51 (S.B. 20), § 5(12), effective September 1, 1987.
(Enacted by Acts 1981, 67th Leg., ch. 388 (H.B. 1436), § 1, effective September 1, 1981.)

### Sec. 143.106. Enforcement.

Each state highway patrolman or county or local law enforcement officer shall enforce this subchapter and may enforce it without the use of a written warrant.
(Enacted by Acts 1981, 67th Leg., ch. 388 (H.B. 1436), § 1, effective September 1, 1981.)

### Sec. 143.107. Conflict with Other Law.

This subchapter prevails to the extent of any conflict with another provision of this chapter.
(Enacted by Acts 1981, 67th Leg., ch. 388 (H.B. 1436), § 1, effective September 1, 1981.)

### Sec. 143.108. Penalty.

(a) A person commits an offense if the person violates Section 143.102 of this code.

(b) An offense under this section is a Class C misdemeanor.

(c) A person commits a separate offense for each day that an animal is permitted to roam at large in violation of Section 143.102 of this code.
(Enacted by Acts 1981, 67th Leg., ch. 388 (H.B. 1436), § 1, effective September 1, 1981; am. Acts 1987, 70th Leg., ch. 51 (S.B. 20), § 4, effective September 1, 1987.)

# CHAPTER 146
# SALE AND SHIPMENT OF LIVESTOCK

**Subchapter A. General Provisions**

## SUBCHAPTER A
## GENERAL PROVISIONS

### Sec. 146.005. Permits to Transport Animals.

(a) A person who drives a vehicle, including a truck or an automobile, containing livestock, domestic fowl, slaughtered livestock or domestic fowl, or butchered portions of livestock or domestic fowl on a highway, public street, or thoroughfare or on property owned or leased by a person other than the driver shall obtain a permit authorizing the movement.

(b) A permit must be signed by the owner or caretaker of the shipment or by the owner or person in control of the land from which the driver began movement. In addition, the permit must state the following information:

(1) the point of origin of the shipment, including the name of the ranch or other place;

(2) the point of destination of the shipment, including the name of the ranch, market center, packinghouse, or other place;

(3) the number of living animals, slaughtered animals, or butchered portions; and

(4) the description of the shipment, including the kind, breed, color, and marks and brands of living or slaughtered animals.

(c) On demand of a peace officer or any other person, the driver shall exhibit the permit required by this section or shall provide a signed, written statement containing all of the information required for a permit under this section.

(d) Failure or refusal of a driver to exhibit a permit or provide a statement in accordance with this section is probable cause for a search of the

**Agriculture Code**

vehicle to determine if it contains stolen property and for detaining the shipment a reasonable length of time to make that determination.
(Enacted by Acts 1981, 67th Leg., ch. 388 (H.B. 1436), § 1, effective September 1, 1981.)

### Sec. 146.006.  Penalty for Driving Stock to Market Without Bill of Sale or Sworn List.

(a) A person commits an offense if the person drives to market animals of a class listed in Section 146.001 of this code without possessing:

(1) a bill of sale or transfer for each animal that shows the marks and brands of the animal and is certified as recorded by the county clerk of the county from which the animals were driven; or

(2) if the person raised the animals, a list of the marks and brands that is certified as recorded by the county clerk of the county from which the animals were driven.

(b) An offense under this section is a misdemeanor punishable by a fine not to exceed $2,000.
(Enacted by Acts 1981, 67th Leg., ch. 388 (H.B. 1436), § 1, effective September 1, 1981.)

### Sec. 146.008.  Penalty for Transporting Animals Without Permit or with Fraudulent Permit.

(a) A person commits an offense if, under Section 146.005 of this code, the person:

(1) transports living animals, slaughtered animals, or butchered portions of animals without possessing a permit;

(2) fails to exhibit a permit or provide a statement on demand;

(3) transports living animals, slaughtered animals, or butchered portions of animals that are not covered by a permit;

(4) possesses a false or forged permit; or

(5) provides a false written statement.

(b) An offense under Subsection (a)(1) or (a)(2) of this section is a misdemeanor punishable by a fine of not less than $25 nor more than $200 for each animal in the shipment.

(c) An offense under Subsection (a)(3) of this section is a misdemeanor punishable by a fine of not less than $25 nor more than $200 for each animal that is not covered by the permit.

(d) An offense under Subsection (a)(4) or (a)(5) of this section is a misdemeanor punishable by:

(1) a fine of not less than $200 nor more than $500;

(2) confinement in county jail for not less than 60 days nor more than 6 months; or

(3) both fine and confinement under this subsection.
(Enacted by Acts 1981, 67th Leg., ch. 388 (H.B. 1436), § 1, effective September 1, 1981.)

Agriculture Code

# Business and Commerce Code

## TITLE 4

## BUSINESS OPPORTUNITIES AND AGREEMENTS

### CHAPTER 35
### MISCELLANEOUS
### [REPEALED]

#### SUBCHAPTER D
#### MISCELLANEOUS
#### [REPEALED]

**Sec. 35.46. Attaching Motor Vehicle Dealer's Name to Vehicle [Repealed].**

Repealed by Acts 2007, 80th Leg., ch. 885 (H.B. 2278), § 2.47(a)(1), effective April 1, 2009. (Enacted by Acts 1987, 70th Leg., ch. 858 (H.B. 152), § 1, effective September 1, 1987; am. Acts 1997, 75th Leg., ch. 165 (S.B. 898), § 30.178, effective September 1, 1997.)

**Sec. 35.54. Use of Crime Victim or Motor Vehicle Accident Information for Certain Purposes Prohibited [Repealed].**

Repealed by Acts 2007, 80th Leg., ch. 885 (H.B. 2278), § 2.47(a)(1), effective April 1, 2009. (Enacted by Acts 1989, 71st Leg., 1st C.S., ch. 4 (S.B. 62), § 1, effective January 1, 1990; am. Acts 1991, 72nd Leg., ch. 860 (H.B. 922), § 1, effective September 1, 1991.)

## TITLE 6

## SALE OR TRANSFER OF GOODS

### CHAPTER 202
### SALES OF MOTOR VEHICLES WITH STOPLAMP COVERINGS

**Sec. 202.001. Sale of Motor Vehicle with Certain Stoplamp Covering Prohibited.**

(a) In this section, "motor vehicle" has the meaning assigned by Section 541.201, Transportation Code.

(b) A person in the business of selling motor vehicles may not sell a motor vehicle with a transparent or semitransparent covering:

(1) placed over a stoplamp that is mounted on the rear center line of the vehicle either in or on the rear window or within six inches from the rear window of the vehicle for the purpose of emitting light when the vehicle's brakes are applied; and

(2) on which is impressed or imprinted a name, trade name, logotype, or other message that a person behind the vehicle can read when the stoplamp is illuminated.

(c) A person who violates this section commits an offense. An offense under this section is a Class C misdemeanor.

(Enacted by Acts 2007, 80th Leg., ch. 885 (H.B. 2278), § 2.01, effective April 1, 2009.)

Business

# TITLE 11
# PERSONAL IDENTITY INFORMATION

## SUBTITLE A
## IDENTIFYING INFORMATION

## CHAPTER 504
## PROHIBITED USE OF CRIME VICTIM OR MOTOR VEHICLE ACCIDENT INFORMATION

**Section**
504.001.  Definitions.
504.002.  Prohibition on Use for Solicitation or Sale of Information.

### Sec. 504.001.  Definitions.
In this chapter:

(1) "Crime victim information" means information that:

(A) is collected or prepared by a law enforcement agency; and

(B) identifies or serves to identify a person who, according to a record of the agency, may have been the victim of a crime in which:

(i) physical injury to the person occurred or was attempted; or

(ii) the offender entered or attempted to enter the dwelling of the person.

(2) "Motor vehicle accident information" means information that:

(A) is collected or prepared by a law enforcement agency; and

(B) identifies or serves to identify a person who, according to a record of the agency, may have been involved in a motor vehicle accident.

(Enacted by Acts 2007, 80th Leg., ch. 885 (H.B. 2278), § 2.01, effective April 1, 2009.)

### Sec. 504.002.  Prohibition on Use for Solicitation or Sale of Information.

(a) A person who possesses crime victim or motor vehicle accident information that the person obtained or knows was obtained from a law enforcement agency may not:

(1) use the information to contact directly any of the following persons for the purpose of soliciting business from the person:

(A) a crime victim;

(B) a person who was involved in a motor vehicle accident; or

(C) a member of the family of a person described by Paragraph (A) or (B); or

(2) sell the information to another person for financial gain.

(b) The attorney general may bring an action against a person who violates Subsection (a) pursuant to Section 17.47.

(c) A person commits an offense if the person violates Subsection (a). An offense under this subsection is a Class C misdemeanor unless the defendant has been previously convicted under this section three or more times, in which event the offense is a felony of the third degree.

(Enacted by Acts 2007, 80th Leg., ch. 885 (H.B. 2278), § 2.01, effective April 1, 2009.)

# Civil Practice and Remedies Code

## TITLE 2
## TRIAL, JUDGMENT, AND APPEAL

### SUBTITLE A
### GENERAL PROVISIONS

### CHAPTER 7
### LIABILITY OF COURT OFFICERS

#### SUBCHAPTER A
#### LIABILITY OF OFFICER

### Sec. 7.003. Liability Regarding Execution of Writs.

(a) Except as provided by Section 34.061, an officer is not liable for damages resulting from the execution of a writ issued by a court of this state if the officer in good faith executes or attempts to execute the writ as provided by law and by the Texas Rules of Civil Procedure.

(b) An officer shall execute a writ issued by a court of this state without requiring that bond be posted for the indemnification of the officer.

(c) An officer shows that the officer acted in good faith when the officer shows that a reasonably prudent officer, under the same or similar circumstances, could have believed that the officer's conduct was justified based on the information the officer possessed when the conduct occurred.

(Enacted by Acts 1985, 69th Leg., ch. 959 (S.B. 797), § 1, effective September 1, 1985; am. Acts 2007, 80th Leg., ch. 421 (S.B. 1269), § 2, effective September 1, 2007.)

### SUBTITLE B
### TRIAL MATTERS

### CHAPTER 22
### WITNESSES

#### SUBCHAPTER B
#### PRIVILEGES

### Sec. 22.011. Privilege from Arrest.

(a) A witness is privileged from arrest while attending, going to, and returning from court.

(b) The privilege provided by this section extends for a period computed by allowing one day of travel for each 150 miles of the distance from the courthouse to the witness's residence.

(c) This section does not apply to an arrest for a felony, treason, or breach of the peace.

(Enacted by Acts 1985, 69th Leg., ch. 959 (S.B. 797), § 1, effective September 1, 1985; am. Acts 1993, 73rd Leg., ch. 103 (H.B. 887), § 1, effective January 1, 1994.)

### SUBTITLE C
### JUDGMENTS

### CHAPTER 34
### EXECUTION ON JUDGMENTS

**Subchapter B. Recovery of Seized Property**

Civil Practice

Section
34.022.    Recovery of Property Value After Sale.

## SUBCHAPTER B
## RECOVERY OF SEIZED PROPERTY

### Sec. 34.021.  Recovery of Property Before Sale.

A person is entitled to recover his property that has been seized through execution of a writ issued by a court if the judgment on which execution is issued is reversed or set aside and the property has not been sold at execution.
(Enacted by Acts 1985, 69th Leg., ch. 959 (S.B. 797), § 1, effective September 1, 1985.)

### Sec. 34.022.  Recovery of Property Value After Sale.

(a) A person is entitled to recover from the judgment creditor the market value of the person's property that has been seized through execution of a writ issued by a court if the judgment on which execution is issued is reversed or set aside but the property has been sold at execution.

(b) The amount of recovery is determined by the market value at the time of sale of the property sold.
(Enacted by Acts 1985, 69th Leg., ch. 959 (S.B. 797), § 1, effective September 1, 1985.)

## TITLE 4
# LIABILITY IN TORT

## CHAPTER 83
## USE OF DEADLY FORCE IN DEFENSE OF PERSON

### Sec. 83.001.  Civil Immunity.

A defendant who uses force or deadly force that is justified under Chapter 9, Penal Code, is immune from civil liability for personal injury or death that results from the defendant's use of force or deadly force, as applicable.
(Acts 1995, 74th Leg., ch. 235, effective September 1, 1995; am. Acts 2007, 80th Leg., ch. 1 (S.B. 378), § 4, effective September 1, 2007.)

### Sec. 83.002.  Liability [Renumbered].

Renumbered to Tex. Civ. Prac. & Rem. Code § 85.002 by Acts 1997, 75th Leg., ch. 165 (S.B. 898), § 31.01(7), effective September 1, 1997.

### Sec. 83.003.  Proof [Renumbered].

Renumbered to Tex. Civ. Prac. & Rem. Code § 85.003 by Acts 1997, 75th Leg., ch. 165 (S.B. 898), § 31.01(7), effective September 1, 1997.

### Sec. 83.004.  Damages [Renumbered].

Renumbered to Tex. Civ. Prac. & Rem. Code § 85.004 by Acts 1997, 75th Leg., ch. 165 (S.B. 898), § 31.01(7), effective September 1, 1997.

### Sec. 83.005.  Defense [Renumbered].

Renumbered to Tex. Civ. Prac. & Rem. Code § 85.005 by Acts 1997, 75th Leg., ch. 165 (S.B. 898), § 31.01(7), effective September 1, 1997.

### Sec. 83.006.  Cause of Action Cumulative [Renumbered].

Renumbered to Tex. Civ. Prac. & Rem. Code § 85.006 by Acts 1997, 75th Leg., ch. 165 (S.B. 898), § 31.01(7), effective September 1, 1997.

## CHAPTER 85
## LIABILITY FOR STALKING

Section
85.001.    Definitions.
85.002.    Liability.
85.003.    Proof.
85.004.    Damages.
85.005.    Defense.
85.006.    Cause of Action Cumulative.

### Sec. 85.001.  Definitions.

In this chapter:

(1) "Claimant" means a party seeking to recover damages under this chapter, including a plaintiff, counterclaimant, cross-claimant, or third-party plaintiff. In an action in which a party seeks recovery of damages under this chapter on behalf of another person, "claimant" includes both that other person and the party seeking recovery of damages.

(2) "Defendant" includes any party from whom a claimant seeks recovery of damages under this chapter.

(3) "Family" has the meaning assigned by Section 71.003, Family Code.

(4) "Harassing behavior" means conduct by the defendant directed specifically toward the claimant, including following the claimant,

that is reasonably likely to harass, annoy, alarm, abuse, torment, or embarrass the claimant.

(Enacted by Acts 1995, 74th Leg., ch. 662 (H.B. 43), § 1, effective June 14, 1995; am. Acts 1997, 75th Leg., ch. 165 (S.B. 898), § 31.01(7), effective September 1, 1997 (renumbered from Sec. 83.001); am. Acts 2003, 78th Leg., ch. 1276 (H.B. 3507), § 7.002(b), effective September 1, 2003.)

## Sec. 85.002. Liability.

A defendant is liable, as provided by this chapter, to a claimant for damages arising from stalking of the claimant by the defendant.

(Enacted by Acts 1995, 74th Leg., ch. 662 (H.B. 43), § 1, effective June 14, 1995; am. Acts 1997, 75th Leg., ch. 165 (S.B. 898), § 31.01(7), effective September 1, 1997 (renumbered from Sec. 83.002).)

## Sec. 85.003. Proof.

(a) A claimant proves stalking against a defendant by showing:

(1) on more than one occasion the defendant engaged in harassing behavior;

(2) as a result of the harassing behavior, the claimant reasonably feared for the claimant's safety or the safety of a member of the claimant's family; and

(3) the defendant violated a restraining order prohibiting harassing behavior or:

(A) the defendant, while engaged in harassing behavior, by acts or words threatened to inflict bodily injury on the claimant or to commit an offense against the claimant, a member of the claimant's family, or the claimant's property;

(B) the defendant had the apparent ability to carry out the threat;

(C) the defendant's apparent ability to carry out the threat caused the claimant to reasonably fear for the claimant's safety or the safety of a family member;

(D) the claimant at least once clearly demanded that the defendant stop the defendant's harassing behavior;

(E) after the demand to stop by the claimant, the defendant continued the harassing behavior; and

(F) the harassing behavior has been reported to the police as a stalking offense.

(b) The claimant must, as part of the proof of the behavior described by Subsection (a)(1), submit evidence other than evidence based on the claimant's own perceptions and beliefs.

(Enacted by Acts 1995, 74th Leg., ch. 662 (H.B. 43), § 1, effective June 14, 1995; am. Acts 1997, 75th Leg., ch. 165 (S.B. 898), § 31.01(7), effective September 1, 1997 (renumbered from Sec. 83.003).)

## Sec. 85.004. Damages.

A claimant who prevails in a suit under this chapter may recover actual damages and, subject to Chapter 41, exemplary damages.

(Enacted by Acts 1995, 74th Leg., ch. 662 (H.B. 43), § 1, effective June 14, 1995; am. Acts 1997, 75th Leg., ch. 165 (S.B. 898), § 31.01(7), effective September 1, 1997 (renumbered from Sec. 83.004).)

## Sec. 85.005. Defense.

It is a defense to an action brought under this chapter that the defendant was engaged in conduct that consisted of activity in support of constitutionally or statutorily protected rights.

(Enacted by Acts 1995, 74th Leg., ch. 662 (H.B. 43), § 1, effective June 14, 1995; am. Acts 1997, 75th Leg., ch. 165 (S.B. 898), § 31.01(7), effective September 1, 1997 (renumbered from Sec. 83.005).)

## Sec. 85.006. Cause of Action Cumulative.

The cause of action created by this chapter is cumulative of any other remedy provided by common law or statute.

(Enacted by Acts 1995, 74th Leg., ch. 662 (H.B. 43), § 1, effective June 14, 1995; am. Acts 1997, 75th Leg., ch. 165 (S.B. 898), § 31.01(7), effective September 1, 1997 (renumbered from Sec. 83.006).)

Civil Practice

# TITLE 6
# MISCELLANEOUS PROVISIONS

## CHAPTER 124
## PRIVILEGE TO INVESTIGATE THEFT

### Sec. 124.001.  Detention.

A person who reasonably believes that another has stolen or is attempting to steal property is privileged to detain that person in a reasonable manner and for a reasonable time to investigate ownership of the property.

(Enacted by Acts 1985, 69th Leg., ch. 959 (S.B. 797), § 1, effective September 1, 1985.)

## CHAPTER 125
## COMMON AND PUBLIC NUISANCES

**Subchapter A. Suit to Abate Certain Common Nuisances**

## SUBCHAPTER A
## SUIT TO ABATE CERTAIN COMMON NUISANCES

### Sec. 125.001.  Definitions.

In this chapter:

(1) "Common nuisance" is a nuisance described by Section 125.0015.

(2) "Public nuisance" is a nuisance described by Section 125.062 or 125.063.

(3) "Multiunit residential property" means improved real property with at least three dwelling units, including an apartment building, condominium, hotel, or motel. The term does not include a single-family home or duplex.

(Enacted by Acts 1985, 69th Leg., ch. 959 (S.B. 797), § 1, effective September 1, 1985; am. Acts 1987, 70th Leg., ch. 959 (S.B. 417), § 1, effective September 1, 1987; am. Acts 1991, 72nd Leg., ch. 14 (S.B. 404), § 284(42), effective September 1, 1991; am. Acts 1993, 73rd Leg., ch. 857 (S.B. 145), § 2, effective September 1, 1993; am. Acts 1993,

73rd Leg., ch. 968 (H.B. 697), § 1, effective August 30, 1993; am. Acts 1995, 74th Leg., ch. 76 (S.B. 959), § 14.03, effective September 1, 1995; am. Acts 1995, 74th Leg., ch. 318 (S.B. 15), § 25, effective September 1, 1995; am. Acts 1995, 74th Leg., ch. 663 (S.B. 68), § 2, effective September 1, 1995; am. Acts 1997, 75th Leg., ch. 1181 (S.B. 642), § 1, effective September 1, 1997; am. Acts 1999, 76th Leg., ch. 1161 (S.B. 56), § 1, effective September 1, 1999; am. Acts 2003, 78th Leg., ch. 1202 (S.B. 1010), § 1, effective September 1, 2003; am. Acts 2005, 79th Leg., ch. 1246 (H.B. 1690), § 1, effective September 1, 2005.)

### Sec. 125.0015.  Common Nuisance.

(a) A person who maintains a place to which persons habitually go for the following purposes and who knowingly tolerates the activity and furthermore fails to make reasonable attempts to abate the activity maintains a common nuisance:

(1) discharge of a firearm in a public place as prohibited by the Penal Code;

(2) reckless discharge of a firearm as prohibited by the Penal Code;

(3) engaging in organized criminal activity as a member of a combination as prohibited by the Penal Code;

(4) delivery, possession, manufacture, or use of a controlled substance in violation of Chapter 481, Health and Safety Code;

(5) gambling, gambling promotion, or communicating gambling information as prohibited by the Penal Code;

(6) prostitution, promotion of prostitution, or aggravated promotion of prostitution as prohibited by the Penal Code;

(7) compelling prostitution as prohibited by the Penal Code;

(8) commercial manufacture, commercial distribution, or commercial exhibition of obscene material as prohibited by the Penal Code;

(9) aggravated assault as described by Section 22.02, Penal Code;

(10) sexual assault as described by Section 22.011, Penal Code;

(11) aggravated sexual assault as described by Section 22.021, Penal Code;

(12) robbery as described by Section 29.02, Penal Code;

(13) aggravated robbery as described by Section 29.03, Penal Code;

Civil Practice

(14) unlawfully carrying a weapon as described by Section 46.02, Penal Code;

(15) murder as described by Section 19.02, Penal Code;

(16) capital murder as described by Section 19.03, Penal Code;

(17) continuous sexual abuse of young child or children as described by Section 21.02, Penal Code;

(18) massage therapy or other massage services in violation of Chapter 455, Occupations Code;

(19) **[2 Versions: As added by Acts 2011, 82nd Leg., ch. 1 (S.B. 24)]** trafficking of persons as described by Section 20A.02, Penal Code;

(19) **[2 Versions: As added by Acts 2011, 82nd Leg., ch. 687 (H.B. 289)]** employing a minor at a sexually oriented business as defined by Section 243.002, Local Government Code;

(20) trafficking of persons as described by Section 20A.02, Penal Code;

(21) sexual conduct or performance by a child as described by Section 43.25, Penal Code; or

(22) employment harmful to a child as described by Section 43.251, Penal Code.

(b) A person maintains a common nuisance if the person maintains a multiunit residential property to which persons habitually go to commit acts listed in Subsection (a) and knowingly tolerates the acts and furthermore fails to make reasonable attempts to abate the acts.

(Enacted by Acts 2003, 78th Leg., ch. 1202 (S.B. 1010), § 1, effective September 1, 2003; am. Acts 2005, 79th Leg., ch. 1246 (H.B. 1690), § 2, effective September 1, 2005; am. Acts 2007, 80th Leg., ch. 593 (H.B. 8), § 3.04, effective September 1, 2007; am. Acts 2007, 80th Leg., ch. 1399 (H.B. 2644), § 6, effective September 1, 2007; am. Acts 2009, 81st Leg., ch. 87 (S.B. 1969), § 5.004, effective September 1, 2009; am. Acts 2011, 82nd Leg., ch. 1 (S.B. 24), § 3.02, effective September 1, 2011; am. Acts 2011, 82nd Leg., ch. 687 (H.B. 289), § 1, effective September 1, 2011.)

## SUBCHAPTER D
## MEMBERSHIP IN CRIMINAL STREET GANG

### Sec. 125.061.  Definitions.

In this subchapter:

(1) "Combination" and "criminal street gang" have the meanings assigned by Section 71.01, Penal Code.

(2) "Continuously or regularly" means at least five times in a period of not more than 12 months.

(3) "Gang activity" means the following types of conduct:

(A) organized criminal activity as described by Section 71.02, Penal Code;

(B) terroristic threat as described by Section 22.07, Penal Code;

(C) coercing, soliciting, or inducing gang membership as described by Section 71.022(a) or (a-1), Penal Code;

(D) criminal trespass as described by Section 30.05, Penal Code;

(E) disorderly conduct as described by Section 42.01, Penal Code;

(F) criminal mischief as described by Section 28.03, Penal Code, that causes a pecuniary loss of $500 or more;

(G) a graffiti offense in violation of Section 28.08, Penal Code;

(H) a weapons offense in violation of Chapter 46, Penal Code; or

(I) unlawful possession of a substance or other item in violation of Chapter 481, Health and Safety Code.

(Enacted by Acts 1993, 73rd Leg., ch. 968 (H.B. 697), § 3, effective August 30, 1993; am. Acts 1995, 74th Leg., ch. 76 (S.B. 959), § 14.10, effective September 1, 1995; am. Acts 1995, 74th Leg., ch. 318 (S.B. 15), § 31, effective September 1, 1995; am. Acts 2003, 78th Leg., ch. 1202 (S.B. 1010), § 9, effective September 1, 2003; am. Acts 2005, 79th Leg., ch. 472 (H.B. 68), § 1, effective September 1, 2005; am. Acts 2011, 82nd Leg., ch. 91 (S.B. 1303), § 5.002, effective September 1, 2011; am. Acts 2011, 82nd Leg., ch. 976 (H.B. 1622), § 1, effective September 1, 2011.)

### Sec. 125.062.  Public Nuisance; Combination.

A combination or criminal street gang that continuously or regularly associates in gang activities is a public nuisance.

(Enacted by Acts 1993, 73rd Leg., ch. 968 (H.B. 697), § 3, effective August 30, 1993; am. Acts 1995, 74th Leg., ch. 76 (S.B. 959), § 14.11, effective September 1, 1995; am. Acts 1995, 74th Leg., ch. 318 (S.B. 15), § 32, effective September 1, 1995; am. Acts 2003, 78th Leg., ch. 1202 (S.B. 1010), § 9, effective September 1, 2003.)

**Civil Practice**

## Sec. 125.063. Public Nuisance; Use of Place.

The habitual use of a place by a combination or criminal street gang for engaging in gang activity is a public nuisance.

(Enacted by Acts 1993, 73rd Leg., ch. 968 (H.B. 697), § 3, effective August 30, 1993; am. Acts 2003, 78th Leg., ch. 1202 (S.B. 1010), § 9, effective September 1, 2003.)

## Sec. 125.070. Civil Action for Violation of Injunction.

(a) In this section, "governmental entity" means a political subdivision of this state, including any city, county, school district, junior college district, levee improvement district, drainage district, irrigation district, water improvement district, water control and improvement district, water control and preservation district, freshwater supply district, navigation district, conservation and reclamation district, soil conservation district, communication district, public health district, and river authority.

(b) A criminal street gang or a member of a criminal street gang is liable to the state or a governmental entity injured by the violation of a temporary or permanent injunctive order under this subchapter.

(c) In an action brought against a member of a criminal street gang, the plaintiff must show that the member violated the temporary or permanent injunctive order.

(d) A district, county, or city attorney or the attorney general may sue for money damages on behalf of the state or a governmental entity. If the state or a governmental entity prevails in a suit under this section, the state or governmental entity may recover:

(1) actual damages;

(2) a civil penalty in an amount not to exceed $20,000 for each violation; and

(3) court costs and attorney's fees.

(e) The property of the criminal street gang or a member of the criminal street gang may be seized in execution on a judgment under this section. Property may not be seized under this subsection if the owner or interest holder of the property proves by a preponderance of the evidence that the owner or interest holder was not a member of the criminal street gang and did not violate the temporary or permanent injunctive order. The owner or interest holder of property that is in the possession of a criminal street gang or a member of the criminal street gang and that is subject to execution under this subsection must show that the property:

(1) was stolen from the owner or interest holder; or

(2) was used or intended to be used without the effective consent of the owner or interest holder by the criminal street gang or a member of the criminal street gang.

(f) The attorney general shall deposit money received under this section for damages or as a civil penalty in the neighborhood and community recovery fund held by the attorney general outside the state treasury. Money in the fund is held by the attorney general in trust for the benefit of the community or neighborhood harmed by the violation of a temporary or permanent injunctive order. Money in the fund may be used only for the benefit of the community or neighborhood harmed by the violation of the injunctive order. Interest earned on money in the fund shall be credited to the fund. The attorney general shall account for money in the fund so that money held for the benefit of a community or neighborhood, and interest earned on that money, are not commingled with money in the fund held for the benefit of a different community or neighborhood.

(g) A district, county, or city attorney who brings suit on behalf of a governmental entity shall deposit money received for damages or as a civil penalty in an account to be held in trust for the benefit of the community or neighborhood harmed by the violation of a temporary or permanent injunctive order. Money in the account may be used only for the benefit of the community or neighborhood harmed by the violation of the injunctive order. Interest earned on money in the account shall be credited to the account. The district, county, or city attorney shall account for money in the account so that money held for the benefit of a community or neighborhood, and interest earned on that money, are not commingled with money in the account held for the benefit of a different community or neighborhood.

(h) An action under this section brought by the state or a governmental entity does not waive sovereign or governmental immunity for any purpose.

(Enacted by Acts 2009, 81st Leg., ch. 1130 (H.B. 2086), § 10, effective September 1, 2009.)

Civil Practice

# Texas Revised Civil Statutes

## TITLE 112

## RAILROADS
### [Repealed April 1, 2011]

### CHAPTER 8
### RESTRICTIONS, DUTIES AND LIABILITIES
### [REPEALED APRIL 1, 2011]

**Sec. 6419a.   Engineer's Operator Permits [Repealed].**
Repealed by Acts 2009, 81st Leg., ch. 85 (S.B. 1540), § 5.01(a)(1), effective April 1, 2011 and Acts

2011, 82nd Leg., ch. 91 (S.B. 1303), § 24.102(1), effective September 1, 2011.

**Sec. 6419b.   Duty to Stop and Render Aid [Repealed].**
Repealed by Acts 2009, 81st Leg., ch. 85 (S.B. 1540), § 5.01(a)(1), effective April 1, 2011.

## TITLE 116

## ROADS, BRIDGES, AND FERRIES

### CHAPTER 1A
### TRAFFIC REGULATIONS

**Sec. 6701j-2.   Railroad and Highway Grade Crossing Safety Instruction.**
(a) All driving safety courses approved by the Department of Public Safety or by a court as authorized by law must include instruction on railroad and highway grade crossing safety.

(b) The Department of Public Safety shall by rule provide minimum standards of course content relating to operation of vehicles at railroad and highway grade crossings.

[Enacted by Acts 1989, 71st Leg., ch. 466 (H.B. 1910), § 1, effective September 1, 1989.]

# Education Code

## TITLE 2
## PUBLIC EDUCATION

### SUBCHAPTER C
### MISSING CHILD PREVENTION AND IDENTIFICATION PROGRAMS

### Sec. 33.051.  Definitions.

In this subchapter:

(1) "Child" and "minor" have the meanings assigned by Section 101.003, Family Code.

(2) "Missing child" means a child whose whereabouts are unknown to the legal custodian of the child and:

(A) the circumstances of whose absence indicate that the child did not voluntarily leave the care and control of the custodian and that the taking of the child was not authorized by law; or

(B) the child has engaged in conduct indicating a need for supervision under Section 51.03(b)(3), Family Code.

(Enacted by Acts 1995, 74th Leg., ch. 260 (S.B. 1), § 1, effective May 30, 1995.)

### Sec. 33.052.  Missing Child Prevention and Identification Programs.

(a) The board of trustees of a school district or of a private school may participate in missing child prevention and identification programs, including fingerprinting and photographing as provided by this subchapter.

(b) The board of trustees of a school district may delegate responsibility for implementation of the program to the district's school administration or to the district's community education services administration.

(c) The chief administrative officer of each private primary or secondary school may participate in the programs and may contract with the regional education service center in which the school is located for operation of all or any part of the program through a shared services arrangement.

(Enacted by Acts 1995, 74th Leg., ch. 260 (S.B. 1), § 1, effective May 30, 1995.)

### Sec. 33.053.  Fingerprints of Children.

(a) A missing child prevention and identification program may include a procedure for taking the fingerprints of each student registered in the school whose parent or legal custodian has consented in writing to the fingerprinting. Fingerprints obtained under this section may be used only for the identification and location of a missing child.

(b) The board of trustees of a school district or the chief administrative officer of a private school may establish a reasonable fee to cover the costs of fingerprinting not provided by volunteer assistance. The fee may not exceed $3 for each child fingerprinted. If the school charges a fee, the school may waive all or a portion of the costs of fingerprinting for educationally disadvantaged children.

(c) A representative of a law enforcement agency of the county or the municipality in which the school district is located or of the Department of Public Safety, or a person trained in fingerprinting technique by a law enforcement agency or the Department of Public Safety, shall make one complete set of fingerprints on a fingerprint card for each child participating in the program. If the school requests, the Department of Public Safety may provide fingerprint training to persons designated by the school.

(d) A fingerprint card shall include a description of the child, including the name, address, date and place of birth, color of eyes and hair, weight, and sex of the child.

(e) Except as provided by Section 33.054(b), the fingerprint card and other materials developed under this subchapter shall be made part of the school's permanent student records.

(f) A state agency, law enforcement agency, or other person may not retain a copy of a child's fingerprints taken under this program.

(Enacted by Acts 1995, 74th Leg., ch. 260 (S.B. 1), § 1, effective May 30, 1995.)

### Sec. 33.054.  Photographs of Children.

(a) A participating school shall retain a current photograph of each child registered in the school whose parent or legal custodian has consented in writing. Photographs retained under this section may be used only for the identification and location of a missing child.

(b) The photograph shall be retained by the participating school until the photograph is replaced by a subsequently made photograph under this section or until the expiration of three years, whichever is earlier.

(c) On the request of a parent or legal custodian of a missing child, or of a peace officer who is engaged in the investigation of a missing child, a participating school may give to the parent, legal custodian, or peace officer a copy of that child's photograph held by the school under this section. Except as provided by this subsection, a photograph held under this section may not be given to any person.

(d) A participating school may charge a fee for making and keeping records of photographs under this section. If the school charges a fee, the school may waive this fee for educationally disadvantaged children.

(Enacted by Acts 1995, 74th Leg., ch. 260 (S.B. 1), § 1, effective May 30, 1995.)

### Sec. 33.055.  Fingerprints and Photographs Not Used As Evidence.

(a) A child's fingerprint card made under Section 33.053 or a photograph of a child made or kept under Section 33.054 may not be used as evidence in any criminal proceeding in which the child is a defendant or in any case under Title 3, Family Code, in which the child is alleged to have engaged in delinquent conduct or in conduct indicating a need for supervision.

(b) This subchapter does not apply to the use by a law enforcement agency for an official purpose of a photograph published in a school annual.

(c) This subchapter does not prevent the use of a videotape or photograph taken to monitor the activity of students for disciplinary reasons or in connection with a criminal prosecution or an action under Title 3, Family Code.

(Enacted by Acts 1995, 74th Leg., ch. 260 (S.B. 1), § 1, effective May 30, 1995.)

### Sec. 33.056.  Liability for Nonperformance.

A person is not liable in any suit for damages for negligent performance or nonperformance of any requirement of this subchapter.

(Enacted by Acts 1995, 74th Leg., ch. 260 (S.B. 1), § 1, effective May 30, 1995.)

### Sec. 33.057.  Destruction of Fingerprints and Photographs.

The agency shall adopt rules relating to the destruction of fingerprints and photographs made or kept under this subchapter.

(Enacted by Acts 1995, 74th Leg., ch. 260 (S.B. 1), § 1, effective May 30, 1995.)

## CHAPTER 34
## TRANSPORTATION

### Sec. 34.002.  Safety Standards.

(a) The Department of Public Safety, with the advice of the Texas Education Agency, shall establish safety standards for school buses used to transport students in accordance with Section 34.003.

(b) Each school district shall meet or exceed the safety standards for school buses established under Subsection (a).

(c) A school district that fails or refuses to meet the safety standards for school buses established under this section is ineligible to share in the transportation allotment under Section 42.155 until the first anniversary of the date the district begins complying with the safety standards.

(Enacted by Acts 1995, 74th Leg., ch. 260 (S.B. 1), § 1, effective May 30, 1995; am. Acts 1997, 75th Leg., ch. 1438 (H.B. 3249), § 2, effective September 1, 1997; am. Acts 2003, 78th Leg., ch. 309 (H.B. 3042), § 9.01, effective June 18, 2003.)

## Sec. 34.003. Operation of School Buses.

(a) School buses or mass transit authority motor buses shall be used for the transportation of students to and from schools on routes having 10 or more students. On those routes having fewer than 10 students, passenger cars may be used for the transportation of students to and from school.

(b) To transport students in connection with school activities other than on routes to and from school:

(1) only school buses or motor buses may be used to transport 15 or more students in any one vehicle; and

(2) passenger cars or passenger vans may be used to transport fewer than 15 students.

(c) In all circumstances in which passenger cars or passenger vans are used to transport students, the operator of the vehicle shall ensure that the number of passengers in the vehicle does not exceed the designed capacity of the vehicle and that each passenger is secured by a safety belt.

(d) In this section, "passenger van" means a motor vehicle other than a motorcycle or passenger car, used to transport persons and designed to transport 15 or fewer passengers, including the driver.

(e) "Motor bus" means a vehicle designed to transport more than 15 passengers, including the driver.

(Enacted by Acts 1995, 74th Leg., ch. 260 (S.B. 1), § 1, effective May 30, 1995; am. Acts 1997, 75th Leg., ch. 1029 (S.B. 517), § 1, effective June 19, 1997; am. Acts 1997, 75th Leg., ch. 1061 (S.B. 1486), § 20, effective September 1, 1997; am. Acts

1997, 75th Leg., ch. 1438 (H.B. 3249), § 3, effective September 1, 1997.)

## Sec. 34.004. Standing Children.

A school district may not require or allow a child to stand on a school bus or passenger van that is in motion.

(Enacted by Acts 1995, 74th Leg., ch. 260 (S.B. 1), § 1, effective May 30, 1995; am. Acts 1997, 75th Leg., ch. 1029 (S.B. 517), § 2, effective June 19, 1997; am. Acts 1997, 75th Leg., ch. 1061 (S.B. 1486), § 21, effective September 1, 1997; am. Acts 1997, 75th Leg., ch. 1438 (H.B. 3249), § 4, effective September 1, 1997.)

## Sec. 34.008. Contract with Transit Authority, Commercial Transportation Company, or Juvenile Board.

(a) A board of county school trustees or school district board of trustees may contract with a mass transit authority, commercial transportation company, or juvenile board for all or any part of a district's public school transportation if the authority, company, or board:

(1) requires its school bus drivers to have the qualifications required by and to be certified in accordance with standards established by the Department of Public Safety; and

(2) uses only those school buses or mass transit authority buses in transporting 15 or more public school students that meet or exceed safety standards for school buses established under Section 34.002.

(b) This section does not prohibit the county or school district board from supplementing the state transportation cost allotment with local funds necessary to provide complete transportation services.

(c) A mass transit authority contracting under this section for daily transportation of pre-primary, primary, or secondary students to or from school shall conduct, in a manner and on a schedule approved by the county or district school board, the following education programs:

(1) a program to inform the public that public school students will be riding on the authority's or company's buses;

(2) a program to educate the drivers of the buses to be used under the contract of the special needs and problems of public school students riding on the buses; and

(3) a program to educate public school students on bus riding safety and any special considerations arising from the use of the authority's or company's buses.

Education

(Enacted by Acts 1995, 74th Leg., ch. 260 (S.B. 1), § 1, effective May 30, 1995; am. Acts 1997, 75th Leg., ch. 1061 (S.B. 1486), § 22, effective September 1, 1997; am. Acts 1997, 75th Leg., ch. 1438 (H.B. 3249), § 5, effective September 1, 1997; am. Acts 2007, 80th Leg., ch. 449 (H.B. 273), §§ 2, 3, effective June 15, 2007.)

### Sec. 34.009.  Contracts for Use, Acquisition, or Lease of School Bus.

(a) As an alternative to purchasing a school bus, a board of county school trustees or school district board of trustees may contract with any person for use, acquisition, or lease with option to purchase of a school bus if the county or school district board determines the contract to be economically advantageous to the county or district. A contract in the form of an installment purchase or any form other than a lease or lease with option to purchase is subject to Section 34.001.

(b) A school bus that is leased or leased with an option to purchase under this section must meet or exceed the safety standards for school buses established under Section 34.002, Education Code.

(c) Each contract that reserves to the county or school district board the continuing right to terminate the contract at the expiration of each budget period of the board during the term of the contract is considered to be a commitment of current revenues only.

(d) Termination penalties may not be included in any contract under this section. The net effective interest rate on any contract must comply with Chapter 1204, Government Code.

(e) The competitive bidding requirements of Subchapter B, Chapter 44, apply to a contract under this section.

(f) The commissioner shall adopt a recommended contract form for the use, acquisition, or lease with option to purchase of school buses. A district is not required to use the contract.

(g) After a contract providing for payment aggregating $100,000 or more by a school district is authorized by the board of trustees, the board may submit the contract and the record relating to the contract to the attorney general for the attorney general's examination as to the validity of the contract. The approval is not required as a term of the contract. If the contract has been made in accordance with the constitution and laws of the state, the attorney general shall approve the contract, and the comptroller shall register the contract. After the contract has been approved by the attorney general and registered by the comptroller, the validity of the contract is incontestable for any cause. The legal obligations of the lessor, vendor, or supplier of the property to the board are not diminished in any respect by the approval and registration of a contract.

(h) The decision of a board of county school trustees or school district board of trustees to use an alternative form of use, acquisition, or purchase of a school bus does not affect a district's eligibility for participation in the transportation funding provisions of the Foundation School Program or any other state funding program.

(i) A contract entered into under this section is a legal and authorized investment for banks, savings banks, trust companies, building and loan associations, savings and loan associations, insurance companies, fiduciaries, and trustees and for the sinking funds of school districts.

(j) A contract under this section may have any lawful term of not less than two or more than 10 years.

(k) A school district may use the provisions of any other law not in conflict with this section to the extent convenient or necessary to carry out any power or authority, express or implied, granted by this section.

(Enacted by Acts 1995, 74th Leg., ch. 260 (S.B. 1), § 1, effective May 30, 1995; am. Acts 1997, 75th Leg., ch. 1438 (H.B. 3249), § 6, effective September 1, 1997; am. Acts 2001, 77th Leg., ch. 1420 (H.B. 2812), art. 8, § 8.206, effective September 1, 2001.)

## SUBTITLE G
## SAFE SCHOOLS

## CHAPTER 37
## DISCIPLINE; LAW AND ORDER

### Subchapter D. Protection of Buildings and Grounds

### Subchapter E. Penal Provisions

## SUBCHAPTER D
## PROTECTION OF BUILDINGS AND GROUNDS

### Sec. 37.107.   Trespass on School Grounds.

An unauthorized person who trespasses on the grounds of any school district of this state commits an offense. An offense under this section is a Class C misdemeanor.
(Enacted by Acts 1995, 74th Leg., ch. 260 (S.B. 1), § 1, effective May 30, 1995.)

### Sec. 37.110.   Information Regarding Gang-Free Zones.

The superintendent of each public school district and the administrator of each private elementary or secondary school located in the public school district shall ensure that the student handbook for each campus in the public school district includes information on gang-free zones and the consequences of engaging in organized criminal activity within those zones.
(Enacted by Acts 2009, 81st Leg., ch. 1130 (H.B. 2086), § 4, effective June 19, 2009.)

## SUBCHAPTER E
## PENAL PROVISIONS

### Sec. 37.121.   Fraternities, Sororities, Secret Societies, and Gangs.

(a) A person commits an offense if the person:
  (1) is a member of, pledges to become a member of, joins, or solicits another person to join or pledge to become a member of a public school fraternity, sorority, secret society, or gang; or
  (2) is not enrolled in a public school and solicits another person to attend a meeting of a public school fraternity, sorority, secret society, or gang or a meeting at which membership in one of those groups is encouraged.
(b) A school district board of trustees or an educator shall recommend placing in a disciplinary alternative education program any student under the person's control who violates Subsection (a).
(c) An offense under this section is a Class C misdemeanor.
(d) In this section, "public school fraternity, sorority, secret society, or gang" means an organization composed wholly or in part of students of public primary or secondary schools that seeks to perpetuate itself by taking in additional members from the students enrolled in school on the basis of the decision of its membership rather than on the free choice of a student in the school who is qualified by the rules of the school to fill the special aims of the organization. The term does not include an agency for public welfare, including Boy Scouts, Hi-Y, Girl Reserves, DeMolay, Rainbow Girls, Pan-American Clubs, scholarship societies, or other similar educational organizations sponsored by state or national education authorities.
(Enacted by Acts 1995, 74th Leg., ch. 260 (S.B. 1), § 1, effective May 30, 1995; am. Acts 2003, 78th Leg., ch. 1055 (H.B. 1314), § 23, effective June 20, 2003.)

### Sec. 37.122.   Possession of Intoxicants on Public School Grounds.

(a) A person commits an offense if the person possesses an intoxicating beverage for consumption, sale, or distribution while:
  (1) on the grounds or in a building of a public school; or
  (2) entering or inside any enclosure, field, or stadium where an athletic event sponsored or participated in by a public school of this state is being held.
(b) An officer of this state who sees a person violating this section shall immediately seize the intoxicating beverage and, within a reasonable time, deliver it to the county or district attorney to be held as evidence until the trial of the accused possessor.
(c) An offense under this section is a Class C misdemeanor.
(Enacted by Acts 1995, 74th Leg., ch. 260 (S.B. 1), § 1, effective May 30, 1995.)

### Sec. 37.123.   Disruptive Activities.

(a) A person commits an offense if the person, alone or in concert with others, intentionally engages in disruptive activity on the campus or property of any private or public school.
(b) For purposes of this section, disruptive activity is:

(1) obstructing or restraining the passage of persons in an exit, entrance, or hallway of a building without the authorization of the administration of the school;

(2) seizing control of a building or portion of a building to interfere with an administrative, educational, research, or other authorized activity;

(3) preventing or attempting to prevent by force or violence or the threat of force or violence a lawful assembly authorized by the school administration so that a person attempting to participate in the assembly is unable to participate due to the use of force or violence or due to a reasonable fear that force or violence is likely to occur;

(4) disrupting by force or violence or the threat of force or violence a lawful assembly in progress; or

(5) obstructing or restraining the passage of a person at an exit or entrance to the campus or property or preventing or attempting to prevent by force or violence or by threats of force or violence the ingress or egress of a person to or from the property or campus without the authorization of the administration of the school.

(c) An offense under this section is a Class B misdemeanor.

(d) Any person who is convicted the third time of violating this section is ineligible to attend any institution of higher education receiving funds from this state before the second anniversary of the third conviction.

(e) This section may not be construed to infringe on any right of free speech or expression guaranteed by the constitution of the United States or of this state.
(Enacted by Acts 1995, 74th Leg., ch. 260 (S.B. 1), § 1, effective May 30, 1995.)

## Sec. 37.124.  Disruption of Classes.

(a) A person commits an offense if the person, on school property or on public property within 500 feet of school property, alone or in concert with others, intentionally disrupts the conduct of classes or other school activities.

(b) An offense under this section is a Class C misdemeanor.

(c) In this section:

(1) "Disrupting the conduct of classes or other school activities" includes:

(A) emitting noise of an intensity that prevents or hinders classroom instruction;

(B) enticing or attempting to entice a student away from a class or other school activity that the student is required to attend;

(C) preventing or attempting to prevent a student from attending a class or other school activity that the student is required to attend; and

(D) entering a classroom without the consent of either the principal or the teacher and, through either acts of misconduct or the use of loud or profane language, disrupting class activities.

(2) "Public property" includes a street, highway, alley, public park, or sidewalk.

(3) "School property" includes a public school campus or school grounds on which a public school is located and any grounds or buildings used by a school for an assembly or other school-sponsored activity.

(d) It is an exception to the application of Subsection (a) that, at the time the person engaged in conduct prohibited under that subsection, the person was a student in the sixth grade or a lower grade level.
(Enacted by Acts 1995, 74th Leg., ch. 260 (S.B. 1), § 1, effective May 30, 1995; am. Acts 2011, 82nd Leg., ch. 691 (H.B. 359), § 4, effective September 1, 2011.)

## Sec. 37.125.  Exhibition of Firearms.

(a) A person commits an offense if, in a manner intended to cause alarm or personal injury to another person or to damage school property, the person intentionally exhibits, uses, or threatens to exhibit or use a firearm:

(1) in or on any property, including a parking lot, parking garage, or other parking area, that is owned by a private or public school; or

(2) on a school bus being used to transport children to or from school-sponsored activities of a private or public school.

(b) An offense under this section is a third degree felony.
(Enacted by Acts 1995, 74th Leg., ch. 260 (S.B. 1), § 1, effective May 30, 1995 am. Acts 2007, 80th Leg., ch. 704 (H.B. 2112), § 1, effective September 1, 2007.)

## Sec. 37.126.  Disruption of Transportation.

(a) Except as provided by Section 37.125, a person commits an offense if the person intentionally disrupts, prevents, or interferes with the lawful transportation of children:

(1) to or from school on a vehicle owned or operated by a county or independent school district; or

(2) to or from an activity sponsored by a school on a vehicle owned or operated by a county or independent school district.

(b) An offense under this section is a Class C misdemeanor.

(c) It is an exception to the application of Subsection (a)(1) that, at the time the person engaged in conduct prohibited under that subdivision, the person was a student in the sixth grade or a lower grade level.

(Enacted by Acts 1995, 74th Leg., ch. 260 (S.B. 1), § 1, effective May 30, 1995; am. Acts 2011, 82nd Leg., ch. 691 (H.B. 359), § 5, effective September 1, 2011.)

## SUBCHAPTER F
## HAZING

### Sec. 37.151.   Definitions.

In this subchapter:

(1) "Educational institution" includes a public or private high school.

(2) "Pledge" means any person who has been accepted by, is considering an offer of membership from, or is in the process of qualifying for membership in an organization.

(3) "Pledging" means any action or activity related to becoming a member of an organization.

(4) "Student" means any person who:

(A) is registered in or in attendance at an educational institution;

(B) has been accepted for admission at the educational institution where the hazing incident occurs; or

(C) intends to attend an educational institution during any of its regular sessions after a period of scheduled vacation.

(5) "Organization" means a fraternity, sorority, association, corporation, order, society, corps, club, or service, social, or similar group, whose members are primarily students.

(6) "Hazing" means any intentional, knowing, or reckless act, occurring on or off the campus of an educational institution, by one person alone or acting with others, directed against a student, that endangers the mental or physical health or safety of a student for the purpose of pledging, being initiated into, affiliating with, holding office in, or maintaining membership in an organization. The term includes:

(A) any type of physical brutality, such as whipping, beating, striking, branding, elec-

tronic shocking, placing of a harmful substance on the body, or similar activity;

(B) any type of physical activity, such as sleep deprivation, exposure to the elements, confinement in a small space, calisthenics, or other activity that subjects the student to an unreasonable risk of harm or that adversely affects the mental or physical health or safety of the student;

(C) any activity involving consumption of a food, liquid, alcoholic beverage, liquor, drug, or other substance that subjects the student to an unreasonable risk of harm or that adversely affects the mental or physical health or safety of the student;

(D) any activity that intimidates or threatens the student with ostracism, that subjects the student to extreme mental stress, shame, or humiliation, that adversely affects the mental health or dignity of the student or discourages the student from entering or remaining registered in an educational institution, or that may reasonably be expected to cause a student to leave the organization or the institution rather than submit to acts described in this subdivision; and

(E) any activity that induces, causes, or requires the student to perform a duty or task that involves a violation of the Penal Code.

(Enacted by Acts 1995, 74th Leg., ch. 260 (S.B. 1), § 1, effective May 30, 1995.)

### Sec. 37.152.   Personal Hazing Offense.

(a) A person commits an offense if the person:

(1) engages in hazing;

(2) solicits, encourages, directs, aids, or attempts to aid another in engaging in hazing;

(3) recklessly permits hazing to occur; or

(4) has firsthand knowledge of the planning of a specific hazing incident involving a student in an educational institution, or has firsthand knowledge that a specific hazing incident has occurred, and knowingly fails to report that knowledge in writing to the dean of students or other appropriate official of the institution.

(b) The offense of failing to report is a Class B misdemeanor.

(c) Any other offense under this section that does not cause serious bodily injury to another is a Class B misdemeanor.

(d) Any other offense under this section that causes serious bodily injury to another is a Class A misdemeanor.

Education

(e) Any other offense under this section that causes the death of another is a state jail felony.

(f) Except if an offense causes the death of a student, in sentencing a person convicted of an offense under this section, the court may require the person to perform community service, subject to the same conditions imposed on a person placed on community supervision under Section 11, Article 42.12, Code of Criminal Procedure, for an appropriate period of time in lieu of confinement in county jail or in lieu of a part of the time the person is sentenced to confinement in county jail.

(Enacted by Acts 1995, 74th Leg., ch. 260 (S.B. 1), § 1, effective May 30, 1995.)

## Sec. 37.153.  Organization Hazing Offense.

(a) An organization commits an offense if the organization condones or encourages hazing or if an officer or any combination of members, pledges, or alumni of the organization commits or assists in the commission of hazing.

(b) An offense under this section is a misdemeanor punishable by:

(1) a fine of not less than $5,000 nor more than $10,000; or

(2) if the court finds that the offense caused personal injury, property damage, or other loss, a fine of not less than $5,000 nor more than double the amount lost or expenses incurred because of the injury, damage, or loss.

(Enacted by Acts 1995, 74th Leg., ch. 260 (S.B. 1), § 1, effective May 30, 1995.)

## Sec. 37.154.  Consent Not a Defense.

It is not a defense to prosecution of an offense under this subchapter that the person against whom the hazing was directed consented to or acquiesced in the hazing activity.

(Enacted by Acts 1995, 74th Leg., ch. 260 (S.B. 1), § 1, effective May 30, 1995.)

## Sec. 37.155.  Immunity from Prosecution Available.

In the prosecution of an offense under this subchapter, the court may grant immunity from prosecution for the offense to each person who is subpoenaed to testify for the prosecution and who does testify for the prosecution. Any person reporting a specific hazing incident involving a student in an educational institution to the dean of students or other appropriate official of the institution is immune from civil or criminal liability that might otherwise be incurred or imposed as a result of the report. Immunity extends to participation in any judicial proceeding resulting from the report. A person reporting in bad faith or with malice is not protected by this section.

(Enacted by Acts 1995, 74th Leg., ch. 260 (S.B. 1), § 1, effective May 30, 1995.)

## Sec. 37.156.  Offenses in Addition to Other Penal Provisions.

This subchapter does not affect or repeal any penal law of this state. This subchapter does not limit or affect the right of an educational institution to enforce its own penalties against hazing.

(Enacted by Acts 1995, 74th Leg., ch. 260 (S.B. 1), § 1, effective May 30, 1995.)

## Sec. 37.157.  Reporting by Medical Authorities.

A doctor or other medical practitioner who treats a student who may have been subjected to hazing activities:

(1) may report the suspected hazing activities to police or other law enforcement officials; and

(2) is immune from civil or other liability that might otherwise be imposed or incurred as a result of the report, unless the report is made in bad faith or with malice.

(Enacted by Acts 1995, 74th Leg., ch. 260 (S.B. 1), § 1, effective May 30, 1995.)

Education

# Election Code

## TITLE 2
## VOTER QUALIFICATIONS AND REGISTRATION

### CHAPTER 20
### VOTER REGISTRATION AGENCIES

### SUBCHAPTER C
### DEPARTMENT OF PUBLIC SAFETY

### Sec. 20.061.   Applicability of Other Provisions.

The other provisions of this chapter apply to the Department of Public Safety except provisions that conflict with this subchapter.

(Enacted by Acts 1995, 74th Leg., ch. 797 (H.B. 127), § 33, effective September 1, 1995.)

### Sec. 20.062.   Department Forms and Procedure.

(a) The Department of Public Safety shall prescribe and use a form and procedure that combines the department's application form for a license or card with an officially prescribed voter registration application form.

(b) The department shall prescribe and use a change of address form and procedure that combines department and voter registration functions. The form must allow a licensee or cardholder to indicate whether the change of address is also to be used for voter registration purposes.

(c) The design, content, and physical characteristics of the department forms must be approved by the secretary of state.

(Enacted by Acts 1995, 74th Leg., ch. 797 (H.B. 127), § 33, effective September 1, 1995.)

### Sec. 20.063.   Registration Procedures.

(a) The Department of Public Safety shall provide to each person who applies in person at the department's offices for an original or renewal of a driver's license, a personal identification card, or a duplicate or corrected license or card an opportunity to complete a voter registration application form.

(b) When the department processes a license or card for renewal by mail, the department shall deliver to the applicant by mail a voter registration application form.

(c) A change of address that relates to a license or card and that is submitted to the department in person or by mail serves as a change of address for voter registration unless the licensee or cardholder indicates that the change is not for voter registration purposes. The date of submission of a change of address to a department employee is considered to be the date of submission to the voter registrar for the purpose of determining the effective date of registration only.

(d) If a completed voter registration application submitted to a department employee does not include the applicant's correct driver's license number or personal identification card number, a department employee shall enter the appropriate information on the application. If a completed application does not include the applicant's correct residence address or mailing address, a department employee shall obtain the appropriate information from the applicant and enter the information on the application.

(Enacted by Acts 1995, 74th Leg., ch. 797 (H.B. 127), § 33, effective September 1, 1995; am. Acts 1997, 75th Leg., ch. 454 (S.B. 500), § 9, effective September 1, 1997.)

Election

### Sec. 20.064. Declination Form Not Required.

The Department of Public Safety is not required to comply with the procedures prescribed by this chapter relating to the form for a declination of voter registration.

(Enacted by Acts 1995, 74th Leg., ch. 797 (H.B. 127), § 33, effective September 1, 1995.)

### Sec. 20.065. Delivery of Applications and Changes of Address.

(a) At the end of each day a Department of Public Safety office is regularly open for business, the manager of the office shall deliver by mail or in person to the voter registrar of the county in which the office is located each completed voter registration application and applicable change of address submitted to a department employee.

(b) Each weekday the department is regularly open for business, the department shall electronically transfer to the secretary of state the name of each person who completes a voter registration application submitted to the department. The secretary shall prescribe procedures necessary to implement this subsection.

(c) On the weekday the secretary of state is regularly open for business following the date the secretary receives information under Subsection (b), the secretary shall inform the appropriate voter registrar of the name of each person who completes a voter registration application submitted to the department. The registrar may verify that the registrar has received each application as indicated by the information provided by the secretary under this subsection.

(Enacted by Acts 1995, 74th Leg., ch. 797 (H.B. 127), § 33, effective September 1, 1995; am. Acts 2001, 77th Leg., ch. 1178 (H.B. 3181), § 5, effective January 1, 2002; am. Acts 2005, 79th Leg., ch. 1105 (H.B. 2280), § 8, effective January 1, 2006.)

### Sec. 20.066. Registration Procedures.

(a) If a person completes a voter registration application as provided by Section 20.063, the Department of Public Safety shall:

(1) input the information provided on the application into the department's electronic data system; and

(2) inform the applicant that the applicant's electronic signature provided to the department will be used for submitting the applicant's voter registration application.

(b) Not later than the fifth day after the date a person completes a voter registration application and provides an electronic signature to the department, the department shall electronically transfer the applicant's voter registration data, including the applicant's signature, to the secretary of state.

(c) The secretary of state shall prescribe additional procedures as necessary to implement this section.

(d), (e) [Expired pursuant to Acts 2005, 79th Leg., ch. 1105 (H.B. 2280), § 9, effective January 2, 2008.]

(Enacted by Acts 2001, 77th Leg., ch. 1136 (H.B. 2691), § 1, effective September 1, 2001; am. Acts 2005, 79th Leg., ch. 1105 (H.B. 2280), § 9, effective January 1, 2006.)

# TITLE 16
# MISCELLANEOUS PROVISIONS

## CHAPTER 276
## MISCELLANEOUS OFFENSES AND OTHER PROVISIONS

### Sec. 276.005. Voter's Privilege from Arrest.

A voter may not be arrested during the voter's attendance at an election and while going to and returning from a polling place except for treason, a felony, or a breach of peace.

(Enacted by Acts 1985, 69th Leg., ch. 211 (S.B. 616), § 1, effective January 1, 1986.)

Election

# Texas Family Code

## TITLE 2
## CHILD IN RELATION TO THE FAMILY

### SUBTITLE A
### LIMITATIONS OF MINORITY

### CHAPTER 32
### CONSENT TO TREATMENT OF CHILD BY NON-PARENT OR CHILD

Subchapter A. Consent to Medical, Dental, Psychological, and Surgical Treatment

### SUBCHAPTER A
### CONSENT TO MEDICAL, DENTAL, PSYCHOLOGICAL, AND SURGICAL TREATMENT

### Sec. 32.001.   Consent by Non-Parent.

(a) The following persons may consent to medical, dental, psychological, and surgical treatment of a child when the person having the right to consent as otherwise provided by law cannot be contacted and that person has not given actual notice to the contrary:

(1) a grandparent of the child;

(2) an adult brother or sister of the child;

(3) an adult aunt or uncle of the child;

(4) an educational institution in which the child is enrolled that has received written authorization to consent from a person having the right to consent;

(5) an adult who has actual care, control, and possession of the child and has written authorization to consent from a person having the right to consent;

(6) a court having jurisdiction over a suit affecting the parent-child relationship of which the child is the subject;

(7) an adult responsible for the actual care, control, and possession of a child under the jurisdiction of a juvenile court or committed by a juvenile court to the care of an agency of the state or county; or

(8) a peace officer who has lawfully taken custody of a minor, if the peace officer has reasonable grounds to believe the minor is in need of immediate medical treatment.

(b) Except as otherwise provided by this subsection, the Texas Youth Commission may consent to the medical, dental, psychological, and surgical treatment of a child committed to the Texas Youth Commission under Title 3 when the person having the right to consent has been contacted and that person has not given actual notice to the contrary. Consent for medical, dental, psychological, and surgical treatment of a child for whom the Department of Family and Protective Services has been appointed managing conservator and who is committed to the Texas Youth Commission is governed by Sections 266.004, 266.009, and 266.010.

(c) This section does not apply to consent for the immunization of a child.

(d) A person who consents to the medical treatment of a minor under Subsection (a)(7) or (8) is immune from liability for damages resulting from the examination or treatment of the minor, except to the extent of the person's own acts of negligence. A physician or dentist licensed to practice in this state, or a hospital or medical facility at which a minor is treated is immune from liability for damages resulting from the examination or treatment of a minor under this section, except to the extent of the person's own acts of negligence. (Enacted by Acts 1995, 74th Leg., ch. 20 (H.B. 655), § 1, effective April 20, 1995; am. Acts 1995,

Family Code

1463

74th Leg., ch. 751 (H.B. 433), § 5, effective September 1, 1995; am. Acts 2009, 81st Leg., ch. 108 (H.B. 1629), § 1, effective May 23, 2009.)

### Sec. 32.002.  Consent Form.

(a) Consent to medical treatment under this subchapter must be in writing, signed by the person giving consent, and given to the doctor, hospital, or other medical facility that administers the treatment.

(b) The consent must include:

(1) the name of the child;

(2) the name of one or both parents, if known, and the consent of any managing conservator or guardian of the child;

(3) the name of the person giving consent and the person's relationship to the child;

(4) a statement of the nature of the medical treatment to be given; and

(5) the date the treatment is to begin.

(Enacted by Acts 1995, 74th Leg., ch. 20 (H.B. 655), § 1, effective April 20, 1995.)

### Sec. 32.003.  Consent to Treatment by Child.

(a) A child may consent to medical, dental, psychological, and surgical treatment for the child by a licensed physician or dentist if the child:

(1) is on active duty with the armed services of the United States of America;

(2) is:

(A) 16 years of age or older and resides separate and apart from the child's parents, managing conservator, or guardian, with or without the consent of the parents, managing conservator, or guardian and regardless of the duration of the residence; and

(B) managing the child's own financial affairs, regardless of the source of the income;

(3) consents to the diagnosis and treatment of an infectious, contagious, or communicable disease that is required by law or a rule to be reported by the licensed physician or dentist to a local health officer or the Texas Department of Health, including all diseases within the scope of Section 81.041, Health and Safety Code;

(4) is unmarried and pregnant and consents to hospital, medical, or surgical treatment, other than abortion, related to the pregnancy;

(5) consents to examination and treatment for drug or chemical addiction, drug or chemical dependency, or any other condition directly related to drug or chemical use;

(6) is unmarried, is the parent of a child, and has actual custody of his or her child and consents to medical, dental, psychological, or surgical treatment for the child; or

(7) is serving a term of confinement in a facility operated by or under contract with the Texas Department of Criminal Justice, unless the treatment would constitute a prohibited practice under Section 164.052(a)(19), Occupations Code.

(b) Consent by a child to medical, dental, psychological, and surgical treatment under this section is not subject to disaffirmance because of minority.

(c) Consent of the parents, managing conservator, or guardian of a child is not necessary in order to authorize hospital, medical, surgical, or dental care under this section.

(d) A licensed physician, dentist, or psychologist may, with or without the consent of a child who is a patient, advise the parents, managing conservator, or guardian of the child of the treatment given to or needed by the child.

(e) A physician, dentist, psychologist, hospital, or medical facility is not liable for the examination and treatment of a child under this section except for the provider's or the facility's own acts of negligence.

(f) A physician, dentist, psychologist, hospital, or medical facility may rely on the written statement of the child containing the grounds on which the child has capacity to consent to the child's medical treatment.

(Enacted by Acts 1995, 74th Leg., ch. 20 (H.B. 655), § 1, effective April 20, 1995; am. Acts 1995, 74th Leg., ch. 751 (H.B. 433), § 6, effective September 1, 1995; am. Acts 2001, 77th Leg., ch. 821 (H.B. 920), § 2.01, effective June 14, 2001; am. Acts 2007, 80th Leg., ch. 1227 (H.B. 2389), § 2, effective June 15, 2007.)

### Sec. 32.004.  Consent to Counseling.

(a) A child may consent to counseling for:

(1) suicide prevention;

(2) chemical addiction or dependency; or

(3) sexual, physical, or emotional abuse.

(b) A licensed or certified physician, psychologist, counselor, or social worker having reasonable grounds to believe that a child has been sexually, physically, or emotionally abused, is contemplating suicide, or is suffering from a chemical or drug addiction or dependency may:

(1) counsel the child without the consent of the child's parents or, if applicable, managing conservator or guardian;

Family Code

(2) with or without the consent of the child who is a client, advise the child's parents or, if applicable, managing conservator or guardian of the treatment given to or needed by the child; and

(3) rely on the written statement of the child containing the grounds on which the child has capacity to consent to the child's own treatment under this section.

(c) Unless consent is obtained as otherwise allowed by law, a physician, psychologist, counselor, or social worker may not counsel a child if consent is prohibited by a court order.

(d) A physician, psychologist, counselor, or social worker counseling a child under this section is not liable for damages except for damages resulting from the person's negligence or wilful misconduct.

(e) A parent, or, if applicable, managing conservator or guardian, who has not consented to counseling treatment of the child is not obligated to compensate a physician, psychologist, counselor, or social worker for counseling services rendered under this section.

(Enacted by Acts 1995, 74th Leg., ch. 20 (H.B. 655), § 1, effective April 20, 1995.)

## Sec. 32.005. Examination Without Consent of Abuse or Neglect of Child.

(a) Except as provided by Subsection (c), a physician, dentist, or psychologist having reasonable grounds to believe that a child's physical or mental condition has been adversely affected by abuse or neglect may examine the child without the consent of the child, the child's parents, or other person authorized to consent to treatment under this subchapter.

(b) An examination under this section may include X-rays, blood tests, photographs, and penetration of tissue necessary to accomplish those tests.

(c) Unless consent is obtained as otherwise allowed by law, a physician, dentist, or psychologist may not examine a child:

(1) 16 years of age or older who refuses to consent; or

(2) for whom consent is prohibited by a court order.

(d) A physician, dentist, or psychologist examining a child under this section is not liable for damages except for damages resulting from the physician's or dentist's negligence.

(Enacted by Acts 1995, 74th Leg., ch. 20 (H.B. 655), § 1, effective April 20, 1995; am. Acts 1997,

75th Leg., ch. 575 (H.B. 1826), § 1, effective September 1, 1997.)

## CHAPTER 34
## AUTHORIZATION AGREEMENT FOR NONPARENT RELATIVE

## Sec. 34.001. Applicability.

This chapter applies only to:

(1) an authorization agreement between a parent of a child and a person who is the child's:

(A) grandparent;

(B) adult sibling; or

(C) adult aunt or uncle; and

(2) an authorization agreement between a parent of a child and the person with whom the child is placed under a parental child safety placement agreement.

(Enacted by Acts 2009, 81st Leg., ch. 815 (S.B. 1598), § 1, effective June 19, 2009; am. Acts 2011, 82nd Leg., ch. 484 (H.B. 848), § 1, effective September 1, 2011.)

## Sec. 34.0015. Definition.

In this chapter, "parent" has the meaning assigned by Section 101.024.

(Enacted by Acts 2011, 82nd Leg., ch. 897 (S.B. 482), § 1, effective September 1, 2011.)

## Sec. 34.002. Authorization Agreement.

(a) A parent or both parents of a child may enter into an authorization agreement with a relative of the child listed in Section 34.001 to authorize the relative to perform the following acts in regard to the child:

(1) to authorize medical, dental, psychological, or surgical treatment and immunization of the child, including executing any consents or authorizations for the release of information as required by law relating to the treatment or immunization;

(2) to obtain and maintain health insurance coverage for the child and automobile insurance coverage for the child, if appropriate;

(3) to enroll the child in a day-care program or preschool or in a public or private primary or secondary school;

(4) to authorize the child to participate in age-appropriate extracurricular, civic, social, or recreational activities, including athletic activities;

(5) to authorize the child to obtain a learner's permit, driver's license, or state-issued identification card;

(6) to authorize employment of the child; and

(7) to apply for and receive public benefits on behalf of the child.

(b) To the extent of any conflict or inconsistency between this chapter and any other law relating to the eligibility requirements other than parental consent to obtain a service under Subsection (a), the other law controls.

(c) An authorization agreement under this chapter does not confer on a relative of the child listed in Section 34.001 or a relative or other person with whom the child is placed under a child safety placement agreement the right to authorize the performance of an abortion on the child or the administration of emergency contraception to the child.

(d) Only one authorization agreement may be in effect for a child at any time. An authorization agreement is void if it is executed while a prior authorization agreement remains in effect.
(Enacted by Acts 2009, 81st Leg., ch. 815 (S.B. 1598), § 1, effective June 19, 2009; am. Acts 2011, 82nd Leg., ch. 897 (S.B. 482), § 2, effective September 1, 2011; am. Acts 2011, 82nd Leg., ch. 484 (H.B. 848), § 2, effective September 1, 2011.)

### Sec. 34.0021. Authorization Agreement by Parent in Child Protective Services Case.

A parent may enter into an authorization agreement with a relative or other person with whom a child is placed under a parental child safety placement agreement approved by the Department of Family and Protective Services to allow the person to perform the acts described by Section 34.002(a) with regard to the child:

(1) during an investigation of abuse or neglect; or

(2) while the department is providing services to the parent.

(Enacted by Acts 2011, 82nd Leg., ch. 484 (H.B. 848), § 3, effective September 1, 2011.)

### Sec. 34.003. Contents of Authorization Agreement.

(a) The authorization agreement must contain:

(1) the following information from the relative of the child to whom the parent is giving authorization:

(A) the name and signature of the relative;

(B) the relative's relationship to the child; and

(C) the relative's current physical address and telephone number or the best way to contact the relative;

(2) the following information from the parent:

(A) the name and signature of the parent; and

(B) the parent's current address and telephone number or the best way to contact the parent;

(3) the information in Subdivision (2) with respect to the other parent, if applicable;

(4) a statement that the relative has been given authorization to perform the functions listed in Section 34.002(a) as a result of a voluntary action of the parent and that the relative has voluntarily assumed the responsibility of performing those functions;

(5) statements that neither the parent nor the relative has knowledge that a parent, guardian, custodian, licensed child-placing agency, or other authorized agency asserts any claim or authority inconsistent with the authorization agreement under this chapter with regard to actual physical possession or care, custody, or control of the child;

(6) statements that:

(A) to the best of the parent's and relative's knowledge:

(i) there is no court order or pending suit affecting the parent-child relationship concerning the child;

(ii) there is no pending litigation in any court concerning:

(a) custody, possession, or placement of the child; or

(b) access to or visitation with the child; and

(iii) the court does not have continuing jurisdiction concerning the child; or

(B) the court with continuing jurisdiction concerning the child has given written approval for the execution of the authorization agreement accompanied by the following information:

    (i) the county in which the court is located;

    (ii) the number of the court; and

    (iii) the cause number in which the order was issued or the litigation is pending;

(7) a statement that to the best of the parent's and relative's knowledge there is no current, valid authorization agreement regarding the child;

(8) a statement that the authorization is made in conformance with this chapter;

(9) a statement that the parent and the relative understand that each party to the authorization agreement is required by law to immediately provide to each other party information regarding any change in the party's address or contact information;

(10) a statement by the parent that establishes the circumstances under which the authorization agreement expires, including that the authorization agreement:

    (A) is valid until revoked;

    (B) continues in effect after the death or during any incapacity of the parent; or

    (C) expires on a date stated in the authorization agreement; and

(11) space for the signature and seal of a notary public.

(b) The authorization agreement must contain the following warnings and disclosures:

(1) that the authorization agreement is an important legal document;

(2) that the parent and the relative must read all of the warnings and disclosures before signing the authorization agreement;

(3) that the persons signing the authorization agreement are not required to consult an attorney but are advised to do so;

(4) that the parent's rights as a parent may be adversely affected by placing or leaving the parent's child with another person;

(5) that the authorization agreement does not confer on the relative the rights of a managing or possessory conservator or legal guardian;

(6) that a parent who is a party to the authorization agreement may terminate the authorization agreement and resume custody, possession, care, and control of the child on demand and that at any time the parent may request the return of the child;

(7) that failure by the relative to return the child to the parent immediately on request may have criminal and civil consequences;

(8) that, under other applicable law, the relative may be liable for certain expenses relating to the child in the relative's care but that the parent still retains the parental obligation to support the child;

(9) that, in certain circumstances, the authorization agreement may not be entered into without written permission of the court;

(10) that the authorization agreement may be terminated by certain court orders affecting the child;

(11) that the authorization agreement does not supersede, invalidate, or terminate any prior authorization agreement regarding the child;

(12) that the authorization agreement is void if a prior authorization agreement regarding the child is in effect and has not expired or been terminated;

(13) that, except as provided by Section 34.005(a-1), the authorization agreement is void unless:

    (A) the parties mail a copy of the authorization agreement by certified mail, return receipt requested, or international registered mail, return receipt requested, as applicable, to a parent who was not a party to the authorization agreement, if the parent is living and the parent's parental rights have not been terminated, not later than the 10th day after the date the authorization agreement is signed; and

    (B) if the parties do not receive a response from the parent who is not a party to the authorization agreement before the 20th day after the date the copy of the authorization agreement is mailed under Paragraph (A), the parties mail a second copy of the authorization agreement by first class mail or international first class mail, as applicable, to the parent not later than the 45th day after the date the authorization agreement is signed; and

(14) that the authorization agreement does not confer on a relative of the child the right to authorize the performance of an abortion on the child or the administration of emergency contraception to the child.

(Enacted by Acts 2009, 81st Leg., ch. 815 (S.B. 1598), § 1, effective June 19, 2009; am. Acts 2011, 82nd Leg., ch. 897 (S.B. 482), § 3, effective September 1, 2011.)

## Sec. 34.004. Execution of Authorization Agreement.

(a) The authorization agreement must be signed and sworn to before a notary public by the parent and the relative.

(b) A parent may not execute an authorization agreement without a written order by the appropriate court if:

(1) there is a court order or pending suit affecting the parent-child relationship concerning the child;

(2) there is pending litigation in any court concerning:

(A) custody, possession, or placement of the child; or

(B) access to or visitation with the child; or

(3) the court has continuing, exclusive jurisdiction over the child.

(c) An authorization agreement obtained in violation of Subsection (b) is void.

(Enacted by Acts 2009, 81st Leg., ch. 815 (S.B. 1598), § 1, effective June 19, 2009.)

## Sec. 34.005. Duties of Parties to Authorization Agreement.

(a) If both parents did not sign the authorization agreement, the parties shall mail a copy of the executed authorization agreement by certified mail, return receipt requested, or international registered mail, return receipt requested, as applicable, to the parent who was not a party to the authorization agreement at the parent's last known address not later than the 10th day after the date the authorization agreement is executed if that parent is living and that parent's parental rights have not been terminated. If the parties do not receive a response from the parent who is not a party to the authorization agreement before the 20th day after the date the copy of the authorization agreement is mailed, the parties shall mail a second copy of the executed authorization agreement by first class mail or international first class mail, as applicable, to the parent at the same address not later than the 45th day after the date the authorization agreement is executed. An authorization agreement is void if the parties fail to comply with this subsection.

(a-1) Subsection (a) does not apply to an authorization agreement if the parent who was not a party to the authorization agreement:

(1) does not have court-ordered possession of or access to the child who is the subject of the authorization agreement; and

(2) has previously committed an act of family violence, as defined by Section 71.004, or assault against the parent who is a party to the authorization agreement, the child who is the subject of the authorization agreement, or another child of the parent who is a party to the authorization agreement, as documented by one or more of the following:

(A) the issuance of a protective order against the parent who was not a party to the authorization agreement as provided under Chapter 85 or under a similar law of another state; or

(B) the conviction of the parent who was not a party to the authorization agreement of an offense under Title 5, Penal Code, or of another criminal offense in this state or in another state an element of which involves a violent act or prohibited sexual conduct.

(b) A party to the authorization agreement shall immediately inform each other party of any change in the party's address or contact information. If a party fails to comply with this subsection, the authorization agreement is voidable by the other party.

(Enacted by Acts 2009, 81st Leg., ch. 815 (S.B. 1598), § 1, effective June 19, 2009; am. Acts 2011, 82nd Leg., ch. 897 (S.B. 482), § 4, effective September 1, 2011.)

## Sec. 34.006. Authorization Voidable.

An authorization agreement is voidable by a party if the other party knowingly:

(1) obtained the authorization agreement by fraud, duress, or misrepresentation; or

(2) made a false statement on the authorization agreement.

(Enacted by Acts 2009, 81st Leg., ch. 815 (S.B. 1598), § 1, effective June 19, 2009.)

## Sec. 34.007. Effect of Authorization Agreement.

(a) A person who is not a party to the authorization agreement who relies in good faith on an authorization agreement under this chapter, without actual knowledge that the authorization agreement is void, revoked, or invalid, is not subject to civil or criminal liability to any person, and is not subject to professional disciplinary action, for that reliance if the agreement is completed as required by this chapter.

(b) The authorization agreement does not affect the rights of the child's parent or legal guardian regarding the care, custody, and control of the child, and does not mean that the relative has legal custody of the child.

(c) An authorization agreement executed under this chapter does not confer or affect standing or a right of intervention in any proceeding under Title 5.

(Enacted by Acts 2009, 81st Leg., ch. 815 (S.B. 1598), § 1, effective June 19, 2009.)

## Sec. 34.008. Termination of Authorization Agreement.

(a) Except as provided by Subsection (b), an authorization agreement under this chapter terminates if, after the execution of the authorization agreement, a court enters an order:

(1) affecting the parent-child relationship;

(2) concerning custody, possession, or placement of the child;

(3) concerning access to or visitation with the child; or

(4) regarding the appointment of a guardian for the child under Section 676, Texas Probate Code.

(b) An authorization agreement may continue after a court order described by Subsection (a) is entered if the court entering the order gives written permission.

(c) An authorization agreement under this chapter terminates on written revocation by a party to the authorization agreement if the party:

(1) gives each party written notice of the revocation;

(2) files the written revocation with the clerk of the county in which:

(A) the child resides;

(B) the child resided at the time the authorization agreement was executed; or

(C) the relative resides; and

(3) files the written revocation with the clerk of each court:

(A) that has continuing, exclusive jurisdiction over the child;

(B) in which there is a court order or pending suit affecting the parent-child relationship concerning the child;

(C) in which there is pending litigation concerning:

(i) custody, possession, or placement of the child; or

(ii) access to or visitation with the child; or

(D) that has entered an order regarding the appointment of a guardian for the child under Section 676, Texas Probate Code.

(d) If an authorization agreement executed under this chapter does not state when the autho-rization agreement expires, the authorization agreement is valid until revoked.

(e) If both parents have signed the authorization agreement, either parent may revoke the authorization agreement without the other parent's consent.

(f) Execution of a subsequent authorization agreement does not by itself supersede, invalidate, or terminate a prior authorization agreement.

(Enacted by Acts 2009, 81st Leg., ch. 815 (S.B. 1598), § 1, effective June 19, 2009; am. Acts 2011, 82nd Leg., ch. 897 (S.B. 482), § 5, effective September 1, 2011.)

## Sec. 34.009. Penalty.

(a) A person commits an offense if the person knowingly:

(1) presents a document that is not a valid authorization agreement as a valid authorization agreement under this chapter;

(2) makes a false statement on an authorization agreement; or

(3) obtains an authorization agreement by fraud, duress, or misrepresentation.

(b) An offense under this section is a Class B misdemeanor.

(Enacted by Acts 2009, 81st Leg., ch. 815 (S.B. 1598), § 1, effective June 19, 2009.)

## SUBTITLE B
## PARENTAL LIABILITY

## CHAPTER 41
## LIABILITY OF PARENTS FOR CONDUCT OF CHILD

## Sec. 41.001. Liability.

A parent or other person who has the duty of control and reasonable discipline of a child is liable for any property damage proximately caused by:

(1) the negligent conduct of the child if the conduct is reasonably attributable to the negligent failure of the parent or other person to exercise that duty; or

(2) the wilful and malicious conduct of a child who is at least 10 years of age but under 18 years of age.

(Enacted by Acts 1995, 74th Leg., ch. 20 (H.B. 655), § 1, effective April 20, 1995; am. Acts 2001, 77th Leg., ch. 587 (S.B. 233), § 1, effective September 1, 2001.)

Family Code

## SUBTITLE C
## CHANGE OF NAME

## CHAPTER 45
## CHANGE OF NAME

**Subchapter B. Change of Name of Adult**

## *SUBCHAPTER B*
## *CHANGE OF NAME OF ADULT*

### Sec. 45.101.  Who May File; Venue.

An adult may file a petition requesting a change of name in the county of the adult's place of residence.

(Enacted by Acts 1995, 74th Leg., ch. 20 (H.B. 655), § 1, effective April 20, 1995.)

### Sec. 45.102.  Requirements of Petition.

(a) A petition to change the name of an adult must be verified and include:

(1) the present name and place of residence of the petitioner;

(2) the full name requested for the petitioner;

(3) the reason the change in name is requested;

(4) whether the petitioner has been the subject of a final felony conviction;

(5) whether the petitioner is subject to the registration requirements of Chapter 62, Code of Criminal Procedure; and

(6) a legible and complete set of the petitioner's fingerprints on a fingerprint card format acceptable to the Department of Public Safety and the Federal Bureau of Investigation.

(b) The petition must include each of the following or a reasonable explanation why the required information is not included:

(1) the petitioner's:

(A) full name;

(B) sex;

(C) race;

(D) date of birth;

(E) driver's license number for any driver's license issued in the 10 years preceding the date of the petition;

(F) social security number; and

(G) assigned FBI number, state identification number, if known, or any other reference number in a criminal history record system that identifies the petitioner;

(2) any offense above the grade of Class C misdemeanor for which the petitioner has been charged; and

(3) the case number and the court if a warrant was issued or a charging instrument was filed or presented for an offense listed in Subsection (b)(2).

(Enacted by Acts 1995, 74th Leg., ch. 20 (H.B. 655), § 1, effective April 20, 1995; am. Acts 2003, 78th Leg., ch. 1003 (H.B. 162), § 1, effective September 1, 2003; am. Acts 2003, 78th Leg., ch. 1300 (S.B. 146), § 7, effective September 1, 2003; am. Acts 2005, 79th Leg., ch. 728 (H.B. 2018), § 6.001, effective September 1, 2005.)

### Sec. 45.103.  Order.

(a) The court shall order a change of name under this subchapter for a person other than a person with a final felony conviction or a person subject to the registration requirements of Chapter 62, Code of Criminal Procedure, if the change is in the interest or to the benefit of the petitioner and in the interest of the public.

(b) A court may order a change of name under this subchapter for a person with a final felony conviction if, in addition to the requirements of Subsection (a), the person has:

(1) received a certificate of discharge by the Texas Department of Criminal Justice or completed a period of community supervision or juvenile probation ordered by a court and not less than two years have passed from the date of the receipt of discharge or completion of community supervision or juvenile probation; or

(2) been pardoned.

(c) A court may order a change of name under this subchapter for a person subject to the registration requirements of Chapter 62, Code of Criminal Procedure, if, in addition to the requirements of Subsection (a), the person provides the court with proof that the person has notified the appropriate local law enforcement authority of the proposed name change. In this subsection, "local law enforcement authority" has the meaning assigned by Article 62.001, Code of Criminal Procedure.

(Enacted by Acts 1995, 74th Leg., ch. 20 (H.B. 655), § 1, effective April 20, 1995; am. Acts 2003, 78th Leg., ch. 1300 (S.B. 146), § 8, effective

September 1, 2003; am. Acts 2005, 79th Leg., ch. 1008 (H.B. 867), § 2.06, effective September 1, 2005; am. Acts 2009, 81st Leg., ch. 87 (S.B. 1969), § 25.057, effective September 1, 2009.)

### Sec. 45.104. Liabilities and Rights Unaffected.

A change of name under this subchapter does not release a person from liability incurred in that person's previous name or defeat any right the person had in the person's previous name. (Enacted by Acts 1995, 74th Leg., ch. 20 (H.B. 655), § 1, effective April 20, 1995.)

# TITLE 3
# JUVENILE JUSTICE CODE

## CHAPTER 51
## GENERAL PROVISIONS

### Sec. 51.01. Purpose and Interpretation.

This title shall be construed to effectuate the following public purposes:

(1) to provide for the protection of the public and public safety;

(2) consistent with the protection of the public and public safety:

  (A) to promote the concept of punishment for criminal acts;

  (B) to remove, where appropriate, the taint of criminality from children committing certain unlawful acts; and

  (C) to provide treatment, training, and rehabilitation that emphasizes the accountability and responsibility of both the parent and the child for the child's conduct;

(3) to provide for the care, the protection, and the wholesome moral, mental, and physical development of children coming within its provisions;

(4) to protect the welfare of the community and to control the commission of unlawful acts by children;

(5) to achieve the foregoing purposes in a family environment whenever possible, separating the child from the child's parents only when necessary for the child's welfare or in the interest of public safety and when a child is removed from the child's family, to give the child the care that should be provided by parents; and

(6) to provide a simple judicial procedure through which the provisions of this title are

**Family Code**

executed and enforced and in which the parties are assured a fair hearing and their constitutional and other legal rights recognized and enforced.

(Enacted by Acts 1973, 63rd Leg., ch. 544 (S.B. 111), § 1, effective September 1, 1973; am. Acts 1995, 74th Leg., ch. 262 (H.B. 327), § 2, effective January 1, 1996.)

## Sec. 51.02.  Definitions.

In this title:

(1) "Aggravated controlled substance felony" means an offense under Subchapter D, Chapter 481, Health and Safety Code, that is punishable by:

(A) a minimum term of confinement that is longer than the minimum term of confinement for a felony of the first degree; or

(B) a maximum fine that is greater than the maximum fine for a felony of the first degree.

(2) "Child" means a person who is:

(A) ten years of age or older and under 17 years of age; or

(B) seventeen years of age or older and under 18 years of age who is alleged or found to have engaged in delinquent conduct or conduct indicating a need for supervision as a result of acts committed before becoming 17 years of age.

(3) "Custodian" means the adult with whom the child resides.

(4) "Guardian" means the person who, under court order, is the guardian of the person of the child or the public or private agency with whom the child has been placed by a court.

(5) "Judge" or "juvenile court judge" means the judge of a juvenile court.

(6) "Juvenile court" means a court designated under Section 51.04 of this code to exercise jurisdiction over proceedings under this title.

(7) "Law-enforcement officer" means a peace officer as defined by Article 2.12, Code of Criminal Procedure.

(8) "Nonoffender" means a child who:

(A) is subject to jurisdiction of a court under abuse, dependency, or neglect statutes under Title 5 for reasons other than legally prohibited conduct of the child; or

(B) has been taken into custody and is being held solely for deportation out of the United States.

(8-a) "Nonsecure correctional facility" means a facility, other than a secure correctional facil-

ity, that accepts only juveniles who are on probation and that is operated by or under contract with a governmental unit, as defined by Section 101.001, Civil Practice and Remedies Code.

(9) "Parent" means the mother or the father of a child, but does not include a parent whose parental rights have been terminated.

(10) "Party" means the state, a child who is the subject of proceedings under this subtitle, or the child's parent, spouse, guardian, or guardian ad litem.

(11) "Prosecuting attorney" means the county attorney, district attorney, or other attorney who regularly serves in a prosecutory capacity in a juvenile court.

(12) "Referral to juvenile court" means the referral of a child or a child's case to the office or official, including an intake officer or probation officer, designated by the juvenile board to process children within the juvenile justice system.

(13) "Secure correctional facility" means any public or private residential facility, including an alcohol or other drug treatment facility, that:

(A) includes construction fixtures designed to physically restrict the movements and activities of juveniles or other individuals held in lawful custody in the facility; and

(B) is used for the placement of any juvenile who has been adjudicated as having committed an offense, any nonoffender, or any other individual convicted of a criminal offense.

(14) "Secure detention facility" means any public or private residential facility that:

(A) includes construction fixtures designed to physically restrict the movements and activities of juveniles or other individuals held in lawful custody in the facility; and

(B) is used for the temporary placement of any juvenile who is accused of having committed an offense, any nonoffender, or any other individual accused of having committed a criminal offense.

(15) "Status offender" means a child who is accused, adjudicated, or convicted for conduct that would not, under state law, be a crime if committed by an adult, including:

(A) truancy under Section 51.03(b)(2);

(B) running away from home under Section 51.03(b)(3);

(C) a fineable only offense under Section 51.03(b)(1) transferred to the juvenile court under Section 51.08(b), but only if the conduct constituting the offense would not have been criminal if engaged in by an adult;

(D) failure to attend school under Section 25.094, Education Code;

(E) a violation of standards of student conduct as described by Section 51.03(b)(5);

(F) a violation of a juvenile curfew ordinance or order;

(G) a violation of a provision of the Alcoholic Beverage Code applicable to minors only; or

(H) a violation of any other fineable only offense under Section 8.07(a)(4) or (5), Penal Code, but only if the conduct constituting the offense would not have been criminal if engaged in by an adult.

(16) "Traffic offense" means:

(A) a violation of a penal statute cognizable under Chapter 729, Transportation Code, except for conduct for which the person convicted may be sentenced to imprisonment or confinement in jail; or

(B) a violation of a motor vehicle traffic ordinance of an incorporated city or town in this state.

(17) "Valid court order" means a court order entered under Section 54.04 concerning a child adjudicated to have engaged in conduct indicating a need for supervision as a status offender. (Enacted by Acts 1973, 63rd Leg., ch. 544 (S.B. 111), § 1, effective September 1, 1973; am. Acts 1975, 64th Leg., ch. 693 (S.B. 247), § 1, effective September 1, 1975; am. Acts 1995, 74th Leg., ch. 262 (H.B. 327), § 3, effective January 1, 1996; am. Acts 1997, 75th Leg., ch. 165 (S.B. 898), §§ 6.06, 30.182, effective September 1, 1997; am. Acts 1997, 75th Leg., ch. 822 (S.B. 81), § 2, effective September 1, 1997; am. Acts 1997, 75th Leg., ch. 1013 (S.B. 35), § 13, effective September 1, 1997; am. Acts 1997, 75th Leg., ch. 1086 (H.B. 1550), §§ 41, 47, effective September 1, 1997; am. Acts 2001, 77th Leg., ch. 821 (H.B. 920), § 2.02, effective June 14, 2001; am. Acts 2001, 77th Leg., ch. 1297 (H.B. 1118), § 1, effective September 1, 2001; am. Acts 2003, 78th Leg., ch. 283 (H.B. 2319), § 1, effective September 1, 2003; am. Acts 2005, 79th Leg., ch. 949 (H.B. 1575), § 1, effective September 1, 2005; am. Acts 2009, 81st Leg., ch. 1187 (H.B. 3689), § 4.004, effective June 19, 2009.)

## Sec. 51.03. Delinquent Conduct; Conduct Indicating a Need for Supervision.

(a) Delinquent conduct is:

(1) conduct, other than a traffic offense, that violates a penal law of this state or of the United States punishable by imprisonment or by confinement in jail;

(2) conduct that violates a lawful order of a court under circumstances that would constitute contempt of that court in:

(A) a justice or municipal court; or

(B) a county court for conduct punishable only by a fine;

(3) conduct that violates Section 49.04, 49.05, 49.06, 49.07, or 49.08, Penal Code; or

(4) conduct that violates Section 106.041, Alcoholic Beverage Code, relating to driving under the influence of alcohol by a minor (third or subsequent offense).

(b) Conduct indicating a need for supervision is:

(1) subject to Subsection (f), conduct, other than a traffic offense, that violates:

(A) the penal laws of this state of the grade of misdemeanor that are punishable by fine only; or

(B) the penal ordinances of any political subdivision of this state;

(2) the absence of a child on 10 or more days or parts of days within a six-month period in the same school year or on three or more days or parts of days within a four-week period from school;

(3) the voluntary absence of a child from the child's home without the consent of the child's parent or guardian for a substantial length of time or without intent to return;

(4) conduct prohibited by city ordinance or by state law involving the inhalation of the fumes or vapors of paint and other protective coatings or glue and other adhesives and the volatile chemicals itemized in Section 485.001, Health and Safety Code;

(5) an act that violates a school district's previously communicated written standards of student conduct for which the child has been expelled under Section 37.007(c), Education Code;

(6) conduct that violates a reasonable and lawful order of a court entered under Section 264.305; or

(7) **[2 Versions: As added by Acts 2011, 82nd Leg., ch. 1150]** notwithstanding Subsection (a)(1), conduct described by Section 43.02(a)(1) or (2), Penal Code.

(7) **[2 Versions: As added by Acts 2011, 82nd Leg., ch. 1322]** conduct that violates Section 43.261, Penal Code.

(c) Nothing in this title prevents criminal proceedings against a child for perjury.

(d) It is an affirmative defense to an allegation of conduct under Subsection (b)(2) that one or more of the absences required to be proven under that subsection have been excused by a school official or by the court or that one or more of the absences were involuntary, but only if there is an insufficient number of unexcused or voluntary absences remaining to constitute conduct under Subsection (b)(2). The burden is on the respondent to show by a preponderance of the evidence that the absence has been or should be excused or that the absence was involuntary. A decision by the court to excuse an absence for purposes of this subsection does not affect the ability of the school district to determine whether to excuse the absence for another purpose.

(e) For the purposes of Subsection (b)(3), "child" does not include a person who is married, divorced, or widowed.

(e-1) Notwithstanding any other law, for purposes of conduct described by Subsection (b)(2), "child" means a person who is:

(1) 10 years of age or older;

(2) alleged or found to have engaged in the conduct as a result of acts committed before becoming 18 years of age; and

(3) required to attend school under Section 25.085, Education Code.

(f) Except as provided by Subsection (g), conduct described under Subsection (b)(1) does not constitute conduct indicating a need for supervision unless the child has been referred to the juvenile court under Section 51.08(b).

(g) In a county with a population of less than 100,000, conduct described by Subsection (b)(1)(A) that violates Section 25.094, Education Code, is conduct indicating a need for supervision.
(Enacted by Acts 1973, 63rd Leg., ch. 544 (S.B. 111), § 1, effective September 1, 1973; am. Acts 1975, 64th Leg., ch. 693 (S.B. 247), §§ 2-4, effective September 1, 1975; am. Acts 1977, 65th Leg., ch. 340 (H.B. 1146), § 1, effective June 6, 1977; am. Acts 1987, 70th Leg., ch. 511 (H.B. 502), § 1, effective September 1, 1987; am. Acts 1987, 70th Leg., ch. 924 (H.B. 1079), § 1, effective September 1, 1987; am. Acts 1987, 70th Leg., ch. 955 (S.B. 225), § 1, effective June 19, 1987; am. Acts 1987, 70th Leg., ch. 1040 (S.B. 17), § 20, effective September 1, 1987; am. Acts 1987, 70th Leg., ch. 1099 (S.B. 33), § 48, effective September 1, 1987; am. Acts 1989, 71st Leg., ch. 1100 (S.B. 1046), § 3.02, effective August 28, 1989; am. Acts 1989,

71st Leg., ch. 1245 (H.B. 535), §§ 1, 4, effective September 1, 1989; am. Acts 1991, 72nd Leg., ch. 14 (S.B. 404), § 284(35), effective September 1, 1991; am. Acts 1991, 72nd Leg., ch. 16 (S.B. 232), § 7.02, effective August 26, 1991; am. Acts 1991, 72nd Leg., ch. 169 (H.B. 944), § 1, effective September 1, 1991; am. Acts 1993, 73rd Leg., ch. 46 (H.B. 323), § 1, effective September 1, 1993; am. Acts 1995, 74th Leg., ch. 76 (S.B. 959), § 14.30, effective September 1, 1995; am. Acts 1995, 74th Leg., ch. 262 (H.B. 327), § 4, effective January 1, 1996; am. Acts 1997, 75th Leg., ch. 165 (S.B. 898), § 6.07, effective September 1, 1997; am. Acts 1997, 75th Leg., ch. 1013 (S.B. 35), § 14, effective September 1, 1997; am. Acts 1997, 75th Leg., ch. 1015 (S.B. 133), § 15, effective June 19, 1997; am. Acts 1997, 75th Leg., ch. 1086 (H.B. 1550), § 1, effective September 1, 1997; am. Acts 2001, 77th Leg., ch. 1297 (H.B. 1118), § 2, effective September 1, 2001; am. Acts 2001, 77th Leg., ch. 1514 (S.B. 1432), § 11, effective September 1, 2001; am. Acts 2003, 78th Leg., ch. 137 (S.B. 358), § 11, effective September 1, 2003; am. Acts 2005, 79th Leg., ch. 949 (H.B. 1575), § 2, effective September 1, 2005; am. Acts 2007, 80th Leg., ch. 908 (H.B. 2884), § 3, effective September 1, 2007; am. Acts 2009, 81st Leg., ch. 311 (H.B. 558), § 3, effective September 1, 2009; am. Acts 2011, 82nd Leg., ch. 1322 (S.B. 407), § 4, effective September 1, 2011; am. Acts 2011, 82nd Leg., ch. 1098 (S.B. 1489), § 2, effective September 1, 2011; am. Acts 2011, 82nd Leg., ch. 1150 (H.B. 2015), § 1, effective September 1, 2011.)

## Sec. 51.031.  Habitual Felony Conduct.

(a) Habitual felony conduct is conduct violating a penal law of the grade of felony, other than a state jail felony, if:

(1) the child who engaged in the conduct has at least two previous final adjudications as having engaged in delinquent conduct violating a penal law of the grade of felony;

(2) the second previous final adjudication is for conduct that occurred after the date the first previous adjudication became final; and

(3) all appeals relating to the previous adjudications considered under Subdivisions (1) and (2) have been exhausted.

(b) For purposes of this section, an adjudication is final if the child is placed on probation or committed to the Texas Youth Commission.

(c) An adjudication based on conduct that occurred before January 1, 1996, may not be considered in a disposition made under this section.

(Enacted by Acts 1995, 74th Leg., ch. 262 (H.B. 327), § 5, effective January 1, 1996; am. Acts 1997, 75th Leg., ch. 1086 (H.B. 1550), § 2, effective September 1, 1997.)

### Sec. 51.04. Jurisdiction.

(a) This title covers the proceedings in all cases involving the delinquent conduct or conduct indicating a need for supervision engaged in by a person who was a child within the meaning of this title at the time the person engaged in the conduct, and, except as provided by Subsection (h), the juvenile court has exclusive original jurisdiction over proceedings under this title.

(b) In each county, the county's juvenile board shall designate one or more district, criminal district, domestic relations, juvenile, or county courts or county courts at law as the juvenile court, subject to Subsections (c) and (d) of this section.

(c) If the county court is designated as a juvenile court, at least one other court shall be designated as the juvenile court. A county court does not have jurisdiction of a proceeding involving a petition approved by a grand jury under Section 53.045 of this code.

(d) If the judge of a court designated in Subsection (b) or (c) of this section is not an attorney licensed in this state, there shall also be designated an alternate court, the judge of which is an attorney licensed in this state.

(e) A designation made under Subsection (b) or (c) of this section may be changed from time to time by the authorized boards or judges for the convenience of the people and the welfare of children. However, there must be at all times a juvenile court designated for each county. It is the intent of the legislature that in selecting a court to be the juvenile court of each county, the selection shall be made as far as practicable so that the court designated as the juvenile court will be one which is presided over by a judge who has a sympathetic understanding of the problems of child welfare and that changes in the designation of juvenile courts be made only when the best interest of the public requires it.

(f) If the judge of the juvenile court or any alternate judge named under Subsection (b) or (c) is not in the county or is otherwise unavailable, any magistrate may make a determination under Section 53.02(f) or may conduct the detention hearing provided for in Section 54.01.

(g) The juvenile board may appoint a referee to make determinations under Section 53.02(f) or to conduct hearings under this title. The referee shall be an attorney licensed to practice law in this state and shall comply with Section 54.10. Payment of any referee services shall be provided from county funds.

(h) In a county with a population of less than 100,000, the juvenile court has concurrent jurisdiction with the justice and municipal courts over conduct engaged in by a child that violates Section 25.094, Education Code.

(Enacted by Acts 1973, 63rd Leg., ch. 544 (S.B. 111), § 1, effective September 1, 1973; am. Acts 1975, 64th Leg., ch. 514, § 1, effective June 19, 1975; am. Acts 1975, 64th Leg., ch. 693 (S.B. 247), § 5 to 7, effective September 1, 1975; am. Acts 1977, 65th Leg., ch. 411 (S.B. 411), § 1, effective June 15, 1977; am. Acts 1987, 70th Leg., ch. 385 (H.B. 682), § 1, effective September 1, 1987; am. Acts 1993, 73rd Leg., ch. 168 (H.B. 793), § 4, effective August 30, 1993; am. Acts 1999, 76th Leg., ch. 232 (H.B. 1269), § 2, effective September 1, 1999; am. Acts 2001, 77th Leg., ch. 1297 (H.B. 1118), § 3, effective September 1, 2001; am. Acts 2001, 77th Leg., ch. 1514 (S.B. 1432), § 12, effective September 1, 2001.)

### Sec. 51.041. Jurisdiction After Appeal.

(a) The court retains jurisdiction over a person, without regard to the age of the person, for conduct engaged in by the person before becoming 17 years of age if, as a result of an appeal by the person or the state under Chapter 56 or by the person under Article 44.47, Code of Criminal Procedure, of an order of the court, the order is reversed or modified and the case remanded to the court by the appellate court.

(b) If the respondent is at least 18 years of age when the order of remand from the appellate court is received by the juvenile court, the juvenile court shall proceed as provided by Sections 54.02(o)—(r) for the detention of a person at least 18 years of age in discretionary transfer proceedings. Pending retrial of the adjudication or transfer proceeding, the juvenile court may:

    (1) order the respondent released from custody;

    (2) order the respondent detained in a juvenile detention facility; or

    (3) set bond and order the respondent detained in a county adult facility if bond is not made.

(Enacted by Acts 1995, 74th Leg., ch. 262 (H.B. 327), § 6, effective January 1, 1996; am. Acts

2001, 77th Leg., ch. 1297 (H.B. 1118), § 4, effective September 1, 2001; am. Acts 2003, 78th Leg., ch. 283 (H.B. 2319), § 2, effective September 1, 2003.)

### Sec. 51.0411.  Jurisdiction for Transfer or Release Hearing.

The court retains jurisdiction over a person, without regard to the age of the person, who is referred to the court under Section 54.11 for transfer to the Texas Department of Criminal Justice or release under supervision.
(Enacted by Acts 1997, 75th Leg., ch. 1086 (H.B. 1550), § 3, effective June 19, 1997.)

### Sec. 51.0412.  Jurisdiction over Incomplete Proceedings.

The court retains jurisdiction over a person, without regard to the age of the person, who is a respondent in an adjudication proceeding, a disposition proceeding, a proceeding to modify disposition, or a motion for transfer of determinate sentence probation to an appropriate district court if:

(1) the petition or motion to modify was filed while the respondent was younger than 18 years of age or the motion for transfer was filed while the respondent was younger than 19 years of age;

(2) the proceeding is not complete before the respondent becomes 18 or 19 years of age, as applicable; and

(3) the court enters a finding in the proceeding that the prosecuting attorney exercised due diligence in an attempt to complete the proceeding before the respondent became 18 or 19 years of age, as applicable.
(Enacted by Acts 2001, 77th Leg., ch. 1297 (H.B. 1118), § 5, effective September 1, 2001; am. Acts 2007, 80th Leg., ch. 908 (H.B. 2884), § 4, effective September 1, 2007; am. Acts 2011, 82nd Leg., ch. 438 (S.B. 1208), § 1, effective September 1, 2011.)

### Sec. 51.042.  Objection to Jurisdiction Because of Age of the Child.

(a) A child who objects to the jurisdiction of the court over the child because of the age of the child must raise the objection at the adjudication hearing or discretionary transfer hearing, if any.

(b) A child who does not object as provided by Subsection (a) waives any right to object to the jurisdiction of the court because of the age of the child at a later hearing or on appeal.
(Enacted by Acts 1995, 74th Leg., ch. 262 (H.B. 327), § 6, effective January 1, 1996.)

### Sec. 51.045.  Juries in County Courts at Law.

If a provision of this title requires a jury of 12 persons, that provision prevails over any other law that limits the number of members of a jury in a particular county court at law. The state and the defense are entitled to the same number of peremptory challenges allowed in a district court.
(Enacted by Acts 1987, 70th Leg., ch. 385 (H.B. 682), § 2, effective September 1, 1987.)

### Sec. 51.05.  Court Sessions and Facilities.

(a) The juvenile court shall be deemed in session at all times. Suitable quarters shall be provided by the commissioners court of each county for the hearing of cases and for the use of the judge, the probation officer, and other employees of the court.

(b) The juvenile court and the juvenile board shall report annually to the commissioners court on the suitability of the quarters and facilities of the juvenile court and may make recommendations for their improvement.
(Enacted by Acts 1973, 63rd Leg., ch. 544 (S.B. 111), § 1, effective September 1, 1973; am. Acts 1975, 64th Leg., ch. 693 (S.B. 247), § 8, effective September 1, 1975.)

### Sec. 51.06.  Venue.

(a) A proceeding under this title shall be commenced in

(1) the county in which the alleged delinquent conduct or conduct indicating a need for supervision occurred; or

(2) the county in which the child resides at the time the petition is filed, but only if:

(A) the child was under probation supervision in that county at the time of the commission of the delinquent conduct or conduct indicating a need for supervision;

(B) it cannot be determined in which county the delinquent conduct or conduct indicating a need for supervision occurred; or

(C) the county in which the child resides agrees to accept the case for prosecution, in writing, prior to the case being sent to the county of residence for prosecution.

(b) An application for a writ of habeas corpus brought by or on behalf of a person who has been committed to an institution under the jurisdiction of the Texas Youth Commission and which attacks the validity of the judgment of commitment shall be brought in the county in which the court that entered the judgment of commitment is located.

(Enacted by Acts 1973, 63rd Leg., ch. 544 (S.B. 111), § 1, effective September 1, 1973; am. Acts 1983, 68th Leg., ch. 44 (S.B. 422), art. 1 § 1, effective April 26, 1983; am. Acts 1995, 74th Leg., ch. 262 (H.B. 327), § 7, effective January 1, 1996; am. Acts 1999, 76th Leg., ch. 488 (S.B. 1571), § 1, effective September 1, 1999.)

## Sec. 51.07. Transfer to Another County for Disposition.

When a child has been found to have engaged in delinquent conduct or conduct indicating a need for supervision under Section 54.03, the juvenile court may transfer the case and transcripts of records and documents to the juvenile court of the county where the child resides for disposition of the case under Section 54.04. Consent by the court of the county where the child resides is not required.

(Enacted by Acts 1973, 63rd Leg., ch. 544 (S.B. 111), § 1, effective September 1, 1973; am. Acts 2005, 79th Leg., ch. 949 (H.B. 1575), § 3, effective September 1, 2005.)

## Sec. 51.071. Transfer of Probation Supervision Between Counties: Courtesy Supervision Prohibited.

Except as provided by Section 51.075, a juvenile court or juvenile probation department may not engage in the practice of courtesy supervision of a child on probation.

(Enacted by Acts 2005, 79th Leg., ch. 949 (H.B. 1575), § 4, effective September 1, 2005.)

## Sec. 51.072. Transfer of Probation Supervision Between Counties: Interim Supervision.

(a) In this section:

(1) "Receiving county" means the county to which a child on probation has moved or intends to move.

(2) "Sending county" means the county that:

(A) originally placed the child on probation; or

(B) assumed permanent supervision of the child under an inter-county transfer of probation supervision.

(b) When a child on probation moves or intends to move from one county to another and intends to remain in the receiving county for at least 60 days, the juvenile probation department of the sending county shall request that the juvenile probation department of the receiving county provide interim supervision of the child. If the receiving county and the sending county are member counties within a judicial district served by one juvenile probation department, then a transfer of probation supervision is not required.

(c) The juvenile probation department of the receiving county may refuse the request to provide interim supervision only if:

(1) the residence of the child in the receiving county is in a residential placement facility arranged by the sending county; or

(2) the residence of the child in the receiving county is in a foster care placement arranged by the Department of Family and Protective Services.

(d) The juvenile probation department of the sending county shall initiate the request for interim supervision by electronic communication to the probation officer designated as the inter-county transfer officer for the juvenile probation department of the receiving county or, in the absence of this designation, to the chief juvenile probation officer.

(e) The juvenile probation department of the sending county shall provide the juvenile probation department of the receiving county with the following information in the request for interim supervision initiated under Subsection (d):

(1) the child's name, sex, age, race, and date of birth;

(2) the name, address, date of birth, and social security or driver's license number, and telephone number, if available, of the person with whom the child proposes to reside or is residing in the receiving county;

(3) the offense for which the child is on probation;

(4) the length of the child's probation term;

(5) a brief summary of the child's history of referrals;

(6) a brief statement of any special needs of the child;

(7) the name and telephone number of the child's school in the receiving county, if available; and

(8) the reason for the child moving or intending to move to the receiving county.

(f) Not later than 10 business days after a receiving county has agreed to provide interim supervision of a child, the juvenile probation department of the sending county shall provide the juvenile probation department of the receiving county with a copy of the following documents:

(1) the petition and the adjudication and disposition orders for the child, including the child's thumbprint;

(2) the child's conditions of probation;

(3) the social history report for the child;

(4) any psychological or psychiatric reports concerning the child;

(5) the Department of Public Safety CR 43J form or tracking incident number concerning the child;

(6) any law enforcement incident reports concerning the offense for which the child is on probation;

(7) any sex offender registration information concerning the child;

(8) any juvenile probation department progress reports concerning the child and any other pertinent documentation for the child's probation officer;

(9) case plans concerning the child;

(10) the Texas Juvenile Probation Commission standard assessment tool results for the child;

(11) the computerized referral and case history for the child, including case disposition;

(12) the child's birth certificate;

(13) the child's social security number or social security card, if available;

(14) the name, address, and telephone number of the contact person in the sending county's juvenile probation department;

(15) Title IV-E eligibility screening information for the child, if available;

(16) the address in the sending county for forwarding funds collected to which the sending county is entitled;

(17) any of the child's school or immunization records that the juvenile probation department of the sending county possesses; and

(18) any victim information concerning the case for which the child is on probation.

(f-1) The inter-county transfer officers in the sending and receiving counties shall agree on the official start date for the period of interim supervision, which must begin no later than three business days after the date the documents required under Subsection (f) have been received and accepted by the receiving county.

(g) The juvenile probation department of the receiving county shall supervise the child under the probation conditions imposed by the sending county and provide services similar to those provided to a child placed on probation under the same conditions in the receiving county. On request of the juvenile probation department of the receiving county, the juvenile court of the receiving county may modify the original probation conditions and impose new conditions using the procedures in Section 54.05. The juvenile court of the receiving county may not modify a financial probation condition imposed by the juvenile court of the sending county or the length of the child's probation term. The juvenile court of the receiving county shall designate a cause number for identifying the modification proceedings.

(h) The juvenile court of the sending county may revoke probation for a violation of a condition imposed by the juvenile court of the sending county only if the condition has not been specifically modified or replaced by the juvenile court of the receiving county. The juvenile court of the receiving county may revoke probation for a violation of a condition of probation that the juvenile court of the receiving county has modified or imposed.

(i) If a child is reasonably believed to have violated a condition of probation imposed by the juvenile court of the sending county, the juvenile court of the sending or receiving county may issue a directive to apprehend or detain the child in a certified detention facility, as in other cases of probation violation. In order to respond to a probation violation under this subsection, the juvenile court of the receiving county may:

(1) modify the conditions of probation or extend the probation term; or

(2) require that the juvenile probation department of the sending county resume direct supervision for the child.

(j) On receiving a directive from the juvenile court of the receiving county under Subsection (i)(2), the juvenile probation department of the sending county shall arrange for the prompt transportation of the child back to the sending county at the expense of the sending county. The juvenile probation department in the receiving county shall provide the sending county with supporting written documentation of the incidents of violation of probation on which the request to resume direct supervision is based.

(k) The juvenile probation department of the receiving county is entitled to any probation supervision fees collected from the child or the child's parent while providing interim supervision for the child. During the period of interim supervision, the receiving county shall collect and distribute to the victim monetary restitution payments in the manner specified by the sending county. At the expiration of the period of interim supervision, the receiving county shall collect and distribute directly to the victim any remaining payments.

(*l*) The sending county is financially responsible for any special treatment program or placement that the juvenile court of the sending county requires as a condition of probation if the child's family is financially unable to pay for the program or placement.

(m) Except as provided by Subsection (n), a period of interim supervision may not exceed 180 days. Permanent supervision automatically transfers to the juvenile probation department of the receiving county after the expiration of the period of interim supervision. The juvenile probation department of the receiving county may request permanent supervision from the juvenile probation department of the sending county at any time before the 180-day interim supervision period expires. After signing and entry of an order of transfer of permanent supervision by the sending county juvenile court, the juvenile probation department shall, in accordance with Section 51.073(b), promptly send the permanent supervision order and related documents to the receiving county.

(m-1) If a child on interim supervision moves to another county of residence or is otherwise no longer in the receiving county before the expiration of 180 days, the receiving county shall direct the sending county to resume supervision of the child.

(n) Notwithstanding Subsection (m), the period of interim supervision of a child who is placed on probation under Section 54.04(q) does not expire until the child has satisfactorily completed the greater of either 180 days or one-third of the term of probation, including one-third of the term of any extension of the probation term ordered under Section 54.05. Permanent supervision automatically transfers to the probation department of the receiving county after the expiration of the period of interim supervision under this subsection. If the state elects to initiate transfer proceedings under Section 54.051, the juvenile court of the sending county may order transfer of the permanent supervision before the expiration of the period of interim supervision under this subsection.

(o) At least once every 90 days during the period of interim supervision, the juvenile probation department of the receiving county shall provide the juvenile probation department of the sending county with a progress report of supervision concerning the child.

(Enacted by Acts 2005, 79th Leg., ch. 949 (H.B. 1575), § 4, effective September 1, 2005; am. Acts 2007, 80th Leg., ch. 908 (H.B. 2884), § 5, effective September 1, 2007.)

### Sec. 51.073. Transfer of Probation Supervision Between Counties: Permanent Supervision.

(a) In this section:

(1) "Receiving county" means the county to which a child on probation has moved or intends to move.

(2) "Sending county" means the county that:

(A) originally placed the child on probation; or

(B) assumed permanent supervision of the child under an inter-county transfer of probation supervision.

(b) On transfer of permanent supervision of a child under Section 51.072(m) or (n), the juvenile court of the sending county shall order the juvenile probation department of the sending county to provide the juvenile probation department of the receiving county with the order of transfer. On receipt of the order of transfer, the juvenile probation department of the receiving county shall ensure that the order of transfer, the petition, the order of adjudication, the order of disposition, and the conditions of probation are filed with the clerk of the juvenile court of the receiving county.

(c) The juvenile court of the receiving county shall require that the child be brought before the court in order to impose new or different conditions of probation than those originally ordered by the sending county or ordered by the receiving county during the period of interim supervision. The child shall be represented by counsel as provided by Section 51.10.

(d) Once permanent supervision is transferred to the juvenile probation department of the receiving county, the receiving county is fully responsible for selecting and imposing conditions of probation, providing supervision, modifying conditions of probation, and revoking probation. The sending county has no further jurisdiction over the child's case.

(d-1) On the final transfer of a case involving a child who has been adjudicated as having committed an offense for which registration is required under Chapter 62, Code of Criminal Procedure, the receiving county shall have jurisdiction to conduct a hearing under that chapter. This subsection does not prohibit the receiving county juvenile court from considering the written recommendations of the sending county juvenile court.

(e) This section does not affect the sending county's jurisdiction over any new offense committed by the child in the sending county.

(Enacted by Acts 2005, 79th Leg., ch. 949 (H.B. 1575), § 4, effective September 1, 2005; am. Acts 2007, 80th Leg., ch. 908 (H.B. 2884), § 6, effective September 1, 2007.)

### Sec. 51.074. Transfer of Probation Supervision Between Counties: Deferred Prosecution.

(a) A juvenile court may transfer interim supervision, but not permanent supervision, to the county where a child on deferred prosecution resides.

(b) On an extension of a previous order of deferred prosecution authorized under Section 53.03(j), the child shall remain on interim supervision for an additional period not to exceed 180 days.

(c) On a violation of the conditions of the original deferred prosecution agreement, the receiving county shall forward the case to the sending county for prosecution or other action in the manner provided by Sections 51.072(i) and (j), except that the original conditions of deferred prosecution may not be modified by the receiving county.

(Enacted by Acts 2005, 79th Leg., ch. 949 (H.B. 1575), § 4, effective September 1, 2005; am. Acts 2007, 80th Leg., ch. 908 (H.B. 2884), § 7, effective September 1, 2007.)

### Sec. 51.075. Collaborative Supervision Between Adjoining Counties.

(a) If a child who is on probation in one county spends substantial time in an adjoining county, including residing, attending school, or working in the adjoining county, the juvenile probation departments of the two counties may enter into a collaborative supervision arrangement regarding the child.

(b) Under a collaborative supervision arrangement, the juvenile probation department of the adjoining county may authorize a probation officer for the county to provide supervision and other services for the child as an agent of the juvenile probation department of the county in which the child was placed on probation. The probation officer providing supervision and other services for the child in the adjoining county shall

provide the probation officer supervising the child in the county in which the child was placed on probation with periodic oral, electronic, or written reports concerning the child.

(c) The juvenile court of the county in which the child was placed on probation retains sole authority to modify, amend, extend, or revoke the child's probation.

(Enacted by Acts 2005, 79th Leg., ch. 949 (H.B. 1575), § 4, effective September 1, 2005.)

### Sec. 51.08. Transfer from Criminal Court.

(a) If the defendant in a criminal proceeding is a child who is charged with an offense other than perjury, a traffic offense, a misdemeanor punishable by fine only, or a violation of a penal ordinance of a political subdivision, unless the child has been transferred to criminal court under Section 54.02, the court exercising criminal jurisdiction shall transfer the case to the juvenile court, together with a copy of the accusatory pleading and other papers, documents, and transcripts of testimony relating to the case, and shall order that the child be taken to the place of detention designated by the juvenile court, or shall release the child to the custody of the child's parent, guardian, or custodian, to be brought before the juvenile court at a time designated by that court.

(b) A court in which there is pending a complaint against a child alleging a violation of a misdemeanor offense punishable by fine only other than a traffic offense or a violation of a penal ordinance of a political subdivision other than a traffic offense:

(1) except as provided by Subsection (d), shall waive its original jurisdiction and refer the child to juvenile court if:

(A) the complaint pending against the child alleges a violation of a misdemeanor offense under Section 43.261, Penal Code, that is punishable by fine only; or

(B) the child has previously been convicted of:

(i) two or more misdemeanors punishable by fine only other than a traffic offense;

(ii) two or more violations of a penal ordinance of a political subdivision other than a traffic offense; or

(iii) one or more of each of the types of misdemeanors described in Subparagraph (i) or (ii); and

(2) may waive its original jurisdiction and refer the child to juvenile court if the child:

    (A) has not previously been convicted of a misdemeanor punishable by fine only other than a traffic offense or a violation of a penal ordinance of a political subdivision other than a traffic offense; or

    (B) has previously been convicted of fewer than two misdemeanors punishable by fine only other than a traffic offense or two violations of a penal ordinance of a political subdivision other than a traffic offense.

(c) A court in which there is pending a complaint against a child alleging a violation of a misdemeanor offense punishable by fine only other than a traffic offense or a violation of a penal ordinance of a political subdivision other than a traffic offense shall notify the juvenile court of the county in which the court is located of the pending complaint and shall furnish to the juvenile court a copy of the final disposition of any matter for which the court does not waive its original jurisdiction under Subsection (b).

(d) A court that has implemented a juvenile case manager program under Article 45.056, Code of Criminal Procedure, may, but is not required to, waive its original jurisdiction under Subsection (b)(1)(B).

(e) A juvenile court may not refuse to accept the transfer of a case brought under Section 25.094, Education Code, for a child described by Subsection (b)(1) if a prosecuting attorney for the court determines under Section 53.012 that the case is legally sufficient under Section 53.01 for adjudication in juvenile court.

(Enacted by Acts 1973, 63rd Leg., ch. 544 (S.B. 111), § 1, effective September 1, 1973; am. Acts 1987, 70th Leg., ch. 1040 (S.B. 17), § 21, effective September 1, 1987; am. Acts 1989, 71st Leg., ch. 1245 (H.B. 535), § 2, effective September 1, 1989; am. Acts 1991, 72nd Leg., ch. 169 (H.B. 944), § 2, effective September 1, 1991; am. Acts 2001, 77th Leg., ch. 1297 (H.B. 1118), § 6, effective September 1, 2001; am. Acts 2003, 78th Leg., ch. 283 (H.B. 2319), § 3, effective September 1, 2003; am. Acts 2005, 79th Leg., ch. 650 (H.B. 3010), § 1, effective September 1, 2005; am. Acts 2009, 81st Leg., ch. 311 (H.B. 558), § 4, effective September 1, 2009; am. Acts 2011, 82nd Leg., ch. 1322 (S.B. 407), § 16, effective September 1, 2011.)

### Sec. 51.09. Waiver of Rights.

Unless a contrary intent clearly appears elsewhere in this title, any right granted to a child by this title or by the constitution or laws of this state or the United States may be waived in proceedings under this title if:

    (1) the waiver is made by the child and the attorney for the child;

    (2) the child and the attorney waiving the right are informed of and understand the right and the possible consequences of waiving it;

    (3) the waiver is voluntary; and

    (4) the waiver is made in writing or in court proceedings that are recorded.

(Enacted by Acts 1973, 63rd Leg., ch. 544 (S.B. 111), § 1, effective September 1, 1973; am. Acts 1975, 64th Leg., ch. 693 (S.B. 247), § 9, effective September 1, 1975; am. Acts 1989, 71st Leg., ch. 84 (S.B. 72), § 1, effective September 1, 1989; am. Acts 1991, 72nd Leg., ch. 64 (H.B. 627), § 1, effective September 1, 1991; am. Acts 1991, 72nd Leg., ch. 429 (S.B. 1401), § 1, effective September 1, 1991; am. Acts 1991, 72nd Leg., ch. 557 (H.B. 653), § 1, effective September 1, 1991; am. Acts 1991, 72nd Leg., ch. 593 (S.B. 885), § 1, effective August 26, 1991; am. Acts 1995, 74th Leg., ch. 262 (H.B. 327), §§ 8, 9, effective January 1, 1996; am. Acts 1997, 75th Leg., ch. 1086 (H.B. 1550), § 4, effective September 1, 1997.)

### Sec. 51.095. Admissibility of a Statement of a Child.

(a) Notwithstanding Section 51.09, the statement of a child is admissible in evidence in any future proceeding concerning the matter about which the statement was given if:

    (1) the statement is made in writing under a circumstance described by Subsection (d) and:

        (A) the statement shows that the child has at some time before the making of the statement received from a magistrate a warning that:

            (i) the child may remain silent and not make any statement at all and that any statement that the child makes may be used in evidence against the child;

            (ii) the child has the right to have an attorney present to advise the child either prior to any questioning or during the questioning;

            (iii) if the child is unable to employ an attorney, the child has the right to have an attorney appointed to counsel with the child before or during any interviews with peace officers or attorneys representing the state; and

            (iv) the child has the right to terminate the interview at any time;

(B) and:

(i) the statement must be signed in the presence of a magistrate by the child with no law enforcement officer or prosecuting attorney present, except that a magistrate may require a bailiff or a law enforcement officer if a bailiff is not available to be present if the magistrate determines that the presence of the bailiff or law enforcement officer is necessary for the personal safety of the magistrate or other court personnel, provided that the bailiff or law enforcement officer may not carry a weapon in the presence of the child; and

(ii) the magistrate must be fully convinced that the child understands the nature and contents of the statement and that the child is signing the same voluntarily, and if a statement is taken, the magistrate must sign a written statement verifying the foregoing requisites have been met;

(C) the child knowingly, intelligently, and voluntarily waives these rights before and during the making of the statement and signs the statement in the presence of a magistrate; and

(D) the magistrate certifies that the magistrate has examined the child independent of any law enforcement officer or prosecuting attorney, except as required to ensure the personal safety of the magistrate or other court personnel, and has determined that the child understands the nature and contents of the statement and has knowingly, intelligently, and voluntarily waived these rights;

(2) the statement is made orally and the child makes a statement of facts or circumstances that are found to be true and tend to establish the child's guilt, such as the finding of secreted or stolen property, or the instrument with which the child states the offense was committed;

(3) the statement was res gestae of the delinquent conduct or the conduct indicating a need for supervision or of the arrest;

(4) the statement is made:

(A) in open court at the child's adjudication hearing;

(B) before a grand jury considering a petition, under Section 53.045, that the child engaged in delinquent conduct; or

(C) at a preliminary hearing concerning the child held in compliance with this code,

other than at a detention hearing under Section 54.01; or

(5) subject to Subsection (f), the statement is made orally under a circumstance described by Subsection (d) and the statement is recorded by an electronic recording device, including a device that records images, and:

(A) before making the statement, the child is given the warning described by Subdivision (1)(A) by a magistrate, the warning is a part of the recording, and the child knowingly, intelligently, and voluntarily waives each right stated in the warning;

(B) the recording device is capable of making an accurate recording, the operator of the device is competent to use the device, the recording is accurate, and the recording has not been altered;

(C) each voice on the recording is identified; and

(D) not later than the 20th day before the date of the proceeding, the attorney representing the child is given a complete and accurate copy of each recording of the child made under this subdivision.

(b) This section and Section 51.09 do not preclude the admission of a statement made by the child if:

(1) the statement does not stem from interrogation of the child under a circumstance described by Subsection (d); or

(2) without regard to whether the statement stems from interrogation of the child under a circumstance described by Subsection (d), the statement is:

(A) voluntary and has a bearing on the credibility of the child as a witness; or

(B) recorded by an electronic recording device, including a device that records images, and is obtained:

(i) in another state in compliance with the laws of that state or this state; or

(ii) by a federal law enforcement officer in this state or another state in compliance with the laws of the United States.

(c) An electronic recording of a child's statement made under Subsection (a)(5) or (b)(2)(B) shall be preserved until all juvenile or criminal matters relating to any conduct referred to in the statement are final, including the exhaustion of all appeals, or barred from prosecution.

(d) Subsections (a)(1) and (a)(5) apply to the statement of a child made:

(1) while the child is in a detention facility or other place of confinement;

(2) while the child is in the custody of an officer; or

(3) during or after the interrogation of the child by an officer if the child is in the possession of the Department of Family and Protective Services and is suspected to have engaged in conduct that violates a penal law of this state.

(e) A juvenile law referee or master may perform the duties imposed on a magistrate under this section without the approval of the juvenile court if the juvenile board of the county in which the statement of the child is made has authorized a referee or master to perform the duties of a magistrate under this section.

(f) A magistrate who provides the warnings required by Subsection (a)(5) for a recorded statement may at the time the warnings are provided request by speaking on the recording that the officer return the child and the recording to the magistrate at the conclusion of the process of questioning. The magistrate may then view the recording with the child or have the child view the recording to enable the magistrate to determine whether the child's statements were given voluntarily. The magistrate's determination of voluntariness shall be reduced to writing and signed and dated by the magistrate. If a magistrate uses the procedure described by this subsection, a child's statement is not admissible unless the magistrate determines that the statement was given voluntarily.

(Enacted by Acts 1997, 75th Leg., ch. 1086 (H.B. 1550), § 4, effective September 1, 1997; am. Acts 1999, 76th Leg., ch. 982 (H.B. 2671), § 1, effective September 1, 1999; am. Acts 1999, 76th Leg., ch. 1477 (H.B. 3517), § 1, effective September 1, 1999; am. Acts 2001, 77th Leg., ch. 1297 (H.B. 1118), § 7, effective September 1, 2001; am. Acts 2001, 77th Leg., ch. 1420 (H.B. 2812), § 21.001(29), effective September 1, 2001; am. Acts 2005, 79th Leg., ch. 949 (H.B. 1575), § 5, effective September 1, 2005; am. Acts 2007, 80th Leg., ch. 908 (H.B. 2884), § 8, effective September 1, 2007; am. Acts 2011, 82nd Leg., ch. 1158 (H.B. 2337), § 1, effective September 1, 2011; am. Acts 2011, 82nd Leg., ch. 110 (H.B. 841), § 3, effective May 21, 2011.)

## Sec. 51.10. Right to Assistance of Attorney; Compensation.

(a) A child may be represented by an attorney at every stage of proceedings under this title, including:

(1) the detention hearing required by Section 54.01 of this code;

(2) the hearing to consider transfer to criminal court required by Section 54.02 of this code;

(3) the adjudication hearing required by Section 54.03 of this code;

(4) the disposition hearing required by Section 54.04 of this code;

(5) the hearing to modify disposition required by Section 54.05 of this code;

(6) hearings required by Chapter 55 of this code;

(7) habeas corpus proceedings challenging the legality of detention resulting from action under this title; and

(8) proceedings in a court of civil appeals or the Texas Supreme Court reviewing proceedings under this title.

(b) The child's right to representation by an attorney shall not be waived in:

(1) a hearing to consider transfer to criminal court as required by Section 54.02 of this code;

(2) an adjudication hearing as required by Section 54.03 of this code;

(3) a disposition hearing as required by Section 54.04 of this code;

(4) a hearing prior to commitment to the Texas Youth Commission as a modified disposition in accordance with Section 54.05(f) of this code; or

(5) hearings required by Chapter 55 of this code.

(c) If the child was not represented by an attorney at the detention hearing required by Section 54.01 of this code and a determination was made to detain the child, the child shall immediately be entitled to representation by an attorney. The court shall order the retention of an attorney according to Subsection (d) or appoint an attorney according to Subsection (f).

(d) The court shall order a child's parent or other person responsible for support of the child to employ an attorney to represent the child, if:

(1) the child is not represented by an attorney;

(2) after giving the appropriate parties an opportunity to be heard, the court determines that the parent or other person responsible for support of the child is financially able to employ an attorney to represent the child; and

(3) the child's right to representation by an attorney:

(A) has not been waived under Section 51.09 of this code; or

Family Code

(B) may not be waived under Subsection (b) of this section.

(e) The court may enforce orders under Subsection (d) by proceedings under Section 54.07 or by appointing counsel and ordering the parent or other person responsible for support of the child to pay a reasonable attorney's fee set by the court. The order may be enforced under Section 54.07.

(f) The court shall appoint an attorney to represent the interest of a child entitled to representation by an attorney, if:

(1) the child is not represented by an attorney;

(2) the court determines that the child's parent or other person responsible for support of the child is financially unable to employ an attorney to represent the child; and

(3) the child's right to representation by an attorney:

(A) has not been waived under Section 51.09 of this code; or

(B) may not be waived under Subsection (b) of this section.

(g) The juvenile court may appoint an attorney in any case in which it deems representation necessary to protect the interests of the child.

(h) Any attorney representing a child in proceedings under this title is entitled to 10 days to prepare for any adjudication or transfer hearing under this title.

(i) Except as provided in Subsection (d) of this section, an attorney appointed under this section to represent the interests of a child shall be paid from the general fund of the county in which the proceedings were instituted according to the schedule in Article 26.05 of the Texas Code of Criminal Procedure, 1965. For this purpose, a bona fide appeal to a court of civil appeals or proceedings on the merits in the Texas Supreme Court are considered the equivalent of a bona fide appeal to the Texas Court of Criminal Appeals.

(j) The juvenile board of a county may make available to the public the list of attorneys eligible for appointment to represent children in proceedings under this title as provided in the plan adopted under Section 51.102. The list of attorneys must indicate the level of case for which each attorney is eligible for appointment under Section 51.102(b)(2).

(k) Subject to Chapter 61, the juvenile court may order the parent or other person responsible for support of the child to reimburse the county for payments the county made to counsel appointed to represent the child under Subsection (f) or (g). The court may:

(1) order payment for each attorney who has represented the child at any hearing, including a detention hearing, discretionary transfer hearing, adjudication hearing, disposition hearing, or modification of disposition hearing;

(2) include amounts paid to or on behalf of the attorney by the county for preparation time and investigative and expert witness costs; and

(3) require full or partial reimbursement to the county.

(*l*) The court may not order payments under Subsection (k) that exceed the financial ability of the parent or other person responsible for support of the child to meet the payment schedule ordered by the court.

(Enacted by Acts 1973, 63rd Leg., ch. 544 (S.B. 111), § 1, effective September 1, 1973; am. Acts 1983, 68th Leg., ch. 44 (S.B. 422), art. 1 § 2, effective April 26, 1983; am. Acts 1995, 74th Leg., ch. 262 (H.B. 327), § 11, effective January 1, 1996; am. Acts 2001, 77th Leg., ch. 1297 (H.B. 1118), § 8, effective September 1, 2001; am. Acts 2003, 78th Leg., ch. 283 (H.B. 2319), § 4, effective September 1, 2003.)

## Sec. 51.101. Appointment of Attorney and Continuation of Representation.

(a) If an attorney is appointed at the initial detention hearing and the child is detained, the attorney shall continue to represent the child until the case is terminated, the family retains an attorney, or a new attorney is appointed by the juvenile court. Release of the child from detention does not terminate the attorney's representation.

(b) If there is an initial detention hearing without an attorney and the child is detained, the attorney appointed under Section 51.10(c) shall continue to represent the child until the case is terminated, the family retains an attorney, or a new attorney is appointed by the juvenile court. Release of the child from detention does not terminate the attorney's representation.

(c) The juvenile court shall determine, on the filing of a petition, whether the child's family is indigent if:

(1) the child is released by intake;

(2) the child is released at the initial detention hearing; or

(3) the case was referred to the court without the child in custody.

(d) A juvenile court that makes a finding of indigence under Subsection (c) shall appoint an attorney to represent the child on or before the fifth working day after the date the petition for adjudication or discretionary transfer hearing was served on the child. An attorney appointed under this subsection shall continue to represent the child until the case is terminated, the family retains an attorney, or a new attorney is appointed by the juvenile court.

(e) The juvenile court shall determine whether the child's family is indigent if a motion or petition is filed under Section 54.05 seeking to modify disposition by committing the child to the Texas Youth Commission or placing the child in a secure correctional facility. A court that makes a finding of indigence shall appoint an attorney to represent the child on or before the fifth working day after the date the petition or motion has been filed. An attorney appointed under this subsection shall continue to represent the child until the court rules on the motion or petition, the family retains an attorney, or a new attorney is appointed.

(Enacted by Acts 2001, 77th Leg., ch. 1297 (H.B. 1118), § 9, effective September 1, 2001.)

## Sec. 51.102.　Appointment of Counsel Plan.

(a) The juvenile board in each county shall adopt a plan that:

(1) specifies the qualifications necessary for an attorney to be included on an appointment list from which attorneys are appointed to represent children in proceedings under this title; and

(2) establishes the procedures for:

(A) including attorneys on the appointment list and removing attorneys from the list; and

(B) appointing attorneys from the appointment list to individual cases.

(b) A plan adopted under Subsection (a) must:

(1) to the extent practicable, comply with the requirements of Article 26.04, Code of Criminal Procedure, except that:

(A) the income and assets of the child's parent or other person responsible for the child's support must be used in determining whether the child is indigent; and

(B) any alternative plan for appointing counsel is established by the juvenile board in the county; and

(2) recognize the differences in qualifications and experience necessary for appointments to cases in which:

(A) the allegation is:

(i) conduct indicating a need for supervision or delinquent conduct, and commit-

ment to the Texas Youth Commission is not an authorized disposition; or

(ii) delinquent conduct, and commitment to the Texas Youth Commission without a determinate sentence is an authorized disposition; or

(B) determinate sentence proceedings have been initiated or proceedings for discretionary transfer to criminal court have been initiated.

(Enacted by Acts 2001, 77th Leg., ch. 906 (S.B. 7), § 11, effective January 1, 2002; Am. Acts 2003, 78th Leg., ch. 283 (H.B. 2319), § 5, effective September 1, 2003 (renumbered from Sec. 51.101); am. Acts 2003, 78th Leg., ch. 1275 (H.B. 3506), § 2(51), effective September 1, 2003 (renumbered from Sec. 51.101).)

## Sec. 51.11.　Guardian Ad Litem.

(a) If a child appears before the juvenile court without a parent or guardian, the court shall appoint a guardian ad litem to protect the interests of the child. The juvenile court need not appoint a guardian ad litem if a parent or guardian appears with the child.

(b) In any case in which it appears to the juvenile court that the child's parent or guardian is incapable or unwilling to make decisions in the best interest of the child with respect to proceedings under this title, the court may appoint a guardian ad litem to protect the interests of the child in the proceedings.

(c) An attorney for a child may also be his guardian ad litem. A law-enforcement officer, probation officer, or other employee of the juvenile court may not be appointed guardian ad litem.

(Enacted by Acts 1973, 63rd Leg., ch. 544 (S.B. 111), § 1, effective September 1, 1973.)

## Sec. 51.115.　Attendance at Hearing: Parent or Other Guardian.

(a) Each parent of a child, each managing and possessory conservator of a child, each court-appointed custodian of a child, and a guardian of the person of the child shall attend each hearing affecting the child held under:

(1) Section 54.02 (waiver of jurisdiction and discretionary transfer to criminal court);

(2) Section 54.03 (adjudication hearing);

(3) Section 54.04 (disposition hearing);

(4) Section 54.05 (hearing to modify disposition); and

(5) Section 54.11 (release or transfer hearing).

(b) Subsection (a) does not apply to:

(1) a person for whom, for good cause shown, the court waives attendance;

(2) a person who is not a resident of this state; or

(3) a parent of a child for whom a managing conservator has been appointed and the parent is not a conservator of the child.

(c) A person required under this section to attend a hearing is entitled to reasonable written or oral notice that includes a statement of the place, date, and time of the hearing and that the attendance of the person is required. The notice may be included with or attached to any other notice required by this chapter to be given the person. Separate notice is not required for a disposition hearing that convenes on the adjournment of an adjudication hearing. If a person required under this section fails to attend a hearing, the juvenile court may proceed with the hearing.

(d) A person who is required by Subsection (a) to attend a hearing, who receives the notice of the hearing, and who fails to attend the hearing may be punished by the court for contempt by a fine of not less than $100 and not more than $1,000. In addition to or in lieu of contempt, the court may order the person to receive counseling or to attend an educational course on the duties and responsibilities of parents and skills and techniques in raising children.

(Enacted by Acts 1995, 74th Leg., ch. 262 (H.B. 327), § 10, effective January 1, 1996.)

## Sec. 51.116.   Right to Reemployment.

(a) An employer may not terminate the employment of a permanent employee because the employee is required under Section 51.115 to attend a hearing.

(b) An employee whose employment is terminated in violation of this section is entitled to return to the same employment that the employee held when notified of the hearing if the employee, as soon as practical after the hearing, gives the employer actual notice that the employee intends to return.

(c) A person who is injured because of a violation of this section is entitled to reinstatement to the person's former position and to damages, but the damages may not exceed an amount equal to six months' compensation at the rate at which the person was compensated when required to attend the hearing.

(d) The injured person is also entitled to reasonable attorney's fees in an amount approved by the court.

(e) It is a defense to an action brought under this section that the employer's circumstances changed while the employee attended the hearing so that reemployment was impossible or unreasonable. To establish a defense under this subsection, an employer must prove that the termination of employment was because of circumstances other than the employee's attendance at the hearing.

(Enacted by Acts 1995, 74th Leg., ch. 262 (H.B. 327), § 10, effective January 1, 1996.)

## Sec. 51.12.   Place and Conditions of Detention.

(a) Except as provided by Subsection (h), a child may be detained only in a:

(1) juvenile processing office in compliance with Section 52.025;

(2) place of nonsecure custody in compliance with Article 45.058, Code of Criminal Procedure;

(3) certified juvenile detention facility that complies with the requirements of Subsection (f);

(4) secure detention facility as provided by Subsection (j); or

(5) county jail or other facility as provided by Subsection (l).

(b) The proper authorities in each county shall provide a suitable place of detention for children who are parties to proceedings under this title, but the juvenile board shall control the conditions and terms of detention and detention supervision and shall permit visitation with the child at all reasonable times.

(b-1) A pre-adjudication secure detention facility may be operated only by:

(1) a governmental unit in this state as defined by Section 101.001, Civil Practice and Remedies Code; or

(2) a private entity under a contract with a governmental unit in this state.

(c) In each county, each judge of the juvenile court and a majority of the members of the juvenile board shall personally inspect all public or private juvenile pre-adjudication secure detention facilities that are located in the county at least annually and shall certify in writing to the authorities responsible for operating and giving financial support to the facilities and to the Texas Juvenile Probation Commission that the facilities are suitable or unsuitable for the detention of children. In determining whether a facility is suitable or unsuitable for the detention of children, the juvenile court judges and juvenile board members shall consider:

(1) current monitoring and inspection reports and any noncompliance citation reports issued by the Texas Juvenile Probation Commission, including the report provided under Subsection (c-1), and the status of any required corrective actions;

(2) current governmental inspector certification regarding the facility's compliance with local fire codes;

(3) current building inspector certification regarding the facility's compliance with local building codes;

(4) for the 12-month period preceding the inspection, the total number of allegations of abuse, neglect, or exploitation reported by the facility and a summary of the findings of any investigations of abuse, neglect, or exploitation conducted by the facility, a local law enforcement agency, and the Texas Juvenile Probation Commission;

(5) the availability of health and mental health services provided to facility residents;

(6) the availability of educational services provided to facility residents; and

(7) the overall physical appearance of the facility, including the facility's security, maintenance, cleanliness, and environment.

(c-1) The Texas Juvenile Probation Commission shall annually inspect each public or private juvenile pre-adjudication secure detention facility. The Texas Juvenile Probation Commission shall provide a report to each juvenile court judge presiding in the same county as an inspected facility indicating whether the facility is suitable or unsuitable for the detention of children in accordance with:

(1) the requirements of Subsections (a), (f), and (g); and

(2) minimum professional standards for the detention of children in pre-adjudication secure confinement promulgated by the Texas Juvenile Probation Commission or, at the election of the juvenile board of the county in which the facility is located, the current standards promulgated by the American Correctional Association.

(d) Except as provided by Subsections (j) and (l), a child may not be placed in a facility that has not been certified under Subsection (c) as suitable for the detention of children and registered under Subsection (i). Except as provided by Subsections (j) and (l), a child detained in a facility that has not been certified under Subsection (c) as suitable

for the detention of children or that has not been registered under Subsection (i) shall be entitled to immediate release from custody in that facility.

(e) If there is no certified place of detention in the county in which the petition is filed, the designated place of detention may be in another county.

(f) A child detained in a building that contains a jail, lockup, or other place of secure confinement, including an alcohol or other drug treatment facility, shall be separated by sight and sound from adults. detained in the same building. Children and adults are separated by. sight and sound only if they are unable to see each other and. conversation between them is not possible. The separation must extend to all areas of the facility, including sally ports and passageways, and. those areas used for admission, counseling, sleeping, toileting, showering, dining, recreational, educational, or vocational activities, and health care. The separation may be accomplished through architectural design. A person who has been transferred for prosecution in criminal court under Section 54.02 and is under 17 years of age is considered a child for the purposes of this subsection.

(g) Except for a child detained in a juvenile processing office, a place of nonsecure custody, a secure detention facility as provided by Subsection (j), or a facility as provided by Subsection (l), a child detained in a building that contains a jail or lockup may not have any contact with:

(1) part-time or full-time security staff, including management, who have contact with adults detained in the same building; or

(2) direct-care staff who have contact with adults detained in the same building.

(h) This section does not apply to a person:

(1) who has been transferred to criminal court for prosecution under Section 54.02 and is at least 17 years of age; or

(2) who is at least 17 years of age and who has been taken into custody after having:

(A) escaped from a juvenile facility operated by or under contract with the Texas Youth Commission; or

(B) violated a condition of release under supervision of the Texas Youth Commission.

(i) Except for a facility as provided by Subsection (l), a governmental unit or private entity that operates or contracts for the operation of a juvenile pre-adjudication secure detention facility under Subsection (b-1) in this state shall:

(1) register the facility annually with the Texas Juvenile Probation Commission; and

**Family Code**

(2) adhere to all applicable minimum standards for the facility.

(j) After being taken into custody, a child may be detained in a secure detention facility until the child is released under Section 53.01, 53.012, or 53.02 or until a detention hearing is held under Section 54.01(a), regardless of whether the facility has been certified under Subsection (c), if:

(1) a certified juvenile detention facility is not available in the county in which the child is taken into custody;

(2) the detention facility complies with:

(A) the short-term detention standards adopted by the Texas Juvenile Probation Commission; and

(B) the requirements of Subsection (f); and

(3) the detention facility has been designated by the county juvenile board for the county in which the facility is located.

(k) If a child who is detained under Subsection (j) or (l) is not released from detention at the conclusion of the detention hearing for a reason stated in Section 54.01(e), the child may be detained after the hearing only in a certified juvenile detention facility.

(l) A child who is taken into custody and required to be detained under Section 53.02(f) may be detained in a county jail or other facility until the child is released under Section 53.02(f) or until a detention hearing is held as required by Section 54.01(p), regardless of whether the facility complies with the requirements of this section, if:

(1) a certified juvenile detention facility or a secure detention facility described by Subsection (j) is not available in the county in which the child is taken into custody or in an adjacent county;

(2) the facility has been designated by the county juvenile board for the county in which the facility is located;

(3) the child is separated by sight and sound from adults detained in the same facility through architectural design or time-phasing;

(4) the child does not have any contact with management or direct-care staff that has contact with adults detained in the same facility on the same work shift;

(5) the county in which the child is taken into custody is not located in a metropolitan statistical area as designated by the United States Bureau of the Census; and

(6) each judge of the juvenile court and a majority of the members of the juvenile board of the county in which the child is taken into custody have personally inspected the facility at least annually and have certified in writing to the Texas Juvenile Probation Commission that the facility complies with the requirements of Subdivisions (3) and (4).

(m) The Texas Juvenile Probation Commission may deny, suspend, or revoke the registration of any facility required to register under Subsection (i) if the facility fails to:

(1) adhere to all applicable minimum standards for the facility; or

(2) timely correct any notice of noncompliance with minimum standards.

(Enacted by Acts 1973, 63rd Leg., ch. 544 (S.B. 111), § 1, effective September 1, 1973; am. Acts 1975, 64th Leg., ch. 693 (S.B. 247), §§ 10, 11, effective September 1, 1975; am. Acts 1985, 69th Leg., ch. 293 (S.B. 253), § 1, effective August 26, 1985; am. Acts 1987, 70th Leg., ch. 149 (S.B. 896), § 31, effective September 1, 1987; am. Acts 1995, 74th Leg., ch. 262 (H.B. 327), § 12, effective January 1, 1996; am. Acts 1997, 75th Leg., ch. 772 (H.B. 1928), § 1, effective September 1, 1997; am. Acts 1997, 75th Leg., ch. 1374 (H.B. 1230), § 1, effective September 1, 1997; am. Acts 1999, 76th Leg., ch. 62 (S.B. 1368), § 6.07, effective September 1, 1999; am. Acts 1999, 76th Leg., ch. 232 (H.B. 1269), § 3, effective September 1, 1999; am. Acts 1999, 76th Leg., ch. 1477 (H.B. 3517), § 2, effective September 1, 1999; am. Acts 2001, 77th Leg., ch. 1297 (H.B. 1118), § 10, effective September 1, 2001; am. Acts 2001, 77th Leg., ch. 1514 (S.B. 1432), § 13, effective September 1, 2001; am. Acts 2007, 80th Leg., ch. 263 (S.B. 103), § 5, effective June 8, 2007; am. Acts 2011, 82nd Leg., ch. 1087 (S.B. 1209), § 1, effective September 1, 2011.)

## Sec. 51.125. Post-Adjudication Correctional Facilities.

(a) A post-adjudication secure correctional facility for juvenile offenders may be operated only by:

(1) a governmental unit in this state as defined by Section 101.001, Civil Practice and Remedies Code; or

(2) a private entity under a contract with a governmental unit in this state.

(b) In each county, each judge of the juvenile court and a majority of the members of the juvenile board shall personally inspect all public or private juvenile post-adjudication secure correctional facilities that are not operated by the Texas Youth Commission and that are located in the county at least annually and shall certify in writing to the authorities responsible for operating and giving financial support to the facilities and to the Texas Juvenile Probation Commission that the facility or facilities are suitable or unsuitable for the confinement of children. In determining whether a facility is suitable or unsuitable for the confinement of children, the juvenile court judges and juvenile board members shall consider:

(1) current monitoring and inspection reports and any noncompliance citation reports issued by the Texas Juvenile Probation Commission, including the report provided under Subsection (c), and the status of any required corrective actions; and

(2) the other factors described under Sections 51.12(c)(2)—(7).

(c) The Texas Juvenile Probation Commission shall annually inspect each public or private juvenile post-adjudication secure correctional facility that is not operated by the Texas Youth Commission. The Texas Juvenile Probation Commission shall provide a report to each juvenile court judge presiding in the same county as an inspected facility indicating whether the facility is suitable or unsuitable for the confinement of children in accordance with minimum professional standards for the confinement of children in post-adjudication secure confinement promulgated by the Texas Juvenile Probation Commission or, at the election of the juvenile board of the county in which the facility is located, the current standards promulgated by the American Correctional Association.

(d) A governmental unit or private entity that operates or contracts for the operation of a juvenile post-adjudication secure correctional facility in this state under Subsection (a), except for a facility operated by or under contract with the Texas Youth Commission, shall:

(1) register the facility annually with the Texas Juvenile Probation Commission; and

(2) adhere to all applicable minimum standards for the facility.

(e) The Texas Juvenile Probation Commission may deny, suspend, or revoke the registration of any facility required to register under Subsection (d) if the facility fails to:

(1) adhere to all applicable minimum standards for the facility; or

(2) timely correct any notice of noncompliance with minimum standards.

(Enacted by Acts 2007, 80th Leg., ch. 263 (S.B. 103), § 6, effective June 8, 2007.)

## Sec. 51.126. Nonsecure Correctional Facilities.

(a) A nonsecure correctional facility for juvenile offenders may be operated only by:

(1) a governmental unit, as defined by Section 101.001, Civil Practice and Remedies Code; or

(2) a private entity under a contract with a governmental unit in this state.

(b) In each county, each judge of the juvenile court and a majority of the members of the juvenile board shall personally inspect, at least annually, all nonsecure correctional facilities that are located in the county and shall certify in writing to the authorities responsible for operating and giving financial support to the facilities and to the Texas Juvenile Justice Department that the facility or facilities are suitable or unsuitable for the confinement of children. In determining whether a facility is suitable or unsuitable for the confinement of children, the juvenile court judges and juvenile board members shall consider:

(1) current monitoring and inspection reports and any noncompliance citation reports issued by the Texas Juvenile Justice Department, including the report provided under Subsection (c), and the status of any required corrective actions; and

(2) the other factors described under Sections 51.12(c)(2)—(7).

(c) The Texas Juvenile Justice Department shall annually inspect each nonsecure correctional facility. The Texas Juvenile Justice Department shall provide a report to each juvenile court judge presiding in the same county as an inspected facility indicating whether the facility is suitable or unsuitable for the confinement of children in accordance with minimum professional standards for the confinement of children in nonsecure confinement promulgated by the Texas Juvenile Justice Department or, at the election of the juvenile board of the county in which the facility is located, the current standards promulgated by the American Correctional Association.

(d) A governmental unit or private entity that operates or contracts for the operation of a juvenile nonsecure correctional facility in this state under Subsection (a), except for a facility operated by or under contract with the Texas Juvenile Justice Department, shall:

(1) register the facility annually with the Texas Juvenile Justice Department; and

(2) adhere to all applicable minimum standards for the facility.

(e) The Texas Juvenile Justice Department may deny, suspend, or revoke the registration of any facility required to register under Subsection (d) if the facility fails to:

(1) adhere to all applicable minimum standards for the facility; or

(2) timely correct any notice of noncompliance with minimum standards.

(f) **[Expires December 1, 2011]** In this section, "Texas Juvenile Justice Department" means the Texas Juvenile Probation Commission. This subsection expires December 1, 2011.

(Enacted by Acts 2009, 81st Leg., ch. 1187 (H.B. 3689), § 4.005, effective June 19, 2009; am. Acts 2011, 82nd Leg., ch. 85 (S.B. 653), § 2.001, effective September 1, 2011.)

### Sec. 51.13. Effect of Adjudication or Disposition.

(a) Except as provided by Subsections (d) and (e), an order of adjudication or disposition in a proceeding under this title is not a conviction of crime. Except as provided by Chapter 841, Health and Safety Code, an order of adjudication or disposition does not impose any civil disability ordinarily resulting from a conviction or operate to disqualify the child in any civil service application or appointment.

(b) The adjudication or disposition of a child or evidence adduced in a hearing under this title may be used only in subsequent:

(1) proceedings under this title in which the child is a party;

(2) sentencing proceedings in criminal court against the child to the extent permitted by the Texas Code of Criminal Procedure, 1965; or

(3) civil commitment proceedings under Chapter 841, Health and Safety Code.

(c) **[2 Versions: As amended by Acts 2011, 82nd Leg., ch. 1087 (S.B. 1209)]** A child may not be committed or transferred to a penal institution or other facility used primarily for the execution of sentences of persons convicted of crime, except:

(1) for temporary detention in a jail or lockup pending juvenile court hearing or disposition under conditions meeting the requirements of Section 51.12;

(2) after transfer for prosecution in criminal court under Section 54.02, unless the juvenile court orders the detention of the child in a certified juvenile detention facility under Section 54.02(h); or

(3) after transfer from the Texas Youth Commission under Section 61.084, Human Resources Code.

(c) **[2 Versions: As amended by Acts 2011, 82nd Leg., ch. 85 (S.B. 653)]** A child may not be committed or transferred to a penal institution or other facility used primarily for the execution of sentences of persons convicted of crime, except:

(1) for temporary detention in a jail or lockup pending juvenile court hearing or disposition under conditions meeting the requirements of Section 51.12 of this code;

(2) after transfer for prosecution in criminal court under Section 54.02 of this code; or

(3) after transfer from the Texas Juvenile Justice Department under Section 245.151(c), Human Resources Code.

(d) An adjudication under Section 54.03 that a child engaged in conduct that occurred on or after January 1, 1996, and that constitutes a felony offense resulting in commitment to the Texas Youth Commission under Section 54.04(d)(2), (d)(3), or (m) or 54.05(f) is a final felony conviction only for the purposes of Sections 12.42(a), (b), (c)(1), and (e), Penal Code.

(e) A finding that a child engaged in conduct indicating a need for supervision as described by Section 51.03(b)(7) is a conviction only for the purposes of Sections 43.261(c) and (d), Penal Code.

(Enacted by Acts 1973, 63rd Leg., ch. 544 (S.B. 111), § 1, effective September 1, 1973; am. Acts 1987, 70th Leg., ch. 385 (H.B. 682), § 3, effective September 1, 1987; am. Acts 1993, 73rd Leg., ch. 799 (H.B. 1493), § 1, effective June 18, 1993; am. Acts 1995, 74th Leg., ch. 262 (H.B. 327), § 13, effective January 1, 1996; am. Acts 1997, 75th Leg., ch. 1086 (H.B. 1550), § 5, effective September 1, 1997; am. Acts 1999, 76th Leg., ch. 1188 (S.B. 365), § 4.02, effective September 1, 1999; am. Acts 2003, 78th Leg., ch. 283 (H.B. 2319), § 6, effective September 1, 2003; am. Acts 2011, 82nd Leg., ch. 1322 (S.B. 407), § 17, effective September 1, 2011; am. Acts 2011, 82nd Leg., ch. 85 (S.B. 653), § 3.004, effective September 1, 2011; am. Acts 2011, 82nd Leg., ch. 1087 (S.B. 1209), § 2, effective September 1, 2011.)

### Sec. 51.14. Files and Records [Repealed].

Repealed by Acts 1995, 74th Leg., ch. 262 (H.B. 327), § 100(a), effective January 1, 1996.

(Enacted by Acts 1973, 63rd Leg., ch. 544 (S.B. 111), § 1, effective September 1, 1973; am. Acts

1983, 68th Leg., ch. 769 (H.B. 475), § 1, effective June 19, 1983; am. Acts 1987, 70th Leg., ch. 385 (H.B. 682), § 4, effective September 1, 1987; am. Acts 1987, 70th Leg., ch. 386 (H.B. 683), § 2, effective September 1, 1987; am. Acts 1987, 70th Leg., ch. 515 (H.B. 593), § 3, effective August 31, 1987; am. Acts 1987, 70th Leg., ch. 576 (H.B. 538), § 1, effective August 31, 1987; am. Acts 1987, 70th Leg., ch. 978 (S.B. 1069), § 1, effective June 19, 1987; am. Acts 1989, 71st Leg., ch. 912 (S.B. 839), § 1, effective June 14, 1989; am. Acts 1993, 73rd Leg., ch. 252 (H.B. 247), § 1, effective May 23, 1993; am. Acts 1993, 73rd Leg., ch. 461 (H.B. 23), § 3, effective September 1, 1993.)

### Sec. 51.15. Fingerprints and Photographs [Repealed].

Repealed by Acts 1995, 74th Leg., ch. 262 (H.B. 327), § 100(a), effective January 1, 1996.
(Enacted by Acts 1973, 63rd Leg., ch. 544 (S.B. 111), § 1, effective September 1, 1973; am. Acts 1975, 64th Leg., ch. 693 (S.B. 247), § 12, effective September 1, 1975; am. Acts 1979, 66th Leg., ch. 517 (S.B. 540), §§ 1 to 3, effective June 11, 1979; am. Acts 1987, 70th Leg., ch. 385 (H.B. 682), § 5, effective September 1, 1987; am. Acts 1987, 70th Leg., ch. 515 (H.B. 593), §§ 1, 2, and 4, effective August 31, 1987; am. Acts 1987, 70th Leg., ch. 576 (H.B. 538), § 2, effective August 31, 1987; am. Acts 1995, 74th Leg., ch. 669 (S.B. 1252), § 4, effective August 28, 1995.)

### Sec. 51.151. Polygraph Examination.

If a child is taken into custody under Section 52.01 of this code, a person may not administer a polygraph examination to the child without the consent of the child's attorney or the juvenile court unless the child is transferred to criminal court for prosecution under Section 54.02 of this code.
(Enacted by Acts 1987, 70th Leg., ch. 708 (H.B. 323), § 1, effective September 1, 1987.)

### Sec. 51.16. Sealing of Files and Records [Repealed].

Repealed by Acts 1995, 74th Leg., ch. 262 (H.B. 327), § 100(a), effective January 1, 1996; Acts 1997 75th Leg., ch. 165 (S.B. 898), § 10.05(b), effective September 1, 1997.
(Enacted by Acts 1973, 63rd Leg., ch. 544 (S.B. 111), § 1, effective September 1, 1973; am. Acts 1975, 64th Leg., ch. 693 (S.B. 247), § 13, effective September 1, 1975; am. Acts 1979, 66th Leg., ch. 307 (S.B. 46), § 1, effective August 27, 1979; am.

Acts 1987, 70th Leg., ch. 385 (H.B. 682), § 6, effective September 1, 1987; am. Acts 1991, 72nd Leg., ch. 682 (H.B. 1050), § 1, effective September 1, 1991; am. Acts 1995, 74th Leg., ch. 229 (S.B. 60), § 5, effective September 1, 1995.)

### Sec. 51.17. Procedure and Evidence.

(a) Except as provided by Section 56.01(b-1) and except for the burden of proof to be borne by the state in adjudicating a child to be delinquent or in need of supervision under Section 54.03(f) or otherwise when in conflict with a provision of this title, the Texas Rules of Civil Procedure govern proceedings under this title.

(b) Discovery in a proceeding under this title is governed by the Code of Criminal Procedure and by case decisions in criminal cases.

(c) Except as otherwise provided by this title, the Texas Rules of Evidence apply to criminal cases and Articles 33.03 and 37.07 and Chapter 38, Code of Criminal Procedure, apply in a judicial proceeding under this title.

(d) When on the motion for appointment of an interpreter by a party or on the motion of the juvenile court, in any proceeding under this title, the court determines that the child, the child's parent or guardian, or a witness does not understand and speak English, an interpreter must be sworn to interpret for the person as provided by Article 38.30, Code of Criminal Procedure.

(e) In any proceeding under this title, if a party notifies the court that the child, the child's parent or guardian, or a witness is deaf, the court shall appoint a qualified interpreter to interpret the proceedings in any language, including sign language, that the deaf person can understand, as provided by Article 38.31, Code of Criminal Procedure.

(f) Any requirement under this title that a document contain a person's signature, including the signature of a judge or a clerk of the court, is satisfied if the document contains the signature of the person as captured on an electronic device or as a digital signature. Article 2.26, Code of Criminal Procedure, applies in a proceeding held under this title.

(g) Articles 21.07, 26.07, 26.08, 26.09, and 26.10, Code of Criminal Procedure, relating to the name of an adult defendant in a criminal case, apply to a child in a proceeding held under this title.

(h) Articles 57.01 and 57.02, Code of Criminal Procedure, relating to the use of a pseudonym by a victim in a criminal case, apply in a proceeding held under this title.

Family Code

(i) Except as provided by Section 56.03(f), the state is not required to pay any cost or fee otherwise imposed for court proceedings in either the trial or appellate courts.

(Enacted by Acts 1973, 63rd Leg., ch. 544 (S.B. 111), § 1, effective September 1, 1973; am. Acts 1995, 74th Leg., ch. 262 (H.B. 327), § 14, effective January 1, 1996; am. Acts 1999, 76th Leg., ch. 1477 (H.B. 3517), § 3, effective September 1, 1999; am. Acts 2003, 78th Leg., ch. 283 (H.B. 2319), § 7, effective September 1, 2003; am. Acts 2005, 79th Leg., ch. 949 (H.B. 1575), § 6, effective September 1, 2005; am. Acts 2007, 80th Leg., ch. 908 (H.B. 2884), § 9, effective September 1, 2007; am. Acts 2009, 81st Leg., ch. 642 (H.B. 1688), § 1, effective September 1, 2009.)

### Sec. 51.18. Election Between Juvenile Court and Alternate Juvenile Court.

(a) This section applies only to a child who has a right to a trial before a juvenile court the judge of which is not an attorney licensed in this state.

(b) On any matter that may lead to an order appealable under Section 56.01 of this code, a child may be tried before either the juvenile court or the alternate juvenile court.

(c) The child may elect to be tried before the alternate juvenile court only if the child files a written notice with that court not later than 10 days before the date of the trial. After the notice is filed, the child may be tried only in the alternate juvenile court. If the child does not file a notice as provided by this subsection, the child may be tried only in the juvenile court.

(d) If the child is tried before the juvenile court, the child is not entitled to a trial de novo before the alternate juvenile court.

(e) The child may appeal any order of the juvenile court or alternate juvenile court only as provided by Section 56.01 of this code.

(Enacted by Acts 1977, 65th Leg., ch. 411 (S.B. 249), § 2, effective June 15, 1977; am. Acts 1993, 73rd Leg., ch. 168 (H.B. 793), § 3, eff. August 30, 1993.)

### Sec. 51.19. Limitation Periods.

(a) The limitation periods and the procedures for applying the limitation periods under Chapter 12, Code of Criminal Procedure, and other statutory law apply to proceedings under this title.

(b) For purposes of computing a limitation period, a petition filed in juvenile court for a transfer or an adjudication hearing is equivalent to an indictment or information and is treated as presented when the petition is filed in the proper court.

(c) The limitation period is two years for an offense or conduct that is not given a specific limitation period under Chapter 12, Code of Criminal Procedure, or other statutory law.

(Enacted by Acts 1997, 75th Leg., ch. 1086 (H.B. 1550), § 6, effective September 1, 1997.)

### Sec. 51.20. Physical or Mental Examination.

(a) At any stage of the proceedings under this title, the juvenile court may order a child who is referred to the juvenile court or who is alleged by a petition or found to have engaged in delinquent conduct or conduct indicating a need for supervision to be examined by a disinterested expert, including a physician, psychiatrist, or psychologist, qualified by education and clinical training in mental health or mental retardation and experienced in forensic evaluation, to determine whether the child has a mental illness as defined by Section 571.003, Health and Safety Code, or is a person with mental retardation as defined by Section 591.003, Health and Safety Code. If the examination is to include a determination of the child's fitness to proceed, an expert may be appointed to conduct the examination only if the expert is qualified under Subchapter B, Chapter 46B, Code of Criminal Procedure, to examine a defendant in a criminal case, and the examination and the report resulting from an examination under this subsection must comply with the requirements under Subchapter B, Chapter 46B, Code of Criminal Procedure, for the examination and resulting report of a defendant in a criminal case.

(b) If, after conducting an examination of a child ordered under Subsection (a) and reviewing any other relevant information, there is reason to believe that the child has a mental illness or mental retardation, the probation department shall refer the child to the local mental health or mental retardation authority for evaluation and services, unless the prosecuting attorney has filed a petition under Section 53.04.

(c) If, while a child is under deferred prosecution supervision or court-ordered probation, a qualified professional determines that the child has a mental illness or mental retardation and the child is not currently receiving treatment services for the mental illness or mental retardation, the probation department shall refer the child to the local mental health or mental retardation authority for evaluation and services.

(d) A probation department shall report each referral of a child to a local mental health or mental retardation authority made under Subsection (b) or (c) to the Texas Juvenile Probation Commission in a format specified by the commission.

(e) At any stage of the proceedings under this title, the juvenile court may order a child who has been referred to the juvenile court or who is alleged by the petition or found to have engaged in delinquent conduct or conduct indicating a need for supervision to be subjected to a physical examination by a licensed physician.
(Enacted by Acts 1999, 76th Leg., ch. 1477 (H.B. 3517), § 4, effective September 1, 1999; am. Acts 2001, 77th Leg., ch. 828 (H.B. 1171), § 5(a), effective September 1, 2001; am. Acts 2003, 78th Leg., ch. 35 (S.B. 1057), § 6, effective January 1, 2004; am. Acts 2005, 79th Leg., ch. 949 (H.B. 1575), § 7, effective September 1, 2005.)

### Sec. 51.21. Mental Health Screening and Referral.

(a) A probation department that administers the mental health screening instrument or clinical assessment required by Section 221.003, Human Resources Code, shall refer the child to the local mental health authority for assessment and evaluation if:

(1) the child's scores on the screening instrument or clinical assessment indicate a need for further mental health assessment and evaluation; and

(2) the department and child do not have access to an internal, contract, or private mental health professional.

(b) A probation department shall report each referral of a child to a local mental health authority made under Subsection (a) to the Texas Juvenile Probation Commission in a format specified by the commission.
(Enacted by Acts 2005, 79th Leg., ch. 949 (H.B. 1575), § 8, effective September 1, 2005; am. Acts

2011, 82nd Leg., ch. 85 (S.B. 653), § 3.005, effective September 1, 2011.)

## CHAPTER 52
## PROCEEDINGS BEFORE AND INCLUDING REFERRAL TO JUVENILE COURT

### Sec. 52.01. Taking into Custody; Issuance of Warning Notice.

(a) A child may be taken into custody:

(1) pursuant to an order of the juvenile court under the provisions of this subtitle;

(2) pursuant to the laws of arrest;

(3) by a law-enforcement officer, including a school district peace officer commissioned under Section 37.081, Education Code, if there is probable cause to believe that the child has engaged in:

(A) conduct that violates a penal law of this state or a penal ordinance of any political subdivision of this state;

(B) delinquent conduct or conduct indicating a need for supervision; or

(C) conduct that violates a condition of probation imposed by the juvenile court;

(4) by a probation officer if there is probable cause to believe that the child has violated a condition of probation imposed by the juvenile court;

(5) pursuant to a directive to apprehend issued as provided by Section 52.015; or

(6) by a probation officer if there is probable cause to believe that the child has violated a condition of release imposed by the juvenile court or referee under Section 54.01.

Family Code

(b) The taking of a child into custody is not an arrest except for the purpose of determining the validity of taking him into custody or the validity of a search under the laws and constitution of this state or of the United States.

(c) A law-enforcement officer authorized to take a child into custody under Subdivisions (2) and (3) of Subsection (a) of this section may issue a warning notice to the child in lieu of taking the child into custody if:

(1) guidelines for warning disposition have been issued by the law-enforcement agency in which the officer works;

(2) the guidelines have been approved by the juvenile board of the county in which the disposition is made;

(3) the disposition is authorized by the guidelines;

(4) the warning notice identifies the child and describes the child's alleged conduct;

(5) a copy of the warning notice is sent to the child's parent, guardian, or custodian as soon as practicable after disposition; and

(6) a copy of the warning notice is filed with the law-enforcement agency and the office or official designated by the juvenile board.

(d) A warning notice filed with the office or official designated by the juvenile board may be used as the basis of further action if necessary.

(e) A law-enforcement officer who has probable cause to believe that a child is in violation of the compulsory school attendance law under Section 25.085, Education Code, may take the child into custody for the purpose of returning the child to the school campus of the child to ensure the child's compliance with compulsory school attendance requirements.

(Enacted by Acts 1973, 63rd Leg., ch. 544 (S.B. 111), § 1, effective September 1, 1973; am. Acts 1993, 73rd Leg., ch. 115 (H.B. 633), § 2, effective May 11, 1993; am. Acts 1995, 74th Leg., ch. 262 (H.B. 327), § 15, effective January 1, 1996; am. Acts 1997, 75th Leg., ch. 165 (S.B. 898), § 6.08, effective September 1, 1997; am. Acts 2001, 77th Leg., ch. 1297 (H.B. 1118), § 11, effective September 1, 2001; am. Acts 2003, 78th Leg., ch. 283 (H.B. 2319), § 8, effective September 1, 2003; am. Acts 2005, 79th Leg., ch. 949 (H.B. 1575), § 9, effective September 1, 2005; am. Acts 2007, 80th Leg., ch. 1058 (H.B. 2237), § 16, effective September 1, 2007.)

## Sec. 52.015. Directive to Apprehend.

(a) On the request of a law-enforcement or probation officer, a juvenile court may issue a directive to apprehend a child if the court finds there is probable cause to take the child into custody under the provisions of this title.

(b) On the issuance of a directive to apprehend, any law-enforcement or probation officer shall take the child into custody.

(c) An order under this section is not subject to appeal.

(Enacted by Acts 1995, 74th Leg., ch. 262 (H.B. 327), § 16, effective January 1, 1996.)

## Sec. 52.0151. Bench Warrant; Attachment of Witness in Custody.

(a) If a witness is in a placement in the custody of the Texas Youth Commission, a juvenile secure detention facility, or a juvenile secure correctional facility, the court may issue a bench warrant or direct that an attachment issue to require a peace officer or probation officer to secure custody of the person at the placement and produce the person in court. Once the person is no longer needed as a witness, the court shall order the peace officer or probation officer to return the person to the placement from which the person was released.

(b) The court may order that the person who is the witness be detained in a certified juvenile detention facility if the person is younger than 17 years of age. If the person is at least 17 years of age, the court may order that the person be detained without bond in an appropriate county facility for the detention of adults accused of criminal offenses.

(Enacted by Acts 2005, 79th Leg., ch. 949 (H.B. 1575), § 10, effective September 1, 2005.)

## Sec. 52.02. Release or Delivery to Court.

(a) Except as provided by Subsection (c), a person taking a child into custody, without unnecessary delay and without first taking the child to any place other than a juvenile processing office designated under Section 52.025, shall do one of the following:

(1) release the child to a parent, guardian, custodian of the child, or other responsible adult upon that person's promise to bring the child before the juvenile court as requested by the court;

(2) bring the child before the office or official designated by the juvenile board if there is probable cause to believe that the child engaged in delinquent conduct, conduct indicating a need for supervision, or conduct that

violates a condition of probation imposed by the juvenile court;

(3) bring the child to a detention facility designated by the juvenile board;

(4) bring the child to a secure detention facility as provided by Section 51.12(j);

(5) bring the child to a medical facility if the child is believed to suffer from a serious physical condition or illness that requires prompt treatment;

(6) dispose of the case under Section 52.03; or

(7) if school is in session and the child is a student, bring the child to the school campus to which the child is assigned if the principal, the principal's designee, or a peace officer assigned to the campus agrees to assume responsibility for the child for the remainder of the school day.

(b) A person taking a child into custody shall promptly give notice of the person's action and a statement of the reason for taking the child into custody, to:

(1) the child's parent, guardian, or custodian; and

(2) the office or official designated by the juvenile board.

(c) A person who takes a child into custody and who has reasonable grounds to believe that the child has been operating a motor vehicle in a public place while having any detectable amount of alcohol in the child's system may, before complying with Subsection (a):

(1) take the child to a place to obtain a specimen of the child's breath or blood as provided by Chapter 724, Transportation Code; and

(2) perform intoxilyzer processing and videotaping of the child in an adult processing office of a law enforcement agency.

(d) Notwithstanding Section 51.09(a), a child taken into custody as provided by Subsection (c) may submit to the taking of a breath specimen or refuse to submit to the taking of a breath specimen without the concurrence of an attorney, but only if the request made of the child to give the specimen and the child's response to that request is videotaped. A videotape made under this subsection must be maintained until the disposition of any proceeding against the child relating to the arrest is final and be made available to an attorney representing the child during that period.

(Enacted by Acts 1973, 63rd Leg., ch. 544 (S.B. 111), § 1, effective September 1, 1973; am. Acts 1991, 72nd Leg., ch. 495 (S.B. 1230), § 1, effective September 1, 1991; am. Acts 1997, 75th Leg., ch.

1013 (S.B. 35), § 15, effective September 1, 1997; am. Acts 1997, 75th Leg., ch. 1374 (H.B. 1230), § 2, effective September 1, 1997; am. Acts 1999, 76th Leg., ch. 62 (S.B. 1368), § 6.08, effective September 1, 1999; am. Acts 1999, 76th Leg., ch. 1477 (H.B. 3517), § 5, effective September 1, 1999; am. Acts 2001, 77th Leg., ch. 1297 (H.B. 1118), § 12, effective September 1, 2001; am. Acts 2003, 78th Leg., ch. 283 (H.B. 2319), § 9, effective September 1, 2003; am. Acts 2007, 80th Leg., ch. 286 (H.B. 776), § 1, effective September 1, 2007.)

### Sec. 52.025. Designation of Juvenile Processing Office.

(a) The juvenile board may designate an office or a room, which may be located in a police facility or sheriff's offices, as the juvenile processing office for the temporary detention of a child taken into custody under Section 52.01. The office may not be a cell or holding facility used for detentions other than detentions under this section. The juvenile board by written order may prescribe the conditions of the designation and limit the activities that may occur in the office during the temporary detention.

(b) A child may be detained in a juvenile processing office only for:

(1) the return of the child to the custody of a person under Section 52.02(a)(1);

(2) the completion of essential forms and records required by the juvenile court or this title;

(3) the photographing and fingerprinting of the child if otherwise authorized at the time of temporary detention by this title;

(4) the issuance of warnings to the child as required or permitted by this title; or

(5) the receipt of a statement by the child under Section 51.095(a)(1), (2), (3), or (5).

(c) A child may not be left unattended in a juvenile processing office and is entitled to be accompanied by the child's parent, guardian, or other custodian or by the child's attorney.

(d) A child may not be detained in a juvenile processing office for longer than six hours.

(Enacted by Acts 1991, 72nd Leg., ch. 495 (S.B. 1230), § 2, effective September 1, 1991; am. Acts 1997, 75th Leg., ch. 1086 (H.B. 1550), § 48, effective September 1, 1997; am. Acts 2001, 77th Leg., ch. 1297 (H.B. 1118), § 13, effective September 1, 2001.)

### Sec. 52.026. Responsibility for Transporting Juvenile Offenders.

(a) It shall be the duty of the law enforcement officer who has taken a child into custody to

**Family Code**

transport the child to the appropriate detention facility or to the school campus to which the child is assigned as provided by Section 52.02(a)(7) if the child is not released to the parent, guardian, or custodian of the child.

(b) If the juvenile detention facility is located outside the county in which the child is taken into custody, it shall be the duty of the law enforcement officer who has taken the child into custody or, if authorized by the commissioners court of the county, the sheriff of that county to transport the child to the appropriate juvenile detention facility unless the child is:

    (1) detained in a secure detention facility under Section 51.12(j); or

    (2) released to the parent, guardian, or custodian of the child.

(c) On adoption of an order by the juvenile board and approval of the juvenile board's order by record vote of the commissioners court, it shall be the duty of the sheriff of the county in which the child is taken into custody to transport the child to and from all scheduled juvenile court proceedings and appearances and other activities ordered by the juvenile court.

(Enacted by Acts 1993, 73rd Leg., ch. 411 (S.B. 588), § 1, effective August 30, 1993; am. Acts 1997, 75th Leg., ch. 1374 (H.B. 1230), § 3, effective September 1, 1997; am. Acts 1999, 76th Leg., ch. 62 (S.B. 1368), § 6.09, effective September 1, 1999; am. Acts 1999, 76th Leg., ch. 1082 (H.B. 3355), § 1, effective June 18, 1999; am. Acts 2007, 80th Leg., ch. 286 (H.B. 776), § 2, effective September 1, 2007.)

### Sec. 52.027. Children Taken into Custody for Traffic Offenses, Other Fineable Only Offenses, or As a Status Offender [Repealed].

Repealed by Acts 2003, 78th Leg., ch. 283 (H.B. 2319), § 61(1), effective September 1, 2003, and Acts 2003, 78th Leg., ch. 1276 (H.B. 3507), § 7.001(a), effective September 1, 2003.

(Enacted by Acts 1995, 74th Leg., ch. 262 (H.B. 327), § 17, effective January 1, 1996; am. Acts 1997, 75th Leg., ch. 822 (S.B. 81), § 3, effective September 1, 1997; am. Acts 1997, 75th Leg., ch. 1374 (H.B. 1230), § 4, effective September 1, 1997; am. Acts 1999, 76th Leg., ch. 76 (H.B. 688), § 1, effective September 1, 1999; am. Acts 1999, 76th Leg., ch. 1545 (S.B. 1230), § 66, effective September 1, 1999; am. Acts 2001, 77th Leg., ch. 1297 (H.B. 1118), §§ 14, 71(1), effective September 1, 2001; am. Acts 2001, 77th Leg., ch. 1514 (S.B. 1432), § 19(b), effective September 1, 2001.)

### Sec. 52.028. Children Taken into Custody for Violation of Juvenile Curfew Ordinance or Order [Repealed].

Repealed by Acts 2001, 77th Leg., ch. 1514 (S.B. 1432), § 19(b), effective September 1, 2001. (Enacted by Acts 1995, 74th Leg., ch. 262 (H.B. 327), § 17, effective May 31, 1995.)

### Sec. 52.03. Disposition Without Referral to Court.

(a) A law-enforcement officer authorized by this title to take a child into custody may dispose of the case of a child taken into custody without referral to juvenile court, if:

    (1) guidelines for such disposition have been adopted by the juvenile board of the county in which the disposition is made as required by Section 52.032;

    (2) the disposition is authorized by the guidelines; and

    (3) the officer makes a written report of the officer's disposition to the law-enforcement agency, identifying the child and specifying the grounds for believing that the taking into custody was authorized.

(b) No disposition authorized by this section may involve:

    (1) keeping the child in law-enforcement custody; or

    (2) requiring periodic reporting of the child to a law-enforcement officer, law-enforcement agency, or other agency.

(c) A disposition authorized by this section may involve:

    (1) referral of the child to an agency other than the juvenile court;

    (2) a brief conference with the child and his parent, guardian, or custodian; or

    (3) referral of the child and the child's parent, guardian, or custodian for services under Section 264.302.

(d) Statistics indicating the number and kind of dispositions made by a law-enforcement agency under the authority of this section shall be reported at least annually to the office or official designated by the juvenile board, as ordered by the board.

(Enacted by Acts 1973, 63rd Leg., ch. 544 (S.B. 111), § 1, effective September 1, 1973; am. Acts 1995, 74th Leg., ch. 262 (H.B. 327), § 18, effective January 1, 1996; am. Acts 1999, 76th Leg., ch. 48 (S.B. 283), § 1, effective September 1, 1999; am. Acts 2001, 77th Leg., ch. 1297 (H.B. 1118), § 15, effective September 1, 2001; am. Acts 2003, 78th

Family Code

Leg., ch. 283 (H.B. 2319), § 10, effective September 1, 2003.)

### Sec. 52.031.  First Offender Program.

(a) A juvenile board may establish a first offender program under this section for the referral and disposition of children taken into custody for:

(1) conduct indicating a need for supervision; or

(2) delinquent conduct other than conduct that constitutes:

(A) a felony of the first, second, or third degree, an aggravated controlled substance felony, or a capital felony; or

(B) a state jail felony or misdemeanor involving violence to a person or the use or possession of a firearm, illegal knife, or club, as those terms are defined by Section 46.01, Penal Code, or a prohibited weapon, as described by Section 46.05, Penal Code.

(b) Each juvenile board in the county in which a first offender program is established shall designate one or more law enforcement officers and agencies, which may be law enforcement agencies, to process a child under the first offender program.

(c) The disposition of a child under the first offender program may not take place until guidelines for the disposition have been adopted by the juvenile board of the county in which the disposition is made as required by Section 52.032.

(d) A law enforcement officer taking a child into custody may refer the child to the law enforcement officer or agency designated under Subsection (b) for disposition under the first offender program and not refer the child to juvenile court only if:

(1) the child has not previously been adjudicated as having engaged in delinquent conduct;

(2) the referral complies with guidelines for disposition under Subsection (c); and

(3) the officer reports in writing the referral to the agency, identifying the child and specifying the grounds for taking the child into custody.

(e) A child referred for disposition under the first offender program may not be detained in law enforcement custody.

(f) The parent, guardian, or other custodian of the child must receive notice that the child has been referred for disposition under the first offender program. The notice must:

(1) state the grounds for taking the child into custody;

(2) identify the law enforcement officer or agency to which the child was referred;

(3) briefly describe the nature of the program; and

(4) state that the child's failure to complete the program will result in the child being referred to the juvenile court.

(g) The child and the parent, guardian, or other custodian of the child must consent to participation by the child in the first offender program.

(h) Disposition under a first offender program may include:

(1) voluntary restitution by the child or the parent, guardian, or other custodian of the child to the victim of the conduct of the child;

(2) voluntary community service restitution by the child;

(3) educational, vocational training, counseling, or other rehabilitative services; and

(4) periodic reporting by the child to the law enforcement officer or agency to which the child has been referred.

(i) The case of a child who successfully completes the first offender program is closed and may not be referred to juvenile court, unless the child is taken into custody under circumstances described by Subsection (j)(3).

(j) The case of a child referred for disposition under the first offender program shall be referred to juvenile court if:

(1) the child fails to complete the program;

(2) the child or the parent, guardian, or other custodian of the child terminates the child's participation in the program before the child completes it; or

(3) the child completes the program but is taken into custody under Section 52.01 before the 90th day after the date the child completes the program for conduct other than the conduct for which the child was referred to the first offender program.

(k) A statement made by a child to a person giving advice or supervision or participating in the first offender program may not be used against the child in any proceeding under this title or any criminal proceeding.

(l) The law enforcement agency must report to the juvenile board in December of each year the following:

(1) the last known address of the child, including the census tract;

(2) the gender and ethnicity of the child referred to the program; and

(3) the offense committed by the child.

(Enacted by Acts 1995, 74th Leg., ch. 262 (H.B. 327), § 19, effective January 1, 1996; am. Acts 1999, 76th Leg., ch. 48 (S.B. 283), § 2, effective September 1, 1999.)

## Sec. 52.032. Informal Disposition Guidelines.

The juvenile board of each county, in cooperation with each law enforcement agency in the county, shall adopt guidelines for the disposition of a child under Section 52.03 or 52.031. The guidelines adopted under this section shall not be considered mandatory.

(Enacted by Acts 1999, 76th Leg., ch. 48 (S.B. 283), § 3, effective September 1, 1999.)

## Sec. 52.04. Referral to Juvenile Court; Notice to Parents.

(a) The following shall accompany referral of a child or a child's case to the office or official designated by the juvenile board or be provided as quickly as possible after referral:

(1) all information in the possession of the person or agency making the referral pertaining to the identity of the child and the child's address, the name and address of the child's parent, guardian, or custodian, the names and addresses of any witnesses, and the child's present whereabouts;

(2) a complete statement of the circumstances of the alleged delinquent conduct or conduct indicating a need for supervision;

(3) when applicable, a complete statement of the circumstances of taking the child into custody; and

(4) when referral is by an officer of a law-enforcement agency, a complete statement of all prior contacts with the child by officers of that law-enforcement agency.

(b) The office or official designated by the juvenile board may refer the case to a law-enforcement agency for the purpose of conducting an investigation to obtain necessary information.

(c) If the office of the prosecuting attorney is designated by the juvenile court to conduct the preliminary investigation under Section 53.01, the referring entity shall first transfer the child's case to the juvenile probation department for statistical reporting purposes only. On the creation of a statistical record or file for the case, the probation department shall within three business days forward the case to the prosecuting attorney for review under Section 53.01.

(d) On referral of the case of a child who has not been taken into custody to the office or official designated by the juvenile board, the office or official designated by the juvenile board shall promptly give notice of the referral and a statement of the reason for the referral to the child's parent, guardian, or custodian.

(Enacted by Acts 1973, 63rd Leg., ch. 544 (S.B. 111), § 1, effective September 1, 1973; am. Acts 1997, 75th Leg., ch. 1091 (H.B. 2065), § 1, effective June 19, 1997; am. Acts 2001, 77th Leg., ch. 136 (H.B. 1790), §§ 1, 2, effective September 1, 2001; am. Acts 2001, 77th Leg., ch. 1297 (H.B. 1118), § 16, effective September 1, 2001; am. Acts 2003, 78th Leg., ch. 283 (H.B. 2319), § 11, effective September 1, 2003.)

## Sec. 52.041. Referral of Child to Juvenile Court After Expulsion.

(a) A school district that expels a child shall refer the child to juvenile court in the county in which the child resides.

(b) The board of the school district or a person designated by the board shall deliver a copy of the order expelling the student and any other information required by Section 52.04 on or before the second working day after the date of the expulsion hearing to the authorized officer of the juvenile court.

(c) Within five working days of receipt of an expulsion notice under this section by the office or official designated by the juvenile board, a preliminary investigation and determination shall be conducted as required by Section 53.01.

(d) The office or official designated by the juvenile board shall within two working days notify the school district that expelled the child if:

(1) a determination was made under Section 53.01 that the person referred to juvenile court was not a child within the meaning of this title;

(2) a determination was made that no probable cause existed to believe the child engaged in delinquent conduct or conduct indicating a need for supervision;

(3) no deferred prosecution or formal court proceedings have been or will be initiated involving the child;

(4) the court or jury finds that the child did not engage in delinquent conduct or conduct indicating a need for supervision and the case has been dismissed with prejudice; or

(5) the child was adjudicated but no disposition was or will be ordered by the court.

(e) In any county where a juvenile justice alternative education program is operated, no student shall be expelled without written notifica-

tion by the board of the school district or its designated agent to the juvenile board's designated representative. The notification shall be made not later than two business days following the board's determination that the student is to be expelled. Failure to timely notify the designated representative of the juvenile board shall result in the child's duty to continue attending the school district's educational program, which shall be provided to that child until such time as the notification to the juvenile board's designated representative is properly made.
(Enacted by Acts 1995, 74th Leg., ch. 262 (H.B. 327), § 20, effective January 1, 1996; am. Acts 1997, 75th Leg., ch. 1015 (S.B. 133), § 16, effective June 19, 1997; am. Acts 2001, 77th Leg., ch. 1297 (H.B. 1118), § 17, effective September 1, 2001.)

## CHAPTER 53
## PROCEEDINGS PRIOR TO JUDICIAL PROCEEDINGS

## Sec. 53.01. Preliminary Investigation and Determinations; Notice to Parents.

(a) On referral of a person believed to be a child or on referral of the person's case to the office or official designated by the juvenile board, the intake officer, probation officer, or other person authorized by the board shall conduct a preliminary investigation to determine whether:

(1) the person referred to juvenile court is a child within the meaning of this title; and

(2) there is probable cause to believe the person:

(A) engaged in delinquent conduct or conduct indicating a need for supervision; or

(B) is a nonoffender who has been taken into custody and is being held solely for deportation out of the United States.

(b) If it is determined that the person is not a child or there is no probable cause, the person shall immediately be released.

(c) When custody of a child is given to the office or official designated by the juvenile board, the intake officer, probation officer, or other person authorized by the board shall promptly give notice of the whereabouts of the child and a statement of the reason the child was taken into custody to the child's parent, guardian, or custodian unless the notice given under Section 52.02(b) provided fair notice of the child's present whereabouts.

(d) Unless the juvenile board approves a written procedure proposed by the office of prosecuting attorney and chief juvenile probation officer which provides otherwise, if it is determined that the person is a child and, regardless of a finding of probable cause, or a lack thereof, there is an allegation that the child engaged in delinquent conduct of the grade of felony, or conduct constituting a misdemeanor offense involving violence to a person or the use or possession of a firearm, illegal knife, or club, as those terms are defined by Section 46.01, Penal Code, or prohibited weapon, as described by Section 46.05, Penal Code, the case shall be promptly forwarded to the office of the prosecuting attorney, accompanied by:

(1) all documents that accompanied the current referral; and

(2) a summary of all prior referrals of the child to the juvenile court, juvenile probation department, or a detention facility.

(e) If a juvenile board adopts an alternative referral plan under Subsection (d), the board shall register the plan with the Texas Juvenile Probation Commission.

(f) A juvenile board may not adopt an alternate referral plan that does not require the forwarding of a child's case to the prosecuting attorney as provided by Subsection (d) if probable cause exists to believe that the child engaged in delinquent conduct that violates Section 19.03, Penal Code (capital murder), or Section 19.02, Penal Code (murder).
(Enacted by Acts 1973, 63rd Leg., ch. 544 (S.B. 111), § 1, effective September 1, 1973; am. Acts 1995, 74th Leg., ch. 262 (H.B. 327), § 21, effective January 1, 1996; am. Acts 1997, 75th Leg., ch. 1374 (H.B. 1230), § 5, effective September 1, 1997; am. Acts 2001, 77th Leg., ch. 1297 (H.B. 1118), § 18, effective September 1, 2001; am. Acts 2003, 78th Leg., ch. 283 (H.B. 2319), § 12, effective September 1, 2003.)

## Sec. 53.012. Review by Prosecutor.

(a) The prosecuting attorney shall promptly review the circumstances and allegations of a referral made under Section 53.01 for legal sufficiency and the desirability of prosecution and may file a petition without regard to whether probable cause was found under Section 53.01.

(b) If the prosecuting attorney does not file a petition requesting the adjudication of the child referred to the prosecuting attorney, the prosecuting attorney shall:

(1) terminate all proceedings, if the reason is for lack of probable cause; or

(2) return the referral to the juvenile probation department for further proceedings.

(c) The juvenile probation department shall promptly refer a child who has been returned to the department under Subsection (b)(2) and who fails or refuses to participate in a program of the department to the prosecuting attorney for review of the child's case and determination of whether to file a petition.

(Enacted by Acts 1995, 74th Leg., ch. 262 (H.B. 327), § 22, effective January 1, 1996.)

## Sec. 53.013. Progressive Sanctions Program.

Each juvenile board may adopt a progressive sanctions program using the model for progressive sanctions in Chapter 59.

(Enacted by Acts 1995, 74th Leg., ch. 262 (H.B. 327), § 22, effective January 1, 1996; am. Acts 1997, 75th Leg., ch. 1086 (H.B. 1550), § 7, effective September 1, 1997; am. Acts 2003, 78th Leg., ch. 479 (H.B. 888), § 1, effective September 1, 2003.)

## Sec. 53.02. Release from Detention.

(a) If a child is brought before the court or delivered to a detention facility as authorized by Sections 51.12(a)(3) and (4), the intake or other authorized officer of the court shall immediately make an investigation and shall release the child unless it appears that his detention is warranted under Subsection (b). The release may be conditioned upon requirements reasonably necessary to insure the child's appearance at later proceedings, but the conditions of the release must be in writing and filed with the office or official designated by the court and a copy furnished to the child.

(b) A child taken into custody may be detained prior to hearing on the petition only if:

(1) the child is likely to abscond or be removed from the jurisdiction of the court;

(2) suitable supervision, care, or protection for the child is not being provided by a parent, guardian, custodian, or other person;

(3) the child has no parent, guardian, custodian, or other person able to return the child to the court when required;

(4) the child may be dangerous to himself or herself or the child may threaten the safety of the public if released;

(5) the child has previously been found to be a delinquent child or has previously been convicted of a penal offense punishable by a term in jail or prison and is likely to commit an offense if released; or

(6) the child's detention is required under Subsection (f).

(c) If the child is not released, a request for detention hearing shall be made and promptly presented to the court, and an informal detention hearing as provided in Section 54.01 of this code shall be held promptly, but not later than the time required by Section 54.01 of this code.

(d) A release of a child to an adult under Subsection (a) must be conditioned on the agreement of the adult to be subject to the jurisdiction of the juvenile court and to an order of contempt by the court if the adult, after notification, is unable to produce the child at later proceedings.

(e) Unless otherwise agreed in the memorandum of understanding under Section 37.011, Education Code, in a county with a population greater than 125,000, if a child being released under this section is expelled under Section 37.007, Education Code, the release shall be conditioned on the child's attending a juvenile justice alternative education program pending a deferred prosecution or formal court disposition of the child's case.

(f) A child who is alleged to have engaged in delinquent conduct and to have used, possessed, or exhibited a firearm, as defined by Section 46.01, Penal Code, in the commission of the offense shall be detained until the child is released at the direction of the judge of the juvenile court, a substitute judge authorized by Section 51.04(f), or a referee appointed under Section 51.04(g), including an oral direction by telephone, or until a detention hearing is held as required by Section 54.01.

(Enacted by Acts 1973, 63rd Leg., ch. 544 (S.B. 111), § 1, effective September 1, 1973; am. Acts 1979, 66th Leg., ch. 518 (S.B. 541), § 1, effective June 11, 1979; am. Acts 1981, 67th Leg., ch. 115 (S.B. 164), § 1, effective August 31, 1981; am. Acts 1995, 74th Leg., ch. 262 (H.B. 327), § 23, effective January 1, 1996; am. Acts 1997, 75th Leg., ch. 1015 (S.B. 133), § 17, effective June 19, 1997; am. Acts 1997, 75th Leg., ch. 1374 (H.B. 1230), § 6, effective September 1, 1997; am. Acts 1999, 76th Leg., ch. 232 (H.B. 1269), § 1, effective September 1, 1999.)

## Sec. 53.03. Deferred Prosecution.

(a) Subject to Subsections (e) and (g), if the preliminary investigation required by Section 53.01 of this code results in a determination that further proceedings in the case are authorized, the probation officer or other designated officer of the court, subject to the direction of the juvenile court, may advise the parties for a reasonable period of time not to exceed six months concerning deferred prosecution and rehabilitation of a child if:

(1) deferred prosecution would be in the interest of the public and the child;

(2) the child and his parent, guardian, or custodian consent with knowledge that consent is not obligatory; and

(3) the child and his parent, guardian, or custodian are informed that they may terminate the deferred prosecution at any point and petition the court for a court hearing in the case.

(b) Except as otherwise permitted by this title, the child may not be detained during or as a result of the deferred prosecution process.

(c) An incriminating statement made by a participant to the person giving advice and in the discussions or conferences incident thereto may not be used against the declarant in any court hearing.

(d) The juvenile board may adopt a fee schedule for deferred prosecution services and rules for the waiver of a fee for financial hardship in accordance with guidelines that the Texas Juvenile Probation Commission shall provide. The maximum fee is $15 a month. If the board adopts a schedule and rules for waiver, the probation officer or other designated officer of the court shall collect the fee authorized by the schedule from the parent, guardian, or custodian of a child for whom a deferred prosecution is authorized under this section or waive the fee in accordance with the rules adopted by the board. The officer shall deposit the fees received under this section in the county treasury to the credit of a special fund that may be used only for juvenile probation or community-based juvenile corrections services or facilities in which a juvenile may be required to

live while under court supervision. If the board does not adopt a schedule and rules for waiver, a fee for deferred prosecution services may not be imposed.

(e) A prosecuting attorney may defer prosecution for any child. A probation officer or other designated officer of the court:

(1) may not defer prosecution for a child for a case that is required to be forwarded to the prosecuting attorney under Section 53.01(d); and

(2) may defer prosecution for a child who has previously been adjudicated for conduct that constitutes a felony only if the prosecuting attorney consents in writing.

(f) The probation officer or other officer designated by the court supervising a program of deferred prosecution for a child under this section shall report to the juvenile court any violation by the child of the program.

(g) Prosecution may not be deferred for a child alleged to have engaged in conduct that:

(1) is an offense under Section 49.04, 49.05, 49.06, 49.07, or 49.08, Penal Code; or

(2) is a third or subsequent offense under Section 106.04 or 106.041, Alcoholic Beverage Code.

(h) If the child is alleged to have engaged in delinquent conduct or conduct indicating a need for supervision that violates Section 28.08, Penal Code, deferred prosecution under this section may include:

(1) voluntary attendance in a class with instruction in self-responsibility and empathy for a victim of an offense conducted by a local juvenile probation department, if the class is available; and

(2) voluntary restoration of the property damaged by the child by removing or painting over any markings made by the child, if the owner of the property consents to the restoration.

(i) The court may defer prosecution for a child at any time:

(1) for an adjudication that is to be decided by a jury trial, before the jury is sworn;

(2) for an adjudication before the court, before the first witness is sworn; or

(3) for an uncontested adjudication, before the child pleads to the petition or agrees to a stipulation of evidence.

(j) The court may add the period of deferred prosecution under Subsection (i) to a previous order of deferred prosecution, except that the court may not place the child on deferred prosecution for a combined period longer than one year.

(k) In deciding whether to grant deferred prosecution under Subsection (i), the court may consider professional representations by the parties concerning the nature of the case and the background of the respondent. The representations made under this subsection by the child or counsel for the child are not admissible against the child at trial should the court reject the application for deferred prosecution.

(Enacted by Acts 1973, 63rd Leg., ch. 544 (S.B. 111), § 1, effective September 1, 1973; am. Acts 1983, 68th Leg., ch. 565 (S.B. 669), § 1, effective September 1, 1983; am. Acts 1987, 70th Leg., ch. 1040 (S.B. 17), § 22, effective September 1, 1987; am. Acts 1995, 74th Leg., ch. 262 (H.B. 327), § 24, effective January 1, 1996; am. Acts 1997, 75th Leg., ch. 593 (S.B. 758), § 6, effective September 1, 1997; am. Acts 1997, 75th Leg., ch. 1013 (S.B. 35), § 16, effective September 1, 1997; am. Acts 1999, 76th Leg., ch. 62 (S.B. 1368), § 19.01(17), effective September 1, 1999; am. Acts 2003, 78th Leg., ch. 283 (H.B. 2319), § 13, effective September 1, 2003; am. Acts 2005, 79th Leg., ch. 949 (H.B. 1575), § 11, effective September 1, 2005.)

### Sec. 53.035.   Grand Jury Referral.

(a) The prosecuting attorney may, before filing a petition under Section 53.04, refer an offense to a grand jury in the county in which the offense is alleged to have been committed.

(b) The grand jury has the same jurisdiction and powers to investigate the facts and circumstances concerning an offense referred to the grand jury under this section as it has to investigate other criminal activity.

(c) If the grand jury votes to take no action on an offense referred to the grand jury under this section, the prosecuting attorney may not file a petition under Section 53.04 concerning the offense unless the same or a successor grand jury approves the filing of the petition.

(d) If the grand jury votes for approval of the prosecution of an offense referred to the grand jury under this section, the prosecuting attorney may file a petition under Section 53.04.

(e) The approval of the prosecution of an offense by a grand jury under this section does not constitute approval of a petition by a grand jury for purposes of Section 53.045.

(Enacted by Acts 1999, 76th Leg., ch. 1477 (H.B. 3517), § 6, effective September 1, 1999.)

### Sec. 53.04.   Court Petition; Answer.

(a) If the preliminary investigation, required by Section 53.01 of this code[,] results in a determination that further proceedings are authorized and warranted, a petition for an adjudication or transfer hearing of a child alleged to have engaged in delinquent conduct or conduct indicating a need for supervision may be made as promptly as practicable by a prosecuting attorney who has knowledge of the facts alleged or is informed and believes that they are true.

(b) The proceedings shall be styled "In the matter of _____."

(c) The petition may be on information and belief.

(d) The petition must state:

(1) with reasonable particularity the time, place, and manner of the acts alleged and the penal law or standard of conduct allegedly violated by the acts;

(2) the name, age, and residence address, if known, of the child who is the subject of the petition;

(3) the names and residence addresses, if known, of the parent, guardian, or custodian of the child and of the child's spouse, if any;

(4) if the child's parent, guardian, or custodian does not reside or cannot be found in the state, or if their places of residence are unknown, the name and residence address of any known adult relative residing in the county or, if there is none, the name and residence address of the known adult relative residing nearest to the location of the court; and

(5) if the child is alleged to have engaged in habitual felony conduct, the previous adjudications in which the child was found to have engaged in conduct violating penal laws of the grade of felony.

(e) An oral or written answer to the petition may be made at or before the commencement of the hearing. If there is no answer, a general denial of the alleged conduct is assumed.

(Enacted by Acts 1973, 63rd Leg., ch. 544 (S.B. 111), § 1, effective September 1, 1973; am. Acts 1995, 74th Leg., ch. 262 (H.B. 327), § 25, effective January 1, 1996.)

### Sec. 53.045.   Violent or Habitual Offenders.

(a) Except as provided by Subsection (e), the prosecuting attorney may refer the petition to the grand jury of the county in which the court in which the petition is filed presides if the petition alleges that the child engaged in delinquent conduct that constitutes habitual felony conduct as described by Section 51.031 or that included the violation of any of the following provisions:

    (1) Section 19.02, Penal Code (murder);

    (2) Section 19.03, Penal Code (capital murder);

    (3) Section 19.04, Penal Code (manslaughter);

    (4) Section 20.04, Penal Code (aggravated kidnapping);

    (5) Section 22.011, Penal Code (sexual assault) or Section 22.021, Penal Code (aggravated sexual assault);

    (6) Section 22.02, Penal Code (aggravated assault);

    (7) Section 29.03, Penal Code (aggravated robbery);

    (8) Section 22.04, Penal Code (injury to a child, elderly individual, or disabled individual), if the offense is punishable as a felony, other than a state jail felony;

    (9) Section 22.05(b), Penal Code (felony deadly conduct involving discharging a firearm);

    (10) Subchapter D, Chapter 481, Health and Safety Code, if the conduct constitutes a felony of the first degree or an aggravated controlled substance felony (certain offenses involving controlled substances);

    (11) Section 15.03, Penal Code (criminal solicitation);

    (12) Section 21.11(a)(1), Penal Code (indecency with a child);

    (13) Section 15.031, Penal Code (criminal solicitation of a minor);

    (14) Section 15.01, Penal Code (criminal attempt), if the offense attempted was an offense under Section 19.02, Penal Code (murder), or Section 19.03, Penal Code (capital murder), or an offense listed by Section 3g(a)(1), Article 42.12, Code of Criminal Procedure;

    (15) Section 28.02, Penal Code (arson), if bodily injury or death is suffered by any person by reason of the commission of the conduct;

    (16) Section 49.08, Penal Code (intoxication manslaughter); or

    (17) Section 15.02, Penal Code (criminal conspiracy), if the offense made the subject of the criminal conspiracy includes a violation of any of the provisions referenced in Subdivisions (1) through (16).

(b) A grand jury may approve a petition submitted to it under this section by a vote of nine members of the grand jury in the same manner that the grand jury votes on the presentment of an indictment.

(c) The grand jury has all the powers to investigate the facts and circumstances relating to a petition submitted under this section as it has to investigate other criminal activity but may not issue an indictment unless the child is transferred to a criminal court as provided by Section 54.02 of this code.

(d) If the grand jury approves of the petition, the fact of approval shall be certified to the juvenile court, and the certification shall be entered in the record of the case. For the purpose of the transfer of a child to the Texas Department of Criminal Justice as provided by Section 245.151(c), Human Resources Code, a juvenile court petition approved by a grand jury under this section is an indictment presented by the grand jury.

(e) The prosecuting attorney may not refer a petition that alleges the child engaged in conduct that violated Section 22.011(a)(2), Penal Code, or Sections 22.021(a)(1)(B) and (2)(B), Penal Code, unless the child is more than three years older than the victim of the conduct.

(Enacted by Acts 1987, 70th Leg., ch. 385 (H.B. 682), § 7, effective September 1, 1987; am. Acts 1991, 72nd Leg., ch. 574 (S.B. 303), § 1, effective September 1, 1991; am. Acts 1995, 74th Leg., ch. 262 (H.B. 327), §§ 26, 27, effective January 1, 1996; am. Acts 1997, 75th Leg., ch. 1086 (H.B. 1550), § 8, effective September 1, 1997; am. Acts 2001, 77th Leg., ch. 1297 (H.B. 1118), § 19, effective September 1, 2001; am. Acts 2007, 80th Leg., ch. 908 (H.B. 2884), § 10, effective September 1, 2007; am. Acts 2011, 82nd Leg., ch. 85 (S.B. 653), § 3.006, effective September 1, 2011.)

### Sec. 53.05.  Time Set for Hearing.

(a) After the petition has been filed, the juvenile court shall set a time for the hearing.

(b) The time set for the hearing shall not be later than 10 working days after the day the petition was filed if:

    (1) the child is in detention; or

    (2) the child will be taken into custody under Section 53.06(d) of this code.

(Enacted by Acts 1973, 63rd Leg., ch. 544 (S.B. 111), § 1, effective September 1, 1973; am. Acts 1995, 74th Leg., ch. 262 (H.B. 327), § 28, effective January 1, 1996.)

### Sec. 53.06.  Summons.

(a) The juvenile court shall direct issuance of a summons to:

(1) the child named in the petition;

(2) the child's parent, guardian, or custodian;

(3) the child's guardian ad litem; and

(4) any other person who appears to the court to be a proper or necessary party to the proceeding.

(b) The summons must require the persons served to appear before the court at the time set to answer the allegations of the petition. A copy of the petition must accompany the summons.

(c) The court may endorse on the summons an order directing the person having the physical custody or control of the child to bring the child to the hearing. A person who violates an order entered under this subsection may be proceeded against under Section 53.08 or 54.07 of this code.

(d) If it appears from an affidavit filed or from sworn testimony before the court that immediate detention of the child is warranted under Section 53.02(b) of this code, the court may endorse on the summons an order that a law-enforcement officer shall serve the summons and shall immediately take the child into custody and bring him before the court.

(e) A party, other than the child, may waive service of summons by written stipulation or by voluntary appearance at the hearing.

(Enacted by Acts 1973, 63rd Leg., ch. 544 (S.B. 111), § 1, effective September 1, 1973; am. Acts 1995, 74th Leg., ch. 262 (H.B. 327), § 29, effective January 1, 1996.)

## Sec. 53.07.  Service of Summons.

(a) If a person to be served with a summons is in this state and can be found, the summons shall be served upon him personally at least two days before the day of the adjudication hearing. If he is in this state and cannot be found, but his address is known or can with reasonable diligence be ascertained, the summons may be served on him by mailing a copy by registered or certified mail, return receipt requested, at least five days before the day of the hearing. If he is outside this state but he can be found or his address is known, or his whereabouts or address can with reasonable diligence be ascertained, service of the summons may be made either by delivering a copy to him personally or mailing a copy to him by registered or certified mail, return receipt requested, at least five days before the day of the hearing.

(b) The juvenile court has jurisdiction of the case if after reasonable effort a person other than the child cannot be found nor his post-office address ascertained, whether he is in or outside this state.

(c) Service of the summons may be made by any suitable person under the direction of the court.

(d) The court may authorize payment from the general funds of the county of the costs of service and of necessary travel expenses incurred by persons summoned or otherwise required to appear at the hearing.

(e) Witnesses may be subpoenaed in accordance with the Texas Code of Criminal Procedure, 1965.

(Enacted by Acts 1973, 63rd Leg., ch. 544 (S.B. 111), § 1, effective September 1, 1973.)

## Sec. 53.08.  Writ of Attachment.

(a) The juvenile court may issue a writ of attachment for a person who violates an order entered under Section 53.06(c).

(b) A writ of attachment issued under this section is executed in the same manner as in a criminal proceeding as provided by Chapter 24, Code of Criminal Procedure.

(Enacted by Acts 1995, 74th Leg., ch. 262 (H.B. 327), § 30, effective January 1, 1996.)

# CHAPTER 54
# JUDICIAL PROCEEDINGS

## Sec. 54.01. Detention Hearing.

(a) Except as provided by Subsection (p), if the child is not released under Section 53.02, a detention hearing without a jury shall be held promptly, but not later than the second working day after the child is taken into custody; provided, however, that when a child is detained on a Friday or Saturday, then such detention hearing shall be held on the first working day after the child is taken into custody.

(b) Reasonable notice of the detention hearing, either oral or written, shall be given, stating the time, place, and purpose of the hearing. Notice shall be given to the child and, if they can be found, to his parents, guardian, or custodian. Prior to the commencement of the hearing, the court shall inform the parties of the child's right to counsel and to appointed counsel if they are indigent and of the child's right to remain silent with respect to any allegations of delinquent conduct, conduct indicating a need for supervision, or conduct that violates an order of probation imposed by a juvenile court.

(c) At the detention hearing, the court may consider written reports from probation officers, professional court employees, or professional consultants in addition to the testimony of witnesses. Prior to the detention hearing, the court shall provide the attorney for the child with access to all written matter to be considered by the court in making the detention decision. The court may order counsel not to reveal items to the child or his parent, guardian, or guardian ad litem if such disclosure would materially harm the treatment and rehabilitation of the child or would substantially decrease the likelihood of receiving information from the same or similar sources in the future.

(d) A detention hearing may be held without the presence of the child's parents if the court has been unable to locate them. If no parent or guardian is present, the court shall appoint counsel or a guardian ad litem for the child.

(e) At the conclusion of the hearing, the court shall order the child released from detention unless it finds that:

(1) he is likely to abscond or be removed from the jurisdiction of the court;

(2) suitable supervision, care, or protection for him is not being provided by a parent, guardian, custodian, or other person;

(3) he has no parent, guardian, custodian, or other person able to return him to the court when required;

(4) he may be dangerous to himself or may threaten the safety of the public if released; or

(5) he has previously been found to be a delinquent child or has previously been convicted of a penal offense punishable by a term in jail or prison and is likely to commit an offense if released.

(f) Unless otherwise agreed in the memorandum of understanding under Section 37.011, Education Code, a release may be conditioned on requirements reasonably necessary to insure the child's appearance at later proceedings, but the conditions of the release must be in writing and a copy furnished to the child. In a county with a population greater than 125,000, if a child being released under this section is expelled under Section 37.007, Education Code, the release shall be conditioned on the child's attending a juvenile justice alternative education program pending a

Family Code

deferred prosecution or formal court disposition of the child's case.

(g) No statement made by the child at the detention hearing shall be admissible against the child at any other hearing.

(h) A detention order extends to the conclusion of the disposition hearing, if there is one, but in no event for more than 10 working days. Further detention orders may be made following subsequent detention hearings. The initial detention hearing may not be waived but subsequent detention hearings may be waived in accordance with the requirements of Section 51.09. Each subsequent detention order shall extend for no more than 10 working days, except that in a county that does not have a certified juvenile detention facility, as described by Section 51.12(a)(3), each subsequent detention order shall extend for no more than 15 working days.

(i) A child in custody may be detained for as long as 10 days without the hearing described in Subsection (a) of this section if:

(1) a written request for shelter in detention facilities pending arrangement of transportation to his place of residence in another state or country or another county of this state is voluntarily executed by the child not later than the next working day after he was taken into custody;

(2) the request for shelter contains:

(A) a statement by the child that he voluntarily agrees to submit himself to custody and detention for a period of not longer than 10 days without a detention hearing;

(B) an allegation by the person detaining the child that the child has left his place of residence in another state or country or another county of this state, that he is in need of shelter, and that an effort is being made to arrange transportation to his place of residence; and

(C) a statement by the person detaining the child that he has advised the child of his right to demand a detention hearing under Subsection (a) of this section; and

(3) the request is signed by the juvenile court judge to evidence his knowledge of the fact that the child is being held in detention.

(j) The request for shelter may be revoked by the child at any time, and on such revocation, if further detention is necessary, a detention hearing shall be held not later than the next working day in accordance with Subsections (a) through (g) of this section.

(k) Notwithstanding anything in this title to the contrary, the child may sign a request for shelter without the concurrence of an adult specified in Section 51.09 of this code.

(l) The juvenile board may appoint a referee to conduct the detention hearing. The referee shall be an attorney licensed to practice law in this state. Such payment or additional payment as may be warranted for referee services shall be provided from county funds. Before commencing the detention hearing, the referee shall inform the parties who have appeared that they are entitled to have the hearing before the juvenile court judge or a substitute judge authorized by Section 51.04(f). If a party objects to the referee conducting the detention hearing, an authorized judge shall conduct the hearing within 24 hours. At the conclusion of the hearing, the referee shall transmit written findings and recommendations to the juvenile court judge or substitute judge. The juvenile court judge or substitute judge shall adopt, modify, or reject the referee's recommendations not later than the next working day after the day that the judge receives the recommendations. Failure to act within that time results in release of the child by operation of law. A recommendation that the child be released operates to secure the child's immediate release, subject to the power of the juvenile court judge or substitute judge to reject or modify that recommendation. The effect of an order detaining a child shall be computed from the time of the hearing before the referee.

(m) The detention hearing required in this section may be held in the county of the designated place of detention where the child is being held even though the designated place of detention is outside the county of residence of the child or the county in which the alleged delinquent conduct, conduct indicating a need for supervision, or probation violation occurred.

(n) An attorney appointed by the court under Section 51.10(c) because a determination was made under this section to detain a child who was not represented by an attorney may request on behalf of the child and is entitled to a de novo detention hearing under this section. The attorney must make the request not later than the 10th working day after the date the attorney is appointed. The hearing must take place not later than the second working day after the date the attorney filed a formal request with the court for a hearing.

(o) The court or referee shall find whether there is probable cause to believe that a child taken into custody without an arrest warrant or a directive to apprehend has engaged in delinquent conduct, conduct indicating a need for supervision, or conduct that violates an order of probation imposed by a juvenile court. The court or referee must make the finding within 48 hours, including weekends and holidays, of the time the child was taken into custody. The court or referee may make the finding on any reasonably reliable information without regard to admissibility of that information under the Texas Rules of Evidence. A finding of probable cause is required to detain a child after the 48th hour after the time the child was taken into custody. If a court or referee finds probable cause, additional findings of probable cause are not required in the same cause to authorize further detention.

(p) If a child is detained in a county jail or other facility as provided by Section 51.12(*l*) and the child is not released under Section 53.02(f), a detention hearing without a jury shall be held promptly, but not later than the 24th hour, excluding weekends and holidays, after the time the child is taken into custody.

(q) If a child has not been released under Section 53.02 or this section and a petition has not been filed under Section 53.04 or 54.05 concerning the child, the court shall order the child released from detention not later than:

(1) the 30th working day after the date the initial detention hearing is held, if the child is alleged to have engaged in conduct constituting a capital felony, an aggravated controlled substance felony, or a felony of the first degree; or

(2) the 15th working day after the date the initial detention hearing is held, if the child is alleged to have engaged in conduct constituting an offense other than an offense listed in Subdivision (1) or conduct that violates an order of probation imposed by a juvenile court.

(q-1) The juvenile board may impose an earlier deadline than the specified deadlines for filing petitions under Subsection (q) and may specify the consequences of not filing a petition by the deadline the juvenile board has established. The juvenile board may authorize but not require the juvenile court to release a respondent from detention for failure of the prosecutor to file a petition by the juvenile board's deadline.

(r) On the conditional release of a child from detention by judicial order under Subsection (f), the court, referee, or detention magistrate may order that the child's parent, guardian, or custodian present in court at the detention hearing engage in acts or omissions specified by the court,

referee, or detention magistrate that will assist the child in complying with the conditions of release. The order must be in writing and a copy furnished to the parent, guardian, or custodian. An order entered under this subsection may be enforced as provided by Chapter 61.

(Enacted by Acts 1973, 63rd Leg., ch. 544 (S.B. 111), § 1, effective September 1, 1973; am. Acts 1975, 64th Leg., ch. 693 (S.B. 247), §§ 14, 15, effective September 1, 1975; am. Acts 1979, 66th Leg., ch. 518 (S.B. 541), § 2, effective June 11, 1979; am. Acts 1995, 74th Leg., ch. 262 (H.B. 327), § 31, effective January 1, 1996; am. Acts 1997, 75th Leg., ch. 922 (S.B. 298), § 1, effective September 1, 1997; am. Acts 1997, 75th Leg., ch. 1015 (S.B. 133), § 18, effective June 19, 1997; am. Acts 1997, 75th Leg., ch. 1086 (H.B. 1550), § 9, effective September 1, 1997; am. Acts 1999, 76th Leg., ch. 232 (H.B. 1269), § 4, effective September 1, 1999; am. Acts 1999, 76th Leg., ch. 1477 (H.B. 3517), § 7, effective September 1, 1999; am. Acts 2001, 77th Leg., ch. 1297 (H.B. 1118), § 20, effective September 1, 2001; am. Acts 2001, 77th Leg., ch. 1420 (H.B. 2812), § 21.001(30), effective September 1, 2001; am. Acts 2003, 78th Leg., ch. 283 (H.B. 2319), § 14, effective September 1, 2003; am. Acts 2005, 79th Leg., ch. 949 (H.B. 1575), § 12, effective September 1, 2005.)

## Sec. 54.011. Detention Hearings for Status Offenders and Nonoffenders; Penalty.

(a) The detention hearing for a status offender or nonoffender who has not been released administratively under Section 53.02 shall be held before the 24th hour after the time the child arrived at a detention facility, excluding hours of a weekend or a holiday. Except as otherwise provided by this section, the judge or referee conducting the detention hearing shall release the status offender or nonoffender from secure detention.

(b) The judge or referee may order a child in detention accused of the violation of a valid court order as defined by Section 51.02 detained not longer than 72 hours after the time the detention order was entered, excluding weekends and holidays, if:

(1) the judge or referee finds at the detention hearing that there is probable cause to believe the child violated the valid court order; and

(2) the detention of the child is justified under Section 54.01(e)(1), (2), or (3).

(c) Except as provided by Subsection (d), a detention order entered under Subsection (b) may be extended for one additional 72-hour period, excluding weekends and holidays, only on a finding of good cause by the juvenile court.

(d) A detention order for a child under this section may be extended on the demand of the child's attorney only to allow the time that is necessary to comply with the requirements of Section 51.10(h), entitling the attorney to 10 days to prepare for an adjudication hearing.

(e) A status offender may be detained for a necessary period, not to exceed five days, to enable the child's return to the child's home in another state under Chapter 60.

(f) Except as provided by Subsection (a), a nonoffender, including a person who has been taken into custody and is being held solely for deportation out of the United States, may not be detained for any period of time in a secure detention facility or secure correctional facility, regardless of whether the facility is publicly or privately operated. A nonoffender who is detained in violation of this subsection is entitled to immediate release from the facility and may bring a civil action for compensation for the illegal detention against any person responsible for the detention. A person commits an offense if the person knowingly detains or assists in detaining a nonoffender in a secure detention facility or secure correctional facility in violation of this subsection. An offense under this subsection is a Class B misdemeanor.

(Enacted by Acts 1995, 74th Leg., ch. 262 (H.B. 327), § 32, effective January 1, 1996; am. Acts 1997, 75th Leg., ch. 1374 (H.B. 1230), § 7, effective September 1, 1997; am. Acts 2003, 78th Leg., ch. 283 (H.B. 2319), §§ 15, 16, effective September 1, 2003.)

## Sec. 54.012. Interactive Video Recording of Detention Hearing.

(a) A detention hearing under Section 54.01 may be held using interactive video equipment if:

(1) the child and the child's attorney agree to the video hearing; and

(2) the parties to the proceeding have the opportunity to cross-examine witnesses.

(b) A detention hearing may not be held using video equipment unless the video equipment for the hearing provides for a two-way communication of image and sound among the child, the court, and other parties at the hearing.

(c) A recording of the communications shall be made. The recording shall be preserved until the earlier of:

(1) the 91st day after the date on which the recording is made if the child is alleged to have engaged in conduct constituting a misdemeanor;

(2) the 120th day after the date on which the recording is made if the child is alleged to have engaged in conduct constituting a felony; or

(3) the date on which the adjudication hearing ends.

(d) An attorney for the child may obtain a copy of the recording on payment of the reasonable costs of reproducing the copy.

(Enacted by Acts 1995, 74th Leg., ch. 262 (H.B. 327), § 33, effective January 1, 1996; am. Acts 2005, 79th Leg., ch. 949 (H.B. 1575), § 13, effective September 1, 2005.)

## Sec. 54.02. Waiver of Jurisdiction and Discretionary Transfer to Criminal Court.

(a) The juvenile court may waive its exclusive original jurisdiction and transfer a child to the appropriate district court or criminal district court for criminal proceedings if:

(1) the child is alleged to have violated a penal law of the grade of felony;

(2) the child was:

(A) 14 years of age or older at the time he is alleged to have committed the offense, if the offense is a capital felony, an aggravated controlled substance felony, or a felony of the first degree, and no adjudication hearing has been conducted concerning that offense; or

(B) 15 years of age or older at the time the child is alleged to have committed the offense, if the offense is a felony of the second or third degree or a state jail felony, and no adjudication hearing has been conducted concerning that offense; and

(3) after a full investigation and a hearing, the juvenile court determines that there is probable cause to believe that the child before the court committed the offense alleged and that because of the seriousness of the offense alleged or the background of the child the welfare of the community requires criminal proceedings.

(b) The petition and notice requirements of Sections 53.04, 53.05, 53.06, and 53.07 of this code must be satisfied, and the summons must state that the hearing is for the purpose of considering discretionary transfer to criminal court.

(c) The juvenile court shall conduct a hearing without a jury to consider transfer of the child for criminal proceedings.

(d) Prior to the hearing, the juvenile court shall order and obtain a complete diagnostic study, social evaluation, and full investigation of the child, his circumstances, and the circumstances of the alleged offense.

(e) At the transfer hearing the court may consider written reports from probation officers, professional court employees, or professional consultants in addition to the testimony of witnesses. At least five days prior to the transfer hearing, the court shall provide the attorney for the child and the prosecuting attorney with access to all written matter to be considered by the court in making the transfer decision. The court may order counsel not to reveal items to the child or the child's parent, guardian, or guardian ad litem if such disclosure would materially harm the treatment and rehabilitation of the child or would substantially decrease the likelihood of receiving information from the same or similar sources in the future.

(f) In making the determination required by Subsection (a) of this section, the court shall consider, among other matters:

(1) whether the alleged offense was against person or property, with greater weight in favor of transfer given to offenses against the person;

(2) the sophistication and maturity of the child;

(3) the record and previous history of the child; and

(4) the prospects of adequate protection of the public and the likelihood of the rehabilitation of the child by use of procedures, services, and facilities currently available to the juvenile court.

(g) If the petition alleges multiple offenses that constitute more than one criminal transaction, the juvenile court shall either retain or transfer all offenses relating to a single transaction. Except as provided by Subsection (g-1), a child is not subject to criminal prosecution at any time for any offense arising out of a criminal transaction for which the juvenile court retains jurisdiction.

(g-1) A child may be subject to criminal prosecution for an offense committed under Chapter 19 or Section 49.08, Penal Code, if:

(1) the offense arises out of a criminal transaction for which the juvenile court retained jurisdiction over other offenses relating to the criminal transaction; and

(2) on or before the date the juvenile court retained jurisdiction, one or more of the elements of the offense under Chapter 19 or Section 49.08, Penal Code, had not occurred.

(h) If the juvenile court waives jurisdiction, it shall state specifically in the order its reasons for waiver and certify its action, including the written order and findings of the court, and shall transfer the person to the appropriate court for criminal proceedings and cause the results of the diagnostic study of the person ordered under Subsection (d), including psychological information, to be transferred to the appropriate criminal prosecutor. On transfer of the person for criminal proceedings, the person shall be dealt with as an adult and in accordance with the Code of Criminal Procedure, except that if detention in a certified juvenile detention facility is authorized under Section 152.0015, Human Resources Code, the juvenile court may order the person to be detained in the facility pending trial or until the criminal court enters an order under Article 4.19, Code of Criminal Procedure. A transfer of custody made under this subsection is an arrest.

(i) A waiver under this section is a waiver of jurisdiction over the child and the criminal court may not remand the child to the jurisdiction of the juvenile court.

(j) The juvenile court may waive its exclusive original jurisdiction and transfer a person to the appropriate district court or criminal district court for criminal proceedings if:

(1) the person is 18 years of age or older;

(2) the person was:

(A) 10 years of age or older and under 17 years of age at the time the person is alleged to have committed a capital felony or an offense under Section 19.02, Penal Code;

(B) 14 years of age or older and under 17 years of age at the time the person is alleged to have committed an aggravated controlled substance felony or a felony of the first degree other than an offense under Section 19.02, Penal Code; or

(C) 15 years of age or older and under 17 years of age at the time the person is alleged to have committed a felony of the second or third degree or a state jail felony;

(3) no adjudication concerning the alleged offense has been made or no adjudication hearing concerning the offense has been conducted;

(4) the juvenile court finds from a preponderance of the evidence that:

(A) for a reason beyond the control of the state it was not practicable to proceed in juvenile court before the 18th birthday of the person; or

(B) after due diligence of the state it was not practicable to proceed in juvenile court before the 18th birthday of the person because:

    (i) the state did not have probable cause to proceed in juvenile court and new evidence has been found since the 18th birthday of the person;

    (ii) the person could not be found; or

    (iii) a previous transfer order was reversed by an appellate court or set aside by a district court; and

  (5) the juvenile court determines that there is probable cause to believe that the child before the court committed the offense alleged.

(k) The petition and notice requirements of Sections 53.04, 53.05, 53.06, and 53.07 of this code must be satisfied, and the summons must state that the hearing is for the purpose of considering waiver of jurisdiction under Subsection (j) of this section.

(*l*) The juvenile court shall conduct a hearing without a jury to consider waiver of jurisdiction under Subsection (j) of this section.

(m) Notwithstanding any other provision of this section, the juvenile court shall waive its exclusive original jurisdiction and transfer a child to the appropriate district court or criminal court for criminal proceedings if:

  (1) the child has previously been transferred to a district court or criminal district court for criminal proceedings under this section, unless:

    (A) the child was not indicted in the matter transferred by the grand jury;

    (B) the child was found not guilty in the matter transferred;

    (C) the matter transferred was dismissed with prejudice; or

    (D) the child was convicted in the matter transferred, the conviction was reversed on appeal, and the appeal is final; and

  (2) the child is alleged to have violated a penal law of the grade of felony.

(n) A mandatory transfer under Subsection (m) may be made without conducting the study required in discretionary transfer proceedings by Subsection (d). The requirements of Subsection (b) that the summons state that the purpose of the hearing is to consider discretionary transfer to criminal court does not apply to a transfer proceeding under Subsection (m). In a proceeding under Subsection (m), it is sufficient that the summons provide fair notice that the purpose of the hearing is to consider mandatory transfer to criminal court.

(o) If a respondent is taken into custody for possible discretionary transfer proceedings under Subsection (j), the juvenile court shall hold a detention hearing in the same manner as provided by Section 54.01, except that the court shall order the respondent released unless it finds that the respondent:

  (1) is likely to abscond or be removed from the jurisdiction of the court;

  (2) may be dangerous to himself or herself or may threaten the safety of the public if released; or

  (3) has previously been found to be a delinquent child or has previously been convicted of a penal offense punishable by a term of jail or prison and is likely to commit an offense if released.

(p) If the juvenile court does not order a respondent released under Subsection (o), the court shall, pending the conclusion of the discretionary transfer hearing, order that the respondent be detained in:

  (1) a certified juvenile detention facility as provided by Subsection (q); or

  (2) an appropriate county facility for the detention of adults accused of criminal offenses.

(q) The detention of a respondent in a certified juvenile detention facility must comply with the detention requirements under this title, except that, to the extent practicable, the person shall be kept separate from children detained in the same facility.

(r) If the juvenile court orders a respondent detained in a county facility under Subsection (p), the county sheriff shall take custody of the respondent under the juvenile court's order. The juvenile court shall set or deny bond for the respondent as required by the Code of Criminal Procedure and other law applicable to the pretrial detention of adults accused of criminal offenses.

(Enacted by Acts 1973, 63rd Leg., ch. 544 (S.B. 111), § 1, effective September 1, 1973; am. Acts 1975, 64th Leg., ch. 693 (S.B. 247), § 16, effective September 1, 1975; am. Acts 1987, 70th Leg., ch. 140 (S.B. 218), § 1 to 3, effective September 1, 1987; am. Acts 1995, 74th Leg., ch. 262 (H.B. 327), § 34, effective January 1, 1996; am. Acts 1999, 76th Leg., ch. 1477 (H.B. 3517), § 8, effective September 1, 1999; am. Acts 2009, 81st Leg., ch. 1354 (S.B. 518), § 1, effective September 1, 2009; am. Acts 2011, 82nd Leg., ch. 1087 (S.B. 1209), § 4, effective September 1, 2011; am. Acts

2011, 82nd Leg., ch. 1103 (S.B. 1617), § 1, effective September 1, 2011.)

## Sec. 54.021. County, Justice, or Municipal Court: Truancy.

(a) **[2 Versions: As amended by Acts 2011, 82nd Leg., ch. 148]** The juvenile court may waive its exclusive original jurisdiction and transfer a child to the constitutional county court, if the county has a population of 1.75 million or more, or to an appropriate justice or municipal court, with the permission of the county, justice, or municipal court, for disposition in the manner provided by Subsection (b) if the child is alleged to have engaged in conduct described in Section 51.03(b)(2). A waiver of jurisdiction under this subsection may be for an individual case or for all cases in which a child is alleged to have engaged in conduct described in Section 51.03(b)(2). The waiver of a juvenile court's exclusive original jurisdiction for all cases in which a child is alleged to have engaged in conduct described in Section 51.03(b)(2) is effective for a period of one year.

(a) **[2 Versions: As amended by Acts 2011, 82nd Leg., ch. 1098]** The juvenile court may waive its exclusive original jurisdiction and transfer a child to the constitutional county court, if the county has a population of two million or more, or to an appropriate justice or municipal court, with the permission of the county, justice, or municipal court, for disposition in the manner provided by Subsection (b) if the child is 12 years of age or older and is alleged to have engaged in conduct described in Section 51.03(b)(2). A waiver of jurisdiction under this subsection may be for an individual case or for all cases in which a child is alleged to have engaged in conduct described in Section 51.03(b)(2). The waiver of a juvenile court's exclusive original jurisdiction for all cases in which a child is alleged to have engaged in conduct described in Section 51.03(b)(2) is effective for a period of one year.

(b) A county, justice, or municipal court may exercise jurisdiction over a person alleged to have engaged in conduct indicating a need for 0 supervision by engaging in conduct described in Section 51.03(b)(2) in a case where:

(1) the person is 12 years of age or older;

(2) the juvenile court has waived its original jurisdiction under this section; and

(3) a complaint is filed by the appropriate authority in the county, justice, or municipal court charging an offense under Section 25.094, Education Code.

(c) A proceeding in a county, justice, or municipal court on a complaint charging an offense under Section 25.094, Education Code, is governed by Chapter 45, Code of Criminal Procedure.

(d) Notwithstanding any other law, the costs assessed in a case filed in or transferred to a constitutional county court for an offense under Section 25.093 or 25.094, Education Code, must be the same as the costs assessed for a case filed in a justice court for an offense under Section 25.093 or 25.094, Education Code.

(e) The proceedings before a constitutional county court related to an offense under Section 25.093 or 25.094, Education Code, may be recorded in any manner provided by Section 30.00010, Government Code, for recording proceedings in a municipal court of record.

(f) to (h) [Repealed by Acts 2001, 77th Leg., ch. 1514, § 19(b), effective September 1, 2001].

(Enacted by Acts 1991, 72nd Leg., ch. 741 (S.B. 1037), § 1, effective September 1, 1991; am. Acts 1993, 73rd Leg., ch. 358 (H.B. 681), § 1, effective September 1, 1993; am. Acts 1995, 74th Leg., ch. 260 (S.B. 1), § 24, effective May 30, 1995; am. Acts 1995, 74th Leg., ch. 262 (H.B. 327), § 35, effective January 1, 1996; am. Acts 1997, 75th Leg., ch. 865 (H.B. 1606), § 1, effective September 1, 1997; am. Acts 1999, 76th Leg., ch. 76 (H.B. 688), § 2, effective September 1, 1999; am. Acts 2001, 77th Leg., ch. 1514 (S.B. 1432), §§ 14, 19(b), effective September 1, 2001; am. Acts 2003, 78th Leg., ch. 137 (S.B. 358), § 12, effective September 1, 2003; am. Acts 2011, 82nd Leg., ch. 148 (H.B. 734), § 3, effective September 1, 2011; am. Acts 2011, 82nd Leg., ch. 1098 (S.B. 1489), § 3, effective September 1, 2011.)

## Sec. 54.022. Justice or Municipal Court: Certain Misdemeanors [Repealed].

Repealed by Acts 2001, 77th Leg., ch. 1297 (H.B. 1118), § 71(2), effective September 1, 2001 and Acts 2001, 77th Leg., ch. 1514 (S.B. 1432), § 19(b), effective September 1, 2001.

(Enacted by Acts 1995, 74th Leg., ch. 262 (H.B. 327), § 36, effective January 1, 1996; am. Acts 1997, 75th Leg., ch. 713 (H.B. 115), § 1, effective September 1, 1997; am. Acts 1999, 76th Leg., ch. 76 (H.B. 688), § 3, effective September 1, 1999.)

## Sec. 54.023. Justice or Municipal Court: Enforcement [Repealed].

Repealed by Acts 2003, 78th Leg., ch. 283 (H.B. 2319), § 61(1), effective September 1, 2003.

(Enacted by Acts 2001, 77th Leg., ch. 1297 (H.B. 1118), § 21, effective September 1, 2001.)

### Sec. 54.03. Adjudication Hearing.

(a) A child may be found to have engaged in delinquent conduct or conduct indicating a need for supervision only after an adjudication hearing conducted in accordance with the provisions of this section.

(b) At the beginning of the adjudication hearing, the juvenile court judge shall explain to the child and his parent, guardian, or guardian ad litem:

(1) the allegations made against the child;

(2) the nature and possible consequences of the proceedings, including the law relating to the admissibility of the record of a juvenile court adjudication in a criminal proceeding;

(3) the child's privilege against self-incrimination;

(4) the child's right to trial and to confrontation of witnesses;

(5) the child's right to representation by an attorney if he is not already represented; and

(6) the child's right to trial by jury.

(c) Trial shall be by jury unless jury is waived in accordance with Section 51.09. If the hearing is on a petition that has been approved by the grand jury under Section 53.045, the jury must consist of 12 persons and be selected in accordance with the requirements in criminal cases. If the hearing is on a petition that alleges conduct that violates a penal law of this state of the grade of misdemeanor, the jury must consist of the number of persons required by Article 33.01(b), Code of Criminal Procedure. Jury verdicts under this title must be unanimous.

(d) Except as provided by Section 54.031, only material, relevant, and competent evidence in accordance with the Texas Rules of Evidence applicable to criminal cases and Chapter 38, Code of Criminal Procedure, may be considered in the adjudication hearing. Except in a detention or discretionary transfer hearing, a social history report or social service file shall not be viewed by the court before the adjudication decision and shall not be viewed by the jury at any time.

(e) A child alleged to have engaged in delinquent conduct or conduct indicating a need for supervision need not be a witness against nor otherwise incriminate himself. An extrajudicial statement which was obtained without fulfilling the requirements of this title or of the constitution of this state or the United States, may not be used in an adjudication hearing. A statement made by the child out of court is insufficient to support a finding of delinquent conduct or conduct indicating a need for supervision unless it is corroborated in whole or in part by other evidence. An adjudication of delinquent conduct or conduct indicating a need for supervision cannot be had upon the testimony of an accomplice unless corroborated by other evidence tending to connect the child with the alleged delinquent conduct or conduct indicating a need for supervision; and the corroboration is not sufficient if it merely shows the commission of the alleged conduct. Evidence illegally seized or obtained is inadmissible in an adjudication hearing.

(f) At the conclusion of the adjudication hearing, the court or jury shall find whether or not the child has engaged in delinquent conduct or conduct indicating a need for supervision. The finding must be based on competent evidence admitted at the hearing. The child shall be presumed to be innocent of the charges against the child and no finding that a child has engaged in delinquent conduct or conduct indicating a need for supervision may be returned unless the state has proved such beyond a reasonable doubt. In all jury cases the jury will be instructed that the burden is on the state to prove that a child has engaged in delinquent conduct or is in need of supervision beyond a reasonable doubt. A child may be adjudicated as having engaged in conduct constituting a lesser included offense as provided by Articles 37.08 and 37.09, Code of Criminal Procedure.

(g) If the court or jury finds that the child did not engage in delinquent conduct or conduct indicating a need for supervision, the court shall dismiss the case with prejudice.

(h) If the finding is that the child did engage in delinquent conduct or conduct indicating a need for supervision, the court or jury shall state which of the allegations in the petition were found to be established by the evidence. The court shall also set a date and time for the disposition hearing.

(i) In order to preserve for appellate or collateral review the failure of the court to provide the child the explanation required by Subsection (b), the attorney for the child must comply with Rule 33.1, Texas Rules of Appellate Procedure, before testimony begins or, if the adjudication is uncontested, before the child pleads to the petition or agrees to a stipulation of evidence.

(j) When the state and the child agree to the disposition of the case, in whole or in part, the prosecuting attorney shall inform the court of the agreement between the state and the child. The court shall inform the child that the court is not required to accept the agreement. The court may delay a decision on whether to accept the agreement until after reviewing a report filed under Section 54.04(b). If the court decides not to accept the agreement, the court shall inform the child of the court's decision and give the child an opportunity to withdraw the plea or stipulation of evidence. If the court rejects the agreement, no document, testimony, or other evidence placed before the court that relates to the rejected agreement may be considered by the court in a subsequent hearing in the case. A statement made by the child before the court's rejection of the agreement to a person writing a report to be filed under Section 54.04(b) may not be admitted into evidence in a subsequent hearing in the case. If the court accepts the agreement, the court shall make a disposition in accordance with the terms of the agreement between the state and the child. (Enacted by Acts 1973, 63rd Leg., ch. 544 (S.B. 111), § 1, effective September 1, 1973; am. Acts 1975, 64th Leg., ch. 693 (S.B. 247), § 17, effective September 1, 1975; am. Acts 1979, 66th Leg., ch. 514 (S.B. 451), § 1, effective August 27, 1979; am. Acts 1985, 69th Leg., ch. 590 (H.B. 579), § 2, effective September 1, 1985; am. Acts 1987, 70th Leg., ch. 385 (H.B. 682), § 8, effective September 1, 1987; am. Acts 1987, 70th Leg., ch. 386 (H.B. 683), § 3, effective September 1, 1987; am. Acts 1995, 74th Leg., ch. 262 (H.B. 327), § 37, effective January 1, 1996; am. Acts 1997, 75th Leg., ch. 1086 (H.B. 1550), § 10, effective September 1, 1997; am. Acts 1999, 76th Leg., ch. 1477 (H.B. 3517), § 9, effective September 1, 1999; am. Acts 2001, 77th Leg., ch. 1297 (H.B. 1118), § 22, effective September 1, 2001; am. Acts 2003, 78th Leg., ch. 283 (H.B. 2319), § 17, effective September 1, 2003; am. Acts 2009, 81st Leg., ch. 28 (H.B. 609), § 1, effective September 1, 2009.)

## Sec. 54.031. Hearsay Statement of Certain Abuse Victims.

(a) This section applies to a hearing under this title in which a child is alleged to be a delinquent child on the basis of a violation of any of the following provisions of the Penal Code, if a child 12 years of age or younger or a person with a disability is the alleged victim of the violation:

(1) Chapter 21 (Sexual Offenses) or 22 (Assaultive Offenses);

(2) Section 25.02 (Prohibited Sexual Conduct);

(3) Section 43.25 (Sexual Performance by a Child);

(4) Section 20A.02(a)(7) or (8) (Trafficking of Persons); or

(5) Section 43.05(a)(2) (Compelling Prostitution).

(b) This section applies only to statements that describe the alleged violation that:

(1) were made by the child or person with a disability who is the alleged victim of the violation; and

(2) were made to the first person, 18 years of age or older, to whom the child or person with a disability made a statement about the violation.

(c) A statement that meets the requirements of Subsection (b) is not inadmissible because of the hearsay rule if:

(1) on or before the 14th day before the date the hearing begins, the party intending to offer the statement:

(A) notifies each other party of its intention to do so;

(B) provides each other party with the name of the witness through whom it intends to offer the statement; and

(C) provides each other party with a written summary of the statement;

(2) the juvenile court finds, in a hearing conducted outside the presence of the jury, that the statement is reliable based on the time, content, and circumstances of the statement; and

(3) the child or person with a disability who is the alleged victim testifies or is available to testify at the hearing in court or in any other manner provided by law.

(d) In this section, "person with a disability" means a person 13 years of age or older who because of age or physical or mental disease, disability, or injury is substantially unable to protect the person's self from harm or to provide food, shelter, or medical care for the person's self. (Enacted by Acts 1985, 69th Leg., ch. 590 (H.B. 579), § 3, effective September 1, 1985; am. Acts 1995, 74th Leg., ch. 76 (S.B. 959), § 14.31, effective September 1, 1995; am. Acts 2009, 81st Leg., ch. 284 (S.B. 643), § 3, effective June 11, 2009; am. Acts 2011, 82nd Leg., ch. 1 (S.B. 24), § 4.01, effective September 1, 2011.)

Family Code

## Sec. 54.032. Deferral of Adjudication and Dismissal of Certain Cases on Completion of Teen Court Program.

(a) A juvenile court may defer adjudication proceedings under Section 54.03 for not more than 180 days if the child:

(1) is alleged to have engaged in conduct indicating a need for supervision that violated a penal law of this state of the grade of misdemeanor that is punishable by fine only or a penal ordinance of a political subdivision of this state;

(2) waives, under Section 51.09, the privilege against self-incrimination and testifies under oath that the allegations are true;

(3) presents to the court an oral or written request to attend a teen court program; and

(4) has not successfully completed a teen court program in the two years preceding the date that the alleged conduct occurred.

(b) The teen court program must be approved by the court.

(c) A child for whom adjudication proceedings are deferred under Subsection (a) shall complete the teen court program not later than the 90th day after the date the teen court hearing to determine punishment is held or the last day of the deferral period, whichever date is earlier. The court shall dismiss the case with prejudice at the time the child presents satisfactory evidence that the child has successfully completed the teen court program.

(d) A case dismissed under this section may not be part of the child's records for any purpose.

(e) The court may require a child who requests a teen court program to pay a fee not to exceed $10 that is set by the court to cover the costs of administering this section. The court shall deposit the fee in the county treasury of the county in which the court is located. A child who requests a teen court program and does not complete the program is not entitled to a refund of the fee.

(f) A court may transfer a case in which proceedings have been deferred as provided by this section to a court in another county if the court to which the case is transferred consents. A case may not be transferred unless it is within the jurisdiction of the court to which it is transferred.

(g) In addition to the fee authorized by Subsection (e), the court may require a child who requests a teen court program to pay a $10 fee to cover the cost to the teen court for performing its duties under this section. The court shall pay the fee to the teen court program, and the teen court program must account to the court for the receipt

and disbursal of the fee. A child who pays a fee under this subsection is not entitled to a refund of the fee, regardless of whether the child successfully completes the teen court program.

(h) Notwithstanding Subsection (e) or (g), a juvenile court that is located in the Texas-Louisiana border region, as defined by Section 2056.002, Government Code, may charge a fee of $20 under those subsections.

(Enacted by Acts 1989, 71st Leg., ch. 1031 (H.B. 198), § 2, effective September 1, 1989; am. Acts 1995, 74th Leg., ch. 748 (H.B. 120), § 1, effective September 1, 1995; am. Acts 2001, 77th Leg., ch. 216 (H.B. 822), § 2, effective September 1, 2001; am. Acts 2003, 78th Leg., ch. 283 (H.B. 2319), § 18, effective September 1, 2003; am. Acts 2007, 80th Leg., ch. 910 (H.B. 2949), § 2, effective September 1, 2007.)

## Sec. 54.0325. Deferral of Adjudication and Dismissal of Certain Cases on Completion of Teen Dating Violence Court Program.

(a) In this section:

(1) "Dating violence" has the meaning assigned by Section 71.0021.

(2) "Family violence" has the meaning assigned by Section 71.004.

(3) "Teen dating violence court program" means a program that includes:

(A) a 12-week program designed to educate children who engage in dating violence and encourage them to refrain from engaging in that conduct;

(B) a dedicated teen victim advocate who assists teen victims by offering referrals to additional services, providing counseling and safety planning, and explaining the juvenile justice system;

(C) a court-employed resource coordinator to monitor children's compliance with the 12-week program;

(D) one judge who presides over all of the cases in the jurisdiction that qualify for the program; and

(E) an attorney in the district attorney's office or the county attorney's office who is assigned to the program.

(b) On the recommendation of the prosecuting attorney, the juvenile court may defer adjudication proceedings under Section 54.03 for not more than 180 days if the child is a first offender who is alleged to have engaged in conduct:

(1) that violated a penal law of this state of the grade of misdemeanor; and

Family Code

(2) involving dating violence.

(c) For the purposes of Subsection (b), a first offender is a child who has not previously been referred to juvenile court for allegedly engaging in conduct constituting dating violence, family violence, or an assault.

(d) Before implementation, the teen dating violence court program must be approved by:

(1) the court; and

(2) the commissioners court of the county.

(e) A child for whom adjudication proceedings are deferred under Subsection (b) shall:

(1) complete the teen dating violence court program not later than the last day of the deferral period; and

(2) appear in court once a month for monitoring purposes.

(f) The court shall dismiss the case with prejudice at the time the child presents satisfactory evidence that the child has successfully completed the teen dating violence court program.

(g) The court may require a child who participates in a teen dating violence court program to pay a fee not to exceed $10 that is set by the court to cover the costs of administering this section. The court shall deposit the fee in the county treasury of the county in which the court is located.

(h) In addition to the fee authorized by Subsection (g), the court may require a child who participates in a teen dating violence court program to pay a fee of $10 to cover the cost to the teen dating violence court program for performing its duties under this section. The court shall pay the fee to the teen dating violence court program, and the teen dating violence court program must account to the court for the receipt and disbursal of the fee.

(i) The court shall track the number of children ordered to participate in the teen dating violence court program, the percentage of victims meeting with the teen victim advocate, and the compliance rate of the children ordered to participate in the program.

(Enacted by Acts 2011, 82nd Leg., ch. 1299 (H.B. 2496), § 1, effective September 1, 2011.)

### Sec. 54.033. Sexually Transmitted Disease, AIDS, and HIV Testing.

(a) A child found at the conclusion of an adjudication hearing under Section 54.03 of this code to have engaged in delinquent conduct that included a violation of Sections 21.11(a)(1), 22.011, or 22.021, Penal Code, shall undergo a medical procedure or test at the direction of the juvenile court designed to show or help show whether the child has a sexually transmitted disease, acquired immune deficiency syndrome (AIDS), human immunodeficiency virus (HIV) infection, antibodies to HIV, or infection with any other probable causative agent of AIDS. The court may direct the child to undergo the procedure or test on the court's own motion or on the request of the victim of the delinquent conduct.

(b) If the child or another person who has the power to consent to medical treatment for the child refuses to submit voluntarily or consent to the procedure or test, the court shall require the child to submit to the procedure or test.

(c) The person performing the procedure or test shall make the test results available to the local health authority. The local health authority shall be required to notify the victim of the delinquent conduct and the person found to have engaged in the delinquent conduct of the test result.

(d) The state may not use the fact that a medical procedure or test was performed on a child under this section or use the results of the procedure or test in any proceeding arising out of the delinquent conduct.

(e) Testing under this section shall be conducted in accordance with written infectious disease control protocols adopted by the Texas Board of Health that clearly establish procedural guidelines that provide criteria for testing and that respect the rights of the child and the victim of the delinquent conduct.

(f) Nothing in this section allows a court to release a test result to anyone other than a person specifically authorized under this section. Section 81.103(d), Health and Safety Code, may not be construed to allow the disclosure of test results under this section except as provided by this section.

(Enacted by Acts 1993, 73rd Leg., ch. 811 (H.B. 2650), § 2, effective September 1, 1993.)

### Sec. 54.034. Limited Right to Appeal: Warning.

Before the court may accept a child's plea or stipulation of evidence in a proceeding held under this title, the court shall inform the child that if the court accepts the plea or stipulation and the court makes a disposition in accordance with the agreement between the state and the child regarding the disposition of the case, the child may not appeal an order of the court entered under Section 54.03, 54.04, or 54.05, unless:

(1) the court gives the child permission to appeal; or

(2) the appeal is based on a matter raised by written motion filed before the proceeding in which the child entered the plea or agreed to the stipulation of evidence.

(Enacted by Acts 1999, 76th Leg., ch. 74 (H.B. 251), § 1, effective September 1, 1999.)

## Sec. 54.04. Disposition Hearing.

(a) The disposition hearing shall be separate, distinct, and subsequent to the adjudication hearing. There is no right to a jury at the disposition hearing unless the child is in jeopardy of a determinate sentence under Subsection (d)(3) or (m), in which case, the child is entitled to a jury of 12 persons to determine the sentence, but only if the child so elects in writing before the commencement of the voir dire examination of the jury panel. If a finding of delinquent conduct is returned, the child may, with the consent of the attorney for the state, change the child's election of one who assesses the disposition.

(b) At the disposition hearing, the juvenile court, notwithstanding the Texas Rules of Evidence or Chapter 37, Code of Criminal Procedure, may consider written reports from probation officers, professional court employees, or professional consultants in addition to the testimony of witnesses. Prior to the disposition hearing, the court shall provide the attorney for the child with access to all written matter to be considered in disposition. The court may order counsel not to reveal items to the child or the child's parent, guardian, or guardian ad litem if such disclosure would materially harm the treatment and rehabilitation of the child or would substantially decrease the likelihood of receiving information from the same or similar sources in the future.

(c) No disposition may be made under this section unless the child is in need of rehabilitation or the protection of the public or the child requires that disposition be made. If the court or jury does not so find, the court shall dismiss the child and enter a final judgment without any disposition. No disposition placing the child on probation outside the child's home may be made under this section unless the court or jury finds that the child, in the child's home, cannot be provided the quality of care and level of support and supervision that the child needs to meet the conditions of the probation.

(d) If the court or jury makes the finding specified in Subsection (c) allowing the court to make a disposition in the case:

(1) the court or jury may, in addition to any order required or authorized under Section 54.041 or 54.042, place the child on probation on such reasonable and lawful terms as the court may determine:

(A) in the child's own home or in the custody of a relative or other fit person; or

(B) subject to the finding under Subsection (c) on the placement of the child outside the child's home, in:

(i) a suitable foster home;

(ii) a suitable public or private residential treatment facility licensed by a state governmental entity or exempted from licensure by state law, except a facility operated by the Texas Youth Commission; or

(iii) a suitable public or private postadjudication secure correctional facility that meets the requirements of Section 51.125, except a facility operated by the Texas Youth Commission;

(2) if the court or jury found at the conclusion of the adjudication hearing that the child engaged in delinquent conduct that violates a penal law of this state or the United States of the grade of felony and if the petition was not approved by the grand jury under Section 53.045, the court may commit the child to the Texas Youth Commission without a determinate sentence;

(3) if the court or jury found at the conclusion of the adjudication hearing that the child engaged in delinquent conduct that included a violation of a penal law listed in Section 53.045(a) and if the petition was approved by the grand jury under Section 53.045, the court or jury may sentence the child to commitment in the Texas Youth Commission with a possible transfer to the Texas Department of Criminal Justice for a term of:

(A) not more than 40 years if the conduct constitutes:

(i) a capital felony;

(ii) a felony of the first degree; or

(iii) an aggravated controlled substance felony;

(B) not more than 20 years if the conduct constitutes a felony of the second degree; or

(C) not more than 10 years if the conduct constitutes a felony of the third degree;

(4) the court may assign the child an appropriate sanction level and sanctions as provided by the assignment guidelines in Section 59.003; or

(5) if applicable, the court or jury may make a disposition under Subsection (m).

(e) The Texas Youth Commission shall accept a person properly committed to it by a juvenile court even though the person may be 17 years of age or older at the time of commitment.

(f) The court shall state specifically in the order its reasons for the disposition and shall furnish a copy of the order to the child. If the child is placed on probation, the terms of probation shall be written in the order.

(g) If the court orders a disposition under Subsection (d)(3) or (m) and there is an affirmative finding that the defendant used or exhibited a deadly weapon during the commission of the conduct or during immediate flight from commission of the conduct, the court shall enter the finding in the order. If there is an affirmative finding that the deadly weapon was a firearm, the court shall enter that finding in the order.

(h) At the conclusion of the dispositional hearing, the court shall inform the child of:

(1) the child's right to appeal, as required by Section 56.01; and

(2) the procedures for the sealing of the child's records under Section 58.003.

(i) If the court places the child on probation outside the child's home or commits the child to the Texas Youth Commission, the court:

(1) shall include in its order its determination that:

(A) it is in the child's best interests to be placed outside the child's home;

(B) reasonable efforts were made to prevent or eliminate the need for the child's removal from the home and to make it possible for the child to return to the child's home; and

(C) the child, in the child's home, cannot be provided the quality of care and level of support and supervision that the child needs to meet the conditions of probation; and

(2) may approve an administrative body to conduct permanency hearings pursuant to 42 U.S.C. Section 675 if required during the placement or commitment of the child.

(j) If the court or jury found that the child engaged in delinquent conduct that included a violation of a penal law of the grade of felony or jailable misdemeanor, the court:

(1) shall require that the child's thumbprint be affixed or attached to the order; and

(2) may require that a photograph of the child be attached to the order.

(k) Except as provided by Subsection (m), the period to which a court or jury may sentence a person to commitment to the Texas Youth Commission with a transfer to the Texas Department of Criminal Justice under Subsection (d)(3) applies without regard to whether the person has previously been adjudicated as having engaged in delinquent conduct.

(l) Except as provided by Subsection (q), a court or jury may place a child on probation under Subsection (d)(1) for any period, except that probation may not continue on or after the child's 18th birthday. Except as provided by Subsection (q), the court may, before the period of probation ends, extend the probation for any period, except that the probation may not extend to or after the child's 18th birthday.

(m) The court or jury may sentence a child adjudicated for habitual felony conduct as described by Section 51.031 to a term prescribed by Subsection (d)(3) and applicable to the conduct adjudicated in the pending case if:

(1) a petition was filed and approved by a grand jury under Section 53.045 alleging that the child engaged in habitual felony conduct; and

(2) the court or jury finds beyond a reasonable doubt that the allegation described by Subdivision (1) in the grand jury petition is true.

(n) A court may order a disposition of secure confinement of a status offender adjudicated for violating a valid court order only if:

(1) before the order is issued, the child received the full due process rights guaranteed by the Constitution of the United States or the Texas Constitution; and

(2) the juvenile probation department in a report authorized by Subsection (b):

(A) reviewed the behavior of the child and the circumstances under which the child was brought before the court;

(B) determined the reasons for the behavior that caused the child to be brought before the court; and

(C) determined that all dispositions, including treatment, other than placement in a secure detention facility or secure correctional facility, have been exhausted or are clearly inappropriate.

(o) In a disposition under this title:

(1) a status offender may not, under any circumstances, be committed to the Texas Youth Commission for engaging in conduct that

would not, under state or local law, be a crime if committed by an adult;

(2) a status offender may not, under any circumstances other than as provided under Subsection (n), be placed in a post-adjudication secure correctional facility; and

(3) a child adjudicated for contempt of a county, justice, or municipal court order may not, under any circumstances, be placed in a post-adjudication secure correctional facility or committed to the Texas Youth Commission for that conduct.

(p) Except as provided by Subsection (*l*), a court that places a child on probation under Subsection (d)(1) for conduct described by Section 54.0405(b) and punishable as a felony shall specify a minimum probation period of two years.

(q) If a court or jury sentences a child to commitment in the Texas Youth Commission under Subsection (d)(3) for a term of not more than 10 years, the court or jury may place the child on probation under Subsection (d)(1) as an alternative to making the disposition under Subsection (d)(3). The court shall prescribe the period of probation ordered under this subsection for a term of not more than 10 years. The court may, before the sentence of probation expires, extend the probationary period under Section 54.05, except that the sentence of probation and any extension may not exceed 10 years. The court may, before the child's 19th birthday, discharge the child from the sentence of probation. If a sentence of probation ordered under this subsection and any extension of probation ordered under Section 54.05 will continue after the child's 19th birthday, the court shall discharge the child from the sentence of probation on the child's 19th birthday unless the court transfers the child to an appropriate district court under Section 54.051.

(r) If the judge orders a disposition under this section and there is an affirmative finding that the victim or intended victim was younger than 17 years of age at the time of the conduct, the judge shall enter the finding in the order.

(s), (t) [Repealed by Acts 2007, 80th Leg., ch. 263 (S.B. 103), § 64(1), effective June 8, 2007.]

(u) For the purposes of disposition under Subsection (d)(2), delinquent conduct that violates a penal law of this state of the grade of felony does not include conduct that violates a lawful order of a county, municipal, justice, or juvenile court under circumstances that would constitute contempt of that court.

(v) If the judge orders a disposition under this section for delinquent conduct based on a viola-

tion of an offense, on the motion of the attorney representing the state the judge shall make an affirmative finding of fact and enter the affirmative finding in the papers in the case if the judge determines that, regardless of whether the conduct at issue is the subject of the prosecution or part of the same criminal episode as the conduct that is the subject of the prosecution, a victim in the trial:

(1) is or has been a victim of a severe form of trafficking in persons, as defined by 22 U.S.C. Section 7102(8); or

(2) has suffered substantial physical or mental abuse as a result of having been a victim of criminal activity described by 8 U.S.C. Section 1101(a)(15)(U)(iii).

(w) That part of the papers in the case containing an affirmative finding under Subsection (v):

(1) must include specific information identifying the victim, as available;

(2) may not include information identifying the victim's location; and

(3) is confidential, unless written consent for the release of the affirmative finding is obtained from the victim or, if the victim is younger than 18 years of age, the victim's parent or guardian.

(x) A child may be detained in an appropriate detention facility following disposition of the child's case under Subsection (d) or (m) pending:

(1) transportation of the child to the ordered placement; and

(2) the provision of medical or other health care services for the child that may be advisable before transportation, including health care services for children in the late term of pregnancy.

(y) A juvenile court conducting a hearing under this section involving a child for whom the Department of Family and Protective Services has been appointed managing conservator may communicate with the court having continuing jurisdiction over the child before the disposition hearing. The juvenile court may allow the parties to the suit affecting the parent-child relationship in which the Department of Family and Protective Services is a party to participate in the communication under this subsection.

(Enacted by Acts 1973, 63rd Leg., ch. 544 (S.B. 111), § 1, effective September 1, 1973; am. Acts 1975, 64th Leg., ch. 693 (S.B. 247), § 23, effective September 1, 1975; am. Acts 1981, 67th Leg., ch. 394 (S.B. 269), § 1, effective August 31, 1981; am. Acts 1983, 68th Leg., ch. 44 (S.B. 422), art. 1, § 3, effective April 26, 1983; am. Acts 1983, 68th Leg., ch. 565 (S.B. 669), § 2, effective September 1, 1983; am. Acts 1987, 70th Leg., ch. 385 (H.B. 682), § 9, effective September 1, 1987; am. Acts 1987, 70th Leg., ch. 1052 (S.B. 298), § 6.11, effective September 1, 1987; am. Acts 1989, 71st Leg., ch. 2 (S.B. 221), § 16.01(17), effective August 28, 1989; am. Acts 1989, 71st Leg., ch. 80 (S.B. 39), § 1, effective September 1, 1989; am. Acts 1991, 72nd Leg., ch. 557 (H.B. 653), § 2, effective September 1, 1991; am. Acts 1991, 72nd Leg., ch. 574 (S.B. 303), § 2, effective September 1, 1991; am. Acts 1991, 72nd Leg., ch. 784 (H.B. 434), § 8, effective September 1, 1991; am. Acts 1993, 73rd Leg., ch. 1048 (H.B. 1731), § 1, effective September 1, 1993; am. Acts 1995, 74th Leg., ch. 262 (H.B. 327), § 38, effective January 1, 1996; am. Acts 1997, 75th Leg., ch. 669 (S.B. 1232), § 2, effective September 1, 1997; am. Acts 1997, 75th Leg., ch. 1086 (H.B. 1550), § 11, effective September 1, 1997; am. Acts 1999, 76th Leg., ch. 1193 (S.B. 399), § 9, effective September 1, 1999; am. Acts 1999, 76th Leg., ch. 1415 (H.B. 2145), § 19, effective September 1, 1999; am. Acts 1999, 76th Leg., ch. 1448 (H.B. 2947), § 1, effective September 1, 1999; am. Acts 1999, 76th Leg., ch. 1477 (H.B. 3517), § 10, effective September 1, 1999; am. Acts 2001, 77th Leg., ch. 1297 (H.B. 1118), § 23, effective September 1, 2001; am. Acts 2001, 77th Leg., ch. 1420 (H.B. 2812), § 5.001, effective September 1, 2001; am. Acts 2003, 78th Leg., ch. 137 (S.B. 358), § 13, effective September 1, 2003; am. Acts 2007, 80th Leg., ch. 263 (S.B. 103), §§ 7, 64(1), effective June 8, 2007; am. Acts 2007, 80th Leg., ch. 849 (H.B. 1121), § 3, effective June 15, 2007; am. Acts 2007, 80th Leg., ch. 908 (H.B. 2884), § 11, effective September 1, 2007; am. Acts 2009, 81st Leg., ch. 87 (S.B. 1969), § 27.001(13), effective September 1, 2009; am. Acts 2009, 81st Leg., ch. 108 (H.B. 1629), § 2, effective May 23, 2009; am. Acts 2011, 82nd Leg., ch. 438 (S.B. 1208), § 2, effective September 1, 2011.)

### Sec. 54.0401. Community-Based Programs.

(a) This section applies only to a county that has a population of at least 335,000.

(b) A juvenile court of a county to which this section applies may require a child who is found to have engaged in delinquent conduct that violates a penal law of the grade of misdemeanor and for whom the requirements of Subsection (c)

are met to participate in a community-based program administered by the county's juvenile board.

(c) A juvenile court of a county to which this section applies may make a disposition under Subsection (b) for delinquent conduct that violates a penal law of the grade of misdemeanor:

(1) if:

(A) the child has been adjudicated as having engaged in delinquent conduct violating a penal law of the grade of misdemeanor on at least two previous occasions;

(B) of the previous adjudications, the conduct that was the basis for one of the adjudications occurred after the date of another previous adjudication; and

(C) the conduct that is the basis of the current adjudication occurred after the date of at least two previous adjudications; or

(2) if:

(A) the child has been adjudicated as having engaged in delinquent conduct violating a penal law of the grade of felony on at least one previous occasion; and

(B) the conduct that is the basis of the current adjudication occurred after the date of that previous adjudication.

(d) The Texas Juvenile Probation Commission shall establish guidelines for the implementation of community-based programs described by this section. The juvenile board of each county to which this section applies shall implement a community-based program that complies with those guidelines.

(e) The Texas Juvenile Probation Commission shall provide grants to selected juvenile boards to assist with the implementation of a system of community-based programs under this section.

(f) [Expired pursuant to Acts 2007, 80th Leg., ch. 263 (S.B. 103), § 8, effective February 1, 2009].

(Enacted by Acts 2007, 80th Leg., ch. 263 (S.B. 103), § 8, effective June 8, 2007.)

### Sec. 54.0402. Dispositional Order for Failure to Attend School.

A dispositional order regarding conduct under Section 51.03(b)(2) is effective for the period specified by the court in the order but may not extend beyond the 180th day after the date of the order or beyond the end of the school year in which the order was entered, whichever period is longer.

(Enacted by Acts 2011, 82nd Leg., ch. 1098 (S.B. 1489), § 4, effective September 1, 2011.)

### Sec. 54.0404. Electronic Transmission of Certain Visual Material Depicting Minor: Educational Programs.

(a) If a child is found to have engaged in conduct indicating a need for supervision described by Section 51.03(b)(7), the juvenile court may enter an order requiring the child to attend and successfully complete an educational program described by Section 37.218, Education Code, or another equivalent educational program.

(b) A juvenile court that enters an order under Subsection (a) shall require the child or the child's parent or other person responsible for the child's support to pay the cost of attending an educational program under Subsection (a) if the court determines that the child, parent, or other person is financially able to make payment.

(Enacted by Acts 2011, 82nd Leg., ch. 1322 (S.B. 407), § 18, effective September 1, 2011.)

### Sec. 54.0405. Child Placed on Probation for Conduct Constituting Sexual Offense.

(a) If a court or jury makes a disposition under Section 54.04 in which a child described by Subsection (b) is placed on probation, the court:

  (1) may require as a condition of probation that the child:

    (A) attend psychological counseling sessions for sex offenders as provided by Subsection (e); and

    (B) submit to a polygraph examination as provided by Subsection (f) for purposes of evaluating the child's treatment progress; and

  (2) shall require as a condition of probation that the child:

    (A) register under Chapter 62, Code of Criminal Procedure; and

    (B) submit a blood sample or other specimen to the Department of Public Safety under Subchapter G, Chapter 411, Government Code, for the purpose of creating a DNA record of the child, unless the child has already submitted the required specimen under other state law.

(b) This section applies to a child placed on probation for conduct constituting an offense for which the child is required to register as a sex offender under Chapter 62, Code of Criminal Procedure.

(c) Psychological counseling required as a condition of probation under Subsection (a) must be with an individual or organization that:

  (1) provides sex offender treatment or counseling;

  (2) is specified by the local juvenile probation department supervising the child; and

  (3) meets minimum standards of counseling established by the local juvenile probation department.

(d) A polygraph examination required as a condition of probation under Subsection (a) must be administered by an individual who is:

  (1) specified by the local juvenile probation department supervising the child; and

  (2) licensed as a polygraph examiner under Chapter 1703, Occupations Code.

(e) A local juvenile probation department that specifies a sex offender treatment provider under Subsection (c) to provide counseling to a child shall:

  (1) establish with the cooperation of the treatment provider the date, time, and place of the first counseling session between the child and the treatment provider;

  (2) notify the child and the treatment provider, not later than the 21st day after the date the order making the disposition placing the child on probation under Section 54.04 becomes final, of the date, time, and place of the first counseling session between the child and the treatment provider; and

  (3) require the treatment provider to notify the department immediately if the child fails to attend any scheduled counseling session.

(f) A local juvenile probation department that specifies a polygraph examiner under Subsection (d) to administer a polygraph examination to a child shall arrange for a polygraph examination to be administered to the child:

  (1) not later than the 60th day after the date the child attends the first counseling session established under Subsection (e); and

  (2) after the initial polygraph examination, as required by Subdivision (1), on the request of the treatment provider specified under Subsection (c).

(g) A court that requires as a condition of probation that a child attend psychological counseling under Subsection (a) may order the parent or guardian of the child to:

  (1) attend four sessions of instruction with an individual or organization specified by the court relating to:

    (A) sexual offenses;

(B) family communication skills;

(C) sex offender treatment;

(D) victims' rights;

(E) parental supervision; and

(F) appropriate sexual behavior; and

(2) during the period the child attends psychological counseling, participate in monthly treatment groups conducted by the child's treatment provider relating to the child's psychological counseling.

(h) A court that orders a parent or guardian of a child to attend instructional sessions and participate in treatment groups under Subsection (g) shall require:

(1) the individual or organization specified by the court under Subsection (g) to notify the court immediately if the parent or guardian fails to attend any scheduled instructional session; and

(2) the child's treatment provider specified under Subsection (c) to notify the court immediately if the parent or guardian fails to attend a session in which the parent or guardian is required to participate in a scheduled treatment group.

(i) A court that requires as a condition of probation that a child attend psychological counseling under Subsection (a) may, before the date the probation period ends, extend the probation for any additional period necessary to complete the required counseling as determined by the treatment provider, except that the probation may not be extended to a date after the date of the child's 18th birthday, or 19th birthday if the child is placed on determinate sentence probation under Section 54.04(q).

(Enacted by Acts 1997, 75th Leg., ch. 669 (S.B. 1232), § 1, effective September 1, 1997; am. Acts 2001, 77th Leg., ch. 211 (S.B. 1380), § 13, effective September 1, 2001; Acts 2001, 77th Leg., ch. 1420 (H.B. 2812), § 14.743, effective September 1, 2001; am. Acts 2011, 82nd Leg., ch. 438 (S.B. 1208), § 3, effective September 1, 2011.)

## Sec. 54.0406. Child Placed on Probation for Conduct Involving a Handgun.

(a) If a court or jury places a child on probation under Section 54.04(d) for conduct that violates a penal law that includes as an element of the offense the possession, carrying, using, or exhibiting of a handgun, as defined by Section 46.01, Penal Code, and if at the adjudication hearing the court or jury affirmatively finds that the child personally possessed, carried, used, or exhibited the handgun, the court shall require as a condition of probation that the child, not later than the 30th day after the date the court places the child on probation, notify the juvenile probation officer who is supervising the child of the manner in which the child acquired the handgun, including the date and place of and any person involved in the acquisition.

(b) On receipt of information described by Subsection (a), a juvenile probation officer shall promptly notify the appropriate local law enforcement agency of the information.

(c) Information provided by a child to a juvenile probation officer as required by Subsection (a) and any other information derived from that information may not be used as evidence against the child in any juvenile or criminal proceeding. (Enacted by Acts 1999, 76th Leg., ch. 1446 (H.B. 2869), § 1, effective September 1, 1999.)

## Sec. 54.0407. Cruelty to Animals: Counseling Required.

If a child is found to have engaged in delinquent conduct constituting an offense under Section 42.09 or 42.092, Penal Code, the juvenile court shall order the child to participate in psychological counseling for a period to be determined by the court.

(Enacted by Acts 2001, 77th Leg., ch. 450 (H.B. 653), § 2, effective September 1, 2001; am. Acts 2007, 80th Leg., ch. 886 (H.B. 2328), § 3, effective September 1, 2007.)

## Sec. 54.0408. Referral of Child Exiting Probation to Mental Health or Mental Retardation Authority.

A juvenile probation officer shall refer a child who has been determined to have a mental illness or mental retardation to an appropriate local mental health or mental retardation authority at least three months before the child is to complete the child's juvenile probation term unless the child is currently receiving treatment from the local mental health or mental retardation authority of the county in which the child resides.

(Enacted by Acts 2005, 79th Leg., ch. 949 (H.B. 1575), § 14, effective September 1, 2005.)

## Sec. 54.0409. DNA Sample Required on Certain Felony Adjudications.

(a) This section applies only to conduct constituting the commission of a felony:

(1) that is listed in Section 3g(a)(1), Article 42.12, Code of Criminal Procedure; or

**Family Code**

(2) for which it is shown that a deadly weapon, as defined by Section 1.07, Penal Code, was used or exhibited during the commission of the conduct or during immediate flight from the commission of the conduct.

(b) If a court or jury makes a disposition under Section 54.04 in which a child is adjudicated as having engaged in conduct constituting the commission of a felony to which this section applies and the child is placed on probation, the court shall require as a condition of probation that the child provide a DNA sample under Subchapter G, Chapter 411, Government Code, for the purpose of creating a DNA record of the child, unless the child has already submitted the required sample under other state law.

(Enacted by Acts 2009, 81st Leg., ch. 1209 (S.B. 727), § 3, effective September 1, 2009.)

## Sec. 54.041.  Orders Affecting Parents and Others.

(a) When a child has been found to have engaged in delinquent conduct or conduct indicating a need for supervision and the juvenile court has made a finding that the child is in need of rehabilitation or that the protection of the public or the child requires that disposition be made, the juvenile court, on notice by any reasonable method to all persons affected, may:

(1) order any person found by the juvenile court to have, by a wilful act or omission, contributed to, caused, or encouraged the child's delinquent conduct or conduct indicating a need for supervision to do any act that the juvenile court determines to be reasonable and necessary for the welfare of the child or to refrain from doing any act that the juvenile court determines to be injurious to the welfare of the child;

(2) enjoin all contact between the child and a person who is found to be a contributing cause of the child's delinquent conduct or conduct indicating a need for supervision;

(3) after notice and a hearing of all persons affected order any person living in the same household with the child to participate in social or psychological counseling to assist in the rehabilitation of the child and to strengthen the child's family environment; or

(4) after notice and a hearing of all persons affected order the child's parent or other person responsible for the child's support to pay all or part of the reasonable costs of treatment programs in which the child is required to partic-

ipate during the period of probation if the court finds the child's parent or person responsible for the child's support is able to pay the costs.

(b) If a child is found to have engaged in delinquent conduct or conduct indicating a need for supervision arising from the commission of an offense in which property damage or loss or personal injury occurred, the juvenile court, on notice to all persons affected and on hearing, may order the child or a parent to make full or partial restitution to the victim of the offense. The program of restitution must promote the rehabilitation of the child, be appropriate to the age and physical, emotional, and mental abilities of the child, and not conflict with the child's schooling. When practicable and subject to court supervision, the court may approve a restitution program based on a settlement between the child and the victim of the offense. An order under this subsection may provide for periodic payments by the child or a parent of the child for the period specified in the order but except as provided by Subsection (h), that period may not extend past the date of the 18th birthday of the child or past the date the child is no longer enrolled in an accredited secondary school in a program leading toward a high school diploma, whichever date is later.

(c) Restitution under this section is cumulative of any other remedy allowed by law and may be used in addition to other remedies; except that a victim of an offense is not entitled to receive more than actual damages under a juvenile court order.

(d) A person subject to an order proposed under Subsection (a) of this section is entitled to a hearing on the order before the order is entered by the court.

(e) An order made under this section may be enforced as provided by Section 54.07 of this code.

(f) If a child is found to have engaged in conduct indicating a need for supervision described under Section 51.03(b)(2) or (g), the court may order the child's parents or guardians to attend a program described by Section 25.093(f), Education Code, if a program is available.

(g) On a finding by the court that a child's parents or guardians have made a reasonable good faith effort to prevent the child from engaging in delinquent conduct or engaging in conduct indicating a need for supervision and that, despite the parents' or guardians' efforts, the child continues to engage in such conduct, the court shall waive any requirement for restitution that may be imposed on a parent under this section.

(h) If the juvenile court places the child on probation in a determinate sentence proceeding initiated under Section 53.045 and transfers supervision on the child's 19th birthday to a district court for placement on community supervision, the district court shall require the payment of any unpaid restitution as a condition of the community supervision. The liability of the child's parent for restitution may not be extended by transfer to a district court for supervision.

(Enacted by Acts 1975, 64th Leg., ch. 693 (S.B. 247), § 18, effective September 1, 1975; am. Acts 1979, 66th Leg., ch. 154 (H.B. 244), § 2, effective September 1, 1979; am. Acts 1983, 68th Leg., ch. 110 (S.B. 99), § 1, effective August 29, 1983; am. Acts 1983, 68th Leg., ch. 565 (S.B. 669), § 3, effective September 1, 1983; am. Acts 1989, 71st Leg., ch. 1170 (H.B. 969), § 3, effective June 16, 1989; am. Acts 1995, 74th Leg., ch. 262 (H.B. 327), § 39, effective January 1, 1996; am. Acts 1997, 75th Leg., ch. 165 (S.B. 898), § 6.09, effective September 1, 1997; am. Acts 2001, 77th Leg., ch. 1297 (H.B. 1118), § 24, effective September 1, 2001; am. Acts 2001, 77th Leg., ch. 1514 (S.B. 1432), § 15, effective September 1, 2001; am. Acts 2003, 78th Leg., ch. 283 (H.B. 2319), § 19, effective September 1, 2003; am. Acts 2011, 82nd Leg., ch. 438 (S.B. 1208), § 4, effective September 1, 2011.)

## Sec. 54.0411. Juvenile Probation Diversion Fund.

(a) If a disposition hearing is held under Section 54.04 of this code, the juvenile court, after giving the child, parent, or other person responsible for the child's support a reasonable opportunity to be heard, shall order the child, parent, or other person, if financially able to do so, to pay a fee as costs of court of $20.

(b) Orders for the payment of fees under this section may be enforced as provided by Section 54.07 of this code.

(c) An officer collecting costs under this section shall keep separate records of the funds collected as costs under this section and shall deposit the funds in the county treasury.

(d) Each officer collecting court costs under this section shall file the reports required under Article 103.005, Code of Criminal Procedure. If no funds due as costs under this section have been collected in any quarter, the report required for each quarter shall be filed in the regular manner, and the report must state that no funds due under this section were collected.

(e) The custodian of the county treasury may deposit the funds collected under this section in interest-bearing accounts. The custodian shall keep records of the amount of funds on deposit collected under this section and not later than the last day of the month following each calendar quarter shall send to the comptroller of public accounts the funds collected under this section during the preceding quarter. A county may retain 10 percent of the funds as a service fee and may retain the interest accrued on the funds if the custodian of a county treasury keeps records of the amount of funds on deposit collected under this section and remits the funds to the comptroller within the period prescribed under this subsection.

(f) Funds collected are subject to audit by the comptroller and funds expended are subject to audit by the State Auditor.

(g) The comptroller shall deposit the funds in a special fund to be known as the juvenile probation diversion fund.

(h) The legislature shall determine and appropriate the necessary amount from the juvenile probation diversion fund to the Texas Juvenile Probation Commission for the purchase of services the commission considers necessary for the diversion of any juvenile who is at risk of commitment to the Texas Youth Commission. The Texas Juvenile Probation Commission shall develop guidelines for the use of the fund. The commission may not purchase the services if a person responsible for the child's support or a local juvenile probation department is financially able to provide the services.

(Enacted by Acts 1987, 70th Leg., ch. 1040 (S.B. 17), § 23, effective September 1, 1987; am. Acts 1989, 71st Leg., ch. 347 (S.B. 1085), § 8, effective October 1, 1989.)

## Sec. 54.042. License Suspension.

(a) A juvenile court, in a disposition hearing under Section 54.04, shall:

(1) order the Department of Public Safety to suspend a child's driver's license or permit, or if the child does not have a license or permit, to deny the issuance of a license or permit to the child if the court finds that the child has engaged in conduct that:

(A) violates a law of this state enumerated in Section 521.342(a), Transportation Code; or

(B) violates a penal law of this state or the United States, an element or elements of which involve a severe form of trafficking in persons, as defined by 22 U.S.C. Section 7102; or

(2) notify the Department of Public Safety of the adjudication, if the court finds that the child has engaged in conduct that violates a law of this state enumerated in Section 521.372(a), Transportation Code.

(b) A juvenile court, in a disposition hearing under Section 54.04, may order the Department of Public Safety to suspend a child's driver's license or permit or, if the child does not have a license or permit, to deny the issuance of a license or permit to the child, if the court finds that the child has engaged in conduct that violates Section 28.08, Penal Code.

(c) The order under Subsection (a)(1) shall specify a period of suspension or denial of 365 days.

(d) The order under Subsection (b) shall specify a period of suspension or denial:

(1) not to exceed 365 days; or

(2) of 365 days if the court finds the child has been previously adjudicated as having engaged in conduct violating Section 28.08, Penal Code.

(e) A child whose driver's license or permit has been suspended or denied pursuant to this section may, if the child is otherwise eligible for, and fulfils [fulfills] the requirements for issuance of, a provisional driver's license or permit under Chapter 521, Transportation Code, apply for and receive an occupational license in accordance with the provisions of Subchapter L of that chapter.

(f) A juvenile court, in a disposition hearing under Section 54.04, may order the Department of Public Safety to suspend a child's driver's license or permit or, if the child does not have a license or permit, to deny the issuance of a license or permit to the child for a period not to exceed 12 months if the court finds that the child has engaged in conduct in need of supervision or delinquent conduct other than the conduct described by Subsection (a).

(g) A juvenile court that places a child on probation under Section 54.04 may require as a reasonable condition of the probation that if the child violates the probation, the court may order the Department of Public Safety to suspend the child's driver's license or permit or, if the child does not have a license or permit, to deny the issuance of a license or permit to the child for a period not to exceed 12 months. The court may make this order if a child that is on probation under this condition violates the probation. A

suspension under this subsection is cumulative of any other suspension under this section.

(h) If a child is adjudicated for conduct that violates Section 49.04, 49.07, or 49.08, Penal Code, and if any conduct on which that adjudication is based is a ground for a driver's license suspension under Chapter 524 or 724, Transportation Code, each of the suspensions shall be imposed. The court imposing a driver's license suspension under this section shall credit a period of suspension imposed under Chapter 524 or 724, Transportation Code, toward the period of suspension required under this section, except that if the child was previously adjudicated for conduct that violates Section 49.04, 49.07, or 49.08, Penal Code, credit may not be given.

(Enacted by Acts 1983, 68th Leg., ch. 303 (S.B. 1), § 25, effective January 1, 1984; am. Acts 1985, 69th Leg., ch. 629 (S.B. 550), § 1, effective September 1, 1985; am. Acts 1991, 72nd Leg., ch. 14 (S.B. 404), § 284(42), effective September 1, 1991; am. Acts 1991, 72nd Leg., ch. 784 (H.B. 434), § 7, effective September 1, 1991; am. Acts 1993, 73rd Leg., ch. 491 (S.B. 387), § 3, effective June 15, 1993; am. Acts 1995, 74th Leg., ch. 76 (S.B. 959), § 14.32, effective September 1, 1995; am. Acts 1995, 74th Leg., ch. 262 (H.B. 327), § 40, effective January 1, 1996; am. Acts 1997, 75th Leg., ch. 165 (S.B. 898), § 30.183, effective September 1, 1997; am. Acts 1997, 75th Leg., ch. 593 (S.B. 758), § 3, effective September 1, 1997; am. Acts 1997, 75th Leg., ch. 1013 (S.B. 35), § 17, effective September 1, 1997; am. Acts 1999, 76th Leg., ch. 62 (S.B. 1368), § 19.01(18), effective September 1, 1999; am. Acts 2003, 78th Leg., ch. 283 (H.B. 2319), § 20, effective September 1, 2003; am. Acts 2009, 81st Leg., ch. 1146 (H.B. 2730), § 18.02, effective September 1, 2009.)

### Sec. 54.043.  Monitoring School Attendance.

If the court places a child on probation under Section 54.04(d) and requires as a condition of probation that the child attend school, the probation officer charged with supervising the child shall monitor the child's school attendance and report to the court if the child is voluntarily absent from school.

(Enacted by Acts 1993, 73rd Leg., ch. 347 (S.B. 7), § 6.02, effective September 1, 1993.)

### Sec. 54.044.  Community Service.

(a) If the court places a child on probation under Section 54.04(d), the court shall require as a condition of probation that the child work a specified number of hours at a community service project approved by the court and designated by the juvenile probation department as provided by Subsection (e), unless the court determines and enters a finding on the order placing the child on probation that:

    (1) the child is physically or mentally incapable of participating in the project;

    (2) participating in the project will be a hardship on the child or the family of the child; or

    (3) the child has shown good cause that community service should not be required.

(b) The court may also order under this section that the child's parent perform community service with the child.

(c) The court shall order that the child and the child's parent perform a total of not more than 500 hours of community service under this section.

(d) A municipality or county that establishes a program to assist children and their parents in rendering community service under this section may purchase insurance policies protecting the municipality or county against claims brought by a person other than the child or the child's parent for a cause of action that arises from an act of the child or parent while rendering community service. The municipality or county is not liable under this section to the extent that damages are recoverable under a contract of insurance or under a plan of self-insurance authorized by statute. The liability of the municipality or county for a cause of action that arises from an action of the child or the child's parent while rendering community service may not exceed $100,000 to a single person and $300,000 for a single occurrence in the case of personal injury or death, and $10,000 for a single occurrence of property damage. Liability may not extend to punitive or exemplary damages. This subsection does not waive a defense, immunity, or jurisdictional bar available to the municipality or county or its officers or employees, nor shall this section be construed to waive, repeal, or modify any provision of Chapter 101, Civil Practice and Remedies Code.

(e) For the purposes of this section, a court may submit to the juvenile probation department a list of organizations or projects approved by the court for community service. The juvenile probation department may:

    (1) designate an organization or project for community service only from the list submitted by the court; and

    (2) reassign or transfer a child to a different organization or project on the list submitted by the court under this subsection without court approval.

(f) A person subject to an order proposed under Subsection (a) or (b) is entitled to a hearing on the order before the order is entered by the court.

(g) On a finding by the court that a child's parents or guardians have made a reasonable good faith effort to prevent the child from engaging in delinquent conduct or engaging in conduct indicating a need for supervision and that, despite the parents' or guardians' efforts, the child continues to engage in such conduct, the court shall waive any requirement for community service that may be imposed on a parent under this section.

(h) An order made under this section may be enforced as provided by Section 54.07.

(i) In a disposition hearing under Section 54.04 in which the court finds that a child engaged in conduct violating Section 521.453, Transportation Code, the court, in addition to any other order authorized under this title and if the court is located in a municipality or county that has established a community service program, may order the child to perform eight hours of community service as a condition of probation under Section 54.04(d) unless the child is shown to have previously engaged in conduct violating Section 521.453, Transportation Code, in which case the court may order the child to perform 12 hours of community service.

(Enacted by Acts 1995, 74th Leg., ch. 262 (H.B. 327), § 41, effective January 1, 1996; am. Acts 1997, 75th Leg., ch. 1358 (H.B. 677), § 2, effective September 1, 1997; am. Acts 2001, 77th Leg., ch. 1297 (H.B. 1118), § 25, effective September 1, 2001.)

## Sec. 54.045. Admission of Unadjudicated Conduct.

(a) During a disposition hearing under Section 54.04, a child may:

    (1) admit having engaged in delinquent conduct or conduct indicating a need for supervision for which the child has not been adjudicated; and

    (2) request the court to take the admitted conduct into account in the disposition of the child.

(b) If the prosecuting attorney agrees in writing, the court may take the admitted conduct into account in the disposition of the child.

(c) A court may take into account admitted conduct over which exclusive venue lies in another county only if the court obtains the written permission of the prosecuting attorney for that county.

(d) A child may not be adjudicated by any court for having engaged in conduct taken into account under this section, except that, if the conduct taken into account included conduct over which exclusive venue lies in another county and the written permission of the prosecuting attorney of that county was not obtained, the child may be adjudicated for that conduct, but the child's admission under this section may not be used against the child in the adjudication.
(Enacted by Acts 1995, 74th Leg., ch. 262 (H.B. 327), § 41, effective January 1, 1996.)

## Sec. 54.046.  Conditions of Probation for Damaging Property with Graffiti.

(a) If a juvenile court places on probation under Section 54.04(d) a child adjudicated as having engaged in conduct in violation of Section 28.08, Penal Code, in addition to other conditions of probation, the court:

(1)  shall order the child to:

(A)  reimburse the owner of the property for the cost of restoring the property; or

(B)  with consent of the owner of the property, restore the property by removing or painting over any markings made by the child on the property; and

(2)  if the child made markings on public property, a street sign, or an official traffic-control device in violation of Section 28.08, Penal Code, shall order the child to:

(A)  make to the political subdivision that owns the public property or erected the street sign or official traffic-control device restitution in an amount equal to the lesser of the cost to the political subdivision of replacing or restoring the public property, street sign, or official traffic-control device; or

(B)  with the consent of the political subdivision, restore the public property, street sign, or official traffic-control device by removing or painting over any markings made by the child on the property, sign, or device.

(a-1)  For purposes of Subsection (a), "official traffic-control device" has the meaning assigned by Section 541.304, Transportation Code.

(b)  In addition to a condition imposed under Subsection (a), the court may require the child as a condition of probation to attend a class with instruction in self-responsibility and empathy for a victim of an offense conducted by a local juvenile probation department.

(c)  If a juvenile court orders a child to make restitution under Subsection (a) and the child, child's parent, or other person responsible for the child's support is financially unable to make the restitution, the court may order the child to perform a specific number of hours of community service, in addition to the hours required under Subsection (d), to satisfy the restitution.

(d)  If a juvenile court places on probation under Section 54.04(d) a child adjudicated as having engaged in conduct in violation of Section 28.08, Penal Code, in addition to other conditions of probation, the court shall order the child to perform:

(1)  at least 15 hours of community service if the amount of pecuniary loss resulting from the conduct is $50 or more but less than $500; or

(2)  at least 30 hours of community service if the amount of pecuniary loss resulting from the conduct is $500 or more.

(e)  The juvenile court shall direct a child ordered to make restitution under this section to deliver the amount or property due as restitution to a juvenile probation department for transfer to the owner. The juvenile probation department shall notify the juvenile court when the child has delivered the full amount of restitution ordered.
(Enacted by Acts 1997, 75th Leg., ch. 593 (S.B. 758), § 7, effective September 1, 1997; am. Acts 2007, 80th Leg., ch. 1053 (H.B. 2151), § 4, effective September 1, 2007; am. Acts 2009, 81st Leg., ch. 639 (H.B. 1633), § 3, effective September 1, 2009.)

## Sec. 54.0461.  Payment of Juvenile Delinquency Prevention Fees.

(a)  If a child is adjudicated as having engaged in delinquent conduct that violates Section 28.08, Penal Code, the juvenile court shall order the child, parent, or other person responsible for the child's support to pay to the court a $50 juvenile delinquency prevention fee as a cost of court.

(b)  The court shall deposit fees received under this section to the credit of the county juvenile delinquency prevention fund provided for under Article 102.0171, Code of Criminal Procedure.

(c)  If the court finds that a child, parent, or other person responsible for the child's support is unable to pay the juvenile delinquency prevention fee required under Subsection (a), the court shall enter into the child's case records a statement of that finding. The court may waive a fee under this section only if the court makes the finding under this subsection.

(Enacted by Acts 1999, 76th Leg., ch. 174 (H.B. 1063), § 1, effective September 1, 1999; am. Acts 2003, 78th Leg., ch. 601 (H.B. 1828), § 3, effective September 1, 2003; am. Acts 2007, 80th Leg., ch. 1053 (H.B. 2151), § 5, effective September 1, 2007.)

## Sec. 54.0462. Payment of Fees for Offenses Requiring DNA Testing.

(a) If a child is adjudicated as having engaged in delinquent conduct that constitutes the commission of a felony and the provision of a DNA sample is required under Section 54.0409 or other law, the juvenile court shall order the child, parent, or other person responsible for the child's support to pay to the court as a cost of court:

(1) a $50 fee if the disposition of the case includes a commitment to a facility operated by or under contract with the Texas Youth Commission; and

(2) a $34 fee if the disposition of the case does not include a commitment described by Subdivision (1) and the child is required to submit a DNA sample under Section 54.0409 or other law.

(b) The clerk of the court shall transfer to the comptroller any funds received under this section. The comptroller shall credit the funds to the Department of Public Safety to help defray the cost of any analyses performed on DNA samples provided by children with respect to whom a court cost is collected under this section.

(c) If the court finds that a child, parent, or other person responsible for the child's support is unable to pay the fee required under Subsection (a), the court shall enter into the child's case records a statement of that finding. The court may waive a fee under this section only if the court makes the finding under this subsection.

(Enacted by Acts 2009, 81st Leg., ch. 1209 (S.B. 727), § 4, effective September 1, 2009.)

## Sec. 54.047. Alcohol-Related Offense.

If the court or jury finds at an adjudication hearing for a child that the child engaged in conduct indicating a need for supervision or delinquent conduct that violates the alcohol-related offenses in Section 106.02, 106.025, 106.04, 106.05, or 106.07, Alcoholic Beverage Code, or Section 49.02, Penal Code, the court shall, subject to a finding under Section 54.04(c), order, in

addition to any other order authorized by this title, that, in the manner provided by Section 106.071(d), Alcoholic Beverage Code:

(1) the child perform community service; and

(2) the child's driver's license or permit be suspended or that the child be denied issuance of a driver's license or permit.

(Enacted by Acts 1997, 75th Leg., ch. 1013 (S.B. 35), § 18, effective September 1, 1997; am. Acts 1999, 76th Leg., ch. 62 (S.B. 1368), § 19.01(19), effective September 1, 1999 (renumbered from Sec. 54.046).)

## Sec. 54.048. Restitution.

(a) A juvenile court, in a disposition hearing under Section 54.04, may order restitution to be made by the child and the child's parents.

(b) This section applies without regard to whether the petition in the case contains a plea for restitution.

(Enacted by Acts 2001, 77th Leg., ch. 1297 (H.B. 1118), § 26, effective September 1, 2001.)

## Sec. 54.0481. Restitution for Damaging Property with Graffiti.

(a) A juvenile court, in a disposition hearing under Section 54.04 regarding a child who has been adjudicated to have engaged in delinquent conduct that violates Section 28.08, Penal Code:

(1) may order the child or a parent or other person responsible for the child's support to make restitution by:

(A) reimbursing the owner of the property for the cost of restoring the property; or

(B) with the consent of the owner of the property, personally restoring the property by removing or painting over any markings the child made; and

(2) if the child made markings on public property, a street sign, or an official traffic-control device in violation of Section 28.08, Penal Code, may order the child or a parent or other person responsible for the child's support to:

(A) make to the political subdivision that owns the public property or erected the street sign or official traffic-control device restitution in an amount equal to the lesser of the cost to the political subdivision of replacing or restoring the public property, street sign, or official traffic-control device; or

(B) with the consent of the political subdivision, restore the public property, street sign, or official traffic-control device by removing or painting over any markings made by the child on the property, sign, or device.

(b) If a juvenile court orders a child to make restitution under Subsection (a) and the child, child's parent, or other person responsible for the child's support is financially unable to make the restitution, the court may order the child to perform a specific number of hours of community service to satisfy the restitution.

(c) For purposes of Subsection (a), "official traffic-control device" has the meaning assigned by Section 541.304, Transportation Code.

(Enacted by Acts 2007, 80th Leg., ch. 1053 (H.B. 2151), § 6, effective September 1, 2007.)

### Sec. 54.0482.   Treatment of Restitution Payments.

(a) A juvenile probation department that receives a payment to a victim as the result of a juvenile court order for restitution shall immediately:

(1) deposit the payment in an interest-bearing account in the county treasury; and

(2) notify the victim by certified mail, sent to the last known address of the victim, that a payment has been received.

(b) The juvenile probation department shall promptly remit the payment to a victim who has been notified under Subsection (a) and makes a claim for payment.

(c) On or before the fifth anniversary of the date the juvenile probation department receives a payment for a victim that is not claimed by the victim, the department shall make and document a good faith effort to locate and notify the victim that an unclaimed payment exists, including:

(1) confirming, if possible, the victim's most recent address with the Department of Public Safety; and

(2) making at least one additional certified mailing to the victim.

(d) A juvenile probation department satisfies the good faith requirement under Subsection (c) by sending by certified mail to the victim, during the period the child is required by the juvenile court order to make payments to the victim, a notice that the victim is entitled to an unclaimed payment.

(e) If a victim claims a payment on or before the fifth anniversary of the date on which the juvenile probation department mailed a notice to the victim under Subsection (a), the juvenile probation department shall pay the victim the amount of the original payment, less any interest earned while holding the payment.

(f) If a victim does not claim a payment on or before the fifth anniversary of the date on which the juvenile probation department mailed a notice to the victim under Subsection (a), the department:

(1) has no liability to the victim or anyone else in relation to the payment; and

(2) shall transfer the payment from the interest-bearing account to a special fund of the county treasury, the unclaimed juvenile restitution fund.

(g) The county may spend money in the unclaimed juvenile restitution fund only for the same purposes for which the county may spend juvenile state aid.

(Enacted by Acts 2007, 80th Leg., ch. 908 (H.B. 2884), § 12, effective September 1, 2007; am. Acts 2009, 81st Leg., ch. 87 (S.B. 1969), § 27.001(14), effective September 1, 2009 (renumbered from Sec. 54.0481).)

### Sec. 54.049.   Conditions of Probation for Desecrating a Cemetery or Abusing a Corpse.

(a) If a juvenile court places on probation under Section 54.04(d) a child adjudicated to have engaged in conduct in violation of Section 28.03(f), Penal Code, involving damage or destruction inflicted on a place of human burial or under Section 42.08, Penal Code, in addition to other conditions of probation, the court shall order the child to make restitution to a cemetery organization operating a cemetery affected by the conduct in an amount equal to the cost to the cemetery of repairing any damage caused by the conduct.

(b) If a juvenile court orders a child to make restitution under Subsection (a) and the child is financially unable to make the restitution, the court may order:

(1) the child to perform a specific number of hours of community service to satisfy the restitution; or

(2) a parent or other person responsible for the child's support to make the restitution in the amount described by Subsection (a).

(c) In this section, "cemetery" and "cemetery organization" have the meanings assigned by Section 711.001, Health and Safety Code.

(Enacted by Acts 2005, 79th Leg., ch. 1025 (H.B. 1012), § 3, effective June 18, 2005.)

### Sec. 54.0491.   Gang-Related Conduct.

(a) In this section:

(1) "Criminal street gang" has the meaning assigned by Section 71.01, Penal Code.

(2) "Gang-related conduct" means conduct that violates a penal law of the grade of Class B misdemeanor or higher and in which a child engages with the intent to:

(A) further the criminal activities of a criminal street gang of which the child is a member;

(B) gain membership in a criminal street gang; or

(C) avoid detection as a member of a criminal street gang.

(b) A juvenile court, in a disposition hearing under Section 54.04 regarding a child who has been adjudicated to have engaged in delinquent conduct that is also gang-related conduct, shall order the child to participate in a criminal street gang intervention program that is appropriate for the child based on the child's level of involvement in the criminal activities of a criminal street gang. The intervention program:

(1) must include at least 12 hours of instruction; and

(2) may include voluntary tattoo removal.

(c) If a child required to attend a criminal street gang intervention program is committed to the Texas Youth Commission as a result of the gang-related conduct, the child must complete the intervention program before being discharged from the custody of or released under supervision by the commission.

(Enacted by Acts 2009, 81st Leg., ch. 1130 (H.B. 2086), § 19, effective September 1, 2009.)

## Sec. 54.05. Hearing to Modify Disposition.

(a) **[2 Versions: As amended by Acts 2011, 82nd Leg., ch. 438]** Any disposition, except a commitment to the Texas Youth Commission, may be modified by the juvenile court as provided in this section until:

(1) the child reaches:

(A) the child's 18th birthday; or

(B) the child's 19th birthday, if the child was placed on determinate sentence probation under Section 54.04(q); or

(2) the child is earlier discharged by the court or operation of law.

(a) **[2 Versions: As amended by Acts 2011, 82nd Leg., ch. 1098]** Except as provided by Subsection (a-1), any disposition, except a commitment to the Texas Youth Commission, may be modified by the juvenile court as provided in this section until:

(1) the child reaches his 18th birthday; or

(2) the child is earlier discharged by the court or operation of law.

(a-1) A disposition regarding conduct under Section 51.03(b)(2) may be modified by the juvenile court as provided by this section until the expiration of the period described by Section 54.0402.

(b) **[2 Versions: As amended by Acts 2011, 82nd Leg., ch. 438]** Except for a commitment to the Texas Youth Commission or a placement on determinate sentence probation under Section 54.04(q), all dispositions automatically terminate when the child reaches the child's 18th birthday.

(b) **[2 Versions: As amended by Acts 2011, 82nd Leg., ch. 1098]** Except for a commitment to the Texas Youth Commission or a disposition under Section 54.0402, all dispositions automatically terminate when the child reaches his 18th birthday.

(c) There is no right to a jury at a hearing to modify disposition.

(d) A hearing to modify disposition shall be held on the petition of the child and his parent, guardian, guardian ad litem, or attorney, or on the petition of the state, a probation officer, or the court itself. Reasonable notice of a hearing to modify disposition shall be given to all parties.

(e) After the hearing on the merits or facts, the court may consider written reports from probation officers, professional court employees, or professional consultants in addition to the testimony of other witnesses. Prior to the hearing to modify disposition, the court shall provide the attorney for the child with access to all written matter to be considered by the court in deciding whether to modify disposition. The court may order counsel not to reveal items to the child or his parent, guardian, or guardian ad litem if such disclosure would materially harm the treatment and rehabilitation of the child or would substantially decrease the likelihood of receiving information from the same or similar sources in the future.

(f) Except as provided by Subsection (j), a disposition based on a finding that the child engaged in delinquent conduct that violates a penal law of this state or the United States of the grade of felony may be modified so as to commit the child to the Texas Youth Commission if the court after a hearing to modify disposition finds by a preponderance of the evidence that the child violated a reasonable and lawful order of the court. A disposition based on a finding that the child engaged in habitual felony conduct as described by Section 51.031 or in delinquent conduct that included a violation of a penal law listed in Section 53.045(a) may be modified to commit the child to the Texas Youth Commission with a possible transfer to the Texas Department of Criminal Justice for a definite term prescribed by Section 54.04(d)(3) if the original petition was approved by the grand jury under Section 53.045 and if after a hearing to modify the disposition the court finds that the child violated a reasonable and lawful order of the court.

(g) Except as provided by Subsection (j), a disposition based solely on a finding that the child engaged in conduct indicating a need for supervision may not be modified to commit the child to the Texas Youth Commission. A new finding in compliance with Section 54.03 must be made that the child engaged in delinquent conduct that meets the requirements for commitment under Section 54.04.

(h) A hearing shall be held prior to placement in a post-adjudication secure correctional facility for a period longer than 30 days or commitment to the Texas Youth Commission as a modified disposition. In other disposition modifications, the child and the child's parent, guardian, guardian ad litem, or attorney may waive hearing in accordance with Section 51.09.

(i) The court shall specifically state in the order its reasons for modifying the disposition and shall furnish a copy of the order to the child.

(j) If, after conducting a hearing to modify disposition without a jury, the court finds by a preponderance of the evidence that a child violated a reasonable and lawful condition of probation ordered under Section 54.04(q), the court may modify the disposition to commit the child to the Texas Youth Commission under Section 54.04(d)(3) for a term that does not exceed the original sentence assessed by the court or jury.

(k) [Repealed by Acts 2007, 80th Leg., ch. 263 (S.B. 103), § 64(2), effective June 8, 2007.]

(l) The court may extend a period of probation under this section at any time during the period of probation or, if a motion for revocation or modification of probation is filed before the period of supervision ends, before the first anniversary of the date on which the period of probation expires.

(m) If the court places the child on probation outside the child's home or commits the child to the Texas Youth Commission, the court:

(1) shall include in the court's order a determination that:

(A) it is in the child's best interests to be placed outside the child's home;

(B) reasonable efforts were made to prevent or eliminate the need for the child's removal from the child's home and to make it possible for the child to return home; and

(C) the child, in the child's home, cannot be provided the quality of care and level of support and supervision that the child needs to meet the conditions of probation; and

(2) may approve an administrative body to conduct a permanency hearing pursuant to 42 U.S.C. Section 675 if required during the placement or commitment of the child.

(Enacted by Acts 1973, 63rd Leg., ch. 544 (S.B. 111), § 1, effective September 1, 1973; am. Acts 1979, 66th Leg., ch. 743 (H.B. 1109), § 1, effective August 27, 1979; am. Acts 1983, 68th Leg., ch. 44 (S.B. 422), art. 1 § 4, effective April 26, 1983; am. Acts 1985, 69th Leg., ch. 45 (S.B. 120), § 3, effective September 1, 1985; am. Acts 1987, 70th Leg., ch. 385 (H.B. 682), § 10, effective September 1, 1987; am. Acts 1991, 72nd Leg., ch. 557 (H.B. 653), § 3, effective September 1, 1991; am. Acts 1995, 74th Leg., ch. 262 (H.B. 327), § 42, effective January 1, 1996; am. Acts 1999, 76th Leg., ch. 1448 (H.B. 2947), § 2, effective September 1, 1999; am. Acts 1999, 76th Leg., ch. 1477 (H.B. 3517), § 11, effective September 1, 1999; am. Acts 2001, 77th Leg., ch. 1297 (H.B. 1118), §§ 27, 28, effective September 1, 2001; am. Acts 2001, 77th Leg., ch. 1420 (H.B. 2812), § 5.002, effective September 1, 2001; am. Acts 2003, 78th Leg., ch. 283 (H.B. 2319), § 21, effective September 1, 2003; am. Acts 2005, 79th Leg., ch. 949 (H.B. 1575), § 15, effective September 1, 2005; am. Acts 2007, 80th Leg., ch. 263 (S.B. 103), §§ 9, 64(2), effective June 8, 2007; am. Acts 2011, 82nd Leg., ch. 438 (S.B. 1208), § 5, effective September 1, 2011; am. Acts 2011, 82nd Leg., ch. 1098 (S.B. 1489), § 5, effective September 1, 2011.)

## Sec. 54.051. Transfer of Determinate Sentence Probation to Appropriate District Court.

(a) On motion of the state concerning a child who is placed on probation under Section 54.04(q) for a period, including any extension ordered under Section 54.05, that will continue after the child's 19th birthday, the juvenile court shall hold a hearing to determine whether to transfer the child to an appropriate district court or discharge the child from the sentence of probation.

(b) The hearing must be conducted before the child's 19th birthday and in the same manner as a hearing to modify disposition under Section 54.05.

(c) If, after a hearing, the court determines to discharge the child, the court shall specify a date on or before the child's 19th birthday to discharge the child from the sentence of probation.

(d) If, after a hearing, the court determines to transfer the child, the court shall transfer the child to an appropriate district court on the child's 19th birthday.

(e) A district court that exercises jurisdiction over a child transferred under Subsection (d) shall place the child on community supervision under Article 42.12, Code of Criminal Procedure, for the remainder of the child's probationary period and under conditions consistent with those ordered by the juvenile court.

(e-1) The restrictions on a judge placing a defendant on community supervision imposed by Section 3g, Article 42.12, Code of Criminal Procedure, do not apply to a case transferred from the juvenile court. The minimum period of community supervision imposed by Section 3(b), Article 42.12, Code of Criminal Procedure, does not apply to a case transferred from the juvenile court.

(e-2) If a child who is placed on community supervision under this section violates a condition of that supervision or if the child violated a condition of probation ordered under Section 54.04(q) and that probation violation was not discovered by the state before the child's 19th birthday, the district court shall dispose of the violation of community supervision or probation, as appropriate, in the same manner as if the court had originally exercised jurisdiction over the case. If the judge revokes community supervision, the judge may reduce the prison sentence to any length without regard to the minimum term imposed by Section 23(a), Article 42.12, Code of Criminal Procedure.

(e-3) The time that a child serves on probation ordered under Section 54.04(q) is the same as time served on community supervision ordered under this section for purposes of determining the child's eligibility for early discharge from community supervision under Section 20, Article 42.12, Code of Criminal Procedure.

(f) The juvenile court may transfer a child to an appropriate district court as provided by this section without a showing that the child violated a condition of probation ordered under Section 54.04(q).

(g) If the juvenile court places the child on probation for an offense for which registration as a sex offender is required by Chapter 62, Code of Criminal Procedure, and defers the registration requirement until completion of treatment for the sex offense under Subchapter H, Chapter 62, Code of Criminal Procedure, the authority under that article to reexamine the need for registration on completion of treatment is transferred to the court to which probation is transferred.

(h) If the juvenile court places the child on probation for an offense for which registration as a sex offender is required by Chapter 62, Code of Criminal Procedure, and the child registers, the authority of the court to excuse further compliance with the registration requirement under Subchapter H, Chapter 62, Code of Criminal Procedure, is transferred to the court to which probation is transferred.

(i) If the juvenile court exercises jurisdiction over a person who is 18 years of age or older under Section 51.041 or 51.0412, the court or jury may, if the person is otherwise eligible, place the person on probation under Section 54.04(q). The juvenile court shall set the conditions of probation and immediately transfer supervision of the person to the appropriate court exercising criminal jurisdiction under Subsection (e).

(Enacted by Acts 1999, 76th Leg., ch. 1477 (H.B. 3517), § 12, effective September 1, 1999; am. Acts 2003, 78th Leg., ch. 283 (H.B. 2319), § 22, effective September 1, 2003; am. Acts 2005, 79th Leg., ch. 1008 (H.B. 867), § 2.07, effective September 1, 2005; am. Acts 2011, 82nd Leg., ch. 438 (S.B. 1208), § 6, effective September 1, 2011.)

## Sec. 54.052. Credit for Time Spent in Detention Facility for Child with Determinate Sentence.

(a) This section applies only to a child who is committed to the Texas Youth Commission under a determinate sentence under Section 54.04(d)(3) or (m) or Section 54.05(f).

(b) The judge of the court in which a child is adjudicated shall give the child credit on the child's sentence for the time spent by the child, in connection with the conduct for which the child was adjudicated, in a secure detention facility before the child's transfer to a Texas Youth Commission facility.

(c) If a child appeals the child's adjudication and is retained in a secure detention facility pending the appeal, the judge of the court in which the child was adjudicated shall give the child credit on the child's sentence for the time spent by the child in a secure detention facility pending disposition of the child's appeal. The court shall endorse on both the commitment and the mandate from the appellate court all credit given the child under this subsection.

(d) The Texas Youth Commission shall grant any credit under this section in computing the child's eligibility for parole and discharge.
(Enacted by Acts 2007, 80th Leg., ch. 263 (S.B. 103), § 10, effective June 8, 2007.)

## Sec. 54.06. Judgments for Support.

(a) At any stage of the proceeding, when a child has been placed outside the child's home, the juvenile court, after giving the parent or other person responsible for the child's support a reasonable opportunity to be heard, shall order the parent or other person to pay in a manner directed by the court a reasonable sum for the support in whole or in part of the child or the court shall waive the payment by order. The court shall order that the payment for support be made to the local juvenile probation department to be used only for residential care and other support for the child unless the child has been committed to the Texas Youth Commission, in which case the court shall order that the payment be made to the Texas Youth Commission for deposit in a special account in the general revenue fund that may be appropriated only for the care of children committed to the commission.

(b) At any stage of the proceeding, when a child has been placed outside the child's home and the parent of the child is obligated to pay support for the child under a court order under Title 5, the juvenile court shall order that the person entitled to receive the support assign the person's right to support for the child placed outside the child's home to the local juvenile probation department to be used for residential care and other support for the child unless the child has been committed to the Texas Youth Commission, in which event the court shall order that the assignment be made to the Texas Youth Commission.

(c) A court may enforce an order for support under this section by ordering garnishment of the wages of the person ordered to pay support or by any other means available to enforce a child support order under Title 5.

(d) [Repealed by Acts 2003, 78th Leg., ch. 283 (H.B. 2319), § 61(1), effective September 1, 2003.]

(e) The court shall apply the child support guidelines under Subchapter C, Chapter 154, in an order requiring the payment of child support under this section. The court shall also require in an order to pay child support under this section that health insurance be provided for the child.

Subchapter D, Chapter 154, applies to an order requiring health insurance for a child under this section.

(f) An order under this section prevails over any previous child support order issued with regard to the child to the extent of any conflict between the orders.
(Enacted by Acts 1973, 63rd Leg., ch. 544 (S.B. 111), § 1, effective September 1, 1973; am. Acts 1983, 68th Leg., ch. 44 (S.B. 422), art. 1, § 5, effective April 26, 1983; am. Acts 1987, 70th Leg., ch. 1040 (S.B. 17), § 24, effective September 1, 1987; am. Acts 1993, 73rd Leg., ch. 798 (H.B. 1433), § 23, effective September 1, 1993; am. Acts 1993, 73rd Leg., ch. 1048 (H.B. 1731), § 2, effective September 1, 1993; am. Acts 1995, 74th Leg., ch. 262 (H.B. 327), § 43, effective January 1, 1996; am. Acts 1997, 75th Leg., ch. 165 (S.B. 898), § 7.11, effective September 1, 1997; am. Acts 2003, 78th Leg., ch. 283 (H.B. 2319), § 61(1), effective September 1, 2003.)

## Sec. 54.061. Payment of Probation Fees.

(a) If a child is placed on probation under Section 54.04(d)(1) of this code, the juvenile court, after giving the child, parent, or other person responsible for the child's support a reasonable opportunity to be heard, shall order the child, parent, or other person, if financially able to do so, to pay to the court a fee of not more than $15 a month during the period that the child continues on probation.

(b) Orders for the payment of fees under this section may be enforced as provided by Section 54.07 of this code.

(c) The court shall deposit the fees received under this section in the county treasury to the credit of a special fund that may be used only for juvenile probation or community-based juvenile corrections services or facilities in which a juvenile may be required to live while under court supervision.

(d) If the court finds that a child, parent, or other person responsible for the child's support is financially unable to pay the probation fee required under Subsection (a), the court shall enter into the records of the child's case a statement of that finding. The court may waive a fee under this section only if the court makes the finding under this subsection.
(Enacted by Acts 1979, 66th Leg., ch. 154 (H.B. 244), § 1, effective September 1, 1979; am. Acts 1981, 67th Leg., ch. 617 (H.B. 1704), § 4, effective

September 1, 1981; am. Acts 1987, 70th Leg., ch. 1040 (S.B. 17), § 25, effective September 1, 1987; am. Acts 1995, 74th Leg., ch. 262 (H.B. 327), § 44, effective January 1, 1996.)

## Sec. 54.07. Enforcement of Order.

(a) Except as provided by Subsection (b) or a juvenile court child support order, any order of the juvenile court may be enforced as provided by Chapter 61.

(b) A violation of any of the following orders of the juvenile court may not be enforced by contempt of court proceedings against the child:

(1) an order setting conditions of probation;

(2) an order setting conditions of deferred prosecution; and

(3) an order setting conditions of release from detention.

(c) This section and Chapter 61 do not preclude a juvenile court from summarily finding a child or other person in direct contempt of the juvenile court for conduct occurring in the presence of the judge of the court. Direct contempt of the juvenile court by a child is punishable by a maximum of 10 days' confinement in a secure juvenile detention facility or by a maximum of 40 hours of community service, or both. The juvenile court may not impose a fine on a child for direct contempt.

(d) This section and Chapter 61 do not preclude a juvenile court in an appropriate case from using a civil or coercive contempt proceeding to enforce an order.

(Enacted by Acts 1973, 63rd Leg., ch. 544 (S.B. 111), § 1, effective September 1, 1973; am. Acts 1979, 66th Leg., ch. 154 (H.B. 244), § 3, effective September 1, 1979; am. Acts 2003, 78th Leg., ch. 283 (H.B. 2319), § 23, effective September 1, 2003.)

## Sec. 54.08. Public Access to Court Hearings.

(a) Except as provided by this section, the court shall open hearings under this title to the public unless the court, for good cause shown, determines that the public should be excluded.

(b) The court may not prohibit a person who is a victim of the conduct of a child, or the person's family, from personally attending a hearing under this title relating to the conduct by the child unless the victim or member of the victim's family is to testify in the hearing or any subsequent hearing relating to the conduct and the court determines that the victim's or family member's testimony would be materially affected if the victim or member of the victim's family hears other testimony at trial.

(c) If a child is under the age of 14 at the time of the hearing, the court shall close the hearing to the public unless the court finds that the interests of the child or the interests of the public would be better served by opening the hearing to the public.

(d) In this section, "family" has the meaning assigned by Section 71.003.

(Enacted by Acts 1973, 63rd Leg., ch. 544 (S.B. 111), § 1, effective September 1, 1973; am. Acts 1987, 70th Leg., ch. 385 (H.B. 682), § 11, effective September 1, 1987; am. Acts 1995, 74th Leg., ch. 262 (H.B. 327), § 45, effective January 1, 1996; am. Acts 1997, 75th Leg., ch. 1086 (H.B. 1550), § 12, effective September 1, 1997.)

## Sec. 54.09. Recording of Proceedings.

All judicial proceedings under this chapter except detention hearings shall be recorded by stenographic notes or by electronic, mechanical, or other appropriate means. Upon request of any party, a detention hearing shall be recorded.

(Enacted by Acts 1973, 63rd Leg., ch. 544 (S.B. 111), § 1, effective September 1, 1973.)

## Sec. 54.10. Hearings Before Referee.

(a) [2 Versions: Effective until January 1, 2012] Except as provided by Subsection (e), a hearing under Section 54.03, 54.04, or 54.05, including a jury trial, a hearing under Chapter 55, including a jury trial, or a hearing under the Interstate Compact for Juveniles (Chapter 60) may be held by a referee appointed in accordance with Section 51.04(g) or a master appointed under Chapter 54, Government Code, provided:

(1) the parties have been informed by the referee or master that they are entitled to have the hearing before the juvenile court judge; and

(2) after each party is given an opportunity to object, no party objects to holding the hearing before the referee or master.

(a) [2 Versions: Effective January 1, 2012] Except as provided by Subsection (e), a hearing under Section 54.03, 54.04, or 54.05, including a jury trial, a hearing under Chapter 55, including a jury trial, or a hearing under the Interstate Compact for Juveniles (Chapter 60) may be held by a referee appointed in accordance with Section 51.04(g) or an associate judge appointed under Chapter 54A, Government Code, provided:

(1) the parties have been informed by the referee or associate judge that they are entitled

Family Code

to have the hearing before the juvenile court judge; and

(2) after each party is given an opportunity to object, no party objects to holding the hearing before the referee or associate judge.

(b) The determination under Section 53.02(f) whether to release a child may be made by a referee appointed in accordance with Section 51.04(g) if:

(1) the child has been informed by the referee that the child is entitled to have the determination made by the juvenile court judge or a substitute judge authorized by Section 51.04(f); or

(2) the child and the attorney for the child have in accordance with Section 51.09 waived the right to have the determination made by the juvenile court judge or a substitute judge.

(c) If a child objects to a referee making the determination under Section 53.02(f), the juvenile court judge or a substitute judge authorized by Section 51.04(f) shall make the determination.

(d) At the conclusion of the hearing or immediately after making the determination, the referee shall transmit written findings and recommendations to the juvenile court judge. The juvenile court judge shall adopt, modify, or reject the referee's recommendations not later than the next working day after the day that the judge receives the recommendations. Failure to act within that time results in release of the child by operation of law and a recommendation that the child be released operates to secure the child's immediate release subject to the power of the juvenile court judge to modify or reject that recommendation.

(e) The hearings provided by Sections 54.03, 54.04, and 54.05 may not be held before a referee if the grand jury has approved of the petition and the child is subject to a determinate sentence.
(Enacted by Acts 1975, 64th Leg., ch. 693 (S.B. 247), § 19, effective September 1, 1975; am. Acts 1979, 66th Leg., ch. 743 (H.B. 1109), § 2, effective August 27, 1979; am. Acts 1987, 70th Leg., ch. 385 (H.B. 682), § 12, effective September 1, 1987; am. Acts 1991, 72nd Leg., ch. 74 (H.B. 626), § 1, effective September 1, 1991; am. Acts 1997, 75th Leg., ch. 1086 (H.B. 1550), § 13, effective September 1, 1997; am. Acts 1999, 76th Leg., ch. 232 (H.B. 1269), § 5, effective September 1, 1999; am. Acts 1999, 76th Leg., ch. 1477 (H.B. 3517), § 13, effective September 1, 1999; am. Acts 2005, 79th Leg., ch. 1007 (H.B. 706), § 2.03, effective August 26, 2008; am. Acts 2011, 82nd Leg., 1st C.S., (H.B. 79), § 6.08, effective January 1, 2012.)

STATUTORY NOTES

**Editor's notes.** — Acts 2005, 79th Leg., ch. 1007 (H.B. 706), § 2.03 amended subsection (a) of this section effective on the day on which the Interstate Compact on Juveniles took effect. The Compact took effect when it was enacted into law by the 35th state. The new compact was adopted by the 35th state, Illinois, on August 26, 2008, making the compact and conforming amendment effective on that date.

## Sec. 54.11. Release or Transfer Hearing.

(a) On receipt of a referral under Section 244.014(a), Human Resources Code, for the transfer to the Texas Department of Criminal Justice of a person committed to the Texas Juvenile Justice Department under Section 54.04(d)(3), 54.04(m), or 54.05(f), or on receipt of a request by the Texas Juvenile Justice Department under Section 245.051(d), Human Resources Code, for approval of the release under supervision of a person committed to the Texas Juvenile Justice Department under Section 54.04(d)(3), 54.04(m), or 54.05(f), the court shall set a time and place for a hearing on the release of the person.

(b) The court shall notify the following of the time and place of the hearing:

(1) the person to be transferred or released under supervision;

(2) the parents of the person;

(3) any legal custodian of the person, including the Texas Youth Commission;

(4) the office of the prosecuting attorney that represented the state in the juvenile delinquency proceedings;

(5) the victim of the offense that was included in the delinquent conduct that was a ground for the disposition, or a member of the victim's family; and

(6) any other person who has filed a written request with the court to be notified of a release hearing with respect to the person to be transferred or released under supervision.

(c) Except for the person to be transferred or released under supervision and the prosecuting attorney, the failure to notify a person listed in Subsection (b) of this section does not affect the validity of a hearing conducted or determination made under this section if the record in the case reflects that the whereabouts of the persons who did not receive notice were unknown to the court and a reasonable effort was made by the court to locate those persons.

(d) At a hearing under this section the court may consider written reports from probation officers, professional court employees, professional consultants, or employees of the Texas Youth Commission, in addition to the testimony of witnesses. At least one day before the hearing, the court shall provide the attorney for the person to be transferred or released under supervision with access to all written matter to be considered by the court.

(e) At the hearing, the person to be transferred or released under supervision is entitled to an attorney, to examine all witnesses against him, to present evidence and oral argument, and to previous examination of all reports on and evaluations and examinations of or relating to him that may be used in the hearing.

(f) A hearing under this section is open to the public unless the person to be transferred or released under supervision waives a public hearing with the consent of his attorney and the court.

(g) A hearing under this section must be recorded by a court reporter or by audio or video tape recording, and the record of the hearing must be retained by the court for at least two years after the date of the final determination on the transfer or release of the person by the court.

(h) The hearing on a person who is referred for transfer under Section 244.014(a), Human Resources Code, shall be held not later than the 60th day after the date the court receives the referral.

(i) On conclusion of the hearing on a person who is referred for transfer under Section 244.014(a), Human Resources Code, the court may order:

(1) the return of the person to the Texas Juvenile Justice Department; or

(2) the transfer of the person to the custody of the Texas Department of Criminal Justice for the completion of the person's sentence.

(j) On conclusion of the hearing on a person who is referred for release under supervision under Section 245.051(c), Human Resources Code, the court may order the return of the person to the Texas Juvenile Justice Department:

(1) with approval for the release of the person under supervision; or

(2) without approval for the release of the person under supervision.

(k) In making a determination under this section, the court may consider the experiences and character of the person before and after commitment to the youth commission, the nature of the penal offense that the person was found to have committed and the manner in which the offense was committed, the abilities of the person to contribute to society, the protection of the victim of the offense or any member of the victim's family, the recommendations of the youth commission and prosecuting attorney, the best interests of the person, and any other factor relevant to the issue to be decided.

(l) Pending the conclusion of a transfer hearing, the juvenile court shall order that the person who is referred for transfer be detained in a certified juvenile detention facility as provided by Subsection (m). If the person is at least 17 years of age, the juvenile court may order that the person be detained without bond in an appropriate county facility for the detention of adults accused of criminal offenses.

(m) The detention of a person in a certified juvenile detention facility must comply with the detention requirements under this title, except that, to the extent practicable, the person must be kept separate from children detained in the same facility.

(n) If the juvenile court orders that a person who is referred for transfer be detained in a county facility under Subsection (l), the county sheriff shall take custody of the person under the juvenile court's order.

(Enacted by Acts 1987, 70th Leg., ch. 385 (H.B. 682), § 13, effective September 1, 1987; am. Acts 1991, 72nd Leg., ch. 574 (S.B. 303), § 3, effective September 1, 1991; am. Acts 1995, 74th Leg., ch. 262 (H.B. 327), § 46, effective January 1, 1996; am. Acts 2001, 77th Leg., ch. 1297 (H.B. 1118), § 29, effective September 1, 2001; am. Acts 2003, 78th Leg., ch. 283 (H.B. 2319), § 24, effective September 1, 2003; am. Acts 2009, 81st Leg., ch. 87 (S.B. 1969), § 25.058, effective September 1, 2009; am. Acts 2011, 82nd Leg., ch. 85 (S.B. 653), § 3.007, effective September 1, 2011.)

# CHAPTER 55
## PROCEEDINGS CONCERNING CHILDREN WITH MENTAL ILLNESS OR MENTAL RETARDATION

### Subchapter A. General Provisions

Family Code

## SUBCHAPTER A
## GENERAL PROVISIONS

### Sec. 55.01. Meaning of "Having a Mental Illness."

For purposes of this chapter, a child who is described as having a mental illness means a child who suffers from mental illness as defined by Section 571.003, Health and Safety Code.
(Enacted by Acts 1999, 76th Leg., ch. 1477 (H.B. 3517), § 14, effective September 1, 1999.)

### Sec. 55.02. Mental Health and Mental Retardation Jurisdiction.

For the purpose of initiating proceedings to order mental health or mental retardation services for a child or for commitment of a child as provided by this chapter, the juvenile court has jurisdiction of proceedings under Subtitle C or D, Title 7, Health and Safety Code.
(Enacted by Acts 1999, 76th Leg., ch. 1477 (H.B. 3517), § 14, effective September 1, 1999.)

### Sec. 55.03. Standards of Care.

(a) Except as provided by this chapter, a child for whom inpatient mental health services is ordered by a court under this chapter shall be cared for as provided by Subtitle C, Title 7, Health and Safety Code.

(b) Except as provided by this chapter, a child who is committed by a court to a residential care facility for mental retardation shall be cared for as provided by Subtitle D, Title 7, Health and Safety Code.
(Enacted by Acts 1999, 76th Leg., ch. 1477 (H.B. 3517), § 14, effective September 1, 1999.)

## CHAPTER 56
## APPEAL

### Sec. 56.01. Right to Appeal.

(a) Except as provided by Subsection (b-1), an appeal from an order of a juvenile court is to a court of appeals and the case may be carried to the Texas Supreme Court by writ of error or upon certificate, as in civil cases generally.

(b) The requirements governing an appeal are as in civil cases generally. When an appeal is sought by filing a notice of appeal, security for costs of appeal, or an affidavit of inability to pay the costs of appeal, and the filing is made in a timely fashion after the date the disposition order is signed, the appeal must include the juvenile court adjudication and all rulings contributing to that adjudication. An appeal of the adjudication may be sought notwithstanding that the adjudication order was signed more than 30 days before the date the notice of appeal, security for costs of appeal, or affidavit of inability to pay the costs of appeal was filed.

(b-1) A motion for new trial seeking to vacate an adjudication is:

(1) timely if the motion is filed not later than the 30th day after the date on which the disposition order is signed; and

(2) governed by Rule 21, Texas Rules of Appellate Procedure.

(c) An appeal may be taken:

(1) except as provided by Subsection (n), by or on behalf of a child from an order entered under:

(A) Section 54.03 with regard to delinquent conduct or conduct indicating a need for supervision;

(B) Section 54.04 disposing of the case;

(C) Section 54.05 respecting modification of a previous juvenile court disposition; or

(D) Chapter 55 by a juvenile court committing a child to a facility for the mentally ill or mentally retarded; or

(2) by a person from an order entered under Section 54.11(i)(2) transferring the person to the custody of the Texas Department of Criminal Justice.

(d) A child has the right to:

(1) appeal, as provided by this subchapter;

(2) representation by counsel on appeal; and

(3) appointment of an attorney for the appeal if an attorney cannot be obtained because of indigency.

(e) On entering an order that is appealable under this section, the court shall advise the child and the child's parent, guardian, or guardian ad litem of the child's rights listed under Subsection (d) of this section.

(f) If the child and his parent, guardian, or guardian ad litem express a desire to appeal, the attorney who represented the child before the juvenile court shall file a notice of appeal with the juvenile court and inform the court whether that attorney will handle the appeal. Counsel shall be appointed under the standards provided in Section 51.10 of this code unless the right to appeal is waived in accordance with Section 51.09 of this code.

(g) An appeal does not suspend the order of the juvenile court, nor does it release the child from the custody of that court or of the person, institution, or agency to whose care the child is committed, unless the juvenile court so orders. However, the appellate court may provide for a personal bond.

(h) If the order appealed from takes custody of the child from his parent, guardian, or custodian, the appeal has precedence over all other cases.

(i) The appellate court may affirm, reverse, or modify the judgment or order, including an order of disposition or modified disposition, from which appeal was taken. It may reverse or modify an order of disposition or modified order of disposition while affirming the juvenile court adjudication that the child engaged in delinquent conduct or conduct indicating a need for supervision. It may remand an order that it reverses or modifies for further proceedings by the juvenile court.

(j) Neither the child nor his family shall be identified in an appellate opinion rendered in an appeal or habeas corpus proceedings related to juvenile court proceedings under this title. The appellate opinion shall be styled, "In the matter of ____," identifying the child by his initials only.

(k) The appellate court shall dismiss an appeal on the state's motion, supported by affidavit showing that the appellant has escaped from custody pending the appeal and, to the affiant's knowledge, has not voluntarily returned to the state's custody on or before the 10th day after the date of the escape. The court may not dismiss an appeal, or if the appeal has been dismissed, shall reinstate the appeal, on the filing of an affidavit of an officer or other credible person showing that the appellant voluntarily returned to custody on or before the 10th day after the date of the escape.

(*l*) The court may order the child, the child's parent, or other person responsible for support of the child to pay the child's costs of appeal, including the costs of representation by an attorney, unless the court determines the person to be ordered to pay the costs is indigent.

(m) For purposes of determining indigency of the child under this section, the court shall consider the assets and income of the child, the child's parent, and any other person responsible for the support of the child.

(n) A child who enters a plea or agrees to a stipulation of evidence in a proceeding held under this title may not appeal an order of the juvenile court entered under Section 54.03, 54.04, or 54.05 if the court makes a disposition in accordance with the agreement between the state and the child regarding the disposition of the case, unless:

(1) the court gives the child permission to appeal; or

(2) the appeal is based on a matter raised by written motion filed before the proceeding in which the child entered the plea or agreed to the stipulation of evidence.

(o) This section does not limit a child's right to obtain a writ of habeas corpus.

(Enacted by Acts 1973, 63rd Leg., ch. 544 (S.B. 111), § 1, effective September 1, 1973; am. Acts 1987, 70th Leg., ch. 385 (H.B. 682), § 14, effective September 1, 1987; am. Acts 1991, 72nd Leg., ch. 680 (H.B. 889), § 1, effective September 1, 1991; am. Acts 1995, 74th Leg., ch. 262 (H.B. 327), § 48, effective January 1, 1996; am. Acts 1997, 75th Leg., ch. 1086 (H.B. 1550), § 15, effective September 1, 1997; am. Acts 1999, 76th Leg., ch. 74 (H.B. 251), § 2, effective September 1, 1999; am. Acts 1999, 76th Leg., ch. 1477 (H.B. 3517), § 15, effective September 1, 1999; am. Acts 2001, 77th Leg., ch. 1297 (H.B. 1118), § 33, effective September 1, 2001; am. Acts 2009, 81st Leg., ch. 87 (S.B. 1969), § 25.059, effective September 1, 2009; am. Acts 2009, 81st Leg., ch. 642 (H.B. 1688), § 2, effective September 1, 2009.)

### Sec. 56.02.   Transcript on Appeal.

(a) An attorney retained to represent a child on appeal who desires to have included in the record on appeal a transcription of notes of the reporter has the responsibility of obtaining and paying for the transcription and furnishing it to the clerk in duplicate in time for inclusion in the record.

(b) The juvenile court shall order the reporter to furnish a transcription without charge to the attorney if the court finds, after hearing or on an affidavit filed by the child's parent or other person responsible for support of the child that the parent or other responsible person is unable to pay or to give security therefor.

(c) On certificate of the court that a transcription has been provided without charge, payment therefor shall be made from the general funds of the county in which the proceedings appealed from occurred.

(d) The court reporter shall report any portion of the proceedings requested by either party or directed by the court and shall report the proceedings in question and answer form unless a narrative transcript is requested.

(Enacted by Acts 1973, 63rd Leg., ch. 544 (S.B. 111), § 1, effective September 1, 1973; am. Acts 1991, 72nd Leg., ch. 674 (H.B. 629), § 1, effective September 1, 1991.)

### Sec. 56.03. Appeal by State in Cases of Violent or Habitual Offender.

(a) In this section, "prosecuting attorney" means the county attorney, district attorney, or criminal district attorney who has the primary responsibility of presenting cases in the juvenile court. The term does not include an assistant prosecuting attorney.

(b) The state is entitled to appeal an order of a court in a juvenile case in which the grand jury has approved of the petition under Section 53.045 if the order:

(1) dismisses a petition or any portion of a petition;

(2) arrests or modifies a judgment;

(3) grants a new trial;

(4) sustains a claim of former jeopardy; or

(5) grants a motion to suppress evidence, a confession, or an admission and if:

(A) jeopardy has not attached in the case;

(B) the prosecuting attorney certifies to the trial court that the appeal is not taken for the purpose of delay; and

(C) the evidence, confession, or admission is of substantial importance in the case.

(c) The prosecuting attorney may not bring an appeal under Subsection (b) later than the 15th day after the date on which the order or ruling to be appealed is entered by the court.

(d) The state is entitled to a stay in the proceedings pending the disposition of an appeal under Subsection (b).

(e) The court of appeals shall give preference in its docket to an appeal filed under Subsection (b).

(f) The state shall pay all costs of appeal under Subsection (b), other than the cost of attorney's fees for the respondent.

(g) If the respondent is represented by appointed counsel, the counsel shall continue to represent the respondent as appointed counsel on the appeal. If the respondent is not represented by appointed counsel, the respondent may seek the appointment of counsel to represent the respondent on appeal. The juvenile court shall determine whether the parent or other person responsible for support of the child is financially able to obtain an attorney to represent the respondent on appeal. If the court determines that the parent or other person is financially unable to obtain counsel for the appeal, the court shall appoint counsel to represent the respondent on appeal.

(h) If the state appeals under this section and the respondent is not detained, the court shall permit the respondent to remain at large subject only to the condition that the respondent appear in court for further proceedings when required by the court. If the respondent is detained, on the state's filing of notice of appeal under this section, the respondent is entitled to immediate release from detention on the allegation that is the subject of the appeal. The court shall permit the respondent to remain at large regarding that allegation subject only to the condition that the respondent appear in court for further proceedings when required by the court.

(i) The Texas Rules of Appellate Procedure apply to a petition by the state to the supreme court for review of a decision of a court of appeals in a juvenile case.

(Enacted by Acts 2003, 78th Leg., ch. 283 (H.B. 2319), § 25, effective September 1, 2003.)

## CHAPTER 57
## RIGHTS OF VICTIMS

### Sec. 57.001. Definitions.

In this chapter:

(1) "Close relative of a deceased victim" means a person who was the spouse of a deceased victim at the time of the victim's death or who is a parent or adult brother, sister, or child of the deceased victim.

(2) "Guardian of a victim" means a person who is the legal guardian of the victim, whether or not the legal relationship between the guardian and victim exists because of the age of the victim or the physical or mental incompetency of the victim.

(3) "Victim" means a person who as the result of the delinquent conduct of a child suffers a pecuniary loss or personal injury or harm.

(Enacted by Acts 1989, 71st Leg., ch. 633 (S.B. 1386), § 1, effective June 14, 1989; am. Acts 1995, 74th Leg., ch. 262 (H.B. 327), § 49, effective January 1, 1996; am. Acts 1997, 75th Leg., ch. 368 (S.B. 170), § 1, effective September 1, 1997.)

### Sec. 57.002. Victim's Rights.

(a) A victim, guardian of a victim, or close relative of a deceased victim is entitled to the following rights within the juvenile justice system:

(1) the right to receive from law enforcement agencies adequate protection from harm and threats of harm arising from cooperation with prosecution efforts;

(2) the right to have the court or person appointed by the court take the safety of the victim or the victim's family into consideration as an element in determining whether the child should be detained before the child's conduct is adjudicated;

(3) the right, if requested, to be informed of relevant court proceedings, including appellate proceedings, and to be informed in a timely manner if those court proceedings have been canceled or rescheduled;

(4) the right to be informed, when requested, by the court or a person appointed by the court concerning the procedures in the juvenile justice system, including general procedures relating to:

(A) the preliminary investigation and deferred prosecution of a case; and

(B) the appeal of the case;

(5) the right to provide pertinent information to a juvenile court conducting a disposition hearing concerning the impact of the offense on the victim and the victim's family by testimony, written statement, or any other manner before the court renders its disposition;

(6) the right to receive information regarding compensation to victims as provided by Subchapter B, Chapter 56, Code of Criminal Procedure, including information related to the costs that may be compensated under that subchapter and the amount of compensation, eligibility for compensation, and procedures for application for compensation under that subchapter, the payment of medical expenses under Section 56.06, Code of Criminal Procedure, for a victim of a sexual assault, and when requested, to referral to available social service agencies that may offer additional assistance;

(7) the right to be informed, upon request, of procedures for release under supervision or transfer of the person to the custody of the Texas Department of Criminal Justice for parole, to participate in the release or transfer for parole process, to be notified, if requested, of the person's release, escape, or transfer for parole proceedings concerning the person, to provide to the Texas Youth Commission for inclusion in the person's file information to be considered by the commission before the release under supervision or transfer for parole of the person, and to be notified, if requested, of the person's release or transfer for parole;

(8) the right to be provided with a waiting area, separate or secure from other witnesses, including the child alleged to have committed the conduct and relatives of the child, before testifying in any proceeding concerning the child, or, if a separate waiting area is not available, other safeguards should be taken to minimize the victim's contact with the child and the child's relatives and witnesses, before and during court proceedings;

(9) the right to prompt return of any property of the victim that is held by a law enforcement agency or the attorney for the state as evidence when the property is no longer required for that purpose;

(10) the right to have the attorney for the state notify the employer of the victim, if requested, of the necessity of the victim's cooperation and testimony in a proceeding that may necessitate the absence of the victim from work for good cause;

(11) the right to be present at all public court proceedings related to the conduct of the child as provided by Section 54.08, subject to that section; and

(12) any other right appropriate to the victim that a victim of criminal conduct has under Article 56.02, Code of Criminal Procedure.

(b) In notifying a victim of the release or escape of a person, the Texas Youth Commission shall use the same procedure established for the notification of the release or escape of an adult offender under Article 56.11, Code of Criminal Procedure.

(Enacted by Acts 1989, 71st Leg., ch. 633 (S.B. 1386), § 1, effective June 14, 1989; am. Acts 1995, 74th Leg., ch. 76 (S.B. 959), § 5.95(110), effective September 1, 1995; am. Acts 1995, 74th Leg., ch. 262 (H.B. 327), § 50, effective January 1, 1996; am. Acts 2001, 77th Leg., ch. 1034 (H.B. 1572), § 8, effective September 1, 2001; am. Acts 2009, 81st Leg., ch. 87 (S.B. 1969), § 25.060, effective September 1, 2009.)

**Family Code**

## Sec. 57.003. Duties of Juvenile Board and Victim Assistance Coordinator.

(a) The juvenile board shall ensure to the extent practicable that a victim, guardian of a victim, or close relative of a deceased victim is afforded the rights granted by Section 57.002 and, on request, an explanation of those rights.

(b) The juvenile board may designate a person to serve as victim assistance coordinator in the juvenile board's jurisdiction for victims of juvenile offenders.

(c) The victim assistance coordinator shall ensure that a victim, or close relative of a deceased victim, is afforded the rights granted victims, guardians, and relatives by Section 57.002 and, on request, an explanation of those rights. The victim assistance coordinator shall work closely with appropriate law enforcement agencies, prosecuting attorneys, the Texas Juvenile Probation Commission, and the Texas Youth Commission in carrying out that duty.

(d) The victim assistance coordinator shall ensure that at a minimum, a victim, guardian of a victim, or close relative of a deceased victim receives:

(1) a written notice of the rights outlined in Section 57.002;

(2) an application for compensation under the Crime Victims' Compensation Act (Subchapter B, Chapter 56, Code of Criminal Procedure); and

(3) a victim impact statement with information explaining the possible use and consideration of the victim impact statement at detention, adjudication, and release proceedings involving the juvenile.

(e) The victim assistance coordinator shall, on request, offer to assist a person receiving a form under Subsection (d) to complete the form.

(f) The victim assistance coordinator shall send a copy of the victim impact statement to the court conducting a disposition hearing involving the juvenile.

(g) The juvenile board, with the approval of the commissioners court of the county, may approve a program in which the victim assistance coordinator may offer not more than 10 hours of posttrial psychological counseling for a person who serves as a juror or an alternate juror in an adjudication hearing involving graphic evidence or testimony and who requests the posttrial psychological counseling not later than the 180th day after the date on which the jury in the adjudication hearing is dismissed. The victim assistance coordinator may provide the counseling using a provider that assists local juvenile justice agencies in providing similar services to victims.

(Enacted by Acts 1989, 71st Leg., ch. 633 (S.B. 1386), § 1, effective June 14, 1989; am. Acts 1995, 74th Leg., ch. 262 (H.B. 327), § 51, effective January 1, 1996; am. Acts 2009, 81st Leg., ch. 93 (H.B. 608), §§ 2, 3, effective September 1, 2009.)

## Sec. 57.0031. Notification of Rights of Victims of Juveniles.

At the initial contact or at the earliest possible time after the initial contact between the victim of a reported crime and the juvenile probation office having the responsibility for the disposition of the juvenile, the office shall provide the victim a written notice:

(1) containing information about the availability of emergency and medical services, if applicable;

(2) stating that the victim has the right to receive information regarding compensation to victims of crime as provided by the Crime Victims' Compensation Act (Subchapter B, Chapter 56, Code of Criminal Procedure), including information about:

(A) the costs that may be compensated and the amount of compensation, eligibility for compensation, and procedures for application for compensation;

(B) the payment for a medical examination for a victim of a sexual assault; and

(C) referral to available social service agencies that may offer additional assistance;

(3) stating the name, address, and phone number of the victim assistance coordinator for victims of juveniles;

(4) containing the following statement: "You may call the crime victim assistance coordinator for the status of the case and information about victims' rights.";

(5) stating the rights of victims of crime under Section 57.002;

(6) summarizing each procedural stage in the processing of a juvenile case, including preliminary investigation, detention, informal adjustment of a case, disposition hearings, release proceedings, restitution, and appeals;

(7) suggesting steps the victim may take if the victim is subjected to threats or intimidation;

(8) stating the case number and assigned court for the case; and

(9) stating that the victim has the right to file a victim impact statement and to have it considered in juvenile proceedings.

(Enacted by Acts 1995, 74th Leg., ch. 262 (H.B. 327), § 51, effective January 1, 1996.)

## Sec. 57.004. Notification.

A court, a person appointed by the court, or the Texas Youth Commission is responsible for notifying a victim, guardian of a victim, or close relative of a deceased victim of a proceeding under this chapter only if the victim, guardian of a victim, or close relative of a deceased victim requests the notification in writing and provides a current address to which the notification is to be sent.

(Enacted by Acts 1989, 71st Leg., ch. 633 (S.B. 1386), § 1, effective June 14, 1989.)

## Sec. 57.005. Liability.

The Texas Youth Commission, a juvenile board, a court, a person appointed by a court, an attorney for the state, a peace officer, or a law enforcement agency is not liable for a failure or inability to provide a right listed under Section 57.002 of this code.

(Enacted by Acts 1989, 71st Leg., ch. 633 (S.B. 1386), § 1, effective June 14, 1989.)

## Sec. 57.006. Appeal.

The failure or inability of any person to provide a right or service listed under Section 57.002 of this code may not be used by a child as a ground for appeal or for a post conviction writ of habeas corpus.

(Enacted by Acts 1989, 71st Leg., ch. 633 (S.B. 1386), § 1, effective June 14, 1989.)

## Sec. 57.007. Standing.

A victim, guardian of a victim, or close relative of a victim does not have standing to participate as a party in a juvenile proceeding or to contest the disposition of any case.

(Enacted by Acts 1989, 71st Leg., ch. 633 (S.B. 1386), § 1, effective June 14, 1989.)

## Sec. 57.008. Court Order for Protection from Juveniles.

(a) A court may issue an order for protection from juveniles directed against a child to protect a victim of the child's conduct who, because of the victim's participation in the juvenile justice system, risks further harm by the child.

(b) In the order, the court may prohibit the child from doing specified acts or require the child to do specified acts necessary or appropriate to prevent or reduce the likelihood of further harm to the victim by the child.

(Enacted by Acts 1995, 74th Leg., ch. 262 (H.B. 327), § 52, effective January 1, 1996.)

# CHAPTER 58
# RECORDS; JUVENILE JUSTICE INFORMATION SYSTEM

### Subchapter A. Records

### Subchapter B. Juvenile Justice Information System

### Subchapter C. Automatic Restriction of Access to Records

## SUBCHAPTER A
## RECORDS

### Sec. 58.001.   Collection of Records of Children.

(a) Law enforcement officers and other juvenile justice personnel shall collect information described by Section 58.104 as a part of the juvenile justice information system created under Subchapter B.

(b) The information is available as provided by Subchapter B.

(c) A law enforcement agency shall forward information, including fingerprints, relating to a child who has been taken into custody under Section 52.01 by the agency to the Department of Public Safety for inclusion in the juvenile justice information system created under Subchapter B, but only if the child is referred to juvenile court on or before the 10th day after the date the child is taken into custody under Section 52.01. If the child is not referred to juvenile court within that time, the law enforcement agency shall destroy all information, including photographs and fingerprints, relating to the child unless the child is placed in a first offender program under Section 52.031 or on informal disposition under Section 52.03. The law enforcement agency may not forward any information to the Department of Public Safety relating to the child while the child is in a first offender program under Section 52.031, or during the 90 days following successful comple-

tion of the program or while the child is on informal disposition under Section 52.03. Except as provided by Subsection (f), after the date the child completes an informal disposition under Section 52.03 or after the 90th day after the date the child successfully completes a first offender program under Section 52.031, the law enforcement agency shall destroy all information, including photographs and fingerprints, relating to the child.

(d) If information relating to a child is contained in a document that also contains information relating to an adult and a law enforcement agency is required to destroy all information relating to the child under this section, the agency shall alter the document so that the information relating to the child is destroyed and the information relating to the adult is preserved.

(e) The deletion of a computer entry constitutes destruction of the information contained in the entry.

(f) A law enforcement agency may maintain information relating to a child after the 90th day after the date the child successfully completes a first offender program under Section 52.031 only to determine the child's eligibility to participate in a first offender program.

(Enacted by Acts 1995, 74th Leg., ch. 262 (H.B. 327), § 53, effective January 1, 1996; am. Acts 1997, 75th Leg., ch. 1086 (H.B. 1550), § 16, effective September 1, 1997; am. Acts 1999, 76th Leg., ch. 1477 (H.B. 3517), § 16, effective September 1, 1999.)

### Sec. 58.002.   Photographs and Fingerprints of Children.

(a) Except as provided by Chapter 63, Code of Criminal Procedure, a child may not be photographed or fingerprinted without the consent of the juvenile court unless the child is taken into custody or referred to the juvenile court for conduct that constitutes a felony or a misdemeanor punishable by confinement in jail.

(b) On or before December 31 of each year, the head of each municipal or county law enforcement agency located in a county shall certify to the juvenile board for that county that the photographs and fingerprints required to be destroyed under Section 58.001 have been destroyed. The juvenile board shall conduct or cause to be conducted an audit of the records of the law enforcement agency to verify the destruction of the photographs and fingerprints and the law enforcement agency shall make its records avail-

**Family Code**

able for this purpose. If the audit shows that the certification provided by the head of the law enforcement agency is false, that person is subject to prosecution for perjury under Chapter 37, Penal Code.

(c) This section does not prohibit a law enforcement officer from photographing or fingerprinting a child who is not in custody if the child's parent or guardian voluntarily consents in writing to the photographing or fingerprinting of the child.

(d) This section does not apply to fingerprints that are required or authorized to be submitted or obtained for an application for a driver's license or personal identification card.

(e) This section does not prohibit a law enforcement officer from fingerprinting or photographing a child as provided by Section 58.0021.

(Enacted by Acts 1995, 74th Leg., ch. 262 (H.B. 327), § 53, effective January 1, 1996; am. Acts 1997, 75th Leg., ch. 1086 (H.B. 1550), § 17, effective September 1, 1997; am. Acts 1999, 76th Leg., ch. 1477 (H.B. 3517), § 17, effective September 1, 1999; am. Acts 2001, 77th Leg., ch. 1297 (H.B. 1118), § 34, effective September 1, 2001.)

## Sec. 58.0021. Fingerprints or Photographs for Comparison in Investigation.

(a) A law enforcement officer may take temporary custody of a child to take the child's fingerprints if:

(1) the officer has probable cause to believe that the child has engaged in delinquent conduct;

(2) the officer has investigated that conduct and has found other fingerprints during the investigation; and

(3) the officer has probable cause to believe that the child's fingerprints will match the other fingerprints.

(b) A law enforcement officer may take temporary custody of a child to take the child's photograph if:

(1) the officer has probable cause to believe that the child has engaged in delinquent conduct; and

(2) the officer has probable cause to believe that the child's photograph will be of material assistance in the investigation of that conduct.

(c) Temporary custody for the purpose described by Subsection (a) or (b):

(1) is not a taking into custody under Section 52.01; and

(2) may not be reported to the juvenile justice information system under Subchapter B.

(d) If a law enforcement officer does not take the child into custody under Section 52.01, the child shall be released from temporary custody authorized under this section as soon as the fingerprints or photographs are obtained.

(e) A law enforcement officer who under this section obtains fingerprints or photographs from a child shall:

(1) immediately destroy them if they do not lead to a positive comparison or identification; and

(2) make a reasonable effort to notify the child's parent, guardian, or custodian of the action taken.

(f) A law enforcement officer may under this section obtain fingerprints or photographs from a child at:

(1) a juvenile processing office; or

(2) a location that affords reasonable privacy to the child.

(Enacted by Acts 2001, 77th Leg., ch. 1297 (H.B. 1118), § 35, effective September 1, 2001.)

## Sec. 58.0022. Fingerprints or Photographs to Identify Runaways.

A law enforcement officer who takes a child into custody with probable cause to believe that the child has engaged in conduct indicating a need for supervision as described by Section 51.03(b)(3) and who after reasonable effort is unable to determine the identity of the child, may fingerprint or photograph the child to establish the child's identity. On determination of the child's identity or that the child cannot be identified by the fingerprints or photographs, the law enforcement officer shall immediately destroy all copies of the fingerprint records or photographs of the child.

(Enacted by Acts 2001, 77th Leg., ch. 1297 (H.B. 1118), § 36, effective September 1, 2001.)

## Sec. 58.003. Sealing of Records.

(a) Except as provided by Subsections (b) and (c), on the application of a person who has been found to have engaged in delinquent conduct or conduct indicating a need for supervision, or a person taken into custody to determine whether the person engaged in delinquent conduct or conduct indicating a need for supervision, on the juvenile court's own motion the court shall order the sealing of the records in the case if the court finds that:

(1) two years have elapsed since final discharge of the person or since the last official action in the person's case if there was no adjudication; and

(2) since the time specified in Subdivision (1), the person has not been convicted of a felony or a misdemeanor involving moral turpitude or found to have engaged in delinquent conduct or conduct indicating a need for supervision and no proceeding is pending seeking conviction or adjudication.

(b) A court may not order the sealing of the records of a person who has received a determinate sentence for engaging in delinquent conduct that violated a penal law listed in Section 53.045 or engaging in habitual felony conduct as described by Section 51.031.

(c) Subject to Subsection (b), a court may order the sealing of records concerning a person adjudicated as having engaged in delinquent conduct that violated a penal law of the grade of felony only if:

(1) the person is 19 years of age or older;

(2) the person was not transferred by a juvenile court under Section 54.02 to a criminal court for prosecution;

(3) the records have not been used as evidence in the punishment phase of a criminal proceeding under Section 3(a), Article 37.07, Code of Criminal Procedure; and

(4) the person has not been convicted of a penal law of the grade of felony after becoming age 17.

(c-1) Notwithstanding Subsections (a) and (c) and subject to Subsection (b), a juvenile court may order the sealing of records concerning a child adjudicated as having engaged in delinquent conduct or conduct indicating a need for supervision that violated a penal law of the grade of misdemeanor or felony if the child successfully completed a drug court program under Chapter 469, Health and Safety Code. The court may:

(1) order the sealing of the records immediately and without a hearing; or

(2) hold a hearing to determine whether to seal the records.

(c-2) If the court orders the sealing of a child's records under Subsection (c-1), a prosecuting attorney or juvenile probation department may maintain until the child's 17th birthday a separate record of the child's name and date of birth and the date the child successfully completed the drug court program. The prosecuting attorney or juvenile probation department, as applicable, shall send the record to the court as soon as

practicable after the child's 17th birthday to be added to the child's other sealed records.

(c-3) **[2 Versions: As added by Acts 2011, 82nd Leg., ch. 1150]** Notwithstanding Subsections (a) and (c) and subject to Subsection (b), a juvenile court, on the court's own motion and without a hearing, shall order the sealing of records concerning a child found to have engaged in conduct indicating a need for supervision described by Section 51.03(b)(7) or taken into custody to determine whether the child engaged in conduct indicating a need for supervision described by Section 51.03(b)(7). This subsection applies only to records related to conduct indicating a need for supervision described by Section 51.03(b)(7).

(c-3) **[2 Versions: As added by Acts 2011, 82nd Leg., ch. 1322]** Notwithstanding Subsections (a) and (c) and subject to Subsection (b), a juvenile court may order the sealing of records concerning a child found to have engaged in conduct indicating a need for supervision that violates Section 43.261, Penal Code, or taken into custody to determine whether the child engaged in conduct indicating a need for supervision that violates Section 43.261, Penal Code, if the child attends and successfully completes an educational program described by Section 37.218, Education Code, or another equivalent educational program. The court may:

(1) order the sealing of the records immediately and without a hearing; or

(2) hold a hearing to determine whether to seal the records.

(c-4) **[2 Versions: As added by Acts 2011, 82nd Leg., ch. 1150]** A prosecuting attorney or juvenile probation department may maintain until a child's 17th birthday a separate record of the child's name and date of birth and the date on which the child's records are sealed, if the child's records are sealed under Subsection (c-3). The prosecuting attorney or juvenile probation department, as applicable, shall send the record to the court as soon as practicable after the child's 17th birthday to be added to the child's other sealed records.

(c-4) **[2 Versions: As added by Acts 2011, 82nd Leg., ch. 1322]** A prosecuting attorney or juvenile probation department may maintain until a child's 17th birthday a separate record of the child's name and date of birth and the date on which the child successfully completed the educational program, if the child's records are sealed under Subsection (c-3). The prosecuting attorney or juvenile probation department, as applicable, shall send the record to the court as soon as practicable after the child's 17th birthday to be added to the child's other sealed records.

(d) **[2 Versions: As amended by Acts 2011, 82nd Leg., ch. 1150]** The court may grant to a child the relief authorized in Subsection (a), (c-1), or (c-3) at any time after final discharge of the child or after the last official action in the case if there was no adjudication, subject, if applicable, to Subsection (e). If the child is referred to the juvenile court for conduct constituting any offense and at the adjudication hearing the child is found to be not guilty of each offense alleged, the court shall immediately and without any additional hearing order the sealing of all files and records relating to the case.

(d) **[2 Versions: As amended by Acts 2011, 82nd Leg., ch. 1322]** The court may grant the relief authorized in Subsection (a), (c-1), or (c-3) at any time after final discharge of the person or after the last official action in the case if there was no adjudication, subject, if applicable, to Subsection(e). If the child is referred to the juvenile court for conduct constituting any offense and at the adjudication hearing the child is found to be not guilty of each offense alleged, the court shall immediately and without any additional hearing order the sealing of all files and records relating to the case.

(e) The court shall hold a hearing before sealing a person's records under Subsection (a) or (c) unless the applicant waives the right to a hearing in writing and the court and the prosecuting attorney for the juvenile court consent. Reasonable notice of the hearing shall be given to:

(1) the person who made the application or who is the subject of the records named in the motion;

(2) the prosecuting attorney for the juvenile court;

(3) the authority granting the discharge if the final discharge was from an institution or from parole;

(4) the public or private agency or institution having custody of records named in the application or motion; and

(5) the law enforcement agency having custody of files or records named in the application or motion.

(f) A copy of the sealing order shall be sent to each agency or official named in the order.

(g) On entry of the order:

(1) all law enforcement, prosecuting attorney, clerk of court, and juvenile court records ordered sealed shall be sent before the 61st day after the date the order is received to the court issuing the order;

(2) all records of a public or private agency or institution ordered sealed shall be sent before the 61st day after the date the order is received to the court issuing the order;

(3) all index references to the records ordered sealed shall be deleted before the 61st day after the date the order is received, and verification of the deletion shall be sent before the 61st day after the date of the deletion to the court issuing the order;

(4) the juvenile court, clerk of court, prosecuting attorney, public or private agency or institution, and law enforcement officers and agencies shall properly reply that no record exists with respect to the person on inquiry in any matter; and

(5) the adjudication shall be vacated and the proceeding dismissed and treated for all purposes other than a subsequent capital prosecution, including the purpose of showing a prior finding of delinquent conduct, as if it had never occurred.

(g-1) Any records collected or maintained by the Texas Juvenile Justice Department, including statistical data submitted under Section 221.007, Human Resources Code, are not subject to a sealing order issued under this section.

(h) Inspection of the sealed records may be permitted by an order of the juvenile court on the petition of the person who is the subject of the records and only by those persons named in the order.

(i) On the final discharge of a child or on the last official action in the case if there is no adjudication, the child shall be given a written explanation of the child's rights under this section and a copy of the provisions of this section.

(j) A person whose records have been sealed under this section is not required in any proceeding or in any application for employment, information, or licensing to state that the person has been the subject of a proceeding under this title and any statement that the person has never been found to be a delinquent child shall never be held against the person in any criminal or civil proceeding.

(k) A prosecuting attorney may, on application to the juvenile court, reopen at any time the files and records of a person adjudicated as having engaged in delinquent conduct that violated a penal law of the grade of felony sealed by the court under this section for the purposes of Sections 12.42(a)—(c) and (e), Penal Code.

*Family Code*

(*l*) On the motion of a person in whose name records are kept or on the court's own motion, the court may order the destruction of records that have been sealed under this section if:

(1) the records relate to conduct that did not violate a penal law of the grade of felony or a misdemeanor punishable by confinement in jail;

(2) five years have elapsed since the person's 16th birthday; and

(3) the person has not been convicted of a felony.

(m) On request of the Department of Public Safety, a juvenile court shall reopen and allow the department to inspect the files and records of the juvenile court relating to an applicant for a license to carry a concealed handgun under Subchapter H, Chapter 411, Government Code.

(n) A record created or maintained under Chapter 62, Code of Criminal Procedure, may not be sealed under this section if the person who is the subject of the record has a continuing obligation to register under that chapter.

(o) An agency or official named in the order that cannot seal the records because the information required in the order under Subsection (p) is incorrect or insufficient shall notify the court issuing the order before the 61st day after the date the agency or official receives the order. The court shall notify the person who made the application or who is the subject of the records named in the motion, or the attorney for that person, before the 61st day after the date the court receives the notice that the agency or official cannot seal the records because there is incorrect or insufficient information in the order.

(p) A person who is eligible to seal records may file an application for the sealing of records in a juvenile court of the county in which the proceedings occurred. The application and sealing order entered on the application must include the following information or an explanation for why one or more of the following is not included:

(1) the applicant's:

(A) full name;

(B) sex;

(C) race or ethnicity;

(D) date of birth;

(E) driver's license or identification card number; and

(F) social security number;

(2) the offense charged against the applicant or for which the applicant was referred to the juvenile justice system;

(3) the date on which and the county where the offense was alleged to have been committed; and

(4) if a petition was filed in the juvenile court, the cause number assigned to the petition and the court and county in which the petition was filed.

(Enacted by Acts 1995, 74th Leg., ch. 262 (H.B. 327), § 53, effective January 1, 1996; am. Acts 1997, 75th Leg., ch. 165 (S.B. 898), § 10.05(a), effective September 1, 1997; am. Acts 1997, 75th Leg., ch. 1086 (H.B. 1550), § 18, effective September 1, 1997; am. Acts 1999, 76th Leg., ch. 62 (S.B. 1368), § 19.01(20), effective September 1, 1999; am. Acts 1999, 76th Leg., ch. 147 (S.B. 422), § 1, effective September 1, 1999; am. Acts 2003, 78th Leg., ch. 283 (H.B. 2319), § 26, effective September 1, 2003; am. Acts 2005, 79th Leg., ch. 949 (H.B. 1575), § 16, effective September 1, 2005; am. Acts 2009, 81st Leg., ch. 189 (H.B. 2386), § 1, effective September 1, 2009; am. Acts 2011, 82nd Leg., ch. 85 (S.B. 653), § 3.008, effective September 1, 2011; am. Acts 2011, 82nd Leg., ch. 731 (H.B. 961), § 3, effective June 17, 2011; am. Acts 2011, 82nd Leg., ch. 1150 (H.B. 2015), § 2, effective September 1, 2011; am. Acts 2011, 82nd Leg., ch. 1322 (S.B. 407), § 19, effective September 1, 2011.)

## Sec. 58.004. Compilation of Information Pertaining to a Criminal Combination [Repealed].

Repealed by Acts 1997, 75th Leg., ch. 1086 (H.B. 1550), § 49(a), effective September 1, 1997. (Enacted by Acts 1995, 74th Leg., ch. 262 (H.B. 327), § 53, effective January 1, 1996.)

## Sec. 58.005. Confidentiality of Records.

(a) Records and files concerning a child, including personally identifiable information, and information obtained for the purpose of diagnosis, examination, evaluation, or treatment or for making a referral for treatment of a child by a public or private agency or institution providing supervision of a child by arrangement of the juvenile court or having custody of the child under order of the juvenile court may be disclosed only to:

(1) the professional staff or consultants of the agency or institution;

(2) the judge, probation officers, and professional staff or consultants of the juvenile court;

(3) an attorney for the child;

Family Code

(4) a governmental agency if the disclosure is required or authorized by law;

(5) a person or entity to whom the child is referred for treatment or services if the agency or institution disclosing the information has entered into a written confidentiality agreement with the person or entity regarding the protection of the disclosed information;

(6) the Texas Department of Criminal Justice and the Texas Juvenile Probation Commission for the purpose of maintaining statistical records of recidivism and for diagnosis and classification; or

(7) with leave of the juvenile court, any other person, agency, or institution having a legitimate interest in the proceeding or in the work of the court.

(b) This section does not apply to information collected under Section 58.104 or under Subchapter D-1.

(Enacted by Acts 1995, 74th Leg., ch. 262 (H.B. 327), § 53, effective January 1, 1996; am. Acts 2003, 78th Leg., ch. 283 (H.B. 2319), § 27, effective September 1, 2003; am. Acts 2007, 80th Leg., ch. 908 (H.B. 2884), § 26(a), effective September 1, 2007.)

## Sec. 58.0051. Interagency Sharing of Educational Records.

(a) In this section:

(1) "Educational records" means records in the possession of a primary or secondary educational institution that contain information relating to a student, including information relating to the student's:

(A) identity;

(B) special needs;

(C) educational accommodations;

(D) assessment or diagnostic test results;

(E) attendance records;

(F) disciplinary records;

(G) medical records; and

(H) psychological diagnoses.

(2) "Juvenile service provider" means a governmental entity that provides juvenile justice or prevention, medical, educational, or other support services to a juvenile. The term includes:

(A) a state or local juvenile justice agency as defined by Section 58.101;

(B) health and human services agencies, as defined by Section 531.001, Government Code, and the Health and Human Services Commission;

(C) the Department of Public Safety;

(D) the Texas Education Agency;

(E) an independent school district;

(F) a juvenile justice alternative education program;

(G) a charter school;

(H) a local mental health or mental retardation authority;

(I) a court with jurisdiction over juveniles;

(J) a district attorney's office;

(K) a county attorney's office; and

(L) a children's advocacy center established under Section 264.402.

(3) "Student" means a person who:

(A) is registered or in attendance at a primary or secondary educational institution; and

(B) is younger than 18 years of age.

(b) At the request of a juvenile service provider, an independent school district or a charter school shall disclose to the juvenile service provider confidential information contained in the student's educational records if the student has been:

(1) taken into custody under Section 52.01; or

(2) referred to a juvenile court for allegedly engaging in delinquent conduct or conduct indicating a need for supervision.

(c) An independent school district or charter school that discloses confidential information to a juvenile service provider under Subsection (b) may not destroy a record of the disclosed information before the seventh anniversary of the date the information is disclosed.

(d) An independent school district or charter school shall comply with a request under Subsection (b) regardless of whether other state law makes that information confidential.

(e) A juvenile service provider that receives confidential information under this section shall:

(1) certify in writing that the juvenile service provider receiving the confidential information has agreed not to disclose it to a third party, other than another juvenile service provider; and

(2) use the confidential information only to:

(A) verify the identity of a student involved in the juvenile justice system; and

(B) provide delinquency prevention or treatment services to the student.

(f) A juvenile service provider may establish an internal protocol for sharing information with other juvenile service providers as necessary to efficiently and promptly disclose and accept the

Family Code

information. The protocol may specify the types of information that may be shared under this section without violating federal law, including any federal funding requirements. A juvenile service provider may enter into a memorandum of understanding with another juvenile service provider to share information according to the juvenile service provider's protocols. A juvenile service provider shall comply with this section regardless of whether the juvenile service provider establishes an internal protocol or enters into a memorandum of understanding under this subsection unless compliance with this section violates federal law.

(g) This section does not affect the confidential status of the information being shared. The information may be released to a third party only as directed by a court order or as otherwise authorized by law. Personally identifiable information disclosed to a juvenile service provider under this section is not subject to disclosure to a third party under Chapter 552, Government Code.

(h) A juvenile service provider that requests information under this section shall pay a fee to the disclosing juvenile service provider in the same amounts charged for the provision of public information under Subchapter F, Chapter 552, Government Code, unless:

(1) a memorandum of understanding between the requesting provider and the disclosing provider:

(A) prohibits the payment of a fee;

(B) provides for the waiver of a fee; or

(C) provides an alternate method of assessing a fee;

(2) the disclosing provider waives the payment of the fee; or

(3) disclosure of the information is required by law other than this subchapter.

(Enacted by Acts 1999, 76th Leg., ch. 217 (H.B. 1749), § 1, effective May 24, 1999; am. Acts 2007, 80th Leg., ch. 908 (H.B. 2884), § 16, effective September 1, 2007; am. Acts 2011, 82nd Leg., ch. 653 (S.B. 1106), § 2, effective June 17, 2011.)

### Sec. 58.0052. Interagency Sharing of Noneducational Records.

(a) In this section:

(1) "Juvenile service provider" has the meaning assigned by Section 58.0051.

(2) "Multi-system youth" means a person who:

(A) is younger than 19 years of age; and

(B) has received services from two or more juvenile service providers.

(3) "Personal health information" means personally identifiable information regarding a multi-system youth's physical or mental health or the provision of or payment for health care services, including case management services, to a multi-system youth. The term does not include clinical psychological notes or substance abuse treatment information.

(b) At the request of a juvenile service provider, another juvenile service provider shall disclose to that provider a multi-system youth's personal health information or a history of governmental services provided to the multi-system youth, including:

(1) identity;

(2) medical records;

(3) assessment results;

(4) special needs;

(5) program placements; and

(6) psychological diagnoses.

(c) A juvenile service provider may disclose personally identifiable information under this section only for the purposes of:

(1) identifying a multi-system youth;

(2) coordinating and monitoring care for a multi-system youth; and

(3) improving the quality of juvenile services provided to a multi-system youth.

(d) To the extent that this section conflicts with another law of this state with respect to confidential information held by a governmental agency, this section controls.

(e) A juvenile service provider may establish an internal protocol for sharing information with other juvenile service providers as necessary to efficiently and promptly disclose and accept the information. The protocol may specify the types of information that may be shared under this section without violating federal law, including any federal funding requirements. A juvenile service provider may enter into a memorandum of understanding with another juvenile service provider to share information according to the juvenile service provider's protocols. A juvenile service provider shall comply with this section regardless of whether the juvenile service provider establishes an internal protocol or enters into a memorandum of understanding under this subsection unless compliance with this section violates federal law.

(f) This section does not affect the confidential status of the information being shared. The information may be released to a third party only as directed by a court order or as otherwise authorized by law. Personally identifiable information disclosed to a juvenile service provider under this section is not subject to disclosure to a third party under Chapter 552, Government Code.

(g) This section does not affect the authority of a governmental agency to disclose to a third party for research purposes information that is not personally identifiable as provided by the governmental agency's protocol.

(h) A juvenile service provider that requests information under this section shall pay a fee to the disclosing juvenile service provider in the same amounts charged for the provision of public information under Subchapter F, Chapter 552, Government Code, unless:

    (1) a memorandum of understanding between the requesting provider and the disclosing provider:

      (A) prohibits the payment of a fee;

      (B) provides for the waiver of a fee; or

      (C) provides an alternate method of assessing a fee;

    (2) the disclosing provider waives the payment of the fee; or

    (3) disclosure of the information is required by law other than this subchapter.

(Enacted by Acts 2011, 82nd Leg., ch. 653 (S.B. 1106), § 2, effective June 17, 2011.)

## Sec. 58.006. Destruction of Certain Records.

The court shall order the destruction of the records relating to the conduct for which a child is taken into custody, including records contained in the juvenile justice information system, if:

    (1) a determination that no probable cause exists to believe the child engaged in the conduct is made under Section 53.01 and the case is not referred to a prosecutor for review under Section 53.012; or

    (2) a determination that no probable cause exists to believe the child engaged in the conduct is made by a prosecutor under Section 53.012.

(Enacted by Acts 1995, 74th Leg., ch. 262 (H.B. 327), § 53, effective January 1, 1996.)

## Sec. 58.007. Physical Records or Files.

(a) This section applies only to the inspection and maintenance of a physical record or file concerning a child and the storage of information, by electronic means or otherwise, concerning the child from which a physical record or file could be generated and does not affect the collection, dissemination, or maintenance of information as provided by Subchapter B. This section does not apply to a record or file relating to a child that is:

    (1) required or authorized to be maintained under the laws regulating the operation of motor vehicles in this state;

    (2) maintained by a municipal or justice court; or

    (3) subject to disclosure under Chapter 62, Code of Criminal Procedure.

(b) Except as provided by Article 15.27, Code of Criminal Procedure, the records and files of a juvenile court, a clerk of court, a juvenile probation department, or a prosecuting attorney relating to a child who is a party to a proceeding under this title are open to inspection only by:

    (1) the judge, probation officers, and professional staff or consultants of the juvenile court;

    (2) a juvenile justice agency as that term is defined by Section 58.101;

    (3) an attorney for a party to the proceeding;

    (4) a public or private agency or institution providing supervision of the child by arrangement of the juvenile court, or having custody of the child under juvenile court order; or

    (5) with leave of the juvenile court, any other person, agency, or institution having a legitimate interest in the proceeding or in the work of the court.

(c) Except as provided by Subsection (d), law enforcement records and files concerning a child and information stored, by electronic means or otherwise, concerning the child from which a record or file could be generated may not be disclosed to the public and shall be:

    (1) if maintained on paper or microfilm, kept separate from adult files and records;

    (2) if maintained electronically in the same computer system as records or files relating to adults, be accessible under controls that are separate and distinct from controls to access electronic data concerning adults; and

    (3) maintained on a local basis only and not sent to a central state or federal depository, except as provided by Subchapters B, D, and E.

(d) The law enforcement files and records of a person who is transferred from the Texas Youth Commission to the Texas Department of Criminal Justice may be transferred to a central state or federal depository for adult records on or after the date of transfer.

(e) Law enforcement records and files concerning a child may be inspected or copied by a juvenile justice agency as that term is defined by Section 58.101, a criminal justice agency as that term is defined by Section 411.082, Government Code, the child, and the child's parent or guardian.

(f) If a child has been reported missing by a parent, guardian, or conservator of that child, information about the child may be forwarded to and disseminated by the Texas Crime Information Center and the National Crime Information Center.

(g) For the purpose of offering a record as evidence in the punishment phase of a criminal proceeding, a prosecuting attorney may obtain the record of a defendant's adjudication that is admissible under Section 3(a), Article 37.07, Code of Criminal Procedure, by submitting a request for the record to the juvenile court that made the adjudication. If a court receives a request from a prosecuting attorney under this subsection, the court shall, if the court possesses the requested record of adjudication, certify and provide the prosecuting attorney with a copy of the record.

(h) The juvenile court may disseminate to the public the following information relating to a child who is the subject of a directive to apprehend or a warrant of arrest and who cannot be located for the purpose of apprehension:

(1) the child's name, including other names by which the child is known;

(2) the child's physical description, including sex, weight, height, race, ethnicity, eye color, hair color, scars, marks, and tattoos;

(3) a photograph of the child; and

(4) a description of the conduct the child is alleged to have committed, including the level and degree of the alleged offense.

(i) In addition to the authority to release information under Subsection (b)(5), a juvenile probation department may release information contained in its records without leave of the juvenile court pursuant to guidelines adopted by the juvenile board.

(j) Before a child or a child's parent or guardian may inspect or copy a record or file concerning the child under Subsection (e), the custodian of the record or file shall redact:

(1) any personally identifiable information about a juvenile suspect, offender, victim, or witness who is not the child; and

(2) any information that is excepted from required disclosure under Chapter 552, Government Code, or other law.

(Enacted by Acts 1995, 74th Leg., ch. 262 (H.B. 327), § 53, effective January 1, 1996; am. Acts 1997, 75th Leg., ch. 1086 (H.B. 1550), § 19, effective September 1, 1997; am. Acts 1997, 75th Leg., ch. 1086 (H.B. 1550), § 20, effective September 1, 1997; am. Acts 1999, 76th Leg., ch. 815 (H.B. 1583), § 1, effective June 18, 1999; am. Acts 1999, 76th Leg., ch. 1415 (H.B. 2145), § 20, effective September 1, 1999; am. Acts 1999, 76th Leg., ch. 1477 (H.B. 3517), § 18, effective September 1, 1999; am. Acts 2001, 77th Leg., ch. 1297 (H.B. 1118), § 37, effective September 1, 2001; am. Acts 2007, 80th Leg., ch. 879 (H.B. 1960), § 1, effective September 1, 2007; am. Acts 2007, 80th Leg., ch. 908 (H.B. 2884), § 17, effective September 1, 2007; am. Acts 2009, 81st Leg., ch. 87 (S.B. 1969), § 25.061, effective September 1, 2009.)

## Sec. 58.0071.　Destruction of Certain Physical Records and Files.

(a) In this section:

(1) "Juvenile case" means:

(A) a referral for conduct indicating a need for supervision or delinquent conduct; or

(B) if a petition was filed, all charges made in the petition.

(2) "Physical records and files" include entries in a computer file or information on microfilm, microfiche, or any other electronic storage media.

(b) The custodian of physical records and files in a juvenile case may destroy the records and files if the custodian duplicates the information in the records and files in a computer file or information on microfilm, microfiche, or any other electronic storage media.

(c) The following persons may authorize, subject to Subsections (d) and (e) and any other restriction the person may impose, the destruction of the physical records and files relating to a closed juvenile case:

(1) a juvenile board in relation to the records and files in the possession of the juvenile probation department;

(2) the head of a law enforcement agency in relation to the records and files in the possession of the agency; and

(3) a prosecuting attorney in relation to the records and files in the possession of the prosecuting attorney's office.

(d) The physical records and files of a juvenile case may only be destroyed if the child who is the respondent in the case:

(1) is at least 18 years of age and:

(A) the most serious allegation adjudicated was conduct indicating a need for supervision;

(B) the most serious allegation was conduct indicating a need for supervision and there was not an adjudication; or

(C) the referral or information did not relate to conduct indicating a need for supervision or delinquent conduct and the juvenile court or the court's staff did not take action on the referral or information for that reason;

(2) is at least 21 years of age and:

(A) the most serious allegation adjudicated was delinquent conduct that violated a penal law of the grade of misdemeanor; or

(B) the most serious allegation was delinquent conduct that violated a penal law of the grade of misdemeanor or felony and there was not an adjudication; or

(3) is at least 31 years of age and the most serious allegation adjudicated was delinquent conduct that violated a penal law of the grade of felony.

(e) If a record or file contains information relating to more than one juvenile case, information relating to each case may only be destroyed if:

(1) the destruction of the information is authorized under this section; and

(2) the information can be separated from information that is not authorized to be destroyed under this section.

(f) This section does not affect the destruction of physical records and files authorized by the Texas State Library Records Retention Schedule. (Enacted by Acts 2001, 77th Leg., ch. 1297 (H.B. 1118), § 38, effective September 1, 2001.)

## Sec. 58.00711. Records Relating to Children Convicted of Fine-Only Misdemeanors.

Except as provided by Article 45.0217(b), Code of Criminal Procedure, all records and files and information stored by electronic means or otherwise, from which a record or file could be generated, relating to a child who is convicted of and has satisfied the judgment for a fine-only misdemeanor offense other than a traffic offense are confidential and may not be disclosed to the public.

(Enacted by Acts 2011, 82nd Leg., ch. 731 (H.B. 961), § 4, effective June 17, 2011.)

## Sec. 58.0072. Dissemination of Juvenile Justice Information.

(a) Except as provided by this section, juvenile justice information collected and maintained by the Texas Juvenile Probation Commission for statistical and research purposes is confidential information for the use of the commission and may not be disseminated by the commission.

(b) Juvenile justice information consists of information of the type described by Section 58.104, including statistical data in any form or medium collected, maintained, or submitted to the Texas Juvenile Justice Department under Section 221.007, Human Resources Code.

(c) The Texas Juvenile Probation Commission may grant the following entities access to juvenile justice information for research and statistical purposes or for any other purpose approved by the commission:

(1) criminal justice agencies as defined by Section 411.082, Government Code;

(2) the Texas Education Agency, as authorized under Section 37.084, Education Code;

(3) any agency under the authority of the Health and Human Services Commission; or

(4) a public or private university.

(d) The Texas Juvenile Probation Commission may grant the following entities access to juvenile justice information only for a purpose beneficial to and approved by the commission to:

(1) a person working on a research or statistical project that:

(A) is funded in whole or in part by state or federal funds; and

(B) meets the requirements of and is approved by the commission; or

(2) a governmental entity that has a specific agreement with the commission, if the agreement:

(A) specifically authorizes access to information;

(B) limits the use of information to the purposes for which the information is given;

(C) ensures the security and confidentiality of the information; and

(D) provides for sanctions if a requirement imposed under Paragraph (A), (B), or (C) is violated.

(e) The Texas Juvenile Probation Commission shall grant access to juvenile justice information for legislative purposes under Section 552.008, Government Code.

(f) The Texas Juvenile Probation Commission may not release juvenile justice information in identifiable form, except for information released under Subsection (c)(1), (2), or (3) or under the terms of an agreement entered into under Subsection (d)(2). For purposes of this subsection, identifiable information means information that contains a juvenile offender's name or other personal identifiers or that can, by virtue of sample size or other factors, be reasonably interpreted as referring to a particular juvenile offender.

(g) The Texas Juvenile Probation Commission is not required to release or disclose juvenile justice information to any person not identified under this section.

(Enacted by Acts 2005, 79th Leg., ch. 949 (H.B. 1575), § 17, effective September 1, 2005; am. Acts 2007, 80th Leg., ch. 908 (H.B. 2884), § 18, effective September 1, 2007; am. Acts 2011, 82nd Leg., ch. 85 (S.B. 653), § 3.009, effective September 1, 2011.)

## SUBCHAPTER B
## JUVENILE JUSTICE INFORMATION SYSTEM

### Sec. 58.101.  Definitions.

In this subchapter:

(1) "Criminal justice agency" has the meaning assigned by Section 411.082, Government Code.

(2) "Department" means the Department of Public Safety of the State of Texas.

(3) "Disposition" means an action that results in the termination, transfer of jurisdiction, or indeterminate suspension of the prosecution of a juvenile offender.

(4) "Incident number" means a unique number assigned to a child during a specific custodial or detention period or for a specific referral to the office or official designated by the juvenile board, if the juvenile offender was not taken into custody before the referral.

(5) "Juvenile justice agency" means an agency that has custody or control over juvenile offenders.

(6) "Juvenile offender" means a child who has been assigned an incident number.

(7) "State identification number" means a unique number assigned by the department to a child in the juvenile justice information system.

(8) "Uniform incident fingerprint card" means a multiple-part form containing a unique incident number with space for information relating to the conduct for which a child has been taken into custody, detained, or referred, the child's fingerprints, and other relevant information.

(Enacted by Acts 1995, 74th Leg., ch. 262 (H.B. 327), § 53, effective January 1, 1996; am. Acts 2001, 77th Leg., ch. 1297 (H.B. 1118), § 39, effective September 1, 2001.)

### Sec. 58.102.   Juvenile Justice Information System.

(a) The department is responsible for recording data and maintaining a database for a computerized juvenile justice information system that serves:

(1) as the record creation point for the juvenile justice information system maintained by the state; and

(2) as the control terminal for entry of records, in accordance with federal law, rule, and policy, into the federal records system maintained by the Federal Bureau of Investigation.

(b) The department shall develop and maintain the system with the cooperation and advice of the:

(1) Texas Youth Commission;

(2) Texas Juvenile Probation Commission;

(3) Criminal Justice Policy Council; and

(4) juvenile courts and clerks of juvenile courts.

(c) The department may not collect or retain information relating to a juvenile if this chapter prohibits or restricts the collection or retention of the information.

(d) The database must contain the information required by this subchapter.

(e) The department shall designate the offense codes and has the sole responsibility for designating the state identification number for each juvenile whose name appears in the juvenile justice system.

(Enacted by Acts 1995, 74th Leg., ch. 262 (H.B. 327), § 53, effective January 1, 1996.)

### Sec. 58.103.   Purpose of System.

The purpose of the juvenile justice information system is to:

(1) provide agencies and personnel within the juvenile justice system accurate information relating to children who come into contact with the juvenile justice system of this state;

(2) provide, where allowed by law, adult criminal justice agencies accurate and easily accessible information relating to children who come into contact with the juvenile justice system;

(3) provide an efficient conversion, where appropriate, of juvenile records to adult criminal records;

(4) improve the quality of data used to conduct impact analyses of proposed legislative changes in the juvenile justice system; and

(5) improve the ability of interested parties to analyze the functioning of the juvenile justice system.

(Enacted by Acts 1995, 74th Leg., ch. 262 (H.B. 327), § 53, effective January 1, 1996.)

### Sec. 58.104. Types of Information Collected.

(a) Subject to Subsection (f), the juvenile justice information system shall consist of information relating to delinquent conduct committed by a juvenile offender that, if the conduct had been committed by an adult, would constitute a criminal offense other than an offense punishable by a fine only, including information relating to:

(1) the juvenile offender;

(2) the intake or referral of the juvenile offender into the juvenile justice system;

(3) the detention of the juvenile offender;

(4) the prosecution of the juvenile offender;

(5) the disposition of the juvenile offender's case, including the name and description of any program to which the juvenile offender is referred; and

(6) the probation or commitment of the juvenile offender.

(b) To the extent possible and subject to Subsection (a), the department shall include in the juvenile justice information system the following information for each juvenile offender taken into custody, detained, or referred under this title for delinquent conduct:

(1) the juvenile offender's name, including other names by which the juvenile offender is known;

(2) the juvenile offender's date and place of birth;

(3) the juvenile offender's physical description, including sex, weight, height, race, ethnicity, eye color, hair color, scars, marks, and tattoos;

(4) the juvenile offender's state identification number, and other identifying information, as determined by the department;

(5) the juvenile offender's fingerprints;

(6) the juvenile offender's last known residential address, including the census tract number designation for the address;

(7) the name and identifying number of the agency that took into custody or detained the juvenile offender;

(8) the date of detention or custody;

(9) the conduct for which the juvenile offender was taken into custody, detained, or referred, including level and degree of the alleged offense;

(10) the name and identifying number of the juvenile intake agency or juvenile probation office;

(11) each disposition by the juvenile intake agency or juvenile probation office;

(12) the date of disposition by the juvenile intake agency or juvenile probation office;

(13) the name and identifying number of the prosecutor's office;

(14) each disposition by the prosecutor;

(15) the date of disposition by the prosecutor;

(16) the name and identifying number of the court;

(17) each disposition by the court, including information concerning custody of a juvenile offender by a juvenile justice agency or probation;

(18) the date of disposition by the court;

(19) any commitment or release under supervision by the Texas Youth Commission;

(20) the date of any commitment or release under supervision by the Texas Youth Commission; and

(21) a description of each appellate proceeding.

(c) The department may designate codes relating to the information described by Subsection (b).

(d) The department shall designate a state identification number for each juvenile offender.

(e) This subchapter does not apply to a disposition that represents an administrative status notice of an agency described by Section 58.102(b).

(f) Records maintained by the department in the depository are subject to being sealed under Section 58.003.

(Enacted by Acts 1995, 74th Leg., ch. 262 (H.B. 327), § 53, effective January 1, 1996; am. Acts 1997, 75th Leg., ch. 1086 (H.B. 1550), § 21, effective September 1, 1997; am. Acts 2005, 79th Leg., ch. 949 (H.B. 1575), § 18, effective September 1, 2005.)

### Sec. 58.105. Duties of Juvenile Board.

Each juvenile board shall provide for:

(1) the compilation and maintenance of records and information needed for reporting information to the department under this subchapter;

(2) the transmittal to the department, in the manner provided by the department, of all

records and information required by the department under this subchapter; and

(3) access by the department to inspect records and information to determine the completeness and accuracy of information reported.

(Enacted by Acts 1995, 74th Leg., ch. 262 (H.B. 327), § 53, effective January 1, 1996.)

### Sec. 58.106. Confidentiality.

(a) Except as otherwise provided by this section, information contained in the juvenile justice information system is confidential information for the use of the department and may not be disseminated by the department except:

(1) with the permission of the juvenile offender, to military personnel of this state or the United States;

(2) to a person or entity to which the department may grant access to adult criminal history records as provided by Section 411.083, Government Code;

(3) to a juvenile justice agency;

(4) to the Texas Youth Commission and the Texas Juvenile Probation Commission for analytical purposes;

(5) to the office of independent ombudsman of the Texas Youth Commission; and

(6) **[2 Versions: As added by Acts 2011, 82nd Leg., ch. 186 and by Acts 2011, 82nd Leg., ch. 1098]** to a county, justice, or municipal court exercising jurisdiction over a juvenile under Section 54.021.

(6) **[2 Versions: As added by Acts 2011, 82nd Leg., ch. 653]** to a county, justice, or municipal court exercising jurisdiction over a juvenile.

(a-1) Information disseminated under Subsection (a) remains confidential after dissemination and may be disclosed by the recipient only as provided by this title.

(b) Subsection (a) does not apply to a document maintained by a juvenile justice agency that is the source of information collected by the department.

(c) The department may, if necessary to protect the welfare of the community, disseminate to the public the following information relating to a juvenile who has escaped from the custody of the Texas Youth Commission or from another secure detention or correctional facility:

(1) the juvenile's name, including other names by which the juvenile is known;

(2) the juvenile's physical description, including sex, weight, height, race, ethnicity, eye color, hair color, scars, marks, and tattoos;

(3) a photograph of the juvenile; and

(4) a description of the conduct for which the juvenile was committed to the Texas Youth Commission or detained in the secure detention or correctional facility, including the level and degree of the alleged offense.

(d) The department may, if necessary to protect the welfare of the community, disseminate to the public the information listed under Subsection (c) relating to a juvenile offender when notified by a law enforcement agency of this state that the law enforcement agency has been issued a directive to apprehend the offender or an arrest warrant for the offender or that the law enforcement agency is otherwise authorized to arrest the offender and that the offender is suspected of having:

(1) committed a felony offense under the following provisions of the Penal Code:

(A) Title 5;

(B) Section 29.02; or

(C) Section 29.03; and

(2) fled from arrest or apprehension for commission of the offense.

(Enacted by Acts 1995, 74th Leg., ch. 262 (H.B. 327), § 53, effective January 1, 1996; am. Acts 1997, 75th Leg., ch. 380 (S.B. 625), § 1, effective September 1, 1997; am. Acts 1999, 76th Leg., ch. 407 (S.B. 187), § 1, effective September 1, 1999; am. Acts 1999, 76th Leg., ch. 1477 (H.B. 3517), § 19, effective September 1, 1999; am. Acts 2007, 80th Leg., ch. 263 (S.B. 103), § 11, effective June 8, 2007; am. Acts 2011, 82nd Leg., ch. 186 (S.B. 1241), § 1, effective September 1, 2011; am. Acts 2011, 82nd Leg., ch. 653 (S.B. 1106), § 3, effective June 17, 2011; am. Acts 2011, 82nd Leg., ch. 1098 (S.B. 1489), § 11, effective September 1, 2011.)

### Sec. 58.107. Compatibility of Data.

Data supplied to the juvenile justice information system must be compatible with the system and must contain both incident numbers and state identification numbers.

(Enacted by Acts 1995, 74th Leg., ch. 262 (H.B. 327), § 53, effective January 1, 1996.)

### Sec. 58.108. Duties of Agencies and Courts.

(a) A juvenile justice agency and a clerk of a juvenile court shall:

(1) compile and maintain records needed for reporting data required by the department;

(2) transmit to the department in the manner provided by the department data required by the department;

(3) give the department or its accredited agents access to the agency or court for the purpose of inspection to determine the completeness and accuracy of data reported; and

(4) cooperate with the department to enable the department to perform its duties under this chapter.

(b) A juvenile justice agency and clerk of a court shall retain documents described by this section.

(Enacted by Acts 1995, 74th Leg., ch. 262 (H.B. 327), § 53, effective January 1, 1996.)

## Sec. 58.109. Uniform Incident Fingerprint Card.

(a) The department may provide for the use of a uniform incident fingerprint card in the maintenance of the juvenile justice information system.

(b) The department shall design, print, and distribute to each law enforcement agency and juvenile intake agency uniform incident fingerprint cards.

(c) The incident cards must:

(1) be serially numbered with an incident number in a manner that allows each incident of referral of a juvenile offender who is the subject of the incident fingerprint card to be readily ascertained; and

(2) be multiple-part forms that can be transmitted with the juvenile offender through the juvenile justice process and that allow each agency to report required data to the department.

(d) Subject to available telecommunications capacity, the department shall develop the capability to receive by electronic means from a law enforcement agency the information on the uniform incident fingerprint card. The information must be in a form that is compatible to the form required of data supplied to the juvenile justice information system.

(Enacted by Acts 1995, 74th Leg., ch. 262 (H.B. 327), § 53, effective January 1, 1996.)

## Sec. 58.110. Reporting.

(a) The department by rule shall develop reporting procedures that ensure that the juvenile offender processing data is reported from the time a juvenile offender is initially taken into custody, detained, or referred until the time a juvenile offender is released from the jurisdiction of the juvenile justice system.

(b) The law enforcement agency or the juvenile intake agency that initiates the entry of the juvenile offender into the juvenile justice information system for a specific incident shall prepare a uniform incident fingerprint card and initiate the reporting process for each incident reportable under this subchapter.

(c) The clerk of the court exercising jurisdiction over a juvenile offender's case shall report the disposition of the case to the department. A clerk of the court who violates this subsection commits an offense. An offense under this subsection is a Class C misdemeanor.

(d) In each county, the reporting agencies may make alternative arrangements for reporting the required information, including combined reporting or electronic reporting, if the alternative reporting is approved by the juvenile board and the department.

(e) Except as otherwise required by applicable state laws or regulations, information required by this chapter to be reported to the department shall be reported promptly. The information shall be reported not later than the 30th day after the date the information is received by the agency responsible for reporting the information, except that a juvenile offender's custody or detention without previous custody shall be reported to the department not later than the seventh day after the date of the custody or detention.

(f) Subject to available telecommunications capacity, the department shall develop the capability to receive by electronic means the information required under this section to be reported to the department. The information must be in a form that is compatible to the form required of data to be reported under this section.

(Enacted by Acts 1995, 74th Leg., ch. 262 (H.B. 327), § 53, effective January 1, 1996; am. Acts 2007, 80th Leg., ch. 908 (H.B. 2884), § 19, effective September 1, 2007.)

## Sec. 58.111. Local Data Advisory Boards.

The commissioners court of each county may create a local data advisory board to perform the same duties relating to the juvenile justice information system as the duties performed by a local data advisory board in relation to the criminal history record system under Article 60.09, Code of Criminal Procedure.

(Enacted by Acts 1995, 74th Leg., ch. 262 (H.B. 327), § 53, effective January 1, 1996.)

## Sec. 58.112. Report to Legislature.

Not later than August 15 of each year, the Texas Juvenile Probation Commission shall submit to the lieutenant governor, the speaker of the house of representatives, and the governor a report that contains the following statistical information relating to children referred to a juvenile court during the preceding year:

(1) the ages, races, and counties of residence of the children transferred to a district court or criminal district court for criminal proceedings; and

(2) the ages, races, and counties of residence of the children committed to the Texas Youth Commission, placed on probation, or discharged without any disposition.

(Enacted by Acts 1995, 74th Leg., ch. 262 (H.B. 327), § 53, effective January 1, 1996; am. Acts 2001, 77th Leg., ch. 1297 (H.B. 1118), § 40, effective September 1, 2001.)

### Sec. 58.113. Warrants.

The department shall maintain in a computerized database that is accessible by the same entities that may access the juvenile justice information system information relating to a warrant of arrest, as that term is defined by Article 15.01, Code of Criminal Procedure, or a directive to apprehend under Section 52.015 for any child, without regard to whether the child has been taken into custody.

(Enacted by Acts 1995, 74th Leg., ch. 262 (H.B. 327), § 53, effective January 1, 1996.)

### SUBCHAPTER C
### AUTOMATIC RESTRICTION OF
### ACCESS TO RECORDS

### Sec. 58.201. Definition.

In this subchapter, "department" means the Department of Public Safety of the State of Texas.

(Enacted by Acts 2001, 77th Leg., ch. 1297 (H.B. 1118), § 41, effective September 1, 2001.)

### Sec. 58.202. Exempted Records.

The following records are exempt from this subchapter:

(1) sex offender registration records maintained by the department or a local law enforcement agency under Chapter 62, Code of Criminal Procedure; and

(2) records relating to a criminal combination or criminal street gang maintained by the department or a local law enforcement agency under Chapter 61, Code of Criminal Procedure.

(Enacted by Acts 2001, 77th Leg., ch. 1297 (H.B. 1118), § 41, effective September 1, 2001.)

### Sec. 58.203. Certification.

(a) The department shall certify to the juvenile probation department to which a referral was made that resulted in information being submitted to the juvenile justice information system that the records relating to a person's juvenile case are subject to automatic restriction of access if:

(1) the person is at least 17 years of age;

(2) the juvenile case did not include violent or habitual felony conduct resulting in proceedings in the juvenile court under Section 53.045; and

(3) the juvenile case was not certified for trial in criminal court under Section 54.02.

(b) If the department's records relate to a juvenile court with multicounty jurisdiction, the department shall issue the certification described by Subsection (a) to each juvenile probation department that serves the court. On receipt of the certification, each juvenile probation department shall determine whether it received the referral and, if it received the referral, take the restrictive action notification required by law.

(c) The department may issue the certification described by Subsection (a) by electronic means, including by electronic mail.

(Enacted by Acts 2001, 77th Leg., ch. 1297 (H.B. 1118), § 41, effective September 1, 2001; am. Acts 2005, 79th Leg., ch. 949 (H.B. 1575), § 19, effective September 1, 2005; am. Acts 2011, 82nd Leg., ch. 731 (H.B. 961), § 5, effective June 17, 2011.)

### Sec. 58.204. Restricted Access on Certification.

(a) On certification of records in a case under Section 58.203, the department, except as provided by Subsection (b):

(1) may not disclose the existence of the records or any information from the records in response to an inquiry from:

(A) a law enforcement agency;

(B) a criminal or juvenile justice agency;

(C) a governmental or other agency given access to information under Chapter 411, Government Code; or

(D) any other person, agency, organization, or entity; and

(2) shall respond to a request for information about the records by stating that the records do not exist.

(b) On certification of records in a case under Section 58.203, the department may permit access to the information in the juvenile justice information system relating to the case of an individual only:

(1) by a criminal justice agency for a criminal justice purpose, as those terms are defined by Section 411.082, Government Code; or

(2) for research purposes, by the Texas Juvenile Probation Commission, the Texas Youth Commission, or the Criminal Justice Policy Council.

(Enacted by Acts 2001, 77th Leg., ch. 1297 (H.B. 1118), § 41, effective September 1, 2001.)

### Sec. 58.205. Request to the Federal Bureau of Investigation on Certification.

On certification of records in a case under Section 58.203, the department shall request the Federal Bureau of Investigation to:

(1) place the information in its files on restricted status, with access only by a criminal justice agency for a criminal justice purpose, as those terms are defined by Section 411.082, Government Code; or

(2) if the action described in Subdivision (1) is not feasible, delete all information in its database concerning the case.

(Enacted by Acts 2001, 77th Leg., ch. 1297 (H.B. 1118), § 41, effective September 1, 2001.)

### Sec. 58.206. Effect of Certification in Relation to the Protected Person.

(a) On certification of records in a case under Section 58.203:

(1) the person who is the subject of the records is not required to state in any proceeding, except as otherwise authorized by law in a criminal proceeding in which the person is testifying as a defendant, or in any application for employment, licensing, or other public or private benefit that the person has been a respondent in a case under this title and may not be punished, by perjury prosecution or otherwise, for denying:

(A) the existence of the records; or

(B) the person's participation in a juvenile proceeding related to the records; and

(2) information from the records may not be admitted against the person who is the subject of the records in a civil or criminal proceeding except a proceeding in which a juvenile adjudication was admitted under:

(A) Section 12.42, Penal Code;

(B) Article 37.07, Code of Criminal Procedure; or

(C) as otherwise authorized by criminal procedural law.

(b) A person who is the subject of records certified under this subchapter may not waive the restricted status of the records or the consequences of the restricted status.

(Enacted by Acts 2001, 77th Leg., ch. 1297 (H.B. 1118), § 41, effective September 1, 2001.)

### Sec. 58.207. Juvenile Court Orders on Certification.

(a) On certification of records in a case under Section 58.203, the juvenile court shall order:

(1) that the following records relating to the case may be accessed only as provided by Section 58.204(b):

(A) if the respondent was committed to the Texas Youth Commission, records maintained by the commission;

(B) records maintained by the juvenile probation department;

(C) records maintained by the clerk of the court;

(D) records maintained by the prosecutor's office; and

(E) records maintained by a law enforcement agency; and

(2) the juvenile probation department to make a reasonable effort to notify the person who is the subject of records for which access has been restricted of the action restricting access and the legal significance of the action for the person, but only if the person has requested the notification in writing and has provided the juvenile probation department with a current address.

(b) On receipt of an order under Subsection (a)(1), the agency maintaining the records:

(1) may allow access only as provided by Section 58.204(b); and

(2) shall respond to a request for information about the records by stating that the records do not exist.

(Enacted by Acts 2001, 77th Leg., ch. 1297 (H.B. 1118), § 41, effective September 1, 2001; am. Acts 2005, 79th Leg., ch. 949 (H.B. 1575), § 20, effective September 1, 2005.)

### Sec. 58.208. Information to Child on Discharge.

On the final discharge of a child from the juvenile system or on the last official action in the case, if there is no adjudication, the appropriate juvenile justice official shall provide to the child:

(1) a written explanation of how automatic restricted access under this subchapter works;

(2) a copy of this subchapter; and

(3) a statement that if the child wishes to receive notification of an action restricting access to the child's records under Section 58.207(a), the child must before the child's 17th birthday provide the juvenile probation department with a current address where the child can receive notification.

(Enacted by Acts 2001, 77th Leg., ch. 1297 (H.B. 1118), § 41, effective September 1, 2001; am. Acts 2005, 79th Leg., ch. 949 (H.B. 1575), § 21, effective September 1, 2005; am. Acts 2011, 82nd Leg., ch. 731 (H.B. 961), § 6, effective June 17, 2011.)

### Sec. 58.209. Information to Child by Probation Officer or Texas Youth Commission.

(a) When a child is placed on probation for an offense that may be eligible for automatic restricted access at age 17 or when a child is received by the Texas Youth Commission on an indeterminate commitment, a probation officer or an official at the Texas Youth Commission reception center, as soon as practicable, shall explain the substance of the following information to the child:

(1) if the child was adjudicated as having committed delinquent conduct for a felony or jailable misdemeanor, that the child probably has a juvenile record with the department and the Federal Bureau of Investigation;

(2) that the child's juvenile record is a permanent record that is not destroyed or erased unless the record is eligible for sealing and the child or the child's family hires a lawyer and files a petition in court to have the record sealed;

(3) that the child's juvenile record, other than treatment records made confidential by law, can be accessed by police, sheriff's officers, prosecutors, probation officers, correctional officers, and other criminal and juvenile justice officials in this state and elsewhere;

(4) that the child's juvenile record, other than treatment records made confidential by law, can be accessed by employers, educational institutions, licensing agencies, and other organizations when the child applies for employment or educational programs;

(5) if the child's juvenile record is placed on restricted access when the child becomes 17 years of age, that access will be denied to employers, educational institutions, and others except for criminal justice agencies; and

(6) that restricted access does not require any action by the child or the child's family, including the filing of a petition or hiring of a lawyer, but occurs automatically at age 17.

(b) The probation officer or Texas Youth Commission official shall:

(1) give the child a written copy of the explanation provided; and

(2) communicate the same information to at least one of the child's parents or, if none can be found, to the child's guardian or custodian.

(c) The Texas Juvenile Probation Commission and the Texas Youth Commission shall adopt rules to implement this section and to facilitate the effective explanation of the information required to be communicated by this section.

(Enacted by Acts 2001, 77th Leg., ch. 1297 (H.B. 1118), § 41, effective September 1, 2001; am. Acts 2011, 82nd Leg., ch. 731 (H.B. 961), § 7, effective June 17, 2011.)

### Sec. 58.210. Sealing or Destruction of Records Not Affected.

(a) This subchapter does not prevent or restrict the sealing or destruction of juvenile records as authorized by law.

(b) Restricted access provided under this subchapter is in addition to sealing or destruction of juvenile records.

(c) A person who is the subject of records certified under this subchapter is entitled to access to the records for the purpose of preparing and presenting a motion to seal or destroy the records.

(Enacted by Acts 2001, 77th Leg., ch. 1297 (H.B. 1118), § 41, effective September 1, 2001.)

### Sec. 58.211. Rescinding Restricted Access.

(a) If the department has notified a juvenile probation department that a record has been placed on restricted access and the department later receives information in the department's criminal history system that the subject of the records has been convicted of or placed on deferred adjudication for a felony or a misdemeanor punishable by confinement in jail for an offense committed after the person reached the age of 17, the person's juvenile records are no longer subject to restricted access. The department shall notify the appropriate local juvenile probation departments in the manner described by Section 58.203

that the person's records are no longer subject to restricted access.

(b) On receipt of the notification described by Subsection (a), the juvenile probation department shall notify the agencies that maintain the person's juvenile records under Section 58.207(b) that the person's records are no longer subject to restricted access.

(Enacted by Acts 2005, 79th Leg., ch. 949 (H.B. 1575), § 22, effective September 1, 2005.)

## SUBCHAPTER D
## LOCAL JUVENILE JUSTICE INFORMATION SYSTEM

### Sec. 58.301. Definitions.

In this subchapter:

(1) "County juvenile board" means a juvenile board created under Chapter 152, Human Resources Code.

(2) "Governmental placement facility" means a juvenile residential placement facility operated by a unit of government.

(3) "Governmental service provider" means a juvenile justice service provider operated by a unit of government.

(4) "Local juvenile justice information system" means a county or multicounty computerized database of information concerning children, with data entry and access by the partner agencies that are members of the system.

(5) "Partner agency" means a governmental service provider or governmental placement facility that is authorized by this subchapter to be a member of a local juvenile justice information system or that has applied to be a member of a local juvenile justice information system and has been approved by the county juvenile board or regional juvenile board committee as a member of the system.

(6) "Regional juvenile board committee" means a committee that is composed of two members from each county juvenile board in a region that comprises a multicounty local juvenile information system.

(Enacted by Acts 2001, 77th Leg., ch. 1297 (H.B. 1118), § 41, effective September 1, 2001; am. Acts 2005, 79th Leg., ch. 949 (H.B. 1575), § 23, effective September 1, 2005.)

### Sec. 58.302. Purposes of System.

The purposes of a local juvenile justice information system are to:

(1) provide accurate information at the county or regional level relating to children who come into contact with the juvenile justice system;

(2) assist in the development and delivery of services to children in the juvenile justice system;

(3) assist in the development and delivery of services to children:

(A) who school officials have reasonable cause to believe have committed an offense for which a report is required under Section 37.015, Education Code; or

(B) who have been expelled, the expulsion of which school officials are required to report under Section 52.041;

(4) provide for an efficient transmission of juvenile records from justice and municipal courts to county juvenile probation departments and the juvenile court and from county juvenile probation departments and juvenile court to the state juvenile justice information system created by Subchapter B;

(5) provide efficient computerized case management resources to juvenile courts, prosecutors, court clerks, county juvenile probation departments, and partner agencies authorized by this subchapter;

(6) provide a directory of services available to children to the partner agencies to facilitate the delivery of services to children;

(7) provide an efficient means for municipal and justice courts to report filing of charges, adjudications, and dispositions of juveniles to the juvenile court as required by Section 51.08; and

(8) provide a method for agencies to fulfill their duties under Section 58.108, including the electronic transmission of information required to be sent to the Department of Public Safety by Section 58.110(f).

(Enacted by Acts 2001, 77th Leg., ch. 1297 (H.B. 1118), § 41, effective September 1, 2001; am. Acts 2007, 80th Leg., ch. 908 (H.B. 2884), § 20, effective September 1, 2007.)

### Sec. 58.303. Local Juvenile Justice Information System.

(a) Juvenile justice agencies in a county or region of this state may jointly create and maintain a local juvenile justice information system to aid in processing the cases of children under this code, to facilitate the delivery of services to children in the juvenile justice system, and to aid in the early identification of at-risk and delinquent children.

(b) A local juvenile justice information system may contain the following components:

(1) case management resources for juvenile courts, court clerks, prosecuting attorneys, and county juvenile probation departments;

(2) reporting systems to fulfill statutory requirements for reporting in the juvenile justice system;

(3) service provider directories and indexes of agencies providing services to children;

(4) victim-witness notices required under Chapter 57;

(5) electronic filing of complaints or petitions, court orders, and other documents filed with the court, including documents containing electronic signatures;

(6) electronic offense and intake processing;

(7) case docket management and calendaring;

(8) communications by email or other electronic communications between partner agencies;

(9) reporting of charges filed, adjudications and dispositions of juveniles by municipal and justice courts and the juvenile court, and transfers of cases to the juvenile court as authorized or required by Section 51.08;

(10) reporting to schools under Article 15.27, Code of Criminal Procedure, by law enforcement agencies, prosecuting attorneys, and juvenile courts;

(11) records of adjudications and dispositions, including probation conditions ordered by the juvenile court; and

(12) warrant management and confirmation capabilities.

(c) [Redesignated as a portion of Tex. Fam. Code § 58.303(b) by Acts 2005, 79th Leg., ch. 949 (H.B. 1575), § 24, effective September 1, 2005.]

(d) Membership in a local juvenile justice information system is determined by this subchapter. Membership in a regional juvenile justice information system is determined by the regional juvenile board committee from among partner agencies that have applied for membership. (Enacted by Acts 2001, 77th Leg., ch. 1297 (H.B. 1118), § 41, effective September 1, 2001; am. Acts 2005, 79th Leg., ch. 949 (H.B. 1575), § 24, effective September 1, 2005; am. Acts 2007, 80th Leg., ch. 908 (H.B. 2884), § 21, effective September 1, 2007.)

### Sec. 58.304. Types of Information Contained in a Local Juvenile Information System.

(a) Subject to Subsection (d), a local juvenile justice information system must consist of:

(1) information relating to all referrals to the juvenile court of any type, including referrals for conduct indicating a need for supervision and delinquent conduct; and

(2) information relating to:

(A) the juvenile;

(B) the intake or referral of the juvenile into the juvenile justice system for any offense or conduct;

(C) the detention of the juvenile;

(D) the prosecution of the juvenile;

(E) the disposition of the juvenile's case, including the name and description of any program to which the juvenile is referred; and

(F) the probation, placement, or commitment of the juvenile.

(b) To the extent possible and subject to Subsections (a) and (d), the local juvenile justice information system may include the following information for each juvenile taken into custody, detained, or referred under this title:

(1) the juvenile's name, including other names by which the juvenile is known;

(2) the juvenile's date and place of birth;

(3) the juvenile's physical description, including sex, weight, height, race, ethnicity, eye color, hair color, scars, marks, and tattoos;

(4) the juvenile's state identification number and other identifying information;

(5) the juvenile's fingerprints and photograph;

(6) the juvenile's last known residential address, including the census tract number designation for the address;

(7) the name, address, and phone number of the juvenile's parent, guardian, or custodian;

(8) the name and identifying number of the agency that took into custody or detained the juvenile;

(9) each date of custody or detention;

(10) a detailed description of the conduct for which the juvenile was taken into custody, detained, or referred, including the level and degree of the alleged offense;

(11) the name and identifying number of the juvenile intake agency or juvenile probation office;

*Family Code*

(12) each disposition by the juvenile intake agency or juvenile probation office;

(13) the date of disposition by the juvenile intake agency or juvenile probation office;

(14) the name and identifying number of the prosecutor's office;

(15) each disposition by the prosecutor;

(16) the date of disposition by the prosecutor;

(17) the name and identifying number of the court;

(18) each disposition by the court, including information concerning custody of a juvenile by a juvenile justice agency or county juvenile probation department;

(19) the date of disposition by the court;

(20) any commitment or release under supervision by the Texas Youth Commission, including the date of the commitment or release;

(21) information concerning each appellate proceeding; and

(22) electronic copies of all documents filed with the court.

(c) If the Department of Public Safety assigns a state identification number for the juvenile, the identification number shall be entered in the local juvenile information system.

(d) Information obtained for the purpose of diagnosis, examination, evaluation, or treatment or for making a referral for treatment of a child by a public or private agency or institution providing supervision of a child by arrangement of the juvenile court or having custody of the child under order of the juvenile court may not be collected under Subsection (a) or (b).

(Enacted by Acts 2001, 77th Leg., ch. 1297 (H.B. 1118), § 41, effective September 1, 2001; am. Acts 2007, 80th Leg., ch. 908 (H.B. 2884), § 22, effective September 1, 2007.)

### Sec. 58.305. Partner Agencies.

(a) A local juvenile justice information system shall to the extent possible include the following partner agencies within that county:

(1) the juvenile court and court clerk;

(2) justice of the peace and municipal courts;

(3) the county juvenile probation department;

(4) the prosecuting attorneys who prosecute juvenile cases in juvenile court, municipal court, or justice court;

(5) law enforcement agencies;

(6) each public school district in the county;

(7) governmental service providers approved by the county juvenile board; and

(8) governmental placement facilities approved by the county juvenile board.

(b) A local juvenile justice information system for a multicounty region shall to the extent possible include the partner agencies listed in Subsections (a)(1)—(6) for each county in the region and the following partner agencies from within the multicounty region that have applied for membership in the system and have been approved by the regional juvenile board committee:

(1) governmental service providers; and

(2) governmental placement facilities.

(Enacted by Acts 2001, 77th Leg., ch. 1297 (H.B. 1118), § 41, effective September 1, 2001; am. Acts 2005, 79th Leg., ch. 949 (H.B. 1575), § 25, effective September 1, 2005; am. Acts 2007, 80th Leg., ch. 908 (H.B. 2884), § 23, effective September 1, 2007.)

### Sec. 58.306. Access to Information; Levels.

(a) This section describes the level of access to information to which each partner agency in a local juvenile justice information system is entitled.

(b) Information is at Access Level 1 if the information relates to a child:

(1) who:

(A) a school official has reasonable grounds to believe has committed an offense for which a report is required under Section 37.015, Education Code; or

(B) has been expelled, the expulsion of which is required to be reported under Section 52.041; and

(2) who has not been charged with a fineable only offense, a status offense, or delinquent conduct.

(c) Information is at Access Level 2 if the information relates to a child who:

(1) is alleged in a justice or municipal court to have committed a fineable only offense, municipal ordinance violation, or status offense; and

(2) has not been charged with delinquent conduct or conduct indicating a need for supervision.

(d) Information is at Access Level 3 if the information relates to a child who is alleged to have engaged in delinquent conduct or conduct indicating a need for supervision.

(e) Level 1 Access is by public school districts in the county or region served by the local juvenile justice information system.

Family Code

(f) Level 2 Access is by:

(1) justice of the peace courts that process juvenile cases; and

(2) municipal courts that process juvenile cases.

(g) Level 3 Access is by:

(1) the juvenile court and court clerk;

(2) the prosecuting attorney;

(3) the county juvenile probation department;

(4) law enforcement agencies;

(5) governmental service providers that are partner agencies; and

(6) governmental placement facilities that are partner agencies.

(h) Access for Level 1 agencies is only to information at Level 1. Access for Level 2 agencies is only to information at Levels 1 and 2. Access for Level 3 agencies is to information at Levels 1, 2, and 3.

(Enacted by Acts 2001, 77th Leg., ch. 1297 (H.B. 1118), § 41, effective September 1, 2001; am. Acts 2007, 80th Leg., ch. 908 (H.B. 2884), § 24, effective September 1, 2007.)

### Sec. 58.307.  Confidentiality of Information.

(a) Information that is part of a local juvenile justice information system is not public information and may not be released to the public, except as authorized by law.

(b) Information that is part of a local juvenile justice information system is for the professional use of the partner agencies that are members of the system and may be used only by authorized employees of those agencies to discharge duties of those agencies.

(c) Information from a local juvenile justice information system may not be disclosed to persons, agencies, or organizations that are not members of the system except to the extent disclosure is authorized or mandated by this title.

(d) Information in a local juvenile justice information system is subject to destruction, sealing, or restricted access as provided by this title.

(e) Information in a local juvenile justice information system, including electronic signature systems, shall be protected from unauthorized access by a system of access security and any access to information in a local juvenile information system performed by browser software shall

be at the level of at least 128-bit encryption. A juvenile board or a regional juvenile board committee shall require all partner agencies to maintain security and restrict access in accordance with the requirements of this title.

(Enacted by Acts 2001, 77th Leg., ch. 1297 (H.B. 1118), § 41, effective September 1, 2001; am. Acts 2007, 80th Leg., ch. 908 (H.B. 2884), § 25, effective September 1, 2007.)

## SUBCHAPTER D-1
## REPORTS ON COUNTY INTERNET WEBSITES

### Sec. 58.351.  Applicability.

This subchapter applies only to a county with a population of 600,000 or more.

(Enacted by Acts 2007, 80th Leg., ch. 908 (H.B. 2884), § 26(b), effective September 1, 2007.)

### Sec. 58.352.  Information Posted on County Website.

(a) A juvenile court judge in a county to which this subchapter applies shall post a report on the Internet website of the county in which the court is located. The report must include:

(1) the total number of children committed by the judge to a correctional facility operated by the Texas Youth Commission; and

(2) for each child committed to a facility described by Subdivision (1):

(A) a general description of the offense committed by the child or the conduct of the child that led to the child's commitment to the facility;

(B) the year the child was committed to the facility; and

(C) the age range, race, and gender of the child.

(b) Not later than the 10th day following the first day of each quarter, a juvenile court judge shall update the information posted on a county Internet website under Subsection (a).

(Enacted by Acts 2007, 80th Leg., ch. 908 (H.B. 2884), § 26(b), effective September 1, 2007.)

### Sec. 58.353.  Confidentiality.

A record posted on a county Internet website under this subchapter may not include any information that personally identifies a child.

(Enacted by Acts 2007, 80th Leg., ch. 908 (H.B. 2884), § 26(b), effective September 1, 2007.)

## SUBCHAPTER E
## STATEWIDE JUVENILE INFORMATION AND CASE MANAGEMENT SYSTEM

### Sec. 58.401. Definitions.

In this subchapter:

(1) "Commission" means the Texas Juvenile Probation Commission.

(2) "Criminal justice agency" has the meaning assigned by Section 411.082, Government Code.

(3) "Juvenile justice agency" means an agency that has custody or control over juvenile offenders.

(4) "Partner agencies" means those agencies described in Section 58.305 as well as private service providers to the juvenile justice system.

(5) "System" means an automated statewide juvenile information and case management system.

(Enacted by Acts 2007, 80th Leg., ch. 908 (H.B. 2884), § 27, effective September 1, 2007.)

### Sec. 58.402. Purposes of System.

The purposes of the system are to:

(1) provide accurate information at the statewide level relating to children who come into contact with the juvenile justice system;

(2) facilitate communication and information sharing between authorized entities in criminal and juvenile justice agencies and partner agencies regarding effective and efficient identification of and service delivery to juvenile offenders; and

(3) provide comprehensive juvenile justice information and case management abilities that will meet the common data collection, reporting, and management needs of juvenile probation departments in this state and provide the flexibility to accommodate individualized requirements.

(Enacted by Acts 2007, 80th Leg., ch. 908 (H.B. 2884), § 27, effective September 1, 2007.)

### Sec. 58.403. Juvenile Information System.

(a) Through the adoption of an interlocal contract under Chapter 791, Government Code, with one or more counties, the commission may participate in and assist counties in the creation, operation, and maintenance of a system that is intended for statewide use to:

(1) aid in processing the cases of children under this title;

(2) facilitate the delivery of services to children in the juvenile justice system;

(3) aid in the early identification of at-risk and delinquent children; and

(4) facilitate cross-jurisdictional sharing of information related to juvenile offenders between authorized criminal and juvenile justice agencies and partner agencies.

(b) The commission may use funds appropriated for the implementation of this section to pay costs incurred under an interlocal contract described by Subsection (a), including license fees, maintenance and operations costs, administrative costs, and any other costs specified in the interlocal contract.

(c) The commission may provide training services to counties on the use and operation of a system created, operated, or maintained by one or more counties under Subsection (a).

(d) Subchapter L, Chapter 2054, Government Code, does not apply to the statewide juvenile information and case management system created under this subchapter.

(Enacted by Acts 2007, 80th Leg., ch. 908 (H.B. 2884), § 27, effective September 1, 2007; am. Acts 2009, 81st Leg., ch. 1337 (S.B. 58), § 1, effective September 1, 2009; am. Acts 2011, 82nd Leg., ch. 85 (S.B. 653), § 2.002, effective September 1, 2011.)

### Sec. 58.404. Information Collected by Commission.

The commission may collect and maintain all information related to juvenile offenders and all offenses committed by a juvenile offender, including all information collected and maintained under Subchapters B and D.

(Enacted by Acts 2007, 80th Leg., ch. 908 (H.B. 2884), § 27, effective September 1, 2007.)

### Sec. 58.405. Authority Cumulative.

The authority granted by this subchapter is cumulative of all other authority granted by this chapter to a county, the commission, or a juvenile justice agency and nothing in this subchapter limits the authority of a county, the commission, or a juvenile justice agency under this chapter to create an information system or to share information related to a juvenile.

(Enacted by Acts 2007, 80th Leg., ch. 908 (H.B. 2884), § 27, effective September 1, 2007.)

Family Code

# CHAPTER 59
# PROGRESSIVE SANCTIONS MODEL

## Sec. 59.001.   Purposes.

The purposes of the progressive sanctions model are to:

(1) ensure that juvenile offenders face uniform and consistent consequences and punishments that correspond to the seriousness of each offender's current offense, prior delinquent history, special treatment or training needs, and effectiveness of prior interventions;

(2) balance public protection and rehabilitation while holding juvenile offenders accountable;

(3) permit flexibility in the decisions made in relation to the juvenile offender to the extent allowed by law;

(4) consider the juvenile offender's circumstances;

(5) recognize that departure of a disposition from this model is not necessarily undesirable and in some cases is highly desirable; and

(6) improve juvenile justice planning and resource allocation by ensuring uniform and consistent reporting of disposition decisions at all levels.

(Enacted by Acts 1995, 74th Leg., ch. 262 (H.B. 327), § 53, effective January 1, 1996; am. Acts 2003, 78th Leg., ch. 479 (H.B. 888), § 3, effective September 1, 2003.)

## Sec. 59.002.   Sanction Level Assignment by Probation Department.

(a) The probation department may assign a sanction level of one to a child referred to the probation department under Section 53.012.

(b) The probation department may assign a sanction level of two to a child for whom deferred prosecution is authorized under Section 53.03.

(Enacted by Acts 1995, 74th Leg., ch. 262 (H.B. 327), § 53, effective January 1, 1996.)

## Sec. 59.003.   Sanction Level Assignment Model.

(a) Subject to Subsection (e), after a child's first commission of delinquent conduct or conduct indicating a need for supervision, the probation department or prosecuting attorney may, or the juvenile court may, in a disposition hearing under Section 54.04 or a modification hearing under Section 54.05, assign a child one of the following sanction levels according to the child's conduct:

(1) for conduct indicating a need for supervision, other than conduct described in Section 51.03(b)(4) or (5) or a Class A or B misdemeanor, the sanction level is one;

(2) for conduct indicating a need for supervision under Section 51.03(b)(4) or (5) or a Class A or B misdemeanor, other than a misdemeanor involving the use or possession of a firearm, or for delinquent conduct under Section 51.03(a)(2), the sanction level is two;

(3) for a misdemeanor involving the use or possession of a firearm or for a state jail felony or a felony of the third degree, the sanction level is three;

(4) for a felony of the second degree, the sanction level is four;

(5) for a felony of the first degree, other than a felony involving the use of a deadly weapon or causing serious bodily injury, the sanction level is five;

(6) for a felony of the first degree involving the use of a deadly weapon or causing serious bodily injury, for an aggravated controlled substance felony, or for a capital felony, the sanction level is six; or

(7) for a felony of the first degree involving the use of a deadly weapon or causing serious bodily injury, for an aggravated controlled substance felony, or for a capital felony, if the petition has been approved by a grand jury under Section 53.045, or if a petition to transfer the child to criminal court has been filed under Section 54.02, the sanction level is seven.

(b) Subject to Subsection (e), if the child subsequently is found to have engaged in delinquent conduct in an adjudication hearing under Section 54.03 or a hearing to modify a disposition under Section 54.05 on two separate occasions and each involves a violation of a penal law of a classification that is less than the classification of the child's previous conduct, the juvenile court may assign the child a sanction level that is one level higher than the previously assigned sanction level, unless the child's previously assigned sanction level is six.

(c) Subject to Subsection (e), if the child's subsequent commission of delinquent conduct or conduct indicating a need for supervision involves a violation of a penal law of a classification that is the same as or greater than the classification of the child's previous conduct, the juvenile court may assign the child a sanction level authorized by law that is one level higher than the previously assigned sanction level.

(d) Subject to Subsection (e), if the child's previously assigned sanction level is four or five and the child's subsequent commission of delinquent conduct is of the grade of felony, the juvenile court may assign the child a sanction level that is one level higher than the previously assigned sanction level.

(e) The probation department may, in accordance with Section 54.05, request the extension of a period of probation specified under sanction levels one through five if the circumstances of the child warrant the extension.

(f) Before the court assigns the child a sanction level that involves the revocation of the child's probation and the commitment of the child to the Texas Youth Commission, the court shall hold a hearing to modify the disposition as required by Section 54.05.

(Enacted by Acts 1995, 74th Leg., ch. 262 (H.B. 327), § 53, effective January 1, 1996; am. Acts 1997, 75th Leg., ch. 1015 (S.B. 133), § 19, effective June 19, 1997; am. Acts 1997, 75th Leg., ch. 1086 (H.B. 1550), § 22, effective September 1, 1997; am. Acts 1999, 76th Leg., ch. 1477 (H.B. 3517), § 20, effective September 1, 1999; am. Acts 2001, 77th Leg., ch. 1297 (H.B. 1118), § 42, effective September 1, 2001; am. Acts 2003, 78th Leg., ch. 479 (H.B. 888), §§ 4, 5, effective September 1, 2003; am. Acts 2007, 80th Leg., ch. 908 (H.B. 2884), § 28, effective September 1, 2007.)

## Sec. 59.004. Sanction Level One.

(a) For a child at sanction level one, the juvenile court or probation department may:

(1) require counseling for the child regarding the child's conduct;

(2) inform the child of the progressive sanctions that may be imposed on the child if the child continues to engage in delinquent conduct or conduct indicating a need for supervision;

(3) inform the child's parents or guardians of the parents' or guardians' responsibility to im-

pose reasonable restrictions on the child to prevent the conduct from recurring;

(4) provide information or other assistance to the child or the child's parents or guardians in securing needed social services;

(5) require the child or the child's parents or guardians to participate in a program for services under Section 264.302, if a program under Section 264.302 is available to the child or the child's parents or guardians;

(6) refer the child to a community-based citizen intervention program approved by the juvenile court;

(7) release the child to the child's parents or guardians; and

(8) require the child to attend and successfully complete an educational program described by Section 37.218, Education Code, or another equivalent educational program.

(b) The probation department shall discharge the child from the custody of the probation department after the provisions of this section are met.

(Enacted by Acts 1995, 74th Leg., ch. 262 (H.B. 327), § 53, effective January 1, 1996; am. Acts 1997, 75th Leg., ch. 1086 (H.B. 1550), § 23, effective September 1, 1997; am. Acts 2011, 82nd Leg., ch. 1322 (S.B. 407), § 20, effective September 1, 2011.)

## Sec. 59.005. Sanction Level Two.

(a) For a child at sanction level two, the juvenile court, the prosecuting attorney, or the probation department may, as provided by Section 53.03:

(1) place the child on deferred prosecution for not less than three months or more than six months;

(2) require the child to make restitution to the victim of the child's conduct or perform community service restitution appropriate to the nature and degree of harm caused and according to the child's ability;

(3) require the child's parents or guardians to identify restrictions the parents or guardians will impose on the child's activities and requirements the parents or guardians will set for the child's behavior;

(4) provide the information required under Sections 59.004(a)(2) and (4);

(5) require the child or the child's parents or guardians to participate in a program for services under Section 264.302, if a program under Section 264.302 is available to the child or the child's parents or guardians;

(6) refer the child to a community-based citizen intervention program approved by the juvenile court; and

(7) if appropriate, impose additional conditions of probation.

(b) The juvenile court or the probation department shall discharge the child from the custody of the probation department on the date the provisions of this section are met or on the child's 18th birthday, whichever is earlier.
(Enacted by Acts 1995, 74th Leg., ch. 262 (H.B. 327), § 53, effective January 1, 1996; am. Acts 1997, 75th Leg., ch. 1086 (H.B. 1550), § 24, effective September 1, 1997; am. Acts 1999, 76th Leg., ch. 1477 (H.B. 3517), § 21, effective September 1, 1999.)

## Sec. 59.006.  Sanction Level Three.

(a) For a child at sanction level three, the juvenile court may:

(1) place the child on probation for not less than six months;

(2) require the child to make restitution to the victim of the child's conduct or perform community service restitution appropriate to the nature and degree of harm caused and according to the child's ability;

(3) impose specific restrictions on the child's activities and requirements for the child's behavior as conditions of probation;

(4) require a probation officer to closely monitor the child's activities and behavior;

(5) require the child or the child's parents or guardians to participate in programs or services designated by the court or probation officer; and

(6) if appropriate, impose additional conditions of probation.

(b) The juvenile court shall discharge the child from the custody of the probation department on the date the provisions of this section are met or on the child's 18th birthday, whichever is earlier.
(Enacted by Acts 1995, 74th Leg., ch. 262 (H.B. 327), § 53, effective January 1, 1996; am. Acts 1997, 75th Leg., ch. 1086 (H.B. 1550), § 25, effective September 1, 1997; am. Acts 2003, 78th Leg., ch. 479 (H.B. 888), § 6, effective September 1, 2003.)

## Sec. 59.007.  Sanction Level Four.

(a) For a child at sanction level four, the juvenile court may:

(1) require the child to participate as a condition of probation for not less than three months or more than 12 months in an intensive services probation program that emphasizes frequent contact and reporting with a probation officer, discipline, intensive supervision services, social responsibility, and productive work;

(2) after release from the program described by Subdivision (1), continue the child on probation supervision;

(3) require the child to make restitution to the victim of the child's conduct or perform community service restitution appropriate to the nature and degree of harm caused and according to the child's ability;

(4) impose highly structured restrictions on the child's activities and requirements for behavior of the child as conditions of probation;

(5) require a probation officer to closely monitor the child;

(6) require the child or the child's parents or guardians to participate in programs or services designed to address their particular needs and circumstances; and

(7) if appropriate, impose additional sanctions.

(b) The juvenile court shall discharge the child from the custody of the probation department on the date the provisions of this section are met or on the child's 18th birthday, whichever is earlier.
(Enacted by Acts 1995, 74th Leg., ch. 262 (H.B. 327), § 53, effective January 1, 1996; am. Acts 1997, 75th Leg., ch. 1086 (H.B. 1550), § 26, effective September 1, 1997; am. Acts 2001, 77th Leg., ch. 1297 (H.B. 1118), § 43, effective September 1, 2001; am. Acts 2003, 78th Leg., ch. 479 (H.B. 888), § 7, effective September 1, 2003.)

## Sec. 59.008.  Sanction Level Five.

(a) For a child at sanction level five, the juvenile court may:

(1) as a condition of probation, place the child for not less than six months or more than 12 months in a post-adjudication secure correctional facility;

(2) after release from the program described by Subdivision (1), continue the child on probation supervision;

(3) require the child to make restitution to the victim of the child's conduct or perform community service restitution appropriate to the nature and degree of harm caused and according to the child's ability;

(4) impose highly structured restrictions on the child's activities and requirements for behavior of the child as conditions of probation;

(5) require a probation officer to closely monitor the child;

(6) require the child or the child's parents or guardians to participate in programs or services designed to address their particular needs and circumstances; and

(7) if appropriate, impose additional sanctions.

(b) The juvenile court shall discharge the child from the custody of the probation department on the date the provisions of this section are met or on the child's 18th birthday, whichever is earlier. (Enacted by Acts 1995, 74th Leg., ch. 262 (H.B. 327), § 53, effective January 1, 1996; am. Acts 1997, 75th Leg., ch. 1086 (H.B. 1550), § 27, effective September 1, 1997; am. Acts 2003, 78th Leg., ch. 479 (H.B. 888), § 8, effective September 1, 2003.)

## Sec. 59.009. Sanction Level Six.

(a) For a child at sanction level six, the juvenile court may commit the child to the custody of the Texas Youth Commission. The commission may:

(1) require the child to participate in a highly structured residential program that emphasizes discipline, accountability, fitness, training, and productive work for not less than nine months or more than 24 months unless the commission extends the period and the reason for an extension is documented;

(2) require the child to make restitution to the victim of the child's conduct or perform community service restitution appropriate to the nature and degree of the harm caused and according to the child's ability, if there is a victim of the child's conduct;

(3) require the child and the child's parents or guardians to participate in programs and services for their particular needs and circumstances; and

(4) if appropriate, impose additional sanctions.

(b) On release of the child under supervision, the Texas Youth Commission parole programs may:

(1) impose highly structured restrictions on the child's activities and requirements for behavior of the child as conditions of release under supervision;

(2) require a parole officer to closely monitor the child for not less than six months; and

(3) if appropriate, impose any other conditions of supervision.

(c) The Texas Youth Commission may discharge the child from the commission's custody on the date the provisions of this section are met or on the child's 19th birthday, whichever is earlier. (Enacted by Acts 1995, 74th Leg., ch. 262 (H.B. 327), § 53, effective January 1, 1996; am. Acts 1997, 75th Leg., ch. 1086 (H.B. 1550), § 28, effective September 1, 1997.)

## Sec. 59.010. Sanction Level Seven.

(a) For a child at sanction level seven, the juvenile court may certify and transfer the child under Section 54.02 or sentence the child to commitment to the Texas Youth Commission under Section 54.04(d)(3), 54.04(m), or 54.05(f). The commission may:

(1) require the child to participate in a highly structured residential program that emphasizes discipline, accountability, fitness, training, and productive work for not less than 12 months or more than 10 years unless the commission extends the period and the reason for the extension is documented;

(2) require the child to make restitution to the victim of the child's conduct or perform community service restitution appropriate to the nature and degree of harm caused and according to the child's ability, if there is a victim of the child's conduct;

(3) require the child and the child's parents or guardians to participate in programs and services for their particular needs and circumstances; and

(4) impose any other appropriate sanction.

(b) On release of the child under supervision, the Texas Youth Commission parole programs may:

(1) impose highly structured restrictions on the child's activities and requirements for behavior of the child as conditions of release under supervision;

(2) require a parole officer to monitor the child closely for not less than 12 months; and

(3) impose any other appropriate condition of supervision.

(Enacted by Acts 1995, 74th Leg., ch. 262 (H.B. 327), § 53, effective January 1, 1996; am. Acts 1997, 75th Leg., ch. 1086 (H.B. 1550), § 29, effective September 1, 1997.)

## Sec. 59.011. Duty of Juvenile Board.

A juvenile board shall require the juvenile probation department to report progressive sanc-

Family Code

tion data electronically to the Texas Juvenile Probation Commission in the format and time frames specified by the commission.

(Enacted by Acts 1995, 74th Leg., ch. 262 (H.B. 327), § 53, effective January 1, 1996; am. Acts 2001, 77th Leg., ch. 1297 (H.B. 1118), § 44, effective September 1, 2001.)

### Sec. 59.012.  Reports by Criminal Justice Policy Council.

(a) The Criminal Justice Policy Council shall analyze trends related to juvenile referrals and the impact of reforms on recidivism rates using standard scientific sampling or appropriate scientific methodologies to represent statewide patterns. The council shall compile other policy studies as determined by the executive director of the council or as requested by the governor, lieutenant governor, or speaker of the house of representatives to assist in policy development.

(b) The Criminal Justice Policy Council shall report its findings and related recommendations to improve juvenile justice policies to the governor and the members of the legislature on or before January 15 of each odd-numbered year.

(c) The Criminal Justice Policy Council may incorporate its findings and recommendations under this section into its report required under Section 413.013, Government Code.

(Enacted by Acts 1995, 74th Leg., ch. 262 (H.B. 327), § 53, effective January 1, 1996; am. Acts 2001, 77th Leg., ch. 1297 (H.B. 1118), § 45, effective September 1, 2001; am. Acts 2003, 78th Leg., ch. 479 (H.B. 888), § 9, effective September 1, 2003.)

### Sec. 59.013.  Liability.

The Texas Youth Commission, a juvenile board, a court, a person appointed by a court, an attorney for the state, a peace officer, or a law enforcement agency is not liable for a failure or inability to provide a service listed under Sections 59.004—59.010.

(Enacted by Acts 1995, 74th Leg., ch. 262 (H.B. 327), § 53, effective January 1, 1996.)

### Sec. 59.014.  Appeal.

A child may not bring an appeal or a postconviction writ of habeas corpus based on:

(1) the failure or inability of any person to provide a service listed under Sections 59.004—59.010;

(2) the failure of a court or of any person to make a sanction level assignment as provided in Section 59.002 or 59.003;

(3) a departure from the sanction level assignment model provided by this chapter; or

(4) the failure of a juvenile court or probation department to report a departure from the model.

(Enacted by Acts 1995, 74th Leg., ch. 262 (H.B. 327), § 53, effective January 1, 1996; am. Acts 1999, 76th Leg., ch. 1011 (H.B. 2870), § 1, effective September 1, 1999; am. Acts 1999, 76th Leg., ch. 1477 (H.B. 3517), § 22, effective September 1, 1999; am. Acts 2003, 78th Leg., ch. 479 (H.B. 888), § 10, effective September 1, 2003.)

### Sec. 59.015.  Waiver of Sanctions on Parents or Guardians.

On a finding by the juvenile court or probation department that a child's parents or guardians have made a reasonable good faith effort to prevent the child from engaging in delinquent conduct or engaging in conduct indicating a need for supervision and that, despite the parents' or guardians' efforts, the child continues to engage in such conduct, the court or probation department shall waive any sanction that may be imposed on the parents or guardians at any sanction level.

(Enacted by Acts 1995, 74th Leg., ch. 262 (H.B. 327), § 53, effective January 1, 1996.)

## CHAPTER 60
## UNIFORM INTERSTATE COMPACT ON JUVENILES

### Sec. 60.001.  Definitions.

In this chapter:

(1) "Commission" means the Interstate Commission for Juveniles.

(2) "Compact" means the Interstate Compact for Juveniles.

(3) "Compact administrator" has the meaning assigned by Article II of the compact.

(Enacted by Acts 1995, 74th Leg., ch. 262 (H.B. 327), § 53, effective January 1, 1996; am. Acts 2005, 79th Leg., ch. 1007 (H.B. 706), § 2.01, effective August 26, 2008.)

STATUTORY NOTES

**Editor's notes.** — Acts 2005, 79th Leg., ch. 1007 (H.B. 706) implemented a significant revision of the original 1955 Interstate Compact on Juveniles, effective on the date that the new version of the compact was adopted by 35 states. The new compact was adopted by the 35th state, Illinois, on August 26, 2008, making the compact and conforming amendment effective on that date.

## Sec. 60.002. Execution of Interstate Compact [Repealed].

Repealed by Acts 2005, 79th Leg., ch. 1007 (H.B. 706), § 3.02, effective August 26, 2008. (Enacted by Acts 1995, 74th Leg., ch. 262 (H.B. 327), § 53, effective January 1, 1996.)

## Sec. 60.003. Execution of Additional Article [Repealed].

Repealed by Acts 2005, 79th Leg., ch. 1007 (H.B. 706), § 3.02, effective August 26, 2008. (Enacted by Acts 1995, 74th Leg., ch. 262 (H.B. 327), § 53, effective January 1, 1996.)

## Sec. 60.004. Execution of Amendment [Repealed].

Repealed by Acts 2005, 79th Leg., ch. 1007 (H.B. 706), § 3.02, effective August 26, 2008. (Enacted by Acts 1995, 74th Leg., ch. 262 (H.B. 327), § 53, effective January 1, 1996.)

## Sec. 60.005. Juvenile Compact Administrator.

Under the compact, the governor may designate an officer as the compact administrator. The administrator, acting jointly with like officers of other party states, shall adopt regulations to carry out more effectively the terms of the compact. The compact administrator serves at the pleasure of the governor. The compact administrator shall cooperate with all departments, agencies, and officers of and in the government of this state and its subdivisions in facilitating the proper administration of the compact or of a supplementary agreement entered into by this state.
(Enacted by Acts 1995, 74th Leg., ch. 262 (H.B. 327), § 53, effective January 1, 1996.)

## Sec. 60.006. Supplementary Agreements.

A compact administrator may make supplementary agreements with appropriate officials of other states pursuant to the compact. If a supplementary agreement requires or contemplates the use of an institution or facility of this state or requires or contemplates the provision of a service of this state, the supplementary agreement has no force or effect until approved by the head of the department or agency under whose jurisdiction the institution is operated, or whose department or agency is charged with performing the service.
(Enacted by Acts 1995, 74th Leg., ch. 262 (H.B. 327), § 53, effective January 1, 1996.)

## Sec. 60.007. Financial Arrangements.

The compact administrator may make or arrange for the payments necessary to discharge the financial obligations imposed upon this state by the compact or by a supplementary agreement made under the compact, subject to legislative appropriations.
(Enacted by Acts 1995, 74th Leg., ch. 262 (H.B. 327), § 53, effective January 1, 1996.)

## Sec. 60.008. Enforcement.

The courts, departments, agencies, and officers of this state and its subdivisions shall enforce this compact and shall do all things appropriate to effectuate its purposes and intent which are within their respective jurisdictions.
(Enacted by Acts 1995, 74th Leg., ch. 262 (H.B. 327), § 53, effective January 1, 1996.)

## Sec. 60.009. Additional Procedures Not Precluded.

In addition to any procedures developed under the compact for the return of a runaway juvenile, the particular states, the juvenile, or his parents, the courts, or other legal custodian involved may agree upon and adopt any plan or procedure legally authorized under the laws of this state and the other respective party states for the return of the runaway juvenile.
(Enacted by Acts 1995, 74th Leg., ch. 262 (H.B. 327), § 53, effective January 1, 1996; am. Acts 2005, 79th Leg., ch. 1007 (H.B. 706), § 2.01, effective August 26, 2008.)

STATUTORY NOTES

**Editor's notes.** — Acts 2005, 79th Leg., ch. 1007 (H.B. 706) implemented a significant revision of the original 1955 Interstate Compact on Juveniles, effective on the date that the new version of the compact was adopted by 35 states. The new compact was adopted by the 35th state, Illinois, on August 26, 2008, making the compact and conforming amendment effective on that date.

Family Code

## Sec. 60.010.   Interstate Compact for Juveniles.

### ARTICLE I PURPOSE

The compacting states to this Interstate Compact recognize that each state is responsible for the proper supervision or return of juveniles, delinquents, and status offenders who are on probation or parole and who have absconded, escaped, or run away from supervision and control and in so doing have endangered their own safety and the safety of others. The compacting states also recognize that each state is responsible for the safe return of juveniles who have run away from home and in doing so have left their state of residence. The compacting states also recognize that congress, by enacting the Crime Control Act, 4 U.S.C. Section 112 (1965), has authorized and encouraged compacts for cooperative efforts and mutual assistance in the prevention of crime.

It is the purpose of this compact, through means of joint and cooperative action among the compacting states to: (A) ensure that the juveniles who are moved under this compact to another state for probation or parole supervision and services are governed in the receiving state by the same standards that apply to juveniles receiving such supervision and services in the receiving state; (B) ensure that the public safety interests of the citizens, including the victims of juvenile offenders, in both the sending and receiving states are adequately protected and balanced with the juvenile's and the juvenile's family's best interests and welfare when an interstate movement is under consideration; (C) return juveniles who have run away, absconded, or escaped from supervision or control or have been accused of an offense to the state requesting their return through a fair and prompt judicial review process that ensures that the requisition is in order and that the transport is properly supervised; (D) make provisions for contracts between member states for the cooperative institutionalization in public facilities in member states for delinquent youth needing special services; (E) provide for the effective tracking of juveniles who move interstate under the compact's provisions; (F) equitably allocate the costs, benefits, and obligations of the compacting states; (G) establish procedures to manage the movement between states of juvenile offenders released to the community under the jurisdiction of courts, juvenile departments, or any other criminal or juvenile justice agency which has jurisdiction over juvenile offenders, ensuring that a receiving state accepts supervision of a juvenile when the juvenile's parent or other person having legal custody resides or is undertaking residence there; (H) ensure immediate notice to jurisdictions where defined offenders are authorized to travel or to relocate across state lines; (I) establish a system of uniform data collection on information pertaining to juveniles who move interstate under this compact that prevents public disclosure of identity and individual treatment information but allows access by authorized juvenile justice and criminal justice officials and regular reporting of compact activities to heads of state executive, judicial, and legislative branches and juvenile and criminal justice administrators; (J) monitor compliance with rules governing interstate movement of juveniles and initiate interventions to address and correct noncompliance; (K) coordinate training and education regarding the regulation of interstate movement of juveniles for officials involved in such activity; and (L) coordinate the implementation and operation of the compact with the Interstate Compact for the Placement of Children, the Interstate Compact for Adult Offender Supervision and other compacts affecting juveniles particularly in those cases where concurrent or overlapping supervision issues arise. It is the policy of the compacting states that the activities conducted by the Interstate Commission created herein are the formation of public policies and therefore are public business. Furthermore, the compacting states shall cooperate and observe their individual and collective duties and responsibilities for the prompt return and acceptance of juveniles subject to the provisions of this compact. The provisions of this compact shall be reasonably and liberally construed to accomplish the purposes and policies of the compact.

### ARTICLE II DEFINITIONS

As used in this compact, unless the context clearly requires a different construction:

A. "Bylaws" means those bylaws established by the Interstate Commission for its governance or for directing or controlling the Interstate Commission's actions or conduct.

B. "Compact administrator" means the individual in each compacting state appointed pursuant to the terms of this compact responsible for the administration and management of the state's supervision and transfer of juveniles subject to the terms of this compact and to the rules adopted by the Interstate Commission under this compact.

C. "Compacting state" means any state which has enacted the enabling legislation for this compact.

D. "Commissioner" means the voting representative of each compacting state appointed pursuant to Article III of this compact.

E. "Court" means any court having jurisdiction over delinquent, neglected, or dependent children.

F. "Deputy compact administrator" means the individual, if any, in each compacting state appointed to act on behalf of a compact administrator pursuant to the terms of this compact, responsible for the administration and management of the state's supervision and transfer of juveniles subject to the terms of this compact and to the rules adopted by the Interstate Commission under this compact.

G. "Interstate Commission" means the Interstate Commission for Juveniles created by Article III of this compact.

H. "Juvenile" means any person defined as a juvenile in any member state or by the rules of the Interstate Commission, including:

(1) Accused Delinquent — a person charged with an offense that, if committed by an adult, would be a criminal offense;

(2) Adjudicated Delinquent — a person found to have committed an offense that, if committed by an adult, would be a criminal offense;

(3) Accused Status Offender — a person charged with an offense that would not be a criminal offense if committed by an adult;

(4) Adjudicated Status Offender — a person found to have committed an offense that would not be a criminal offense if committed by an adult; and

(5) Nonoffender — a person in need of supervision who has not been accused or adjudicated a status offender or delinquent.

I. "Noncompacting state" means any state which has not enacted the enabling legislation for this compact.

J. "Probation or parole" means any kind of supervision or conditional release of juveniles authorized under the laws of the compacting states.

K. "Rule" means a written statement by the Interstate Commission promulgated pursuant to Article VI of this compact that is of general applicability, implements, interprets, or prescribes a policy or provision of the compact, or an organizational, procedural, or practice requirement of the Interstate Commission, and has the force and effect of statutory law in a compacting state, and includes the amendment, repeal, or suspension of an existing rule.

L. "State" means a state of the United States, the District of Columbia (or its designee), the Commonwealth of Puerto Rico, the U.S. Virgin Islands, Guam, American Samoa, and the Northern Marianas Islands.

## ARTICLE III INTERSTATE COMMISSION FOR JUVENILES

A. The compacting states hereby create the Interstate Commission for Juveniles. The Interstate Commission shall be a body corporate and joint agency of the compacting states. The commission shall have all the responsibilities, powers, and duties set forth herein, and such additional powers as may be conferred upon it by subsequent action of the respective legislatures of the compacting states in accordance with the terms of this compact.

B. The Interstate Commission shall consist of commissioners appointed by the appropriate appointing authority in each state pursuant to the rules and requirements of each compacting state. The commissioner shall be the compact administrator, deputy compact administrator, or designee from that state who shall serve on the Interstate Commission in such capacity under or pursuant to the applicable law of the compacting state.

C. In addition to the commissioners who are the voting representatives of each state, the Interstate Commission shall include individuals who are not commissioners, but who are members of interested organizations. Such noncommissioner members must include a member of the national organizations of governors, legislators, state chief justices, attorneys general, Interstate Compact for Adult Offender Supervision, Interstate Compact for the Placement of Children, juvenile justice and juvenile corrections officials, and crime victims. All noncommissioner members of the Interstate Commission shall be ex officio (nonvoting) members. The Interstate Commission may provide in its bylaws for such additional ex officio (nonvoting) members, including members of other national organizations, in such numbers as shall be determined by the commission.

D. Each compacting state represented at any meeting of the Interstate Commission is entitled to one vote. A majority of the compacting states shall constitute a quorum for the transaction of business, unless a larger quorum is required by the bylaws of the Interstate Commission.

E. The Interstate Commission shall meet at least once each calendar year. The chairperson may call additional meetings and, upon the request of a simple majority of the compacting states, shall call additional meetings. Public notice shall be given of all meetings and meetings shall be open to the public.

F. The Interstate Commission shall establish an executive committee, which shall include commission officers, members, and others as determined by the bylaws. The executive committee shall have the power to act on behalf of the Interstate Commission during periods when the Interstate Commission is not in session, with the exception of rulemaking or amendment to the compact. The executive committee shall oversee the day-to-day activities of the administration of the compact managed by an executive director and Interstate Commission staff; administers enforcement and compliance with the provisions of the compact, its bylaws and rules, and performs such other duties as directed by the Interstate Commission or set forth in the bylaws.

G. Each member of the Interstate Commission shall have the right and power to cast a vote to which that compacting state is entitled and to participate in the business and affairs of the Interstate Commission. A member shall vote in person and shall not delegate a vote to another compacting state. However, a commissioner shall appoint another authorized representative, in the absence of the commissioner from that state, to cast a vote on behalf of the compacting state at a specified meeting. The bylaws may provide for members' participation in meetings by telephone or other means of telecommunication or electronic communication.

H. The Interstate Commission's bylaws shall establish conditions and procedures under which the Interstate Commission shall make its information and official records available to the public for inspection or copying. The Interstate Commission may exempt from disclosure any information or official records to the extent they would adversely affect personal privacy rights or proprietary interests.

I. Public notice shall be given of all meetings and all meetings shall be open to the public, except as set forth in the rules or as otherwise provided in the compact. The Interstate Commission and any of its committees may close a meeting to the public when it determines by two-thirds vote that an open meeting would be likely to:

1. Relate solely to the Interstate Commission's internal personnel practices and procedures;

2. Disclose matters specifically exempted from disclosure by statute;

3. Disclose trade secrets or commercial or financial information which is privileged or confidential;

4. Involve accusing any person of a crime or formally censuring any person;

5. Disclose information of a personal nature where disclosure would constitute a clearly unwarranted invasion of personal privacy;

6. Disclose investigative records compiled for law enforcement purposes;

7. Disclose information contained in or related to examination, operating or condition reports prepared by, or on behalf of or for the use of, the Interstate Commission with respect to a regulated person or entity for the purpose of regulation or supervision of such person or entity;

8. Disclose information, the premature disclosure of which would significantly endanger the stability of a regulated person or entity; or

9. Specifically relate to the Interstate Commission's issuance of a subpoena, or its participation in a civil action or other legal proceeding.

J. For every meeting closed pursuant to this provision, the Interstate Commission's legal counsel shall publicly certify that, in the legal counsel's opinion, the meeting may be closed to the public, and shall reference each relevant exemptive provision. The Interstate Commission shall keep minutes which shall fully and clearly describe all matters discussed in any meeting and shall provide a full and accurate summary of any actions taken, and the reasons therefore, including a description of each of the views expressed on any item and the record of any roll call vote (reflected in the vote of each member on the question). All documents considered in connection with any action shall be identified in such minutes.

K. The Interstate Commission shall collect standardized data concerning the interstate movement of juveniles as directed through its rules which shall specify the data to be collected, the means of collection and data exchange, and reporting requirements. Such methods of data collection, exchange, and reporting shall insofar as is reasonably possible conform to up-to-date technology and coordinate the Interstate Commission's information functions with the appropriate repository of records.

## ARTICLE IV POWERS AND DUTIES OF THE INTERSTATE COMMISSION

The commission shall have the following powers and duties:

1. To provide for dispute resolution among compacting states.

2. To promulgate rules to effect the purposes and obligations as enumerated in this compact, which shall have the force and effect of statutory law and shall be binding in the compacting states to the extent and in the manner provided in this compact.

3. To oversee, supervise, and coordinate the interstate movement of juveniles subject to the terms of this compact and any bylaws adopted and rules promulgated by the Interstate Commission.

4. To enforce compliance with the compact provisions, the rules promulgated by the Interstate Commission, and the bylaws, using all necessary and proper means, including but not limited to the use of judicial process.

5. To establish and maintain offices which shall be located within one or more of the compacting states.

6. To purchase and maintain insurance and bonds.

7. To borrow, accept, hire, or contract for services of personnel.

8. To establish and appoint committees and hire staff which it deems necessary for the carrying out of its functions including, but not limited to, an executive committee as required by Article III of this compact, which shall have the power to act on behalf of the Interstate Commission in carrying out its powers and duties hereunder.

9. To elect or appoint officers, attorneys, employees, agents, or consultants, and to fix their compensation, define their duties, and determine their qualifications, and to establish the Interstate Commission's personnel policies and programs relating to, inter alia, conflicts of interest, rates of compensation, and qualifications of personnel.

10. To accept any and all donations and grants of money, equipment, supplies, materials, and services, and to receive, utilize, and dispose of same.

11. To lease, purchase, accept contributions or donations of, or otherwise to own, hold, improve, or use any property, whether real, personal, or mixed.

12. To sell, convey, mortgage, pledge, lease, exchange, abandon, or otherwise dispose of any property, whether real, personal, or mixed.

13. To establish a budget and make expenditures and levy dues as provided in Article VIII of this compact.

14. To sue and be sued.

15. To adopt a seal and bylaws governing the management and operation of the Interstate Commission.

16. To perform such functions as may be necessary or appropriate to achieve the purposes of this compact.

17. To report annually to the legislatures, governors, and judiciary of the compacting states concerning the activities of the Interstate Commission during the preceding year. Such reports shall also include any recommendations that may have been adopted by the Interstate Commission.

18. To coordinate education, training, and public awareness regarding the interstate movement of juveniles for officials involved in such activity.

19. To establish uniform standards of the reporting, collecting, and exchanging of data.

20. The Interstate Commission shall maintain its corporate books and records in accordance with the bylaws.

## ARTICLE V ORGANIZATION AND OPERATION OF THE INTERSTATE COMMISSION

Sec. A. Bylaws

1. The Interstate Commission shall, by a majority of the members present and voting, within 12 months of the first Interstate Commission meeting, adopt bylaws to govern its conduct as may be necessary or appropriate to carry out the purposes of the compact, including, but not limited to:

    a. Establishing the fiscal year of the Interstate Commission;

    b. Establishing an executive committee and such other committees as may be necessary;

    c. Providing for the establishment of committees governing any general or specific delegation of any authority or function of the Interstate Commission;

d. Providing reasonable procedures for calling and conducting meetings of the Interstate Commission and ensuring reasonable notice of each such meeting;

e. Establishing the titles and responsibilities of the officers of the Interstate Commission;

f. Providing a mechanism for concluding the operations of the Interstate Commission and the return of any surplus funds that may exist upon the termination of the compact after the payment or reserving of all of its debts and obligations;

g. Providing start-up rules for initial administration of the compact; and

h. Establishing standards and procedures for compliance and technical assistance in carrying out the compact.

Sec. B. Officers and Staff

1. The Interstate Commission shall, by a majority of the members, elect annually from among its members a chairperson and a vice chairperson, each of whom shall have such authority and duties as may be specified in the bylaws. The chairperson or, in the chairperson's absence or disability, the vice chairperson shall preside at all meetings of the Interstate Commission. The officers so elected shall serve without compensation or remuneration from the Interstate Commission, provided that, subject to the availability of budgeted funds, the officers shall be reimbursed for any ordinary and necessary costs and expenses incurred by them in the performance of their duties and responsibilities as officers of the Interstate Commission.

2. The Interstate Commission shall, through its executive committee, appoint or retain an executive director for such period, upon such terms and conditions, and for such compensation as the Interstate Commission may deem appropriate. The executive director shall serve as secretary to the Interstate Commission, but shall not be a member and shall hire and supervise such other staff as may be authorized by the Interstate Commission.

Sec. C. Qualified Immunity, Defense, and Indemnification

1. The Interstate Commission's executive director and employees shall be immune from suit and liability, either personally or in their official capacity, for any claim for damage to or loss of property or personal injury or other civil liability caused or arising out of or relating to any actual or alleged act, error, or omission that occurred, or that such person had a reasonable basis for believing occurred, within the scope of Interstate Commission employment, duties, or responsibilities, provided that any such person shall not be protected from suit or liability for any damage, loss, injury, or liability caused by the intentional or wilful and wanton misconduct of any such person.

2. The liability of any commissioner, or the employee or agent of a commissioner, acting within the scope of such person's employment or duties for acts, errors, or omissions occurring within such person's state may not exceed the limits of liability set forth under the constitution and laws of that state for state officials, employees, and agents. Nothing in this subsection shall be construed to protect any such person from suit or liability for any damage, loss, injury, or liability caused by the intentional or wilful and wanton misconduct of any such person.

3. The Interstate Commission shall defend the executive director or the employees or representatives of the Interstate Commission and, subject to the approval of the attorney general of the state represented by any commissioner of a compacting state, shall defend such commissioner or the commissioner's representatives or employees in any civil action seeking to impose liability arising out of any actual or alleged act, error, or omission that occurred within the scope of Interstate Commission employment, duties, or responsibilities, or that the defendant had a reasonable basis for believing occurred within the scope of Interstate Commission employment, duties, or responsibilities, provided that the actual or alleged act, error, or omission did not result from intentional or wilful and wanton misconduct on the part of such person.

4. The Interstate Commission shall indemnify and hold the commissioner of a compacting state, or the commissioner's representatives or employees, or the Interstate Commission's representatives or employees, harmless in the amount of any settlement or judgment obtained against such persons arising out of any actual or alleged act, error, or omission that occurred within the scope of Interstate Commission employment, duties, or responsibilities, or that such persons had a reasonable basis for believing occurred within the scope of Interstate Commission employment, duties, or responsibilities, provided that the actual or alleged act, error, or omission did not result

from intentional or wilful and wanton misconduct on the part of such persons.

## ARTICLE VI RULEMAKING FUNCTIONS OF THE INTERSTATE COMMISSION

A. The Interstate Commission shall promulgate and publish rules in order to effectively and efficiently achieve the purposes of the compact.

B. Rulemaking shall occur pursuant to the criteria set forth in this article and the bylaws and rules adopted pursuant thereto. Such rulemaking shall substantially conform to the principles of the "Model State Administrative Procedures Act," 1981 Act, Uniform Laws Annotated, Vol. 15, p.1 (2000), or such other administrative procedures act, as the Interstate Commission deems appropriate consistent with due process requirements under the United States Constitution as now or hereafter interpreted by the United States Supreme Court. All rules and amendments shall become binding as of the date specified, as published with the final version of the rule as approved by the Interstate Commission.

C. When promulgating a rule, the Interstate Commission shall, at a minimum:

1. Publish the proposed rule's entire text stating the reason or reasons for that proposed rule;

2. Allow and invite persons to submit written data, facts, opinions, and arguments, which information shall be added to the record and be made publicly available;

3. Provide an opportunity for an informal hearing, if petitioned by 10 or more persons; and

4. Promulgate a final rule and its effective date, if appropriate, based on input from state or local officials, or interested parties.

D. Allow, not later than 60 days after a rule is promulgated, any interested person to file a petition in the United States District Court for the District of Columbia or in the federal district court where the Interstate Commission's principal office is located for judicial review of the rule. If the court finds that the Interstate Commission's action is not supported by substantial evidence in the rulemaking record, the court shall hold the rule unlawful and set it aside. For purposes of this subsection, evidence is substantial if it would be considered substantial evidence under the Model State Administrative Procedures Act.

E. If a majority of the legislatures of the compacting states rejects a rule, those states may, by enactment of a statute or resolution in the same manner used to adopt the compact, cause that such rule shall have no further force and effect in any compacting state.

F. The existing rules governing the operation of the Interstate Compact on Juveniles superceded by this Act shall be null and void 12 months after the first meeting of the Interstate Commission created under this compact.

G. Upon determination by the Interstate Commission that an emergency exists, the Interstate Commission may promulgate an emergency rule which shall become effective immediately upon adoption, provided that the usual rulemaking procedures provided hereunder shall be retroactively applied to said rule as soon as reasonably possible, but no later than 90 days after the effective date of the emergency rule.

## ARTICLE VII OVERSIGHT, ENFORCEMENT, AND DISPUTE RESOLUTION BY THE INTERSTATE COMMISSION

Sec. A. Oversight

1. The Interstate Commission shall oversee the administration and operations of the interstate movement of juveniles subject to this compact in the compacting states and shall monitor such activities being administered in noncompacting states which may significantly affect compacting states.

2. The courts and executive agencies in each compacting state shall enforce this compact and shall take all actions necessary and appropriate to effectuate the compact's purposes and intent. The provisions of this compact and the rules promulgated hereunder shall be received by all the judges, public officers, commissions, and departments of the state government as evidence of the authorized statute and administrative rules. All courts shall take judicial notice of the compact and the rules. In any judicial or administrative proceeding in a compacting state pertaining to the subject matter of this compact which may affect the powers, responsibilities, or actions of the Interstate Commission, the Interstate Commission shall be entitled to receive all service of process in any such proceeding, and shall have standing to intervene in the proceeding for all purposes.

Sec. B. Dispute Resolution

1. The compacting states shall report to the Interstate Commission on all issues and activities necessary for the administration of the compact as well as issues and activities pertaining to compliance with the provisions of the compact and its bylaws and rules.

2. The Interstate Commission shall attempt, upon the request of a compacting state, to resolve any disputes or other issues which are subject to the compact and which may arise among compacting states and between compacting and noncompacting states. The Interstate Commission shall promulgate a rule providing for both mediation and binding dispute resolution for disputes among the compacting states.

3. The Interstate Commission, in the reasonable exercise of its discretion, shall enforce the provisions and rules of this compact using any or all means set forth in Article X of this compact.

## ARTICLE VIII FINANCE

A. The Interstate Commission shall pay or provide for the payment of the reasonable expenses of its establishment, organization, and ongoing activities.

B. The Interstate Commission shall levy on and collect an annual assessment from each compacting state to cover the cost of the internal operations and activities of the Interstate Commission and its staff which must be in a total amount sufficient to cover the Interstate Commission's annual budget as approved each year. The aggregate annual assessment amount shall be allocated based upon a formula to be determined by the Interstate Commission, taking into consideration the population of each compacting state and the volume of interstate movement of juveniles in each compacting state. The Interstate Commission shall promulgate a rule binding upon all compacting states that governs said assessment.

C. The Interstate Commission shall not incur any obligations of any kind prior to securing the funds adequate to meet the same, nor shall the Interstate Commission pledge the credit of any of the compacting states, except by and with the authority of the compacting state.

D. The Interstate Commission shall keep accurate accounts of all receipts and disbursements. The receipts and disbursements of the Interstate Commission shall be subject to the audit and accounting procedures established under its by-laws. However, all receipts and disbursements of funds handled by the Interstate Commission shall be audited yearly by a certified or licensed public accountant and the report of the audit shall be included in and become part of the annual report of the Interstate Commission.

## ARTICLE IX COMPACTING STATES, EFFECTIVE DATE, AND AMENDMENT

A. Any state, as defined in Article II of this compact, is eligible to become a compacting state.

B. The compact shall become effective and binding upon legislative enactment of the compact into law by no less than 35 of the states. The initial effective date shall be the later of July 1, 2004, or upon enactment into law by the 35th jurisdiction. Thereafter, the compact shall become effective and binding, as to any other compacting state, upon enactment of the compact into law by that state. The governors of noncompacting states or their designees shall be invited to participate in Interstate Commission activities on a nonvoting basis prior to adoption of the compact by all states.

C. The Interstate Commission may propose amendments to the compact for enactment by the compacting states. No amendment shall become effective and binding upon the Interstate Commission and the compacting states unless and until it is enacted into law by unanimous consent of the compacting states.

## ARTICLE X WITHDRAWAL, DEFAULT, TERMINATION, AND JUDICIAL ENFORCEMENT

Sec. A. Withdrawal

1. Once effective, the compact shall continue in force and remain binding upon each and every compacting state, provided that a compacting state may withdraw from the compact by specifically repealing the statute which enacted the compact into law.

2. The effective date of withdrawal is the effective date of the repeal.

3. The withdrawing state shall immediately notify the chairperson of the Interstate Commission in writing upon the introduction of legislation repealing this compact in the withdrawing state. The Interstate Commission shall notify the other compacting states of the withdrawing state's intent to withdraw within 60 days of its receipt thereof.

4. The withdrawing state is responsible for all assessments, obligations, and liabilities incurred through the effective date of withdrawal, including any obligations, the performance of which extend beyond the effective date of withdrawal.

5. Reinstatement following withdrawal of any compacting state shall occur upon the withdrawing state reenacting the compact or upon such later date as determined by the Interstate Commission.

Sec. B. Technical Assistance, Fines, Suspension, Termination, and Default

1. If the Interstate Commission determines that any compacting state has at any time defaulted in the performance of any of its obligations or responsibilities under this compact, or the bylaws or duly promulgated rules, the Interstate Commission may impose any or all of the following penalties:

a. Remedial training and technical assistance as directed by the Interstate Commission;

b. Alternative dispute resolution;

c. Fines, fees, and costs in such amounts as are deemed to be reasonable as fixed by the Interstate Commission; and

d. Suspension or termination of membership in the compact, which shall be imposed only after all other reasonable means of securing compliance under the bylaws and rules have been exhausted and the Interstate Commission has determined that the offending state is in default. Immediate notice of suspension shall be given by the Interstate Commission to the governor, the chief justice or the chief judicial officer of the state, and the majority and minority leaders of the defaulting state's legislature. The grounds for default include, but are not limited to, failure of a compacting state to perform such obligations or responsibilities imposed upon it by this compact, the bylaws or duly promulgated rules, and any other grounds designated in commission bylaws and rules. The Interstate Commission shall immediately notify the defaulting state in writing of the penalty imposed by the Interstate Commission and of the default pending a cure of the default. The Interstate Commission shall stipulate the conditions and the time period within which the defaulting state must cure its default. If the defaulting state fails to cure the default within the time period specified

by the Interstate Commission, the defaulting state shall be terminated from the compact upon an affirmative vote of a majority of the compacting states and all rights, privileges, and benefits conferred by this compact shall be terminated from the effective date of termination.

2. Within 60 days of the effective date of termination of a defaulting state, the Interstate Commission shall notify the governor, the chief justice or chief judicial officer of the state, and the majority and minority leaders of the defaulting state's legislature of such termination.

3. The defaulting state is responsible for all assessments, obligations, and liabilities incurred through the effective date of termination including any obligations, the performance of which extends beyond the effective date of termination.

4. The Interstate Commission shall not bear any costs relating to the defaulting state unless otherwise mutually agreed upon in writing between the Interstate Commission and the defaulting state.

5. Reinstatement following termination of any compacting state requires both a reenactment of the compact by the defaulting state and the approval of the Interstate Commission pursuant to the rules.

Sec. C. Judicial Enforcement

The Interstate Commission may, by majority vote of the members, initiate legal action in the United States District Court for the District of Columbia or, at the discretion of the Interstate Commission, in the federal district where the Interstate Commission has its offices, to enforce compliance with the provisions of the compact, its duly promulgated rules and bylaws, against any compacting state in default. In the event judicial enforcement is necessary the prevailing party shall be awarded all costs of such litigation including reasonable attorney's fees.

Sec. D. Dissolution of Compact

1. The compact dissolves effective upon the date of the withdrawal or default of the compacting state, which reduces membership in the compact to one compacting state.

2. Upon the dissolution of this compact, the compact becomes null and void and shall be of no further force or effect, and the business and affairs of the Interstate Commission shall be concluded and any surplus funds shall be distributed in accordance with the bylaws.

Family Code

## ARTICLE XI SEVERABILITY AND CONSTRUCTION

A. The provisions of this compact shall be severable, and if any phrase, clause, sentence, or provision is deemed unenforceable, the remaining provisions of the compact shall be enforceable.

B. The provisions of this compact shall be liberally construed to effectuate its purposes.

## ARTICLE XII BINDING EFFECT OF COMPACT AND OTHER LAWS

Sec. A. Other Laws

1. Nothing herein prevents the enforcement of any other law of a compacting state that is not inconsistent with this compact.

2. All compacting states' laws other than state constitutions and other interstate compacts conflicting with this compact are superseded to the extent of the conflict.

Sec. B. Binding Effect of the Compact

1. All lawful actions of the Interstate Commission, including all rules and bylaws promulgated by the Interstate Commission, are binding upon the compacting states.

2. All agreements between the Interstate Commission and the compacting states are binding in accordance with their terms.

3. Upon the request of a party to a conflict over meaning or interpretation of Interstate Commission actions, and upon a majority vote of the compacting states, the Interstate Commission may issue advisory opinions regarding such meaning or interpretation.

4. In the event any provision of this compact exceeds the constitutional limits imposed on the legislature of any compacting state, the obligations, duties, powers, or jurisdiction sought to be conferred by such provision upon the Interstate Commission shall be ineffective and such obligations, duties, powers, or jurisdiction shall remain in the compacting state and shall be exercised by the agency thereof to which such obligations, duties, powers, or jurisdiction are delegated by law in effect at the time this compact becomes effective.

(Enacted by Acts 2005, 79th Leg., ch. 1007 (H.B. 706), § 1.01, effective September 1, 2005.)

STATUTORY NOTES

Editor's notes. — Acts 2005, 79th Leg., ch. 1007 (H.B. 706) implemented a significant revision of the original 1955 Interstate Compact on Juveniles, effective on the date that the new version of the compact was adopted by 35 states. The new compact was adopted by the 35th state, Illinois, on August 26, 2008, making the compact and conforming amendment effective on that date.

## Sec. 60.011. Effect of Texas Laws.

If the laws of this state conflict with the compact, the compact controls, except that in the event of a conflict between the compact and the Texas Constitution, as determined by the courts of this state, the Texas Constitution controls.

(Enacted by Acts 2005, 79th Leg., ch. 1007 (H.B. 706), § 2.02, effective August 26, 2008.)

STATUTORY NOTES

Editor's notes. — Acts 2005, 79th Leg., ch. 1007 (H.B. 706) implemented a significant revision of the original 1955 Interstate Compact on Juveniles, effective on the date that the new version of the compact was adopted by 35 states. The new compact was adopted by the 35th state, Illinois, on August 26, 2008, making the compact and conforming amendment effective on that date.

## Sec. 60.012. Liabilities for Certain Commission Agents.

The compact administrator and each member, officer, executive director, employee, or agent of the commission acting within the scope of the person's employment or duties is, for the purpose of acts or omissions occurring within this state, entitled to the same protections under Chapter 104, Civil Practice and Remedies Code, as an employee, a member of the governing board, or any other officer of a state agency, institution, or department.

(Enacted by Acts 2005, 79th Leg., ch. 1007 (H.B. 706), § 2.02, effective August 26, 2008.)

STATUTORY NOTES

Editor's notes. — Acts 2005, 79th Leg., ch. 1007 (H.B. 706) implemented a significant revision of the original 1955 Interstate Compact on Juveniles, effective on the date that the new version of the compact was adopted by 35 states. The new compact was adopted by the 35th state, Illinois, on August 26, 2008, making the compact and conforming amendment effective on that date.

Family Code

# CHAPTER 61
## RIGHTS AND RESPONSIBILITIES OF PARENTS AND OTHER ELIGIBLE PERSONS

### Subchapter A. Entry of Orders Against Parents and Other Eligible Persons

## SUBCHAPTER A
## ENTRY OF ORDERS AGAINST PARENTS AND OTHER ELIGIBLE PERSONS

### Sec. 61.001. Definitions.

In this chapter:

(1) "Juvenile court order" means an order by a juvenile court in a proceeding to which this chapter applies requiring a parent or other eligible person to act or refrain from acting.

(2) "Other eligible person" means the respondent's guardian, the respondent's custodian, or any other person described in a provision under this title authorizing the court order.

(Enacted by Acts 2003, 78th Leg., ch. 283 (H.B. 2319), § 28, effective September 1, 2003.)

### Sec. 61.002. Applicability.

(a) Except as provided by Subsection (b), this chapter applies to a proceeding to enter a juvenile court order:

(1) for payment of probation fees under Section 54.061;

(2) for restitution under Sections 54.041(b) and 54.048;

(3) for payment of graffiti eradication fees under Section 54.0461;

(4) for community service under Section 54.044(b);

(5) for payment of costs of court under Section 54.0411 or other provisions of law;

(6) requiring the person to refrain from doing any act injurious to the welfare of the child under Section 54.041(a)(1);

(7) enjoining contact between the person and the child who is the subject of a proceeding under Section 54.041(a)(2);

(8) ordering a person living in the same household with the child to participate in counseling under Section 54.041(a)(3);

(9) requiring a parent or guardian of a child found to be truant to participate in an available program addressing truancy under Section 54.041(f);

(10) requiring a parent or other eligible person to pay reasonable attorney's fees for representing the child under Section 51.10(e);

(11) requiring the parent or other eligible person to reimburse the county for payments the county has made to an attorney appointed to represent the child under Section 51.10(j);

(12) requiring payment of deferred prosecution supervision fees under Section 53.03(d);

(13) requiring a parent or other eligible person to attend a court hearing under Section 51.115;

(14) requiring a parent or other eligible person to act or refrain from acting to aid the child in complying with conditions of release from detention under Section 54.01(r);

(15) requiring a parent or other eligible person to act or refrain from acting under any law imposing an obligation of action or omission on a parent or other eligible person because of the parent's or person's relation to the child who is the subject of a proceeding under this title;

(16) for payment of fees under Section 54.0462; or

(17) for payment of the cost of attending an educational program under Section 54.0404.

(b) This subchapter does not apply to the entry and enforcement of a child support order under Section 54.06.

(Enacted by Acts 2003, 78th Leg., ch. 283 (H.B. 2319), § 28, effective September 1, 2003; am. Acts 2009, 81st Leg., ch. 1209 (S.B. 727), § 5, effective

September 1, 2009; am. Acts 2011, 82nd Leg., ch. 1322 (S.B. 407), § 21, effective September 1, 2011.)

## Sec. 61.003.  Entry of Juvenile Court Order Against Parent or Other Eligible Person.

(a) To comply with the requirements of due process of law, the juvenile court shall:

(1) provide sufficient notice in writing or orally in a recorded court hearing of a proposed juvenile court order; and

(2) provide a sufficient opportunity for the parent or other eligible person to be heard regarding the proposed order.

(b) A juvenile court order must be in writing and a copy promptly furnished to the parent or other eligible person.

(c) The juvenile court may require the parent or other eligible person to provide suitable identification to be included in the court's file. Suitable identification includes fingerprints, a driver's license number, a social security number, or similar indicia of identity.

(Enacted by Acts 2003, 78th Leg., ch. 283 (H.B. 2319), § 28, effective September 1, 2003.)

## Sec. 61.0031.  Transfer of Order Affecting Parent or Other Eligible Person to County of Child's Residence.

(a) This section applies only when:

(1) a juvenile court has placed a parent or other eligible person under a court order under this chapter;

(2) the child who was the subject of the juvenile court proceedings in which the order was entered:

(A) resides in a county other than the county in which the order was entered;

(B) has moved to a county other than the county in which the order was entered and intends to remain in that county for at least 60 days; or

(C) intends to move to a county other than the county in which the order was entered and to remain in that county for at least 60 days; and

(3) the parent or other eligible person resides or will reside in the same county as the county in which the child now resides or to which the child has moved or intends to move.

(b) A juvenile court that enters an order described by Subsection (a)(1) may transfer the order to the juvenile court of the county in which the parent now resides or to which the parent has moved or intends to move.

(c) The juvenile court shall provide the parent or other eligible person written notice of the transfer. The notification must identify the court to which the order has been transferred.

(d) The juvenile court to which the order has been transferred shall require the parent or other eligible person to appear before the court to notify the person of the existence and terms of the order. Failure to do so renders the order unenforceable.

(e) If the notice required by Subsection (d) is provided, the juvenile court to which the order has been transferred may modify, extend, or enforce the order as though the court originally entered the order.

(Enacted by Acts 2005, 79th Leg., ch. 949 (H.B. 1575), § 26, effective September 1, 2005.)

## Sec. 61.004.  Appeal.

(a) The parent or other eligible person against whom a final juvenile court order has been entered may appeal as provided by law from judgments entered in civil cases.

(b) The movant may appeal from a judgment denying requested relief regarding a juvenile court order as provided by law from judgments entered in civil cases.

(c) The pendency of an appeal initiated under this section does not abate or otherwise affect the proceedings in juvenile court involving the child.

(Enacted by Acts 2003, 78th Leg., ch. 283 (H.B. 2319), § 28, effective September 1, 2003.)

## SUBCHAPTER B
## ENFORCEMENT OF ORDER AGAINST PARENT OR OTHER ELIGIBLE PERSON

## Sec. 61.051.  Motion for Enforcement.

(a) A party initiates enforcement of a juvenile court order by filing a written motion. In ordinary and concise language, the motion must:

(1) identify the provision of the order allegedly violated and sought to be enforced;

(2) state specifically and factually the manner of the person's alleged noncompliance;

(3) state the relief requested; and

(4) contain the signature of the party filing the motion.

(b) The movant must allege in the same motion for enforcement each violation by the person of the juvenile court orders described by Section 61.002(a) that the movant had a reasonable basis for believing the person was violating when the motion was filed.

(c) The juvenile court retains jurisdiction to enter a contempt order if the motion for enforcement is filed not later than six months after the child's 18th birthday.

(Enacted by Acts 2003, 78th Leg., ch. 283 (H.B. 2319), § 28, effective September 1, 2003.)

## Sec. 61.052. Notice and Appearance.

(a) On the filing of a motion for enforcement, the court shall by written notice set the date, time, and place of the hearing and order the person against whom enforcement is sought to appear and respond to the motion.

(b) The notice must be given by personal service or by certified mail, return receipt requested, on or before the 10th day before the date of the hearing on the motion. The notice must include a copy of the motion for enforcement. Personal service must comply with the Code of Criminal Procedure.

(c) If a person moves to strike or specially excepts to the motion for enforcement, the court shall rule on the exception or motion to strike before the court hears evidence on the motion for enforcement. If an exception is sustained, the court shall give the movant an opportunity to replead and continue the hearing to a designated date and time without the requirement of additional service.

(d) If a person who has been personally served with notice to appear at the hearing does not appear, the juvenile court may not hold the person in contempt, but may issue a capias for the arrest of the person. The court shall set and enforce bond as provided by Subchapter C, Chapter 157. If a person served by certified mail, return receipt requested, with notice to appear at the hearing does not appear, the juvenile court may require immediate personal service of notice.

(Enacted by Acts 2003, 78th Leg., ch. 283 (H.B. 2319), § 28, effective September 1, 2003.)

## Sec. 61.053. Attorney for the Person.

(a) In a proceeding on a motion for enforcement where incarceration is a possible punishment against a person who is not represented by an attorney, the court shall inform the person of the right to be represented by an attorney and, if the person is indigent, of the right to the appointment of an attorney.

(b) If the person claims indigency and requests the appointment of an attorney, the juvenile court

may require the person to file an affidavit of indigency. The court may hear evidence to determine the issue of indigency.

(c) The court shall appoint an attorney to represent the person if the court determines that the person is indigent.

(d) The court shall allow an appointed or retained attorney at least 10 days after the date of the attorney's appointment or retention to respond to the movant's pleadings and to prepare for the hearing. The attorney may waive the preparation time or agree to a shorter period for preparation.

(Enacted by Acts 2003, 78th Leg., ch. 283 (H.B. 2319), § 28, effective September 1, 2003.)

## Sec. 61.054. Compensation of Appointed Attorney.

(a) An attorney appointed to represent an indigent person is entitled to a reasonable fee for services to be paid from the general fund of the county according to the schedule for compensation adopted by the county juvenile board. The attorney must meet the qualifications required of attorneys for appointment to Class B misdemeanor cases in juvenile court.

(b) For purposes of compensation, a proceeding in the supreme court is the equivalent of a proceeding in the court of criminal appeals.

(c) The juvenile court may order the parent or other eligible person for whom it has appointed counsel to reimburse the county for the fees the county pays to appointed counsel.

(Enacted by Acts 2003, 78th Leg., ch. 283 (H.B. 2319), § 28, effective September 1, 2003.)

## Sec. 61.055. Conduct of Enforcement Hearing.

(a) The juvenile court shall require that the enforcement hearing be recorded as provided by Section 54.09.

(b) The movant must prove beyond a reasonable doubt that the person against whom enforcement is sought engaged in conduct constituting contempt of a reasonable and lawful court order as alleged in the motion for enforcement.

(c) The person against whom enforcement is sought has a privilege not to be called as a witness or otherwise to incriminate himself or herself.

(d) The juvenile court shall conduct the enforcement hearing without a jury.

(e) The juvenile court shall include in its judgment findings as to each violation alleged in the motion for enforcement and the punishment, if any, to be imposed.

(f) If the person against whom enforcement is sought was not represented by counsel during any previous court proceeding involving a motion for enforcement, the person may through counsel raise any defense or affirmative defense to the proceeding that could have been lodged in the previous court proceeding but was not because the person was not represented by counsel.

(g) It is an affirmative defense to enforcement of a juvenile court order that the juvenile court did not provide the parent or other eligible person with due process of law in the proceeding in which the court entered the order.

(Enacted by Acts 2003, 78th Leg., ch. 283 (H.B. 2319), § 28, effective September 1, 2003.)

## Sec. 61.056.  Affirmative Defense of Inability to Pay.

(a) In an enforcement hearing in which the motion for enforcement alleges that the person against whom enforcement is sought failed to pay restitution, court costs, supervision fees, or any other payment ordered by the court, it is an affirmative defense that the person was financially unable to pay.

(b) The burden of proof to establish the affirmative defense of inability to pay is on the person asserting it.

(c) In order to prevail on the affirmative defense of inability to pay, the person asserting it must show that the person could not have reasonably paid the court-ordered obligation after the person discharged the person's other important financial obligations, including payments for housing, food, utilities, necessary clothing, education, and preexisting debts.

(Enacted by Acts 2003, 78th Leg., ch. 283 (H.B. 2319), § 28, effective September 1, 2003.)

## Sec. 61.057.  Punishment for Contempt.

(a) On a finding of contempt, the juvenile court may commit the person to the county jail for a term not to exceed six months or may impose a fine in an amount not to exceed $500, or both.

(b) The court may impose only a single jail sentence not to exceed six months or a single fine not to exceed $500, or both, during an enforcement proceeding, without regard to whether the court has entered multiple findings of contempt.

(c) On a finding of contempt in an enforcement proceeding, the juvenile court may, instead of issuing a commitment to jail, enter an order requiring the person's future conduct to comply with the court's previous orders.

(d) Violation of an order entered under Subsection (c) may be the basis of a new enforcement proceeding.

(e) The juvenile court may assign a juvenile probation officer to assist a person in complying with a court order issued under Subsection (c).

(f) A juvenile court may reduce a term of incarceration or reduce payment of all or part of a fine at any time before the sentence is fully served or the fine fully paid.

(g) A juvenile court may reduce the burden of complying with a court order issued under Subsection (c) at any time before the order is fully satisfied, but may not increase the burden except following a new finding of contempt in a new enforcement proceeding.

(Enacted by Acts 2003, 78th Leg., ch. 283 (H.B. 2319), § 28, effective September 1, 2003.)

## SUBCHAPTER C
## RIGHTS OF PARENTS

## Sec. 61.101.  Definition.

In this subchapter, "parent" includes the guardian or custodian of a child.

(Enacted by Acts 2003, 78th Leg., ch. 283 (H.B. 2319), § 28, effective September 1, 2003.)

## Sec. 61.102.  Right to Be Informed of Proceeding.

(a) The parent of a child referred to a juvenile court is entitled as soon as practicable after the referral to be informed by staff designated by the juvenile board, based on the information accompanying the referral to the juvenile court, of:

(1) the date and time of the offense;

(2) the date and time the child was taken into custody;

(3) the name of the offense and its penal category;

(4) the type of weapon, if any, that was used;

(5) the type of property taken or damaged and the extent of damage, if any;

(6) the physical injuries, if any, to the victim of the offense;

(7) whether there is reason to believe that the offense was gang-related;

(8) whether there is reason to believe that the offense was related to consumption of alcohol or use of an illegal controlled substance;

(9) if the child was taken into custody with adults or other juveniles, the names of those persons;

**Family Code**

(10) the aspects of the juvenile court process that apply to the child;

(11) if the child is in detention, the visitation policy of the detention facility that applies to the child;

(12) the child's right to be represented by an attorney and the local standards and procedures for determining whether the parent qualifies for appointment of counsel to represent the child; and

(13) the methods by which the parent can assist the child with the legal process.

(b) If the child was released on field release citation, or from the law enforcement station by the police, by intake, or by the judge or associate judge at the initial detention hearing, the information required by Subsection (a) may be communicated to the parent in person, by telephone, or in writing.

(c) If the child is not released before or at the initial detention hearing, the information required by Subsection (a) shall be communicated in person to the parent unless that is not feasible, in which event it may be communicated by telephone or in writing.

(d) Information disclosed to a parent under Subsection (a) is not admissible in a judicial proceeding under this title as substantive evidence or as evidence to impeach the testimony of a witness for the state.

(Enacted by Acts 2003, 78th Leg., ch. 283 (H.B. 2319), § 28, effective September 1, 2003.)

### Sec. 61.103. Right of Access to Child.

(a) The parent of a child taken into custody for delinquent conduct, conduct indicating a need for supervision, or conduct that violates a condition of probation imposed by the juvenile court has the right to communicate in person privately with the child for reasonable periods of time while the child is in:

(1) a juvenile processing office;

(2) a secure detention facility;

(3) a secure correctional facility;

(4) a court-ordered placement facility; or

(5) the custody of the Texas Youth Commission.

(b) The time, place, and conditions of the private, in-person communication may be regulated to prevent disruption of scheduled activities and to maintain the safety and security of the facility. (Enacted by Acts 2003, 78th Leg., ch. 283 (H.B. 2319), § 28, effective September 1, 2003.)

### Sec. 61.104. Parental Written Statement.

(a) When a petition for adjudication, a motion or petition to modify disposition, or a motion or petition for discretionary transfer to criminal court is served on a parent of the child, the parent must be provided with a form prescribed by the Texas Juvenile Probation Commission on which the parent can make a written statement about the needs of the child or family or any other matter relevant to disposition of the case.

(b) The parent shall return the statement to the juvenile probation department, which shall transmit the statement to the court along with the discretionary transfer report authorized by Section 54.02(e), the disposition report authorized by Section 54.04(b), or the modification of disposition report authorized by Section 54.05(e), as applicable. The statement shall be disclosed to the parties as appropriate and may be considered by the court at the disposition, modification, or discretionary transfer hearing. (Enacted by Acts 2003, 78th Leg., ch. 283 (H.B. 2319), § 28, effective September 1, 2003.)

### Sec. 61.105. Parental Oral Statement.

(a) After all the evidence has been received but before the arguments of counsel at a hearing for discretionary transfer to criminal court, a disposition hearing without a jury, or a modification of disposition hearing, the court shall give a parent who is present in court a reasonable opportunity to address the court about the needs or strengths of the child or family or any other matter relevant to disposition of the case.

(b) The parent may not be required to make the statement under oath and may not be subject to cross-examination, but the court may seek clarification or expansion of the statement from the person giving the statement.

(c) The court may consider and act on the statement as the court considers appropriate. (Enacted by Acts 2003, 78th Leg., ch. 283 (H.B. 2319), § 28, effective September 1, 2003.)

### Sec. 61.106. Appeal or Collateral Challenge.

The failure or inability of a person to perform an act or to provide a right or service listed under this subchapter may not be used by the child or any party as a ground for:

(1) appeal;

(2) an application for a post-adjudication writ of habeas corpus; or

(3) exclusion of evidence against the child in any proceeding or forum.

(Enacted by Acts 2003, 78th Leg., ch. 283 (H.B. 2319), § 28, effective September 1, 2003.)

### Sec. 61.107.  Liability.

The Texas Youth Commission, a juvenile board, a court, a person appointed by the court, an employee of a juvenile probation department, an attorney for the state, a peace officer, or a law enforcement agency is not liable for a failure or inability to provide a right listed in this chapter. (Enacted by Acts 2003, 78th Leg., ch. 283 (H.B. 2319), § 28, effective September 1, 2003.)

# TITLE 4
# PROTECTIVE ORDERS AND FAMILY VIOLENCE

## SUBTITLE A
## GENERAL PROVISIONS

## CHAPTER 71
## DEFINITIONS

### Sec. 71.001.  Applicability of Definitions.

(a) Definitions in this chapter apply to this title.

(b) If, in another part of this title, a term defined by this chapter has a meaning different from the meaning provided by this chapter, the meaning of that other provision prevails.

(c) Except as provided by this chapter, the definitions in Chapter 101 apply to terms used in this title.

(Enacted by Acts 1997, 75th Leg., ch. 34 (S.B. 797), § 1, effective May 5, 1997.)

### Sec. 71.002.  Court.

"Court" means the district court, court of domestic relations, juvenile court having the jurisdiction of a district court, statutory county court, constitutional county court, or other court expressly given jurisdiction under this title.

(Enacted by Acts 1997, 75th Leg., ch. 34 (S.B. 797), § 1, effective May 5, 1997; am. Acts 1997, 75th Leg., ch. 1220 (H.B. 308), § 1, effective September 1, 1997.)

### Sec. 71.0021.  Dating Violence.

(a) "Dating violence" means an act, other than a defensive measure to protect oneself, by an actor that:

(1) is committed against a victim:

(A) with whom the actor has or has had a dating relationship; or

(B) because of the victim's marriage to or dating relationship with an individual with whom the actor is or has been in a dating relationship or marriage; and

(2) is intended to result in physical harm, bodily injury, assault, or sexual assault or that is a threat that reasonably places the victim in fear of imminent physical harm, bodily injury, assault, or sexual assault.

(b) For purposes of this title, "dating relationship" means a relationship between individuals who have or have had a continuing relationship of a romantic or intimate nature. The existence of such a relationship shall be determined based on consideration of:

(1) the length of the relationship;

(2) the nature of the relationship; and

(3) the frequency and type of interaction between the persons involved in the relationship.

(c) A casual acquaintanceship or ordinary fraternization in a business or social context does not constitute a "dating relationship" under Subsection (b).

(Enacted by Acts 2001, 77th Leg., ch. 91 (S.B. 68), § 1, effective September 1, 2001; am. Acts 2011, 82nd Leg., ch. 872 (S.B. 116), § 2, effective June 17, 2011.)

### Sec. 71.003.  Family.

"Family" includes individuals related by consanguinity or affinity, as determined under Sections 573.022 and 573.024, Government Code,

individuals who are former spouses of each other, individuals who are the parents of the same child, without regard to marriage, and a foster child and foster parent, without regard to whether those individuals reside together.
(Enacted by Acts 1997, 75th Leg., ch. 34 (S.B. 797), § 1, effective May 5, 1997; am. Acts 2001, 77th Leg., ch. 821 (H.B. 920), § 2.03, effective June 14, 2001.)

### Sec. 71.004. Family Violence.
"Family violence" means:
(1) an act by a member of a family or household against another member of the family or household that is intended to result in physical harm, bodily injury, assault, or sexual assault or that is a threat that reasonably places the member in fear of imminent physical harm, bodily injury, assault, or sexual assault, but does not include defensive measures to protect oneself;
(2) abuse, as that term is defined by Sections 261.001(1)(C), (E), and (G), by a member of a family or household toward a child of the family or household; or
(3) dating violence, as that term is defined by Section 71.0021.
(Enacted by Acts 1997, 75th Leg., ch. 34 (S.B. 797), § 1, effective May 5, 1997; am. Acts 2001, 77th Leg., ch. 91 (S.B. 68), § 2, effective September 1, 2001.)

### Sec. 71.005. Household.
"Household" means a unit composed of persons living together in the same dwelling, without regard to whether they are related to each other.
(Enacted by Acts 1997, 75th Leg., ch. 34 (S.B. 797), § 1, effective May 5, 1997.)

### Sec. 71.006. Member of a Household.
"Member of a household" includes a person who previously lived in a household.
(Enacted by Acts 1997, 75th Leg., ch. 34 (S.B. 797), § 1, effective May 5, 1997.)

### Sec. 71.007. Prosecuting Attorney.
"Prosecuting attorney" means the attorney, determined as provided in this title, who represents the state in a district or statutory county court in the county in which venue of the application for a protective order is proper.
(Enacted by Acts 1997, 75th Leg., ch. 34 (S.B. 797), § 1, effective May 5, 1997.)

### Sec. 71.008. Protective Order from

**Another Jurisdiction [Repealed].**
Repealed by Acts 2001, 77th Leg., ch. 48 (H.B. 919), § 3, effective September 1, 2001.
(Enacted by Acts 1997, 75th Leg., ch. 1193 (S.B. 1253), § 2, effective September 1, 1997.)

## SUBTITLE B
## PROTECTIVE ORDERS

## CHAPTER 82
## APPLYING FOR PROTECTIVE ORDER

## SUBCHAPTER A
## APPLICATION FOR PROTECTIVE ORDER

### Sec. 82.001. Application.
A proceeding under this subtitle is begun by filing "An Application for a Protective Order" with the clerk of the court.
(Enacted by Acts 1997, 75th Leg., ch. 34 (S.B. 797), § 1, effective May 5, 1997.)

### Sec. 82.002. Who May File Application.
(a) With regard to family violence under Section 71.004(1) or (2), an adult member of the family or household may file an application for a

**Family Code**

protective order to protect the applicant or any other member of the applicant's family or household.

(b) **[2 Versions: As amended by Acts 2011, 82nd Leg., ch. 632 (S.B. 819)]** With regard to family violence under Section 71.004(3), an application for a protective order to protect the applicant may be filed by a member of the dating relationship, regardless of whether the member is an adult or a child.

(b) **[2 Versions: As amended by Acts 2011, 82nd Leg., ch. 872 (S.B. 116)]** With regard to family violence under Section 71.004(3), an application for a protective order to protect the applicant may be filed by:

(1) an adult member of the dating relationship; or

(2) an adult member of the marriage, if the victim is or was married as described by Section 71.0021(a)(1)(B).

(c) Any adult may apply for a protective order to protect a child from family violence.

(d) In addition, an application may be filed for the protection of any person alleged to be a victim of family violence by:

(1) a prosecuting attorney; or

(2) the Department of Family and Protective Services.

(e) The person alleged to be the victim of family violence in an application filed under Subsection (c) or (d) is considered to be the applicant for a protective order under this subtitle.

(Enacted by Acts 1997, 75th Leg., ch. 34 (S.B. 797), § 1, effective May 5, 1997; am. Acts 1997, 75th Leg., ch. 1193 (S.B. 1253), § 8, effective September 1, 1997; am. Acts 2001, 77th Leg., ch. 91 (S.B. 68), § 3, effective September 1, 2001; am. Acts 2011, 82nd Leg., ch. 110 (H.B. 841), § 7, effective May 21, 2011; am. Acts 2011, 82nd Leg., ch. 632 (S.B. 819), § 2, effective September 1, 2011.am. Acts 2011, 82nd Leg., ch. 872 (S.B. 116), § 3, effective June 17, 2011.)

### Sec. 82.003.  Venue.

An application may be filed in:

(1) the county in which the applicant resides; or

(2) the county in which the respondent resides.

(Enacted by Acts 1997, 75th Leg., ch. 34 (S.B. 797), § 1, effective May 5, 1997.)

### Sec. 82.004.   Contents of Application.

An application must state:

(1) the name and county of residence of each applicant;

(2) the name and county of residence of each individual alleged to have committed family violence;

(3) the relationships between the applicants and the individual alleged to have committed family violence; and

(4) a request for one or more protective orders.

(Enacted by Acts 1997, 75th Leg., ch. 34 (S.B. 797), § 1, effective May 5, 1997; am. Acts 2001, 77th Leg., ch. 296 (H.B. 593), § 1, effective September 1, 2001.)

### Sec. 82.005.  Application Filed During Suit for Dissolution of Marriage or Suit Affecting Parent-Child Relationship.

A person who wishes to apply for a protective order with respect to the person's spouse and who is a party to a suit for the dissolution of a marriage or a suit affecting the parent-child relationship that is pending in a court must file the application as required by Subchapter D, Chapter 85.

(Enacted by Acts 1997, 75th Leg., ch. 34 (S.B. 797), § 1, effective May 5, 1997; am. Acts 1997, 75th Leg., ch. 1193 (S.B. 1253), § 9, effective September 1, 1997.)

### Sec. 82.006.  Application Filed After Dissolution of Marriage.

If an applicant for a protective order is a former spouse of the individual alleged to have committed family violence, the application must include:

(1) a copy of the decree dissolving the marriage; or

(2) a statement that the decree is unavailable to the applicant and that a copy of the decree will be filed with the court before the hearing on the application.

(Enacted by Acts 1997, 75th Leg., ch. 34 (S.B. 797), § 1, effective May 5, 1997.)

### Sec. 82.007.  Application Filed for Child Subject to Continuing Jurisdiction.

An application that requests a protective order for a child who is subject to the continuing exclusive jurisdiction of a court under Title 5 or alleges that a child who is subject to the continuing exclusive jurisdiction of a court under Title 5 has committed family violence must include:

Family Code

(1) a copy of each court order affecting the conservatorship, support, and possession of or access to the child; or

(2) a statement that the orders affecting the child are unavailable to the applicant and that a copy of the orders will be filed with the court before the hearing on the application.

(Enacted by Acts 1997, 75th Leg., ch. 34 (S.B. 797), § 1, effective May 5, 1997.)

### Sec. 82.008. Application Filed After Expiration of Former Protective Order.

(a) An application for a protective order that is filed after a previously rendered protective order has expired must include:

(1) a copy of the expired protective order attached to the application or, if a copy of the expired protective order is unavailable, a statement that the order is unavailable to the applicant and that a copy of the order will be filed with the court before the hearing on the application;

(2) a description of either:

(A) the violation of the expired protective order, if the application alleges that the respondent violated the expired protective order by committing an act prohibited by that order before the order expired; or

(B) the threatened harm that reasonably places the applicant in fear of imminent physical harm, bodily injury, assault, or sexual assault; and

(3) if a violation of the expired order is alleged, a statement that the violation of the expired order has not been grounds for any other order protecting the applicant that has been issued or requested under this subtitle.

(b) The procedural requirements for an original application for a protective order apply to a protective order requested under this section.

(Enacted by Acts 1997, 75th Leg., ch. 34 (S.B. 797), § 1, effective May 5, 1997; am. Acts 1999, 76th Leg., ch. 1160 (S.B. 50), § 1, effective September 1, 1999.)

### Sec. 82.0085. Application Filed Before Expiration of Previously Rendered Protective Order.

(a) If an application for a protective order alleges that an unexpired protective order applicable to the respondent is due to expire not later than the 30th day after the date the application was filed, the application for the subsequent protective order must include:

(1) a copy of the previously rendered protective order attached to the application or, if a copy of the previously rendered protective order is unavailable, a statement that the order is unavailable to the applicant and that a copy of the order will be filed with the court before the hearing on the application; and

(2) a description of the threatened harm that reasonably places the applicant in fear of imminent physical harm, bodily injury, assault, or sexual assault.

(b) The procedural requirements for an original application for a protective order apply to a protective order requested under this section.

(Enacted by Acts 1999, 76th Leg., ch. 1160 (S.B. 50), § 2, effective September 1, 1999.)

### Sec. 82.009. Application for Temporary Ex Parte Order.

(a) An application that requests the issuance of a temporary ex parte order under Chapter 83 must:

(1) contain a detailed description of the facts and circumstances concerning the alleged family violence and the need for the immediate protective order; and

(2) be signed by each applicant under an oath that the facts and circumstances contained in the application are true to the best knowledge and belief of each applicant.

(b) For purposes of this section, a statement signed under oath by a child is valid if the statement otherwise complies with this chapter.

(Enacted by Acts 1997, 75th Leg., ch. 34 (S.B. 797), § 1, effective May 5, 1997; am. Acts 2011, 82nd Leg., ch. 632 (S.B. 819), § 3, effective September 1, 2011.)

### Sec. 82.010. Confidentiality of Application.

(a) This section applies only in a county with a population of 3.4 million or more.

(b) Except as otherwise provided by law, an application for a protective order is confidential, is excepted from required public disclosure under Chapter 552, Government Code, and may not be released to a person who is not a respondent to the application until after the date of service of notice of the application or the date of the hearing on the application, whichever date is sooner.

(c) Except as otherwise provided by law, an application requesting the issuance of a temporary ex parte order under Chapter 83 is confidential, is excepted from required public disclosure under Chapter 552, Government Code, and may not be released to a person who is not a respondent to the application until after the date that the court or law enforcement informs the respondent of the court's order.

(Enacted by Acts 2003, 78th Leg., ch. 1314 (H.B. 1391), § 2, effective September 1, 2003.)

## SUBCHAPTER B
## PLEADINGS BY RESPONDENT

### Sec. 82.021.  Answer.

A respondent to an application for a protective order who is served with notice of an application for a protective order may file an answer at any time before the hearing. A respondent is not required to file an answer to the application.

(Enacted by Acts 1997, 75th Leg., ch. 34 (S.B. 797), § 1, effective May 5, 1997.)

### Sec. 82.022.  Request by Respondent for Protective Order.

To apply for a protective order, a respondent to an application for a protective order must file a separate application.

(Enacted by Acts 1997, 75th Leg., ch. 34 (S.B. 797), § 1, effective May 5, 1997.)

## SUBCHAPTER C
## NOTICE OF APPLICATION FOR PROTECTIVE ORDER

### Sec. 82.041.  Contents of Notice of Application.

(a) A notice of an application for a protective order must:

(1) be styled "The State of Texas";

(2) be signed by the clerk of the court under the court's seal;

(3) contain the name and location of the court;

(4) show the date the application was filed;

(5) show the date notice of the application for a protective order was issued;

(6) show the date, time, and place of the hearing;

(7) show the file number;

(8) show the name of each applicant and each person alleged to have committed family violence;

(9) be directed to each person alleged to have committed family violence;

(10) show the name and address of the attorney for the applicant or the mailing address of

the applicant, if the applicant is not represented by an attorney; and

(11) contain the address of the clerk of the court.

(b) The notice of an application for a protective order must state: "An application for a protective order has been filed in the court stated in this notice alleging that you have committed family violence. You may employ an attorney to defend you against this allegation. You or your attorney may, but are not required to, file a written answer to the application. Any answer must be filed before the hearing on the application. If you receive this notice within 48 hours before the time set for the hearing, you may request the court to reschedule the hearing not later than 14 days after the date set for the hearing. If you do not attend the hearing, a default judgment may be taken and a protective order may be issued against you."

(Enacted by Acts 1997, 75th Leg., ch. 34 (S.B. 797), § 1, effective May 5, 1997; am. Acts 1997, 75th Leg., ch. 1193 (S.B. 1253), § 10, effective September 1, 1997.)

### Sec. 82.042.  Issuance of Notice of Application.

(a) On the filing of an application, the clerk of the court shall issue a notice of an application for a protective order and deliver the notice as directed by the applicant.

(b) On request by the applicant, the clerk of the court shall issue a separate or additional notice of an application for a protective order.

(Enacted by Acts 1997, 75th Leg., ch. 34 (S.B. 797), § 1, effective May 5, 1997.)

### Sec. 82.043.  Service of Notice of Application.

(a) Each respondent to an application for a protective order is entitled to service of notice of an application for a protective order.

(b) An applicant for a protective order shall furnish the clerk with a sufficient number of copies of the application for service on each respondent.

(c) Notice of an application for a protective order must be served in the same manner as citation under the Texas Rules of Civil Procedure, except that service by publication is not authorized.

(d) Service of notice of an application for a protective order is not required before the issuance of a temporary ex parte order under Chapter 83.

(e) The requirements of service of notice under this subchapter do not apply if the application is filed as a motion in a suit for dissolution of a marriage. Notice for the motion is given in the same manner as any other motion in a suit for dissolution of a marriage.

(Enacted by Acts 1997, 75th Leg., ch. 34 (S.B. 797), § 1, effective May 5, 1997.)

# CHAPTER 83
# TEMPORARY EX PARTE ORDERS

**Section**

## Sec. 83.001. Requirements for Temporary Ex Parte Order.

(a) If the court finds from the information contained in an application for a protective order that there is a clear and present danger of family violence, the court, without further notice to the individual alleged to have committed family violence and without a hearing, may enter a temporary ex parte order for the protection of the applicant or any other member of the family or household of the applicant.

(b) In a temporary ex parte order, the court may direct a respondent to do or refrain from doing specified acts.

(Enacted by Acts 1997, 75th Leg., ch. 34 (S.B. 797), § 1, effective May 5, 1997; am. Acts 2001, 77th Leg., ch. 91 (S.B. 68), § 4, effective September 1, 2001.)

## Sec. 83.002. Duration of Order; Extension.

(a) A temporary ex parte order is valid for the period specified in the order, not to exceed 20 days.

(b) On the request of an applicant or on the court's own motion, a temporary ex parte order may be extended for additional 20-day periods.

(Enacted by Acts 1997, 75th Leg., ch. 34 (S.B. 797), § 1, effective May 5, 1997.)

## Sec. 83.003. Bond Not Required.

The court, at the court's discretion, may dispense with the necessity of a bond for a temporary ex parte order.

(Enacted by Acts 1997, 75th Leg., ch. 34 (S.B. 797), § 1, effective May 5, 1997.)

## Sec. 83.004. Motion to Vacate.

Any individual affected by a temporary ex parte order may file a motion at any time to vacate the order. On the filing of the motion to vacate, the court shall set a date for hearing the motion as soon as possible.

(Enacted by Acts 1997, 75th Leg., ch. 34 (S.B. 797), § 1, effective May 5, 1997; am. Acts 2001, 77th Leg., ch. 91 (S.B. 68), § 5, effective September 1, 2001.)

## Sec. 83.005. Conflicting Orders.

During the time the order is valid, a temporary ex parte order prevails over any other court order made under Title 5 to the extent of any conflict between the orders.

(Enacted by Acts 1997, 75th Leg., ch. 34 (S.B. 797), § 1, effective May 5, 1997; am. Acts 1997, 75th Leg., ch. 1193 (S.B. 1253), § 11, effective September 1, 1997.)

## Sec. 83.006. Exclusion of Party from Residence.

(a) Subject to the limitations of Section 85.021(2), a person may only be excluded from the occupancy of the person's residence by a temporary ex parte order under this chapter if the applicant:

(1) files a sworn affidavit that provides a detailed description of the facts and circumstances requiring the exclusion of the person from the residence; and

(2) appears in person to testify at a temporary ex parte hearing to justify the issuance of the order without notice.

(b) Before the court may render a temporary ex parte order excluding a person from the person's residence, the court must find from the required affidavit and testimony that:

(1) the applicant requesting the excluding order either resides on the premises or has resided there within 30 days before the date the application was filed;

(2) the person to be excluded has within the 30 days before the date the application was filed committed family violence against a member of the household; and

(3) there is a clear and present danger that the person to be excluded is likely to commit family violence against a member of the household.

(c) The court may recess the hearing on a temporary ex parte order to contact the respondent by telephone and provide the respondent the opportunity to be present when the court resumes the hearing. Without regard to whether the respondent is able to be present at the hearing, the court shall resume the hearing before the end of the working day.

(Enacted by Acts 1997, 75th Leg., ch. 34 (S.B. 797), § 1, effective May 5, 1997; am. Acts 2011, 82nd Leg., ch. 632 (S.B. 819), § 4, effective September 1, 2011.)

### Sec. 83.007. Recess of Hearing to Contact Respondent [Repealed].

Repealed by Acts 2011, 82nd Leg., ch. 632 (S.B. 819), § 6(1), effective September 1, 2011.

(Enacted by Acts 1997, 75th Leg., ch. 34 (S.B. 797), § 1, effective May 5, 1997.)

## CHAPTER 84
## HEARING

### Sec. 84.001. Time Set for Hearing.

(a) On the filing of an application for a protective order, the court shall set a date and time for the hearing unless a later date is requested by the applicant. Except as provided by Section 84.002, the court may not set a date later than the 14th day after the date the application is filed.

(b) The court may not delay a hearing on an application in order to consolidate it with a hearing on a subsequently filed application.

(Enacted by Acts 1997, 75th Leg., ch. 34 (S.B. 797), § 1, effective May 5, 1997.)

### Sec. 84.002. Extended Time for Hearing in District Court in Certain Counties.

(a) On the request of the prosecuting attorney in a county with a population of more than two million or in a county in a judicial district that is composed of more than one county, the district court shall set the hearing on a date and time not later than 20 days after the date the application

is filed or 20 days after the date a request is made to reschedule a hearing under Section 84.003.

(b) The district court shall grant the request of the prosecuting attorney for an extended time in which to hold a hearing on a protective order either on a case-by-case basis or for all cases filed under this subtitle.

(Enacted by Acts 1997, 75th Leg., ch. 34 (S.B. 797), § 1, effective May 5, 1997; am. Acts 1997, 75th Leg., ch. 1193 (S.B. 1253), § 12, effective September 1, 1997; am. Acts 2011, 82nd Leg., ch. 1163 (H.B. 2702), § 17, effective September 1, 2011.)

### Sec. 84.003. Hearing Rescheduled for Failure of Service.

(a) If a hearing set under this chapter is not held because of the failure of a respondent to receive service of notice of an application for a protective order, the applicant may request the court to reschedule the hearing.

(b) Except as provided by Section 84.002, the date for a rescheduled hearing shall be not later than 14 days after the date the request is made.

(Enacted by Acts 1997, 75th Leg., ch. 34 (S.B. 797), § 1, effective May 5, 1997.)

### Sec. 84.004. Hearing Rescheduled for Insufficient Notice.

(a) If a respondent receives service of notice of an application for a protective order within 48 hours before the time set for the hearing, on request by the respondent, the court shall reschedule the hearing for a date not later than 14 days after the date set for the hearing.

(b) The respondent is not entitled to additional service for a hearing rescheduled under this section.

(Enacted by Acts 1997, 75th Leg., ch. 34 (S.B. 797), § 1, effective May 5, 1997.)

### Sec. 84.005. Legislative Continuance.

If a proceeding for which a legislative continuance is sought under Section 30.003, Civil Practice and Remedies Code, includes an application for a protective order, the continuance is discretionary with the court.

(Enacted by Acts 1999, 76th Leg., ch. 62 (S.B. 1368), § 6.10(a), effective September 1, 1999.)

### Sec. 84.006. Hearsay Statement of Child Victim of Family Violence.

In a hearing on an application for a protective order, a statement made by a child 12 years of age or younger that describes alleged family violence against the child is admissible as evidence in the same manner that a child's statement regarding alleged abuse against the child is admissible under Section 104.006 in a suit affecting the parent-child relationship.

(Enacted by Acts 2011, 82nd Leg., ch. 59 (H.B. 905), § 1, effective September 1, 2011.)

# CHAPTER 85
# ISSUANCE OF PROTECTIVE ORDER

### Subchapter A. Findings and Orders

## SUBCHAPTER A
## FINDINGS AND ORDERS

## Sec. 85.001. Required Findings and Orders.

(a) At the close of a hearing on an application for a protective order, the court shall find whether:

(1) family violence has occurred; and

(2) family violence is likely to occur in the future.

(b) If the court finds that family violence has occurred and that family violence is likely to occur in the future, the court:

(1) shall render a protective order as provided by Section 85.022 applying only to a person found to have committed family violence; and

(2) may render a protective order as provided by Section 85.021 applying to both parties that is in the best interest of the person protected by the order or member of the family or household of the person protected by the order.

(c) A protective order that requires the first applicant to do or refrain from doing an act under Section 85.022 shall include a finding that the first applicant has committed family violence and is likely to commit family violence in the future.

(d) If the court renders a protective order for a period of more than two years, the court must include in the order a finding described by Section 85.025(a-1).

(Enacted by Acts 1997, 75th Leg., ch. 34 (S.B. 797), § 1, effective May 5, 1997; am. Acts 2001, 77th Leg., ch. 91 (S.B. 68), § 6, effective September 1, 2001; am. Acts 2011, 82nd Leg., ch. 627 (S.B. 789), § 1, effective September 1, 2011.)

## Sec. 85.002. Exception for Violation of Expired Protective Order.

If the court finds that a respondent violated a protective order by committing an act prohibited by the order as provided by Section 85.022, that the order was in effect at the time of the violation, and that the order has expired after the date that the violation occurred, the court, without the necessity of making the findings described by Section 85.001(a), shall render a protective order as provided by Section 85.022 applying only to the respondent and may render a protective order as provided by Section 85.021.

(Enacted by Acts 1997, 75th Leg., ch. 34 (S.B. 797), § 1, effective May 5, 1997; am. Acts 1997, 75th Leg., ch. 1193 (S.B. 1253), § 13, effective September 1, 1997.)

## Sec. 85.003. Separate Protective Orders Required.

(a) A court that renders separate protective orders that apply to both parties and require both parties to do or refrain from doing acts under

Section 85.022 shall render two distinct and separate protective orders in two separate documents that reflect the appropriate conditions for each party.

(b) A court that renders protective orders that apply to both parties and require both parties to do or refrain from doing acts under Section 85.022 shall render the protective orders in two separate documents. The court shall provide one of the documents to the applicant and the other document to the respondent.

(c) A court may not render one protective order under Section 85.022 that applies to both parties. (Enacted by Acts 1997, 75th Leg., ch. 34 (S.B. 797), § 1, effective May 5, 1997.)

### Sec. 85.004. Protective Order in Suit for Dissolution of Marriage.

A protective order in a suit for dissolution of a marriage must be in a separate document entitled "PROTECTIVE ORDER." (Enacted by Acts 1997, 75th Leg., ch. 34 (S.B. 797), § 1, effective May 5, 1997.)

### Sec. 85.005. Agreed Order.

(a) To facilitate settlement, the parties to a proceeding may agree in writing to the terms of a protective order as provided by Section 85.021. An agreement under this subsection is subject to the approval of the court.

(b) To facilitate settlement, a respondent may agree in writing to the terms of a protective order as provided by Section 85.022, subject to the approval of the court. The court may not approve an agreement that requires the applicant to do or refrain from doing an act under Section 85.022. The agreed order is enforceable civilly or criminally.

(c) If the court approves an agreement between the parties, the court shall render an agreed protective order that is in the best interest of the applicant, the family or household, or a member of the family or household.

(d) An agreed protective order is not enforceable as a contract.

(e) An agreed protective order expires on the date the court order expires. (Enacted by Acts 1997, 75th Leg., ch. 34 (S.B. 797), § 1, effective May 5, 1997; am. Acts 2005, 79th Leg., ch. 541 (H.B. 1059), § 1, effective June 17, 2005.)

### Sec. 85.006. Default Order.

(a) A court may render a protective order that is binding on a respondent who does not attend a hearing if the respondent received service of the application and notice of the hearing.

(b) If the court reschedules the hearing under Chapter 84, a protective order may be rendered if the respondent does not attend the rescheduled hearing. (Enacted by Acts 1997, 75th Leg., ch. 34 (S.B. 797), § 1, effective May 5, 1997.)

### Sec. 85.007. Confidentiality of Certain Information.

(a) On request by a person protected by an order or member of the family or household of a person protected by an order, the court may exclude from a protective order the address and telephone number of:

(1) a person protected by the order, in which case the order shall state the county in which the person resides;

(2) the place of employment or business of a person protected by the order; or

(3) the child-care facility or school a child protected by the order attends or in which the child resides.

(b) On granting a request for confidentiality under this section, the court shall order the clerk to:

(1) strike the information described by Subsection (a) from the public records of the court; and

(2) maintain a confidential record of the information for use only by the court. (Enacted by Acts 1997, 75th Leg., ch. 34 (S.B. 797), § 1, effective May 5, 1997; am. Acts 2001, 77th Leg., ch. 91 (S.B. 68), § 7, effective September 1, 2001.)

### Sec. 85.008. Dismissal of Application Prohibited If Divorce Filed; Exception [Repealed].

Repealed by Acts 1997, 75th Leg., ch. 1193 (S.B. 1253), § 24, effective September 1, 1997. (Enacted by Acts 1997, 75th Leg., ch. 34 (S.B. 797), § 1, effective May 5, 1997.)

### Sec. 85.009. Order Valid Until Superseded.

A protective order rendered under this chapter is valid and enforceable pending further action by the court that rendered the order until the order is properly superseded by another court with jurisdiction over the order. (Enacted by Acts 1997, 75th Leg., ch. 34 (S.B. 797), § 1, effective May 5, 1997.)

Family Code

## SUBCHAPTER B
## CONTENTS OF PROTECTIVE ORDER

### Sec. 85.021. Requirements of Order Applying to Any Party.

In a protective order, the court may:

(1) prohibit a party from:

(A) removing a child who is a member of the family or household from:

(i) the possession of a person named in the order; or

(ii) the jurisdiction of the court;

(B) transferring, encumbering, or otherwise disposing of property, other than in the ordinary course of business, that is mutually owned or leased by the parties; or

(C) removing a pet, companion animal, or assistance animal, as defined by Section 121.002, Human Resources Code, from the possession of a person named in the order;

(2) grant exclusive possession of a residence to a party and, if appropriate, direct one or more parties to vacate the residence if the residence:

(A) is jointly owned or leased by the party receiving exclusive possession and a party being denied possession;

(B) is owned or leased by the party retaining possession; or

(C) is owned or leased by the party being denied possession and that party has an obligation to support the party or a child of the party granted possession of the residence;

(3) provide for the possession of and access to a child of a party if the person receiving possession of or access to the child is a parent of the child;

(4) require the payment of support for a party or for a child of a party if the person required to make the payment has an obligation to support the other party or the child; or

(5) award to a party the use and possession of specified property that is community property or jointly owned or leased property.

(Enacted by Acts 1997, 75th Leg., ch. 34 (S.B. 797), § 1, effective May 5, 1997; am. Acts 2011, 82nd Leg., ch. 136 (S.B. 279), § 1, effective September 1, 2011.)

### Sec. 85.022. Requirements of Order Applying to Person Who Committed Family Violence.

(a) In a protective order, the court may order the person found to have committed family violence to perform acts specified by the court that the court determines are necessary or appropriate to prevent or reduce the likelihood of family violence and may order that person to:

(1) complete a battering intervention and prevention program accredited under Article 42.141, Code of Criminal Procedure;

(2) beginning on September 1, 2008, if the referral option under Subdivision (1) is not available, complete a program or counsel with a provider that has begun the accreditation process described by Subsection (a-1); or

(3) if the referral option under Subdivision (1) or, beginning on September 1, 2008, the referral option under Subdivision (2) is not available, counsel with a social worker, family service agency, physician, psychologist, licensed therapist, or licensed professional counselor who has completed family violence intervention training that the community justice assistance division of the Texas Department of Criminal Justice has approved, after consultation with the licensing authorities described by Chapters 152, 501, 502, 503, and 505, Occupations Code, and experts in the field of family violence.

(a-1) Beginning on September 1, 2009, a program or provider serving as a referral option for the courts under Subsection (a)(1) or (2) must be accredited under Section 4A, Article 42.141, Code of Criminal Procedure, as conforming to program guidelines under that article.

(b) In a protective order, the court may prohibit the person found to have committed family violence from:

(1) committing family violence;

(2) communicating:

(A) directly with a person protected by an order or a member of the family or household of a person protected by an order, in a threatening or harassing manner;

(B) a threat through any person to a person protected by an order or a member of the family or household of a person protected by an order; and

(C) if the court finds good cause, in any manner with a person protected by an order or a member of the family or household of a person protected by an order, except through the party's attorney or a person appointed by the court;

(3) going to or near the residence or place of employment or business of a person protected by an order or a member of the family or household of a person protected by an order;

(4) going to or near the residence, child-care facility, or school a child protected under the order normally attends or in which the child normally resides;

(5) engaging in conduct directed specifically toward a person who is a person protected by an order or a member of the family or household of a person protected by an order, including following the person, that is reasonably likely to harass, annoy, alarm, abuse, torment, or embarrass the person;

(6) possessing a firearm, unless the person is a peace officer, as defined by Section 1.07, Penal Code, actively engaged in employment as a sworn, full-time paid employee of a state agency or political subdivision; and

(7) harming, threatening, or interfering with the care, custody, or control of a pet, companion animal, or assistance animal, as defined by Section 121.002, Human Resources Code, that is possessed by a person protected by an order or by a member of the family or household of a person protected by an order.

(c) In an order under Subsection (b)(3) or (4), the court shall specifically describe each prohibited location and the minimum distances from the location, if any, that the party must maintain. This subsection does not apply to an order in which Section 85.007 applies.

(d) In a protective order, the court shall suspend a license to carry a concealed handgun issued under Subchapter H, Chapter 411, Government Code, that is held by a person found to have committed family violence.

(e) In this section, "firearm" has the meaning assigned by Section 46.01, Penal Code.

(Enacted by Acts 1997, 75th Leg., ch. 34 (S.B. 797), § 1, effective May 5, 1997; am. Acts 1997, 75th Leg., ch. 1193 (S.B. 1253), § 14, effective September 1, 1997; am. Acts 1999, 76th Leg., ch. 1412 (H.B. 2124), § 3, effective September 1, 1999; am. Acts 2001, 77th Leg., ch. 23 (S.B. 199), § 3, effective September 1, 2001; am. Acts 2001, 77th Leg., ch. 91 (S.B. 68), § 8, effective September 1, 2001; am. Acts 2007, 80th Leg., ch. 113 (S.B. 44), § 4, effective September 1, 2007; am. Acts 2009, 81st Leg., ch. 1146 (H.B. 2730), § 11.21, effective September 1, 2009; am. Acts 2011, 82nd Leg., ch. 136 (S.B. 279), § 2, effective September 1, 2011.)

## Sec. 85.023.  Effect on Property Rights.

A protective order or an agreement approved by the court under this subtitle does not affect the title to real property.

(Enacted by Acts 1997, 75th Leg., ch. 34 (S.B. 797), § 1, effective May 5, 1997.)

## Sec. 85.024.  Enforcement of Counseling Requirement.

(a) A person found to have engaged in family violence who is ordered to attend a program or counseling under Section 85.022(a)(1), (2), or (3) shall file with the court an affidavit before the 60th day after the date the order was rendered stating either that the person has begun the program or counseling or that a program or counseling is not available within a reasonable distance from the person's residence. A person who files an affidavit that the person has begun the program or counseling shall file with the court before the date the protective order expires a statement that the person completed the program or counseling not later than the 30th day before the expiration date of the protective order or the 30th day before the first anniversary of the date the protective order was issued, whichever date is earlier. An affidavit under this subsection must be accompanied by a letter, notice, or certificate from the program or counselor that verifies the person's completion of the program or counseling. A person who fails to comply with this subsection may be punished for contempt of court under Section 21.002, Government Code.

(b) A protective order under Section 85.022 must specifically advise the person subject to the order of the requirement of this section and the possible punishment if the person fails to comply with the requirement.

(Enacted by Acts 1997, 75th Leg., ch. 34 (S.B. 797), § 1, effective May 5, 1997; am. Acts 1997, 75th Leg., ch. 1193 (S.B. 1253), § 15, effective September 1, 1997; am. Acts 2007, 80th Leg., ch. 113 (S.B. 44), § 5, effective September 1, 2007; am. Acts 2007, 80th Leg., ch. 770 (H.B. 3593), § 1, effective September 1, 2007.)

## Sec. 85.025.  Duration of Protective Order.

(a) Except as otherwise provided by this section, an order under this subtitle is effective:

(1) for the period stated in the order, not to exceed two years; or

(2) if a period is not stated in the order, until the second anniversary of the date the order was issued.

(a-1) The court may render a protective order sufficient to protect the applicant and members of the applicant's family or household that is effective for a period that exceeds two years if the court finds that the person who is the subject of the protective order:

(1) caused serious bodily injury to the applicant or a member of the applicant's family or household; or

(2) was the subject of two or more previous protective orders rendered:

(A) to protect the person on whose behalf the current protective order is sought; and

(B) after a finding by the court that the subject of the protective order:

(i) has committed family violence; and

(ii) is likely to commit family violence in the future.

(b) A person who is the subject of a protective order may file a motion not earlier than the first anniversary of the date on which the order was rendered requesting that the court review the protective order and determine whether there is a continuing need for the order. A person who is the subject of a protective order under Subsection (a-1) that is effective for a period that exceeds two years may file a subsequent motion requesting that the court review the protective order and determine whether there is a continuing need for the order not earlier than the first anniversary of the date on which the court rendered an order on a previous motion by the person under this subsection. After a hearing on the motion, if the court does not make a finding that there is no continuing need for the protective order, the protective order remains in effect until the date the order expires under this section. Evidence of the movant's compliance with the protective order does not by itself support a finding by the court that there is no continuing need for the protective order. If the court finds there is no continuing need for the protective order, the court shall order that the protective order expires on a date set by the court.

(c) If a person who is the subject of a protective order is confined or imprisoned on the date the protective order would expire under Subsection (a) or (a-1), the period for which the order is effective is extended, and the order expires on the first anniversary of the date the person is released from confinement or imprisonment.

(Enacted by Acts 1997, 75th Leg., ch. 34 (S.B. 797), § 1, effective May 5, 1997; am. Acts 1999, 76th Leg., ch. 1160 (S.B. 50), § 3, effective September 1, 1999; am. Acts 2011, 82nd Leg., ch. 627 (S.B. 789), § 2, effective September 1, 2011.)

## Sec. 85.026.  Warning on Protective Order.

(a) Each protective order issued under this subtitle, including a temporary ex parte order, must contain the following prominently displayed statements in boldfaced type, capital letters, or underlined:

"A PERSON WHO VIOLATES THIS ORDER MAY BE PUNISHED FOR CONTEMPT OF COURT BY A FINE OF AS MUCH AS $500 OR BY CONFINEMENT IN JAIL FOR AS LONG AS SIX MONTHS, OR BOTH."

"NO PERSON, INCLUDING A PERSON WHO IS PROTECTED BY THIS ORDER, MAY GIVE PERMISSION TO ANYONE TO IGNORE OR VIOLATE ANY PROVISION OF THIS ORDER. DURING THE TIME IN WHICH THIS ORDER IS VALID, EVERY PROVISION OF THIS ORDER IS IN FULL FORCE AND EFFECT UNLESS A COURT CHANGES THE ORDER."

"IT IS UNLAWFUL FOR ANY PERSON, OTHER THAN A PEACE OFFICER, AS DEFINED BY SECTION 1.07, PENAL CODE, ACTIVELY ENGAGED IN EMPLOYMENT AS A SWORN, FULL-TIME PAID EMPLOYEE OF A STATE AGENCY OR POLITICAL SUBDIVISION, WHO IS SUBJECT TO A PROTECTIVE ORDER TO POSSESS A FIREARM OR AMMUNITION."

"A VIOLATION OF THIS ORDER BY COMMISSION OF AN ACT PROHIBITED BY THE ORDER MAY BE PUNISHABLE BY A FINE OF AS MUCH AS $4,000 OR BY CONFINEMENT IN JAIL FOR AS LONG AS ONE YEAR, OR BOTH. AN ACT THAT RESULTS IN FAMILY VIOLENCE MAY BE PROSECUTED AS A SEPARATE MISDEMEANOR OR FELONY OFFENSE. IF THE ACT IS PROSECUTED AS A SEPARATE FELONY OFFENSE, IT IS PUNISHABLE BY CONFINEMENT IN PRISON FOR AT LEAST TWO YEARS."

(b) [Repealed by Acts 2011, 82nd Leg., ch. 632 (S.B. 819), § 6, effective September 1, 2011.]

(c) Each protective order issued under this subtitle, including a temporary ex parte order, must contain the following prominently displayed statement in boldfaced type, capital letters, or underlined:

"NO PERSON, INCLUDING A PERSON WHO IS PROTECTED BY THIS ORDER, MAY GIVE PERMISSION TO ANYONE TO IGNORE OR VIOLATE ANY PROVISION OF THIS ORDER. DURING THE TIME IN WHICH THIS ORDER

Family Code

IS VALID, EVERY PROVISION OF THIS ORDER IS IN FULL FORCE AND EFFECT UNLESS A COURT CHANGES THE ORDER."
(Enacted by Acts 1997, 75th Leg., ch. 34 (S.B. 797), § 1, effective May 5, 1997; am. Acts 1999, 76th Leg., ch. 178 (H.B. 1209), § 3, effective August 30, 1999; am. Acts 1999, 76th Leg., ch. 1160 (S.B. 50), § 4, effective September 1, 1999; am. Acts 2001, 77th Leg., ch. 23 (S.B. 199), § 5, effective September 1, 2001; am. Acts 2011, 82nd Leg., ch. 632 (S.B. 819), §§ 5, 6(2), effective September 1, 2011.)

## SUBCHAPTER C
## DELIVERY OF PROTECTIVE ORDER

### Sec. 85.041.  Delivery to Respondent.

(a) A protective order rendered under this subtitle shall be:

(1) delivered to the respondent as provided by Rule 21a, Texas Rules of Civil Procedure;

(2) served in the same manner as a writ of injunction; or

(3) served in open court at the close of the hearing as provided by this section.

(b) The court shall serve an order in open court to a respondent who is present at the hearing by giving to the respondent a copy of the order, reduced to writing and signed by the judge or master. A certified copy of the signed order shall be given to the applicant at the time the order is given to the respondent. If the applicant is not in court at the conclusion of the hearing, the clerk of the court shall mail a certified copy of the order to the applicant not later than the third business day after the date the hearing is concluded.

(c) If the order has not been reduced to writing, the court shall give notice orally to a respondent who is present at the hearing of the part of the order that contains prohibitions under Section 85.022 or any other part of the order that contains provisions necessary to prevent further family violence. The clerk of the court shall mail a copy of the order to the respondent and a certified copy of the order to the applicant not later than the third business day after the date the hearing is concluded.

(d) If the respondent is not present at the hearing and the order has been reduced to writing at the conclusion of the hearing, the clerk of the court shall immediately provide a certified copy of the order to the applicant and mail a copy of the order to the respondent not later than the third business day after the date the hearing is concluded.
(Enacted by Acts 1997, 75th Leg., ch. 34 (S.B. 797), § 1, effective May 5, 1997.)

### Sec. 85.042.  Delivery of Order to Other Persons.

(a) The clerk of the court issuing an original or modified protective order under this subtitle shall send a copy of the order, along with the information provided by the applicant or the applicant's attorney that is required under Section 411.042(b)(6), Government Code, to the chief of police of the municipality in which the person protected by the order resides, if the person resides in a municipality, or to the appropriate constable and the sheriff of the county in which the person resides, if the person does not reside in a municipality.

(a-1) This subsection applies only if the respondent, at the time of issuance of an original or modified protective order under this subtitle, is a member of the state military forces or is serving in the armed forces of the United States in an active-duty status. In addition to complying with Subsection (a), the clerk of the court shall also provide a copy of the protective order and the information described by that subsection to the staff judge advocate at Joint Force Headquarters or the provost marshal of the military installation to which the respondent is assigned with the intent that the commanding officer will be notified, as applicable.

(b) If a protective order made under this chapter prohibits a respondent from going to or near a child-care facility or school, the clerk of the court shall send a copy of the order to the child-care facility or school.

(c) The clerk of a court that vacates an original or modified protective order under this subtitle shall notify each individual or entity who received a copy of the original or modified order from the clerk under this section that the order is vacated.

(d) The applicant or the applicant's attorney shall provide to the clerk of the court:

(1) the name and address of each law enforcement agency, child-care facility, school, and other individual or entity to which the clerk is required to mail a copy of the order under this section; and

(2) any other information required under Section 411.042(b)(6), Government Code.

(e) The clerk of the court issuing an original or modified protective order under Section 85.022 that suspends a license to carry a concealed handgun shall send a copy of the order to the appropriate division of the Department of Public Safety at its Austin headquarters. On receipt of the order suspending the license, the department shall:

(1) record the suspension of the license in the records of the department;

(2) report the suspension to local law enforcement agencies, as appropriate; and

(3) demand surrender of the suspended license from the license holder.

(Enacted by Acts 1997, 75th Leg., ch. 34 (S.B. 797), § 1, effective May 5, 1997; am. Acts 1997, 75th Leg., ch. 614 (S.B. 712), § 3, effective September 1, 1997; am. Acts 1999, 76th Leg., ch. 1412 (H.B. 2124), § 4, effective September 1, 1999; am. Acts 2001, 77th Leg., ch. 35 (S.B. 479), § 1, effective September 1, 2001; am. Acts 2001, 77th Leg., ch. 91 (S.B. 68), § 9, effective September 1, 2001; am. Acts 2011, 82nd Leg., ch. 327 (H.B. 2624), § 1, effective September 1, 2011.)

## SUBCHAPTER D
## RELATIONSHIP BETWEEN PROTECTIVE ORDER AND SUIT FOR DISSOLUTION OF MARRIAGE AND SUIT AFFECTING PARENT-CHILD RELATIONSHIP

### Sec. 85.061. Dismissal of Application Prohibited; Subsequently Filed Suit for Dissolution of Marriage or Suit Affecting Parent-Child Relationship.

If an application for a protective order is pending, a court may not dismiss the application or delay a hearing on the application on the grounds that a suit for dissolution of marriage or suit affecting the parent-child relationship is filed after the date the application was filed. (Enacted by Acts 1997, 75th Leg., ch. 1193 (S.B. 1253), § 16, effective September 1, 1997.)

### Sec. 85.062. Application Filed While Suit for Dissolution of Marriage or Suit Affecting Parent-Child Relationship Pending.

(a) If a suit for dissolution of a marriage or suit affecting the parent-child relationship is pending, a party to the suit may apply for a protective order against another party to the suit by filing an application:

(1) in the court in which the suit is pending; or

(2) in a court in the county in which the applicant resides if the applicant resides outside the jurisdiction of the court in which the suit is pending.

(b) An applicant subject to this section shall inform the clerk of the court that renders a protective order that a suit for dissolution of a marriage or a suit affecting the parent-child relationship is pending in which the applicant is party.

(c) If a final protective order is rendered by a court other than the court in which a suit for dissolution of a marriage or a suit affecting the parent-child relationship is pending, the clerk of the court that rendered the protective order shall:

(1) inform the clerk of the court in which the suit is pending that a final protective order has been rendered; and

(2) forward a copy of the final protective order to the court in which the suit is pending.

(d) A protective order rendered by a court in which an application is filed under Subsection (a)(2) is subject to transfer under Section 85.064. (Enacted by Acts 1997, 75th Leg., ch. 1193 (S.B. 1253), § 16, effective September 1, 1997.)

### Sec. 85.063. Application Filed After Final Order Rendered in Suit for Dissolution of Marriage or Suit Affecting Parent-Child Relationship.

(a) If a final order has been rendered in a suit for dissolution of marriage or suit affecting the parent-child relationship, an application for a protective order by a party to the suit against another party to the suit filed after the date the final order was rendered, and that is:

(1) filed in the county in which the final order was rendered, shall be filed in the court that rendered the final order; and

(2) filed in another county, shall be filed in a court having jurisdiction to render a protective order under this subtitle.

(b) A protective order rendered by a court in which an application is filed under Subsection (a)(2) is subject to transfer under Section 85.064. (Enacted by Acts 1997, 75th Leg., ch. 1193 (S.B. 1253), § 16, effective September 1, 1997.)

### Sec. 85.064. Transfer of Protective Order.

(a) If a protective order was rendered before the filing of a suit for dissolution of marriage or suit affecting the parent-child relationship or while the suit is pending as provided by Section 85.062, the court that rendered the order may, on the motion of a party or on the court's own motion, transfer the protective order to the court having jurisdiction of the suit if the court makes the finding prescribed by Subsection (c).

(b) If a protective order that affects a party's right to possession of or access to a child is rendered after the date a final order was rendered in a suit affecting the parent-child relationship, on the motion of a party or on the court's own motion, the court may transfer the protective order to the court of continuing, exclusive jurisdiction if the court makes the finding prescribed by Subsection (c).

(c) A court may transfer a protective order under this section if the court finds that the transfer is:

(1) in the interest of justice; or

(2) for the safety or convenience of a party or a witness.

(d) The transfer of a protective order under this section shall be conducted according to the procedures provided by Section 155.207.

(e) Except as provided by Section 81.002, the fees or costs associated with the transfer of a protective order shall be paid by the movant.
(Enacted by Acts 1997, 75th Leg., ch. 1193 (S.B. 1253), § 16, effective September 1, 1997.)

### Sec. 85.065.  Effect of Transfer.

(a) [Repealed by Acts 2011, 82nd Leg., ch. 632 (S.B. 819), § 6(3), effective September 1, 2011.]

(b) [Repealed by Acts 2011, 82nd Leg., ch. 632 (S.B. 819), § 6(3), effective September 1, 2011.]

(c) A protective order that is transferred is subject to modification by the court that receives the order to the same extent modification is permitted under Chapter 87 by a court that rendered the order.
(Enacted by Acts 1997, 75th Leg., ch. 1193 (S.B. 1253), § 16, effective September 1, 1997; am. Acts 2011, 82nd Leg., ch. 632 (S.B. 819), § 6(3), effective September 1, 2011.)

# CHAPTER 86
# LAW ENFORCEMENT DUTIES RELATING TO PROTECTIVE ORDERS

### Sec. 86.001.  Adoption of Procedures by Law Enforcement Agency.

(a) To ensure that law enforcement officers responding to calls are aware of the existence and terms of protective orders issued under this subtitle, each law enforcement agency shall establish procedures in the agency to provide adequate information or access to information for law enforcement officers of the names of each person protected by an order issued under this subtitle and of each person against whom protective orders are directed.

(b) A law enforcement agency may enter a protective order in the agency's computer records of outstanding warrants as notice that the order has been issued and is currently in effect. On receipt of notification by a clerk of court that the court has vacated or dismissed an order, the law enforcement agency shall remove the order from the agency's computer record of outstanding warrants.
(Enacted by Acts 1997, 75th Leg., ch. 34 (S.B. 797), § 1, effective May 5, 1997.)

### Sec. 86.0011.  Duty to Enter Information into Statewide Law Enforcement Information System.

On receipt of an original or modified protective order from the clerk of the issuing court, a law enforcement agency shall immediately, but not later than the 10th day after the date the order is received, enter the information required by Section 411.042(b)(6), Government Code, into the statewide law enforcement information system maintained by the Department of Public Safety. (Enacted by Acts 2001, 77th Leg., ch. 35 (S.B. 479), § 2, effective September 1, 2001.)

### Sec. 86.002. Duty to Provide Information to Firearms Dealers.

(a) On receipt of a request for a law enforcement information system record check of a prospective transferee by a licensed firearms dealer under the Brady Handgun Violence Prevention Act, 18 U.S.C. Section 922, the chief law enforcement officer shall determine whether the Department of Public Safety has in the department's law enforcement information system a record indicating the existence of an active protective order directed to the prospective transferee.

(b) If the department's law enforcement information system indicates the existence of an active protective order directed to the prospective transferee, the chief law enforcement officer shall immediately advise the dealer that the transfer is prohibited.

(Enacted by Acts 1997, 75th Leg., ch. 34 (S.B. 797), § 1, effective May 5, 1997.)

### Sec. 86.003. Court Order for Law Enforcement Assistance Under Temporary Order.

On request by an applicant obtaining a temporary ex parte protective order that excludes the respondent from the respondent's residence, the court granting the temporary order shall render a written order to the sheriff, constable, or chief of police to provide a law enforcement officer from the department of the chief of police, constable, or sheriff to:

(1) accompany the applicant to the residence covered by the order;

(2) inform the respondent that the court has ordered that the respondent be excluded from the residence;

(3) protect the applicant while the applicant takes possession of the residence; and

(4) protect the applicant if the respondent refuses to vacate the residence while the applicant takes possession of the applicant's necessary personal property.

(Enacted by Acts 1997, 75th Leg., ch. 34 (S.B. 797), § 1, effective May 5, 1997; am. Acts 1997, 75th Leg., ch. 852 (H.B. 1192), § 1, effective June 18, 1997.)

### Sec. 86.004. Court Order for Law Enforcement Assistance Under Final Order.

On request by an applicant obtaining a final protective order that excludes the respondent from the respondent's residence, the court granting the final order shall render a written order to the sheriff, constable, or chief of police to provide a law enforcement officer from the department of the chief of police, constable, or sheriff to:

(1) accompany the applicant to the residence covered by the order;

(2) inform the respondent that the court has ordered that the respondent be excluded from the residence;

(3) protect the applicant while the applicant takes possession of the residence and the respondent takes possession of the respondent's necessary personal property; and

(4) if the respondent refuses to vacate the residence:

(A) remove the respondent from the residence; and

(B) arrest the respondent for violating the court order.

(Enacted by Acts 1997, 75th Leg., ch. 34 (S.B. 797), § 1, effective May 5, 1997; am. Acts 1997, 75th Leg., ch. 852 (H.B. 1192), § 2, effective June 18, 1997.)

### Sec. 86.005. Protective Order from Another Jurisdiction.

To ensure that law enforcement officers responding to calls are aware of the existence and terms of a protective order from another jurisdiction, each law enforcement agency shall establish procedures in the agency to provide adequate information or access to information for law enforcement officers regarding the name of each person protected by an order rendered in another jurisdiction and of each person against whom the protective order is directed.

(Enacted by Acts 1997, 75th Leg., ch. 1193 (S.B. 1253), § 17, effective September 1, 1997; am. Acts 2001, 77th Leg., ch. 48 (H.B. 919), § 1, effective September 1, 2001.)

# CHAPTER 87
## MODIFICATION OF PROTECTIVE ORDERS

### Sec. 87.001.  Modification of Protective Order.

On the motion of any party, the court, after notice and hearing, may modify an existing protective order to:

(1)  exclude any item included in the order; or

(2)  include any item that could have been included in the order.

(Enacted by Acts 1997, 75th Leg., ch. 34 (S.B. 797), § 1, effective May 5, 1997.)

### Sec. 87.002.  Modification May Not Extend Duration of Order.

A protective order may not be modified to extend the period of the order's validity beyond the second anniversary of the date the original order was rendered or beyond the date the order expires under Section 85.025(a-1) or (c), whichever date occurs later.

(Enacted by Acts 1997, 75th Leg., ch. 34 (S.B. 797), § 1, effective May 5, 1997; am. Acts 1999, 76th Leg., ch. 1160 (S.B. 50), § 5, effective September 1, 1999; am. Acts 2011, 82nd Leg., ch. 627 (S.B. 789), § 3, effective September 1, 2011.)

### Sec. 87.003.  Notification of Motion to Modify.

Notice of a motion to modify a protective order is sufficient if delivery of the motion is attempted on the respondent at the respondent's last known address by registered or certified mail as provided by Rule 21a, Texas Rules of Civil Procedure.

(Enacted by Acts 1997, 75th Leg., ch. 34 (S.B. 797), § 1, effective May 5, 1997.)

### Sec. 87.004.  Change of Address or Telephone Number.

(a)  If a protective order contains the address or telephone number of a person protected by the order, of the place of employment or business of the person, or of the child-care facility or school of a child protected by the order and that information is not confidential under Section 85.007, the person protected by the order may file a notification of change of address or telephone number with the court that rendered the order to modify the information contained in the order.

(b)  The clerk of the court shall attach the notification of change to the protective order and shall deliver a copy of the notification to the respondent by registered or certified mail as provided by Rule 21a, Texas Rules of Civil Procedure.

(c)  The filing of a notification of change of address or telephone number and the attachment of the notification to a protective order does not affect the validity of the order.

(Enacted by Acts 1997, 75th Leg., ch. 1193 (S.B. 1253), § 18, effective September 1, 1997.)

# CHAPTER 88
## UNIFORM INTERSTATE ENFORCEMENT OF DOMESTIC-VIOLENCE PROTECTION ORDERS ACT

### Sec. 88.001.  Short Title.

This chapter may be cited as the Uniform Interstate Enforcement of Domestic Violence Protection Orders Act.

(Enacted by Acts 1997, 75th Leg., ch. 1193 (S.B. 1253), § 19, effective September 1, 1997; am. Acts 2001, 77th Leg., ch. 48 (H.B. 919), § 2, effective September 1, 2001.)

### Sec. 88.002.  Definitions.

In this chapter:

(1)  "Foreign protective order" means a protective order issued by a tribunal of another state.

(2)  "Issuing state" means the state in which a tribunal issues a protective order.

(3)  "Mutual foreign protective order" means a foreign protective order that includes provisions issued in favor of both the protected individual seeking enforcement of the order and the respondent.

(4)  "Protected individual" means an individual protected by a protective order.

(5) "Protective order" means an injunction or other order, issued by a tribunal under the domestic violence or family violence laws or another law of the issuing state, to prevent an individual from engaging in violent or threatening acts against, harassing, contacting or communicating with, or being in physical proximity to another individual.

(6) "Respondent" means the individual against whom enforcement of a protective order is sought.

(7) "State" means a state of the United States, the District of Columbia, the Commonwealth of Puerto Rico, the United States Virgin Islands, or a territory or insular possession subject to the jurisdiction of the United States. The term includes a military tribunal of the United States, an Indian tribe or band, and an Alaskan native village that has jurisdiction to issue protective orders.

(8) "Tribunal" means a court, agency, or other entity authorized by law to issue or modify a protective order.

(Enacted by Acts 1997, 75th Leg., ch. 1193 (S.B. 1253), § 19, effective September 1, 1997; am. Acts 2001, 77th Leg., ch. 48 (H.B. 919), § 2, effective September 1, 2001.)

## Sec. 88.003. Judicial Enforcement of Order.

(a) A tribunal of this state shall enforce the terms of a foreign protective order, including a term that provides relief that a tribunal of this state would not have power to provide but for this section. The tribunal shall enforce the order regardless of whether the order was obtained by independent action or in another proceeding, if the order is an order issued in response to a complaint, petition, or motion filed by or on behalf of an individual seeking protection. In a proceeding to enforce a foreign protective order, the tribunal shall follow the procedures of this state for the enforcement of protective orders.

(b) A tribunal of this state shall enforce the provisions of the foreign protective order that govern the possession of and access to a child if the provisions were issued in accordance with the jurisdictional requirements governing the issuance of possession and access orders in the issuing state.

(c) A tribunal of this state may enforce a provision of the foreign protective order relating to child support if the order was issued in accordance with the jurisdictional requirements of Chapter 159 and the federal Full Faith and Credit for Child Support Orders Act, 28 U.S.C. Section 1738B, as amended.

(d) A foreign protective order is valid if the order:

(1) names the protected individual and the respondent;

(2) is currently in effect;

(3) was rendered by a tribunal that had jurisdiction over the parties and the subject matter under the law of the issuing state; and

(4) was rendered after the respondent was given reasonable notice and an opportunity to be heard consistent with the right to due process, either:

(A) before the tribunal issued the order; or

(B) in the case of an ex parte order, within a reasonable time after the order was rendered.

(e) A protected individual seeking enforcement of a foreign protective order establishes a prima facie case for its validity by presenting an order that is valid on its face.

(f) It is an affirmative defense in an action seeking enforcement of a foreign protective order that the order does not meet the requirements for a valid order under Subsection (d).

(g) A tribunal of this state may enforce the provisions of a mutual foreign protective order that favor a respondent only if:

(1) the respondent filed a written pleading seeking a protective order from the tribunal of the issuing state; and

(2) the tribunal of the issuing state made specific findings in favor of the respondent.

(Enacted by Acts 1997, 75th Leg., ch. 1193 (S.B. 1253), § 19, effective September 1, 1997; am. Acts 2001, 77th Leg., ch. 48 (H.B. 919), § 2, effective September 1, 2001.)

## Sec. 88.004. Nonjudicial Enforcement of Order.

(a) A law enforcement officer of this state, on determining that there is probable cause to believe that a valid foreign protective order exists and that the order has been violated, shall enforce the foreign protective order as if it were an order of a tribunal of this state. A law enforcement officer has probable cause to believe that a foreign protective order exists if the protected individual presents a foreign protective order that identifies both the protected individual and the respondent and on its face, is currently in effect.

(b) For the purposes of this section, a foreign protective order may be inscribed on a tangible medium or may be stored in an electronic or other medium if it is retrievable in a perceivable form. Presentation of a certified copy of a protective order is not required for enforcement.

(c) If a protected individual does not present a foreign protective order, a law enforcement officer may determine that there is probable cause to believe that a valid foreign protective order exists by relying on any relevant information.

(d) A law enforcement officer of this state who determines that an otherwise valid foreign protective order cannot be enforced because the respondent has not been notified or served with the order shall inform the respondent of the order and make a reasonable effort to serve the order on the respondent. After informing the respondent and attempting to serve the order, the officer shall allow the respondent a reasonable opportunity to comply with the order before enforcing the order.

(e) The registration or filing of an order in this state is not required for the enforcement of a valid foreign protective order under this chapter. (Enacted by Acts 1997, 75th Leg., ch. 1193 (S.B. 1253), § 19, effective September 1, 1997; am. Acts 2001, 77th Leg., ch. 48 (H.B. 919), § 2, effective September 1, 2001.)

### Sec. 88.005. Registration of Order.

(a) An individual may register a foreign protective order in this state. To register a foreign protective order, an individual shall:

(1) present a certified copy of the order to a sheriff, constable, or chief of police responsible for the registration of orders in the local computer records and in the statewide law enforcement system maintained by the Texas Department of Public Safety; or

(2) present a certified copy of the order to the Department of Public Safety and request that the order be registered in the statewide law enforcement system maintained by the Department of Public Safety.

(b) On receipt of a foreign protective order, the agency responsible for the registration of protective orders shall register the order in accordance with this section and furnish to the individual registering the order a certified copy of the registered order.

(c) The agency responsible for the registration of protective orders shall register a foreign pro-

tective order on presentation of a copy of a protective order that has been certified by the issuing state. A registered foreign protective order that is inaccurate or not currently in effect shall be corrected or removed from the registry in accordance with the law of this state.

(d) An individual registering a foreign protective order shall file an affidavit made by the protected individual that, to the best of the protected individual's knowledge, the order is in effect.

(e) A foreign protective order registered under this section may be entered in any existing state or federal registry of protective orders, in accordance with state or federal law.

(f) A fee may not be charged for the registration of a foreign protective order. (Enacted by Acts 2001, 77th Leg., ch. 48 (H.B. 919), § 2, effective September 1, 2001.)

### Sec. 88.006. Immunity.

A state or local governmental agency, law enforcement officer, prosecuting attorney, clerk of court, or any state or local governmental official acting in an official capacity is immune from civil and criminal liability for an act or omission arising from the registration or enforcement of a foreign protective order or the detention or arrest of a person alleged to have violated a foreign protective order if the act or omission was done in good faith in an effort to comply with this chapter. (Enacted by Acts 2001, 77th Leg., ch. 48 (H.B. 919), § 2, effective September 1, 2001.)

### Sec. 88.007. Other Remedies.

A protected individual who pursues a remedy under this chapter is not precluded from pursuing other legal or equitable remedies against the respondent. (Enacted by Acts 2001, 77th Leg., ch. 48 (H.B. 919), § 2, effective September 1, 2001.)

### Sec. 88.008. Uniformity of Application and Construction.

In applying and construing this chapter, consideration shall be given to the need to promote uniformity of the law with respect to its subject matter among the states that enact the Uniform Interstate Enforcement of Domestic Violence Protection Orders Act. (Enacted by Acts 2001, 77th Leg., ch. 48 (H.B. 919), § 2, effective September 1, 2001.)

## SUBTITLE C
## REPORTING FAMILY VIOLENCE

## CHAPTER 91
## REPORTING FAMILY VIOLENCE

### Sec. 91.001. Definitions.

In this subtitle:

(1) "Family violence" has the meaning assigned by Section 71.004.

(2) "Medical professional" means a licensed doctor, nurse, physician assistant, or emergency medical technician.

(Enacted by Acts 1997, 75th Leg., ch. 34 (S.B. 797), § 1, effective May 5, 1997.)

### Sec. 91.002. Reporting by Witnesses Encouraged.

A person who witnesses family violence is encouraged to report the family violence to a local law enforcement agency.

(Enacted by Acts 1997, 75th Leg., ch. 34 (S.B. 797), § 1, effective May 5, 1997.)

### Sec. 91.003. Information Provided by Medical Professionals.

A medical professional who treats a person for injuries that the medical professional has reason to believe were caused by family violence shall:

(1) immediately provide the person with information regarding the nearest family violence shelter center;

(2) document in the person's medical file:

(A) the fact that the person has received the information provided under Subdivision (1); and

(B) the reasons for the medical professional's belief that the person's injuries were caused by family violence; and

(3) give the person a written notice in substantially the following form, completed with the required information, in both English and Spanish:

## "NOTICE TO ADULT VICTIMS OF FAMILY VIOLENCE

"It is a crime for any person to cause you any physical injury or harm even if that person is a member or former member of your family or household.

"You may report family violence to a law enforcement officer by calling the following telephone numbers: _____.

"If you, your child, or any other household resident has been injured or if you feel you are going to be in danger after a law enforcement officer investigating family violence leaves your residence or at a later time, you have the right to:

"Ask the local prosecutor to file a criminal complaint against the person committing family violence; and

"Apply to a court for an order to protect you. You may want to consult with a legal aid office, a prosecuting attorney, or a private attorney. A court can enter an order that:

"(1) prohibits the abuser from committing further acts of violence;

"(2) prohibits the abuser from threatening, harassing, or contacting you at home;

"(3) directs the abuser to leave your household; and

"(4) establishes temporary custody of the children or any property.

"A VIOLATION OF CERTAIN PROVISIONS OF COURT-ORDERED PROTECTION MAY BE A FELONY.

"CALL THE FOLLOWING VIOLENCE SHELTERS OR SOCIAL ORGANIZATIONS IF YOU NEED PROTECTION: _____."

(Enacted by Acts 1997, 75th Leg., ch. 34 (S.B. 797), § 1, effective May 5, 1997.)

### Sec. 91.004. Application of Subtitle.

This subtitle does not affect a duty to report child abuse under Chapter 261.

(Enacted by Acts 1997, 75th Leg., ch. 34 (S.B. 797), § 1, effective May 5, 1997.)

## CHAPTER 92
## IMMUNITY

### Sec. 92.001. Immunity.

(a) Except as provided by Subsection (b), a person who reports family violence under Section 91.002 or provides information under Section 91.003 is immune from civil liability that might otherwise be incurred or imposed.

(b) A person who reports the person's own conduct or who otherwise reports family violence in bad faith is not protected from liability under this section.

(Enacted by Acts 1997, 75th Leg., ch. 34 (S.B. 797), § 1, effective May 5, 1997.)

# TITLE 5

# THE PARENT-CHILD RELATIONSHIP AND THE SUIT AFFECTING THE PARENT-CHILD RELATIONSHIP

## SUBTITLE A
## GENERAL PROVISIONS

## CHAPTER 105
## SETTINGS, HEARINGS, AND ORDERS

### Sec. 105.0011.  Information Regarding Protective Orders.

At any time while a suit is pending, if the court believes, on the basis of any information received by the court, that a party to the suit or a member of the party's family or household may be a victim of family violence, the court shall inform that party of the party's right to apply for a protective order under Title 4.

(Enacted by Acts 2005, 79th Leg., ch. 361 (S.B. 1275), § 3, effective June 17, 2005.)

## SUBTITLE B
## SUITS AFFECTING THE PARENT-CHILD RELATIONSHIP

## CHAPTER 151
## RIGHTS AND DUTIES IN PARENT-CHILD RELATIONSHIP

**Section**
151.001.   Rights and Duties of Parent.
151.003.   Limitation on State Agency Action.

### Sec. 151.001.  Rights and Duties of Parent.

(a) A parent of a child has the following rights and duties:

(1) the right to have physical possession, to direct the moral and religious training, and to designate the residence of the child;

(2) the duty of care, control, protection, and reasonable discipline of the child;

(3) the duty to support the child, including providing the child with clothing, food, shelter, medical and dental care, and education;

(4) the duty, except when a guardian of the child's estate has been appointed, to manage the estate of the child, including the right as an agent of the child to act in relation to the child's estate if the child's action is required by a state, the United States, or a foreign government;

(5) except as provided by Section 264.0111, the right to the services and earnings of the child;

(6) the right to consent to the child's marriage, enlistment in the armed forces of the United States, medical and dental care, and psychiatric, psychological, and surgical treatment;

(7) the right to represent the child in legal action and to make other decisions of substantial legal significance concerning the child;

(8) the right to receive and give receipt for payments for the support of the child and to hold or disburse funds for the benefit of the child;

(9) the right to inherit from and through the child;

(10) the right to make decisions concerning the child's education; and

(11) any other right or duty existing between a parent and child by virtue of law.

(b) The duty of a parent to support his or her child exists while the child is an unemancipated minor and continues as long as the child is fully enrolled in a secondary school in a program leading toward a high school diploma and complies with attendance requirements described by Section 154.002(a)(2).

(c) A parent who fails to discharge the duty of support is liable to a person who provides necessaries to those to whom support is owed.

(d) The rights and duties of a parent are subject to:

(1) a court order affecting the rights and duties;

(2) an affidavit of relinquishment of parental rights; and

(3) an affidavit by the parent designating another person or agency to act as managing conservator.

(e) Only the following persons may use corporal punishment for the reasonable discipline of a child:

(1) a parent or grandparent of the child;

(2) a stepparent of the child who has the duty of control and reasonable discipline of the child; and

(3) an individual who is a guardian of the child and who has the duty of control and reasonable discipline of the child.

Family Code

(Enacted by Acts 1995, 74th Leg., ch. 20 (H.B. 655), § 1, effective April 20, 1995; am. Acts 1995, 74th Leg., ch. 751 (H.B. 433), § 23, effective September 1, 1995; am. Acts 2001, 77th Leg., ch. 821 (H.B. 920), § 2.13, effective June 14, 2001 (renumbered from Sec. 151.003); am. Acts 2001, 77th Leg., ch. 964 (S.B. 1683), § 2, effective September 1, 2001; am. Acts 2003, 78th Leg., ch. 1036 (H.B. 913), § 3, effective September 1, 2003; am. Acts 2005, 79th Leg., ch. 924 (H.B. 383), § 1, effective September 1, 2005; am. Acts 2007, 80th Leg., ch. 972 (S.B. 228), § 6, effective September 1, 2007.)

## Sec. 151.003. Limitation on State Agency Action.

A state agency may not adopt rules or policies or take any other action that violates the fundamental right and duty of a parent to direct the upbringing of the parent's child.
(Enacted by Acts 1999, 76th Leg., ch. 62 (S.B. 1368), § 6.18(a), effective September 1, 1999; am. Acts 2001, 77th Leg., ch. 821 (H.B. 920), § 2.13, effective June 14, 2001 (renumbered from Sec. 151.005).)

# CHAPTER 153
# CONSERVATORSHIP, POSSESSION, AND ACCESS

## SUBCHAPTER A
## GENERAL PROVISIONS

### Sec. 153.013. False Report of Child Abuse.

(a) If a party to a pending suit affecting the parent-child relationship makes a report alleging child abuse by another party to the suit that the reporting party knows lacks a factual foundation, the court shall deem the report to be a knowingly false report.

(b) Evidence of a false report of child abuse is admissible in a suit between the involved parties regarding the terms of conservatorship of a child.

(c) If the court makes a finding under Subsection (a), the court shall impose a civil penalty not to exceed $500.

(Enacted by Acts 1995, 74th Leg., ch. 751 (H.B. 433), § 28, effective September 1, 1995; am. Acts 1997, 75th Leg., ch. 786 (H.B. 2615), § 2, effective September 1, 1997.)

## SUBCHAPTER B
## PARENT APPOINTED AS
## CONSERVATOR: IN GENERAL

### Sec. 153.074. Rights and Duties During Period of Possession.

Unless limited by court order, a parent appointed as a conservator of a child has the following rights and duties during the period that the parent has possession of the child:

(1) the duty of care, control, protection, and reasonable discipline of the child;

(2) the duty to support the child, including providing the child with clothing, food, shelter, and medical and dental care not involving an invasive procedure;

(3) the right to consent for the child to medical and dental care not involving an invasive procedure; and

(4) the right to direct the moral and religious training of the child.

(Enacted by Acts 1995, 74th Leg., ch. 20 (H.B. 655), § 1, effective April 20, 1995; am. Acts 1995, 74th Leg., ch. 751 (H.B. 433), § 30, effective September 1, 1995; am. Acts 2003, 78th Leg., ch. 1036 (H.B. 913), § 7, effective September 1, 2003.)

# CHAPTER 157
# ENFORCEMENT

## SUBCHAPTER B
## PROCEDURE

### Sec. 157.066. Failure to Appear.

If a respondent who has been personally served with notice to appear at a hearing does not appear at the designated time, place, and date to respond to a motion for enforcement of an existing court order, regardless of whether the motion is joined with other claims or remedies, the court may not hold the respondent in contempt but may, on proper proof, grant a default judgment for the relief sought and issue a capias for the arrest of the respondent.

(Enacted by Acts 1995, 74th Leg., ch. 20 (H.B. 655), § 1, effective April 20, 1995; am. Acts 1995, 74th Leg., ch. 751 (H.B. 433), § 50, effective September 1, 1995.)

## SUBCHAPTER C
## FAILURE TO APPEAR; BOND OR SECURITY

### Sec. 157.102.   Capias or Warrant; Duty of Law Enforcement Officials.

Law enforcement officials shall treat a capias or arrest warrant ordered under this chapter in the same manner as an arrest warrant for a criminal offense and shall enter the capias or warrant in the computer records for outstanding warrants maintained by the local police, sheriff, and Department of Public Safety. The capias or warrant shall be forwarded to and disseminated by the Texas Crime Information Center and the National Crime Information Center.

(Enacted by Acts 1995, 74th Leg., ch. 20 (H.B. 655), § 1, effective April 20, 1995; am. Acts 1997, 75th Leg., ch. 702 (S.B. 1594), § 3, effective September 1, 1997; am. Acts 1999, 76th Leg., ch. 556 (S.B. 368), § 16, effective September 1, 1999; am. Acts 2007, 80th Leg., ch. 972 (S.B. 228), § 19, effective September 1, 2007.)

### Sec. 157.114.   Failure to Appear.

The court may order a capias to be issued for the arrest of the respondent if:

   (1) the motion for enforcement requests contempt;

   (2) the respondent was personally served; and

   (3) the respondent fails to appear.

(Enacted by Acts 1995, 74th Leg., ch. 20 (H.B. 655), § 1, effective April 20, 1995.)

## CHAPTER 160
## UNIFORM PARENTAGE ACT

### SUBCHAPTER F
### GENETIC TESTING

### Sec. 160.512.   Offense: Falsification of Specimen.

(a) A person commits an offense if the person alters, destroys, conceals, fabricates, or falsifies genetic evidence in a proceeding to adjudicate parentage, including inducing another person to provide a specimen with the intent to affect the outcome of the proceeding.

(b) An offense under this section is a felony of the third degree.

(c) An order excluding a man as the biological father of a child based on genetic evidence shown to be altered, fabricated, or falsified is void and unenforceable.

(Enacted by Acts 2011, 82nd Leg., ch. 1221 (S.B. 502), § 7, effective September 1, 2011.)

## SUBTITLE C
## JUDICIAL RESOURCES AND SERVICES

## CHAPTER 203
## DOMESTIC RELATIONS OFFICES

### Sec. 203.007.   Access to Records; Offense.

(a) A domestic relations office may obtain the records described by Subsections (b), (c), (d), and (e) that relate to a person who has:

   (1) been ordered to pay child support;

   (2) been designated as a conservator of a child;

   (3) been designated to be the father of a child;

   (4) executed an acknowledgment of paternity;

   (5) court-ordered possession of a child; or

   (6) filed suit to adopt a child.

(b) A domestic relations office is entitled to obtain from the Department of Public Safety records that relate to:

   (1) a person's date of birth;

   (2) a person's most recent address;

   (3) a person's current driver's license status;

   (4) motor vehicle accidents involving a person;

   (5) reported traffic-law violations of which a person has been convicted; and

   (6) a person's criminal history record information.

(c) A domestic relations office is entitled to obtain from the Texas Workforce Commission records that relate to:

   (1) a person's address;

   (2) a person's employment status and earnings;

   (3) the name and address of a person's current or former employer; and

(4) unemployment compensation benefits received by a person.

(d) To the extent permitted by federal law, a domestic relations office is entitled to obtain from the national directory of new hires established under 42 U.S.C. Section 653(i), as amended, records that relate to a person described by Subsection (a), including records that relate to:

(1) the name, telephone number, and address of the person's employer;

(2) information provided by the person on a W-4 form; and

(3) information provided by the person's employer on a Title IV-D form.

(e) To the extent permitted by federal law, a domestic relations office is entitled to obtain from the state case registry records that relate to a person described by Subsection (a), including records that relate to:

(1) the street and mailing address and the social security number of the person;

(2) the name, telephone number, and address of the person's employer;

(3) the location and value of real and personal property owned by the person; and

(4) the name and address of each financial institution in which the person maintains an account and the account number for each account.

(f) An agency required to provide records under this section may charge a domestic relations office a fee for providing the records in an amount that does not exceed the amount paid for those records by the agency responsible for Title IV-D cases.

(g) The Department of Public Safety, the Texas Workforce Commission, or the office of the secretary of state may charge a domestic relations office a fee not to exceed the charge paid by the Title IV-D agency for furnishing records under this section.

(h) Information obtained by a domestic relations office under this section that is confidential under a constitution, statute, judicial decision, or rule is privileged and may be used only by that office.

(i) A person commits an offense if the person releases or discloses confidential information obtained under this section without the consent of the person to whom the information relates. An offense under this subsection is a Class C misdemeanor.

(j) A domestic relations office is entitled to obtain from the office of the secretary of state the following information about a registered voter to the extent that the information is available:

(1) complete name;

(2) current and former street and mailing address;

(3) sex;

(4) date of birth;

(5) social security number; and

(6) telephone number.

(Enacted by Acts 1995, 74th Leg., ch. 20 (H.B. 655), § 1, effective April 20, 1995; am. Acts 1995, 74th Leg., ch. 475 (S.B. 622), § 1, effective September 1, 1995 (renumbered from Sec. 203.012); am. Acts 1995, 74th Leg., ch. 803 (H.B. 1274), § 1, effective September 1, 1995; am. Acts 1997, 75th Leg., ch. 165 (S.B. 898), § 7.18, effective September 1, 1997; am. Acts 1999, 76th Leg., ch. 556 (S.B. 368), § 49, effective September 1, 1999; am. Acts 1999, 76th Leg., ch. 859 (H.B. 1884), § 4, effective September 1, 1999; am. Acts 1999, 76th Leg., ch. 1191 (S.B. 391), § 2, effective June 18, 1999; am. Acts 2007, 80th Leg., ch. 832 (H.B. 772), § 9, effective September 1, 2007.)

## SUBTITLE D
## ADMINISTRATIVE SERVICES

## CHAPTER 232
## SUSPENSION OF LICENSE

## Sec. 232.001. Definitions.

In this chapter:

(1) "License" means a license, certificate, registration, permit, or other authorization that:

    (A) is issued by a licensing authority;

    (B) is subject before expiration to renewal, suspension, revocation, forfeiture, or termination by a licensing authority; and

    (C) a person must obtain to:

        (i) practice or engage in a particular business, occupation, or profession;

        (ii) operate a motor vehicle on a public highway in this state; or

        (iii) engage in any other regulated activity, including hunting, fishing, or other recreational activity for which a license or permit is required.

(2) "Licensing authority" means a department, commission, board, office, or other agency of the state or a political subdivision of the state that issues or renews a license or that otherwise has authority to suspend or refuse to renew a license.

(3) "Order suspending license" means an order issued by the Title IV-D agency or a court directing a licensing authority to suspend or refuse to renew a license.

(4) "Subpoena" means a judicial or administrative subpoena issued in a parentage determination or child support proceeding under this title.

(Enacted by Acts 1995, 74th Leg., ch. 655 (H.B. 1863), § 5.03, effective September 1, 1995; enacted by Acts 1995, 74th Leg., ch. 751 (H.B. 433), § 85, effective September 1, 1995; am. Acts 1997, 75th Leg., ch. 911 (S.B. 29), § 82, effective September 1, 1997; am. Acts 2001, 77th Leg., ch. 1023 (H.B. 1365), § 58, effective September 1, 2001; am. Acts 2007, 80th Leg., ch. 972 (S.B. 228), § 50, effective September 1, 2007.)

### Sec. 232.002. Licensing Authorities Subject to Chapter.

Unless otherwise restricted or exempted, all licensing authorities are subject to this chapter. (Enacted by Acts 1995, 74th Leg., ch. 655 (H.B. 1863), § 5.03, effective September 1, 1995; enacted by Acts 1995, 74th Leg., ch. 751 (H.B. 433), § 85, effective September 1, 1995; am. Acts 1997, 75th Leg., ch. 165 (S.B. 898), § 7.22, effective September 1, 1997; am. Acts 1997, 75th Leg., ch. 1280 (S.B. 84), § 1(1.02), effective September 1, 1997; am. Acts 1997, 75th Leg., ch. 1288 (S.B. 291), § 2, effective September 1, 1997; am. Acts 1999, 76th Leg., ch. 1477 (H.B. 3517), § 23,

effective September 1, 1999; am. Acts 2001, 77th Leg., ch. 394 (H.B. 965), § 2, effective September 1, 2001; am. Acts 2003, 78th Leg., ch. 553 (H.B. 1483), § 2.003, effective February 1, 2004; am. Acts 2005, 79th Leg., ch. 798 (S.B. 411), § 4.01, effective September 1, 2005; am. Acts 2007, 80th Leg., ch. 889 (H.B. 2426), § 53, effective September 1, 2007; am. Acts 2007, 80th Leg., ch. 890 (H.B. 2458), § 2.02, effective September 1, 2007; am. Acts 2007, 80th Leg., ch. 921 (H.B. 3167), § 6.001, effective September 1, 2007; am. Acts 2007, 80th Leg., ch. 972 (S.B. 228), § 51, effective September 1, 2007.)

### Sec. 232.0021. Application of Chapter to Texas Lottery Commission.

With respect to the Texas Lottery Commission, this chapter applies only to a lottery ticket sales agent license issued under Chapter 466, Government Code.

(Enacted by Acts 2001, 77th Leg., ch. 394 (H.B. 965), § 3, effective September 1, 2001.)

### Sec. 232.0022. Suspension or Nonrenewal of Motor Vehicle Registration.

(a) The Texas Department of Motor Vehicles is the appropriate licensing authority for suspension or nonrenewal of a motor vehicle registration under this chapter.

(b) The suspension or nonrenewal of a motor vehicle registration under this chapter does not:

    (1) encumber the title to the motor vehicle or otherwise affect the transfer of the title to the vehicle; or

    (2) affect the sale, purchase, or registration of the motor vehicle by a person who holds a general distinguishing number issued under Chapter 503, Transportation Code.

(Acts 2007, 80th Leg., ch. 972 (S.B. 228), § 52, effective September 1, 2007; am. Acts 2009, 81st Leg., ch. 933 (H.B. 3097), § 3C.02, effective September 1, 2009.)

### Sec. 232.003. Suspension of License.

(a) A court or the Title IV-D agency may issue an order suspending a license as provided by this chapter if an individual who is an obligor:

    (1) owes overdue child support in an amount equal to or greater than the total support due for three months under a support order;

    (2) has been provided an opportunity to make payments toward the overdue child support under a court-ordered or agreed repayment schedule; and

(3) has failed to comply with the repayment schedule.

(b) A court or the Title IV-D agency may issue an order suspending a license as provided by this chapter if a parent or alleged parent has failed, after receiving appropriate notice, to comply with a subpoena.

(c) A court may issue an order suspending license as provided by this chapter for an individual for whom a court has rendered an enforcement order under Chapter 157 finding that the individual has failed to comply with the terms of a court order providing for the possession of or access to a child.

(Enacted by Acts 1995, 74th Leg., ch. 655 (H.B. 1863), § 5.03, effective September 1, 1995; enacted by Acts 1995, 74th Leg., ch. 751 (H.B. 433), § 85, effective September 1, 1995; am. Acts 1997, 75th Leg., ch. 420 (H.B. 3281), §§ 22, 23, effective September 1, 1997; am. Acts 1997, 75th Leg., ch. 911 (S.B. 29), § 83, effective September 1, 1997; am. Acts 1999, 76th Leg., ch. 556 (S.B. 368), § 59, effective September 1, 1999; am. Acts 2001, 77th Leg., ch. 724 (S.B. 700), § 2, effective September 1, 2001; am. Acts 2001, 77th Leg., ch. 1023 (H.B. 1365), § 59, effective September 1, 2001.)

### Sec. 232.004. Petition for Suspension of License.

(a) A child support agency or obligee may file a petition to suspend, as provided by this chapter, a license of an obligor who has an arrearage equal to or greater than the total support due for three months under a support order.

(b) In a Title IV-D case, the petition shall be filed with the Title IV-D agency, the court of continuing jurisdiction, or the tribunal in which a child support order has been registered under Chapter 159. The tribunal in which the petition is filed obtains jurisdiction over the matter.

(c) In a case other than a Title IV-D case, the petition shall be filed in the court of continuing jurisdiction or the court in which a child support order has been registered under Chapter 159.

(d) A proceeding in a case filed with the Title IV-D agency under this chapter is governed by the contested case provisions of Chapter 2001, Government Code, except that Section 2001.054 does not apply to the proceeding. The director of the Title IV-D agency or the director's designee may render a final decision in a contested case proceeding under this chapter.

(Enacted by Acts 1995, 74th Leg., ch. 655 (H.B. 1863), § 5.03, effective September 1, 1995; en-

acted by Acts 1995, 74th Leg., ch. 751 (H.B. 433), § 85, effective September 1, 1995; am. Acts 1997, 75th Leg., ch. 420 (H.B. 3281), § 24, effective September 1, 1997; am. Acts 1997, 75th Leg., ch. 911 (S.B. 29), § 84, effective September 1, 1997; am. Acts 1999, 76th Leg., ch. 556 (S.B. 368), § 60, effective September 1, 1999; am. Acts 2007, 80th Leg., ch. 972 (S.B. 228), § 53, effective September 1, 2007.)

### Sec. 232.005. Contents of Petition.

(a) A petition under this chapter must state that license suspension is required under Section 232.003 and allege:

(1) the name and, if known, social security number of the individual;

(2) the name of the licensing authority that issued a license the individual is believed to hold; and

(3) the amount of arrearages owed under the child support order or the facts associated with the individual's failure to comply with:

    (A) a subpoena; or

    (B) the terms of a court order providing for the possession of or access to a child.

(b) A petition under this chapter may include as an attachment a copy of:

(1) the record of child support payments maintained by the Title IV-D registry or local registry;

(2) the subpoena with which the individual has failed to comply, together with proof of service of the subpoena; or

(3) with respect to a petition for suspension under Section 232.003(c):

    (A) the enforcement order rendered under Chapter 157 describing the manner in which the individual was found to have not complied with the terms of a court order providing for the possession of or access to a child; and

    (B) the court order containing the provisions that the individual was found to have violated.

(Enacted by Acts 1995, 74th Leg., ch. 655 (H.B. 1863), § 5.03, effective September 1, 1995; enacted by Acts 1995, 74th Leg., ch. 751 (H.B. 433), § 85, effective September 1, 1995; am. Acts 1997, 75th Leg., ch. 911 (S.B. 29), § 85, effective September 1, 1997; am. Acts 2001, 77th Leg., ch. 724 (S.B. 700), § 3, effective September 1, 2001; am. Acts 2001, 77th Leg., ch. 1023 (H.B. 1365), § 60, effective September 1, 2001; am. Acts 2009, 81st Leg., ch. 767 (S.B. 865), § 29, effective June 19, 2009.)

## Sec. 232.006. Notice.

(a) On the filing of a petition under Section 232.004, the clerk of the court or the Title IV-D agency shall deliver to the individual:

(1) notice of the individual's right to a hearing before the court or agency;

(2) notice of the deadline for requesting a hearing; and

(3) a hearing request form if the proceeding is in a Title IV-D case.

(b) Notice under this section may be served:

(1) if the party has been ordered under Chapter 105 to provide the court and registry with the party's current mailing address, by mailing a copy of the notice to the respondent, together with a copy of the petition, by first class mail to the last mailing address of the respondent on file with the court and the state case registry; or

(2) as in civil cases generally.

(c) The notice must contain the following prominently displayed statement in boldfaced type, capital letters, or underlined:

"AN ACTION TO SUSPEND ONE OR MORE LICENSES ISSUED TO YOU HAS BEEN FILED AS PROVIDED BY CHAPTER 232, TEXAS FAMILY CODE. YOU MAY EMPLOY AN ATTORNEY TO REPRESENT YOU IN THIS ACTION. IF YOU OR YOUR ATTORNEY DO NOT REQUEST A HEARING BEFORE THE 21ST DAY AFTER THE DATE OF SERVICE OF THIS NOTICE, AN ORDER SUSPENDING YOUR LICENSE MAY BE RENDERED."

(Enacted by Acts 1995, 74th Leg., ch. 655 (H.B. 1863), § 5.03, effective September 1, 1995; enacted by Acts 1995, 74th Leg., ch. 751 (H.B. 433), § 85, effective September 1, 1995; am. Acts 1997, 75th Leg., ch. 911 (S.B. 29), § 86, effective September 1, 1997; am. Acts 1997, 75th Leg., ch. 976 (H.B. 2273), § 7, effective September 1, 1997; am. Acts 1999, 76th Leg., ch. 178 (H.B. 1209), § 11, effective August 30, 1999; am. Acts 2007, 80th Leg., ch. 972 (S.B. 228), § 54, effective September 1, 2007.)

## Sec. 232.007. Hearing on Petition to Suspend License.

(a) A request for a hearing and motion to stay suspension must be filed with the court or Title IV-D agency by the individual not later than the 20th day after the date of service of the notice under Section 232.006.

(b) If a request for a hearing is filed, the court or Title IV-D agency shall:

(1) promptly schedule a hearing;

(2) notify each party of the date, time, and location of the hearing; and

(3) stay suspension pending the hearing.

(c) In a case involving support arrearages, a record of child support payments made by the Title IV-D agency or a local registry is evidence of whether the payments were made. A copy of the record appearing regular on its face shall be admitted as evidence at a hearing under this chapter, including a hearing on a motion to revoke a stay. Either party may offer controverting evidence.

(d) In a case in which an individual has failed to comply with a subpoena, proof of service is evidence of delivery of the subpoena.

(Enacted by Acts 1995, 74th Leg., ch. 655 (H.B. 1863), § 5.03, effective September 1, 1995; enacted by Acts 1995, 74th Leg., ch. 751 (H.B. 433), § 85, effective September 1, 1995; am. Acts 1997, 75th Leg., ch. 911 (S.B. 29), § 87, effective September 1, 1997.)

## Sec. 232.008. Order Suspending License for Failure to Pay Child Support.

(a) On making the findings required by Section 232.003, the court or Title IV-D agency shall render an order suspending the license unless the individual:

(1) proves that all arrearages and the current month's support have been paid;

(2) shows good cause for failure to comply with the subpoena or the terms of the court order providing for the possession of or access to a child; or

(3) establishes an affirmative defense as provided by Section 157.008(c).

(b) The court or Title IV-D agency may stay an order suspending a license conditioned on the individual's compliance with:

(1) a reasonable repayment schedule that is incorporated in the order;

(2) the requirements of a reissued and delivered subpoena; or

(3) the requirements of any court order pertaining to the possession of or access to a child.

(c) An order suspending a license with a stay of the suspension may not be served on the licensing authority unless the stay is revoked as provided by this chapter.

(d) A final order suspending license rendered by a court or the Title IV-D agency shall be forwarded to the appropriate licensing authority

Family Code

by the clerk of the court or Title IV-D agency. The clerk shall collect from an obligor a fee of $5 for each order mailed.

(e) If the court or Title IV-D agency renders an order suspending license, the individual may also be ordered not to engage in the licensed activity.

(f) If the court or Title IV-D agency finds that the petition for suspension should be denied, the petition shall be dismissed without prejudice, and an order suspending license may not be rendered. (Enacted by Acts 1995, 74th Leg., ch. 655 (H.B. 1863), § 5.03, effective September 1, 1995; enacted by Acts 1995, 74th Leg., ch. 751 (H.B. 433), § 85, effective September 1, 1995; am. Acts 1997, 75th Leg., ch. 911 (S.B. 29), § 88, effective September 1, 1997; am. Acts 1997, 75th Leg., ch. 976 (H.B. 2273), § 8, effective September 1, 1997; am. Acts 1999, 76th Leg., ch. 556 (S.B. 368), § 61, effective September 1, 1999; am. Acts 2001, 77th Leg., ch. 724 (S.B. 700), § 4, effective September 1, 2001.)

## Sec. 232.009.  Default Order.

The court or Title IV-D agency shall consider the allegations of the petition for suspension to be admitted and shall render an order suspending the license of an obligor without the requirement of a hearing if the court or Title IV-D agency determines that the individual failed to respond to a notice issued under Section 232.006 by:

(1) requesting a hearing; or

(2) appearing at a scheduled hearing.

(Enacted by Acts 1995, 74th Leg., ch. 655 (H.B. 1863), § 5.03, effective September 1, 1995; enacted by Acts 1995, 74th Leg., ch. 751 (H.B. 433), § 85, effective September 1, 1995; am. Acts 1997, 75th Leg., ch. 420 (H.B. 3281), § 25, effective September 1, 1997; am. Acts 1997, 75th Leg., ch. 911 (S.B. 29), § 89, effective September 1, 1997; am. Acts 2001, 77th Leg., ch. 1023 (H.B. 1365), § 61, effective September 1, 2001.)

## Sec. 232.010.  Review of Final Administrative Order.

An order issued by a Title IV-D agency under this chapter is a final agency decision and is subject to review under the substantial evidence rule as provided by Chapter 2001, Government Code.

(Enacted by Acts 1995, 74th Leg., ch. 655 (H.B. 1863), § 5.03, effective September 1, 1995; enacted by Acts 1995, 74th Leg., ch. 751 (H.B. 433), § 85, effective September 1, 1995.)

## Sec. 232.011.  Action by Licensing Authority.

(a) On receipt of a final order suspending license, the licensing authority shall immediately determine if the authority has issued a license to the individual named on the order and, if a license has been issued:

(1) record the suspension of the license in the licensing authority's records;

(2) report the suspension as appropriate; and

(3) demand surrender of the suspended license if required by law for other cases in which a license is suspended.

(b) A licensing authority shall implement the terms of a final order suspending license without additional review or hearing. The authority may provide notice as appropriate to the license holder or to others concerned with the license.

(c) A licensing authority may not modify, remand, reverse, vacate, or stay an order suspending license issued under this chapter and may not review, vacate, or reconsider the terms of a final order suspending license.

(d) An individual who is the subject of a final order suspending license is not entitled to a refund for any fee or deposit paid to the licensing authority.

(e) An individual who continues to engage in the business, occupation, profession, or other licensed activity after the implementation of the order suspending license by the licensing authority is liable for the same civil and criminal penalties provided for engaging in the licensed activity without a license or while a license is suspended that apply to any other license holder of that licensing authority.

(f) A licensing authority is exempt from liability to a license holder for any act authorized under this chapter performed by the authority.

(g) Except as provided by this chapter, an order suspending license or dismissing a petition for the suspension of a license does not affect the power of a licensing authority to grant, deny, suspend, revoke, terminate, or renew a license.

(h) The denial or suspension of a driver's license under this chapter is governed by this chapter and not by the general licensing provisions of Chapter 521, Transportation Code.

(i) An order issued under this chapter to suspend a license applies to each license issued by the licensing authority subject to the order for which the obligor is eligible. The licensing authority may not issue or renew any other license for the obligor until the court or the Title IV-D agency renders an order vacating or staying an order suspending license.

(Enacted by Acts 1995, 74th Leg., ch. 655 (H.B. 1863), § 5.03, effective September 1, 1995; enacted by Acts 1995, 74th Leg., ch. 751 (H.B. 433), § 85, effective September 1, 1995; am. Acts 1997, 75th Leg., ch. 165 (S.B. 898), § 30.184, effective September 1, 1997; am. Acts 1997, 75th Leg., ch. 911 (S.B. 29), § 90, effective September 1, 1997; am. Acts 2001, 77th Leg., ch. 1023 (H.B. 1365), § 62, effective September 1, 2001.)

### Sec. 232.012.  Motion to Revoke Stay.

(a) The obligee, support enforcement agency, court, or Title IV-D agency may file a motion to revoke the stay of an order suspending license if the individual who is subject of an order suspending license does not comply with:

(1) the terms of a reasonable repayment plan entered into by the individual;

(2) the requirements of a reissued subpoena; or

(3) the terms of any court order pertaining to the possession of or access to a child.

(b) Notice to the individual of a motion to revoke stay under this section may be given by personal service or by mail to the address provided by the individual, if any, in the order suspending license. The notice must include a notice of hearing. The notice must be provided to the individual not less than 10 days before the date of the hearing.

(c) A motion to revoke stay must allege the manner in which the individual failed to comply with the repayment plan, the reissued subpoena, or the court order pertaining to possession of or access to a child.

(d) If the court or Title IV-D agency finds that the individual is not in compliance with the terms of the repayment plan, reissued subpoena, or court order pertaining to possession of or access to a child, the court or agency shall revoke the stay of the order suspending license and render a final order suspending license.

(Enacted by Acts 1995, 74th Leg., ch. 655 (H.B. 1863), § 5.03, effective September 1, 1995; enacted by Acts 1995, 74th Leg., ch. 751 (H.B. 433), § 85, effective September 1, 1995; am. Acts 1997, 75th Leg., ch. 911 (S.B. 29), § 91, effective September 1, 1997; am. Acts 2001, 77th Leg., ch. 724 (S.B. 700), § 5, effective September 1, 2001.)

### Sec. 232.013.  Vacating or Staying Order Suspending License.

(a) The court or Title IV-D agency may render an order vacating or staying an order suspending an individual's license if:

(1) the individual has:

(A) paid all delinquent child support or has established a satisfactory payment record;

(B) complied with the requirements of a reissued subpoena; or

(C) complied with the terms of any court order providing for the possession of or access to a child; or

(2) the court or Title IV-D agency determines that good cause exists for vacating or staying the order.

(b) The clerk of the court or Title IV-D agency shall promptly deliver an order vacating or staying an order suspending license to the appropriate licensing authority. The clerk shall collect from an obligor a fee of $5 for each order mailed.

(c) On receipt of an order vacating or staying an order suspending license, the licensing authority shall promptly issue the affected license to the individual if the individual is otherwise qualified for the license.

(d) An order rendered under this section does not affect the right of the child support agency or obligee to any other remedy provided by law, including the right to seek relief under this chapter. An order rendered under this section does not affect the power of a licensing authority to grant, deny, suspend, revoke, terminate, or renew a license as otherwise provided by law.

(Enacted by Acts 1995, 74th Leg., ch. 655 (H.B. 1863), § 5.03, effective September 1, 1995; enacted by Acts 1995, 74th Leg., ch. 751 (H.B. 433), § 85, effective September 1, 1995; am. Acts 1997, 75th Leg., ch. 911 (S.B. 29), § 92, effective September 1, 1997; am. Acts 1997, 75th Leg., ch. 976 (H.B. 2273), § 9, effective September 1, 1997; am. Acts 2001, 77th Leg., ch. 724 (S.B. 700), § 6, effective September 1, 2001; am. Acts 2003, 78th Leg., ch. 610 (H.B. 1878), § 16, effective September 1, 2003.)

### Sec. 232.0135.  Denial of License Issuance or Renewal.

(a) A child support agency, as defined by Section 101.004, may provide notice to a licensing authority concerning an obligor who has failed to pay child support for six months or more that

Family Code

requests the authority to refuse to accept an application for issuance of a license to the obligor or renewal of an existing license of the obligor.

(b) A licensing authority that receives the information described by Subsection (a) shall refuse to accept an application for issuance of a license to the obligor or renewal of an existing license of the obligor until the authority is notified by the child support agency that the obligor has:

(1) paid all child support arrearages;

(2) established with the agency a satisfactory repayment schedule or is in compliance with a court order for payment of the arrearages;

(3) been granted an exemption from this subsection as part of a court-supervised plan to improve the obligor's earnings and child support payments; or

(4) successfully contested the denial of issuance or renewal of license under Subsection (d).

(c) On providing a licensing authority with the notice described by Subsection (a), the child support agency shall send a copy to the obligor by first class mail and inform the obligor of the steps the obligor must take to permit the authority to accept the obligor's application for license issuance or renewal.

(d) An obligor receiving notice under Subsection (c) may request a review by the child support agency to resolve any issue in dispute regarding the identity of the obligor or the existence or amount of child support arrearages. The agency shall promptly provide an opportunity for a review, either by telephone or in person, as appropriate to the circumstances. After the review, if appropriate, the agency may notify the licensing authority that it may accept the obligor's application for issuance or renewal of license. If the agency and the obligor fail to resolve any issue in dispute, the obligor, not later than the 30th day after the date of receiving notice of the agency's determination from the review, may file a motion with the court to direct the agency to withdraw the notice under Subsection (a) and request a hearing on the motion. The obligor's application for license issuance or renewal may not be accepted by the licensing authority until the court rules on the motion. If, after a review by the agency or a hearing by the court, the agency withdraws the notice under Subsection (a), the agency shall reimburse the obligor the amount of any fee charged the obligor under Section 232.014.

(e) If an obligor enters into a repayment agreement with the child support agency under this section, the agency may incorporate the agreement in an order to be filed with and confirmed by the court in the manner provided for agreed orders under Chapter 233.

(f) In this section, "licensing authority" does not include the State Securities Board.
(Acts 2007, 80th Leg., ch. 972 (S.B. 228), § 55, effective September 1, 2007; am. Acts 2011, 82nd Leg., ch. 508 (H.B. 1674), §§ 15, 16, effective September 1, 2011.)

## Sec. 232.014. Fee by Licensing Authority.

(a) A licensing authority may charge a fee to an individual who is the subject of an order suspending license or of an action of a child support agency under Section 232.0135 to deny issuance or renewal of license in an amount sufficient to recover the administrative costs incurred by the authority under this chapter.

(b) A fee collected by the Texas Department of Motor Vehicles or the Department of Public Safety shall be deposited to the credit of the state highway fund.
(Enacted by Acts 1995, 74th Leg., ch. 655 (H.B. 1863), § 5.03, effective September 1, 1995; enacted by Acts 1995, 74th Leg., ch. 751 (H.B. 433), § 85, effective September 1, 1995; am. Acts 1997, 75th Leg., ch. 911 (S.B. 29), § 93, effective September 1, 1997; am. Acts 2007, 80th Leg., ch. 972 (S.B. 228), § 56, effective September 1, 2007; am. Acts 2009, 81st Leg., ch. 933 (H.B. 3097), § 3C.03, effective September 1, 2009; am. Acts 2011, 82nd Leg., ch. 508 (H.B. 1674), § 17, effective September 1, 2011.)

## Sec. 232.015. Cooperation Between Licensing Authorities and Title IV-D Agency.

(a) The Title IV-D agency may request from each licensing authority the name, address, social security number, license renewal date, and other identifying information for each individual who holds, applies for, or renews a license issued by the authority.

(b) A licensing authority shall provide the requested information in the form and manner identified by the Title IV-D agency.

(c) The Title IV-D agency may enter into a cooperative agreement with a licensing authority to administer this chapter in a cost-effective manner.

(d) The Title IV-D agency may adopt a reasonable implementation schedule for the requirements of this section.

(e) The Title IV-D agency, the comptroller, and the Texas Alcoholic Beverage Commission shall by rule specify additional prerequisites for the suspension of licenses relating to state taxes collected under Title 2, Tax Code. The joint rules must be adopted not later than March 1, 1996. (Enacted by Acts 1995, 74th Leg., ch. 655 (H.B. 1863), § 5.03, effective September 1, 1995; enacted by Acts 1995, 74th Leg., ch. 751 (H.B. 433), § 85, effective September 1, 1995; am. Acts 2001, 77th Leg., ch. 1023 (H.B. 1365), § 63, effective September 1, 2001.)

### Sec. 232.016. Rules, Forms, and Procedures.

The Title IV-D agency by rule shall prescribe forms and procedures for the implementation of this chapter.
(Enacted by Acts 1995, 74th Leg., ch. 655 (H.B. 1863), § 5.03, effective September 1, 1995; enacted by Acts 1995, 74th Leg., ch. 751 (H.B. 433), § 85, effective September 1, 1995.)

## SUBTITLE E
## PROTECTION OF THE CHILD

## CHAPTER 261
## INVESTIGATION OF REPORT OF CHILD ABUSE OR NEGLECT

### Subchapter A. General Provisions

## SUBCHAPTER A
## GENERAL PROVISIONS

### Sec. 261.001. Definitions.

In this chapter:

(1) "Abuse" includes the following acts or omissions by a person:

(A) mental or emotional injury to a child that results in an observable and material impairment in the child's growth, development, or psychological functioning;

(B) causing or permitting the child to be in a situation in which the child sustains a mental or emotional injury that results in an observable and material impairment in the child's growth, development, or psychological functioning;

(C) physical injury that results in substantial harm to the child, or the genuine threat of substantial harm from physical injury to the child, including an injury that is at variance with the history or explanation given and excluding an accident or reasonable discipline by a parent, guardian, or managing or possessory conservator that does not expose the child to a substantial risk of harm;

(D) failure to make a reasonable effort to prevent an action by another person that results in physical injury that results in substantial harm to the child;

(E) sexual conduct harmful to a child's mental, emotional, or physical welfare, including conduct that constitutes the offense of continuous sexual abuse of young child or children under Section 21.02, Penal Code, indecency with a child under Section 21.11, Penal Code, sexual assault under Section 22.011, Penal Code, or aggravated sexual assault under Section 22.021, Penal Code;

(F) failure to make a reasonable effort to prevent sexual conduct harmful to a child;

(G) compelling or encouraging the child to engage in sexual conduct as defined by Section 43.01, Penal Code, including conduct that constitutes an offense of trafficking of persons under Section 20A.02(a)(7) or (8), Penal Code, prostitution under Section 43.02(a)(2), Penal Code, or compelling prostitution under Section 43.05(a)(2), Penal Code;

(H) causing, permitting, encouraging, engaging in, or allowing the photographing, filming, or depicting of the child if the person knew or should have known that the resulting photograph, film, or depiction of the child is obscene as defined by Section 43.21, Penal Code, or pornographic;

(I) the current use by a person of a controlled substance as defined by Chapter 481,

Health and Safety Code, in a manner or to the extent that the use results in physical, mental, or emotional injury to a child;

(J) causing, expressly permitting, or encouraging a child to use a controlled substance as defined by Chapter 481, Health and Safety Code;

(K) causing, permitting, encouraging, engaging in, or allowing a sexual performance by a child as defined by Section 43.25, Penal Code; or

(L) knowingly causing, permitting, encouraging, engaging in, or allowing a child to be trafficked in a manner punishable as an offense under Section 20A.02(a)(5), (6), (7), or (8), Penal Code, or the failure to make a reasonable effort to prevent a child from being trafficked in a manner punishable as an offense under any of those sections.

(2) "Department" means the Department of Family and Protective Services.

(3) "Designated agency" means the agency designated by the court as responsible for the protection of children.

(4) "Neglect" includes:

(A) the leaving of a child in a situation where the child would be exposed to a substantial risk of physical or mental harm, without arranging for necessary care for the child, and the demonstration of an intent not to return by a parent, guardian, or managing or possessory conservator of the child;

(B) the following acts or omissions by a person:

(i) placing a child in or failing to remove a child from a situation that a reasonable person would realize requires judgment or actions beyond the child's level of maturity, physical condition, or mental abilities and that results in bodily injury or a substantial risk of immediate harm to the child;

(ii) failing to seek, obtain, or follow through with medical care for a child, with the failure resulting in or presenting a substantial risk of death, disfigurement, or bodily injury or with the failure resulting in an observable and material impairment to the growth, development, or functioning of the child;

(iii) the failure to provide a child with food, clothing, or shelter necessary to sustain the life or health of the child, excluding failure caused primarily by financial inability unless relief services had been offered and refused;

(iv) placing a child in or failing to remove the child from a situation in which the child would be exposed to a substantial risk of sexual conduct harmful to the child; or

(v) placing a child in or failing to remove the child from a situation in which the child would be exposed to acts or omissions that constitute abuse under Subdivision (1)(E), (F), (G), (H), or (K) committed against another child; or

(C) the failure by the person responsible for a child's care, custody, or welfare to permit the child to return to the child's home without arranging for the necessary care for the child after the child has been absent from the home for any reason, including having been in residential placement or having run away.

(5) "Person responsible for a child's care, custody, or welfare" means a person who traditionally is responsible for a child's care, custody, or welfare, including:

(A) a parent, guardian, managing or possessory conservator, or foster parent of the child;

(B) a member of the child's family or household as defined by Chapter 71;

(C) a person with whom the child's parent cohabits;

(D) school personnel or a volunteer at the child's school; or

(E) personnel or a volunteer at a public or private child-care facility that provides services for the child or at a public or private residential institution or facility where the child resides.

(6) "Report" means a report that alleged or suspected abuse or neglect of a child has occurred or may occur.

(7) "Board" means the Board of Protective and Regulatory Services.

(8) "Born addicted to alcohol or a controlled substance" means a child:

(A) who is born to a mother who during the pregnancy used a controlled substance, as defined by Chapter 481, Health and Safety Code, other than a controlled substance legally obtained by prescription, or alcohol; and

(B) who, after birth as a result of the mother's use of the controlled substance or alcohol:

(i) experiences observable withdrawal from the alcohol or controlled substance;

(ii) exhibits observable or harmful effects in the child's physical appearance or functioning; or

(iii) exhibits the demonstrable presence of alcohol or a controlled substance in the child's bodily fluids.

(Enacted by Acts 1995, 74th Leg., ch. 20 (H.B. 655), § 1, effective April 20, 1995; am. Acts 1995, 74th Leg., ch. 751 (H.B. 433), § 86, effective September 1, 1995; am. Acts 1997, 75th Leg., ch. 575 (H.B. 1826), § 10, effective September 1, 1997; am. Acts 1997, 75th Leg., ch. 1022 (S.B. 359), § 63, effective September 1, 1997; am. Acts 1999, 76th Leg., ch. 62 (S.B. 1368), § 19.01(26), effective September 1, 1999; am. Acts 2001, 77th Leg., ch. 59 (H.B. 360), § 1, effective September 1, 2001; am. Acts 2005, 79th Leg., ch. 268 (S.B. 6), § 1.11, effective September 1, 2005; am. Acts 2007, 80th Leg., ch. 593 (H.B. 8), § 3.32, effective September 1, 2007; am. Acts 2011, 82nd Leg., ch. 1 (S.B. 24), § 4.03, effective September 1, 2011.)

## Sec. 261.002.  Central Registry.

(a) The department shall establish and maintain in Austin a central registry of reported cases of child abuse or neglect.

(b) The department may adopt rules necessary to carry out this section. The rules shall provide for cooperation with local child service agencies, including hospitals, clinics, and schools, and cooperation with other states in exchanging reports to effect a national registration system.

(c) The department may enter into agreements with other states to allow for the exchange of reports of child abuse and neglect in other states' central registry systems. The department shall use information obtained under this subsection in performing the background checks required under Section 42.056, Human Resources Code. The department shall cooperate with federal agencies and shall provide information and reports of child abuse and neglect to the appropriate federal agency that maintains the national registry for child abuse and neglect, if a national registry exists.

(Enacted by Acts 1995, 74th Leg., ch. 20 (H.B. 655), § 1, effective April 20, 1995; am. Acts 2005, 79th Leg., ch. 268 (S.B. 6), § 1.12, effective September 1, 2005.)

## Sec. 261.003.  Application to Students in School for Deaf or School for Blind and Visually Impaired.

This chapter applies to the investigation of a report of abuse or neglect of a student, without

regard to the age of the student, in the Texas School for the Deaf or the Texas School for the Blind and Visually Impaired.
(Enacted by Acts 1995, 74th Leg., ch. 20 (H.B. 655), § 1, effective April 20, 1995.)

## Sec. 261.004. Statistics of Abuse and Neglect of Children.

(a) The department shall prepare and disseminate statistics by county relating to the department's activities under this subtitle and include the information specified in Subsection (b) in an annual report available to the public.

(b) The department shall report the following information:

(1) the number of initial phone calls received by the department alleging abuse and neglect;

(2) the number of children reported to the department as having been abused and neglected;

(3) the number of reports received by the department alleging abuse or neglect and assigned by the department for investigation;

(4) of the children to whom Subdivision (2) applies:

(A) the number for whom the report was substantiated;

(B) the number for whom the report was unsubstantiated;

(C) the number for whom the report was determined to be false;

(D) the number who did not receive services from the department under a state or federal program;

(E) the number who received services, including preventative services, from the department under a state or federal program; and

(F) the number who were removed from the child's home during the preceding year;

(5) the number of families in which the child was not removed, but the child or family received services from the department;

(6) the number of children who died during the preceding year as a result of child abuse or neglect;

(7) of the children to whom Subdivision (6) applies, the number who were in foster care at the time of death;

(8) the number of child protective services workers responsible for report intake, assessment, or investigation;

(9) the response time by the department with respect to conducting an initial investigation of a report of child abuse or neglect;

(10) the response time by the department with respect to commencing services to families and children for whom an allegation of abuse or neglect has been made;

(11) the number of children who were returned to their families or who received family preservation services and who, before the fifth anniversary of the date of return or receipt, were the victims of substantiated reports of child abuse or neglect, including abuse or neglect resulting in the death of the child;

(12) the number of cases pursued by the department in each stage of the judicial process, including civil and criminal proceedings and the results of each proceeding; and

(13) the number of children for whom a person was appointed by the court to represent the best interests of the child and the average number of out-of-court contacts between the person and the child.

(c) The department shall compile the information specified in Subsection (b) for the preceding year in a report to be submitted to the legislature and the general public not later than February 1 of each year.
(Enacted by Acts 1997, 75th Leg., ch. 1022 (S.B. 359), § 64, effective September 1, 1997.)

## SUBCHAPTER B
## REPORT OF ABUSE OR NEGLECT; IMMUNITIES

## Sec. 261.101. Persons Required to Report; Time to Report.

(a) A person having cause to believe that a child's physical or mental health or welfare has been adversely affected by abuse or neglect by any person shall immediately make a report as provided by this subchapter.

(b) If a professional has cause to believe that a child has been abused or neglected or may be abused or neglected, or that a child is a victim of an offense under Section 21.11, Penal Code, and the professional has cause to believe that the child has been abused as defined by Section 261.001 or 261.401, the professional shall make a report not later than the 48th hour after the hour the professional first suspects that the child has been or may be abused or neglected or is a victim of an offense under Section 21.11, Penal Code. A professional may not delegate to or rely on another person to make the report. In this subsection, "professional" means an individual who is licensed or certified by the state or who is an employee of a facility licensed, certified, or operated by the state and who, in the normal course of official duties or duties for which a license or certification is required, has direct contact with children. The term includes teachers, nurses, doctors, day-care employees, employees of a clinic or health care facility that provides reproductive services, juvenile probation officers, and juvenile detention or correctional officers.

(c) The requirement to report under this section applies without exception to an individual whose personal communications may otherwise be privileged, including an attorney, a member of the clergy, a medical practitioner, a social worker, a mental health professional, and an employee of a clinic or health care facility that provides reproductive services.

(d) Unless waived in writing by the person making the report, the identity of an individual making a report under this chapter is confidential and may be disclosed only:

(1) as provided by Section 261.201; or

(2) to a law enforcement officer for the purposes of conducting a criminal investigation of the report.

(Enacted by Acts 1995, 74th Leg., ch. 20 (H.B. 655), § 1, effective April 20, 1995; am. Acts 1995, 74th Leg., ch. 751 (H.B. 433), § 87, effective September 1, 1995; am. Acts 1997, 75th Leg., ch. 162 (H.B. 1929), § 1, effective September 1, 1997; am. Acts 1997, 75th Leg., ch. 575 (H.B. 1826), § 11, effective September 1, 1997; am. Acts 1997, 75th Leg., ch. 1022 (S.B. 359), § 65, effective September 1, 1997; am. Acts 1999, 76th Leg., ch. 62 (S.B. 1368), § 6.29, effective September 1, 1999; am. Acts 1999, 76th Leg., ch. 1150 (H.B. 3838), § 2, effective September 1, 1999; am. Acts 1999, 76th Leg., ch. 1390 (H.B. 1622), § 21, effective September 1, 1999; am. Acts 2001, 77th Leg., ch. 1420 (H.B. 2812), § 5.003, effective September 1, 2001; am. Acts 2005, 79th Leg., ch. 949 (H.B. 1575), § 27, effective September 1, 2005.)

### Sec. 261.102. Matters to Be Reported.

A report should reflect the reporter's belief that a child has been or may be abused or neglected or has died of abuse or neglect.

(Enacted by Acts 1995, 74th Leg., ch. 20 (H.B. 655), § 1, effective April 20, 1995; am. Acts 1995, 74th Leg., ch. 751 (H.B. 433), § 88, effective September 1, 1995.)

### Sec. 261.103. Report Made to Appropriate Agency.

(a) Except as provided by Subsections (b) and (c) and Section 261.405, a report shall be made to:

(1) any local or state law enforcement agency;

(2) the department;

(3) the state agency that operates, licenses, certifies, or registers the facility in which the alleged abuse or neglect occurred; or

(4) the agency designated by the court to be responsible for the protection of children.

(b) A report may be made to the Texas Youth Commission instead of the entities listed under Subsection (a) if the report is based on information provided by a child while under the supervision of the commission concerning the child's alleged abuse of another child.

(c) Notwithstanding Subsection (a), a report, other than a report under Subsection (a)(3) or Section 261.405, must be made to the department if the alleged or suspected abuse or neglect involves a person responsible for the care, custody, or welfare of the child.

(Enacted by Acts 1995, 74th Leg., ch. 20 (H.B. 655), § 1, effective April 20, 1995; am. Acts 1995, 74th Leg., ch. 751 (H.B. 433), § 89, effective September 1, 1995; am. Acts 1999, 76th Leg., ch. 1477 (H.B. 3517), § 24, effective September 1, 1999; am. Acts 2001, 77th Leg., ch. 1297 (H.B. 1118), § 46, effective September 1, 2001; am. Acts 2005, 79th Leg., ch. 213 (H.B. 1970), § 1, effective September 1, 2005.)

### Sec. 261.104. Contents of Report.

The person making a report shall identify, if known:

(1) the name and address of the child;

(2) the name and address of the person responsible for the care, custody, or welfare of the child; and

(3) any other pertinent information concerning the alleged or suspected abuse or neglect.

(Enacted by Acts 1995, 74th Leg., ch. 20 (H.B. 655), § 1, effective April 20, 1995; am. Acts 1995, 74th Leg., ch. 751 (H.B. 433), § 90, effective September 1, 1995.)

### Sec. 261.105. Referral of Report by Department or Law Enforcement.

(a) All reports received by a local or state law enforcement agency that allege abuse or neglect by a person responsible for a child's care, custody, or welfare shall be referred immediately to the department or the designated agency.

(b) The department or designated agency shall immediately notify the appropriate state or local law enforcement agency of any report it receives, other than a report from a law enforcement agency, that concerns the suspected abuse or neglect of a child or death of a child from abuse or neglect.

(c) In addition to notifying a law enforcement agency, if the report relates to a child in a facility operated, licensed, certified, or registered by a state agency, the department shall refer the report to the agency for investigation.

(c-1) Notwithstanding Subsections (b) and (c), if a report under this section relates to a child with mental retardation receiving services in a state supported living center as defined by Section 531.002, Health and Safety Code, or the ICF-MR component of the Rio Grande State Center, the department shall proceed with the investigation of the report as provided by Section 261.404.

(d) If the department initiates an investigation and determines that the abuse or neglect does not involve a person responsible for the child's care, custody, or welfare, the department shall refer the report to a law enforcement agency for further investigation. If the department determines that the abuse or neglect involves an employee of a public primary or secondary school, and that the child is a student at the school, the department shall orally notify the superintendent of the school district in which the employee is employed about the investigation.

(e) In cooperation with the department, the Texas Youth Commission by rule shall adopt guidelines for identifying a report made to the commission under Section 261.103(b) that is appropriate to refer to the department or a law enforcement agency for investigation. Guidelines adopted under this subsection must require the commission to consider the severity and immediacy of the alleged abuse or neglect of the child victim.
(Enacted by Acts 1995, 74th Leg., ch. 20 (H.B. 655), § 1, effective April 20, 1995; am. Acts 1997, 75th Leg., ch. 1022 (S.B. 359), § 66, effective September 1, 1997; am. Acts 1999, 76th Leg., ch. 1477 (H.B. 3517), § 25, effective September 1, 1999; am. Acts 2003, 78th Leg., ch. 374 (S.B. 1488), § 3, effective June 18, 2003; am. Acts 2009, 81st Leg., ch. 284 (S.B. 643), § 4, effective June 11, 2009.)

## Sec. 261.1055. Notification of District Attorneys.

(a) A district attorney may inform the department or designated agency that the district attorney wishes to receive notification of some or all reports of suspected abuse or neglect of children who were in the county at the time the report was made or who were in the county at the time of the alleged abuse or neglect.

(b) If the district attorney makes the notification under this section, the department or designated agency shall, on receipt of a report of suspected abuse or neglect, immediately notify the district attorney as requested and the department or designated agency shall forward a copy of the reports to the district attorney on request.
(Enacted by Acts 1997, 75th Leg., ch. 1022 (S.B. 359), § 67, effective September 1, 1997.)

## Sec. 261.106. Immunities.

(a) A person acting in good faith who reports or assists in the investigation of a report of alleged child abuse or neglect or who testifies or otherwise participates in a judicial proceeding arising from a report, petition, or investigation of alleged child abuse or neglect is immune from civil or criminal liability that might otherwise be incurred or imposed.

(b) Immunity from civil and criminal liability extends to an authorized volunteer of the department or a law enforcement officer who participates at the request of the department in an investigation of alleged or suspected abuse or neglect or in an action arising from an investigation if the person was acting in good faith and in the scope of the person's responsibilities.

(c) A person who reports the person's own abuse or neglect of a child or who acts in bad faith or with malicious purpose in reporting alleged child abuse or neglect is not immune from civil or criminal liability.
(Enacted by Acts 1995, 74th Leg., ch. 20 (H.B. 655), § 1, effective April 20, 1995; am. Acts 1995, 74th Leg., ch. 751 (H.B. 433), § 91, effective September 1, 1995.)

## Sec. 261.107. False Report; Criminal Penalty; Civil Penalty.

(a) A person commits an offense if, with the intent to deceive, the person knowingly makes a report as provided in this chapter that is false. An offense under this subsection is a state jail felony unless it is shown on the trial of the offense that the person has previously been convicted under this section, in which case the offense is a felony of the third degree.

(b) A finding by a court in a suit affecting the parent-child relationship that a report made under this chapter before or during the suit was false or lacking factual foundation may be grounds for the court to modify an order providing for possession of or access to the child who was the subject of the report by restricting further access to the child by the person who made the report.

(c) The appropriate county prosecuting attorney shall be responsible for the prosecution of an offense under this section.

(d) The court shall order a person who is convicted of an offense under Subsection (a) to pay any reasonable attorney's fees incurred by the person who was falsely accused of abuse or neglect in any proceeding relating to the false report.

(e) A person who engages in conduct described by Subsection (a) is liable to the state for a civil penalty of $1,000. The attorney general shall bring an action to recover a civil penalty authorized by this subsection.
(Enacted by Acts 1995, 74th Leg., ch. 20 (H.B. 655), § 1, effective April 20, 1995; am. Acts 1995, 74th Leg., ch. 751 (H.B. 433), § 92, effective September 1, 1995; am. Acts 1997, 75th Leg., ch. 575 (H.B. 1826), § 2, effective September 1, 1997; am. Acts 1997, 75th Leg., ch. 1022 (S.B. 359), § 68, effective September 1, 1997; am. Acts 1999, 76th Leg., ch. 62 (S.B. 1368), § 6.30, effective September 1, 1999; am. Acts 2005, 79th Leg., ch. 268 (S.B. 6), §§ 1.13, 1.14(a), effective September 1, 2005.)

## Sec. 261.108. Frivolous Claims Against Person Reporting.

(a) In this section:

(1) "Claim" means an action or claim by a party, including a plaintiff, counterclaimant, cross-claimant, or third-party plaintiff, requesting recovery of damages.

(2) "Defendant" means a party against whom a claim is made.

(b) A court shall award a defendant reasonable attorney's fees and other expenses related to the defense of a claim filed against the defendant for damages or other relief arising from reporting or assisting in the investigation of a report under this chapter or participating in a judicial proceeding resulting from the report if:

(1) the court finds that the claim is frivolous, unreasonable, or without foundation because

the defendant is immune from liability under Section 261.106; and

(2) the claim is dismissed or judgment is rendered for the defendant.

(c) To recover under this section, the defendant must, at any time after the filing of a claim, file a written motion stating that:

(1) the claim is frivolous, unreasonable, or without foundation because the defendant is immune from liability under Section 261.106; and

(2) the defendant requests the court to award reasonable attorney's fees and other expenses related to the defense of the claim.
(Enacted by Acts 1995, 74th Leg., ch. 20 (H.B. 655), § 1, effective April 20, 1995.)

## Sec. 261.109. Failure to Report; Penalty.

(a) A person commits an offense if the person has cause to believe that a child's physical or mental health or welfare has been or may be adversely affected by abuse or neglect and knowingly fails to report as provided in this chapter.

(b) An offense under this section is a Class A misdemeanor, except that the offense is a state jail felony if it is shown on the trial of the offense that the child was a person with mental retardation who resided in a state supported living center, the ICF-MR component of the Rio Grande State Center, or a facility licensed under Chapter 252, Health and Safety Code, and the actor knew that the child had suffered serious bodily injury as a result of the abuse or neglect.
(Enacted by Acts 1995, 74th Leg., ch. 20 (H.B. 655), § 1, effective April 20, 1995; am. Acts 2009, 81st Leg., ch. 284 (S.B. 643), § 5, effective June 11, 2009.)

## Sec. 261.110. Employer Retaliation Prohibited.

(a) In this section, "professional" has the meaning assigned by Section 261.101(b).

(b) An employer may not suspend or terminate the employment of, or otherwise discriminate against, a person who is a professional and who in good faith:

(1) reports child abuse or neglect to:

(A) the person's supervisor;

(B) an administrator of the facility where the person is employed;

(C) a state regulatory agency; or

(D) a law enforcement agency; or

(2) initiates or cooperates with an investigation or proceeding by a governmental entity

relating to an allegation of child abuse or neglect.

(c) A person whose employment is suspended or terminated or who is otherwise discriminated against in violation of this section may sue for injunctive relief, damages, or both.

(d) A plaintiff who prevails in a suit under this section may recover:

(1) actual damages, including damages for mental anguish even if an injury other than mental anguish is not shown;

(2) exemplary damages under Chapter 41, Civil Practice and Remedies Code, if the employer is a private employer;

(3) court costs; and

(4) reasonable attorney's fees.

(e) In addition to amounts recovered under Subsection (d), a plaintiff who prevails in a suit under this section is entitled to:

(1) reinstatement to the person's former position or a position that is comparable in terms of compensation, benefits, and other conditions of employment;

(2) reinstatement of any fringe benefits and seniority rights lost because of the suspension, termination, or discrimination; and

(3) compensation for wages lost during the period of suspension or termination.

(f) A public employee who alleges a violation of this section may sue the employing state or local governmental entity for the relief provided for by this section. Sovereign immunity is waived and abolished to the extent of liability created by this section. A person having a claim under this section may sue a governmental unit for damages allowed by this section.

(g) In a suit under this section against an employing state or local governmental entity, a plaintiff may not recover compensatory damages for future pecuniary losses, emotional pain, suffering, inconvenience, mental anguish, loss of enjoyment of life, and other nonpecuniary losses in an amount that exceeds:

(1) $50,000, if the employing state or local governmental entity has fewer than 101 employees in each of 20 or more calendar weeks in the calendar year in which the suit is filed or in the preceding year;

(2) $100,000, if the employing state or local governmental entity has more than 100 and fewer than 201 employees in each of 20 or more calendar weeks in the calendar year in which the suit is filed or in the preceding year;

(3) $200,000, if the employing state or local governmental entity has more than 200 and fewer than 501 employees in each of 20 or more calendar weeks in the calendar year in which the suit is filed or in the preceding year; and

(4) $250,000, if the employing state or local governmental entity has more than 500 employees in each of 20 or more calendar weeks in the calendar year in which the suit is filed or in the preceding year.

(h) If more than one subdivision of Subsection (g) applies to an employing state or local governmental entity, the amount of monetary damages that may be recovered from the entity in a suit brought under this section is governed by the applicable provision that provides the highest damage award.

(i) A plaintiff suing under this section has the burden of proof, except that there is a rebuttable presumption that the plaintiff's employment was suspended or terminated or that the plaintiff was otherwise discriminated against for reporting abuse or neglect if the suspension, termination, or discrimination occurs before the 61st day after the date on which the person made a report in good faith.

(j) A suit under this section may be brought in a district or county court of the county in which:

(1) the plaintiff was employed by the defendant; or

(2) the defendant conducts business.

(k) It is an affirmative defense to a suit under Subsection (b) that an employer would have taken the action against the employee that forms the basis of the suit based solely on information, observation, or evidence that is not related to the fact that the employee reported child abuse or neglect or initiated or cooperated with an investigation or proceeding relating to an allegation of child abuse or neglect.

(*l*) A public employee who has a cause of action under Chapter 554, Government Code, based on conduct described by Subsection (b) may not bring an action based on that conduct under this section.

(m) This section does not apply to a person who reports the person's own abuse or neglect of a child or who initiates or cooperates with an investigation or proceeding by a governmental entity relating to an allegation of the person's own abuse or neglect of a child.

(Enacted by Acts 2001, 77th Leg., ch. 896 (H.B. 3476), § 1, effective September 1, 2001.)

### Sec. 261.111.  Refusal of Psychiatric or Psychological Treatment of Child.

(a) In this section, "psychotropic drug" means a substance that is:

Family Code

(1) used in the diagnosis, treatment, or prevention of a disease or as a component of a medication; and

(2) intended to have an altering effect on perception, emotion, or behavior.

(b) The refusal of a parent, guardian, or managing or possessory conservator of a child to administer or consent to the administration of a psychotropic drug to the child, or to consent to any other psychiatric or psychological treatment of the child, does not by itself constitute neglect of the child unless the refusal to consent:

(1) presents a substantial risk of death, disfigurement, or bodily injury to the child; or

(2) has resulted in an observable and material impairment to the growth, development, or functioning of the child.

(Enacted by Acts 2003, 78th Leg., ch. 1008 (H.B. 320), § 3, effective June 20, 2003.)

## SUBCHAPTER C
## CONFIDENTIALITY AND
## PRIVILEGED COMMUNICATION

### Sec. 261.201. Confidentiality and Disclosure of Information.

(a) Except as provided by Section 261.203, the following information is confidential, is not subject to public release under Chapter 552, Government Code, and may be disclosed only for purposes consistent with this code and applicable federal or state law or under rules adopted by an investigating agency:

(1) a report of alleged or suspected abuse or neglect made under this chapter and the identity of the person making the report; and

(2) except as otherwise provided in this section, the files, reports, records, communications, audiotapes, videotapes, and working papers used or developed in an investigation under this chapter or in providing services as a result of an investigation.

(b) A court may order the disclosure of information that is confidential under this section if:

(1) a motion has been filed with the court requesting the release of the information;

(2) a notice of hearing has been served on the investigating agency and all other interested parties; and

(3) after hearing and an in camera review of the requested information, the court determines that the disclosure of the requested information is:

(A) essential to the administration of justice; and

(B) not likely to endanger the life or safety of:

(i) a child who is the subject of the report of alleged or suspected abuse or neglect;

(ii) a person who makes a report of alleged or suspected abuse or neglect; or

(iii) any other person who participates in an investigation of reported abuse or neglect or who provides care for the child.

(b-1) On a motion of one of the parties in a contested case before an administrative law judge relating to the license or certification of a professional, as defined by Section 261.101(b), or an educator, as defined by Section 5.001, Education Code, the administrative law judge may order the disclosure of information that is confidential under this section that relates to the matter before the administrative law judge after a hearing for which notice is provided as required by Subsection (b)(2) and making the review and determination required by Subsection (b)(3). Before the department may release information under this subsection, the department must edit the information to protect the confidentiality of the identity of any person who makes a report of abuse or neglect.

(c) In addition to Subsection (b), a court, on its own motion, may order disclosure of information that is confidential under this section if:

(1) the order is rendered at a hearing for which all parties have been given notice;

(2) the court finds that disclosure of the information is:

(A) essential to the administration of justice; and

(B) not likely to endanger the life or safety of:

(i) a child who is the subject of the report of alleged or suspected abuse or neglect;

(ii) a person who makes a report of alleged or suspected abuse or neglect; or

(iii) any other person who participates in an investigation of reported abuse or neglect or who provides care for the child; and

(3) the order is reduced to writing or made on the record in open court.

(d) The adoptive parents of a child who was the subject of an investigation and an adult who was the subject of an investigation as a child are entitled to examine and make copies of any report, record, working paper, or other information in the possession, custody, or control of the state that pertains to the history of the child. The department may edit the documents to protect the identity of the biological parents and any other person whose identity is confidential, unless this information is already known to the adoptive parents or is readily available through other sources, including the court records of a suit to terminate the parent-child relationship under Chapter 161.

(e) Before placing a child who was the subject of an investigation, the department shall notify the prospective adoptive parents of their right to examine any report, record, working paper, or other information in the possession, custody, or control of the state that pertains to the history of the child.

(f) The department shall provide prospective adoptive parents an opportunity to examine information under this section as early as practicable before placing a child.

(f-1) The department shall provide to a relative or other individual with whom a child is placed any information the department considers necessary to ensure that the relative or other individual is prepared to meet the needs of the child. The information required by this subsection may include information related to any abuse or neglect suffered by the child.

(g) Notwithstanding Subsection (b), the department, on request and subject to department rule, shall provide to the parent, managing conservator, or other legal representative of a child who is the subject of reported abuse or neglect information concerning the reported abuse or neglect that would otherwise be confidential under this section if the department has edited the information to protect the confidentiality of the identity of the person who made the report and any other person whose life or safety may be endangered by the disclosure.

(h) This section does not apply to an investigation of child abuse or neglect in a home or facility regulated under Chapter 42, Human Resources Code.

(i) Notwithstanding Subsection (a), the Texas Youth Commission shall release a report of alleged or suspected abuse or neglect made under this chapter if:

(1) the report relates to a report of abuse or neglect involving a child committed to the commission during the period that the child is committed to the commission; and

(2) the commission is not prohibited by Chapter 552, Government Code, or other law from disclosing the report.

(j) The Texas Youth Commission shall edit any report disclosed under Subsection (i) to protect the identity of:

(1) a child who is the subject of the report of alleged or suspected abuse or neglect;

(2) the person who made the report; and

(3) any other person whose life or safety may be endangered by the disclosure.

(k) Notwithstanding Subsection (a), an investigating agency, other than the department or the Texas Youth Commission, on request, shall provide to the parent, managing conservator, or other legal representative of a child who is the subject of reported abuse or neglect, or to the child if the child is at least 18 years of age, information concerning the reported abuse or neglect that would otherwise be confidential under this section. The investigating agency shall withhold information under this subsection if the parent, managing conservator, or other legal representative of the child requesting the information is alleged to have committed the abuse or neglect.

(*l*) Before a child or a parent, managing conservator, or other legal representative of a child may inspect or copy a record or file concerning the child under Subsection (k), the custodian of the record or file must redact:

(1) any personally identifiable information about a victim or witness under 18 years of age unless that victim or witness is:

(A) the child who is the subject of the report; or

(B) another child of the parent, managing conservator, or other legal representative requesting the information;

(2) any information that is excepted from required disclosure under Chapter 552, Government Code, or other law; and

(3) the identity of the person who made the report.

(Enacted by Acts 1995, 74th Leg., ch. 20 (H.B. 655), § 1, effective April 20, 1995; am. Acts 1995, 74th Leg., ch. 751 (H.B. 433), § 93, effective September 1, 1995; am. Acts 1997, 75th Leg., ch. 575 (H.B. 1826), § 12, effective September 1, 1997; am. Acts 1997, 75th Leg., ch. 1022 (S.B. 359), § 69, effective September 1, 1997; am. Acts 1999, 76th Leg., ch. 1150 (H.B. 3838), § 3, effective September 1, 1999; am. Acts 1999, 76th Leg., ch. 1390 (H.B. 1622), § 22, effective September 1, 1999; am. Acts 2003, 78th Leg., ch. 68 (S.B. 579), § 2, effective September 1, 2003; am. Acts 2005, 79th Leg., ch. 268 (S.B. 6), § 1.15, effective September 1, 2005; am. Acts 2007, 80th Leg., ch. 263

(S.B. 103), § 12, effective June 8, 2007; am. Acts 2009, 81st Leg., ch. 713 (H.B. 2876), § 1, effective June 19, 2009; am. Acts 2009, 81st Leg., ch. 779 (S.B. 1050), § 1, effective September 1, 2009; am. Acts 2009, 81st Leg., ch. 1377 (S.B. 1182), § 13, effective September 1, 2009.)

## Sec. 261.202. Privileged Communication.

In a proceeding regarding the abuse or neglect of a child, evidence may not be excluded on the ground of privileged communication except in the case of communications between an attorney and client.

(Enacted by Acts 1995, 74th Leg., ch. 20 (H.B. 655), § 1, effective April 20, 1995.)

## Sec. 261.203. Information Relating to Child Fatality.

(a) Not later than the fifth day after the date the department receives a request for information about a child fatality with respect to which the department is conducting an investigation of alleged abuse or neglect, the department shall release:

(1) the age and sex of the child;

(2) the date of death;

(3) whether the state was the managing conservator of the child at the time of the child's death; and

(4) whether the child resided with the child's parent, managing conservator, guardian, or other person entitled to possession of the child at the time of the child's death.

(b) If, after a child abuse or neglect investigation is completed, the department determines a child's death was caused by abuse or neglect, the department shall promptly release the following information on request:

(1) the information described by Subsection (a), if not previously released to the person requesting the information;

(2) for cases in which the child's death occurred while the child was living with the child's parent, managing conservator, guardian, or other person entitled to possession of the child:

(A) a summary of any previous reports of abuse or neglect of the deceased child or another child made while the child was living with that parent, managing conservator, guardian, or other person entitled to possession of the child;

(B) the disposition of any report under Paragraph (A);

(C) a description of the services, if any, that were provided by the department to the child or the child's family as a result of any report under Paragraph (A); and

(D) the results of any risk or safety assessment completed by the department relating to the deceased child; and

(3) for a case in which the child's death occurred while the child was in substitute care with the department or with a residential child-care provider regulated under Chapter 42, Human Resources Code, the following information:

(A) the date the substitute care provider with whom the child was residing at the time of death was licensed or verified;

(B) a summary of any previous reports of abuse or neglect investigated by the department relating to the substitute care provider, including the disposition of any investigation resulting from a report;

(C) any reported licensing violations, including notice of any action taken by the department regarding a violation; and

(D) records of any training completed by the substitute care provider while the child was placed with the provider.

(c) If the department is unable to release the information required by Subsection (b) before the 11th day after the date the department receives a request for the information or the date the investigation of the child fatality is completed, whichever is later, the department shall inform the person requesting the information of the date the department will release the information.

(d) After receiving a request for information required by Subsection (b), the department shall notify and provide a copy of the request to the attorney ad litem for the deceased child, if any.

(e) Before the department releases any information under Subsection (b), the department shall redact from the records any information the release of which would:

(1) identify:

(A) the individual who reported the abuse or neglect; or

(B) any other individual other than the deceased child or an alleged perpetrator of the abuse or neglect;

(2) jeopardize an ongoing criminal investigation or prosecution;

(3) endanger the life or safety of any individual; or

(4) violate other state or federal law.

(f) The executive commissioner of the Health and Human Services Commission shall adopt rules to implement this section. (Enacted by Acts 2009, 81st Leg., ch. 779 (S.B. 1050), § 2, effective September 1, 2009.)

## SUBCHAPTER D
## INVESTIGATIONS

### Sec. 261.301. Investigation of Report.

(a) With assistance from the appropriate state or local law enforcement agency as provided by this section, the department or designated agency shall make a prompt and thorough investigation of a report of child abuse or neglect allegedly committed by a person responsible for a child's care, custody, or welfare. The investigation shall be conducted without regard to any pending suit affecting the parent-child relationship.

(b) A state agency shall investigate a report that alleges abuse or neglect occurred in a facility operated, licensed, certified, or registered by that agency as provided by Subchapter E. In conducting an investigation for a facility operated, licensed, certified, registered, or listed by the department, the department shall perform the investigation as provided by:

(1) Subchapter E; and

(2) the Human Resources Code.

(c) The department is not required to investigate a report that alleges child abuse or neglect by a person other than a person responsible for a child's care, custody, or welfare. The appropriate state or local law enforcement agency shall investigate that report if the agency determines an investigation should be conducted.

(d) The department shall by rule assign priorities and prescribe investigative procedures for investigations based on the severity and immediacy of the alleged harm to the child. The primary purpose of the investigation shall be the protection of the child. The rules must require the department, subject to the availability of funds, to:

(1) immediately respond to a report of abuse and neglect that involves circumstances in which the death of the child or substantial bodily harm to the child would result unless the department immediately intervenes;

(2) respond within 24 hours to a report of abuse and neglect that is assigned the highest priority, other than a report described by Subdivision (1); and

(3) respond within 72 hours to a report of abuse and neglect that is assigned the second highest priority.

(e) As necessary to provide for the protection of the child, the department or designated agency shall determine:

(1) the nature, extent, and cause of the abuse or neglect;

(2) the identity of the person responsible for the abuse or neglect;

(3) the names and conditions of the other children in the home;

(4) an evaluation of the parents or persons responsible for the care of the child;

(5) the adequacy of the home environment;

(6) the relationship of the child to the persons responsible for the care, custody, or welfare of the child; and

(7) all other pertinent data.

(f) An investigation of a report to the department that alleges that a child has been or may be the victim of conduct that constitutes a criminal offense that poses an immediate risk of physical or sexual abuse of a child that could result in the death of or serious harm to the child shall be conducted jointly by a peace officer, as defined by Article 2.12, Code of Criminal Procedure, from the appropriate local law enforcement agency and the department or the agency responsible for conducting an investigation under Subchapter E.

(g) The inability or unwillingness of a local law enforcement agency to conduct a joint investigation under this section does not constitute grounds to prevent or prohibit the department from performing its duties under this subtitle. The department shall document any instance in which a law enforcement agency is unable or unwilling to conduct a joint investigation under this section.

(h) The department and the appropriate local law enforcement agency shall conduct an investigation, other than an investigation under Subchapter E, as provided by this section and Article 2.27, Code of Criminal Procedure, if the investigation is of a report that alleges that a child has been or may be the victim of conduct that constitutes a criminal offense that poses an immediate risk of physical or sexual abuse of a child that could result in the death of or serious harm to the child. Immediately on receipt of a report described by this subsection, the department shall notify the appropriate local law enforcement agency of the report.

(Enacted by Acts 1995, 74th Leg., ch. 20 (H.B. 655), § 1, effective April 20, 1995; am. Acts 1995, 74th Leg., ch. 751 (H.B. 433), § 94, effective September 1, 1995; am. Acts 1995, 74th Leg., ch. 943 (H.B. 2569), § 2, effective September 1, 1995;

am. Acts 1997, 75th Leg., ch. 1022 (S.B. 359), § 70, effective September 1, 1997; am. Acts 1997, 75th Leg., ch. 1137 (H.B. 3345), § 1, effective September 1, 1997; am. Acts 1999, 76th Leg., ch. 1150 (H.B. 3838), § 4, effective September 1, 1999; am. Acts 1999, 76th Leg., ch. 1390 (H.B. 1622), § 23, effective September 1, 1999; am. Acts 2003, 78th Leg., ch. 867 (S.B. 669), § 1, effective September 1, 2003; am. Acts 2005, 79th Leg., ch. 268 (S.B. 6), § 1.16(a), effective September 1, 2005.)

### Sec. 261.3011.  Joint Investigation Guidelines and Training.

(a) The department shall, in consultation with the appropriate law enforcement agencies, develop guidelines and protocols for joint investigations by the department and the law enforcement agency under Section 261.301. The guidelines and protocols must:

(1) clarify the respective roles of the department and law enforcement agency in conducting the investigation;

(2) require that mutual child protective services and law enforcement training and agreements be implemented by both entities to ensure the integrity and best outcomes of joint investigations; and

(3) incorporate the use of forensic methods in determining the occurrence of child abuse and neglect.

(b) The department shall collaborate with law enforcement agencies to provide to department investigators and law enforcement officers responsible for investigating reports of abuse and neglect joint training relating to methods to effectively conduct joint investigations under Section 261.301. The training must include information on interviewing techniques, evidence gathering, and testifying in court for criminal investigations, as well as instruction on rights provided by the Fourth Amendment to the United States Constitution.

(Enacted by Acts 2005, 79th Leg., ch. 268 (S.B. 6), § 1.17, effective September 1, 2005.)

### Sec. 261.3012.  Completion of Paperwork.

An employee of the department who responds to a report that is assigned the highest priority in accordance with department rules adopted under Section 261.301(d) shall identify, to the extent reasonable under the circumstances, forms and other paperwork that can be completed by mem-

bers of the family of the child who is the subject of the report. The department employee shall request the assistance of the child's family members in completing that documentation but remains responsible for ensuring that the documentation is completed in an appropriate manner.

(Enacted by Acts 2005, 79th Leg., ch. 55 (H.B. 802), § 1, effective May 17, 2005; enacted by Acts 2005, 79th Leg., ch. 268 (S.B. 6), § 1.18, effective September 1, 2005.)

### Sec. 261.3013.  Case Closure Agreements Prohibited.

(a) Except as provided by Subsection (b), on closing a case, the department may not enter into a written agreement with a child's parent or another adult with whom the child resides that requires the parent or other adult to take certain actions after the case is closed to ensure the child's safety.

(b) This section does not apply to an agreement that is entered into by a parent or other adult:

(1) following the removal of a child and that is subject to the approval of a court with continuing jurisdiction over the child;

(2) as a result of the person's participation in family group conferencing; or

(3) as part of a formal case closure plan agreed to by the person who will continue to care for a child as a result of a parental child safety placement.

(c) The department shall develop policies to guide caseworkers in the development of case closure agreements authorized under Subsections (b)(2) and (3).

(Enacted by Acts 2011, 82nd Leg., ch. 598 (S.B. 218), § 1, effective September 1, 2011.)

### Sec. 261.3015.  Flexible Response System.

(a) In assigning priorities and prescribing investigative procedures based on the severity and immediacy of the alleged harm to a child under Section 261.301(d), the department shall establish a flexible response system to allow the department to make the most effective use of resources by investigating serious cases of abuse and neglect and by screening out less serious cases of abuse and neglect if the department determines, after contacting a professional or other credible source, that the child's safety can be assured without further investigation. The department may administratively close the less serious cases without providing services or making a referral to another entity for assistance.

(a-1) For purposes of Subsection (a), a case is considered to be a less serious case of abuse or neglect if the circumstances of the case do not indicate an immediate risk of abuse or neglect that could result in the death of or serious harm to the child who is the subject of the case.

(b) The classification under the flexible response system of a case may be changed as warranted by the circumstances.

(c) The department may implement the flexible response system by establishing a pilot program in a single department service region. The department shall study the results of the system in the region in determining the method by which to implement the system statewide.

(Enacted by Acts 1997, 75th Leg., ch. 1022 (S.B. 359), § 71, effective September 1, 1997; am. Acts 2005, 79th Leg., ch. 268 (S.B. 6), § 1.19(a), effective September 1, 2005.)

## Sec. 261.3016. Training of Personnel Receiving Reports of Abuse and Neglect.

The department shall develop, in cooperation with local law enforcement officials and the Commission on State Emergency Communications, a training program for department personnel who receive reports of abuse and neglect. The training program must include information on:

(1) the proper methods of screening reports of abuse and neglect; and

(2) ways to determine the seriousness of a report, including determining whether a report alleges circumstances that could result in the death of or serious harm to a child or whether the report is less serious in nature.

(Enacted by Acts 2005, 79th Leg., ch. 54 (H.B. 801), § 1, effective September 1, 2005; enacted by Acts 2005, 79th Leg., ch. 268 (S.B. 6), § 1.20, effective September 1, 2005.)

## Sec. 261.3019. Pilot Programs for Investigations of Child Abuse [Expired].

Expired pursuant to Acts 1997, 75th Leg., ch. 1022 (S.B. 359), § 72, effective September 1, 2001.

(Enacted by Acts 1997, 75th Leg., ch. 1022 (S.B. 359), § 72, effective September 1, 1997; am. Acts 1999, 76th Leg., ch. 907 (H.B. 2170), § 38, effective September 1, 1999.)

## Sec. 261.302. Conduct of Investigation.

(a) The investigation may include:

(1) a visit to the child's home, unless the alleged abuse or neglect can be confirmed or clearly ruled out without a home visit; and

(2) an interview with and examination of the subject child, which may include a medical, psychological, or psychiatric examination.

(b) The interview with and examination of the child may:

(1) be conducted at any reasonable time and place, including the child's home or the child's school;

(2) include the presence of persons the department or designated agency determines are necessary; and

(3) include transporting the child for purposes relating to the interview or investigation.

(b-1) Before the department may transport a child as provided by Subsection (b)(3), the department shall attempt to notify the parent or other person having custody of the child of the transport.

(c) The investigation may include an interview with the child's parents and an interview with and medical, psychological, or psychiatric examination of any child in the home.

(d) If, before an investigation is completed, the investigating agency believes that the immediate removal of a child from the child's home is necessary to protect the child from further abuse or neglect, the investigating agency shall file a petition or take other action under Chapter 262 to provide for the temporary care and protection of the child.

(e) An interview with a child conducted by the department during the investigation stage shall be audiotaped or videotaped. An interview with a child alleged to be a victim of physical abuse or sexual abuse conducted by an investigating agency other than the department shall be audiotaped or videotaped unless the investigating agency determines that good cause exists for not audiotaping or videotaping the interview in accordance with rules of the agency. Good cause may include, but is not limited to, such considerations as the age of the child and the nature and seriousness of the allegations under investigation. Nothing in this subsection shall be construed as prohibiting the investigating agency from audiotaping or videotaping an interview of a child on any case for which such audiotaping or videotaping is not required under this subsection. The fact that the investigating agency failed to audiotape or videotape an interview is admissible at the trial of the offense that is the subject of the interview.

(f) A person commits an offense if the person is notified of the time of the transport of a child by the department and the location from which the transport is initiated and the person is present at the location when the transport is initiated and attempts to interfere with the department's investigation. An offense under this subsection is a Class B misdemeanor. It is an exception to the application of this subsection that the department requested the person to be present at the site of the transport.

(Enacted by Acts 1995, 74th Leg., ch. 20 (H.B. 655), § 1, effective April 20, 1995; am. Acts 1995, 74th Leg., ch. 751 (H.B. 433), § 95, effective September 1, 1995; am. Acts 1997, 75th Leg., ch. 575 (H.B. 1826), §§ 13, 14, effective September 1, 1997; am. Acts 1997, 75th Leg., ch. 1022 (S.B. 359), § 73, effective September 1, 1997; am. Acts 2005, 79th Leg., ch. 268 (S.B. 6), § 1.21, effective September 1, 2005.)

### Sec. 261.3021.  Casework Documentation and Management.

Subject to the appropriation of money for these purposes, the department shall:

(1) identify critical investigation actions that impact child safety and require department caseworkers to document those actions in a child's case file not later than the day after the action occurs;

(2) identify and develop a comprehensive set of casework quality indicators that must be reported in real time to support timely management oversight;

(3) provide department supervisors with access to casework quality indicators and train department supervisors on the use of that information in the daily supervision of caseworkers;

(4) develop a case tracking system that notifies department supervisors and management when a case is not progressing in a timely manner;

(5) use current data reporting systems to provide department supervisors and management with easier access to information; and

(6) train department supervisors and management on the use of data to monitor cases and make decisions.

(Enacted by Acts 2005, 79th Leg., ch. 268 (S.B. 6), § 1.22, effective September 1, 2005.)

### Sec. 261.3022.  Child Safety Check Alert List.

(a) Subject to the availability of funds, the Department of Public Safety of the State of Texas shall create a child safety check alert list as part of the Texas Crime Information Center to help locate a family for purposes of investigating a report of child abuse or neglect.

(b) If the child safety check alert list is established and the department is unable to locate a family for purposes of investigating a report of child abuse or neglect, after the department has exhausted all means available to the department for locating the family, the department may seek assistance under this section from the appropriate county attorney, district attorney, or criminal district attorney with responsibility for representing the department as provided by Section 264.009.

(c) If the department requests assistance, the county attorney, district attorney, or criminal district attorney, as applicable, may file an application with the court requesting the issuance of an ex parte order requiring the Texas Crime Information Center to place the members of the family the department is attempting to locate on a child safety check alert list. The application must include a summary of:

(1) the report of child abuse or neglect the department is attempting to investigate; and

(2) the department's efforts to locate the family.

(d) If the court determines after a hearing that the department has exhausted all means available to the department for locating the family, the court shall approve the application and order the appropriate law enforcement agency to notify the Texas Crime Information Center to place the family on a child safety check alert list. The alert list must include:

(1) the name of the family member alleged to have abused or neglected a child according to the report the department is attempting to investigate;

(2) the name of the child who is the subject of the report;

(3) a code identifying the type of child abuse or neglect alleged to have been committed against the child;

(4) the family's last known address; and

(5) the minimum criteria for an entry as established by the center.

(Enacted by Acts 2005, 79th Leg., ch. 268 (S.B. 6), § 1.22, effective September 1, 2005.)

### Sec. 261.3023.  Law Enforcement Response to Child Safety Check Alert.

(a) If a law enforcement officer encounters a person listed on the Texas Crime Information

Center's child safety check alert list who is alleged to have abused or neglected a child, or encounters a child listed on the alert list who is the subject of a report of child abuse or neglect the department is attempting to investigate, the officer shall request information from the person or the child regarding the child's well-being and current residence.

(b) If the law enforcement officer determines that the circumstances described by Section 262.104 exist, the officer may take possession of the child without a court order as authorized by that section if the officer is able to locate the child. If the circumstances described by Section 262.104 do not exist, the officer shall obtain the child's current address and any other relevant information and report that information to the department.

(Enacted by Acts 2005, 79th Leg., ch. 268 (S.B. 6), § 1.22, effective September 1, 2005.)

## Sec. 261.3024. Removal from Child Safety Check Alert List.

(a) A law enforcement officer who locates a child listed on the Texas Crime Information Center's child safety check alert list who is the subject of a report of child abuse or neglect the department is attempting to investigate and who reports the child's current address and other relevant information to the department under Section 261.3023 shall report to the Texas Crime Information Center that the child has been located.

(b) If the department locates a child described by Subsection (a) through a means other than information reported by a law enforcement officer under Subsection (a), the department shall report to the Texas Crime Information Center that the child has been located.

(c) On receipt of notice under this section that a child has been located, the Texas Crime Information Center shall remove the child and the child's family from the child safety check alert list.

(Enacted by Acts 2005, 79th Leg., ch. 268 (S.B. 6), § 1.22, effective September 1, 2005.)

## Sec. 261.303. Interference with Investigation; Court Order.

(a) A person may not interfere with an investigation of a report of child abuse or neglect conducted by the department or designated agency.

(b) If admission to the home, school, or any place where the child may be cannot be obtained,

then for good cause shown the court having family law jurisdiction shall order the parent, the person responsible for the care of the children, or the person in charge of any place where the child may be to allow entrance for the interview, examination, and investigation.

(c) If a parent or person responsible for the child's care does not consent to release of the child's prior medical, psychological, or psychiatric records or to a medical, psychological, or psychiatric examination of the child that is requested by the department or designated agency, the court having family law jurisdiction shall, for good cause shown, order the records to be released or the examination to be made at the times and places designated by the court.

(d) A person, including a medical facility, that makes a report under Subchapter B shall release to the department or designated agency, as part of the required report under Section 261.103, records that directly relate to the suspected abuse or neglect without requiring parental consent or a court order. If a child is transferred from a reporting medical facility to another medical facility to treat the injury or condition that formed the basis for the original report, the transferee medical facility shall, at the department's request, release to the department records relating to the injury or condition without requiring parental consent or a court order.

(e) A person, including a utility company, that has confidential locating or identifying information regarding a family that is the subject of an investigation under this chapter shall release that information to the department on request. The release of information to the department as required by this subsection by a person, including a utility company, is not subject to Section 552.352, Government Code, or any other law providing liability for the release of confidential information.

(Enacted by Acts 1995, 74th Leg., ch. 20 (H.B. 655), § 1, effective April 20, 1995; am. Acts 1995, 74th Leg., ch. 751 (H.B. 433), § 96, effective September 1, 1995; am. Acts 1999, 76th Leg., ch. 1150 (H.B. 3838), § 5, effective September 1, 1999; am. Acts 1999, 76th Leg., ch. 1390 (H.B. 1622), § 24, effective September 1, 1999; am. Acts 2007, 80th Leg., ch. 1406 (S.B. 758), § 6, effective September 1, 2007.)

## Sec. 261.3031. Failure to Cooperate with Investigation; Department Response.

(a) If a parent or other person refuses to cooperate with the department's investigation of the alleged abuse or neglect of a child and the refusal poses a risk to the child's safety, the department shall seek assistance from the appropriate county attorney or district attorney or criminal district attorney with responsibility for representing the department as provided by Section 264.009 to obtain a court order as described by Section 261.303.

(b) A person's failure to report to an agency authorized to investigate abuse or neglect of a child within a reasonable time after receiving proper notice constitutes a refusal by the person to cooperate with the department's investigation. A summons may be issued to locate the person.

(Enacted by Acts 2005, 79th Leg., ch. 268 (S.B. 6), § 1.23, effective September 1, 2005; am. Acts 2007, 80th Leg., ch. 1406 (S.B. 758), § 7, effective September 1, 2007.)

## Sec. 261.3032.  Interference with Investigation; Criminal Penalty.

(a) A person commits an offense if, with the intent to interfere with the department's investigation of a report of abuse or neglect of a child, the person relocates the person's residence, either temporarily or permanently, without notifying the department of the address of the person's new residence or conceals the child and the person's relocation or concealment interferes with the department's investigation.

(b) An offense under this section is a Class B misdemeanor.

(c) If conduct that constitutes an offense under this section also constitutes an offense under any other law, the actor may be prosecuted under this section or the other law.

(Enacted by Acts 2005, 79th Leg., ch. 268 (S.B. 6), § 1.24, effective September 1, 2005.)

## Sec. 261.304.  Investigation of Anonymous Report.

(a) If the department receives an anonymous report of child abuse or neglect by a person responsible for a child's care, custody, or welfare, the department shall conduct a preliminary investigation to determine whether there is any evidence to corroborate the report.

(b) An investigation under this section may include a visit to the child's home and an interview with and examination of the child and an interview with the child's parents. In addition, the department may interview any other person the department believes may have relevant information.

(c) Unless the department determines that there is some evidence to corroborate the report of abuse, the department may not conduct the thorough investigation required by this chapter or take any action against the person accused of abuse.

(Enacted by Acts 1995, 74th Leg., ch. 20 (H.B. 655), § 1, effective April 20, 1995.)

## Sec. 261.305.  Access to Mental Health Records.

(a) An investigation may include an inquiry into the possibility that a parent or a person responsible for the care of a child who is the subject of a report under Subchapter B has a history of medical or mental illness.

(b) If the parent or person does not consent to an examination or allow the department or designated agency to have access to medical or mental health records requested by the department or agency, the court having family law jurisdiction, for good cause shown, shall order the examination to be made or that the department or agency be permitted to have access to the records under terms and conditions prescribed by the court.

(c) If the court determines that the parent or person is indigent, the court shall appoint an attorney to represent the parent or person at the hearing. The fees for the appointed attorney shall be paid as provided by Chapter 107.

(d) A parent or person responsible for the child's care is entitled to notice and a hearing when the department or designated agency seeks a court order to allow a medical, psychological, or psychiatric examination or access to medical or mental health records.

(e) This access does not constitute a waiver of confidentiality.

(Enacted by Acts 1995, 74th Leg., ch. 20 (H.B. 655), § 1, effective April 20, 1995; am. Acts 1997, 75th Leg., ch. 575 (H.B. 1826), § 15, effective September 1, 1997; am. Acts 1999, 76th Leg., ch. 1150 (H.B. 3838), § 6, effective September 1, 1999; am. Acts 1999, 76th Leg., ch. 1390 (H.B. 1622), § 25, effective September 1, 1999.)

## Sec. 261.306.  Removal of Child from State.

(a) If the department or designated agency has reason to believe that a person responsible for the care, custody, or welfare of the child may remove the child from the state before the investigation is completed, the department or designated agency may file an application for a temporary restraining order in a district court without regard to continuing jurisdiction of the child as provided in Chapter 155.

(b) The court may render a temporary restraining order prohibiting the person from removing the child from the state pending completion of the investigation if the court:

(1) finds that the department or designated agency has probable cause to conduct the investigation; and

(2) has reason to believe that the person may remove the child from the state.

(Enacted by Acts 1995, 74th Leg., ch. 20 (H.B. 655), § 1, effective April 20, 1995.)

## Sec. 261.307. Information Relating to Investigation Procedure.

(a) As soon as possible after initiating an investigation of a parent or other person having legal custody of a child, the department shall provide to the person:

(1) a summary that:

(A) is brief and easily understood;

(B) is written in a language that the person understands, or if the person is illiterate, is read to the person in a language that the person understands; and

(C) contains the following information:

(i) the department's procedures for conducting an investigation of alleged child abuse or neglect, including:

(a) a description of the circumstances under which the department would request to remove the child from the home through the judicial system; and

(b) an explanation that the law requires the department to refer all reports of alleged child abuse or neglect to a law enforcement agency for a separate determination of whether a criminal violation occurred;

(ii) the person's right to file a complaint with the department or to request a review of the findings made by the department in the investigation;

(iii) the person's right to review all records of the investigation unless the review would jeopardize an ongoing criminal investigation or the child's safety;

(iv) the person's right to seek legal counsel;

(v) references to the statutory and regulatory provisions governing child abuse

and neglect and how the person may obtain copies of those provisions; and

(vi) the process the person may use to acquire access to the child if the child is removed from the home;

(2) if the department determines that removal of the child may be warranted, a proposed child placement resources form that:

(A) instructs the parent or other person having legal custody of the child to:

(i) complete and return the form to the department or agency; and

(ii) identify in the form three individuals who could be relative caregivers or designated caregivers, as those terms are defined by Section 264.751; and

(B) informs the parent or other person of a location that is available to the parent or other person to submit the information in the form 24 hours a day either in person or by facsimile machine or e-mail; and

(3) an informational manual required by Section 261.3071.

(b) The child placement resources form described by Subsection (a)(2) must include information on the periods of time by which the department must complete a background check.
(Enacted by Acts 1995, 74th Leg., ch. 20 (H.B. 655), § 1, effective April 20, 1995; am. Acts 2005, 79th Leg., ch. 268 (S.B. 6), § 1.25(a), effective September 1, 2005.)

## Sec. 261.3071. Informational Manuals.

(a) In this section:

(1) "Designated caregiver" and "relative caregiver" have the meanings assigned those terms by Section 264.751.

(2) "Voluntary caregiver" means a person who voluntarily agrees to provide temporary care for a child:

(A) who is the subject of an investigation by the department or whose parent, managing conservator, possessory conservator, guardian, caretaker, or custodian is receiving family-based safety services from the department;

(B) who is not in the conservatorship of the department; and

(C) who is placed in the care of the person by the parent or other person having legal custody of the child.

(b) The department shall develop and publish informational manuals that provide information for:

(1) a parent or other person having custody of a child who is the subject of an investigation under this chapter;

(2) a person who is selected by the department to be the child's relative or designated caregiver; and

(3) a voluntary caregiver.

(c) Information provided in the manuals must be in both English and Spanish and must include, as appropriate:

(1) useful indexes of information such as telephone numbers;

(2) the information required to be provided under Section 261.307(a)(1);

(3) information describing the rights and duties of a relative or designated caregiver;

(4) information regarding the relative and other designated caregiver program under Subchapter I, Chapter 264; and

(5) information regarding the role of a voluntary caregiver, including information on how to obtain any documentation necessary to provide for a child's needs.

(Enacted by Acts 2005, 79th Leg., ch. 268 (S.B. 6), § 1.26, effective September 1, 2005; am. Acts 2009, 81st Leg., ch. 825 (S.B. 1723), § 1, effective June 19, 2009.)

## Sec. 261.308. Submission of Investigation Report.

(a) The department or designated agency shall make a complete written report of the investigation.

(b) If sufficient grounds for filing a suit exist, the department or designated agency shall submit the report, together with recommendations, to the court, the district attorney, and the appropriate law enforcement agency.

(c) On receipt of the report and recommendations, the court may direct the department or designated agency to file a petition requesting appropriate relief as provided in this title.

(d) The department shall release information regarding a person alleged to have committed abuse or neglect to persons who have control over the person's access to children, including, as appropriate, the Texas Education Agency, the State Board for Educator Certification, the local school board or the school's governing body, the superintendent of the school district, or the school principal or director if the department determines that:

(1) he person alleged to have committed abuse or neglect poses a substantial and imme-

diate risk of harm to one or more children outside the family of a child who is the subject of the investigation; and

(2) the release of the information is necessary to assist in protecting one or more children from the person alleged to have committed abuse or neglect.

(e) On request, the department shall release information about a person alleged to have committed abuse or neglect to the State Board for Educator Certification if the board has a reasonable basis for believing that the information is necessary to assist the board in protecting children from the person alleged to have committed abuse or neglect.

(Enacted by Acts 1995, 74th Leg., ch. 20 (H.B. 655), § 1, effective April 20, 1995; am. Acts 1995, 74th Leg., ch. 751 (H.B. 433), § 97, effective September 1, 1995; am. Acts 2007, 80th Leg., ch. 1372 (S.B. 9), § 13, effective June 15, 2007.)

## Sec. 261.309. Review of Department Investigations.

(a) The department shall by rule establish policies and procedures to resolve complaints relating to and conduct reviews of child abuse or neglect investigations conducted by the department.

(b) If a person under investigation for allegedly abusing or neglecting a child requests clarification of the status of the person's case or files a complaint relating to the conduct of the department's staff or to department policy, the department shall conduct an informal review to clarify the person's status or resolve the complaint. The immediate supervisor of the employee who conducted the child abuse or neglect investigation or against whom the complaint was filed shall conduct the informal review as soon as possible but not later than the 14th day after the date the request or complaint is received.

(c) If, after the department's investigation, the person who is alleged to have abused or neglected a child disputes the department's determination of whether child abuse or neglect occurred, the person may request an administrative review of the findings. A department employee in administration who was not involved in or did not directly supervise the investigation shall conduct the review. The review must sustain, alter, or reverse the department's original findings in the investigation.

(d) Unless a civil or criminal court proceeding or an ongoing criminal investigation relating to the alleged abuse or neglect investigated by the department is pending, the department employee shall conduct the review prescribed by Subsection (c) as soon as possible but not later than the 45th day after the date the department receives the request. If a civil or criminal court proceeding or an ongoing criminal investigation is pending, the department may postpone the review until the court proceeding is completed.

(e) A person is not required to exhaust the remedies provided by this section before pursuing a judicial remedy provided by law.

(f) This section does not provide for a review of an order rendered by a court.

(Enacted by Acts 1995, 74th Leg., ch. 20 (H.B. 655), § 1, effective April 20, 1995.)

## Sec. 261.310. Investigation Standards.

(a) The department shall by rule develop and adopt standards for persons who investigate suspected child abuse or neglect at the state or local level. The standards shall encourage professionalism and consistency in the investigation of suspected child abuse or neglect.

(b) The standards must provide for a minimum number of hours of annual professional training for interviewers and investigators of suspected child abuse or neglect.

(c) The professional training curriculum developed under this section shall include:

(1) information concerning:

(A) physical abuse and neglect, including distinguishing physical abuse from ordinary childhood injuries;

(B) psychological abuse and neglect;

(C) available treatment resources; and

(D) the incidence and types of reports of child abuse and neglect that are received by the investigating agencies, including information concerning false reports;

(2) law-enforcement-style training, including training relating to forensic interviewing and investigatory techniques and the collection of physical evidence; and

(3) training regarding applicable federal law, including the Adoption and Safe Families Act of 1997 (Pub. L. No. 105-89) and the Child Abuse Prevention and Treatment Act (Pub. L. No. 93-247) and its subsequent amendments by the Keeping Children and Families Safe Act of 2003 (Pub. L. No. 108-36).

(d) The standards shall:

(1) recommend that videotaped and audiotaped interviews be uninterrupted;

(2) recommend a maximum number of interviews with and examinations of a suspected victim;

(3) provide procedures to preserve evidence, including the original recordings of the intake telephone calls, original notes, videotapes, and audiotapes, for one year; and

(4) provide that an investigator of suspected child abuse or neglect make a reasonable effort to locate and inform each parent of a child of any report of abuse or neglect relating to the child.

(e) The department, in conjunction with the Department of Public Safety, shall provide to the department's residential child-care facility licensing investigators advanced training in investigative protocols and techniques.

(Enacted by Acts 1995, 74th Leg., ch. 20 (H.B. 655), § 1, effective April 20, 1995; am. Acts 2005, 79th Leg., ch. 268 (S.B. 6), § 1.27, effective September 1, 2005.)

## Sec. 261.3101. Forensic Investigation Support.

The department shall, subject to the availability of money:

(1) employ or contract with medical and law enforcement professionals who shall be strategically placed throughout the state to provide forensic investigation support and to assist caseworkers with assessment decisions and intervention activities;

(2) employ or contract with subject matter experts to serve as consultants to department caseworkers in all aspects of their duties; and

(3) designate persons who shall act as liaisons within the department whose primary functions are to develop relationships with local law enforcement agencies and courts.

(Enacted by Acts 2005, 79th Leg., ch. 268 (S.B. 6), § 1.28, effective September 1, 2005.)

## Sec. 261.311. Notice of Report.

(a) When during an investigation of a report of suspected child abuse or neglect a representative of the department or the designated agency conducts an interview with or an examination of a child, the department or designated agency shall make a reasonable effort before 24 hours after the time of the interview or examination to notify each parent of the child and the child's legal guardian, if one has been appointed, of the nature of the allegation and of the fact that the interview or examination was conducted.

Family Code

(b) If a report of suspected child abuse or neglect is administratively closed by the department or designated agency as a result of a preliminary investigation that did not include an interview or examination of the child, the department or designated agency shall make a reasonable effort before the expiration of 24 hours after the time the investigation is closed to notify each parent and legal guardian of the child of the disposition of the investigation.

(c) The notice required by Subsection (a) or (b) is not required if the department or agency determines that the notice is likely to endanger the safety of the child who is the subject of the report, the person who made the report, or any other person who participates in the investigation of the report.

(d) The notice required by Subsection (a) or (b) may be delayed at the request of a law enforcement agency if notification during the required time would interfere with an ongoing criminal investigation.

(Enacted by Acts 1995, 74th Leg., ch. 20 (H.B. 655), § 1, effective April 20, 1995; am. Acts 1997, 75th Leg., ch. 1022 (S.B. 359), § 74, effective September 1, 1997.)

## Sec. 261.312. Review Teams; Offense.

(a) The department shall establish review teams to evaluate department casework and decision-making related to investigations by the department of child abuse or neglect. The department may create one or more review teams for each region of the department for child protective services. A review team is a citizen review panel or a similar entity for the purposes of federal law relating to a state's child protection standards.

(b) A review team consists of at least five members who serve staggered two-year terms. Review team members are appointed by the director of the department and consist of volunteers who live in and are broadly representative of the region in which the review team is established and have expertise in the prevention and treatment of child abuse and neglect. At least two members of a review team must be parents who have not been convicted of or indicted for an offense involving child abuse or neglect, have not been determined by the department to have engaged in child abuse or neglect, and are not under investigation by the department for child abuse or neglect. A member of a review team is a department volunteer for the purposes of Section 411.114, Government Code.

(c) A review team conducting a review of an investigation may conduct the review by examining the facts of the case as outlined by the department caseworker and law enforcement personnel. A review team member acting in the member's official capacity may receive information made confidential under Section 40.005, Human Resources Code, or Section 261.201.

(d) A review team shall report to the department the results of the team's review of an investigation. The review team's report may not include confidential information. The findings contained in a review team's report are subject to disclosure under Chapter 552, Government Code. This section does not require a law enforcement agency to divulge information to a review team that the agency believes would compromise an ongoing criminal case, investigation, or proceeding.

(e) A member of a review team commits an offense if the member discloses confidential information. An offense under this subsection is a Class C misdemeanor.

(Enacted by Acts 1995, 74th Leg., ch. 943 (H.B. 2569), § 3, effective September 1, 1995; am. Acts 1997, 75th Leg., ch. 575 (H.B. 1826), § 16, effective September 1, 1997; am. Acts 2009, 81st Leg., ch. 1372 (S.B. 939), § 3, effective June 19, 2009.)

## Sec. 261.3125. Child Safety Specialists.

(a) The department shall employ in each of the department's administrative regions at least one child safety specialist. The job responsibilities of the child safety specialist must focus on child abuse and neglect investigation issues, including reports of child abuse required by Section 261.101, to achieve a greater compliance with that section, and on assessing and improving the effectiveness of the department in providing for the protection of children in the region.

(b) The duties of a child safety specialist must include the duty to:

(1) conduct staff reviews and evaluations of cases determined to involve a high risk to the health or safety of a child, including cases of abuse reported under Section 261.101, to ensure that risk assessment tools are fully and correctly used;

(2) review and evaluate cases in which there have been multiple referrals to the department of child abuse or neglect involving the same family, child, or person alleged to have committed the abuse or neglect; and

(3) approve decisions and assessments related to investigations of cases of child abuse or neglect that involve a high risk to the health or safety of a child.

(Enacted by Acts 1999, 76th Leg., ch. 1490 (H.B. 3778), § 1, effective September 1, 1999; am. Acts 2005, 79th Leg., ch. 268 (S.B. 6), § 1.29, effective September 1, 2005.)

### Sec. 261.3126. Colocation of Investigators.

(a) In each county, to the extent possible, the department and the local law enforcement agencies that investigate child abuse in the county shall colocate in the same offices investigators from the department and the law enforcement agencies to improve the efficiency of child abuse investigations. With approval of the local children's advocacy center and its partner agencies, in each county in which a children's advocacy center established under Section 264.402 is located, the department shall attempt to locate investigators from the department and county and municipal law enforcement agencies at the center.

(b) A law enforcement agency is not required to comply with the colocation requirements of this section if the law enforcement agency does not have a full-time peace officer solely assigned to investigate reports of child abuse and neglect.

(c) If a county does not have a children's advocacy center, the department shall work with the local community to encourage one as provided by Section 264.402.

(Enacted by Acts 2005, 79th Leg., ch. 268 (S.B. 6), § 1.30, effective September 1, 2005.)

### Sec. 261.314. Testing.

(a) The department shall provide testing as necessary for the welfare of a child who the department believes, after an investigation under this chapter, has been sexually abused, including human immunodeficiency virus (HIV) testing of a child who was abused in a manner by which HIV may be transmitted.

(b) Except as provided by Subsection (c), the results of a test under this section are confidential.

(c) If requested, the department shall report the results of a test under this section to:

(1) a court having jurisdiction of a proceeding involving the child or a proceeding involving a person suspected of abusing the child;

(2) a person responsible for the care and custody of the child as a foster parent; and

(3) a person seeking to adopt the child.

(Enacted by Acts 1995, 74th Leg., ch. 943 (H.B. 2569), § 7, effective September 1, 1995.)

### Sec. 261.315. Removal of Certain Investigation Information from Records.

(a) At the conclusion of an investigation in which the department determines that the person alleged to have abused or neglected a child did not commit abuse or neglect, the department shall notify the person of the person's right to request the department to remove information about the person's alleged role in the abuse or neglect report from the department's records.

(b) On request under Subsection (a) by a person whom the department has determined did not commit abuse or neglect, the department shall remove information from the department's records concerning the person's alleged role in the abuse or neglect report.

(c) The board shall adopt rules necessary to administer this section.

(Enacted by Acts 1997, 75th Leg., ch. 1022 (S.B. 359), § 75, effective September 1, 1997.)

### Sec. 261.316. Exemption from Fees for Medical Records.

The department is exempt from the payment of a fee otherwise required or authorized by law to obtain a medical record from a hospital or health care provider if the request for a record is made in the course of an investigation by the department.

(Enacted by Acts 1997, 75th Leg., ch. 575 (H.B. 1826), § 17, effective September 1, 1997; am. Acts 1999, 76th Leg., ch. 62 (S.B. 1368), § 19.01(27), effective September 1, 1999 (renumbered from Sec. 261.315).)

### SUBCHAPTER E
### INVESTIGATIONS OF ABUSE, NEGLECT, OR EXPLOITATION IN CERTAIN FACILITIES

### Sec. 261.401. Agency Investigation.

(a) Notwithstanding Section 261.001, in this section:

(1) "Abuse" means an intentional, knowing, or reckless act or omission by an employee, volunteer, or other individual working under the auspices of a facility or program that causes or may cause emotional harm or physical injury to, or the death of, a child served by the facility or program as further described by rule or policy.

(2) "Exploitation" means the illegal or improper use of a child or of the resources of a child for monetary or personal benefit, profit, or gain by an employee, volunteer, or other individual working under the auspices of a facility or program as further described by rule or policy.

(3) "Neglect" means a negligent act or omission by an employee, volunteer, or other individual working under the auspices of a facility or program, including failure to comply with an individual treatment plan, plan of care, or individualized service plan, that causes or may cause substantial emotional harm or physical injury to, or the death of, a child served by the facility or program as further described by rule or policy.

(b) **[2 Versions: As amended by Acts 2009, 81st Leg., ch. 284]** Except as provided by Section 261.404, a state agency that operates, licenses, certifies, or registers a facility in which children are located or provides oversight of a program that serves children shall make a prompt, thorough investigation of a report that a child has been or may be abused, neglected, or exploited in the facility or program. The primary purpose of the investigation shall be the protection of the child.

(b) **[2 Versions: As amended by Acts 2009, 81st Leg., ch. 720]** A state agency that operates, licenses, certifies, registers, or lists a facility in which children are located or provides oversight of a program that serves children shall make a prompt, thorough investigation of a report that a child has been or may be abused, neglected, or exploited in the facility or program. The primary purpose of the investigation shall be the protection of the child.

(c) A state agency shall adopt rules relating to the investigation and resolution of reports received as provided by this subchapter. The Health and Human Services Commission shall review and approve the rules of agencies other than the Texas Department of Criminal Justice, Texas Youth Commission, or Texas Juvenile Probation Commission to ensure that those agencies implement appropriate standards for the conduct of investigations and that uniformity exists among agencies in the investigation and resolution of reports.

(d) The Texas School for the Blind and Visually Impaired and the Texas School for the Deaf shall adopt policies relating to the investigation and resolution of reports received as provided by this subchapter. The Health and Human Services

Commission shall review and approve the policies to ensure that the Texas School for the Blind and Visually Impaired and the Texas School for the Deaf adopt those policies in a manner consistent with the minimum standards adopted by the Health and Human Services Commission under Section 261.407.

(Enacted by Acts 1995, 74th Leg., ch. 20 (H.B. 655), § 1, effective April 20, 1995; am. Acts 1995, 74th Leg., ch. 751 (H.B. 433), § 98, effective September 1, 1995; am. Acts 2001, 77th Leg., ch. 355 (S.B. 664), § 2, effective September 1, 2001; am. Acts 2007, 80th Leg., ch. 908 (H.B. 2884), § 29, effective September 1, 2007; am. Acts 2009, 81st Leg., ch. 284 (S.B. 643), § 6, effective June 11, 2009; am. Acts 2009, 81st Leg., ch. 720 (S.B. 68), § 18, effective September 1, 2009.)

### Sec. 261.402.   Investigative Reports.

(a) A state agency shall prepare and keep on file a complete written report of each investigation conducted by the agency under this subchapter.

(b) A state agency shall immediately notify the appropriate state or local law enforcement agency of any report the agency receives, other than a report from a law enforcement agency, that concerns the suspected abuse, neglect, or exploitation of a child or the death of a child from abuse or neglect. If the state agency finds evidence indicating that a child may have been abused, neglected, or exploited, the agency shall report the evidence to the appropriate law enforcement agency.

(c) A state agency that licenses, certifies, or registers a facility in which children are located shall compile, maintain, and make available statistics on the incidence of child abuse, neglect, and exploitation in the facility.

(d) A state agency shall compile, maintain, and make available statistics on the incidence of child abuse, neglect, and exploitation in a facility operated by the state agency.

(Enacted by Acts 1995, 74th Leg., ch. 20 (H.B. 655), § 1, effective April 20, 1995; am. Acts 1995, 74th Leg., ch. 751 (H.B. 433), § 99, effective September 1, 1995; am. Acts 2001, 77th Leg., ch. 355 (S.B. 664), § 3, effective September 1, 2001.)

### Sec. 261.403.   Complaints.

(a) If a state agency receives a complaint relating to an investigation conducted by the agency concerning a facility operated by that agency in which children are located, the agency shall refer the complaint to the agency's board.

Family Code

(b) The board of a state agency that operates a facility in which children are located shall ensure that the procedure for investigating abuse, neglect, and exploitation allegations and inquiries in the agency's facility is periodically reviewed under the agency's internal audit program required by Chapter 2102, Government Code.

(Enacted by Acts 1995, 74th Leg., ch. 20 (H.B. 655), § 1, effective April 20, 1995; am. Acts 2001, 77th Leg., ch. 355 (S.B. 664), § 4, effective September 1, 2001.)

### Sec. 261.404. Investigations Regarding Certain Children with Mental Illness or Mental Retardation.

(a) The department shall investigate a report of abuse, neglect, or exploitation of a child receiving services:

(1) in a facility operated by the Department of Aging and Disability Services or a mental health facility operated by the Department of State Health Services;

(2) in or from a community center, a local mental health authority, or a local mental retardation authority;

(3) through a program providing services to that child by contract with a facility operated by the Department of Aging and Disability Services, a mental health facility operated by the Department of State Health Services, a community center, a local mental health authority, or a local mental retardation authority;

(4) from a provider of home and community-based services who contracts with the Department of Aging and Disability Services; or

(5) in a facility licensed under Chapter 252, Health and Safety Code.

(b) The department shall investigate the report under rules developed by the executive commissioner of the Health and Human Services Commission with the advice and assistance of the department, the Department of Aging and Disability Services, and the Department of State Health Services.

(c) If a report under this section relates to a child with mental retardation receiving services in a state supported living center or the ICF-MR component of the Rio Grande State Center, the department shall, within one hour of receiving the report, notify the facility in which the child is receiving services of the allegations in the report.

(d) If during the course of the department's investigation of reported abuse, neglect, or exploitation a caseworker of the department or the caseworker's supervisor has cause to believe that a child with mental retardation described by Subsection (c) has been abused, neglected, or exploited by another person in a manner that constitutes a criminal offense under any law, including Section 22.04, Penal Code, the caseworker shall immediately notify the Health and Human Services Commission's office of inspector general and promptly provide the commission's office of inspector general with a copy of the department's investigation report.

(e) The definitions of "abuse" and "neglect" prescribed by Section 261.001 do not apply to an investigation under this section.

(f) In this section:

(1) "Community center," "local mental health authority," "local mental retardation authority," and "state supported living center" have the meanings assigned by Section 531.002, Health and Safety Code.

(2) "Provider" has the meaning assigned by Section 48.351, Human Resources Code.

(Enacted by Acts 1995, 74th Leg., ch. 751 (H.B. 433), § 100, effective September 1, 1995; am. Acts 1999, 76th Leg., ch. 907 (H.B. 2170), § 39, effective September 1, 1999; am. Acts 2009, 81st Leg., ch. 284 (S.B. 643), § 7, effective June 11, 2009.)

### Sec. 261.405. Investigations in Juvenile Justice Programs and Facilities.

(a) In this section:

(1) "Juvenile justice facility" means a facility operated wholly or partly by the juvenile board, by another governmental unit, or by a private vendor under a contract with the juvenile board, county, or other governmental unit that serves juveniles under juvenile court jurisdiction. The term includes:

(A) a public or private juvenile pre-adjudication secure detention facility, including a holdover facility;

(B) a public or private juvenile post-adjudication secure correctional facility except for a facility operated solely for children committed to the Texas Youth Commission; and

(C) a public or private non-secure juvenile post-adjudication residential treatment facility that is not licensed by the Department of Protective and Regulatory Services or the Texas Commission on Alcohol and Drug Abuse.

(2) "Juvenile justice program" means a program or department operated wholly or partly by the juvenile board or by a private vendor

Family Code

under a contract with a juvenile board that serves juveniles under juvenile court jurisdiction. The term includes:

 (A) a juvenile justice alternative education program;

 (B) a non-residential program that serves juvenile offenders under the jurisdiction of the juvenile court; and

 (C) a juvenile probation department.

(b) A report of alleged abuse, neglect, or exploitation in any juvenile justice program or facility shall be made to the Texas Juvenile Probation Commission and a local law enforcement agency for investigation.

(c) The Texas Juvenile Probation Commission shall conduct an investigation as provided by this chapter if the commission receives a report of alleged abuse, neglect, or exploitation in any juvenile justice program or facility.

(d) In an investigation required under this section, the investigating agency shall have access to medical and mental health records as provided by Subchapter D.

(e) As soon as practicable after a child is taken into custody or placed in a juvenile justice facility or juvenile justice program, the facility or program shall provide the child's parents with:

 (1) information regarding the reporting of suspected abuse, neglect, or exploitation of a child in a juvenile justice facility or juvenile justice program to the Texas Juvenile Probation Commission; and

 (2) the commission's toll-free number for this reporting.

(Enacted by Acts 1995, 74th Leg., ch. 751 (H.B. 433), § 100, effective September 1, 1995; am. Acts 1997, 75th Leg., ch. 162 (H.B. 1929), § 2, effective September 1, 1997; am. Acts 1997, 75th Leg., ch. 1374 (H.B. 1230), § 8, effective September 1, 1997; am. Acts 1999, 76th Leg., ch. 1150 (H.B. 3838), § 7, effective September 1, 1999; am. Acts 1999, 76th Leg., ch. 1390 (H.B. 1622), § 26, effective September 1, 1999; am. Acts 1999, 76th Leg., ch. 1477 (H.B. 3517), § 26, effective September 1, 1999; am. Acts 2001, 77th Leg., ch. 1297 (H.B. 1118), § 47, effective September 1, 2001; am. Acts 2003, 78th Leg., ch. 283 (H.B. 2319), § 29, effective September 1, 2003; am. Acts 2005, 79th Leg., ch. 949 (H.B. 1575), § 28, effective September 1, 2005; am. Acts 2007, 80th Leg., ch. 908 (H.B. 2884), § 30, effective September 1, 2007.)

## Sec. 261.406. Investigations in Schools.

(a) On receipt of a report of alleged or suspected abuse or neglect of a child in a public or private school under the jurisdiction of the Texas Education Agency, the department shall perform an investigation as provided by this chapter.

(b) The department shall send a copy of the completed report of the department's investigation to the Texas Education Agency, the State Board for Educator Certification, the local school board or the school's governing body, the superintendent of the school district, and the school principal or director, unless the principal or director is alleged to have committed the abuse or neglect, for appropriate action. On request, the department shall provide a copy of the report of investigation to the parent, managing conservator, or legal guardian of a child who is the subject of the investigation and to the person alleged to have committed the abuse or neglect. The report of investigation shall be edited to protect the identity of the persons who made the report of abuse or neglect. Other than the persons authorized by the section to receive a copy of the report, Section 261.201(b) applies to the release of the report relating to the investigation of abuse or neglect under this section and to the identity of the person who made the report of abuse or neglect.

(c) Nothing in this section may prevent a law enforcement agency from conducting an investigation of a report made under this section.

(d) The Board of Protective and Regulatory Services shall adopt rules necessary to implement this section.

(Enacted by Acts 1995, 74th Leg., ch. 751 (H.B. 433), § 100, effective September 1, 1995; am. Acts 1997, 75th Leg., ch. 575 (H.B. 1826), § 18, effective September 1, 1997; am. Acts 1999, 76th Leg., ch. 1150 (H.B. 3838), § 8, effective September 1, 1999; am. Acts 1999, 76th Leg., ch. 1390 (H.B. 1622), § 27, effective September 1, 1999; am. Acts 2005, 79th Leg., ch. 213 (H.B. 1970), § 2, effective September 1, 2005; Acts 2007, 80th Leg., ch. 1372 (S.B. 9), § 14, effective June 15, 2007.)

## Sec. 261.407. Minimum Standards.

(a) The Health and Human Services Commission by rule shall adopt minimum standards for the investigation under Section 261.401 of suspected child abuse, neglect, or exploitation in a facility.

(b) A rule or policy adopted by a state agency or institution under Section 261.401 must be consistent with the minimum standards adopted by the Health and Human Services Commission.

(c) This section does not apply to a facility under the jurisdiction of the Texas Department of Criminal Justice, Texas Youth Commission, or Texas Juvenile Probation Commission.

(Enacted by Acts 2001, 77th Leg., ch. 355 (S.B. 664), § 5, effective September 1, 2001.)

### Sec. 261.408. Information Collection.

(a) The Health and Human Services Commission by rule shall adopt uniform procedures for collecting information under Section 261.401, including procedures for collecting information on deaths that occur in facilities.

(b) The department shall receive and compile information on investigations in facilities. An agency submitting information to the department is responsible for ensuring the timeliness, accuracy, completeness, and retention of the agency's reports.

(c) This section does not apply to a facility under the jurisdiction of the Texas Department of Criminal Justice, Texas Youth Commission, or Texas Juvenile Probation Commission.

(Enacted by Acts 2001, 77th Leg., ch. 355 (S.B. 664), § 5, effective September 1, 2001.)

### Sec. 261.409. Investigations in Facilities Under Texas Youth Commission Jurisdiction.

The board of the Texas Youth Commission by rule shall adopt standards for:

(1) the investigation under Section 261.401 of suspected child abuse, neglect, or exploitation in a facility under the jurisdiction of the Texas Youth Commission; and

(2) compiling information on those investigations.

(Enacted by Acts 2001, 77th Leg., ch. 355 (S.B. 664), § 6, effective September 1, 2001.)

### Sec. 261.410. Report of Abuse by Other Children.

(a) In this section:

(1) "Physical abuse" means:

(A) physical injury that results in substantial harm to the child requiring emergency medical treatment and excluding an accident or reasonable discipline by a parent, guardian, or managing or possessory conservator that does not expose the child to a substantial risk of harm; or

(B) failure to make a reasonable effort to prevent an action by another person that results in physical injury that results in substantial harm to the child.

(2) "Sexual abuse" means:

(A) sexual conduct harmful to a child's mental, emotional, or physical welfare; or

(B) failure to make a reasonable effort to prevent sexual conduct harmful to a child.

(b) An agency that operates, licenses, certifies, or registers a facility shall require a residential child-care facility to report each incident of physical or sexual abuse committed by a child against another child.

(c) Using information received under Subsection (b), the agency that operates, licenses, certifies, or registers a facility shall, subject to the availability of funds, compile a report that includes information:

(1) regarding the number of cases of physical and sexual abuse committed by a child against another child;

(2) identifying the residential child-care facility;

(3) regarding the date each allegation of abuse was made;

(4) regarding the date each investigation was started and concluded;

(5) regarding the findings and results of each investigation; and

(6) regarding the number of children involved in each incident investigated.

(Enacted by Acts 2005, 79th Leg., ch. 268 (S.B. 6), § 1.31, effective September 1, 2005.)

# CHAPTER 262
## PROCEDURES IN SUIT BY GOVERNMENTAL ENTITY TO PROTECT HEALTH AND SAFETY OF CHILD

### Subchapter A. General Provisions

## SUBCHAPTER A
## GENERAL PROVISIONS

### Sec. 262.001.  Authorized Actions by Governmental Entity.

(a) A governmental entity with an interest in the child may file a suit affecting the parent-child relationship requesting an order or take possession of a child without a court order as provided by this chapter.

(b) In determining the reasonable efforts that are required to be made with respect to preventing or eliminating the need to remove a child from the child's home or to make it possible to return a child to the child's home, the child's health and safety is the paramount concern.

(Enacted by Acts 1995, 74th Leg., ch. 20 (H.B. 655), § 1, effective April 20, 1995; am. Acts 1999, 76th Leg., ch. 1150 (H.B. 2838), § 10, effective September 1, 1999; am. Acts 1999, 76th Leg., ch. 1390 (H.B. 1622), § 29, effective September 1, 1999.)

### Sec. 262.002.  Jurisdiction.

A suit brought by a governmental entity requesting an order under this chapter may be filed in a court with jurisdiction to hear the suit in the county in which the child is found.

(Enacted by Acts 1995, 74th Leg., ch. 20 (H.B. 655), § 1, effective April 20, 1995; am. Acts 1999, 76th Leg., ch. 1150 (H.B. 3838), § 11, effective September 1, 1999; am. Acts 1999, 76th Leg., ch. 1390 (H.B. 1622), § 30, effective September 1, 1999.)

### Sec. 262.003.  Civil Liability.

A person who takes possession of a child without a court order is immune from civil liability if, at the time possession is taken, there is reasonable cause to believe there is an immediate danger to the physical health or safety of the child.

(Enacted by Acts 1995, 74th Leg., ch. 20 (H.B. 655), § 1, effective April 20, 1995.)

### Sec. 262.004.  Accepting Voluntary Delivery of Possession of Child.

A law enforcement officer or a juvenile probation officer may take possession of a child without a court order on the voluntary delivery of the child by the parent, managing conservator, possessory conservator, guardian, caretaker, or custodian who is presently entitled to possession of the child.

(Enacted by Acts 1995, 74th Leg., ch. 20 (H.B. 655), § 1, effective April 20, 1995; am. Acts 1995, 74th Leg., ch. 751 (H.B. 433), § 101, effective September 1, 1995.)

### Sec. 262.005. Filing Petition After Accepting Voluntary Delivery of Possession of Child.

When possession of the child has been acquired through voluntary delivery of the child to a law enforcement officer or juvenile probation officer, the law enforcement officer or juvenile probation officer taking the child into possession shall cause a suit to be filed not later than the 60th day after the date the child is taken into possession.

(Enacted by Acts 1995, 74th Leg., ch. 20 (H.B. 655), § 1, effective April 20, 1995; am. Acts 1995, 74th Leg., ch. 751 (H.B. 433), § 102, effective September 1, 1995.)

### Sec. 262.006. Living Child After Abortion.

(a) An authorized representative of the Department of Protective and Regulatory Services may assume the care, control, and custody of a child born alive as the result of an abortion as defined by Chapter 161.

(b) The department shall file a suit and request an emergency order under this chapter.

(c) A child for whom possession is assumed under this section need not be delivered to the court except on the order of the court.

(Enacted by Acts 1995, 74th Leg., ch. 20 (H.B. 655), § 1, effective April 20, 1995.)

### Sec. 262.007. Possession and Delivery of Missing Child.

(a) A law enforcement officer who, during a criminal investigation relating to a child's custody, discovers that a child is a missing child and believes that a person may flee with or conceal the child shall take possession of the child and provide for the delivery of the child as provided by Subsection (b).

(b) An officer who takes possession of a child under Subsection (a) shall deliver or arrange for the delivery of the child to a person entitled to possession of the child.

(c) If a person entitled to possession of the child is not immediately available to take possession of the child, the law enforcement officer shall deliver the child to the Department of Protective and Regulatory Services. Until a person entitled to possession of the child takes possession of the child, the department may, without a court order, retain possession of the child not longer than five days after the date the child is delivered to the department. While the department retains possession of a child under this subsection, the department may place the child in foster home care. If a parent or other person entitled to possession of the child does not take possession of the child before the sixth day after the date the child is delivered to the department, the department shall proceed under this chapter as if the law enforcement officer took possession of the child under Section 262.104.

(Enacted by Acts 1995, 74th Leg., ch. 776 (S.B. 789), § 1, effective September 1, 1995; am. Acts 1999, 76th Leg., ch. 685 (H.B. 668), § 6, effective September 1, 1999; am. Acts 1999, 76th Leg., ch. 1150 (H.B. 3838), § 12, effective September 1, 1999; am. Acts 1999, 76th Leg., ch. 1390 (H.B. 1622), § 31, effective September 1, 1999.)

### Sec. 262.008. Abandoned Children.

(a) An authorized representative of the Department of Protective and Regulatory Services may assume the care, control, and custody of a child:

(1) who is abandoned without identification or a means for identifying the child; and

(2) whose identity cannot be ascertained by the exercise of reasonable diligence.

(b) The department shall immediately file a suit to terminate the parent-child relationship of a child under Subsection (a).

(c) A child for whom possession is assumed under this section need not be delivered to the court except on the order of the court.

(Enacted by Acts 1997, 75th Leg., ch. 600 (S.B. 34), § 4, effective January 1, 1998.)

### Sec. 262.009. Temporary Care of Child Taken into Possession.

An employee of or volunteer with a law enforcement agency who successfully completes a background and criminal history check approved by the law enforcement agency may assist a law enforcement officer or juvenile probation officer with the temporary care of a child who is taken into possession by a governmental entity without a court order under this chapter until further arrangements regarding the custody of the child can be made.

Family Code

(Enacted by Acts 2003, 78th Leg., ch. 970 (S.B. 1665), § 1, effective June 20, 2003.)

## Sec. 262.010.  Child with Sexually Transmitted Disease.

(a) If during an investigation by the Department of Family and Protective Services the department discovers that a child younger than 11 years of age has a sexually transmitted disease, the department shall:

(1) appoint a special investigator to assist in the investigation of the case; and

(2) file an original suit requesting an emergency order under this chapter for possession of the child unless the department determines, after taking the following actions, that emergency removal is not necessary for the protection of the child:

(A) reviewing the medical evidence to determine whether the medical evidence supports a finding that abuse likely occurred;

(B) interviewing the child and other persons residing in the child's home;

(C) conferring with law enforcement;

(D) determining whether any other child in the home has a sexually transmitted disease and, if so, referring the child for a sexual abuse examination;

(E) if the department determines a forensic interview is appropriate based on the child's age and development, ensuring that each child alleged to have been abused undergoes a forensic interview by a children's advocacy center established under Section 264.402 or another professional with specialized training in conducting forensic interviews if a children's advocacy center is not available in the county in which the child resides;

(F) consulting with a department staff nurse or other medical expert to obtain additional information regarding the nature of the sexually transmitted disease and the ways the disease is transmitted and an opinion as to whether abuse occurred based on the facts of the case;

(G) contacting any additional witness who may have information relevant to the investigation, including other individuals who had access to the child; and

(H) if the department determines after taking the actions described by Paragraphs (A)—(G) that a finding of sexual abuse is not supported, obtaining an opinion from the Forensic Assessment Center Network as to whether the evidence in the case supports a finding that abuse likely occurred.

(b) If the department determines that abuse likely occurred, the department shall work with law enforcement to obtain a search warrant to require an individual the department reasonably believes may have sexually abused the child to undergo medically appropriate diagnostic testing for sexually transmitted diseases.

(Enacted by Acts 2011, 82nd Leg., ch. 598 (S.B. 218), § 2, effective September 1, 2011.)

## SUBCHAPTER B
## TAKING POSSESSION OF CHILD

## Sec. 262.101.  Filing Petition Before Taking Possession of Child.

An original suit filed by a governmental entity that requests permission to take possession of a child without prior notice and a hearing must be supported by an affidavit sworn to by a person with personal knowledge and stating facts sufficient to satisfy a person of ordinary prudence and caution that:

(1) there is an immediate danger to the physical health or safety of the child or the child has been a victim of neglect or sexual abuse and that continuation in the home would be contrary to the child's welfare;

(2) there is no time, consistent with the physical health or safety of the child, for a full adversary hearing under Subchapter C; and

(3) reasonable efforts, consistent with the circumstances and providing for the safety of the child, were made to prevent or eliminate the need for the removal of the child.

(Enacted by Acts 1995, 74th Leg., ch. 20 (H.B. 655), § 1, effective April 20, 1995; am. Acts 1995, 74th Leg., ch. 751 (H.B. 433), § 103, effective September 1, 1995; am. Acts 1997, 75th Leg., ch. 752 (H.B. 1336), § 1, effective June 17, 1997; am. Acts 1999, 76th Leg., ch. 1150 (H.B. 3838), § 14, effective September 1, 1999; am. Acts 1999, 76th Leg., ch. 1390 (H.B. 1622), § 33, effective September 1, 1999; am. Acts 2001, 77th Leg., ch. 849 (H.B. 1566), § 1, effective September 1, 2001.)

## Sec. 262.1015.  Removal of Alleged Perpetrator; Offense.

(a) If the department determines after an investigation that child abuse has occurred and that the child would be protected in the child's home by the removal of the alleged perpetrator of the abuse, the department shall file a petition for the removal of the alleged perpetrator from the residence of the child rather than attempt to remove the child from the residence.

(a-1) Notwithstanding Subsection (a), if the Department of Family and Protective Services determines that a protective order issued under Title 4 provides a reasonable alternative to obtaining an order under that subsection, the department may:

(1) file an application for a protective order on behalf of the child instead of or in addition to obtaining a temporary restraining order under this section; or

(2) assist a parent or other adult with whom a child resides in obtaining a protective order.

(b) A court may issue a temporary restraining order in a suit by the department for the removal of an alleged perpetrator under Subsection (a) if the department's petition states facts sufficient to satisfy the court that:

(1) there is an immediate danger to the physical health or safety of the child or the child has been a victim of sexual abuse;

(2) there is no time, consistent with the physical health or safety of the child, for an adversary hearing;

(3) the child is not in danger of abuse from a parent or other adult with whom the child will continue to reside in the residence of the child;

(4) the parent or other adult with whom the child will continue to reside in the child's home is likely to:

(A) make a reasonable effort to monitor the residence; and

(B) report to the department and the appropriate law enforcement agency any attempt by the alleged perpetrator to return to the residence; and

(5) the issuance of the order is in the best interest of the child.

(c) The order shall be served on the alleged perpetrator and on the parent or other adult with whom the child will continue to reside.

(d) A temporary restraining order under this section expires not later than the 14th day after the date the order was rendered.

(e) A temporary restraining order under this section and any other order requiring the removal of an alleged perpetrator from the residence of a child shall require that the parent or other adult with whom the child will continue to reside in the child's home make a reasonable effort to monitor the residence and report to the department and the appropriate law enforcement

agency any attempt by the alleged perpetrator to return to the residence.

(f) The court shall order the removal of an alleged perpetrator if the court finds that the child is not in danger of abuse from a parent or other adult with whom the child will continue to reside in the child's residence and that:

(1) the presence of the alleged perpetrator in the child's residence constitutes a continuing danger to the physical health or safety of the child; or

(2) the child has been the victim of sexual abuse and there is a substantial risk that the child will be the victim of sexual abuse in the future if the alleged perpetrator remains in the residence.

(g) A person commits an offense if the person is a parent or other person with whom a child resides, the person is served with an order containing the requirement specified by Subsection (e), and the person fails to make a reasonable effort to monitor the residence of the child or to report to the department and the appropriate law enforcement agency an attempt by the alleged perpetrator to return to the residence. An offense under this section is a Class A misdemeanor.

(h) A person commits an offense if, in violation of a court order under this section, the person returns to the residence of the child the person is alleged to have abused. An offense under this subsection is a Class A misdemeanor, except that the offense is a felony of the third degree if the person has previously been convicted under this subsection.

(Enacted by Acts 1995, 74th Leg., ch. 943 (H.B. 2569), § 4, effective September 1, 1995; am. Acts 1997, 75th Leg., ch. 575 (H.B. 1826), § 19, effective September 1, 1997; am. Acts 2011, 82nd Leg., ch. 598 (S.B. 218), § 3, effective September 1, 2011; am. Acts 2011, 82nd Leg., ch. 222 (H.B. 253), § 2, effective September 1, 2011.)

## Sec. 262.102. Emergency Order Authorizing Possession of Child.

(a) Before a court may, without prior notice and a hearing, issue a temporary restraining order or attachment of a child in a suit brought by a governmental entity, the court must find that:

(1) there is an immediate danger to the physical health or safety of the child or the child has been a victim of neglect or sexual abuse and that continuation in the home would be contrary to the child's welfare;

(2) there is no time, consistent with the physical health or safety of the child and the

nature of the emergency, for a full adversary hearing under Subchapter C; and

(3) reasonable efforts, consistent with the circumstances and providing for the safety of the child, were made to prevent or eliminate the need for removal of the child.

(b) In determining whether there is an immediate danger to the physical health or safety of a child, the court may consider whether the child's household includes a person who has:

(1) abused or neglected another child in a manner that caused serious injury to or the death of the other child; or

(2) sexually abused another child.

(c) If, based on the recommendation of or a request by the department, the court finds that child abuse or neglect has occurred and that the child requires protection from family violence by a member of the child's family or household, the court shall render a temporary order under Chapter 71 for the protection of the child. In this subsection, "family violence" has the meaning assigned by Section 71.004.

(Enacted by Acts 1995, 74th Leg., ch. 20 (H.B. 655), § 1, effective April 20, 1995; am. Acts 1995, 74th Leg., ch. 751 (H.B. 433), § 104, effective September 1, 1995; am. Acts 1997, 75th Leg., ch. 752 (H.B. 1336), § 2, effective June 17, 1997; am. Acts 1999, 76th Leg., ch. 1150 (H.B. 3838), § 15, effective September 1, 1999; am. Acts 1999, 76th Leg., ch. 1390 (H.B. 1622), § 34, effective September 1, 1999; am. Acts 2001, 77th Leg., ch. 849 (H.B. 1566), § 2, effective September 1, 2001; am. Acts 2003, 78th Leg., ch. 1276 (H.B. 3507), § 7.002(m), effective September 1, 2003.)

## Sec. 262.103. Duration of Temporary Restraining Order and Attachment.

A temporary restraining order or attachment of the child issued under this chapter expires not later than 14 days after the date it is issued unless it is extended as provided by the Texas Rules of Civil Procedure.

(Enacted by Acts 1995, 74th Leg., ch. 20 (H.B. 655), § 1, effective April 20, 1995.)

## Sec. 262.104. Taking Possession of a Child in Emergency Without a Court Order.

(a) If there is no time to obtain a temporary restraining order or attachment before taking possession of a child consistent with the health and safety of that child, an authorized representative of the Department of Family and Protective Services, a law enforcement officer, or a juvenile probation officer may take possession of a child without a court order under the following conditions, only:

(1) on personal knowledge of facts that would lead a person of ordinary prudence and caution to believe that there is an immediate danger to the physical health or safety of the child;

(2) on information furnished by another that has been corroborated by personal knowledge of facts and all of which taken together would lead a person of ordinary prudence and caution to believe that there is an immediate danger to the physical health or safety of the child;

(3) on personal knowledge of facts that would lead a person of ordinary prudence and caution to believe that the child has been the victim of sexual abuse;

(4) on information furnished by another that has been corroborated by personal knowledge of facts and all of which taken together would lead a person of ordinary prudence and caution to believe that the child has been the victim of sexual abuse; or

(5) on information furnished by another that has been corroborated by personal knowledge of facts and all of which taken together would lead a person of ordinary prudence and caution to believe that the parent or person who has possession of the child is currently using a controlled substance as defined by Chapter 481, Health and Safety Code, and the use constitutes an immediate danger to the physical health or safety of the child.

(b) An authorized representative of the Department of Family and Protective Services, a law enforcement officer, or a juvenile probation officer may take possession of a child under Subsection (a) on personal knowledge or information furnished by another, that has been corroborated by personal knowledge, that would lead a person of ordinary prudence and caution to believe that the parent or person who has possession of the child has permitted the child to remain on premises used for the manufacture of methamphetamine.

(Enacted by Acts 1995, 74th Leg., ch. 20 (H.B. 655), § 1, effective April 20, 1995; am. Acts 1997, 75th Leg., ch. 575 (H.B. 1826), § 20, effective

September 1, 1997; am. Acts 2005, 79th Leg., ch. 282 (H.B. 164), § 2, effective August 1, 2005.)

### Sec. 262.1041. Release of Child by Law Enforcement or Juvenile Probation Officer.

(a) A law enforcement or juvenile probation officer who takes possession of a child under this chapter may release the child to:

(1) a child-placing agency licensed by the Department of Family and Protective Services under Chapter 42, Human Resources Code, if the agency is authorized by the department to take possession of the child;

(2) the Department of Family and Protective Services; or

(3) any other person authorized by law to take possession of the child.

(b) A child-placing agency or other authorized person who takes possession of a child under this section shall:

(1) immediately notify the Department of Family and Protective Services that the agency or other authorized person has taken possession of the child; and

(2) with the assistance of the law enforcement or juvenile probation officer who releases the child to the agency or other authorized person, complete a form prescribed by the Department of Family and Protective Services that contains basic information regarding the child and the circumstances under which the officer took possession of the child and promptly submit the completed form to the department.

(Enacted by Acts 2005, 79th Leg., ch. 268 (S.B. 6), § 1.32, effective September 1, 2005; enacted by Acts 2005, 79th Leg., ch. 516 (H.B. 798), § 1, effective June 17, 2005.)

### Sec. 262.105. Filing Petition After Taking Possession of Child in Emergency.

(a) When a child is taken into possession without a court order, the person taking the child into possession, without unnecessary delay, shall:

(1) file a suit affecting the parent-child relationship;

(2) request the court to appoint an attorney ad litem for the child; and

(3) request an initial hearing to be held by no later than the first working day after the date the child is taken into possession.

(b) If the Department of Protective and Regulatory Services files a suit affecting the parent-child relationship required under Subsection (a)(1) seeking termination of the parent-child relationship, the department shall file the suit not later than the 45th day after the date the department assumes the care, control, and custody of a child under Section 262.303.

(Enacted by Acts 1995, 74th Leg., ch. 20 (H.B. 655), § 1, effective April 20, 1995; am. Acts 2001, 77th Leg., ch. 809 (H.B. 706), § 2, effective September 1, 2001.)

### Sec. 262.106. Initial Hearing After Taking Possession of Child in Emergency Without Court Order.

(a) The court in which a suit has been filed after a child has been taken into possession without a court order by a governmental entity shall hold an initial hearing on or before the first working day after the date the child is taken into possession. The court shall render orders that are necessary to protect the physical health and safety of the child. If the court is unavailable for a hearing on the first working day, then, and only in that event, the hearing shall be held no later than the first working day after the court becomes available, provided that the hearing is held no later than the third working day after the child is taken into possession.

(b) The initial hearing may be ex parte and proof may be by sworn petition or affidavit if a full adversary hearing is not practicable.

(c) If the initial hearing is not held within the time required, the child shall be returned to the parent, managing conservator, possessory conservator, guardian, caretaker, or custodian who is presently entitled to possession of the child.

(d) For the purpose of determining under Subsection (a) the first working day after the date the child is taken into possession, the child is considered to have been taken into possession by the Department of Protective and Regulatory Services on the expiration of the five-day period permitted under Section 262.007(c) or 262.110(b), as appropriate.

(Enacted by Acts 1995, 74th Leg., ch. 20 (H.B. 655), § 1, effective April 20, 1995; am. Acts 1999, 76th Leg., ch. 1150 (H.B. 3838), § 16, effective September 1, 1999; am. Acts 1999, 76th Leg., ch. 1390 (H.B. 1622), § 35, effective September 1, 1999.)

Family Code

### Sec. 262.107. Standard for Decision at Initial Hearing After Taking Possession of Child Without a Court Order in Emergency.

(a) The court shall order the return of the child at the initial hearing regarding a child taken in possession without a court order by a governmental entity unless the court is satisfied that:

(1) there is a continuing danger to the physical health or safety of the child if the child is returned to the parent, managing conservator, possessory conservator, guardian, caretaker, or custodian who is presently entitled to possession of the child or the evidence shows that the child has been the victim of sexual abuse on one or more occasions and that there is a substantial risk that the child will be the victim of sexual abuse in the future;

(2) continuation of the child in the home would be contrary to the child's welfare; and

(3) reasonable efforts, consistent with the circumstances and providing for the safety of the child, were made to prevent or eliminate the need for removal of the child.

(b) In determining whether there is a continuing danger to the physical health or safety of a child, the court may consider whether the household to which the child would be returned includes a person who has:

(1) abused or neglected another child in a manner that caused serious injury to or the death of the other child; or

(2) sexually abused another child.

(Enacted by Acts 1995, 74th Leg., ch. 20 (H.B. 655), § 1, effective April 20, 1995; am. Acts 1995, 74th Leg., ch. 751 (H.B. 433), § 105, effective September 1, 1995; am. Acts 2001, 77th Leg., ch. 849 (H.B. 1566), § 3, effective September 1, 2001.)

### Sec. 262.108. Unacceptable Facilities for Housing Child.

When a child is taken into possession under this chapter, that child may not be held in isolation or in a jail, juvenile detention facility, or other secure detention facility.

(Enacted by Acts 1995, 74th Leg., ch. 20 (H.B. 655), § 1, effective April 20, 1995; am. Acts 1997, 75th Leg., ch. 1374 (H.B. 1230), § 9, effective September 1, 1997.)

### Sec. 262.109. Notice to Parent, Conservator, or Guardian.

(a) The department or other agency must give written notice as prescribed by this section to each parent of the child or to the child's conservator or legal guardian when a representative of the Department of Protective and Regulatory Services or other agency takes possession of a child under this chapter.

(b) The written notice must be given as soon as practicable, but in any event not later than the first working day after the date the child is taken into possession.

(c) The written notice must include:

(1) the reasons why the department or agency is taking possession of the child and the facts that led the department to believe that the child should be taken into custody;

(2) the name of the person at the department or agency that the parent, conservator, or other custodian may contact for information relating to the child or a legal proceeding relating to the child;

(3) a summary of legal rights of a parent, conservator, guardian, or other custodian under this chapter and an explanation of the probable legal procedures relating to the child; and

(4) a statement that the parent, conservator, or other custodian has the right to hire an attorney.

(d) The written notice may be waived by the court at the initial hearing:

(1) on a showing that:

(A) the parents, conservators, or other custodians of the child could not be located; or

(B) the department took possession of the child under Subchapter D; or

(2) for other good cause.

(Enacted by Acts 1995, 74th Leg., ch. 20 (H.B. 655), § 1, effective April 20, 1995; am. Acts 1997, 75th Leg., ch. 1022 (S.B. 359), § 76, effective January 1, 1998; am. Acts 1999, 76th Leg., ch. 1150 (H.B. 3838), § 17, effective September 1, 1999; am. Acts 1999, 76th Leg., ch. 1390 (H.B. 1622), § 36, effective September 1, 1999; am. Acts 2001, 77th Leg., ch. 809 (H.B. 706), § 3, effective September 1, 2001.)

### Sec. 262.1095. Information Provided to Relatives and Certain Individuals; Investigation.

(a) When the Department of Family and Protective Services or another agency takes possession of a child under this chapter, the department:

(1) shall provide information as prescribed by this section to each adult the department is able to identify and locate who:

(A) is related to the child within the third degree by consanguinity as determined under Chapter 573, Government Code, or is an adult relative of the alleged father of the child who the department determines is most likely to be the child's biological father; and

(B) is identified as a potential relative or designated caregiver, as defined by Section 264.751, on the proposed child placement resources form provided under Section 261.307; and

(2) may provide information as prescribed by this section to each adult the department is able to identify and locate who has a long-standing and significant relationship with the child.

(b) The information provided under Subsection (a) must:

(1) state that the child has been removed from the child's home and is in the temporary managing conservatorship of the department;

(2) explain the options available to the individual to participate in the care and placement of the child and the support of the child's family;

(3) state that some options available to the individual may be lost if the individual fails to respond in a timely manner; and

(4) include, if applicable, the date, time, and location of the hearing under Subchapter C, Chapter 263.

(c) The department is not required to provide information to an individual if the individual has received service of citation under Section 102.009 or if the department determines providing information is inappropriate because the individual has a criminal history or a history of family violence.

(d) The department shall use due diligence to identify and locate all individuals described by Subsection (a) not later than the 30th day after the date the department files a suit affecting the parent-child relationship. In order to identify and locate the individuals described by Subsection (a), the department shall seek information from:

(1) each parent, relative, and alleged father of the child; and

(2) the child in an age-appropriate manner.

(e) The failure of a parent or alleged father of the child to complete the proposed child placement resources form does not relieve the department of its duty to seek information about the person under Subsection (d).

(Enacted by Acts 2011, 82nd Leg., ch. 490 (S.B. 993), § 2, effective September 1, 2011.)

### Sec. 262.110. Taking Possession of Child in Emergency with Intent to Return Home.

(a) An authorized representative of the Department of Protective and Regulatory Services, a law enforcement officer, or a juvenile probation officer may take temporary possession of a child without a court order on discovery of a child in a situation of danger to the child's physical health or safety when the sole purpose is to deliver the child without unnecessary delay to the parent, managing conservator, possessory conservator, guardian, caretaker, or custodian who is presently entitled to possession of the child.

(b) Until a parent or other person entitled to possession of the child takes possession of the child, the department may retain possession of the child without a court order for not more than five days. On the expiration of the fifth day, if a parent or other person entitled to possession does not take possession of the child, the department shall take action under this chapter as if the department took possession of the child under Section 262.104.

(Enacted by Acts 1995, 74th Leg., ch. 20 (H.B. 655), § 1, effective April 20, 1995; am. Acts 1999, 76th Leg., ch. 1150 (H.B. 3838), § 18, effective September 1, 1999; am. Acts 1999, 76th Leg., ch. 1390 (H.B. 1622), § 37, effective September 1, 1999.)

### Sec. 262.111. Finding That Child Cannot Remain in or Be Returned to Home [Repealed].

Repealed by Acts 2001, 77th Leg., ch. 849 (H.B. 1566), § 10, effective September 1, 2001.
(Enacted by Acts 1995, 74th Leg., ch. 751 (H.B. 433), § 106, effective September 1, 1995.)

### Sec. 262.112. Expedited Hearing and Appeal.

(a) The Department of Protective and Regulatory Services is entitled to an expedited hearing under this chapter in any proceeding in which a hearing is required if the department determines that a child should be removed from the child's home because of an immediate danger to the physical health or safety of the child.

(b) In any proceeding in which an expedited hearing is held under Subsection (a), the department, parent, guardian, or other party to the proceeding is entitled to an expedited appeal on a ruling by a court that the child may not be removed from the child's home.

(c) If a child is returned to the child's home after a removal in which the department was entitled to an expedited hearing under this section and the child is the subject of a subsequent allegation of abuse or neglect, the department or any other interested party is entitled to an expedited hearing on the removal of the child from the child's home in the manner provided by Subsection (a) and to an expedited appeal in the manner provided by Subsection (b).

(Enacted by Acts 1995, 74th Leg., ch. 943 (H.B. 2569), § 1, effective September 1, 1995; am. Acts 1997, 75th Leg., ch. 165 (S.B. 898), § 31.01(29), effective September 1, 1997 (renumbered from Sec. 262.111).)

## Sec. 262.113.  Filing Suit Without Taking Possession of Child.

An original suit filed by a governmental entity that requests to take possession of a child after notice and a hearing must be supported by an affidavit sworn to by a person with personal knowledge and stating facts sufficient to satisfy a person of ordinary prudence and caution that:

(1) reasonable efforts have been made to prevent or eliminate the need to remove the child from the child's home; and

(2) allowing the child to remain in the home would be contrary to the child's welfare.

(Enacted by Acts 1999, 76th Leg., ch. 1150 (H.B. 3838), § 19, effective September 1, 1999; enacted by Acts 1999, 76th Leg., ch. 1390 (H.B. 1622), § 38, effective September 1, 1999.)

## Sec. 262.114.  Evaluation of Identified Relatives and Other Designated Individuals; Placement.

(a) Before a full adversary hearing under Subchapter C, the Department of Family and Protective Services must perform a background and criminal history check of the relatives or other designated individuals identified as a potential relative or designated caregiver, as defined by Section 264.751, on the proposed child placement resources form provided under Section 261.307. The department shall evaluate each person listed on the form to determine the relative or other designated individual who would be the most appropriate substitute caregiver for the child and must complete a home study of the most appropriate substitute caregiver, if any, before the full adversary hearing. Until the department identifies a relative or other designated individual qualified to be a substitute caregiver, the depart-

ment must continue to explore substitute caregiver options. The time frames in this subsection do not apply to a relative or other designated individual located in another state.

(a-1) At the full adversary hearing under Section 262.201, the department shall, after redacting any social security numbers, file with the court:

(1) a copy of each proposed child placement resources form completed by the parent or other person having legal custody of the child;

(2) a copy of any completed home study performed under Subsection (a); and

(3) the name of the relative or other designated caregiver, if any, with whom the child has been placed.

(a-2) If the child has not been placed with a relative or other designated caregiver by the time of the full adversary hearing under Section 262.201, the department shall file with the court a statement that explains:

(1) the reasons why the department has not placed the child with a relative or other designated caregiver listed on the proposed child placement resources form; and

(2) the actions the department is taking, if any, to place the child with a relative or other designated caregiver.

(b) The department may place a child with a relative or other designated individual identified on the proposed child placement resources form if the department determines that the placement is in the best interest of the child. The department may place the child with the relative or designated individual before conducting the background and criminal history check or home study required under Subsection (a). The department shall provide a copy of an informational manual required under Section 261.3071 to the relative or other designated caregiver at the time of the child's placement.

(c) The department shall consider placing a child who has previously been in the managing conservatorship of the department with a foster parent with whom the child previously resided if:

(1) the department determines that placement of the child with a relative or designated caregiver is not in the child's best interest; and

(2) the placement is available and in the child's best interest.

(Enacted by Acts 2005, 79th Leg., ch. 268 (S.B. 6), § 1(1.33), effective September 1, 2005; am. Acts 2009, 81st Leg., ch. 527 (S.B. 1332), § 1, effective September 1, 2009; am. Acts 2009, 81st Leg., ch. 856 (S.B. 2385), § 1, effective September 1, 2009.)

## SUBCHAPTER C
## ADVERSARY HEARING

### Sec. 262.201. Full Adversary Hearing; Findings of the Court.

(a) Unless the child has already been returned to the parent, managing conservator, possessory conservator, guardian, caretaker, or custodian entitled to possession and the temporary order, if any, has been dissolved, a full adversary hearing shall be held not later than the 14th day after the date the child was taken into possession by the governmental entity.

(b) At the conclusion of the full adversary hearing, the court shall order the return of the child to the parent, managing conservator, possessory conservator, guardian, caretaker, or custodian entitled to possession unless the court finds sufficient evidence to satisfy a person of ordinary prudence and caution that:

(1) there was a danger to the physical health or safety of the child which was caused by an act or failure to act of the person entitled to possession and for the child to remain in the home is contrary to the welfare of the child;

(2) the urgent need for protection required the immediate removal of the child and reasonable efforts, consistent with the circumstances and providing for the safety of the child, were made to eliminate or prevent the child's removal; and

(3) reasonable efforts have been made to enable the child to return home, but there is a substantial risk of a continuing danger if the child is returned home.

(c) If the court finds sufficient evidence to satisfy a person of ordinary prudence and caution that there is a continuing danger to the physical health or safety of the child and for the child to remain in the home is contrary to the welfare of the child, the court shall issue an appropriate temporary order under Chapter 105. The court shall require each parent, alleged father, or relative of the child before the court to complete the proposed child placement resources form provided under Section 261.307 and file the form with the court, if the form has not been previously filed with the court, and provide the Department of Family and Protective Services with information necessary to locate any other absent parent, alleged father, or relative of the child. The court shall inform each parent, alleged father, or relative of the child before the court that the person's failure to submit the proposed child placement resources form will not delay any court proceedings relating to the child. The court shall inform each parent in open court that parental and custodial rights and duties may be subject to restriction or to termination unless the parent or parents are willing and able to provide the child with a safe environment. If the court finds that the child requires protection from family violence by a member of the child's family or household, the court shall render a protective order under Title 4 for the child. In this subsection, "family violence" has the meaning assigned by Section 71.004.

(d) In determining whether there is a continuing danger to the physical health or safety of the child, the court may consider whether the household to which the child would be returned includes a person who:

(1) has abused or neglected another child in a manner that caused serious injury to or the death of the other child; or

(2) has sexually abused another child.

(e) The court shall place a child removed from the child's custodial parent with the child's noncustodial parent or with a relative of the child if placement with the noncustodial parent is inappropriate, unless placement with the noncustodial parent or a relative is not in the best interest of the child.

(f) When citation by publication is needed for a parent or alleged or probable father in an action brought under this chapter because the location of the parent, alleged father, or probable father is unknown, the court may render a temporary order without delay at any time after the filing of the action without regard to whether notice of the citation by publication has been published.

(g) For the purpose of determining under Subsection (a) the 14th day after the date the child is taken into possession, a child is considered to have been taken into possession by the department on the expiration of the five-day period permitted under Section 262.007(c) or 262.110(b), as appropriate.

(Enacted by Acts 1995, 74th Leg., ch. 20 (H.B. 655), § 1, effective April 20, 1995; am. Acts 1995, 74th Leg., ch. 751 (H.B. 433), § 107, effective September 1, 1995; am. Acts 1997, 75th Leg., ch. 575 (H.B. 1826), § 21, effective September 1, 1997; am. Acts 1997, 75th Leg., ch. 600 (S.B. 34), § 5, effective January 1, 1998; am. Acts 1997, 75th Leg., ch. 603 (S.B. 181), § 1, effective January 1, 1998; am. Acts 1997, 75th Leg., ch. 752 (H.B. 1336), § 3, effective June 17, 1997; am. Acts 1997, 75th Leg., ch. 1022 (S.B. 359), § 77, effective January 1, 1998; am. Acts 1997, 75th Leg., ch. 1022 (S.B. 359), § 78, effective September 1, 1997; am. Acts 1999, 76th Leg., ch. 62 (S.B. 1368), § 6.31(a), (b), effective September 1, 1999; am. Acts 1999, 76th Leg., ch. 1150 (H.B. 3838), § 20, effective September 1, 1999; am. Acts 1999, 76th Leg., ch. 1390 (H.B. 1622), § 39, effective September 1, 1999; am. Acts 2001, 77th Leg., ch. 306 (H.B. 1266), § 1, effective September 1, 2001; am. Acts 2001, 77th Leg., ch. 849 (H.B. 1566), § 4, effective September 1, 2001; am. Acts 2005, 79th Leg., ch. 268 (S.B. 6), § 1.34(a), effective September 1, 2005; am. Acts 2009, 81st Leg., ch. 856 (S.B. 2385), § 2, effective September 1, 2009.)

### Sec. 262.2015.  Aggravated Circumstances.

(a) The court may waive the requirement of a service plan and the requirement to make reasonable efforts to return the child to a parent and may accelerate the trial schedule to result in a final order for a child under the care of the department at an earlier date than provided by Subchapter D, Chapter 263, if the court finds that the parent has subjected the child to aggravated circumstances.

(b) The court may find under Subsection (a) that a parent has subjected the child to aggravated circumstances if:

(1) the parent abandoned the child without identification or a means for identifying the child;

(2) the child is a victim of serious bodily injury or sexual abuse inflicted by the parent or by another person with the parent's consent;

(3) the parent has engaged in conduct against the child that would constitute an offense under the following provisions of the Penal Code:

(A) Section 19.02 (murder);

(B) Section 19.03 (capital murder);

(C) Section 19.04 (manslaughter);

(D) Section 21.11 (indecency with a child);

(E) Section 22.011 (sexual assault);

(F) Section 22.02 (aggravated assault);

(G) Section 22.021 (aggravated sexual assault);

(H) Section 22.04 (injury to a child, elderly individual, or disabled individual);

(I) Section 22.041 (abandoning or endangering child);

(J) Section 25.02 (prohibited sexual conduct);

(K) Section 43.25 (sexual performance by a child);

(L) Section 43.26 (possession or promotion of child pornography);

(M) Section 21.02 (continuous sexual abuse of young child or children);

(N) Section 43.05(a)(2) (compelling prostitution); or

(O) Section 20A.02(a)(7) or (8) (trafficking of persons);

(4) the parent voluntarily left the child alone or in the possession of another person not the parent of the child for at least six months without expressing an intent to return and without providing adequate support for the child;

(5) the parent's parental rights with regard to another child have been involuntarily terminated based on a finding that the parent's conduct violated Section 161.001(1)(D) or (E) or a substantially equivalent provision of another state's law;

(6) the parent has been convicted for:

(A) the murder of another child of the parent and the offense would have been an offense under 18 U.S.C. Section 1111(a) if the offense had occurred in the special maritime or territorial jurisdiction of the United States;

(B) the voluntary manslaughter of another child of the parent and the offense would have been an offense under 18 U.S.C. Section 1112(a) if the offense had occurred in the special maritime or territorial jurisdiction of the United States;

(C) aiding or abetting, attempting, conspiring, or soliciting an offense under Subdivision (A) or (B); or

(D) the felony assault of the child or another child of the parent that resulted in serious bodily injury to the child or another child of the parent; or

(7) the parent's parental rights with regard to two other children have been involuntarily terminated.

(c) On finding that reasonable efforts to make it possible for the child to safely return to the child's home are not required, the court shall at any time before the 30th day after the date of the finding, conduct an initial permanency hearing under Subchapter D, Chapter 263. Separate notice of the permanency plan is not required but may be given with a notice of a hearing under this section.

(d) The Department of Protective and Regulatory Services shall make reasonable efforts to finalize the permanent placement of a child for whom the court has made the finding described by Subsection (c). The court shall set the suit for trial on the merits as required by Subchapter D, Chapter 263, in order to facilitate final placement of the child.

(Enacted by Acts 1997, 75th Leg., ch. 1022 (S.B. 359), § 79, effective September 1, 1997; am. Acts 1999, 76th Leg., ch. 1150 (H.B. 3838), § 21, effective September 1, 1999; am. Acts 1999, 76th Leg., ch. 1390 (H.B. 1622), § 40, effective September 1, 1999; am. Acts 2001, 77th Leg., ch. 849 (H.B. 1566), § 5, effective September 1, 2001; am. Acts 2005, 79th Leg., ch. 268 (S.B. 6), § 1.35, effective September 1, 2005; am. Acts 2007, 80th Leg., ch. 593 (H.B. 8), § 3.33, effective September 1, 2007; am. Acts 2011, 82nd Leg., ch. 1 (S.B. 24), § 4.04, effective September 1, 2011.)

### Sec. 262.202. Identification of Court of Continuing, Exclusive Jurisdiction.

If at the conclusion of the full adversary hearing the court renders a temporary order, the governmental entity shall request identification of a court of continuing, exclusive jurisdiction as provided by Chapter 155.

(Enacted by Acts 1995, 74th Leg., ch. 20 (H.B. 655), § 1, effective April 20, 1995.)

### Sec. 262.203. Transfer of Suit.

(a) On the motion of a party or the court's own motion, if applicable, the court that rendered the temporary order shall in accordance with procedures provided by Chapter 155:

(1) transfer the suit to the court of continuing, exclusive jurisdiction, if any;

(2) if grounds exist for mandatory transfer from the court of continuing, exclusive jurisdiction under Section 155.201, order transfer of the suit from that court; or

(3) if grounds exist for transfer based on improper venue, order transfer of the suit to the court having venue of the suit under Chapter 103.

(b) Notwithstanding Section 155.204, a motion to transfer relating to a suit filed under this chapter may be filed separately from the petition and is timely if filed while the case is pending.

(c) Notwithstanding Sections 6.407 and 103.002, a court exercising jurisdiction under this chapter is not required to transfer the suit to a court in which a parent has filed a suit for dissolution of marriage before a final order for the protection of the child has been rendered under Subchapter E, Chapter 263.

(Enacted by Acts 1995, 74th Leg., ch. 20 (H.B. 655), § 1, effective April 20, 1995; am. Acts 1997, 75th Leg., ch. 575 (H.B. 1826), § 22, effective September 1, 1997; am. Acts 1999, 76th Leg., ch. 1150 (H.B. 3838), § 22, effective September 1, 1999; am. Acts 1999, 76th Leg., ch. 1390 (H.B. 1622), § 41, effective September 1, 1999.)

### Sec. 262.204. Temporary Order in Effect Until Superseded.

(a) A temporary order rendered under this chapter is valid and enforceable until properly superseded by a court with jurisdiction to do so.

(b) A court to which the suit has been transferred may enforce by contempt or otherwise a temporary order properly issued under this chapter.

(Enacted by Acts 1995, 74th Leg., ch. 20 (H.B. 655), § 1, effective April 20, 1995.)

### Sec. 262.205. Hearing When Child Not in Possession of Governmental Entity.

(a) In a suit requesting possession of a child after notice and hearing, the court may render a temporary restraining order as provided by Section 105.001. The suit shall be promptly set for hearing.

(b) After the hearing, the court may grant the request to remove the child from the parent, managing conservator, possessory conservator, guardian, caretaker, or custodian entitled to possession of the child if the court finds sufficient evidence to satisfy a person of ordinary prudence and caution that:

(1) reasonable efforts have been made to prevent or eliminate the need to remove the child from the child's home; and

(2) allowing the child to remain in the home would be contrary to the child's welfare.

(c) If the court orders removal of the child from the child's home, the court shall:

(1) issue an appropriate temporary order under Chapter 105; and

(2) inform each parent in open court that parental and custodial rights and duties may be subject to restriction or termination unless the parent is willing and able to provide a safe environment for the child.

(d) If citation by publication is required for a parent or alleged or probable father in an action under this chapter because the location of the person is unknown, the court may render a temporary order without regard to whether notice of the citation has been published.

(e) Unless it is not in the best interest of the child, the court shall place a child who has been removed under this section with:

(1) the child's noncustodial parent; or

(2) another relative of the child if placement with the noncustodial parent is inappropriate.

(f) If the court finds that the child requires protection from family violence by a member of the child's family or household, the court shall render a protective order for the child under Title 4.

(Enacted by Acts 1999, 76th Leg., ch. 1150 (H.B. 3838), § 23, effective September 1, 1999; enacted by Acts 1999, 76th Leg., ch. 1390 (H.B. 1622), § 42, effective September 1, 1999.)

## SUBCHAPTER D
## EMERGENCY POSSESSION OF CERTAIN ABANDONED CHILDREN

### Sec. 262.301. Definitions.

In this chapter:

(1) "Designated emergency infant care provider" means:

(A) an emergency medical services provider;

(B) a hospital; or

(C) a child-placing agency licensed by the Department of Protective and Regulatory Services under Chapter 42, Human Resources Code, that:

(i) agrees to act as a designated emergency infant care provider under this subchapter; and

(ii) has on staff a person who is licensed as a registered nurse under Chapter 301, Occupations Code, or who provides emergency medical services under Chapter 773, Health and Safety Code, and who will examine and provide emergency medical services to a child taken into possession by the agency under this subchapter.

(2) "Emergency medical services provider" has the meaning assigned that term by Section 773.003, Health and Safety Code.

(Enacted by Acts 1999, 76th Leg., ch. 1087 (H.B. 3423), § 2, effective September 1, 1999; am. Acts 2001, 77th Leg., ch. 809 (H.B. 706), § 4, effective September 1, 2001.)

### Sec. 262.302. Accepting Possession of Certain Abandoned Children.

(a) A designated emergency infant care provider shall, without a court order, take possession of a child who appears to be 60 days old or younger if the child is voluntarily delivered to the provider by the child's parent and the parent did not express an intent to return for the child.

(b) A designated emergency infant care provider who takes possession of a child under this section has no legal duty to detain or pursue the parent and may not do so unless the child appears to have been abused or neglected. The designated emergency infant care provider has no legal duty to ascertain the parent's identity and the parent may remain anonymous. However, the parent may be given a form for voluntary disclosure of the child's medical facts and history.

(c) A designated emergency infant care provider who takes possession of a child under this section shall perform any act necessary to protect the physical health or safety of the child. The designated emergency infant care provider is not liable for damages related to the provider's taking possession of, examining, or treating the child, except for damages related to the provider's negligence.

(Enacted by Acts 1999, 76th Leg., ch. 1087 (H.B. 3423), § 2, effective September 1, 1999; am. Acts 2001, 77th Leg., ch. 809 (H.B. 706), § 4, effective September 1, 2001 (renumbered from Sec. 262.301).)

### Sec. 262.303. Notification of Possession of Abandoned Child.

(a) Not later than the close of the first business day after the date on which a designated emergency infant care provider takes possession of a child under Section 262.302, the provider shall notify the Department of Protective and Regulatory Services that the provider has taken possession of the child.

(b) The department shall assume the care, control, and custody of the child immediately on receipt of notice under Subsection (a).

(Enacted by Acts 1999, 76th Leg., ch. 1087 (H.B. 3423), § 2, effective September 1, 1999; am. Acts 2001, 77th Leg., ch. 809 (H.B. 706), § 4, effective September 1, 2001 (renumbered from Sec. 262.302).)

### Sec. 262.304. Filing Petition After Accepting Possession of Abandoned Child.

A child for whom the Department of Protective and Regulatory Services assumes care, control, and custody under Section 262.303 shall be

treated as a child taken into possession without a court order, and the department shall take action as required by Section 262.105 with regard to the child.
(Enacted by Acts 1999, 76th Leg., ch. 1087 (H.B. 3423), § 2, effective September 1, 1999; am. Acts 2001, 77th Leg., ch. 809 (H.B. 706), § 4, effective September 1, 2001 (renumbered from Sec. 262.303).)

### Sec. 262.305. Report to Law Enforcement Agency; Investigation.

(a) Immediately after assuming care, control, and custody of a child under Section 262.303, the Department of Protective and Regulatory Services shall report the child to appropriate state and local law enforcement agencies as a potential missing child.

(b) A law enforcement agency that receives a report under Subsection (a) shall investigate whether the child is reported as missing.
(Enacted by Acts 2001, 77th Leg., ch. 809 (H.B. 706), § 4, effective September 1, 2001.)

### Sec. 262.306. Notice.

Each designated emergency infant care provider shall post in a conspicuous location a notice stating that the provider is a designated emergency infant care provider location and will accept possession of a child in accordance with this subchapter.
(Enacted by Acts 2001, 77th Leg., ch. 809 (H.B. 706), § 4, effective September 1, 2001.)

### Sec. 262.307. Reimbursement for Care of Abandoned Child.

The department shall reimburse a designated emergency infant care provider that takes possession of a child under Section 262.302 for the cost to the provider of assuming the care, control, and custody of the child.
(Enacted by Acts 2001, 77th Leg., ch. 809 (H.B. 706), § 4, effective September 1, 2001.)

### Sec. 262.308. Confidentiality.

(a) All identifying information, documentation, or other records regarding a person who voluntarily delivers a child to a designated emergency infant care provider under this subchapter is confidential and not subject to release to any individual or entity except as provided by Subsection (b).

(b) Any pleading or other document filed with a court under this subchapter is confidential, is not public information for purposes of Chapter 552, Government Code, and may not be released to a person other than to a party in a suit regarding the child, the party's attorney, or an attorney ad litem or guardian ad litem appointed in the suit.

(c) In a suit concerning a child for whom the Department of Family and Protective Services assumes care, control, and custody under this subchapter, the court shall close the hearing to the public unless the court finds that the interests of the child or the public would be better served by opening the hearing to the public.

(d) Unless the disclosure, receipt, or use is permitted by this section, a person commits an offense if the person knowingly discloses, receives, uses, or permits the use of information derived from records or files described by this section or knowingly discloses identifying information concerning a person who voluntarily delivers a child to a designated emergency infant care provider. An offense under this subsection is a Class B misdemeanor.
(Enacted by Acts 2005, 79th Leg., ch. 620 (H.B. 2331), § 1, effective September 1, 2005.)

### Sec. 262.309. Search for Relatives Not Required.

The Department of Family and Protective Services is not required to conduct a search for the relatives of a child for whom the department assumes care, control, and custody under this subchapter.
(Enacted by Acts 2005, 79th Leg., ch. 620 (H.B. 2331), § 1, effective September 1, 2005.)

## CHAPTER 264
## CHILD WELFARE SERVICES

### SUBCHAPTER F
### CHILD FATALITY REVIEW AND INVESTIGATION

### Sec. 264.513. Report of Death of Child.

(a) A person who knows of the death of a child younger than six years of age shall immediately report the death to the medical examiner of the county in which the death occurs or, if the death occurs in a county that does not have a medical examiner's office or that is not part of a medical examiner's district, to a justice of the peace in that county.

Family Code

(b) The requirement of this section is in addition to any other reporting requirement imposed by law, including any requirement that a person report child abuse or neglect under this code.

(c) A person is not required to report a death under this section that is the result of a motor vehicle accident. This subsection does not affect a duty imposed by another law to report a death that is the result of a motor vehicle accident.

(Enacted by Acts 1995, 74th Leg., ch. 255 (S.B. 81), § 2, effective September 1, 1995; enacted by Acts 1995, 74th Leg., ch. 878 (S.B. 1485), § 1, effective September 1, 1995.)

# Finance Code

## TITLE 3
## FINANCIAL INSTITUTIONS AND BUSINESSES

### SUBTITLE E
### OTHER FINANCIAL BUSINESSES

### CHAPTER 151
### REGULATION OF MONEY SERVICES BUSINESSES

## SUBCHAPTER A
## GENERAL PROVISIONS

### Sec. 151.001.  Short Title.

This chapter may be cited as the Money Services Act.

(Enacted by Acts 2005, 79th Leg., ch. 1099 (H.B. 2218), § 1, effective September 1, 2005.)

### Sec. 151.002.  Definitions.

(a) This section defines general terms that apply to an applicant for or holder of a money services license issued under this chapter, regardless of whether the license is a money transmission license or a currency exchange license. Additional terms that apply specifically to money transmission are defined in Section 151.301. Additional terms that apply specifically to currency exchange are defined in Section 151.501.

(b) In this chapter:

(1) "Applicant" means a person that files an application for a license under this chapter.

(2) "Authorized delegate" means a person a license holder appoints under Section 151.402 to conduct money transmission on behalf of the license holder.

(3) "Bank Secrecy Act" means the Bank Secrecy Act (31 U.S.C. Section 5311 et seq.), and its implementing regulations set forth at 31 C.F.R. Part 103.

(4) "Commission" means the Finance Commission of Texas.

(5) "Commissioner" means the Banking Commissioner of Texas or a person designated by the banking commissioner and acting under the banking commissioner's direction and authority.

(6) "Control" means ownership of, or the power to directly or indirectly vote, 25 percent or more of the outstanding voting interests of a license holder or applicant, and includes an individual whose ownership is through one or more legal entities.

(7) "Currency exchange" has the meaning assigned by Section 151.501.

(8) "Currency exchange license" means a license issued under Subchapter F.

(9) "Department" means the Texas Department of Banking.

(10) "Executive officer" means a president, a presiding officer of the executive committee, a treasurer or chief financial officer, or any other individual who performs similar functions.

(11) "License holder" means a person that holds a money transmission license or a currency exchange license.

(12) "Location" means a place at which activity regulated by this chapter occurs.

(13) "Material litigation" means any litigation that, according to generally accepted accounting principles, is considered significant to an applicant's or license holder's financial health and would be required to be referenced in that entity's audited financial statements, report to shareholders, or similar documents.

(14) "Money services" means money transmission or currency exchange.

(15) "Money transmission" has the meaning assigned by Section 151.301.

(16) "Money transmission license" means a license issued under Subchapter D.

(17) "Person" means an individual or legal entity.

(18) "Principal" means:

(A) with respect to a sole proprietorship, an owner; or

(B) with respect to a legal entity other than a sole proprietorship, an executive officer, director, general partner, trustee, or manager, as applicable.

(19) "Record" means information that is:

(A) inscribed on a tangible medium; or

(B) stored in an electronic or other medium and retrievable in perceivable form.

(20) "Responsible individual" means an individual who has direct control over or significant management policy and decision-making authority with respect to a license holder's ongoing, daily money services operations in this state.

(21) "USA PATRIOT ACT" means the Uniting and Strengthening America by Providing Appropriate Tools Required to Intercept and Obstruct Terrorism (USA PATRIOT ACT) Act of 2001 (Pub. L. No. 107-56, 115 Stat. 272).

(Enacted by Acts 2005, 79th Leg., ch. 1099 (H.B. 2218), § 1, effective September 1, 2005.)

### Sec. 151.003.  Exclusions.

The following persons are not required to be licensed under this chapter:

(1) the United States or an instrumentality of the United States, including the United States Post Office or a contractor acting on behalf of the United States Post Office;

(2) a state or an agency, political subdivision, or other instrumentality of a state;

(3) a federally insured financial institution, as that term is defined by Section 201.101, that is organized under the laws of this state, another state, or the United States;

Finance

(4) a foreign bank branch or agency in the United States established under the federal International Banking Act of 1978 (12 U.S.C. Section 3101 et seq.);

(5) a person acting as an agent for an entity excluded under Subdivision (3) or (4), to the extent of the person's actions in that capacity, provided that:

(A) the entity is liable for satisfying the money services obligation owed to the purchaser on the person's receipt of the purchaser's money; and

(B) the entity and person enter into a written contract that appoints the person as the entity's agent and the person acts only within the scope of authority conferred by the contract;

(6) a person that, on behalf of the United States or a department, agency, or instrumentality of the United States, or a state or county, city, or any other governmental agency or political subdivision of a state, provides electronic funds transfer services of governmental benefits for a federal, state, county, or local governmental agency;

(7) a person that acts as an intermediary on behalf of and at the direction of a license holder in the process by which the license holder, after receiving money or monetary value from a purchaser, either directly or through an authorized delegate, transmits the money or monetary value to the purchaser's designated recipient, provided that the license holder is liable for satisfying the obligation owed to the purchaser;

(8) an attorney or title company that in connection with a real property transaction receives and disburses domestic currency or issues an escrow or trust fund check only on behalf of a party to the transaction;

(9) a person engaged in the business of currency transportation who is both a registered motor carrier under Chapter 643, Transportation Code, and a licensed armored car company or courier company under Chapter 1702, Occupations Code, provided that the person does not engage in the money transmission or currency exchange business without a license issued under this chapter; and

(10) any other person, transaction, or class of persons or transactions exempted by commission rule or any other person or transaction exempted by the commissioner's order on a finding that the licensing of the person is not

necessary to achieve the purposes of this chapter.
(Enacted by Acts 2005, 79th Leg., ch. 1099 (H.B. 2218), § 1, effective September 1, 2005.)

### Sec. 151.051. Incorporation Requirement [Repealed].

Repealed by Acts 1999, 76th leg., ch. 62 (S.B. 1368), § 7.17, effective September 1, 1999.
(Enacted by Acts 1997, 75th Leg., ch. 1008 (H.B. 10), § 1, effective September 1, 1997; repealed by Acts 1999, 76th Leg., ch. 62 (S.B. 1368), § 7.17(b), effective September 1, 1999.)

### Sec. 151.052. Purposes of Incorporation [Repealed].

Repealed by Acts 1999, 76th leg., ch. 62 (S.B. 1368), § 7.17, effective September 1, 1999.
(Enacted by Acts 1997, 75th Leg., ch. 1008 (H.B. 10), § 1, effective September 1, 1997; repealed by Acts 1999, 76th Leg., ch. 62 (S.B. 1368), § 7.17(b), effective September 1, 1999.)

### Sec. 151.053. Paid-In Capital [Repealed].

Repealed by Acts 1999, 76th leg., ch. 62 (S.B. 1368), § 7.17, effective September 1, 1999.
(Enacted by Acts 1997, 75th Leg., ch. 1008 (H.B. 10), § 1, effective September 1, 1997; repealed by Acts 1999, 76th Leg., ch. 62 (S.B. 1368), § 7.17(b), effective September 1, 1999.)

### Sec. 151.054. Determination of Application for Charter; Appeal [Repealed].

Repealed by Acts 1999, 76th leg., ch. 62 (S.B. 1368), § 7.17, effective September 1, 1999.
(Enacted by Acts 1997, 75th Leg., ch. 1008 (H.B. 10), § 1, effective September 1, 1997; repealed by Acts 1999, 76th Leg., ch. 62 (S.B. 1368), § 7.17(b), effective September 1, 1999.)

## SUBCHAPTER B
## ADMINISTRATIVE PROVISIONS

### Sec. 151.101. Administration.

The department shall administer this chapter.
(Enacted by Acts 2005, 79th Leg., ch. 1099 (H.B. 2218), § 1, effective September 1, 2005.)

### Sec. 151.102. Rules.

(a) The commission may adopt rules to administer and enforce this chapter, including rules necessary or appropriate to:

(1) implement and clarify this chapter;

Finance

(2) preserve and protect the safety and soundness of money services businesses;

(3) protect the interests of purchasers of money services and the public;

(4) protect against drug trafficking, terrorist funding, and money laundering, structuring, or a related financial crime; and

(5) recover the cost of maintaining and operating the department and the cost of administering and enforcing this chapter and other applicable law by imposing and collecting proportionate and equitable fees and costs for notices, applications, examinations, investigations, and other actions required to achieve the purposes of this chapter.

(b) The presence or absence of a specific reference in this chapter to a rule regarding a particular subject is not intended to and does not limit the general rulemaking authority granted to the commission by this section.

(Enacted by Acts 2005, 79th Leg., ch. 1099 (H.B. 2218), § 1, effective September 1, 2005.)

### Sec. 151.103. Commissioner's General Authority.

(a) Each power granted to the commissioner under this chapter is in addition to, and not in limitation of, each other power granted under this chapter. The fact that the commissioner possesses, or has exercised, a power under a provision of this chapter does not preclude the commissioner from exercising a power under any other provision of this chapter.

(b) Each power granted to the commissioner under this chapter is in addition to, and not in limitation of, powers granted to the commissioner under other law. The fact that the commissioner possesses, or has exercised, a power under any other provision of law does not preclude the commissioner from exercising any power under this chapter. The fact that the commissioner possesses, or has exercised, a power under a provision of this chapter does not preclude the commissioner from exercising a power under any other law.

(c) The commissioner may impose on any authority, approval, exemption, license, or order issued or granted under this chapter any condition the commissioner considers reasonably necessary or appropriate to carry out and achieve the purposes of this chapter.

(Enacted by Acts 2005, 79th Leg., ch. 1099 (H.B. 2218), § 1, effective September 1, 2005.)

### Sec. 151.104. Investigations.

(a) The commissioner may conduct investigations in or outside this state and the United States as the commissioner considers necessary or appropriate to administer and enforce this chapter, including investigations to:

(1) determine whether to approve an application for or renewal of a license or a request for approval or exemption filed under this chapter or a rule adopted or order issued under this chapter;

(2) determine whether a person has violated or is likely to violate this chapter or a rule adopted or order issued under this chapter;

(3) determine whether a license or authorized delegate designation should be revoked or suspended;

(4) otherwise aid in the enforcement of this chapter or a rule adopted or order issued under this chapter; and

(5) aid in the adoption of rules or issuance of orders under this chapter.

(b) For purposes of an investigation, examination, or other proceeding under this chapter, the commissioner may administer or cause to be administered oaths, subpoena witnesses, compel the attendance of witnesses, take evidence, and require the production of any document that the commissioner determines to be relevant to the inquiry.

(c) If a person refuses to obey a subpoena, a district court of Travis County, on application by the commissioner, may issue an order requiring the person to appear before the commissioner and produce documents or give evidence regarding the matter under investigation.

(d) The commissioner may employ a person or request the attorney general, the Department of Public Safety, or any other state, federal, or local law enforcement agency to assist in enforcing this chapter.

(e) The commissioner may recover the reasonable costs incurred in connection with an investigation conducted under this chapter from the person that is the subject of the investigation.

(Enacted by Acts 2005, 79th Leg., ch. 1099 (H.B. 2218), § 1, effective September 1, 2005.)

### Sec. 151.105. Regulatory Cooperation.

(a) To efficiently and effectively administer and enforce this chapter and to minimize regulatory burden, the commissioner may cooperate, coordinate, and share information with another state, federal, or foreign governmental agency that:

(1) regulates or supervises persons engaged in money services businesses or activities subject to this chapter; or

(2) is authorized to investigate or prosecute violations of a state, federal, or foreign law related to persons engaged in money services businesses or activities subject to this chapter, including a state attorney general's office.

(b) The commissioner, with respect to an agency described by and for the purposes set forth in Subsection (a), may:

(1) enter into a written cooperation, coordination, or information-sharing contract or agreement with the agency;

(2) share information with the agency, subject to the confidentiality provisions of Section 151.606(b)(3);

(3) conduct a joint or concurrent on-site examination or other investigation or enforcement action with the agency;

(4) accept a report of examination or investigation by, or a report submitted to, the agency, in which event the accepted report is an official report of the commissioner for all purposes;

(5) engage the services of the agency to assist the commissioner in performing or discharging a duty or responsibility imposed by this chapter or other law and pay a reasonable fee for the services;

(6) share with the agency any supervisory or examination fees assessed against a license holder or authorized delegate under this chapter and receive a portion of supervisory or examination fees assessed by the agency against a license holder or authorized delegate; and

(7) take other action as the commissioner considers reasonably necessary or appropriate to carry out and achieve the purposes of this chapter.

(c) The commissioner may not waive, and nothing in this section constitutes a waiver of, the commissioner's authority to conduct an examination or investigation or otherwise take independent action authorized by this chapter or a rule adopted or order issued under this chapter to enforce compliance with applicable state or federal law.

(d) A joint examination or investigation, or acceptance of an examination or investigation report, does not waive an examination assessment provided for in this chapter.

(e) Chapter 2254, Government Code, does not apply to a contract or agreement entered into under this section.

(Enacted by Acts 2005, 79th Leg., ch. 1099 (H.B. 2218), § 1, effective September 1, 2005.)

### Sec. 151.106. Consent to Service of Process.

A license holder, an authorized delegate, or a person who knowingly engages in activities that are regulated and require a license under this chapter, with or without filing an application for a license or holding a license under this chapter, is considered to have consented to the jurisdiction of the courts of this state for all actions arising under this chapter.

(Enacted by Acts 2005, 79th Leg., ch. 1099 (H.B. 2218), § 1, effective September 1, 2005.)

### Sec. 151.107. Compliance with the Securities Act [Repealed].

Repealed by Acts 1999, 76th Leg., ch. 62 (S.B. 1368), § 7.17, effective September 1, 1999.

(Enacted by Acts 1997, 75th Leg., ch. 1008 (H.B. 10), § 1, effective September 1, 1997; repealed by Acts 1999, 76th Leg., ch. 62 (S.B. 1368), § 7.17(b), effective September 1, 1999.)

### Sec. 151.151. Restrictions on Foreign Trust Companies and Corporations [Repealed].

Repealed by Acts 1999, 76th Leg., ch. 62 (S.B. 1368), § 7.17, effective September 1, 1999.

(Enacted by Acts 1997, 75th Leg., ch. 1008 (H.B. 10), § 1, effective September 1, 1997; repealed by Acts 1999, 76th Leg., ch. 62 (S.B. 1368), § 7.17(b), effective September 1, 1999.)

### Sec. 151.152. Examination [Repealed].

Repealed by Acts 1999, 76th Leg., ch. 62 (S.B. 1368), § 7.17, effective September 1, 1999.

(Enacted by Acts 1997, 75th Leg., ch. 1008 (H.B. 10), § 1, effective September 1, 1997; repealed by Acts 1999, 76th Leg., ch. 62 (S.B. 1368), § 7.17(b), effective September 1, 1999.)

### Sec. 151.153. Applicability of Provisions to Certain Foreign Corporations [Repealed].

Repealed by Acts 1999, 76th Leg., ch. 62 (S.B. 1368), § 7.17, effective September 1, 1999.

(Enacted by Acts 1997, 75th Leg., ch. 1008 (H.B. 10), § 1, effective September 1, 1997; repealed by Acts 1999, 76th Leg., ch. 62 (S.B. 1368), § 7.17(b), effective September 1, 1999.)

### Sec. 151.154. Acquisition or Control of Trust Company by Foreign Trust Company or Corporation [Repealed].

Repealed by Acts 1999, 76th Leg., ch. 62 (S.B. 1368), § 7.17, effective September 1, 1999.

(Enacted by Acts 1997, 75th Leg., ch. 1008 (H.B. 10), § 1, effective September 1, 1997; repealed by Acts 1999, 76th Leg., ch. 62 (S.B. 1368), § 7.17(b), effective September 1, 1999.)

### Sec. 151.155. Establishment of Trust Relationship Regardless of Domicile [Repealed].

Repealed by Acts 1999, 76th Leg., ch. 62 (S.B. 1368), § 7.17, effective September 1, 1999.

(Enacted by Acts 1997, 75th Leg., ch. 1008 (H.B. 10), § 1, effective September 1, 1997; repealed by Acts 1999, 76th Leg., ch. 62 (S.B. 1368), § 7.17(b), effective September 1, 1999.)

## SUBCHAPTER C
## GENERAL QUALIFICATIONS AND PROVISIONS APPLICABLE TO MONEY SERVICES LICENSES

### Sec. 151.201. Scope.

This subchapter sets out the general qualifications and provisions that apply to a money services license, regardless of whether the license is a money transmission license or a currency exchange license. Subchapters D and E set forth the additional qualifications and provisions that apply specifically to a money transmission license. Subchapter F sets forth the additional qualifications and provisions that apply specifically to a currency exchange license.

(Enacted by Acts 2005, 79th Leg., ch. 1099 (H.B. 2218), § 1, effective September 1, 2005.)

### Sec. 151.202. Qualifications for License.

(a) Subject to Subsections (b) and (c), to qualify for a license under this chapter, an applicant must demonstrate to the satisfaction of the commissioner that:

(1) the financial responsibility and condition, financial and business experience, competence, character, and general fitness of the applicant justify the confidence of the public and warrant the belief that the applicant will conduct business in compliance with this chapter and the rules adopted under this chapter and other applicable state and federal law;

(2) the issuance of the license is in the public interest;

(3) the applicant, a principal of the applicant, or a person in control of the applicant does not owe the department a delinquent fee, assessment, administrative penalty, or other amount imposed under this chapter or a rule adopted or order issued under this chapter;

(4) the applicant, if a partnership, and any partner that would generally be liable for the obligations of the partnership, does not owe a delinquent federal tax;

(5) the applicant, if a corporation:

(A) is in good standing and statutory compliance in the state or country of incorporation;

(B) is authorized to engage in business in this state; and

(C) does not owe any delinquent franchise or other taxes to this state;

(6) the applicant, if not a corporation, is properly registered under the laws of this state or another state or country and, if required, is authorized to engage in business in this state; and

(7) the applicant, a principal of the applicant, or a principal of a person in control of the applicant is not listed on the specifically designated nationals and blocked persons list prepared by the United States Department of the Treasury, or designated successor agency, as a potential threat to commit or fund terrorist acts.

(b) In determining whether an applicant has demonstrated satisfaction of the qualifications identified in Subsection (a)(1), the commissioner shall consider the financial responsibility and condition, financial and business experience, competence, character, and general fitness of each principal of, person in control of, principal of a person in control of, and proposed responsible individual of the applicant and may deny approval of the application on the basis that the applicant has failed to demonstrate satisfaction of the requisite qualifications with respect to one or more of those persons.

(c) The commissioner may not issue a license to an applicant if the applicant or one of the following persons has been convicted within the preceding 10 years of a criminal offense specified in Subsection (e):

(1) if the applicant is an individual, the spouse or proposed responsible individual or individuals of the applicant;

(2) if the applicant is an entity that is wholly owned, directly or indirectly, by a single individual, the spouse of the individual; or

(3) if the applicant is a person other than an individual, a principal of, person in control of, principal of a person in control of, or proposed responsible individual or individuals of the applicant.

(d) The commissioner, on a finding that the conviction does not reflect adversely on the present likelihood that the applicant will conduct business in compliance with this chapter, rules adopted under this chapter, and other applicable state and federal law, may waive a disqualification under Subsection (c) based on the conviction of a spouse or a corporate applicant or corporate person in control of an applicant.

(e) For purposes of Subsection (c), a disqualifying conviction is a conviction for a felony criminal offense:

(1) under state or federal law that involves or relates to:

(A) deception, dishonesty, or defalcation;

(B) money transmission or other money services, including a reporting, recordkeeping or registration requirement of the Bank Secrecy Act, the USA PATRIOT ACT, or Chapter 271;

(C) money laundering, structuring, or a related financial crime;

(D) drug trafficking; or

(E) terrorist funding; and

(2) under a similar law of a foreign country unless the applicant demonstrates to the satisfaction of the commissioner that the conviction was based on extenuating circumstances unrelated to the person's reputation for honesty and obedience to law.

(f) For purposes of Subsection (c), a person is considered to have been convicted of an offense if the person has been found guilty or pleaded guilty or nolo contendere to the charge or has been placed on probation or deferred adjudication without regard to whether a judgment of conviction has been entered by the court.

(Enacted by Acts 2005, 79th Leg., ch. 1099 (H.B. 2218), § 1, effective September 1, 2005.)

## Sec. 151.203. Application for License.

(a) An application for a license under this chapter must be made under oath and in the form and medium required by the commissioner. The application must contain:

(1) the legal name and residential and business address of the applicant and each principal of the applicant;

(2) the taxpayer identification number, social security number, driver's license number, or other identifying information the commissioner requires of the applicant and each principal of the applicant; and

(3) any other information or documentation the commissioner reasonably requires to determine whether the applicant qualifies for and should be issued the license for which application is made.

(b) The commissioner, at the time the application is submitted or in connection with an investigation of the application under Section 151.204, may require the applicant, the spouse of the applicant, a principal of, individual who is a person in control of, or proposed responsible individual of the applicant, or any other individual associated with the applicant and the proposed licensed activities, to provide the department a complete set of fingerprints for purposes of a criminal background investigation.

(c) An applicant must certify in writing on the application that the applicant and each principal of, person in control of, and proposed responsible individual of the applicant:

(1) is familiar with and agrees to fully comply with all applicable state and federal laws and regulations pertaining to the applicant's proposed money services business, including this chapter, relevant provisions of the Bank Secrecy Act, the USA PATRIOT ACT, and Chapter 271;

(2) has not within the preceding three years knowingly failed to file or evaded the obligation to file a report, including a currency transaction or suspicious activity report required by the Bank Secrecy Act, the USA PATRIOT ACT, or Chapter 271; and

(3) has not knowingly accepted money for transmission or exchange in which a portion of the money was derived from an illegal transaction or activity.

(d) The commissioner may waive an application requirement or permit the submission of substituted information in lieu of the information generally required in an application, either with respect to a specific applicant or a category of applicants, if the commissioner determines that the waiver or substitution of information is con-

Finance

sistent with achievement of the purposes of this chapter.
(Enacted by Acts 2005, 79th Leg., ch. 1099 (H.B. 2218), § 1, effective September 1, 2005.)

### Sec. 151.204.  Processing and Investigation of Application.

(a) An application for a license under this chapter shall be processed and acted on according to the time periods established by commission rule.

(b) On receipt of an application that meets the requirements of Section 151.203 and Section 151.304 or 151.504, as applicable, the commissioner shall investigate the applicant to determine whether the prescribed qualifications have been met. The commissioner may:

(1) conduct an on-site investigation of the applicant;

(2) employ a screening service to assist with the investigation;

(3) to the extent the commissioner considers reasonably necessary to evaluate the application and the applicant's qualifications, investigate the financial responsibility and condition, financial and business experience, character and general fitness of each principal of, person in control of, principal of a person in control of, or proposed responsible individual of the applicant or any other person that is or will be associated with the applicant's licensed activities in this state; or

(4) require additional information and take other action the commissioner considers reasonably necessary.

(c) The commissioner may collect from the applicant the reasonable expenses of an on-site examination or third-party investigation. Additionally, depending on the nature and extent of the investigation required in connection with a particular application, the commissioner may require an applicant to pay a nonrefundable investigation fee in an amount established by commission rule.

(d) The commissioner may suspend consideration of an application for a license if the applicant or a principal of, person in control of, or proposed responsible individual of the applicant is the subject of a pending state or federal criminal prosecution, state or federal government enforcement action, or state or federal asset forfeiture proceeding until the conclusion of the prosecution, action, or proceeding.
(Enacted by Acts 2005, 79th Leg., ch. 1099 (H.B. 2218), § 1, effective September 1, 2005.)

### Sec. 151.205.  Issuance of License.

(a) The commissioner shall issue a license if the commissioner, with respect to the license for which application has been made, finds that:

(1) the applicant meets the prescribed qualifications and it is reasonable to believe that the applicant's business will be conducted fairly and lawfully, according to applicable state and federal law, and in a manner commanding the public's trust and confidence;

(2) the issuance of the license is in the public interest;

(3) the documentation and forms required to be submitted by the applicant are acceptable; and

(4) the applicant has satisfied all requirements for licensure.

(b) If the commissioner finds that the applicant for any reason fails to possess the qualifications or satisfy the requirements for the license for which application is made, the commissioner shall inform the applicant in writing that the application is denied and state the reasons for the denial. The applicant may appeal the denial by filing a written request for a hearing with the commissioner not later than the 30th day after the date the notice is mailed. A hearing on the denial must be held not later than the 45th day after the date the commissioner receives the written request unless the administrative law judge extends the period for good cause or the parties agree to a later hearing date. The hearing is considered a contested case hearing and is subject to Section 151.801.
(Enacted by Acts 2005, 79th Leg., ch. 1099 (H.B. 2218), § 1, effective September 1, 2005.)

### Sec. 151.206.  Transfer or Assignment of License.

A license issued under this chapter may not be transferred or assigned.
(Enacted by Acts 2005, 79th Leg., ch. 1099 (H.B. 2218), § 1, effective September 1, 2005.)

### Sec. 151.207.  Renewal of License.

(a) Regardless of the date on which a license under this chapter is issued, the license expires on August 15 of each year unless the license is renewed in accordance with this section or is previously surrendered by the license holder or suspended or revoked by the commissioner.

(b) As a condition of renewal, a license holder must continue to possess the qualifications and satisfy the requirements that apply to an applicant for a new money transmission license or currency exchange license, as applicable. Additionally, not later than July 1 of each year, a license holder must:

(1) pay an annual renewal fee in an amount established by commission rule; and

(2) submit a renewal report that is under oath, is in the form and medium required by the commissioner, and contains:

(A) if the license is a money transmission license, an audited unconsolidated financial statement dated as of the last day of the license holder's fiscal year that ended in the immediately preceding calendar year;

(B) if the license is a currency exchange license, a financial statement, audited or unaudited, dated as of the last day of the license holder's fiscal year that ended in the immediately preceding calendar year; and

(C) documentation and certification, or any other information the commissioner reasonably requires to determine the security, net worth, permissible investments, and other requirements the license holder must satisfy and whether the license holder continues to meet the qualifications and requirements for licensure.

(c) If the department does not receive a license holder's renewal fee and complete renewal report on or before July 1, the commissioner shall notify the license holder in writing that:

(1) the license holder has until August 15 to submit the renewal report and pay the renewal fee; and

(2) the license holder must pay a late fee, in an amount that is established by commission rule and not subject to appeal, for each business day after July 1 that the commissioner does not receive the completed renewal report and renewal fee.

(d) If the license holder fails to submit the completed renewal report and pay the renewal fee and any late fee due, the license expires effective 5 p.m. central daylight time on August 15, and the license holder must cease and desist from engaging in the business of money transmission or currency exchange, as applicable, as of that time. The expiration of a license is not subject to appeal.

(e) On timely receipt of a license holder's complete renewal report, renewal fee, and any late fee due, the department shall review the report and, if necessary, investigate the business and records of the license holder. On completion of the review and investigation, if any, the commissioner may:

(1) renew the license;

(2) impose conditions on the renewal of the license the commissioner may consider reasonably necessary or appropriate; or

(3) suspend or revoke the license on the basis of a ground specified in Section 151.703.

(f) On written application and for good cause shown, the commissioner may extend the time for filing the fee and report required under this section.

(g) The holder or principal of or the person in control of the holder of an expired license, or the holder or principal of or person in control of the holder of a license surrendered under Section 151.208, that wishes to conduct activities for which a license is required under this chapter must file a new license application and satisfy all requirements for licensure that apply at the time the new application is filed.

(Enacted by Acts 2005, 79th Leg., ch. 1099 (H.B. 2218), § 1, effective September 1, 2005.)

### Sec. 151.208.  Surrender of License.

(a) A license holder may surrender the license holder's license by delivering the original license to the commissioner along with a written notice of surrender that includes the location at which the license holder's records will be stored and the name, address, telephone number, and other contact information for an individual who is authorized to provide access to the records.

(b) A license holder shall surrender the license holder's license if the license holder becomes ineligible for a license under Section 151.202(c).

(c) The surrender of a license does not reduce or eliminate a license holder's civil or criminal liability arising from any acts or omissions before the surrender of the license, including any administrative action undertaken by the commissioner to deny the renewal of a license, to revoke or suspend a license, to assess an administrative penalty, to order the payment of restitution, or to exercise any other authority under this chapter. Further, the surrender of a license does not release the security required of the license holder under Section 151.308 or 151.506.

(Enacted by Acts 2005, 79th Leg., ch. 1099 (H.B. 2218), § 1, effective September 1, 2005.)

### Sec. 151.209.  Refunds.

A fee or cost paid under this chapter in connection with an application or renewal is not refundable.

(Enacted by Acts 2005, 79th Leg., ch. 1099 (H.B. 2218), § 1, effective September 1, 2005.)

### Sec. 151.251. Administrative Penalty [Repealed].

Repealed by Acts 1999, 76th Leg., ch. 62 (S.B. 1368), § 7.17, effective September 1, 1999. (Enacted by Acts 1997, 75th Leg., ch. 1008 (H.B. 10), § 1, effective September 1, 1997; repealed by Acts 1999, 76th Leg., ch. 62 (S.B. 1368), § 7.17(b), effective September 1, 1999.)

### Sec. 151.252. Revocation of Certificate of Foreign Corporation [Repealed].

Repealed by Acts 1999, 76th Leg., ch. 62 (S.B. 1368), § 7.17, effective September 1, 1999. (Enacted by Acts 1997, 75th Leg., ch. 1008 (H.B. 10), § 1, effective September 1, 1997; repealed by Acts 1999, 76th Leg., ch. 62 (S.B. 1368), § 7.17(b), effective September 1, 1999.)

### Sec. 151.253. Forfeiture of Charter of Trust Company [Repealed].

Repealed by Acts 1999, 76th Leg., ch. 62 (S.B. 1368), § 7.17, effective September 1, 1999. (Enacted by Acts 1997, 75th Leg., ch. 1008 (H.B. 10), § 1, effective September 1, 1997; repealed by Acts 1999, 76th Leg., ch. 62 (S.B. 1368), § 7.17(b), effective September 1, 1999.)

### Sec. 151.254. Enforcement Order [Repealed].

Repealed by Acts 1999, 76th Leg., ch. 62 (S.B. 1368), § 7.17, effective September 1, 1999. (Enacted by Acts 1997, 75th Leg., ch. 1008 (H.B. 10), § 1, effective September 1, 1997; repealed by Acts 1999, 76th Leg., ch. 62 (S.B. 1368), § 7.17(b), effective September 1, 1999.)

### Sec. 151.255. Supervision or Conservatorship [Repealed].

Repealed by Acts 1999, 76th Leg., ch. 62 (S.B. 1368), § 7.17, effective September 1, 1999. (Enacted by Acts 1997, 75th Leg., ch. 1008 (H.B. 10), § 1, effective September 1, 1997; repealed by Acts 1999, 76th Leg., ch. 62 (S.B. 1368), § 7.17(b), effective September 1, 1999.)

### Sec. 151.256. Priority of Claims on Liquidation [Repealed].

Repealed by Acts 1999, 76th Leg., ch. 62 (S.B. 1368), § 7.17, effective September 1, 1999.

(Enacted by Acts 1997, 75th Leg., ch. 1008 (H.B. 10), § 1, effective September 1, 1997; repealed by Acts 1999, 76th Leg., ch. 62 (S.B. 1368), § 7.17(b), effective September 1, 1999.)

### Sec. 151.257. Venue for Liquidation Action [Repealed].

Repealed by Acts 1999, 76th Leg., ch. 62 (S.B. 1368), § 7.17, effective September 1, 1999. (Enacted by Acts 1997, 75th Leg., ch. 1008 (H.B. 10), § 1, effective September 1, 1997; repealed by Acts 1999, 76th Leg., ch. 62 (S.B. 1368), § 7.17(b), effective September 1, 1999.)

## SUBCHAPTER D
## MONEY TRANSMISSION LICENSE

### Sec. 151.301. Definitions.

(a) This section defines terms that apply to an applicant for or holder of a money transmission license issued under this subchapter.

(b) In this subchapter:

(1) "Currency" means the coin and paper money of the United States or another country that is designated as legal tender and circulates and is customarily used and accepted as a medium of exchange in the country of issuance.

(2) "Electronic instrument" means a card or other tangible object for the transmission, transfer, or payment of money or monetary value, that contains an electronic chip or strip for the storage of information or that provides access to information.

(3) "Money" or "monetary value" means currency or a claim that can be converted into currency through a financial institution, electronic payments network, or other formal or informal payment system.

(4) "Money transmission" means the receipt of money or monetary value by any means in exchange for a promise to make the money or monetary value available at a later time or different location. The term:

(A) includes:

(i) selling or issuing stored value or payment instruments, including checks, money orders, and traveler's checks;

(ii) receiving money or monetary value for transmission, including by payment instrument, wire, facsimile, electronic transfer, or ACH debit;

(iii) providing third-party bill paying services; or

(iv) receiving currency or an instrument payable in currency to physically transport the currency or its equivalent from one location to another by motor vehicle or other means of transportation or through the use of the mail or a shipping, courier, or other delivery service; and

(B) does not include the provision solely of online or telecommunication services or connection services to the Internet.

(5) "Outstanding" means:

(A) with respect to a payment instrument or stored value, a payment instrument or stored value that has been issued and sold in the United States directly by the license holder, or sold by an authorized delegate of the license holder in the United States and reported to the license holder, that has not yet been paid by or for the license holder; or

(B) with respect to transmission, a money transmission for which the license holder, directly or through an authorized delegate of the license holder, has received money or monetary value from the customer for transmission, but has not yet completed the money transmission by delivering the money or monetary value to the person designated by the customer or refunded the money or monetary value to the customer.

(6) "Payment instrument" means a written or electronic equivalent of a check, draft, money order, traveler's check, or other written or electronic instrument, service, or device for the transmission or payment of money or monetary value, sold or issued to one or more persons, regardless of whether negotiable. The term does not include an instrument, service, or device that:

(A) transfers money directly from a purchaser to a creditor of the purchaser or to an agent of the creditor;

(B) is redeemed by the issuer in goods or services or a cash or credit refund under circumstances not designed to evade the obligations and responsibilities imposed by this chapter; or

(C) is a credit card voucher or letter of credit.

(7) "Receive" means to obtain possession of money or monetary value in a manner that cannot be reversed through the exercise of routine contractual or statutory rights.

(8) "Stored value" means monetary value evidenced by an electronic record that is prefunded and for which value is reduced on each use. The term does not include an electronic record that is:

(A) loaded with points, miles, or other nonmonetary value; or

(B) not sold to the public but distributed as a reward or charitable donation.

(9) "Unsafe or unsound act or practice" means a practice of or conduct by a license holder or an authorized delegate of the license holder that creates the likelihood of material loss, insolvency, or dissipation of the license holder's assets, or that otherwise materially prejudices the interests of the license holder or the license holder's customers.

(Enacted by Acts 2005, 79th Leg., ch. 1099 (H.B. 2218), § 1, effective September 1, 2005.)

## Sec. 151.302.  License Required.

(a)  A person may not engage in the business of money transmission or advertise, solicit, or hold itself out as a person that engages in the business of money transmission unless the person:

(1) is licensed under this subchapter;

(2) is an authorized delegate of a person licensed under this subchapter, appointed by the license holder in accordance with Section 151.402;

(3) is excluded from licensure under Section 151.003; or

(4) has been granted an exemption under Subsection (c).

(b) For purposes of this chapter:

(1) a person engages in the business of money transmission if the person conducts money transmission for persons located in this state and receives compensation or expects to receive compensation, directly or indirectly, for conducting the transmissions; and

(2) a person solicits, advertises, or holds itself out as a person that engages in the business of money transmission if the person represents that the person will conduct money transmission for persons located in this state.

(c) On application and a finding that the exemption is in the public interest, the commissioner may exempt a person that:

(1) incidentally engages in the money transmission business only to the extent reasonable and necessary to accomplish a primary business objective unrelated to the money transmission business;

(2) does not advertise or offer money transmission services to the public except to the extent reasonable and necessary to fairly advertise or offer the person's primary business services; and

(3) either transmits money exclusively in connection with commercial contracts in interstate commerce or does not charge a fee to transmit money or transmits money without a fee as an inducement for customer participation in the person's primary business.

(d) A license holder may engage in the money transmission business at one or more locations in this state owned, directly or indirectly, by the license holder, or through one or more authorized delegates, or both, under a single license granted to the license holder.

(Enacted by Acts 2005, 79th Leg., ch. 1099 (H.B. 2218), § 1, effective September 1, 2005.)

## Sec. 151.303. Additional Qualifications.

In addition to the general qualifications for licensure set forth in Section 151.202, an applicant for a money transmission license must demonstrate to the satisfaction of the commissioner that:

(1) the applicant has and will maintain the minimum net worth required under Section 151.307;

(2) the applicant's financial condition will enable the applicant to safely and soundly engage in the business of money transmission; and

(3) the applicant does not engage in any activity or practice that adversely affects the applicant's safety and soundness.

(Enacted by Acts 2005, 79th Leg., ch. 1099 (H.B. 2218), § 1, effective September 1, 2005.)

## Sec. 151.304. Application and Accompanying Fee, Statements, and Security.

(a) An applicant for a money transmission license must submit an application in accordance with Section 151.203.

(b) At the time an application for a money transmission license is submitted, an applicant must file with the department:

(1) an application fee in the amount established by commission rule;

(2) audited financial statements that are satisfactory to the commissioner for purposes of determining whether the applicant has the minimum net worth required under Section 151.307 and is likely to maintain the required minimum net worth if a license is issued; and

(3) security in the amount of $300,000, that meets the requirements of Section 151.308, and an undertaking or agreement that the appli-

cant will increase or supplement the security to equal the aggregate security required by the commissioner under that section before the issuance of the license and the start of operations.

(Enacted by Acts 2005, 79th Leg., ch. 1099 (H.B. 2218), § 1, effective September 1, 2005.)

## Sec. 151.305. Investigation and Action on Application.

The commissioner shall investigate the applicant and act on the application in accordance with Sections 151.204 and 151.205.

(Enacted by Acts 2005, 79th Leg., ch. 1099 (H.B. 2218), § 1, effective September 1, 2005.)

## Sec. 151.306. Temporary License.

(a) The commissioner may issue a temporary license to a person that is engaging in money transmission, but has not obtained a license under this subchapter, if the person:

(1) certifies in writing that the person qualifies for the license and will submit a completed license application not later than the 60th day after the date the temporary license is issued;

(2) submits a recent financial statement acceptable to the commissioner that reflects the minimum net worth required under Section 151.307;

(3) provides security that meets the requirements of Section 151.308 in an amount specified by the commissioner, but not less than $300,000;

(4) agrees in writing that, until a permanent license is issued, the person will engage only in activities being conducted at existing locations; and

(5) pays the application fee and a nonrefundable temporary license fee in the amount established by commission rule.

(b) The effective period for a temporary license may not exceed 90 days from the date the license is issued, provided that the commissioner may extend the period for not more than an additional 30 days if necessary to complete the processing of a timely filed application for which approval is likely.

(Enacted by Acts 2005, 79th Leg., ch. 1099 (H.B. 2218), § 1, effective September 1, 2005.)

## Sec. 151.307. Net Worth.

(a) An applicant for a money transmission license must possess, and a money transmission license holder must maintain at all times, a

Finance

minimum net worth computed in accordance with generally accepted accounting principles of:

    (1) $100,000, if business is proposed to be or is conducted, directly or through an authorized delegate, at four or fewer locations; or

    (2) $500,000, if business is proposed to be or is conducted, directly or through an authorized delegate, at five or more locations.

(b) The commissioner may increase the amount of net worth required of an applicant or license holder, up to a maximum of $1 million, if the commissioner determines, with respect to the applicant or license holder, that a higher net worth is necessary to achieve the purposes of this chapter based on:

    (1) the nature and volume of the projected or established business;

    (2) the number of locations at or through which money transmission is or will be conducted;

    (3) the amount, nature, quality, and liquidity of its assets;

    (4) the amount and nature of its liabilities;

    (5) the history of its operations and prospects for earning and retaining income;

    (6) the quality of its operations;

    (7) the quality of its management;

    (8) the nature and quality of its principals and persons in control;

    (9) the history of its compliance with applicable state and federal law; and

    (10) any other factor the commissioner considers relevant.

(Enacted by Acts 2005, 79th Leg., ch. 1099 (H.B. 2218), § 1, effective September 1, 2005.)

## Sec. 151.308. Security.

(a) An applicant for a money transmission license must provide, and a money transmission license holder must maintain at all times, security consisting of a surety bond, an irrevocable letter of credit, or a deposit instead of a bond in accordance with this section.

(b) The amount of the required security is the greater of $300,000 or an amount equal to one percent of the license holder's total yearly dollar volume of money transmission business in this state or the applicant's projected total volume of business in this state for the first year of licensure, up to a maximum of $2 million. When the amount of the required security exceeds $1 million, the applicant or license holder may, in the alternative, provide security in the amount of $1 million, plus a dollar for dollar increase in the net worth of the applicant or license holder over the amount required under Section 151.307, up to a total amount of $2 million.

(c) The security must:

    (1) be in a form satisfactory to the commissioner;

    (2) be payable to any claimant or to the commissioner, on behalf of a claimant or this state, for any liability arising out of the license holder's money transmission business in this state, incurred under, subject to, or by virtue of this chapter;

    (3) be conditioned on the faithful compliance of the license holder or the principals, responsible individuals, employees and authorized delegates of the license holder with this chapter or any rule adopted or order issued under this chapter; and

    (4) if the security is a bond, be issued by a qualified surety company authorized to engage in business in this state and acceptable to the commissioner or, if the security is an irrevocable letter of credit, be issued by a financial institution acceptable to the commissioner.

(d) A claimant may bring suit directly on the security, or the commissioner may bring suit on behalf of the claimant or the state, either in one action or in successive actions.

(e) The commissioner may collect from the security or proceeds of the security any delinquent fee, assessment, cost, penalty, or other amount imposed on and owed by a license holder. If the security is a surety bond, the commissioner shall give the surety reasonable prior notice of a hearing to impose an administrative penalty against the license holder, provided that a surety may not be considered an interested, aggrieved, or affected person for purposes of an administrative proceeding under Section 151.801 or Chapter 2001, Government Code.

(f) The security remains in effect until canceled, which may occur only after providing 30 days' written notice to the commissioner. Cancellation does not affect any liability incurred or accrued during the period covered by the security.

(g) The security shall cover claims for at least five years after the license holder surrenders its license or otherwise ceases to engage in activities for which a license is required under this subchapter. However, the commissioner may permit the amount of the security to be reduced or eliminated before that time to the extent that the amount of the license holder's obligations to the department and to purchasers in this state is reduced. The commissioner may permit a license holder to substitute another form of security when the license holder ceases to provide money transmission in this state.

(h) If the commissioner at any time reasonably determines that the required security is insecure, deficient in amount, or exhausted in whole or in part, the commissioner by written order shall require the license holder to file or make new or additional security to comply with this section.

(i) Instead of providing all or part of the amount of the security required by this section, an applicant or license holder may deposit, with a financial institution possessing trust powers that is authorized to conduct a trust business in this state and is acceptable to the commissioner, an aggregate amount of United States currency, certificates of deposit, or other cash equivalents that equals the total amount of the required security or the remaining part of the security. The deposit:

(1) must be held in trust in the name of and be pledged to the commissioner;

(2) must secure the same obligations as the security; and

(3) is subject to other conditions and terms the commissioner may reasonably require.

(j) The security is considered by operation of law to be held in trust for the benefit of this state and any individual to whom an obligation arising under this chapter is owed, and may not be considered an asset or property of the license holder in the event of bankruptcy, receivership, or a claim against the license holder unrelated to the license holder's obligations under this chapter.

(Enacted by Acts 2005, 79th Leg., ch. 1099 (H.B. 2218), § 1, effective September 1, 2005.)

## Sec. 151.309. Permissible Investments.

(a) A money transmission license holder must maintain at all times permissible investments that have an aggregate market value computed in accordance with generally accepted accounting principles in an amount not less than:

(1) if the license holder has a net worth of less than $5 million, the aggregate face amount of the license holder's average outstanding money transmission obligations in the United States, computed in the manner prescribed by commission rule; or

(2) if the license holder has a net worth of $5 million or more, 50 percent of the amount required by Subdivision (1).

(b) Except to the extent limited by Subsection (d), the following constitute a permissible investment for purposes of this section:

(1) 40 percent of the receivables due a license holder from authorized delegates resulting from money transmission under this chapter that is not past due or doubtful of collection;

(2) cash in demand or interest-bearing accounts with a federally insured depository institution, including certificates of deposit;

(3) certificates of deposit or senior debt obligations of a domestic federally insured depository institution that are readily marketable and insured by an agency of the federal government;

(4) investment grade bonds and other legally created general obligations of a state, an agency or political subdivision of a state, the United States, or an instrumentality of the United States;

(5) obligations that a state, an agency or political subdivision of a state, the United States, or an instrumentality of the United States has unconditionally agreed to purchase, insure, or guarantee and that bear a rating of one of the three highest grades as defined by a nationally recognized organization that rates securities;

(6) shares in a money market mutual fund if the mutual fund, under the terms of the mutual fund's governing documents, is authorized to invest only in securities of the type described by Subdivisions (4) and (5) or permitted by commission rule; and

(7) other assets and investments permitted by rule of the commission or approved by the commissioner in writing, based on a determination that the assets or investments have a safety substantially equivalent to other permissible investments.

(c) In addition to investments listed in Subsection (b), a permissible investment for purposes of Subsection (a) includes:

(1) the security provided under Section 151.308;

(2) a surety bond or letter of credit in addition to the security provided under Section 151.308, if the additional surety bond or letter of credit satisfies the requirements of Section 151.308; and

(3) that portion of a surety bond maintained for the benefit of the purchasers of the license holder's outstanding money transmission obligations in another state that is not in excess of the amount of the outstanding obligations in that state, provided:

(A) the license holder maintains a surety bond or letter of credit or has on hand other permissible investments, or a combination of investments, in an amount sufficient to satisfy the requirements of Subsection (a) with respect to the outstanding money transmission obligations in this state; and

(B) the surety bond is issued by a surety rated within the top two rating categories of a nationally recognized United States rating service.

(d) The commissioner, with respect to a license holder, may limit or disallow for purposes of determining compliance with Subsection (a) an investment, surety bond, or letter of credit otherwise permitted by this section if the commissioner determines it to be unsatisfactory for investment purposes or to pose a significant supervisory concern.

(e) A permissible investment subject to this section, even if commingled with other assets of the license holder, is considered by operation of law to be held in trust for the benefit of any individual to whom an obligation arising under this chapter is owed, and may not be considered an asset or property of the license holder in the event of bankruptcy, receivership, or a claim against the license holder unrelated to any of the license holder's obligations under this chapter. (Enacted by Acts 2005, 79th Leg., ch. 1099 (H.B. 2218), § 1, effective September 1, 2005.)

## SUBCHAPTER E
## CONDUCT OF MONEY
## TRANSMISSION BUSINESS

### Sec. 151.401. Liability of License Holder.

A money transmission license holder is liable for the payment of all money or monetary value received for transmission either directly or through an authorized delegate appointed in accordance with Section 151.402. (Enacted by Acts 2005, 79th Leg., ch. 1099 (H.B. 2218), § 1, effective September 1, 2005.)

### Sec. 151.402. Conduct of Business Through Authorized Delegate.

(a) A money transmission license holder may conduct business regulated under this chapter through an authorized delegate appointed by the license holder in accordance with this section. A license holder is responsible for the acts of the authorized delegate, of which the license holder has or reasonably should have knowledge, that are conducted pursuant to the authority granted by the license holder and that relate to the license holder's money transmission business.

(b) Before a license holder is authorized to conduct business through an authorized delegate or allows a person to act as the license holder's authorized delegate, the license holder must:

(1) adopt, and update as necessary, written policies and procedures designed to ensure that the license holder's authorized delegate complies with applicable state and federal law;

(2) enter into a written contract that complies with Subsection (c); and

(3) conduct a reasonable risk-based background investigation sufficient for the license holder to determine whether the authorized delegate has complied with applicable state and federal law.

(c) The written contract required by Subsection (b)(2) must be signed by the license holder and the authorized delegate and, at a minimum, must:

(1) appoint the person signing the contract as the license holder's authorized delegate with the authority to conduct money transmission on behalf of the license holder;

(2) set forth the nature and scope of the relationship between the license holder and the authorized delegate and the respective rights and responsibilities of the parties;

(3) require the authorized delegate to certify that the delegate is familiar with and agrees to fully comply with all applicable state and federal laws, rules, and regulations pertaining to money transmission, including this chapter and rules adopted under this chapter, relevant provisions of the Bank Secrecy Act and the USA PATRIOT ACT, and Chapter 271;

(4) require the authorized delegate to remit and handle money and monetary value in accordance with Sections 151.403(b) and (c);

(5) impose a trust on money and monetary value received in accordance with Section 151.404;

(6) require the authorized delegate to prepare and maintain records as required by this chapter or a rule adopted under this chapter or as reasonably requested by the commissioner;

(7) acknowledge that the authorized delegate consents to examination or investigation by the commissioner;

(8) state that the license holder is subject to regulation by the commissioner and that, as part of that regulation, the commissioner may suspend or revoke an authorized delegate des-

ignation or require the license holder to terminate an authorized delegate designation;

(9) acknowledge receipt of the written policies and procedures required under Subsection (b)(1); and

(10) acknowledge that the authorized delegate has been provided regulatory website addresses through which the authorized delegate can access this chapter and rules adopted under this chapter and the Bank Secrecy Act, the USA PATRIOT ACT, and Chapter 271.

(d) A license holder must report to the commissioner the theft or loss of payment instruments or stored value from the license holder or an authorized delegate in this state if the total value of the instruments or stored value exceeds $10,000. The license holder must make the report as soon as the license holder has knowledge of the theft or loss.

(e) A license holder must notify the license holder's authorized delegates and require the delegates to take any action required by the commissioner if the license holder:

(1) fails to renew the license holder's license; or

(2) is subject to an emergency or final order that affects the conduct of the license holder's business through an authorized delegate.

(f) A license holder must maintain a current list of authorized delegates located in this state that includes the name and business address of each delegate and must provide the list to the commissioner on request. A license holder that engages in business through 11 or more authorized delegates located in this state must include on the license holder's website a list of the names and addresses of the authorized delegates of the license holder located in this state and the delegates' business addresses. The license holder must update the list quarterly.

(g) The commission by rule may exempt from one or more of the requirements of this chapter an authorized delegate that is a federally insured financial institution excluded under Section 151.003(3) or a foreign bank branch or agency excluded under Section 151.003(4).

(Enacted by Acts 2005, 79th Leg., ch. 1099 (H.B. 2218), § 1, effective September 1, 2005.)

### Sec. 151.403. Authorized Delegate Conduct.

(a) An authorized delegate of a license holder:

(1) is under a duty to and must act only as authorized under the contract with the license holder and in strict compliance with the license holder's written policies and procedures;

(2) must not commit fraud or misrepresentation or make any fraudulent or false statement or misrepresentation to a license holder or the commissioner;

(3) must cooperate with an investigation or examination conducted by the commissioner and is considered to have consented to the commissioner's examination of the delegate's books and records;

(4) must not commit an unsafe or unsound act or practice or conduct business in an unsafe and unsound manner;

(5) must, on discovery, immediately report to the license holder the theft or loss of payment instruments or stored value;

(6) must prominently display on the form prescribed by the commissioner a notice that indicates that the person is an authorized delegate of the license holder under this subchapter; and

(7) must cease to provide money services as an authorized delegate of a license holder or take other required action immediately on receipt of notice from the commissioner or the license holder as provided by Section 151.402(e).

(b) An authorized delegate shall remit all money owed to the license holder:

(1) not later than the 10th business day after the date the authorized delegate receives the money;

(2) in accordance with the contract between the license holder and the authorized delegate; or

(3) as directed by the commissioner.

(c) Notwithstanding Subsection (b)(1), an authorized delegate may remit the money at a later date if the authorized delegate maintains on deposit with an office of a federally insured financial institution located in the United States an amount that:

(1) is in an account solely in the name of the license holder; and

(2) for each day by which the period before the remittance exceeds 10 business days, is not less than the outstanding obligations of the license holder routinely incurred by the authorized delegate on a daily basis.

(d) Any business for which a license is required under this subchapter that is conducted by an authorized delegate outside the scope of authority conferred in the contract between the autho-

Finance

rized delegate and the license holder is unlicensed activity.

(Enacted by Acts 2005, 79th Leg., ch. 1099 (H.B. 2218), § 1, effective September 1, 2005.)

### Sec. 151.404. Trust Imposed.

(a) A license holder shall hold in trust all money received for transmission directly or from an authorized delegate from the time of receipt until the time the transmission obligation is discharged. A trust resulting from the license holder's actions is in favor of the persons to whom the related money transmission obligations are owed.

(b) A license holder's authorized delegate shall hold in trust all money received for transmission by or for the license holder from the time of receipt until the time the money is remitted by the authorized delegate to the license holder. A trust resulting from the authorized delegate's actions is in favor of the license holder.

(c) A license holder's authorized delegate may not commingle the money received for transmission by or for the license holder with the authorized delegate's own money or other property, except to use in the ordinary course of the delegate's business for the purpose of making change, if the money is accounted for at the end of each business day.

(d) If a license holder or the license holder's authorized delegate commingles any money received for transmission with money or other property owned or controlled by the license holder or delegate, all commingled money and other property are impressed with a trust as provided by this section in an amount equal to the amount of money received for transmission, less the amount of fees paid for the transmission.

(e) If the commissioner revokes a license holder's license under Section 151.703, all money held in trust by the license holder and the license holder's authorized delegates is assigned to the commissioner for the benefit of the persons to whom the related money transmission obligations are owed.

(f) Money of a license holder or authorized delegate impressed with a trust under this section may not be considered an asset or property of the license holder or authorized delegate in the event of bankruptcy, receivership, or a claim against the license holder or authorized delegate unrelated to the license holder's or delegate's obligations under this chapter.

(Enacted by Acts 2005, 79th Leg., ch. 1099 (H.B. 2218), § 1, effective September 1, 2005.)

### Sec. 151.405. Disclosure Requirements.

(a) A license holder's name and mailing address or telephone number must be provided to the purchaser in connection with each money transmission transaction conducted by the license holder directly or through an authorized delegate.

(b) A license holder receiving currency or an instrument payable in currency for transmission must comply with Chapter 278.

(Enacted by Acts 2005, 79th Leg., ch. 1099 (H.B. 2218), § 1, effective September 1, 2005.)

## SUBCHAPTER F
## CURRENCY EXCHANGE LICENSE

### Sec. 151.501. Definitions.

(a) This section defines terms that apply specifically to an applicant for or holder of a currency exchange license issued under this subchapter.

(b) In this subchapter:

(1) "Currency" means the coin and paper money of the United States or any country that is designated as legal tender and circulates and is customarily used and accepted as a medium of exchange in the country of issuance.

(2) "Currency exchange" means exchanging the currency of one government for the currency of another government.

(Enacted by Acts 2005, 79th Leg., ch. 1099 (H.B. 2218), § 1, effective September 1, 2005.)

### Sec. 151.502. License Required.

(a) A person may not engage in the business of currency exchange or advertise, solicit, or hold itself out as providing currency exchange unless the person:

(1) is licensed under this subchapter;

(2) is licensed for money transmission under Subchapter D;

(3) is an authorized delegate of a person licensed for money transmission under Subchapter D;

(4) is excluded under Section 151.003; or

(5) has been granted an exemption under Subsection (d).

(b) For purposes of this chapter, a person engages in the business of currency exchange if the person exchanges currency and receives compensation or expects to receive compensation, directly or indirectly, for the currency exchange.

(c) A license holder may engage in the currency exchange business at one or more locations in this

Finance

state owned, directly or indirectly by the license holder, under a single license.

(d) On application and a finding that the exemption is in the public interest, the commissioner may exempt a retailer, wholesaler, or service provider that in the ordinary course of business accepts currency of a foreign country or government as payment for goods or services, provided that a person is not eligible for the exemption if:

(1) the value of the goods or services purchased in a single transaction exceeds $10,000;

(2) the change given or made as a result of the transaction exceeds $100;

(3) an attempt is made to structure a transaction in a manner that evades the licensing requirements of this subchapter or avoids using a business licensed under this chapter;

(4) the person is engaged in the business of cashing checks, drafts, or other payment instruments for consideration and is not otherwise exempt from licensing under this chapter; or

(5) the person would not be eligible for a license under this chapter.

(e) In accordance with the investigation provisions of this chapter, the commissioner may examine a person to verify the person's exempt status under Subsection (d).

(Enacted by Acts 2005, 79th Leg., ch. 1099 (H.B. 2218), § 1, effective September 1, 2005.)

### Sec. 151.503. Qualifications.

An applicant for a currency exchange license must have the qualifications set forth in Section 151.202.

(Enacted by Acts 2005, 79th Leg., ch. 1099 (H.B. 2218), § 1, effective September 1, 2005.)

### Sec. 151.504. Application and Accompanying Fee and Security.

(a) An applicant for a currency exchange license must submit an application in accordance with Section 151.203.

(b) At the time an application for a currency exchange license is submitted, an applicant must file with the department:

(1) an application fee in the amount established by commission rule; and

(2) security in the amount of $2,500 that meets the requirements of Section 151.506.

(Enacted by Acts 2005, 79th Leg., ch. 1099 (H.B. 2218), § 1, effective September 1, 2005.)

### Sec. 151.505. Investigation and Action on Application.

The commissioner shall investigate the applicant and act on the application in accordance with Sections 151.204 and 151.205.

(Enacted by Acts 2005, 79th Leg., ch. 1099 (H.B. 2218), § 1, effective September 1, 2005.)

### Sec. 151.506. Security.

An applicant for a currency exchange license must provide and a currency exchange license holder must maintain at all times security in the amount of $2,500 that satisfies the requirements of and is subject to Sections 151.308(c)—(j).

(Enacted by Acts 2005, 79th Leg., ch. 1099 (H.B. 2218), § 1, effective September 1, 2005.)

## SUBCHAPTER G
## EXAMINATIONS, REPORTS, AND RECORDS

### Sec. 151.601. Examinations.

(a) The commissioner may examine a license holder or authorized delegate of a license holder as reasonably necessary or appropriate to administer and enforce this chapter and rules adopted and orders issued under this chapter and other applicable law, including the Bank Secrecy Act, the USA PATRIOT ACT, and Chapter 271.

(b) The commissioner may:

(1) conduct an examination annually or at other times as the commissioner may reasonably require;

(2) conduct an on-site examination or an off-site review of records;

(3) conduct an examination in conjunction with an examination conducted by representatives of other state agencies or agencies of another state or of the federal government;

(4) accept the examination report of another state agency or an agency of another state or of the federal government, or a report prepared by an independent accounting firm, which on being accepted is considered for all purposes as an official report of the commissioner; and

(5) summon and examine under oath a principal, responsible individual, or employee of a license holder or authorized delegate of a license holder and require the person to produce records regarding any matter related to the condition and business of the license holder or authorized delegate.

(c) A license holder or authorized delegate of a license holder shall provide, and the commissioner shall have full and complete access to, all records the commissioner may reasonably require to conduct a complete examination. The records must be provided at the location and in the format specified by the commissioner.

(d) Unless otherwise directed by the commissioner, a license holder shall pay all costs reasonably incurred in connection with an examination of the license holder or the license holder's authorized delegate.

(e) Disclosure of information to the commissioner under an examination request does not waive or otherwise affect or diminish confidentiality or a privilege to which the information is otherwise subject. Information disclosed to the commissioner in connection with an examination is confidential under Section 151.606.

(Enacted by Acts 2005, 79th Leg., ch. 1099 (H.B. 2218), § 1, effective September 1, 2005.)

## Sec. 151.602. Records.

(a) A license holder must prepare, maintain, and preserve the following books, accounts, and other records for at least five years or another period as may be prescribed by rule of the commission:

(1) a record of each money transmission transaction or currency exchange transaction, as applicable;

(2) a general ledger posted in accordance with generally accepted accounting principles containing all asset, liability, capital, income, and expense accounts, unless directed otherwise by the commissioner;

(3) bank statements and bank reconciliation records;

(4) all records and reports required by applicable state and federal law, including the reporting and recordkeeping requirements imposed by the Bank Secrecy Act, the USA PATRIOT ACT, and Chapter 271, and other federal and state laws pertaining to money laundering, drug trafficking, or terrorist funding; and

(5) any other records required by commission rule or reasonably requested by the commissioner to determine compliance with this chapter.

(b) The records required under this section may be:

(1) maintained in a photographic, electronic, or other similar form; and

(2) maintained at the license holder's principal place of business or another location as may be reasonably requested by the commissioner.

(c) An authorized delegate must prepare, maintain, and preserve the records required by commission rule or reasonably requested by the commissioner.

(d) The records required under this section are subject to inspection by the commissioner under Section 151.601.

(e) The records required under this section and the reports required under Section 151.603 must be in English and the financial information contained in the records and reports must be denominated in United States dollars.

(Enacted by Acts 2005, 79th Leg., ch. 1099 (H.B. 2218), § 1, effective September 1, 2005.)

## Sec. 151.603. Reports.

(a) An applicant or license holder shall file a written report with the commissioner not later than the 15th day after the date the applicant or license holder knows or has reason to know of a material change in the information reported in an application or renewal report. The report must describe the change and the anticipated impact of the change on the activities of the applicant or license holder in this state.

(b) A money transmission license holder shall prepare written reports and statements as follows:

(1) the renewal report required by Section 151.207(b)(2), including an audited unconsolidated financial statement that is dated as of the last day of the license holder's fiscal year that ended in the immediately preceding calendar year;

(2) a quarterly interim financial statement and report regarding the permissible investments required to be maintained under Section 151.309 that reflect the license holder's financial condition and permissible investments as of the last day of the calendar quarter to which the statement and report relate and that are prepared not later than the 45th day after the last day of the calendar quarter; and

(3) any other report required by rule of the commission or reasonably requested by the commissioner to determine compliance with this chapter.

(c) A currency exchange license holder shall prepare a written report or statement as follows:

(1) the renewal report required by Section 151.207(b)(2), including a financial statement

that may be audited or unaudited and that is dated as of the last day of the license holder's fiscal year that ended in the immediately preceding calendar year;

(2) a quarterly interim financial statement and transaction report that reflects the license holder's financial condition and currency exchange business as of the last day of the calendar quarter to which the statement and report relate and that are prepared not later than the 45th day after the last day of the calendar quarter; and

(3) any other report required by rule of the commission or reasonably requested by the commissioner to determine compliance with this chapter.

(d) A license holder shall file the statements and reports required under this section with the commissioner as required by this chapter, by commission rule, or as requested by the commissioner.

(e) On written application and for good cause shown, the commissioner may extend the time for preparing or filing a statement or report required under this section.

(Enacted by Acts 2005, 79th Leg., ch. 1099 (H.B. 2218), § 1, effective September 1, 2005.)

## Sec. 151.604. Extraordinary Reporting Requirements.

(a) A license holder shall file a written report with the commissioner not later than the 15th day after the date the license holder knows or has reason to know of a material change in the information reported in an application or renewal report. The report must describe the change and the anticipated impact of the change on the license holder's activities in this state.

(b) A license holder must file a written report with the commissioner not later than 24 hours after the license holder knows or has reason to know of:

(1) the filing of a petition by or against the license holder for bankruptcy or reorganization;

(2) the filing of a petition by or against the license holder for receivership, the commencement of any other judicial or administrative proceeding for its dissolution or reorganization, or the making of a general assignment for the benefit of the license holder's creditors;

(3) the institution of a proceeding to revoke or suspend the license holder's license, or to enjoin or otherwise require the license holder to cease and desist from engaging in an activity related to money transmission, by a state or country in which the license holder engages in business or is licensed;

(4) the felony indictment or conviction of the license holder or a principal of, person in control of, responsible individual of, or authorized delegate of the license holder for an offense identified in Section 151.202(e);

(5) the cancellation or other impairment of the license holder's security; or

(6) the inability to meet the license holder's transmission obligations under this chapter for a period of 24 hours or longer.

(Enacted by Acts 2005, 79th Leg., ch. 1099 (H.B. 2218), § 1, effective September 1, 2005.)

## Sec. 151.605. Change of Control.

(a) This section applies to a proposed change of control of a license holder that results in a person or group of persons acting in concert, a "proposed person in control," after consummation of the acquisition transaction, controlling the license holder or a person in control of a license holder.

(b) A person may not directly or indirectly acquire control of a license holder or a person in control of a license holder without the prior written approval of the commissioner, except as provided by this section.

(c) A license holder or proposed person in control shall:

(1) give the commissioner written notice of a proposed change of control at least 45 days before the date the proposed transaction is to be consummated;

(2) request approval of the proposed change of control; and

(3) submit a nonrefundable fee in an amount established by commission rule.

(d) A proposed person in control is subject to the same standards and qualifications that apply to a principal of an applicant for a new license under this chapter. The commissioner may require the license holder or proposed person in control to provide the same type of information, documentation, and certifications and may conduct the same type of investigation the commissioner requires and conducts in connection with a new license application.

(e) The commissioner shall approve a proposed change of control if the commissioner determines that the proposed person in control has the financial responsibility, financial condition, business experience, competence, character, and general fitness to warrant the belief that the business of the license holder will be conducted in compliance with this chapter, rules adopted under this chapter, and other applicable state and federal law and that the change of control will not jeopardize the public interest.

(f) If the commissioner determines that the proposed person in control fails to meet the qualifications, standards, and requirements of this chapter, the commissioner shall inform the license holder and the proposed person in control in writing that the application is denied and state the reasons for the denial. The license holder or the proposed person in control may appeal the denial by filing a written request for a hearing with the commissioner not later than the 30th day after the date the notice is mailed. A hearing on the denial must be held not later than the 45th day after the date the commissioner receives the written request unless the administrative law judge extends the period for good cause or the parties agree to a later hearing date. The hearing is considered a contested case hearing and is subject to Section 151.801.

(g) The following persons are exempt from the requirements of Subsection (a), but the license holder must notify the commissioner not later than the 15th day after the date the change of control becomes effective:

(1) a person that acts as proxy for the sole purpose of voting at a designated meeting of the security holders or holders of voting interests of a license holder or controlling person;

(2) a person that acquires control of a license holder by devise or descent;

(3) a person that acquires control as a personal representative, custodian, guardian, conservator, or trustee, or as an officer appointed by a court or by operation of law;

(4) a person exempted in the public interest by rule of the commission or by order of the commissioner; and

(5) a person that has previously complied with and received approval under this chapter or that was identified as a person in control in a prior application filed with and approved by the commissioner.

(h) Subsection (b) does not apply to a public offering of securities.

(i) Before filing an application for approval of a proposed change of control, a license holder may submit a written request asking the commissioner to determine whether a person would be considered a proposed person in control of the license holder and whether the requirements of

this section apply to the proposed transaction. The request must be accompanied by a fee in an amount established by commission rule and must correctly and fully represent the facts relevant to the person and the proposed transaction. If the commissioner determines that the person would not be a person in control of the license holder for purposes of this section, the commissioner shall advise the license holder in writing that this section does not apply to the proposed person and transaction.

(Enacted by Acts 2005, 79th Leg., ch. 1099 (H.B. 2218), § 1, effective September 1, 2005.)

### Sec. 151.606. Confidentiality.

(a) Except as otherwise provided by Subsection (b) or by rule of the commission, all financial information and all other personal information obtained by the commissioner under this chapter through application, examination, investigation, or otherwise, and any related file or record of the department, is confidential and not subject to disclosure.

(b) The commissioner may disclose confidential information if:

(1) the applicant, license holder, or authorized delegate consents to the release of the information or has published the information contained in the release;

(2) the commissioner finds that release of the information is necessary to protect the public or purchasers or potential purchasers of money services from the license holder or authorized delegate from immediate and irreparable harm;

(3) the information is disclosed to an agency identified in Section 151.105(a), in which event the information remains confidential and the agency must take appropriate measures to maintain that confidentiality;

(4) the commissioner finds that release of the information is required for an administrative hearing; or

(5) the commissioner discloses the information to a person acting on behalf of or for the commissioner for regulatory or enforcement purposes, subject to an agreement that maintains the confidentiality of the information.

(c) This section does not prohibit the commissioner from disclosing to the public:

(1) a list of license holders or authorized delegates, including addresses and the names of contact individuals;

(2) the identity of a license holder or authorized delegate subject to an emergency or final

order of the commissioner and the basis for the commissioner's action; or

(3) information regarding or included in a consumer complaint against a license holder or authorized delegate.

(Enacted by Acts 2005, 79th Leg., ch. 1099 (H.B. 2218), § 1, effective September 1, 2005.)

## SUBCHAPTER H
## ENFORCEMENT

### Sec. 151.701.  Injunctive Relief.

(a) Whenever it appears that a person has violated, or that reasonable cause exists to believe that a person is likely to violate, this chapter or a rule adopted under this chapter, the following persons may bring an action for injunctive relief to enjoin the violation or enforce compliance with the provision:

(1) the commissioner, through the attorney general;

(2) the attorney general;

(3) the district attorney of Travis County; or

(4) the prosecuting attorney of the county in which the violation is alleged to have occurred.

(b) In addition to the authority granted to the commissioner under Subsection (a), the commissioner, through the attorney general, may bring an action for injunctive relief if the commissioner has reason to believe that a person has violated or is likely to violate an order of the commissioner issued under this chapter.

(c) An action for injunctive relief brought by the commissioner, the attorney general, or the district attorney of Travis County under Subsection (a), or brought by the commissioner under Subsection (b), must be brought in a district court in Travis County. An action brought by a prosecuting attorney under Subsection (a)(4) must be brought in a district court in the county in which all or part of the violation is alleged to have occurred.

(d) On a proper showing, the court may issue a restraining order, an order freezing assets, a preliminary or permanent injunction, or a writ of mandate, or may appoint a receiver for the defendant or the defendant's assets.

(e) A receiver appointed by the court under Subsection (d) may, with approval of the court, exercise all of the powers of the defendant's directors, officers, partners, trustees, or persons who exercise similar powers and perform similar duties.

(f) An action brought under this section may include a claim for ancillary relief, including a claim by the commissioner for costs or civil penalties authorized under this chapter, or for restitution or damages on behalf of the persons injured by the act constituting the subject matter of the action, and the court has jurisdiction to award that relief.

(Enacted by Acts 2005, 79th Leg., ch. 1099 (H.B. 2218), § 1, effective September 1, 2005.)

### Sec. 151.702.  Unlicensed Persons.

If the commissioner has reason to believe that an unlicensed person has engaged or is likely to engage in an activity for which a license is required under this chapter, the commissioner may order the person to cease and desist from the violation until the person is issued a license under this chapter. The commissioner's order is subject to Section 151.709, unless the order is issued as an emergency order. The commissioner may issue an emergency cease and desist order in accordance with Section 151.710 if the commissioner finds that the person's violation or likely violation threatens immediate and irreparable harm to the public.

(Enacted by Acts 2005, 79th Leg., ch. 1099 (H.B. 2218), § 1, effective September 1, 2005.)

### Sec. 151.703.  Suspension and Revocation of License.

(a) The commissioner must revoke a license if the commissioner finds that:

(1) the net worth of the license holder is less than the amount required under this chapter; or

(2) the license holder does not provide the security required under this chapter.

(b) The commissioner may suspend or revoke a license or order a license holder to revoke the designation of an authorized delegate if the commissioner has reason to believe that:

(1) the license holder has violated this chapter, a rule adopted or order issued under this chapter, a written agreement entered into with the department or commissioner, or any other state or federal law applicable to the license holder's money services business;

(2) the license holder has refused to permit or has not cooperated with an examination or investigation authorized by this chapter;

(3) the license holder has engaged in fraud, knowing misrepresentation, deceit, or gross negligence in connection with the operation of the license holder's money services business or any transaction subject to this chapter;

(4) an authorized delegate of the license holder has knowingly violated this chapter, a rule adopted or order issued under this chapter, or a state or federal anti-money-laundering or terrorist funding law, and the license holder knows or should have known of the violation and has failed to make a reasonable effort to prevent or correct the violation;

(5) the competence, experience, character, or general fitness of the license holder or an authorized delegate of the license holder, or a principal of, person in control of, or responsible person of a license holder or authorized delegate, indicates that it is not in the public interest to permit the license holder or authorized delegate to provide money services;

(6) the license holder has engaged in an unsafe or unsound act or practice or has conducted business in an unsafe or unsound manner;

(7) the license holder has suspended payment of the license holder's obligations, made a general assignment for the benefit of the license holder's creditors, or admitted in writing the license holder's inability to pay debts of the license holder as they become due;

(8) the license holder has failed to terminate the authority of an authorized delegate after the commissioner has issued and served on the license holder a final order finding that the authorized delegate has violated this chapter;

(9) a fact or condition exists that, if it had been known at the time the license holder applied for the license, would have been grounds for denying the application;

(10) the license holder has engaged in false, misleading, or deceptive advertising;

(11) the license holder has failed to pay a judgment entered in favor of a claimant or creditor in an action arising out of the license holder's activities under this chapter not later than the 30th day after the date the judgment becomes final or not later than the 30th day after the date the stay of execution expires or is terminated, as applicable;

(12) the license holder has knowingly made a material misstatement or has suppressed or withheld material information on an application, request for approval, report, or other document required to be filed with the department under this chapter; or

(13) the license holder has committed a breach of trust or of a fiduciary duty.

(c) In determining whether a license holder has engaged in an unsafe or unsound act or practice or has conducted business in an unsafe or unsound manner, the commissioner may consider factors that include:

(1) the size and condition of the license holder's provision of money services;

(2) the magnitude of the loss or potential loss;

(3) the gravity of the violation of this chapter or rule adopted or order issued under this chapter;

(4) any action taken against the license holder by this state, another state, or the federal government; and

(5) the previous conduct of the license holder.

(d) The commissioner's order suspending or revoking a license or directing a license holder to revoke the designation of an authorized delegate is subject to Section 151.709, unless the order is issued as an emergency order. The commissioner may issue an emergency order suspending a license or directing a license holder to revoke the designation of an authorized delegate in accordance with Section 151.710 if the commissioner finds that the factors identified in Section 151.710(b) exist.

(Enacted by Acts 2005, 79th Leg., ch. 1099 (H.B. 2218), § 1, effective September 1, 2005.)

## Sec. 151.704. Suspension and Revocation of Authorized Delegate Designation.

(a) The commissioner may suspend or revoke the designation of an authorized delegate if the commissioner has reason to believe that:

(1) the authorized delegate has violated this chapter, a rule adopted or order issued under this chapter, a written agreement entered into with the commissioner or the department, or any other state or federal law applicable to a money services business;

(2) the authorized delegate has refused to permit or has not cooperated with an examination or investigation under this chapter;

(3) the authorized delegate has engaged in fraud, knowing misrepresentation, deceit, gross negligence, or an unfair or deceptive act or practice in connection with the operation of the delegate's business on behalf of the license holder or any transaction subject to this chapter;

(4) the competence, experience, character, or general fitness of the authorized delegate, or a principal of, person in control of, or responsible

**Finance**

person of the authorized delegate, indicates that it is not in the public interest to permit the authorized delegate to provide money services;

(5) the authorized delegate has engaged in an unsafe or unsound act or practice or conducted business in an unsafe and unsound manner;

(6) the authorized delegate, or a principal or responsible person of the authorized delegate, is listed on the specifically designated nationals and blocked persons list prepared by the United States Department of the Treasury as a potential threat to commit terrorist acts or to fund terrorist acts; or

(7) the authorized delegate, or a principal or responsible person of the authorized delegate, has been convicted of a state or federal anti-money-laundering or terrorist funding law.

(b) In determining whether an authorized delegate has engaged in an unsafe or unsound act or practice or conducted business in an unsafe or unsound manner, the commissioner may consider factors that include:

(1) the size and condition of the authorized delegate's provision of money services;

(2) the magnitude of the loss or potential loss;

(3) the gravity of the violation of this chapter or rule adopted or order issued under this chapter;

(4) any action taken against the authorized delegate by this state, another state, or the federal government; and

(5) the previous conduct of the authorized delegate.

(c) The commissioner's order suspending or revoking the designation of an authorized delegate is subject to Section 151.709, unless the order is issued as an emergency order. The commissioner may issue an emergency order suspending the designation of an authorized delegate in accordance with Section 151.710 if the commissioner finds that the factors identified in Section 151.710(b) exist.

(Enacted by Acts 2005, 79th Leg., ch. 1099 (H.B. 2218), § 1, effective September 1, 2005.)

### Sec. 151.705.  Cease and Desist Orders.

(a) The commissioner may issue an order to cease and desist if the commissioner finds that:

(1) an action, violation, or condition listed in Section 151.703 or 151.704 exists with respect to a license holder or authorized delegate; and

(2) a cease and desist order is necessary to protect the interests of the license holder, the purchasers of the license holder's money services, or the public.

(b) A cease and desist order may require a license holder or authorized delegate to cease and desist from the action or violation or to take affirmative action to correct any condition resulting from or contributing to the action or violation, and the requirements of the order may apply to a principal or responsible person of the license holder or authorized delegate.

(c) The cease and desist order is subject to Section 151.709, unless the order is issued as an emergency order. The commissioner may issue an emergency cease and desist order in accordance with Section 151.710 if the commissioner finds that the factors identified in Section 151.710(b) exist.

(Enacted by Acts 2005, 79th Leg., ch. 1099 (H.B. 2218), § 1, effective September 1, 2005.)

### Sec. 151.706.  Consent Orders.

(a) The commissioner may enter into a consent order at any time with a person to resolve a matter arising under this chapter or a rule adopted or order issued under this chapter.

(b) A consent order must be signed by the person to whom the order is issued or by the person's authorized representative and must indicate agreement with the terms contained in the order. However, a consent order may provide that the order does not constitute an admission by a person that this chapter or a rule adopted or order issued under this chapter has been violated.

(c) A consent order is a final order and may not be appealed.

(Enacted by Acts 2005, 79th Leg., ch. 1099 (H.B. 2218), § 1, effective September 1, 2005.)

### Sec. 151.707.  Administrative Penalty.

(a) After notice and hearing, the commissioner may assess an administrative penalty against a person that:

(1) has violated this chapter or a rule adopted or order issued under this chapter and has failed to correct the violation not later than the 30th day after the date the department sends written notice of the violation to the person;

(2) if the person is a license holder, has engaged in conduct specified in Section 151.703;

(3) has engaged in a pattern of violations; or

(4) has demonstrated wilful disregard for the requirements of this chapter, the rules adopted under this chapter, or an order issued under this chapter.

(b) A violation corrected after a person receives written notice from the department of the violation may be considered for purposes of determining whether a person has engaged in a pattern of violations under Subsection (a)(3) or demonstrated wilful disregard under Subsection (a)(4).

(c) The amount of the penalty may not exceed $5,000 for each violation or, in the case of a continuing violation, $5,000 for each day that the violation continues. Each transaction in violation of this chapter and each day that a violation continues is a separate violation.

(d) In determining the amount of the penalty, the commissioner shall consider factors that include the seriousness of the violation, the person's compliance history, and the person's good faith in attempting to comply with this chapter, provided that if the person is found to have demonstrated wilful disregard under Subsection (a)(4), the trier of fact shall recommend that the commissioner impose the maximum administrative penalty permitted under Subsection (c).

(e) A hearing to assess an administrative penalty is considered a contested case hearing and is subject to Section 151.801.

(f) An order imposing an administrative penalty after notice and hearing becomes effective and is final for purposes of collection and appeal immediately on issuance.

(g) The commissioner may collect an administrative penalty assessed under this section:

(1) in the same manner that a money judgment is enforced in court; or

(2) if the penalty is imposed against a license holder or a license holder's authorized delegate, from the proceeds of the license holder's security in accordance with Section 151.308(e).

(Enacted by Acts 2005, 79th Leg., ch. 1099 (H.B. 2218), § 1, effective September 1, 2005.)

## Sec. 151.708. Criminal Penalty.

(a) A person commits an offense if the person:

(1) intentionally makes a false statement, misrepresentation, or certification in a record or application filed with the department or required to be maintained under this chapter or a rule adopted or order issued under this chapter, or intentionally makes a false entry or omits a material entry in the record or application; or

(2) knowingly engages in an activity for which a license is required under Subchapter D or F without being licensed under this chapter.

(b) An offense under this section is a felony of the third degree.

(c) If the commissioner has reason to believe that a person has committed an offense under this section or any other state or federal law, the commissioner may file a criminal referral with the district attorney of Travis County or an appropriate prosecuting attorney of the county in which the offense is alleged to have been committed.

(d) Nothing in this section limits the power of the state to punish a person for an act that constitutes an offense under this or any other law. (Enacted by Acts 2005, 79th Leg., ch. 1099 (H.B. 2218), § 1, effective September 1, 2005.)

## Sec. 151.709. Notice, Hearing, and Other Procedures for Nonemergency Orders.

(a) This section applies to an order issued by the commissioner under this subchapter that is not an emergency order.

(b) An order to which this section applies becomes effective only after notice and an opportunity for hearing. The order must:

(1) state the grounds on which the order is based;

(2) to the extent applicable, state the action or violation from which the person subject to the order must cease and desist or the affirmative action the person must take to correct a condition resulting from the violation or that is otherwise appropriate;

(3) be delivered by personal delivery or sent by certified mail, return receipt requested, to the person against whom the order is directed at the person's last known address;

(4) state the effective date of the order, which may not be before the 21st day after the date the order is delivered or mailed; and

(5) include a notice that a person may file a written request for a hearing on the order with the commissioner not later than the 20th day after the date the order is delivered or mailed.

(c) Unless the commissioner receives a written request for hearing from the person against whom the order is directed not later than the 20th day after the date the order is delivered or mailed, the order takes effect as stated in the order and is final against and nonappealable by that person from that date.

Finance

(d) A hearing on the order must be held not later than the 45th day after the date the commissioner receives the written request for the hearing unless the administrative law judge extends the period for good cause or the parties agree to a later hearing date.

(e) An order that has been affirmed or modified after a hearing becomes effective and is final for purposes of enforcement and appeal immediately on issuance. The order may be appealed to the district court of Travis County as provided by Section 151.801(b).

(Enacted by Acts 2005, 79th Leg., ch. 1099 (H.B. 2218), § 1, effective September 1, 2005.)

### Sec. 151.710.  Requirements and Notice and Hearing Procedures for Emergency Orders.

(a) This section applies to an emergency order issued by the commissioner under this subchapter.

(b) The commissioner may issue an emergency order, without prior notice and an opportunity for hearing, if the commissioner finds that:

(1) the action, violation, or condition that is the basis for the order:

(A) has caused or is likely to cause the insolvency of the license holder;

(B) has caused or is likely to cause the substantial dissipation of the license holder's assets or earnings;

(C) has seriously weakened or is likely to seriously weaken the condition of the license holder; or

(D) has seriously prejudiced or is likely to seriously prejudice the interests of the license holder, a purchaser of the license holder's money services, or the public; and

(2) immediate action is necessary to protect the interests of the license holder, a purchaser of the license holder's money services, or the public.

(c) In connection with and as directed by an emergency order, the commissioner may seize the records and assets of a license holder or authorized delegate that relate to the license holder's money services business.

(d) An emergency order must:

(1) state the grounds on which the order is based;

(2) advise the person against whom the order is directed that the order takes effect immediately, and, to the extent applicable, require the person to immediately cease and desist from the conduct or violation that is the subject of the order or to take the affirmative action stated in the order as necessary to correct a condition resulting from the conduct or violation or as otherwise appropriate;

(3) be delivered by personal delivery or sent by certified mail, return receipt requested, to the person against whom the order is directed at the person's last known address; and

(4) include a notice that a person may request a hearing on the order by filing a written request for hearing with the commissioner not later than the 15th day after the date the order is delivered or mailed.

(e) An emergency order takes effect as soon as the person against whom the order is directed has actual or constructive knowledge of the issuance of the order.

(f) A license holder or authorized delegate against whom an emergency order is directed must submit a written certification to the commissioner, signed by the license holder or authorized delegate, and their principals and responsible individuals, as applicable, and each person named in the order, stating that each person has received a copy of and has read and understands the order.

(g) Unless the commissioner receives a written request for a hearing from a person against whom an emergency order is directed not later than the 15th day after the date the order is delivered or mailed, the order is final and nonappealable as to that person on the 16th day after the date the order is delivered or mailed.

(h) A request for a hearing does not stay an emergency order.

(i) A hearing on an emergency order takes precedence over any other matter pending before the commissioner, and must be held not later than the 10th day after the date the commissioner receives the written request for hearing unless the administrative law judge extends the period for good cause or the parties agree to a later hearing date.

(j) An emergency order that has been affirmed or modified after a hearing is final for purposes of enforcement and appeal. The order may be appealed to the district court of Travis County as provided in Section 151.801(b).

(Enacted by Acts 2005, 79th Leg., ch. 1099 (H.B. 2218), § 1, effective September 1, 2005.)

## SUBCHAPTER I
## ADMINISTRATIVE PROCEDURES AND JUDICIAL REVIEW

### Sec. 151.801. Administrative Procedures.

(a) All administrative proceedings under this chapter must be conducted in accordance with Chapter 2001, Government Code, and Title 7, Chapter 9, Texas Administrative Code.

(b) A person affected by a final order of the commissioner issued under this chapter after a hearing may appeal the order by filing a petition for judicial review in a district court of Travis County. A petition for judicial review filed in the district court under this subsection does not stay or vacate the appealed order unless the court, after notice and hearing, specifically stays or vacates the order.

(Enacted by Acts 2005, 79th Leg., ch. 1099 (H.B. 2218), § 1, effective September 1, 2005.)

## SUBTITLE Z
## MISCELLANEOUS PROVISIONS RELATING TO FINANCIAL INSTITUTIONS AND BUSINESSES

## CHAPTER 271
## FINANCIAL TRANSACTION REPORTING REQUIREMENTS

### Sec. 271.001. Reporting Requirement for Crimes and Suspected Crimes and Currency and Foreign Transactions.

(a) A financial institution that is required to file a report with respect to a transaction in this state under the Currency and Foreign Transactions Reporting Act (31 U.S.C. Section 5311 et seq.), 31 C.F.R. Part 103, or 12 C.F.R. Section 21.11, and their subsequent amendments, shall file a copy of the report with the attorney general.

(b) A financial institution that timely files the report described by Subsection (a) with the appropriate federal agency as required by federal law complies with that subsection unless the attorney general:

(1) notifies the financial institution that the report is not of a type that is regularly and comprehensively transmitted by the federal agency to the attorney general following the attorney general's request to that agency;

(2) requests that the financial institution provide the attorney general with a copy of the report; and

(3) reimburses the financial institution for the actual cost of duplicating and delivering the report or 25 cents for each page, whichever is less.

(c) In this section, "financial institution" has the meaning assigned by 31 U.S.C. Section 5312 and its subsequent amendments.

(Enacted by Acts 1997, 75th Leg., ch. 1008 (H.B. 10), § 1, effective September 1, 1997; am. Acts 1999, 76th Leg., ch. 344 (H.B. 2066), § 2.028, effective September 1, 1999.)

### Sec. 271.002. Reporting Requirement for Cash Receipts of More Than $10,000.

(a) A person engaged in a trade or business who, in the course of the trade or business, receives more than $10,000 in one transaction or in two or more related transactions in this state and who is required to file a return under Section 6050I, Internal Revenue Code of 1986 (26 U.S.C. Section 6050I), or 26 C.F.R. Section 1.6050I-1, and their subsequent amendments, shall file a copy of the return with the attorney general.

(b) A person who timely files the return described by Subsection (a) with the appropriate federal agency as required by federal law complies with that subsection unless the attorney general:

(1) notifies the person that the return is not of a type that is regularly and comprehensively transmitted by the federal agency to the attorney general; and

(2) requests that the person provide the attorney general with a copy of the return.

(Enacted by Acts 1997, 75th Leg., ch. 1008 (H.B. 10), § 1, effective September 1, 1997; am. Acts

Finance

1999, 76th Leg., ch. 344 (H.B. 2066), § 2.029, effective September 1, 1999.)

### Sec. 271.003.  Use of Reported Information.

The attorney general may report a possible violation indicated by analysis of a report or return described by this chapter or information obtained under this chapter to an appropriate law enforcement agency for use in the proper discharge of the agency's official duties.
(Enacted by Acts 1997, 75th Leg., ch. 1008 (H.B. 10), § 1, effective September 1, 1997.)

### Sec. 271.004.  Failure to Comply with Reporting Requirements; Criminal Penalty.

(a) A person commits an offense if the person:
   (1) is requested by the attorney general to submit information required by Section 271.001 or 271.002 to the attorney general; and
   (2) knowingly fails to provide the requested information to the attorney general before the 30th day after the date of the request.
(b) An offense under this section is a Class A misdemeanor.
(Enacted by Acts 1997, 75th Leg., ch. 1008 (H.B. 10), § 1, effective September 1, 1997.)

### Sec. 271.005.  Suppression of Physical Evidence; Criminal Penalty.

(a) A person commits an offense if the person knowingly suppresses physical evidence connected with information contained in a report or return required by this chapter through concealment, alteration, or destruction.
(b) An offense under this section is a Class A misdemeanor.
(Enacted by Acts 1997, 75th Leg., ch. 1008 (H.B. 10), § 1, effective September 1, 1997.)

### Sec. 271.006.  Notification to Target of Criminal Investigation; Criminal Penalty.

(a) A person commits an offense if the person:
   (1) is required to submit a report or return under this chapter; and
   (2) knowingly notifies an individual who is the target of a criminal investigation involving an offense under Chapter 34, Penal Code, that:
      (A) the attorney general has requested the person to provide information required by this chapter related to the targeted individual; or
      (B) the individual may be subject to impending criminal prosecution.
(b) An offense under this section is a Class A misdemeanor.
(Enacted by Acts 1997, 75th Leg., ch. 1008 (H.B. 10), § 1, effective September 1, 1997.)

# TITLE 5

# PROTECTION OF CONSUMERS OF FINANCIAL SERVICES

## CHAPTER 391
## FURNISHING FALSE CREDIT INFORMATION

**Section**
391.001.  Definition.
391.002.  Furnishing False Information; Penalty.

### Sec. 391.001.  Definition.

In this chapter, "credit reporting bureau" means a person who engages in the practice of assembling or reporting credit information about individuals for the purpose of furnishing the information to a third party.
(Enacted by Acts 1997, 75th Leg., ch. 1008 (H.B. 10), § 1, effective September 1, 1997.)

### Sec. 391.002.  Furnishing False Information; Penalty.

(a) A person commits an offense if the person knowingly furnishes false information about another person's creditworthiness, credit standing, or credit capacity to a credit reporting bureau.
(b) A credit reporting bureau commits an offense if the credit reporting bureau knowingly furnishes false information about a person's creditworthiness, credit standing, or credit capacity to a third party.
(c) An offense under this section is a misdemeanor punishable by a fine of not more than $200.
(Enacted by Acts 1997, 75th Leg., ch. 1008 (H.B. 10), § 1, effective September 1, 1997.)

# Government Code

## TITLE 2

## JUDICIAL BRANCH

### SUBCHAPTER B
### COURT COSTS ON CONVICTION

### Sec. 102.0211. Court Costs on Conviction: Government Code.

A person convicted of an offense shall pay the following under the Government Code, in addition to all other costs:

(1) court costs on certain convictions in statutory county courts (Sec. 51.702, Government Code) . . . $15; and

(2) court costs on certain convictions in certain county courts (Sec. 51.703, Government Code) . . . $15.

(Enacted by Acts 2003, 78th Leg., ch. 1278 (S.B. 1180), § 1, effective June 21, 2003; am. Acts 2007, 80th Leg., ch. 921 (H.B. 3167), § 7.109(a), effective September 1, 2007 (renumbered from Sec. 102.021(4) and (5).)

### Sec. 102.0212. Court Costs on Conviction: Local Government Code.

A person convicted of an offense shall pay the following under the Local Government Code, in addition to all other costs:

(1) court costs on conviction of a felony (Sec. 133.102, Local Government Code)... $133;

(2) court costs on conviction of a Class A or Class B misdemeanor (Sec. 133.102, Local Government Code)... $83;

(3) court costs on conviction of a nonjailable misdemeanor offense, including a criminal violation of a municipal ordinance, other than a conviction of an offense relating to a pedestrian or the parking of a motor vehicle (Sec. 133.102, Local Government Code)... $40;

(4) a time payment fee if convicted of a felony or misdemeanor for paying any part of a fine, court costs, or restitution on or after the 31st day after the date on which a judgment is entered assessing the fine, court costs, or restitution (Sec. 133.103, Local Government Code)... $25;

(5) a cost on conviction of any offense, other than an offense relating to a pedestrian or the parking of a motor vehicle (Sec. 133.105, Local Government Code)... $6; and

(6) a cost on conviction of any offense, other than an offense relating to a pedestrian or the parking of a motor vehicle (Sec. 133.107, Local Government Code)... $2.

(Enacted by Acts 2003, 78th Leg., ch. 1278 (S.B. 1180), § 1, effective June 21, 2003; am. Acts 2007, 80th Leg., ch. 921 (H.B. 3167), § 7.109(a), effective September 1, 2007 (renumbered from Sec. 102.021(1)—(3) and (6); am. Acts 2009, 81st Leg., ch. 87 (S.B. 1969), § 11.112(a), effective September 1, 2009.)

### Sec. 102.0213. Court Costs on Conviction: Transportation Code.

A person convicted of an offense shall pay the following under the Transportation Code, in addition to all other costs:

(1) court cost on conviction of a misdemeanor under Subtitle C, Title 7, Transportation Code (Sec. 542.403, Transportation Code) . . . $3;

(2) cost for impoundment of vehicle (Sec. 601.263, Transportation Code) . . . $15 per day; and

(3) a civil and criminal enforcement cost on conviction of an offense of, or related to, the nonpayment of a toll in certain counties (Sec. 284.2031, Transportation Code) . . . $1.

(Enacted by Acts 2003, 78th Leg., ch. 1278 (S.B. 1180), § 1, effective June 21, 2003; am. Acts 2007, 80th Leg., ch. 921 (H.B. 3167), § 7.109(a), effective September 1, 2007 (renumbered from 102.021(19)—(21).)

### Sec. 102.0214. Court Costs on Conviction: Parks and Wildlife Code.

A person convicted of an offense shall pay under Section 12.110, Parks and Wildlife Code, in addition to all other costs, the actual cost of any storage, care, feeding, cold storage, or processing necessary for an unlawfully taken, shipped, or possessed game bird, fowl, animal, game fish, or exotic animal.

(Enacted by Acts 2005, 79th Leg., ch. 992 (H.B. 2026), § 29, effective June 18, 2005; am. Acts 2007, 80th Leg., ch. 921 (H.B. 3167), § 7.109(a), effective September 1, 2007 (renumbered from Sec. 102.021(22).)

### Sec. 102.0215. Additional Court Costs on Conviction: Code of Criminal Procedure [Repealed].

Repealed by Acts 2009, 81st Leg., ch. 87 (S.B. 1969), § 11.111(b), effective September 1, 2009; Acts 2009, 81st Leg., ch. 902 (H.B. 666), § 2(b), effective September 1, 2009; and Acts 2009 81st Leg., ch. 1209 (S.B. 727), § 7(b), effective September 1, 2009.

(Enacted by Acts 2007, 80th Leg., ch. 625 (H.B. 530), § 10, effective June 15, 2007.)

## SUBCHAPTER F
## CRIMINAL COURT COSTS IN JUSTICE COURT

### Sec. 102.102. Additional Court Costs on Conviction in Justice Court: Business & Commerce Code.

The clerk of a justice court shall collect from a defendant a court cost not to exceed $30 under Section 3.506, Business & Commerce Code, on conviction of certain offenses involving issuing or passing a subsequently dishonored check.

(Enacted by Acts 2007, 80th Leg., ch. 921 (H.B. 3167), § 7.113, effective September 1, 2007.)

## TITLE 4
# EXECUTIVE BRANCH

## SUBTITLE B
## LAW ENFORCEMENT AND PUBLIC PROTECTION

## CHAPTER 411
## DEPARTMENT OF PUBLIC SAFETY OF THE STATE OF TEXAS

### Subchapter A. General Provisions and Administration

## SUBCHAPTER A
## GENERAL PROVISIONS AND ADMINISTRATION

### Sec. 411.0132. Use of Funds to Support Peace Officer Training.

The department, subject to director approval, may use appropriated funds to purchase food and beverages for training functions required of peace officers of the department.

(Enacted by Acts 2011, 82nd Leg., ch. 1270 (H.B. 78), § 2, effective June 17, 2011.)

## Sec. 411.017.  Unauthorized Acts Involving Department Name, Insignia, or Division Name.

(a)  A person commits an offense if, without the director's authorization, the person:

(1)  manufactures, sells, or possesses a badge, identification card, or other item bearing a department insignia or an insignia deceptively similar to the department's;

(2)  makes a copy or likeness of a badge, identification card, or department insignia, with intent to use or allow another to use the copy or likeness to produce an item bearing the department insignia or an insignia deceptively similar to the department's; or

(3)  uses the term "Texas Department of Public Safety," "Department of Public Safety," "Texas Ranger," or "Texas Highway Patrol" in connection with an object, with the intent to create the appearance that the object belongs to or is being used by the department.

(b)  In this section, "department insignia" means an insignia or design prescribed by the director for use by officers and employees of the department in connection with their official activities. An insignia is deceptively similar to the department's if it is not prescribed by the department but a reasonable person would presume that it was prescribed by the department.

(c)  A district or county court, on application of the attorney general or of the district attorney or prosecuting attorney performing the duties of district attorney for the district in which the court is located, may enjoin a violation or threatened violation of this section on a showing that a violation has occurred or is likely to occur.

(d)  It is an affirmative defense to a prosecution under this section that the object is used exclusively:

(1)  for decorative purposes, maintained or preserved in a decorative state, and not offered for sale; or

(2)  in an artistic or dramatic presentation, and before the use of the object the producer of the presentation notifies the director in writing of the intended use, the location where the use will occur, and the period during which the use will occur.

(e)  An offense under this section is a Class A misdemeanor, unless the object is shipped by

United States mail or by any type of commercial carrier from a point outside the State of Texas to a point inside the state if the shipper or his agent has been sent notification by registered United States mail of this section prior to the shipment, in which event the offense is a felony of the third degree.

(Enacted by Acts 1987, 70th Leg., ch. 147 (S.B. 894), § 1, effective September 1, 1987; am. Acts 1989, 71st Leg., ch. 496 (H.B. 2162), § 1, effective September 1, 1989.)

## Sec. 411.0175.  Accident Reports [Repealed].

Repealed by Acts 2007, 80th Leg., ch. 1407 (S.B. 766), § 6, effective September 1, 2007.

(Enacted by Acts 1995, 74th Leg., ch. 165 (S.B. 971), § 5, effective September 1, 1995; am. Acts 2001, 77th Leg., ch. 1085 (H.B. 2204), § 2, effective September 1, 2001.)

## Sec. 411.019.  Toll-Free Number.

(a)  The department shall provide a 24-hour toll-free telephone number for use by the public in reporting traffic offenses, including driving while intoxicated, suspected criminal activity, and traffic accidents and other emergencies.

(b)  On receiving a report of an offense, the department shall contact the law enforcement agency of the jurisdiction where the reported suspected driver or incident was observed or shall dispatch department officers.

(Enacted by Acts 1989, 71st Leg., ch. 1251 (H.B. 1633), § 1, effective June 16, 1989.)

## Sec. 411.0201.  Reproduction of Records.

(a)  Except as provided by Subsection (b), the department may photograph, microphotograph, or film any record in connection with the issuance of a driver's license or commercial driver's license and any record of any division of the department.

(b)  None of the following may be photographed or filmed to dispose of the original record:

(1)  an original fingerprint card;

(2)  any evidence submitted in connection with a criminal case; or

(3)  a confession or statement made by the defendant in a criminal case.

(c)  The department may create original records in micrographic form on media, such as computer output microfilm.

(d)  A photograph, microphotograph, or film of a record reproduced under Subsection (a) is equivalent to the original record for all purposes, including introduction as evidence in all courts and administrative agency proceedings. A certified or authenticated copy of such a photograph, microphotograph, or film is admissible as evidence equally with the original photograph, microphotograph, or film.

(e) The director or an authorized representative may certify the authenticity of a photograph, microphotograph, or film of a record reproduced under this section and shall charge a fee for the certified photograph, microphotograph, or film as provided by law.

(f) Certified records shall be furnished to any person who is authorized by law to receive them. (Enacted by Acts 1995, 74th Leg., ch. 165 (S.B. 971), § 6, effective September 1, 1995; am. Acts 1997, 75th Leg., ch. 1187 (S.B. 1069), § 3, effective September 1, 1997.)

### Sec. 411.0206. Abatement or Deferral for Victims of Identity Theft.

(a) In this section:

(1) "License" means a license, certificate, permit, or other authorization issued by the department.

(2) "Victim of identity theft" means an individual who has filed a criminal complaint alleging the commission of an offense under Section 32.51, Penal Code, other than a person who is convicted of an offense under Section 37.08, Penal Code, with respect to that complaint.

(b) The department may abate or defer a mandatory suspension or revocation of a license if the license holder presents evidence acceptable to the department that:

(1) the license holder is the victim of identity theft; and

(2) the person against whom a criminal complaint alleging the commission of an offense under Section 32.51, Penal Code, has been filed, and not the license holder, engaged in the act or omission that mandates the suspension or revocation.

(Enacted by Acts 2003, 78th Leg., ch. 698 (H.B. 2703), § 4, effective June 20, 2003; am. Acts 2011, 82nd Leg., ch. 796 (H.B. 2256), § 1, effective June 17, 2011.)

### Sec. 411.0207. Public Corruption Unit.

(a) In this section, "organized criminal activ-

ity" means conduct that constitutes an offense under Section 71.02, Penal Code.

(b) A public corruption unit is created within the department to investigate and assist in the management of allegations of participation in organized criminal activity by:

(1) an individual elected, appointed, or employed to serve as a peace officer for a governmental entity of this state under Article 2.12, Code of Criminal Procedure; or

(2) a federal law enforcement officer while performing duties in this state.

(c) The unit shall:

(1) assist district attorneys and county attorneys in the investigation and prosecution of allegations described by Subsection (b);

(2) if requested by the agency, assist a state or local law enforcement agency with the investigation of such allegations against law enforcement officers in the agency;

(3) assist the United States Department of Justice or any other appropriate federal department or agency in the investigation and prosecution of allegations described by Subsection (b);

(4) if requested by the agency, assist a federal law enforcement agency with the investigation of such allegations against law enforcement officers in the agency;

(5) serve as a clearinghouse for information relating to the investigation and prosecution of allegations described by Subsection (b); and

(6) report to the highest-ranking officer of the Texas Rangers division of the department.

(d) On written approval of the director or of the chair of the commission, the highest-ranking officer of the Texas Rangers division of the department may initiate an investigation of an allegation of participation in organized criminal activity by a law enforcement officer described by Subsection (b)(1). Written approval under this subsection must be based on cause.

(e) To the extent allowed by law, a state or local law enforcement agency shall cooperate with the public corruption unit by providing information requested by the unit as necessary to carry out the purposes of this section. Information described by this subsection is excepted from required disclosure under Chapter 552 in the manner provided by Section 552.108.

(Enacted by Acts 2009, 81st Leg., ch. 1130 (H.B. 2086), § 41, effective September 1, 2009.)

## SUBCHAPTER B
## TEXAS RANGERS

### Sec. 411.022.   Authority of Officers.

(a) An officer of the Texas Rangers is governed by the law regulating and defining the powers and duties of sheriffs performing similar duties, except that the officer may make arrests, execute process in a criminal case in any county and, if specially directed by the judge of a court of record, execute process in a civil case.

(b) An officer of the Texas Rangers who arrests a person charged with a criminal offense shall immediately convey the person to the proper officer of the county where the person is charged and shall obtain a receipt. The state shall pay all necessary expenses incurred under this subsection.

(Enacted by Acts 1987, 70th Leg., ch. 147 (S.B. 894), § 1, effective September 1, 1987.)

## SUBCHAPTER C
## TEXAS HIGHWAY PATROL

### Sec. 411.032.   Powers and Duties of Officers.

In addition to the powers and duties provided by law for the officers, noncommissioned officers, and enlisted persons of the Texas Highway Patrol, they have the powers and authority provided by law for members of the Texas Rangers force. (Enacted by Acts 1987, 70th Leg., ch. 147 (S.B. 894), § 1, effective September 1, 1987.)

## SUBCHAPTER D
## ADMINISTRATIVE DIVISION

### Sec. 411.047.   Reporting Related to Concealed Handgun Incidents.

(a) The department may maintain statistics on its website related to responses by law enforcement agencies to incidents in which a person licensed to carry a handgun under Subchapter H is convicted of an offense only if the offense is prohibited under Subchapter H or under Title 5, Chapter 29, Chapter 46, or Section 30.02, Penal Code.

(b) Such statistics shall be drawn and reported annually from the Department of Public Safety computerized criminal history file on persons 21 years of age and older and shall be compared in numerical and graphical format to all like offenses committed in the state for the reporting period as a percentage of the total of such reported offenses.

(c) The department by rule shall adopt procedures for local law enforcement to make reports to the department described by Subsection (a). (Enacted by Acts 1995, 74th Leg., ch. 229 (S.B. 60), § 6, effective September 1, 1995; am. Acts 1997, 75th Leg., ch. 165 (S.B. 898), § 10.06, effective September 1, 1997; am. Acts 1999, 76th Leg., ch. 1189 (S.B. 370), § 12, effective September 1, 1999; am. Acts 2001, 77th Leg., ch. 1146 (H.B. 2784), § 1, effective September 1, 2001.)

### Sec. 411.049.   Report Related to Certain Intoxication Offenses.

(a) In this section, "offense relating to the operating of a motor vehicle while intoxicated" has the meaning assigned by Section 49.09, Penal Code.

(b) The department shall compile and maintain statistical information on the prosecution of offenses relating to the operating of a motor vehicle while intoxicated, including:

(1) the number of arrests;

(2) the number of arrests resulting in release with no charges;

(3) the number of charges resulting in a plea of not guilty and a trial;

(4) the number of charges resulting in a plea of guilty or nolo contendere;

(5) the number of charges resulting in a conviction of the offense charged in the original information, indictment, complaint, or other charging instrument;

(6) the number of charges resulting in a conviction of an offense other than the offense charged in the original information, indictment, complaint, or other charging instrument; and

(7) the number of charges resulting in a dismissal.

(c) Each law enforcement agency that enforces Chapter 49, Penal Code, and each appropriate prosecuting attorney's office and court in this state shall report in the manner and on a form prescribed by the department the information necessary for the department to compile the information required by Subsection (b).

(d) The department shall identify law enforcement agencies, prosecuting attorney's offices, and courts required to report under Subsection (c) that fail to timely report or that report incomplete information to the department.

(e) The department shall submit to the legislature not later than February 15 of each year a report of the statistical information described in Subsection (b) compiled for the preceding calendar year. The report must include a list of the law enforcement agencies, prosecuting attorney's offices, and courts identified by the department under Subsection (d).

(f) The department may adopt rules to implement this section.

(Enacted by Acts 2011, 82nd Leg., ch. 889 (S.B. 364), § 1, effective September 1, 2011.)

## Sec. 411.052.    Federal Firearm Reporting.

(a) In this section, "federal prohibited person information" means information that identifies an individual as:

(1) a person ordered by a court to receive inpatient mental health services under Chapter 574, Health and Safety Code;

(2) a person acquitted in a criminal case by reason of insanity or lack of mental responsibility, regardless of whether the person is ordered by a court to receive inpatient treatment or residential care under Chapter 46C, Code of Criminal Procedure;

(3) a person determined to have mental retardation and committed by a court for long-term placement in a residential care facility under Chapter 593, Health and Safety Code;

(4) an incapacitated adult individual for whom a court has appointed a guardian of the individual under Chapter XIII, Probate Code, based on the determination that the person lacks the mental capacity to manage the person's affairs; or

(5) a person determined to be incompetent to stand trial under Chapter 46B, Code of Criminal Procedure.

(b) The department by rule shall establish a procedure to provide federal prohibited person information to the Federal Bureau of Investigation for use with the National Instant Criminal Background Check System. Except as otherwise provided by state law, the department may disseminate federal prohibited person information under this subsection only to the extent necessary to allow the Federal Bureau of Investigation to collect and maintain a list of persons who are prohibited under federal law from engaging in certain activities with respect to a firearm.

(c) The department shall grant access to federal prohibited person information to the person who is the subject of the information.

(d) Federal prohibited person information maintained by the department is confidential

information for the use of the department and, except as otherwise provided by this section and other state law, may not be disseminated by the department.

(e) The department by rule shall establish a procedure to correct department records and transmit those corrected records to the Federal Bureau of Investigation when a person provides:

(1) a copy of a judicial order or finding that a person is no longer an incapacitated adult or is entitled to relief from disabilities under Section 574.088, Health and Safety Code; or

(2) proof that the person has obtained notice of relief from disabilities under 18 U.S.C. Section 925.

(Enacted by Acts 2009, 81st Leg., ch. 950 (H.B. 3352), § 1, effective September 1, 2009.)

## Sec. 411.0521.    Report to Department Concerning Certain Persons' Access to Firearms.

(a) The clerk of the court shall prepare and forward to the department the information described by Subsection (b) not later than the 30th day after the date the court:

(1) orders a person to receive inpatient mental health services under Chapter 574, Health and Safety Code;

(2) acquits a person in a criminal case by reason of insanity or lack of mental responsibility, regardless of whether the person is ordered to receive inpatient treatment or residential care under Chapter 46C, Code of Criminal Procedure;

(3) commits a person determined to have mental retardation for long-term placement in a residential care facility under Chapter 593, Health and Safety Code;

(4) appoints a guardian of the incapacitated adult individual under Chapter XIII, Probate Code, based on the determination that the person lacks the mental capacity to manage the person's affairs;

(5) determines a person is incompetent to stand trial under Chapter 46B, Code of Criminal Procedure; or

(6) finds a person is entitled to relief from disabilities under Section 574.088, Health and Safety Code.

(b) The clerk of the court shall prepare and forward the following information under Subsection (a):

(1) the complete name, race, and sex of the person;

Government

(2) any known identifying number of the person, including social security number, driver's license number, or state identification number;

(3) the person's date of birth; and

(4) the federal prohibited person information that is the basis of the report required by this section.

(c) If practicable, the clerk of the court shall forward to the department the information described by Subsection (b) in an electronic format prescribed by the department.

(d) If an order previously reported to the department under Subsection (a) is reversed by order of any court, the clerk shall notify the department of the reversal not later than 30 days after the clerk receives the mandate from the appellate court.

(e) The duty of a clerk to prepare and forward information under this section is not affected by:

(1) any subsequent appeal of the court order;

(2) any subsequent modification of the court order; or

(3) the expiration of the court order.

(Enacted by Acts 2009, 81st Leg., ch. 950 (H.B. 3352), § 1, effective September 1, 2009.)

## Sec. 411.053. Preservation of Evidence Containing Biological Material.

(a) The department:

(1) shall maintain a storage space for the preservation of evidence containing biological material that is delivered to the department under Article 38.43(f), Code of Criminal Procedure; and

(2) may maintain a storage space for the preservation of evidence of a sexual assault or other sex offense.

(b) The department shall adopt rules relating to the delivery, cataloging, and preservation of evidence stored under this section.

(Enacted by Acts 2009, 81st Leg., ch. 1179 (H.B. 3594), § 2, effective September 1, 2009; am. Acts 2011, 82nd Leg., ch. 91 (S.B. 1303), § 27.001(15), effective September 1, 2011, (renumbered from Sec. 411.052).)

## SUBCHAPTER D-1
## CENTRAL INDEX OF CERTAIN ADDITIONAL OFFENSES SUSPECTED TO HAVE BEEN COMMITTED BY CRIMINAL DEFENDANTS

## Sec. 411.0601. Definition.

In this subchapter, "criminal justice agency" has the meaning assigned by Article 60.01, Code of Criminal Procedure.

(Enacted by Acts 2009, 81st Leg., ch. 1152 (H.B. 2932), § 1, effective September 1, 2009.)

## Sec. 411.0602. Establishment of Central Index; Entry of Information.

(a) In the law enforcement information system maintained by the department, the bureau of identification and records shall establish and maintain a central index to collect and disseminate information regarding additional offenses that forensic DNA test results indicate may have been committed by a defendant who has been arrested for or charged with any felony or misdemeanor offense, other than a misdemeanor offense punishable by fine only.

(b) Information relating to a defendant described by Subsection (a) may be entered in the central index only if the information is based on forensic DNA test results indicating that the DNA profile of the defendant cannot be excluded as a donor to the DNA profile of a person suspected to have committed an offense, regardless of whether the defendant has been or will be arrested for or charged with that offense. The information must be:

(1) submitted in the form of an affidavit signed by a representative of an investigating criminal justice agency and approved by a district judge; and

(2) accompanied by a set of the defendant's fingerprints.

(Enacted by Acts 2009, 81st Leg., ch. 1152 (H.B. 2932), § 1, effective September 1, 2009.)

## Sec. 411.0603. Confidentiality and Dissemination of Information in Central Index.

(a) Information maintained by the department in the central index established under this subchapter is confidential. The department may not disseminate the information except as otherwise provided by this section.

(b) On proper inquiry, the department shall disseminate to a criminal justice agency the information collected under Section 411.0602. The criminal justice agency may disseminate the information to any other criminal justice agency if the dissemination of that information is for a criminal justice purpose.

(c) A criminal justice agency or an employee of a criminal justice agency is not liable for an act or omission relating to the collection, use, or dissemination of information collected under Section 411.0602 if that collection, use, or dissemination is performed in accordance with rules adopted by the director.

(Enacted by Acts 2009, 81st Leg., ch. 1152 (H.B. 2932), § 1, effective September 1, 2009.)

## Sec. 411.0604. Rules.

The director shall adopt rules to implement and enforce this subchapter.

(Enacted by Acts 2009, 81st Leg., ch. 1152 (H.B. 2932), § 1, effective September 1, 2009.)

## Sec. 411.0605. Right to Request Notice of Entry in Central Index.

(a) A defendant described by Section 411.0602(a) may submit to the bureau of identification and records a request to determine whether the bureau has entered information relating to the defendant in the central index established under Section 411.0602. The bureau shall respond to the request not later than the 10th business day after the date the bureau receives the request.

(b) Before responding to a request under Subsection (a), the bureau may require reasonable written verification of the identity of the defendant submitting the request, including written verification of an address, date of birth, driver's license number, state identification card number, or social security number.

(Enacted by Acts 2009, 81st Leg., ch. 1152 (H.B. 2932), § 1, effective September 1, 2009.)

## Sec. 411.0606. Right to Request Review of Entry in Central Index.

(a) On receipt by the bureau of identification and records of a written request that is submitted by a defendant described by Section 411.0602(a), that is accompanied by a set of the defendant's fingerprints, and that alleges that the bureau may have entered inaccurate information relating to the defendant in the central index established under Section 411.0602, the head of the bureau or that person's designee and the head of the department's crime laboratory in Austin each shall review the information to determine whether there is a high likelihood that the information is accurate.

(b) If after review the head of the bureau or that person's designee or the head of the department's crime laboratory in Austin determines there is not a high likelihood that the information relating to the defendant is accurate, the bureau shall:

(1) promptly remove that information from the central index; and

(2) notify other appropriate divisions of the department, the investigating criminal justice agency, and the defendant of the bureau's determination and the removal of the information.

(c) If after review the head of the bureau or that person's designee and the head of the department's crime laboratory in Austin jointly determine there is a high likelihood that the information relating to the defendant is accurate, the bureau shall notify the defendant of that determination.

(Enacted by Acts 2009, 81st Leg., ch. 1152 (H.B. 2932), § 1, effective September 1, 2009.)

## SUBCHAPTER E
## CAPITOL COMPLEX

## Sec. 411.0625. Pass for Expedited Access to Capitol.

(a) The department shall allow a person to enter the Capitol and the Capitol Extension, including any public space in the Capitol or Capitol Extension, in the same manner as the department allows entry to a person who presents a concealed handgun license under Subchapter H if the person:

(1) obtains from the department a Capitol access pass; and

(2) presents the pass to the appropriate law enforcement official when entering the building or a space within the building.

(b) To be eligible for a Capitol access pass, a person must meet the eligibility requirements applicable to a license to carry a concealed hand-

**Government**

gun under Subchapter H, other than require-ments regarding evidence of handgun proficiency.

(c) The department shall adopt rules to estab-lish a procedure by which a resident of the state may apply for and be issued a Capitol access pass. Rules adopted under this section must include provisions for eligibility, application, approval, issuance, and renewal that:

(1) require the department to conduct the same background check on an applicant for a Capitol access pass that is conducted on an applicant for a concealed handgun license un-der Subchapter H;

(2) enable the department to conduct the background check described by Subdivision (1); and

(3) establish application and renewal fees in amounts sufficient to cover the cost of admin-istering this section, not to exceed the amounts of similar fees required for a concealed hand-gun license under Section 411.174.

(Enacted by Acts 2011, 82nd Leg., ch. 205 (H.B. 2131), § 1, effective May 30, 2011.)

## SUBCHAPTER F
## CRIMINAL HISTORY RECORD INFORMATION

### Sec. 411.0971. Access to Criminal His-tory Record Information: Teacher Re-tirement System of Texas.

(a) The Teacher Retirement System of Texas is entitled to obtain from the department, the Fed-eral Bureau of Investigation Criminal Justice Information Services Division, or another law enforcement agency criminal history record infor-mation maintained by the department, division, or agency that relates to a person who:

(1) is an employee or an applicant for em-ployment with the retirement system;

(2) is a consultant, contract employee, inde-pendent contractor, intern, or volunteer for the retirement system or an applicant to serve in one of those positions;

(3) proposes to enter into a contract with or has a contract with the retirement system to perform services for or supply goods to the retirement system; or

(4) is an employee or subcontractor, or an applicant to be an employee or subcontractor, of a contractor that provides services to the retire-ment system.

(b) Criminal history record information ob-tained by the Teacher Retirement System of

Texas under Subsection (a) may not be released or disclosed to any person except:

(1) on court order;

(2) with the consent of the person who is the subject of the criminal history record informa-tion; or

(3) to a federal agency as required by federal law or executive order.

(c) The Teacher Retirement System of Texas shall destroy criminal history record information obtained under this section after the information is used for the purposes authorized by this sec-tion.

(d) The Teacher Retirement System of Texas may provide a copy of the criminal history record information obtained from the department, the Federal Bureau of Investigation Criminal Justice Information Services Division, or other law en-forcement agency to the individual who is the subject of the information.

(e) The failure or refusal of an employee or applicant to provide the following on request constitutes good cause for dismissal or refusal to hire:

(1) a complete set of fingerprints;

(2) a true and complete name; or

(3) other information necessary for a law enforcement entity to obtain criminal history record information.

(Enacted by Acts 2011, 82nd Leg., ch. 455 (S.B. 1667), § 2, effective September 1, 2011.)

### Sec. 411.135. Access to Certain Infor-mation by Public.

(a) Any person is entitled to obtain from the department:

(1) any information described as public in-formation under Chapter 62, Code of Criminal Procedure, as added by Chapter 668, Acts of the 75th Legislature, Regular Session, 1997, in-cluding, to the extent available, a recent pho-tograph of each person subject to registration under that chapter; and

(2) criminal history record information maintained by the department that relates to the conviction of or a grant of deferred adjudi-cation to a person for any criminal offense, including arrest information that relates to the conviction or grant of deferred adjudication.

(b) The department by rule shall design and implement a system to respond to electronic inquiries and other inquiries for information de-scribed by Subsection (a).

(c) A person who obtains information from the department under Subsection (a) may:

(1) use the information for any purpose; or

(2) release the information to any other person.

(Enacted by Acts 1997, 75th Leg., ch. 747 (H.B. 1176), § 2, effective September 1, 1997; am. Acts 1999, 76th Leg., ch. 1415 (H.B. 2145), § 21, effective September 1, 1999.)

## SUBCHAPTER H
## LICENSE TO CARRY A CONCEALED HANDGUN

### Sec. 411.171.　Definitions.

In this subchapter:

(1) "Action" means single action, revolver, or semi-automatic action.

(2) "Chemically dependent person" means a person who frequently or repeatedly becomes intoxicated by excessive indulgence in alcohol or uses controlled substances or dangerous drugs so as to acquire a fixed habit and an involuntary tendency to become intoxicated or use those substances as often as the opportunity is presented.

(3) "Concealed handgun" means a handgun, the presence of which is not openly discernible to the ordinary observation of a reasonable person.

(4) "Convicted" means an adjudication of guilt or, except as provided in Section 411.1711, an order of deferred adjudication entered against a person by a court of competent jurisdiction whether or not the imposition of the sentence is subsequently probated and the person is discharged from community supervision. The term does not include an adjudication of guilt or an order of deferred adjudication that has been subsequently:

(A) expunged;

(B) pardoned under the authority of a state or federal official; or

(C) otherwise vacated, set aside, annulled, invalidated, voided, or sealed under any state or federal law.

(4-a) "Federal judge" means:

(A) a judge of a United States court of appeals;

(B) a judge of a United States district court;

(C) a judge of a United States bankruptcy court; or

(D) a magistrate judge of a United States district court.

(4-b) "State judge" means:

(A) the judge of an appellate court, a district court, or a county court at law of this state;

(B) an associate judge appointed under Chapter 201, Family Code; or

(C) a justice of the peace.

(5) "Handgun" has the meaning assigned by Section 46.01, Penal Code.

(6) "Intoxicated" has the meaning assigned by Section 49.01, Penal Code.

(7) "Qualified handgun instructor" means a person who is certified to instruct in the use of handguns by the department.

(8) [Repealed by Acts 1999, 76th Leg., ch. 62 (S.B. 1368), § 9.02(a), effective September 1, 1999.]

(Enacted by Acts 1997, 75th Leg., ch. 165 (S.B. 898), § 10.01(a), effective September 1, 1997; am. Acts 1999, 76th Leg., ch. 62 (S.B. 1368), §§ 9.01(a), 9.02(a), effective September 1, 1999; am. Acts 2005, 79th Leg., ch. 1084 (H.B. 1831), § 1, effective September 1, 2005; am. Acts 2007, 80th Leg., ch. 594 (H.B. 41), § 8, effective September 1, 2007; am. Acts 2009, 81st Leg., ch. 1146 (H.B. 2730), §§ 6.06, 11.02, effective September 1, 2009; am. Acts 2009, 81st Leg., ch. 1259 (H.B. 559), § 2, effective September 1, 2009.)

### Sec. 411.1711.　Certain Exemptions from Convictions.

A person is not convicted, as that term is defined by Section 411.171, if an order of deferred adjudication was entered against the person on a date not less than 10 years preceding the date of the person's application for a license under this subchapter unless the order of deferred adjudication was entered against the person for:

(1) a felony offense under:

(A) Title 5, Penal Code;

(B) Chapter 29, Penal Code;

(C) Section 25.07, Penal Code; or

(D) Section 30.02, Penal Code, if the offense is punishable under Subsection (c)(2) or (d) of that section; or

(2) an offense under the laws of another state if the offense contains elements that are substantially similar to the elements of an offense listed in Subdivision (1).

(Enacted by Acts 2005, 79th Leg., ch. 1084 (H.B. 1831), § 2, effective September 1, 2005; am. Acts 2009, 81st Leg., ch. 1146 (H.B. 2730), § 11.01, effective September 1, 2009.)

### Sec. 411.172.　Eligibility.

(a) A person is eligible for a license to carry a concealed handgun if the person:

(1) is a legal resident of this state for the six-month period preceding the date of application under this subchapter or is otherwise eligible for a license under Section 411.173(a);

(2) is at least 21 years of age;

(3) has not been convicted of a felony;

(4) is not charged with the commission of a Class A or Class B misdemeanor or equivalent offense, or of an offense under Section 42.01, Penal Code, or equivalent offense, or of a felony under an information or indictment;

(5) is not a fugitive from justice for a felony or a Class A or Class B misdemeanor or equivalent offense;

(6) is not a chemically dependent person;

(7) is not incapable of exercising sound judgment with respect to the proper use and storage of a handgun;

(8) has not, in the five years preceding the date of application, been convicted of a Class A or Class B misdemeanor or equivalent offense or of an offense under Section 42.01, Penal Code, or equivalent offense;

(9) is fully qualified under applicable federal and state law to purchase a handgun;

(10) has not been finally determined to be delinquent in making a child support payment administered or collected by the attorney general;

(11) has not been finally determined to be delinquent in the payment of a tax or other money collected by the comptroller, the tax collector of a political subdivision of the state, or any agency or subdivision of the state;

(12) is not currently restricted under a court protective order or subject to a restraining order affecting the spousal relationship, other than a restraining order solely affecting property interests;

(13) has not, in the 10 years preceding the date of application, been adjudicated as having engaged in delinquent conduct violating a penal law of the grade of felony; and

(14) has not made any material misrepresentation, or failed to disclose any material fact, in an application submitted pursuant to Section 411.174.

(b) For the purposes of this section, an offense under the laws of this state, another state, or the United States is:

(1) except as provided by Subsection (b-1), a felony if the offense, at the time the offense is committed:

(A) is designated by a law of this state as a felony;

(B) contains all the elements of an offense designated by a law of this state as a felony; or

(C) is punishable by confinement for one year or more in a penitentiary; and

(2) a Class A misdemeanor if the offense is not a felony and confinement in a jail other than a state jail felony facility is affixed as a possible punishment.

(b-1) An offense is not considered a felony for purposes of Subsection (b) if, at the time of a person's application for a license to carry a concealed handgun, the offense:

(1) is not designated by a law of this state as a felony; and

(2) does not contain all the elements of any offense designated by a law of this state as a felony.

(c) An individual who has been convicted two times within the 10-year period preceding the date on which the person applies for a license of an offense of the grade of Class B misdemeanor or greater that involves the use of alcohol or a controlled substance as a statutory element of the offense is a chemically dependent person for purposes of this section and is not qualified to receive a license under this subchapter. This subsection does not preclude the disqualification of an individual for being a chemically dependent person if other evidence exists to show that the person is a chemically dependent person.

(d) For purposes of Subsection (a)(7), a person is incapable of exercising sound judgment with respect to the proper use and storage of a handgun if the person:

(1) has been diagnosed by a licensed physician as suffering from a psychiatric disorder or condition that causes or is likely to cause substantial impairment in judgment, mood, perception, impulse control, or intellectual ability;

(2) suffers from a psychiatric disorder or condition described by Subdivision (1) that:

(A) is in remission but is reasonably likely to redevelop at a future time; or

(B) requires continuous medical treatment to avoid redevelopment;

(3) has been diagnosed by a licensed physician, determined by a review board or similar authority, or declared by a court to be incompetent to manage the person's own affairs; or

(4) has entered in a criminal proceeding a plea of not guilty by reason of insanity.

(e) The following constitutes evidence that a person has a psychiatric disorder or condition described by Subsection (d)(1):

(1) involuntary psychiatric hospitalization;

(2) psychiatric hospitalization;

(3) inpatient or residential substance abuse treatment in the preceding five-year period;

(4) diagnosis in the preceding five-year period by a licensed physician that the person is dependent on alcohol, a controlled substance, or a similar substance; or

(5) diagnosis at any time by a licensed physician that the person suffers or has suffered from a psychiatric disorder or condition consisting of or relating to:

(A) schizophrenia or delusional disorder;

(B) bipolar disorder;

(C) chronic dementia, whether caused by illness, brain defect, or brain injury;

(D) dissociative identity disorder;

(E) intermittent explosive disorder; or

(F) antisocial personality disorder.

(f) Notwithstanding Subsection (d), a person who has previously been diagnosed as suffering from a psychiatric disorder or condition described by Subsection (d) or listed in Subsection (e) is not because of that disorder or condition incapable of exercising sound judgment with respect to the proper use and storage of a handgun if the person provides the department with a certificate from a licensed physician whose primary practice is in the field of psychiatry stating that the psychiatric disorder or condition is in remission and is not reasonably likely to develop at a future time.

(g) Notwithstanding Subsection (a)(2), a person who is at least 18 years of age but not yet 21 years of age is eligible for a license to carry a concealed handgun if the person:

(1) is a member or veteran of the United States armed forces, including a member or veteran of the reserves or national guard;

(2) was discharged under honorable conditions, if discharged from the United States armed forces, reserves, or national guard; and

(3) meets the other eligibility requirements of Subsection (a) except for the minimum age required by federal law to purchase a handgun.

(h) The issuance of a license to carry a concealed handgun to a person eligible under Subsection (g) does not affect the person's ability to purchase a handgun or ammunition under federal law.

(Enacted by Acts 1997, 75th Leg., ch. 165 (S.B. 898), § 10.01(a), effective September 1, 1997; am. Acts 1999, 76th Leg., ch. 62 (S.B. 1368), §§ 9.03(a), 9.04(a), effective September 1, 1999; am. Acts 2003, 78th Leg., ch. 255 (H.B. 1704), § 1, effective September 1, 2003; am. Acts 2005,

79th Leg., ch. 486 (H.B. 322), § 1, effective September 1, 2005; am. Acts 2009, 81st Leg., ch. 1146 (H.B. 2730), § 11.03, effective September 1, 2009.)

## Sec. 411.173. Nonresident License.

(a) The department by rule shall establish a procedure for a person who meets the eligibility requirements of this subchapter other than the residency requirement established by Section 411.172(a) (1) to obtain a license under this subchapter if the person is a legal resident of another state or if the person relocates to this state with the intent to establish residency in this state. The procedure must include payment of a fee in an amount sufficient to recover the average cost to the department of obtaining a criminal history record check and investigation on a nonresident applicant. A license issued in accordance with the procedure established under this subsection:

(1) remains in effect until the license expires under Section 411.183; and

(2) may be renewed under Section 411.185.

(a-1) [Repealed by Acts 2005, 79th Leg., ch. 915 (H.B. 225), § 4, effective September 1, 2005.]

(b) The governor shall negotiate an agreement with any other state that provides for the issuance of a license to carry a concealed handgun under which a license issued by the other state is recognized in this state or shall issue a proclamation that a license issued by the other state is recognized in this state if the attorney general of the State of Texas determines that a background check of each applicant for a license issued by that state is initiated by state or local authorities or an agent of the state or local authorities before the license is issued. For purposes of this subsection, "background check" means a search of the National Crime Information Center database and the Interstate Identification Index maintained by the Federal Bureau of Investigation.

(c) The attorney general of the State of Texas shall annually:

(1) submit a report to the governor, lieutenant governor, and speaker of the house of representatives listing the states the attorney general has determined qualify for recognition under Subsection (b); and

(2) review the statutes of states that the attorney general has determined do not qualify for recognition under Subsection (b) to determine the changes to their statutes that are necessary to qualify for recognition under that subsection.

**Government**

(d) The attorney general of the State of Texas shall submit the report required by Subsection (c)(1) not later than January 1 of each calendar year.

(Enacted by Acts 1997, 75th Leg., ch. 165 (S.B. 898), § 10.01(a), effective September 1, 1997; am. Acts 1999, 76th Leg., ch. 62 (S.B. 1368), § 9.05(a), effective September 1, 1999; am. Acts 2003, 78th Leg., ch. 255 (H.B. 1704), § 2, effective September 1, 2003; am. Acts 2003, 78th Leg., ch. 752 (H.B. 3477), § 1, effective September 1, 2003; am. Acts 2005, 79th Leg., ch. 915 (H.B. 225), §§ 1, 2, 4, effective September 1, 2005.)

### Sec. 411.174. Application.

(a) An applicant for a license to carry a concealed handgun must submit to the director's designee described by Section 411.176:

(1) a completed application on a form provided by the department that requires only the information listed in Subsection (b);

(2) one or more photographs of the applicant that meet the requirements of the department;

(3) a certified copy of the applicant's birth certificate or certified proof of age;

(4) proof of residency in this state;

(5) two complete sets of legible and classifiable fingerprints of the applicant taken by a person appropriately trained in recording fingerprints who is employed by a law enforcement agency or by a private entity designated by a law enforcement agency as an entity qualified to take fingerprints of an applicant for a license under this subchapter;

(6) a nonrefundable application and license fee of $140 paid to the department;

(7) evidence of handgun proficiency, in the form and manner required by the department;

(8) an affidavit signed by the applicant stating that the applicant:

(A) has read and understands each provision of this subchapter that creates an offense under the laws of this state and each provision of the laws of this state related to use of deadly force; and

(B) fulfills all the eligibility requirements listed under Section 411.172; and

(9) a form executed by the applicant that authorizes the director to make an inquiry into any noncriminal history records that are necessary to determine the applicant's eligibility for a license under Section 411.172(a).

(b) An applicant must provide on the application a statement of the applicant's:

(1) full name and place and date of birth;

(2) race and sex;

(3) residence and business addresses for the preceding five years;

(4) hair and eye color;

(5) height and weight;

(6) driver's license number or identification certificate number issued by the department;

(7) criminal history record information of the type maintained by the department under this chapter, including a list of offenses for which the applicant was arrested, charged, or under an information or indictment and the disposition of the offenses; and

(8) history, if any, of treatment received by, commitment to, or residence in:

(A) a drug or alcohol treatment center licensed to provide drug or alcohol treatment under the laws of this state or another state, but only if the treatment, commitment, or residence occurred during the preceding five years; or

(B) a psychiatric hospital.

(c) The department shall distribute on request a copy of this subchapter and application materials.

(Enacted by Acts 1997, 75th Leg., ch. 165 (S.B. 898), § 10.01(a), effective September 1, 1997; am. Acts 1999, 76th Leg., ch. 62 (S.B. 1368), § 9.06(a), effective September 1, 1999; am. Acts 2005, 79th Leg., ch. 486 (H.B. 322), § 2, effective September 1, 2005; am. Acts 2009, 81st Leg., ch. 1146 (H.B. 2730), § 11.04, effective September 1, 2009.)

### Sec. 411.175. Request for Application Materials [Repealed].

Repealed by Acts 2009, 81st Leg., ch. 1146 (H.B. 2730), § 11.25, effective September 1, 2009. (Enacted by Acts 1997, 75th Leg., ch. 165 (S.B. 898), § 10.01(a), effective September 1, 1997.)

### Sec. 411.176. Review of Application Materials.

(a) On receipt of application materials by the department at its Austin headquarters, the department shall conduct the appropriate criminal history record check of the applicant through its computerized criminal history system. Not later than the 30th day after the date the department receives the application materials, the department shall forward the materials to the director's designee in the geographical area of the applicant's residence so that the designee may conduct the investigation described by Subsection (b). For purposes of this section, the director's designee may be a noncommissioned employee of the department.

(b) The director's designee as needed shall conduct an additional criminal history record check of the applicant and an investigation of the applicant's local official records to verify the accuracy of the application materials. The director's designee may access any records necessary for purposes of this subsection. The scope of the record check and the investigation are at the sole discretion of the department, except that the director's designee shall complete the record check and investigation not later than the 60th day after the date the department receives the application materials. The department shall send a fingerprint card to the Federal Bureau of Investigation for a national criminal history check of the applicant. On completion of the investigation, the director's designee shall return all materials and the result of the investigation to the appropriate division of the department at its Austin headquarters.

(c) The director's designee may submit to the appropriate division of the department, at the department's Austin headquarters, along with the application materials a written recommendation for disapproval of the application, accompanied by an affidavit stating personal knowledge or naming persons with personal knowledge of a ground for denial under Section 411.172. The director's designee may also submit the application and the recommendation that the license be issued.

(d) On receipt at the department's Austin headquarters of the application materials and the result of the investigation by the director's designee, the department shall conduct any further record check or investigation the department determines is necessary if a question exists with respect to the accuracy of the application materials or the eligibility of the applicant, except that the department shall complete the record check and investigation not later than the 180th day after the date the department receives the application materials from the applicant.

(Enacted by Acts 1997, 75th Leg., ch. 165 (S.B. 898), § 10.01(a), effective September 1, 1997; am. Acts 1999, 76th Leg., ch. 62 (S.B. 1368), § 9.07(a), effective September 1, 1999; am. Acts 2009, 81st Leg., ch. 1146 (H.B. 2730), § 11.05, effective September 1, 2009.)

## Sec. 411.177. Issuance or Denial of License.

(a) The department shall issue a license to carry a concealed handgun to an applicant if the applicant meets all the eligibility requirements and submits all the application materials. The department may issue a license to carry handguns only of the categories for which the applicant has demonstrated proficiency in the form and manner required by the department. The department shall administer the licensing procedures in good faith so that any applicant who meets all the eligibility requirements and submits all the application materials shall receive a license. The department may not deny an application on the basis of a capricious or arbitrary decision by the department.

(b) The department shall, not later than the 60th day after the date of the receipt by the director's designee of the completed application materials:

(1) issue the license;

(2) notify the applicant in writing that the application was denied:

    (A) on the grounds that the applicant failed to qualify under the criteria listed in Section 411.172;

    (B) based on the affidavit of the director's designee submitted to the department under Section 411.176(c); or

    (C) based on the affidavit of the qualified handgun instructor submitted to the department under Section 411.188(k); or

(3) notify the applicant in writing that the department is unable to make a determination regarding the issuance or denial of a license to the applicant within the 60-day period prescribed by this subsection and include in that notification an explanation of the reason for the inability and an estimation of the amount of time the department will need to make the determination.

(c) Failure of the department to issue or deny a license for a period of more than 30 days after the department is required to act under Subsection (b) constitutes denial.

(d) A license issued under this subchapter is effective from the date of issuance.

(Enacted by Acts 1997, 75th Leg., ch. 165 (S.B. 898), § 10.01(a), effective September 1, 1997; am. Acts 1999, 76th Leg., ch. 62 (S.B. 1368), § 9.08(a), effective September 1, 1999; am. Acts 2009, 81st

Leg., ch. 1146 (H.B. 2730), § 11.06, effective September 1, 2009.)

## Sec. 411.178. Notice to Local Law Enforcement.

On request of a local law enforcement agency, the department shall notify the agency of the licenses that have been issued to license holders who reside in the county in which the agency is located.

(Enacted by Acts 1997, 75th Leg., ch. 165 (S.B. 898), § 10.01(a), effective September 1, 1997; am. Acts 1999, 76th Leg., ch. 1189 (S.B. 370), § 14, effective September 1, 1999.)

## Sec. 411.179. Form of License.

(a) The department by rule shall adopt the form of the license. A license must include:

(1) a number assigned to the license holder by the department;

(2) a statement of the period for which the license is effective;

(3) a statement of the category or categories of handguns the license holder may carry as provided by Subsection (b);

(4) a color photograph of the license holder;

(5) the license holder's full name, date of birth, hair and eye color, height, weight, and signature;

(6) the license holder's residence address or, as provided by Subsection (d), the street address of the courthouse in which the license holder or license holder's spouse serves as a federal judge or the license holder serves as a state judge; and

(7) the number of a driver's license or an identification certificate issued to the license holder by the department.

(b) A category of handguns contains handguns that are not prohibited by law and are of certain actions. The categories of handguns are:

(1) SA: any handguns, whether semi-automatic or not; and

(2) NSA: handguns that are not semi-automatic.

(c) In adopting the form of the license under Subsection (a), the department shall establish a procedure for the license of a federal judge, a state judge, or the spouse of a federal judge or state judge to omit the license holder's residence address and to include, in lieu of that address, the street address of the courthouse in which the license holder or license holder's spouse serves as a federal judge or state judge. In establishing the

procedure, the department shall require sufficient documentary evidence to establish the license holder's status as a federal judge, a state judge, or the spouse of a federal judge or state judge.

(d) In adopting the form of the license under Subsection (a), the department shall establish a procedure for the license of a judge, justice, prosecuting attorney, or assistant prosecuting attorney, as described by Section 46.15(a)(4) or (6), Penal Code, to indicate on the license the license holder's status as a judge, justice, district attorney, criminal district attorney, or county attorney. In establishing the procedure, the department shall require sufficient documentary evidence to establish the license holder's status under this subsection.

(Enacted by Acts 1997, 75th Leg., ch. 165 (S.B. 898), § 10.01(a), effective September 1, 1997; am. Acts 2007, 80th Leg., ch. 594 (H.B. 41), § 9, effective September 1, 2007; am. Acts 2007, 80th Leg., ch. 1222 (H.B. 2300), § 1, effective June 15, 2007; am. Acts 2009, 81st Leg., ch. 87 (S.B. 1969), §§ 27.001(25), 27.002(6), effective September 1, 2009; am. Acts 2009, 81st Leg., ch. 316 (H.B. 598), § 5, effective September 1, 2009; am. Acts 2009, 81st Leg., ch. 1146 (H.B. 2730), § 11.07, effective September 1, 2009.)

## Sec. 411.180. Notification of Denial, Revocation, or Suspension of License; Review.

(a) The department shall give written notice to each applicant for a handgun license of any denial, revocation, or suspension of that license. Not later than the 30th day after the notice is received by the applicant, according to the records of the department, the applicant or license holder may request a hearing on the denial, revocation, or suspension. The applicant must make a written request for a hearing addressed to the department at its Austin address. The request for hearing must reach the department in Austin prior to the 30th day after the date of receipt of the written notice. On receipt of a request for hearing from a license holder or applicant, the department shall promptly schedule a hearing in the appropriate justice court in the county of residence of the applicant or license holder. The justice court shall conduct a hearing to review the denial, revocation, or suspension of the license. In a proceeding under this section, a justice of the peace shall act as an administrative hearing officer. A hearing under this section is not subject to Chapter 2001 (Administrative Procedure Act). A district attorney or county attorney, the attorney general, or a designated member of the department may represent the department.

(b) The department, on receipt of a request for hearing, shall file the appropriate petition in the justice court selected for the hearing and send a copy of that petition to the applicant or license holder at the address contained in departmental records. A hearing under this section must be scheduled within 30 days of receipt of the request for a hearing. The hearing shall be held expeditiously but in no event more than 60 days after the date that the applicant or license holder requested the hearing. The date of the hearing may be reset on the motion of either party, by agreement of the parties, or by the court as necessary to accommodate the court's docket.

(c) The justice court shall determine if the denial, revocation, or suspension is supported by a preponderance of the evidence. Both the applicant or license holder and the department may present evidence. The court shall affirm the denial, revocation, or suspension if the court determines that denial, revocation, or suspension is supported by a preponderance of the evidence. If the court determines that the denial, revocation, or suspension is not supported by a preponderance of the evidence, the court shall order the department to immediately issue or return the license to the applicant or license holder.

(d) A proceeding under this section is subject to Chapter 105, Civil Practice and Remedies Code, relating to fees, expenses, and attorney's fees.

(e) A party adversely affected by the court's ruling following a hearing under this section may appeal the ruling by filing within 30 days after the ruling a petition in a county court at law in the county in which the applicant or license holder resides or, if there is no county court at law in the county, in the county court of the county. A person who appeals under this section must send by certified mail a copy of the person's petition, certified by the clerk of the court in which the petition is filed, to the appropriate division of the department at its Austin headquarters. The trial on appeal shall be a trial de novo without a jury. A district or county attorney or the attorney general may represent the department.

(f) A suspension of a license may not be probated.

(g) If an applicant or a license holder does not petition the justice court, a denial becomes final and a revocation or suspension takes effect on the 30th day after receipt of written notice.

(h) The department may use and introduce into evidence certified copies of governmental records to establish the existence of certain events that could result in the denial, revocation, or suspension of a license under this subchapter, including records regarding convictions, judicial findings regarding mental competency, judicial findings regarding chemical dependency, or other matters that may be established by governmental records that have been properly authenticated.

(i) This section does not apply to a suspension of a license under Section 85.022, Family Code, or Article 17.292, Code of Criminal Procedure. (Enacted by Acts 1997, 75th Leg., ch. 165 (S.B. 898), § 10.01(a), effective September 1, 1997; am. Acts 1999, 76th Leg., ch. 1412 (H.B. 2124), § 5, effective September 1, 1999.)

## Sec. 411.181. Notice of Change of Address or Name.

(a) If a person who is a current license holder moves from any residence address stated on the license, if the name of the person is changed by marriage or otherwise, or if the person's status becomes inapplicable for purposes of the information required to be displayed on the license under Section 411.179, the person shall, not later than the 30th day after the date of the address, name, or status change, notify the department and provide the department with the number of the person's license and, as applicable, the person's:

(1) former and new addresses;

(2) former and new names; or

(3) former and new status.

(b) If the name of the license holder is changed by marriage or otherwise, or if the person's status becomes inapplicable as described by Subsection (a), the person shall apply for a duplicate license. The duplicate license must reflect the person's current name, residence address, and status.

(c) If a license holder moves from the address stated on the license, the person shall apply for a duplicate license.

(d) The department shall charge a license holder a fee of $25 for a duplicate license.

(e) The department shall make the forms available on request.

(f) On request of a local law enforcement agency, the department shall notify the agency of changes made under Subsection (a) by license holders who reside in the county in which the agency is located.

(g) If a license is lost, stolen, or destroyed, the license holder shall apply for a duplicate license

Government

not later than the 30th day after the date of the loss, theft, or destruction of the license.

(h) If a license holder is required under this section to apply for a duplicate license and the license expires not later than the 60th day after the date of the loss, theft, or destruction of the license, the applicant may renew the license with the modified information included on the new license. The applicant must pay only the nonrefundable renewal fee.

(i) A license holder whose application fee for a duplicate license under this section is dishonored or reversed may reapply for a duplicate license at any time, provided the application fee and a dishonored payment charge of $25 is paid by cashier's check or money order made payable to the "Texas Department of Public Safety."
(Enacted by Acts 1997, 75th Leg., ch. 165 (S.B. 898), § 10.01(a), effective September 1, 1997; am. Acts 1999, 76th Leg., ch. 1189 (S.B. 370), § 15, effective September 1, 1999; am. Acts 2005, 79th Leg., ch. 1065 (H.B. 1483), § 3, effective September 1, 2005; am. Acts 2007, 80th Leg., ch. 594 (H.B. 41), § 10, effective September 1, 2007; am. Acts 2007, 80th Leg., ch. 1222 (H.B. 2300), § 2, effective June 15, 2007; am. Acts 2009, 81st Leg., ch. 316 (H.B. 598), § 6, effective September 1, 2009; am. Acts 2009, 81st Leg., ch. 1146 (H.B. 2730), § 11.08, effective September 1, 2009.)

## Sec. 411.182.  Notice.

(a) For the purpose of a notice required by this subchapter, the department may assume that the address currently reported to the department by the applicant or license holder is the correct address.

(b) A written notice meets the requirements under this subchapter if the notice is sent by certified mail to the current address reported by the applicant or license holder to the department.

(c) If a notice is returned to the department because the notice is not deliverable, the department may give notice by publication once in a newspaper of general interest in the county of the applicant's or license holder's last reported address. On the 31st day after the date the notice is published, the department may take the action proposed in the notice.
(Enacted by Acts 1997, 75th Leg., ch. 165 (S.B. 898), § 10.01(a), effective September 1, 1997.)

## Sec. 411.183.  Expiration.

(a) A license issued under this subchapter expires on the first birthday of the license holder occurring after the fourth anniversary of the date of issuance.

(b) A renewed license expires on the license holder's birthdate, five years after the date of the expiration of the previous license.

(c) A duplicate license expires on the date the license that was duplicated would have expired.

(d) A modified license expires on the date the license that was modified would have expired.

(e) [Expired pursuant to Acts 1997, 75th Leg., ch. 165 (S.B. 898), § 10.01, effective January 1, 2005.]
(Enacted by Acts 1997, 75th Leg., ch. 165 (S.B. 898), § 10.01 (a), effective September 1, 1997; am. Acts 2005, 79th Leg., ch. 915 (H.B. 225), § 3, effective September 1, 2005.)

## Sec. 411.184.  Modification.

(a) To modify a license to allow a license holder to carry a handgun of a different category than the license indicates, the license holder must:

(1) complete a proficiency examination as provided by Section 411.188(e); and

(2) submit to the department:

(A) an application for a modified license on a form provided by the department;

(B) evidence of handgun proficiency, in the form and manner required by the department;

(C) payment of a modified license fee of $25; and

(D) one or more photographs of the license holder that meet the requirements of the department.

(b) The director by rule shall adopt a modified license application form requiring an update of the information on the original completed application.

(c) The department may modify the license of a license holder who meets all the eligibility requirements and submits all the modification materials. Not later than the 45th day after receipt of the modification materials, the department shall issue the modified license or notify the license holder in writing that the modified license application was denied.

(d) On receipt of a modified license, the license holder shall return the previously issued license to the department.

(e) A license holder whose application fee for a modified license under this section is dishonored or reversed may reapply for a modified license at any time, provided the application fee and a dishonored payment charge of $25 is paid by cashier's check or money order made payable to the "Texas Department of Public Safety."

(Enacted by Acts 1997, 75th Leg., ch. 165 (S.B. 898), § 10.01(a), effective September 1, 1997; am. Acts 2005, 79th Leg., ch. 486 (H.B. 322), § 3, effective September 1, 2005; am. Acts 2005, 79th Leg., ch. 1065 (H.B. 1483), § 4, effective September 1, 2005; am. Acts 2009, 81st Leg., ch. 1146 (H.B. 2730), § 11.09, effective September 1, 2009.)

### Sec. 411.185. Renewal.

(a) To renew a license, a license holder must:

(1) complete a continuing education course in handgun proficiency under Section 411.188(c) within the six-month period preceding:

(A) the date of application for renewal, for a first or second renewal; and

(B) the date of application for renewal or the date of application for the preceding renewal, for a third or subsequent renewal, to ensure that the license holder is not required to complete the course more than once in any 10-year period; and

(2) submit to the department:

(A) an application for renewal on a form provided by the department;

(B) evidence of handgun proficiency, in the form and manner required by the department;

(C) payment of a nonrefundable renewal fee as set by the department; and

(D) one or more photographs of the applicant that meet the requirements of the department.

(b) The director by rule shall adopt a renewal application form requiring an update of the information on the original completed application. The director by rule shall set the renewal fee in an amount that is sufficient to cover the actual cost to the department to renew a license. Not later than the 60th day before the expiration date of the license, the department shall mail to each license holder a written notice of the expiration of the license and a renewal form.

(c) The department shall renew the license of a license holder who meets all the eligibility requirements and submits all the renewal materials. Not later than the 45th day after receipt of the renewal materials, the department shall issue the renewal or notify the license holder in writing that the renewal application was denied.

(d) The director by rule shall adopt a procedure by which a license holder who satisfies the eligibility criteria may renew a license by mail. The materials for renewal by mail must include a form to be signed and returned to the department by the applicant that describes state law regarding:

(1) the use of deadly force; and

(2) the places where it is unlawful for the holder of a license issued under this subchapter to carry a concealed handgun.

(Enacted by Acts 1997, 75th Leg., ch. 165 (S.B. 898), § 10.01(a), effective September 1, 1997; am. Acts 2007, 80th Leg., ch. 694 (H.B. 1839), § 1, effective September 1, 2007; am. Acts 2009, 81st Leg., ch. 1146 (H.B. 2730), § 11.10, effective September 1, 2009.)

### Sec. 411.186. Revocation.

(a) The department shall revoke a license under this section if the license holder:

(1) was not entitled to the license at the time it was issued;

(2) made a material misrepresentation or failed to disclose a material fact in an application submitted under this subchapter;

(3) subsequently becomes ineligible for a license under Section 411.172, unless the sole basis for the ineligibility is that the license holder is charged with the commission of a Class A or Class B misdemeanor or equivalent offense, or of an offense under Section 42.01, Penal Code, or equivalent offense, or of a felony under an information or indictment;

(4) is convicted of an offense under Section 46.035, Penal Code;

(5) is determined by the department to have engaged in conduct constituting a reason to suspend a license listed in Section 411.187(a) after the person's license has been previously suspended twice for the same reason; or

(6) submits an application fee that is dishonored or reversed if the applicant fails to submit a cashier's check or money order made payable to the "Department of Public Safety of the State of Texas" in the amount of the dishonored or reversed fee, plus $25, within 30 days of being notified by the department that the fee was dishonored or reversed.

(b) If a peace officer believes a reason listed in Subsection (a) to revoke a license exists, the officer shall prepare an affidavit on a form provided by the department stating the reason for the revocation of the license and giving the department all of the information available to the officer at the time of the preparation of the form.

Government

The officer shall attach the officer's reports relating to the license holder to the form and send the form and attachments to the appropriate division of the department at its Austin headquarters not later than the fifth working day after the date the form is prepared. The officer shall send a copy of the form and the attachments to the license holder. If the license holder has not surrendered the license or the license was not seized as evidence, the license holder shall surrender the license to the appropriate division of the department not later than the 10th day after the date the license holder receives the notice of revocation from the department, unless the license holder requests a hearing from the department. The license holder may request that the justice court in the justice court precinct in which the license holder resides review the revocation as provided by Section 411.180. If a request is made for the justice court to review the revocation and hold a hearing, the license holder shall surrender the license on the date an order of revocation is entered by the justice court.

(c) A license holder whose license is revoked for a reason listed in Subsections (a)(1)—(5) may reapply as a new applicant for the issuance of a license under this subchapter after the second anniversary of the date of the revocation if the cause for revocation does not exist on the date of the second anniversary. If the cause for revocation exists on the date of the second anniversary after the date of revocation, the license holder may not apply for a new license until the cause for revocation no longer exists and has not existed for a period of two years.

(d) A license holder whose license is revoked under Subsection (a)(6) may reapply for an original or renewed license at any time, provided the application fee and a dishonored payment charge of $25 is paid by cashier's check or money order made payable to the "Texas Department of Public Safety."

(Enacted by Acts 1997, 75th Leg., ch. 165 (S.B. 898), § 10.01(a), effective September 1, 1997; am. Acts 1999, 76th Leg., ch. 62 (S.B. 1368), § 9.09(a), effective September 1, 1999; am. Acts 2005, 79th Leg., ch. 1065 (H.B. 1483), § 2, effective September 1, 2005; am. Acts 2009, 81st Leg., ch. 1146 (H.B. 2730), § 11.11, effective September 1, 2009.)

## Sec. 411.187. Suspension of License.

(a) The department shall suspend a license under this section if the license holder:

(1) is charged with the commission of a Class A or Class B misdemeanor or equivalent offense, or of an offense under Section 42.01, Penal Code, or equivalent offense, or of a felony under an information or indictment;

(2) fails to notify the department of a change of address, name, or status as required by Section 411.181;

(3) carries a concealed handgun under the authority of this subchapter of a different category than the license holder is licensed to carry;

(4) fails to return a previously issued license after a license is modified as required by Section 411.184(d);

(5) commits an act of family violence and is the subject of an active protective order rendered under Title 4, Family Code; or

(6) is arrested for an offense involving family violence or an offense under Section 42.072, Penal Code, and is the subject of an order for emergency protection issued under Article 17.292, Code of Criminal Procedure.

(b) If a peace officer believes a reason listed in Subsection (a) to suspend a license exists, the officer shall prepare an affidavit on a form provided by the department stating the reason for the suspension of the license and giving the department all of the information available to the officer at the time of the preparation of the form. The officer shall attach the officer's reports relating to the license holder to the form and send the form and the attachments to the appropriate division of the department at its Austin headquarters not later than the fifth working day after the date the form is prepared. The officer shall send a copy of the form and the attachments to the license holder. If the license holder has not surrendered the license or the license was not seized as evidence, the license holder shall surrender the license to the appropriate division of the department not later than the 10th day after the date the license holder receives the notice of suspension from the department unless the license holder requests a hearing from the department. The license holder may request that the justice court in the justice court precinct in which the license holder resides review the suspension as provided by Section 411.180. If a request is made for the justice court to review the suspension and hold a hearing, the license holder shall surrender the license on the date an order of suspension is entered by the justice court.

(c) The department shall suspend a license under this section:

(1) for 30 days, if the person's license is subject to suspension for a reason listed in Subsection (a)(2), (3), or (4), except as provided by Subdivision (2);

(2) for not less than one year and not more than three years, if the person's license:

(A) is subject to suspension for a reason listed in Subsection (a), other than the reason listed in Subsection (a)(1); and

(B) has been previously suspended for the same reason;

(3) until dismissal of the charges, if the person's license is subject to suspension for the reason listed in Subsection (a)(1); or

(4) for the duration of or the period specified by:

(A) the protective order issued under Title 4, Family Code, if the person's license is subject to suspension for the reason listed in Subsection (a)(5); or

(B) the order for emergency protection issued under Article 17.292, Code of Criminal Procedure, if the person's license is subject to suspension for the reason listed in Subsection (a)(6).

(Enacted by Acts 1997, 75th Leg., ch. 165 (S.B. 898), § 10.01(a), effective September 1, 1997; am. Acts 1999, 76th Leg., ch. 62 (S.B. 1368), § 9.10(a), effective September 1, 1999; am. Acts 1999, 76th Leg., ch. 1412 (H.B. 2124), § 6, effective September 1, 1999; am. Acts 2009, 81st Leg., ch. 316 (H.B. 598), § 7, effective September 1, 2009; am. Acts 2009, 81st Leg., ch. 1146 (H.B. 2730), §§ 11.12, 12A.01, effective September 1, 2009.)

## Sec. 411.188. Handgun Proficiency Requirement.

(a) The director by rule shall establish minimum standards for handgun proficiency and shall develop a course to teach handgun proficiency and examinations to measure handgun proficiency. The course to teach handgun proficiency must contain training sessions divided into two parts. One part of the course must be classroom instruction and the other part must be range instruction and an actual demonstration by the applicant of the applicant's ability to safely and proficiently use the applicable category of handgun. An applicant must be able to demonstrate, at a minimum, the degree of proficiency that is required to effectively operate a handgun of .32 caliber or above. The department shall distribute the standards, course requirements, and examinations on request to any qualified handgun instructor.

(b) Only a qualified handgun instructor may administer a handgun proficiency course. The handgun proficiency course must include at least 10 hours and not more than 15 hours of instruction on:

(1) the laws that relate to weapons and to the use of deadly force;

(2) handgun use, proficiency, and safety;

(3) nonviolent dispute resolution; and

(4) proper storage practices for handguns with an emphasis on storage practices that eliminate the possibility of accidental injury to a child.

(c) The department by rule shall develop a continuing education course in handgun proficiency for a license holder who wishes to renew a license. Only a qualified handgun instructor may administer the continuing education course. The course must include:

(1) at least four hours of instruction on one or more of the subjects listed in Subsection (b); and

(2) other information the director determines is appropriate.

(d) Only a qualified handgun instructor may administer the proficiency examination to obtain or to renew a license. The proficiency examination must include:

(1) a written section on the subjects listed in Subsection (b); and

(2) a physical demonstration of proficiency in the use of one or more handguns of specific categories and in handgun safety procedures.

(e) Only a qualified handgun instructor may administer the proficiency examination to modify a license. The proficiency examination must include a physical demonstration of the proficiency in the use of one or more handguns of specific categories and in handgun safety procedures.

(f) The department shall develop and distribute directions and materials for course instruction, test administration, and recordkeeping. All test results shall be sent to the department, and the department shall maintain a record of the results.

(g) A person who wishes to obtain or renew a license to carry a concealed handgun must apply in person to a qualified handgun instructor to take the appropriate course in handgun proficiency and demonstrate handgun proficiency as required by the department.

(h) A license holder who wishes to modify a license to allow the license holder to carry a handgun of a different category than the license indicates must apply in person to a qualified handgun instructor to demonstrate the required knowledge and proficiency in that category.

(i) A certified firearms instructor of the department may monitor any class or training presented by a qualified handgun instructor. A qualified handgun instructor shall cooperate with the department in the department's efforts to monitor the presentation of training by the qualified handgun instructor. A qualified handgun instructor shall make available for inspection to the department any and all records maintained by a qualified handgun instructor under this subchapter. The qualified handgun instructor shall keep a record of all information required by department rule.

(j) The department may offer online, or allow a qualified handgun instructor to offer online, the continuing education instruction course and written section of the proficiency examination required to renew a license.

(k) A qualified handgun instructor may submit to the department a written recommendation for disapproval of the application for a license, renewal, or modification of a license, accompanied by an affidavit stating personal knowledge or naming persons with personal knowledge of facts that lead the instructor to believe that an applicant does not possess the required handgun proficiency. The department may use a written recommendation submitted under this subsection as the basis for denial of a license only if the department determines that the recommendation is made in good faith and is supported by a preponderance of the evidence. The department shall make a determination under this subsection not later than the 45th day after the date the department receives the written recommendation. The 60-day period in which the department must take action under Section 411.177(b) is extended one day for each day a determination is pending under this subsection.
(Enacted by Acts 1997, 75th Leg., ch. 165 (S.B. 898), § 10.01(a), effective September 1, 1997; am. Acts 1999, 76th Leg., ch. 62 (S.B. 1368), § 9.11(a), effective September 1, 1999; am. Acts 2009, 81st Leg., ch. 1146 (H.B. 2730), §§ 5.10, 11.13, effective September 1, 2009.)

### Sec. 411.1881. Exemption from Instruction for Certain Persons.

(a) Notwithstanding any other provision of this subchapter, a person may not be required to complete the range instruction portion of a handgun proficiency course to obtain or renew a concealed handgun license issued under this subchapter if the person:

(1) is currently serving in or is honorably discharged from:

(A) the army, navy, air force, coast guard, or marine corps of the United States or an auxiliary service or reserve unit of one of those branches of the armed forces; or

(B) the state military forces, as defined by Section 431.001; and

(2) has, within the five years preceding the date of the person's application for an original or renewed license, as applicable, completed a course of training in handgun proficiency or familiarization as part of the person's service with the armed forces or state military forces.

(b) The director by rule shall adopt a procedure by which a license holder who is exempt under Subsection (a) from the range instruction portion of the handgun proficiency requirement may submit a form demonstrating the license holder's qualification for an exemption under that subsection. The form must provide sufficient information to allow the department to verify whether the license holder qualifies for the exemption.
(Enacted by Acts 2005, 79th Leg., ch. 132 (H.B. 685), § 1, effective September 1, 2005.)

### Sec. 411.1882. Evidence of Handgun Proficiency for Certain Persons.

(a) A person who is serving in this state as a judge or justice of a federal court, as an active judicial officer, as defined by Section 411.201, or as a district attorney, assistant district attorney, criminal district attorney, assistant criminal district attorney, county attorney, or assistant county attorney may establish handgun proficiency for the purposes of this subchapter by obtaining from a handgun proficiency instructor approved by the Commission on Law Enforcement Officer Standards and Education for purposes of Section 1702.1675, Occupations Code, a sworn statement that:

(1) indicates that the person, during the 12-month period preceding the date of the person's application to the department, demonstrated to the instructor proficiency in the use of handguns; and

(2) designates the categories of handguns with respect to which the person demonstrated proficiency.

(b) The director by rule shall adopt a procedure by which a person described under Subsection (a) may submit a form demonstrating the person's qualification for an exemption under that subsection. The form must provide sufficient information to allow the department to verify whether the person qualifies for the exemption.

(c) A license issued under this section automatically expires on the six-month anniversary of the date the person's status under Subsection (a) becomes inapplicable. A license that expires under this subsection may be renewed under Section 411.185.

(Enacted by Acts 2007, 80th Leg., ch. 1222 (H.B. 2300), § 3, effective June 15, 2007; am. Acts 2009, 81st Leg., ch. 1146 (H.B. 2730), § 11.14, effective September 1, 2009.)

### Sec. 411.189.  Handgun Proficiency Certificate [Repealed].

Repealed by Acts 2009, 81st Leg., ch. 1146 (H.B. 2730), § 11.25, effective September 1, 2009. (Enacted by Acts 1997, 75th Leg., ch. 165 (S.B. 898), § 10.01(a), effective September 1, 1997; am. Acts 1999, 76th Leg., ch. 62 (S.B. 1368), § 9.12(a), effective September 1, 1999.)

### Sec. 411.190.  Qualified Handgun Instructors.

(a) The director may certify as a qualified handgun instructor a person who:

(1) is certified by the Commission on Law Enforcement Officer Standards and Education or under Chapter 1702, Occupations Code, to instruct others in the use of handguns;

(2) regularly instructs others in the use of handguns and has graduated from a handgun instructor school that uses a nationally accepted course designed to train persons as handgun instructors; or

(3) is certified by the National Rifle Association of America as a handgun instructor.

(b) In addition to the qualifications described by Subsection (a), a qualified handgun instructor must be qualified to instruct persons in:

(1) the laws that relate to weapons and to the use of deadly force;

(2) handgun use, proficiency, and safety;

(3) nonviolent dispute resolution; and

(4) proper storage practices for handguns, including storage practices that eliminate the possibility of accidental injury to a child.

(c) In the manner applicable to a person who applies for a license to carry a concealed handgun, the department shall conduct a background check of a person who applies for certification as a qualified handgun instructor. If the background check indicates that the applicant for certification would not qualify to receive a handgun license, the department may not certify the applicant as a qualified handgun instructor. If the background check indicates that the applicant for certification would qualify to receive a handgun license, the department shall provide handgun instructor training to the applicant. The applicant shall pay a fee of $100 to the department for the training. The applicant must take and successfully complete the training offered by the department and pay the training fee before the department may certify the applicant as a qualified handgun instructor. The department shall issue a license to carry a concealed handgun under the authority of this subchapter to any person who is certified as a qualified handgun instructor and who pays to the department a fee of $100 in addition to the training fee. The department by rule may prorate or waive the training fee for an employee of another governmental entity.

(d) The certification of a qualified handgun instructor expires on the second anniversary after the date of certification. To renew a certification, the qualified handgun instructor must pay a fee of $100 and take and successfully complete the retraining courses required by department rule.

(d-1) The department shall ensure that an applicant may renew certification under Subsection (d) from any county in this state by using an online format to complete the required retraining courses if:

(1) the applicant is renewing certification for the first time; or

(2) the applicant completed the required retraining courses in person the previous time the applicant renewed certification.

(e) After certification, a qualified handgun instructor may conduct training for applicants for a license under this subchapter.

(f) If the department determines that a reason exists to revoke, suspend, or deny a license to carry a concealed handgun with respect to a person who is a qualified handgun instructor or an applicant for certification as a qualified handgun instructor, the department shall take that action against the person's:

(1) license to carry a concealed handgun if the person is an applicant for or the holder of a license issued under this subchapter; and

(2) certification as a qualified handgun instructor.

(Enacted by Acts 1997, 75th Leg., ch. 165 (S.B. 898), § 10.01(a), effective September 1, 1997; am.

Acts 1999, 76th Leg., ch. 62 (S.B. 1368), § 9.13(a), effective September 1, 1999; am. Acts 1999, 76th Leg., ch. 199 (H.B. 592), § 1, effective September 1, 1999; am. Acts 2001, 77th Leg., ch. 1420 (H.B. 2812), § 14.758, effective September 1, 2001; am. Acts 2009, 81st Leg., ch. 1146 (H.B. 2730), §§ 5.11, 11.15, effective September 1, 2009; am. Acts 2011, 82nd Leg., ch. 91 (S.B. 1303), § 11.007, effective September 1, 2011.)

### Sec. 411.191. Review of Denial, Revocation, or Suspension of Certification As Qualified Handgun Instructor.

The procedures for the review of a denial, revocation, or suspension of a license under Section 411.180 apply to the review of a denial, revocation, or suspension of certification as a qualified handgun instructor. The notice provisions of this subchapter relating to denial, revocation, or suspension of handgun licenses apply to the proposed denial, revocation, or suspension of a certification of a qualified handgun instructor or an applicant for certification as a qualified handgun instructor.
(Enacted by Acts 1997, 75th Leg., ch. 165 (S.B. 898), § 10.01(a), effective September 1, 1997.)

### Sec. 411.192. Confidentiality of Records.

(a) The department shall disclose to a criminal justice agency information contained in its files and records regarding whether a named individual or any individual named in a specified list is licensed under this subchapter. Information on an individual subject to disclosure under this section includes the individual's name, date of birth, gender, race, zip code, telephone number, e-mail address, and Internet website address. Except as otherwise provided by this section and by Section 411.193, all other records maintained under this subchapter are confidential and are not subject to mandatory disclosure under the open records law, Chapter 552.

(b) An applicant or license holder may be furnished a copy of disclosable records regarding the applicant or license holder on request and the payment of a reasonable fee.

(c) The department shall notify a license holder of any request that is made for information relating to the license holder under this section and provide the name of the agency making the request.

(d) The department shall make public and distribute to the public at no cost lists of individ-

uals who are certified as qualified handgun instructors by the department and who request to be included as provided by Subsection (e). The department shall include on the lists each individual's name, telephone number, e-mail address, and Internet website address. The department shall make the list available on the department's Internet website.

(e) An individual who is certified as a qualified handgun instructor may request in writing that the department disclose all or part of the information described by Subsection (d) regarding the individual. The department shall include all or part of the individual's information on the list as requested.
(Enacted by Acts 1997, 75th Leg., ch. 165 (S.B. 898), § 10.01(a), effective September 1, 1997; am. Acts 2007, 80th Leg., ch. 172 (H.B. 991), § 1, effective May 23, 2007; am. Acts 2009, 81st Leg., ch. 1146 (H.B. 2730), § 6.03, effective September 1, 2009.)

### Sec. 411.193. Statistical Report.

The department shall make available, on request and payment of a reasonable fee to cover costs of copying, a statistical report that includes the number of licenses issued, denied, revoked, or suspended by the department during the preceding month, listed by age, gender, race, and zip code of the applicant or license holder.
(Enacted by Acts 1997, 75th Leg., ch. 165 (S.B. 898), § 10.01(a), effective September 1, 1997.)

### Sec. 411.194. Reduction of Fees Due to Indigency.

(a) Notwithstanding any other provision of this subchapter, the department shall reduce by 50 percent any fee required for the issuance of an original, duplicate, modified, or renewed license under this subchapter if the department determines that the applicant is indigent.

(b) The department shall require an applicant requesting a reduction of a fee to submit proof of indigency with the application materials.

(c) For purposes of this section, an applicant is indigent if the applicant's income is not more than 100 percent of the applicable income level established by the federal poverty guidelines.
(Enacted by Acts 1997, 75th Leg., ch. 165 (S.B. 898), § 10.01(a), effective September 1, 1997.)

### Sec. 411.195. Reduction of Fees for Senior Citizens.

Notwithstanding any other provision of this subchapter, the department shall reduce by 50

Government

percent any fee required for the issuance of an original, duplicate, modified, or renewed license under this subchapter if the applicant for the license is 60 years of age or older.

(Enacted by Acts 1997, 75th Leg., ch. 165 (S.B. 898), § 10.01(a), effective September 1, 1997; am. Acts 2005, 79th Leg., ch. 289 (H.B. 1038), § 1, effective September 1, 2005.)

### Sec. 411.1951. Waiver or Reduction of Fees for Members or Veterans of United States Armed Forces.

(a) In this section, "veteran" means a person who:

(1) has served in:

(A) the army, navy, air force, coast guard, or marine corps of the United States;

(B) the state military forces as defined by Section 431.001; or

(C) an auxiliary service of one of those branches of the armed forces; and

(2) has been honorably discharged from the branch of the service in which the person served.

(b) Notwithstanding any other provision of this subchapter, the department shall waive any fee required for the issuance of an original, duplicate, modified, or renewed license under this subchapter if the applicant for the license is:

(1) a member of the United States armed forces, including a member of the reserves, national guard, or state guard; or

(2) a veteran who, within 365 days preceding the date of the application, was honorably discharged from the branch of service in which the person served.

(c) Notwithstanding any other provision of this subchapter, the department shall reduce by 50 percent any fee required for the issuance of an original, duplicate, modified, or renewed license under this subchapter if the applicant for the license is a veteran who, more than 365 days preceding the date of the application, was honorably discharged from the branch of the service in which the person served.

(Enacted by Acts 2005, 79th Leg., ch. 486 (H.B. 322), § 4, effective September 1, 2005; am. Acts 2007, 80th Leg., ch. 200 (H.B. 233), § 1, effective September 1, 2007.)

### Sec. 411.196. Method of Payment.

A person may pay a fee required by this subchapter by cash, credit card, personal check, cashier's check, or money order. A person who pays a fee required by this subchapter by cash must pay the fee in person. Checks or money orders must be made payable to the "Texas Department of Public Safety." A person whose payment for a fee required by this subchapter is dishonored or reversed must pay any future fees required by this subchapter by cashier's check or money order made payable to the "Texas Department of Public Safety." A fee received by the department under this subchapter is nonrefundable.

(Enacted by Acts 1997, 75th Leg., ch. 165 (S.B. 898), § 10.01(a), effective September 1, 1997; am. Acts 2005, 79th Leg., ch. 1065 (H.B. 1483), § 1, effective September 1, 2005.)

### Sec. 411.197. Rules.

The director shall adopt rules to administer this subchapter.

(Enacted by Acts 1997, 75th Leg., ch. 165 (S.B. 898), § 10.01(a), effective September 1, 1997.)

### Sec. 411.198. Law Enforcement Officer Alias Handgun License.

(a) On written approval of the director, the department may issue to a law enforcement officer an alias license to carry a concealed handgun to be used in supervised activities involving criminal investigations.

(b) It is a defense to prosecution under Section 46.035, Penal Code, that the actor, at the time of the commission of the offense, was the holder of an alias license issued under this section.

(Enacted by Acts 1997, 75th Leg., ch. 165 (S.B. 898), § 10.01(a), effective September 1, 1997.)

### Sec. 411.199. Honorably Retired Peace Officers.

(a) A person who is licensed as a peace officer under Chapter 1701, Occupations Code, and who has been employed full-time as a peace officer by a law enforcement agency may apply for a license under this subchapter at any time after retirement.

(b) The person shall submit two complete sets of legible and classifiable fingerprints and a sworn statement from the head of the law enforcement agency employing the applicant. A head of a law enforcement agency may not refuse to issue a statement under this subsection. If the applicant alleges that the statement is untrue, the department shall investigate the validity of the statement. The statement must include:

(1) the name and rank of the applicant;

(2) the status of the applicant before retirement;

(3) whether or not the applicant was accused of misconduct at the time of the retirement;

(4) the physical and mental condition of the applicant;

(5) the type of weapons the applicant had demonstrated proficiency with during the last year of employment;

(6) whether the applicant would be eligible for reemployment with the agency, and if not, the reasons the applicant is not eligible; and

(7) a recommendation from the agency head regarding the issuance of a license under this subchapter.

(c) The department may issue a license under this subchapter to an applicant under this section if the applicant is honorably retired and physically and emotionally fit to possess a handgun. In this subsection, "honorably retired" means the applicant:

(1) did not retire in lieu of any disciplinary action;

(2) was eligible to retire from the law enforcement agency or was ineligible to retire only as a result of an injury received in the course of the applicant's employment with the agency; and

(3) is entitled to receive a pension or annuity for service as a law enforcement officer or is not entitled to receive a pension or annuity only because the law enforcement agency that employed the applicant does not offer a pension or annuity to its employees.

(d) An applicant under this section must pay a fee of $25 for a license issued under this subchapter.

(e) A retired peace officer who obtains a license under this subchapter must maintain, for the category of weapon licensed, the proficiency required for a peace officer under Section 1701.355, Occupations Code. The department or a local law enforcement agency shall allow a retired peace officer of the department or agency an opportunity to annually demonstrate the required proficiency. The proficiency shall be reported to the department on application and renewal.

(f) A license issued under this section expires as provided by Section 411.183.

(g) A retired officer of the United States who was eligible to carry a firearm in the discharge of the officer's official duties is eligible for a license under this section. An applicant described by this subsection may submit the application at any time after retirement. The applicant shall submit with the application proper proof of retired status by presenting the following documents prepared by the agency from which the applicant retired:

(1) retirement credentials; and

(2) a letter from the agency head stating the applicant retired in good standing.

(Enacted by Acts 1997, 75th Leg., ch. 165 (S.B. 898), § 10.01(a), effective September 1, 1997; am. Acts 1999, 76th Leg., ch. 25 (S.B. 404), § 1, effective May 3, 1999; am. Acts 1999, 76th Leg., ch. 62 (S.B. 1368), § 9.14(a), effective September 1, 1999; am. Acts 2001, 77th Leg., ch. 196 (H.B. 780), § 1, effective September 1, 2001; am. Acts 2009, 81st Leg., ch. 1146 (H.B. 2730), § 11.16, effective September 1, 2009.)

## Sec. 411.1991. Active Peace Officers.

(a) A person who is licensed as a peace officer under Chapter 1701, Occupations Code, and is employed full-time as a peace officer by a law enforcement agency may apply for a license under this subchapter. The person shall submit to the department two complete sets of legible and classifiable fingerprints and a sworn statement of the head of the law enforcement agency employing the applicant. A head of a law enforcement agency may not refuse to issue a statement under this subsection. If the applicant alleges that the statement is untrue, the department shall investigate the validity of the statement. The statement must include:

(1) the name and rank of the applicant;

(2) whether the applicant has been accused of misconduct at any time during the applicant's period of employment with the agency and the disposition of that accusation;

(3) a description of the physical and mental condition of the applicant;

(4) a list of the types of weapons the applicant has demonstrated proficiency with during the preceding year; and

(5) a recommendation from the agency head that a license be issued to the person under this subchapter.

(b) The department may issue a license under this subchapter to an applicant under this section if the statement from the head of the law enforcement agency employing the applicant complies with Subsection (a) and indicates that the applicant is qualified and physically and mentally fit to carry a handgun.

(c) An applicant under this section shall pay a fee of $25 for a license issued under this subchapter.

Government

(d) A license issued under this section expires as provided by Section 411.183.
(Enacted by Acts 1999, 76th Leg., ch. 62 (S.B. 1368), § 9.15(a), effective September 1, 1999; am. Acts 2009, 81st Leg., ch. 1146 (H.B. 2730), § 11.17, effective September 1, 2009.)

## Sec. 411.200. Application to Licensed Security Officers.

This subchapter does not exempt a license holder who is also employed as a security officer and licensed under Chapter 1702, Occupations Code, from the duty to comply with Chapter 1702, Occupations Code, or Section 46.02, Penal Code.
(Enacted by Acts 1997, 75th Leg., ch. 165 (S.B. 898), § 10.01(a), effective September 1, 1997; am. Acts 2001, 77th Leg., ch. 1420 (H.B. 2812), § 14.759, effective September 1, 2001.)

## Sec. 411.201. Active and Retired Judicial Officers.

(a) In this section:
(1) "Active judicial officer" means:
(A) a person serving as a judge or justice of the supreme court, the court of criminal appeals, a court of appeals, a district court, a criminal district court, a constitutional county court, a statutory county court, a justice court, or a municipal court;
(B) a federal judge who is a resident of this state; or
(C) **[Effective September 28, 2011]** a person appointed and serving as an associate judge under Chapter 201, Family Code.
(2) "Retired judicial officer" means:
(A) a special judge appointed under Section 26.023 or 26.024; or
(B) a senior judge designated under Section 75.001 or a judicial officer as designated or defined by Section 75.001, 831.001, or 836.001.
(b) Notwithstanding any other provision of this subchapter, the department shall issue a license under this subchapter to an active or retired judicial officer who meets the requirements of this section.
(c) An active judicial officer is eligible for a license to carry a concealed handgun under the authority of this subchapter. A retired judicial officer is eligible for a license to carry a concealed handgun under the authority of this subchapter if the officer:
(1) has not been convicted of a felony;
(2) has not, in the five years preceding the date of application, been convicted of a Class A or Class B misdemeanor or equivalent offense;

(3) is not charged with the commission of a Class A or Class B misdemeanor or equivalent offense or of a felony under an information or indictment;
(4) is not a chemically dependent person; and
(5) is not a person of unsound mind.
(d) An applicant for a license who is an active or retired judicial officer must submit to the department:
(1) a completed application, including all required affidavits, on a form prescribed by the department;
(2) one or more photographs of the applicant that meet the requirements of the department;
(3) two complete sets of legible and classifiable fingerprints of the applicant, including one set taken by a person employed by a law enforcement agency who is appropriately trained in recording fingerprints;
(4) evidence of handgun proficiency, in the form and manner required by the department for an applicant under this section;
(5) a nonrefundable application and license fee set by the department in an amount reasonably designed to cover the administrative costs associated with issuance of a license to carry a concealed handgun under this subchapter; and
(6) if the applicant is a retired judicial officer, a form executed by the applicant that authorizes the department to make an inquiry into any noncriminal history records that are necessary to determine the applicant's eligibility for a license under this subchapter.
(e) On receipt of all the application materials required by this section, the department shall:
(1) if the applicant is an active judicial officer, issue a license to carry a concealed handgun under the authority of this subchapter; or
(2) if the applicant is a retired judicial officer, conduct an appropriate background investigation to determine the applicant's eligibility for the license and, if the applicant is eligible, issue a license to carry a concealed handgun under the authority of this subchapter.
(f) Except as otherwise provided by this subsection, an applicant for a license under this section must satisfy the handgun proficiency requirements of Section 411.188. The classroom instruction part of the proficiency course for an active judicial officer is not subject to a minimum hour requirement. The instruction must include instruction only on:
(1) handgun use, proficiency, and safety; and

(2) proper storage practices for handguns with an emphasis on storage practices that eliminate the possibility of accidental injury to a child.

(g) A license issued under this section expires as provided by Section 411.183 and, except as otherwise provided by this subsection, may be renewed in accordance with Section 411.185 of this subchapter. An active judicial officer is not required to attend the classroom instruction part of the continuing education proficiency course to renew a license.

(h) The department shall issue a license to carry a concealed handgun under the authority of this subchapter to an elected attorney representing the state in the prosecution of felony cases who meets the requirements of this section for an active judicial officer. The department shall waive any fee required for the issuance of an original, duplicate, or renewed license under this subchapter for an applicant who is an attorney elected or employed to represent the state in the prosecution of felony cases.

(Enacted by Acts 1997, 75th Leg., ch. 165 (S.B. 898), § 10.01(a), effective September 1, 1997; am. Acts 2007, 80th Leg., ch. 402 (S.B. 835), § 1, effective June 15, 2007; am. Acts 2007, 80th Leg., ch. 1222 (H.B. 2300), § 4, effective June 15, 2007; am. Acts 2009, 81st Leg., ch. 1146 (H.B. 2730), § 11.18, effective September 1, 2009; am. Acts 2011, 82nd Leg., 1st C.S., (H.B. 79), § 13.01, effective September 28, 2011.)

### Sec. 411.202.   License a Benefit.

The issuance of a license under this subchapter is a benefit to the license holder for purposes of those sections of the Penal Code to which the definition of "benefit" under Section 1.07, Penal Code, applies.

(Enacted by Acts 1997, 75th Leg., ch. 165 (S.B. 898), § 10.01(a), effective September 1, 1997.)

### Sec. 411.203.   Rights of Employers.

This subchapter does not prevent or otherwise limit the right of a public or private employer to prohibit persons who are licensed under this subchapter from carrying a concealed handgun on the premises of the business. In this section, "premises" has the meaning assigned by Section 46.035(f)(3), Penal Code.

(Enacted by Acts 1997, 75th Leg., ch. 165 (S.B. 898), § 10.01(a), effective September 1, 1997; am. Acts 2011, 82nd Leg., ch. 1058 (S.B. 321), § 2, effective September 1, 2011.)

### Sec. 411.204.   Notice Required on Certain Premises.

(a) A business that has a permit or license issued under Chapter 25, 28, 32, 69, or 74, Alcoholic Beverage Code, and that derives 51 percent or more of its income from the sale of alcoholic beverages for on-premises consumption as determined by the Texas Alcoholic Beverage Commission under Section 104.06, Alcoholic Beverage Code, shall prominently display at each entrance to the business premises a sign that complies with the requirements of Subsection (c).

(b) A hospital licensed under Chapter 241, Health and Safety Code, or a nursing home licensed under Chapter 242, Health and Safety Code, shall prominently display at each entrance to the hospital or nursing home, as appropriate, a sign that complies with the requirements of Subsection (c) other than the requirement that the sign include on its face the number "51".

(c) The sign required under Subsections (a) and (b) must give notice in both English and Spanish that it is unlawful for a person licensed under this subchapter to carry a handgun on the premises. The sign must appear in contrasting colors with block letters at least one inch in height and must include on its face the number "51" printed in solid red at least five inches in height. The sign shall be displayed in a conspicuous manner clearly visible to the public.

(d) A business that has a permit or license issued under the Alcoholic Beverage Code and that is not required to display a sign under this section may be required to display a sign under Section 11.041 or 61.11, Alcoholic Beverage Code.

(e) This section does not apply to a business that has a food and beverage certificate issued under the Alcoholic Beverage Code.

(Enacted by Acts 1997, 75th Leg., ch. 165 (S.B. 898), § 10.01(a), effective September 1, 1997; am. Acts 1999, 76th Leg., ch. 62 (S.B. 1368), § 9.16(a), effective September 1, 1999; am. Acts 1999, 76th Leg., ch. 523 (S.B. 131), § 1, effective June 18, 1999.)

### Sec. 411.205.   Requirement to Display License.

If a license holder is carrying a handgun on or about the license holder's person when a magistrate or a peace officer demands that the license holder display identification, the license holder shall display both the license holder's driver's license or identification certificate issued by the department and the license holder's handgun license.

(Enacted by Acts 1997, 75th Leg., ch. 165 (S.B. 898), § 10.01(a), effective September 1, 1997; am. Acts 1999, 76th Leg., ch. 62 (S.B. 1368), § 9.17(a), effective September 1, 1999; am. Acts 2009, 81st Leg., ch. 1146 (H.B. 2730), § 12A.02, effective September 1, 2009.)

## Sec. 411.206. Seizure of Handgun and License.

(a) If a peace officer arrests and takes into custody a license holder who is carrying a handgun under the authority of this subchapter, the officer shall seize the license holder's handgun and license as evidence.

(b) The provisions of Article 18.19, Code of Criminal Procedure, relating to the disposition of weapons seized in connection with criminal offenses, apply to a handgun seized under this subsection.

(c) Any judgment of conviction entered by any court for an offense under Section 46.035, Penal Code, must contain the handgun license number of the convicted license holder. A certified copy of the judgment is conclusive and sufficient evidence to justify revocation of a license under Section 411.186(a)(4).

(Enacted by Acts 1997, 75th Leg., ch. 165 (S.B. 898), § 10.01(a), effective September 1, 1997.)

## Sec. 411.207. Authority of Peace Officer to Disarm.

(a) A peace officer who is acting in the lawful discharge of the officer's official duties may disarm a license holder at any time the officer reasonably believes it is necessary for the protection of the license holder, officer, or another individual. The peace officer shall return the handgun to the license holder before discharging the license holder from the scene if the officer determines that the license holder is not a threat to the officer, license holder, or another individual and if the license holder has not violated any provision of this subchapter or committed any other violation that results in the arrest of the license holder.

(b) A peace officer who is acting in the lawful discharge of the officer's official duties may temporarily disarm a license holder when a license holder enters a nonpublic, secure portion of a law enforcement facility, if the law enforcement agency provides a gun locker where the peace officer can secure the license holder's handgun. The peace officer shall secure the handgun in the locker and shall return the handgun to the license holder immediately after the license holder leaves the nonpublic, secure portion of the law enforcement facility.

(c) A law enforcement facility shall prominently display at each entrance to a nonpublic, secure portion of the facility a sign that gives notice in both English and Spanish that, under this section, a peace officer may temporarily disarm a license holder when the license holder enters the nonpublic, secure portion of the facility. The sign must appear in contrasting colors with block letters at least one inch in height. The sign shall be displayed in a clearly visible and conspicuous manner.

(d) In this section:

(1) "Law enforcement facility" means a building or a portion of a building used exclusively by a law enforcement agency that employs peace officers as described by Articles 2.12(1) and (3), Code of Criminal Procedure, and support personnel to conduct the official business of the agency. The term does not include:

(A) any portion of a building not actively used exclusively to conduct the official business of the agency; or

(B) any public or private driveway, street, sidewalk, walkway, parking lot, parking garage, or other parking area.

(2) "Nonpublic, secure portion of a law enforcement facility" means that portion of a law enforcement facility to which the general public is denied access without express permission and to which access is granted solely to conduct the official business of the law enforcement agency.

(Enacted by Acts 1997, 75th Leg., ch. 165 (S.B. 898), § 10.01(a), effective September 1, 1997; am. Acts 2007, 80th Leg., ch. 572 (S.B. 1709), § 1, effective September 1, 2007.)

## Sec. 411.208. Limitation of Liability.

(a) A court may not hold the state, an agency or subdivision of the state, an officer or employee of the state, a peace officer, or a qualified handgun instructor liable for damages caused by:

(1) an action authorized under this subchapter or a failure to perform a duty imposed by this subchapter; or

(2) the actions of an applicant or license holder that occur after the applicant has received a license or been denied a license under this subchapter.

(b) A cause of action in damages may not be brought against the state, an agency or subdivision of the state, an officer or employee of the state, a peace officer, or a qualified handgun instructor for any damage caused by the actions of an applicant or license holder under this subchapter.

(c) The department is not responsible for any injury or damage inflicted on any person by an applicant or license holder arising or alleged to have arisen from an action taken by the department under this subchapter.

(d) The immunities granted under Subsections (a), (b), and (c) do not apply to an act or a failure to act by the state, an agency or subdivision of the state, an officer of the state, or a peace officer if the act or failure to act was capricious or arbitrary.

(e) The immunities granted under Subsection (a) to a qualified handgun instructor do not apply to a cause of action for fraud or a deceptive trade practice.

(Enacted by Acts 1997, 75th Leg., ch. 165 (S.B. 898), § 10.01(a), effective September 1, 1997; am. Acts 2009, 81st Leg., ch. 1146 (H.B. 2730), § 11.19, effective September 1, 2009.)

## SUBCHAPTER L
## STATEWIDE AMERICA'S MISSING: BROADCAST EMERGENCY RESPONSE (AMBER) ALERT SYSTEM FOR ABDUCTED CHILDREN AND MISSING PERSONS WITH INTELLECTUAL DISABILITIES

### Sec. 411.351.   Definitions.

In this subchapter:

(1) "Abducted child" means a child 17 years of age or younger whose whereabouts are unknown and whose disappearance poses a credible threat to the safety and health of the child, as determined by a local law enforcement agency.

(2) "Alert system" means the statewide America's Missing: Broadcast Emergency Response (AMBER) alert system for abducted children and missing persons with intellectual disabilities.

(2-a) "Intellectual disability" means significantly subaverage general intellectual functioning that is concurrent with deficits in adaptive behavior and originates during the developmental period. The term includes a pervasive developmental disorder.

(3) "Local law enforcement agency" means a local law enforcement agency with jurisdiction over the investigation of:

(A) the abduction of a child; or

(B) a missing person with an intellectual disability.

(3-a) "Pervasive developmental disorder" means a disorder that meets the criteria for a pervasive developmental disorder established in the most recent Diagnostic and Statistical Manual of Mental Disorders published by the American Psychiatric Association.

(4) "Serious bodily injury" has the meaning assigned by Section 1.07, Penal Code.

(Enacted by Acts 2003, 78th Leg., ch. 789 (S.B. 57), § 1, effective June 20, 2003; am. Acts 2011, 82nd Leg., ch. 737 (H.B. 1075), § 2, effective September 1, 2011.)

### Sec. 411.352.   Statewide America's Missing: Broadcast Emergency Response (AMBER) Alert System for Abducted Children and Missing Persons with Intellectual Disabilities.

With the cooperation of the Texas Department of Transportation, the office of the governor, and other appropriate law enforcement agencies in this state, the department shall develop and implement a statewide alert system to be activated on behalf of an abducted child or a missing person with an intellectual disability.

(Enacted by Acts 2003, 78th Leg., ch. 789 (S.B. 57), § 1, effective June 20, 2003; am. Acts 2011, 82nd Leg., ch. 737 (H.B. 1075), § 3, effective September 1, 2011.)

### Sec. 411.353.   Administration.

(a) The director is the statewide coordinator of the alert system.

(b) The director shall adopt rules and issue directives as necessary to ensure proper implementation of the alert system. The rules and directives must include instructions on the procedures for activating and deactivating the alert system.

(c) The director shall prescribe forms for use by local law enforcement agencies in requesting activation of the alert system.

(Enacted by Acts 2003, 78th Leg., ch. 789 (S.B. 57), § 1, effective June 20, 2003.)

### Sec. 411.354.   Department to Recruit Participants.

(a) The department shall recruit public and commercial television and radio broadcasters, private commercial entities, state or local governmental entities, the public, and other appropriate persons to assist in developing and implementing the alert system.

(b) The department may enter into agreements with participants in the alert system to provide necessary support for the alert system. (Enacted by Acts 2003, 78th Leg., ch. 789 (S.B. 57), § 1, effective June 20, 2003.)

### Sec. 411.355. Activation.

(a) On the request of a local law enforcement agency regarding an abducted child, the department shall activate the alert system and notify appropriate participants in the alert system, as established by rule, if:

(1) the local law enforcement agency believes that a child has been abducted, including a child who:

(A) is younger than 14 years of age; and

(B) regardless of whether the child departed willingly with the other person, has been taken from the care and custody of the child's parent or legal guardian without the permission of the parent or legal guardian by another person who is:

(i) more than three years older than the child; and

(ii) not related to the child by any degree of consanguinity or affinity as defined under Subchapter B, Chapter 573, Government Code;

(2) the local law enforcement agency believes that the abducted child is in immediate danger of serious bodily injury or death or of becoming the victim of a sexual assault;

(3) the local law enforcement agency confirms that a preliminary investigation has taken place that verifies the abduction and eliminates alternative explanations for the child's disappearance; and

(4) sufficient information is available to disseminate to the public that could assist in locating the child, a person suspected of abducting the child, or a vehicle suspected of being used in the abduction.

(b) On the request of a local law enforcement agency regarding a missing person with an intellectual disability, the department shall activate the alert system and notify appropriate participants in the alert system, as established by rule, if:

(1) the local law enforcement agency receives notice of a missing person with an intellectual disability;

(2) the local law enforcement agency verifies that at the time the person is reported missing:

(A) the person has an intellectual disability, as determined according to the procedure provided by Section 593.005, Health and Safety Code; and

(B) the person's location is unknown;

(3) the local law enforcement agency determines that the person's disappearance poses a credible threat to the person's health and safety; and

(4) sufficient information is available to disseminate to the public that could assist in locating the person.

(c) The department may modify the criteria described by Subsection (a) or (b) as necessary for the proper implementation of the alert system. (Enacted by Acts 2003, 78th Leg., ch. 789 (S.B. 57), § 1, effective June 20, 2003; am. Acts 2009, 81st Leg., ch. 1404 (H.B. 3385), § 1, effective June 19, 2009; am. Acts 2011, 82nd Leg., ch. 737 (H.B. 1075), § 4, effective September 1, 2011.)

### Sec. 411.356. Local Law Enforcement Agencies.

Before requesting activation of the alert system, a local law enforcement agency must verify that the criteria described by Section 411.355(a) or (b), as applicable, have been satisfied. On verification of the applicable criteria, the local law enforcement agency shall immediately contact the department to request activation and shall supply the necessary information on the forms prescribed by the director. (Enacted by Acts 2003, 78th Leg., ch. 789 (S.B. 57), § 1, effective June 20, 2003; am. Acts 2011, 82nd Leg., ch. 737 (H.B. 1075), § 5, effective September 1, 2011.)

### Sec. 411.357. State Agencies.

(a) A state agency participating in the alert system shall:

(1) cooperate with the department and assist in developing and implementing the alert system; and

(2) establish a plan for providing relevant information to its officers, investigators, or employees, as appropriate, once the alert system has been activated.

(b) In addition to its duties as a state agency under Subsection (a), the Texas Department of Transportation shall establish a plan for providing relevant information to the public through an existing system of dynamic message signs located across the state. (Enacted by Acts 2003, 78th Leg., ch. 789 (S.B. 57), § 1, effective June 20, 2003.)

**Government**

## Sec. 411.358. Termination.

The director shall terminate any activation of the alert system with respect to a particular abducted child or a particular missing person with an intellectual disability if:

    (1) the abducted child or missing person is recovered or the situation is otherwise resolved; or

    (2) the director determines that the alert system is no longer an effective tool for locating and recovering the abducted child or missing person.

(Enacted by Acts 2003, 78th Leg., ch. 789 (S.B. 57), § 1, effective June 20, 2003; am. Acts 2011, 82nd Leg., ch. 737 (H.B. 1075), § 6, effective September 1, 2011.)

## Sec. 411.359. System Name.

The director by rule may assign a name other than America's Missing: Broadcast Emergency Response (AMBER) to the alert system when the system is activated regarding a missing person with an intellectual disability.

(Enacted by Acts 2011, 82nd Leg., ch. 737 (H.B. 1075), § 7, effective September 1, 2011.)

## SUBCHAPTER M
## SILVER ALERT FOR MISSING SENIOR CITIZENS

## Sec. 411.381. Definitions.

In this subchapter:

    (1) "Alert" means the statewide silver alert for missing senior citizens developed and implemented under this subchapter.

    (2) "Local law enforcement agency" means a local law enforcement agency with jurisdiction over the investigation of a missing senior citizen.

    (3) "Senior citizen" means a person who is 65 years of age or older.

(Enacted by Acts 2007, 80th Leg., ch. 69 (S.B. 1315), § 1, effective September 1, 2007.)

## Sec. 411.382. Silver Alert for Missing Senior Citizens.

With the cooperation of the Texas Department of Transportation, the office of the governor, and other appropriate law enforcement agencies in this state, the department shall develop and implement a statewide silver alert to be activated on behalf of a missing senior citizen.

(Enacted by Acts 2007, 80th Leg., ch. 69 (S.B. 1315), § 1, effective September 1, 2007.)

## Sec. 411.383. Administration.

(a) The director is the statewide coordinator of the alert.

(b) The director shall adopt rules and issue directives as necessary to ensure proper implementation of the alert. The rules and directives must include:

    (1) the procedures to be used by a local law enforcement agency to verify whether a senior citizen:

        (A) is missing; and

        (B) has an impaired mental condition;

    (2) a description of the circumstances under which a local law enforcement agency is required to report a missing senior citizen to the department; and

    (3) the procedures to be used by an individual or entity to report information about a missing senior citizen to designated media outlets in Texas.

(Enacted by Acts 2007, 80th Leg., ch. 69 (S.B. 1315), § 1, effective September 1, 2007.)

## Sec. 411.384. Department to Recruit Participants.

The department shall recruit public and commercial television and radio broadcasters, private commercial entities, state or local governmental entities, the public, and other appropriate persons to assist in developing and implementing the alert.

(Enacted by Acts 2007, 80th Leg., ch. 69 (S.B. 1315), § 1, effective September 1, 2007.)

## Sec. 411.385. Duties of Texas Department of Transportation.

The Texas Department of Transportation shall:

    (1) cooperate with the department and assist in developing and implementing the alert; and

    (2) establish a plan for providing relevant information to the public through an existing system of dynamic message signs located across the state.

(Enacted by Acts 2007, 80th Leg., ch. 69 (S.B. 1315), § 1, effective September 1, 2007.)

## Sec. 411.387. Activation of Silver Alert.

(a) When a local law enforcement agency notifies the department under Section 411.386, the department shall confirm the accuracy of the information and, if confirmed, immediately issue an alert under this subchapter in accordance with department rules.

Government

(b) In issuing the alert, the department shall send the alert to designated media outlets in Texas. Following receipt of the alert, participating radio stations, television stations, and other media outlets may issue the alert at designated intervals to assist in locating the missing senior citizen.

(Enacted by Acts 2007, 80th Leg., ch. 69 (S.B. 1315), § 1, effective September 1, 2007.)

### Sec. 411.389. Termination of Silver Alert.

(a) The director shall terminate any activation of the alert with respect to a particular missing senior citizen not later than the earlier of the date on which:

(1) the missing senior citizen is located or the situation is otherwise resolved; or

(2) the notification period ends, as determined by department rule.

(b) A local law enforcement agency that locates a missing senior citizen who is the subject of an alert under this subchapter shall notify the department as soon as possible that the missing senior citizen has been located.

(Enacted by Acts 2007, 80th Leg., ch. 69 (S.B. 1315), § 1, effective September 1, 2007.)

### SUBCHAPTER N
### PREVENTION OF SCRAP METAL THEFT GRANT PROGRAM
### [AS ADDED BY ACTS 2011, 82ND LEG., CH. 1234]

### Sec. 411.421. Definition.

In this subchapter, "regulated material" has the meaning assigned by Section 1956.001, Occupations Code.

(Enacted by Acts 2011, 82nd Leg., ch. 1234 (S.B. 694), § 20, effective September 1, 2011.)

### Sec. 411.422. Grants to Fund Scrap Metal Theft Prevention.

(a) From fines collected and distributed to the department under Sections 1956.040(a-2) and (a-4), Occupations Code, the commission by rule shall establish and implement a grant program to provide funding to assist local law enforcement agencies in preventing the theft of regulated material.

(b) To be eligible for a grant, a recipient must be a local law enforcement agency that has established a program designed to prevent the theft of regulated material.

(c) Rules adopted under this section must:

(1) include accountability measures for grant recipients and provisions for loss of eligibility for grant recipients that fail to comply with the measures; and

(2) require grant recipients to provide to the department information on program outcomes.

(Enacted by Acts 2011, 82nd Leg., ch. 1234 (S.B. 694), § 20, effective September 1, 2011.)

### CHAPTER 420A
### OFFICE OF VIOLENT SEX OFFENDER MANAGEMENT

### Sec. 420A.001. Definitions.

In this chapter:

(1) "Board" means the governing board of the Office of Violent Sex Offender Management.

(2) "Office" means the Office of Violent Sex Offender Management.

(Enacted by Acts 2011, 82nd Leg., ch. 1201 (S.B. 166), § 2, effective September 1, 2011.)

### Sec. 420A.002. Office; Governing Board.

(a) The Office of Violent Sex Offender Management is a state agency.

(b) The office is governed by a board composed of the following three members appointed by the governor:

(1) one member experienced in the management of sex offenders;

(2) one member experienced in the investigation or prosecution of sex offenses; and

(3) one member experienced in counseling or advocating on behalf of victims of sexual assault.

(c) Members of the board serve staggered two-year terms. Two members' terms expire February 1 of each even-numbered year and one member's term expires February 1 of each odd-numbered year.

(d) A member of the board is entitled to travel expenses incurred in performing official duties and to a per diem equal to the maximum amount allowed on January 1 of that year for federal employees per diem for federal income tax purposes, subject to the same limitations provided for members of state boards and commissions in the General Appropriations Act.
(Enacted by Acts 2011, 82nd Leg., ch. 1201 (S.B. 166), § 2, effective September 1, 2011.)

### Sec. 420A.003. Presiding Officer; Meetings.

(a) The governor shall designate a member of the board as presiding officer. The presiding officer serves at the discretion of the governor.

(b) The board shall meet at least quarterly and at other times at the call of the presiding officer.
(Enacted by Acts 2011, 82nd Leg., ch. 1201 (S.B. 166), § 2, effective September 1, 2011.)

### Sec. 420A.004. Sunset Provision.

The Office of Violent Sex Offender Management is subject to Chapter 325 (Texas Sunset Act). Unless continued in existence as provided by that chapter, the office is abolished and this chapter expires September 1, 2023.
(Enacted by Acts 2011, 82nd Leg., ch. 1201 (S.B. 166), § 2, effective September 1, 2011.)

### Sec. 420A.005. Grants and Donations.

On behalf of the state, the office may apply for and accept grants and donations from any source to be used by the office in the performance of the duties of the office.
(Enacted by Acts 2011, 82nd Leg., ch. 1201 (S.B. 166), § 2, effective September 1, 2011.)

### Sec. 420A.006. Public Interest Information.

The office shall prepare information of public interest describing the functions of the office and the procedures by which complaints are filed with and resolved by the office. The office shall make the information available to the public and appropriate state agencies.
(Enacted by Acts 2011, 82nd Leg., ch. 1201 (S.B. 166), § 2, effective September 1, 2011.)

### Sec. 420A.007. Biennial Report.

Not later than December 1 of each even-numbered year, the office shall submit to the governor, the lieutenant governor, and the speaker of the house of representatives a report concerning the operation of the office. The office may include in the report any recommendations that the office considers appropriate.
(Enacted by Acts 2011, 82nd Leg., ch. 1201 (S.B. 166), § 2, effective September 1, 2011.)

### Sec. 420A.008. Staff.

The office may select and employ a general counsel, staff attorneys, and other staff necessary to perform the office's functions.
(Enacted by Acts 2011, 82nd Leg., ch. 1201 (S.B. 166), § 2, effective September 1, 2011.)

### Sec. 420A.009. Salary Career Ladder for Case Managers.

(a) The board shall adopt a salary career ladder for case managers. The salary career ladder must base a case manager's salary on the manager's classification and years of service with the office.

(b) For purposes of the salary schedule, the office shall classify all case manager positions as Case Manager I, Case Manager II, Case Manager III, Case Manager IV, or Case Manager V.

(c) Under the salary career ladder adopted under Subsection (a), a case manager to whom the schedule applies and who received an overall evaluation of at least satisfactory in the case manager's most recent annual evaluation is entitled to an annual salary increase, during each of the case manager's first 10 years of service in a designated case manager classification as described by Subsection (b), equal to one-tenth of the difference between:

(1) the case manager's current annual salary; and

(2) the minimum annual salary of a case manager in the next highest classification.
(Enacted by Acts 2011, 82nd Leg., ch. 1201 (S.B. 166), § 2, effective September 1, 2011.)

### Sec. 420A.010. Powers and Duties.

The office shall perform appropriate functions related to the sex offender civil commitment program provided under Chapter 841, Health and Safety Code, including functions related to the provision of treatment and supervision to civilly committed sex offenders.
(Enacted by Acts 2011, 82nd Leg., ch. 1201 (S.B. 166), § 2, effective September 1, 2011.)

## Sec. 420A.011.　Administrative Attachment; Support.

(a) The office is administratively attached to the Department of State Health Services.

(b) The Department of State Health Services shall provide administrative support services, including human resources, budgetary, accounting, purchasing, payroll, information technology, and legal support services, to the office as necessary to carry out the purposes of this chapter.

(c) The office, in accordance with the rules and procedures of the Legislative Budget Board, shall prepare, approve, and submit a legislative appropriations request that is separate from the legislative appropriations request for the Department of State Health Services and is used to develop the office's budget structure. The office shall maintain the office's legislative appropriations request and budget structure separately from those of the department.

(Enacted by Acts 2011, 82nd Leg., ch. 1201 (S.B. 166), § 2, effective September 1, 2011.)

## SUBTITLE C
## STATE MILITARY FORCES AND VETERANS

## CHAPTER 431
## STATE MILITIA

## SUBCHAPTER F
## SERVICE AND DUTIES

## Sec. 431.086.　Exemption from Arrest.

(a) A member of the state military forces may not be arrested, except for treason, felony, or breach of the peace, while the person is going to or coming from a place that the person was required to be for military duty.

(b) This section does not prevent a peace officer from issuing a traffic summons or citation to appear in court at a later date that does not conflict with the member's duty hours.

(Enacted by Acts 1987, 70th Leg., ch. 147 (S.B. 894), § 1, effective September 1, 1987.)

## SUBTITLE G
## CORRECTIONS

## CHAPTER 508
## PAROLE AND MANDATORY SUPERVISION

### Subchapter F. Mandatory Conditions of Parole or Mandatory Supervision

### Subchapter G. Discretionary Conditions of Parole or Mandatory Supervision

### Subchapter H. Warrants

### Subchapter I. Hearings and Sanctions

### Subchapter J. Miscellaneous

Government

## SUBCHAPTER F
## MANDATORY CONDITIONS OF PAROLE OR MANDATORY SUPERVISION

### Sec. 508.181.   Residence During Release.

(a) Except as provided by Subsections (b) and (c), a parole panel shall require as a condition of parole or mandatory supervision that the releasee reside in the county in which:

(1) the releasee resided at the time of committing the offense for which the releasee was sentenced to the institutional division; or

(2) the releasee committed the offense for which the releasee was sentenced to the institutional division, if the releasee was not a resident of this state at the time of committing the offense.

(b) A parole panel may require a releasee to reside in a county other than the county required under Subsection (a) to:

(1) protect the life or safety of:

(A) a victim of the releasee's offense;

(B) the releasee;

(C) a witness in the case; or

(D) any other person; or

(2) increase the likelihood of the releasee's successful completion of parole or mandatory supervision, because of:

(A) written expressions of significant public concern in the county in which the releasee would otherwise be required to reside;

(B) the presence of family members or friends in the other county who have expressed a willingness to assist the releasee in successfully completing the conditions of the releasee's parole or mandatory supervision;

(C) the verified existence of a job offer in the other county; or

(D) the availability of a treatment program, educational program, or other social service program in the other county that is not available in the county in which the releasee is otherwise required to reside under Subsection (a).

(c) At any time after a releasee is released on parole or to mandatory supervision, a parole panel may modify the conditions of parole or mandatory supervision to require the releasee to reside in a county other than the county required by the original conditions. In making a decision under this subsection, a parole panel must consider the factors listed under Subsection (b).

(d) If a parole panel initially requires the releasee to reside in a county other than the county required under Subsection (a), the parole panel shall subsequently require the releasee to reside in the county described under Subsection (a) if the requirement that the releasee reside in the other county was based on:

(1) the verified existence of a job offer under Subsection (b)(2)(C) and the releasee is no longer employed or actively seeking employment; or

(2) the availability of a treatment program, educational program, or other social service program under Subsection (b)(2)(D) and the releasee:

(A) no longer regularly participates in the program as required by a condition of parole or mandatory supervision; or

(B) has successfully completed the program but has violated another condition of the releasee's parole or mandatory supervision.

(e) If a parole panel requires the releasee to reside in a county other than the county required under Subsection (a), the panel shall:

(1) state in writing the reason for the panel's decision; and

(2) place the statement in the releasee's permanent record.

(f) This section does not apply to a decision by a parole panel to require a releasee to serve the period of parole or mandatory supervision in another state.

(g) The division shall, on the first working day of each month, notify the sheriff of any county in which the total number of sex offenders under the supervision and control of the division residing in the county exceeds 10 percent of the total number of sex offenders in the state under the supervision and control of the division. The notice must be provided by e-mail or other electronic communication. If the total number of sex offenders under the supervision and control of the division residing in a county exceeds 22 percent of the total number of sex offenders in the state under the supervision and control of the division, a parole panel may require a sex offender to reside in that county only as required by Subsection (a) or for the reason stated in Subsection (b)(2)(B). In this subsection, "sex offender" means a person who is released on parole or to mandatory supervision after serving a sentence for an offense described by Section 508.187(a).

(h) If a parole panel requires a releasee to reside in a county other than the county required under Subsection (a), the division shall include the reason for residency exemption in the required notification to the sheriff of the county in which the defendant is to reside, the chief of police of the municipality in which the halfway house is located, and the attorney who represents the state in the prosecution of felonies in that county.

(Enacted by Acts 1997, 75th Leg., ch. 165 (S.B. 898), § 12.01, effective September 1, 1997; am. Acts 1999, 76th Leg., ch. 62 (S.B. 1368), §§ 10.23, 10.24, effective September 1, 1999; am. Acts 2011, 82nd Leg., ch. 1123 (H.B. 200), § 6, effective September 1, 2011.)

## Sec. 508.182.  Parole Supervision Fee; Administrative Fee.

(a) A parole panel shall require as a condition of parole or mandatory supervision that a releasee pay to the division for each month during which the releasee is under parole supervision:

(1) a parole supervision fee of $10; and

(2) an administrative fee of $8.

(b) A fee under this section applies to an inmate released in another state who is required as a condition of the inmate's release to report to a parole officer or supervisor in this state for parole supervision.

(c) On the request of the releasee, a parole panel may allow the releasee to defer one or more payments under this section. The releasee remains responsible for payment of the fee and shall pay the amount of the deferred payment not later than the second anniversary of the date the payment becomes due.

(d) The Texas Board of Criminal Justice shall adopt rules relating to the method of payment required of the releasee.

(e) The division shall remit fees collected under this section to the comptroller. The comptroller shall deposit the fees collected under:

(1) Subsection (a)(1) in the general revenue fund; and

(2) Subsection (a)(2) in the compensation to victims of crime fund.

(f) In a parole or mandatory supervision revocation hearing under Section 508.281 at which it is alleged only that the releasee failed to make a payment under this section, it is an affirmative defense to revocation that the releasee is unable to pay the amount as ordered by a parole panel. The releasee must prove the affirmative defense by a preponderance of the evidence.

(Enacted by Acts 1997, 75th Leg., ch. 165 (S.B. 898), § 12.01, effective September 1, 1997.)

## Sec. 508.183.  Educational Skill Level.

(a) A parole panel shall require as a condition of release on parole or release to mandatory supervision that an inmate demonstrate to the parole panel whether the inmate has an educational skill level that is equal to or greater than the average skill level of students who have completed the sixth grade in a public school in this state.

(b) If the parole panel determines that the inmate has not attained that skill level, the parole panel shall require as a condition of parole or mandatory supervision that the inmate as a releasee attain that level of educational skill, unless the parole panel determines that the inmate lacks the intellectual capacity or the learning ability to ever achieve that level of skill.

(Enacted by Acts 1997, 75th Leg., ch. 165 (S.B. 898), § 12.01, effective September 1, 1997.)

## Sec. 508.184.  Controlled Substance Testing.

(a) A parole panel shall require as a condition of parole or mandatory supervision that a releasee submit to testing for controlled substances on evidence that:

(1) a controlled substance is present in the releasee's body;

(2) the releasee has used a controlled substance; or

(3) the use of a controlled substance is related to the offense for which the releasee was convicted.

(b) The Texas Board of Criminal Justice by rule shall adopt procedures for the administration of a test required under this section.

(Enacted by Acts 1997, 75th Leg., ch. 165 (S.B. 898), § 12.01, effective September 1, 1997.)

Government

## Sec. 508.185. Substance Abuse Treatment.

(a) A parole panel shall require as a condition of release on parole or release to mandatory supervision that an inmate who immediately before release is a participant in the program established under Section 501.0931 participate as a releasee in a drug or alcohol abuse continuum of care treatment program.

(b) The Texas Commission on Alcohol and Drug Abuse shall develop the continuum of care treatment program.

(Enacted by Acts 1997, 75th Leg., ch. 165 (S.B. 898), § 12.01, effective September 1, 1997.)

## Sec. 508.186. Sex Offender Registration.

A parole panel shall require as a condition of parole or mandatory supervision that a releasee required to register as a sex offender under Chapter 62, Code of Criminal Procedure:

(1) register under that chapter; and

(2) submit a blood sample or other specimen to the Department of Public Safety under Subchapter G, Chapter 411, for the purpose of creating a DNA record of the releasee, unless the releasee has already submitted the required specimen under other state law.

(Enacted by Acts 1997, 75th Leg., ch. 165 (S.B. 898), § 12.01, effective September 1, 1997; am. Acts 1999, 76th Leg., ch. 62 (S.B. 1368), § 10.25, effective September 1, 1999; am. Acts 2001, 77th Leg., ch. 211 (S.B. 1380), § 16, effective September 1, 2001; am. Acts 2003, 78th Leg., ch. 1300 (S.B. 146), § 9, effective September 1, 2003; am. Acts 2005, 79th Leg., ch. 1008 (H.B. 867), § 1.06, effective September 1, 2005.)

## Sec. 508.1861. Prohibitions on Internet Access for Certain Sex Offenders.

(a) This section applies only to a person who, on release, will be required to register as a sex offender under Chapter 62, Code of Criminal Procedure, by court order or otherwise, and:

(1) is serving a sentence for an offense under Section 21.11, 22.011(a)(2), 22.021(a)(1)(B), 33.021, or 43.25, Penal Code;

(2) used the Internet or any other type of electronic device used for Internet access to commit the offense or engage in the conduct for which the person is required to register under Chapter 62, Code of Criminal Procedure; or

(3) is assigned a numeric risk level of three based on an assessment conducted under Article 62.007, Code of Criminal Procedure.

(b) If the parole panel releases on parole or to mandatory supervision a person described by Subsection (a), the parole panel as a condition of parole or mandatory supervision shall prohibit the releasee from using the Internet to:

(1) access material that is obscene as defined by Section 43.21, Penal Code;

(2) access a commercial social networking site, as defined by Article 62.0061(f), Code of Criminal Procedure;

(3) communicate with any individual concerning sexual relations with an individual who is younger than 17 years of age; or

(4) communicate with another individual the releasee knows is younger than 17 years of age.

(c) The parole panel may modify at any time the condition described by Subsection (b)(4) if:

(1) the condition interferes with the releasee's ability to attend school or become or remain employed and consequently constitutes an undue hardship for the releasee; or

(2) the releasee is the parent or guardian of an individual who is younger than 17 years of age and the releasee is not otherwise prohibited from communicating with that individual.

(Enacted by Acts 2009, 81st Leg., ch. 755 (S.B. 689), § 10, effective September 1, 2009.)

## Sec. 508.187. Child Safety Zone.

(a) This section applies only to a releasee serving a sentence for an offense under:

(1) Section 43.25 or 43.26, Penal Code;

(2) Section 21.02, 21.11, 22.011, 22.021, or 25.02, Penal Code;

(3) Section 20.04(a)(4), Penal Code, if the releasee committed the offense with the intent to violate or abuse the victim sexually;

(4) Section 30.02, Penal Code, punishable under Subsection (d) of that section, if the releasee committed the offense with the intent to commit a felony listed in Subdivision (2) or (3);

(5) Section 43.05(a)(2), Penal Code; or

(6) Section 20A.02, Penal Code, if the defendant:

(A) trafficked the victim with the intent or knowledge that the victim would engage in sexual conduct, as defined by Section 43.25, Penal Code; or

(B) benefited from participating in a venture that involved a trafficked victim engaging in sexual conduct, as defined by Section 43.25, Penal Code.

(b) A parole panel shall establish a child safety zone applicable to a releasee if the panel determines that a child as defined by Section 22.011(c), Penal Code, was the victim of the offense, by requiring as a condition of parole or mandatory supervision that the releasee:

(1) not:

(A) supervise or participate in any program that includes as participants or recipients persons who are 17 years of age or younger and that regularly provides athletic, civic, or cultural activities; or

(B) go in, on, or within a distance specified by the panel of premises where children commonly gather, including a school, day-care facility, playground, public or private youth center, public swimming pool, or video arcade facility; and

(2) attend for a period of time determined necessary by the panel psychological counseling sessions for sex offenders with an individual or organization that provides sex offender treatment or counseling as specified by the parole officer supervising the releasee after release.

(c) A parole officer who under Subsection (b)(2) specifies a sex offender treatment provider to provide counseling to a releasee shall:

(1) contact the provider before the releasee is released;

(2) establish the date, time, and place of the first session between the releasee and the provider; and

(3) request the provider to immediately notify the officer if the releasee fails to attend the first session or any subsequent scheduled session.

(d) At any time after the imposition of a condition under Subsection (b)(1), the releasee may request the parole panel to modify the child safety zone applicable to the releasee because the zone as created by the panel:

(1) interferes with the releasee's ability to attend school or hold a job and consequently constitutes an undue hardship for the releasee; or

(2) is broader than necessary to protect the public, given the nature and circumstances of the offense.

(e) A parole officer supervising a releasee may permit the releasee to enter on an event-by-event basis into the child safety zone that the releasee is otherwise prohibited from entering if:

(1) the releasee has served at least two years of the period of supervision imposed on release;

(2) the releasee enters the zone as part of a program to reunite with the releasee's family;

(3) the releasee presents to the parole officer a written proposal specifying:

(A) where the releasee intends to go within the zone;

(B) why and with whom the releasee is going; and

(C) how the releasee intends to cope with any stressful situations that occur;

(4) the sex offender treatment provider treating the releasee agrees with the officer that the releasee should be allowed to attend the event; and

(5) the officer and the treatment provider agree on a chaperon to accompany the releasee, and the chaperon agrees to perform that duty.

(f) In this section, "playground," "premises," "school," "video arcade facility," and "youth center" have the meanings assigned by Section 481.134, Health and Safety Code.

(Enacted by Acts 1997, 75th Leg., ch. 165 (S.B. 898), § 12.01, effective September 1, 1997; am. Acts 2001, 77th Leg., ch. 978 (H.B. 223), § 2, effective September 1, 2001; am. Acts 2007, 80th Leg., ch. 593 (H.B. 8), § 3.41, effective September 1, 2007; am. Acts 2011, 82nd Leg., ch. 515 (H.B. 2014), § 3.03, effective September 1, 2011.)

## Sec. 508.188. Community Service for Certain Releasees.

A parole panel shall require as a condition of parole or mandatory supervision that a releasee for whom the court has made an affirmative finding under Article 42.014, Code of Criminal Procedure, perform not less than 300 hours of community service at a project designated by the parole panel that primarily serves the person or group that was the target of the releasee.

(Enacted by Acts 1997, 75th Leg., ch. 165 (S.B. 898), § 12.01, effective September 1, 1997.)

## Sec. 508.189. Parole Fee for Certain Releasees.

(a) A parole panel shall require as a condition of parole or mandatory supervision that a releasee convicted of an offense under Section 21.02, 21.08, 21.11, 22.011, 22.021, 25.02, 43.25, or 43.26, Penal Code, pay to the division a parole supervision fee of $5 each month during the period of parole supervision.

(b) The division shall send fees collected under this section to the comptroller. The comptroller shall deposit the fees in the general revenue fund to the credit of the sexual assault program fund established under Section 44.0061, Health and Safety Code.

(Enacted by Acts 1997, 75th Leg., ch. 165 (S.B. 898), § 12.01, effective September 1, 1997; am. Acts 2007, 80th Leg., ch. 593 (H.B. 8), § 3.42, effective September 1, 2007.)

### Sec. 508.190.   Avoiding Victim of Stalking Offense.

(a) A parole panel shall require as a condition of parole or mandatory supervision that a relasee serving a sentence for an offense under Section 42.072, Penal Code, not:

(1) communicate directly or indirectly with the victim;

(2) go to or near the residence, place of employment, or business of the victim; or

(3) go to or near a school, day-care facility, or similar facility where a dependent child of the victim is in attendance.

(b) If a parole panel requires the prohibition contained in Subsection (a)(2) or (3) as a condition of parole or mandatory supervision, the parole panel shall specifically describe the prohibited locations and the minimum distances, if any, that the releasee must maintain from the locations.

(Enacted by Acts 1999, 76th Leg., ch. 62 (S.B. 1368), § 10.26, effective September 1, 1999.)

### Sec. 508.191.   No Contact with Victim.

(a) If a parole panel releases a defendant on parole or to mandatory supervision, the panel shall require as a condition of parole or mandatory supervision that the defendant not intentionally or knowingly communicate directly or indirectly with a victim of the offense or intentionally or knowingly go near a residence, school, place of employment, or business of a victim. At any time after the defendant is released on parole or to mandatory supervision, a victim of the offense may petition the panel for a modification of the conditions of the defendant's parole or mandatory supervision allowing the defendant contact with the victim subject to reasonable restrictions.

(b) Notwithstanding Subsection (a), a defendant may participate in victim-offender mediation authorized by Section 508.324 on the request of the victim or a guardian of the victim or a close relative of a deceased victim.

(c) In this section, "victim" has the meaning assigned by Article 56.01(3), Code of Criminal Procedure.

(Enacted by Acts 1999, 76th Leg., ch. 62 (S.B. 1368), § 10.27, effective September 1, 1999.)

### Sec. 508.192.   Reentry into the United States Prohibited.

(a) In this section, "illegal criminal alien" has the meaning assigned by Section 493.015.

(b) A parole panel shall require as a condition of parole or mandatory supervision that an illegal criminal alien released to the custody of United States Immigration and Customs Enforcement:

(1) regardless of whether a final order of deportation is issued with reference to the illegal criminal alien, leave the United States as soon as possible after release; and

(2) not unlawfully return to or unlawfully reenter the United States in violation of the Immigration Reform and Control Act of 1986 (8 U.S.C. Section 1101 et seq.).

(Enacted by Acts 2011, 82nd Leg., ch. 1025 (H.B. 2734), § 1, effective September 1, 2011.)

## SUBCHAPTER G

## DISCRETIONARY CONDITIONS OF PAROLE OR MANDATORY SUPERVISION

### Sec. 508.221.   Conditions Permitted Generally.

A parole panel may impose as a condition of parole or mandatory supervision any condition that a court may impose on a defendant placed on community supervision under Article 42.12, Code of Criminal Procedure, including the condition that a releasee submit to testing for controlled substances or submit to electronic monitoring if the parole panel determines that without testing for controlled substances or participation in an electronic monitoring program the inmate would not be released on parole.

(Enacted by Acts 1997, 75th Leg., ch. 165 (S.B. 898), § 12.01, effective September 1, 1997.)

### Sec. 508.222.   Payment of Certain Damages.

A parole panel may require as a condition of parole or mandatory supervision that a releasee make payments in satisfaction of damages for which the releasee is liable under Section 500.002.

(Enacted by Acts 1997, 75th Leg., ch. 165 (S.B. 898), § 12.01, effective September 1, 1997.)

## Sec. 508.223. Psychological Counseling.

A parole panel may require as a condition of parole or mandatory supervision that a releasee serving a sentence for an offense under Section 42.072, Penal Code, attend psychological counseling sessions of a type and for a duration as specified by the parole panel, if the parole panel determines in consultation with a local mental health services provider that appropriate mental health services are available through the Texas Department of Mental Health and Mental Retardation in accordance with Section 534.053, Health and Safety Code, or through another mental health services provider.
(Enacted by Acts 1997, 75th Leg., ch. 165 (S.B. 898), § 12.01, effective September 1, 1997; am. Acts 1999, 76th Leg., ch. 62 (S.B. 1368), § 10.28, effective September 1, 1999.)

## Sec. 508.224. Substance Abuse Counseling.

A parole panel may require as a condition of parole or mandatory supervision that the releasee attend counseling sessions for substance abusers or participate in substance abuse treatment services in a program or facility approved or licensed by the Texas Commission on Alcohol and Drug Abuse if:

(1) the releasee was sentenced for an offense involving a controlled substance; or

(2) the panel determines that the releasee's substance abuse was related to the commission of the offense.
(Enacted by Acts 1997, 75th Leg., ch. 165 (S.B. 898), § 12.01, effective September 1, 1997.)

## Sec. 508.225. Child Safety Zone.

(a) If the nature of the offense for which an inmate is serving a sentence warrants the establishment of a child safety zone, a parole panel may establish a child safety zone applicable to an inmate serving a sentence for an offense listed in Section 3g(a)(1), Article 42.12, Code of Criminal Procedure, or for which the judgment contains an affirmative finding under Section 3g(a)(2), Article 42.12, Code of Criminal Procedure, by requiring as a condition of parole or release to mandatory supervision that the inmate not:

(1) supervise or participate in any program that includes as participants or recipients persons who are 17 years of age or younger and that regularly provides athletic, civic, or cultural activities; or

(2) go in or on, or within a distance specified by the panel of, a premises where children commonly gather, including a school, day-care facility, playground, public or private youth center, public swimming pool, or video arcade facility.

(b) At any time after the imposition of a condition under Subsection (a), the inmate may request the parole panel to modify the child safety zone applicable to the inmate because the zone as created by the panel:

(1) interferes with the ability of the inmate to attend school or hold a job and consequently constitutes an undue hardship for the inmate; or

(2) is broader than is necessary to protect the public, given the nature and circumstances of the offense.

(c) This section does not apply to an inmate described by Section 508.187.

(d) In this section, "playground," "premises," "school," "video arcade facility," and "youth center" have the meanings assigned by Section 481.134, Health and Safety Code.
(Enacted by Acts 1999, 76th Leg., ch. 56 (S.B. 660), § 2, effective September 1, 1999.)

## Sec. 508.226. Orchiectomy As Condition Prohibited.

A parole panel may not require an inmate to undergo an orchiectomy as a condition of release on parole or to mandatory supervision.
(Enacted by Acts 1999, 76th Leg., ch. 62 (S.B. 1368), § 10.29, effective September 1, 1999; am. Acts 2001, 77th Leg., ch. 1420 (H.B. 2812), § 21.001(45), effective September 1, 2001 (renumbered from Sec. 508.225).)

## Sec. 508.227. Electronic Monitoring of Certain Members of Criminal Street Gang.

(a) This section applies only to a releasee who:

(1) is identified as a member of a criminal street gang in an intelligence database established under Chapter 61, Code of Criminal Procedure; and

(2) has three or more times been convicted of, or received a grant of deferred adjudication community supervision or another functionally equivalent form of community supervision or probation for, a felony offense under the laws of this state, another state, or the United States.

(b) A parole panel may require as a condition of release on parole or to mandatory supervision

that a releasee described by Subsection (a) submit to tracking under an electronic monitoring service or other appropriate technological service designed to track a person's location.
(Enacted by Acts 2009, 81st Leg., ch. 1130 (H.B. 2086), § 20, effective September 1, 2009.)

## SUBCHAPTER H
## WARRANTS

### Sec. 508.251.  Issuance of Warrant or Summons.

(a) In a case of parole or mandatory supervision, the director or a designated agent of the director or, in another case, the board on order by the governor, may issue a warrant as provided by Section 508.252 for the return of:

(1) a releasee;

(2) an inmate released although not eligible for release;

(3) a resident released to a preparole or work program;

(4) an inmate released on emergency reprieve or on emergency absence under escort; or

(5) a person released on a conditional pardon.

(b) A warrant issued under Subsection (a) must require the return of the person to the institution from which the person was paroled or released.

(c) Instead of the issuance of a warrant under this section, the division:

(1) may issue to the person a summons requiring the person to appear for a hearing under Section 508.281 if the person is not a releasee who is:

(A) on intensive supervision or superintensive supervision;

(B) an absconder; or

(C) determined by the division to be a threat to public safety; and

(2) shall issue to the person a summons requiring the person to appear for a hearing under Section 508.281 if the person:

(A) is charged only with committing an administrative violation of release that is alleged to have been committed after the third anniversary of the date the person was released on parole or to mandatory supervision;

(B) is not serving a sentence for, and has not been previously convicted of, an offense listed in or described by Article 62.001(5), Code of Criminal Procedure; and

(C) is not a releasee with respect to whom a summons may not be issued under Subdivision (1).

(c-1) A summons issued under Subsection (c) must state the time, date, place, and purpose of the hearing.

(d) A designated agent of the director acts independently from a parole officer and must receive specialized training as determined by the director.
(Enacted by Acts 1997, 75th Leg., ch. 165 (S.B. 898), § 12.01, effective September 1, 1997; am. Acts 2003, 78th Leg., ch. 264 (H.B. 1849), § 1, effective September 1, 2003; am. Acts 2011, 82nd Leg., ch. 546 (H.B. 2735), § 1, effective September 1, 2011.)

### Sec. 508.252.  Grounds for Issuance of Warrant or Summons.

A warrant or summons may be issued under Section 508.251 if:

(1) there is reason to believe that the person has been released although not eligible for release;

(2) the person has been arrested for an offense;

(3) there is a document that is self-authenticating as provided by Rule 902, Texas Rules of Evidence, stating that the person violated a rule or condition of release; or

(4) there is reliable evidence that the person has exhibited behavior during the person's release that indicates to a reasonable person that the person poses a danger to society that warrants the person's immediate return to custody.
(Enacted by Acts 1997, 75th Leg., ch. 165 (S.B. 898), § 12.01, effective September 1, 1997; am. Acts 1999, 76th Leg., ch. 62 (S.B. 1368), § 10.30, effective September 1, 1999; am. Acts 2003, 78th Leg., ch. 264 (H.B. 1849), § 2, effective September 1, 2003.)

### Sec. 508.253.  Effect on Sentence After Issuance of Warrant.

If it appears a releasee has violated a condition or provision of the releasee's parole or mandatory supervision, the date of the issuance of the warrant to the date of the releasee's arrest is not counted as a part of the time served under the releasee's sentence.
(Enacted by Acts 1997, 75th Leg., ch. 165 (S.B. 898), § 12.01, effective September 1, 1997.)

## Sec. 508.254.  Detention Under Warrant.

(a) A person who is the subject of a warrant may be held in custody pending a determination of all facts surrounding the alleged offense, violation of a rule or condition of release, or dangerous behavior.

(b) A warrant authorizes any officer named by the warrant to take custody of the person and detain the person until a parole panel orders the return of the person to the institution from which the person was released.

(c) Pending a hearing on a charge of parole violation, ineligible release, or violation of a condition of mandatory supervision, a person returned to custody shall remain confined.

(Enacted by Acts 1997, 75th Leg., ch. 165 (S.B. 898), § 12.01, effective September 1, 1997.)

## Sec. 508.255.  Status As Fugitive from Justice.

(a) After the issuance of a warrant, a person for whose return a warrant was issued is a fugitive from justice.

(b) The law relating to the right of the state to extradite a person and return a fugitive from justice and Article 42.11, Code of Criminal Procedure, relating to the waiver of all legal requirements to obtain extradition of a fugitive from justice from another state to this state, are not impaired by this chapter and remain in full force and effect.

(Enacted by Acts 1997, 75th Leg., ch. 165 (S.B. 898), § 12.01, effective September 1, 1997.)

## Sec. 508.256.  Withdrawal of Warrant.

At any time before setting a revocation hearing date under Section 508.282, the division may withdraw a warrant and continue supervision of a releasee.

(Enacted by Acts 1997, 75th Leg., ch. 165 (S.B. 898), § 12.01, effective September 1, 1997.)

## SUBCHAPTER I
## HEARINGS AND SANCTIONS

## Sec. 508.281.  Hearing.

(a) A releasee, a person released although ineligible for release, or a person granted a conditional pardon is entitled to a hearing before a parole panel or a designated agent of the board under the rules adopted by the board and within a period that permits a parole panel, a designee of the board, or the department to dispose of the charges within the periods established by Sections 508.282(a) and (b) if the releasee or person:

(1) is accused of a violation of the releasee's parole or mandatory supervision or the person's conditional pardon, on information and complaint by a peace officer or parole officer; or

(2) is arrested after an ineligible release.

(b) If a parole panel or designated agent of the board determines that a releasee or person granted a conditional pardon has been convicted of a felony offense committed while an administrative releasee and has been sentenced to a term of confinement in a penal institution, the determination is considered to be a sufficient hearing to revoke the parole or mandatory supervision or recommend to the governor revocation of a conditional pardon without further hearing, except that the parole panel or designated agent shall conduct a hearing to consider mitigating circumstances if requested by the releasee or person granted a conditional pardon.

(c) If a hearing before a designated agent of the board is held under this section for a releasee who appears in compliance with a summons, the sheriff of the county in which the releasee is required to appear shall provide the designated agent with a place at the county jail to hold the hearing. Immediately on conclusion of a hearing in which the designated agent determines that a releasee has violated a condition of release, a warrant may be issued requiring the releasee to be held in the county jail pending:

(1) the action of a parole panel on any recommendations made by the designated agent; and

(2) if subsequently ordered by the parole panel, the return of the releasee to the institution from which the releasee was released.

(d) If a parole panel or designated agent of the board determines that a releasee has violated a condition of release required under Section 508.192 and confirms the violation with a peace officer or other law enforcement officer of this state who is authorized under federal law to verify a person's immigration status or, in accordance with 8 U.S.C. Section 1373(c), with a federal law enforcement officer, the determination is considered to be a sufficient hearing to revoke the parole or mandatory supervision without further hearing or determination, except that the parole panel or designated agent shall conduct a hearing to consider mitigating circumstances, if requested by the releasee.

(Enacted by Acts 1997, 75th Leg., ch. 165 (S.B. 898), § 12.01, effective September 1, 1997; am.

Acts 1999, 76th Leg., ch. 62 (S.B. 1368), § 10.31, effective September 1, 1999; am. Acts 2003, 78th Leg., ch. 264 (H.B. 1849), § 3, effective September 1, 2003; am. Acts 2003, 78th Leg., 3rd C.S., ch. 3 (H.B. 7), § 11.20, effective January 11, 2004; am. Acts 2011, 82nd Leg., ch. 1025 (H.B. 2734), § 2, effective September 1, 2011.)

## Sec. 508.2811. Preliminary Hearing.

A parole panel or a designee of the board shall provide within a reasonable time to an inmate or person described by Section 508.281(a) a preliminary hearing to determine whether probable cause or reasonable grounds exist to believe that the inmate or person has committed an act that would constitute a violation of a condition of release, unless the inmate or person:

   (1) waives the preliminary hearing; or

   (2) after release:

     (A) has been charged only with an administrative violation of a condition of release; or

     (B) has been adjudicated guilty of or has pleaded guilty or nolo contendere to an offense committed after release, other than an offense punishable by fine only involving the operation of a motor vehicle, regardless of whether the court has deferred disposition of the case, imposed a sentence in the case, or placed the inmate or person on community supervision.

(Enacted by Acts 1999, 76th Leg., ch. 62 (S.B. 1368), § 10.32, effective September 1, 1999.)

## Sec. 508.282. Deadlines.

(a) Except as provided by Subsection (b), a parole panel, a designee of the board, or the department shall dispose of the charges against an inmate or person described by Section 508.281(a):

   (1) before the 41st day after the date on which:

     (A) a warrant issued as provided by Section 508.251 is executed, if the inmate or person is arrested only on a charge that the inmate or person has committed an administrative violation of a condition of release, and the inmate or person is not charged before the 41st day with the commission of an offense described by Section 508.2811(2)(B); or

     (B) the sheriff having custody of an inmate or person alleged to have committed an offense after release notifies the department that:

     (i) the inmate or person has discharged the sentence for the offense; or

     (ii) the prosecution of the alleged offense has been dismissed by the attorney representing the state in the manner provided by Article 32.02, Code of Criminal Procedure; or

   (2) within a reasonable time after the date on which the inmate or person is returned to the custody of the department, if:

     (A) immediately before the return the inmate or person was in custody in another state or in a federal correctional system; or

     (B) the inmate or person is transferred to the custody of the department under Section 508.284.

(b) A parole panel, a designee of the board, or the department is not required to dispose of the charges against an inmate or person within the period required by Subsection (a) if:

   (1) the inmate or person is in custody in another state or a federal correctional institution;

   (2) the parole panel or a designee of the board is not provided a place by the sheriff to hold the hearing, in which event the department, parole panel, or designee is not required to dispose of the charges against the inmate or person until the 30th day after the date on which the sheriff provides a place to hold the hearing; or

   (3) the inmate or person is granted a continuance by a parole panel or a designee of the board in the inmate's or person's hearing under Section 508.281(a), but in no event may a parole panel, a designee of the board, or the department dispose of the charges against the person later than the 15th day after the date on which the parole panel, designee, or department would otherwise be required to dispose of the charges under this section, unless the inmate or person is released from custody and a summons is issued under Section 508.251 requiring the inmate or person to appear for a hearing under Section 508.281.

(c) In Subsections (a), (b), and (f), charges against an inmate or person are disposed of when:

   (1) the inmate's or person's conditional pardon, parole, or release to mandatory supervision is:

     (A) revoked; or

     (B) continued or modified and the inmate or person is released from the county jail;

Government

(2) the warrant for the inmate or person issued under Section 508.251 is withdrawn; or

(3) the inmate or person is transferred to a facility described by Section 508.284 for further proceedings.

(d) A sheriff, not later than the 10th day before the date on which the sheriff intends to release from custody an inmate or person described by Section 508.281(a) or transfer the inmate or person to the custody of an entity other than the department, shall notify the department of the intended release or transfer.

(e) If a warrant for an inmate or person issued under Section 508.251 is withdrawn, a summons may be issued requiring the inmate or person to appear for a hearing under Section 508.281.

(f) A parole panel, a designee of the board, or the department shall dispose of the charges against a releasee for whom a warrant is issued under Section 508.281(c) not later than the 31st day after the date on which the warrant is issued. (Enacted by Acts 1997, 75th Leg., ch. 165 (S.B. 898), § 12.01, effective September 1, 1997; am. Acts 1999, 76th Leg., ch. 62 (S.B. 1368), § 10.33, effective September 1, 1999; am. Acts 2003, 78th Leg., ch. 264 (H.B. 1849), § 4, effective September 1, 2003; am. Acts 2003, 78th Leg., ch. 1194 (S.B. 880), § 1, effective September 1, 2003.)

### Sec. 508.283.   Sanctions.

(a) After a parole panel or designated agent of the board has held a hearing under Section 508.281, in any manner warranted by the evidence:

(1) the board may recommend to the governor to continue, revoke, or modify the conditional pardon; and

(2) a parole panel may continue, revoke, or modify the parole or mandatory supervision.

(b) If the parole, mandatory supervision, or conditional pardon of a person described by Section 508.149(a) is revoked, the person may be required to serve the remaining portion of the sentence on which the person was released. The remaining portion is computed without credit for the time from the date of the person's release to the date of revocation.

(c) If the parole, mandatory supervision, or conditional pardon of a person other than a person described by Section 508.149(a) is revoked, the person may be required to serve the remaining portion of the sentence on which the person was released. For a person who on the date of issuance of a warrant or summons initi-

ating the revocation process is subject to a sentence the remaining portion of which is greater than the amount of time from the date of the person's release to the date of issuance of the warrant or summons, the remaining portion is to be served without credit for the time from the date of the person's release to the date of revocation. For a person who on the date of issuance of the warrant or summons is subject to a sentence the remaining portion of which is less than the amount of time from the date of the person's release to the date of issuance of the warrant or summons, the remaining portion is to be served without credit for an amount of time equal to the remaining portion of the sentence on the date of issuance of the warrant or citation.

(d) If a warrant is issued charging a violation of a release condition or a summons is issued for a hearing under Section 508.281, the sentence time credit may be suspended until a determination is made in the case. The suspended time credit may be reinstated if the parole, mandatory supervision, or conditional pardon is continued.

(e) If a person's parole or mandatory supervision is modified after it is established that the person violated conditions of release, the board may require the releasee to remain under custodial supervision in a county jail for a period of not less than 60 days or more than 180 days. A sheriff is required to accept an inmate sanctioned under this subsection only if the commissioners court of the county in which the sheriff serves and the Texas Department of Criminal Justice have entered into a contract providing for the housing of persons sanctioned under this subsection. (Enacted by Acts 1997, 75th Leg., ch. 165 (S.B. 898), § 12.01, effective September 1, 1997; am. Acts 1999, 76th Leg., ch. 62 (S.B. 1368), § 10.34, effective September 1, 1999; am. Acts 2001, 77th Leg., ch. 856 (H.B. 1649), § 7, effective September 1, 2001; am. Acts 2001, 77th Leg., ch. 1197 (H.B. 3504), § 1, effective September 1, 2001; am. Acts 2003, 78th Leg., ch. 1275 (H.B. 3506), § 2(62), effective September 1, 2003.)

### Sec. 508.284.   Transfer Pending Revocation Hearing.

The department, as provided by Section 508.282(c), may authorize a facility that is otherwise required to detain and house an inmate or person to transfer the inmate or person to a correctional facility operated by the department or under contract with the department if:

(1) the department determines that adequate space is available in the facility to which the inmate or person is to be transferred; and

Government

(2) the facility to which the inmate or person is to be transferred is located not more than 150 miles from the facility from which the inmate or person is to be transferred.

(Enacted by Acts 1999, 76th Leg., ch. 62 (S.B. 1368), § 10.35, effective September 1, 1999.)

## SUBCHAPTER J
## MISCELLANEOUS

### Sec. 508.311.  Duty to Provide Information.

On request of a member of the board or employee of the board or department, a public official of the state, including a judge, district attorney, county attorney, or police officer, who has information relating to an inmate eligible for parole shall send to the department in writing the information in the official's possession or under the official's control.

(Enacted by Acts 1997, 75th Leg., ch. 165 (S.B. 898), § 12.01, effective September 1, 1997.)

### Sec. 508.312.  Information on Recidivism of Releasees.

The Texas Board of Criminal Justice shall collect information on recidivism of releasees under the supervision of the division and shall use the information to evaluate operations.

(Enacted by Acts 1997, 75th Leg., ch. 165 (S.B. 898), § 12.01, effective September 1, 1997.)

### Sec. 508.313.  Confidential Information.

(a) All information obtained and maintained, including a victim protest letter or other correspondence, a victim impact statement, a list of inmates eligible for release on parole, and an arrest record of an inmate, is confidential and privileged if the information relates to:

(1) an inmate of the institutional division subject to release on parole, release to mandatory supervision, or executive clemency;

(2) a releasee; or

(3) a person directly identified in any proposed plan of release for an inmate.

(b) Statistical and general information relating to the parole and mandatory supervision system, including the names of releasees and data recorded relating to parole and mandatory supervision services, is not confidential or privileged and must be made available for public inspection at any reasonable time.

(c) The department, on request or in the normal course of official business, shall provide information that is confidential and privileged under Subsection (a) to:

(1) the governor;

(2) a member of the board or a parole commissioner;

(3) the Criminal Justice Policy Council in performing duties of the council under Section 413.017; or

(4) an eligible entity requesting information for a law enforcement, prosecutorial, correctional, clemency, or treatment purpose.

(d) In this section, "eligible entity" means:

(1) a government agency, including the office of a prosecuting attorney;

(2) an organization with which the department contracts or an organization to which the department provides a grant; or

(3) an organization to which inmates are referred for services by the department.

(e) This section does not apply to information relating to a sex offender that is authorized for release under Chapter 62, Code of Criminal Procedure.

(f) This section does not apply to information that is subject to required public disclosure under Section 552.029.

(Enacted by Acts 1997, 75th Leg., ch. 165 (S.B. 898), § 12.01, effective September 1, 1997; am. Acts 1999, 76th Leg., ch. 62 (S.B. 1368), § 10.36, effective September 1, 1999; am. Acts 1999, 76th Leg., ch. 783 (H.B. 1379), § 3, effective August 30, 1999; am. Acts 2001, 77th Leg., ch. 856 (H.B. 1649), § 8, effective September 1, 2001; am. Acts 2003, 78th Leg., ch. 6 (S.B. 519), § 3, effective April 10, 2003; am. Acts 2003, 78th Leg., 3rd C.S., ch. 3 (H.B. 7), § 11.21, effective January 11, 2004.)

### Sec. 508.314.  Access to Inmates.

The department shall:

(1) grant to a member or employee of the board access at all reasonable times to any inmate;

(2) provide for the member or employee or a representative of the member or employee facilities for communicating with or observing an inmate; and

(3) furnish to the member or employee:

(A) any report the member or employee requires relating to the conduct or character of an inmate; or

(B) other facts a parole panel considers pertinent in determining whether an inmate will be released on parole.

(Enacted by Acts 1997, 75th Leg., ch. 165 (S.B. 898), § 12.01, effective September 1, 1997.)

## Sec. 508.315. Electronic Monitoring Programs.

(a) To establish and maintain an electronic monitoring program under this chapter, the department may:

(1) fund an electronic monitoring program in a parole office;

(2) develop standards for the operation of an electronic monitoring program in a parole office; and

(3) fund the purchase, lease, or maintenance of electronic monitoring equipment.

(b) In determining whether electronic monitoring equipment should be leased or purchased, the department shall consider the rate at which technological change makes electronic monitoring equipment obsolete.

(Enacted by Acts 1997, 75th Leg., ch. 165 (S.B. 898), § 12.01, effective September 1, 1997.)

## Sec. 508.316. Special Programs.

(a) The department may contract for services for releasees if funds are appropriated to the department for the services, including services for releasees who have a history of:

(1) mental impairment or mental retardation;

(2) substance abuse; or

(3) sexual offenses.

(b) The department shall seek funding for a contract under this section as a priority item.

(Enacted by Acts 1997, 75th Leg., ch. 165 (S.B. 898), § 12.01, effective September 1, 1997.)

## Sec. 508.317. Intensive Supervision Program; Super-Intensive Supervision Program.

(a) The department shall establish a program to provide intensive supervision to inmates released under Subchapter B, Chapter 499, and other inmates determined by a parole panel or the department to require intensive supervision.

(b) The Texas Board of Criminal Justice shall adopt rules that establish standards for determining which inmates require intensive supervision.

(c) The program must provide the level of supervision the department provides that is higher than any level of supervision other than the level of supervision described by Subsection (d).

(d) The department shall establish a program to provide super-intensive supervision to inmates released on parole or mandatory supervision and determined by parole panels to require super-intensive supervision. The program must provide the highest level of supervision provided by the department.

(Enacted by Acts 1997, 75th Leg., ch. 165 (S.B. 898), § 12.01, effective September 1, 1997; am. Acts 1999, 76th Leg., ch. 62 (S.B. 1368), § 10.37, effective September 1, 1999.)

## Sec. 508.318. Continuing Education Program.

(a) The Texas Board of Criminal Justice and the Texas Education Agency shall adopt a memorandum of understanding that establishes the respective responsibilities of the board and the agency in implementing a continuing education program to increase the literacy of releasees.

(b) The Texas Board of Criminal Justice and the agency shall coordinate the development of the memorandum of understanding and each by rule shall adopt the memorandum.

(Enacted by Acts 1997, 75th Leg., ch. 165 (S.B. 898), § 12.01, effective September 1, 1997.)

## Sec. 508.319. Program to Assess and Enhance Educational and Vocational Skills.

(a) The department, with the assistance of public school districts, community and public junior colleges, public and private institutions of higher education, and other appropriate public and private entities, may establish a developmental program based on information obtained under Section 508.183 for an inmate to be released to the supervision of the division.

(b) The developmental program may provide the inmate with the educational and vocational training necessary to:

(1) meet the average skill level required under Section 508.183; and

(2) acquire employment while in the custody of the division to lessen the likelihood that the inmate will return to the institutional division.

(c) To decrease state expense for a program established under this section, the Texas Workforce Commission shall provide to the department and the other entities described by Subsection (a) information relating to obtaining financial assistance under applicable programs of public or private entities.

(d) The department may establish a developmental program similar to the program described

by Subsection (a) for inmates released from the institutional division who will not be supervised by the department.
(Enacted by Acts 1997, 75th Leg., ch. 165 (S.B. 898), § 12.01, effective September 1, 1997.)

### Sec. 508.320.  Contracts for Lease of Federal Facilities.

(a) The department may contract with the federal government for the lease of a military base or other federal facility that is not being used by the federal government.

(b) The department may use a facility leased under this section to house releasees in the custody of the division.

(c) The department may not enter into a contract under this section unless funds have been appropriated specifically to make payments on a contract under this section.

(d) The department shall attempt to enter into contracts that will provide the department with facilities located in various parts of the state.
(Enacted by Acts 1997, 75th Leg., ch. 165 (S.B. 898), § 12.01, effective September 1, 1997.)

### Sec. 508.321.  Reporting, Management, and Collection Services.

The department, with the approval of the Texas Board of Criminal Justice, may contract with a public or private vendor to provide telephone reporting, automated caseload management, or collection services for:

(1) fines, fees, restitution, or other costs ordered to be paid by a court; or

(2) fees collected by the division.
(Enacted by Acts 1997, 75th Leg., ch. 165 (S.B. 898), § 12.01, effective September 1, 1997.)

### Sec. 508.322.  Releasee Restitution Fund.

(a) The releasee restitution fund is a fund outside the treasury and consists of restitution payments made by releasees. Money in the fund may be used only to pay restitution as required by a condition of parole or mandatory supervision to victims of criminal offenses.

(b) The comptroller is the trustee of the releasee restitution fund as provided by Section 404.073.

(c) When a parole panel orders the payment of restitution from a releasee as provided by Article

42.037(h), Code of Criminal Procedure, the department shall:

(1) collect the payment for disbursement to the victim;

(2) deposit the payment in the releasee restitution fund; and

(3) transmit the payment to the victim as soon as practicable.

(d) If a victim who is entitled to restitution cannot be located, immediately after receiving a final payment in satisfaction of an order of restitution for the victim, the department shall attempt to notify the victim of that fact by certified mail, mailed to the last known address of the victim. If a victim then makes a claim for payment, the department promptly shall remit the payment to the victim.

(e) Money that remains unclaimed shall be transferred to the compensation to victims of crime auxiliary fund on the fifth anniversary of the date the money was deposited to the credit of the releasee restitution fund.
(Enacted by Acts 1997, 75th Leg., ch. 165 (S.B. 898), § 12.01, effective September 1, 1997; am. Acts 2001, 77th Leg., ch. 856 (H.B. 1649), § 9, effective September 1, 2001.)

### Sec. 508.323.  Audit.

The financial transactions of the division and the board are subject to audit by the state auditor in accordance with Chapter 321.
(Enacted by Acts 1997, 75th Leg., ch. 165 (S.B. 898), § 12.01, effective September 1, 1997.)

### Sec. 508.324.  Victim-Offender Mediation.

If the pardons and paroles division receives notice from the victim services office of the department that a victim of the defendant, or the victim's guardian or close relative, wishes to participate in victim-offender mediation with a person released on parole or to mandatory supervision, the division shall cooperate and assist the person if the person chooses to participate in the mediation program provided by the office. The pardons and paroles division may not require the defendant to participate and may not reward the person for participation by modifying conditions of release or the person's level of supervision or by granting any other benefit to the person.
(Enacted by Acts 1999, 76th Leg., ch. 62 (S.B. 1368), § 10.38, effective September 1, 1999.)

Government

# TITLE 5
# OPEN GOVERNMENT; ETHICS

## SUBTITLE A
## OPEN GOVERNMENT

## CHAPTER 552
## PUBLIC INFORMATION

### Subchapter I. Criminal Violations

## SUBCHAPTER I
## CRIMINAL VIOLATIONS

### Sec. 552.351.  Destruction, Removal, or Alteration of Public Information.

(a) A person commits an offense if the person wilfully destroys, mutilates, removes without permission as provided by this chapter, or alters public information.

(b) An offense under this section is a misdemeanor punishable by:

(1) a fine of not less than $25 or more than $4,000;

(2) confinement in the county jail for not less than three days or more than three months; or

(3) both the fine and confinement.

(c) It is an exception to the application of Subsection (a) that the public information was transferred under Section 441.204.

(Enacted by Acts 1993, 73rd Leg., ch. 268 (S.B. 248), § 1, effective September 1, 1993; am. Acts 1995, 74th Leg., ch. 1035 (H.B. 1718), § 25, effective September 1, 1995; am. Acts 2001, 77th Leg., ch. 771 (S.B. 1800), § 2, effective June 13, 2001.)

### Sec. 552.352.  Distribution or Misuse of Confidential Information.

(a) A person commits an offense if the person distributes information considered confidential under the terms of this chapter.

(a-1) An officer or employee of a governmental body who obtains access to confidential information under Section 552.008 commits an offense if the officer or employee knowingly:

(1) uses the confidential information for a purpose other than the purpose for which the information was received or for a purpose unrelated to the law that permitted the officer or employee to obtain access to the information, including solicitation of political contributions or solicitation of clients;

(2) permits inspection of the confidential information by a person who is not authorized to inspect the information; or

(3) discloses the confidential information to a person who is not authorized to receive the information.

(a-2) For purposes of Subsection (a-1), a member of an advisory committee to a governmental body who obtains access to confidential information in that capacity is considered to be an officer or employee of the governmental body.

(b) An offense under this section is a misdemeanor punishable by:

(1) a fine of not more than $1,000;

(2) confinement in the county jail for not more than six months; or

(3) both the fine and confinement.

(c) A violation under this section constitutes official misconduct.

(Enacted by Acts 1993, 73rd Leg., ch. 268 (S.B. 248), § 1, effective September 1, 1993; am. Acts 2003, 78th Leg., ch. 249 (H.B. 1606), §§ 7.01, 7.02, effective September 1, 2003; am. Acts 2003, 78th Leg., ch. 1089 (H.B. 2032), § 2, effective September 1, 2003.)

### Sec. 552.353.  Failure or Refusal of Officer for Public Information to Provide Access to or Copying of Public Information.

(a) An officer for public information, or the officer's agent, commits an offense if, with criminal negligence, the officer or the officer's agent fails or refuses to give access to, or to permit or provide copying of, public information to a requestor as provided by this chapter.

(b) It is an affirmative defense to prosecution

under Subsection (a) that the officer for public information reasonably believed that public access to the requested information was not required and that:

    (1) the officer acted in reasonable reliance on a court order or a written interpretation of this chapter contained in an opinion of a court of record or of the attorney general issued under Subchapter G;

    (2) the officer requested a decision from the attorney general in accordance with Subchapter G, and the decision is pending; or

    (3) not later than the 10th calendar day after the date of receipt of a decision by the attorney general that the information is public, the officer or the governmental body for whom the defendant is the officer for public information filed a petition for a declaratory judgment against the attorney general in a Travis County district court seeking relief from compliance with the decision of the attorney general, as provided by Section 552.324, and the cause is pending.

    (c) It is an affirmative defense to prosecution under Subsection (a) that a person or entity has, not later than the 10th calendar day after the date of receipt by a governmental body of a decision by the attorney general that the information is public, filed a cause of action seeking relief from compliance with the decision of the attorney general, as provided by Section 552.325, and the cause is pending.

    (d) It is an affirmative defense to prosecution under Subsection (a) that the defendant is the agent of an officer for public information and that the agent reasonably relied on the written instruction of the officer for public information not to disclose the public information requested.

    (e) An offense under this section is a misdemeanor punishable by:

    (1) a fine of not more than $1,000;

    (2) confinement in the county jail for not more than six months; or

    (3) both the fine and confinement.

    (f) A violation under this section constitutes official misconduct.

(Enacted by Acts 1993, 73rd Leg., ch. 268 (S.B. 248), § 1, effective September 1, 1993; am. Acts 1995, 74th Leg., ch. 1035 (H.B. 1718), § 25, effective September 1, 1995; am. Acts 2009, 81st Leg., ch. 1377 (S.B. 1182), § 12, effective September 1, 2009.)

# CHAPTER 557
# SEDITION, SABOTAGE, AND COMMUNISM

### Subchapter A. Sedition

## SUBCHAPTER A
## SEDITION

### Sec. 557.001. Sedition.

    (a) A person commits an offense if the person knowingly:

    (1) commits, attempts to commit, or conspires with one or more persons to commit an act intended to overthrow, destroy, or alter the constitutional form of government of this state or of any political subdivision of this state by force or violence;

    (2) under circumstances that constitute a clear and present danger to the security of this state or a political subdivision of this state, advocates, advises, or teaches or conspires with one or more persons to advocate, advise, or teach a person to commit or attempt to commit an act described in Subdivision (1); or

    (3) participates, with knowledge of the nature of the organization, in the management of an organization that engages in or attempts to engage in an act intended to overthrow, destroy, or alter the constitutional form of government of this state or of any political subdivision of this state by force or violence.

    (b) An offense under this section is a felony punishable by:

    (1) a fine not to exceed $20,000;

    (2) confinement in the Texas Department of Criminal Justice for a term of not less than one year or more than 20 years; or

(3) both fine and imprisonment.

(c) A person convicted of an offense under this section may not receive probation under Article 42.12, Code of Criminal Procedure.

(Enacted by Acts 1993, 73rd Leg., ch. 268 (S.B. 248), § 1, effective September 1, 1993; am. Acts 2009, 81st Leg., ch. 87 (S.B. 1969), § 25.072, effective September 1, 2009.)

### Sec. 557.002.　Disqualification.

A person who is finally convicted of an offense under Section 557.001 may not hold office or a position of profit, trust, or employment with the state or any political subdivision of the state.

(Enacted by Acts 1993, 73rd Leg., ch. 268 (S.B. 248), § 1, effective September 1, 1993.)

### Sec. 557.003.　Seditious Organizations.

(a) An organization, either incorporated or unincorporated, may not engage in or have as a purpose activities intended to overthrow, destroy, or alter the constitutional form of government of this state or a political subdivision of this state by force or violence.

(b) An organization that violates Subsection (a):

(1) may not lawfully exist, function, or operate in this state; and

(2) is not entitled to the rights, privileges, and immunities granted to organizations under the law of this state.

(c) A district attorney, criminal district attorney, or county attorney may bring an action against an organization in a court of competent jurisdiction. If the court finds that the organization has violated Subsection (a), the court shall order:

(1) the organization dissolved;

(2) if the organization is incorporated in the state or has a permit to do business in the state, the organization's charter or permit revoked;

(3) all funds, records, and property of the organization forfeited to the state; and

(4) all books, records, and files of the organization turned over to the attorney general.

(d) It is prima facie evidence that an organization engages in or has as a purpose engaging in activities intended to overthrow, destroy, or alter the constitutional form of the government of this state or a political subdivision of this state by force or violence if it is shown that the organization has a parent or superior organization that engages in or has as a purpose engaging in activities intended to overthrow, destroy, or alter the constitutional form of the government of this state or a political subdivision of this state by force or violence.

(Enacted by Acts 1993, 73rd Leg., ch. 268 (S.B. 248), § 1, effective September 1, 1993.)

### Sec. 557.004.　Enforcement.

(a) A district court may, on application by a district attorney, criminal district attorney, or county attorney, order injunctive or other equitable relief appropriate to enforce this subchapter.

(b) The procedure for relief sought under Subsection (a) of this section is the same as that for other similar relief in the district court except that the proceeding may not be instituted unless the director of the Department of Public Safety of the State of Texas or the director's assistant in charge is notified by telephone, telegraph, or in person that injunctive or other equitable relief will be sought.

(c) An affidavit that states that the notice described in Subsection (b) was given and that accompanies the application for relief is sufficient to permit filing of the application.

(d) Injunctive or other equitable relief sought to enforce this subchapter may not be granted in a labor dispute.

(e) The internal security section of the Department of Public Safety of the State of Texas shall assist in the enforcement of this subchapter.

(Enacted by Acts 1993, 73rd Leg., ch. 268 (S.B. 248), § 1, effective September 1, 1993.)

### Sec. 557.005.　Judicial Powers in Labor Disputes.

This subchapter does not affect the powers of the courts of this state or of the United States under the law of this state in a labor dispute.

(Enacted by Acts 1993, 73rd Leg., ch. 268 (S.B. 248), § 1, effective September 1, 1993.)

### SUBCHAPTER B
### SABOTAGE

### Sec. 557.011.　Sabotage.

(a) A person commits an offense if the person, with the intent to injure the United States, this state, or any facility or property used for national defense sabotages or attempts to sabotage any property or facility used or to be used for national defense.

(b) An offense under this section is a felony punishable by confinement in the Texas Department of Criminal Justice for a term of not less than two years or more than 20 years.

(c) If conduct constituting an offense under this section also constitutes an offense under another provision of law, the actor may be prosecuted under both sections.

(d) In this section, "sabotage" means to wilfully and maliciously damage or destroy property.
(Enacted by Acts 1993, 73rd Leg., ch. 268 (S.B. 248), § 1, effective September 1, 1993; am. Acts 2009, 81st Leg., ch. 87 (S.B. 1969), § 25.073, effective September 1, 2009.)

### Sec. 557.012.  Capital Sabotage.

(a) A person commits an offense if the person commits an offense under Section 557.011(a) and the sabotage or attempted sabotage causes the death of an individual.

(b) An offense under this section is punishable by:

(1) death; or

(2) confinement in the Texas Department of Criminal Justice for:

(A) life; or

(B) a term of not less than two years.

(c) If conduct constituting an offense under this section also constitutes an offense under other law, the actor may be prosecuted under both sections.
(Enacted by Acts 1993, 73rd Leg., ch. 268 (S.B. 248), § 1, effective September 1, 1993; am. Acts 2009, 81st Leg., ch. 87 (S.B. 1969), § 25.074, effective September 1, 2009.)

### Sec. 557.013.  Enforcement.

The attorney general, a district or county attorney, the department, and any law enforcement officer of this state shall enforce this subchapter.

(Enacted by Acts 1993, 73rd Leg., ch. 268 (S.B. 248), § 1, effective September 1, 1993.)

### SUBCHAPTER C
### COMMUNISM

### Sec. 557.021.  Definitions.

In this subchapter:

(1) "Communist" means a person who commits an act reasonably calculated to further the overthrow of the government:

(A) by force or violence; or

(B) by unlawful or unconstitutional means and replace it with a communist government.

(2) "Department" means the Department of Public Safety of the State of Texas.

(3) "Government" means the government of this state or any of its political subdivisions.
(Enacted by Acts 1993, 73rd Leg., ch. 268 (S.B. 248), § 1, effective September 1, 1993.)

### Sec. 557.022.  Restrictions.

(a) The name of a communist may not be printed on the ballot for any primary or general election in this state or a political subdivision of this state.

(b) A person may not hold a nonelected office or position with the state or any political subdivision of the state if:

(1) any of the compensation for the office or position comes from public funds of this state or a political subdivision of this state; and

(2) the employer or superior of the person has reasonable grounds to believe that the person is a communist.
(Enacted by Acts 1993, 73rd Leg., ch. 268 (S.B. 248), § 1, effective September 1, 1993.)

### Sec. 557.023.  Enforcement.

The attorney general, a district or county attorney, the department, and any law enforcement officer of this state shall enforce this subchapter.
(Enacted by Acts 1993, 73rd Leg., ch. 268 (S.B. 248), § 1, effective September 1, 1993.)

Government

# Health and Safety Code

## TITLE 2

## HEALTH

### SUBTITLE A
### TEXAS DEPARTMENT OF HEALTH

### CHAPTER 12
### POWERS AND DUTIES OF TEXAS DEPARTMENT OF HEALTH

**Subchapter H. Medical Advisory Board**

### SUBCHAPTER H
### MEDICAL ADVISORY BOARD

### Sec. 12.091.  Definitions.

In this subchapter:

(1) "Medical standards division" means the Medical Standards on Motor Vehicle Operations Division of the department.

(2) "Panel" means a panel of the medical advisory board.

(Enacted by Acts 1995, 74th Leg., ch. 165 (S.B. 971), § 9, effective September 1, 1995.)

### Sec. 12.092.  Medical Advisory Board; Board Members.

(a) The commissioner shall appoint the medical advisory board members from:

(1) persons licensed to practice medicine in this state, including physicians who are board certified in internal medicine, psychiatry, neurology, physical medicine, or ophthalmology and who are jointly recommended by the Texas Department of Health and the Texas Medical Association; and

(2) persons licensed to practice optometry in this state who are jointly recommended by the department and the Texas Optometric Association.

(b) The medical advisory board shall assist the Department of Public Safety of the State of Texas in determining whether:

(1) an applicant for a driver's license or a license holder is capable of safely operating a motor vehicle; or

(2) an applicant for or holder of a license to carry a concealed handgun under the authority of Subchapter H, Chapter 411, Government Code, is capable of exercising sound judgment with respect to the proper use and storage of a handgun.

(Enacted by Acts 1995, 74th Leg., ch. 165 (S.B. 971), § 9, effective September 1, 1995; am. Acts 1997, 75th Leg., ch. 1261 (H.B. 2909), § 21, effective September 1, 1997; am. Acts 1999, 76th Leg., ch. 62 (S.B. 1368), § 9.23, effective September 1, 1999.)

### Sec. 12.093.  Administration; Rules.

(a) The medical advisory board is administratively attached to the medical standards division.

(b) The medical standards division:

(1) shall provide administrative support for the medical advisory board and panels of the medical advisory board; and

(2) may collect and maintain the individual medical records necessary for use by the medical advisory board and the panels under this section from a physician, hospital, or other health care provider.

(Enacted by Acts 1995, 74th Leg., ch. 165 (S.B. 971), § 9, effective September 1, 1995.)

Health

## Sec. 12.094. Rules Relating to Medical Advisory Board Members.

(a) The board:

(1) may adopt rules to govern the activities of the medical advisory board;

(2) by rule may establish a reasonable fee to pay a member of the medical advisory board for the member's professional consultation services; and

(3) if appropriate, may authorize per diem and travel allowances for each meeting a member attends, not to exceed the amounts authorized for state employees by the General Appropriations Act.

(b) The fee under Subsection (a)(2) may not be less than $75 or more than $150 for each meeting that the member attends.

(Enacted by Acts 1995, 74th Leg., ch. 165 (S.B. 971). § 9, effective September 1, 1995.)

## Sec. 12.095. Board Panels; Powers and Duties.

(a) If the Department of Public Safety of the State of Texas requests an opinion or recommendation from the medical advisory board as to the ability of an applicant or license holder to operate a motor vehicle safely or to exercise sound judgment with respect to the proper use and storage of a handgun, the commissioner or a person designated by the commissioner shall convene a panel to consider the case or question submitted by that department.

(b) To take action as a panel, at least three members of the medical advisory board must be present.

(c) Each panel member shall prepare an individual independent written report for the Department of Public Safety of the State of Texas that states the member's opinion as to the ability of the applicant or license holder to operate a motor vehicle safely or to exercise sound judgment with respect to the proper use and storage of a handgun, as appropriate. In the report the panel member may also make recommendations relating to that department's subsequent action.

(d) In its deliberations, a panel may examine any medical record or report that contains material that may be relevant to the ability of the applicant or license holder.

(e) The panel may require the applicant or license holder to undergo a medical or other examination at the applicant's or holder's expense. A person who conducts an examination under this subsection may be compelled to testify before the panel and in any subsequent proceedings under Subchapter H, Chapter 411, Government Code, or Subchapter N, Chapter 521, Transportation Code, as applicable, concerning the person's observations and findings.

(Enacted by Acts 1995, 74th Leg., ch. 165 (S.B. 971), § 9, effective September 1, 1995; am. Acts 1997, 75th Leg., ch. 1261 (H.B. 2909), § 22, effective September 1, 1997; am. Acts 2009, 81st Leg., ch. 1146 (H.B. 2730), § 11.22, effective September 1, 2009.)

## Sec. 12.096. Physician Report.

(a) A physician licensed to practice medicine in this state may inform the Department of Public Safety of the State of Texas or the medical advisory board, orally or in writing, of the name, date of birth, and address of a patient older than 15 years of age whom the physician has diagnosed as having a disorder or disability specified in a rule of the Department of Public Safety of the State of Texas.

(b) The release of information under this section is an exception to the patient-physician privilege requirements imposed under Section 159.002, Occupations Code.

(Enacted by Acts 1995, 74th Leg., ch. 165 (S.B. 971), § 9, effective September 1, 1995; am. Acts 2001, 77th Leg., ch. 1420 (H.B. 2812), § 14.768, effective September 1, 2001.)

## Sec. 12.097. Confidentiality Requirements.

(a) All records, reports, and testimony relating to the medical condition of an applicant or license holder:

(1) are for the confidential use of the medical advisory board, a panel, or the Department of Public Safety of the State of Texas;

(2) are privileged information; and

(3) may not be disclosed to any person or used as evidence in a trial except as provided by Subsection (b).

(b) In a subsequent proceeding under Subchapter H, Chapter 411, Government Code, or Subchapter N, Chapter 521, Transportation Code, the medical standards division may provide a copy of the report of the medical advisory board or panel and a medical record or report relating to an applicant or license holder to:

(1) the Department of Public Safety of the State of Texas;

(2) the applicant or license holder; and

(3) the officer who presides at the hearing.

(Enacted by Acts 1995, 74th Leg., ch. 165 (S.B. 971), § 9, effective September 1, 1995; am. Acts 2009, 81st Leg., ch. 1146 (H.B. 2730), § 11.23, effective September 1, 2009.)

### Sec. 12.098.  Liability.

A member of the medical advisory board, a member of a panel, a person who makes an examination for or on the recommendation of the medical advisory board, or a physician who reports to the medical advisory board or a panel under Section 12.096 is not liable for a professional opinion, recommendation, or report made under this subchapter.

(Enacted by Acts 1995, 74th Leg., ch. 165 (S.B. 971), § 9, effective September 1, 1995.)

## SUBTITLE G
## LICENSES

## CHAPTER 142
## HOME AND COMMUNITY SUPPORT SERVICES

**Subchapter A. Home and Community Support Services License**

Section
142.0061.  Possession of Sterile Water or Saline.
142.0062.  Possession of Certain Vaccines or Tuberculin.
142.0063.  Possession of Certain Dangerous Drugs.

**Subchapter B. Permits to Administer Medication**

142.021.  Administration of Medication.
142.022.  Exemptions for Nursing Students and Medication Aide Trainees.
142.029.  Administration of Medication; Criminal Penalty.
142.030.  Dispensing Dangerous Drugs or Controlled Substances; Criminal Penalty.

## SUBCHAPTER A
## HOME AND COMMUNITY SUPPORT SERVICES LICENSE

### Sec. 142.0061.  Possession of Sterile Water or Saline.

A home and community support services agency or its employees who are registered nurses or licensed vocational nurses may purchase, store, or transport for the purpose of administering to their home health or hospice patients under physician's orders:

(1) sterile water for injection and irrigation; and

(2) sterile saline for injection and irrigation. (Enacted by Acts 1993, 73rd Leg., ch. 16 (S.B. 310), § 1, effective April 2, 1993; am. Acts 1993, 73rd Leg., ch. 789 (S.B. 472), § 23, effective September 1, 1993; am. Acts 1995, 74th Leg., ch. 307 (H.B. 1408), § 1, effective September 1, 1995; am. Acts 1997, 75th Leg., ch. 1129 (H.B. 3075), § 1, effective September 1, 1997.)

### Sec. 142.0062.  Possession of Certain Vaccines or Tuberculin.

(a) A home and community support services agency or its employees who are registered nurses or licensed vocational nurses may purchase, store, or transport for the purpose of administering to the agency's employees, home health or hospice patients, or patient family members under physician's standing orders the following dangerous drugs:

(1) hepatitis B vaccine;

(2) influenza vaccine;

(3) tuberculin purified protein derivative for tuberculosis testing; and

(4) pneumococcal polysaccharide vaccine.

(b) A home and community support services agency that purchases, stores, or transports a vaccine or tuberculin under this section shall ensure that any standing order for the vaccine or tuberculin:

(1) is signed and dated by the physician;

(2) identifies the vaccine or tuberculin covered by the order;

(3) indicates that the recipient of the vaccine or tuberculin has been assessed as an appropriate candidate to receive the vaccine or tuberculin and has been assessed for the absence of any contraindication;

(4) indicates that appropriate procedures are established for responding to any negative reaction to the vaccine or tuberculin; and

(5) orders that a specific medication or category of medication be administered if the recipient has a negative reaction to the vaccine or tuberculin.

(Enacted by Acts 1997, 75th Leg., ch. 1129 (H.B. 3075), § 1, effective September 1, 1997; am. Acts 2003, 78th Leg., ch. 198 (H.B. 2292), § 2.195, effective September 1, 2003.)

### Sec. 142.0063.  Possession of Certain Dangerous Drugs.

(a) A home and community support services agency in compliance with this section or its employees who are registered nurses or licensed

Health

vocational nurses may purchase, store, or transport for the purpose of administering to their home health or hospice patients in accordance with Subsection (c) the following dangerous drugs:

(1) any of the following items in a sealed portable container of a size determined by the dispensing pharmacist:

(A) 1,000 milliliters of 0.9 percent sodium chloride intravenous infusion;

(B) 1,000 milliliters of five percent dextrose in water injection; or

(C) sterile saline; or

(2) not more than five dosage units of any of the following items in an individually sealed, unused portable container:

(A) heparin sodium lock flush in a concentration of 10 units per milliliter or 100 units per milliliter;

(B) epinephrine HCl solution in a concentration of 1 to 1,000;

(C) diphenhydramine HCl solution in a concentration of 50 milligrams per milliliter;

(D) methylprednisolone in a concentration of 125 milligrams per two milliliters;

(E) naloxone in a concentration of one milligram per milliliter in a two-milliliter vial;

(F) promethazine in a concentration of 25 milligrams per milliliter;

(G) glucagon in a concentration of one milligram per milliliter;

(H) furosemide in a concentration of 10 milligrams per milliliter;

(I) lidocaine 2.5 percent and prilocaine 2.5 percent cream in a five-gram tube; or

(J) lidocaine HCl solution in a concentration of one percent in a two-milliliter vial.

(b) A home and community support services agency or the agency's authorized employees may purchase, store, or transport dangerous drugs in a sealed portable container under this section only if the agency has established policies and procedures to ensure that:

(1) the container is handled properly with respect to storage, transportation, and temperature stability;

(2) a drug is removed from the container only on a physician's written or oral order;

(3) the administration of any drug in the container is performed in accordance with a specific treatment protocol; and

(4) the agency maintains a written record of the dates and times the container is in the possession of a registered nurse or licensed vocational nurse.

(c) A home and community support services agency or the agency's authorized employee who administers a drug listed in Subsection (a) may administer the drug only in the patient's residence under physician's orders in connection with the provision of emergency treatment or the adjustment of:

(1) parenteral drug therapy; or

(2) vaccine or tuberculin administration.

(d) If a home and community support services agency or the agency's authorized employee administers a drug listed in Subsection (a) pursuant to a physician's oral order, the physician shall promptly send a signed copy of the order to the agency, and the agency shall:

(1) not later than 24 hours after receipt of the order, reduce the order to written form and send a copy of the form to the dispensing pharmacy by mail or facsimile transmission; and

(2) not later than 20 days after receipt of the order, send a copy of the order as signed by and received from the physician to the dispensing pharmacy.

(e) A pharmacist that dispenses a sealed portable container under this section shall ensure that the container:

(1) is designed to allow access to the contents of the container only if a tamper-proof seal is broken;

(2) bears a label that lists the drugs in the container and provides notice of the container's expiration date, which is the earlier of:

(A) the date that is six months after the date on which the container is dispensed; or

(B) the earliest expiration date of any drug in the container; and

(3) remains in the pharmacy or under the control of a pharmacist, registered nurse, or licensed vocational nurse.

(f) If a home and community support services agency or the agency's authorized employee purchases, stores, or transports a sealed portable container under this section, the agency shall deliver the container to the dispensing pharmacy for verification of drug quality, quantity, integrity, and expiration dates not later than the earlier of:

(1) the seventh day after the date on which the seal on the container is broken; or

(2) the date for which notice is provided on the container label.

(g) A pharmacy that dispenses a sealed portable container under this section shall take reasonable precautionary measures to ensure that the home and community support services agency

receiving the container complies with Subsection (f). On receipt of a container under Subsection (f), the pharmacy shall perform an inventory of the drugs used from the container and shall restock and reseal the container before delivering the container to the agency for reuse.
(Enacted by Acts 1997, 75th Leg., ch. 1129 (H.B. 3075), § 1, effective September 1, 1997.)

## SUBCHAPTER B
## PERMITS TO ADMINISTER MEDICATION

### Sec. 142.021. Administration of Medication.

A person may not administer medication to a client of a home and community support services agency unless the person:

(1) holds a license under state law that authorizes the person to administer medication;

(2) holds a permit issued under Section 142.025 and acts under the delegated authority of a person who holds a license under state law that authorizes the person to administer medication;

(3) administers a medication to a client of a home and community support service agency in accordance with rules of the Texas Board of Nursing that permit delegation of the administration of medication to a person not holding a permit under Section 142.025; or

(4) administers noninjectable medication under circumstances authorized by the memorandum of understanding adopted under Section 142.016.
(Enacted by Acts 1990, 71st Leg., 6th C.S., ch. 31 (S.B. 46), § 3, effective June 19, 1990; am. Acts 1993, 73rd Leg., ch. 800 (H.B. 1551), § 19, effective September 1, 1993; am. Acts 1997, 75th Leg., ch. 1191 (S.B. 1247), § 8, effective September 1, 1997; am. Acts 2007, 80th Leg., ch. 889 (H.B. 2426), § 65, effective September 1, 2007.)

### Sec. 142.022. Exemptions for Nursing Students and Medication Aide Trainees.

(a) Sections 142.021 and 142.029 do not apply to:

(1) a graduate nurse holding a temporary permit issued by the Texas Board of Nursing;

(2) a student enrolled in an accredited school of nursing or program for the education of registered nurses who is administering medications as part of the student's clinical experience;

(3) a graduate vocational nurse holding a temporary permit issued by the Texas Board of Nursing;

(4) a student enrolled in an accredited school of vocational nursing or program for the education of vocational nurses who is administering medications as part of the student's clinical experience; or

(5) a trainee in a medication aide training program approved by the department under Section 142.024 who is administering medications as part of the trainee's clinical experience.

(b) The administration of medications by persons exempted under Subdivisions (1) through (4) of Subsection (a) is governed by the terms of the memorandum of understanding executed by the department and the Texas Board of Nursing.
(Enacted by Acts 1990, 71st Leg., 6th C.S., ch. 31 (S.B. 46), § 4, effective June 19, 1990; am. Acts 2003, 78th Leg., ch. 553 (H.B. 1483), § 2.009, effective February 1, 2004; am. Acts 2007, 80th Leg., ch. 889 (H.B. 2426), § 66, effective September 1, 2007.)

### Sec. 142.029. Administration of Medication; Criminal Penalty.

(a) A person commits an offense if the person knowingly administers medication to a client of a home and community support services agency and the person is not authorized to administer the medication under Section 142.021 or 142.022.

(b) An offense under this section is a Class B misdemeanor.
(Enacted by Acts 1990, 71st Leg., 6th C.S., ch. 31 (S.B. 46), § 3, effective June 19, 1990; am. Acts 1993, 73rd Leg., ch. 800 (H.B. 1551), § 27, effective September 1, 1993.)

### Sec. 142.030. Dispensing Dangerous Drugs or Controlled Substances; Criminal Penalty.

(a) A person authorized by this subchapter to administer medication to a client of a home and community support services agency may not dispense dangerous drugs or controlled substances without complying with Subtitle J, Title 3, Occupations Code.

(b) An offense under this section is a Class A misdemeanor.
(Enacted by Acts 1990, 71st Leg., 6th C.S., ch. 31 (S.B. 46), § 3, effective June 19, 1990; am. Acts 1993, 73rd Leg., ch. 800 (H.B. 1551), § 28, effec-

Health

tive September 1, 1993; am. Acts 2001, 77th Leg., ch. 1420 (H.B. 2812), § 14.779, effective September 1, 2001.)

## SUBTITLE H
## PUBLIC HEALTH PROVISIONS

## CHAPTER 161
## PUBLIC HEALTH PROVISIONS

### Subchapter H. Distribution of Cigarettes or Tobacco Products

## SUBCHAPTER H
## DISTRIBUTION OF CIGARETTES OR TOBACCO PRODUCTS

### Sec. 161.081.  Definitions.

In this subchapter:

(1) "Cigarette" has the meaning assigned by Section 154.001, Tax Code.

(2) "Permit holder" has the meaning assigned by Section 154.001 or 155.001, Tax Code, as applicable.

(3) "Retail sale" means a transfer of possession from a retailer to a consumer in connection with a purchase, sale, or exchange for value of cigarettes or tobacco products.

(4) "Retailer" has the meaning assigned by Section 154.001 or 155.001, Tax Code, as applicable.

(5) "Tobacco product" has the meaning assigned by Section 155.001, Tax Code.

(6) "Wholesaler" has the meaning assigned by Section 154.001 or 155.001, Tax Code, as applicable.

(Enacted by Acts 1989, 71st Leg., ch. 678 (H.B. 2136), § 1, effective September 1, 1989; am. Acts 1997, 75th Leg., ch. 671 (S.B. 55), § 1.01, effective September 1, 1997.)

### Sec. 161.082.  Sale of Cigarettes or Tobacco Products to Persons Younger Than 18 Years of Age Prohibited; Proof of Age Required.

(a) A person commits an offense if the person, with criminal negligence:

(1) sells, gives, or causes to be sold or given a cigarette or tobacco product to someone who is younger than 18 years of age; or

(2) sells, gives, or causes to be sold or given a cigarette or tobacco product to another person who intends to deliver it to someone who is younger than 18 years of age.

(b) If an offense under this section occurs in connection with a sale by an employee of the owner of a store in which cigarettes or tobacco products are sold at retail, the employee is criminally responsible for the offense and is subject to prosecution.

(c) An offense under this section is a Class C misdemeanor.

(d) It is a defense to prosecution under Subsection (a)(1) that the person to whom the cigarette or tobacco product was sold or given presented to the defendant apparently valid proof of identification.

(e) A proof of identification satisfies the requirements of Subsection (d) if it contains a physical description and photograph consistent with the person's appearance, purports to establish that the person is 18 years of age or older, and was issued by a governmental agency. The proof of identification may include a driver's license issued by this state or another state, a passport, or an identification card issued by a state or the federal government.

(Enacted by Acts 1989, 71st Leg., ch. 678 (H.B. 2136), § 1, effective September 1, 1989; am. Acts 1991, 72nd Leg., ch. 14 (S.B. 404), § 50, effective September 1, 1991; am. Acts 1997, 75th Leg., ch. 671 (S.B. 55), § 1.01, effective September 1, 1997 (renumbered from Sec. 161.081).)

## Sec. 161.0825. Use of Certain Electronically Readable Information.

(a) In this section, "transaction scan device" means a device capable of deciphering electronically readable information on a driver's license, commercial driver's license, or identification certificate.

(b) A person may access electronically readable information on a driver's license, commercial driver's license, or identification certificate for the purpose of complying with Section 161.082.

(c) Information accessed under this section may not be sold or otherwise disseminated to a third party for any purpose, including any marketing, advertising, or promotional activities. The information may be obtained by court order or on proper request by the comptroller, a law enforcement officer, or a law enforcement agency.

(d) A person who violates this section commits an offense. An offense under this section is a Class A misdemeanor.

(e) It is an affirmative defense to prosecution under Section 161.082 that:

(1) a transaction scan device identified a license or certificate as valid and the defendant accessed the information and relied on the results in good faith; or

(2) if the defendant is the owner of a store in which cigarettes or tobacco products are sold at retail, the offense under Section 161.082 occurs in connection with a sale by an employee of the owner, and the owner had provided the employee with:

(A) a transaction scan device in working condition; and

(B) adequate training in the use of the transaction scan device.

(Enacted by Acts 2005, 79th Leg., ch. 391 (S.B. 1465), § 1, effective September 1, 2005.)

## Sec. 161.083. Sale of Cigarettes or Tobacco Products to Persons Younger Than 27 Years of Age.

(a) Pursuant to federal regulation under 21 C.F.R. Section 897.14(b), a person may not sell, give, or cause to be sold or given a cigarette or tobacco product to someone who is younger than 27 years of age unless the person to whom the cigarette or tobacco product was sold or given presents an apparently valid proof of identification.

(b) A retailer shall adequately supervise and train the retailer's agents and employees to prevent a violation of Subsection (a).

(c) A proof of identification described by Section 161.082(e) satisfies the requirements of Subsection (a).

(d) Notwithstanding any other provision of law, a violation of this section is not a violation of this subchapter for purposes of Section 154.1142 or 155.0592, Tax Code.

(Enacted by Acts 1997, 75th Leg., ch. 671 (S.B. 55), § 1.01, effective January 1, 1998.)

## Sec. 161.084. Warning Notice.

(a) Each person who sells cigarettes or tobacco products at retail or by vending machine shall post a sign in a location that is conspicuous to all employees and customers and that is close to the place at which the cigarettes or tobacco products may be purchased.

(b) The sign must include the statement:

PURCHASING OR ATTEMPTING TO PURCHASE TOBACCO PRODUCTS BY A MINOR UNDER 18 YEARS OF AGE IS PROHIBITED BY LAW. SALE OR PROVISION OF TOBACCO PRODUCTS TO A MINOR UNDER 18 YEARS OF AGE IS PROHIBITED BY LAW. UPON CONVICTION, A CLASS C MISDEMEANOR, INCLUDING A FINE OF UP TO $500, MAY BE IMPOSED. VIOLATIONS MAY BE REPORTED TO THE TEXAS COMPTROLLER'S OFFICE BY CALLING (insert toll-free telephone number). PREGNANT WOMEN SHOULD NOT SMOKE. SMOKERS ARE MORE LIKELY TO HAVE BABIES WHO ARE BORN PREMATURE OR WITH LOW BIRTH WEIGHT.

(c) The comptroller by rule shall determine the design and size of the sign.

(d) The comptroller on request shall provide the sign without charge to any person who sells cigarettes or tobacco products. The comptroller may provide the sign without charge to distributors of cigarettes or tobacco products or wholesale dealers of cigarettes or tobacco products in this state for distribution to persons who sell cigarettes or tobacco products. A distributor or wholesale dealer may not charge for distributing a sign under this subsection.

(e) A person commits an offense if the person fails to display a sign as prescribed by this section. An offense under this subsection is a Class C misdemeanor.

(f) The comptroller may accept gifts or grants from any public or private source to perform the comptroller's duties under this section.

(Enacted by Acts 1991, 72nd Leg., ch. 14 (S.B. 404), § 50, effective September 1, 1991; am. Acts

Health

1997, 75th Leg., ch. 671 (S.B. 55), § 1.01, effective September 1, 1997 (renumbered from Sec. 161.082); am. Acts 2001, 77th Leg., ch. 1141 (H.B. 2767), § 1, effective September 1, 2001; am. Acts 2007, 80th Leg., ch. 62 (S.B. 91), § 1, effective September 1, 2007; am. Acts 2007, 80th Leg., ch. 488 (S.B. 143), § 2, effective September 1, 2007.)

### Sec. 161.085.  Notification of Employees and Agents.

(a) Each retailer shall notify each individual employed by that retailer who is to be engaged in retail sales of cigarettes or tobacco products that state law:

(1) prohibits the sale or distribution of cigarettes or tobacco products to any person who is younger than 18 years of age as provided by Section 161.082 and that a violation of that section is a Class C misdemeanor; and

(2) requires each person who sells cigarettes or tobacco products at retail or by vending machine to post a warning notice as provided by Section 161.084, requires each employee to ensure that the appropriate sign is always properly displayed while that employee is exercising the employee's duties, and provides that a violation of Section 161.084 is a Class C misdemeanor.

(b) The notice required by Subsection (a) must be provided within 72 hours of the date an individual begins to engage in retail sales of tobacco products. The individual shall signify that the individual has received the notice required by Subsection (a) by signing a form stating that the law has been fully explained, that the individual understands the law, and that the individual, as a condition of employment, agrees to comply with the law.

(c) Each form signed by an individual under this section shall indicate the date of the signature and the current address and social security number of the individual. The retailer shall retain the form signed by each individual employed as a retail sales clerk until the 60th day after the date the individual has left the employer's employ.

(d) A retailer required by this section to notify employees commits an offense if the retailer fails, on demand of a peace officer or an agent of the comptroller, to provide the forms prescribed by this section. An offense under this section is a Class C misdemeanor.

(e) It is a defense to prosecution under Subsection (d) to show proof that the employee did

complete, sign, and date the forms required by Subsections (b) and (c). Proof must be shown to the comptroller or an agent of the comptroller not later than the seventh day after the date of a demand under Subsection (d).

(Enacted by Acts 1997, 75th Leg., ch. 671 (S.B. 55), § 1.01, effective January 1, 1998; am. Acts 2001, 77th Leg., ch. 1141 (H.B. 2767), § 2, effective September 1, 2001.)

### Sec. 161.086.  Vendor Assisted Sales Required; Vending Machines.

(a) Except as provided by Subsection (b), a retailer or other person may not:

(1) offer cigarettes or tobacco products for sale in a manner that permits a customer direct access to the cigarettes or tobacco products; or

(2) install or maintain a vending machine containing cigarettes or tobacco products.

(b) Subsection (a) does not apply to:

(1) a facility or business that is not open to persons younger than 18 years of age at any time;

(2) that part of a facility or business that is a humidor or other enclosure designed to store cigars in a climate-controlled environment; or

(3) a premises for which a person holds a package store permit issued under the Alcoholic Beverage Code.

(c) The comptroller or a peace officer may, with or without a warrant, seize, seal, or disable a vending machine installed or maintained in violation of this section. Property seized under this subsection must be seized in accordance with, and is subject to forfeiture to the state in accordance with, Subchapter H, Chapter 154, Tax Code, and Subchapter E, Chapter 155, Tax Code.

(d) A person commits an offense if the person violates Subsection (a). An offense under this subsection is a Class C misdemeanor.

(Enacted by Acts 1997, 75th Leg., ch. 671 (S.B. 55), § 1.01, effective January 1, 1998; am. Acts 1999, 76th Leg., ch. 567 (S.B. 451), § 1, effective September 1, 1999.)

### Sec. 161.087.  Distribution of Cigarettes or Tobacco Products.

(a) A person may not distribute to persons younger than 18 years of age:

(1) a free sample of a cigarette or tobacco product; or

(2) a coupon or other item that the recipient may use to receive a free or discounted cigarette or tobacco product or a sample cigarette or tobacco product.

(b) Except as provided by Subsection (c), a permit holder may not accept or redeem, offer to accept or redeem, or hire a person to accept or redeem a coupon or other item that the recipient may use to receive a free or discounted cigarette or tobacco product or a sample cigarette or to-bacco product if the recipient is younger than 18 years of age. A coupon or other item that such a recipient may use to receive a free or discounted cigarette or tobacco product or a sample cigarette or tobacco product may not be redeemable through mail or courier delivery.

(c) Subsections (a)(2) and (b) do not apply to a transaction between permit holders unless the transaction is a retail sale.

(d) A person commits an offense if the person violates this section. An offense under this sub-section is a Class C misdemeanor.

(Enacted by Acts 1997, 75th Leg., ch. 671 (S.B. 55), § 1.01, effective September 1, 1997.)

## Sec. 161.088. Enforcement; Unan-nounced Inspections.

(a) The comptroller shall enforce this subchap-ter in partnership with local law enforcement agencies and with their cooperation and shall ensure the state's compliance with Section 1926 of the federal Public Health Service Act (42 U.S.C. Section 300x-26) and any implementing regulations adopted by the United States Depart-ment of Health and Human Services. Except as expressly authorized by law, the comptroller may not adopt any rules governing the subject matter of this subchapter or Subchapter K, N, or O.

(b) The comptroller may make block grants to counties and municipalities to be used by local law enforcement agencies to enforce this sub-chapter in a manner that can reasonably be expected to reduce the extent to which cigarettes and tobacco products are sold or distributed to persons who are younger than 18 years of age. At least annually, random unannounced inspections shall be conducted at various locations where cigarettes and tobacco products are sold or dis-tributed to ensure compliance with this subchap-ter. The comptroller shall rely, to the fullest extent possible, on local law enforcement agen-cies to enforce this subchapter.

(c) To facilitate the effective administration and enforcement of this subchapter, the comptrol-ler may enter into interagency contracts with other state agencies, and those agencies may assist the comptroller in the administration and enforcement of this subchapter.

(d) The use of a person younger than 18 years of age to act as a minor decoy to test compliance with this subchapter shall be conducted in a fashion that promotes fairness. A person may be enlisted by the comptroller or a local law enforce-ment agency to act as a minor decoy only if the following requirements are met:

(1) written parental consent is obtained for the use of a person younger than 18 years of age to act as a minor decoy to test compliance with this subchapter;

(2) at the time of the inspection, the minor decoy is younger than 17 years of age;

(3) the minor decoy has an appearance that would cause a reasonably prudent seller of cigarettes or tobacco products to request iden-tification and proof of age;

(4) the minor decoy carries either the mi-nor's own identification showing the minor's correct date of birth or carries no identification, and a minor decoy who carries identification presents it on request to any seller of cigarettes or tobacco products; and

(5) the minor decoy answers truthfully any questions about the minor's age.

(e) The comptroller shall annually prepare for submission by the governor to the secretary of the United States Department of Health and Human Services the report required by Section 1926 of the federal Public Health Service Act (42 U.S.C. Section 300x-26).

(Enacted by Acts 1997, 75th Leg., ch. 671 (S.B. 55), § 1.01, effective September 1, 1997; am. Acts 1999, 76th Leg., ch. 1156 (S.B. 16), § 1, effective September 1, 1999.)

## Sec. 161.089. Preemption of Local Law.

This subchapter does not preempt a local reg-ulation of the sale, distribution, or use of ciga-rettes or tobacco products or affect the authority of a political subdivision to adopt or enforce an ordinance or requirement relating to the sale, distribution, or use of cigarettes or tobacco prod-ucts if the regulation, ordinance, or requirement:

(1) is compatible with and equal to or more stringent than a requirement prescribed by this subchapter; or

(2) relates to an issue that is not specifically addressed by this subchapter or Chapter 154 or 155, Tax Code.

(Enacted by Acts 1997, 75th Leg., ch. 671 (S.B. 55), § 1.01, effective September 1, 1997.)

Health

## Sec. 161.090.   Reports of Violation.

A local or state law enforcement agency or other governmental unit shall notify the comptroller, on the 10th day of each month, or the first working day after that date, of any violation of this subchapter that occurred in the preceding month that the agency or unit detects, investigates, or prosecutes.

(Enacted by Acts 1997, 75th Leg., ch. 671 (S.B. 55), § 1.01, effective September 1, 1997.)

## Sec. 161.0901.   Report of Office of Smoking and Health.

(a) Not later than January 5th of each odd-numbered year the Office of Smoking and Health of the department shall report to the governor, lieutenant governor, and the speaker of the house of representatives on the status of smoking and the use of tobacco and tobacco products in this state.

(b) The report must include, at a minimum:

(1) a baseline of statistics and analysis regarding retail compliance with this subchapter, Subchapter K, and Chapters 154 and 155, Tax Code;

(2) a baseline of statistics and analysis regarding illegal tobacco sales, including:

(A) sales to minors;

(B) enforcement actions concerning minors; and

(C) sources of citations;

(3) tobacco controls and initiatives by the Office of Smoking and Health of the department, or any other state agency, including an evaluation of the effectiveness of the controls and initiatives;

(4) the future goals and plans of the Office of Smoking and Health of the department to decrease the use of tobacco and tobacco products;

(5) the educational programs of the Office of Smoking and Health of the department and the effectiveness of those programs; and

(6) the incidence of use of tobacco and tobacco products by regions in this state, including use of cigarettes and tobacco products by ethnicity.

(Enacted by Acts 1997, 75th Leg., ch. 671 (S.B. 55), § 1.01, effective September 1, 1997.)

## SUBCHAPTER N
## TOBACCO USE BY MINORS

## Sec. 161.251.   Definitions.

In this subchapter:

(1) "Cigarette" has the meaning assigned by Section 154.001, Tax Code.

(2) "Tobacco product" has the meaning assigned by Section 155.001, Tax Code.

(Enacted by Acts 1997, 75th Leg., ch. 671 (S.B. 55), § 3.01, effective January 1, 1998.)

## Sec. 161.252.   Possession, Purchase, Consumption, or Receipt of Cigarettes or Tobacco Products by Minors Prohibited.

(a) An individual who is younger than 18 years of age commits an offense if the individual:

(1) possesses, purchases, consumes, or accepts a cigarette or tobacco product; or

(2) falsely represents himself or herself to be 18 years of age or older by displaying proof of age that is false, fraudulent, or not actually proof of the individual's own age in order to obtain possession of, purchase, or receive a cigarette or tobacco product.

(b) It is an exception to the application of this section that the individual younger than 18 years of age possessed the cigarette or tobacco product in the presence of:

(1) an adult parent, a guardian, or a spouse of the individual; or

(2) an employer of the individual, if possession or receipt of the tobacco product is required in the performance of the employee's duties as an employee.

(c) It is an exception to the application of this section that the individual younger than 18 years of age is participating in an inspection or test of compliance in accordance with Section 161.088.

(d) An offense under this section is punishable by a fine not to exceed $250.

(Enacted by Acts 1997, 75th Leg., ch. 671 (S.B. 55), § 3.01, effective January 1, 1998.)

## Sec. 161.253.   Tobacco Awareness Program; Community Service.

(a) On conviction of an individual for an offense under Section 161.252, the court shall suspend execution of sentence and shall require the defendant to attend a tobacco awareness program approved by the commissioner. The court may require the parent or guardian of the defendant to attend the tobacco awareness program with the defendant.

(b) On request, a tobacco awareness program may be taught in languages other than English.

(c) If the defendant resides in a rural area of this state or another area of this state in which access to a tobacco awareness program is not readily available, the court shall require the defendant to perform eight to 12 hours of tobacco-related community service instead of attending the tobacco awareness program.

(d) The tobacco awareness program and the tobacco-related community service are remedial and are not punishment.

(e) Not later than the 90th day after the date of a conviction under Section 161.252, the defendant shall present to the court, in the manner required by the court, evidence of satisfactory completion of the tobacco awareness program or the tobacco-related community service.

(f) On receipt of the evidence required under Subsection (e), the court shall:

(1) if the defendant has been previously convicted of an offense under Section 161.252, execute the sentence, and at the discretion of the court, reduce the fine imposed to not less than half the fine previously imposed by the court; or

(2) if the defendant has not been previously convicted of an offense under Section 161.252, discharge the defendant and dismiss the complaint or information against the defendant.

(g) If the court discharges the defendant under Subsection (f)(2), the defendant is released from all penalties and disabilities resulting from the offense except that the defendant is considered to have been convicted of the offense if the defendant is subsequently convicted of an offense under Section 161.252 committed after the dismissal under Subsection (f)(2).

(Enacted by Acts 1997, 75th Leg., ch. 671 (S.B. 55), § 3.01, effective January 1, 1998.)

## Sec. 161.254. Driver's License Suspension or Denial.

(a) If the defendant does not provide the evidence required under Section 161.253(e) within the period specified by that subsection, the court shall order the Department of Public Safety to suspend or deny issuance of any driver's license or permit to the defendant. The order must specify the period of the suspension or denial, which may not exceed 180 days after the date of the order.

(b) The Department of Public Safety shall send to the defendant notice of court action under

Subsection (a) by first class mail. The notice must include the date of the order and the reason for the order and must specify the period of the suspension or denial.

(Enacted by Acts 1997, 75th Leg., ch. 671 (S.B. 55), § 3.01, effective January 1, 1997; am. Acts 1999, 76th Leg., ch. 1409 (H.B. 2031), § 8, effective September 1, 1999.)

## Sec. 161.255. Expungement of Conviction.

(a) An individual convicted of an offense under Section 161.252 may apply to the court to have the conviction expunged. If the court finds that the individual satisfactorily completed the tobacco awareness program or tobacco-related community service ordered by the court, the court shall order the conviction and any complaint, verdict, sentence, or other document relating to the offense to be expunged from the individual's record and the conviction may not be shown or made known for any purpose.

(b) The court shall charge an applicant a fee in the amount of $30 for each application for expungement filed under this section to defray the cost of notifying state agencies of orders of expungement under this section.

(Enacted by Acts 1997, 75th Leg., ch. 671 (S.B. 55), § 3.01, effective January 1, 1998; am. Acts 2005, 79th Leg., ch. 886 (S.B. 1426), § 5, effective September 1, 2005.)

## Sec. 161.256. Jurisdiction of Courts.

A justice court or municipal court may exercise jurisdiction over any matter in which a court under this subchapter may:

(1) impose a requirement that a defendant attend a tobacco awareness program or perform tobacco-related community service; or

(2) order the suspension or denial of a driver's license or permit.

(Enacted by Acts 1997, 75th Leg., ch. 671 (S.B. 55), § 3.01, effective January 1, 1998.)

## Sec. 161.257. Application of Other Law.

Title 3, Family Code, does not apply to a proceeding under this subchapter.

(Enacted by Acts 1997, 75th Leg., ch. 671 (S.B. 55), § 3.01, effective January 1, 1998.)

# CHAPTER 166
## ADVANCE DIRECTIVES

### SUBCHAPTER B
### DIRECTIVE TO PHYSICIANS

## Sec. 166.048.   Criminal Penalty; Prosecution.

(a) A person commits an offense if the person intentionally conceals, cancels, defaces, obliterates, or damages another person's directive without that person's consent. An offense under this subsection is a Class A misdemeanor.

(b) A person is subject to prosecution for criminal homicide under Chapter 19, Penal Code, if the person, with the intent to cause life-sustaining treatment to be withheld or withdrawn from another person contrary to the other person's desires, falsifies or forges a directive or intentionally conceals or withholds personal knowledge of a revocation and thereby directly causes life-sustaining treatment to be withheld or withdrawn from the other person with the result that the other person's death is hastened.

(Acts 1989, 71st Leg. ch. 678 (H.B. 2136), § 1, effective September 1, 1989; am. Acts 1999, 76th Leg., ch. 450 (S.B. 1260), § 1.03, effective September 1, 1999 (renumbered from Sec. 672.018).)

# CHAPTER 167
## FEMALE GENITAL MUTILATION

## Sec. 167.001.   Female Genital Mutilation Prohibited.

(a) A person commits an offense if the person knowingly circumcises, excises, or infibulates any part of the labia majora or labia minora or clitoris of another person who is younger than 18 years of age.

(b) An offense under this section is a state jail felony.

(c) It is a defense to prosecution under Subsection (a) that:

(1) the person performing the act is a physician or other licensed health care professional and the act is within the scope of the person's license; and

(2) the act is performed for medical purposes.

(Enacted by Acts 1999, 76th Leg., ch. 642 (H.B. 91), § 1, effective August 30, 1999; am. Acts 2001, 77th Leg., ch. 1420 (H.B. 2812), § 21.001(75), effective September 1, 2001 (renumbered from Sec. 166.001).)

# CHAPTER 169
## FIRST OFFENDER PROSTITUTION PREVENTION PROGRAM

Section

## Sec. 169.001.   First Offender Prostitution Prevention Program; Procedures for Certain Defendants.

(a) In this chapter, "first offender prostitution prevention program" means a program that has the following essential characteristics:

(1) the integration of services in the processing of cases in the judicial system;

(2) the use of a nonadversarial approach involving prosecutors and defense attorneys to promote public safety, to reduce the demand for the commercial sex trade and trafficking of persons by educating offenders, and to protect the due process rights of program participants;

(3) early identification and prompt placement of eligible participants in the program;

(4) access to information, counseling, and services relating to sex addiction, sexually transmitted diseases, mental health, and substance abuse;

(5) a coordinated strategy to govern program responses to participant compliance;

(6) monitoring and evaluation of program goals and effectiveness;

(7) continuing interdisciplinary education to promote effective program planning, implementation, and operations; and

(8) development of partnerships with public agencies and community organizations.

(b) If a defendant successfully completes a first offender prostitution prevention program, regardless of whether the defendant was convicted of the offense for which the defendant entered the program or whether the court deferred further proceedings without entering an adjudication of guilt, after notice to the state and a hearing on whether the defendant is otherwise entitled to the petition, including whether the required time period has elapsed, and whether issuance of the order is in the best interest of justice, the court shall enter an order of nondisclosure under Section 411.081, Government Code, as if the defen-

Health

dant had received a discharge and dismissal under Section 5(c), Article 42.12, Code of Criminal Procedure, with respect to all records and files related to the defendant's arrest for the offense for which the defendant entered the program if the defendant:

(1) has not been previously convicted of a felony offense; and

(2) is not convicted of any other felony offense before the second anniversary of the defendant's successful completion of the program.

(Enacted by Acts 2011, 82nd Leg., ch. 1289 (H.B. 1994), § 1, effective June 17, 2011.)

### Sec. 169.002. Authority to Establish Program; Eligibility.

(a) The commissioners court of a county or governing body of a municipality may establish a first offender prostitution prevention program for defendants charged with an offense under Section 43.02(a)(2), Penal Code, in which the defendant offered or agreed to hire a person to engage in sexual conduct.

(b) A defendant is eligible to participate in a first offender prostitution prevention program established under this chapter only if:

(1) the attorney representing the state consents to the defendant's participation in the program; and

(2) the court in which the criminal case is pending finds that the defendant has not been previously convicted of:

(A) an offense under Section 20A.02, 43.02, 43.03, 43.04, or 43.05, Penal Code;

(B) an offense listed in Section 3g(a)(1), Article 42.12, Code of Criminal Procedure; or

(C) an offense punishable as a felony under Chapter 481.

(c) For purposes of Subsection (b), a defendant has been previously convicted of an offense listed in that subsection if:

(1) the defendant was adjudged guilty of the offense or entered a plea of guilty or nolo contendere in return for a grant of deferred adjudication, regardless of whether the sentence for the offense was ever imposed or whether the sentence was probated and the defendant was subsequently discharged from community supervision; or

(2) the defendant was convicted under the laws of another state for an offense containing

elements that are substantially similar to the elements of an offense listed in Subsection (b).

(d) A defendant is not eligible to participate in the first offender prostitution prevention program if the defendant offered or agreed to hire a person to engage in sexual conduct and the person was younger than 18 years of age at the time of the offense.

(e) The court in which the criminal case is pending shall allow an eligible defendant to choose whether to participate in the first offender prostitution prevention program or otherwise proceed through the criminal justice system.

(f) If a defendant who chooses to participate in the first offender prostitution prevention program fails to attend any portion of the program, the court in which the defendant's criminal case is pending shall issue a warrant for the defendant's arrest and proceed on the criminal case as if the defendant had chosen not to participate in the program.

(Enacted by Acts 2011, 82nd Leg., ch. 1289 (H.B. 1994), § 1, effective June 17, 2011.)

### Sec. 169.003. Program Powers and Duties.

(a) A first offender prostitution prevention program established under this chapter must:

(1) ensure that a person eligible for the program is provided legal counsel before volunteering to proceed through the program and while participating in the program;

(2) allow any participant to withdraw from the program at any time before a trial on the merits has been initiated;

(3) provide each participant with information, counseling, and services relating to sex addiction, sexually transmitted diseases, mental health, and substance abuse; and

(4) provide each participant with classroom instruction related to the prevention of prostitution.

(b) To provide each program participant with information, counseling, and services described by Subsection (a)(3), a program established under this chapter may employ a person or solicit a volunteer who is:

(1) a health care professional;

(2) a psychologist;

(3) a licensed social worker or counselor;

(4) a former prostitute;

(5) a family member of a person arrested for soliciting prostitution;

**Health**

(6) a member of a neighborhood association or community that is adversely affected by the commercial sex trade or trafficking of persons; or

(7) an employee of a nongovernmental organization specializing in advocacy or laws related to sex trafficking or human trafficking or in providing services to victims of those offenses.

(c) A program established under this chapter shall establish and publish local procedures to promote maximum participation of eligible defendants in programs established in the county or municipality in which the defendants reside.

(Enacted by Acts 2011, 82nd Leg., ch. 1289 (H.B. 1994), § 1, effective June 17, 2011.)

### Sec. 169.004.  Oversight.

(a) The lieutenant governor and the speaker of the house of representatives may assign to appropriate legislative committees duties relating to the oversight of first offender prostitution prevention programs established under this chapter.

(b) A legislative committee or the governor may request the state auditor to perform a management, operations, or financial or accounting audit of a first offender prostitution prevention program established under this chapter.

(c) A first offender prostitution prevention program established under this chapter shall:

(1) notify the criminal justice division of the governor's office before or on implementation of the program; and

(2) provide information regarding the performance of the program to the division on request.

(Enacted by Acts 2011, 82nd Leg., ch. 1289 (H.B. 1994), § 1, effective June 17, 2011.)

### Sec. 169.005.  Fees.

(a) A first offender prostitution prevention program established under this chapter may collect from a participant in the program a nonrefundable program fee in a reasonable amount not to exceed $1,000, from which the following must be paid:

(1) a counseling and services fee in an amount necessary to cover the costs of the counseling and services provided by the program;

(2) a victim services fee in an amount equal to 10 percent of the amount paid under Subdivision (1), to be deposited to the credit of the general revenue fund to be appropriated only to cover costs associated with the grant program described by Section 531.383, Government Code; and

(3) a law enforcement training fee, in an amount equal to five percent of the total amount paid under Subdivision (1), to be deposited to the credit of the treasury of the county or municipality that established the program to cover costs associated with the provision of training to law enforcement personnel on domestic violence, prostitution, and the trafficking of persons.

(b) Fees collected under this section may be paid on a periodic basis or on a deferred payment schedule at the discretion of the judge, magistrate, or program director administering the first offender prostitution prevention program. The fees must be based on the participant's ability to pay.

(Enacted by Acts 2011, 82nd Leg., ch. 1289 (H.B. 1994), § 1, effective June 17, 2011.)

### Sec. 169.006.  Suspension or Dismissal of Community Service Requirement.

(a) To encourage participation in a first offender prostitution prevention program established under this chapter, the judge or magistrate administering the program may suspend any requirement that, as a condition of community supervision, a participant in the program work a specified number of hours at a community service project.

(b) On a participant's successful completion of a first offender prostitution prevention program, a judge or magistrate may excuse the participant from any condition of community supervision previously suspended under Subsection (a).

(Enacted by Acts 2011, 82nd Leg., ch. 1289 (H.B. 1994), § 1, effective June 17, 2011.)

Health

# TITLE 3
# VITAL STATISTICS

## CHAPTER 192
## BIRTH RECORDS

### SUBCHAPTER A
### GENERAL REGISTRATION PROVISIONS

**Sec. 192.0021. Heirloom Birth Certificate.**

(a) The department shall promote and sell copies of an heirloom birth certificate. The department shall solicit donated designs for the certificate from Texas artists and select the best donated designs for the form of the certificate. An heirloom birth certificate must contain the same information as, and have the same effect of, a certified copy of another birth record. The department shall prescribe a fee for the issuance of an heirloom birth certificate in an amount that does not exceed $50. The heirloom birth certificate must be printed on high-quality paper with the appearance of parchment not smaller than 11 inches by 14 inches.

(b) The department shall deposit 50 percent of the proceeds from the sale of heirloom birth certificates to the credit of the childhood immunization account and the other 50 percent to the credit of the undedicated portion of the general revenue fund. The childhood immunization account is an account in the general revenue fund. Money in the account may be used only by the Department of State Health Services for:

(1) making grants to fund childhood immunizations and related education programs; and

(2) administering this section.

(c) The department may sell an heirloom birth certificate only for an individual born in this state.

(Enacted by Acts 1993, 73rd Leg., ch. 941 (H.B. 1641), § 1, effective August 30, 1993; am. Acts 2005, 79th Leg., ch. 1265 (H.B. 2101), § 1, effective September 1, 2005.)

# TITLE 5
# SANITATION AND ENVIRONMENTAL QUALITY

### SUBTITLE B
### SOLID WASTE, TOXIC CHEMICALS, SEWAGE, LITTER, AND WATER

## CHAPTER 365
## LITTER

### Subchapter A. General Provisions

### SUBCHAPTER A
### GENERAL PROVISIONS

**Sec. 365.001. Short Title.**

This chapter may be cited as the Texas Litter Abatement Act.

Health

(Enacted by Acts 1989, 71st Leg., ch. 678 (H.B. 2136), § 1, effective September 1, 1989.)

### Sec. 365.002.  Water Pollution Controlled by Water Code.

The pollution of water in the state is controlled by Chapter 26, Water Code, and other applicable law.

(Enacted by Acts 1989, 71st Leg., ch. 678 (H.B. 2136), § 1, effective September 1, 1989.)

### Sec. 365.003.  Litter on Beaches Controlled by Natural Resources Code.

The regulation of litter on public beaches is controlled by Subchapters C and D, Chapter 61, Natural Resources Code.

(Enacted by Acts 1989, 71st Leg., ch. 678 (H.B. 2136), § 1, effective September 1, 1989.)

### Sec. 365.004.  Disposal of Garbage, Refuse, and Sewage in Certain Areas Under Control of Parks and Wildlife Department.

The Parks and Wildlife Commission may adopt rules to govern the disposal of garbage, refuse, and sewage in state parks, public water in state parks, historic sites, scientific areas, and forts under the control of the Parks and Wildlife Department.

(Enacted by Acts 1989, 71st Leg., ch. 678 (H.B. 2136), § 1, effective September 1, 1989.)

### Sec. 365.005.  Venue and Recovery of Costs.

(a) Venue for the prosecution of a criminal offense under Subchapter B or Section 365.032 or 365.033 or for a suit for injunctive relief under any of those provisions is in the county in which the defendant resides, in the county in which the offense or the violation occurs, or in Travis County.

(b) If the attorney general or a local government brings a suit for injunctive relief under Subchapter B or Section 365.032 or 365.033, a prevailing party may recover its reasonable attorney fees, court costs, and reasonable investigative costs incurred in relation to the proceeding.

## SUBCHAPTER B
## CERTAIN ACTIONS PROHIBITED

### Sec. 365.011.  Definitions.

In this subchapter:

(1) "Approved solid waste site" means:

(A) a solid waste site permitted or registered by the Texas Natural Resource Conservation Commission;

(B) a solid waste site licensed by a county under Chapter 361; or

(C) a designated collection area for ultimate disposal at a permitted or licensed municipal solid waste site.

(2) "Boat" means a vehicle, including a barge, airboat, motorboat, or sailboat, used for transportation on water.

(3) "Commercial purpose" means the purpose of economic gain.

(4) "Commercial vehicle" means a vehicle that is operated by a person for a commercial purpose or that is owned by a business or commercial enterprise.

(5) "Dispose" and "dump" mean to discharge, deposit, inject, spill, leak, or place litter on or into land or water.

(6) "Litter" means:

(A) decayable waste from a public or private establishment, residence, or restaurant, including animal and vegetable waste material from a market or storage facility handling or storing produce or other food products, or the handling, preparation, cooking, or consumption of food, but not including sewage, body wastes, or industrial by-products; or

(B) nondecayable solid waste, except ashes, that consists of:

(i) combustible waste material, including paper, rags, cartons, wood, excelsior, furniture, rubber, plastics, yard trimmings, leaves, or similar materials;

(ii) noncombustible waste material, including glass, crockery, tin or aluminum cans, metal furniture, and similar materials that do not burn at ordinary incinerator temperatures of 1800 degrees Fahrenheit or less; and

(iii) discarded or worn-out manufactured materials and machinery, including motor vehicles and parts of motor vehicles, tires, aircraft, farm implements, building or construction materials, appliances, and scrap metal.

(7) "Motor vehicle" has the meaning assigned by Section 541.201, Transportation Code.

(8) "Public highway" means the entire width between property lines of a road, street, way, thoroughfare, bridge, public beach, or park in this state, not privately owned or controlled, if

any part of the road, street, way, thoroughfare, bridge, public beach, or park:

    (A) is opened to the public for vehicular traffic;

    (B) is used as a public recreational area; or

    (C) is under the state's legislative jurisdiction through its police power.

    (9) "Solid waste" has the meaning assigned by Section 361.003.

(Enacted by Acts 1991, 72nd Leg., 1st C.S., ch. 3 (S.B. 2), § 8.161, effective September 1, 1991; am. Acts 1993, 73rd Leg., ch. 740 (H.B. 1951), § 1, effective September 1, 1993; am. Acts 1995, 74th Leg., ch. 76 (S.B. 959), § 11.111, effective September 1, 1995; am. Acts 1997, 75th Leg., ch. 165 (S.B. 898), § 30.206, effective September 1, 1997; am. Acts 1997, 75th Leg., ch. 286 (H.B. 717), § 1, effective May 26, 1997.)

## Sec. 365.012. Illegal Dumping; Discarding Lighted Materials; Criminal Penalties.

(a) A person commits an offense if the person disposes or allows or permits the disposal of litter or other solid waste at a place that is not an approved solid waste site, including a place on or within 300 feet of a public highway, on a right-of-way, on other public or private property, or into inland or coastal water of the state.

(a-1) A person commits an offense if:

    (1) the person discards lighted litter, including a match, cigarette, or cigar, onto open-space land, a private road or the right-of-way of a private road, a public highway or other public road or the right-of-way of a public highway or other public road, or a railroad right-of-way; and

    (2) a fire is ignited as a result of the conduct described by Subdivision (1).

(b) A person commits an offense if the person receives litter or other solid waste for disposal at a place that is not an approved solid waste site, regardless of whether the litter or other solid waste or the land on which the litter or other solid waste is disposed is owned or controlled by the person.

(c) A person commits an offense if the person transports litter or other solid waste to a place that is not an approved solid waste site for disposal at the site.

(d) An offense under Subsection (a), (b), or (c) is a Class C misdemeanor if the litter or other solid waste to which the offense applies weighs five pounds or less or has a volume of five gallons or less.

(d-1) An offense under Subsection (a-1) is a misdemeanor under this subsection if the litter or other solid waste to which the offense applies weighs less than 500 pounds or has a volume of less than 100 cubic feet and is punishable by:

    (1) a fine not to exceed $500;

    (2) confinement in jail for a term not to exceed 30 days; or

    (3) both such fine and confinement.

(e) An offense under Subsection (a), (b), or (c) is a Class B misdemeanor if the litter or other solid waste to which the offense applies weighs more than five pounds but less than 500 pounds or has a volume of more than five gallons but less than 100 cubic feet.

(f) An offense under this section is a Class A misdemeanor if:

    (1) the litter or other solid waste to which the offense applies weighs 500 pounds or more but less than 1,000 pounds or has a volume of 100 cubic feet or more but less than 200 cubic feet; or

    (2) the litter or other solid waste is disposed for a commercial purpose and weighs more than five pounds but less than 200 pounds or has a volume of more than five gallons but less than 200 cubic feet.

(g) An offense under this section is a state jail felony if the litter or solid waste to which the offense applies:

    (1) weighs 1,000 pounds or more or has a volume of 200 cubic feet or more;

    (2) is disposed of for a commercial purpose and weighs 200 pounds or more or has a volume of 200 cubic feet or more; or

    (3) is contained in a closed barrel or drum.

(h) If it is shown on the trial of the defendant for an offense under this section that the defendant has previously been convicted of an offense under this section, the punishment for the offense is increased to the punishment for the next highest category.

(i) On conviction for an offense under this section, the court shall provide to the defendant written notice that a subsequent conviction for an offense under this section may result in the forfeiture under Chapter 59, Code of Criminal Procedure, of the vehicle used by the defendant in committing the offense.

(j) The offenses prescribed by this section include the unauthorized disposal of litter or other solid waste in a dumpster or similar receptacle.

(k) This section does not apply to the temporary storage for future disposal of litter or other solid waste by a person on land owned by that person, or by that person's agent. The commission by rule shall regulate temporary storage for future disposal of litter or other solid waste by a person on land owned by the person or the person's agent.

(*l*) This section does not apply to an individual's disposal of litter or other solid waste if:

(1) the litter or waste is generated on land the individual owns;

(2) the litter or waste is not generated as a result of an activity related to a commercial purpose;

(3) the disposal occurs on land the individual owns; and

(4) the disposal is not for a commercial purpose.

(m) A municipality or county may offer a reward of $50 for reporting a violation of this section that results in a prosecution under this section.

(n) An offense under this section may be prosecuted without alleging or proving any culpable mental state, unless the offense is a state jail felony.

(o) For purposes of a prosecution under Subsection (g), a generator creates a rebuttable presumption of lack of culpable mental state if the generator of the solid waste to be disposed of secures, prior to the hauler's receipt of the solid waste, a signed statement from the hauler that the solid waste will be disposed of legally. The statement shall include the hauler's valid Texas driver's license number.

(p) It is an affirmative defense to prosecution under Subsection (a-1) that the person discarded the lighted litter in connection with controlled burning the person was conducting in the area into which the lighted litter was discarded.

(q) The operator of a public conveyance in which smoking tobacco is allowed shall post a sign stating the substance of Subsections (a-1) and (d-1) in a conspicuous place within any portion of the public conveyance in which smoking is allowed.

(r) If conduct that constitutes an offense under Subsection (a-1) also constitutes an offense under Subsection (a), the actor may be prosecuted only under Subsection (a-1). If conduct that constitutes an offense under Subsection (a-1) also constitutes an offense under Chapter 28, Penal Code, the actor may be prosecuted under Subsection (a-1) or Chapter 28, Penal Code, but not both.

(Enacted by Acts 1991, 72nd Leg., 1st C.S., ch. 3 (S.B. 2), § 8.161, effective September 1, 1991; am. Acts 1993, 73rd Leg., ch. 740 (H.B. 1951), § 2,

effective September 1, 1993; am. Acts 1993, 73rd Leg., ch. 828 (S.B. 1285), § 3, effective September 1, 1993; am. Acts 1995, 74th Leg., ch. 76 (S.B. 959), § 17.01(28), effective September 1, 1995; am. Acts 1997, 75th Leg., ch. 286 (H.B. 717), § 2, effective May 26, 1997; am. Acts 2001, 77th Leg., ch. 995 (H.B. 631), § 1, effective September 1, 2001; am. Acts 2011, 82nd Leg., ch. 430 (S.B. 1043), §§ 1, 2, effective September 1, 2011.)

## Sec. 365.013.  Rules and Standards; Criminal Penalty.

(a) The Texas Natural Resource Conservation Commission shall adopt rules and standards regarding processing and treating litter disposed in violation of this subchapter.

(b) A person commits an offense if the person violates a rule adopted under this section.

(c) An offense under this section is a Class A misdemeanor.

(Enacted by Acts 1991, 72nd Leg., 1st C.S., ch. 3 (S.B. 2), § 8.161, effective September 1, 1991; am. Acts 1995, 74th Leg., ch. 76 (S.B. 959), § 11.112, effective September 1, 1995.)

## Sec. 365.014.  Application of Subchapter; Defenses; Presumptions.

(a) This subchapter does not apply to farmers:

(1) in handling anything necessary to grow, handle, and care for livestock; or

(2) in erecting, operating, and maintaining improvements necessary to handle, thresh, and prepare agricultural products or for conservation projects.

(b) A person who dumps more than five pounds or 13 gallons of litter or other solid waste from a commercial vehicle in violation of this subchapter is presumed to be dumping the litter or other solid waste for a commercial purpose.

(c) It is an affirmative defense to prosecution under Section 365.012 that:

(1) the storage, processing, or disposal took place on land owned or leased by the defendant;

(2) the defendant received the litter or other solid waste from another person;

(3) the defendant, after exercising due diligence, did not know and reasonably could not have known that litter or other solid waste was involved; and

(4) the defendant did not receive, directly or indirectly, compensation for the receipt, storage, processing, or treatment.

(Enacted by Acts 1991, 72nd Leg., 1st C.S., ch. 3 (S.B. 2), § 8.161, effective September 1, 1991; am.

Acts 1993, 73rd Leg., ch. 740 (H.B. 1951), § 3, effective September 1, 1993.)

### Sec. 365.015. Injunction; Venue; Recovery of Costs.

(a) A district attorney, a county attorney, or the attorney general may bring a civil suit for an injunction to prevent or restrain a violation of this subchapter. A person affected or to be affected by a violation is entitled to seek injunctive relief to enjoin the violation.

(b) Venue for a prosecution of a criminal offense under this subchapter or for a civil suit for injunctive relief under this subchapter is in the county in which the defendant resides, the county in which the offense or violation occurred, or in Travis County.

(c) In a suit for relief under this section, the prevailing party may recover its reasonable attorney fees, court costs, and reasonable investigative costs incurred in relation to the proceeding. (Enacted by Acts 1991, 72nd Leg., 1st C.S., ch. 3 (S.B. 2), § 8.161, effective September 1, 1991.)

### Sec. 365.016. Disposal of Litter in a Cave; Criminal Penalty.

(a) A person commits an offense if the person disposes litter, a dead animal, sewage, or any chemical in a cave.

(b) An offense under this section is a Class C misdemeanor unless:

   (1) it is shown on the trial of the defendant that the defendant previously has been convicted once of an offense under this section, in which event the offense is a Class A misdemeanor; or

   (2) it is shown on the trial of the defendant that the defendant previously has been convicted two or more times of an offense under this section, in which event the offense is a felony of the third degree.

(Enacted by Acts 1991, 72nd Leg., 1st C.S., ch. 3 (S.B. 2), § 8.161, effective September 1, 1991.)

### Sec. 365.017. Regulation of Litter in Certain Counties.

(a) The commissioners court of a county may adopt regulations to control the disposal of litter and the removal of illegally dumped litter from private property in unincorporated areas of that county. The commissioners court may not adopt regulations under this section concerning the disposal of recyclable materials as defined in Chapter 361 of the Health and Safety Code.

(b) Prior to the adoption of regulations the commissioners court of a county must find that the proposed regulations are necessary to promote the public health, safety, and welfare of the residents of that county.

(c) The definitions of Section 365.011 apply in this Act. "Illegally dumped litter" means litter dumped anywhere other than in an approved solid waste site. "Litter" has the meaning assigned by Section 365.011, except that the term does not include equipment used for agricultural purposes.

(d) The regulations adopted by the commissioners court may require the record property owners to pay for the cost of removal after the commissioners court has given the record property owner 30 days written notice to remove the illegally dumped litter.

(e) Regulations adopted under this section are in addition to any other law regarding this issue and the stricter law shall apply.

(f) In addition to any other remedy provided by law, a district attorney, a county attorney, or the attorney general may bring a civil suit to enjoin violation of regulations adopted under this section and to recover the costs of removal of illegally dumped litter. In such a suit the prevailing party may recover its reasonable attorney fees, court fees, and reasonable investigative costs incurred in relation to that proceeding. (Enacted by Acts 1993, 73rd Leg., ch. 828 (S.B. 1285), § 4, effective September 1, 1993; am. Acts 1995, 74th Leg., ch. 439 (H.B. 160), § 1, effective June 9, 1995.)

## SUBCHAPTER C
## SPECIAL PROVISIONS

### Sec. 365.031. Litter, Garbage, Refuse, and Rubbish in Lake Sabine.

The governing body of Port Arthur by ordinance may prohibit the depositing or placing of litter, garbage, refuse, or rubbish into or on the waters of Lake Sabine within the municipal limits.

(Enacted by Acts 1989, 71st Leg., ch. 678 (H.B. 2136), § 1, effective September 1, 1989.)

### Sec. 365.032. Throwing Certain Substances in or Near Lake Lavon; Criminal Penalty.

(a) The definitions provided by Section 365.011 apply to this section.

(b) A person commits an offense if the person throws, leaves, or causes to be thrown or left

Health

wastepaper, glass, metal, a tin can, refuse, garbage, waste, discarded or soiled personal property, or any other noxious or poisonous substance in the water of or near Lake Lavon in Collin County if the substance is detrimental to fish or to a person fishing in Lake Lavon.

(c) An offense under this section is a Class C misdemeanor unless it is shown on the trial of the defendant that the defendant has previously been convicted of an offense under this section, in which event the offense is a Class A misdemeanor.

(Enacted by Acts 1989, 71st Leg., ch. 678 (H.B. 2136), § 1, effective September 1, 1989.)

## Sec. 365.033.  Discarding Refuse in Certain County Parks; Criminal Penalty.

(a) The definitions provided by Section 365.011 apply to this section.

(b) In this section, "beach" means an area in which the public has acquired a right of use or an easement and that borders on the seaward shore of the Gulf of Mexico or extends from the line of mean low tide to the line of vegetation bordering on the Gulf of Mexico.

(c) This section applies only to a county park located in a county that has the Gulf of Mexico as one boundary, but does not apply to a beach located in that park.

(d) A person commits an offense if the person discards in a county park any junk, garbage, rubbish, or other refuse in a place that is not an officially designated refuse container or disposal unit.

(e) An offense under this section is a Class C misdemeanor unless it is shown on the trial of the defendant that the defendant has previously been convicted of an offense under this section, in which event the offense is a Class A misdemeanor.

(Enacted by Acts 1989, 71st Leg., ch. 678 (H.B. 2136), § 1, effective September 1, 1989.)

## Sec. 365.034.  County Regulation of Litter Near Public Highway; Criminal Penalty.

(a) The commissioners court of a county may:

(1) by order prohibit the accumulation of litter for more than 30 days on a person's property within 50 feet of a public highway in the county;

(2) provide for the removal and disposition of litter accumulated near a public highway in

violation of an order adopted under this section; and

(3) provide for the assessment against a person who owns the property from which litter is removed under Subdivision (2) of the costs incurred by the county in removing and disposing of the litter.

(b) Before the commissioners court takes any action to remove or dispose of litter under this section, the court shall send a notice by certified mail to the record owners of the property on which the litter is accumulated in violation of an order adopted under this section. The court may not remove or dispose of the litter or assess the costs of the removal or disposition against a property owner before the 30th day after the date the notice is sent under this subsection.

(c) If a person assessed costs under this section does not pay the costs within 60 days after the date of assessment:

(1) a lien in favor of the county attaches to the property from which the litter was removed to secure the payment of the costs and interest accruing at an annual rate of 10 percent on any unpaid part of the costs; and

(2) the commissioners court shall file a record of the lien in the office of the county clerk.

(d) The violation of an order adopted under this section is a Class C misdemeanor.

(e) In this section:

(1) "Litter" has the meaning assigned by Section 365.011 except that the term does not include equipment used for agricultural purposes.

(2) "Public highway" has the meaning assigned by Section 365.011.

(Enacted by Acts 1991, 72nd Leg., ch. 14 (S.B. 404), § 126, effective September 1, 1991; am. Acts 1991, 72nd Leg., 1st C.S., ch. 3 (S.B. 2), § 8.162, effective September 1, 1991.)

## Sec. 365.035.  Prohibition on Possessing Glass Containers Within Boundary of State-Owned Riverbed; Penalties.

(a) In this section, "glass container" means a glass container designed to contain a beverage, including a bottle or jar.

(b) A person commits an offense if the person knowingly possesses a glass container within the boundaries of a state-owned riverbed in a county:

(1) that is located within 85 miles of an international border; and

(2) in which at least four rivers are located.

(c) An offense under this section is a Class C misdemeanor.

(d) It is a defense to prosecution under Subsection (b) that the person who possessed the glass container:

(1) did not transport the glass container into the boundaries of the riverbed;

(2) possessed the glass container only for the purpose of lawfully disposing of the glass container in a designated waste receptacle; or

(3) is the owner of property adjacent to the section of the riverbed in which the person possessed the glass container.

(e) It is an exception to the application of Subsection (b) that the person possessed the glass container only for the purpose of water sampling or conducting scientific research as authorized by:

(1) a governmental entity;

(2) a utility as defined by Section 11.004, Utilities Code;

(3) a retail public utility as defined by Section 13.002, Water Code;

(4) a power generation company as defined by Section 31.002, Utilities Code;

(5) a surface coal mining and reclamation operation, as defined by Section 134.004, Natural Resources Code; or

(6) a school-sponsored or university-sponsored educational activity.

(Enacted by Acts 2011, 82nd Leg., ch. 1124 (H.B. 218), § 1, effective September 1, 2011.)

## SUBTITLE C
## AIR QUALITY

## CHAPTER 382
## CLEAN AIR ACT

### Subchapter G. Vehicle Emissions

## SUBCHAPTER G
## VEHICLE EMISSIONS

### Sec. 382.201.  Definitions.

In this subchapter:

(1) "Affected county" means a county with a motor vehicle emissions inspection and maintenance program established under Section 548.301, Transportation Code.

(2) "Commercial vehicle" means a vehicle that is owned or leased in the regular course of business of a commercial or business entity.

(3) "Fleet vehicle" means a motor vehicle operated as one of a group that consists of more than 10 motor vehicles and that is owned and operated by a public or commercial entity or by a private entity other than a single household.

(4) "Participating county" means an affected county in which the commissioners court by resolution has chosen to implement a low-income vehicle repair assistance, retrofit, and accelerated vehicle retirement program authorized by Section 382.209.

(5) "Retrofit" means to equip, or the equipping of, an engine or an exhaust or fuel system with new, emissions-reducing parts or equipment designed to reduce air emissions and improve air quality, after the manufacture of the original engine or exhaust or fuel system, so long as the parts or equipment allow the vehicle to meet or exceed state and federal air emissions reduction standards.

(6) "Retrofit equipment" means emissions-reducing equipment designed to reduce air emissions and improve air quality that is installed after the manufacture of the original engine or exhaust or fuel system.

(7) "Vehicle" includes a fleet vehicle.

(Enacted by Acts 2001, 77th Leg., ch. 1075 (H.B. 2134), § 1, effective September 1, 2001.)

## Sec. 382.202. Vehicle Emissions Inspection and Maintenance Program.

(a) The commission by resolution may request the Public Safety Commission to establish a vehicle emissions inspection and maintenance program under Subchapter F, Chapter 548, Transportation Code, in accordance with this section and rules adopted under this section. The commission by rule may establish, implement, and administer a program requiring emissions-related inspections of motor vehicles to be performed at inspection facilities consistent with the requirements of the federal Clean Air Act (42 U.S.C. Section 7401 et seq.) and its subsequent amendments.

(b) The commission by rule may require emissions-related inspection and maintenance of land vehicles, including testing exhaust emissions, examining emission control devices and systems, verifying compliance with applicable standards, and other requirements as provided by federal law or regulation.

(c) If the program is established under this section, the commission:

(1) shall adopt vehicle emissions inspection and maintenance requirements for certain areas as required by federal law or regulation; and

(2) shall adopt vehicle emissions inspection and maintenance requirements for counties not subject to a specific federal requirement in response to a formal request by resolutions adopted by the county and the most populous municipality within the county according to the most recent federal decennial census.

(d) On adoption of a resolution by the commission and after proper notice, the Department of Public Safety of the State of Texas shall implement a system that requires, as a condition of obtaining a safety inspection certificate issued under Subchapter C, Chapter 548, Transportation Code, in a county that is included in a vehicle emissions inspection and maintenance program under Subchapter F of that chapter, that the vehicle, unless the vehicle is not covered by the system, be annually or biennially inspected under the vehicle emissions inspection and maintenance program as required by the state's air quality state implementation plan. The Department of Public Safety shall implement such a system when it is required by any provision of federal or state law, including any provision of the state's air quality state implementation plan.

(e) The commission may assess fees for vehicle emissions-related inspections performed at inspection or reinspection facilities authorized and licensed by the commission in amounts reasonably necessary to recover the costs of developing, administering, evaluating, and enforcing the vehicle emissions inspection and maintenance program. If the program relies on privately operated or contractor-operated inspection or reinspection stations, an appropriate portion of the fee as determined by commission rule may be retained by the station owner, contractor, or operator to recover the cost of performing the inspections and provide for a reasonable margin of profit. Any portion of the fee collected by the commission is a Clean Air Act fee under Section 382.0622.

(f) The commission:

(1) shall, no less frequently than biennially, review the fee established under Subsection (e); and

(2) may use part of the fee collected under Subsection (e) to provide incentives, including financial incentives, for participation in the testing network to ensure availability of an adequate number of testing stations.

(g) The commission shall:

(1) use part of the fee collected under Subsection (e) to fund low-income vehicle repair assistance, retrofit, and accelerated vehicle retirement programs created under Section 382.209; and

(2) to the extent practicable, distribute available funding created under Subsection (e) to participating counties in reasonable proportion to the amount of fees collected under Subsection (e) in those counties or in the regions in which those counties are located.

(h) Regardless of whether different tests are used for different vehicles as determined under Section 382.205, the commission may:

(1) set fees assessed under Subsection (e) at the same rate for each vehicle in a county or region; and

(2) set different fees for different counties or regions.

(i) The commission shall examine the efficacy of annually inspecting diesel vehicles for compliance with applicable federal emission standards, compliance with an opacity or other emissions-related standard established by commission rule, or both and shall implement that inspection program if the commission determines the program would minimize emissions. For purposes of this subsection, a diesel engine not used in a vehicle registered for use on public highways is not a diesel vehicle.

(j) The commission may not establish, before January 1, 2004, vehicle fuel content standards to provide for vehicle fuel content for clean motor vehicle fuels for any area of the state that are more stringent or restrictive than those standards promulgated by the United States Environmental Protection Agency applicable to that area except as provided in Subsection (o) unless the fuel is specifically authorized by the legislature.

(k) The commission by rule may establish classes of vehicles that are exempt from vehicle emissions inspections and by rule may establish procedures to allow and review petitions for the exemption of individual vehicles, according to criteria established by commission rule. Rules adopted by the commission under this subsection must be consistent with federal law. The commission by rule may establish fees to recover the costs of administering this subsection. Fees collected under this subsection shall be deposited to the credit of the clean air account, an account in the general revenue fund, and may be used only for the purposes of this section.

(*l*) Except as provided by this subsection, a person who sells or transfers ownership of a motor vehicle for which a vehicle emissions inspection certificate has been issued is not liable for the cost of emission control system repairs that are required for the vehicle subsequently to receive an emissions inspection certificate. This subsection does not apply to repairs that are required because emission control equipment or devices on the vehicle were removed or tampered with before the sale or transfer of the vehicle.

(m) The commission may conduct audits to determine compliance with this section.

(n) The commission may suspend the emissions inspection program as it applies to pre-1996 vehicles in an affected county if:

(1) the department certifies that the number of pre-1996 vehicles in the county subject to the program is 20 percent or less of the number of those vehicles that were in the county on September 1, 2001; and

(2) an alternative testing methodology that meets or exceeds United States Environmental Protection Agency requirements is available.

(o) The commission may not require the distribution of Texas low-emission diesel as described in revisions to the State Implementation Plan for the control of ozone air pollution prior to February 1, 2005.

(p) The commission may consider, as an alternative method of compliance with Subsection (o), fuels to achieve equivalent emissions reductions.

(q), (r) [Repealed by Acts 2007, 80th Leg., ch. 262 (S.B. 12), § 1.10(2), effective June 8, 2007.] (Enacted by Acts 1989, 71st Leg., ch. 678 (H.B. 2136), § 1, effective September 1, 1989; am. Acts 1991, 72nd Leg., 1st C.S., ch. 3 (S.B. 2), § 2.25, effective September 1, 1991; am. Acts 1993, 73rd Leg., ch. 547 (H.B. 1969), § 1, effective August 30, 1993; am. Acts 1995, 74th Leg., ch. 1 (S.B. 19), § 1, effective January 31, 1995; am. Acts 1995, 74th Leg., ch. 34 (S.B. 178), § 9(1), (3), effective May 1, 1995; am. Acts 1995, 74th Leg., ch. 76 (S.B. 959), § 11.157, effective September 1, 1995; am. Acts 1997, 75th Leg., ch. 165 (S.B. 971), § 30.207, effective September 1, 1997; am. Acts 1997, 75th Leg., ch. 333 (H.B. 3231), § 73, effective Setpember 1, 1997; am. Acts 1997, 75th Leg., ch. 1069 (S.B. 1856), § 1, effective June 19, 1997; am. Acts 2001, 77th Leg., ch. 1075 (H.B. 2134), § 1, effective September 1, 2001 (renumbered from Sec. 382.037); am. Acts 2003, 78th Leg., ch. 1276 (H.B. 3507), § 10.008(a), effective September 1, 2003; am. Acts 2005, 79th Leg., ch. 958 (H.B. 1611), § 2, effective June 18, 2005; am. Acts 2007, 80th Leg., ch. 262 (S.B. 12), § 1.10(2), effective June 8, 2007.)

### Sec. 382.203. Vehicles Subject to Program; Exemptions.

(a) The inspection and maintenance program applies to any gasoline-powered vehicle that is:

(1) required to be registered in and is primarily operated in an affected county; and

(2) at least two and less than 25 years old; or

(3) subject to test-on-resale requirements under Section 548.3011, Transportation Code.

(b) In addition to a vehicle described by Subsection (a), the program applies to:

(1) a vehicle with United States governmental plates primarily operated in an affected county;

(2) a vehicle operated on a federal facility in an affected county; and

(3) a vehicle primarily operated in an affected county that is exempt from motor vehicle registration requirements or eligible under Chapter 502, Transportation Code, to display an "exempt" license plate.

(c) The Department of Public Safety of the State of Texas by rule may waive program requirements, in accordance with standards adopted by the commission, for certain vehicles and vehicle owners, including:

(1) the registered owner of a vehicle who cannot afford to comply with the program, based on reasonable income standards;

(2) a vehicle that cannot be brought into compliance with emissions standards by performing repairs;

(3) a vehicle:

(A) on which at least $100 has been spent to bring the vehicle into compliance; and

(B) that the department:

(i) can verify was driven fewer than 5,000 miles since the last safety inspection; and

(ii) reasonably determines will be driven fewer than 5,000 miles during the period before the next safety inspection is required; and

(4) a vehicle for which parts are not readily available.

(d) The program does not apply to a:

(1) motorcycle;

(2) slow-moving vehicle as defined by Section 547.001, Transportation Code; or

(3) vehicle that is registered but not operated primarily in a county or group of counties subject to a motor vehicle emissions inspection program established under Subchapter F, Chapter 548, Transportation Code.

(Enacted by Acts 1997, 75th Leg., ch. 106 (H.B. 2274), § 2, effective June 19, 1997; am. Acts 2001, 77th Leg., ch. 1075 (H.B. 2134), § 1, effective September 1, 2001 (renumbered from Sec. 382.0372).)

## Sec. 382.204. Remote Sensing Program Component.

(a) The commission and the Department of Public Safety of the State of Texas jointly shall develop a program component for enforcing vehicle emissions testing and standards by use of remote or automatic emissions detection and analysis equipment.

(b) The program component may be employed in any county designated as a nonattainment area within the meaning of Section 107(d) of the Clean Air Act (42 U.S.C. Section 7407) and its subsequent amendments, in any affected county, or in any county adjacent to an affected county.

(c) If a vehicle registered in a county adjacent to an affected county is detected under the program component authorized by this section as operating and exceeding acceptable emissions limitations in an affected county, the department shall provide notice of the violation under Section 548.306, Transportation Code.

(Enacted by Acts 1997, 75th Leg., ch. 1069 (H.B. 2274), § 2, effective June 19, 1997; am. Acts

2001, 77th Leg., ch. 1075 (H.B. 2134), § 1, effective September 1, 2001 (renumbered from Sec. 382.0373).)

## Sec. 382.205. Inspection Equipment and Procedures.

(a) The commission by rule may adopt:

(1) standards and specifications for motor vehicle emissions testing equipment;

(2) recordkeeping and reporting procedures; and

(3) measurable emissions standards a vehicle must meet to pass the inspection.

(b) In adopting standards and specifications under Subsection (a), the commission may require different types of tests for different vehicle models.

(c) In consultation with the Department of Public Safety of the State of Texas, the commission may contract with one or more private entities to provide testing equipment, training, and related services to inspection stations in exchange for part of the testing fee. A contract under this subsection may apply to one specified area of the state or to the entire state. The commission at least once during each year shall review each contract entered into under this subsection to determine whether the contracting entity is performing satisfactorily under the terms of the contract. Immediately after completing the review, the commission shall prepare a report summarizing the review and send a copy of the report to the speaker of the house of representatives, the lieutenant governor, and the governor.

(d) The Department of Public Safety of the State of Texas by rule shall adopt:

(1) testing procedures in accordance with motor vehicle emissions testing equipment specifications; and

(2) procedures for issuing or denying an emissions inspection certificate.

(e) The commission and the Department of Public Safety of the State of Texas by joint rule may adopt procedures to encourage a stable private market for providing emissions testing to the public in all areas of an affected county, including:

(1) allowing facilities to perform one or more types of emissions tests; and

(2) any other measure the commission and the Department of Public Safety consider appropriate.

(f) Rules and procedures under this section must ensure that approved repair facilities participating in a low-income vehicle repair assistance, retrofit, and accelerated vehicle retirement program established under Section 382.209 have access to adequate testing equipment.

(g) Subject to Subsection (h), the commission and the Department of Public Safety of the State of Texas by rule may allow alternative vehicle emissions testing if:

(1) the technology provides accurate and reliable results;

(2) the technology is widely and readily available to persons interested in performing alternative vehicle emissions testing; and

(3) the use of alternative testing is not likely to substantially affect federal approval of the state's air quality state implementation plan.

(h) A rule adopted under Subsection (g) may not be more restrictive than federal regulations governing vehicle emissions testing.

(Enacted by Acts 1997, 75th Leg., ch. 1069 (S.B. 1856), § 2, effective June 19, 1997; am. Acts 1999, 76th Leg., ch. 1189 (S.B. 370), § 42, effective September 1, 1999; am. Acts 2001, 77th Leg., ch. 1075 (H.B. 2134), § 1, effective September 1, 2001 (renumbered from Sec. 382.0374).)

### Sec. 382.206. Collection of Data; Report.

(a) The commission and the Department of Public Safety of the State of Texas may collect inspection and maintenance information derived from the emissions inspection and maintenance program, including:

(1) inspection results;

(2) inspection station information;

(3) information regarding vehicles operated on federal facilities;

(4) vehicle registration information; and

(5) other data the United States Environmental Protection Agency requires.

(b) The commission shall:

(1) report the information to the United States Environmental Protection Agency; and

(2) compare the information on inspection results with registration information for enforcement purposes.

(Enacted by Acts 1997, 75th Leg., ch. 1069 (S.B. 1856), § 2, effective June 19, 1997; am. Acts 2001, 77th Leg., ch. 1075 (H.B. 2134), § 1, effective September 1, 2001 (renumbered from Sec. 382.0375).)

### Sec. 382.207. Inspection Stations; Quality Control Audits.

(a) The Department of Public Safety of the State of Texas by rule shall adopt standards and procedures for establishing vehicle emissions inspection stations authorized and licensed by the state.

(b) A vehicle emissions inspection may be performed at a decentralized independent inspection station or at a centralized inspection facility operated or licensed by the state. In developing the program for vehicle emissions inspections, the Department of Public Safety shall make all reasonable efforts to preserve the present decentralized system.

(c) After consultation with the Texas Department of Transportation, the commission shall require state and local transportation planning entities designated by the commission to prepare long-term projections of the combined impact of significant planned transportation system changes on emissions and air quality. The projections shall be prepared using air pollution estimation methodologies established jointly by the commission and the Texas Department of Transportation. This subsection does not restrict the Texas Department of Transportation's function as the transportation planning body for the state or its role in identifying and initiating specific transportation-related projects in the state.

(d) The Department of Public Safety may authorize enforcement personnel or other individuals to remove, disconnect, adjust, or make inoperable vehicle emissions control equipment, devices, or systems and to operate a vehicle in the tampered condition in order to perform a quality control audit of an inspection station or other quality control activities as necessary to assess and ensure the effectiveness of the vehicle emissions inspection and maintenance program.

(e) The Department of Public Safety shall develop a challenge station program to provide for the reinspection of a motor vehicle at the option of the owner of the vehicle to ensure quality control of a vehicle emissions inspection and maintenance system.

(f) The commission may contract with one or more private entities to operate a program established under this section.

(g) In addition to other procedures established by the commission, the commission shall establish procedures by which a private entity with whom the commission has entered into a contract to operate a program established under this section may agree to perform:

(1) testing at a fleet facility or dealership using mobile test equipment;

(2) testing at a fleet facility or dealership using test equipment owned by the fleet or

dealership but calibrated and operated by the private entity's personnel; or

(3) testing at a fleet facility or dealership using test equipment owned and operated by the private entity and installed at the fleet or dealership facility.

(h) The fee for a test conducted as provided by Subsection (g) shall be set by the commission in an amount not to exceed twice the fee otherwise provided by law or by rule of the commission. An appropriate portion of the fee, as determined by the commission, may be remitted by the private entity to the fleet facility or dealership.

(Enacted by Acts 1991, 72nd Leg., 1st C.S., ch. 3 (S.B. 2), § 2.26, effective September 1, 1991; am. Acts 1993, 73rd Leg., ch. 547 (H.B. 1969), § 2, effective August 30, 1993; am. Acts 1995, 74th Leg., ch. 34 (S.B. 178), § 3, effective May 1, 1995; am. Acts 1995, 74th Leg., ch. 76 (S.B. 959), § 11.158, effective September 1, 1995; am. Acts 1995, 74th Leg., ch. 165 (S.B. 971), § 22(41), effective September 1, 1995; am. Acts 2001, 77th Leg., ch. 1075 (H.B. 2134), § 1, effective September 1, 2001 (renumbered from Sec. 382.038).)

### Sec. 382.208. Attainment Program.

(a) Except as provided by Section 382.202(j) or another provision of this chapter, the commission shall coordinate with federal, state, and local transportation planning agencies to develop and implement transportation programs and other measures necessary to demonstrate and maintain attainment of national ambient air quality standards and to protect the public from exposure to hazardous air contaminants from motor vehicles.

(b) Participating agencies include the Texas Department of Transportation and metropolitan planning organizations designated by the governor.

(Enacted by Acts 1991, 72nd Leg., 1st C.S., ch. 3 (S.B. 2), § 2.26, effective September 1, 1991; am. Acts 1995, 74th Leg., ch. 76 (S.B. 959), § 11.158, effective September 1, 1995; am. Acts 1995, 74th Leg., ch. 165 (S.B. 971), § 22(42), effective September 1, 1995; am. Acts 2001, 77th Leg., ch. 965 (H.B. 2912), § 15.03, effective September 1, 2001; am. Acts 2001, 77th Leg., ch. 1075 (H.B. 2134), § 1, effective September 1, 2001 (renumbered from Sec. 382.039); am. Acts 2003, 78th Leg., ch. 1276 (H.B. 3507), § 10.008(c), effective September 1, 2003.)

### Sec. 382.209. Low-Income Vehicle Repair Assistance, Retrofit, and Accelerated Vehicle Retirement Program.

(a) The commission and the Public Safety Commission by joint rule shall establish and authorize the commissioners court of a participating county to implement a low-income vehicle repair assistance, retrofit, and accelerated vehicle retirement program subject to agency oversight that may include reasonable periodic commission audits.

(b) The commission shall provide funding for local low-income vehicle repair assistance, retrofit, and accelerated vehicle retirement programs with available funds collected under Section 382.202, 382.302, or other designated and available funds. The programs shall be administered in accordance with Chapter 783, Government Code. Program costs may include call center management, application oversight, invoice analysis, education, outreach, and advertising. Not more than 10 percent of the money provided to a local low-income vehicle repair assistance, retrofit, and accelerated vehicle retirement program under this section may be used for the administration of the programs, including program costs.

(c) The rules adopted under Subsection (a) must provide procedures for ensuring that a program implemented under authority of that subsection does not apply to a vehicle that is:

(1) registered under Section 504.501 or 504.502, Transportation Code; and

(2) not regularly used for transportation during the normal course of daily activities.

(d) Subject to the availability of funds, a low-income vehicle repair assistance, retrofit, and accelerated vehicle retirement program established under this section shall provide monetary or other compensatory assistance for:

(1) repairs directly related to bringing certain vehicles that have failed a required emissions test into compliance with emissions requirements;

(2) a replacement vehicle or replacement assistance for a vehicle that has failed a required emissions test and for which the cost of repairs needed to bring the vehicle into compliance is uneconomical; and

(3) installing retrofit equipment on vehicles that have failed a required emissions test, if practically and economically feasible, in lieu of or in combination with repairs performed un-

der Subdivision (1). The commission and the Department of Public Safety of the State of Texas shall establish standards and specifications for retrofit equipment that may be used under this section.

(e) A vehicle is not eligible to participate in a low-income vehicle repair assistance, retrofit, and accelerated vehicle retirement program established under this section unless:

(1) the vehicle is capable of being operated;

(2) the registration of the vehicle:

(A) is current; and

(B) reflects that the vehicle has been registered in the county implementing the program for at least 12 of the 15 months preceding the application for participation in the program;

(3) the commissioners court of the county administering the program determines that the vehicle meets the eligibility criteria adopted by the commission, the Texas Department of Motor Vehicles, and the Public Safety Commission;

(4) if the vehicle is to be repaired, the repair is done by a repair facility recognized by the Department of Public Safety, which may be an independent or private entity licensed by the state; and

(5) if the vehicle is to be retired under this subsection and Section 382.213, the replacement vehicle is a qualifying motor vehicle.

(f) A fleet vehicle, a vehicle owned or leased by a governmental entity, or a commercial vehicle is not eligible to participate in a low-income vehicle repair assistance, retrofit, and accelerated vehicle retirement program established and implemented under this section.

(g) A participating county may contract with any appropriate entity, including the regional council of governments or the metropolitan planning organization in the appropriate region, or with another county for services necessary to implement the participating county's low-income vehicle repair assistance, retrofit, and accelerated vehicle retirement program. The participating counties in a nonattainment region or counties participating in an early action compact under Subchapter H may agree to have the money collected in any one county be used in any other participating county in the same region.

(h) Participation by an affected county in a low-income vehicle repair assistance, retrofit, and accelerated vehicle retirement program is not mandatory. To the extent allowed by federal law, any emissions reductions attributable to a low-income vehicle repair assistance, retrofit, and accelerated vehicle retirement program in a county that are attained during a period before the county is designated as a nonattainment county shall be considered emissions reductions credit if the county is later determined to be a nonattainment county.

(i) Notwithstanding the vehicle replacement requirements provided by Subsection (d)(2), the commission by rule may provide monetary or other compensatory assistance under the low-income vehicle repair assistance, retrofit, and accelerated vehicle retirement program, subject to the availability of funds, for the replacement of a vehicle that meets the following criteria:

(1) the vehicle is gasoline-powered and is at least 10 years old;

(2) the vehicle owner meets applicable financial eligibility criteria;

(3) the vehicle meets the requirements provided by Subsections (e)(1) and (2); and

(4) the vehicle has passed a Department of Public Safety motor vehicle safety inspection or safety and emissions inspection within the 15-month period before the application is submitted.

(j) The commission may provide monetary or other compensatory assistance under the low-income vehicle repair assistance, retrofit, and accelerated vehicle retirement program for a replacement vehicle or replacement assistance for a pre-1996 model year replacement vehicle that passes the required United States Environmental Protection Agency Start-Up Acceleration Simulation Mode Standards emissions test but that would have failed the United States Environmental Protection Agency Final Acceleration Simulation Mode Standards emissions test or failed to meet some other criterion determined by the commission; provided, however, that a replacement vehicle under this subsection must be a qualifying motor vehicle.

(Enacted by Acts 2001, 77th Leg., ch. 1075 (H.B. 2134), § 1, effective September 1, 2001; am. Acts 2005, 79th Leg., ch. 958 (H.B. 1611), § 3, effective June 18, 2005; am. Acts 2007, 80th Leg., ch. 262 (S.B. 12), § 1.03, effective June 8, 2007; am. Acts 2009, 81st Leg., ch. 933 (H.B. 3097), § 3F.01, effective September 1, 2009; am. Acts 2011, 82nd Leg., ch. 91 (S.B. 1303), § 12.004, effective September 1, 2011; am. Acts 2011, 82nd Leg., ch. 347 (H.B. 3272), § 2, effective September 1, 2011.)

Health

## Sec. 382.210. Implementation Guidelines and Requirements.

(a) The commission by rule shall adopt guidelines to assist a participating county in implementing a low-income vehicle repair assistance, retrofit, and accelerated vehicle retirement program authorized under Section 382.209. The guidelines at a minimum shall recommend:

(1) a minimum and maximum amount for repair assistance;

(2) a minimum and maximum amount toward the purchase price of a replacement vehicle qualified for the accelerated retirement program, based on vehicle type and model year, with the maximum amount not to exceed:

(A) $3,000 for a replacement car of the current model year or the previous three model years, except as provided by Paragraph (C);

(B) $3,000 for a replacement truck of the current model year or the previous two model years, except as provided by Paragraph (C); and

(C) $3,500 for a replacement vehicle of the current model year or the previous three model years that:

(i) is a hybrid vehicle, electric vehicle, or natural gas vehicle; or

(ii) has been certified to meet federal Tier 2, Bin 3 or a cleaner Bin certification under 40 C.F.R. Section 86.1811-04, as published in the February 10, 2000, Federal Register;

(3) criteria for determining eligibility, taking into account:

(A) the vehicle owner's income, which may not exceed 300 percent of the federal poverty level;

(B) the fair market value of the vehicle; and

(C) any other relevant considerations;

(4) safeguards for preventing fraud in the repair, purchase, or sale of a vehicle in the program; and

(5) procedures for determining the degree and amount of repair assistance a vehicle is allowed, based on:

(A) the amount of money the vehicle owner has spent on repairs;

(B) the vehicle owner's income; and

(C) any other relevant factors.

(b) A replacement vehicle described by Subsection (a)(2) must:

(1) except as provided by Subsection (c), be a vehicle in a class or category of vehicles that has been certified to meet federal Tier 2, Bin 5 or a cleaner Bin certification under 40 C.F.R. Section 86.1811-04, as published in the February 10, 2000, Federal Register;

(2) have a gross vehicle weight rating of less than 10,000 pounds;

(3) have an odometer reading of not more than 70,000 miles; and

(4) be a vehicle the total cost of which does not exceed:

(A) for a vehicle described by Subsection (a)(2)(A) or (B), $35,000; or

(B) for a vehicle described by Subsection (a)(2)(C), $45,000.

(c) The commission may adopt any revisions made by the federal government to the emissions standards described by Subsection (b)(1).

(d) A participating county shall provide an electronic means for distributing vehicle repair or replacement funds once all program criteria have been met with regard to the repair or replacement. The county shall ensure that funds are transferred to a participating dealer under this section not later than the 10th business day after the date the county receives proof of the sale and any required administrative documents from the participating dealer.

(e) In rules adopted under this section, the commission shall require a mandatory procedure that:

(1) produces a document confirming that a person is eligible to purchase a replacement vehicle in the manner provided by this chapter, and the amount of money available to the participating purchaser;

(2) provides that a person who seeks to purchase a replacement vehicle in the manner provided by this chapter is required to have the document required by Subdivision (1) before the person enters into negotiation for a replacement vehicle in the manner provided by this chapter; and

(3) provides that a participating dealer who relies on a document issued as required by Subdivision (1) has no duty to otherwise confirm the eligibility of a person to purchase a replacement vehicle in the manner provided by this chapter.

(f) In this section, "total cost" means the total amount of money paid or to be paid for the purchase of a motor vehicle as set forth as "sales price" in the form entitled "Application for Texas Certificate of Title" promulgated by the Texas Department of Motor Vehicles. In a transaction that does not involve the use of that form, the term means an amount of money that is equivalent, or substantially equivalent, to the amount that would appear as "sales price" on the Application for Texas Certificate of Title if that form were involved.

(Enacted by Acts 2001, 77th Leg., ch. 1075 (H.B. 2134), § 1, effective September 1, 2001; am. Acts 2007, 80th Leg., ch. 262 (S.B. 12), § 1.04, effective June 8, 2007; am. Acts 2009, 81st Leg., ch. 933 (H.B. 3097), § 3F.02, effective September 1, 2009; am. Acts 2009, 81st Leg., ch. 1125 (H.B. 1796), § 12, effective September 1, 2009; am. Acts 2011, 82nd Leg., ch. 347 (H.B. 3272), § 3, effective September 1, 2011.)

### Sec. 382.211.  Local Advisory Panel.

(a) The commissioners court of a participating county may appoint one or more local advisory panels consisting of representatives of automobile dealerships, the automotive repair industry, safety inspection facilities, the public, antique and vintage car clubs, local nonprofit organizations, and locally affected governments to advise the county regarding the operation of the county's low-income vehicle repair assistance, retrofit, and accelerated vehicle retirement program, including the identification of a vehicle make or model with intrinsic value as an existing or future collectible.

(b) The commissioners court may delegate all or part of the administrative and financial matters to one or more local advisory panels established under Subsection (a).

(Enacted by Acts 2001, 77th Leg., ch. 1075 (H.B. 2134), § 1, effective September 1, 2001.)

### Sec. 382.212.  Emissions Reduction Credit.

(a) In this section, "emissions reduction credit" means an emissions reduction certified by the commission that is:

(1) created by eliminating future emissions, quantified during or before the period in which emissions reductions are made;

(2) expressed in tons or partial tons per year; and

(3) banked by the commission in accordance with commission rules relating to emissions banking.

(b) To the extent allowable under federal law, the commission by rule shall authorize:

(1) the assignment of a percentage of emissions reduction credit to a private, commercial, or business entity that purchases, for acceler-

ated retirement, a qualified vehicle under a low-income vehicle repair assistance, retrofit, and accelerated vehicle retirement program;

(2) the transferability of an assigned emissions reduction credit;

(3) the use of emissions reduction credit by the holder of the credit against any state or federal emissions requirements applicable to a facility owned or operated by the holder of the credit;

(4) the assignment of a percentage of emissions reduction credit, on the retirement of a fleet vehicle, a vehicle owned or leased by a governmental entity, or a commercial vehicle, to the owner or lessor of the vehicle; and

(5) other actions relating to the disposition or use of emissions reduction credit that the commission determines will benefit the implementation of low-income vehicle repair assistance, retrofit, and accelerated vehicle retirement programs established under Section 382.209.

(Enacted by Acts 2001, 77th Leg., ch. 1075 (H.B. 2134), § 1, effective September 1, 2001.)

### Sec. 382.213.  Disposition of Retired Vehicle.

(a) Except as provided by Subsection (c) and Subdivision (5) of this subsection, a vehicle retired under an accelerated vehicle retirement program authorized by Section 382.209 may not be resold or reused in its entirety in this or another state. Subject to the provisions of Subsection (i), the automobile dealer who takes possession of the vehicle must submit to the program administrator proof, in a manner adopted by the commission, that the vehicle has been retired. The vehicle must be:

(1) destroyed;

(2) recycled;

(3) dismantled and its parts sold as used parts or used in the program;

(4) placed in a storage facility of a program established under Section 382.209 and subsequently destroyed, recycled, or dismantled and its parts sold or used in the program; or

(5) repaired, brought into compliance, and used as a replacement vehicle under Section 382.209(d)(2).

(a-1) The commission shall establish a partnership with representatives of the steel industry, automobile dismantlers, and the scrap metal recycling industry to ensure that:

(1) vehicles retired under Section 382.209 are scrapped or recycled; and

(2) proof of scrapping or recycling is provided to the commission.

(b) Not more than 10 percent of all vehicles eligible for retirement under this section may be used as replacement vehicles under Subsection (a)(5).

(c) A vehicle identified by a local advisory panel as an existing or future collectible vehicle under Section 382.211 may be sold to an individual if the vehicle:

(1) is repaired and brought into compliance;

(2) is removed from the state;

(3) is removed from an affected county; or

(4) is stored for future restoration and cannot be registered in an affected county except under Section 504.501 or 504.502, Transportation Code.

(d) Notwithstanding Subsection (a)(3), the dismantler of a vehicle shall scrap the emissions control equipment and engine. The dismantler shall certify that the equipment and engine have been scrapped and not resold into the marketplace. A person who causes, suffers, allows, or permits a violation of this subsection or of a rule adopted under this section is subject to a civil penalty under Subchapter D, Chapter 7, Water Code, for each violation. For purposes of this subsection, a separate violation occurs with each fraudulent certification or prohibited resale.

(e) Notwithstanding Subsection (d), vehicle parts not related to emissions control equipment or the engine may be resold in any state. The only cost to be paid by a recycler for the residual scrap metal of a vehicle retired under this section shall be the cost of transportation of the residual scrap metal to the recycling facility.

(f) Any dismantling of vehicles or salvaging of steel under this section must be performed at a facility located in this state.

(g) In dismantling a vehicle under this section, the dismantler shall remove any mercury switches in accordance with state and federal law.

(h) The commission shall adopt rules:

(1) defining "emissions control equipment" and "engine" for the purposes of this section; and

(2) providing a procedure for certifying that emissions control equipment and vehicle engines have been scrapped or recycled.

(i) Notwithstanding any other provision of this section, and except as provided by this subsection, a dealer is in compliance with this section and incurs no civil or criminal liability as a result of the disposal of a replaced vehicle if the dealer produces proof of transfer of the replaced vehicle by the dealer to a dismantler. The defense provided by this subsection is not available to a dealer who knowingly and intentionally conspires with another person to violate this section. (Enacted by Acts 2001, 77th Leg., ch. 1075 (H.B. 2134), § 1, effective September 1, 2001; am. Acts 2007, 80th Leg., ch. 262 (S.B. 12), § 1.05, effective June 8, 2007; am. Acts 2011, 82nd Leg., ch. 91 (S.B. 1303), § 12.005, effective September 1, 2011; am. Acts 2011, 82nd Leg., ch. 347 (H.B. 3272), § 4, effective September 1, 2011.)

## Sec. 382.214. Sale of Vehicle with Intent to Defraud.

(a) A person who with intent to defraud sells a vehicle in an accelerated vehicle retirement program established under Section 382.209 commits an offense that is a third degree felony.

(b) Sale of a vehicle in an accelerated vehicle retirement program includes:

(1) sale of the vehicle to retire the vehicle under the program; and

(2) sale of a vehicle purchased for retirement under the program.

(Enacted by Acts 2001, 77th Leg., ch. 1075 (H.B. 2134), § 1, effective September 1, 2001.)

## Sec. 382.215. Sale of Vehicle Not Required.

Nothing in this subchapter may be construed to require a vehicle that has failed a required emissions test to be sold or destroyed by the owner. (Enacted by Acts 2001, 77th Leg., ch. 1075 (H.B. 2134), § 1, effective September 1, 2001.)

## Sec. 382.216. Incentives for Voluntary Participation in Vehicle Emissions Inspection and Maintenance Program.

The commission, the Texas Department of Transportation, and the Public Safety Commission may, subject to federal limitations:

(1) encourage counties likely to exceed federal clean air standards to implement voluntary:

(A) motor vehicle emissions inspection and maintenance programs; and

(B) low-income vehicle repair assistance, retrofit, and accelerated vehicle retirement programs;

(2) establish incentives for counties to voluntarily implement motor vehicle emissions inspection and maintenance programs and low-income vehicle repair assistance, retrofit, and accelerated vehicle retirement programs; and

(3) designate a county that voluntarily implements a motor vehicle emissions inspection and maintenance program or a low-income vehicle repair assistance, retrofit, and accelerated vehicle retirement program as a "Clean Air County" and give preference to a county designated as a Clean Air County in any federal or state clean air grant program.
(Enacted by Acts 2001, 77th Leg., ch. 1075 (H.B. 2134), § 1, effective September 1, 2001.)

### Sec. 382.217. Use of Unexpended Vehicle Repair Assistance, Retrofit, and Retirement Money [Repealed].
Repealed by Acts 2007, 80th Leg., ch. 262 (S.B. 12), § 1.10(3), effective June 8, 2007.
(Enacted by Acts 2005, 79th Leg., ch. 958 (H.B. 1611), § 4, effective June 18, 2005.)

### Sec. 382.218. Required Participation by Certain Counties.
(a) This section applies only to a county with a population of 800,000 or more that borders the United Mexican States.
(b) A county that was at any time required, because of the county's designation as a nonattainment area under Section 107(d) of the federal Clean Air Act (42 U.S.C. Section 7407), to participate in the vehicle emissions inspection and maintenance program under this subchapter and Subchapter F, Chapter 548, Transportation Code, shall continue to participate in the program even if the county is designated as an attainment area under the federal Clean Air Act.
(Enacted by Acts 2005, 79th Leg., ch. 958 (H.B. 1611), § 4, effective June 18, 2005; am. Acts 2011, 82nd Leg., ch. 1163 (H.B. 2702), § 47, effective September 1, 2011.)

### Sec. 382.219. Purchase of Replacement Vehicle; Automobile Dealerships.
(a) An amount described by Section 382.210(a)(2) may be used as a down payment toward the purchase of a replacement vehicle.
(b) An automobile dealer that participates in the procedures and programs offered by this chapter must be located in the state. No dealer is required to participate in the procedures and programs provided by this chapter.
(Enacted by Acts 2007, 80th Leg., ch. 262 (S.B. 12), § 1.06, effective June 8, 2007.)

### Sec. 382.220. Use of Funding for Local Initiative Projects.
(a) Money that is made available to participating counties under Section 382.202(g) or 382.302

may be appropriated only for programs administered in accordance with Chapter 783, Government Code, to improve air quality. A participating county may agree to contract with any appropriate entity, including a metropolitan planning organization or a council of governments to implement a program under Section 382.202, 382.209, or this section.
(b) A program under this section must be implemented in consultation with the commission and may include a program to:
(1) expand and enhance the AirCheck Texas Repair and Replacement Assistance Program;
(2) develop and implement programs or systems that remotely determine vehicle emissions and notify the vehicle's operator;
(3) develop and implement projects to implement the commission's smoking vehicle program;
(4) develop and implement projects for coordinating with local law enforcement officials to reduce the use of counterfeit state inspection stickers by providing local law enforcement officials with funds to identify vehicles with counterfeit state inspection stickers and to carry out appropriate actions;
(5) develop and implement programs to enhance transportation system improvements; or
(6) develop and implement new air control strategies designed to assist local areas in complying with state and federal air quality rules and regulations.
(c) Money that is made available for the implementation of a program under Subsection (b) may not be expended for local government fleet or vehicle acquisition or replacement, call center management, application oversight, invoice analysis, education, outreach, or advertising purposes.
(d) Fees collected under Sections 382.202 and 382.302 may be used, in an amount not to exceed $5 million per fiscal year, for projects described by Subsection (b). The fees shall be made available only to counties participating in the low-income vehicle repair assistance, retrofit, and accelerated vehicle retirement programs created under Section 382.209 and only on a matching basis, whereby the commission provides money to a county in the same amount that the county dedicates to a project authorized by Subsection (b). The commission may reduce the match requirement for a county that proposes to develop and implement independent test facility fraud detection programs, including the use of remote sensing technology for coordinating with law en-

Health

forcement officials to detect, prevent, and prosecute the use of counterfeit state inspection stickers.
(Enacted by Acts 2007, 80th Leg., ch. 262 (S.B. 12), § 1.07, effective June 8, 2007; am. Acts 2009, 81st Leg., ch. 1125 (H.B. 1796), § 13, effective September 1, 2009.)

## SUBCHAPTER H
## VEHICLE EMISSIONS PROGRAMS IN CERTAIN COUNTIES

### Sec. 382.301. Definitions.

In this subchapter:

(1) "Early action compact" means an agreement entered into before January 1, 2003, by the United States Environmental Protection Agency, the commission, the governing body of a county that is in attainment of the one-hour national ambient air quality standard for ozone but that has incidents approaching, or monitors incidents that exceed, the eight-hour national ambient air quality standard for ozone, and the governing body of the most populous municipality in that county that results in the submission of:

(A) an early action plan to the commission that the commission finds to be adequate; and

(B) a state implementation plan revision to the United States Environmental Protection Agency on or before December 31, 2004, that provides for attainment of the eight-hour national ambient air quality standard for ozone on or before December 31, 2007.

(2) "Participating county" means a county that is a party to an early action compact.
(Enacted by Acts 2003, 78th Leg., ch. 203 (S.B. 1159), § 1, effective June 10, 2003.)

### Sec. 382.302. Inspection and Maintenance Program.

(a) A participating county whose early action plan contains provisions for a motor vehicle emissions inspection and maintenance program and has been found adequate by the commission may formally request the commission to adopt motor vehicle emissions inspection and maintenance program requirements for the county. The request must be made by a resolution adopted by the governing body of the participating county and the governing body of the most populous municipality in the county.

(b) After approving a request made under Subsection (a), the commission by resolution may request the Public Safety Commission to establish motor vehicle emissions inspection and maintenance program requirements for the participating county under Subchapter F, Chapter 548, Transportation Code, in accordance with this section and rules adopted under this section. The motor vehicle emissions inspection and maintenance program requirements for the participating county may include exhaust emissions testing, emissions control devices and systems inspections, or other testing methods that meet or exceed United States Environmental Protection Agency requirements, and a remote sensing component as provided by Section 382.204. The motor vehicle emissions inspection and maintenance program requirements adopted for the participating county may apply to all or to a defined subset of vehicles described by Section 382.203.

(c) The commission may assess a fee for a vehicle inspection performed in accordance with a program established under this section. The fee must be in an amount reasonably necessary to recover the costs of developing, administering, evaluating, and enforcing the participating county's motor vehicle emissions inspection and maintenance program. An appropriate part of the fee as determined by commission rule may be retained by the station owner, contractor, or operator to recover the cost of performing the inspection and provide for a reasonable margin of profit.

(d) The incentives for voluntary participation established under Section 382.216 shall be made available to a participating county.

(e) A participating county may participate in the program established under Section 382.209.
(Enacted by Acts 2003, 78th Leg., ch. 203 (S.B. 1159), § 1, effective June 10, 2003.)

# TITLE 6
# FOOD, DRUGS, ALCOHOL, AND HAZARDOUS SUBSTANCES

## SUBTITLE A
## FOOD AND DRUG HEALTH REGULATIONS

## CHAPTER 431
## TEXAS FOOD, DRUG, AND COSMETIC ACT

## SUBCHAPTER A
## GENERAL PROVISIONS

## Sec. 431.001. Short Title.

This chapter may be cited as the Texas Food, Drug, and Cosmetic Act.

(Enacted by Acts 1989, 71st Leg., ch. 678 (H.B. 2136), § 1, effective September 1, 1989.)

## Sec. 431.002.　Definitions.

In this chapter:

(1) "Advertising" means all representations disseminated in any manner or by any means, other than by labeling, for the purpose of inducing, or that are likely to induce, directly or indirectly, the purchase of food, drugs, devices, or cosmetics.

(2) "Animal feed," as used in Subdivision (23), in Section 512 of the federal Act, and in provisions of this chapter referring to those paragraphs or sections, means an article intended for use as food for animals other than man as a substantial source of nutrients in the diet of the animals. The term is not limited to a mixture intended to be the sole ration of the animals.

(3) "Authorized agent" means an employee of the department who is designated by the commissioner to enforce the provisions of this chapter.

(4) "Board" means the Texas Board of Health.

(5) "Butter" means the food product usually known as butter that is made exclusively from milk or cream, or both, with or without common salt or additional coloring matter, and containing not less than 80 percent by weight of milk fat, after allowing for all tolerances.

(6) (A) "Color additive" means a material that:

(i) is a dye, pigment, or other substance made by a process of synthesis or similar artifice, or extracted, isolated, or otherwise derived, with or without intermediate or final change of identity from a vegetable, animal, mineral, or other source; and

(ii) when added or applied to a food, drug, or cosmetic, or to the human body or any part of the human body, is capable, alone or through reaction with other substance, of imparting color. The term does not include any material exempted under the federal Act.

(B) "Color" includes black, white, and intermediate grays.

(C) Paragraph (A) does not apply to any pesticide chemical, soil or plant nutrient, or other agricultural chemical solely because of its effect in aiding, retarding, or otherwise affecting, directly or indirectly, the growth or other natural physiological processes of produce of the soil and thereby affecting its color, whether before or after harvest.

(7) "Commissioner" means the commissioner of health.

(8) "Consumer commodity," except as otherwise provided by this subdivision, means any food, drug, device, or cosmetic, as those terms are defined by this chapter or by the federal Act, and any other article, product, or commodity of any kind or class that is customarily produced or distributed for sale through retail sales agencies or instrumentalities for consumption by individuals, or for use by individuals for purposes of personal care or in the performance of services ordinarily rendered within the household, and that usually is consumed or expended in the course of the consumption or use. The term does not include:

(A) a meat or meat product, poultry or poultry product, or tobacco or tobacco product;

(B) a commodity subject to packaging or labeling requirements imposed under the Federal Insecticide, Fungicide, and Rodenticide Act (7 U.S.C. 136), or The Virus-Serum-Toxin Act (21 U.S.C. 151 et seq.);

(C) a drug subject to the provisions of Section 431.113(c)(1) or 431.112(j), or Section 503(b)(1) of the federal Act;

(D) a beverage subject to or complying with packaging or labeling requirements imposed under the Federal Alcohol Administration Act (27 U.S.C. 205(e)); or

(E) a commodity subject to the provisions of Chapter 61, Agriculture Code, relating to the inspection, labeling, and sale of agricultural and vegetable seed.

(9) "Contaminated with filth" applies to any food, drug, device, or cosmetic not securely protected from dust, dirt, and as far as may be necessary by all reasonable means, from all foreign or injurious contaminations.

(10) "Cosmetic" means articles intended to be rubbed, poured, sprinkled, or sprayed on, introduced into, or otherwise applied to the human body or any part of the human body for cleaning, beautifying, promoting attractiveness, or altering the appearance, and articles intended for use as a component of those articles. The term does not include soap.

(11) "Counterfeit drug" means a drug, or the container or labeling of a drug, that, without authorization, bears the trademark, trade name or other identifying mark, imprint, or

device of a drug manufacturer, processor, packer, or distributor other than the person who in fact manufactured, processed, packed, or distributed the drug, and that falsely purports or is represented to be the product of, or to have been packed or distributed by, the other drug manufacturer, processor, packer, or distributor.

(12) "Department" means the Texas Department of Health.

(13) "Device," except when used in Sections 431.003, 431.021(*l*), 431.082(g), 431.112(c) and 431.142(c), means an instrument, apparatus, implement, machine, contrivance, implant, in vitro reagent, or other similar or related article, including any component, part, or accessory, that is:

    (A) recognized in the official United States Pharmacopoeia National Formulary or any supplement to it;

    (B) intended for use in the diagnosis of disease or other conditions, or in the cure, mitigation, treatment, or prevention of disease in man or other animals; or

    (C) intended to affect the structure or any function of the body of man or other animals and that does not achieve any of its principal intended purposes through chemical action within or on the body of man or other animals and is not dependent on metabolization for the achievement of any of its principal intended purposes.

(14) "Drug" means articles recognized in the official United States Pharmacopoeia National Formulary, or any supplement to it, articles designed or intended for use in the diagnosis, cure, mitigation, treatment, or prevention of disease in man or other animals, articles, other than food, intended to affect the structure or any function of the body of man or other animals, and articles intended for use as a component of any article specified in this subdivision. The term does not include devices or their components, parts, or accessories. A food for which a claim is made in accordance with Section 403(r) of the federal Act, and for which the claim is approved by the secretary, is not a drug solely because the label or labeling contains such a claim.

(15) "Federal Act" means the Federal Food, Drug and Cosmetic Act (Title 21 U.S.C. 301 et seq.).

(16) "Food" means:

    (A) articles used for food or drink for man;

    (B) chewing gum; and

    (C) articles used for components of any such article.

(17) "Food additive" means any substance the intended use of which results or may reasonably be expected to result, directly or indirectly, in its becoming a component or otherwise affecting the characteristics of any food (including any substance intended for use in producing, manufacturing, packing, processing, preparing, treating, packaging, transporting, or holding food; and including any source of radiation intended for any use), if such substance is not generally recognized, among experts qualified by scientific training and experience to evaluate its safety, as having been adequately shown through scientific procedures (or, in the case of a substance used in food prior to January 1, 1958, through either scientific procedures or experience based on common use in food) to be safe under the conditions of its intended use; except that such term does not include:

    (A) a pesticide chemical in or on a raw agricultural commodity;

    (B) a pesticide chemical to the extent that it is intended for use or is used in the production, storage, or transportation of any raw agricultural commodity;

    (C) a color additive;

    (D) any substance used in accordance with a sanction or approval granted prior to the enactment of the Food Additives Amendment of 1958, Pub. L. No. 85-929, 52 Stat. 1041 (codified as amended in various sections of 21 U.S.C.), pursuant to the federal Act, the Poultry Products Inspection Act (21 U.S.C. 451 et seq.) or the Meat Inspection Act of 1907 (21 U.S.C. 603); or

    (E) a new animal drug.

(18) "Health authority" means a physician designated to administer state and local laws relating to public health.

(19) "Immediate container" does not include package liners.

(20) "Infant formula" means a food that is represented for special dietary use solely as a food for infants by reason of its simulation of human milk or its suitability as a complete or partial substitute for human milk.

(21) "Label" means a display of written, printed, or graphic matter upon the immediate container of any article; and a requirement made by or under authority of this chapter that any word, statement, or other information that appears on the label shall not be considered to

Health

be complied with unless the word, statement, or other information also appears on the outside container or wrapper, if any, of the retail package of the article, or is easily legible through the outside container or wrapper.

(22) "Labeling" means all labels and other written, printed, or graphic matter (1) upon any article or any of its containers or wrappers, or (2) accompanying such article.

(23) "Manufacture" means:

(A) the process of combining or purifying food or packaging food for sale to a person at wholesale or retail, and includes repackaging, labeling, or relabeling of any food;

(B) the process of preparing, propagating, compounding, processing, packaging, repackaging, labeling, testing, or quality control of a drug or drug product, but does not include compounding that is done within the practice of pharmacy and pursuant to a prescription drug order or initiative from a practitioner for a patient or prepackaging that is done in accordance with Section 562.154, Occupations Code;

(C) the process of preparing, fabricating, assembling, processing, packing, repacking, labeling, or relabeling a device; or

(D) the making of any cosmetic product by chemical, physical, biological, or other procedures, including manipulation, sampling, testing, or control procedures applied to the product.

(24) "New animal drug" means any drug intended for use for animals other than man, including any drug intended for use in animal feed:

(A) the composition of which is such that the drug is not generally recognized among experts qualified by scientific training and experience to evaluate the safety and effectiveness of animal drugs as safe and effective for use under the conditions prescribed, recommended, or suggested in the labeling of the drug (except that such an unrecognized drug is not deemed to be a "new animal drug" if at any time before June 25, 1938, it was subject to the Food and Drug Act of June 30, 1906, and if at that time its labeling contained the same representations concerning the conditions of its use);

(B) the composition of which is such that the drug, as a result of investigations to determine its safety and effectiveness for use under those conditions, has become recognized but that has not, otherwise than in the investigations, been used to a material extent or for a material time under those conditions; or

(C) is composed wholly or partly of penicillin, streptomycin, chloratetracycline, chloramphenicol, or bacitracin, or any derivative of those substances, unless:

(i) a published order of the secretary is in effect that declares the drug not to be a new animal drug on the grounds that the requirement of certification of batches of the drug, as provided by Section 512(n) of the federal Act, is not necessary to ensure that the objectives specified in Section 512(n)(3) of that Act are achieved; and

(ii) Paragraph (A) or (B) of this subdivision does not apply to the drug.

(25) "New drug" means:

(A) any drug, except a new animal drug, the composition of which is such that such drug is not generally recognized among experts qualified by scientific training and experience to evaluate the safety and effectiveness of drugs, as safe and effective for use under the conditions prescribed, recommended, or suggested in the labeling thereof (except that such an unrecognized drug is not a "new drug" if at any time before May 26, 1985, it was subject to the Food and Drug Act of June 30, 1906, and if at that time its labeling contained the same representations concerning the conditions of its use); or

(B) any drug, except a new animal drug, the composition of which is such that such drug, as a result of investigations to determine its safety and effectiveness for use under such conditions, has become so recognized, but which has not, otherwise than in such investigations, been used to a material extent or for a material time under such conditions.

(26) "Official compendium" means the official United States Pharmacopoeia National Formulary, or any supplement to it.

(27) "Package" means any container or wrapping in which a consumer commodity is enclosed for use in the delivery or display of that consumer commodity to retail purchasers. The term includes wrapped meats enclosed in papers or other materials as prepared by the manufacturers thereof for sale. The term does not include:

(A) shipping containers or wrappings used solely for the transportation of a consumer commodity in bulk or in quantity to manu-

Health

facturers, packers, or processors, or to wholesale or retail distributors;

(B) shipping containers or outer wrappings used by retailers to ship or deliver a commodity to retail customers if the containers and wrappings do not bear printed matter relating to any particular commodity; or

(C) containers subject to the provisions of the Standard Barrel Act (Apple Barrels) (15 U.S.C. 231, 21 U.S.C. 20) or the Standard Barrel Act (Fruits and Vegetables) (15 U.S.C. 234—236).

(28) "Person" includes individual, partnership, corporation, and association.

(29) "Pesticide chemical" means any substance which, alone, in chemical combination or in formulation with one or more other substances, is a "pesticide" within the meaning of the Federal Insecticide, Fungicide, and Rodenticide Act (7 U.S.C. 136(u)), as now in force or as amended, and that is used in the production, storage, or transportation of raw agricultural commodities.

(30) "Principal display panel" means that part of a label that is most likely to be displayed, presented, shown, or examined under normal and customary conditions of display for retail sale.

(31) "Raw agricultural commodity" means any food in its raw or natural state, including all fruits that are washed, colored, or otherwise treated in their unpeeled natural form prior to marketing.

(32) "Saccharin" includes calcium saccharin, sodium saccharin, and ammonium saccharin.

(33) "Safe" refers to the health of humans or animals.

(34) "Secretary" means the secretary of the United States Department of Health and Human Services.

(Enacted by Acts 1989, 71st Leg., ch. 678 (H.B. 2136), § 1, effective September 1, 1989; am. Acts 1991, 72nd Leg., ch. 14 (S.B. 404), § 149, effective September 1, 1991; am. Acts 1991, 72nd Leg., ch. 539 (S.B. 873), § 1, effective September 1, 1991; am. Acts 1993, 73rd Leg., ch. 459 (S.B. 558), § 1, effective September 1, 1993; am. Acts 1997, 75th Leg., ch. 629 (H.B. 492), § 1, effective September 1, 1997; am. Acts 2003, 78th Leg., ch. 111 (S.B. 1400), § 1, effective September 1, 2003; am. Acts 2003, 78th Leg., ch. 383 (S.B. 1803), § 1, effective September 1, 2003; am. Acts 2003, 78th Leg., ch. 982 (S.B. 1826), § 1, effective September 1, 2003; am. Acts 2003, 78th Leg., ch. 1099 (H.B. 2192), § 1, effective September 1, 2003; am. Acts 2005,

79th Leg., ch. 28 (S.B. 492), § 5, effective September 1, 2005.)

### Sec. 431.003. Article Misbranded Because of Misleading Labeling or Advertising.

If an article is alleged to be misbranded because the labeling or advertising is misleading, then in determining whether the labeling or advertising is misleading, there shall be taken into account, among other things, not only representations made or suggested by statement, word, design, device, sound, or any combination of these, but also the extent to which the labeling or advertising fails to reveal facts material in the light of such representations or material with respect to consequences which may result from the use of the article to which the labeling or advertising relates under the conditions of use prescribed in the labeling or advertising thereof, or under such conditions of use as are customary or usual.

(Enacted by Acts 1989, 71st Leg., ch. 678 (H.B. 2136), § 1, effective September 1, 1989; am. Acts 1991, 72nd Leg., ch. 14 (S.B. 404), § 150, effective September 1, 1991.)

### Sec. 431.004. Representation of Drug As Antiseptic.

The representation of a drug, in its labeling, as an antiseptic shall be considered to be a representation that the drug is a germicide, except in the case of a drug purporting to be, or represented as, an antiseptic for inhibitory use as a wet dressing, ointment, dusting powder, or such other use as involves prolonged contact with the body.

(Enacted by Acts 1989, 71st Leg., ch. 678 (H.B. 2136), § 1, effective September 1, 1989.)

### Sec. 431.005. Provisions Regarding Sale of Food, Drugs, Devices, or Cosmetics.

The provisions of this chapter regarding the selling of food, drugs, devices, or cosmetics, shall be considered to include the manufacture, production, processing, packaging, exposure, offer, possession, and holding of any such article for sale; and the sale, dispensing, and giving of any such article, and the supplying or applying of any such articles in the conduct of any food, drug, or cosmetic establishment.

(Enacted by Acts 1989, 71st Leg., ch. 678 (H.B. 2136), § 1, effective September 1, 1989.)

## Sec. 431.006.　Certain Combination Products.

If the United States Food and Drug Administration determines, with respect to a product that is a combination of a drug and a device, that:

(1) the primary mode of action of the product is as a drug, a person who engages in wholesale distribution of the product is subject to licensure under Subchapter I; and

(2) the primary mode of action of the product is as a device, a distributor or manufacturer of the product is subject to licensure under Subchapter L.

(Enacted by Acts 1999, 76th Leg., ch. 132 (S.B. 1236), § 1, effective May 20, 1999.)

## Sec. 431.007.　Compliance with Other Law; Molluscan Shellfish.

A person who is subject to this chapter and who handles molluscan shellfish, as that term is defined by Section 436.002, shall comply with Section 436.105.

(Enacted by Acts 1999, 76th Leg., ch. 1298, effective June 18, 1999; am. Acts 2001, 77th Leg., ch. 1420 (H.B. 2812), § 21.001(78), effective September 1, 2001 (renumbered from Sec. 431.006).)

## Sec. 431.008.　Applicability of Chapter to Distressed or Reconditioned Merchandise and Certain Licensed Entities.

(a) This chapter applies to a food, drug, device, or cosmetic that is distressed merchandise for purposes of Chapter 432 or that has been subject to reconditioning in accordance with Chapter 432.

(b) Except as provided by Subsection (c), this chapter applies to the conduct of a person licensed under Chapter 432.

(c) A person who holds a license under Chapter 432 and is engaging in conduct within the scope of that license is not required to hold a license as a wholesale drug distributor under Subchapter I, a food wholesaler under Subchapter J, or a device distributor under Subchapter L.

(Enacted by Acts 2001, 77th Leg., ch. 265 (S.B. 1080), § 1, effective May 22, 2001.)

## Sec. 431.009.　Applicability of Chapter to Frozen Desserts.

(a) This chapter applies to a frozen dessert, an imitation frozen dessert, a product sold in semblance of a frozen dessert, or a mix for one of those products subject to Chapter 440. A frozen dessert, an imitation frozen dessert, a product sold in semblance of a frozen dessert, or a mix for one of those products is food for purposes of this chapter.

(b) Except as provided by Subsection (c), this chapter applies to the conduct of a person licensed under Chapter 440.

(c) A person who holds a license under Chapter 440 related to the manufacturing of a product regulated under that chapter and is engaging in conduct within the scope of that license is not required to hold a license as a food manufacturer or food wholesaler under Subchapter J.

(Enacted by Acts 2003, 78th Leg., ch. 112 (S.B. 1454), § 1, effective September 1, 2003.)

## Sec. 431.010.　Applicability of Chapter to Milk and Milk Products.

(a) This chapter applies to milk or a milk product subject to Chapter 435. Milk or a milk product is a food for purposes of this chapter.

(b) Except as provided by Subsection (c), this chapter applies to the conduct of a person who holds a permit under Chapter 435.

(c) A person who holds a permit under Chapter 435 related to the processing, producing, bottling, receiving, transferring, or transporting of Grade A milk or milk products and who is engaging in conduct within the scope of that permit is not required to hold a license as a food manufacturer or food wholesaler under Subchapter J.

(Enacted by Acts 2003, 78th Leg., ch. 757 (H.B. 3542), § 1, effective September 1, 2003.)

## SUBCHAPTER B
## PROHIBITED ACTS

## Sec. 431.021.　Prohibited Acts.

The following acts and the causing of the following acts within this state are unlawful and prohibited:

(a) the introduction or delivery for introduction into commerce of any food, drug, device, or cosmetic that is adulterated or misbranded;

(b) the adulteration or misbranding of any food, drug, device, or cosmetic in commerce;

(c) the receipt in commerce of any food, drug, device, or cosmetic that is adulterated or misbranded, and the delivery or proffered delivery thereof for pay or otherwise;

(d) the distribution in commerce of a consumer commodity, if such commodity is contained in a package, or if there is affixed to that commodity a label that does not conform to the provisions of this chapter and of rules adopted under the authority of this chapter; provided, however, that this prohibition shall not apply to persons engaged in business as wholesale or retail distributors of consumer commodities except to the extent that such persons:

(1) are engaged in the packaging or labeling of such commodities; or

(2) prescribe or specify by any means the manner in which such commodities are packaged or labeled;

(e) the introduction or delivery for introduction into commerce of any article in violation of Section 431.084, 431.114, or 431.115;

(f) the dissemination of any false advertisement;

(g) the refusal to permit entry or inspection, or to permit the taking of a sample or to permit access to or copying of any record as authorized by Sections 431.042—431.044; or the failure to establish or maintain any record or make any report required under Section 512(j), (*l*), or (m) of the federal Act, or the refusal to permit access to or verification or copying of any such required record;

(h) the manufacture within this state of any food, drug, device, or cosmetic that is adulterated or misbranded;

(i) the giving of a guaranty or undertaking referred to in Section 431.059, which guaranty or undertaking is false, except by a person who relied on a guaranty or undertaking to the same effect signed by, and containing the name and address of the person residing in this state from whom the person received in good faith the food, drug, device, or cosmetic; or the giving of a guaranty or undertaking referred to in Section 431.059, which guaranty or undertaking is false;

(j) the use, removal, or disposal of a detained or embargoed article in violation of Section 431.048;

(k) the alteration, mutilation, destruction, obliteration, or removal of the whole or any part of the labeling of, or the doing of any other act with respect to a food, drug, device, or cosmetic, if such act is done while such article is held for sale after shipment in commerce and results in such article being adulterated or misbranded;

(*l*) (1) forging, counterfeiting, simulating, or falsely representing, or without proper authority using any mark, stamp, tag, label, or other identification device authorized or required by rules adopted under this chapter or

the regulations promulgated under the provisions of the federal Act;

(2) making, selling, disposing of, or keeping in possession, control, or custody, or concealing any punch, die, plate, stone, or other thing designed to print, imprint, or reproduce the trademark, trade name, or other identifying mark, imprint, or device of another or any likeness of any of the foregoing on any drug or container or labeling thereof so as to render such drug a counterfeit drug;

(3) the doing of any act that causes a drug to be a counterfeit drug, or the sale or dispensing, or the holding for sale or dispensing, of a counterfeit drug;

(m) the using by any person to the person's own advantage, or revealing, other than to the commissioner, an authorized agent, a health authority or to the courts when relevant in any judicial proceeding under this chapter, of any information acquired under the authority of this chapter concerning any method or process that as a trade secret is entitled to protection;

(n) the using, on the labeling of any drug or device or in any advertising relating to such drug or device, of any representation or suggestion that approval of an application with respect to such drug or device is in effect under Section 431.114 or Section 505, 515, or 520(g) of the federal Act, as the case may be, or that such drug or device complies with the provisions of such sections;

(o) the using, in labeling, advertising or other sales promotion of any reference to any report or analysis furnished in compliance with Sections 431.042—431.044 or Section 704 of the federal Act;

(p) in the case of a prescription drug distributed or offered for sale in this state, the failure of the manufacturer, packer, or distributor of the drug to maintain for transmittal, or to transmit, to any practitioner licensed by applicable law to administer such drug who makes written request for information as to such drug, true and correct copies of all printed matter that is required to be included in any package in which that drug is distributed or sold, or such other printed matter as is approved under the federal Act. Nothing in this subsection shall be construed to exempt any person from any labeling requirement imposed by or under other provisions of this chapter;

(q) (1) placing or causing to be placed on any drug or device or container of any drug or device, with intent to defraud, the trade name or other identifying mark, or imprint of another or any likeness of any of the foregoing;

(2) selling, dispensing, disposing of or causing to be sold, dispensed, or disposed of, or concealing or keeping in possession, control, or custody, with intent to sell, dispense, or dispose of, any drug, device, or any container of any drug or device, with knowledge that the trade name or other identifying mark or imprint of another or any likeness of any of the foregoing has been placed thereon in a manner prohibited by Subdivision (1) of this subsection; or

(3) making, selling, disposing of, causing to be made, sold, or disposed of, keeping in possession, control, or custody, or concealing with intent to defraud any punch, die, plate, stone, or other thing designed to print, imprint, or reproduce the trademark, trade name, or other identifying mark, imprint, or device of another or any likeness of any of the foregoing on any drug or container or labeling of any drug or container so as to render such drug a counterfeit drug;

(r) dispensing or causing to be dispensed a different drug in place of the drug ordered or prescribed without the express permission in each case of the person ordering or prescribing;

(s) the failure to register in accordance with Section 510 of the federal Act, the failure to provide any information required by Section 510(j) or (k) of the federal Act, or the failure to provide a notice required by Section 510(j)(2) of the federal Act;

(t) (1) the failure or refusal to:

(A) comply with any requirement prescribed under Section 518 or 520(g) of the federal Act; or

(B) furnish any notification or other material or information required by or under Section 519 or 520(g) of the federal Act;

(2) with respect to any device, the submission of any report that is required by or under this chapter that is false or misleading in any material respect;

(u) the movement of a device in violation of an order under Section 304(g) of the federal Act or the removal or alteration of any mark or label required by the order to identify the device as detained;

(v) the failure to provide the notice required by Section 412(b) or 412(c), the failure to make the reports required by Section 412(d)(1)(B), or

the failure to meet the requirements prescribed under Section 412(d)(2) of the federal Act;

(w) except as provided under Subchapter M of this chapter and Section 562.1085, Occupations Code, the acceptance by a person of an unused prescription or drug, in whole or in part, for the purpose of resale, after the prescription or drug has been originally dispensed, or sold;

(x) engaging in the wholesale distribution of drugs or operating as a distributor or manufacturer of devices in this state without obtaining a license issued by the department under Subchapter I, L, or N, as applicable;

(y) engaging in the manufacture of food in this state or operating as a warehouse operator in this state without having a license as required by Section 431.222 or operating as a food wholesaler in this state without having a license under Section 431.222 or being registered under Section 431.2211, as appropriate;

(z) unless approved by the United States Food and Drug Administration pursuant to the federal Act, the sale, delivery, holding, or offering for sale of a self-testing kit designed to indicate whether a person has a human immunodeficiency virus infection, acquired immune deficiency syndrome, or a related disorder or condition;

(aa) making a false statement or false representation in an application for a license or in a statement, report, or other instrument to be filed with or requested by the department under this chapter;

(bb) failing to comply with a requirement or request to provide information or failing to submit an application, statement, report, or other instrument required by the department;

(cc) performing, causing the performance of, or aiding and abetting the performance of an act described by Subdivision (x);

(dd) purchasing or otherwise receiving a prescription drug from a pharmacy in violation of Section 431.411(a);

(ee) selling, distributing, or transferring a prescription drug to a person who is not authorized under state or federal law to receive the prescription drug in violation of Section 431.411(b);

(ff) failing to deliver prescription drugs to specified premises as required by Section 431.411(c);

(gg) failing to maintain or provide pedigrees as required by Section 431.412 or 431.413;

(hh) failing to obtain, pass, or authenticate a pedigree as required by Section 431.412 or 431.413;

(ii) the introduction or delivery for introduction into commerce of a drug or prescription device at a flea market;

(jj) the receipt of a prescription drug that is adulterated, misbranded, stolen, obtained by fraud or deceit, counterfeit, or suspected of being counterfeit, and the delivery or proffered delivery of such a drug for payment or otherwise; or

(kk) the alteration, mutilation, destruction, obliteration, or removal of all or any part of the labeling of a prescription drug or the commission of any other act with respect to a prescription drug that results in the prescription drug being misbranded.

(Enacted by Acts 1989, 71st Leg., ch. 678 (H.B. 2136), § 1, effective September 1, 1989; am. Acts 1991, 72nd Leg., ch. 14 (S.B. 404), § 151, effective September 1, 1991; am. Acts 1991, 72nd Leg., ch. 539 (S.B. 873), § 2, effective September 1, 1991; am. Acts 1993, 73rd Leg., ch. 440 (S.B. 564), § 1, effective September 1, 1993; am. Acts 1995, 74th Leg., ch. 1047 (H.B. 2550), § 6, effective September 1, 1995; am. Acts 1997, 75th Leg., ch. 282 (H.B. 358), § 1, effective September 1, 1997; am. Acts 2001, 77th Leg., ch. 262 (S.B. 1046), § 1, effective September 1, 2001; am. Acts 2001, 77th Leg., ch. 1138 (H.B. 2729), § 2, effective January 1, 2002; am. Acts 2003, 78th Leg., ch. 198 (H.B. 2292), § 2.71, effective September 1, 2003; am. Acts 2003, 78th Leg., ch. 321 (H.B. 3486), § 2, effective June 18, 2003; am. Acts 2003, 78th Leg., ch. 383 (S.B. 1803), § 2, effective September 1, 2003; am. Acts 2003, 78th Leg., ch. 982 (S.B. 1826), § 2, effective September 1, 2003; am. Acts 2005, 79th Leg., ch. 282 (H.B. 164), § 3(i), effective March 1, 2006; am. Acts 2007, 80th Leg., ch. 980 (S.B. 943), § 1, effective September 1, 2007.)

## Sec. 431.0211. Exception.

Any provision of Section 431.021 that relates to a prescription drug does not apply to a prescription drug manufacturer, or an agent of a prescription drug manufacturer, who is obtaining or attempting to obtain a prescription drug for the sole purpose of testing the prescription drug for authenticity.

(Enacted by Acts 2007, 80th Leg., ch. 980 (S.B. 943), § 2, effective September 1, 2007.)

## Sec. 431.022. Offense: Transfer of Product Containing Ephedrine.

(a) A person commits an offense if the person knowingly sells, transfers, or otherwise furnishes a product containing ephedrine to a person 17 years of age or younger, unless:

(1) the actor is:

(A) a practitioner or other health care provider licensed by this state who has obtained, as required by law, consent to the treatment of the person to whom the product is furnished; or

(B) the parent, guardian, or managing conservator of the person to whom the product is furnished;

(2) the person to whom the product is furnished has had the disabilities of minority removed for general purposes under Chapter 31, Family Code; or

(3) the product is a drug.

(b) An offense under this section is a Class C misdemeanor unless it is shown on the trial of the offense that the defendant has been previously convicted of an offense under this section, in which event the offense is a Class B misdemeanor.

(c) A product containing ephedrine that is not described in Subsection (a)(3) must be labeled in accordance with rules adopted by the Texas Department of Health to indicate that sale to persons 17 years of age or younger is prohibited.

(Enacted by Acts 1999, 76th Leg., ch. 151 (S.B. 656), § 1, effective September 1, 1999.)

## Sec. 431.023. Limited Exemption for Distressed Food, Drugs, Devices, or Cosmetics.

In relation to a food, drug, device, or cosmetic that is distressed merchandise for purposes of Chapter 432, Sections 431.021(a), (c), and (d) do not prohibit:

(1) the introduction or delivery for introduction into commerce of the merchandise for the purpose of reconditioning in accordance with Chapter 432 and not for sale to the ultimate consumer;

(2) the receipt in commerce of the merchandise for the purpose of reconditioning in accordance with Chapter 432 and not for sale to the ultimate consumer;

(3) the holding of merchandise for the purpose of reconditioning in accordance with

Chapter 432 and not for resale to the ultimate consumer; or

(4) the reconditioning of the merchandise in accordance with Chapter 432.

(Enacted by Acts 2001, 77th Leg., ch. 265 (S.B. 1080), § 2, effective May 22, 2001.)

## SUBCHAPTER C
## ENFORCEMENT

### Sec. 431.041.  Definition.

In this subchapter, "detained or embargoed article" means a food, drug, device, cosmetic, or consumer commodity that has been detained or embargoed under Section 431.048.

(Enacted by Acts 1989, 71st Leg., ch. 678 (H.B. 2136), § 1, effective September 1, 1989.)

### Sec. 431.042.  Inspection.

(a) To enforce this chapter, the commissioner, an authorized agent, or a health authority may, on presenting appropriate credentials to the owner, operator, or agent in charge:

(1) enter at reasonable times an establishment, including a factory or warehouse, in which a food, drug, device, or cosmetic is manufactured, processed, packed, or held for introduction into commerce or held after the introduction;

(2) enter a vehicle being used to transport or hold the food, drug, device, or cosmetic in commerce; or

(3) inspect at reasonable times, within reasonable limits, and in a reasonable manner, the establishment or vehicle and all equipment, finished and unfinished materials, containers, and labeling of any item and obtain samples necessary for the enforcement of this chapter.

(b) The inspection of an establishment, including a factory, warehouse, or consulting laboratory, in which a prescription drug or restricted device is manufactured, processed, packed, or held for introduction into commerce extends to any place or thing, including a record, file, paper, process, control, or facility, in order to determine whether the drug or device:

(1) is adulterated or misbranded;

(2) may not be manufactured, introduced into commerce, sold, or offered for sale under this chapter; or

(3) is otherwise in violation of this chapter.

(c) An inspection under Subsection (b) may not extend to:

(1) financial data;

(2) sales data other than shipment data;

(3) pricing data;

(4) personnel data other than data relating to the qualifications of technical and professional personnel performing functions under this chapter;

(5) research data other than data:

(A) relating to new drugs, antibiotic drugs, and devices; and

(B) subject to reporting and inspection under regulations issued under Section 505(i) or (j), 519, or 520(g) of the federal Act; or

(6) data relating to other drugs or devices that, in the case of a new drug, would be subject to reporting or inspection under regulations issued under Section 505(j) of the federal Act.

(d) An inspection under Subsection (b) shall be started and completed with reasonable promptness.

(e) This section does not apply to:

(1) a pharmacy that:

(A) complies with Subtitle J, Title 3, Occupations Code;

(B) regularly engages in dispensing prescription drugs or devices on prescriptions of practitioners licensed to administer the drugs or devices to their patients in the course of their professional practice; and

(C) does not, through a subsidiary or otherwise, manufacture, prepare, propagate, compound, or process a drug or device for sale other than in the regular course of its business of dispensing or selling drugs or devices at retail;

(2) a practitioner licensed to prescribe or administer a drug who manufactures, prepares, propagates, compounds, or processes the drug solely for use in the course of the practitioner's professional practice;

(3) a practitioner licensed to prescribe or use a device who manufactures or processes the device solely for use in the course of the practitioner's professional practice; or

(4) a person who manufactures, prepares, propagates, compounds, or processes a drug or manufactures or processes a device solely for use in research, teaching, or chemical analysis and not for sale.

(f) The board may exempt a class of persons from inspection under this section if the board finds that inspection as applied to the class is not necessary for the protection of the public health.

(g) An authorized agent or health authority who makes an inspection under this section to enforce the provisions of this chapter applicable to infant formula shall be permitted, at all reasonable times, to have access to and to copy and verify records:

(1) in order to determine whether the infant formula manufactured or held in the inspected facility meets the requirements of this chapter; or

(2) that are required by this chapter.

(h) An authorized agent or health authority who makes an inspection of an establishment, including a factory or warehouse, and obtains a sample during or on completion of the inspection and before leaving the establishment, shall give to the owner, operator, or the owner's or operator's agent a receipt describing the sample.

(Enacted by Acts 1989, 71st Leg., ch. 678 (H.B. 2136), § 1, effective September 1, 1989; am. Acts 2001, 77th Leg., ch. 1420 (H.B. 2812), § 14.793, effective September 1, 2001; am. Acts 2003, 78th Leg., ch. 111 (S.B. 1400), § 2, effective September 1, 2003.)

### Sec. 431.043.　Access to Records.

A person who is required to maintain records under this chapter or Section 519 or 520(g) of the federal Act or a person who is in charge or custody of those records shall, at the request of an authorized agent or health authority, permit the authorized agent or health authority at all reasonable times access to and to copy and verify the records.

(Enacted by Acts 1989, 71st Leg., ch. 678 (H.B. 2136), § 1, effective September 1, 1989.)

### Sec. 431.044.　Access to Records Showing Movement in Commerce.

(a) To enforce this chapter, a carrier engaged in commerce or other person receiving a food, drug, device, or cosmetic in commerce or holding a food, drug, device, or cosmetic received in commerce shall, at the request of an authorized agent or health authority, permit the authorized agent or health authority at all reasonable times to have access to and to copy all records showing:

(1) the movement in commerce of the food, drug, device, or cosmetic;

(2) the holding of the food, drug, device, or cosmetic after movement in commerce; and

(3) the quantity, shipper, and consignee of the food, drug, device, or cosmetic.

(b) The carrier or other person may not refuse access to and copying of the requested record if the request is accompanied by a written statement that specifies the nature or kind of food, drug, device, or cosmetic to which the request relates.

(c) Evidence obtained under this section or evidence that is directly or indirectly derived from the evidence obtained under this section may not be used in a criminal prosecution of the person from whom the evidence is obtained.

(d) A carrier is not subject to other provisions of this chapter because of the carrier's receipt, carriage, holding, or delivery of a food, drug, device, or cosmetic in the usual course of business as a carrier.

(Enacted by Acts 1989, 71st Leg., ch. 678 (H.B. 2136), § 1, effective September 1, 1989.)

### Sec. 431.045.　Emergency Order.

(a) The commissioner or a person designated by the commissioner may issue an emergency order, either mandatory or prohibitory in nature, in relation to the manufacture or distribution of a food, drug, device, or cosmetic in the department's jurisdiction if the commissioner or the person designated by the commissioner determines that:

(1) the manufacture or distribution of the food, drug, device, or cosmetic creates or poses an immediate and serious threat to human life or health; and

(2) other procedures available to the department to remedy or prevent the occurrence of the situation will result in unreasonable delay.

(b) The commissioner or a person designated by the commissioner may issue the emergency order without notice and hearing if the commissioner or a person designated by the commissioner determines this is practicable under the circumstances.

(c) If an emergency order is issued without a hearing, the department shall determine a time and place for a hearing at which the emergency order is affirmed, modified, or set aside. The hearing shall be held under the contested case provisions of Chapter 2001, Government Code, and the board's formal hearing rules.

(d) This section prevails over Sections 11.013 and 12.001.

(Enacted by Acts 1989, 71st Leg., ch. 678 (H.B. 2136), § 1, effective September 1, 1989; am. Acts 1997, 75th Leg., ch. 629 (H.B. 492), § 4, effective September 1, 1997; am. Acts 2001, 77th Leg., ch. 262 (S.B. 1046), § 2, effective September 1, 2001.)

### Sec. 431.046.　Violation of Rules.

A violation of a rule adopted under this chapter is a violation of this chapter.

(Enacted by Acts 1989, 71st Leg., ch. 678 (H.B. 2136), § 1, effective September 1, 1989.)

Health

## Sec. 431.047.  Violation; Injunction.

(a) The commissioner, an authorized agent, or a health authority may petition the district court for a temporary restraining order to restrain a continuing violation of Subchapter B or a threat of a continuing violation of Subchapter B if the commissioner, authorized agent, or health authority finds that:

(1) a person has violated, is violating, or is threatening to violate Subchapter B; and

(2) the violation or threatened violation creates an immediate threat to the health and safety of the public.

(b) A district court, on petition of the commissioner, an authorized agent, or a health authority, and on a finding by the court that a person is violating or threatening to violate Subchapter B shall grant any injunctive relief warranted by the facts.

(c) Venue for a suit brought under this section is in the county in which the violation or threat of violation is alleged to have occurred or in Travis County.

(d) The commissioner and the attorney general may each recover reasonable expenses incurred in obtaining injunctive relief under this section, including investigative costs, court costs, reasonable attorney fees, witness fees, and deposition expenses. The expenses recovered by the commissioner are hereby appropriated to the department for the administration and enforcement of this chapter. The expenses recovered by the attorney general are hereby appropriated to the attorney general.

(Enacted by Acts 1989, 71st Leg., ch. 678 (H.B. 2136), § 1, effective September 1, 1989; am. Acts 1991, 72nd Leg., ch. 539 (S.B. 873), § 3, effective September 1, 1991.)

## Sec. 431.048.  Detained or Embargoed Article.

(a) The commissioner or an authorized agent shall affix to an article that is a food, drug, device, cosmetic, or consumer commodity a tag or other appropriate marking that gives notice that the article is, or is suspected of being, adulterated or misbranded and that the article has been detained or embargoed if the commissioner or the authorized agent finds or has probable cause to believe that the article:

(1) is adulterated;

(2) is misbranded so that the article is dangerous or fraudulent under this chapter; or

(3) violates Section 431.084, 431.114, or 431.115.

(b) The tag or marking on a detained or embargoed article must warn all persons not to use the article, remove the article from the premises, or dispose of the article by sale or otherwise until permission for use, removal, or disposal is given by the commissioner, the authorized agent, or a court.

(c) A person may not use a detained or embargoed article, remove a detained or embargoed article from the premises, or dispose of a detained or embargoed article by sale or otherwise without permission of the commissioner, the authorized agent, or a court. The commissioner or the authorized agent may permit perishable goods to be moved to a place suitable for proper storage.

(d) The commissioner or an authorized agent shall remove the tag or other marking from an embargoed or detained article if the commissioner or an authorized agent finds that the article is not adulterated or misbranded.

(e) The commissioner or an authorized agent may not detain or embargo an article, including an article that is distressed merchandise, that is in the possession of a person licensed under Chapter 432 and that is being held for the purpose of reconditioning in accordance with Chapter 432, unless the commissioner or an authorized agent finds or has probable cause to believe that the article cannot be adequately reconditioned in accordance with that chapter and applicable rules.

(Enacted by Acts 1989, 71st Leg., ch. 678 (H.B. 2136), § 1, effective September 1, 1989; am. Acts 1997, 75th Leg., ch. 282 (H.B. 358), § 2, effective September 1, 1997; am. Acts 2001, 77th Leg., ch. 265 (S.B. 1080), § 3, effective May 22, 2001.)

## Sec. 431.049.  Removal Order for Detained or Embargoed Article.

(a) If the claimant of the detained or embargoed articles or the claimant's agent fails or refuses to transfer the articles to a secure place after the tag or other appropriate marking has been affixed as provided by Section 431.048, the commissioner or an authorized agent may order the transfer of the articles to one or more secure storage areas to prevent their unauthorized use, removal, or disposal.

(b) The commissioner or an authorized agent may provide for the transfer of the article if the claimant of the article or the claimant's agent does not carry out the transfer order in a timely manner. The costs of the transfer shall be assessed against the claimant of the article or the claimant's agent.

Health

(c) The claimant of the article or the claimant's agent shall pay the costs of the transfer.

(d) The commissioner may request the attorney general to bring an action in the district court in Travis County to recover the costs of the transfer. In a judgment in favor of the state, the court may award costs, attorney fees, court costs, and interest from the time the expense was incurred through the date the department is reimbursed.

(Enacted by Acts 1989, 71st Leg., ch. 678 (H.B. 2136), § 1, effective September 1, 1989; am. Acts 1991, 72nd Leg., ch. 14 (S.B. 404), § 152, effective September 1, 1991; am. Acts 1997, 75th Leg., ch. 282 (H.B. 358), § 3, effective September 1, 1997.)

## Sec. 431.0495.　Recall Orders.

(a) In conjunction with the issuance of an emergency order under Section 431.045 or the detention or embargo of an article under Section 431.048, the commissioner may order a food, drug, device, cosmetic, or consumer commodity to be recalled from commerce.

(b) The commissioner's recall order may require the articles to be removed to one or more secure areas approved by the commissioner or an authorized agent.

(c) The recall order must be in writing and signed by the commissioner.

(d) The recall order may be issued before or in conjunction with the affixing of the tag or other appropriate marking as provided by Section 431.048(a) or in conjunction with the commissioner's issuance of an emergency order under Section 431.045.

(e) The recall order is effective until the order:

(1) expires on its own terms;

(2) is withdrawn by the commissioner;

(3) is reversed by a court in an order denying condemnation under Section 431.050; or

(4) is set aside at the hearing provided to affirm, modify, or set aside an emergency order under Section 431.045.

(f) The claimant of the articles or the claimant's agent shall pay the costs of the removal and storage of the articles removed.

(g) If the claimant or the claimant's agent fails or refuses to carry out the recall order in a timely manner, the commissioner may provide for the recall of the articles. The costs of the recall shall be assessed against the claimant of the articles or the claimant's agent.

(h) The commissioner may request the attorney general to bring an action in the district court

of Travis County to recover the costs of the recall. In a judgment in favor of the state, the court may award costs, attorney fees, court costs, and interest from the time the expense was incurred through the date the department is reimbursed.

## Sec. 431.050.　Condemnation.

An action for the condemnation of an article may be brought before a court in whose jurisdiction the article is located, detained, or embargoed if the article is adulterated, misbranded, or in violation of Section 431.084, 431.114, or 431.115. (Enacted by Acts 1989, 71st Leg., ch. 678 (H.B. 2136), § 1, effective September 1, 1989.)

## Sec. 431.051.　Destruction of Article.

(a) A court shall order the destruction of a sampled article or a detained or embargoed article if the court finds that the article is adulterated or misbranded.

(b) After entry of the court's order, an authorized agent shall supervise the destruction of the article.

(c) The claimant of the article shall pay the cost of the destruction of the article.

(d) The court shall tax against the claimant of the article or the claimant's agent all court costs and fees, and storage and other proper expenses. (Enacted by Acts 1989, 71st Leg., ch. 678 (H.B. 2136), § 1, effective September 1, 1989.)

## Sec. 431.052.　Correction by Proper Labeling or Processing.

(a) A court may order the delivery of a sampled article or a detained or embargoed article that is adulterated or misbranded to the claimant of the article for labeling or processing under the supervision of an agent of the commissioner or an authorized agent if:

(1) the decree has been entered in the suit;

(2) the costs, fees, and expenses of the suit have been paid;

(3) the adulteration or misbranding can be corrected by proper labeling or processing; and

(4) a good and sufficient bond, conditioned on the correction of the adulteration or misbranding by proper labeling or processing, has been executed.

(b) The claimant shall pay the costs of the supervision.

(c) The court shall order that the article be returned to the claimant and the bond discharged on the representation to the court by the commissioner or an authorized agent that the article no

longer violates this chapter and that the expenses of the supervision are paid.
(Enacted by Acts 1989, 71st Leg., ch. 678 (H.B. 2136), § 1, effective September 1, 1989.)

### Sec. 431.053.  Condemnation of Perishable Articles.

(a) The commissioner or an authorized agent shall immediately condemn or render by any means unsalable as human food an article that is a nuisance under Subsection (b) and that the commissioner or authorized agent finds in any room, building, or other structure or in a vehicle.

(b) Any meat, seafood, poultry, vegetable, fruit, or other perishable article is a nuisance if it:

(1) is unsound;

(2) contains a filthy, decomposed, or putrid substance; or

(3) may be poisonous or deleterious to health or otherwise unsafe.

(Enacted by Acts 1989, 71st Leg., ch. 678 (H.B. 2136), § 1, effective September 1, 1989.)

### Sec. 431.054.  Administrative Penalty.

(a) The commissioner may assess an administrative penalty against a person who violates Subchapter B or an order adopted or registration issued under this chapter.

(b) In determining the amount of the penalty, the commissioner shall consider:

(1) the person's previous violations;

(2) the seriousness of the violation;

(3) any hazard to the health and safety of the public;

(4) the person's demonstrated good faith; and

(5) such other matters as justice may require.

(c) The penalty may not exceed $25,000 a day for each violation.

(d) Each day a violation continues may be considered a separate violation.

(Enacted by Acts 1989, 71st Leg., ch. 678 (H.B. 2136), § 1, effective September 1, 1989; am. Acts 1991, 72nd Leg., ch. 539 (S.B. 873), § 4, effective September 1, 1991.)

### Sec. 431.055.  Administrative Penalty Assessment Procedure.

(a) An administrative penalty may be assessed only after a person charged with a violation is given an opportunity for a hearing.

(b) If a hearing is held, the commissioner shall make findings of fact and shall issue a written decision regarding the occurrence of the violation and the amount of the penalty that may be warranted.

(c) If the person charged with the violation does not request a hearing, the commissioner may assess a penalty after determining that a violation has occurred and the amount of the penalty that may be warranted.

(d) After making a determination under this section that a penalty is to be assessed against a person, the commissioner shall issue an order requiring that the person pay the penalty.

(e) The commissioner may consolidate a hearing held under this section with another proceeding.

(Enacted by Acts 1989, 71st Leg., ch. 678 (H.B. 2136), § 1, effective September 1, 1989.)

### Sec. 431.056.  Payment of Administrative Penalty.

(a) Not later than the 30th day after the date an order finding that a violation has occurred is issued, the commissioner shall inform the person against whom the order is issued of the amount of the penalty for the violation.

(b) Not later than the 30th day after the date on which a decision or order charging a person with a penalty is final, the person shall:

(1) pay the penalty in full; or

(2) if the person seeks judicial review of the amount of the penalty, the fact of the violation, or both:

(A) send the amount of the penalty to the commissioner for placement in an escrow account; or

(B) post with the commissioner a bond for the amount of the penalty.

(c) A bond posted under this section must be in a form approved by the commissioner and be effective until all judicial review of the order or decision is final.

(d) A person who does not send money to the commissioner or post the bond within the period prescribed by Subsection (b) waives all rights to contest the violation or the amount of the penalty.

(Enacted by Acts 1989, 71st Leg., ch. 678 (H.B. 2136), § 1, effective September 1, 1989.)

### Sec. 431.057.  Refund of Administrative Penalty.

Not later than the 30th day after the date of a judicial determination that an administrative penalty against a person should be reduced or not assessed, the commissioner shall:

Health

(1) remit to the person the appropriate amount of any penalty payment plus accrued interest; or

(2) execute a release of the bond if the person has posted a bond.

(Enacted by Acts 1989, 71st Leg., ch. 678 (H.B. 2136), § 1, effective September 1, 1989.)

### Sec. 431.058. Recovery of Administrative Penalty by Attorney General.

The attorney general at the request of the commissioner may bring a civil action to recover an administrative penalty under this subchapter. (Enacted by Acts 1989, 71st Leg., ch. 678 (H.B. 2136), § 1, effective September 1, 1989.)

### Sec. 431.0585. Civil Penalty.

(a) At the request of the commissioner, the attorney general or a district, county, or city attorney shall institute an action in district court to collect a civil penalty from a person who has violated Section 431.021.

(b) The civil penalty may not exceed $25,000 a day for each violation. Each day of violation constitutes a separate violation for purposes of the penalty assessment.

(c) The court shall consider the following in determining the amount of the penalty:

(1) the person's history of any previous violations of Section 431.021;

(2) the seriousness of the violation;

(3) any hazard posed to the public health and safety by the violation; and

(4) demonstrations of good faith by the person charged.

(d) Venue for a suit brought under this section is in the city or county in which the violation occurred or in Travis County.

(e) A civil penalty recovered in a suit instituted by a local government under this section shall be paid to that local government.

(Enacted by Acts 1991, 72nd Leg., ch. 14 (S.B. 404), § 154, effective September 1, 1991.)

### Sec. 431.059. Criminal Penalty; Defenses.

(a) A person commits an offense if the person violates any of the provisions of Section 431.021 relating to unlawful or prohibited acts. A first offense under this subsection is a Class A misdemeanor unless it is shown on the trial of an offense under this subsection that the defendant was previously convicted of an offense under this subsection, in which event the offense is a state jail felony. In a criminal proceeding under this section, it is not necessary to prove intent, knowledge, recklessness, or criminal negligence of the defendant beyond the degree of culpability, if any, stated in Subsection (a-2) or Section 431.021, as applicable, to establish criminal responsibility for the violation.

(a-1), (a-2) [Repealed by Acts 2007, 80th Leg., ch. 980 (S.B. 943), § 14, effective September 1, 2007.]

(b) A person is not subject to the penalties of Subsection (a):

(1) for having received an article in commerce and having delivered or offered delivery of the article, if the delivery or offer was made in good faith, unless the person refuses to furnish on request of the commissioner, an authorized agent, or a health authority, the name and address of the person from whom the article was received and copies of any documents relating to the receipt of the article;

(2) for having violated Section 431.021(a) or (e) if the person establishes a guaranty or undertaking signed by, and containing the name and address of, the person residing in this state from whom the person received in good faith the article, to the effect that:

(A) in the case of an alleged violation of Section 431.021(a), the article is not adulterated or misbranded within the meaning of this chapter; and

(B) in the case of an alleged violation of Section 431.021(e), the article is not an article that may not, under the provisions of Section 404 or 405 of the federal Act or Section 431.084 or 431.114, be introduced into commerce;

(3) for having violated Section 431.021, if the violation exists because the article is adulterated by reason of containing a color additive not from a batch certified in accordance with regulations promulgated under the federal Act, if the person establishes a guaranty or undertaking signed by, and containing the name and address of, the manufacturer of the color additive, to the effect that the color additive was from a batch certified in accordance with the applicable regulations promulgated under the federal Act;

(4) for having violated Section 431.021(b), (c), or (k) by failure to comply with Section 431.112(i) with respect to an article received in commerce to which neither Section 503(a) nor Section 503(b)(1) of the federal Act applies if the delivery or offered delivery was made in

good faith and the labeling at the time of the delivery or offer contained the same directions for use and warning statements as were contained in the labeling at the same time of the receipt of the article; or

(5) for having violated Section 431.021(*l*)(2) if the person acted in good faith and had no reason to believe that use of the punch, die, plate, stone, or other thing would result in a drug being a counterfeit drug, or for having violated Section 431.021(*l*)(3) if the person doing the act or causing it to be done acted in good faith and had no reason to believe that the drug was a counterfeit drug.

(c) A publisher, radio-broadcast licensee, or agency or medium for the dissemination of an advertisement, except the manufacturer, packer, distributor, or seller of the article to which a false advertisement relates, is not liable under this section for the dissemination of the false advertisement, unless the person has refused, on the request of the commissioner to furnish the commissioner the name and post-office address of the manufacturer, packer, distributor, seller, or advertising agency, residing in this state who caused the person to disseminate the advertisement.

(d) A person is not subject to the penalties of Subsection (a) for a violation of Section 431.021 involving misbranded food if the violation exists solely because the food is misbranded under Section 431.082 because of its advertising, and a person is not subject to the penalties of Subsection (a) for such a violation unless the violation is committed with the intent to defraud or mislead.

(e) It is an affirmative defense to prosecution under Subsection (a) that the conduct charged is exempt, in accordance with Section 431.023, from the application of Section 431.021.

(Enacted by Acts 1989, 71st Leg., ch. 678 (H.B. 2136), § 1, effective September 1, 1989; am. Acts 1991, 72nd Leg., ch. 14 (S.B. 404), § 155, effective September 1, 1991; am. Acts 2001, 77th Leg., ch. 265 (S.B. 1080), § 4, effective May 22, 2001; am. Acts 2003, 78th Leg., ch. 111 (S.B. 1400), § 3, effective September 1, 2003; am. Acts 2003, 78th Leg., ch. 383 (S.B. 1803), § 3, effective September 1, 2003; am. Acts 2003, 78th Leg., ch. 982 (S.B. 1826), § 3, effective September 1, 2003; am. Acts 2005, 79th Leg., ch. 282 (H.B. 164), § 3(h), effec-

tive March 1, 2006; am. Acts 2007, 80th Leg., ch. 980 (S.B. 943), § 14, effective September 1, 2007.)

## Sec. 431.060. Initiation of Proceedings.

(a) The attorney general, or a district, county, or municipal attorney to whom the commissioner, an authorized agent, or a health authority reports a violation of this chapter, shall initiate and prosecute appropriate proceedings without delay.

(b) The commissioner, the commissioner's authorized agent, or the attorney general may, as authorized by Section 307 of the federal Act, bring in the name of this state a suit for civil penalties or to restrain a violation of Section 401 or Section 403(b) through (i), (k), (q), or (r) of the federal Act if the food that is the subject of the proceedings is located in this state.

(c) The commissioner, the commissioner's authorized agent, or the attorney general may not bring a proceeding under Subsection (b):

(1) before the 31st day after the date on which the state has given notice to the secretary of its intent to bring a suit;

(2) before the 91st day after the date on which the state has given notice to the secretary of its intent to bring a suit if the secretary has, not later than the 30th day after receiving notice from the state, commenced an informal or formal enforcement action pertaining to the food that would be the subject of the suit brought by the state; or

(3) if the secretary is diligently prosecuting a suit in court pertaining to that food, has settled a suit pertaining to that food, or has settled the informal or formal enforcement action pertaining to that food.

(Enacted by Acts 1989, 71st Leg., ch. 678 (H.B. 2136), § 1, effective September 1, 1989; am. Acts 1993, 73rd Leg., ch. 459 (S.B. 558), § 2, effective September 1, 1993.)

## Sec. 431.061. Minor Violation.

This chapter does not require the commissioner, an authorized agent, or a health authority to report for prosecution or the institution of proceedings under this chapter a minor violation of this chapter if the commissioner, authorized agent, or health authority believes that the public interest is adequately served by a suitable written notice or warning.

(Enacted by Acts 1989, 71st Leg., ch. 678 (H.B. 2136), § 1, effective September 1, 1989.)

## SUBCHAPTER E
## DRUGS AND DEVICES

### Sec. 431.111. Adulterated Drug or Device.

A drug or device shall be deemed to be adulterated:

(a) (1) if it consists in whole or in part of any filthy, putrid, or decomposed substance; or

(2) (A) if it has been prepared, packed, or held under insanitary conditions whereby it may have been contaminated with filth, or whereby it may have been rendered injurious to health; or

(B) if it is a drug and the methods used in, or the facilities or controls used for, its manufacture, processing, packing, or holding do not conform to or are not operated or administered in conformity with current good manufacturing practice to assure that such drug meets the requirements of this chapter as to safety and has the identity and strength, and meets the quality and purity characteristics, which it purports or is represented to possess; or

(3) if its container is composed, in whole or in part, of any poisonous or deleterious substance which may render the contents injurious to health; or

(4) if it:

(A) bears or contains, for purposes of coloring only, a color additive that is unsafe under Section 431.161(a); or

(B) is a color additive, the intended use of which in or on drugs or devices is for purposes of coloring only, and is unsafe under Section 431.161(a); or

(5) if it is a new animal drug that is unsafe under Section 512 of the federal Act;

(b) if it purports to be or is represented as a drug, the name of which is recognized in an official compendium, and its strength differs from, or its quality or purity falls below, the standards set forth in such compendium. Such determination as to strength, quality or purity shall be made in accordance with the tests or methods of assay set forth in such compendium, or in the absence of or inadequacy of such tests or methods of assay, those prescribed under the authority of the federal Act. No drug defined in an official compendium shall be deemed to be adulterated under this paragraph because it differs from the standards of strength, quality, or purity therefor set forth in such compendium, if its difference in strength, quality, or purity from such standards is plainly stated on its label. Whenever a drug is recognized in the United States Pharmacopoeia National Formulary, it shall be subject to the requirements of the United States Pharmacopoeia National Formulary;

(c) if it is not subject to the provision of Paragraph (b) and its strength differs from, or its purity or quality falls below, that which it purports or is represented to possess;

(d) if it is a drug and any substance has been:

(1) mixed or packed therewith so as to reduce its quality or strength; or

(2) substituted wholly or in part therefor;

(e) if it is, or purports to be or is represented as, a device that is subject to a performance standard established under Section 514 of the federal Act, unless the device is in all respects in conformity with the standard;

(f) (1) if it is a class III device:

(A) (i) that is required by a regulation adopted under Section 515(b) of the federal Act to have an approval under that section of an application for premarket approval and that is not exempt from Section 515 as provided by Section 520(g) of the federal Act; and

(ii) (I) for which an application for premarket approval or a notice of completion of a product development protocol was not filed with the United States Food and Drug Administration by the 90th day after the date of adoption of the regulation; or

(II) for which that application was filed and approval was denied or withdrawn, for which that notice was filed and was declared incomplete, or for which approval of the device under the protocol was withdrawn;

(B) that was classified under Section 513(f) of the federal Act into class III, which under Section 515(a) of the federal Act is required to have in effect an approved application for premarket approval, that is not exempt from Section 515 as provided by Section 520(g) of the federal Act, and that does not have the application in effect; or

(C) that was classified under Section 520(*l*) of the federal Act into class III, which under that section is required to have in effect an approved application under Section 515 of the federal Act, and that does not have the application in effect, except that:

(2) (A) in the case of a device classified under Section 513(f) of the federal Act into class III and intended solely for investigational use, Subdivision (1)(B) does not apply to the device during the period ending on the 90th day after the date of adoption of the regulations prescribing the procedures and conditions required by Section 520(g)(2) of the federal Act; and

(B) in the case of a device subject to a regulation adopted under Section 515(b) of the federal Act, Subdivision (1) does not apply to the device during the period ending on whichever of the following dates occurs later:

(i) the last day of the 30-day calendar month beginning after the month in which the classification of the device into class III became effective under Section 513 of the federal Act; or

(ii) the 90th day after the date of adoption of the regulation;

(g) if it is a banned device;

(h) if it is a device and the methods used in, or the facilities or controls used for its manufacture, packing, storage, or installations are not in conformity with applicable requirements under Section 520(f)(1) of the federal Act or an applicable condition as prescribed by an order under Section 520(f)(2) of the federal Act; or

(i) if it is a device for which an exemption has been granted under Section 520(g) of the federal Act for investigational use and the person who was granted the exemption or any investigator who uses the device under the exemption fails to comply with a requirement prescribed by or under that section.

(Enacted by Acts 1989, 71st Leg., ch. 678 (H.B. 2136), § 1, effective September 1, 1989; am. Acts 1993, 73rd Leg., ch. 440 (S.B. 564), § 2, effective September 1, 1993.)

## Sec. 431.112.  Misbranded Drug or Device.

A drug or device shall be deemed to be misbranded:

(a) (1) if its labeling is false or misleading in any particular; or

(2) if its labeling or packaging fails to conform with the requirements of Section 431.181.

(b) if in a package form unless it bears a label containing (1) the name and place of business of the manufacturer, packer, or distributor; and (2) an accurate statement of the quantity of the contents in terms of weight, measure, or numerical count; provided, that under Subdivision (2) reasonable variations shall be permitted, and exemptions as to small packages shall be allowed in accordance with regulations prescribed by the secretary under the federal Act;

(c) if any word, statement, or other information required by or under authority of this chapter to appear on the label or labeling is not prominently placed thereon with such conspicuousness (as compared with other words, statements, designs, or devices, in the labeling) and in such terms as to render it likely to be read and understood by the ordinary individual under customary conditions of purchase and use;

(d) (1) if it is a drug, unless:

(A) its label bears, to the exclusion of any other nonproprietary name (except the applicable systematic chemical name or the chemical formula):

(i) the established name (as defined in Subdivision (3)) of the drug, if any; and

(ii) in case it is fabricated from two or more ingredients, the established name and quantity of each active ingredient, including the quantity, kind, and proportion of any alcohol, and also including, whether active or not, the established name and quantity or proportion of any bromides, ether, chloroform, acetanilid, acetphenetidin, amidopyrine, antipyrine, atropine, hyoscine, hyoscyamine, arsenic, digitalis, digitalis glucosides, mercury, ouabain, strophanthin, strychnine, thyroid, or any derivative or preparation of any such substances, contained therein; provided, that the requirement for stating the quantity of the active ingredients, other than the quantity of those specifically named in this subparagraph shall apply only to prescription drugs; and

(B) for any prescription drug the established name of the drug or ingredient, as the case may be, on the label (and on any labeling on which a name for such drug or ingredient is used) is printed prominently and in type at least half as large as that used thereon for any proprietary name or designation for such drug or ingredient; and provided, that to the extent that compliance with the requirements of Paragraph (A)(ii) or this paragraph is impracticable, exemptions shall be allowed under regulations promulgated by the secretary under the federal Act;

(2) if it is a device and it has an established name, unless its label bears, to the exclusion of any other nonproprietary name, its established name (as defined in Subdivision (4)) prominently printed in type at least half as large as that used thereon for any proprietary name or designation for such device, except that to the extent compliance with this subdivision is impracticable, exemptions shall be allowed under regulations promulgated by the secretary under the federal Act;

(3) as used in Subdivision (1), the term "established name," with respect to a drug or ingredient thereof, means:

(A) the applicable official name designated pursuant to Section 508 of the federal Act; or

(B) if there is no such name and such drug, or such ingredient, is an article recognized in an official compendium, then the official title thereof in such compendium; or

(C) if neither Paragraph (A) nor Paragraph (B) applies, then the common or usual name, if any, of such drug or of such ingredient; provided further, that where Paragraph (B) applies to an article recognized in the United States Pharmacopoeia National Formulary, the official title used in the United States Pharmacopoeia National Formulary shall apply;

(4) as used in Subdivision (2), the term "established name" with respect to a device means:

(A) the applicable official name of the device designated pursuant to Section 508 of the federal Act;

(B) if there is no such name and such device is an article recognized in an official compendium, then the official title thereof in such compendium; or

(C) if neither Paragraph (A) nor Paragraph (B) applies, then any common or usual name of such device;

(e) unless its labeling bears:

(1) adequate directions for use; and

(2) such adequate warnings against use in those pathological conditions or by children where its use may be dangerous to health, or against unsafe dosage or methods or durations of administration or application, in such manner and form, as are necessary for the protection of users unless the drug or device has been exempted from those requirements by the regulations adopted by the secretary;

(f) if it purports to be a drug the name of which is recognized in an official compendium, unless it is packaged and labeled as prescribed therein unless the method of packing has been modified with the consent of the secretary. Whenever a drug is recognized in the United States Pharmacopoeia National Formulary, it shall be subject to the requirements of the United States Pharmacopoeia National Formulary with respect to packaging and labeling. If there is an inconsistency between the requirements of this subsection and those of Subsection (d) as to the name by which the drug or its ingredients shall be designated, the requirements of Subsection (d) prevail;

(g) if it has been found by the secretary to be a drug liable to deterioration, unless it is packaged in such form and manner, and its label bears a statement of such precautions, as the secretary shall by regulations require as necessary for the protection of public health;

(h) if:

(1) it is a drug and its container is so made, formed, or filled as to be misleading; or

(2) it is an imitation of another drug; or

(3) it is offered for sale under the name of another drug;

(i) if it is dangerous to health when used in the dosage, or manner or with the frequency or duration prescribed, recommended, or suggested in the labeling thereof;

(j) if it is a color additive, the intended use of which is for the purpose of coloring only, unless its packaging and labeling are in conformity with such packaging and labeling requirements applicable to such color additive, as may be contained in rules issued under Section 431.161(b);

(k) in the case of any prescription drug distributed or offered for sale in this state, unless the manufacturer, packer, or distributor thereof includes in all advertisements and other descriptive printed matter issued or caused to be issued by the manufacturer,

Health

packer, or distributor with respect to that drug a true statement of:

(1) the established name as defined in Subsection (d), printed prominently and in type at least half as large as that used for any trade or brand name;

(2) the formula showing quantitatively each ingredient of the drug to the extent required for labels under Subsection (d); and

(3) other information in brief summary relating to side effects, contraindications, and effectiveness as required in regulations issued under Section 701(e) of the federal Act;

(*l*) if it was manufactured, prepared, propagated, compounded, or processed in an establishment in this state not registered under Section 510 of the federal Act, if it was not included in a list required by Section 510(j) of the federal Act, if a notice or other information respecting it was not provided as required by that section or Section 510(k) of the federal Act, or if it does not bear symbols from the uniform system for identification of devices prescribed under Section 510(e) of the federal Act as required by regulation;

(m) if it is a drug and its packaging or labeling is in violation of an applicable regulation issued under Section 3 or 4 of the federal Poison Prevention Packaging Act of 1970 (15 U.S.C. 1472 or 1473);

(n) if a trademark, trade name, or other identifying mark, imprint or device of another, or any likeness of the foregoing has been placed thereon or on its container with intent to defraud;

(o) in the case of any restricted device distributed or offered for sale in this state, if:

(1) its advertising is false or misleading in any particular; or

(2) it is sold, distributed, or used in violation of regulations prescribed under Section 520(e) of the federal Act;

(p) in the case of any restricted device distributed or offered for sale in this state, unless the manufacturer, packer, or distributor thereof includes in all advertisements and other descriptive printed matter issued by the manufacturer, packer, or distributor with respect to that device:

(1) a true statement of the device's established name as defined in Section 502(e) of the federal Act, printed prominently and in type at least half as large as that used for any trade or brand name thereof; and

(2) a brief statement of the intended uses of the device and relevant warnings, precautions, side effects, and contraindications and in the case of specific devices made subject to regulations issued under the federal Act, a full description of the components of such device or the formula showing quantitatively each ingredient of such device to the extent required in regulations under the federal Act;

(q) if it is a device subject to a performance standard established under Section 514 of the federal Act, unless it bears such labeling as may be prescribed in such performance standard; or

(r) if it is a device and there was a failure or refusal:

(1) to comply with any requirement prescribed under Section 518 of the federal Act respecting the device; or

(2) to furnish material required by or under Section 519 of the federal Act respecting the device.

(Enacted by Acts 1989, 71st Leg., ch. 678 (H.B. 2136), § 1, effective September 1, 1989; am. Acts 1997, 75th Leg., ch. 282 (H.B. 358), § 4, effective September 1, 1997; am. Acts 2003, 78th Leg., ch. 111 (S.B. 1400), § 4, effective September 1, 2003; am. Acts 2003, 78th Leg., ch. 1099 (H.B. 2192), § 2, effective September 1, 2003.)

## Sec. 431.113. Exemption for Certain Drugs and Devices.

(a) The board is directed to adopt rules exempting from any labeling or packaging requirement of this chapter drugs and devices that are, in accordance with the practice of the trade, to be processed, labeled, or repacked in substantial quantities at establishments other than those where originally processed or packaged on condition that such drugs and devices are not adulterated or misbranded under the provisions of this chapter on removal from such processing, labeling, or repacking establishment.

(b) Drugs and device labeling or packaging exemptions adopted under the federal Act shall apply to drugs and devices in this state except insofar as modified or rejected by rules of the board.

(c) (1) A drug intended for use by man that:

(A) because of its toxicity or other potentiality for harmful effect, or the method of its use, or the collateral measures necessary to its use, is not safe for use except under the supervision of a practitioner licensed by law to administer such drug; or

(B) is limited by an approved application under Section 505 of the federal Act to use under the professional supervision of a practitioner licensed by law to administer such drug shall be dispensed only:

(i) on a written prescription of a practitioner licensed by law to administer such drug; or

(ii) on an oral prescription of such practitioner that is reduced promptly to writing and filed by the pharmacist; or

(iii) by refilling any such written or oral prescription if such refilling is authorized by the prescriber either in the original prescription or by oral order that is reduced promptly to writing and filed by the pharmacist. The act of dispensing a drug contrary to the provisions of this paragraph shall be deemed to be an act that results in a drug being misbranded while held for sale.

(2) Any drug dispensed by filling or refilling a written or oral prescription of a practitioner licensed by law to administer such drug shall be exempt from the requirements of Section 431.112, except Sections 431.112(a)(1), (h)(2), and (h)(3), and the packaging requirements of Sections 431.112(f), (g), and (m), if the drug bears a label containing the name and address of the dispenser, the serial number and date of the prescription or of its filling, the name of the prescriber, and, if stated in the prescription, the name of the patient, and the directions for use and cautionary statements, if any, contained in such prescription. This exemption shall not apply to any drugs dispensed in the course of the conduct of business of dispensing drugs pursuant to diagnosis by mail, or to a drug dispensed in violation of Subdivision (1).

(3) A drug that is subject to Subdivision (1) shall be deemed to be misbranded if at any time prior to dispensing its label fails to bear at a minimum, the symbol "RX Only." A drug to which Subdivision (1) does not apply shall be deemed to be misbranded if at any time prior to dispensing its label bears the caution statement quoted in the preceding sentence. (Enacted by Acts 1989, 71st Leg., ch. 678 (H.B. 2136), § 1, effective September 1, 1989; am. Acts 2003, 78th Leg., ch. 111 (S.B. 1400), § 5, effective September 1, 2003; am. Acts 2003, 78th Leg., ch. 1099 (H.B. 2192), § 3, effective September 1, 2003.)

## Sec. 431.114. New Drugs.

(a) A person shall not sell, deliver, offer for sale, hold for sale or give away any new drug unless:

(1) an application with respect thereto has been approved and the approval has not been withdrawn under Section 505 of the federal Act; and

(2) a copy of the letter of approval or approvability issued by the Federal Food and Drug Administration is on file with the commissioner if the product is manufactured in this state.

(b) A person shall not use in or on human beings or animals a new drug or new animal drug limited to investigational use unless the person has filed with the Federal Food and Drug Administration a completed and signed "Notice of claimed investigational exemption for a new drug" form in accordance with 21 C.F.R. 312.1 (1980) and the exemption has not been terminated. The drug shall be plainly labeled in compliance with Section 505(i) of the federal Act.

(c) This section shall not apply:

(1) to any drug that is not a new drug as defined in the federal Act;

(2) to any drug that is licensed under the Public Health Services Act of July 1, 1944 (42 U.S.C. 201 et seq.); or

(3) to any drug approved by the commissioner by the authority of any prior law.

(Enacted by Acts 1989, 71st Leg., ch. 678 (H.B. 2136), § 1, effective September 1, 1989; am. Acts 1991, 72nd Leg., ch. 14 (S.B. 404), § 157, effective September 1, 1991; am. Acts 2003, 78th Leg., ch. 111 (S.B. 1400), § 6, effective September 1, 2003.)

## Sec. 431.115. New Animal Drugs.

(a) A new animal drug shall, with respect to any particular use or intended use of the drug, be deemed unsafe for the purposes of this chapter unless:

(1) there is in effect an approval of an application filed pursuant to Section 512(b) of the federal Act with respect to the use or intended use of the drug; and

(2) the drug, its labeling, and the use conforms to the approved application.

(b) A new animal drug shall not be deemed unsafe for the purposes of this chapter if the article is for investigational use and conforms to the terms of an exemption in effect with respect thereto under Section 512(j) of the federal Act.

Health

(c) This section does not apply to any drug:

(1) licensed under the virus-serum-toxin law of March 4, 1913 (21 U.S.C. 151—159);

(2) approved by the United States Department of Agriculture; or

(3) approved by the commissioner by the authority of any prior law.

(Enacted by Acts 1989, 71st Leg., ch. 678 (H.B. 2136), § 1, effective September 1, 1989; am. Acts 1991, 72nd Leg., ch. 14 (S.B. 404), § 158, effective September 1, 1991.)

## Sec. 431.116.   Average Manufacturer Price.

(a) In this section, "average manufacturer price" has the meaning assigned by 42 U.S.C. Section 1396r-8(k), as amended.

(b) A person who manufactures a drug, including a person who manufactures a generic drug, that is sold in this state shall file with the department:

(1) the average manufacturer price for the drug; and

(2) the price that each wholesaler in this state pays the manufacturer to purchase the drug.

(c) The information required under Subsection (b) must be filed annually or more frequently as determined by the department.

(d) The department and the attorney general may investigate the manufacturer to determine the accuracy of the information provided under Subsection (b). The attorney general may take action to enforce this section.

(e) [Repealed by Acts 2005, 79th Leg., ch. 349 (S.B. 1188), § 29, effective September 1, 2007.]

(f) Notwithstanding any other state law, pricing information disclosed by manufacturers or labelers under this section may be provided by the department only to the Medicaid vendor drug purchase program for its sole use. The Medicaid vendor drug purchase program may use the information only as necessary to administer its drug programs, including Medicaid drug programs.

(g) Notwithstanding any other state law, pricing information disclosed by manufacturers or labelers under this section is confidential and, except as necessary to permit the attorney general to enforce state and federal laws, may not be disclosed by the Health and Human Services Commission or any other state agency in a form that discloses the identity of a specific manufacturer or labeler or the prices charged by a specific manufacturer or labeler for a specific drug.

(h) The attorney general shall treat information obtained under this section in the same manner as information obtained by the attorney general through a civil investigative demand under Section 36.054, Human Resources Code.

(i) Notwithstanding any other state law, the penalties for unauthorized disclosure of confidential information under Chapter 552, Government Code, apply to unauthorized disclosure of confidential information under this section.

(Enacted by Acts 2001, 77th Leg., ch. 1003 (H.B. 915), § 2, effective September 1, 2001; am. Acts 2003, 78th Leg., ch. 198 (H.B. 2292), § 2.199, effective September 1, 2003; am. Acts 2005, 79th Leg., ch. 349 (S.B. 1188), § 29, effective September 1, 2007.)

## Sec. 431.117.   Priority for Health Care Providers in Distribution of Influenza Vaccine.

The executive commissioner of the Health and Human Services Commission shall study the wholesale distribution of influenza vaccine in this state to determine the feasibility of implementing a system that requires giving a priority in filling orders for influenza vaccine to physicians and other licensed health care providers authorized to administer influenza vaccine over retail establishments. The executive commissioner may implement such a system if it is determined to be feasible.

(Enacted by Acts 2007, 80th Leg., ch. 922 (H.B. 3184), § 2, effective June 15, 2007.)

## SUBCHAPTER H
## FAIR PACKAGING AND LABELING; FALSE ADVERTISING

## Sec. 431.181.   Fair Packaging and Labeling.

(a) All labels of consumer commodities, as defined by this chapter, shall conform with the requirements for the declaration of net quantity of contents of Section 4 of the Fair Packaging and Labeling Act (15 U.S.C. 1451 et seq.) and the regulations promulgated pursuant thereto; provided, that consumer commodities exempted from the requirements of Section 4 of the Fair Packaging and Labeling Act shall also be exempt from this subsection.

(b) The label of any package of a consumer commodity that bears a representation as to the number of servings of the commodity contained in the package shall bear a statement of the net quantity (in terms of weight, measure, or numerical count) of each serving.

(c) No person shall distribute or cause to be distributed in commerce any packaged consumer commodity if any qualifying words or phrases appear in conjunction with the separate statement of the net quantity of contents required by Subsection (a), but nothing in this subsection shall prohibit supplemental statements at other places on the package describing in nondeceptive terms the net quantity of contents; provided, that the supplemental statements of net quantity of contents shall not include any term qualifying a unit of weight, measure, or count that tends to exaggerate the amount of the commodity contained in the package.

(d) Whenever the board determines that rules containing prohibitions or requirements other than those prescribed by Subsection (a) are necessary to prevent the deception of consumers or to facilitate value comparisons as to any consumer commodity, the board shall adopt with respect to that commodity rules effective to:

(1) establish and define standards for the characterization of the size of a package enclosing any consumer commodity, which may be used to supplement the label statement of net quantity of contents of packages containing such commodity, but this paragraph shall not be construed as authorizing any limitation on the size, shape, weight, dimensions, or number of packages that may be used to enclose any commodity;

(2) regulate the placement on any package containing any commodity, or on any label affixed to the commodity, of any printed matter stating or representing by implication that such commodity is offered for retail sale at a price lower than the ordinary and customary retail sale price or that a retail sale price advantage is accorded to purchasers thereof by reason of the size of that package or the quantity of its contents;

(3) require that the label on each package of a consumer commodity (other than one which is a food within the meaning of Section 431.002(15)) bear:

(A) the common or usual name of the consumer commodity, if any; and

(B) in case the consumer commodity consists of two or more ingredients, the common or usual name of each ingredient listed in order of decreasing predominance, but nothing in this paragraph shall be deemed to require that any trade secret be divulged; or

(4) prevent the nonfunctional slack-fill of packages containing consumer commodities. For the purpose of this subdivision, a package shall be deemed to be nonfunctionally slack-filled if it is filled of substantially less than its capacity for reasons other than:

(A) protection of the contents of the package; or

(B) the requirements of the machine used for enclosing the contents in the package.

(Enacted by Acts 1989, 71st Leg., ch. 678 (H.B. 2136), § 1, effective September 1, 1989.)

## Sec. 431.182.  False Advertisement.

(a) An advertisement of a food, drug, device, or cosmetic shall be deemed to be false if it is false or misleading in any particular.

(b) The advertising of a food that incorporates a health claim not in conformance with or defined by Section 403(r) of the federal Act is deemed to be false or misleading for the purposes of this chapter.

(Enacted by Acts 1989, 71st Leg., ch. 678 (H.B. 2136), § 1, effective September 1, 1989; am. Acts 1993, 73rd Leg., ch. 459 (S.B. 558), § 5, effective September 1, 1993.)

## Sec. 431.183.  False Advertisement of Drug or Device.

(a) An advertisement of a drug or device is false if the advertisement represents that the drug or device affects:

(1) infectious and parasitic diseases;

(2) neoplasms;

(3) endocrine, nutritional, and metabolic diseases and immunity disorders;

(4) diseases of blood and blood-forming organs;

(5) mental disorders;

(6) diseases of the nervous system and sense organs;

(7) diseases of the circulatory system;

(8) diseases of the respiratory system;

(9) diseases of the digestive system;

(10) diseases of the genitourinary system;

(11) complications of pregnancy, childbirth, and the puerperium;

(12) diseases of the skin and subcutaneous tissue;

(13) diseases of the musculoskeletal system and connective tissue;

(14) congenital anomalies;

(15) certain conditions originating in the perinatal period;

(16) symptoms, signs, and ill-defined conditions; or

(17) injury and poisoning.

(b) Subsection (a) does not apply to an advertisement of a drug or device if the advertisement does not violate Section 431.182 and is disseminated:

(1) to the public for self-medication and is consistent with the labeling claims permitted by the federal Food and Drug Administration;

(2) only to members of the medical, dental, and veterinary professions and appears only in the scientific periodicals of those professions; or

(3) only for the purpose of public health education by a person not commercially interested, directly or indirectly, in the sale of the drug or device.

(c) The board by rule shall authorize the advertisement of a drug having a curative or therapeutic effect for a disease listed under Subsection (a) if the board determines that an advance in medical science has made any type of self-medication safe for the disease. The board may impose conditions and restrictions on the advertisement of the drug necessary in the interest of public health.

(d) This section does not indicate that self-medication for a disease other than a disease listed under Subsection (a) is safe or effective.
(Enacted by Acts 1989, 71st Leg., ch. 678 (H.B. 2136), § 1, effective September 1, 1989; am. Acts 1991, 72nd Leg., ch. 14 (S.B. 404), § 160, effective September 1, 1991.)

## SUBCHAPTER I
## WHOLESALE DISTRIBUTORS OF NONPRESCRIPTION DRUGS

### Sec. 431.201.  Definitions.

In this subchapter:

(1) "Nonprescription drug" means any drug that is not a prescription drug as defined by Section 431.401.

(2) "Place of business" means each location at which a drug for wholesale distribution is located.

(3) "Wholesale distribution" means distribution to a person other than a consumer or patient, and includes distribution by a manufacturer, repackager, own label distributor, broker, jobber, warehouse, or wholesaler.
(Enacted by Acts 1989, 71st Leg., ch. 678 (H.B. 2136), § 1, effective September 1, 1989; am. Acts 2005, 79th Leg., ch. 282 (H.B. 164), § 3(b), effective March 1, 2006.)

### Sec. 431.2011.  Applicability of Subchapter.

This subchapter applies only to the wholesale distribution of nonprescription drugs.
(Enacted by Acts 2005, 79th Leg., ch. 282 (H.B. 164), § 3(c), effective March 1, 2006.)

### Sec. 431.202.  License Required.

(a) A person may not engage in wholesale distribution of nonprescription drugs in this state unless the person holds a wholesale drug distribution license issued by the department under this subchapter or Subchapter N.

(b) An applicant for a license under this subchapter must submit an application to the department on the form prescribed by the department or electronically on the state electronic Internet portal.

(c) A license issued under this subchapter expires on the second anniversary of the date of issuance.
(Enacted by Acts 1989, 71st Leg., ch. 678 (H.B. 2136), § 1, effective September 1, 1989; am. Acts 1991, 72nd Leg., ch. 14 (S.B. 404), § 161, effective September 1, 1991; am. Acts 1991, 72nd Leg., ch. 539 (S.B. 873), § 5, effective September 1, 1991; am. Acts 2005, 79th Leg., ch. 282 (H.B. 164), § 3(d), effective March 1, 2006; am. Acts 2011, 82nd Leg., ch. 973 (H.B. 1504), § 28, effective June 17, 2011.)

### Sec. 431.2021.  Exemption from Licensing.

(a) A person who engages in wholesale distribution of prescription drugs in this state for use in humans is exempt from this subchapter if the person is exempt under:

(1) the Prescription Drug Marketing Act of 1987, as amended (21 U.S.C. Section 353(c)(3)(B));

(2) the regulations adopted by the secretary to administer and enforce that Act;

(3) the interpretations of that Act set out in the compliance policy manual of the United States Food and Drug Administration; or

(4) Section 562.154, Occupations Code.

(b) [Repealed by Acts 2005, 79th Leg., ch. 282 (H.B. 164), § 3(k), effective August 1, 2005.]
(Acts 1991, 72nd Leg., ch. 539 (S.B. 873), effective September 1, 1991; am. Acts 1993, 73rd Leg., ch. 375 (S.B. 561), effective June 2, 1993; am. Acts 2005, 79th Leg., ch. 28 (S.B. 492), § 6, effective September 1, 2005; am. Acts 2005, 79th Leg., ch. 282 (H.B. 164), § 3(k), effective August 1, 2005.)

Health

## Sec. 431.203. Contents of License Statement.

The license statement must contain:

(1) the name under which the business is conducted;

(2) the address of each place of business that is licensed;

(3) the name and residence address of:

(A) the proprietor, if the business is a proprietorship;

(B) all partners, if the business is a partnership; or

(C) all principals, if the business is an association;

(4) the date and place of incorporation, if the business is a corporation;

(5) the names and residence addresses of the individuals in an administrative capacity showing:

(A) the managing proprietor, if the business is a proprietorship;

(B) the managing partner, if the business is a partnership;

(C) the officers and directors, if the business is a corporation; or

(D) the persons in a managerial capacity, if the business is an association; and

(6) the residence address of an individual in charge of each place of business.

(Enacted by Acts 1989, 71st Leg., ch. 678 (H.B. 2136), § 1, effective September 1, 1989; am. Acts 1991, 72nd Leg., ch. 539 (S.B. 873), § 7, effective September 1, 1991.)

## Sec. 431.2031. Effect of Operation in Other Jurisdictions; Reports.

(a) A person who engages in the wholesale distribution of drugs outside this state may engage in the wholesale distribution of drugs in this state if the person holds a license issued by the department.

(b) The department may accept reports from authorities in other jurisdictions to determine the extent of compliance with this chapter and the minimum standards adopted under this chapter.

(c) The department may issue a license to a person who engages in the wholesale distribution of drugs outside this state to engage in the wholesale distribution of drugs in this state, if after an examination of the reports of the person's compliance history and current compliance record, the department determines that the person is in compliance with this subchapter and the board's rules.

(d) The department shall consider each licensing statement filed by a person who wishes to engage in wholesale distribution of drugs in this state on an individual basis.

(Enacted by Acts 1991, 72nd Leg., ch. 539 (S.B. 873), § 8, effective September 1, 1991.)

## Sec. 431.204. Fees.

(a) The department shall collect fees for:

(1) a license that is filed or renewed;

(2) a license that is amended, including a notification of a change in the location of a licensed place of business required under Section 431.206; and

(3) an inspection performed in enforcing this subchapter and rules adopted under this subchapter.

(b) The executive commissioner of the Health and Human Services Commission by rule shall set the fees in amounts that allow the department to recover the biennial expenditures of state funds by the department in:

(1) reviewing and acting on a license;

(2) amending and renewing a license;

(3) inspecting a licensed facility; and

(4) implementing and enforcing this subchapter, including a rule or order adopted or a license issued under this subchapter.

(c) Fees collected under this section shall be deposited to the credit of the food and drug registration fee account of the general revenue fund and appropriated to the department to carry out the administration and enforcement of this chapter.

(Enacted by Acts 1989, 71st Leg., ch. 678 (H.B. 2136), § 1, effective September 1, 1989; am. Acts 1991, 72nd Leg., ch. 539 (S.B. 873), § 9, effective September 1, 1991; am. Acts 2005, 79th Leg., ch. 282 (H.B. 164), § 3(e), effective March 1, 2006.)

## Sec. 431.205. Expiration Date [Repealed].

Repealed by Acts 2005, 79th Leg., ch. 282 (H.B. 164), § 3(k), effective September 1, 2005.

(Acts 1989, 71st Leg., ch. 678 (S.B. 2136), effective September 1, 1989; am. Acts 1991, 72nd Leg., ch. 539 (S.B. 873), effective September 1, 1991.)

## Sec. 431.206. Change of Location of Place of Business.

(a) Not fewer than 30 days in advance of the change, the licensee shall notify the department in writing of the licensee's intent to change the location of a licensed place of business.

(b) The notice shall include the address of the new location, and the name and residence address of the individual in charge of the business at the new location.

(c) Not more than 10 days after the completion of the change of location, the licensee shall notify the department in writing to confirm the completion of the change of location and provide verification of the information previously provided or correct and confirm any information that has changed since providing the notice of intent.

(d) The notice and confirmation required by this section are deemed adequate if the licensee sends the notices by certified mail, return receipt requested, to the central office of the department or submits them electronically through the state electronic Internet portal.

(Enacted by Acts 1989, 71st Leg., ch. 678 (H.B. 2136), § 1, effective September 1, 1989; am. Acts 1991, 72nd Leg., ch. 539 (S.B. 873), § 9, effective September 1, 1991; am. Acts 2005, 79th Leg., ch. 282 (H.B. 164), § 3(f), effective March 1, 2006; am. Acts 2011, 82nd Leg., ch. 973 (H.B. 1504), § 29, effective June 17, 2011.)

### Sec. 431.207. Refusal to License; Suspension or Revocation of License.

(a) The commissioner of state health services may refuse an application for a license or may suspend or revoke a license if the applicant or licensee:

(1) has been convicted of a felony or misdemeanor that involves moral turpitude;

(2) is an association, partnership, or corporation and the managing officer has been convicted of a felony or misdemeanor that involves moral turpitude;

(3) has been convicted in a state or federal court of the illegal use, sale, or transportation of intoxicating liquors, narcotic drugs, barbiturates, amphetamines, desoxyephedrine, their compounds or derivatives, or any other dangerous or habit-forming drugs;

(4) is an association, partnership, or corporation and the managing officer has been convicted in a state or federal court of the illegal use, sale, or transportation of intoxicating liquors, narcotic drugs, barbiturates, amphetamines, desoxyephedrine, their compounds or derivatives, or any other dangerous or habit-forming drugs;

(5) has not complied with this chapter or the rules implementing this chapter;

(6) has violated Section 431.021(*l*)(3), relating to the counterfeiting of a drug or the sale or holding for sale of a counterfeit drug;

(7) has violated Chapter 481 or 483;

(8) has violated the rules of the director of the Department of Public Safety, including being responsible for a significant discrepancy in the records that state law requires the applicant or licensee to maintain; or

(9) fails to complete a license application or submits an application that contains false, misleading, or incorrect information or contains information that cannot be verified by the department.

(b) The executive commissioner of the Health and Human Services Commission by rule shall establish minimum standards required for the issuance or renewal of a license under this subchapter.

(c) The refusal to license an applicant or the suspension or revocation of a license by the department and the appeal from that action are governed by the procedures for a contested case hearing under Chapter 2001, Government Code.

(Enacted by Acts 1989, 71st Leg., ch. 678 (H.B. 2136), § 1, effective September 1, 1989; am. Acts 1991, 72nd Leg., ch. 539 (S.B. 873), § 9, effective September 1, 1991; am. Acts 1995, 74th Leg., ch. 76 (S.B. 959), § 5.95(49), effective September 1, 1995; am. Acts 2005, 79th Leg., ch. 282 (H.B. 164), § 3(f), effective March 1, 2006.)

### Sec. 431.208. Reporting of Purchase Price.

(a) On the department's request, a person who engages in the wholesale distribution of drugs in this state shall file with the department information showing the actual price at which the wholesale distributor sells a particular drug to a retail pharmacy.

(b) The department shall adopt rules to implement this section.

(c) The department and the attorney general may investigate the distributor to determine the accuracy of the information provided under Subsection (a). The attorney general may take action to enforce this section.

(d) [Repealed by Acts 2005, 79th Leg., ch. 349 (S.B. 1188), § 29, effective September 1, 2007.]

(Enacted by Acts 2001, 77th Leg., ch. 1003 (H.B. 915), § 3, effective September 1, 2001; am. Acts 2005, 79th Leg., ch. 349 (S.B. 1188), § 29, effective September 1, 2007.)

Health

## SUBCHAPTER K
## GENERAL ADMINISTRATIVE PROVISIONS AND RULEMAKING AUTHORITY

### Sec. 431.241. Rulemaking Authority.

(a) The board may adopt rules for the efficient enforcement of this chapter.

(b) The board may conform its rules, if practicable, with regulations adopted under the federal Act.

(c) The enumeration of specific federal laws and regulations in Sections 431.244 and 431.245 does not limit the general authority granted to the board in Subsection (b) to conform its rules to those adopted under the federal Act.

(d) The board may adopt the federal regulations issued by the secretary pursuant to the Prescription Drug Marketing Act of 1987 (21 U.S.C. Sections 331, 333, 353, and 381), as necessary or desirable so that the state wholesale drug distributor licensing program in Subchapter I of this chapter may achieve compliance with that Act.

(e) The board and the Texas Department of Human Services shall not establish a drug formulary that restricts by any prior or retroactive approval process a physician's ability to treat a patient with a prescription drug that has been approved and designated as safe and effective by the United States Food and Drug Administration, in compliance with federal law and subject to review by the Texas Department of Human Services, Vendor Drug Advisory Subcommittee.

(f) Nothing in this section shall effect a prior approval program in operation on the effective date of this section nor shall any portion of this chapter prohibit a prior approval process on any federally exempted products.

(g) The department may assess a fee for the issuance of a certificate of free sale and another certification issued under this chapter. The board by rule shall set each fee in an amount sufficient to recover the cost to the department of issuing the particular certificate.

(Enacted by Acts 1989, 71st Leg., ch. 678 (H.B. 2136), § 1, effective September 1, 1989; am. Acts 1991, 72nd Leg., ch. 539 (S.B. 873), § 11, effective September 1, 1991; am. Acts 1993, 73rd Leg., ch. 675 (S.B. 1058), § 7, effective September 1, 1993.)

### Sec. 431.242. Contested Case Hearings and Appeals.

A hearing under this chapter or an appeal from a final administrative decision shall be conducted under Chapter 2001, Government Code.

(Enacted by Acts 1989, 71st Leg., ch. 678 (H.B. 2136), § 1, effective September 1, 1989; am. Acts 1995, 74th Leg., ch. 76 (S.B. 959), § 5.95(49), effective September 1, 1995.)

### Sec. 431.243. Persons to Conduct Hearings.

The commissioner or an officer, agent, or employee designated by the commissioner shall conduct a hearing authorized or required under this chapter.

(Enacted by Acts 1989, 71st Leg., ch. 678 (H.B. 2136), § 1, effective September 1, 1989.)

### Sec. 431.244. Federal Regulations Adopted As State Rules.

(a) A regulation adopted by the secretary under the federal Act concerning pesticide chemicals, food additives, color additives, special dietary use, processed low acid food, acidified food, infant formula, bottled water, or vended bottled water is a rule for the purposes of this chapter, unless the board modifies or rejects the rule.

(b) A regulation adopted under the Fair Packaging and Labeling Act (15 U.S.C. 1451 et seq.) is a rule for the purposes of this chapter, unless the board modifies or rejects the rule. The board may not adopt a rule that conflicts with the labeling requirements for the net quantity of contents required under Section 4 of the Fair Packaging and Labeling Act (15 U.S.C. 1453) and the regulations adopted under that Act.

(c) A regulation adopted by the secretary under Sections 403(b) through (i) of the federal Act is a rule for the purposes of this chapter unless the board modifies or rejects the rule. The board may not adopt a rule that conflicts with the limitations provided by Sections 403(q) and (r) of the federal Act.

(d) A federal regulation that this section provides as a rule for the purposes of this chapter is effective:

(1) on the date that the regulation becomes effective as a federal regulation; and

(2) whether or not the department has fulfilled the rulemaking provisions of Chapter 2001, Government Code.

(e) If the board modifies or rejects a federal regulation, the board shall comply with the rule-making provisions of Chapter 2001, Government Code.

(f) For any federal regulation adopted as a state rule under this chapter, including a regulation considered to be a rule for purposes of this chapter under Subsection (a), (b), or (c), the Department of State Health Services shall provide on its Internet website:

(1) a link to the text of the federal regulation;

(2) a clear explanation of the substance of and purpose for the regulation; and

(3) information on providing comments in response to any proposed or pending federal regulation, including an address to which and the manner in which comments may be submitted.

(Enacted by Acts 1989, 71st Leg., ch. 678 (H.B. 2136), § 1, effective September 1, 1989; am. Acts 1991, 72nd Leg., ch. 539 (S.B. 873), § 12, effective September 1, 1991; am. Acts 1993, 73rd Leg., ch. 459 (S.B. 558), § 6, effective September 1, 1993; am. Acts 1995, 74th Leg., ch. 76 (S.B. 959), § 5.95(49), effective September 1, 1995; am. Acts 2011, 82nd Leg., ch. 1317 (S.B. 81), § 4, effective September 1, 2011.)

### Sec. 431.245.  Definition or Standard of Identity, Quality, or Fill of Container.

(a) A definition or standard of identity, quality, or fill of container of the federal Act is a definition or standard of identity, quality, or fill of container in this chapter, except as modified by board rules.

(b) The board by rule may establish definitions and standards of identity, quality, and fill of container for a food if:

(1) a federal regulation does not apply to the food; and

(2) the board determines that adopting the rules will promote honest and fair dealing in the interest of consumers.

(c) A temporary permit granted for interstate shipment of an experimental pack of food that varies from the requirements of federal definitions and standards of identity is automatically effective in this state under the conditions of the permit.

(d) The commissioner may issue additional permits if the commissioner determines that:

(1) it is necessary for the completion of an otherwise adequate investigation; and

(2) the interests of consumers are safeguarded.

(e) A permit issued under Subsection (d) is subject to the terms and conditions of board rules. (Enacted by Acts 1989, 71st Leg., ch. 678 (H.B. 2136), § 1, effective September 1, 1989.)

### Sec. 431.246.  Removal of Adulterated Item from Stores.

The board shall adopt rules that provide a system for removing adulterated items from the shelves of a grocery store or other retail establishment selling those items.
(Enacted by Acts 1989, 71st Leg., ch. 678 (H.B. 2136), § 1, effective September 1, 1989.)

### Sec. 431.247.  Delegation of Powers or Duties.

(a) The board by rule may delegate a power or duty imposed on the commissioner by this chapter to a designee of the board, including the power or duty to issue an emergency rule, an emergency manufacturing permit, or an order or to render a final administrative decision.

(b) A health authority may, unless otherwise restricted by law, delegate a power or duty imposed on the health authority by this chapter to an employee of the local health department, the local health unit, or the public health district in which the health authority serves.
(Enacted by Acts 1989, 71st Leg., ch. 678 (H.B. 2136), § 1, effective September 1, 1989.)

### Sec. 431.2471.  Texas Department of Health Peace Officers.

(a) The department may employ a peace officer to administer and enforce this chapter.

(b) The department may not employ a peace officer under this section unless:

(1) the employee will enforce the food and drug portions of this chapter;

(2) the Commission on Law Enforcement Officer Standards and Education certifies the employee as qualified to be a peace officer;

(3) the commissioner recommends the employee to the department as being qualified to enforce the food and drug laws within the jurisdiction of the department; and

(4) the employee also serves simultaneously as the director of the food and drugs division of the department.

(c) A person employed as a peace officer under this section has the powers, privileges, and immunities of a peace officer while carrying out the employee's duties under this chapter.

(Enacted by Acts 1993, 73rd Leg., ch. 339 (S.B. 563), § 1, effective September 1, 1993.)

### Sec. 431.248. Memorandum of Understanding with Department of Agriculture.

(a) The department and the Department of Agriculture shall execute a memorandum of understanding that:

(1) requires each agency to disclose to the other agency any positive results of testing conducted by the agency for pesticides in food; and

(2) specifies how each agency will assist the other in performing its duties regarding pesticides in food.

(b) The department and the Department of Agriculture shall adopt the memorandum of understanding as a rule.

(c) The department and the Department of Agriculture shall request the federal Food and Drug Administration to join in execution of the memorandum of understanding.

(Enacted by Acts 1989, 71st Leg., ch. 678 (H.B. 2136), § 1, effective September 1, 1989.)

### Sec. 431.249. Dissemination of Information.

(a) The commissioner may publish reports summarizing the judgments, decrees, and court orders rendered under this chapter, including the nature and disposition of the charge.

(b) The commissioner may disseminate information regarding a food, drug, device, or cosmetic in a situation that the commissioner determines to involve imminent danger to health or gross deception of consumers.

(c) This section does not prohibit the commissioner from collecting, reporting, and illustrating the results of an investigation by the commissioner.

(Enacted by Acts 1989, 71st Leg., ch. 678 (H.B. 2136), § 1, effective September 1, 1989.)

## SUBTITLE B
## ALCOHOL AND SUBSTANCE ABUSE PROGRAMS

## CHAPTER 462
## TREATMENT OF CHEMICALLY DEPENDENT PERSONS

### SUBCHAPTER C
### EMERGENCY DETENTION

### Sec. 462.041. Apprehension by Peace Officer Without Warrant.

(a) A peace officer, without a warrant, may take a person into custody if the officer:

(1) has reason to believe and does believe that:

(A) the person is chemically dependent; and

(B) because of that chemical dependency there is a substantial risk of harm to the person or to others unless the person is immediately restrained; and

(2) believes that there is not sufficient time to obtain a warrant before taking the person into custody.

(b) A substantial risk of serious harm to the person or others under Subsection (a)(1)(B) may be demonstrated by:

(1) the person's behavior; or

(2) evidence of severe emotional distress and deterioration in the person's mental or physical condition to the extent that the person cannot remain at liberty.

(c) The peace officer may form the belief that the person meets the criteria for apprehension:

(1) from a representation of a credible person; or

(2) on the basis of the conduct of the apprehended person or the circumstances under which the apprehended person is found.

(d) A peace officer who takes a person into custody under Subsection (a) shall immediately transport the apprehended person to:

(1) the nearest appropriate inpatient treatment facility; or

(2) if an appropriate inpatient treatment facility is not available, a facility considered suitable by the county's health authority.

(e) A person may not be detained in a jail or similar detention facility except in an extreme

Health

emergency. A person detained in a jail or a non-medical facility shall be kept separate from any person who is charged with or convicted of a crime.

(f) A peace officer shall immediately file an application for detention after transporting a person to a facility under this section. The application for detention must contain:

(1) a statement that the officer has reason to believe and does believe that the person evidences chemical dependency;

(2) a statement that the officer has reason to believe and does believe that the person evidences a substantial risk of serious harm to himself or others;

(3) a specific description of the risk of harm;

(4) a statement that the officer has reason to believe and does believe that the risk of harm is imminent unless the person is immediately restrained;

(5) a statement that the officer's beliefs are derived from specific recent behavior, overt acts, attempts, or threats that were observed by or reliably reported to the officer;

(6) a detailed description of the specific behavior, acts, attempts, or threats; and

(7) the name and relationship to the apprehended person of any person who reported or observed the behavior, acts, attempts, or threats.

(g) The person shall be released on completion of a preliminary examination conducted under Section 462.044 unless the examining physician determines that emergency detention is necessary and provides the statement prescribed by Section 462.044(b). If a person is not admitted to a facility, is not arrested, and does not object, arrangements shall be made to immediately return the person to:

(1) the location of the person's apprehension;

(2) the person's residence in this state; or

(3) another suitable location.

(h) The county in which the person was apprehended shall pay the costs of the person's return.

(i) A treatment facility may provide to a person medical assistance regardless of whether the facility admits the person or refers the person to another facility.

(Am. Acts 1991, 72nd Leg., ch. 14 (S.B. 404), § 175, effective September 1, 1991.)

# CHAPTER 463
# CONTRIBUTING TO DELINQUENCY OF HABITUAL DRUNKARD OR NARCOTIC ADDICT

**Subchapter A. Contributing to Delinquency of Habitual Drunkard**

## SUBCHAPTER A
## CONTRIBUTING TO DELINQUENCY OF HABITUAL DRUNKARD

### Sec. 463.001.   Contributing to Delinquency of Habitual Drunkard; Criminal Penalty.

(a) In this section, "delinquency" means any act that tends to debase or injure the morals, health, or welfare of a habitual drunkard and includes:

(1) drinking intoxicating liquor;

(2) entering or remaining in any bawdy house, assignation house, disorderly house, roadhouse, hotel, or public dance hall where prostitutes, gamblers, or thieves are permitted to enter and ply their trade;

(3) entering a place where intoxicating liquors are kept, drunk, used, or sold;

(4) associating with thieves and immoral persons;

(5) causing a habitual drunkard to leave home or to leave the custody of the drunkard's parents, guardian, or person acting for the drunkard's parents or guardian without first receiving their consent or against their will; or

(6) causing the habitual drunkard, by undue influence, to unlawfully cohabit with a person known by the actor to be a habitual drunkard.

(b) A person commits an offense if the person by any act or in any manner encourages, causes, acts in conjunction with, or contributes to the delinquency, dependency, or neglect of a habitual drunkard, regardless of the drunkard's previous convictions.

(c) An offense under this section is punishable by a fine of not more than $500, confinement in jail for not more than one year, or both.
(Enacted by Acts 1991, 72nd Leg., ch. 14 (S.B. 404), § 177, effective September 1, 1991.)

### Sec. 463.002. Conflicting Offenses.

To the extent of any conflict, the offenses prescribed by the Penal Code or other law enacted after June 9, 1949, prevail over the offense prescribed by Section 463.001.
(Am. Acts 1991, 72nd Leg., ch. 14 (S.B. 404), § 177, effective September 1, 1991.)

## SUBCHAPTER B
## CONTRIBUTING TO NARCOTIC ADDICTION

### Sec. 463.011. Contributing to Delinquency of Narcotic Addict; Criminal Penalty.

(a) In this section, "delinquency" means any act that tends to debase or injure the morals, health, or welfare of a narcotic addict, and includes:

(1) drinking intoxicating liquor;

(2) going into or remaining in any bawdy house, assignation house, disorderly house, roadhouse, hotel, or public dance hall where prostitutes, gamblers, or thieves are permitted to enter and ply their trade;

(3) going into a place where intoxicating liquors are kept, drunk, used, or sold;

(4) associating with thieves and immoral persons;

(5) causing a narcotic addict to leave home or to leave the custody of the addict's parents, guardian, or person acting for the addict's parent or guardian without first receiving that person's consent or against that person's will; or

(6) causing the addict, by undue influence, to unlawfully cohabit with a person known by the actor to be a narcotic addict.

(b) A person commits an offense if the person, by any act or in any manner, encourages, causes, acts in conjunction with, or contributes to the delinquency, dependency, or neglect of a narcotic addict, regardless of the addict's previous convictions.

(c) An offense under this section is punishable by a fine of not more than $500, confinement in jail for not more than one year, or both.
(Enacted by Acts 1989, 71st Leg., ch. 678 (H.B. 2136), § 1, effective September 1, 1989; am. Acts 1991, 72nd Leg., ch. 14 (S.B. 404), § 179, effective September 1, 1991 (renumbered from Sec. 463.121).)

### Sec. 463.012. Conflicting Offenses.

To the extent of any conflict, the offenses defined by the Penal Code or other law enacted after June 9, 1949, prevail over the offense defined by Section 463.011.
(Enacted by Acts 1989, 71st Leg., ch. 678 (H.B. 2136), § 1, effective September 1, 1989; am. Acts 1991, 72nd Leg., ch. 14 (S.B. 404), § 179, effective September 1, 1991 (renumbered from Sec. 463.122).)

### Sec. 463.013. Exception.

(a) In this section, "informant" means a person who has communicated information to a law enforcement official in connection with a law enforcement function.

(b) It is an exception to the application of Section 463.011(b) that the person is a law enforcement official and the narcotic addict is an informant.
(Enacted by Acts 1999, 76th Leg., ch. 422 (S.B. 1116), § 1, effective September 1, 1999.)

### Sec. 463.014. Mental Health Facility Requirements [Repealed].

Repealed by Acts 1991, 72nd Leg., ch. 14 (S.B. 404), § 178, effective September 1, 1991.

### Sec. 463.015. Appointment of Attorney Ad Litem; Notice of Hearing [Repealed].

Repealed by Acts 1991, 72nd Leg., ch. 14 (S.B. 404), § 178, effective September 1, 1991.

### Sec. 463.016. Time for Probable Cause Hearing [Repealed].

Repealed by Acts 1991, 72nd Leg., ch. 14 (S.B. 404), § 178, effective September 1, 1991.

### Sec. 463.017. Probable Cause Hearing [Repealed].

Repealed by Acts 1991, 72nd Leg., ch. 14 (S.B. 404), § 178, effective September 1, 1991.

Health

**Sec. 463.018. Order for Release or Detention After Probable Cause Hearing [Repealed].**
Repealed by Acts 1991, 72nd Leg., ch. 14 (S.B. 404), § 178, effective September 1, 1991.

**Sec. 463.019. Notification of Probable Cause Hearing [Repealed].**
Repealed by Acts 1991, 72nd Leg., ch. 14 (S.B. 404), § 178, effective September 1, 1991.

**Sec. 463.020. Detention Pending Commitment Hearing [Repealed].**
Repealed by Acts 1991, 72nd Leg., ch. 14 (S.B. 404), § 178, effective September 1, 1991.

**Sec. 463.021. Appropriate Detention Facilities [Repealed].**
Repealed by Acts 1991, 72nd Leg., ch. 14 (S.B. 404), § 178, effective September 1, 1991.

**Secs. 463.022 to 463.040 [Reserved for expansion].**

### SUBCHAPTER C
### COMMITMENT OF DRUG-DEPENDENT PERSON TO MENTAL HEALTH FACILITY
### [REPEALED]

**Sec. 463.041. Definition [Repealed].**
Repealed by Acts 1991, 72nd Leg., ch. 14 (S.B. 404), § 178, effective September 1, 1991.

**Sec. 463.042. Application for Extended Commitment [Repealed].**
Repealed by Acts 1991, 72nd Leg., ch. 14 (S.B. 404), § 178, effective September 1, 1991.

**Sec. 463.043. Physician's Certificate Filed with Application [Repealed].**
Repealed by Acts 1991, 72nd Leg., ch. 14 (S.B. 404), § 178, effective September 1, 1991.

**Sec. 463.044. Certificates Required [Repealed].**
Repealed by Acts 1991, 72nd Leg., ch. 14 (S.B. 404), § 178, effective September 1, 1991.

**Sec. 463.045. Time for Commitment Hearing; Continuance [Repealed].**
Repealed by Acts 1991, 72nd Leg., ch. 14 (S.B.

404), § 178, effective September 1, 1991.

**Sec. 463.046. Attorney Ad Litem; Attorney Access to Patient's Files [Repealed].**
Repealed by Acts 1991, 72nd Leg., ch. 14 (S.B. 404), § 178, effective September 1, 1991.

**Sec. 463.047. Jury [Repealed].**
Repealed by Acts 1991, 72nd Leg., ch. 14 (S.B. 404), § 178, effective September 1, 1991.

**Sec. 463.048. Burden of Proof; Hearing Evidence [Repealed].**
Repealed by Acts 1991, 72nd Leg., ch. 14 (S.B. 404), § 178, effective September 1, 1991.

**Sec. 463.049. Transfer [Repealed].**
Repealed by Acts 1991, 72nd Leg., ch. 14 (S.B. 404), § 178, effective September 1, 1991.

**Sec. 463.050. Findings [Repealed].**
Repealed by Acts 1991, 72nd Leg., ch. 14 (S.B. 404), § 178, effective September 1, 1991.

**Sec. 463.051. Order for Release or Commitment [Repealed].**
Repealed by Acts 1991, 72nd Leg., ch. 14 (S.B. 404), § 178, effective September 1, 1991.

**Sec. 463.052. Order for Outpatient Care or Services [Repealed].**
Repealed by Acts 1991, 72nd Leg., ch. 14 (S.B. 404), § 178, effective September 1, 1991.

**Sec. 463.053. New Trial [Repealed].**
Repealed by Acts 1991, 72nd Leg., ch. 14 (S.B. 404), § 178, effective September 1, 1991.

**Sec. 463.054. Appeal [Repealed].**
Repealed by Acts 1991, 72nd Leg., ch. 14 (S.B. 404), § 178, effective September 1, 1991.

**Sec. 463.055. Place of Commitment [Repealed].**
Repealed by Acts 1991, 72nd Leg., ch. 14 (S.B. 404), § 178, effective September 1, 1991.

**Sec. 463.056. Commitment to Private Mental Health Facility [Repealed].**
Repealed by Acts 1991, 72nd Leg., ch. 14 (S.B. 404), § 178, effective September 1, 1991.

Health

**Sec. 463.057. Commitment to Federal Agency [Repealed].**
Repealed by Acts 1991, 72nd Leg., ch. 14 (S.B. 404), § 178, effective September 1, 1991.

**Sec. 463.058. Patient Transport [Repealed].**
Repealed by Acts 1991, 72nd Leg., ch. 14 (S.B. 404), § 178, effective September 1, 1991.

**Sec. 463.059. Duties of Clerk Concerning Patient Transport [Repealed].**
Repealed by Acts 1991, 72nd Leg., ch. 14 (S.B. 404), § 178, effective September 1, 1991.

**Sec. 463.060. Receipt of Patient [Repealed].**
Repealed by Acts 1991, 72nd Leg., ch. 14 (S.B. 404), § 178, effective September 1, 1991.

## SUBCHAPTER D
## COSTS, LIABILITY, AND VIOLATIONS: EXTENDED COMMITMENTS AND PROTECTIVE CUSTODY
## [REPEALED]

**Sec. 463.071. Costs Relating to Detention or Commitment [Repealed].**
Repealed by Acts 1991, 72nd Leg., ch. 14 (S.B. 404), § 178, effective September 1, 1991.

**Sec. 463.072. Immunity from Liability [Repealed].**
Repealed by Acts 1991, 72nd Leg., ch. 14 (S.B. 404), § 178, effective September 1, 1991.

**Sec. 463.073. Unwarranted Commitment; Criminal Penalty [Repealed].**
Repealed by Acts 1991, 72nd Leg., ch. 14 (S.B. 404), § 178, effective September 1, 1991.

**Sec. 463.074. Criminal Penalty [Repealed].**
Repealed by Acts 1991, 72nd Leg., ch. 14 (S.B. 404), § 178, effective September 1, 1991.

**Sec. 463.075. Prosecution of Violation [Repealed].**
Repealed by Acts 1991, 72nd Leg., ch. 14 (S.B. 404), § 178, effective September 1, 1991.

## SUBCHAPTER E
## VOLUNTARY ADMISSION TO STATE HOSPITAL
## [REPEALED]

**Sec. 463.081. Eligibility for Voluntary Admission to State Hospital [Repealed].**
Repealed by Acts 1991, 72nd Leg., ch. 14 (S.B. 404), § 178, effective September 1, 1991.

**Sec. 463.082. Admission to State Hospital; Certification [Repealed].**
Repealed by Acts 1991, 72nd Leg., ch. 14 (S.B. 404), § 178, effective September 1, 1991.

**Sec. 463.083. Denial of Admission [Repealed].**
Repealed by Acts 1991, 72nd Leg., ch. 14 (S.B. 404), § 178, effective September 1, 1991.

**Sec. 463.084. Costs of Treatment [Repealed].**
Repealed by Acts 1991, 72nd Leg., ch. 14 (S.B. 404), § 178, effective September 1, 1991.

**Sec. 463.085. Treatment and Release [Repealed].**
Repealed by Acts 1991, 72nd Leg., ch. 14 (S.B. 404), § 178, effective September 1, 1991.

**Sec. 463.086. Commitment of Child to State Hospital [Repealed].**
Repealed by Acts 1991, 72nd Leg., ch. 14 (S.B. 404), § 178, effective September 1, 1991.

## SUBCHAPTER F
## TREATMENT OF CHILDREN FOR DRUG ABUSE
## [REPEALED]

**Sec. 463.101. Consent to Medical Treatment for Drug Use [Repealed].**
Repealed by Acts 1991, 72nd Leg., ch. 14 (S.B. 404), § 178, effective September 1, 1991.

**Sec. 463.102. Commitment of Child to Approved Treatment Program [Repealed].**
Repealed by Acts 1991, 72nd Leg., ch. 14 (S.B. 404), § 178, effective September 1, 1991.

Health

## SUBCHAPTER G
## CONTRIBUTING TO NARCOTIC
## ADDICTION
## [RENUMBERED]

### Sec. 463.121. Contributing to Delinquency of Narcotic Addict; Criminal Penalty [Renumbered].

Renumbered to Tex. Health & Safety Code § 463.011 by Acts 1991, 72nd Leg., ch. 14 (S.B. 404), § 179, effective September 1, 1991.

### Sec. 463.122. Conflicting Offenses [Renumbered].

Renumbered to Tex. Health & Safety Code § 463.012 by Acts 1991, 72nd Leg., ch. 14 (S.B. 404), § 179, effective September 1, 1991.

## CHAPTER 465
## LOCAL DRUG AND ALCOHOL
## EDUCATION PROGRAMS

### Sec. 465.001. Commission.

A municipality or county may create and support with public funds a commission to:

(1) educate the public on drug and alcohol abuse;

(2) promote drug and alcohol education at all levels of the schools;

(3) study the effectiveness of efforts, including the commission's efforts, in reducing drug and alcohol abuse; and

(4) create and administer a program to counsel or treat drug and alcohol abusers or to provide both counseling and treatment.

(Enacted by Acts 1989, 71st Leg., ch. 678 (H.B. 2136), § 1, effective September 1, 1989; am. Acts 1991, 72nd Leg., ch. 14 (S.B. 404), § 191, effective September 1, 1991.)

### Sec. 465.002. Individual or Joint Action.

The municipality or county may create the commission by its own action or jointly by agreement with another municipality or county or a private foundation, nonprofit organization, church, or other entity. If the commission is created by agreement, all matters regarding the creation and operation of the commission are governed as provided by the agreement.

(Enacted by Acts 1989, 71st Leg., ch. 678 (H.B. 2136), § 1, effective September 1, 1989; am. Acts 1991, 72nd Leg., ch. 14 (S.B. 404), § 191, effective September 1, 1991.)

### Sec. 465.003. Report.

The commission shall report annually to each entity that participates in the creation of the commission regarding the commission's activities.

(Am. Acts 1991, 72nd Leg., ch. 14 (S.B. 404), § 191, effective September 1, 1991.)

## CHAPTER 466
## REGULATION OF NARCOTIC DRUG
## TREATMENT PROGRAMS

## SUBCHAPTER A
## GENERAL PROVISIONS

### Sec. 466.001. Legislative Intent.

(a) It is the intent of the legislature that the department exercise its administrative powers and regulatory authority to ensure the proper use of approved narcotic drugs in the treatment of narcotic dependent persons.

(b) Treatment of narcotic addiction by permitted treatment programs is recognized as a specialty chemical dependency treatment area using the medical model.

(c) Short-term goals should have an emphasis of personal and public health, crime prevention,

Health

reintegration of narcotic addicted persons into the public work force, and social and medical stabilization. Narcotic treatment programs are an important component of the state's effort to prevent the further proliferation of the AIDS virus. Total drug abstinence is recognized as a long-term goal of treatment, subject to medical determination of the medical appropriateness and prognosis of the narcotic addicted person.
(Enacted by Acts 1989, 71st Leg., ch. 678 (H.B. 2136), § 1, effective September 1, 1989; am. Acts 1991, 72nd Leg., ch. 14 (S.B. 404), § 193, effective September 1, 1991; am. Acts 1999, 76th Leg., ch. 1411 (H.B. 2085), § 1.12, effective September 1, 1999.)

### Sec. 466.002. Definitions.

In this chapter:

(1) "Approved narcotic drug" means a drug approved by the United States Food and Drug Administration for maintenance or detoxification of a person physiologically addicted to the opiate class of drugs.

(2) "Authorized agent" means an employee of the department who is designated by the commissioner to enforce this chapter.

(3) "Board" means the Texas Board of Health.

(4) "Commissioner" means the commissioner of public health.

(5) "Department" means the Texas Department of Health.

(6) "Facility" includes a medical office, an outpatient clinic, a general or special hospital, a community mental health center, and any other location in which a structured narcotic dependency program is conducted.

(7) "Narcotic drug" has the meaning assigned by Chapter 481 (Texas Controlled Substances Act).
(Enacted by Acts 1989, 71st Leg., ch. 678 (H.B. 2136), § 1, effective September 1, 1989; am. Acts 1991, 72nd Leg., ch. 14 (S.B. 404), § 193, effective September 1, 1991; am. Acts 1999, 76th Leg., ch. 1411 (H.B. 2085), § 1.13, effective September 1, 1999.)

### Sec. 466.003. Exclusion of Cocaine.

Cocaine is excluded for the purpose of this chapter.
(Enacted by Acts 1989, 71st Leg., ch. 678 (H.B. 2136), § 1, effective September 1, 1989; am. Acts

1991, 72nd Leg., ch. 14 (S.B. 404), § 193, effective September 1, 1991.)

### Sec. 466.004. Powers and Duties of Board and Department.

(a) The board shall adopt and the department shall administer and enforce rules to ensure the proper use of approved narcotic drugs in the treatment of narcotic drug-dependent persons, including rules that:

(1) require an applicant or a permit holder to make annual, periodic, and special reports that the department determines are necessary;

(2) require an applicant or permit holder to keep records that the department determines are necessary;

(3) provide for investigations that the department determines are necessary; and

(4) provide for the coordination of the approval of narcotic drug treatment programs by the United States Food and Drug Administration and the United States Drug Enforcement Administration.

(b) The board shall adopt rules for the issuance of permits to operate narcotic drug treatment programs including rules:

(1) governing the submission and review of applications;

(2) establishing the criteria for the issuance and renewal of permits; and

(3) establishing the criteria for the suspension and revocation of permits.
(Enacted by Acts 1989, 71st Leg., ch. 678 (H.B. 2136), § 1, effective September 1, 1989; am. Acts 1991, 72nd Leg., ch. 14 (S.B. 404), § 193, effective September 1, 1991; am. Acts 1999, 76th Leg., ch. 1411 (H.B. 2085), § 1.14, effective September 1, 1999.)

### Sec. 466.005. Administration by Commission and Department [Repealed].

Repealed by Acts 1999, 76th Leg., ch. 1411 (H.B. 2085), § 1.18, effective September 1, 1999.

### SUBCHAPTER B
### PERMIT

### Sec. 466.021. Permit Required.

A person may not operate a narcotic drug treatment program unless the person has a permit issued under this chapter.

Health

(Am. Acts 1991, 72nd Leg., ch. 14 (S.B. 404), § 193, effective September 1, 1991 (renumbered from Sec. 466.003).)

## Sec. 466.022.   Limitation on Prescription, Order, or Administration of Narcotic Drug.

A physician may not prescribe, order, or administer a narcotic drug for the purpose of treating drug dependency unless the physician prescribes, orders, or administers an approved narcotic drug for the maintenance or detoxification of drug-dependent persons as part of a program permitted by the department.

(Enacted by Acts 1991, 72nd Leg., ch. 14 (S.B. 404), § 193, effective September 1, 1991; am. Acts 1999, 76th Leg., ch. 1411 (H.B. 2085), § 1.15, effective September 1, 1999.)

## Sec. 466.023.   Application for Permit; Fees.

(a) The department shall issue a permit to an applicant who qualifies under rules and standards adopted by the board.

(b) A permit issued under this section is valid until suspended or revoked by the department or surrendered by the permit holder in accordance with board rules.

(c) A person must obtain a permit for each facility that the person operates.

(d) A permit issued by the department is not transferable from one facility to another facility and must be returned to the department if the permit holder sells or otherwise conveys the facility to another person.

(e) The board by rule shall establish and collect a nonrefundable application fee to defray the cost to the department of processing each application for a permit. The application fee must be submitted with the application. An application may not be considered unless the application is accompanied by the application fee.

(f) The board shall adopt rules that set permit fees in amounts sufficient for the department to recover not less than half of the actual annual expenditures of state funds by the department to:

(1) amend permits;

(2) inspect facilities operated by permit holders; and

(3) implement and enforce this chapter.

(g) Fees collected by the department shall be deposited in the state treasury to the credit of the narcotic treatment permitting fee fund.

(Am. Acts 1991, 72nd Leg., ch. 14 (S.B. 404), § 193, effective September 1, 1991 (renumbered from Sec. 466.004).)

## Sec. 466.024.   Permit Limitations.

(a) The department may issue a permit to:

(1) a person constituting a legal entity organized and operating under the laws of this state; or

(2) a physician.

(b) The department may issue a permit to a person other than a physician only if the person provides health care services under the supervision of one or more physicians licensed by the Texas State Board of Medical Examiners.

(Am. Acts 1991, 72nd Leg., ch. 14 (S.B. 404), § 193, effective September 1, 1991.)

## Sec. 466.025.   Inspection.

(a) An authorized agent may enter the facility of a person who is an applicant for a permit or who is a permit holder during any hours in which the facility is in operation for the purpose of inspecting the facility to determine:

(1) if the person meets the standards set in the rules of the board for the issuance of a permit; or

(2) if a person who holds a permit is in compliance with this chapter, the standards set in the rules of the board for the operation of a facility, any special provisions contained in the permit, or an order of the commissioner or the department.

(b) The inspection may be conducted without prior notice to the applicant or the permit holder.

(c) The authorized agent shall provide the applicant or permit holder with a copy of the inspection report. An inspection report shall be made a part of the applicant's submission file or the permit holder's compliance record.

(Am. Acts 1991, 72nd Leg., ch. 14 (S.B. 404), § 193, effective September 1, 1991.)

## Sec. 466.026.   Multiple Enrollment Prevention.

The department shall work with representatives from permitted narcotic treatment programs in this state to develop recommendations for a plan to prevent the simultaneous multiple enrollment of persons in narcotic treatment programs. The board may adopt rules to implement these recommendations.

(Am. Acts 1991, 72nd Leg., ch. 14 (S.B. 404), § 193, effective September 1, 1991.)

## Sec. 466.027.   Denial, Suspension, or Revocation of Permit.

(a) After notice to an applicant or a permit holder and after the opportunity for a hearing, the department may:

Health

(1) deny an application of the person if the person fails to comply with this chapter or the rules establishing minimum standards for the issuance of a permit adopted under this chapter; or

(2) suspend or revoke the permit of a person who has violated this chapter, an order issued under this chapter, or a minimum standard required for the issuance of a permit.

(b) The board may adopt rules that establish the criteria for the denial, suspension, or revocation of a permit.

(c) Hearings, appeals from, and judicial review of final administrative decisions under this section shall be conducted according to the contested case provisions of Chapter 2001, Government Code and the board's formal hearing rules.

(d) This section does not prevent the informal reconsideration of a case before the setting of a hearing or before the issuance of the final administrative decision under this section. The program rules must contain provisions establishing the procedures for the initiation and conduct of the informal reconsideration by the department. (Am. Acts 1991, 72nd Leg., ch. 14 (S.B. 404), § 193, effective September 1, 1991(renumbered from Sec. 466.005); am. Acts 1995, 74th Leg., ch. 76 (S.B. 959), § 5.95(49), effective September 1, 1995.)

### SUBCHAPTER C
### ENFORCEMENT

### Sec. 466.041. Emergency Orders.

(a) The commissioner or the commissioner's designee may issue an emergency order, either mandatory or prohibitory in nature, in relation to the operation of a permitted facility or the treatment of patients by the facility staff, in the department's jurisdiction. The order may be issued if the commissioner or the commissioner's designee determines that the treatment of patients by the staff of the permit holder creates or poses an immediate and serious threat to human life or health and other procedures available to the department to remedy or prevent the occurrence of the situation will result in an unreasonable delay.

(b) The commissioner or the commissioner's designee may issue the emergency order, including an emergency order suspending or revoking a permit issued by the department, without notice and hearing, if the commissioner or the commissioner's designee determines that action to be practicable under the circumstances.

(c) If an emergency order is issued without a hearing, the department shall determine a time and place for a hearing at which the emergency order is affirmed, modified, or set aside. The hearing shall be held under the contested case provisions of Chapter 2001, Government Code and the board's formal hearing rules.

(d) If an emergency order is issued to suspend or revoke the permit, the department shall ensure that treatment services for the patients are maintained at the same location until appropriate referrals to an alternate treatment program are made. (Am. Acts 1991, 72nd Leg., ch. 14 (S.B. 404), § 193, effective September 1, 1991 (renumbered from Sec. 466.006); am. Acts 1995, 74th Leg., ch. 76 (S.B. 959), § 5.95(49), effective September 1, 1995.)

### Sec. 466.042. Injunction.

(a) The commissioner, the commissioner's designee, or an authorized agent may request the attorney general or a district, county, or municipal attorney to petition the district court for a temporary restraining order to restrain:

(1) a continuing violation of this chapter, a rule adopted under this chapter, or an order or permit issued under this chapter; or

(2) a threat of a continuing violation of this chapter, a rule, or an order or permit.

(b) To request a temporary restraining order, the commissioner, commissioner's designee, or an authorized agent must find that a person has violated, is violating, or is threatening to violate this chapter, a rule adopted under this chapter, or an order or permit issued under this chapter and:

(1) the violation or threatened violation creates an immediate threat to the health and safety of the public; or

(2) there is reasonable cause to believe that the permit holder or the staff of the permit holder is party to the diversion of a narcotic drug or drugs in violation of Chapter 481 (Texas Controlled Substances Act).

(c) On finding by the court that a person is violating or threatening to violate this chapter, a rule adopted under this chapter, or an order or permit issued under this chapter, the court shall grant the injunctive relief warranted by the facts.

(d) Venue for a suit brought under this section is in the county in which the violation or threat of violation is alleged to have occurred or in Travis County. (Am. Acts 1991, 72nd Leg., ch. 14 (S.B. 404), § 193, effective September 1, 1991 (renumbered from Sec. 466.007).)

Health

## Sec. 466.043. Administrative Penalty.

If a person violates this chapter, a rule adopted under this chapter, or an order or permit issued under this chapter, the commissioner may assess an administrative penalty against the person as provided by Chapter 431 (Texas Food, Drug, and Cosmetic Act).

(Am. Acts 1991, 72nd Leg., ch. 14 (S.B. 404), § 193, effective September 1, 1991 (renumbered from Sec. 466.008).)

## Sec. 466.044. Criminal Penalty.

(a) A person commits an offense if the person operates a narcotic drug treatment program without a permit issued by the department.

(b) An offense under this section is a Class A misdemeanor.

(Am. Acts 1991, 72nd Leg., ch. 14 (S.B. 404), § 193, effective September 1, 1991 (renumbered from Sec. 466.009).)

## Sec. 466.045. Civil Penalty.

(a) If it appears that a person has violated this chapter, a rule adopted under this chapter, or an order or permit issued under this chapter, the commissioner may request the attorney general or the district, county, or municipal attorney of the municipality or county in which the violation occurred to institute a civil suit for the assessment and recovery of a civil penalty.

(b) The penalty may be in an amount not to exceed $10,000 for each violation.

(c) In determining the amount of the penalty, the court shall consider:

(1) the person's history of previous violations;

(2) the seriousness of the violation;

(3) any hazard to the health and safety of the public; and

(4) the demonstrated good faith of the person charged.

(d) A civil penalty recovered in a suit instituted by the attorney general under this chapter shall be deposited in the state treasury to the credit of the General Revenue Fund. A civil penalty recovered in a suit instituted by a local government under this chapter shall be paid to the local government.

(Am. Acts 1991, 72nd Leg., ch. 14 (S.B. 404), § 193, effective September 1, 1991 (renumbered from Sec. 466.010).)

# SUBTITLE C
# SUBSTANCE ABUSE REGULATION AND CRIMES

# CHAPTER 481
# TEXAS CONTROLLED SUBSTANCES ACT

### Subchapter A. General Provisions

Health

## SUBCHAPTER A
## GENERAL PROVISIONS

### Sec. 481.001.   Short Title.

This chapter may be cited as the Texas Controlled Substances Act.

(Enacted by Acts 1989, 71st Leg., ch. 678 (H.B. 2136), § 1, effective September 1, 1989.)

### Sec. 481.002.   Definitions.

In this chapter:

(1) "Administer" means to directly apply a controlled substance by injection, inhalation, ingestion, or other means to the body of a patient or research subject by:

(A) a practitioner or an agent of the practitioner in the presence of the practitioner; or

(B) the patient or research subject at the direction and in the presence of a practitioner.

(2) "Agent" means an authorized person who acts on behalf of or at the direction of a manufacturer, distributor, or dispenser. The term does not include a common or contract carrier, public warehouseman, or employee of a carrier or warehouseman acting in the usual and lawful course of employment.

(3) "Commissioner" means the commissioner of public health or the commissioner's designee.

(4) "Controlled premises" means:

(A) a place where original or other records or documents required under this chapter are kept or are required to be kept; or

(B) a place, including a factory, warehouse, other establishment, or conveyance, where a person registered under this chapter may lawfully hold, manufacture, distribute, dispense, administer, possess, or otherwise dispose of a controlled substance or other item governed by this chapter, including a chemical precursor and a chemical laboratory apparatus.

(5) "Controlled substance" means a substance, including a drug, an adulterant, and a dilutant, listed in Schedules I through V or Penalty Groups 1, 1-A, or 2 through 4. The term includes the aggregate weight of any mixture, solution, or other substance containing a controlled substance.

(6) "Controlled substance analogue" means:

(A) a substance with a chemical structure substantially similar to the chemical structure of a controlled substance in Schedule I or II or Penalty Group 1, 1-A, or 2; or

(B) a substance specifically designed to produce an effect substantially similar to, or greater than, the effect of a controlled substance in Schedule I or II or Penalty Group 1, 1-A, or 2.

(7) "Counterfeit substance" means a controlled substance that, without authorization, bears or is in a container or has a label that bears an actual or simulated trademark, trade name, or other identifying mark, imprint, number, or device of a manufacturer, distributor, or dispenser other than the person who in fact manufactured, distributed, or dispensed the substance.

(8) "Deliver" means to transfer, actually or constructively, to another a controlled substance, counterfeit substance, or drug paraphernalia, regardless of whether there is an agency relationship. The term includes offering to sell a controlled substance, counterfeit substance, or drug paraphernalia.

(9) "Delivery" or "drug transaction" means the act of delivering.

(10) "Designated agent" means an individual designated under Section 481.073 to communicate a practitioner's instructions to a pharmacist.

(11) "Director" means the director of the Department of Public Safety or an employee of the department designated by the director.

(12) "Dispense" means the delivery of a controlled substance in the course of professional practice or research, by a practitioner or person acting under the lawful order of a practitioner, to an ultimate user or research subject. The term includes the prescribing, administering, packaging, labeling, or compounding necessary to prepare the substance for delivery.

(13) "Dispenser" means a practitioner, institutional practitioner, pharmacist, or pharmacy that dispenses a controlled substance.

(14) "Distribute" means to deliver a controlled substance other than by administering or dispensing the substance.

(15) "Distributor" means a person who distributes.

(16) "Drug" means a substance, other than a device or a component, part, or accessory of a device, that is:

(A) recognized as a drug in the official United States Pharmacopoeia, official Homeopathic Pharmacopoeia of the United States, official National Formulary, or a supplement to either pharmacopoeia or the formulary;

(B) intended for use in the diagnosis, cure, mitigation, treatment, or prevention of disease in man or animals;

(C) intended to affect the structure or function of the body of man or animals but is not food; or

(D) intended for use as a component of a substance described by Paragraph (A), (B), or (C).

(17) "Drug paraphernalia" means equipment, a product, or material that is used or intended for use in planting, propagating, cultivating, growing, harvesting, manufacturing, compounding, converting, producing, processing, preparing, testing, analyzing, packaging, repackaging, storing, containing, or concealing a controlled substance in violation of this chapter or in injecting, ingesting, inhaling, or otherwise introducing into the human body a controlled substance in violation of this chapter. The term includes:

(A) a kit used or intended for use in planting, propagating, cultivating, growing, or harvesting a species of plant that is a controlled substance or from which a controlled substance may be derived;

(B) a material, compound, mixture, preparation, or kit used or intended for use in manufacturing, compounding, converting, producing, processing, or preparing a controlled substance;

(C) an isomerization device used or intended for use in increasing the potency of a species of plant that is a controlled substance;

(D) testing equipment used or intended for use in identifying or in analyzing the strength, effectiveness, or purity of a controlled substance;

(E) a scale or balance used or intended for use in weighing or measuring a controlled substance;

(F) a dilutant or adulterant, such as quinine hydrochloride, mannitol, inositol, nicotinamide, dextrose, lactose, or absorbent, blotter-type material, that is used or intended to be used to increase the amount or weight of or to transfer a controlled substance regardless of whether the dilutant or adulterant diminishes the efficacy of the controlled substance;

(G) a separation gin or sifter used or intended for use in removing twigs and seeds from or in otherwise cleaning or refining marihuana;

(H) a blender, bowl, container, spoon, or mixing device used or intended for use in compounding a controlled substance;

(I) a capsule, balloon, envelope, or other container used or intended for use in packaging small quantities of a controlled substance;

(J) a container or other object used or intended for use in storing or concealing a controlled substance;

(K) a hypodermic syringe, needle, or other object used or intended for use in parenterally injecting a controlled substance into the human body; and

(L) an object used or intended for use in ingesting, inhaling, or otherwise introducing marihuana, cocaine, hashish, or hashish oil into the human body, including:

(i) a metal, wooden, acrylic, glass, stone, plastic, or ceramic pipe with or without a screen, permanent screen, hashish head, or punctured metal bowl;

(ii) a water pipe;

(iii) a carburetion tube or device;

(iv) a smoking or carburetion mask;

(v) a chamber pipe;

(vi) a carburetor pipe;

(vii) an electric pipe;

(viii) an air-driven pipe;

(ix) a chillum;

(x) a bong; or

(xi) an ice pipe or chiller.

(18) "Federal Controlled Substances Act" means the Federal Comprehensive Drug Abuse Prevention and Control Act of 1970 (21 U.S.C. Section 801 et seq.) or its successor statute.

(19) "Federal Drug Enforcement Administration" means the Drug Enforcement Administration of the United States Department of Justice or its successor agency.

(20) "Hospital" means:

(A) a general or special hospital as defined by Section 241.003 (Texas Hospital Licensing Law); or

(B) an ambulatory surgical center licensed by the Texas Department of Health and approved by the federal government to perform surgery paid by Medicaid on patients admitted for a period of not more than 24 hours.

(21) "Human consumption" means the injection, inhalation, ingestion, or application of a substance to or into a human body.

(22) "Immediate precursor" means a substance the director finds to be and by rule designates as being:

(A) a principal compound commonly used or produced primarily for use in the manufacture of a controlled substance;

(B) a substance that is an immediate chemical intermediary used or likely to be used in the manufacture of a controlled substance; and

(C) a substance the control of which is necessary to prevent, curtail, or limit the manufacture of a controlled substance.

(23) "Institutional practitioner" means an intern, resident physician, fellow, or person in an equivalent professional position who:

(A) is not licensed by the appropriate state professional licensing board;

(B) is enrolled in a bona fide professional training program in a base hospital or institutional training facility registered by the Federal Drug Enforcement Administration; and

(C) is authorized by the base hospital or institutional training facility to administer, dispense, or prescribe controlled substances.

(24) "Lawful possession" means the possession of a controlled substance that has been obtained in accordance with state or federal law.

(25) "Manufacture" means the production, preparation, propagation, compounding, conversion, or processing of a controlled substance other than marihuana, directly or indirectly by extraction from substances of natural origin, independently by means of chemical synthesis, or by a combination of extraction and chemical synthesis, and includes the packaging or repackaging of the substance or labeling or relabeling of its container. However, the term does not include the preparation, compounding, packaging, or labeling of a controlled substance:

(A) by a practitioner as an incident to the practitioner's administering or dispensing a controlled substance in the course of professional practice; or

(B) by a practitioner, or by an authorized agent under the supervision of the practitioner, for or as an incident to research, teaching, or chemical analysis and not for delivery.

(26) "Marihuana" means the plant Cannabis sativa L., whether growing or not, the seeds of that plant, and every compound, manufacture, salt, derivative, mixture, or preparation of that plant or its seeds. The term does not include:

(A) the resin extracted from a part of the plant or a compound, manufacture, salt, derivative, mixture, or preparation of the resin;

(B) the mature stalks of the plant or fiber produced from the stalks;

(C) oil or cake made from the seeds of the plant;

(D) a compound, manufacture, salt, derivative, mixture, or preparation of the mature stalks, fiber, oil, or cake; or

(E) the sterilized seeds of the plant that are incapable of beginning germination.

(27) "Medical purpose" means the use of a controlled substance for relieving or curing a mental or physical disease or infirmity.

(28) "Medication order" means an order from a practitioner to dispense a drug to a patient in a hospital for immediate administration while the patient is in the hospital or for emergency use on the patient's release from the hospital.

(29) "Narcotic drug" means any of the following, produced directly or indirectly by extraction from substances of vegetable origin, independently by means of chemical synthesis, or by a combination of extraction and chemical synthesis:

(A) opium and opiates, and a salt, compound, derivative, or preparation of opium or opiates;

(B) a salt, compound, isomer, derivative, or preparation of a salt, compound, isomer, or derivative that is chemically equivalent or identical to a substance listed in Paragraph (A) other than the isoquinoline alkaloids of opium;

(C) opium poppy and poppy straw; or

(D) cocaine, including:

(i) its salts, its optical, position, or geometric isomers, and the salts of those isomers;

(ii) coca leaves and a salt, compound, derivative, or preparation of coca leaves; and

(iii) a salt, compound, derivative, or preparation of a salt, compound, or derivative that is chemically equivalent or identical to a substance described by Subparagraph (i) or (ii), other than decocainized coca leaves or extractions of coca leaves that do not contain cocaine or ecgonine.

(30) "Opiate" means a substance that has an addiction-forming or addiction-sustaining liability similar to morphine or is capable of conversion into a drug having addiction-forming or addiction-sustaining liability. The term includes its racemic and levorotatory forms. The term does not include, unless specifically designated as controlled under Subchapter B, the dextrorotatory isomer of 3-methoxy-n-methylmorphinan and its salts (dextromethorphan).

(31) "Opium poppy" means the plant of the species Papaver somniferum L., other than its seeds.

(32) "Patient" means a human for whom or an animal for which a drug is administered, dispensed, delivered, or prescribed by a practitioner.

(33) "Person" means an individual, corporation, government, business trust, estate, trust, partnership, association, or any other legal entity.

(34) "Pharmacist" means a person licensed by the Texas State Board of Pharmacy to practice pharmacy and who acts as an agent for a pharmacy.

(35) "Pharmacist-in-charge" means the pharmacist designated on a pharmacy license as the pharmacist who has the authority or responsibility for the pharmacy's compliance with this chapter and other laws relating to pharmacy.

(36) "Pharmacy" means a facility licensed by the Texas State Board of Pharmacy where a prescription for a controlled substance is received or processed in accordance with state or federal law.

(37) "Poppy straw" means all parts, other than the seeds, of the opium poppy, after mowing.

(38) "Possession" means actual care, custody, control, or management.

(39) "Practitioner" means:

(A) a physician, dentist, veterinarian, podiatrist, scientific investigator, or other person licensed, registered, or otherwise permitted to distribute, dispense, analyze, conduct research with respect to, or administer a controlled substance in the course of professional practice or research in this state;

(B) a pharmacy, hospital, or other institution licensed, registered, or otherwise permitted to distribute, dispense, conduct research with respect to, or administer a

controlled substance in the course of professional practice or research in this state;

(C) a person practicing in and licensed by another state as a physician, dentist, veterinarian, or podiatrist, having a current Federal Drug Enforcement Administration registration number, who may legally prescribe Schedule II, III, IV, or V controlled substances in that state; or

(D) an advanced practice nurse or physician assistant to whom a physician has delegated the authority to carry out or sign prescription drug orders under Section 157.0511, 157.052, 157.053, 157.054, 157.0541, or 157.0542, Occupations Code.

(40) "Prescribe" means the act of a practitioner to authorize a controlled substance to be dispensed to an ultimate user.

(41) "Prescription" means an order by a practitioner to a pharmacist for a controlled substance for a particular patient that specifies:

(A) the date of issue;

(B) the name and address of the patient or, if the controlled substance is prescribed for an animal, the species of the animal and the name and address of its owner;

(C) the name and quantity of the controlled substance prescribed with the quantity shown numerically followed by the number written as a word if the order is written or, if the order is communicated orally or telephonically, with the quantity given by the practitioner and transcribed by the pharmacist numerically;

(D) directions for the use of the drug;

(E) the intended use of the drug unless the practitioner determines the furnishing of this information is not in the best interest of the patient; and

(F) the legibly printed or stamped name, address, Federal Drug Enforcement Administration registration number, and telephone number of the practitioner at the practitioner's usual place of business.

(42) "Principal place of business" means a location where a person manufactures, distributes, dispenses, analyzes, or possesses a controlled substance. The term does not include a location where a practitioner dispenses a controlled substance on an outpatient basis unless the controlled substance is stored at that location.

(43) "Production" includes the manufacturing, planting, cultivating, growing, or harvesting of a controlled substance.

Health

(44) "Raw material" means a compound, material, substance, or equipment used or intended for use, alone or in any combination, in manufacturing a controlled substance.

(45) "Registrant" means a person who is registered under Section 481.063.

(46) "Substitution" means the dispensing of a drug or a brand of drug other than that which is ordered or prescribed.

(47) "Official prescription form" means a prescription form that contains the prescription information required by Section 481.075.

(48) "Ultimate user" means a person who has lawfully obtained and possesses a controlled substance for the person's own use, for the use of a member of the person's household, or for administering to an animal owned by the person or by a member of the person's household.

(49) "Adulterant or dilutant" means any material that increases the bulk or quantity of a controlled substance, regardless of its effect on the chemical activity of the controlled substance.

(50) "Abuse unit" means:

(A) except as provided by Paragraph (B):

(i) a single unit on or in any adulterant, dilutant, or similar carrier medium, including marked or perforated blotter paper, a tablet, gelatin wafer, sugar cube, or stamp, or other medium that contains any amount of a controlled substance listed in Penalty Group 1-A, if the unit is commonly used in abuse of that substance; or

(ii) each quarter-inch square section of paper, if the adulterant, dilutant, or carrier medium is paper not marked or perforated into individual abuse units; or

(B) if the controlled substance is in liquid form, 40 micrograms of the controlled substance including any adulterant or dilutant.

(51) "Chemical precursor" means:

(A) Methylamine;

(B) Ethylamine;

(C) D-lysergic acid;

(D) Ergotamine tartrate;

(E) Diethyl malonate;

(F) Malonic acid;

(G) Ethyl malonate;

(H) Barbituric acid;

(I) Piperidine;

(J) N-acetylanthranilic acid;

(K) Pyrrolidine;

(L) Phenylacetic acid;

(M) Anthranilic acid;

(N) Ephedrine;

(O) Pseudoephedrine;

(P) Norpseudoephedrine; or

(Q) Phenylpropanolamine.

(52) "Department" means the Department of Public Safety.

(53) "Chemical laboratory apparatus" means any item of equipment designed, made, or adapted to manufacture a controlled substance or a controlled substance analogue, including:

(A) a condenser;

(B) a distilling apparatus;

(C) a vacuum drier;

(D) a three-neck or distilling flask;

(E) a tableting machine;

(F) an encapsulating machine;

(G) a filter, Buchner, or separatory funnel;

(H) an Erlenmeyer, two-neck, or single-neck flask;

(I) a round-bottom, Florence, thermometer, or filtering flask;

(J) a Soxhlet extractor;

(K) a transformer;

(L) a flask heater;

(M) a heating mantel; or

(N) an adaptor tube.

(54), (55) [Repealed by Acts 1999, 76th Leg., ch. 145 (S.B. 254), § 5(1), effective September 1, 1999.]

(Enacted by Acts 1989, 71st Leg., ch. 678 (H.B. 2136), § 1, effective September 1, 1989; am. Acts 1989, 71st Leg., ch. 1100 (S.B. 1046), § 5.02(b), effective September 1, 1989; am. Acts 1993, 73rd Leg., ch. 351 (S.B. 621), § 27, effective September 1, 1993; am. Acts 1993, 73rd Leg., ch. 789 (S.B. 472), § 15, effective September 1, 1993; am. Acts 1993, 73rd Leg., ch. 900 (S.B. 1067), § 2.01, effective September 1, 1994; am. Acts 1997, 75th Leg., ch. 745 (H.B. 1070), §§ 1, 2, effective January 1, 1998; am. Acts 1999, 76th Leg., ch. 145 (S.B. 254), §§ 1, 5(1), effective September 1, 1999; am. Acts 2001, 77th Leg., ch. 251 (S.B. 753), § 1, effective September 1, 2001; am. Acts 2001, 77th Leg., ch. 1188 (H.B. 3351), § 1, effective September 1, 2001; am. Acts 2003, 78th Leg., ch. 88 (H.B. 1095), § 9, effective May 20, 2003; am. Acts 2003, 78th Leg., ch. 1099 (H.B. 2192), § 4, effective September 1, 2003.)

## Sec. 481.003.   Rules.

(a) The director may adopt rules to administer and enforce this chapter.

(b) The director by rule shall prohibit a person in this state, including a person regulated by the

Texas Department of Insurance under the Insurance Code or the other insurance laws of this state, from using a practitioner's Federal Drug Enforcement Administration number for a purpose other than a purpose described by federal law or by this chapter. A person who violates a rule adopted under this subsection commits a Class C misdemeanor.
(Enacted by Acts 1997, 75th Leg., ch. 745 (H.B. 1070), § 3, effective January 1, 1998; am. Acts 1999, 76th Leg., ch. 1266 (S.B. 1235), § 1, effective September 1, 1999.)

## SUBCHAPTER B
## SCHEDULES

### Sec. 481.031. Nomenclature.

Controlled substances listed in Schedules I through V and Penalty Groups 1 through 4 are included by whatever official, common, usual, chemical, or trade name they may be designated.
(Enacted by Acts 1989, 71st Leg., ch. 678 (H.B. 2136), § 1, effective September 1, 1989; am. Acts 1997, 75th Leg., ch. 745 (H.B. 1070), § 4, effective January 1, 1998.)

### Sec. 481.032. Schedules.

(a) The commissioner shall establish and modify the following schedules of controlled substances under this subchapter: Schedule I, Schedule II, Schedule III, Schedule IV, and Schedule V.

(b) A reference to a schedule in this chapter means the most current version of the schedule established or altered by the commissioner under this subchapter and published in the Texas Register on or after January 1, 1998.
(Enacted by Acts 1989, 71st Leg., ch. 678 (H.B. 2136), § 1, effective September 1, 1989; am. Acts 1997, 75th Leg., ch. 745 (H.B. 1070), § 4, effective January 1, 1998; am. Acts 2001, 77th Leg., ch. 251 (S.B. 753), § 2, effective September 1, 2001.)

### Sec. 481.033. Exclusion from Schedules and Application of Act.

(a) A nonnarcotic substance is excluded from Schedules I through V if the substance may lawfully be sold over the counter without a prescription, under the Federal Food, Drug, and Cosmetic Act (21 U.S.C. Section 301 et seq.).

(b) The commissioner may not include in the schedules:

(1) a substance described by Subsection (a); or

(2) distilled spirits, wine, malt beverages, or tobacco.

(c) A compound, mixture, or preparation containing a stimulant substance listed in Schedule II and having a potential for abuse associated with a stimulant effect on the central nervous system is excepted from the application of this chapter if the compound, mixture, or preparation contains one or more active medicinal ingredients not having a stimulant effect on the central nervous system and if the admixtures are included in combinations, quantity, proportions, or concentrations that vitiate the potential for abuse of the substance having a stimulant effect on the central nervous system.

(d) A compound, mixture, or preparation containing a depressant substance listed in Schedule III or IV and having a potential for abuse associated with a depressant effect on the central nervous system is excepted from the application of this chapter if the compound, mixture, or preparation contains one or more active medicinal ingredients not having a depressant effect on the central nervous system and if the admixtures are included in combinations, quantity, proportions, or concentrations that vitiate the potential for abuse of the substance having a depressant effect on the central nervous system.

(e) A nonnarcotic prescription substance is exempted from Schedules I through V and the application of this chapter to the same extent that the substance has been exempted from the application of the Federal Controlled Substances Act, if the substance is listed as an exempt prescription product under 21 C.F.R. Section 1308.32 and its subsequent amendments.

(f) A chemical substance that is intended for laboratory, industrial, educational, or special research purposes and not for general administration to a human being or other animal is exempted from Schedules I through V and the application of this chapter to the same extent that the substance has been exempted from the application of the Federal Controlled Substances Act, if the substance is listed as an exempt chemical preparation under 21 C.F.R. Section 1308.24 and its subsequent amendments.

(g) An anabolic steroid product, which has no significant potential for abuse due to concentration, preparation, mixture, or delivery system, is exempted from Schedules I through V and the application of this chapter to the same extent that the substance has been exempted from the application of the Federal Controlled Substances Act, if the substance is listed as an exempt

anabolic steroid product under 21 C.F.R. Section 1308.34 and its subsequent amendments.
(Enacted by Acts 1989, 71st Leg., ch. 678 (H.B. 2136), § 1, effective September 1, 1989; am. Acts 1993, 73rd Leg., ch. 532 (S.B. 1197), § 1, effective September 1, 1993; am. Acts 1997, 75th Leg., ch. 745 (H.B. 1070), § 4, effective January 1, 1998 (renumbered from Sec. 481.037).)

## Sec. 481.034. Establishment and Modification of Schedules by Commissioner.

(a) The commissioner shall annually establish the schedules of controlled substances. These annual schedules shall include the complete list of all controlled substances from the previous schedules and modifications in the federal schedules of controlled substances as required by Subsection (g). Any further additions to and deletions from these schedules, any rescheduling of substances and any other modifications made by the commissioner to these schedules of controlled substances shall be made:

(1) in accordance with Section 481.035;

(2) in a manner consistent with this subchapter; and

(3) with approval of the Texas Board of Health.

(b) Except for alterations in schedules required by Subsection (g), the commissioner may not make an alteration in a schedule unless the commissioner holds a public hearing on the matter in Austin and obtains approval from the Texas Board of Health.

(c) The commissioner may not:

(1) add a substance to the schedules if the substance has been deleted from the schedules by the legislature;

(2) delete a substance from the schedules if the substance has been added to the schedules by the legislature; or

(3) reschedule a substance if the substance has been placed in a schedule by the legislature.

(d) In making a determination regarding a substance, the commissioner shall consider:

(1) the actual or relative potential for its abuse;

(2) the scientific evidence of its pharmacological effect, if known;

(3) the state of current scientific knowledge regarding the substance;

(4) the history and current pattern of its abuse;

(5) the scope, duration, and significance of its abuse;

(6) the risk to the public health;

(7) the potential of the substance to produce psychological or physiological dependence liability; and

(8) whether the substance is a controlled substance analogue, chemical precursor, or an immediate precursor of a substance controlled under this chapter.

(e) After considering the factors listed in Subsection (d), the commissioner shall make findings with respect to those factors and adopt a rule controlling the substance if the commissioner finds the substance has a potential for abuse.

(f) [Repealed by Acts 2003, 78th Leg., ch. 1099 (H.B. 2192), § 17, effective September 1, 2003.]

(g) Except as otherwise provided by this subsection, if a substance is designated, rescheduled, or deleted as a controlled substance under federal law and notice of that fact is given to the commissioner, the commissioner similarly shall control the substance under this chapter. After the expiration of a 30-day period beginning on the day after the date of publication in the Federal Register of a final order designating a substance as a controlled substance or rescheduling or deleting a substance, the commissioner similarly shall designate, reschedule, or delete the substance, unless the commissioner objects during the period. If the commissioner objects, the commissioner shall publish the reasons for the objection and give all interested parties an opportunity to be heard. At the conclusion of the hearing, the commissioner shall publish a decision, which is final unless altered by statute. On publication of an objection by the commissioner, control as to that particular substance under this chapter is stayed until the commissioner publishes the commissioner's decision.

(h) Not later than the 10th day after the date on which the commissioner designates, deletes, or reschedules a substance under Subsection (a), the commissioner shall give written notice of that action to the director and to each state licensing agency having jurisdiction over practitioners.
(Enacted by Acts 1989, 71st Leg., ch. 678 (H.B. 2136), § 1, effective September 1, 1989; am. Acts 1997, 75th Leg., ch. 745 (H.B. 1070), § 4, effective January 1, 1998 (renumbered from Sec. 481.038);

am. Acts 2003, 78th Leg., ch. 1099 (H.B. 2192), §§ 5, 17, effective September 1, 2003.)

### Sec. 481.035. Findings.

(a) The commissioner shall place a substance in Schedule I if the commissioner finds that the substance:

(1) has a high potential for abuse; and

(2) has no accepted medical use in treatment in the United States or lacks accepted safety for use in treatment under medical supervision.

(b) The commissioner shall place a substance in Schedule II if the commissioner finds that:

(1) the substance has a high potential for abuse;

(2) the substance has currently accepted medical use in treatment in the United States; and

(3) abuse of the substance may lead to severe psychological or physical dependence.

(c) The commissioner shall place a substance in Schedule III if the commissioner finds that:

(1) the substance has a potential for abuse less than that of the substances listed in Schedules I and II;

(2) the substance has currently accepted medical use in treatment in the United States; and

(3) abuse of the substance may lead to moderate or low physical dependence or high psychological dependence.

(d) The commissioner shall place a substance in Schedule IV if the commissioner finds that:

(1) the substance has a lower potential for abuse than that of the substances listed in Schedule III;

(2) the substance has currently accepted medical use in treatment in the United States; and

(3) abuse of the substance may lead to a more limited physical or psychological dependence than that of the substances listed in Schedule III.

(e) The commissioner shall place a substance in Schedule V if the commissioner finds that the substance:

(1) has a lower potential for abuse than that of the substances listed in Schedule IV;

(2) has currently accepted medical use in treatment in the United States; and

(3) may lead to a more limited physical or psychological dependence liability than that of the substances listed in Schedule IV.

(Enacted by Acts 1989, 71st Leg., ch. 678 (H.B. 2136), § 1, effective September 1, 1989; am. Acts 1997, 75th Leg., ch. 745 (H.B. 1070), § 4, effective January 1, 1998 (renumbered from Sec. 481.039).)

### Sec. 481.036. Publication of Schedules.

(a) The commissioner shall publish the schedules by filing a certified copy of the schedules with the secretary of state for publication in the Texas Register not later than the fifth working day after the date the commissioner takes action under this subchapter.

(b) Each published schedule must show changes, if any, made in the schedule since its latest publication.

(c) An action by the commissioner that establishes or modifies a schedule under this subchapter may take effect not earlier than the 21st day after the date on which the schedule or modification is published in the Texas Register unless an emergency exists that necessitates earlier action to avoid an imminent hazard to the public safety. (Enacted by Acts 1989, 71st Leg., ch. 678 (H.B. 2136), § 1, effective September 1, 1989; am. Acts 1997, 75th Leg., ch. 745 (H.B. 1070), § 4, effective January 1, 1998 (renumbered from Sec. 481.040).)

### Sec. 481.037. Carisoprodol.

Schedule IV includes carisoprodol. (Enacted by Acts 2009, 81st Leg., ch. 774 (S.B. 904), § 4, effective June 19, 2009.)

### Sec. 481.038. Alteration of Schedules by Commission [Renumbered].

Renumbered to Tex. Health & Safety Code § 481.034 by Acts 1997, 75th Leg., ch. 745 (H.B. 1070), § 4, effective January 1, 1998.

### Sec. 481.039. Findings [Renumbered].

Renumbered to Tex. Health & Safety Code § 481.035 by Acts 1997, 75th Leg., ch. 745 (H.B. 1070), § 4, effective January 1, 1998.

### Sec. 481.040. Publication of Schedules [Renumbered].

Renumbered to Tex. Health & Safety Code § 481.036 by Acts 1997, 75th Leg., ch. 745 (H.B. 1070), § 4, effective January 1, 1998.

Health

### SUBCHAPTER C
### REGULATION OF MANUFACTURE, DISTRIBUTION, AND DISPENSATION OF CONTROLLED SUBSTANCES, CHEMICAL PRECURSORS, AND CHEMICAL LABORATORY APPARATUS

### Sec. 481.061.  Registration Required.

(a) Except as otherwise provided by this chapter, a person who is not a registrant may not manufacture, distribute, prescribe, possess, analyze, or dispense a controlled substance in this state.

(b) A person who is registered by the director to manufacture, distribute, analyze, dispense, or conduct research with a controlled substance may possess, manufacture, distribute, analyze, dispense, or conduct research with that substance to the extent authorized by the person's registration and in conformity with this chapter.

(c) A separate registration is required at each principal place of business or professional practice where the applicant manufactures, distributes, analyzes, dispenses, or possesses a controlled substance. However, the director may not require separate registration for a practitioner engaged in research with a nonnarcotic controlled substance listed in Schedules II through V if the registrant is already registered under this subchapter in another capacity.

(d) A person shall provide the department with the person's Federal Drug Enforcement Administration number not later than the 45th day after the director issues a registration to the person under this subchapter.
(Enacted by Acts 1989, 71st Leg., ch. 678 (H.B. 2136), § 1, effective September 1, 1989; am. Acts 1997, 75th Leg., ch. 745 (H.B. 1070), § 5, effective January 1, 1998; am. Acts 2011, 82nd Leg., ch. 1228 (S.B. 594), § 1, effective September 1, 2011; am. Acts 2011, 82nd Leg., ch. 1342 (S.B. 1273), § 1, effective September 1, 2011.)

### Sec. 481.062.  Exemptions.

(a) The following persons are not required to register and may possess a controlled substance under this chapter:

(1) an agent or employee of a registered manufacturer, distributor, analyzer, or dispenser of the controlled substance acting in the usual course of business or employment;

(2) a common or contract carrier, a warehouseman, or an employee of a carrier or warehouseman whose possession of the controlled substance is in the usual course of business or employment;

(3) an ultimate user or a person in possession of the controlled substance under a lawful order of a practitioner or in lawful possession of the controlled substance if it is listed in Schedule V;

(4) an officer or employee of this state, another state, a political subdivision of this state or another state, or the United States who is lawfully engaged in the enforcement of a law relating to a controlled substance or drug or to a customs law and authorized to possess the controlled substance in the discharge of the person's official duties; or

(5) if the substance is tetrahydrocannabinol or one of its derivatives:

(A) a Texas Department of Health official, a medical school researcher, or a research program participant possessing the substance as authorized under Subchapter G; or

(B) a practitioner or an ultimate user possessing the substance as a participant in a federally approved therapeutic research program that the commissioner has reviewed and found, in writing, to contain a medically responsible research protocol.

(b) The director by rule may waive the requirement for registration of certain manufacturers, distributors, or dispensers if the director finds it consistent with the public health and safety and if the attorney general of the United States has issued a similar waiver under the Federal Controlled Substances Act.
(Enacted by Acts 1989, 71st Leg., ch. 678 (H.B. 2136), § 1, effective September 1, 1989; am. Acts 1997, 75th Leg., ch. 745 (H.B. 1070), § 6, effective January 1, 1998; am. Acts 2001, 77th Leg., ch. 251 (S.B. 753), § 3, effective September 1, 2001; am. Acts 2001, 77th Leg., ch. 1420 (H.B. 2812), § 21.001(79), effective September 1, 2001.)

### Sec. 481.0621.  Exceptions.

(a) This subchapter does not apply to an educational or research program of a school district or a public or private institution of higher education. This subchapter does not apply to a manufacturer, wholesaler, retailer, or other person who sells, transfers, or furnishes materials covered by this subchapter to those educational or research programs.

(b) The department and the Texas Higher Education Coordinating Board shall adopt a memorandum of understanding that establishes the responsibilities of the board, the department, and the public or private institutions of higher education in implementing and maintaining a program for reporting information concerning controlled substances, controlled substance analogues, chemical precursors, and chemical laboratory apparatus used in educational or research activities of institutions of higher education.

(c) The department and the Texas Education Agency shall adopt a memorandum of understanding that establishes the responsibilities of the agency, the department, and school districts in implementing and maintaining a program for reporting information concerning controlled substances, controlled substance analogues, chemical precursors, and chemical laboratory apparatus used in educational or research activities of those schools and school districts.
(Enacted by Acts 1989, 71st Leg., ch. 1100 (S.B. 1046), § 5.02(e), effective September 1, 1989; am. Acts 1997, 75th Leg., ch. 165 (S.B. 898), § 6.45, effective September 1, 1997; am. Acts 1997, 75th Leg., ch. 745 (H.B. 1070), § 7, effective January 1, 1998.)

## Sec. 481.063. Registration Application; Issuance or Denial.

(a) The director may refuse to issue a registration to a person to manufacture, distribute, analyze, or conduct research with a controlled substance if the person fails or refuses to provide to the director a consent form signed by the person granting the director the right to inspect the person's controlled premises and any record, controlled substance, or other item covered by this chapter.

(b) The director may not issue a registration to a person to dispense a controlled substance unless the director receives a consent form signed by the person granting the director the right to inspect records as required by this chapter.

(c) The director shall register a person to manufacture, distribute, or analyze a controlled substance listed in Schedules II through V if:

(1) the person furnishes the director evidence that the person is registered for that purpose under the Federal Controlled Substances Act;

(2) the person has made proper application and paid the applicable fee; and

(3) the person has not been found by the director to have violated a provision of Subsection (e).

(d) The director shall register a person to dispense or conduct research with a controlled substance listed in Schedules II through V if the person:

(1) is a practitioner licensed under the laws of this state;

(2) has made proper application and paid the applicable fee; and

(3) has not been found by the director to have violated a provision of Subsection (e).

(e) An application for registration to manufacture, distribute, analyze, dispense, or conduct research with a controlled substance may be denied on a finding that the applicant:

(1) has furnished material information in an application filed under this chapter that the applicant knows is false or fraudulent;

(2) has been convicted of or placed on community supervision or other probation for:

(A) a felony;

(B) a violation of this chapter or of Chapters 482—485; or

(C) an offense reasonably related to the registration sought;

(3) has voluntarily surrendered or has had suspended, denied, or revoked a registration or application for registration to manufacture, distribute, analyze, or dispense controlled substances under the Federal Controlled Substances Act;

(4) has had suspended, probated, or revoked a registration or a practitioner's license under the laws of this state or another state;

(5) has intentionally or knowingly failed to establish and maintain effective security controls against diversion of controlled substances into other than legitimate medical, scientific, or industrial channels as provided by federal regulations or laws, this chapter, or a rule adopted under this chapter;

(6) has intentionally or knowingly failed to maintain records required to be kept by this chapter or a rule adopted under this chapter;

(7) has refused to allow an inspection authorized by this chapter or a rule adopted under this chapter;

(8) has intentionally or knowingly violated this chapter or a rule adopted under this chapter; or

(9) has voluntarily surrendered a registration that has not been reinstated.

(f) The director may inspect the premises or establishment of an applicant for registration in accordance with this chapter.

Health

(g) A registration is valid until the first anniversary of the date of issuance and may be renewed annually under rules adopted by the director, unless a rule provides for a longer period of validity or renewal.

(h) Chapter 2001, Government Code, does not apply to a denial of a registration under Subsection (e)(2)(A) or (B), (e)(3), (e)(4), or (e)(9).

(i) For good cause shown, the director may probate the denial of an application for registration. If a denial of an application is probated, the director may require the person to report regularly to the department on matters that are the basis of the probation or may limit activities of the person to those prescribed by the director, or both.

(Enacted by Acts 1989, 71st Leg., ch. 678 (H.B. 2136), § 1, effective September 1, 1989; am. 1989, 71st Leg., ch. 1100 (S.B. 1046), § 5.02(f), effective September 1, 1989; am. Acts 1993, 73rd Leg., ch. 790 (S.B. 510), § 19, effective September 1, 1993; am. Acts 1995, 74th Leg., ch. 76 (S.B. 959), § 5.95(49), effective September 1, 1995; am. Acts 1997, 75th Leg., ch. 745 (H.B. 1070), § 8, effective January 1, 1998; am. Acts 2001, 77th Leg., ch. 251 (S.B. 753), § 4, effective September 1, 2001.)

### Sec. 481.064.  Registration Fees.

(a) The director may charge a nonrefundable fee of not more than $25 before processing an application for annual registration and may charge a late fee of not more than $50 for each application for renewal the department receives after the date the registration expires. The director by rule shall set the amounts of the fees at the amounts that are necessary to cover the cost of administering and enforcing this subchapter. Except as provided by Subsection (b), registrants shall pay the fees to the director. Not later than 60 days before the date the registration expires, the director shall send a renewal notice to the registrant at the last known address of the registrant according to department records.

(b) The director may authorize a contract between the department and an appropriate state agency for the collection and remittance of the fees. The director by rule may provide for remittance of the fees collected by state agencies for the department.

(c) The director shall deposit the collected fees to the credit of the operator's and chauffeur's license account in the general revenue fund. The fees may be used only by the department in the administration or enforcement of this subchapter.

(Enacted by Acts 1989, 71st Leg., ch. 678 (H.B. 2136), § 1, effective September 1, 1989; am. Acts 1997, 75th Leg., ch. 745 (H.B. 1070), § 9, effective January 1, 1998; am. Acts 2001, 77th Leg., ch. 251 (S.B. 753), § 5, effective September 1, 2001; am. Acts 2007, 80th Leg., ch. 1391 (S.B. 1879), § 1, effective September 1, 2007.)

### Sec. 481.065.  Authorization for Certain Activities.

(a) The director may authorize the possession, distribution, planting, and cultivation of controlled substances by a person engaged in research, training animals to detect controlled substances, or designing or calibrating devices to detect controlled substances. A person who obtains an authorization under this subsection does not commit an offense involving the possession or distribution of controlled substances to the extent that the possession or distribution is authorized.

(b) A person may conduct research with or analyze substances listed in Schedule I in this state only if the person is a practitioner registered under federal law to conduct research with or analyze those substances and the person provides the director with evidence of federal registration.

(Enacted by Acts 1989, 71st Leg., ch. 678 (H.B. 2136), § 1, effective September 1, 1989.)

### Sec. 481.066.  Voluntary Surrender, Cancellation, Suspension, Probation, or Revocation of Registration.

(a) The director may accept a voluntary surrender of a registration.

(b) The director may cancel, suspend, or revoke a registration, place on probation a person whose license has been suspended, or reprimand a registrant for a cause described by Section 481.063(e).

(c) The director may cancel a registration that was issued in error.

(d) The director may limit the cancellation, suspension, probation, or revocation to the particular schedule or controlled substance within a schedule for which grounds for cancellation, suspension, probation, or revocation exist.

(e) After accepting the voluntary surrender of a registration or ordering the cancellation, suspension, probation, or revocation of a registration, the director may seize or place under seal all controlled substances owned or possessed by the registrant under the authority of that registration. If the director orders the cancellation, suspension, probation, or revocation of a registration, a disposition may not be made of the seized or sealed substances until the time for administrative appeal of the order has elapsed or until all appeals have been concluded, except that the director may order the sale of perishable substances and deposit of the proceeds of the sale in a special interest-bearing account in the general revenue fund. When a surrender or cancellation, suspension, probation, or revocation order becomes final, all controlled substances may be forfeited to the state as provided under Subchapter E.

(f) The operation of a registrant in violation of this section is a public nuisance, and the director may apply to any court of competent jurisdiction for an injunction suspending the registration of the registrant.

(g) Chapter 2001, Government Code, applies to a proceeding under this section to the extent that that chapter does not conflict with this subchapter. Chapter 2001, Government Code, does not apply to a cancellation, suspension, probation, or revocation of a registration for a cause described by Section 481.063(e)(2)(A) or (B), (e)(3), (e)(4), or (e)(9).

(h) The director shall promptly notify appropriate state agencies of an order accepting a voluntary surrender or canceling, suspending, probating, or revoking a registration and the forfeiture of controlled substances.

(i) The director shall give written notice to the applicant or registrant of the acceptance of a voluntary surrender of a registration, or of the cancellation, suspension, probation, revocation, or denial of a registration. The notice shall be sent by certified mail, return receipt requested, to the most current address of the applicant or registrant contained in department files.

(j) After a voluntary surrender, cancellation, suspension, probation, revocation, or denial of a registration, on petition of the applicant or former registrant, the director may issue or reinstate the registration for good cause shown by the petitioner.

(Enacted by Acts 1989, 71st Leg., ch. 678 (H.B. 2136), § 1, effective September 1, 1989; am. Acts 1997, 75th Leg., ch. 745 (H.B. 1070), § 10, effective January 1, 1998; am. Acts 2001, 77th Leg., ch. 251 (S.B. 753), § 6, effective September 1, 2001.)

## Sec. 481.067. Records.

(a) A person who is registered to manufacture, distribute, analyze, or dispense a controlled sub-

stance shall keep records and maintain inventories in compliance with recordkeeping and inventory requirements of federal law and with additional rules the director adopts.

(b) The pharmacist-in-charge of a pharmacy shall maintain the records and inventories required by this section.

(c) A record required by this section must be made at the time of the transaction that is the basis of the record. A record or inventory required by this section must be kept or maintained for at least two years after the date the record or inventory is made.

(Enacted by Acts 1989, 71st Leg., ch. 678 (H.B. 2136), § 1, effective September 1, 1989; am. Acts 2001, 77th Leg., ch. 251 (S.B. 753), § 7, effective September 1, 2001.)

## Sec. 481.068. Confidentiality.

(a) The director may authorize a person engaged in research on the use and effects of a controlled substance to withhold the names and other identifying characteristics of individuals who are the subjects of the research. A person who obtains the authorization may not be compelled in a civil, criminal, administrative, legislative, or other proceeding to identify the individuals who are the subjects of the research for which the authorization is obtained.

(b) Except as provided by Sections 481.074 and 481.075, a practitioner engaged in authorized medical practice or research may not be required to furnish the name or identity of a patient or research subject to the department, the director of the Texas Commission on Alcohol and Drug Abuse, or any other agency, public official, or law enforcement officer. A practitioner may not be compelled in a state or local civil, criminal, administrative, legislative, or other proceeding to furnish the name or identity of an individual that the practitioner is obligated to keep confidential.

(c) The director may not provide to a federal, state, or local law enforcement agency the name or identity of a patient or research subject whose identity could not be obtained under Subsection (b).

(Enacted by Acts 1989, 71st Leg., ch. 678 (H.B. 2136), § 1, effective September 1, 1989; am. Acts 2001, 77th Leg., ch. 251 (S.B. 753), § 8, effective September 1, 2001.)

## Sec. 481.069. Order Forms.

A registrant may not distribute or order a controlled substance listed in Schedule I or II to

or from another registrant except under an order form. A registrant complying with the federal law concerning order forms is in compliance with this section.
(Enacted by Acts 1989, 71st Leg., ch. 678 (H.B. 2136), § 1, effective September 1, 1989; am. 1989, 71st Leg., ch. 1100 (S.B. 1046), § 5.02(g), effective September 1, 1989.)

## Sec. 481.070.  Administering or Dispensing Schedule I Controlled Substance.

Except as permitted by this chapter, a person may not administer or dispense a controlled substance listed in Schedule I.
(Enacted by Acts 1989, 71st Leg., ch. 678 (H.B. 2136), § 1, effective September 1, 1989.)

## Sec. 481.071.  Medical Purpose Required Before Prescribing, Dispensing, Delivering, or Administering Controlled Substance.

(a) A practitioner defined by Section 481.002(39)(A) may not prescribe, dispense, deliver, or administer a controlled substance or cause a controlled substance to be administered under the practitioner's direction and supervision except for a valid medical purpose and in the course of medical practice.

(b) An anabolic steroid or human growth hormone listed in Schedule III may only be:

(1) dispensed, prescribed, delivered, or administered by a practitioner, as defined by Section 481.002(39)(A), for a valid medical purpose and in the course of professional practice; or

(2) dispensed or delivered by a pharmacist according to a prescription issued by a practitioner, as defined by Section 481.002(39)(A) or (C), for a valid medical purpose and in the course of professional practice.

(c) For the purposes of Subsection (b), body-building, muscle enhancement, or increasing muscle bulk or strength through the use of an anabolic steroid or human growth hormone listed in Schedule III by a person who is in good health is not a valid medical purpose.
(Enacted by Acts 1989, 71st Leg., ch. 678 (H.B. 2136), § 1, effective September 1, 1989; am. 1989, 71st Leg., ch. 1100 (S.B. 1046), § 5.03(b), effective September 1, 1989; am. Acts 1997, 75th Leg., ch. 745 (H.B. 1070), § 11, effective January 1, 1998.)

## Sec. 481.072.  Medical Purpose Required Before Distributing or Dispensing Schedule V Controlled Substance.

A person may not distribute or dispense a controlled substance listed in Schedule V except for a valid medical purpose.
(Enacted by Acts 1989, 71st Leg., ch. 678 (H.B. 2136), § 1, effective September 1, 1989.)

## Sec. 481.073.  Communication of Prescriptions by Agent.

(a) Only a practitioner defined by Section 481.002(39)(A) and an agent designated in writing by the practitioner in accordance with rules adopted by the department may communicate a prescription by telephone. A pharmacy that receives a telephonically communicated prescription shall promptly write the prescription and file and retain the prescription in the manner required by this subchapter. A practitioner who designates an agent to communicate prescriptions shall maintain the written designation of the agent in the practitioner's usual place of business and shall make the designation available for inspection by investigators for the Texas State Board of Medical Examiners, the State Board of Dental Examiners, the State Board of Veterinary Medical Examiners, and the department. A practitioner who designates a different agent shall designate that agent in writing and maintain the designation in the same manner in which the practitioner initially designated an agent under this section.

(b) On the request of a pharmacist, a practitioner shall furnish a copy of the written designation authorized under Subsection (a).

(c) This section does not relieve a practitioner or the practitioner's designated agent from the requirement of Subchapter A, Chapter 562, Occupations Code. A practitioner is personally responsible for the actions of the designated agent in communicating a prescription to a pharmacist.
(Enacted by Acts 1989, 71st Leg., ch. 678 (H.B. 2136), § 1, effective September 1, 1989; am. Acts 2001, 77th Leg., ch. 251 (S.B. 753), § 9, effective September 1, 2001; am. Acts 2001, 77th Leg., ch. 1420 (H.B. 2812), § 14.794, effective September 1, 2001.)

## Sec. 481.074.  Prescriptions.

(a) A pharmacist may not:

(1) dispense or deliver a controlled substance or cause a controlled substance to be

dispensed or delivered under the pharmacist's direction or supervision except under a valid prescription and in the course of professional practice;

(2) dispense a controlled substance if the pharmacist knows or should have known that the prescription was issued without a valid patient-practitioner relationship;

(3) fill a prescription that is not prepared or issued as prescribed by this chapter;

(4) permit or allow a person who is not a licensed pharmacist or pharmacist intern to dispense, distribute, or in any other manner deliver a controlled substance even if under the supervision of a pharmacist, except that after the pharmacist or pharmacist intern has fulfilled his professional and legal responsibilities, a nonpharmacist may complete the actual cash or credit transaction and delivery; or

(5) permit the delivery of a controlled substance to any person not known to the pharmacist, the pharmacist intern, or the person authorized by the pharmacist to deliver the controlled substance without first requiring identification of the person taking possession of the controlled substance, except as provided by Subsection (n).

(b) Except in an emergency as defined by rule of the director or as provided by Subsection (o) or Section 481.075(j) or (m) a person may not dispense or administer a controlled substance listed in Schedule II without a written prescription of a practitioner on an official prescription form or without an electronic prescription that meets the requirements of and is completed by the practitioner in accordance with Section 481.075. In an emergency, a person may dispense or administer a controlled substance listed in Schedule II on the oral or telephonically communicated prescription of a practitioner. The person who administers or dispenses the substance shall:

(1) if the person is a prescribing practitioner or a pharmacist, promptly comply with Subsection (c); or

(2) if the person is not a prescribing practitioner or a pharmacist, promptly write the oral or telephonically communicated prescription and include in the written record of the prescription the name, address, and Federal Drug Enforcement Administration number issued for prescribing a controlled substance in this state of the prescribing practitioner, all information required to be provided by a practitioner under Section 481.075(e)(1), and all information re-

quired to be provided by a dispensing pharmacist under Section 481.075(e)(2).

(c) Not later than the seventh day after the date a prescribing practitioner authorizes an emergency oral or telephonically communicated prescription, the prescribing practitioner shall cause a written or electronic prescription, completed in the manner required by Section 481.075, to be delivered to the dispensing pharmacist at the pharmacy where the prescription was dispensed. A written prescription may be delivered in person or by mail. The envelope of a prescription delivered by mail must be postmarked not later than the seventh day after the date the prescription was authorized. On receipt of a written prescription, the dispensing pharmacy shall file the transcription of the telephonically communicated prescription and the pharmacy copy and shall send information to the director as required by Section 481.075. On receipt of an electronic prescription, the pharmacist shall annotate the electronic prescription record with the original authorization and date of the emergency oral or telephonically communicated prescription.

(d) Except as specified in Subsections (e) and (f), the director, by rule and in consultation with the Texas Medical Board and the Texas State Board of Pharmacy, shall establish the period after the date on which the prescription is issued that a person may fill a prescription for a controlled substance listed in Schedule II. A person may not refill a prescription for a substance listed in Schedule II.

(d-1) Notwithstanding Subsection (d), a prescribing practitioner may issue multiple prescriptions authorizing the patient to receive a total of up to a 90-day supply of a Schedule II controlled substance if:

(1) each separate prescription is issued for a legitimate medical purpose by a prescribing practitioner acting in the usual course of professional practice;

(2) the prescribing practitioner provides instructions on each prescription to be filled at a later date indicating the earliest date on which a pharmacy may fill each prescription;

(3) the prescribing practitioner concludes that providing the patient with multiple prescriptions in this manner does not create an undue risk of diversion or abuse; and

(4) the issuance of multiple prescriptions complies with other applicable state and federal laws.

(e) The partial filling of a prescription for a controlled substance listed in Schedule II is permissible, if the pharmacist is unable to supply the full quantity called for in a written or electronic prescription or emergency oral prescription and the pharmacist makes a notation of the quantity supplied on the face of the written prescription, on the written record of the emergency oral prescription, or in the electronic prescription record. The remaining portion of the prescription may be filled within 72 hours of the first partial filling; however, if the remaining portion is not or cannot be filled within the 72-hour period, the pharmacist shall so notify the prescribing individual practitioner. No further quantity may be supplied beyond 72 hours without a new prescription.

(f) A prescription for a Schedule II controlled substance for a patient in a long-term care facility (LTCF) or for a patient with a medical diagnosis documenting a terminal illness may be filled in partial quantities to include individual dosage units. If there is any question about whether a patient may be classified as having a terminal illness, the pharmacist must contact the practitioner before partially filling the prescription. Both the pharmacist and the practitioner have a corresponding responsibility to assure that the controlled substance is for a terminally ill patient. The pharmacist must record the prescription on an official prescription form or in the electronic prescription record and must indicate on the official prescription form or in the electronic prescription record whether the patient is "terminally ill" or an "LTCF patient." A prescription that is partially filled and does not contain the notation "terminally ill" or "LTCF patient" is considered to have been filled in violation of this chapter. For each partial filling, the dispensing pharmacist shall record on the back of the official prescription form or in the electronic prescription record the date of the partial filling, the quantity dispensed, the remaining quantity authorized to be dispensed, and the identification of the dispensing pharmacist. Before any subsequent partial filling, the pharmacist must determine that the additional partial filling is necessary. The total quantity of Schedule II controlled substances dispensed in all partial fillings may not exceed the total quantity prescribed. Schedule II prescriptions for patients in a long-term care facility or patients with a medical diagnosis documenting a terminal illness are valid for a period not to exceed 60 days following the issue date

unless sooner terminated by discontinuance of the medication.

(g) A person may not dispense a controlled substance in Schedule III or IV that is a prescription drug under the Federal Food, Drug, and Cosmetic Act (21 U.S.C. Section 301 et seq.) without a written, electronic, oral, or telephonically communicated prescription of a practitioner defined by Section 481.002(39)(A) or (D), except that the practitioner may dispense the substance directly to an ultimate user. A prescription for a controlled substance listed in Schedule III or IV may not be filled or refilled later than six months after the date on which the prescription is issued and may not be refilled more than five times, unless the prescription is renewed by the practitioner. A prescription under this subsection must comply with other applicable state and federal laws.

(h) A pharmacist may dispense a controlled substance listed in Schedule III, IV, or V under a written, electronic, oral, or telephonically communicated prescription issued by a practitioner defined by Section 481.002(39)(C) and only if the pharmacist determines that the prescription was issued for a valid medical purpose and in the course of professional practice. A prescription issued under this subsection may not be filled or refilled later than six months after the date the prescription is issued and may not be refilled more than five times, unless the prescription is renewed by the practitioner.

(i) A person may not dispense a controlled substance listed in Schedule V and containing 200 milligrams or less of codeine, or any of its salts, per 100 milliliters or per 100 grams, or containing 100 milligrams or less of dihydrocodeine, or any of its salts, per 100 milliliters or per 100 grams, without the prescription of a practitioner defined by Section 481.002(39)(A), except that a practitioner may dispense the substance directly to an ultimate user. A prescription issued under this subsection may not be filled or refilled later than six months after the date the prescription is issued and may not be refilled more than five times, unless the prescription is renewed by the practitioner.

(j) A practitioner or institutional practitioner may not allow a patient, on the patient's release from the hospital, to possess a controlled substance prescribed by the practitioner unless:

(1) the substance was dispensed under a medication order while the patient was admitted to the hospital;

(2) the substance is in a properly labeled container; and

(3) the patient possesses not more than a seven-day supply of the substance.

(k) A prescription for a controlled substance must show:

(1) the quantity of the substance prescribed:

(A) numerically, followed by the number written as a word, if the prescription is written;

(B) numerically, if the prescription is electronic; or

(C) if the prescription is communicated orally or telephonically, as transcribed by the receiving pharmacist;

(2) the date of issue;

(2-a) if the prescription is issued for a Schedule II controlled substance to be filled at a later date under Subsection (d-1), the earliest date on which a pharmacy may fill the prescription;

(3) the name, address, and date of birth or age of the patient or, if the controlled substance is prescribed for an animal, the species of the animal and the name and address of its owner;

(4) the name and strength of the controlled substance prescribed;

(5) the directions for use of the controlled substance;

(6) the intended use of the substance prescribed unless the practitioner determines the furnishing of this information is not in the best interest of the patient;

(7) the name, address, Federal Drug Enforcement Administration number, and telephone number of the practitioner at the practitioner's usual place of business, which must be legibly printed or stamped on a written prescription; and

(8) if the prescription is handwritten, the signature of the prescribing practitioner.

(l) A pharmacist may exercise his professional judgment in refilling a prescription for a controlled substance in Schedule III, IV, or V without the authorization of the prescribing practitioner provided:

(1) failure to refill the prescription might result in an interruption of a therapeutic regimen or create patient suffering;

(2) either:

(A) a natural or manmade disaster has occurred which prohibits the pharmacist from being able to contact the practitioner; or

(B) the pharmacist is unable to contact the practitioner after reasonable effort;

(3) the quantity of prescription drug dispensed does not exceed a 72-hour supply;

(4) the pharmacist informs the patient or the patient's agent at the time of dispensing that the refill is being provided without such authorization and that authorization of the practitioner is required for future refills; and

(5) the pharmacist informs the practitioner of the emergency refill at the earliest reasonable time.

(l-1) Notwithstanding Subsection (l), in the event of a natural or manmade disaster, a pharmacist may dispense not more than a 30-day supply of a prescription drug, other than a controlled substance listed in Schedule II, without the authorization of the prescribing practitioner if:

(1) failure to refill the prescription might result in an interruption of a therapeutic regimen or create patient suffering;

(2) the natural or manmade disaster prohibits the pharmacist from being able to contact the practitioner;

(3) the governor has declared a state of disaster under Chapter 418, Government Code; and

(4) the Texas State Board of Pharmacy, through its executive director, has notified pharmacies in this state that pharmacists may dispense up to a 30-day supply of a prescription drug.

(l-2) The prescribing practitioner is not liable for an act or omission by a pharmacist in dispensing a prescription drug under Subsection (l-1).

(m) A pharmacist may permit the delivery of a controlled substance by an authorized delivery person, by a person known to the pharmacist, a pharmacist intern, or the authorized delivery person, or by mail to the person or address of the person authorized by the prescription to receive the controlled substance. If a pharmacist permits delivery of a controlled substance under this subsection, the pharmacist shall retain in the records of the pharmacy for a period of not less than two years:

(1) the name of the authorized delivery person, if delivery is made by that person;

(2) the name of the person known to the pharmacist, a pharmacist intern, or the authorized delivery person if delivery is made by that person; or

(3) the mailing address to which delivery is made, if delivery is made by mail.

(n) A pharmacist may permit the delivery of a controlled substance to a person not known to the pharmacist, a pharmacist intern, or the authorized delivery person without first requiring the identification of the person to whom the controlled substance is delivered if the pharmacist determines that an emergency exists and that the controlled substance is needed for the immediate well-being of the patient for whom the controlled substance is prescribed. If a pharmacist permits delivery of a controlled substance under this subsection, the pharmacist shall retain in the records of the pharmacy for a period of not less than two years all information relevant to the delivery known to the pharmacist, including the name, address, and date of birth or age of the person to whom the controlled substance is delivered.

(o) A pharmacist may dispense a Schedule II controlled substance pursuant to a facsimile copy of an official prescription completed in the manner required by Section 481.075 and transmitted by the practitioner or the practitioner's agent to the pharmacy if:

(1) the prescription is written for:

(A) a Schedule II narcotic or nonnarcotic substance for a patient in a long-term care facility (LTCF), and the practitioner notes on the prescription "LTCF patient";

(B) a Schedule II narcotic product to be compounded for the direct administration to a patient by parenteral, intravenous, intramuscular, subcutaneous, or intraspinal infusion; or

(C) a Schedule II narcotic substance for a patient with a medical diagnosis documenting a terminal illness or a patient enrolled in a hospice care program certified or paid for by Medicare under Title XVIII, Social Security Act (42 U.S.C. Section 1395 et seq.), as amended, by Medicaid, or by a hospice program that is licensed under Chapter 142, and the practitioner or the practitioner's agent notes on the prescription "terminally ill" or "hospice patient"; and

(2) after transmitting the prescription, the prescribing practitioner or the practitioner's agent:

(A) writes across the face of the official prescription "VOID—sent by fax to (name and telephone number of receiving pharmacy)"; and

(B) files the official prescription in the patient's medical records instead of delivering it to the patient.

(p) On receipt of the prescription, the dispensing pharmacy shall file the facsimile copy of the prescription and shall send information to the director as required by Section 481.075.

(q) Each dispensing pharmacist shall send all information required by the director, including any information required to complete the Schedule III through V prescription forms, to the director by electronic transfer or another form approved by the director not later than the seventh day after the date the prescription is completely filled.

(Enacted by Acts 1989, 71st Leg., ch. 678 (H.B. 2136), § 1, effective September 1, 1989; am. Acts 1989, 71st Leg., ch. 1100 (S.B. 1046), § 5.02, effective September 1, 1989; am. Acts 1991, 72nd, Leg., ch. 615 (S.B. 1497), § 10, effective September 1, 1991; am. Acts 1991, 72nd Leg., ch. 761 (S.B. 314), § 6, effective September 1, 1991; am. Acts 1993, 73rd Leg., ch. 351 (S.B. 621), § 28, effective September 1, 1993; am. Acts 1993, 73rd Leg., ch. 789 (S.B. 472), § 16, effective September 1, 1993; am. Acts 1997, 75th Leg., ch. 745 (H.B. 1070), §§ 12, 13, effective January 1, 1998; am. Acts 1999, 76th Leg., ch. 145 (S.B. 254), § 2, effective September 1, 1999; am. Acts 2001, 77th Leg., ch. 251 (S.B. 753), § 10, effective September 1, 2001; am. Acts 2001, 77th Leg., ch. 1254 (S.B. 768), § 10, effective September 1, 2001; am. Acts 2005, 79th Leg., ch. 349 (S.B. 1188), § 21(a), effective September 1, 2005; am. Acts 2005, 79th Leg., ch. 1345 (S.B. 410), § 44(a), effective June 18, 2005; am. Acts 2007, 80th Leg., ch. 535 (S.B. 994), § 1, effective September 1, 2007; am. Acts 2007, 80th Leg., ch. 567 (S.B. 1658), § 2, effective September 1, 2007; am. Acts 2007, 80th Leg., ch. 1391 (S.B. 1879), § 2, effective September 1, 2007 (subsections (k) and (q) effective September 1, 2008); am. Acts 2009, 81st Leg., ch. 774 (S.B. 904), § 1, effective June 19, 2009; am. Acts 2011, 82nd Leg., ch. 91 (S.B. 1303), § 12.007, effective September 1, 2011; am. Acts 2011, 82nd Leg., ch. 1228 (S.B. 594), § 2, effective September 1, 2011; am. Acts 2011, 82nd Leg., ch. 1342 (S.B. 1273), § 2, effective September 1, 2011.)

### Sec. 481.075.   Official Prescription Program.

(a) A practitioner who prescribes a controlled substance listed in Schedule II shall, except as provided by rule adopted under Section 481.0761, record the prescription on an official prescription form or in an electronic prescription that includes the information required by this section.

(b) Each official prescription form must be sequentially numbered.

(c) The director shall issue official prescription forms to practitioners for a fee covering the actual cost of printing, processing, and mailing the forms at 100 a package. Before mailing or otherwise delivering prescription forms to a practitioner, the director shall print on each form the number of the form and any other information the director determines is necessary.

(d) A person may not obtain an official prescription form unless the person is a practitioner as defined by Section 481.002(39)(A) or an institutional practitioner.

(e) Each official prescription form or electronic prescription used to prescribe a Schedule II controlled substance must contain:

(1) information provided by the prescribing practitioner, including:

(A) the date the prescription is issued;

(B) the controlled substance prescribed;

(C) the quantity of controlled substance prescribed, shown:

(i) numerically, followed by the number written as a word, if the prescription is written; or

(ii) numerically, if the prescription is electronic;

(D) the intended use of the controlled substance or the diagnosis for which it is prescribed and the instructions for use of the substance;

(E) the practitioner's name, address, and Federal Drug Enforcement Administration number issued for prescribing a controlled substance in this state;

(F) the name, address, and date of birth or age of the person for whom the controlled substance is prescribed; and

(G) if the prescription is issued to be filled at a later date under Section 481.074(d-1), the earliest date on which a pharmacy may fill the prescription;

(2) information provided by the dispensing pharmacist, including the date the prescription is filled; and

(3) for a written prescription, the signatures of the prescribing practitioner and the dispensing pharmacist or for an electronic prescription, the prescribing practitioner's electronic signature or other secure method of validation authorized by federal law.

(f) Not more than one prescription may be recorded on an official prescription form, except as provided by rule adopted under Section 481.0761.

(g) Except for an oral prescription prescribed under Section 481.074(b), the prescribing practitioner shall:

(1) legibly fill in, or direct a designated agent to legibly fill in, on the official prescription form or in the electronic prescription, each item of information required to be provided by the prescribing practitioner under Subsection (e)(1), unless the practitioner determines that:

(A) under rule adopted by the director for this purpose, it is unnecessary for the practitioner or the practitioner's agent to provide the patient identification number; or

(B) it is not in the best interest of the patient for the practitioner or practitioner's agent to provide information regarding the intended use of the controlled substance or the diagnosis for which it is prescribed; and

(2) sign the official prescription form and give the form to the person authorized to receive the prescription or, in the case of an electronic prescription, electronically sign or validate the electronic prescription as authorized by federal law and transmit the prescription to the dispensing pharmacy.

(h) In the case of an oral prescription prescribed under Section 481.074(b), the prescribing practitioner shall give the dispensing pharmacy the information needed to complete the official prescription form or electronic prescription record.

(i) Each dispensing pharmacist shall:

(1) fill in on the official prescription form or note in the electronic prescription record each item of information given orally to the dispensing pharmacy under Subsection (h) and the date the prescription is filled, and:

(A) for a written prescription, fill in the dispensing pharmacist's signature; or

(B) for an electronic prescription, appropriately record the identity of the dispensing pharmacist in the electronic prescription record;

(2) retain with the records of the pharmacy for at least two years:

(A) the official prescription form or the electronic prescription record, as applicable; and

(B) the name or other patient identification required by Section 481.074(m) or (n); and

(3) send all information required by the director, including any information required to complete an official prescription form or electronic prescription record, to the director by

electronic transfer or another form approved by the director not later than the seventh day after the date the prescription is completely filled.

(j) A medication order written for a patient who is admitted to a hospital at the time the medication order is written and filled is not required to be on an official prescription form or in an electronic prescription record that meets the requirements of this section.

(k) Not later than the 30th day after the date a practitioner's department registration number, Federal Drug Enforcement Administration number, or license to practice has been denied, suspended, canceled, surrendered, or revoked, the practitioner shall return to the department all official prescription forms in the practitioner's possession that have not been used for prescriptions.

(l) Each prescribing practitioner:

(1) may use an official prescription form only to prescribe a controlled substance;

(2) shall date or sign an official prescription form only on the date the prescription is issued; and

(3) shall take reasonable precautionary measures to ensure that an official prescription form issued to the practitioner is not used by another person to violate this subchapter or a rule adopted under this subchapter.

(m) A pharmacy in this state may fill a prescription for a controlled substance listed in Schedule II issued by a practitioner in another state if:

(1) a share of the pharmacy's business involves the dispensing and delivery or mailing of controlled substances;

(2) the prescription is issued by a prescribing practitioner in the other state in the ordinary course of practice; and

(3) the prescription is filled in compliance with a written plan providing the manner in which the pharmacy may fill a Schedule II prescription issued by a practitioner in another state that:

(A) is submitted by the pharmacy to the director; and

(B) is approved by the director in consultation with the Texas State Board of Pharmacy.

(n) [Repealed by Acts 1999, 76th Leg., ch. 145 (S.B. 254), § 5(2), effective September 1, 1999.] (Enacted by Acts 1989, 71st Leg., ch. 678 (H.B. 2136), § 1, effective September 1, 1989; am. Acts 1989, 71st Leg., ch. 1100 (S.B. 1046), § 5.02(i),

effective September 1, 1989; am. Acts 1993, 73rd Leg., ch. 789 (S.B. 472), § 17, effective September 1, 1993; am. Acts 1997, 75th Leg., ch. 745 (H.B. 1070), § 14, effective January 1, 1998; am. Acts 1999, 76th Leg., ch. 145 (S.B. 254), §§ 3, 5(2), effective September 1, 1999; am. Acts 2001, 77th Leg., ch. 251 (S.B. 753), § 11, effective September 1, 2001; am. Acts 2009, 81st Leg., ch. 774 (S.B. 904), § 2, effective June 19, 2009; am. Acts 2011, 82nd Leg., ch. 1228 (S.B. 594), § 3, effective September 1, 2011; am. Acts 2011, 82nd Leg., ch. 1342 (S.B. 1273), § 3, effective September 1, 2011.)

## Sec. 481.076.  Official Prescription Information.

(a) The director may not permit any person to have access to information submitted to the director under Section 481.074(q) or 481.075 except:

(1) an investigator for the Texas Medical Board, the Texas State Board of Podiatric Medical Examiners, the State Board of Dental Examiners, the State Board of Veterinary Medical Examiners, the Texas Board of Nursing, or the Texas State Board of Pharmacy;

(2) an authorized officer or member of the department engaged in the administration, investigation, or enforcement of this chapter or another law governing illicit drugs in this state or another state; or

(3) if the director finds that proper need has been shown to the director:

(A) a law enforcement or prosecutorial official engaged in the administration, investigation, or enforcement of this chapter or another law governing illicit drugs in this state or another state;

(B) a pharmacist or practitioner who is a physician, dentist, veterinarian, podiatrist, or advanced practice nurse or physician assistant described by Section 481.002(39)(D) and is inquiring about a recent Schedule II, III, IV, or V prescription history of a particular patient of the practitioner; or

(C) a pharmacist or practitioner who is inquiring about the person's own dispensing or prescribing activity.

(b) This section does not prohibit the director from creating, using, or disclosing statistical data about information received by the director under this section if the director removes any information reasonably likely to reveal the identity of each patient, practitioner, or other person who is a subject of the information.

(c) The director by rule shall design and implement a system for submission of information to the director by electronic or other means and for retrieval of information submitted to the director under this section and Sections 481.074 and 481.075. The director shall use automated information security techniques and devices to preclude improper access to the information. The director shall submit the system design to the Texas State Board of Pharmacy and the Texas Medical Board for review and approval or comment a reasonable time before implementation of the system and shall comply with the comments of those agencies unless it is unreasonable to do so.

(d) Information submitted to the director under this section may be used only for:

(1) the administration, investigation, or enforcement of this chapter or another law governing illicit drugs in this state or another state;

(2) investigatory or evidentiary purposes in connection with the functions of an agency listed in Subsection (a)(1); or

(3) dissemination by the director to the public in the form of a statistical tabulation or report if all information reasonably likely to reveal the identity of each patient, practitioner, or other person who is a subject of the information has been removed.

(e) The director shall remove from the information retrieval system, destroy, and make irretrievable the record of the identity of a patient submitted under this section to the director not later than the end of the 12th calendar month after the month in which the identity is entered into the system. However, the director may retain a patient identity that is necessary for use in a specific ongoing investigation conducted in accordance with this section until the 30th day after the end of the month in which the necessity for retention of the identity ends.

(f) If the director permits access to information under Subsection (a)(2) relating to a person licensed or regulated by an agency listed in Subsection (a)(1), the director shall notify and cooperate with that agency regarding the disposition of the matter before taking action against the person, unless the director determines that notification is reasonably likely to interfere with an administrative or criminal investigation or prosecution.

(g) If the director permits access to information under Subsection (a)(3)(A) relating to a person licensed or regulated by an agency listed in

Subsection (a)(1), the director shall notify that agency of the disclosure of the information not later than the 10th working day after the date the information is disclosed.

(h) If the director withholds notification to an agency under Subsection (f), the director shall notify the agency of the disclosure of the information and the reason for withholding notification when the director determines that notification is no longer likely to interfere with an administrative or criminal investigation or prosecution.

(i) Information submitted to the director under Section 481.074(q) or 481.075 is confidential and remains confidential regardless of whether the director permits access to the information under this section.

(j) [Repealed by Acts 1999, 76th Leg., ch. 145 (S.B. 254), § 5(3), effective September 1, 1999.] (Enacted by Acts 1989, 71st Leg., ch. 678 (H.B. 2136), § 1, effective September 1, 1989; am. Acts 1995, 74th Leg., ch. 965 (S.B. 673), § 81, effective June 16, 1995; am. Acts 1997, 75th Leg., ch. 745 (H.B. 1070), § 15, effective January 1, 1998; am. Acts 1999, 76th Leg., ch. 145 (S.B. 254), §§ 4, 5(3), effective September 1, 1999; am. Acts 2007, 80th Leg., ch. 1391 (S.B. 1879), § 3, effective September 1, 2008; am. Acts 2011, 82nd Leg., ch. 1228 (S.B. 594), § 4, effective September 1, 2011; am. Acts 2011, 82nd Leg., ch. 1342 (S.B. 1273), § 4, effective September 1, 2011.)

### Sec. 481.0761. Rules; Authority to Contract.

(a) The director shall consult with the Texas State Board of Pharmacy and by rule establish and revise as necessary a standardized database format that may be used by a pharmacy to transmit the information required by Sections 481.074(q) and 481.075(i) to the director electronically or to deliver the information on storage media, including disks, tapes, and cassettes.

(b) The director shall consult with the Department of State Health Services, the Texas State Board of Pharmacy, and the Texas Medical Board and by rule may:

(1) remove a controlled substance listed in Schedules II through V from the official prescription program, if the director determines that the burden imposed by the program substantially outweighs the risk of diversion of the particular controlled substance; or

(2) return a substance previously removed from Schedules II through V to the official prescription program, if the director deter-

mines that the risk of diversion substantially outweighs the burden imposed by the program on the particular controlled substance.

(c) The director by rule may:

(1) permit more than one prescription to be administered or dispensed and recorded on one prescription form for a Schedule III through V controlled substance;

(1-a) establish a procedure for the issuance of multiple prescriptions of a Schedule II controlled substance under Section 481.074(d-1);

(2) remove from or return to the official prescription program any aspect of a practitioner's or pharmacist's hospital practice, including administering or dispensing;

(3) waive or delay any requirement relating to the time or manner of reporting;

(4) establish compatibility protocols for electronic data transfer hardware, software, or format;

(5) establish a procedure to control the release of information under Sections 481.074, 481.075, and 481.076; and

(6) establish a minimum level of prescription activity below which a reporting activity may be modified or deleted.

(d) The director by rule shall authorize a practitioner to determine whether it is necessary to obtain a particular patient identification number and to provide that number on the official prescription form or in the electronic prescription record.

(e) In adopting a rule relating to the electronic transfer of information under this subchapter, the director shall consider the economic impact of the rule on practitioners and pharmacists and, to the extent permitted by law, act to minimize any negative economic impact, including the imposition of costs related to computer hardware or software or to the transfer of information. The director may not adopt a rule relating to the electronic transfer of information under this subchapter that imposes a fee in addition to the fees authorized by Section 481.064.

(f) The director may authorize a contract between the department and another agency of this state or a private vendor as necessary to ensure the effective operation of the official prescription program.

(g) [Repealed by Acts 1999, 76th Leg., ch. 145 (S.B. 254), § 5(4), effective September 1, 1999.] (Enacted by Acts 1997, 75th Leg., ch. 745 (H.B. 1070), § 16, effective September 1, 1997; am. Acts 1999, 76th Leg., ch. 145 (S.B. 254), § 5(4), effective September 1, 1999; am. Acts 2007, 80th Leg.,

ch. 1391 (S.B. 1879), § 4, effective September 1, 2007; am. Acts 2009, 81st Leg., ch. 774 (S.B. 904), § 3, effective June 19, 2009; am. Acts 2011, 82nd Leg., ch. 1228 (S.B. 594), § 5, effective September 1, 2011.)

## Sec. 481.077. Chemical Precursor Records and Reports.

(a) Except as provided by Subsection (*l*), a person who sells, transfers, or otherwise furnishes a chemical precursor to another person shall make an accurate and legible record of the transaction and maintain the record for at least two years after the date of the transaction.

(b) The director by rule may:

(1) name an additional chemical substance as a chemical precursor for purposes of Subsection (a) if the director determines that public health and welfare are jeopardized by evidenced proliferation or use of the chemical substance in the illicit manufacture of a controlled substance or controlled substance analogue; or

(2) exempt a chemical precursor from the requirements of Subsection (a) if the director determines that the chemical precursor does not jeopardize public health and welfare or is not used in the illicit manufacture of a controlled substance or a controlled substance analogue.

(b-1) If the director names a chemical substance as a chemical precursor for purposes of Subsection (a) or designates a substance as an immediate precursor, a substance that is a precursor of the chemical precursor or the immediate precursor is not subject to control solely because it is a precursor of the chemical precursor or the immediate precursor.

(c) This section and Section 481.078 do not apply to a person to whom a registration has been issued under Section 481.063.

(d) Before selling, transferring, or otherwise furnishing to a person in this state a chemical precursor subject to Subsection (a), a manufacturer, wholesaler, retailer, or other person shall:

(1) if the recipient does not represent a business, obtain from the recipient:

(A) the recipient's driver's license number or other personal identification certificate number, date of birth, and residential or mailing address, other than a post office box number, from a driver's license or personal identification certificate issued by the department that contains a photograph of the recipient;

(B) the year, state, and number of the motor vehicle license of the motor vehicle owned or operated by the recipient;

(C) a complete description of how the chemical precursor is to be used; and

(D) the recipient's signature; or

(2) if the recipient represents a business, obtain from the recipient:

(A) a letter of authorization from the business that includes the business license or comptroller tax identification number, address, area code, and telephone number and a complete description of how the chemical precursor is to be used; and

(B) the recipient's signature; and

(3) for any recipient, sign as a witness to the signature and identification of the recipient.

(e) If the recipient does not represent a business, the recipient shall present to the manufacturer, wholesaler, retailer, or other person a permit issued in the name of the recipient by the department under Section 481.078.

(f) Except as provided by Subsection (h), a manufacturer, wholesaler, retailer, or other person who sells, transfers, or otherwise furnishes to a person in this state a chemical precursor subject to Subsection (a) shall submit, at least 21 days before the delivery of the chemical precursor, a report of the transaction on a form obtained from the director that includes the information required by Subsection (d).

(g) The director shall supply to a manufacturer, wholesaler, retailer, or other person who sells, transfers, or otherwise furnishes a chemical precursor subject to Subsection (a) a form for the submission of:

(1) the report required by Subsection (f);

(2) the name and measured amount of the chemical precursor delivered; and

(3) any other information required by the director.

(h) The director may authorize a manufacturer, wholesaler, retailer, or other person to submit a comprehensive monthly report instead of the report required by Subsection (f) if the director determines that:

(1) there is a pattern of regular supply and purchase of the chemical precursor between the furnisher and the recipient; or

(2) the recipient has established a record of use of the chemical precursor solely for a lawful purpose.

(i) A manufacturer, wholesaler, retailer, or other person who receives from a source outside this state a chemical precursor subject to Subsec-

tion (a) or who discovers a loss or theft of a chemical precursor subject to Subsection (a) shall:

(1) submit a report of the transaction to the director in accordance with department rule; and

(2) include in the report:

(A) any difference between the amount of the chemical precursor actually received and the amount of the chemical precursor shipped according to the shipping statement or invoice; or

(B) the amount of the loss or theft.

(j) A report under Subsection (i) must:

(1) be made not later than the third day after the date that the manufacturer, wholesaler, retailer, or other person learns of the discrepancy, loss, or theft; and

(2) if the discrepancy, loss, or theft occurred during a shipment of the chemical precursor, include the name of the common carrier or person who transported the chemical precursor and the date that the chemical precursor was shipped.

(k) Unless the person is the holder of only a permit issued under Section 481.078(b)(1), a manufacturer, wholesaler, retailer, or other person who sells, transfers, or otherwise furnishes any chemical precursor subject to Subsection (a) or a permit holder, commercial purchaser, or other person who receives a chemical precursor subject to Subsection (a):

(1) shall maintain records and inventories in accordance with rules established by the director;

(2) shall allow a member of the department or a peace officer to conduct audits and inspect records of purchases and sales and all other records made in accordance with this section at any reasonable time; and

(3) may not interfere with the audit or with the full and complete inspection or copying of those records.

(*l*) This section does not apply to the sale or transfer of any compound, mixture, or preparation containing ephedrine, pseudoephedrine, or norpseudoephedrine that is in liquid, liquid capsule, or liquid gel capsule form.

(Enacted by Acts 1989, 71st Leg., ch. 678 (H.B. 2136), § 1, effective September 1, 1989; am. Acts 1989, 71st Leg., ch. 1100 (S.B. 1046), § 5.02(k), effective September 1, 1989; am. Acts 1997, 75th Leg., ch. 745 (H.B. 1070), § 17, effective January 1, 1998; am. Acts 2001, 77th Leg., ch. 251 (S.B. 753), § 12, effective September 1, 2001; am. Acts

Health

2003, 78th Leg., ch. 570 (H.B. 1629), § 1, effective September 1, 2003; am. Acts 2003, 78th Leg., ch. 1099 (H.B. 2192), § 6, effective September 1, 2003; am. Acts 2005, 79th Leg., ch. 282 (H.B. 164), § 4, effective August 1, 2005.)

## Sec. 481.0771.   Records and Reports on Pseudoephedrine.

(a) A wholesaler who sells, transfers, or otherwise furnishes a product containing ephedrine, pseudoephedrine, or norpseudoephedrine to a retailer shall:

(1) before delivering the product, obtain from the retailer the retailer's address, area code, and telephone number; and

(2) make an accurate and legible record of the transaction and maintain the record for at least two years after the date of the transaction.

(b) The wholesaler shall make all records available to the director in accordance with department rule, including:

(1) the information required by Subsection (a)(1);

(2) the amount of the product containing ephedrine,        pseudoephedrine,        or norpseudoephedrine delivered; and

(3) any other information required by the director.

(c) Not later than 10 business days after receipt of an order for a product containing ephedrine, pseudoephedrine, or norpseudoephedrine that requests delivery of a suspicious quantity of the product as determined by department rule, a wholesaler shall submit to the director a report of the order in accordance with department rule.

(d) A wholesaler who, with reckless disregard for the duty to report, fails to report as required by Subsection (c) may be subject to disciplinary action in accordance with department rule.
(Enacted by Acts 2005, 79th Leg., ch. 282 (H.B. 164), § 5, effective August 1, 2005.)

## Sec. 481.078.   Chemical Precursor Transfer Permit.

(a) A person must obtain a chemical precursor transfer permit from the department to be eligible:

(1) to sell, transfer, or otherwise furnish a chemical precursor subject to Section 481.077(a) to a person in this state;

(2) to receive a chemical precursor subject to Section 481.077(a) from a source outside this state; or

(3) to receive a chemical precursor subject to Section 481.077(a) if the person, in receiving the chemical precursor, does not represent a business.

(b) The director by rule shall adopt procedures and standards for the issuance and renewal or the voluntary surrender, cancellation, suspension, probation, or revocation of:

(1) a permit for one sale, transfer, receipt, or otherwise furnishing of a chemical precursor; or

(2) a permit for more than one sale, transfer, receipt, or otherwise furnishing of a chemical precursor.

(c) A permit issued or renewed under Subsection (b)(1) is valid only for the transaction indicated on the permit. A permit issued or renewed under Subsection (b)(2) is valid for one year after the date of issuance or renewal.

(d) A permit holder must report in writing or by telephone to the director a change in the holder's business name, address, area code, and telephone number not later than the seventh day after the date of the change.

(e) The director may not issue a permit under this section unless the person applying for the permit delivers to the director a written consent to inspect signed by the person that grants to the director the right to inspect any controlled premises, record, chemical precursor, or other item governed by this chapter in the care, custody, or control of the person. After the director receives the consent, the director may inspect any controlled premises, record, chemical precursor, or other item to which the consent applies.

(f) The director may adopt rules to establish security controls and provide for the inspection of a place, entity, or item to which a chemical precursor transfer permit applies.
(Enacted by Acts 1989, 71st Leg., ch. 1100 (S.B. 1046), § 5.02(*l*), effective September 1, 1989; am. Acts 1997, 75th Leg., ch. 745 (H.B. 1070), § 18, effective January 1, 1998; am. Acts 2001, 77th Leg., ch. 251 (S.B. 753), § 13, effective September 1, 2001.)

## Sec. 481.079.   Offense: Unlawful Transfer or Receipt of Chemical Precursor [Repealed].

Repealed by Acts 1997, 75th Leg., ch. 745 (H.B. 1070), § 37, effective January 1, 1998.

Health

## Sec. 481.080. Chemical Laboratory Apparatus Record-Keeping Requirements and Penalties.

(a) A manufacturer, wholesaler, retailer, or other person who sells, transfers, or otherwise furnishes a chemical laboratory apparatus shall make an accurate and legible record of the transaction and maintain the record for at least two years after the date of the transaction.

(b) The director may adopt rules to implement this section.

(c) The director by rule may:

(1) name an additional item of equipment as a chemical laboratory apparatus for purposes of Subsection (a) if the director determines that public health and welfare are jeopardized by evidenced proliferation or use of the item of equipment in the illicit manufacture of a controlled substance or controlled substance analogue; or

(2) exempt a chemical laboratory apparatus from the requirement of Subsection (a) if the director determines that the apparatus does not jeopardize public health and welfare or is not used in the illicit manufacture of a controlled substance or a controlled substance analogue.

(d) This section and Section 481.081 do not apply to a person to whom a registration has been issued under Section 481.063.

(e) Before selling, transferring, or otherwise furnishing to a person in this state a chemical laboratory apparatus subject to Subsection (a), a manufacturer, wholesaler, retailer, or other person shall:

(1) if the recipient does not represent a business, obtain from the recipient:

(A) the recipient's driver's license number or other personal identification certificate number, date of birth, and residential or mailing address, other than a post office box number, from a driver's license or personal identification certificate issued by the department that contains a photograph of the recipient;

(B) the year, state, and number of the motor vehicle license of the motor vehicle owned or operated by the recipient;

(C) a complete description of how the apparatus is to be used; and

(D) the recipient's signature; or

(2) if the recipient represents a business, obtain from the recipient:

(A) a letter of authorization from the business that includes the business license or comptroller tax identification number, address, area code, and telephone number and a complete description of how the apparatus is to be used; and

(B) the recipient's signature; and

(3) for any recipient, sign as a witness to the signature and identification of the recipient.

(f) If the recipient does not represent a business, the recipient shall present to the manufacturer, wholesaler, retailer, or other person a permit issued in the name of the recipient by the department under Section 481.081.

(g) Except as provided by Subsection (i), a manufacturer, wholesaler, retailer, or other person who sells, transfers, or otherwise furnishes to a person in this state a chemical laboratory apparatus subject to Subsection (a) shall, at least 21 days before the delivery of the apparatus, submit a report of the transaction on a form obtained from the director that includes the information required by Subsection (e).

(h) The director shall supply to a manufacturer, wholesaler, retailer, or other person who sells, transfers, or otherwise furnishes a chemical laboratory apparatus subject to Subsection (a) a form for the submission of:

(1) the report required by Subsection (g);

(2) the name and number of apparatus delivered; and

(3) any other information required by the director.

(i) The director may authorize a manufacturer, wholesaler, retailer, or other person to submit a comprehensive monthly report instead of the report required by Subsection (g) if the director determines that:

(1) there is a pattern of regular supply and purchase of the apparatus between the furnisher and the recipient; or

(2) the recipient has established a record of use of the apparatus solely for a lawful purpose.

(j) A manufacturer, wholesaler, retailer, or other person who receives from a source outside this state a chemical laboratory apparatus subject to Subsection (a) or who discovers a loss or theft of such an apparatus shall:

(1) submit a report of the transaction to the director in accordance with department rule; and

(2) include in the report:

(A) any difference between the number of the apparatus actually received and the number of the apparatus shipped according to the shipping statement or invoice; or

(B) the number of the loss or theft.

(k) A report under Subsection (j) must:

(1) be made not later than the third day after the date that the manufacturer, wholesaler, retailer, or other person learns of the discrepancy, loss, or theft; and

(2) if the discrepancy, loss, or theft occurred during a shipment of the apparatus, include the name of the common carrier or person who transported the apparatus and the date that the apparatus was shipped.

(*l*) This subsection applies to a manufacturer, wholesaler, retailer, or other person who sells, transfers, or otherwise furnishes any chemical laboratory apparatus subject to Subsection (a) and to a permit holder, commercial purchaser, or other person who receives such an apparatus unless the person is the holder of only a permit issued under Section 481.081(b)(1). A person covered by this subsection:

(1) shall maintain records and inventories in accordance with rules established by the director;

(2) shall allow a member of the department or a peace officer to conduct audits and inspect records of purchases and sales and all other records made in accordance with this section at any reasonable time; and

(3) may not interfere with the audit or with the full and complete inspection or copying of those records.

(Enacted by Acts 1989, 71st Leg., ch. 1100 (S.B. 1046), § 5.02(*l*), effective September 1, 1989; am. Acts 1997, 75th Leg., ch. 745 (H.B. 1070), § 19, effective January 1, 1998; am. Acts 2001, 77th Leg., ch. 251 (S.B. 753), § 14, effective September 1, 2001.)

## Sec. 481.081. Chemical Laboratory Apparatus Transfer Permit.

(a) A person must obtain a chemical laboratory apparatus transfer permit from the department to be eligible:

(1) to sell, transfer, or otherwise furnish an apparatus subject to Section 481.080(a) to a person in this state;

(2) to receive an apparatus subject to Section 481.080(a) from a source outside this state; or

(3) to receive an apparatus subject to Section 481.080(a) if the person, in receiving the apparatus, does not represent a business.

(b) The director by rule shall adopt procedures and standards for the issuance and renewal or the voluntary surrender, cancellation, suspension, probation, or revocation of:

(1) a permit for one sale, transfer, receipt, or otherwise furnishing of a chemical laboratory apparatus; or

(2) a permit for more than one sale, transfer, receipt, or otherwise furnishing of a chemical laboratory apparatus.

(c) A permit issued or renewed under Subsection (b)(1) is valid only for the transaction indicated on the permit. A permit issued or renewed under Subsection (b)(2) is valid for one year after the date of issuance or renewal.

(d) A permit holder must report in writing or by telephone to the director a change in the holder's business name, address, area code, and telephone number not later than the seventh day after the date of the change.

(e) The director may not issue a permit under this section unless the person applying for the permit delivers to the director a written consent to inspect signed by the person that grants to the director the right to inspect any controlled premises, record, chemical laboratory apparatus, or other item governed by this chapter in the care, custody, or control of the person. After the director receives the consent, the director may inspect any controlled premises, record, chemical laboratory apparatus, or other item to which the consent applies.

(f) The director may by rule establish security controls and provide for the inspection of a place, entity, or item to which a chemical laboratory apparatus transfer permit applies.

(Enacted by Acts 1989, 71st Leg., ch. 1100 (S.B. 1046), § 5.02(*l*), effective September 1, 1989; am. Acts 1997, 75th Leg., ch. 745 (H.B. 1070), § 20, effective January 1, 1998; am. Acts 2001, 77th Leg., ch. 251 (S.B. 753), § 15, effective September 1, 2001.)

## Sec. 481.082. Unlawful Transfer or Receipt of Chemical Laboratory Apparatus [Repealed].

Repealed by Acts 1997, 75th Leg., ch. 745 (H.B. 1070), § 37, effective January 1, 1998.

(Enacted by Acts 1989, 71st Leg., ch. 1100 (S.B. 1046), § 5.02(*l*), effective September 1, 1989.)

## SUBCHAPTER D
## OFFENSES AND PENALTIES

## Sec. 481.101. Criminal Classification.

For the purpose of establishing criminal penalties for violations of this chapter, controlled substances, including a material, compound, mixture, or preparation containing the controlled substance, are divided into Penalty Groups 1 through 4.

(Enacted by Acts 1989, 71st Leg., ch. 678 (H.B. 2136), § 1, effective September 1, 1989; am. Acts 1989, 71st Leg., ch. 1100 (S.B. 1046), § 5.02(n), effective September 1, 1989.)

## Sec. 481.102. Penalty Group 1.

Penalty Group 1 consists of:

(1) the following opiates, including their isomers, esters, ethers, salts, and salts of isomers, esters, and ethers, unless specifically excepted, if the existence of these isomers, esters, ethers, and salts is possible within the specific chemical designation:

Alfentanil;
Allylprodine;
Alphacetylmethadol;
Benzethidine;
Betaprodine;
Clonitazene;
Diampromide;
Diethylthiambutene;
Difenoxin not listed in Penalty Group 3 or 4;
Dimenoxadol;
Dimethylthiambutene;
Dioxaphetyl butyrate;
Dipipanone;
Ethylmethylthiambutene;
Etonitazene;
Etoxeridine;
Furethidine;
Hydroxypethidine;
Ketobemidone;
Levophenacylmorphan;
Meprodine;
Methadol;
Moramide;
Morpheridine;
Noracymethadol;
Norlevorphanol;
Normethadone;
Norpipanone;
Phenadoxone;
Phenampromide;
Phenomorphan;
Phenoperidine;
Piritramide;
Proheptazine;
Properidine;
Propiram;
Sufentanil;

Tilidine; and
Trimeperidine;

(2) the following opium derivatives, their salts, isomers, and salts of isomers, unless specifically excepted, if the existence of these salts, isomers, and salts of isomers is possible within the specific chemical designation:

Acetorphine;
Acetyldihydrocodeine;
Benzylmorphine;
Codeine methylbromide;
Codeine-N-Oxide;
Cyprenorphine;
Desomorphine;
Dihydromorphine;
Drotebanol;
Etorphine, except hydrochloride salt;
Heroin;
Hydromorphinol;
Methyldesorphine;
Methyldihydromorphine;
Monoacetylmorphine;
Morphine methylbromide;
Morphine methylsulfonate;
Morphine-N-Oxide;
Myrophine;
Nicocodeine;
Nicomorphine;
Normorphine;
Pholcodine; and
Thebacon;

(3) the following substances, however produced, except those narcotic drugs listed in another group:

(A) Opium and opiate not listed in Penalty Group 3 or 4, and a salt, compound, derivative, or preparation of opium or opiate, other than thebaine derived butorphanol, nalmefene and its salts, naloxone and its salts, and naltrexone and its salts, but including:

Codeine not listed in Penalty Group 3 or 4;
Dihydroetorphine;
Ethylmorphine not listed in Penalty Group 3 or 4;
Granulated opium;
Hydrocodone not listed in Penalty Group 3;
Hydromorphone;
Metopon;
Morphine not listed in Penalty Group 3;
Opium extracts;
Opium fluid extracts;
Oripavine;
Oxycodone;

Oxymorphone;

Powdered opium;

Raw opium;

Thebaine; and

Tincture of opium;

(B) a salt, compound, isomer, derivative, or preparation of a substance that is chemically equivalent or identical to a substance described by Paragraph (A), other than the isoquinoline alkaloids of opium;

(C) Opium poppy and poppy straw;

(D) Cocaine, including:

(i) its salts, its optical, position, and geometric isomers, and the salts of those isomers;

(ii) coca leaves and a salt, compound, derivative, or preparation of coca leaves;

(iii) a salt, compound, derivative, or preparation of a salt, compound, or derivative that is chemically equivalent or identical to a substance described by Subparagraph (i) or (ii), other than decocainized coca leaves or extractions of coca leaves that do not contain cocaine or ecgonine; and

(E) concentrate of poppy straw, meaning the crude extract of poppy straw in liquid, solid, or powder form that contains the phenanthrine alkaloids of the opium poppy;

(4) the following opiates, including their isomers, esters, ethers, salts, and salts of isomers, if the existence of these isomers, esters, ethers, and salts is possible within the specific chemical designation:

Acetyl-alpha-methylfentanyl (N-[1-(1-methyl-2- phenethyl)-4-piperidinyl]-N-phenyl-acetamide);

Alpha-methylthiofentanyl (N-[1-methyl-2-(2- thienyl)ethyl-4-piperidinyl]-N-phenyl-propanamide);

Alphaprodine;

Anileridine;

Beta-hydroxyfentanyl (N-[1-(2-hydroxy-2-phenethyl)-4-piperidinyl]          -N-phenyl-propanamide);

Beta-hydroxy-3-methylfentanyl;

Bezitramide;

Carfentanil;

Dihydrocodeine not listed in Penalty Group 3 or 4;

Diphenoxylate not listed in Penalty Group 3 or 4;

Fentanyl or alpha-methylfentanyl, or any other derivative of Fentanyl;

Isomethadone;

Levomethorphan;

Levorphanol;

Metazocine;

Methadone;

Methadone-Intermediate,     4-cyano-2-di-methylamino-4, 4-diphenyl butane;

3-methylfentanyl(N-[3-methyl-1-(2-phenylethyl)- 4-piperidyl]-N-phenylpropanamide);

3-methylthiofentanyl(N-[3-methyl-1-(2-thienyl) ethyl-4-piperidinyl]-N-phenylpro-panamide);

Moramide-Intermediate,     2-methyl-3-morpholino-1, 1-diphenyl-propane-carboxylic acid;

Para-fluorofentanyl(N-(4-fluorophenyl)-N-1-(2- phenylethyl)-4-piperidinylpropana-mide);

PEPAP     (1-(2-phenethyl)-4-phenyl-4-acetoxypiperidine);

Pethidine (Meperidine);

Pethidine-Intermediate-A,     4-cyano-1-methyl-4- phenylpiperidine;

Pethidine-Intermediate-B, ethyl-4-phenyl-piperidine-4 carboxylate;

Pethidine-Intermediate-C,     1-methyl-4-phenylpiperidine-4-carboxylic acid;

Phenazocine;

Piminodine;

Racemethorphan;

Racemorphan;

Remifentanil; and

Thiofentanyl(N-phenyl-N-[1-(2-thienyl)ethyl-4-piperidinyl]-prop anamide);

(5) Flunitrazepam (trade or other name: Rohypnol);

(6) Methamphetamine, including its salts, optical isomers, and salts of optical isomers;

(7) Phenylacetone and methylamine, if possessed together with intent to manufacture methamphetamine;

(8) Phencyclidine, including its salts;

(9) Gamma hydroxybutyric acid (some trade or other names: gamma hydroxybutyrate, GHB), including its salts; and

(10) Ketamine.

(Enacted by Acts 1989, 71st Leg., ch. 678 (H.B. 2136), § 1, effective September 1, 1989; am. Acts 1989, 71st Leg., ch. 1100 (S.B. 1046), § 5.02(n), effective September 1, 1989; am. Acts 1991, 72nd Leg., ch. 761 (S.B. 314), § 1, effective September 1, 1991; am. Acts 1997, 75th Leg., ch. 745 (H.B. 1070), § 21, effective January 1, 1998; am. Acts 2001, 77th Leg., ch. 251 (S.B. 753), § 16, effective September 1, 2001; am. Acts 2001, 77th Leg., ch.

459 (H.B. 139), § 1, effective September 1, 2001; am. Acts 2003, 78th Leg., ch. 1099 (H.B. 2192), § 7, effective September 1, 2003; am. Acts 2009, 81st Leg., ch. 739 (S.B. 449), § 1, effective September 1, 2009.)

## Sec. 481.1021.  Penalty Group 1-A.

Penalty Group 1-A consists of lysergic acid diethylamide (LSD), including its salts, isomers, and salts of isomers.
(Enacted by Acts 1997, 75th Leg., ch. 745 (H.B. 1070), § 22, effective January 1, 1998.)

## Sec. 481.103.  Penalty Group 2.

(a) Penalty Group 2 consists of:

(1) any quantity of the following hallucinogenic substances, their salts, isomers, and salts of isomers, unless specifically excepted, if the existence of these salts, isomers, and salts of isomers is possible within the specific chemical designation:

alpha-ethyltryptamine;

alpha-methyltryptamine;

4-bromo-2, 5-dimethoxyamphetamine (some trade or other names: 4-bromo-2, 5-dimethoxy-alpha-methylphenethylamine; 4-bromo-2, 5-DMA);

4-bromo-2, 5-dimethoxyphenethylamine;

Bufotenine (some trade and other names: 3-(beta- Dimethylaminoethyl)-5-hydroxyindole; 3-(2-dimethylaminoethyl)- 5- indolol; N, N-dimethylserotonin; 5-hydroxy-N, N- dimethyltryptamine; mappine);

Diethyltryptamine (some trade and other names: N, N-Diethyltryptamine, DET);

2, 5-dimethoxyamphetamine (some trade or other names: 2, 5-dimethoxy-alpha-methylphenethylamine; 2, 5-DMA);

2, 5-dimethoxy-4-ethylamphetamine (trade or other name: DOET);

2, 5-dimethoxy-4-(n)-propylthiophenethylamine (trade or other name: 2C-T-7);

Dimethyltryptamine (trade or other name: DMT);

Dronabinol (synthetic) in sesame oil and encapsulated in a soft gelatin capsule in a U.S. Food and Drug Administration approved drug product (some trade or other names for Dronabinol: (a6aR-trans)-6a,7,8,10a-tetrahydro- 6,6, 9- trimethyl-3-pentyl-6H- dibenzo [b,d]pyran-1-ol or (-)-delta-9-(trans)- tetrahydrocannabinol);

Ethylamine Analog of Phencyclidine (some trade or other names: N-ethyl-1-phenylcyclo-

hexylamine, (1- phenylcyclohexyl) ethylamine, N-(1-phenylcyclohexyl) ethylamine, cyclohexamine, PCE);

Ibogaine (some trade or other names: 7-Ethyl-6, 6, beta 7, 8, 9, 10, 12, 13-octahydro-2-methoxy-6, 9-methano-5H- pyrido [1', 2':1, 2] azepino [5, 4-b] indole; tabernanthe iboga.);

Mescaline;

5-methoxy-N, N-diisopropyltryptamine;

5-methoxy-3, 4-methylenedioxy amphetamine;

4-methoxyamphetamine (some trade or other names: 4-methoxy-alpha-methylphenethylamine; paramethoxyamphetamine; PMA);

1-methyl- 4-phenyl-4-propionoxypiperidine (MPPP, PPMP);

4-methyl-2, 5-dimethoxyamphetamine (some trade and other names: 4-methyl-2, 5-dimethoxy-alpha- methylphenethylamine; "DOM"; "STP");

3,4-methylenedioxy methamphetamine (MDMA, MDM);

3,4-methylenedioxy amphetamine;

3,4-methylenedioxy N-ethylamphetamine (Also known as N-ethyl MDA);

Nabilone (Another name for nabilone: (+)-trans- 3-(1,1-dimethylheptyl)- 6,6a, 7,8,10,10a-hexahydro-1-hydroxy- 6, 6-dimethyl-9H-dibenzo[b,d] pyran-9-one;

N-benzylpiperazine (some trade or other names: BZP; 1-benzylpiperazine);

N-ethyl-3-piperidyl benzilate;

N-hydroxy-3,4-methylenedioxyamphetamine (Also known as N-hydroxy MDA);

4-methylaminorex;

N-methyl-3-piperidyl benzilate;

Parahexyl (some trade or other names: 3-Hexyl-1- hydroxy-7, 8, 9, 10-tetrahydro-6, 6, 9-trimethyl-6H-dibenzo [b, d] pyran; Synhexyl);

1-Phenylcyclohexylamine;

1-Piperidinocyclohexanecarbonitrile (PCC);

Psilocin;

Psilocybin;

Pyrrolidine Analog of Phencyclidine (some trade or other names: 1-(1-phenylcyclohexyl)- pyrrolidine, PCPy, PHP);

Tetrahydrocannabinols, other than marihuana, and synthetic equivalents of the substances contained in the plant, or in the resinous extractives of Cannabis, or synthetic substances, derivatives, and their isomers with similar chemical structure and pharmacological activity such as:

delta-1 cis or trans tetrahydrocannabinol, and their optical isomers;

delta-6 cis or trans tetrahydrocannabinol, and their optical isomers;

delta-3, 4 cis or trans tetrahydrocannabinol, and its optical isomers;

compounds of these structures, regardless of numerical designation of atomic positions, since nomenclature of these substances is not internationally standardized;

Thiophene Analog of Phencyclidine (some trade or other names: 1-[1-(2-thienyl) cyclohexyl] piperidine; 2-Thienyl Analog of Phencyclidine; TPCP, TCP);

1-pyrrolidine (some trade or other name: TCPy);

1-(3-trifluoromethylphenyl)piperazine (trade or other name: TFMPP); and

3,4,5-trimethoxy amphetamine;

(2) Phenylacetone (some trade or other names: Phenyl-2-propanone; P2P, Benzymethyl ketone, methyl benzyl ketone);

(3) unless specifically excepted or unless listed in another Penalty Group, a material, compound, mixture, or preparation that contains any quantity of the following substances having a potential for abuse associated with a depressant or stimulant effect on the central nervous system:

Aminorex (some trade or other names: aminoxaphen; 2-amino-5-phenyl-2-oxazoline; 4,5-dihydro-5- phenyl-2-oxazolamine);

Amphetamine, its salts, optical isomers, and salts of optical isomers;

Cathinone (some trade or other names: 2-amino-1- phenyl-1-propanone, alpha-aminopropiophenone, 2- aminopropiophenone);

Etorphine Hydrochloride;

Fenethylline and its salts;

Lisdexamfetamine, including its salts, isomers, and salts of isomers;

Mecloqualone and its salts;

Methaqualone and its salts;

Methcathinone (some trade or other names: 2-methylamino-propiophenone; alpha-(methylamino)propriophenone; 2-(methyl-amino)-1-phenylpropan-1-one; alpha-N-methylaminopropriophenone; monomethylpropion; ephedrone, N-methylcathinone; methylcathinone; AL-464; AL-422; AL-463; and UR 1431);

N-Ethylamphetamine, its salts, optical isomers, and salts of optical isomers; and

N,N-dimethylamphetamine (some trade or other names: N,N,alpha-trimethylbenzeneethaneamine; N,N,alpha-

trimethylphenethylamine), its salts, optical isomers, and salts of optical isomers; and

(4) any compound structurally derived from 2-aminopropanal by substitution at the 1-position with any monocyclic or fused-polycyclic ring system, including:

(A) compounds further modified by:

(i) substitution in the ring system to any extent (including alkyl, alkoxy, alkylenedioxy, haloalkyl, or halide substituents), whether or not further substituted in the ring system by other substituents;

(ii) substitution at the 3-position with an alkyl substituent; or

(iii) substitution at the 2-amino nitrogen atom with alkyl or dialkyl groups, or inclusion of the 2-amino nitrogen atom in a cyclic structure; and

(B) by example, compounds such as:

4-Methylmethcathinone (Also known as Mephedrone);

3,4-Dimethylmethcathinone (Also known as 3,4-DMMC);

3-Fluoromethcathinone (Also known as 3-FMC);

4-Fluoromethcathinone (Also known as Flephedrone);

3,4-Methylenedioxy-N-methylcathinone (Also known as Methylone);

3,4-Methylenedioxypyrovalerone (Also known as MDPV);

alpha-Pyrrolidinopentiophenone (Also known as alpha-PVP);

Naphthylpyrovalerone (Also known as Naphyrone);

beta-Keto-N-methylbenzodioxolylpropylamine (Also known as Butylone);

beta-Keto-N-methylbenzodioxolylpentanamine (Also known as Pentylone);

beta-Keto-Ethylbenzodioxolylbutanamine (Also known as Eutylone); and

3,4-methylenedioxy-N-ethylcathinone (Also known as Ethylone).

(b) For the purposes of Subsection (a)(1) only, the term "isomer" includes an optical, position, or geometric isomer.

(c) To the extent Subsection (a)(4) conflicts with this subtitle or another law, the subtitle or other law prevails.

(Enacted by Acts 1989, 71st Leg., ch. 678 (H.B. 2136), § 1, effective September 1, 1989; am. Acts 1989, 71st Leg., ch. 1100 (S.B. 1046), § 5.02(n), effective September 1, 1989; am. Acts 1991, 72nd

Leg., ch. 761 (S.B. 314), § 2, effective September 1, 1991; am. Acts 1997, 75th Leg., ch. 745 (H.B. 1070), § 23, effective January 1, 1998; am. Acts 2001, 77th Leg., ch. 251 (S.B. 753), § 17, effective September 1, 2001; am. Acts 2003, 78th Leg., ch. 1099 (H.B. 2192), § 8, effective September 1, 2003; am. Acts 2009, 81st Leg., ch. 739 (S.B. 449), § 2, effective September 1, 2009; am. Acts 2011, 82nd Leg., ch. 784 (H.B. 2118), § 1, effective September 1, 2011.)

### Sec. 481.1031.   Penalty Group 2-A.

Penalty Group 2-A consists of any quantity of a synthetic chemical compound that is a cannabinoid receptor agonist and mimics the pharmacological effect of naturally occurring cannabinoids, including:

naphthoylindoles structurally derived from 3-(1-naphthoyl)indole by substitution at the nitrogen atom of the indole ring by alkyl, alkenyl, cycloalkylmethyl, cycloalkylethyl, or 2-(4-morpholinyl)ethyl, whether or not further substituted in the indole ring to any extent, whether or not substituted in the napthyl ring to any extent, including:

AM-2201;
JWH-004;
JWH-007;
JWH-009;
JWH-015;
JWH-016;
JWH-018;
JWH-019;
JWH-020;
JWH-046;
JWH-047;
JWH-048;
JWH-049;
JWH-050;
JWH-073;
JWH-076;
JWH-079;
JWH-080;
JWH-081;
JWH-082;
JWH-083;
JWH-093;
JWH-094;
JWH-095;
JWH-096;
JWH-097;
JWH-098;
JWH-099;
JWH-100;

JWH-116;
JWH-122;
JWH-148;
JWH-149;
JWH-153;
JWH-159;
JWH-164;
JWH-165;
JWH-166;
JWH-180;
JWH-181;
JWH-182;
JWH-189;
JWH-193;
JWH-198;
JWH-200;
WH-210;
JWH-211;
JWH-212;
JWH-213;
JWH-234;
JWH-235;
JWH-239;
JWH-240;
JWH-241;
JWH-242;
JWH-258;
JWH-259;
JWH-260;
JWH-262;
JWH-267;
JWH-386;
JWH-387;
JWH-394;
JWH-395;
JWH-397;
JWH-398;
JWH-399;
JWH-400;
JWH-412;
JWH-413; and
JWH-414;

naphthylmethylindones structurally derived from 1H-indol-3-yl-(1-naphthyl)methane by substitution at the nitrogen atom of the indole ring by alkyl, alkenyl, cycloalkylmethyl, cycloalkylethyl, or 2-(4-morpholinyl)ethyl, whether or not further substituted in the indole ring to any extent, whether or not substituted in the naphthyl ring to any extent, including:

JWH-175;
JWH-184;
JWH-185;
JWH-192;
JWH-194;

JWH-195;

JWH-196;

JWH-197; and

JWH-199;

naphthoylpyrroles structurally derived from 3-(1-naphthoyl)pyrrole by substitution at the nitrogen atom of the pyrrole ring by alkyl, alkenyl, cycloalkylmethyl, cycloalkylethyl, or 2-(4-morpholinyl)ethyl, whether or not further substituted in the pyrrole ring to any extent, whether or not substituted in the naphthyl ring to any extent, including:

JWH-030;

JWH-145;

JWH-146;

JWH-147;

JWH-150;

JWH-156;

JWH-243;

JWH-244;

JWH-245;

JWH-246;

JWH-292;

JWH-293;

JWH-307;

JWH-308;

JWH-309;

JWH-346;

JWH-347;

JWH-348;

JWH-363;

JWH-364;

JWH-365;

JWH-366;

JWH-367;

JWH-368;

JWH-369;

JWH-370;

JWH-371;

JWH-372;

JWH-373; and

JWH-392;

naphthylmethylindenes structurally derived from 1-(1-naphthylmethyl)indene by substitution at the 3-position of the indene ring by alkyl, alkenyl, cycloalkylmethyl, cycloalkylethyl, or 2-(4-morpholinyl)ethyl, whether or not further substituted in the indene ring to any extent, whether or not substituted in the naphthyl ring to any extent, including:

JWH-171;

JWH-172;

JWH-173; and

JWH-176;

phenylacetylindoles structurally derived from 3-phenylacetylindole by substitution at the nitrogen atom of the indole ring with alkyl, alkenyl, cycloalkylmethyl, cycloalkylethyl, or 2-(4-morpholinyl)ethyl, whether or not further substituted in the indole ring to any extent, whether or not substituted in the phenyl ring to any extent, including:

AM-694;

AM-1241;

JWH-167;

JWH-203;

JWH-204;

JWH-205;

JWH-206;

JWH-208;

JWH-237;

JWH-248;

JWH-249;

JWH-250;

JWH-251;

JWH-252;

JWH-253;

JWH-302;

JWH-303;

JWH-305;

JWH-306;

JWH-311;

JWH-312;

JWH-313;

JWH-314; and

JWH-315;

cyclohexylphenols structurally derived from 2-(3-hydroxycyclohexyl)phenol by substitution at the 5-position of the phenolic ring by alkyl, alkenyl, cycloalkylmethyl, cycloalkylethyl, or 2-(4-morpholinyl)ethyl, whether or not substituted in the cyclohexyl ring to any extent, including:

CP-55,940;

CP-47,497;

analogues of CP-47,497, including VII, V, VIII, I, II, III, IV, IX, X, XI, XII, XIII, XV, and XVI;

JWH-337;

JWH-344;

JWH-345; and

JWH-405; and

cannabinol derivatives, except where contained in marihuana, including tetrahydro derivatives of cannabinol and 3-alkyl homologues of cannabinol or of its tetrahydro derivatives, such as:

Nabilone;

HU-210;

HU-211; and

WIN-55,212-2.
(Enacted by Acts 2011, 82nd Leg., ch. 170 (S.B. 331), § 1, effective September 1, 2011.)

## Sec. 481.104. Penalty Group 3.

(a) Penalty Group 3 consists of:

(1) a material, compound, mixture, or preparation that contains any quantity of the following substances having a potential for abuse associated with a stimulant effect on the central nervous system:

Methylphenidate and its salts; and

Phenmetrazine and its salts;

(2) a material, compound, mixture, or preparation that contains any quantity of the following substances having a potential for abuse associated with a depressant effect on the central nervous system:

a substance that contains any quantity of a derivative of barbituric acid, or any salt of a derivative of barbituric acid not otherwise described by this subsection;

a compound, mixture, or preparation containing amobarbital, secobarbital, pentobarbital, or any salt of any of these, and one or more active medicinal ingredients that are not listed in any penalty group;

a suppository dosage form containing amobarbital, secobarbital, pentobarbital, or any salt of any of these drugs, and approved by the United States Food and Drug Administration for marketing only as a suppository;

Alprazolam;

Amobarbital;

Bromazepam;

Camazepam;

Chlordiazepoxide;

Chlorhexadol;

Clobazam;

Clonazepam;

Clorazepate;

Clotiazepam;

Cloxazolam;

Delorazepam;

Diazepam;

Estazolam;

Ethyl loflazepate;

Fludiazepam;

Flurazepam;

Glutethimide;

Halazepam;

Haloxzolam;

Ketazolam;

Loprazolam;

Lorazepam;

Lormetazepam;

Lysergic acid, including its salts, isomers, and salts of isomers;

Lysergic acid amide, including its salts, isomers, and salts of isomers;

Mebutamate;

Medazepam;

Methyprylon;

Midazolam;

Nimetazepam;

Nitrazepam;

Nordiazepam;

Oxazepam;

Oxazolam;

Pentazocine, its salts, derivatives, or compounds or mixtures thereof;

Pentobarbital;

Pinazepam;

Prazepam;

Quazepam;

Secobarbital;

Sulfondiethylmethane;

Sulfonethylmethane;

Sulfonmethane;

Temazepam;

Tetrazepam;

Tiletamine and zolazepam in combination, and its salts. (some trade or other names for a tiletamine-zolazepam combination product: Telazol, for tiletamine: 2-(ethylamino)-2-(2-thienyl)-cyclohexanone, and for zolazepam: 4-(2-fluorophenyl)-6, 8-dihydro-1,3,8,-trimethylpyrazolo-[3,4--e](1,4)-d diazepin-7(1H)-one, flupyrazapon);

Triazolam;

Zaleplon;

Zolpidem; and

Zopiclone;

(3) Nalorphine;

(4) a material, compound, mixture, or preparation containing limited quantities of the following narcotic drugs, or any of their salts:

not more than 1.8 grams of codeine, or any of its salts, per 100 milliliters or not more than 90 milligrams per dosage unit, with an equal or greater quantity of an isoquinoline alkaloid of opium;

not more than 1.8 grams of codeine, or any of its salts, per 100 milliliters or not more than 90 milligrams per dosage unit, with one or more active, nonnarcotic ingredients in recognized therapeutic amounts;

not more than 300 milligrams of dihydrocodeinone (hydrocodone), or any of its salts, per 100 milliliters or not more than 15 milligrams per dosage unit, with a fourfold or greater quantity of an isoquinoline alkaloid of opium;

not more than 300 milligrams of dihydrocodeinone (hydrocodone), or any of its salts, per 100 milliliters or not more than 15 milligrams per dosage unit, with one or more active, nonnarcotic ingredients in recognized therapeutic amounts;

not more than 1.8 grams of dihydrocodeine, or any of its salts, per 100 milliliters or not more than 90 milligrams per dosage unit, with one or more active, nonnarcotic ingredients in recognized therapeutic amounts;

not more than 300 milligrams of ethylmorphine, or any of its salts, per 100 milliliters or not more than 15 milligrams per dosage unit, with one or more active, nonnarcotic ingredients in recognized therapeutic amounts;

not more than 500 milligrams of opium per 100 milliliters or per 100 grams, or not more than 25 milligrams per dosage unit, with one or more active, nonnarcotic ingredients in recognized therapeutic amounts;

not more than 50 milligrams of morphine, or any of its salts, per 100 milliliters or per 100 grams with one or more active, nonnarcotic ingredients in recognized therapeutic amounts; and

not more than 1 milligram of difenoxin and not less than 25 micrograms of atropine sulfate per dosage unit;

(5) a material, compound, mixture, or preparation that contains any quantity of the following substances:

Barbital;

Chloral betaine;

Chloral hydrate;

Ethchlorvynol;

Ethinamate;

Meprobamate;

Methohexital;

Methylphenobarbital (Mephobarbital);

Paraldehyde;

Petrichloral; and

Phenobarbital;

(6) Peyote, unless unharvested and growing in its natural state, meaning all parts of the plant classified botanically as Lophophora, whether growing or not, the seeds of the plant, an extract from a part of the plant, and every compound, manufacture, salt, derivative, mix-

ture, or preparation of the plant, its seeds, or extracts;

(7) unless listed in another penalty group, a material, compound, mixture, or preparation that contains any quantity of the following substances having a stimulant effect on the central nervous system, including the substance's salts, optical, position, or geometric isomers, and salts of the substance's isomers, if the existence of the salts, isomers, and salts of isomers is possible within the specific chemical designation:

Benzphetamine;

Cathine [(+)-norpseudoephedrine];

Chlorphentermine;

Clortermine;

Diethylpropion;

Fencamfamin;

Fenfluramine;

Fenproporex;

Mazindol;

Mefenorex;

Modafinil;

Pemoline (including organometallic complexes and their chelates);

Phendimetrazine;

Phentermine;

Pipradrol;

Sibutramine; and

SPA　　　　　　[(-)-1-dimethylamino-1,2-diphenylethane];

(8) unless specifically excepted or unless listed in another penalty group, a material, compound, mixture, or preparation that contains any quantity of the following substance, including its salts:

Dextropropoxyphene (Alpha-(+)-4-dimethylamino-　　　1,2-diphenyl-3-methyl-2-propionoxybutane); and

(9) an anabolic steroid, including any drug or hormonal substance, or any substance that is chemically or pharmacologically related to testosterone, other than an estrogen, progestin, dehydroepiandrosterone, or corticosteroid, and promotes muscle growth, including the following drugs and substances and any salt, ester, or ether of the following drugs and substances:

Androstanediol;

Androstanedione;

Androstenediol;

Androstenedione;

Bolasterone;

Boldenone;

Calusterone;

Clostebol;

Dehydrochlormethyltestosterone;

Delta-1-dihydrotestosterone;

Dihydrotestosterone (4-dihydrotestosterone);

Drostanolone;

Ethylestrenol;

Fluoxymesterone;

Formebulone;

Furazabol;

13beta-ethyl-17beta-hydroxygon-4-en-3-one;

4-hydroxytestosterone;

4-hydroxy-19-nortestosterone;

Mestanolone;

Mesterolone;

Methandienone;

Methandriol;

Methenolone;

17alpha-methyl-3beta, 17 beta-dihydroxy-5alpha- androstane;

17alpha-methyl-3alpha, 17 beta-dihydroxy-5alpha- androstane;

17alpha-methyl-3beta, 17beta-dihydroxyandrost-4- ene;

17alpha-methyl-4-hydroxynandrolone;

Methyldienolone;

Methyltestosterone;

Methyltrienolone;

17alpha-methyl-delta-1-dihydrotestosterone;

Mibolerone;

Nandrolone;

Norandrostenediol;

Norandrostenedione;

Norbolethone;

Norclostebol;

Norethandrolone;

Normethandrolone;

Oxandrolone;

Oxymesterone;

Oxymetholone;

Stanozolol;

Stenbolone;

Testolactone;

Testosterone;

Tetrahydrogestrinone; and

Trenbolone.

(b) Penalty Group 3 does not include a compound, mixture, or preparation containing a stimulant substance listed in Subsection (a)(1) if the compound, mixture, or preparation contains one or more active medicinal ingredients not having a stimulant effect on the central nervous system and if the admixtures are included in combinations, quantity, proportion, or concentration that vitiate the potential for abuse of the substances that have a stimulant effect on the central nervous system.

(c) Penalty Group 3 does not include a compound, mixture, or preparation containing a depressant substance listed in Subsection (a)(2) or (a)(5) if the compound, mixture, or preparation contains one or more active medicinal ingredients not having a depressant effect on the central nervous system and if the admixtures are included in combinations, quantity, proportion, or concentration that vitiate the potential for abuse of the substances that have a depressant effect on the central nervous system.

(Enacted by Acts 1989, 71st Leg., ch. 678 (H.B. 2136), § 1, effective September 1, 1989; am. Acts 1989, 71st Leg., ch. 1100 (S.B. 1046), § 5.02(n), effective September 1, 1989; am. Acts 1991, 72nd Leg., ch. 761 (S.B. 314), § 3, effective September 1, 1991; am. Acts 1997, 75th Leg., ch. 745 (H.B. 1070), § 24, effective January 1, 1998; am. Acts 2001, 77th Leg., ch. 251 (S.B. 753), § 18, effective September 1, 2001; am. Acts 2009, 81st Leg., ch. 739 (S.B. 449), § 3, effective September 1, 2009.)

## Sec. 481.105.  Penalty Group 4.

Penalty Group 4 consists of:

(1) a compound, mixture, or preparation containing limited quantities of any of the following narcotic drugs that includes one or more nonnarcotic active medicinal ingredients in sufficient proportion to confer on the compound, mixture, or preparation valuable medicinal qualities other than those possessed by the narcotic drug alone:

not more than 200 milligrams of codeine per 100 milliliters or per 100 grams;

not more than 100 milligrams of dihydrocodeine per 100 milliliters or per 100 grams;

not more than 100 milligrams of ethylmorphine per 100 milliliters or per 100 grams;

not more than 2.5 milligrams of diphenoxylate and not less than 25 micrograms of atropine sulfate per dosage unit;

not more than 15 milligrams of opium per 29.5729 milliliters or per 28.35 grams; and

not more than 0.5 milligram of difenoxin and not less than 25 micrograms of atropine sulfate per dosage unit;

(2) unless specifically excepted or unless listed in another penalty group, a material, compound, mixture, or preparation containing any quantity of the narcotic drug Buprenorphine or Butorphanol or a salt of either; and

(3) unless specifically exempted or excluded or unless listed in another penalty group, any material, compound, mixture, or preparation that contains any quantity of pyrovalerone, a substance having a stimulant effect on the central nervous system, including its salts, isomers, and salts of isomers.

(Enacted by Acts 1989, 71st Leg., ch. 678 (H.B. 2136), § 1, effective September 1, 1989; am. Acts 1989, 71st Leg., ch. 1100 (S.B. 1046), § 5.04(a), effective September 1, 1989; am. Acts 1991, 72nd Leg., ch. 761 (S.B. 314), § 4, effective September 1, 1991; am. Acts 1997, 75th Leg., ch. 745 (H.B. 1070), § 25, effective January 1, 1998; am. Acts 2001, 77th Leg., ch. 251 (S.B. 753), § 19, effective September 1, 2001.)

### Sec. 481.106.  Classification of Controlled Substance Analogue.

For the purposes of the prosecution of an offense under this subchapter involving the manufacture, delivery, or possession of a controlled substance, Penalty Groups 1, 1-A, and 2 include a controlled substance analogue that:

(1) has a chemical structure substantially similar to the chemical structure of a controlled substance listed in the applicable penalty group; or

(2) is specifically designed to produce an effect substantially similar to, or greater than, a controlled substance listed in the applicable penalty group.

(Enacted by Acts 2003, 78th Leg., ch. 1099 (H.B. 2192), § 9, effective September 1, 2003.)

### Sec. 481.107.  Repeat Offenders [Repealed].

Repealed by Acts 1993, 73rd Leg., ch. 900 (S.B. 1067), § 2.07, effective September 1, 1994.

### Sec. 481.108.  Preparatory Offenses.

Title 4, Penal Code, applies to an offense under this chapter.

(Enacted by Acts 1989, 71st Leg., ch. 678 (H.B. 2136), § 1, effective September 1, 1989; am. Acts 1993, 73rd Leg., ch. 900 (S.B. 1067), § 2.02, effective September 1, 1994; am. Acts 1995, 74th Leg., ch. 318 (S.B. 15), § 36, effective September 1, 1995.)

### Sec. 481.109.  Conditional Discharge [Repealed].

Repealed by Acts 1991, 72nd Leg., ch. 141 (S.B.

11), § 6, effective September 1, 1991.

### Sec. 481.110.  Resentencing [Repealed].

Repealed by Acts 1991, 72nd Leg., ch. 141 (S.B. 11), § 6, effective September 1, 1991.

### Sec. 481.111.  Exemptions.

(a) The provisions of this chapter relating to the possession and distribution of peyote do not apply to the use of peyote by a member of the Native American Church in bona fide religious ceremonies of the church. However, a person who supplies the substance to the church must register and maintain appropriate records of receipts and disbursements in accordance with rules adopted by the director. An exemption granted to a member of the Native American Church under this section does not apply to a member with less than 25 percent Indian blood.

(b) The provisions of this chapter relating to the possession of denatured sodium pentobarbital do not apply to possession by personnel of a humane society or an animal control agency for the purpose of destroying injured, sick, homeless, or unwanted animals if the humane society or animal control agency is registered with the Federal Drug Enforcement Administration. The provisions of this chapter relating to the distribution of denatured sodium pentobarbital do not apply to a person registered as required by Subchapter C, who is distributing the substance for that purpose to a humane society or an animal control agency registered with the Federal Drug Enforcement Administration.

(c) A person does not violate Section 481.113, 481.116, 481.1161, 481.121, or 481.125 if the person possesses or delivers tetrahydrocannabinols or their derivatives, or drug paraphernalia to be used to introduce tetrahydrocannabinols or their derivatives into the human body, for use in a federally approved therapeutic research program.

(d) The provisions of this chapter relating to the possession and distribution of anabolic steroids do not apply to the use of anabolic steroids that are administered to livestock or poultry.

(Enacted by Acts 1989, 71st Leg., ch. 678 (H.B. 2136), § 1, effective September 1, 1989; am. Acts 1989, 71st Leg., ch. 1100 (S.B. 1046), § 5.03(d), effective September 1, 1989; am. Acts 2011, 82nd Leg., ch. 170 (S.B. 331), § 2, effective September 1, 2011.)

Health

## Sec. 481.112. Offense: Manufacture or Delivery of Substance in Penalty Group 1.

(a) Except as authorized by this chapter, a person commits an offense if the person knowingly manufactures, delivers, or possesses with intent to deliver a controlled substance listed in Penalty Group 1.

(b) An offense under Subsection (a) is a state jail felony if the amount of the controlled substance to which the offense applies is, by aggregate weight, including adulterants or dilutants, less than one gram.

(c) An offense under Subsection (a) is a felony of the second degree if the amount of the controlled substance to which the offense applies is, by aggregate weight, including adulterants or dilutants, one gram or more but less than four grams.

(d) An offense under Subsection (a) is a felony of the first degree if the amount of the controlled substance to which the offense applies is, by aggregate weight, including adulterants or dilutants, four grams or more but less than 200 grams.

(e) An offense under Subsection (a) is punishable by imprisonment in the Texas Department of Criminal Justice for life or for a term of not more than 99 years or less than 10 years, and a fine not to exceed $100,000, if the amount of the controlled substance to which the offense applies is, by aggregate weight, including adulterants or dilutants, 200 grams or more but less than 400 grams.

(f) An offense under Subsection (a) is punishable by imprisonment in the Texas Department of Criminal Justice for life or for a term of not more than 99 years or less than 15 years, and a fine not to exceed $250,000, if the amount of the controlled substance to which the offense applies is, by aggregate weight, including adulterants or dilutants, 400 grams or more.

(Enacted by Acts 1989, 71st Leg., ch. 678 (H.B. 2136), § 1, effective September 1, 1989; am. Acts 1993, 73rd Leg., ch. 900 (S.B. 1067), § 2.02, effective September 1, 1994; am. Acts 2001, 77th Leg., ch. 1188 (H.B. 3351), § 2, effective September 1, 2001; am. Acts 2009, 81st Leg., ch. 87 (S.B. 1969), § 25.095, effective September 1, 2009.)

## Sec. 481.1121. Offense: Manufacture or Delivery of Substance in Penalty Group 1-A.

(a) Except as provided by this chapter, a person commits an offense if the person knowingly manufactures, delivers, or possesses with intent to deliver a controlled substance listed in Penalty Group 1-A.

(b) An offense under this section is:

(1) a state jail felony if the number of abuse units of the controlled substance is fewer than 20;

(2) a felony of the second degree if the number of abuse units of the controlled substance is 20 or more but fewer than 80;

(3) a felony of the first degree if the number of abuse units of the controlled substance is 80 or more but fewer than 4,000; and

(4) punishable by imprisonment in the Texas Department of Criminal Justice for life or for a term of not more than 99 years or less than 15 years and a fine not to exceed $250,000, if the number of abuse units of the controlled substance is 4,000 or more.

(Enacted by Acts 1997, 75th Leg., ch. 745 (H.B. 1070), § 26, effective January 1, 1998; am. Acts 2001, 77th Leg., ch. 1188 (H.B. 3351), § 3, effective September 1, 2001; am. Acts 2009, 81st Leg., ch. 87 (S.B. 1969), § 25.096, effective September 1, 2009.)

## Sec. 481.1122. Manufacture of Substance in Penalty Group 1: Presence of Child.

If it is shown at the punishment phase of a trial for the manufacture of a controlled substance listed in Penalty Group 1 that when the offense was committed a child younger than 18 years of age was present on the premises where the offense was committed:

(1) the punishments specified by Sections 481.112(b) and (c) are increased by one degree;

(2) the minimum term of imprisonment specified by Section 481.112(e) is increased to 15 years and the maximum fine specified by that section is increased to $150,000; and

(3) the minimum term of imprisonment specified by Section 481.112(f) is increased to 20 years and the maximum fine specified by that section is increased to $300,000.

(Enacted by Acts 2007, 80th Leg., ch. 840 (H.B. 946), § 1, effective September 1, 2007.)

## Sec. 481.113. Offense: Manufacture or Delivery of Substance in Penalty Group 2 or 2-A.

(a) Except as authorized by this chapter, a person commits an offense if the person knowingly manufactures, delivers, or possesses with

Health

intent to deliver a controlled substance listed in Penalty Group 2 or 2-A.

(b) An offense under Subsection (a) is a state jail felony if the amount of the controlled substance to which the offense applies is, by aggregate weight, including adulterants or dilutants, less than one gram.

(c) An offense under Subsection (a) is a felony of the second degree if the amount of the controlled substance to which the offense applies is, by aggregate weight, including adulterants or dilutants, one gram or more but less than four grams.

(d) An offense under Subsection (a) is a felony of the first degree if the amount of the controlled substance to which the offense applies is, by aggregate weight, including adulterants or dilutants, four grams or more but less than 400 grams.

(e) An offense under Subsection (a) is punishable by imprisonment in the Texas Department of Criminal Justice for life or for a term of not more than 99 years or less than 10 years, and a fine not to exceed $100,000, if the amount of the controlled substance to which the offense applies is, by aggregate weight, including adulterants or dilutants, 400 grams or more.

(Enacted by Acts 1989, 71st Leg., ch. 678 (H.B. 2136), § 1, effective September 1, 1989; am. Acts 1993, 73rd Leg., ch. 900 (S.B. 1067), § 2.02, effective September 1, 1994; am. Acts 2001, 77th Leg., ch. 1188 (H.B. 3351), § 4, effective September 1, 2001; am. Acts 2009, 81st Leg., ch. 87 (S.B. 1969), § 25.097, effective September 1, 2009; am. Acts 2011, 82nd Leg., ch. 170 (S.B. 331), §§ 3, 4, effective September 1, 2011.)

### Sec. 481.114.   Offense: Manufacture or Delivery of Substance in Penalty Group 3 or 4.

(a) Except as authorized by this chapter, a person commits an offense if the person knowingly manufactures, delivers, or possesses with intent to deliver a controlled substance listed in Penalty Group 3 or 4.

(b) An offense under Subsection (a) is a state jail felony if the amount of the controlled substance to which the offense applies is, by aggregate weight, including adulterants or dilutants, less than 28 grams.

(c) An offense under Subsection (a) is a felony of the second degree if the amount of the controlled substance to which the offense applies is, by aggregate weight, including adulterants or

dilutants, 28 grams or more but less than 200 grams.

(d) An offense under Subsection (a) is a felony of the first degree, if the amount of the controlled substance to which the offense applies is, by aggregate weight, including adulterants or dilutants, 200 grams or more but less than 400 grams.

(e) An offense under Subsection (a) is punishable by imprisonment in the Texas Department of Criminal Justice for life or for a term of not more than 99 years or less than 10 years, and a fine not to exceed $100,000, if the amount of the controlled substance to which the offense applies is, by aggregate weight, including any adulterants or dilutants, 400 grams or more.

(Enacted by Acts 1989, 71st Leg., ch. 678 (H.B. 2136), § 1, effective September 1, 1989; am. Acts 1993, 73rd Leg., ch. 900 (S.B. 1067), § 2.02, effective September 1, 1994; am. Acts 2001, 77th Leg., ch. 1188 (H.B. 3351), § 5, effective September 1, 2001; am. Acts 2009, 81st Leg., ch. 87 (S.B. 1969), § 25.098, effective September 1, 2009.)

### Sec. 481.115.   Offense: Possession of Substance in Penalty Group 1.

(a) Except as authorized by this chapter, a person commits an offense if the person knowingly or intentionally possesses a controlled substance listed in Penalty Group 1, unless the person obtained the substance directly from or under a valid prescription or order of a practitioner acting in the course of professional practice.

(b) An offense under Subsection (a) is a state jail felony if the amount of the controlled substance possessed is, by aggregate weight, including adulterants or dilutants, less than one gram.

(c) An offense under Subsection (a) is a felony of the third degree if the amount of the controlled substance possessed is, by aggregate weight, including adulterants or dilutants, one gram or more but less than four grams.

(d) An offense under Subsection (a) is a felony of the second degree if the amount of the controlled substance possessed is, by aggregate weight, including adulterants or dilutants, four grams or more but less than 200 grams.

(e) An offense under Subsection (a) is a felony of the first degree if the amount of the controlled substance possessed is, by aggregate weight, including adulterants or dilutants, 200 grams or more but less than 400 grams.

(f) An offense under Subsection (a) is punishable by imprisonment in the Texas Department of

Criminal Justice for life or for a term of not more than 99 years or less than 10 years, and a fine not to exceed $100,000, if the amount of the controlled substance possessed is, by aggregate weight, including adulterants or dilutants, 400 grams or more.

(Enacted by Acts 1989, 71st Leg., ch. 678 (H.B. 2136), § 1, effective September 1, 1989; am. Acts 1993, 73rd Leg., ch. 900 (S.B. 1067), § 2.02, effective September 1, 1994; am. Acts 2009, 81st Leg., ch. 87 (S.B. 1969), § 25.099, effective September 1, 2009.)

## Sec. 481.1151.  Offense: Possession of Substance in Penalty Group 1-A.

(a) Except as provided by this chapter, a person commits an offense if the person knowingly possesses a controlled substance listed in Penalty Group 1-A.

(b) An offense under this section is:

(1) a state jail felony if the number of abuse units of the controlled substance is fewer than 20;

(2) a felony of the third degree if the number of abuse units of the controlled substance is 20 or more but fewer than 80;

(3) a felony of the second degree if the number of abuse units of the controlled substance is 80 or more but fewer than 4,000;

(4) a felony of the first degree if the number of abuse units of the controlled substance is 4,000 or more but fewer than 8,000; and

(5) punishable by imprisonment in the Texas Department of Criminal Justice for life or for a term of not more than 99 years or less than 15 years and a fine not to exceed $250,000, if the number of abuse units of the controlled substance is 8,000 or more.

(Enacted by Acts 1997, 75th Leg., ch. 745 (H.B. 1070), § 26, effective January 1, 1998; am. Acts 2009, 81st Leg., ch. 87 (S.B. 1969), § 25.100, effective September 1, 2009.)

## Sec. 481.116.  Offense: Possession of Substance in Penalty Group 2.

(a) Except as authorized by this chapter, a person commits an offense if the person knowingly or intentionally possesses a controlled substance listed in Penalty Group 2, unless the person obtained the substance directly from or under a valid prescription or order of a practitioner acting in the course of professional practice.

(b) An offense under Subsection (a) is a state jail felony if the amount of the controlled substance possessed is, by aggregate weight, including adulterants or dilutants, less than one gram.

(c) An offense under Subsection (a) is a felony of the third degree if the amount of the controlled substance possessed is, by aggregate weight, including adulterants or dilutants, one gram or more but less than four grams.

(d) An offense under Subsection (a) is a felony of the second degree if the amount of the controlled substance possessed is, by aggregate weight, including adulterants or dilutants, four grams or more but less than 400 grams.

(e) An offense under Subsection (a) is punishable by imprisonment in the Texas Department of Criminal Justice for life or for a term of not more than 99 years or less than five years, and a fine not to exceed $50,000, if the amount of the controlled substance possessed is, by aggregate weight, including adulterants or dilutants, 400 grams or more.

(Enacted by Acts 1989, 71st Leg., ch. 678 (H.B. 2136), § 1, effective September 1, 1989; am. Acts 1993, 73rd Leg., ch. 900 (S.B. 1067), § 2.02, effective September 1, 1994; am. Acts 2009, 81st Leg., ch. 87 (S.B. 1969), § 25.101, effective September 1, 2009.)

## Sec. 481.1161.  Offense: Possession of Substance in Penalty Group 2-A.

(a) Except as authorized by this chapter, a person commits an offense if the person knowingly possesses a controlled substance listed in Penalty Group 2-A, unless the person obtained the substance directly from or under a valid prescription or order of a practitioner acting in the course of professional practice.

(b) An offense under this section is:

(1) a Class B misdemeanor if the amount of the controlled substance possessed is, by aggregate weight, including adulterants or dilutants, two ounces or less;

(2) a Class A misdemeanor if the amount of the controlled substance possessed is, by aggregate weight, including adulterants or dilutants, four ounces or less but more than two ounces;

(3) a state jail felony if the amount of the controlled substance possessed is, by aggregate weight, including adulterants or dilutants, five pounds or less but more than four ounces;

(4) a felony of the third degree if the amount of the controlled substance possessed is, by aggregate weight, including adulterants or dilutants, 50 pounds or less but more than 5 pounds;

(5) a felony of the second degree if the amount of the controlled substance possessed is, by aggregate weight, including adulterants or dilutants, 2,000 pounds or less but more than 50 pounds; and

(6) punishable by imprisonment in the Texas Department of Criminal Justice for life or for a term of not more than 99 years or less than 5 years, and a fine not to exceed $50,000, if the amount of the controlled substance possessed is, by aggregate weight, including adulterants or dilutants, more than 2,000 pounds.

(Enacted by Acts 2011, 82nd Leg., ch. 170 (S.B. 331), § 5, effective September 1, 2011.)

## Sec. 481.117. Offense: Possession of Substance in Penalty Group 3.

(a) Except as authorized by this chapter, a person commits an offense if the person knowingly or intentionally possesses a controlled substance listed in Penalty Group 3, unless the person obtains the substance directly from or under a valid prescription or order of a practitioner acting in the course of professional practice.

(b) An offense under Subsection (a) is a Class A misdemeanor if the amount of the controlled substance possessed is, by aggregate weight, including adulterants or dilutants, less than 28 grams.

(c) An offense under Subsection (a) is a felony of the third degree if the amount of the controlled substance possessed is, by aggregate weight, including adulterants or dilutants, 28 grams or more but less than 200 grams.

(d) An offense under Subsection (a) is a felony of the second degree, if the amount of the controlled substance possessed is, by aggregate weight, including adulterants or dilutants, 200 grams or more but less than 400 grams.

(e) An offense under Subsection (a) is punishable by imprisonment in the Texas Department of Criminal Justice for life or for a term of not more than 99 years or less than five years, and a fine not to exceed $50,000, if the amount of the controlled substance possessed is, by aggregate weight, including adulterants or dilutants, 400 grams or more.

(Enacted by Acts 1989, 71st Leg., ch. 678 (H.B. 2136), § 1, effective September 1, 1989; am. Acts 1993, 73rd Leg., ch. 900 (S.B. 1067), § 2.02, effective September 1, 1994; am. Acts 2009, 81st Leg., ch. 87 (S.B. 1969), § 25.102, effective September 1, 2009.)

## Sec. 481.118. Offense: Possession of Substance in Penalty Group 4.

(a) Except as authorized by this chapter, a person commits an offense if the person knowingly or intentionally possesses a controlled substance listed in Penalty Group 4, unless the person obtained the substance directly from or under a valid prescription or order of a practitioner acting in the course of practice.

(b) An offense under Subsection (a) is a Class B misdemeanor if the amount of the controlled substance possessed is, by aggregate weight, including adulterants or dilutants, less than 28 grams.

(c) An offense under Subsection (a) is a felony of the third degree if the amount of the controlled substance possessed is, by aggregate weight, including adulterants or dilutants, 28 grams or more but less than 200 grams.

(d) An offense under Subsection (a) is a felony of the second degree, if the amount of the controlled substance possessed is, by aggregate weight, including adulterants or dilutants, 200 grams or more but less than 400 grams.

(e) An offense under Subsection (a) is punishable by imprisonment in the Texas Department of Criminal Justice for life or for a term of not more than 99 years or less than five years, and a fine not to exceed $50,000, if the amount of the controlled substance possessed is, by aggregate weight, including adulterants or dilutants, 400 grams or more.

(Enacted by Acts 1989, 71st Leg., ch. 678 (H.B. 2136), § 1, effective September 1, 1989; am. Acts 1993, 73rd Leg., ch. 900 (S.B. 1067), § 2.02, effective September 1, 1994; am. Acts 2009, 81st Leg., ch. 87 (S.B. 1969), § 25.103, effective September 1, 2009.)

## Sec. 481.119. Offense: Manufacture, Delivery, or Possession of Miscellaneous Substances.

(a) A person commits an offense if the person knowingly manufactures, delivers, or possesses with intent to deliver a controlled substance listed in a schedule by an action of the commissioner under this chapter but not listed in a penalty group. An offense under this subsection is a Class A misdemeanor.

(b) A person commits an offense if the person knowingly or intentionally possesses a controlled substance listed in a schedule by an action of the commissioner under this chapter but not listed in a penalty group. An offense under this subsection is a Class B misdemeanor.

(Enacted by Acts 1989, 71st Leg., ch. 678 (H.B. 2136), § 1, effective September 1, 1989; am. Acts 2001, 77th Leg., ch. 1188 (H.B. 3351), § 6, effective September 1, 2001.)

## Sec. 481.120.  Offense: Delivery of Marihuana.

(a) Except as authorized by this chapter, a person commits an offense if the person knowingly or intentionally delivers marihuana.

(b) An offense under Subsection (a) is:

(1) a Class B misdemeanor if the amount of marihuana delivered is one-fourth ounce or less and the person committing the offense does not receive remuneration for the marihuana;

(2) a Class A misdemeanor if the amount of marihuana delivered is one-fourth ounce or less and the person committing the offense receives remuneration for the marihuana;

(3) a state jail felony if the amount of marihuana delivered is five pounds or less but more than one-fourth ounce;

(4) a felony of the second degree if the amount of marihuana delivered is 50 pounds or less but more than five pounds;

(5) a felony of the first degree if the amount of marihuana delivered is 2,000 pounds or less but more than 50 pounds; and

(6) punishable by imprisonment in the Texas Department of Criminal Justice for life or for a term of not more than 99 years or less than 10 years, and a fine not to exceed $100,000, if the amount of marihuana delivered is more than 2,000 pounds.

(Enacted by Acts 1989, 71st Leg., ch. 678 (H.B. 2136), § 1, effective September 1, 1989; am. Acts 1993, 73rd Leg., ch. 900 (S.B. 1067), § 2.02, effective September 1, 1994; am. Acts 2009, 81st Leg., ch. 87 (S.B. 1969), § 25.104, effective September 1, 2009.)

## Sec. 481.121.  Offense: Possession of Marihuana.

(a) Except as authorized by this chapter, a person commits an offense if the person knowingly or intentionally possesses a usable quantity of marihuana.

(b) An offense under Subsection (a) is:

(1) a Class B misdemeanor if the amount of marihuana possessed is two ounces or less;

(2) a Class A misdemeanor if the amount of marihuana possessed is four ounces or less but more than two ounces;

(3) a state jail felony if the amount of marihuana possessed is five pounds or less but more than four ounces;

(4) a felony of the third degree if the amount of marihuana possessed is 50 pounds or less but more than 5 pounds;

(5) a felony of the second degree if the amount of marihuana possessed is 2,000 pounds or less but more than 50 pounds; and

(6) punishable by imprisonment in the Texas Department of Criminal Justice for life or for a term of not more than 99 years or less than 5 years, and a fine not to exceed $50,000, if the amount of marihuana possessed is more than 2,000 pounds.

(Enacted by Acts 1989, 71st Leg., ch. 678 (H.B. 2136), § 1, effective September 1, 1989; am. Acts 1993, 73rd Leg., ch. 900 (S.B. 1067), § 2.02, effective September 1, 1994; am. Acts 2009, 81st Leg., ch. 87 (S.B. 1969), § 25.105, effective September 1, 2009.)

## Sec. 481.122.  Offense: Delivery of Controlled Substance or Marihuana to Child.

(a) A person commits an offense if the person knowingly delivers a controlled substance listed in Penalty Group 1, 1-A, 2, or 3 or knowingly delivers marihuana and the person delivers the controlled substance or marihuana to a person:

(1) who is a child;

(2) who is enrolled in a public or private primary or secondary school; or

(3) who the actor knows or believes intends to deliver the controlled substance or marihuana to a person described by Subdivision (1) or (2).

(b) It is an affirmative defense to prosecution under this section that:

(1) the actor was a child when the offense was committed; or

(2) the actor:

(A) was younger than 21 years of age when the offense was committed;

(B) delivered only marihuana in an amount equal to or less than one-fourth ounce; and

(C) did not receive remuneration for the delivery.

(c) An offense under this section is a felony of the second degree.

(d) In this section, "child" means a person younger than 18 years of age.

(e) If conduct that is an offense under this section is also an offense under another section of this chapter, the actor may be prosecuted under either section or both.

Health

(Enacted by Acts 1989, 71st Leg., ch. 678 (H.B. 2136), § 1, effective September 1, 1989; am. Acts 1993, 73rd Leg., ch. 900 (S.B. 1067), § 2.02, effective September 1, 1994; am. Acts 1997, 75th Leg., ch. 745 (H.B. 1070), § 27, effective January 1, 1998; am. Acts 2001, 77th Leg., ch. 251 (S.B. 753), § 20, effective September 1, 2001.)

## Sec. 481.123. Defense to Prosecution for Offense Involving Controlled Substance Analogue.

(a) It is an affirmative defense to the prosecution of an offense under this subchapter involving the manufacture, delivery, or possession of a controlled substance analogue that the analogue:

(1) was not in any part intended for human consumption;

(2) was a substance for which there is an approved new drug application under Section 505 of the Federal Food, Drug, and Cosmetic Act (21 U.S.C. Section 355); or

(3) was a substance for which an exemption for investigational use has been granted under Section 505 of the Federal Food, Drug, and Cosmetic Act (21 U.S.C. Section 355), if the actor's conduct with respect to the substance is in accord with the exemption.

(b) For the purposes of this section, Section 505 of the Federal Food, Drug, and Cosmetic Act (21 U.S.C. Section 355) applies to the introduction or delivery for introduction of any new drug into intrastate, interstate, or foreign commerce. (Enacted by Acts 1989, 71st Leg., ch. 678 (H.B. 2136), § 1, effective September 1, 1989; am. Acts 1997, 75th Leg., ch. 745 (H.B. 1070), § 28, effective January 1, 1998; am. Acts 2003, 78th Leg., ch. 1099 (H.B. 2192), § 10, effective September 1, 2003.)

## Sec. 481.124. Offense: Possession or Transport of Certain Chemicals with Intent to Manufacture Controlled Substance.

(a) A person commits an offense if, with intent to unlawfully manufacture a controlled substance, the person possesses or transports:

(1) anhydrous ammonia;

(2) an immediate precursor; or

(3) a chemical precursor or an additional chemical substance named as a precursor by the director under Section 481.077(b)(1).

(b) For purposes of this section, an intent to unlawfully manufacture the controlled substance methamphetamine is presumed if the actor possesses or transports:

(1) anhydrous ammonia in a container or receptacle that is not designed and manufactured to lawfully hold or transport anhydrous ammonia;

(2) lithium metal removed from a battery and immersed in kerosene, mineral spirits, or similar liquid that prevents or retards hydration; or

(3) in one container, vehicle, or building, phenylacetic acid, or more than nine grams, three containers packaged for retail sale, or 300 tablets or capsules of a product containing ephedrine or pseudoephedrine, and:

(A) anhydrous ammonia;

(B) at least three of the following categories of substances commonly used in the manufacture of methamphetamine:

(i) lithium or sodium metal or red phosphorus, iodine, or iodine crystals;

(ii) lye, sulfuric acid, hydrochloric acid, or muriatic acid;

(iii) an organic solvent, including ethyl ether, alcohol, or acetone;

(iv) a petroleum distillate, including naphtha, paint thinner, or charcoal lighter fluid; or

(v) aquarium, rock, or table salt; or

(C) at least three of the following items:

(i) an item of equipment subject to regulation under Section 481.080, if the person is not registered under Section 481.063; or

(ii) glassware, a plastic or metal container, tubing, a hose, or other item specially designed, assembled, or adapted for use in the manufacture, processing, analyzing, storing, or concealing of methamphetamine.

(c) For purposes of this section, a substance is presumed to be anhydrous ammonia if the substance is in a container or receptacle that is:

(1) designed and manufactured to lawfully hold or transport anhydrous ammonia; or

(2) not designed and manufactured to lawfully hold or transport anhydrous ammonia, if:

(A) a properly administered field test of the substance using a testing device or instrument designed and manufactured for that purpose produces a positive result for anhydrous ammonia; or

(B) a laboratory test of a water solution of the substance produces a positive result for ammonia.

(d) An offense under this section is:

(1) a felony of the second degree if the controlled substance is listed in Penalty Group 1 or 1-A;

(2) a felony of the third degree if the controlled substance is listed in Penalty Group 2;

(3) a state jail felony if the controlled substance is listed in Penalty Group 3 or 4; or

(4) a Class A misdemeanor if the controlled substance is listed in a schedule by an action of the commissioner under this chapter but not listed in a penalty group.

(e) If conduct constituting an offense under this section also constitutes an offense under another section of this code, the actor may be prosecuted under either section or under both sections.

(f) This section does not apply to a chemical precursor exempted by the director under Section 481.077(b)(2) from the requirements of that section.

(Enacted by Acts 2001, 77th Leg., ch. 1188 (H.B. 3351), § 7, effective September 1, 2001; am. Acts 2003, 78th Leg., ch. 570 (H.B. 1629), § 2, effective September 1, 2003; am. Acts 2005, 79th Leg., ch. 282 (H.B. 164), § 6, effective August 1, 2005.)

## Sec. 481.1245. Offense: Possession or Transport of Anhydrous Ammonia; Use of or Tampering with Equipment.

(a) A person commits an offense if the person:

(1) possesses or transports anhydrous ammonia in a container or receptacle that is not designed or manufactured to hold or transport anhydrous ammonia;

(2) uses, transfers, or sells a container or receptacle that is designed or manufactured to hold anhydrous ammonia without the express consent of the owner of the container or receptacle; or

(3) tampers with equipment that is manufactured or used to hold, apply, or transport anhydrous ammonia without the express consent of the owner of the equipment.

(b) An offense under this section is a felony of the third degree.

(Enacted by Acts 2005, 79th Leg., ch. 282 (H.B. 164), § 7, effective August 1, 2005.)

## Sec. 481.125. Offense: Possession or Delivery of Drug Paraphernalia.

(a) A person commits an offense if the person knowingly or intentionally uses or possesses with intent to use drug paraphernalia to plant, propagate, cultivate, grow, harvest, manufacture,

compound, convert, produce, process, prepare, test, analyze, pack, repack, store, contain, or conceal a controlled substance in violation of this chapter or to inject, ingest, inhale, or otherwise introduce into the human body a controlled substance in violation of this chapter.

(b) A person commits an offense if the person knowingly or intentionally delivers, possesses with intent to deliver, or manufactures with intent to deliver drug paraphernalia knowing that the person who receives or who is intended to receive the drug paraphernalia intends that it be used to plant, propagate, cultivate, grow, harvest, manufacture, compound, convert, produce, process, prepare, test, analyze, pack, repack, store, contain, or conceal a controlled substance in violation of this chapter or to inject, ingest, inhale, or otherwise introduce into the human body a controlled substance in violation of this chapter.

(c) A person commits an offense if the person commits an offense under Subsection (b), is 18 years of age or older, and the person who receives or who is intended to receive the drug paraphernalia is younger than 18 years of age and at least three years younger than the actor.

(d) An offense under Subsection (a) is a Class C misdemeanor.

(e) An offense under Subsection (b) is a Class A misdemeanor, unless it is shown on the trial of a defendant that the defendant has previously been convicted under Subsection (b) or (c), in which event the offense is punishable by confinement in jail for a term of not more than one year or less than 90 days.

(f) An offense under Subsection (c) is a state jail felony.

(Enacted by Acts 1989, 71st Leg., ch. 678 (H.B. 2136), § 1, effective September 1, 1989; am. Acts 1993, 73rd Leg., ch. 900 (S.B. 1067), § 2.02, effective September 1, 1994.)

## Sec. 481.126. Offense: Illegal Barter, Expenditure, or Investment.

(a) A person commits an offense if the person:

(1) barters property or expends funds the person knows are derived from the commission of an offense under this chapter punishable by imprisonment in the Texas Department of Criminal Justice for life;

(2) barters property or expends funds the person knows are derived from the commission of an offense under Section 481.121(a) that is punishable under Section 481.121(b)(5);

(3) barters property or finances or invests funds the person knows or believes are in-

tended to further the commission of an offense for which the punishment is described by Subdivision (1); or

(4) barters property or finances or invests funds the person knows or believes are intended to further the commission of an offense under Section 481.121(a) that is punishable under Section 481.121(b)(5).

(b) An offense under Subsection (a)(1) or (3) is a felony of the first degree. An offense under Subsection (a)(2) or (4) is a felony of the second degree.

(Enacted by Acts 1989, 71st Leg., ch. 678 (H.B. 2136), § 1, effective September 1, 1989; am. Acts 1993, 73rd Leg., ch. 900 (S.B. 1067), § 2.02, effective September 1, 1994; am. Acts 1995, 74th Leg., ch. 318 (S.B. 15), § 37, effective September 1, 1995; am. Acts 2001, 77th Leg., ch. 251 (S.B. 753), § 21, effective September 1, 2001; am. Acts 2003, 78th Leg., ch. 712 (H.B. 2892), § 1, effective September 1, 2003; am. Acts 2009, 81st Leg., ch. 87 (S.B. 1969), § 25.106, effective September 1, 2009.)

## Sec. 481.127. Offense: Unauthorized Disclosure of Information.

(a) A person commits an offense if the person knowingly gives, permits, or obtains unauthorized access to information submitted to the director under Section 481.075.

(b) An offense under this section is a state jail felony.

(Enacted by Acts 1989, 71st Leg., ch. 678 (H.B. 2136), § 1, effective September 1, 1989; am. Acts 1993, 73rd Leg., ch. 900 (S.B. 1067), § 2.02, effective September 1, 1994; am. Acts 1997, 75th Leg., ch. 745 (H.B. 1070), § 29, effective January 1, 1998.)

## Sec. 481.128. Offense and Civil Penalty: Commercial Matters.

(a) A registrant or dispenser commits an offense if the registrant or dispenser knowingly:

(1) distributes, delivers, administers, or dispenses a controlled substance in violation of Sections 481.070—481.075;

(2) manufactures a controlled substance not authorized by the person's registration or distributes or dispenses a controlled substance not authorized by the person's registration to another registrant or other person;

(3) refuses or fails to make, keep, or furnish a record, report, notification, order form, statement, invoice, or information required by this chapter;

(4) prints, manufactures, possesses, or produces an official prescription form without the approval of the director;

(5) delivers or possesses a counterfeit official prescription form;

(6) refuses an entry into a premise for an inspection authorized by this chapter;

(7) refuses or fails to return an official prescription form as required by Section 481.075(k);

(8) refuses or fails to make, keep, or furnish a record, report, notification, order form, statement, invoice, or information required by a rule adopted by the director; or

(9) refuses or fails to maintain security required by this chapter or a rule adopted under this chapter.

(b) If the registrant or dispenser knowingly refuses or fails to make, keep, or furnish a record, report, notification, order form, statement, invoice, or information or maintain security required by a rule adopted by the director, the registrant or dispenser is liable to the state for a civil penalty of not more than $5,000 for each act.

(c) An offense under Subsection (a) is a state jail felony.

(d) If a person commits an act that would otherwise be an offense under Subsection (a) except that it was committed without the requisite culpable mental state, the person is liable to the state for a civil penalty of not more than $1,000 for each act.

(e) A district attorney of the county where the act occurred may file suit in district court in that county to collect a civil penalty under this section, or the district attorney of Travis County or the attorney general may file suit in district court in Travis County to collect the penalty.

(Enacted by Acts 1993, 73rd Leg., ch. 900 (S.B. 1067), § 2.02, effective September 1, 1994; am. Acts 1997, 75th Leg., ch. 745 (H.B. 1070), § 30, effective January 1, 1998; am. Acts 2001, 77th Leg., ch. 251 (S.B. 753), § 22, effective September 1, 2001.)

## Sec. 481.1285. Offense: Diversion of Controlled Substance by Registrants, Dispensers, and Certain Other Persons.

(a) This section applies only to a registrant, a dispenser, or a person who, pursuant to Section 481.062(a)(1) or (2), is not required to register under this subchapter.

(b) A person commits an offense if the person knowingly:

(1) converts to the person's own use or benefit a controlled substance to which the person has access by virtue of the person's profession or employment; or

(2) diverts to the unlawful use or benefit of another person a controlled substance to which the person has access by virtue of the person's profession or employment.

(c) An offense under Subsection (b)(1) is a state jail felony. An offense under Subsection (b)(2) is a felony of the third degree.

(d) If conduct that constitutes an offense under this section also constitutes an offense under any other law, the actor may be prosecuted under this section, the other law, or both.

(Enacted by Acts 2011, 82nd Leg., ch. 1200 (S.B. 158), § 1, effective September 1, 2011.)

## Sec. 481.129.   Offense: Fraud.

(a) A person commits an offense if the person knowingly:

(1) distributes as a registrant or dispenser a controlled substance listed in Schedule I or II, unless the person distributes the controlled substance under an order form as required by Section 481.069;

(2) uses in the course of manufacturing, prescribing, or distributing a controlled substance a registration number that is fictitious, revoked, suspended, or issued to another person;

(3) issues a prescription bearing a forged or fictitious signature;

(4) uses a prescription issued to another person to prescribe a Schedule II controlled substance;

(5) possesses, obtains, or attempts to possess or obtain a controlled substance or an increased quantity of a controlled substance:

(A) by misrepresentation, fraud, forgery, deception, or subterfuge;

(B) through use of a fraudulent prescription form; or

(C) through use of a fraudulent oral or telephonically communicated prescription; or

(6) furnishes false or fraudulent material information in or omits material information from an application, report, record, or other document required to be kept or filed under this chapter.

(a-1) A person commits an offense if the person, with intent to obtain a controlled substance or combination of controlled substances that is not medically necessary for the person or an amount of a controlled substance or substances that is not medically necessary for the person, obtains or attempts to obtain from a practitioner a controlled substance or a prescription for a controlled substance by misrepresentation, fraud, forgery, deception, subterfuge, or concealment of a material fact. For purposes of this subsection, a material fact includes whether the person has an existing prescription for a controlled substance issued for the same period of time by another practitioner.

(b) A person commits an offense if the person knowingly or intentionally:

(1) makes, distributes, or possesses a punch, die, plate, stone, or other thing designed to print, imprint, or reproduce an actual or simulated trademark, trade name, or other identifying mark, imprint, or device of another on a controlled substance or the container or label of a container for a controlled substance, so as to make the controlled substance a counterfeit substance; or

(2) manufactures, delivers, or possesses with intent to deliver a counterfeit substance.

(c) A person commits an offense if the person knowingly or intentionally:

(1) delivers a prescription or a prescription form for other than a valid medical purpose in the course of professional practice; or

(2) possesses a prescription for a controlled substance or a prescription form unless the prescription or prescription form is possessed:

(A) during the manufacturing or distribution process;

(B) by a practitioner, practitioner's agent, or an institutional practitioner for a valid medical purpose during the course of professional practice;

(C) by a pharmacist or agent of a pharmacy during the professional practice of pharmacy;

(D) under a practitioner's order made by the practitioner for a valid medical purpose in the course of professional practice; or

(E) by an officer or investigator authorized to enforce this chapter within the scope of the officer's or investigator's official duties.

(d) An offense under Subsection (a) is:

(1) a felony of the second degree if the controlled substance that is the subject of the offense is listed in Schedule I or II;

(2) a felony of the third degree if the controlled substance that is the subject of the offense is listed in Schedule III or IV; and

(3) a Class A misdemeanor if the controlled substance that is the subject of the offense is listed in Schedule V.

Health

(d-1) An offense under Subsection (a-1) is:

(1) a felony of the second degree if any controlled substance that is the subject of the offense is listed in Schedule I or II;

(2) a felony of the third degree if any controlled substance that is the subject of the offense is listed in Schedule III or IV; and

(3) a Class A misdemeanor if any controlled substance that is the subject of the offense is listed in Schedule V.

(e) An offense under Subsection (b) is a Class A misdemeanor.

(f) An offense under Subsection (c)(1) is:

(1) a felony of the second degree if the defendant delivers:

(A) a prescription form; or

(B) a prescription for a controlled substance listed in Schedule II; and

(2) a felony of the third degree if the defendant delivers a prescription for a controlled substance listed in Schedule III, IV, or V.

(g) An offense under Subsection (c)(2) is:

(1) a state jail felony if the defendant possesses:

(A) a prescription form; or

(B) a prescription for a controlled substance listed in Schedule II or III; and

(2) a Class B misdemeanor if the defendant possesses a prescription for a controlled substance listed in Schedule IV or V.

(Enacted by Acts 1989, 71st Leg., ch. 678 (H.B. 2136), § 1, effective September 1, 1989; am. Acts 1989, 71st Leg., ch. 1100 (S.B. 1046), § 5.02(p), effective September 1, 1989; am. Acts 1993, 73rd Leg., ch. 900 (S.B. 1067), § 2.02, effective September 1, 1994; am. Acts 1997, 75th Leg., ch. 745 (H.B. 1070), § 31, effective January 1, 1998; am. Acts 2001, 77th Leg., ch. 251 (S.B. 753), § 23, effective September 1, 2001; am. Acts 2011, 82nd Leg., ch. 1200 (S.B. 158), § 2, effective September 1, 2011.)

## Sec. 481.130.  Penalties Under Other Law.

A penalty imposed for an offense under this chapter is in addition to any civil or administrative penalty or other sanction imposed by law. (Enacted by Acts 1989, 71st Leg., ch. 678 (H.B. 2136), § 1, effective September 1, 1989.)

## Sec. 481.131.  Offense: Diversion of Controlled Substance Property or Plant.

(a) A person commits an offense if the person intentionally or knowingly:

(1) converts to the person's own use or benefit a controlled substance property or plant seized under Section 481.152 or 481.153; or

(2) diverts to the unlawful use or benefit of another person a controlled substance property or plant seized under Section 481.152 or 481.153.

(b) An offense under this section is a state jail felony.

(Enacted by Acts 1991, 72nd Leg., ch. 141 (S.B. 11), § 2, effective September 1, 1991; am. Acts 1993, 73rd Leg., ch. 900 (S.B. 1067), § 2.02, effective September 1, 1994.)

## Sec. 481.132.  Multiple Prosecutions.

(a) In this section, "criminal episode" means the commission of two or more offenses under this chapter under the following circumstances:

(1) the offenses are committed pursuant to the same transaction or pursuant to two or more transactions that are connected or constitute a common scheme, plan, or continuing course of conduct; or

(2) the offenses are the repeated commission of the same or similar offenses.

(b) A defendant may be prosecuted in a single criminal action for all offenses arising out of the same criminal episode. If a single criminal action is based on more than one charging instrument within the jurisdiction of the trial court, not later than the 30th day before the date of the trial, the state shall file written notice of the action.

(c) If a judgment of guilt is reversed, set aside, or vacated and a new trial is ordered, the state may not prosecute in a single criminal action in the new trial any offense not joined in the former prosecution unless evidence to establish probable guilt for that offense was not known to the appropriate prosecution official at the time the first prosecution began.

(d) If the accused is found guilty of more than one offense arising out of the same criminal episode prosecuted in a single criminal action, sentence for each offense for which the accused has been found guilty shall be pronounced, and those sentences run concurrently.

(e) If it appears that a defendant or the state is prejudiced by a joinder of offenses, the court may order separate trials of the offenses or provide other relief as justice requires.

(f) This section provides the exclusive method for consolidation and joinder of prosecutions for offenses under this chapter. This section is not a limitation of Article 36.09 or 36.10, Code of Criminal Procedure.

(Enacted by Acts 1991, 72nd Leg., ch. 193 (S.B. 148), § 1, effective September 1, 1991; am. Acts 1991, 72nd Leg., 1st C.S., ch. 14 (H.B. 169), § 8.01(17)(a), effective November 12, 1991 (renumbered from Sec. 481.131).)

## Sec. 481.133. Offense: Falsification of Drug Test Results.

(a) A person commits an offense if the person knowingly or intentionally uses or possesses with intent to use any substance or device designed to falsify drug test results.

(b) A person commits an offense if the person knowingly or intentionally delivers, possesses with intent to deliver, or manufactures with intent to deliver a substance or device designed to falsify drug test results.

(c) In this section, "drug test" means a lawfully administered test designed to detect the presence of a controlled substance or marihuana.

(d) An offense under Subsection (a) is a Class B misdemeanor.

(e) An offense under Subsection (b) is a Class A misdemeanor.

(Enacted by Acts 1991, 72nd Leg., ch. 274 (H.B. 268), § 1, effective September 1, 1991; am. Acts 1991, 72nd Leg., 1st C.S., ch. 14 (H.B. 169), § 8.01(17)(b), effective November 12, 1991 (renumbered from Sec. 481.131).)

## Sec. 481.134. Drug-Free Zones.

(a) In this section:

(1) "Minor" means a person who is younger than 18 years of age.

(2) "Institution of higher education" means any public or private technical institute, junior college, senior college or university, medical or dental unit, or other agency of higher education as defined by Section 61.003, Education Code.

(3) "Playground" means any outdoor facility that is not on the premises of a school and that:

(A) is intended for recreation;

(B) is open to the public; and

(C) contains three or more play stations intended for the recreation of children, such as slides, swing sets, and teeterboards.

(4) "Premises" means real property and all buildings and appurtenances pertaining to the real property.

(5) "School" means a private or public elementary or secondary school or a day-care center, as defined by Section 42.002, Human Resources Code.

(6) "Video arcade facility" means any facility that:

(A) is open to the public, including persons who are 17 years of age or younger;

(B) is intended primarily for the use of pinball or video machines; and

(C) contains at least three pinball or video machines.

(7) "Youth center" means any recreational facility or gymnasium that:

(A) is intended primarily for use by persons who are 17 years of age or younger; and

(B) regularly provides athletic, civic, or cultural activities.

(b) An offense otherwise punishable as a state jail felony under Section 481.112, 481.113, 481.114, or 481.120 is punishable as a felony of the third degree, and an offense otherwise punishable as a felony of the second degree under any of those sections is punishable as a felony of the first degree, if it is shown at the punishment phase of the trial of the offense that the offense was committed:

(1) in, on, or within 1,000 feet of premises owned, rented, or leased by an institution of higher learning, the premises of a public or private youth center, or a playground; or

(2) in, on, or within 300 feet of the premises of a public swimming pool or video arcade facility.

(c) The minimum term of confinement or imprisonment for an offense otherwise punishable under Section 481.112(c), (d), (e), or (f), 481.113(c), (d), or (e), 481.114(c), (d), or (e), 481.115(c)-(f), 481.116(c), (d), or (e), 481.1161(b)(4), (5), or (6), 481.117(c), (d), or (e), 481.118(c), (d), or (e), 481.120(b)(4), (5), or (6), or 481.121(b)(4), (5), or (6) is increased by five years and the maximum fine for the offense is doubled if it is shown on the trial of the offense that the offense was committed:

(1) in, on, or within 1,000 feet of the premises of a school, the premises of a public or private youth center, or a playground; or

(2) on a school bus.

(d) An offense otherwise punishable under Section 481.112(b), 481.113(b), 481.114(b), 481.115(b), 481.116(b), 481.1161(b)(3), 481.120(b)(3), or 481.121(b)(3) is a felony of the third degree if it is shown on the trial of the offense that the offense was committed:

(1) in, on, or within 1,000 feet of any real property that is owned, rented, or leased to a school or school board, the premises of a public or private youth center, or a playground; or

(2) on a school bus.

(e) An offense otherwise punishable under Section 481.117(b), 481.119(a), 481.120(b)(2), or 481.121(b)(2) is a state jail felony if it is shown on the trial of the offense that the offense was committed:

(1) in, on, or within 1,000 feet of any real property that is owned, rented, or leased to a school or school board, the premises of a public or private youth center, or a playground; or

(2) on a school bus.

(f) An offense otherwise punishable under Section 481.118(b), 481.119(b), 481.120(b)(1), or 481.121(b)(1) is a Class A misdemeanor if it is shown on the trial of the offense that the offense was committed:

(1) in, on, or within 1,000 feet of any real property that is owned, rented, or leased to a school or school board, the premises of a public or private youth center, or a playground; or

(2) on a school bus.

(g) Subsection (f) does not apply to an offense if:

(1) the offense was committed inside a private residence; and

(2) no minor was present in the private residence at the time the offense was committed.

(h) Punishment that is increased for a conviction for an offense listed under this section may not run concurrently with punishment for a conviction under any other criminal statute.

(Enacted by Acts 1993, 73rd Leg., ch. 888 (S.B. 16), § 1, effective September 1, 1993; am. Acts 1995, 74th Leg., ch. 260 (S.B. 1), § 39, effective May 30, 1995; am. Acts 1995, 74th Leg., ch. 318 (S.B. 15), § 38, effective September 1, 1995; am. Acts 1997, 75th Leg., ch. 1063 (S.B. 1539), § 9, effective September 1, 1997; am. Acts 2003, 78th Leg., ch. 570 (H.B. 1629), § 3, effective September 1, 2003; am. Acts 2009, 81st Leg., ch. 452 (H.B. 2467), §§ 1, 2, effective September 1, 2009; am. Acts 2011, 82nd Leg., ch. 170 (S.B. 331), § 6, effective September 1, 2011.)

### Sec. 481.135.  Maps As Evidence of Location or Area.

(a) In a prosecution under Section 481.134, a map produced or reproduced by a municipal or county engineer for the purpose of showing the location and boundaries of drug-free zones is admissible in evidence and is prima facie evidence of the location or boundaries of those areas if the governing body of the municipality or county adopts a resolution or ordinance approving the map as an official finding and record of the location or boundaries of those areas.

(b) A municipal or county engineer may, on request of the governing body of the municipality or county, revise a map that has been approved by the governing body of the municipality or county as provided by Subsection (a).

(c) A municipal or county engineer shall file the original or a copy of every approved or revised map approved as provided by Subsection (a) with the county clerk of each county in which the area is located.

(d) This section does not prevent the prosecution from:

(1) introducing or relying on any other evidence or testimony to establish any element of an offense for which punishment is increased under Section 481.134; or

(2) using or introducing any other map or diagram otherwise admissible under the Texas Rules of Evidence.

(Enacted by Acts 1993, 73rd Leg., ch. 888 (S.B. 16), § 3, effective September 1, 1993; am. Acts 2005, 79th Leg., ch. 728 (H.B. 2018), § 9.004, effective September 1, 2005.)

### Sec. 481.136.  Offense: Unlawful Transfer or Receipt of Chemical Precursor.

(a) A person commits an offense if the person sells, transfers, furnishes, or receives a chemical precursor subject to Section 481.077(a) and the person:

(1) does not hold a chemical precursor transfer permit as required by Section 481.078 at the time of the transaction;

(2) does not comply with Section 481.077 or 481.0771;

(3) knowingly makes a false statement in a report or record required by Section 481.077, 481.0771, or 481.078; or

(4) knowingly violates a rule adopted under Section 481.077, 481.0771, or 481.078.

(b) An offense under this section is a state jail felony, unless it is shown on the trial of the offense that the defendant has been previously convicted of an offense under this section or Section 481.137, in which event the offense is a felony of the third degree.

(Enacted by Acts 1997, 75th Leg., ch. 745 (H.B. 1070), § 32, effective January 1, 1998; am. Acts 2001, 77th Leg., ch. 251 (S.B. 753), § 24, effective September 1, 2001; am. Acts 2005, 79th Leg., ch. 282 (H.B. 164), § 8, effective August 1, 2005.)

Health

## Sec. 481.137. Offense: Transfer of Precursor Substance for Unlawful Manufacture.

(a) A person commits an offense if the person sells, transfers, or otherwise furnishes a chemical precursor subject to Section 481.077(a) with the knowledge or intent that the recipient will use the chemical precursor to unlawfully manufacture a controlled substance or controlled substance analogue.

(b) An offense under this section is a felony of the third degree.

(Enacted by Acts 1997, 75th Leg., ch. 745 (H.B. 1070), § 32, effective January 1, 1998; am. Acts 2001, 77th Leg., ch. 251 (S.B. 753), § 25, effective September 1, 2001.)

## Sec. 481.138. Offense: Unlawful Transfer or Receipt of Chemical Laboratory Apparatus.

(a) A person commits an offense if the person sells, transfers, furnishes, or receives a chemical laboratory apparatus subject to Section 481.080(a) and the person:

(1) does not have a chemical laboratory apparatus transfer permit as required by Section 481.081 at the time of the transaction;

(2) does not comply with Section 481.080;

(3) knowingly makes a false statement in a report or record required by Section 481.080 or 481.081; or

(4) knowingly violates a rule adopted under Section 481.080 or 481.081.

(b) An offense under this section is a state jail felony, unless it is shown on the trial of the offense that the defendant has been previously convicted of an offense under this section, in which event the offense is a felony of the third degree.

(Enacted by Acts 1997, 75th Leg., ch. 745 (H.B. 1070), § 32, effective January 1, 1998; am. Acts 2001, 77th Leg., ch. 251 (S.B. 753), § 26, effective September 1, 2001.)

## Sec. 481.139. Offense: Transfer of Chemical Laboratory Apparatus for Unlawful Manufacture.

(a) A person commits an offense if the person sells, transfers, or otherwise furnishes a chemical laboratory apparatus with the knowledge or intent that the recipient will use the apparatus to unlawfully manufacture a controlled substance or controlled substance analogue.

(b) An offense under Subsection (a) is a felony of the third degree.

(Enacted by Acts 1997, 75th Leg., ch. 745 (H.B. 1070), § 32, effective January 1, 1998; am. Acts 2001, 77th Leg., ch. 251 (S.B. 753), § 27, effective September 1, 2001.)

## Sec. 481.140. Use of Child in Commission of Offense.

(a) If it is shown at the punishment phase of the trial of an offense otherwise punishable as a state jail felony, felony of the third degree, or felony of the second degree under Section 481.112, 481.1121, 481.113, 481.114, 481.120, or 481.122 that the defendant used or attempted to use a child younger than 18 years of age to commit or assist in the commission of the offense, the punishment is increased by one degree, unless the defendant used or threatened to use force against the child or another to gain the child's assistance, in which event the punishment for the offense is a felony of the first degree.

(b) Notwithstanding Article 42.08, Code of Criminal Procedure, if punishment for a defendant is increased under this section, the court may not order the sentence for the offense to run concurrently with any other sentence the court imposes on the defendant.

(Enacted by Acts 2001, 77th Leg., ch. 786 (H.B. 156), § 1, effective June 14, 2001.)

## Sec. 481.141. Manufacture or Delivery of Controlled Substance Causing Death or Serious Bodily Injury.

(a) If at the guilt or innocence phase of the trial of an offense described by Subsection (b), the judge or jury, whichever is the trier of fact, determines beyond a reasonable doubt that a person died or suffered serious bodily injury as a result of injecting, ingesting, inhaling, or introducing into the person's body any amount of the controlled substance manufactured or delivered by the defendant, regardless of whether the controlled substance was used by itself or with another substance, including a drug, adulterant, or dilutant, the punishment for the offense is increased by one degree.

(b) This section applies to an offense otherwise punishable as a state jail felony, felony of the third degree, or felony of the second degree under Section 481.112, 481.1121, 481.113, 481.114, or 481.122.

(c) Notwithstanding Article 42.08, Code of Criminal Procedure, if punishment for a defendant is increased under this section, the court may not order the sentence for the offense to run

Health

concurrently with any other sentence the court imposes on the defendant.

(Enacted by Acts 2003, 78th Leg., ch. 712 (H.B. 2892), § 2, effective September 1, 2003.)

## SUBCHAPTER E
## FORFEITURE

### Sec. 481.151.  Definitions.

In this subchapter:

(1) "Controlled substance property" means a controlled substance, mixture containing a controlled substance, controlled substance analogue, counterfeit controlled substance, drug paraphernalia, chemical precursor, chemical laboratory apparatus, or raw material.

(2) "Controlled substance plant" means a species of plant from which a controlled substance listed in Schedule I or II may be derived.

(3) "Summary destruction" or "summarily destroy" means destruction without the necessity of any court action, a court order, or further proceedings.

(4) "Summary forfeiture" or "summarily forfeit" means forfeiture without the necessity of any court action, a court order, or further proceedings.

(Enacted by Acts 1991, 72nd Leg., ch. 141 (S.B. 11), § 1, effective September 1, 1991; am. Acts 2001, 77th Leg., ch. 251 (S.B. 753), § 28, effective September 1, 2001; am. Acts 2007, 80th Leg., ch. 152 (S.B. 722), § 1, effective May 21, 2007.)

### Sec. 481.152.  Seizure, Summary Forfeiture, and Summary Destruction of Controlled Substance Plants.

(a) Controlled substance plants are subject to seizure and summary forfeiture to the state if:

(1) the plants have been planted, cultivated, or harvested in violation of this chapter;

(2) the plants are wild growths; or

(3) the owners or cultivators of the plants are unknown.

(b) Subsection (a) does not apply to unharvested peyote growing in its natural state.

(c) If a person who occupies or controls land or premises on which the plants are growing fails on the demand of a peace officer to produce an appropriate registration or proof that the person is the holder of the registration, the officer may seize and summarily forfeit the plants.

(d) If a controlled substance plant is seized and forfeited under this section, a court may order the disposition of the plant under Section 481.159, or

the department or a peace officer may summarily destroy the property under the rules of the department.

(Enacted by Acts 1989, 71st Leg., ch. 678 (H.B. 2136), § 1, effective September 1, 1989; am. Acts 1991, 72nd Leg., ch. 141 (S.B. 11), § 1, effective September 1, 1991; am. Acts 2007, 80th Leg., ch. 152 (S.B. 722), §§ 2, 3, effective May 21, 2007.)

### Sec. 481.153.  Seizure, Summary Forfeiture, and Summary Destruction of Controlled Substance Property.

(a) Controlled substance property that is manufactured, delivered, or possessed in violation of this chapter is subject to seizure and summary forfeiture to the state.

(b) If an item of controlled substance property is seized and forfeited under this section, a court may order the disposition of the property under Section 481.159, or the department or a peace officer may summarily destroy the property under the rules of the department.

(Enacted by Acts 1991, 72nd Leg., ch. 141 (S.B. 11), § 1, effective September 1, 1991; am. Acts 2007, 80th Leg., ch. 152 (S.B. 722), §§ 4, 5, effective May 21, 2007.)

### Sec. 481.154.  Rules.

(a) The director may adopt reasonable rules and procedures, not inconsistent with the provisions of this chapter, concerning:

(1) summary forfeiture and summary destruction of controlled substance property or plants;

(2) establishment and operation of a secure storage area;

(3) delegation by a law enforcement agency head of the authority to access a secure storage area; and

(4) minimum tolerance for and the circumstances of loss or destruction during an investigation.

(b) The rules for the destruction of controlled substance property or plants must require:

(1) more than one person to witness the destruction of the property or plants;

(2) the preparation of an inventory of the property or plants destroyed; and

(3) the preparation of a statement that contains the names of the persons who witness the destruction and the details of the destruction.

(c) A document prepared under a rule adopted under this section must be completed, retained, and made available for inspection by the director.

(Enacted by Acts 1991, 72nd Leg., ch. 141 (S.B. 11), § 1, effective September 1, 1991; am. Acts 2007, 80th Leg., ch. 152 (S.B. 722), § 6, effective May 21, 2007.)

### Sec. 481.155. Replevy [Repealed].

Repealed by Acts 1989, 71st Leg., 1st C.S., ch. 12 (H.B. 65), § 6, effective October 18, 1989.

### Sec. 481.156. Deposit of Money Pending Disposition [Repealed].

Repealed by Acts 1989, 71st Leg., 1st C.S., ch. 12 (H.B. 65), § 6, effective October 18, 1989.

### Sec. 481.157. Forfeiture Hearing [Repealed].

Repealed by Acts 1989, 71st Leg., 1st C.S., ch. 12 (H.B. 65), § 6, effective October 18, 1989; Acts 1991, 72nd Leg., ch. 14 (S.B. 404), § 198, effective September 1, 1991.

### Sec. 481.158. Disposition of Money or Other Things of Value [Repealed].

Repealed by Acts 1989, 71st Leg., 1st C.S., ch. 12 (H.B. 65), § 6, effective October 18, 1989.

### Sec. 481.159. Disposition of Controlled Substance Property or Plant.

(a) If a district court orders the forfeiture of a controlled substance property or plant under Chapter 59, Code of Criminal Procedure, or under this code, the court shall also order a law enforcement agency to:

(1) retain the property or plant for its official purposes, including use in the investigation of offenses under this code;

(2) deliver the property or plant to a government agency for official purposes;

(3) deliver the property or plant to a person authorized by the court to receive it;

(4) deliver the property or plant to a person authorized by the director to receive it for a purpose described by Section 481.065(a); or

(5) destroy the property or plant that is not otherwise disposed of in the manner prescribed by this subchapter.

(b) The district court may not require the department to receive, analyze, or retain a controlled substance property or plant forfeited to a law enforcement agency other than the department.

(c) In order to ensure that a controlled substance property or plant is not diluted, substituted, diverted, or tampered with while being used in the investigation of offenses under this code, law enforcement agencies using the property or plant for this purpose shall:

(1) employ a qualified individual to conduct qualitative and quantitative analyses of the property or plant before and after their use in an investigation;

(2) maintain the property or plant in a secure storage area accessible only to the law enforcement agency head and the individual responsible for analyzing, preserving, and maintaining security over the property or plant; and

(3) maintain a log documenting:

(A) the date of issue, date of return, type, amount, and concentration of property or plant used in an investigation; and

(B) the signature and the printed or typed name of the peace officer to whom the property or plant was issued and the signature and the printed or typed name of the individual issuing the property or plant.

(d) A law enforcement agency may contract with another law enforcement agency to provide security that complies with Subsection (c) for controlled substance property or plants.

(e) A law enforcement agency may adopt a written policy with more stringent requirements than those required by Subsection (c). The director may enter and inspect, in accordance with Section 481.181, a location at which an agency maintains records or controlled substance property or plants as required by this section.

(f) If a law enforcement agency uses a controlled substance property or plant in the investigation of an offense under this code and the property or plant has been transported across state lines before the forfeiture, the agency shall cooperate with a federal agency in the investigation if requested to do so by the federal agency.

(g) Under the rules of the department, a law enforcement agency head may grant to another person access to a secure storage facility under Subsection (c)(2).

(h) A county, justice, or municipal court may order forfeiture of a controlled substance property or plant, unless the lawful possession of and title to the property or plant can be ascertained. If the court determines that a person had lawful possession of and title to the controlled substance property or plant before it was seized, the court shall order the controlled substance property or plant returned to the person, if the person so desires. The court may only order the destruction of a controlled substance property or plant that is

not otherwise disposed of in the manner prescribed by Section 481.160.

(i) If a controlled substance property or plant
seized under this chapter was forfeited to an
agency for the purpose of destruction or for any
purpose other than investigation, the property or
plant may not be used in an investigation unless
a district court orders disposition under this
section and permits the use of the property or
plant in the investigation.

(Enacted by Acts 1989, 71st Leg., ch. 678 (H.B.
2136), § 1, effective September 1, 1989; am. Acts
1989, 71st Leg., 1st C.S., ch. 12 (H.B. 65), § 5(a),
effective October 18, 1989; am. Acts 1991, 72nd
Leg., ch. 141 (S.B. 11), § 1, effective September 1,
1991.)

## Sec. 481.160. Destruction of Excess Quantities.

(a) If a controlled substance property or plant
is forfeited under this code or under Chapter 59,
Code of Criminal Procedure, the law enforcement
agency that seized the property or plant or to
which the property or plant is forfeited may
summarily destroy the property or plant without
a court order before the disposition of a case
arising out of the forfeiture if the agency ensures
that:

(1) at least five random and representative
samples are taken from the total amount of the
property or plant and a sufficient quantity is
preserved to provide for discovery by parties
entitled to discovery;

(2) photographs are taken that reasonably
depict the total amount of the property or
plant; and

(3) the gross weight or liquid measure of the
property or plant is determined, either by actually weighing or measuring the property or
plant or by estimating its weight or measurement after making dimensional measurements
of the total amount seized.

(b) If the property consists of a single container
of liquid, taking and preserving one representative sample complies with Subsection (a)(1).

(c) A representative sample, photograph, or
record made under this section is admissible in
civil or criminal proceedings in the same manner
and to the same extent as if the total quantity of
the suspected controlled substance property or
plant was offered in evidence, regardless of
whether the remainder of the property or plant
has been destroyed. An inference or presumption
of spoliation does not apply to a property or plant
destroyed under this section.

(d) If hazardous waste, residuals, contaminated glassware, associated equipment, or by-
products from illicit chemical laboratories or similar operations that create a health or
environmental hazard or are not capable of being
safely stored are forfeited, those items may be
disposed of under Subsection (a) or may be seized
and summarily forfeited and destroyed by a law
enforcement agency without a court order before
the disposition of a case arising out of the forfeiture if current environmental protection standards are followed.

(e) A law enforcement agency seizing and destroying or disposing of materials described in
Subsection (d) shall ensure that photographs are
taken that reasonably depict the total amount of
the materials seized and the manner in which the
materials were physically arranged or positioned
before seizure.

(f) [Repealed by Acts 2005, 79th Leg., ch. 1224
(H.B. 1068), § 19(2), effective September 1,
2005.]

(Enacted by Acts 1989, 71st Leg., ch. 678 (H.B.
2136), § 1, effective September 1, 1989; am. Acts
1989, 71st Leg., ch. 1100 (S.B. 1046), § 5.02(r),
effective September 1, 1989; am. Acts 1991, 72nd
Leg., ch. 14 (S.B. 404), § 199, effective September
1, 1991; am. Acts 1991, 72nd Leg., ch. 141 (S.B.
11), § 1, effective September 1, 1991; am. Acts
1991, 72nd Leg., ch. 285 (S.B. 853), § 2, effective
September 1, 1991; am. Acts 1997, 75th Leg., ch.
745 (H.B. 1070), § 33, effective January 1, 1998;
am. Acts 2001, 77th Leg., ch. 251 (S.B. 753), § 29,
effective September 1, 2001; am. Acts 2005, 79th
Leg., ch. 1224 (H.B. 1068), § 19(2), effective September 1, 2005.)

## SUBCHAPTER F
## INSPECTIONS, EVIDENCE, AND MISCELLANEOUS LAW ENFORCEMENT PROVISIONS

## Sec. 481.181. Inspections.

(a) The director may enter controlled premises
at any reasonable time and inspect the premises
and items described by Subsection (b) in order to
inspect, copy, and verify the correctness of a
record, report, or other document required to be
made or kept under this chapter and to perform
other functions under this chapter. For purposes
of this subsection, "reasonable time" means any
time during the normal business hours of the
person or activity regulated under this chapter or
any time an activity regulated under this chapter
is occurring on the premises. The director shall:

(1) state the purpose of the entry;

(2) display to the owner, operator, or agent in charge of the premises appropriate credentials; and

(3) deliver to the owner, operator, or agent in charge of the premises a written notice of inspection authority.

(b) The director may:

(1) inspect and copy a record, report, or other document required to be made or kept under this chapter;

(2) inspect, within reasonable limits and in a reasonable manner, the controlled premises and all pertinent equipment, finished and unfinished drugs, other substances, and materials, containers, labels, records, files, papers, processes, controls, and facilities as appropriate to verify a record, report, or document required to be kept under this chapter or to administer this chapter;

(3) examine and inventory stock of a controlled substance and obtain samples of the controlled substance;

(4) examine a hypodermic syringe, needle, pipe, or other instrument, device, contrivance, equipment, control, container, label, or facility relating to a possible violation of this chapter; and

(5) examine a material used, intended to be used, or capable of being used to dilute or adulterate a controlled substance.

(c) Unless the owner, operator, or agent in charge of the controlled premises consents in writing, the director may not inspect:

(1) financial data;

(2) sales data other than shipment data; or

(3) pricing data.

(Enacted by Acts 1989, 71st Leg., ch. 678 (H.B. 2136), § 1, effective September 1, 1989; am. Acts 2003, 78th Leg., ch. 1099 (H.B. 2192), § 11, effective September 1, 2003.)

### Sec. 481.182. Evidentiary Rules Relating to Offer of Delivery.

For the purpose of establishing a delivery under this chapter, proof of an offer to sell must be corroborated by:

(1) a person other than the person to whom the offer is made; or

(2) evidence other than a statement of the person to whom the offer is made.

(Enacted by Acts 1989, 71st Leg., ch. 678 (H.B. 2136), § 1, effective September 1, 1989; am. Acts 2003, 78th Leg., ch. 1099 (H.B. 2192), § 12, effective September 1, 2003.)

### Sec. 481.183. Evidentiary Rules Relating to Drug Paraphernalia.

(a) In considering whether an item is drug paraphernalia under this chapter, a court or other authority shall consider, in addition to all other logically relevant factors, and subject to rules of evidence:

(1) statements by an owner or person in control of the object concerning its use;

(2) the existence of any residue of a controlled substance on the object;

(3) direct or circumstantial evidence of the intent of an owner or other person in control of the object to deliver it to a person whom the person knows or should reasonably know intends to use the object to facilitate a violation of this chapter;

(4) oral or written instructions provided with the object concerning its use;

(5) descriptive material accompanying the object that explains or depicts its use;

(6) the manner in which the object is displayed for sale;

(7) whether the owner or person in control of the object is a supplier of similar or related items to the community, such as a licensed distributor or dealer of tobacco products;

(8) direct or circumstantial evidence of the ratio of sales of the object to the total sales of the business enterprise;

(9) the existence and scope of uses for the object in the community;

(10) the physical design characteristics of the item; and

(11) expert testimony concerning the item's use.

(b) The innocence of an owner or other person in charge of an object as to a direct violation of this chapter does not prevent a finding that the object is intended or designed for use as drug paraphernalia.

(Enacted by Acts 1989, 71st Leg., ch. 678 (H.B. 2136), § 1, effective September 1, 1989; am. Acts 2003, 78th Leg., ch. 1099 (H.B. 2192), § 13, effective September 1, 2003.)

### Sec. 481.184. Burden of Proof; Liabilities.

(a) The state is not required to negate an exemption or exception provided by this chapter in a complaint, information, indictment, or other pleading or in any trial, hearing, or other proceeding under this chapter. A person claiming the benefit of an exemption or exception has the

Health

burden of going forward with the evidence with respect to the exemption or exception.

(b) In the absence of proof that a person is the duly authorized holder of an appropriate registration or order form issued under this chapter, the person is presumed not to be the holder of the registration or form. The presumption is subject to rebuttal by a person charged with an offense under this chapter.

(c) This chapter does not impose a liability on an authorized state, county, or municipal officer engaged in the lawful performance of official duties.

(Enacted by Acts 1989, 71st Leg., ch. 678 (H.B. 2136), § 1, effective September 1, 1989; am. Acts 2003, 78th Leg., ch. 1099 (H.B. 2192), § 14, effective September 1, 2003.)

### Sec. 481.185.  Arrest Reports.

(a) Each law enforcement agency in this state shall file monthly with the director a report of all arrests made for drug offenses and quantities of controlled substances seized during the preceding month. The agency shall make the report on a form provided by the director and shall provide the information required by the form.

(b) The director shall publish an annual summary of all drug arrests and controlled substances seized in the state.

(Enacted by Acts 1989, 71st Leg., ch. 678 (H.B. 2136), § 1, effective September 1, 1989.)

### Sec. 481.186.  Cooperative Arrangements.

(a) The director shall cooperate with federal and state agencies in discharging the director's responsibilities concerning traffic in controlled substances and in suppressing the abuse of controlled substances. The director may:

(1) arrange for the exchange of information among government officials concerning the use and abuse of controlled substances;

(2) cooperate in and coordinate training programs concerning controlled substances law enforcement at local and state levels;

(3) cooperate with the Federal Drug Enforcement Administration and state agencies by establishing a centralized unit to accept, catalog, file, and collect statistics, including records on drug-dependent persons and other controlled substance law offenders in this state and, except as provided by Section 481.068, make the information available for federal, state, and local law enforcement purposes; and

(4) conduct programs of eradication aimed at destroying wild or illegal growth of plant species from which controlled substances may be extracted.

(b) In the exercise of regulatory functions under this chapter, the director may rely on results, information, and evidence relating to the regulatory functions of this chapter received from the Federal Drug Enforcement Administration or a state agency.

(Enacted by Acts 1989, 71st Leg., ch. 678 (H.B. 2136), § 1, effective September 1, 1989; am. Acts 2003, 78th Leg., ch. 1099 (H.B. 2192), § 15, effective September 1, 2003.)

## SUBCHAPTER G
## THERAPEUTIC RESEARCH
## PROGRAM

### Sec. 481.201.  Research Program; Review Board.

(a) The Texas Board of Health may establish a controlled substance therapeutic research program for the supervised use of tetrahydrocannabinols for medical and research purposes to be conducted in accordance with this chapter.

(b) If the Texas Board of Health establishes the program, the board shall create a research program review board. The review board members are appointed by the Texas Board of Health and serve at the will of the board.

(c) The review board shall be composed of:

(1) a licensed physician certified by the American Board of Ophthalmology;

(2) a licensed physician certified by the American Board of Internal Medicine and certified in the subspecialty of medical oncology;

(3) a licensed physician certified by the American Board of Psychiatry;

(4) a licensed physician certified by the American Board of Surgery;

(5) a licensed physician certified by the American Board of Radiology; and

(6) a licensed attorney with experience in law pertaining to the practice of medicine.

(d) Members serve without compensation but are entitled to reimbursement for actual and necessary expenses incurred in performing official duties.

(Enacted by Acts 1989, 71st Leg., ch. 678 (H.B. 2136), § 1, effective September 1, 1989.)

### Sec. 481.202.  Review Board Powers and Duties.

(a) The review board shall review research proposals submitted and medical case histories of

Health

persons recommended for participation in a research program and determine which research programs and persons are most suitable for the therapy and research purposes of the program. The review board shall approve the research programs, certify program participants, and conduct periodic reviews of the research and participants.

(b) The review board, after approval of the Texas Board of Health, may seek authorization to expand the research program to include diseases not covered by this subchapter.

(c) The review board shall maintain a record of all persons in charge of approved research programs and of all persons who participate in the program as researchers or as patients.

(d) The Texas Board of Health may terminate the distribution of tetrahydrocannabinols and their derivatives to a research program as it determines necessary.

(Enacted by Acts 1989, 71st Leg., ch. 678 (H.B. 2136), § 1, effective September 1, 1989.)

## Sec. 481.203. Patient Participation.

(a) A person may not be considered for participation as a recipient of tetrahydrocannabinols and their derivatives through a research program unless the person is recommended to a person in charge of an approved research program and the review board by a physician who is licensed by the Texas State Board of Medical Examiners and is attending the person.

(b) A physician may not recommend a person for the research program unless the person:

    (1) has glaucoma or cancer;

    (2) is not responding to conventional treatment for glaucoma or cancer or is experiencing severe side effects from treatment; and

    (3) has symptoms or side effects from treatment that may be alleviated by medical use of tetrahydrocannabinols or their derivatives.

(Enacted by Acts 1989, 71st Leg., ch. 678 (H.B. 2136), § 1, effective September 1, 1989.)

## Sec. 481.204. Acquisition and Distribution of Controlled Substances.

(a) The Texas Board of Health shall acquire the tetrahydrocannabinols and their derivatives for use in the research program by contracting with the National Institute on Drug Abuse to receive tetrahydrocannabinols and their derivatives that are safe for human consumption according to the regulations adopted by the institute, the Food and Drug Administration, and the Federal Drug Enforcement Administration.

(b) The Texas Board of Health shall supervise the distribution of the tetrahydrocannabinols and their derivatives to program participants. The tetrahydrocannabinols and derivatives of tetrahydrocannabinols may be distributed only by the person in charge of the research program to physicians caring for program participant patients, under rules adopted by the Texas Board of Health in such a manner as to prevent unauthorized diversion of the substances and in compliance with all requirements of the Federal Drug Enforcement Administration. The physician is responsible for dispensing the substances to patients.

(Enacted by Acts 1989, 71st Leg., ch. 678 (H.B. 2136), § 1, effective September 1, 1989.)

## Sec. 481.205. Rules; Reports.

(a) The Texas Board of Health shall adopt rules necessary for implementing the research program.

(b) If the Texas Board of Health establishes a program under this subchapter, the commissioner shall publish a report not later than January 1 of each odd-numbered year on the medical effectiveness of the use of tetrahydrocannabinols and their derivatives and any other medical findings of the research program.

(Enacted by Acts 1989, 71st Leg., ch. 678 (H.B. 2136), § 1, effective September 1, 1989.)

## SUBCHAPTER H
## ADMINISTRATIVE PENALTY

## Sec. 481.301. Imposition of Penalty.

The department may impose an administrative penalty on a person who violates Section 481.061, 481.066, 481.067, 481.069, 481.074, 481.075, 481.077, 481.0771, 481.078, 481.080, or 481.081 or a rule or order adopted under any of those sections.

(Enacted by Acts 2007, 80th Leg., ch. 1391 (S.B. 1879), § 5, effective September 1, 2007.)

## Sec. 481.302. Amount of Penalty.

(a) The amount of the penalty may not exceed $1,000 for each violation, and each day a violation continues or occurs is a separate violation for purposes of imposing a penalty. The total amount of the penalty assessed for a violation continuing or occurring on separate days under this subsection may not exceed $20,000.

(b) The amount shall be based on:

Health

(1) the seriousness of the violation, including the nature, circumstances, extent, and gravity of the violation;

(2) the threat to health or safety caused by the violation;

(3) the history of previous violations;

(4) the amount necessary to deter a future violation;

(5) whether the violator demonstrated good faith, including when applicable whether the violator made good faith efforts to correct the violation; and

(6) any other matter that justice may require.

(Enacted by Acts 2007, 80th Leg., ch. 1391 (S.B. 1879), § 5, effective September 1, 2007.)

## Sec. 481.303.  Report and Notice of Violation and Penalty.

(a) If the department initially determines that a violation occurred, the department shall give written notice of the report to the person by certified mail, registered mail, personal delivery, or another manner of delivery that records the person's receipt of the notice.

(b) The notice must:

(1) include a brief summary of the alleged violation;

(2) state the amount of the recommended penalty; and

(3) inform the person of the person's right to a hearing on the occurrence of the violation, the amount of the penalty, or both.

(Enacted by Acts 2007, 80th Leg., ch. 1391 (S.B. 1879), § 5, effective September 1, 2007.)

## Sec. 481.304.  Penalty to Be Paid or Informal Hearing Requested.

(a) Before the 21st day after the date the person receives notice under Section 481.303, the person in writing may:

(1) accept the determination and recommended penalty; or

(2) make a request for an informal hearing held by the department on the occurrence of the violation, the amount of the penalty, or both.

(b) At the conclusion of an informal hearing requested under Subsection (a), the department may modify the amount of the recommended penalty.

(c) If the person accepts the determination and recommended penalty, including any modification of the amount, or if the person fails to timely respond to the notice, the director by order shall approve the determination and impose the recommended penalty.

(Enacted by Acts 2007, 80th Leg., ch. 1391 (S.B. 1879), § 5, effective September 1, 2007.)

## Sec. 481.305.  Formal Hearing.

(a) The person may request a formal hearing only after participating in an informal hearing.

(b) The request must be submitted in writing and received by the department before the 21st day after the date the person is notified of the decision from the informal hearing.

(c) If a timely request for a formal hearing is not received, the director by order shall approve the determination from the informal hearing and impose the recommended penalty.

(d) If the person timely requests a formal hearing, the director shall refer the matter to the State Office of Administrative Hearings, which shall promptly set a hearing date and give written notice of the time and place of the hearing to the director and to the person. An administrative law judge of the State Office of Administrative Hearings shall conduct the hearing.

(e) The administrative law judge shall make findings of fact and conclusions of law and promptly issue to the director a proposal for a decision about the occurrence of the violation and the amount of any proposed penalty.

(f) If a penalty is proposed under Subsection (e), the administrative law judge shall include in the proposal for a decision a finding setting out costs, fees, expenses, and reasonable and necessary attorney's fees incurred by the state in bringing the proceeding. The director may adopt the finding and impose the costs, fees, and expenses on the person as part of the final order entered in the proceeding.

(Enacted by Acts 2007, 80th Leg., ch. 1391 (S.B. 1879), § 5, effective September 1, 2007.)

## Sec. 481.306.  Decision.

(a) Based on the findings of fact, conclusions of law, and proposal for a decision, the director by order may:

(1) find that a violation occurred and impose a penalty; or

(2) find that a violation did not occur.

(b) The notice of the director's order under Subsection (a) that is sent to the person in the manner provided by Chapter 2001, Government Code, must include a statement of the right of the person to judicial review of the order.

(Enacted by Acts 2007, 80th Leg., ch. 1391 (S.B. 1879), § 5, effective September 1, 2007.)

## Sec. 481.307.　Options Following Decision: Pay or Appeal.

Before the 31st day after the date the order under Section 481.306 that imposes an administrative penalty becomes final, the person shall:

(1) pay the penalty; or

(2) file a petition for judicial review of the order contesting the occurrence of the violation, the amount of the penalty, or both.

(Enacted by Acts 2007, 80th Leg., ch. 1391 (S.B. 1879), § 5, effective September 1, 2007.)

## Sec. 481.308.　Stay of Enforcement of Penalty.

(a) Within the period prescribed by Section 481.307, a person who files a petition for judicial review may:

(1) stay enforcement of the penalty by:

(A) paying the penalty to the court for placement in an escrow account; or

(B) giving the court a supersedeas bond approved by the court that:

(i) is for the amount of the penalty; and

(ii) is effective until all judicial review of the order is final; or

(2) request the court to stay enforcement of the penalty by:

(A) filing with the court a sworn affidavit of the person stating that the person is financially unable to pay the penalty and is financially unable to give the supersedeas bond; and

(B) sending a copy of the affidavit to the director by certified mail.

(b) Following receipt of a copy of an affidavit under Subsection (a)(2), the director may file with the court, before the sixth day after the date of receipt, a contest to the affidavit. The court shall hold a hearing on the facts alleged in the affidavit as soon as practicable and shall stay the enforcement of the penalty on finding that the alleged facts are true. The person who files an affidavit has the burden of proving that the person is financially unable to pay the penalty or to give a supersedeas bond.

(Enacted by Acts 2007, 80th Leg., ch. 1391 (S.B. 1879), § 5, effective September 1, 2007.)

## Sec. 481.309.　Collection of Penalty.

(a) If the person does not pay the penalty and the enforcement of the penalty is not stayed, the penalty may be collected.

(b) The attorney general may sue to collect the penalty.

(Enacted by Acts 2007, 80th Leg., ch. 1391 (S.B. 1879), § 5, effective September 1, 2007.)

## Sec. 481.310.　Decision by Court.

(a) If the court sustains the finding that a violation occurred, the court may uphold or reduce the amount of the penalty and order the person to pay the full or reduced amount of the penalty.

(b) If the court does not sustain the finding that a violation occurred, the court shall order that a penalty is not owed.

(Enacted by Acts 2007, 80th Leg., ch. 1391 (S.B. 1879), § 5, effective September 1, 2007.)

## Sec. 481.311.　Remittance of Penalty and Interest.

(a) If the person paid the penalty and if the amount of the penalty is reduced or the penalty is not upheld by the court, the court shall order, when the court's judgment becomes final, that the appropriate amount plus accrued interest be remitted to the person before the 31st after the date that the judgment of the court becomes final.

(b) The interest accrues at the rate charged on loans to depository institutions by the New York Federal Reserve Bank.

(c) The interest shall be paid for the period beginning on the date the penalty is paid and ending on the date the penalty is remitted.

(Enacted by Acts 2007, 80th Leg., ch. 1391 (S.B. 1879), § 5, effective September 1, 2007.)

## Sec. 481.312.　Release of Bond.

(a) If the person gave a supersedeas bond and the penalty is not upheld by the court, the court shall order, when the court's judgment becomes final, the release of the bond.

(b) If the person gave a supersedeas bond and the amount of the penalty is reduced, the court shall order the release of the bond after the person pays the reduced amount.

(Enacted by Acts 2007, 80th Leg., ch. 1391 (S.B. 1879), § 5, effective September 1, 2007.)

## Sec. 481.313.　Administrative Procedure.

A proceeding to impose the penalty is considered to be a contested case under Chapter 2001, Government Code.

(Enacted by Acts 2007, 80th Leg., ch. 1391 (S.B. 1879), § 5, effective September 1, 2007.)

## Sec. 481.314.　Disposition of Penalty.

The department shall send any amount collected as a penalty under this subchapter to the comptroller for deposit to the credit of the general revenue fund.

(Enacted by Acts 2007, 80th Leg., ch. 1391 (S.B. 1879), § 5, effective September 1, 2007.)

# CHAPTER 482
# SIMULATED CONTROLLED SUBSTANCES

## Sec. 482.001.   Definitions.

In this chapter:

(1) "Controlled substance" has the meaning assigned by Section 481.002 (Texas Controlled Substances Act).

(2) "Deliver" means to transfer, actually or constructively, from one person to another a simulated controlled substance, regardless of whether there is an agency relationship. The term includes offering to sell a simulated controlled substance.

(3) "Manufacture" means to make a simulated controlled substance and includes the preparation of the substance in dosage form by mixing, compounding, encapsulating, tableting, or any other process.

(4) "Simulated controlled substance" means a substance that is purported to be a controlled substance, but is chemically different from the controlled substance it is purported to be.

(Enacted by Acts 1989, 71st Leg., ch. 678 (H.B. 2136), § 1, effective September 1, 1989.)

## Sec. 482.002.   Unlawful Delivery or Manufacture with Intent to Deliver; Criminal Penalty.

(a) A person commits an offense if the person knowingly or intentionally manufactures with the intent to deliver or delivers a simulated controlled substance and the person:

(1) expressly represents the substance to be a controlled substance;

(2) represents the substance to be a controlled substance in a manner that would lead a reasonable person to believe that the substance is a controlled substance; or

(3) states to the person receiving or intended to receive the simulated controlled substance that the person may successfully represent the

substance to be a controlled substance to a third party.

(b) It is a defense to prosecution under this section that the person manufacturing with the intent to deliver or delivering the simulated controlled substance was:

(1) acting in the discharge of the person's official duties as a peace officer;

(2) manufacturing the substance for or delivering the substance to a licensed medical practitioner for use as a placebo in the course of the practitioner's research or practice; or

(3) a licensed medical practitioner, pharmacist, or other person authorized to dispense or administer a controlled substance, and the person was acting in the legitimate performance of the person's professional duties.

(c) It is not a defense to prosecution under this section that the person manufacturing with the intent to deliver or delivering the simulated controlled substance believed the substance to be a controlled substance.

(d) An offense under this section is a state jail felony.

(Enacted by Acts 1989, 71st Leg., ch. 678 (H.B. 2136), § 1, effective September 1, 1989; am. Acts 1993, 73rd Leg., ch. 900 (S.B. 1067), § 2.03, effective September 1, 1994.)

## Sec. 482.003.   Evidentiary Rules.

(a) In determining whether a person has represented a simulated controlled substance to be a controlled substance in a manner that would lead a reasonable person to believe the substance was a controlled substance, a court may consider, in addition to all other logically relevant factors, whether:

(1) the simulated controlled substance was packaged in a manner normally used for the delivery of a controlled substance;

(2) the delivery or intended delivery included an exchange of or demand for property as consideration for delivery of the substance and the amount of the consideration was substantially in excess of the reasonable value of the simulated controlled substance; and

(3) the physical appearance of the finished product containing the substance was substantially identical to a controlled substance.

(b) Proof of an offer to sell a simulated controlled substance must be corroborated by a person other than the offeree or by evidence other than a statement of the offeree.

(Enacted by Acts 1989, 71st Leg., ch. 678 (H.B. 2136), § 1, effective September 1, 1989.)

## Sec. 482.004. Summary Forfeiture.

A simulated controlled substance seized as a result of an offense under this chapter is subject to summary forfeiture and to destruction or disposition in the same manner as is a controlled substance property under Subchapter E, Chapter 481.

(Enacted by Acts 1989, 71st Leg., ch. 678 (H.B. 2136), § 1, effective September 1, 1989; am. Acts 1991, 72nd Leg., ch. 141 (S.B. 11), § 3, effective September 1, 1991.)

## Sec. 482.005. Preparatory Offenses.

Title 4, Penal Code, applies to an offense under this chapter.

(Enacted by Acts 1995, 74th Leg., ch. 318 (S.B. 15), § 39, effective September 1, 1995.)

# CHAPTER 483
# DANGEROUS DRUGS

### Subchapter A. General Provisions

## SUBCHAPTER A
## GENERAL PROVISIONS

### Sec. 483.0001. Short Title.

This Act may be cited as the Texas Dangerous Drug Act.

(Enacted by Acts 1993, 73rd Leg., ch. 789 (S.B. 472), § 18, effective September 1, 1993.)

### Sec. 483.001. Definitions.

In this chapter:

(1) "Board" means the Texas State Board of Pharmacy.

(2) "Dangerous drug" means a device or a drug that is unsafe for self-medication and that is not included in Schedules I through V or Penalty Groups 1 through 4 of Chapter 481 (Texas Controlled Substances Act). The term includes a device or a drug that bears or is required to bear the legend:

(A) "Caution: federal law prohibits dispensing without prescription" or "Rx only" or another legend that complies with federal law; or

(B) "Caution: federal law restricts this drug to use by or on the order of a licensed veterinarian."

(3) "Deliver" means to sell, dispense, give away, or supply in any other manner.

(4) "Designated agent" means:

(A) a licensed nurse, physician assistant, pharmacist, or other individual designated by a practitioner to communicate prescription drug orders to a pharmacist;

(B) a licensed nurse, physician assistant, or pharmacist employed in a health care facility to whom the practitioner communicates a prescription drug order; or

(C) a registered nurse or physician assistant authorized by a practitioner to carry out a prescription drug order for dangerous drugs under Subchapter B, Chapter 157, Occupations Code.

(5) "Dispense" means to prepare, package, compound, or label a dangerous drug in the course of professional practice for delivery under the lawful order of a practitioner to an ultimate user or the user's agent.

(6) "Manufacturer" means a person, other than a pharmacist, who manufactures dangerous drugs. The term includes a person who prepares dangerous drugs in dosage form by mixing, compounding, encapsulating, entableting, or any other process.

(7) "Patient" means:

(A) an individual for whom a dangerous drug is prescribed or to whom a dangerous drug is administered; or

(B) an owner or the agent of an owner of an animal for which a dangerous drug is prescribed or to which a dangerous drug is administered.

(8) "Person" includes an individual, corporation, partnership, and association.

(9) "Pharmacist" means a person licensed by the Texas State Board of Pharmacy to practice pharmacy.

(10) "Pharmacy" means a facility where prescription drug or medication orders are received, processed, dispensed, or distributed under this chapter, Chapter 481 of this code, and Subtitle J, Title 3, Occupations Code. The term does not include a narcotic drug treatment program that is regulated by Chapter 466, Health and Safety Code.

(11) "Practice of pharmacy" means:

(A) provision of those acts or services necessary to provide pharmaceutical care;

(B) interpretation and evaluation of prescription drug orders or medication orders;

(C) participation in drug and device selection as authorized by law, drug administration, drug regimen review, or drug or drug-related research;

(D) provision of patient counseling;

(E) responsibility for:

(i) dispensing of prescription drug orders or distribution of medication orders in the patient's best interest;

(ii) compounding and labeling of drugs and devices, except labeling by a manufacturer, repackager, or distributor of nonprescription drugs and commercially packaged prescription drugs and devices;

(iii) proper and safe storage of drugs and devices; or

(iv) maintenance of proper records for drugs and devices. In this subdivision, "device" has the meaning assigned by Subtitle J, Title 3, Occupations Code; or

(F) performance of a specific act of drug therapy management for a patient delegated to a pharmacist by a written protocol from a physician licensed by the state under Subtitle B, Title 3, Occupations Code.

(12) "Practitioner" means a person licensed:

(A) by the Texas State Board of Medical Examiners, State Board of Dental Examiners, Texas State Board of Podiatric Medical Examiners, Texas Optometry Board, or State Board of Veterinary Medical Examiners to prescribe and administer dangerous drugs;

(B) by another state in a health field in which, under the laws of this state, a licensee may legally prescribe dangerous drugs;

(C) in Canada or Mexico in a health field in which, under the laws of this state, a licensee may legally prescribe dangerous drugs; or

(D) an advanced practice nurse or physician assistant to whom a physician has delegated the authority to carry out or sign prescription drug orders under Section 157.0511, 157.052, 157.053, 157.054, 157.0541, or 157.0542, Occupations Code.

(13) "Prescription" means an order from a practitioner, or an agent of the practitioner designated in writing as authorized to communicate prescriptions, or an order made in accordance with Subchapter B, Chapter 157, Occupations Code, or Section 203.353, Occupations Code, to a pharmacist for a dangerous drug to be dispensed that states:

(A) the date of the order's issue;

(B) the name and address of the patient;

(C) if the drug is prescribed for an animal, the species of the animal;

(D) the name and quantity of the drug prescribed;

(E) the directions for the use of the drug;

(F) the intended use of the drug unless the practitioner determines the furnishing of this information is not in the best interest of the patient;

(G) the name, address, and telephone number of the practitioner at the practitioner's usual place of business, legibly printed or stamped; and

(H) the name, address, and telephone number of the licensed midwife, registered nurse, or physician assistant, legibly printed or stamped, if signed by a licensed midwife, registered nurse, or physician assistant.

(14) "Warehouseman" means a person who stores dangerous drugs for others and who has no control over the disposition of the drugs except for the purpose of storage.

(15) "Wholesaler" means a person engaged in the business of distributing dangerous drugs to a person listed in Sections 483.041(c)(1)—(6). (Enacted by Acts 1989, 71st Leg., ch. 678 (H.B. 2136), § 1, effective September 1, 1989; am. Acts 1989, 71st Leg., ch. 1100 (S.B. 1046), §§ 5.03(h), 5.04(b), effective September 1, 1989; am. Acts 1991, 72nd Leg., ch. 14 (S.B. 404), § 200, effective September 1, 1991; am. Acts 1991, 72nd Leg., ch. 237 (H.B. 1495), § 10, effective September 1, 1991; am. Acts 1991, 72nd Leg., ch. 588 (S.B. 774), § 26, effective September 1, 1991; am. Acts 1993, 73rd Leg., ch. 351 (S.B. 621), § 29, effective September 1, 1993; am. Acts 1993, 73rd Leg., ch. 789 (S.B. 472), § 18, effective September 1, 1993; am. Acts 1995, 74th Leg., ch. 965 (S.B. 673), §§ 6, 82, effective June 16, 1995; am. Acts 1997, 75th Leg., ch. 1095 (H.B. 2088), § 18, effective September 1, 1997; am. Acts 1997, 75th Leg., ch. 1180 (S.B. 609), § 22, effective September 1, 1997; am. Acts 2001, 77th Leg., ch. 112 (S.B. 1166), § 6, effective May 11, 2001; am. Acts 2001, 77th Leg., ch. 1254 (S.B. 768), § 11, effective September 1, 2001; am. Acts 2001, 77th Leg., ch. 1420 (H.B. 2812), § 14.795, effective September 1, 2001; am. Acts 2003, 78th Leg., ch. 88 (H.B. 1095), § 10, effective May 20, 2003; am. Acts 2005, 79th Leg., ch. 1240 (H.B. 1535), § 54, effective September 1, 2005.)

### Sec. 483.002.   Rules.

The board may adopt rules for the proper administration and enforcement of this chapter. (Enacted by Acts 1989, 71st Leg., ch. 678 (H.B. 2136), § 1, effective September 1, 1989.)

### Sec. 483.003.   Board of Health Hearings Regarding Certain Dangerous Drugs.

(a) The Texas Board of Health may hold public hearings in accordance with Chapter 2001, Government Code to determine whether there is compelling evidence that a dangerous drug has been abused, either by being prescribed for nontherapeutic purposes or by the ultimate user.

(b) On making that finding, the Texas Board of Health may limit the availability of the abused drug by permitting its dispensing only on the prescription of a practitioner described by Section 483.001(12)(A), (B), or (D). (Enacted by Acts 1989, 71st Leg., ch. 678 (H.B. 2136), § 1, effective September 1, 1989; am. Acts 1995, 74th Leg., ch. 76 (S.B. 959), § 5.95(49),

effective September 1, 1995; am. Acts 1997, 75th Leg., ch. 1180 (S.B. 609), § 23, effective September 1, 1997; am. Acts 2001, 77th Leg., ch. 112 (S.B. 1166), § 7, effective May 11, 2001.)

### Sec. 483.004.   Commissioner of Health Emergency Authority Relating to Dangerous Drugs.

If the commissioner of health has compelling evidence that an immediate danger to the public health exists as a result of the prescription of a dangerous drug by practitioners described by Section 483.001(12)(C), the commissioner may use the commissioner's existing emergency authority to limit the availability of the drug by permitting its prescription only by practitioners described by Section 483.001(12)(A), (B), or (D). (Enacted by Acts 1989, 71st Leg., ch. 678 (H.B. 2136), § 1, effective September 1, 1989; am. Acts 2001, 77th Leg., ch. 112 (S.B. 1166), § 8, effective May 11, 2001.)

### SUBCHAPTER B
### DUTIES OF PHARMACISTS, PRACTITIONERS, AND OTHER PERSONS

### Sec. 483.021.   Determination by Pharmacist on Request to Dispense Drug.

(a) A pharmacist who is requested to dispense a dangerous drug under a prescription issued by a practitioner shall determine, in the exercise of the pharmacist's professional judgment, that the prescription is a valid prescription. A pharmacist may not dispense a dangerous drug if the pharmacist knows or should have known that the prescription was issued without a valid patient-practitioner relationship.

(b) A pharmacist who is requested to dispense a dangerous drug under a prescription issued by a therapeutic optometrist shall determine, in the exercise of the pharmacist's professional judgment, whether the prescription is for a dangerous drug that a therapeutic optometrist is authorized to prescribe under Section 351.358, Occupations Code. (Enacted by Acts 1989, 71st Leg., ch. 678 (H.B. 2136), § 1, effective September 1, 1989; am. Acts 1991, 72nd Leg., ch. 588 (S.B. 774), § 27, effective September 1, 1991; am. Acts 2001, 77th Leg., ch. 1254 (S.B. 768), § 12, effective September 1, 2001; am. Acts 2001, 77th Leg., ch. 1420 (H.B. 2812), § 14.796, effective September 1, 2001.)

Health

### Sec. 483.022. Practitioner's Designated Agent; Practitioner's Responsibilities.

(a) A practitioner shall provide in writing the name of each designated agent as defined by Section 483.001(4)(A) and (C), and the name of each healthcare facility which employs persons defined by Section 483.001(4)(B).

(b) The practitioner shall maintain at the practitioner's usual place of business a list of the designated agents or healthcare facilities as defined by Section 483.001(4).

(c) The practitioner shall provide a pharmacist with a copy of the practitioner's written authorization for a designated agent as defined by Section 483.001(4) on the pharmacist's request.

(d) This section does not relieve a practitioner or the practitioner's designated agent from the requirements of Subchapter A, Chapter 562, Occupations Code.

(e) A practitioner remains personally responsible for the actions of a designated agent who communicates a prescription to a pharmacist.

(f) A practitioner may designate a person who is a licensed vocational nurse or has an education equivalent to or greater than that required for a licensed vocational nurse to communicate prescriptions of an advanced practice nurse or physician assistant authorized by the practitioner to sign prescription drug orders under Subchapter B, Chapter 157, Occupations Code.

(Enacted by Acts 1989, 71st Leg., ch. 678 (H.B. 2136), § 1, effective September 1, 1989; am. Acts 1991, 72nd Leg., ch. 14 (S.B. 404), § 201, effective September 1, 1991; am. Acts 1991, 72nd Leg., ch. 237 (H.B. 1495), § 11, effective September 1, 1991; am. Acts 1993, 73rd Leg., ch. 789 (S.B. 472), § 19, effective September 1, 1993; am. Acts 1999, 76th Leg., ch. 428 (S.B. 1131), § 4, effective September 1, 1999; am. Acts 2001, 77th Leg., ch. 1420 (H.B. 2812), § 14.797, effective September 1, 2001.)

### Sec. 483.023. Retention of Prescriptions.

A pharmacy shall retain a prescription for a dangerous drug dispensed by the pharmacy for two years after the date of the initial dispensing or the last refilling of the prescription, whichever date is later.

(Enacted by Acts 1989, 71st Leg., ch. 678 (H.B. 2136), § 1, effective September 1, 1989.)

### Sec. 483.024. Records of Acquisition or Disposal.

The following persons shall maintain a record of each acquisition and each disposal of a dangerous drug for two years after the date of the acquisition or disposal:

(1) a pharmacy;

(2) a practitioner;

(3) a person who obtains a dangerous drug for lawful research, teaching, or testing purposes, but not for resale;

(4) a hospital that obtains a dangerous drug for lawful administration by a practitioner; and

(5) a manufacturer or wholesaler registered with the commissioner of health under Chapter 431 (Texas Food, Drug, and Cosmetic Act).

(Enacted by Acts 1989, 71st Leg., ch. 678 (H.B. 2136), § 1, effective September 1, 1989.)

### Sec. 483.025. Inspections; Inventories.

A person required to keep records relating to dangerous drugs shall:

(1) make the records available for inspection and copying at all reasonable hours by any public official or employee engaged in enforcing this chapter; and

(2) allow the official or employee to inventory all stocks of dangerous drugs on hand.

(Enacted by Acts 1989, 71st Leg., ch. 678 (H.B. 2136), § 1, effective September 1, 1989.)

### Sec. 483.026. Requirements Relating to Anabolic Steroids and Human Growth Hormones [Repealed].

Repealed by Acts 1989, 71st Leg., ch. 1100 (S.B. 1046), § 5.03(h), effective September 1, 1989.

### SUBCHAPTER C
### CRIMINAL PENALTIES

### Sec. 483.041. Possession of Dangerous Drug.

(a) A person commits an offense if the person possesses a dangerous drug unless the person obtains the drug from a pharmacist acting in the manner described by Section 483.042(a)(1) or a practitioner acting in the manner described by Section 483.042(a)(2).

(b) Except as permitted by this chapter, a person commits an offense if the person possesses a dangerous drug for the purpose of selling the drug.

(c) Subsection (a) does not apply to the possession of a dangerous drug in the usual course of business or practice or in the performance of official duties by the following persons or an agent or employee of the person:

(1) a pharmacy licensed by the board;

(2) a practitioner;

(3) a person who obtains a dangerous drug for lawful research, teaching, or testing, but not for resale;

(4) a hospital that obtains a dangerous drug for lawful administration by a practitioner;

(5) an officer or employee of the federal, state, or local government;

(6) a manufacturer or wholesaler licensed by the Department of State Health Services under Chapter 431 (Texas Food, Drug, and Cosmetic Act);

(7) a carrier or warehouseman;

(8) a home and community support services agency licensed under and acting in accordance with Chapter 142;

(9) a licensed midwife who obtains oxygen for administration to a mother or newborn or who obtains a dangerous drug for the administration of prophylaxis to a newborn for the prevention of ophthalmia neonatorum in accordance with Section 203.353, Occupations Code;

(10) a salvage broker or salvage operator licensed under Chapter 432; or

(11) a certified laser hair removal professional under Subchapter M, Chapter 401, who possesses and uses a laser or pulsed light device approved by and registered with the department and in compliance with department rules for the sole purpose of cosmetic nonablative hair removal.

(d) An offense under this section is a Class A misdemeanor.

(Enacted by Acts 1989, 71st Leg., ch. 678 (H.B. 2136), § 1, effective September 1, 1989; am. Acts 1989, 71st Leg., ch. 1100 (S.B. 1046), § 5.03(f), effective September 1, 1989; am. Acts 1993, 73rd Leg., ch. 16 (S.B. 310), § 2, effective April 2, 1993; am. Acts 1993, 73rd Leg., ch. 789 (S.B. 472), § 20, effective September 1, 1993; am. Acts 1995, 74th Leg., ch. 307 (H.B. 1408), § 2, effective September 1, 1995; am. Acts 1995, 74th Leg., ch. 318 (S.B. 15), § 41, effective September 1, 1995; am. Acts 1997, 75th Leg., ch. 1095 (H.B. 2088), § 19, effective September 1, 1997; am. Acts 1997, 75th Leg., ch. 1129 (H.B. 3075), § 2, effective September 1, 1997; am. Acts 2001, 77th Leg., ch. 265

(S.B. 1080), § 9, effective May 22, 2001; am. Acts 2001, 77th Leg., ch. 1420 (H.B. 2812), § 14.798, effective September 1, 2001; am. Acts 2005, 79th Leg., ch. 1240 (H.B. 1535), § 55, effective September 1, 2005; am. Acts 2009, 81st Leg., ch. 303 (H.B. 449), § 2, effective September 1, 2010.)

### Sec. 483.042. Delivery or Offer of Delivery of Dangerous Drug.

(a) A person commits an offense if the person delivers or offers to deliver a dangerous drug:

(1) unless:

(A) the dangerous drug is delivered or offered for delivery by a pharmacist under:

(i) a prescription issued by a practitioner described by Section 483.001(12)(A) or (B);

(ii) a prescription signed by a registered nurse or physician assistant in accordance with Subchapter B, Chapter 157, Occupations Code; or

(iii) an original written prescription issued by a practitioner described by Section 483.001(12)(C); and

(B) a label is attached to the immediate container in which the drug is delivered or offered to be delivered and the label contains the following information:

(i) the name and address of the pharmacy from which the drug is delivered or offered for delivery;

(ii) the date the prescription for the drug is dispensed;

(iii) the number of the prescription as filed in the prescription files of the pharmacy from which the prescription is dispensed;

(iv) the name of the practitioner who prescribed the drug and, if applicable, the name of the registered nurse or physician assistant who signed the prescription;

(v) the name of the patient and, if the drug is prescribed for an animal, a statement of the species of the animal; and

(vi) directions for the use of the drug as contained in the prescription; or

(2) unless:

(A) the dangerous drug is delivered or offered for delivery by:

(i) a practitioner in the course of practice; or

(ii) a registered nurse or physician assistant in the course of practice in accordance with Subchapter B, Chapter 157, Occupations Code; and

Health

(B) a label is attached to the immediate container in which the drug is delivered or offered to be delivered and the label contains the following information:

(i) the name and address of the practitioner who prescribed the drug, and if applicable, the name and address of the registered nurse or physician assistant;

(ii) the date the drug is delivered;

(iii) the name of the patient and, if the drug is prescribed for an animal, a statement of the species of the animal; and

(iv) the name of the drug, the strength of the drug, and directions for the use of the drug.

(b) Subsection (a) does not apply to the delivery or offer for delivery of a dangerous drug to a person listed in Section 483.041(c) for use in the usual course of business or practice or in the performance of official duties by the person.

(c) Proof of an offer to sell a dangerous drug must be corroborated by a person other than the offeree or by evidence other than a statement by the offeree.

(d) An offense under this section is a state jail felony.

(e) The labeling provisions of Subsection (a) do not apply to a dangerous drug prescribed or dispensed for administration to a patient who is institutionalized. The board shall adopt rules for the labeling of such a drug.

(f) Provided all federal requirements are met, the labeling provisions of Subsection (a) do not apply to a dangerous drug prescribed or dispensed for administration to food production animals in an agricultural operation under a written medical directive or treatment guideline from a veterinarian licensed under Chapter 801, Occupations Code.

(Enacted by Acts 1989, 71st Leg., ch. 678 (H.B. 2136), § 1, effective September 1, 1989; am. Acts 1989, 71st Leg., ch. 1100 (S.B. 1046), § 5.03(g), effective September 1, 1989; am. Acts 1993, 73rd Leg., ch. 287 (S.B. 623), § 3, effective September 1, 1993; am. Acts 1993, 73rd Leg., ch. 789 (S.B. 472), § 21, effective September 1, 1993; am. Acts 1993, 73rd Leg., ch. 900 (S.B. 1067), § 2.04, effective September 1, 1994; am. Acts 1995, 74th Leg., ch. 965 (S.B. 673), § 7, effective June 16, 1995; am. Acts 1997, 75th Leg., ch. 1180 (S.B. 609), § 24, effective September 1, 1997; am. Acts 1999, 76th Leg., ch. 1404 (H.B. 1975), § 1, effective September 1, 1999; am. Acts 2001, 77th Leg., ch. 1420 (H.B. 2812), § 14.799, effective September 1, 2001.)

### Sec. 483.043. Manufacture of Dangerous Drug.

(a) A person commits an offense if the person manufactures a dangerous drug and the person is not authorized by law to manufacture the drug.

(b) An offense under this section is a state jail felony.

(Enacted by Acts 1989, 71st Leg., ch. 678 (H.B. 2136), § 1, effective September 1, 1989; am. Acts 1993, 73rd Leg., ch. 900 (S.B. 1067), § 2.05, effective September 1, 1994.)

### Sec. 483.044. Prescribing, Delivering, and Administering Steroids and Growth Hormones [Repealed].

Repealed by Acts 1989, 71st Leg., ch. 1100 (S.B. 1046), § 5.03(h), effective September 1, 1989.

### Sec. 483.045. Forging or Altering Prescription.

(a) A person commits an offense if the person:

(1) forges a prescription or increases the prescribed quantity of a dangerous drug in a prescription;

(2) issues a prescription bearing a forged or fictitious signature;

(3) obtains or attempts to obtain a dangerous drug by using a forged, fictitious, or altered prescription;

(4) obtains or attempts to obtain a dangerous drug by means of a fictitious or fraudulent telephone call; or

(5) possesses a dangerous drug obtained by a forged, fictitious, or altered prescription or by means of a fictitious or fraudulent telephone call.

(b) An offense under this section is a Class B misdemeanor unless it is shown on the trial of the defendant that the defendant has previously been convicted of an offense under this chapter, in which event the offense is a Class A misdemeanor.

(Enacted by Acts 1989, 71st Leg., ch. 678 (H.B. 2136), § 1, effective September 1, 1989.)

### Sec. 483.046. Failure to Retain Prescription.

(a) A pharmacist commits an offense if the pharmacist:

(1) delivers a dangerous drug under a prescription; and

(2) fails to retain the prescription as required by Section 483.023.

(b) An offense under this section is a Class B misdemeanor unless it is shown on the trial of the defendant that the defendant has previously been convicted of an offense under this chapter, in which event the offense is a Class A misdemeanor.

(Enacted by Acts 1989, 71st Leg., ch. 678 (H.B. 2136), § 1, effective September 1, 1989.)

## Sec. 483.047. Refilling Prescription Without Authorization.

(a) Except as authorized by Subsection (b), a pharmacist commits an offense if the pharmacist refills a prescription unless:

(1) the prescription contains an authorization by the practitioner for the refilling of the prescription, and the pharmacist refills the prescription in the manner provided by the authorization; or

(2) at the time of refilling the prescription, the pharmacist is authorized to do so by the practitioner who issued the prescription.

(b) A pharmacist may exercise his professional judgment in refilling a prescription for a dangerous drug without the authorization of the prescribing practitioner provided:

(1) failure to refill the prescription might result in an interruption of a therapeutic regimen or create patient suffering;

(2) either:

(A) a natural or manmade disaster has occurred which prohibits the pharmacist from being able to contact the practitioner; or

(B) the pharmacist is unable to contact the practitioner after reasonable effort;

(3) the quantity of drug dispensed does not exceed a 72-hour supply;

(4) the pharmacist informs the patient or the patient's agent at the time of dispensing that the refill is being provided without such authorization and that authorization of the practitioner is required for future refills; and

(5) the pharmacist informs the practitioner of the emergency refill at the earliest reasonable time.

(c) An offense under this section is a Class B misdemeanor unless it is shown on the trial of the defendant that the defendant has previously been convicted under this chapter, in which event the offense is a Class A misdemeanor.

(Enacted by Acts 1989, 71st Leg., ch. 678 (H.B. 2136), § 1, effective September 1, 1989; am. Acts 1993, 73rd Leg., ch. 789 (S.B. 472), § 22, effective September 1, 1993.)

## Sec. 483.048. Unauthorized Communication of Prescription.

(a) An agent of a practitioner commits an offense if the agent communicates by telephone a prescription unless the agent is designated in writing under Section 483.022 as authorized by the practitioner to communicate prescriptions by telephone.

(b) An offense under this section is a Class B misdemeanor unless it is shown on the trial of the defendant that the defendant has previously been convicted of an offense under this chapter, in which event the offense is a Class A misdemeanor.

(Enacted by Acts 1989, 71st Leg., ch. 678 (H.B. 2136), § 1, effective September 1, 1989.)

## Sec. 483.049. Failure to Maintain Records.

(a) A person commits an offense if the person is required to maintain a record under Section 483.023 or 483.024 and the person fails to maintain the record in the manner required by those sections.

(b) An offense under this section is a Class B misdemeanor unless it is shown on the trial of the defendant that the defendant has previously been convicted of an offense under this chapter, in which event the offense is a Class A misdemeanor.

(Enacted by Acts 1989, 71st Leg., ch. 678 (H.B. 2136), § 1, effective September 1, 1989.)

## Sec. 483.050. Refusal to Permit Inspection.

(a) A person commits an offense if the person is required to permit an inspection authorized by Section 483.025 and fails to permit the inspection in the manner required by that section.

(b) An offense under this section is a Class B misdemeanor unless it is shown on the trial of the defendant that the defendant has previously been convicted of an offense under this chapter, in which event the offense is a Class A misdemeanor.

(Enacted by Acts 1989, 71st Leg., ch. 678 (H.B. 2136), § 1, effective September 1, 1989.)

## Sec. 483.051. Using or Revealing Trade Secret.

(a) A person commits an offense if the person uses for the person's advantage or reveals to another person, other than to an officer or employee of the board or to a court in a judicial proceeding relevant to this chapter, information relating to dangerous drugs required to be kept under this chapter, if that information concerns a method or process subject to protection as a trade secret.

(b) An offense under this section is a Class B misdemeanor unless it is shown on the trial of the defendant that the defendant has previously been convicted of an offense under this chapter, in which event the offense is a Class A misdemeanor.

(Enacted by Acts 1989, 71st Leg., ch. 678 (H.B. 2136), § 1, effective September 1, 1989.)

### Sec. 483.052.   Violation of Other Provision.

(a) A person commits an offense if the person violates a provision of this chapter other than a provision for which a specific offense is otherwise described by this chapter.

(b) An offense under this section is a Class B misdemeanor, unless it is shown on the trial of the defendant that the defendant has previously been convicted of an offense under this chapter, in which event the offense is a Class A misdemeanor.

(Enacted by Acts 1989, 71st Leg., ch. 678 (H.B. 2136), § 1, effective September 1, 1989.)

### Sec. 483.053.   Preparatory Offenses.

Title 4, Penal Code, applies to an offense under this subchapter.

(Enacted by Acts 1995, 74th Leg., ch. 318 (S.B. 15), § 40, effective September 1, 1995.)

## SUBCHAPTER D
## CRIMINAL AND CIVIL PROCEDURE

### Sec. 483.071.   Exceptions; Burden of Proof.

(a) In a complaint, information, indictment, or other action or proceeding brought for the enforcement of this chapter, the state is not required to negate an exception, excuse, proviso, or exemption contained in this chapter.

(b) The defendant has the burden of proving the exception, excuse, proviso, or exemption.

(Enacted by Acts 1989, 71st Leg., ch. 678 (H.B. 2136), § 1, effective September 1, 1989.)

### Sec. 483.072.   Uncorroborated Testimony.

A conviction under this chapter may be obtained on the uncorroborated testimony of a party to the offense.

(Enacted by Acts 1989, 71st Leg., ch. 678 (H.B. 2136), § 1, effective September 1, 1989.)

### Sec. 483.073.   Search Warrant.

A peace officer may apply for a search warrant to search for dangerous drugs possessed in violation of this chapter. The peace officer must apply for and execute the search warrant in the manner prescribed by the Code of Criminal Procedure.

(Enacted by Acts 1989, 71st Leg., ch. 678 (H.B. 2136), § 1, effective September 1, 1989.)

### Sec. 483.074.   Seizure and Destruction.

(a) A dangerous drug that is manufactured, sold, or possessed in violation of this chapter is contraband and may be seized by an employee of the board or by a peace officer authorized to enforce this chapter and charged with that duty.

(b) If a dangerous drug is seized under Subsection (a), the board may direct an employee of the board or an authorized peace officer to destroy the drug. The employee or authorized peace officer directed to destroy the drug must act in the presence of another employee of the board or authorized peace officer and shall destroy the drug in any manner designated as appropriate by the board.

(c) Before the dangerous drug is destroyed, an inventory of the drug must be prepared. The inventory must be accompanied by a statement that the dangerous drug is being destroyed at the direction of the board, by an employee of the board or an authorized peace officer, and in the presence of another employee of the board or authorized peace officer. The statement must also contain the names of the persons in attendance at the time of destruction, state the capacity in which each of those persons acts, be signed by those persons, and be sworn to by those persons that the statement is correct. The statement shall be filed with the board.

(Enacted by Acts 1989, 71st Leg., ch. 678 (H.B. 2136), § 1, effective September 1, 1989; am. Acts 1991, 72nd Leg., ch. 237 (H.B. 1495), § 12, effective September 1, 1991.)

### Sec. 483.075.   Injunction.

The board may institute an action in its own name to enjoin a violation of this chapter.

(Enacted by Acts 1989, 71st Leg., ch. 678 (H.B. 2136), § 1, effective September 1, 1989.)

### Sec. 483.076.   Legal Representation of Board.

(a) If the board institutes a legal proceeding under this chapter, the board may be represented only by a county attorney, a district attorney, or the attorney general.

(b) The board may not employ private counsel in any legal proceeding instituted by or against the board under this chapter.
(Enacted by Acts 1989, 71st Leg., ch. 678 (H.B. 2136), § 1, effective September 1, 1989.)

## CHAPTER 484
## VOLATILE CHEMICALS
## [REPEALED]

**Sec. 484.001. Definitions [Repealed].**
Repealed by Acts 2001, 77th Leg., ch. 1463 (H.B. 2950), § 4, effective September 1, 2001. (Enacted by Acts 1989, 71st Leg., ch. 678 (H.B. 2136), § 1, effective September 1, 1989.)

**Sec. 484.002. Volatile Chemicals [Repealed].**
Repealed by Acts 2001, 77th Leg., ch. 1463 (H.B. 2950), § 4, effective September 1, 2001, and Acts 2005, 79th Leg., ch. 848 (S.B. 910), § 1, effective June 17, 2005.
(Enacted by Acts 1989, 71st Leg., ch. 678 (H.B. 2136), § 1, effective September 1, 1989; am. Acts 2001, 77th Leg., ch. 459 (H.B. 139), § 2, effective September 1, 2001.)

**Sec. 484.003. Possession and Use; Criminal Penalty [Repealed].**
Repealed by Acts 2001, 77th Leg., ch. 1463 (H.B. 2950), § 4, effective September 1, 2001, and Acts 2005, 79th Leg., ch. 848 (S.B. 910), § 1, effective June 17, 2005.
(Enacted by Acts 1989, 71st Leg., ch. 678 (H.B. 2136), § 1, effective September 1, 1989; am. Acts 2001, 77th Leg., ch. 459 (H.B. 139), § 3, effective September 1, 2001.)

**Sec. 484.004. Inhalant Paraphernalia; Criminal Penalty [Repealed].**
Repealed by Acts 2001, 77th Leg., ch. 1463 (H.B. 2950), § 4, effective September 1, 2001. (Enacted by Acts 1989, 71st Leg., ch. 678 (H.B. 2136), § 1, effective September 1, 1989; am. Acts 1991, 72nd Leg., ch. 14 (H.B. 11), § 202, effective September 1, 1991.)

**Sec. 484.005. Delivery to a Minor; Criminal Penalty [Repealed].**
Repealed by Acts 2001, 77th Leg., ch. 1463 (H.B. 2950), § 4, effective September 1, 2001, and

Acts 2005, 79th Leg., ch. 848 (S.B. 910), § 1, effective June 17, 2005.
(Enacted by Acts 1989, 71st Leg., ch. 678 (H.B. 2136), § 1, effective September 1, 1989; am. Acts 1999, 76th Leg., ch. 684 (H.B. 656), § 1, effective September 1, 1999; am. Acts 2001, 77th Leg., ch. 459 (H.B. 139), § 4, effective September 1, 2001.)

**Sec. 484.006. Proof of Offer to Sell or Deliver [Repealed].**
Repealed by Acts 2001, 77th Leg., ch. 1463 (H.B. 2950), § 4, effective September 1, 2001. (Enacted by Acts 1989, 71st Leg., ch. 678 (H.B. 2136), § 1, effective September 1, 1989.)

**Sec. 484.007. Summary Forfeiture [Repealed].**
Repealed by Acts 2001, 77th Leg., ch. 1463 (H.B. 2950), § 4, effective September 1, 2001. (Enacted by Acts 1991, 72nd Leg., ch. 141 (S.B. 11), § 4, effective September 1, 1989.)

**Sec. 484.008. Preparatory Offenses [Repealed].**
Repealed by Acts 2001, 77th Leg., ch. 1463 (H.B. 2950), § 4, effective September 1, 2001. (Enacted by Acts 1995, 74th Leg., ch. 318 (S.B. 15), § 42, effective September 1, 1995.)

## CHAPTER 485
## ABUSABLE VOLATILE CHEMICALS

### Subchapter A. General Provisions

**Health**

## SUBCHAPTER A
## GENERAL PROVISIONS

### Sec. 485.001.  Definitions.

In this chapter:

(1) "Abusable volatile chemical" means:

(A) a chemical, including aerosol paint, that:

(i) is packaged in a container subject to the labeling requirements concerning precautions against inhalation established under the Federal Hazardous Substances Act (15 U.S.C. Section 1261 et seq.), as amended, and regulations adopted under that Act and is labeled with the statement of principal hazard on the principal display panel "VAPOR HARMFUL" or other labeling requirement subsequently established under that Act or those regulations;

(ii) when inhaled, ingested, or otherwise introduced into a person's body, may:

(a) affect the person's central nervous system;

(b) create or induce in the person a condition of intoxication, hallucination, or elation; or

(c) change, distort, or disturb the person's eyesight, thinking process, balance, or coordination; and

(iii) is not:

(a) a pesticide subject to Chapter 76, Agriculture Code, or to the Federal Environmental Pesticide Control Act of 1972 (7 U.S.C. Section 136 et seq.), as amended;

(b) a food, drug, or cosmetic subject to Chapter 431 or to the Federal Food, Drug, and Cosmetic Act (21 U.S.C. Section 301 et seq.), as amended; or

(c) a beverage subject to the Federal Alcohol Administration Act (27 U.S.C. Section 201 et seq.), as amended; or

(B) nitrous oxide that is not:

(i) a pesticide subject to Chapter 76, Agriculture Code, or to the Federal Environmental Pesticide Control Act of 1972 (7 U.S.C. Section 136 et seq.), as amended;

(ii) a food, drug, or cosmetic subject to Chapter 431 or to the Federal Food, Drug, and Cosmetic Act (21 U.S.C. Section 301 et seq.), as amended; or

(iii) a beverage subject to the Federal Alcohol Administration Act (27 U.S.C. Section 201 et seq.), as amended.

(2) "Aerosol paint" means an aerosolized paint product, including a clear or pigmented lacquer or finish.

(3) "Board" means the Texas Board of Health.

(4) "Commissioner" means the commissioner of health.

(5) "Deliver" means to make the actual or constructive transfer from one person to another of an abusable volatile chemical, regardless of whether there is an agency relationship. The term includes an offer to sell an abusable volatile chemical.

(6) "Delivery" means the act of delivering.

(7) "Department" means the Texas Department of Health.

(8) "Inhalant paraphernalia" means equipment or materials of any kind that are intended for use in inhaling, ingesting, or otherwise introducing into the human body an abusable volatile chemical. The term includes a tube, balloon, bag, fabric, bottle, or other container used to concentrate or hold in suspension an abusable volatile chemical or vapors of the chemical.

(9) "Sell" includes a conveyance, exchange, barter, or trade.

(Enacted by Acts 1989, 71st Leg., ch. 678 (H.B. 2136), § 1, effective September 1, 1989; am. Acts 2001, 77th Leg., ch. 1463 (H.B. 2950), § 2, effective September 1, 2001.)

### Sec. 485.002.  Rules.

The board may adopt rules necessary to comply with any labeling requirements concerning precautions against inhalation of an abusable volatile chemical established under the Federal Hazardous Substances Act (15 U.S.C. Section 1261 et seq.), as amended, or under regulations adopted under that Act.

(Enacted by Acts 2001, 77th Leg., ch. 1463 (H.B. 2950), § 2, effective September 1, 2001.)

Health

## SUBCHAPTER B
## SALES PERMITS AND SIGNS

### Sec. 485.011. Permit Required.

A person may not sell an abusable volatile chemical at retail unless the person or the person's employer holds, at the time of the sale, a volatile chemical sales permit for the location of the sale.

(Enacted by Acts 1989, 71st Leg., ch. 678 (H.B. 2136), § 1, effective September 1, 1989; am. Acts 2001, 77th Leg., ch. 1463 (H.B. 2950), § 2, effective September 1, 2001 (renumbered from Sec. 485.012).)

### Sec. 485.012. Issuance and Renewal of Permit.

(a) To be eligible for the issuance or renewal of a volatile chemical sales permit, a person must:

(1) hold a sales tax permit that has been issued to the person;

(2) complete and return to the department an application as required by the department; and

(3) pay to the department the application fee established under Section 485.013 for each location at which an abusable volatile chemical may be sold by the person holding a volatile chemical sales permit.

(b) The board shall adopt rules as necessary to administer this chapter, including application procedures and procedures by which the department shall give each permit holder reasonable notice of permit expiration and renewal requirements.

(c) The department shall issue or deny a permit and notify the applicant of the department's action not later than the 60th day after the date on which the department receives the complete application and appropriate fee. If the department denies an application, the department shall include in the notice the reasons for the denial.

(d) A permit issued or renewed under this chapter is valid for one year from the date of issuance or renewal.

(e) A permit is not valid if the permit holder has been convicted more than once in the preceding year of an offense committed:

(1) at a location for which the permit is issued; and

(2) under Section 485.031, 485.032, or 485.033.

(f) A permit issued by the department is the property of the department and must be surrendered on demand by the department.

(g) The department shall prepare an annual roster of permit holders.

(h) The department shall monitor and enforce compliance with this chapter.

(Enacted by Acts 1989, 71st Leg., ch. 678 (H.B. 2136), § 1, effective September 1, 1989; am. Acts 1991, 72nd Leg., ch. 14 (S.B. 404), § 203, effective September 1, 1991; am. Acts 2001, 77th Leg., ch. 1463 (H.B. 2950), § 2, effective September 1, 2001 (renumbered from Sec. 485.013).)

### Sec. 485.013. Fee.

The board by rule may establish fees in amounts not to exceed $25 for the issuance of a permit under this chapter.

(Enacted by Acts 2001, 77th Leg., ch. 1463 (H.B. 2950), § 2, effective September 1, 2001.)

### Sec. 485.014. Permit Available for Inspection.

A permit holder must have the volatile chemical sales permit or a copy of the permit available for inspection by the public at each location where the permit holder sells an abusable volatile chemical.

(Enacted by Acts 1989, 71st Leg., ch. 678 (H.B. 2136), § 1, effective September 1, 1989; am. Acts 2001, 77th Leg., ch. 1463 (H.B. 2950), § 2, effective September 1, 2001.)

### Sec. 485.015. Refusal to Issue or Renew Permit.

A proceeding for the failure to issue or renew a volatile chemical sales permit under Section 485.012 or for an appeal from that proceeding is governed by the contested case provisions of Chapter 2001, Government Code.

(Enacted by Acts 1989, 71st Leg., ch. 678 (H.B. 2136), § 1, effective September 1, 1989; am. Acts 1995, 74th Leg., ch. 76 (S.B. 959), § 5.95(49), effective September 1, 1995; am. Acts 2001, 77th Leg., ch. 1463 (H.B. 2950), § 2, effective September 1, 2001.)

### Sec. 485.016. Disposition of Funds; Education and Prevention Programs.

(a) The department shall account for all amounts received under Section 485.013 and send those amounts to the comptroller.

(b) The comptroller shall deposit the amounts received under Subsection (a) in the state treasury to the credit of the general revenue fund to be used only by the department to:

(1) administer, monitor, and enforce this chapter; and

Health

(2) finance statewide education projects concerning the hazards of abusable volatile chemicals and the prevention of inhalant abuse.
(Enacted by Acts 1989, 71st Leg., ch. 678 (H.B. 2136), § 1, effective September 1, 1989; am. Acts 1991, 72nd Leg., ch. 14 (S.B. 404), § 204, effective September 1, 1991; am. Acts 2001, 77th Leg., ch. 1463 (H.B. 2950), § 2, effective September 1, 2001.)

## Sec. 485.017.  Signs.

A business establishment that sells an abusable volatile chemical at retail shall display a conspicuous sign, in English and Spanish, that states the following:

It is unlawful for a person to sell or deliver an abusable volatile chemical to a person under 18 years of age. Except in limited situations, such an offense is a state jail felony.

It is also unlawful for a person to abuse a volatile chemical by inhaling, ingesting, applying, using, or possessing with intent to inhale, ingest, apply, or use a volatile chemical in a manner designed to affect the central nervous system. Such an offense is a Class B misdemeanor.
(Enacted by Acts 1989, 71st Leg., ch. 678 (H.B. 2136), § 1, effective September 1, 1989; am. Acts 2001, 77th Leg., ch. 1463 (H.B. 2950), § 2, effective September 1, 2001.)

## Sec. 485.018.  Prohibited Ordinance and Rule.

(a) A political subdivision or an agency of this state may not enact an ordinance or rule that requires a business establishment to display an abusable volatile chemical, other than aerosol paint, in a manner that makes the chemical accessible to patrons of the business only with the assistance of personnel of the business.

(b) This section does not apply to an ordinance or rule that was enacted before September 1, 1989.
(Enacted by Acts 1991, 72nd Leg., ch. 14 (S.B. 404), § 205, effective September 1, 1991; am. Acts 2001, 77th Leg., ch. 1463 (H.B. 2950), § 2, effective September 1, 2001; am. Acts 2009, 81st Leg., ch. 1130 (H.B. 2086), § 28, effective September 1, 2009.)

## Sec. 485.019.  Restriction of Access to Aerosol Paint.

(a) A business establishment that holds a permit under Section 485.012 and that displays aerosol paint shall display the paint:

(1) in a place that is in the line of sight of a cashier or in the line of sight from a workstation normally continuously occupied during business hours;

(2) in a manner that makes the paint accessible to a patron of the business establishment only with the assistance of an employee of the establishment; or

(3) in an area electronically protected, or viewed by surveillance equipment that is monitored, during business hours.

(b) This section does not apply to a business establishment that has in place a computerized checkout system at the point of sale for merchandise that alerts the cashier that a person purchasing aerosol paint must be over 18 years of age.

(c) A court may issue a warning to a business establishment or impose a civil penalty of $50 on the business establishment for a first violation of this section. After receiving a warning or penalty for the first violation, the business establishment is liable to the state for a civil penalty of $100 for each subsequent violation.

(d) For the third violation of this section in a calendar year, a court may issue an injunction prohibiting the business establishment from selling aerosol paint for a period of not more than two years. A business establishment that violates the injunction is liable to the state for a civil penalty of $100, in addition to any other penalty authorized by law, for each day the violation continues.

(e) If a business establishment fails to pay a civil penalty under this section, the court may issue an injunction prohibiting the establishment from selling aerosol paint until the establishment pays the penalty, attorney's fees, and court costs.

(f) The district or county attorney for the county in which a violation of this section is alleged to have occurred, or the attorney general, if requested by the district or county attorney for that county, may file suit for the issuance of a warning, the collection of a penalty, or the issuance of an injunction.

(g) A penalty collected under this section shall be sent to the comptroller for deposit in the state treasury to the credit of the general revenue fund.

(h) This section applies only to a business establishment that is located in a county with a population of 75,000 or more.
(Enacted by Acts 1997, 75th Leg., ch. 593 (S.B. 758), § 4, effective September 1, 1997; am. Acts 2001, 77th Leg., ch. 1463 (H.B. 2950), § 2, effective September 1, 2001.)

Health

## SUBCHAPTER C
## CRIMINAL PENALTIES

### Sec. 485.031. Possession and Use.

(a) A person commits an offense if the person inhales, ingests, applies, uses, or possesses an abusable volatile chemical with intent to inhale, ingest, apply, or use the chemical in a manner:

(1) contrary to directions for use, cautions, or warnings appearing on a label of a container of the chemical; and

(2) designed to:

(A) affect the person's central nervous system;

(B) create or induce a condition of intoxication, hallucination, or elation; or

(C) change, distort, or disturb the person's eyesight, thinking process, balance, or coordination.

(b) An offense under this section is a Class B misdemeanor.

(Enacted by Acts 1989, 71st Leg., ch. 678 (H.B. 2136), § 1, effective September 1, 1989; am. Acts 2001, 77th Leg., ch. 1463 (H.B. 2950), § 2, effective September 1, 2001.)

### Sec. 485.032. Delivery to a Minor.

(a) A person commits an offense if the person knowingly delivers an abusable volatile chemical to a person who is younger than 18 years of age.

(b) It is a defense to prosecution under this section that:

(1) the abusable volatile chemical that was delivered contains additive material that effectively discourages intentional abuse by inhalation; or

(2) the person making the delivery is not the manufacturer of the chemical and the manufacturer of the chemical failed to label the chemical with the statement of principal hazard on the principal display panel "VAPOR HARMFUL" or other labeling requirement subsequently established under the Federal Hazardous Substances Act (15 U.S.C. Section 1261 et seq.), as amended, or regulations subsequently adopted under that Act.

(c) It is an affirmative defense to prosecution under this section that:

(1) the person making the delivery is an adult having supervisory responsibility over the person younger than 18 years of age and:

(A) the adult permits the use of the abusable volatile chemical only under the adult's direct supervision and in the adult's presence and only for its intended purpose; and

(B) the adult removes the chemical from the person younger than 18 years of age on completion of that use; or

(2) the person to whom the abusable volatile chemical was delivered presented to the defendant an apparently valid Texas driver's license or an identification certificate, issued by the Department of Public Safety of the State of Texas and containing a physical description consistent with the person's appearance, that purported to establish that the person was 18 years of age or older.

(d) Except as provided by Subsections (e) and (f), an offense under this section is a state jail felony.

(e) An offense under this section is a Class B misdemeanor if it is shown on the trial of the defendant that at the time of the delivery the defendant or the defendant's employer held a volatile chemical sales permit for the location of the sale.

(f) An offense under this section is a Class A misdemeanor if it is shown on the trial of the defendant that at the time of the delivery the defendant or the defendant's employer:

(1) did not hold a volatile chemical sales permit but did hold a sales tax permit for the location of the sale; and

(2) had not been convicted previously under this section for an offense committed after January 1, 1988.

(Enacted by Acts 1989, 71st Leg., ch. 678 (H.B. 2136), § 1, effective September 1, 1989; am. Acts 1993, 73rd Leg., ch. 900 (S.B. 1067), § 2.06, effective September 1, 1994; am. Acts 2001, 77th Leg., ch. 1463 (H.B. 2950), § 2, effective September 1, 2001 (renumbered from Sec. 485.033).)

### Sec. 485.033. Inhalant Paraphernalia.

(a) A person commits an offense if the person knowingly uses or possesses with intent to use inhalant paraphernalia to inhale, ingest, or otherwise introduce into the human body an abusable volatile chemical in violation of Section 485.031.

(b) A person commits an offense if the person:

(1) knowingly:

(A) delivers or sells inhalant paraphernalia;

(B) possesses, with intent to deliver or sell, inhalant paraphernalia; or

(C) manufactures, with intent to deliver or sell, inhalant paraphernalia; and

(2) at the time of the act described by Subdivision (1), knows that the person who re-

ceives or is intended to receive the paraphernalia intends that it be used to inhale, ingest, apply, use, or otherwise introduce into the human body a volatile chemical in violation of Section 485.031.

(c) An offense under Subsection (a) is a Class B misdemeanor, and an offense under Subsection (b) is a Class A misdemeanor.

(Enacted by Acts 1989, 71st Leg., ch. 678 (H.B. 2136), § 1, effective September 1, 1989; am. Acts 1991, 72nd Leg., ch. 14 (S.B. 404), § 206, effective September 1, 1991; am. Acts 2001, 77th Leg., ch. 1463 (H.B. 2950), § 2, effective September 1, 2001 (renumbered from Sec. 485.034).)

### Sec. 485.034.   Failure to Post Sign.

(a) A person commits an offense if the person sells an abusable volatile chemical in a business establishment and the person does not display the sign required by Section 485.017.

(b) An offense under this section is a Class C misdemeanor.

(Enacted by Acts 1989, 71st Leg., ch. 678 (H.B. 2136), § 1, effective September 1, 1989; am. Acts 2001, 77th Leg., ch. 1463 (H.B. 2950), § 2, effective September 1, 2001 (renumbered from Sec. 485.035).)

### Sec. 485.035.   Sale Without Permit.

(a) A person commits an offense if the person sells an abusable volatile chemical in violation of Section 485.011 and the purchaser is 18 years of age or older.

(b) An offense under this section is a Class B misdemeanor.

(Enacted by Acts 1989, 71st Leg., ch. 678 (H.B. 2136), § 1, effective September 1, 1989; am. Acts 2001, 77th Leg., ch. 1463 (H.B. 2950), § 2, effective September 1, 2001 (renumbered from Sec. 485.036).)

### Sec. 485.036.   Proof of Offer to Sell.

Proof of an offer to sell an abusable volatile chemical must be corroborated by a person other than the offeree or by evidence other than a statement of the offeree.

(Enacted by Acts 1989, 71st Leg., ch. 678 (H.B. 2136), § 1, effective September 1, 1989; am. Acts 2001, 77th Leg., ch. 1463 (H.B. 2950), § 2, effective September 1, 2001 (renumbered from Sec. 485.037).)

### Sec. 485.037.   Summary Forfeiture.

An abusable volatile chemical or inhalant paraphernalia seized as a result of an offense under this chapter is subject to summary forfeiture and to destruction or disposition in the same manner as controlled substance property under Subchapter E, Chapter 481.

(Enacted by Acts 1991, 72nd Leg., ch. 141 (S.B. 11), § 5, effective September 1, 1991; am. Acts 2001, 77th Leg., ch. 1463 (H.B. 2950), § 2, effective September 1, 2001 (renumbered from Sec. 485.038).)

### Sec. 485.038.   Preparatory Offenses.

Title 4, Penal Code, applies to an offense under this subchapter.

(Enacted by Acts 1995, 74th Leg., ch. 318 (S.B. 15), § 43, effective September 1, 1995; am. Acts 2001, 77th Leg., ch. 1463 (H.B. 2950), § 2, effective September 1, 2001 (renumbered from Sec. 485.039).)

### Sec. 485.039.   Preparatory Offense [Renumbered].

Renumbered to Tex. Health & Safety Code § 485.038 by Acts 2001, 77th Leg., ch. 1463 (H.B. 2950), § 2, effective September 1, 2001.

(Enacted by Acts 1995, 74th Leg., ch. 318 (S.B. 15), § 43, effective September 1, 1995.)

## SUBCHAPTER D
## ADMINISTRATIVE PENALTY

### Sec. 485.101.   Imposition of Penalty.

(a) The department may impose an administrative penalty on a person who sells abusable glue or aerosol paint at retail who violates this chapter or a rule or order adopted under this chapter.

(b) A penalty collected under this subchapter shall be deposited in the state treasury in the general revenue fund.

(Enacted by Acts 1999, 76th Leg., ch. 1411 (H.B. 2085), § 6.01, effective September 1, 1999.)

### Sec. 485.102.   Amount of Penalty.

(a) The amount of the penalty may not exceed $1,000 for each violation, and each day a violation continues or occurs is a separate violation for purposes of imposing a penalty. The total amount of the penalty assessed for a violation continuing or occurring on separate days under this subsection may not exceed $5,000.

(b) The amount shall be based on:

(1) the seriousness of the violation, including the nature, circumstances, extent, and gravity of the violation;

Health

(2) the threat to health or safety caused by the violation;

(3) the history of previous violations;

(4) the amount necessary to deter a future violation;

(5) whether the violator demonstrated good faith, including when applicable whether the violator made good faith efforts to correct the violation; and

(6) any other matter that justice may require.

(Enacted by Acts 1999, 76th Leg., ch. 1411 (H.B. 2085), § 6.01, effective September 1, 1999.)

### Sec. 485.103. Report and Notice of Violation and Penalty.

(a) If the department initially determines that a violation occurred, the department shall give written notice of the report by certified mail to the person.

(b) The notice must:

(1) include a brief summary of the alleged violation;

(2) state the amount of the recommended penalty; and

(3) inform the person of the person's right to a hearing on the occurrence of the violation, the amount of the penalty, or both.

(Enacted by Acts 1999, 76th Leg., ch. 1411 (H.B. 2085), § 6.01, effective September 1, 1999.)

### Sec. 485.104. Penalty to Be Paid or Hearing Requested.

(a) Within 20 days after the date the person receives the notice sent under Section 485.103, the person in writing may:

(1) accept the determination and recommended penalty of the department; or

(2) make a request for a hearing on the occurrence of the violation, the amount of the penalty, or both.

(b) If the person accepts the determination and recommended penalty or if the person fails to respond to the notice, the commissioner by order shall approve the determination and impose the recommended penalty.

(Enacted by Acts 1999, 76th Leg., ch. 1411 (H.B. 2085), § 6.01, effective September 1, 1999.)

### Sec. 485.105. Hearing.

(a) If the person requests a hearing, the commissioner shall refer the matter to the State Office of Administrative Hearings, which shall promptly set a hearing date and give written notice of the time and place of the hearing to the person. An administrative law judge of the State Office of Administrative Hearings shall conduct the hearing.

(b) The administrative law judge shall make findings of fact and conclusions of law and promptly issue to the commissioner a proposal for a decision about the occurrence of the violation and the amount of a proposed penalty.

(Enacted by Acts 1999, 76th Leg., ch. 1411 (H.B. 2085), § 6.01, effective September 1, 1999.)

### Sec. 485.106. Decision by Commissioner.

(a) Based on the findings of fact, conclusions of law, and proposal for a decision, the commissioner by order may:

(1) find that a violation occurred and impose a penalty; or

(2) find that a violation did not occur.

(b) The notice of the commissioner's order under Subsection (a) that is sent to the person in accordance with Chapter 2001, Government Code, must include a statement of the right of the person to judicial review of the order.

(Enacted by Acts 1999, 76th Leg., ch. 1411 (H.B. 2085), § 6.01, effective September 1, 1999.)

### Sec. 485.107. Options Following Decision: Pay or Appeal.

Within 30 days after the date the order of the commissioner under Section 485.106 that imposes an administrative penalty becomes final, the person shall:

(1) pay the penalty; or

(2) file a petition for judicial review of the commissioner's order contesting the occurrence of the violation, the amount of the penalty, or both.

(Enacted by Acts 1999, 76th Leg., ch. 1411 (H.B. 2085), § 6.01, effective September 1, 1999.)

### Sec. 485.108. Stay of Enforcement of Penalty.

(a) Within the 30-day period prescribed by Section 485.107, a person who files a petition for judicial review may:

(1) stay enforcement of the penalty by:

(A) paying the penalty to the court for placement in an escrow account; or

(B) giving the court a supersedeas bond approved by the court that:

(i) is for the amount of the penalty; and

(ii) is effective until all judicial review of the commissioner's order is final; or

(2) request the court to stay enforcement of the penalty by:

    (A) filing with the court a sworn affidavit of the person stating that the person is financially unable to pay the penalty and is financially unable to give the supersedeas bond; and

    (B) sending a copy of the affidavit to the commissioner by certified mail.

(b) If the commissioner receives a copy of an affidavit under Subsection (a)(2), the commissioner may file with the court, within five days after the date the copy is received, a contest to the affidavit. The court shall hold a hearing on the facts alleged in the affidavit as soon as practicable and shall stay the enforcement of the penalty on finding that the alleged facts are true. The person who files an affidavit has the burden of proving that the person is financially unable to pay the penalty or to give a supersedeas bond.
(Enacted by Acts 1999, 76th Leg., ch. 1411 (H.B. 2085), § 6.01, effective September 1, 1999.)

### Sec. 485.109. Collection of Penalty.

(a) If the person does not pay the penalty and the enforcement of the penalty is not stayed, the penalty may be collected.

(b) The attorney general may sue to collect the penalty.
(Enacted by Acts 1999, 76th Leg., ch. 1411 (H.B. 2085), § 6.01, effective September 1, 1999.)

### Sec. 485.110. Decision by Court.

(a) If the court sustains the finding that a violation occurred, the court may uphold or reduce the amount of the penalty and order the person to pay the full or reduced amount of the penalty.

(b) If the court does not sustain the finding that a violation occurred, the court shall order that a penalty is not owed.
(Enacted by Acts 1999, 76th Leg., ch. 1411 (H.B. 2085), § 6.01, effective September 1, 1999.)

### Sec. 485.111. Remittance of Penalty and Interest.

(a) If the person paid the penalty and if the amount of the penalty is reduced or the penalty is not upheld by the court, the court shall order, when the court's judgment becomes final, that the appropriate amount plus accrued interest be remitted to the person within 30 days after the date that the judgment of the court becomes final.

(b) The interest accrues at the rate charged on loans to depository institutions by the New York Federal Reserve Bank.

(c) The interest shall be paid for the period beginning on the date the penalty is paid and ending on the date the penalty is remitted.
(Enacted by Acts 1999, 76th Leg., ch. 1411 (H.B. 2085), § 6.01, effective September 1, 1999.)

### Sec. 485.112. Release of Bond.

(a) If the person gave a supersedeas bond and the penalty is not upheld by the court, the court shall order, when the court's judgment becomes final, the release of the bond.

(b) If the person gave a supersedeas bond and the amount of the penalty is reduced, the court shall order the release of the bond after the person pays the reduced amount.
(Enacted by Acts 1999, 76th Leg., ch. 1411 (H.B. 2085), § 6.01, effective September 1, 1999.)

### Sec. 485.113. Administrative Procedure.

A proceeding to impose the penalty is considered to be a contested case under Chapter 2001, Government Code.
(Enacted by Acts 1999, 76th Leg., ch. 1411 (H.B. 2085), § 6.01, effective September 1, 1999.)

# CHAPTER 486
## OVER-THE-COUNTER SALES OF EPHEDRINE, PSEUDOEPHEDRINE, AND NORPSEUDOEPHEDRINE

### Subchapter A. General Provisions

## SUBCHAPTER A
## GENERAL PROVISIONS

### Sec. 486.001. Definitions.

(a) In this chapter:

(1) "Commissioner" means the commissioner of state health services.

(2) "Council" means the State Health Services Council.

(3) "Department" means the Department of State Health Services.

(4) "Ephedrine," "pseudoephedrine," and "norpseudoephedrine" mean any compound, mixture, or preparation containing any detectable amount of that substance, including its salts, optical isomers, and salts of optical isomers. The term does not include any compound, mixture, or preparation that is in liquid, liquid capsule, or liquid gel capsule form.

(5) "Sale" includes a conveyance, exchange, barter, or trade.

(6) "Real-time electronic logging system" means a system intended to be used by law enforcement agencies and pharmacies or other business establishments that:

(A) is installed, operated, and maintained free of any one-time or recurring charge to the business establishment or to the state;

(B) is able to communicate in real time with similar systems operated in other states and similar systems containing information submitted by more than one state;

(C) complies with the security policy of the Criminal Justice Information Services division of the Federal Bureau of Investigation;

(D) complies with information exchange standards adopted by the National Information Exchange Model;

(E) uses a mechanism to prevent the completion of a sale of a product containing ephedrine, pseudoephedrine, or norpseudoephedrine that would violate state or federal law regarding the purchase of a product containing those substances; and

(F) is equipped with an override of the mechanism described in Paragraph (E) that:

(i) may be activated by an employee of a business establishment; and

(ii) creates a record of each activation of the override.

(b) A term that is used in this chapter but is not defined by Subsection (a) has the meaning assigned by Section 481.002.

(Enacted by Acts 2005, 79th Leg., ch. 282 (H.B. 164), § 9, effective August 1, 2005; am. Acts 2011, 82nd Leg., ch. 742 (H.B. 1137), § 1, effective September 1, 2011.)

### Sec. 486.002. Applicability.

This chapter does not apply to the sale of any product dispensed or delivered by a pharmacist according to a prescription issued by a practitioner for a valid medical purpose and in the course of professional practice.

(Enacted by Acts 2005, 79th Leg., ch. 282 (H.B. 164), § 9, effective August 1, 2005.)

### Sec. 486.003. Rules.

The council shall adopt rules necessary to implement and enforce this chapter.

(Enacted by Acts 2005, 79th Leg., ch. 282 (H.B. 164), § 9, effective August 1, 2005.)

### Sec. 486.004. Fees.

(a) The department shall collect fees for:

(1) the issuance of a certificate of authority under this chapter; and

(2) an inspection performed in enforcing this chapter and rules adopted under this chapter.

(b) The commissioner by rule shall set the fees in amounts that allow the department to recover the biennial expenditures of state funds by the department in:

(1) reviewing applications for the issuance of a certificate of authority under this chapter;

(2) issuing certificates of authority under this chapter;

(3) inspecting and auditing a business establishment that is issued a certificate of authority under this chapter; and

(4) otherwise implementing enforcing this chapter.

(c) Fees collected under this section shall be deposited to the credit of a special account in the general revenue fund and appropriated to the department to implement and enforce this chapter.

Health

(Enacted by Acts 2005, 79th Leg., ch. 282 (H.B. 164), § 9, effective August 1, 2005.)

### Sec. 486.005. Statewide Application and Uniformity.

(a) To ensure uniform and equitable implementation and enforcement throughout this state, this chapter constitutes the whole field of regulation regarding over-the-counter sales of products that contain ephedrine, pseudoephedrine, or norpseudoephedrine.

(b) This chapter preempts and supersedes a local ordinance, rule, or regulation adopted by a political subdivision of this state pertaining to over-the-counter sales of products that contain ephedrine, pseudoephedrine, or norpseudoephedrine.

(c) This section does not preclude a political subdivision from imposing administrative sanctions on the holder of a business or professional license or permit issued by the political subdivision who engages in conduct that violates this chapter.

(Enacted by Acts 2005, 79th Leg., ch. 282 (H.B. 164), § 9, effective August 1, 2005.)

## SUBCHAPTER B
## OVER-THE-COUNTER SALES

### Sec. 486.011. Sales by Pharmacies.

A business establishment that operates a pharmacy licensed by the Texas State Board of Pharmacy may engage in over-the-counter sales of ephedrine, pseudoephedrine, and norpseudoephedrine.

(Enacted by Acts 2005, 79th Leg., ch. 282 (H.B. 164), § 9, effective August 1, 2005.)

### Sec. 486.012. Sales by Establishments Other Than Pharmacies; Certificate of Authority.

(a) A business establishment that does not operate a pharmacy licensed by the Texas State Board of Pharmacy may engage in over-the-counter sales of ephedrine, pseudoephedrine, or norpseudoephedrine only if the establishment holds a certificate of authority issued under this section.

(b) The department may issue a certificate of authority to engage in over-the-counter sales of ephedrine, pseudoephedrine, and norpseudoephedrine to a business establishment that does not operate a pharmacy licensed by the Texas State Board of Pharmacy if the establishment:

(1) applies to the department for the certificate in accordance with department rule; and

(2) complies with the requirements established by the department for issuance of a certificate.

(c) The department by rule shall establish requirements for the issuance of a certificate of authority under this section. The rules must include a consideration by the department of whether the establishment:

(1) complies with the requirements of the Texas State Board of Pharmacy for the issuance of a license to operate a pharmacy;

(2) sells a wide variety of healthcare products; and

(3) employs sales techniques and other measures designed to deter the theft of products containing ephedrine, pseudoephedrine, or norpseudoephedrine and other items used in the manufacture of methamphetamine.

(d) The department may inspect or audit a business establishment that is issued a certificate of authority under this section at any time the department determines necessary.

(Enacted by Acts 2005, 79th Leg., ch. 282 (H.B. 164), § 9, effective August 1, 2005.)

### Sec. 486.013. Restriction of Access to Ephedrine, Pseudoephedrine, and Norpseudoephedrine.

A business establishment that engages in over-the-counter sales of products containing ephedrine, pseudoephedrine, or norpseudoephedrine shall:

(1) if the establishment operates a pharmacy licensed by the Texas State Board of Pharmacy, maintain those products:

(A) behind the pharmacy counter; or

(B) in a locked case within 30 feet and in a direct line of sight from a pharmacy counter staffed by an employee of the establishment; or

(2) if the establishment does not operate a pharmacy licensed by the Texas State Board of Pharmacy, maintain those products:

(A) behind a sales counter; or

(B) in a locked case within 30 feet and in a direct line of sight from a sales counter continuously staffed by an employee of the establishment.

Health

(Enacted by Acts 2005, 79th Leg., ch. 282 (H.B. 164), § 9, effective August 1, 2005.)

### Sec. 486.014. Prerequisites to and Restrictions on Sale.

(a) Before completing an over-the-counter sale of a product containing ephedrine, pseudoephedrine, or norpseudoephedrine, a business establishment that engages in those sales shall:

(1) require the person making the purchase to:

(A) display a driver's license or other form of government-issued identification containing the person's photograph and indicating that the person is 16 years of age or older; and

(B) sign for the purchase;

(2) make a record of the sale, including the name and date of birth of the person making the purchase, the address of the purchaser, the date and time of the purchase, the type of identification displayed by the person and the identification number, and the item and number of grams purchased; and

(3) transmit the record of sale as required by Section 486.0141.

(b) A business establishment may not sell to a person who makes over-the-counter purchases of one or more products containing ephedrine, pseudoephedrine, or norpseudoephedrine:

(1) within any calendar day, more than 3.6 grams of ephedrine, pseudoephedrine, norpseudoephedrine, or a combination of those substances; and

(2) within any 30-day period, more than nine grams of ephedrine, pseudoephedrine, norpseudoephedrine, or a combination of those substances.

(Enacted by Acts 2005, 79th Leg., ch. 282 (H.B. 164), § 9, effective August 1, 2005; am. Acts 2011, 82nd Leg., ch. 742 (H.B. 1137), § 2, effective September 1, 2011.)

### Sec. 486.0141. Transmission of Sales Information to Real-Time Electronic Logging System.

(a) Before completing an over-the-counter sale of a product containing ephedrine, pseudoephedrine, or norpseudoephedrine, a business establishment that engages in those sales shall transmit the information in the record made under Section 486.014(a)(2) to a real-time electronic logging system.

(b) Except as provided by Subsection (c), a business establishment may not complete an over-the-counter sale of a product containing ephedrine, pseudoephedrine, or norpseudoephedrine if the real-time electronic logging system returns a report that the completion of the sale would result in the person obtaining an amount of ephedrine, pseudoephedrine, norpseudoephedrine, or a combination of those substances greater than the amount described by Section 486.014(b), regardless of whether all or some of the products previously obtained by the buyer were sold at the establishment or another business establishment.

(c) An employee of a business establishment may complete a sale prohibited by Subsection (b) by using the override mechanism described by Section 486.001(a)(6)(F) only if the employee has a reasonable fear of imminent bodily injury or death from the person attempting to obtain ephedrine, pseudoephedrine, or norpseudoephedrine.

(d) On request of the Department of Public Safety, the administrators of a real-time electronic logging system shall make available to the department a copy of each record of an over-the-counter sale of a product containing ephedrine, pseudoephedrine, or norpseudoephedrine that is submitted by a business establishment located in this state.

(Enacted by Acts 2011, 82nd Leg., ch. 742 (H.B. 1137), § 3, effective September 1, 2011.)

### Sec. 486.0142. Temporary Exemption.

(a) On application by a business establishment that operates a pharmacy and engages in over-the-counter sales of products containing ephedrine, pseudoephedrine, or norpseudoephedrine as authorized by Section 486.011, the State Board of Pharmacy may grant that business establishment a temporary exemption, not to exceed 180 days, from the requirement of using a real-time electronic logging system under this chapter.

(b) On application by a business establishment that engages in over-the-counter sales of products containing ephedrine, pseudoephedrine, or norpseudoephedrine in accordance with a certificate of authority issued under Section 486.012, the department may grant that business establishment a temporary exemption, not to exceed 180 days, from the requirement of using a real-time electronic logging system under this chapter.

(c) A business establishment granted a temporary exemption under this section must keep records of sales in the same manner required under Section 486.0143 for a business establish-

Health

ment that experiences a mechanical or electronic failure of the real-time electronic logging system.

(d) An exemption granted under this section does not relieve a business establishment of any duty under this chapter other than the duty to use a real-time electronic logging system.
(Enacted by Acts 2011, 82nd Leg., ch. 742 (H.B. 1137), § 3, effective September 1, 2011.)

## Sec. 486.0143.  Written Log or Other Electronic Recordkeeping.

If a business establishment that engages in over-the-counter sales of a product containing ephedrine, pseudoephedrine, or norpseudo-ephedrine experiences a mechanical or electronic failure of the real-time electronic logging system, the business shall:

(1) maintain a written record or an electronic record made by any means that satisfies the requirements of Section 486.014(a)(2); and

(2) enter the information in the real-time electronic logging system as soon as practicable after the system becomes operational.
(Enacted by Acts 2011, 82nd Leg., ch. 742 (H.B. 1137), § 3, effective September 1, 2011.)

## Sec. 486.0144.  Online Portal.

The administrators of a real-time electronic logging system shall provide real-time access to the information in the system to the Department of Public Safety if the department executes a memorandum of understanding with the administrators.
(Enacted by Acts 2011, 82nd Leg., ch. 742 (H.B. 1137), § 3, effective September 1, 2011.)

## Sec. 486.0145.  Limitation on Civil Liability.

A person is not liable for an act done or omission made in compliance with the requirements of Section 486.014 or 486.0141.
(Enacted by Acts 2011, 82nd Leg., ch. 742 (H.B. 1137), § 3, effective September 1, 2011.)

## Sec. 486.0146.  Privacy Protections.

(a) The privacy protections provided an individual under 21 C.F.R. Section 1314.45 apply to information entered or stored in a real-time electronic logging system.

(b) A business establishment that engages in over-the-counter sales of a product containing ephedrine, pseudoephedrine, or norpseudo-ephedrine may disclose information entered or stored in a real-time electronic logging system

only to the United States Drug Enforcement Administration and other federal, state, and local law enforcement agencies.

(c) A business establishment that engages in over-the-counter sales of a product containing ephedrine, pseudoephedrine, or norpseudo-ephedrine may not use information entered or stored in a real-time electronic logging system for any purpose other than for a disclosure authorized by Subsection (b) or to comply with the requirements of this chapter.

(d) Notwithstanding Subsection (c), a business establishment that engages in over-the-counter sales of a product containing ephedrine, pseu-doephedrine, or norpseudoephedrine or an employee or agent of the business establishment is not civilly liable for the release of information entered or stored in a real-time electronic logging system unless the release constitutes negligence, recklessness, or wilful misconduct.
(Enacted by Acts 2011, 82nd Leg., ch. 742 (H.B. 1137), § 3, effective September 1, 2011.)

## Sec. 486.015.  Maintenance of Records.

(a) Except as provided by Subsection (b), a business establishment shall maintain each record made under Section 486.014(a)(2) until at least the second anniversary of the date the record is made and shall make each record available on request by the department or any local, state, or federal law enforcement agency, including the United States Drug Enforcement Administration.

(b) Subsection (a) does not apply to a business establishment that has used a real-time electronic logging system for longer than two years.

(c) A business establishment that has used a real-time electronic logging system for longer than two years shall destroy all paper records maintained under this section unless the destruction is otherwise prohibited by law.
(Enacted by Acts 2005, 79th Leg., ch. 282 (H.B. 164), § 9, effective August 1, 2005; am. Acts 2011, 82nd Leg., ch. 742 (H.B. 1137), § 4, effective September 1, 2011.)

## *SUBCHAPTER C*
## *ADMINISTRATIVE PENALTY*

## Sec. 486.021.  Imposition of Penalty.

The department may impose an administrative penalty on a person who violates this chapter.
(Enacted by Acts 2005, 79th Leg., ch. 282 (H.B. 164), § 9, effective August 1, 2005.)

### Sec. 486.022. Amount of Penalty.

(a) The amount of the penalty may not exceed $1,000 for each violation, and each day a violation continues or occurs is a separate violation for purposes of imposing a penalty. The total amount of the penalty assessed for a violation continuing or occurring on separate days under this subsection may not exceed $20,000.

(b) The amount shall be based on:

(1) the seriousness of the violation, including the nature, circumstances, extent, and gravity of the violation;

(2) the threat to health or safety caused by the violation;

(3) the history of previous violations;

(4) the amount necessary to deter a future violation;

(5) whether the violator demonstrated good faith, including when applicable whether the violator made good faith efforts to correct the violation; and

(6) any other matter that justice may require.

(Enacted by Acts 2005, 79th Leg., ch. 282 (H.B. 164), § 9, effective August 1, 2005.)

### Sec. 486.023. Report and Notice of Violation and Penalty.

(a) If the department initially determines that a violation occurred, the department shall give written notice of the report by certified mail to the person.

(b) The notice must:

(1) include a brief summary of the alleged violation;

(2) state the amount of the recommended penalty; and

(3) inform the person of the person's right to a hearing on the occurrence of the violation, the amount of the penalty, or both.

(Enacted by Acts 2005, 79th Leg., ch. 282 (H.B. 164), § 9, effective August 1, 2005.)

### Sec. 486.024. Penalty to Be Paid or Hearing Requested.

(a) Before the 21st day after the date the person receives notice under Section 486.023, the person in writing may:

(1) accept the determination and recommended penalty; or

(2) make a request for a hearing on the occurrence of the violation, the amount of the penalty, or both.

(b) If the person accepts the determination and recommended penalty or if the person fails to respond to the notice, the commissioner by order shall approve the determination.

(Enacted by Acts 2005, 79th Leg., ch. 282 (H.B. 164), § 9, effective August 1, 2005.)

### Sec. 486.025. Hearing.

(a) If the person requests a hearing, the commissioner shall refer the matter to the State Office of Administrative Hearings, which shall promptly set a hearing date and give written notice of the time and place of the hearing to the person. An administrative law judge of the State Office of Administrative Hearings shall conduct the hearing.

(b) The administrative law judge shall make findings of fact and conclusions of law and promptly issue to the commissioner a proposal for a decision about the occurrence of the violation and the amount of a proposed penalty.

(Enacted by Acts 2005, 79th Leg., ch. 282 (H.B. 164), § 9, effective August 1, 2005.)

### Sec. 486.026. Decision.

(a) Based on the findings of fact, conclusions of law, and proposal for a decision, the commissioner by order may:

(1) find that a violation occurred and impose a penalty; or

(2) find that a violation did not occur.

(b) The notice of the commissioner's order under Subsection (a) that is sent to the person in the manner provided by Chapter 2001, Government Code, must include a statement of the right of the person to judicial review of the order.

(Enacted by Acts 2005, 79th Leg., ch. 282 (H.B. 164), § 9, effective August 1, 2005.)

### Sec. 486.027. Options Following Decision: Pay or Appeal.

Before the 31st day after the date the order under Section 486.026 that imposes an administrative penalty becomes final, the person shall:

(1) pay the penalty; or

(2) file a petition for judicial review of the order contesting the occurrence of the violation, the amount of the penalty, or both.

(Enacted by Acts 2005, 79th Leg., ch. 282 (H.B. 164), § 9, effective August 1, 2005.)

### Sec. 486.028. Stay of Enforcement of Penalty.

(a) Within the period prescribed by Section 486.027, a person who files a petition for judicial review may:

(1) stay enforcement of the penalty by:

(A) paying the amount of the penalty to the court for placement in an escrow account; or

(B) giving the court a supersedeas bond approved by the court that:

(i) is for the amount of the penalty; and

(ii) is effective until all judicial review of the order is final; or

(2) request the court to stay enforcement of the penalty by:

(A) filing with the court an affidavit of the person stating that the person is financially unable to pay the penalty and is financially unable to give the supersedeas bond; and

(B) sending a copy of the affidavit to the commissioner by certified mail.

(b) Following receipt of a copy of an affidavit under Subsection (a)(2), the commissioner may file with the court, before the sixth day after the date of receipt, a contest to the affidavit. The court shall hold a hearing on the facts alleged in the affidavit as soon as practicable and shall stay the enforcement of the penalty on finding that the alleged facts are true. The person who files an affidavit has the burden of proving that the person is financially unable to pay the penalty or to give a supersedeas bond.

(Enacted by Acts 2005, 79th Leg., ch. 282 (H.B. 164), § 9, effective August 1, 2005.)

### Sec. 486.029.   Collection of Penalty.

(a) If the person does not pay the penalty and the enforcement of the penalty is not stayed, the penalty may be collected.

(b) The attorney general may sue to collect the penalty.

(Enacted by Acts 2005, 79th Leg., ch. 282 (H.B. 164), § 9, effective August 1, 2005.)

### Sec. 486.030.   Decision by Court.

(a) If the court sustains the finding that a violation occurred, the court may uphold or reduce the amount of the penalty and order the person to pay the full or reduced amount of the penalty.

(b) If the court does not sustain the finding that a violation occurred, the court shall order that a penalty is not owed.

(Enacted by Acts 2005, 79th Leg., ch. 282 (H.B. 164), § 9, effective August 1, 2005.)

### Sec. 486.031.   Remittance of Penalty and Interest.

(a) If the person paid the penalty and if the amount of the penalty is reduced or the penalty is not upheld by the court, the court shall order, when the court's judgment becomes final, that the appropriate amount plus accrued interest be remitted to the person before the 31st day after the date that the judgment of the court becomes final.

(b) The interest accrues at the rate charged on loans to depository institutions by the New York Federal Reserve Bank.

(c) The interest shall be paid for the period beginning on the date the penalty is paid and ending on the date the penalty is remitted.

(Enacted by Acts 2005, 79th Leg., ch. 282 (H.B. 164), § 9, effective August 1, 2005.)

### Sec. 486.032.   Release of Bond.

(a) If the person gave a supersedeas bond and the penalty is not upheld by the court, the court shall order, when the court's judgment becomes final, the release of the bond.

(b) If the person gave a supersedeas bond and the amount of the penalty is reduced, the court shall order the release of the bond after the person pays the reduced amount.

(Enacted by Acts 2005, 79th Leg., ch. 282 (H.B. 164), § 9, effective August 1, 2005.)

### Sec. 486.033.   Administrative Procedure.

A proceeding to impose the penalty under this subchapter is considered to be a contested case under Chapter 2001, Government Code.

(Enacted by Acts 2005, 79th Leg., ch. 282 (H.B. 164), § 9, effective August 1, 2005.)

Health

# TITLE 7
# MENTAL HEALTH AND MENTAL RETARDATION

## SUBTITLE C
## TEXAS MENTAL HEALTH CODE

### CHAPTER 573
### EMERGENCY DETENTION

**Subchapter A. Apprehension by Peace Officer or Transportation for Emergency Detention by Guardian**

Section
573.001.   Apprehension by Peace Officer Without Warrant.
573.002.   Peace Officer's Application for Detention.

### SUBCHAPTER A
### APPREHENSION BY PEACE OFFICER OR TRANSPORTATION FOR EMERGENCY DETENTION BY GUARDIAN

## Sec. 573.001. Apprehension by Peace Officer Without Warrant.

(a) A peace officer, without a warrant, may take a person into custody if the officer:

(1) has reason to believe and does believe that:

(A) the person is mentally ill; and

(B) because of that mental illness there is a substantial risk of serious harm to the person or to others unless the person is immediately restrained; and

(2) believes that there is not sufficient time to obtain a warrant before taking the person into custody.

(b) A substantial risk of serious harm to the person or others under Subsection (a)(1)(B) may be demonstrated by:

(1) the person's behavior; or

(2) evidence of severe emotional distress and deterioration in the person's mental condition to the extent that the person cannot remain at liberty.

(c) The peace officer may form the belief that the person meets the criteria for apprehension:

(1) from a representation of a credible person; or

(2) on the basis of the conduct of the apprehended person or the circumstances under which the apprehended person is found.

(d) A peace officer who takes a person into custody under Subsection (a) shall immediately transport the apprehended person to:

(1) the nearest appropriate inpatient mental health facility; or

(2) a mental health facility deemed suitable by the local mental health authority, if an appropriate inpatient mental health facility is not available.

(e) A jail or similar detention facility may not be deemed suitable except in an extreme emergency.

(f) A person detained in a jail or a nonmedical facility shall be kept separate from any person who is charged with or convicted of a crime.
(Enacted by Acts 1991, 72nd Leg., ch. 76 (H.B. 902), § 1, effective September 1, 1991; am. Acts 2001, 77th Leg., ch. 367 (S.B. 1386), § 5, effective September 1, 2001.)

## Sec. 573.002. Peace Officer's Application for Detention.

(a) A peace officer shall immediately file an application for detention after transporting a person to a facility under Section 573.001.

(b) The application for detention must contain:

(1) a statement that the officer has reason to believe and does believe that the person evidences mental illness;

(2) a statement that the officer has reason to believe and does believe that the person evidences a substantial risk of serious harm to himself or others;

(3) a specific description of the risk of harm;

(4) a statement that the officer has reason to believe and does believe that the risk of harm is imminent unless the person is immediately restrained;

(5) a statement that the officer's beliefs are derived from specific recent behavior, overt acts, attempts, or threats that were observed by or reliably reported to the officer;

(6) a detailed description of the specific behavior, acts, attempts, or threats; and

(7) the name and relationship to the apprehended person of any person who reported or observed the behavior, acts, attempts, or threats.
(Enacted by Acts 1991, 72nd Leg., ch. 76 (H.B. 902), § 1, effective September 1, 1991.)

Health

# TITLE 9
# SAFETY

## SUBTITLE A
## PUBLIC SAFETY

## CHAPTER 751
## MASS GATHERINGS

## Sec. 751.001.   Short Title.

This chapter may be cited as the Texas Mass Gatherings Act.

(Enacted by Acts 1989, 71st Leg., ch. 678 (H.B. 2136), § 1, effective September 1, 1989.)

## Sec. 751.002.   Definitions.

In this chapter:

(1) "Mass gathering" means a gathering:

(A) that is held outside the limits of a municipality;

(B) that attracts or is expected to attract:

(i) more than 2,500 persons; or

(ii) more than 500 persons, if 51 percent or more of those persons may reasonably be expected to be younger than 21 years of age and it is planned or may reasonably be expected that alcoholic beverages will be sold, served, or consumed at or around the gathering; and

(C) at which the persons will remain:

(i) for more than five continuous hours; or

(ii) for any amount of time during the period beginning at 10 p.m. and ending at 4 a.m.

(2) "Person" means an individual, group of individuals, firm, corporation, partnership, or association.

(3) "Promote" includes organize, manage, finance, or hold.

(4) "Promoter" means a person who promotes a mass gathering.

(Enacted by Acts 1989, 71st Leg., ch. 678 (H.B. 2136), § 1, effective September 1, 1989; am. Acts 1999, 76th Leg., ch. 553 (S.B. 339), § 1, effective June 18, 1999; am. Acts 2005, 79th Leg., ch. 692 (S.B. 270), § 1, effective June 17, 2005.)

## Sec. 751.003.   Permit Requirement.

A person may not promote a mass gathering without a permit issued under this chapter.

(Enacted by Acts 1989, 71st Leg., ch. 678 (H.B. 2136), § 1, effective September 1, 1989.)

## Sec. 751.004.   Application Procedure.

(a) At least 45 days before the date on which a mass gathering will be held, the promoter shall file a permit application with the county judge of the county in which the mass gathering will be held.

(b) The application must include:

(1) the promoter's name and address;

(2) a financial statement that reflects the funds being supplied to finance the mass gathering and each person supplying the funds;

(3) the name and address of the owner of the property on which the mass gathering will be held;

(4) a certified copy of the agreement between the promoter and the property owner;

(5) the location and a description of the property on which the mass gathering will be held;

(6) the dates and times that the mass gathering will be held;

(7) the maximum number of persons the promoter will allow to attend the mass gathering and the plan the promoter intends to use to limit attendance to that number;

(8) the name and address of each performer who has agreed to appear at the mass gathering and the name and address of each performer's agent;

(9) a description of each agreement between the promoter and a performer;

(10) a description of each step the promoter has taken to ensure that minimum standards of sanitation and health will be maintained during the mass gathering;

(11) a description of all preparations being made to provide traffic control, to ensure that

the mass gathering will be conducted in an orderly manner, and to protect the physical safety of the persons who attend the mass gathering;

(12) a description of the preparations made to provide adequate medical and nursing care; and

(13) a description of the preparations made to supervise minors who may attend the mass gathering.

(Enacted by Acts 1989, 71st Leg., ch. 678 (H.B. 2136), § 1, effective September 1, 1989.)

## Sec. 751.005.  Investigation.

(a) After a permit application is filed with the county judge, the county judge shall send a copy of the application to the county health authority, the county fire marshal or the person designated under Subsection (c), and the sheriff.

(b) The county health authority shall inquire into preparations for the mass gathering. At least five days before the date on which the hearing prescribed by Section 751.006 is held, the county health authority shall submit to the county judge a report stating whether the health authority believes that the minimum standards of health and sanitation prescribed by state and local laws, rules, and orders will be maintained.

(c) The county fire marshal shall investigate preparations for the mass gathering. If there is no county fire marshal in that county, the commissioners court shall designate a person to act under this section. At least five days before the date on which the hearing prescribed by Section 751.006 is held, the county fire marshal or the commissioners court designee shall submit to the county judge a report stating whether the fire marshal or designee believes that the minimum standards for ensuring public fire safety and order as prescribed by state and local laws, rules, and orders will be maintained.

(d) The sheriff shall investigate preparations for the mass gathering. At least five days before the date on which the hearing prescribed by Section 751.006 is held, the sheriff shall submit to the county judge a report stating whether the sheriff believes that the minimum standards for ensuring public safety and order that are prescribed by state and local laws, rules, and orders will be maintained.

(e) The county judge may conduct any additional investigation that the judge considers necessary.

(f) The county health authority, county fire marshal or commissioners court designee, and

sheriff shall be available at the hearing prescribed by Section 751.006 to give testimony relating to their reports.

(Enacted by Acts 1989, 71st Leg., ch. 678 (H.B. 2136), § 1, effective September 1, 1989; am. Acts 1999, 76th Leg., ch. 553 (S.B. 339), § 2, effective June 18, 1999.)

## Sec. 751.0055.  Delegation of Duties of County Judge.

(a) The county judge of a county may file an order with the commissioners court of the county delegating to another county officer the duty to hear applications for a permit under this chapter. The order may provide for allowing the county officer to revoke a permit under Section 751.008.

(b) An order of a county officer acting under the delegated authority of the county judge in regard to a permit has the same effect as an order of the county judge.

(c) During the period in which the order is in effect, the county judge may withdraw the authority delegated in relation to an application and the county judge may hear the application.

(d) The county judge may at any time revoke an order delegating duties under this section.

(Enacted by Acts 2001, 77th Leg., ch. 1 (S.B. 286), § 1, effective March 26, 2001.)

## Sec. 751.006.  Hearing.

(a) Not later than the 10th day before the date on which a mass gathering will begin, the county judge shall hold a hearing on the application. The county judge shall set the date and time of the hearing.

(b) Notice of the time and place of the hearing shall be given to the promoter and to each person who has an interest in whether the permit is granted or denied.

(c) At the hearing, any person may appear and testify for or against granting the permit.

(Enacted by Acts 1989, 71st Leg., ch. 678 (H.B. 2136), § 1, effective September 1, 1989.)

## Sec. 751.007.  Findings and Decision of County Judge.

(a) After the completion of the hearing prescribed by Section 751.006, the county judge shall enter his findings in the record and shall either grant or deny the permit.

(b) The county judge may deny the permit if he finds that:

(1) the application contains false or misleading information or omits required information;

(2) the promoter's financial backing is insufficient to ensure that the mass gathering will be conducted in the manner stated in the application;

(3) the location selected for the mass gathering is inadequate for the purpose for which it will be used;

(4) the promoter has not made adequate preparations to limit the number of persons attending the mass gathering or to provide adequate supervision for minors attending the mass gathering;

(5) the promoter does not have assurance that scheduled performers will appear;

(6) the preparations for the mass gathering do not ensure that minimum standards of sanitation and health will be maintained;

(7) the preparations for the mass gathering do not ensure that the mass gathering will be conducted in an orderly manner and that the physical safety of persons attending will be protected;

(8) adequate arrangements for traffic control have not been provided; or

(9) adequate medical and nursing care will not be available.

(Enacted by Acts 1989, 71st Leg., ch. 678 (H.B. 2136), § 1, effective September 1, 1989.)

### Sec. 751.008.  Permit Revocation.

(a) The county judge may revoke a permit issued under this chapter if the county judge finds that preparations for the mass gathering will not be completed by the time the mass gathering will begin or that the permit was obtained by fraud or misrepresentation.

(b) The county judge must give notice to the promoter that the permit will be revoked at least 24 hours before the revocation. If requested by the promoter, the county judge shall hold a hearing on the revocation.

(Enacted by Acts 1989, 71st Leg., ch. 678 (H.B. 2136), § 1, effective September 1, 1989.)

### Sec. 751.009.  Appeal.

A promoter or a person affected by the granting, denying, or revoking of a permit may appeal that action to a district court having jurisdiction in the county in which the mass gathering will be held.

(Enacted by Acts 1989, 71st Leg., ch. 678 (H.B. 2136), § 1, effective September 1, 1989; am. Acts 2001, 77th Leg., ch. 1 (S.B. 286), § 2, effective March 26, 2001.)

### Sec. 751.010.  Rules.

(a) After notice and a public hearing, the Texas Board of Health shall adopt rules relating to minimum standards of health and sanitation to be maintained at mass gatherings.

(b) After notice and a public hearing, the Department of Public Safety shall adopt rules relating to minimum standards that must be maintained at a mass gathering to protect public safety and maintain order.

(Enacted by Acts 1989, 71st Leg., ch. 678 (H.B. 2136), § 1, effective September 1, 1989.)

### Sec. 751.011.  Criminal Penalty.

(a) A person commits an offense if the person violates Section 751.003.

(b) An offense under this section is a misdemeanor punishable by a fine of not more than $1,000, confinement in the county jail for not more than 90 days, or both.

(Enacted by Acts 1989, 71st Leg., ch. 678 (H.B. 2136), § 1, effective September 1, 1989.)

### Sec. 751.012.  Inspections.

(a) The county health authority may inspect a mass gathering during the mass gathering to ensure that the minimum standards of health and sanitation prescribed by state and local laws, rules, and orders are being maintained. If the county health authority determines a violation of the minimum standards is occurring, the health authority may order the promoter of the mass gathering to correct the violation.

(b) The county fire marshal or the person designated under Section 751.005(c) may inspect a mass gathering during the mass gathering to ensure that the minimum standards for ensuring public fire safety and order as prescribed by state and local laws, rules, and orders are being maintained. If the marshal or commissioners court designee determines a violation of the minimum standards is occurring, the marshal or designee may order the promoter of the mass gathering to correct the violation.

(c) The sheriff may inspect a mass gathering during the mass gathering to ensure that the minimum standards for ensuring public safety and order prescribed by state and local laws, rules, and orders are being maintained. If the sheriff determines a violation of the minimum standards is occurring, the sheriff may order the promoter of the mass gathering to correct the violation.

(d) A promoter who fails to comply with an order issued under this section commits an offense. An offense under this section is a Class C misdemeanor.

(Enacted by Acts 1999, 76th Leg., ch. 553 (S.B. 339), § 3, effective June 18, 1999.)

## Sec. 751.013.  Inspection Fees.

(a) A commissioners court may establish and collect a fee for an inspection performed under Section 751.012. The fee may not exceed the amount necessary to defray the costs of performing the inspections. The fee shall be deposited into the general fund of the county.

(b) A commissioners court may use money collected under this section to reimburse the county department or, if a state agency performs the inspection on behalf of the county, the state agency, the cost of performing the inspection.

(Enacted by Acts 1999, 76th Leg., ch. 553 (S.B. 339), § 3, effective June 18, 1999.)

## SUBTITLE B
## EMERGENCIES

## CHAPTER 784
## CRITICAL INCIDENT STRESS MANAGEMENT AND CRISIS RESPONSE SERVICES

Section
784.001.   Definitions.
784.002.   Closed Meetings.
784.003.   Confidentiality.
784.004.   Limitation on Liability.

## Sec. 784.001.  Definitions.

In this chapter:

(1) "Crisis response service" means consultation, risk assessment, referral, and on-site crisis intervention services provided by an emergency response team member to an emergency service provider affected by a crisis or disaster.

(2) "Critical incident stress" means the acute or cumulative psychological stress or trauma that an emergency service provider may experience in providing emergency services in response to a critical incident, including a crisis, disaster, or emergency. The stress or trauma is an unusually strong emotional, cognitive, or physical reaction that has the potential to interfere with normal functioning, including:

(A) physical and emotional illness;

(B) failure of usual coping mechanisms;

(C) loss of interest in the job;

(D) personality changes; and

(E) loss of ability to function.

(3) "Critical incident stress management service" means a service providing a process of crisis intervention designed to assist an emergency service provider in coping with critical incident stress. The term includes consultation, counseling, debriefing, defusing, intervention services, case management services, prevention, and referral.

(4) "Emergency response team member" means an individual providing critical incident stress management services or crisis response services, or both, who is designated by an appropriate state or local governmental unit to provide those services as a member of an organized team or in association with the governmental unit.

(5) "Emergency service provider" means an individual who provides emergency response services, including a law enforcement officer, firefighter, emergency medical services provider, dispatcher, or rescue service provider.

(Enacted by Acts 2011, 82nd Leg., ch. 651 (S.B. 1065), § 1, effective September 1, 2011.)

## Sec. 784.002.  Closed Meetings.

(a) Except as provided by Subsection (b) and notwithstanding Chapter 551, Government Code, or any other law, a meeting in which critical incident stress management services or crisis response services are provided to an emergency service provider:

(1) is closed to the general public; and

(2) may be closed to any individual who was not directly involved in the critical incident or crisis.

(b) Subsection (a) does not apply if:

(1) the emergency service provider or the legal representative of the provider expressly agrees that the meeting may be open to the general public or to certain individuals; or

(2) the emergency service provider is deceased.

(Enacted by Acts 2011, 82nd Leg., ch. 651 (S.B. 1065), § 1, effective September 1, 2011.)

## Sec. 784.003.  Confidentiality.

(a) Except as otherwise provided by this section:

(1) a communication made by an emergency service provider to an emergency response team member while the provider receives critical incident stress management services or crisis response services is confidential and may not be disclosed in a civil, criminal, or administrative proceeding; and

Health

(2) a record kept by an emergency response team member relating to the provision of critical incident stress management services or crisis response services to an emergency service provider by the team is confidential and is not subject to subpoena, discovery, or introduction into evidence in a civil, criminal, or administrative proceeding.

(b) A court in a civil or criminal case or the decision-making entity in an administrative proceeding may allow disclosure of a communication or record described by Subsection (a) if the court or entity finds that the benefit of allowing disclosure of the communication or record is more important than protecting the privacy of the individual.

(c) A communication or record described by Subsection (a) is not confidential if:

(1) the emergency response team member reasonably needs to make an appropriate referral of the emergency service provider to or consult about the provider with another member of the team or an appropriate professional associated with the team;

(2) the communication conveys information that the emergency service provider is or appears to be an imminent threat to the provider or anyone else;

(3) the communication conveys information relating to a past, present, or future criminal act that does not directly relate to the critical incident or crisis;

(4) the emergency service provider or the legal representative of the provider expressly agrees that the communication or record is not confidential; or

(5) the emergency service provider is deceased.

(d) A communication or record described by Subsection (a) is not confidential to the extent that it conveys information concerning the services and care provided to or withheld by the emergency service provider to an individual injured in the critical incident or during the crisis. (Enacted by Acts 2011, 82nd Leg., ch. 651 (S.B. 1065), § 1, effective September 1, 2011.)

## Sec. 784.004.  Limitation on Liability.

(a) Except as provided by Subsection (b), an emergency response team or an emergency response team member providing critical incident stress management services or crisis response services is not liable for damages, including personal injury, wrongful death, property damage, or other loss related to the team's or member's act, error, or omission in the performance of the services, unless the act, error, or omission constitutes wanton, wilful, or intentional misconduct.

(b) Subsection (a) limits liability for damages in any civil action, other than an action under Chapter 74, Civil Practice and Remedies Code. (Enacted by Acts 2011, 82nd Leg., ch. 651 (S.B. 1065), § 1, effective September 1, 2011.)

# TITLE 10

# HEALTH AND SAFETY OF ANIMALS

## CHAPTER 821
## TREATMENT AND DISPOSITION OF ANIMALS

### SUBCHAPTER B
### DISPOSITION OF CRUELLY TREATED ANIMALS

### Sec. 821.022.  Seizure of Cruelly Treated Animal.

(a) If a peace officer or an officer who has responsibility for animal control in a county or municipality has reason to believe that an animal has been or is being cruelly treated, the officer may apply to a justice court or magistrate in the county or to a municipal court in the municipality

in which the animal is located for a warrant to seize the animal.

(b) On a showing of probable cause to believe that the animal has been or is being cruelly treated, the court or magistrate shall issue the warrant and set a time within 10 calendar days of the date of issuance for a hearing in the appropriate justice court or municipal court to determine whether the animal has been cruelly treated.

(c) The officer executing the warrant shall cause the animal to be impounded and shall give written notice to the owner of the animal of the time and place of the hearing. (Enacted by Acts 1989, 71st Leg., ch. 678 (H.B. 2136), § 1, effective September 1, 1989; am. Acts 1991, 72nd Leg., ch. 387 (H.B. 2300), § 1, effective June 7, 1991; am. Acts 2003, 78th Leg., ch. 1043 (H.B. 1119), § 2, effective September 1, 2003.)

# CHAPTER 822
# REGULATION OF ANIMALS

## SUBCHAPTER A
## GENERAL PROVISIONS; DOGS THAT ATTACK PERSONS OR ARE A DANGER TO PERSONS

### Sec. 822.001. Definitions.

In this subchapter:

(1) "Animal control authority" means a municipal or county animal control office with authority over the area in which the dog is kept or the county sheriff in an area that does not have an animal control office.

(2) "Serious bodily injury" means an injury characterized by severe bite wounds or severe ripping and tearing of muscle that would cause a reasonably prudent person to seek treatment from a medical professional and would require hospitalization without regard to whether the person actually sought medical treatment.

(3) "Dangerous dog," "dog," "owner," and "secure enclosure" have the meanings assigned by Section 822.041.

(4) "Secure" means to take steps that a reasonable person would take to ensure a dog remains on the owner's property, including confining the dog in an enclosure that is capable of preventing the escape or release of the dog.

(Enacted by Acts 1997, 75th Leg., ch. 99 (H.B. 991), § 1, effective September 1, 1997; am. Acts 2007, 80th Leg., ch. 669 (H.B. 1355), § 3, effective September 1, 2007.)

### Sec. 822.0011. Application to Certain Property.

For purposes of this subchapter, a person's property includes property the person is entitled to possess or occupy under a lease or other agreement.

Health

(Enacted by Acts 2007, 80th Leg., ch. 669 (H.B. 1355), § 4, effective September 1, 2007.)

### Sec. 822.002.  Seizure of a Dog Causing Death of or Serious Bodily Injury to a Person.

(a) A justice court, county court, or municipal court shall order the animal control authority to seize a dog and shall issue a warrant authorizing the seizure:

(1) on the sworn complaint of any person, including the county attorney, the city attorney, or a peace officer, that the dog has caused the death of or serious bodily injury to a person by attacking, biting, or mauling the person; and

(2) on a showing of probable cause to believe that the dog caused the death of or serious bodily injury to the person as stated in the complaint.

(b) The animal control authority shall seize the dog or order its seizure and shall provide for the impoundment of the dog in secure and humane conditions until the court orders the disposition of the dog.

(Enacted by Acts 1989, 71st Leg., ch. 678 (H.B. 2136), § 1, effective September 1, 1989; am. Acts 1997, 75th Leg., ch. 99 (H.B. 991), § 1, effective September 1, 1997 (renumbered from Sec. 822.001).)

### Sec. 822.003.  Hearing.

(a) The court shall set a time for a hearing to determine whether the dog caused the death of or serious bodily injury to a person by attacking, biting, or mauling the person. The hearing must be held not later than the 10th day after the date on which the warrant is issued.

(b) The court shall give written notice of the time and place of the hearing to:

(1) the owner of the dog or the person from whom the dog was seized; and

(2) the person who made the complaint.

(c) Any interested party, including the county attorney or city attorney, is entitled to present evidence at the hearing.

(d) The court shall order the dog destroyed if the court finds that the dog caused the death of a person by attacking, biting, or mauling the person. If that finding is not made, the court shall order the dog released to:

(1) its owner;

(2) the person from whom the dog was seized; or

(3) any other person authorized to take possession of the dog.

(e) The court may order the dog destroyed if the court finds that the dog caused serious bodily injury to a person by attacking, biting, or mauling the person. If that finding is not made, the court shall order the dog released to:

(1) its owner;

(2) the person from whom the dog was seized; or

(3) any other person authorized to take possession of the dog.

(f) The court may not order the dog destroyed if the court finds that the dog caused the serious bodily injury to a person by attacking, biting, or mauling the person and:

(1) the dog was being used for the protection of a person or person's property, the attack, bite, or mauling occurred in an enclosure in which the dog was being kept, and:

(A) the enclosure was reasonably certain to prevent the dog from leaving the enclosure on its own and provided notice of the presence of a dog; and

(B) the injured person was at least eight years of age, and was trespassing in the enclosure when the attack, bite, or mauling occurred;

(2) the dog was not being used for the protection of a person or person's property, the attack, bite, or mauling occurred in an enclosure in which the dog was being kept, and the injured person was at least eight years of age and was trespassing in the enclosure when the attack, bite, or mauling occurred;

(3) the attack, bite, or mauling occurred during an arrest or other action of a peace officer while the peace officer was using the dog for law enforcement purposes;

(4) the dog was defending a person from an assault or person's property from damage or theft by the injured person; or

(5) the injured person was younger than eight years of age, the attack, bite, or mauling occurred in an enclosure in which the dog was being kept, and the enclosure was reasonably certain to keep a person younger than eight years of age from entering.

(Enacted by Acts 1989, 71st Leg., ch. 678 (H.B. 2136), § 1, effective September 1, 1989; am. Acts 1997, 75th Leg., ch. 99 (H.B. 991), § 1, effective September 1, 1997 (renumbered from Sec. 822.002).)

### Sec. 822.004.  Destruction of Dog.

The destruction of a dog under this subchapter must be performed by:

(1) a licensed veterinarian;

(2) personnel of a recognized animal shelter or humane society who are trained in the humane destruction of animals; or

(3) personnel of a governmental agency responsible for animal control who are trained in the humane destruction of animals.

(Enacted by Acts 1989, 71st Leg., ch. 678 (H.B. 2136), § 1, effective September 1, 1989; am. Acts 1997, 75th Leg., ch. 99 (H.B. 991), § 1, effective September 1, 1997 (renumbered from Sec. 822.003).)

### Sec. 822.005. Attack by Dog.

(a) A person commits an offense if the person is the owner of a dog and the person:

(1) with criminal negligence, as defined by Section 6.03, Penal Code, fails to secure the dog and the dog makes an unprovoked attack on another person that occurs at a location other than the owner's real property or in or on the owner's motor vehicle or boat and that causes serious bodily injury, as defined by Section 1.07, Penal Code, or death to the other person; or

(2) knows the dog is a dangerous dog by learning in a manner described by Section 822.042(g) that the person is the owner of a dangerous dog, and the dangerous dog makes an unprovoked attack on another person that occurs at a location other than a secure enclosure in which the dog is restrained in accordance with Subchapter D and that causes serious bodily injury, as defined by Section 822.001, or death to the other person.

(b) An offense under this section is a felony of the third degree unless the attack causes death, in which event the offense is a felony of the second degree.

(c) If a person is found guilty of an offense under this section, the court may order the dog destroyed by a person listed in Section 822.004.

(d) A person who is subject to prosecution under this section and under any other law may be prosecuted under this section, the other law, or both.

(Enacted by Acts 1989, 71st Leg., ch. 678 (H.B. 2136), § 1, effective September 1, 1989; am. Acts 1997, 75th Leg., ch. 99 (H.B. 991), § 1, effective September 1, 1997 (renumbered from Sec. 822.004); am. Acts 2007, 80th Leg., ch. 669 (H.B. 1355), § 5, effective September 1, 2007.)

### Sec. 822.006. Defenses.

(a) It is a defense to prosecution under Section 822.005(a) that the person is a veterinarian, a veterinary clinic employee, a peace officer, a person employed by a recognized animal shelter, or a person employed by this state or a political subdivision of this state to deal with stray animals and has temporary ownership, custody, or control of the dog in connection with that position.

(b) It is a defense to prosecution under Section 822.005(a) that the person is an employee of the Texas Department of Criminal Justice or a law enforcement agency and trains or uses dogs for law enforcement or corrections purposes and is training or using the dog in connection with the person's official capacity.

(c) It is a defense to prosecution under Section 822.005(a) that the person is a dog trainer or an employee of a guard dog company under Chapter 1702, Occupations Code, and has temporary ownership, custody, or control of the dog in connection with that position.

(d) It is a defense to prosecution under Section 822.005(a) that the person is disabled and uses the dog to provide assistance, the dog is trained to provide assistance to a person with a disability, and the person is using the dog to provide assistance in connection with the person's disability.

(e) It is a defense to prosecution under Section 822.005(a) that the person attacked by the dog was at the time of the attack engaged in conduct prohibited by Chapters 19, 20, 21, 22, 28, 29, and 30, Penal Code.

(f) It is an affirmative defense to prosecution under Section 822.005(a) that, at the time of the conduct charged, the person and the dog are participating in an organized search and rescue effort at the request of law enforcement.

(g) It is an affirmative defense to prosecution under Section 822.005(a) that, at the time of the conduct charged, the person and the dog are participating in an organized dog show or event sponsored by a nationally recognized or state-recognized kennel club.

(h) It is an affirmative defense to prosecution under Section 822.005(a) that, at the time of the conduct charged, the person and the dog are engaged in:

(1) a lawful hunting activity; or

(2) a farming or ranching activity, including herding livestock, typically performed by a working dog on a farm or ranch.

(i) It is a defense to prosecution under Section 822.005(a) that, at the time of the conduct charged, the person's dog was on a leash and the person:

(1) was in immediate control of the dog; or

Health

(2) if the person was not in control of the dog, the person was making immediate and reasonable attempts to regain control of the dog.
(Enacted by Acts 2007, 80th Leg., ch. 669 (H.B. 1355), § 6, effective September 1, 2007.)

### Sec. 822.007.  Local Regulation of Dogs.

This subchapter does not prohibit a municipality or county from adopting leash or registration requirements applicable to dogs.
(Enacted by Acts 2007, 80th Leg., ch. 669 (H.B. 1355), § 6, effective September 1, 2007.)

## SUBCHAPTER B
## DOGS AND COYOTES THAT ARE A DANGER TO ANIMALS

### Sec. 822.011.  Definitions.

In this subchapter:
(1) "Dog or coyote" includes a crossbreed between a dog and a coyote.
(2) "Livestock" includes exotic livestock as defined by Section 161.001, Agriculture Code.
(Enacted by Acts 2003, 78th Leg., ch. 1002 (H.B. 151), § 1, effective September 1, 2003.)

### Sec. 822.012.  Certain Dogs and Coyotes Prohibited from Running at Large; Criminal Penalty.

(a) The owner, keeper, or person in control of a dog or coyote that the owner, keeper, or person knows is accustomed to run, worry, or kill livestock, domestic animals, or fowls may not permit the dog or coyote to run at large.
(b) A person who violates this section commits an offense. An offense under this subsection is punishable by a fine of not more than $100.
(c) Each time a dog or coyote runs at large in violation of this section constitutes a separate offense.
(Enacted by Acts 1989, 71st Leg., ch. 678 (H.B. 2136), § 1, effective September 1, 1989; am. Acts 2003, 78th Leg., ch. 1002 (H.B. 151), § 1, effective September 1, 2003 (renumbered from Sec. 822.011).)

### Sec. 822.013.  Dogs or Coyotes That Attack Animals.

(a) A dog or coyote that is attacking, is about to attack, or has recently attacked livestock, domestic animals, or fowls may be killed by:
(1) any person witnessing the attack; or

(2) the attacked animal's owner or a person acting on behalf of the owner if the owner or person has knowledge of the attack.
(b) A person who kills a dog or coyote as provided by this section is not liable for damages to the owner, keeper, or person in control of the dog or coyote.
(c) A person who discovers on the person's property a dog or coyote known or suspected of having killed livestock, domestic animals, or fowls may detain or impound the dog or coyote and return it to its owner or deliver the dog or coyote to the local animal control authority. The owner of the dog or coyote is liable for all costs incurred in the capture and care of the dog or coyote and all damage done by the dog or coyote.
(d) The owner, keeper, or person in control of a dog or coyote that is known to have attacked livestock, domestic animals, or fowls shall control the dog or coyote in a manner approved by the local animal control authority.
(e) A person is not required to acquire a hunting license under Section 42.002, Parks and Wildlife Code, to kill a dog or coyote under this section.
(Enacted by Acts 1989, 71st Leg., ch. 678 (H.B. 2136), § 1, effective September 1, 1989; am. Acts 2003, 78th Leg., ch. 1002 (H.B. 151), § 1, effective September 1, 2003 (renumbered from Sec. 822.033).)

## SUBCHAPTER C
## COUNTY REGISTRATION AND REGULATION OF DOGS

### Sec. 822.021.  Application to Counties That Adopt Subchapter.

This subchapter applies only to a county that adopts this subchapter by a majority vote of the qualified voters of the county voting at an election held under this subchapter. This subchapter shall not apply to any county or municipality that enacts or has enacted registration or restraint laws pursuant to Chapter 826 (Rabies Control Act of 1981).
(Enacted by Acts 1989, 71st Leg., ch. 678 (H.B. 2136), § 1, effective September 1, 1989; am. Acts 1995, 74th Leg., ch. 489 (S.B. 1437), § 1, effective August 28, 1995.)

### Sec. 822.022.  Petition for Election.

(a) On receiving a petition signed by at least 100 qualified property taxpaying voters of the county or a majority of the qualified property taxpaying voters of the county, whichever is less, the commissioners court of a county shall order an election to determine whether the registration of and registration fee for dogs will be required in the county.

(b) The election shall be held on the first authorized uniform election date prescribed by the Election Code that allows sufficient time to comply with other requirements of law.

(Enacted by Acts 1989, 71st Leg., ch. 678 (H.B. 2136), § 1, effective September 1, 1989.)

### Sec. 822.023. Notice.

In addition to the notice required by Section 4.003, Election Code, notice of an election under this subchapter shall be published at least once in an English language newspaper of general circulation in the county. If there is no English language newspaper of general circulation in the county, the notice shall be posted at the courthouse door for at least one week before the election.

(Enacted by Acts 1989, 71st Leg., ch. 678 (H.B. 2136), § 1, effective September 1, 1989.)

### Sec. 822.024. Ballot Proposition.

The ballot for an election under this subchapter shall be printed to provide for voting for or against the proposition: "Registration of and registration fee for dogs."

(Enacted by Acts 1989, 71st Leg., ch. 678 (H.B. 2136), § 1, effective September 1, 1989.)

### Sec. 822.025. Election Result.

(a) If a majority of those voting at the election vote in favor of the measure, the requirement that dogs be registered takes effect in the county on the 10th day after the date on which the result of the election is declared.

(b) The county judge shall issue a proclamation declaring the result of the election if the vote is in favor of the measure. The proclamation shall be published at least once in an English language newspaper of general circulation in the county or, if there is no English language newspaper of general circulation in the county, the proclamation shall be posted at the courthouse door.

(Enacted by Acts 1989, 71st Leg., ch. 678 (H.B. 2136), § 1, effective September 1, 1989.)

### Sec. 822.026. Interval Between Elections.

(a) If the result of an election is against the registration of and registration fee for dogs, another election on that subject may not be held for six months after the date of the election.

(b) If the result of an election is for the registration of and registration fee for dogs, an election to repeal the registration and fee may not be held for two years from the date of the election.

(Enacted by Acts 1989, 71st Leg., ch. 678 (H.B. 2136), § 1, effective September 1, 1989.)

### Sec. 822.027. Registration Tags and Certificate.

(a) The commissioners court of a county shall furnish the county treasurer the necessary dog identification tags.

(b) The tags must be numbered consecutively and must be printed or impressed with the name of the county issuing the tags.

(c) The county treasurer shall assign a registration number to each dog registered with the county and shall give the owner or person having control of the dog the identification tag and a registration certificate.

(d) The county treasurer shall record the registration of a dog, including the age, breed, color, sex, and registration date of the dog. If the registration information is not recorded on microfilm, as may be permitted under other law, it shall be recorded in a book kept for that purpose.

(e) If the ownership of a dog is transferred, the dog's registration certificate shall be transferred to the new owner.

(Enacted by Acts 1989, 71st Leg., ch. 678 (H.B. 2136), § 1, effective September 1, 1989.)

### Sec. 822.028. Registration Fee.

(a) An owner of a dog registered under this subchapter must pay a registration fee of $1. However, the commissioners court of the county may set the fee in an amount of more than $1 but not more than $5, and if the court sets the amount of the fee the owner must pay that amount.

(b) Registration is valid for one year from the date of registration.

(c) If a dog is moved to another county, the owner may present the registration certificate to the county treasurer of the county to which the dog is moved and receive without additional cost a registration certificate. The new registration certificate is valid for one year from the date of registration in the county from which the dog was moved.

(Enacted by Acts 1989, 71st Leg., ch. 678 (H.B. 2136), § 1, effective September 1, 1989; am. Acts 2001, 77th Leg., ch. 870 (H.B. 1863), § 1, effective June 14, 2001.)

Health

### Sec. 822.029.  Disposition of Fee.

(a) The fee collected for the registration of a dog shall be deposited to the credit of a special fund of the county and used only to:

(1) defray the cost of administering this subchapter in the county, including the costs of registration and the identification tags; and

(2) reimburse the owner of any sheep, goats, calves, or other domestic animals or fowls killed in the county by a dog not owned by the person seeking reimbursement.

(b) Reimbursement under Subsection (a)(2) shall be made on the order of the commissioners court only on satisfactory proof of the killing.

(c) The commissioners court shall determine the amount and time of reimbursement. If there is insufficient money in the fund to reimburse all injured persons in full, reimbursement shall be made on a pro rata basis.

(d) The county treasurer shall keep an accurate record showing all amounts received into and paid from the fund.

(Enacted by Acts 1989, 71st Leg., ch. 678 (H.B. 2136), § 1, effective September 1, 1989.)

### Sec. 822.030.  Registration Required; Exception for Temporary Visits.

(a) The owner or person having control of a dog six months of age or older in a county that has adopted this subchapter must register the dog not later than the 30th day after the date on which the proclamation is published or adopted.

(b) A dog brought into a county for not more than 10 days for breeding purposes, trial, or show is not required to be registered.

(Enacted by Acts 1989, 71st Leg., ch. 678 (H.B. 2136), § 1, effective September 1, 1989.)

### Sec. 822.031.  Unregistered Dogs Prohibited from Running at Large.

The owner or person having control of a dog at least six months of age in a county adopting this subchapter may not allow the dog to run at large unless the dog:

(1) is registered under this subchapter with the county in which the dog runs at large; and

(2) has fastened about its neck a dog identification tag issued by the county.

(Enacted by Acts 1989, 71st Leg., ch. 678 (H.B. 2136), § 1, effective September 1, 1989.)

### Sec. 822.032.  Unmuzzled Dogs Prohibited from Running at Large [Re-

pealed].

Repealed by Acts 2003, 78th Leg., ch. 1002 (H.B. 151), § 2, effective September 1, 2003.
(Enacted by Acts 1989, 71st Leg., ch. 678 (H.B. 2136), § 1, effective September 1, 1989.)

### Sec. 822.033.  Dogs That Attack Domestic Animals [Renumbered].

Renumbered to Tex. Health & Safety Code § 822.013 by Acts 2003, 78th Leg., ch. 1002 (H.B. 151), § 1, effective September 1, 2003.
(Enacted by Acts 1989, 71st Leg., ch. 678 (H.B. 2136), § 1, effective September 1, 1989.)

### Sec. 822.034.  Protection of Domestic Animals [Repealed].

Repealed by Acts 2003, 78th Leg., ch. 1002 (H.B. 151), § 2, effective September 1, 2003.
(Enacted by Acts 1989, 71st Leg., ch. 678 (H.B. 2136), § 1, effective September 1, 1989.)

### Sec. 822.035.  Criminal Penalty.

(a) A person commits an offense if the person intentionally:

(1) fails or refuses to register a dog required to be registered under this subchapter;

(2) fails or refuses to allow a dog to be killed when ordered by the proper authorities to do so; or

(3) violates this subchapter.

(b) An offense under this section is a misdemeanor punishable by a fine of not more than $100, confinement in the county jail for not more than 30 days, or both.

(Enacted by Acts 1989, 71st Leg., ch. 678 (H.B. 2136), § 1, effective September 1, 1989.)

## SUBCHAPTER D
## DANGEROUS DOGS

### Sec. 822.041.  Definitions.

In this subchapter:

(1) "Animal control authority" means a municipal or county animal control office with authority over the area where the dog is kept or a county sheriff in an area with no animal control office.

(2) "Dangerous dog" means a dog that:

(A) makes an unprovoked attack on a person that causes bodily injury and occurs in a place other than an enclosure in which the dog was being kept and that was reasonably certain to prevent the dog from leaving the enclosure on its own; or

(B) commits unprovoked acts in a place other than an enclosure in which the dog was being kept and that was reasonably certain to prevent the dog from leaving the enclosure on its own and those acts cause a person to reasonably believe that the dog will attack and cause bodily injury to that person.

(3) "Dog" means a domesticated animal that is a member of the canine family.

(4) "Secure enclosure" means a fenced area or structure that is:

    (A) locked;

    (B) capable of preventing the entry of the general public, including children;

    (C) capable of preventing the escape or release of a dog;

    (D) clearly marked as containing a dangerous dog; and

    (E) in conformance with the requirements for enclosures established by the local animal control authority.

(5) "Owner" means a person who owns or has custody or control of the dog.

(Enacted by Acts 1991, 72nd Leg., ch. 916 (H.B. 2065), § 1, effective September 1, 1991.)

## Sec. 822.042. Requirements for Owner of Dangerous Dog.

(a) Not later than the 30th day after a person learns that the person is the owner of a dangerous dog, the person shall:

    (1) register the dangerous dog with the animal control authority for the area in which the dog is kept;

    (2) restrain the dangerous dog at all times on a leash in the immediate control of a person or in a secure enclosure;

    (3) obtain liability insurance coverage or show financial responsibility in an amount of at least $100,000 to cover damages resulting from an attack by the dangerous dog causing bodily injury to a person and provide proof of the required liability insurance coverage or financial responsibility to the animal control authority for the area in which the dog is kept; and

    (4) comply with an applicable municipal or county regulation, requirement, or restriction on dangerous dogs.

(b) The owner of a dangerous dog who does not comply with Subsection (a) shall deliver the dog to the animal control authority not later than the 30th day after the owner learns that the dog is a dangerous dog.

(c) If, on application of any person, a justice court, county court, or municipal court finds, after notice and hearing as provided by Section 822.0423, that the owner of a dangerous dog has failed to comply with Subsection (a) or (b), the court shall order the animal control authority to seize the dog and shall issue a warrant authorizing the seizure. The authority shall seize the dog or order its seizure and shall provide for the impoundment of the dog in secure and humane conditions.

(d) The owner shall pay any cost or fee assessed by the municipality or county related to the seizure, acceptance, impoundment, or destruction of the dog. The governing body of the municipality or county may prescribe the amount of the fees.

(e) The court shall order the animal control authority to humanely destroy the dog if the owner has not complied with Subsection (a) before the 11th day after the date on which the dog is seized or delivered to the authority. The court shall order the authority to return the dog to the owner if the owner complies with Subsection (a) before the 11th day after the date on which the dog is seized or delivered to the authority.

(f) The court may order the humane destruction of a dog if the owner of the dog has not been located before the 15th day after the seizure and impoundment of the dog.

(g) For purposes of this section, a person learns that the person is the owner of a dangerous dog when:

    (1) the owner knows of an attack described in Section 822.041(2)(A) or (B);

    (2) the owner receives notice that a justice court, county court, or municipal court has found that the dog is a dangerous dog under Section 822.0423; or

    (3) the owner is informed by the animal control authority that the dog is a dangerous dog under Section 822.0421.

(Enacted by Acts 1991, 72nd Leg., ch. 916 (H.B. 2065), § 1, effective September 1, 1991; am. Acts 1997, 75th Leg., ch. 99 (H.B. 991), § 2, effective September 1, 1997; am. Acts 1999, 76th Leg., ch. 96 (S.B. 221), § 1, effective May 17, 1999.)

## Sec. 822.0421. Determination That Dog Is Dangerous.

(a) If a person reports an incident described by Section 822.041(2), the animal control authority may investigate the incident. If, after receiving the sworn statements of any witnesses, the animal control authority determines the dog is a dangerous dog, it shall notify the owner of that fact.

Health

(b) An owner, not later than the 15th day after the date the owner is notified that a dog owned by the owner is a dangerous dog, may appeal the determination of the animal control authority to a justice, county, or municipal court of competent jurisdiction. An owner may appeal the decision of the justice, county, or municipal court in the same manner as appeal for other cases from the justice, county, or municipal court.

(Enacted by Acts 1997, 75th Leg., ch. 99 (H.B. 991), § 2, effective September 1, 1997.)

## Sec. 822.0422.  Reporting of Incident in Certain Counties and Municipalities.

(a) This section applies only to a county with a population of more than 2,800,000, to a county in which the commissioners court has entered an order electing to be governed by this section, and to a municipality in which the governing body has adopted an ordinance electing to be governed by this section.

(b) A person may report an incident described by Section 822.041(2) to a municipal court, a justice court, or a county court. The owner of the dog shall deliver the dog to the animal control authority not later than the fifth day after the date on which the owner receives notice that the report has been filed. The authority may provide for the impoundment of the dog in secure and humane conditions until the court orders the disposition of the dog.

(c) If the owner fails to deliver the dog as required by Subsection (b), the court shall order the animal control authority to seize the dog and shall issue a warrant authorizing the seizure. The authority shall seize the dog or order its seizure and shall provide for the impoundment of the dog in secure and humane conditions until the court orders the disposition of the dog. The owner shall pay any cost incurred in seizing the dog.

(d) The court shall determine, after notice and hearing as provided in Section 822.0423, whether the dog is a dangerous dog.

(e) The court, after determining that the dog is a dangerous dog, may order the animal control authority to continue to impound the dangerous dog in secure and humane conditions until the court orders disposition of the dog under Section 822.042 and the dog is returned to the owner or destroyed.

(f) The owner shall pay a cost or fee assessed under Section 822.042(d).

(Enacted by Acts 1997, 75th Leg., ch. 99 (H.B. 991), § 2, effective September 1, 1997; am. Acts 1999, 76th Leg., ch. 96 (S.B. 221), § 2, effective May 17, 1999.)

## Sec. 822.0423.  Hearing.

(a) The court, on receiving a report of an incident under Section 822.0422 or on application under Section 822.042(c), shall set a time for a hearing to determine whether the dog is a dangerous dog or whether the owner of the dog has complied with Section 822.042. The hearing must be held not later than the 10th day after the date on which the dog is seized or delivered.

(b) The court shall give written notice of the time and place of the hearing to:

(1) the owner of the dog or the person from whom the dog was seized; and

(2) the person who made the complaint.

(c) Any interested party, including the county or city attorney, is entitled to present evidence at the hearing.

(d) An owner or person filing the action may appeal the decision of the municipal court, justice court, or county court in the manner provided for the appeal of cases from the municipal, justice, or county court.

(Enacted by Acts 1997, 75th Leg., ch. 99 (H.B. 991), § 2, effective September 1, 1997.)

## Sec. 822.043.  Registration.

(a) An animal control authority for the area in which the dog is kept shall annually register a dangerous dog if the owner:

(1) presents proof of:

(A) liability insurance or financial responsibility, as required by Section 822.042;

(B) current rabies vaccination of the dangerous dog; and

(C) the secure enclosure in which the dangerous dog will be kept; and

(2) pays an annual registration fee of $50.

(b) The animal control authority shall provide to the owner registering a dangerous dog a registration tag. The owner must place the tag on the dog's collar.

(c) If an owner of a registered dangerous dog sells or moves the dog to a new address, the owner, not later than the 14th day after the date of the sale or move, shall notify the animal control authority for the area in which the new address is located. On presentation by the current owner of the dangerous dog's prior registration tag and payment of a fee of $25, the animal control authority shall issue a new registration tag to be placed on the dangerous dog's collar.

(d) An owner of a registered dangerous dog shall notify the office in which the dangerous dog was registered of any attacks the dangerous dog makes on people.

(Enacted by Acts 1991, 72nd Leg., ch. 916 (H.B. 2065), § 1, effective September 1, 1991.)

## Sec. 822.044. Attack by Dangerous Dog.

(a) A person commits an offense if the person is the owner of a dangerous dog and the dog makes an unprovoked attack on another person outside the dog's enclosure and causes bodily injury to the other person.

(b) An offense under this section is a Class C misdemeanor.

(c) If a person is found guilty of an offense under this section, the court may order the dangerous dog destroyed by a person listed in Section 822.004.

(d) [Repealed by Acts 2007, 80th Leg., ch. 669 (H.B. 1355), § 8, effective September 1, 2007.]

(Enacted by Acts 1991, 72nd Leg., ch. 916 (H.B. 2065), § 1, effective September 1, 1991; am. Acts 2007, 80th Leg., ch. 669 (H.B. 1355), §§ 7, 8, effective September 1, 2007.)

## Sec. 822.045. Violations.

(a) A person who owns or keeps custody or control of a dangerous dog commits an offense if the person fails to comply with Section 822.042 or Section 822.0422(b) or an applicable municipal or county regulation relating to dangerous dogs.

(b) Except as provided by Subsection (c), an offense under this section is a Class C misdemeanor.

(c) An offense under this section is a Class B misdemeanor if it is shown on the trial of the offense that the defendant has previously been convicted under this section.

(Enacted by Acts 1991, 72nd Leg., ch. 916 (H.B. 2065), § 1, effective September 1, 1991; am. Acts 1997, 75th Leg., ch. 99 (H.B. 991), § 2, effective September 1, 1997.)

## Sec. 822.046. Defense.

(a) It is a defense to prosecution under Section 822.044 or Section 822.045 that the person is a veterinarian, a peace officer, a person employed by a recognized animal shelter, or a person employed by the state or a political subdivision of the state to deal with stray animals and has

temporary ownership, custody, or control of the dog in connection with that position.

(b) It is a defense to prosecution under Section 822.044 or Section 822.045 that the person is an employee of the institutional division of the Texas Department of Criminal Justice or a law enforcement agency and trains or uses dogs for law enforcement or corrections purposes.

(c) It is a defense to prosecution under Section 822.044 or Section 822.045 that the person is a dog trainer or an employee of a guard dog company under Chapter 1702, Occupations Code.

(Enacted by Acts 1991, 72nd Leg., ch. 916 (H.B. 2065), § 1, effective September 1, 1991; am. Acts 2001, 77th Leg., ch. 1420 (H.B. 2812), § 14.809, effective September 1, 2001.)

## Sec. 822.047. Local Regulation of Dangerous Dogs.

A county or municipality may place additional requirements or restrictions on dangerous dogs if the requirements or restrictions:

(1) are not specific to one breed or several breeds of dogs; and

(2) are more stringent than restrictions provided by this subchapter.

(Enacted by Acts 1991, 72nd Leg., ch. 916 (H.B. 2065), § 1, effective September 1, 1991.)

## SUBCHAPTER E
## DANGEROUS WILD ANIMALS

## Sec. 822.101. Definitions.

In this subchapter:

(1) "Animal registration agency" means the municipal or county animal control office with authority over the area where a dangerous wild animal is kept or a county sheriff in an area that does not have an animal control office.

(2) "Board" means the Texas Board of Health.

(3) "Commercial activity" means:

(A) an activity involving a dangerous wild animal conducted for profit that is not inherent to the animal's nature;

(B) an activity for which a fee is charged and that is entertainment using or an exhibition of the animal; or

(C) the selling, trading, bartering, or auctioning of a dangerous wild animal or a dangerous wild animal's body parts.

(4) "Dangerous wild animal" means:

(A) a lion;

(B) a tiger;

(C) an ocelot;

(D) a cougar;

(E) a leopard;

(F) a cheetah;

(G) a jaguar;

(H) a bobcat;

(I) a lynx;

(J) a serval;

(K) a caracal;

(L) a hyena;

(M) a bear;

(N) a coyote;

(O) a jackal;

(P) a baboon;

(Q) a chimpanzee;

(R) an orangutan;

(S) a gorilla; or

(T) any hybrid of an animal listed in this subdivision.

(5) "Owner" means any person who owns, harbors, or has custody or control of a dangerous wild animal.

(6) "Person" means an individual, partnership, corporation, trust, estate, joint stock company, foundation, or association of individuals.

(7) "Primary enclosure" means any structure used to immediately restrict an animal to a limited amount of space, including a cage, pen, run, room, compartment, or hutch.

(Enacted by Acts 2001, 77th Leg., ch. 54 (H.B. 1362), § 1, effective September 1, 2001.)

## Sec. 822.102. Applicability of Subchapter.

(a) This subchapter does not apply to:

(1) a county, municipality, or agency of the state or an agency of the United States or an agent or official of a county, municipality, or agency acting in an official capacity;

(2) a research facility, as that term is defined by Section 2(e), Animal Welfare Act (7 U.S.C. Section 2132), and its subsequent amendments, that is licensed by the secretary of agriculture of the United States under that Act;

(3) an organization that is an accredited member of the American Zoo and Aquarium Association;

(4) an injured, infirm, orphaned, or abandoned dangerous wild animal while being transported for care or treatment;

(5) an injured, infirm, orphaned, or abandoned dangerous wild animal while being rehabilitated, treated, or cared for by a licensed veterinarian, an incorporated humane society or animal shelter, or a person who holds a rehabilitation permit issued under Subchapter C, Chapter 43, Parks and Wildlife Code;

(6) a dangerous wild animal owned by and in the custody and control of a transient circus company that is not based in this state if:

(A) the animal is used as an integral part of the circus performances; and

(B) the animal is kept within this state only during the time the circus is performing in this state or for a period not to exceed 30 days while the circus is performing outside the United States;

(7) a dangerous wild animal while in the temporary custody or control of a television or motion picture production company during the filming of a television or motion picture production in this state;

(8) a dangerous wild animal owned by and in the possession, custody, or control of a college or university solely as a mascot for the college or university;

(9) a dangerous wild animal while being transported in interstate commerce through the state in compliance with the Animal Welfare Act (7 U.S.C. Section 2131 et seq.) and its subsequent amendments and the regulations adopted under that Act;

(10) a nonhuman primate owned by and in the control and custody of a person whose only business is supplying nonhuman primates directly and exclusively to biomedical research facilities and who holds a Class "A" or Class "B" dealer's license issued by the secretary of agriculture of the United States under the Animal Welfare Act (7 U.S.C. Section 2131 et seq.) and its subsequent amendments;

(11) a dangerous wild animal that is:

(A) owned by or in the possession, control, or custody of a person who is a participant in a species survival plan of the American Zoo and Aquarium Association for that species; and

(B) an integral part of that species survival plan; and

(12) in a county west of the Pecos River that has a population of less than 25,000, a cougar, bobcat, or coyote in the possession, custody, or control of a person that has trapped the cougar, bobcat, or coyote as part of a predator or depredation control activity.

(b) This subchapter does not require a municipality that does not have an animal control office to create that office.

(Enacted by Acts 2001, 77th Leg., ch. 54 (H.B. 1362), § 1, effective September 1, 2001; am. Acts 2005, 79th Leg., ch. 992 (H.B. 2026), § 31, effective June 18, 2005.)

## Sec. 822.103. Certificate of Registration; Fees.

(a) A person may not own, harbor, or have custody or control of a dangerous wild animal for any purpose unless the person holds a certificate of registration for that animal issued by an animal registration agency.

(b) A certificate of registration issued under this subchapter is not transferrable and is valid for one year after its date of issuance or renewal unless revoked.

(c) The animal registration agency may establish and charge reasonable fees for application, issuance, and renewal of a certificate of registration in order to recover the costs associated with the administration and enforcement of this subchapter. The fee charged to an applicant may not exceed $50 for each animal registered and may not exceed $500 for each person registering animals, regardless of the number of animals owned by the person. The fees collected under this section may be used only to administer and enforce this subchapter.

(Enacted by Acts 2001, 77th Leg., ch. 54 (H.B. 1362), § 1, effective September 1, 2001.)

## Sec. 822.104. Certificate of Registration Application.

(a) An applicant for an original or renewal certificate of registration for a dangerous wild animal must file an application with an animal registration agency on a form provided by the animal registration agency.

(b) The application must include:

(1) the name, address, and telephone number of the applicant;

(2) a complete identification of each animal, including species, sex, age, if known, and any distinguishing marks or coloration that would aid in the identification of the animal;

(3) the exact location where each animal is to be kept;

(4) a sworn statement that:

(A) all information in the application is complete and accurate; and

(B) the applicant has read this subchapter and that all facilities used by the applicant to confine or enclose the animal comply with the requirements of this subchapter; and

(5) any other information the animal registration agency may require.

(c) An applicant shall include with each application:

(1) the nonrefundable fee;

(2) proof, in a form acceptable by the animal registration agency, that the applicant has liability insurance, as required by Section 822.107;

(3) a color photograph of each animal being registered taken not earlier than the 30th day before the date the application is filed;

(4) a photograph and a statement of the dimensions of the primary enclosure in which each animal is to be kept and a scale diagram of the premises where each animal will be kept, including the location of any perimeter fencing and any residence on the premises; and

(5) if an applicant holds a Class "A" or Class "B" dealer's license or Class "C" exhibitor's license issued by the secretary of agriculture of the United States under the Animal Welfare Act (7 U.S.C. Section 2131 et seq.) and its subsequent amendments, a clear and legible photocopy of the license.

(d) In addition to the items required under Subsection (c), an application for renewal must include a statement signed by a veterinarian licensed to practice in this state stating that the veterinarian:

(1) inspected each animal being registered not earlier than the 30th day before the date of the filing of the renewal application; and

(2) finds that the care and treatment of each animal by the owner meets or exceeds the standards prescribed under this subchapter.

(Enacted by Acts 2001, 77th Leg., ch. 54 (H.B. 1362), § 1, effective September 1, 2001.)

## Sec. 822.105. Denial or Revocation of Certificate of Registration; Appeal.

(a) If the animal registration agency finds that an application for an original or renewal certificate of registration under this subchapter does not meet the requirements of Section 822.104 or, after inspection, that an applicant has not complied with this subchapter, the animal registration agency shall deny the applicant a certificate of registration and give the applicant written notice of the denial and the reasons for the denial.

(b) If the animal registration agency finds, after inspection, that a registered owner provided false information in or in connection with the application or has not complied with this subchapter, the animal registration agency shall revoke the certificate of registration and give the owner written notice of the revocation and the reasons for the revocation.

(c) A person may appeal the denial of an original or renewal certificate of registration or the revocation of a certificate of registration to the justice court for the precinct in which the animal is located or the municipal court in the municipality in which the animal is located not later than the 15th day after the date the certificate of registration is denied or revoked. Either party may appeal the decision of the justice or municipal court to a county court or county court at law in the county in which the justice or municipal court is located. The decision of the county court or county court at law may not be appealed.

(d) The filing of an appeal of the denial or revocation of a certificate of registration under Subsection (c) stays the denial or revocation until the court rules on the appeal.
(Enacted by Acts 2001, 77th Leg., ch. 54 (H.B. 1362), § 1, effective September 1, 2001.)

## Sec. 822.106. Display of Certificate of Registration.

(a) A holder of a certificate of registration shall prominently display the certificate at the premises where each animal that is the subject of the certificate of registration is kept.

(b) Not later than the 10th day after the date a person receives a certificate of registration, the person shall file a clear and legible copy of the certificate of registration with the Texas Department of Health. The department shall establish a procedure for filing a certificate of registration and shall charge a reasonable fee in an amount sufficient to recover the cost associated with filing a certificate of registration under this subsection.
(Enacted by Acts 2001, 77th Leg., ch. 54 (H.B. 1362), § 1, effective September 1, 2001.)

## Sec. 822.107. Liability Insurance.

An owner of a dangerous wild animal shall maintain liability insurance coverage in an amount of not less than $100,000 for each occurrence for liability for damages for destruction of or damage to property and death or bodily injury to a person caused by the dangerous wild animal.
(Enacted by Acts 2001, 77th Leg., ch. 54 (H.B. 1362), § 1, effective September 1, 2001.)

## Sec. 822.108. Inspection.

An owner of a dangerous wild animal, at all reasonable times, shall allow the animal registra-

tion agency, its staff, its agents, or a designated licensed veterinarian to enter the premises where the animal is kept and to inspect the animal, the primary enclosure for the animal, and the owner's records relating to the animal to ensure compliance with this subchapter.
(Enacted by Acts 2001, 77th Leg., ch. 54 (H.B. 1362), § 1, effective September 1, 2001.)

## Sec. 822.109. Relocation or Disposition of Animal.

(a) An owner of a dangerous wild animal may not permanently relocate the animal unless the owner first notifies the animal registration agency in writing of the exact location to which the animal will be relocated and provides the animal registration agency, with respect to the new location, the information required by Section 822.104.

(b) Within 10 days after the death, sale, or other disposition of the animal, the owner of the animal shall notify the animal registration agency in writing of the death, sale, or other disposition.
(Enacted by Acts 2001, 77th Leg., ch. 54 (H.B. 1362), § 1, effective September 1, 2001.)

## Sec. 822.110. Attack by Animal; Escape of Animal; Liability.

(a) An owner of a dangerous wild animal shall notify the animal registration agency of any attack of a human by the animal within 48 hours of the attack.

(b) An owner of a dangerous wild animal shall immediately notify the animal registration agency and the local law enforcement agency of any escape of the animal.

(c) An owner of a dangerous wild animal that escapes is liable for all costs incurred in apprehending and confining the animal.

(d) An animal registration agency, a law enforcement agency, or an employee of an animal registration agency or law enforcement agency is not liable to an owner of a dangerous wild animal for damages arising in connection with the escape of a dangerous wild animal, including liability for damage, injury, or death caused by the animal during or after the animal's escape, or for injury to or death of the animal as a result of apprehension or confinement of the animal after escape.
(Enacted by Acts 2001, 77th Leg., ch. 54 (H.B. 1362), § 1, effective September 1, 2001.)

## Sec. 822.111. Powers and Duties of Board; Caging Requirements and Standards.

(a) The board by rule shall establish caging requirements and standards for the keeping and confinement of a dangerous wild animal to ensure that the animal is kept in a manner and confined in a primary enclosure that:

(1) protects and enhances the public's health and safety;

(2) prevents escape by the animal; and

(3) provides a safe, healthy, and humane environment for the animal.

(b) An owner of a dangerous wild animal shall keep and confine the animal in accordance with the caging requirements and standards established by the board.

(c) An animal registration agency may approve a deviation from the caging requirements and standards established by the board, only if:

(1) the animal registration agency has good cause for the deviation; and

(2) the deviation:

(A) does not compromise the public's health and safety;

(B) does not reduce the total area of the primary enclosure below that established by the board; and

(C) does not otherwise adversely affect the overall welfare of the animal involved.

(Enacted by Acts 2001, 77th Leg., ch. 54 (H.B. 1362), § 1, effective September 1, 2001.)

## Sec. 822.112. Care, Treatment, and Transportation of Animal.

(a) For each dangerous wild animal, the owner shall comply with all applicable standards of the Animal Welfare Act (7 U.S.C. Section 2131 et seq.) and its subsequent amendments and the regulations adopted under that Act relating to:

(1) facilities and operations;

(2) animal health and husbandry; and

(3) veterinary care.

(b) An owner of a dangerous wild animal shall maintain a separate written log for each dangerous wild animal documenting the animal's veterinary care and shall make the log available to the animal registration agency or its agent on request. The log must:

(1) identify the animal treated;

(2) provide the date of treatment;

(3) describe the type or nature of treatment; and

(4) provide the name of the attending veterinarian, if applicable.

(c) When transporting a dangerous wild animal, the owner of the animal, or a designated carrier or intermediate handler of the animal, shall comply with all transportation standards that apply to that animal under the Animal Welfare Act (7 U.S.C. Section 2131 et seq.) and its subsequent amendments or the regulations adopted under that Act.

(d) A person is exempt from the requirements of this section if the person is caring for, treating, or transporting an animal for which the person holds a Class "A" or Class "B" dealer's license or a Class "C" exhibitor's license issued by the secretary of agriculture of the United States under the Animal Welfare Act (7 U.S.C. Section 2131 et seq.) and its subsequent amendments.

(Enacted by Acts 2001, 77th Leg., ch. 54 (H.B. 1362), § 1, effective September 1, 2001.)

## Sec. 822.113. Offense and Penalty.

(a) A person commits an offense if the person violates Section 822.103(a), Section 822.106, or Section 822.110(a) or (b). Each animal with respect to which there is a violation and each day that a violation continues is a separate offense.

(b) A person commits an offense if the person knowingly sells or otherwise transfers ownership of a dangerous wild animal to a person who does not have a certificate of registration for that animal as required by this subchapter.

(c) An offense under this section is a Class C misdemeanor.

(Enacted by Acts 2001, 77th Leg., ch. 54 (H.B. 1362), § 1, effective September 1, 2001.)

## Sec. 822.114. Civil Penalty.

(a) A person who violates Section 822.103(a) is liable for a civil penalty of not less than $200 and not more than $2,000 for each animal with respect to which there is a violation and for each day the violation continues.

(b) The county or municipality in which the violation occurs may sue to collect a civil penalty. A civil penalty collected under this subsection may be retained by the county or municipality.

(c) The county or municipality in which the violation occurs may also recover the reasonable costs of investigation, reasonable attorney's fees, and reasonable expert witness fees incurred by the animal registration agency in the civil action. Costs or fees recovered under this subsection shall be credited to the operating account from which payment for the animal registration agency's expenditures was made.

Health

(Enacted by Acts 2001, 77th Leg., ch. 54 (H.B. 1362), § 1, effective September 1, 2001.)

### Sec. 822.115.  Injunction.

Any person who is directly harmed or threatened with harm by a violation of this subchapter or a failure to enforce this subchapter may sue an owner of a dangerous wild animal to enjoin a violation of this subchapter or to enforce this subchapter.

(Enacted by Acts 2001, 77th Leg., ch. 54 (H.B. 1362), § 1, effective September 1, 2001.)

### Sec. 822.116.  Effect of Subchapter on Other Law.

(a) This subchapter does not affect the applicability of any other law, rule, order, ordinance, or other legal requirement of this state or a political subdivision of this state.

(b) This subchapter does not prevent a municipality or county from prohibiting or regulating by ordinance or order the ownership, possession, confinement, or care of a dangerous wild animal.

(Enacted by Acts 2001, 77th Leg., ch. 54 (H.B. 1362), § 1, effective September 1, 2001.)

## CHAPTER 825
## PREDATORY ANIMALS AND ANIMAL PESTS

**Subchapter A. Cooperation Between State and Federal Agencies in Controlling Predatory Animals and Rodents**

## SUBCHAPTER A
## COOPERATION BETWEEN STATE AND FEDERAL AGENCIES IN CONTROLLING PREDATORY ANIMALS AND RODENTS

### Sec. 825.008.  Tampering with Traps; Criminal Penalty.

(a) A person commits an offense if the person maliciously or wilfully tampers with all or any part of a trap set under this subchapter or removes a trap from the position in which it is placed by a hunter or trapper acting under this subchapter.

(b) An offense under this section is punishable by a fine of not less than $50 or more than $200.

(Enacted by Acts 1989, 71st Leg., ch. 678 (H.B. 2136), § 1, effective September 1, 1989.)

### Sec. 825.009.  Stealing Traps; Criminal Penalty.

(a) A person commits an offense if the person steals or fraudulently takes a trap belonging to the state or the United States Department of the Interior.

(b) An offense under this section is a misdemeanor punishable by a fine of not less than $100 or more than $200.

(Enacted by Acts 1989, 71st Leg., ch. 678 (H.B. 2136), § 1, effective September 1, 1989.)

### Sec. 825.010.  Stealing Animals from Traps; Criminal Penalty.

(a) A person commits an offense if the person steals an animal listed in Section 825.001 from a trap set under this subchapter or takes the animal from the trap without authority.

(b) An offense under this section is a misdemeanor punishable by a fine of not less than $100 or more than $200.

(c) An animal stolen or taken in violation of this section is the property of the state. A complaint alleging a violation of this section must allege that the animal is owned by the state, and the only proof necessary to establish ownership shall consist of proving that the animal was taken from a trap that had been set by a hunter or trapper acting under this subchapter.

(Enacted by Acts 1989, 71st Leg., ch. 678 (H.B. 2136), § 1, effective September 1, 1989.)

## CHAPTER 826
## RABIES

**Subchapter C. Rabies Vaccinations**

**Subchapter D. Registration and Restraint of Dogs and Cats**

**Subchapter E. Reports and Quarantine**

## SUBCHAPTER C
## RABIES VACCINATIONS

### Sec. 826.021.  Vaccination of Dogs and Cats Required.

(a) Except as otherwise provided by board rule, the owner of a dog or cat shall have the animal vaccinated against rabies by the time the animal is four months of age and at regular intervals thereafter as prescribed by board rule.

(b) A veterinarian who vaccinates a dog or cat against rabies shall issue to the animal's owner a vaccination certificate in a form that meets the minimum standards approved by the board.

(c) A county or municipality may not register or license an animal that has not been vaccinated in accordance with this section.

(Enacted by Acts 1989, 71st Leg., ch. 678 (H.B. 2136), § 1, effective September 1, 1989.)

### Sec. 826.022. Vaccination; Criminal Penalty.

(a) A person commits an offense if the person fails or refuses to have each dog or cat owned by the person vaccinated against rabies and the animal is required to be vaccinated under:

(1) Section 826.021 and board rules; or

(2) ordinances or rules adopted under this chapter by a county or municipality within whose jurisdiction the act occurs.

(b) An offense under this section is a Class C misdemeanor.

(c) If on the trial of an offense under this section the court finds that the person has been previously convicted of an offense under this section, the offense is a Class B misdemeanor.

(Enacted by Acts 1989, 71st Leg., ch. 678 (H.B. 2136), § 1, effective September 1, 1989; am. Acts 1995, 74th Leg., ch. 44 (H.B. 721), § 3, effective May 5, 1995.)

### SUBCHAPTER D
### REGISTRATION AND RESTRAINT OF DOGS AND CATS

### Sec. 826.034. Restraint; Criminal Penalty.

(a) A person commits an offense if:

(1) the person fails or refuses to restrain a dog or cat owned by the person; and

(2) the animal is required to be restrained under the ordinances or rules adopted under this chapter by a county or municipality within whose jurisdiction the act occurs.

(b) An offense under this section is a Class C misdemeanor.

(Enacted by Acts 1989, 71st Leg., ch. 678 (H.B. 2136), § 1, effective September 1, 1989.)

### SUBCHAPTER E
### REPORTS AND QUARANTINE

### Sec. 826.042. Quarantine of Animals.

(a) The board shall adopt rules governing the testing of quarantined animals and the procedure for and method of quarantine.

(b) The local rabies control authority or a veterinarian shall quarantine or test in accordance with board rules any animal that the local rabies control authority or veterinarian has probable cause to believe is rabid, may have been exposed to rabies, or may have exposed a person to rabies.

(c) An owner shall submit for quarantine an animal that:

(1) is reported to be rabid or to have exposed an individual to rabies; or

(2) the owner knows or suspects is rabid or has exposed an individual to rabies.

(d) The owner shall submit the animal to the local rabies control authority of the county or municipality in which the exposure occurs.

(e) A veterinarian shall quarantine an animal that:

(1) is in the possession of the veterinarian; and

(2) the veterinarian knows or suspects is rabid or has exposed an individual to rabies.

(Enacted by Acts 1989, 71st Leg., ch. 678 (H.B. 2136), § 1, effective September 1, 1989; am. Acts 1995, 74th Leg., ch. 44 (H.B. 721), § 8, effective May 5, 1995.)

### Sec. 826.044. Quarantine; Criminal Penalty.

(a) A person commits an offense if the person fails or refuses to quarantine or present for quarantine or testing an animal that:

(1) is required to be placed in quarantine or presented for testing under Section 826.042 and board rules; or

(2) is required to be placed in quarantine under ordinances or rules adopted under this chapter by a county or municipality within whose jurisdiction the act occurs.

(b) An offense under this section is a Class C misdemeanor.

(Enacted by Acts 1989, 71st Leg., ch. 678 (H.B. 2136), § 1, effective September 1, 1989.)

Health

# TITLE 11
# CIVIL COMMITMENT OF SEXUALLY VIOLENT PREDATORS

## CHAPTER 841
## CIVIL COMMITMENT OF SEXUALLY VIOLENT PREDATORS

### Subchapter A. General Provisions

### Subchapter B. Notice of Potential Predator; Initial Determinations

### Subchapter C. Petition Alleging Predator Status

### Subchapter D. Trial

### Subchapter E. Civil Commitment

### Subchapter F. Commitment Review

### Subchapter G. Petition for Release

### Subchapter H. Miscellaneous Provisions

## SUBCHAPTER A
## GENERAL PROVISIONS

### Sec. 841.001.  Legislative Findings.

The legislature finds that a small but extremely dangerous group of sexually violent predators exists and that those predators have a behavioral abnormality that is not amenable to traditional mental illness treatment modalities and that makes the predators likely to engage in repeated predatory acts of sexual violence. The legislature finds that the existing involuntary commitment provisions of Subtitle C, Title 7, are inadequate to address the risk of repeated predatory behavior that sexually violent predators pose to society. The legislature further finds that treatment modalities for sexually violent predators are different from the traditional treatment modalities for persons appropriate for involuntary commitment under Subtitle C, Title 7. Thus, the legislature finds that a civil commitment procedure for the long-term supervision and treatment of sexually violent predators is necessary and in the interest of the state.
(Enacted by Acts 1999, 76th Leg., ch. 1188 (S.B. 365), § 4.01, effective September 1, 1999.)

### Sec. 841.002.  Definitions.

In this chapter:
(1) "Attorney representing the state" means an attorney employed by the civil division of the special prosecution unit to initiate and pursue a civil commitment proceeding under this chapter.
(2) "Behavioral abnormality" means a congenital or acquired condition that, by affecting a person's emotional or volitional capacity, pre-

disposes the person to commit a sexually violent offense, to the extent that the person becomes a menace to the health and safety of another person.

(3) "Case manager" means a person employed by or under contract with the office to perform duties related to outpatient treatment and supervision of a person committed under this chapter.

(3-a) "Civil commitment proceeding" means a trial or hearing conducted under Subchapter D, F, or G.

(4) "Office" means the Office of Violent Sex Offender Management.

(5) "Predatory act" means an act directed toward individuals, including family members, for the primary purpose of victimization.

(6) "Repeat sexually violent offender" has the meaning assigned by Section 841.003.

(7) "Secure correctional facility" means a county jail or a confinement facility operated by or under contract with any division of the Texas Department of Criminal Justice.

(7-a) "Sexually motivated conduct" means any conduct involving the intent to arouse or gratify the sexual desire of any person immediately before, during, or immediately after the commission of an offense.

(8) "Sexually violent offense" means:

(A) an offense under Section 21.02, 21.11(a)(1), 22.011, or 22.021, Penal Code;

(B) an offense under Section 20.04(a)(4), Penal Code, if the person committed the offense with the intent to violate or abuse the victim sexually;

(C) an offense under Section 30.02, Penal Code, if the offense is punishable under Subsection (d) of that section and the person committed the offense with the intent to commit an offense listed in Paragraph (A) or (B);

(D) an offense under Section 19.02 or 19.03, Penal Code, that, during the guilt or innocence phase or the punishment phase for the offense, during the adjudication or disposition of delinquent conduct constituting the offense, or subsequently during a civil commitment proceeding under Subchapter D, is determined beyond a reasonable doubt to have been based on sexually motivated conduct;

(E) an attempt, conspiracy, or solicitation, as defined by Chapter 15, Penal Code, to commit an offense listed in Paragraph (A), (B), (C), or (D);

(F) an offense under prior state law that contains elements substantially similar to the elements of an offense listed in Paragraph (A), (B), (C), (D), or (E); or

(G) an offense under the law of another state, federal law, or the Uniform Code of Military Justice that contains elements substantially similar to the elements of an offense listed in Paragraph (A), (B), (C), (D), or (E).

(9) "Sexually violent predator" has the meaning assigned by Section 841.003.

(10) "Tracking service" means an electronic monitoring service, global positioning satellite service, or other appropriate technological service that is designed to track a person's location.

(Enacted by Acts 1999, 76th Leg., ch. 1188 (S.B. 365), § 4.01, effective September 1, 1999; am. Acts 2003, 78th Leg., ch. 347 (S.B. 871), § 16, effective September 1, 2003; am. Acts 2005, 79th Leg., ch. 849 (S.B. 912), § 1, effective September 1, 2005; am. Acts 2007, 80th Leg., ch. 593 (H.B. 8), § 3.45, effective September 1, 2007; am. Acts 2007, 80th Leg., ch. 1219 (H.B. 2034), § 5, effective September 1, 2007; am. Acts 2011, 82nd Leg., ch. 1201 (S.B. 166), § 3, effective September 1, 2011.)

## Sec. 841.003. Sexually Violent Predator.

(a) A person is a sexually violent predator for the purposes of this chapter if the person:

(1) is a repeat sexually violent offender; and

(2) suffers from a behavioral abnormality that makes the person likely to engage in a predatory act of sexual violence.

(b) A person is a repeat sexually violent offender for the purposes of this chapter if the person is convicted of more than one sexually violent offense and a sentence is imposed for at least one of the offenses or if:

(1) the person:

(A) is convicted of a sexually violent offense, regardless of whether the sentence for the offense was ever imposed or whether the sentence was probated and the person was subsequently discharged from community supervision;

(B) enters a plea of guilty or nolo contendere for a sexually violent offense in return for a grant of deferred adjudication;

(C) is adjudged not guilty by reason of insanity of a sexually violent offense; or

Health

(D) is adjudicated by a juvenile court as having engaged in delinquent conduct constituting a sexually violent offense and is committed to the Texas Youth Commission under Section 54.04(d)(3) or (m), Family Code; and

(2) after the date on which under Subdivision (1) the person is convicted, receives a grant of deferred adjudication, is adjudged not guilty by reason of insanity, or is adjudicated by a juvenile court as having engaged in delinquent conduct, the person commits a sexually violent offense for which the person:

(A) is convicted, but only if the sentence for the offense is imposed; or

(B) is adjudged not guilty by reason of insanity.

(Enacted by Acts 1999, 76th Leg., ch. 1188 (S.B. 365), § 4.01, effective September 1, 1999.)

### Sec. 841.004.  Special Prosecution Unit.

The civil division of the special prosecution unit, separate from that part of the unit responsible for prosecuting criminal cases, is responsible for initiating and pursuing a civil commitment proceeding under this chapter.

(Enacted by Acts 1999, 76th Leg., ch. 1188 (S.B. 365), § 4.01, effective September 1, 1999; am. Acts 2007, 80th Leg., ch. 1219 (H.B. 2034), § 6, effective September 1, 2007.)

### Sec. 841.005.  Office of State Counsel for Offenders.

(a) Except as provided by Subsection (b), the Office of State Counsel for Offenders shall represent an indigent person subject to a civil commitment proceeding under this chapter.

(b) If for any reason the Office of State Counsel for Offenders is unable to represent an indigent person described by Subsection (a) at a civil commitment proceeding under this chapter, the court shall appoint other counsel to represent the indigent person.

(Enacted by Acts 1999, 76th Leg., ch. 1188 (S.B. 365), § 4.01, effective September 1, 1999; am. Acts 2003, 78th Leg., ch. 347 (S.B. 871), § 17, effective September 1, 2003.)

### Sec. 841.006.  Application of Chapter.

This chapter does not:

(1) prohibit a person committed under this chapter from filing at any time a petition for release under this chapter; or

(2) create for the committed person a cause of action against another person for failure to give notice within a period required by Subchapter B, C, or D.

(Enacted by Acts 1999, 76th Leg., ch. 1188 (S.B. 365), § 4.01, effective September 1, 1999; am. Acts 2003, 78th Leg., ch. 347 (S.B. 871), § 17, effective September 1, 2003.)

### Sec. 841.007.  Duties of Office of Violent Sex Offender Management.

The Office of Violent Sex Offender Management is responsible for providing appropriate and necessary treatment and supervision through the case management system.

(Enacted by Acts 1999, 76th Leg., ch. 1188 (S.B. 365), § 4.01, effective September 1, 1999; am. Acts 2003, 78th Leg., ch. 347 (S.B. 871), § 17, effective September 1, 2003; am. Acts 2011, 82nd Leg., ch. 1201 (S.B. 166), § 4, effective September 1, 2011.)

### SUBCHAPTER B
### NOTICE OF POTENTIAL PREDATOR; INITIAL DETERMINATIONS

### Sec. 841.021.  Notice of Potential Predator.

(a) Before the person's anticipated release date, the Texas Department of Criminal Justice shall give to the multidisciplinary team established under Section 841.022 written notice of the anticipated release of a person who:

(1) is serving a sentence for:

(A) a sexually violent offense described by Section 841.002(8)(A), (B), or (C); or

(B) what is, or as described by this chapter what the department reasonably believes may be determined to be, a sexually violent offense described by Section 841.002(8)(D); and

(2) may be a repeat sexually violent offender.

(b) Before the person's anticipated discharge date, the Department of State Health Services shall give to the multidisciplinary team established under Section 841.022 written notice of the anticipated discharge of a person who:

(1) is committed to the department after having been adjudged not guilty by reason of insanity of:

(A) a sexually violent offense described by Section 841.002(8)(A), (B), or (C); or

(B) what is, or as described by this chapter what the department reasonably believes may be determined to be, a sexually violent offense described by Section 841.002(8)(D); and

(2) may be a repeat sexually violent offender.

(c) The Texas Department of Criminal Justice or the Department of State Health Services, as appropriate, shall give the notice described by Subsection (a) or (b) not later than the first day of the 16th month before the person's anticipated release or discharge date, but under exigent circumstances may give the notice at any time before the anticipated release or discharge date. The notice must contain the following information:

(1) the person's name, identifying factors, anticipated residence after release or discharge, and criminal history;

(2) documentation of the person's institutional adjustment and actual treatment; and

(3) an assessment of the likelihood that the person will commit a sexually violent offense after release or discharge.

(Enacted by Acts 1999, 76th Leg., ch. 1188 (S.B. 365), § 4.01, effective September 1, 1999; am. Acts 2005, 79th Leg., ch. 849 (S.B. 912), § 2, effective September 1, 2005; am. Acts 2011, 82nd Leg., ch. 1201 (S.B. 166), § 5, effective September 1, 2011.)

### Sec. 841.022. Multidisciplinary Team.

(a) The executive director of the Texas Department of Criminal Justice and the commissioner of the Department of State Health Services jointly shall establish a multidisciplinary team to review available records of a person referred to the team under Section 841.021. The team must include:

(1) one person from the Department of State Health Services;

(2) two persons from the Texas Department of Criminal Justice, one of whom must be from the victim services office of that department;

(3) one person from the Department of Public Safety;

(4) two persons from the office or office personnel; and

(5) one person from the Council on Sex Offender Treatment.

(b) The multidisciplinary team may request the assistance of other persons in making an assessment under this section.

(c) Not later than the 60th day after the date the multidisciplinary team receives notice under Section 841.021(a) or (b), the team shall:

(1) assess whether the person is a repeat sexually violent offender and whether the person is likely to commit a sexually violent offense after release or discharge;

(2) give notice of that assessment to the Texas Department of Criminal Justice or the Texas Department of Mental Health and Mental Retardation, as appropriate; and

(3) recommend the assessment of the person for a behavioral abnormality, as appropriate.

(Enacted by Acts 1999, 76th Leg., ch. 1188 (S.B. 365), § 4.01, effective September 1, 1999; am. Acts 2003, 78th Leg., ch. 347 (S.B. 871), § 18, effective September 1, 2003; am. Acts 2011, 82nd Leg., ch. 1201 (S.B. 166), § 6, effective September 1, 2011.)

### Sec. 841.023. Assessment for Behavioral Abnormality.

(a) Not later than the 60th day after the date of a recommendation under Section 841.022(c), the Texas Department of Criminal Justice or the Department of State Health Services, as appropriate, shall assess whether the person suffers from a behavioral abnormality that makes the person likely to engage in a predatory act of sexual violence. To aid in the assessment, the department required to make the assessment shall use an expert to examine the person. That department may contract for the expert services required by this subsection. The expert shall make a clinical assessment based on testing for psychopathy, a clinical interview, and other appropriate assessments and techniques to aid the department in its assessment.

(b) If as a result of the assessment the Texas Department of Criminal Justice or the Department of State Health Services believes that the person suffers from a behavioral abnormality, the department making the assessment shall give notice of that assessment and provide corresponding documentation to the attorney representing the state not later than the 60th day after the date of a recommendation under Section 841.022(c).

(Enacted by Acts 1999, 76th Leg., ch. 1188 (S.B. 365), § 4.01, effective September 1, 1999; am. Acts 2003, 78th Leg., ch. 347 (S.B. 871), § 19, effective September 1, 2003; am. Acts 2011, 82nd Leg., ch. 1201 (S.B. 166), § 7, effective September 1, 2011.)

Health

## SUBCHAPTER C
## PETITION ALLEGING PREDATOR STATUS

### Sec. 841.041. Petition Alleging Predator Status.

(a) If a person is referred to the attorney representing the state under Section 841.023, the attorney may file, in a Montgomery County district court other than a family district court, a petition alleging that the person is a sexually violent predator and stating facts sufficient to support the allegation.

(b) A petition described by Subsection (a) must be:

(1) filed not later than the 90th day after the date the person is referred to the attorney representing the state; and

(2) served on the person as soon as practicable after the date the petition is filed.

(Enacted by Acts 1999, 76th Leg., ch. 1188 (S.B. 365), § 4.01, effective September 1, 1999; am. Acts 2003, 78th Leg., ch. 347 (S.B. 871), § 20, effective September 1, 2003.)

## SUBCHAPTER D
## TRIAL

### Sec. 841.061. Trial.

(a) Not later than the 270th day after the date a petition is served on the person under Section 841.041, the judge shall conduct a trial to determine whether the person is a sexually violent predator.

(b) The person or the state is entitled to a jury trial on demand. A demand for a jury trial must be filed in writing not later than the 10th day before the date the trial is scheduled to begin.

(c) The person and the state are each entitled to an immediate examination of the person by an expert. All components of the examination must be completed not later than the 90th day before the date the trial begins.

(d) Additional rights of the person at the trial include the following:

(1) the right to appear at the trial;

(2) except as provided by Subsection (f), the right to present evidence on the person's behalf;

(3) the right to cross-examine a witness who testifies against the person; and

(4) the right to view and copy all petitions and reports in the court file.

(e) The attorney representing the state may rely on the petition filed under Section 841.041 and supplement the petition with documentary evidence or live testimony.

(f) A person who is on trial to determine the person's status as a sexually violent predator is required to submit to all expert examinations that are required or permitted of the state to prepare for the person's trial. A person who fails to submit to expert examination on the state's behalf as required by this subsection is subject to the following consequences:

(1) the person's failure to participate may be used as evidence against the person at trial;

(2) the person may be prohibited from offering into evidence the results of an expert examination performed on the person's behalf; and

(3) the person may be subject to contempt proceedings if the person violates a court order by failing to submit to an expert examination on the state's behalf.

(g) A judge assigned to preside over a trial under this subchapter is not subject to an objection under Section 74.053, Government Code, other than an objection made under Section 74.053(d), Government Code.

(Enacted by Acts 1999, 76th Leg., ch. 1188 (S.B. 365), § 4.01, effective September 1, 1999; am. Acts 2003, 78th Leg., ch. 347 (S.B. 871), § 21, effective September 1, 2003; am. Acts 2007, 80th Leg., ch. 1219 (H.B. 2034), § 7, effective June 15, 2007.)

### Sec. 841.062. Determination of Predator Status.

(a) The judge or jury shall determine whether, beyond a reasonable doubt, the person is a sexually violent predator. Either the state or the person is entitled to appeal the determination.

(b) A jury determination that the person is a sexually violent predator must be by unanimous verdict.

(Enacted by Acts 1999, 76th Leg., ch. 1188 (S.B. 365), § 4.01, effective September 1, 1999.)

### Sec. 841.063. Continuance.

The judge may continue a trial or hearing conducted under this chapter if the person is not substantially prejudiced by the continuance and:

(1) on the request of either party and a showing of good cause; or

(2) on the judge's own motion in the due administration of justice.

(Enacted by Acts 1999, 76th Leg., ch. 1188 (S.B. 365), § 4.01, effective September 1, 1999; am. Acts 2003, 78th Leg., ch. 347 (S.B. 871), § 22, effective September 1, 2003.)

Health

## Sec. 841.064. Mistrial.

A trial following a mistrial must begin not later than the 90th day after the date a mistrial was declared in the previous trial, unless the later trial is continued as provided by Section 841.063. (Enacted by Acts 1999, 76th Leg., ch. 1188 (S.B. 365), § 4.01, effective September 1, 1999.)

### SUBCHAPTER E
### CIVIL COMMITMENT

## Sec. 841.081. Civil Commitment of Predator.

(a) If at a trial conducted under Subchapter D the judge or jury determines that the person is a sexually violent predator, the judge shall commit the person for outpatient treatment and supervision to be coordinated by the case manager. The commitment order is effective immediately on entry of the order, except that the outpatient treatment and supervision begins on the person's release from a secure correctional facility or discharge from a state hospital and continues until the person's behavioral abnormality has changed to the extent that the person is no longer likely to engage in a predatory act of sexual violence.

(b) At any time after entry of a commitment order under Subsection (a), the case manager may provide to the person instruction regarding the requirements associated with the order, regardless of whether the person is incarcerated at the time of the instruction. (Enacted by Acts 1999, 76th Leg., ch. 1188 (S.B. 365), § 4.01, effective September 1, 1999; am. Acts 2003, 78th Leg., ch. 347 (S.B. 871), § 23, effective September 1, 2003.)

## Sec. 841.082. Commitment Requirements.

(a) Before entering an order directing a person's outpatient civil commitment, the judge shall impose on the person requirements necessary to ensure the person's compliance with treatment and supervision and to protect the community. The requirements shall include:

(1) requiring the person to reside in a Texas residential facility under contract with the office or at another location or facility approved by the office;

(2) prohibiting the person's contact with a victim or potential victim of the person;

(3) prohibiting the person's possession or use of alcohol, inhalants, or a controlled substance;

(4) requiring the person's participation in and compliance with a specific course of treat-

ment provided by the office and compliance with all written requirements imposed by the case manager or otherwise by the office;

(5) requiring the person to:

(A) submit to tracking under a particular type of tracking service and to any other appropriate supervision; and

(B) refrain from tampering with, altering, modifying, obstructing, or manipulating the tracking equipment;

(6) prohibiting the person from changing the person's residence without prior authorization from the judge and from leaving the state without that prior authorization;

(7) if determined appropriate by the judge, establishing a child safety zone in the same manner as a child safety zone is established by a judge under Section 13B, Article 42.12, Code of Criminal Procedure, and requiring the person to comply with requirements related to the safety zone; and

(8) any other requirements determined necessary by the judge.

(b) A tracking service to which a person is required to submit under Subsection (a)(5) must:

(1) track the person's location in real time;

(2) be able to provide a real-time report of the person's location to the case manager at the case manager's request; and

(3) periodically provide a cumulative report of the person's location to the case manager.

(c) The judge shall provide a copy of the requirements imposed under Subsection (a) to the person and to the office. The office shall provide a copy of those requirements to the case manager and to the service providers.

(d) The court retains jurisdiction of the case with respect to a civil commitment proceeding conducted under Subchapters F and G.

(e) The requirements imposed under Subsection (a) may be modified at any time after notice to each affected party to the proceedings and a hearing. (Enacted by Acts 1999, 76th Leg., ch. 1188 (S.B. 365), § 4.01, effective September 1, 1999; am. Acts 2003, 78th Leg., ch. 347 (S.B. 871), § 24, effective September 1, 2003; am. Acts 2005, 79th Leg., ch. 849 (S.B. 912), §§ 3, 7(1), effective September 1, 2005; am. Acts 2007, 80th Leg., ch. 593 (H.B. 8), § 1.12, effective September 1, 2007; am. Acts 2011, 82nd Leg., ch. 1201 (S.B. 166), § 8, effective September 1, 2011.)

## Sec. 841.083. Treatment; Supervision.

(a) The office shall approve and contract for the provision of a treatment plan for the committed person to be developed by the treatment provider. A treatment plan may include the monitoring of the person with a polygraph or plethysmograph. The treatment provider may receive annual compensation in an amount not to exceed $10,000 for providing the required treatment.

(b) The case manager shall provide supervision to the person. The provision of supervision must include a tracking service and, if required by court order, supervised housing.

(c) The office shall enter into appropriate memoranda of understanding with the Department of Public Safety for the provision of a tracking service and with the Department of Public Safety and local law enforcement authorities for assistance in the preparation of criminal complaints, warrants, and related documents and in the apprehension and arrest of a person.

(d) The office shall enter into appropriate memoranda of understanding for any necessary supervised housing. The office shall reimburse the applicable provider for housing costs under this section.

(e) The case manager shall:

(1) coordinate the outpatient treatment and supervision required by this chapter, including performing a periodic assessment of the success of that treatment and supervision;

(2) make timely recommendations to the judge on whether to allow the committed person to change residence or to leave the state and on any other appropriate matters; and

(3) provide a report to the office, semiannually or more frequently as necessary, which must include:

(A) any known change in the person's status that affects proper treatment and supervision; and

(B) any recommendations made to the judge.

(Enacted by Acts 1999, 76th Leg., ch. 1188 (S.B. 365), § 4.01, effective September 1, 1999; am. Acts 2003, 78th Leg., ch. 347 (S.B. 871), § 25, effective September 1, 2003; am. Acts 2005, 79th Leg., ch. 849 (S.B. 912), § 4, effective September 1, 2005; am. Acts 2007, 80th Leg., ch. 937 (H.B. 3560), § 1.94, effective September 1, 2007; am. Acts 2011, 82nd Leg., ch. 1201 (S.B. 166), § 9, effective September 1, 2011.)

## Sec. 841.084.  Cost of Tracking Service.

Notwithstanding Section 841.146(c), a civilly committed person who is not indigent is responsible for the cost of the tracking service required by Section 841.082 and monthly shall pay to the office the amount that the office determines will be necessary to defray the cost of operating the service with respect to the person during the subsequent month. The office immediately shall transfer the money to the appropriate service provider.

(Enacted by Acts 2007, 80th Leg., ch. 593 (H.B. 8), § 1.13, effective September 1, 2007; am. Acts 2011, 82nd Leg., ch. 1201 (S.B. 166), § 10, effective September 1, 2011.)

## Sec. 841.085.  Criminal Penalty; Prosecution of Offense.

(a) A person commits an offense if, after having been adjudicated and civilly committed as a sexually violent predator under this chapter, the person violates a civil commitment requirement imposed under Section 841.082.

(b) An offense under this section is a felony of the third degree.

(c) At the request of the local prosecuting attorney, an attorney employed by the civil division of the special prosecution unit described by Section 841.004 may assist in the trial of an offense under this section.

(Enacted by Acts 1999, 76th Leg., ch. 1188 (S.B. 365), § 4.01, effective September 1, 1999; am. Acts 2007, 80th Leg., ch. 1219 (H.B. 2034), § 8, effective September 1, 2007.)

## SUBCHAPTER F
## COMMITMENT REVIEW

## Sec. 841.101.  Biennial Examination.

(a) A person committed under Section 841.081 shall receive a biennial examination. The office shall contract for an expert to perform the examination.

(b) In preparation for a judicial review conducted under Section 841.102, the case manager shall provide a report of the biennial examination to the judge. The report must include consideration of whether to modify a requirement imposed on the person under this chapter and whether to release the person from all requirements imposed on the person under this chapter. The case manager shall provide a copy of the report to the office.

(Enacted by Acts 1999, 76th Leg., ch. 1188 (S.B. 365), § 4.01, effective September 1, 1999; am. Acts 2011, 82nd Leg., ch. 1201 (S.B. 166), § 11, effective September 1, 2011.)

### Sec. 841.102.  Biennial Review.

(a) The judge shall conduct a biennial review of the status of the committed person.

(b) The person is entitled to be represented by counsel at the biennial review, but the person is not entitled to be present at that review.

(c) The judge shall set a hearing if the judge determines at the biennial review that:

(1) a requirement imposed on the person under this chapter should be modified; or

(2) probable cause exists to believe that the person's behavioral abnormality has changed to the extent that the person is no longer likely to engage in a predatory act of sexual violence. (Enacted by Acts 1999, 76th Leg., ch. 1188 (S.B. 365), § 4.01, effective September 1, 1999.)

### Sec. 841.103.  Hearing.

(a) At a hearing set by the judge under Section 841.102, the person and the state are entitled to an immediate examination of the person by an expert.

(b) If the hearing is set under Section 841.102(c)(1), hearsay evidence is admissible if it is considered otherwise reliable by the judge.

(c) If the hearing is set under Section 841.102(c)(2), the committed person is entitled to be present and to have the benefit of all constitutional protections provided to the person at the initial civil commitment proceeding. On the request of the person or the attorney representing the state, the court shall conduct the hearing before a jury. The burden of proof at that hearing is on the state to prove beyond a reasonable doubt that the person's behavioral abnormality has not changed to the extent that the person is no longer likely to engage in a predatory act of sexual violence. (Enacted by Acts 1999, 76th Leg., ch. 1188 (S.B. 365), § 4.01, effective September 1, 1999.)

### SUBCHAPTER G
### PETITION FOR RELEASE

### Sec. 841.121.  Authorized Petition for Release.

(a) If the case manager determines that the committed person's behavioral abnormality has changed to the extent that the person is no longer likely to engage in a predatory act of sexual violence, the case manager shall authorize the person to petition the court for release.

(b) The petitioner shall serve a petition under this section on the court and the attorney representing the state.

(c) The judge shall set a hearing on a petition under this section not later than the 30th day after the date the judge receives the petition. The petitioner and the state are entitled to an immediate examination of the petitioner by an expert.

(d) On request of the petitioner or the attorney representing the state, the court shall conduct the hearing before a jury.

(e) The burden of proof at the hearing is on the state to prove beyond a reasonable doubt that the petitioner's behavioral abnormality has not changed to the extent that the petitioner is no longer likely to engage in a predatory act of sexual violence. (Enacted by Acts 1999, 76th Leg., ch. 1188 (S.B. 365), § 4.01, effective September 1, 1999.)

### Sec. 841.122.  Right to File Unauthorized Petition for Release.

On a person's commitment and annually after that commitment, the case manager shall provide the person with written notice of the person's right to file with the court and without the case manager's authorization a petition for release. (Enacted by Acts 1999, 76th Leg., ch. 1188 (S.B. 365), § 4.01, effective September 1, 1999.)

### Sec. 841.123.  Review of Unauthorized Petition for Release.

(a) If the committed person files a petition for release without the case manager's authorization, the person shall serve the petition on the court and the attorney representing the state.

(b) On receipt of a petition for release filed by the committed person without the case manager's authorization, the judge shall attempt as soon as practicable to review the petition.

(c) Except as provided by Subsection (d), the judge shall deny without a hearing a petition for release filed without the case manager's authorization if the petition is frivolous or if:

(1) the petitioner previously filed without the case manager's authorization another petition for release; and

(2) the judge determined on review of the previous petition or following a hearing that:

(A) the petition was frivolous; or

(B) the petitioner's behavioral abnormality had not changed to the extent that the petitioner was no longer likely to engage in a predatory act of sexual violence.

(d) The judge is not required to deny a petition under Subsection (c) if probable cause exists to believe that the petitioner's behavioral abnormality has changed to the extent that the petitioner is no longer likely to engage in a predatory act of sexual violence.

(Enacted by Acts 1999, 76th Leg., ch. 1188 (S.B. 365), § 4.01, effective September 1, 1999.)

## Sec. 841.124. Hearing on Unauthorized Petition for Release.

(a) If as authorized by Section 841.123 the judge does not deny a petition for release filed by the committed person without the case manager's authorization, the judge shall conduct as soon as practicable a hearing on the petition.

(b) The petitioner and the state are entitled to an immediate examination of the person by an expert.

(c) On request of the petitioner or the attorney representing the state, the court shall conduct the hearing before a jury.

(d) The burden of proof at the hearing is on the state to prove beyond a reasonable doubt that the petitioner's behavioral abnormality has not changed to the extent that the petitioner is no longer likely to engage in a predatory act of sexual violence.

(Enacted by Acts 1999, 76th Leg., ch. 1188 (S.B. 365), § 4.01, effective September 1, 1999.)

## SUBCHAPTER H
## MISCELLANEOUS PROVISIONS

## Sec. 841.141. Rulemaking Authority.

(a) The office by rule shall administer this chapter. Rules adopted by the office under this section must be consistent with the purposes of this chapter.

(b) The office by rule shall develop standards of care and case management for persons committed under this chapter.

(Enacted by Acts 1999, 76th Leg., ch. 1188 (S.B. 365), § 4.01, effective September 1, 1999; am. Acts 2011, 82nd Leg., ch. 1201 (S.B. 166), § 12, effective September 1, 2011.)

## Sec. 841.142. Release or Exchange of Information.

(a) To protect the public and to enable an assessment or determination relating to whether a person is a sexually violent predator, any entity that possesses relevant information relating to the person shall release the information to an entity charged with making an assessment or determination under this chapter.

(b) To protect the public and to enable the provision of supervision and treatment to a person who is a sexually violent predator, any entity that possesses relevant information relating to the person shall release the information to the case manager.

(c) On the written request of any attorney for another state or for a political subdivision in another state, the Texas Department of Criminal Justice, the office, a service provider contracting with one of those agencies, the multidisciplinary team, and the attorney representing the state shall release to the attorney any available information relating to a person that is sought in connection with an attempt to civilly commit the person as a sexually violent predator in another state.

(d) To protect the public and to enable an assessment or determination relating to whether a person is a sexually violent predator or to enable the provision of supervision and treatment to a person who is a sexually violent predator, the Texas Department of Criminal Justice, the office, a service provider contracting with one of those agencies, the multidisciplinary team, and the attorney representing the state may exchange any available information relating to the person.

(e) Information subject to release or exchange under this section includes information relating to the supervision, treatment, criminal history, or physical or mental health of the person, as appropriate, regardless of whether the information is otherwise confidential and regardless of when the information was created or collected. The person's consent is not required for release or exchange of information under this section.

(Enacted by Acts 1999, 76th Leg., ch. 1188 (S.B. 365), § 4.01, effective September 1, 1999; am. Acts 2003, 78th Leg., ch. 347 (S.B. 871), § 27, effective September 1, 2003; am. Acts 2011, 82nd Leg., ch. 1201 (S.B. 166), § 13, effective September 1, 2011.)

## Sec. 841.143. Report, Record, or Statement Submitted to Court.

(a) A psychological report, drug and alcohol report, treatment record, diagnostic report, medical record, or victim impact statement submitted to the court under this chapter is part of the record of the court.

(b) Notwithstanding Subsection (a), the report, record, or statement must be sealed and may be opened only:

(1) on order of the judge;

(2) as provided by this chapter; or

(3) in connection with a criminal proceeding as otherwise provided by law.

(Enacted by Acts 1999, 76th Leg., ch. 1188 (S.B. 365), § 4.01, effective September 1, 1999.)

## Sec. 841.144. Counsel.

(a) Immediately after the filing of a petition under Section 841.041, a person subject to a civil commitment proceeding under this chapter is entitled to the assistance of counsel at all stages of the proceeding.

(b) If the person is indigent, the court shall appoint counsel as appropriate under Section 841.005 to assist the person.

(Enacted by Acts 1999, 76th Leg., ch. 1188 (S.B. 365), § 4.01, effective September 1, 1999; am. Acts 2003, 78th Leg., ch. 347 (S.B. 871), § 28, effective September 1, 2003.)

## Sec. 841.145. Expert.

(a) At the person's own expense, a person who is examined under this chapter may retain an expert to perform an examination or participate in a civil commitment proceeding on the person's behalf, including a biennial examination or other civil commitment proceeding to assess the person's status as a sexually violent predator.

(b) On the request of an indigent person examined under this chapter, the judge shall determine whether expert services for the person are necessary. If the judge determines that the services are necessary, the judge shall appoint an expert to perform an examination or participate in a civil commitment proceeding on the person's behalf and shall approve compensation for the expert as appropriate under Subsection (c).

(c) The court shall approve reasonable compensation for expert services rendered on behalf of an indigent person on the filing of a certified compensation claim supported by a written statement specifying:

(1) time expended on behalf of the person;

(2) services rendered on behalf of the person;

(3) expenses incurred on behalf of the person; and

(4) compensation received in the same case or for the same services from any other source.

(d) The court shall ensure that an expert retained or appointed under this section has for purposes of examination reasonable access to a person examined under this chapter, as well as to all relevant medical and psychological records and reports.

(Enacted by Acts 1999, 76th Leg., ch. 1188 (S.B. 365), § 4.01, effective September 1, 1999; am. Acts 2005, 79th Leg., ch. 849 (S.B. 912), § 5, effective September 1, 2005.)

## Sec. 841.146. Civil Commitment Proceeding; Procedure and Costs.

(a) On request, a person subject to a civil commitment proceeding under this chapter and the attorney representing the state are entitled to a jury trial or a hearing before a jury for that proceeding, except for a proceeding set by the judge under Section 841.102(c)(1). The number and selection of jurors are governed by Chapter 33, Code of Criminal Procedure.

(b) Except as otherwise provided by this subsection, a civil commitment proceeding is subject to the rules of procedure and appeal for civil cases. To the extent of any conflict between this chapter and the rules of procedure and appeal for civil cases, this chapter controls.

(c) In an amount not to exceed $2,500, the State of Texas shall pay all costs associated with a civil commitment proceeding conducted under Subchapter D. The State of Texas shall pay the reasonable costs of state or appointed counsel or experts for any other civil commitment proceeding conducted under this chapter and shall pay the reasonable costs of the person's outpatient treatment and supervision.

(Enacted by Acts 1999, 76th Leg., ch. 1188 (S.B. 365), § 4.01, effective September 1, 1999; am. Acts 2003, 78th Leg., ch. 347 (S.B. 871), § 29, effective September 1, 2003.)

## Sec. 841.1461. Certain Expert Testimony Not Required for Civil Commitment of Sexually Violent Predator.

A person who suffers from a behavioral abnormality as determined under this chapter is not because of that abnormality a person of unsound mind for purposes of Section 15-a, Article I, Texas Constitution.

(Enacted by Acts 2003, 78th Leg., ch. 347 (S.B. 871), § 30, effective September 1, 2003.)

## Sec. 841.1462. Privilege for Personal Information That Identifies Victim.

Personal information, including a home address, home telephone number, and social security account number, that identifies the victim of a person subject to a civil commitment proceeding under this chapter is privileged from discovery by that person.

Health

(Enacted by Acts 2003, 78th Leg., ch. 347 (S.B. 871), § 30, effective September 1, 2003.)

### Sec. 841.1463.  Failure to Give Notice Within Relevant Period Not Jurisdictional Error.

The periods within which notice must be given under this chapter are binding on all appropriate persons as provided by this chapter, but a failure to give notice within the relevant period is not a jurisdictional error.

(Enacted by Acts 2003, 78th Leg., ch. 347 (S.B. 871), § 30, effective September 1, 2003.)

### Sec. 841.147.  Immunity.

The following persons are immune from liability for good faith conduct under this chapter:

(1) an employee or officer of the Texas Department of Criminal Justice, the Department of State Health Services, the Department of Aging and Disability Services, or the office;

(2) a member of the multidisciplinary team established under Section 841.022;

(3) an employee of the civil division of the special prosecution unit charged with initiating and pursuing civil commitment proceedings under this chapter; and

(4) a person providing, or contracting, appointed, or volunteering to perform, a tracking service or another service under this chapter.

(Enacted by Acts 1999, 76th Leg., ch. 1188 (S.B. 365), § 4.01, effective September 1, 1999; am. Acts 2003, 78th Leg., ch. 347 (S.B. 871), § 31, effective September 1, 2003; am. Acts 2007, 80th Leg., ch. 1219 (H.B. 2034), § 9, effective September 1, 2007; am. Acts 2011, 82nd Leg., ch. 1201 (S.B. 166), § 14, effective September 1, 2011.)

### Sec. 841.148.  [Blank].

### Sec. 841.149.  [Blank].

### Sec. 841.150.  Effect of Subsequent Commitment or Confinement on Order of Civil Commitment.

(a) The duties imposed by this chapter are suspended for the duration of any confinement of a person, or if applicable any other commitment of a person to a community center, mental health facility, or state school, by governmental action.

(b) In this section:

(1) "Community center" means a center established under Subchapter A, Chapter 534.

(2) "Mental health facility" has the meaning assigned by Section 571.003.

(3) "State school" has the meaning assigned by Section 531.002.

(Enacted by Acts 2003, 78th Leg., ch. 347 (S.B. 871), § 30, effective September 1, 2003; am. Acts 2005, 79th Leg., ch. 849 (S.B. 912), § 6, effective September 1, 2005; am. Acts 2011, 82nd Leg., ch. 1201 (S.B. 166), § 15, effective September 1, 2011.)

### Sec. 841.151.  Notice of Release of Sexually Violent Predator.

(a) In this section:

(1) "Correctional facility" has the meaning assigned by Section 1.07, Penal Code.

(2) "Secure correctional facility" and "secure detention facility" have the meanings assigned by Section 51.02, Family Code.

(b) This section applies to a person who has been civilly committed under this chapter and who is detained or confined in a correctional facility, secure correctional facility, or secure detention facility as a result of violating:

(1) a civil commitment requirement imposed under Section 841.082; or

(2) a law of this state.

(c) Not later than the day preceding the date a correctional facility, secure correctional facility, or secure detention facility releases a person who, at the time of the person's detention or confinement, was civilly committed under this chapter as a sexually violent predator, the facility shall notify the person's case manager in writing of the anticipated date and time of the person's release.

(d) A case manager, on request, shall provide a correctional facility, a secure correctional facility, or a secure detention facility with the case manager's appropriate contact information for notification under Subsection (c).

(Enacted by Acts 2011, 82nd Leg., ch. 1201 (S.B. 166), § 16, effective September 1, 2011.)

# Local Government Code

## TITLE 4

## FINANCES

## SUBCHAPTER C
## CRIMINAL FEES

### Sec. 133.105.  Fee for Support of Court-Related Purposes.

(a) A person convicted of any offense, other than an offense relating to a pedestrian or the parking of a motor vehicle, shall pay as a court cost, in addition to all other costs, a fee of $6 to be used for court-related purposes for the support of the judiciary.

(b) The treasurer shall deposit 60 cents of each fee collected under this section in the general fund of the municipality or county to promote the efficient operation of the municipal or county courts and the investigation, prosecution, and enforcement of offenses that are within the jurisdiction of the courts.

(c) The treasurer shall remit the remainder of the fees collected under this section to the comptroller in the manner provided by Subchapter B. The comptroller shall deposit the fees in the judicial fund.

(Enacted by Acts 2005, 79th Leg., 2nd C.S., ch. 3 (H.B. 11), § 12, effective December 1, 2005; am. Acts 2007, 80th Leg., ch. 1301 (S.B. 600), § 3, effective October 1, 2007.)

### Sec. 133.107.  Fee for Support of Indigent Defense Representation.

(a) A person convicted of any offense, other than an offense relating to a pedestrian or the parking of a motor vehicle, shall pay as a court cost, in addition to other costs, a fee of $2 to be used to fund indigent defense representation through the fair defense account established under Section 79.031, Government Code.

(b) The treasurer shall remit a fee collected under this section to the comptroller in the manner provided by Subchapter B. The comptroller shall credit the remitted fees to the credit of the fair defense account established under Section 79.031, Government Code.

(Enacted by Acts 2007, 80th Leg., ch. 1014 (H.B. 1267), § 6, effective September 1, 2007; am. Acts 2011, 82nd Leg., ch. 984 (H.B. 1754), § 14, effective September 1, 2011.)

Local Government Code

# TITLE 11
# PUBLIC SAFETY

## SUBTITLE B
## COUNTY PUBLIC SAFETY

## CHAPTER 351
## COUNTY JAILS AND LAW ENFORCEMENT

### SUBCHAPTER Z
### MISCELLANEOUS LAW ENFORCEMENT PROVISIONS

### Sec. 351.904.  Electronic Monitoring Program.

(a) A commissioners court of a county may establish and operate an electronic monitoring program for the purpose of monitoring defendants required by a court of the county to participate in an electronic monitoring program under:

(1) Article 43.09, Code of Criminal Procedure, to discharge a fine or costs; or

(2) Article 42.035, Code of Criminal Procedure, as an alternative to serving all or part of a sentence of confinement in county jail.

(b) The commissioners court shall provide for the sheriff or the community supervision and corrections department serving the county, under an agreement with the commissioners court, to oversee and operate, or, if the program is operated by a private vendor under Subsection (c), oversee the operation of, an electronic monitoring program established under this section.

(c) A commissioners court may contract with a private vendor to operate an electronic monitoring program under this section, including by enrolling and tracking participants in the program and performing periodic reviews with participants regarding compliance with the program.

(d) A commissioners court may use money that a defendant is ordered to pay to a county under Article 42.035(c), Code of Criminal Procedure, to pay for the services of a private vendor that operates an electronic monitoring program under Subsection (c).

(e) A commissioners court may subsidize all or part of the cost of a defendant's participation in an electronic monitoring program under this section if the defendant is indigent.

(f) A commissioners court may contract for any available electronic monitoring technology, including a technology that provides continuous positional tracking of the participant, that meets the approval of the commissioners court and either the sheriff or the community supervision and corrections department, as appropriate. (Enacted by Acts 2009, 81st Leg., ch. 854 (S.B. 2340), § 6, effective June 19, 2009.)

## SUBTITLE C
## PUBLIC SAFETY PROVISIONS APPLYING TO MORE THAN ONE TYPE OF LOCAL GOVERNMENT

## CHAPTER 370
## MISCELLANEOUS PROVISIONS RELATING TO MUNICIPAL AND COUNTY HEALTH AND PUBLIC SAFETY

### Sec. 370.004.  Notice of Damaged Fence.

(a) A peace officer employed by a political subdivision of this state who investigates or responds to an incident in which a motor vehicle damages a fence shall, if the peace officer reasonably believes that the fence is intended to contain livestock or other animals:

(1) immediately determine the owner of the land on which the damaged fence is located; and

(2) notify the owner of the type and extent of the damage, if the owner has registered with the political subdivision in accordance with Subsection (c).

(b) A peace officer is not liable to an owner of land or any other person for damage resulting from the peace officer's failure to notify the owner under Subsection (a).

(c) A landowner must provide an agency or department of a political subdivision that employs peace officers with the following information if the landowner would like a peace officer of that agency or department to notify the landowner of damage under Subsection (a):

(1) the landowner's name, address, and telephone number; and

(2) the location and a description of the landowner's property.

(Enacted by Acts 2007, 80th Leg., ch. 330 (H.B. 2931), § 2, effective September 1, 2007.)

Local Government Code

# Natural Resources Code

## TITLE 3
## OIL AND GAS

**SUBTITLE B**
**CONSERVATION AND REGULATION OF OIL AND GAS**

### CHAPTER 85
### CONSERVATION OF OIL AND GAS

#### SUBCHAPTER K
#### PENALTIES, IMPRISONMENT, AND CONFINEMENT

### Sec. 85.389. Criminal Penalty.

(a) A person who is not the owner or operator of an oil well, gas well, or oil and gas well, a purchaser under contract of oil, gas, or oil and gas from a well, a gatherer with written authorization from the owner, operator, or purchaser, or an authorized representative of the commission who knowingly destroys, breaks, removes, or otherwise tampers with or attempts to destroy, break, remove, or otherwise tamper with any cap, seal, or other device placed on an oil well, gas well, oil and gas well, or associated oil or gas gathering equipment by the owner or operator for the purpose of controlling or limiting the operation of the well or associated equipment commits an offense.

(b) An offense under this section is a felony of the third degree.

(Enacted by Acts 1983, 68th Leg., ch. 960 (H.B. 1914), § 1, effective September 1, 1983.)

**SUBTITLE D**
**REGULATION OF SPECIFIC BUSINESSES AND OCCUPATIONS**

### CHAPTER 112
### USED OIL FIELD EQUIPMENT DEALERS

#### SUBCHAPTER A
#### GENERAL PROVISIONS

### Sec. 112.001. Definitions.

In this chapter:

(1) "Pipeline equipment" means all pipe, fittings, pumps, telephone and telegraph lines, and all other material and equipment used as part of or incident to the construction, maintenance, and operation of a pipeline for the trans-

**Natural Resources**

1919

portation of oil, gas, water, or other liquid or gaseous substance.

(2) "Oil and gas equipment" means equipment and materials that are part of or incident to the exploration, development, maintenance, and operation of oil and gas properties and includes equipment and materials that are part of or incident to the construction, maintenance, and operation of oil and gas wells, oil and gas leases, gasoline plants, and refineries.

(3) "Used materials" means pipeline equipment or oil and gas equipment after the equipment has once been placed in the use for which it first was manufactured and intended.

(4) "Dealer" means every person whose primary business is buying, selling, or otherwise dealing in used materials and who has a fixed, designated place or places of business within the state.

(5) "Broker" means every person whose primary business is buying, selling, or otherwise dealing in used materials as agent for the seller of the used materials, or as agent for the buyer of the used materials, or as agent for both.

(6) "Peddler" means every person who is not a dealer or broker and whose primary business is buying, selling, or otherwise dealing in used materials.

(Enacted by Acts 1977, 65th Leg., ch. 871 (S.B. 1207), art. I, § 1, effective September 1, 1977; am. Acts 1981, 67th Leg., ch. 573 (S.B. 677), § 1, effective August 31, 1981.)

## Sec. 112.002.  Applicability.

The provisions of this chapter shall not apply if the reasonable market value of the purchase made is less than $25.

(Enacted by Acts 1977, 65th Leg., ch. 871 (S.B. 1207), art. I, § 1, effective September 1, 1977.)

## SUBCHAPTER B
## SALE OF USED EQUIPMENT

## Sec. 112.011.  Bill of Sale.

Before purchasing or acquiring by exchange used materials, a dealer, broker, or peddler shall require that a bill of sale for the used materials be executed by the seller or the person who exchanges the materials. The dealer, broker, or peddler shall keep a copy of each bill of sale at his place of business.

(Enacted by Acts 1977, 65th Leg., ch. 871 (S.B. 1207), art. I, § 1, effective September 1, 1977; am. Acts 1981, 67th Leg., ch. 573 (S.B. 677), § 2, effective August 31, 1981.)

## Sec. 112.012.  Required Information.

(a) The bill of sale shall include:

(1) the name and address of the dealer, broker, or peddler;

(2) the serial number, if any;

(3) the kind, make, size, weight, length, and quantity of the used materials purchased or acquired by exchange;

(4) the date of the purchase or acquisition by exchange, if different from the date of the bill of sale;

(5) the name and address of the seller or person who exchanged the materials;

(6) the place of location of the property at the time purchased or acquired by exchange;

(7) the license number of each motor vehicle used in transporting a purchased or exchanged item to the dealer's, broker's, or peddler's place of business; and

(8) the driver's license number of the seller or person who exchanged the materials.

(b) A dealer, broker, or peddler under this chapter shall keep at his regular place of business all records required to be kept by this chapter for two years after the date of the purchase or acquisition by exchange of the materials.

(Enacted by Acts 1977, 65th Leg., ch. 871 (S.B. 1207), art. I, § 1, effective September 1, 1977; am. Acts 1981, 67th Leg., ch. 573 (S.B. 677), § 3, effective August 31, 1981.)

## SUBCHAPTER C
## ENFORCEMENT; PENALTY

## Sec. 112.031.  Injunctive Relief.

In the name and on behalf of the State of Texas, the attorney general or any district attorney or county attorney in this state may enjoin a dealer, peddler, or broker from continuing in business in this state as a dealer, peddler, or broker on violation of any of the provisions of this chapter.

(Enacted by Acts 1977, 65th Leg., ch. 871 (S.B. 1207), art. I, § 1, effective September 1, 1977.)

## Sec. 112.032.  Criminal Penalty.

A person, dealer, peddler, or broker who violates any of the provisions of this chapter is guilty of a misdemeanor and on conviction is subject to a fine of not less than $500 for each violation.

(Enacted by Acts 1977, 65th Leg., ch. 871 (S.B. 1207), art. I, § 1, effective September 1, 1977; am. Acts 1981, 67th Leg., ch. 573 (S.B. 677), § 4, effective August 31, 1981.)

Natural Resources

## Sec. 112.033. Inspection.

(a) Any Texas Ranger or other officer commissioned by the Department of Public Safety, any sheriff or deputy sheriff, or any municipal police officer may enter the business premises of a dealer, broker, or peddler under this chapter during normal business hours to inspect the premises and the records of the dealer, broker, or peddler to determine whether the dealer, broker, or peddler is in compliance with this chapter.

(b) A dealer, broker, or peddler under this chapter must allow and shall not interfere with inspections conducted pursuant to this chapter.

(c) Each inspection conducted under this chapter shall be commenced and completed with reasonable promptness and shall be conducted in a reasonable manner.

(Enacted by Acts 1981, 67th Leg., ch. 573 (S.B. 677), § 5, effective August 31, 1981; am. Acts 1983, 68th Leg., ch. 741 (H.B. 171), § 3, effective September 1, 1983.)

# CHAPTER 115
## REGULATION OF CERTAIN TRANSPORTERS OF OIL OR PETROLEUM PRODUCTS

# SUBCHAPTER A
## GENERAL PROVISIONS

## Sec. 115.001. Definitions.

In this chapter:

(1) "Commission" means the Railroad Commission of Texas.

(2) "Commission order" includes a rule or order adopted by the commission under the oil and gas conservation statutes of this state, including this title and Subtitle B, Title 3, Utilities Code.

(3) "Gas" includes natural gas, bradenhead gas, casinghead gas, or gas produced from an oil or gas well.

(4) "Manifest" includes a document issued by a shipper that covers oil or a petroleum product transported by motor vehicle.

(5) "Oil" includes crude petroleum oil:

(A) in its natural state as produced; or

(B) from which only the basic sediment and water have been removed.

(6) "Person" includes an individual, corporation, association, partnership, receiver, trustee, guardian, executor, administrator, or representative.

(7) "Petroleum product" includes:

(A) refined crude oil;

(B) crude tops;

(C) topped crude;

(D) processed crude petroleum;

(E) residue from crude petroleum;

(F) cracking stock;

(G) uncracked fuel oil;

(H) fuel oil;

(I) treated crude oil;

(J) residuum;

(K) gas oil;

(L) casinghead gasoline;

(M) natural gas gasoline;

(N) naphtha;

(O) distillate;

(P) gasoline;

(Q) kerosene;

(R) benzine;

(S) wash oil;

(T) waste oil;

(U) blended gasoline;

(V) lubricating oil;

(W) blends or mixtures of petroleum; or

(X) any other liquid petroleum product or byproduct derived from crude petroleum oil or gas.

(8) "Shipping papers" includes:

(A) a bill of lading that covers oil or a petroleum product transported by railway;

(B) a manifest; or

(C) a document that covers oil or a petroleum product by pipeline, boat, or barge.

(9) "Tender" means a permit or certificate of clearance for the transportation of oil or a petroleum product that is approved and issued or registered under the authority of the commission.

(10) "Unlawful gas" includes gas produced or transported in violation of a law of this state or commission order.

(11) "Unlawful petroleum product" includes a petroleum product:

(A) any part of which was processed or derived in whole or in part from:

(i) unlawful oil;

(ii) a product of unlawful oil; or

(iii) unlawful gas; or

(B) transported in violation of a law of this state or commission order.

(Enacted by Acts 1997, 75th Leg., ch. 166 (S.B. 1751), § 7, effective September 1, 1997.)

### Sec. 115.002.   Exception.

This chapter does not apply to the retail purchase of a petroleum product if that product is:

(1) contained in the ordinary equipment of a motor vehicle; and

(2) used only to operate the motor vehicle in which it is contained.

(Enacted by Acts 1997, 75th Leg., ch. 166 (S.B. 1751), § 7, effective September 1, 1997.)

### Sec. 115.003.   Definition of Unlawful Oil; Presumption.

(a) For purposes of this chapter, oil is unlawful if the oil is:

(1) produced in this state from a well in excess of the amount allowed by a commission order or otherwise in violation of a law of this state or commission order; or

(2) transported in violation of a law of this state or commission order.

(b) It is presumed that oil is "unlawful oil" for purposes of this chapter if the oil is retained in storage for more than six years without being used, consumed, or moved into regular commercial channels.

(c) The presumption under Subsection (b) may be rebutted by proof that the oil:

(1) was produced from a well within the production allowable then applying to that well;

(2) was not produced in violation of a law of this state or commission order; and

(3) if transported from the lease from which it was produced, was not transported in violation of a law of this state or commission order.

(Enacted by Acts 1997, 75th Leg., ch. 166 (S.B. 1751), § 7, effective September 1, 1997.)

## SUBCHAPTER B
## TENDERS AND MANIFESTS

### Sec. 115.011.   Tender Requirements.

The commission by order may require that a tender be obtained before oil or a petroleum product may be transported or received for transportation by pipeline, railway, boat, or barge.

(Enacted by Acts 1997, 75th Leg., ch. 166 (S.B. 1751), § 7, effective September 1, 1997.)

### Sec. 115.012.   Tender; Application Requirements.

(a) The commission by order shall prescribe the form of a tender and a tender application.

(b) The form must show:

(1) the name and address of the shipper or other person who tenders oil or a petroleum product for transportation;

(2) the name and address of the transporter if the commission order requires the transporter to be designated;

(3) the quantity and classification of each commodity authorized to be transported;

(4) each location at which delivery is to be made to the transporter; and

(5) other related information as prescribed by commission order.

(c) Each tender must:

(1) bear a date and serial number;

(2) state the expiration date of the tender; and

(3) be executed by an agent authorized by the commission to deny, approve, or register tenders.

(d) An agent may not approve or register a tender for the transportation of unlawful oil or an unlawful petroleum product.

(Enacted by Acts 1997, 75th Leg., ch. 166 (S.B. 1751), § 7, effective September 1, 1997.)

Natural Resources

### Sec. 115.013. Action on Tender Application.

(a) If an agent of the commission rejects an application for a tender, the agent shall return a copy of the application to the applicant with the reasons for the rejection indicated on the copy.

(b) A person whose tender application is not acted on before the 21st day after the date on which the application is filed is entitled to judicial review in the manner provided by Section 115.014 for the appeal of a rejection of a tender application.

(Enacted by Acts 1997, 75th Leg., ch. 166 (S.B. 1751), § 7, effective September 1, 1997.)

### Sec. 115.014. Judicial Review.

(a) A person whose tender application is rejected may appeal that action by filing a petition against the commission in a district court of Travis County for review of the agent's decision.

(b) The clerk of the court shall issue to the commission a notice setting forth briefly the cause of action stated in the petition. The court may not enter an order on the petition until the court conducts a hearing. The court must conduct the hearing not later than the fifth day after the date of issuance of the notice.

(c) The court may sustain, modify, or overrule the agent's decision and may issue a restraining order or injunction as warranted by the facts.

(d) A person dissatisfied with the decision of the district court may appeal to the court of appeals.

(Enacted by Acts 1997, 75th Leg., ch. 166 (S.B. 1751), § 7, effective September 1, 1997.)

### Sec. 115.015. Transfer Under Tender.

(a) A person who obtains a tender may not transport or deliver, or cause or permit to be transported or delivered, any more or any different commodity than that authorized by the tender.

(b) A connecting carrier or consignee who receives oil or a petroleum product from another transporter by pipeline, railway, boat, or barge under authority of shipping papers executed by the initial transporter that bear the date and serial number of a tender issued to that initial transporter is considered to receive the oil or petroleum product by authority of that tender if the commission order provides that a connecting carrier or consignee may rely on the shipping papers.

(Enacted by Acts 1997, 75th Leg., ch. 166 (S.B. 1751), § 7, effective September 1, 1997.)

### Sec. 115.016. Issuance of Manifest.

(a) A person who obtains a tender required under this subchapter shall sign and issue a manifest to the operator of each motor vehicle used to transport the oil or petroleum product that is covered by the tender.

(b) The person shall issue a separate manifest for each load carried by the motor vehicle.

(Enacted by Acts 1997, 75th Leg., ch. 166 (S.B. 1751), § 7, effective September 1, 1997.)

### Sec. 115.017. Form of Manifest.

(a) The commission by order may prescribe the form of a manifest.

(b) A manifest must:

(1) bear a certificate signed by the shipper that states the amount of oil or petroleum products to be transported and specifies each petroleum product to be transported; and

(2) include, if required by commission order:

(A) the date and serial number of the tender that authorizes the transportation or a seal, number, or other evidence of the tender, if a tender is required;

(B) the amount and classification of each petroleum product to be transported;

(C) the name and address of the transporter, the name and address of the shipper, and the name and address of the consignee, if known;

(D) the name and address of the operator of the motor vehicle;

(E) the license plate number of the motor vehicle;

(F) the date, time, and place at which the motor vehicle was loaded and the destination, if known, of the load; and

(G) other related information as required by commission order.

(c) If the form of the manifest is not prescribed by commission order, each shipper required to issue a manifest to a transporter shall use a form of manifest that is:

(1) commonly used in commercial transactions; or

(2) required by another state agency to accompany the movement of gasoline.

(Enacted by Acts 1997, 75th Leg., ch. 166 (S.B. 1751), § 7, effective September 1, 1997.)

### Sec. 115.018. Transfer Under Manifest; Restrictions.

(a) A person authorized to transport oil or a petroleum product on a manifest issued by a shipper may not receive:

Natural Resources

(1) a commodity for transportation that is different from the commodity described in the manifest; or

(2) oil or a petroleum product in an amount exceeding the amount authorized by the manifest.

(b) A person authorized to transport oil or a petroleum product by a shipper-issued manifest that bears on its face the date and serial number of the tender may rely on the manifest delivered to that person and each consignee or person to whom the transporter delivers oil or a petroleum product covered by that manifest may rely on the manifest as authority to receive the commodity delivered if the manifest:

(1) appears to be valid on its face;

(2) is signed by the shipper; and

(3) bears the certificate of the shipper that the transportation of the oil or petroleum product is authorized by the tender.

(c) If the commission by order prohibits the transportation of oil or a petroleum product by motor vehicle without a manifest that shows the date and serial number of a tender authorizing the transportation, a person may not ship or transport or cause to be shipped or transported by motor vehicle oil or a petroleum product unless the person furnishes the manifest to the operator of the motor vehicle. The person transporting the oil or petroleum product shall maintain the manifest in the vehicle at all times during the shipment. If the person to whom the tender is issued is the operator of the motor vehicle and the tender identifies the motor vehicle by license number and covers one load, the person may carry the tender in the vehicle in lieu of a manifest.

(Enacted by Acts 1997, 75th Leg., ch. 166 (S.B. 1751), § 7, effective September 1, 1997.)

### Sec. 115.019. Receipt Required.

A person who transports oil or a petroleum product by motor vehicle under conditions that require a tender or manifest shall obtain a receipt from each person to whom any part of the oil or petroleum product is delivered. The receipt must be on the reverse side of the tender or manifest and must indicate:

(1) the number of gallons of oil or of each petroleum product delivered;

(2) the date of delivery; and

(3) the signature and address of the purchaser or consignee of the oil or petroleum product.

(Enacted by Acts 1997, 75th Leg., ch. 166 (S.B. 1751), § 7, effective September 1, 1997.)

### Sec. 115.020. Records; Inspection.

(a) A person who transports by motor vehicle and delivers oil or a petroleum product shall keep in this state for two years each tender or manifest issued to the person, together with the receipts and endorsements on the tender or manifest.

(b) A tender or manifest is at all times subject to inspection by the commission or an agent or inspector of the commission.

(Enacted by Acts 1997, 75th Leg., ch. 166 (S.B. 1751), § 7, effective September 1, 1997.)

## SUBCHAPTER C
## FORFEITURE OF UNLAWFUL OIL OR PETROLEUM PRODUCT

### Sec. 115.031. Forfeiture Authorized.

Unlawful oil and unlawful petroleum products, regardless of the date of production or manufacture, are declared to be a nuisance and shall be forfeited to this state as provided by this subchapter.

(Enacted by Acts 1997, 75th Leg., ch. 166 (S.B. 1751), § 7, effective September 1, 1997.)

### Sec. 115.032. Report to Attorney General.

On the discovery of unlawful oil or an unlawful petroleum product, a member of the commission, an agent or employee of the commission, or a peace officer shall immediately file with the attorney general a report that describes the unlawful oil or unlawful petroleum product. The report must state the ownership, party in possession, amount, location, and classification of the oil or petroleum product.

(Enacted by Acts 1997, 75th Leg., ch. 166 (S.B. 1751), § 7, effective September 1, 1997.)

### Sec. 115.033. Action in Rem.

(a) If the attorney general is advised of the presence of unlawful oil or an unlawful petroleum product, the attorney general shall bring an action in rem in the name of the state in Travis County or in the county in which the oil or petroleum product is located against the unlawful oil or petroleum product and against each person who owns, claims, or is in possession of the oil or petroleum product.

(b) If it appears to the court from an examination of the petition or after hearing evidence on the petition at a preliminary hearing that the unlawful oil or petroleum product mentioned in the petition is in danger of being removed, wasted, lost, or destroyed, the court shall:

(1) issue restraining orders or injunctive relief, either mandatory or prohibitive;

(2) appoint a receiver to take charge of the oil or petroleum product; or

(3) direct the sheriff of the county in which the unlawful oil or petroleum product is located to seize and impound the oil or petroleum product pending further orders of the court.

(c) A party to the action may demand a trial by jury on any issue of fact raised by the pleadings, and the case shall proceed to trial in the manner provided for other civil cases.

(Enacted by Acts 1997, 75th Leg., ch. 166 (S.B. 1751), § 7, effective September 1, 1997.)

## Sec. 115.034. Forfeiture Sale.

(a) If, on the trial of the action, the oil or petroleum product in controversy is found to be unlawful, the court shall render judgment forfeiting the oil or petroleum product to this state. The court shall issue an order of sale directing the sheriff or a constable of the county in which the oil or petroleum product is located to seize and sell the oil or petroleum product in the same manner as personal property is sold under execution. The court may order the oil or petroleum product sold in whole or in part.

(b) The sale shall be conducted at the courthouse door of the county in which the oil or petroleum product is located.

(c) The court shall apply the money realized from the sale first to the payment of the costs of the action and expenses incident to the sale of the oil or petroleum product. The court may then use not more than one-half of the money to compensate a person for expenses incurred in storing the unlawful oil or petroleum product. Any balance remaining shall be remitted to the comptroller.

(d) The officers of the court shall receive the same fees provided by law for other civil actions. The sheriff who executes the sale shall issue a bill of sale or certificate to the purchaser of the oil or petroleum product, and the commission, on presentation of that certificate of clearance, shall issue a tender, if a tender is required, permitting the purchaser of the oil or petroleum product to move the oil or petroleum product into commerce.

(Enacted by Acts 1997, 75th Leg., ch. 166 (S.B. 1751), § 7, effective September 1, 1997.)

## SUBCHAPTER D
## ENFORCEMENT AND PENALTIES

## Sec. 115.041. Enforcement; Arrests.

(a) To enforce this chapter, an agent of the commission or a peace officer of this state who has probable cause and reasonable grounds to believe that a motor vehicle is transporting unlawful oil or an unlawful petroleum product may stop the vehicle to take samples of the cargo and to inspect the shipping papers.

(b) If, on examination of the motor vehicle, the agent or officer finds that the vehicle is transporting unlawful oil or an unlawful petroleum product or is transporting oil or a petroleum product without a required tender, the agent or officer, with or without a warrant, shall arrest the operator of the vehicle and file a complaint against the operator under this chapter.

(c) In a criminal action under this chapter, the agent or officer is not entitled to a fee for executing a warrant of arrest or capias or for making an arrest with or without a warrant.

(Enacted by Acts 1997, 75th Leg., ch. 166 (S.B. 1751), § 7, effective September 1, 1997.)

## Sec. 115.042. Publication of Commission Order Prior to Enforcement.

A criminal action may not be maintained against a person involving the violation of a rule or order that the commission adopts, modifies, or amends until the commission publishes a complete copy of the rule or order.

(Enacted by Acts 1997, 75th Leg., ch. 166 (S.B. 1751), § 7, effective September 1, 1997.)

## Sec. 115.043. Certificate As Evidence.

(a) A certificate that sets forth the terms of a commission order and states that the order has been adopted and published and was in effect on a specified date or during a specified period is prima facie evidence of those facts if the certificate is:

(1) made under the seal of the commission; and

(2) executed by a member or the secretary of the commission.

(b) The certificate is admissible in evidence in any civil or criminal action that involves the order without further proof of the adoption, publication, or contents of the order.

(Enacted by Acts 1997, 75th Leg., ch. 166 (S.B. 1751), § 7, effective September 1, 1997.)

Natural Resources

## Sec. 115.044.  Service of Process.

(a) In an action or proceeding that involves the enforcement of this chapter or a commission order, a Texas Ranger or agent of the commission may serve any judicial process, warrant, subpoena, or writ as directed by the court issuing the process and shall serve the process in the same manner as a peace officer.

(b) The ranger or agent may serve the process, warrant, or subpoena anywhere in this state although it may be directed to the sheriff or a constable of a particular county.

(c) The ranger or agent shall make the same return as any other officer, sign the return, and add under the name the title "State Ranger" or "Agent, Railroad Commission of Texas," as appropriate, which is sufficient to make the writ valid if the writ is otherwise properly prepared.

(d) A Texas Ranger or agent of the commission is not entitled to a fee in addition to that person's regular compensation for a service provided under this section.

(Enacted by Acts 1997, 75th Leg., ch. 166 (S.B. 1751), § 7, effective September 1, 1997.)

## Sec. 115.045.  Pleading; Proof.

(a) In a complaint, information, or indictment that alleges a violation of a commission order, it is unnecessary to set forth fully the terms of the order and sufficient to allege the substance of the order or the pertinent terms of the order that are alleged to have been violated.

(b) In a criminal action filed under this chapter, a certificate executed by a member or the secretary of the commission that shows the amount of allowable oil that may be produced per day or during a stated period from an oil well, proof of production from which is involved in the criminal action, is admissible and is prima facie evidence of the facts stated in the certificate.

(c) This section does not limit the power of the commission to adopt rules or orders under the oil and gas conservation statutes of this state, including this title and Subtitle B, Title 3, Utilities Code.

(Enacted by Acts 1997, 75th Leg., ch. 166 (S.B. 1751), § 7, effective September 1, 1997.)

## Sec. 115.046.  Venue.

A criminal action maintained under this chapter must be brought in:

(1) the county in which the oil or petroleum product involved in the criminal action is received or delivered; or

(2) any county in or through which that oil or petroleum product is transported.

(Enacted by Acts 1997, 75th Leg., ch. 166 (S.B. 1751), § 7, effective September 1, 1997.)

## Sec. 115.047.  Penalties.

(a) A person commits an offense if the person is the operator of a motor vehicle that transports oil or a petroleum product and the person:

(1) intentionally fails to stop the vehicle on the command of an agent of the commission or peace officer; or

(2) intentionally fails to permit inspection by the agent or officer of the contents of or the shipping papers accompanying the vehicle.

(b) A person commits an offense if the person:

(1) knowingly violates Section 115.011, 115.015(a), 115.016, 115.018, 115.019, or 115.020;

(2) knowingly ships or transports or causes to be shipped or transported unlawful oil or an unlawful petroleum product by motor vehicle over a public highway in this state;

(3) knowingly ships or transports or causes to be shipped or transported by motor vehicle oil or a petroleum product without the authority of a tender if a tender is required by a commission order; or

(4) if a tender is required by a commission order, knowingly receives from a motor vehicle or knowingly delivers to a motor vehicle oil or a petroleum product that is not covered by a tender authorizing the transportation of the oil or petroleum product.

(c) A person commits an offense if the person:

(1) knowingly ships or transports or causes or permits to be shipped or transported by pipeline, railway, boat, or barge unlawful oil or an unlawful petroleum product;

(2) knowingly receives or delivers for transportation by pipeline, railway, boat, or barge unlawful oil or an unlawful petroleum product;

(3) knowingly ships or transports or causes or permits to be shipped or transported by pipeline, railway, boat, or barge oil or a petroleum product without authority of a tender if a tender is required by a commission order; or

(4) knowingly receives or delivers by pipeline, railway, boat, or barge oil or a petroleum product without authority of a tender if a tender is required by a commission order.

(d) An offense under this section is punishable by a fine of not less than $50 or more than $200.

(Enacted by Acts 1997, 75th Leg., ch. 166 (S.B. 1751), § 7, effective September 1, 1997.)

# TITLE 6
# TIMBER

## CHAPTER 151
## PROVISIONS GENERALLY APPLICABLE

### SUBCHAPTER B
### UNAUTHORIZED HARVESTING OF TIMBER

### Sec. 151.052. Criminal Offense.

(a) A person commits an offense if the person:

(1) harvests standing timber with knowledge that the harvesting is without the permission of the owner of the standing timber; or

(2) causes another person to harvest standing timber without the permission of the owner of the standing timber.

(b) An offense under this section is:

(1) a state jail felony if it is shown on the trial of the offense that the value of the timber harvested is at least $500 but less than $20,000;

(2) a felony of the third degree if it is shown on the trial of the offense that the value of the timber harvested is at least $20,000 but less than $100,000;

(3) a felony of the second degree if it is shown on the trial of the offense that the value of the timber harvested is at least $100,000 but less than $200,000; or

(4) a felony of the first degree if it is shown on the trial of the offense that the value of the timber harvested is at least $200,000.

(Enacted by Acts 2011, 82nd Leg., ch. 23 (H.B. 613), § 2, effective September 1, 2011.)

# Occupations Code

## TITLE 3
## HEALTH PROFESSIONS

### SUBCHAPTER A
### GENERAL PROVISIONS

## Sec. 107.001.  Short Title.
This chapter may be cited as the Intractable Pain Treatment Act.

(Enacted by Acts 2003, 78th Leg., ch. 1276 (H.B. 3507), § 14.002(a), effective September 1, 2003.)

## Sec. 107.002.  Definitions.
In this chapter:

(1) "Board" means the Texas State Board of Medical Examiners.

(2) "Intractable pain" means a state of pain for which:

(A) the cause of the pain cannot be removed or otherwise treated; and

(B) in the generally accepted course of medical practice, relief or cure of the cause of the pain:

(i) is not possible; or

(ii) has not been found after reasonable efforts.

(3) "Physician" means a physician licensed by the board.

(Enacted by Acts 2003, 78th Leg., ch. 1276 (H.B. 3507), § 14.002(a), effective September 1, 2003.)

## Sec. 107.003.  Nonapplicability of Chapter to Certain Chemically Dependent Persons.
Except as provided by Subchapter C, this chapter does not apply to a person being treated by a physician for chemical dependency because of the person's use of a dangerous drug or controlled substance.

(Enacted by Acts 2003, 78th Leg., ch. 1276 (H.B. 3507), § 14.002(a), effective September 1, 2003.)

## Sec. 107.004.  Rules [Renumbered].
Renumbered to Tex. Occ. Code § 111.004 by Acts 2005, 79th Leg., ch. 728 (H.B. 2018), § 23.001(69), effective September 1, 2005.

Occupations

## SUBCHAPTER B
## PRESCRIPTION AND ADMINISTRATION OF DANGEROUS DRUGS AND CONTROLLED SUBSTANCES

### Sec. 107.051. Authority to Prescribe or Administer Dangerous Drug or Controlled Substance.

Notwithstanding any other law, a physician may prescribe or administer a dangerous drug or controlled substance to a person in the course of the physician's treatment of the person for intractable pain.

(Enacted by Acts 2003, 78th Leg., ch. 1276 (H.B. 3507), § 14.002(a), effective September 1, 2003.)

### Sec. 107.052. Limitations on Prescription or Administration of Dangerous Drug or Controlled Substance.

This chapter does not authorize a physician to prescribe or administer to a person a dangerous drug or controlled substance:

(1) for a purpose that is not a legitimate medical purpose as defined by the board; and

(2) if the physician knows or should know the person is using drugs for a nontherapeutic purpose.

(Enacted by Acts 2003, 78th Leg., ch. 1276 (H.B. 3507), § 14.002(a), effective September 1, 2003.)

### Sec. 107.053. Limitation on Authority of Hospital or Other Health Care Facility Regarding Use of Dangerous Drug or Controlled Substance.

A hospital or other health care facility may not prohibit or restrict the use of a dangerous drug or controlled substance prescribed or administered by a physician who holds staff privileges at the hospital or facility for a person diagnosed and treated by a physician for intractable pain.

(Enacted by Acts 2003, 78th Leg., ch. 1276 (H.B. 3507), § 14.002(a), effective September 1, 2003.)

## SUBCHAPTER C
## TREATMENT OF CERTAIN PATIENTS

### Sec. 107.101. Patient.

In this subchapter, "patient" includes a person who:

(1) is currently abusing a dangerous drug or controlled substance;

(2) is not currently abusing such a drug or substance but has a history of such abuse; or

(3) lives in an environment that poses a risk for misuse or diversion to illegitimate use of such a drug or substance.

(Enacted by Acts 2003, 78th Leg., ch. 1276 (H.B. 3507), § 14.002(a), effective September 1, 2003.)

### Sec. 107.102. Authority to Treat.

This chapter authorizes a physician to treat a patient with an acute or chronic painful medical condition with a dangerous drug or controlled substance to relieve the patient's pain using appropriate doses, for an appropriate length of time, and for as long as the pain persists.

(Enacted by Acts 2003, 78th Leg., ch. 1276 (H.B. 3507), § 14.002(a), effective September 1, 2003.)

### Sec. 107.103. Duty to Monitor Patient.

A physician who treats a patient under this subchapter shall monitor the patient to ensure that a prescribed dangerous drug or controlled substance is used only for the treatment of the patient's painful medical condition.

(Enacted by Acts 2003, 78th Leg., ch. 1276 (H.B. 3507), § 14.002(a), effective September 1, 2003.)

### Sec. 107.104. Documentation and Consultation Required.

To ensure that a prescribed dangerous drug or controlled substance is not diverted to another use and to ensure the appropriateness of the treatment of the patient's targeted symptoms, the physician shall:

(1) specifically document:

(A) the understanding between the physician and patient about the patient's prescribed treatment;

(B) the name of the drug or substance prescribed;

(C) the dosage and method of taking the prescribed drug or substance;

(D) the number of dose units prescribed; and

(E) the frequency of prescribing and dispensing the drug or substance; and

(2) consult with a psychologist, psychiatrist, expert in the treatment of addictions, or other health care professional, as appropriate.

(Enacted by Acts 2003, 78th Leg., ch. 1276 (H.B. 3507), § 14.002(a), effective September 1, 2003.)

## SUBCHAPTER D
## DISCIPLINARY ACTION

### Sec. 107.151. Disciplinary Action Prohibited.

A physician is not subject to disciplinary action by the board for prescribing or administering a dangerous drug or controlled substance in the course of treatment of a person for intractable pain.

(Enacted by Acts 2003, 78th Leg., ch. 1276 (H.B. 3507), § 14.002(a), effective September 1, 2003.)

### Sec. 107.152. Authority of Board to Revoke or Suspend License.

(a) This chapter does not affect the authority of the board to revoke or suspend the license of a physician who:

(1) prescribes, administers, or dispenses a drug or treatment:

(A) for a purpose that is not a legitimate medical purpose as defined by the board; and

(B) that is nontherapeutic in nature or nontherapeutic in the manner the drug or treatment is administered or prescribed;

(2) fails to keep a complete and accurate record of the purchase and disposal of:

(A) a drug listed in Chapter 481, Health and Safety Code; or

(B) a controlled substance scheduled in the Comprehensive Drug Abuse Prevention and Control Act of 1970 (21 U.S.C. Section 801 et seq.);

(3) writes a false or fictitious prescription for:

(A) a dangerous drug as defined by Chapter 483, Health and Safety Code;

(B) a controlled substance listed in a schedule under Chapter 481, Health and Safety Code; or

(C) a controlled substance scheduled in the Comprehensive Drug Abuse Prevention and Control Act of 1970 (21 U.S.C. Section 801 et seq.); or

(4) prescribes, administers, or dispenses in a manner inconsistent with public health and welfare:

(A) a dangerous drug as defined by Chapter 483, Health and Safety Code;

(B) a controlled substance listed in a schedule under Chapter 481, Health and Safety Code; or

(C) a controlled substance scheduled in the Comprehensive Drug Abuse Prevention

and Control Act of 1970 (21 U.S.C. Section 801 et seq.).

(b) For purposes of Subsection (a)(2), the physician's records must include a record of:

(1) the date of purchase;

(2) the sale or disposal of the drug or substance by the physician;

(3) the name and address of the person receiving the drug or substance; and

(4) the reason for the disposal or dispensing of the drug or substance to the person.

(Enacted by Acts 2003, 78th Leg., ch. 1276 (H.B. 3507), § 14.002(a), effective September 1, 2003.)

## SUBCHAPTER E
## PAIN TREATMENT REVIEW COMMITTEE

### Sec. 107.201. Pain Treatment Review Committee [Expired].

Expired pursuant to Acts 2007, 80th Leg., ch. 1391 (S.B. 1879), § 6, effective July 1, 2009.

(Enacted by Acts 2007, 80th Leg., ch. 1391 (S.B. 1879), § 6, effective September 1, 2007.)

## SUBTITLE B
## PHYSICIANS

## CHAPTER 158
## AUTHORITY OF PHYSICIAN TO PROVIDE CERTAIN DRUGS AND SUPPLIES

**Section**

---

### Sec. 158.001. Provision of Drugs and Other Supplies.

(a) A physician licensed under this subtitle may supply a patient with any drug, remedy, or clinical supply necessary to meet the patient's immediate needs.

(b) This section does not permit a physician to operate a retail pharmacy without complying with Chapter 558.

(c) This chapter does not prohibit a physician from supplying to a patient, free of charge, a drug provided to the physician by a drug manufacturer for an indigent pharmaceutical program if, in the physician's opinion, it is advantageous to the patient, in adhering to a course of treatment prescribed by the physician, to receive the drug. (Enacted by Acts 1999, 76th Leg., ch. 388 (H.B. 3155), § 1, effective September 1, 1999; am. Acts 2001, 77th Leg., ch. 700 (S.B. 332), § 1, effective June 13, 2001.)

### Sec. 158.002.   Provision of Free Samples.

(a) This chapter does not prohibit a physician from supplying a pharmaceutical sample to a patient free of charge if, in the physician's opinion, it is advantageous to the patient, in adhering to a course of treatment prescribed by the physician, to receive the sample.

(b) A pharmaceutical sample provided under this section must be:

(1) provided to the physician from the manufacturer free of charge and delivered to a patient free of any direct or indirect charge;

(2) prepackaged by the original manufacturer and not repackaged; and

(3) marked on the immediate container to indicate that it is a sample or recorded in records that indicate it is a sample.

(c) Each state and federal labeling and recordkeeping requirement must be followed and documented. A record maintained under Subsection (b)(3) must be accessible as provided under state and federal law. (Enacted by Acts 1999, 76th Leg., ch. 388 (H.B. 3155), § 1, effective September 1, 1999.)

### Sec. 158.003.   Dispensing of Dangerous Drugs in Certain Rural Areas.

(a) In this section, "reimbursement for cost" means an additional charge, separate from that imposed for the physician's professional services, that includes the cost of the drug product and all other actual costs to the physician incidental to providing the dispensing service. The term does not include a separate fee imposed for the act of dispensing the drug itself.

(b) This section applies to an area located in a county with a population of 5,000 or less, or in a municipality or an unincorporated town with a population of less than 2,500, that is within a 15-mile radius of the physician's office and in which a pharmacy is not located. This section does not apply to a municipality or an unincorporated town that is adjacent to a municipality with a population of 2,500 or more.

(c) A physician who practices medicine in an area described by Subsection (b) may:

(1) maintain a supply of dangerous drugs in the physician's office to be dispensed in the course of treating the physician's patients; and

(2) be reimbursed for the cost of supplying those drugs without obtaining a license under Chapter 558.

(d) A physician who dispenses dangerous drugs under Subsection (c) shall:

(1) comply with each labeling provision under Subtitle J applicable to that class of drugs; and

(2) oversee compliance with packaging and recordkeeping provisions applicable to that class of drugs.

(e) A physician who desires to dispense dangerous drugs under this section shall notify both the Texas State Board of Pharmacy and the board that the physician practices in an area described by Subsection (b). The physician may continue to dispense dangerous drugs in the area until the Texas State Board of Pharmacy determines, after notice and hearing, that the physician no longer practices in an area described by Subsection (b). (Enacted by Acts 1999, 76th Leg., ch. 388 (H.B. 3155), § 1, effective September 1, 1999.)

## SUBTITLE J
## PHARMACY AND PHARMACISTS

## CHAPTER 551
## GENERAL PROVISIONS

### Sec. 551.001.   Short Title.

The chapters of this subtitle, other than Chapter 567, may be cited as the Texas Pharmacy Act. (Enacted by Acts 1999, 76th Leg., ch. 388 (H.B. 3155), § 1, effective September 1, 1999.)

### Sec. 551.002.   Legislative Declaration; Purpose.

(a) This subtitle shall be liberally construed to regulate in the public interest the practice of pharmacy in this state as a professional practice that affects the public health, safety, and welfare.

(b) It is a matter of public interest and concern that the practice of pharmacy merits and receives the confidence of the public and that only qualified persons be permitted to engage in the practice of pharmacy in this state.

Occupations

(c) The purpose of this subtitle is to promote, preserve, and protect the public health, safety, and welfare through:

(1) effectively controlling and regulating the practice of pharmacy; and

(2) licensing pharmacies engaged in the sale, delivery, or distribution of prescription drugs and devices used in diagnosing and treating injury, illness, and disease.

(Enacted by Acts 1999, 76th Leg., ch. 388 (H.B. 3155), § 1, effective September 1, 1999.)

## Sec. 551.003. Definitions.

In Chapters 551-566:

(1) "Administer" means to directly apply a prescription drug to the body of a patient by any means, including injection, inhalation, or ingestion, by:

(A) a person authorized by law to administer the drug, including a practitioner or an authorized agent under a practitioner's supervision; or

(B) the patient at the direction of a practitioner.

(2) "Board" means the Texas State Board of Pharmacy.

(3) "Class A pharmacy license" or "community pharmacy license" means a license described by Section 560.051.

(4) "Class B pharmacy license" or "nuclear pharmacy license" means a license described by Section 560.051.

(5) "Class C pharmacy license" or "institutional pharmacy license" means a license described by Section 560.051.

(6) "Class D pharmacy license" or "clinic pharmacy license" means a license described by Section 560.051.

(7) "Class E pharmacy license" or "nonresident pharmacy license" means a license described by Section 560.051.

(8) "College of pharmacy" means a school, university, or college of pharmacy that:

(A) satisfies the accreditation standards of the American Council on Pharmaceutical Education as adopted by the board; or

(B) has degree requirements that meet the standards of accreditation set by the board.

(9) "Compounding" means the preparation, mixing, assembling, packaging, or labeling of a drug or device:

(A) as the result of a practitioner's prescription drug order based on the practitioner-patient-pharmacist relationship in the course of professional practice;

(B) for administration to a patient by a practitioner as the result of a practitioner's initiative based on the practitioner-patient-pharmacist relationship in the course of professional practice;

(C) in anticipation of a prescription drug order based on a routine, regularly observed prescribing pattern; or

(D) for or as an incident to research, teaching, or chemical analysis and not for selling or dispensing, except as allowed under Section 562.154 or Chapter 563.

(10) "Confidential record" means a health-related record, including a patient medication record, prescription drug order, or medication order, that:

(A) contains information that identifies an individual; and

(B) is maintained by a pharmacy or pharmacist.

(11) "Controlled substance" means a substance, including a drug:

(A) listed in Schedule I, II, III, IV, or V, as established by the commissioner of public health under Chapter 481, Health and Safety Code, or in Penalty Group 1, 1-A, 2, 3, or 4, Chapter 481; or

(B) included in Schedule I, II, III, IV, or V of the Comprehensive Drug Abuse Prevention and Control Act of 1970 (21 U.S.C. Section 801 et seq.).

(12) "Dangerous drug" means a drug or device that:

(A) is not included in Penalty Group 1, 2, 3, or 4, Chapter 481, Health and Safety Code, and is unsafe for self-medication; or

(B) bears or is required to bear the legend:

(i) "Caution: federal law prohibits dispensing without prescription" or "Rx only" or another legend that complies with federal law; or

(ii) "Caution: federal law restricts this drug to use by or on the order of a licensed veterinarian."

(13) "Deliver" or "delivery" means the actual, constructive, or attempted transfer of a prescription drug or device or controlled substance from one person to another, with or without consideration.

(14) "Designated agent" means:

(A) an individual, including a licensed nurse, physician assistant, or pharmacist:

(i) who is designated by a practitioner and authorized to communicate a prescription drug order to a pharmacist; and

(ii) for whom the practitioner assumes legal responsibility;

(B) a licensed nurse, physician assistant, or pharmacist employed in a health care facility to whom a practitioner communicates a prescription drug order; or

(C) a registered nurse or physician assistant authorized by a practitioner to administer a prescription drug order for a dangerous drug under Subchapter B, Chapter 157.

(15) "Device" means an instrument, apparatus, implement, machine, contrivance, implant, in vitro reagent, or other similar or related article, including a component part or accessory, that is required under federal or state law to be ordered or prescribed by a practitioner.

(16) "Dispense" means to prepare, package, compound, or label, in the course of professional practice, a prescription drug or device for delivery to an ultimate user or the user's agent under a practitioner's lawful order.

(17) "Distribute" means to deliver a prescription drug or device other than by administering or dispensing.

(18) "Drug" means:

(A) a substance recognized as a drug in a drug compendium, including the current official United States Pharmacopoeia, official National Formulary, or official Homeopathic Pharmacopoeia, or in a supplement to a drug compendium;

(B) a substance intended for use in the diagnosis, cure, mitigation, treatment, or prevention of disease in a human or another animal;

(C) a substance, other than food, intended to affect the structure or a function of the body of a human or another animal;

(D) a substance intended for use as a component of a substance specified in Paragraph (A), (B), or (C);

(E) a dangerous drug; or

(F) a controlled substance.

(19) "Drug regimen review" includes evaluation of prescription drug or medication orders and a patient medication record for:

(A) a known allergy;

(B) a rational therapy-contraindication;

(C) a reasonable dose and route of administration;

(D) reasonable directions for use;

(E) duplication of therapy;

(F) a drug-drug interaction;

(G) drug-food interaction;

(H) drug-disease interaction;

(I) adverse drug reaction; and

(J) proper use, including overuse or underuse.

(20) "Internship" means a practical experience program that is approved by the board.

(21) "Label" means written, printed, or graphic matter on the immediate container of a drug or device.

(22) "Labeling" means the process of affixing a label, including all information required by federal and state statute or regulation, to a drug or device container. The term does not include:

(A) the labeling by a manufacturer, packer, or distributor of a nonprescription drug or commercially packaged prescription drug or device; or

(B) unit dose packaging.

(23) "Manufacturing" means the production, preparation, propagation, conversion, or processing of a drug or device, either directly or indirectly, by extraction from a substance of natural origin or independently by a chemical or biological synthesis. The term includes packaging or repackaging a substance or labeling or relabeling a container and promoting and marketing the drug or device and preparing and promoting a commercially available product from a bulk compound for resale by a person, including a pharmacy or practitioner. The term does not include compounding.

(24) "Medication order" means an order from a practitioner or a practitioner's designated agent for administration of a drug or device.

(25) "Nonprescription drug" means a nonnarcotic drug or device that may be sold without a prescription and that is labeled and packaged in compliance with state or federal law.

(26) "Patient counseling" means communication by a pharmacist of information, as specified by board rule, to a patient or caregiver to improve therapy by ensuring proper use of a drug or device.

(27) "Pharmaceutical care" means providing drug therapy and other pharmaceutical services defined by board rule and intended to assist in curing or preventing a disease, eliminating or reducing a patient's symptom, or arresting or slowing a disease process.

(28) "Pharmacist" means a person licensed by the board to practice pharmacy.

(29) "Pharmacist-in-charge" means the pharmacist designated on a pharmacy license as the pharmacist who has the authority or

Occupations

responsibility for the pharmacy's compliance with statutes and rules relating to the practice of pharmacy.

(30) "Pharmacist-intern" means:

(A) an undergraduate student who is enrolled in the professional sequence of a college of pharmacy approved by the board and who is participating in a board-approved internship program; or

(B) a graduate of a college of pharmacy who is participating in a board-approved internship.

(31) "Pharmacy" means a facility at which a prescription drug or medication order is received, processed, or dispensed under this subtitle, Chapter 481 or 483, Health and Safety Code, or the Comprehensive Drug Abuse Prevention and Control Act of 1970 (21 U.S.C. Section 801 et seq.). The term does not include a narcotic drug treatment program that is regulated under Chapter 466, Health and Safety Code.

(32) "Pharmacy technician" means an individual employed by a pharmacy whose responsibility is to provide technical services that do not require professional judgment regarding preparing and distributing drugs and who works under the direct supervision of and is responsible to a pharmacist.

(33) "Practice of pharmacy" means:

(A) providing an act or service necessary to provide pharmaceutical care;

(B) interpreting or evaluating a prescription drug order or medication order;

(C) participating in drug or device selection as authorized by law, and participating in drug administration, drug regimen review, or drug or drug-related research;

(D) providing patient counseling;

(E) being responsible for:

(i) dispensing a prescription drug order or distributing a medication order;

(ii) compounding or labeling a drug or device, other than labeling by a manufacturer, repackager, or distributor of a nonprescription drug or commercially packaged prescription drug or device;

(iii) properly and safely storing a drug or device; or

(iv) maintaining proper records for a drug or device;

(F) performing for a patient a specific act of drug therapy management delegated to a pharmacist by a written protocol from a physician licensed in this state in compliance with Subtitle B; or

(G) administering an immunization or vaccination under a physician's written protocol.

(34) "Practitioner" means:

(A) a person licensed or registered to prescribe, distribute, administer, or dispense a prescription drug or device in the course of professional practice in this state, including a physician, dentist, podiatrist, or veterinarian but excluding a person licensed under this subtitle;

(B) a person licensed by another state, Canada, or the United Mexican States in a health field in which, under the law of this state, a license holder in this state may legally prescribe a dangerous drug;

(C) a person practicing in another state and licensed by another state as a physician, dentist, veterinarian, or podiatrist, who has a current federal Drug Enforcement Administration registration number and who may legally prescribe a Schedule II, III, IV, or V controlled substance, as specified under Chapter 481, Health and Safety Code, in that other state; or

(D) an advanced practice nurse or physician assistant to whom a physician has delegated the authority to carry out or sign prescription drug orders under Section 157.0511, 157.052, 157.053, 157.054, 157.0541, or 157.0542.

(35) "Preceptor" has the meaning assigned by Section 558.057.

(36) "Prescription drug" means:

(A) a substance for which federal or state law requires a prescription before the substance may be legally dispensed to the public;

(B) a drug or device that under federal law is required, before being dispensed or delivered, to be labeled with the statement:

(i) "Caution: federal law prohibits dispensing without prescription" or "Rx only" or another legend that complies with federal law; or

(ii) "Caution: federal law restricts this drug to use by or on the order of a licensed veterinarian"; or

(C) a drug or device that is required by federal or state statute or regulation to be dispensed on prescription or that is restricted to use by a practitioner only.

(37) "Prescription drug order" means:

Occupations

(A) an order from a practitioner or a practitioner's designated agent to a pharmacist for a drug or device to be dispensed; or

(B) an order under Subchapter B, Chapter 157.

(38) "Prospective drug use review" means the review of a patient's drug therapy and prescription drug order or medication order, as defined by board rule, before dispensing or distributing a drug to the patient.

(39) "Provide" means to supply one or more unit doses of a nonprescription drug or dangerous drug to a patient.

(40) "Radioactive drug" means a drug that exhibits spontaneous disintegration of unstable nuclei with the emission of nuclear particles or photons, including a nonradioactive reagent kit or nuclide generator that is intended to be used in the preparation of the substance.

(41) "Substitution" means the dispensing of a drug or a brand of drug other than the drug or brand of drug ordered or prescribed.

(42) "Texas trade association" means a cooperative and voluntarily joined statewide association of business or professional competitors in this state designed to assist its members and its industry or profession in dealing with mutual business or professional problems and in promoting their common interest.

(42-a) "Therapeutic contact lens" means a contact lens that contains one or more drugs and that delivers the drugs into the wearer's eye.

(43) "Ultimate user" means a person who obtains or possesses a prescription drug or device for the person's own use or for the use of a member of the person's household or for administering to an animal owned by the person or by a member of the person's household.

(44) "Unit dose packaging" means the ordered amount of drug in a dosage form ready for administration to a particular patient, by the prescribed route at the prescribed time, and properly labeled with the name, strength, and expiration date of the drug.

(45) "Written protocol" means a physician's order, standing medical order, standing delegation order, or other order or protocol as defined by rule of the Texas State Board of Medical Examiners under Subtitle B.

(Enacted by Acts 1999, 76th Leg., ch. 388 (H.B. 3155), § 1, effective September 1, 1999; am. Acts 2001, 77th Leg., ch. 112 (S.B. 1166), § 5, effective May 11, 2001; am. Acts 2001, 77th Leg., ch. 1254 (S.B. 768), § 1, effective September 1, 2001; am.

Acts 2003, 78th Leg., ch. 88 (H.B. 1095), § 8, effective May 20, 2003; am. Acts 2005, 79th Leg., ch. 28 (S.B. 492), § 1, effective September 1, 2005; am. Acts 2005, 79th Leg., ch. 1345 (S.B. 410), § 2, effective September 1, 2005; am. Acts 2009, 81st Leg., ch. 396 (H.B. 1740), § 1, effective June 19, 2009.)

## Sec. 551.004.  Applicability of Subtitle.

(a) This subtitle does not apply to:

(1) a practitioner licensed by the appropriate state board who supplies a patient of the practitioner with a drug in a manner authorized by state or federal law and who does not operate a pharmacy for the retailing of prescription drugs;

(2) a member of the faculty of a college of pharmacy recognized by the board who is a pharmacist and who performs the pharmacist's services only for the benefit of the college;

(3) a person who procures prescription drugs for lawful research, teaching, or testing and not for resale; or

(4) a home and community support services agency that possesses a dangerous drug as authorized by Section 142.0061, 142.0062, or 142.0063, Health and Safety Code.

(b) This subtitle does not prevent a practitioner from administering a drug to a patient of the practitioner.

(c) This subtitle does not prevent the sale by a person, other than a pharmacist, firm, joint stock company, partnership, or corporation, of:

(1) a nonprescription drug that is harmless if used according to instructions on a printed label on the drug's container and that does not contain a narcotic;

(2) an insecticide, a fungicide, or a chemical used in the arts if the insecticide, fungicide, or chemical is properly labeled; or

(3) an insecticide or fungicide that is mixed or compounded only for an agricultural purpose.

(d) A wholesaler or manufacturer may distribute a prescription drug as provided by state or federal law.

(e) This subtitle does not prevent a physician or therapeutic optometrist from dispensing and charging for therapeutic contact lenses. This subsection does not authorize a therapeutic optometrist to prescribe, administer, or dispense a drug that is otherwise outside the therapeutic optometrist's scope of practice.

(Enacted by Acts 1999, 76th Leg., ch. 388 (H.B. 3155), § 1, effective September 1, 1999; am. Acts 2009, 81st Leg., ch. 396(H.B. 1740), § 2, effective June 19, 2009.)

## Sec. 551.005. Application of Sunset Act.

The Texas State Board of Pharmacy is subject to Chapter 325, Government Code (Texas Sunset Act). Unless continued in existence as provided by that chapter, the board is abolished and this subtitle expires September 1, 2017.

(Enacted by Acts 1999, 76th Leg., ch. 388 (H.B. 3155), § 1, effective September 1, 1999; am. Acts 2005, 79th Leg., ch. 1345 (S.B. 410), § 1, effective September 1, 2005.)

# CHAPTER 563
# PRESCRIPTION REQUIREMENTS; DELEGATION OF ADMINISTRATION AND PROVISION OF DANGEROUS DRUGS

**Subchapter B. Delegation of Administration and Provision of Dangerous Drugs**

## SUBCHAPTER A
## PRESCRIPTION REQUIREMENTS FOR PRACTITIONERS [REPEALED]

### Sec. 563.001. Prescription Issued by Practitioner [Repealed].

Repealed by Acts 2001, 77th Leg., ch. 1254 (S.B. 768), § 13(a)(2), effective June 1, 2002. (Enacted by Acts 1999, 76th Leg., ch. 388 (H.B. 3155), § 1, effective September 1, 1999.)

### Sec. 563.002. Requirements Related to Prescription Forms [Repealed].

Repealed by Acts 2001, 77th Leg., ch. 1254 (S.B. 768), § 13(a)(2), effective June 1, 2002. (Enacted by Acts 1999, 76th Leg., ch. 388 (H.B. 3155), § 1, effective September 1, 1999.)

## SUBCHAPTER B
## DELEGATION OF ADMINISTRATION AND PROVISION OF DANGEROUS DRUGS

### Sec. 563.051. General Delegation of Administration and Provision of Dangerous Drugs.

(a) A physician may delegate to any qualified and properly trained person acting under the physician's supervision the act of administering or providing dangerous drugs in the physician's office, as ordered by the physician, that are used or required to meet the immediate needs of the physician's patients. The administration or provision of the dangerous drugs must be performed in compliance with laws relating to the practice of medicine and state and federal laws relating to those dangerous drugs.

(b) A physician may also delegate to any qualified and properly trained person acting under the physician's supervision the act of administering or providing dangerous drugs through a facility licensed by the board, as ordered by the physician, that are used or required to meet the needs of the physician's patients. The administration of those dangerous drugs must be in compliance with laws relating to the practice of medicine, professional nursing, and pharmacy and state and federal drug laws. The provision of those dangerous drugs must be in compliance with:

(1) laws relating to the practice of medicine, professional nursing, and pharmacy;

(2) state and federal drug laws; and

(3) rules adopted by the board.

(c) The administration or provision of the drugs may be delegated through a physician's order, a standing medical order, a standing delegation order, or another order defined by the Texas State Board of Medical Examiners.

(d) This section does not authorize a physician or a person acting under the supervision of a physician to keep a pharmacy, advertised or otherwise, for the retail sale of dangerous drugs, other than as authorized under Section 158.003, without complying with the applicable laws relating to the dangerous drugs.

(e) A practitioner may designate a licensed vocational nurse or a person having education equivalent to or greater than that required for a licensed vocational nurse to communicate the prescriptions of an advanced practice nurse or physician assistant authorized by the practitioner to sign prescription drug orders under Subchapter B, Chapter 157.

(Enacted by Acts 1999, 76th Leg., ch. 388 (H.B. 3155), § 1, effective September 1, 1999; am. Acts 2001, 77th Leg., ch. 1420 (H.B. 2812), § 14.308(a), effective September 1, 2001.)

### Sec. 563.052. Suitable Container Required.

A drug or medicine provided under this subchapter must be supplied in a suitable container labeled in compliance with applicable drug laws. A qualified and trained person, acting under the supervision of a physician, may specify at the time of the provision of the drug the inclusion on the container of the date of the provision and the patient's name and address.

(Enacted by Acts 1999, 76th Leg., ch. 388 (H.B. 3155), § 1, effective September 1, 1999.)

### Sec. 563.053. Dispensing of Dangerous Drugs in Certain Rural Areas.

(a) In this section, "reimbursement for cost" means an additional charge, separate from that imposed for the physician's professional services, that includes the cost of the drug product and all other actual costs to the physician incidental to providing the dispensing service. The term does not include a separate fee imposed for the act of dispensing the drug itself.

(b) This section applies to an area located in a county with a population of 5,000 or less, or in a municipality or an unincorporated town with a population of less than 2,500, that is within a 15-mile radius of the physician's office and in which a pharmacy is not located. This section does not apply to a municipality or an unincorporated town that is adjacent to a municipality with a population of 2,500 or more.

(c) A physician who practices medicine in an area described by Subsection (b) may:

(1) maintain a supply of dangerous drugs in the physician's office to be dispensed in the course of treating the physician's patients; and

(2) be reimbursed for the cost of supplying those drugs without obtaining a license under Chapter 558.

(d) A physician who dispenses dangerous drugs under Subsection (c) shall:

(1) comply with each labeling provision under this subtitle applicable to that class of drugs; and

(2) oversee compliance with packaging and recordkeeping provisions applicable to that class of drugs.

(e) A physician who desires to dispense dangerous drugs under this section shall notify both the board and the Texas State Board of Medical Examiners that the physician practices in an area described by Subsection (b). The physician may continue to dispense dangerous drugs in the area until the board determines, after notice and hearing, that the physician no longer practices in an area described by Subsection (b).

(Enacted by Acts 1999, 76th Leg., ch. 388 (H.B. 3155), § 1, effective September 1, 1999.)

### Sec. 563.054. Administration of Dangerous Drugs.

(a) A veterinarian may:

(1) administer or provide dangerous drugs to a patient in the veterinarian's office, or on the patient's premises, if the drugs are used or required to meet the needs of the veterinarian's patients;

(2) delegate the administration or provision of dangerous drugs to a person who:

(A) is qualified and properly trained; and

(B) acts under the veterinarian's supervision; and

(3) itemize and receive compensation for the administration or provision of the dangerous drugs under Subdivision (1).

(b) This section does not permit a veterinarian to maintain a pharmacy for the retailing of drugs without complying with applicable laws.

(c) The administration or provision of dangerous drugs must comply with:

(1) laws relating to the practice of veterinary medicine; and

(2) state and federal laws relating to dangerous drugs.

(Enacted by Acts 1999, 76th Leg., ch. 388 (H.B. 3155), § 1, effective September 1, 1999.)

## CHAPTER 1701
## LAW ENFORCEMENT OFFICERS

**Subchapter G. License Requirements; Disqualifications and Exemptions**

## SUBCHAPTER G
## LICENSE REQUIREMENTS; DISQUALIFICATIONS AND EXEMPTIONS

### Sec. 1701.301. License Required.

Except as provided by Sections 1701.310 and 1701.311, a person may not appoint a person to serve as an officer, county jailer, or public security officer unless the person appointed holds an appropriate license issued by the commission.

(Enacted by Acts 1999, 76th Leg., ch. 388 (H.B. 3155), § 1, effective September 1, 1999.)

### Sec. 1701.302. Certain Elected Law Enforcement Officers; License Required.

(a) An officer, including a sheriff, elected under the Texas Constitution or a statute or appointed to fill a vacancy in an elective office must obtain a license from the commission not later than the second anniversary of the date the officer takes office.

(b) The commission shall establish requirements for issuing the license and for revocation, suspension, or denial of the license.

(c) An officer to whom this section applies who does not obtain the license by the required date or does not remain licensed is incompetent and is subject to removal from office under Section

Occupations

665.052, Government Code, or another removal statute.

(Enacted by Acts 1999, 76th Leg., ch. 388 (H.B. 3155), § 1, effective September 1, 1999.)

### Sec. 1701.303.  License Application; Duties of Appointing Entity.

(a) A law enforcement agency or governmental entity that hires a person for whom a license is sought must file an application with the commission as provided by commission rule.

(b) A person who appoints an officer or county jailer licensed by the commission shall notify the commission not later than the 30th day after the date of the appointment. If the person appoints an individual who previously served as an officer or county jailer and the appointment occurs after the 180th day after the last date of service as an officer or county jailer, the person must have on file for the officer or county jailer in a form readily accessible to the commission:

(1) new criminal history record information;

(2) a new declaration of psychological and emotional health and lack of drug dependency or illegal drug use; and

(3) two completed fingerprint cards.

(Enacted by Acts 1999, 76th Leg., ch. 388 (H.B. 3155), § 1, effective September 1, 1999.)

### Sec. 1701.304.  Examination.

(a) The commission shall conduct an examination for each type of license issued by the commission at least four times each year at times and places designated by the commission. The commission shall:

(1) prescribe the content of an examination for each type of license;

(2) include in each examination a written examination that tests the applicant's knowledge of the appropriate occupation; and

(3) prescribe standards for acceptable performance on each examination.

(b) The commission by rule shall establish minimum qualifications for a person to be examined under this section. A person who is disqualified by law to be an officer or county jailer may not take an examination under this section.

(c) A law enforcement agency may request the commission to conduct examinations required by this chapter in the jurisdiction served by the agency. The commission may conduct the examinations in the jurisdiction if:

(1) the commission determines that doing so will not place a significant hardship on the commission's resources; and

(2) the requesting law enforcement agency reimburses the commission for additional costs incurred in conducting the examination in the agency's jurisdiction.

(Enacted by Acts 1999, 76th Leg., ch. 388 (H.B. 3155), § 1, effective September 1, 1999.)

### Sec. 1701.305.  Examination Results.

(a) The commission shall notify each examinee of the examination results not later than the 30th day after the date the examination is administered. If an examination is graded or reviewed by a national testing service, the commission shall notify each examinee of the examination results not later than the 14th day after the date the commission receives the results from the testing service.

(b) If notice of the results of an examination graded or reviewed by a national testing service will be delayed for longer than 90 days after the examination date, the commission shall notify each examinee of the reason for the delay before the 90th day.

(c) If requested in writing by a person who fails an examination, the commission shall provide to the person an analysis of the person's performance on the examination.

(Enacted by Acts 1999, 76th Leg., ch. 388 (H.B. 3155), § 1, effective September 1, 1999.)

### Sec. 1701.306.  Psychological and Physical Examination.

(a) The commission may not issue a license to a person unless the person is examined by:

(1) a licensed psychologist or by a psychiatrist who declares in writing that the person is in satisfactory psychological and emotional health to serve as the type of officer for which a license is sought; and

(2) a licensed physician who declares in writing that the person does not show any trace of drug dependency or illegal drug use after a blood test or other medical test.

(b) An agency hiring a person for whom a license is sought shall select the examining physician and the examining psychologist or psychiatrist. The agency shall prepare a report of each declaration required by Subsection (a) and shall maintain a copy of the report on file in a format readily accessible to the commission. A declaration is not public information.

(c) The commission shall adopt rules that:

(1) relate to appropriate standards and measures to be used by a law enforcement agency

in reporting the declarations made under Subsection (a); and

(2) provide for exceptional circumstances in the administration of the examination of the applicant's psychological and emotional health, including permitting the examination to be made by a qualified licensed physician instead of a psychologist or psychiatrist.

(d) The commission may order an applicant to submit to an examination described by Subsection (a) by a psychologist, psychiatrist, or physician appointed by the commission if the commission:

(1) has cause to believe that a law enforcement agency failed to follow commission rules relating to an examination; or

(2) discovers that the applicant has submitted a false declaration.

(Enacted by Acts 1999, 76th Leg., ch. 388 (H.B. 3155), § 1, effective September 1, 1999; am. Acts 2011, 82nd Leg., ch. 1224 (S.B. 542), § 2, effective September 1, 2011.)

### Sec. 1701.307. Issuance of License.

(a) The commission shall issue an appropriate license to a person who, as required by this chapter:

(1) submits an application;

(2) completes the required training;

(3) passes the required examination;

(4) is declared to be in satisfactory psychological and emotional health and free from drug dependency or illegal drug use; and

(5) demonstrates weapons proficiency.

(b) The commission may issue a permanent license to a person who meets the requirements of this chapter and the rules prescribed by the commission to serve as an officer.

(c) The commission may issue a temporary or permanent license to a person to serve as a county jailer.

(Enacted by Acts 1999, 76th Leg., ch. 388 (H.B. 3155), § 1, effective September 1, 1999; am. Acts 2007, 80th Leg., R.S., ch. 878 (H.B. 1955), § 2, effective June 15, 2007.)

### Sec. 1701.3075. Qualified Applicant Awaiting Appointment.

(a) A person who meets the requirements set forth in Section 1701.307(a) has the same reporting responsibilities toward the commission under rules adopted by the commission as a license holder who has already been appointed as a peace officer.

(b) The commission may determine that a person who meets the requirements under Section 1701.307(a) is ineligible for appointment as a peace officer based on events that occur after the person meets the requirements in Section 1701.307(a) but before the person is appointed. (Enacted by Acts 2009, 81st Leg., ch. 701 (H.B. 2799), § 1, effective September 1, 2009.)

### Sec. 1701.308. Weapons Proficiency.

The commission shall require a person applying for a peace officer license to demonstrate weapons proficiency.

(Enacted by Acts 1999, 76th Leg., ch. 388 (H.B. 3155), § 1, effective September 1, 1999.)

### Sec. 1701.309. Age Requirement.

The commission by rule shall set 21 years of age as the minimum age for obtaining a license as an officer. The rules must provide that a person at least 18 years of age may be issued a license as an officer if the person has:

(1) completed and received credit for at least 60 hours of study at an accredited college or university or received an associate degree from an accredited college or university; or

(2) received an honorable discharge from the United States armed forces after at least two years of service.

(Enacted by Acts 1999, 76th Leg., ch. 388 (H.B. 3155), § 1, effective September 1, 1999.)

### Sec. 1701.310. Appointment of County Jailer; Training Required.

(a) Except as provided by Subsection (e), a person may not be appointed as a county jailer, except on a temporary basis, unless the person has satisfactorily completed a preparatory training program, as required by the commission, in the operation of a county jail at a school operated or licensed by the commission.

(b) A county jailer appointed on a temporary basis who does not satisfactorily complete the preparatory training program before the first anniversary of the date that the person is appointed shall be removed from the position. A temporary appointment may not be renewed, except that not earlier than the first anniversary of the date that a person is removed under this subsection, the sheriff may petition the commission for reinstatement of the person to a temporary appointment.

(c) A county jailer serving under permanent appointment before September 1, 1979, regardless of whether the person's employment was terminated before that date because of failure to satisfy standards adopted under Chapter 511, Government Code, is not required to meet a requirement of this section as a condition of continued employment or promotion unless:

(1) in an attempt to meet the standards the person took an examination and failed or was not allowed to finish the examination because the person acted dishonestly in regard to the examination;

(2) the person forged a document purporting to show that the person meets the standards; or

(3) the person seeks a new appointment as a county jailer on or after September 1, 1984.

(d) A county jailer serving under permanent appointment before September 1, 1979, is eligible to attend training courses in the operation of a county jail, subject to commission rules.

(e) A person trained and certified by the Texas Department of Criminal Justice to serve as a corrections officer in that agency's correctional institutions division is not required to complete the training requirements of this section to be appointed a part-time county jailer. Examinations under Section 1701.304 and psychological examinations under Section 1701.306 apply.

(Enacted by Acts 1999, 76th Leg., ch. 388 (H.B. 3155), § 1, effective September 1, 1999; am. Acts 2001, 77th Leg., ch. 1420 (H.B. 2812), § 14.502(a), effective September 1, 2001; am. Acts 2009, 81st Leg., R.S., ch. 87 (S.B. 1969), § 25.142, effective September 1, 2009; am. Acts 2011, 82nd Leg., ch. 1224 (S.B. 542), § 3, effective September 1, 2011.)

### Sec. 1701.311.  Provisional License for Workforce Shortage.

(a) The commission shall adopt rules to allow a law enforcement agency to petition for issuance of a provisional license for an officer if the agency proves that it has a workforce shortage.

(b) Except in an emergency, a peace officer holding a provisional license may not be required to work at the peace officer's employing agency and attend a commission-approved basic preparatory school for more than a total of 40 hours a week.

(c) An agency employing a peace officer who holds a provisional license may contract with the peace officer for reimbursement of the cost of a basic preparatory training course if the peace officer voluntarily resigns from the agency before a date specified in the contract that is not later

than the first anniversary of the date the officer is appointed. The contract must state the cost of the course.

(Enacted by Acts 1999, 76th Leg., ch. 388 (H.B. 3155), § 1, effective September 1, 1999.)

### Sec. 1701.312.  Disqualification: Felony Conviction or Placement on Community Supervision.

(a) A person who has been convicted of a felony is disqualified to be an officer, public security officer, telecommunicator, or county jailer, and the commission may not issue a license to, and a law enforcement agency may not appoint or employ, the person.

(b) For purposes of this section and Section 1701.502, a person is convicted of a felony if a court enters an adjudication of guilt against the person on a felony offense under the laws of this or another state or the United States, regardless of whether:

(1) the sentence is subsequently probated and the person is discharged from community supervision;

(2) the accusation, complaint, information, or indictment against the person is dismissed and the person is released from all penalties and disabilities resulting from the offense; or

(3) the person is pardoned for the offense, unless the pardon is granted expressly for subsequent proof of innocence.

(c) The commission, on receipt of a certified copy of a court's judgment under Article 42.011, Code of Criminal Procedure, shall note on the person's licensing records the conviction or community supervision indicated by the judgment.

(Enacted by Acts 1999, 76th Leg., ch. 388 (H.B. 3155), § 1, effective September 1, 1999; am. Acts 2011, 82nd Leg., ch. 855 (H.B. 3823), § 6, effective September 1, 2011.)

### Sec. 1701.313.  Disqualification: Conviction of Barratry.

(a) A person who has been convicted of barratry under Section 38.12, Penal Code, is disqualified to be an officer, telecommunicator, or county jailer, and the commission may not issue a license to the person.

(b) For purposes of this section and Section 1701.503, a person is convicted of barratry if a court enters an adjudication of guilt against the person regardless of whether:

(1) the sentence is subsequently probated and the person is discharged from community supervision;

(2) the accusation, complaint, information, or indictment against the person is dismissed following community supervision; or

(3) the person is pardoned for the offense, unless the pardon is granted expressly for subsequent proof of innocence.

(Enacted by Acts 1999, 76th Leg., ch. 388 (H.B. 3155), § 1, effective September 1, 1999; am. Acts 2011, 82nd Leg., ch. 855 (H.B. 3823), § 7, effective September 1, 2011.)

### Sec. 1701.314. Exemption: Officer Appointed Before September 1, 1970.

A peace officer serving under a permanent appointment before September 1, 1970, is not required to obtain a license as a condition of tenure, continued employment, or promotion unless the officer seeks a new appointment. The officer is eligible to attend peace officer training courses subject to commission rules.

(Enacted by Acts 1999, 76th Leg., ch. 388 (H.B. 3155), § 1, effective September 1, 1999.)

### Sec. 1701.315. Records [Repealed].

Repealed by Acts 2009, 81st Leg., ch. 1172 (H.B. 3389), § 35, effective September 1, 2009. (Enacted by Acts 1999, 76th Leg., ch. 388 (H.B. 3155), § 1, effective September 1, 1999.)

### Sec. 1701.316. Reactivation of Peace Officer License.

(a) The commission shall adopt rules establishing requirements for reactivation of a peace officer's license after a break in employment.

(b) The commission may consider employment as a peace officer in another state in determining whether the person is required to obtain additional training or testing.

(Enacted by Acts 1999, 76th Leg., ch. 388 (H.B. 3155), § 1, effective September 1, 1999.)

### Sec. 1701.3161. Reactivation of Peace Officer License: Retired Peace Officers.

(a) In this section, "retired peace officer" means a person who served as a peace officer in this state who:

(1) is not currently serving as an elected, appointed, or employed peace officer under Article 2.12, Code of Criminal Procedure, or other law;

(2) was eligible to retire from a law enforcement agency in this state or was ineligible to retire only as a result of an injury received in the course of the officer's employment with the law enforcement agency; and

(3) is eligible to receive a pension or annuity for service as a law enforcement officer in this state or is ineligible to receive a pension or annuity only because the law enforcement agency that employed the officer does not offer a pension or annuity to its employees.

(b) The commission shall adopt rules for the reactivation of a retired peace officer's license after a break in employment. The rules must allow a retired peace officer to reactivate the officer's license by completing the continuing education requirements prescribed by Section 1701.351 and completing any other continuing education requirement imposed by law in lieu of successfully completing any examination required by the commission for reactivation.

(c) The commission may waive the reinstatement fee established for the reactivation of a peace officer's license for a retired peace officer who is eligible for reactivation as provided by Subsection (b).

(Enacted by Acts 2007, 80th Leg., ch. 878 (H.B. 1955), § 3, effective June 15, 2007.)

### Sec. 1701.317. Limitation on Information Required for License Renewal.

The requirements and procedures adopted by the commission for the renewal of a license issued under this chapter:

(1) may not require an applicant to provide unchanged criminal history information already included in one or more of the applicant's previous applications for licensure or for license renewal filed with the commission; and

(2) may require the applicant to provide only information relevant to the period occurring since the date of the applicant's last application for licensure or for license renewal, as applicable, including information relevant to any new requirement applicable to the license held by the applicant.

(Enacted by Acts 2009, 81st Leg., ch. 332 (H.B. 846), § 2, effective September 1, 2009.)

## SUBCHAPTER H
## CONTINUING EDUCATION AND YEARLY WEAPONS PROFICIENCY

### Sec. 1701.351. Continuing Education Required for Peace Officers.

(a) Each peace officer shall complete at least 40 hours of continuing education programs once every 24 months. The commission may suspend

Occupations

the license of a peace officer who fails to comply with this requirement.

(a-1) As part of the continuing education programs under Subsection (a), a peace officer must complete a training and education program that covers recent changes to the laws of this state and of the United States pertaining to peace officers.

(b) The commission by rule shall provide for waiver of the requirements of this section when mitigating circumstances exist.

(c) The commission shall credit a peace officer with meeting the continuing education requirements of this section if during the relevant 24-month period the peace officer serves on active duty as a member of the United States military for at least 12 months or serves as an elected member of the legislature. Credit for continuing education under this subsection does not affect any requirement to demonstrate continuing weapons proficiency under Section 1701.355.

(d) A peace officer who is second in command to a police chief of a law enforcement agency and who attends a continuing education program for command staff provided by the Bill Blackwood Law Enforcement Management Institute of Texas under Section 96.641, Education Code, is exempt from the continuing education requirements of this subchapter.

(Enacted by Acts 1999, 76th Leg., ch. 388 (H.B. 3155), § 1, effective September 1, 1999; am. Acts 2001, 77th Leg., ch. 1157 (H.B. 2881), § 1, effective September 1, 2001; am. Acts 2005, 79th Leg., ch. 1236 (H.B. 1438), § 1, effective June 18, 2005; am. Acts 2009, 81st Leg., R.S., ch. 1172 (H.B. 3389), § 15, effective September 1, 2009; am. Acts 2011, 82nd Leg., ch. 602 (S.B. 244), § 3, effective September 1, 2011.)

### Sec. 1701.352. Continuing Education Programs.

(a) The commission shall recognize, prepare, or administer continuing education programs for officers and county jailers.

(b) The commission shall require a state, county, special district, or municipal agency that appoints or employs peace officers to provide each peace officer with a training program at least once every 48 months that is approved by the commission and consists of:

(1) topics selected by the agency; and

(2) for an officer holding only a basic proficiency certificate, not more than 20 hours of education and training that contain curricula incorporating the learning objectives developed by the commission regarding:

(A) civil rights, racial sensitivity, and cultural diversity;

(B) de-escalation and crisis intervention techniques to facilitate interaction with persons with mental impairments; and

(C) unless determined by the agency head to be inconsistent with the officer's assigned duties:

(i) the recognition and documentation of cases that involve child abuse or neglect, family violence, and sexual assault; and

(ii) issues concerning sex offender characteristics.

(c) A course provided under Subsection (b) may use instructional materials developed by the agency or its trainers or by entities having training agreements with the commission in addition to materials included in curricula developed by the commission.

(d) A peace officer appointed to the officer's first supervisory position must receive in-service training on supervision as part of the course provided for the officer under Subsection (b) during the 24-month period after the date of that appointment.

(e) The commission may require a state, county, special district, or municipal agency that appoints or employs a reserve law enforcement officer, county jailer, or public security officer to provide each of those persons with education and training in civil rights, racial sensitivity, and cultural diversity at least once every 48 months.

(f) Training in documentation of cases required by Subsection (b) shall include instruction in:

(1) making a written account of the extent of injuries sustained by the victim of an alleged offense;

(2) recording by photograph or videotape the area in which an alleged offense occurred and the victim's injuries; and

(3) recognizing and recording a victim's statement that may be admissible as evidence in a proceeding concerning the matter about which the statement was made.

(g) The training and education program on de-escalation and crisis intervention techniques to facilitate interaction with persons with mental impairments under Subsection (b)(2)(B) may not be provided as an online course. The commission shall:

(1) determine best practices for interacting with persons with mental impairments, in consultation with the Bill Blackwood Law Enforcement Management Institute of Texas; and

(2) review the education and training program under Subsection (b)(2)(B) at least once every 24 months.

(h) The commission shall require a state, county, special district, or municipal agency that employs telecommunicators to provide each telecommunicator with 24 hours of crisis communications instruction approved by the commission. The instruction must be provided on or before the first anniversary of the telecommunicator's first day of employment.

(Enacted by Acts 1999, 76th Leg., ch. 388 (H.B. 3155), § 1, effective September 1, 1999; am. Acts 2001, 77th Leg., ch. 1157 (H.B. 2881), § 2, effective September 1, 2001; am. Acts 2009, 81st Leg., R.S., ch. 1172 (H.B. 3389), § 16, effective September 1, 2009; am. Acts 2011, 82nd Leg., ch. 855 (H.B. 3823), § 8, effective September 1, 2011.)

### Sec. 1701.353. Continuing Education Procedures.

(a) The commission by rule shall adopt procedures to:

(1) ensure the timely and accurate reporting by agencies and persons licensed under this chapter of information related to training programs offered under this subchapter, including procedures for creating training records for license holders; and

(2) provide adequate notice to agencies and license holders of impending noncompliance with the training requirements of this subchapter so that the agencies and license holders may comply within the 24-month period or 48-month period, as appropriate.

(b) The commission shall require agencies to report to the commission in a timely manner the reasons that a license holder is in noncompliance after the agency receives notice by the commission of the license holder's noncompliance. The commission shall, following receipt of an agency's report or on a determination that the agency has failed to report in a timely manner, notify the license holder by certified mail of the reasons the license holder is in noncompliance and that the commission at the request of the license holder will hold a hearing as provided by this subsection if the license holder fails to obtain the required training within 60 days after the date the license holder receives notice under this subsection. The commission shall conduct a hearing consistent with Section 1701.504 if the license holder claims that:

(1) mitigating circumstances exist; or

(2) the license holder failed to complete the required training because the license holder's employing agency did not provide an adequate opportunity for the license holder to attend the required training course.

(Enacted by Acts 1999, 76th Leg., ch. 388 (H.B. 3155), § 1, effective September 1, 1999; am. Acts 2005, 79th Leg., ch. 1236 (H.B. 1438), § 2, effective June 18, 2005; am. Acts 2011, 82nd Leg., ch. 1224 (S.B. 542), § 4, effective September 1, 2011.)

### Sec. 1701.354. Continuing Education for Deputy Constables.

(a) If the commission requires a state, county, special district, or municipal agency that employs a deputy constable to provide the deputy constable with a training program under Section 1701.352, the commission shall require the deputy constable to attend at least 20 hours of instruction in civil process.

(b) The commission shall adopt rules and procedures concerning a civil process course, including rules providing for:

(1) approval of course content and standards; and

(2) issuance of course credit.

(c) The commission may waive the instruction requirements for a deputy constable under this section:

(1) if a constable requests a waiver for the deputy constable based on a representation that the deputy constable's duty assignment does not involve civil process responsibilities; or

(2) if the deputy constable requests a waiver because of hardship and the commission determines that a hardship exists.

(Enacted by Acts 1999, 76th Leg., ch. 388 (H.B. 3155), § 1, effective September 1, 1999; am. Acts 2005, 79th Leg., ch. 735 (H.B. 2574), § 1, effective June 17, 2005; am. Acts 2005, 79th Leg., ch. 954 (H.B. 1588), § 3, effective June 18, 2005; am. Acts 2007, 80th Leg., ch. 921 (H.B. 3167), § 12.001, effective September 1, 2007.)

### Sec. 1701.3545. Initial Training and Continuing Education for Constables.

(a) A public institution of higher education selected by the commission shall establish and offer a program of initial training and a program of continuing education for constables. The curriculum for each program must relate to law enforcement management and civil process issues. The institution selected under this subsec-

Occupations

tion shall develop the curriculum for the programs. The curriculum must be approved by the commission.

(b) Each constable must complete at least 40 hours of continuing education provided by the selected institution under this section each 48-month period. The commission by rule shall establish a uniform 48-month continuing education training period.

(c) An individual appointed or elected to that individual's first position as constable must complete at least 40 hours of initial training for new constables in accordance with Subsections (d) and (e).

(d) A newly appointed or elected constable shall complete the initial training program for new constables not later than the second anniversary of that individual's appointment or election as constable. The initial training program for new constables is in addition to the initial training required by this chapter. The commission by rule shall establish that the first continuing education training period for an individual under Subsection (b) begins on the first day of the first uniform continuing education training period that follows the date the individual completed the initial training program.

(e) The institution selected under Subsection (a) by rule may provide for the waiver of:

(1) all or part of the required 40 hours of initial training for new constables to the extent the new constable has satisfactorily completed equivalent training during the 24 months preceding the individual's appointment or election; or

(2) the continuing education requirements of Subsection (b) for an individual who has satisfactorily completed equivalent continuing education during the preceding 24 months.

(f) An individual who is subject to the continuing education requirements of Subsection (b) is exempt from other continuing education requirements under this subchapter.

(g) The commission shall establish procedures to annually determine the status of the peace officer license of each elected constable and to ensure that constables comply with this section. The commission shall forward to the attorney general's office documentation for each constable who does not comply with this section. A constable who does not comply with this section forfeits the office and the attorney general shall institute a quo warranto proceeding under Chapter 66, Civil Practice and Remedies Code, to remove the constable from office.

(h) To the extent of a conflict between this section and any other law, this section controls. (Enacted by Acts 2005, 79th Leg., ch. 954 (H.B. 1588), § 2, effective June 18, 2005; am. Acts 2007, 80th Leg., ch. 622 (H.B. 487), § 1, effective June 15, 2007.)

## Sec. 1701.355. Continuing Demonstration of Weapons Proficiency.

(a) An agency that employs one or more peace officers shall designate a firearms proficiency officer and require each peace officer the agency employs to demonstrate weapons proficiency to the firearms proficiency officer at least annually. The agency shall maintain records of the weapons proficiency of the agency's peace officers.

(b) On request, the commission may waive the requirement that a peace officer demonstrate weapons proficiency on a determination by the commission that the requirement causes a hardship.

(c) The commission by rule shall define weapons proficiency for purposes of this section. (Enacted by Acts 1999, 76th Leg., ch. 388 (H.B. 3155), § 1, effective September 1, 1999; am. Acts 2009, 81st Leg., R.S., ch. 222 (S.B. 1303), § 1, effective September 1, 2009; am. Acts 2009, 81st Leg., R.S., ch. 1172 (H.B. 3389), § 18, effective September 1, 2009.)

## Sec. 1701.356. Certain Officers: Reactivation and Continuing Education Not Required.

(a) An honorably retired commissioned officer of the Department of Public Safety who is a special ranger under Section 411.023, Government Code, may not be required to undergo training under Section 1701.352(b).

(b) An honorably retired commissioned officer of the Department of Public Safety who is a special ranger under Section 411.023, Government Code, or a retired state employee and who holds a permanent license issued before January 1981 and that was current on January 1, 1995:

(1) has the same rights and privileges as any other peace officer of this state;

(2) holds, notwithstanding Section 1701.316, an active license unless the license is revoked, suspended, or probated by the commission for a violation of this chapter; and

(3) is not subject to Section 1701.351.

(c) An honorably retired commissioned officer of the Department of Public Safety who is a special ranger under Section 411.023, Government Code, or who is a special Texas Ranger under Section 411.024, Government Code, may not be required to undergo training under Section 1701.253(j).

(Enacted by Acts 1999, 76th Leg., ch. 388 (H.B. 3155), § 1, effective September 1, 1999; am. Acts 2003, 78th Leg., ch. 1276 (H.B. 3507), § 14.009, effective September 1, 2003; am. Acts 2009, 81st Leg., R.S., ch. 920 (H.B. 2991), § 2, effective June 19, 2009.)

### Sec. 1701.357. Weapons Proficiency for Certain Retired Peace Officers and Federal Law Enforcement Officers.

(a) This section applies only to:

(1) a peace officer;

(2) a federal criminal investigator designated as a special investigator under Article 2.122, Code of Criminal Procedure; and

(3) a qualified retired law enforcement officer who is entitled to carry a concealed firearm under 18 U.S.C. Section 926C and is not otherwise described by Subdivision (1) or (2).

(b) The head of a state or local law enforcement agency may allow an honorably retired peace officer an opportunity to demonstrate weapons proficiency if the retired officer provides to the agency a sworn affidavit stating that:

(1) the officer honorably retired after not less than a total of 15 years of service as a commissioned officer with one or more state or local law enforcement agencies;

(2) the officer's license as a commissioned officer was not revoked or suspended for any period during the officer's term of service as a commissioned officer; and

(3) the officer has no psychological or physical disability that would interfere with the officer's proper handling of a handgun.

(c) The agency shall establish written procedures for the issuance or denial of a certificate of proficiency under this section. The agency shall issue the certificate to a retired officer who satisfactorily demonstrates weapons proficiency under Subsection (b), provides proof that the officer is entitled to receive a pension or annuity for service with a state or local law enforcement agency or is not entitled to receive a pension or annuity only because the law enforcement agency that employed the retired officer does not offer a pension or annuity to its retired employees, and satisfies the written procedures established by the agency. The agency shall maintain records of any retired officer who holds a certificate issued

under this section. For purposes of this subsection, proof that a retired officer is entitled to receive a pension or annuity or is not entitled to receive a pension or annuity only because the agency that last employed the retired officer does not offer a pension or annuity may include a retired peace officer identification card issued under Subchapter H, Chapter 614, Government Code.

(d) A certificate issued under this section expires on the second anniversary of the date the certificate was issued. A retired officer to whom this section applies may request an annual evaluation of weapons proficiency and issuance of a certificate of proficiency as needed to comply with applicable federal or other laws.

(e) The head of a state or local law enforcement agency may set and collect fees to recover the expenses the agency incurs in performing duties under this section.

(f) The amount of a fee set by a county law enforcement agency under Subsection (e) is subject to the approval of the commissioners court of the county. A county law enforcement agency that collects a fee under Subsection (e) shall deposit the amounts collected to the credit of the general fund of the county.

(g) A county law enforcement agency must obtain approval of the program authorized by this section from the commissioners court of the county before issuing a certificate of proficiency under this section.

(h) The head of a state law enforcement agency may allow an honorably retired federal criminal investigator or a qualified retired law enforcement officer to whom this section applies an opportunity to demonstrate weapons proficiency in the same manner as, and subject to the same requirements applicable to, an honorably retired peace officer as described by this section. The agency shall issue a certificate of proficiency to an honorably retired federal criminal investigator or a qualified retired law enforcement officer who otherwise meets the requirements of this section and shall maintain records regarding the issuance of that certificate.

(i) On request of an honorably retired officer who holds a certificate of proficiency under this section, the head of the state or local law enforcement agency from which the officer retired shall issue to the retired officer identification that indicates that the officer honorably retired from the agency. An identification under this subsection must include a photograph of the retired officer.

(Enacted by Acts 2003, 78th Leg., ch. 325 (S.B. 117), § 1, effective September 1, 2003; am. Acts 2005, 79th Leg., ch. 1093 (H.B. 2110), § 2, effective September 1, 2005; am. Acts 2005, 79th Leg., ch. 1179 (S.B. 578), § 1, effective September 1, 2005; am. Acts 2007, 80th Leg., R.S., ch. 1187 (H.B. 638), §§ 1, 2, effective September 1, 2007; am. Acts 2009, 81st Leg., R.S., ch. 428 (H.B. 2068), § 1, effective June 19, 2009.)

### Sec. 1701.358. Initial Training and Continuing Education for Police Chiefs.

A police chief shall complete the initial training and continuing education required under Section 96.641, Education Code.

(Enacted by Acts 2011, 82nd Leg., ch. 1224 (S.B. 542), § 5, effective September 1, 2011.)

## SUBCHAPTER I
## PROFESSIONAL TRAINING AND RECOGNITION

### Sec. 1701.401. Professional Achievement.

(a) In this section:

(1) "Professional achievement" includes an instance in which an individual through personal initiative, fixity of purpose, persistence, or endeavor creates a program or system that has a significant positive impact on the law enforcement profession that exceeds the normal expectations of job performance.

(2) "Public service" includes an instance in which an individual through initiative creates or participates in a program or system that has a significant positive impact on the general population of a community that exceeds the normal expectations of job performance.

(3) "Valor" includes an act of personal heroism or bravery that exceeds the normal expectations of job performance, including placing one's own life in jeopardy to save another person's life, to prevent serious bodily injury to another, or to prevent the consequences of a criminal act.

(b) The commission shall issue certificates that recognize professional achievement. For this purpose the commission shall use the employment records of the employing agency.

(c) The commission shall adopt rules for issuing achievement awards to peace officers, reserve peace officers, jailers, or custodial officers who are licensed by the commission. The commission's rules shall require recommendations from an elected official of this state or a political subdivision, an administrator of a law enforcement agency, or a person holding a license issued by the commission.

(d) The awards shall be given in the name of this state and presented at the State Capitol during May of each year. At a minimum the award shall consist of a document, an appropriate medal, and a ribbon suitable for wearing on a uniform.

(e) The awards shall be issued in three areas: valor, public service, and professional achievement.

(f) The commission may present awards relating to not more than a total of 20 incidents and accomplishments each year.

(Enacted by Acts 1999, 76th Leg., ch. 388 (H.B. 3155), § 1, effective September 1, 1999; am. Acts 2009, 81st Leg., R.S., ch. 174 (H.B. 1492), § 1, effective May 27, 2009.)

### Sec. 1701.402. Proficiency Certificates.

(a) The commission shall issue certificates that recognize proficiency based on law enforcement training, education, and experience. For this purpose the commission shall use the employment records of the employing agency.

(b) As a requirement for a basic proficiency certificate, the commission shall require completion of local courses or programs of instruction on federal and state statutes that relate to employment issues affecting peace officers, telecommunicators, and county jailers, including:

(1) civil service;

(2) compensation, including overtime compensation, and vacation time;

(3) personnel files and other employee records;

(4) management-employee relations in law enforcement organizations;

(5) work-related injuries;

(6) complaints and investigations of employee misconduct; and

(7) disciplinary actions and the appeal of disciplinary actions.

(c) An employing agency is responsible for providing the training required by this section.

(d) As a requirement for an intermediate proficiency certificate, an officer must complete an education and training program on asset forfeiture established by the commission under Section 1701.253(g).

Occupations

(e) As a requirement for an intermediate proficiency certificate, an officer must complete an education and training program on racial profiling established by the commission under Section 1701.253(h).

(f) As a requirement for an intermediate proficiency certificate, an officer must complete an education and training program on identity theft established by the commission under Section 1701.253(i).

(g) As a requirement for an intermediate proficiency certificate or an advanced proficiency certificate, an officer must complete the education and training program described by Section 1701.253 regarding de-escalation and crisis intervention techniques to facilitate interaction with persons with mental impairments.

(h) As a requirement for an intermediate proficiency certificate, an officer must complete an education and training program on investigative topics established by the commission under Section 1701.253(b).

(i) As a requirement for an intermediate proficiency certificate, an officer must complete an education and training program on civil rights, racial sensitivity, and cultural diversity established by the commission under Section 1701.253(c).

(j) As a requirement for an intermediate or advanced proficiency certificate issued by the commission on or after January 1, 2011, an officer must complete the basic education and training program on the trafficking of persons described by Section 1701.258(a).
(Enacted by Acts 1999, 76th Leg., ch. 388 (H.B. 3155), § 1, effective September 1, 1999; am. Acts 2001, 77th Leg., ch. 929 (S.B. 563), § 6, effective September 1, 2001; am. Acts 2001, 77th Leg., ch. 947 (S.B. 1074), § 5, effective September 1, 2001; am. Acts 2003, 78th Leg., ch. 1276 (H.B. 3507), § 14.008, effective September 1, 2003; am. Acts 2003, 78th Leg., ch. 1326 (S.B. 473), § 9, effective September 1, 2003; am. Acts 2005, 79th Leg., ch. 393 (S.B. 1473), § 4, effective September 1, 2005; am. Acts 2009, 81st Leg., R.S., ch. 1002 (H.B. 4009), § 6, effective September 1, 2009; am. Acts 2009, 81st Leg., R.S., ch. 1172 (H.B. 3389), § 17, effective September 1, 2009; am. Acts 2011, 82nd Leg., ch. 91 (S.B. 1303), § 27.001(48), effective September 1, 2011; am. Acts 2011, 82nd Leg., ch. 855 (H.B. 3823), § 9, effective September 1, 2011.)

### Sec. 1701.403. Investigative Hypnosis.

(a) The commission may establish minimum requirements for the training, testing, and certification of peace officers who use investigative hypnosis.

(b) A peace officer may not use a hypnotic interview technique unless the officer:

(1) completes a training course approved by the commission; and

(2) passes an examination administered by the commission that is designed to test the officer's knowledge of investigative hypnosis.

(c) The commission may issue a professional achievement or proficiency certificate to an officer who meets the requirements of Subsection (b).
(Enacted by Acts 1999, 76th Leg., ch. 388 (H.B. 3155), § 1, effective September 1, 1999.)

### Sec. 1701.404. Certification of Officers for Mental Health Assignments.

(a) The commission by rule may establish minimum requirements for the training, testing, and certification of special officers for offenders with mental impairments.

(b) The commission may certify a sheriff, sheriff's deputy, constable, other peace officer, county jailer, or justice of the peace as a special officer for offenders with mental impairments if the person:

(1) completes a training course in emergency first aid and lifesaving techniques approved by the commission;

(2) completes a training course administered by the commission on mental health issues and offenders with mental impairments; and

(3) passes an examination administered by the commission that is designed to test the person's:

(A) knowledge and recognition of the characteristics and symptoms of mental illness, mental retardation, and mental disabilities; and

(B) knowledge of mental health crisis intervention strategies for people with mental impairments.

(c) The commission may issue a professional achievement or proficiency certificate to an officer, county jailer, or justice of the peace who meets the requirements of Subsection (b).
(Enacted by Acts 1999, 76th Leg., ch. 388 (H.B. 3155), § 1, effective September 1, 1999; am. Acts 2009, 81st Leg., R.S., ch. 1131 (H.B. 2093), § 1, effective September 1, 2009.)

### Sec. 1701.405. Telecommunicators.

(a) In this section:

(1) [Repealed by Acts 2011, 82 Leg., ch. 855 (H.B. 3823), § 12, effective September 1, 2011.]

(2) "Emergency" means the occurrence or imminent threat of damage, injury, or loss of life or property resulting from an extraordinary natural or man-made cause.

(3) [Repealed by Acts 2011, 82 Leg., ch. 855 (H.B. 3823), § 12, effective September 1, 2011.]

(b) This state or a political subdivision of this state may not employ a person to act as a telecommunicator unless the person:

(1) has had at least 40 hours of telecommunicator training as determined by the commission;

(2) is at least 18 years of age; and

(3) holds a high school diploma or high school equivalency certificate.

(c) The commission shall accredit telecommunicator training programs that fulfill the minimum requirements for a telecommunicator. The commission shall adopt rules providing for the accreditation of telecommunicator training programs developed and taught by the Department of Public Safety, an institution of higher education, including a junior college, community college, or technical school, or any other entity approved by the commission.

(d) A person who completes an accredited training program under this section may, by letter to the commission, request a written acknowledgment from the commission that the person has met the minimum requirements for a telecommunicator as determined by the commission. The request must be accompanied, in accordance with commission rules, by evidence of satisfactory completion of an accredited telecommunicator training program. On a determination by the commission that the person meets the minimum requirements for a telecommunicator, the commission shall issue the written acknowledgment to the person.

(e) [Repealed by Acts 2011, 82 Leg., ch. 855 (H.B. 3823), § 12, effective September 1, 2011.]

(f) A person performing the duties of a telecommunicator and serving under permanent appointment on and before September 1, 1987, is not required to meet the requirements of this section as a condition of continued employment.

(g) Notwithstanding this section, a person may be appointed or serve as a telecommunicator on a temporary or probationary basis or may perform the duties of a telecommunicator in an emergency.

(h) A person appointed on a temporary or probationary basis after September 1, 1987, who does not satisfactorily complete an accredited telecommunicator training program before the first anniversary of the date the person is originally appointed shall be removed from the position. The person's temporary or probationary appointment may not be extended for more than one year except that not earlier than the first anniversary of the date the person is removed under this subsection, the employing agency may petition the commission for reinstatement of the person to temporary or probationary employment.

(Enacted by Acts 1999, 76th Leg., ch. 388 (H.B. 3155), § 1, effective September 1, 1999; am. Acts 2011, 82nd Leg., ch. 855 (H.B. 3823), §§ 10, 12, effective September 1, 2011.)

## Sec. 1701.406. County Jail Personnel [Repealed].

Repealed by Acts 2009, 81st Leg., ch. 1172 (H.B. 3389), § 35, effective September 1, 2009. (Enacted by Acts 1999, 76th Leg., ch. 388 (H.B. 3155), § 1, effective September 1, 1999.)

## SUBCHAPTER J
## EMPLOYMENT RECORDS

## Sec. 1701.451. Preemployment Request for Employment Termination Report and Submission of Background Check Confirmation Form.

(a) Before a law enforcement agency may hire a person licensed under this chapter, the agency head or the agency head's designee must:

(1) make a request to the commission for any employment termination report regarding the person that is maintained by the commission under this subchapter; and

(2) submit to the commission on the form prescribed by the commission confirmation that the agency:

(A) conducted in the manner prescribed by the commission a criminal background check regarding the person;

(B) obtained the person's written consent on a form prescribed by the commission for the agency to view the person's employment records;

(C) obtained from the commission any service or education records regarding the person maintained by the commission; and

(D) contacted each of the person's previous law enforcement employers.

(a-1) A law enforcement agency that obtains a consent form described by Subsection (a)(2)(B) shall make the person's employment records available to a hiring law enforcement agency on request.

(b) The commission by rule shall establish a system for verifying an electronically submitted request required by Subsection (a)(1).

(c) If the commission receives from a law enforcement agency a request that complies with Subsections (a)(1) and (b), the commission employee having the responsibility to maintain any employment termination report regarding the person who is the subject of the request shall release the report to the agency.

(Enacted by Acts 1999, 76th Leg., ch. 388 (H.B. 3155), § 1, effective September 1, 1999; am. Acts 2005, 79th Leg., ch. 1298 (H.B. 2677), § 1, effective September 1, 2005; am. Acts 2007, 80th Leg., R.S., ch. 1068 (H.B. 2445), § 1, effective September 1, 2007; am. Acts 2009, 81st Leg., R.S., ch. 1172 (H.B. 3389), § 19, effective September 1, 2009.)

## Sec. 1701.452.  Employment Termination Report.

(a) The head of a law enforcement agency or the head's designee shall submit a report to the commission on a form prescribed by the commission regarding a person licensed under this chapter who resigns or retires from employment with the law enforcement agency, whose appointment with the law enforcement agency is terminated, or who separates from the law enforcement agency for any other reason. The report must be submitted by the head or the designee not later than the seventh business day after the date the license holder:

(1) resigns, retires, is terminated, or separates from the agency; and

(2) exhausts all administrative appeals available to the license holder, if applicable.

(b) The head of a law enforcement agency or the head's designee shall include in the report required under Subsection (a) a statement on whether the license holder was honorably discharged, generally discharged, or dishonorably discharged and, as required by the commission, an explanation of the circumstances under which the person resigned, retired, or was terminated. For purposes of this subsection:

(1) "Honorably discharged" means a license holder who, while in good standing and not because of pending or final disciplinary actions or a documented performance problem, retired, resigned, or separated from employment with or died while employed by a law enforcement agency.

(2) "Generally discharged" means a license holder who:

(A) was terminated by, retired or resigned from, or died while in the employ of a law enforcement agency and the separation was related to a disciplinary investigation of conduct that is not included in the definition of dishonorably discharged; or

(B) was terminated by or retired or resigned from a law enforcement agency and the separation was for a documented performance problem and was not because of a reduction in workforce or an at-will employment decision.

(3) "Dishonorably discharged" means a license holder who:

(A) was terminated by a law enforcement agency or retired or resigned in lieu of termination by the agency in relation to allegations of criminal misconduct; or

(B) was terminated by a law enforcement agency or retired or resigned in lieu of termination by the agency for insubordination or untruthfulness.

(c) The commission by rule may further specify the circumstances that constitute honorably discharged, dishonorably discharged, and generally discharged within the definitions provided by Subsection (b).

(d) The head of the law enforcement agency from which a license holder resigns, retires, is terminated, or separates for reasons other than death, or the head's designee, shall provide to the license holder a copy of the report. The report must be provided to the license holder not later than the seventh business day after the date the license holder:

(1) resigns, retires, is terminated, or separates from the agency; and

(2) exhausts all administrative appeals available to the license holder, if applicable.

(e) If the person who is the subject of the employment termination report is deceased, the head of the law enforcement agency or the head's designee on request shall provide a copy of the report to the person's next of kin not later than the seventh business day after the date of the request.

(f) The head of a law enforcement agency or the head's designee satisfies the obligation to provide the report required under Subsection (d) or (e) by sending by certified mail:

(1) the report required under Subsection (d) to the last known address of the license holder if the license holder is not otherwise available; or

(2) the report required under Subsection (e) to the last known address of the next of kin if the next of kin who requested the report is not otherwise available.

(g) The head of a law enforcement agency or the head's designee must submit a report under this section each time a person licensed under this chapter resigns, retires, is terminated, or separates for any other reason from the agency. The report is an official government document.

(Enacted by Acts 1999, 76th Leg., ch. 388 (H.B. 3155), § 1, effective September 1, 1999; am. Acts 2005, 79th Leg., ch. 1298 (H.B. 2677), § 2, effective September 1, 2005; am. Acts 2007, 80th Leg., ch. 1068 (H.B. 2445), § 2, effective September 1, 2007; am. Acts 2011, 82nd Leg., ch. 399 (S.B. 545), § 1, effective September 1, 2011.)

### Sec. 1701.4521. License Suspension for Officer Dishonorably Discharged.

(a) The commission shall suspend the license of an officer licensed under this chapter on notification that the officer has been dishonorably discharged if the officer has previously been dishonorably discharged from another law enforcement agency.

(b) An officer whose license is suspended under this section may appeal the suspension in writing to the commission not later than the 30th day after the date the officer is suspended.

(c) After a commission determination, the commission may revoke or reinstate the officer's license in accordance with rules or procedures adopted by the commission under this chapter related to revocation or reinstatement of a license. The commission shall revoke the officer's license if the officer does not appeal the suspension before the 30th day after the date the officer is suspended.

(d) The commission's decision does not affect:

(1) the employment relationship between an officer licensed under this chapter and a law enforcement agency; or

(2) any disciplinary action taken against an officer licensed under this chapter by a law enforcement agency.

(Enacted by Acts 2007, 80th Leg., ch. 1068 (H.B. 2445), § 3, effective September 1, 2007.)

### Sec. 1701.4525. Petition for Correction of Report; Hearing; Administrative Penalty.

(a) A person who is the subject of an employment termination report maintained by the commission under this subchapter may contest information contained in the report by submitting to the law enforcement agency and to the commission a written petition on a form prescribed by the commission for a correction of the report not later than the 30th day after the date the person receives a copy of the report. On receipt of the petition, the commission shall refer the petition to the State Office of Administrative Hearings.

(b) , (c) [Repealed by Acts 2011, 82nd Leg., ch. 399 (S.B. 545), § 6, effective September 1, 2011.]

(d) A proceeding to contest information in an employment termination report is a contested case under Chapter 2001, Government Code.

(e) In a proceeding to contest information in an employment termination report for a report based on alleged misconduct, an administrative law judge shall determine if the alleged misconduct occurred by a preponderance of the evidence regardless of whether the person who is the subject of the report was terminated or the person resigned, retired, or separated in lieu of termination. If the alleged misconduct is not supported by a preponderance of the evidence, the administrative law judge shall order the report to be changed.

(e-1) The commission may assess an administrative penalty against an agency head who fails to make a correction to an employment termination report following an order by the State Office of Administrative Hearings after all appeals available to the agency head have been exhausted.

(f) The commission shall adopt rules for the administration of this section.

(g) The commission is not considered a party in a proceeding conducted by the State Office of Administrative Hearings under this section.

(Enacted by Acts 2005, 79th Leg., ch. 1298 (H.B. 2677), § 3, effective September 1, 2005; am. Acts 2007, 80th Leg., R.S., ch. 1068 (H.B. 2445), § 4, effective September 1, 2007; am. Acts 2009, 81st Leg., R.S., ch. 1172 (H.B. 3389), § 20, effective September 1, 2009; am. Acts 2011, 82nd Leg., ch. 399 (S.B. 545), §§ 2, 3, 6, effective September 1, 2011.)

Occupations

### Sec. 1701.453.  Maintenance of Reports and Statements.

The commission shall maintain a copy of each report and statement submitted to the commission under this subchapter until at least the 10th anniversary of the date on which the report or statement is submitted.

(Enacted by Acts 1999, 76th Leg., ch. 388 (H.B. 3155), § 1, effective September 1, 1999; am. Acts 2009, 81st Leg., R.S., ch. 1172 (H.B. 3389), § 21, effective September 1, 2009.)

### Sec. 1701.454.  Confidentiality.

(a) All information submitted to the commission under this subchapter is confidential and is not subject to disclosure under Chapter 552, Government Code, unless the person resigned or was terminated due to substantiated incidents of excessive force or violations of the law other than traffic offenses.

(b) Except as provided by this subchapter, a commission member or other person may not release information submitted under this subchapter.

(Enacted by Acts 1999, 76th Leg., ch. 388 (H.B. 3155), § 1, effective September 1, 1999; am. Acts 2001, 77th Leg., ch. 182 (S.B. 1583), § 1, effective September 1, 2001; am. Acts 2005, 79th Leg., ch. 1298 (H.B. 2677), § 4, effective September 1, 2005; am. Acts 2011, 82nd Leg., ch. 399 (S.B. 545), § 4, effective September 1, 2011.)

### Sec. 1701.455.  Subpoena.

Information submitted to the commission under this subchapter is subject to subpoena only in a judicial proceeding.

(Enacted by Acts 1999, 76th Leg., ch. 388 (H.B. 3155), § 1, effective September 1, 1999; am. Acts 2011, 82nd Leg., ch. 399 (S.B. 545), § 5, effective September 1, 2011.)

### Sec. 1701.456.  Immunity from Liability.

(a) The commission is not liable for civil damages for providing information contained in a report or statement maintained by the commission under this subchapter if the commission released the information as provided by this subchapter.

(b) A law enforcement agency, agency head, or other law enforcement official is not liable for civil damages for a report made by that agency or person if the report is made in good faith.

(Enacted by Acts 1999, 76th Leg., ch. 388 (H.B. 3155), § 1, effective September 1, 1999; am. Acts

2005, 79th Leg., ch. 1298 (H.B. 2677), § 5, effective September 1, 2005.)

### Sec. 1701.457.  Limitation on Commission Authority.

This subchapter does not authorize the commission to review disciplinary action taken by a law enforcement agency against a person licensed under this chapter or to issue a subpoena to compel the production of a document prepared or maintained by the agency in connection with a disciplinary matter.

(Enacted by Acts 1999, 76th Leg., ch. 388 (H.B. 3155), § 1, effective September 1, 1999.)

### Sec. 1701.458.  Venue.

Venue for the prosecution of an offense under Section 37.10, Penal Code, that arises from a report required under this subchapter lies in the county where the offense occurred or in Travis County.

(Enacted by Acts 2007, 80th Leg., ch. 1068 (H.B. 2445), § 5, effective September 1, 2007.)

## SUBCHAPTER K
## DISCIPLINARY PROCEDURES

### Sec. 1701.501.  Disciplinary Action.

(a) Except as provided by Subsection (d), the commission shall revoke or suspend a license, place on probation a person whose license has been suspended, or reprimand a license holder for a violation of:

(1) this chapter;

(2) the reporting requirements provided by Articles 2.132 and 2.134, Code of Criminal Procedure; or

(3) a commission rule.

(b) The commission may establish procedures for the revocation of a license issued under this chapter.

(c) The commission by rule may adopt other necessary enforcement procedures.

(d) The commission may revoke a license issued under this chapter to an officer elected under the Texas Constitution only if the officer is convicted of:

(1) a felony; or

(2) a criminal offense directly involving the person's duties as an officer.

(Enacted by Acts 1999, 76th Leg., ch. 388 (H.B. 3155), § 1, effective September 1, 1999; am. Acts 2007, 80th Leg., R.S., ch. 279 (H.B. 488), § 1, effective September 1, 2007; am. Acts 2009, 81st

Leg., R.S., ch. 1172 (H.B. 3389), § 22, effective September 1, 2009.)

### Sec. 1701.502.  Felony Conviction or Placement on Community Supervision.

(a) The commission shall immediately revoke the license of a person licensed under this chapter who is convicted of a felony.

(b) The commission shall immediately suspend the license of a person licensed under this chapter who is charged with a felony and is placed on community supervision regardless of whether the court defers further proceedings without entering an adjudication of guilt.

(c) The commission may reinstate, as provided by commission rules, a license that is suspended under Subsection (b) when the license holder is released from community supervision.
(Enacted by Acts 1999, 76th Leg., ch. 388 (H.B. 3155), § 1, effective September 1, 1999.)

### Sec. 1701.503.  Barratry Conviction.

The commission shall immediately revoke the license of a person licensed under this chapter who is convicted of barratry under Section 38.12, Penal Code.
(Enacted by Acts 1999, 76th Leg., ch. 388 (H.B. 3155), § 1, effective September 1, 1999.)

### Sec. 1701.504.  Hearing.

(a) Except as provided by Sections 1701.502 and 1701.503, if the commission proposes to suspend or revoke a person's license, the person is entitled to a hearing conducted by the State Office of Administrative Hearings.

(b) If the commission proposes to refuse to renew a person's license, the person is entitled to a hearing conducted by the State Office of Administrative Hearings.
(Enacted by Acts 1999, 76th Leg., ch. 388 (H.B. 3155), § 1, effective September 1, 1999.)

### Sec. 1701.505.  Administrative Procedure.

(a) Proceedings for a disciplinary action are governed by Chapter 2001, Government Code.

(b) Rules of practice adopted by the commission under Section 2001.004, Government Code, applicable to the proceedings for a disciplinary action may not conflict with rules adopted by the State Office of Administrative Hearings.
(Enacted by Acts 1999, 76th Leg., ch. 388 (H.B. 3155), § 1, effective September 1, 1999.)

### Sec. 1701.506.  Appeal.

(a) A person dissatisfied with an action of the commission may appeal the action under Chapter 2001, Government Code. The court shall set the matter for hearing not earlier than 10 days after written notice of the appeal is given to the commission and the commission's attorney.

(b) The court may suspend an action of the commission pending a hearing. The order suspending the action takes effect when served on the commission. The commission shall provide its attorney a copy of the petition and order.

(c) The attorney general or the district or county attorney shall represent the commission in the appeal.
(Enacted by Acts 1999, 76th Leg., ch. 388 (H.B. 3155), § 1, effective September 1, 1999.)

### Sec. 1701.507.  Administrative Penalties.

(a) In addition to other penalties imposed by law, a law enforcement agency or governmental entity that violates this chapter or a rule adopted under this chapter is subject to an administrative penalty in an amount set by the commission not to exceed $1,000 per day per violation. The administrative penalty shall be assessed in a proceeding conducted in accordance with Chapter 2001, Government Code.

(b) The amount of the penalty shall be based on:

(1) the seriousness of the violation;

(2) the respondent's history of violations;

(3) the amount necessary to deter future violations;

(4) efforts made by the respondent to correct the violation; and

(5) any other matter that justice may require.

(c) The commission by rule shall establish a written enforcement plan that provides notice of the specific ranges of penalties that apply to specific alleged violations and the criteria by which the commission determines the amount of a proposed administrative penalty.
(Enacted by Acts 2009, 81st Leg., ch. 1172 (H.B. 3389), § 23, effective September 1, 2009.)

## SUBCHAPTER L
## CRIMINAL PENALTY

### Sec. 1701.551.  Criminal Penalty for Appointment or Retention of Certain Persons.

(a) A person commits an offense if the person appoints or retains another person as an officer or county jailer in violation of Section 1701.301, 1701.303, or 1701.306.

(b) An offense under Subsection (a) is a misdemeanor punishable by a fine of not less than $100 and not more than $1,000.

(Enacted by Acts 1999, 76th Leg., ch. 388 (H.B. 3155), § 1, effective September 1, 1999.)

## Sec. 1701.552. Criminal Penalty for Appointment of Person Not Certified for Investigative Hypnosis.

(a) A person commits an offense if the person appoints or retains another person in violation of Section 1701.403.

(b) An offense under Subsection (a) is a misdemeanor punishable by a fine of not less than $100 and not more than $1,000.

(Enacted by Acts 1999, 76th Leg., ch. 388 (H.B. 3155), § 1, effective September 1, 1999.)

## Sec. 1701.553. Criminal Penalty for Appointment or Retention of Persons with Certain Convictions.

(a) A person commits an offense if the person appoints, employs, or retains an individual as an officer, public security officer, telecommunicator, or county jailer in violation of Section 1701.312 or 1701.313.

(b) An offense under Subsection (a) is a state jail felony.

(Enacted by Acts 1999, 76th Leg., ch. 388 (H.B. 3155), § 1, effective September 1, 1999; am. Acts 2011, 82nd Leg., ch. 855 (H.B. 3823), § 11, effective September 1, 2011.)

## Sec. 1701.554. Venue.

Venue for the prosecution of an offense that arises from a violation of this chapter or in connection with the administration of this chapter lies in the county where the offense occurred or in Travis County.

(Enacted by Acts 2009, 81st Leg., ch. 1172 (H.B. 3389), § 24, effective September 1, 2009.)

## SUBCHAPTER M
## VISITING RESOURCE OFFICER IN PUBLIC SCHOOL

## Sec. 1701.601. Definition.

In this subchapter, "school resource officer" means a peace officer who is assigned by the officer's employing political subdivision to provide:

(1) a police presence at a public school;

(2) safety or drug education to students of a public school; or

(3) other similar services.

(Enacted by Acts 2001, 77th Leg., ch. 923 (S.B. 430), § 2, effective September 1, 2001.)

## Sec. 1701.602. License Required.

A peace officer who is a visiting school resource officer in a public school must be licensed as provided by this chapter.

(Enacted by Acts 2001, 77th Leg., ch. 923 (S.B. 430), § 2, effective September 1, 2001.)

## Sec. 1701.603. Firearms Accident Prevention Program.

(a) A peace officer who is a visiting school resource officer in a public elementary school shall at least once each school year offer to provide instruction to students in a firearms accident prevention program, as determined by the school district.

(b) A firearms accident prevention program must include the safety message, "Stop! Don't Touch. Leave the Area. Tell an Adult.", and may include instructional materials from the National Rifle Association Eddie Eagle GunSafe Program, including animated videos and activity books.

(Enacted by Acts 2001, 77th Leg., ch. 923 (S.B. 430), § 2, effective September 1, 2001.)

Occupations

# TITLE 12
# PRACTICES AND TRADES RELATED TO WATER, HEALTH, AND SAFETY

## SUBTITLE B
## PRACTICES RELATED TO HEALTH AND SAFETY

## CHAPTER 1956
## METAL RECYCLING ENTITIES

## SUBCHAPTER A
## GENERAL PROVISIONS

# Sec. 1956.001.  Definitions.

In this chapter:

(1) "Aluminum material" means a product made from aluminum, an aluminum alloy, or an aluminum by-product. The term includes aluminum wiring and an aluminum beer keg but does not include another type of aluminum can used to contain a food or beverage.

(2) "Bronze material" means:

(A) a cemetery vase, receptacle, or memorial made from bronze;

(B) bronze statuary; or

(C) material readily identifiable as bronze, including bronze wiring.

(3) "Commission" means the Public Safety Commission.

(4) "Copper or brass material" means:

(A) insulated or noninsulated copper wire or cable of the type used by a public utility or common carrier that contains copper or an alloy of copper or zinc;

(B) a copper or brass item of a type commonly used in construction or by a public utility; or

(C) copper pipe or copper tubing.

(5) "Department" means the Texas Department of Public Safety.

(6) "Director" means the public safety director.

(7) "Metal recycling entity" means a business that is operated from a fixed location and is predominantly engaged in:

(A) performing the manufacturing process by which scrap, used, or obsolete ferrous or nonferrous metal is converted into raw material products consisting of prepared grades and having an existing or potential economic value, by a method that in part requires the use of powered tools and equipment, including processes that involve processing, sorting, cutting, classifying, cleaning, baling, wrapping, shredding, shearing, or changing the physical form of that metal;

(B) the use of raw material products described under Paragraph (A) in the manufacture of producer or consumer goods; or

(C) purchasing or otherwise acquiring scrap, used, or obsolete ferrous or nonferrous metals for the eventual use of the metal for the purposes described by Paragraph (A) or (B).

(8) "Personal identification document" means:

(A) a valid driver's license issued by a state in the United States;

(B) a United States military identification card; or

(C) a personal identification certificate issued by the department under Section 521.101, Transportation Code, or a corresponding card or certificate issued by another state.

(9) "Regulated material" means:

(A) aluminum material;

(B) bronze material;

(C) copper or brass material; or

(D) regulated metal.

(10) "Regulated metal" means:

(A) manhole covers;

(B) guardrails;

(C) metal cylinders designed to contain compressed air, oxygen, gases, or liquids;

(D) beer kegs made from metal other than aluminum;

(E) historical markers or cemetery vases, receptacles, or memorials made from metal other than aluminum;

(F) unused rebar;

(G) street signs;

(H) drain gates;

(I) safes;

(J) communication, transmission, and service wire or cable;

(K condensing or evaporator coils for central heating or air conditioning units;

(L) utility structures, including the fixtures and hardware;

(M) aluminum or stainless steel containers designed to hold propane for fueling forklifts;

(N) metal railroad equipment, including tie plates, signal houses, control boxes, signs, signals, traffic devices, traffic control devices, traffic control signals, switch plates, e-clips, and rail tie functions;

(O) catalytic converters not attached to a vehicle;

(P) fire hydrants;

(Q) metal bleachers or other seating facilities used in recreational areas or sporting arenas;

(R) any metal item clearly and conspicuously marked with any form of the name, initials, or logo of a governmental entity, utility, cemetery, or railroad;

(S) insulated utility, communications, or electrical wire that has been burned in whole or in part to remove the insulation;

(T) backflow valves; and

(U) metal in the form of commonly recognized products of the industrial metals recycling process, including bales, briquettes, bil-

lets, sows, ingots, pucks, and chopped or shredded metals.
(Enacted by Acts 2001, 77th Leg., ch. 1421 (H.B. 2813), § 4, effective June 1, 2003; am. Acts 2007, 80th Leg., ch. 1316 (S.B. 1154), § 2, effective September 1, 2007; am. Acts 2011, 82nd Leg., ch. 1234 (S.B. 694), § 1, effective September 1, 2011.)

### Sec. 1956.002.  Exception.

This chapter does not apply to:

(1) a purchase of regulated material from a public utility or a manufacturing, industrial, commercial, retail, or other seller that sells regulated material in the ordinary course of the seller's business;

(2) a purchase of regulated material by a manufacturer whose primary business is the manufacture of iron and steel products made from melting scrap iron and scrap steel; or

(3) the transport or hauling of recyclable materials to or from the metal recycling entity.
(Enacted by Acts 2001, 77th Leg., ch. 1421 (H.B. 2813), § 4, effective June 1, 2003; am. Acts 2007, 80th Leg., ch. 1316 (S.B. 1154), § 2, effective September 1, 2007.)

### Sec. 1956.003.  Local Law; Criminal Penalty.

(a) A county, municipality, or political subdivision of this state may adopt a rule, charter, or ordinance or issue an order or impose standards that are more stringent than but do not conflict with this chapter or rules adopted under this chapter.

(a-1) A county, municipality, or other political subdivision may require the record of purchase described under Section 1956.033 to contain a clear and legible thumbprint of a seller of regulated material.

(a-2) A county, municipality, or other political subdivision that, as authorized under Subsection (a), requires a metal recycling entity to report to the county, municipality, or political subdivision information relating to a sale of regulated material shall:

(1) include in any contract entered into by the county, municipality, or political subdivision relating to the reporting of the information a provision that:

(A) requires any contractor, subcontractor, or third party that has access to, comes into possession of, or otherwise obtains information relating to a sale of regulated material to maintain the confidentiality of all informa-

tion received, including the name of the seller, the price paid for a purchase of regulated material, and the quantity of regulated material purchased; and

(B) allows the county, municipality, or political subdivision to terminate the contract of any contractor, subcontractor, or third party that violates the confidentiality provision required by Paragraph (A); and

(2) investigate a complaint alleging that a contractor, subcontractor, or third party has failed to maintain the confidentiality of information relating to a sale of regulated material.

(b) A county, municipality, or political subdivision of this state may issue a license or permit to a business to allow the business to act as a metal recycling entity in that county or municipality and may impose a fee not to exceed $250 for the issuance or renewal of the license or permit.

(b-1) [Expired pursuant to Acts 2007, 80th Leg., ch. 1316 (S.B. 1154), § 2, effective January 1, 2010.]

(c) A county, municipality, or political subdivision of this state that issues a license or permit to a business as authorized under Subsection (b) shall submit to the department in the manner required by the department information on each business that is issued a license or permit.

(d) A municipality or political subdivision of this state, other than a county, may not increase the local license or permit fee imposed on a metal recycling facility unless the increase is approved by the local governing body. A request for an increase in the local license or permit fee must be based on the costs associated with law enforcement and administration of the licensing or permitting program. The municipality or political subdivision must submit a report to the department on the law enforcement and administrative costs associated with the fee increase.

(e) A county may increase the local license or permit fee imposed on a metal recycling facility one additional time before the second anniversary of the date of the initial fee increase. The fee increase must be based on the average cost charged by municipalities statewide.

(f) **[Effective March 1, 2012]** A person commits an offense if the person owns or operates a metal recycling entity and does not hold a license or permit required by a county, municipality, or other political subdivision as authorized under Subsection (b). An offense under this subsection is a Class B misdemeanor unless it is shown on the trial of the offense that the person has been previously convicted under this subsection, in which event the offense is a Class A misdemeanor.

(f-1) **[Expires March 1, 2013]** It is an exception to the application of Subsection (f) that:

(1) the person held a license or permit issued by the appropriate county, municipality, or other political subdivision at one point during the 12-month period preceding the date of the alleged offense; and

(2) the person obtains or submits an application for the appropriate license or permit not later than the 15th day after the date the person receives notice from the appropriate county, municipality, or other political subdivision informing the person that the metal recycling entity is operating without the required license or permit.

(f-2) **[Expires March 1, 2013]** This subsection and Subsection (f-1) expire March 1, 2013.

(g) Notwithstanding any other law, a county, municipality, or other political subdivision must provide a minimum 30-day notice followed by a public hearing prior to enacting a prohibition on the sale or use of a recyclable product.

(Enacted by Acts 2001, 77th Leg., ch. 1421 (H.B. 2813), § 4, effective June 1, 2003; am. by Acts 2007, 80th Leg., ch. 1316 (S.B. 1154), § 2, effective September 1, 2007; am. Acts 2011, 82nd Leg., ch. 1234 (S.B. 694), §§ 2, 3, effective September 1, 2011.)

### Sec. 1956.004. [Effective March 1, 2012] Civil Penalty.

(a) A person who owns or operates a metal recycling entity and does not hold a license or permit required by a county, municipality, or other political subdivision as authorized under Section 1956.003(b) is subject to a civil penalty of not more than $1,000 for each violation. In determining the amount of the civil penalty, the court shall consider:

(1) any other violations by the person; and

(2) the amount necessary to deter future violations.

(b) A district attorney, county attorney, or municipal attorney may institute an action to collect the civil penalty provided by this section.

(c) Each day a violation occurs or continues to occur is a separate violation.

(d) The district attorney, county attorney, or municipal attorney may recover reasonable expenses incurred in obtaining a civil penalty under this section, including court costs, reasonable attorney's fees, investigative costs, witness fees, and deposition expenses.

(e) **[Expires March 1, 2013]** It is an exception to the application of this section that:

(1) the person held a license or permit issued by the appropriate county, municipality, or other political subdivision at one point during the 12-month period preceding the date of the alleged violation; and

(2) the person obtains or submits an application for the appropriate license or permit not later than the 15th day after the date the person receives notice from the appropriate county, municipality, or other political subdivision informing the person that the metal recycling entity is operating without the required license or permit.

(f) **[Expires March 1, 2013]** This subsection and Subsection (e) expire March 1, 2013.

(Enacted by Acts 2001, 77th Leg., ch. 1421 (H.B. 2813), § 4, effective June 1, 2003; am. Acts 2011, 82nd Leg., ch. 1234 (S.B. 694), § 4, effective March 1, 2012.)

### Sec. 1956.005. Record of Purchase [Renumbered].

Renumbered to Tex. Occ. Code § 1956.033 by Acts 2007, 80th Leg., ch. 1316 (S.B. 1154), § 2, effective September 1, 2007.

### Sec. 1956.006. Preservation of Records [Renumbered].

Renumbered to Tex. Occ. Code § 1956.034 by Acts 2007, 80th Leg., ch. 1316 (S.B. 1154), § 2, effective September 1, 2007.

### Sec. 1956.007. Inspection of Records by Peace Officer [Renumbered].

Renumbered to Tex. Occ. Code § 1956.035 by Acts 2007, 80th Leg., ch. 1316 (S.B. 1154), § 2, effective September 1, 2007.

### Sec. 1956.008. Furnishing of Report to Department [Renumbered].

Renumbered to Tex. Occ. Code § 1956.036 by Acts 2007, 80th Leg., ch. 1316 (S.B. 1154), § 2, effective September 1, 2007.

### Sec. 1956.009. Placement of Items on Hold [Renumbered].

Renumbered to Tex. Occ. Code § 1956.037 by Acts 2007, 80th Leg., ch. 1316 (S.B. 1154), § 2, effective September 1, 2007.

### Sec. 1956.010. Prohibited Acts [Renumbered].

Renumbered to Tex. Occ. Code § 1956.038 by Acts 2007, 80th Leg., ch. 1316 (S.B. 1154), § 2, effective September 1, 2007.

Occupations

## SUBCHAPTER A-1
## POWERS AND DUTIES

### Sec. 1956.011.  Administration of Chapter.

The department shall administer this chapter. (am. Acts 2007, 80th Leg., ch. 890 (H.B. 2458), § 1.04, effective September 1, 2007.)

### Sec. 1956.012.  Department Staff.

The department may employ administrative and clerical staff as necessary to carry out this chapter.

(Enacted by Acts 2007, 80th Leg., ch. 1316 (S.B. 1154), § 2, effective September 1, 2007.)

### Sec. 1956.013.  Rules.

The commission may adopt rules to administer this chapter, including rules:

(1) establishing minimum requirements for registration under this chapter; and

(2) adopting forms required by this chapter.

(Enacted by Acts 2007, 80th Leg., ch. 1316 (S.B. 1154), § 2, effective September 1, 2007.)

### Sec. 1956.014.  Fees; Reports.

(a) The commission by rule shall prescribe fees in reasonable amounts sufficient to cover the costs of administering this chapter, including fees for:

(1) an initial application for a certificate of registration;

(2) issuance of a certificate of registration;

(3) issuance of a renewal certificate of registration; and

(4) issuance of a duplicate certificate of registration or duplicate renewal certificate of registration.

(b) The commission may not impose a fee for issuance of a certificate of registration that exceeds $250 annually. The department shall report annually to the legislature, not later than December 1, any costs associated with administering this chapter that are not covered by the fees assessed under this chapter.

(c) The department annually shall submit to both houses of the legislature a report on the number of metal recycling entities who have complied with the registration requirements under this chapter and the total number of metal recycling entities identified statewide. The report must include the information on metal recycling entities submitted to the department by municipalities, counties, and other political subdivisions of this state.

(d) [Expired pursuant to Acts 2007, 80th Leg., ch. 1316 (S.B. 1154), § 2, effective January 1, 2009.]

(Enacted by Acts 2007, 80th Leg., ch. 1316 (S.B. 1154), § 2, effective September 1, 2007.)

### Sec. 1956.015.  Statewide Electronic Reporting System.

(a) The department shall establish a statewide electronic reporting system to track the sales of regulated metal reported to the department under Section 1956.036.

(b) The department shall post a summary of the reports provided to the department under Section 1956.036 on the department's Internet website. The summary must include by county or region the frequency with which a person presents regulated materials for sale to a metal recycling entity. The summary may not identify any person to which the metal recycling entity sells the regulated materials.

(c) Subsection (b) does not apply to regulated material sold by a utility company, municipality, manufacturer, railroad, cemetery, cable or satellite entity, or other business entity that routinely has access to regulated metal.

(d) Information provided under this section is not subject to disclosure under Chapter 552, Government Code. The department may use information provided under this section for law enforcement purposes. Except as provided by this subsection, the department shall maintain the confidentiality of all information provided under this section, including the name of the seller, the price paid for a purchase of regulated material, and the quantity of regulated material purchased.

(e) The department may enter into contracts relating to the operation of the statewide electronic reporting system established by this section. A contract under this subsection must:

(1) require that any contractor, subcontractor, or third party that has access to, comes into possession of, or otherwise obtains information provided under this section maintain the confidentiality of all information provided under this section, including the name of the seller, the price paid for a purchase of regulated material, and the quantity of regulated material purchased; and

(2) provide that the department may terminate the contract of any contractor, subcontrac-

Occupations

tor, or third party that violates the confidentiality provision required by Subdivision (1).

(f) The department shall investigate a complaint alleging that a contractor, subcontractor, or third party has failed to maintain the confidentiality of information relating to a sale of regulated material.

(Enacted by Acts 2007, 80th Leg., ch. 1316 (S.B. 1154), § 2, effective September 1, 2007; am. Acts 2011, 82nd Leg., ch. 1234 (S.B. 694), § 5, effective September 1, 2011.)

### Sec. 1956.016. Registration Database.

The department shall make available on its Internet website a publicly accessible list of all registered metal recycling entities. The list must contain the following for each registered metal recycling entity:

(1) the entity's name;

(2) the entity's physical address; and

(3) the name of and contact information for a representative of the entity.

(Enacted by Acts 2011, 82nd Leg., ch. 1234 (S.B. 694), § 6, effective September 1, 2011.)

### Sec. 1956.017. Advisory Committee.

(a) The department shall establish an advisory committee to advise the department on matters related to the department's regulation of metal recycling entities under this chapter.

(b) The advisory committee consists of 12 members appointed by the director as follows:

(1) one representative of the department;

(2) two representatives of local law enforcement agencies located in different municipalities, each with a population of 500,000 or more;

(3) two representatives of local law enforcement agencies located in different municipalities, each with a population of 200,000 or more but less than 500,000;

(4) one representative of a local law enforcement agency located in a municipality with a population of less than 200,000;

(5) four representatives of metal recycling entities; and

(6) two members who represent industries that are impacted by theft of regulated material.

(c) The director shall ensure that the members of the advisory committee reflect the diverse geographic regions of this state.

(d) The advisory committee shall elect a presiding officer from among its members to serve a two-year term. A member may serve more than one term as presiding officer.

(e) The advisory committee shall meet annually and at the call of the presiding officer or the director.

(f) An advisory committee member is not entitled to compensation or reimbursement of expenses.

(g) Chapter 2110, Government Code, does not apply to the size, composition, or duration of the advisory committee or to the appointment of the committee's presiding officer.

(Enacted by Acts 2011, 82nd Leg., ch. 1234 (S.B. 694), § 6, effective September 1, 2011.)

## SUBCHAPTER A-2
## CERTIFICATE OF REGISTRATION

### Sec. 1956.021. Registration Required.

A person may not act as a metal recycling entity or represent to the public that the person is a metal recycling entity unless the person is registered under this chapter.

(Enacted by Acts 2007, 80th Leg., ch. 1316 (S.B. 1154), § 2, effective September 1, 2007.)

### Sec. 1956.022. Issuance of Certificate; Qualifications.

(a) The department shall issue a certificate of registration to an applicant who:

(1) applies and pays a registration fee; and

(2) presents any relevant evidence relating to the applicant's qualifications as required by commission rule.

(b) The commission by rule may establish qualifications for the holder of a certificate of registration under this chapter, which may include accepting copies of a license or permit issued by a county or municipality authorizing a metal recycling entity to conduct business in that county or municipality.

(Enacted by Acts 2007, 80th Leg., ch. 1316 (S.B. 1154), § 2, effective September 1, 2007.)

### Sec. 1956.023. Term of Certificate.

(a) A certificate of registration is valid for two years after the date of issuance.

(b) The department shall adopt a system under which certificates of registration expire and are renewed on various dates.

(c) Not later than the 45th day before the date a person's certificate of registration is scheduled to expire, the department shall send written notice of the impending expiration to the person at the person's last known address according to the records of the department.

(d) A person whose certificate of registration has expired may not make a representation for which a certificate of registration is required under Section 1956.021 or perform collections services until the certificate has been renewed. (Enacted by Acts 2007, 80th Leg., ch. 1316 (S.B. 1154), § 2, effective September 1, 2007.)

## Sec. 1956.024.  Renewal of Certificate.

(a) To renew a certificate of registration, a person must submit an application for renewal in the manner prescribed by the department.

(b) A person who is otherwise eligible to renew a certificate of registration may renew an unexpired certificate by paying the required renewal fee to the department before the expiration date of the certificate.

(c) A person whose certificate of registration has been expired for 90 days or less may renew the certificate by paying to the department a renewal fee that is equal to 1-½ times the normally required renewal fee.

(d) A person whose certificate of registration has been expired for more than 90 days but less than one year may renew the certificate by paying to the department a renewal fee that is equal to two times the normally required renewal fee.

(e) A person whose certificate of registration has been expired for one year or more may not renew the certificate. The person may obtain a new certificate of registration by complying with the requirements and procedures, including the examination requirements, for an original certificate. (Enacted by Acts 2007, 80th Leg., ch. 1316 (S.B. 1154), § 2, effective September 1, 2007.)

## SUBCHAPTER A-3
## PRACTICE BY CERTIFICATE HOLDERS

## Sec. 1956.031.  Notice to Sellers.

(a) A metal recycling entity shall at all times maintain in a prominent place in the entity's place of business, in open view to a seller of regulated material, a notice in two-inch lettering that:

(1) includes the following language:

"A PERSON ATTEMPTING TO SELL ANY REGULATED MATERIAL MUST PRESENT SUFFICIENT IDENTIFICATION AND WRITTEN PROOF OF OWNERSHIP REQUIRED BY STATE LAW."

"WARNING: STATE LAW PROVIDES A CRIMINAL PENALTY FOR A PERSON WHO INTENTIONALLY PROVIDES A FALSE DOCUMENT OF IDENTIFICATION OR OTHER FALSE INFORMATION TO A METAL RECYCLING ENTITY WHILE ATTEMPTING TO SELL ANY REGULATED MATERIAL."; and

(2) states the metal recycling entity's usual business hours.

(b) The notice required by this section may be contained on a sign that contains another notice if the metal recycling entity is required to display another notice under applicable law. (Enacted by Acts 2001, 77th Leg., ch. 1421, effective June 1, 2003; am. Acts 2007, 80th Leg., ch. 1316 (S.B. 1154), § 2, effective September 1, 2007 (renumbered from Sec. 1956.003).)

## Sec. 1956.032.  Information Regarding Seller.

(a) Except as provided by Subsection (f), a person attempting to sell regulated material to a metal recycling entity shall:

(1) display to the metal recycling entity the person's personal identification document;

(2) provide to the metal recycling entity the make, model, color, and license plate number of the motor vehicle used to transport the regulated material and the name of the state issuing the license plate;

(3) either:

(A) present written documentation evidencing that the person is the legal owner or is lawfully entitled to sell the regulated material; or

(B) sign a written statement provided by the metal recycling entity that the person is the legal owner of or is lawfully entitled to sell the regulated material offered for sale;

(4) if the regulated material includes condensing or evaporator coils for central heating or air conditioning units, display to the metal recycling entity:

(A) the person's air conditioning and refrigeration contractor license issued under Subchapter F or G, Chapter 1302;

(B) the person's air conditioning and refrigeration technician registration issued under Subchapter K, Chapter 1302;

(C) a receipt, bill of sale, or other documentation showing that the seller purchased the coils the seller is attempting to sell; or

(D) a receipt, bill of sale, or other documentation showing that the seller has purchased a replacement central heating or air conditioning unit; and

(5) **[Effective January 1, 2012]** if the regulated material includes insulated communications wire that has been burned wholly or partly to remove the insulation, display to the metal recycling entity documentation acceptable under the rules adopted under Subsection (h) that states that the material was salvaged from a fire.

(b) A person required by a municipality to prepare a signed statement consisting of the information required by Subsection (a)(3) may use the statement required by the municipality to comply with Subsection (a)(3).

(c) The metal recycling entity or the entity's agent shall visually verify the accuracy of the identification presented by the seller at the time of the purchase of regulated material and make a copy of the identification to be maintained by the entity in the entity's records, except as otherwise provided by Subsection (f).

(d) The metal recycling entity or the entity's agent for recordkeeping purposes may photograph the seller's entire face, not including any hat, and obtain the name of the seller's employer.

(e) The metal recycling entity or the entity's agent for recordkeeping purposes may take a photograph of the motor vehicle of the seller in which the make, model, and license plate number of the motor vehicle are identifiable in lieu of the information required under Subsection (a)(3).

(f) The metal recycling entity is not required to make a copy of the identification as required under Subsection (c) or collect the information required under Subsection (a)(3) if:

(1) the seller signs the written statement as required under Subsection (a)(3);

(2) the seller has previously provided the information required under Subsection (a); and

(3) the previously provided information has not changed.

(g) Notwithstanding Section 1956.002, the metal recycling entity shall verify the registration of a person attempting to sell regulated material who represents that the person is a metal recycling entity as follows:

(1) by using the database described by Section 1956.016; or

(2) by obtaining from the person a copy of the person's certificate of registration issued under Section 1956.022 in addition to the information required under Subsection (a).

(h) The commission shall adopt rules establishing the type of documentation that a seller of insulated communications wire described by Subsection (a)(5) must provide to a metal recycling entity to establish that the wire was salvaged from a fire.

(Enacted by Acts 2001, 77th Leg., ch. 1421, effective June 1, 2003; am. Acts 2007, 80th Leg., ch. 1316 (S.B. 1154), § 2, effective September 1, 2007 (renumbered from Sec. 1956.004); am. Acts 2011, 82nd Leg., ch. 1234 (S.B. 694), §§ 7, 8, effective September 1, 2011.)

### Sec. 1956.033. Record of Purchase.

(a) Each metal recycling entity in this state shall keep an accurate electronic record or an accurate and legible written record of each purchase of regulated material made in the course of the entity's business from an individual.

(b) The record must be in English and include:

(1) the place and date of the purchase;

(2) the name and address of the seller in possession of the regulated material purchased;

(3) the identifying number of the seller's personal identification document;

(4) a description made in accordance with the custom of the trade of the commodity type and quantity of regulated material purchased;

(5) the information required by Sections 1956.032(a)(2) and (3);

(6) as applicable:

(A) the identifying number of the seller's air conditioning and refrigeration contractor license displayed under Section 1956.032(a)(4)(A);

(B) a copy of the seller's air conditioning and refrigeration technician registration displayed under Section 1956.032(a)(4)(B);

(C) a copy of the documentation described by Section 1956.032(a)(4)(C); or

(D) a copy of the documentation described by Section 1956.032(a)(4)(D);

(7) if applicable, a copy of the documentation described by Section 1956.032(a)(5); and

(8) a copy of the documentation described by Section 1956.032(g).

(Enacted by Acts 2001, 77th Leg., ch. 1421, effective June 1, 2003; am. Acts 2007, 80th Leg., ch. 1316 (S.B. 1154), § 2, effective September 1, 2007 (renumbered from Sec. 1956.005); am. Acts 2011, 82nd Leg., ch. 1234 (S.B. 694), § 9, effective September 1, 2011.)

Occupations

## Sec. 1956.0331. Photograph or Recording Requirement for Regulated Metal Transaction.

(a) In addition to the requirements of Sections 1956.032 and 1956.033, for each purchase by a metal recycling entity of an item of regulated metal, the entity shall obtain a digital photograph or video recording that accurately depicts the seller's entire face and each type of regulated metal purchased.

(b) A metal recycling entity shall preserve a photograph or recording required under Subsection (a) as follows:

(1) for a video recording, until the 91st day after the date of the transaction; and

(2) for a digital photograph, until the 181st day after the date of the transaction.

(c) The photograph or recording must be made available for inspection as provided by Section 1956.035 not later than 72 hours after the time of purchase.

(Enacted by Acts 2011, 82nd Leg., ch. 1234 (S.B. 694), § 10, effective September 1, 2011.)

## Sec. 1956.034. Preservation of Records.

A metal recycling entity shall preserve each record required by Sections 1956.032 and 1956.033 until the second anniversary of the date the record was made. The records must be kept in an easily retrievable format and must be available for inspection as provided by Section 1956.035 not later than 72 hours after the time of purchase.

(Enacted by Acts 2001, 77th Leg., ch. 1421, effective June 1, 2003; am. Acts 2007, 80th Leg., ch. 1316 (S.B. 1154), § 2, effective September 1, 2007 (renumbered from Sec. 1956.006); am. Acts 2011, 82nd Leg., ch. 1234 (S.B. 694), § 11, effective September 1, 2011.)

## Sec. 1956.035. Inspection of Records.

(a) On request, a metal recycling entity shall permit a peace officer of this state, a representative of the department, or a representative of a county, municipality, or other political subdivision that issues a license or permit under Section 1956.003(b) to inspect, during the entity's usual business hours:

(1) a record required by Section 1956.033;

(2) a digital photograph or video recording required by Section 1956.0331; or

(3) regulated material in the entity's possession.

(b) The person seeking to inspect a record or material shall:

(1) inform the entity of the officer's status as a peace officer; or

(2) if the person is a representative of the department or a representative of a county, municipality, or other political subdivision, inform the entity of the person's status and display to the entity an identification document or other appropriate documentation establishing the person's status as a representative of the department or of the appropriate county, municipality, or political subdivision.

(Enacted by Acts 2001, 77th Leg., ch. 1421, effective June 1, 2003; am. Acts 2007, 80th Leg., ch. 1316 (S.B. 1154), § 2, effective September 1, 2007 (renumbered from Sec. 1956.007); am. Acts 2011, 82nd Leg., ch. 1234 (S.B. 694), § 12, effective September 1, 2011.)

## Sec. 1956.036. Furnishing of Report to Department.

(a) Except as provided by Subsections (b) and (d), not later than the close of business on a metal recycling entity's second working day after the date of the purchase or other acquisition of material for which a record is required under Section 1956.033, the entity shall send an electronic transaction report to the department via the department's Internet website. The report must contain the information required to be recorded under Section 1956.033.

(b) If a metal recycling entity purchases bronze material that is a cemetery vase, receptacle, memorial, or statuary or a pipe that can reasonably be identified as aluminum irrigation pipe, the entity shall:

(1) not later than the close of business on the entity's first working day after the purchase date, notify the department by telephone, by e-mail, or via the department's Internet website; and

(2) not later than the close of business on the entity's second working day after the purchase date, submit to the department electronically via the department's Internet website or file with the department a report containing the information required to be recorded under Section 1956.033.

(c) Subsection (b) does not apply to a purchase from:

(1) the manufacturer or fabricator of the material or pipe;

(2) a seller bearing a bill of sale for the material or pipe; or

(3) the owner of the material or pipe.

(d) A metal recycling entity may submit the transaction report required under Subsection (a) by facsimile if:

(1) the entity submits to the department annually:

(A) an application requesting an exception to the electronic reporting requirement; and

(B) an affidavit stating that the entity does not have an available and reliable means of submitting the transaction report electronically; and

(2) the department approves the entity's application under this subsection.

(e) The department, after notice and an opportunity for a hearing, may prohibit a metal recycling entity from paying cash for a purchase of regulated material for a period determined by the department if the department finds that the entity has failed to comply with this section.
(Enacted by Acts 2001, 77th Leg., ch. 1421, effective June 1, 2003; am. Acts 2007, 80th Leg., ch. 1316 (S.B. 1154), § 2, effective September 1, 2007 (renumbered from Sec. 1956.008); am. Acts 2011, 82nd Leg., ch. 1234 (S.B. 694), § 13, effective September 1, 2011.)

### Sec. 1956.037. Placement of Items on Hold.

(a) A metal recycling entity may not dispose of, process, sell, or remove from the premises an item of regulated metal unless:

(1) the entity acquired the item more than:

(A) eight days, excluding weekends and holidays, before the disposal, processing, sale, or removal, if the item is a cemetery vase, receptacle, or memorial made from a regulated material other than aluminum material; or

(B) 72 hours, excluding weekends and holidays, before the disposal, processing, sale, or removal, if the item is not an item described by Paragraph (A); or

(2) the entity purchased the item from a manufacturing, industrial, commercial, retail, or other seller that sells regulated material in the ordinary course of its business.

(b) A peace officer who has reasonable suspicion to believe that an item of regulated material in the possession of a metal recycling entity is stolen may place the item on hold by issuing to the entity a written notice that:

(1) specifically identifies the item alleged to be stolen and subject to the hold; and

(2) informs the entity of the requirements of Subsection (c).

(c) On receiving the notice, the entity may not, except as provided by Subsection (e), process or remove from the entity's premises the identified item before the 60th day after the date the notice is issued unless the hold is released at an earlier time in writing by a peace officer of this state or a court order.

(d) After the holding period expires, the entity may dispose of the item unless disposition violates a court order.

(e) If a hold is placed on a purchase of regulated material, a metal recycling entity may not dispose of, process, sell, or remove from the premises any item from the purchased material unless the hold on the material is released.
(Enacted by Acts 2001, 77th Leg., ch. 1421, effective June 1, 2003; am. Acts 2007, 80th Leg., ch. 1316 (S.B. 1154), § 2, effective September 1, 2007 (renumbered from Sec. 1956.009); am. Acts 2011, 82nd Leg., ch. 1234 (S.B. 694), § 14, effective September 1, 2011.)

### Sec. 1956.038. Prohibited Acts.

(a) A person may not, with the intent to deceive:

(1) display to a metal recycling entity a false or invalid personal identification document in connection with the person's attempted sale of regulated material;

(2) make a false, material statement or representation to a metal recycling entity in connection with:

(A) that person's execution of a written statement required by Section 1956.032(a)(3); or

(B) the entity's efforts to obtain the information required under Section 1956.033(b);

(3) display or provide to a metal recycling entity any information required under Section 1956.032 that the person knows is false or invalid; or

(4) display another individual's personal identification document in connection with the sale of regulated material.

(b) **[Effective March 1, 2012]** A metal recycling entity may not pay for a purchase of regulated material in cash if:

(1) the entity does not hold a certificate of registration under Subchapter A-2 and, if applicable, a license or permit required by a county, municipality, or other political subdivision as authorized under Section 1956.003(b); or

**Occupations**

(2) the entity has been prohibited by the department from paying cash under Section 1956.036(e).

(c) Notwithstanding Section 1956.003(a) or any other law, a county, municipality, or other political subdivision may not adopt or enforce a rule, charter, or ordinance or issue an order or impose standards that limit the use of cash by a metal recycling entity in a manner more restrictive than that provided by Subsection (b).

(d) Subsection (c) does not apply to a rule, charter, ordinance, or order of a county, municipality, or other political subdivision in effect on January 1, 2011.

(d-1) **[Expires March 1, 2012]** Not later than January 1, 2012, the department shall issue a notice to each known owner or operator of a metal recycling entity in this state informing the owner or operator of the requirement to obtain a certificate of registration under Subchapter A-2 and, if applicable, to obtain a license or permit required by a county, municipality, or other political subdivision under Section 1956.003. The notice must also state:

(1) that the owner or operator shall submit an application for a certificate of registration and the appropriate license or permit required by a county, municipality, or other political subdivision on or before March 1, 2012; and

(2) the penalties under this chapter for failure to comply with Subdivision (1).

(d-2) **[Expires March 1, 2012]** This subsection and Subsection (d-1) expire March 1, 2012.

(e) **[Effective March 1, 2012]** The department or a county, municipality, or other political subdivision may bring an action in the county in which a metal recycling entity is located to enjoin the business operations of the owner or operator of the metal recycling entity for a period of not less than 30 days and not more than 90 days if the owner or operator has not submitted an application for a certificate of registration or the appropriate license or permit required by a county, municipality, or other political subdivision.

(f) An action under Subsection (e) must be brought in the name of the state. If judgment is in favor of the state, the court shall:

(1) enjoin the owner or operator from maintaining or participating in the business of a metal recycling entity for a definite period of not less than 30 days and not more than 90 days, as determined by the court; and

(2) order that the place of business of the owner or operator be closed for the same period.

(Enacted by Acts 2001, 77th Leg., ch. 1421, effective June 1, 2003; am. Acts 2007, 80th Leg., ch. 1316 (S.B. 1154), § 2, effective September 1, 2007 (renumbered from Sec. 1956.010); am. Acts 2011, 82nd Leg., ch. 1234 (S.B. 694), § 15, effective September 1, 2011.)

## Sec. 1956.039.  Hours for Purchasing Material.

(a) Subject to Subsection (b), a county, municipality, or political subdivision may establish the hours during which a metal recycling entity may purchase regulated material.

(b) A metal recycling entity may not purchase from the general public regulated material:

(1) more than 15 consecutive hours in one day; or

(2) later than 9 p.m.

(Enacted by Acts 2007, 80th Leg., ch. 1316 (S.B. 1154), § 2, effective September 1, 2007.)

## Sec. 1956.040.  Criminal Penalty.

(a) A person commits an offense if the person knowingly violates Section 1956.038.

An offense under this subsection is a Class A misdemeanor unless it is shown on trial of the offense that the person has previously been convicted of a violation of this subchapter, in which event the offense is a state jail felony.

(a-1) A person commits an offense if the person knowingly violates Section 1956.021, 1956.023(d), 1956.036(a), or 1956.039.

(a-2) An offense under Subsection (a-1) is a misdemeanor punishable by a fine not to exceed $10,000, unless it is shown on trial of the offense that the person has previously been convicted of a violation of Subsection (a-1), in which event the offense is a state jail felony.

(a-3) It is an affirmative defense to prosecution of a violation of Section 1956.021 or 1956.023(d) that the person made a diligent effort to obtain or renew a certificate of registration at the time of the violation.

(a-4) A municipality or county may retain 10 percent of the money collected from a fine for a conviction of an offense under Subsection (a-1) as a service fee for that collection and the clerk of the court shall remit the remainder of the fine collected for conviction of an offense under Subsection (a-1) to the comptroller in the manner provided for the remission of fees to the comptroller under Subchapter B, Chapter 133, Local Government Code. The comptroller shall deposit proceeds received under this subsection to the credit of an account in the general revenue fund, and those proceeds may be appropriated only to the department and used to:

(1) finance the department's administration of Subchapters A, A-1, A-2, and A-3; and

(2) fund grants distributed under the prevention of scrap metal theft grant program established under Subchapter N, Chapter 411, Government Code.

(b) A person commits an offense if the person knowingly buys:

(1) stolen regulated material; or

(2) **[Effective January 1, 2012]** insulated communications wire that has been burned wholly or partly to remove the insulation, unless the wire is accompanied by documentation acceptable under the rules adopted under Section 1956.032(h) that states that the material was salvaged from a fire.

(b-1) An offense under Subsection (b) is a Class A misdemeanor unless it is shown on trial of the offense that the person has previously been convicted under Subsection (b), in which event the offense is a state jail felony.

(c) A person commits an offense if the person knowingly sells stolen regulated material. An offense under this subsection is a state jail felony unless it is shown on trial of the offense that the person has previously been convicted under this subsection, in which event the offense is a third degree felony.

(d) On the conviction of a metal recycling entity for an offense punishable under Subsection (b), a court, in addition to imposing any other applicable penalty, may order that the entity cease doing business as a metal recycling entity for a period not to exceed:

(1) 30 days from the date of the order for each violation that forms the basis of the conviction for a first offense; and

(2) 180 days from the date of the order for each violation that forms the basis of the conviction if it is shown on trial of the offense that the person has previously been convicted under this section.

(e) If conduct that constitutes an offense under this section also constitutes an offense under any other law, the actor may be prosecuted under this section or the other law.

(Enacted by Acts 2001, 77th Leg., ch. 1421, effective June 1, 2003; am. Acts 2007, 80th Leg., ch. 1316 (S.B. 1154), § 2, effective September 1, 2007 (renumbered from Sec. 1956.011); am. Acts 2011,

82nd Leg., ch. 1234 (S.B. 694), § 16, effective September 1, 2011.)

## SUBCHAPTER B
## SALE OF CRAFTED PRECIOUS METAL TO DEALERS

### Sec. 1956.051. Definitions.

In this subchapter:

(1) "Commission" means the Finance Commission of Texas.

(2) "Commissioner" means the consumer credit commissioner.

(3) "Crafted precious metal" means jewelry, silverware, an art object, or another object, made wholly or partly from precious metal, other than a coin, a bar, a commemorative medallion, or scrap or a broken item selling at five percent or more than the scrap value of the item.

(4) "Dealer" means a person registered to engage in the business of purchasing and selling crafted precious metal, including purchases or sales made through the mail.

(5) "Department" means the Texas Department of Public Safety.

(6) "Precious metal" means gold, silver, platinum, palladium, iridium, rhodium, osmium, ruthenium, or an alloy of those metals.

(Enacted by Acts 2001, 77th Leg., ch. 1421 (H.B. 2813), § 4, effective June 1, 2003; am. Acts 2011, 82nd Leg., ch. 1298 (H.B. 2490), § 1, effective September 1, 2011.)

### Sec. 1956.0511. Administration by Commission.

(a) Notwithstanding any other provision of this chapter, the commission shall administer and enforce this subchapter, unless the context clearly requires another state agency to perform a specific duty.

(b) To the extent of any conflict between this subchapter and other provisions of this chapter, this subchapter prevails.

(Enacted by Acts 2011, 82nd Leg., ch. 1298 (H.B. 2490), § 2, effective September 1, 2011.)

### Sec. 1956.052. Applicability of Subchapter.

This subchapter applies only to crafted precious metal that has been sold or used primarily for personal, family, or household purposes.

**Occupations**

(Enacted by Acts 2001, 77th Leg., ch. 1421 (H.B. 2813), § 4, effective June 1, 2003.)

## Sec. 1956.053. Exception: Precious Metal Extracted, Recovered, or Salvaged from Industrial By-Products or Industrial Waste Products.

This subchapter does not apply to a person whose purchase or sale of precious metal or a product made of precious metal is merely incidental to the person's business of extracting, recovering, or salvaging precious metal from industrial by-products or industrial waste products.
(Enacted by Acts 2001, 77th Leg., ch. 1421 (H.B. 2813), § 4, effective June 1, 2003.)

## Sec. 1956.054. Exception: Dental, Pharmaceutical, or Medical Application of Crafted Precious Metal.

This subchapter does not apply to a dental, pharmaceutical, or medical application of crafted precious metal.
(Enacted by Acts 2001, 77th Leg., ch. 1421 (H.B. 2813), § 4, effective June 1, 2003.)

## Sec. 1956.055. Exception: Crafted Precious Metal Acquired from Another Dealer Who Previously Made Required Reports.

This subchapter does not apply to crafted precious metal acquired in good faith in a transaction involving the stock-in-trade of another dealer who previously made the reports concerning that metal as required by this subchapter if:

(1) the selling dealer delivers to the acquiring dealer a written document stating that the reports have been made;

(2) the acquiring dealer submits a copy of the statement to the chief of police of the municipality or the sheriff of the county in which the selling dealer is located; and

(3) each dealer involved in the transaction retains a copy of the statement until the third anniversary of the date of the transaction.
(Enacted by Acts 2001, 77th Leg., ch. 1421 (H.B. 2813), § 4, effective June 1, 2003.)

## Sec. 1956.056. Exception: Crafted Precious Metal Acquired in Dissolution or Liquidation Sale.

This subchapter does not apply to crafted precious metal acquired in a nonjudicial sale, transfer, assignment, assignment for the benefit of creditors, or consignment of the assets or stock-in-trade, in bulk, or a substantial part of those assets, of an industrial or commercial enterprise, other than a dealer, for the voluntary dissolution or liquidation of the seller's business, or for disposing of an excessive quantity of personal property, or property that has been acquired in a nonjudicial sale or transfer from an owner other than a dealer, the seller's entire household of personal property, or a substantial part of that property, if the dealer:

(1) gives written notice to the chief of police of the municipality or the sheriff of the county in which the dealer's business is located that a reporting exemption is being claimed under this section;

(2) retains in the dealer's place of business, until the third anniversary of the date of the transaction, a copy of the bill of sale, receipt, inventory list, or other transfer document; and

(3) makes the record retained available for inspection by a peace officer.
(Enacted by Acts 2001, 77th Leg., ch. 1421 (H.B. 2813), § 4, effective June 1, 2003.)

## Sec. 1956.057. Exception: Crafted Precious Metal Acquired in Judicial Sale.

This subchapter does not apply to crafted precious metal acquired in a sale made:

(1) by any public officer in the officer's official capacity as a trustee in bankruptcy, executor, administrator, receiver, or public official acting under judicial process or authority; or

(2) on the execution of, or by virtue of, any process issued by a court.
(Enacted by Acts 2001, 77th Leg., ch. 1421 (H.B. 2813), § 4, effective June 1, 2003.)

## Sec. 1956.058. Exception: Crafted Precious Metal Acquired As Payment for Other Crafted Precious Metal by Person in Business of Selling to Consumers.

This subchapter does not apply to crafted precious metal acquired in good faith as part or complete payment for other crafted precious metal by a person whose principal business is primarily that of selling directly to the consumer crafted precious metal that has not been subject to a prior sale.

(Enacted by Acts 2001, 77th Leg., ch. 1421 (H.B. 2813), § 4, effective June 1, 2003.)

## Sec. 1956.059. Exception: Crafted Precious Metal Acquired from or Reported to Governmental Agency.

This subchapter does not apply to crafted precious metal:

(1) acquired as surplus property from the United States, a state, a subdivision of a state, or a municipal corporation; or

(2) reported by a dealer as an acquisition or a purchase, or reported as destroyed or otherwise disposed of, to:

(A) a state agency under another law of this state; or

(B) a municipal or county office or agency under another law of this state or a municipal ordinance.

(Enacted by Acts 2001, 77th Leg., ch. 1421 (H.B. 2813), § 4, effective June 1, 2003.)

## Sec. 1956.060. Exception: Crafted Precious Metal Acquired by Person Licensed Under Texas Pawnshop Act.

This subchapter does not apply to crafted precious metal acquired by:

(1) a person licensed under Chapter 371, Finance Code; or

(2) an entity affiliated with a person licensed under Chapter 371, Finance Code, if the entity's recordkeeping practices satisfy the requirements of that chapter.

(Enacted by Acts 2001, 77th Leg., ch. 1421 (H.B. 2813), § 4, effective June 1, 2003; am. Acts 2011, 82nd Leg., ch. 1298 (H.B. 2490), § 3, effective September 1, 2011.)

## Sec. 1956.061. Effect on Other Laws and Ordinances.

This subchapter does not:

(1) excuse noncompliance with another state law or municipal ordinance covering the reporting, holding, or releasing of crafted precious metal;

(2) prohibit a municipality from enacting, amending, or enforcing an ordinance relating to a dealer; or

(3) supersede a municipal ordinance except to the extent the ordinance does not require reporting for transactions involving crafted precious metal.

(Enacted by Acts 2001, 77th Leg., ch. 1421 (H.B. 2813), § 4, effective June 1, 2003.)

## Sec. 1956.0611. Rulemaking.

The commission may adopt rules necessary to implement and enforce this subchapter.

(Enacted by Acts 2011, 82nd Leg., ch. 1298 (H.B. 2490), § 4, effective September 1, 2011.)

## Sec. 1956.0612. [Effective January 1, 2012] Registration As Dealer.

(a) A person may not engage in the business of purchasing and selling crafted precious metal unless the person is registered with the commissioner as a dealer under this section.

(b) To register as a dealer, a person must provide to the commissioner, on or before December 31 preceding each calendar year in which the person seeks to act as a dealer:

(1) a list of each location in this state at which the person will conduct business as a dealer; and

(2) a processing fee for each location included on the list furnished under Subdivision (1).

(c) The commissioner shall prescribe the processing fee in an amount necessary to cover the costs of administering this section.

(d) After the December 31 deadline, a dealer may amend the registration required under Subsection (a) to reflect any change in the information provided by the registration.

(e) The commissioner shall make available to the public a list of dealers registered under this section.

(f) The commissioner may prescribe the registration form.

(g) A reference to a registration in another subchapter of this chapter does not apply to a person to the extent the person is registered under this subchapter.

(Enacted by Acts 2011, 82nd Leg., ch. 1298 (H.B. 2490), § 4, effective January 1, 2012.)

## Sec. 1956.0613. Investigation by Commissioner.

The commissioner shall:

(1) monitor the operations of a dealer to ensure compliance with this chapter; and

(2) receive and investigate complaints against a dealer or a person acting as a dealer.

(Enacted by Acts 2011, 82nd Leg., ch. 1298 (H.B. 2490), § 4, effective September 1, 2011.)

## Sec. 1956.0614. Revocation of Registration.

(a) The commissioner may revoke the registration of a dealer if the commissioner concludes

**Occupations**

that the dealer has violated this chapter. The commissioner shall recite the basis of the decision in an order revoking the registration.

(b) If the commissioner proposes to revoke a registration, the dealer is entitled to a hearing before the commissioner or a hearings officer, who shall propose a decision to the commissioner. The commissioner or hearings officer shall prescribe the time and place of the hearing. The hearing is governed by Chapter 2001, Government Code.

(c) A dealer aggrieved by a ruling, order, or decision of the commissioner is entitled to appeal to a district court in the county in which the hearing was held. An appeal under this subsection is governed by Chapter 2001, Government Code.

(Enacted by Acts 2011, 82nd Leg., ch. 1298 (H.B. 2490), § 4, effective September 1, 2011.)

## Sec. 1956.0615.    Administrative Penalty.

The commissioner may assess an administrative penalty not to exceed $500 against a person for each knowing and wilful violation of this chapter.

(Enacted by Acts 2011, 82nd Leg., ch. 1298 (H.B. 2490), § 4, effective September 1, 2011.)

## Sec. 1956.062.    Report of Purchase Required.

(a) A dealer shall, as required by Section 1956.063, report all identifiable crafted precious metal that the dealer purchases, takes in trade, accepts for sale on consignment, or accepts for auction.

(b) Before crafted precious metal is offered for sale or exchange, a dealer must notify each person intending to sell or exchange the metal that, before the dealer may accept any of the person's property, the person must file with the dealer a list describing all of the person's crafted precious metal to be accepted by the dealer. The list must contain:

(1) the proposed seller's name and address;

(2) a complete and accurate description of the crafted precious metal; and

(3) the proposed seller's certification that the information is true and complete.

(c) The dealer shall record the proposed seller's driver's license number or department personal identification certificate number on physical presentation of the license or personal identification certificate by the seller. The record must accompany the list.

(d) The dealer shall:

(1) provide to a peace officer, on demand, the list required by Subsection (b); and

(2) mail or deliver a complete copy of the list to the chief of police or the sheriff as provided by Section 1956.063 not later than 48 hours after the list is filed with the dealer.

(Enacted by Acts 2001, 77th Leg., ch. 1421 (H.B. 2813), § 4, effective June 1, 2003.)

## Sec. 1956.063.    Form of Report; Filing.

(a) A report required by this subchapter must comply with this section unless a similar report is required by another state law or a municipal ordinance, in which event the required report must comply with the applicable law or ordinance.

(b) If a transaction regulated by this subchapter occurs in a municipality that maintains a police department, the original and a copy of the report required by this subchapter shall be submitted to the municipality's chief of police. If the transaction does not occur in such a municipality, the original and a copy of the report shall be submitted to the sheriff of the county in which the transaction occurs.

(c) For each transaction regulated by this subchapter, the dealer shall submit a report on a preprinted and prenumbered form prescribed by the commissioner. The form must include the following:

(1) the date of the transaction;

(2) a description of the crafted precious metal purchased by the dealer;

(3) the name and physical address of the dealer; and

(4) the name, physical description, and physical address of the seller or transferor.

(d) The dealer shall retain a copy of the report until the third anniversary of the date the report is filed.

(Enacted by Acts 2001, 77th Leg., ch. 1421 (H.B. 2813), § 4, effective June 1, 2003; am. Acts 2011, 82nd Leg., ch. 1298 (H.B. 2490), § 5, effective September 1, 2011.)

## Sec. 1956.064.    Required Retention of Crafted Precious Metal.

(a) A dealer may not melt, deface, alter, or dispose of crafted precious metal that is the subject of a report required by this subchapter before the 11th day after the date the report is filed unless:

(1) the peace officer to whom the report is submitted, for good cause, authorizes disposition of the metal;

(2) the dealer obtains the name, address, and description of the buyer and retains a record of that information; or

(3) the dealer is a pawnbroker and the disposition is the redemption of pledged property by the pledgor.

(b) A peace officer who has reasonable suspicion to believe that an item of crafted precious metal in the possession of a dealer is stolen may place the item on hold for a period not to exceed 60 days by issuing to the dealer a written notice that:

(1) specifically identifies the item alleged to be stolen and subject to the hold; and

(2) informs the dealer of the requirements of Subsection (c).

(c) On receiving the notice, the dealer may not melt, deface, alter, or dispose of the identified crafted precious metal until the hold is released in writing by a peace officer of this state or a court order.

(Enacted by Acts 2001, 77th Leg., ch. 1421 (H.B. 2813), § 4, effective June 1, 2003; am. Acts 2011, 82nd Leg., ch. 1298 (H.B. 2490), § 6, effective September 1, 2011.)

## Sec. 1956.065.  Inspection of Crafted Precious Metal by Peace Officer.

(a) A dealer shall make crafted precious metal purchased by the dealer available for inspection by a peace officer during regular business hours while in the dealer's possession.

(b) Information obtained under this section is confidential except for use in a criminal investigation or prosecution or a civil court proceeding. (Enacted by Acts 2001, 77th Leg., ch. 1421 (H.B. 2813), § 4, effective June 1, 2003.)

## Sec. 1956.066.  Purchase from Minor.

(a) A dealer may not purchase crafted precious metal from a person younger than 18 years of age unless the seller delivers to the dealer before the purchase a written statement from the seller's parent or legal guardian consenting to the transaction.

(b) The dealer shall retain the statement with the records required to be kept under this subchapter. The dealer may destroy the statement after the later of:

(1) the date the item is sold; or

(2) the first anniversary of the date the dealer purchased the item.

(Enacted by Acts 2001, 77th Leg., ch. 1421 (H.B. 2813), § 4, effective June 1, 2003.)

## Sec. 1956.067.  Purchase at Temporary Location of Dealer.

(a) **[2 Versions: Effective Until January 1, 2012]** A dealer who conducts business at a temporary location for a period of less than 90 days may not engage in the business of buying precious metal or used items made of precious metal unless, within a 12-month period at least 30 days before the date on which each purchase is made, the person has filed:

(1) a registration statement with the department; and

(2) a copy of the registration statement with the local law enforcement agency of:

(A) the municipality in which the temporary location is located; or

(B) if the temporary location is not located in a municipality, the county in which the temporary location is located.

(a) **[2 Versions: Effective January 1, 2012]** A dealer who conducts business at a temporary location for a period of less than one year may not engage in the business of buying precious metal or used items made of precious metal unless, within a 12-month period at least 30 days before the date on which each purchase is made, the dealer has filed:

(1) a registration statement with the department;

(2) a copy of the registration statement and a copy of the dealer's certificate of registration issued under this subchapter with the local law enforcement agency of:

(A) the municipality in which the temporary location is located; or

(B) if the temporary location is not located in a municipality, the county in which the temporary location is located; and

(3) a copy of the dealer's certificate of registration issued under this subchapter with the county and, if applicable, the municipality in which the temporary location is located.

(b) The registration statement must contain:

(1) the name and address of the dealer;

(2) the location where business is to be conducted;

(3) if the dealer is an association, the name and address of each member of the association;

(4) if the dealer is a corporation, the name and address of each officer and director of the corporation; and

(5) other relevant information required by the department.

(Enacted by Acts 2001, 77th Leg., ch. 1421 (H.B. 2813), § 4, effective June 1, 2003; am. Acts 2011,

82nd Leg., ch. 1298 (H.B. 2490), § 7, effective January 1, 2012.)

### Sec. 1956.068.   Purchase of Melted Items.

A dealer, in the course of business, may not purchase from a person other than a manufacturer of or a regular dealer in crafted precious metal an object formed as the result of the melting of crafted precious metal.

(Enacted by Acts 2001, 77th Leg., ch. 1421 (H.B. 2813), § 4, effective June 1, 2003.)

### Sec. 1956.069.   Criminal Penalty.

(a) **[2 Versions: Effective Until January 1, 2012]** A dealer commits an offense if the dealer:

(1) fails to make or permit inspection of a report as required by Section 1956.062 or 1956.063;

(2) disposes of crafted precious metal or fails to make a record available for inspection by a peace officer as required by Section 1956.064;

(3) fails to obtain or retain a statement as required by Section 1956.066;

(4) fails to file a registration statement as required by Section 1956.067; or

(5) purchases an object in violation of Section 1956.068.

(a) **[2 Versions: Effective January 1, 2012]** A person commits an offense if the person:

(1) fails to make or permit inspection of a report as required by Section 1956.062 or 1956.063;

(2) violates Section 1956.0612 or 1956.064;

(3) fails to obtain or retain a statement as required by Section 1956.066;

(4) fails to file a registration statement as required by Section 1956.067; or

(5) purchases an object in violation of Section 1956.068.

(b) An offense under this section is a Class B misdemeanor.

(Enacted by Acts 2001, 77th Leg., ch. 1421 (H.B. 2813), § 4, effective June 1, 2003; am. Acts 2011, 82nd Leg., ch. 1298 (H.B. 2490), § 8, effective January 1, 2012.)

### SUBCHAPTER C
### RESTRICTIONS ON SALE OF CERTAIN ITEMS TO METAL RECYCLING ENTITIES

### Sec. 1956.101.   Definitions.

In this subchapter:

(1) [Repealed by Acts 2007, 80th Leg., ch. 1316 (S.B. 1154), § 5, effective September 1, 2007.]

(2) "Motor vehicle" has the meaning assigned by Section 541.201, Transportation Code.

(3) "PCB-containing capacitor" means a capacitor that contains polychlorinated biphenyls and is regulated under the federal Toxic Substances Control Act (15 U.S.C. Section 2601 et seq.).

(4) "Person" means an individual, corporation, partnership, sole proprietorship, or other business entity.

(Enacted by Acts 2001, 77th Leg., ch. 1421 (H.B. 2813), § 4, effective June 1, 2003; am. Acts 2007, 80th Leg., ch. 1316 (S.B. 1154), § 5, effective September 1, 2007.)

### Sec. 1956.102.   Exception.

This subchapter does not apply to a sale or transfer by or on behalf of a metal recycling entity.

(Enacted by Acts 2001, 77th Leg., ch. 1421 (H.B. 2813), § 4, effective June 1, 2003.)

### Sec. 1956.103.   Restrictions on Transfer of Certain Property.

(a) A person may not sell or otherwise transfer to a metal recycling entity:

(1) a lead-acid battery, fuel tank, or PCB-containing capacitor that is included with another type of scrap, used, or obsolete metal without first obtaining from the metal recycling entity a written and signed acknowledgment that the scrap, used, or obsolete metal includes one or more lead-acid batteries, fuel tanks, or PCB-containing capacitors;

(2) any of the following items that contain or enclose a lead-acid battery, fuel tank, or PCB-containing capacitor or of which a lead-acid battery, fuel tank, or PCB-containing capacitor is a part:

(A) a motor vehicle;

(B) a motor vehicle that has been junked, flattened, dismantled, or changed so that it has lost its character as a motor vehicle;

(C) an appliance; or

(D) any other item of scrap, used, or obsolete metal;

(3) a motor vehicle or a motor vehicle that has been junked, flattened, dismantled, or changed so that it has lost its character as a motor vehicle if the motor vehicle includes, contains, or encloses a tire or scrap tire; or

(4) a metal alcoholic beverage keg, regardless of condition, unless the seller is the manufacturer of the keg, the brewer or distiller of the beverage that was contained in the keg, or an authorized representative of the manufacturer, brewer, or distiller.

(b) Subsection (a)(3) does not apply to the sale or other transfer of a motor vehicle or a junked, flattened, dismantled, or changed motor vehicle from another state.

(c) Subsection (a) does not apply to a fuel tank that has been completely drained and rendered unusable in accordance with Texas Commission on Environmental Quality rules regardless of whether the fuel tank is attached to a motor vehicle.

(Enacted by Acts 2001, 77th Leg., ch. 1421 (H.B. 2813), § 4, effective June 1, 2003; am. Acts 2005, 79th Leg., ch. 47 (S.B. 1298), § 1, effective September 1, 2005; am. Acts 2011, 82nd Leg., ch. 1234 (S.B. 694), § 17, effective September 1, 2011.)

### Sec. 1956.104. Notice of Restrictions.

A metal recycling entity shall post in a conspicuous location a notice that:

(1) is readily visible to a person selling material to the metal recycling entity;

(2) is at least 24 inches horizontally by 18 inches vertically; and

(3) contains the following language:

### TEXAS LAW PROHIBITS:

1. THE SALE OF A WHOLE, FLATTENED, OR JUNKED MOTOR VEHICLE, AN APPLIANCE, OR ANY OTHER SCRAP METAL ITEM CONTAINING A LEAD-ACID BATTERY, FUEL TANK THAT HAS NOT BEEN COMPLETELY DRAINED AND RENDERED UNUSABLE, OR PCB-CONTAINING CAPACITOR; AND

2. THE SALE OF LEAD-ACID BATTERIES, FUEL TANKS THAT HAVE NOT BEEN COMPLETELY DRAINED AND RENDERED UNUSABLE, OR PCB-CONTAINING CAPACITORS INCLUDED WITH OTHER SCRAP METALS WITHOUT OUR PRIOR WRITTEN ACKNOWLEDGMENT.

### VIOLATION OF THIS LAW IS A MISDEMEANOR.

(Enacted by Acts 2001, 77th Leg., ch. 1421 (H.B. 2813), § 4, effective June 1, 2003; am. Acts 2005,

79th Leg., ch. 47 (S.B. 1298), § 2, effective September 1, 2005.)

### Sec. 1956.105. Criminal Penalty.

(a) A person commits an offense if the person violates this subchapter.

(b) An offense under this section is a misdemeanor punishable by:

(1) a fine of not more than $1,000;

(2) confinement in the county jail for not more than 60 days; or

(3) both the fine and the confinement.

(Enacted by Acts 2001, 77th Leg., ch. 1421 (H.B. 2813), § 4, effective June 1, 2003.)

## SUBCHAPTER D
## DISCIPLINARY PROCEDURES

### Sec. 1956.151. Denial of Certificate; Disciplinary Action.

The department shall deny an application for a certificate of registration, suspend or revoke a certificate of registration, or reprimand a person who is registered under this chapter if the person:

(1) obtains a certificate of registration by means of fraud, misrepresentation, or concealment of a material fact;

(2) sells, barters, or offers to sell or barter a certificate of registration;

(3) violates a provision of this chapter or a rule adopted under this chapter; or

(4) violates Section 1956.021.

(Enacted by Acts 2007, 80th Leg., ch. 1316 (S.B. 1154), § 4, effective September 1, 2007; am. Acts 2011, 82nd Leg., ch. 1234 (S.B. 694), § 18, effective September 1, 2011.)

### Sec. 1956.152. Investigation.

Within the limits of available resources, the department may investigate:

(1) a person who engages in a practice that violates this chapter; and

(2) a complaint filed with the department against a person registered under this chapter.

(Enacted by Acts 2007, 80th Leg., ch. 1316 (S.B. 1154), § 4, effective September 1, 2007.)

### Sec. 1956.153. Hearing.

(a) A person whose application for a certificate of registration is denied, whose certificate of registration is suspended or revoked, or who is reprimanded is entitled to a hearing before the department if the person submits to the department a written request for the hearing.

(b) A hearing is governed by department rules for a contested hearing and by Chapter 2001, Government Code.
(Enacted by Acts 2007, 80th Leg., ch. 1316 (S.B. 1154), § 4, effective September 1, 2007.)

## SUBCHAPTER E
## OTHER PENALTIES AND
## ENFORCEMENT PROVISIONS

### Sec. 1956.201. Enforcement Proceedings; Injunction.

(a) The department, the attorney general, or the district, county, or city attorney for the county or municipality in which an alleged violation of this chapter occurs may, on receipt of a verified complaint, bring an appropriate administrative or judicial proceeding to enforce this chapter or a rule adopted under this chapter.

(b) The attorney general or an attorney representing the state may initiate an action for an injunction to prohibit a person from violating this chapter or a rule adopted under this chapter.
(Enacted by Acts 2007, 80th Leg., ch. 1316 (S.B. 1154), § 4, effective September 1, 2007.)

### Sec. 1956.202. Civil Penalty.

(a) Except as provided by Subsection (d), a person who violates this chapter or a rule adopted under this chapter is liable to this state for a civil penalty of not more than $1,000 for each violation.

(b) The amount of the penalty shall be based on:

(1) the seriousness of the violation;
(2) the history of previous violations;
(3) the amount necessary to deter a future violation; and
(4) any other matter that justice may require.

(c) The attorney general may sue to collect a civil penalty under this section. In the suit the attorney general may recover, on behalf of the state, the reasonable expenses incurred in obtaining the penalty, including investigation and court costs, reasonable attorney's fees, witness fees, and other expenses.

(d) A civil penalty may not be assessed under this section for conduct described by Section 1956.021, 1956.023(d), 1956.036(a), 1956.038, or 1956.039.
(Enacted by Acts 2007, 80th Leg., ch. 1316 (S.B. 1154), § 4, effective September 1, 2007; am. Acts 2011, 82nd Leg., ch. 1234 (S.B. 694), § 19, effective September 1, 2011.)

### Sec. 1956.203. Criminal Penalty for Certain Solicitation.

(a) A person commits an offense if the person solicits the purchase of regulated material at a location other than a business location at which the material is produced as a by-product in the ordinary course of that business.

(b) An offense under this section is a Class B misdemeanor.
(Enacted by Acts 2007, 80th Leg., ch. 1316 (S.B. 1154), § 4, effective September 1, 2007.)

# TITLE 13
# SPORTS, AMUSEMENTS, ENTERTAINMENT

## SUBTITLE A
## GAMING

## CHAPTER 2002
## CHARITABLE RAFFLES

### Subchapter A. General Provisions

## SUBCHAPTER A
## GENERAL PROVISIONS

### Sec. 2002.001. Short Title.

This chapter may be cited as the Charitable Raffle Enabling Act.

(Enacted by Acts 1999, 76th Leg., ch. 388 (H.B. 3155), § 1, effective September 1, 1999.)

## Sec. 2002.002. Definitions.

In this chapter:

(1) "Charitable purposes" means:

(A) benefitting needy or deserving persons in this state, indefinite in number, by:

(i) enhancing their opportunities for religious or educational advancement;

(ii) relieving them from disease, suffering, or distress;

(iii) contributing to their physical well-being;

(iv) assisting them in establishing themselves in life as worthy and useful citizens; or

(v) increasing their comprehension of and devotion to the principles on which this nation was founded and enhancing their loyalty to their government;

(B) initiating, performing, or fostering worthy public works in this state; or

(C) enabling or furthering the erection or maintenance of public structures in this state.

(1-a) "Money" means coins, paper currency, or a negotiable instrument that represents and is readily convertible to coins or paper currency.

(2) "Qualified organization" means a qualified religious society, qualified volunteer fire department, qualified volunteer emergency medical service, or qualified nonprofit organization.

(3) "Qualified religious society" means a church, synagogue, or other organization or association organized primarily for religious purposes that:

(A) has been in existence in this state for at least 10 years; and

(B) does not distribute any of its income to its members, officers, or governing body, other than as reasonable compensation for services or for reimbursement of expenses.

(4) "Qualified volunteer emergency medical service" means an association that:

(A) is organized primarily to provide and actively provides emergency medical, rescue, or ambulance services;

(B) does not pay its members compensation other than nominal compensation; and

(C) does not distribute any of its income to its members, officers, or governing body other than for reimbursement of expenses.

(5) "Qualified volunteer fire department" means an association that:

(A) operates fire-fighting equipment;

(B) is organized primarily to provide and actively provides fire-fighting services;

(C) does not pay its members compensation other than nominal compensation; and

(D) does not distribute any of its income to its members, officers, or governing body, other than for reimbursement of expenses.

(6) "Raffle" means the award of one or more prizes by chance at a single occasion among a single pool or group of persons who have paid or promised a thing of value for a ticket that represents a chance to win a prize.

(7) "Reverse raffle" means a raffle in which the last ticket or tickets drawn are considered the winning tickets.

(Enacted by Acts 1999, 76th Leg., ch. 388 (H.B. 3155), § 1, effective September 1, 1999; am. Acts 2005, 79th Leg., ch. 929 (H.B. 541), § 1, effective June 18, 2005; am. Acts 2005, 79th Leg., ch. 1006 (H.B. 659), § 1, effective September 1, 2005.)

## Sec. 2002.003. Qualified Nonprofit Organization.

(a) An organization incorporated or holding a certificate of authority under the Texas Non-Profit Corporation Act (Article 1396-1.01 et seq., Vernon's Texas Civil Statutes) is a qualified nonprofit organization for the purposes of this chapter if the organization:

(1) does not distribute any of its income to its members, officers, or governing body, other than as reasonable compensation for services;

(2) has existed for the three preceding years;

(3) does not devote a substantial part of its activities to attempting to influence legislation and does not participate or intervene in any political campaign on behalf of any candidate for public office in any manner, including by publishing or distributing statements or making campaign contributions;

(4) qualifies for and has obtained an exemption from federal income tax from the Internal Revenue Service under Section 501(c), Internal Revenue Code of 1986; and

(5) does not have or recognize any local chapter, affiliate, unit, or subsidiary organization in this state.

(b) An organization that is formally recognized as and that operates as a local chapter, affiliate, unit, or subsidiary organization of a parent organization incorporated or holding a certificate of authority under the Texas Non-Profit Corporation Act (Article 1396-1.01 et seq., Vernon's Texas Civil Statutes) is a qualified nonprofit organization if:

(1) neither the local organization nor the parent organization distributes any of its income to its members, officers, or governing body, other than as reasonable compensation for services;

(2) the local organization has existed for the three preceding years and during those years has been formally recognized as a local chapter, affiliate, unit, or subsidiary organization of the parent organization;

(3) neither the local organization nor the parent organization:

(A) devotes a substantial part of its activities to attempting to influence legislation; or

(B) participates or intervenes in any political campaign on behalf of any candidate for public office in any manner, including by publishing or distributing statements or making campaign contributions; and

(4) either the local organization or the parent organization qualifies for and has obtained an exemption from federal income tax from the Internal Revenue Service under Section 501(c), Internal Revenue Code of 1986.

(b-1) An organization that is formally recognized as and that operates as a local chapter, affiliate, unit, or subordinate lodge of a grand lodge or other institution or order incorporated under Title 32, Revised Statutes, as authorized by Article 1399, Revised Statutes, is a qualified nonprofit organization if:

(1) neither the local organization nor the incorporated grand lodge or other institution or order distributes any of its income to its members, officers, or governing body, other than as reasonable compensation for services;

(2) the local organization has existed for the three preceding years and during those years:

(A) has had a governing body or officers elected by a vote of its members or by a vote of delegates elected by its members; or

(B) has been formally recognized as a local chapter, affiliate, unit, or subordinate lodge of the grand lodge or other institution or order;

(3) neither the local organization nor the incorporated grand lodge or other institution or order:

(A) devotes a substantial part of its activities to attempting to influence legislation; or

(B) participates or intervenes in any political campaign on behalf of any candidate for public office in any manner, including by publishing or distributing statements or making campaign contributions; and

(4) either the local organization or the incorporated grand lodge or other institution or order qualifies for and has obtained an exemption from federal income tax from the Internal Revenue Service under Section 501(c), Internal Revenue Code of 1986, or other applicable provision.

(c) An unincorporated organization, association, or society is a qualified nonprofit organization if it:

(1) does not distribute any of its income to its members, officers, or governing body, other than as reasonable compensation for services;

(2) for the three preceding years has been affiliated with a state or national organization organized to perform the same purposes as the unincorporated organization, association, or society;

(3) does not devote a substantial part of its activities to attempting to influence legislation and does not participate or intervene in any political campaign on behalf of any candidate for public office in any manner, including by publishing or distributing statements or making campaign contributions; and

(4) qualifies for and has obtained an exemption from federal income tax from the Internal Revenue Service under Section 501(c), Internal Revenue Code of 1986.

(d) An organization, association, or society is considered to devote a substantial part of its activities to attempting to influence legislation for purposes of this section if, in any 12-month period in the preceding three years, more than 10 percent of the organization's expenditures were made to influence legislation.

(e) A nonprofit wildlife conservation association and its local chapters, affiliates, wildlife cooperatives, or units are qualified nonprofit organizations under this chapter if the parent association meets the eligibility criteria under this section other than the requirement prescribed by Subsection (a)(3), (b)(3), (b-1)(3), or (c)(3), as applicable. An association or a local chapter, affiliate, wildlife cooperative, or unit that is eligible under this subsection may not use any proceeds from a raffle conducted under this chapter to attempt to influence legislation or participate or intervene in a political campaign on behalf of a candidate for public office in any manner, includ-

ing by publishing or distributing a statement or making a campaign contribution. A nonprofit wildlife conservation association may conduct two raffles each year and each local chapter, affiliate, wildlife cooperative, or unit may conduct two raffles each year under this chapter. For purposes of this section, a nonprofit wildlife conservation association includes an association that supports wildlife, fish, or fowl.
(Enacted by Acts 1999, 76th Leg., ch. 388 (H.B. 3155), § 1, effective September 1, 1999; am. Acts 2005, 79th Leg., ch. 34 (S.B. 766), § 1, effective May 9, 2005; am. Acts 2005, 79th Leg., ch. 929 (H.B. 541), § 2, effective June 18, 2005; am. Acts 2009, 81st Leg., ch. 936 (H.B. 3113), § 1, effective June 19, 2009.)

### Sec. 2002.004.  Imputed Actions of Organization.

For purposes of this chapter, an organization performs an act if a member, officer, or agent of the organization performs the act with the consent or authorization of the organization.
(Enacted by Acts 1999, 76th Leg., ch. 388 (H.B. 3155), § 1, effective September 1, 1999.)

## SUBCHAPTER B
## OPERATION OF RAFFLE

### Sec. 2002.051.  Raffle Authorized.

A qualified organization may conduct a raffle subject to the conditions imposed by this subchapter.
(Enacted by Acts 1999, 76th Leg., ch. 388 (H.B. 3155), § 1, effective September 1, 1999.)

### Sec. 2002.052.  Time and Frequency Restrictions.

(a) In this section, "calendar year" means a period beginning January 1 and ending on the succeeding December 31.

(b) A raffle is not authorized by this chapter if the organization sells or offers to sell tickets for or awards prizes in the raffle in a calendar year in which the organization has previously sold or offered to sell tickets for or awarded prizes in two or more other raffles.

(c) The organization may not sell or offer to sell tickets for a raffle during a period in which the organization sells or offers to sell tickets for another raffle. If an organization violates this subsection, neither of the raffles is authorized.

(d) Before selling or offering to sell tickets for a raffle, a qualified organization shall set a date on which the organization will award the prize or prizes in a raffle. The organization must award the prize or prizes on that date unless the organization becomes unable to award the prize or prizes on that date.

(e) A qualified organization that is unable to award a prize or prizes on the date set under Subsection (d) may set another date not later than 30 days from the date originally set on which the organization will award the prize or prizes.

(f) If the prize or prizes are not awarded within the 30 days as required by Subsection (e), the organization must refund or offer to refund the amount paid by each person who purchased a ticket for the raffle.
(Enacted by Acts 1999, 76th Leg., ch. 388 (H.B. 3155), § 1, effective September 1, 1999; am. Acts 2003, 78th Leg., ch. 597 (H.B. 1813), § 1, effective September 1, 2003.)

### Sec. 2002.053.  Use of Raffle Proceeds.

All proceeds from the sale of tickets for a raffle must be spent for the charitable purposes of the qualified organization.
(Enacted by Acts 1999, 76th Leg., ch. 388 (H.B. 3155), § 1, effective September 1, 1999; am. Acts 2005, 79th Leg., ch. 929 (H.B. 541), § 3, effective June 18, 2005.)

### Sec. 2002.054.  Restrictions on Raffle Promotion and Ticket Sales.

(a) The organization may not:

(1) directly or indirectly, by the use of paid advertising, promote a raffle through a medium of mass communication, including television, radio, or newspaper;

(2) promote or advertise a raffle statewide, other than on the organization's Internet website or through a publication or solicitation, including a newsletter, social media, or electronic mail, provided only to previously identified supporters of the organization; or

(3) sell or offer to sell tickets for a raffle statewide.

(b) Except as provided by this subsection, the organization may not compensate a person directly or indirectly for organizing or conducting a raffle or for selling or offering to sell tickets to a raffle. A member of the organization who is employed by the organization may organize and conduct a raffle, but the member's work organizing or conducting a raffle may not be more than a de minimis portion of the member's employment with the organization.

(c) Except as provided by Section 2002.0541, the organization may not permit a person who is not authorized by the organization to sell or offer to sell raffle tickets.
(Enacted by Acts 1999, 76th Leg., ch. 388 (H.B. 3155), § 1, effective September 1, 1999; am. Acts 2005, 79th Leg., ch. 929 (H.B. 541), § 4, effective June 18, 2005; am. Acts 2005, 79th Leg., ch. 1006 (H.B. 659), § 2, effective September 1, 2005; am. Acts 2007, 80th Leg., ch. 921 (H.B. 3167), § 12.003, effective September 1, 2007; am. Acts 2011, 82nd Leg., ch. 124 (H.B. 457), § 1, effective May 27, 2011.)

### Sec. 2002.0541.   Reverse Raffle.

(a) A qualified organization may conduct a reverse raffle as provided by this section.

(b) Notwithstanding Section 2002.056(a), a refund of the purchase price of a ticket may be awarded as a raffle prize in a reverse raffle.

(c) Notwithstanding Section 2002.055(3), after the drawing of tickets in a reverse raffle has begun, the qualified organization conducting the raffle may auction off additional tickets to persons who are present at the drawing for a price other than the price printed on the ticket.

(d) After the drawing of tickets in a reverse raffle has begun, the qualified organization may permit a ticket holder present at the drawing to resell the ticket to another person present at the drawing for an amount greater than the original purchase price of the ticket. The sale must be made through a designated representative of the organization, and not less than 10 percent of the sale proceeds must be retained by the organization.

(e) Notwithstanding Section 2002.055(3), after the drawing of tickets in a reverse raffle has begun, the qualified organization may permit the holder of a previously drawn ticket:

(1) to purchase additional chances for the ticket to be selected to win a prize; or

(2) to purchase additional tickets for the raffle.

(f) Only the portion of the proceeds from the resale of a ticket under Subsection (d) retained by the organization are subject to Section 2002.053. All proceeds from the sale of additional chances for a ticket under Subsection (e) are considered to be proceeds from the sale of the ticket for purposes of Section 2002.053.
(Enacted by Acts 2005, 79th Leg., ch. 1006 (H.B. 659), § 3, effective September 1, 2005.)

### Sec. 2002.055.   Ticket Disclosures.

The following information must be printed on each raffle ticket sold or offered for sale:

(1) the name of the organization conducting the raffle;

(2) the address of the organization or of a named officer of the organization;

(3) the ticket price;

(4) a general description of each prize having a value of more than $10 to be awarded in the raffle; and

(5) the date on which the raffle prize or prizes will be awarded.
(Enacted by Acts 1999, 76th Leg., ch. 388 (H.B. 3155), § 1, effective September 1, 1999; am. Acts 2003, 78th Leg., ch. 597 (H.B. 1813), § 2, effective September 1, 2003.)

### Sec. 2002.056.   Restrictions on Prizes.

(a) A prize offered or awarded at a raffle may not be money.

(b) Except as provided by Subsections (b-1) and (c), the value of a prize offered or awarded at a raffle that is purchased by the organization or for which the organization provides any consideration may not exceed $50,000.

(b-1) The value of a residential dwelling offered or awarded as a prize at a raffle that is purchased by the organization or for which the organization provides any consideration may not exceed $250,000.

(c) A raffle prize may consist of one or more tickets in the state lottery authorized by Chapter 466, Government Code, with a face value of $50,000 or less, without regard to whether a prize in the lottery game to which the ticket or tickets relate exceeds $50,000.

(d) A raffle is not authorized by this chapter unless the organization:

(1) has the prize to be offered in the raffle in its possession or ownership; or

(2) posts bond with the county clerk of the county in which the raffle is to be held for the full amount of the money value of the prize.
(Enacted by Acts 1999, 76th Leg., ch. 388 (H.B. 3155), § 1, effective September 1, 1999; am. Acts 2005, 79th Leg., ch. 929 (H.B. 541), § 5, effective June 18, 2005.)

### Sec. 2002.057.   Ticket Sale on University Property.

An institution of higher education, as defined by Section 61.003, Education Code, shall allow a

qualified organization that is a student organization recognized by the institution to sell raffle tickets at any facility of the institution, subject to reasonable restrictions on the time, place, and manner of the sale.
(Enacted by Acts 1999, 76th Leg., ch. 388 (H.B. 3155), § 1, effective September 1, 1999.)

### Sec. 2002.058. Injunctive Action Against Unauthorized Raffle.

(a) A county attorney, district attorney, criminal district attorney, or the attorney general may bring an action in county or district court for a permanent or temporary injunction or a temporary restraining order prohibiting conduct involving a raffle or similar procedure that:

(1) violates or threatens to violate state law relating to gambling; and

(2) is not authorized by this chapter or other law.

(b) Venue for an action under this section is in the county in which the conduct occurs or in which a defendant in the action resides.
(Enacted by Acts 1999, 76th Leg., ch. 388 (H.B. 3155), § 1, effective September 1, 1999.)

# CHAPTER 2003
# INSPECTION AND REGULATION OF GAMBLING VESSELS

### Subchapter A. General Provisions

## SUBCHAPTER A
## GENERAL PROVISIONS

### Sec. 2003.001. Definition.

In this chapter, "department" means the Department of Public Safety of the State of Texas.
(Enacted by Acts 1999, 76th Leg., ch. 388 (H.B. 3155), § 1, effective September 1, 1999.)

### Sec. 2003.002. Application of Chapter.

This chapter applies only to a vessel on which activity described by Section 47.02(a), Penal Code, is regularly conducted, whether or not the activity occurs in this state.
(Enacted by Acts 1999, 76th Leg., ch. 388 (H.B. 3155), § 1, effective September 1, 1999.)

## SUBCHAPTER B
## STATE INSPECTION AND REGULATION

### Sec. 2003.051. Criminal History Record Information.

(a) The department may request criminal history record information from the Federal Bureau of Investigation or any other law enforcement agency relating to a person who owns, has a financial interest in, operates, or is employed by a person who operates a vessel in this state, including the territorial waters of this state, whether or not the operation of the vessel is in violation of law.

(b) The department may maintain records of information obtained under Subsection (a).
(Enacted by Acts 1999, 76th Leg., ch. 388 (H.B. 3155), § 1, effective September 1, 1999.)

### Sec. 2003.052. Inspection.

The department may inspect a vessel located in this state, including the territorial waters of this state, to ensure that the vessel is operated in compliance with state or other law.
(Enacted by Acts 1999, 76th Leg., ch. 388 (H.B. 3155), § 1, effective September 1, 1999.)

## SUBCHAPTER C
## MUNICIPAL INSPECTION AND REGULATION

### Sec. 2003.101. Regulation.

(a) A municipality, by ordinance, may impose regulations for the protection of the health and safety of the passengers or crew of a vessel that:

(1) regularly boards passengers in the municipality; or

(2) is regularly loaded, fueled, repaired, stored, or docked in the municipality.

(b) A municipal ordinance may not prohibit an activity relating to a vessel that is expressly permitted under Chapter 47, Penal Code, or other state law.
(Enacted by Acts 1999, 76th Leg., ch. 388 (H.B. 3155), § 1, effective September 1, 1999.)

### Sec. 2003.102. Inspection.

A municipality may inspect a vessel docked in the municipality to determine if the vessel is

operated in compliance with Chapter 47, Penal Code, a municipal ordinance, or other law.
(Enacted by Acts 1999, 76th Leg., ch. 388 (H.B. 3155), § 1, effective September 1, 1999.)

## SUBTITLE D
## OTHER AMUSEMENTS AND ENTERTAINMENT

## CHAPTER 2154
## REGULATION OF FIREWORKS AND FIREWORKS DISPLAYS

### SUBCHAPTER F
### PROHIBITED ACTS

**Sec. 2154.254. Employment of Minors.**
(a) Except as provided by Subsection (c), a person may not employ or allow a person younger than 16 years of age to manufacture, distribute, sell, or purchase fireworks in the course of the person's business.

(b) Except as provided by Subsection (c), a person may not employ a person 16 years of age or older but younger than 18 years of age to sell fireworks at a retail sales location unless the person selling fireworks at that location is accompanied by another person who is at least 18 years of age.

(c) An owner of a retail sales location may employ a person who is otherwise prohibited from engaging in that activity by Subsection (a) or (b) to sell fireworks at the owner's retail sales location if the person employed is:

    (1) a member of the owner's immediate family;

    (2) 12 years of age or older; and

    (3) accompanied by another person who is at least 18 years of age while the person is engaged in selling fireworks at that location.
(Enacted by Acts 2007, 80th Leg., ch. 1179 (H.B. 539), § 5, effective June 15, 2007.)

# TITLE 14
# REGULATION OF MOTOR VEHICLES AND TRANSPORTATION

## SUBTITLE A
## REGULATIONS RELATED TO MOTOR VEHICLES

## CHAPTER 2302
## SALVAGE VEHICLE DEALERS

## SUBCHAPTER A
## GENERAL PROVISIONS

### Sec. 2302.001.　Definitions.

In this chapter:

(1) "Casual sale," "damage," "insurance company," "major component part," "metal recycler," "motor vehicle," "nonrepairable motor vehicle," "nonrepairable vehicle title," "out-of-state buyer," "salvage motor vehicle," "salvage vehicle title," "salvage vehicle dealer," and "used part" have the meanings assigned by Section 501.091, Transportation Code.

(2) "Board" means the board of the Texas Department of Motor Vehicles.

(3) "Department" means the Texas Department of Motor Vehicles.

(4) "Federal safety certificate" means the label or tag required under 49 U.S.C. Section 30115 that certifies that a motor vehicle or equipment complies with applicable federal motor vehicle safety standards.

(5) "Salvage pool operator" means a person who engages in the business of selling nonrepairable motor vehicles or salvage motor vehicles at auction, including wholesale auction, or otherwise.

(6) "Salvage vehicle agent" means a person who acquires, sells, or otherwise deals in nonrepairable or salvage motor vehicles in this state as directed by the salvage vehicle dealer under whose license the person operates. The term does not include a person who:

(A) is a licensed salvage vehicle dealer or a licensed used automotive parts recycler;

(B) is a partner, owner, or officer of a business entity that holds a salvage vehicle dealer license or a used automotive parts recycler license;

(C) is an employee of a licensed salvage vehicle dealer or a licensed used automotive parts recycler; or

(D) only transports salvage motor vehicles for a licensed salvage vehicle dealer or a licensed used automotive parts recycler.

(Enacted by Acts 2001, 77th Leg., ch. 1421 (H.B. 2813), § 5, effective June 1, 2003; am. Acts 2003, 78th Leg., ch. 1325 (H.B. 3588), § 17.03, effective September 1, 2003; am. Acts 2009, 81st Leg., ch. 783 (S.B. 1095), § 1, effective September 1, 2009; am. Acts 2009, 81st Leg., ch. 933 (H.B. 3097), §§ 3I.04, 4.01, effective September 1, 2009.)

### Sec. 2302.0015.　Consent to Entry and Inspection.

(a) A person consents to an entry or inspection described by Subsection (b) by:

(1) accepting a license under this chapter; or

(2) engaging in a business or activity regulated under this chapter.

(b) For the purpose of enforcing or administering this chapter or Chapter 501 or 502, Transportation Code, a member of the board, an employee or agent of the board or department, a member of the Public Safety Commission, an officer of the Department of Public Safety, or a peace officer may at a reasonable time:

(1) enter the premises of a business regulated under one of those chapters; and

(2) inspect or copy any document, record, vehicle, part, or other item regulated under one of those chapters.

(c) A person described by Subsection (a):

(1) may not refuse or interfere with an entry or inspection under this section; and

(2) shall cooperate fully with a person conducting an inspection under this section to assist in the recovery of stolen motor vehicles and parts and to prevent the sale or transfer of stolen motor vehicles and parts.

(d) An entry or inspection occurs at a reasonable time for purposes of Subsection (b) if the entry or inspection occurs:

(1) during normal business hours of the person or activity regulated under this chapter; or

(2) while an activity regulated under this chapter is occurring on the premises.

(Enacted by Acts 2003, 78th Leg., ch. 1325 (H.B. 3588), § 17.04, effective September 1, 2003; am. Acts 2009, 81st Leg., ch. 933 (H.B. 3097), § 3I.05, effective September 1, 2009.)

### Sec. 2302.002.　Classification of Vehicles [Repealed].

Repealed by Acts 2003, 78th Leg., ch. 1325 (H.B. 3588), § 17.09(2), effective September 1, 2003.

(Enacted by Acts 2001, 77th Leg., ch. 1421 (H.B. 2813), § 5, effective June 1, 2003.)

### Sec. 2302.003. Classification As Metal Recycler [Repealed].

Repealed by Acts 2003, 78th Leg., ch. 1325 (H.B. 3588), § 17.09(2), effective September 1, 2003.

(Enacted by Acts 2001, 77th Leg., ch. 1421 (H.B. 2813), § 5, effective June 1, 2003.)

### Sec. 2302.004. Sale of Certain Water-Damaged Vehicles [Repealed].

Repealed by Acts 2003, 78th Leg., ch. 1325 (H.B. 3588), § 17.09(2), effective September 1, 2003.

(Enacted by Acts 2001, 77th Leg., ch. 1421 (H.B. 2813), § 5, effective June 1, 2003.)

### Sec. 2302.005. Applicability of Certain Municipal Ordinances, Licenses, and Permits.

This chapter:

(1) is in addition to any municipal ordinance relating to the regulation of a person who deals in nonrepairable or salvage motor vehicles or used parts; and

(2) does not prohibit the enforcement of a requirement of a municipal license or permit that is related to an activity regulated under this chapter.

(Enacted by Acts 2001, 77th Leg., ch. 1421 (H.B. 2813), § 5, effective June 1, 2003; am. Acts 2003, 78th Leg., ch. 1325 (H.B. 3588), § 17.05, effective September 1, 2003.)

### Sec. 2302.006. Application of Chapter to Metal Recyclers.

(a) Except as provided by Subsections (b) and (c), this chapter does not apply to a transaction in which a metal recycler is a party.

(b) This chapter applies to a transaction in which a motor vehicle:

(1) is sold, transferred, released, or delivered to a metal recycler for the purpose of reuse or resale as a motor vehicle; and

(2) is used for that purpose.

(c) Sections 2302.0015 and 2302.205 apply to a metal recycler.

(Enacted by Acts 2001, 77th Leg., ch. 1421 (H.B. 2813), § 5, effective June 1, 2003; am. Acts 2003, 78th Leg., ch. 1325 (H.B. 3588), § 17.05, effective September 1, 2003; am. Acts 2009, 81st Leg., ch. 783 (S.B. 1095), § 2, effective September 1, 2009;

am. Acts 2009, 81st Leg., ch. 933 (H.B. 3097), § 4.02, effective September 1, 2009.)

### Sec. 2302.007. Application of Chapter to Insurance Companies.

This chapter does not apply to an insurance company.

(Enacted by Acts 2001, 77th Leg., ch. 1421 (H.B. 2813), § 5, effective June 1, 2003; am. Acts 2003, 78th Leg., ch. 1325 (H.B. 3588), § 17.05, effective September 1, 2003.)

### Sec. 2302.008. Applicability of Chapter to Used Automotive Parts Recyclers.

This chapter does not apply to a used automotive parts recycler licensed under Chapter 2309.

(Enacted by Acts 2009, 81st Leg., ch. 783 (S.B. 1095), § 3, effective September 1, 2009; Enacted by Acts 2009, 81st Leg., ch. 933 (H.B. 3097), § 4.03, effective September 1, 2009.)

## SUBCHAPTER B
## BOARD POWERS AND DUTIES

### Sec. 2302.051. Rules and Enforcement Powers.

The board shall adopt rules as necessary to administer this chapter and may take other action as necessary to enforce this chapter.

(Enacted by Acts 2001, 77th Leg., ch. 1421 (H.B. 2813), § 5, effective June 1, 2003; am. Acts 2003, 78th Leg., ch. 1325 (H.B. 3588), § 17.05, effective September 1, 2003; am. Acts 2009, 81st Leg., ch. 933 (H.B. 3097), § 3I.07, effective September 1, 2009.)

### Sec. 2302.052. Duty to Set Fees.

The board shall set application fees, license fees, renewal fees, and other fees as required to implement this chapter. The board shall set the fees in amounts reasonable and necessary to implement and enforce this chapter.

(Enacted by Acts 2001, 77th Leg., ch. 1421 (H.B. 2813), § 5, effective June 1, 2003; am. Acts 2003, 78th Leg., ch. 1325 (H.B. 3588), § 17.05, effective September 1, 2003; am. Acts 2009, 81st Leg., ch. 933 (H.B. 3097), § 3I.07, effective September 1, 2009.)

### Sec. 2302.053. Rules Restricting Advertising or Competitive Bidding.

(a) The board may not adopt a rule under Section 2302.051 restricting advertising or competitive bidding by a person who holds a license issued under this chapter except to prohibit false, misleading, or deceptive practices by the person.

(b) The board may not include in its rules to prohibit false, misleading, or deceptive practices a rule that:

(1) restricts the use of any advertising medium;

(2) restricts the person's personal appearance or use of the person's voice in an advertisement;

(3) relates to the size or duration of an advertisement by the person; or

(4) restricts the use of a trade name in advertising by the person.

(Enacted by Acts 2001, 77th Leg., ch. 1421 (H.B. 2813), § 5, effective June 1, 2003; am. Acts 2009, 81st Leg., ch. 933 (H.B. 3097), § 3I.07, effective September 1, 2009.)

## SUBCHAPTER C
## LICENSE REQUIREMENTS

### Sec. 2302.101. License Required for Salvage Vehicle Dealer.

Unless a person holds a salvage vehicle dealer license issued under this chapter, the person may not:

(1) act as a salvage vehicle dealer or rebuilder; or

(2) store or display a motor vehicle as an agent or escrow agent of an insurance company.

(Enacted by Acts 2001, 77th Leg., ch. 1421 (H.B. 2813), § 5, effective June 1, 2003; am. Acts 2003, 78th Leg., ch. 1325 (H.B. 3588), § 17.05, effective September 1, 2003.)

### Sec. 2302.102. Salvage Vehicle Dealer License Classification.

(a) The department shall classify a salvage vehicle dealer according to the type of activity performed by the dealer.

(b) A salvage vehicle dealer may not engage in activities of a particular classification unless the dealer holds a license with an endorsement in that classification.

(Enacted by Acts 2001, 77th Leg., ch. 1421 (H.B. 2813), § 5, effective June 1, 2003.)

### Sec. 2302.103. Application for Salvage Vehicle Dealer License.

(a) To apply for a salvage vehicle dealer license, a person must submit to the department an application on a form prescribed by the de-

partment. The application must be signed by the applicant and accompanied by the application fee.

(b) An applicant may apply for a salvage vehicle dealer license with an endorsement in one or more of the following classifications:

(1) new automobile dealer;

(2) used automobile dealer;

(3) salvage pool operator;

(4) salvage vehicle broker; or

(5) salvage vehicle rebuilder.

(Enacted by Acts 2001, 77th Leg., ch. 1421 (H.B. 2813), § 5, effective June 1, 2003; am. Acts 2009, 81st Leg., ch. 783 (S.B. 1095), § 4, effective September 1, 2009; am. Acts 2009, 81st Leg., ch. 933 (H.B. 3097), § 4.04, effective September 1, 2009.)

### Sec. 2302.104. Contents of Application.

(a) An application for a salvage vehicle dealer license must include:

(1) the name, business address, and business telephone number of the applicant;

(2) the name under which the applicant proposes to conduct business;

(3) the location, by number, street, and municipality, of each office at which the applicant proposes to conduct business;

(4) a statement indicating whether the applicant previously applied for a license under this chapter and, if so, a statement indicating the result of the previous application and indicating whether the applicant has ever been the holder of a license issued under this chapter that was revoked or suspended;

(5) a statement of the previous history, record, and associations of the applicant to the extent sufficient to establish, to the satisfaction of the department, the business reputation and character of the applicant;

(6) the applicant's federal tax identification number, if any;

(7) the applicant's state sales tax number; and

(8) any other information required by rules adopted under this chapter.

(b) In addition to the information required by Subsection (a), the application of a corporation must include:

(1) the state of its incorporation;

(2) the name, address, date of birth, and social security number of each principal officer or director of the corporation;

(3) a statement of the previous history, record, and associations of each officer and each director to the extent sufficient to establish, to the satisfaction of the department, the business reputation and character of the applicant; and

(4) a statement showing whether an officer, director, or employee of the applicant has been refused a license as a salvage vehicle dealer or has been the holder of a license issued under this chapter that was revoked or suspended.

(c) In addition to the information required by Subsection (a), the application of a partnership must include:

(1) the name, address, date of birth, and social security number of each owner or partner;

(2) a statement of the previous history, record, and associations of each owner and each partner to the extent sufficient to establish, to the satisfaction of the department, the business reputation and character of the applicant; and

(3) a statement showing whether an owner, partner, or employee of the applicant has been refused a license as a salvage vehicle dealer or has been the holder of a license issued under this chapter that was revoked or suspended.

(Enacted by Acts 2001, 77th Leg., ch. 1421 (H.B. 2813), § 5, effective June 1, 2003.)

### Sec. 2302.105.  Department Investigation.

(a) The department may not issue a license under this chapter until the department completes an investigation of the applicant's qualifications.

(b) The department shall conduct the investigation not later than the 15th day after the date the department receives the application. The department shall report to the applicant the results of the investigation.

(Enacted by Acts 2001, 77th Leg., ch. 1421 (H.B. 2813), § 5, effective June 1, 2003.)

### Sec. 2302.106.  License Issuance.

(a) The department shall issue a license to an applicant who meets the license qualifications adopted under this chapter and pays the required fees.

(b) A license may not be issued in a fictitious name that may be confused with or is similar to that of a governmental entity or that is otherwise deceptive or misleading to the public.

(Enacted by Acts 2001, 77th Leg., ch. 1421 (H.B. 2813), § 5, effective June 1, 2003.)

### Sec. 2302.107.  Salvage Vehicle Agent License.

(a) A person may not act as a salvage vehicle agent unless the person holds a salvage vehicle agent license issued under this chapter.

(b) A person is entitled to a salvage vehicle agent license on application to the department, payment of the required fee, and authorization from a salvage vehicle dealer to operate under the dealer's license.

(c) A salvage vehicle dealer may authorize not more than five persons to operate as salvage vehicle agents under the dealer's license.

(d) A salvage vehicle agent may acquire, sell, or otherwise deal in, nonrepairable or salvage motor vehicles as directed by the authorizing dealer.

(Enacted by Acts 2001, 77th Leg., ch. 1421 (H.B. 2813), § 5, effective June 1, 2003; am. Acts 2003, 78th Leg., ch. 1325 (H.B. 3588), § 17.06, effective September 1, 2003; am. Acts 2009, 81st Leg., ch. 783 (S.B. 1095), § 5, effective September 1, 2009; am. Acts 2009, 81st Leg., ch. 933 (H.B. 3097), § 4.05, effective September 1, 2009.)

### Sec. 2302.108.  Disciplinary Action.

(a) The department may deny, suspend, revoke, or reinstate a license issued under this chapter.

(b) The board by rule shall establish the grounds for denial, suspension, revocation, or reinstatement of a license issued under this chapter and the procedures for disciplinary action. A rule adopted under this subsection may not conflict with a rule adopted by the State Office of Administrative Hearings.

(c) A proceeding under this section is subject to Chapter 2001, Government Code.

(d) A person whose license is revoked may not apply for a new license before the first anniversary of the date of the revocation.

(Enacted by Acts 2001, 77th Leg., ch. 1421 (H.B. 2813), § 5, effective June 1, 2003; am. Acts 2009, 81st Leg., ch. 933 (H.B. 3097), § 3I.08, effective September 1, 2009.)

### SUBCHAPTER D
### LICENSE EXPIRATION AND RENEWAL

### Sec. 2302.151.  License Expiration.

(a) A license issued under this chapter expires on the first anniversary of the date of issuance.

Occupations

(b) A person whose license has expired may not engage in the activities that require a license until the license has been renewed under this subchapter.
(Enacted by Acts 2001, 77th Leg., ch. 1421 (H.B. 2813), § 5, effective June 1, 2003.)

### Sec. 2302.152.  Notice of Expiration.

Not later than the 31st day before the expiration date of a person's license, the department shall send written notice of the impending expiration to the person at the person's last known address according to department records.
(Enacted by Acts 2001, 77th Leg., ch. 1421 (H.B. 2813), § 5, effective June 1, 2003.)

### Sec. 2302.153.  Procedures for Renewal.

(a) A person who is otherwise eligible to renew a license issued under this chapter may renew an unexpired license by paying the required renewal fee to the department on or before the expiration date of the license.

(b) A person whose license has been expired for 90 days or less may renew the license by paying to the department a renewal fee that is equal to 1-½ times the normally required renewal fee.

(c) A person whose license has been expired for more than 90 days but less than one year may renew the license by paying to the department a renewal fee that is equal to two times the normally required renewal fee.

(d) A person whose license has been expired for one year or longer may not renew the license. The person may obtain a new license by complying with the requirements and procedures for obtaining an original license.

(e) A person who was licensed in this state, moved to another state, and has been doing business in the other state for the two years preceding the date of application may renew an expired license. The person must pay to the department a renewal fee that is equal to two times the normally required renewal fee.
(Enacted by Acts 2001, 77th Leg., ch. 1421 (H.B. 2813), § 5, effective June 1, 2003.)

## SUBCHAPTER E
## CONDUCTING BUSINESS

### Sec. 2302.201.  Duties on Acquisition of Salvage Motor Vehicle.

(a) Except as provided by Section 501.0935, Transportation Code, a salvage vehicle dealer who acquires ownership of a salvage motor vehicle from an owner must receive from the owner a properly assigned title.

(b) The dealer shall comply with Subchapter E, Chapter 501, Transportation Code.
(Enacted by Acts 2001, 77th Leg., ch. 1421 (H.B. 2813), § 5, effective June 1, 2003; am. Acts 2003, 78th Leg., ch. 1325 (H.B. 3588), § 17.07, effective September 1, 2003; am. Acts 2011, 82nd Leg., ch. 1136 (H.B. 1422), § 6, effective September 1, 2011.)

### Sec. 2302.202.  Records of Purchases.

A salvage vehicle dealer shall maintain a record of each salvage motor vehicle purchased or sold by the dealer.
(Enacted by Acts 2001, 77th Leg., ch. 1421 (H.B. 2813), § 5, effective June 1, 2003; am. Acts 2003, 78th Leg., ch. 1325 (H.B. 3588), § 17.07, effective September 1, 2003; am. Acts 2009, 81st Leg., ch. 783 (S.B. 1095), § 6, effective September 1, 2009; am. Acts 2009, 81st Leg., ch. 933 (H.B. 3097), § 4.06, effective September 1, 2009.)

### Sec. 2302.203.  Registration of New Business Location.

Before moving a place of business or opening an additional place of business, a salvage vehicle dealer must register the new location with the department.
(Enacted by Acts 2001, 77th Leg., ch. 1421 (H.B. 2813), § 5, effective June 1, 2003.)

### Sec. 2302.204.  [2 Versions: Effective Until January 1, 2012] Casual Sales.

This chapter does not apply to a person who purchases fewer than three nonrepairable motor vehicles or salvage motor vehicles from a salvage vehicle dealer, an insurance company or salvage pool operator in a casual sale at auction, except that:

(1) the board shall adopt rules as necessary to regulate casual sales by salvage vehicle dealers, insurance companies, or salvage pool operators and to enforce this section; and

(2) a salvage vehicle dealer, insurance company, or salvage pool operator who sells a motor vehicle in a casual sale shall comply with those rules and Subchapter E, Chapter 501, Transportation Code.
(Enacted by Acts 2001, 77th Leg., ch. 1421 (H.B. 2813), § 5, effective June 1, 2003; am. Acts 2003, 78th Leg., ch. 1325 (H.B. 3588), § 17.07, effective September 1, 2003; am. Acts 2009, 81st Leg., ch.

Occupations

933 (H.B. 3097), § 3I.09, effective September 1, 2009.)

### Sec. 2302.204.  [2 Versions: Effective January 1, 2012] Casual Sales.

This chapter does not apply to a person who purchases fewer than five nonrepairable motor vehicles or salvage motor vehicles from a salvage vehicle dealer, an insurance company or salvage pool operator in a casual sale at auction, except that:

(1) the board shall adopt rules as necessary to regulate casual sales by salvage vehicle dealers, insurance companies, or salvage pool operators and to enforce this section; and

(2) a salvage vehicle dealer, insurance company, or salvage pool operator who sells a motor vehicle in a casual sale shall comply with those rules and Subchapter E, Chapter 501, Transportation Code.

(Enacted by Acts 2001, 77th Leg., ch. 1421 (H.B. 2813), § 5, effective June 1, 2003; am. Acts 2003, 78th Leg., ch. 1325 (H.B. 3588), § 17.07, effective September 1, 2003; am. Acts 2009, 81st Leg., ch. 933 (H.B. 3097), § 3I.09, effective September 1, 2009; am. Acts 2011, 82nd Leg., ch. 1296 (H.B. 2357), § 245, effective January 1, 2012.)

### Sec. 2302.205.  Duty of Metal Recycler.

A metal recycler who purchases a motor vehicle shall submit a regular certificate of title or a nonrepairable or salvage vehicle title or comparable out-of-state ownership document to the department and comply with Subchapter E, Chapter 501, Transportation Code.

(Enacted by Acts 2001, 77th Leg., ch. 1421 (H.B. 2813), § 5, effective June 1, 2003; am. Acts 2003, 78th Leg., ch. 1325 (H.B. 3588), § 17.07, effective September 1, 2003.)

### SUBCHAPTER F
### ADDITIONAL DUTIES OF SALVAGE VEHICLE DEALER IN CONNECTION WITH MOTOR VEHICLE COMPONENT PARTS

### Sec. 2302.251.  Definitions.

In this subchapter:

(1) "Component part" means a major component part as defined in Section 501.091, Transportation Code, or a minor component part.

(2) "Interior component part" means a seat or radio of a motor vehicle.

(3) "Minor component part" means an interior component part, a special accessory part, or a motor vehicle part that displays or should display one or more of the following:

(A) a federal safety certificate;

(B) a motor number;

(C) a serial number or a derivative; or

(D) a manufacturer's permanent vehicle identification number or a derivative.

(4) "Special accessory part" means a tire, wheel, tailgate, or removable glass top of a motor vehicle.

(Enacted by Acts 2001, 77th Leg., ch. 1421 (H.B. 2813), § 5, effective June 1, 2003; am. Acts 2003, 78th Leg., ch. 1325 (H.B. 3588), § 17.07, effective September 1, 2003.)

### Sec. 2302.252.  Removal of License Plates; Inventory.

(a) Immediately on receipt of a motor vehicle, a salvage vehicle dealer shall remove any unexpired license plates from the vehicle and place the license plates in a secure, locked place.

(b) A salvage vehicle dealer shall maintain on a form provided by the department an inventory of unexpired license plates removed under Subsection (a). The inventory must include:

(1) each license plate number;

(2) the make of the motor vehicle from which the license plate was removed;

(3) the motor number of that vehicle; and

(4) the vehicle identification number of that vehicle.

(Enacted by Acts 2001, 77th Leg., ch. 1421 (H.B. 2813), § 5, effective June 1, 2003.)

### Sec. 2302.253.  Receipt of Motor Vehicle by Holder of Endorsement As Used Vehicle Parts Dealer [Repealed].

Repealed by Acts 2009, 81st Leg., ch. 783 (S.B. 1095), § 12, effective September 1, 2009 and by Acts 2009, 81st Leg., ch. 933 (H.B. 3097), § 4.12, effective September 1, 2009.

(Enacted by Acts 2001, 77th Leg., ch. 1421 (H.B. 2813), § 5, effective June 1, 2003.)

### Sec. 2302.254.  Record of Purchase; Inventory of Parts.

(a) A salvage vehicle dealer shall keep an accurate and legible inventory of each used component part purchased by or delivered to the dealer. The inventory must contain a record of each part that includes:

(1) the date of purchase or delivery;

(2) the name, age, address, sex, and driver's license number of the seller and a legible photocopy of the seller's driver's license;

(3) the license plate number of the motor vehicle in which the part was delivered;

(4) a complete description of the part, including the type of material and, if applicable, the make, model, color, and size of the part; and

(5) the vehicle identification number of the motor vehicle from which the part was removed.

(b) Instead of the information required by Subsection (a), a salvage vehicle dealer may record:

(1) the name of the person who sold the part or the motor vehicle from which the part was obtained; and

(2) the Texas certificate of inventory number or the federal taxpayer identification number of that person.

(c) The department shall prescribe the form of the record required under Subsection (a) and shall make the form available to salvage vehicle dealers.

(d) This section does not apply to:

(1) an interior component part or special accessory part that is from a motor vehicle more than 10 years of age; or

(2) a part delivered to a salvage vehicle dealer by a commercial freight line or commercial carrier.

(Enacted by Acts 2001, 77th Leg., ch. 1421 (H.B. 2813), § 5, effective June 1, 2003.)

### Sec. 2302.255. Assignment of Inventory Number.

(a) A salvage vehicle dealer shall:

(1) assign a unique inventory number to each transaction in which the dealer purchases or takes delivery of a component part;

(2) attach the unique inventory number to each component part the dealer obtains in the transaction; and

(3) retain each component part in its original condition on the business premises of the dealer for at least three calendar days, excluding Sundays, after the date the dealer obtains the part.

(b) An inventory number attached to a component part under Subsection (a) may not be removed while the part remains in the inventory of the salvage vehicle dealer.

(c) A salvage vehicle dealer shall record a component part on an affidavit bill of sale if:

(1) the component part does not have a vehicle identification number or the vehicle identification number has been removed; or

(2) the vehicle identification number of the vehicle from which the component part was removed is not available.

(d) The department shall prescribe and make available the form for the affidavit bill of sale.

(e) This section does not apply to the purchase by a salvage vehicle dealer of a nonoperational engine, transmission, or rear axle assembly from another salvage vehicle dealer or an automotive-related business.

(Enacted by Acts 2001, 77th Leg., ch. 1421 (H.B. 2813), § 5, effective June 1, 2003.)

### Sec. 2302.256. Maintenance of Records.

A salvage vehicle dealer shall keep a record required under this subchapter on a form prescribed by the department. The dealer shall maintain two copies of each record required under this subchapter until the first anniversary of the date the dealer sells or disposes of the item for which the record is maintained.

(Enacted by Acts 2001, 77th Leg., ch. 1421 (H.B. 2813), § 5, effective June 1, 2003.)

### Sec. 2302.257. Surrender of Certain Documents or License Plates.

(a) On demand, a salvage vehicle dealer shall surrender to the department for cancellation a certificate of title or authority, sales receipt or transfer document, license plate, or inventory list that the dealer is required to possess or maintain.

(b) The department shall provide a signed receipt for a surrendered certificate of title or license plate.

(Enacted by Acts 2001, 77th Leg., ch. 1421 (H.B. 2813), § 5, effective June 1, 2003.)

### Sec. 2302.258. Inspection of Records.

(a) A peace officer at any reasonable time may inspect a record required to be maintained under this subchapter, including an inventory record and affidavit bill of sale.

(b) On demand of a peace officer, a salvage vehicle dealer shall give to the officer a copy of a record required to be maintained under this subchapter.

(c) A peace officer may inspect the inventory on the premises of a salvage vehicle dealer at any reasonable time in order to verify, check, or audit the records required to be maintained under this subchapter.

(d) A salvage vehicle dealer or an employee of the dealer shall allow and may not interfere with

Occupations

a peace officer's inspection of the dealer's inventory, premises, or required inventory records or affidavit bills of sale.
(Enacted by Acts 2001, 77th Leg., ch. 1421 (H.B. 2813), § 5, effective June 1, 2003.)

## SUBCHAPTER G
### MOTOR VEHICLE SALVAGE YARDS IN CERTAIN COUNTIES

### Sec. 2302.301.  Application of Subchapter.

This subchapter applies only to a motor vehicle salvage yard located in a county with a population of 2.8 million or more.
(Enacted by Acts 2001, 77th Leg., ch. 1421 (H.B. 2813), § 5, effective June 1, 2003.)

### Sec. 2302.302.  Limits on Operation of Heavy Machinery.

(a) A salvage vehicle dealer may not operate heavy machinery in a motor vehicle salvage yard between the hours of 7 p.m. of one day and 7 a.m. of the following day.

(b) This section does not apply to conduct necessary to a sale or purchase by the dealer.
(Enacted by Acts 2001, 77th Leg., ch. 1421 (H.B. 2813), § 5, effective June 1, 2003; am. Acts 2003, 78th Leg., ch. 1325 (H.B. 3588), § 17.07, effective September 1, 2003.)

## SUBCHAPTER H
### PENALTIES AND ENFORCEMENT

### Sec. 2302.351.  Injunctions.

(a) The prosecutor in the county where a motor vehicle salvage yard is located or the city attorney in the municipality where the salvage yard is located may bring suit to enjoin for a period of less than one year a violation of this chapter.

(b) If a salvage vehicle dealer, an employee of the dealer acting in the course of employment, or a salvage vehicle agent operating under the dealer's license is convicted of more than one offense under Section 2302.353(a), the district attorney for a county in which the dealer's salvage business is located may bring an action in that county to enjoin the dealer's business operations for a period of at least one year.

(c) An action under Subsection (b) must be brought in the name of the state. If judgment is in favor of the state, the court shall:

(1) enjoin the dealer from maintaining or participating in the business of a salvage vehi-

cle dealer for a definite period of at least one year or indefinitely, as determined by the court; and

(2) order that the dealer's place of business be closed for the same period.
(Enacted by Acts 2001, 77th Leg., ch. 1421 (H.B. 2813), § 5, effective June 1, 2003; am. Acts 2003, 78th Leg., ch. 1325 (H.B. 3588), § 17.07, effective September 1, 2003.)

### Sec. 2302.352.  Seizure of Vehicle or Part [Repealed].

Repealed by Acts 2003, 78th Leg., ch. 1325 (H.B. 3588), § 17.09(2), effective September 1, 2003.
(Enacted by Acts 2001, 77th Leg., ch. 1421 (H.B. 2813), § 5, effective June 1, 2003.)

### Sec. 2302.353.  Offenses.

(a) A person commits an offense if the person knowingly violates:

(1) a provision of this chapter other than Subchapter G; or

(2) a rule adopted under a provision of this chapter other than Subchapter G.

(b) A person commits an offense if the person knowingly violates Subchapter G.

(c) An offense under Subsection (a) is a Class A misdemeanor unless it is shown on the trial of the offense that the defendant has been previously convicted of an offense under that subsection, in which event the offense is punishable as a state jail felony.

(d) An offense under Subsection (b) is a Class C misdemeanor.
(Enacted by Acts 2001, 77th Leg., ch. 1421 (H.B. 2813), § 5, effective June 1, 2003; am. Acts 2003, 78th Leg., ch. 1325 (H.B. 3588), § 17.07, effective September 1, 2003.)

### Sec. 2302.354.  Administrative Penalty.

(a) The department may impose an administrative penalty against a person licensed under this chapter who violates this chapter or a rule or order adopted under this chapter.

(b) The penalty may not be less than $50 or more than $1,000, and each day a violation continues or occurs is a separate violation for the purpose of imposing a penalty. The amount of the penalty shall be based on:

(1) the seriousness of the violation, including the nature, circumstances, extent, and gravity of the violation;

Occupations

(2) the economic harm caused by the violation;

(3) the history of previous violations;

(4) the amount necessary to deter a future violation;

(5) efforts to correct the violation; and

(6) any other matter that justice requires.

(c) The person may stay enforcement during the time the order is under judicial review if the person pays the penalty to the court clerk or files a supersedeas bond with the court in the amount of the penalty. A person who cannot afford to pay the penalty or file the bond may stay enforcement by filing an affidavit in the manner required by the Texas Rules of Civil Procedure for a party who cannot afford to file security for costs, subject to the right of the department to contest the affidavit as provided by those rules.

(d) A proceeding to impose an administrative penalty is subject to Chapter 2001, Government Code.

(Enacted by Acts 2011, 82nd Leg., ch. 1296 (H.B. 2357), § 246(a), effective September 1, 2011.)

# CHAPTER 2303
# VEHICLE STORAGE FACILITIES

### Subchapter A. General Provisions

## SUBCHAPTER A
## GENERAL PROVISIONS

### Sec. 2303.001. Short Title.

This chapter may be cited as the Vehicle Storage Facility Act.

(Enacted by Acts 2001, 77th Leg., ch. 1421 (H.B. 2813), § 5, effective June 1, 2003.)

### Sec. 2303.002. Definitions.

In this chapter:

(1) "Abandoned nuisance vehicle" means a motor vehicle that is:

(A) at least 10 years old; and

(B) of a condition only to be demolished, wrecked, or dismantled.

(2) "Commission" means the Texas Commission of Licensing and Regulation.

(3) "Department" means the Texas Department of Licensing and Regulation.

(4) "Executive director" means the executive director of the department.

(5) "Owner of a vehicle" means a person:

(A) named as the purchaser or transferee in the certificate of title issued for the vehicle under Chapter 501, Transportation Code;

(B) in whose name the vehicle is registered under Chapter 502, Transportation Code, or a member of the person's immediate family;

(C) who holds the vehicle through a lease agreement;

(D) who is an unrecorded lienholder entitled to possess the vehicle under the terms of a chattel mortgage; or

(E) who is a lienholder, holds an affidavit of repossession, and is entitled to repossess the vehicle.

(6) "Principal" means an individual who:

(A) personally or constructively holds, including as the beneficiary of a trust:

(i) at least 10 percent of a corporation's outstanding stock; or

(ii) more than $25,000 of the fair market value of a business entity;

(B) has the controlling interest in a business entity;

(C) has a direct or indirect participating interest through shares, stock, or otherwise, regardless of whether voting rights are included, of more than 10 percent of the profits, proceeds, or capital gains of a business entity;

(D) is a member of the board of directors or other governing body of a business entity; or

(E) serves as an elected officer of a business entity.

(7) "Vehicle" means:

(A) a motor vehicle for which the issuance of a certificate of title is required under Chapter 501, Transportation Code; or

(B) any other device designed to be self-propelled or transported on a public highway.

(8) "Vehicle storage facility" means a garage, parking lot, or other facility that is:

(A) owned by a person other than a governmental entity; and

(B) used to store or park at least 10 vehicles each year.

(Enacted by Acts 2001, 77th Leg., ch. 1421 (H.B. 2813), § 5, effective June 1, 2003; am. Acts 2003, 78th Leg., ch. 1276 (H.B. 3507), § 14A.626(a), effective September 1, 2003; am. Acts 2007, 80th Leg., ch. 1046 (H.B. 2094), § 1.01, effective September 1, 2007.)

### Sec. 2303.003.   Exemptions.

(a) This chapter does not apply to a vehicle stored or parked at a vehicle storage facility with the consent of the owner of the vehicle.

(b) This chapter does not apply to a vehicle storage facility operated by a person licensed under Chapter 2301.

(Enacted by Acts 2001, 77th Leg., ch. 1421 (H.B. 2813), § 5, effective June 1, 2003.)

## SUBCHAPTER B
## POWERS AND DUTIES OF COMMISSION AND DEPARTMENT

### Sec. 2303.051.   Rulemaking: License Requirements.

The commission shall adopt rules that:

(1) establish the requirements for a person to be licensed to operate a vehicle storage facility to ensure that the facility maintains adequate standards for the care of stored vehicles;

(2) relate to the administrative sanctions that may be imposed on a person licensed under this chapter;

(3) govern the administration of this chapter.

(Enacted by Acts 2001, 77th Leg., ch. 1421 (H.B. 2813), § 5, effective June 1, 2003; am. Acts 2007, 80th Leg., ch. 1046 (H.B. 2094), § 1.02, effective September 1, 2007.)

### Sec. 2303.052.   Issuance of License; Fees.

(a) The department may issue licenses to operate vehicle storage facilities.

(b) The department may impose and collect a fee for a license in an amount sufficient to cover the costs incurred by the department in administering this chapter.

(Enacted by Acts 2001, 77th Leg., ch. 1421 (H.B. 2813), § 5, effective June 1, 2003.)

### Sec. 2303.053.   Rules Regarding Payment of Fee.

(a) The commission may adopt rules regarding the method of payment of a fee under this chapter.

(b) The rules may authorize the use of:

(1) electronic funds transfer; or

(2) a credit card issued by a financial institution chartered by:

(A) a state or the federal government; or

(B) a nationally recognized credit organization approved by the department.

(c) The rules may require the payment of a discount or a service charge for a credit card payment in addition to the fee.

(Enacted by Acts 2001, 77th Leg., ch. 1421 (H.B. 2813), § 5, effective June 1, 2003.)

## Sec. 2303.054. Rules Restricting Advertising or Competitive Bidding.

(a) The commission may not adopt a rule restricting advertising or competitive bidding by a person licensed under this chapter except to prohibit a false, misleading, or deceptive practice.

(b) In its rules to prohibit a false, misleading, or deceptive practice, the commission may not include a rule that:

(1) restricts the person's use of any advertising medium;

(2) restricts the person's personal appearance or the use of the person's voice in an advertisement;

(3) relates to the size or duration of an advertisement by the person; or

(4) restricts the person's advertisement under a trade name.

(Enacted by Acts 2001, 77th Leg., ch. 1421 (H.B. 2813), § 5, effective June 1, 2003.)

## Sec. 2303.055. Examination of Criminal Conviction.

The department may conduct an examination of any criminal conviction of an applicant, including by obtaining any criminal history record information permitted by law.

(Enacted by Acts 2007, 80th Leg., ch. 1046 (H.B. 2094), § 1.03, effective September 1, 2007.)

## Sec. 2303.056. Periodic and Risk-Based Inspections.

(a) The department may enter and inspect at any time during business hours:

(1) the place of business of any person regulated under this chapter; or

(2) any place in which the department has reasonable cause to believe that a license holder is in violation of this chapter or in violation of a rule or order of the commission or executive director.

(b) At least once every two years, the department shall inspect a vehicle storage facility that holds a license under this chapter.

(c) The department shall conduct additional inspections based on a schedule of risk-based inspections using the following criteria:

(1) the type and nature of the vehicle storage facility;

(2) the inspection history of the vehicle storage facility;

(3) any history of violations involving the vehicle storage facility; and

(4) any other factor determined by the commission by rule.

(d) The vehicle storage facility shall pay a fee for each risk-based inspection performed under Subsection (c). The commission by rule shall set the amount of the fee.

(Enacted by Acts 2007, 80th Leg., ch. 1046 (H.B. 2094), § 1.03, effective September 1, 2007.)

## Sec. 2303.057. Personnel.

The department may employ personnel necessary to administer and enforce this chapter.

(Enacted by Acts 2007, 80th Leg., ch. 1046 (H.B. 2094), § 1.03, effective September 1, 2007.)

## Sec. 2303.058. Advisory Board.

The Towing, Storage, and Booting Advisory Board under Chapter 2308 shall advise the commission in adopting vehicle storage rules under this chapter.

(Enacted by Acts 2007, 80th Leg., ch. 1046 (H.B. 2094), § 1.03, effective September 1, 2007; am. Acts 2009, 81st Leg., ch. 845 (S.B. 2153), § 30, effective September 1, 2009.)

## SUBCHAPTER C

## LICENSE REQUIREMENTS, ISSUANCE, AND RENEWAL

## Sec. 2303.101. Facility License Required.

(a) A person may not operate a vehicle storage facility unless the person holds a license issued under this chapter.

(b) A license issued under this chapter:

(1) is valid only for the person who applied for the license; and

(2) applies only to a single vehicle storage facility named on the license.

(Enacted by Acts 2001, 77th Leg., ch. 1421 (H.B. 2813), § 5, effective June 1, 2003; am. Acts 2007, 80th Leg., ch. 1046 (H.B. 2094), § 1.04, effective September 1, 2007.)

## Sec. 2303.1015. Employee License Required.

(a) A person may not work at a vehicle storage facility unless the person holds a license issued under this chapter.

(b) The commission shall adopt rules governing the application for and issuance of a license under this section.

(Enacted by Acts 2007, 80th Leg., ch. 1046 (H.B. 2094), § 1.05, effective September 1, 2007.)

Occupations

### Sec. 2303.1016.  Vehicle Storage Facility Employee and Towing Operator; Dual License.

(a) The commission shall adopt rules for the issuance of a dual license for a person who is a vehicle storage facility employee and towing operator. The department shall issue the license to an applicant who:

(1) meets the requirements established under:

(A) Section 2303.1015;

(B) Section 2308.153, 2308.154, or 2308.155; and

(C) any applicable rules adopted under this subchapter or Subchapter D, Chapter 2308; and

(2) submits to the department:

(A) an application on a department-approved form; and

(B) the required license fee.

(b) A person holding a license issued under this section may:

(1) work at a vehicle storage facility; and

(2) perform towing operations.

(Enacted by Acts 2009, 81st Leg., ch. 757 (S.B. 702), § 1, effective June 1, 2010.)

### Sec. 2303.102.  License Application.

(a) The commission by rule shall determine the types of information to be included in an application for a license under this chapter on a form prescribed by the executive director.

(b) The rules adopted under this section must require an application for a facility license to list:

(1) the name and address of each partner, if the applicant is a partnership; and

(2) the name and address of the president, secretary, and treasurer of the corporation, if the applicant is a corporation.

(c) A corporation's application must be signed and sworn to by the president and secretary of the corporation.

(Enacted by Acts 2001, 77th Leg., ch. 1421 (H.B. 2813), § 5, effective June 1, 2003; am. Acts 2007, 80th Leg., ch. 1046 (H.B. 2094), § 1.06, effective September 1, 2007.)

### Sec. 2303.103.  Eligibility.

The department shall approve an application submitted as provided by Section 2303.102 unless the department determines that:

(1) the applicant knowingly supplied false or incomplete information on the application;

(2) in the three years preceding the date of application, the applicant, a partner, principal,

or officer of the applicant, or the general manager of the applicant, was convicted of:

(A) a felony; or

(B) a misdemeanor punishable by confinement in jail or by a fine exceeding $500; or

(3) the vehicle storage facility for which the license is sought does not meet the standards for storage facilities established by commission rules.

(Enacted by Acts 2001, 77th Leg., ch. 1421 (H.B. 2813), § 5, effective June 1, 2003.)

### Sec. 2303.104.  Notice of Denial; Opportunity to Comply.

(a) If the department denies an application for a license under this chapter, the department shall send written notice of the decision to the applicant at the address shown on the application by certified mail, return receipt requested.

(b) The notice must state the reason for the department's decision and that the applicant is entitled to a hearing before the department under Subchapter E.

(c) The notice may state that the decision is temporary pending compliance by the applicant. If the decision is temporary and the applicant complies with this chapter and commission rules not later than the 14th day after the date the applicant receives the notice, the department shall approve the application.

(Enacted by Acts 2001, 77th Leg., ch. 1421 (H.B. 2813), § 5, effective June 1, 2003.)

### Sec. 2303.105.  Term of License; Notice of Expiration.

(a) A license issued under this chapter is valid for the period set by the department.

(b) Not later than the 30th day before the expiration date of a person's license, the department shall send written notice of the impending license expiration to the person at the person's last known address according to the department's records.

(Enacted by Acts 2001, 77th Leg., ch. 1421 (H.B. 2813), § 5, effective June 1, 2003.)

### Sec. 2303.106.  Procedure for Renewal.

(a) A person may apply to the department to renew the person's license. The application for renewal must be:

(1) made on a form approved by the department;

(2) submitted to the department before the expiration date of the license; and

(3) accompanied by a nonrefundable fee.

(b) A person whose license expires and is not renewed under this section may apply for a new license under Section 2303.102.

(Enacted by Acts 2001, 77th Leg., ch. 1421 (H.B. 2813), § 5, effective June 1, 2003.)

## SUBCHAPTER D
## PRACTICE BY LICENSE HOLDER

### Sec. 2303.151. Notice to Vehicle Owner or Lienholder.

(a) The operator of a vehicle storage facility who receives a vehicle that is registered in this state and that is towed to the facility for storage shall send a written notice to the registered owner and the primary lienholder of the vehicle not later than the fifth day after the date but not earlier than 24 hours after the date the operator receives the vehicle.

(b) Except as provided by Section 2303.152, the operator of a vehicle storage facility who receives a vehicle that is registered outside this state shall send a written notice to the registered owner and each recorded lienholder of the vehicle not later than the 14th day after the date but not earlier than 24 hours after the date the operator receives the vehicle.

(c) It is a defense to an action initiated by the department for a violation of this section that the operator of the facility unsuccessfully attempted in writing or electronically to obtain information from the governmental entity with which the vehicle is registered.

(d) A notice under this section must:

(1) be correctly addressed;

(2) carry sufficient postage; and

(3) be sent by certified mail, return receipt requested or electronic certified mail.

(e) A notice under this section is considered to have been given on the date indicated on the postmark and to be timely filed if:

(1) the postmark indicates that the notice was mailed within the period described by Subsection (a) or (b), as applicable; or

(2) the notice was published as provided by Section 2303.152.

(Enacted by Acts 2001, 77th Leg., ch. 1421 (H.B. 2813), § 5, effective June 1, 2003; am. Acts 2003, 78th Leg., ch. 1034 (H.B. 849), § 1, effective September 1, 2003; am. Acts 2007, 80th Leg., ch. 1046 (H.B. 2094), § 1.07, effective September 1, 2007.)

### Sec. 2303.1511. Vehicle Storage Facility's Duty to Report After Accepting Unauthorized Vehicle.

(a) A vehicle storage facility accepting a vehicle that is towed under this chapter shall, within two hours after receiving the vehicle, report to the local law enforcement agency with jurisdiction over the area from which the vehicle was towed:

(1) a general description of the vehicle;

(2) the state and number of the vehicle's license plate, if any;

(3) the vehicle identification number of the vehicle, if it can be ascertained;

(4) the location from which the vehicle was towed; and

(5) the name and location of the vehicle storage facility where the vehicle is being stored.

(b) The report required by this section must be made by telephone or electronically or delivered personally or by facsimile.

(c) This section does not apply to a vehicle received as a result of an incident management tow requested by a law enforcement agency unless the law enforcement agency requests a report of incident management tows within the jurisdiction of the agency. In this subsection, "incident management tow" has the meaning assigned by Section 2308.002.

(Enacted by Acts 2009, 81st Leg., ch. 757 (S.B. 702), § 2, effective September 1, 2009; am. Acts 2011, 82nd Leg., ch. 353 (H.B. 3510), § 1, effective September 1, 2011.)

### Sec. 2303.152. Notice by Publication.

(a) Notice to the registered owner and the primary lienholder of a vehicle towed to a vehicle storage facility may be provided by publication in a newspaper of general circulation in the county in which the vehicle is stored if:

(1) the vehicle is registered in another state;

(2) the operator of the storage facility submits to the governmental entity with which the vehicle is registered a written request for information relating to the identity of the registered owner and any lienholder of record;

(3) the identity of the registered owner cannot be determined;

(4) the registration does not contain an address for the registered owner; or

(5) the operator of the storage facility cannot reasonably determine the identity and address of each lienholder.

(b) The written request must:

(1) be correctly addressed;

(2) carry sufficient postage; and

(3) be sent by certified mail, return receipt requested.

(c) Notice by publication is not required if each notice sent as provided by Section 2303.151 is returned because:

(1) the notice was unclaimed or refused; or

(2) the person to whom the notice was sent moved without leaving a forwarding address.

(d) Only one notice is required to be published for an abandoned nuisance vehicle.

(e) Notice to the registered owner and the primary lienholder of a vehicle towed to a vehicle storage facility may be provided by publication in a newspaper of general circulation in the county in which the vehicle is stored if:

(1) the vehicle does not display a license plate or a vehicle inspection certificate indicating the state of registration;

(2) the identity of the registered owner cannot reasonably be determined by the operator of the storage facility; or

(3) the operator of the storage facility cannot reasonably determine the identity and address of each lienholder.

(Enacted by Acts 2001, 77th Leg., ch. 1421 (H.B. 2813), § 5, effective June 1, 2003; am. Acts 2003, 78th Leg., ch. 1276 (H.B. 3507), § 14A.627(a), effective September 1, 2003; am. Acts 2005, 79th Leg., ch. 737 (H.B. 2630), § 9, effective September 1, 2005.)

## Sec. 2303.153. Contents of Notice.

(a) A notice by mail provided under Section 2303.151 must include:

(1) the date the vehicle was accepted for storage;

(2) the first day for which a storage fee is assessed;

(3) the daily storage rate;

(4) the type and amount of any other charge to be paid when the vehicle is claimed;

(5) the full name, street address, and telephone number of the vehicle storage facility;

(6) the hours during which the owner may claim the vehicle; and

(7) the facility license number preceded by "Texas Department of Transportation Vehicle Storage Facility License Number."

(b) A notice by publication provided under Section 2303.152 must include:

(1) the vehicle description;

(2) the total charges;

(3) the full name, street address, and telephone number of the facility; and

(4) the department registration number.

(c) Notice by publication is not required to include any information other than that listed in Subsection (b).

(d) Notice by publication may include a list of more than one vehicle, watercraft, or outboard motor.

(Enacted by Acts 2001, 77th Leg., ch. 1421 (H.B. 2813), § 5, effective June 1, 2003; am. Acts 2003, 78th Leg., ch. 1276 (H.B. 3507), § 14A.627(b), effective September 1, 2003.)

## Sec. 2303.154. Second Notice; Consent to Sale.

(a) If a vehicle is not claimed by a person permitted to claim the vehicle or a law enforcement agency has not taken an action in response to a notice under Section 683.031(c), Transportation Code, before the 15th day after the date notice is mailed or published under Section 2303.151 or 2303.152, the operator of the vehicle storage facility shall send a second notice to the registered owner and the primary lienholder of the vehicle.

(a-1) If a vehicle is not claimed by a person permitted to claim the vehicle before the 10th day after the date notice is mailed or published under Section 2303.151 or 2303.152, the operator of the vehicle storage facility shall consider the vehicle to be abandoned and send notice of abandonment to a law enforcement agency under Chapter 683, Transportation Code.

(b) Notice under this section must include:

(1) the information listed in Section 2303.153(a);

(2) a statement of the right of the facility to dispose of the vehicle under Section 2303.157; and

(3) a statement that the failure of the owner or lienholder to claim the vehicle before the 30th day after the date the notice is provided is:

(A) a waiver by that person of all right, title, or interest in the vehicle; and

(B) a consent to the sale of the vehicle at a public sale.

(c) Notwithstanding Subsection (b), if publication is required for notice under this section, the notice must include:

(1) the information listed in Section 2303.153(b); and

(2) a statement that the failure of the owner or lienholder to claim the vehicle before the date of sale is:

(A) a waiver of all right, title, and interest in the vehicle; and

(B) a consent to the sale of the vehicle at a public sale.

(Enacted by Acts 2001, 77th Leg., ch. 1421 (H.B. 2813), § 5, effective June 1, 2003; am. Acts 2003, 78th Leg., ch. 1276 (H.B. 3507), § 14A.627(c), effective September 1, 2003; am. Acts 2005, 79th Leg., ch. 737 (H.B. 2630), § 10, effective September 1, 2005; am. Acts 2011, 82nd Leg., ch. 353 (H.B. 3510), § 2, effective September 1, 2011.)

## Sec. 2303.1545. Disposition of Abandoned Nuisance Vehicle.

(a) A vehicle storage facility that holds an abandoned nuisance vehicle is not required to send or publish a second notice and is entitled to dispose of the vehicle on the 30th day after the date the notice is mailed or published under Section 2303.151 or 2303.152.

(b) The facility may:

(1) notify the department that notices under Chapter 683, Transportation Code, have been provided and shall pay a fee of $10 to the department; or

(2) in the alternative, notify the appropriate law enforcement agency and pay a fee of $10 to that agency.

(c) A law enforcement agency described by Subsection (b)(2) may sign a document issued by the department.

(Enacted by Acts 2003, 78th Leg., ch. 1276 (H.B. 3507), § 14A.627(d), effective September 1, 2003.)

## Sec. 2303.155. Charges Related to Storage.

(a) For the purposes of this section, "governmental vehicle storage facility" means a garage, parking lot, or other facility that is:

(A) owned by a governmental entity; and

(B) used to store or park at least 10 vehicles each year.

(b) The operator of a vehicle storage facility or governmental vehicle storage facility may charge the owner of a vehicle stored or parked at the facility:

(1) a notification fee set in a reasonable amount for providing notice under this subchapter, including notice under Section 2303.154(c);

(2) an impoundment fee of $20 for any action that:

(A) is taken by or at the direction of the owner or operator of the facility; and

(B) is necessary to preserve, protect, or service a vehicle stored or parked at the facility;

(3) a daily storage fee of:

(A) not less than $5 and not more than $20 for each day or part of a day the vehicle is stored at the facility if the vehicle is not longer than 25 feet; or

(B) $35 for each day or part of a day the vehicle is stored at the facility if the vehicle is longer than 25 feet;

(4) any fee that is required to be submitted to a law enforcement agency, the agency's authorized agent, or a governmental entity; and

(5) a fee in an amount set by the commission for the remediation, recovery, or capture of an environmental or biological hazard.

(c) A notification fee under Subsection (b) may not exceed $50, except that if notice by publication is required by this chapter and the cost of publication exceeds 50 percent of the notification fee, the vehicle storage facility may recover the additional amount of the cost of publication from the vehicle owner or agent.

(d) For purposes of imposing a daily storage fee, a day is considered to begin at midnight and to end at the next following midnight. A daily storage fee may be charged regardless of whether the vehicle is stored for 24 hours of the day, except that a daily storage fee may not be charged for more than one day if the vehicle remains at the facility for less than 12 hours.

(e) The operator of a vehicle storage facility or governmental vehicle storage facility may charge a daily storage fee under Subsection (b):

(1) for not more than five days before the date notice is mailed or published under this subchapter, if the vehicle is registered in this state;

(2) for not more than five days before the date the request for owner information is sent to the appropriate governmental entity as required by this subchapter, if the vehicle is registered in another state; and

(3) for each day the vehicle is in storage after the date the notice is mailed or published until the vehicle is removed and all accrued charges are paid.

(f) The operator of a vehicle storage facility or governmental vehicle storage facility may not charge an additional fee related to the storage of a vehicle other than a fee authorized by this section or a towing fee authorized by Chapter 2308.

Occupations

(g) This section controls over any conflicting municipal ordinance or charter provision.

(Enacted by Acts 2001, 77th Leg., ch. 1421 (H.B. 2813), § 5, effective June 1, 2003; am. Acts 2003, 78th Leg., ch. 1034 (H.B. 849), § 2, effective September 1, 2003; am. Acts 2003, 78th Leg., ch. 1276 (H.B. 3507), § 14A.627(e), effective September 1, 2003; am. Acts 2005, 79th Leg., ch. 737 (H.B. 2630), § 11, effective September 1, 2005; am. Acts 2005, 79th Leg., ch. 1197 (H.B. 480), § 2, effective September 1, 2005; am. Acts 2007, 80th Leg., ch. 1046 (H.B. 2094), §§ 1.08, 3.04, effective September 1, 2007.)

### Sec. 2303.1551.  Required Posting.

(a) All storage fees shall be posted at the licensed vehicle storage facility to which the motor vehicle has been delivered and shall be posted in view of the person who claims the vehicle.

(b) A vehicle storage facility accepting a nonconsent towed vehicle shall post a sign in one inch letters stating "Nonconsent tow fees schedules available on request." The vehicle storage facility shall provide a copy of a nonconsent towing fees schedule on request.

(Enacted by Acts 2009, 81st Leg., ch. 757 (S.B. 702), § 2, effective September 1, 2009.)

### Sec. 2303.156.  Payment by Lienholder or Insurance Company.

(a) A lienholder who repossesses a vehicle delivered to a vehicle storage facility is liable to the operator of the facility for any money owed to the operator in relation to delivery of the vehicle to or storage of the vehicle in the facility regardless of whether an amount accrued before the lienholder repossessed the vehicle.

(b) An insurance company that pays a claim of total loss on a vehicle in a vehicle storage facility is liable to the operator of the facility for any money owed to the operator in relation to delivery of the vehicle to or storage of the vehicle in the facility regardless of whether an amount accrued before the insurance company paid the claim.

(Enacted by Acts 2001, 77th Leg., ch. 1421 (H.B. 2813), § 5, effective June 1, 2003.)

### Sec. 2303.157.  Disposal of Certain Abandoned Vehicles.

(a) The operator of a vehicle storage facility may dispose of a vehicle for which notice is given under Section 2303.154 if, before the 30th day after the date notice is mailed, the vehicle is not:

(1) claimed by a person entitled to claim the vehicle; or

(2) taken into custody by a law enforcement agency under Chapter 683, Transportation Code.

(b) An operator entitled to dispose of a vehicle under this section may sell the vehicle at a public sale without obtaining a release or discharge of any lien on the vehicle, regardless of whether notice was provided by mail or by publication under this chapter. The proceeds from the sale of the vehicle shall be applied to the charges incurred for the vehicle under Section 2303.155. The operator shall pay any excess proceeds to the person entitled to those proceeds.

(c) Notwithstanding Subsection (a), the operator of a vehicle storage facility may dispose of a vehicle for which notice was given under this subchapter as provided by this section if:

(1) the vehicle is an abandoned nuisance vehicle; and

(2) before the 30th day after the date the notice was sent, the facility submits an application to the department for disposal of the vehicle.

(Enacted by Acts 2001, 77th Leg., ch. 1421 (H.B. 2813), § 5, effective June 1, 2003; am. Acts 2003, 78th Leg., ch. 1276 (H.B. 3507), § 14A.628(a), effective September 1, 2003.)

### Sec. 2303.158.  Access to Glove Compartment, Console, or Other Interior Storage Area to Establish Identity or Ownership.

The operator of a vehicle storage facility or a governmental vehicle storage facility must allow a person claiming to be the owner of a vehicle stored or parked at the facility to have access to the vehicle's glove compartment, console, or other interior storage area if documents necessary to establish the person's identity or ownership of the vehicle are located in the glove compartment, console, or other interior storage area.

(Enacted by Acts 2005, 79th Leg., ch. 1197 (H.B. 480), § 3, effective September 1, 2005.)

### Sec. 2303.159.  Forms of Payment of Charges.

(a) The operator of a vehicle storage facility shall accept payment by an electronic check, debit card, or credit card for any charge associated with delivery or storage of a vehicle. The facility shall conspicuously post a sign that states: "This vehicle storage facility must accept payment by an electronic check, credit card, or debit card for any fee or charge associated with delivery or storage of a vehicle." The operator of a vehicle storage facility may not refuse to release a vehicle based on the inability of the facility to accept payment by electronic check, debit card, or credit card of a fee or charge associated with delivery or storage of the vehicle unless the operator, through no fault of the operator, is unable to accept the electronic check, debit card, or credit card because of a power outage or a machine malfunction.

(b) In this section, "vehicle storage facility" includes a governmental vehicle storage facility as defined by Section 2303.155.

(Enacted by Acts 2005, 79th Leg., ch. 1197 (H.B. 480), § 4, effective September 1, 2005; am. Acts 2009, 81st Leg., ch. 1310 (H.B. 2571), § 21, effective September 1, 2009.)

### Sec. 2303.160. Release of Vehicles.

(a) A vehicle storage facility may not refuse to release a vehicle to the owner or operator of the vehicle or require a sworn affidavit of the owner or operator of the vehicle solely because the owner or operator presents valid photo identification issued by this state, another state, or a federal agency that includes a different address than the address contained in the title and registration records of the vehicle.

(b) A vehicle storage facility must accept evidence of financial responsibility, as required by Section 601.051, Transportation Code, as an additional form of identification that establishes ownership or right of possession or control of the vehicle.

(c) Subsection (b) does not require a vehicle storage facility to release a vehicle to the owner or operator of the vehicle if the owner or operator of the vehicle does not:

(1) pay the charges for services regulated under this chapter or Chapter 2308, including charges for an incident management tow, as defined by Section 2308.002; and

(2) present valid photo identification issued by this state, another state, a federal agency, or a foreign government.

(Enacted by Acts 2007, 80th Leg., ch. 271 (H.B. 90), § 1, effective September 1, 2007; am. Acts 2011, 82nd Leg., ch. 353 (H.B. 3510), § 3, effective September 1, 2011.)

### Sec. 2303.161. Drug Testing of Employees.

(a) A license holder shall establish a drug testing policy for employees of the vehicle storage facility operated by the license holder. A license holder that establishes a drug testing policy under this subsection may adopt the model drug testing policy adopted by the commission or may use another drug testing policy that the department determines is at least as stringent as the policy adopted by the commission.

(b) The commission by rule shall adopt a model drug testing policy for use by license holders. The model drug testing policy must be designed to ensure the safety of the public through appropriate drug testing and to protect the rights of employees. The model drug testing policy must:

(1) require at least one scheduled drug test each year for each employee of a vehicle storage facility who has direct contact with the public; and

(2) authorize random, unannounced drug testing for employees described by Subdivision (1).

(Enacted by Acts 2007, 80th Leg., ch. 1046 (H.B. 2094), § 1.09, effective September 1, 2007; am. Acts 2009, 81st Leg., ch. 87 (S.B. 1969), § 27.001(75), effective September 1, 2009 (renumbered from Sec. 2303.160).)

## SUBCHAPTER E
## DISCIPLINARY ACTION AND PROCEDURES
## [REPEALED]

### Sec. 2303.201. Disciplinary Action Based on Violation of Chapter [Repealed].

Repealed by Acts 2007, 80th Leg., ch. 1046 (H.B. 2094), § 5.01(b), effective September 1, 2007.

(Enacted by Acts 2001, 77th Leg., ch. 1421 (H.B. 2813), § 5, effective June 1, 2003.)

### Sec. 2303.202. Disciplinary Action Based on Certain Criminal Convictions [Repealed].

Repealed by Acts 2007, 80th Leg., ch. 1046 (H.B. 2094), § 5.01(b), effective September 1, 2007.

(Enacted by Acts 2001, 77th Leg., ch. 1421 (H.B. 2813), § 5, effective June 1, 2003.)

### Sec. 2303.203. Right to Hearing [Repealed].

Repealed by Acts 2007, 80th Leg., ch. 1046 (H.B. 2094), § 5.01(b), effective September 1, 2007.

(Enacted by Acts 2001, 77th Leg., ch. 1421 (H.B. 2813), § 5, effective June 1, 2003.)

### Sec. 2303.204.  Hearing; Decision by Director [Repealed].

Repealed by Acts 2007, 80th Leg., ch. 1046 (H.B. 2094), § 5.01(b), effective September 1, 2007.

(Enacted by Acts 2001, 77th Leg., ch. 1421 (H.B. 2813), § 5, effective June 1, 2003.)

### Sec. 2303.205.  Administrative Procedure [Repealed].

Repealed by Acts 2007, 80th Leg., ch. 1046 (H.B. 2094), § 5.01(b), effective September 1, 2007.

(Enacted by Acts 2001, 77th Leg., ch. 1421 (H.B. 2813), § 5, effective June 1, 2003.)

## SUBCHAPTER F
## ADMINISTRATIVE PENALTY
## [REPEALED]

### Sec. 2303.251.  Imposition of Administrative Penalty [Repealed].

Repealed by Acts 2007, 80th Leg., ch. 1046 (H.B. 2094), § 5.01(b), effective September 1, 2007.

(Enacted by Acts 2001, 77th Leg., ch. 1421 (H.B. 2813), § 5, effective June 1, 2003.)

### Sec. 2303.252.  Amount of Administrative Penalty [Repealed].

Repealed by Acts 2007, 80th Leg., ch. 1046 (H.B. 2094), § 5.01(b), effective September 1, 2007.

(Enacted by Acts 2001, 77th Leg., ch. 1421 (H.B. 2813), § 5, effective June 1, 2003.)

### Sec. 2303.253.  Opportunity for Hearing [Repealed].

Repealed by Acts 2007, 80th Leg., ch. 1046 (H.B. 2094), § 5.01(b), effective September 1, 2007.

(Enacted by Acts 2001, 77th Leg., ch. 1421 (H.B. 2813), § 5, effective June 1, 2003.)

### Sec. 2303.254.  Hearing [Repealed].

Repealed by Acts 2007, 80th Leg., ch. 1046 (H.B. 2094), § 5.01(b), effective September 1, 2007.

(Enacted by Acts 2001, 77th Leg., ch. 1421 (H.B. 2813), § 5, effective June 1, 2003.)

### Sec. 2303.255.  Decision by Director [Repealed].

Repealed by Acts 2007, 80th Leg., ch. 1046 (H.B. 2094), § 5.01(b), effective September 1, 2007.

(Enacted by Acts 2001, 77th Leg., ch. 1421 (H.B. 2813), § 5, effective June 1, 2003.)

### Sec. 2303.256.  Options Following Decision: Pay or Appeal [Repealed].

Repealed by Acts 2007, 80th Leg., ch. 1046 (H.B. 2094), § 5.01(b), effective September 1, 2007.

(Enacted by Acts 2001, 77th Leg., ch. 1421 (H.B. 2813), § 5, effective June 1, 2003.)

### Sec. 2303.257.  Collection of Penalty [Repealed].

Repealed by Acts 2007, 80th Leg., ch. 1046 (H.B. 2094), § 5.01(b), effective September 1, 2007.

(Enacted by Acts 2001, 77th Leg., ch. 1421 (H.B. 2813), § 5, effective June 1, 2003.)

### Sec. 2303.258.  Remittance of Penalty and Interest [Repealed].

Repealed by Acts 2007, 80th Leg., ch. 1046 (H.B. 2094), § 5.01(b), effective September 1, 2007.

(Enacted by Acts 2001, 77th Leg., ch. 1421 (H.B. 2813), § 5, effective June 1, 2003.)

## SUBCHAPTER G
## OTHER PENALTIES AND
## ENFORCEMENT PROVISIONS

### Sec. 2303.301.  Injunction; Civil Penalty.

(a) If a person has violated, is violating, or is threatening to violate this chapter or a rule or order adopted under this chapter, the department or the attorney general at the request of the department may institute an action for:

(1) injunctive relief;

(2) a civil penalty not to exceed $1,000 for each violation; or

(3) both injunctive relief and the civil penalty.

(b) If the department or the attorney general prevails in an action under this section, the department or the attorney general is entitled to recover reasonable attorney's fees and court costs.

(Enacted by Acts 2001, 77th Leg., ch. 1421 (H.B. 2813), § 5, effective June 1, 2003.)

### Sec. 2303.302. Criminal Penalties.

(a) A person commits an offense if the person:

(1) violates the licensing requirements of this chapter; or

(2) employs an individual who does not hold an appropriate license required by this chapter.

(b) An offense under this section is a Class C misdemeanor.

(Enacted by Acts 2001, 77th Leg., ch. 1421 (H.B. 2813), § 5, effective June 1, 2003; am. Acts 2007, 80th Leg., ch. 1046 (H.B. 2094), § 1.10, effective September 1, 2007.)

### Sec. 2303.303. Authority to Arrest.

A peace officer or license and weight inspector for the Department of Public Safety may make an arrest for a violation of a rule adopted under this chapter.

(Enacted by Acts 2001, 77th Leg., ch. 1421 (H.B. 2813), § 5, effective June 1, 2003.)

### Sec. 2303.304. Administrative Penalty.

(a) The commission may impose an administrative penalty on a person under Subchapter F, Chapter 51, regardless of whether the person holds a registration, permit, or license under this chapter, if the person violates:

(1) this chapter or a rule adopted under this chapter; or

(2) a rule or order of the executive director or commission.

(b) An administrative penalty may not be imposed unless the person charged with a violation is provided the opportunity for a hearing.

(Enacted by Acts 2007, 80th Leg., ch. 1046 (H.B. 2094), § 1.11, effective September 1, 2007.)

### Sec. 2303.305. Cease and Desist Order; Injunction; Civil Penalty.

(a) The executive director may issue a cease and desist order as necessary to enforce this chapter if the executive director determines that the action is necessary to prevent a violation of this chapter and to protect public health and safety.

(b) The attorney general or executive director may institute an action for an injunction or a civil penalty under this chapter as provided by Section 51.352.

(Enacted by Acts 2007, 80th Leg., ch. 1046 (H.B. 2094), § 1.11, effective September 1, 2007.)

# CHAPTER 2304
# NONMECHANICAL REPAIRS TO MOTOR VEHICLES

### Subchapter A. General Provisions

## SUBCHAPTER A
## GENERAL PROVISIONS

### Sec. 2304.001. Definitions.

In this chapter:

(1) "Commission" means the Texas Natural Resource Conservation Commission.

(2) "Executive director" means the executive director of the Texas Natural Resource Conservation Commission.

(3) "Motor vehicle" means a vehicle with at least four wheels that is self-propelled and that can transport a person or property on a public street or highway. The term does not include a vehicle that is used exclusively on stationary tracks.

(4) "Repair facility" means a person that engages in the business of repairing or replacing the nonmechanical exterior or interior body parts of a damaged motor vehicle.

(Enacted by Acts 2001, 77th Leg., ch. 1421 (H.B. 2813), § 5, effective June 1, 2003.)

### Sec. 2304.002. Application of Chapter.

This chapter does not apply to a repair facility located in a county with a population of 50,000 or less.

(Enacted by Acts 2001, 77th Leg., ch. 1421 (H.B. 2813), § 5, effective June 1, 2003.)

## SUBCHAPTER B
## CERTIFICATE OF REGISTRATION

### Sec. 2304.051.  Registration Required.

A repair facility shall register with the commission as provided by this chapter and the rules adopted by the commission.
(Enacted by Acts 2001, 77th Leg., ch. 1421 (H.B. 2813), § 5, effective June 1, 2003.)

### Sec. 2304.052.  Application.

(a) The commission by rule shall:

(1) prescribe an application form for the issuance or renewal of a certificate of registration; and

(2) determine the information to be disclosed on the application.

(b) The application must include:

(1) the name, street address, and mailing address of each location at which the applicant operates a repair facility;

(2) the name and address of:

(A) each owner, partner, officer, or director of the applicant; and

(B) if the applicant is a corporation, each shareholder holding 10 percent or more of the outstanding shares;

(3) the identification number assigned by, or a statement of other evidence of compliance with any applicable requirements of:

(A) the United States Environmental Protection Agency;

(B) the United States Occupational Safety and Health Administration;

(C) the commission;

(D) the Texas Department of Health;

(E) the comptroller; and

(F) a municipality or county; and

(4) a statement of each conviction obtained against the applicant or a partner or officer of the applicant during the three years preceding the date of the application of:

(A) a felony; or

(B) a misdemeanor punishable by confinement in jail or by a fine exceeding $200.
(Enacted by Acts 2001, 77th Leg., ch. 1421 (H.B. 2813), § 5, effective June 1, 2003.)

### Sec. 2304.053.  Issuance and Renewal of Certificate.

(a) An applicant for the issuance or renewal of a certificate of registration shall submit to the executive director a sworn application on the form prescribed by the commission accompanied by a $50 fee.

(b) On receipt of the application and required fee, the executive director shall issue a certificate of registration to the applicant.

(c) A certificate of registration expires on the first anniversary of the date of issuance and may be renewed annually in the manner prescribed by the commission. An application for renewal must be submitted to the executive director within 30 days before the expiration date of the certificate.
(Enacted by Acts 2001, 77th Leg., ch. 1421 (H.B. 2813), § 5, effective June 1, 2003.)

### Sec. 2304.054.  Form of Certificate; Transferability.

A certificate of registration:

(1) must contain a unique number;

(2) applies only to the person whose name appears on the certificate or an employee of that person; and

(3) is not transferable.
(Enacted by Acts 2001, 77th Leg., ch. 1421 (H.B. 2813), § 5, effective June 1, 2003.)

### Sec. 2304.055.  Replacement Certificate.

(a) If a certificate of registration is lost or destroyed, the certificate holder may apply to the executive director for a replacement certificate of registration.

(b) The certificate holder must submit:

(1) an affidavit verifying that the certificate of registration was lost or destroyed; and

(2) a $25 replacement fee.

(c) The executive director shall issue a replacement certificate of registration on receipt of the affidavit and replacement fee.

(d) A replacement certificate of registration must be clearly identified as a replacement certificate on the certificate and in the records of the commission.
(Enacted by Acts 2001, 77th Leg., ch. 1421 (H.B. 2813), § 5, effective June 1, 2003.)

### Sec. 2304.056.  Voluntary Surrender of Certificate.

A certificate holder may terminate a certificate of registration at any time by voluntarily surrendering the certificate.
(Enacted by Acts 2001, 77th Leg., ch. 1421 (H.B. 2813), § 5, effective June 1, 2003.)

### Sec. 2304.057.  Cancellation of Certificate.

(a) On the expiration, termination, or surrender of a certificate of registration, the certificate holder shall deliver the certificate to the executive director.

(b) The executive director shall:

(1) cancel the certificate; or

(2) endorse on the certificate the date of expiration, termination, or surrender.

(Enacted by Acts 2001, 77th Leg., ch. 1421 (H.B. 2813), § 5, effective June 1, 2003.)

### Sec. 2304.058.  Maintenance of Registration Information.

(a) The executive director shall maintain each application for a certificate of registration and a copy of each certificate of registration in a convenient form that is available to the public.

(b) The executive director shall annually publish a list of:

(1) the name and address of each person registered under this chapter; and

(2) the name of each person whose registration has been revoked, suspended, or surrendered during the period and the specific date of the suspension, revocation, or surrender.

(Enacted by Acts 2001, 77th Leg., ch. 1421 (H.B. 2813), § 5, effective June 1, 2003.)

### SUBCHAPTER C
### PRACTICE BY CERTIFICATE HOLDER

### Sec. 2304.101.  Display of Certificate.

A certificate holder shall publicly display the current certificate of registration at the certificate holder's place of business in a location readily visible to a customer paying for repairs.

(Enacted by Acts 2001, 77th Leg., ch. 1421 (H.B. 2813), § 5, effective June 1, 2003.)

### Sec. 2304.102.  Registration Number.

A certificate holder shall include the certificate holder's registration number:

(1) on each repair estimate, repair order, or correspondence; and

(2) in each advertisement for motor vehicle repairs by the repair facility.

(Enacted by Acts 2001, 77th Leg., ch. 1421 (H.B. 2813), § 5, effective June 1, 2003.)

### Sec. 2304.103.  False Statements.

A certificate holder may not make a false or fraudulent statement in connection with:

(1) a repair; or

(2) an attempt to collect compensation for a repair.

(Enacted by Acts 2001, 77th Leg., ch. 1421 (H.B. 2813), § 5, effective June 1, 2003.)

### Sec. 2304.104.  Record of Vehicle Repairs.

(a) A certificate holder shall maintain in a convenient place a record of each motor vehicle that enters the certificate holder's premises for a repair. Except as provided by Subsection (b), the certificate holder shall include in the record:

(1) a description of the vehicle;

(2) the vehicle identification number;

(3) the date the vehicle entered the certificate holder's premises;

(4) the odometer reading at the time the vehicle is received;

(5) the name and address of the person from whom the vehicle is received; and

(6) a signed authorization for the work to be performed on the vehicle.

(b) If a motor vehicle is towed to the certificate holder's repair facility without the consent of the owner of the vehicle, the information in the record is the information provided by the law enforcement agency that initiated the towing process.

(Enacted by Acts 2001, 77th Leg., ch. 1421 (H.B. 2813), § 5, effective June 1, 2003.)

### SUBCHAPTER D
### ENFORCEMENT PROVISIONS

### Sec. 2304.151.  Inspection of Premises and Record.

The executive director or an employee of the commission may, at any time, inspect:

(1) a record maintained under Section 2304.104; and

(2) the premises of a certificate holder's place of business.

(Enacted by Acts 2001, 77th Leg., ch. 1421 (H.B. 2813), § 5, effective June 1, 2003.)

### Sec. 2304.152.  Administrative Disciplinary Action and Procedures.

(a) The commission shall adopt rules establishing:

(1) grounds for suspension, revocation, or reinstatement of a certificate of registration; and

(2) procedures for taking disciplinary action.

Occupations

(b) The executive director may suspend or revoke a certificate of registration based on a ground established under this section.

(c) Procedures for the suspension or revocation of a certificate of registration are governed by Chapter 2001, Government Code.

(Enacted by Acts 2001, 77th Leg., ch. 1421 (H.B. 2813), § 5, effective June 1, 2003.)

### Sec. 2304.153.  Failure to Register; Civil Penalty.

(a) A repair facility that fails to register under this chapter is liable to the state for a civil penalty of $250.

(b) The executive director shall waive the penalty if the repair facility applies for registration not later than the 10th day after the date of notice of the violation.

(Enacted by Acts 2001, 77th Leg., ch. 1421 (H.B. 2813), § 5, effective June 1, 2003.)

### Sec. 2304.154.  Violation of Chapter; Civil Penalty.

Except as provided by Section 2304.153, a person that violates this chapter is liable to the state for a civil penalty in an amount not to exceed $100.

(Enacted by Acts 2001, 77th Leg., ch. 1421 (H.B. 2813), § 5, effective June 1, 2003.)

# CHAPTER 2305
## RECORDS OF CERTAIN VEHICLE REPAIRS, SALES, AND PURCHASES

### Subchapter A. Records Maintained by Certain Entities

## SUBCHAPTER A
## RECORDS MAINTAINED BY CERTAIN ENTITIES

### Sec. 2305.001.  Definitions.

In this subchapter:

(1) "Person" means an individual, corporation, or firm.

(2) "Repair" includes the rebuilding of a motor vehicle, the installation of a new or used part or accessory on a motor vehicle, and the performance of electrical work in connection with the repair of a motor vehicle. The term does not include a repair covered by Chapter 2304.

(3) "Used motor vehicle" includes a second-hand motor vehicle.

(4) "Motor vehicle" has the meaning assigned by Section 501.002, Transportation Code.

(Enacted by Acts 2001, 77th Leg., ch. 1421 (H.B. 2813), § 5, effective June 1, 2003; am. Acts 2005, 79th Leg., ch. 761 (H.B. 3221), § 1, effective September 1, 2005.)

### Sec. 2305.002.  Application of Subchapter.

This subchapter applies to any person who:

(1) operates a shop or garage that is engaged in the business of repairing motor vehicles; or

(2) engages in the business of purchasing or selling used motor vehicles in this state.

(Enacted by Acts 2001, 77th Leg., ch. 1421 (H.B. 2813), § 5, effective June 1, 2003; am. Acts 2005, 79th Leg., ch. 761 (H.B. 3221), § 2, effective September 1, 2005.)

### Sec. 2305.003.  Register of Repairs.

(a) A person subject to this subchapter shall maintain a register of each repair the person makes to a motor vehicle. The register must contain a substantially complete and accurate description of each motor vehicle that is repaired.

(b) This section does not apply to a repair having a value of $1 or less.

(Enacted by Acts 2001, 77th Leg., ch. 1421 (H.B. 2813), § 5, effective June 1, 2003; am. Acts 2005, 79th Leg., ch. 761 (H.B. 3221), § 3, effective September 1, 2005.)

### Sec. 2305.004.  Register of Used Motor Vehicle Sales and Purchases.

(a) A person subject to this subchapter shall maintain a register of each sale or purchase the person makes of a used motor vehicle.

(b) If the person buys a used motor vehicle, the register must contain:

(1) the make and model, the number of cylinders, the motor number, the vehicle identification number, and the passenger capacity of the motor vehicle, if applicable;

(2) the name, date of birth, usual place of address, and official identification number of each person claiming to be the owner of the motor vehicle; and

(3) the state registration number of the motor vehicle, if applicable.

(c) If the person sells a used motor vehicle, in addition to the requirements of Subsection (b), the register must contain the name and address of the purchaser of the motor vehicle.

(Enacted by Acts 2001, 77th Leg., ch. 1421 (H.B. 2813), § 5, effective June 1, 2003; am. Acts 2005, 79th Leg., ch. 761 (H.B. 3221), § 4, effective September 1, 2005.)

### Sec. 2305.005. Record of Replaced Cylinder Block.

The owner of the garage or repair shop that installs a replacement cylinder block and stamps the original engine number on the block as required by Section 2305.051 shall record in a substantially bound book:

(1) the name and address of the vehicle's owner; and

(2) the engine number and registration number of the vehicle.

(Enacted by Acts 2001, 77th Leg., ch. 1421 (H.B. 2813), § 5, effective June 1, 2003.)

### Sec. 2305.006. Maintenance of Records.

(a) All records required to be maintained under this subchapter shall be kept until at least the first anniversary of the date the record is made.

(b) The registers required by Sections 2305.003 and 2305.004 shall be maintained in a clear and intelligent manner in a well-bound book or an electronic recordkeeping system and kept in a secure place in the office or place of business where the work is performed or the business is conducted.

(Enacted by Acts 2001, 77th Leg., ch. 1421 (H.B. 2813), § 5, effective June 1, 2003; am. Acts 2005, 79th Leg., ch. 761 (H.B. 3221), § 5, effective September 1, 2005.)

### Sec. 2305.007. Entry and Inspection.

(a) Except as provided by Subsection (b), for the purpose of enforcing or administering this chapter, Chapter 2302 of this code, or Chapter 501 or 502, Transportation Code, a member of the Texas Transportation Commission, an employee of the Texas Transportation Commission or Texas Department of Transportation, a member of the Public Safety Commission, an officer of the Department of Public Safety, or another peace officer who is interested in tracing or locating a stolen motor vehicle may at a reasonable time:

(1) enter the premises of a business regulated under one of those chapters; and

(2) inspect or copy any document, record, vehicle, part, or other item regulated under one of those chapters.

(b) For the purposes of tracing or locating a stolen motor vehicle on the premises of a person engaging in a business or activity regulated under this chapter who is also licensed under Chapter 348 or 353, Finance Code, only an officer of the Department of Public Safety may at a reasonable time:

(1) enter the premises of the person's business; and

(2) inspect or copy any document, record, vehicle, part, or other item regulated under:

(A) this chapter; or

(B) Chapter 348 or 353, Finance Code.

(c) A person engaging in a business or activity regulated under this chapter shall cooperate with a person conducting an inspection under this section to assist in the recovery of stolen motor vehicles and parts and to prevent the sale or transfer of stolen motor vehicles and parts.

(d) An entry or inspection occurs at a reasonable time for purposes of Subsection (a) or (b) if the entry or inspection occurs:

(1) during normal business hours of the person or activity regulated under a chapter listed in Subsection (a) or (b); or

(2) while an activity regulated under a chapter listed in Subsection (a) or (b) is occurring on the premises.

(Enacted by Acts 2005, 79th Leg., ch. 761 (H.B. 3221), § 6, effective September 1, 2005; am. Acts 2011, 82nd Leg., ch. 117 (H.B. 2559), § 21, effective September 1, 2011.)

### SUBCHAPTER B
### REQUIREMENT APPLICABLE TO OWNERS OF CERTAIN MOTOR VEHICLES

### Sec. 2305.051. Replacement of Cylinder Block.

The owner of a motor vehicle registered under Chapter 502, Transportation Code, that has a damaged cylinder block replaced shall have the original engine number of the motor vehicle stamped with a steel die on the replacement cylinder block.

(Enacted by Acts 2001, 77th Leg., ch. 1421 (H.B. 2813), § 5, effective June 1, 2003.)

## SUBCHAPTER C
## ENFORCEMENT

### Sec. 2305.101.  Criminal Penalty.

(a) A person commits an offense if the person violates this chapter or a rule adopted under this chapter.

(b) Except as provided by Subsection (c), an offense under this section is punishable by a fine of not less than $10 and not more than $100.

(c) An offense under this chapter that consists of the violation of Section 2305.007 is a Class A misdemeanor.

(Enacted by Acts 2001, 77th Leg., ch. 1421 (H.B. 2813), § 5, effective June 1, 2003; am. Acts 2005, 79th Leg., ch. 761 (H.B. 3221), § 7, effective September 1, 2005.)

## CHAPTER 2308
## VEHICLE TOWING AND BOOTING

## SUBCHAPTER A
## GENERAL PROVISIONS

### Sec. 2308.001. Short Title.

This chapter may be cited as the Texas Towing and Booting Act.

(Enacted by Acts 2007, 80th Leg., ch. 1046 (H.B. 2094), § 1.12, effective September 1, 2007; am. Acts 2009, 81st Leg., ch. 845 (S.B. 2153), § 2, effective September 1, 2009.)

### Sec. 2308.002. Definitions.

In this chapter:

(1) "Advisory board" means the Towing, Storage, and Booting Advisory Board.

(1-a) "Boot" means a lockable road wheel clamp or similar vehicle immobilization device that is designed to immobilize a parked vehicle and prevent its movement until the device is unlocked or removed.

(1-b) "Booting company" means a person that controls, installs, or directs the installation and removal of one or more boots.

(1-c) "Boot operator" means an individual who installs or removes a boot on or from a vehicle.

(2) "Commission" means the Texas Commission of Licensing and Regulation.

(3) "Consent tow" means any tow of a motor vehicle in which the tow truck is summoned by the owner or operator of the vehicle or by a person who has possession, custody, or control of the vehicle. The term does not include an incident management tow or a private property tow.

(4) "Department" means the Texas Department of Licensing and Regulation.

(5) "Driver's license" has the meaning assigned by Section 521.001, Transportation Code.

(5-a) "Incident management tow" means any tow of a vehicle in which the tow truck is summoned to the scene of a traffic accident or to an incident, including the removal of a vehicle, commercial cargo, and commercial debris from an accident or incident scene.

(6) "Nonconsent tow" means any tow of a motor vehicle that is not a consent tow, including:

(A) an incident management tow; and

(B) a private property tow.

(7) "Parking facility" means public or private property used, wholly or partly, for restricted or paid vehicle parking. The term includes:

(A) a restricted space on a portion of an otherwise unrestricted parking facility; and

(B) a commercial parking lot, a parking garage, and a parking area serving or adjacent to a business, church, school, home that charges a fee for parking, apartment com-

*Occupations*

plex, property governed by a property owners' association, or government-owned property leased to a private person, including:

    (i) a portion of the right-of-way of a public roadway that is leased by a governmental entity to the parking facility owner; and

    (ii) the area between the facility's property line abutting a county or municipal public roadway and the center line of the roadway's drainage way or the curb of the roadway, whichever is farther from the facility's property line.

(7-a) "Parking facility authorized agent" means an employee or agent of a parking facility owner with the authority to:

    (A) authorize the removal of a vehicle from the parking facility on behalf of the parking facility owner; and

    (B) accept service on behalf of the parking facility owner of a notice of hearing requested under this chapter.

(8) "Parking facility owner" means:

    (A) an individual, corporation, partnership, limited partnership, limited liability company, association, trust, or other legal entity owning or operating a parking facility;

    (B) a property owners' association having control under a dedicatory instrument, as that term is defined in Section 202.001, Property Code, over assigned or unassigned parking areas; or

    (C) a property owner having an exclusive right under a dedicatory instrument, as that term is defined in Section 202.001, Property Code, to use a parking space.

(8-a) "Private property tow" means any tow of a vehicle authorized by a parking facility owner without the consent of the owner or operator of the vehicle.

(9) "Property owners' association" has the meaning assigned by Section 202.001, Property Code.

(10) "Public roadway" means a public street, alley, road, right-of-way, or other public way, including paved and unpaved portions of the right-of-way.

(11) "Tow truck" means a motor vehicle, including a wrecker, equipped with a mechanical device used to tow, winch, or otherwise move another motor vehicle. The term does not include:

    (A) a motor vehicle owned and operated by a governmental entity, including a public school district;

    (B) a motor vehicle towing:

       (i) a race car;

       (ii) a motor vehicle for exhibition; or

       (iii) an antique motor vehicle;

    (C) a recreational vehicle towing another vehicle;

    (D) a motor vehicle used in combination with a tow bar, tow dolly, or other mechanical device if the vehicle is not operated in the furtherance of a commercial enterprise;

    (E) a motor vehicle that is controlled or operated by a farmer or rancher and used for towing a farm vehicle; or

    (F) a motor vehicle that:

       (i) is owned or operated by an entity the primary business of which is the rental of motor vehicles; and

       (ii) only tows vehicles rented by the entity.

(12) "Towing company" means an individual, association, corporation, or other legal entity that controls, operates, or directs the operation of one or more tow trucks over a public roadway in this state but does not include a political subdivision of the state.

(13) "Unauthorized vehicle" means a vehicle parked, stored, or located on a parking facility without the consent of the parking facility owner.

(14) "Vehicle" means a device in, on, or by which a person or property may be transported on a public roadway. The term includes an operable or inoperable automobile, truck, motorcycle, recreational vehicle, or trailer but does not include a device moved by human power or used exclusively on a stationary rail or track.

(15) "Vehicle owner" means a person:

    (A) named as the purchaser or transferee in the certificate of title issued for the vehicle under Chapter 501, Transportation Code;

    (B) in whose name the vehicle is registered under Chapter 502, Transportation Code, or a member of the person's immediate family;

    (C) who holds the vehicle through a lease agreement;

    (D) who is an unrecorded lienholder entitled to possess the vehicle under the terms of a chattel mortgage; or

    (E) who is a lienholder holding an affidavit of repossession and entitled to repossess the vehicle.

(16) "Vehicle storage facility" means a vehicle storage facility, as defined by Section

2303.002, that is operated by a person who holds a license issued under Chapter 2303 to operate the facility.

(Enacted by Acts 2007, 80th Leg., ch. 1046 (H.B. 2094), § 1.12, effective September 1, 2007; am. Acts 2009, 81st Leg., ch. 757 (S.B. 702), § 3, effective September 1, 2009; am. Acts 2009, 81st Leg., ch. 845 (S.B. 2153), § 3, effective September 1, 2009; am. Acts 2009, 81st Leg., ch. 1310 (H.B. 2571), § 1, effective September 1, 2009; am. Acts 2011, 82nd Leg., ch. 353 (H.B. 3510), § 4, effective September 1, 2011.)

### Sec. 2308.003.  Study of Nonconsent Towing Fees [Expired].

Expired pursuant to Acts 2007, 80th Leg., ch. 1046 (H.B. 2094), § 1.12, effective September 1, 2009.

### Sec. 2308.004.  Exemption.

(a) This chapter does not apply to a person who, while exercising a statutory or contractual lien right with regard to a vehicle:

(1) installs or removes a boot; or

(2) controls, installs, or directs the installation and removal of one or more boots.

(b) This chapter does not apply to a commercial office building owner or manager who installs or removes a boot in the building's parking facility.

(Enacted by Acts 2009, 81st Leg., ch. 845 (S.B. 2153), § 4, effective September 1, 2009.)

## SUBCHAPTER B
## ADVISORY BOARD

### Sec. 2308.051.  Towing, Storage, and Booting Advisory Board.

(a) The advisory board consists of the following members appointed by the presiding officer of the commission with the approval of the commission:

(1) one representative of a towing company operating in a county with a population of less than one million;

(2) one representative of a towing company operating in a county with a population of one million or more;

(3) one owner of a vehicle storage facility located in a county with a population of less than one million;

(4) one owner of a vehicle storage facility located in a county with a population of one million or more;

(5) one parking facility owner;

(6) one law enforcement officer from a county with a population of less than one million;

(7) one law enforcement officer from a county with a population of one million or more;

(8) one representative of property and casualty insurers who write automobile insurance in this state; and

(9) **[2 Versions: As added by Acts 2009, 81st Leg., ch. 457]** one public member.

(9) **[2 Versions: As added by Acts 2009, 81st Leg., ch. 845]** one representative of a booting company.

(b) The advisory board must include representation for each classification of towing.

(c) An appointment to the advisory board shall be made without regard to the race, color, disability, sex, religion, age, or national origin of the appointee.

(Enacted by Acts 2007, 80th Leg., ch. 1046 (H.B. 2094), § 1.12, effective September 1, 2007; am. Acts 2009, 81st Leg., ch. 457 (H.B. 2548), § 7, effective September 1, 2009; am. Acts 2009, 81st Leg., ch. 845 (S.B. 2153), §§ 5, 6, effective September 1, 2009.)

### Sec. 2308.052.  Terms; Vacancies.

(a) Advisory board members serve terms of six years, with the terms of two or three members, as appropriate, expiring on February 1 of each odd-numbered year.

(b) A member may not serve more than two full consecutive terms.

(c) If a vacancy occurs during a term, the presiding officer of the commission shall appoint a replacement who meets the qualifications of the vacated position to serve for the remainder of the term.

(Enacted by Acts 2007, 80th Leg., ch. 1046 (H.B. 2094), § 1.12, effective September 1, 2007.)

### Sec. 2308.053.  Presiding Officer.

The presiding officer of the commission shall appoint one of the advisory board members to serve as presiding officer of the advisory board for a term of one year. The presiding officer of the advisory board may vote on any matter before the advisory board.

(Enacted by Acts 2007, 80th Leg., ch. 1046 (H.B. 2094), § 1.12, effective September 1, 2007.)

### Sec. 2308.054.  Compensation; Reimbursement of Expenses.

Advisory board members may not receive compensation but are entitled to reimbursement for

Occupations

actual and necessary expenses incurred in performing the functions of the advisory board, subject to the General Appropriations Act.
(Enacted by Acts 2007, 80th Leg., ch. 1046 (H.B. 2094), § 1.12, effective September 1, 2007.)

### Sec. 2308.055. Meetings.

The advisory board shall meet twice annually and may meet at other times at the call of the presiding officer of the commission or the executive director.
(Enacted by Acts 2007, 80th Leg., ch. 1046 (H.B. 2094), § 1.12, effective September 1, 2007.)

### Sec. 2308.056. General Powers and Duties.

The executive director or commission, as appropriate, may take action as necessary to administer and enforce this chapter.
(Enacted by Acts 2007, 80th Leg., ch. 1046 (H.B. 2094), § 1.12, effective September 1, 2007.)

### Sec. 2308.057. Rules.

(a) The commission shall adopt rules for permitting tow trucks and licensing towing operators, towing companies, booting companies, and boot operators. The commission may adopt different rules applicable to each type of permit or license.

(a-1) The commission shall adopt rules for denial of applications and permits if the applicant, a partner, principal, officer, or general manager of the applicant, or other license or permit holder has:

(1) a criminal conviction, or has pleaded guilty or nolo contendere to an offense, before the date of the application, for:

(A) a felony; or

(B) a misdemeanor punishable by confinement in jail or by a fine in an amount that exceeds $500;

(2) violated an order of the commission or executive director, including an order for sanctions or administrative penalties;

(3) failed to submit a license or permit bond in an amount established by the commission;

(4) knowingly submitted false or incomplete information on the application; or

(5) filed an application to permit a tow truck previously permitted by a license or permit holder.

(b) The commission by rule shall adopt:

(1) standards of conduct for license and permit holders under this chapter; and

(2) requirements for a consent tow, private property tow, and incident management tow.
(Enacted by Acts 2007, 80th Leg., ch. 1046 (H.B. 2094), § 1.12, effective September 1, 2007; am. Acts 2009, 81st Leg., ch. 845 (S.B. 2153), § 7, effective September 1, 2009; am. Acts 2009, 81st Leg., ch. 1310 (H.B. 2571), § 2, effective September 1, 2009; am. Acts 2011, 82nd Leg., ch. 353 (H.B. 3510), § 5, effective September 1, 2011.)

### Sec. 2308.0575. Rules on Fees; Contract for Study; Confidential Information.

(a) To protect the public health and safety, the commission by rule shall establish:

(1) the fees that may be charged in connection with a private property tow;

(2) the maximum amount that may be charged for fees, other than tow fees, that may be assessed by a towing company in connection with a private property tow; and

(3) a maximum amount that may be charged for the following private property tows:

(A) standard light-duty tows of motor vehicles with a gross weight rating of 10,000 pounds or less;

(B) medium-duty tows of motor vehicles with a gross weight rating of more than 10,000 pounds, but less than 25,000 pounds; and

(C) heavy-duty tows of motor vehicles with a gross weight rating that exceeds 25,000 pounds.

(b) In adopting rules under Subsection (a), the commission shall contract for a study that:

(1) examines towing fee studies conducted by municipalities in this state; and

(2) analyzes the cost of towing services by company, the consumer price index, the geographic area, and individual cost components.

(c) The commission may structure the maximum amounts that may be charged for private property tows based on hourly or flat fees or by geographic location.

(d) The commission shall maintain the confidentiality of information contained in a study conducted under this section that is claimed to be confidential for competitive purposes and may not release information that identifies a person or company. The confidential information is exempt from disclosure under Chapter 552, Government Code.

(e) To protect the confidentiality of the information, the commission shall aggregate the information to the maximum extent possible considering the purpose of the study.

(f) The department shall contract to conduct a study on private property towing fees under this section at least once every two years.
(Enacted by Acts 2009, 81st Leg., ch. 1310 (H.B. 2571), § 3, effective September 1, 2010.)

### Sec. 2308.058. Fees.

The commission shall establish and collect reasonable and necessary fees in amounts sufficient to cover the costs of administering this chapter.
(Enacted by Acts 2007, 80th Leg., ch. 1046 (H.B. 2094), § 1.12, effective September 1, 2007.)

### Sec. 2308.059. Periodic and Risk-Based Inspections.

(a) The department may enter and inspect at any time during business hours:

(1) the place of business of any person regulated under this chapter; or

(2) any place in which the department has reasonable cause to believe that a license or permit holder is in violation of this chapter or in violation of a rule or order of the commission or executive director.

(b) The department shall conduct additional inspections based on a schedule of risk-based inspections using the following criteria:

(1) the type and nature of the towing company or operator;

(2) the inspection history;

(3) any history of complaints involving the towing company or operator; and

(4) any other factor determined by the commission by rule.

(c) The towing company shall pay a fee for each risk-based inspection performed under this section. The commission by rule shall set the amount of the fee.

(d) In conducting an inspection under this section, the department may inspect a vehicle, a facility, business records, or any other place or thing reasonably required to enforce this chapter or a rule or order adopted under this chapter.
(Enacted by Acts 2007, 80th Leg., ch. 1046 (H.B. 2094), § 1.12, effective September 1, 2007.)

### Sec. 2308.060. Powers and Duties of Advisory Board.

The advisory board shall provide advice and recommendations to the department on technical matters relevant to the administration and enforcement of this chapter, including examination content, licensing standards, continuing education requirements, and maximum amounts that may be charged for fees related to private property tows.
(Enacted by Acts 2007, 80th Leg., ch. 1046 (H.B. 2094), § 1.12, effective September 1, 2007; am. Acts 2009, 81st Leg., ch. 1310 (H.B. 2571), § 4, effective September 1, 2009.)

### Sec. 2308.061. Personnel.

The department may employ personnel necessary to administer and enforce this chapter.
(Enacted by Acts 2007, 80th Leg., ch. 1046 (H.B. 2094), § 1.12, effective September 1, 2007.)

## SUBCHAPTER C
## TOW TRUCK PERMIT REQUIREMENTS

### Sec. 2308.101. Permit Required.

A tow truck may not be used for consent towing or nonconsent towing on a public roadway in this state unless an appropriate permit has been issued for the tow truck under this subchapter. Each tow truck requires a separate permit.
(Enacted by Acts 2007, 80th Leg., ch. 1046 (H.B. 2094), § 1.12, effective September 1, 2008.)

### Sec. 2308.102. Application Requirements.

(a) An applicant for a permit under this subchapter must submit to the department:

(1) a completed application on a form prescribed by the executive director;

(2) evidence of insurance or financial responsibility required under this subchapter;

(3) the required fees; and

(4) any other information required by the executive director.

(b) The department may conduct an examination of any criminal conviction of an applicant, including by obtaining any criminal history record information permitted by law.
(Enacted by Acts 2007, 80th Leg., ch. 1046 (H.B. 2094), § 1.12, effective September 1, 2008.)

### Sec. 2308.103. Requirements for Incident Management Towing Permit.

(a) An incident management towing permit is required for a tow truck used to perform any nonconsent tow initiated by a peace officer, including a tow authorized under Section 545.3051, Transportation Code.

(b) To be eligible for an incident management towing permit, an applicant must submit evidence that:

(1) the tow truck is equipped to tow light-duty or heavy-duty vehicles according to the manufacturer's towing guidelines;

(2) the applicant has at least $500,000 of liability insurance for the tow truck; and

(3) the applicant has at least $50,000 of cargo insurance for the tow truck.

(c) A tow truck permitted under this section may also be used for private property towing and consent towing.

(d) When a tow truck is used for a nonconsent tow initiated by a peace officer under Section 545.3051, Transportation Code, the permit holder is an agent of law enforcement and is subject to Section 545.3051(e), Transportation Code.

(Enacted by Acts 2007, 80th Leg., ch. 1046 (H.B. 2094), § 1.12, effective September 1, 2008.)

## Sec. 2308.104.  Requirements for Private Property Towing Permit.

(a) A private property towing permit is required for a tow truck used to perform a nonconsent tow authorized by a parking facility owner under this chapter.

(b) To be eligible for a private property towing permit, an applicant must submit evidence that:

(1) the tow truck is equipped to tow light-duty or heavy-duty vehicles according to the manufacturer's towing guidelines;

(2) the applicant has at least $300,000 of liability insurance for the tow truck; and

(3) the applicant has at least $50,000 of cargo insurance for the tow truck.

(c) A tow truck permitted under this section may also be used for consent towing but not for incident management towing.

(Enacted by Acts 2007, 80th Leg., ch. 1046 (H.B. 2094), § 1.12, effective September 1, 2008.)

## Sec. 2308.105.  Requirements for Consent Towing Permit.

(a) A consent towing permit is required for a tow truck used to perform a consent tow authorized by the vehicle owner.

(b) To be eligible for a consent towing permit, an applicant must submit evidence that:

(1) the tow truck is equipped to tow light-duty or heavy-duty vehicles according to the manufacturer's towing guidelines; and

(2) the applicant has at least $300,000 of liability insurance for the tow truck.

(c) A tow truck permitted under this section may not be used for nonconsent towing, including incident management towing and private property towing.

(Enacted by Acts 2007, 80th Leg., ch. 1046 (H.B. 2094), § 1.12, effective September 1, 2008.)

## Sec. 2308.106.  Department Approval; Issuance of Permit.

(a) The department shall issue a permit under this subchapter to an applicant who meets the requirements for a permit. The department may deny an application if the applicant has had a permit revoked under this chapter.

(b) The department shall issue a certificate containing a single unique permit number for each tow truck, regardless of whether the permit holder holds more than one permit.

(Enacted by Acts 2007, 80th Leg., ch. 1046 (H.B. 2094), § 1.12, effective September 1, 2008.)

## Sec. 2308.107.  Permit Renewal.

(a) A permit issued under this chapter is valid for one year. The department may adopt a system under which permits expire at different times during the year.

(b) The department shall notify the permit holder at least 30 days before the date a permit expires. The notice must be in writing and sent to the permit holder's last known address according to the records of the department.

(c) A permit holder may renew a permit under this chapter by:

(1) paying a fee for each tow truck; and

(2) providing to the department evidence of continuing insurance or financial responsibility in an amount required by this chapter.

(Enacted by Acts 2007, 80th Leg., ch. 1046 (H.B. 2094), § 1.12, effective September 1, 2008.)

## Sec. 2308.108.  Cab Cards.

(a) The department shall issue a cab card for each tow truck issued a permit. The cab card must:

(1) show the permit number of the certificate issued under Section 2308.106(b);

(2) show the type of permit issued;

(3) show the vehicle unit number;

(4) show the vehicle identification number; and

(5) contain a statement that the vehicle has been issued a permit under this subchapter.

(b) The department shall issue a cab card when the department issues or renews a permit under this subchapter.

(c) A permit holder must keep the cab card in the cab of each permitted tow truck.

(d) The department may order a permit holder to surrender a cab card if the permit is suspended or revoked under this chapter.

(e) If the department determines that the cab card system described by Subsections (a) through (c) is not an efficient means of enforcing this subchapter, the executive director by rule may adopt an alternative method that is accessible by law enforcement personnel in the field and provides for the enforcement of the permit requirements of this subchapter.

(f) A cab card or a permit issued under the alternative method described in Subsection (e) must be valid for the same duration as a certificate issued under Section 2308.106.

(Enacted by Acts 2007, 80th Leg., ch. 1046 (H.B. 2094), § 1.12, effective September 1, 2008.)

## Sec. 2308.109. Display of Information on Tow Truck.

(a) A permit holder shall display on each permitted tow truck:

(1) the permit holder's name;

(2) the permit holder's telephone number;

(3) the city and state where the permit holder is located; and

(4) the permit number for the tow truck.

(b) The information required to be displayed must be:

(1) printed in letters and numbers that are at least two inches high and in a color that contrasts with the color of the background surface; and

(2) permanently affixed in conspicuous places on both sides of the tow truck.

(Enacted by Acts 2007, 80th Leg., ch. 1046 (H.B. 2094), § 1.12, effective September 1, 2008.)

## Sec. 2308.110. Financial Responsibility.

(a) A permit holder shall maintain liability insurance for each tow truck according to the requirements under this subchapter.

(b) Unless state law permits a tow truck to be self-insured, any insurance required for a tow truck must be obtained from an insurer authorized to do business in this state.

(c) An applicant or permit holder must file with the department evidence of insurance as required by this subchapter.

(d) A permit holder shall keep evidence of insurance in a form approved by the department in the cab of each permitted tow truck.

(Enacted by Acts 2007, 80th Leg., ch. 1046 (H.B. 2094), § 1.12, effective September 1, 2008.)

## SUBCHAPTER D
## LICENSE REQUIREMENTS

### Sec. 2308.151. License Required.

Unless the person holds an appropriate license under this subchapter, a person may not:

(1) perform towing operations;

(2) operate a towing company;

(3) perform booting operations; or

(4) operate a booting company.

(Enacted by Acts 2007, 80th Leg., ch. 1046 (H.B. 2094), § 1.12, effective September 1, 2008; am. Acts 2009, 81st Leg., ch. 845 (S.B. 2153), § 8, effective September 1, 2009.)

### Sec. 2308.152. General License Application Requirements.

An applicant for a license under this subchapter must submit to the department:

(1) a completed application on a form prescribed by the executive director;

(2) the required fees; and

(3) any other information required by commission rule.

(Enacted by Acts 2007, 80th Leg., ch. 1046 (H.B. 2094), § 1.12, effective September 1, 2008.)

### Sec. 2308.1521. Vehicle Storage Facility Employee and Towing Operator; Dual License.

(a) The commission shall adopt rules for the issuance of a dual license for a person who is a vehicle storage facility employee and towing operator. The department shall issue the license to an applicant who:

(1) meets the requirements established under:

(A) Section 2308.153, 2308.154, or 2308.155;

(B) Section 2303.1015; and

(C) any applicable rules adopted under this subchapter or Subchapter C, Chapter 2303; and

(2) submits to the department:

(A) an application on a department-approved form; and

(B) the required license fee.

(b) A person holding a license issued under this section may:

(1) work at a vehicle storage facility; and

(2) perform towing operations.

Occupations

(c) The fee for a license issued under this section may not be:

(1) less than the fee for a license issued under this subchapter or Section 2303.1015; or

(2) more than the sum of the fees for a license issued under this subchapter and a license issued under Section 2303.1015.

(Enacted by Acts 2009, 81st Leg., ch. 757 (S.B. 702), § 4, effective June 1, 2010.)

## Sec. 2308.153.   Incident Management Towing Operator's License.

(a) An incident management towing operator's license is required to operate a tow truck permitted under Section 2308.103.

(b) An applicant for an incident management towing operator's license must:

(1) hold a valid driver's license issued by a state in the United States; and

(2) be certified by a program approved by the department.

(Enacted by Acts 2007, 80th Leg., ch. 1046 (H.B. 2094), § 1.12, effective September 1, 2008; am. Acts 2009, 81st Leg., ch. 757 (S.B. 702), § 5, effective September 1, 2009.)

## Sec. 2308.154.   Private Property Towing Operator's License.

(a) A private property towing operator's license is required to operate a tow truck permitted under Section 2308.104.

(b) An applicant for a private property towing operator's license must:

(1) hold a valid driver's license issued by a state in the United States; and

(2) be certified by a program approved by the department.

(Enacted by Acts 2007, 80th Leg., ch. 1046 (H.B. 2094), § 1.12, effective September 1, 2008; am. Acts 2009, 81st Leg., ch. 757 (S.B. 702), § 6, effective September 1, 2009.)

## Sec. 2308.155.   Consent Towing Operator's License.

(a) A consent towing operator's license is required to operate a tow truck permitted under Section 2308.105.

(b) An applicant for a consent towing operator's license must hold a valid driver's license issued by a state in the United States.

(Enacted by Acts 2007, 80th Leg., ch. 1046 (H.B. 2094), § 1.12, effective September 1, 2008; am. Acts 2009, 81st Leg., ch. 757 (S.B. 702), § 7, effective September 1, 2009.)

## Sec. 2308.1551.   Training License.

(a) The department may issue a training license to an applicant for a license under this subchapter if the applicant:

(1) holds a valid driver's license issued by a state in the United States;

(2) meets the qualifications established by rule by the commission; and

(3) is engaged in the process of learning and assisting in the operation of a tow truck under the supervision of a licensed tow truck operator.

(b) Notwithstanding Subsection (a), an applicant for a license under Section 2308.153 may be supervised by an operator who holds a license issued under Section 2308.153, 2308.154, or 2308.155.

(c) A training license issued under this section expires on the 91st day after the date of issuance and may not be renewed.

(d) The commission by rule shall set the fee, establish the qualifications, and provide for the issuance of a training license under this section.

(Enacted by Acts 2009, 81st Leg., ch. 757 (S.B. 702), § 8, effective June 1, 2010.)

## Sec. 2308.1555.   Boot Operator's License.

(a) A boot operator's license is required to install or remove a boot from a vehicle.

(b) An applicant for a boot operator's license must be at least 18 years of age.

(Enacted by Acts 2009, 81st Leg., ch. 845 (S.B. 2153), § 9, effective September 1, 2009.)

## Sec. 2308.1556.   Booting Company License.

(a) A booting company license is required for a person to operate a booting company.

(b) To be eligible for a booting company license, an applicant must submit evidence that the applicant is covered by:

(1) a general liability insurance policy on a broad form with:

(A) a combined single limit for bodily injury and property damage for each occurrence of at least $500,000; and

(B) an aggregate limit for all occurrences for each policy year of at least $500,000; and

(2) an automobile liability insurance policy covering the applicant and the applicant's employees for vehicles owned, hired, or otherwise used in the applicant's business, with a combined single limit for each occurrence of at least $500,000.

Occupations

(Enacted by Acts 2009, 81st Leg., ch. 845 (S.B. 2153), § 9, effective September 1, 2009.)

### Sec. 2308.156. Nontransferability of License.

A license issued by the executive director is valid throughout this state and is not transferable.

(Enacted by Acts 2007, 80th Leg., ch. 1046 (H.B. 2094), § 1.12, effective September 1, 2008.)

### Sec. 2308.157. Continuing Education.

(a) The commission by rule shall recognize, prepare, or administer continuing education programs for license holders. Except as provided by Subsection (c), each license holder must complete a continuing education program before the license holder may renew the license holder's license.

(b) A person recognized by the commission to offer a continuing education program must:

(1) register with the department; and

(2) comply with rules adopted by the commission relating to continuing education.

(c) To renew an incident management towing operator's license the first time, a license holder must complete a professional development course relating to incident management towing that is approved and administered by the department under this section.

(Enacted by Acts 2007, 80th Leg., ch. 1046 (H.B. 2094), § 1.12, effective September 1, 2008; am. Acts 2009, 81st Leg., ch. 757 (S.B. 702), § 9, effective September 1, 2009.)

### Sec. 2308.158. Alcohol and Drug Testing of Towing Operators.

(a) A towing company shall establish an alcohol and drug testing policy for towing operators. A towing company that establishes an alcohol and drug testing policy under this subsection may adopt the model alcohol and drug testing policy adopted by the commission or may use another alcohol and drug testing policy that the department determines is at least as stringent as the policy adopted by the commission.

(b) The commission by rule shall adopt a model alcohol and drug testing policy for use by a towing company. The model alcohol and drug testing policy must be designed to ensure the safety of the public through appropriate alcohol and drug testing and to protect the rights of employees. The model alcohol and drug testing policy must:

(1) require at least one scheduled drug test each year for each towing operator; and

(2) authorize random, unannounced alcohol and drug testing for towing operators.

(Enacted by Acts 2007, 80th Leg., ch. 1046 (H.B. 2094), § 1.12, effective September 1, 2008; am. Acts 2009, 81st Leg., ch. 757 (S.B. 702), § 10, effective September 1, 2009.)

### Sec. 2308.159. License Renewal.

(a) A license issued under this subchapter is valid for one year. The department may adopt a system under which licenses expire at different times during the year.

(b) The department shall notify the license holder at least 30 days before the date a license expires. The notice must be in writing and sent to the license holder's last known address according to the records of the department.

(c) A license holder may renew a license issued under this chapter by:

(1) submitting an application on a form prescribed by the executive director;

(2) submitting evidence demonstrating compliance with the requirements for the license type as required by this chapter or commission rule;

(3) paying a renewal fee; and

(4) completing continuing education as required by Section 2308.157.

(Enacted by Acts 2007, 80th Leg., ch. 1046 (H.B. 2094), § 1.12, effective September 1, 2008; am. Acts 2011, 82nd Leg., ch. 353 (H.B. 3510), § 6, effective September 1, 2011.)

### SUBCHAPTER E
### LOCAL REGULATION OF TOWING AND BOOTING

### Sec. 2308.201. Tow Truck Regulation by Political Subdivisions.

(a) A political subdivision of this state may regulate the operation of a tow truck to the extent allowed by federal law, except that a political subdivision may not issue a more restrictive regulation for the use of lighting equipment on a tow truck than is imposed by Title 7, Transportation Code.

(b) A political subdivision may not require the registration of a tow truck that performs consent tows in the political subdivision unless the owner of the tow truck has a place of business in the territory of the political subdivision.

(c) A political subdivision may require the registration of a tow truck that performs a nonconsent tow in the political subdivision, regardless of

Occupations

whether the owner of the tow truck has a place of business in the territory of the political subdivision.

(d) A political subdivision may not require a person who holds a driver's license or commercial driver's license to obtain a license or permit for operating a tow truck unless the person performs nonconsent tows in the territory of the political subdivision. A fee charged for a license or permit may not exceed $15.

(Enacted by Acts 1997, 75th Leg., ch. 165 (S.B. 898), § 30.150(a), effective September 1, 1997; am. Acts 2001, 77th Leg., ch. 1303 (H.B. 1681), § 1, effective September 1, 2001; am. Acts 2003, 78th Leg., ch. 1034 (H.B. 849), § 9, effective September 1, 2003; am. Acts 2007, 80th Leg., ch. 1046 (H.B. 2094), § 2.01, effective September 1, 2007 (renumbered from Transportation Code Sec. 643.201).)

## Sec. 2308.202.  Regulation by Political Subdivisions of Fees for Nonconsent Tows.

The governing body of a political subdivision may regulate the fees that may be charged or collected in connection with a nonconsent tow originating in the territory of the political subdivision if the private property tow fees:

(1) are authorized by commission rule; and

(2) do not exceed the maximum amount authorized by commission rule.

(Enacted by Acts 2003, 78th Leg., ch. 1034 (H.B. 849), § 10, effective September 1, 2003; am. Acts 2007, 80th Leg., ch. 1046 (H.B. 2094), § 2.01, effective September 1, 2007 (renumbered from Transportation Code Sec. 643.203); am. Acts 2009, 81st Leg., ch. 1310 (H.B. 2571), § 5, effective September 1, 2010.)

## Sec. 2308.203.  Towing Fee Studies.

(a) The governing body of a political subdivision that regulates nonconsent tow fees shall establish procedures by which a towing company may request that a towing fee study be performed.

(b) The governing body of the political subdivision shall establish or amend the allowable fees for nonconsent tows at amounts that represent the fair value of the services of a towing company and are reasonably related to any financial or accounting information provided to the governing body.

(Enacted by Acts 2003, 78th Leg., ch. 1034 (H.B. 849), § 10, effective September 1, 2003; am. Acts

2007, 80th Leg., ch. 1046 (H.B. 2094), § 2.01, effective September 1, 2007 (renumbered from Transportation Code Sec. 643.204).)

## Sec. 2308.204.  Fees for Private Property Tows in Other Areas [Repealed].

Repealed by Acts 2011, 82nd Leg., ch. 353 (H.B. 3510), § 19(a)(1), effective September 1, 2011. (Enacted by Acts 2003, 78th Leg., ch. 1034 (H.B. 849), § 10, effective September 1, 2003; am. Acts 2007, 80th Leg., ch. 1046 (H.B. 2094), § 2.01, effective September 1, 2007 (renumbered from Transportation Code Sec. 643.205); am. Acts 2009, 81st Leg., ch. 1310 (H.B. 2571), § 6, effective September 1, 2010.)

## Sec. 2308.205.  Storage of Towed Vehicles.

(a) A towing company that makes a nonconsent tow shall tow the vehicle to a vehicle storage facility that is operated by a person who holds a license to operate the facility under Chapter 2303, unless the towing company agrees to take the vehicle to a location designated by the vehicle's owner.

(b) A storage or notification fee imposed in connection with a motor vehicle towed to a vehicle storage facility is governed by Chapter 2303.

(c) Except as provided by this chapter, Article 18.23, Code of Criminal Procedure, or Chapter 2303, a fee may not be charged or collected without the prior written consent of the vehicle owner or operator.

(Enacted by Acts 2003, 78th Leg., ch. 1034 (H.B. 849), § 10, effective September 1, 2003; am. Acts 2005, 79th Leg., ch. 1197 (H.B. 480), § 5, effective September 1, 2005; am. Acts 2007, 80th Leg., ch. 1046 (H.B. 2094), § 2.01, effective September 1, 2007 (renumbered from Transportation Code Sec. 643.206).)

## Sec. 2308.206.  Required Filing [Repealed].

Repealed by Acts 2011, 82nd Leg., ch. 353 (H.B. 3510), § 19(a)(2), effective September 1, 2011. (Enacted by Acts 2003, 78th Leg., ch. 1034 (H.B. 849), § 10, effective September 1, 2003; am. Acts 2007, 80th Leg., ch. 1046 (H.B. 2094), § 2.01, effective September 1, 2007 (renumbered from Transportation Code Sec. 643.207); am. Acts 2009, 81st Leg., ch. 1310 (H.B. 2571), § 7, effective September 1, 2009.)

## Sec. 2308.2065.  Fees for Nonconsent Tows; Refunds.

(a) A license or permit holder may not charge a fee for a nonconsent tow that is greater than:

(1) the fee for a nonconsent tow established under Section 2308.0575; or

(2) a fee for a nonconsent tow authorized by a political subdivision.

(b) A license or permit holder may not charge a fee for a service related to a nonconsent tow that is not included in the list of fees established:

(1) under Section 2308.0575; or

(2) by a political subdivision.

(c) The department may require a license or permit holder to refund to a vehicle owner or operator the:

(1) amount charged to the owner or operator in excess of the amounts established by commission rule or by a political subdivision; or

(2) total amount of the charges for a service not listed in the amounts established by commission rule or by a political subdivision.

(Enacted by Acts 2011, 82nd Leg., ch. 353 (H.B. 3510), § 7, effective September 1, 2011.)

## Sec. 2308.207.  Required Posting [Repealed].

Repealed by Acts 2009, 81st Leg., ch. 757 (S.B. 702), § 13, effective September 1, 2009.

(Acts 2003, 78th Leg., ch. 1034, effective September 1, 2003; am. Acts 2007, 80th Leg., ch. 1046 (H.B. 2094), § 2.01, effective September 1, 2007 (renumbered from Transportation Code Sec. 643.208).)

## Sec. 2308.208.  Municipal or County Ordinance Regulating Unauthorized Vehicles and Towing of Motor Vehicles.

The governing body of a municipality or the commissioners court of a county may adopt an ordinance that is identical to this chapter or that imposes additional requirements that exceed the minimum standards of this chapter but may not adopt an ordinance conflicting with this chapter. (Enacted by Acts 1995, 74th Leg., ch. 165 (S.B. 971), § 1, effective September 1, 1995; am. Acts 2007, 80th Leg., ch. 1046 (H.B. 2094), § 2.02, effective September 1, 2007 (renumbered from Transportation Code Sec. 684.101); am. Acts 2009, 81st Leg., ch. 1310 (H.B. 2571), § 8, effective September 1, 2009.)

## Sec. 2308.2085.  Municipal Ordinance Regulating Booting Companies and Operators.

(a) A municipality may adopt an ordinance that is identical to the booting provisions in this chapter or that imposes additional requirements that exceed the minimum standards of the booting provisions in this chapter but may not adopt an ordinance that conflicts with the booting provisions in this chapter.

(b) A municipality may regulate the fees that may be charged in connection with the booting of a vehicle, including associated parking fees.

(c) A municipality may require booting companies to obtain a permit to operate in the municipality.

(Enacted by Acts 2009, 81st Leg., ch. 845 (S.B. 2153), § 11, effective September 1, 2009.)

## Sec. 2308.209.  Tow Rotation List in Certain Counties.

(a) [Repealed by Acts 2009, 81st Leg., ch. 87 (S.B. 1969), § 27.002(37), effective September 1, 2009.]

(b) This section applies only to the unincorporated area of a county:

(1) with a population of 550,000 or more that is adjacent to a county with a population of 3.3 million or more;

(2) with a population of less than 10,000 that is located in a national forest; or

(3) adjacent to a county described by Subdivision (2) that has a population of less than 75,000.

(c) The sheriff's office may maintain a list of towing companies to perform nonconsent tows of motor vehicles initiated by a peace officer investigating a traffic accident or a traffic incident. The towing companies must operate in a county to which this section applies.

(d) A peace officer initiating a nonconsent tow of a motor vehicle involved in a traffic accident or traffic incident that the officer is investigating shall notify the sheriff's office that the tow is being initiated. The sheriff's office shall contact successive towing companies on the tow rotation list until a company agrees to carry out the tow.

(e) The sheriff's office may assess a towing company an administrative fee to be included on the tow rotation list in an amount not to exceed the amount necessary to implement this section.

(f) The commissioners court of a county in which a list is maintained under Subsection (c) shall adopt policies to implement this section in a manner that ensures:

(1) equal distribution of nonconsent tows among the towing companies that perform nonconsent tows in the county; and

(2) consumer protection, including fair pricing, for owners or operators of motor vehicles

towed by towing companies on the tow rotation list.

(g) The sheriff's office shall make a list maintained under this section available for public inspection.

(h) In a county in which a list is maintained under Subsection (c), a person commits an offense if:

(1) the person arrives at the scene of a traffic accident or traffic incident to perform a nonconsent tow of a motor vehicle without first being contacted by the sheriff's office;

(2) the person directly or indirectly solicits, on streets located in the county, towing services, including towing, removing, repairing, wrecking, storing, trading, selling, or purchasing related to a vehicle that has been damaged in an accident to the extent that it cannot be normally and safely driven; or

(3) the person enters the scene of a traffic accident, traffic incident, or other area under the control of a peace officer without the permission of the peace officer.

(i) An offense under Subsection (h) is a misdemeanor punishable by a fine of not less than $1 or more than $200.

(Enacted by Acts 2007, 80th Leg., ch. 162 (S.B. 500), § 1, effective September 1, 2007; am. Acts 2009, 81st Leg., ch. 87 (S.B. 1969), §§ 27.001(109), 27.002(37), effective September 1, 2009 (renumbered from Transportation Code Sec. 643.209); am. Acts 2011, 82nd Leg., ch. 1163 (H.B. 2702), § 108, effective September 1, 2011.)

## SUBCHAPTER F
## UNAUTHORIZED VEHICLES

### Sec. 2308.251. Prohibition Against Unattended Vehicles in Certain Areas.

(a) The owner or operator of a vehicle may not leave unattended on a parking facility a vehicle that:

(1) is in or obstructs a vehicular traffic aisle, entry, or exit of the parking facility;

(2) prevents a vehicle from exiting a parking space in the facility;

(3) is in or obstructs a fire lane marked according to Subsection (c);

(4) does not display the special license plates issued under Section 504.201, Transportation Code, or the disabled parking placard issued under Chapter 681, Transportation Code, for a vehicle transporting a disabled person and is in a parking space that is designated for the

exclusive use of a vehicle transporting a disabled person; or

(5) is leaking a fluid that presents a hazard or threat to persons or property.

(b) Subsection (a) does not apply to an emergency vehicle that is owned by, or the operation of which is authorized by, a governmental entity.

(c) If a government regulation governing the marking of a fire lane applies to a parking facility, a fire lane in the facility must be marked as provided by the regulation. If a government regulation on the marking of a fire lane does not apply to the parking facility, all curbs of fire lanes must be painted red and be conspicuously and legibly marked with the warning "FIRE LANE—TOW AWAY ZONE" in white letters at least three inches tall, at intervals not exceeding 50 feet.

(Enacted by Acts 1995, 74th Leg., ch. 165 (S.B. 971), § 1, effective September 1, 1995; am. Acts 2005, 79th Leg., ch. 728 (H.B. 2018), § 20.003, effective September 1, 2005; am. Acts 2007, 80th Leg., ch. 1046 (H.B. 2094), § 2.03, effective September 1, 2007 (renumbered from Transportation Code Sec. 684.011); am. Acts 2009, 81st Leg., ch. 757 (S.B. 702), § 11, effective September 1, 2009.)

### Sec. 2308.252. Removal and Storage of Unauthorized Vehicle.

(a) A parking facility owner may, without the consent of the owner or operator of an unauthorized vehicle, cause the vehicle and any property on or in the vehicle to be removed and stored at a vehicle storage facility at the vehicle owner's or operator's expense if:

(1) signs that comply with Subchapter G prohibiting unauthorized vehicles are located on the parking facility at the time of towing and for the preceding 24 hours and remain installed at the time of towing;

(2) the owner or operator of the vehicle has received actual notice from the parking facility owner that the vehicle will be towed at the vehicle owner's or operator's expense if it is in or not removed from an unauthorized space;

(3) the parking facility owner gives notice to the owner or operator of the vehicle under Subsection (b); or

(4) on request the parking facility owner provides to the owner or operator of the vehicle information on the name of the towing company and vehicle storage facility that will be used to remove and store the vehicle and the vehicle is:

(A) left in violation of Section 2308.251 or 2308.253; or

(B) in or obstructing a portion of a paved driveway or abutting public roadway used for entering or exiting the facility.

(b) A parking facility owner is considered to have given notice under Subsection (a)(3) if:

(1) a conspicuous notice has been attached to the vehicle's front windshield or, if the vehicle has no front windshield, to a conspicuous part of the vehicle stating:

(A) that the vehicle is in a parking space in which the vehicle is not authorized to be parked;

(B) a description of all other unauthorized areas in the parking facility;

(C) that the vehicle will be towed at the expense of the owner or operator of the vehicle if it remains in an unauthorized area of the parking facility; and

(D) a telephone number that is answered 24 hours a day to enable the owner or operator of the vehicle to locate the vehicle; and

(2) a notice is mailed after the notice is attached to the vehicle as provided by Subdivision (1) to the owner of the vehicle by certified mail, return receipt requested, to the last address shown for the owner according to the vehicle registration records of the Texas Department of Transportation, or if the vehicle is registered in another state, the appropriate agency of that state.

(c) The notice under Subsection (b)(2) must:

(1) state that the vehicle is in a space in which the vehicle is not authorized to park;

(2) describe all other unauthorized areas in the parking facility;

(3) contain a warning that the unauthorized vehicle will be towed at the expense of the owner or operator of the vehicle if it is not removed from the parking facility before the 15th day after the postmark date of the notice; and

(4) state a telephone number that is answered 24 hours a day to enable the owner or operator to locate the vehicle.

(d) The mailing of a notice under Subsection (b)(2) is not required if after the notice is attached under Subsection (b)(1) the owner or operator of the vehicle leaves the vehicle in another location where parking is unauthorized for the vehicle according to the notice.

(Enacted by Acts 1995, 74th Leg., ch. 165 (S.B. 971), § 1, effective September 1, 1995; am. Acts 2003, 78th Leg., ch. 442 (H.B. 560), § 1, effective January 1, 2004; am. Acts 2005, 79th Leg., ch. 1197 (H.B. 480), § 6, effective September 1, 2005;

am. Acts 2007, 80th Leg., ch. 1046 (H.B. 2094), § 2.03, effective September 1, 2007 (renumbered from Transportation Code Sec. 684.012); am. Acts 2009, 81st Leg., ch. 1310 (H.B. 2571), § 9, effective September 1, 2009.)

### Sec. 2308.253. Unattended Vehicles on Parking Facility of Apartment Complex; Removal and Storage of Vehicles.

(a) This section applies only to a parking facility serving or adjacent to an apartment complex consisting of one or more residential apartment units and any adjacent real property serving the apartment complex.

(b) The owner or operator of a vehicle may not leave unattended on a parking facility a vehicle that:

(1) obstructs a gate that is designed or intended for the use of pedestrians or vehicles;

(2) obstructs pedestrian or vehicular access to an area that is used for the placement of a garbage or refuse receptacle used in common by residents of the apartment complex;

(3) is in or obstructs a restricted parking area or parking space designated under Subchapter G, including a space designated for the use of employees or maintenance personnel of the parking facility or apartment complex;

(4) is in a tow away zone, other than a fire lane covered by Section 2308.251(c), that is brightly painted and is conspicuously and legibly marked with the warning "TOW AWAY ZONE" in contrasting letters at least three inches tall;

(5) is a semitrailer, trailer, or truck-tractor, as defined by Chapter 502, Transportation Code, unless the owner or operator of the vehicle is permitted under the terms of a rental or lease agreement with the apartment complex to leave the unattended vehicle on the parking facility; or

(6) is leaking a fluid that presents a hazard or threat to persons or property.

(c) A parking facility owner may not have an emergency vehicle described by Section 2308.251(b) removed from the parking facility.

(d) Except as provided by a contract described by Subsection (e), a parking facility owner may not have a vehicle removed from the parking facility merely because the vehicle does not display:

(1) an unexpired license plate or registration insignia issued for the vehicle under Chapter

502, Transportation Code, or the vehicle registration law of another state or country; or

(2) a valid vehicle inspection certificate issued under Chapter 548, Transportation Code, or the vehicle inspection law of another state or country.

(e) A contract provision providing for the removal from a parking facility of a vehicle that does not display an unexpired license plate or registration insignia or a valid inspection certificate is valid only if the provision requires the owner or operator of the vehicle to be given at least 10 days' written notice that the vehicle will be towed from the facility at the vehicle owner's or operator's expense if it is not removed from the parking facility. The notice must be:

(1) delivered in person to the owner or operator of the vehicle; or

(2) sent by certified mail, return receipt requested, to that owner or operator.

(f) This section may not be construed:

(1) to authorize the owner or operator of a vehicle to leave an unattended vehicle on property that is not designed or intended for the parking of vehicles; or

(2) to limit or restrict the enforcement of Chapter 683, Transportation Code, the abandoned motor vehicle law.

(g) A provision of an apartment lease or rental agreement entered into or renewed on or after January 1, 2004, that is in conflict or inconsistent with this section is void and may not be enforced. (Enacted by Acts 2003, 78th Leg., ch. 442 (H.B. 560), § 2, effective January 1, 2004; am. Acts 2007, 80th Leg., ch. 1046 (H.B. 2094), § 2.03, effective September 1, 2007 (renumbered from Transportation Code Sec. 684.0125).)

## Sec. 2308.254. Limitation on Parking Facility Owner's Authority to Remove Unauthorized Vehicle.

A parking facility owner may not have an unauthorized vehicle removed from the facility except:

(1) as provided by this chapter or a municipal ordinance that complies with Section 2308.208; or

(2) under the direction of a peace officer or the owner or operator of the vehicle.

(Enacted by Acts 1995, 74th Leg., ch. 165 (S.B. 971), § 1, effective September 1, 1995; am. Acts 2007, 80th Leg., ch. 1046 (H.B. 2094), § 2.03, effective September 1, 2007 (renumbered from Transportation Code Sec. 684.013).)

## Sec. 2308.255. Towing Company's or Boot Operator's Authority to Remove and Store or Boot Unauthorized Vehicle.

(a) A towing company that is insured as provided by Subsection (c) may, without the consent of an owner or operator of an unauthorized vehicle, remove and store the vehicle at a vehicle storage facility at the expense of the owner or operator of the vehicle if:

(1) the towing company has received written verification from the parking facility owner that:

(A) the parking facility owner has installed the signs required by Section 2308.252(a)(1); or

(B) the owner or operator received notice under Section 2308.252(a)(2) or the parking facility owner gave notice complying with Section 2308.252(a)(3); or

(2) on request the parking facility owner provides to the owner or operator of the vehicle information on the name of the towing company and vehicle storage facility that will be used to remove and store the vehicle and the vehicle is:

(A) left in violation of Section 2308.251;

(B) in or obstructing a portion of a paved driveway; or

(C) on a public roadway used for entering or exiting the facility and the removal is approved by a peace officer.

(b) A towing company may not remove an unauthorized vehicle except under:

(1) this chapter;

(2) a municipal ordinance that complies with Section 2308.208; or

(3) the direction of a peace officer or the owner or operator of the vehicle.

(c) Only a towing company that is insured against liability for property damage incurred in towing a vehicle may remove and store an unauthorized vehicle under this section.

(d) A towing company may remove and store a vehicle under Subsection (a) and a boot operator may boot a vehicle under Section 2308.257 only if the parking facility owner:

(1) requests that the towing company remove and store or that the boot operator boot the specific vehicle; or

(2) has a standing written agreement with the towing company or boot operator to enforce parking restrictions in the parking facility.

(Enacted by Acts 1995, 74th Leg., ch. 165 (S.B. 971), § 1, effective September 1, 1995; am. Acts

2005, 79th Leg., ch. 1197 (H.B. 480), § 7, effective September 1, 2005; am. Acts 2007, 80th Leg., ch. 1046 (H.B. 2094), § 2.03, effective September 1, 2007 (renumbered from Transportation Code Sec. 684.014); am. Acts 2009, 81st Leg., ch. 1310 (H.B. 2571), § 10, effective September 1, 2009; am. Acts 2011, 82nd Leg., ch. 353 (H.B. 3510), §§ 8, 9, effective September 1, 2011.)

## Sec. 2308.2555. Removal of Certain Unauthorized Vehicles in Rural Areas.

(a) This section applies only to an abandoned vehicle that has damaged a fence on private property in a rural area.

(b) A law enforcement agency directing a towing company or tow operator to remove an abandoned vehicle that is located on private property shall provide the towing company or tow operator with the name and telephone number of the property owner or the owner's agent if the owner or agent has provided the information to the law enforcement agency.

(c) A towing company or tow operator provided with information under Subsection (b) shall contact the property owner or the owner's agent before entering private property to tow a vehicle described by Subsection (a).

(Enacted by Acts 2009, 81st Leg., ch. 757 (S.B. 702), § 12, effective September 1, 2009; am. Acts 2011, 82nd Leg., ch. 91 (S.B. 1303), § 27.001(49), effective September 1, 2011, (renumbered from Sec. 2308.257); am. Acts 2011, 82nd Leg., ch. 353 (H.B. 3510), § 10, effective September 1, 2011, (renumbered from Sec. 2308.257).)

## Sec. 2308.256. Vehicle Storage Facility's Duty to Report After Accepting Unauthorized Vehicle [Repealed].

Repealed by Acts 2009, 81st Leg., ch. 757 (S.B. 702), § 13, effective September 1, 2009; Acts 2011, 82nd Leg., ch. 91 (S.B. 1303), § 18.005, effective September 1, 2011; and Acts 2011, 82nd Leg., ch. 353 (H.B. 3510), § 19(b), effective September 1, 2011.

(Enacted by Acts 1995, 74th Leg., ch. 165 (S.B. 971), § 1, effective September 1, 1995; am. Acts 2007, 80th Leg., ch. 1046 (H.B. 2094), § 2.03, effective September 1, 2007 (renumbered from Transportation Code Sec. 684.015); am. Acts 2009, 81st Leg., ch. 757 (S.B. 702), § 13, effective September 1, 2009; am. Acts 2009, 81st Leg., ch. 1310 (H.B. 2571), § 11, effective September 1, 2009; am. Acts 2011, 82nd Leg., ch. 91 (S.B. 1303), § 18.005, effective September 1, 2011.)

## Sec. 2308.2565. Vehicle Storage Facility Duty to Report After Accepting Unauthorized Vehicle.

(a) Except for an incident management tow requested by a law enforcement agency, a vehicle storage facility accepting a vehicle that is towed under this chapter shall within two hours after receiving the vehicle report to the police department of the municipality from which the vehicle was towed or, if the vehicle was towed from a location that is not in a municipality with a police department, to the sheriff of the county from which the vehicle was towed:

(1) a general description of the vehicle;

(2) the state and number of the vehicle's license plate, if any;

(3) the vehicle identification number of the vehicle, if it can be ascertained;

(4) the location from which the vehicle was towed; and

(5) the name and location of the vehicle storage facility in which the vehicle is being stored.

(b) A law enforcement agency may request a vehicle storage facility to provide a report, in a manner prescribed by the law enforcement agency, of incident management tows within the jurisdiction of the agency. A vehicle storage facility must provide the report not later than 48 hours after the time the facility receives the request.

(Enacted by Acts 2011, 82nd Leg., ch. 353 (H.B. 3510), § 11, effective September 1, 2011.)

## Sec. 2308.257. Booting of Unauthorized Vehicle.

(a) A parking facility owner may, without the consent of the owner or operator of an unauthorized vehicle, cause a boot to be installed on the vehicle in the parking facility if signs that comply with Subchapter G prohibiting unauthorized vehicles are located on the parking facility at the time of the booting and for the preceding 24 hours and remain installed at the time of the booting.

(b) A boot operator that installs a boot on a vehicle must affix a conspicuous notice to the vehicle's front windshield or driver's side window stating:

(1) that the vehicle has been booted and damage may occur if the vehicle is moved;

(2) the date and time the boot was installed;

(3) the name, address, and telephone number of the booting company;

(4) a telephone number that is answered 24 hours a day to enable the owner or operator of the vehicle to arrange for removal of the boot;

Occupations

(5) the amount of the fee for removal of the boot and any associated parking fees; and

(6) notice of the right of a vehicle owner or vehicle operator to a hearing under Subchapter J.

(c) On removal of a boot, the boot operator shall provide a receipt to the vehicle owner or operator stating:

(1) the name of the person who removed the boot;

(2) the date and time the boot was removed;

(3) the name of the person to whom the vehicle was released;

(4) the amount of fees paid for removal of the boot and any associated parking fees; and

(5) the right of the vehicle owner or operator to a hearing under Subchapter J.

(d) The booting company shall maintain a copy of the receipt at its place of business for a period of three years. A peace officer has the right, on request, to inspect and copy the records to determine compliance with the requirements of this section.

(e) A booting company shall accept payment by an electronic check, debit card, or credit card for any fee or charge associated with the removal of a boot. A booting company may not collect a fee for any charge associated with the removal of a boot from a person who offers to pay the charge with an electronic check, debit card, or credit card form of payment that the booting company is not equipped to accept.

(Enacted by Acts 2009, 81st Leg., ch. 845 (S.B. 2153), § 12, effective September 1, 2009.)

## SUBCHAPTER G
### SIGNS PROHIBITING UNAUTHORIZED VEHICLES AND DESIGNATING RESTRICTED AREAS

### Sec. 2308.301. General Requirements for Sign Prohibiting Unauthorized Vehicles.

(a) Except as provided by Subsection (a)(2)(B) and Section 2308.304 or 2308.305, an unauthorized vehicle may not be towed under Section 2308.252(a)(1) or booted under Section 2308.257 unless a sign prohibiting unauthorized vehicles on a parking facility is:

(1) facing and conspicuously visible to the driver of a vehicle that enters the facility;

(2) located:

(A) on the right or left side of each driveway or curb-cut through which a vehicle can enter the facility, including an entry from an alley abutting the facility; or

(B) at intervals along the entrance so that no entrance is farther than 25 feet from a sign if:

(i) curbs, access barriers, landscaping, or driveways do not establish definite vehicle entrances onto a parking facility from a public roadway other than an alley; and

(ii) the width of an entrance exceeds 35 feet;

(3) permanently mounted on a pole, post, permanent wall, or permanent barrier;

(4) installed on the parking facility; and

(5) installed so that the bottom edge of the sign is no lower than five feet and no higher than eight feet above ground level.

(b) Except as provided by Section 2308.305, an unauthorized vehicle may be towed under Section 2308.252(a)(1) or booted under Section 2308.257 only if each sign prohibiting unauthorized vehicles:

(1) is made of weather-resistant material;

(2) is at least 18 inches wide and 24 inches tall;

(3) contains the international symbol for towing vehicles;

(4) contains a statement describing who may park in the parking facility and prohibiting all others;

(5) bears the words, as applicable:

(A) "Unauthorized Vehicles Will Be Towed or Booted at Owner's or Operator's Expense";

(B) "Unauthorized Vehicles Will Be Towed at Owner's or Operator's Expense"; or

(C) "Unauthorized Vehicles Will Be Booted at Owner's or Operator's Expense";

(6) contains a statement of the days and hours of towing and booting enforcement; and

(7) contains a number, including the area code, of a telephone that is answered 24 hours a day to enable an owner or operator of a vehicle to locate a towed vehicle or to arrange for removal of a boot from a vehicle.

(Enacted by Acts 1995, 74th Leg., ch. 165 (S.B. 971), § 1, effective September 1, 1995; am. Acts 2007, 80th Leg., ch. 1046 (H.B. 2094), § 2.04, effective September 1, 2007 (renumbered from Transportation Code Sec. 684.031); am. Acts 2009, 81st Leg., ch. 845 (S.B. 2153), § 13, effective September 1, 2009; am. Acts 2011, 82nd Leg.,

Occupations

ch. 353 (H.B. 3510), § 12, effective September 1, 2011.)

## Sec. 2308.302. Color, Layout, and Lettering Height Requirements.

(a) Except as provided by Section 2308.305, each sign required by this chapter must comply with the color, layout, and lettering height requirements of this section.

(b) A bright red international towing symbol, which is a solid silhouette of a tow truck towing a vehicle on a generally rectangular white background, at least four inches in height, must be on the uppermost portion of a sign or on a separate sign placed immediately above the sign.

(c) The portion of the sign immediately below the international towing symbol must:

(1) in lettering at least two inches in height, contain the words, as applicable:

(A) "Towing and Booting Enforced";

(B) "Towing Enforced"; or

(C) "Booting Enforced"; and

(2) consist of white letters on a bright red background.

(d) Except as provided by Subsection (e), the next lower portion of the sign must contain the remaining information required by Section 2308.301(b) displayed in bright red letters at least one inch in height on a white background.

(e) The bottommost portion of the sign must contain the telephone numbers required by Section 2308.301(b), in lettering at least one inch in height and may, if the facility owner chooses or if an applicable municipal ordinance requires, include the name and address of the storage facility to which an unauthorized vehicle will be removed. The lettering on this portion of the sign must consist of white letters on a bright red background.

(Enacted by Acts 1995, 74th Leg., ch. 165 (S.B. 971), § 1, effective September 1, 1995; am. Acts 2007, 80th Leg., ch. 1046 (H.B. 2094), § 2.04, effective September 1, 2007 (renumbered from Transportation Code Sec. 684.032); am. Acts 2009, 81st Leg., ch. 845 (S.B. 2153), § 14, effective September 1, 2009; am. Acts 2011, 82nd Leg., ch. 353 (H.B. 3510), § 13, effective September 1, 2011.)

## Sec. 2308.303. Telephone Number for Locating Towed Vehicle Required.

If a parking facility owner posts a sign described by Sections 2308.301 and 2308.302, the owner of a vehicle that is towed from the facility under this chapter must be able to locate the vehicle by calling the telephone number on the sign.

(Enacted by Acts 1995, 74th Leg., ch. 165 (S.B. 971), § 1, effective September 1, 1995; am. Acts 2007, 80th Leg., ch. 1046 (H.B. 2094), § 2.04, effective September 1, 2007 (renumbered from Transportation Code Sec. 684.033).)

## Sec. 2308.304. Designation of Restricted Parking Spaces on Otherwise Unrestricted Parking Facility.

A parking facility owner may designate one or more spaces as restricted parking spaces on a portion of an otherwise unrestricted parking facility. Instead of installing a sign at each entrance to the parking facility as provided by Section 2308.301(a)(2), an owner may place a sign that prohibits unauthorized vehicles from parking in designated spaces and that otherwise complies with Sections 2308.301 and 2308.302:

(1) at the right or left side of each entrance to a designated area or group of parking spaces located on the restricted portion of the parking facility; or

(2) at the end of a restricted parking space so that the sign, the top of which must not be higher than seven feet above the ground, is in front of a vehicle that is parked in the space and the rear of which is at the entrance of the space.

(Enacted by Acts 1995, 74th Leg., ch. 165 (S.B. 971), § 1, effective September 1, 1995; am. Acts 2007, 80th Leg., ch. 1046 (H.B. 2094), § 2.04, effective September 1, 2007 (renumbered from Transportation Code Sec. 684.034).)

## Sec. 2308.305. Individual Parking Restrictions in Restricted Area.

(a) A parking facility owner who complies with Sections 2308.301 and 2308.302 may impose further specific parking restrictions in an area to which the signs apply for individual spaces by installing or painting a weather-resistant sign or notice on a curb, pole, post, permanent wall, or permanent barrier so that the sign is in front of a vehicle that is parked in the space and the rear of which is at the entrance of the space.

(b) The top of the sign or notice may not be higher than seven feet above the ground.

(c) The sign or notice must include an indication that the space is reserved for a particular unit number, person, or type of person.

(d) The letters on the sign or notice must be at least two inches in height and must contrast to the color of the curb, wall, or barrier so they can be read during the day and at night. The letters are not required to be illuminated or made of reflective material.

(Enacted by Acts 1995, 74th Leg., ch. 165 (S.B. 971), § 1, effective September 1, 1995; am. Acts 2007, 80th Leg., ch. 1046 (H.B. 2094), § 2.04, effective September 1, 2007 (renumbered from Transportation Code Sec. 684.035).)

## SUBCHAPTER H
## REGULATION OF PARKING ON CERTAIN PUBLIC ROADWAY AREAS

### Sec. 2308.351.   Removal of Unauthorized Vehicle from Leased Right-of-Way.

Unless prohibited by the lease, a parking facility owner or towing company may remove an unauthorized vehicle parked in a leased area described by Section 2308.002(7)(B)(i) if the owner or towing company gives notice under Section 2308.252(a)(1), (2), or (3) and otherwise complies with this chapter.

(Enacted by Acts 1995, 74th Leg., ch. 165 (S.B. 971), § 1, effective September 1, 1995; am. Acts 2007, 80th Leg., ch. 1046 (H.B. 2094), § 2.05, effective September 1, 2007 (renumbered from Transportation Code Sec. 684.051).)

### Sec. 2308.352.   Removal of Unauthorized Vehicle from Area Between Parking Facility and Public Roadway.

Unless prohibited by a municipal ordinance, a parking facility owner or towing company may remove an unauthorized vehicle any part of which is in an area described by Section 2308.002(7)(B)(ii) if notice provided by Section 2308.252(a)(2) or (3) is given and the owner or towing company has otherwise complied with this chapter.

(Enacted by Acts 1995, 74th Leg., ch. 165 (S.B. 971), § 1, effective September 1, 1995; am. Acts 2007, 80th Leg., ch. 1046 (H.B. 2094), § 2.05, effective September 1, 2007 (renumbered from Transportation Code Sec. 684.052).)

### Sec. 2308.353.   Removal Under Governmental Entity's Authority of Unauthorized Vehicle Parked in Right-of-Way.

(a) A governmental entity that has jurisdiction over a public roadway and that has posted one or more signs in the right-of-way stating that parking is prohibited in the right-of-way may:

(1) remove or contract with a towing company to remove an unauthorized vehicle parked in the right-of-way of the public roadway; or

(2) grant written permission to an abutting parking facility owner to:

(A) post one or more "No parking in R.O.W." signs along a common property line of the facility and the roadway; and

(B) remove vehicles from the right-of-way of the public roadway under this chapter.

(b) A sign under Subsection (a)(2) must:

(1) state that a vehicle parked in the right-of-way may be towed at the expense of the owner or operator of the vehicle;

(2) be placed facing the public roadway:

(A) on the parking facility owner's property not more than two feet from the common boundary line; and

(B) at intervals so that no point in the boundary line is less than 25 feet from a sign posted under this subsection; and

(3) in all other respects comply with Subchapter G.

(c) After signs have been posted under Subsection (b), the parking facility owner or a towing company may remove an unauthorized vehicle from the right-of-way subject to the governmental entity's written permission given under Subsection (a)(2).

(Enacted by Acts 1995, 74th Leg., ch. 165 (S.B. 971), § 1, effective September 1, 1995; am. Acts 2007, 80th Leg., ch. 1046 (H.B. 2094), § 2.05, effective September 1, 2007 (renumbered from Transportation Code Sec. 684.053).)

### Sec. 2308.354.   Authority for Removal of Vehicle from Public Roadway.

(a) Under an ordinance of a municipality regulating the parking of vehicles in the municipality, to aid in the enforcement of the ordinance, an employee designated by the municipality may be authorized to:

(1) immobilize a vehicle parked in the municipality; and

(2) remove an immobilized vehicle from a public roadway in the municipality.

(b) A parking facility owner or towing company may not remove a vehicle from a public roadway except under:

(1) this chapter or a municipal ordinance that complies with Section 2308.208; or

Occupations

(2) the direction of a peace officer or the owner or operator of the vehicle.

(c) In addition to the authority granted under Subsection (a) and to aid in the enforcement of an ordinance regulating the parking of vehicles, a municipality with a population of 1.9 million or more may authorize a designated employee to request the removal of a vehicle parked illegally in an area designated as a tow-away zone in a residential area where on-street parking is regulated by the ordinance.

(d) Subsections (a) and (c) do not apply to a vehicle owned by an electric, gas, water, or telecommunications utility while the vehicle is parked for the purpose of conducting work on a facility of the utility that is located below, above, or adjacent to the street.

(Enacted by Acts 1995, 74th Leg., ch. 165 (S.B. 971), § 1, effective September 1, 1995; am. Acts 2001, 77th Leg., ch. 301 (H.B. 996), § 1, effective September 1, 2001; am. Acts 2007, 80th Leg., ch. 1046 (H.B. 2094), § 2.05, effective September 1, 2007 (renumbered from Transportation Code Sec. 684.054); am. Acts 2009, 81st Leg., ch. 1298 (H.B. 2346), § 1, effective September 1, 2009.)

## SUBCHAPTER I
## REGULATION OF TOWING COMPANIES, BOOTING COMPANIES, AND PARKING FACILITY OWNERS

### Sec. 2308.401. Parking Facility Owner Prohibited from Receiving Financial Gain from Towing Company or Booting Company.

(a) A parking facility owner may not directly or indirectly accept anything of value from:

(1) a towing company in connection with the removal of a vehicle from a parking facility; or

(2) a booting company in connection with booting a vehicle in a parking facility.

(b) A parking facility owner may not have a direct or indirect monetary interest in:

(1) a towing company that for compensation removes unauthorized vehicles from a parking facility in which the parking facility owner has an interest; or

(2) a booting company that for compensation boots vehicles in a parking facility in which the parking facility owner has an interest.

(c) This section does not apply to a sign required under Section 2308.301 provided by a towing or booting company to a parking facility owner.

(Enacted by Acts 1995, 74th Leg., ch. 165 (S.B. 971), § 1, effective September 1, 1995; am. Acts 2007, 80th Leg., ch. 1046 (H.B. 2094), § 2.06, effective September 1, 2007 (renumbered from Transportation Code Sec. 684.081); am. Acts 2009, 81st Leg., ch. 845 (S.B. 2153), § 16, effective September 1, 2009; am. Acts 2011, 82nd Leg., ch. 353 (H.B. 3510), § 14, effective September 1, 2011.)

### Sec. 2308.402. Towing Company and Booting Company Prohibited from Financial Involvement with Parking Facility Owner.

(a) A towing company or booting company may not directly or indirectly give anything of value to a parking facility owner in connection with:

(1) the removal of a vehicle from a parking facility; or

(2) the booting of a vehicle in a parking facility.

(b) A towing company or booting company may not have a direct or indirect monetary interest in a parking facility:

(1) from which the towing company for compensation removes unauthorized vehicles; or

(2) in which the booting company for compensation installs boots on unauthorized vehicles.

(c) This section does not apply to a sign required under Section 2308.301 provided by a towing or booting company to a parking facility owner.

(Enacted by Acts 1995, 74th Leg., ch. 165 (S.B. 971), § 1, effective September 1, 1995; am. Acts 2007, 80th Leg., ch. 1046 (H.B. 2094), § 2.06, effective September 1, 2007 (renumbered from Transportation Code Sec. 684.082); am. Acts 2009, 81st Leg., ch. 845 (S.B. 2153), § 17, effective September 1, 2009; am. Acts 2011, 82nd Leg., ch. 353 (H.B. 3510), § 15, effective September 1, 2011.)

### Sec. 2308.403. Limitation on Liability of Parking Facility Owner for Removal or Storage of Unauthorized Vehicle.

A parking facility owner who causes the removal of an unauthorized vehicle is not liable for damages arising from the removal or storage of the vehicle if the vehicle:

(1) was removed in compliance with this chapter; and

(2) is:

(A) removed by a towing company insured against liability for property damage incurred in towing a vehicle; and

(B) stored by a vehicle storage facility insured against liability for property damage incurred in storing a vehicle.

(Enacted by Acts 1995, 74th Leg., ch. 165 (S.B. 971), § 1, effective September 1, 1995; am. Acts 2007, 80th Leg., ch. 1046 (H.B. 2094), § 2.06, effective September 1, 2007 (renumbered from Transportation Code Sec. 684.083).)

### Sec. 2308.404. Civil Liability of Towing Company, Booting Company, or Parking Facility Owner for Violation of Chapter.

(a) A towing company, booting company, or parking facility owner who violates this chapter is liable to the owner or operator of the vehicle that is the subject of the violation for:

(1) damages arising from the removal, storage, or booting of the vehicle; and

(2) towing, storage, or booting fees assessed in connection with the vehicle's removal, storage, or booting.

(b) A vehicle's owner or operator is not required to prove negligence of a parking facility owner, towing company, or booting company to recover under Subsection (a).

(c) A towing company, booting company, or parking facility owner who intentionally, knowingly, or recklessly violates this chapter is liable to the owner or operator of the vehicle that is the subject of the violation for $1,000 plus three times the amount of fees assessed in the vehicle's removal, towing, storage, or booting.

(d) [Repealed by Acts 2011, 82nd Leg., ch. 353 (H.B. 3510), § 19(a)(3), effective September 1, 2011.]

(Enacted by Acts 1995, 74th Leg., ch. 165 (S.B. 971), § 1, effective September 1, 1995; am. Acts 2007, 80th Leg., ch. 1046 (H.B. 2094), § 2.06, effective September 1, 2007 (renumbered from Transportation Code Sec. 684.084); am. Acts 2009, 81st Leg., ch. 845 (S.B. 2153), §§ 18, 19, effective September 1, 2009; am. Acts 2009, 81st Leg., ch. 1310 (H.B. 2571), § 12, effective September 1, 2009; am. Acts 2011, 82nd Leg., ch. 353 (H.B. 3510), § 19(a)(3), effective September 1, 2011.)

### Sec. 2308.405. Criminal Penalty.

A person commits an offense if the person violates this chapter. An offense under this section is a misdemeanor punishable by a fine of not less than $500 or more than $1,500 unless it is shown on trial of the offense that the person knowingly or intentionally violated this chapter, in which event the offense is a Class B misdemeanor.

(Enacted by Acts 1995, 74th Leg., ch. 165 (S.B. 971), § 1, effective September 1, 1995; am. Acts 2005, 79th Leg., ch. 1197 (H.B. 480), § 8, effective September 1, 2005; am. Acts 2007, 80th Leg., ch. 1046 (H.B. 2094), § 2.06, effective September 1, 2007 (renumbered from Transportation Code Sec. 684.085); am. Acts 2009, 81st Leg., ch. 1310 (H.B. 2571), § 13, effective September 1, 2009.)

### Sec. 2308.406. Violation of Chapter; Injunction.

A violation of this chapter may be enjoined under Subchapter E, Chapter 17, Business & Commerce Code.

(Enacted by Acts 1995, 74th Leg., ch. 165 (S.B. 971), § 1, effective September 1, 1995; am. Acts 2007, 80th Leg., ch. 1046 (H.B. 2094), § 2.06, effective September 1, 2007 (renumbered from Transportation Code Sec. 684.086).)

### Sec. 2308.407. Minor Sign or Lettering Height Variations.

A minor variation of a required or minimum height of a sign or lettering is not a violation of this chapter.

(Enacted by Acts 1995, 74th Leg., ch. 165 (S.B. 971), § 1, effective September 1, 1995; am. Acts 2007, 80th Leg., ch. 1046 (H.B. 2094), § 2.06, effective September 1, 2007 (renumbered from Transportation Code Sec. 684.087).)

### SUBCHAPTER J
### RIGHTS OF OWNERS AND OPERATORS OF STORED OR BOOTED VEHICLES

### Sec. 2308.451. Payment of Cost of Removal, Storage, and Booting of Vehicle.

(a) If in a hearing held under this chapter the court finds that a person or law enforcement agency authorized, with probable cause, the removal and storage in a vehicle storage facility of a vehicle, the person who requested the hearing shall pay the costs of the removal and storage.

(b) If in a hearing held under this chapter the court does not find that a person or law enforcement agency authorized, with probable cause, the removal and storage in a vehicle storage facility of a vehicle, the towing company, vehicle storage facility, or parking facility owner or law enforcement agency that authorized the removal shall:

    (1) pay the costs of the removal and storage; or

    (2) reimburse the owner or operator for the cost of the removal and storage paid by the owner or operator.

(c) If in a hearing held under this chapter the court finds that a person authorized, with probable cause, the booting of a vehicle in a parking facility, the person who requested the hearing shall pay the costs of the booting.

(c-1) If, in a hearing held under this chapter, regardless of whether the court finds that there was probable cause for the removal and storage of a vehicle, the court finds that the towing charge collected exceeded fees regulated by a political subdivision or authorized by this chapter or Chapter 2303, the towing company shall reimburse the owner or operator of the vehicle an amount equal to the overcharge.

(d) If in a hearing held under this chapter the court does not find that a person authorized, with probable cause, the booting of a vehicle, the person that authorized the booting shall:

    (1) pay the costs of the booting and any related parking fees; or

    (2) reimburse the owner or operator for the cost of the booting and any related parking fees paid by the owner or operator.

(Enacted by Acts 1995, 74th Leg., ch. 165 (S.B. 971), § 1, effective September 1, 1995; am. Acts 1997, 75th Leg., ch. 165 (S.B. 898), § 30.159(a), effective September 1, 1997; am. Acts 2007, 80th Leg., ch. 1046 (H.B. 2094), § 2.07, effective September 1, 2007 (renumbered from Transportation Code Sec. 685.002); am. Acts 2009, 81st Leg., ch. 845 (S.B. 2153), § § 21, 22, effective September 1, 2009; am. Acts 2009, 81st Leg., ch. 1310 (H.B. 2571), § 14, effective September 1, 2009; am. Acts 2011, 82nd Leg., ch. 91 (S.B. 1303), § 27.001(50), effective September 1, 2011.)

### Sec. 2308.452. Right of Owner or Operator of Vehicle to Hearing.

The owner or operator of a vehicle that has been removed and placed in a vehicle storage facility or booted without the consent of the owner or operator of the vehicle is entitled to a hearing on whether probable cause existed for the removal and placement or booting.

(Enacted by Acts 1995, 74th Leg., ch. 165 (S.B. 971), § 1, effective September 1, 1995; am. Acts

1997, 75th Leg., ch. 165 (S.B. 898), § 30.159(a), effective September 1, 1997; am. Acts 2007, 80th Leg., ch. 1046 (H.B. 2094), § 2.07, effective September 1, 2007 (renumbered from Transportation Code Sec. 685.003); am. Acts 2009, 81st Leg., ch. 845 (S.B. 2153), § 23, effective September 1, 2009.)

### Sec. 2308.453. Jurisdiction.

A hearing under this chapter shall be in the justice court having jurisdiction in:

    (1) the precinct from which the motor vehicle was towed; or

    (2) for booted vehicles, the precinct in which the parking facility is located.

(Enacted by Acts 1995, 74th Leg., ch. 165 (S.B. 971), § 1, effective September 1, 1995; am. Acts 1997, 75th Leg., ch. 165 (S.B. 898), § 30.159(a), effective September 1, 1997; am. Acts 2001, 77th Leg., ch. 669 (H.B. 2810), § 144, effective September 1, 2001; am. Acts 2005, 79th Leg., ch. 737 (H.B. 2630), § 4, effective September 1, 2005; am. Acts 2007, 80th Leg., ch. 1046 (H.B. 2094), § 2.07, effective September 1, 2007 (renumbered from Transportation Code Sec. 685.004); am. Acts 2009, 81st Leg., ch. 845 (S.B. 2153), § 24, effective September 1, 2009 am. Acts 2009, 81st Leg., ch. 1310 (H.B. 2571), § 15, effective September 1, 2009; am. Acts 2011, 82nd Leg., ch. 91 (S.B. 1303), § 18.006, effective September 1, 2011.)

### Sec. 2308.454. Notice to Vehicle Owner or Operator.

(a) If before a hearing held under this chapter the owner or operator of a vehicle pays the costs of the vehicle's removal or storage, the towing company or vehicle storage facility that received the payment shall at the time of payment give the owner or operator written notice of the person's rights under this chapter.

(b) The operator of a vehicle storage facility that sends a notice under Subchapter D, Chapter 2303, shall include with that notice a notice of the person's rights under this chapter.

(c) If before a hearing held under this chapter the owner or operator of a vehicle pays the costs for removal of a boot, the booting company shall at the time of payment give the owner or operator written notice of the person's rights under this chapter.

(d) The booting operator that places a notice on a booted vehicle under Section 2308.257 shall include with that notice a notice of the person's rights under this chapter.

**Occupations**

(e) If the towing company or vehicle storage facility that received the payment fails to furnish to the owner or operator of the vehicle the name, address, and telephone number of the parking facility owner or law enforcement agency that authorized the removal of the vehicle, the towing company or vehicle storage facility that received the payment is liable if the court, after a hearing, does not find probable cause for the removal and storage of the vehicle.

(Enacted by Acts 1997, 75th Leg., ch. 165 (S.B. 898), § 30.159(a), effective September 1, 1997; am. Acts 2003, 78th Leg., ch. 1276 (H.B. 3507), § 14A.841, effective September 1, 2003; am. Acts 2007, 80th Leg., ch. 1046 (H.B. 2094), § 2.07, effective September 1, 2007 (renumbered from Transportation Code Sec. 685.005); am. Acts 2009, 81st Leg., ch. 845 (S.B. 2153), § 25, effective September 1, 2009; am. Acts 2009, 81st Leg., ch. 1310 (H.B. 2571), § 16, effective September 1, 2009; am. Acts 2011, 82nd Leg., ch. 91 (S.B. 1303), § 27.001(51), effective September 1, 2011.)

### Sec. 2308.455.  Contents of Notice.

The notice under Section 2308.454 must include:

(1) a statement of:

(A) the person's right to submit a request within 14 days for a court hearing to determine whether probable cause existed to remove, or install a boot on, the vehicle;

(B) the information that a request for a hearing must contain; and

(C) any filing fee for the hearing;

(2) the name, address, and telephone number of the towing company that removed the vehicle or the booting company that booted the vehicle;

(3) the name, address, and telephone number of the vehicle storage facility in which the vehicle was placed;

(4) the name, street address including city, state, and zip code, and telephone number of the person, parking facility owner, or law enforcement agency that authorized the removal of the vehicle; and

(5) the name, address, and telephone number of the justice court having jurisdiction in the precinct in which the parking facility is located.

(Enacted by Acts 1997, 75th Leg., ch. 165 (S.B. 898), § 30.159(a), effective September 1, 1997; am. Acts 2005, 79th Leg., ch. 737 (H.B. 2630), § 5, effective September 1, 2005; am. Acts 2007,

80th Leg., ch. 1046 (H.B. 2094), § 2.07, effective September 1, 2007 (renumbered from Transportation Code Sec. 685.006); am. Acts 2009, 81st Leg., ch. 845 (S.B. 2153), § 26, effective September 1, 2009; am. Acts 2009, 81st Leg., ch. 1310 (H.B. 2571), § 17, effective September 1, 2009; am. Acts 2011, 82nd Leg., ch. 91 (S.B. 1303), § 18.007, effective September 1, 2011.)

### Sec. 2308.456.  Request for Hearing.

(a) Except as provided by Subsections (c) and (c-1), a person entitled to a hearing under this chapter must deliver a written request for the hearing to the court before the 14th day after the date the vehicle was removed and placed in the vehicle storage facility or booted, excluding Saturdays, Sundays, and legal holidays.

(b) A request for a hearing must contain:

(1) the name, address, and telephone number of the owner or operator of the vehicle;

(2) the location from which the vehicle was removed or in which the vehicle was booted;

(3) the date when the vehicle was removed or booted;

(4) the name, address, and telephone number of the person or law enforcement agency that authorized the removal or booting;

(5) the name, address, and telephone number of the vehicle storage facility in which the vehicle was placed;

(6) the name, address, and telephone number of the towing company that removed the vehicle or of the booting company that installed a boot on the vehicle;

(7) a copy of any receipt or notification that the owner or operator received from the towing company, the booting company, or the vehicle storage facility; and

(8) if the vehicle was removed from or booted in a parking facility:

(A) one or more photographs that show the location and text of any sign posted at the facility restricting parking of vehicles; or

(B) a statement that no sign restricting parking was posted at the parking facility.

(c) If notice was not given under Section 2308.454, the 14-day deadline for requesting a hearing under Subsection (a) does not apply, and the owner or operator of the vehicle may deliver a written request for a hearing at any time.

(c-1) The 14-day period for requesting a hearing under Subsection (a) does not begin until the date on which the towing company or vehicle storage facility provides to the vehicle owner or operator the information necessary for the vehicle owner or operator to complete the material for the request for hearing required under Subsections (b)(2) through (6).

(d) A person who fails to deliver a request in accordance with Subsection (a) waives the right to a hearing.

(Enacted by Acts 1995, 74th Leg., ch. 165 (S.B. 971), § 1, effective September 1, 1995; am. Acts 1997, 75th Leg., ch. 165 (S.B. 898), § 30.159(a), effective September 1, 1997; am. Acts 2007, 80th Leg., ch. 1046 (H.B. 2094), § 2.07, effective September 1, 2007 (renumbered from Transportation Code Sec. 685.007); am. Acts 2009, 81st Leg., ch. 845 (S.B. 2153), § 27, effective September 1, 2009; am. Acts 2009, 81st Leg., ch. 1310 (H.B. 2571), § 18, effective September 1, 2009; am. Acts 2011, 82nd Leg., ch. 91 (S.B. 1303), § 18.008, effective September 1, 2011.)

### Sec. 2308.457. Filing Fee Authorized.

The court may charge a filing fee of $20 for a hearing under this chapter.

(Enacted by Acts 1995, 74th Leg., ch. 165 (S.B. 971), § 1, effective September 1, 1995; am. Acts 1997, 75th Leg., ch. 165 (S.B. 898), § 30.159(a), effective September 1, 1997; am. Acts 2005, 79th Leg., ch. 737 (H.B. 2630), § 6, effective September 1, 2005; am. Acts 2007, 80th Leg., ch. 1046 (H.B. 2094), § 2.07, effective September 1, 2007 (renumbered from Transportation Code Sec. 685.008).)

### Sec. 2308.458. Hearing.

(a) A hearing under this chapter shall be held before the 21st calender day after the date the court receives the request for the hearing.

(b) The court shall notify the person who requested the hearing for a towed vehicle, the parking facility owner or law enforcement agency that authorized the removal of the vehicle, the towing company, and the vehicle storage facility in which the vehicle was placed of the date, time, and place of the hearing in a manner provided by Rule 21a, Texas Rules of Civil Procedure. The notice of the hearing to the towing company and the parking facility owner or law enforcement agency that authorized the removal of the vehicle must include a copy of the request for hearing. Notice to the law enforcement agency that authorized the removal of the vehicle is sufficient as notice to the political subdivision in which the law enforcement agency is located.

(b-1) At a hearing under this section:

(1) the burden of proof is on the person who requested the hearing; and

(2) hearsay evidence is admissible if it is considered otherwise reliable by the justice of the peace.

(b-2) The court shall notify the person who requested the hearing for a booted vehicle, the parking facility in which the vehicle was booted, and the booting company of the date, time, and place of the hearing in a manner provided by Rule 21a, Texas Rules of Civil Procedure. The notice of hearing to the person that authorized the booting of the vehicle must include a copy of the request for hearing.

(c) The issues in a hearing regarding a towed vehicle under this chapter are:

(1) whether probable cause existed for the removal and placement of the vehicle;

(2) whether a towing charge imposed or collected in connection with the removal or placement of the vehicle was greater than the amount authorized by the political subdivision under Section 2308.201 or 2308.202;

(3) whether a towing charge imposed or collected in connection with the removal or placement of the vehicle was greater than the amount authorized under Section 2308.203; or

(4) whether a towing charge imposed or collected in connection with the removal or placement of the vehicle was greater than the amount authorized under Section 2308.0575.

(c-1) The issues in a hearing regarding a booted vehicle under this chapter are:

(1) whether probable cause existed for the booting of the vehicle; and

(2) whether a boot removal charge imposed or collected in connection with the removal of the boot from the vehicle was greater than the amount authorized by the political subdivision under Section 2308.2085.

(d) The court shall make written findings of fact and a conclusion of law.

(e) The court may award:

(1) court costs and attorney's fees to the prevailing party;

(2) the reasonable cost of photographs submitted under Section 2308.456(b)(8) to a vehicle owner or operator who is the prevailing party;

(3) an amount equal to the amount that the towing charge or booting removal charge and associated parking fees exceeded fees regulated by a political subdivision or authorized by this code or by Chapter 2303; and

(4) reimbursement of fees paid for vehicle towing, storage, or removal of a boot.

(Enacted by Acts 1995, 74th Leg., ch. 165 (S.B. 971), § 1, effective September 1, 1995; am. Acts 1997, 75th Leg., ch. 165 (S.B. 898), § 30.159(a), effective September 1, 1997; am. Acts 2003, 78th Leg., ch. 1034 (H.B. 849), § 17, effective September 1, 2003; am. Acts 2005, 79th Leg., ch. 737 (H.B. 2630), § 7, effective September 1, 2005; am. Acts 2007, 80th Leg., ch. 1046 (H.B. 2094), § 2.07, effective September 1, 2007 (renumbered from Transportation Code Sec. 685.009); am. Acts 2009, 81st Leg., ch. 845 (S.B. 2153), § 28, effective September 1, 2009; am. Acts 2009, 81st Leg., ch. 1310 (H.B. 2571), § 19, effective September 1, 2009; am. Acts 2011, 82nd Leg., ch. 353 (H.B. 3510), § 16, effective September 1, 2011.)

### Sec. 2308.459.  Appeal.

An appeal from a hearing under this chapter is governed by the rules of procedure applicable to civil cases in justice court, except that no appeal bond may be required by the court.

(Enacted by Acts 2005, 79th Leg., ch. 737 (H.B. 2630), § 8, effective September 1, 2005; am. Acts 2007, 80th Leg., ch. 1046 (H.B. 2094), § 2.07, effective September 1, 2007 (renumbered from Transportation Code Sec. 685.010).)

### Sec. 2308.460.  Enforcement of Award.

(a) An award under this chapter may be enforced by any means available for the enforcement of a judgment for a debt.

(b) The department shall suspend a license holder's license on the license holder's failure to pay a final judgment awarded to an owner or operator of a vehicle before the 60th day after the date of the final judgment. The department must provide notice of the suspension to the license holder at least 30 days before the date the license is to be suspended.

(c) The owner or operator of the vehicle shall submit a certified copy of the final judgment to the department.

(d) On receipt of the certified copy of the unpaid final judgment, the department shall disqualify a person from renewing a license or permit or deny the person the opportunity of taking a licensing examination on the grounds that the person, towing company, or vehicle storage facility has not paid a final judgment awarded to an owner or operator of a vehicle.

(e) The department shall reinstate the license on submission of evidence satisfactory to the department of payment of the final judgment by the person, towing company, or vehicle storage facility.

(Enacted by Acts 2007, 80th Leg., ch. 1046 (H.B. 2094), § 2.08, effective September 1, 2007; am. Acts 2009, 81st Leg., ch. 1310 (H.B. 2571), § 20, effective September 1, 2009.)

### SUBCHAPTER K
### ENFORCEMENT

### Sec. 2308.501.  Administrative Penalty.

(a) The commission may impose an administrative penalty on a person under Subchapter F, Chapter 51, regardless of whether the person holds a registration, permit, or license under this chapter, if the person violates:

(1) this chapter or a rule adopted under this chapter; or

(2) a rule or order of the executive director or commission.

(b) An administrative penalty may not be imposed unless the person charged with a violation is provided the opportunity for a hearing.

(Enacted by Acts 2007, 80th Leg., ch. 1046 (H.B. 2094), § 2.09, effective September 1, 2007.)

### Sec. 2308.502.  Cease and Desist Order; Injunction; Civil Penalty.

(a) The executive director may issue a cease and desist order as necessary to enforce this chapter if the executive director determines that the action is necessary to prevent a violation of this chapter and to protect public health and safety.

(b) The attorney general or executive director may institute an action for an injunction or a civil penalty under this chapter as provided by Section 51.352.

(Enacted by Acts 2007, 80th Leg., ch. 1046 (H.B. 2094), § 2.09, effective September 1, 2007.)

### Sec. 2308.503.  Sanctions.

The department may impose sanctions as provided by Section 51.353.

(Enacted by Acts 2007, 80th Leg., ch. 1046 (H.B. 2094), § 2.09, effective September 1, 2007.)

### Sec. 2308.504.  Criminal Penalty; Licensing.

(a) A person commits an offense if the person:

(1) violates the permitting or licensing requirements of this chapter;

(2) performs towing without a license to perform towing in this state;

(3) employs an individual who does not hold the appropriate license required by this chapter; or

(4) falsifies a certification or training.

(b) An offense under this section is a Class C misdemeanor. An offense under this section is enforceable by law enforcement.

(Enacted by Acts 2007, 80th Leg., ch. 1046 (H.B. 2094), § 2.09, effective September 1, 2008; am. Acts 2011, 82nd Leg., ch. 353 (H.B. 3510), § 17, effective September 1, 2011.)

## Sec. 2308.505. Criminal Penalty; Towing.

(a) A person commits an offense if the person:

(1) violates an ordinance, resolution, order, rule, or regulation of a political subdivision adopted under Section 2308.201, 2308.202, or 2308.2085 for which the political subdivision does not prescribe the penalty;

(2) charges or collects a fee in a political subdivision that regulates the operation of tow trucks under Section 2308.201 or 2308.202 or booting under Section 2308.2085 that is not authorized or is greater than the authorized amount of the fee;

(3) charges or collects a fee greater than the amount authorized under Section 2308.204;

(4) charges or collects a fee in excess of the amount filed with the department under Section 2308.206;

(5) violates Section 2308.205; or

(6) violates a rule of the department applicable to a tow truck, towing company, or booting company.

(b) An offense under this section is a misdemeanor punishable by a fine of not less than $200 or more than $1,000 per violation. An offense under this section is enforceable by law enforcement.

(Am. Acts 2007, 80th Leg., ch. 1046 (H.B. 2094), § 2.10, effective September 1, 2007 (renumbered from Transportation Code Sec. 643.253(d)); am. Acts 2009, 81st Leg., ch. 845 (S.B. 2153), § 29, effective September 1, 2009; am. Acts 2011, 82nd Leg., ch. 353 (H.B. 3510), § 18, effective September 1, 2011.)

# CHAPTER 2309
# USED AUTOMOTIVE PARTS RECYCLERS

## SUBCHAPTER A
## GENERAL PROVISIONS

### Sec. 2309.001.  Short Title.

This chapter may be cited as the Texas Used Automotive Parts Recycling Act.
(Enacted by Acts 2009, 81st Leg., ch. 783 (S.B. 1095), § 7, effective September 1, 2009; Enacted by Acts 2009, 81st Leg., ch. 933 (H.B. 3097), § 4.07, effective September 1, 2009.)

### Sec. 2309.002.  Definitions.

In this chapter:

(1) "Insurance company," "metal recycler," "motor vehicle," "nonrepairable motor vehicle," "nonrepairable vehicle title," "salvage motor vehicle," "salvage vehicle title," and "salvage vehicle dealer" have the meanings assigned by Section 501.091, Transportation Code.

(2) "Commission" means the Texas Commission of Licensing and Regulation.

(3) "Department" means the Texas Department of Licensing and Regulation.

(4) "Executive director" means the executive director of the department.

(5) "Used automotive part" has the meaning assigned to "used part" by Section 501.091, Transportation Code.

(6) "Used automotive parts recycler" means a person licensed under this chapter to operate a used automotive parts recycling business.

(7) "Used automotive parts recycling" means the dismantling and reuse or resale of used automotive parts and the safe disposal of salvage motor vehicles or nonrepairable motor vehicles, including the resale of those vehicles.
(Enacted by Acts 2009, 81st Leg., ch. 783 (S.B. 1095), § 7, effective September 1, 2009; Enacted by Acts 2009, 81st Leg., ch. 933 (H.B. 3097), § 4.07, effective September 1, 2009.)

### Sec. 2309.003.  Applicability of Chapter to Metal Recyclers.

(a) Except as provided by Subsection (b), this chapter does not apply to a transaction to which a metal recycler is a party.

(b) This chapter applies to a transaction in which a motor vehicle:

(1) is sold, transferred, released, or delivered to a metal recycler as a source of used automotive parts; and

(2) is used as a source of used automotive parts.
(Enacted by Acts 2009, 81st Leg., ch. 783 (S.B. 1095), § 7, effective September 1, 2009; Enacted by Acts 2009, 81st Leg., ch. 933 (H.B. 3097), § 4.07, effective September 1, 2009.)

### Sec. 2309.004.  Applicability of Chapter to Salvage Vehicle Dealers.

(a) Except as provided by Subsection (b), this chapter does not apply to a transaction in which a salvage vehicle dealer is a party.

(b) This chapter applies to a salvage vehicle dealer who deals in used automotive parts as more than an incidental part of the salvage vehicle dealer's primary business.
(Enacted by Acts 2009, 81st Leg., ch. 783 (S.B. 1095), § 7, effective September 1, 2009; Enacted by Acts 2009, 81st Leg., ch. 933 (H.B. 3097), § 4.07, effective September 1, 2009.)

### Sec. 2309.005.  Applicability of Chapter to Insurance Companies.

This chapter does not apply to an insurance company.
(Enacted by Acts 2009, 81st Leg., ch. 783 (S.B. 1095), § 7, effective September 1, 2009; Enacted by Acts 2009, 81st Leg., ch. 933 (H.B. 3097), § 4.07, effective September 1, 2009.)

## SUBCHAPTER B
## ADVISORY BOARD

### Sec. 2309.051.  Used Automotive Parts Recycling Advisory Board.

(a) The advisory board consists of five members representing the used automotive parts in-

Occupations

dustry in this state appointed by the presiding officer of the commission with the approval of the commission.

(b) The advisory board shall include members who represent used automotive parts businesses owned by domestic entities, as defined by Section 1.002, Business Organizations Code.

(c) The advisory board shall include one member who represents a used automotive parts business owned by a foreign entity, as defined by Section 1.002, Business Organizations Code.

(d) The advisory board may not include more than one member from any one used automotive parts business entity.

(e) Appointments to the advisory board shall be made without regard to the race, color, disability, sex, religion, age, or national origin of the appointee.

(Enacted by Acts 2009, 81st Leg., ch. 783 (S.B. 1095), § 7, effective September 1, 2009; Enacted by Acts 2009, 81st Leg., ch. 933 (H.B. 3097), § 4.07, effective September 1, 2009.)

### Sec. 2309.052. Terms; Vacancies.

(a) Advisory board members serve terms of six years, with the terms of one or two members expiring on February 1 of each odd-numbered year.

(b) A member may not serve more than two full consecutive terms.

(c) If a vacancy occurs during a term, the presiding officer of the commission shall appoint a replacement who meets the qualifications of the vacated position to serve for the remainder of the term.

(Enacted by Acts 2009, 81st Leg., ch. 783 (S.B. 1095), § 7, effective September 1, 2009; Enacted by Acts 2009, 81st Leg., ch. 933 (H.B. 3097), § 4.07, effective September 1, 2009.)

### Sec. 2309.053. Presiding Officer.

The presiding officer of the commission shall appoint one of the advisory board members to serve as presiding officer of the advisory board for a term of one year. The presiding officer of the advisory board may vote on any matter before the advisory board.

(Enacted by Acts 2009, 81st Leg., ch. 783 (S.B. 1095), § 7, effective September 1, 2009; Enacted by Acts 2009, 81st Leg., ch. 933 (H.B. 3097), § 4.07, effective September 1, 2009.)

### Sec. 2309.054. Powers and Duties of Advisory Board.

The advisory board shall provide advice and recommendations to the department on technical matters relevant to the administration and enforcement of this chapter, including licensing standards.

(Enacted by Acts 2009, 81st Leg., ch. 783 (S.B. 1095), § 7, effective September 1, 2009; Enacted by Acts 2009, 81st Leg., ch. 933 (H.B. 3097), § 4.07, effective September 1, 2009.)

### Sec. 2309.055. Compensation; Reimbursement of Expenses.

Advisory board members may not receive compensation but are entitled to reimbursement for actual and necessary expenses incurred in performing the functions of the advisory board, subject to the General Appropriations Act.

(Enacted by Acts 2009, 81st Leg., ch. 783 (S.B. 1095), § 7, effective September 1, 2009; Enacted by Acts 2009, 81st Leg., ch. 933 (H.B. 3097), § 4.07, effective September 1, 2009.)

### Sec. 2309.056. Meetings.

The advisory board shall meet twice annually and may meet at other times at the call of the presiding officer of the commission or the executive director.

(Enacted by Acts 2009, 81st Leg., ch. 783 (S.B. 1095), § 7, effective September 1, 2009; Enacted by Acts 2009, 81st Leg., ch. 933 (H.B. 3097), § 4.07, effective September 1, 2009.)

### SUBCHAPTER C
### POWERS AND DUTIES OF COMMISSION AND DEPARTMENT

### Sec. 2309.101. General Powers and Duties.

The executive director or commission, as appropriate, may take action as necessary to administer and enforce this chapter.

(Enacted by Acts 2009, 81st Leg., ch. 783 (S.B. 1095), § 7, effective September 1, 2009; Enacted by Acts 2009, 81st Leg., ch. 933 (H.B. 3097), § 4.07, effective September 1, 2009.)

### Sec. 2309.102. Rules.

(a) The commission shall adopt rules for licensing used automotive parts recyclers and used automotive parts employees.

(b) The commission by rule shall adopt standards of conduct for license holders under this chapter.

(Enacted by Acts 2009, 81st Leg., ch. 783 (S.B. 1095), § 7, effective September 1, 2009; Enacted by Acts 2009, 81st Leg., ch. 933 (H.B. 3097), § 4.07, effective September 1, 2009.)

### Sec. 2309.103.   Rules Regarding Licensing and Standards of Conduct.

(a) The commission shall adopt rules for licensing applicants, including rules for denial of an application if the applicant, a partner, principal, officer, or general manager of the applicant, or another license or permit holder with a connection to the applicant, has:

(1) before the application date, been convicted of, pleaded guilty or nolo contendere to, or been placed on deferred adjudication for:

(A) a felony; or

(B) a misdemeanor punishable by confinement in jail or by a fine exceeding $500;

(2) violated an order of the commission or executive director, including an order for sanctions or administrative penalties; or

(3) knowingly submitted false information on the application.

(b) The commission by rule shall adopt standards of conduct for license holders under this chapter.

(Enacted by Acts 2009, 81st Leg., ch. 783 (S.B. 1095), § 7, effective September 1, 2009; Enacted by Acts 2009, 81st Leg., ch. 933 (H.B. 3097), § 4.07, effective September 1, 2009.)

### Sec. 2309.104.   Fees.

The commission shall establish and collect reasonable and necessary fees in amounts sufficient to cover the costs of administering this chapter.

(Enacted by Acts 2009, 81st Leg., ch. 783 (S.B. 1095), § 7, effective September 1, 2009; Enacted by Acts 2009, 81st Leg., ch. 933 (H.B. 3097), § 4.07, effective September 1, 2009.)

### Sec. 2309.105.   Rules Restricting Advertising or Competitive Bidding.

(a) The commission may not adopt a rule restricting advertising or competitive bidding by a person who holds a license issued under this chapter except to prohibit false, misleading, or deceptive practices by the person.

(b) The commission may not include in its rules to prohibit false, misleading, or deceptive practices a rule that:

(1) restricts the use of any advertising medium;

(2) restricts the person's personal appearance or use of the person's voice in an advertisement;

(3) relates to the size or duration of an advertisement by the person; or

(4) restricts the use of a trade name in advertising by the person.

(Enacted by Acts 2009, 81st Leg., ch. 783 (S.B. 1095), § 7, effective September 1, 2009; Enacted by Acts 2009, 81st Leg., ch. 933 (H.B. 3097), § 4.07, effective September 1, 2009.)

### Sec. 2309.106.   Periodic and Risk-Based Inspections.

(a) The department shall inspect each used automotive parts recycling facility at least once every two years.

(b) The department may enter and inspect at any time during business hours:

(1) the place of business of any person regulated under this chapter; or

(2) any place in which the department has reasonable cause to believe that a license holder is in violation of this chapter or in violation of a rule or order of the commission or executive director.

(c) The department shall conduct additional inspections based on a schedule of risk-based inspections using the following criteria:

(1) the inspection history;

(2) any history of complaints involving a used automotive parts recycler; and

(3) any other factor determined by the commission by rule.

(d) A used automotive parts recycler shall pay a fee for each risk-based inspection performed under this section. The commission by rule shall set the amount of the fee.

(e) In conducting an inspection under this section, the department may inspect a facility, a used automotive part, a business record, or any other place or thing reasonably required to enforce this chapter or a rule or order adopted under this chapter.

(Enacted by Acts 2009, 81st Leg., ch. 783 (S.B. 1095), § 7, effective September 1, 2009; Enacted by Acts 2009, 81st Leg., ch. 933 (H.B. 3097), § 4.07, effective September 1, 2009.)

### Sec. 2309.107.   Personnel.

The department may employ personnel necessary to administer and enforce this chapter.

(Enacted by Acts 2009, 81st Leg., ch. 783 (S.B. 1095), § 7, effective September 1, 2009; Enacted by Acts 2009, 81st Leg., ch. 933 (H.B. 3097), § 4.07, effective September 1, 2009.)

Occupations

## SUBCHAPTER D
## LICENSE REQUIREMENTS

### Sec. 2309.151. Used Automotive Parts Recycler License Required.

(a) Unless the person holds a used automotive parts recycler license issued under this chapter, a person may not own or operate a used automotive parts recycling business or sell used automotive parts.

(b) A used automotive parts recycler license:

(1) is valid only with respect to the person who applied for the license; and

(2) authorizes the license holder to operate a used automotive parts recycling business only at the one facility listed on the license.

(Enacted by Acts 2009, 81st Leg., ch. 783 (S.B. 1095), § 7, effective September 1, 2010; Enacted by Acts 2009, 81st Leg., ch. 933 (H.B. 3097), § 4.07, effective September 1, 2010.)

### Sec. 2309.152. General License Application Requirements.

An applicant for a used automotive parts recycler license under this chapter must submit to the department:

(1) a completed application on a form prescribed by the executive director;

(2) the required fees; and

(3) any other information required by commission rule.

(Enacted by Acts 2009, 81st Leg., ch. 783 (S.B. 1095), § 7, effective September 1, 2009; Enacted by Acts 2009, 81st Leg., ch. 933 (H.B. 3097), § 4.07, effective September 1, 2009.)

### Sec. 2309.153. License Requirements.

An applicant for a used automotive parts recycler license under this chapter must provide in a manner prescribed by the executive director:

(1) a federal tax identification number;

(2) proof of general liability insurance in an amount not less than $250,000; and

(3) proof of a storm water permit if the applicant is required by the Texas Commission on Environmental Quality to obtain a permit.

(Enacted by Acts 2009, 81st Leg., ch. 783 (S.B. 1095), § 7, effective September 1, 2009; Enacted by Acts 2009, 81st Leg., ch. 933 (H.B. 3097), § 4.07, effective September 1, 2009.)

### Sec. 2309.154. Used Automotive Parts Employee License Required.

(a) A person employed by a used automotive parts recycler may not in the scope of the person's employment acquire a vehicle or used automotive parts and may not sell used automotive parts unless the person holds a used automotive parts employee license issued under this chapter.

(b) The commission by rule shall adopt requirements for the application for and issuance of a used automotive parts employee license under this chapter.

(Enacted by Acts 2009, 81st Leg., ch. 783 (S.B. 1095), § 7, effective September 1, 2010; Enacted by Acts 2009, 81st Leg., ch. 933 (H.B. 3097), § 4.07, effective September 1, 2010.)

### Sec. 2309.155. Nontransferability of License.

A license issued by the executive director is valid throughout this state and is not transferable.

(Enacted by Acts 2009, 81st Leg., ch. 783 (S.B. 1095), § 7, effective September 1, 2009; Enacted by Acts 2009, 81st Leg., ch. 933 (H.B. 3097), § 4.07, effective September 1, 2009.)

### Sec. 2309.156. License Renewal.

(a) A license issued under this chapter is valid for one year. The department may adopt a system under which licenses expire at different times during the year.

(b) The department shall notify the license holder at least 30 days before the date a license expires. The notice must be in writing and sent to the license holder's last known address according to the records of the department.

(c) The commission by rule shall adopt requirements to renew a license issued under this chapter.

(Enacted by Acts 2009, 81st Leg., ch. 783 (S.B. 1095), § 7, effective September 1, 2009; Enacted by Acts 2009, 81st Leg., ch. 933 (H.B. 3097), § 4.07, effective September 1, 2009.)

## SUBCHAPTER E
## LOCAL REGULATION

### Sec. 2309.201. Applicability of Certain Municipal Ordinances, Licenses, and Permits.

(a) The requirements of this chapter apply in addition to the requirements of any applicable municipal ordinance relating to the regulation of a person who deals in used automotive parts.

(b) This chapter does not prohibit the enforcement of an applicable municipal license or permit

requirement that is related to an activity regulated under this chapter.
(Enacted by Acts 2009, 81st Leg., ch. 783 (S.B. 1095), § 7, effective September 1, 2009; Enacted by Acts 2009, 81st Leg., ch. 933 (H.B. 3097), § 4.07, effective September 1, 2009.)

## SUBCHAPTER F
## ENFORCEMENT

### Sec. 2309.251.   Administrative Penalty.

(a) The commission may impose an administrative penalty on a person under Subchapter F, Chapter 51, regardless of whether the person holds a license under this chapter, if the person violates:

(1) this chapter or a rule adopted under this chapter; or

(2) a rule or order of the executive director or commission.

(b) An administrative penalty may not be imposed unless the person charged with a violation is provided the opportunity for a hearing.
(Enacted by Acts 2009, 81st Leg., ch. 783 (S.B. 1095), § 7, effective September 1, 2010; Enacted by Acts 2009, 81st Leg., ch. 933 (H.B. 3097), § 4.07, effective September 1, 2010.)

### Sec. 2309.252.   Cease and Desist Order; Injunction; Civil Penalty.

(a) The executive director may issue a cease and desist order as necessary to enforce this chapter if the executive director determines that the action is necessary to prevent a violation of this chapter and to protect public health and safety.

(b) The attorney general or executive director may institute an action for an injunction or a civil penalty under this chapter as provided by Section 51.352.
(Enacted by Acts 2009, 81st Leg., ch. 783 (S.B. 1095), § 7, effective September 1, 2010; Enacted by Acts 2009, 81st Leg., ch. 933 (H.B. 3097), § 4.07, effective September 1, 2010.)

### Sec. 2309.253.   Sanctions.

The department may impose sanctions as provided by Section 51.353.
(Enacted by Acts 2009, 81st Leg., ch. 783 (S.B. 1095), § 7, effective September 1, 2010; Enacted by Acts 2009, 81st Leg., ch. 933 (H.B. 3097), § 4.07, effective September 1, 2010.)

### Sec. 2309.254.   Criminal Penalty; Licensing.

(a) A person commits an offense if the person:

(1) violates the licensing requirements of this chapter;

(2) deals in used parts without a license required by this chapter; or

(3) employs an individual who does not hold the appropriate license required by this chapter.

(b) An offense under this section is a Class C misdemeanor.
(Enacted by Acts 2009, 81st Leg., ch. 783 (S.B. 1095), § 7, effective September 1, 2010; Enacted by Acts 2009, 81st Leg., ch. 933 (H.B. 3097), § 4.07, effective September 1, 2010.)

## SUBCHAPTER G
## CONDUCTING BUSINESS

### Sec. 2309.301.   Duties on Acquisition of Salvage Motor Vehicle.

(a) A used automotive parts recycler who acquires ownership of a salvage motor vehicle shall obtain a properly assigned title from the previous owner of the vehicle.

(b) A used automotive parts recycler who acquires ownership of a motor vehicle, nonrepairable motor vehicle, or salvage motor vehicle for the purpose of dismantling, scrapping, or destroying the motor vehicle, shall, before the 31st day after the date of acquiring the motor vehicle, submit to the Texas Department of Transportation a properly assigned manufacturer's certificate of origin, regular certificate of title, nonrepairable vehicle title, salvage vehicle title, other ownership document, or comparable out-of-state ownership document for the motor vehicle.

(c) After receiving the title or document, the Texas Department of Transportation shall issue the used automotive parts recycler a receipt for the manufacturer's certificate of origin, regular certificate of title, nonrepairable vehicle title, salvage vehicle title, other ownership document, or comparable out-of-state ownership document.

(d) The recycler shall comply with Subchapter E, Chapter 501, Transportation Code.
(Enacted by Acts 2009, 81st Leg., ch. 783 (S.B. 1095), § 7, effective September 1, 2009; Enacted by Acts 2009, 81st Leg., ch. 933 (H.B. 3097), § 4.07, effective September 1, 2009.)

### Sec. 2309.302.   Records of Purchases.

A used automotive parts recycler shall maintain a record of or sales receipt for each motor vehicle, salvage motor vehicle, nonrepairable motor vehicle, and used automotive part purchased. (Enacted by Acts 2009, 81st Leg., ch. 783 (S.B. 1095), § 7, effective September 1, 2009; Enacted by Acts 2009, 81st Leg., ch. 933 (H.B. 3097), § 4.07, effective September 1, 2009.)

### Sec. 2309.303. Registration of New Business Location.

Before moving a place of business, a used automotive parts recycler must notify the department of the new location. The used automotive parts recycler shall provide a storm water permit for the location if a permit is required by the Texas Commission on Environmental Quality. (Enacted by Acts 2009, 81st Leg., ch. 783 (S.B. 1095), § 7, effective September 1, 2009; Enacted by Acts 2009, 81st Leg., ch. 933 (H.B. 3097), § 4.07, effective September 1, 2009.)

### SUBCHAPTER H
### ADDITIONAL DUTIES OF USED AUTOMOTIVE PARTS RECYCLER IN CONNECTION WITH MOTOR VEHICLE COMPONENT PARTS

### Sec. 2309.351. Definitions.

In this subchapter:

(1) "Component part" means a major component part as defined by Section 501.091, Transportation Code, or a minor component part.

(2) "Interior component part" means a motor vehicle's seat or radio.

(3) "Minor component part" means an interior component part, a special accessory part, or a motor vehicle part that displays or should display at least one of the following:

(A) a federal safety certificate;

(B) a motor number;

(C) a serial number or a derivative; or

(D) a manufacturer's permanent vehicle identification number or a derivative.

(4) "Special accessory part" means a motor vehicle's tire, wheel, tailgate, or removable glass top.

(Enacted by Acts 2009, 81st Leg., ch. 783 (S.B. 1095), § 7, effective September 1, 2009; Enacted by Acts 2009, 81st Leg., ch. 933 (H.B. 3097), § 4.07, effective September 1, 2009.)

### Sec. 2309.352. Removal of License Plates.

Immediately on receipt of a motor vehicle, a used automotive parts recycler shall:

(1) remove any unexpired license plates from the vehicle; and

(2) place the license plates in a secure place until destroyed by the used automotive parts recycler.

(Enacted by Acts 2009, 81st Leg., ch. 783 (S.B. 1095), § 7, effective September 1, 2009; Enacted by Acts 2009, 81st Leg., ch. 933 (H.B. 3097), § 4.07, effective September 1, 2009.)

### Sec. 2309.353. Dismantlement or Disposition of Motor Vehicle.

A used automotive parts recycler may not dismantle or dispose of a motor vehicle unless the recycler first obtains:

(1) a certificate of authority to dispose of the vehicle, a sales receipt, or a transfer document for the vehicle issued under Chapter 683, Transportation Code; or

(2) a certificate of title showing that there are no liens on the vehicle or that all recorded liens have been released.

(Enacted by Acts 2009, 81st Leg., ch. 783 (S.B. 1095), § 7, effective September 1, 2009; Enacted by Acts 2009, 81st Leg., ch. 933 (H.B. 3097), § 4.07, effective September 1, 2009.)

### Sec. 2309.354. Record of Purchase; Inventory of Parts.

(a) A used automotive parts recycler shall keep an accurate and legible record of each used component part purchased by or delivered to the recycler. The record must include:

(1) the date of purchase or delivery;

(2) the driver's license number of the seller and a legible photocopy of the seller's driver's license; and

(3) a description of the part and, if applicable, the make and model of the part.

(b) As an alternative to the information required by Subsection (a), a used automotive parts recycler may record:

(1) the name of the person who sold the part or the motor vehicle from which the part was obtained; and

(2) the Texas certificate of inventory number or the federal taxpayer identification number of the person.

(c) The department shall prescribe the form of the record required by Subsection (a) and shall make the form available to used automotive parts recyclers.

(d) This section does not apply to:

(1) an interior component part or special accessory part from a motor vehicle more than 10 years old; or

(2) a part delivered to a used automotive parts recycler by a commercial freight line, commercial carrier, or licensed used automotive parts recycler.

(Enacted by Acts 2009, 81st Leg., ch. 783 (S.B. 1095), § 7, effective September 1, 2009; Enacted by Acts 2009, 81st Leg., ch. 933 (H.B. 3097), § 4.07, effective September 1, 2009.)

### Sec. 2309.355.  Retention of Component Parts.

(a) A used automotive parts recycler shall retain each component part in its original condition on the business premises of the recycler for at least three calendar days, excluding Sundays, after the date the recycler obtains the part.

(b) This section does not apply to the purchase by a used automotive parts recycler of a nonoperational engine, transmission, or rear axle assembly from another used automotive parts recycler or an automotive-related business.

(Enacted by Acts 2009, 81st Leg., ch. 783 (S.B. 1095), § 7, effective September 1, 2009; Enacted by Acts 2009, 81st Leg., ch. 933 (H.B. 3097), § 4.07, effective September 1, 2009.)

### Sec. 2309.356.  Maintenance of Records.

A used automotive parts recycler shall maintain copies of each record required under this subchapter until the first anniversary of the purchase date of the item for which the record is maintained.

(Enacted by Acts 2009, 81st Leg., ch. 783 (S.B. 1095), § 7, effective September 1, 2009; Enacted by Acts 2009, 81st Leg., ch. 933 (H.B. 3097), § 4.07, effective September 1, 2009.)

### Sec. 2309.357.  Surrender of Certain Documents or License Plates.

(a) A used automotive parts recycler shall surrender to the Texas Department of Transportation for cancellation a certificate of title or authority, sales receipt, or transfer document, as required by the department.

(b) The Texas Department of Transportation shall provide a signed receipt for a surrendered certificate of title.

(Enacted by Acts 2009, 81st Leg., ch. 783 (S.B. 1095), § 7, effective September 1, 2009; Enacted

by Acts 2009, 81st Leg., ch. 933 (H.B. 3097), § 4.07, effective September 1, 2009.)

### Sec. 2309.358.  Inspection of Records.

(a) A peace officer at any reasonable time may inspect a record required to be maintained under this subchapter, including an inventory record.

(b) On demand by a peace officer, a used automotive parts recycler shall provide to the officer a copy of a record required to be maintained under this subchapter.

(c) A peace officer may inspect the inventory on the premises of a used automotive parts recycler at any reasonable time to verify, check, or audit the records required to be maintained under this subchapter.

(d) A used automotive parts recycler or an employee of the recycler shall allow and may not interfere with a peace officer's inspection of the recycler's inventory, premises, or required inventory records.

(Enacted by Acts 2009, 81st Leg., ch. 783 (S.B. 1095), § 7, effective September 1, 2009; Enacted by Acts 2009, 81st Leg., ch. 933 (H.B. 3097), § 4.07, effective September 1, 2009.)

## SUBCHAPTER I
## MOTOR VEHICLE SALVAGE YARDS IN CERTAIN COUNTIES

### Sec. 2309.401.  Applicability of Subchapter.

This subchapter applies only to a used automotive parts facility located in a county with a population of 2.8 million or more.

(Enacted by Acts 2009, 81st Leg., ch. 783 (S.B. 1095), § 7, effective September 1, 2009; Enacted by Acts 2009, 81st Leg., ch. 933 (H.B. 3097), § 4.07, effective September 1, 2009.)

### Sec. 2309.402.  Limits on Operation of Heavy Machinery.

(a) A used automotive parts recycler may not operate heavy machinery in a used automotive parts recycling facility between the hours of 7 p.m. of one day and 7 a.m. of the following day.

(b) This section does not apply to conduct necessary to a sale or purchase by the recycler.

(Enacted by Acts 2009, 81st Leg., ch. 783 (S.B. 1095), § 7, effective September 1, 2009; Enacted by Acts 2009, 81st Leg., ch. 933 (H.B. 3097), § 4.07, effective September 1, 2009.)

Occupations

# Parks and Wildlife

## TITLE 5
## WILDLIFE AND PLANT CONSERVATION

### SUBTITLE I
### PROTECTED FRESHWATER AREAS

### CHAPTER 90
### ACCESS TO PROTECTED
### FRESHWATER AREAS

### Sec. 90.001.  Definitions.

In this chapter:

(1) "Emergency" means a condition or circumstance in which a person reasonably believes that an individual has sustained serious bodily injury or is in imminent danger of serious bodily injury or that property has sustained significant damage or destruction or is in imminent danger of significant damage or destruction.

(2) "Motor vehicle" means any wheeled or tracked vehicle, machine, tractor, trailer, or semitrailer propelled or drawn by mechanical power and used to transport a person or thing.

(3) "Navigable river or stream" means a river or stream that retains an average width of 30 or more feet from the mouth or confluence up.

(4) "Protected freshwater area" means that portion of the bed, bottom, or bank of any navigable river or stream that lies at or below the gradient boundary of the river or stream. The term does not include that portion of a bed, bottom, or bank that lies below tidewater limits.

(Enacted by Acts 2003, 78th Leg., ch. 800 (S.B. 155), § 2, effective September 1, 2003.)

### Sec. 90.002.  Operation of Motor Vehicle in Protected Freshwater Area Prohibited.

Except as provided by Section 90.003 or 90.004, a person may not operate a motor vehicle in or on a protected freshwater area on or after January 1, 2004.

(Enacted by Acts 2003, 78th Leg., ch. 800 (S.B. 155), § 2, effective September 1, 2003.)

### Sec. 90.003.  Exemptions.

(a) Section 90.002 does not apply to:

(1) a state, county, or municipal road right-of-way;

(2) a private road crossing established on or before December 31, 2003; or

(3) operation of a motor vehicle by:

(A) a federal, state, or local government employee if operation of a motor vehicle is necessary for conducting official business;

(B) a person if operation of a motor vehicle is necessary for reasonable purposes related to usual and customary agricultural activities;

(C) a person if operation of a motor vehicle is necessary to and is authorized by a mineral lease;

(D) a person if operation of a motor vehicle is necessary to and authorized by a crossing easement granted by the General Land Office under the Natural Resources Code;

(E) a person if operation of a motor vehicle is necessary to an activity authorized by Chapter 86;

(F) a person in response to an emergency;

(G) a person if operation of a motor vehicle is necessary for the lawful construction, operation, or maintenance of equipment, facilities, or structures used for:

(i) the production, transportation, transmission, or distribution of electric power;

(ii) the provision of telecommunications services or other services delivered through a cable system;

(iii) the transportation of aggregates, oil, natural gas, coal, or any product of oil, natural gas, or coal;

(iv) the production, treatment, or transportation of water or wastewater; or

(v) dredge material disposal placement;

(H) an owner of the uplands adjacent to a protected freshwater area, the owner's agent, lessee, sublessee, or the lessee or sublessee's agent, representative, licensee, invitee, or guest for reasonable purposes related to usual and customary operation of:

(i) a camp regulated under Chapter 141, Health and Safety Code; or

(ii) a retreat facility owned and operated by a nonprofit corporation chartered under the laws of this state before January 1, 1970; or

(I) an owner of the adjacent uplands on both sides of a protected freshwater area and the owner's agents, employees, representatives, and lessees only for the purpose of accessing the owner's property on the opposite side of the protected freshwater area when no reasonable alternate access is available.

(b) This chapter does not apply to any river with headwaters in a state other than Texas and a mouth or confluence in a state other than Texas.

(c) A person exempt under this section who operates a motor vehicle in or on a protected freshwater area shall do so in a manner that avoids, to the extent reasonably possible, harming or disturbing vegetation, wildlife, or wildlife habitat within the protected freshwater area. A person exempt under this section who is crossing a protected freshwater area shall cross by the most direct feasible route.

(Enacted by Acts 2003, 78th Leg., ch. 800 (S.B. 155), § 2, effective September 1, 2003.)

## Sec. 90.004. Local River Access Plan.

(a) A county, municipality, or river authority may adopt a written local plan to provide access to a protected freshwater area located within the county's geographical boundaries or the river authority's or municipality's jurisdiction.

(b) A local plan adopted under Subsection (a) may:

(1) notwithstanding Section 90.002, allow limited motor vehicle use in a protected freshwater area;

(2) provide for the county, municipality, or river authority to collect a fee from a person accessing a protected freshwater area, the amount of which may not exceed the estimated cost that the county, municipality, or river authority incurs by allowing the limited use of motorized vehicles in protected freshwater areas within its jurisdiction; or

(3) establish other measures consistent with the policy and purposes of this chapter.

(c) Before a local plan adopted under Subsection (a) may take effect, a county, municipality, or river authority must file the plan with the department. A local plan does not take effect until the plan is approved in writing by the department.

(d) The department may approve, disapprove, or modify a local plan filed under Subsection (c). In determining whether to approve, disapprove, or modify a local plan, the department shall consider whether the plan:

(1) protects fish, wildlife, water quality, and other natural resources;

(2) protects public safety;

(3) provides for adequate enforcement;

(4) coordinates with adjacent and overlapping jurisdictions;

(5) provides for and publicizes adequate public access to a protected freshwater area;

(6) provides for adequate public services relating to access to a protected freshwater area; and

(7) protects private property rights.

(e) The department by rule may adopt additional criteria or procedures to govern approval of local plans. Lack of rules adopted under this section alone is not a sufficient basis for rejecting a local plan.

(f) The department may conduct periodic reviews of a local plan filed under Subsection (c) to monitor the effectiveness of the plan.

(g) A person who has reason to believe that a local plan filed under Subsection (c) does not comply with this section may file a petition for revocation of the plan with the department.

(h) The department shall revoke approval of a local plan if the department finds, as a result of a periodic review conducted under Subsection (f) or a petition for revocation filed under Subsection (g), that the plan as implemented fails to meet any of the criteria for approval established by Subsection (d).

(i) The department may adopt rules necessary to implement this section and Section 90.002, including rules relating to locations from which a person may launch or retrieve a vessel by trailer from the banks of a protected freshwater area. For purposes of this subsection, "vessel" has the meaning assigned by Section 12.101.
(Enacted by Acts 2003, 78th Leg., ch. 800 (S.B. 155), § 2, effective September 1, 2003.)

## Sec. 90.010.　Enforcement.

All peace officers of this state shall enforce the provisions of this chapter.
(Enacted by Acts 2003, 78th Leg., ch. 800 (S.B. 155), § 2, effective September 1, 2003.)

## Sec. 90.011.　Penalty.

(a) A person commits an offense if the person violates Section 90.002 or 90.008.

(b) Except as provided by Subsection (c), an offense under Subsection (a) is a Class C misdemeanor.

(c) If it is shown on the trial of an offense under this section that the defendant was previously convicted two or more times under Section 90.002 or 90.008, on conviction the defendant shall be punished for a Class B misdemeanor.

(d) Each violation under this section is a separate offense.

(e) Notwithstanding Section 12.403 of this code, Subchapter B, Chapter 12, Penal Code, applies to punishments under this section.
(Enacted by Acts 2003, 78th Leg., ch. 800 (S.B. 155), § 2, effective September 1, 2003.)

# Tax Code

## TITLE 2
## STATE TAXATION

### SUBTITLE B
### ENFORCEMENT AND COLLECTION

### CHAPTER 111
### COLLECTION PROCEDURES

#### SUBCHAPTER A
#### COLLECTION DUTIES AND POWERS

**Sec. 111.021. Notice to Holders of and Levy upon Assets Belonging to Delinquent.**

(a) If a person is delinquent in the payment of an amount required to be paid or has not paid an amount claimed in a determination made against the person, the comptroller may notify personally, by mail, or by means of facsimile or electronic transmission any other person who:

(1) possesses or controls a credit, bank or savings account, deposit, or other intangible or personal property belonging to the delinquent or the person against whom the unpaid determination is made, hereafter referred to as "assets"; or

(2) owes a debt to the delinquent or person against whom the unpaid determination is made.

(b) A notice under this section to a state officer, department, or agency must be given before the officer, department, or agency presents to the comptroller the claim of the delinquent or person to whom the unpaid determination applies.

(c) A notice under this section may be given at any time within three years after the payment becomes delinquent or within three years after the last recording of a lien filed under this title, but not thereafter. The notice must state the amount of taxes, penalties and interest due and owing, and an additional amount of penalties and interest that will accrue by operation of law in a period not to exceed 30 days and, in the case of a credit, bank or savings account or deposit, is effective only up to that amount.

(d) On receipt of a notice given under this section, the person receiving the notice:

(1) within 20 days after receiving the notice shall advise the comptroller of each such asset belonging to the delinquent or person to whom an unpaid determination applies that is possessed or controlled by the person receiving the notice and of each debt owed by the person receiving the notice to the delinquent person or person to whom an unpaid determination applies;

(2) may not transfer or dispose of the asset or debt possessed, controlled, or owed by the person at the time the person received the notice for a period of 60 days after receipt of the notice, unless the comptroller consents to an earlier disposal; and

(3) may not avoid or attempt to avoid compliance with this section by filing an interpleader action in court and depositing the delinquent's or person's funds or other assets into the registry of the court.

(e) A notice under this section that attempts to prohibit the transfer or disposal of an asset possessed or controlled by a bank or other financial institution is governed by Section 59.008, Finance Code, and also is effective if it is delivered or mailed to the principal or any branch office of the bank or other financial institution including any office of the bank or other financial institution at which the deposit is carried or the credit or property is held.

(f) A person who has received a notice under this section and who violates Subdivision (2) of Subsection (d) of this section is liable to the state for the amount of indebtedness of the person with respect to whose obligation the notice was given to the extent of the value of the asset or debt transferred or disposed of.

(f-1) A person who fails or refuses to comply with this section after receiving a notice of freeze or levy is liable for a penalty in an amount equal to 50 percent of the amount sought to be frozen or levied. This penalty is in addition to the liability imposed under Subsection (f). The penalty may be assessed and collected by the comptroller using any remedy available to collect other amounts under this title.

(g) At any time during the 60-day period as stated in Subdivision (2) of Subsection (d) of this section, the comptroller may levy upon the asset or debt. The levy shall be accomplished by delivery of a notice of levy, upon receipt of which the person possessing the asset or debt shall transfer the asset to the comptroller or pay to the comptroller the amount owed to the delinquent or to the person against whom the unpaid determination is made.

(h) A notice delivered under this section is effective:

(1) at the time of delivery against all property, rights to property, credits, and/or debts involving the delinquent taxpayer which are not at the time of the notice subject to an attachment, garnishment, or execution issued through a judicial process; and

(2) against all property, rights to property, credits and/or debts involving the delinquent taxpayer that come into the possession or control of the person served with the notice within the 60-day period provided by Subdivision (2) of Subsection (d) of this section.

(i) Any person acting in accordance with the terms of the notice of freeze or levy issued by the comptroller is discharged from any obligation or liability to the delinquent taxpayer with respect to such property or rights to property, credits, and/or debts of the taxpayer affected by compliance with the notice of freeze or levy.

(j) For purposes of collecting delinquent taxes imposed under Chapter 159, the term "asset" includes the contents of a safe deposit box. The comptroller shall issue regulations specifying procedures for accomplishing a levy upon the contents of a safe deposit box, including rules relating to inventory of the box contents, delivery of the contents, and reimbursement to the financial institution or other safe deposit box facility for drilling and other costs.
(Enacted by Acts 1987, 70th Leg., 2nd C.S., ch. 1 (S.B. 28), § 6, effective July 21, 1987; am. Acts

1993, 73rd Leg., ch. 362 (H.B. 365), § 1, effective September 1, 1993; am. Acts 1993, 73rd Leg., ch. 486 (S.B. 82), § 1.03, effective September 1, 1993; am. Acts 1999, 76th Leg., ch. 344 (H.B. 2066), § 7.009, effective September 1, 1999; am. Acts 2001, 77th Leg., ch. 442 (S.B. 1123), § 4, effective September 1, 2001 am. Acts 2007, 80th Leg., ch. 931 (H.B. 3314), § 4, effective June 15, 2007.)

# SUBTITLE E
## SALES, EXCISE, AND USE TAXES

# CHAPTER 159
## CONTROLLED SUBSTANCES TAX

### Subchapter A. General Provisions

## SUBCHAPTER A
## GENERAL PROVISIONS

### Sec. 159.001.   Definitions.

In this chapter:

(1) "Controlled substance" has the meaning assigned by Section 481.002, Health and Safety Code.

(2) "Counterfeit substance" has the meaning assigned by Section 481.002, Health and Safety Code.

(3) "Dealer" means a person who in violation of the law of this state imports into this state or manufactures, produces, acquires, or possesses in this state:

(A) seven grams or more of a taxable substance consisting of or containing a con-

*Tax Code*

trolled substance, counterfeit substance, or simulated controlled substance;

　(B) fifty dosage units or more of a taxable substance not commonly sold by weight, consisting of or containing a controlled substance, counterfeit substance, or simulated controlled substance; or

　(C) more than four ounces of a taxable substance consisting of or containing marihuana.

　(4) "Marihuana" has the meaning assigned by Section 481.002, Health and Safety Code.

　(5) "Simulated controlled substance" has the meaning assigned by Section 482.001, Health and Safety Code.

　(6) "Tax payment certificate" means a stamp or other device provided by the comptroller under Section 159.003 of this code for use under this chapter.

　(7) "Taxable substance" means a controlled substance, a counterfeit substance, a simulated controlled substance, or marihuana, or a mixture of any materials that contains a controlled substance, counterfeit substance, simulated controlled substance, or marihuana.

　(8) "Dosage unit" means a tablet, pill, capsule, vial, ampule, or other identifiable or separated unit designed or packaged to be used, taken, or ingested at one time.

(Enacted by Acts 1989, 71st Leg., ch. 1152 (H.B. 24), § 1, effective September 1, 1989; am. Acts 1991, 72nd Leg., ch. 14, § 284(45), (65), effective September 1, 1991; am. Acts 1991, 72nd Leg., ch. 705 (H.B. 1814), § 20, effective September 1, 1991; am. Acts 1993, 73rd Leg., ch. 1031 (S.B. 893), § 23, effective September 1, 1993.)

## Sec. 159.002.　Measurements.

For purposes of this chapter, the weight of a taxable substance is its weight in the possession of the dealer.

(Enacted by Acts 1989, 71st Leg., ch. 1152 (H.B. 24), § 1, effective September 1, 1989.)

## Sec. 159.003.　Tax Payment Certificates.

　(a) The comptroller shall adopt a uniform system for providing, affixing, and displaying official tax payment certificates to be attached to a taxable substance as evidence that the tax imposed by this chapter has been paid.

　(b) A tax payment certificate may not be used more than once.

(Enacted by Acts 1989, 71st Leg., ch. 1152 (H.B. 24), § 1, effective September 1, 1989.)

## Sec. 159.004.　No Defense or Immunity.

Nothing in this chapter provides a defense or affirmative defense to, exception to, or immunity from prosecution under the penal laws of this state relating to controlled substances, counterfeit substances, simulated controlled substances, or marihuana.

(Enacted by Acts 1989, 71st Leg., ch. 1152 (H.B. 24), § 1, effective September 1, 1989.)

## Sec. 159.005.　Confidential Information.

　(a) Information provided by a person in a report or return made for purposes of paying a tax imposed by this chapter is confidential.

　(b) The comptroller or any other public official or employee commits an offense if he reveals information made confidential by this section to any person other than:

　(1) to the comptroller or a public official or employee whose duties involve the administration or collection of the taxes imposed by this chapter; or

　(2) in a judicial proceeding involving a tax imposed by this chapter.

　(c) An offense under Subsection (b) of this section is a Class A misdemeanor.

　(d) Except in a prosecution directly related to a tax imposed by this chapter, information made confidential by this section may not be used in any way in a prosecution of the dealer for whom the report or return is made unless the information is obtained independently of the report or return.

(Enacted by Acts 1989, 71st Leg., ch. 1152 (H.B. 24), § 1, effective September 1, 1989.)

## SUBCHAPTER B
## IMPOSITION, RATE, AND PAYMENT OF TAX

## Sec. 159.101.　Tax Imposed; Rate of Tax.

　(a) A tax is imposed on the possession, purchase, acquisition, importation, manufacture, or production by a dealer of a taxable substance on which a tax has not previously been paid under this chapter.

　(b) The rate of the tax is:

　(1) $200 for each gram of a taxable substance consisting of or containing a controlled substance, counterfeit substance, or simulated controlled substance;

Tax Code

(2) $3.50 for each gram of a taxable substance consisting of or containing marihuana; and

(3) $2,000 on each 50 dosage units, or portion of 50 dosage units, if the total amount is less than 50 dosage units, of a controlled substance that is not sold by weight.

(c) The tax becomes due immediately when a dealer possesses, purchases, acquires, manufactures, or produces in this state or imports into this state the taxable substance on which the tax has not previously been paid.

(d) In determining the total weight of taxable substance, a part of a gram remaining after the measurement of whole grams is considered as one gram.

(e) For purposes of this section, if a taxable substance consists of a mixture containing both marihuana and another substance listed in the definition of taxable substance provided by Section 159.001 of this code, the taxable substance is taxable under Subsection (b)(1) of this section and not under Subsection (b)(2) of this section.

(f) If a determination made under this chapter becomes final without payment of the amount of the determination being made, the comptroller shall add to the amount a penalty of 10 percent of the amount of the tax and interest.

(g) In a redetermination proceeding held or a judicial proceeding brought under this chapter, a certificate from the comptroller that shows the issued determination is prima facie evidence of:

(1) the determination of the stated tax or amount of the tax;

(2) the stated amount of the penalties and interest; and

(3) the compliance of the comptroller with this chapter in computing and determining the amount due.

(h) The suppression of evidence on any ground in a criminal case that arises out of facts on which a determination is made under this chapter or the dismissal of criminal charges in such a case does not affect a determination made under this chapter.

(Enacted by Acts 1989, 71st Leg., ch. 1152 (H.B. 24), § 1, effective September 1, 1989; am. Acts 1991, 72nd Leg., ch. 484 (H.B. 2595), § 1, effective September 1, 1991; am. Acts 1991, 72nd Leg., ch. 705 (H.B. 1814), § 21, effective September 1, 1991; am. Acts 1995, 74th Leg., ch. 1000 (S.B. 640), § 57, effective October 1, 1995.)

## Sec. 159.102.   Tax Payment Certificate Required.

(a) A dealer who pays a tax imposed by this chapter shall securely affix in the manner required by the comptroller to the taxable substance the appropriate tax payment certificate to show payment of the tax.

(b) A dealer shall obtain the necessary tax payment certificates before the tax becomes due as provided by Section 159.101 of this code. The possession of a taxable substance without the possession of the requisite amount or number of certificates is prima facie evidence that and is notice that the tax has not been paid as required by this chapter.

(c) The comptroller's rules shall provide for the return of unused certificates and for the refund of money for returned certificates.

(Enacted by Acts 1989, 71st Leg., ch. 1152 (H.B. 24), § 1, effective September 1, 1989.)

## Sec. 159.103.   Exemption.

The possession, purchase, acquisition, importation, manufacture, or production of a taxable substance is exempt from the tax imposed by this chapter if the activity is authorized by law.

(Enacted by Acts 1989, 71st Leg., ch. 1152 (H.B. 24), § 1, effective September 1, 1989; am. Acts 1995, 74th Leg., ch. 1000 (S.B. 640), § 58, effective October 1, 1995.)

## SUBCHAPTER C
## CRIMINAL PROVISIONS

## Sec. 159.201.   Possession of Item If Tax Unpaid.

(a) A dealer commits an offense if the dealer possesses a taxable substance on which the tax imposed by this chapter has not been paid.

(b) An offense under this section is a felony of the third degree. In addition to the fine provided by law for a felony of the third degree, a person convicted of an offense under this section shall be fined an amount equal to the amount of tax due and unpaid on the taxable substance that is the subject of the offense.

(c) An indictment for an offense under this section may be presented within six years from the date of the offense and not afterward.

(Enacted by Acts 1989, 71st Leg., ch. 1152 (H.B. 24), § 1, effective September 1, 1989.)

## Sec. 159.202. Counterfeit Tax Payment Certificates.

(a) A person commits an offense if the person:

(1) prints, engraves, makes, issues, sells, or circulates a counterfeit tax payment certificate;

(2) possesses with intent to use, sell, circulate, or pass a counterfeit tax payment certificate; or

(3) places or causes to be placed a counterfeit tax payment certificate on a taxable substance.

(b) An offense under this section is a felony of the third degree.

(c) Venue of a prosecution under this section is in Travis County.

(Enacted by Acts 1989, 71st Leg., ch. 1152 (H.B. 24), § 1, effective September 1, 1989.)

## Sec. 159.203. Previously Used Certificates.

(a) A person commits an offense if the person:

(1) uses, sells, offers for sale, or possesses for use or sale previously used tax payment certificates; or

(2) attaches or causes to be attached a previously used tax payment certificate to a taxable substance.

(b) An offense under this section is a felony of the third degree.

(c) Venue of a prosecution under this section is in Travis County.

(Enacted by Acts 1989, 71st Leg., ch. 1152 (H.B. 24), § 1, effective September 1, 1989; am. Acts 1995, 74th Leg., ch. 1000 (S.B. 640), § 60, effective October 1, 1995.)

## Sec. 159.204. Property Subject to Seizure [Repealed].

Repealed by Acts 1995, 74th Leg., ch. 1000 (S.B. 640), § 73, effective October 1, 1995.

(Enacted by Acts 1989, 71st Leg., ch. 1152 (H.B. 24), § 1, effective September 1, 1989.)

## Sec. 159.205. Right to Collect Subordinate to Other Laws.

(a) The right of the comptroller to collect the tax imposed by this chapter, including applicable penalty and interest, is subordinate to the right of a federal, state, or local law enforcement authority to seize, forfeit, and retain property under Chapter 481, Health and Safety Code; Chapter 59, Code of Criminal Procedure; or any other criminal forfeiture law of this state or of the United States. A lien filed by the comptroller as a result of the failure of a dealer to pay the tax, penalty, or interest due under this chapter is also subordinate to those rights.

(b) This section does not affect the validity of a lien or a collection action relating to the tax imposed by this chapter under any other circumstance.

(Enacted by Acts 1989, 71st Leg., ch. 1152 (H.B. 24), § 1, effective September 1, 1989; am. Acts 1991, 72nd Leg., ch. 14, § 284(54), effective September 1, 1991; am. Acts 1991, 72nd Leg., ch. 705 (H.B. 1814), § 22, effective September 1, 1991; am. Acts 1995, 74th Leg., ch. 1000 (S.B. 640), § 61, effective October 1, 1995.)

## Sec. 159.206. Settlement or Compromise of Tax.

The comptroller may settle or compromise a tax, penalty, or interest imposed under this chapter only if:

(1) the prosecutor of a criminal offense under this chapter or of another offense arising out of the same incident or transaction requests in writing that the comptroller settle or compromise and specifies the reasons for the request; and

(2) the comptroller determines that the settlement or compromise is in the best interest of the state.

(Enacted by Acts 1991, 72nd Leg., ch. 705 (H.B. 1814), § 23, effective September 1, 1991; am. Acts 1995, 74th Leg., ch. 1000 (S.B. 640), § 62, effective October 1, 1995.)

## SUBCHAPTER D
## DISPOSITION OF PROCEEDS

## Sec. 159.301. Disposition of Proceeds.

All proceeds from the collection of the tax, penalty, and interest imposed by this chapter shall be deposited to the credit of the general revenue fund. The fine imposed by Section 159.201(b) of this code and the fine provided by law for a felony shall be deposited to the credit of the county treasury of the county in which the offense occurred.

(Enacted by Acts 1989, 71st Leg., ch. 1152 (H.B. 24), § 1, effective September 1, 1989; am. Acts 1991, 72nd Leg., ch. 705 (H.B. 1814), § 24, effective September 1, 1991.)

# Utilities Code

## TITLE 2
## PUBLIC UTILITY REGULATORY ACT

### SUBTITLE C
### TELECOMMUNICATIONS UTILITIES

### CHAPTER 55
### REGULATION OF
### TELECOMMUNICATIONS SERVICES

#### Subchapter E. Caller Identification Service

### SUBCHAPTER E
### CALLER IDENTIFICATION SERVICE

### Sec. 55.101. Definitions.

In this subchapter:

(1) "Caller identification information" means any information that may be used to identify the specific originating number or originating location of a wire or electronic communication transmitted by a telephone, including the telephone listing number or the name of the customer from whose telephone a telephone number is dialed.

(2) "Caller identification service" means a service that provides caller identification information to a device that can display the information.

(3) "Per-call blocking" means a telecommunications service that prevents caller identification information from being transmitted to a called party on an individual call when the calling party affirmatively acts to prevent the transmission.

(4) "Per-line blocking" means a telecommunications service that prevents caller identification information from being transmitted to a called party on each call unless the calling party affirmatively acts to permit the transmission.

(Enacted by Acts 1997, 75th Leg., ch. 166 (S.B. 1751), § 1, effective September 1, 1997.)

### Sec. 55.102. Applicability.

(a) This subchapter applies only to the provision of caller identification service.

(b) This subchapter does not apply to:

(1) an identification service that is used in a limited system, including a central office based PBX-type system;

(2) information that is used on a public agency's emergency telephone line or on a line that receives the primary emergency telephone number (911);

(3) information exchanged between telecommunications utilities, enhanced service providers, or other entities that is necessary for the setting up, processing, transmission, or billing of telecommunications or related services;

(4) information provided in compliance with applicable law or legal process; or

(5) an identification service provided in connection with a 700, 800, or 900 access code telecommunications service.

(Enacted by Acts 1997, 75th Leg., ch. 166 (S.B. 1751), § 1, effective September 1, 1997.)

### Sec. 55.103. Provision of Service.

(a) A telecommunications utility may offer caller identification services under this subchapter only if the utility obtains written authorization from the commission.

(b) A commercial mobile service provider may offer caller identification services in accordance with Sections 55.104, 55.105, 55.106, 55.1065, and 55.107.

(Enacted by Acts 1997, 75th Leg., ch. 166 (S.B. 1751), § 1, effective September 1, 1997; am. Acts 1999, 76th Leg., ch. 62 (S.B. 1368), § 18.05(a), effective September 1, 1999.)

### Sec. 55.104.   Use of Information.

(a) A person may not use a caller identification service to compile and sell specific local call information without the affirmative approval of the originating telephone customer.

(b) This section does not prohibit a provider of caller identification service from:

(1) verifying network performance or testing the caller identification service;

(2) compiling, using, and disclosing aggregate caller identification information; or

(3) complying with applicable law or legal process.

(Enacted by Acts 1997, 75th Leg., ch. 166 (S.B. 1751), § 1, effective September 1, 1997.)

### Sec. 55.105.   Per-Call Blocking.

Except as provided by Section 55.1065, the commission shall require that a provider of caller identification service offer free per-call blocking to each telephone subscriber in the specific area in which the service is offered.

(Enacted by Acts 1997, 75th Leg., ch. 166 (S.B. 1751), § 1, effective September 1, 1997; am. Acts 1999, 76th Leg., ch. 62 (S.B. 1368), § 18.05(b), effective September 1, 1999.)

### Sec. 55.106.   Per-Line Blocking.

(a) Except as provided by Section 55.1065, the commission shall require that a provider of caller identification service offer free per-line blocking to a particular customer if the commission receives from the customer written certification that the customer has a compelling need for per-line blocking.

(b) A provider who is ordered to offer per-line blocking under this section shall notify the customer by mail of the date the blocking will begin.

(c) If a customer removes and later reinstates the per-line block, the provider may assess a service order charge in an amount approved by the commission for the provider's administrative expenses relating to the reinstatement.

(d) The commission may impose a fee or assessment on a provider in an amount sufficient to cover the additional expenses the commission incurs in implementing the customer certification provisions of this section.

(e) Information received under this section by the commission or by a provider is confidential and may be used only to administer this section.

(Enacted by Acts 1997, 75th Leg., ch. 166 (S.B. 1751), § 1, effective September 1, 1997; am. Acts 1999, 76th Leg., ch. 62 (S.B. 1368), § 18.05(c), effective September 1, 1999.)

### Sec. 55.1065.   Use of Blocking by Telephone Solicitor [Repealed].

Repealed by Acts 2001, 77th Leg., ch. 1429 (H.B. 472), § 3, effective June 17, 2001.

(Enacted by Acts 1999, 76th Leg., ch. 62 (S.B. 1368), § 18.05(d), effective September 1, 1999.)

### Sec. 55.107.   Limitation on Commission Authority.

The commission may prescribe in relation to blocking only a requirement authorized by Sections 55.105, 55.106, and 55.1065.

(Enacted by Acts 1997, 75th Leg., ch. 166 (S.B. 1751), § 1, effective September 1, 1997; am. Acts 1999, 76th Leg., ch. 62 (S.B. 1368), § 18.05(e), effective September 1, 1999.)

### Sec. 55.108.   Caller ID Consumer Education Panel [Expired].

Expired pursuant to Acts 1997, 75th Leg., ch. 166 (S.B. 1751), § 1, effective September 1, 1997.

(Enacted by Acts 1997, 75th Leg., ch. 166 (S.B. 1751), § 1, effective September 1, 1997.)

### Sec. 55.109.   Implementation of Panel Recommendations.

The commission may implement the recommendations of the Caller ID Consumer Education Panel and interested parties to the extent consistent with the public interest.

(Enacted by Acts 1997, 75th Leg., ch. 166 (S.B. 1751), § 1, effective September 1, 1997.)

### Sec. 55.110.   Report of Blocking Failure.

(a) A provider of caller ID services who becomes aware of the failure of per-call or per-line blocking to block identification of a customer shall report that failure to the commission, the Caller ID Consumer Education Panel, and the customer whose identification was not blocked.

(b) The provider shall make a reasonable effort to notify the customer within 24 hours after the

Utilities

provider becomes aware of the failure. The provider is not required to notify the customer if the customer reported the failure.

(c) In this section, "caller ID service" means a service that permits the called party to determine the identity, telephone number, or address of the calling party. The term does not include 911 services.

(Enacted by Acts 1997, 75th Leg., ch. 166 (S.B. 1751), § 1, effective September 1, 1997.)

# TITLE 4
# DELIVERY OF UTILITY SERVICES

## SUBTITLE B
## PROVISIONS REGULATING DELIVERY OF SERVICES

## CHAPTER 186
## PROVISIONS TO ENSURE THE RELIABILITY AND INTEGRITY OF UTILITY SERVICE

## SUBCHAPTER B
## MANIPULATION OF SERVICE FOR CERTAIN LAW ENFORCEMENT PURPOSES

### Sec. 186.021. Emergency Involving Hostage or Armed Suspect.

(a) In an emergency in which the supervising law enforcement official having jurisdiction in the geographical area has probable cause to believe that an armed and barricaded suspect or a person holding a hostage is committing a crime, the supervising law enforcement official may order a designated telephone company security official to cut or otherwise control telephone lines to prevent telephone communication by the armed suspect or the hostage holder with a person other than a peace officer or person authorized by a peace officer.

(b) The serving telephone company in the geographical area of a law enforcement unit shall designate a telephone company security official and an alternate to provide all required assistance to law enforcement officials to carry out this section.

(c) Good faith reliance on an order given by a supervising law enforcement official under this section is a complete defense to a civil or criminal action brought against a telephone company or the company's director, officer, agent, or employee as a result of compliance with the order.

(Enacted by Acts 1997, 75th Leg., ch. 166 (S.B. 1751), § 1, effective September 1, 1997.)

## SUBCHAPTER C
## FRAUDULENT OBTAINING OF SERVICE

### Sec. 186.031. Definitions.

In this subchapter:

(1) "Publish" means to communicate information to another by any means.

(2) "Telecommunications service" means the transmission of a message or other information by a public utility, including a telephone or telegraph company.

(Enacted by Acts 1997, 75th Leg., ch. 166 (S.B. 1751), § 1, effective September 1, 1997.)

### Sec. 186.032. Fraudulently Obtaining Telecommunications Services.

(a) A person commits an offense if:

(1) knowing that another will use the published information to avoid payment of a charge for telecommunications service, the person publishes:

(A) an existing, cancelled, revoked, or nonexistent telephone number;

(B) a credit number or other credit device; or

(C) a method of numbering or coding that is used in issuing telephone numbers or credit devices, including credit numbers; or

(2) the person makes or possesses equipment specifically designed to be used fraudulently to avoid charges for telecommunications service.

(b) An offense under this section is a misdemeanor punishable by a fine of not more than $500, by confinement in jail for not more than 60 days, or by both, unless the person has been previously convicted of an offense under this section. A second or subsequent offense is a felony punishable by a fine of not more than $5,000, by imprisonment in the Texas Department of Criminal Justice for not less than two years and not more than five years, or by both.

(c) This section does not apply to an employee of a public utility who provides telecommunications service while acting in the course of employment.

(Enacted by Acts 1997, 75th Leg., ch. 166 (S.B. 1751), § 1, effective September 1, 1997; am. Acts 2009, 81st Leg., ch. 87 (S.B. 1969), § 25.156, effective September 1, 2009.)

### Sec. 186.033.  Disposition of Certain Equipment.

(a) A peace officer may seize equipment described by Section 186.032(a)(2) under a warrant or incident to a lawful arrest.

(b) If the person who possessed equipment seized under Subsection (a) is convicted under Section 186.032, the court entering the judgment of conviction shall order the sheriff to destroy the equipment.

(Enacted by Acts 1997, 75th Leg., ch. 166 (S.B. 1751), § 1, effective September 1, 1997.)

## SUBCHAPTER D
## AVAILABILITY OF EMERGENCY TELEPHONE SERVICE

### Sec. 186.041.  Definitions.

In this subchapter:

(1) "Emergency" means a situation in which property or human life is in jeopardy and the prompt summoning of aid is essential.

(2) "Party line" means a subscriber's telephone circuit, consisting of two or more main telephone stations connected with the circuit, each station with a distinctive ring or telephone number.

(Enacted by Acts 1997, 75th Leg., ch. 166 (S.B. 1751), § 1, effective September 1, 1997.)

### Sec. 186.042.  Obstruction of Emergency Telephone Call; Penalty.

(a) A person commits an offense if:

(1) the person wilfully refuses to relinquish a party line immediately on being informed that the line is needed for an emergency call described by Subdivision (2); and

(2) the party line is needed for an emergency call:

(A) to a fire or police department; or

(B) for medical aid or an ambulance service.

(b) An offense under this section is a misdemeanor punishable by:

(1) a fine of not less than $25 and not more than $500;

(2) confinement in the county jail for not more than one month; or

(3) both fine and confinement.

(Enacted by Acts 1997, 75th Leg., ch. 166 (S.B. 1751), § 1, effective September 1, 1997.)

### Sec. 186.043.  Falsification of Emergency Telephone Call; Penalty.

(a) A person commits an offense if the person secures the use of a party line by falsely stating that the line is needed for an emergency call:

(1) to a fire or police department; or

(2) for medical aid or an ambulance service.

(b) An offense under this section is a misdemeanor punishable by:

(1) a fine of not less than $25 and not more than $500;

(2) confinement in the county jail for not more than one month; or

(3) both fine and confinement.

(Enacted by Acts 1997, 75th Leg., ch. 166 (S.B. 1751), § 1, effective September 1, 1997.)

### Sec. 186.044.  Notice of Certain Offenses Required.

(a) A telephone directory distributed to the public in this state that lists the telephone numbers of an exchange located in this state must contain a notice explaining the offenses under Sections 186.042 and 186.043. The notice must be:

(1) printed in type not smaller than the smallest type on the same page; and

Utilities

(2) preceded by the word "warning" printed in type at least as large as the largest type on the same page.

(b) At least once each year, a person providing telephone service shall enclose in the telephone bill mailed to each person who uses a party line telephone a notice of Sections 186.042 and 186.043.

(c) This section does not apply to a directory, commonly known as a classified directory, that is distributed solely for business advertising purposes.

(Enacted by Acts 1997, 75th Leg., ch. 166 (S.B. 1751), § 1, effective September 1, 1997.)

## Sec. 186.045. Failure to Provide Notice; Penalty.

(a) A person providing telephone service commits an offense if the person:

(1) distributes copies of a telephone directory subject to Section 186.044(a) from which the notice required by that section is wilfully omitted; or

(2) wilfully fails to enclose in telephone bills the notice required by Section 186.044(b).

(b) An offense under this section is a misdemeanor punishable by a fine of not less than $25 and not more than $500.

(Enacted by Acts 1997, 75th Leg., ch. 166 (S.B. 1751), § 1, effective September 1, 1997.)

# Water Code

## TITLE 2
## WATER ADMINISTRATION

### SUBTITLE D
### WATER QUALITY CONTROL

### CHAPTER 26
### WATER QUALITY CONTROL

#### SUBCHAPTER I
#### UNDERGROUND AND
#### ABOVEGROUND STORAGE TANKS

**Sec. 26.3574. Fee on Delivery of Certain Petroleum Products.**

(a) In this section:

(1) "Bulk facility" means a facility, including pipeline terminals, refinery terminals, rail and barge terminals, and associated underground and aboveground tanks, connected or separate, from which petroleum products are withdrawn from bulk and delivered into a cargo tank or a barge used to transport those products. This term does not include petroleum products consumed at an electric generating facility.

(2) "Cargo tank" means an assembly that is used for transporting, hauling, or delivering liquids and that consists of a tank having one or more compartments mounted on a wagon, truck, trailer, railcar, or wheels.

(3) "Withdrawal from bulk" means the removal of a petroleum product from a bulk facility storage tank for delivery directly into a cargo tank or a barge to be transported to another location other than another bulk facility for distribution or sale in this state.

(b) A fee is imposed on the delivery of a petroleum product on withdrawal from bulk of that product as provided by this subsection. Each operator of a bulk facility on withdrawal from bulk of a petroleum product shall collect from the person who orders the withdrawal a fee in an amount determined as follows:

(1) not more than $3.75 for each delivery into a cargo tank having a capacity of less than 2,500 gallons;

(2) not more than $7.50 for each delivery into a cargo tank having a capacity of 2,500 gallons or more but less than 5,000 gallons;

(3) not more than $11.75 for each delivery into a cargo tank having a capacity of 5,000 gallons or more but less than 8,000 gallons;

(4) not more than $15.00 for each delivery into a cargo tank having a capacity of 8,000 gallons or more but less than 10,000 gallons; and

(5) not more than $7.50 for each increment of 5,000 gallons or any part thereof delivered into a cargo tank having a capacity of 10,000 gallons or more.

(b-1) The commission by rule shall set the amount of the fee in Subsection (b) in an amount not to exceed the amount necessary to cover the agency's costs of administering this subchapter, as indicated by the amount appropriated by the legislature from the petroleum storage tank remediation account for that purpose.

(c) The fee collected under Subsection (b) of this section shall be computed on the net amount of a petroleum product delivered into a cargo tank.

(d) A person who imports a petroleum product in a cargo tank or a barge destined for delivery into an underground or aboveground storage tank, regardless of whether or not the tank is exempt from regulation under Section 26.344 of this code, other than a storage tank connected to or part of a bulk facility in this state, shall pay to the comptroller a fee on the number of gallons imported, computed as provided by Subsections (b) and (c) of this section. If a bulk facility operator imports a petroleum product in a cargo tank or a barge, the bulk facility operator is not required to pay the fee on that imported petroleum product if the petroleum product is delivered to a bulk facility from which the petroleum product will be withdrawn from bulk.

(e) A bulk facility operator who receives petroleum products on which the fee has been paid may take credit for the fee paid on monthly reports.

(f) Subsection (b) of this section does not apply to a delivery of a petroleum product destined for export from this state if the petroleum product is in continuous movement to a destination outside this state.

(g) Each operator of a bulk facility and each person covered by Subsection (d) of this section shall file an application with the comptroller for a permit to deliver a petroleum product into a cargo tank destined for delivery to an underground or aboveground storage tank, regardless of whether or not the tank is exempt from regulation under Section 26.344 of this code. A permit issued by the comptroller under this subsection is valid on and after the date of its issuance and until the permit is surrendered by the holder or canceled by the comptroller. An applicant for a permit issued under this subsection must use a form adopted or approved by the comptroller that contains:

(1) the name under which the applicant transacts or intends to transact business;

(2) the principal office, residence, or place of business in this state of the applicant;

(3) if the applicant is not an individual, the names of the principal officers of an applicant corporation, or the name of the member of an applicant partnership, and the office, street, or post office address of each; and

(4) any other information required by the comptroller.

(h) A permit must be posted in a conspicuous place or kept available for inspection at the principal place of business of the owner. A copy of the permit must be kept at each place of business or other place of storage from which petroleum products are delivered into cargo tanks and in each motor vehicle used by the permit holder to transport petroleum products by him for delivery into petroleum storage tanks in this state.

(i) Each operator of a bulk facility and each person covered by Subsection (d) of this section shall:

(1) list, as a separate line item on an invoice or cargo manifest required under this section, the amount of the delivery fee due under this section; and

(2) on or before the 25th day of the month following the end of each calendar month, file a report with the comptroller and remit the amount of fees required to be collected or paid during the preceding month.

(j) Each operator of a bulk facility or his representative and each person covered by Subsection (d) of this section shall prepare the report required under Subsection (i) of this section on a form provided or approved by the comptroller.

(k) The cargo manifests or invoices or copies of the cargo manifests or invoices and any other records required under this section or rules of the comptroller must be maintained for a period of four years after the date on which the document or other record is prepared and be open for inspection by the comptroller at all reasonable times.

(*l*) As provided by the rules of the comptroller, the owner or lessee of a cargo tank or a common or contract carrier transporting a petroleum product shall possess a cargo manifest or an invoice showing the delivery point of the product, the amount of the required fee, and other information as required by rules of the comptroller.

(m) The comptroller shall adopt rules necessary for the administration, collection, reporting, and payment of the fees payable or collected under this section.

(n) A person who fails to file a report as provided by Subsection (i) of this section or who possesses a fee collected or payable under this section and who fails to remit the fee to the comptroller at the time and in the manner required by this section and rules of the comptroller shall pay a penalty of five percent of the amount of the fee due and payable. If the person fails to file the report or pay the fee before the 30th day after the date on which the fee or report is due, the person shall pay a penalty of an additional five percent of the amount of the fee due and payable.

(o) Chapters 101 and 111-113, and Sections 162.005, 162.007, and 162.111(b)-(k), Tax Code, apply to the administration, payment, collection, and enforcement of fees under this section in the same manner that those chapters apply to the administration, payment, collection, and enforcement of taxes under Title 2, Tax Code.

(p) The comptroller may add a penalty of 75 percent of the amount of the fee, penalty, and interest due if failure to file the report or pay the fee when it comes due is attributable to fraud or an intent to evade the application of this section or a rule made under this section or Chapter 111, Tax Code.

(q) The comptroller may require a bond or other security from a permittee and may establish the amount of the bond or other security.

(r) A person forfeits to the state a civil penalty of not less than $25 nor more than $200 if the person:

(1) refuses to stop and permit the inspection and examination of a motor vehicle transporting petroleum products on demand of a peace officer or the comptroller;

(2) fails or refuses to comply with or violates a provision of this section; or

(3) fails or refuses to comply with or violates a comptroller's rule for administering or enforcing this section.

(s) A person commits an offense if the person:

(1) refuses to stop and permit the inspection and examination of a motor vehicle transporting petroleum products on the demand of a peace officer or the comptroller;

(2) makes a delivery of petroleum products into cargo tanks on which he knows the fee is required to be collected, if at the time the delivery is made he does not hold a valid permit issued under this section;

(3) makes a delivery of petroleum products imported into this state on which he knows a fee is required to be collected, if at the time the delivery is made he does not hold a valid permit issued under this section;

(4) refuses to permit the comptroller or the attorney general to inspect, examine, or audit a book or record required to be kept by any person required to hold a permit under this section;

(5) refuses to permit the comptroller or the attorney general to inspect or examine any plant, equipment, or premises where petroleum products are stored or delivered into cargo tanks;

(6) refuses to permit the comptroller or the attorney general to measure or gauge the contents of or take samples from a storage tank or container on premises where petroleum products are stored or delivered into cargo tanks;

(7) is required to hold a permit under this section and fails or refuses to make or deliver to the comptroller a report required by this section to be made and delivered to the comptroller;

(8) refuses, while transporting petroleum products, to stop the motor vehicle he is operating when called on to do so by a person authorized to stop the motor vehicle;

(9) transports petroleum products for which a cargo manifest is required to be carried without possessing or exhibiting on demand by an officer authorized to make the demand a cargo manifest containing the information required to be shown on the manifest;

(10) mutilates, destroys, or secretes a book or record required by this section to be kept by any person required to hold a permit under this section;

(11) is required to hold a permit under this section or is the agent or employee of that person and makes a false entry or fails to make an entry in the books and records required under this section to be made by the person;

(12) transports in any manner petroleum products under a false cargo manifest;

(13) engages in a petroleum products transaction that requires that the person have a permit under this section without then and there holding the required permit;

(14) makes and delivers to the comptroller a report required under this section to be made and delivered to the comptroller, if the report contains false information;

(15) forges, falsifies, or alters an invoice or manifest prescribed by law; or

(16) fails to remit any fees collected by any person required to hold a permit under this section.

(t) The following criminal penalties apply to the offenses enumerated in Subsection (s) of this section:

(1) an offense under Subdivision (1) is a Class C misdemeanor;

(2) an offense under Subdivisions (2) through (7) is a Class B misdemeanor;

(3) an offense under Subdivisions (8) and (9) is a Class A misdemeanor;

(4) an offense under Subdivisions (10) through (15) is a felony of the third degree;

(5) an offense under Subdivision (16) is a felony of the second degree; and

(6) violations of three or more separate offenses under Subdivisions (10) through (15) committed pursuant to one scheme or continuous course of conduct may be considered as one offense and are punished as a felony of the second degree.

(u) The court may not fine a corporation or association under Section 12.51(c), Penal Code, unless the amount of the fine under that subsection is greater than the amount that could be fixed by the court under Section 12.51(b), Penal Code.

(v) In addition to a sentence imposed on a corporation, the court shall give notice of the conviction to the attorney general as required by Article 17A.09, Code of Criminal Procedure.

(w) The comptroller shall deduct two percent of the amount collected under this section as the state's charge for its services and shall credit the amount deducted to the general revenue fund. The balance of the fees, penalties, and interest collected by the comptroller shall be deposited in the state treasury to the credit of the petroleum storage tank remediation account.

(x) The commission shall report to the Legislative Budget Board at the end of each fiscal quarter on the financial status of the petroleum storage tank remediation account.

(Enacted by Acts 1989, 71st Leg., ch. 228 (H.B. 1588), § 17, effective May 31, 1989; am. Acts 1995, 74th Leg., ch. 315 (H.B. 2587), § 13, effective September 1, 1995; am. Acts 1997, 75th Leg., ch. 333 (H.B. 3231), § 26, effective September 1, 1997; am. Acts 1999, 76th Leg., ch. 1442 (H.B. 2816), § 2, effective September 1, 1999; am. Acts 2001, 77th Leg., ch. 965 (H.B. 2912), § 14.09, effective September 1, 2001; am. Acts 2001, 77th Leg., ch. 1135 (H.B. 2687), § 9, effective September 1, 2001; am. Acts 2005, 79th Leg., ch. 899 (S.B. 1863), § 5.05, effective September 1, 2005; Acts 2007, 80th Leg., ch. 1109 (H.B. 3554), § 3, effective August 27, 2007; am. Acts 2009, 81st Leg., ch. 1227 (S.B. 1495), § 40, effective September 1, 2009; am. Acts 2011, 82nd Leg., ch. 1021 (H.B. 2694), § 4.19, effective September 1, 2011.)

# TITLE 4
# GENERAL LAW DISTRICTS

## CHAPTER 49
## PROVISIONS APPLICABLE TO ALL DISTRICTS

### SUBCHAPTER H
### POWERS AND DUTIES

### Sec. 49.217.   Operation of Certain Motor Vehicles on or Near Public Facilities.

(a) In this section, "motor vehicle" means a self-propelled device in, upon, or by which a person or property is or may be transported or drawn on a road or highway.

(b) Except as provided in Subsections (c) and (d), a person may not operate a motor vehicle on a levee, in a drainage ditch, or on land adjacent to a levee, canal, ditch, exposed conduit, pipeline, pumping plant, storm water facility, or other facility for the transmission, storage, treatment, or distribution of water, sewage, or storm water owned or controlled by a district.

(c) A district may authorize the use of motor vehicles on land that it owns or controls by posting signs on the property.

(d) This section does not prohibit a person from:

(1) driving on a public road or highway; or

(2) operating a motor vehicle used for repair or maintenance of public water, sewer, or storm water facilities.

(e) A person who operates a motor vehicle in violation of Subsection (b) commits an offense. An offense under this section is a Class C misdemeanor, except that if a person has been convicted of an offense under this section, a subsequent offense is a Class B misdemeanor.

(Enacted by Acts 1995, 74th Leg., ch. 715 (S.B. 626), § 2, effective September 1, 1995.)

Water Code

# TEXAS RULES OF EVIDENCE

## IN THE SUPREME COURT OF TEXAS

Misc. Docket No. 97-____

## FINAL APPROVAL OF REVISIONS TO THE
## TEXAS RULES OF EVIDENCE IN CIVIL CASES

### ORDERED that:

1. The Texas Rules of Civil Evidence, amended by Order in Misc. Docket No. 97-9184, dated October 20, 1997, 60 Tex. Bar J. 1129 (Dec. 1997), and now changed after public comments, are attached. The format and style of these amended rules are part of the official promulgation.

2. These amended rules take effect March 1, 1998, and apply to all proceedings on or after that date.

3. With the exception of the notes and comments to Rules 509 and 510, the notes and comments appended to these changes are incomplete, are included only for the convenience of the bench and bar, and are not a part of the rules. The notes and comments to Rules 509 and 510 are intended to inform the construction and application of those rules.

4. Pursuant to Section 22.004(c) of the Texas Government Code, Section 611.006(a)(6) of the Texas Health and Safety Code is deemed to be repealed insofar as it conflicts with Rule 510 of the Texas Rules of Evidence.

5. The Clerk is directed to file a copy of this Order with the Secretary of State forthwith, and to cause a copy of this Order to be mailed to each registered member of the State Bar of Texas by publication in the *Texas Bar Journal*.

### SIGNED AND ENTERED this 25th day of February, 1998.

Thomas R. Phillips, Chief Justice
Raul A. Gonzalez, Justice
Nathan L. Hecht, Justice
Craig T. Enoch, Justice
Rose Spector, Justice
Priscilla R. Owen, Justice
James A. Baker, Justice
Greg Abbott, Justice
Deborah G. Hankinson, Justice

**Texas Rules**

# ARTICLE I. GENERAL PROVISIONS

## Rule 101. Title and Scope.

(a) *Title.* These rules shall be known and cited as the Texas Rules of Evidence.

(b) *Scope.* Except as otherwise provided by statute, these rules govern civil and criminal proceedings (including examining trials before magistrates) in all courts of Texas, except small claims courts.

(c) *Hierarchical Governance in Criminal Proceedings.* Hierarchical governance shall be in the following order: the Constitution of the United States, those federal statutes that control states under the supremacy clause, the Constitution of Texas, the Code of Criminal Procedure and the Penal Code, civil statutes, these rules, and the common law. Where possible, inconsistency is to be removed by reasonable construction.

(d) *Special Rules of Applicability in Criminal Proceedings.*

(1) Rules Not Applicable in Certain Proceedings. These rules, except with respect to privileges, do not apply in the following situations:

(A) the determination of questions of fact preliminary to admissibility of evidence when the issue is to be determined by the court under Rule 104;

(B) proceedings before grand juries;

(C) proceedings in an application for habeas corpus in extradition, rendition, or interstate detainer;

(D) a hearing under Code of Criminal Procedure article 46.02, by the court out of the presence of a jury, to determine whether there is sufficient evidence of incompetency to require a jury determination of the question of incompetency;

(E) proceedings regarding bail except hearings to deny, revoke or increase bail;

(F) a hearing on justification for pretrial detention not involving bail;

(G) proceedings for the issuance of a search or arrest warrant; or

(H) proceedings in a direct contempt determination.

(2) Applicability of Privileges. These rules with respect to privileges apply at all stages of all actions, cases, and proceedings.

(3) Military Justice Hearings. Evidence in hearings under the Texas Code of Military Justice, Tex. Gov't Code §§ 432.001—432.195, shall be governed by that Code.

## Rule 102. Purpose and Construction.

These rules shall be construed to secure fairness in administration, elimination of unjustifiable expense and delay, and promotion of growth and development of the law of evidence to the end that the truth may be ascertained and proceedings justly determined.

## Rule 103. Rulings on Evidence.

(a) *Effect of Erroneous Ruling.* Error may not be predicated upon a ruling which admits or excludes evidence unless a substantial right of the party is affected, and

(1) Objection. In case the ruling is one admitting evidence, a timely objection or motion to strike appears of record, stating the specific ground of objection, if the specific ground was not apparent from the context. When the court hears objections to offered evidence out of the presence of the jury and rules that such evidence be admitted, such objections shall be deemed to apply to such evidence when it is admitted before the jury without the necessity of repeating those objections.

(2) Offer of Proof. In case the ruling is one excluding evidence, the substance of the evidence was made known to the court by offer, or was apparent from the context within which questions were asked.

(b) *Record of Offer and Ruling.* The offering party shall, as soon as practicable, but before the court's charge is read to the jury, be allowed to make, in the absence of the jury, its offer of proof. The court may add any other or further statement which shows the character of the evidence, the form in which it was offered, the objection made, and the ruling thereon. The court may, or at the request of a party shall, direct the making of an offer in question and answer form.

(c) *Hearing of Jury.* In jury cases, proceedings shall be conducted, to the extent practicable, so as to prevent inadmissible evidence from being suggested to the jury by any means, such as making statements or offers of proof or asking questions in the hearing of the jury.

(d) *Fundamental Error in Criminal Cases.* In a criminal case, nothing in these rules precludes taking notice of fundamental errors affecting substantial rights although they were not brought to the attention of the court.

## Rule 104. Preliminary Questions.

(a) *Questions of Admissibility Generally.* Preliminary questions concerning the qualification of a person to be a witness, the existence of a privilege, or the admissibility of evidence shall be determined by the court, subject to the provisions of subdivision (b). In making its determination the court is not bound by the rules of evidence except those with respect to privileges.

(b) *Relevancy Conditioned on Fact.* When the relevancy of evidence depends upon the fulfillment of a condition of fact, the court shall admit it upon, or subject to, the introduction of evidence sufficient to support a finding of the fulfillment of the condition.

(c) *Hearing of Jury.* In a criminal case, a hearing on the admissibility of a confession shall be conducted out of the hearing of the jury. All other civil or criminal hearings on preliminary matters shall be conducted out of the hearing of the jury when the interests of justice so require or in a criminal case when an accused is a witness and so requests.

(d) *Testimony by Accused Out of the Hearing of the Jury.* The accused in a criminal case does not, by testifying upon a preliminary matter out of the hearing of the jury, become subject to cross-examination as to other issues in the case.

(e) *Weight and Credibility.* This rule does not limit the right of a party to introduce before the jury evidence relevant to weight or credibility.

## Rule 105. Limited Admissibility.

(a) *Limiting Instruction.* When evidence which is admissible as to one party or for one purpose but not admissible as to another party or for another purpose is admitted, the court, upon request, shall restrict the evidence to its proper scope and instruct the jury accordingly; but, in the absence of such request the court's action in admitting such evidence without limitation shall not be a ground for complaint on appeal.

(b) *Offering Evidence for Limited Purpose.* When evidence referred to in paragraph (a) is excluded, such exclusion shall not be a ground for complaint on appeal unless the proponent expressly offers the evidence for its limited, admissible purpose or limits its offer to the party against whom it is admissible.

## Rule 106. Remainder of or Related Writings or Recorded Statements.

When a writing or recorded statement or part thereof is introduced by a party, an adverse party may at that time introduce any other part or any other writing or recorded statement which ought in fairness to be considered contemporaneously with it. "Writing or recorded statement" includes depositions.

## Rule 107. Rule of Optional Completeness.

When part of an act, declaration, conversation, writing or recorded statement is given in evidence by one party, the whole on the same subject may be inquired into by the other, and any other act, declaration, writing or recorded statement which is necessary to make it fully understood or to explain the same may also be given in evidence, as when a letter is read, all letters on the same subject between the same parties may be given. "Writing or recorded statement" includes depositions.

# ARTICLE II. JUDICIAL NOTICE

## Rule 201. Judicial Notice of Adjudicative Facts.

(a) *Scope of Rule.* This rule governs only judicial notice of adjudicative facts.

(b) *Kinds of Facts.* A judicially noticed fact must be one not subject to reasonable dispute in that it is either (1) generally known within the territorial jurisdiction of the trial court or (2) capable of accurate and ready determination by resort to sources whose accuracy cannot reasonably be questioned.

**Texas Rules**

(c) *When Discretionary*. A court may take judicial notice, whether requested or not.

(d) *When Mandatory*. A court shall take judicial notice if requested by a party and supplied with the necessary information.

(e) *Opportunity to Be Heard*. A party is entitled upon timely request to an opportunity to be heard as to the propriety of taking judicial notice and the tenor of the matter noticed. In the absence of prior notification, the request may be made after judicial notice has been taken.

(f) *Time of Taking Notice*. Judicial notice may be taken at any stage of the proceeding.

(g) *Instructing Jury*. In civil cases, the court shall instruct the jury to accept as conclusive any fact judicially noticed. In criminal cases, the court shall instruct the jury that it may, but is not required to, accept as conclusive any fact judicially noticed.

## Rule 202. Determination of Law of Other States.

A court upon its own motion may, or upon the motion of a party shall, take judicial notice of the constitutions, public statutes, rules, regulations, ordinances, court decisions, and common law of every other state, territory, or jurisdiction of the United States. A party requesting that judicial notice be taken of such matter shall furnish the court sufficient information to enable it properly to comply with the request, and shall give all parties such notice, if any, as the court may deem necessary, to enable all parties fairly to prepare to meet the request. A party is entitled upon timely request to an opportunity to be heard as to the propriety of taking judicial notice and the tenor of the matter noticed. In the absence of prior notification, the request may be made after judicial notice has been taken. Judicial notice of such matters may be taken at any stage of the proceeding. The court's determination shall be subject to review as a ruling on a question of law.

## Rule 203. Determination of the Laws of Foreign Countries.

A party who intends to raise an issue concerning the law of a foreign country shall give notice in the pleadings or other reasonable written notice, and at least 30 days prior to the date of trial such party shall furnish all parties copies of any written materials or sources that the party intends to use as proof of the foreign law. If the materials or sources were originally written in a language other than English, the party intending to rely upon them shall furnish all parties both a copy of the foreign language text and an English translation. The court, in determining the law of a foreign nation, may consider any material or source, whether or not submitted by a party or admissible under the rules of evidence, including but not limited to affidavits, testimony, briefs, and treatises. If the court considers sources other than those submitted by a party, it shall give all parties notice and a reasonable opportunity to comment on the sources and to submit further materials for review by the court. The court, and not a jury, shall determine the laws of foreign countries. The court's determination shall be subject to review as a ruling on a question of law.

## Rule 204. Determination of Texas City and County Ordinances, the Contents of the Texas Register, and the Rules of Agencies Published in the Administrative Code.

A court upon its own motion may, or upon the motion of a party shall, take judicial notice of the ordinances of municipalities and counties of Texas, of the contents of the Texas Register, and of the codified rules of the agencies published in the Administrative Code. Any party requesting that judicial notice be taken of such matter shall furnish the court sufficient information to enable it properly to comply with the request, and shall give all parties such notice, if any, as the court may deem necessary, to enable all parties fairly to prepare to meet the request. A party is entitled upon timely request to an opportunity to be heard as to the propriety of taking judicial notice and the tenor of the matter noticed. In the absence of prior notification, the request may be made after judicial notice has been taken. The court's determination shall be subject to review as a ruling on a question of law.

# ARTICLE III. PRESUMPTIONS

[No rules adopted at this time.]

# ARTICLE IV. RELEVANCY AND ITS LIMITS

Rule
401. Definition of "Relevant Evidence".
402. Relevant Evidence Generally Admissible; Irrelevant Evidence Inadmissible.

## Rule 401. Definition of "Relevant Evidence".

"Relevant evidence" means evidence having any tendency to make the existence of any fact that is of consequence to the determination of the action more probable or less probable than it would be without the evidence.

## Rule 402. Relevant Evidence Generally Admissible; Irrelevant Evidence Inadmissible.

All relevant evidence is admissible, except as otherwise provided by Constitution, by statute, by these rules, or by other rules prescribed pursuant to statutory authority. Evidence which is not relevant is inadmissible.

## Rule 403. Exclusion of Relevant Evidence on Special Grounds.

Although relevant, evidence may be excluded if its probative value is substantially outweighed by the danger of unfair prejudice, confusion of the issues, or misleading the jury, or by considerations of undue delay, or needless presentation of cumulative evidence.

## Rule 404. Character Evidence Not Admissible to Prove Conduct; Exceptions; Other Crimes.

(a) *Character Evidence Generally.* Evidence of a person's character or character trait is not admissible for the purpose of proving action in conformity therewith on a particular occasion, except:

(1) Character of Accused. Evidence of a pertinent character trait offered:

(A) by an accused in a criminal case, or by the prosecution to rebut the same, or

(B) by a party accused in a civil case of conduct involving moral turpitude, or by the accusing party to rebut the same;

(2) Character of Victim. In a criminal case and subject to Rule 412, evidence of a pertinent character trait of the victim of the crime offered by an accused, or by the prosecution to rebut the same, or evidence of peaceable character of the victim offered by the prosecution in a homicide case to rebut evidence that the victim was the first aggressor; or in a civil case, evidence of character for violence of the alleged victim of assaultive conduct offered on the issue of self-defense by a party accused of the assaultive conduct, or evidence of peaceable character to rebut the same;

(3) Character of Witness. Evidence of the character of a witness, as provided in rules 607, 608 and 609.

(b) *Other Crimes, Wrongs or Acts.* Evidence of other crimes, wrongs or acts is not admissible to prove the character of a person in order to show action in conformity therewith. It may, however, be admissible for other purposes, such as proof of motive, opportunity, intent, preparation, plan, knowledge, identity, or absence of mistake or accident, provided that upon timely request by the accused in a criminal case, reasonable notice is given in advance of trial of intent to introduce in the State's case-in-chief such evidence other than that arising in the same transaction.

## Rule 405. Methods of Proving Character.

(a) *Reputation or Opinion.* In all cases in which evidence of a person's character or character trait is admissible, proof may be made by testimony as to reputation or by testimony in the form of an opinion. In a criminal case, to be qualified to testify at the guilt stage of trial concerning the character or character trait of an accused, a witness must have been familiar with the reputation, or with the underlying facts or information upon which the opinion is based, prior to the day of the offense. In all cases where testimony is admitted under this rule, on cross-examination inquiry is allowable into relevant specific instances of conduct.

(b) *Specific Instances of Conduct.* In cases in which a person's character or character trait is an essential element of a charge, claim or defense,

Texas Rules

proof may also be made of specific instances of that person's conduct.

## Rule 406. Habit; Routine Practice.

Evidence of the habit of a person or of the routine practice of an organization, whether corroborated or not and regardless of the presence of eyewitnesses, is relevant to prove that the conduct of the person or organization on a particular occasion was in conformity with the habit or routine practice.

## Rule 407. Subsequent Remedial Measures; Notification of Defect.

(a) *Subsequent Remedial Measures.* When, after an injury or harm allegedly caused by an event, measures are taken that, if taken previously, would have made the injury or harm less likely to occur, evidence of the subsequent remedial measures is not admissible to prove negligence, culpable conduct, a defect in a product, a defect in a product's design, or a need for a warning or instruction. This rule does not require the exclusion of evidence of subsequent remedial measures when offered for another purpose, such as proving ownership, control, or feasibility of precautionary measures, if controverted, or impeachment.

(b) *Notification of Defect.* A written notification by a manufacturer of any defect in a product produced by such manufacturer to purchasers thereof is admissible against the manufacturer on the issue of existence of the defect to the extent that it is relevant.

## Rule 408. Compromise and Offers to Compromise.

Evidence of (1) furnishing or offering or promising to furnish or (2) accepting or offering or promising to accept, a valuable consideration in compromising or attempting to compromise a claim which was disputed as to either validity or amount is not admissible to prove liability for or invalidity of the claim or its amount. Evidence of conduct or statements made in compromise negotiations is likewise not admissible. This rule does not require the exclusion of any evidence otherwise discoverable merely because it is presented in the course of compromise negotiations. This rule also does not require exclusion when the evidence is offered for another purpose, such as proving bias or prejudice or interest of a witness

or a party, negativing a contention of undue delay, or proving an effort to obstruct a criminal investigation or prosecution.

## Rule 409. Payment of Medical and Similar Expenses.

Evidence of furnishing or offering or promising to pay medical, hospital, or similar expenses occasioned by an injury is not admissible to prove liability for the injury.

## Rule 410. Inadmissibility of Pleas, Plea Discussions and Related Statements.

Except as otherwise provided in this rule, evidence of the following is not admissible against the defendant who made the plea or was a participant in the plea discussions:

(1) a plea of guilty that was later withdrawn;

(2) in civil cases, a plea of *nolo contendere*, and in criminal cases, a plea of *nolo contendere* that was later withdrawn;

(3) any statement made in the course of any proceedings under Rule 11 of the Federal Rules of Criminal Procedure or comparable state procedure regarding, in a civil case, either a plea of guilty that was later withdrawn or a plea of *nolo contendere*, or in a criminal case, either a plea of guilty that was later withdrawn or a plea of *nolo contendere* that was later withdrawn; or

(4) any statement made in the course of plea discussions with an attorney for the prosecuting authority, in a civil case, that do not result in a plea of guilty or that result in a plea of guilty later withdrawn, or in a criminal case, that do not result in a plea of guilty or a plea of *nolo contendere* or that results in a plea, later withdrawn, of guilty or *nolo contendere*.

However, such a statement is admissible in any proceeding wherein another statement made in the course of the same plea or plea discussions has been introduced and the statement ought in fairness be considered contemporaneously with it.

## Rule 411. Liability Insurance.

Evidence that a person was or was not insured against liability is not admissible upon the issue whether the person acted negligently or otherwise wrongfully. This rule does not require the exclusion of evidence of insurance against liability when offered for another issue, such as proof of agency, ownership, or control, if disputed, or bias or prejudice of a witness.

## Rule 412. Evidence of Previous Sexual Conduct in Criminal Cases.

(a) *Reputation or Opinion Evidence.* In a prosecution for sexual assault or aggravated sexual assault, or attempt to commit sexual assault or aggravated sexual assault, reputation or opinion evidence of the past sexual behavior of an alleged victim of such crime is not admissible.

(b) *Evidence of Specific Instances.* In a prosecution for sexual assault or aggravated sexual assault, or attempt to commit sexual assault or aggravated sexual assault, evidence of specific instances of an alleged victim's past sexual behavior is also not admissible, unless:

(1) such evidence is admitted in accordance with paragraphs (c) and (d) of this rule;

(2) it is evidence:

(A) that is necessary to rebut or explain scientific or medical evidence offered by the State;

(B) of past sexual behavior with the accused and is offered by the accused upon the issue of whether the alleged victim consented to the sexual behavior which is the basis of the offense charged;

(C) that relates to the motive or bias of the alleged victim;

(D) is admissible under Rule 609; or

(E) that is constitutionally required to be admitted; and

(3) its probative value outweighs the danger of unfair prejudice.

(c) *Procedure for Offering Evidence.* If the defendant proposes to introduce any documentary evidence or to ask any question, either by direct examination or cross-examination of any witness, concerning specific instances of the alleged victim's past sexual behavior, the defendant must inform the court out of the hearing of the jury prior to introducing any such evidence or asking any such question. After this notice, the court shall conduct an in camera hearing, recorded by the court reporter, to determine whether the proposed evidence is admissible under paragraph (b) of this rule. The court shall determine what evidence is admissible and shall accordingly limit the questioning. The defendant shall not go outside these limits or refer to any evidence ruled inadmissible in camera without prior approval of the court without the presence of the jury.

(d) *Record Sealed.* The court shall seal the record of the in camera hearing required in paragraph (c) of this rule for delivery to the appellate court in the event of an appeal.

(e) *Sexual Conduct of Child As Defense.* [Deleted by Texas Court of Criminal Appeals, Misc. Docket No. 06-101, effective January 1, 2007.] (Amended effective January 1, 2007, Texas Court of Criminal Appeals, Misc. Docket No. 06-101, December 13, 2006.)

# ARTICLE V. PRIVILEGES

## Rule 501. Privileges Recognized Only As Provided.

Except as otherwise provided by Constitution, by statute, by these rules, or by other rules prescribed pursuant to statutory authority, no person has a privilege to:

(1) refuse to be a witness;

(2) refuse to disclose any matter;

(3) refuse to produce any object or writing; or

(4) prevent another from being a witness or disclosing any matter or producing any object or writing.

## Rule 502. Required Reports Privileged by Statute.

A person, corporation, association, or other organization or entity, either public or private, making a return or report required by law to be made has a privilege to refuse to disclose and to prevent any other person from disclosing the return or report, if the law requiring it to be made so provides. A public officer or agency to whom a return or report is required by law to be made has a privilege to refuse to disclose the return or report if the law requiring it to be made so

Texas Rules

provides. No privilege exists under this rule in actions involving perjury, false statements, fraud in the return or report, or other failure to comply with the law in question.

## Rule 503. Lawyer-Client Privilege.

(a) *Definitions.* As used in this rule:

(1) A "client" is a person, public officer, or corporation, association, or other organization or entity, either public or private, who is rendered professional legal services by a lawyer, or who consults a lawyer with a view to obtaining professional legal services from that lawyer.

(2) A "representative of the client" is:

(A) a person having authority to obtain professional legal services, or to act on advice thereby rendered, on behalf of the client, or

(B) any other person who, for the purpose of effectuating legal representation for the client, makes or receives a confidential communication while acting in the scope of employment for the client.

(3) A "lawyer" is a person authorized, or reasonably believed by the client to be authorized, to engage in the practice of law in any state or nation.

(4) A "representative of the lawyer" is:

(A) one employed by the lawyer to assist the lawyer in the rendition of professional legal services; or

(B) an accountant who is reasonably necessary for the lawyer's rendition of professional legal services.

(5) A communication is "confidential" if not intended to be disclosed to third persons other than those to whom disclosure is made in furtherance of the rendition of professional legal services to the client or those reasonably necessary for the transmission of the communication.

(b) *Rules of Privilege.*

(1) General Rule of Privilege. A client has a privilege to refuse to disclose and to prevent any other person from disclosing confidential communications made for the purpose of facilitating the rendition of professional legal services to the client:

(A) between the client or a representative of the client and the client's lawyer or a representative of the lawyer;

(B) between the lawyer and the lawyer's representative;

(C) by the client or a representative of the client, or the client's lawyer or a representa-

tive of the lawyer, to a lawyer or a representative of a lawyer representing another party in a pending action and concerning a matter of common interest therein;

(D) between representatives of the client or between the client and a representative of the client; or

(E) among lawyers and their representatives representing the same client.

(2) Special Rule of Privilege in Criminal Cases. In criminal cases, a client has a privilege to prevent the lawyer or lawyer's representative from disclosing any other fact which came to the knowledge of the lawyer or the lawyer's representative by reason of the attorney-client relationship.

(c) *Who May Claim the Privilege.* The privilege may be claimed by the client, the client's guardian or conservator, the personal representative of a deceased client, or the successor, trustee, or similar representative of a corporation, association, or other organization, whether or not in existence. The person who was the lawyer or the lawyer's representative at the time of the communication is presumed to have authority to claim the privilege but only on behalf of the client.

(d) *Exceptions.* There is no privilege under this rule:

(1) Furtherance of Crime or Fraud. If the services of the lawyer were sought or obtained to enable or aid anyone to commit or plan to commit what the client knew or reasonably should have known to be a crime or fraud;

(2) Claimants Through Same Deceased Client. As to a communication relevant to an issue between parties who claim through the same deceased client, regardless of whether the claims are by testate or intestate succession or by *inter vivos* transactions;

(3) Breach of Duty by a Lawyer or Client. As to a communication relevant to an issue of breach of duty by a lawyer to the client or by a client to the lawyer;

(4) Document Attested by a Lawyer. As to a communication relevant to an issue concerning an attested document to which the lawyer is an attesting witness; or

(5) Joint Clients. As to a communication relevant to a matter of common interest between or among two or more clients if the communication was made by any of them to a lawyer retained or consulted in common, when offered in an action between or among any of the clients.

## Rule 504. Husband-Wife Privileges.

(a) *Confidential Communication Privilege.*

(1) Definition. A communication is confidential if it is made privately by any person to the person's spouse and it is not intended for disclosure to any other person.

(2) Rule of Privilege. A person, whether or not a party, or the guardian or representative of an incompetent or deceased person, has a privilege during marriage and afterwards to refuse to disclose and to prevent another from disclosing a confidential communication made to the person's spouse while they were married.

(3) Who May Claim the Privilege. The confidential communication privilege may be claimed by the person or the person's guardian or representative, or by the spouse on the person's behalf. The authority of the spouse to do so is presumed.

(4) Exceptions. There is no confidential communication privilege:

(A) Furtherance of Crime or Fraud. If the communication was made, in whole or in part, to enable or aid anyone to commit or plan to commit a crime or fraud.

(B) Proceeding Between Spouses in Civil Cases. In (A) a proceeding brought by or on behalf of one spouse against the other spouse, or (B) a proceeding between a surviving spouse and a person who claims through the deceased spouse, regardless of whether the claim is by testate or intestate succession or by *inter vivos* transaction.

(C) Crime Against Spouse or Minor Child. In a proceeding in which the party is accused of conduct which, if proved, is a crime against the person of the spouse, any minor child, or any member of the household of either spouse, or, in a criminal proceeding, when the offense charged is under Section 25.01, Penal Code (Bigamy).

(D) Commitment or Similar Proceeding. In a proceeding to commit either spouse or otherwise to place that person or that person's property, or both, under the control of another because of an alleged mental or physical condition.

(E) Proceeding to Establish Competence. In a proceeding brought by or on behalf of either spouse to establish competence.

(b) *Privilege Not to Testify in Criminal Case.*

(1) Rule of Privilege. In a criminal case, the spouse of the accused has a privilege not to be called as a witness for the state. This rule does not prohibit the spouse from testifying voluntarily for the state, even over objection by the accused. A spouse who testifies on behalf of an accused is subject to cross-examination as provided in rule 611(b).

(2) Failure to Call As Witness. Failure by an accused to call the accused's spouse as a witness, where other evidence indicates that the spouse could testify to relevant matters, is a proper subject of comment by counsel.

(3) Who May Claim the Privilege. The privilege not to testify may be claimed by the person or the person's guardian or representative but not by that person's spouse.

(4) Exceptions. The privilege of a person's spouse not to be called as a witness for the state does not apply:

(A) Certain Criminal Proceedings. In any proceeding in which the person is charged with a crime against the person's spouse, a member of the household of either spouse, or any minor, or in an offense charged under Section 25.01, Penal Code (Bigamy).

(B) Matters Occurring Prior to Marriage. As to matters occurring prior to the marriage.

(Amended effective January 1, 2007, Texas Court of Criminal Appeals, Misc. Docket No. 06-101, December 13, 2006.)

## Rule 505. Communication to Members of the Clergy.

(a) *Definitions.* As used in this rule:

(1) A "member of the clergy" is a minister, priest, rabbi, accredited Christian Science Practitioner, or other similar functionary of a religious organization or an individual reasonably believed so to be by the person consulting with such individual.

(2) A communication is "confidential" if made privately and not intended for further disclosure except to other persons present in furtherance of the purpose of the communication.

(b) *General Rule of Privilege.* A person has a privilege to refuse to disclose and to prevent another from disclosing a confidential communication by the person to a member of the clergy in the member's professional character as spiritual adviser.

(c) *Who May Claim the Privilege.* The privilege may be claimed by the person, by the person's guardian or conservator, or by the personal representative of the person if the person is deceased. The member of the clergy to whom the communication was made is presumed to have authority to claim the privilege but only on behalf of the communicant.

## Rule 506. Political Vote.

Every person has a privilege to refuse to disclose the tenor of the person's vote at a political election conducted by secret ballot unless the vote was cast illegally.

## Rule 507. Trade Secrets.

A person has a privilege, which may be claimed by the person or the person's agent or employee, to refuse to disclose and to prevent other persons from disclosing a trade secret owned by the person, if the allowance of the privilege will not tend to conceal fraud or otherwise work injustice. When disclosure is directed, the judge shall take such protective measure as the interests of the holder of the privilege and of the parties and the furtherance of justice may require.

## Rule 508. Identity of Informer.

(a) *Rule of Privilege.* The United States or a state or subdivision thereof has a privilege to refuse to disclose the identity of a person who has furnished information relating to or assisting in an investigation of a possible violation of a law to a law enforcement officer or member of a legislative committee or its staff conducting an investigation.

(b) *Who May Claim.* The privilege may be claimed by an appropriate representative of the public entity to which the information was furnished, except the privilege shall not be allowed in criminal cases if the state objects.

(c) *Exceptions.*

(1) Voluntary Disclosure; Informer a Witness. No privilege exists under this rule if the identity of the informer or the informer's interest in the subject matter of the communication has been disclosed to those who would have cause to resent the communication by a holder of the privilege or by the informer's own action, or if the informer appears as a witness for the public entity.

(2) Testimony on Merits. If it appears from the evidence in the case or from other showing by a party that an informer may be able to give testimony necessary to a fair determination of a material issue on the merits in a civil case to which the public entity is a party, or on guilt or innocence in a criminal case, and the public entity invokes the privilege, the court shall give the public entity an opportunity to show in camera facts relevant to determining whether the informer can, in fact, supply that testimony. The showing will ordinarily be in the form of affidavits, but the court may direct that testimony be taken if it finds that the matter cannot be resolved satisfactorily upon affidavit. If the court finds that there is a reasonable probability that the informer can give the testimony, and the public entity elects not to disclose the informer's identity, the court in a civil case may make any order that justice requires, and in a criminal case shall, on motion of the defendant, and may, on the court's own motion, dismiss the charges as to which the testimony would relate. Evidence submitted to the court shall be sealed and preserved to be made available to the appellate court in the event of an appeal, and the contents shall not otherwise be revealed without consent of the public entity. All counsel and parties shall be permitted to be present at every stage of proceedings under this subdivision except a showing in camera, at which no counsel or party shall be permitted to be present.

(3) Legality of Obtaining Evidence. If information from an informer is relied upon to establish the legality of the means by which evidence was obtained and the court is not satisfied that the information was received from an informer reasonably believed to be reliable or credible, it may require the identity of the informer to be disclosed. The court shall, on request of the public entity, direct that the disclosure be made in camera. All counsel and parties concerned with the issue of legality shall be permitted to be present at every stage of proceedings under this subdivision except a disclosure in camera, at which no counsel or party shall be permitted to be present. If disclosure of the identity of the informer is made in camera, the record thereof shall be sealed and preserved to be made available to the appellate court in the event of an appeal, and the contents shall not otherwise be revealed without consent of the public entity.

## Rule 509. Physician-Patient Privilege.

(a) *Definitions.* As used in this rule:

(1) A "patient" means any person who consults or is seen by a physician to receive medical care.

(2) A "physician" means a person licensed to practice medicine in any state or nation, or reasonably believed by the patient so to be.

(3) A communication is "confidential" if not intended to be disclosed to third persons other than those present to further the interest of the patient in the consultation, examination, or interview, or those reasonably necessary for the transmission of the communication, or those who are participating in the diagnosis and treatment under the direction of the physician, including members of the patient's family.

(b) *Limited Privilege in Criminal Proceedings.* There is no physician-patient privilege in criminal proceedings. However, a communication to any person involved in the treatment or examination of alcohol or drug abuse by a person being treated voluntarily or being examined for admission to treatment for alcohol or drug abuse is not admissible in a criminal proceeding.

(c) *General Rule of Privilege in Civil Proceedings.* In a civil proceeding:

(1) Confidential communications between a physician and a patient, relative to or in connection with any professional services rendered by a physician to the patient are privileged and may not be disclosed.

(2) Records of the identity, diagnosis, evaluation, or treatment of a patient by a physician that are created or maintained by a physician are confidential and privileged and may not be disclosed.

(3) The provisions of this rule apply even if the patient received the services of a physician prior to the enactment of the Medical Liability and Insurance Improvement Act, Tex. Rev. Civ. Stat. art. 4590i.

(d) *Who May Claim the Privilege in a Civil Proceeding.* In a civil proceeding:

(1) The privilege of confidentiality may be claimed by the patient or by a representative of the patient acting on the patient's behalf.

(2) The physician may claim the privilege of confidentiality, but only on behalf of the patient. The authority to do so is presumed in the absence of evidence to the contrary.

(e) *Exceptions in a Civil Proceeding.* Exceptions to confidentiality or privilege in administrative proceedings or in civil proceedings in court exist:

(1) when the proceedings are brought by the patient against a physician, including but not limited to malpractice proceedings, and in any license revocation proceeding in which the patient is a complaining witness and in which

disclosure is relevant to the claims or defense of a physician;

(2) when the patient or someone authorized to act on the patient's behalf submits a written consent to the release of any privileged information, as provided in paragraph (f);

(3) when the purpose of the proceedings is to substantiate and collect on a claim for medical services rendered to the patient;

(4) as to a communication or record relevant to an issue of the physical, mental or emotional condition of a patient in any proceeding in which any party relies upon the condition as a part of the party's claim or defense;

(5) in any disciplinary investigation or proceeding of a physician conducted under or pursuant to the Medical Practice Act, Tex. Rev. Civ. Stat. art. 4495b, or of a registered nurse under or pursuant to Tex. Rev. Civ. Stat. arts. 4525, 4527a, 4527b, and 4527c, provided that the board shall protect the identity of any patient whose medical records are examined, except for those patients covered under subparagraph (e)(1) or those patients who have submitted written consent to the release of their medical records as provided by paragraph (f);

(6) in an involuntary civil commitment proceeding, proceeding for court-ordered treatment, or probable cause hearing under Tex. Health & Safety Code ch. 462; tit. 7, subtit. C; and tit. 7, subtit. D;

(7) in any proceeding regarding the abuse or neglect, or the cause of any abuse or neglect, of the resident of an "institution" as defined in Tex. Health & Safety Code § 242.002.

(f) *Consent.*

(1) Consent for the release of privileged information must be in writing and signed by the patient, or a parent or legal guardian if the patient is a minor, or a legal guardian if the patient has been adjudicated incompetent to manage personal affairs, or an attorney ad litem appointed for the patient, as authorized by Tex. Health & Safety Code tit. 7, subtits. C and D; Tex. Prob. Code ch. V; and Tex. Fam. Code § 107.011; or a personal representative if the patient is deceased, provided that the written consent specifies the following:

(A) the information or medical records to be covered by the release;

(B) the reasons or purposes for the release; and

(C) the person to whom the information is to be released.

(2) The patient, or other person authorized to consent, has the right to withdraw consent to the release of any information. Withdrawal of consent does not affect any information disclosed prior to the written notice of the withdrawal.

(3) Any person who received information made privileged by this rule may disclose the information to others only to the extent consistent with the authorized purposes for which consent to release the information was obtained.

## Rule 510. Confidentiality of Mental Health Information in Civil Cases.

(a) *Definitions.* As used in this rule:

(1) "Professional" means any person:

(A) authorized to practice medicine in any state or nation;

(B) licensed or certified by the State of Texas in the diagnosis, evaluation or treatment of any mental or emotional disorder;

(C) involved in the treatment or examination of drug abusers; or

(D) reasonably believed by the patient to be included in any of the preceding categories.

(2) "Patient" means any person who:

(A) consults, or is interviewed by, a professional for purposes of diagnosis, evaluation, or treatment of any mental or emotional condition or disorder, including alcoholism and drug addiction; or

(B) is being treated voluntarily or being examined for admission to voluntary treatment for drug abuse.

(3) A representative of the patient is:

(A) any person bearing the written consent of the patient;

(B) a parent if the patient is a minor;

(C) a guardian if the patient has been adjudicated incompetent to manage the patient's personal affairs; or

(D) the patient's personal representative if the patient is deceased.

(4) A communication is "confidential" if not intended to be disclosed to third persons other than those present to further the interest of the patient in the diagnosis, examination, evaluation, or treatment, or those reasonably necessary for the transmission of the communication, or those who are participating in the diagnosis, examination, evaluation, or treat-

ment under the direction of the professional, including members of the patient's family.

(b) *General Rule of Privilege.*

(1) Communication between a patient and a professional is confidential and shall not be disclosed in civil cases.

(2) Records of the identity, diagnosis, evaluation, or treatment of a patient which are created or maintained by a professional are confidential and shall not be disclosed in civil cases.

(3) Any person who received information from confidential communications or records as defined herein, other than a representative of the patient acting on the patient's behalf, shall not disclose in civil cases the information except to the extent that disclosure is consistent with the authorized purposes for which the information was first obtained.

(4) The provisions of this rule apply even if the patient received the services of a professional prior to the enactment of Tex. Rev. Civ. Stat. art. 5561h (Vernon Supp. 1984)(now codified as Tex. Health & Safety Code §§ 611.001—611.008).

(c) *Who May Claim the Privilege.*

(1) The privilege of confidentiality may be claimed by the patient or by a representative of the patient acting on the patient's behalf.

(2) The professional may claim the privilege of confidentiality but only on behalf of the patient. The authority to do so is presumed in the absence of evidence to the contrary.

(d) *Exceptions.* Exceptions to the privilege in court or administrative proceedings exist:

(1) when the proceedings are brought by the patient against a professional, including but not limited to malpractice proceedings, and in any license revocation proceedings in which the patient is a complaining witness and in which disclosure is relevant to the claim or defense of a professional;

(2) when the patient waives the right in writing to the privilege of confidentiality of any information, or when a representative of the patient acting on the patient's behalf submits a written waiver to the confidentiality privilege;

(3) when the purpose of the proceeding is to substantiate and collect on a claim for mental or emotional health services rendered to the patient;

(4) when the judge finds that the patient after having been previously informed that communications would not be privileged, has made communications to a professional in the

course of a court-ordered examination relating to the patient's mental or emotional condition or disorder, providing that such communications shall not be privileged only with respect to issues involving the patient's mental or emotional health. On granting of the order, the court, in determining the extent to which any disclosure of all or any part of any communication is necessary, shall impose appropriate safeguards against unauthorized disclosure;

(5) as to a communication or record relevant to an issue of the physical, mental or emotional condition of a patient in any proceeding in which any party relies upon the condition as a part of the party's claim or defense;

(6) in any proceeding regarding the abuse or neglect, or the cause of any abuse or neglect, of the resident of an institution as defined in Tex. Health and Safety Code § 242.002.

## Rule 511. Waiver of Privilege by Voluntary Disclosure.

A person upon whom these rules confer a privilege against disclosure waives the privilege if:

(1) the person or a predecessor of the person while holder of the privilege voluntarily discloses or consents to disclosure of any significant part of the privileged matter unless such disclosure itself is privileged; or

(2) the person or a representative of the person calls a person to whom privileged communications have been made to testify as to the person's character or character trait insofar as such communications are relevant to such character or character trait.

## Rule 512. Privileged Matter Disclosed Under Compulsion or Without Opportunity to Claim Privilege.

A claim of privilege is not defeated by a disclosure which was (1) compelled erroneously or (2) made without opportunity to claim the privilege.

## Rule 513. Comment upon or Inference from Claim of Privilege; Instruction.

(a) *Comment or Inference Not Permitted.* Except as permitted in Rule 504(b)(2), the claim of a privilege, whether in the present proceeding or upon a prior occasion, is not a proper subject of comment by judge or counsel, and no inference may be drawn therefrom.

(b) *Claiming Privilege Without Knowledge of Jury.* In jury cases, proceedings shall be conducted, to the extent practicable, so as to facilitate the making of claims of privilege without the knowledge of the jury.

(c) *Claim of Privilege Against Self-Incrimination in Civil Cases.* Paragraphs (a) and (b) shall not apply with respect to a party's claim, in the present civil proceeding, of the privilege against self-incrimination.

(d) *Jury Instruction.* Except as provided in Rule 504(b)(2) and in paragraph (c) of this Rule, upon request any party against whom the jury might draw an adverse inference from a claim of privilege is entitled to an instruction that no inference may be drawn therefrom.

# ARTICLE VI. WITNESSES

## Rule 601. Competency and Incompetency of Witnesses.

(a) *General Rule.* Every person is competent to be a witness except as otherwise provided in these rules. The following witnesses shall be incompetent to testify in any proceeding subject to these rules:

(1) Insane Persons. Insane persons who, in the opinion of the court, are in an insane condition of mind at the time when they are offered as a witness, or who, in the opinion of the court, were in that condition when the events happened of which they are called to testify.

(2) Children. Children or other persons who, after being examined by the court, appear not to possess sufficient intellect to relate transac-

*Texas Rules*

tions with respect to which they are interrogated.

(b) *"Dead Man's Rule" in Civil Actions.* In civil actions by or against executors, administrators, or guardians, in which judgment may be rendered for or against them as such, neither party shall be allowed to testify against the others as to any oral statement by the testator, intestate or ward, unless that testimony to the oral statement is corroborated or unless the witness is called at the trial to testify thereto by the opposite party; and, the provisions of this article shall extend to and include all actions by or against the heirs or legal representatives of a decedent based in whole or in part on such oral statement. Except for the foregoing, a witness is not precluded from giving evidence of or concerning any transaction with, any conversations with, any admissions of, or statement by, a deceased or insane party or person merely because the witness is a party to the action or a person interested in the event thereof. The trial court shall, in a proper case, where this rule prohibits an interested party or witness from testifying, instruct the jury that such person is not permitted by the law to give evidence relating to any oral statement by the deceased or ward unless the oral statement is corroborated or unless the party or witness is called at the trial by the opposite party.

## Rule 602. Lack of Personal Knowledge.

A witness may not testify to a matter unless evidence is introduced sufficient to support a finding that the witness has personal knowledge of the matter. Evidence to prove personal knowledge may, but need not, consist of the testimony of the witness. This rule is subject to the provisions of Rule 703, relating to opinion testimony by expert witnesses.

## Rule 603. Oath or Affirmation.

Before testifying, every witness shall be required to declare that the witness will testify truthfully, by oath or affirmation administered in a form calculated to awaken the witness' conscience and impress the witness' mind with the duty to do so.

## Rule 604. Interpreters.

An interpreter is subject to the provisions of these rules relating to qualification as an expert and the administration of an oath or affirmation to make a true translation.

## Rule 605. Competency of Judge As a Witness.

The judge presiding at the trial may not testify in that trial as a witness. No objection need be made in order to preserve the point.

## Rule 606. Competency of Juror As a Witness.

(a) *At the Trial.* A member of the jury may not testify as a witness before that jury in the trial of the case in which the juror is sitting as a juror. If the juror is called so to testify, the opposing party shall be afforded an opportunity to object out of the presence of the jury.

(b) *Inquiry into Validity of Verdict or Indictment.* Upon an inquiry into the validity of a verdict or indictment, a juror may not testify as to any matter or statement occurring during the jury's deliberations, or to the effect of anything on any juror's mind or emotions or mental processes, as influencing any juror's assent to or dissent from the verdict or indictment. Nor may a juror's affidavit or any statement by a juror concerning any matter about which the juror would be precluded from testifying be admitted in evidence for any of these purposes. However, a juror may testify: (1) whether any outside influence was improperly brought to bear upon any juror; or (2) to rebut a claim that the juror was not qualified to serve.

## Rule 607. Who May Impeach.

The credibility of a witness may be attacked by any party, including the party calling the witness.

## Rule 608. Evidence of Character and Conduct of a Witness.

(a) *Opinion and Reputation Evidence of Character.* The credibility of a witness may be attacked or supported by evidence in the form of opinion or reputation, but subject to these limitations:

(1) the evidence may refer only to character for truthfulness or untruthfulness; and

(2) evidence of truthful character is admissible only after the character of the witness for truthfulness has been attacked by opinion or reputation evidence or otherwise.

(b) *Specific Instances of Conduct.* Specific instances of the conduct of a witness, for the purpose of attacking or supporting the witness' credibility, other than conviction of crime as provided in Rule 609, may not be inquired into on cross-examination of the witness nor proved by extrinsic evidence.

## Rule 609. Impeachment by Evidence of Conviction of Crime.

(a) *General Rule.* For the purpose of attacking the credibility of a witness, evidence that the witness has been convicted of a crime shall be admitted if elicited from the witness or established by public record but only if the crime was a felony or involved moral turpitude, regardless of punishment, and the court determines that the probative value of admitting this evidence outweighs its prejudicial effect to a party.

(b) *Time Limit.* Evidence of a conviction under this rule is not admissible if a period of more than ten years has elapsed since the date of the conviction or of the release of the witness from the confinement imposed for that conviction, whichever is the later date, unless the court determines, in the interests of justice, that the probative value of the conviction supported by specific facts and circumstances substantially outweighs its prejudicial effect.

(c) *Effect of Pardon, Annulment, or Certificate of Rehabilitation.* Evidence of a conviction is not admissible under this rule if:

(1) based on the finding of the rehabilitation of the person convicted, the conviction has been the subject of a pardon, annulment, certificate of rehabilitation, or other equivalent procedure, and that person has not been convicted of a subsequent crime which was classified as a felony or involved moral turpitude, regardless of punishment;

(2) probation has been satisfactorily completed for the crime for which the person was convicted, and that person has not been convicted of a subsequent crime which was classified as a felony or involved moral turpitude, regardless of punishment; or

(3) based on a finding of innocence, the conviction has been the subject of a pardon, annulment, or other equivalent procedure.

(d) *Juvenile Adjudications.* Evidence of juvenile adjudications is not admissible, except for proceedings conducted pursuant to Title III, Family Code, in which the witness is a party, under this rule unless required to be admitted by the Constitution of the United States or Texas.

(e) *Pendency of Appeal.* Pendency of an appeal renders evidence of a conviction inadmissible.

(f) *Notice.* Evidence of a conviction is not admissible if after timely written request by the adverse party specifying the witness or witnesses, the proponent fails to give to the adverse party sufficient advance written notice of intent to use such evidence to provide the adverse party with a fair opportunity to contest the use of such evidence.

## Rule 610. Religious Beliefs or Opinions.

Evidence of the beliefs or opinions of a witness on matters of religion is not admissible for the purpose of showing that by reason of their nature the witness' credibility is impaired or enhanced.

## Rule 611. Mode and Order of Interrogation and Presentation.

(a) *Control by Court.* The court shall exercise reasonable control over the mode and order of interrogating witnesses and presenting evidence so as to (1) make the interrogation and presentation effective for the ascertainment of the truth, (2) avoid needless consumption of time, and (3) protect witnesses from harassment or undue embarrassment.

(b) *Scope of Cross-Examination.* A witness may be cross-examined on any matter relevant to any issue in the case, including credibility.

(c) *Leading Questions.* Leading questions should not be used on the direct examination of a witness except as may be necessary to develop the testimony of the witness. Ordinarily leading questions should be permitted on cross-examination. When a party calls a hostile witness, an adverse party, or a witness identified with an adverse party, interrogation may be by leading questions.

## Rule 612. Writing Used to Refresh Memory.

If a witness uses a writing to refresh memory for the purpose of testifying either

(1) while testifying;

(2) before testifying, in civil cases, if the court in its discretion determines it is necessary in the interests of justice; or

(3) before testifying, in criminal cases;

an adverse party is entitled to have the writing produced at the hearing, to inspect it, to cross-examine the witness thereon, and to introduce in evidence those portions which relate to the testi-

**Texas Rules**

mony of the witness. If it is claimed that the writing contains matters not related to the subject matter of the testimony the court shall examine the writing in camera, excise any portion not so related, and order delivery of the remainder to the party entitled thereto. Any portion withheld over objections shall be preserved and made available to the appellate court in the event of an appeal. If a writing is not produced or delivered pursuant to order under this rule, the court shall make any order justice requires, except that in criminal cases when the prosecution elects not to comply, the order shall be one striking the testimony or, if the court in its discretion determines that the interests of justice so require, declaring a mistrial.

## Rule 613. Prior Statements of Witnesses: Impeachment and Support.

(a) *Examining Witness Concerning Prior Inconsistent Statement.* In examining a witness concerning a prior inconsistent statement made by the witness, whether oral or written, and before further cross-examination concerning, or extrinsic evidence of, such statement may be allowed, the witness must be told the contents of such statement and the time and place and the person to whom it was made, and must be afforded an opportunity to explain or deny such statement. If written, the writing need not be shown to the witness at that time, but on request the same shall be shown to opposing counsel. If the witness unequivocally admits having made such statement, extrinsic evidence of same shall not be admitted. This provision does not apply to admissions of a party-opponent as defined in Rule 801(e)(2).

(b) *Examining Witness Concerning Bias or Interest.* In impeaching a witness by proof of circumstances or statements showing bias or interest on the part of such witness, and before further cross-examination concerning, or extrinsic evidence of, such bias or interest may be allowed, the circumstances supporting such claim or the details of such statement, including the contents and where, when and to whom made, must be made known to the witness, and the witness must be given an opportunity to explain or to deny such circumstances or statement. If written, the writing need not be shown to the witness at that time, but on request the same shall be shown to opposing counsel. If the witness unequivocally admits such bias or interest, extrinsic evidence of same shall not be admitted. A party shall be permitted

to present evidence rebutting any evidence impeaching one of said party's witnesses on grounds of bias or interest.

(c) *Prior Consistent Statements of Witnesses.* A prior statement of a witness which is consistent with the testimony of the witness is inadmissible except as provided in Rule 801(e)(1)(B).

## Rule 614. Exclusion of Witnesses.

At the request of a party the court shall order witnesses excluded so that they cannot hear the testimony of other witnesses, and it may make the order of its own motion. This rule does not authorize exclusion of:

(1) a party who is a natural person or in civil cases the spouse of such natural person;

(2) an officer or employee of a party in a civil case or a defendant in a criminal case that is not a natural person designated as its representative by its attorney;

(3) a person whose presence is shown by a party to be essential to the presentation of the party's cause; or

(4) the victim in a criminal case, unless the victim is to testify and the court determines that the victim's testimony would be materially affected if the victim hears other testimony at the trial.

## Rule 615. Production of Statements of Witnesses in Criminal Cases.

(a) *Motion for Production.* After a witness other than the defendant has testified on direct examination, the court, on motion of a party who did not call the witness, shall order the attorney for the state or the defendant and defendant's attorney, as the case may be, to produce, for the examination and use of the moving party, any statement of the witness that is in their possession and that relates to the subject matter concerning which the witness has testified.

(b) *Production of Entire Statement.* If the entire contents of the statement relate to the subject matter concerning which the witness has testified, the court shall order that the statement be delivered to the moving party.

(c) *Production of Excised Statement.* If the other party claims that the statement contains matter that does not relate to the subject matter concerning which the witness has testified, the court shall order that it be delivered to the court in camera. Upon inspection, the court shall excise the portions of the statement that do not relate to the subject matter concerning which the witness has testified, and shall order that the statement, with such material excised, be delivered to the moving party. Any portion withheld over objection shall be preserved and made available to the appellate court in the event of appeal.

(d) *Recess for Examination of Statement.* Upon delivery of the statement to the moving party, the court, upon application of that party, shall recess proceedings in the trial for a reasonable examination of such statement and for preparation for its use in the trial.

(e) *Sanction for Failure to Produce Statement.* If the other party elects not to comply with an order to deliver a statement to the moving party, the court shall order that the testimony of the witness be stricken from the record and that the trial proceed, or, if it is the attorney for the state who elects not to comply, shall declare a mistrial if required by the interest of justice.

(f) *Definition.* As used in this rule, a "statement" of a witness means:

(1) a written statement made by the witness that is signed or otherwise adopted or approved by the witness;

(2) a substantially verbatim recital of an oral statement made by the witness that is recorded contemporaneously with the making of the oral statement and that is contained in a stenographic, mechanical, electrical, or other recording or a transcription thereof; or

(3) a statement, however taken or recorded, or a transcription thereof, made by the witness to a grand jury.

# ARTICLE VII. OPINIONS AND EXPERT TESTIMONY

Rule
701. Opinion Testimony by Lay Witnesses.
702. Testimony by Experts.
703. Bases of Opinion Testimony by Experts.
704. Opinion on Ultimate Issue.
705. Disclosure of Facts or Data Underlying Expert Opinion.
706. Audit in Civil Cases.

## Rule 701. Opinion Testimony by Lay Witnesses.

If the witness is not testifying as an expert, the witness' testimony in the form of opinions or inferences is limited to those opinions or inferences which are (a) rationally based on the perception of the witness and (b) helpful to a clear understanding of the witness' testimony or the determination of a fact in issue.

## Rule 702. Testimony by Experts.

If scientific, technical, or other specialized knowledge will assist the trier of fact to understand the evidence or to determine a fact in issue, a witness qualified as an expert by knowledge, skill, experience, training, or education may testify thereto in the form of an opinion or otherwise.

## Rule 703. Bases of Opinion Testimony by Experts.

The facts or data in the particular case upon which an expert bases an opinion or inference may be those perceived by, reviewed by, or made known to the expert at or before the hearing. If of a type reasonably relied upon by experts in the particular field in forming opinions or inferences upon the subject, the facts or data need not be admissible in evidence.

## Rule 704. Opinion on Ultimate Issue.

Testimony in the form of an opinion or inference otherwise admissible is not objectionable because it embraces an ultimate issue to be decided by the trier of fact.

## Rule 705. Disclosure of Facts or Data Underlying Expert Opinion.

(a) *Disclosure of Facts or Data.* The expert may testify in terms of opinion or inference and give the expert's reasons therefor without prior disclosure of the underlying facts or data, unless the court requires otherwise. The expert may in any event disclose on direct examination, or be required to disclose on cross-examination, the underlying facts or data.

(b) *Voir Dire.* Prior to the expert giving the expert's opinion or disclosing the underlying facts or data, a party against whom the opinion is offered upon request in a criminal case shall, or in a civil case may, be permitted to conduct a *voir dire* examination directed to the underlying facts or data upon which the opinion is based. This examination shall be conducted out of the hearing of the jury.

(c) *Admissibility of Opinion.* If the court determines that the underlying facts or data do not provide a sufficient basis for the expert's opinion under Rule 702 or 703, the opinion is inadmissible.

Texas Rules

(d) *Balancing Test; Limiting Instructions.* When the underlying facts or data would be inadmissible in evidence, the court shall exclude the underlying facts or data if the danger that they will be used for a purpose other than as explanation or support for the expert's opinion outweighs their value as explanation or support or are unfairly prejudicial. If otherwise inadmissible facts or data are disclosed before the jury, a limiting instruction by the court shall be given upon request.

### Rule 706. Audit in Civil Cases.

Despite any other evidence rule to the contrary, verified reports of auditors prepared pursuant to Rule of Civil Procedure 172, whether in the form of summaries, opinions, or otherwise, shall be admitted in evidence when offered by any party whether or not the facts or data in the reports are otherwise admissible and whether or not the reports embrace the ultimate issues to be decided by the trier of fact. Where exceptions to the reports have been filed, a party may contradict the reports by evidence supporting the exceptions.

# ARTICLE VIII. HEARSAY

Rule

### Rule 801. Definitions.

The following definitions apply under this article:

(a) *Statement.* A "statement" is (1) an oral or written verbal expression or (2) nonverbal conduct of a person, if it is intended by the person as a substitute for verbal expression.

(b) *Declarant.* A "declarant" is a person who makes a statement.

(c) *Matter Asserted.* "Matter asserted" includes any matter explicitly asserted, and any matter implied by a statement, if the probative value of the statement as offered flows from declarant's belief as to the matter.

(d) *Hearsay.* "Hearsay" is a statement, other than one made by the declarant while testifying at the trial or hearing, offered in evidence to prove the truth of the matter asserted.

(e) *Statements Which Are Not Hearsay.* A statement is not hearsay if:

(1) Prior Statement by Witness. The declarant testifies at the trial or hearing and is subject to cross-examination concerning the statement, and the statement is:

(A) inconsistent with the declarant's testimony, and was given under oath subject to the penalty of perjury at a trial, hearing, or other proceeding except a grand jury proceeding in a criminal case, or in a deposition;

(B) consistent with the declarant's testimony and is offered to rebut an express or implied charge against the declarant of recent fabrication or improper influence or motive;

(C) one of identification of a person made after perceiving the person; or

(D) taken and offered in a criminal case in accordance with Code of Criminal Procedure article 38.071.

(2) Admission by Party-Opponent. The statement is offered against a party and is:

(A) the party's own statement in either an individual or representative capacity;

(B) a statement of which the party has manifested an adoption or belief in its truth;

(C) a statement by a person authorized by the party to make a statement concerning the subject;

(D) a statement by the party's agent or servant concerning a matter within the scope of the agency or employment, made during the existence of the relationship; or

(E) a statement by a co-conspirator of a party during the course and in furtherance of the conspiracy.

(3) Depositions. In a civil case, it is a deposition taken in the same proceeding, as same proceeding is defined in Rule of Civil Procedure 203.6(b). Unavailability of deponent is not a requirement for admissibility.

### Rule 802. Hearsay Rule.

Hearsay is not admissible except as provided by statute or these rules or by other rules prescribed pursuant to statutory authority. Inadmissible hearsay admitted without objection shall not be denied probative value merely because it is hearsay.

## Rule 803. Hearsay Exceptions; Availability of Declarant Immaterial.

The following are not excluded by the hearsay rule, even though the declarant is available as a witness:

(1) *Present Sense Impression.* A statement describing or explaining an event or condition made while the declarant was perceiving the event or condition, or immediately thereafter.

(2) *Excited Utterance.* A statement relating to a startling event or condition made while the declarant was under the stress of excitement caused by the event or condition.

(3) *Then Existing Mental, Emotional, or Physical Condition.* A statement of the declarant's then existing state of mind, emotion, sensation, or physical condition (such as intent, plan, motive, design, mental feeling, pain, or bodily health), but not including a statement of memory or belief to prove the fact remembered or believed unless it relates to the execution, revocation, identification, or terms of declarant's will.

(4) *Statements for Purposes of Medical Diagnosis or Treatment.* Statements made for purposes of medical diagnosis or treatment and describing medical history, or past or present symptoms, pain, or sensations, or the inception or general character of the cause or external source thereof insofar as reasonably pertinent to diagnosis or treatment.

(5) *Recorded Recollection.* A memorandum or record concerning a matter about which a witness once had personal knowledge but now has insufficient recollection to enable the witness to testify fully and accurately, shown to have been made or adopted by the witness when the matter was fresh in the witness' memory and to reflect that knowledge correctly, unless the circumstances of preparation cast doubt on the document's trustworthiness. If admitted, the memorandum or record may be read into evidence but may not itself be received as an exhibit unless offered by an adverse party.

(6) *Records of Regularly Conducted Activity.* A memorandum, report, record, or data compilation, in any form, of acts, events, conditions, opinions, or diagnoses, made at or near the time by, or from information transmitted by, a person with knowledge, if kept in the course of a regularly conducted business activity, and if it was the regular practice of that business activity to make the memorandum, report, record, or data compilation, all as shown by the testimony of the custodian or other qualified witness, or by affidavit that complies with Rule 902(10), unless the source of information or the method or circumstances of preparation indicate lack of trustworthiness. "Business" as used in this paragraph includes any and every kind of regular organized activity whether conducted for profit or not.

(7) *Absence of Entry in Records Kept in Accordance with the Provisions of Paragraph (6).* Evidence that a matter is not included in the memoranda, reports, records, or data compilations, in any form, kept in accordance with the provisions of paragraph (6), to prove the nonoccurrence or nonexistence of the matter, if the matter was of a kind of which a memorandum, report, record, or data compilation was regularly made and preserved, unless the sources of information or other circumstances indicate lack of trustworthiness.

(8) *Public Records and Reports.* Records, reports, statements, or data compilations, in any form, of public offices or agencies setting forth:

(A) the activities of the office or agency;

(B) matters observed pursuant to duty imposed by law as to which matters there was a duty to report, excluding in criminal cases matters observed by police officers and other law enforcement personnel; or

(C) in civil cases as to any party and in criminal cases as against the state, factual findings resulting from an investigation made pursuant to authority granted by law;

unless the sources of information or other circumstances indicate lack of trustworthiness.

(9) *Records of Vital Statistics.* Records or data compilations, in any form, of births, fetal deaths, deaths, or marriages, if the report thereof was made to a public office pursuant to requirements of law.

(10) *Absence of Public Record or Entry.* To prove the absence of a record, report, statement, or data compilation, in any form, or the nonoccurrence or nonexistence of a matter of which a record, report, statement, or data compilation, in any form, was regularly made and preserved by a public office or agency, evidence in the form of a certification in accordance with Rule 902, or testimony, that diligent search failed to disclose the record, report statement, or data compilation, or entry.

(11) *Records of Religious Organizations.* Statements of births, marriages, divorces,

deaths, legitimacy, ancestry, relationship by blood or marriage, or other similar facts of personal or family history, contained in a regularly kept record of a religious organization.

(12) *Marriage, Baptismal, and Similar Certificates.* Statements of fact contained in a certificate that the maker performed a marriage or other ceremony or administered a sacrament, made by a member of the clergy, public official, or other person authorized by the rules or practices of a religious organization or by law to perform the act certified, and purporting to have been issued at the time of the act or within a reasonable time thereafter.

(13) *Family Records.* Statements of fact concerning personal or family history contained in family Bibles, genealogies, charts, engravings on rings, inscriptions on family portraits, engravings on urns, crypts, or tombstones, or the like.

(14) *Records of Documents Affecting an Interest in Property.* The record of a document purporting to establish or affect an interest in property, as proof of the content of the original recorded document and its execution and delivery by each person by whom it purports to have been executed, if the record is a record of a public office and an applicable statute authorizes the recording of documents of that kind in that office.

(15) *Statements in Documents Affecting an Interest in Property.* A statement contained in a document purporting to establish or affect an interest in property if the matter stated was relevant to the purpose of the document, unless dealings with the property since the document was made have been inconsistent with the truth of the statement or the purport of the document.

(16) *Statements in Ancient Documents.* Statements in a document in existence twenty years or more the authenticity of which is established.

(17) *Market Reports, Commercial Publications.* Market quotations, tabulations, lists, directories, or other published compilations, generally used and relied upon by the public or by persons in particular occupations.

(18) *Learned Treatises.* To the extent called to the attention of an expert witness upon cross-examination or relied upon by the expert in direct examination, statements contained in published treatises, periodicals, or pamphlets on a subject of history, medicine, or other science or art established as a reliable authority by the testimony or admission of the witness or by other expert testimony or by judicial notice. If admitted, the statements may be read into evidence but may not be received as exhibits.

(19) *Reputation Concerning Personal or Family History.* Reputation among members of a person's family by blood, adoption, or marriage, or among a person's associates, or in the community, concerning a person's birth, adoption, marriage, divorce, death, legitimacy, relationship by blood, adoption, or marriage, ancestry, or other similar fact of personal or family history.

(20) *Reputation Concerning Boundaries or General History.* Reputation in a community, arising before the controversy, as to boundaries of or customs affecting lands in the community, and reputation as to events of general history important to the community or state or nation in which located.

(21) *Reputation As to Character.* Reputation of a person's character among associates or in the community.

(22) *Judgment of Previous Conviction.* In civil cases, evidence of a judgment, entered after a trial or upon a plea of guilty (but not upon a plea of *nolo contendere*), judging a person guilty of a felony, to prove any fact essential to sustain the judgment of conviction. In criminal cases, evidence of a judgment, entered after a trial or upon a plea of guilty or *nolo contendere*, adjudging a person guilty of a criminal offense, to prove any fact essential to sustain the judgment of conviction, but not including, when offered by the state for purposes other than impeachment, judgments against persons other than the accused. In all cases, the pendency of an appeal renders such evidence inadmissible.

(23) *Judgment As to Personal, Family, or General History, or Boundaries.* Judgments as proof of matters of personal, family or general history, or boundaries, essential to the judgment, if the same would be provable by evidence of reputation.

(24) *Statement Against Interest.* A statement which was at the time of its making so far contrary to the declarant's pecuniary or proprietary interest, or so far tended to subject the declarant to civil or criminal liability, or to render invalid a claim by the declarant against another, or to make the declarant an object of hatred, ridicule, or disgrace, that a reasonable person in declarant's position would not have made the statement unless believing it to be

true. In criminal cases, a statement tending to expose the declarant to criminal liability is not admissible unless corroborating circumstances clearly indicate the trustworthiness of the statement.

## Rule 804. Hearsay Exceptions; Declarant Unavailable.

(a) *Definition of Unavailability.* "Unavailability as a witness" includes situations in which the declarant:

(1) is exempted by ruling of the court on the ground of privilege from testifying concerning the subject matter of the declarant's statement;

(2) persists in refusing to testify concerning the subject matter of the declarant's statement despite an order of the court to do so;

(3) testifies to a lack of memory of the subject matter of the declarant's statement;

(4) is unable to be present or to testify at the hearing because of death or then existing physical or mental illness or infirmity; or

(5) is absent from the hearing and the proponent of the declarant's statement has been unable to procure the declarant's attendance or testimony by process or other reasonable means.

A declarant is not unavailable as a witness if the declarant's exemption, refusal, claim of lack of memory, inability, or absence is due to the procurement or wrong-doing of the proponent of the declarant's statement for the purpose of preventing the witness from attending or testifying.

(b) *Hearsay Exceptions.* The following are not excluded if the declarant is unavailable as a witness:

(1) Former Testimony. In civil cases, testimony given as a witness at another hearing of the same or a different proceeding, or in a deposition taken in the course of another proceeding, if the party against whom the testimony is now offered, or a person with a similar interest, had an opportunity and similar motive to develop the testimony by direct, cross, or redirect examination. In criminal cases, testimony given as a witness at another hearing of the same or a different proceeding, if the party against whom the testimony is now offered had an opportunity and similar motive to develop the testimony by direct, cross, or redirect examination. In criminal cases the use of depositions is controlled by Chapter 39 of the Code of Criminal Procedure.

(2) Dying Declarations. A statement made by a declarant while believing that the declarant's death was imminent, concerning the cause or circumstances of what the declarant believed to be impending death.

(3) Statement of Personal or Family History.

(A) A statement concerning the declarant's own birth, adoption, marriage, divorce, legitimacy, relationship by blood, adoption, or marriage, ancestry, or other similar fact of personal or family history even though declarant had no means of acquiring personal knowledge of the matter stated; or

(B) A statement concerning the foregoing matters, and death also, of another person, if the declarant was related to the other by blood, adoption, or marriage or was so intimately associated with the other's family as to be likely to have accurate information concerning the matter declared.

## Rule 805. Hearsay Within Hearsay.

Hearsay included within hearsay is not excluded under the hearsay rule if each part of the combined statements conforms with an exception to the hearsay rule provided in these rules.

## Rule 806. Attacking and Supporting Credibility of Declarant.

When a hearsay statement, or a statement defined in Rule 801(e)(2)(C), (D), or (E), or in civil cases a statement defined in Rule 801(e)(3), has been admitted in evidence, the credibility of the declarant may be attacked, and if attacked may be supported by any evidence which would be admissible for those purposes if declarant had testified as a witness. Evidence of a statement or conduct by the declarant at any time, offered to impeach the declarant, is not subject to any requirement that the declarant may have been afforded an opportunity to deny or explain. If the party against whom a hearsay statement has been admitted calls the declarant as a witness, the party is entitled to examine the declarant on the statement as if under cross-examination.

# ARTICLE IX.
# AUTHENTICATION AND IDENTIFICATION

Texas Rules

## Rule 901. Requirement of Authentication or Identification.

(a) *General Provision.* The requirement of authentication or identification as a condition precedent to admissibility is satisfied by evidence sufficient to support a finding that the matter in question is what its proponent claims.

(b) *Illustrations.* By way of illustration only, and not by way of limitation, the following are examples of authentication or identification conforming with the requirements of this rule:

(1) Testimony of Witness with Knowledge. Testimony that a matter is what it is claimed to be.

(2) Nonexpert Opinion on Handwriting. Nonexpert opinion as to the genuineness of handwriting, based upon familiarity not acquired for purposes of the litigation.

(3) Comparison by Trier or Expert Witness. Comparison by the trier of fact or by expert witness with specimens which have been found by the court to be genuine.

(4) Distinctive Characteristics and the Like. Appearance, contents, substance, internal patterns, or other distinctive characteristics, taken in conjunction with circumstances.

(5) Voice Identification. Identification of a voice, whether heard firsthand or through mechanical or electronic transmission or recording, by opinion based upon hearing the voice at anytime under circumstances connecting it with the alleged speaker.

(6) Telephone Conversations. Telephone conversations, by evidence that a call was made to the number assigned at the time by the telephone company to a particular person or business, if:

(A) in the case of a person, circumstances, including self-identification, show the person answering to be the one called; or

(B) in the case of a business, the call was made to a place of business and the conversation related to business reasonably transacted over the telephone.

(7) Public Records or Reports. Evidence that a writing authorized by law to be recorded or filed and in fact recorded or filed in a public office, or a purported public record, report, statement, or data compilation, in any form, is from the public office where items of this nature are kept.

(8) Ancient Documents or Data Compilation. Evidence that a document or data compilation, in any form, (A) is in such condition as to create no suspicion concerning its authenticity, (B) was in a place where it, if authentic, would likely be, and (C) has been in existence twenty years or more at the time it is offered.

(9) Process or System. Evidence describing a process or system used to produce a result and showing that the process or system produces an accurate result.

(10) Methods Provided by Statute or Rule. Any method of authentication or identification provided by statute or by other rule prescribed pursuant to statutory authority.

## Rule 902. Self-Authentication.

Extrinsic evidence of authenticity as a condition precedent to admissibility is not required with respect to the following:

(1) *Domestic Public Documents Under Seal.* A document bearing a seal purporting to be that of the United States, or of any State, district, Commonwealth, territory, or insular possession thereof, or the Panama Canal Zone, or the Trust Territory of the Pacific Islands, or of a political subdivision, department, officer, or agency thereof, and a signature purporting to be an attestation or execution.

(2) *Domestic Public Documents Not Under Seal.* A document purporting to bear the signature in the official capacity of an officer or employee of any entity included in paragraph (1) hereof, having no seal, if a public officer having a seal and having official duties in the district or political subdivision of the officer or employee certifies under seal that the signer has the official capacity and that the signature is genuine.

(3) *Foreign Public Documents.* A document purporting to be executed or attested in an official capacity by a person, authorized by the laws of a foreign country to make the execution or attestation, and accompanied by a final certification as to the genuineness of the signature and official position (A) of the executing or attesting person, or (B) of any foreign official whose certificate of genuineness of signature and official position relates to the execution or attestation or is in a chain of certificates of genuineness of signature and official position relating to the execution or attestation. A final certification may be made by a secretary of embassy or legation, consul general, consul, vice consul, or consular agent of the United States, or a diplomatic or consular official of the foreign country assigned or accredited to the

United States. If reasonable opportunity has been given to all parties to investigate the authenticity and accuracy of official documents, the court may, for good cause shown, order that they be treated as presumptively authentic without final certification or permit them to be evidenced by an attested summary with or without final certification. The final certification shall be dispensed with whenever both the United States and the foreign country in which the official record is located are parties to a treaty or convention that abolishes or displaces such requirement, in which case the record and the attestation shall be certified by the means provided in the treaty or convention.

(4) *Certified Copies of Public Records.* A copy of an official record or report or entry therein, or of a document authorized by law to be recorded or filed and actually recorded or filed in a public office, including data compilations in any form certified as correct by the custodian or other person authorized to make the certification, by certificate complying with paragraph (1), (2) or (3) of this rule or complying with any statute or other rule prescribed pursuant to statutory authority.

(5) *Official Publications.* Books, pamphlets, or other publications purporting to be issued by public authority.

(6) *Newspapers and Periodicals.* Printed materials purporting to be newspapers or periodicals.

(7) *Trade Inscriptions and the Like.* Inscriptions, signs, tags, or labels purporting to have been affixed in the course of business and indicating ownership, control, or origin.

(8) *Acknowledged Documents.* Documents accompanied by a certificate of acknowledgment executed in the manner provided by law by a notary public or other officer authorized by law to take acknowledgments.

(9) *Commercial Paper and Related Documents.* Commercial paper, signatures thereon, and documents relating thereto to the extent provided by general commercial law.

(10) *Business Records Accompanied by Affidavit.*

(a) Records or Photocopies; Admissibility; Affidavit; Filing. Any record or set of records or photographically reproduced copies of such records, which would be admissible under Rule 803(6) or (7) shall be admissible in evidence in any court in this state upon the affidavit of the person who would otherwise provide the prerequisites of Rule 803(6) or

(7), that such records attached to such affidavit were in fact so kept as required by Rule 803(6) or (7), provided further, that such record or records along with such affidavit are filed with the clerk of the court for inclusion with the papers in the cause in which the record or records are sought to be used as evidence at least fourteen days prior to the day upon which trial of said cause commences, and provided the other parties to said cause are given prompt notice by the party filing same of the filing of such record or records and affidavit, which notice shall identify the name and employer, if any, of the person making the affidavit and such records shall be made available to the counsel for other parties to the action or litigation for inspection and copying. The expense for copying shall be borne by the party, parties or persons who desire copies and not by the party or parties who file the records and serve notice of said filing, in compliance with this rule. Notice shall be deemed to have been promptly given if it is served in the manner contemplated by Rule of Civil Procedure 21a fourteen days prior to commencement of trial in said cause.

(b) Form of Affidavit. A form for the affidavit of such person as shall make such affidavit as is permitted in paragraph (a) above shall be sufficient if it follows this form though this form shall not be exclusive, and an affidavit which substantially complies with the provisions of this rule shall suffice, to-wit:

No. _____

| John Doe (Name of Plaintiff) v. John Roe (Name of Defendant) | IN THE _____ COURT IN AND FOR _____ COUNTY, TEXAS |

## AFFIDAVIT

Before me, the undersigned authority, personally appeared _____, who, being by me duly sworn, deposed as follows:

My name is _____, I am of sound mind, capable of making this affidavit, and personally acquainted with the facts herein stated:

I am the custodian of the records of _____. Attached hereto are _____ pages of records from _____. These said _____ pages of records are kept by _____ in the regular course of business, and it was the regular course of business of _____ for an employee or representative of _____, with knowledge of the act, event, condition, opinion, or diagnosis, recorded to make the record or to transmit information thereof to be included in such record; and the record was made at or near the time or reasonably soon thereafter. The records attached hereto are the original or exact duplicates of the original.

_____
Affiant

SWORN TO AND SUBSCRIBED before me on the ____ day of ____, 19 [20] ___.

_____
Notary Public, State of Texas
Notary's printed name:

_____
My commission expires:

(11) *Presumptions Under Statutes or Other Rules.* Any signature, document, or other matter declared by statute or by other rules prescribed pursuant to statutory authority to be presumptively or prima facie genuine or authentic.

## Rule 903. Subscribing Witness' Testimony Unnecessary.

The testimony of a subscribing witness is not necessary to authenticate a writing unless required by the laws of the jurisdiction whose laws govern the validity of the writing.

# ARTICLE X. CONTENTS OF WRITINGS, RECORDINGS, AND PHOTOGRAPHS

Rule
1001. Definitions.
1002. Requirement of Originals.
1003. Admissibility of Duplicates.
1004. Admissibility of Other Evidence of Contents.
1005. Public Records.
1006. Summaries.
1007. Testimony or Written Admission of Party.
1008. Functions of Court and Jury.
1009. Translation of Foreign Language Documents.

## Rule 1001. Definitions.

For purposes of this article the following definitions are applicable:

(a) *Writings and Recordings.* "Writings" and "recordings" consist of letters, words, or numbers or their equivalent, set down by handwriting, typewriting, printing, photostating, photographing, magnetic impulse, mechanical or electronic recording, or other form of data compilation.

(b) *Photographs.* "Photographs" include still photographs, X-ray films, video tapes, and motion pictures.

(c) *Original.* An "original" of a writing or recording is the writing or recording itself or any counterpart intended to have the same effect by a person executing or issuing it. An "original" of a photograph includes the negative or any print therefrom. If data are stored in a computer or similar device, any printout or other output readable by sight, shown to reflect the data accurately, is an "original."

(d) *Duplicate.* A "duplicate" is a counterpart produced by the same impression as the original, or from the same matrix, or by means of photography, including enlargements and miniatures, or by mechanical or electronic re-recording, or by chemical reproduction, or by other equivalent techniques which accurately reproduce the original.

## Rule 1002. Requirement of Originals.

To prove the content of a writing, recording, or photograph, the original writing, recording, or photograph is required except as otherwise provided in these rules or by law.

## Rule 1003. Admissibility of Duplicates.

A duplicate is admissible to the same extent as an original unless (1) a question is raised as to the authenticity of the original or (2) in the circumstances it would be unfair to admit the duplicate in lieu of the original.

## Rule 1004. Admissibility of Other Evidence of Contents.

The original is not required, and other evidence of the contents of a writing, recording, or photograph is admissible if:

(a) *Originals Lost or Destroyed.* All originals are lost or have been destroyed, unless the proponent lost or destroyed them in bad faith;

(b) *Original Not Obtainable.* No original can be obtained by any available judicial process or procedure;

(c) *Original Outside the State.* No original is located in Texas;

(d) *Original in Possession of Opponent.* At a time when an original was under the control of the party against whom offered, that party was put on notice, by the pleadings or otherwise, that the content would be a subject of proof at the hearing, and that party does not produce the original at the hearing; or

(e) *Collateral Matters.* The writing, recording or photograph is not closely related to a controlling issue.

## Rule 1005. Public Records.

The contents of an official record or of a document authorized to be recorded or filed and actually recorded or filed, including data compilations in any form, if otherwise admissible, may be proved by copy, certified as correct in accordance with Rule 902 or testified to be correct by a witness who has compared it with the original. If a copy which complies with the foregoing cannot be obtained by the exercise of reasonable diligence, then other evidence of the contents may be given.

## Rule 1006. Summaries.

The contents of voluminous writings, recordings, or photographs, otherwise admissible, which cannot conveniently be examined in court may be presented in the form of a chart, summary, or calculation. The originals, or duplicates, shall be made available for examination or copying, or both, by other parties at a reasonable time and place. The court may order that they be produced in court.

## Rule 1007. Testimony or Written Admission of Party.

Contents of writings, recordings, or photographs may be proved by the testimony or deposition of the party against whom offered or by that party's written admission, without accounting for the nonproduction of the original.

## Rule 1008. Functions of Court and Jury.

When the admissibility of other evidence of contents of writings, recordings, or photographs under these rules depends upon the fulfillment of a condition of fact, the question whether the condition has been fulfilled is ordinarily for the court to determine in accordance with the provisions of Rule 104. However, when an issue is raised (a) whether the asserted writing ever existed, or (b) whether another writing, recording, or photograph produced at the trial is the original, or (c) whether other evidence of contents correctly reflects the contents, the issue is for the trier of fact to determine as in the case of other issues of fact.

## Rule 1009. Translation of Foreign Language Documents.

(a) *Translations.* A translation of foreign language documents shall be admissible upon the affidavit of a qualified translator setting forth the qualifications of the translator and certifying that the translation is fair and accurate. Such affidavit, along with the translation and the underlying foreign language documents, shall be served upon all parties at least 45 days prior to the date of trial.

(b) *Objections.* Any party may object to the accuracy of another party's translation by pointing out the specific inaccuracies of the translation and by stating with specificity what the objecting party contends is a fair and accurate translation. Such objection shall be served upon all parties at least 15 days prior to the date of trial.

(c) *Effect of Failure to Object or Offer Conflicting Translation.* If no conflicting translation or objection is timely served, the court shall admit a translation submitted under paragraph (a) without need of proof, provided however that the underlying foreign language documents are otherwise admissible under the Texas Rules of Evidence. Failure to serve a conflicting translation under paragraph (a) or failure to timely and properly object to the accuracy of a translation under paragraph (b) shall preclude a party from attacking or offering evidence contradicting the accuracy of such translation at trial.

(d) *Effect of Objections or Conflicting Translations.* In the event of conflicting translations under paragraph (a) or if objections to another party's translation are served under paragraph (b), the court shall determine whether there is a genuine issue as to the accuracy of a material part of the translation to be resolved by the trier of fact.

(e) *Expert Testimony of Translator.* Except as provided in paragraph (c), this Rule does not preclude the admission of a translation of foreign language documents at trial either by live testimony or by deposition testimony of a qualified expert translator.

(f) *Varying of Time Limits.* The court, upon motion of any party and for good cause shown, may enlarge or shorten the time limits set forth in this Rule.

(g) *Court Appointment.* The court, if necessary, may appoint a qualified translator, the reasonable value of whose services shall be taxed as court costs.

# CONSTITUTION OF THE UNITED STATES OF AMERICA

## ARTICLE I. LEGISLATIVE DEPARTMENT

### Sec. 6, Cl 1.  Compensation and privileges of members.

The Senators and Representatives shall receive a Compensation for their Services, to be ascertained by Law, and paid out of the Treasury of the United States. They shall in all Cases, except Treason, Felony and Breach of the Peace, be privileged from Arrest during their Attendance at the Session of their respective Houses, and in going to and returning from the same; and for any Speech or Debate in either House, they shall not be questioned in any other Place.

### Sec. 9, Cl 2.  Habeas corpus.

The Privilege of the Writ of Habeas Corpus shall not be suspended, unless when in Cases of Rebellion or Invasion the public Safety may require it.

U.S. Constitution

# AMENDMENTS

## Amendment 1. Religious and political freedom.

Congress shall make no law respecting an establishment of religion, or prohibiting the free exercise thereof; or abridging the freedom of speech, or of the press; or the right of the people peaceably to assemble, and to petition the Government for a redress of grievances.

## Amendment 2. Right to bear arms.

A well regulated Militia, being necessary to the security of a free State, the right of the people to keep and bear Arms, shall not be infringed.

## Amendment 3. Quartering soldiers.

No Soldier shall, in time of peace be quartered in any house, without the consent of the Owner, nor in time of war, but in a manner to be prescribed by law.

## Amendment 4. Unreasonable searches and seizures.

The right of the people to be secure in their persons, houses, papers, and effects, against unreasonable searches and seizures, shall not be violated, and no Warrants shall issue, but upon probable cause, supported by Oath or affirmation, and particularly describing the place to be searched, and the persons or things to be seized.

## Amendment 5. Criminal actions—Provisions concerning—Due process of law and just compensation clauses.

No person shall be held to answer for a capital, or otherwise infamous crime, unless on a presentment or indictment of a Grand Jury, except in cases arising in the land or naval forces, or in the Militia, when in actual service in time of War or public danger; nor shall any person be subject for the same offence to be twice put in jeopardy of life or limb; nor shall be compelled in any criminal case to be a witness against himself, nor be deprived of life, liberty, or property, without due process of law; nor shall private property be taken for public use, without just compensation.

## Amendment 6. Rights of the accused.

In all criminal prosecutions, the accused shall enjoy the right to a speedy and public trial, by an impartial jury of the State and district wherein the crime shall have been committed, which district shall have been previously ascertained by law, and to be informed of the nature and cause of the accusation; to be confronted with the witnesses against him; to have compulsory process for obtaining witnesses in his favor, and to have the Assistance of Counsel for his defence.

## Amendment 7. Trial by jury in civil cases.

In Suits at common law, where the value in controversy shall exceed twenty dollars, the right

Amendments

of trial by jury shall be preserved, and no fact tried by a jury, shall be otherwise re-examined in any Court of the United States, than according to the rules of the common law.

## Amendment 8.
## Bail—Punishment.

Excessive bail shall not be required, nor excessive fines imposed, nor cruel and unusual punishments inflicted.

## Amendment 9. Rights retained by people.

The enumeration in the Constitution, of certain rights, shall not be construed to deny or disparage others retained by the people.

## Amendment 10. Powers reserved to states or people

The powers not delegated to the United States by the Constitution, nor prohibited by it to the States, are reserved to the States respectively, or to the people.

## Amendment 14.
## Citizenship—Due process of law—Equal protection

Section 1. All persons born or naturalized in the United States, and subject to the jurisdiction thereof, are citizens of the United States and of the State wherein they reside. No State shall make or enforce any law which shall abridge the privileges or immunities of citizens of the United States; nor shall any State deprive any person of life, liberty, or property, without due process of law; nor deny to any person within its jurisdiction the equal protection of the laws.

Amendments

# UNITED STATES CODE SERVICE

## TITLE 18
## CRIMES AND CRIMINAL PROCEDURE

Part I Crimes

## CHAPTER 44
## FIREARMS

## Sec. 926B. Carrying of concealed firearms by qualified law enforcement officers

(a) Notwithstanding any other provision of the law of any State or any political subdivision thereof, an individual who is a qualified law enforcement officer and who is carrying the identification required by subsection (d) may carry a concealed firearm that has been shipped or transported in interstate or foreign commerce, subject to subsection (b).

(b) This section shall not be construed to supersede or limit the laws of any State that--

(1) permit private persons or entities to prohibit or restrict the possession of concealed firearms on their property; or

(2) prohibit or restrict the possession of firearms on any State or local government property, installation, building, base, or park.

(c) As used in this section, the term "qualified law enforcement officer" means an employee of a governmental agency who--

(1) is authorized by law to engage in or supervise the prevention, detection, investigation, or prosecution of, or the incarceration of any person for, any violation of law, and has statutory powers of arrest;

(2) is authorized by the agency to carry a firearm;

(3) is not the subject of any disciplinary action by the agency which could result in suspension or loss of police powers;

(4) meets standards, if any, established by the agency which require the employee to regularly qualify in the use of a firearm;

(5) is not under the influence of alcohol or another intoxicating or hallucinatory drug or substance; and

(6) is not prohibited by Federal law from receiving a firearm.

(d) The identification required by this subsection is the photographic identification issued by the governmental agency for which the individual is employed as a law enforcement officer.

(e) As used in this section, the term "firearm"--

(1) except as provided in this subsection, has the same meaning as in section 921 of this title [26 USCS § 921];

(2) includes ammunition not expressly prohibited by Federal law or subject to the provisions of the National Firearms Act [26 USCS §§ 5801 et seq.] and

(3) does not include--

(A) any machinegun (as defined in section 5845 of the National Firearms Act [26 USCS § 5845]);

(B) any firearm silencer (as defined in section 921 of this title [26 USCS § 921]); and

(C) any destructive device (as defined in section 921 of this title [26 USCS § 921]).

(f) For the purposes of this section, a law enforcement officer of the Amtrak Police Department, a law enforcement officer of the Federal Reserve, or a law enforcement or police officer of the executive branch of the Federal Government qualifies as an employee of a governmental agency who is authorized by law to engage in or supervise the prevention, detection, investigation, or prosecution of, or the incarceration of any person for, any violation of law, and has statutory powers of arrest.

HISTORY: (Added July 22, 2004, P. L. 108-277, § 2(a), 118 Stat. 865; Oct. 12, 2010, P. L. 111-272, § 2(a), (b), 124 Stat. 2855.)

## Sec. 926C. Carrying of concealed firearms by qualified retired law enforcement officers

(a) Notwithstanding any other provision of the law of any State or any political subdivision thereof, an individual who is a qualified retired law enforcement officer and who is carrying the identification required by subsection (d) may carry a concealed firearm that has been shipped or transported in interstate or foreign commerce, subject to subsection (b).

(b) This section shall not be construed to supersede or limit the laws of any State that--

(1) permit private persons or entities to prohibit or restrict the possession of concealed firearms on their property; or

(2) prohibit or restrict the possession of firearms on any State or local government property, installation, building, base, or park.

(c) As used in this section, the term "qualified retired law enforcement officer" means an individual who--

(1) separated from service in good standing from service with a public agency as a law enforcement officer;

(2) before such separation, was authorized by law to engage in or supervise the prevention, detection, investigation, or prosecution of, or the incarceration of any person for, any violation of law, and had statutory powers of arrest;

(3)(A) before such separation, served as a law enforcement officer for an aggregate of 10 years or more; or

(B) separated from service with such agency, after completing any applicable probationary period of such service, due to a service-connected disability, as determined by such agency;

(4) during the most recent 12-month period, has met, at the expense of the individual, the standards for qualification in firearms training for active law enforcement officers, as determined by the former agency of the individual, the State in which the individual resides or, if the State has not established such standards, either a law enforcement agency within the State in which the individual resides or the standards used by a certified firearms instructor that is qualified to

conduct a firearms qualification test for active duty officers within that State;

(5)(A) has not been officially found by a qualified medical professional employed by the agency to be unqualified for reasons relating to mental health and as a result of this finding will not be issued the photographic identification as described in subsection (d)(1); or

(B) has not entered into an agreement with the agency from which the individual is separating from service in which that individual acknowledges he or she is not qualified under this section for reasons relating to mental health and for those reasons will not receive or accept the photographic identification as described in subsection (d)(1);

(6) is not under the influence of alcohol or another intoxicating or hallucinatory drug or substance; and

(7) is not prohibited by Federal law from receiving a firearm.

(d) The identification required by this subsection is--

(1) a photographic identification issued by the agency from which the individual separated from service as a law enforcement officer that indicates that the individual has, not less recently than one year before the date the individual is carrying the concealed firearm, been tested or otherwise found by the agency to meet the active duty standards for qualification in firearms training as established by the agency to carry a firearm of the same type as the concealed firearm; or

(2)(A) a photographic identification issued by the agency from which the individual separated from service as a law enforcement officer; and

(B) a certification issued by the State in which the individual resides or by a certified firearms instructor that is qualified to conduct a firearms qualification test for active duty officers within that State that indicates that the individual has, not less than 1 year before the date the individual is carrying the concealed firearm, been tested or otherwise found by the State or a certified firearms instructor that is qualified to conduct a firearms qualification test for active duty officers within that State to have met--

(I) the active duty standards for qualification in firearms training, as established by the State, to carry a firearm of the same type as the concealed firearm; or

(II) if the State has not established such standards, standards set by any law enforcement agency within that State to carry a firearm of the same type as the concealed firearm.

(e) As used in this section--

(1) the term "firearm";

(A) except as provided in this paragraph, has the same meaning as in section 921 of this title [18 USCS § 921];

(B) includes ammunition not expressly prohibited by Federal law or subject to the provisions of the National Firearms Act [26 USCS §§ 5801 et seq.]; and

(C) does not include--

(i) any machinegun (as defined in section 5845 of the National Firearms Act [26 USCS § 5845]);

(ii) any firearm silencer (as defined in section 921 of this title [18 USCS § 921]); and

(iii) any destructive device (as defined in section 921 of this title [18 USCS § 921]); and

(2) the term "service with a public agency as a law enforcement officer" includes service as a law enforcement officer of the Amtrak Police Department, service as a law enforcement officer of the Federal Reserve, or service as a law enforcement or police officer of the executive branch of the Federal Government.

HISTORY: (Added July 22, 2004, P. L. 108-277, § 3(a), 118 Stat. 866; Oct. 12, 2010, P. L. 111-272, § 2(c), 124 Stat. 2855.)

# TITLE 22
# FOREIGN RELATIONS AND INTERCOURSE

## CHAPTER 6
## FOREIGN DIPLOMATIC AND CONSULAR OFFICERS

## Sec. 254a.   Definitions

As used in this Act--

(1) the term "members of a mission" means--

(A) the head of a mission and those members of a mission who are members of the diplomatic staff or who, pursuant to law, are granted equivalent privileges and immunities,

(B) members of the administrative and technical staff of a mission, and

(C) members of the service staff of a mission, as such terms are defined in Article 1 of the Vienna Convention;

(2) the term "family" means--

(A) the members of the family of a member of a mission described in paragraph (1)(A) who form part of his or her household if they are not nationals of the United States, and

(B) the members of the family of a member of a mission described in paragraph (1)(B) who form part of his or her household if they are not nationals or permanent residents of the United States, within the meaning of Article 37 of the Vienna Convention;

(3) the term "mission" includes missions within the meaning of the Vienna Convention and any missions representing foreign governments, individually or collectively, which are extended the same privileges and immunities, pursuant to law, as are enjoyed by missions under the Vienna Convention; and

(4) the term "Vienna Convention" means the Vienna Convention on Diplomatic Relations of April 18, 1961 (T.I.A.S. numbered 7502; 23 U.S.T. 3227), entered into force with respect to the United States on December 13, 1972.

HISTORY: (Sept. 30, 1978, P.L. 95-393, § 2, 92 Stat. 808; Aug. 24, 1982, P.L. 97-241, Title II, § 203(b)(1), 96 Stat. 290.)

## Sec. 254b.   Privileges and immunities of members of mission of a state not ratifying Vienna Convention

With respect to a nonparty to the Vienna Convention, the mission, the members of the mission, their families, and diplomatic couriers shall enjoy the privileges and immunities specified in the Vienna Convention.

HISTORY: (Sept. 30, 1978, P.L. 95-393, § 3(b), 92 Stat. 808; Aug. 24, 1982, P.L. 97-241, Title II, § 203(b)(2), 96 Stat. 291.)

## Sec. 254c.   Extension of more favorable or less favorable treatment than provided under Vienna Convention; authority of President

The President may, on the basis of reciprocity and under such terms and conditions as he may determine, specify privileges and immunities for the mission, the members of the mission, their families, and the diplomatic couriers which result in more favorable treatment or less favorable treatment than is provided under the Vienna Convention.

HISTORY: (Sept. 30, 1978, P.L. 95-393, § 4, 92 Stat. 809; Aug. 24, 1982, P.L. 97-241, Title II, § 203(b)(3), 96 Stat. 291.)

# TRAFFIC OFFENSE TITLES

BASED ON CHANGES FROM THE 82nd LEGISLATURE, REGULAR AND
FIRST CALLED SPECIAL SESSION

(Do not use for citation purposes – use CJIS Offense Codes.)

| TITLE | PENALTY | TRAFFIC CODE SECTION *(unless otherwise noted)* |
|---|---|---|
| **ALL-TERRAIN VEHICLE VIOLATIONS** | | |
| Carry Passenger on ATV/Recreational Off-Highway Vehicle on Public Property | MC | 663.036 |
| Child < 14 years old Operating ATV/Recreational Off-Highway Vehicle w/o Adult Supervision | MC | 663.032 |
| Operate ATV/Recreational Off-Highway Vehicle in Reckless Manner that Endangerous Others | MC | 663.035 |
| Operate ATV/Recreational Off-Highway Vehicle on Public Roadway | MC | 663.037; 663.003 |
| Operate ATV/Recreational Off-Highway Vehicle w/Modified Exhaust System or Spark Arrester | MC | 633.034(c) |
| Operate ATV/Recreational Off-Highway Vehicle w/o Proper Lights; Brakes; Muffler; Spark Arrester | MC | 633.034(a);(b) |
| Operate ATV/Recreational Off-Highway Vehicle w/o Safety Apparel | MC | 663.034 |
| Operate ATV/Recreational Off-Highway Vehicle w/o Safety Certificate | MC | 663.031(a) |
| **BICYCLE VIOLATIONS** | | |
| Carried Articles that Interfered With Handling of Bicycle | M | 551.102(c) |
| Commission of Other Hazardous Traffic Violation Applicable by Definition to Bycicle Rider | M | 551.101 |
| Electric Bicycles, Regulation by Local Authority | M | 551.106 |
| Failure to Ride on Right Side of Roadway | M | 551.103(a) |
| Failure to Ride in Single Lane When Riding Two Abreast | M | 551.103(c) |
| No Brake or Defective Brake | M | 551.104(a) |
| No Red Taillight or Red Rear Reflector at Nighttime | M | 551.104(b) |
| Rode Improperly | M | 551.102(a);(b) |
| Towed by Vehicle while Using Bicycle, Coaster, Roller Skates, Sled, or Toy Vehicle on Roadway | M | 551.102(d) |
| **COMMERCIAL MOTOR VEHICLE VIOLATIONS** | | |
| Driving a Commercial Motor Vehicle w/Multiple DL | MC | 522.026 |
| Driving Commercial Vehicle during Period of Suspension | M | 522.071 |

| TITLE | PENALTY | TRAFFIC CODE SECTION *(unless otherwise noted)* |
|---|---|---|
| Driving Commercial Vehicle in Violation of Restriction | MC | 522.043(c) |
| Driving Vehicle w/o Proper Endorsements | MC | 522.042 |
| Driving w/o DL Appropriate for Class of Vehicle | MC | 522.011 |
| Employing Unlicensed Driver for a Commercial Vehicle | MB | 522.072 |
| Failure to Comply with Regulation of Operation of Commercial Vehicles | MC | 644.151(a)(1) |
| Failure to Keep Cab Card in Cab | MC | 643.253(a)(3) |
| Failure to Provide Bond to TX DMV | MC | 646.004 |
| Failure to Register Vehicle as Required by Unified Carrier System | MC | 645.004(a)(2) |
| Failure to Register Vehicle w/DMV | MC | 643.253(a)(1) |
| Failure to Report Change of Address or Name for Commercial DL | MC | 522.032 |
| Operate Foreign Commercial Vehicle w/o Proper Annual Permit | M | 502.093; 502.476 |
| Provide False/Fraudulent Information on Commercial DL Application | MC | 522.021(d) |
| Refusal to Allow Vehicle Inspection | MC | 644.151(a)(2) |
| Unregistered Solicitation to Transport Household Goods for Compensation | MC | 643.253(b) |
| Unregistered Solicitation to Transport Household Goods for Compensation - One Previous Conviction | MB | 643.253(e)(1) |
| Unregistered Solicitation to Transport Household Goods for Compensation - Two or More Previous Convictions | MA | 643.253(e)(2) |

## DRIVER LICENSE VIOLATIONS

| TITLE | PENALTY | TRAFFIC CODE SECTION |
|---|---|---|
| Accesses Electronically Readable Information from DL w/Intent to Sell/Disseminate to Third Party | MA | HSC § 161.0825 |
| Accesses/Uses/Compiles a Database of Electronically Readable Information Derived from DL | MA | 521.126(b) |
| Allow Person w/Suspended DL Because of Dangerous Driving to Borrow Vehicle | MC | 705.001 |
| Conspiring to Manufacture Counterfeit DL/ID | FS | 521.4565 |
| Conspiring to Manufacture Counterfeit DL/ID - Public Servant | F3 | 521.4565(c) |
| Display Another's DL as Person's Own | MA | 521.451(a)(3) |
| Display/Possess DL Known to be Fictitious or Altered | MA | 521.451(a)(1) |
| Driving Common Carrier when Less than 18 Years Old | M | 521.024 |
| Driving in Violation of Restriction | M | 521.221(c) |
| Driving w/an Expired DL | M | 521.021; 521.026 |
| Driving w/Occupational License in Violation of Restriction | MB | 521.253(a)(1) |
| Driving w/Out-of-State DL for More than 90 Days | M | 521.029 |
| Driving w/o DL | M | 521.021 |
| Driving w/o DL during Period of Suspension | MC | 521.457 |
| Driving w/o DL during Period of Suspension: Due to Intoxication | MB | 521.457(f-1) |

| TITLE | PENALTY | TRAFFIC CODE SECTION *(unless otherwise noted)* |
|---|---|---|
| Driving w/o DL during Period of Suspension: Due to No Insurance | MB | 521.457(f)(2) |
| Driving w/o DL during Period of Suspension: Due to No Insurance - Caused Death/Serious Bodily Injury | MA | 521.457(f-2) |
| Employing Unlicensed Driver | M | 521.459 |
| Failure to Display Court Order for Occupation License | MB | 521.253(a)(2) |
| Failure to Have/Display DL While Driving | M | 521.025 |
| Failure to Have/Display DL While Driving and Caused Death/Serious Bodily Injury While w/o Insurance | MA | 521.025(c)(3) |
| Failure to Report Change of Address or Name | M | 521.054 |
| Failure to Surrender Suspended/Cancelled/Revoked DL | MB | 521.315 |
| Improper DL for Type of Vehicle | M | 521.085 |
| Passenger Sleeps/Is Intoxicated/Cannot Observe Driver when Driver is Holder of Instruction Permit | M | 521.222(g) |
| Permit Unauthorized Person to Drive | M | 521.458 |
| Permit Unlawful Use of DL | MA | 521.451(a)(2) |
| Possess More than One Valid DL/ID | MA | 521.451(a)(4) |
| Possess/Manufacture/Produce w/Intent to Sell Forged/Counterfeit DL/ID | MA | 521.456 |
| Possess w/Intent to Represent False DL/ID when Less Than 21 Years Old | MC | 521.453 |
| Provide False/Fraudulent Information on a DL Application | MA | 521.451(a)(5); 521.454 |
| Rent Vehicle to Unlicensed Driver | M | 521.460 |
| Unauthorized Driving of School Bus | M | 521.022 |
| Use of Illegal DL w/Intent to Harm/Defraud | MA | 521.455 |

## DRIVERS – MISCELLANEOUS VIOLATIONS

| TITLE | PENALTY | TRAFFIC CODE SECTION |
|---|---|---|
| Aggravated Assault w/Motor Vehicle | F2 | PC § 22.02 |
| Aggravated Assault w/Motor Vehicle: Knowingly Discharges a Firearm at Habitation/Building/Vehicle | F1 | PC § 22.02(b)(3) |
| Assault w/Motor Vehicle | MA | PC § 22.01 |
| Backing Vehicle in Unsafe Manner or Interfered w/Traffic | M | 545.415(a) |
| Backing Vehicle on Shoulder/Roadway of Limited-Access Highway | M | 545.415(b) |
| Bus Carrying Passengers: Shifting Gears While Crossing RR Track | M | 545.253(b) |
| Bus Carrying Passengers; Vehicle Containing Flammable/Explosive Material/Heavy Equipment: Failure to Stop at RR Grade Crossing | M | 545.253; 545.254; 545.255(c) |
| Coasting in Truck/Tractor/Bus in Neutral on Downgrade w/Clutch Disengaged | M | 545.406(b) |
| Coasting w/Gear in Neutral on Downgrade | M | 545.406(a) |
| Criminally Negligent Homicide w/Motor Vehicle | FS | PC § 19.05 |
| Crossing RR Grade w/o Sufficient Undercarriage Clearance | M | 545.427 |

| TITLE | PENALTY | TRAFFIC CODE SECTION *(unless otherwise noted)* |
|---|---|---|
| Driving > 30 mph in Park in County Bordering Gulf of Mexico | M | 750.002 |
| Driving On or Across Streetcar Tracks When Prohibited | M | 547.203 |
| Driving on Restricted Access Roadway | M | 545.064 |
| Driving on Right-of-Way Designated for Rapid Transit System | MC | 451.113 |
| Driving on Sidewalk | M | 545.422 |
| Driving Through Safety Zone | M | 545.403 |
| Driving Vehicle Modified/Weighted to Lower Clearance Between Roadway and Lowest Rim of Wheel | M | 727.001 |
| Driving Vehicle when < 18 yrs. old in Violation of Restrictions During 12-month Restricted Period | M | 545.424(a-1) |
| Driving Vehicle when < 18 yrs. old While Using Wireless Communications Device | M | 545.424(a) |
| Driving When ≥ 15 yrs. and Not Wearing Safety Belt | M | 545.413(a) |
| Driving While Child < 18 Years Old is a Passenger of Towed Boat or Watercraft | M | 545.4145 |
| Driving w/Load or > 3 Persons in Front Seat that Obstructs Control/View of Driver | M | 545.417 |
| Failure to Make Written Report of Accident | M | 550.061 |
| Failure to Notify of Damage to Fixture/Structure/Landscaping Next to Roadway when < $200 | MC | 550.025(b)(1) |
| Failure to Notify of Damage to Fixture/Structure/Landscaping Next to Roadway when ≥ $200 | MB | 550.025(b)(2) |
| Failure to Notify of Damage to Unattended Vehicle when < $200 | MC | 550.024(b)(1) |
| Failure to Notify of Damage to Unattended Vehicle when ≥ $200 | MB | 550.024(b)(2) |
| Failure to Obey Lawful Order of Police Officer/School Crossing Guard | M | 542.501 |
| Failure to Pay Toll on Toll Road M 228.054(b) | | |
| Failure to Pay Toll to Collection Agency of Turnpike Project | M | 370.177 |
| Failure to Remove Drivable Vehicle from Freeway After Accident | MC | 550.022(b) |
| Failure to Report Serious Accident to Authorities | M | 550.026 |
| Failure to Stop or Permit Inspection by Patroleum Transport Vehicle | M | NRC § 115.047 |
| Failure to Stop When Involved in Accident Resulting in Death/Serious Bodily Injury | F3 | 550.021 |
| Failure to Stop When Involved in Accident where Damage < $200 | MC | 550.022(c)(1) |
| Failure to Stop When Involved in Accident where Damage > $200 | MB | 550.022(c)(2) |
| Fleeing From Police Officer | MB | 545.421 |
| Fleeing From Police Officer and Recklessly Endangerous Others | MA | 545.421(d) |
| Manslaughter w/Motor Vehicle | F2 | PC § 19.04 |
| Opening/Leaving Open Door on Side of Vehicle w/Moving Traffic | M | 545.418 |

| TITLE | PENALTY | TRAFFIC CODE SECTION *(unless otherwise noted)* |
|---|---|---|
| Operate Electric Vehicle on Roadway w/Speed Limit > 45 mph | M | 551.303 |
| Operate Motor-Assisted Scooter on Roadway w/Speed Lmit > 35 mph | M | 551.352 |
| Operate Motor Vehicle in Protected Freshwater Area | MC | PWC § 90.002 |
| Operate Motor Vehicle in Protected Freshwater Area w/2 Prev. Conv. | MB | PWC §§ 90.002; 90.011(c) |
| Operate Personal Assistance Mobility Device on Roadway | M | 551.202 |
| Operate Vehicle on Dune Seaward of Dune Protection Line | MC | 750.003 |
| Operate Vehicle w/Passenger in Drawn Trailer or Semitrailer | M | 545.4191 |
| Reckless Driving | M | 545.401 |
| Reckless Driving Causing Serious Bodily Injury or Death | MB | 545.401(e) |
| Tow Trucks: Charges Fee Greater Than Authorized; Violates Company Rule | M | OCC § 2308.505 |
| Tow Trucks: Tows w/o Consent; Solicits Towing; Enters Scene of Incident w/o Permission when on County Tow Rotation List | M | OCC § 2308.209(h) |
| Transport Child < 8 yrs. w/o Securing in Safety Seat (Unless Child is Taller than 4 ft., 9 in.) | M | 545.412 |
| Transport Child < 17 yrs. but Not Required to be Secured in Safety Seat when Not Wearing Safety Belt | M | 545.413(b);(b-1) |
| Transport Child < 18 yrs. in Open Bed of Truck or Trailer | M | 545.414 |
| Transport Manufactured House w/o Permit | M | 623.092 |
| Transport Special Mobile Equipment w/Insufficient Identifying Marks | M | 622.073 |
| Unnecessary Use of Horn | M | 547.501(c) |
| Use of Wireless Communications Device in School Zone | M | 545.425(b) |
| Use of Wireless Communications Device While Operating Passenger Bus w/Minor Passenger | M | 545.425(c) |
| Vehicle Moving Heavy Equipment: Crossed RR Track w/o Giving Notice | M | 545.255(b) |

### DRIVING WHILE INTOXICATED (DWI)

| | | |
|---|---|---|
| DWI | MB | PC § 49.04 |
| DWI w/2 or More Prev. Convictions | F3 | PC § 49.09(b)(2) |
| DWI w/BAC 0.15 or Greater | MA | PC § 49.04(d) |
| DWI w/Passenger < 15 years old | FS | PC § 49.045 |
| DWI w/Previous Conviction | MA | PC § 49.09(a) |
| DWI w/Previous Conviction of Intoxication Manslaughter | F3 | PC § 49.09(b)(1) |
| Intoxication Assault w/Motor Vehicle | F3 | PC § 49.07 |
| Intoxication Assault w/Motor Vehicle Injuring Police/Firefighter/EMS | F2 | PC § 49.09(b-1) |
| Intoxication Manslaughter Causing Death of Police/Firefighter/EMS | F1 | PC § 49.09(b-2) |

| TITLE | PENALTY | TRAFFIC CODE SECTION *(unless otherwise noted)* |
|---|---|---|
| Intoxication Assault w/Motor Vehicle Causing Brain Injury that Results in Persistent Vegetative State | F2 | PC § 49.09(b-4) |
| Intoxication Manslaughter w/Motor Vehicle | F2 | PC § 49.08 |
| Open Container of Alcohol | MC | PC § 49.031 |

## LANE POSITION, PASSING, AND FOLLOWING

| TITLE | PENALTY | |
|---|---|---|
| Changing Lanes when Unsafe | M | 545.060(a)(2) |
| Driving in Center Lane on 3-Lane Road w/2 Directions of Traffic | M | 545.060(b) |
| Driving in Multiple Lanes | M | 545.060(a)(1) |
| Driving Left of Rotary Traffic Island | M | 545.059(c) |
| Driving on Improved Shoulder | M | 545.058 |
| Driving on Wrong Side of Roadway | M | 545.051(a)(1) |
| Driving Wrong Way in Lane where Direction is Designated by Device | M | 545.060(b)(3) |
| Driving Wrong Way on One-Way Roadway | M | 545.059(b) |
| Failure to Give Way to Vehicle Passing Left | M | 545.053(b)(1) |
| Failure to Keep Right on Mountain Road | M | 545.405(a) |
| Failure to Yield One-Half of Roadway on One-Lane Road | M | 545.052(2)(A) |
| Following Closer than 500 ft. from Fire Engine or Ambulance | M | 545.407(a);(b)(1) |
| Following too Closely | M | 545.062(a) |
| Following too Closely when in a Caravan | M | 545.062(c) |
| Following too Closely when Operating a Vehicle Towing a Trailer | M | 545.062(b) |
| Increased Speed While Being Overtaken | M | 545.053(b)(2) |
| Passing Left of a Streetcar | M | 545.201(a) |
| Passing Left of a Streetcar w/o Reducing Speed or w/o Caution | M | 545.201(b) |
| Passing Left w/Insufficient Clearance | M | 545.054 |
| Passing Left w/in 100 ft. of Railroad Grade Crossing; Intersection; Bridge/Viaduct/Tunnel | M | 545.056(a)(1);(2); (3) |
| Passing Left when Awaiting Access to Ferry Operated by TX TC | M | 545.056(a)(4) |
| Passing Right of a Streetcar When Passengers are Boarding/Descending | M | 545.202 |
| Passing Right under Unsafe Conditions | M | 545.057 |
| Passing Stationary Emergency Vehicle or Tow Truck w/o Vacating Lane and Slowing | M | 545.157 |
| Passing Stationary Emergency Vehicle or Tow Truck w/o Vacating Lane and Slowing that Results in Bodily Injury | MB | 545.157(b)(3) |
| Passing Vehicle Stopped for Pedestrian | M | 552.003(c) |
| Slower Vehicle Failed to Keep Right | M | 545.051(b) |

## MISCELLANEOUS VIOLATIONS

| TITLE | PENALTY | |
|---|---|---|
| Allow Livestock to Roam Unattended on Highway | MC | AGC § 143.102 |
| Causes Fire w/Lighted Litter: < 500 lbs. or < 100 cubic ft. | M | HSC § 365.012(d-1) |
| Crossing Fire Hose w/o Permission | M | 545.205; 545.408 |

| TITLE | PENALTY | TRAFFIC CODE SECTION (unless otherwise noted) |
|---|---|---|
| Failure to Appear in Court | M | 543.009 |
| Failure to Display Certificate When Hauling Citrus Fruits | MB | AGC § 102.102 |
| Failure to Pay Penalty Received for HOV Lane Violation | MC | 462.0613(d) |
| Failure to Properly Identify Vehicle Hauling Citrus Fruits | MB | AGC § 102.101 |
| Failure to Remove Injurious Material from Highway | M | 600.001(a) |
| Failure to Surrender DL or Registration when Required Because of Lack of Liability Insurance | M | 601.373 |
| Illegal Dumping: < 5 lbs. or < 5 gallons | MC | HSC § 365.012(d) |
| Illegal Dumping: > 5 lbs. or > 5 gallons | MB | HSC § 365.012(e) |
| Illegal Dumping: > 5 lbs. or > 5 gallons w/Commercial Purpose | MA | HSC § 365.012(f)(2) |
| Illegal Dumping: > 200 lbs. or > 200 cubic ft. w/Commercial Purpose | FS | HSC § 365.012(g)(2) |
| Illegal Dumping: > 500 lbs. or > 100 cubic ft. | MA | HSC § 365.012(f)(1) |
| Illegal Dumping: > 1,000 lbs.; > 200 cubic ft.; or in Barrel/Drum | FS | HSC § 365.012(g)(1);(3) |
| Left Child < 7 yrs. old in Vehicle Unattended by Person > 14 | MC | PC § 22.10 |
| Maintain Junkyard w/in 1,000 ft. of Right-of-Way of Highway | M | 391.121 |
| Maintain Unlicensed Vehicle Storage Facility or Employee at Facility | MC | OCC § 2303.302 |
| Passenger in Vehicle when > 15 yrs. and Not Wearing Safety Belt | M | 545.413(a) |
| Passenger Obstructing View of Driver in Streetcar | M | 545.206 |
| Person that Removed Wrecked Vehicle Failed to Remove Glass and Other Injurious Substances from Highway | M | 600.001(b) |
| Provides Compensation for Illegal Movement of Manufactured House | M | 623.105 |
| Opening/Leaving Open Door on Side of Vehicle w/Moving Traffic | M | 545.418 |
| Requires or Knowingly Permits Driver to Commit an Offense | M | 542.302 |
| Riding in House Trailer | M | 545.419 |
| Staying Longer Than Permitted or Erecting Tent or Shelter at Rest Area | M | 545.411 |
| Train Obstructs Public Roadway for More Than 10 Minutes | M | 471.007 |
| Train Operator Fails to Stop and Render Aid After Accident | MC | 112.103 |
| Transporting Farm Products Over Greater Distance than Allowed by Permit | M | 502.477 |
| Transporting Livestock w/o Permit or with Fraudulent Permit | M | AGC § 146.008 |
| Use of Public Transportation System w/o Paying Appropriate Fare | M | 460.1091(d) |
| Use of Registered Farm Vehicle for Impermissible Purpose | M | 502.478 |
| Use of Seasonal Agricultural Vehicle for Impermissible Purpose | M | 502.479 |

| TITLE | PENALTY | TRAFFIC CODE SECTION *(unless otherwise noted)* |
|---|---|---|
| Use/Sale/Possession of Traffic-Control Signal Preemption Device | MC | 544.0055(b) |
| Violation of Local Regulation of Roadside Vendor or Solicitor | MC | 285.004 |

### MOTORCYCLE VIOLATIONS

| TITLE | PENALTY | TRAFFIC CODE SECTION |
|---|---|---|
| Carry Motorcycle Passenger w/o Approved Headgear | M | 661.003(b) |
| Driving Motorcycle/Moped When < 17 years old at Night or While Using Wireless Communications Device | M | 545.424(b) |
| Driving Motorcycle/Moped When < 17 years old in Violation of Restrictions During 12-month Restricted Period | M | 545.424(b-1) |
| Driving or Riding as Passenger on Motorcycle w/o Approved Headgear | M | 661.003(a) |
| Driving Motorcylce w/Passenger < 5 years old | M | 545.416(d) |
| Sitting Improperly or Carring Too Many Riders on Motorcycle | M | 545.416(a);(b) |

### OVERSIZE VIOLATIONS

| TITLE | PENALTY | TRAFFIC CODE SECTION |
|---|---|---|
| Combination of > 3 Vehicles | M | 621.205(a) |
| Height of Vehicle > 14" | M | 621.207 |
| Length of Non-Truck-Tractor w/Combination of Vehicles > 65 ft. | M | 621.205(a) |
| Length of Semitrailer or Trailer in Violation of Limit | M | 621.204 |
| Length of Vehicle > 45 ft. | M | 621.203 |
| Load Extension > 3" in Front or 4" in Rear of Vehicle | M | 621.206 |
| Load Extension > 6" to Left or Right of Vehicle | M | 621.201(c) |
| Width of Passenger Vehicle > 96" | M | 621.201(b) |
| Width of Vehicle > 102" | M | 621.201(a) |
| Vehicle w/< 2500 lbs. Coupled w/Multiple Vehicles or Towing Devices | M | 621.205(b) |

### PARKING VIOLATIONS

| TITLE | PENALTY | TRAFFIC CODE SECTION |
|---|---|---|
| Lending Disabled Parking Placard to Another for Unlawful Purpose | M | 681.011(d) |
| Overnight Parking of Commercial Vehicle near Residential Area | M | 545.307(b) |
| Stand or Park: w/in 15 ft. of Fire Hydrant | M | 545.302(b)(2) |
| Stand or Park: w/in 20 ft. of a Crosswalk at an Intersection | M | 545.302(b)(3) |
| Stand or Park: w/in 20 ft. of Driveway Entrance to Fire Station or w/in 75 ft. Opposite Entrance | M | 545.302(b)(5) |
| Stand or Park: w/in 30 ft. of Traffic Signal at Side of Roadway | M | 545.302(b)(4) |
| Stand or Park: Where Prohibited by Official Sign | M | 545.302(b)(6) |
| Stop, Stand, or Park: Alongside or Opposite Excavation/Construction | M | 545.302(a)(6) |
| Stop, Stand, or Park: Between Safety Zone and Curb | M | 545.302(a)(5) |
| Stand or Park: In Front of Public or Private Driveway | M | 545.302(b)(1) |
| Stop, Stand, or Park: In Intersection | M | 545.302(a)(3) |

Traffic Offense Titles

| TITLE | PENALTY | TRAFFIC CODE SECTION *(unless otherwise noted)* |
|---|---|---|
| Stop, Stand, or Park: On Bridge or Tunnel | M | 545.302(a)(7) |
| Stop, Stand, or Park: On Crosswalk | M | 545.302(a)(4) |
| Stop, Stand, or Park: On Main Travelled Part of Highway | M | 545.301 |
| Stop, Stand, or Park: On Railroad Track | M | 545.302(a)(8) |
| Stop, Stand, or Park: On Roadway Side of Vehicle Parked at Curb | M | 545.302(a)(1) |
| Stop, Stand, or Park: On Sidewalk | M | 545.302(a)(2) |
| Stop, Stand, or Park: Where Prohibited by Official Sign | M | 545.302(a)(9) |
| Parking at Angle Where Not Permitted | M | 545.303(c) |
| Parking Facing Traffic or Wheels > 18" from Curb | M | 545.303(a);(b) |
| Parking in Block where Fire Engine has Stopped to Answer Alarm | M | 545.407(a) |
| Parking Vehicle in Disabled Parking Area when Not Authorized | M | 681.011(a);(b) |
| Parking Vehicle that Blocks Disability Access Architecture | M | 681.011(c) |
| Parking w/in 50 ft. of RR Crossing | M | 545.302(c)(1) |
| Parking where Ambulance has been Summoned w/Intent to Interfere | M | 545.407(b)(2) |
| Parking where Prohibited by Official Sign | M | 545.302(c)(2) |
| Unattended Vehicle: Engine Running | M | 545.404(1) |
| Unattended Vehicle: Ignition Unlocked or Key in Ignition | M | 545.404(2);(3) |
| Unattended Vehicle: Failed to Set Parking Brake | M | 545.404(4) |
| Unattended Vehicle: Failed to Turn Front Wheels when Parked on Grade | M | 545.404(5) |
| Unlawful Parking of Another's Vehicle | M | 545.304 |
| Unsafe Start from Parked Position | M | 545.402 |
| Valet Parking w/o Financial Responsibility via Bond/Insurance | M | 686.002 |

## PEDESTRIANS – VIOLATIONS AGAINST

| TITLE | PENALTY | TRAFFIC CODE SECTION |
|---|---|---|
| Failure to Use Due Care for Pedestrian | M | 552.008 |
| Failure to Yield ROW to Pedestrian Lawfully in Roadway w/Green Traffic Signal | M | 544.007(b);(c) |
| Failure to Yield ROW to Pedestrian on Sidewalk when Emerging from Driveway | M | 552.006(c) |
| Failure to Yield ROW to Pedestrian when No Traffic Control Signal | M | 552.003(a) |
| Failure to Yield ROW to Pedestrian with "Walk" Control Signal | M | 552.002(b) |
| Failure to Yield ROW w/Red Signal for Right or Lawful Left Turn | M | 544.007(d) |
| Failure to Use Due Care for Blind Pedestrian | M | 552.010(b) |

## PEDESTRIANS – VIOLATIONS BY

| TITLE | PENALTY | TRAFFIC CODE SECTION |
|---|---|---|
| Carried White Cane when Not Blind | M | 552.010(a) |
| Crossing Between Intersections Other than on Marked Crosswalk | M | 552.005(b) |
| Crossing Intersection Diagonally | M | 552.005(c) |
| Disregarded Green Arrow Turn Signal | M | 552.001(b) |
| Disregarded Pedestrian Control Signal | M | 552.002 |
| Disregarded Red or Yellow Turn Signal | M | 552.001(c) |

| TITLE | PENALTY | TRAFFIC CODE SECTION (unless otherwise noted) |
|---|---|---|
| Failure to Obey Lawful Order of Police Officer/School Crossing Guard | M | 542.501 |
| Failure to Use Right Half of Crosswalk when Possible | M | 552.004 |
| Failure to Walk of Left Side of Roadway when Possible when No Sidewalk | M | 552.006(b) |
| Failure to Yield ROW to Vehicle when Crossing Not at Marked Crosswalk | M | 552.005(a)(1) |
| Failure to Yield ROW to Vehicle when Pedestrian Bridge/Tunnel Provided | M | 552.005(a)(2) |
| Pedestrian Entering Path of Vehicle | M | 552.003(b) |
| Presence on Restricted Access Roadway | M | 545.065(a);(c) |
| Public Intoxication: Pedestrian On or Adjacent to Public Highway | MC | PC § 49.02 |
| Stood in or Near Highway to Solicit Guarding Vehicle | M | 552.007(b) |
| Stood in Roadway to Solicit Vehicles | M | 552.007(a) |
| Walking on Roadway Where Sidewalk is Provided | M | 552.006(a) |

## REGISTRATION AND TITLE VIOLATIONS

| TITLE | PENALTY | SECTION |
|---|---|---|
| Alteration of Certificate/Title/Receipt | M | 501.154 |
| Applying for Registration for Vehicle w/o Motor Number | M | 501.0331 |
| Applying for Title w/Knowledge that Vehicle is Stolen | M | 501.153 |
| Displays Fictitioius License Plate | MB | 504.945(e) |
| Displays License Plate that is Wrong, Altered, or Obscured | M | 504.945(a) |
| Displays License Plate that is Knowingly Altered or Obscured | MB | 504.945(b) |
| Displays Fictitious Registration Insignia | MB | 502.475(a)(4) |
| Displays Registration Insignia that is Wrong, Altered, or Obscured | M | 502.475(a) |
| Failure to File Application when Motor Number is Removed/Destroyed | M | 501.0332 |
| Failure to Display Two License Plates on Motor Vehicle | M | 504.943(a) |
| Failure to Display One License Plate on Tractor, Motorcycle, Trailer, or Semitrailer | M | 504.943(b) |
| Failure to Display Specialty License Plate on Exhibition Vehicle | M | 504.502; 504.941 |
| Failure to Display Specialty License Plate on Log-Loader Vehicle | M | 504.506; 504.942 |
| Failure to Display Vehicle Registration Receipt for Heavy Vehicle | M | 621.501 |
| False/Incorrect Information or Signing w/o Legal Authority on Title | F3 | 501.155 |
| Displays Registration Insignia that Owner Knowingly Altered | MB | 502.475(b) |
| Knowingly Provide False/Incorrect Information or Forgery on Application for Registration | F3 | 502.410 |
| Offering Vehicle for Sale or Security w/o Valid Title | M | 501.152 |
| Operate Vehicle that is Unregistered/Registered for Improper Class | M | 502.472(a) |

| TITLE | PENALTY | TRAFFIC CODE SECTION (unless otherwise noted) |
|---|---|---|
| Operate a tractor, motorcycle, trailer, or semitrailer without Registration | M | 502.472(b) |
| Operate Vehicle in Violation of Registration Suspension | M | 601.371 |
| Operate Vehicle in Violation of Registration Suspension - Prev. Conv. | MA | 601.371(d) |
| Operate Vehicle That Requires One-Trip Permit w/o Registration Receipt and Properly Displayed Tag | M | 502.474 |
| Operate Vehicle w/Expired License Plates after 5th day of Expiration | M | 502.407 |
| Operate Vehicle w/License Plate or Insignia of Different Vehicle | M | 504.944 |
| Operate Vehicle w/o Registration Insignia Establishing Vehicle Registration | M | 502.473 |
| Placing Serial Number on Vehicle w/Intent to Change Identity of Vehicle | F3 | 501.151 |
| Purchase or Operate Vehicle w/Unauthorized Temporary Tag | MC | 503.067(b);(c) |
| Purchase, Sale, or Operate Vehicle w/Unauthorized Temporary Tag as Part of Organized Criminal Activity | FS | 503.094(d)(4) |
| Sale of Unauthorized Temporary Tag | MA | 503.067(d) |
| Reproduce Temporary Tag w/Purpose of Distribution | FS | 503.067(a) |
| Use of Unregistered Soil Conservation Equipment on Highway | M | 502.435(e) |
| Use of Vehicle w/Improperly Displayed or No In-Transit License | M | 503.023; 503.069 |
| Transfer of Specialty License Plate to Another Person or Vehicle | M | 504.008(h) |
| Transfer of Vehicle: Buyer Accepts Incomplete Documents or Alters/Mutilates Documents | M | 501.161(b) |
| Transfer of Vehicle: Failure to Deliver Receipt and Title to Purchaser of Used Motor Vehicle | M | 501.0721 |
| Transfer of Vehicle: w/Incomplete Documents | M | 501.161(a) |

**RIGHT OF WAY**

| TITLE | PENALTY | SECTION |
|---|---|---|
| Failure to Stop/Yield in Obedience to Official Traffic Control Device | M | 545.151(a)(1)(A) |
| Failure to Stop/Yield when Approaching a Divided Highway w/> 2 Lanes from a Single- or Two-Lane Roadway | M | 545.151(b) |
| Failure to Stop/Yield when Approaching a Paved Roadway from an Unpaved Roadway | M | 545.151(c) |
| Failure to Stop/Yield when Approaching from Roadway that Terminates at the Intersection | M | 545.151(e) |
| Failure to Stop/Yield when Traffic Control Device Displays No Signal | M | 545.151(a)(1)(B) |
| Failure to Stop/Yield when Turning from an Alleyway/Driveway | M | 545.155; 545.256 |
| Failure to Yield ROW at Stop or Yield Intersection | M | 545.153 |
| Failure to Yield ROW on Left when Avoiding Obstruction | M | 545.051(a)(2) |
| Failure to Yield ROW on One-Way Roadway | M | 545.061 |

Traffic Offense Titles

| TITLE | PENALTY | TRAFFIC CODE SECTION (unless otherwise noted) |
|---|---|---|
| Failure to Yield ROW to Emergency Vehicle | M | 545.156 |
| Failure to Yield ROW to Streetcar Approaching from Behind on Tracks | M | 545.203(a) |
| Failure to Yield ROW to Traffic Approaching from Opposite Direction when Turning Left | M | 545.152 |
| Failure to Yield ROW to Train at RR Crossing w/o Crossbar or Signal | M | 545.251(c) |
| Failure to Yield ROW to Vehicle Exiting Highway when on Access Road | M | 545.154 |
| Failure to Yield ROW w/Green Signal for Left Turn | M | 544.007(b);(c) |
| Failure to Yield ROW w/Red Signal for Right or Lawful Left Turn | M | 544.007(d) |
| **SCHOOL BUSES** | | |
| Changing Gears While Crossing RR Track | M | 545.2535(b) |
| Driving Overcrowded School Bus | M | 545.426(a)(2) |
| Driving School Bus While Door is Open; Passenger is Standing or Sitting in Improper Place | M | 545.426(a)(1);(b) |
| Driving School Bus While not Secured by Safety Belt | M | 545.413(a)(2) |
| Failure to Activate Warning Signal Equipment | M | 547.701(c) |
| Failure to Stop at RR Grade Crossing | M | 545.2535 |
| Failure to Stop for School Bus | M | 545.066 |
| Failure to Stop for School Bus: Causes Serious Bodily Injury | MA | 545.066(c)(1) |
| Failure to Stop for School Bus: Causes Serious Bodily Injury - Prev. Conv. | FS | 545.066(c)(2) |
| Inappropriate Activation of Warning Signal Equipment | M | 547.701(c) |
| Unauthorized Driving of School Bus | M | 521.022 |
| **SIGNAL INTENTION** | | |
| Failure to Signal Intention to Start from a Parked Position | M | 545.104(a) |
| Failure to Signal Intention to Stop or Decrease Speed | M | 545.105 |
| Failure to Signal Intention to Turn for at Least 100 ft. Before Turn | M | 545.104(a);(b) |
| Failure to Signal Lane Change | M | 545.104(a) |
| Failure to Sound Horn on Mountain Road | M | 545.405(2) |
| Improper Method of Signalling | M | 545.106(b) |
| Improper Use of Turn Indicator | M | 545.104(c) |
| **SPEEDING** | | |
| Driving at Unsafe Speed | M | 545.351; 545.352 |
| Driving Below Posted Minimum Speed | M | 545.363(c) |
| Driving Speed in Violation of Limit Set by Government Authority | M | 545.353 et seq. |
| Failure to Control Speed Necessary to Avoid Collision w/Another Vehicle | M | 545.351(b)(2) |
| Failure to Reduce Speed when Required by Road Conditions | M | 545.351(c) |
| Impeding Traffic by Driving Slowly | M | 545.363(a) |
| Racing: Caused Bodily Injury | F3 | 545.420(g) |
| Racing: Caused Serious Bodily Injury or Death | F2 | 545.420(h) |

Traffic Offense Titles

| TITLE | PENALTY | TRAFFIC CODE SECTION *(unless otherwise noted)* |
|---|---|---|
| Racing: One Previous Conviction | MA | 545.420(e)(1) |
| Racing: On Highway | MB | 545.420 |
| Racing: Two Previous Convictions | FS | 545.420(f) |
| Racing: While Intoxicated or In Possession of Open Container | MA | 545.420(e)(2) |
| Speeding: Manufactured House Towed in Excess of Limit or > 55 mph. | M | 623.101 |
| Speeding: Motorcycle w/o Headlamp > 35 mph. | M | 545.361(a) |
| Speeding: Over Bridge in Violation of Maximum Speed Limitation | M | 545.361(c) |
| Speeding: Oversized/Overweight Vehicle in Excess of County or Port Authority Limit | M | 623.217; 623.237; 623.257; 623.286; 623.308 |
| Speeding: Unregistered Transportion of Agricultural Chemicals > 30 mph. | M | 545.361(d) |
| Speeding: Vehicle w/o Solid Rubber or Cushion Tires > 10 mph. | M | 545.361(b) |

## TRAFFIC SIGNS, SIGNALS AND ROAD MARKINGS

| TITLE | PENALTY | TRAFFIC CODE SECTION |
|---|---|---|
| Disregarded Lane-Direction-Control Signals on Highway | M | 544.009 |
| Disregarded No Passing Zone | M | 545.055(b) |
| Disregarded Offical Traffic Control Device | M | 544.004 |
| Disregarded Red or Green Traffic Signal | M | 544.007(b);(d) |
| Disregarded RR Crossing Gate, Signal, Flagger, or Other Indication of Approaching Train | M | 545.251 |
| Disregarded Warning Sign/Barricade | M | 472.022 |
| Disregarded Warning Sign/Barricade b/c of Water Covering Road | MB | 472.022(d)(2) |
| Failure to Proceed w/Caution for Flashing Yellow Signal | M | 544.008(b) |
| Failure to Stop at Designated Point for Stop Sign | M | 544.010 |
| Failure to Stop at Designated Point for Yield Sign if Safety Requires | M | 544.010(b) |
| Failure to Stop at Proper Place at Traffic Light/Intersection | M | 544.007(d);(g); 544.008(a) |
| Failure to Stop at RR Grade Crossing Designated as Dangerous | M | 545.252(b) |
| Failure to Stop for Flashing Red Signal | M | 544.008(a) |
| Lack of Caution on Green Arrow Signal | M | 544.007(c) |
| Obsuring or Interfering With Official Traffic Control Device or RR Sign | M | 544.005 |
| Place Off-Premise Sign w/o License on Rural Road | M | 394.0201 |
| Place Unauthorized Flashing Light or Sign w/in 1,000 ft. of Intersection | M | 544.006(c) |
| Place Unauthorized Traffic Sign, Marking, or Device on Highway | M | 544.006(a) |
| Place Unauthorized Sign on Highway Right-of-Way | MC | 392.032 |

## TURNING MOVEMENTS

| TITLE | PENALTY | TRAFFIC CODE SECTION |
|---|---|---|
| Crossed Barrier/Space Between Divided Highway | M | 545.063(b) |

| TITLE | PENALTY | TRAFFIC CODE SECTION *(unless otherwise noted)* |
|---|---|---|
| Crossing Sidewalk, Parking Lot, Business, or Residental Enterance to Make Turn | M | 545.423(b) |
| Failure to Make Left Turn from Extreme Left-Hand Lane Available | M | 545.101(b);(c);(d) |
| Failure to Make Right Turn as Close as Possible to Right-Hand Curb | M | 545.101(a) |
| Made U-Turn on Curve or Hill | M | 545.102 |
| Turned in Front of Streetcar | M | 545.203(c) |
| Turned When Unsafe | M | 545.103 |

### VEHICLE – BRAKES

| | | |
|---|---|---|
| Brakes Inadequate to Control Vehicle | M | 547.402(a)(2) |
| Brakes Not Maintained in Good Working Order | M | 547.402(d) |
| Brakes Not On All Wheels | M | 547.402(a) |
| Brakes Operate Unequally on Wheels | M | 547.402(d) |
| Defective/Inadequate Brake Reservoir for Air Brakes | M | 547.406(a) |
| Defective/Inadequate Brake Reservoir for Vacuum Brakes | M | 547.406(b) |
| Inadequate Braking Performance | M | 547.408 |
| Inadequate Reservoir Safeguard for Air or Vacuum Brakes | M | 547.406(c) |
| No Automatic Brakes on Trailer, Semitrailer, or Pole Trailer | M | 547.405(d) |
| No Emergency Device for Air-Controlled Brakes on Towed Vehicle | M | 547.405(a) |
| No Second Control Device for Vacuum Brakes on Towed Vehicle | M | 547.405(b) |
| No Service Brakes in Case of Breakaway on Towed Vehicle | M | 547.405(e) |
| No Single Control for All Brakes | M | 547.402(b) |
| No Warning Signal on Vacuum Brakes | M | 547.407(b) |
| No Working Parking Brake | M | 547.404 |
| No Working Warning Signal or Pressure Gauge on Air Brakes | M | 547.407(a) |

### VEHICLE – EQUIPMENT

| | | |
|---|---|---|
| Airbags: Altering or Failed or Improper Installation that Caused Bodily Injury | F2 | 547.614(d) |
| Airbags: Failure to Install; Improper Installation; Altering Airbag | MA | 547.614 |
| Airbags: Previous Conviction | F3 | 547.614(c) |
| Emissions System: Does Not Prevent Crankcase Emissions | M | 547.605(b) |
| Emissions System: Does Not Prevent Excessive Smoke or Fumes | M | 547.605(a) |
| Emissions System: Removed or Non-Functioning System | M | 547.605(c) |
| Horn: Not Equipped w/Horn in Good Working Condition | M | 547.501(a) |
| Horn: Unauthorized Type or Sound | M | 547.501(b);(d) |
| Improper Use of Slow-Moving Vehicle or School Bus Emblem | M | 547.005 |
| Improper Safety Glazing Material | M | 547.608 |
| Improper Sunscreening Device | M | 547.609 |

| TITLE | PENALTY | TRAFFIC CODE SECTION (unless otherwise noted) |
|---|---|---|
| Insufficient Identifying Markings on Commercial Motor Vehicle | M | 642.002 |
| Insufficient Identifying Markings on Special Mobile Equipment | M | 622.072 |
| No Fire Extinguisher in Vehicle that Transports Passengers | M | 547.607 |
| No Proper Mud Flaps on Large Towing Vehicle | M | 547.606 |
| No Safety Belts | M | 547.601 |
| No Mirror that Reflects View of Highway from Rear of Vehicle | M | 547.602 |
| No Working Muffler System | M | 547.604 |
| No Working Windsheild Wipers | M | 547.603 |
| Obstructed View Through Windshield, Side, or Rear Windows | M | 547.613(a) |
| Operate/Permit Another to Operate Vehicle Equipped in Manner Non-Compliant or Prohibited | M | 547.004(a)(2);(3) |
| Operate/Permit Another to Operate Vehicle that is Unsafe | M | 547.004(a)(1) |
| Operate/Sell/Install Radar Interference Device | MC | 547.616 |
| Operate Vehicle w/Equipment in Violation of Compliance Proceeding | M | 547.004(b) |
| Tampering w/Odometer | M | 727.002 |
| Television/Video Receiver Visible to Driver when Vehicle is in Motion | M | 547.611 |
| Tires: Improper Preturbance Beyond Tread of Traction Surface | M | 547.612(c) |
| Tires: Improper Use of Metal Tires | M | 547.612(b) |
| Tires: Insufficient Rubber on Traction Surface | M | 547.612(a) |
| Tires: Operating Vehicle w/Removed Pneumatic Tires or Tires of Insufficient Thickness | M | 727.003 |
| Tires: Sells/Purchases for Sale Tires of Insufficient Width | M | 727.004 |
| Towing: > 3 Vehicles Attached by Triple Saddle-Mount Method | M | 545.409(c) |
| Towing: Drawbar Insufficiently Strong or > 15 feet | M | 545.409(a) |
| Towing: No White Flag on Tow Chain | M | 545.409(b) |
| Unsafe Air Conditioning Equipment | M | 547.610(b) |
| Vehicle w/Loose Cargo: Bed Not Properly Enclosed | M | 725.021(b)(2) |
| Vehicle w/Loose Cargo: Failure to Remove Spilled Material on Vehicle when Loading/Unloading | M | 725.022 |
| Vehicle w/Loose Cargo: Hole, Crack, or Opening in Vehicle Bed | M | 725.021(b)(1) |
| Vehicle w/Loose Cargo: Improperly Secured Tailgate | M | 725.021(d) |
| Vehicle w/Loose Cargo: Load Not Covered and Secured | M | 725.021(c);(e) |

## VEHICLE – INSPECTION AND INSURANCE

| | | |
|---|---|---|
| Displays Certificate Not in Compliance w/Emissions Requirements | MB | 548.603(a)(3); (4); (5) |
| Displays Counterfeit, Tampered With, Altered, or Fictitious Inspection Certificate or Insurance Document | MB | 548.603(a)(1) |

| TITLE | PENALTY | TRAFFIC CODE SECTION (*unless otherwise noted*) |
|---|---|---|
| Displays Inspection Certificate or Insurance Document that was Issued for Another Vehicle | MB | 548.603(a)(1);(2) |
| Driving w/Expired Inspection Certificate | M | 548.602 |
| Makes/Possesses w/Intent to Circulate Counterfeit Certificate or Insurance Document | F3 | 548.603(b)(1) |
| Makes/Possesses w/Intent to Circulate or Possesses Device Used to Counterfeit w/Intent to Defraud | F2 | 548.603(d) |
| Operating Commercial Motor Vehicle w/o Proper Liability Insurance | MC | 643.104(d); 643.253(a)(2) |
| Operating Vehicle w/o Proper Liability Insurance | M | 601.191 |
| Possesses Any Part of Device Used to Counterfeit Certificates/Documents | F3 | 548.603(b)(2) |
| Transporting Manufactured House w/o Sufficient Liability Insurance | M | 623.103 |

## VEHICLE – LIGHTS AND WARNING DEVICES

| TITLE | PENALTY | TRAFFIC CODE SECTION |
|---|---|---|
| Driving Lighting-Exempt Vehicle w/o Minimum Lighting Equipment | M | 547.326 |
| Driving Service Equipment w/o Lamps | M | 547.305(e) |
| Driving w/< 1 or > 4 Lighted Lamps on Front of Vehicle | M | 547.302(d) |
| Driving w/o Lamps at Nighttime or in Unfavorable Weather Conditions | M | 547.302(a) |
| Driving w/o Proper Clearance, Marker, or Hazard Lamps or Reflectors on Vehicle that is Overwide or Overlong | M | 547.352 |
| Driving w/o Proper Headlamps | M | 547.321 |
| Driving w/o Proper Reflectors | M | 547.325 |
| Driving w/o Proper Stoplamps | M | 547.323 |
| Driving w/o Proper Taillamps | M | 547.322 |
| Driving w/o Proper Turn Signal Lamps | M | 547.324 |
| Driving w/o Rear License Plate Lamp | M | 547.322(f) |
| Failure to Use Proper Headlight Beam | M | 547.333(c) |
| Failure to Dim Headlights when Approaching Oncoming Vehicle or From Rear of Vehicle | M | 547.333(c)(1);(2) |
| Failure to Display Hazard Lights/Lighted Lanterns/Flags/Reflectors Under Required Conditions for Overwide or Overlong Vehicle | M | 547.503; 547.504; 547.505; 547.506; 547.507 |
| Improper Lamps or Reflectors on Farm/Husbandry Equipment or Combination Vehicle | M | 547.371; 547.372 |
| Improperly Intense Light Directed at Roadway: > 300 Candlepower | M | 547.305(a) |
| Improper Mounting or Visibility of Clearance Lamp, Side Marker Lamp, or Reflector | M | 547.354; 547.355 |
| Improper Number or Direction of Spotlamps; Foglamps; Auxiliary Driving or Passing Lamps; Hazard Lamps; Cowl or Fender Lamps | M | 547.327; 327.328; 327.329; 327.330; 327.331; 327.332 |
| Manufactured House: Escort Flag Vehicle w/o Proper Lights, Beacons, Flags, or Signs | M | 623.099(c) |

| TITLE | PENALTY | TRAFFIC CODE SECTION *(unless otherwise noted)* |
|---|---|---|
| Mobile Home: No Escort Flag Vehicle | M | 623.099(a);(b) |
| Mobile Home: No Rotating Beacon on Top of Towing Vehicle | M | 623.098 |
| Mobile Home: No Wiring Harness Equipped w/Turn Signal, Braking and Parking Lights | M | 623.102(b) |
| Mobile Home: Operating w/o Rotating Beacons or Flashing Lights | M | 623.098 |
| Motorcycle/Motor-Driven Cycle: No Proper Headlamps, Taillamps, License Plate Lamp, Stoplamp, or Rear Reflector | M | 547.801(a) |
| Motorcycle: No Multiple-Beam Lighting Equipment | M | 547.801(b) |
| Motorcycle: Operating w/o Headlamp Illuminated | M | 547.801(d) |
| Motor-Driven Cycle: No Proper Multiple-Beam or Single-Beam Lighting Equipment | M | 547.801(c) |
| No Multiple-Beam Lighting Equipment | M | 547.333 |
| No Parking Lights When Required | M | 547.383 |
| No Signal Lamps When Required | M | 545.106(b) |
| No Visible Flags/Lights/Flares on Vehicle Towing House Trailer or Explosive Cargo | M | 547.502 |
| Parked w/Head Lamps Not Dimmed | M | 547.383(d) |
| Public Transportation: Not Equipped w/Hazard Lamps and Exiting Sign | M | 547.7011 |
| School Bus: Not Equipped w/Convex Mirror, Signal Lamps, Rooftop Warning Lamps, Movable Stop Arms | M | 547.701(a);(b) |
| Slow-Moving Vehicle: Emblem in Non-Reflective Condition | M | 547.703(a) |
| Slow-Moving Vehicle: No Properly Affixed Reflective Emblem | M | 547.703 |
| Taillamps not Illuminated when Headlights are Illuminated | M | 547.322(g) |
| Unauthorized Use of Flashing Red, White, and Blue Lights | M | 547.305(c) |
| Unauthorized Use of Red Light in Front Center of Vehicle | M | 547.305(b) |
| Vehicle w/Projecting Load: No Flags on Rear | M | 547.382(b) |
| Vehicle w/Projecting Load: No Lamps or Reflectors on Side and Rear | M | 547.382(a) |
| Wrong Color of Clearance, Marker, or Identification Lamp or Reflector | M | 547.353 |
| Wrong Color of Lighting Device, Reflector, or Signaling Device | M | 547.303 |

## WEIGHT VIOLATIONS

| TITLE | PENALTY | TRAFFIC CODE SECTION |
|---|---|---|
| Axle Weight: 2 or more Consecutive Axles; > 34,000 lbs. | M | 621.101(b) |
| Axle Weight: Improper Weight Based on Formula for Gross Weight on 2 or more Consecutive Axles | M | 621.101(a)(3) |
| Axle Weight: Single > 20,000 lbs. | M | 621.101(a)(1) |
| Axle Weight: Tandem > 34,000 lbs. | M | 621.101(a)(2) |
| Axle Weight - Cement Truck: Gross Weight > 69,000 lbs. | M | 622.012(b) |
| Axle Weight - Cement Truck: Tandem > 46,000 lbs. or Single > 23,000 lbs. | M | 622.012(a) |
| Axle Weight - Vehicle w/Recyclable Materials or Solid Waste: Gross Weight > 64,000 lbs. | M | 622.133; 623.162 |

| TITLE | PENALTY | TRAFFIC CODE SECTION (unless otherwise noted) |
|---|---|---|
| Axle Weight - Vehicle w/Recyclable Materials or Solid Waste: Single > 21,000 lbs.; Tandem > 44,000 lbs. | M | 622.133; 623.162 |
| Failure to Carry/Present Surety Bond for Commercial Vehicle w/Tandem Axle Weight > 34,000 lbs. | M | 622.013; 622.134; 623.163 |
| Failure to Maintain Weight Record of Cargo Transported Commercially | MC | 621.509 |
| Load or Cause to be Loaded Vehicle in Excess of Weight Limitations | M | 621.503 |
| Tire Weight: Heavier than Weight Specified on Tire | M | 621.101(a)(4) |
| Use of Vehicle w/Weight > Statement in Application for Registration | M | 502.412 |

# PENAL CODE OFFENSE TITLES

BASED ON CHANGES FROM THE 82<sup>nd</sup> LEGISLATURE, REGULAR AND
FIRST CALLED SPECIAL SESSION

(Do not use for citation purposes – use CJIS Offense Codes.)

| PENAL CODE TITLE | PENALTY | PENALTY SECTION |
|---|---|---|
| Aband./Endang. Child: < 15 w/Intent to Return | FS | 22.041(d)(1) |
| Aband./Endang. Child: < 15 w/o Intent to Return | F3 | 22.041(d)(2) |
| Aband./Endang. Child: < 15 w/or w/o Intent to Return - Imminent Danger | F2 | 22.041(e) |
| Aband./Endang. Child: < 15 - Child in Imminent Danger/Bodily Injury/Physical or Mental Impairment - Presumed by Manufacturing/Possessing/Introducing into the Body of any Person - Methamphetamine in the Presence/Proximity of Child | FS | 22.041(c-1) (1);(2);(3) |
| Abuse of Corpse / Vandalizes Grounds | MA | 42.08 |
| Abuse of Official Capacity | MA | 39.02(a)(1) |
| Abuse of Official Capacity < $20 | MC | 39.02(c)(1) |
| Abuse of Official Capacity > $20 | MB | 39.02(c)(2) |
| Abuse of Official Capacity > $500 | MA | 39.02(c)(3) |
| Abuse of Official Capacity > $1,500 | FS | 39.02(c)(4) |
| Abuse of Official Capacity > $20,000 | F3 | 39.02(c)(5) |
| Abuse of Official Capacity > $100,000 | F2 | 39.02(c)(6) |
| Abuse of Official Capacity > $200,000 | F1 | 39.02(c)(7) |
| Academic Product: Deceptive Marketing/Preparation | MC | 32.50 |
| Acceptance of Honorarium | MA | 36.07 |
| Accident Report Information and Other Info. for Pecuniary Gain | MB | 38.18 |
| Advertising Placement of Child | MA | 25.09 |
| Advertising Placement of Child: 2 or more Previous Convictions | F3 | 25.09(c) |
| Agreement to Abduct Child for Renumeration: < 17 | FS | 25.031 |
| Aiding Suicide | MC | 22.08 |
| Aiding Suicide: Serious Bodily Injury/Death | FS | 22.08(b) |
| Alcoholic Beverage: Possession of in Motor Vehicle | MC | 49.031 |
| Arson | F2 | 28.02(a) |
| Arson: Causes Bodily Injury/Death | F1 | 28.02(d)(1) |
| Arson: Causes Damage to Habitation or Place of Worship | F1 | 28.02(d)(2) |
| Arson: Intentionally Starts a Fire that Recklessly Damages Propery or Causes Injury/Death | FS | 28.02(a-2) |

| PENAL CODE TITLE | PENALTY | PENALTY SECTION |
|---|---|---|
| Arson: Recklessly Starts a Fire while Attempting to Manufacture Controlled Substance | FS | 28.02(a-1) |
| Arson: Recklessly Starts a Fire while Attempting to Manufacture Controlled Substance - Causes Bodily Injury/Death | F3 | 28.02(e) |
| Assault: Bodily Injury | MA | 22.01(a)(1) |
| Assault: Bodily Injury against - Public Servant; Correctional Facility Contractor; Security Officer; Emergency Services Personnel while providing emergency services | F3 | 22.01(b)(1);(3);(4);(5) |
| Assault: Bodily Injury against Family/Household Member - 2 times or more w/in a 12-month period | F3 | 25.11 |
| Assault: Bodily Injury against Family/Household Member - Intentionally/Knowingly/Recklessly impeding normal Breathing or Circulation | F3 | 22.01(b)(2)(B) |
| Assault: Bodily Injury against Family/Household Member - Prev. Conv. | F3 | 22.01(b)(2)(A) |
| Assault: Bodily Injury against Family/Household Member - Prev. Conv. and Intentionally/Knowingly/Recklessly impeding normal Breathing or Circulation | F2 | 22.01(b-1) |
| Assault: Threatens Bodily Injury or Offensive/Provocative Contact | MC | 22.01(a)(2);(3) |
| Assault: Threatens Bodily Injury or Offensive/Provocative Contact - Against a Sport Participant | MB | 22.01(c)(2) |
| Assault: Threatens Bodily Injury or Offensive/Provocative Contact - Against the Elderly/Disabled | MA | 22.01(c)(1) |
| Agg. Assault: Against Public Servant; Security Officer | F1 | 22.02(b)(2)(B);(D) |
| Agg. Assault: Against Witness/Informant | F1 | 22.02(b)(2)(C) |
| Agg. Assault: By Public Servant | F1 | 22.02(b)(2)(A) |
| Agg. Assault: Causes Serious Bodily Injury | F2 | 22.02(a)(1) |
| Agg. Assault: In a Motor Vehicle - Knowingly discharges a firearm at habitation/building/vehicle - Recklessly w/respect to occupancy - Causes Serious Bodily Injury | F1 | 22.02(b)(3) |
| Agg. Assault: w/Deadly Weapon | F2 | 22.02(a)(2) |
| Agg. Assault: w/Deadly Weapon - Causes Serious Bodily Injury to Family Member | F1 | 22.02(b)(1) |
| Assembling/Operating Amusement Ride while Intoxicated | MB (min. 72 hrs.) | 49.065 |
| Assembling/Operating Amusement Ride while Intoxicated: One Prev. Conviction - Intoxication | MA (min. 30 days) | 49.09(a) |
| Assembling/Operating Amusement Ride while Intoxicated: One Prev. Conv. - Intoxication Manslaughter | F3 | 49.09(b)(1) |
| Assembling/Operating Amusement Ride while Intoxicated: Two Prev. Convictions - Intoxication | F3 | 49.09(b)(2) |
| Assembling/Operating Amusement Ride while Intoxicated: w/Open Container of Alcohol | MB (min. 6 days) | 49.065(c) |
| Bad Check Issuance | MC | 32.41 |
| Bad Check Issuance: Child Support | MB | 32.41(f) |
| Bail Jumping and Failure to Appear | MA | 38.10 |
| Bail Jumping and Failure to Appear: From Pun. by Fine Only | MC | 38.10(e) |
| Bail Jumping and Failure to Appear: From Pun. by Felony | F3 | 38.10(f) |

| PENAL CODE TITLE | PENALTY | PENALTY SECTION |
|---|---|---|
| Barratry: Aiding/Assisting/Investing | F3 | 38.12(b) |
| Barratry: Economic Benefit | F3 | 38.12(a) |
| Barratry: Licensed Professional Illicitly Solicits Employment | MA | 38.12(d) |
| Barratry: Licensed Professional Illicitly Solicits Employment - Prev. Conv. | F3 | 38.12(h) |
| Bigamy | F3 | 25.01 |
| Bigamy: Purported Spouse is 17 Years Old | F2 | 25.01(e)(1) |
| Bigamy: Purported Spouse is ≤ 16 Years Old | F1 | 25.01(e)(2) |
| Boating While Intoxicated | MB (min. 72 hrs.) | 49.06 |
| Boating While Intoxicated: One Previous Conviction - Intoxication | MA (min. 30 days) | 49.09(a) |
| Boating While Intoxicated: One Previous Conviction - Intoxication Manslaughter | F3 | 49.09(b)(1) |
| Boating While Intoxicated: Two Previous Convictions - Intoxication | F3 | 49.09(b)(2) |
| Bribery | F2 | 36.02 |
| Bribery: Commercial | FS | 32.43(b);(c) |
| Burglary: Building - Habitation | F2 | 30.02(c)(2) |
| Burglary: Building - Habitation and Intended or Committed Other Felony | F1 | 30.02(d) |
| Burglary: Building - Not a Habitation | FS | 30.02(c)(1) |
| Burglary: Coin Operated or Coin Collection Machine | MA | 30.03 |
| Burglary: Vehicle | MA | 30.04 |
| Burglary: Vehicle - 2 or more Convs. | FS | 30.04(d)(2)(A) |
| Burglary: Vehicle - Prev. Conv. | MA (min. 6 mos.) | 30.04(d)(1) |
| Burglary: Vehicle - Rail Car | FS | 30.04(d)(2)(B) |
| Capital Murder: Multiple Murders | FC | 19.03(7) |
| Capital Murder: Child < 10 Years Old | FC | 19.03(8) |
| Capital Murder: Judge | FC | 19.03(9) |
| Capital Murder: Police Officer/Fireman | FC | 19.03(a)(1) |
| Capital Murder: Remuneration | FC | 19.03(a)(3) |
| Capital Murder: While Committing a Cited Offense | FC | 19.03(a)(2) |
| Capital Murder: While Escaping a Penal Institution | FC | 19.03(a)(4) |
| Capital Murder: While Incarcerated in Penal Institution or for Murder/Life/99 Years | FC | 19.03(a)(5);(6) |
| Child Custody: Interference | FS | 25.03 |
| Child Left in Vehicle: < 7 Years Old - Not Attended by Individual ≥14 | MC | 22.10 |
| Child Pornography: Possession | F3 | 43.26 |
| Child Pornography: Promotion | F2 | 43.26(e) |
| Child Pornography: Electronic Transmission of Visual Material Depicting Minor | MC | 43.261(b)(1) |
| Child Pornography: Possession of Electronic Format Visual Material Depicting Minor | MC | 43.261(b)(2) |
| Child, Sell/Purchase | F3 | 25.08 |
| Child, Sell/Purchase: w/Intent to Commit Sexual Performance | F2 | 25.08(c) |
| Child, Sell/Purchase: Child > 14 Years but < 18 Years Old at Time of Offense | F3 | 25.08(c) |

Penal Offense Titles

| PENAL CODE TITLE | PENALTY | PENALTY SECTION |
|---|---|---|
| Child, Sell/Purchase: Child < 14 Years Old At Time of Offense | F2 | 25.08(c) |
| Cigarettes, Certain Types Prohibited | MA | 48.015 |
| Civil Rights of Person in Custody: Violation of Rights | MA | 39.04(a)(1) |
| Civil Process: Preventing Execution | MC | 38.16 |
| Cockfighting: Causes a Cock to Fight/Participates in Earnings | FS | 42.105(b)(1); (2) |
| Cockfighting: Provides Building or Property; Owns or Trains Cock for Cockfight; Manufactures Equipment to be Used in Cockfight | MA | 42.105(b)(3); (4);(5) |
| Cockfighting: Spectator | MC | 42.105(b)(6) |
| Coercion: Public Servant/Voter | MA | 36.03 |
| Coercion: Public Servant/Voter - Threat is a Felony | F3 | 36.03(b) |
| Community Corrections Facility/Center: Unauthorized Absence | FS | 38.113 |
| Components of Explosives: Possession w/Intent to Use | F3 | 46.09 |
| Computer Security Breach | MB | 33.02(a) |
| Computer Security Breach: 2 or More Previous Convictions | FS | 33.02(b)(1) |
| Computer Security Breach: Aggregate Benefit < $20,000 | FS | 33.02(b-2)(1) |
| Computer Security Breach: Aggregate Benefit > $20,000 | F3 | 33.02(b-2)(2) |
| Computer Security Breach: Aggregate Benefit > $100,000 | F2 | 33.02(b-2)(3)(A) |
| Computer Security Breach: Aggregate Benefit < $200,000 - Government Owned Computer/Network | F2 | 33.02(b-2)(3)(B) |
| Computer Security Breach: Aggregate Benefit > $200,000 | F1 | 33.02(b)(A) |
| Computer Security Breach: Computer/Network Owned by Government | FS | 33.02(b)(2) |
| Computer Security Breach: Obtain Identifying Records of Another | F2 | 33.02(b-2)(3)(C) |
| Computer Security Breach: Obtain Identifying Records of Another - by Accessing Multiple Computers/Networks | F1 | 33.02(b)(4)(B) |
| Contraband in Correctional Facility | MC | 38.114 |
| Contraband in Correctional Facility: By an Employee or Volunteer | MB | 38.114(c) |
| Counterfeiting Trademarks: Retail Value < $20 | MC | 32.23(e)(1) |
| Counterfeiting Trademarks: Retail Value ≥ $20 | MB | 32.23(e)(2) |
| Counterfeiting Trademarks: Retail Value ≥ $500 | MA | 32.23(e)(3) |
| Counterfeiting Trademarks: Retail Value ≥ $1500 | FS | 32.23(e)(4) |
| Counterfeiting Trademarks: Retail Value ≥ $20,000 | F3 | 32.23(e)(5) |
| Counterfeiting Trademarks: Retail Value ≥ $100,000 | F2 | 32.23(e)(6) |
| Counterfeiting Trademarks: Retail Value ≥ $200,000 | F1 | 32.23(3)(7) |
| Credit or Debit Card Abuse | FS | 32.31 |
| Credit or Debit Card Abuse: Against an Elderly Person | F3 | 32.31(d) |
| Credit Card Transaction Laundering: < $20 | MC | 32.35(e)(1) |

| PENAL CODE TITLE | PENALTY | PENALTY SECTION |
|---|---|---|
| Credit Card Transaction Laundering: >$20 | MB | 32.35(e)(2) |
| Credit Card Transaction Laundering: >$500 | MA | 32.35(e)(3) |
| Credit Card Transaction Laundering: >$1,500 | FS | 32.35(e)(4) |
| Credit Card Transaction Laundering: >$20,000 | F3 | 32.35(e)(5) |
| Credit Card Transaction Laundering: >$100,000 | F2 | 32.35(e)(6) |
| Credit Card Transaction Laundering: >$200,000 | F1 | 32.35(e)(7) |
| Criminal Attempt | One level lower than attempt offense | 15.01 |
| Criminal Conspiracy | One level lower than most serious felony that is the object of conspir. | 15.02 |
| Criminal Instrument/Mechanical Security Device: Possesses w/Intent to Use in Commission of an Offense | One level lower than offense intended | 16.01(a)(1) |
| Criminal Instrument/Mechanical Security Device: Manufactures/Adapts/Sells/Installs w/Intent to Use in Commission of an Offense | FS | 16.01(a)(2) |
| Criminal Mischief: < $50 | MC | 28.03(b)(1)(A) |
| Criminal Mischief: > $50 | MB | 28.03(b)(2) |
| Criminal Mischief: > $500 | MA | 28.03(b)(3)(A) |
| Criminal Mischief: > $1,500 | FS | 28.03(b)(4)(A) |
| Criminal Mischief: > $20,000 | F3 | 28.03(b)(5) |
| Criminal Mischief: > $100,000 | F2 | 28.03(b)(6) |
| Criminal Mischief: > $200,000 | F1 | 28.03(b)(7) |
| Criminal Mischief: < $1,500 - Damage to Habitation by Firearm/Explosive | FS | 28.03(b)(4)(B) |
| Criminal Mischief: < $1,500 - Damage to Fence Confining Animals | FS | 28.03(b)(4)(C) |
| Criminal Mischief: > $1500 but < $20,000 - Damage to Educational Institution | SF | 28.03(h) |
| Criminal Mischief: < $20,000 - Damage to Church/Cemetery/Community Building | FS | 28.03(f) |
| Criminal Mischief: < $20,000 - Impair/Interrupt Public Service | FS | 28.03(b)(4)(D) |
| Criminal Mischief: < $100,000 - Damage to Transportation Communications Equipment/Device | F3 | 28.03(j) |
| Criminal Mischief: Causes Substantial Inconvenience | MC | 28.03(b)(1)(B) |
| Criminal Mischief: Impair/Interrupt Public Service | MA | 28.03(b)(3)(B) |
| Criminal Mischief: Introducing Mad Cow Disease to Livestock | F1 | 28.03(i) |
| Criminal Nonsupport | FS | 25.05 |
| Criminal Simulation | MA | 32.22 |
| Criminal Solicitation: Offense Solicited is Capital Offense | F1 | 15.03(d)(1) |
| Criminal Solicitation: Offense Solicited is F1 | F2 | 15.03(d)(2) |
| Criminal Solicitation of Minor | One level lower than offense solicited | 15.031 |
| Criminal Solicitation of Minor: When > 17 Years Old and a Member of a Criminal Gang | Same level as | 15.031(e)(1) |

Penal Offense Titles

| PENAL CODE TITLE | PENALTY | PENALTY SECTION |
|---|---|---|
| | offense solicited | |
| Criminal Trespass: Agricultural Land w/in 100 ft. of the Boundary | MC | 30.05(d)(2)(A) |
| Criminal Trespass: by Holder of Lisence to Carry Concealed Handgun | MA | 30.06 |
| Criminal Trespass: Habitation/Shelter Center; Superfund Site; Critical Infrastructure Facility | MA | 30.05(d)(3)(A) |
| Criminal Trespass: Property; Building; Aircraft; Vehicle | MB | 30.05(a) |
| Criminal Trepass: Residential w/in 100 ft. of a protected freshwater area | MC | 30.05(d)(2)(B) |
| Criminal Trespass: w/Deadly Weapon | MA | 30.05(d)(3)(B) |
| Criminally Negligent Homicide | FS | 19.05 |
| Cruelty - Attack on Assistance Animal: Attacks an assistance animal | MA | 42.091(c)(1) |
| Cruelty - Attack on Assistance Animal: Injures an assistance animal | FS | 42.091(c)(2) |
| Cruelty - Attack on Assistance Animal: Kills an assistance animal | F3 | 42.091(c)(3) |
| Cruelty - Livestock Animals: Fails to Provide; Abandons; Confines; Overworks | MA | 42.09(c) |
| Cruelty - Livestock Animals: Fails to Provide; Abandons; Confines; Overworks - w/2 Prev. Convictions | FS | 42.09(c) |
| Cruelty - Livestock Animals: Tortures; Poisons; Causes to Fight; Uses as Lure; Trips a Horse | FS | 42.09(c) |
| Cruelty - Livestock Animals: Tortures; Poisons; Causes to Fight; Uses as Lure; Trips a Horse - w/2 Prev. Convictions | F3 | 42.09(c) |
| Cruelty - Non-Livestock Animals: Fails to Provide; Abandons; Confines; Injures; Seriously Overworks | MA | 42.092(c) |
| Cruelty - Non-Livestock Animals: Fails to Provide; Abandons; Confines; Injures; Seriously Overworks - w/2 Previous Convictions | FS | 42.092(c) |
| Cruelty - Non-Livestock Animals: Tortures; Kills/seriously injures; Causes to Fight; Uses as Lure | FS | 42.092(c) |
| Cruelty - Non-Livestock Animals: Tortures; Poisons/kills/seriously injures; Causes to Fight; Uses as Lure - w/2 Prev. Convictions | F3 | 42.092(c) |
| Deadly Conduct | MA | 22.05(a) |
| Deadly Conduct: Discharge Firearm at Individual | F3 | 22.05(b)(1) |
| Deadly Conduct: Discharge Firearm at Vehicle/Building/Habitation | F3 | 22.05(b)(2) |
| Deadly Weapon in a Penal Institution | F3 | 46.10 |
| Deceptive Business Practice: Committed with Criminal Neg. - No Prior Conviction | MC | 32.42(c)(1) |
| Deceptive Business Practice: Committed Intentionally/Knowingly/Recklessly or w/a Prior MB/MC Conviction | MA | 32.42(c)(2) |
| Deceptive Business Practice: False Advertising or Misrepresentation | MA | 32.42(b)(7)-(12) |
| Destruction of Flag | MA | 42.11 |

| PENAL CODE TITLE | PENALTY | PENALTY SECTION |
|---|---|---|
| Disorderly Conduct – does not apply to students in 6th grade or lower | MC | 42.01(a)(1)-(6), (9)–(11) |
| Disorderly Conduct: Discharges/Displays Firearm in a Public Place | MB | 42.01(a)(7),(8) |
| Disrupting Meeting/Procession | MB | 42.05 |
| Document Execution by Deception: < $20 | MC | 32.46(b)(1) |
| Document Execution by Deception: >$20 | MB | 32.46(b)(2) |
| Document Execution by Deception: >$500 | MA | 32.46(b)(3) |
| Document Execution by Deception: >$1,500 | FS | 32.46(b)(4) |
| Document Execution by Deception: >$20,000 | F3 | 32.46(b)(5) |
| Document Execution by Deception: >$100,000 | F2 | 32.46(b)(6) |
| Document Execution by Deception: >$200,000 | F1 | 32.46(b)(7) |
| Document Execution by Deception: Committed against Elderly Person | One level higher than offense | 32.46(b)(1)–(6) |
| Document Execution by Deception: Public Servant | FS | 32.46(c) |
| Dog Fighting: Owns/Possesses dog-fighting equipment | MA | 42.10(a)(4) |
| Dog Fighting: Owns/Trains a Dog to be used for Dog Fighting | MA | 42.10(a)(5) |
| Dog Fighting: Participates in the Earnings; Causes a Dog to Fight; Provides Building or Property | FS | 42.10(a)(1),(2),(3) |
| Dog Fighting: Spectator | MA | 42.10(a)(5) |
| Driving While Intoxicated | MB (min. 72 hrs.) | 49.04 |
| Driving While Intoxicated: One Prev. Conviction - Intoxication | MA (min. 30 days) | 49.09(a) |
| Driving While Intoxicated: One Prev. Conv. - Intoxication Manslaughter | F3 | 49.09(b)(1) |
| Driving While Intoxicated: Open Alcoholic Container in Possession | MB (min. 6 days) | 49.04(c) |
| Driving While Intoxicated: Two Prev. Convictions - Intoxication | F3 | 49.09(b)(2) |
| Driving While Intoxicated: w/BAC 0.15 or Greater | MA | 49.04(d) |
| Driving While Intoxicated: w/Child Younger than 15 years old | FS | 49.045 |
| Employment Harmful to Children | F2 | 43.251(c) |
| Employment Harmful to Children: Child < 14 Years at time of Offense | F1 | 43.251(c) |
| Enticing a Child | MB | 25.04 |
| Enticing a Child: w/Intent to Commit a Felony against the Child | F3 | 25.04(b) |
| Escape | MA | 38.06(a) |
| Escape: Causes Bodily Injury | F2 | 38.06(d) |
| Escape: Causes Serious Bodily Injury; Threatens/Uses Deadly Weapon | F1 | 38.06(e) |
| Escape: While Arrested/Charged w/Felony; In Secure Correctional | F3 | 38.06(c) |
| Escape, Implements for: Introduce/Provide Tools for Escape | F3 | 38.09(a) |
| Escape, Implements for: What is Provided is a Deadly Weapon | F2 | 38.09(b) |
| Escape, Permitting/Facilitating | MA | 38.07(c) |

| PENAL CODE TITLE | PENALTY | PENALTY SECTION |
|---|---|---|
| Escape, Permitting/Facilitating: Charged/Convicted Felon; Inmate of Non-Secure Correctional Facility | F3 | 38.07(d)(1) |
| Escape, Permitting/Facilitating: Inmate Threatened/Used Deadly Weapon | F2 | 38.07(e)(1) |
| Escape, Permitting/Facilitating: Inmate of Secure Correctional Facility | F2 | 38.07(e)(2) |
| Evading Arrest/Detention | MA | 38.04 |
| Evading Arrest/Detention: Causes Death of Another | F2 | 38.04(b)(3)(A) |
| Evading Arrest/Detention: Causes Serious Bodily Injury of Another Due to Tire Deflation Device | F2 | 38.04(b)(3)(B) |
| Evading Arrest/Detention: Prev. Conviction | FS | 38.04(b)(1) |
| Evading Arrest/Detention: Using Vehicle or Watercraft | F3 | 38.04(b)(2)(A) |
| Evading Arrest/Detention: Serious Bodily Injury of Another | F3 | 38.04(b)(2)(B) |
| Evading Arrest/Detention: Use Tire Deflation Device Against Officer | F3 | 38.04(b)(2)(C) |
| Exploitation of Child/Elderly/Disabled | F3 | 32.53 |
| Failure to Identify | MC | 38.02(a) |
| Failure to Identify: Fugitive | MB | 38.02(d)(1) |
| Failure to Identify: Intentionally gives False Information | MB | 38.02(b) |
| Failure to Identify: Intentionally gives False Information - Fugitive | MA | 38.02(d)(2) |
| Failure to Report Death of Prisoner | MB | 39.05 |
| Failure to Report Felony: When Felony may have caused Serious Bodily Injury/Death | MA | 38.171 |
| False Alarm/Report | MA | 42.06 |
| False Alarm/Report: Involves Utilities/Public Transportation/School | FS | 42.06(b) |
| False ID as Peace Officer | MB | 37.12 |
| False Report: Missing Child/Person | MC | 37.081 |
| False Report: To Peace Officer, Federal Special Investigator, or Law Enforcement Employee | MB | 37.08 |
| False Statement for Property or Credit: Property or Credit is < $50 | MC | 32.32(c)(1) |
| False Statement for Property or Credit: Property or Credit is ≥ $50 | MB | 32.32(c)(2) |
| False Statement for Property or Credit: Property or Credit is ≥ $500 | MA | 32.32(c)(3) |
| False Statement for Property or Credit: Property or Credit is ≥ $1500 | FS | 32.32(c)(4) |
| False Statement for Property or Credit: Property or Credit is ≥ $20,000 | F3 | 32.32(c)(5) |
| False Statement for Property or Credit: Property or Credit is ≥ $100,000 | F2 | 32.32(c)(6) |
| False Statement for Property or Credit: Property or Credit is ≥ $200,000 | F1 | 32.32(c)(7) |
| False Statement Regarding Child Custody Determination Made in Foreign Country | F3 | 37.14 |
| Firearm, Accessible to a Child | MC | 46.13 |
| Firearm, Accessible to a Child: Causes Death/Serious Bodily Injury | MA | 46.13(e) |

| PENAL CODE TITLE | PENALTY | PENALTY SECTION |
|---|---|---|
| Firearm Smuggling | F3 | 46.14 |
| Firearm Smuggling: 3 or more Firearms in a Single Episode | F2 | 46.14(b) |
| Firearm, Unlawful Possession | F3 | 46.04 |
| Firearm, Unlawful Possession: By Person Convicted of Assault - Involves Family/Household Member - Before 5 years have passed | MA | 46.04(b) |
| Firearm, Unlawful Possession: Agency Employee - Possession after receiving Notice of Order and before Expiration of Order | MA | 46.04(c) |
| Flying While Intoxicated | MB (min. 72 hrs.) | 49.05 |
| Flying While Intoxicated: One Prev. Conviction - Intoxication | MA (min. 30 days) | 49.09(a) |
| Flying While Intoxicated: One Prev. Conv. - Intoxication Manslaughter | F3 | 49.09(b)(1) |
| Flying While Intoxicated: Two Prev. Convictions - Intoxication | F3 | 49.09(b)(2) |
| Forgery | MA | 32.21 |
| Forgery: Committed against Elderly Person | Next higher category of offense | 32.21(e-1) |
| Forgery: Checks; Wills; Contracts; Deeds; Financial Instruments | FS | 32.21(d) |
| Forgery: Money; Securities; Postage; Gov't Financial Instruments | F3 | 32.21(e) |
| Fraudulent Postsecondary Degree: Substandard or Fictitious | MB | 32.52 |
| Fraudulent Destruction/Removal/Concealment of Writing | MA | 32.47 |
| Fraudulent Destruction/Removal/Concealment of Writing: Will; Financial Instrument | FS | 32.47(d) |
| Fraudulent Finance Statement: Forgery | F3 | 37.101(a)(1) |
| Fraudulent Finance Statement: Forgery - Two or More Prev. Convictions | F2 | 37.101(b) |
| Fraudulent Finance Statement: False or Groundless Statement | MA | 37.101(a)(2)(3) |
| Fraudulent Finance Statement: False or Groundless Statement - w/Intent to Defraud/Harm | FS | 37.101(b) |
| Fraudulent Lien/Claim: Refusal to Release | MA | 32.49 |
| Fraudulent Court Record | MA | 37.13 |
| Fraudulent Court Record: Two or More Previous Convictions | F3 | 37.13(b) |
| Fraudulent Military Record | MC | 32.54 |
| Fraudulent Transfer of a Motor Vehicle: < $20,000 | FS | 32.34(f)(1) |
| Fraudulent Transfer of a Motor Vehicle: > $20,000 | F3 | 32.34(f)(2) |
| Fraudulent Transfer of a Motor Vehicle: Failure to Disclose Location | MA | 32.34(b)(4) |
| Funeral Service Disruption: Pickets w/in 1000 ft. of Funeral Facility Between 3 hrs. Before/After Service | MB | 42.055(b) |
| Gambling | MC | 47.02 |
| Gambling: Communicating Information | MA | 47.05 |

| PENAL CODE TITLE | PENALTY | PENALTY SECTION |
|---|---|---|
| Gambling: Promotion | MA | 47.03 |
| Gambling: Keeping a Gambling Place | MA | 47.04 |
| Gambling: Possession of Paraphernalia | MA | 47.06 |
| Gangs: Causes/Solicits/Recruits Another to Join - Condition of Gang Membership is Felony or MA Offense | F3 | 71.022(a) |
| Gangs: Solicits a Child to Participate - by Threatening or Causing Bodily Injury to the Child or Child's Family | F3 | 71.022(a-1) |
| Gangs: Solicits Another to Join - Second or Subsequent Offense | F2 | 71.022(c) |
| Gangs: Initiates/Organizes/Plans Gang Activity w/Intent to Further Activity | F1 | 71.023 |
| Gift to Public Servant by Person Subject to Jurisdiction | MA | 36.08 |
| Graffiti: Pecuniary Loss < $500 | MB | 28.08(b)(1) |
| Graffiti: Pecuniary Loss > $500 | MA | 28.08(b)(2) |
| Graffiti: Pecuniary Loss > $1500 | FS | 28.08(b)(3) |
| Graffiti: Pecuniary Loss > $20,000 | F3 | 28.08(b)(4) |
| Graffiti: Pecuniary Loss > $100,000 | F2 | 28.08(b)(5) |
| Graffiti: Pecuniary Loss > $200,000 | F1 | 28.08(b)(6) |
| Graffiti: Place of Worship, Burial, Public Monument - < $20,000 | FS | 28.08(d) |
| Handgun, Unlawful Carrying by License Holder | MA | 46.035 |
| Handgun, Unlawful Carrying of by License Holder: Correction Facility/ABC Licensed Premises | F3 | 46.035(b)(1); (3) |
| Harassment | MB | 42.07 |
| Harassment: by Persons in Correctional Facilities; of Public Servant | F3 | 22.11 |
| Harassment: Previous Conviction | MA | 42.07(c) |
| Harboring Runaway | MA | 25.06 |
| Hindering Apprehension/Prosecution | MA | 38.05 |
| Hindering Apprehension/Prosecution: of a Convicted Felon; of Person who Failed to Register as Sex Offender | F3 | 38.05 (d) |
| Hindering of Official Proceedings by Disorderly Conduct | MA | 38.13 |
| Hindering Secured Creditors: Loss of Property < $20 | MC | 32.33(d)(1) |
| Hindering Secured Creditors: Loss of Property > $20 | MB | 32.33(d)(2) |
| Hindering Secured Creditors: Loss of Property > $500 | MA | 32.33(d)(3) |
| Hindering Secured Creditors: Loss of Property > $1500 | FS | 32.33(d)(4) |
| Hindering Secured Creditors: Loss of Property > $20,000 | F3 | 32.33(d)(5) |
| Hindering Secured Creditors: Loss of Property > $100,000 | F2 | 32.33(d)(6) |
| Hindering Secured Creditors: Loss of Property > $200,000 | F1 | 32.33(d)(7) |
| Hindering Secured Creditors: Proceeds from Sale < $20 | MC | 32.33(e)(1) |
| Hindering Secured Creditors: Proceeds from Sale > $20 | MB | 32.33(e)(2) |

| PENAL CODE TITLE | PENALTY | PENALTY SECTION |
|---|---|---|
| Hindering Secured Creditors: Proceeds from Sale ≥ $500 | MA | 32.33(e)(3) |
| Hindering Secured Creditors: Proceeds from Sale ≥ $1500 | FS | 32.33(e)(4) |
| Hindering Secured Creditors: Proceeds from Sale ≥ $20,000 | F3 | 32.33(e)(5) |
| Hindering Secured Creditors: Proceeds from Sale ≥ $100,000 | F2 | 32.33(e)(6) |
| Hindering Secured Creditors: Proceeds from Sale ≥ $200,000 | F1 | 32.33(e)(7) |
| Hoax Bombs | MA | 46.08 |
| Homosexual Conduct | MC | 21.06 |
| Honorarium, Acceptance | MA | 36.07 |
| Identifying Information, Fraudulent Use/Possession: Number of Items Possessed/Used/Obtained < 5 | FS | 32.51(c)(1) |
| Identifying Information, Fraudulent Use/Possession: Number of Items Possessed/Used/Obtained ≥ 5 | F3 | 32.51(c)(2) |
| Identifying Information, Fraudulent Use/Possession: Number of Items Possessed/Used/Obtained ≥ 10 | F2 | 32.51(c)(3) |
| Identifying Information, Fraudulent Use/Possession: Number of Items Possessed/Used/Obtained ≥ 50 | F1 | 32.51(c)(4) |
| Identifying Information, Fraudulent Use/Possession: Number of Items Possessed/Used/Obtained < 5 - Committed Against the Elderly | F3 | 32.51(c-1) |
| Identifying Information, Fraudulent Use/Possession: Number of Items Possessed/Used/Obtained ≥ 5 - Committed Against the Elderly | F2 | 32.51(c-1) |
| Identifying Information, Fraudulent Use/Possession: Number of Items Possessed/Used/Obtained ≥ 10 - Committed Against the Elderly | F1 | 32.51(c-1) |
| Illumination of Aircraft: Intense Light | MC | 42.14 |
| Illumination of Aircraft: by Intense Light that Impairs Operator's Ability | MA | 42.14(c) |
| Improper Contact with Victim: Charged or Convicted of Offense under CCP Art. 62.001(5) | MA | 38.111 |
| Improper Contact with Victim: Convicted of Felony under CCP Art. 62.001(5) | F3 | 38.111(d) |
| Improper Influence | MA | 36.04 |
| Improper Photography or Visual Recording | FS | 21.15 |
| Improper Relationship Between Educator and Student | F2 | 21.12 |
| Indecency w/Child: Engages or Causes Child to Engage in Sexual Conduct | F2 | 21.11(a)(1) |
| Indecency w/Child: Exposes or Causes Child to Expose | F3 | 21.11(a)(2) |
| Indecent Exposure | MB | 21.08 |
| Injury to Child/Elderly/Disabled: by Owner/Employee of Care Facility - Bodily Injury - Intentional/Knowingly by Omission | F3 | 22.04(f) |
| Injury to Child/Elderly/Disabled: by Owner/Employee of Care Facility - Serious Bodily/Mental Injury - Intentional/Knowingly by Omission | F1 | 22.04(e) |

Penal Offense Titles

| PENAL CODE TITLE | PENALTY | PENALTY SECTION |
|---|---|---|
| Injury to Child/Elderly/Disabled: by Owner/Employee of Care Facility - Serious Bodily/Mental Injury - Recklessly by Omission | F2 | 22.04(e) |
| Injury to Child/Elderly/Disabled: by Owner/Employee of Care Facility - Serious Bodily/Mental Injury; Bodily Injury - Criminal Negligence by Omission | FS | 22.04(g) |
| Injury to Child/Elderly/Disabled: by Owner/Employee of Care Facility - where Victim is Resident - Bodily Injury - Intentionally/Knowingly | F2 | 22.04(f) |
| Injury to Child/Elderly/Disabled: by Owner/Employee of Care Facility - where Victim is Resident - Bodily Injury - Recklessly | FS | 22.04(f) |
| Injury to Child/Elderly/Disabled: Bodily Injury - Intentionally/Knowingly by Act or Omission | F3 | 22.04(f) |
| Injury to Child/Elderly/Disabled: Serious Bodily/Mental Injury - Intentionally/Knowingly by Act or Omission | F1 | 22.04(e) |
| Injury to Child/Elderly/Disabled: Serious Bodily/Mental Injury - Recklessly by Act or Omission | F2 | 22.04(e) |
| Injury to Child/Elderly/Disabled: Serious Bodily/Mental Injury; Bodily Injury - Criminal Negligence by Act or Omission | FS | 22.04(g) |
| Insurance Fraud: Claim < $50 | MC | 35.02(c)(1) |
| Insurance Fraud: Claim ≥ $50 | MB | 35.02(c)(2) |
| Insurance Fraud: Claim ≥ $500 | MA | 35.02(c)(3) |
| Insurance Fraud: Claim ≥ $1500 | FS | 35.02(c)(4) |
| Insurance Fraud: Claim ≥ $20,000 | F3 | 35.02(c)(5) |
| Insurance Fraud: Claim ≥ $100,000 | F2 | 35.02(c)(6) |
| Insurance Fraud: Claim ≥ $200,000 | F1 | 35.02(c)(7)(A) |
| Insurance Fraud: Places a Person at Risk of Death/Serious Bodily Injury | F1 | 35.02(c)(7)(B) |
| Insurance Fraud: w/Intent to Defraud, Prepares/Presents False/Misleading Statement in support of an Application for a Policy | FS | 35.02(a-1) |
| Interference w/Duties: Public Servant; Animal Control Officer | MB | 38.15 |
| Interference with Emergency Telephone Call | MA | 42.062 |
| Interference with Emergency Telephone Call: Prev. Conviction | FS | 42.062(c) |
| Interference w/Police Service Animals: Taunts; Torments; Strikes | MC | 38.151(c)(1) |
| Interference with Police Service Animals: Throws Object/Substance | MB | 38.151.(c)(2) |
| Interference with Police Service Animals: Interferes/Obstructs Animal or Handler; Releases; Enters Area of Control w/o Consent | MA | 38.151(c)(3) |
| Interference with Police Service Animals: Injures; Engages in Conduct likely to Injure | FS | 38.151(c)(4) |
| Interference with Police Service Animals: Permanently Injures; Kills; Engages in Conduct likely to Kill or Permanently Injure | F2 | 38.151(c)(5) |
| Interference w/Government Radio Frequency | MA | 38.152 |
| Interference w/Government Radio Frequency: w/Intent to Facilitate another offense; w/Intent to Interfere with Emergency Response Capability | FS | 38.152(b) |
| Interference With Rights of Guardian of the Person | FS | 25.10 |

| PENAL CODE TITLE | PENALTY | PENALTY SECTION |
|---|---|---|
| Intoxication Assault: Causes Serious Bodily Injury - while Operating Amusement Ride; Vehicle; Aircraft; Watercraft | F3 | 49.07(a)(1) |
| Intoxication Assault: Causes Serious Bodily Injury - while Assembling Amusement Ride | F3 | 49.07(a)(2) |
| Intoxication Assault: Causes Serious Bodily Injury that Results in Traumatic Brain Injury/Persistent Vegetative State | F2 | 49.09(b-4) |
| Intoxication Assault: Causes Serious Bodily Injury to Peace Officer, Firefighter, EMS Personnel | F2 | 49.09(b-1) |
| Intoxication Manslaughter: Causes Death of Peace Officer, Firefighter, EMS Personnel | F1 | 49.09(b-2) |
| Intoxication Manslaughter: Causes Death while Operating Amusement Ride/Vehicle/Aircraft/ Watercraft or while Assembling Amusement Ride | F2 | 49.08 |
| Kidnapping | F3 | 20.03 |
| Kidnapping, Aggravated | F1 | 20.04 |
| Kidnapping, Aggravated: Voluntarily Released Victim in Safe Place | F2 | 20.04(d) |
| Law, Unauthorized Practice of | MA | 38.123 |
| Law, Unauthorized Practice of: Previous Conviction | F3 | 38.123(d) |
| Lawyer, False Representation As | F3 | 38.122 |
| Legal Process, Simulating | MA | 32.48(e) |
| Legal Process, Simulating: Prev. Conv. | FS | 32.48(f) |
| Manslaughter | F2 | 19.04 |
| Medicaid Fraud: Benefit < $50 | MC | 35A.02(b)(1) |
| Medicaid Fraud: Benefit > $50 | MB | 35A.02(b)(2) |
| Medicaid Fraud: Benefit > $500 | MA | 35A.02(b)(3) |
| Medicaid Fraud: Benefit > $1500 | FS | 35A.02(b)(4) |
| Medicaid Fraud: Benefit > $20,000 | F3 | 35A.02(b)(5)(A) |
| Medicaid Fraud: Benefit > $100,000 | F2 | 35A.02(b)(6)(B) |
| Medicare Fraud: > 25 Fraudulent Claims | F3 | 35A.02(b)(5)(B) |
| Medicare Fraud: > 50 Fraudulent Claims | F2 | 35A.02(b)(6)(B) |
| Medicaid Fraud: Benefit > $200,000 | F1 | 35A.02(b)(7) |
| Medicaid Fraud: Value of Benefit Cannot be Ascertained; Obstructs Investigation by AG | FS | 35A.02(a)(11); (b)(4) (B) |
| Misapplication, Fiduciary/Financial Institution Property: < $20 | MC | 32.45(c)(1) |
| Misapplication, Fiduciary/Financial Institution Property: > $20 | MB | 32.45(c)(2) |
| Misapplication, Fiduciary/Financial Institution Property: > $500 | MA | 32.45(c)(3) |
| Misapplication, Fiduciary/Financial Institution Property: > $1,500 | FS | 32.45(c)(4) |
| Misapplication, Fiduciary/Financial Institution Property: > $20,000 | F3 | 32.45(c)(5) |
| Misapplication, Fiduciary/Financial Institution Property: > $100,000 | F2 | 32.45(c)(6) |
| Misapplication, Fiduciary/Financial Institution Property: > $200,000 | F1 | 32.45(c)(7) |
| Misapplication, Fiduciary/Financial Institution Property: < $200,000 -Committed Against the Elderly | One level higher than offense | 32.45(d) |

| PENAL CODE TITLE | PENALTY | PENALTY SECTION |
|---|---|---|
| Misuse of Official Information | F3 | 39.06 |
| Misuse of Official Information: Coerces Another to Suppress or Fail to Report Information | MC | 39.06(a)(3) |
| Money Laundering: ≥ $1,500 | FS | 34.02(e)(1) |
| Money Laundering: ≥ $20,000 | F3 | 34.02(e)(2) |
| Money Laundering: ≥ $100,000 | F2 | 34.02(e)(3) |
| Money Laundering: ≥ $200,000 | F1 | 34.02(e)(4) |
| Multichannel Video/Information Service: Theft/Tampering | MC | 31.12(a) |
| Multichannel Video/Information Service: Theft/Tampering - One Previous Conviction | MB | 31.12(d)(1) |
| Multichannel Video/Information Service: Theft/Tampering - Two or More Previous Convictions | MA | 31.12(d)(1) |
| Multichannel Video/Information Service: Theft/Tampering for Remun. | MA | 31.12(d)(2) |
| Multichannel Video/Information Service: Theft/Tampering for Remun. - Two or More Prev. Convictions | MA (min 180 days + $2000) | 31.12(d)(2) |
| Multichannel Video/Information Service Manuf/Distribute/Advertises | MA | 31.13 |
| Multichannel Video/Information Service Devices: Sale or Lease | MA | 31.14 |
| Murder | F1 | 19.02 |
| Murder: Under the Influence of a Sudden Passion | F2 | 19.02(d) |
| Obscene Display/Distribution | MC | 43.22 |
| Obscenity: Wholesale Promotion | FS | 43.23(a) |
| Obscenity, Wholesale Promotion that Depicts | F3 | a Child 43.23(h) |
| Obscenity: Promotes/Produces/Possesses | MA | 43.23(c) |
| Obscenity: Promotes/Produces/Possesses - Depicts a Child | FS | 43.23(h) |
| Obstructing Highway/Passageway | MB | 42.03 |
| Obstruction/Retaliation | F3 | 36.06 |
| Obstruction/Retaliation: Because of Status as Juror | F2 | 36.06(c) |
| Offering Gift to Public Servant | MA | 36.09 |
| Official Oppression | MA | 39.03 |
| Online Impersonation: Uses Name/Persona of Another w/Intent to Harm/Defraud/Intimidate/Threaten w/Other's Consent | F3 | 33.07(a) |
| Online Impersonation: Sends Electronic Communication containing Identifying Information of Another | MA | 33.07(b) |
| Online Impersonation: Sends Electronic Communication containing Identifying Information of Another - w/Intent to Solicit Response from Emergency Personnel | F3 | 33.07(b) |
| Online Solicitation of Minor: Person ≥ 17 - by Electronic Communication - Communicates/ Distributes Sexually Explicit Material | F3 | 33.021(b) |

| PENAL CODE TITLE | PENALTY | PENALTY SECTION |
|---|---|---|
| Online Solicitation of Minor: Person > 17 - by Electronic Communication - Communicates/ Distributes Sexually Explicit Material - Minor is or is Believed to be < 14 years old | F2 | 33.021(f) |
| Online Solicitation of Minor: by Electronic Communication - Solicits Minor to Meet w/Intent that Minor will Engage in Sexual Activity | F2 | 33.021(c) |
| Organized Criminal Activity: Commits Offense | One level higher than most serious offense | 71.02(b) |
| Organized Criminal Activity: Conspires to Commit Offense | Same level as most serious offense | 71.02(c) |
| Organized Criminal Activity: Violation of Court Order Enjoining from | MA | 71.021 |
| Organized Retail Theft: < $50 | MB | 31.16(c)(1) |
| Organized Retail Theft: > $50 but < $500 | MA | 31.16(c)(2) |
| Organized Retail Theft: > $500 but < $1500 | FS | 31.16(c)(3) |
| Organized Retail Theft: > $1,500 but < $20,000 | F3 | 31.16(c)(4) |
| Organized Retail Theft: > $20,000 but < $100,000 | F2 | 31.16(c)(5) |
| Organized Retail Theft: > $100,000 or more | F1 | 31.16(c)(6) |
| Organized Retail Theft: Organized/Supervised/Financed/Managed Theft | One level higher than offense | 31.16(d)(1) |
| Organized Retail Theft: Caused Alarm to Sound as Distraction; Deactivated or Prevented Fire/Theft Alarm | One level higher than offense | 31.16(d)(2) |
| Pen Register or Trap and Trace Device, Unlawful Use | FS | 16.03 |
| Perjury | MA | 37.02 |
| Perjury, Aggravated | F3 | 37.03 |
| Prohibited Substances and Items in Correctional Facility | F3 | 38.11 |
| Prostitution | MB | 43.02 |
| Prostitution: < 2 Prev. Convictions | MA | 43.02(c)(1) |
| Prostitution: > 3 Prev. Convictions | FS | 43.02(c)(2) |
| Prostitution: Person Solicited > 14 but < 18 Years Old | F3 | 43.02(c)(3) |
| Prostitution: Person Solicited < 14 Years Old | F2 | 43.02(c)(4) |
| Prostitution: Compelling Another by Force/Threat/Fraud | F2 | 43.05(a)(1) |
| Prostitution: Compelling Child < 18 Years Old | F1 | 43.05(a)(2) |
| Prostitution: Promotion | MA | 43.03 |
| Prostitution: Promotion - Aggravated | F3 | 43.04 |
| Public Comm., Illegal Divulgence | FS | 16.05(b) |
| Public Comm., Illegal Divulgence: Unencrypted Communication - Mobile/Paging Service Commun. | MC | 16.05(e)(2) |
| Public Comm., Illegal Divulgence: Unencrypted Communication - Not Mobile/Paging Service Commun. | MA | 16.05(e)(1) |
| Public Intoxication | MC | 49.02 |
| Public Intoxication: < 21 Years Old | Same level as if under ABC 106.071 | 49.02(e) |

| PENAL CODE TITLE | PENALTY | PENALTY SECTION |
|---|---|---|
| Public Lewdness | MA | 21.07 |
| Railroad Property: Uses Weapon | MB | 28.07(b)(1) |
| Railroad Property: Uses Weapon - Causes Bodily Injury | F3 | 28.07(c) |
| Railroad Property: Enters w/o Consent | MC | 28.07(b)(2)(A) |
| Railroad Property: Tampers/Obstructs/Derails | MC | 28.07(e) |
| Railroad Property: Tampers/Obstructs/Derails - Pecuniary Loss $\geq$ $20 | MB | 28.07(e)(1) |
| Railroad Property: Tampers/Obstructs/Derails - Pecuniary Loss $\geq$ $500 | MA | 28.07(e)(2) |
| Railroad Property: Tampers/Obstructs/Derails - Pecuniary Loss $\geq$ $1500 | FS | 28.07(e)(3) |
| Railroad Property: Tampers/Obstructs/Derails - Pecuniary Loss $\geq$ $20,000 | F3 | 28.07(e)(4) |
| Railroad Property: Tampers/Obstructs/Derails - Pecuniary Loss $\geq$ $100,000 | F2 | 28.07(e)(5) |
| Railroad Property: Tampers/Obstructs/Derails - Pecuniary Loss $\geq$ $200,000 | F1 | 28.07(e)(6) |
| Reckless Damage or Destruction | MC | 28.04 |
| Recruitment of Athlete: Illegal Benefit < $20 | MC | 32.441(e)(1) |
| Recruitment of Athlete: Illegal Benefit $\geq$ $20 | MB | 32.441(e)(2) |
| Recruitment of Athlete: Illegal Benefit $\geq$ $500 | MA | 32.441(e)(3) |
| Recruitment of Athlete: Illegal Benefit $\geq$ $1,500 | FS | 32.441(e)(4) |
| Recruitment of Athlete: Illegal Benefit $\geq$ $20,000 | F3 | 32.441(e)(5) |
| Recruitment of Athlete: Illegal Benefit $\geq$ $100,000 | F2 | 32.441(e)(6) |
| Recruitment of Athlete: Illegal Benefit $\geq$ $200,000 | F1 | 32.441(e)(7) |
| Resisting Arrest/Search/Transportation | MA | 38.03 |
| Resisting Arrest/Search/Transportation: Use of Deadly Weapon | F3 | 38.03(d) |
| Rigging Publicly Exhibited Contest | MA | 32.44 |
| Riot, Participation | MB | 42.02(b) |
| Riot, Participation: If Offense More Serious than MB Committed | Same level as other offense | 42.02(f) |
| Robbery | F2 | 29.02 |
| Robbery, Aggravated | F1 | 29.03 |
| Sell/Distrib/Display Harmful Material to Minor | MA | 43.24(b) |
| Sell/Distrib/Display Harmful Material to Minor - Hires Minor to Sell | F3 | 43.24(d) |
| Sexual Abuse of Young Child(ren): 2 or More Acts - Actor $\geq$ 17 - Victim < 14 | F1 (min. 25 yrs.) | 21.02 |
| Sexual Assault | F2 | 22.011 |
| Sexual Assault: Bigamy | F1 | 22.011(f) |
| Sexual Assault: Aggravated | F1 | 22.021 |
| Sexual Assault: Failure to Stop/Report Aggravated Assault of a Child | MA | 38.17 |
| Sexual Conduct, Prohibited | F3 | 25.02 |
| Sexual Conduct, Prohibited: Ancestor or Descendant by Blood or Adoption | F2 | 25.02(c) |

| PENAL CODE TITLE | PENALTY | PENALTY SECTION |
|---|---|---|
| Sexual Conduct: w/Person in Custody | FS | 39.04(a)(2) |
| Sexual Conduct: w/Person in Custody - Juvenile Offender | F2 | 39.04(b) |
| Sexual Conduct: by Texas Employee w/Person Under Supervision | FS | 39.04(f) |
| Sexual Performance by Child: Directs/Produces/Promotes | F3 | 43.25(d) |
| Sexual Performance by Child: Directs/Produces/Promotes - < 14 yrs | F2 | 43.25(e) |
| Sexual Performance by Child: Employ/Induce/Authorize | F2 | 43.25(b) |
| Sexual Performance by Child: Employ/Induce/Authorize - < 14 yrs | F1 | 43.25(c) |
| Silent/Abusive Calls to 9-1-1 Service | MB | 42.061 |
| Smoking Tobacco: Prohibited Area | MC | 48.01 |
| Smuggling of Persons | FS | 20.05 |
| Smuggling of Persons: For monetary gain or smuggling results in serious injury or death | F3 | 20.05(c) |
| Stored Comm., Unlawful Access | MA | 16.04(b) |
| Stored Comm., Unlawful Access: For Benefit/Harm to Another | FS | 16.04(d) |
| Stalking | F3 | 42.072 |
| Stalking: Previous Conviction | F2 | 42.072(b) |
| Tampering w/Consumer Product | F2 | 22.09(b) |
| Tampering w/Consumer Product: Serious Bodily Injury | F1 | 22.09(d) |
| Tampering w/Consumer Product: Threatens to Tamper | F3 | 22.09(c) |
| Tampering: w/Direct Recording Electronic Voting Machine | F1 | 33.05 |
| Tampering: w/ID Number | MA | 31.11 |
| Tampering: w/Witness | F3 | 36.05 |
| Tampering/Fabricating Physical Evidence | F3 | 37.09(a) |
| Tampering/Fabricating Physical Evidence: w/Intent to Impair as Evidence | F3 | 37.09(d)(1) |
| Tampering/Fabricating Physical Evidence: Human Corpse | F2 | 37.09(c) |
| Tampering/Fabricating Physical Evidence: Fails to Report Human Corpse | MA | 37.09(d)(2) |
| Tampering w/Gov't Record | MA | 37.10 |
| Tampering w/Gov't Record: Intent to Defraud/Harm | FS | 37.10(c)(1) |
| Tampering w/Gov't Record: School Record or Gov't Issued Certificate | F3 | 37.10(c)(2)(A) |
| Tampering w/Gov't Record: School Record or Gov't Issued Certificate - Intent to Defraud/Harm | F2 | 37.10(c)(2)(A) |
| Tampering w/Gov't Record: Written Report of Examination of Physical Evidence for Criminal Case | F3 | 37.10(c)(2)(B) |
| Tampering w/Gov't Record: Written Report of Device used for Examination of Criminal Evidence | F3 | 37.10(c)(2)(C) |
| Tampering w/Gov't Record: School Enrollment | MC | 37.10(c)(3) |
| Tampering w/Gov't Record: Written Appraisal | MB | 37.10(c)(4) |

| PENAL CODE TITLE | PENALTY | PENALTY SECTION |
|---|---|---|
| Telecomm. Device: Unlawful Manufacture/Possession/Delivery | F3 | 33A.03 |
| Telecomm. Access Device: Publication | MA | 33A.05 |
| Telecomm. Access Device: Publication - Previous Conviction | F3 | 33A.05(b) |
| Telecomm. Service: Theft < $500 | MB | 33A.04(b)(1) |
| Telecomm. Service: Theft ≥ $500 | MA | 33A.04(b)(2)(A) |
| Telecomm. Service: Theft < $500 - Previous Conviction | MA | 33A.04(b)(2)(B) |
| Telecomm. Service: Theft ≥ $1500 | FS | 33A.04(b)(3)(A) |
| Telecomm. Service: Theft < $1500 - Two or More Prev. Convictions | FS | 33A.04(b)(3)(B) |
| Telecomm. Service: Theft ≥ $20,000 | F3 | 33A.04(b)(4) |
| Telecomm. Service: Theft ≥ $100,000 | F2 | 33A.04(b)(5) |
| Telecomm. Service: Theft ≥ $200,000 | F1 | 33A.04(b)(6) |
| Telecomm. Service: Unauthorized Use < $500 | MB | 33A.02(b)(1) |
| Telecomm. Service: Unauthorized Use ≥ $500 | MA | 33A.02(b)(2) (A) |
| Telecomm. Service: Unauthorized Use < $500 - Previous Conviction | MA | 33A.02(b)(2) (B) |
| Telecomm. Service: Unauthorized Use ≥ $1500 | FS | 33A.02(b)(3) (A) |
| Telecomm. Service: Unauthorized Use < $1500 - Two or More Prev. Conv. | FS | 33A.02(b)(3) (B) |
| Telecomm. Service: Unauthorized Use ≥ $20,000 | F3 | 33A.02(b)(4) |
| Telecomm. Service: Unauthorized Use ≥ $100,000 | F2 | 33A.02(b)(5) |
| Telecomm. Service: Unauthorized Use ≥ $200,000 | F1 | 33A.02(b)(6) |
| Terroristic Threat | MB | 22.07(a)(1);(2) |
| Terroristic Threat: Causes Fear of Serious Bodily Injury - Against Person's Family/Household or Public Servant | MA | 22.07(c) |
| Terroristic Threat: Prevent Use of Public Place | MA | 22.07(a)(3) |
| Terroristic Threat: Prevent Use of Public Place - Damage ≥ $1500 | FS | 22.07(d) |
| Terroristic Threat: Interrupt Public Service; Public Fear of Bodily Injury; Influence Government | F3 | 22.07(e) |
| Theft: < $20 - by Check | MC | 31.03(e)(1)(B) |
| Theft: ≥ $20 - by Check | MB | 31.03(e)(2)(A)(ii) |
| Theft: < $20 - by Check - Prev. Conv. | MB | 31.03(e)(2)(B)(ii) |
| Theft: < $50 | MC | 31.03(e)(1)(A) |
| Theft: < $50 - Previous Conviction | MB | 31.03(e)(2)(B)(i) |
| Theft: ≥ $50 | MB | 31.03(e)(2)(A)(i) |
| Theft: ≥ $500 | MA | 31.03(e)(3) |
| Theft: < $1500 - Two or More Prev. Convictions | FS | 31.03(e)(4)(D) |
| Theft: ≥ $1500 | FS | 31.03(e)(4) |
| Theft: < $20,000 - Livestock | FS | 31.03(e)(4) |
| Theft: < $20,000 - Wire/Cable ≥ 50% Aluminum/Bronze/Copper/Brass | FS | 31.03(e)(4)(F) |
| Theft: ≥ $20,000 | F3 | 31.03(e)(5) |
| Theft: < $100,000 - Livestock | F3 | 31.03(e)(5)(A);(B) |
| Theft: ≥ $100,000 | F2 | 31.03(e)(6) |
| Theft: ≥ $200,000 | F1 | 31.03(e)(7) |
| Theft: Against the Elderly or Nonprofit Organization | Next higher level of offense | 31.03(f)(3) |
| Theft: Caused Alarm to Sound as Distraction; Deactivated or Prevented Fire/Theft Alarm | Next higher level of offense | 31.03(f)(5) |

| PENAL CODE TITLE | PENALTY | PENALTY SECTION |
|---|---|---|
| Theft: Firearm; From the Person of Another; From Corpse/Grave; Election Ballot/Envelope | FS | 31.03(e)(4)(B);(C);(E) |
| Theft: of Trade Secrets | F3 | 31.05 |
| Theft: of Service < $20 | MC | 31.04(e)(1) |
| Theft: of Service > $20 | MB | 31.04(e)(2) |
| Theft: of Service > $500 | MA | 31.04(e)(3) |
| Theft: of Service > $1,500 | FS | 31.04(e)(4) |
| Theft: of Service > $20,000 | F3 | 31.04(e)(5) |
| Theft: of Service > $100,000 | F2 | 31.04(e)(6) |
| Theft: of Service > $200,000 | F1 | 31.04(e)(7) |
| Theft: Personal ID Issued by Gov't | MB | 31.03(e)(2)(C) |
| Theft: Stolen Property Obtained by Virtue of Actor's Status as Public Servant or Gov't Contractor | Next higher level of offense | 31.03(f)(1);(2); (4) |
| Theft: Steals/Receives Stolen Check/Sight Order | MA | 32.24 |
| Theft: Unauthorized Acquisition of Financial Information | MB | 31.17(b)(1) |
| Theft: Unauthorized Transfer of Financial Information | MA | 31.17(b)(2) |
| Tracking Device: Unlawful Installation | MA | 16.06 |
| Trafficking of Persons | F2 | 20A.02 |
| Trafficking of Persons: < 18 Years Old - For the Purpose of Prostitution/Forced Labor | F1 | 20A.02(b)(1) |
| Trafficking of Persons: Continuous Trafficking of Persons | F1 | 20A.03 |
| Trafficking of Persons: Results in Death of Person Trafficked | F1 | 20A.02(b)(2) |
| Unlawful Restraint | MA | 20.02 |
| Unlawful Restraint: < 17 Years Old | FS | 20.02(c)(1) |
| Unlawful Restraint: Exposes Victim to Risk of Serious Bodily Injury | F3 | 20.02(c)(2)(A) |
| Unlawful Restraint: of Public Servant in Retaliation to Victim's Exercise of Power/Duty | F3 | 20.02(c)(2)(B) |
| Unlawful Restratint: While in Custody | F3 | 20.02(c)(2)(C) |
| Use of Laser Pointers: at Uniformed Officer | MC | 42.13 |
| Vehicle, Unauthorized Use | FS | 31.07 |
| Violation of Protective Order: In Family Violence Case | MA | 25.07 |
| Violation of Protective Order: In Family Violence Case - Two or More Previous Convictions | F3 | 25.07(g) |
| Violation of Protective Order: In Family Violence Case - Assault/Stalking | F3 | 25.07(g) |
| Violation of Protective Order | MA | 25.071 |
| Violation of Protective Order: Two or More Prev. Convictions | F3 | 25.071(d) |
| Violation of Protective Order: Assault | F3 | 25.071(d) |
| Violation of Protective Order: Issued on Basis of Sexual Assault | MA | 38.112 |
| Weapons: An Attempt to Take from Officer, Federal Special Investigator, or Employee of Correctional Facility | FS | 38.14(b) |
| Weapons: A Successful Attempt to Take from Officer, Federal Special Investigator, or Employee of Correctional Facility | F3 | 38.14(e) |

| PENAL CODE TITLE | PENALTY | PENALTY SECTION |
|---|---|---|
| Weapons: Carrying in Prohibited Place | F3 | 46.03 |
| Weapons: Unlawful Carrying | MA | 46.02 |
| Weapons: Unlawful Carrying - on ABC Licensed Premises | F3 | 46.02(c) |
| Weapons: Unlawful Transfer | MA | 46.06 |
| Weapons: Unlawful Transfer of Handgun - to Child < 18 Years Old | FS | 46.06(d) |
| Weapons, Prohibited | F3 | 46.05(a) |
| Weapons, Prohibited: Switchblade/Knuckles | MA | 46.05(a)(5);(6) |
| Weapons, Prohibited: Tire Deflation Device | FS | 46.05(a)(10) =te |

# Introduction to Appendix

We are happy to provide you with **The Supreme Court on Selected Criminal and Traffic Issues**. This appendix is designed to provide the reader with a concise overview of U.S. Supreme Court decisions relating to criminal and traffic law. Prepared by the publisher's staff of lawyer-editors, selected case notes from the **United States Supreme Court Reports, Lawyers' Edition 2d** provide succinct summaries of Supreme Court holdings based on the Court's own language. The aim of the appendix is to efficiently inform the reader of governing decisions relating to criminal and traffic issues and to enrich the understanding of the true spirit and nature of the law.

The appendix is organized by subject, with case notes listed in paragraph form. Under each specific subject heading, case notes are listed in reverse chronological order. Thus, using the Analysis at the front of the appendix, it is possible to focus upon an area of interest and quickly scan a handful of case notes to gain a valuable overview of the Court's history of decisions on a specific topic. Selected from decisions reaching back to 1956, case law is current as of June 30, 2011.

Also included in this appendix are Practice Pointers, which draw from the Supreme Court's decisions to provide practical, real world advice for both officers and attorneys. Finally, references to relevant Lawyer's Edition Annotations are included as an aid to continued research. Written in a clear, narrative format, these Annotations (available electronically) guide the reader through the progression of cases that constitute the Supreme Court's body of decisions on selected key points of constitutional law.

Due to the concise nature of the case notes and the limited scope of this appendix, the serious researcher is encouraged to broaden their research and to retrieve the full text of each relevant case. For those publications that are packaged with a companion CD, a full text version of each case summarized in the appendix is provided in a searchable and linked electronic format. Similarly, full text versions of all Annotations referenced are provided. Full text versions of the cases and Annotations are also available online via LexisNexis. com, and through electronic and print versions of the **United States Supreme Court Reports, Lawyer's Edition.**

Concise and accessible enough to be read in a single sitting, yet optimized for quick reference, any officer or attorney who uses this appendix will undoubtedly find that it is an efficient way of enriching their comprehension of the complex constitutional issues surrounding criminal and traffic laws.

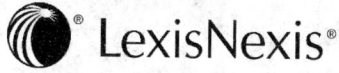

# THE SUPREME COURT ON SELECT CRIMINAL AND TRAFFIC ISSUES

(Derived from the United States Supreme Court Reports, Lawyers' Edition)

———————

## Arrests

### § 1. In General

Although a warrant presumptively is required for a felony arrest in a suspect's home, the Federal Constitution's Fourth Amendment permits warrantless arrests in public places where an officer has probable cause to believe that a felony has occurred. Florida v White (1999) 526 US 559, 143 L Ed 2d 748, 1999 US LEXIS 3172, 119 S Ct 1555.

To say that an arrest—a seizure of the person for the purposes of the Federal Constitution's Fourth Amendment—is effected by the slightest application of physical force, despite the arrestee's escape, is not to say that for Fourth Amendment purposes there is a continuing arrest during the period of fugitivity; if, for example, a police officer lays his hands upon a fleeing person to arrest him, but the fugitive breaks away and then discards contraband, it is not realistic to say that the contraband was discovered during the course of an arrest. California v Hodari D. (1991) 499 US 621, 113 L Ed 2d 690, 1991 US LEXIS 2397, 111 S Ct 1547.

To constitute a seizure of the person, just as to constitute an arrest—the quintessential "seizure of the person" under Fourth Amendment jurisprudence—there must be either the application of physical force, however slight, or, where that is absent, submission to an officer's "show of authority" to restrain the subject's liberty. California v Hodari D. (1991) 499 US 621, 113 L Ed 2d 690, 1991 US LEXIS 2397, 111 S Ct 1547.

Every arrest, and every seizure having the essential attributes of a formal arrest, is unreasonable, within the meaning of the Fourth Amendment, unless it is supported by probable cause, but an exception for limited intrusions that may be justified by special law enforcement interests is not confined to the momentary, on-the-street detention accompanied by a frisk for weapons. Michigan v Summers (1981) 452 US 692, 69 L Ed 2d 340, 1981 US LEXIS 118, 101 S Ct 2587.

### § 2. Exclusionary Rule

Suppression of evidence seized in violation of the Federal Constitution's Fourth Amendment is not required by the exclusionary rule where the evidence was seized incident to an arrest made on the basis of erroneous information—a computer check of a driver stopped for a routine traffic violation revealed the existence of an outstanding misdemeanor warrant for the driver's arrest, when in fact the warrant had been quashed 2 weeks earlier—which in turn resulted from a clerical error of court employees. Arizona v Evans (1995) 514 US 1, 131 L Ed 2d 34, 1995 US LEXIS 1806, 115 S Ct 1185.

The indirect fruits of an illegal arrest should be suppressed when they bear a sufficiently close relationship to the underlying illegality; however, such attenuation analysis is appropriate only where, as a threshold matter, courts determine that the challenged evidence is in some sense the product of illegal governmental activity. New York v Harris (1990) 495 US 14, 109 L Ed 2d 13, 1990 US LEXIS 2037, 110 S Ct 1640.

The Fourth Amendment exclusionary rule does not bar a state's use in a criminal trial of a written inculpatory statement made by a murder suspect at a police station—even though the statement was taken after the suspect was arrested by the police in his home without a warrant and without consent to their entry—where (1) the statement was not the product of being in unlawful custody, inasmuch as the police had probable cause to arrest the suspect; (2) the police had a justification to question the suspect prior to his arrest, so that the suspect's subsequent statement was not an exploitation of the illegal entry into the suspect's home; and (3) the statement was not the fruit of having been arrested in the home rather than someplace else. New York v Harris (1990) 495 US 14, 109 L Ed 2d 13, 1990 US LEXIS 2037, 110 S Ct 1640.

### § 3. Media Accompaniment

A "media ride-along"—in which a print reporter and a photographer for a newspaper accompany a team of federal and county police officers during an attempt to execute arrest warrants in a private home—violates the Federal Constitution's Fourth Amendment. Wilson v Layne (1999) 526 US 603, 143 L Ed 2d 818, 119 S Ct 1692, 1999 US LEXIS 3633.

### § 4. Probable Cause

Officer had probable cause to believe that defendant had committed the crime of possession of a controlled substance where in addition to the driver and a back set passenger, defendant was a front seat passenger in a vehicle which was stopped for speeding in the early morning hours; upon a consensual search, a significant amount of cash was found in the glove compartment of the vehicle and drugs were discovered between the back-seat armrest and the back seat; and although defendant subsequently admitted that the drugs and cash were his, none of the vehicle occupants admitted to ownership of the drugs at the time of the search, and all three occupants were arrested. It was an entirely reasonable inference that any or all three of the occupants had knowledge of, and exercised dominion and control over, the drugs, and thus a reasonable officer could conclude that there was probable cause to believe defendant committed the crime of possession of drugs, either solely or jointly. It was also reasonable for the officer to infer a common enterprise among the three occupants, in view of the likelihood of drug dealing in which an innocent party was unlikely to be involved. Maryland v Pringle (2003) 540 US 366, 157 L Ed 2d 769, **2003** US LEXIS 9198, 124 S Ct 795.

Under the Federal Constitution's Fourth Amendment, police officers need either a warrant, or probable cause plus exigent circumstances, in order to make a lawful entry into a home. Thus, a state court erred in failing to assess whether exigent circumstances were present when some police officers entered an individual's home without either an arrest warrant or a search warrant, arrested him, and searched him. Exigent circumstances were required to justify the officers' conduct even if, as the state court ruled, the officers had probable cause to arrest the individual. Kirk v Louisiana (2002) 536 US 635, 153 L Ed 2d 599, 2002 US LEXIS 4682, 122 S Ct 2458.

A jurisdiction that provides judicial determinations of probable cause within 48 hours of a warrantless arrest will, as a general matter, comply with the requirement, under the Federal Constitution's Fourth Amendment, that such determinations be provided promptly, and such a jurisdiction will therefore be immune from systemic challenges to its probable cause determination procedures. County of Riverside v McLaughlin (1991) 500 US 44, 114 L Ed 2d 49, 1991 US LEXIS 2528, 111 S Ct 1661.

Although a county is entitled to combine probable cause determinations following warrantless arrests with the arrestees' arraignment, the county's policy of excluding weekends and holidays in computing the 2-day period within which the combined proceedings must be offered—which exclusion could result in delays of up to 7 days—means that the county's regular practice exceeds the 48-hour period that will generally satisfy the promptness requirement for probable cause determinations that is imposed by the Federal Constitution's Fourth Amendment. County of Riverside v McLaughlin (1991) 500 US 44, 114 L Ed 2d 49, 1991 US LEXIS 2528, 111 S Ct 1661.

Before agents of the government may invade the sanctity of the home without a search or arrest warrant, the burden is on the government to demonstrate exigent circumstances that overcome the presumption of unreasonableness that attaches to all warrantless home entries; when the government's interest is only to arrest for a minor offense, that presumption is difficult to rebut, and the government usually should be allowed to make such arrests only with a warrant issued upon probable cause by a neutral and detached magistrate. Welsh v Wisconsin (1984) 466 US 740, 80 L Ed 2d 732, 1984 US LEXIS 82, 104 S Ct 2091.

Probable cause which will justify an arrest without a warrant by police officers exists where the facts and circumstances within the officers' knowledge and of which they have reasonably trustworthy information are sufficient in themselves to warrant a man of reasonable caution in the belief that an offense has been or is being committed by the person to be arrested. Dunaway v New York (1979) 442 US 200, 60 L Ed 2d 824, 1979 US LEXIS 126, 99 S Ct 2248.

Under the Fourth Amendment, a person arrested without a warrant and charged by information with a state offense is entitled to a timely judicial determination by a neutral magistrate of probable cause for pretrial restraint of liberty, and may not be jailed or subjected to other significant restraints pending trial without any opportunity for such a probable cause determination; the state prosecutor's decision to file an information does not alone meet the requirements of the Fourth Amendment as constituting a determination of probable cause that furnishes sufficient reason for detention pending trial. Gerstein v Pugh (1975) 420 US 103, 43 L Ed 2d 54, 95 S Ct 854, 1975 US LEXIS 29.

## § 5. Search Incident to Arrest

Evidence obtained during a search incident to arrest of a vehicle that would violate the holding of Arizona v Gant is not subject to the exclusionary rule if the search was conducted before the Gant decision was announced and was lawful under the previous standard set in New York v Belton. Suppressing such evidence would do nothing to deter police misconduct, which is the sole purpose of the Exclusionary Rule. Davis v U.S. (2011) 2011 US LEXIS 4560.

When police arrest the driver of or a passenger in a vehicle, officers may search the passenger compartment of the vehicle incident to the arrest, but only if the arrestee is within "reaching distance" of the passenger compartment at the time of the search, *or* it is reasonable to believe the vehicle contains evidence of the offense of arrest. If the arrestee has already been handcuffed and placed in the back of a patrol car, then a search of the vehicle is no longer justified because the arrestee is no longer capable of accessing any weapon potentially hidden inside, unless police reasonable expect to find evidence of the crime for which the arrest was made in the vehicle. While police can generally expect to find evidence following a drug arrest (e.g. more drugs, paraphernalia), a search is not allowed following a traffic violation (for example, driving with a suspended license) as no evidence of such offenses could be concealed inside the vehicle. Arizona v Gant (2009) 556 US __, 173 L Ed 2d 485, 2009 US LEXIS 3120, 129 S Ct 1710.

For a search incident to arrest to be valid, the underlying arrest need only be "lawful" in terms of the Fourth Amendment, not necessarily whatever local state statute applies. Although an arrest for driving under suspension was not valid under Virginia state law (such a traffic offense is not an "arrestable offense" in that state unless the arrestee fails or refuses to continue driving, or the officer reasonable believes the arrestee will likely disregard a summons or harm himself or others, and neither circumstance applied), a subsequent search incident to arrest was nevertheless valid under the Fourth Amendment, because the arrest was supported by probable cause. Virginia v Moore (2008) 553 US 164, 170 L Ed 2d 559, 128 S Ct 1598, 2008 US LEXIS 3674, 2008 US LEXIS 3674.

When a police officer has made a lawful custodial arrest of the occupant of an automobile, the officer may, as a contemporaneous incident of that arrest, search the passenger compartment of the automobile and examine the contents of any containers found within the passenger compartment—the same probable cause to believe that a container holds drugs will allow the police to arrest the person transporting the container and search it. California v Acevedo (1991) 500 US 565, 114 L Ed 2d 619, 1991 US LEXIS 3016, 111 S Ct 1982.

In the case of a search incident to a lawful arrest, if the police stray outside the permissible scope of the search, they are in violation of the Fourth Amendment, and evidence so seized will be excluded. Horton v California (1990) 496 US 128, 110 L Ed 2d 112, 1990 US LEXIS 2937, 110 S Ct 2301.

As an incident to an in-home arrest, police may, as a precautionary measure and without a search warrant, probable cause, or reasonable suspicion, look in closets and other spaces immediately adjoining the place of arrest from which an attack could be immediately launched; beyond that, however, the Fourth Amendment permits a protective sweep, without a search warrant, in conjunction with an in-home arrest—extending only to a cursory inspection of those spaces where a person may be found, lasting no longer than is necessary to dispel the reasonable suspicion of danger, and in any event no longer than it takes to complete the arrest and depart the premises—when the searching officer possesses a reasonable belief based on specific and articulable facts which, taken together with the rational inferences from those facts, would warrant a reasonably prudent officer in believing that the area to be swept harbors an individual posing a danger to those on the arrest scene. Maryland v Buie (1990) 494 US 325, 108 L Ed 2d 276, 1990 US LEXIS 1176, 110 S Ct 1093.

Police officers possessing an arrest warrant and probable cause to believe that the person to be arrested is in his or her home are entitled, under the Fourth Amendment, to enter the home and search anywhere in the home in which the person might be found; once the person is found, however, the search for the person is over, and there is no longer that particular justification for entering any rooms that have not yet been searched; that the person has an expectation of privacy in those remaining areas of the house, however, does not mean such rooms are immune from entry. Maryland v Buie (1990) 494 US 325, 108 L Ed 2d 276, 1990 US LEXIS 1176, 110 S Ct 1093.

If police officers arrest a person for speeding or for driving while intoxicated, they can search the passenger compartment of the car, and they can search the trunk if they have probable cause to believe that the trunk contains contraband. Michigan v Long (1983) 463 US 1032, 77 L Ed 2d 1201, 1983 US LEXIS 7, 103 S Ct 3469.

A policeman who has made a lawful custodial arrest of the occupant of an automobile may, as a contemporaneous incident of that arrest, search the passenger compartment of the automobile and may examine the contents of any containers found within the passenger compartment, the term "container" denoting any object capable of holding another object and including closed or open glove compartments, consoles, or other receptacles, as well as luggage, boxes, bags, clothing, and the like. New York v Belton (1981) 453 US 454, 69 L Ed 2d 768, 1981 US LEXIS 13, 101 S Ct 2860, reh den 453 US 950, 69 L Ed 2d 1036, 102 S Ct 26.

A law enforcement officer may not, consistent with the Fourth Amendment, search for the subject of an arrest warrant in the home of a third party without first obtaining a search warrant, absent consent or exigent circumstances, for (1) the requirement of a search warrant does not significantly impede effective law enforcement efforts when weighed against the constitutional interests at stake, (2) the third party has a Fourth Amendment privacy interest in being free from an unreasonable invasion and search of his home, and (3) the arrest warrant serves to protect only those named in the warrant from an unreasonable seizure, but does nothing to safeguard the third party's interest in the privacy of his home and possessions against the unjustified intrusion of the police. Steagald v United States (1981) 451 US 204, 68 L Ed 2d 38, 1981 US LEXIS 89, 101 S Ct 1642.

The search of a locked footlocker by federal agents acting without a search warrant but upon a probable cause belief that the footlocker contained contraband—which search is conducted in a federal building to which the footlocker had been brought by federal agents after being lawfully seized at the time of the arrests of those who had been in possession of the footlocker—cannot be justified as being incident to the arrests or on the basis of any other exigency, where the search is conducted more than an hour after federal agents had gained exclusive control of the footlocker and long after those from whom it had been seized were securely in custody. United States v Chadwick (1977) 433 US 1, 53 L Ed 2d 538, 1977 US LEXIS 133, 97 S Ct 2476.

A search incident to a lawful arrest is a traditional exception to the warrant requirement of the Fourth Amendment; such a search may be made (1) of the person of the arrestee by virtue of the lawful arrest, and (2) of the area within the arrestee's control. United States v Robinson (1973) 414 US 218, 38 L Ed 2d 427, 1973 US LEXIS 21, 94 S Ct 467.

After a police officer lawfully places a suspect under arrest for the purpose of taking him into custody, the officer may proceed to fully search the prisoner, and is not limited—as in the case of a stop-and-frisk search incident to an investigative stop based on less than probable cause to arrest—to conducting a frisk of outer clothing only and removing such weapons that he may, as a result of such limited frisk, reasonably believe the suspect has in his possession. United States v Robinson (1973) 414 US 218, 38 L Ed 2d 427, 1973 US LEXIS 21, 94 S Ct 467.

Limits imposed by the Fourth Amendment are not offended by a full search of the defendant's person by a District of Columbia police officer pursuant to established police department practice after a lawful, full custody arrest of the defendant for operating a motor vehicle after revocation of the defendant's operator's permit, or by the officer's seizure of heroin capsules found in a crumpled cigarette package in the defendant's coat pocket and introduced in evidence in a narcotics prosecution which resulted in conviction, it being immaterial that the officer did not indicate any subjective fear of the defendant, that he did not suspect that the defendant was armed, that he was not specifically looking for weapons or anything else, or that no further evidence of the crime of driving while one's permit was revoked could be obtained in the search; having in the course of a lawful search come upon the crumpled cigarette package, the officer was entitled to inspect it, and when his inspection revealed the heroin capsules, he was entitled to seize them as fruits, instrumentalities, or contraband probative of criminal conduct. United States v Robinson (1973) 414 US 218, 38 L Ed 2d 427, 1973 US LEXIS 21, 94 S Ct 467.

While a search incident to an arrest, although justified in part by the acknowledged necessity to protect the arresting officer from assault with a concealed weapon, is also justified on other grounds and can therefore involve a relatively extensive exploration of the person, a search for weapons in the absence of probable cause to arrest must, like any other search, be strictly circumscribed by the exigencies justifying its initiation; thus it must be limited to that which is necessary for the discovery of weapons which might be used to harm the officer or others nearby, and may realistically be characterized as something less than a "full" search, even though it remains a serious intrusion. Terry v Ohio (1968) 392 US 1, 20 L Ed 2d 889, 1968 US LEXIS 1345, 88 S Ct 1868.

## § 6. Warrant Requirement for Arrest

An arrest pursuant to a warrant that was wrongfully included in a county database due to an isolated incidence of police negligence did not trigger the Exclusionary Rule. Other officers, not the arresting officers, negligently failed to enter the recall of the arrest warrant in the database. Because the error was nonrecurring—not a result of systematic negligence—and attenuated from the arrest, application of the Exclusionary Rule would not have resulted in appreciable deterrence of future violations. Herring v United States (2009) 555 US 135, 172 L Ed 2d 496, 2009 US LEXIS 581, 129 S Ct 695.

For purposes of determining whether a warrantless arrest is lawful under the Fourth Amendment, the criminal offense for which there is probable cause to arrest does not have to be "closely related" to the offense stated by the arresting officer at the time of arrest. Devenpeck v Alford (2004) 543 US 146, 160 L Ed 2d 537, 125 S Ct 588, 2004 US LEXIS 8272.

Under the Federal Constitution's Fourth Amendment, police officers need either a warrant, or probable cause plus exigent circumstances, in order to make a lawful entry into a home. Thus, a state court erred in failing to assess whether exigent circumstances were present when some police officers entered an individual's home without either an arrest warrant or a search warrant, arrested him, and searched him. Exigent circumstances were required to justify the officers' conduct even if, as the state court ruled, the officers had probable cause to arrest the individual. Kirk v Louisiana (2002) 536 US 635, 153 L Ed 2d 599, 2002 US LEXIS 4682, 122 S Ct 2458.

The Fourth Amendment does not forbid a warrantless arrest for a minor criminal offense, such as a misdemeanor seatbelt violation punishable only by a fine. Atwater v Lago Vista (2001) 532 US 318, 149 L Ed 2d 549, 2001 US LEXIS 3366, 121 S Ct 1536.

Warrantless arrests are permitted under the Federal Constitution's Fourth Amendment, but persons arrested without a warrant must promptly be brought before a neutral magistrate for a judicial determination of probable cause. County of Riverside v McLaughlin (1991) 500 US 44, 114 L Ed 2d 49, 1991 US LEXIS 2528, 111 S Ct 1661.

A routine felony arrest by the police of a murder suspect in his home without an arrest warrant and by means of a nonconsensual entry violates the Fourth Amendment. New York v Harris (1990) 495 US 14, 109 L Ed 2d 13, 1990 US LEXIS 2037, 110 S Ct 1640.

Police officers acting without probable cause and without a warrant violate the Fourth Amendment, made applicable to the states by the Fourteenth Amendment, by forcibly removing a person from his home or other place where he is entitled to be and transporting him to the police station for fingerprinting; such seizures, at least where not under judicial supervision, are sufficiently like arrests to invoke the traditional rule that arrests may constitutionally be made only on probable cause, and fingerprints taken under these circumstances are thus the inadmissible fruits of an illegal detention. Hayes v Florida (1985) 470 US 811, 84 L Ed 2d 705, 1985 US LEXIS 1523, 105 S Ct 1643.

A warrantless home arrest for driving while intoxicated is not justified by the need to preserve evidence of the offender's blood-alcohol level, the imminent destruction of evidence being an exigent circumstance exception to the warrant requirement of the Fourth Amendment, where a state has chosen to classify the first offense for driving while intoxicated as a noncriminal, civil forfeiture offense for which no imprisonment is possible; given this expression of the state's interest in precipitating an arrest, a warrantless home arrest cannot be upheld simply because evidence of the offender's blood-alcohol level might have dissipated while the police obtained a warrant. Welsh v Wisconsin (1984) 466 US 740, 80 L Ed 2d 732, 1984 US LEXIS 82, 104 S Ct 2091.

While an arrest warrant and a search warrant both serve to subject the probable-cause determination of the police to judicial review, the interests protected by the two warrants differ, for (1) an arrest warrant is issued by a magistrate upon a showing that probable cause exists to believe that the subject of the warrant has committed an offense and thus the warrant primarily serves to protect an individual from an unreasonable seizure; while (2) a search warrant, in contrast, is issued upon a showing of probable cause to believe that the legitimate object of a search is located in a particular place, and therefore safeguards an individual's interest in the privacy of his home and possessions against the unjustified intrusion of the police. Steagald v United States (1981) 451 US 204, 68 L Ed 2d 38, 1981 US LEXIS 89, 101 S Ct 1642.

The Fourth Amendment prohibits the police from making a warrantless and nonconsensual entry into a suspect's home in order to make a routine felony arrest. Payton v New York (1980) 445 US 573, 63 L Ed 2d 639, 1980 US LEXIS 13, 100 S Ct 1371.

City police violate the Fourth and Fourteenth Amendments when, without probable cause to arrest, they take an individual into custody, transport him to the police station, and detain him there for interrogation without making a formal arrest. Dunaway v New York (1979) 442 US 200, 60 L Ed 2d 824, 1979 US LEXIS 126, 99 S Ct 2248.

The usual rule is that a police officer may arrest without a warrant one believed by the officer upon reasonable cause to have been guilty of a felony; the lawfulness of the arrest without a warrant must be based upon probable cause. United States v Watson (1976) 423 US 411, 46 L Ed 2d 598, 1976 US LEXIS 121, 96 S Ct 820.

Good faith on the part of an arresting officer is not sufficient to establish the validity of an arrest without a warrant. Terry v Ohio (1968) 392 US 1, 20 L Ed 2d 889, 1968 US LEXIS 1345, 88 S Ct 1868.

### § 7. Transporting Subject Without Warrant

Within the meaning of the Federal Constitution's Fourth Amendment, an individual, who was then a suspect in a murder investigation and who was then 17 years old, was illegally arrested before he was questioned, when officers of a county sheriff's department transported the individual involuntarily from his home to the sheriff's headquarters for questioning, as: (1) There was evidence that (a) the officers, who did not have a warrant and concededly lacked probable cause at that time, awakened the individual in his home at approximately 3 a.m.; (b) one of the officers told the individual that "we need to go and talk"; (c) the individual replied "Okay"; (d) the officers (i) handcuffed the individual, who was in his underwear, and (ii) took him the scene of the crime and then to headquarters; and (e) once at headquarters, the officers removed the handcuffs, after which the individual was given Miranda warnings and interrogated. (2) On this evidence, the circumstances which indicated that a seizure occurred included (a) the threatening presence of several officers, (b) some physical touching of the individual, (c) the use of language or tone of voice indicating that compliance with the officers' request might be compelled, and (d) possibly, a display of a weapon by at least one officer. (3) There was no reason to think the individual's "Okay" answer was anything more than a mere submission to a claim of lawful authority. (4) Even if there were doubt on this point, the ensuing events resolved it, where, once the individual was taken to headquarters and the officers began to question the individual, a reasonable person in this situation would not have thought that the person was sitting in the interview room as a matter of choice, free to change the person's mind and to go home to bed. (5) It was not significant that the sheriff's department assertedly "routinely" transported persons, including this individual on one prior occasion, while handcuffed for the safety of the officers, as stressing the officers' motivation of self-protection did not speak to how their actions would reasonably be understood. (6) Moreover, it was not significant that the individual assertedly did not resist the use of handcuffs or act in a manner consistent with anything other than full cooperation, as failure to struggle with a cohort of deputy sheriffs was not a waiver of Fourth Amendment protection, which did not require the perversity of resisting arrest or assaulting a police officer. Kaupp v Texas (2003) 538 US 626, 155 L Ed 2d 814, 123 S Ct 1843, 2003 US LEXIS 3670.

## § 8. Foreign Nationals

Failure to inform an arrested foreign national of the right under Article 36 of the Vienna Convention to contact a consular officer of his or her home country does not require suppression of subsequent statements made by the foreign national under the Exclusionary Rule. Sanchez-Llamas v Oregon (2006) 548 US 331, 165 L Ed 2d 557, 126 S Ct 2669, 2006 US LEXIS 5177.

# Stop and Frisk; Temporary Detention

## § 1. In General

Under the Fourth Amendment, a policeman who lacks probable cause, but whose observations lead him reasonably to suspect that a particular person has committed, is committing, or is about to commit a crime, may detain that person briefly in order to investigate the circumstances that provoke suspicion; the stop and inquiry must be reasonably related in scope to the justification for their initiation. Berkemer v McCarty (1984) 468 US 420, 82 L Ed 2d 317, 1984 US LEXIS 140, 104 S Ct 3138.

The governmental interest of effective crime prevention and detection underlies the recognition that a police officer may in appropriate circumstances and in an appropriate manner approach a person for purposes of investigating possibly criminal behavior even though there is no probable cause to make an arrest, as where a police officer observed defendant and two other men go through a series of acts, each of them perhaps innocent in itself, but which, taken together, warranted further investigation, in the instant case the investigation of daytime robbery. Terry v Ohio (1968) 392 US 1, 20 L Ed 2d 889, 1968 US LEXIS 1345, 88 S Ct 1868.

The police "stop and frisk" practice is not outside the purview of the Fourth Amendment, which governs "seizures" of the person not eventuating in "arrests" in traditional terminology; whenever a police officer accosts an individual and restrains his freedom to walk away, he has "seized" that person, and a careful exploration of the outer surfaces of a person's clothing all over his body in an attempt to find weapons is a "search," a serious intrusion upon the sanctity of the person, which is not to be undertaken lightly. Terry v Ohio (1968) 392 US 1, 20 L Ed 2d 889, 1968 US LEXIS 1345, 88 S Ct 1868.

Not all personal intercourse between policemen and citizens involves "seizures" of persons within the meaning of the Fourth Amendment; only where the officer, by means of physical force or show of authority, has in some way restrained the liberty of a citizen is the inference that a "seizure" has occurred justifiable. While the police must, whenever practicable, obtain advance judicial approval of searches and seizures through the warrant procedure, and in most instances failure to comply with the warrant requirement can only be excused by exigent circumstances, the police "stop and frisk" procedure—necessarily swift action predicated upon the on-the-spot observations of the officer on the beat—cannot be subjected to the warrant procedure; instead, the conduct involved must be tested by the Fourth Amendment's general proscription against unreasonable searches and seizures. Terry v Ohio (1968) 392 US 1, 20 L Ed 2d 889, 1968 US LEXIS 1345, 88 S Ct 1868.

## § 2. Airport Travelers

Officers have adequate grounds for suspecting a person of carrying drugs and for temporarily detaining the suspect and his luggage at an airport where the officers discovered that the suspect was traveling under an assumed name and where the suspect's appearance, mannerisms, luggage, and actions fit the so-called "drug courier profile." Florida v Royer (1983) 460 US 491, 75 L Ed 2d 229, 1983 US LEXIS 151, 103 S Ct 1319.

## § 3. Anonymous Tips

Although an anonymous tip—unlike a tip from a known informant whose reputation can be assessed and who can be held responsible if the informant's allegations turn out to be fabricated—alone seldom demonstrates the informant's basis of knowledge or veracity, there are situations in which an anonymous tip, suitably corroborated, exhibits sufficient indicia of reliability, under the Fourth Amendment, to provide reasonable suspicion to make an investigatory stop of a person; however, an anonymous tip that a person is carrying a gun is not, without more, sufficient to justify a police officer's stop and frisk of that person. Florida v J.L. (2000) 529 US 266, 146 L Ed 2d 254, 2000 US LEXIS 2345, 120 S Ct 1375.

A police officer violates the Fourth Amendment by stopping and frisking an accused, when (1) an anonymous caller reports to the police that a young black male standing at a particular bus stop and wearing a plaid shirt is carrying a gun; (2) a police officer, in response to the tip, goes to the bus stop, where the officer sees the accused, who is a 15-year-old black male wearing a plaid shirt; and (3) apart from the tip, the officer has no reason to suspect the accused of illegal conduct, as (a) the officer does not see a firearm, and (b) the accused makes no threatening or otherwise unusual movements. Florida v J.L. (2000) 529 US 266, 146 L Ed 2d 254, 2000 US LEXIS 2345, 120 S Ct 1375.

As a general rule, something more than an anonymous tip is required to provide the reasonable suspicion necessary to make a valid investigatory stop of a person suspected of criminal activity; standing alone, an anonymous tip seldom demonstrates the informant's basis of knowledge or veracity, so as to warrant a man of reasonable caution in the belief that an investigatory stop is appropriate, given that (1) ordinary citizens generally do not provide extensive recitations of the basis of their everyday observations, and (2) the veracity of persons supplying anonymous tips is by hypothesis largely unknown and unknowable. Alabama v White (1990) 496 US 325, 110 L Ed 2d 301, 1990 US LEXIS 3053, 110 S Ct 2412.

An anonymous telephone tip received by a police officer that a person possesses cocaine, as corroborated by independent police work, exhibits sufficient indicia of reliability to provide reasonable suspicion for the police to make an investigatory stop of the person's station wagon, and therefore such stop does not violate the Fourth Amendment, where (1) the anonymous caller states that the person (a) will be leaving a certain apartment within an apartment complex at a particular time in a brown Plymouth station wagon with the right taillight lens broken, (b) will be going to a certain motel, and (c) will be in possession of cocaine, (2) after receiving the call, the officer and his partner proceed to the apartment complex, where (a) they see a brown Plymouth station wagon with a broken right taillight in the parking lot in front of the building which contains the apartment identified by the caller, and (b) they see the person leave the building, carrying nothing in her hands, and enter the station wagon, and (3) police officers (a) follow the vehicle as it drives for a distance of 4 miles, including several turns, along the most direct route to the motel which the caller has identified, and (b) arrange for a patrol unit to stop the vehicle just short of the motel. Alabama v White (1990) 496 US 325, 110 L Ed 2d 301, 1990 US LEXIS 3053, 110 S Ct 2412.

## § 4. Automobile Passengers

During a lawful routine traffic stop, an officer may conduct a pat-down search of the driver and any passengers upon reasonable suspicion that they may be armed and dangerous. In such cases, the officer is not constitutionally required to give the passenger an opportunity to depart the scene without first ensuring that, in so doing, the officer is not permitting a dangerous person to get behind him or her. Arizona v Johnson (2009) 555 US 323, 172 L Ed 2d 694, 2009 US LEXIS 868, 129 S Ct 781.

When police make a traffic stop, a passenger in the car, like the driver, is seized for Fourth Amendment purposes and so may challenge the stop's constitutionality. Brendlin v California (2007) 551 US 249, 168 L Ed 2d 132, 127 S Ct 2400, 2007 US LEXIS 7897.

Temporary detention of individuals during the stop of an automobile by the police, even if only for a brief period and for a limited purpose, constitutes a seizure of persons within the meaning of the Fourth Amendment; thus, an automobile stop is subject to the constitutional imperative that the stop not be unreasonable under the circumstances. Whren v United States (1996) 517 US 806, 135 L Ed 2d 89, 1996 US LEXIS 3720, 116 S Ct 1769.

A police officer's order to a motorist to get out of the car, issued after the vehicle was lawfully stopped for a traffic violation, is reasonable and thus is permissible under the Fourth Amendment even though the officer had no reason to suspect foul play from the particular driver at the time of the stop, since (1) the officer's interest in protection against an unsuspected assault by the driver and against accidental injury from passing traffic is both legitimate and weighty, (2) the intrusion into the driver's personal liberty occasioned by the order to get out of the car, after the car was lawfully stopped, is de minimis, not constituting a serious intrusion upon the sanctity of the person and hardly rising to the level of a petty indignity, and (3) thus, what is at most a mere inconvenience to the driver cannot prevail when balanced against legitimate concerns for the officer's safety. Pennsylvania v Mimms (1977) 434 US 106, 54 L Ed 2d 331, 1977 US LEXIS 157, 98 S Ct 330.

## § 5. Concomitant with Execution of Search Warrant

The initial detention of the occupant of a home subject to a valid search warrant, while the police execute the warrant to search his home for contraband, does not violate the occupant's Fourth Amendment right to be secure against an unreasonable seizure of his person, since the warrant, founded on probable cause where the evidence that the occupant's residence is harboring contraband is sufficient to persuade a judicial officer that an invasion of the occupant's privacy is justified, implicitly carries with it the limited authority to detain the occupants of the premises while a proper search is conducted; because it is lawful to require the occupant to re-enter and to remain in the house until evidence establishing probable cause to arrest him is found, his arrest and the search incident thereto, resulting in the discovery of heroin on his person, are constitutionally permissible. Michigan v Summers (1981) 452 US 692, 69 L Ed 2d 340, 1981 US LEXIS 118, 101 S Ct 2587.

## § 6. Duration

In assessing whether a detention is too long in duration to be justified as an investigative stop, it is appropriate to examine whether the police diligently pursued a means of investigation that was likely to confirm or dispel their suspicions quickly, during which time it was necessary to detain the defendant; the question is not simply whether some other alternative was available, but whether the police acted unreasonably in failing to recognize or to pursue it. United States v Sharpe (1985) 470 US 675, 84 L Ed 2d 605, 1985 US LEXIS 74, 105 S Ct 1568.

## § 7. Investigatory Stops

Terry stop, the request for identification, and the State's requirement of a response did not contravene the guarantees of the Fourth Amendment, because the request for identity had an immediate relation to the purpose, rationale, and practical demands of the Terry stop. Also, the request for identification was reasonably related in scope to the circumstances which justified the Terry stop. The Court also determined that defendant's conviction did not violate the Fifth Amendment's prohibition on compelled self-incrimination, because disclosure of his name presented no reasonable danger of incrimination. Hiibel v Sixth Judicial Dist. Court (2004) 542 US 177, 159 L Ed 2d 292, 2004 US LEXIS 4385, 124 S Ct 2451.

With respect to a federal border patrol agent's investigatory stop of a minivan in a remote area of southeastern Arizona, which stop resulted in a search of the minivan that found marijuana—when considering the totality of the circumstances and when giving due weight to the factual inferences drawn by the agent and by a Federal District Court judge in Arizona—the agent had a reasonable suspicion, which sufficed to make the stop reasonable within the meaning of the Fourth Amendment, to believe that the minivan's driver was engaged in illegal activity, where, among other factors, (1) the driver had set out from a border city along a little-traveled route used by smugglers; (2) the likelihood that the driver and his passengers, a woman and three children, were merely on a family picnic outing was diminished by the fact that the vehicle turned away from some known recreational areas. United States v Arvizu (2002) 534 US 266, 151 L Ed 2d 740, 2002 US LEXIS 490, 122 S Ct 744.

For purposes of determining the validity of an investigatory stop of a person's automobile under the Federal Constitution's Fourth Amendment, based on an anonymous caller's tip that the person is engaged in criminal activity, it is not unreasonable to conclude that (1) the independent corroboration by the police of significant aspects of the caller's predictions about some facts imparts some degree of reliability to the other allegations made by the caller, including the claim that the person is engaged in criminal activity, (2) if the anonymous tip contains a range of details relating not just to easily obtained facts and conditions existing at the time of the tip, but also to future actions of third parties ordinarily not easily predicted, someone with access to such information is likely also to have access to reliable information about the person's illegal activities, and (3) where significant aspects of the caller's predictions are verified, the caller is honest and at least well enough informed to justify the stop. Alabama v White (1990) 496 US 325, 110 L Ed 2d 301, 1990 US LEXIS 3053, 110 S Ct 2412.

A 20-minute detention of a driver reasonably suspected of transporting marijuana in a pickup truck meets the Fourth Amendment's standard of reasonableness for investigative stops, where the investigation is pursued in a diligent and reasonable manner by a drug enforcement agent and where the complained of delay is attributable almost entirely to the evasive actions of the suspect; accordingly, marijuana discovered in the course of the investigation is admissible in evidence in a subsequent prosecution. United States v Sharpe (1985) 470 US 675, 84 L Ed 2d 605, 1985 US LEXIS 74, 105 S Ct 1568.

The rule for evaluating the reasonableness under the Fourth Amendment of an investigative stop—whether the officer's action was justified at its inception, and whether it was reasonably related in scope to the circumstances which justified the interference in the first place—imposes no rigid time limits on such stops; although the brevity of an invasion of an individual's Fourth Amendment interests is an important factor in determining whether a seizure is so minimally intrusive as to be justifiable on reasonable suspicion, it is also necessary to consider the law enforcement purposes to be served by the stop as well as the time reasonably needed to effectuate those purposes. United States v Sharpe (1985) 470 US 675, 84 L Ed 2d 605, 1985 US LEXIS 74, 105 S Ct 1568.

An investigatory stop of a suspected robber by police officers in reliance on a "wanted flyer" issued by a neighboring police department is reasonable under the Fourth Amendment, and handguns uncovered in the course of the stop are admissible in evidence in a subsequent criminal prosecution, where the detention is brief, where a reasonable suspicion underlies and supports issuance of the flyer, and where the stop is reasonable in objective reliance on the flyer and is not significantly more intrusive than a stop that the issuing department would have been permitted to make. United States v Hensley (1985) 469 US 221, 83 L Ed 2d 604, 1985 US LEXIS 34, 105 S Ct 675.

### § 8. Pedestrians

With respect to the prohibition under the Federal Constitution's Fourth Amendment against unreasonable searches and seizures, when a police officer, without reasonable suspicion or probable cause, approaches an individual, any refusal to cooperate, without more, does not furnish the minimal level of objective justification needed for a detention or seizure; however, unprovoked flight is the opposite of the going about one's business that the United States Supreme Court has held the individual has a right to do; although flight is not necessarily indicative of ongoing criminal activity, this fact does not establish a Fourth Amendment violation by officers who, when confronted with such flight, stop the fugitive and investigate further. Illinois v Wardlow (2000) 528 US 119, 145 L Ed 2d 570, 2000 US LEXIS 504, 120 S Ct 673.

A police officer does not violate the Federal Constitution's Fourth Amendment prohibition against unreasonable searches and seizures when the officer stops an accused after the accused flees upon seeing a police caravan patrolling an area known for heavy narcotics trafficking, where the accused is convicted of unlawful use of the handgun that is discovered during a pat-down search immediately following the stop. Illinois v Wardlow (2000) 528 US 119, 145 L Ed 2d 570, 2000 US LEXIS 504, 120 S Ct 673.

The conduct of police officers in accelerating a marked patrol car to catch up with a man who ran around a street corner upon seeing the patrol car's approach, followed by the car's short drive alongside the man until he discarded packets—which were later found to contain illegal drugs—and then shortly stopped running, did not constitute a seizure within the meaning of the Federal Constitution's Fourth Amendment, since such conduct—where the record in the case did not reflect that the police activated a siren or flashers, commanded the man to halt, displayed any weapons, or operated the car in an aggressive manner to block the man's course or otherwise control the direction or speed of his movement—was not so intimidating that it would have communicated to a reasonable person that he was not at liberty to ignore the police presence and go about his business. Michigan v Chesternut (1988) 486 US 567, 100 L Ed 2d 565, 1988 US LEXIS 2582, 108 S Ct 1975.

A state criminal statute that requires persons who loiter or wander on the streets to provide a credible and reliable identification and to account for their presence when requested by a peace officer under circumstances that would justify a valid stop is unconstitutionally vague on its face within the meaning of the due process clause of the Fourteenth Amendment because it encourages arbitrary enforcement by failing to clarify what is contemplated by the requirement that a suspect provide a credible and reliable identification. Kolender v Lawson (1983) 461 US 352, 75 L Ed 2d 903, 1983 US LEXIS 159, 103 S Ct 1855.

### § 9. Protective Search

When a police officer is justified in believing that the individual whose suspicious behavior the officer is investigating at close range is armed and presently dangerous to the officer or to others, the officer may, under the Federal Constitution's Fourth Amendment, conduct a patdown search to determine whether the person is in fact carrying a weapon; such protective search—permitted without a warrant and on the basis of reasonable suspicion less than probable cause—must be strictly limited to that which is necessary for the discovery of weapons which might be used to harm the officer or others nearby; if the protective search goes beyond what is necessary to determine if the suspect is armed, the search is no longer valid and its fruits will be suppressed. Minnesota v Dickerson (1993) 508 US 366, 124 L Ed 2d 334, 1993 US LEXIS 4018, 113 S Ct 2130.

The Fourth Amendment does not permit the seizure of a small plastic bag containing one fifth of one gram of crack cocaine, which was detected through a police officer's sense of touch during a protective patdown search of a person for weapons which was justified under Terry v Ohio (1968) 392 US 1, 20 L Ed 2d 889, 1968 US LEXIS 1345, 88 S Ct 1868, where (1) the officer determined that a small lump in the front pocket of the person's nylon jacket was contraband only after squeezing, sliding, and otherwise manipulating the contents of the pocket, which the officer already knew contained no weapon; and (2) because the officer's further search of the pocket was constitutionally invalid in that it was not authorized by Terry v Ohio or any other exception to the Fourth Amendment's warrant requirement, the seizure of the cocaine that followed likewise is unconstitutional. Minnesota v Dickerson (1993) 508 US 366, 124 L Ed 2d 334, 1993 US LEXIS 4018, 113 S Ct 2130.

Supreme Court

A protective search of the passenger compartment of an automobile, limited to those areas in which a weapon may be placed or hidden, is permissible during an investigative detention, even though there is no probable cause to arrest, if the police officer possesses a reasonable belief based on specific and articulable facts which, taken together with the rational inferences from those facts, reasonably warrant the officer in believing that the suspect is dangerous and the suspect may gain immediate control of weapons. Michigan v Long (1983) 463 US 1032, 77 L Ed 2d 1201, 1983 US LEXIS 7, 103 S Ct 3469.

### § 10. Reasonable Suspicion

While reasonable suspicion is a less demanding standard than probable cause and requires a showing considerably less than a preponderance of the evidence, the Federal Constitution's Fourth Amendment, which prohibits unreasonable searches and seizures, requires at least a minimal level of objective justification for making the stop; the officer must be able to articulate more than an inchoate and unparticularized suspicion or hunch of criminal activity. Illinois v Wardlow (2000) 528 US 119, 145 L Ed 2d 570, 2000 US LEXIS 504, 120 S Ct 673.

Where a police officer observes unusual conduct which leads the officer reasonably to conclude in light of the officer's experience that criminal activity may be afoot, the officer may, under the Fourth Amendment, briefly stop the suspicious person and make reasonable inquiries aimed at confirming or dispelling the officer's suspicions. Minnesota v Dickerson (1993) 508 US 366, 124 L Ed 2d 334, 1993 US LEXIS 4018, 113 S Ct 2130.

The standard of reasonable suspicion—satisfaction of which is necessary to justify an investigatory stop of a person, consistent with the Fourth Amendment—is less demanding than the probable cause standard for an arrest or for issuance of a search warrant under the Fourth Amendment, not only in the sense that reasonable suspicion can be established with information that is different in quantity or content than that required to establish probable cause, but also in the sense that reasonable suspicion can arise from information that is less reliable than that required to show probable cause; reasonable suspicion, like probable cause, is dependent upon both the content of information possessed by police and its degree of reliability; the quantity and the quality of information are considered in the totality of the circumstances that must be taken into account when evaluating whether there is reasonable suspicion; thus, if an informant's tip has a relatively low degree of reliability, more information will be required to establish the requisite quantum of suspicion than would be required if the tip were more reliable; a totality-of-the-circumstances approach applies in the reasonable suspicion context as well as in the probable cause context, the only difference being the level of suspicion that must be established. Alabama v White (1990) 496 US 325, 110 L Ed 2d 301, 1990 US LEXIS 3053, 110 S Ct 2412.

Some seizures involving detention of persons, while admittedly covered by the Fourth Amendment, constitute such limited intrusions on the personal security of those detained and are justified by such substantial law enforcement interests that they may be made on less than probable cause, so long as the police have an articulable basis for suspecting criminal activity. Michigan v Summers (1981) 452 US 692, 69 L Ed 2d 340, 1981 US LEXIS 118, 101 S Ct 2587.

In determining whether the Fourth Amendment was violated by a police officer's seizure of a person by way of stopping him for interrogation, the notions which underlie both the warrant procedure and the requirement of probable cause remain fully relevant; in order to assess the reasonableness of the police officer's conduct as a general proposition, it is necessary first to focus upon the governmental interest which allegedly justifies official intrusion upon the constitutionally protected interests of the private citizen, and in justifying the particular intrusion the police officer must be able to point to specific and articulable facts which, taken together with rational inferences from those facts, reasonably warrant that intrusion. Terry v Ohio (1968) 392 US 1, 20 L Ed 2d 889, 1968 US LEXIS 1345, 88 S Ct 1868.

## Search and Seizure

### § 1. In General

A warrantless entry by police into a home based on exigent circumstances (e.g. a belief that evidence is being destroyed) is reasonable when the police do not create the exigency by engaging or threatening to engage in conduct violating the Fourth Amendment. This is true even if it was reasonably foreseeable that the investigative tactics employed by the police would prompt the people inside the residence to destroy evidence. Thus, when police smelled an odor of marijuana coming from defendant's apartment, then knocked on the front door and identified themselves—lawful conduct under the Fourth Amendment—exigent circumstances still justified entry when they heard people moving about inside. "Occupants who choose not to stand on their constitutional rights but instead elect to attempt to destroy evidence have only themselves to blame for the warrantless exigent-circumstances search that may ensue." Kentucky v King (2011) 131 S Ct 1849, 179 L Ed 2d 865, 2011 US LEXIS 3541.

Use of a thermal-imaging device aimed at a private home from a public street to detect relative amounts of heat within the home constitutes a search within the meaning of the Fourth Amendment—and use of such imaging without a warrant is unlawful under the Fourth Amendment—notwithstanding that (1) the device detects only heat radiating from the external surface of the home, (2) the measurements made by the device merely provide the basis for inferences as to what is inside the home, and (3) the device does not detect private activities occurring in private areas. Kyllo v United States (2001) 533 US 27, 150 L Ed 2d 94, 2001 US LEXIS 4487, 121 S Ct 2038.

The exclusionary rule does not require suppression of evidence seized in violation of the Fourth Amendment where the erroneous information resulted from clerical errors of court employees. Arizona v Evans (1995) 514 US 1, 131 L Ed 2d 34, 1995 US LEXIS 1806, 115 S Ct 1185.

For purposes of the Fourth Amendment's protection against unreasonable seizures, the word "seizure" readily bears the meaning of a laying on of hands or application of physical force to restrain movement, even when it is ultimately unsuccessful, but there is no seizure when a police officer merely yells "Stop, in the name of the law!" at a fleeing form that continues to flee, and neither usage nor common-law tradition makes an attempted seizure a "seizure." California v Hodari D. (1991) 499 US 621, 113 L Ed 2d 690, 1991 US LEXIS 2397, 111 S Ct 1547.

A search which is reasonable at its inception may violate the Fourth Amendment by virtue of its intolerable intensity and scope; the scope of the search must be strictly tied to and justified by the circumstances which rendered its initiation permissible. Terry v Ohio (1968) 392 US 1, 20 L Ed 2d 889, 1968 US LEXIS 1345, 88 S Ct 1868.

A police officer "seizes" a person and subjects him to a "search" when the officer takes hold of the person and pats down the outer surfaces of his clothing; the decisive issue is whether at this point it is reasonable for the officer to interfere with the person's security, and in determining the reasonableness of the seizure and search, the court's inquiry is a dual one: whether the officer's action is justified at its inception, and whether it is reasonably related in scope to the circumstances justifying the interference in the first place. Terry v Ohio (1968) 392 US 1, 20 L Ed 2d 889, 1968 US LEXIS 1345, 88 S Ct 1868.

## § 2. Administrative Inspection

For purposes of the administrative-inspection exemption from the need for probable cause and a warrant under the Fourth Amendment guarantee against unreasonable searches and seizures, an "administrative inspection" is the inspection of business premises conducted by authorities responsible for enforcing a pervasive regulatory scheme—for example, the unannounced inspection of a mine for compliance with health and safety standards; the administrative-inspection exemption is not accorded to a search that is not made for the purpose of administrative regulation. Whren v United States (1996) 517 US 806, 135 L Ed 2d 89, 1996 US LEXIS 3720, 116 S Ct 1769.

## § 3. Automobiles, Generally

A dog sniff conducted during a concededly lawful traffic stop that reveals no information other than the location of a substance that no individual has any right to possess does not violate the Fourth Amendment. Illinois v Caballes (2005) 543 US 405, 160 L Ed 2d 842, 2005 US LEXIS 769, 125 S Ct 834.

Officer was allowed to search the passenger compartment of defendant's vehicle incident to the lawful custodial arrest of defendant as a recent occupant of the vehicle. The authority for the vehicle search was not limited to arrests of persons actually occupying vehicles at the time of initial contacts with officers, since the same interests in the safety of the officer and preservation of evidence applied to both occupants and recent occupants of a vehicle. Thornton v United States (2004) 541 US 615, 158 L Ed 2d 905, **2004** US LEXIS 3681, 124 S Ct 2127.

A highway patrol officer does not violate the Fourth Amendment right of a front seat automobile passenger to be free from unreasonable searches—where, after the officer stops the car for speeding and driving with a faulty brake light, the driver admits that the driver uses a hypodermic syringe, that the officer notices in the driver's shirt pocket, to take drugs—by searching the passenger's purse that the officer finds on the back seat. Wyoming v Houghton (1999) 526 US 295, 143 L Ed 2d 408, 1999 US LEXIS 2347, 119 S Ct 1297.

Police officers with probable cause to conduct a warrantless search of a car for contraband may search a passenger's personal belongings in the car that are capable of concealing contraband. Wyoming v Houghton (1999) 526 US 295, 143 L Ed 2d 408, 1999 US LEXIS 2347, 119 S Ct 1297.

Police officers making a routine traffic stop may (1) order out of a vehicle both the driver and any passengers, (2) perform a "patdown" of a driver and any passenger upon reasonable suspicion that they may be armed and dangerous, (3) conduct a "Terry patdown" of the passenger compartment of a vehicle upon reasonable suspicion that an occupant is dangerous and may gain immediate control of a weapon, and (4) even conduct a full search of the passenger compartment, including any containers therein, pursuant to a custodial arrest. Knowles v Iowa (1998) 525 US 113, 142 L Ed 2d 492, 1998 US LEXIS 8068, 119 S Ct 484.

The full search of an automobile, with neither the automobile driver's consent nor probable cause to conduct the search, by a police officer who stops the driver for speeding and issues the driver a citation rather than arresting the driver, as authorized by state statute, violates the Fourth Amendment. Knowles v Iowa (1998) 525 US 113, 142 L Ed 2d 492, 1998 US LEXIS 8068, 119 S Ct 484.

Consistent with the Federal Constitution's Fourth Amendment proscription of unreasonable seizures, a police officer making a traffic stop may order passengers to get out of the car pending completion of the stop. Maryland v Wilson (1997) 519 US 408, 137 L Ed 2d 41, 1997 US LEXIS 1271, 117 S Ct 882.

For purposes of the Fourth Amendment guarantee against unreasonable searches and seizures, a police officer is objectively justified in asking an accused to get out of a car where there was probable cause to stop the accused's car for speeding. Ohio v Robinette (1996) 519 US 33, 136 L Ed 2d 347, 1996 US LEXIS 6971, 117 S Ct 417.

The automobile exception to the Fourth Amendment's warrant requirement requires only that there be probable cause to conduct a search; if a vehicle is readily mobile and probable cause exists to believe that the vehicle contains contraband, then the Fourth Amendment permits police to search the vehicle. Pennsylvania v Labron (1996) 518 US 938, 135 L Ed 2d 1031, 1996 US LEXIS 4268, 116 S Ct 2485.

Police officers may, under the Fourth Amendment, conduct a warrantless search of a paper bag found in an automobile trunk where they have probable cause to believe the bag contains marijuana. California v Acevedo (1991) 500 US 565, 114 L Ed 2d 619, 1991 US LEXIS 3016, 111 S Ct 1982.

A police officer's stopping an automobile and detaining the driver in order to check the driver's license and the registration of the automobile constitute an unreasonable seizure under the Fourth and Fourteenth Amendments, where the police officer has no articulable and reasonable suspicion that a motorist is unlicensed or that an automobile is not registered, or that either the vehicle or an occupant is otherwise subject to seizure for violation of law, there being no justification for subjecting every occupant of every vehicle on the roads to a seizure at the unbridled discretion of law-enforcement officials on the basis of a state interest in promoting roadway safety. Delaware v Prouse (1979) 440 US 648, 59 L Ed 2d 660, 1979 US LEXIS 80, 99 S Ct 1391.

The rule that a police officer's stopping an automobile and detaining the driver in order to check his driver's license and the registration of the automobile constitute an unreasonable seizure under the Fourth Amendment when there is no articulable and reasonable suspicion that a motorist is unlicensed or that an automobile is not registered, or that either the vehicle or an occupant is otherwise subject to seizure for violation of law, does not preclude the state from developing methods for spot checks that involve less intrusion or that do not involve the unconstrained exercise of discretion, the questioning of all oncoming traffic at roadblock-type stops being one possible alternative. Delaware v Prouse (1979) 440 US 648, 59 L Ed 2d 660, 1979 US LEXIS 80, 99 S Ct 1391.

## § 4. Bus Passengers

The Federal Constitution's Fourth Amendment permits police officers to approach passengers on a bus at random to ask questions and to request their consent to searches, provided that a reasonable person would understand that he or she is free to refuse. Police officers do not need to advise bus passengers during these encounters of their right to refuse to cooperate. The proper inquiry in such cases—which inquiry necessitates a consideration of all the circumstances surrounding the encounter—is whether a reasonable person would feel free to decline the officers' requests or otherwise terminate the encounter. United States v Drayton (2002) 536 US 194, 153 L Ed 2d 242, 2002 US LEXIS 4420, 122 S Ct 2105.

For purposes of the Fourth Amendment, police officers who boarded a bus and began questioning passengers did not seize two passengers who were later arrested for possession of cocaine, where (1) the officers gave none of the passengers reason to believe that they were required to answer the officers' questions; (2) when one of the officers approached the two passengers, he displayed his badge but did not brandish a weapon or make any intimidating movements; (3) this officer (a) left the aisle free so that passengers could exit, and (b) spoke to passengers one by one and in a polite, quiet voice; (4) there were thus ample grounds to conclude there was nothing coercive or confrontational about the encounter between this officer and the two passengers; and (5) the other officer was positioned at the front of the bus, but he (a) did nothing to intimidate passengers, (b) said nothing to suggest that people could not exit, and (c) left the aisle clear. United States v Drayton (2002) 536 US 194, 153 L Ed 2d 242, 2002 US LEXIS 4420, 122 S Ct 2105.

A border patrol agent's physical manipulation of a bus passenger's carry-on luggage violates the Fourth Amendment's prohibition against unreasonable searches, as (1) the accused's luggage is an effect protected by the Fourth

Amendment; (2) cases in which the Supreme Court has held that matters open to public observation were not protected by the Fourth Amendment have involved only visual, as opposed to tactile, observation; (3) physically invasive inspection is more intrusive than purely visual inspection; (4) the accused exhibits an actual expectation of privacy by using an opaque bag and placing that bag directly above his seat; and (5) the accused's expectation of privacy is one that society is prepared to recognize as reasonable. Bond v United States (2000) 529 US 334, 146 L Ed 2d 365, 2000 US LEXIS 2520, 120 S Ct 1462.

A state's highest court errs in adopting a per se rule that an impermissible seizure results when police mount a drug search on buses during scheduled stops and question boarded passengers without articulable reasons for doing so, thereby obtaining consent to search the passengers' luggage. Florida v Bostick (1991) 501 US 429, 115 L Ed 2d 389, 1991 US LEXIS 3625, 111 S Ct 2382.

## § 5. Commercial Enterprises

With respect to the Fourth Amendment's prohibition against unreasonable searches and seizures, an owner or operator of a business has a reasonable expectation of privacy in commercial property which is different from, and less than, the expectation of privacy in an individual's home; this expectation is particularly attenuated in commercial property employed in "closely regulated" industries; certain industries have such a history of government oversight that no reasonable expectation of privacy can exist for a proprietor over the stock of such an enterprise. New York v Burger (1987) 482 US 691, 96 L Ed 2d 601, 1987 US LEXIS 2725, 107 S Ct 2636.

A warrantless inspection of a pervasively regulated business will be deemed to be reasonable, for purposes of the Fourth Amendment's prohibition against unreasonable searches and seizures, as long as (1) there is a substantial government interest that informs the regulatory scheme pursuant to which the inspection is made, (2) the warrantless inspection is necessary to further the regulatory scheme, and (3) the statute's inspection program, in terms of the certainty and regularity of its application, provides a constitutionally adequate substitute for a warrant—it must (a) advise the owner of the commercial premises that the property will be subject to periodic inspections undertaken for specific purposes, and (b) limit the discretion of the inspecting officers by carefully limiting the inspection in time, place, and scope. New York v Burger (1987) 482 US 691, 96 L Ed 2d 601, 1987 US LEXIS 2725, 107 S Ct 2636.

## § 6. Consent

A warrantless, suspicionless search of a parolee did not offend the Fourth Amendment when the parolee had agreed unambiguously to such searches at any time as a condition of release. Samson v California (2006) 547 US 843, 165 L Ed 2d 250, 126 S Ct 2193, 2006 US LEXIS 4885.

When one co-occupant of a residence consents to a search, but another co-occupant is also physically present and expressly objects to the search, then any subsequent search and seizure is unreasonable and invalid as to the objecting party. Georgia v Randolph (2006) 547 US 103, 164 L Ed 2d 208, 126 S Ct 1515, 2006 US LEXIS 2498.

Since a co-tenant wishing to open the door to a third party has no recognized authority in law or social practice to prevail over a present and objecting co-tenant, his disputed invitation, without more, gives a **police** officer no better claim to reasonableness in entering than the officer would have in the absence of any consent at all. Accordingly, in the balancing of competing individual and governmental interests entailed by the bar to unreasonable searches, the cooperative occupant's invitation adds nothing to the government's side to counter the force of an objecting individual's claim to security against the government's intrusion into his dwelling place. Georgia v Randolph (2006) 547 US 103, 164 L Ed 2d 208, 2006 US LEXIS 2498.

A physically present inhabitant's express refusal of consent to a **police** search is dispositive as to him, regardless of the consent of a fellow occupant. Thus, in the circumstances here at issue, a physically present co-occupant's stated refusal to permit entry renders warrantless entry and search unreasonable and invalid as to him. Georgia v Randolph (2006) 547 US 103, 164 L Ed 2d 208, 2006 US LEXIS 2498.

Two bus passengers' consent to a suspicionless search by a police officer was voluntary under the totality of the circumstances—and thus the passengers were not subjected to an unreasonable search for purposes of the Federal Constitution's Fourth Amendment—notwithstanding that the officer did not inform the passengers of their right to refuse the search, where (1) under the circumstances, the passengers had not been seized for Fourth Amendment purposes; (2) nothing that the officer said indicated a command to consent to the search; (3) when the passengers informed the officer that they had a bag on the bus, the officer asked for their permission to check the bag; (4) when the officer requested to search the passengers' persons, he asked first if they objected, thus indicating to a reasonable person that he or she was free to refuse; and (5) even after arresting one of the passengers, the officer provided the second passenger with no indication that he was required to consent to a search. United States v Drayton (2002) 536 US 194, 153 L Ed 2d 242, 2002 US LEXIS 4420, 122 S Ct 2105.

A warrantless search of a probationer's apartment was reasonable under the totality of the circumstances, for purposes of the Fourth Amendment, where (1) as a condition of probation for a drug offense, the probationer had signed an order stating that he would submit to a search at any time, with or without a warrant or reasonable cause, by any probation officer or law enforcement officer; (2) the order's search condition did not mention anything about the purpose of such a search; and (3) the police detective who conducted the search had reasonable suspicion to believe that the probationer was involved with incendiary materials. United States v Knights (2001) 534 US 112, 151 L Ed 2d 497, 2001 US LEXIS 10950, 122 S Ct 587.

The Federal Constitution's Fourth Amendment does not require that a lawfully seized defendant be advised that the defendant is "free to go" before the defendant's consent to search will be recognized as voluntary, because (1) the Fourth Amendment test for a valid consent to search is that the consent be voluntary; (2) voluntariness is a question of fact to be determined from all the circumstances; (3) while knowledge of the right to refuse consent is one factor to be taken into account, the government need not establish such knowledge as the sine qua non of an effective consent; and (4) just as it would be thoroughly impractical to impose on the normal consent search the detailed requirements of an effective warning, so too would it be unrealistic to require police officers to always inform detainees that they are free to go before a consent to search may be deemed voluntary. Ohio v Robinette (1996) 519 US 33, 136 L Ed 2d 347, 1996 US LEXIS 6971, 117 S Ct 417.

For the purposes of the Federal Constitution's Fourth Amendment, a bus passenger's decision to cooperate with law enforcement officers who request the passenger's consent to search his or her luggage authorizes the officers to conduct a search without first obtaining a warrant only if the cooperation is voluntary; "consent" that is the product of official intimidation or harassment is not consent at all, and citizens do not forfeit their constitutional rights when they are coerced to comply with a request that they would prefer to refuse. Florida v Bostick (1991) 501 US 429, 115 L Ed 2d 389, 1991 US LEXIS 3625, 111 S Ct 2382.

A seizure does not occur, for the purposes of the Federal Constitution's Fourth Amendment, simply because police officers approach an individual, ask a few questions, ask to examine the individual's identification, and request consent to search his or her luggage—so long as the officers do not convey a message that compliance with their requests is required; so long as a reasonable person would feel free to disregard the police and go about his business, the encounter is consensual and no reasonable suspicion is required; and the encounter is not a seizure and will not trigger Fourth Amendment scrutiny unless it loses its consensual nature. Florida v Bostick (1991) 501 US 429, 115 L Ed 2d 389, 1991 US LEXIS 3625, 111 S Ct 2382.

For purposes of determining whether consent to enter a person's home has been obtained from a third party who possesses "common authority" over the premises—so as to validate a search of the premises under the Fourth Amendment—the requisite common authority rests on mutual use of the property by persons generally having joint access or control for most purposes; the burden of establishing such common authority rests upon the state. Illinois v Rodriguez (1990) 497 US 177, 111 L Ed 2d 148, 1990 US LEXIS 3295, 110 S Ct 2793.

A warrantless entry by law enforcement officers onto a person's premises does not violate the proscription of unreasonable searches and seizures under the Fourth Amendment, where such entry is based upon the consent of a third party whom the officers, at the time of the entry, reasonably believe to possess common authority over the premises, but who in fact does not possess such authority; whether the basis for a person's authority to consent to a search exists is the sort of recurring factual question to which law enforcement officials must be expected to apply their judgment; determination of a person's consent to enter premises must be judged against an objective standard of whether the facts available to the officer at the moment warrant a person of reasonable caution in the belief that the consenting party has authority over the premises. Illinois v Rodriguez (1990) 497 US 177, 111 L Ed 2d 148, 1990 US LEXIS 3295, 110 S Ct 2793.

A suspect's consent to the search of his two suitcases is tainted by an illegal detention and is ineffective to justify the search, where (1) the suspect was approached at an airport by detectives who asked for the suspect's airline ticket and driver's license, (2) the detectives, without returning the ticket and license, asked the suspect to accompany them to a small room, (3) the detectives retrieved the suspect's luggage from the airline without the suspect's consent, (4) the suspect produced a key and unlocked one of the suitcases, in which drugs were found, and did not object when the detectives pried open the second suitcase in which more marijuana was found, and (5) the suspect was then told that he was under arrest. Florida v Royer (1983) 460 US 491, 75 L Ed 2d 229, 1983 US LEXIS 151, 103 S Ct 1319.

## § 7. Inventory Search

A state's highest court erred in upholding a state trial court's grant of an accused's motion to suppress some drug-related evidence obtained by a police officer from an inventory search of the accused's car—after the officer had (1) stopped the accused for speeding and for having an improperly tinted windshield, (2) noticed a rusted roofing hatchet on the floorboard of the accused's car, and (3) arrested the accused for speeding, some other traffic violations, and carrying a weapon (the hatchet)—where the state's highest court erroneously held that (1) the arrest, although supported by probable cause, nonetheless violated the Fourth Amendment because the arresting officer had an improper subjective motivation for making the stop; and alternatively (2) the Federal Constitution could be interpreted by the state's highest court to provide greater protection than the Supreme Court's own federal constitutional precedents provided. Arkansas v Sullivan (2001) 532 US 769, 149 L Ed 2d 994, 2001 US LEXIS 4118, 121 S Ct 1876.

For purposes of the inventory-search exemption from the need for probable cause and a warrant under the Federal Constitution's Fourth Amendment guarantee against unreasonable searches and seizures, an "inventory search" is the search of property lawfully seized and detained, in order (1) to insure that it is harmless, (2) to secure valuable items, such as might be kept in a towed car, and (3) to protect against false claims of loss or damage; the inventory-search exemption is not accorded to a search that is not made for the purpose of inventory. Whren v United States (1996) 517 US 806, 135 L Ed 2d 89, 1996 US LEXIS 3720, 116 S Ct 1769.

Under the Federal Constitution's Fourth Amendment, an inventory search must not be a ruse for a general rummaging by the police in order to discover incriminating evidence; the policy or practice governing inventory searches should be designed to produce an inventory, and an individual police officer must not be allowed so much latitude that inventory searches are turned into a purposeful and general means of discovering evidence of crime. Florida v Wells (1990) 495 US 1, 109 L Ed 2d 1, 1990 US LEXIS 2035, 110 S Ct 1632.

An inventory search of an accused's impounded car is not sufficiently regulated to satisfy the Fourth Amendment, and thus marijuana, which is discovered when employees of an impoundment facility—at the direction of a state highway patrol trooper—force open a locked suitcase found in the car's trunk, is properly suppressed, where the highway patrol has no policy whatever with respect to the opening of closed containers encountered during an inventory search. Florida v Wells (1990) 495 US 1, 109 L Ed 2d 1, 1990 US LEXIS 2035, 110 S Ct 1632.

The Fourth Amendment is not violated where the police, following an individual's arrest for driving while under the influence of alcohol, impound the individual's van and, while inventorying the van's contents without a search warrant, open a sealed backpack and certain containers therein and discover narcotics which are used as evidence in a subsequent prosecution of the individual, given (1) that there was no showing that the police, who followed standardized procedures, acted in bad faith or for the sole purpose of investigation; (2) that the police were potentially responsible for the property taken into their custody; (3) that local police procedures governing inventory searches mandated the opening of closed containers and the listing of their contents; and (4) that those procedures established standardized criteria to govern an officer's choice between impounding a vehicle and simply parking and locking it. Colorado v Bertine (1987) 479 US 367, 93 L Ed 2d 739, 1987 US LEXIS 286, 107 S Ct 738.

Consistent with the Fourth Amendment, it is reasonable for police to search the personal effects of a person under lawful arrest as part of the routine administrative procedure at a police station incident to booking and jailing the suspect. Illinois v Lafayette (1983) 462 US 640, 77 L Ed 2d 65, 1983 US LEXIS 71, 103 S Ct 2605.

The Fourth Amendment's prohibition of unreasonable search and seizures is not violated by a local police warrantless routine inventory search, following standard procedures, of an accused's automobile impounded for violations of municipal parking ordinances, where (1) the police standard procedure was not a pretext concealing an investigatory police motive, and (2) the inventory, including matters in the unlocked glove compartment, was not unreasonable in scope. South Dakota v Opperman (1976) 428 US 364, 49 L Ed 2d 1000, 1976 US LEXIS 15, 96 S Ct 3092.

## § 8. Knock and Announce

Evidence seized pursuant to an otherwise valid search warrant is not subject to suppression under the Exclusionary Rule solely because the officers executing the warrant entered in violation of the knock-and-announce requirement. The deterrence of knock-and-announce violations is not worth the "substantial social costs" of the Exclusionary Rule. However, officers who violate the rule still face the threat of possible civil remedies (such as a lawsuit under 42 U.S.C. §1983) or internal discipline by their employer. Hudson v Michigan (2006) 547 US 586, 165 L Ed 2d 56, 126 S Ct 2159, 2006 US LEXIS 4677.

Violation of the "knock-and-announce" rule did not require suppression of evidence found in a search. Hudson v Michigan (2006) 547 US 586, 165 L Ed 2d 56, 126 S Ct 2159, 2006 US LEXIS 4677

For purposes of determining whether some **police** officers' warrantless entry of a residence without first knocking on the front door was valid under the Federal Constitution's Fourth Amendment, the entry was reasonable, for: (1) The officers were responding at 3 a.m. to complaints about a loud party; (2) As the officers approached the house, they heard from within "an altercation occurring, some kind of a fight," "thumping and crashing," and people yelling "stop, stop" and "get off me."; and (3) It was obvious that knocking on the front door would have been futile, for (a) the noise seemed to be coming from the back of the house; (b) after looking in the front window and seeing nothing, the officers proceeded around back to investigate further; (c) they found two juveniles drinking beer in the backyard; and (d) from there, the officers could see that a fracas was taking place in the kitchen, where (i) a juvenile, fists clenched, was being held back by several adults, and (ii) as the officers watched, the juvenile broke free and stuck one of the adults in the face, sending the adult to the sink spitting blood. **Police** may enter a home without a warrant when they have an objectively reasonable basis for believing that an occupant is seriously injured or imminently threatened with such injury. Brigham City v Stuart (2006) 547 US 398, 164 L Ed 2d 650, 2006 US LEXIS 4155

A 15-to-20 second wait by federal and local law-enforcement officers—who (1) had a warrant to search for cocaine in an accused's two-bedroom apartment, (2) called out "police search warrant," and (3) knocked on the apartment's front door—before, having received no response, breaking open the door with a battering ram satisfied the guarantee in the Federal **Constitution's** Fourth Amendment against unreasonable searches and seizures, even without refusal of admittance, as: (1) after 15 or 20 seconds without a response, the officers could fairly have suspected that cocaine would be gone if the officers were reticent any longer. Federal Courts of Appeals had routinely held similar wait times to be reasonable in drug cases with similar facts including easily disposable evidence, and some courts had found even shorter waits to be reasonable enough; (2) the fact that the accused had been in the shower and had not heard the officers was not to the point, for, as for the shower (a) it was enough to say that the facts known to the officers were what counted in judging reasonable waiting time; and (b) there was no indication that the officers had known that the accused was in the shower and thus unaware of an impending search that the accused would otherwise have tried to frustrate; (3) the accused's claim that it might have taken the accused longer than 20 seconds to answer the door if the accused had heard the knock and headed straight for the door also was not to the point, for (a) the officers claimed exigent need to enter; and (b) the crucial fact in examining their actions was not time to reach the door, but the particular exigency claimed; (4) on the record in the case at hand, what mattered was the opportunity to get rid of cocaine, which a prudent dealer would have kept near a commode or kitchen sink; (5) the significant circumstances included (a) the arrival of the officers during the day, when anyone inside probably would have been up and around; and (b) the sufficiency of to 20 seconds for getting to the bathroom or the kitchen to start flushing the cocaine down the drain; (6) 15 to 20 seconds did not seem an unrealistic guess about the time someone would need to get in a position to rid one's quarters of cocaine; and (7) once the exigency had matured, the officers were not bound to learn anything more or wait any longer before going in, even though their entry entailed some harm to the building, for (a) a prior United States Supreme Court case had held that the exigent need of law enforcement trumped a resident's interest in avoiding all property damage; and (b) there was no reason to treat a post-knock exigency differently from the no-knock counterpart that had been involved in the prior case. United States v Banks (2003) 540 US 31, 157 L Ed 2d 343, **2003** US LEXIS 8966, 124 S Ct 521.

The Federal Constitution's Fourth Amendment does not permit a blanket exception for felony drug investigations to the requirement that police officers entering a dwelling must knock on the door and announce their identity and purpose before attempting forcible entry. Richards v Wisconsin (1997) 520 US 385, 137 L Ed 2d 615, 1997 US LEXIS 2794, 117 S Ct 1416.

The decision by some police officers—in executing a warrant in a felony drug investigation to search an individual's hotel room for drugs and related paraphernalia—not to knock and announce the officers' identity and purpose is reasonable under the circumstances and, hence, does not violate the Federal Constitution's Fourth Amendment, in that the officers have a reasonable suspicion that the individual may destroy evidence if given further opportunity to do so, where (1) the individual, after opening the door to the room after one of the officers states that the officer is a maintenance man, quickly slams the door when the individual sees that one of the officers is in a police uniform, and (2) the drugs are of an easily disposable nature. Richards v Wisconsin (1997) 520 US 385, 137 L Ed 2d 615, 1997 US LEXIS 2794, 117 S Ct 1416.

In order to justify a "no-knock" entry under the Federal Constitution's Fourth Amendment, the police must have a reasonable suspicion that knocking and announcing their presence, under the particular circumstances, would (1) be dangerous or futile, or (2) inhibit the effective investigation of the crime by, for example, allowing the destruction of evidence. Richards v Wisconsin (1997) 520 US 385, 137 L Ed 2d 615, 1997 US LEXIS 2794, 117 S Ct 1416.

### § 9. Mobile Homes

Law enforcement agents do not violate the Fourth Amendment when they conduct a warrantless search, based on probable cause, of a fully mobile motor home located in a public place, even though the vehicle possesses some, if not many of the attributes of a home. California v Carney (1985) 471 US 386, 85 L Ed 2d 406, 1985 US LEXIS 8, 105 S Ct 2066.

Among the factors that might be relevant in determining whether the vehicle exception to the warrant requirement is applicable to a motor home that is situated in a way or place that objectively indicates that it is being used as a residence are its location, whether the vehicle is readily mobile or instead, for instance, elevated on blocks, whether the vehicle is licensed, whether it is connected to utilities, and whether it has convenient access to a public road. California v Carney (1985) 471 US 386, 85 L Ed 2d 406, 1985 US LEXIS 8, 105 S Ct 2066.

A warrantless search by law enforcement agents of a fully mobile motor home located in a public place is not unreasonable, not withstanding the motor home's possible use as a dwelling place, where the agents have probable cause to enter and search the motor home based on direct and uncontradicted evidence that the occupant of the motor home was distributing a controlled substance from the motor home. California v Carney (1985) 471 US 386, 85 L Ed 2d 406, 1985 US LEXIS 8, 105 S Ct 2066.

### § 10. Plain View Doctrine

Under the "plain-view" doctrine, police officers may seize an object without a warrant if (1) the officers are lawfully in a position from which they view the object, (2) the object's incriminating character is immediately apparent, and (3) the officers have a lawful right of access to the object; if contraband is left in open view and is observed by a police officer from a lawful vantage point, there has been no invasion of a legitimate expectation of privacy and thus no "search" within the meaning of the Federal Constitution's Fourth Amendment, or at least no search independent of the initial intrusion that gave the officers their vantage point; however, the plain-view doctrine cannot justify the seizure of an object in plain view if the police lack probable cause to believe that the object is contraband without conducting some further search of the object, that is, if its incriminating character is not immediately apparent. Minnesota v Dickerson (1993) 508 US 366, 124 L Ed 2d 334, 1993 US LEXIS 4018, 113 S Ct 2130.

It is important to distinguish "plain view," as used to justify seizure of an object, from an officer's mere observation of an item left in plain view; whereas the latter generally involves no Fourth Amendment search, the former generally implicates the Fourth Amendment's limitations upon seizures of personal property; if an article is already in plain view, neither its observation nor its seizure would involve any invasion of privacy, but a seizure of the article would invade the owner's possessory interest. Horton v California (1990) 496 US 128, 110 L Ed 2d 112, 1990 US LEXIS 2937, 110 S Ct 2301.

It is an essential predicate to any valid warrantless seizure of incriminating evidence under the "plain view" doctrine that the police officer did not violate the Fourth Amendment in arriving at the place from which the evidence could be plainly viewed; there are, moreover, two additional conditions that must be satisfied: first, not only must the item be in plain view, but also its incriminating character must be immediately apparent; second, not only must the officer be lawfully located in a place from which the object can be plainly seen, but also he or she must have a lawful right of access to the object itself. Horton v California (1990) 496 US 128, 110 L Ed 2d 112, 1990 US LEXIS 2937, 110 S Ct 2301.

For purposes of the "plain view" doctrine, a police officer's seizure without a warrant of a balloon, later found to contain heroin, at a routine driver's license checkpoint, after the officer saw the balloon fall from the driver's hand to his seat, and saw several small plastic vials, quantities of loose white powder and an open bag of party balloons in the glove compartment, does not violate the Fourth Amendment, where the police officer had probable cause to believe that the balloon contained an illegal substance, even though the substance itself was not visible. Texas v Brown (1983) 460 US 730, 75 L Ed 2d 502, 1983 US LEXIS 143, 103 S Ct 1535.

### § 11. Probable Cause

In the context of safety and administrative regulations, a search unsupported by probable cause may sometimes be reasonable for Fourth Amendment purposes when special needs, beyond the normal need for law enforcement, make the warrant and probable-cause requirement impracticable. Board of Education v Earls (2002) 536 US 822, 153 L Ed 2d 735, 2002 US LEXIS 4882, 122 S Ct 2559.

The fact that a police officer does not have the state of mind which is hypothecated by the reasons which provide the legal justification for the officer's action does not invalidate the action under the Fourth Amendment, as long as the circumstances, viewed objectively, justify that action; subjective intentions play no role in ordinary, probable-cause analysis under the Fourth Amendment. Ohio v Robinette (1996) 519 US 33, 136 L Ed 2d 347, 1996 US LEXIS 6971, 117 S Ct 417.

Search warrants need only be supported by probable cause, which demands no more than a proper assessment of probabilities in particular factual contexts. Illinois v Rodriguez (1990) 497 US 177, 111 L Ed 2d 148, 1990 US LEXIS 3295, 110 S Ct 2793.

Probable cause is a fluid concept—turning on the assessment of probabilities in particular contexts—not readily, or even usefully, reduced to a neat set of rules; informant's tips vary in their value and reliability and rigid legal rules are ill-suited to an area of such diversity. Illinois v Gates (1983) 462 US 213, 76 L Ed 2d 527, 1983 US LEXIS 54, 103 S Ct 2317.

Police officers with probable cause to search an automobile on the scene where it was stopped may constitutionally do so later at the station house without first obtaining a warrant, where the probable cause factor that developed on the scene still obtains at the station house. Texas v White (1975) 423 US 67, 46 L Ed 2d 209, 1975 US LEXIS 98, 96 S Ct 304, reh den 423 US 1081, 47 L Ed 2d 91, 96 S Ct 869.

For purposes of the automobile exception to the search warrant requirement of the Fourth Amendment, a probable cause determination must be based on objective facts that would justify the issuance of a warrant by a magistrate and not merely on the subjective good faith of the police officers involved, since good faith does not constitute probable cause, but rather must be grounded on facts within the officer's knowledge which, within a court's judgment, would make his faith reasonable. United States v Ross (1982) 456 US 798, 72 L Ed 2d 572, 1982 US LEXIS 18, 102 S Ct 2157.

Police officers, though having no warrant, have probable cause to stop a light blue compact station wagon carrying four men, to arrest the occupants, one of whom was wearing a green sweater and one of whom had a trench coat with him in the automobile, and to search the automobile for guns and stolen money, and probable cause for such a search still exists after the automobile is taken to a police station, where (1) a robbery victim had told the police that one of the men who robbed him was wearing a green sweater and the other was wearing a trench coat, and (2) other witnesses had told the police that a blue compact station wagon was at the scene of the robbery, that four men were in the station wagon, and that one of them was wearing a green sweater. Chambers v Maroney (1970) 399 US 42, 26 L Ed 2d 419, 1970 US LEXIS 19, 90 S Ct 1975, reh den 400 US 856, 27 L Ed 2d 94, 91 S Ct 23.

## § 12. Reasonableness

The touchstone of the Federal Constitution's Fourth Amendment is reasonableness, and the reasonableness of a search is determined by assessing, on the one hand, the degree to which the search intrudes upon an individual's privacy and, on the other, the degree to which the search is needed for the promotion of legitimate governmental interests. United States v Knights (2001) 534 US 112, 151 L Ed 2d 497, 2001 US LEXIS 10950, 122 S Ct 587.

Under the Federal Constitution's Fourth Amendment, the ultimate measure of the constitutionality of a governmental search is reasonableness; at least in a case involving the type of search for which there was no clear practice, either approving or disapproving the type of search, at the time the Fourth Amendment was adopted, whether a particular search meets the reasonableness standard is judged by balancing the search's intrusion on the individual's Fourth Amendment interests against the search's promotion of legitimate governmental interests. Vernonia Sch. Dist. 47J v Acton (1995) 515 US 646, 132 L Ed 2d 564, 1995 US LEXIS 4275, 115 S Ct 2386.

The touchstone of the United States Supreme Court's analysis of the legality of a search and seizure under the Fourth Amendment is always the reasonableness in all the circumstances of the particular governmental invasion of a citizen's personal security; reasonableness depends on a balance between the public interest and the individual's right to personal security free from arbitrary interference by law officers. Pennsylvania v Mimms (1977) 434 US 106, 54 L Ed 2d 331, 1977 US LEXIS 157, 98 S Ct 330.

The scheme of the Fourth Amendment becomes meaningful only when it is assured that at some point the conduct of those charged with enforcing the laws can be subjected to the more detached, neutral scrutiny of a judge who must evaluate the reasonableness of a particular search or seizure in the light of the particular circumstances; in making that assessment it is imperative that the facts be judged against an objective standard, namely, whether the facts available to the officer at the moment of the seizure or the search warrant a man of reasonable caution in the belief that the action taken was appropriate, and anything less would invite intrusions upon constitutionally guaranteed rights based on nothing more substantial than irrelevant inarticulate hunches. Terry v Ohio (1968) 392 US 1, 20 L Ed 2d 889, 1968 US LEXIS 1345, 88 S Ct 1868.

There is no ready test for determining reasonableness of a search or seizure other than by balancing the need to search or seize against the invasion which the search or seizure entails. Terry v Ohio (1968) 392 US 1, 20 L Ed 2d 889, 1968 US LEXIS 1345, 88 S Ct 1868.

## § 13. Search Warrant

Deputies serving a search warrant relating to crimes committed by four African-American suspects did not violate the Fourth Amendment by detaining two Caucasian residents of the home (who were ultimately determined to be unconnected to the crimes) found in bed, even though they were of a different race than the suspects. When the deputies ordered the couple from their bed, they had no way of knowing whether or not the African-American suspects were elsewhere in the house-"[t]he presence of some Caucasians in the residence did not eliminate the possibility that the suspects lived there as well." It is not uncommon for people of different races to live together-"[j]ust as people of different races live and work together, so too might they engage in joint criminal activity." The deputies' actions were necessary to ensure their safety. Los Angeles County v Rettele (2007) 550 US 609, 167 L Ed 2d 974, 127 S Ct 1989, 2007 US LEXIS 5900.

An anticipatory warrant is a warrant based upon a showing of probable cause that at some future time (but not presently) certain evidence of crime will be located at a specified place. Anticipatory warrants are no different in principle form from ordinary warrants and are therefore constitutional. To obtain an anticipatory warrant, the supporting affidavit must provide facts establishing a fair probability that evidence of a crime or contraband will be found at the place to be searched if the triggering condition occurs, and probable cause to believe that the triggering condition will occur. The Fourth Amendment does not require that the triggering condition be set forth in the warrant itself. United States v Grubbs (2006) 547 US 90, 164 L Ed 2d 195, 126 S Ct 1494, 2006 US LEXIS 2496.

Warrant was invalid, and the search was clearly unreasonable, in violation of the Fourth Amendment, for among other matters, (a) the warrant failed altogether to comply with the Fourth Amendment's unambiguous requirement that a warrant particularly describe the persons or things to be seized; (b) the fact that the application for the warrant adequately described the things to be seized did not save the warrant from its facial invalidity; (c) by not describing the items to be seized at all, the warrant was so obviously deficient that the search had to be regarded as "warrantless"; (d) searches and seizures inside a home without a warrant were presumptively unreasonable; and (e) the presumptive rule against warrantless searches applied with equal force to searches whose only defect was a lack of particularity in the warrant. And, in such circumstances, the agent was not entitled to qualified immunity, for among other matters, (a) no reasonable officer could have believed that a warrant that plainly did not comply with the Fourth Amendment's particularity requirement was valid; and (b) because the agent had prepared the invalid warrant, he could not properly argue that he reasonably had relied on the Magistrate's assurance that the warrant contained an adequate description of the things to be seized. Groh v Ramirez (2004) 540 US 551, 157 L Ed 2d 1068, **2004** US LEXIS 1624, 124 S Ct 1284.

Under the Federal Constitution's Fourth Amendment, police officers need either a warrant, or probable cause plus exigent circumstances, in order to make a lawful entry into a home. Thus, a state court erred in failing to assess whether exigent circumstances were present when some police officers entered an individual's home without either an arrest warrant or a search warrant, arrested him, and searched him. Exigent circumstances were required to justify the officers' conduct even if, as the state court ruled, the officers had probable cause to arrest the individual. Kirk v Louisiana (2002) 536 US 635, 153 L Ed 2d 599, 2002 US LEXIS 4682, 122 S Ct 2458.

If a magistrate, based upon seemingly reliable but factually inaccurate information, issues a warrant for the search of a house in which a sought-after felon is not present, has never been present, and was never likely to have been present, the owner of the house suffers one of the inconveniences all expose themselves to as the cost of living in a safe society, but does not suffer a violation of the Federal Constitution's Fourth Amendment. Illinois v Rodriguez (1990) 497 US 177, 111 L Ed 2d 148, 1990 US LEXIS 3295, 110 S Ct 2793.

If a police officer investigating an armed robbery conducts a search of a dwelling pursuant to a search warrant authorizing a search for only the property stolen in the robbery, and if the items named in the warrant are found at the outset of the search—or if the resident of the dwelling has them in his possession and responds to the warrant by producing them immediately—no search for the weapons used in the robbery may take place. Horton v California (1990) 496 US 128, 110 L Ed 2d 112, 1990 US LEXIS 2937, 110 S Ct 2301.

The manifest purpose of the Fourth Amendment's requirement that a search warrant particularly describe the place to be searched and the persons or things to be seized is to prevent general searches; this particularity requirement insures that the search will be carefully tailored to its justifications, and will not take on the character of the wide-ranging exploratory searches the Framers intended to prohibit. Maryland v Garrison (1987) 480 US 79, 94 L Ed 2d 72, 1987 US LEXIS 559, 107 S Ct 1013.

The validity of a search warrant must be assessed on the basis of the information that the requesting officers disclose, or have a duty to discover and to disclose, to the issuing magistrate; the constitutionality of the officers' conduct must be judged in light of the information available to them at the time they request the warrant; those items of evidence that emerge after the warrant is issued have no bearing on whether a warrant was validly issued. Maryland v Garrison (1987) 480 US 79, 94 L Ed 2d 72, 1987 US LEXIS 559, 107 S Ct 1013.

A warrant to search "the premises known as 2036 Park Avenue third floor apartment," insofar as it authorizes a search that is ambiguous in scope, is valid under the Fourth Amendment when issued, even though the description of the place to be searched is broader than appropriate because it is based on the mistaken belief that there is only one apartment on the third floor of the building in question, where (1) the police officer who obtains the warrant reasonably believes that the person whose apartment is intended to be searched is the only tenant on the third floor, and (2) the discovery that there are two separate apartments on that floor—one occupied by the person named in the warrant and the other occupied by another tenant—is made by the officers executing the warrant only after they enter, and find contraband in, the apartment of the tenant not named in the warrant. Maryland v Garrison (1987) 480 US 79, 94 L Ed 2d 72, 1987 US LEXIS 559, 107 S Ct 1013.

## § 14. Checkpoints

Highway checkpoint where police stopped motorists to ask them for information about a recent hit-and-run accident was reasonable, hence, constitutional. The checkpoint stop's primary law enforcement purpose was to ask vehicle occupants for their help in providing information about a crime committed, in all likelihood, by others. The police expected the information elicited to help them apprehend, not the vehicle's occupants, but other individuals. An information-seeking stop was not the kind of event that involved suspicion, or lack of suspicion, of the relevant individual. A presumptive rule of unconstitutionality did not apply. Thus, the instant court had to judge the stop's reasonableness, hence, its constitutionality, on the basis of the individual circumstances. The relevant public concern was grave because police were investigating a crime that had resulted in a human death. The stop advanced the grave public concern to a significant degree, and the police appropriately tailored their checkpoint stops to fit important **criminal** investigatory needs. The stops interfered only minimally with liberty of the sort the Fourth Amendment sought to protect. Each stop required only a brief wait in line. Police contact consisted simply of a request for information and the distribution of a flyer. Illinois v Lidster (2004) 540 US 419, 157 L Ed 2d 843, 2004 US LEXIS 656, 124 S Ct 885.

A city police department's highway checkpoint program whose primary purpose is the discovery and interdiction of illegal narcotics—which purpose is ultimately indistinguishable from the general interest in crime control—violates the Fourth Amendment, where, under the program, (1) the police, acting without individualized suspicion, stop a predetermined number of vehicles at roadblocks in various locations, (2) at least one officer (a) approaches each stopped vehicle, (b) advises the driver that he or she is being stopped briefly at a drug checkpoint, (c) asks the driver to produce a driver's license and the vehicle's registration, (d) looks for signs of impairment, and (e) conducts an open-view examination of the vehicle from the outside, and (3) a narcotics-detection dog walks around the outside of each stopped vehicle; such a checkpoint program cannot be justified under the Fourth Amendment by (1) the severe and intractable nature of the illegal drug problem, (2) a highway safety concern, or (3) the secondary purposes of (a) keeping impaired motorists off the road, and (b) verifying licenses and registrations. City of Indianapolis v Edmond (2000) 531 US 32, 148 L Ed 2d 333, 2000 US LEXIS 8084, 121 S Ct 447.

The initial stop of each motorist passing through a highway sobriety checkpoint and the associated preliminary questioning and observation by checkpoint officers—under state police guidelines which govern checkpoint operation, site selection, and publicity, and which provide in part that (1) checkpoints will be set up at selected sites along state roads, (2) all vehicles passing through a checkpoint will be stopped and their drivers briefly examined for signs of intoxication, (3) drivers in which such signs are detected will be directed to a location out of the traffic flow for further checks, after which drivers who are found to be intoxicated will be arrested, and (4) all other drivers will be permitted to resume their journeys immediately—constitute a "reasonable" seizure which is consistent with the Federal Constitution's Fourth Amendment. Michigan Dep't of State Police v Sitz (1990) 496 US 444, 110 L Ed 2d 412, 1990 US LEXIS 3144, 110 S Ct 2481.

## § 15. Students on School Premises

A 13-year-old student's Fourth Amendment rights were violated when she was subjected to a search of her bra and underpants by school officials acting on reasonable suspicion that she had brought forbidden prescription and over-the-counter drugs to school. The content of the suspicion failed to match the degree of intrusion. There was no reason to believe the drugs sought (common pain relievers equivalent to two Advil, or one Aleve, caplet) were dangerous; they presented only a limited threat. Moreover, there was no reason to believe the student had hidden the drugs in her underwear—neither of her accusers alleged she hid the pills there, nor evidence that hiding contraband in underwear was the general practice among students at the school. Safford Unified Sch. Dist. #1 v Redding (2009) 557 US __, 174 L Ed 2d 354, 2009 US LEXIS 4735, 129 S Ct 2633.

While public schoolchildren do not shed their federal constitutional rights when they enter the schoolhouse, rights under the Federal Constitution's Fourth Amendment are different in public schools than elsewhere; the inquiry as to whether a search of students on school premises is reasonable cannot disregard the schools' custodial tutelary responsibility for children. A student's Fourth Amendment privacy interest is limited in a public school environment, where the state is responsible for maintaining discipline, health, and safety. Board of Education v Earls (2002) 536 US 822, 153 L Ed 2d 735, 2002 US LEXIS 4882, 122 S Ct 2559.

A public school district's policy that required all students who participated in any of the district's competitive extracurricular activities to submit to urinalysis drug testing did not violate the Fourth Amendment prohibition against unreasonable searches and seizures, because (1) the students affected by the policy had a limited expectation of privacy; (2) the sample-collection procedure in the instant case was virtually identical to—and to the extent of difference, even less intrusive than—a collection method that had been determined by the court not to violate the Fourth Amendment in an earlier Supreme Court case that involved high school athletes; (3) the invasion of the students' privacy was not significant, as the results neither (a) were turned over to any law enforcement authority, (b) led to the imposition of discipline, nor (c) had any academic consequences; (4) the policy was a reasonably effective means of addressing the district's legitimate concerns in preventing, deterring, and detecting drug use; and (5) the court had never required a particularized or pervasive drug problem before allowing the government to conduct suspicionless drug testing. Board of Education v Earls (2002) 536 US 822, 153 L Ed 2d 735, 2002 US LEXIS 4882, 122 S Ct 2559.

A public school district's urinalysis drug testing policy for student athletes, under which policy all students wishing to participate in interscholastic athletics were tested at the beginning of the season for their sport and random testing of 10 percent of the athletes was done weekly during the season, did not violate the Fourth Amendment right, of a seventh grader who wished to participate in the school district's football program, to be free from unreasonable searches—where the record showed no objection to the policy by any parents other than the parents of the student in question, and where a Federal District Court had found that student drug problems in the school district, particularly with respect to students involved in interscholastic athletics, were severe enough to demonstrate a need to address such problems—because the policy was reasonable under the circumstances, taking into account (1) the decreased expectation of privacy with regard to students, particularly student athletes, (2) the relative unobtrusiveness of the search, and (3) the severity of the need met by the search. Vernonia Sch. Dist. 47J v Acton (1995) 515 US 646, 132 L Ed 2d 564, 1995 US LEXIS 4275, 115 S Ct 2386.

Although children do not shed their federal constitutional rights at the schoolhouse gate, the nature of those rights is what is appropriate for children in school; the Federal Constitution's Fourth Amendment rights, no less than the Constitution's First and Fourteenth Amendment rights, are different in public schools than elsewhere. Vernonia Sch. Dist. 47J v Acton (1995) 515 US 646, 132 L Ed 2d 564, 1995 US LEXIS 4275, 115 S Ct 2386.

For purposes of determining the reasonableness of a search under the Federal Constitution's Fourth Amendment, public school students who voluntarily participate in school athletics have reason to expect intrusions upon normal rights and privileges, including privacy; the reasonableness inquiry cannot disregard the schools' custodial and tutelary responsibility for children; particularly with regard to medical examinations and procedures, students within the school environment have a lesser expectation of privacy than members of the population generally; legitimate privacy expectations are even less with regard to student athletes, who, by choosing to go out for a team, voluntarily subject themselves to a degree of regulation even higher than that imposed on students generally. Vernonia Sch. Dist. 47J v Acton (1995) 515 US 646, 132 L Ed 2d 564, 1995 US LEXIS 4275, 115 S Ct 2386.

Under ordinary circumstances, a search of a student by a teacher or other school official will be justified at its inception when there are reasonable grounds for suspecting that the search will turn up evidence that the student has violated or is violating either the law or the rule of the school, and such a search will be permissible in its scope when the measures adopted are reasonably related to the objectives of the search and not excessively intrusive in light of the age and sex of the student and the nature of the infraction. New Jersey v T.L.O. (1985) 469 US 325, 83 L Ed 2d 720, 1985 US LEXIS 41, 105 S Ct 733.

The accommodation of the privacy interests of schoolchildren with the substantial need of teachers and administrators for freedom to maintain order in the schools does not require strict adherence to the requirement that searches be based on probable cause to believe that the subject of the search has violated or is violating the law; rather, the legality of a search of a student should depend simply on the reasonableness, under all the circumstances, of the search. New Jersey v T.L.O. (1985) 469 US 325, 83 L Ed 2d 720, 1985 US LEXIS 41, 105 S Ct 733.

The search of a female student's purse by a public school official is not unreasonable under the Fourth Amendment where: (1) the student was discovered smoking in a lavatory in violation of a school rule, but when questioned at the principal's office by the school official, denied that she had been smoking and claimed that she did not smoke at all, (2) the school official demanded to see her purse, opened the purse, found a pack of cigarettes, and, upon removing the cigarettes, noticed a package of cigarette rolling papers, which is closely associated with the use of marijuana; and (3) suspecting that a closer examination of the purse might yield further evidence of drug use, the school official proceeded to search the purse thoroughly and found a small amount of marijuana, a pipe, a number of empty plastic bags, a substantial quantity of money, an index card that appeared to be a list of those who owed the student money, and two letters implicating the student in marijuana dealing. New Jersey v T.L.O. (1985) 469 US 325, 83 L Ed 2d 720, 1985 US LEXIS 41, 105 S Ct 733.

### § 16. Warrantless Search: Protection of Others

Brownstown, Michigan, officers responded to a complaint of a disturbance—a man was reportedly "going crazy" at a residence. Upon arrival, the officers found a household in considerable chaos: a pickup truck in the driveway with its front smashed, damaged fenceposts along the side of the property, and three broken house windows, the glass still on the ground outside. The officers also noticed blood on the hood of the pickup and on clothes inside of it, as well as on one of the doors to the house. Through a window, the officers could see defendant inside, screaming and throwing things. The back door was locked, and a couch had been placed to block the front door. The officers knocked, but defendant would not answer. They saw defendant had a cut on his hand and asked if he needed medical help, but defendant ignored these questions and demanded, with accompanying profanity, that they get a search warrant. One of the officers then pushed his way inside. The U.S. Supreme Court ruled that this warrantless entry was justified under the "Emergency Aid" doctrine because of defendant's violent behavior. Although the officers had not seen defendant hit anyone, they did see him throwing things, and it was objectively reasonable to believe that these projectiles might have a human target (perhaps a spouse or a child), or that defendant would hurt himself in the course of his rage. Michigan v Fisher (2009) 558 US __, 175 L Ed 2d 410, 2009 US LEXIS 8773, 130 S Ct 546.

Police made a lawful warrantless entry into a residence when, through a screen door and an open window, they observed four adults fighting with a juvenile. Law enforcement officers may enter a home without a warrant to render emergency assistance to an injured occupant or to protect an occupant from imminent injury, and need not wait until someone is unconscious (or semi-conscious) before entering. "The role of a peace officer includes preventing violence and restoring order, not simply rendering first aid to casualties; an officer is not like a boxing (or hockey) referee, poised to stop a bout only if it becomes too one-sided." Brigham City v Stuart (2006) 547 US 398, 164 L Ed 2d 650, 126 S Ct 1943, 2006 US LEXIS 4155.

### § 17. Warrantless Search: Exclusionary Rule

Violation of the "knock-and-announce" rule did not require suppression of evidence found in a search. Hudson v Michigan (2006) 547 US 586, 165 L Ed 2d 56, 126 S Ct 2159, 2006 US LEXIS 4677

The indirect fruits of an illegal search should be suppressed when they bear a sufficiently close relationship to the underlying illegality; however, such attenuation analysis is appropriate only where, as a threshold matter, courts determine that the challenged evidence is in some sense the product of illegal governmental activity. New York v Harris (1990) 495 US 14, 109 L Ed 2d 13, 1990 US LEXIS 2037, 110 S Ct 1640.

A state constitutional amendment eliminating the exclusionary rule for evidence seized in violation of state but not federal law does not violate the due process clause of the Federal Constitution's Fourteenth Amendment; a state has the power to eliminate the exclusionary rule as a remedy for violations of a state constitutional right against warrantless searches of trash. California v Greenwood (1988) 486 US 35, 100 L Ed 2d 30, 1988 US LEXIS 2279, 108 S Ct 1625.

Evidence obtained by a law enforcement officer during a warrantless administrative search authorized by, and in objectively reasonable reliance upon, a statute which is later declared to violate the Fourth Amendment to the Federal Constitution is admissible in a criminal prosecution against the person from whom the evidence is obtained. Illinois v Krull (1987) 480 US 340, 94 L Ed 2d 364, 1987 US LEXIS 1061, 107 S Ct 1160.

As a matter of due process, evidence obtained by a search and seizure in violation of the Fourth Amendment is inadmissible in a state court as it is in a federal court. Mapp v Ohio (1961) 367 US 643, 6 L Ed 2d 1081, 1961 US LEXIS 812, 81 S Ct 1684.

### § 18. Warrantless Search: Scope

After a homicide crime scene is secured for police investigation, the police are not entitled to make a warrantless search of anything and everything found within the crime scene area, where none of the exceptions to the warrant requirement of the Federal Constitution's Fourth Amendment are invoked. Flippo v West Virginia (1999) 528 US 11, 145 L Ed 2d 16, 1999 US LEXIS 6924, 120 S Ct 7.

The scope of a warrantless search of an automobile which is permissible under the Federal Constitution's Fourth Amendment is not defined by the nature of the container in which the contraband is secreted; rather, it is defined by the object of the search and the places in which there is probable cause to believe that it may be found; probable cause to believe that a container placed in the trunk of a taxi contains contraband or evidence does not justify a search of the entire taxi. California v Acevedo (1991) 500 US 565, 114 L Ed 2d 619, 1991 US LEXIS 3016, 111 S Ct 1982.

The object of a warrantless search of an automobile also defines its scope; just as probable cause to believe that a stolen lawnmower may be found in a garage will not support a warrant to search an upstairs bedroom, probable cause to believe that undocumented aliens are being transported in a van will not justify a warrantless search of a suitcase; probable cause to believe that a container placed in the trunk of a taxi contains contraband or evidence does not justify a search of the entire cab. Horton v California (1990) 496 US 128, 110 L Ed 2d 112, 1990 US LEXIS 2937, 110 S Ct 2301.

The Fourth Amendment does not prohibit the warrantless search and seizure of garbage which has been left for collection outside the curtilage of a home; thus, the Fourth Amendment rights of accused narcotics traffickers are not violated where (1) the accused, as occupants of a house, place their garbage in opaque plastic bags and put those bags out on the street curb for collection at a fixed time, with the expectation that the garbage collector will pick up the bags, mingle them with the trash of others, and deposit them at the garbage dump, but (2) the garbage collector instead, at the request of a police investigator, picks up the accused's garbage bags after cleaning his truck bin of other garbage and turns the bags over to the investigator, and (3) the investigator, acting without a warrant, searches through the garbage bags and uses evidence found therein to support an application for a warrant to search the house. California v Greenwood (1988) 486 US 35, 100 L Ed 2d 30, 1988 US LEXIS 2279, 108 S Ct 1625.

### § 19. Handcuffs

Individual's detention during the search of the premises was plainly permissible because a warrant existed to search a particular residence and the individual was an occupant of that residence at the time of the search. The officers' use of handcuffs to effectuate the detention was reasonable where the warrant authorized a search for weapons and a wanted gang member resided on the premises. Thus, the use of handcuffs minimized the inherent safety risk involved in the search. Moreover, the need to detain multiple occupants of the premises made the use of handcuffs all the more reasonable. The two to three hour detention in handcuffs was not unreasonable given that the case involved the detention of four people by two officers during a search of a gang house for dangerous weapons. Muehler v Mena (2005) 544 US 93, 161 L Ed 2d 299, 2005 US LEXIS 2755, 125 S Ct 1465.

### § 20. Parolees

The Fourth Amendment does not render states powerless to address recidivism concerns effectively. California's ability to conduct suspicionless searches of parolees serves its interest in reducing recidivism in a manner that aids, rather than hinders, the reintegration of parolees into productive society. Samson v California (2006) 547 US 843, 165 L Ed 2d 250, 126 S Ct 2193, 2006 US LEXIS 4885

Suspicionless search, conducted under the authority of California statute providing that every prisoner eligible for release on state parole shall agree in writing to be subject to search or seizure by a parole officer or other peace officer at any time of the day or night, with or without a search warrant and with or without cause, did not violate the United States Constitution. Samson v California (2006) 547 US 843, 165 L Ed 2d 250, 126 S Ct 2193, 2006 US LEXIS 4885

### § 21. Anticipatory Warrants

Anticipatory warrants are no different in principle from ordinary warrants. They require the magistrate to determine (1) that it is now probable that (2) contraband, evidence of a crime, or a fugitive will be on the described premises (3) when the warrant is executed. It should be noted, however, that where the anticipatory warrant places a condition (other than the mere passage of time) upon its execution, the first of these determinations goes not merely to what will probably be found if the condition is met. (If that were the extent of the probability determination, an anticipatory warrant could be issued for every house in the country, authorizing search and seizure if contraband should be delivered—though for any single location there is no likelihood that contraband will be delivered.) Rather, the probability determination for a conditioned anticipatory warrant looks also to the likelihood that the condition will occur, and thus that a proper object of seizure will be on the described premises. United States v Grubbs (2006) 547 US 90, 164 L Ed 2d 195, 126 S Ct 1494, 2006 US LEXIS 2496

For a conditioned anticipatory warrant to comply with the Fourth Amendment's requirement of probable cause, two prerequisites of probability must be satisfied. It must be true not only that if the triggering condition occurs there is a fair probability that contraband or evidence of a crime will be found in a particular place, but also that there is probable cause to believe the triggering condition will occur. The supporting affidavit must provide the magistrate with sufficient information to evaluate both aspects of the probable-cause determination. United States v Grubbs (2006) 547 US 90, 164 L Ed 2d 195, 126 S Ct 1494, 2006 US LEXIS 2496

Anticipatory warrants are not categorically unconstitutional under the Fourth Amendment's provision that no warrants shall issue, but upon probable cause. Probable cause exists when there is a fair probability that contraband or evidence of a crime will be found in a particular place. When an anticipatory warrant is issued, the fact that the contraband is not presently at the place described is immaterial so long as there is probable cause to believe it will be there when the warrant is executed. Anticipatory warrants are, therefore, no different in principle from ordinary warrants: They require the magistrate to determine (1) that it is now probable that (2) contraband, evidence of a crime, or a fugitive will be on the described premises (3) when the warrant is executed. Where the anticipatory warrant places a condition (other than the mere passage of time) upon its execution, the first of these determinations goes not merely to what will probably be found if the condition is met, but also to the likelihood that the condition will be met, and thus that a proper object of seizure will be on the described premises. Here, the occurrence of the triggering condition—successful delivery of the videotape—would plainly establish probable cause for the search, and the affidavit established probable cause to believe the triggering condition would be satisfied. United States v Grubbs (2006) 547 US 90, 164 L Ed 2d 195, 126 S Ct 1494, 2006 US LEXIS 2496

# Right to Counsel, Privilege Against Self-Incrimination; Confrontation of Witnesses

### § 1. In General

Like an invocation of the Fifth Amendment right to counsel, a suspect's invocation of the right to remain silent must be unambiguous and unequivocal before police are required to halt questioning. Berghuis v Thompkins (2010) 560 US __, 176 L Ed 2d 1098, 2010 US LEXIS 4379, 130 S Ct 2250.

Failure to give a suspect Miranda warnings does not require suppression of the physical fruits of the suspect's unwarned but voluntary statements. United States v Patane (2004) 542 US 630, 159 L Ed 2d 667, 2004 US LEXIS 4577, 124 S Ct 2620.

This case tests a **police** protocol for custodial interrogation that calls for giving no warnings of the rights to silence and counsel until interrogation has produced a confession. Although such a statement is generally inadmissible, since taken in violation of, the interrogating officer follows it with Miranda warnings and then leads the suspect to cover the same ground a second time. The question here is the admissibility of the repeated statement. Because this midstream recitation of warnings after interrogation and unwarned confession could not effectively comply with Miranda's constitutional requirement, we hold that a statement repeated after a warning in such circumstances is inadmissible. Missouri v Seibert (2004) 542 US 600, 159 L Ed 2d 643, 2004 US LEXIS 4578, 124 S Ct 2601.

With respect to an accused who does not have the assistance of counsel at a plea hearing, the Federal **Constitution's** Sixth Amendment is satisfied when the trial court, before accepting a guilty plea, informs the accused of (1) the nature of the charges against the accused, (2) the accused's right to be counseled regarding the plea, and (3) the range of allowable punishments attendant upon the entry of a guilty plea. The Sixth Amendment does not require the trial court to warn the accused that (1) waiving the assistance of counsel in deciding whether to plead guilty entails the risk that a viable defense will be overlooked; or (2) by waiving the right to an attorney, the accused will lose the opportunity to obtain an independent opinion on whether, under the facts and applicable law, it is wise to plead guilty. Iowa v Tovar (2004) 541 US 77, 158 L Ed 2d 209, 2004 US LEXIS 1837, 124 S Ct 1379.

A criminal defendant's Sixth Amendment right to self-representation at trial is not absolute, for (1) the defendant must voluntarily and intelligently elect to conduct his or her own defense; (2) the defendant must first be made aware of the dangers and disadvantages of self-representation; (3) a trial judge may properly terminate self-representation if necessary, even over the defendant's objection; and (4) the trial judge is under no duty to provide personal instruction on courtroom procedure or to perform any legal "chores" for the defendant that counsel would normally carry out. Moreover, a lay appellant who had represented himself at a state criminal trial and who wished to do so on direct appeal from conviction was not deprived of a federal constitutional right, where state courts required him to accept a state-appointed attorney on appeal. Martinez v Court of Appeal (2000) 528 US 152, 145 L Ed 2d 597, 2000 US LEXIS 502, 120 S Ct 684.

The right to counsel under the Federal Constitution's Sixth Amendment attaches only at the initiation of adversary criminal proceedings; before proceedings are initiated, a suspect in a criminal investigation has no constitutional right to the assistance of counsel. Davis v United States (1994) 512 US 452, 129 L Ed 2d 362, 1994 US LEXIS 4827, 114 S Ct 2350.

Invocation, regarding one offense, of the right—derived by Miranda v Arizona (1966) 384 US 436, 16 L Ed 2d 694, 1966 US LEXIS 2817, 86 S Ct 1602, from the Federal Constitution's Fifth Amendment privilege against self-incrimination—to the assistance of counsel during custodial interrogation is not offense-specific; once an accused invokes the Miranda Fifth Amendment right to the assistance of counsel for interrogation regarding one offense, the accused may not be reapproached regarding any offense unless counsel is present. McNeil v Wisconsin (1991) 501 US 171, 115 L Ed 2d 158, 1991 US LEXIS 3483, 111 S Ct 2204.

Under the Federal Constitution's Fifth Amendment privilege against self-incrimination, persons questioned must be warned, prior to any custodial questioning, that they have a right to remain silent, that any statement they do make may be used in evidence against them, and that they have a right to the presence of an attorney, either retained or appointed. Pennsylvania v Muniz (1990) 496 US 582, 110 L Ed 2d 528, 1990 US LEXIS 3211, 110 S Ct 2638.

Unless a suspect voluntarily, knowingly, and intelligently waives his or her rights, under the Federal Constitution's Fifth Amendment privilege against self-incrimination, to remain silent and to have an attorney present during custodial questioning, any incriminating responses to questioning may not be introduced into evidence in the prosecution's case in chief in a subsequent criminal proceeding. Pennsylvania v Muniz (1990) 496 US 582, 110 L Ed 2d 528, 1990 US LEXIS 3211, 110 S Ct 2638.

The Federal Constitution's Fifth Amendment privilege against self-incrimination protects persons accused of crimes only from being compelled to testify against themselves or to otherwise provide the state with evidence of a testimonial or communicative nature; in order to be testimonial, an accused's communication must itself, explicitly or implicitly, relate a factual assertion or disclose information, as only then are persons compelled to be witnesses against themselves. Pennsylvania v Muniz (1990) 496 US 582, 110 L Ed 2d 528, 1990 US LEXIS 3211, 110 S Ct 2638.

Under the Federal Constitution's Fifth Amendment privilege against self-incrimination, confessions remain a proper element in law enforcement, and any statement given freely and voluntarily without compelling influences is admissible into evidence. Illinois v Perkins (1990) 496 US 292, 110 L Ed 2d 243, 1990 US LEXIS 2885, 110 S Ct 2394.

Statements taken during legal custody are inadmissible if they are the product of coercion, if Miranda warnings are not given, or if interrogation does not cease when an accused requests counsel. New York v Harris (1990) 495 US 14, 109 L Ed 2d 13, 1990 US LEXIS 2037, 110 S Ct 1640.

A more searching or formal inquiry is required before permitting an accused to waive the right, under the Federal Constitution's Sixth Amendment, to counsel at trial than is required for a Sixth Amendment waiver during postindictment questioning, not because postindictment questioning is less important than a trial, but because the full dangers and disadvantages of self-representation during questioning are less substantial and more obvious to an accused than they are at trial. Patterson v Illinois (1988) 487 US 285, 101 L Ed 2d 261, 1988 US LEXIS 2876, 108 S Ct 2389.

In order to protect the Fifth Amendment privilege against self-incrimination in custodial interrogations, the police are required, prior to the initiation of questioning, to fully apprise a suspect of the state's intention to use his statements to secure a conviction, and must inform him of his rights to remain silent and to have counsel present if he so desires; also, the police must respect the suspect's decision to exercise the rights outlined in these warnings, so that if the suspect indicates in any manner, at any time prior to or during questioning, that he wishes to remain silent, or states that he wants an attorney, the interrogation must cease. Moran v Burbine (1986) 475 US 412, 89 L Ed 2d 410, 1986 US LEXIS 32, 106 S Ct 1135.

The Miranda exclusionary rule may be triggered even in the absence of a violation of the Fifth Amendment, which prohibits use by the prosecution in its case in chief only of compelled testimony; failure to administer Miranda warnings creates a presumption of compulsion, and consequently unwarned statements that are otherwise voluntary within the meaning of the Fifth Amendment must nevertheless be excluded from evidence under Miranda, even as to a defendant who has suffered no identifiable constitutional harm. Oregon v Elstad (1985) 470 US 298, 84 L Ed 2d 222, 1985 US LEXIS 60, 105 S Ct 1285.

## § 2. Coercion

A state department of corrections' rehabilitation program for sex-offender inmates and the consequences for an inmate's nonparticipation in the program did not combine to create a compulsion that violated the inmate's privilege against self-incrimination under the Federal Constitution's Fifth Amendment, where (1) inmates participating in the program were required, among other matters, to (a) complete and sign an "Admission of Responsibility" form, in which they discussed and accepted responsibility for the crime for which they had been sentenced, and (b) complete a sexual history form detailing all prior sexual activities, regardless of whether such activities constituted uncharged criminal offenses; (2) information obtained from participants could be used against them in future criminal proceedings; and (3) if an inmate refused to participate, then (a) the inmate's privilege status would be reduced so as to curtail visitation rights, earnings, work opportunities, ability to send money to family, canteen expenditures, access to a personal television, and other privileges; and (b) the inmate would be transferred to a maximum-security unit. McKune v Lile (2002) 536 US 24, 153 L Ed 2d 47, 2002 US LEXIS 4206, 122 S Ct 2017.

For purposes of determining, under the due process clause of the Federal Constitution's Fourteenth Amendment, whether a state criminal defendant's confession has been coerced, (1) a finding of coercion need not depend upon actual violence by a government agent; (2) a credible threat is sufficient; (3) coercion can be mental as well as physical; and (4) the blood of the accused is not the only hallmark of an unconstitutional inquisition. Arizona v Fulminante (1991) 499 US 279, 113 L Ed 2d 302, 1991 US LEXIS 1854, 111 S Ct 1246.

The admission at a state criminal trial, in violation of the due process clause of the Federal Constitution's Fourteenth Amendment, of a defendant's involuntary—that is, coerced—confession is subject to harmless-error analysis. Arizona v Fulminante (1991) 499 US 279, 113 L Ed 2d 302, 1991 US LEXIS 1854, 111 S Ct 1246.

Absent deliberately coercive or improper tactics by police in obtaining an initial statement, the mere fact that a suspect has made an unwarned admission does not warrant a presumption of compulsion; a subsequent administration of Miranda warnings to a suspect who has given a voluntary but unwarned statement ordinarily should suffice to remove the conditions that precluded admission of the earlier statement; in such circumstances, the finder of fact may reasonably conclude that the suspect made a rational and intelligent choice whether to waive or invoke his rights. Oregon v Elstad (1985) 470 US 298, 84 L Ed 2d 222, 1985 US LEXIS 60, 105 S Ct 1285.

## § 3. Collaboration with Other Officers

For purposes of the rule that a confession obtained during a period of detention by state or local officers must be suppressed if an accused can demonstrate the existence of improper collaboration between federal officers and the state or local officers, the action of a local sheriff's department in informing agents of the United States Secret Service that counterfeit currency had been found in an accused's possession is routine cooperation between local and federal authorities which by itself is wholly unobjectionable. United States v Alvarez-Sanchez (1994) 511 US 350, 128 L Ed 2d 319, 1994 US LEXIS 3300, 114 S Ct 1599.

## § 4. Custody

Two discrete inquiries are essential to the determination whether a suspect being interrogated by the police is in custody: (1) what are the circumstances surrounding the interrogation, and (2) given those circumstances, would a reasonable person feel that he or she is not at liberty to terminate the interrogation and leave. Thompson v Keohane (1995) 516 US 99, 133 L Ed 2d 383, 1995 US LEXIS 8315, 116 S Ct 457.

A law enforcement officer's subjective and undisclosed view concerning whether a person being interrogated by law enforcement officers is a criminal suspect is irrelevant to the assessment whether the interrogatee is in custody and thus entitled to Miranda warnings as to the right to counsel and as to the privilege against self-incrimination, because the initial determination as to the custody issue depends on the objective circumstances of the interrogation, not on the views harbored by either the interrogating officers or the interrogatee, where under Miranda (1) a police officer's unarticulated plan has no bearing on the question whether a suspect was in custody at a particular time, (2) the only relevant inquiry is how a reasonable person in the suspect's shoes would have understood the situation, and (3) save as they are communicated or otherwise manifested to the interrogatee, an officer's evolving but unarticulated suspicions do not affect the objective circumstances of an interrogation or interview, as one cannot expect the interrogatee to probe the officer's innermost thoughts. Stansbury v California (1994) 511 US 318, 128 L Ed 2d 293, 1994 US LEXIS 3293, 114 S Ct 1526.

A law enforcement officer's obligation to administer Miranda warnings—as to the right to counsel and as to the privilege against self-incrimination—attaches only where there has been such a restriction on a person's freedom as to render the person in custody; in determining whether an individual was in custody, a court must examine all the circumstances surrounding an interrogation, but the ultimate inquiry is simply whether there was a formal arrest or restraint on freedom of movement of the degree associated with a formal arrest. Stansbury v California (1994) 511 US 318, 128 L Ed 2d 293, 1994 US LEXIS 3293, 114 S Ct 1526.

For purposes of the assessment whether a person being interrogated by a police officer was in custody and thus entitled to Miranda warnings as to the right to counsel and as to the privilege against self-incrimination, the officer's views concerning the nature of the interrogation, or beliefs concerning the potential culpability of the interrogatee, may be one among many relevant factors, but only if the officer's views or beliefs were somehow manifested by words or deeds to the interrogatee and would have affected how a reasonable person in the interrogatee's position would perceive his or her freedom to leave; even a clear statement from an officer that an interrogatee is a prime criminal suspect is not, in itself, dispositive of the custody issue, for some suspects are free to come and go until the police decide to make an arrest; the weight and pertinence of any communications regarding the officer's degree of suspicion will depend upon the facts and circumstances of the particular case. Stansbury v California (1994) 511 US 318, 128 L Ed 2d 293, 1994 US LEXIS 3293, 114 S Ct 1526.

The custodial interrogation of an accused must cease when the accused requests counsel, and where there has been such a request, police officials may not reinitiate the interrogation without counsel present, regardless of whether the accused has consulted with counsel. Minnick v Mississippi (1990) 498 US 146, 112 L Ed 2d 489, 1990 US LEXIS 6118, 111 S Ct 486.

A person subjected to custodial interrogation is entitled to the benefit of the Miranda procedural safeguards, regardless of the nature or severity of the offense of which he is suspected or for which he was arrested. Berkemer v McCarty (1984) 468 US 420, 82 L Ed 2d 317, 1984 US LEXIS 140, 104 S Ct 3138.

## § 5. Fifth, Sixth Amendment Rights Distinguished

The rule established in Edwards v Arizona (1981) 451 US 477, 68 L Ed 2d 378, 1981 US LEXIS 96, 101 S Ct 1880—that once an accused asserts the right, derived by Miranda v Arizona (1966) 384 US 436, 16 L Ed 2d 694, 1966 US LEXIS 2817, 86 S Ct 1602, from the Federal Constitution's Fifth Amendment privilege against self-incrimination, to the assistance of counsel during custodial interrogation, not only must the current interrogation cease, but also the accused may not be approached for further interrogation until counsel has been made available to the accused—no longer applies when a suspect who has requested an attorney is released from pretrial custody for 14 days or more. After a 14-day break in custody, police may attempt to once again initiate questioning even though the suspect is not accompanied by an attorney. Maryland v Shatzer (2010) 559 US __, 175 L Ed 2d 1045, 2010 US LEXIS 1899, 130 S Ct 1213.

An accused's invocation, during a judicial proceeding, of the right, under the Federal Constitution's Sixth Amendment, to the assistance of counsel in a criminal prosecution does not constitute an invocation of the Fifth Amendment right to the assistance of counsel during custodial interrogation—which right was derived by Miranda v Arizona (1966) 384 US 436, 16 L Ed 2d 694, 1966 US LEXIS 2817, 86 S Ct 1602, from the Fifth Amendment privilege against self-incrimination. McNeil v Wisconsin (1991) 501 US 171, 115 L Ed 2d 158, 1991 US LEXIS 3483, 111 S Ct 2204.

The right, under the Federal Constitution's Sixth Amendment, to the assistance of counsel in all criminal prosecutions is offense-specific; the right cannot be invoked once for all future prosecutions, since it does not attach until the initiation of adversary judicial criminal proceedings by formal charge, preliminary hearing, indictment, information, or arraignment; just as the right is offense-specific, so also its effect of invalidating, subsequent to the attachment and invocation of the right, any waivers of the right during police-initiated custodial interviews is offense-specific. McNeil v Wisconsin (1991) 501 US 171, 115 L Ed 2d 158, 1991 US LEXIS 3483, 111 S Ct 2204.

The interest protected by the right—derived by Miranda v Arizona (1966) 384 US 436, 16 L Ed 2d 694, 1966 US LEXIS 2817, 86 S Ct 1602, from the Federal Constitution's Fifth Amendment privilege against self-incrimination—to the assistance of counsel during custodial interrogation is (1) in one respect narrower than the interest protected by the Sixth Amendment right to the assistance of counsel in all criminal prosecutions, because the Miranda Fifth Amendment right relates to only custodial interrogation; and (2) in another respect broader than the interest protected by the Sixth Amendment right to the assistance of counsel, because the Miranda Fifth Amendment right relates to interrogation regarding any suspected crime and attaches regardless of whether the adversarial relationship produced by a pending prosecution has yet arisen. McNeil v Wisconsin (1991) 501 US 171, 115 L Ed 2d 158, 1991 US LEXIS 3483, 111 S Ct 2204.

The rule established in Edwards v Arizona (1981) 451 US 477, 68 L Ed 2d 378, 1981 US LEXIS 96, 101 S Ct 1880—that once an accused asserts the right, derived by Miranda v Arizona (1966) 384 US 436, 16 L Ed 2d 694, 1966 US LEXIS 2817, 86 S Ct 1602, from the Federal Constitution's Fifth Amendment privilege against self-incrimination, to the assistance of counsel during custodial interrogation, not only must the current interrogation cease, but also the accused may not be approached for further interrogation until counsel has been made available to the accused—applies only when the accused has expressed a wish for the particular sort of lawyerly assistance that is the subject of Miranda; the rule requires, at a minimum, some statement that reasonably can be construed to be expression of a desire for the assistance of an attorney in dealing with custodial interrogation by the police; however, a request for the assistance of an attorney at a bail hearing, under the Sixth Amendment provision for the assistance of counsel in all criminal prosecutions, does not bear the same construction. McNeil v Wisconsin (1991) 501 US 171, 115 L Ed 2d 158, 1991 US LEXIS 3483, 111 S Ct 2204.

Because the protection of the attorney-client relationship under the Federal Constitution's Sixth Amendment—the right to rely on counsel as a medium between the accused and the state—extends beyond the protection of the Fifth Amendment right to counsel afforded by the Miranda rule, there are cases where a waiver which would be valid under Miranda will not suffice for Sixth Amendment purposes. Patterson v Illinois (1988) 487 US 285, 101 L Ed 2d 261, 1988 US LEXIS 2876, 108 S Ct 2389.

## § 6. Traffic Stop

A motorist detained pursuant to a traffic stop is not taken into custody for purposes of the Miranda doctrine, and Miranda warnings are not required to be given, where a single police officer asked the motorist a modest number of questions and requested him to perform a simple balancing test at a location visible to passing motorists, and where only a short period of time elapsed between the stop and his arrest, and at no point during the interval was the motorist informed that his detention would not be temporary; statements made by the motorist prior to his arrest are therefore admissible against him. Berkemer v McCarty (1984) 468 US 420, 82 L Ed 2d 317, 1984 US LEXIS 140, 104 S Ct 3138.

The initial stop of a motorist's car by a law enforcement officer, by itself, does not render the motorist "in custody" for purposes of the Miranda doctrine. Berkemer v McCarty (1984) 468 US 420, 82 L Ed 2d 317, 1984 US LEXIS 140, 104 S Ct 3138.

Statements made during custodial interrogation by a suspect accused of a misdemeanor traffic offense are inadmissible where the suspect was not informed of his Miranda rights when he was formally placed under arrest. Berkemer v McCarty (1984) 468 US 420, 82 L Ed 2d 317, 1984 US LEXIS 140, 104 S Ct 3138.

## § 7. Undercover Officers

An undercover law enforcement officer posing as a fellow jail inmate is not required, under the Federal Constitution's Fifth Amendment privilege against self-incrimination, to give the warnings required by Miranda v Arizona (1966) 384 US 436, 16 L Ed 2d 694, 1966 US LEXIS 2817, 86 S Ct 1602, to an incarcerated suspect before the officer asks questions that may elicit an incriminating response, and incriminating statements made by a suspect in such circumstances are thus not inadmissible at trial. Illinois v Perkins (1990) 496 US 292, 110 L Ed 2d 243, 1990 US LEXIS 2885, 110 S Ct 2394.

Under the Federal Constitution's Fifth Amendment privilege against self-incrimination, the warnings required by Miranda v Arizona (1966) 384 US 436, 16 L Ed 2d 694, 1966 US LEXIS 2817, 86 S Ct 1602, are not required when a suspect is unaware that the suspect is speaking to a law enforcement officer and gives a voluntary statement. Illinois v Perkins (1990) 496 US 292, 110 L Ed 2d 243, 1990 US LEXIS 2885, 110 S Ct 2394.

## § 8. Jailhouse Informants

A defendant's incriminating statement to a jailhouse informant, even though taken in violation of the Sixth Amendment, is nevertheless admissible at trial to impeach the defendant's conflicting statements. Kansas v Ventris (2009) 556 US __, 173 L Ed 2d 801, 2009 US LEXIS 3299, 129 S Ct 1841.

## § 9. Waiver

If a suspect, after receiving the Miranda warnings, effectively waives the Miranda right to have counsel present during custodial interrogation, then law enforcement officers are free to question the suspect; however, under the rule of Edwards v Arizona (1981) 451 US 477, 68 L Ed 2d 378, 1981 US LEXIS 96, 101 S Ct 1880, if the suspect requests counsel at any time during the interview, then the suspect is not subject to further questioning until a lawyer has been made available or the suspect reinitiates conversation; this second layer of prophylaxis for the Miranda right to counsel (1) is designed to prevent police from badgering a suspect into waiving previously asserted Miranda rights, (2) like other aspects of Miranda, is not itself required by the Federal Constitution's Fifth Amendment prohibition on coerced confessions, and (3) is instead justified only by reference to its prophylactic purpose. Davis v United States (1994) 512 US 452, 129 L Ed 2d 362, 1994 US LEXIS 4827, 114 S Ct 2350.

The rule of Edwards v Arizona (1981) 451 US 477, 68 L Ed 2d 378, 1981 US LEXIS 96, 101 S Ct 1880—under which an accused who invokes the right to counsel while undergoing custodial interrogation is not subject to further interrogation until counsel has been "made available" to the accused—does not foreclose a waiver by the accused, after counsel has been requested, of protections afforded by the Edwards v Arizona rule as to the accused's privilege against self-incrimination under the Federal Constitution's Fifth Amendment, provided that the accused has initiated the conversation or discussions with the authorities. Minnick v Mississippi (1990) 498 US 146, 112 L Ed 2d 489, 1990 US LEXIS 6118, 111 S Ct 486.

An accused's waiver of the right to counsel during questioning must be knowing and intelligent and voluntary; where the accused has waived the right under the Federal Constitution's Sixth Amendment to have counsel present during postindictment questioning, the key inquiry is whether the accused was made sufficiently aware of this right and of the possible consequences of a decision to forgo the aid of counsel. Patterson v Illinois (1988) 487 US 285, 101 L Ed 2d 261, 1988 US LEXIS 2876, 108 S Ct 2389.

If an accused who waives the right to counsel under the Federal Constitution's Sixth Amendment lacks a full and complete appreciation of all of the consequences flowing from such a waiver, despite having been warned that any statement that the accused might make could be used against him or her in subsequent criminal proceedings, such a lack of appreciation does not defeat a showing by the prosecution that the information provided to the accused regarding the waiver satisfied the constitutional minimum. Patterson v Illinois (1988) 487 US 285, 101 L Ed 2d 261, 1988 US LEXIS 2876, 108 S Ct 2389.

An accused's waiver of the right under the Federal Constitution's Sixth Amendment to have counsel present during postindictment questioning is not valid where the accused is not told that his or her lawyer is trying to reach the accused during questioning. Patterson v Illinois (1988) 487 US 285, 101 L Ed 2d 261, 1988 US LEXIS 2876, 108 S Ct 2389.

An accused who has been admonished, during postindictment questioning, with the Miranda warnings—that he or she has the right to remain silent, to consult with an attorney, to have an attorney present during questioning, and to have an attorney appointed if the accused cannot afford to retain one, and that any statement by the accused can be used against him or her in subsequent criminal proceedings—has been sufficiently apprised of the nature of the right to counsel at such questioning under the Federal Constitution's Sixth Amendment, and of the possible consequences of going without counsel during such questioning, so that the accused's waiver of that right is a knowing and intelligent one, and the interrogation does not violate that right. Patterson v Illinois (1988) 487 US 285, 101 L Ed 2d 261, 1988 US LEXIS 2876, 108 S Ct 2389.

Waiver of a suspect's Miranda self-incrimination right, once the suspect has requested during custodial interrogation that an attorney be present, requires a finding that the suspect (1) initiated further discussions with the police and (2) knowingly and intelligently waived the right he had invoked. Connecticut v Barrett (1987) 479 US 523, 93 L Ed 2d 920, 1987 US LEXIS 419, 107 S Ct 828.

A defendant may waive effectuation of the rights conveyed in the Miranda warnings provided the waiver is made voluntarily, knowingly, and intelligently; this inquiry has two distinct dimensions, first, that the relinquishment of the right must be voluntary in the sense that it is the product of a free and deliberate choice rather than intimidation, coercion, or deception, and second, that the waiver must be made with a full awareness both of the nature of the right being abandoned and the consequences of the decision to abandon it; only if the totality of the circumstances surrounding the interrogation reveals both an uncoerced choice and the requisite level of comprehension may a court properly conclude that the Miranda rights have been waived. Moran v Burbine (1986) 475 US 412, 89 L Ed 2d 410, 1986 US LEXIS 32, 106 S Ct 1135.

The conduct of the police in failing to inform a suspect in custody that counsel has been retained for him and is trying to reach him, and in misinforming counsel that the suspect will not be questioned or placed in a lineup on the night in question, does not invalidate the suspect's ensuing waiver of his right to remain silent and to have counsel present during questioning after he has been properly advised of his rights under the Miranda rule, regardless of the culpability or state of mind of the police in so acting; thus, the Fifth Amendment does not require that inculpatory statements made by the suspect during questioning which follows that waiver be excluded from evidence at his subsequent trial. Moran v Burbine (1986) 475 US 412, 89 L Ed 2d 410, 1986 US LEXIS 32, 106 S Ct 1135.

A suspect who has responded to uncoercive questioning by a police officer while in custody and without being given Miranda warnings is not thereby disabled from waiving his rights and confessing after he has been given the requisite Miranda warnings, and his confession is not, solely on account of the prior, unwarned admission, rendered inadmissible as "fruit of the poisonous tree"; the relevant inquiry is whether, in fact, the second statement was also voluntarily made in view of the surrounding circumstances and the entire course of police conduct with respect to the suspect. Oregon v Elstad (1985) 470 US 298, 84 L Ed 2d 222, 1985 US LEXIS 60, 105 S Ct 1285.

Supreme Court

## § 10. Illegal Arrest

Under the Federal Constitution's Fourth Amendment, a confession obtained by exploitation of an illegal arrest may not properly be used against a criminal defendant. Thus, where the United States Supreme Court held that a suspect had been arrested, by officers of a county sheriff's department who had lacked a warrant, before the suspect had been questioned—and where the state did not even claim that the department had had probable cause to detain the individual at that point—the individual's subsequent confession had to be suppressed, unless that confession was an act of free will sufficient to purge the primary taint of the unlawful invasion. Demonstrating such purgation was a function of circumstantial evidence, with the burden of persuasion on the state. For such purposes, the relevant considerations included (1) the observance of Miranda warnings, (2) the temporal proximity of the arrest and the confession, (3) the presence of intervening circumstances, and (4) particularly, the purpose and flagrancy of the official misconduct. Kaupp v Texas (2003) 538 US 626, 155 L Ed 2d 814, 123 S Ct 1843, 2003 US LEXIS 3670.

## § 11. Admissible Statements

The Confrontation Clause did not bar admission of statements made during a domestic dispute by the victim to a 911 emergency operator identifying the defendant as her attacker. Statements are nontestimonial when made in the course of police interrogation under circumstances objectively indicating that the primary purpose of the interrogation is to enable police assistance to meet an ongoing emergency. They are testimonial when the circumstances objectively indicate that there is no such ongoing emergency, and that the primary purpose of the interrogation is to establish or prove past events potentially relevant to later criminal prosecution. In this case, the victim was speaking about events as they were happening, not relating past events; moreover, the 911 dispatcher's questions were necessary to resolve the present emergency faced by the victim, and were not directed simply at learning what had happened in the past. Davis v Washington (2006) 547 US 813, 165 L Ed 2d 224, 126 S Ct 2266, 2006 US LEXIS 4886.

A motorist charged with driving under the influence of alcohol cannot successfully challenge, as a violation of his rights under the Federal Constitution's Fifth Amendment privilege against self-incrimination, the introduction into evidence at his state court trial of his refusal to take a breathalyzer test, because, since submission to such a test could itself be compelled, a state's decision to permit a suspect to refuse to take the test but then to comment on that refusal at trial does not "compel" the suspect to incriminate himself and hence does not violate the privilege. Pennsylvania v Muniz (1990) 496 US 582, 110 L Ed 2d 528, 1990 US LEXIS 3211, 110 S Ct 2638.

A videotape of part of the booking proceedings following the arrest of a drunk-driving suspect—in which part the suspect, who had not yet been given a Miranda warning, was asked by a police officer to give the suspect's name, address, height, weight, eye color, date of birth, and current age, and the date of the suspect's sixth birthday—is not rendered inadmissible, at the suspect's state court trial for driving under the influence of alcohol, as a violation of the suspect's rights under the Federal Constitution's Fifth Amendment privilege against self-incrimination merely because the slurred nature of the suspect's speech in responding to the questions is incriminating, since any slurring of speech and other evidence of lack of muscular coordination revealed by the suspect's responses to the officer's direct questions constitute nontestimonial components of those responses; requiring suspects to reveal the physical manner in which they articulate words, like requiring them to reveal the physical properties of the sounds produced by their voices, does not, without more, compel them to provide "testimonial" responses for purposes of the privilege against self-incrimination. Pennsylvania v Muniz (1990) 496 US 582, 110 L Ed 2d 528, 1990 US LEXIS 3211, 110 S Ct 2638.

A trial court does not err in permitting an accused's confessions to be used against him in a murder trial where, during postindictment questioning, the accused was informed by law enforcement officials of his right to counsel, and of the consequences of any choice not to exercise that right, by means of the Miranda warnings, but where on two separate occasions he elected to forgo the assistance of counsel and to speak directly to officials concerning his role in the murder, and thus made a knowing and intelligent waiver of his right to counsel under the Federal Constitution's Sixth Amendment. Patterson v Illinois (1988) 487 US 285, 101 L Ed 2d 261, 1988 US LEXIS 2876, 108 S Ct 2389.

The self-incrimination privilege of the Fifth Amendment to the Federal Constitution does not forbid the use, at a suspect's criminal trial, of incriminating statements made by the suspect to his wife in the presence of a police officer, and the suspect is not subjected to such compelling influences, psychological ploys, or direct questioning as would constitute "interrogation," or the functional equivalent of interrogation, for Fifth Amendment purposes—even though the statements are made after the suspect has been placed in custody and given his Miranda warnings, and after the suspect has refused to make any more statements without a lawyer present—where (1) during the discussion between the suspect and his wife, the officer asked the suspect no questions about the crime or the suspect's conduct; (2) the suspect, with knowledge that the police were listening and that a tape recorder was being used, chose to speak; (3) the police did not send the wife to see the suspect for the purpose of eliciting incriminating statements, but instead yielded to the wife's insistent demands to talk to her husband; (4) under the circumstances, the police acted reasonably and lawfully, for the police were not required (a) to adopt inflexible rules barring suspects from speaking with their spouses, or (b) to ignore legitimate concerns—such as security— by allowing such spouses to meet in private; (5) the suspect, told by police that his wife would be allowed to speak to him, was not likely to feel that he was being coerced to incriminate himself in any way; (6) even though the police were aware that there was a possibility that the suspect might incriminate himself, the police did not interrogate the suspect simply by hoping that he would incriminate himself, and the suspect's volunteered statements could not properly be considered the result of police interrogation; and (7) the police actions in the case did not implicate the Supreme Court's purpose of preventing government officials from using the coercive nature of confinement to extract confessions that would not be given in an unrestrained environment. Arizona v Mauro (1987) 481 US 520, 95 L Ed 2d 458, 1987 US LEXIS 1933, 107 S Ct 1931.

## § 12. Inadmissible Statements

While States are free to impose whatever specific rules they see fit to ensure that criminal defendants are well represented, the Federal Constitution imposes only one general requirement: that counsel make objectively reasonable choices. Standards promulgated by the American Bar Association are "only guides" to what reasonableness means, not its definition—an attorney's failure to comply with such standards does not constitute proof that the attorney was ineffective. Bobby v Van Hook (2009) 558 US __, 130 S Ct 13, 175 L Ed 2d 255, 2009 US LEXIS 7976.

A state's playing, for the jury at a trial for assault and attempted murder, of a tape-recorded statement in which the accused's wife—who, because of the state marital privilege that generally barred one spouse from testifying against the other without the other's consent, did not testify at trial—during police interrogation, had described her husband's stabbing of the victim, violated the husband's right, under the Federal Constitution's Sixth Amendment, to be confronted by the witnesses against him. Crawford v Washington (2004) 541 US 36, 158 L Ed 2d 177, 2004 US LEXIS 1838, 124 S Ct 1354.

An accused's right, under the Federal Constitution's Sixth Amendment, to be confronted with the witnesses against him is violated where the entire confession of the accused's nontestifying alleged accomplice—which confession contains some statements against the accomplice's penal interest and others that inculpate the accused— is admitted into evidence at the accused's state criminal trial. Lilly v Virginia (1999) 527 US 116, 144 L Ed 2d 117, 1999 US LEXIS 4006, 119 S Ct 1887.

The custodial confession of a criminally accused's alleged accomplice that inculpates the accused is not within a firmly rooted exception to the hearsay rule such that the admission of the confession into evidence at the accused's trial will not violate the accused's right, under the Federal Constitution's Sixth Amendment, to be confronted with the witnesses against him. Lilly v Virginia (1999) 527 US 116, 144 L Ed 2d 117, 1999 US LEXIS 4006, 119 S Ct 1887.

Assuming that there has been no break in the custody of an accused subsequent to the accused's assertion of the right—derived by Miranda v Arizona (1966) 384 US 436, 16 L Ed 2d 694, 1966 US LEXIS 2817, 86 S Ct 1602, from the Federal Constitution's Fifth Amendment privilege against self-incrimination—to the assistance of counsel during custodial interrogation, if the police initiate an encounter with the accused in the absence of counsel subsequent to the accused's assertion of the right, the accused's statements made during the encounter are presumed involuntary and therefore inadmissible as substantive evidence at trial, even where the accused executes a waiver and the accused's statements would be considered voluntary under traditional standards; this rule is designed to prevent police from badgering an accused into waiving the accused's previously asserted Miranda rights. McNeil v Wisconsin (1991) 501 US 171, 115 L Ed 2d 158, 1991 US LEXIS 3483, 111 S Ct 2204.

Where a motorist arrested on suspicion of driving under the influence of alcohol is not advised of his Miranda rights until after the videotaped proceedings at the booking center are completed, any verbal statements on the videotape that are both testimonial in nature and elicited during custodial interrogation are inadmissible as evidence in the motorist's state court trial. Pennsylvania v Muniz (1990) 496 US 582, 110 L Ed 2d 528, 1990 US LEXIS 3211, 110 S Ct 2638.

## § 13. Ineffective Assistance of Counsel

There was no Sixth Amendment violation when defendant's attorney appeared at a plea hearing via speaker phone rather than in person. The physical absence of the defendant's attorney from his plea hearing did not constitute a "complete denial of counsel." Wright v Van Patten (2008) 552 US 120, 169 L Ed 2d 583, 2008 US LEXIS 200, 128 S Ct 743.

Even when a capital defendant's family members and the defendant himself have suggested that no mitigating evidence is available, his lawyer is bound to make reasonable efforts to obtain and review material that counsel knows the prosecution will probably rely on as evidence of aggravation at the sentencing phase of trial. It flouts prudence to deny that a defense lawyer should try to look at a file he knows the prosecution will cull for aggravating evidence, let alone when the file is sitting in the trial courthouse, open for the asking. No reasonable lawyer would forgo examination of the file thinking he could do as well by asking the defendant or family relations whether they recalled anything helpful or damaging in the prior victim's testimony. Nor would a reasonable lawyer compare possible searches for school reports, juvenile records, and evidence of drinking habits to the opportunity to take a look at a file disclosing what the prosecutor knows and even plans to read from in his case. Questioning a few more family members and searching for old records can promise less than looking for a needle in a haystack, when a lawyer truly has reason to doubt there is any needle there. But looking at a file the prosecution says it will use is a sure bet: whatever may be in that file is going to tell defense counsel something about what the prosecution can produce. Rompilla v Beard (2005) **545 US 374,** 162 L Ed 2d 360, 125 S Ct 2456, 2005 US LEXIS 4846.

### § 14. Confrontation

A defendant's right to confrontation was violated when a technician other than the one who signed the laboratory report certifying that his blood-alcohol concentration (BAC) was well above the threshold for aggravated DWI was called as a witness. This other analyst had neither participated in nor observed the test on defendant's blood sample, and therefore could not convey what the testing analyst knew or observed about the events he certified, nor expose any lapses or lies on that analyst's part. Bullcoming v New Mexico (2011) 2011 US LEXIS 4790.

When police asked a shooting victim "what had happened, who had shot him, and where the shooting had occurred," the primary purpose of the questions was to enable them to assist him in the face of an ongoing emergency. Thus, the shooting victim's responses were non-testimonial, and were therefore not barred at trial by the Confrontation Clause. Michigan v Bryant (2011) 179 L Ed 2d 93, 2011 US LEXIS 1713, 131 S Ct 1143.

The Confrontation Clause bars admission of testimonial statements of a witness who did not appear at trial unless he was unavailable to testify, and the defendant had a prior opportunity for cross-examination. These cases require the Court to determine which **police** "interrogations" produce statements that fall within this prohibition. Without attempting to produce an exhaustive classification of all conceivable statements as either testimonial or nontestimonial, it suffices to decide the present cases to hold that statements are nontestimonial when made in the course of **police** interrogation under circumstances objectively indicating that the primary purpose of interrogation is to enable **police** assistance to meet an ongoing emergency. They are testimonial when the circumstances objectively indicate that there is no such ongoing emergency, and that the primary purpose of the interrogation is to establish or prove past events potentially relevant to later criminal prosecution. Davis v Washington (2006) 547 US 813, 165 L Ed 2d 224, 126 S Ct 2266, 2006 US LEXIS 4886

The question in the instant case is whether, objectively considered, the interrogation during the 911 call produced testimonial statements. In contrast to Crawford, where the interrogation took place at a **police** station and was directed solely at establishing a past crime, a 911 call is ordinarily designed primarily to describe current circumstances requiring **police** assistance. The difference is apparent here. Domestic violence complainant was speaking of events as they were actually happening, while Crawford's interrogation took place hours after the events occurred. Moreover, complainant was facing an ongoing emergency. Further, the statements elicited were necessary to enable the **police** to resolve the present emergency rather than simply to learn what had happened in the past. Finally, the difference in the level of formality is striking. Crawford calmly answered questions at a station house, with an officer-interrogator taping and taking notes, while the frantic answers in the instant case were provided over the phone, in an environment that was not tranquil, or even safe. Thus, the circumstances of her interrogation objectively indicate that its primary purpose was to enable **police** assistance to meet an ongoing emergency. She was not acting as a witness or testifying. Davis v Washington (2006) 547 US 813, 165 L Ed 2d 224, 126 S Ct 2266, 2006 US LEXIS 4886

A criminal defendant's federal constitutional rights are violated by an evidence rule under which the defendant may not introduce evidence of third-party guilt if the prosecution has introduced forensic evidence that, if believed, strongly supports a guilty verdict. State and federal rulemakers have broad latitude under the Constitution to establish rules excluding evidence from criminal trials. This latitude, however, has limits. Whether rooted directly in the Due Process Clause of the Fourteenth Amendment or in the Compulsory Process or Confrontation clauses of the Sixth Amendment, the Constitution guarantees criminal defendants a meaningful opportunity to present a complete defense. This right is abridged by evidence rules that infringe upon a weighty interest of the accused and are arbitrary or disproportionate to the purposes they are designed to serve. Holmes v South Carolina (2006) 547 US 319, 164 L Ed 2d 503, 126 S Ct 1727, 2006 US LEXIS 3454

## Liability

### § 1. Police

While a two-step procedure for resolving whether officers have qualified immunity—(1) whether the facts alleged or shown by the plaintiff make out a violation of a constitutional right, and (2) if so, whether that right was "clearly established" at the time of the defendant's alleged misconduct—remains useful for courts, it is no longer mandatory. Courts now have the discretion to decide whether that procedure is worthwhile in particular cases. Pearson v Callahan (2009) 555 US 223, 172 L Ed 2d 565, 2009 US LEXIS 591, 129 S Ct 808.

Actions undertaken by police to terminate a dangerous high-speed car chase that threatens the lives of innocent by-standers—such as bumping the fleeing vehicle—do not create liability under §1983 even when such actions place the fleeing motorist at risk of death or serious bodily injury. Scott v Harris (2007) 550 US 372, 167 L Ed 2d 686, 127 S Ct 1769, 2007 US LEXIS 4748.

The statute of limitations upon a §1983 claim seeking damages for a false arrest in violation of the Fourth Amendment, where the arrest is followed by criminal proceedings, begins to run at the time the claimant becomes detained pursuant to legal process. Wallace v Kato (2007) 549 US 384, 166 L Ed 2d 973, 127 S Ct 1091, 2007 US LEXIS 2650.

There was no liability under 42 USCS §1983 when police failed to arrest the plaintiff's husband for violation of a temporary restraining order, even though he later went on to kill the couple's daughters (which he could not have done had he been in custody). It is not clear that an individual entitlement to enforcement of a restraining order could constitute a "property" interest for purposes of the Due Process Clause. Moreover, prior Supreme Court cases had recognized that a benefit is not a protected entitlement if government officials have discretion to grant or deny it; there is a well-established tradition of police discretion with regard to whether or not to make arrests. Town of Castle Rock v Gonzales (2005) 545 US 748, 162 L Ed 2d 658, 125 S Ct 2796, 2005 US LEXIS 5214.

Warrant was invalid, and the search was clearly unreasonable, in violation of the Fourth Amendment, for among other matters, (a) the warrant failed altogether to comply with the Fourth Amendment's unambiguous requirement that a warrant particularly describe the persons or things to be seized; (b) the fact that the application for the warrant adequately described the things to be seized did not save the warrant from its facial invalidity; (c) by not describing the items to be seized at all, the warrant was so obviously deficient that the search had to be regarded as "warrantless"; (d) searches and seizures inside a home without a warrant were presumptively unreasonable; and (e) the presumptive rule against warrantless searches applied with equal force to searches whose only defect was a lack of particularity in the warrant. And, in such circumstances, the agent was not entitled to qualified immunity, for among other matters, (a) no reasonable officer could have believed that a warrant that plainly did not comply with the Fourth Amendment's particularity requirement was valid; and (b) because the agent had prepared the invalid warrant, he could not properly argue that he reasonably had relied on the Magistrate's assurance that the warrant contained an adequate description of the things to be seized. Groh v Ramirez (2004) 540 US 551, 157 L Ed 2d 1068, **2004** US LEXIS 1624, 124 S Ct 1284.

With respect to an arrestee's 42 USCS § 1983 claims against a police supervisor—which claims arose out of the supervisor's allegedly coercive interrogation of the arrestee, without giving Miranda warnings, while the arrestee had been receiving medical treatment at a hospital after having been shot by another police officer during the altercation which had resulted in the arrest—the arrestee's allegations failed to state a valid § 1983 claim for a violation of the arrestee's privilege against self-incrimination, under the Federal Constitution's Fifth Amendment as made applicable to the states by the Constitution's Fourteenth Amendment, where (1) the arrestee had never been charged with any crime related to the altercation; and (2) thus, the arrestee's answers to the supervisor's interrogation had never been used against the arrestee in any subsequent criminal prosecution. Chavez v Martinez (2003) 538 US 760, 155 L Ed 2d 984, 2003 US LEXIS 4274.

On certiorari to review a Federal Court of Appeals' judgment upholding a Federal District Court's denial, to a police supervisor, of qualified immunity from some 42 USCS § 1983 claims by an arrestee—which claims arose out of the supervisor's allegedly coercive interrogation of the arrestee, without giving Miranda warnings, while the arrestee had been receiving medical treatment at a hospital after having been shot by another police officer during the altercation which had resulted in the arrest—the United States Supreme Court held that the issue whether the arrestee could properly pursue a claim of liability for a substantive due process violation, under the Federal Constitution's Fourteenth Amendment, was an issue that ought to be addressed on remand, along with the scope and merits of any such action that might be found open to the arrestee. Chavez v Martinez (2003) 538 US 760, 155 L Ed 2d 984, 2003 US LEXIS 4274.

High-speed police chases with no intent to harm suspects physically or to worsen their legal plight do not give rise to liability under the substantive due process guarantee of the Federal Constitution's Fourteenth Amendment, redressable by an action under 42 USCS § 1983 for violation of a federal right, as (1) a police officer deciding whether to give chase must balance the need to stop a suspect and show that flight from the law is no way to freedom against the high-speed threat to everyone within stopping range, be they suspects, their passengers, other drivers, or bystanders, (2) when unforeseen circumstances demand an officer's instant judgment, even precipitate recklessness fails to inch close enough to harmful purpose to spark the shock that implicates the large concerns of the governors and the governed, and (3) just as a purpose to cause harm is needed for liability under the Constitution's Eighth Amendment in a prison riot case, so it ought to be needed for due process liability in a pursuit case. County of Sacramento v Lewis (1998) 523 US 833, 140 L Ed 2d 1043, 1998 US LEXIS 3404, 118 S Ct 1708.

All claims brought under 42 USCS § 1983 in which it is alleged that law enforcement officers used excessive force—deadly or not—in the course of an arrest, investigatory stop, or other seizure of a free citizen are properly analyzed under the "objective reasonableness" standard of the Federal Constitution's Fourth Amendment, rather than under the more generalized standard of "substantive due process" pursuant to the due process clause of the Fourteenth Amendment, because the Fourth Amendment provides an explicit textual source of federal constitutional protection against such physically intrusive governmental conduct. Graham v Connor (1989) 490 US 386, 104 L Ed 2d 443, 1989 US LEXIS 2467, 109 S Ct 1865.

The right of law enforcement officers to make an arrest or investigatory stop of an individual, as a "reasonable" seizure under the Federal Constitution's Fourth Amendment, necessarily carries with it the right to use some degree of physical coercion or threat thereof to effect such arrest or stop. Graham v Connor (1989) 490 US 386, 104 L Ed 2d 443, 1989 US LEXIS 2467, 109 S Ct 1865.

With respect to a claim brought under 42 USCS § 1983 that a police officer has used excessive force in seizing an individual in violation of the Federal Constitution's Fourth Amendment, the inquiry as to the officer's "reasonableness" is an objective one, with the question being whether the officer's actions are objectively reasonable in light of the facts and circumstances confronting the officer, without regard to the officer's underlying intent or motivation; such reasonableness must be judged from the perspective of a reasonable officer on the scene, rather than with the 20/20 vision of hindsight; not every push or shove, even if it may later seem unnecessary in the peace of a judge's chambers, violates the Fourth Amendment, and the calculus of reasonableness must embody allowance for the fact that police officers are often forced to make split-second judgments about the amount of force that is necessary in a particular situation in circumstances that are tense, uncertain, and rapidly evolving; an officer's evil intentions will not make a Fourth Amendment violation out of an objectively reasonable use of force, nor will an officer's good intentions make an objectively unreasonable use of force constitutional. Graham v Connor (1989) 490 US 386, 104 L Ed 2d 443, 1989 US LEXIS 2467, 109 S Ct 1865.

In an action under 42 USCS § 1983, whereby the relatives of an individual who fatally crashed into a police roadblock following a high-speed nighttime chase by county police seek to hold the county and other defendants liable on the ground that they unreasonably seized the individual in violation of his rights under the Federal Constitution's Fourth Amendment, a determination that the use of the roadblock constitutes a "seizure" is not enough for 1983 liability, as the seizure must be "unreasonable". Brower v County of Inyo (1989) 489 US 593, 103 L Ed 2d 628, 1989 US LEXIS 1569, 109 S Ct 1378.

A federal law enforcement officer who conducts a warrantless search in violation of the Fourth Amendment will not be held personally liable for money damages if it is found that a reasonable officer could have believed the search to be lawful under the Fourth Amendment in light of clearly established law and the information possessed by the searching officer. Anderson v Creighton (1987) 483 US 635, 97 L Ed 2d 523, 1987 US LEXIS 2894, 107 S Ct 3034.

A police officer who applies for a search warrant that is not supported by reasonable cause is immune from liability for damages if a reasonable officer could have believed that there was probable cause to support the application. Anderson v Creighton (1987) 483 US 635, 97 L Ed 2d 523, 1987 US LEXIS 2894, 107 S Ct 3034.

Public officials, including state and federal law enforcement officers, are immune from personal liability for their allegedly unlawful official actions unless the law clearly proscribes the actions they took; such qualified immunity protects all but the plainly incompetent or those who knowingly violate the law; whether an official protected by qualified immunity may be held personally liable generally turns on the objective legal reasonableness of the allegedly unlawful action, assessed in the light of the legal rules that were clearly established at the time it was taken; in addition, the contours of the right that the official is alleged to have violated must be sufficiently clear that a reasonable official would understand that what he or she is doing violates that right; the unlawfulness of the contested action must be apparent in the light of pre-existing law, although the very action in question need not have been previously held unlawful. Anderson v Creighton (1987) 483 US 635, 97 L Ed 2d 523, 1987 US LEXIS 2894, 107 S Ct 3034.

In an action under 42 USCS § 1983 against a police officer whose successful request for a warrant allegedly causes an unconstitutional arrest because his complaint and supporting affidavit fail to establish probable cause, the officer is not entitled to absolute immunity from liability for damages, but is entitled only to a qualified immunity which depends on the objective reasonableness of his actions; the officer will not be immune if, on an objective basis, the application is so lacking in indicia of probable cause that no reasonably competent officer would have concluded that a warrant should issue, but immunity should be recognized if officers of reasonable competence could disagree on this issue; the officer is not shielded from damages liability on the theory that the act of applying for a warrant is per se objectively reasonable if the officer believes that the facts alleged in his affidavit are true. Malley v Briggs (1986) 475 US 335, 89 L Ed 2d 271, 1986 US LEXIS 29, 106 S Ct 1092.

### § 2. Prosecutors

Prosecutors involved in supervision or training of attorneys or information-system management focused upon administrative obligations directly related with the conduct of a trial enjoy absolute immunity. Immunity applies whether the training given was general or specific to a certain case. Van De Kamp v Goldstein (2009) 555 US 335, 172 L Ed 2d 706, 2009 US LEXIS 1003, 129 S Ct 855.

The conduct of a county prosecuting attorney in making allegedly false statements of fact in a certification for determination of probable cause—a document that summarizes the evidence supporting an application for an arrest warrant—is not protected by the doctrine of absolute prosecutorial immunity, where (1) although state law, in compliance with the command of the Federal Constitution's Fourth Amendment, requires an arrest warrant to be supported by either an affidavit or sworn testimony establishing the grounds for issuing the warrant, neither federal nor state law makes it necessary for the prosecutor to make such certification, (2) even if the prosecutor may be following a practice that has been routinely employed by the prosecutor's colleagues and predecessors, the practice is not prevalent in other parts of the country and is not mandated by law in the county, (3) the prosecutor, in making the certification, thus performs a function of a witness rather than an advocate, and (4) denying the prosecutor absolute immunity will not have a chilling effect on prosecutors in the administration of justice; thus, 42 USCS § 1983, under some circumstances, provide a damages remedy against such a prosecutor insofar as the prosecutor performs the function of a complaining witness. Kalina v Fletcher (1997) 522 US 118, 139 L Ed 2d 471, 1997 US LEXIS 7498, 118 S Ct 502.

A prosecutor is fully protected by absolute immunity when performing the traditional functions of an advocate; such absolute immunity (1) is not grounded in any special esteem for those who perform these functions, and (2) does not stem from a desire to shield abuses of office, but (3) is given because any lesser degree of immunity could impair the judicial process itself. Kalina v Fletcher (1997) 522 US 118, 139 L Ed 2d 471, 1997 US LEXIS 7498, 118 S Ct 502.

A state prosecutor is not entitled to absolute immunity from an accused's claim seeking damages for the prosecutor's allegedly false statements at a press conference announcing the return of an indictment against the accused concerning a rape and murder, which claim is brought under 42 USCS § 1983—which provides a private right of action against a person who, under color of state law, violates another person's federal rights. Buckley v Fitzsimmons (1993) 509 US 259, 125 L Ed 2d 209, 1993 US LEXIS 4400, 113 S Ct 2606.

With respect to being sued under 42 USCS § 1983, which provides a private right of action against a person who, under color of state law, violates another person's federal rights, most public officials are entitled to only qualified immunity—that is, such officials are not subject to damages liability for the performance of their discretionary functions when their conduct does not violate clearly established federal statutory or constitutional rights of which a reasonable person would have known—which immunity, in most cases, is sufficient to protect (1) officials who are required to exercise their discretion, and (2) the related public interest in encouraging the vigorous exercise of official authority. Buckley v Fitzsimmons (1993) 509 US 259, 125 L Ed 2d 209, 1993 US LEXIS 4400, 113 S Ct 2606.

Acts which are undertaken by a prosecutor in preparing for the initiation of judicial proceedings or for trial and occur in the course of the prosecutor's rule as an advocate for the state are entitled to the protections of absolute immunity from a suit seeking damages under 42 USCS § 1983, which provides a private right of action against a person who, under color of state law, violates another person's federal rights; such acts by a prosecutor include (1) the professional evaluation of evidence assembled by the police, and (2) appropriate preparation for presentation of the evidence at trial and before a grand jury after a decision to seek an indictment has been made. Buckley v Fitzsimmons (1993) 509 US 259, 125 L Ed 2d 209, 1993 US LEXIS 4400, 113 S Ct 2606.

A determination of probable cause to arrest a person does not guarantee a prosecutor absolute immunity from liability for all actions taken by the prosecutor after such a determination, because, even after such a determination, a prosecutor may engage in "police investigative work" that is entitled to only qualified immunity. Buckley v Fitzsimmons (1993) 509 US 259, 125 L Ed 2d 209, 1993 US LEXIS 4400, 113 S Ct 2606.

A local prosecutor is entitled to absolute immunity from liability for damages under 42 USCS § 1983 for the prosecutor's appearance as a lawyer for the state in a probable cause hearing in which the prosecutor examines a witness and successfully supports an application for a search warrant. Burns v Reed (1991) 500 US 478, 114 L Ed 2d 547, 1991 US LEXIS 3018, 111 S Ct 1934.

For purposes of liability for damages under 42 USCS § 1983, a local prosecutor has not met his burden of showing that the relevant factors justify an extension of absolute immunity to the prosecutorial function of giving legal advice to the police in the investigative phase of a criminal case, and thus the prosecutor is entitled to only qualified immunity for giving such advice. Burns v Reed (1991) 500 US 478, 114 L Ed 2d 547, 1991 US LEXIS 3018, 111 S Ct 1934.

### § 3. Municipality

An award of damages under 42 USCS § 1983, for an arrest allegedly without probable cause and with excessive force, is not authorized against a municipal corporation based on the actions of one of its officers, when the jury has concluded that the officer inflicted no constitutional harm, and the fact that departmental regulations might have authorized the use of constitutionally excessive force is beside the point. Los Angeles v Heller (1986) 475 US 796, 89 L Ed 2d 806, 1986 US LEXIS 99, 106 S Ct 1571.

# Forfeiture

### § 1. In General

A seizure of property by the government must comply with the due process clauses of the Federal Constitution's Fifth and Fourteenth Amendments, where the property is seized not to preserve evidence of wrongdoing but to assert ownership and control over the property itself; although the Constitution's Fourth Amendment places restrictions on seizures conducted for purposes of civil forfeiture, the Fourth Amendment does not provide the sole measure of constitutional protection that must be afforded property owners in civil forfeiture proceedings. United States v James Daniel Good Real Property (1993) 510 US 43, 126 L Ed 2d 490, 1993 US LEXIS 7941, 114 S Ct 492.

### § 2. Automobiles

The Federal Constitution's Fourth Amendment does not require the police to obtain a warrant before seizing an automobile from a public place when the police have probable cause to believe that the vehicle itself is forfeitable contraband, since (1) the recognized need to seize readily movable contraband before it is taken away is equally weighty when the automobile itself, as opposed to its contents, is the contraband that police seek to secure, and (2) the seizure, which occurs in a public place, does not involve any invasion of the vehicle owner's privacy. Florida v White (1999) 526 US 559, 143 L Ed 2d 748, 1999 US LEXIS 3172, 119 S Ct 1555.

The Fourth Amendment does not require a warrant to seize an individual's automobile where the police, while arresting the individual on unrelated charges, seize the automobile from his employer's parking lot without a warrant, on the ground that (1) the individual was previously been observed using the vehicle to deliver narcotics, and (2) the vehicle was therefore allegedly subject to forfeiture as contraband under a state statute. Florida v White (1999) 526 US 559, 143 L Ed 2d 748, 1999 US LEXIS 3172, 119 S Ct 1555.

A state's forfeiture of an automobile as a public nuisance—under the state's nuisance abatement statute, without an offset for the interest of an innocent co-owner—does not offend the due process clause of the Federal Constitution's Fourteenth Amendment or the takings clause of the Constitution's Fifth Amendment where an owner of the vehicle is convicted of gross indecency as a result of his engaging in a sexual act in the vehicle with a prostitute, without the knowledge of the co-owner, his spouse, that the vehicle was to be utilized for illegal activity. Bennis v Michigan (1996) 516 US 442, 134 L Ed 2d 68, 116 S Ct 994.

### § 3. Drug-Related

With respect to the administrative forfeiture, pursuant to a provision of the Controlled Substances Act (21 USCS § 881(a)(6)), of a federal prisoner's property that had been seized during the execution of a search warrant for the residence where the prisoner had been arrested, the means employed to provide notice to the prisoner were reasonably calculated, under all the circumstances, to apprise the prisoner of the forfeiture—and thus such notice satisfied the due process clause of the Federal Constitution's Fifth Amendment, even if the prisoner did not actually receive notice—where (1) federal agents sent notice by certified mail (a) addressed to the prisoner care of the prison where the prisoner was incarcerated, (b) to the address of the residence where the prisoner had been arrested, and (c) to an address in the town where the prisoner's mother lived; and (2) according to a prison officer's testimony, (a) the officer signed the certified mail receipt for the notice, and (b) the prison's procedure would normally have been for the officer to log the mail in, for a "Unit Team" of the federal Bureau of Prisons to sign for the mail, and for the mail to be given to the prisoner. Dusenbery v United States (2002) 534 US 161, 151 L Ed 2d 597, 2002 US LEXIS 401, 122 S Ct 694.

In order to show exigent circumstances which, for purposes of the due process clause of the Federal Constitution's Fifth Amendment, would justify the Federal Government's seizure of real property—pursuant to 21 USCS § 881(a)(7), which generally authorizes the civil forfeiture of property used to commit or facilitate the commission of a drug offense—without affording the owner prior notice and an opportunity to be heard, the government must show that less restrictive measures, such as a lis pendens, restraining order, or bond, would not suffice to protect the government's interests in preventing the sale, destruction, or continued unlawful use of the real property. United States v James Daniel Good Real Property (1993) 510 US 43, 126 L Ed 2d 490, 1993 US LEXIS 7941, 114 S Ct 492.

The Federal Government's seizure, pursuant to a federal drug forfeiture statute (21 USCS § 881(a)(7)), of a person's home and the 4-acre parcel of land on which the home is situated deprives the person of property interests protected by the due process clause of the Federal Constitution's Fifth Amendment, where the seizure gives the government the right to charge rent, to condition occupancy, and to evict the occupants. United States v James Daniel Good Real Property (1993) 510 US 43, 126 L Ed 2d 490, 1993 US LEXIS 7941, 114 S Ct 492.

In an in rem action for the forfeiture of property to the United States pursuant to 21 USCS § 881(a)(6) (a provision of the Comprehensive Drug Abuse Prevention and Control Act of 1970), a bona fide purchaser for value of the property is entitled to assert an "innocent owner" defense, under the provision of 881(a)(6) that no property shall be forfeited to the extent of the interest of an owner by reason of any act or omission established by that owner to have been committed or omitted "without the knowledge or consent of that owner." United States v 92 Buena Vista Ave. (1993) 507 US 111, 122 L Ed 2d 469, 1993 US LEXIS 1782, 113 S Ct 1126.

# Juveniles

## § 1. In General

The due process clause applies in juvenile proceedings, but a juvenile proceeding is fundamentally different from an adult criminal trial so that a court must respect the informality and flexibility that characterize juvenile proceedings while insuring that such proceedings comport with the fundamental fairness demanded by the due process clause. Schall v Martin (1984) 467 US 253, 81 L Ed 2d 207, 1984 US LEXIS 96, 104 S Ct 2403.

Proof beyond a reasonable doubt is among the essentials of due process and fair treatment required during the adjudicatory stage when a juvenile is charged with an act which would constitute a crime if committed by an adult, and a state statue permitting a determination of delinquency on a preponderance of the evidence is unconstitutional. In re Winship (1970) 397 US 358, 25 L Ed 2d 368, 1970 US LEXIS 56, 90 S Ct 1068.

## § 2. Death Penalty Eligibility

The Eighth and Fourteenth Amendments forbid imposition of the death penalty on offenders who were under the age of 18 when their crimes were committed. Roper v Simmons (2005) 543 US 551, 161 L Ed 2d 1, 2005 US LEXIS 2200, 125 S Ct 1183.

There is some age below which a juvenile's crimes can never, consistently with the Federal Constitution, be punished by death. Thompson v Oklahoma (1988) 487 US 815, 101 L Ed 2d 702, 1988 US LEXIS 3028, 108 S Ct 2687.

## § 3. Determination of Delinquency

Although the Fourteenth Amendment does not require that a hearing at which a determination is made as to whether a juvenile is a delinquent, subjecting him to commitment to a state institution, conform with all the requirements of a criminal trial or even of the usual administrative proceeding, the due process clause does require application during the adjudicatory hearing of the essentials of due process and fair treatment. In re Winship (1970) 397 US 358, 25 L Ed 2d 368, 1970 US LEXIS 56, 90 S Ct 1068.

Juveniles, like adults, are constitutionally entitled, under the due process clause, to proof beyond a reasonable doubt when they are charged with violation of a criminal law, and the constitutionality of a state statute permitting a determination of delinquency on a preponderance of the evidence cannot be sustained on the grounds that (1) a delinquency adjudication is not a "conviction" and affects no right or privilege, including the right to hold public office or to obtain a license; (2) a cloak of protective confidentiality is thrown around all the proceedings; (3) the delinquency status is not made a crime and the proceedings are not criminal; or (4) juvenile proceedings are designed not to punish but to save the child. In re Winship (1970) 397 US 358, 25 L Ed 2d 368, 1970 US LEXIS 56, 90 S Ct 1068.

### § 4. Pre-Trial Detention

A state statute authorizing pretrial detention of an accused juvenile delinquent, based on a finding that there is a serious risk that the child may before the return date commit an act which if committed by an adult would constitute a crime, serves a legitimate state objective of protecting the child and society from the potential consequences of his criminal acts, and thereby is compatible with the fundamental fairness required by due process, and satisfies the procedural safeguards of due process where the detention is limited to 17 days and the accused juvenile is given full notice of the charges against him and is given a hearing at which he is informed of his rights, may be accompanied by a parent or guardian, may be represented by counsel chosen by him or by a law guardian assigned by the court, and may call witnesses and offer evidence, and at which probable cause must be established to believe that the juvenile committed the offense. Schall v Martin (1984) 467 US 253, 81 L Ed 2d 207, 1984 US LEXIS 96, 104 S Ct 2403.

## Practice Pointers

### Selected from legal analysts' annotations in
### United States Supreme Court Reports, L Ed 2d

**From Validity, under Federal Constitution's Fourth Amendment, of searches of parolees or probationers on asserted basis of their status—Supreme Court cases, 165 L Ed 2d 1055**

Defense counsel seeking to challenge the validity of a warrantless search of a probationer or a parolee may want to consider the type of proceeding in which evidence discovered during a search is being offered. If a revocation of parole or probation is involved, then the evidence may be admissible regardless of the validity of the search, as the exclusionary rule of the Federal Constitution's Fourth Amendment has been held inapplicable to parole revocation proceedings.

If evidence uncovered in a warrantless search is offered in support of new criminal charges against a probationer or a parolee, then a relevant consideration in determining validity of the search may include whether any agreed-upon condition of parole or probation or any applicable regulation or statute purports to authorize warrantless searches of probationers or parolees, with or without probable cause. Absent such express authorization for warrantless searches regardless of probable cause, it may be possible for defense counsel to argue that the probationer or parolee has a greater expectation of privacy that should factor into the determination of whether the search was reasonable (§§ 3 and 4). Also, in the event of a warrantless search of a probationer without any individualized suspicion, defense counsel may wish to note the Supreme Court's finding that probationers have a greater expectation of privacy than do parolees because parole is more akin to imprisonment than is probation (§4).

A prosecutor who seeks admission of evidence obtained in a warrantless search of the person or property of a probationer or a parolee may wish to determine whether the search could be supported by some additional basis, such as express consent to the particular search, in order to provide a possible alternative approach to an expectation-of-privacy analysis.

**From Validity, under Federal Constitution's Fourth Amendment, of investigative stop of motor vehicle by roving federal border patrol—Supreme Court cases, 151 L Ed 2d 1111**

When a case might involve the validity, under the Federal Constitution's Fourth Amendment, of an investigative stop of a motor vehicle by a roving federal border patrol, counsel for either side should be prepared properly to raise and to preserve any appropriate issues. For example, United States v Brignoni-Ponce (1975) 422 US 873, 45 L Ed 2d 607, 95 S Ct 2574, infra §§ 3 and 4[b], the record indicated that an individual had been convicted, on a federal immigration charge, after his car had been pursued and stopped by some United States Border Patrol officers, who initially had been parked at the side of a road near a Border Patrol checkpoint, in southern California, that had been closed due to the weather. The Supreme Court treated the stop in question as one by a roving patrol, rather than one involving a checkpoint, as the court observed that this "factual conclusion" by the Federal Court of Appeals below was unchallenged by the Federal Government. Moreover, the Supreme Court said that it declined "at this stage of the case" to give any weight to the stop's location as a basis for justifying the stop, as the Supreme Court noted that (1) the stop's location appeared to be an after-the-fact justification; (2) at trial, the officers had given no reason for the stop except the apparent Mexican ancestry of the car's occupants; and (3) it was not even clear that the Federal Government had presented the broader justification to the Court of Appeals.

**From Accused's right, under Federal Constitution, to be present at accused's own trial—Supreme Court cases, 146 L Ed 2d 985**

When asserting an accused's right to be present at trial, defense counsel may find it advisable-instead of, or in addition to, relying upon the Federal Constitution-to rely upon such possible alternative bases of the right to be present as (1) federal statutes or court rules,6 or (2) constitutional provisions, statutes, or court rules of states, territories, or possessions of the United States.

Although a disruptive defendant may, under some circumstances, properly be removed from the trial courtroom (see §4[a]), defense counsel may wish to suggest alternatives to such removal where, for example, the defendant may have a propensity to escape or has threatened to do harm. Some alternative measures-which would preserve the defendant's right to be present and at the same time might help maintain decorum and security in the courtroom-could include various modern methods of restraint that are less cumbersome and visible than traditional handcuffs or chains.

In some cases involving alleged child abuse, the prosecution may seek to avoid face-to-face courtroom contact between the accused and the alleged victim, as by means of closed circuit television testimony. In order to preserve the accused's right to be present at the trial, defense counsel may find it advisable to agree to such technological methods only if (1) there is a particularized showing of need to protect the child witness because of actual trauma, intimidation, or the like; and (2) the chosen procedure does not deny the accused a meaningful opportunity to confront the accusers, assist in cross-examination, or otherwise assist in the defense.

### From Right, under Federal Constitution, of accused to represent himself or herself in criminal proceedings—Supreme Court cases, 145 L Ed 2d 1177:

Where a criminal defendant chooses to represent himself or herself at trial, the judge may wish to determine, among other matters, whether the defendant has the mental capacity to present a coherent defense. Also, the judge may find it advisable to appoint standby counsel, especially if the case is expected to be long or complicated, or if there are multiple defendants.

Counsel who has been asked by a pro se criminal defendant to aid in the defense, or who has been appointed standby counsel by the trial court without the defendant's solicitation, should be aware that the role of counsel in such a situation is a sensitive and sometimes difficult one. Thus, although counsel may expect to take part in such tasks as investigating the facts and law of the case, preparing and presenting pretrial motions, helping the defendant present the case in court, and assembling and presenting information relevant to sentencing, counsel may find it prudent to keep in mind that it is the defendant who still has the right to control all strategic decisions and speak for the defense unless the court specifically directs otherwise.

### From Validity, under Federal Constitution, of warrantless search of motor vehicle—Supreme Court cases, 142 L Ed 2d 993:

When preparing a Fourth Amendment challenge to a warrantless motor vehicle search, it may be prudent for counsel to review the relevant police reports to see whether such records appear to be incomplete or fail to articulate a specific ground for the search. In the case of a search that was purportedly consented to by the accused, a careful examination of any available records may support an argument that (1) the consent had been revoked prior to the search; or (2) the accused had given only limited consent, which was exceeded by the scope of the search as actually carried out.

In contesting the validity of a warrantless motor vehicle search that was conducted under the "automobile exception" to the requirement of a search warrant, counsel may wish to consider a factor that has been held to be significant with respect to searches incident to arrest, namely, the timing of the search. If it appears that the search was not conducted quickly or as soon as practicable after the vehicle was stopped, counsel may choose to argue that the police (1) had time to obtain a search warrant, and (2) ought to have done so under the circumstances presented.

In a case involving the warrantless search of an automobile's passenger compartment incident to arrest, counsel may find it advisable to argue, where possible, that even though the search may have been permissible as a matter of federal constitutional law, the applicable state's own law has been—or ought to be—interpreted so as to invalidate such a search. Similar arguments may possibly be employed with respect to other categories of warrantless motor vehicle searches. For example, if a state's constitution has been authoritatively interpreted to the effect that a search under the automobile exception requires not only probable cause but exigent circumstances—which rule is stricter than the United States Supreme Court's interpretation of the Fourth Amendment—then counsel may wish to invoke such a rule of state law.

### From Prejudicial effect of admitting at criminal trial evidence of confession or other self-incriminating statement obtained from accused in violation of federal constitution—Supreme Court cases, 113 L Ed 2d 757:

Whenever a self-incriminating, unconstitutionally obtained statement is introduced into evidence at a criminal trial, it would seem advisable for the defense counsel to make a timely objection and to move for the exclusion of the statement in order to preserve the issue for appeal, notwithstanding early Supreme Court decisions which indicated that the admission in evidence of an involuntary confession was so fundamental a constitutional error that the accused could not properly be considered to have waived the right to challenge, on appeal, the voluntariness of the confession and its admission in evidence.

### From Supreme Court's views as to constitutionality of inventory searches, 109 L Ed 2d 776:

Although an inventory search may be "reasonable" for purposes of the Federal Constitution's Fourth Amendment, counsel for an accused in a state criminal case may be successful in invalidating the search on the ground that the search violated a state constitutional provision—even where such provision is closely analogous to the Fourth Amendment—given the power of state courts to provide an individual with greater protection under the state constitution than that afforded by the Federal Constitution. Furthermore, while the Supreme Court has upheld the validity of police inventories of impounded vehicles in accordance with standard inventory procedures, counsel for an accused should consider challenging the lawfulness of the initial impounding of the vehicle where the evidence warrants such contention.

**From Constitutionality of searching premises without warrant as incident to valid arrest—Supreme Court cases, 108 L Ed 2d 987:**

Besides making themselves aware of the holdings contained in Supreme Court decisions restricting the permissible scope of a search of premises as an incident to a valid arrest, federal and state prosecuting attorneys should seek to assure that law enforcement officers are made aware of these restrictions and comply with them when they conduct searches and seizures. For example, law enforcement officers should be forewarned that if they are concerned about the possible presence of weapons or evidence in areas of the premises beyond the reach of an arrestee, they should not make a nonconsensual search without a warrant, but should remove the arrestee from the premises or handcuff him immediately after arresting him, and, while keeping the premises under close surveillance, should obtain a search warrant.

**From Supreme Court's views as to what constitutes valid waiver of accused's federal constitutional right to counsel, 101 L Ed 2d 1017:**

Counsel prosecuting a case against an accused who is not being represented by counsel, or was not represented or assisted by counsel at any time at which the accused had the federal constitutional right to such representation or assistance, should be certain that the record of the legal proceedings against the accused shows that (1) the accused was made aware of this right at all stages of the proceedings at which the right existed, (2) if the accused is indigent, he or she was offered the assistance of appointed counsel, and (3) the accused waived the right to the assistance of counsel at all stages at which he or she had the right and was not assisted by counsel. Failure to insure that such evidence is entered into the record may result in a conviction's being overturned in a later proceeding in which the waiver issue arises, because the Supreme Court has said that presuming an accused's waiver of the right to the assistance of counsel from a silent record is impermissible, and that the record must show, or there must be an allegation and evidence which show, that the accused was offered counsel but intelligently and understandingly rejected the offer.

**From What constitutes "seizure" within meaning of Federal Constitution's Fourth Amendment—Supreme Court cases, 100 L Ed 2d 981:**

Counsel for a party who is aggrieved by an official search or seizure (1) should bear in mind that the party's remedies are not limited to challenging the use of any resulting evidence in subsequent criminal proceedings, and (2) may wish to advise such a party to institute a civil action for damages against one responsible for an unlawful search and seizure in contravention of the Federal Constitution's Fourth Amendment. For example, under 42 USCS § 1983, a civil cause of action may be brought against state officials for deprivation of the right to be free from unreasonable searches and seizures; and although § 1983 has been held not applicable if evidence resulting from such search or seizure is excluded at trial in a criminal proceeding and if the would-be civil plaintiff, as defendant therein, is nevertheless convicted, relief may be available in that situation through a common-law action for damages against errant law enforcement officials, such as an action for trespass, replevin of articles taken by the officials, or false imprisonment.

Counsel for a party who wishes to claim that a police roadblock constituted an unreasonable seizure should take particular care to establish the physical and operational circumstances of the roadblock, such as the physical structure of any barrier that was used, the presence of uniformed officers, the manner of selection of automobiles to be stopped, the existence and use of safety measures, and the visibility of the roadblock. Although the United States Supreme Court has eschewed consideration of such factors in resolving the question whether the use of a roadblock constitutes a "seizure" within the meaning of the Fourth Amendment, it has indicated that the circumstances of the roadblock may be decisive on the issue as to whether such a seizure is "reasonable."

**From What constitutes probable cause for arrest—Supreme Court cases, 28 L Ed 2d 978:**

If the attorney for a person who has been arrested wishes to contend that the arrest was made without probable cause, a common method of raising this contention is to challenge the arrest in the course of defending a criminal prosecution, for example, by means of a motion to suppress evidence obtained through a search conducted after the arrest, but other methods which the attorney may wish to use as a means of challenging an arrest for lack of probable cause include: (1) Instituting habeas corpus proceedings for the purpose of obtaining the arrestee's release from custody, (2) instituting a common-law action for false imprisonment, or a statutory action for violation of civil rights, or both.

## Annotation References

Validity, under Federal Constitution, of imposing death penalty on particular categories of offenders—Supreme Court cases. 161 L Ed 2d 1173

Validity, under Federal Constitution's Fourth Amendment, of investigative stop of motor vehicle by roving federal border patrol—Supreme Court cases. 151 L Ed 2d 1111.

Accused's right, under Federal Constitution, to be present at accused's own trial—Supreme Court cases. 146 L Ed 2d 985.

Right, under Federal Constitution, of accused to represent himself or herself in criminal proceedings—Supreme Court cases. 145 L Ed 2d 1177.

Validity, under Federal Constitution, of warrantless search of motor vehicle—Supreme Court cases. 142 L Ed 2d 993.

Applicability and application, to questions concerning what violates Federal Constitution's Fourth Amendment guarantee against unreasonable searches and seizures, of "knock and announce" doctrine that law enforcement officers, before entering premises, must knock and announce some matters—Supreme Court cases. 140 L Ed 2d 1111.

Requirement, under Federal Constitution's Fourth Amendment guarantee against unreasonable searches and seizures, that warrants, when issued upon probable cause, must be supported "by Oath or affirmation"—Supreme Court cases. 139 L Ed 2d 971.

Conviction or acquittal in criminal prosecution as bar to particular actions for forfeiture of property or for statutory damages or penalties—Supreme Court cases. 135 L Ed 2d 1133.

Taking of individual's bodily fluid or material for analysis or comparison as violating individual's rights under Federal Constitution—Supreme Court cases. 132 L Ed 2d 1021.

Requirement, under Federal constitution, that law enforcement officer's custodial interrogation cease after suspect requests assistance of counsel—Supreme Court cases. 129 L Ed 2d 955.

Supreme Court's views as to due process requirements, under Federal Constitution's Fifth and Fourteenth Amendments, concerning forfeitures of property to government as result of unlawful conduct. 126 L Ed 2d 799.

Prejudicial effect of admitting at criminal trial evidence of confession or other self-incriminating statement obtained from accused in violation of federal constitution—Supreme Court cases. 113 L Ed 2d 757.

Applicability of "plain view" doctrine and its relation to Fourth Amendment prohibition against unreasonable searches and seizures—Supreme Court cases. 110 L Ed 2d 704.

Supreme Court's views as to constitutionality of inventory searches. 109 L Ed 2d 776.

Constitutionality of searching premises without warrant as incident to valid arrest—Supreme Court cases. 108 L Ed 2d 987.

Law enforcement officer's authority, under Federal Constitution's Fourth Amendment, to stop and briefly detain, and to conduct limited protective search of or "frisk," for investigative purposes, person suspected of criminal activity—Supreme Court cases. 104 L Ed 2d 1046.

Supreme Court's views as to accused's federal constitutional right to counsel on appeal. 102 L Ed 2d 1049.

Supreme Court's views as to what constitutes valid waiver of accused's federal constitutional right to counsel. 101 L Ed 2d 1017.

What constitutes "seizure" within meaning of Federal Constitution's Fourth Amendment—Supreme Court cases. 100 L Ed 2d 981.

Fourth Amendment's prohibition of unreasonable search and seizure as applied to administrative inspections of private property—Supreme Court cases. 69 L Ed 2d 1078.

The Progeny of Miranda v Arizona in the Supreme Court. 46 L Ed 2d 903.

Validity, under Federal Constitution, of consent to search—Supreme Court cases. 36 L Ed 2d 1143.

What constitutes probable cause for arrest—Supreme Court cases. 28 L Ed 2d 978.

Supreme Court

Admissibility of evidence obtained by illegal search and seizure—Supreme Court cases. 6 L Ed 2d 1544.

Accused's right to counsel under the Federal Constitution—Supreme Court cases. 2 L Ed 2d 1644, 9 L Ed 2d 1260.

Admissibility of pretrial confession in criminal case—Supreme Court cases. 1 L Ed 2d 1735, 4 L Ed 2d 1833, 12 L Ed 2d 1340, 16 L Ed 2d 1294, 22 L Ed 2d 872.

# User's Guide to the Index

Two guidelines for using this index are:

(1) *Consult the most pertinent subject.* For example, if you were looking in an evidence book for information about depositions, you would start with DEPOSITIONS rather than broader headings like EVIDENCE, TESTIMONY or WITNESSES. The broader headings may also exist, but to find the material more quickly, look for the specific subject first.

(2) *Cross references.* Pay close attention to and make full use of the index cross references. An index cross reference directs the index user to go to another part of the index to find treatment.

The index benefits from customer suggestions. Especially helpful are popular names or legal terms specific to your area of practice. We are grateful for your assistance in the ongoing improvement of the index.

To make comments or suggestions to improve this index or for assistance in locating material within this index, please use one of the following methods:

- Toll Free Number: 1-800-897-7922.
- Email: LNG-CHO-Indexing@lexisnexis.com

For issues not directly related to the Index, such as missing pages, ordering or other customer service information, you may contact Customer Service via a toll-free number, 1-800-833-9844, or by toll-free fax at 1-800-828-8341.

# Index

## A

**ABANDONED PROPERTY.**
**Seized under search warrant.**
Disposition of property, Crim Proc 18.17.
**ABANDONED VEHICLES,** Transp 683.001 to
683.078.
**Conflict of laws,** Transp 683.003.
**Definitions,** Transp 683.001.
**Demolition,** Transp 683.051 to 683.057.
Application for authorization, Transp 683.051,
683.052.
Certificate of authority, Transp 683.054.
Duties of demolisher, Transp 683.056.
Notice by department, Transp 683.053.
Records of demolisher, Transp 683.057.
Rules and forms, Transp 683.055.
**Junked vehicles,** Transp 683.071 to 683.078.
Authority to abate nuisance, Transp 683.074.
Declaration as public nuisance, Transp
683.072.
Definition, Transp 683.071, 683.0711.
Disposal, Transp 683.078.
Hearings, Transp 683.076, 683.0765.
Inapplicability of provisions, Transp 683.077.
Notice of nuisance abatement, Transp
683.075.
Offense of maintaining public nuisance,
Transp 683.073.
**Seizure and auction,** Transp 683.011 to
683.016.
Auction procedures, Transp 683.015.
Authority to seize, Transp 683.011.
Notice of auction, Transp 683.014.
Notice of taking into custody, Transp 683.012.
Proceeds from auction, Transp 683.015.
Storage fees, Transp 683.013.
Use of vehicle by law enforcement agency,
Transp 683.016.
Waiver of right to title, Transp 683.014.
**Storage facilities, abandoned in,** Transp
683.031 to 683.034.
Disposal of vehicle, Occ 2303.157, 2303.1545,
Transp 683.034.
Duty of garagekeeper, Transp 683.031.
Fees and charges, Transp 683.032.
Unauthorized storage fee, Transp 683.033.
**Unattended vehicles,** Occ 2308.251 to
2308.407, Transp 545.404.
See UNATTENDED VEHICLES.
**When deemed abandoned,** Transp 683.002.

**ABANDONING A CHILD,** Penal 22.041.
**Governmental actions to protect child,**
Fam 262.008.
Emergency possession of abandoned child,
Fam 262.301 to 262.309.
Generally, Fam 262.001 to 262.309.
See GOVERNMENTAL ACTIONS TO
PROTECT CHILD.
**Leaving in vehicle,** Penal 22.10.
**Limitation of actions,** Crim Proc 12.01.
**ABANDONMENT/ENDANGERMENT OF**
**CHILD,** Penal 22.041.
**ABDUCTION.**
**Agreement to abduct from custody for**
**remuneration,** Penal 25.031.
**Definitions,** Penal 20.01.
**Enticing of child,** Penal 25.04.
**Guardian's rights, interfering with,** Penal
25.10.
**Interference with child custody,** Penal
25.03.
**Kidnapping,** Penal 20.03.
Aggravated kidnapping, Penal 20.04.
**Limitation of actions,** Crim Proc 12.01.
**Murder committed during,** Penal 19.03.
**Sentence and punishment.**
Restitution, Crim Proc 42.0371.
**Smuggling of persons,** Penal 20.05.
**Unlawful restraint,** Penal 20.02.
**Venue of prosecution,** Crim Proc 13.12.
**ABORTION.**
**Assaultive offenses, inapplicability of**
**chapter,** Penal 22.12.
**Governmental actions to protect child.**
Abortion, child living as result of, Fam
262.006.
**Homicide, applicability of chapter,** Penal
19.06.
**ABUSABLE VOLATILE CHEMICALS,** HS
485.001 to 485.113.
**Administrative penalty.**
Action for collection, HS 485.109.
Amount, HS 485.102.
Appeal, HS 485.107.
Contested case status, HS 485.113.
Decision of court, HS 485.110.
Findings of commissioner, HS 485.106.
Hearing, HS 485.105.
Imposition, HS 485.101.
Notice of violation, HS 485.103.
Payment or appeal, HS 485.107.
Payment or request for hearing, HS 485.104.

## ABUSABLE VOLATILE CHEMICALS
—Cont'd

**Administrative penalty** —Cont'd
Release of supersedeas bond, HS 485.112.
Remittance to payee, HS 485.111.
Stay of enforcement, HS 485.108.
**Aerosol paint, restricted access,** HS 485.019.
**Corroboration of proof,** HS 485.036.
**Definitions,** HS 485.001.
**Education and prevention programs,** HS 485.016.
**Forfeiture,** HS 485.037.
**Inhalant paraphernalia,** HS 485.033.
**Minor, delivery to,** HS 485.032.
**Ordinances or rules prohibited,** HS 485.018.
**Permits for sale.**
Fees, HS 485.013.
Inspection, HS 485.014.
Issuance and renewal, HS 485.012.
Refusal to issue, HS 485.015.
Required, HS 485.011.
Sale without, HS 485.035.
**Possession and use,** HS 485.031.
**Preparatory offenses,** HS 485.038.
**Rulemaking,** HS 485.002.
**Signs at retail establishments,** HS 485.017.
Failure to post, HS 485.034.

## ABUSE OF CHILD.
See CHILD ABUSE.

## ABUSE OF CORPSE, Penal 42.08.
**Juvenile probation,** Fam 54.049.

## ABUSE OF CREDIT OR DEBIT CARD,
Penal 32.31.

## ABUSE OF OFFICE, Penal 39.01 to 39.06.
**Death of prisoner, failure to report,** Penal 39.05.
**Definitions,** Penal 39.01.
**Detainees, violation of rights,** Penal 39.04.
**Misuse of official information,** Penal 39.06.
**Official capacity,** Penal 39.02.
**Oppression by official,** Penal 39.03.

## ABUSE OF OFFICIAL CAPACITY, Penal 39.02.

## ACADEMIC DEGREE, FRAUDULENT OR FICTITIOUS, Penal 32.52.
**Venue of prosecution,** Crim Proc 13.30.

## ACADEMIC PRODUCTS.
**Deceptive preparation and marketing,** Penal 32.50.

## ACCEPTANCE OF HONORARIUM, Penal 36.07.

## ACCESS TO STORED COMMUNICATIONS,
Penal 16.04.
**Order to obtain,** Crim Proc 18.21.

## ACCIDENT REPORT INFORMATION AND OTHER INFORMATION, USING FOR PECUNIARY GAIN, Penal 38.18.

## ACCIDENTS, Transp 550.001 to 550.081.
**Applicability of provisions,** Transp 550.001.
**Collision rate statistics compilation and publication,** Transp 521.206.
**Coroner's report,** Transp 550.081.
**Drivers' licenses.**
Records of department.
Accident and conviction reports, Transp 521.042.
Disclosures, Transp 521.046.
**Duties after an accident.**
Damage to vehicle involved, Transp 550.022.
Immediate reporting, Transp 550.026.
Information to be given, Transp 550.023.
Personal injury or death involved, Transp 550.021.
Rendering of aid, Transp 550.023.
Striking structure adjacent to highway, fixture or highway landscaping, Transp 550.025.
Striking unattended vehicle, Transp 550.024.
**Failing to comply with requirements on striking structures next to highways, fixtures or landscaping on highway,** Transp 550.025.
**Failing to comply with requirements on striking unattended vehicle,** Transp 550.024.
**Failing to make written report of accident,** Transp 550.061.
**Failing to report accident,** Transp 601.004.
**Failing to report injury accident at once,** Transp 550.026.
**Failing to stop and render aid, felony,** Transp 550.021.
**Failing to stop and render aid, misdemeanor,** Transp 550.022.
**Failure to remove driveable vehicle after accident on freeway in metropolitan area,** Transp 550.022.
**Failure to yield right of way resulting in accident,** Transp 542.4045.
**Information in accident report, dispatch log, 911 service, etc.**
Sale of information, Bus 504.002.
Using for pecuniary gain, Penal 38.18.
Using for solicitation of business, Bus 504.002.
**Investigation by peace officer,** Transp 550.041.
**Photographic traffic signal enforcement system.**
Report of frequency and type of accidents at intersection, Transp 707.004.
**Railroads.**
Engineers' operator or train operator permits, Transp 192.001 to 192.005.

**ACCIDENTS** —Cont'd
**Reports.**
Admissibility of information, Transp 550.066.
Change or modification or written report,
    Transp 550.068.
Coroner's report, Transp 550.081.
Definition of department, Transp 550.0601.
Duty to report immediately, Transp 550.026.
Form for reporting, Transp 550.063, 550.064.
Municipal authority to require, Transp
    550.067.
Officer's report, Transp 550.062.
Operator's report, Transp 550.061.
Railroads.
    Engineers' operator or train operator
        permits, Transp 192.001 to 192.005.
    Release of information, Transp 550.065.
    Safety responsibility act requirements,
        Transp 601.004.
    Using information for pecuniary gain, Penal
        38.18.
**Security following accident,** Transp 601.151
    to 601.170.
    See MOTOR VEHICLE SAFETY
        RESPONSIBILITY.
**Speed limits.**
Vehicular accident reconstruction site,
    authority to temporarily lower, Transp
    545.3561.
**Use of victim's information to solicit
    business,** Bus 35.54.

**ACCOMPLICES AND ACCESSORIES.**
**Evidence.**
Accomplice testimony, Crim Proc 38.14.
**Prostitution, witness testimony and
    immunity,** Penal 43.06.

**ACCOUNT NUMBERS.**
**Personal identifying information,
    fraudulent use or possession,** Penal
    32.51.
Report required by peace officer, Crim Proc
    2.29.
Venue of prosecution, Crim Proc 13.29.

**ACQUITTAL.**
**Double jeopardy,** Crim Proc 1.10.
Constitutional provisions, US Const Amd 5.
Pleadings.
    Former acquittal or conviction, Crim Proc
        28.13.
Verdict.
    Acquittal of higher offense, Crim Proc
        37.14.

**ACQUITTAL OF OFFENSE.**
**Responsibility for conduct of another.**
Defenses excluded, Penal 7.03.

**ADDRESS CONFIDENTIALITY PROGRAM.**
**Victims of crime,** Crim Proc 56.81 to Crim
    Proc 56.93.

**ADJUNCT POLICE OFFICERS,** Crim Proc
    2.123.

**ADMINISTRATION OF MEDICATION.**
**Unlawful,** HS 142.029.

**ADMITTING TO UNADJUDICATED
    OFFENSE,** Penal 12.45.

**ADOPTION.**
**Advertising placement of or solicitation of
    child for adoption,** Penal 25.09.
**Sale or purchase of child, exceptions,** Penal
    25.08.

**ADULTERATED FOOD OR DRUGS.**
**Food, drugs and cosmetics generally.**
See FOOD, DRUGS AND COSMETICS.

**ADVANCE DIRECTIVES.**
**Criminal penalties regarding,** HS 166.048.

**ADVERTISING.**
**Academic products, deceptive preparation
    and marketing,** Penal 32.50.
**Adoption, placement of or solicitation of
    child,** Penal 25.09.
**Automobile club services,** Transp 722.012.
**Deceptive business practices,** Penal 32.42.
**Drivers' licenses.**
Advertising in drivers' handbook and drivers'
    license mailings, Transp 521.006.
**Food, drug and cosmetics.**
Advertising causing misbranding, HS
    431.003.
Fair packaging and labeling, HS 431.181 to
    431.183.
**Motor carrier registration.**
Economic regulation, Transp 643.156.
**Solicitation of professional employment,**
    Penal 38.12.

**ADVERTISING PLACEMENT OF CHILD,**
    Penal 25.09.

**AEROSOL PAINT.**
**Abusable volatile chemicals.**
Restriction of access, HS 485.019.

**AEROSPACE COMMISSION LICENSE
    PLATES,** Transp 504.610.

**AFFIDAVITS.**
**Bail, sufficiency of security,** Crim Proc 17.13,
    Crim Proc 17.14.
**Commercial drivers' licenses.**
Driving under the influence.
    Affidavit of breath test results, Transp
        522.106.
**Drivers' licenses.**
Administrative suspension for failure to pass
    intoxication test.
    Reliability of instrument used in analysis,
        Transp 524.038.
**Evidence.**
Chain of custody affidavit, Crim Proc 38.42.

**AGGRAVATED ROBBERY,** Penal 29.03.
**Protection of one's own property.**
  Use of deadly force to prevent offense, Penal 9.42.

**AGGRAVATED SEXUAL ASSAULT,** Penal 22.021.
**Child, failure to stop or report assault of,** Penal 38.17.
**Continuous sexual abuse of young child or children,** Penal 21.02.
**Limitation of actions,** Crim Proc 12.01.
**Murder committed during,** Penal 19.03.
**Report required by peace officer,** Crim Proc 2.30.

**AGREEING TO ABDUCT CHILD FOR REMUNERATION,** Penal 25.031.

**AGRICULTURAL LAND.**
**Criminal trespass,** Penal 30.05.

**AGRICULTURAL PRODUCTS AND EQUIPMENT TRANSPORTERS.**
**Oversize and overweight vehicles,** Transp 622.101.

**AGRICULTURAL PRODUCTS LICENSE PLATES,** Transp 504.625.

**AGRICULTURAL WORKERS, TRANSPORTATION OF,** Transp 647.001 to 647.019.
See MIGRANT AGRICULTURAL WORKERS, TRANSPORTATION OF.

**AIDING AND ABETTING, HINDERING ARREST OR PROSECUTION,** Penal 38.05.

**AIDING AND ABETTING ON WEIGHT VIOLATIONS,** Transp 621.503.

**AIDING SUICIDE,** Penal 22.08.

**AIDS.**
**Bail conditions.**
  AIDS and HIV educational instruction, Crim Proc 17.45.
**Indictments.**
  Testing for diseases for certain offenses, Crim Proc 21.31.
**Jails, testing in,** Crim Proc 46A.01.
**Juvenile proceedings, testing,** Fam 54.033.
**Testing for communicable diseases following arrest,** Crim Proc 18.22.

**AIRBAG RESTRICTIONS,** Transp 547.614.

**AIRBAGS, MAKES/SELLS COUNTERFEIT OR INTENTIONALLY ALTERS,** Transp 547.614.

**AIR BRAKES.**
**Defective air brake reservoir,** Transp 547.406.
**Inadequate air brake reservoir,** Transp 547.406.

**AIR BRAKES** —Cont'd
**Inadequate reservoir safeguard,** Transp 547.406.
**No warning signal or warning devices on brakes,** Transp 547.407.

**AIR CONDITIONING.**
**Motor vehicle equipment standards,** Transp 547.103, 547.610.

**AIRCRAFT.**
**Abandoned vehicles,** Transp 683.001 to 683.078.
  See ABANDONED VEHICLES.
**Criminal trespass,** Penal 30.05.
**Flying while intoxicated,** Penal 49.05.
  Enhanced offenses and penalties, Penal 49.09.
  Intoxication assault, Penal 49.07.
  Intoxication manslaughter, Penal 49.08.
  Unborn children, death or injury due to conduct of mother.
    Nonapplicability of certain provisions, Penal 49.12.
**Forfeiture of contraband,** Crim Proc 59.11.
**Fuel containers, offenses,** Transp 24.013.
**Identification numbers, failure to display,** Transp 24.012.
**Intoxication manslaughter,** Penal 49.08.
**Involuntary manslaughter (DWI),** Penal 49.08.
**Junked vehicles,** Transp 683.071 to 683.078.
  See ABANDONED VEHICLES.
**Lights, pointing at,** Penal 42.14.
**Registration.**
  Failure to register, Transp 24.011.
**Use of public roads,** Transp 24.021, 24.022.

**AIR FORCE ASSOCIATION.**
**License plates,** Transp 504.630.

**AIR FORCE CROSS RECIPIENTS.**
**License plates,** Transp 504.315.

**AIR POLLUTION.**
**Vehicle emissions,** HS 382.201 to 382.302.
  See EMISSIONS FROM MOTOR VEHICLES.

**AIRPORTS.**
**Weapons, places where prohibited,** Penal 46.03.

**ALABAMA-COUSHATTA INDIAN TRIBE.**
**Peace officers.**
  Officers employed to enforce state law within the boundaries of the tribal reservation, Crim Proc 2.126.

**ALCOHOLIC BEVERAGE POSSESSION IN A MOTOR VEHICLE,** Penal 49.031.

**ALCOHOLIC BEVERAGES.**
**Alcohol content limits,** ABC 101.66.
**Amusement rides, assembling or operating while intoxicated,** Penal 49.065.
**Arrest without warrant,** ABC 101.02.
  Emergency detention for substance abuse, HS 462.041.

**ANIMALS** —Cont'd

**Dangerous wild animals,** HS 822.101 to 822.116.

**Dogs.**

Dangerous dogs generally, HS 822.041 to 822.047.

Danger to animals, HS 822.011 to 822.013.

Danger to persons, HS 822.001 to 822.007.

Dog fighting, Penal 42.10.

Property seized under search warrant, disposition of, Crim Proc 18.18.

Registration and regulation, HS 822.021 to 822.035.

**Food, drug and cosmetics.**

New animal drugs, HS 431.115.

**Permitting livestock to roam,** Agric 143.108.

**Pets.**

Harming, threatening or interfering with control of.

Violation of bond in family violence case, Penal 25.07.

**Predatory animals and rodents,** HS 825.008 to 825.010.

**Rabies.**

Quarantine of animal, HS 826.042, 826.044.

Restraint of pet, HS 826.034.

Vaccinations, HS 826.021, 826.022.

**Rodents and predatory pests,** HS 825.008 to 825.010.

**Running at large.**

Dogs.

Danger to animals, HS 822.012.

Unregistered dogs, HS 822.031.

Highways, on, Agric 143.101 to 143.108.

Turkeys or cattle, Agric 143.082.

**Sale and shipment of livestock,** Agric 146.005 to 146.008.

**Seizure of cruelly treated animal,** HS 821.022.

**Service animals.**

Attack of assistance animal, Penal 42.091.

Supervised by law enforcement officials.

Interference with, Penal 38.15.

**Service animals supervised by law enforcement officials.**

Interference with, Penal 38.151.

**Traffic regulation.**

Applicability of rules, Transp 542.003.

**Transporting animals without permit or with fraudulent permit,** Agric 146.008.

**Wild animals,** HS 822.101 to 822.116.

**ANKLE BRACELETS.**

**Bail conditions.**

Home curfew and electronic monitoring, Crim Proc 17.43, Crim Proc 17.44.

**Parole and mandatory supervision.**

Electronic monitoring, Gov 508.315.

**ANKLE BRACELETS** —Cont'd

**Sentencing.**

Electronic monitoring and house arrest, Crim Proc 42.035.

**ANTIQUE VEHICLES.**

**Exhibition and parade vehicles.**

Effective January 1, 2012.

License plates, Transp 504.502.

Offenses and penalties, Transp 504.941.

**ANTIQUITIES.**

**Criminal simulation,** Penal 32.22.

**ANTISEPTICS, REPRESENTING DRUGS AS,** HS 431.004.

**ANTITRUST.**

**Motor carrier registration.**

Economic regulation, Transp 643.154.

**APARTMENT COMPLEXES.**

**Removal and storage of unauthorized vehicles,** Occ 2308.253.

**APPEALS.**

**Abusable volatile chemicals.**

Administrative penalty, HS 485.107.

**Bail forfeitures,** Crim Proc 44.42, Crim Proc 44.44.

**Blood alcohol testing.**

Suspension of license on refusal, Transp 724.047.

**Bond pending appeal,** Crim Proc 44.04.

Conditions in lieu of bond, Crim Proc 44.041.

Habeas corpus appeal, Crim Proc 44.35.

Justice and municipal courts, Crim Proc 45.0425.

Effect of appeal, Crim Proc 45.043.

Forfeiture of bond in satisfaction of fine, Crim Proc 45.044.

Perfecting appeal, Crim Proc 45.0426.

New bond, Crim Proc 44.15.

Procedure, Crim Proc 44.12.

Rules, Crim Proc 44.20.

Time for giving, Crim Proc 44.16.

Who may take, Crim Proc 44.41.

**Capital case.**

Reformation of sentence, Crim Proc 44.251, Crim Proc 44.2511.

**Certificates of title.**

Refusal, revocation or suspension, Transp 501.052.

**County court, procedures,** Crim Proc 44.17.

**Court of criminal appeals.**

Jurisdiction, Crim Proc 4.04.

Review by, Crim Proc 44.45.

**Courts of appeal.**

Jurisdiction, Crim Proc 4.03.

**Defective complaint, trial de novo,** Crim Proc 44.181.

**CAMPGROUNDS.**
**Theft of services.**
Intent to avoid payment, Penal 31.04.

**CANALS.**
**Operating vehicle in or near,** Water 49.217.

**CAPIAS,** Crim Proc 23.01 to Crim Proc 23.18.
**Capital cases,** Crim Proc 23.15.
Arrest in another county, Crim Proc 23.16.
**Defined,** Crim Proc 23.01, Crim Proc 43.015.
**Electronic issuance,** Crim Proc 23.031, Crim Proc 43.021.
**Felony cases,** Crim Proc 23.03.
Bail where prosecution pending, Crim Proc 23.10.
Court to fix bail, Crim Proc 23.12.
Execution, Crim Proc 23.13.
New bail, Crim Proc 23.06.
Sheriff may take bail, Crim Proc 23.11.
**Forfeiture of bail, after,** Crim Proc 23.05.
**Justice and municipal courts.**
Capias pro fine, Crim Proc 45.045.
**Misdemeanor cases,** Crim Proc 23.04.
Bail, Crim Proc 23.14.
**Multiple counties, issuance to,** Crim Proc 23.09.
**Not executed,** Crim Proc 23.07.
**Requisites,** Crim Proc 23.02.
**Retention, list of reasons,** Crim Proc 23.08.
**Return of bail and capias,** Crim Proc 23.17, Crim Proc 23.18.
**Sentence and punishment.**
Defined, Crim Proc 43.015.
Electronic form, issuance in, Crim Proc 43.021.
Fine against absent defendant, Crim Proc 43.06.
**Surrender of defendant, after,** Crim Proc 23.05.
**Who may execute,** Crim Proc 23.13.

**CAPITAL FELONIES,** Penal 12.31.
**Appeals.**
Reformation of sentence, Crim Proc 44.251, Crim Proc 44.2511.
**Arraignment.**
Appointment of counsel, Crim Proc 26.052.
**Capias, arrest under,** Crim Proc 23.15.
Arrest in another county, Crim Proc 23.16.
**Continuances.**
Bail in capital cases when multiple continuances granted to state, Crim Proc 29.12.
**Execution of death sentence.**
Competency to be executed, Crim Proc 46.05.
Designation of executioner, Crim Proc 43.18.
Embalming of body, Crim Proc 43.25.
Generally, Crim Proc 43.14.
Persons present, Crim Proc 43.20.
Place, Crim Proc 43.19.

**CAPITAL FELONIES** —Cont'd
**Execution of death sentence** —Cont'd
Return of warrant of execution, Crim Proc 42.23.
Scheduling, Crim Proc 43.141.
Transport of prisoner to department, Crim Proc 43.16.
Treatment of condemned, Crim Proc 43.24.
Visitors, Crim Proc 43.17.
Warrant of execution, Crim Proc 43.15.
**Habeas corpus.**
Hearing before indictment, Crim Proc 11.58.
Hearing before judge, Crim Proc 11.41.
Procedure in death penalty cases, Crim Proc 11.071.
**Jury trial, selection of jury generally.**
See JURY TRIAL.
**Jury trial, special venire,** Crim Proc 34.01.
Additional names drawn, Crim Proc 34.02.
Exemptions from service by consent of both parties, Crim Proc 35.05.
Instructions to sheriff, Crim Proc 34.03.
Notice of list to defendant, Crim Proc 34.04.
Selection method, Crim Proc 34.05.
**Murder,** Penal 19.03.
**Preliminary hearings.**
Who may discharge capital offenses, Crim Proc 16.15.
**Sabotage,** Gov 557.012.
**Verdict,** Crim Proc 37.071, Crim Proc 37.0711.
Repeat sex offenders, Crim Proc 37.072.
**Waiver of trial by jury,** Crim Proc 1.13.

**CAPITAL MURDER,** Penal 19.03.

**CARDBOARD TAGS, UNAUTHORIZED REPRODUCTION, PURCHASE, USE OR SALE,** Transp 503.067.

**CARISOPRODOL.**
**Schedules of controlled substances,** HS 481.037.

**CARRIED ARTICLES INTERFERING WITH HANDLING OF BICYCLE,** Transp 551.102.

**CARRIERS.**
**Motor carriers.**
See MOTOR CARRIERS.

**CARRYING MOTORCYCLE PASSENGER WITHOUT APPROVED HEADGEAR,** Transp 661.003.

**CARRYING WEAPONS UNLAWFULLY,** Penal 46.02.
**Handgun license holders,** Penal 46.035.

**CASTRATION.**
**Parole and mandatory supervision.**
Orchiectomy as condition, prohibited, Gov 508.226.

**CATTLE RAISERS ASSOCIATION, SPECIAL RANGERS OF,** Crim Proc 2.125.

**CONFIDENTIAL INFORMATION** —Cont'd
**Controlled substances and other drugs.**
Registration for manufacturers, distributors and dispensers, HS 481.068.
Taxation, Tax 159.005.
**Criminal history record system,** Crim Proc 60.03.
**Critical incident stress management and crisis response services,** HS 784.003.
**Distribution of misuse,** Gov 552.352.
**Family violence victims.**
Address confidentiality program, Crim Proc 56.81 to Crim Proc 56.93.
Identifying information, Crim Proc 57B.01 to Crim Proc 57B.05.
**Governmental actions to protect child.**
Emergency possession of abandoned child. Identifying information, Fam 262.308.
**Grand jury.**
Personal information, Crim Proc 19.42.
**Juvenile justice information system,** Fam 58.106.
**Juvenile records,** Fam 58.001 to 58.307.
See JUVENILE RECORDS.
**Medical advisory board,** HS 12.097.
**Mental health information in criminal cases,** TRE 510.
**Minors.**
Crimes committed by children.
Records relating to children convicted of fine-only misdemeanors, confidentiality, Crim Proc 44.2811.
Records relating to conviction of child, confidentiality, Crim Proc 45.0217.
**Missing persons DNA database.**
Voluntary provision of samples, Crim Proc 63.062.
**Missing persons information clearinghouse.**
Confidential records, Crim Proc 63.017.
**Misuse of official information,** Penal 39.06.
**Parole and mandatory supervision,** Gov 508.313.
**Peace officers.**
Employment records, Occ 1701.454.
**Protective orders.**
Applications, Fam 82.010.
Certain information contained in, Fam 85.007.
**Sexually violent predators, civil commitment.**
Victim identifying information, privilege, HS 841.1462.
**Stalking victims.**
Address confidentiality program, Crim Proc 56.81 to Crim Proc 56.93.
**Street gang intelligence database.**
Compilation of information pertaining to criminal combinations and street gangs.
Unauthorized use or release of information, Crim Proc 61.05.

**CONFIDENTIAL INFORMATION** —Cont'd
**Trafficking of persons.**
Victims, identifying information, Crim Proc 57D.01 to Crim Proc 57D.03.
**Victims of sexual offenses,** Crim Proc 57.01 to Crim Proc 57.03.
Address confidentiality program, Crim Proc 56.81 to Crim Proc 56.93.

**CONFINEMENT.**
**Justified use of force,** Penal 9.03.

**CONGRESS.**
**License plates,** Transp 504.402.

**CONGRESSIONAL MEDAL OF HONOR RECIPIENTS.**
**License plates,** Transp 504.315.

**CONQUER CANCER.**
**License plates,** Transp 504.620.

**CONSENT.**
**Abuse of office offenses.**
Concurrent jurisdiction to prosecute, consent to, Penal 39.015.
**Alcoholic beverages.**
Consent to inspection, ABC 101.04.
**Assaultive conduct, consent as defense to,** Penal 22.06.
**Autopsies.**
Informed consent, Crim Proc 49.31 to Crim Proc 49.35.
**Autopsies for inquests,** Crim Proc 49.13.
**Blood alcohol testing,** Transp 724.001 to 724.064.
See BLOOD ALCOHOL TESTING.
**Hazing.**
Consent as defense, Educ 37.154.
**Medical treatment of child by non-parent or child,** Fam 32.001 to 32.005.
Authorization agreement for nonparent relative, Fam 34.001 to 34.009.
**State property, offenses involving.**
Concurrent jurisdiction, consent to, Penal 1.09.
**Venue, consent to,** Crim Proc 13.20.

**CONSERVATION LICENSE PLATES,** Transp 504.618.

**CONSERVATORS OF THE PEACE.**
**Peace officers generally.**
See PEACE OFFICERS.
**Sheriffs,** Crim Proc 2.17.

**CONSIGNMENT SALES.**
**Alcoholic beverages,** ABC 101.68.

**CONSOLIDATION OF OFFENSES,** Penal 3.02.

**CONSPIRACY.**
**Attempt to carry out felony where another felony committed.**
Responsibility of all conspirators, Penal 7.02.

**DROVE WRONG WAY ON ONE-WAY ROAD,**
Transp 545.059.

**DRUG-FREE ZONES,** HS 481.134, 481.135.

**DRUG PARAPHERNALIA.**
**Evidentiary rules,** HS 481.183.
**Inhalant paraphernalia,** HS 485.033.
**Possession or delivery,** HS 481.125.

**DRUGS.**
See CONTROLLED SUBSTANCES AND
OTHER DRUGS.

**DRUG TESTING.**
**Bail conditions.**
Generally, Crim Proc 17.44.
Personal bond of defendant, Crim Proc 17.03.
**Falsification of drug test results,** HS
481.133.
**Parole and mandatory supervision,** Gov
508.184.
**Vehicle storage facilities.**
Drug testing of employees, Occ 2303.161.

**DRUNK DRIVING,** Penal 49.04.
**Blood alcohol testing,** Transp 724.001 to
724.064.
See BLOOD ALCOHOL TESTING.
**Child passenger,** Penal 49.045.
**Community supervision,** Crim Proc 42.12.
**Convictions surcharges,** Transp 708.102.
**Costs for breath alcohol testing program,**
Crim Proc 102.016.
**Drivers' licenses.**
Commercial drivers' licenses, Transp 522.101
to 522.106.
Occupational licenses, Transp 521.241 to
521.253.
**Enhanced offenses and penalties,** Penal
49.09.
**Ignition interlock devices.**
Condition of bail, Crim Proc 17.441.
Occupational licenses, Transp 521.246 to
521.2476.
**Implied consent law,** Transp 724.001 to
724.064.
See BLOOD ALCOHOL TESTING.
**Intoxication assault,** Penal 49.07.
**Intoxication manslaughter,** Penal 49.08.
**Minors,** ABC 106.041.
**Unborn children, death or injury due to
conduct of mother.**
Nonapplicability of certain provisions, Penal
49.12.

**DRUNK IN PUBLIC,** Penal 49.02.

**DRY AREAS, OFFENSES IN,** ABC 101.31,
101.32.

**DUE COURSE OF LAW.**
**Code of criminal procedure,** Crim Proc 1.04.

**DUE DILIGENCE.**
**Corporations, criminal responsibility.**
Defenses, Penal 7.24.

**DUE PROCESS.**
**Constitutional provisions,** US Const Amds 5,
14.

**DUI.**
See DRIVING UNDER THE INFLUENCE.

**DUNE PROTECTION.**
**Operating vehicle on dune seaward of
dune protection line,** Transp 750.003.

**DURESS.**
**Defenses,** Penal 8.05.

**DUTY TO RETREAT.**
**Law enforcement, justification for, when
retreat not required,** Penal 9.51.

**DVD PLAYERS IN MOTOR VEHICLES,**
Transp 547.611.

**DWI.**
See DRIVING UNDER THE INFLUENCE.

**DWI, FIRST OFFENSE,** Penal 49.04.

**DWI, SECOND OR SUBSEQUENT
OFFENSES,** Penal 49.09.

**DYING DECLARATION.**
**Hearsay exceptions,** TRE 804.

**E**

**EAGLE SCOUTS.**
**License plates,** Transp 504.654.

**EAVESDROPPING.**
**Access to stored communications,** Penal
16.04.
Order to obtain, Crim Proc 18.21.
**Divulging of communications,** Penal 16.05.
**Order for interception of communications,**
Crim Proc 18.20.
**Pen registers and trap and trace devices,**
Penal 16.03.
Order for, Crim Proc 18.21.
**Unlawful interception of communications,**
Penal 16.02.

**EDUCATION.**
See SCHOOLS.

**EDUCATOR-STUDENT RELATIONSHIPS,
IMPROPER,** Penal 21.12.

**EFFECT OF CODE.**
**Code of criminal procedure,** Crim Proc 1.02.
**Penal code,** Penal 1.03.

**ELDERLY PERSONS.**
**Abuse of credit or debit card.**
Classification of offense commited against
elderly person, Penal 32.31.
**Assault of,** Penal 22.01.
Report required by peace officer, Crim Proc
2.30.
**Concealed weapons licenses.**
Fee reductions, Gov 411.195.

**ELDERLY PERSONS** —Cont'd

**Depositions,** Crim Proc 39.025.

Medicaid fraud, Crim Proc 39.026.

**Document execution by deception,** Penal 32.46.

**Execution of documents, securing by deception,** Penal 32.46.

**Exploitation of children, elderly or disabled persons,** Penal 32.53.

**Forgery, commited against elderly person.**

Classification of offense, Penal 32.21.

**Injury to children, elderly or disabled persons,** Penal 22.04.

Limitation of action, Crim Proc 12.01.

**Robbery, aggravated,** Penal 29.03.

**ELECTIONS.**

**Dispersing of riots and unlawful assemblies.**

Appointment of special constables, Crim Proc 8.08.

Powers of special constables, Crim Proc 8.09.

**Dogs, county registration and regulation.**

Election to determine, HS 822.021 to 822.026.

**Identification.**

Election identification certificates, Transp 521A.001.

**Tampering with direct recording electronic voting machine,** Penal 33.05.

**Theft of election ballot/envelopes,** Penal 31.03.

**Voter privilege from arrest,** Elec 276.005, TX Const §6-5.

**Voter registration by department of public safety,** Elec 20.061 to 20.066.

**Voting in secret,** TRE 506.

**Weapons, places where prohibited,** Penal 46.03.

**ELECTRIC BICYCLES,** Transp 551.106.

**Registration of motor vehicles.**

Effective January 1, 2012, Transp 502.143.

**ELECTRIC PERSONAL ASSISTIVE MOBILITY DEVICES.**

**Applicability of traffic rules,** Transp 542.009.

**Defined,** Transp 551.201.

**Operation on roadway,** Transp 551.202.

**Operation on sidewalks,** Transp 551.203.

**ELECTRIC POWER TRANSMISSION POLES, TRANSPORTING.**

**Oversize and overweight vehicles,** Transp 622.051 to 622.053.

**ELECTRIC TRAFFIC-CONTROL SIGNALS.**

**Traffic-actuated signals,** Transp 544.0075.

**ELECTRIC VEHICLES, OPERATION OF,** Transp 551.202, 551.302.

**ELECTRONICALLY READABLE INFORMATION ON DRIVER'S LICENSE.**

**Accesses or uses,** Transp 521.126.

**ELECTRONICALLY READABLE INFORMATION ON DRIVER'S LICENSE** —Cont'd

**Compiles database,** Transp 521.126.

**Sold or disseminated to third party,** HS 161.0825.

**ELECTRONIC INTERCEPTION OF COMMUNICATIONS,** Penal 16.02.

**Access to stored communications,** Penal 16.04.

Order to obtain, Crim Proc 18.21.

**Divulging of communications,** Penal 16.05.

**Order for,** Crim Proc 18.20.

**Pen registers or trap and trace devices,** Penal 16.03.

Order for, Crim Proc 18.21.

**ELECTRONIC MONITORING.**

**Bail conditions,** Crim Proc 17.43, Crim Proc 17.44.

**Commissioners court program,** Loc Gov 351.904.

**Parole and mandatory supervision,** Gov 508.315.

Gang member, electronic monitoring upon release, Gov 508.227.

**Sentencing.**

Electronic monitoring and house arrest, Crim Proc 42.035.

**ELECTRONIC TAGS.**

**Shoplifting, use of shielding or deactivation device.**

Classification of offense, Penal 31.03.

**ELECTRONIC TITLING SYSTEM, MOTOR VEHICLES.**

**Effective January 1, 2012,** Transp 501.171 to 501.179.

**ELECTRONIC TRANSMISSION OF DOCUMENTS,** Crim Proc 2.26.

**Capias,** Crim Proc 23.031, Crim Proc 43.021.

**Indictments and other charging papers,** Crim Proc 21.011.

**ELEVATORS.**

**Obstructing highways or passageways,** Penal 42.03.

**EL PASO MISSION VALLEY.**

**License plates,** Transp 504.635.

**E-MAIL.**

**Harassing communications,** Penal 42.07.

Online harassment, Penal 33.07.

**Online solicitation of a minor,** Penal 33.021.

Internet service providers.

Preserving information, Crim Proc 24A.051.

Subpoenas, search warrants, or other court orders, responding to, Crim Proc 24A.001 to Crim Proc 24A.003.

**EVIDENCE** —Cont'd

**Tampering with physical evidence,** Penal 37.09.

**Texas forensic science commission,** Crim Proc 38.01.

**Theft, photographic evidence,** Crim Proc 38.34.

**Title of rules provisions,** TRE 101.

**Trade secrets,** TRE 507.

**Treason cases.**
Inadmissible evidence, Crim Proc 38.16.
Two witnesses, Crim Proc 38.15.
Requirement not fulfilled, Crim Proc 38.17.

**Undercover officers or special investigators,** Crim Proc 38.141.

**Voting in secret,** TRE 506.

**Waiver of privilege by voluntary disclosure,** TRE 511.

**Weapon-free school zones.**
Map as evidence of location, Penal 46.12.

**Witnesses.**
See WITNESSES.

**Writings.**
Contents generally, TRE 1001 to 1009.
Handwriting evidence, Crim Proc 38.27.
Instrument partly written and partly printed, Crim Proc 38.25.

**EXAMINING COURT.**

**Magistrates sitting to inquire into criminal accusation,** Crim Proc 2.11.

**EXAMINING TRIALS.**
See PRELIMINARY HEARINGS.

**EXCEPTIONS TO OFFENSES.**
**Burden of proof,** Penal 2.02.

**EXCESSIVE BAIL,** Crim Proc 1.09.

**Constitutional provisions,** TX Const §§1-11, 1-11a, US Const Amd 8.

**EXCITED UTTERANCE.**
**Hearsay exceptions,** TRE 803.

**EXCLUSION OF WITNESSES,** TRE 614.

**EXECUTION OF DEATH SENTENCE,** Crim Proc 43.14 to Crim Proc 43.25.
See DEATH PENALTY.

**EXECUTION OF DOCUMENTS, SECURING BY DECEPTION,** Penal 32.46.

**EXECUTION OF JUDGMENT.**
**Recovery of seized property,** Civil Prac 34.021, Civil Prac 34.022.
**Victims of crime.**
Compensation.
Exemptions from execution, Crim Proc 56.49.

**EXECUTION OF PROCESS.**
**County jailers,** Crim Proc 2.31.
**Preventing,** Penal 38.16.

**EXHIBITION VEHICLES.**
**License plates,** Transp 504.502.
Offenses and penalties.
Effective January 1, 2012, Transp 504.941.

**EXHIBITS.**
**Court reporters.**
Release of items for safekeeping, Crim Proc 2.21.
**Disposal of,** Crim Proc 2.21.
**Jury trial.**
Deliberations.
Exhibits requested by jury, Crim Proc 36.25.

**EXILE PROHIBITED,** Crim Proc 1.18.

**EXOTIC ANIMALS.**
**Theft.**
Classification of offense, Penal 31.03.
**Wild animals generally,** HS 822.101 to 822.116.
See WILD ANIMALS.

**EX PARTE ORDERS.**
**Protective orders.**
Application for temporary ex parte order, Fam 82.009.
Temporary ex parte orders generally, Fam 83.001 to 83.006.
Trafficking of persons, Crim Proc 7B.02.
Victims of sexual assault, Crim Proc 7A.02.

**EXPERT WITNESSES,** TRE 702 to 705.

**EXPIRED DRIVER'S LICENSE,** Transp 521.021, 521.026.

**EXPLOITATION.**
**Children, elderly or disabled persons,** Penal 32.53.
**Injury to children, elderly or disabled persons.**
Limitation of action, Crim Proc 12.01.

**EXPLOSIVES.**
**Arson,** Penal 28.02.
**Fertilizer.**
Explosive components, possession, Penal 46.09.
**Fireworks.**
Minors.
Employment of minors to manufacture or sell, Occ 2154.254.
**Railroad crossings.**
Flammable or explosive substances, vehicles carrying, Transp 545.254.
**Seized under search warrant.**
Disposition, Crim Proc 18.181.
**Warning devices not installed or defective,** Transp 547.001, 547.502.
**Warning devices on explosive cargo vehicles,** Transp 547.502.
**Weapons offenses generally.**
See WEAPONS.

**FINES** —Cont'd
**Trapping of predatory animals and rodents.**
Tampering or interfering with traps, HS 825.008 to 825.010.
**Unattended vehicles.**
Regulation of parking facilities and towing companies, Occ 2308.404, 2308.405.
**Used oil field equipment dealers,** Natur 112.032.
**Victims of crime.**
Compensation.
Penalty for false claims, Crim Proc 56.63.
**Wild animals.**
Dangerous wild animals, HS 822.114.
**Witnesses.**
Attachment to secure attendance.
Fine of out-of-county witness, Crim Proc 24.22.

**FINGERPRINTS.**
**Criminal history record system.**
Fingerprint and arrest information, Crim Proc 60.12.
Generally, Crim Proc 60.01 to Crim Proc 60.21.
See CRIMINAL HISTORY RECORD SYSTEM.
Uniform incident fingerprint card, Crim Proc 60.07.
**Drivers' licenses.**
Records of department.
Image verification system, Transp 521.059.
**Juvenile justice information system.**
Uniform incident fingerprint card, Fam 58.109.
**Juvenile records.**
Fingerprints of child, Fam 58.002 to 58.0022.
**Misdemeanors, preservation and use of evidence,** Crim Proc 38.33.
**Missing child prevention and identification,** Educ 33.053, 33.055, 33.057.
**Personal identifying information, fraudulent use or possession,** Penal 32.51.
Report required by peace officer, Crim Proc 2.29.
Venue of prosecution, Crim Proc 13.29.

**FIRE ALARMS.**
**Theft, disabling or activating during commission of offense,** Penal 31.03.

**FIREARM, ACCESSIBLE TO A CHILD,** Penal 46.13.

**FIREARM, UNLAWFUL POSSESSION,** Penal 46.04.

**FIREARMS.**
**Licenses to carry concealed weapons,** Gov 411.171 to 411.208.
See CONCEALED WEAPONS LICENSES.

**FIREARMS** —Cont'd
**Weapons offenses generally.**
See WEAPONS.

**FIREARM SMUGGLING,** Penal 46.14.

**FIRE CODE.**
**Search warrants for inspections,** Crim Proc 18.05.

**FIRE EXTINGUISHERS IN CERTAIN VEHICLES,** Transp 547.607.

**FIRE EXTINGUISHER VIOLATION, HAZARDOUS MATERIALS,** Transp 644.151.

**FIREFIGHTERS.**
**Capital murder,** Penal 19.03.
**Closure of road or highway, authority,** Transp 546.007.
**Interference with public duties,** Penal 38.15.
**Interference with radio frequency licensed by government entity,** Penal 38.152.
**Intoxication manslaughter, causes death to,** Penal 49.09.
**Laser pointers, pointing at certain persons,** Penal 42.13.
**License plates.**
Effective until January 1, 2012.
Fire-fighting vehicles, Transp 502.202.
Volunteer firefighters, Transp 504.409.
Professional firefighters, Transp 504.414.
Volunteer firefighters.
Effective January 1, 2012, Transp 504.513.
**Murder of.**
Capital murder, Penal 19.03.
**Mutual aid organizations supplying fire-fighting equipment,** Transp 546.021.
**Streetcars crossing fire hose.**
Permission required, Transp 545.205.

**FIRE HOSE, CROSSING,** Transp 545.408.
**Streetcars,** Transp 545.205.

**FIRE INQUESTS,** Crim Proc 50.01 to Crim Proc 50.07.

**FIRE TRUCKS.**
See EMERGENCY VEHICLES.

**FIREWORKS.**
**Minors.**
Employment of minor to manufacture or sell, Occ 2154.254.

**FIRST DEGREE FELONIES,** Penal 12.32.
**Habitual and repeat offenders,** Penal 12.42, 12.425.

**FIXING PUBLIC CONTESTS,** Penal 32.44.

**FLAGS.**
**Destruction of flag,** Penal 42.11.

**FLASHERS.**
**Indecency with a child,** Penal 21.11.
Limitation of actions, Crim Proc 12.01.

**HIGHWAYS** —Cont'd
**Off-premises signs,** Transp 391.251 to
391.255.
**One-way roads,** Transp 545.059.
**Pedestrian on prohibited roadway,** Transp
545.065.
**Prohibiting use of, powers,** Transp 201.901.
County traffic regulations, Transp 251.157.
**Removal of property from state highways,**
Transp 472.011 to 472.015.
**Removing material dropped onto highway,**
Transp 600.001.
**Signs on right-of-way,** Transp 392.032 to
392.036.
Off-premises signs, Transp 391.251 to
391.255.
**Speed limit signs,** Transp 201.904.
**Tolls.**
Controlled-access toll roads, Transp 370.179.
Failure to pay on certain county roads,
Transp 284.070 to 284.0702.
Failure to pay on state highways, Transp
228.054.
Failure to pay turnpike project toll, Transp
370.177.
Use and return of transponders, Transp
370.178.
Unauthorized use of toll roads in certain
counties, Transp 284.201 to 284.213.
**Traffic control devices.**
Highways, designation as through highways,
Transp 544.003.
**Transportation projects of regional
authorities,** Transp 370.177 to 370.191.
**Turning across dividing section,** Transp
545.063.
**Warning signs and devices.**
Disobeying, Transp 472.022.
Tampering with, Transp 472.021.
**Work zones.**
Penalties for offense committed in, Transp
542.404.
**Wrecker driver failed to remove glass from
highway,** Transp 600.001.

**HINDERING
APPREHENSION/PROSECUTION,**
Penal 38.05.

**HINDERING OFFICIAL PROCEEDINGS.**
**Disorderly conduct,** Penal 38.13.
**Inquests,** Crim Proc 49.06.

**HINDERING OF FINAL PROCEEDINGS
BY DISORDERLY CONDUCT,** Penal
38.13.

**HINDERING SECURED CREDITORS.**
**Disposal of secured property,** Penal 32.33.
**Venue of prosecution,** Crim Proc 13.09.

**HIT AND RUN.**
**Limitation of action if resulted in death,**
Crim Proc 12.01.

**HIV.**
**Bail conditions.**
AIDS and HIV educational instruction, Crim
Proc 17.45.
**Indictments.**
Testing for diseases for certain offenses, Crim
Proc 21.31.
**Jails, testing in,** Crim Proc 46A.01.
**Juvenile proceedings, testing,** Fam 54.033.
**Testing for communicable diseases
following arrest,** Crim Proc 18.22.

**HOAX BOMBS,** Penal 46.08.

**HOAXES.**
**False alarms or reports of emergencies,**
Penal 42.06.
**Hoax bombs,** Penal 46.08.
**Terroristic threats,** Penal 22.07.
Report required by peace officer, Crim Proc
2.30.

**HOLDING OVER OF PROPERTY.**
**Theft of services,** Penal 31.04.

**HOME AND COMMUNITY SUPPORT
SERVICES,** HS 142.0061 to 142.0063.
**Administration of medication,** HS 142.021.

**HOME CURFEW.**
**Bail conditions,** Crim Proc 17.43, Crim Proc
17.44.

**HOME INVASION.**
**Burglary,** Penal 30.01 to 30.06.
**Robbery,** Penal 29.01 to 29.03.

**HOMICIDE,** Penal 19.01 to 19.06.
**Body found in state.**
Jurisdiction under penal code, Penal 1.04.
**Criminally negligent homicide,** Penal 19.05.
**Definition,** Penal 19.01.
**Limitation of action,** Crim Proc 12.01.
**Manslaughter,** Penal 19.04.
Intoxication manslaughter, Penal 49.08.
**Murder,** Penal 19.02.
Capital murder, Penal 19.03.
Evidence, Crim Proc 38.36.
**Unborn children, applicability of chapter,**
Penal 19.06.
**Venue of prosecution.**
Homicide committed outside state, Crim Proc
13.05.
Injury in one county and death in another,
Crim Proc 13.07.

**HOMOSEXUAL CONDUCT.**
**Deviate sexual intercourse,** Penal 21.01,
21.06.

**HONORARIUM, ACCEPTANCE OF,** Penal
36.07.

**HONORARY CONSULS.**
**License plates.**
Effective January 1, 2012, Transp 504.515.

**INJURY TO ANOTHER** —Cont'd
**Dogs.**
Danger to persons.
Seizure of dog causing death or serious
bodily injury, HS 822.002.
**Innocent bystanders.**
Reckless injury of innocent third person.
Justification as no defense for, Penal 9.05.
**Search warrants.**
Photographing injured child, Crim Proc
18.021.
**Venue of prosecution.**
Child injured in one county and residing in
another, Crim Proc 13.075.
Injury in one county and death in another,
Crim Proc 13.07.

**INJURY TO CHILD, ELDERLY OR
DISABLED,** Penal 22.04.

**INNOCENCE, PRESUMPTION OF,** Crim
Proc 38.03, Penal 2.01.

**INNOCENT BYSTANDERS.**
**Reckless injury of innocent third person,
justification as no defense for,** Penal
9.05.

**INQUESTS,** Crim Proc 49.01 to Crim Proc
49.25.
**Applicability of provisions,** Crim Proc 49.02.
**Arrest warrants.**
Authority to order, Crim Proc 49.19.
Fire inquests, Crim Proc 50.05.
Sufficiency, Crim Proc 49.20.
**Autopsies,** Crim Proc 49.10.
Consent to, Crim Proc 49.13.
Immunity of person performing, Crim Proc
49.12.
Informed consent, Crim Proc 49.31 to Crim
Proc 49.35.
Medical examiners, duties, Crim Proc 49.25.
**Chemical analysis to determine cause of
death,** Crim Proc 49.11.
**Commitment of homicide suspect,** Crim
Proc 49.21.
**Cremation of body subject to investigation,**
Crim Proc 49.09.
**Death certificate to be signed by justice,**
Crim Proc 49.16.
**Deaths requiring,** Crim Proc 49.04.
**Definitions,** Crim Proc 49.01.
**Disinterment of body,** Crim Proc 49.09.
Medical examiners, duties, Crim Proc 49.25.
**Disposal of unidentified body.**
Medical examiners, duties, Crim Proc 49.25.
**Evidence, safekeeping of,** Crim Proc 49.17.
**Fire inquests,** Crim Proc 50.01 to Crim Proc
50.07.
**Forensic anthropologist, use of,** Crim Proc
49.25.
**Hearing,** Crim Proc 49.14.

**INQUESTS** —Cont'd
**Hindering, offense of,** Crim Proc 49.06.
**Information leading to,** Crim Proc 49.08.
**Institutional resident, death of,** Crim Proc
49.24.
**Medical examiners, duties,** Crim Proc 49.25.
**Notice to justice of the peace,** Crim Proc
49.07.
**Office of death investigator,** Crim Proc
49.23.
**Powers and duties of justice of the peace,**
Crim Proc 49.03.
**Prisoner, death of,** Crim Proc 49.18.
**Record of,** Crim Proc 49.15.
**Reopening,** Crim Proc 49.041.
**Sealing of premises where body found,**
Crim Proc 49.22.
**Time and place,** Crim Proc 49.05.
**Violation of provisions.**
Medical examiners, Crim Proc 49.25.

**INSANITY DEFENSE,** Crim Proc 46C.001 to
Crim Proc 46C.270, Penal 8.01.
**Acquittal by reason of insanity, disposition
following.**
Appeal of judgment, Crim Proc 46C.270.
Dangerous offense, Crim Proc 46C.251 to
Crim Proc 46C.270. See within this
heading, "Dangerous offense."
Nondangerous offense, Crim Proc 46C.201,
Crim Proc 46C.202.
Victim notification of release, Crim Proc
46.03.
**Dangerous offense.**
Determination of issue of sanity.
Continuing jurisdiction over defendant,
Crim Proc 46C.158.
Determination of nature of offense, Crim Proc
46C.157.
Disposition following acquittal, Crim Proc
46C.251 to Crim Proc 46C.270.
Appeal of judgment, Crim Proc 46C.270.
Commitment for evaluation and treatment,
Crim Proc 46C.251.
Facility responsibilities, Crim Proc 46C.258.
Hearing on disposition, Crim Proc 46C.253.
Inpatient or residential care, order for,
Crim Proc 46C.256.
Discharge, Crim Proc 46C.268.
Order for outpatient or community-based
treatment after inpatient
commitment, Crim Proc 46C.262.
Renewal of order, Crim Proc 46C.261.
Jury, proceedings requiring, Crim Proc
46C.255.
Outpatient or community-based treatment,
Crim Proc 46C.257.
Discharge, Crim Proc 46C.268.
Location, Crim Proc 46C.264.

## K

**KEEP TEXAS BEAUTIFUL.**
License plates, Transp 504.602.

**KEYS.**
Sale of master key for motor vehicle
    ignitions, Transp 728.011.

**KIDNAPPING,** Penal 20.03.
**Aggravated kidnapping,** Penal 20.04.
    Continuous sexual abuse of young child or
        children, Penal 21.02.
**Agreement to abduct from custody for
    remuneration,** Penal 25.031.
**Definitions,** Penal 20.01.
**Enticing of child,** Penal 25.04.
**Guardian's rights, interfering with,** Penal
    25.10.
**Interference with child custody,** Penal
    25.03.
**Limitation of actions,** Crim Proc 12.01.
**Murder committed during,** Penal 19.03.
**Sentence and punishment.**
    Restitution, Crim Proc 42.0371.
**Smuggling of persons,** Penal 20.05.
**Unlawful restraint,** Penal 20.02.
**Venue of prosecution,** Crim Proc 13.12.

**KIDNEYS.**
Purchase and sale of human organs, Penal
    48.02.

**KNIGHTS OF COLUMBUS.**
License plates, Transp 504.638.

**KNIVES.**
Weapons offenses generally.
    See WEAPONS.

**KNOWLEDGE.**
Culpability requirement, Penal 6.02.
    Definition of knowingly, Penal 6.03.

**KNUCKLES.**
Weapons offenses generally.
    See WEAPONS.

**KOREAN WAR VETERANS.**
License plates, Transp 504.311.

## L

**LABELS.**
Food, drug and cosmetics.
    Fair packaging and labeling, HS 431.181 to
        431.183.
    Labeling causing misbranding, HS 431.003.
    Labeling to correct item, HS 431.052.

**LABORATORIES.**
Controlled substances and other drugs.
    Chemical laboratory apparatus.
        Records requirements, HS 481.080.

**LABORATORIES** —Cont'd
**Controlled substances and other drugs**
    —Cont'd
    Chemical laboratory apparatus —Cont'd
        Transfer for unlawful manufacture, HS
            481.139.
        Transfer permit, HS 481.081.
        Unlawful transfer or receipt, HS 481.138.

**LACK OF CAUTION ON GREEN ARROW
    SIGNAL,** Transp 544.007.

**LAKE LAVON.**
Littering, HS 365.032.

**LAKE SABINE.**
Littering, HS 365.031.

**LANE DIRECTION CONTROL SIGNALS,**
    Transp 544.009.

**LANE USE SIGNS,** Transp 544.011.

**LARCENY.**
See THEFT.

**LASER POINTERS.**
Aircraft, pointing bright lights at, Penal
    42.14.
Pointing at certain officials, Penal 42.13.

**LAUNDERING.**
Credit card transaction record laundering,
    Penal 32.35.
Financial transaction reporting, Fin
    271.001 to 271.006.
Money laundering, Penal 34.01 to 34.03.
Notice of conviction to insurance
    department, Crim Proc 42.0181.

**LAW, UNAUTHORIZED PRACTICE,** Penal
    38.123.

**LAW ENFORCEMENT OFFICERS.**
See PEACE OFFICERS.

**LAWYER, FALSELY HOLDING ONESELF
    OUT AS,** Penal 38.122.

**LAWYER-CLIENT PRIVILEGE,** TRE 503.

**LEARNED TREATISES.**
Hearsay exceptions, TRE 803.

**LEARNERS' PERMIT,** Transp 521.222.
**Commercial drivers' licenses,** Transp
    522.014.
    Limitations on issuance, Transp 522.025.

**LEASE OF WEAPONS.**
Unlawful transfer, Penal 46.06.

**LEAVING CHILD IN VEHICLE,** Penal 22.10.

**LEAVING REFUSE ON HIGHWAY,** HS
    365.013.

**LEAVING THE SCENE OF AN ACCIDENT.**
Limitation of action if resulted in death,
    Crim Proc 12.01.

**MAGISTRATES** —Cont'd
**Duties generally,** Crim Proc 2.10.
**Examining court,** Crim Proc 2.11.
**Examining trial.**
  See PRELIMINARY HEARINGS.
**Fugitives from justice.**
  Magistrate's warrant, Crim Proc 51.03.
**Habeas corpus.**
  Summoning of magistrate by court, Crim Proc
    11.47.
**Orders of, violating,** Penal 25.07, 25.071.
**Protection, ordering peace officer to
    provide,** Crim Proc 7.15.
**Rules of the road.**
  Arrest and charging procedures, Transp
    543.001 to 543.011.
**Search warrants.**
  Certification of record to court, Crim Proc
    18.15.
  Examination upon return, Crim Proc 18.12.
  Examining trial, Crim Proc 18.14.
  Issuance, Crim Proc 18.01.
**Threats, duty upon hearing,** Crim Proc 6.01.
  Taking of life, threats of, Crim Proc 6.02.
**Violation of condition of bond,** Crim Proc
    7.18.
**Who are magistrates,** Crim Proc 2.09.

**MAGNETIC DEVICES.**
**Retail theft, possession, manufacture or
    distribution of instruments used to
    commit,** Penal 31.15.

**MAKING U-TURN ON CURVE OR HILL,**
  Transp 545.102.

**MANDAMUS.**
**Missing persons.**
  Enforcement of compliance with provisions,
    Crim Proc 63.010.

**MANDATORY CONDITIONS OF PAROLE,**
  Gov 508.181 to 508.192.

**MANDATORY SUPERVISION.**
**Parole and mandatory supervision,** Gov
    508.181 to 508.324.
  See PAROLE AND MANDATORY
    SUPERVISION.

**MANSLAUGHTER,** Penal 19.04.
**Intoxication manslaughter,** Penal 49.08.
**Limitation of action,** Crim Proc 12.01.
**Unborn children, applicability of chapter,**
  Penal 19.06.

**MANUAL LABOR.**
**Sentence and punishment,** Crim Proc 43.10.
  Voluntary work, Crim Proc 43.101.

**MANUFACTURED HOUSING.**
**Mobile home, compensation for unlawful
    movement,** Transp 623.105.
**No escort vehicle, mobile home,** Transp
  623.099.

**MANUFACTURED HOUSING** —Cont'd
**No liability insurance as required, mobile
    home,** Transp 623.103.
**No red flags, escort, mobile homes,** Transp
  623.099.
**No valid permit for transporting,** Transp
  623.092.
**No wide load signs, mobile homes,** Transp
  623.099.
**Permits for oversize and overweight
    vehicles,** Transp 623.091 to 623.105.
**Registration of motor vehicles.**
  Effective January 1, 2012, Transp 502.142.
  Effective until January 1, 2012, Transp
    502.0072.

**MANUFACTURE OR DELIVERY OF
    CONTROLLED SUBSTANCE.**
**Chemicals, possession with intent to
    manufacture substance,** HS 481.124.
**Dangerous drugs.**
  Delivery or offer of delivery, HS 483.042.
  Manufacture, HS 483.043.
**Death or serious bodily injury caused,** HS
  481.141.
**Drug paraphernalia,** HS 481.125.
**Evidence to establish delivery,** HS 481.182.
**Marihuana, delivery of,** HS 481.120.
**Penalty group 1,** HS 481.112.
  Child present of premises, HS 481.1122.
**Penalty group 1-a,** HS 481.1121.
**Penalty group 2,** HS 481.113.
**Penalty group 3,** HS 481.114.
**Penalty group 4,** HS 481.114.
**Simulated substances,** HS 482.002.
**Substances not listed in penalty group,** HS
  481.119.

**MANUFACTURERS.**
**Motor vehicle dealers and manufacturers,**
  Transp 503.001 to 503.095.
  See MOTOR VEHICLE DEALERS AND
    MANUFACTURERS.

**MAPS.**
**Gang-free zones.**
  Evidence of location, Penal 71.029.
**Weapon-free school zones.**
  Evidence of location, Penal 46.12.

**MARCH OF DIMES.**
**License plates,** Transp 504.651.

**MARIHUANA.**
**Possession and delivery,** HS 481.120,
  481.121.
  Child, delivery to, HS 481.122.
  Venue of prosecution, Crim Proc 13.22.
**Therapeutic research program,** HS 481.201
  to 481.205.
  Acquisition and distribution of substances,
    HS 481.204.
  Patient participation, HS 481.203.

MARIHUANA —Cont'd
**Therapeutic research program** —Cont'd
Reports and rules, HS 481.205.
Review board, HS 481.201, 481.202.

**MARINE LAW ENFORCEMENT VEHICLES.**
**License plates.**
Effective January 1, 2012, Transp 502.453.
Effective until January 1, 2012, Transp 502.202.

**MARINE MAMMAL RECOVERY.**
**License plates,** Transp 504.644.

**MARRIAGE.**
**Bigamy,** Penal 25.01.
Venue of prosecution, Crim Proc 13.14.

**MARSHALS.**
**Peace officers.**
Generally.
See PEACE OFFICERS.
Who are peace officers, Crim Proc 2.12.

**MASSAGE PARLORS.**
**Employment harmful to minors,** Penal 43.251.

**MASS GATHERINGS,** HS 751.001 to 751.013.
**Definitions,** HS 751.002.
**Inspections,** HS 751.012.
Fees, HS 751.013.
**Offenses and penalties,** HS 751.011.
**Permits.**
Appeal of actions on, HS 751.009.
Applications, HS 751.004.
Delegation of duties by county judge, HS 751.0055.
Findings and decision, HS 751.007.
Hearing on application, HS 751.006.
Investigation by county authorities, HS 751.005.
Required, HS 751.003.
Revocation, HS 751.008.
**Rules adoption,** HS 751.010.
**Title of act,** HS 751.001.

**MASTER GARDENER.**
**License plates,** Transp 504.652.

**MEAT PACKERS.**
**Presumption of inducement of consent by deception,** Penal 31.03.

**MECHANICAL SECURITY DEVICES.**
**Unlawful use,** Penal 16.01.

**MEDIATION.**
**Family violence prevention,** Crim Proc 5.08.
**Victim-offender mediation,** Crim Proc 56.13.
Parole and mandatory supervision, Gov 508.324.

**MEDICAID FRAUD,** Penal 35A.01, 35A.02.
**Aggregation prosecution, numerous recipients.**
Evidence, Crim Proc 38.46.

**MEDICAID FRAUD** —Cont'd
**Depositions.**
Witnesses.
Elderly persons, Crim Proc 39.026.
**Limitation of action,** Crim Proc 12.01.

**MEDICAL ADVISORY BOARD,** HS 12.091 to 12.098.
**Administration,** HS 12.093.
**Confidentiality,** HS 12.097.
**Definitions,** HS 12.091.
**Immunity of members,** HS 12.098.
**Members,** HS 12.092.
**Panels,** HS 12.095.
**Physician reports to,** HS 12.096.
**Rules adoption,** HS 12.094.

**MEDICAL DIRECTIVES.**
**Criminal penalties regarding,** HS 166.048.

**MEDICAL EXAMINERS.**
**Accidents.**
Coroner's report, Transp 550.081.
**Inquests,** Crim Proc 49.01 to Crim Proc 49.25.
See INQUESTS.

**MEDICAL MARIHUANA.**
**Therapeutic research program,** HS 481.201 to 481.205.
Acquisition and distribution of substances, HS 481.204.
Patient participation, HS 481.203.
Reports and rules, HS 481.205.
Review board, HS 481.201, 481.202.

**MEDICAL RECORDS.**
**Missing persons.**
Release of dental records, Crim Proc 63.006.
Release of medical records, Crim Proc 63.007.
**Sealing medical records of child victim,** Crim Proc 57C.01, Crim Proc 57C.02.

**MEETINGS.**
**Disrupting meeting or procession,** Penal 42.05.

**MEGAN'S LAW.**
**Sex offender registration.**
Community notification, Crim Proc 62.056.
Generally, Crim Proc 62.001 to Crim Proc 62.408.
See SEX OFFENDER REGISTRATION.

**MENTAL HEALTH AND MENTALLY ILL.**
**Apprehension without warrant,** HS 573.001.
Peace officer application for detention, HS 573.002.
**Child abuse.**
Investigations in mental health facilities, Fam 261.404.
**Confidential information.**
Mental health information in criminal cases, TRE 510.
**Execution of sentence.**
Competency to be executed, Crim Proc 46.05.

**MILITARY PERSONNEL.**
**Concealed weapons.**
Licenses to carry.
Fee reductions, Gov 411.1951.
**Drivers' licenses,** Transp 521.028.
Selective service registration on application,
Transp 521.147.
**Execution of process.**
Military assistance to peace officers, Crim
Proc 8.02.
**Family violence prevention.**
Notice of family violence offenses provided by
clerk of court, Crim Proc 42.0182.
Peace officers' duties.
Report to commanding officer, Crim Proc
5.05.
**Fraudulent or fictitious military record,**
Penal 32.54.
**License plates.**
Effective January 1, 2012, Transp 504.301 to
504.317.
Effective until January 1, 2012, Transp
504.301 to 504.316.
**Quartering of soldiers,** US Const Amd 3.
**Registration of motor vehicles.**
Effective January 1, 2012.
Military service, effect on requirement,
Transp 502.090.
Used vehicle transfers.
Active duty military, Transp 502.457.
Effective until January 1, 2012.
Military service, effect on requirement,
Transp 502.0025.
Used vehicle transfers.
Active duty military, Transp 520.0225.
**Sentence and punishment.**
Presentence investigation report, information
included, Crim Proc 42.12.
**Speed limits.**
Authority to alter.
United States military reservation
commanding officer, Transp 545.358.
**State militia privilege from arrest,** Gov
431.086.
**Suppression of riots and disturbances.**
Military assistance to peace officers, Crim
Proc 8.02, Crim Proc 8.03.
**Weapons, places where prohibited.**
Exceptions, Penal 46.03.
**MILITARY VEHICLES.**
**Certificates of title.**
Former military vehicles, Transp 501.035.

**MILK AND MILK PRODUCTS.**
**Regulation of food, drugs and cosmetics,**
HS 431.010.

**MILK TRANSPORTERS.**
**Oversize and overweight vehicles,** Transp
622.031, 622.032.

**MINES.**
**Weapons offenses generally.**
See WEAPONS.

**MINIMOTORBIKES.**
**Applicability of provisions,** Transp 551.353.
**Definitions,** Transp 551.301, 551.351.
**Operation on roadways,** Transp 551.303.
**Registration,** Transp 551.302.

**MINORS.**
**Abandonment of child,** Penal 22.041.
**Abusable volatile chemicals.**
Delivery to minor, HS 485.032.
**Age affecting criminal responsibility,** Penal
8.07.
**Aggravated assault of child, failure to stop
or report,** Penal 38.17.
**Alcoholic beverages,** ABC 106.01 to 106.15.
Alcohol awareness course, ABC 106.115.
Attempt to purchase, ABC 106.025.
Boating under the influence, ABC 106.041.
Consumption of alcohol, ABC 106.04.
Definition of minor, ABC 106.01.
Drivers' licenses.
Automatic suspension, Transp 521.351.
Purchasing for or furnishing alcohol to
minor, Transp 521.351.
Failure to attend alcohol awareness course,
ABC 106.115.
Driving under the influence, ABC 106.041.
Employment to handle liquor, ABC 106.09.
Expungement of conviction, ABC 106.12.
Fake identification, ABC 106.07.
Furnishing to, ABC 106.06.
Guilty pleas, ABC 106.10.
Importation of alcohol, ABC 106.08.
Juvenile proceedings.
Alcohol-related offenses, Fam 54.047.
Misrepresentation of age, ABC 106.07.
Notice of convictions, ABC 106.116.
Penalties for offenses, ABC 106.15, 106.071.
Possession of alcohol, ABC 106.05.
Purchase by, ABC 106.02.
Purchase for, ABC 106.06.
Reports of court, ABC 106.116, 106.117.
Sale to, ABC 106.03.
**Arraignment.**
Cost of employing counsel for, Crim Proc
26.057.
State training school for delinquent children,
counties with.
State contributions to defense, Crim Proc
26.056.
**Assault.**
Child injured in one county and residing in
another, venue, Crim Proc 13.075.
Injury to children, elderly or disabled
persons, Penal 22.04.
Limitation of action, Crim Proc 12.01.
**Authorization agreement for nonparent
relative,** Fam 34.001 to 34.009.
Applicability of chapter, Fam 34.001.

## MOTOR VEHICLES —Cont'd

**Size and weight of vehicles,** Transp 621.001 to 623.310.
　See SIZE AND WEIGHT OF VEHICLES.

**Slow-moving vehicles.**
　Display of emblem, Transp 547.703.
　Emblem standards, Transp 547.104.
　Violation of special-use provisions, Transp 547.005.

**Tail lamp improperly located on motorcycle,** Transp 547.801.

**Tail lamps improperly located,** Transp 547.322.

**Tampering with equipment,** Transp 727.001 to 727.004.

**Tampering with identification number,** Penal 31.11.

**Television receiver or video equipment improperly located,** Transp 547.611.

**Theft.**
　Certificates of title.
　　Application for stolen or concealed vehicle, Transp 501.153.
　　Record of stolen or concealed vehicle, Transp 501.135.
　　Seizure of stolen vehicle or vehicle with altered serial number.
　　　Effective until January 1, 2012, Transp 501.158.
　　Seizure of stolen vehicle or vehicle with altered vehicle identification number.
　　　Effective January 1, 2012, Transp 501.158.
　Scrap and salvage yards, presumption of knowledge of stolen property, Penal 31.03.

**Tire restrictions,** Transp 547.612.

**Too many auxiliary passing lamps,** Transp 547.329.

**Too many fog lamps,** Transp 547.328.

**Too many spot lamps,** Transp 547.327.

**Towing and storage of motor vehicle, expenses,** Crim Proc 18.23.

**Tracking devices.**
　Unlawful installation, Penal 16.06.

**Tractor brakes not protected in case of breakaway,** Transp 547.405.

**Transferring motor vehicle with papers blank or partially blank.**
　Effective January 1, 2012, Transp 501.161.
　Effective until January 1, 2012, Transp 520.035.

**Trucks.**
　See TRAILERS AND TRUCKS.

**Turn signals,** Transp 547.324.

**Unauthorized use of,** Penal 31.07.
　Venue of prosecution, Crim Proc 13.23.

**Unauthorized use of flashing red, white or blue lights,** Transp 547.305.

## MOTOR VEHICLES —Cont'd

**Unauthorized use of siren, whistle or bell,** Transp 547.501.

**Unnecessary use of horn,** Transp 547.501.

**Unsafe air conditioning equipment,** Transp 547.001, 547.103, 547.610.

**Used vehicles.**
　See USED CARS.

**Using equipment not approved,** Transp 547.101, 547.201.

**Vehicle with defective required equipment or in unsafe condition,** Transp 548.004, 548.104, 548.401, 548.405 to 548.408, 548.502, 548.603, 548.604.

**Warning devices,** Transp 547.501 to 547.508.

**Windows and doors.**
　Obstructed view, Transp 547.613.
　Safety glazing, Transp 547.608.
　Sunscreening devices, Transp 547.609.

**Windshield wipers,** Transp 547.603.

**Wrong color lamps,** Transp 547.353.

**Wrong color lights,** Transp 547.303, 547.322, 547.332.

**Wrong use of school bus signal,** Transp 547.701.

## MOTOR VEHICLE SAFETY RESPONSIBILITY, Transp 601.001 to 601.454.

**Accidents.**
　Reporting, Transp 601.004.
　Security following, Transp 601.151 to 601.170.
　　See within this heading, "Security following accident."

**Administration by department,** Transp 601.021, 601.023.

**Alternative methods of establishing.**
　Deposits with comptroller, Transp 601.122.
　Deposits with county judge, Transp 601.123.
　Self-insurance, Transp 601.124.
　Surety bond, Transp 601.121.

**Appeal of department action,** Transp 601.401.

**Database interface verification system,** Transp 601.451 to 601.453.

**Definitions,** Transp 601.002.

**Drivers' license applications.**
　Evidence of financial responsibility, Transp 521.143.

**Effect of suspension,** Transp 601.371 to 601.376.
　Cooperation with other jurisdictions, Transp 601.375.
　Operation in violation of suspension, Transp 601.371.
　Reinstatement fee, Transp 601.376.
　Return of license to department, Transp 601.372, 601.373.
　Transfer of registration prohibited, Transp 601.374.

PHYSICIANS AND SURGEONS —Cont'd
**Solicitation of professional employment,** Penal 38.12.
**Vaccinations.**
Influenza vaccine.
Priority in distribution to health care providers, HS 431.117.

PICKETING.
**Disorderly conduct, defense,** Penal 42.04.
**Funerals, disrupting,** Penal 42.055.

PIMPING.
**Compelling prostitution,** Penal 43.05.
**Promoting prostitution,** Penal 43.03.
Aggravated, Penal 43.04.

PIPELINES.
**Operating vehicle in or near,** Water 49.217.

**PLACED INSPECTION CERTIFICATE ON WRONG VEHICLE,** Transp 548.603.

**PLACING OR MAINTAINING UNAUTHORIZED SIGN, SIGNAL OR DEVICE,** Transp 544.006.

**PLACING UNAUTHORIZED MOTOR NUMBER ON MOTOR VEHICLE,** Transp 501.151.

PLAGIARISM.
**Academic products, deceptive preparation and marketing,** Penal 32.50.

PLAYGROUNDS.
**Gang-free zones.**
Enhanced punishment for offenses within, Penal 71.028.
Map as evidence of location of area, Penal 71.029.
Information in student handbook, Educ 37.110.

PLEADINGS.
**Defendant's pleadings enumerated,** Crim Proc 27.02.
**Dismissal of case.**
Barred by limitation, Crim Proc 28.06.
Delay, Crim Proc 28.061.
No offense charged, Crim Proc 28.07.
**Double jeopardy,** Crim Proc 28.13.
**Exception to form of indictment,** Crim Proc 27.09.
Amendment, Crim Proc 28.09 to Crim Proc 28.11.
**Exception to substance of indictment,** Crim Proc 27.08.
Amendment, Crim Proc 28.09 to Crim Proc 28.11.
No offense charged, Crim Proc 28.07.
**Former acquittal or conviction,** Crim Proc 28.13.
**Guilty pleas.**
Change of venue to plead guilty, Crim Proc 27.15.

PLEADINGS —Cont'd
**Guilty pleas** —Cont'd
Entering on arraignment, Crim Proc 26.13, Crim Proc 26.14.
Felony cases, Crim Proc 27.13.
Misdemeanor cases, Crim Proc 27.14.
**Indictment or information as primary pleading,** Crim Proc 27.01.
**Judgment against defendant on outcome of pleading,** Crim Proc 28.14.
**Justice and municipal courts,** Crim Proc 45.021.
Nolo contendere pleas, Crim Proc 45.022.
**Motion to set aside indictment,** Crim Proc 27.03.
Sustained, but defendant held by court, Crim Proc 28.08.
Trial by judge, Crim Proc 27.04.
**Nolo contendere pleas.**
Felony cases, Crim Proc 27.13.
Inmates in penal institutions, Crim Proc 27.19.
Justice and municipal courts, Crim Proc 45.022.
Misdemeanor cases, Crim Proc 27.14.
**Not guilty pleas.**
Construed as denial of material allegations, Crim Proc 27.17.
Entering on arraignment, Crim Proc 26.12.
Manner of making, Crim Proc 27.16.
**Order of argument,** Crim Proc 28.02.
**Petroleum product transporters.**
Enforcement of provisions, Natur 115.045.
**Pre-trial motions and hearings,** Crim Proc 28.01.
**Protective orders.**
Pleadings in response to application, Fam 82.021, 82.022.
**Quashing charge in misdemeanor,** Crim Proc 28.04.
**Quashing indictment in felony,** Crim Proc 28.05.
**Signing of papers filed on behalf of defendant,** Crim Proc 1.052.
**Special plea of defendant,** Crim Proc 27.05.
Exception by state, Crim Proc 28.12.
Trial of, Crim Proc 27.07, Crim Proc 28.12.
Verification, Crim Proc 27.06.
**Testimony on,** Crim Proc 28.03.
**Time for filing,** Crim Proc 27.11.
After service, Crim Proc 27.12.
**Video teleconferencing, pleas or waiver of rights by,** Crim Proc 27.18.
**Writing, pleas and motions to be in,** Crim Proc 27.10.

POCKET BIKES.
**Applicability of provisions,** Transp 551.353.
**Definitions,** Transp 551.301, 551.351.
**Operation on roadways,** Transp 551.303.
**Registration,** Transp 551.302.

**PUBLIC LEWDNESS,** Penal 21.07.

**PUBLIC NUISANCES.**
**Gangs, membership in,** Civil Prac 125.061 to
    Civil Prac 125.063.
**Junked vehicles,** Transp 683.071 to 683.078.
    See ABANDONED VEHICLES.

**PUBLIC ORDER AND DECENCY,**
    **OFFENSES AGAINST.**
**Disorderly conduct and related offenses,**
    Penal 42.01 to 42.14.
    See DISORDERLY CONDUCT AND
        RELATED OFFENSES.
**Obscenity,** Penal 43.21 to 43.27.
**Prostitution,** Penal 43.01 to 43.06.

**PUBLIC RECORDS.**
**Contents of writings, recordings and**
    **photographs,** TRE 1005.
**Destruction, removal or alteration of**
    **public information,** Gov 552.351.
**Hearsay exceptions,** TRE 803.
**Officer refusal to provide access,** Gov
    552.353.
**Release of information to defense counsel**
    **not considered voluntary release of**
    **public information,** Crim Proc 38.02.

**PUBLIC TRANSPORTATION.**
**Criminal mischief,** Penal 28.03.

**PUBLIC TRIAL,** Crim Proc 1.24.

**PUBLIC UTILITIES.**
**Caller identification service,** Util 55.101 to
    55.110.
**Criminal mischief,** Penal 28.03.
**Emergency telephone services,** Util 186.041
    to 186.045.
**Fraudulently obtaining service,** Util 186.031
    to 186.033.
**Manipulation of service for law**
    **enforcement purposes,** Util 186.021.
**Telecommunications crimes,** Penal 33A.01 to
    33A.06.
    Venue of prosecution, Crim Proc 13.26.

**PULLING AWAY, UNSAFE START FROM**
    **PARKED POSITION,** Transp 545.402.

**PULLING MORE THAN ONE TRAILER OR**
    **OTHER VEHICLE,** Transp 545.409.

**PULLING MORE THAN TWO TRAILERS**
    **OR VEHICLES,** Transp 621.205.

**PUNISHMENT.**
See SENTENCE AND PUNISHMENT.

**PURCHASE OF ALCOHOL FOR MINOR**
    **OR FURNISHING ALCOHOL TO**
    **MINOR,** Transp 521.351.

**PURCHASE OF CHILD,** Penal 25.08.

**PURPLE HEART RECIPIENTS.**
**License plates,** Transp 504.315.

**PURPOSE OF CODE.**
**Code of criminal procedure,** Crim Proc 1.03,
    Crim Proc 101.001.
**Penal code,** Penal 1.02.

## Q

**QUARANTINE OF RABID ANIMAL,** HS
    826.042, 826.044.

**QUARTERING OF SOLDIERS,** US Const
    Amd 3.

**QUASH, MOTION TO.**
**Felony indictment,** Crim Proc 28.05.
**Misdemeanor charges,** Crim Proc 28.04.

**QUOTAS.**
**Prohibition on traffic offense quotas,**
    Transp 720.002.

## R

**RABIES.**
**Quarantine of animal,** HS 826.042, 826.044.
**Restraint of pet,** HS 826.034.
**Vaccinations,** HS 826.021, 826.022.

**RACETRACKS.**
**Weapons, places where prohibited,** Penal
    46.03.

**RACIAL PROFILING BY PEACE**
    **OFFICERS,** Crim Proc 2.131.
**Adoption of rules to implement provisions,**
    Crim Proc 2.138.
**Definition,** Crim Proc 3.05.
**Enforcement of policy against,** Crim Proc
    2.132.
**Funding for installation of audio and**
    **video equipment,** Crim Proc 2.137.
**Reports required for pedestrian and traffic**
    **stops,** Crim Proc 2.133.
    Compilation and analysis of data collected,
        Crim Proc 2.134.
    Exemption from reporting and analysis if
        using audio and video equipment, Crim
        Proc 2.135.
    Failure to submit incident-based data, Crim
        Proc 2.1385.
    Immunity of officer regarding, Crim Proc
        2.136.

**RACING, DRAG RACING, ACCELERATION**
    **CONTEST,** Transp 545.420.

**RACING OF BICYCLES,** Transp 551.105.

**RACING OF MOTOR VEHICLES.**
**Drivers' licenses.**
    Automatic suspension, Transp 521.350.
**Rules of the road,** Transp 545.420.

**RACING OR DRAG RACING, DRIVER'S**
    **LICENSE SUSPENSION,** Transp
    521.350.

## VEHICLE WITH DEFECTIVE REQUIRED EQUIPMENT OR IN UNSAFE CONDITION, Transp 548.004.

## VENDING MACHINES.
**Burglary,** Penal 30.03.
**Tobacco products,** HS 161.086.

## VENUE.
**Absence, unauthorized,** Crim Proc 13.28.
**Academic degrees, fraudulent or fictitious,** Crim Proc 13.30.
**Allegation of venue,** Crim Proc 13.17.
**Athletes, illegal recruitment,** Crim Proc 13.24.
**Authority of state, persons exercising outside of state,** Crim Proc 13.10.
**Bigamy,** Crim Proc 13.14.
**Boats, offenses committed on board,** Crim Proc 13.11.
**Boundaries of counties, offenses committed on,** Crim Proc 13.04.
**Boundaries of municipalities, offenses committed on,** Crim Proc 13.045.
**Boundary stream or river, offenses committed on,** Crim Proc 13.06.
**Burden of proof,** Crim Proc 13.17.
**Change of name,** Fam 45.101.
**Change of venue.**
Challenge of motion, Crim Proc 31.04.
Court's own motion, Crim Proc 31.01.
Defendant in custody, Crim Proc 31.06.
Defendant motion for, Crim Proc 31.03.
Duties of clerk, Crim Proc 31.05.
Maintenance of existing services and facilities, Crim Proc 31.09.
Return to original venue, Crim Proc 31.08.
State request for, Crim Proc 31.02.
Witnesses not resummoned, Crim Proc 31.07.
**Child injured in one county and residing in another,** Crim Proc 13.075.
**Computer crimes,** Crim Proc 13.25.
Telecommunications crimes, Crim Proc 13.26.
**Consent to venue,** Crim Proc 13.20.
**Conspiracy,** Crim Proc 13.13.
**Degrees, fraudulent or fictitious,** Crim Proc 13.30.
**Escape,** Crim Proc 13.28.
**False imprisonment,** Crim Proc 13.12.
**Family violence prevention.**
Protective order offenses, Crim Proc 5.07.
**Forgery,** Crim Proc 13.02.
**Guilty pleas.**
Change of venue to plead guilty, Crim Proc 27.15.
**Hindering secured creditors,** Crim Proc 13.09.
**Homicide committed outside state,** Crim Proc 13.05.
**Identifying information, fraudulent use or possession,** Crim Proc 13.29.

## VENUE —Cont'd
**Indictment, alleging venue,** Crim Proc 21.06.
**Injured in one county and dying in another,** Crim Proc 13.07.
**Juvenile proceedings,** Fam 51.06.
**Kidnapping,** Crim Proc 13.12.
**Littering prosecution,** HS 365.005, 365.015.
**Marihuana, possession and delivery,** Crim Proc 13.22.
**Misapplication of fiduciary or financial property,** Crim Proc 13.32.
**Money laundering,** Crim Proc 13.35.
**Motor vehicle, unauthorized use,** Crim Proc 13.23.
**Nonsupport, criminal,** Crim Proc 13.16.
**Offenses committed outside state,** Crim Proc 13.01.
**Offenses not specifically set out,** Crim Proc 13.18.
**Organized crime,** Crim Proc 13.21.
**Perjury,** Crim Proc 13.03.
**Petroleum product transporters.**
Enforcement of provisions, Natur 115.046.
**Proof of venue,** Crim Proc 13.17.
**Protective orders.**
Application for, Fam 82.003.
**Recruiting athletes illegally,** Crim Proc 13.24.
**Sex offender registration, noncompliance,** Crim Proc 13.31.
**Sexual assault,** Crim Proc 13.15.
**Sexually violent predator civil commitment, noncompliance,** Crim Proc 13.315.
**Simulating legal process,** Crim Proc 13.27.
**Smuggling of persons,** Crim Proc 13.12.
**Stalking,** Crim Proc 13.36.
**Stolen property.**
Disposition of stolen property.
Hearing on restoration to owner, Crim Proc 47.01a.
**Telecommunications crimes,** Crim Proc 13.26.
**Texas youth council, offenses against child committed to,** Crim Proc 13.34.
**Theft,** Crim Proc 13.08.
Unauthorized acquisition of financial information, Crim Proc 13.295.
**Trafficking of persons,** Crim Proc 13.12.
**Unable to determine,** Crim Proc 13.19.
**Vessels, offenses committed on board,** Crim Proc 13.11.

## VERBAL PROVOCATION.
**Self-defense, use of force not justified,** Penal 9.31.

## VERDICT.
**Acquittal of higher offense,** Crim Proc 37.14.
**Capital cases,** Crim Proc 37.071, Crim Proc 37.0711.
Repeat sex offenders, Crim Proc 37.072.

## VICTIMS OF CRIME —Cont'd

**Release of defendant** —Cont'd

Family violence offenders, Crim Proc 42.21.

Notice generally, Crim Proc 56.11.

**Rights generally,** Crim Proc 56.02.

**Rulemaking,** Crim Proc 56.93.

**Sealing medical records of child victim,** Crim Proc 57C.01, Crim Proc 57C.02.

**Sentence and punishment.**

Prohibiting contact with victim, Crim Proc 42.24.

**Sexually violent predators, civil commitment.**

Victim identifying information, privilege, HS 841.1462.

**Sexual offenses.**

Address confidentiality program, Crim Proc 56.81 to Crim Proc 56.93. See within this heading, "Address confidentiality program."

Confidentiality of identifying information, Crim Proc 57.01 to Crim Proc 57.03.

Evidence, corroboration of victim, Crim Proc 38.07.

Medical examination of victim, Crim Proc 56.06, Crim Proc 56.065.

**Statistical reporting,** Crim Proc 56.05.

**Trafficking of persons.**

Confidentiality of identifying information, Crim Proc 57D.01 to Crim Proc 57D.03.

Restitution for child victims, mandatory, Crim Proc 42.0372.

**Transfer of defendant.**

Notice generally, Crim Proc 56.12.

**Use of victim's information to solicit business,** Bus 35.54.

**Victim impact statement,** Crim Proc 56.03.

## VICTORIA COUNTY NAVIGATION DISTRICT.

**Permits for oversize and overweight vehicles,** Transp 623.230 to 623.239.

## VICTORIA COUNTY NAVIGATION DISTRICT OVERWEIGHT PERMITS, Transp 623.230.

## VIDEO ARCADES.

**Gang-free zones.**

Enhanced punishment for offenses within, Penal 71.028.

Map as evidence of location of area, Penal 71.029.

Information in student handbook, Educ 37.110.

## VIDEOTAPES AND VIDEO EQUIPMENT.

**Child pornography.**

Evidence.

Discovery, Crim Proc 39.15.

Restriction of access, Crim Proc 38.45.

Possession or promotion, Penal 43.26.

## VIDEOTAPES AND VIDEO EQUIPMENT —Cont'd

**Evidence from child victims,** Crim Proc 38.071.

**Evidence from inmate witnesses,** Crim Proc 38.073.

**Grand jury.**

Witnesses, testimony by video teleconferencing, Crim Proc 20.151.

**Improper photography or visual recording,** Penal 21.15.

**Motor vehicles, equipment mounted in,** Transp 547.611.

**Peace officers.**

Racial profiling enforcement of policy, Crim Proc 2.132.

Funding for installation of audio and video equipment, Crim Proc 2.137.

Reports required for pedestrian and traffic stops.

Exemption from reporting and analysis if using audio and video equipment, Crim Proc 2.135.

**Pleas or waiver of rights by video teleconferencing,** Crim Proc 27.18.

**Sexual conduct.**

Material depicting sexual conduct by child or minor.

Discovery, Crim Proc 39.15.

Educational program required, Crim Proc 6.09, Crim Proc 45.061, Fam 54.0404.

Expunction of conviction records of children, Crim Proc 45.0216.

Juvenile proceedings, Penal 43.261.

Restriction of access, Crim Proc 38.45.

**Shoplifting.**

Use of shielding or deactivation device, Penal 31.03.

**Taping of another without consent,** Penal 21.15.

**Television receiver or video equipment improperly located,** Transp 547.611.

## VIETNAM VETERANS.

**License plates,** Transp 504.312.

## VIOLATING DRIVER'S LICENSE RESTRICTION, Transp 521.221.

## VIOLATING DRIVER'S LICENSE RESTRICTION ON OCCUPATIONAL LICENSE, Transp 521.253.

## VIOLATING MOTOR CARRIER REGISTRATION, Transp 643.253.

## VIOLATING MOTOR CARRIER REGISTRATION, ADMINISTRATIVE SANCTIONS, Transp 643.252.

## VIOLATING MOTOR CARRIER SAFETY STANDARDS, Transp 644.001.

## VIOLATING PROMISE TO APPEAR, Transp 543.009.

**WRONG USE OF SCHOOL BUS SIGNAL,**
Transp 547.701.

## Y

**YIELD SIGNS,** Transp 544.010.

**YMCA.**
License plates, Transp 504.623.

**YOUNG LAWYERS ASSOCIATION.**
License plates, Transp 504.612.

**YOUTH CENTERS.**
Gang-free zones.
  Enhanced punishment for offenses within, Penal 71.028.
  Map as evidence of location of area, Penal 71.029.

**YOUTH COMMISSION.**
Child abuse.
  Investigations in youth commission facilities, Fam 261.409.
**Venue for prosecution of offenses against child committed to,** Crim Proc 13.34.

## Z

**ZIP GUNS.**
Weapons offenses generally.
  See WEAPONS.

# Notes

# Notes

# Notes

# Notes

# Notes

# Notes

# Notes

# Notes

# Notes

# Notes

# Notes

# Notes

# Notes

# Notes

# Notes

# Notes

# Notes

# Notes

# Notes

# Notes

# Notes

**Notes**

**Notes**

# Notes

# Notes

# Notes

# Notes

**Notes**